The
Medical
Disability
Advisor

Fourth Edition

¤

First Edition, 1991

Second Edition, 1994

Third Edition, 1997

Fourth Edition, 2001

A Practical Reference
for Diagnoses and Procedures

The Medical Disability Advisor

Workplace Guidelines
for Disability Duration

Fourth Edition

Presley Reed, MD

Editor-in-Chief

**Reed Group, Ltd.
Boulder, CO
Reed Group Holdings, Ltd.
Singapore**

This publication is designed to provide accurate and authoritative information in regard to the subject matter covered. It is published with the understanding that the author, editors and publisher are *not* engaged in rendering medical, legal, accounting or other professional service. If medical, legal, or other expert assistance is required, the service of a competent professional should be sought.

Editor-in-Chief: Presley Reed, MD
MAB Chairman: Christopher R. Brigham, MD
Consulting Editor: Stacey Grace
Project Manager/Text Editor: Rebecca Wiard, MA
Data Collection/Analysis: Kathi Dangerfield, MS
Database Engineer: Mike Hellem
Web Interface Programmer: Kamolrat Therawat
Book Design/Production: Louis Burkhardt, PhD
Illustrators: Frank Forney, Laurie O'Keefe
Cover Design: PageWorks Communications

Library of Congress Control Number: 2001089027

THE MEDICAL DISABILITY ADVISOR: WORKPLACE GUIDELINES FOR DISABILITY DURATION, Fourth Edition
ISBN 1-889010-02-2

Copyright © 2001 Reed Group Holdings, Ltd. and Reed Group, Ltd. All Rights Reserved.
No part of this publication may be used, reproduced, stored, or transmitted in any form or by any means—graphic, electronic, mechanical, including photocopying, recording, taping, information storage and retrieval systems, or otherwise—without the prior writtenpermission of the copyright owner.

Also available as Software for Windows, MDA Internet, and MDA Data License.

Direct comments or inquiries to:
Reed Group, Ltd.
4041 Hanover Ave., Second Floor
Boulder, Colorado 80305 USA
303-247-1860
303-247-1863 FAX
800-347-7443
www.presleyreed.com

Third Edition published by Reed Group, Ltd.
Boulder, Colorado
ISBN 1-889010-01-4

First and Second Editions published by LRP Publications
An Axon Group Company, Horsham, Pennsylvania
ISBN 0-934753-52-0

Additional copies may be purchased from:
Reed Group, Ltd. 800-347-7443 or 303-247-1860

Printed on acid-free paper.
Manufactured in the United States of America.
Fourth Edition.
99 98 97 96 95 94

6 5 4 3 2 1

The Medical Disability Advisor is dedicated

to all of the men and women

around the world who remain productive

despite significant emotional and physical pain.

PR

Table of Contents

Medical Advisory Board ix

Contributors xiii

Foreword xv

Preface xix

Acknowledgments xxi

Overview xxiii

Development Process xxiii

Understanding The Medical Disability Advisor xxiv

Disability Duration Tables xxvi

Normative Data Graphs xxvii

Diagnoses and Procedures 1

Managing Medical Absences 2309

Glossary 2319

Translation of ICD-9 CM to ICD-10 2383

Index of ICD-9 CM 2461

Index 2507

Medical Advisory Board

Chair

Christopher R. Brigham, MD, MMS, FACOEM, FAADEP, CIME
President, Brigham and Associates, Inc., Portland, ME; President, eMedicoLegal, Inc.; Founder, American Board of Independent Medical Examiners; Editor, AMA *Guides Newsletter*

Associate Chairs

William F. Boucher, MD, MPH, FACOEM, CIME
Chair, Section on Work Fitness and Disability for the American College of Occupational and Environmental Medicine; Medical Director, WorkWell, Biddeford, ME

Charles N. Brooks, MD, PC
President, Washington Association of Independent Medical Examiners, Bellevue, WA; Clinical Instructor, University of Washington Department of Orthopedics; Reviewer, AMA *Guides to the Evaluation of Permanent Impairment,* Fifth Edition

Leon Ensalada, MD, MPH, FAADEP, FACPM, CIME
President, Leon Ensalada & Associates; Member of Board of Directors, American Academy of Disability Evaluating Physicians, Waitsfield, VT

Norma J. Leclair, RN, PhD
Executive Director, DCG Research Institute, Disability Consulting Group, LLC, Portland, ME

Gideon Letz, MD, MPH
Medical Director, State Compensation Insurance Fund, California, San Francisco, CA

James B. Talmage, MD, FAADEP
Occupational Health Center, A Division of Cookeville Regional Medical Center; Associate Editor, AMA *Guides Newsletter*, Cookeville, TN

Reviewers

Harvey Alpern, MD, FACC, FAADEP
Past President and Member of Board of Directors, American Academy of Disability Evaluating Physicians; Assistant Clinical Professor, Medicine, University of California, Los Angeles

Ahmad K. S. Al-Shatti, MD, MFOM
Chairman, General Medical Council, Ministry of Health, State of Kuwait

Edward L. Anderson, MD
President, Nucleus Technologies, Inc., Arlington, VA

Gunnar Bengt Johan Andersson, MD, PhD
Editor, AMA *Guides to the Evaluation of Permanent Impairment,* Fifth Edition; Professor and Chairman, Department of Orthopedic Surgery, Rush - Presbyterian - St. Luke's Medical Center, Chicago, IL

Gerald M. Aronoff, MD, FAADEP, DABPM
Medical Director, North American Pain and Disability Group, Charlotte, NC; Past President, American Academy of Pain Medicine; Assistant Clinical Professor, Tufts Medical School; Member of the Board of Directors, American Academy of Disability Evaluating Physicians

Douglas Allen Benner, MD, FACOEM
Coordinator, Occupational Health, Kaiser Permanente, San Francisco, CA

Bernard R. Blais MD, FAAO, FACOEM, FACS
President, Blais Consulting, Ltd.; Chair, Eye and Vision Committee, American College of Occupational and Environmental Medicine; ACOEM Liaison to AAO Committee on Eye Safety and Sports Ophthalmology; Clinical Professor, Ophthalmology, Albany Medical College, Clifton Park, NY

E. Richard Blonsky, MD
Director, Pain and Rehabilitation Clinic of Chicago; Associate Professor of Clinical Neurology, Northwestern University Medical School, Evanston, IL

Peter Blumenthal, MD, MPH, FACOEM, CIME
IME Specialist, Concentra Medical Evaluations, Maplewood, NJ

William B. Bunn III, MD, JD, MPH
Vice President, Health and Safety and Productivity, International Truck and Engine Corporation, Chicago, IL

Samuel Dan Caughron, MD, FACOEM, FACPM
Family Physician, Charlottesville Wellness Center Family Practice, Charlotteville, VA

John L. Chase, MD, FACS
President and Medical Director, Benchmark Administrative Consultants, Berkeley, CA

Cherryl Christensen, DO, MS
Medical Director North America, The Procter & Gamble Company, Cincinnati, OH

Jennifer Christian MD, MPH
President, Webility Corporation, Wayland, MA

Ronald Seth Citron, MD
Medical Oncologist, San Francisco, CA

Alan Colledge, MD
Medical Director, Utah State Industrial Commission, Salt Lake City, UT

William Craig, MD
Principal, William M. Mercer, Incorporated, San Francisco, CA

Timothy Crimmins, MD, FACEP
Vice President, Director, Health Safety and Environment, General Mills, Inc., Minneapolis, MN

John A. Davis, MD
Director, Davis Occupational Medicine, Norwood, MA

Stephen Demeter, MD, MPH, FACP, FCCP, FAADEP, FACOEM
Professor and Chairman, Department of Pulmonary and Critical Care Medicine, Northeastern Ohio Universities College of Medicine, Akron, OH; President, American Academy of Disability Evaluating Physicians

Robert Dennis, MD
Seaview Orthopedic and Medical Associates, Neptune City, NJ

David Dickison, DO
Consultant, Disability and Occupational Medicine, Freeport, ME

Lorne K. Direnfeld MD, FRCP(C)
Neurologist/Medical Director, Maui Occupational Health Center, Kahului, Maui, HI; Assistant Clinical Professor, University of Hawaii School of Medicine

Anthony J. Dorto, DC, MD, FAAPM, FAADEP
Medical Director, Disability Assessment Center, PA, Miami, FL; Past President and Member of the Board of Directors, American Academy of Disability Evaluating Physicians

Paul E. Epstein, MD
Clinical Professor of Medicine, University of Pennsylvania, Pulmonary and Critical Care Medicine, Philadelphia, PA

Michael Erdil, MD, FACOEM
Medical Director, Eastern Rehabilitation Network, Connecticut Occupational Health Network, Newington, CT

Robert Stephen Falcone, MD
Corporate Medical Director, Merck & Co., Inc., Whitehouse Station, NJ

Gerald A. M. Finerman, MD
Professor and Chairman, University of California, Los Angeles, Department of Orthopaedic Surgery, Los Angeles, CA

David Fishbain, MD
Professor of Psychiatry and Adjunct Professor Neurological Surgery and Anesthesiology, University of Miami School of Medicine, Miami Beach, FL

Shepard Fountaine, MD
Medical Director, Employment Development Department, State of California, Sacramento, CA

Martin Daniel Fritzhand, MD
Occupational Health Consultants, Cincinnati, OH

Ian Robert Gardner, MD, MBBS, MPH, FAFOM
President, Australasian Faculty of Occupational Medicine, Lindfield, NSW, Australia

Lynn Garvey Kirby, RN, BSN, NP, COHN-S
Occupational Health Nurse Practitioner, Malvern, PA

L. Barton Goldman, MD
Medical Director, HealthONE Clinic Services, Denver, CO

Annette B. Haag, MA, RN, COHN-S/CM
Annette B. Haag & Associates, Inc.; Past President, American Association of Occupational Health Nurses, Simi Valley, CA

Constance Hanna, MD
Corporate Director, Health Services and Product Safety, Honeywell, International

Christine C. Hansen, MD
Boulder Women's Clinic, Boulder, CO

Robert H. Haralson III, MD, MBA, FAADEP
Editor, Musculoskeletal Chapter, AMA *Guides to the Evaluation of Permanent Impairment*, Fourth Edition; Editor, Spine Chapter, AMA *Guides*, Fifth Edition; Associate Clinical Professor, University of Tennessee Center for the Health Sciences; Medical Director, Southeastern Orthopaedics, Knoxville, TN

Stephen H. Heidel, MD
CEO, Integrated Insights; Assoc. Clinical Professor, Dept. of Psychiatry, University of California San Diego Medical School; Founding Member, Past President and Board Member Academy of Organizational and Occupational Psychiatry, San Diego, CA

Craig S. Heligman, MD, MS
Medical Director/Second Vice President, Fortis Benefits Insurance Company, Kansas City, MO

Jennifer Hone, MD, FACE
Associate Clinical Professor, University of Colorado Health Sciences Center; Center for Diabetes and Endocrinology, Arvada, CO

Gwilym Hughes MB, FRCP, FFOM, FACOEM
Consultant Occupational Physician, Middlesex, UK

Oregon Kenneth Hunter, Jr., MD
Lead Physician, Rehabilitation Medicine Associates, Ocala FL

Fikry Isaac, MD, MPH
Director, Occupational Medicine, Johnson & Johnson, New Brunswick, NJ

Gary Jacob, DC, LAc, DipMDT, CICE
Associated Faculty Member, Southern California University of Health Sciences, Clinical Sciences and Clinical Intern Division; Private Practice, Los Angeles, CA

Richard E. Johns, Jr., MD, MSPH
Medical Director, Alliant Techsystems, Magna, UT

Jeffrey Kahn MD, FAAPMR, CIME
Medical Director, rehabwoRx Physical Medicine and Rehabilitation, PLLC, Syracuse, NY

Charles W. Kennedy Jr., MD
Orthopaedic Associates of Corpus Christi, TX

Edwin Herbert Klimek, MD, FRCPC Neurology
Medical Director, Disability Assessment Center, St. Catherines, Ontario, Canada

Steven W. Leclair, PhD
Senior Vice President, Ability Management, Disability Consulting Group, LLC, Portland, ME

Wayne M. Lednar MD, PhD
Corporate Medical Director, Eastman Kodak Company, Rochester, NY

Michael Chun-Leng Lim, MD, MBBS, FRCP
Consultant Cardiologist, Mt. Elizabeth Medical Centre; Member, Advisory Panel, Asian Pacific Society of Interventional Cardiology, Singapore

Barton G. Margoshes, MD
Vice President, National Medical Director, Liberty Mutual Insurance Group, Boston, MA

Leonard Matheson, PhD
Director, Work Performance Clinical Laboratory, Washington University School of Medicine, St. Louis, MO

Laurence Mercer McKinley, MD, MB, BCh, BAO (Honors), CIME
Pacific Spine Clinic, Inc., Escondido, CA

Laurence A. Miller, MD
President and Founder, Risk Quality Management Consulting Associates, La Jolla, CA

John H. Mitchell, MD, MPH, FACOEM
Consultant, Wilmette, IL

Vert Mooney, MD
Medical Director, U.S. Spine & Sport, San Diego, CA

Kathryn Mueller, MD
Littleton, CO

Nancy H. Nelson, MD, FACOG
Nelson Consulting: Disability Consulting and Education; Fellow of the American College of Obstetrics and Gynecology, Damariscotta, ME

Ronald Pawl, MD
Medical Director, Center for Rehabilitation, Lake Forest Hospital, Lake Forest IL; Assoc. Professor Neurosurgery, University of Illinois at Chicago

John Thomas Pessoney, MD, MPH, CIME
Medical Director, Finley Business Health, Debuke, IA

Kent W. Peterson, MD, CIME, MRO, FACOEM
President and CEO, Occupational Health Strategies, Inc.; Past President, American College of Occupational and Environmental Medicine; Senior Vice President, Institute for Health and Productivity Management

Patricia Posey, BSN, MA, RN, LPC
Nurse Coordinator/Rehabilitation Consultant, US Postal Service, Appalachian District, Charleston, WV

John Dennis Pro, MD
Midwest Psychiatric Consultants; Member of Board of Directors, American Academy of Disability Evaluating Physicians, Kansas City, MO

Luiz Fernando Ribeiro Macatti, MD
Manager, Occupational Medicine and Life Quality, 3M, Campinas SP, Brasil

Jack Richman, MD
Executive Vice President and Medical Director, AssessMed, Inc., Mississauga, Ontario, Canada

Henry Roth, MD
Medical Director, Integrated Health Management; CEO and Co-Founder of eMedicoLegal, Inc., Denver, CO

Marcia Satlow, MD
Vice President of Claims, Medical for Hartford Insurance Group, Hartford, CT

Brian Schulman, MD, CIME
President, Occupational Psychiatry, Bethesda, MD

James L. Schuppert, MD
Director of Health Services, Worldwide Health & Benefits, Corning, Incorporated, Corning, NY

Adam L. Seidner, MD, MPH
National Medical Director, Travelers Property Casualty, Hartford, CT

Gabriel Eugen Sella, MD
Independent Medical Examiner, Worker's Compensation Bureau, Department of Human Resources, Charleston, WV

Jorge Serrano MD, MPH, MOH, CPEA
Medical Director/Occupational Medicine Consultant, Servicios En Salud Ocupacional, Bogota, Colombia

Suzanne T. Smith, RN, COHN-S/CM, FAAOHN
Vice President, Operations, Occupational Health Division, Liberty Healthcare Corporation, Bala Cynwyd, PA

Gordon C. Steinagle, DO, MPH
Occupational Physician, Buffalo, NY

Laura Stewart Welch, MD
Director, Occupational and Environmental Health, Washington Hospital Center, Washington, DC

Ryszard Szozda, MD,PhD
Head, Occupational Health Care Unit, GPBP Building Company, Gliwice, Poland

Dennis C. Turk, PhD
John and Emma Bonica Professor of Anesthesiology and Pain Research, University of Washington School of Medicine, Seattle, WA

Nathan D. Zasler, MD, FAAPM&R, FAADEP, CIME, DAAPM
CEO and Medical Director, Concussion Care Centre of Virginia, Ltd.; Tree of Life, LLC; Medical Consultant, Pinnacle Rehabilitation, Inc., Glen Allen, VA

Contributors

Adrianne E. Avillion, DEd

Susan Baguisi, RN

Laurie Barclay, MD

Bethanne Black, MHT

Jeanne Bottroff, RNC, BSN

Teddi Bryant-Ruiz, BA, ACSM, CPT

Louis Burkhardt, PhD

Patrick Charbonneau, MD

Sherri Chasin Calvo, MBA

Cecile Childrose, RN, COHN-S/CM, CCM

Deborah Chrey, RN, MSN

William E. Dale, PhD

Carl D. Emerson, MS, MBA

Carol Evans, RN, COHN-S

Cali M. Fidopiastis, MA

Frank Forney, Medical Illustrator

Mildred Fuller, RN

Thomas R. Gatliffe, MSc

P.J. Gieseman

Robert D. Goldhamer, MD, MA

Stacey Grace

Marilyn Haddrill, BS

Rita Harris, RN

Katherine Hasal, M.S.

Margaret Heeran, RN

Mike Hellem

Lori Holohan, BA

Rebecca Horn, RN, MSN

Cindy Jones, PhD

Linda Stuart Koopmann, RN, BA

Helen Lamothe, RN BSN ONC

Ginny Landes

Nancy Lane, RNC, BSN

Jeffrey P. Larson, PT, ATC

Dot Mace, RN

Denise Mayrer, RN, BSN, CCM

Nancy J. Nordenson, MT (ASCP) CLS (NCA)

Laurie O'Keefe, Medical Illustrator

Philip B. Oliva, MD

Kerstin M. Palombaro, MS, PT

Deborah A. Pennett, MA

Charles R. Perakis, DO

Nancy Pugh, RN, MS

Randy Roark, MFA

Scott R. Rossi, BA

Belinda M. Rowland, PhD

Carol Ryan, RN, BSN

Lucy Shannon

Kathi Solt Dangerfield, MS

Arthur W. Stange, PhD

Sharon Sweet, RN, COHN-S

Carole Swenson Fisher, RN, JD

Kamolrat Therawat, MSIS

Laleh T. Varasteh, RPh, MSF

Elaine H. Wacholtz, PhD

Kathleen Wallace, MD

Rebecca Wiard, MA

Richard C. Wilson, DPM, FACFAS

Paula J. Wun, BS

Jennifer Ziedses des Plantes, BS

Contributors

Adrianne E. Avillion, DEd
Susan Bagwell, RN
Laurie Barclay, MD
bethanne Black, MHT
Jeanne Bofforf, RNC, BSN
Teddi Bryant-Ruiz, BA, ACSM, CPT
Louis Burkhardt, PhD
Patrick Charbonneau, MD
Sherri Chastin Galvo, MBA
Cecile Childress, RN, COHN-S/CM, CCM
Deborah Chrey, RN, MSN
William E. Dale, PhD
Carl D. Emerson, MS, MBA
Carol Evans, RN, COHN-S
Gail M. Ficocielllo, MA
Frank Forney, Medical Illustrator
Mildred Fuller, RN
Thomas R. Gatliffe, MSc
P.J. Giesselman
Robert D. Goldhamer, MD, MA
Sidney Grace
Marilyn Haddrill, BS
Rita Hema, RN
Katharine Hazel, M.S
Margaret Heeran, RN
Mike Helfer
Lori Halloran, BA
Rebecca Horn, RN, MSN
Cindy Jones, PhD
Linda Stuart Koopmann, RN, BA

Helen Lanoltre, RN BSN ONC
Ginny Landes
Nancy Lane, RNC, BSN
Jeffrey P. Larson, PT, ATC
Dot Mace, RN
Denise Mayner, RN, BSN, CCM
Nancy J. Nordenson, MT (ASCP) CLS (NCA)
Laurie O'Keefe, Medical Illustrator
Philip B. Oliva, MD
Kerstin M. Palombaro, MS, PT
Deborah A. Pernarl, MA
Charles R. Perakis, DO
Nancy Pugh, RN, MS
Randy Roarh, MFA
Scott R. Rossi, BA
Belinda M. Howland, PhD
Carol Ryan, RN, BSN
Lucy Shannon
Kathi Soli Dangerfield, MS
Arthur W. Stange, PhD
Sharon Sweet, RN, CCHN-C
Carole Svensson Fisher, RN, JD
Kamichet Theravat, MSIS
Laleh T. Varasteh, RPh, MSP
Elaine H. Wacholtz, PhD
Kathleen Wallace, MD
Rebecca Ward, MA
Richard O. Wilson, DPM, FACFAS
Paula J. Wuh, BS
Jennifer Ziadeses des Plantes, BS

Foreword

Fourth Edition

Over the past decade employers, insurers and health care providers designed a variety of programs and benefit systems to minimize the impact illness, injury and disability had in the work place. Employers moved from passive recipients of services provided by insurers and health care providers to active stakeholders who assumed greater responsibility for directing this process. They expressed concerns about the impact that absenteeism has on productivity, customer satisfaction, the cost of benefits and the morale of the workforce. Insurers responded to these concerns by improving risk assessment strategies, plan and benefit designs, and claim management practices. Health care providers, asked to make clinical decisions about impairment and work ability, questioned whether they have the essential information necessary to make such decisions.

At the center of this activity are individuals (employees, patients, claimants) experiencing an illness or injury. They are concerned about whether their symptoms will diminish and their conditions will resolve over time. If the condition persists, they must learn to adapt to changes in the way their bodies' function. These individuals think about how treatment and medications may affect their overall wellbeing, and whether they can meet family responsibilities and financial obligations. They wonder about their ability to maintain or resume a productive work role. They expect their health care provider to clarify whether they can safely perform the requirements of their job. They wonder about how their employer, supervisor and co-workers will respond to temporary or permanent changes they may require in the way they perform work activities. They wonder about their health, worker's compensation and disability benefits.

The intentions and inherent values of each of these groups (employees, employers, health care providers and insurers) shape their response to a work disrupting illness or injury. The relationship they establish with one another and the influence of state and federal regulations further define this response. Conflicting self-interests extend the duration of disability and escalate personal, employer and insurer costs. Partnership and cooperative interaction among these groups minimize conflict and promote safe and timely return to work. Tools and procedures that promote cooperation are essential to the work return process and the management of disability.

The Medical Disability Advisor is a valuable tool and resource for promoting a successful communication exchange and working partnership among these groups. This fourth edition of the Medical Disability Advisor reflects the continued commitment of Presley Reed, MD, his colleagues at Reed Group, Ltd., and the Medical Advisory Board to provide vital information about physical and psychological conditions that may result in a disabling condition. Employers, health care providers, insurers and employees need a valid and reliable tool that helps define the expected duration of specific physical or psychological conditions. The content of this book establishes a common language and reference point for strategic information about a wide range of illnesses and injuries. The duration guidelines allow for reasonable variability and individual differences in response to an illness or injury. The Medical Disability Advisor helps guide these groups through the challenging landscapes of employee illness and injury, health care intervention, and the prevention of work disability.

Norma J. Leclair, RN, Ph.D
Executive Director
DCG Research Institute
Steven W. Leclair, Ph.D
Senior Vice President
Ability Management
Disability Consulting Group
Portland, Maine
2001

Third Edition

Increasingly, employers recognize the connection between healthy workers and company productivity. The health and productivity connection is reflected in employer concerns about the impact of absenteeism on worker productivity, company morale, and customer satisfaction as well as costs of benefits, replacement workers, recruitment, and training.

One manifestation of this new awareness is employer focus on minimizing disability and encouraging appropriate return to work behaviors through disability management programs. These programs range from integration of traditional benefits such as short-term disability, long-term disability, and workers compensation to sophisticated approaches that include wellness programs, prevention programs, and work/family solutions. An underlying philosophy driving innovations in disability management is recognition of the importance of appropriate and timely interventions that help employees regain functional abilities. Equally important are partnerships that include employers, employees, health plans, and health providers working together to achieve gains in function and to encourage return to work outcomes.

To have effective partnerships around disability management and return to work goals, there must be tools that assist employers, providers, and other participants in the disability management process to be successful in their efforts to minimize disability impact on the workplace. These tools must incorporate current quality standards, be clear and easy-to-use and reliable. The disability duration guidelines provided in *The Medical Disability Advisor* are an excellent example of such tools. These guidelines help assure a consistent approach to determining disability duration for purposes of benefits decisions. These guidelines provide a starting point from which to build a disability management program that incorporates job requirements and individual functional abilities.

The Medical Disability Advisor has been used by more than 10,000 disability management practitioners over the last seven years. These practitioners include managed care companies, insurance carriers, physicians, disability determination companies, and third party administrators, among others. This Third Edition represents an ongoing commitment to continuous improvement of tools for disability management to reflect an emphasis on function and to recognize the emergence of new disability categories. This effort makes an important contribution by providing a common basis for various stakeholders in the disability management process to discuss disability duration assessments as one component of a disability management program.

Mary Jane England, M.D.
President
Washington Business Group on Health
Washington, DC
1997

Second Edition

Disability is a challenging concept that reflects perceptions of individuals and society. *The Medical Disability Advisor* empowers its users to proactively manage disability, through an understanding of potentially disabling conditions and usual recovery times.

The costs of disability, both human and financial, are enormous. About one in every seven Americans has a disabling condition that interferes with their life activities. More than nine million people have conditions that keep them from being able to work, attend school, or maintain a household. The inability to work often results in loss of purpose and altered self-esteem. The annual disability-related costs to the nation total more than $170 billion.

The experience of disability is more related to society's willingness to accommodate and individual motivation than to any underlying impairment or limitation. Our narrow concepts of health and disability limit our potential. Lacking an adequate understanding of disease and function, we have often created barriers to recovery and self-fulfilling prophecies of an individual's inability to function.

Over the years, I have been impressed by the relative lack of correlation between impairment and disability. An individual with chronic low back pain without any objective findings may have been defined as "totally disabled," whereas another individual with profound impairments and limitations is actively involved with life and gainfully employed. Much of disability results from learned experiences, lack of adaptive skills and reinforcements from physicians, family members, attorneys, employers, and others. We can no longer accept this societal illness; the costs are too enormous.

The Medical Disability Advisor is an extraordinary resource to the understanding of injuries, illness, and the potential for disability. The use of this tool facilitates the needed paradigm shift in disability evaluation and management from a reactive model based on lack of knowledge to a proactive approach in creating futures of ability. I am tremendously impressed by the dedication and deep commitment of Presley Reed, M.D. to this process.

Many difficulties have arisen due to confusion over diagnoses and appropriateness of clinical management. *The Medical Disability Advisor* exemplifies the crucial need to translate medical knowledge into a framework usable by employers, insurers, health care organizations, and others involved in case management. It is written with its readership in mind. It provides descriptions, case management information, and disability times for the vast majority of diagnoses and procedures. Knowledge is needed for quality case management. Distinctions exist among the concepts of health, impairment, function, disability, and pain. The presence of a specific diagnosis does not imply disability. Disability refers to an activity or task that an individual cannot accomplish. It arises out of the interaction between impairment and external requirements, and the motivation of the individual and society.

The Americans with Disabilities Act, Title I has brought into focus the potential of individuals with disabilities and the roles of health care providers, employers, insurers and case managers. Physicians are to facilitate functional recovery and provide information on impairment and functioning, e.g., ability. Most physicians lack the skills needed to define disability for specific tasks, and therefore should not define disability. It is the role of the employer to provide reasonable accommodation for an individual with a disability to perform the essential functions of a job. *The Medical Disability Advisor* serves as a tool in this process. The specified recovery guidelines help in establishing a period during which individuals recover the function needed to carry out job demands. Classification levels of the U.S. Department of Labor Dictionary of Occupational Titles provide a basic frame of reference. It is incumbent upon the employer to provide reasonable accommodation. This is based on the specific functional abilities of the worker and functional demands of the essential functions of the job.

The establishment of disability duration guidelines by Dr. Reed and his Medical Advisory Board is an enormous undertaking. There is significant variability in an individual's physical experience with an illness, other conditions or health factors may make the burden of an illness more difficult, and behavioral and psychosocial issues are very important. Employers vary widely in their attitudes to employees, especially those with disabilities, and willingness to accommodate. Dr. Reed emphasizes that the disability guidelines are just that, guidelines, and that good case management is required in any disability situation.

Dr. Reed's book should be appreciated as a labor of love, a gracious gift to this field, and a powerful instrument in facilitating needed change. Our approach to disability should not be limited by our past ignorance; it should be based on knowledge and influencing the future. We are responsible for honoring the integrity of the human spirit and taking deliberate steps to fulfill potential. Through these efforts, and resources such as *The Medical Disability Advisor*, we can disable the disability process and create a future of ability for both the individual and society.

Christopher R. Brigham, M.D.
Vice President - Medical Affairs
Occupational Health Resources, Inc.
Falmouth, Maine
1994

Preface

In 1981, while working in psychiatric practice, I accepted an invitation to serve as a consultant to a pain control center. During the course of this work, I became fascinated with individuals who were away from work on extended leaves of disability when, in my opinion, subject to only minor illness or injury with little or no positive findings of organic pathology. I later had the opportunity to serve as a contract occupational physician to a large multinational corporation where my interest in the issues of medical disability, absenteeism, and employee morale in the workplace increased. I founded Reed Group, Ltd. to provide proprietary research on these issues. This work is the basis for the development of this reference text.

Disability is a complicated psychosocial problem that extends beyond the sole question of illness or injury. Many factors contribute to the complexity of the problem. They include, but are not limited to an individual's values and beliefs; the role of illness in the individual's childhood/family experience; the specific symbolic meaning of illness or injury to the individual; the individual's relationship with his/her employer; occupational alternatives available to the individual; the individual's financial situation; economic issues (the local economy, incentives associated with illness and disability); motivation and ethics of the treating health care professional; the occupational health professional or case manager's role and level of involvement; the quality of medical care and case management provided; workplace accommodations made available by the employer; and the employer's policies/practices, culture, and values

Disability is a relational concept; it does not equal functional impairment. It speaks to the issue of one's relationship to real or perceived functional impairment with other aspects of one's life. When most people think of people with disabilities, they envision individuals with dramatic functional limitations (e.g., a survivor of a catastrophic accident). This is not the case. The vast majority of people with disabilities have minimal objective findings on careful medical evaluation and appear to the outside observer to be "whole." Pain for example, the most common disabling condition, is impossible for another person to observe or measure directly.

In assessing a potential "disability" case, one must examine not only the individual but also the context in which the problem is occurring. Managing medical disability by utilizing disability duration guidelines based upon diagnosis or procedure is, admittedly, an imperfect approach. However, when used judicially, taking into account the totality of information about the employee's medical condition and the work environment, as well as the accommodations available, their use can yield surprising results. The benefits accrue not just to the employer, but to the employee as well. It results in better, more timely medical care, earlier return to productive endeavor, and more satisfied, productive employees.

Reed Group's research and experience in the workplace repeatedly demonstrates that workers who feel valued as people and for their contributions are more reliable and productive. Workers who are treated with respect and who are recognized for their efforts, continually work to reconfirm their value within the organization, even in the event of illness or injury. In so doing, they strengthen their own self-worth and self-esteem as workers. This is substantiated by the fact that millions of men and women continue to perform productive work in spite of significant emotional or physical discomfort and/or impairments. On the other hand, workers who feel "used" and unappreciated make few strides to return to productive endeavor when disabling illnesses or injuries occur.

Employees better understand their value, and respond accordingly when employers demonstrate sincere concern about the worker's well being. The employer's concern can be communicated in all areas of the business and may be manifested in many different forms. An attentive employer might provide a recovering employee with additional days off, beyond the normal guidelines, to insure full recovery. The employer might make provisions to allow an employee to return to work early with medical consultation and specific accommodations for the employee's medical condition (e.g., a temporary, less physically demanding job or part-time position). Workplace accommodations offer proven dividends to both the employer and the employee.

The multifaceted nature of medical disability made the development and revision of a comprehensive reference tool challenging. Degree of disability can be greatly influenced by the individual's state of mind. These guidelines cannot measure one of the most important "state of mind" variables in the determination of disability, the individual's motivation. Motivational factors are commonly overlooked when assessing disability. As a result, disability evaluations seldom reflect the employee's motivation to return to full-time, productive endeavor. We have all seen and admired workers who have significant physical disabilities and perform to the limits of their capacities. Likewise, we have seen workers who are seemingly normal on examination, but are unable to perform any productive work.

These guidelines are not intended to be used as a device to coerce workers back to work when, for whatever reason, they are unable to perform their normal duties. Moreover, it is hoped that this tool will not be used to legitimize disability for those who lack motivation to reassume their workplace responsibilities.

The Medical Disability Advisor is intended to be used as a tool against which the user should weigh the totality of his or her available knowledge and the specific case information. These guidelines should always be used in conjunction with the combined information available regarding the individual case (e.g., specific medical condition, the ongoing medical record and treatment program, the nature of the job itself, availability of employer-provided workplace accommodations) when attempting to determine the appropriate length of disability.

October 1994

The wide acceptance of the First and Second Editions encouraged our development of a much more detailed and precise document. The improvements in the Third Edition represent input from MDA users and many thousands of hours of research. It is our hope that all users of these guidelines will continue to provide us with comments and suggestions, and participate in ongoing research designed to further improve, refine, and validate this tool.

Medicine is an inexact and ever changing science. New medical technologies and more effective treatments, as well as better understanding of the most important psychosocial factors that affect disability, will alter our future perceptions and expectations of the disability phenomenon and render our current thinking obsolete.

The Medical Disability Advisor reflects current knowledge and will continue to expand and improve in successive editions. *The Medical Disability Advisor* is a tool and a tool is only as good as its user. Please use this tool judiciously, tempering your decisions with thoughtfulness and compassion.

November 1997

It has been ten years since Reed Group published the First Edition of *The Medical Disability Advisor*. Over the years, much has changed, though much has remained the same.

Employers continue to struggle with employee absenteeism from all causes, and with the associated challenges of maintaining productivity.

Employees continue to search for meaning and relevance in their work, while trying to balance the multiple demands of a faster paced technological society.

In the United States, new regulations have been passed to assist workers. The Americans with Disabilities Act requires employers to reasonably accommodate workers at their job. Likewise, the Family Medical Leave Act provides opportunity for workers to care for themselves or their family members in circumstances of serious illness.

Disability management programs have become the norm and *The Medical Disability Advisor* has become an integral tool within the industry. Nevertheless, lost time incidence and average length of disability have not significantly changed.

Social forces, economic incentives (and disincentives), home life issues, the economy, safety and ergonomic conditions, employee morale, labor relations conditions, and employee motivation continue to be major factors that have an impact on disability experience.

The Fourth Edition offers many new additions and improvements, and although *The Medical Disability Advisor* is the most comprehensive resource available, it is still only a tool. *The MDA*, like any other tool, has its limitations.

No reference text can take into account all of the important variables that may potentially have an impact on any individual medical case. No text can (or should) attempt to mandate the recommendations of the treating caregiver. No text can (or should) substitute for the strategy agreed upon by the patient and their caregiver.

We urge you to use this tool in the manner in which it was conceived—with prudence, compassion, and thoughtfulness. When using this tool, treat everyone the way you, yourself, would like to be treated.

March, 2001

Acknowledgments

I wish to thank the talented group of dedicated individuals who put forth extraordinary efforts to produce *The Medical Disability Advisor*, Fourth Edition. As with previous editions, Stacey Grace served as a consulting editor on this project and took responsibility to oversee many of the interrelated details associated with this ambitious undertaking. She worked closely with Rebecca Wiard who, once again, contributed her invaluable management and professional editing skills to this project. The Fourth Edition would not have been as comprehensive without Rebecca's devoted commitment, admirable work ethic, and tireless service. Mike Hellem designed and engineered the MDA database, into which all contributors submitted their work via the Internet. He worked with Kamolrat Therawat who developed the web pages that interfaced with the MDA database. Mike developed automated merge protocols to "programmagically" transport the information from the database onto the printed page. He and Louis Burkhardt devised the means to take this compiled information into the book publishing software, in consultation with Larry Prado and Rick Quatro. Additionally, Louis contributed his expertise to the overall design and final page layout of the book—a layout that was guided in its early stages by the artistic sensibility of Bo Hick. Louis' excellent work is evident on every page. Kathi Solt Dangerfield coordinated the collection, compilation and analysis of the normative data graphs. The reader will appreciate her significant contribution to the Fourth Edition and the notable improvements in this regard. She worked closely with Tom Gatliffe and Bill Stange on the data analysis and graph presentation. Cecile Childrose, Denise Mayrer, and members of their nurse case management team provided invaluable consultation and research to greatly improve the Fourth Edition's content and continuity. Ginny Landes, Lucy Shannon, and PJ Gieseman coordinated the draft manuscript distribution to the members of the Medical Advisory Board and provided necessary support to bring the project to completion. Jennifer Ziedses des Plantes and Randy Roark proofread this work with painstaking attention to detail. Laurie O'Keefe and Frank Forney provided exceptional illustrations that add beauty to this work. Jeff Katz worked with PageWorks Communications on the cover design. I also wish to acknowledge all of the Reed Group staff members who attended to the other lines of business to ensure that the guidelines team could focus on completion of the Fourth Edition. Thank you.

My friend and colleague, Chris Brigham, MD, graciously agreed to serve as Chairman of the Medical Advisory Board for the Fourth Edition. He assembled an international, multidisciplinary team of medical professionals to review and improve this work. He coordinated their advice and recommendations. He oversaw six Associate Chairpersons, Doctors Bill Boucher, Charley Brooks, Leon Ensalada, Norma Leclair, Gideon Letz, and Jim Talmage, who performed meritoriously under his supervision in the face of difficult deadlines. The members of the Medical Advisory Board gave graciously of their time and exponentially improved this edition. I wish to thank Alan Koral for his clear, concise and comprehensive section on the FMLA, ADA, and workers' compensation.

Finally, it is you, our customers, we ultimately wish to thank. Your important ideas and suggestions continue to improve the MDA guidelines with each new edition. It is our sincere hope that we have met your highest expectations.

Overview

The Medical Disability Advisor: Workplace Guidelines for Disability Duration (MDA) developed and revised by Reed Group, is the world's most comprehensive set of disability management guidelines. This single-source reference provides disability duration figures for normal recovery periods and natural language descriptions on the most common illnesses and injuries of working people.

The Fourth Edition provides comprehensive information on each diagnosis and procedure including:

- Injury, illness or treatment name in alphabetical order with ICD-9 code(s)
- Descriptive text written in concise, straightforward language and displayed in a user-friendly format
- Diagnostic criteria (history, physical exam, tests)
- Potential treatment protocols for medical conditions or a list of reasons why specific procedures are performed
- Possible complications
- Predicted outcome or prognosis
- Suggestions for appropriate work restrictions and accommodations
- Other diagnoses (differential diagnoses)
- Recommendations on appropriate rehabilitation therapies, frequency, and duration of treatment
- Appropriate specialists for treatment, referral, and independent medical examination
- Comorbid conditions that may impact disability duration
- Important factors that may influence length of disability
- Complementary and alternative therapies
- MDA duration tables that provide minimum, optimum, and maximum disability duration expectancies based on job classifications
- Summarized normative data displayed in bar graphs and line graphs for more than 200 of the most common injuries and illnesses
- Illustrations to assist the user in understanding the anatomy of an injury, or why the medical condition may be disabling
- List of questions the reader may wish to reference when an individual fails to recover within the maximum duration
- List of references for each topic

Development Process

Reed Group is committed to the continuous improvement of *The Medical Disability Advisor*. During the time between publication of editions, Reed Group collects information from the users of this tool in order to improve and refine this reference. A description of the research and development process follows:

Data collection and topic identification.

Building on the content of previous editions, Reed Group collects data and solicits input from its users to identify high frequency injuries, illnesses and medical/surgical procedures (affecting working people) to be researched and included in the next edition.

Research and writing of descriptive copy.

Clinical researchers and writers draft material for review by medical editors to ensure medical accuracy, and text editors review each topic to ensure consistent writing style.

Cleansing, and analysis of duration data.

Reed Group's Fourth Edition database contains more than 3.5 million disability cases. The methodology for cleansing and analyzing these data is described in greater detail under "Development of the Disability Duration Tables."

Development of draft duration tables.

Based on the data analysis findings and the Third Edition tables, draft duration tables for each diagnosis and procedure are developed by Reed Group.

Production of draft manuscripts.

Draft manuscripts are produced by merging text and draft duration tables from the writers/editors database into diagnostic categories for distribution to the members of the Medical Advisory Board.

Medical Advisory Board review of draft manuscripts.

Nearly 100 physicians, occupational health nurses, and adjunct health care professionals participated in the review process. Attention was focused on consistency, completeness, and accuracy. Dr. Chris Brigham served as MAB Chair for the Fourth Edition.

Consolidation of Medical Advisory Boards input.

Six Associate Chairs reviewed the edits and comments from the Medical Advisory Board members. Each Associate Chair consolidated the modifications, recommendations, and edits from these reviewers into a single draft. Their drafts were reviewed by Doctors Reed and Brigham for inclusion in this edition.

Publication of the final manuscript.

After all edits were completed, the book was assembled by integrating the text, duration tables, illustrations, and normative data graphs. Indexes, appendix, and other sections were then added.

The information published in *The Medical Disability Advisor* represents the combined efforts of many individuals and may not necessarily represent the opinions of individual contributors or reviewers.

Understanding *The Medical Disability Advisor*

The Medical Disability Advisor is designed for use by medical and nonmedical professionals whose positions require familiarity with the injuries and illnesses of working people. This reference provides general guidelines that can be used to alert those working in the areas of medical disability to important points in time during the recovery process when review of the individual's case is desirable (such as to ensure delivery of appropriate, timely medical care to assist individuals return to productive endeavors when and if they are medically able to do so).

The Medical Disability Advisor, Fourth Edition provides information in a predictable order within each topic. Specific information is set apart in color-coded boxes to help the reader identify those entries at a glance. The following illustrations provide a guide to the structure of a sample topic:

1 Topic Name: Descriptive name of each diagnosis or procedure
Other Names / Synonyms: List of common names for each diagnosis or procedure
ICD-9-CM: List of applicable International Classification of Disease Codes for the topic

2 Definition
Descriptive text that defines each illness, injury or treatment including basic epidemiological information, possible causative agent, basic signs and symptoms, and the prevalence of the condition.

3 Illustration (where appropriate)
Full-color line drawing depicting relevant anatomy of the medical condition, procedure, or injury.

4 Diagnosis (for Diagnoses) or **Reason for Procedure** (for Procedures)
For each Diagnosis topic, desciption of diagnostic criteria (history, physical exam, tests) used to confirm the diagnosis. For each Procedure topic, a description of why a specific procedure or therapy is used.

5 Treatment (for Diagnoses) or **Description** (for Procedures)
Description of the procedures that may be utilized to treat the condition including occupational or physical therapy or surgical repair or removal. For Procedures, a description of how the medical or surgical procedure is performed.

6 Prognosis
Description of predicted outcome or expectation for recovery when the individual follows the prescribed treatment. When applicable, the prognosis section also includes survival or mortality rates.

7 Differential Diagnosis (Diagnoses only)
Examples of other medical conditions that may present with similar signs and symptoms.

8 Specialists
List of specialists that may be involved in the diagnosis, treatment, or independent medical examination for any medical condition, or may be qualified to perform the medical or surgical procedure.

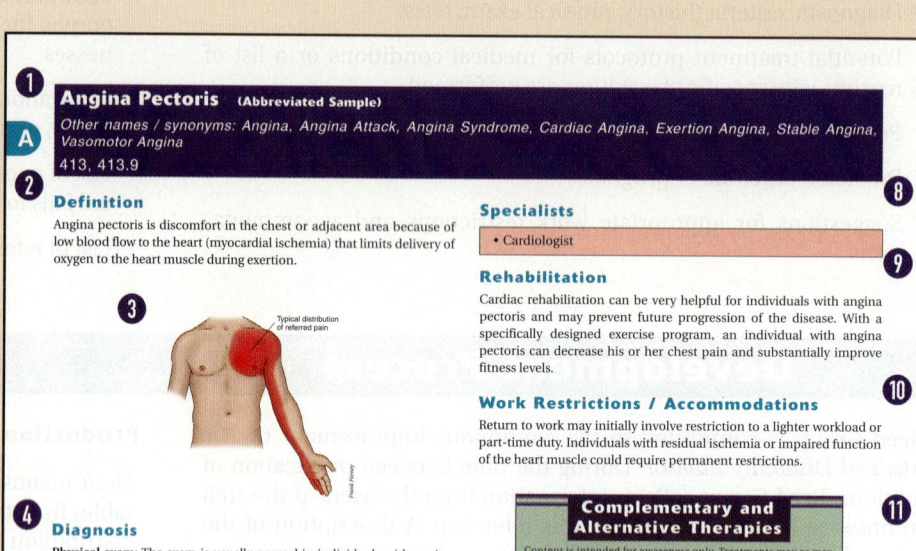

⑨ Rehabilitation
Description of applicable rehabilitation methods that may be employed to assist in successful recovery and return to work. Information on the frequency and duration of rehabilitation therapies is also included.

⑩ Work Restrictions / Accommodations
List of possible work restrictions and accommodations that may be employed when an individual is medically able to return to work in a modified duty capacity.

⑪ Complementary and Alternative Therapies (where appropriate)
Description of therapies intended for awareness purposes only. Treatments may or may not be effective. Scientific evidence may be lacking and some substances have potentially toxic effects. The editors do not endorse the use of these therapies in the absence of consultation with a licensed medical professional.

⑫ Comorbid Conditions
List of coexisting or pre-existing medical conditions that may adversely impact the individual's ability to recover and may lengthen disability.

⑬ Complications
List of complications for each medical condition or procedure that may possibly occur and/or influence recovery time.

⑭ Factors Influencing Duration
The ability to return to work depends on the type and outcome of treatment, complications from treatment, severity of any residual symptom, or any other medical conditions, and demands of the individual's occupation.

⑮ Length of Disability
Description of issues that may impact the expected recovery period or when a disability may be permanent.

⑯ Duration Tables
Minimum, optimum, and maximum disability duration expectancy figures based on the amount of physical effort required to perform a job

⑰ Duration Graphs
Graphs depict actual observed experience of individuals across the spectrum of physical conditions, in various industries, with or without case management. Also, the percent of cases that progressed to long term disability.

⑱ Failure to Recover
List of questions the reader may wish to reference to assist in better understanding the specifics of an individual's medical condition when they fail to recover within the maximum duration expectancy period.

⑲ References
Bibliography of textbooks, journals, Internet web sites, and other resources used to develop the material for each topic.

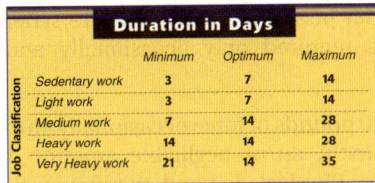

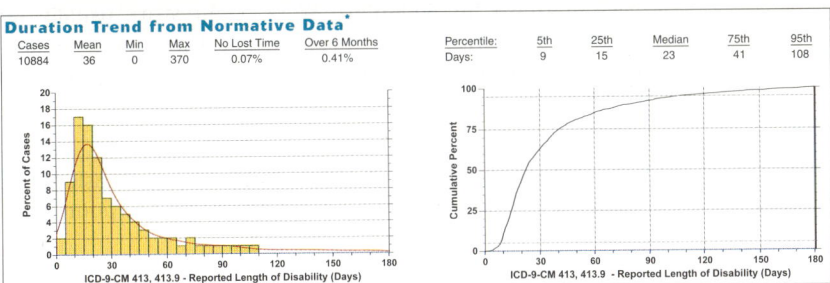

⑱ Failure to Recover
If an individual fails to recover within the maximum duration expectancy period, the reader may wish to reference the following questions to assist in better understanding the specifics of an individual's medical case.

Regarding diagnosis:
- Does individual have a history of coronary artery disease? Other risk factors for angina? Is there a family history of heart disease?
- Has individual worn an ambulatory Holter monitor to record the ECG for a 24-hour period?
- Have perfusion scintigraphy, radionuclide angiography, or two-dimensional echocardiography been performed?
- Was selective coronary angiography required to confirm the diagnosis?

- Was the diagnosis of angina pectoris confirmed?

Regarding treatment:
- Does individual sit down as soon as discomfort begins and remains quiet until pain stops?
- Could individual benefit from a less demanding job situation, either physically or emotionally? Would individual benefit from participation in a cardiac rehabilitation program?

Regarding prognosis:
- Has individual developed worsening symptoms (unstable angina)?
- How severe is the ischemia and how many vessels are involved?
- Have any complications occurred such as heart attack or arrhythmia?

⑲ References

Ades, Philip A. "Cardiac Rehabilitation and Secondary Prevention." Textbook of Cardiovascular Medicine. Topol, Eric J., ed. Philadelphia: Lippincott-Raven Publishers, 1998. 263-282.

Anderson, D.J., C. Jenkins, and C. McInally. "Using Spinal Cord Stimulation to Manage Angina Pain." Dimensions of Critical Care Nursing 18.3 (1999): 12-13.

Loop, Floyd D. "Coronary Artery Bypass Surgery." Textbook of Cardiovascular Medicine. Topol, Eric J., ed. Philadelphia: Lippincott-Raven Publishers, 1998. 2011-2031.

Luckmann, J., and K.C. Sorensen. Medical-Surgical Nursing. Philadelphia: W.B. Saunders Company, 1987.

Angina Pectoris (Abbreviate Sample) 3

Disability Duration Tables

For more than a decade, Reed Group has developed and published *The Medical Disability Advisor* containing its highly regarded duration tables. As in previous editions, the Fourth Edition provides disability duration tables whenever practical, based on the nature of the disease or procedure. The revised disability duration tables in this edition provide benchmark information on expected lengths of disability.

The duration tables in *The Medical Disability Advisor* are physiologically-based. The disability duration figures do not merely reflect actuarial experience, but rather provide expectancy figures for normal recovery from a medical condition, injury or procedure. *The Medical Disability Advisor* is so widely used and accepted based on this important distinction. The terms used in these tables are defined below for the reader's reference:

Example:

Job Classification	Duration in Days		
	Minimum	Optimum	Maximum
Sedentary work	42	56	112
Light work	42	56	112
Medium work	56	70	140
Heavy work	56	84	140
Very Heavy work	56	112	168

MDA Guidelines

The MDA guideline tables provide minimum, optimum, and maximum recovery time by job classification. The duration data is most useful when envisioned as a continuum in the case management process. The continuum extends from the minimum time required for most individuals to return to work to the maximum time when additional information should be obtained from the treating physician.

These values do not represent the absolute minimum or maximum lengths of disability at which an individual must or should return to work. Rather, they represent important points in time at which, if full recovery has not occurred, additional evaluation should take place. These values are designed to allow for individual differences in recovery time based on the numerous variables that impact disability duration. The duration-specific terms are defined below:

Minimum The minimum recovery time most individuals require to return to work at the same performance level as prior to injury or illness. In some cases, individuals may be medically able to return to work in a lesser amount of time (such as with job accommodations provided by the employer, with medical supervision, availability of modified duty assignments, company policies and practices).

Optimum The point in time when most individuals who do not experience significant complications or comorbid medical conditions and whose cases are optimally managed by their provider, are likely to be able to return to work.

Maximum The recommended point in time at which (or before) additional case information should be requested from the treating physician to determine when (and if) the disabled individual may be able to return to work. Suggested information to be collected includes specific information on the presence of comorbid conditions or complications, work accommodations available, and medical treatment administered. The maximum length of disability is not a definitive cutoff point beyond which individuals must return to work at the same level of efficiency as prior to their injury or illness.

Job Classification

In many duration tables, five job classifications are displayed. These job classifications are based on the amount of physical effort required to perform the work. The classifications correspond to the Strength Factor classifications described in the United States Department of Labor's *Dictionary of Occupational Titles*. The following definitions are quoted directly from that publication.

Sedentary Work Exerting up to 10 pounds of force occasionally and/or a negligible amount of force frequently or constantly to lift, carry, push, pull, or otherwise move objects, including the human body. Sedentary work involves sitting most of the time, but may involve walking or standing for brief periods of time. Jobs are sedentary if walking and standing are required only occasionally and other sedentary criteria are met.

Light Work Exerting up to 20 pounds of force occasionally an/or up to 10 pounds of force frequently, an/or negligible amount of force constantly to move objects. Physical demand requirements are in excess of those for Sedentary Work. Light Work usually requires walking or standing to a significant degree. However, if the use of the arm and/or leg controls requires exertion of forces greater than that for Sedentary Work and the worker sits most the time, the job is rated Light Work.

Medium Work Exerting up to 50 pounds of force occasionally, an/or up to 20 pounds of force frequently, and/or up to 10 pounds of forces constantly to move objects.

Heavy Work Exerting up to 100 pounds of force occasionally, an/or in excess of 50 pounds of force frequently, an/or in excess of 20 pounds of force constantly to move objects.

Very Heavy Work Exerting in excess of 100 pounds of force occasionally, and/or in excess of 50 pounds of force frequently, and/or in excess of 20 pounds of force constantly to move objects.

The Department of Labor job classifications focus on physical effort only. This may not be relevant to the duration of some disability.

In addition to pounds of force, other important factors contribute to the definition of an individual's job classification. These factors include posture, biomechanics (size, shape, and manageability of the object being moved), height from and to which the object is lifted, and frequency of exertion. Each of these factors (and any other job-specific requirements) should be considered when determining expected length of disability.

The MDA duration table guidelines represent a unique combination of methodologies that have resulted in the development of practical, usable guidelines. In edition to the MDA guideline tables, the Fourth Edition also provides graphical representation of the normative data. These graphs are described on the next page for the reader's reference.

Normative Data Graphs

Disability duration graphs were created for approximately 300 different ICD-9-CM codes. Specific ICD-9 codes (or, in some cases, ICD-9 code groups) were selected for display in the normative data graphs based on both their relative frequency and overall significance to workplace absence.

A bar graph and a line graph are provided for each of the selected conditions and procedures. One graph depicts the density of cases per duration; the other represents the cumulative percentage of the cases.

Differences may exist between the expected duration tables and the normative graphs. Duration tables provide expected recovery periods based on the type of work performed by the individual. The normative graphs reflect the actual observed experience of many individuals across the spectrum of physical conditions, in a variety of industries, and with varying levels of case management.

The sample graphs below provide explanation for the statistical values they utilize.

Bar Graph

The bar graph shows the percent of total cases at each duration value in the normative dataset. Each bar represents a 5-day period, and the line demonstrates the relative density of the data.

In the example, 4% of the cases for ICD-9-CM codes 490 and 491.9 had a disability duration between 1 and 5 days.

❶ "Cases" .... The total number of cases in the normative dataset with this clinical diagnosis or procedure.

❷ "Mean" .... The average duration of the total cases for the clinical diagnosis or procedure.

❸ "Min"/"Max" .... The lowest and highest durations found in the normative data for this clinical diagnosis or procedure.

❹ "No Lost Time" .... Percent of cases in the dataset that recorded no lost time.

❺ "Over 6 Months" ..... Percent of cases that had a duration of greater than 6 months. In some instances, the case may have progressed to long-term disability.

Line Graph

The line graph shows the cumulative frequency distribution and plots the percentage of cases falling in or below a specific duration. In the example, although the range of durations is between 0 and 352 days, 95% of the cases had a duration of less than 67 days.

❻ "Percentile" .... The percentiles show the average duration for the 5th, 25th, 50th, 75th and 95th percent of the cases in the normative database for this diagnosis or procedure.

❼ "Median" .... The median represents the 50%, or middle value, of the dataset arranged in numerical order. The median value is important as it is not affected by cases with disability durations that may be significantly higher or lower then normally expected.

Sample Normative Data Graphs

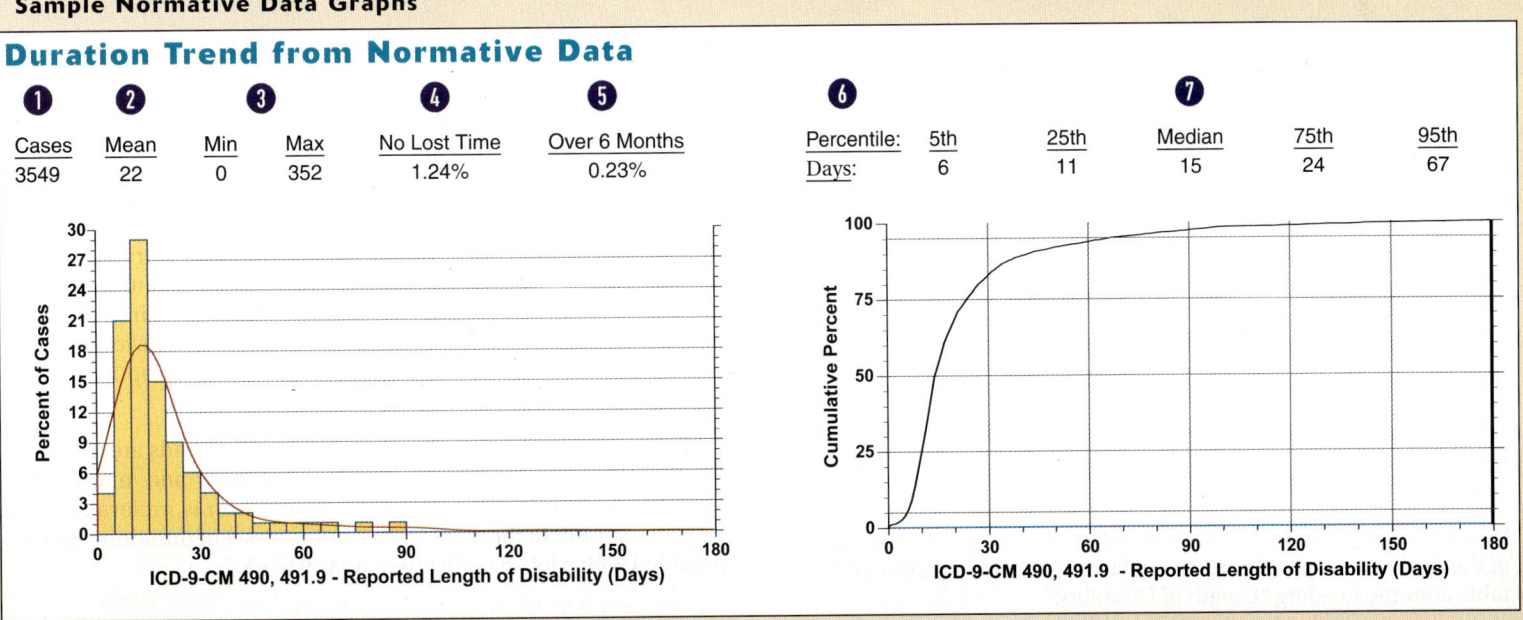

Development of the Disability Duration Tables

Reed Group used a two-step process in the development of the MDA disability duration tables.

Draft Duration Table Development

Reed Group collected data on more than 3.5 million workplace absence cases from multinational companies and government organizations to compile the normative database for the Fourth Edition. Reed Group's database consists of actual workplace absence data from a wide range of industries and geographic locations. In order to represent the most objective, accurate, and reliable view of disability duration, Reed Group's data set includes organizations that manage disability as well as those without case management services.

The respective data sets were integrated into one common database after extensive data quality investigation and normalizing to ensure compatibility of data elements and record constructs. The goal was to capture high integrity measures of total days per disability absence by clinical condition; therefore the focus was on the accuracy of day accounting and consistency in diagnostic and procedural coding.

Various types of records were excluded from the combined database based on the following criteria: family medical leave cases, disqualified cases, cases without an end date, records with incomplete days or clinical information, and cases opened and/or closed outside of the reporting period. The resulting data covered absences from a 10-year time span (1990-2000).

Reed Group's diagnostic grouper featured a hierarchical topology, with the ability to capture broad to very specific clinical coding detail. In a mutually exclusive process, the clinical information in the absence record was matched on one or more grouper levels. A full complement of statistics was produced for statistically significant groups with at least 150 absences or more.

The normative data was used as a "starting point" for development of the clinical recovery expectancy figures featured in the disability duration tables. In some instances, the normative data corresponds to the clinical recommendations in the disability duration tables. However, in other cases the normative data shows a considerably longer recovery period than would normally be expected for individuals with a specific medical condition and appropriate case management. We can speculate that these differences relate to the medical specifics of a case and to the other factors influencing disability, as described in each topic. In addition, variations in or lack of case management services between organizations can greatly affect individual disability duration.

Medical Advisory Board Review

Reed Group duration guidelines are based on clinical judgment and experience informed by statistical data, rather than being simply derived from statistical profiling. Clinical assessment as to the minimum, optimum, and maximum expectancies of a disability duration is the most constant variable in predicting a length of disability.

Other variables, such as an individual's motivation, benefit structure, and corporate culture (discussed below), may also affect the duration of a disability absence, but cannot be fully accounted for in evaluating normative data sets. Thus, using normative data to establish duration guidelines (such as at the 75th percentile) does not adequately address the issue of "the appropriate duration" for a specific case. Instead, it provides a profile of historical durations without regard to the many factors affecting the duration of a disability.

Despite its limitations, statistical profiling can provide important information in establishing guidelines. Duration tables for the relevant diagnoses and procedures were developed using the information from Reed Group's database. These data were then reviewed and modified by the members of the Medical Advisory Board, whose input was used to establish the final disability duration guidelines.

Cumulative percentile graphs on disability duration for more than 300 diagnostic codes or groups are included to assist the reader evaluate disability management effectiveness. The graphs include a calculated mean and median for the diagnostic group. The percentage of cases that exceeded 182 days and may have progressed to long term disability cases is also displayed.

MDA Duration Table Notes

Expected Length of Disability

"Calendar days" are represented by the number of days provided in each disability duration table.

A minimum length of disability of "0" days indicates that, in some cases, an individual may not need to miss any work based on the diagnosis or procedure. Individuals may miss work for diagnosis and treatment of a medical condition, but this may not result in a disability event.

When a medical condition or treatment requires hospitalization, the length of disability starts after hospital discharge unless otherwise noted above the duration table.

When disability duration cannot be established based on the nature of the diagnosis or procedure, an explanatory note is substituted for a table after the heading "Length of Disability."

Psychiatric Diagnoses

Some Medical Advisory Board members expressed concerns about using the terms "minimum," "optimal," and "maximum" duration for the psychiatric diagnoses. Unfortunately, the MDA duration figures are sometimes used in a manner that is inconsistent with their intended use, as defined above. The terminology used in the psychiatric duration tables remains consistent with others. However, we ask that the reader to review the definitions of minimum, optimum, and maximum duration expectancies.

Additionally, it was determined that physical demands are irrelevant to disability duration for psychiatric diagnoses and many other medical conditions where strength classification is irrelevant to the recovery period. In those instances, only one set of duration figures is provided with a job classification of "Any Work."

Factors That Influence Length of Disability

The disability duration guidelines provided in this work are just that, guidelines. There are many factors that may influence length of disability for a specific diagnosis or procedure. While it is impossible to take into account all of the factors that may affect the course of recovery and/or ultimate outcome of a disease process for an individual, some of the most important factors to consider are listed below:

Psychological Factors

An individual's motivation to return to work is critically important to determining length of disability and the final recovery outcome. Factors such as the individual's work environment, the type of work, the attitude of the employer toward employees, the individual's coworkers, and the meaning of work to the individual, will all influence an individual's motivation to return to work. Pre-existing psychological conditions, meaning of the illness or injury to the individual, and prior experience with illness or injury may also influence the length of disability.

Finally, an individual who is highly motivated to return to work should not be permitted to return until he or she is medically able to do so. Returning too early to one's job after an illness or injury may result in a recurrence of the disability and ultimately prolong the disability period.

Variability within a Diagnosis

Often times, there are discrepancies in disability recovery periods among individuals with the same illness, injury, or undergoing the same procedure or surgery. Some reasons for the variability may be:

- severity of the illness
- individual's response to treatment
- course of recovery
- stage at which the illness is detected and treated
- availability of effective treatment
- whether the treatment is medical or surgical
- individual's motivation

Age

An individual's age may be an important contributing factor to the course and prognosis of many injuries and diseases. Age and its relation to an individual's retirement eligibility may also affect the length of disability resulting from an injury or illness.

Complications

The presence of medical complications resulting from the primary diagnosis may significantly influence the length of disability and the predicted outcome. Possible complications are enumerated within each topic, together with the potential influence on the length of disability.

Medication

An individual may be disabled by the medical condition and/or by the medications used for treatment of the condition. Particularly with the psychiatric diagnoses, a number of medications render the individual less capable of working around heavy machinery or from heights. Narcotic analgesics, antihistamines, decongestants, muscle relaxants, and many other medications will restrict the type of work individuals can perform and may lengthen disability.

Benefit Structure

The type and structure of disability benefits available to the individual may influence an individual's motivation to return to work and, therefore, the length of disability. For example, companies with rich disability benefits may experience longer durations than companies with similar job types but less generous benefits.

Job Stability

Companies that are considering (or have announced) layoffs or downsizing are more likely to experience both an increase in the number of disabilities and potentially longer lengths of disability.

Job Demands

Disability duration may be significantly impacted by the demands put on the affected body part based on the individual's job functions.

Return to Work Programs, Availability of Modified Duty

Companies with return to work programs or policies are likely to be more effective in reducing disability duration than companies without such programs or policies. Also, the availability of modified duty can be helpful in the reduction of disability durations.

Managed Disability Programs

Managed disability programs focusing on early notification, intervention, case management, and information sharing have proven to be effective in reducing disability durations. Additional reductions in durations may be possible when managed disability programs are coordinated with medical plans.

Workplace Factors

Numerous other workplace factors may significantly influence when and if an individual can return to a job performed prior to illness or injury. These factors include the work environment (such as noise levels, exposure to weather, heat, cold, or vibration), sensory requirements associated with the job (such as hearing, visual acuity, color vision, verbal abilities), and special physical activities (such as kneeling, balancing, fingering, and climbing).

The factors that may influence disability are not included in the duration table data because to do so would be unwieldy. It would imply that a reasonable estimate of disability could be derived for a given individual from a formula containing all of these variables weighted according to their relative importance. This is not the case. Every medical disability case is unique and must be evaluated as such.

These guidelines are not a substitute for quality case management of any medical disability situation. The appropriate employer/provider interface should be in contact with the disabled worker before the maximum disability duration date is realized. When appropriate, frequent contacts with the disabled worker should be made to ensure a smooth transition from disability to maximum medical improvement and return to productive endeavor.

Terms and Conventions Used

ICD-9-CM Codes

Abbreviation for the *International Classification of Diseases, 9th Revision, Clinical Modifications.* Codes used in industry to identify diagnoses and procedures.

Disability

"Disability" refers to a state in which the individual is unable to perform his or her job at the same level of efficiency as before the illness or injury occurred. Disability is not necessarily correlated to the presence or absence of pain or other symptoms.

Length of Disability

The periods of disability enumerated in this book describe significant points in time during an evaluation and treatment process designed to return an individual to productive endeavor. The duration figures are not arbitrary times that denote how long an individual should be away from work or when an individual should absolutely return to the workplace.

Indefinite

This term replaces duration figures in some tables. It is intended to describe a length of disability that may be greater than 365 days. Additional information should be obtained from the treating physician regarding the individual's medical case. Determination of permanent disability may be made at any time within the 365 day period.

Vague Diagnosis

Refers to a diagnosis which, by itself, is insufficient to determine an expected length of disability; a more definitive diagnosis must be requested from the treating physician before a length of disability can be determined.

Reference to "Blacks"

Because of the international nature of this reference text, the term "blacks" is used instead of "African-Americans." This is consistent with the medical literature.

Features

Alphabetical Listings of Diagnoses and Procedures

Topics are displayed in alphabetical order beginning on page one of the textbook. The descriptive name coincides with the ICD-9 code(s) listed below the name. Often times, the ICD-9 descriptive name is not the name most commonly used to describe the medical condition or procedure. An example of this is Lou Gehrig's Disease which is listed in the MDA under Amyotrophic Lateral Sclerosis.

Alphabetical Index

The Alphabetical Index includes all topic names and synonyms for the diagnoses and procedures covered in this edition. An example of its usefulness is that a user can locate Reflex Sympathetic Dystrophy which is described as Complex Regional Pain Syndrome.

ICD-9 Code Numerical Index

When you only know the ICD-9 code for the condition or procedure, use the ICD-9 index to locate the diagnosis or procedure from the numeric list. ICD-9 codes are listed in numerical order. Each line contains the ICD-9 code, the descriptive name, and the corresponding page number(s). CPT codes are not cross-referenced in the Fourth Edition.

ICD-9-CM to ICD-10 Codes Translator Index

This index provides a direct translation of the ICD-9-CM codes to the corresponding ICD-10 codes for the user's reference. The ICD-10 codes are in active use outside the US at the time of publication.

Complementary / Alternative Therapies

Content in this new section is intended for awareness purposes only. Increasingly, patients are seeking non-traditional or alternative forms of treatment that are listed within relevant topics. The treatments described may or may not be effective. Scientific evidence may be lacking and some substances have potentially toxic effects. The editors and reviewers of this work do not endorse the use of these therapies in the absence of consultation with a licensed medical professional.

Failure to Recover

In the Fourth Edition, a list of reference questions is provided for use in the event that an individual fails to recover within the maximum duration expectancy period. They are intended to be used to assist the reader gain a better understanding of the individual's medical case specifics.

Glossary of Terms

Whenever possible, straightforward language has been used in the text, sometimes followed by the corresponding medical term in parentheses. For individuals who may not understand a medical term used in the guidelines, an extensive glossary provides definitions for medical terminology used in this edition.

Managing Medical Absence

An appendix written by Alan Koral on the interaction among ADA, FMLA, Workers' Compensation and Disability Benefits Law is provided in this edition. It provides a comprehensive summary of these important legislative concerns.

Common Usage

More than 10,000 multinational employers, insurance carriers, workers' compensation boards, government agencies, third party administration firms, labor organizations, occupational health professionals, and others use *The Medical Disability Advisor* in the US and in sixteen countries. Following is general information on the use of *The Medical Disability Advisor* guidelines:

Disability Duration Tables

To make projections on case or claim duration

Compare actual estimated return to work date (prognosis date) to duration expectancy data

Calculate days saved against duration expectancy data

Assess risk and risk pooling

Normative Case Experience

Display actual case duration data with the MDA normative data as well as the duration expectancy figures

Estimate the percentage of cases that may progress to long term disability based on normative data percentages

Factors that Influence Disability

A discussion of the factors that may influence length of disability is included under each diagnosis and procedure. This general information is important to consider in the context of the data displayed in the disability duration tables. It may be helpful to insert portions of this information in reports whenever duration data is included.

Provider Experience Profiles

Track actual case experience by provider versus MDA guidelines to demonstrate on a case-by-case basis which providers may consistently exceed normal duration expectancies.

Treatment

Information in the Treatment section may be used to evaluate the treatment plan provided by the attending physician. This section provides general information on the treatment of a medical condition. It may be helpful to insert portions of this information in the treatment section of reports. Treatment methods are constantly changing for many medical conditions. As such, this published information should only be used as a guideline in the assessment of individual treatment.

Prognosis

Information in the Prognosis section may be used to evaluate the predicted outcome provided by the attending physician. This section provides general prognosis information for a medical condition. It may be helpful to include portions of this information in the medical outlook section of reports.

Work Restrictions and Accommodations

Users may reference the information in this section to make suggestions for return-to-work to the work site contact. This section provides general information on possible work restrictions that may be appropriate and accommodations that may be recommended for a given medical condition. It may be helpful to insert portions of this information in the vocational section of a report.

Differential Diagnosis

Based on the specifics of the case provided by the patient or others, a diagnosis may not seem reasonable. Information in the differential diagnosis section may provide suggestions to the user on other possible diagnoses to explore with the individuals involved in the case or to an independent medical examiner.

Rehabilitation

This section provides general rehabilitation information for a medical condition. Information in this section may be used to evaluate the rehabilitation plan provided by the attending physician or to help assist in scheduling appropriate rehabilitation therapies for the injured or ill patient.

Medical Specialists

A list of appropriate specialists for treatment, referral or independent medical examination is provided for diagnoses and procedures in this edition. A comprehensive description of each of the specialties is also provided on the following pages.

Patient Education

The Fourth Edition is written in straightforward language and can be used for patient education after diagnosis. Some of the descriptions include illustrations that can help the injured or ill individual better understand the medical condition. In some cases, users may wish to provide the individual with the written text and exclude the disability duration tables.

Provider Education

It is most often helpful to work cooperatively with the attending physician to resolve case issues and to address cases in a non-adversarial manner. For some cases, it may be helpful to provide the treating physician with a copy of *The Medical Disability Advisor* write-up so that you can both "read from the same page" in the resolution of the case. It is our experience that the treating physician is usually receptive to receiving a copy of the guidelines. This gives the user an opportunity to open up a dialogue about secondary diagnoses and/or comorbid conditions that may be having an adverse impact on an individual's ability to return to work. Likewise, providers have shared with us that the information is helpful to them as they can present it to those patients (the physician's customers, after all) who may be asking them to extend a period of disability beyond what they believe is reasonable for the circumstances of the case.

Specialists

The appropriate specialists for treatment, referral, or independent examination are listed for the reader within each topic. Following are descriptions of the specialties and sub-specialties for the reader's reference.

Some of the following definitions have been reprinted with permission of the American Board of Medical Specialties (ABMS) in Evanston, Illinois. The ABMS produces and distributes a brochure entitled *Which Medical Specialist for You?* You may obtain a copy of the brochure by contacting the ABMS at 847-491-9091.

A "medical doctor" is a physician who has had years of training to understand the diagnosis, treatment, and prevention of disease. The basic training of a physician specialist includes four years of premedical education in a college or university, four years of medical school, and after receiving the MD degree, at least three years of specialty training under supervision (called a "residency"). Training in additional subspecialties can take an additional two to three years.

Specialists are doctors who concentrate on certain body systems, specific age groups, or on complex scientific techniques developed to diagnose or treat certain types of disorders. Specialties in medicine developed because of the rapidly expanding body of knowledge about health and illness and the constantly evolving new treatment techniques for disease. Today, no one doctor can hope to master the total field of knowledge or maintain skills in all diagnostic tests, treatments, and procedures.

A subspecialist is a physician who has completed training in a general medical specialty and then take additional training in a more specific subarea of that specialty in that particular field. For example, cardiology is a subspecialty of internal medicine. The training of a subspecialist within a specialty requires an additional one or more years of full-time education.

Abdominal Surgeon: An abdominal surgeon is a general surgeon who surgically treats complex abdominal problems. Abdominal surgeons establish the diagnosis and provide the preoperative, operative, and postoperative care to surgical patients and are usually responsible for the comprehensive management of trauma victims and the critically ill. These surgeons treat abdominal compartment syndrome (ACS), trauma requiring damage control procedures, severe intra-abdominal infections pancreatitis (IPN), and other complex abdominal problems. They use a variety of diagnostic techniques, including endoscopy, for observing internal structures, and may use specialized instruments during operative procedures.

Advanced Practice Registered Nurse: An advanced practice nurse is a registered nurse who has a license to practice professional nursing and is specialized in one of the following areas: nurse practitioner, certified nurse-midwife, certified registered nurse anesthetist or clinical nurse specialist. Registered nurses hold a master's degree in nursing or a related health field.

Alcohol Abuse Counselor: Alcohol and drug counseling is the application of general counseling theories and treatment methods adapted to specific alcohol and drug theory for the purpose of treating alcohol and drug problems. Alcohol and drug counseling is based on pharmacology and psychopharmacology of alcohol and drugs including the effects of these drugs on violence and aggression, learning and memory, sensation and perception, sleep, sexual behavior, human growth and development, and psychiatric conditions. These counselors use various treatment models and methods including: models of treatment, relapse prevention, and continuing care; impact of treatment on problems associated with addiction; the importance of community, social, family and self-help systems. Alcohol and drug counselors are involved in clinical evaluation of drug and alcohol issues, treatment planning, counseling, and education and prevention.

Allergist-Immunologist: An allergist-immunologist is a certified internist or pediatrician with expertise in the evaluation, physical and laboratory diagnosis, and management of disorders potentially involving the immune system. Selected examples of such conditions include asthma, anaphylaxis, rhinitis, eczema, and adverse reactions to drugs, foods, and insect stings as well as immune deficiency diseases (both acquired and congenital), defects in host defense, and problems related to autoimmune disease, organ transplant or malignancies of the immune system. The scope of this specialty is ever-widening as our understanding of the immune system develops. Selected experts may receive special certification in clinical and laboratory procedures required to analyze both the function and malfunction of the immune system.

Anesthesiologist: The anesthesiologist is a physician specialist who, following medical school graduation and at least four years of postgraduate training, has the principal task of providing pain relief and maintenance, or restoration, of a stable condition during and immediately following an operation, an obstetric, or diagnostic procedure. The anesthesiologist assesses the risk of the patient undergoing surgery and optimizes the patient's condition prior to, during, and after the surgery. Anesthesiologists direct resuscitation in the care of patients with cardiac or respiratory emergencies, including the provision of artificial ventilation. They also supervise and teach others involved in anesthesia, respiratory and intensive care. Anesthesiologists may specialize in critical care and intensive care units, postanesthesia recovery rooms, and other settings.

Audiologist: Audiologists are specialists in hearing loss. They are involved in comprehensive hearing evaluations for all age groups, including hearing aid assessment, selection, and fitting. They provide ear plugs for swimming, noise reduction, and hunting. They also perform hearing conservation and industrial screenings, and tympanometry to assess middle ear function.

Cardiologist: Cardiology is a subspecialty of internal medicine. Cardiologists specialize in diseases of the heart, and circulatory system, and manage complex cardiac conditions such as heart attacks and life-threatening, abnormal heartbeat rhythms. They often perform complicated diagnostic procedures such as cardiac catheterization and consult with surgeons prior to heart surgery. The core of the specialty is the diagnosis and medical treatment of heart disease.

Cardiothoracic Surgeon: Cardiothoracic surgeon, also known as a cardiovascular surgeon, is a medical doctor who has devoted at least five years to training in general surgery after medical school, followed by an additional two to three years of specialty training in cardiothoracic surgery. Cardiothoracic surgery is surgery of the chest area, most commonly the heart and lungs. Cardiothoracic surgeons have expertise in the management of diseases of the airways, lung, esophagus, and chest wall. Typical diseases treated by cardiothoracic surgery include coronary artery disease; tumors and cancers of the lung, esophagus and chest wall; heart vessel and valve abnormalities; and birth defects involving the chest or heart. Usually, a cardiothoracic surgeon will become involved in patient care at the request of the primary care physician or specialist, typically a cardiologist or pulmonologist. These surgeons may be asked to assist in the diagnosis of a patient's condition, or to determine whether or not surgery is indicated. The surgeon reviews heart catheterization (for heart patients) or CT scans (for lung patients) and discusses the patient's case with the referring physician.

Cardiovascular Surgeon: Cardiovascular surgeons are specialized to operatively treat diseases and injuries of the heart, lungs, mediastinum, esophagus, chest wall, diaphragm, and great vessels. The most common procedure that cardiovascular surgeons perform is coronary artery bypass grafting. They are also specialized in the postoperative care of critically ill patients. Other major vascular surgery procedures such as carotid endarterectomy and aneurysm repair are performed by cardiovascular surgeons. Cardiovascular surgeons also perform heart valve replacement surgery.

Certified Nurse Midwife: A Certified Nurse-Midwife is an individual educated in the two disciplines of nursing and midwifery. They are involved in the independent management of women's health care, focusing particularly on pregnancy, childbirth, the postpartum period, care of the newborn, and the family planning and gynecological needs of women. The Certified Nurse-Midwife practices within a health care system that provides for consultation, collaborative management or referral as indicated by the health status of the client.

Chiropractor: Chiropractics is a therapy that focuses on the role of the spine and nervous system in maintaining health. Chiropractors are specialists in detecting and correcting by manual or mechanical means structural imbalance, distortion, or subluxations in the human body for the purpose of removing nerve interference. They use joint adjustments to correct structural or mechanical imbalances.

Cognitive Rehabilitation Specialist: Cognitive rehabilitation specialists are dedicated to the rehabilitation needs of adults and children with traumatic brain injury and other neurological diagnoses. They specifically address patients'' unique physical, cognitive, and adjustment difficulties that can interfere with successful living. They also assist in family education, and development of community supports and resources. Services are provided within the individual's home, school, workplace, and/or community to ensure effective intervention, immediate feedback, and successful transfer of skills in the real life settings in which the patient will engage. Cognitive rehabilitation therapy emphasizes the continuous, integrative practice of daily skills and routines in the individual's residential and community setting based on physical, cognitive, emotional and social needs of the individual through a holistic approach.

Colorectal Surgeon: A board-certified colon and rectal surgeon has completed at least five years of residency training in surgery and one additional year devoted entirely to colon and rectal surgery Colon and rectal surgeons diagnose and treat various diseases of the internal tract, colon, rectum, and anal canal by medical and surgical means. A colon and rectal surgeon can diagnose and manage anorectal conditions such as hemorrhoids, fissures (painful tears in the anal lining), abscesses and fistulae (infections located around the anus and rectum). Colon and rectal surgeons also treat problems of the intestine and colon, and perform endoscopic procedures to detect and treat conditions of the bowel lining. Polyps can often be removed during endoscopy without abdominal surgery. If cancers are detected, colon and rectal surgeons plan the surgical treatment programs and follow up with endoscopic techniques. The management of intestinal infections such as diverticulitis, bacterial colon infections and intestinal parasites is also within the proficiency of the colon and rectal surgeon.

Critical Care Specialist: Critical care training involves one to three additional years after completion of a residency in internal medicine, anesthesiology, or surgery. A critical care specialist has expertise in the management and care of critically ill patients, usually in the setting of intensive care units. These specialists have broad knowledge of the medical and surgical conditions that cause patients to be in the intensive care unit, and a specialized knowledge of the respiratory, fluid, and cardiovascular management needed to maintain these patients.

Dental Surgeon: A dental surgeon, also known as an oral surgeon, is a dentist with training in the surgical treatment of conditions of the mouth and teeth. They are often consulted for the repair of facial trauma or broken jawbones and perform more complicated tooth extractions such as wisdom tooth extraction, and the removal of broken or cracked teeth.

Dentist: A dentist is a specialist in the care of the teeth and associated structures of the oral cavity. They are concerned with prevention, diagnosis, and treatment of diseases of the teeth and gums. Dentists extract teeth, fill cavities, perform root canals, and place crowns. With additional education, some dentists further specialize in oral surgery, orthodontics or periodontics.

Dermatologist: A dermatologist is a physician who has expertise in the diagnosis and treatment of skin cancers, melanomas, moles, and other tumors of the skin, contact dermatitis, and other allergic and non allergic disorders, and in the recognition of the skin manifestations of systemic and infectious diseases. The dermatologist also has expertise in the management of cosmetic disorders of the skin such as hair loss and scars. Dermatologists perform many specialized diagnostic procedures including microscopic examination of skin biopsy specimens, cytological smears, patch tests, photo tests, potassium hydroxide (KOH) preparations, fungus cultures and other microbiologic examination of skin scrapings and secretions. Treatment methods used by dermatologists include externally applied, injected, and internal medicine, selected x-ray and ultraviolet light therapy, and a range of dermatologic surgical procedures. Among some of the techniques used by dermatologists for the correction of cosmetic defects are dermabrasion, chemical face peels, hair transplants, injections of materials into the skin for scar revision, sclerosis of vein, and laser surgery of vascular lesions of the skin, including certain birth marks.

Diagnostic Radiologist: Diagnostic radiology is a branch of radiology that deals with the utilization of all modalities of radiant energy in medical diagnoses and therapeutic procedures utilizing radiologic guidance. This includes, but is not restricted to, imaging techniques and methodologies utilizing radiations emitted by x-ray tubes, radionuclides, ultrasonographic devices, and the radiofrequency electromagnetic radiation emitted by atoms. Diagnostic radiologists are trained to read x-rays, ultrasound, CT scans, MRI, and PET scans.

Dietary Advisor: Dietary advisors oversee the diets of individuals from hospital patients to those in the community. They evaluate dietetic standards, sanitation, and safety. They work closely with professional and administrative representatives of medical facilities to coordinate their nutritional medicine operations. They also act as nutritional consultants to nursing homes, schools and child care centers. They work with physicians and their patients to develop nutritionally balanced and therapeutic menus, and track patients' progress.

Emergency Medicine Physician: Emergency medicine physicians are trained to manage acute illness and injury in all age groups. Physical diagnosis and the use of medical and surgical therapeutic modalities are an integral part of this specialty. Emergency medicine physicians are trained to stabilize patients with acute injuries and deal with life-threatening conditions. Emergency medicine physicians have a broad knowledge of medical, surgical, neurologic, gynecologic, and pediatric disorders.

Endocrinologist: Endocrinologists receive two year of additional training following an internal medicine residency. The endocrinologist concentrates on disorders of the endocrine glands such as the thyroid and adrenal glands. Endocrinology also deals with disorders such as diabetes, metabolic and nutritional disorders, pituitary diseases, and menstrual and reproductive problems. Patients are often referred to endocrinologists for failure to grow, early or late puberty, excess hair growth, high calcium levels, osteoporosis, pituitary tumors, or reproductive problems.

Endodontist: An endodontist is a dentist who specializes in root canal treatment. As a specialist, endodontists limit their practice to endodontic procedures. Endodontists have advanced surgical and nonsurgical skills that make them uniquely qualified to treat routine as well as complex cases. The care that an endodontist provides is supported by intensive education on how to perform the very best endodontics. After completing dental school, endodontists attend a two- or three-year advanced dental school program that focuses only on endodontic science and procedures.

Exercise Physiologist: An Exercise Physiologist is concerned with the body's responses and adaptations to exercise. Exercise includes anything from a cardiac rehabilitation program to the training program of an elite athlete. Essentially, the role of the exercise physiologist is to firstly assess the current state of fitness of the individual, then write a program of exercise that enhances the fitness or well-being of that individual. They also teach and conduct research in Universities. Exercise physiologists work in a variety of occupational settings including fitness centres, universities, hospitals and sports academies.

Family Practice Physician: Family physicians are trained to prevent, diagnose, and treat a wide variety of ailments in patients of all ages. They have received a broad range of training that includes surgery, psychiatry, internal medicine, obstetrics and gynecology, pediatrics, and geriatrics. They place special emphasis on care of families on a continuing basis, utilizing consultations and community resources when appropriate. They are able to apply modern techniques to prevention, diagnosis, and treatment of the vast majority of common illnesses and injuries.

Fertility Specialist: Also known as reproductive endocrinologist, these physicians receive additional training after a residency in obstetrics and gynecology. These physicians have a broad knowledge of hormonal function and environmental factors that impair conception. They are trained to diagnose, treat, and manage disorders that impact fertility. They can perform tests, diagnostic procedures, administer medications and perform specialized surgical procedures to assist patients in becoming pregnant. Both male and female fertility problems can be addressed by these physicians.

Gastroenterologist: This is a subspecialty of internal medicine that focuses on the digestive organs, including the stomach, bowels, liver, and gallbladder. A gastroenterologist diagnoses and treats conditions such as abdominal pain, ulcers, diarrhea, cancer, and jaundice. They have expertise in the administration of medication used to treat nearly any condition of the gastrointestinal tract. Gastroenterologists can also perform complex diagnostic and therapeutic procedures such as endoscopy, colonoscopy, ERCP, treatment of esophageal varices and ulcers. They consult with surgeons when abdominal operations are indicated.

General Surgeon: A general surgeon is a specialist prepared to manage a broad spectrum of surgical conditions affecting almost any area of the body. The surgeon establishes the diagnosis and provides the preoperative, operative, and postoperative care to surgical patients and is usually responsible for the comprehensive management of the trauma victim and the critically ill. During at least a five-year educational period after obtaining a medical degree, the surgeon has acquired knowledge and technical skills in congenital, infectious, metabolic and neoplastic problems relating to the head and neck, breast, abdomen, extremities, including the hand, and the gastrointestinal, vascular and endocrine systems. The surgeon uses a variety of diagnostic techniques, including endoscopy, for observing internal structures, and may use specialized instruments during operative procedures. A general surgeon is expected to be familiar with salient features of other surgical specialties in order to recognize problems in those areas and to know when to refer a patient to another specialist.

Genetics Specialist: Medical geneticists work in association with medical specialists. Genetics specialists are trained in eliciting and interpreting individual and family histories, heterogeneity, variability, and the natural history of the medical disorder in question. They have expertise in specialized laboratory and clinical procedures, genetic and mathematical principles to perform complex risk assessments, interpreting pedigree analysis (both segregation and linkage), and an understanding of the principals of genetic etiology.

Gerontologist: A gerontologist has additional training beyond a residency in internal medicine or family practice. They have expertise in the diagnosis, management, and treatment of disorders that affect the elderly. They are responsible for deriving treatment plans for their patients and making appropriate referrals for specialized procedures.

Gynecologic Oncologist: Gynecologic oncologists receive additional training beyond their residency in obstetrics and gynecology. They provide consultation and comprehensive management of patients with gynecologic cancer. Management of these patients includes diagnostic and therapeutic procedures necessary for the total care of the patient with gynecologic cancer. These physicians have extensive training in the surgical treatment of cancer. They are also trained in the chemotherapeutic and radiation use in the treatment of gynecologic cancers.

Gynecologist: A gynecologist is a physician who has completed a residency training program in obstetrics and gynecology and specializes in diseases of the female genital tract and women's health. They treat diseases of the uterus, fallopian tubes, ovaries, cervix, vagina, and vulva. Gynecologists also specialize in menstrual problems, contraception, sexuality, menopause, and infertility. These physicians also perform routine pelvic exams and may sometimes provide prenatal care.

Hand Surgeon: Specialists in hand surgery receive additional training after a residency in orthopedic surgery or plastic surgery. They have expertise in the investigation, preservation and restoration of the hand and wrist. They are trained in the medical, surgical, and rehabilitative modalities that affect the form and function of the hand and wrist.

Hand Therapist: Hand Therapy is the art and science of rehabilitation of the upper extremity. Hand Therapy has developed from the professions of Occupational Therapy and Physical Therapy. The hand therapist combines comprehensive knowledge of the upper extremity with special skills in assessment and treatment to prevent dysfunction, restore function or reverse the advancement of pathology in the upper extremity. In addition to the usual history taking, general observation and careful subjective examination including pain scores, that is part of most clinical practice, the Hand Therapist takes careful measurements of relevant factors such as range of movement, grip strength, and sensibility. They assess and record swelling, joint stiffness, the state of scars and wound healing, and establish a diagnosis on which to plan treatment. Treatment can include the fitting of gloves or the manufacture of Lycra finger stalls to control swelling, scar management by stretch, compression or silicone gel products, home program including specific exercises to be done regularly, the use of heat and cold, electrotherapy, the manufacture and/or fitting of splints and braces, posture education, pain management techniques, joint protection advice, massage and triggerpoint therapy, passive mobilization of stiff and painful joints, assessment of the workplace or home for aid requirements, and functional capacity evaluation. In private practice, hand therapists receive referred patients from surgeons, general practitioners, and other physicians.

Hematologist: A hematologist is a type of pathologist with expertise in diseases that affect blood cells, blood clotting mechanisms, bone marrow, and lymph nodes. This specialist has the knowledge and technical skills essential for the laboratory diagnosis of anemias, leukemias, lymphomas, bleeding disorders, and blood clotting disorders. They perform special types of transfusions and biopsy the bone marrow for analysis. The hematologist/pathologist functions as a consultant to all physicians and works closely with clinical hematologists and oncologists.

Hepatologist: A Hepatologist is a physician who has specialized in the diagnosis and treatment of disorders of the liver. Hepatologists are often consulted for patients in the hospital who have developed complications related to the liver. They can also manage patients with chronic liver disease.

Home Health Care Specialist: Under the direction of a physician, home health care specialists provide care on a short-term, intermittent basis for patients confined to their home due to illness, injury, or surgery. They are trained to provide blood pressure monitoring, wound care, catheter, colostomy and ileostomy care, blood draws and injections, diabetic management, medication and pain control, respiratory monitoring and care, and education for the patient, family or caregiver.

Immunologist: An immunologist is one who studies the immunology of diseases. Some immunologists are scientific researchers and others are physicians with an immunology-allergy practice. These physicians receive training in internal medicine or pediatrics, and complete allergy and immunology fellowships. Allergist-Immunologists diagnosis and treat problems dealing with the immune system, such as allergies and susceptibility to infections. Because an allergist and clinical immunologist is also an internist or a pediatrician, he or she has the capability of a primary care physician as well as the added expertise required to care for patients with asthma, allergies and other problems of the immune system. Frequently immunologists are consulted about problems related to seasonal or year-round allergies, asthma, sinus problems, eczema, contact dermatitis, recurrent infections, food allergies, bee sting allergies, drug allergies, and chemical or environmental sensitivity.

Industrial Hygienist: Industrial hygienists are occupational health professionals who have expertise and strong specialization in one or more phases of biological, chemical, or toxicological factors, effects, and control measures or in the area of engineering and mechanical control operations and industrial processes encountered in work places. They investigate and recommend corrections for industrial hygiene problems through recognition, evaluation, and control of environmental hazards, which adversely affect the health of workers. They are involved in conducting inspections and investigations in work places, provide consultation and assistance to agencies, and interested groups. They are responsible for the enforcement of industrial hygiene and occupational health standards; developing and evaluating proposed standards; and providing training in methods and techniques in meeting and enforcing standards.

Infectious Disease Physician: Infectious disease specialists have extensive knowledge of infectious diseases of all types, including bacterial, viral, and parasitic diseases. They are trained in the selective use of antibiotics. These specialists often work with patients in the intensive care unit, AIDS patients, and patients with fevers, which have not been explained. Infectious disease specialists are also experienced in preventive medicine and the treatment of infectious diseases associated with travel.

Internist: The general internist is a personal physician who provides long-term, comprehensive care in the office and the hospital, managing both common illnesses and complex problems for adolescents, adults, and the elderly. General internists are trained in the essentials of primary care internal medicine, which incorporates an understanding of disease prevention, wellness, substance abuse, mental health, and effective treatment of common problems of the eyes, ears, skin, nervous system, and reproductive organs. All internists are trained in the subspecialty areas of internal medicine including emergency medicine and critical care. Care by an internist is characterized by extensive knowledge and skill in diagnosis and treatment by the humanistic qualities of integrity, support, sensitivity, and compassion, and by personal commitment of patients. Internists consult with surgeons when surgical management is indicated. Well-trained internists are unique in their ability to deliver care with great professional expertise and often act as consultants to other specialists.

Licensed Clinical Psychotherapist: Psychotherapists are psychiatrists or psychologists who are specialized in the area of psychotherapy. Psychotherapy addresses the patient's problems through an exploration of historical factors that influence current beliefs and behaviors. It involves a series of meetings with the psychotherapist in which the patient discusses current and past problems.

Licensed Clinical Social Worker: Social workers manage the social and relationship factors that impact a patient's well-being. They are trained in counseling, and often serve as a referral source for more specialized care. Social workers aid individuals and families in obtaining medical care and social services support.

Licensed Professional Counselor: A counselor is a psychologist or other individual with training in counseling psychology. Counselors provide guidance for patients with mental disorders, and patients undergoing life stressors such as grief, loss, depression, illness, and addiction. Counselors often work with psychiatrists and other health care specialists.

Medical Toxicologist: Medical toxicology focuses on the evaluation and management of patients with accidental or intentional poisoning through exposure to prescription and nonprescription medications, drugs of abuse, household or industrial toxins, and environmental toxins. These physicians provide consultation through affiliations with regional poison control centers, or work in medical institutions. Medical toxicologists treat acute pediatric and adult drug ingestion; drug abuse, addiction and withdrawal.

Neonatologist: Neonatology is a subspecialty of pediatrics that is primarily concerned with newborns. A neonatologist specializes in the care and development of newborn infants as well as the treatment of ailments and conditions common to newborns.

Nephrologist: Nephrologists diagnose and treat disorders of the kidney, including high blood pressure, fluid and mineral imbalance. They are also trained to provide dialysis when the kidneys do not function properly. Nephrologists also consult with surgeons regarding kidney transplantation.

Neurologist: The specialty of neurology is concerned with the diagnosis and treatment of all categories of disease or impaired function of the brain, spinal cord, peripheral nerves, muscles, and automatic nervous system, and the blood vessels that relate to these structures. The neurologist serves as a consultant to other physicians, but is often also the principal or primary physician. This may include continuing care of outpatients and/or inpatients. The neurologist will often perform and interpret certain tests that relate to the central or peripheral nervous system or muscles.

Neuro-ophthalmologist: A neuro-ophthalmologist is an ophthalmologist who specializes in the diagnosis and treatment of neurologic conditions that affect the eye and vision. Neuro-Ophthalmology deals with diagnostically challenging cases. Theses physicians examine patients with rheumatologic, toxic, oncologic, metabolic, endocrine, infectious, and other medical diseases. They have expertise in differentiating medical conditions from intrinsic neurologic or ophthalmic diseases that affect the eye and brain leading to neuro-ophthalmic problems. The evaluate the etiology of vision and visual field loss, unusual eye complaints or visual phenomena, ptosis, diplopia, abnormal pupils and eye movements, ocular, periocular and associated head pain.

Neurophysiologist: Neurophysiologists study the functions of the nervous system in the clinical setting, for diagnostics, intensive care, and intraoperative monitoring. They utilize techniques such as electroencephalography (EEG), electromyography (EMG), somatosensory evoked potentials (SSEP), motor evoked potentials (MEP), and brainstem auditory evoked responses (BAER). Neurophysiologists are concerned with the diagnosis, management, and treatment of disorders such as epilepsy, autonomic dysfunction, movement disorders, neuromuscular disorders, sleep disorders, and spinal cord and nerve dysfunction.

Neuropsychologist: A neuropsychologist is a psychologist who specializes in studying brain behavior relationships. Neuropsychologists have extensive training in the anatomy, physiology, and pathology of the nervous system. Some neuropsychologists specialize in research while other neuropsychologists specialize in evaluating and treating people who are thought to have something wrong with the way in which their nervous system is functioning. Neuropsychologists study brain behavior relationships under very specific circumstances, which are both controlled and standardized.

Neuroradiologist: A neuroradiologist is a radiologist who specializes in the use of radioactive substances, x-rays and scanning devices for the diagnosis of diseases of the nervous system. Radiologists use x-rays, ultrasound, magnetic fields, and other forms of energy to make diagnoses. They interpret nuclear scans, PET scans, CT scans and MRI images.

Neurosurgeon: Neurosurgeons provide operative and nonoperative management of disorders of the central, peripheral, and autonomic nervous systems. This includes the prevention, diagnosis, evaluation, treatment, critical care, and rehabilitation of neurologic disorders. Neurologic surgery encompasses disorders of the nervous system; the brain, meninges, skull, and their blood supply, including the extracranial carotid and vertebral arteries; disorders of the pituitary gland; disorders of the spinal cord, meninges, and spine, including treatment by fusion or instrumentation; and disorders of the cranial and spinal nerves throughout their distribution.

Nuclear Medicine Physician: Nuclear medicine is the medical specialty that employs the nuclear properties of radioactive and stable nuclides in diagnosis, therapy, and research. These properties are used to evaluate metabolic, physiologic, and pathologic conditions in both the clinical and laboratory setting. Nuclear medicine physicians are trained in the diagnostic and therapeutic use of radionuclides including therapy with radioisotopically labeled antibodies; positron emission tomography (PET), and single proton emission computerized tomography (SPECT). Additionally, the nuclear medicine physician has knowledge in the biologic effects of radiation exposure, the principles of radiation safety and protection, and the management of patients who have been exposed to ionizing radiation. The nuclear medicine specialist serves as a consultant to physicians, obtaining pertinent information from patients as necessary by means of history and physical examination and selecting and carrying out appropriate diagnostic or therapeutic uses of radionuclides.

Obstetrics and Gynecology: Obstetrics and Gynecology (OB/GYN) is a field of medicine concerned with women's health. OB/GYN physicians are trained in the medical and surgical care of the female reproductive system and associated disorders. They diagnose and treat gynecologic and reproductive disorders. They can also perform surgeries related to the female reproductive tract. In addition, these physicians manage pregnancy and deliver babies.

Occupational Medicine Physician: Occupational medicine is a subspecialty of medicine which focuses on the investigation, prevention, and treatment of diseases particular to people in the working environment. They also provide consultant services to business, industry, government, legal and private agencies. These services may include Independent Medical Examinations (IME), Permanent Impairment Ratings (PIR), case reviews and expert witness services. Preventative services include onsite evaluations to industry as well as the implementation of surveillance programs to help meet OSHA requirements.

Occupational Therapist: An occupational therapist is trained to help people manage the daily activities of living, such as dressing, grooming or cooking, and regaining vocational skills. Occupational therapists help people improve their ability to perform tasks in their daily living and working environments. They work with individuals who have conditions that are mentally, physically, developmentally, or emotionally disabling. They also help them to develop, recover, or maintain daily living and work skills. Occupational therapists not only help clients improve basic motor functions and reasoning abilities, but also compensate for permanent loss of function. Their goal is to help clients have independent, productive, and satisfying lives. Occupational therapists assist clients in performing activities of all types, ranging from using a computer, to caring for daily needs such as dressing, cooking, and eating. Physical exercises may be used to increase strength and dexterity, while paper and pencil exercises may be chosen to improve visual acuity and the ability to discern patterns. For those with permanent functional disabilities, such as spinal cord injuries, cerebral palsy, or muscular dystrophy, therapists instruct in the use of adaptive equipment such as wheelchairs, splints, and aids for eating and dressing. They also design or make special equipment needed at home or at work. Therapists develop computer-aided adaptive equipment and teach clients with severe limitations how to use it. This equipment enables clients to communicate better and to control other aspects of their environment.

Oncologist: The medical oncologist specializes in the diagnosis and treatment of all types of cancer and other benign and malignant tumors. These specialists select and administer chemotherapy for malignancy, as well as consult with surgeons and radiotherapists on other treatments for cancer.

Ophthalmologist: Ophthalmologists provide comprehensive eye and vision care. They diagnose, monitor and medically or surgically treat all eyelid and orbital problems affecting the eye and visual pathways. They often prescribe vision services such as glasses and contact lenses. The ophthalmologist also serves as a consultant to physicians and other professionals.

Oral Surgeon: Oral surgery is a subspecialty of dentistry that is concerned with surgical treatment of diseases of the mouth, teeth, and gums. Oral surgeons are frequently consulted for the repair of facial trauma or broken jawbones. They also perform more complicated tooth extractions such as wisdom tooth extraction, and the removal of broken or cracked teeth.

Orthopedic Surgeon: Orthopedic surgery is a surgical specialty that involves the preservation and restoration of the extremities and spine by medical, surgical, and physical means. Orthopedic surgeons treat congenital deformities, trauma, infections, tumors, and metabolic disturbances of the musculoskeletal system. These musculoskeletal problems include deformities, injuries, and degenerative diseases of the spine, hands, feet, knees, hips, shoulders, and elbows in both children and adults. They are also involved in the care of patients who manifest the effects of central or peripheral nervous system lesions of the musculoskeletal system.

Orthopedist: An orthopedist, also known as an orthopedic surgeon, treats diseases and injuries of the spine and extremities. Using surgery, medications, and physical therapy, their goal is to preserve maximal function of the musculoskeletal system. Orthopedic Surgery is a medical specialty devoted to the diagnosis, treatment, rehabilitation and prevention of injuries and diseases of the body's musculoskeletal system. This complex system includes the bones, joints, ligaments, tendons, muscles and nerves. Orthopedic surgeons can place a joint prosthesis in people with broken hips who were once limited to wheelchairs, and perform arthroscopic surgery which allows them to look inside joints and perform complex procedures without having to undergo a more serious open-joint operation. Orthopedists may specialize in in fields such as, musculoskeletal oncology, reconstructive orthopedics, sports medicine, pediatric orthopedics, orthopedic trauma, and spine surgery.

Osteopath: An osteopath is a physician who practices osteopathy. Osteopathy is a system of medicine based upon the theory that the human body is a vital mechanical organism in which the structural and functional states are of equal importance. They believe that the body is able to rectify itself against toxic conditions when it has favorable environmental circumstances and satisfactory nourishment. Therefore, it is the osteopathic physician's responsibility to remove any internal or external abnormalities of the system. Osteopaths rely upon physical, medical, and surgical methods.

Otolaryngologist: An otolaryngologist (ENT) provides comprehensive medical and surgical care for patients with diseases and disorders that affect the ears, the respiratory and upper alimentary systems and related structures, and the head and neck. Surgery of the head and neck is a major component of this specialty. These physicians also have knowledge of audiology and speech-language pathology; the chemical senses and allergy, endocrinology, and neurology, as they relate to the head and neck. Head and neck oncology and facial plastic and reconstructive surgery are fundamental areas of expertise.

Otologist: Otology is a subspecialty of otolaryngology. An otologist is a specialist in diseases of the ear. They are knowledgeable in the anatomy, physiology, and pathology of the ear. Otologists diagnose and treat conditions such as hearing and balance disorders.

Otorhinolaryngologist: Otorhinolaryngologists are physicians trained in the medical and surgical management and treatment of patients with diseases and disorders of the ear, nose, throat (ENT), and related structures of the head and neck. They are commonly referred to as ENT physicians. Their special skills include diagnosing and managing diseases of the sinuses, larynx, oral cavity, and upper pharynx, as well as structures of the neck and face. Otorhinolaryngologists diagnose, treat, and manage specialty-specific disorders as well as many primary care problems in both children and adults. Some of the conditions they treat are allergies, sleep apnea, sinusitis, and head and neck cancer. They are trained in both the medical and surgical treatment of hearing, ear infections, balance disorders, ear noise (tinnitus), nerve pain, and facial and cranial nerve disorders. Otorhinolaryngologists also manage congenital disorders of the outer and inner ear. Care of the nasal cavity and sinuses is one of the primary skills of otolaryngologists. Management of the nasal area includes allergies and sense of smell. Breathing and the appearance of the nose are also part of otorhinolaryngologists expertise. Also specific to these physicians is expertise in managing diseases of the larynx and the upper aero-digestive tract or esophagus, including voice and swallowing disorders. In the head and neck area, otorhinolaryngologists are trained to treat infectious diseases, both benign and malignant tumors, facial trauma, and deformities of the face. They perform both cosmetic plastic and reconstructive surgery. They may subspecialize in pediatric otolaryngology, otology/neurotology, allergy, facial plastic and reconstructive surgery, head and neck, laryngology, and rhinology.

Pain Management Specialist: The anesthesiologist who specializes in pain management is a physician who must receive additional training in pain management after the completion of anesthesiology training. The pain management specialist can be the primary physician or a consultant for patients experiencing problems with acute or chronic pain in both hospital and ambulatory settings, and can coordinate a multidisciplinary approach toward pain management of patients with pain. In addition to providing direct patient care, they may also coordinate the patient care needs with other primary care physicians and other specialists.

Pathologist: Pathology is a specialty of medicine dealing with the causes and nature of disease. Pathologists contribute to diagnosis, prognosis, and treatment through knowledge gained by the laboratory application of the biologic, chemical, and physical sciences to man, or materials obtained from man. Pathologists use their skills and knowledge for the diagnosis, exclusion, and monitoring of disease by means of information gathered from the microscopic examination of tissue specimens, cells, and body fluids, and from clinical laboratory tests on the body fluids, and from clinical laboratory tests on the body fluids and secretions.

Perinatologist: Perinatologists specialize in diagnosing and managing complications of pregnancy. They are also known as high-risk pregnancy specialists or maternal-fetal medicine specialists. They complete a residency in OB/GYN and then a two-year subspecialty training program in Maternal-Fetal Medicine. Women are usually referred to a perinatologist for conditions that are unusual or that require care by a team of trained individuals. They provide different levels of care, depending on individual circumstances, including routine ultrasound or advanced ultrasound, consultation, co-management with the regular care provider, and complete pregnancy care.

Physiatrist: Physical medicine and rehabilitation, also referred to as rehabilitation medicine, is the medical specialty concerned with diagnosing, evaluating, and treating patients with impairments and/or disabilities that involve musculoskeletal, neurologic, cardiovascular, or other body systems. The primary focus is on maximal restoration of physical, psychological, social, and vocational function and on alleviation of pain. For diagnosis and evaluation, a physiatrist may include the techniques of electromyography and electrodiagnosis as supplements to the standard history, physical, x-ray, and laboratory examinations. In addition to traditional treatment modes, the specialist in physical medicine and rehabilitation may use therapeutic exercise, prosthetics, orthotics, and mechanical and electrical devices.

Physical Therapist: A physical therapist is an individual trained to assist people in restoring muscle function. Physical therapists work in a variety of settings including hospitals, nursing homes, schools, outpatient clinics, fitness facilities, the home environment and many industrial companies. Physical therapists evaluate and treat those with musculoskeletal disorders, neurological dysfunctions and those with other types of disease, injury or illness. Manual therapy, joint mobilization, myofascial release and neurodevelopmental (NDT) techniques are some of the special skills used by therapists to treat patients to help lessen disability, pain and improve overall function and quality of life. Therapists use special equipment called modalities when treating patients which help aid in the healing and recovery of an injury. Electrical stimulation, hot packs, cold packs, infrared and ultrasound are some of the modalities one may require during a treatment session with a physical therapist. As part of treatment and the rehabilitation process, a physical therapist will often stretch, strengthen, facilitate muscles, challenge balance, test coordination abilities, teach home exercise programs and enhance basic mobility skills. Physical therapists coordinate treatment plans with doctors, nurses, social workers and occupational therapists. This multidisciplinary approach helps achieve patient goals and individual treatment outcomes as quickly and as effectively as possible. Physical therapists may specialize in pediatrics, sports medicine, neurology, home health, geriatrics, orthopedics, aquatic therapy, wound care, electrotherapy, occupational health, women's health, acute care, education, administration, research and cardiopulmonary rehabilitation.

Plastic Surgeon: Plastic surgery deals with the repair, reconstruction, or replacement of physical defects of form or function involving the skin, musculoskeletal system, craniomaxillofacial structures, hand, extremities, breast and trunk, and external genitalia. It uses aesthetic surgical principles not only to improve undesirable qualities of normal structures but in all reconstructive procedures as well. Special knowledge and skill in the design and surgery of grafts, flaps, free tissue transfer and replantation is necessary. Competence in the management of complex wounds, the use of implantable materials, and in tumor surgery is required. Plastic surgery has been prominent in the development of innovative techniques such as microvascular and craniomaxillofacial surgery, liposuction, and tissue transfer. A foundation in surgical anatomy, physiology, pathology, and other basic sciences is fundamental to this specialty. Competency in plastic surgery implies a special combination of basic knowledge, surgical judgment, technical expertise, ethics, and interpersonal skills in order to achieve satisfactory patient relationships and problem resolution.

Podiatrist: Podiatrists are specialized to treat foot problems of patients. A full podiatric practice includes podiatry, podopediatrics, podiatric orthopedics, trauma and surgery. Podiatrists examine patients and determine appropriate treatments. They track their progress and, if necessary, refer patients to other practitioners.

Poison Control Center Personnel: This is an individual who works at a poison control center. These centers give information on, or treatment to, patients suffering from poisoning. They are commonly associated with large hospitals or medical schools.

Preventive Medicine Physician: Preventive medicine is a specialty that focuses on the health of individuals and defined populations in order to protect, promote and maintain health and well-being and to prevent disease, disability and premature death. The distinctive components of preventive medicine include biostatistics; epidemiology; health services administration; environmental and occupational influences on health; social and behavioral influences on health; and measures, which prevent the occurrence, progression and disabling effects of disease or injury. Preventive medicine physicians may be specialists in general preventive medicine, public health, occupational medicine, or aerospace medicine. They work with large population groups as well as with the individual patients to promote health and understanding the risks of disease, injury disability, and death, seeking modify and eliminate these risks.In addition to providing clinical care, physicians trained in preventive medicine work in various settings: public health agencies and managed care systems, often managing large health care systems; occupational health settings to treat patients at the work site and to assess and modify work site conditions to reduce work-related risks and improve employee health; and clinical settings to enhance the health and performance of aviators and astronauts.

Primary Care Physician: A primary care physician is the physician to whom a family or individual goes initially for medical care, and the management of their care even if eventually referred to other physicians. Family practitioners, internists, general practitioners, and OB/GYN physicians can all fulfill the role of primary care physician.

Proctologist: Proctologists, also known as colorectal surgeons, are specialists in diseases of the colon, rectum, and anus. They diagnose and treat, often surgically, cancer, hemorrhoids, colitis, fistulas, fissures, ulcers, tumors, polyposis, parasites, and condylomas. When cancers are detected, proctologists plan the surgical treatment programs and follow up with endoscopic techniques.

Psychiatrist: A psychiatrist specializes in the prevention, diagnosis, and treatment of mental, addictive, and emotional disorders, e.g., psychoses, depression, anxiety disorders, substance abuse disorders, developmental disabilities, sexual dysfunctions, and adjustment reactions. Psychiatrists understand the biological, psychological, and social components of illness, and can order diagnostic laboratory tests and prescribe medications, as well as evaluate and treat psychological and interpersonal problems. Psychiatrists also intervene with individuals and families who are coping with stress, crises, and other problems. Some psychiatrists have also had further training in specialized areas such as psychoanalysis, psychiatric aspects of general medicine, psychoanalysis, alcohol and substance abuse, geriatrics, neuropsychiatry, and forensic psychiatry.

Pulmonologist: Pulmonology is a subspecialty of internal medicine concerned with diseases of the lungs and airways. Pulmonologists diagnose and treat cancer, pneumonia, pleurisy, asthma, occupational diseases, bronchitis, sleep disorders, emphysema, and other complex disorders of the lungs. Pulmonologists test lung functions in many ways, endoscope the bronchial airways and prescribe and monitor mechanical assistance to ventilation. Many pulmonologists are also experts in critical care.

Psychologist: Psychologists are concerned with the study of behavior. Clinical psychology is a broad field of practice and research within the discipline of psychology, which applies psychological principles to the assessment, prevention, amelioration, and rehabilitation of psychological distress, disability, dysfunctional behavior, and health-risk behavior, and to the enhancement of psychological and physical well-being. The role of a psychologist includes both scientific research, focusing on the search for general principles, and clinical service, focusing on the study and care of clients, and information gathered from each of these activities influences practice and research. These professionals apply a broad approach to human problems consisting of assessment, diagnosis, consultation, treatment, program development, administration, and research with regard to numerous populations, including children, adolescents, adults, the elderly, families, groups, and disadvantaged persons. There is overlap between some areas of clinical psychology and other professional fields of psychology such as counseling psychology and clinical neuropsychology, as well as some professional fields outside of psychology, such as psychiatry and social work.

Pulmonologist: Pulmonology is classified as an internal medicine subspecialty. A pulmonologist is a physician who possesses specialized knowledge and skill in the diagnosis and treatment of pulmonary (lung) conditions and diseases. These physicians diagnose and treat acute respiratory distress syndrome, asbestosis, asthma, bronchitis, chronic cough, chronic obstructive pulmonary disease, emphysema, hemoptysis, lung cancer, obstructive sleep apnea, pleural effusion, sarcoidosis, solitary pulmonary nodule, and tuberculosis. They are often critical care specialists as well.

Radiation Oncologist: Radiation oncology is a branch of radiology that deals with the therapeutic applications of radiant energy and its modifiers and the study and management of disease. Radiation oncologists are experts in treating malignant tumors, and are most often consultants in a multi-disciplinary approach to treating cancer.

Radiation Therapist: Radiation therapy uses high doses of ionizing radiation for the treatment of benign and malignant tumors. The radiation therapist is responsible for the daily treatment of patients, using radiation-producing equipment, such as linear accelerators or cobalt machines. Radiation therapists observe the patient's clinical progress, and observe the first signs of complications. The therapist can assist in the initial examination of the patient, simulations of the area to be treated, calculations of the radiation dosage, and the construction of patient immobilization and beam shaping devices.

Radiologist: Radiology is a branch of medicine that utilizes radiologic methodologies in diagnosis and treatment of disease. Radiologists use x-rays, ultrasound, magnetic fields, and other forms of energy to make diagnoses. They interpret nuclear scans, PET scans, ultrasonography images, CT scans and MRI images. They can also perform diagnostic interventional procedures, such as angiography, guided biopsy drainage procedures, and non-coronary angioplasty. These physicians often specialize in diagnostic radiology, radiation oncology, neuroradiology, nuclear radiology, pediatric radiology, or vascular and interventional radiology.

Rectal Surgeon: A rectal surgeon, also known as a colorectal surgeon, is a physician who has received specialized training in colon and rectal surgery following a residency in general surgery. These surgeons are experts in the surgical and non-surgical treatment of colon and rectal problems. They treat colon and rectal cancer, chronic ulcerative colitis, Crohn's disease, and diverticulitis. Surgical conditions such as hemorrhoids, anal fissures, fistulas, condolomata, sphincter injuries, rectal prolapse and anal incontinence are conditions that are also within the scope of this specialty.

Reproductive Endocrinologist: Reproductive endocrinologists are obstetrician-gynecologists with advanced education and research in the field of reproductive endocrinology. These physicians treat reproductive disorders that affect both men and women. Their practices typically include infertility evaluation, endometriosis treatment, ovulation induction, artificial insemination, operative laparoscopy, operative hysteroscopy, microsurgery, donor insemination, in vitro fertilization (IVF), oocyte donation, intracytoplasmic sperm injection (ICSI), cryopreservation of embryos, and gestational carrier arrangements.

Registered Nurse: A registered nurse is a nurse who has passed the state board exam. Nurses provide health care ranging from simple patient care tasks to the most expert professional techniques necessary in acute life-threatening situations.

Respiratory Therapist: Respiratory therapists provide treatment to preserve or improve pulmonary function. The care provided includes evaluation, treatment of those with breathing disorders, patient and family education, and rehabilitation instruction. They may work in hospitals, intensive care units, nursing homes, physicians' offices, home health agencies, and patient's homes. Responsibilities of respiratory therapists include obtaining and analyzing breath sounds and sputum specimens, taking blood specimens and analyzing them to determine levels of oxygen, carbon dioxide, and other gases, measuring the capacity of a patient's lungs to determine if there is impaired function, and performing stress tests and other studies of the cardiopulmonary system. Responsibilities also include operating and maintaining various types of highly sophisticated equipment to administer oxygen or to assist with breathing, monitoring and managing therapy that will help a patient recover lung function, administering medications in aerosol form to help alleviate breathing problems and to help prevent respiratory infections.

Rheumatologist: Rheumatologists are concerned with diseases of joints, muscle, bones, and tendons. They diagnose and treat arthritis, back strain, muscle strains, common athletic injuries, and "collagen" diseases. Often they work closely with other specialists such as physical therapists and orthopedic surgeons.

Sleep Disorder Specialist: Sleep disorder specialists diagnose and treat patients with sleep related disorders. They care for patients who have sleep related breathing disorders, abnormal daytime sleepiness, chronic insomnia, or unusual behaviors during sleep, or medical problems that might be exacerbated during sleep. Treatments might include medication changes, schedule changes, weight loss, use of nocturnal appliances (e.g., CPAP for sleep apnea), behavioral recommendations, and specific medications.

Speech Pathologist: A speech pathologist is an individual educated and trained to plan, direct, and conduct programs to improve communicative skills of children and adults with language and speech impairments arising from physiologic disturbances, defective articulation, or dialect. Speech-language pathologists are educated in the study of human communication, its development, and its disorders. By evaluating the speech, language, cognitive-communication, and swallowing skills of children and adults, the speech-language pathologist determines what communication or swallowing problems exist and the best way to treat them. They can evaluate programs and may perform research related to speech and language problems.

Speech Therapist: A speech therapist assesses and treats children and/or adults who have a communication disability. This may include difficulties with speech, language, cognition (thought processes), voice, fluency or swallowing.

Spine Surgeon: Spine surgeons are orthopedic surgeons or neurosurgeons whose specialty is in the operative treatment of spinal disorders. These physicians have received special training in the diagnosis and treatment of the spine including problems with the neck (cervical spine), mid back (thoracic spine) and low back (lumbar spine). They provide evaluation and surgical services to adults and children for the entire spine, for correction of spine deformity (scoliosis and kyphosis), for reconstruction when needed due to trauma or tumors, and for diseases that accompany aging. They are involved in the correction and/or treatment of fractures, spinal fixations, trauma to the spine, spinal infections, and spinal deformities. They may use video assisted surgery, DET (IntraDiscal Electro-Thermal Therapy), and microsurgical techniques.

Sports Medicine Specialist: Sports medicine specialists are trained in the enhancement of health and fitness, and in the prevention of injury and illness. These physicians are experts in exercise physiology, biomechanics, nutrition, psychology, physical rehabilitation, epidemiology, physical evaluation, injuries (treatment and prevention and referral practice), and the role of exercise in promoting a healthy lifestyle. Sports Medicine physicians are involved in the health care of individuals engaged in physical exercise and sports.

Surgeon: A surgeon is a physician who specializes in the surgical treatment of disease or injury. Depending on their training, surgeons may practice in a variety of specialties including general surgery, cardiothoracic surgery, urologic surgery, gynecologic-obstetric surgery, otolaryngologic surgery, plastic and reconstructive surgery, orthopedic surgery, transplant surgery, hand surgery, neurosurgery, and others.

Thoracic Surgeon: Thoracic surgeons surgically treat diseases of the chest including coronary artery disease; cancers of the lung, esophagus, and chest wall; abnormalities of the great vessels and heart valves; birth defects of the chest and heart; tumors in the organs contained in the chest cavity; and transplantation of the heart and lungs. They surgically manage diseases of the blood supply to the heart, heart valves, and the arteries and veins in the chest as well as treating esophageal swallowing problems and gastroesophageal reflux. In addition, these surgeons can sometimes correct heart defects, and furnish cardiovascular support to infants and children.

Transplant Surgeon: A transplant surgeon is a surgeon who has completed additional training in the technical, physiologic, and anatomic areas pertaining to the transplantation of organs. Prior training can be in general surgery, pediatric surgery, cardiac surgery, or urologic surgery. Transplant surgeons require extensive knowledge in the immunology involved in organ rejection and the medications used to prevent rejection. The most commonly transplanted organs include heart, kidneys, liver, and lungs.

Trauma Surgeon: Trauma surgeons manage patients who have sustained traumatic injury. They perform emergency procedures including endotracheal tube intubation, tube thoracostomy, pericardiocentesis, ultrasonographic evaluation, and peritoneal lavage. Usually trauma surgeons initiate contact with the operating room when an urgent surgical procedure is needed. Trauma surgeons determine the priority of operations. After initial emergency room resuscitation and operations, trauma surgeons follow the patient to the intensive care unit. After the general conditions of the trauma patients are stabilized, they are transferred to the trauma ward to continue the comprehensive plan of care and prepare for discharge. After discharge, trauma patients are followed-up at outpatient clinics, which are specialized for wound care. Trauma surgeons are specialists at managing injuries, including avoiding preventable prehospital early trauma death, normalizing hemodynamic status during resuscitation, decreasing severe complications during the intensive care and rehabilitating the patient back to the community.

Tropical Disease Specialist: Tropical disease specialists are concerned with the diagnosis, treatment and prevention of tropical illness. They treat patients with a broad spectrum of infectious and non-infectious disease problems. Patients usually are tourists, expatriates, missionaries, volunteers, immigrants and refugees. Tropical disease specialists are concerned with the treatment of unusual, exotic, and tropical diseases and provide medical care that specifically addresses the concerns of travelers. These physicians are able to assist the traveler or expatriate in maintaining their health during all phases of travel. This requires expert knowledge and dedication to continuing education on international diseases and health risks.

Urologist: Urologists manage benign and malignant medical and surgical disorders of the adrenal gland and of the genitourinary system. Urologists are skilled in endoscopic, percutaneous, and open surgery of congenital and acquired conditions of the reproductive and urinary systems and their contiguous structures. Disorders of the kidneys, bladder, and prostate gland are the most frequently treated disorders.

Vascular Surgeon: Vascular surgeons are general surgeons with additional training in the management of surgical disorders of the blood vessels, excluding those immediately adjacent to the heart, lungs or brain. These physicians operatively treat diseases such as peripheral and abdominal aneurysms, varicose veins, claudication, arterial occlusion, and injuries to blood vessels. They also are consulted for the placement of dialysis access grafts, and the management of diabetic ulcers.

Vocational Rehabilitation Counselor: Vocational rehabilitation counselors seek to enable those with disabilities to prepare for, achieve and maintain competitive employment. The vocational rehabilitation counselor understands the effects of disabilities on employment and helps clients identify their strengths and weaknesses. They also work with clients to identify needed vocational rehabilitation services. Together, the counselor and client develop an organized plan of action with a goal of competitive employment. They also coordinate a medical or psychological evaluation to identify the physical and/or mental disability. Evaluation may identify job-related functions the individual can and cannot perform and help the client establish an employment goal. Clients sometimes need to learn to deal with day-to-day situations and problems, and how to get along on the job and in the community. During rehabilitation the client may receive adjustment training to develop social and coping skills as well as job interviewing and job survival skills. This training may be given individually or in a group setting. Many clients spend time in our work training centers to build work tolerance, endurance and job skills. In addition to hands-on work experience in the work training centers, these professionals may sponsor clients' course work or special skills training through colleges, technical schools, trade schools or even employer training sites. This course work or training equips the client with the skills needed to improve his or her marketability. Sponsorship for skills training is always coordinated with federal and other grants (such as Pell) that the client may be eligible to receive. If a client needs a worksite or vehicle modification, wheelchair, limb, brace, hearing aid or other type of artificial appliance to perform satisfactorily on the job, the counselor may help provide it.

Wound Care Specialist: Wound care specialists, usually registered nurses, are concerned with the treatment of wounds to promote healing and to restore patients' quality of life. Their responsibilities include diagnosis, taking medical and clinical history, photographing, tracing and documenting the patient's wound. The assessment may involve blood tests, microbiological examinations, and investigations which involve both venous and arterial studies including duplex ultrasound assessment, venography and arteriography. Patient education is also a major component of their role in patient care.

WARNING

These guidelines are not to be used for the diagnosis and treatment of any medical condition.

Diagnostic and treatment methods are constantly changing and improving.

The final opinion regarding any medical condition should rest with the treating or consulting health care professional.

WARNING

These guidelines are not to be used for the diagnosis and treatment of any medical condition.

Diagnostic and treatment methods are constantly changing and improving.

The final opinion regarding any medical condition should rest with the treating or consulting health care professional.

Abdominal Adhesions

Other names / synonyms: Diaphragm Adhesions, Mesenteric Adhesions, Omentum Adhesions, Peritoneal Adhesions, Stomach Adhesions

568.0

Definition

Abdominal adhesions are bands of scar tissue that have formed inside the abdomen. The adhesions can form between the inside of the abdominal wall and the small intestine (the omentum), between loops of small intestine, or between any of the abdominal organs.

Abdominal adhesions can form in response to surgery, bleeding, or an inflammatory disease in the abdomen. Adhesions are the most common cause of bowel obstruction, particularly in the small bowel, because the intestine wraps itself around the adhesion blocking a portion of the bowel. In women, they may form on or adhere to the ovaries and fallopian tubes (pelvic adhesions) resulting in obstruction of reproductive functions and often leading to infertility.

Other causes of adhesions include radiation treatment to the abdomen or a foreign substance or object left in the abdomen after surgery. Some adhesions are formed from perforated ulcers, appendicitis, endometriosis, or infections in the fallopian tubes. Any trauma to the abdomen may result in adhesions. Adhesion formation remains a major complication after lower abdominal and gynecologic operations. Although more of these procedures are now being done through use of a small incision and a scope (laparoscopy), the rate of adhesion formation has not significantly decreased.

Approximately 15-20% of all cases of female infertility are due to adhesions. The incidence of abdominal adhesions requiring surgical correction (adhesiolysis) in the US is 400,000 individuals a year.

Diagnosis

History: Individuals usually report prior abdominal surgery particularly if postoperative infection developed. Cramping and intense abdominal pain are the primary symptoms of adhesions that are causing partial intestinal obstruction. Nausea followed by vomiting that may occur in waves is also reported if the adhesion causes complete intestinal obstruction.

Physical exam: The exam may reveal a surgical scar. Abdominal distention may be seen if complete intestinal obstruction has occurred. Listening to the abdomen with a stethoscope (auscultation) may reveal abnormal bowel sounds.

Tests: Plain abdominal x-rays or contrast films (upper GI or barium enema) may document small bowel obstruction. If pain is the only symptom and there is no evidence of intestinal obstruction, many other tests may be done. Visually examining the various areas and levels of the gastrointestinal tract with various scopes (endoscope, colonoscope, sigmoidoscope, proctoscope) can identify adhesions. MRI evaluation may be useful in some cases. In cases where the diagnosis is questionable, surgical exploration either by laparoscopy or laparotomy may be the final diagnostic test.

Treatment

Surgical release of adhesions (adhesiolysis) is the only effective treatment of adhesions. This treatment may be problematic since surgery may have been the original cause of adhesions and 11-21% of individuals will re-form new adhesions. Adhesiolysis of both abdominal and pelvic adhesions can often be performed through a scope inserted through a small skin incision (laparoscopy). Through the laparoscope or via open procedure the adhesions will be cut (sharp dissection), electrically coagulated, or laser treated (ablation).

Newer surgical techniques have been developed where membranes made of cellulose, polytetrafluoroethylene (PTFE), or sodium hyaluronate/carboxymethylcellulose (HA/CMC) are inserted between organs during surgery. These reduce the tendency for adhesions to develop. Adhesiolysis of small adhesions in the colon can be performed through a scope (colonoscope, sigmoidoscope).

Prognosis

Surgical removal of the adhesions produces a good outcome with full recovery in the majority of individuals however in about 11-21% of cases, the adhesions will re-form within weeks to years after the surgery.

Differential Diagnosis

There are many other causes of abdominal pain including gastroenteritis, irritable bowel syndrome, kidney stone, urinary tract infection, constipation, hernia, inflamed gallbladder (cholecystitis), mesenteric infarct, cancer in the abdomen, ectopic pregnancy, tubo-ovarian abscess, pelvic inflammatory disease, and ovarian cyst.

Specialists

- Gastroenterologist
- General Surgeon
- Gynecologist

Work Restrictions / Accommodations

If the individual has had surgical treatment, time off from work to recover from surgery is needed. If sedentary duties are available, the individual may return to work during the latter weeks of recovery, but lifting and climbing activities may not be permitted until postoperative recovery is complete.

Comorbid Conditions

Coexisting conditions that may impact recovery and lengthen disability include ischemic tissue, abscess, trauma, foreign bodies, and inflammatory disease in the abdomen such as peritonitis.

Complications

More adhesions may develop following the surgery to remove the original adhesions. Bleeding, infection, and mechanical injury may occur as complications after any surgery.

Factors Influencing Duration

Complications from surgery lengthen the time of disability, as does recurrence of adhesions.

Length of Disability

Surgery without colostomy.

Duration in Days

Job Classification	Minimum	Optimum	Maximum
Sedentary work	7	14	21
Light work	14	21	28
Medium work	21	28	35
Heavy work	42	49	56
Very Heavy work	42	49	56

Surgery with colostomy.

Duration in Days

Job Classification	Minimum	Optimum	Maximum
Sedentary work	14	21	28
Light work	21	28	35
Medium work	28	42	56
Heavy work	42	49	63
Very Heavy work	42	56	70

Failure to Recover

If an individual fails to recover within the maximum duration expectancy period, the reader may wish to reference the following questions to assist in better understanding the specifics of an individual's medical case.

Regarding diagnosis:

- What is the suspected cause of the adhesions? Previous surgery? Bleeding? Inflammatory disease?
- Was radiation treatment to the abdomen performed?
- Does individual have a history of a perforated ulcer, appendicitis, or endometriosis or infections in the fallopian tubes?
- On exam, were there abnormal bowel sounds? Was abdominal distension evident?
- Were plain abdominal x-rays or upper GI or barium enema done to rule out a bowel obstruction?
- Was endoscopic examination of the GI tract done?
- Was MRI done?
- Was it necessary to do surgical exploration?
- Were conditions with similar symptoms ruled out?

Regarding treatment:

- Were the adhesions released through the laparoscope or open procedure?
- Were the adhesions cut, electrically coagulated, or laser treated?
- What kind of membrane was used during the current surgery?

Regarding prognosis:

- Does individual have any comorbid conditions that could impact recovery?
- Did adhesions re-form?

References

Bane, C.L., and C. Jennings. "Adhesion Reduction as a New Treatment Innovation." AORN Journal 67 4 1998: 774-782.

Medicine for the Practicing Physician. Hurst, J.W., ed. Stamford: Appleton & Lange, 1996.

Ray, N.F., et al. "Abdominal Adhesiolysis: Inpatient Care and Expenditures in the United States 1994." Journal of the American College of Surgeons 186 11 1998: 1-9.

Scott, James R. "Endoscopic Surgery." Danforth's Obstetrics and Gynecology, 7th ed. Scott, James R., et al Philadelphia: J.B. Lippincott, 1994. 827-835.

Abdominal Aneurysm

Other names / synonyms: Abdominal Aortic Aneurysm, Fusiform Abdominal Aneurysm, Saccular Aneurysm

441.02, 441.03, 441.3, 441.4, 441.6, 441.7

Definition

An abdominal aortic aneurysm (AAA) refers to a localized weakness and ballooning (dilation) of the aorta in the segment between the kidneys and the branches in the legs (iliac arteries). The aneurysm is termed saccular when it consists of an out pouching on one side of the arterial wall. The aneurysm is termed fusiform when the dilation extends around the circumference of the vessel. When there is actual separation within the wall of the aorta, the aneurysm is termed dissecting. Dissecting aneurysms of the abdominal aorta are rare and usually represent an extension of a process beginning in the thoracic aorta.

AAAs begin as small pea-sized swellings. They grow at a rate of about one-quarter to one-half inch per year. AAAs under 6 cms in diameter are considered small. The likelihood of rupture increases as the aneurysm increases in size. As the aneurysm expands, increasing pressure is exerted against neighboring structures and may result in potentially lethal complications.

So-called "hardening of the arteries" (atherosclerosis) is the cause of about 95% of AAAs. It causes the wall of the aorta to become weak and dilated. High blood pressure (hypertension) may contribute to the progressive expansion. Other less common causes are trauma, syphilis, and connective tissue diseases such as systemic lupus erythematosus.

The prevalence of AAAs is 2-3% in individuals over the age of 50 and are 8 times more common in men than in women.

Diagnosis

History: An individual may not have any symptoms (asymptomatic) and may not be aware of the condition for quite some time, especially if the aneurysm is small. Some individuals, however, may report an abnormally prominent throbbing (pulsating) lump or mass in the abdomen that is easily seen and felt. Constant pain in the lower back region as a result of pressure on the lumbar nerves may be present. The individual may also describe the pain as a steady, gnawing discomfort in the lower back or abdomen. Severe pain in the lower abdomen or back that radiates to the buttocks, groin, or legs may signal an imminent rupture of the aneurysm. Individuals experiencing severe, abrupt, persistent back and/or abdominal pain may have an aneurysm that has already ruptured. Additional symptoms indicating that rupture has occurred include low blood pressure, weakness, sweating, and fast heart rate (tachycardia).

Physical exam: In non-obese individuals, a pulsating mass or swelling in the umbilical area may be evident. Approximately 80% of all abdominal aneurysms are felt (palpated) and diagnosed during a routine physical examination. Ninety percent of these originate below the renal arteries and often involve the iliac arteries. A blowing murmur (bruit) can be heard when a stethoscope is placed over the mass. Abdominal aneurysms do not cause diminished pulses in the arms. However, diminished pulses in the legs (peripheral pulses) may be present due to atherosclerotic narrowing of the iliac, femoral, or more distal arteries and thereby mimicking a dissecting aneurysm.

Tests: Routine x-rays of the abdomen may demonstrate an AAA by revealing the calcification that exists in the wall of the aneurysm in 75% of instances. Aortography is a more detailed x-ray procedure that depicts the inside of an aneurysm and permits precise measurement of its size and location. Aortography can also differentiate a dissecting aneurysm from a saccular or fusiform aneurysm. Abdominal ultrasound is a noninvasive alternative to aortography. Serial ultrasound examinations permit following the size of an AAA to ascertain when elective surgery should be performed. Serial CT scans and MRI examinations are equally valuable, though more expensive techniques to obtain the same information.

Treatment

Treatment is directed at reducing the risk of aneurysm rupture by timely surgical resection of the aneurysm and replacement of the damaged aortic section with a graft. If the aneurysm is small and produces no symptoms, surgery may be delayed, however, even small aneurysms may rupture. The risk of rupture of smaller (less than 6 cms in diameter) aneurysms is about 4% per year. The risk of rupture of larger aneurysms is 3 to 5 times higher.

Medications called beta-blockers may be taken to decrease the rate of growth of an AAA. Regular physical examinations and ultrasound studies are used to detect enlargement that may precede rupture. Rupture of an AAA constitutes a medical emergency necessitating immediate surgery.

Emergency surgery involves the same procedure to resect the aneurysm and repair the damaged section of the aorta as in nonemergency situations with the possible addition of the stabilizing measures. These measures include the administration of medications to lower blood pressure (antihypertensives), medications to decrease the force of blood vessel contractions (beta-blockers), oxygen for difficulty in breathing, narcotics for pain relief, administration of fluids directly into a vein (intravenous) and, if necessary, whole blood transfusions.

Urgent but not emergency surgical repair is recommended for aneurysms 6 cm or larger in individuals without other significant medical problems. Elective surgical repair is often considered for aneurysms between 4 and 6 cm. The operative mortality rate for elective repair of an AAA is 2-5%. In contrast, the operative mortality for ruptured AAAs is 50% or more.

Surgical repair of an AAA consists of cutting out the part of the artery affected by the aneurysm (aneurysm resection) and restoration of blood flow using a synthetic or composite graft replacement. This procedure is used in emergency as well as elective situations. High-risk cardiac patients are poor surgical risks. Heart problems should be addressed prior to surgery.

Prognosis

Approximately half the individuals with an AAA larger than 6 cm in diameter die from rupture within 2 years of diagnosis if elective surgical repair is not performed. Among individuals with a leaking or ruptured AAA, the perioperative death rate is about 50%. Among individuals with smaller, unruptured aneurysms the perioperative mortality is only 2-5%.

Differential Diagnosis

The differential diagnosis of a ruptured AAA includes an acute myocardial infarction, unstable, intestinal ischemia, renal colic, mesenteric thrombosis, appendicitis, intestinal obstruction, and peptic ulcer disease.

Specialists

- Cardiologist
- Gastroenterologist
- Vascular Surgeon

Work Restrictions / Accommodations

Before and after surgery for an AAA, contact sports and activities that require lifting more than 25 pounds should be avoided. Associated atherosclerotic cardiovascular disease involving the heart or legs causing effort angina and/or claudication may limit activity or require work accommodations in addition to those necessitated by an AAA.

Comorbid Conditions

Existing conditions that can impact the individual's ability to recover include obesity, heart disease, respiratory disease, additional vascular disease, and gastrointestinal disease.

Complications

The major complication of an AAA is rupture. Rupture may result in hypovolemic shock, a heart attack, stroke, or death.

Factors Influencing Duration

Factors that may lengthen disability include the location and size of the aneurysm, extent of surgical repair necessary, whether underlying cardiovascular diseases such as hypertension or arteriosclerosis are present, and whether postoperative heart attack (myocardial infarction) or renal failure occurs.

Length of Disability

The length of disability depends on job requirements and how rapidly the individual recovers from the surgical procedure. If the job is one of primarily strenuous physical labor, the disability will last longer than if requirements are more sedentary. Other factors that may influence length of disability include age and any other chronic illness such as heart or respiratory disease. Disability may be permanent.

Non-ruptured.

Duration in Days

Job Classification	Minimum	Optimum	Maximum
Sedentary work	3	5	15
Light work	3	5	15
Medium work	3	5	Indefinite
Heavy work	5	10	Indefinite
Very Heavy work	5	10	Indefinite

Surgical treatment. Aneurysmectomy.

Duration in Days

Job Classification	Minimum	Optimum	Maximum
Sedentary work	56	70	Indefinite
Light work	56	84	Indefinite
Medium work	56	105	Indefinite
Heavy work	84	140	Indefinite
Very Heavy work	84	140	Indefinite

Duration Trend from Normative Data*

Cases	Mean	Min	Max	No Lost Time	Over 6 Months
551	66	0	559	0.73%	0.73%

Percentile:	5th	25th	Median	75th	95th
Days:	14	39	56	83	147

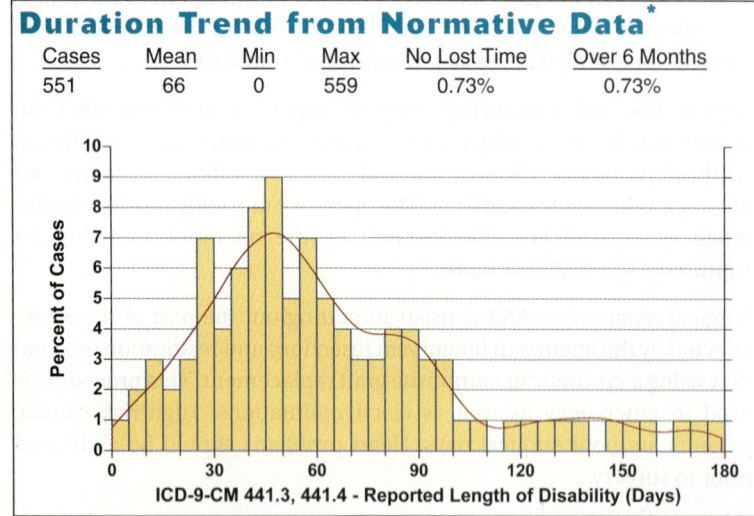
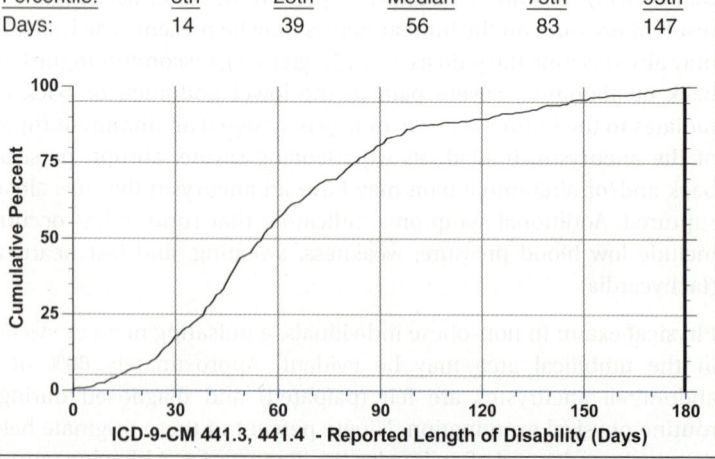

ICD-9-CM 441.3, 441.4 - Reported Length of Disability (Days)

* Differences may exist between the expected duration tables and the normative graphs. Duration tables provide expected recovery periods based on the type of work performed by the individual. The normative graphs reflect the actual observed experience of many individuals across the spectrum of physical conditions, in a variety of industries, and with varying levels of case management.

The Medical Disability Advisor—Fourth Edition

Failure to Recover

If an individual fails to recover within the maximum duration expectancy period, the reader may wish to reference the following questions to assist in better understanding the specifics of an individual's medical case.

Regarding diagnosis:

- What type of AAA does individual have? Saccular, fusiform, or dissecting?
- What was the cause of the AAA?
- Did individual present with a clinical history and symptoms consistent with the diagnosis of abdominal aortic aneurysm?
- Did individual have symptoms of shock or symptoms suggestive of aneurysm rupture?
- Was the diagnosis confirmed with a physical exam and diagnostic x-rays?
- Was the diagnosis determined promptly?
- If the diagnosis was uncertain, were other conditions with similar symptoms ruled out?
- Would individual benefit from consultation with a specialist (cardiologist, vascular surgeon, gastroenterologist)?

Regarding treatment:

- Was the treatment appropriate for the size and nature of the aneurysm?
- Was there any unnecessary delay in treatment?
- Did individual require emergency surgery?

Regarding prognosis:

- Based on the size of the aneurysm and the presenting symptoms (rupture vs. non rupture), what was the expected outcome?
- Does individual have any comorbid conditions that may impact surgical risk or ability to recover?
- Did individual have any complications that may impact recovery and prognosis?

References

Eagle, Kim A., MD, and William F. Armstrong, MD. Diseases of the Aorta. Scientific American 01 May 1999 24 July 2000 <http://www.samed.com/sam/forms/index.htm>.

Kang, S.S., et al. "Higher Prevalence of Abdominal Aortic Aneurysms in Patients With Carotid Stenosis but Without Diabetes." Surgery 126.4 1999 1. 18 May 2000 <http://www.pch@caregroup.harvard.edu>.

Abdominal Muscle Strain

Other names / synonyms: Abdominal Strain, Abdominal-Wall Strain, Pulled Abdominal Muscle, Strained Abdominal Muscle

848.8

Definition

Abdominal muscle strain occurs when muscles of the abdominal wall, or their tendons, are stretched or torn due to excessive force. Abdominal wall muscles include the rectus abdominis, external and internal oblique, and the transversus abdominis. Of these, the rectus is the most commonly strained.

Muscle strains may be classified as first, second, or third degree (mild, moderate, and severe, respectively). In a first-degree strain, the muscle is stretched but not torn. Further stretching results in partial tearing, a second-degree strain. In third-degree strain, the muscle or tendon by which it is attached to bone is completely torn (ruptured).

In an employment setting, abdominal muscle strains most often result from heavy lifting or sudden twisting. Athletic activities such as weightlifting or sit-ups are also common causes of such strains. Abdominal muscles may be stretched or torn when an overweight or out of condition individual begins to exercise. The risk of abdominal strain increases when cardiovascular problems impede circulation to the muscles.

Diagnosis

History: The individual complains of abdominal pain, worse when the muscle contracts and less when it is relaxed. There may also be spasms, particularly when moving.

Physical exam: There is tenderness (generally localized), muscle guarding, and some loss of strength except with a mild "pulled" muscle. Swelling may be apparent. When pressed with the fingers, the injured area may have a crackling feeling (crepitation) that may be audible.

Tests: X-rays may show calcification in the muscle or associated tendon.

Treatment

Treatment of mild to moderate (first to second degree) abdominal strains consists of ice, rest, and nonsteroidal anti-inflammatory drugs for the first 36 to 48 hours. If stronger pain relief is necessary, an oral narcotic or injection of a long-acting local anesthetic may be appropriate. After 48 hours, moist heat or whirlpool heat may be applied to the area if symptoms persist. Between treatments, a loosely wrapped elastic bandage or corset may be worn. Any activity involving lifting, twisting, or sudden stretching should be avoided. Severe (third degree) strains require surgical repair or reconstruction of the torn abdominal wall muscle or tendon.

Prognosis

Complete recovery is expected. In most cases, conservative treatment with ice, rest, and medication yields results in recovery of function and resolution of pain. For the most severe strains surgical repair or reconstruction generally restores function and relieves the discomfort. Compliance with the physician's instructions, particularly activity restrictions, is important to avoid prolonging healing time. The individual may be prone to repeated injury of the same area.

Differential Diagnosis

Symptoms may be similar to those from blunt trauma (e.g., a lap belt contusion in an automobile accident or crush injury). However, in addition to bruising of abdominal wall muscles, such blunt trauma may damage organs in the abdominal cavity.

Abdominal muscle strain may also be confused with intra-abdominal diseases such as appendicitis. However, unlike a muscle strain, the pain from appendicitis is usually not significantly increased by muscle contraction and vice versa.

Specialists

- General Surgeon
- Orthopedic Surgeon
- Physiatrist
- Sports Medicine Physician

Rehabilitation

The basic goals in rehabilitation of abdominal strains are to decrease pain and swelling, and regain full motion, flexibility, strength, and endurance of the muscle, so the individual can return to unrestricted work and recreational activities with minimal risk of reinjury. The severity of the strain determines treatment methods chosen by the physical therapist, and length of the therapy.

If the abdominal strain produces severe pain and a collection of blood (hematoma), ice with an elastic wrap compress is often initially used. The cold helps stop bleeding and diminish pain. Thereafter heat treatments are often used to diminish pain, promote circulation and healing, and facilitate stretching the abdominal muscles. Forms of heat treatment include moist hot packs and ultrasound, the latter using high frequency sound waves that penetrate deep into the involved muscles. Electrical stimulation may also diminish pain and muscle guarding, and strengthen weak muscles.

After 48 hours, stretching and strengthening exercises of the abdominal muscles may be initiated, staying within pain-free limits. In an abdominal stretch, the individual stands with feet apart and bends the trunk to one side (laterally) without any backward (extension) or forward motion (flexion).

There are several exercises to strengthen the abdominal muscles. In a pelvic tilt, the individual lies on their back (supine) on a firm surface, and attempts to push the small of lower back into the floor by tilting the upper pelvis rearward. Sit-ups, with knees bent or straight, also help strengthen abdominal muscles. Another popular abdominal strengthening exercise is lying supine and performing circles with the legs as if riding a bicycle. Physical therapists or exercise physiologists also teach resistance exercises using a pulley system with combined rotation and bending of the trunk.

The therapist may need to modify the program depending on the severity of the abdominal muscle strain. With a significant tear, healing generally takes longer, and requires more stretching and strengthening before return to work. Once back on the job, it is important to initially minimize bending, lifting, and twisting of the trunk.

Work Restrictions / Accommodations

Temporary reassignment to duties that do not involve lifting, bending, twisting, or prolonged standing may be required. For example, a childcare employee who often lifts or carries toddlers might be reassigned to work with older children who do not require such care. Delivery drivers, warehouse workers, and others whose jobs involve repetitive lifting may need to be assigned to modified duty until the strain heals.

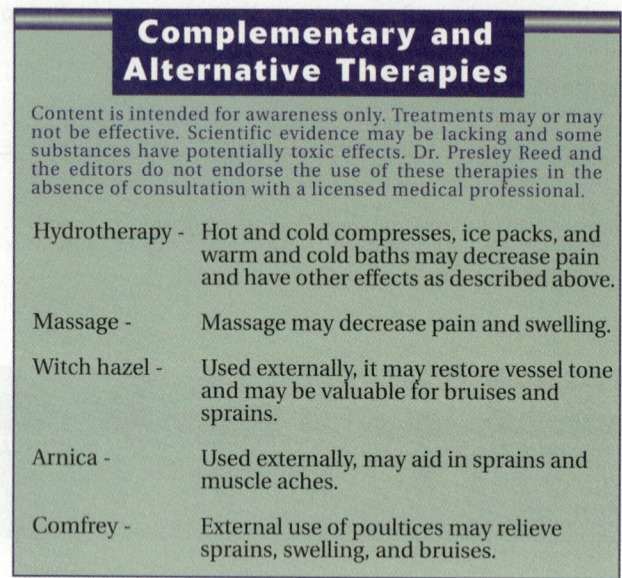

Complementary and Alternative Therapies

Content is intended for awareness only. Treatments may or may not be effective. Scientific evidence may be lacking and some substances have potentially toxic effects. Dr. Presley Reed and the editors do not endorse the use of these therapies in the absence of consultation with a licensed medical professional.

Hydrotherapy - Hot and cold compresses, ice packs, and warm and cold baths may decrease pain and have other effects as described above.

Massage - Massage may decrease pain and swelling.

Witch hazel - Used externally, it may restore vessel tone and may be valuable for bruises and sprains.

Arnica - Used externally, may aid in sprains and muscle aches.

Comfrey - External use of poultices may relieve sprains, swelling, and bruises.

Comorbid Conditions

Coexisting conditions that may delay recovery and lengthen disability include structural abnormalities that inordinately stress the abdominal wall, fractures of associated bones such as ribs or hips, malnutrition, obesity, and cardiovascular disease.

Complications

Extreme overstretching may rupture of the muscle-tendon-bone attachment. Inflammation may occur where the tendon attaches to the bone (periostitis).

Factors Influencing Duration

Length of disability depends on the severity of the muscle or tendon strain, which muscle(s) is involved, and physical demands of the individual's work. Disability duration will be increased if the individual does not comply with instructions regarding activity restrictions for a sufficient time. If muscles or tendons were torn, it will take about as long to heal as a fracture. If surgery is required, additional postoperative recovery will be necessary.

Length of Disability

Duration depends on severity and which muscle(s) is involved. The individual may need to be reassigned to duties that require no bending, lifting, or twisting until the injury heals.

Duration in Days

Job Classification	Minimum	Optimum	Maximum
Sedentary work	0	2	5
Light work	0	3	7
Medium work	2	5	7
Heavy work	2	7	21
Very Heavy work	3	10	28

Failure to Recover

If an individual fails to recover within the maximum duration expectancy period, the reader may wish to reference the following questions to assist in better understanding the specifics of an individual's medical case.

Regarding diagnosis:
- Was diagnosis of muscle strain confirmed?
- Were other causes of abdominal pain and/or swelling ruled out?
- Were x-rays performed to rule out additional injuries such as fractures?
- Was there inflammation at tendon attachment to bone (periostitis)? If so, what was done?

Regarding treatment:
- Have rest, ice, and nonsteroidal anti-inflammatory drugs relieved symptoms?
- Has heat in some form been added to the treatment regimen?
- Has individual been instructed to avoid excessive lifting, bending, or twisting, as well as sudden stretching?

Regarding prognosis:
- Does excessive soreness persist despite treatment?
- Has individual resumed activity too soon?
- Is he or she prone to repeated injury? If so, was individual instructed in safe body mechanics?

References

"Common Sports Injuries." Merck Manual of Diagnosis and Therapy, 17th ed. Beers, Mark H., and Robert Berkow, MD Whitehouse Station, NJ: Merck & Co., Inc, 1999 07 Nov 2000 <http://www.merck.com/pubs/mmanual/section5/chapter62/62a.htm>.

DerMarderosian, Ara. The Review of Natural Products. St. Louis: Facts and Comparisons, 2000.

Abdominal Pain
Other names / synonyms: Acute Abdomen
789.0, 789.3

Definition

Abdominal pain is a symptom that occurs during the course of many acute and chronic illnesses.

Abdominal pain may vary in severity and length of duration. It may be indicative of a severe, life-threatening condition or may resolve before a diagnosis can be made. Abdominal pain may have a rapid, severe onset (acute) that requires hospitalization to control symptoms and diagnose the condition, or it may be chronic and not require hospitalization for treatment or diagnosis. The source of abdominal pain is sometimes difficult to identify.

Acute abdomen refers to an episode of severe abdominal pain that lasts for several hours or longer, possibly accompanied by other significant signs and symptoms, and requires immediate medical attention. Examples of acute abdomen include gastrointestinal tract disorders (appendicitis, bowel obstruction, bowel perforation, perforated peptic ulcer, acute gastritis, gastroenteritis, incarcerated hernia); liver, spleen, and biliary tract disorders (acute cholecystitis, acute cholangitis, hepatic abscess, acute hepatitis, splenic infarct or rupture); pancreatic disorders (acute pancreatitis); urinary tract disorders (renal colic, acute pyelonephritis, acute cystitis); gynecological disorders (ruptured ectopic pregnancy, twisted ovarian cyst or tumor, acute salpingitis, endometriosis); vascular disorders (ruptured aortic aneurysms, mesenteric thrombosis); and peritoneal disorders (peritonitis and intra-abdominal abscesses). An acute abdomen may also occur with the worsening of chronic abdominal conditions.

Recurrent milder abdominal pain may suggest chronic illness such as chronic gastritis, pancreatitis, cholecystitis, hepatitis, peptic and duodenal ulcers, abdominal tumors, diverticulosis, Crohn's disease, ulcerative colitis, irritable bowel syndrome, gynecologic problems, or psychosomatic pain.

Males and females may be equally affected and incidence varies with the underlying cause or diagnosis.

Diagnosis

History: Abdominal pain differs in its location, mode of onset, progression, and character. The individual may complain of slow onset, dull, poorly localized abdominal pain, or acute, sharper, and better-localized pain. Abdominal pain can spread or shift. Onset may be rapid (within seconds), rapidly progressive (within 1 to 2 hours), or gradual (over several hours or days). Character of pain can be constant or recurrent, vague, crampy, "stabbing," or "breathtaking." Individuals may also complain of fever, loss of appetite, nausea and vomiting, constipation, or diarrhea. In many cases, other symptoms help identify the cause of abdominal pain.

Physical exam: Physical findings vary depending on the cause of the abdominal pain. The abdomen can be tense, rigid, generally or locally tender, distended, with visible contractions, or diminished bowel sounds. Abdominal masses can be detected by deep touch (palpation). Pain experienced with gentle pressure on the abdomen may become suddenly worse when the pressure is released (rebound tenderness). Other findings may include pale complexion (pallor), low blood pressure (hypotension), fever, rapid heartbeat, shallow breathing, sweating, and shock. Other findings include yellow tinge to the skin and whites of the eyes (jaundice) and blood in the urine, stool, or vomit. Rectal and pelvic examinations help identify location and source of the pain.

Tests: Laboratory tests include blood studies such as a complete blood count, liver function, kidney function, pregnancy test, amylase, and lipase. Urinalysis tests may be performed for infections, pregnancy, kidney function, and urinary tract disorders. The stool may be tested for blood, amebae, parasites, or other abnormalities. Imaging depends on indication and may include plain chest and abdominal x-rays, contrast x-rays, intravenous pyelogram, angiography, ultrasound, CT, and radionuclide scan. Endoscopy studies may be indicated (colonoscopy, gastroduodenoscopy, proctosigmoidoscopy), as well as paracentesis and laparoscopy. In females, diagnostic laparoscopy may be necessary.

Treatment

Treatment depends on symptoms, their severity, and the specific diagnosis when identified. Hospitalization is often necessary for individuals experiencing acute abdomen. Treatment of acute abdomen may include medications to reduce pain and stomach acid secretions that may contribute to esophagitis or peptic ulcer symptoms. Antibiotics may also be given to treat pain secondary to an infectious cause (e.g., pelvic inflammatory disease). Medications may be given to help stabilize vital signs (blood pressure or heart rate) that are adversely affected by the pain or the underlying condition causing it. Individuals with an acute abdomen are not given anything to eat or drink and are placed on intravenous fluids. Bed rest may also be ordered until improvement is noted.

Prognosis

Outcome depends on diagnosis, severity of symptoms, and the promptness and effectiveness of treatment. Surgical outcome depends on the underlying condition that requires surgical repair. Prognosis for the majority of surgeries is good (i.e., appendicitis or cholecystectomy). When a malignancy is the underlying cause, however, prognosis may be variable. Outcome may also be guarded if there is a severe or widespread infection (i.e., peritonitis, sepsis) especially in older individuals or individuals with increased risk of complications (i.e., obesity, diabetes).

Differential Diagnosis

Other possibilities include endocrine and metabolic disorders, hematologic disorders (leukemia), toxins and drugs (lead and heavy metal poisoning, narcotic withdrawal, black widow spider bite), infections and inflammatory disorders, and referred pain from thoracic region, hip, or back. In women, abdominal pain (lower abdominal) may be gynecologic in origin.

Specialists

- Emergency Medicine
- Gastroenterologist
- General Surgeon
- Gynecologist
- Internist

Work Restrictions / Accommodations

Restrictions and accommodations depend on type of abdominal pain (acute or chronic), severity of symptoms, specific diagnosis, and type of treatment (i.e., medication or surgery).

Comorbid Conditions

If surgical repair is necessary, comorbid conditions that may impact recovery include obesity, diabetes, and cardiovascular and pulmonary diseases.

Complications

Complications include rupture of an inflamed organ (e.g., ruptured appendix), puncture (perforation) that causes leakage of digestive tract contents into the abdominal cavity, bleeding (hemorrhage), bowel obstruction, or overwhelming infection (sepsis). In women, a ruptured fallopian tube from an ectopic pregnancy can be a life-threatening emergency.

Factors Influencing Duration

Length of disability may be influenced by the severity of the symptoms, specific diagnosis, type of treatment, response to treatment, and the development of complications.

Length of Disability

Vague diagnosis. Duration depends on cause. Contact physician for more information.

Duration in Days			
Job Classification	Minimum	Optimum	Maximum
Any work	0	3	7

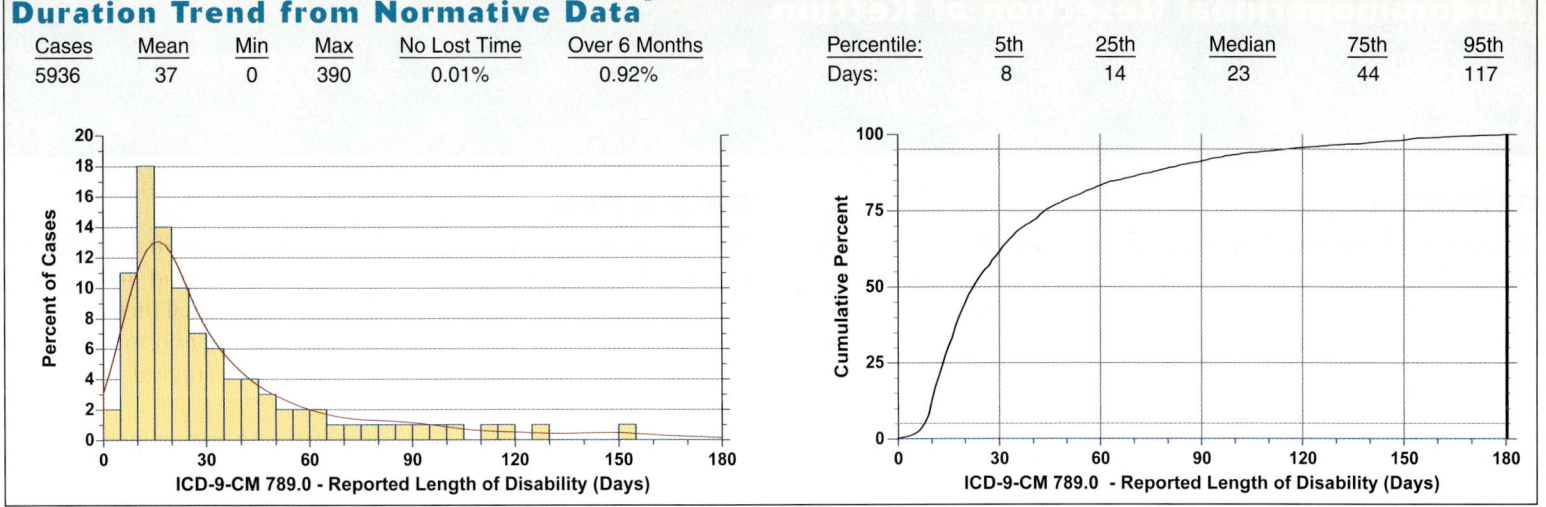

Failure to Recover

If an individual fails to recover within the maximum duration expectancy period, the reader may wish to reference the following questions to assist in better understanding the specifics of an individual's medical case.

Regarding diagnosis:

- Did individual complain of slow onset, dull, poorly localized abdominal pain or acute, sharper, and better-localized pain? Did pain spread or shift? What was the character of the pain? Constant or recurrent? Vague, crampy, stabbing, or breathtaking?
- Did individual have fever, loss of appetite, nausea and vomiting, constipation, or diarrhea?
- Was abdomen tense, rigid, generally or locally tender, distended, with visible contractions, or diminished bowel sounds?
- Did individual have pale complexion (pallor), low blood pressure (hypotension), fever, rapid heartbeat, shallow breathing, sweating, or shock? Was there a yellow tinge to the skin and whites of eyes (jaundice)? Was there blood in the urine, stool, or vomit?
- Were diagnostic tests performed to help identify cause of abdominal pain?
- Was underlying cause of abdominal pain identified?
- Was specific diagnosis confirmed?

Regarding treatment:

- Has underlying cause of pain been identified and resolved? Infection eliminated? Condition surgically repaired?
- If caused by a malignancy, is malignancy operable? If not, what other modes of treatment are available?
- Did individual respond as expected to treatment? If not, what further or alternative treatment options are planned?

Regarding prognosis:

- What is the expected outcome for this diagnosis?
- Why or in what ways does individual's course differ?
- What is expected prognosis for this diagnosis?
- What accommodations can be made to assist individual?
- Would individual benefit from referral to a pain clinic?
- Has individual experienced any complications?
- Were underlying conditions identified that may impact course of illness or recovery?

References

DerMarderosian, Ara, ed. The Review of Natural Products. St. Louis: Facts and Comparisons, 2000.

Huang, William Y. "Gastrointestinal Symptoms." Saunders Manual of Medical Practice, 2nd ed. Rakel, Robert E., ed. Philadelphia: W.B. Saunders Company, 2000. 390-392.

Abdominoperineal Resection of Rectum

Other names / synonyms: Abdomino Endorectal Resection, Bowel Resection, Excision of Distal Sigmoid, Excision of Rectosigmoid, Excision of Rectum, Segmental Resection

48.35, 48.5

Definition

Abdominoperineal resection of the rectum is an extensive operation that involves removal of the far end (distal) section of the intestinal tract, including the far end of the colon, rectum, and anus. This part of the intestinal tract is called by many terms, including the large intestine, large bowel, and colon. It is called abdominoperineal because two incisions are needed to complete the surgery, one in the abdomen and one in the perineal area.

A general term for surgery on the colon is a segmental resection, because only segments of the intestine are removed.

The large intestine and rectum are the far ends of the muscular tube that makes up the intestinal tract. The colon and rectum remove nutrients from foods and store the waste material (stool or feces) until it is expelled from the body.

In this procedure, the cancerous tumor and a length of normal tissue on either side of the tumor are removed. Generally, in an abdominoperineal resection, a permanent opening is made through the wall of the abdomen through which waste products can be removed (colostomy). Sometimes the muscles that allow voluntary control and passage of stool can be preserved (sphincter saving or preserving) and a permanent colostomy is not necessary.

An abdominoperineal resection is most often performed to remove cancerous tumors from the colon, rectum (often referred to as colorectal cancer), and anus. Colorectal cancer is the third most common cancer in the US. It is the second most common cause of cancer death in both men and women in the US. About 150,000 cases of colorectal cancer occur every year in the US. About 75% of all cases of colorectal cancer occur in the parts of the colon closest to the rectum (the descending colon and the sigmoid colon) and the rectum.

Only about 2-3% of all cancers of the gastrointestinal tract involve the anus. Abdominoperineal resection is generally reserved for these cancers that involve or are closest to the anus.

Reason for Procedure

An abdominoperineal resection is generally performed to remove (excise) a cancerous tumor from the lower end of the rectum or the anus. This procedure is part of the treatment for cancer of the rectum that has not spread (metastasized) beyond the limits of the rectum.

An abdominoperineal resection is sometimes performed to remove parts of the large intestine that are diseased due to inflammatory diseases of the lower colon, rectum, and anus such as ulcerative colitis and Crohn's disease.

Sometimes the tumor is too advanced for potential cure, but the procedure may be undertaken to remove as much tumor as possible and prevent the tumor from obstructing the intestinal tract in order to prolong life.

Description

The operation is performed through two incisions, one in the abdomen and one through the region between the anus and the genitals (perineum). Surgery may proceed from the abdominal incision to the perineal incision, or sometimes the operation is performed through both incisions simultaneously with two sets of surgical teams and equipment.

The individual is anesthetized, and the abdomen and perineum are cleansed with an antibiotic surgical scrub solution. A drainage tube is placed into the bladder to drain urine (Foley catheter) and a tube is placed through the nose and into the stomach to drain secretions. An incision is made through the abdomen, and the entire abdominal cavity is examined to identify spread of the tumor (tumor staging). The surgeon gently works through membranes and tissues that line the abdominal and perineal organs (peritoneum). Abdominal and peritoneal arteries and nerves are identified and protected. The perineal incision is also made. The rectum is freed from surrounding tissue and removed. The bowel is also freed from surrounding tissue and cut loose. The end of the bowel that is to remain is examined to be certain that all cancer cells have been removed, and the end of the bowel is attached to an artificial opening in the abdominal wall (colostomy). The anus is removed and the area is sutured closed. Tubes may be placed in the incisions to drain blood and other secretions during healing. Dressings are applied to both incisions, and a drainage bag is placed over the colostomy.

Prognosis

The 10-year survival rate for individuals who undergo surgical resection is also about 50 percent. Unfortunately, about 20-30% of individuals develop a recurrence of the tumor. Ninety-eight percent of these recurrences occur in the first 4 years. The outcome is much poorer following recurrence of the tumor.

The extent and spread of cancer, especially at the time of diagnosis, is the main factor determining the outcome of cancer of the colon and rectum (colorectal cancer). About 50% of all individuals with colorectal cancer are alive at 5 years. However, with early detection and treatment, the 5-year survival rate is higher, at about 80%, compared with only 5% in cases where the disease had already spread at the time of diagnosis.

If surgery was performed for palliative purposes, the average length of survival is 7 months.

Specialists

- Colorectal Surgeon
- Surgeon

Work Restrictions / Accommodations

As with all operations that involve abdominal incisions, there is a period when moderate to heavy lifting should be avoided until there is satisfactory healing of the operative sites. Until there is satisfactory adjustment of the diet, more frequent restroom breaks may be necessary. Development of complications may increase the recovery time and the amount of time needed off of work. Increased recovery time may also be needed for chemotherapy or radiation therapy. Individuals undergoing chemotherapy may be at increased risk of infection, and may need to avoid individuals with infective illnesses.

There are profound psychological factors involved with undergoing this operation. Individuals must cope with the knowledge that they have cancer, and there is a period of adjustment to having the colostomy. There are support groups of individuals who have undergone these types of operations, and the individual should be aware that there is help available apart from the traditional medical community.

Comorbid Conditions

Comorbid conditions may include diabetes mellitus and heart or lung disease. Obesity can cause prolapse of the stoma.

Procedure Complications

Complications include bleeding, infection, wound healing problems, problems with the colostomy, and cardiopulmonary complications. In some cases, even though all of the tumor was removed at the time of surgery, it may recur and spread (metastasis). Another complication that may occur is damage to nerves, which may result in "dry" orgasms and release of semen into the bladder (retrograde ejaculation) in men. Other complications may occur as a result of additional cancer therapy (adjuvant therapy), such as treatment with anticancer medications (chemotherapy) and radiation therapy. Chemotherapy may cause nausea, vomiting, loss of appetite, loss of hair, rashes, and mouth sores. Chemotherapy can also cause a severe decrease in the number of red blood cells (anemia) and white blood cells. A reduction in the number of white blood cells may make the individual at increased risk of infection. Radiation therapy may cause mild skin irritation, nausea, diarrhea, rectal irritation, bladder irritation, and fatigue.

Factors Influencing Duration

Physical limitations that might lengthen the period of disability include the underlying diseases associated with aging (including diabetes) that may slow healing of the surgical wounds, heart and lung disease, and mental infirmity.

Length of Disability

Duration in Days

Job Classification	Minimum	Optimum	Maximum
Sedentary work	28	35	42
Light work	28	35	42
Medium work	42	49	56
Heavy work	56	70	84
Very Heavy work	56	70	84

References

Colon and Rectum Cancer. American Cancer Society 24 Feb 2000 11 Jan 2001 <http://www3.cancer.org/cancerinfo/load_cont.asp?ct=10&st=tr>.

DerMarderosian, Ara. The Review of Natural Products. St. Louis: Facts and Comparisons, 2000.

Ewert-Flannagan, Patricia, and Bernard Levin. "Colorectal Cancer." Primary Care Oncology. Boyer, Kathryn L., et al Philadelphia: W.B. Saunders Company, 1999. 141-155.

Kodner, J. II, et al. "Colon, Rectum, and Anus." Principles of Surgery, Companion Handbook, 7th ed. Schwartz, Seymour I New York: McGraw-Hill, 1999. 631-658.

Levin, Bernard. "Neoplasms of the Large and Small Intestines." Cecil Textbook of Medicine, 20th ed. Bennett, J. Claude, and Fred Plum Philadelphia: W.B. Saunders Company, 1996. 721-729.

Livstone, Elliot M. "Tumors of the Gastrointestinal Tract." The Merck Manual of Diagnosis and Therapy, 17th ed. Beers, Mark H., and Robert Berkow, eds. Whitehouse Station, NJ: Merck Research Laboratories, 1999. 320-335.

Mailliard, James A. "Carcinoma of the Rectum." Current Therapy in Cancer, 2nd ed. Foley, John F., Julie M. Vose, and James O. Armitage, eds. Philadelphia: W.B. Saunders Company, 1999. 101-103.

Markman, Maurie. "Colon Cancer." Basic Cancer Medicine. Markman, Maurie, ed. Philadelphia: W.B. Saunders Company, 1997. 78-79.

McQuaid, Kenneth R. "Alimentary Tract." Current Medical Diagnosis and Treatment, 39th ed. Tierney, Lawrence M., Stephen J. McPhee, and Maxine A. Papadakis, eds. New York: Lange Medical Books/McGraw-Hill, 2000. 553-655.

O'Connell, Michael J. "Carcinoma of the Colon." Current Therapy in Cancer, 2nd ed. Foley, John F., Julie M. Vose, and James O. Armitage, eds. Philadelphia: W.B. Saunders Company, 1999. 97-100.

Petty, Lynda. "Gastrointestinal Surgery." Alexander's Care of the Patient in Surgery, 11th ed. Meeker, Margaret H. and Jane C. Rothrock, eds. St. Louis: Mosby, 1999. 313-370.

Way, L.W., ed. Current Surgical Diagnosis and Treatment. Norwalk: Appleton & Lange, 1994.

Abortion by Dilation and Curettage for Termination of Pregnancy
Other names / synonyms: Elective Abortion, TOP
69.01

Definition

Abortion by dilation and curettage (D & C abortion) is a surgical procedure used to terminate pregnancies between 12 to 16 weeks' duration. The D & C abortion procedure is similar to the D & C procedure used to evaluate abnormal uterine bleeding for any cause. In both procedures, the opening to a woman's uterus (cervix) is enlarged (dilated) and the lining of the uterus (endometrium) is scraped with a special instrument (curette). In the D & C abortion, the curette is also used to remove the products of conception.

The D & C abortion procedure takes slightly more time than the suction curettage abortion procedure. More dilation is required for the cervix, more cramping occurs, and there is a slightly greater risk of complications than with the suction curettage abortion procedure, the most common abortion procedure for pregnancies of 12 to 14 weeks' duration in the US.

Reports issued by Centers for Disease Control and Prevention (CDC) for 1993 and 1994 revealed 20,106 D & C abortion procedures were performed on women in non-Federal, short-stay hospitals in the US. The states with the highest number of procedures were New Jersey (13,791), New York (1,033), and Georgia (4,142). When considered in light of the total curettage abortion procedures performed, D & C abortion comprised 2.6% of the total number of procedures.

Reason for Procedure

The D & C method of early abortion is performed to terminate pregnancy in situations of rape, unplanned pregnancy, or when adverse medical conditions are present. Clinical investigations show that fewer than 5 to 1,000 women experience serious complications.

Description

The D & C abortion is performed with the woman in the same position as that of a pelvic examination (lying on an examination table with legs externally rotated and knees flexed and supported in stirrups). When the individual is anesthetized (local or general anesthesia), a dilator is inserted and as the cervix stretches open (dilates), the gynecologist keeps inserting larger and larger dilators of increasing thickness until an opening is large enough to begin the second phase of surgery. In the second phase, a loop-shaped steel knife (curette) is inserted into the uterus. The walls of the uterus are then scraped to ascertain the removal of any remaining tissue. The entire procedure takes about 15 minutes. Most individuals can go home after a few hours of observation.

Specialists

• Gynecologist	• Primary Care Provider

Prognosis

Predicted outcome after a D & C abortion is good. Most individuals recover with no problems associated with the anesthesia or the procedure. Aftereffects are minimal and a few individuals experience some bleeding and mild period-like cramping for a day or two following the procedure. Hospitalization is usually not required. Although duration of bleeding varies widely, volume of bleeding is similar to a menstrual cycle. If bleeding soaks more than one pad per hour the woman should consult her physician.

The most common problems that develop after an abortion are infection and bleeding. Infection or clots in the uterus can cause cramping. If there is fever, bleeding, or excessive cramps, the individual should request care from her physician.

It is important for the individual to schedule an appointment with her physician 2-4 weeks after the abortion to make sure there are no problems or complications and that all pregnancy tissue was removed. The individual and her physician should discuss the possibility of psychological counseling, as the decision and the actual procedure of abortion are potentially traumatic.

Work Restrictions / Accommodations

Restrictions or accommodations are usually not required because most individuals can return to regular activities and the work environment soon after the procedure. However, if complications arise, extended sick leave may be required. Strenuous physical activity should also be temporarily modified. Returning to work on a part-time basis may be advised until the woman regains her normal strength and stamina.

During the time the individual regains her strength and stamina, accommodations may include the option of relaxed work hours for a few days after returning to work with time allotted for rest periods in a comfortable, quiet, on-site environment.

Comorbid Conditions

Comorbid conditions that might influence length of disability after a D & C abortion include heart, kidney, liver, or lung disorders, or insulin dependent diabetes (IDDM). Some psychiatric conditions (depression) may influence the length of disability.

Procedure Complications

Complications include perforation of the uterus, excessive bleeding (hemorrhage) due to incomplete removal of the products of conception, trauma to abdominal organs (e.g., rupture of bowel or bladder), pelvic infection and inflammation, and laceration or damage to the cervix. Laceration or damage to the uterus often results in the inability of the cervix to retain the fetus within the uterus (cervical incompetence) in future pregnancies, resulting in spontaneous abortion (miscarriage) or premature birth.

Factors Influencing Duration

Length of disability may be influenced by the stage of pregnancy and the presence or absence of complications.

Length of Disability

Duration depends on stage of pregnancy and method. The length of disability varies from 1 to 7 days depending on the level of physical energy required for work duties and whether or not there were any complications from the procedure.

Duration in Days

Job Classification	Minimum	Optimum	Maximum
Sedentary work	2	3	7
Light work	2	3	7
Medium work	3	4	7
Heavy work	3	4	7
Very Heavy work	3	4	7

References

Koonin, Lisa M., MN, MPH, et al. "Abortion Surveillance - United States, 1993 and 1994." Division of Reproductive Health National Center for Chronic Disease Prevention and Health Promotion 08 Aug 1997 30 Sept 2000 <http://www.cdc.gov/mmwr/preview/mmwrhtml/00049084.htm>.

What Is Surgical Abortion? (Fact Sheet). National Abortion Federation 1996 28 Sept 2000 <http://www.prochoice.org/default2.htm>.

Abortion, Medical Induction

Other names / synonyms: Therapeutic Abortion, Medical Termination of Pregnancy

75.0, 96.49

Definition

An abortion by medical induction (medical termination of pregnancy) is the ending or termination of a pregnancy by a means other than surgery. Medical abortions are often performed using agents that induce abortion (prostaglandins, RU 486).

A medical abortion allows the woman to have an abortion without undergoing a surgical procedure, thus reducing the risk of puncturing (perforating) the uterus or tearing (lacerating) the cervix. The medical abortion can, however, be a slow and potentially ineffective method compared to surgical abortion.

There are approximately 1.4 million abortions performed each year in the US. Approximately 1% of all abortions are performed medically or nonsurgically. Maternal or fetal health problems account for 6% of all abortions.

Reason for Procedure

Medical abortion may be recommended for conditions affecting either the woman or the fetus. Maternal indications for medical abortion include autoimmune disease, severe heart disease, cystic fibrosis, chronic kidney disease, sickle cell disease, diabetic retinopathy, cancer, intrauterine infection, premature rupture of membranes, and psychiatric illness. Medical abortion may be indicated if the fetus suffers from severe developmental defects that are incompatible with life such as absence of brain or spinal cord (anencephaly), heart defects, or absence of kidneys (renal agenesis).

Description

Medical abortion methods appropriate for early pregnancy (first trimester) involve giving agents that induce abortion (abortifacients) orally, intramuscularly, or vaginally. Before giving any medications, however, gestational age is verified by ultrasound, and a laminaria (a type of tightly rolled seaweed that slowly dilates the cervix) is inserted into the cervix. Once the cervix has dilated, the laminaria is removed and abortifacients are given. Prostaglandins are a group of fatty acid derivatives that have a marked effect on the uterus and can induce abortion. These are usually administered vaginally every 3 to 4 hours until abortion occurs.

Another agent that induces abortion is called RU 486. This agent competes against the hormone progesterone required to sustain early pregnancy. RU 486 is often used in combination with a prostaglandin and is administered vaginally or intramuscularly 36 to 60 hours after the administration of RU 486. The abortion usually occurs within 24 hours following prostaglandin administration. Methotrexate is a drug that affects rapidly dividing cells such as those within an embryo or early fetus and can be used in combination with a prostaglandin. Methotrexate is administered intramuscularly and followed within 1 to 7 days by vaginal administration of prostaglandin. The abortion should occur in 1 to 2 days but may take up to 4 weeks.

When the pregnancy is between 3 to 6 months (second trimester), an abortion can be initiated by injecting an abortifacient into the fluid-filled sac (amniotic sac) that holds the fetus (intra-amniotic instillation). Abortifacients used for intra-amniotic instillation include solutions of glucose, urea, saline, or prostaglandins. Spontaneous labor and expulsion of the fetus and placenta occurs within 16 to 22 hours after injection of the abortifacient.

Prognosis

Prostaglandins have an excellent effectiveness rate for inducing abortion. Over 85% of women on the mifepristone (RU 486) and prostaglandin regimen abort within 24 hours. Fewer than 1% require surgical intervention (suction curettage).

The methotrexate and prostaglandin regimen has a success rate of 90-93%. Approximately 5% will require surgical abortion because of a failed or incomplete abortion. Intra-amniotic instillation has a high success rate.

Aside from those who develop complications, most women recover physically within a few days.

Specialists

- Gynecologist
- Internist
- Obstetrician
- Psychiatrist
- Psychologist

Work Restrictions / Accommodations

Time off for follow-up medical appointments may be necessary, especially with RU 486. The woman may need to temporarily refrain from engaging in strenuous physical activity. The psychological impact of therapeutic abortion can be considerable and may temporarily affect work performance. Psychotherapeutic counseling may be necessary. A temporary part-time work schedule may also be beneficial in some situations.

Comorbid Conditions

Depression can lengthen the disability. The underlying condition that necessitated the abortion (e.g., heart disease, diabetes, cancer, or autoimmune disease) can influence the length of disability.

Procedure Complications

Complications include excessive or long-term bleeding (hemorrhaging), infection, retention of tissue in the uterus, delivery of a live fetus, and failure to terminate the pregnancy. Uterine infection (endometritis) occurs in 5% of intra-amniotic instillations and can lead to infertility. Prostaglandins can cause vomiting and diarrhea. Methotrexate can cause nausea, diarrhea, and vomiting and, rarely, hair loss (alopecia) and bone marrow suppression. High doses of methotrexate can damage the kidneys or gastrointestinal lining. Abortions generally may have a severe psychological impact on the involved individuals.

Factors Influencing Duration

Length of disability may be influenced by the reason for the procedure, stage of pregnancy, type of procedure used, and any complications.

Length of Disability

Duration of disability depends on type of induction, stage of pregnancy, and job requirements. More lengthy disability may be necessary if the job requires heavy lifting.

Medical induction (saline injection, prostaglandins).

Job Classification	Minimum	Optimum	Maximum
Sedentary work	2	3	7
Light work	2	3	7
Medium work	3	4	7
Heavy work	3	4	7
Very Heavy work	3	4	7

Duration in Days

References

DerMarderosian, Ara, ed. The Review of Natural Products. St. Louis: Facts and Comparisons, 2000.

Ethical Considerations Concerning the Use of Anti-progestins. The FIGO Committee for the Study of Ethical Aspects of Human Reproduction 1994 30 May 2000 <http://www.md.huji.ac.il/figo/figo14.htm>.

Trupin, Suzanne. "Induced Abortion." Danforth's Obstetrics and Gynecology. Scott, James, et al Philadelphia: Lippincott Williams & Wilkins, 1999. 567-578.

Trussel, J., and C. Ellerston. "Estimating the Efficacy of Medical Abortion." Contraception 60 3 1999: 119-135.

Abrasions
919.0, 919.1

Definition

An abrasion is an open wound caused when the topmost layers of skin are rubbed or scraped off. Rope burns, floor burns, and skinned knees or elbows are common examples of abrasions. Abrasions can result from falls or handling coarse objects. In addition, individuals who work on floors or carpets or in tight, confined spaces are at greater risk of sustaining abrasion wounds as a result of skinning the knees, elbows, or knuckles along the floor or rough surfaces.

This type of wound tends to ooze blood or clear fluid. Abrasions can easily become infected because dirt and germs are usually ground into the tissues. However, since abrasions have minimal bleeding, the wound is rarely life-threatening.

Diagnosis

History: Individuals may report a recent injury or accident. History should include information regarding where the injury or accident occurred (on a tar, cement, sand, or gravel surface). Individuals may report a recent scraping of skin over the area involved. Individuals may have had a fall or brushed up against the surface of something rough.

Physical exam: The exam may reveal an area where the skin surface has been rubbed down to bright pink or red tissue with little or no bleeding. Instead, there may be oozing of clear-colored fluid. A slight swelling may be seen around the site and is tender to the touch.

Tests: There are generally no tests indicated in the diagnosis of abrasion wounds. If the wound is old and infection is suspected, a complete blood count and wound culture may be ordered to detect the presence of a wound infection.

Treatment

Abrasions are rarely serious. Applying direct pressure to the wound may be necessary to control bleeding. Dressing and bandaging may be sufficient but the wound should be monitored for signs of infection. If deeper layers of tissue are involved or when the damaged area is large, wound débridement, antibiotic therapy, and possible plastic or reconstructive surgery may be required.

Prognosis

Outcome is good for most individuals. Proper care should be taken to guard against infection.

Differential Diagnosis

Presentation of an abrasion is definitive.

Specialists

- Emergency Medicine
- General Surgeon
- Plastic Surgeon
- Primary Care Provider

Work Restrictions / Accommodations

Work restrictions and accommodations are determined based on the site and size of the abrasion and if it interferes with the individual's job responsibilities.

Complementary and Alternative Therapies

Content is intended for awareness only. Treatments may or may not be effective. Scientific evidence may be lacking and some substances have potentially toxic effects. Dr. Presley Reed and the editors do not endorse the use of these therapies in the absence of consultation with a licensed medical professional.

Electric stimulation -	Said to stimulate healing.
Hyperbaric oxygen therapy -	Increases oxygen to the tissues and may encourage healing.
Ultrasound -	May promote healing.
Whirlpool -	Stimulates circulation and may encourage healing.
Aloe -	Inhibits infection and may promote healing of minor wounds.
Arnica -	Said to stimulate healing of wounds.
Echinacea -	Topical application may stimulate healing of wounds and taken internally, it may stimulate immune system.
Gotu kola -	Used in traditional Eastern medicine, it may help in the promotion of wound healing particularly in chronic lesions.

Comorbid Conditions

Coexisting conditions that may impact recovery and lengthen disability include circulatory disorders or diabetes in which poor circulation causes poor wound healing. Any condition that lowers the immune system and increases the risk of infection can lengthen disability.

Complications

Infection is the primary complication. Scarring may follow deeper abrasions.

Factors Influencing Duration

Primary factors that can lengthen disability time are the location (especially face, hand, and foot), extent, and depth of injury. Deep abrasions involving muscle tissue and bleeding (hemorrhage) may mean a longer period of disability. An abrasion involving a dominant arm or hand requires more time to regain normal functioning. Any abrasion involving a leg or foot may take longer to heal, especially in the presence of vascular compromise.

Length of Disability

Duration in Days

Job Classification	Minimum	Optimum	Maximum
Sedentary work	0	1	1
Light work	0	1	1
Medium work	0	1	1
Heavy work	0	1	3
Very Heavy work	0	1	3

Failure to Recover

If an individual fails to recover within the maximum duration expectancy period, the reader may wish to reference the following questions to assist in better understanding the specifics of an individual's medical case.

Regarding diagnosis:
- What was the mechanism of the injury?
- Did the exam reveal skin surface that has been rubbed down to bright pink or red tissue?
- Was there any bleeding? Oozing of clear-colored fluid?
- Was there swelling around the site? Was it tender to the touch?
- Did infection occur?

Regarding treatment:
- Were strong antiseptics applied such as iodine, methylate, Mercurochrome, or alcohol to clean abrasion?
- Is individual monitoring the wound for infection?
- Were wound debridement or antibiotic therapy needed?
- Was plastic or reconstructive surgery necessary?
- When did individual last have a tetanus booster?

Regarding prognosis:
- Does individual have diabetes or any other condition that can affect circulation or the immune system?
- Where is the abrasion on the body?
- Does individual use that part of the body when performing job responsibilities? If so, is this putting individual at risk for infection?
- Was the abrasion deep and did it involve muscle tissue?
- Does the abrasion affect the dominant hand or arm?

References

Current Medical Diagnosis and Treatment, 39th ed. Tierney, Lawrence M., Stephen J. McPhee, and Maxine Papadakis, eds. New York: Lange Medical Books/McGraw-Hill, 2000.

The Review of Natural Products. DerMarderosian, Ara, ed. St. Louis: Facts and Comparisons, 2000.

Abruptio Placentae

Other names / synonyms: Ablatio Placentae, Accidental Antepartum Hemorrhage, Couvelaire Uterus, Placental Abruption

641.2, 641.20, 641.21, 641.23

Definition

Placental abruption (abruptio placentae) is the premature separation of the placenta from the inside of the uterus during pregnancy. It can occur at 20 weeks (or later) in a pregnancy or during labor. Most often the condition is mild and requires bed rest and careful monitoring of the mother and fetus. In severe cases (complex separation), it can result in severe hemorrhage and shock with death occurring in minutes.

The cause of placental separation is not known, however, increased rates are associated with high blood pressure (hypertension) and an abnormal condition of pregnancy (preeclampsia) that results in acute hypertension.

It is estimated that abruptio placentae occur in approximately 1 in 200 deliveries in the US. Of these US cases, excessive bleeding from the placental abruption accounted for 15% of stillbirths in the last 3 months of pregnancy and 35% of newborn deaths.

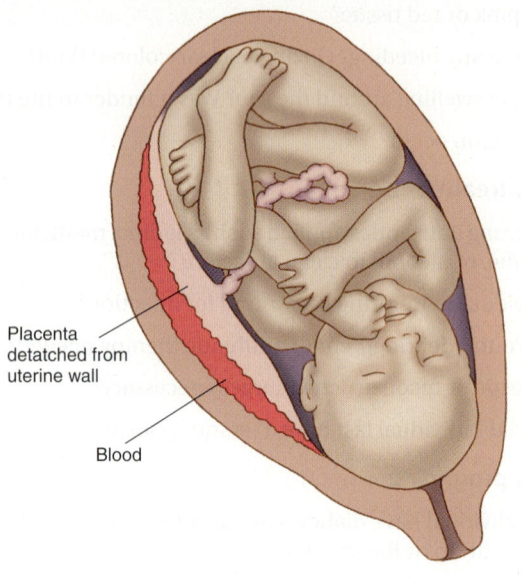

Placenta detached from uterine wall

Blood

Frank Forney

Diagnosis

History: Individuals with complaints of abdominal pain between uterine contractions, a tender uterus, or vaginal bleeding (bleeding is contained underneath the placenta and not seen in a minority of such cases) must be presumed to have abruptio placentae. In severe cases, the individual suddenly hemorrhages heavily. The bleeding causes abdominal pain and uterine tenderness.

Physical exam: Vaginal bleeding is noted in most cases. Signs of major blood loss may be present such as a high heart rate and low blood pressure. The uterus is usually tender.

Tests: Since ultrasonography has a high false-negative rate for abruptio placentae, this condition is typically diagnosed by clinical symptoms. Blood tests include hematocrit, hemoglobin and coagulation studies to screen for disseminated intravascular coagulation (overstimulation of blood clotting processes due to injury or disease).

Treatment

Treatment varies according to the severity of the abruption as well as the fetus' condition. A premature pregnancy may be allowed to continue under close observation of the mother who may be restricted to complete bed rest, however only in the case of a stable nonprogressive abruption with no fetal or maternal compromise.

Mild cases in the third trimester may involve continuous fetal monitoring and may require hospitalization with aggressive hydration. If the pregnancy is near term, labor may be permitted or induced.

In some cases abruption is followed by rapid progression of labor and precipitous vaginal delivery. In severe cases regardless of the stage of pregnancy, an emergency cesarean section may be performed. In some cases, hysterectomy may be necessary due to hemorrhage or coagulopathy. Blood transfusions or medication to aid blood clotting may also be required.

Prognosis

Mild cases have a favorable outcome with slight or no long-term effects to the mother or baby. In some cases, the placenta does not become further detached and the remainder of the pregnancy proceeds without additional complication. Bleeding can cause contractions to occur. However, because the underlying cause of abruption is unknown and the potential for progression is always present, these pregnancies may be considered high risk.

In severe cases when the mother hemorrhages suddenly, fetal mortality rate is 50-80%. In cases that involve emergency delivery, surviving infants often require intensive care and may have serious neurological impairment.

Differential Diagnosis

Bleeding may result from placental abnormalities (e.g., placenta previa or vasa previa), an inflamed cervix, or vaginal blood flow. Abruptio placentae may initially resemble premature labor and be misdiagnosed. Uterine rupture may resemble placental abruption as the signs and symptoms include vaginal bleeding and uterine pain.

Specialists

- Neonatologist
- Perinatologist
- Obstetrician

Work Restrictions / Accommodations

Women with placental abruption cannot usually work without severe risk to themselves and their fetuses. In some cases where the abruption spontaneously heals itself, the woman may return to work on a limited schedule provided she is under frequent observation by her doctor. Women confined to bed may be allowed to perform some sedentary work such as handling telephone calls, working on a laptop computer, or routine paperwork.

Comorbid Conditions

Hypertension, kidney (renal) insufficiency, diabetes, and poor general health may impact the ability to recover.

Complications

A blood clotting defect, acute renal failure, a flaccid uterus, transfusion reaction, amniotic fluid embolus and acute right heart failure are possible complications. The mother can also experience massive hemorrhage and/or death.

Factors Influencing Duration

Severity of hemorrhage, the need for an emergency cesarean section, and any complications all influence the length of disability. In rare cases where the abruption heals itself, the individual may be considered for return to work. In most cases, a woman with placental abruption is confined to bed for the rest of the pregnancy, but may return to work after a normal maternity leave. In severe cases, additional convalescent time will be necessary. In cases where the fetus is stillborn, the woman may be physically able to return to work within a few weeks, but needs more leave time for emotional factors.

Length of Disability

Duration of disability depends on circumstances of abruption and complications and if the mother had a cesarean section. In most cases, the mother can return to work at normal maternity leave time.

Failure to Recover

If an individual fails to recover within the maximum duration expectancy period, the reader may wish to reference the following questions to assist in better understanding the specifics of an individual's medical case.

Regarding diagnosis:

- Did individual present with clinical symptoms consistent with the diagnosis of abruptio placentae?
- Was the diagnosis confirmed with physical exam?
- If the diagnosis was uncertain, were other disorders with similar symptoms ruled out?
- Was the pregnancy near term?
- Was there evidence of severe bleeding or associated shock noted?
- Was any bleeding disturbance confirmed with coagulation studies?
- Was fetal monitoring done? If so, was fetal distress detected?

Regarding treatment:

- Was the treatment appropriate for the severity of the bleeding and condition of the fetus?
- Did the mother have a normal labor and vaginal delivery?
- Was emergency cesarean delivery required?
- Was a blood transfusion required?
- Was a hysterectomy required?

Regarding prognosis:

- What was the expected outcome?
- Was there evidence of severe bleeding?
- Did the mother have any complications or pre-existing conditions that may influence prognosis and length of disability?
- Was fetal death or demise associated with the abruptio placentae? If so, does the mother have psychological counseling and appropriate support systems (family, friends, etc) to foster healthy coping and emotional recovery?

References

DeCherney, Alan H., ed. Current Obstetric and Gynecologic Diagnosis and Treatment. Norwalk: Lange, 1994.

Morrison, Elizabeth H. "Common Peripartum Emergencies." American Family Physician 4 11 1998: 5-10.

Peleg, David., Colleen M. Kennedy, and Stephen K. Hunter. "Intrauterine Growth Restriction; Identification and Management." American Family Physician 4 11 1998: 2-5.

Pritchard, J.A., et al. "On Reducing the Frequency of Severe Abruptio Placentae." American Journal of Obstetrics and Gynecology 165 5 Pt 1 1991: 1345-1351.

Saftlas, A.F., et al. "National Trends in the Incidence of Abruptio Placentae." Obstetrics and Gynecology 78 6 1991: 1081-1086.

Williams, M.A., et al. "Risk Factors for Abruptio Placentae." American Journal of Epidemiology 134 9 1991: 965-972.

Abscess
682, 682.0, 682.1, 682.2, 682.3, 682.4, 682.5, 682.6, 682.7, 682.8, 682.9

Definition

An abscess is a localized infection (usually bacterial) that has been walled off by a protective lining called a pyogenic membrane. The abscess is a defense mechanism designed to prevent the spread of the infectious organism to other parts of the body. The abscess contains pus made up of destroyed tissue cells, white blood cells (leukocytes) that have been carried to the area to fight the infection, and microorganisms (dead and alive). Whether the abscess enlarges or subsides depends on whether the microorganisms or the leukocytes gain the upper hand. Fungi or single-celled parasites called ameba can also cause abscesses.

Although an abscess may occur in any organ or tissue of the body, common sites include the breast (mammary abscess), gums (dental abscess), armpit, and groin. Less common sites include the liver, lung, gastrointestinal tract, kidney, spleen, pancreas, brain, and spinal cord. The infecting organism is usually transported through the bloodstream (hematogenous spread) to the affected organ. Abscesses are classified according to location, i.e., the abdominal cavity (intraperitoneal abscess), near the kidney or spine (retroperitoneal abscess), or within abdominal organs (visceral abscess).

Intra-abdominal abscesses most often form when gastrointestinal contents (including bacteria) are released into the abdominal cavity. Conditions such as appendicitis, diverticulitis, perforated peptic ulcers, and abdominal surgery can cause intra-abdominal abscesses. Brain abscesses often originate from an ear or sinus infection. Abscesses can also form under the skin from several different routes including external (from a wound or an infected hair root), a distant source through the bloodstream, or directly from an internal organ (lung or gastrointestinal system).

Injection drug users have an increased risk of developing skin abscesses. Individuals with cancer, diabetes, alcoholism, and those who use corticosteroids or have had abdominal surgery are at increased risk of developing intraperitoneal abscesses. Alcoholics and individuals with gallstones are at increased risk of developing pancreatic abscesses. Risk factors for developing a kidney abscess include kidney stones (calculi), diabetes mellitus, abnormalities of the urinary tract, and a history of surgery to the urinary tract. Risk factors for developing a lung abscess include gum disease, alcoholism, lung cancer, diabetes mellitus, and inhalation (aspiration) of stomach contents due to heartburn (gastroesophageal reflux). Individuals at risk for spinal epidural abscess include those with diabetes mellitus, alcoholism, kidney failure, and cancer; and those who have had a spinal tap (lumbar puncture), spinal anesthesia, or spinal surgery. Immunocompromised individuals are generally at an increased risk of developing abscesses.

Abscesses of internal organs are rare. The incidence of brain abscess is 0.18-1.3% and that of splenic abscess is 0.14-0.7%. Common superficial abscesses occur in the breast, mouth, and skin.

Diagnosis

History: Individuals with an abscess close to the skin (cutaneous or subcutaneous) may complain of heat, swelling, tenderness, redness over the affected site, and possibly fever. Internal abscesses produce local pain and tenderness, fever, chills, weight loss, fatigue, and loss of appetite. Intra-abdominal abscesses can also cause vomiting, diarrhea, or constipation. Symptoms of a lung abscess include a cough, foul-smelling material coughed up from the lungs, fever, chills, chest pain, weakness, fatigue, and a vague feeling of discomfort or illness (malaise). A spinal epidural abscess causes back pain, fever, and weakness. Brain abscess may cause headache, fever, speech disorder, muscle weakness, impaired vision, seizures, nausea, and vomiting.

Physical exam: Physical findings will depend on the location of the abscess. An intraabdominal abscess may cause tenderness localized to a particular abdominal quadrant and a mass may be detected by touch (palpation). Lung abscess may cause crackling (rales), wheezing, abnormal breath sounds, and dullness to percussion. In some individuals, the presenting symptom is abnormal functioning of the organ in which the abscess has formed.

Tests: Because most abscesses are caused by bacterial infection, material removed from the abscess and blood samples are cultured in the laboratory to identify the causative organism(s). Mucous material coughed up from the lungs (sputum) of individuals with a suspected lung abscess would be cultured. Antibiotic susceptibility tests may also be performed. Complete blood count (CBC), erythrocyte sedimentation rate (ESR), liver enzymes, and amebic serologic tests may be performed. If amebic abscess is suspected, stool samples will be analyzed for the presence of ameba. Tuberculin test (PPD test) may be performed on individuals with lung abscess.

The diagnosis may be confirmed by plain x-rays, ultrasound exams, CT scanning, or MRI imaging techniques. Radionuclide scanning, in which radioactively labeled white blood cells (or the element gallium) concentrate in the region where pus has recently formed, may also be used.

Complementary and Alternative Therapies

Content is intended for awareness only. Treatments may or may not be effective. Scientific evidence may be lacking and some substances have potentially toxic effects. Dr. Presley Reed and the editors do not endorse the use of these therapies in the absence of consultation with a licensed medical professional.

Slippery Elm -	Used as an emollient, it may protect irritated skin in wounds and abscesses.
Soaks in warm water -	May improve circulation and reduce inflammation.
Echinacea -	Said to be effective when used for topical wound healing. Said to aid in internal stimulation of the immune system.
Goldenseal -	May be of use in topical infections. Contraindicated in pregnancy and hypertension.
Gotu Kola -	Used topically in traditional Eastern medicine, may aid in wound healing, particularly in chronic lesions.

Treatment

A minor abscess can sometimes heal without intervention, however drugs are usually necessary to combat the infection. Antibiotics are used for bacterial infections, antifungal drugs for fungal infections, and antiamebic drugs for amebic infections. Drainage is usually necessary either through an open surgical procedure or directly through the skin (percutaneous). Intra-abdominal abscesses almost always require drainage. Exceptions include mild diverticulitis, enteritis, mild cholangitis, and primary peritonitis. Repair of a gastrointestinal defect may involve closure of a hole or removal of the appendix. Spinal abscesses are usually treated with surgical drainage and removal of the lamina (laminectomy) to relieve pressure on the spinal cord.

Prognosis

Early intervention and appropriate treatment of minor abscesses result in an effective cure. The outcome of a deep-seated abscess depends on the location of the abscess, the age of the individual, and the timing and effectiveness of treatment. An abscess within a vital organ (i.e., liver or brain) may occasionally cause enough pressure or damage to surrounding tissue that some permanent loss of function results. Percutaneous drainage of intra-abdominal abscess has an 80% success rate.

Surgical repair of a gastrointestinal defect (e.g., closure of a hole) usually has a good outcome. A ruptured intra-abdominal abscess, however, has a high mortality rate. Pancreatic abscesses have a high mortality rate if surgical drainage is not performed. Although brain abscess has only a 10% mortality rate, 30-55% of these survivors suffer from nervous system effects (sequelae). In spinal abscess, laminectomy and drainage can prevent, reverse, or improve developing paralysis however they will probably not improve established nervous system deficits.

Differential Diagnosis

Cysts and tumors can mimic an abscess. Conditions with signs and symptoms similar to a brain abscess include complicated migraine headache, meningitis, encephalitis, bleeding (hemorrhage), clot (thrombosis), stroke (cerebral infarction), or multiple sclerosis.

Specialists

- Dermatologist
- General Surgeon
- Infectious Disease Physician
- Internist

Work Restrictions / Accommodations

Work restrictions and accommodations require individual consideration. Abscess in an internal organ (e.g., liver, lung, gastrointestinal tract, kidney, spleen, pancreas, brain, or spinal cord) may require a temporary limit on heavy lifting or activities that involve physical exertion. Temporary reassignment to sedentary duties may be necessary.

An armpit or groin abscess may temporarily limit the use of the affected limb. An individual with a complicated brain or spinal epidural abscess may require more extensive accommodations or restrictions depending on the severity of the nervous system deficits. An individual with a complicated spinal epidural abscess for example, may be confined to a wheelchair and so requires wheelchair accessibility in the workplace. An individual with speech impairment because of a complicated brain abscess may need reasonable accommodations or reassignment.

Comorbid Conditions

Coexisting conditions that may impact recovery and lengthen disability include impaired blood supply as occurring in diabetes, or impaired immune system function as found in individuals with AIDS.

Complications

Bacterial infection of the blood (sepsis) may spread the infection to other body sites. Other complications include rupture into adjacent tissue, bleeding from vessels eroded by inflammation, and impaired function of a vital organ. Spinal abscess can cause paralysis. Brain abscess can cause nervous system defects.

Factors Influencing Duration

Length of disability may be influenced by the type and location of the abscess, the individual's age and overall health, early intervention, whether surgical or percutaneous drainage was performed, and response to treatment.

Length of Disability

Duration depends on site, comorbidities, and complications.

Duration in Days

Job Classification	Minimum	Optimum	Maximum
Sedentary work	0	1	7
Light work	0	1	7
Medium work	0	2	7
Heavy work	0	3	7
Very Heavy work	0	3	7

Duration Trend from Normative Data*

Cases	Mean	Min	Max	No Lost Time	Over 6 Months
10198	26	0	349	0.06%	0.07%

Percentile:	5th	25th	Median	75th	95th
Days:	8	12	17	29	87

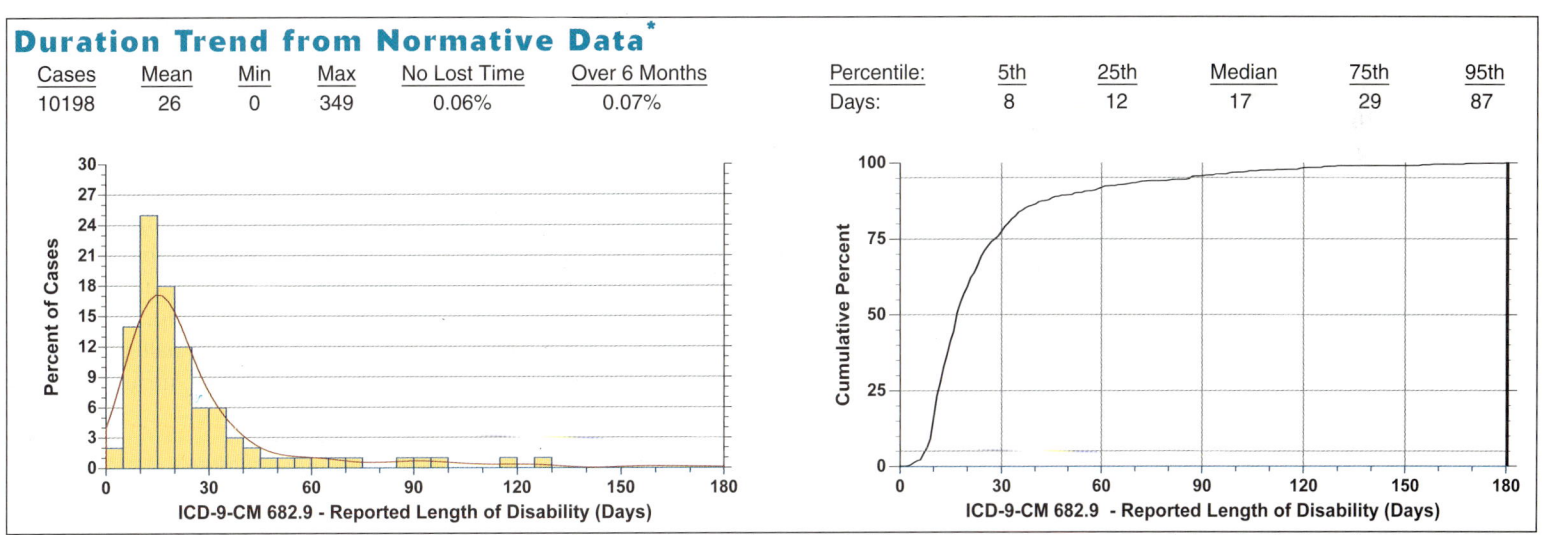

ICD-9-CM 682.9 - Reported Length of Disability (Days)

* Differences may exist between the expected duration tables and the normative graphs. Duration tables provide expected recovery periods based on the type of work performed by the individual. The normative graphs reflect the actual observed experience of many individuals across the spectrum of physical conditions, in a variety of industries, and with varying levels of case management.

Failure to Recover

If an individual fails to recover within the maximum duration expectancy period, the reader may wish to reference the following questions to assist in better understanding the specifics of an individual's medical case.

Regarding diagnosis:

- Where was the abscess located? Was a vital organ involved?
- Did physical findings confirm individual's report?
- Were there nonspecific symptoms such as weight loss, fatigue, or loss of appetite?

- Did a blood test confirm an abnormally large number of white blood cells indicative of infection?
- Were x-rays, ultrasound scanning, CT, or MRI used to determine size and position of abscess?
- Was microscopic examination done to identify causative organism?
- Do culture results confirm diagnosis?

Regarding treatment:

- Was surgical drainage necessary?

- Was laboratory analysis of pus used to select the most effective antibiotic, antifungal, or antiamebic drug?
- Is there evidence of response to treatment?
- Is there a possibility of antibiotic-resistant bacteria?
- Is change of antibiotic warranted?
- Has individual recently used any alternative medication or health practices?

Regarding prognosis:

- What is the overall health of individual?

References

Dellinger, E. "Peritonitis and Intraabdominal Abscesses." Clinical Infectious Diseases. Root, Richard, et al., eds. New York: Oxford University Press, 1999. 613-619.

DerMarderosian, Ara, ed. The Review of Natural Products. St. Louis: Facts and Comparisons, 2000.

Galil, K. Miller, et al. "Abscesses Due to Mycobacterium Abscessus Linked to Infection of Unapproved Alternative Medication." Emerging Infectious Diseases 5 5 1999: 681-687.

Scheld, Michael. "Bacterial Meningitis, Brain Abscess, and Other Suppurative Intracranial Infections." Harrison's Principles of Internal Medicine. Fauci, Anthony, et al., eds. New York: McGraw-Hill, 1998. 2419-2433.

Tunkel, Allan, and Michael Scheld. "Focal Central Nervous System Infections." Clinical Infectious Diseases. Root, Richard, et al New York: Oxford University Press, 1999. 723-731.

Zaleznik, Dori, and Dennis Kasper. "Intraabdominal Infections and Abscesses." Harrison's Principles of Internal Medicine. Fauci, Anthony, et al., eds. New York: McGraw-Hill, 1998. 792-796.

Abscess, Anorectal

Other names / synonyms: Anal Abscess, Ischiorectal Abscess, Perianal Abscess, Perirectal Abscess, Rectal Abscess

566

Definition

An anorectal abscess is a tender pus-filled swelling in the region of the anal or rectal opening.

It is caused by an infection that develops from injury to the anal tissue such as a cut or scratch, in an anal gland that becomes obstructed, or as a sexually transmitted infection. The abscess can be superficial or deep within the tissues around the anus. Crohn's disease, diverticulitis, or other intestinal disorders may sometimes cause deep abscesses. Adults with intestinal disorders such as inflammatory bowel disease may be predisposed to the condition.

Anorectal abscesses are about twice as common in men than women. In adults and adolescents, the infection may be sexually transmitted particularly among male homosexuals.

Diagnosis

History: An anorectal abscess may cause persistent, throbbing pain in and around the anal opening. Surface (superficial) abscesses are usually the most painful especially while sitting and walking and during bowel movements. Constipation may develop. Abscesses deeper in the anorectal tissues may bring on fever and chills, loss of appetite, and a general feeling of illness (malaise) but localized pain may not be severe. With abscesses high in the rectum, the individual may experience lower abdominal pain and fever with minimal or no anorectal symptoms.

Physical exam: Superficial abscesses that are swollen, red, hard, tender lumps or nodules at the edge of the anus may be evident upon exam. In the case of deeper anorectal abscesses, an exam is performed placing a gloved finger into the anus (digital rectal exam). This may reveal tender swelling and the presence of an abscess. Pus may discharge from the rectum. Proctosigmoidoscopy may be used to more completely visualize the entire upper rectal area as well as the sigmoid (lower) portion of the large intestine.

Tests: Blood test results indicate an increase in white blood cell count (leukocytosis).

Treatment

Treatment of an anorectal abscess involves making an incision in it (lancing) that allows the pus to drain. Unless the abscess is deep within the rectum, the procedure is usually performed on an outpatient basis. If the abscess is very deep, surgery may be indicated. Antibiotics may be prescribed orally or by injection. Pain medication may also be prescribed. Warm sitz baths may help the abscess to drain. An abnormal tunnel into nearby tissues (fistula) develops about half the time in individuals with an anorectal abscess. This fistula is removed surgically by a procedure called a fistulotomy.

Prognosis

For an uncomplicated anorectal abscess with no fistula, incision and drainage yields good results. If a fistula develops and is not removed, however, the condition will recur in approximately two-thirds of cases. Recurrent disease predisposes an individual to some degree of incontinence. A recent study found that a fistulotomy reduces the risk of recurrence to approximately four percent.

Differential Diagnosis

Anorectal abscesses should be distinguished from other causes of anorectal pain including hemorrhoids, anal fissure, and proctitis. Higher anorectal abscesses are usually associated with lower abdominal pain. Other causes of such discomfort include urinary tract infection, pelvic inflammatory disease, Crohn's disease, and irritable bowel syndrome.

Specialists

- General Surgeon
- Rectal Surgeon

Work Restrictions / Accommodations

Return to work may be delayed if individual's occupation involves prolonged sitting or walking. This is particularly relevant in occupations such as truck driving where changes in position are difficult. Recovery from a fistulectomy may take weeks or months.

Complementary and Alternative Therapies

Content is intended for awareness only. Treatments may or may not be effective. Scientific evidence may be lacking and some substances have potentially toxic effects. Dr. Presley Reed and the editors do not endorse the use of these therapies in the absence of consultation with a licensed medical professional.

Sitz bath -	Improves circulation and reduces inflammation.
Echinacea -	May be used for topical wound healing and internal stimulation of the immune system.
Goldenseal -	May be of use in topical infections. Contraindicated in pregnancy and hypertension.
Gota Kola -	Used topically in traditional eastern medicine for promotion of wound healing particularly in chronic lesions.

Comorbid Conditions

Pre-existing conditions that may impact recovery and lengthen disability include impaired blood supply as occurring in diabetes or impaired immune system function as in AIDS.

Complications

The infection associated with anorectal abscess may extend into surrounding tissues. The condition may also be associated with an anorectal fistula. With recurrent abscesses, the individual may experience an inability to control the passage of stool (incontinence) or flatulence.

Factors Influencing Duration

Other underlying conditions, severity of symptoms, and need for surgical exploration influence the length of disability. Recurrent disease leading to incontinence may impair an individual's ability to return to work.

Length of Disability

The duration of disability depends on job requirements, particularly sitting requirements, severity of the condition, and type of treatment. In the work environment, the availability of convenient sanitary facilities may influence the ability of an individual experiencing some incontinence.

Surgical drainage.

Duration in Days

Job Classification	Minimum	Optimum	Maximum
Any work	7	14	21

Failure to Recover

If an individual fails to recover within the maximum duration expectancy period, the reader may wish to reference the following questions to assist in better understanding the specifics of an individual's medical case.

Regarding diagnosis:

- Was a microscopic examination done to identify the organism(s) causing infection?
- Did culture results confirm the diagnosis?
- Was this a recurring infection?
- Has individual experienced any complications?
- Does individual have an underlying condition that may impact recovery?
- Were other contributing factors ruled out such as an infected internal hemorrhoid or foreign body?

Regarding treatment:

- Was the abscess drained?
- If the abscess was drained, how long ago was the procedure done?
- Is individual on antibiotic therapy?
- Was laboratory analysis of pus used to select the most effective antibiotic?
- Are systemic antibiotics being used?
- Is there a possibility of antibiotic-resistant bacteria?
- Is change of antibiotic warranted?
- Has individual recently used any alternative medication or health practices?
- Was a fistulotomy performed?

Regarding prognosis:

- What is the overall health of individual?
- Are coexisting conditions being addressed such as diabetes or infection elsewhere in the body?
- Does individual have a history of constipation, diarrhea, or other condition?
- Does abscess recur?
- Has fistula been ruled out?
- If an anal fistula was present, why wasn't a fistulotomy performed?

References

Beers, Mark H., and Robert Berkow. The Merck Manual of Diagnosis and Therapy. Whitehouse Station, NJ: Merck & Co., Inc, 1999.

Janicke, D.M., and M.R. Pundt. "Anorectal Disorders." Emergency Medicine Clinics of North America 14 4 1996: 757-788.

Abscess, Breast

Other names / synonyms: Breast Abscess, Breast Infection, Infective Mastitis, Inflammatory Disease of Breast, Mammary Abscess, Mammillary Fistula, Mastitis, Retromammary Mastitis

611.0

Definition

A breast abscess is a localized pocket of infection containing pus in the breast tissue. When bacteria invade through an irritated or cracked (fissured) nipple in a woman who recently gave birth, the resulting infection that spreads through the tissues (cellulitis) is called postpartum mastitis.

In nursing women, a single type of bacteria (either Staphylococcus aureus or different streptococcus species) is most commonly found in breast abscesses. Abscesses in women who are not nursing usually contain a mixture of bacteria including S. aureus, streptococci, and bacteria that grow best in the absence of oxygen (anaerobes).

In one study, abscess behind the nipple (subareolar abscess) is linked to cigarette smoking.

Breast abscess is more common in women who are not nursing (lactating). In one 10-year study, only 8.5% of 72 women with breast abscess were nursing. Postpartum mastitis occurs in 1-5% of nursing women.

Diagnosis

History: The individual complains of a hard, red, warm, painful spot on her breast. There may be a history of recent mastitis or a previous breast abscess. The individual may feel generally ill and tired and experience fever, chills, and vomiting. There may be discharge from the mass or the nipple. The nipple of the affected breast may be turned inward (inverted).

Physical exam: The exam reveals a firm, red, hard, swollen, painful, warm breast mass usually near or around the nipple. When the mass is felt beneath the skin, it may seem to move (fluctuans). There may be visible cracks (fissures) on the nipple and it may be inverted. The lymph glands in the armpit near the breast may be swollen and tender. The woman may have fever or an increased pulse rate. Discharge may be noted coming from the nipple or mass.

Tests: Cultures of breast milk and breast skin, and discharge from the mass and/or the nipple should be taken. A complete blood count (CBC) and sedimentation rate may be administered. A mammogram or ultrasound may help in viewing the mass and surrounding breast tissue. Ultrasound may also help distinguish solid from fluid-containing (cystic) structures in the breast, and direct the path of a fine needle used to remove fluid from the abscess for culture. A mammogram is standard for breast mass evaluation.

Treatment

Using a needle to remove fluid from a breast abscess may be beneficial but in most cases the abscess needs to be cut open (incised) and drained (incision and drainage [I & D]). A simple I & D does not treat the underlying cause of the breast abscess, so surgery that creates a passage from the abscess to the skin (fistulectomy) may be necessary. Hospitalization may be required for I & D, fistulectomy, and medication such as intravenous antibiotics.

Medications taken by mouth include antibiotics, anti-inflammatories, analgesics, and antipyretics. Antibiotics fight the bacteria causing the infection and anti-inflammatories decrease the warmth and redness. Analgesics relieve pain and antipyretics reduce the fever that may occur as a result of the infection. Warm or cold water soaks to the infected breast may help relieve pain and hasten healing. If the individual is breast-feeding, she may be advised to discontinue on the infected breast until it heals. The breast may need to be pumped regularly by hand or with mechanical suction devices to empty it completely of milk.

Prognosis

Complete recovery is expected usually within 8 to 10 days with treatment. A subareolar abscess may recur unless the involved milk (lactiferous) duct is removed. Recurrence rate of abscess is 40-50% following standard incision and drainage, and is lower following fistulectomy. Drainage guided by ultrasound may improve success rate to about eighty percent. In a 1991 study of 13 fistulectomies, two required reoperation. In a 1995 study at the State University of New York, all individuals treated with antibiotics and I & D had recurrence of subareolar breast abscess (around the nipple). When the abscess and plugged milk duct were removed, the condition did not recur.

Differential Diagnosis

Inflammatory carcinoma of the breast, other types of breast cancer, fibroadenoma, fibrocystic disease, and fat necrosis may present with similar symptoms and exam findings.

Specialists

- Gynecologist
- Surgeon

Work Restrictions / Accommodations

In women who are breast-feeding, scheduled breaks and a private room may be needed to periodically empty the breast.

Comorbid Conditions

Conditions that impede recovery may include other breast diseases or infections or a compromised immune system.

Complications

Complications may include recurring or chronic breast infections, pain, and scarring of breast tissue.

Factors Influencing Duration

Factors that may influence disability include age, response to treatment, pain, recurring infection, and treatment noncompliance.

Length of Disability

The length of disability depends on job requirements. Although a complete recovery is expected, response to treatment and compliance with treatment guidelines may influence the length of disability. For individuals with incision and drainage with or without biopsy, duration depends on site and size of abscess.

Incision and drainage (with or without biopsy).

Duration in Days

Job Classification	Minimum	Optimum	Maximum
Any work	1	7	14

Failure to Recover

If an individual fails to recover within the maximum duration expectancy period, the reader may wish to reference the following questions to assist in better understanding the specifics of an individual's medical case.

Regarding diagnosis:

- Does individual complain of a hard, red, warm, painful spot on her breast?
- Is there a history of recent mastitis or a previous breast abscess?
- Does individual feel generally ill and tired? Has there been fever, chills, or vomiting?
- Does she complain of discharge from the mass or the nipple, or that the nipple is turned inward (inverted)?
- Is there a firm, red, swollen, warm area near or around the nipple that moves when palpated? Are lymph nodes in the armpit nearest the affected breast swollen and tender?
- Were skin, breast milk, and discharge cultures obtained? If so, what type of bacterium is causing the infection?
- Was a complete blood count (CBC) and sedimentation rate done?
- Was a mammogram or ultrasound done? Did either or both of these tests confirm the diagnosis?

Regarding treatment:

- Was the appropriate antibiotic therapy ordered?
- Does individual take all medications exactly as prescribed?
- Has individual applied warm or cold compresses as directed?
- Has she stopped breastfeeding from the infected breast and pumping the breast as directed?
- Was individual hospitalized for treatment?
- Was the mass incised and drained or is a fistulectomy needed?

Regarding prognosis:

- Did the abscess respond to medical management or was I & D or fistulectomy required?
- Is there scarring, chronic pain, or recurrent infection? How are these being treated and what is the expected outcome with treatment?

References

Breast Abscess. RxMed 17 May 2000 <http://www.rxmed.com/illnesses/breast_abscess.html>.

Bundred, N.J., D.J. Webster, and R.E. Mansel. "Management of Mammillary Fistulae." Journal of the Royal College of Surgeons of Edinburgh 36 6 1991: 381-383.

Eckman, Margaret, and Nancy Prif, eds. Diseases. Springhouse, PA: Springhouse Corporation, 1997.

Kneece, Judy, C. Solving the Mystery of Breast Pain. Columbia: EduCare Publishing, 1996.

Meguid, M.M., et al. "Pathogenesis-based Treatment of Recurring Subareolar Breast Abscesses." Surgery 118 4 1995: 775-782.

Schantz, Amy K., and Howard Blumstein, MD. "Breast Abscess and Masses." eMedicine.com 13 Jan 2001 24 Feb 2001 <http://www.emedicine.com/emerg/topic68.htm>.

Abscess, Ischiorectal

Other names / synonyms: Anal Cellulitis, Anorectal Abscess, Anorectal Suppuration, Perianal Abscess, Perirectal Abscess, Perirectal Cellulitis, Rectal Cellulitis

Definition

An ischiorectal abscess is when an infection occurs in the tissues around the rectum. The infection results in the formation of pus between the rectum and the pelvic bone (ischiorectal space).

Ischiorectal abscess is classified as a type of anorectal abscess and it is sometimes mistakenly referred to as one of the three other types (perianal, intersphincteric, or supralevator abscess). Ischiorectal abscess occurs deeper in the tissue than any of the other three types and it usually originates from one of the six to eight anal glands that lie near the ischiorectal space. Ischiorectal abscess can spread to both the right and left ischiorectal spaces and form a horseshoe-shaped abscess. Also, an abnormal channel (fistula) can develop between the site of infection and the rectum.

Risk factors for ischiorectal abscess include blood (hematologic) diseases such as leukemia, diseases where the immune system is compromised such as human immunodeficiency virus (HIV), Crohn's disease, diabetes mellitus, anal fissure, prolapsed internal hemorrhoid, traumatic injury to the anal region, high blood pressure (hypertension), inflammatory bowel disease, heart disease, or any sort of infection within the anal glands.

Ischiorectal abscess is the second most common form of anorectal abscess and it accounts for approximately 23% of all anorectal abscesses. The average age at diagnosis of ischiorectal abscess is 45 years and there is a male to female ratio of more than 2:1. Fistula formation between the abscess and the rectum occurs in approximately 25% of cases.

Diagnosis

History: Individuals complain of a throbbing, constant pain in or around the anal (perianal) region. Pain may sometimes be reported in the lower abdomen. Swelling in the anal region, drainage of pus from the anus, bleeding, constipation, or diarrhea may also be reported. The pain may not be aggravated by defecation. The individual may report having a fever and a general feeling of ill health (malaise) prior to experiencing any rectal symptoms. As the infection worsens, the abscess can result in chills and fever.

Physical exam: The exam may not show any external signs. However, an examination done by placing a gloved finger inside the anus (digital rectal exam) with the individual lying on the side (SIMM's position) may detect the abscess as a tender, soft mass. Probing of potential internal openings with the proper instrumentation (crypt hook or Hill-Ferguson retractor) may also reveal fistula openings. Examination may reveal redness (erythema), tenderness, swelling, or drainage of pus over the infected area.

Tests: Tests are not needed for the diagnosis however a complete blood count (CBC) with white blood cell differential may show an increase in the white blood cell count. A sample of pus from the abscess cavity may be tested for aerobic and anaerobic cultures.

Treatment

Prompt surgical drainage under general anesthesia is the treatment for ischiorectal abscess. Drainage can be done with an incision (radial stab incision). For ischiorectal abscess that has spread to both ischiorectal spaces (horseshoe abscess), separate stab incisions may be made to allow complete drainage. The wound may then be packed with medicated gauze that can be removed 24 hours after the procedure.

If a fistula is present, an incision (anal fistulotomy) may be made using an electrically heated needle (electrocautery) that allows the fistula to heal. Systemic, broad-spectrum antibiotics may be prescribed.

Prognosis

Ischiorectal abscess treated with drainage and antibiotics usually heals promptly in otherwise healthy individuals. Without prompt drainage treatment, there is a high risk of progression to a horseshoe abscess. Recurrence rates of ischiorectal abscess range from 35-95%, however, recent studies report recurrence rates as low as 30%. These same studies show that recurrence is generally high in individuals with diabetes mellitus (40%) or Crohn's disease (42%). Uncontrollable intestinal gas (incontinence of flatus) occurs approximately 5-10% of the time in those treated for ischiorectal abscess. Twenty percent of individuals treated for this condition will have incontinence of liquids and solids from the intestine. Recurrence rate for fistula formation following anal fistulotomy ranges from 21-40%.

Differential Diagnosis

Conditions that present with similar symptoms include pilonidal sinus; hidradenitis suppurativa; colorectal cancer; Bartholin's gland abscess; and pelvirectal, perianal, intersphincteric, or supralevator abscess.

Specialists

- Colorectal Surgeon
- General Surgeon

Work Restrictions / Accommodations

Prolonged sitting, standing, or walking may be particularly uncomfortable until complete healing has occurred.

Comorbid Conditions

Existing conditions that may impact an individual's ability to recover and further lengthen disability include Crohn's disease, ulcerative colitis, diabetes, and previous treatment for ischiorectal abscess.

Complications

Complications of ischiorectal abscess include progression of the infection to the point where tissue death occurs (necrotizing infection). Extensive anal and perianal skin infection (cellulitis) is characterized by local heat, redness, pain, swelling, and on occasion with fever, malaise, chills, and headache. This may be accompanied by production of fetid gas just underneath the skin (crepitation) that is considered a surgical emergency. Ischiorectal abscess left untreated in immunocompromised individuals can be deadly.

Factors Influencing Duration

Factors that may influence the length of disability include the severity of symptoms and extent of the infection, individual's response to treatment, and older age. Complications of bacteremia or sepsis can also influence the length of disability. If the abscess is not drained adequately, there is an increased risk of recurrence and longer disability.

Length of Disability

Remission of this condition is not uncommon.

Surgical drainage.

Duration in Days

Job Classification	Minimum	Optimum	Maximum
Any work	7	14	21

Failure to Recover

If an individual fails to recover within the maximum duration expectancy period, the reader may wish to reference the following questions to assist in better understanding the specifics of an individual's medical case.

Regarding diagnosis:
- Does individual have a throbbing, constant pain in or around the perianal region?
- Does individual have any risk factors (i.e., immune suppression, inflammatory bowel disorders, rectal inflammation or trauma, diabetes mellitus) for the disease?
- Was the diagnosis confirmed with a rectal exam? Was evidence of a rectal fistula or abscess noted? If so, was a culture obtained?
- If the diagnosis was uncertain, were conditions with similar symptoms ruled out?

Regarding treatment:
- Was the abscess surgically drained?
- Was fistula treated with electrocautery?
- Is individual on appropriate antibiotic therapy?

Regarding prognosis:
- Was prompt drainage performed?
- Did individual have recurrence of abscess?
- Does individual have any conditions (i.e., inflammatory bowel disease) that may impact recovery?
- Did the ischiorectal abscess progress to necrotizing infection?
- Was fetid gas produced, requiring emergency surgery?
- Did other complications occur?

References

Bleday, R. "Hemorrhoids and Other Anorectal Disorders." Therapy of Digestive Disorders. Wolfe, M.M., ed. Philadelphia: W.B. Saunders Company, 2000. 701-707.

Ramanujam, P.S., et al. "Perianal Abscesses and Fistulas." Diseases of the Colon and Rectum 27 1984: 593-597.

Abscess, Larynx
478.79

Definition

An abscess of the larynx (the voice box - located where the back of the throat connects to top of the trachea) is a collection of pus formed as the result of an infection. The pus is composed of destroyed (necrotic) tissue cells, living and dead white blood cells (leukocytes) brought to the area to fight the infection, body fluids, and both dead and live microorganisms. Abscesses occur when the body walls off small area of infection to keep it from spreading.

A larynx abscess may be associated with inflammation of the supportive membranes of the larynx (perichondritis), cancer, previous injury to the larynx occurring when instruments were used to establish an airway, or a pre-existing abnormal air sac connected to the larynx (laryngocele).

An abscess of the larynx is a serious and potentially lethal condition that requires emergency treatment. Since the development of antibiotics, abscesses of the larynx are rare. Recent literature reports only 6 cases in the US, all in the late 1970s. Generally, bacterial laryngitis is effectively treated with antibiotics long before an abscess can develop.

Diagnosis

History: The individual may complain of hoarseness, fever, and difficulty or pain in swallowing (dysphagia). Swelling at the site may interfere with breathing. Coughing may occur.

Physical exam: The neck and external throat area may be swollen and tender to touch (palpation). The examiner will try to elicit the individual's gag and swallowing reflexes; these may be diminished or absent because of swelling. The examiner may hear a high-pitched, whistling sound when the individual breathes (stridor). Inspection of the larynx using a mirror held against the back roof of the mouth (indirect laryngoscopy) may reveal redness and swelling of the larynx.

Tests: A viewing instrument (laryngoscope) may be passed down the throat or nose in order to view the larynx directly (direct laryngoscopy) or to take a biopsy for microscopic analysis. The presence of an abscess is confirmed by removing pus from the larynx by suction (aspiration) and culturing it to identify the organism causing the infection. X-ray, CT scan, or MRI may be done to assess extent of the condition or to rule out a tumor.

Treatment

Treatment consists of antibiotics given intravenously (IV). Even with antibiotic therapy, the abscess may need to be surgically drained (incision and drainage procedure) using a scope (laryngoscopy); this will provide an escape route for the pus. In severe cases with a large formation of abnormal tissue around the abscess (granuloma formation), reducing the size of this enlargement (debulking) is done with a laser. If respiratory distress occurs, it may be necessary to perform an immediate surgical incision into the windpipe (tracheostomy) in order to establish an airway.

Complementary and Alternative Therapies

Content is intended for awareness only. Treatments may or may not be effective. Scientific evidence may be lacking and some substances have potentially toxic effects. Dr. Presley Reed and the editors do not endorse the use of these therapies in the absence of consultation with a licensed medical professional.

Echinacea - Said to stimulate the immune system.

Goldenseal - Has been used orally for its anticatarrhal (anti-inflammatory) effects, but little evidence supports this use and effects are debatable. Contraindicated in pregnancy and hypertension.

Prognosis

Complete recovery is expected with appropriate antibiotic and possible surgical treatment. Without prompt treatment, an abscess on the larynx can be a serious condition, and may result in death.

Differential Diagnosis

Conditions with similar symptoms include cancer of the larynx and granulomatous diseases, as well as several tumors of the larynx.

Specialists

- Otolaryngologist

Work Restrictions / Accommodations

Work restrictions or accommodations are not usually associated with this procedure. Individuals may have to limit using their voices excessively (public speaking, singing, telephone operator, telemarketer, receptionist) while recovering from surgery.

Comorbid Conditions

Coexisting conditions that may impact recovery and lengthen disability include impaired blood supply, as occurs in diabetes, or impaired immune system function, as occurs in AIDS.

Complications

Complications include respiratory distress due to tissue swelling in the trachea (windpipe), or spread of the infection into adjacent structures.

Factors Influencing Duration

Length of disability may be influenced by the extent of the infection, severity of the symptoms, method of treatment, response to treatment, or the development of complications.

Length of Disability

With tracheostomy, disability may be permanent.

Medical treatment.

Duration in Days

Job Classification	Minimum	Optimum	Maximum
Sedentary work	0	2	3
Light work	0	2	3
Medium work	0	2	3
Heavy work	0	2	3
Very Heavy work	0	2	3

Surgical drainage.

Duration in Days

Job Classification	Minimum	Optimum	Maximum
Sedentary work	14	21	42
Light work	14	21	42
Medium work	14	28	49
Heavy work	21	28	49
Very Heavy work	21	28	56

Tracheostomy.

Duration in Days

Job Classification	Minimum	Optimum	Maximum
Sedentary work	14	21	Indefinite
Light work	14	21	Indefinite
Medium work	14	35	Indefinite
Heavy work	21	35	Indefinite
Very Heavy work	21	42	Indefinite

Failure to Recover

If an individual fails to recover within the maximum duration expectancy period, the reader may wish to reference the following questions to assist in better understanding the specifics of an individual's medical case.

Regarding diagnosis:

- Was fiber-optic laryngoscopy or biopsy done to rule out other conditions with similar symptoms?
- Was a tumor ruled out? Was pneumonia ruled out?
- Has individual recently used any alternative medication or health practices?
- Was microscopic examination done to identify causative organism?
- Was x-ray or CT/MRI performed to assess extent of abscess?
- Has infection spread to adjacent structures? Is there lymph node involvement?
- Was abscess of larynx confirmed?

Regarding treatment:

- Was laboratory analysis of pus used to select the most effective antibiotic?
- Has individual responded to treatment?
- Are systemic antibiotics being used? IV or oral?
- Is there a possibility of antibiotic-resistant bacteria? Is change of antibiotic warranted?
- Was incision and drainage required? Debulking?
- Was tracheostomy necessary? Was individual compliant with care and hygiene of tracheostomy site?

Regarding prognosis:

- Did individual receive prompt, appropriate treatment?
- Was recovery delayed as a result of incision and drainage, tracheostomy, or laser debulking?
- What is the overall health of individual? How does this impact recovery?
- Does individual have an underlying condition that may impact recovery?

References

Beers, Mark H., and Robert Berkow, MD, eds. "Larynx." Merck Manual of Diagnosis and Therapy, 17th ed. Whitehouse Station, NJ: Merck & Co. Inc, 1999 10 Nov 2000 <http://www.merck.com/pubs/manual>.

Galil, K., et al. "Abscesses Due to Mycobacterium." Emerging Infectious Diseases 5 5 1999: 681-687.

Abscess, Liver
Other names / synonyms: Hepatic Abscess, Visceral Abscess
572.0

Definition

A liver abscess is an enclosed localized infection buried within the tissues of the liver.

The two principle types of liver abscesses are amebic liver abscess from parasites in water and food of some foreign countries, and pus-filled (pyogenic) abscess usually from a bacterial infection. Amebic liver abscess is caused by the same organism in the intestinal infection called amebiasis. It is carried through the blood to the liver where the abscess is formed.

An amebic abscess is usually caused by an amebic parasite typically picked up during an individual's recent trip abroad to tropical regions or underdeveloped countries. Transmission occurs through ingestion of cysts in fecally contaminated food or water, use of human excrement as fertilizer, and individual-to-individual contact. It is contracted in areas where poor sanitation exists, water is unpurified, and when uncooked vegetables or unpeeled fruit are eaten. The abscess can develop weeks or months after the original amebic infection and, because symptoms are usually intermittent, many individuals suffer up to 30 days before seeking treatment. Because routine diagnostic tests are typically normal, these abscesses are difficult to diagnose.

Bacterial abscesses usually develop by one of five mechanisms: infection of the liver (portal) vein from an intra-abdominal infection, systemic bacterial infection where the infection spread to the liver via the circulatory system, spread of infection from the gallbladder or bile ducts up to the liver (ascending cholangitis), spread of infection from the lung to the liver, or direct trauma to the liver. Consequently, individuals who have had some sort of systemic infection or infections of structures near the liver (lung, gallbladder, or abdomen) or those with liver trauma are at greatest risk of developing this type of abscess.

Malnutrition, alcoholism, and immunosuppression predisposes an individual to more severe disease.

The exact prevalence of bacterial liver abscesses is difficult to ascertain.

The incidence for amebic liver abscess is 1 in 100,000. It seems to occur with equal frequency in both genders but men tend to have amebic abscesses more often than women. Most individuals are under the age of 50. The infection occurs worldwide but is most common in areas with crowded living conditions and poor sanitation. Africa, Latin America, Southeast Asia, and India have significant health problems associated with this disease.

Diagnosis

History: Individuals should be questioned about recent travel abroad. Individuals may complain of recurrent high fever, sweating (diaphoresis), chills, severe headaches, nausea, vomiting, a general feeling of illness (malaise), loss of appetite (anorexia), unintentional weight loss, diarrhea, and pain.

Physical exam: Individuals may present with intense, continuous, stabbing pain in the area of the right lung and upper-right abdomen (from the enlarged, tender liver), and fever. The skin may have a yellow tinge (jaundice).

Tests: A multiple-panel blood test is necessary to screen for presence and identification of ameba and bacteria. A complete blood count (CBC) is done and an increase in white blood cells is a sign of infection. Liver function tests are performed and liver enzymes levels measured. The abscess may be cultured using a needle (needle aspiration) to identify the disease-producing organism (pathogen) and the antimicrobial medication that the pathogens are sensitive to. A liver biopsy helps determine the exact nature of liver pathology. Imaging tests such as an abdominal MRI, CT, or ultrasound help the doctor pinpoint the location and number of abscesses. Radionuclide liver scans may also be used to demonstrate areas of abscess formation.

Treatment

Initially, the individual is treated with drugs to kill the specific bacteria or parasite (antibiotics or antimicrobials). After the acute symptoms have cleared, the individual must continue to take oral antimicrobial drugs for 20 days to kill any bacteria or parasites in the intestines.

Treatment then consists of draining the abscess(es) either surgically (incision and drainage) or via needle (percutaneous catheter drainage) to help relieve some of the abdominal pain associated with the abscess. In addition, appropriate antibiotic therapy is necessary. If the exact infecting organism is not identified, then antibiotics covering many common pathogens (broad-spectrum) are used. Antibiotics are continued for several weeks. Occasionally, single, pyogenic abscesses may be treated solely with antibiotics.

Prognosis

If correctly diagnosed and treated, most individuals with liver abscesses respond well to treatment. The overall mortality for liver abscesses (either parasitic or bacterial) is 20-40%. Those with multiple abscesses have a higher mortality rate than those with isolated single abscesses.

Differential Diagnosis

The nonspecific symptoms of liver abscesses (fever, chills, anorexia, weight loss, nausea, and vomiting) can be from a number of diseases therefore an extensive workup is required. More specific symptoms can result from diseases of the gallbladder and pancreas and from acute hepatitis.

Specialists

- Gastroenterologist
- Infectious Disease Physician

Work Restrictions / Accommodations

After full recovery, the individual may return to work with no restrictions or accommodations.

Comorbid Conditions

Comorbid conditions of liver disease, bleeding disorders, diabetes, malnutrition, alcoholism, or immune suppression can impact the ability to recover and further lengthen disability.

Complications

With or without treatment, the abscess may rupture into the lungs, the lining of the lungs (pleural cavity), abdominal (peritoneal) cavity, or sac around the heart (pericardium), raising the individual's risk of systemic infection (sepsis) and/or death.

Factors Influencing Duration

Approximately 75% of the cases have a prior infection that has spread to the liver causing the abscess to form. The primary infection and other involved organ systems must be treated. This is the major factor determining the length of disability.

Length of Disability

Percutaneous drainage. Needle aspiration.

Duration in Days

Job Classification	Minimum	Optimum	Maximum
Sedentary work	7	9	14
Light work	7	9	14
Medium work	14	21	28
Heavy work	14	21	28
Very Heavy work	14	21	28

Surgical drainage.

Duration in Days

Job Classification	Minimum	Optimum	Maximum
Sedentary work	14	21	28
Light work	14	21	28
Medium work	28	35	42
Heavy work	42	49	56
Very Heavy work	42	49	56

Failure to Recover

If an individual fails to recover within the maximum duration expectancy period, the reader may wish to reference the following questions to assist in better understanding the specifics of an individual's medical case.

Regarding diagnosis:

- Was individual's liver abscess amebic or pyogenic?
- Has individual traveled out of the country in the past year?
- Did individual complain of recurrent high fevers, sweating, chills, severe headaches, nausea, vomiting, diarrhea or pain?
- Was individual generally ill, with no appetite, or with unintentional weight loss?

- Did individual have continuous stabbing pain in the upper right abdomen and lung?
- Was individual's skin yellowish?
- When did symptoms first occur?
- Did individual have any trauma to the liver?
- Did individual recently have a systemic infection?
- Did individual recently have an infection in the lung, gallbladder, or abdomen?
- Is individual immunosuppressed?
- Does individual have malnutrition or alcoholism?

Regarding treatment:
- Is individual receiving medication appropriate for the abscess pathogen (antibiotics and/or antimicrobials)?
- Were broad-spectrum antibiotics necessary?

Regarding prognosis:
- Have there been any complications such as rupture of the abscess into adjacent lung, heart, or abdominal cavities?
- Is there evidence of some prior infection and other organ system involvement? If so, has it been treated?

References

"Amebic Liver Abscess." dr.koop.com 4 Feb 2001 <http://www.drkoop.com/conditions/ency/article/000211.htm>.

Tierney, Lawrence M., Stephen J. McPhee, and Maxine Papadakis, eds. Current Medical Diagnosis and Treatment, 39th ed. New York: Lange Medical Books/McGraw-Hill, 2000.

Abscess, Lung
Other names / synonyms: Lung Abscess, Pulmonary Abscess, Pulmonary Necrosis
513, 513.0

Definition

A lung abscess is a pocket of pus that collects where lung tissue was destroyed.

Lung tissue can be destroyed by aspiration pneumonia, obstruction of an airway by a foreign body, or from a tumor in the lung. The dead tissue provides a breeding ground for many types of microorganisms. As the organisms multiply, they further destroy the tissue and create a cavity in the lung that fills with very foul smelling pus. Lung abscesses can occur singularly or in groups. They are often accompanied by pus in the space between the lungs and chest wall (empyema).

The most common organisms to cause abscess formation are bacteria that multiply in places without oxygen (anaerobic bacteria). Bacteria from the nose and mouth that are normally inactive (dormant) because of the high oxygen level there can be aspirated into the lung where they become active. Dental problems (poor dentition) can lead to an overgrowth of various bacteria that can also be aspirated into the lungs. Although almost everyone aspirates very small amounts of oral secretions, lung abscesses generally occur when a large amount of secretion is aspirated. This type of aspiration can occur during anesthesia, impaired consciousness, seizure disorders, alcohol intoxication, or in those with poor control of their swallowing such as the elderly or individuals with neurological impairment. Individuals with immune system deficiencies (immunocompromised) or with a chronic disruption of airflow into or out of the lungs (COPD) are also at greater risk of developing a lung abscess.

If a lung abscess arises in an individual without any of these predisposing conditions, a lung tumor or some type of bronchial obstruction may be the cause of the abscess formation.

The mortality rate for lung abscesses is approximately 4-7% but varies with the type of material aspirated. Aspiration of fluids with mixed gram-negative flora approaches 20% mortality, while aspiration of acidic materials is even higher.

Diagnosis

History: Symptoms may include fever, a vague feeling of illness (malaise), cough, weight loss, a foul taste in the mouth, and increased sputum production that is foul smelling or possibly bloody. Individuals may also complain of shortness of breath, diminished appetite (anorexia), night sweats, and chest pains near the ribs. The individual may report a history of some predisposing factors such as tooth decay and periodontal disease, recent anesthesia, or a history of swallowing difficulty. Many individuals have history of recent diagnosis and treatment for pneumonia. A recent penetrating chest trauma should raise a clinical suspicion for empyema.

Physical exam: The individual may be feverish (temperature frequently elevated but usually not greater than 102 degrees F), appear to lack vigor, have a weight loss since last seen, and a foul mouth odor. There may also be evidence of poor dental care and hygiene. Listening to breath sounds through a stethoscope (auscultation) usually reveals a decrease in breath sounds in the area of the abscess and abnormal breath sounds similar to pneumonia in other parts of the lung.

Tests: A chest x-ray is the cornerstone for diagnosis of lung abscess. Other tests that determine the type of organisms present in the lungs include sputum culture and culture of fluid withdrawn through the trachea (transtracheal aspiration). A complete blood count (CBC) with differential may reveal a leukocytosis. Bronchoscopy (using a viewing instrument passed down through the trachea to examine the bronchi air passages) may be necessary to rule out bronchial obstruction or tumor. A blood culture or a culture of the pleural fluid may be done acquired by a needle puncture through the chest wall (thoracentesis). An arterial blood gas determination helps assess respiratory adequacy.

Treatment

Treatment consists of antibiotic therapy and drainage of the pus. In general, antibiotics are given intravenously for the first week then followed by oral antibiotics for 4 to 8 weeks. Treatment is continued until the individual's chest x-ray is cleared even though symptoms may have resolved much earlier. The use of a diagnostic bronchoscopy is reserved for individuals who do not respond well to treatment.

Chest physical therapy is often recommended to promote drainage of the lung. This involves vibrating over specific areas of the chest with hands or a special machine to loosen secretions. If there is a significant collection of pus in the pleural cavity (empyema), a drainage tube (tube thoracostomy) may need to be surgically inserted between the lung and chest wall.

Treatment may also include fever-reducing medication (antipyretics) and cough suppressants, increased fluid intake, rest, and a program to increase nutritional intake if the individual has lost a significant amount of weight. Dental or swallowing problems need to be addressed on an individual basis to prevent recurrence. If the abscess appears to be caused by severe periodontal disease, the teeth may need to be removed and dentures built.

If a lung abscess is resistant to treatment (refractory) or the area begins to hemorrhage massively, surgery may be necessary to remove the segment or lobe of the lung involved (segmentectomy or lobectomy). Surgery may also be necessary if the abscess is caused by bronchial obstruction or a tumor.

Prognosis

Once antibiotic treatment is initiated, the individual begins to feel better. Although symptoms usually resolve within 2 weeks, the total resolution of the abscess takes 4 to 8 weeks. Healing may take longer if the abscess is extremely large, the individual has compromised healing or immune system, or the abscess requires surgical drainage. Before the advent of antibiotics, the mortality rate for lung abscess was approximately 33%. Mortality is now reduced to about 10%.

Drainage of the fluids associated with the abscess helps individual recover from the effects of the disease and may speed the healing process.

Differential Diagnosis

Conditions with similar symptoms include pneumonia, empyema, lung cancer, tuberculosis, aspiration of a foreign body, and COPD.

Specialists

- Infectious Disease Physician
- Thoracic Surgeon
- Pulmonologist

Rehabilitation

Individuals typically undergo chest physical therapy to promote drainage of the lung. Chest physical therapy uses a combination of techniques. Individuals sit or lie in different postures (i.e., seated in a forward bend or lying on the back with the feet elevated above the head) to target different areas of the lung. A physical therapist then uses percussion techniques where the chest wall is clapped by the therapist's cupped hands. Vibrations are created when the therapist places his or her hands on the chest wall to compress it while the individual breathes out. In addition to chest physical therapy, the individual learns how to produce an effective cough through techniques such as huffing where the individual breathes out while making a sound like the letter "h." This technique helps vibrate the lining of the lungs and yields a more productive cough. Individuals may also use an incentive spirometer. This device measures the volume of inspired air and encourages deep breathing.

Work Restrictions / Accommodations

Moderate to heavy physical activity may need to be modified during the recovery period. Dust and fumes also need to be avoided during this time due to the individual's compromised lung function. Respiratory protection may be necessary.

Comorbid Conditions

Pre-existing respiratory disease, a deficient immune system, and cardiopulmonary disease may worsen the effects of lung abscesses.

Complications

Complications occur when the organisms breeding in the lung abscess break free, infecting other areas of the lung and forming more abscesses. Pus can collect within the pleural cavity (empyema). The destruction of lung tissue by microorganisms can cause damage to large blood vessels in the lungs and lead to a life-threatening hemorrhage. They can also cause a hole to develop between a large airway of the lungs and the space between the lungs and chest (bronchopleural fistula). Of even greater concern is the possibility of the organisms migrating to the lining of the brain and forming a brain abscess.

Factors Influencing Duration

Length of disability may be influenced by the cause of the abscess, location and number of abscesses, how early the abscess was diagnosed and treatment begun, individual compliance with treatment regimens, type and effectiveness of treatment, or any complications. Length of disability may also be influenced by individual's age, general health, or underlying chronic medical conditions especially chronic pulmonary disease and/or a compromised immune system.

Response of the lungs depends on the characteristics and amount of the aspirated substance, e.g., the more acidic the material, the greater the degree of lung injury.

Length of Disability

Depends on extent of resection (lobectomy, segmental or pneumonectomy). Duration reflects recovery from procedure. Disability may be permanent.

Medical treatment.[1]

Duration in Days

Job Classification	Minimum	Optimum	Maximum
Sedentary work	14	21	28
Light work	14	21	28
Medium work	21	28	42
Heavy work	42	63	84
Very Heavy work	42	63	84

Surgical treatment.

Job Classification	Duration in Days		
	Minimum	Optimum	Maximum
Sedentary work	56	84	182
Light work	56	84	182
Medium work	56	84	182
Heavy work	Indefinite	Indefinite	Indefinite
Very Heavy work	Indefinite	Indefinite	Indefinite

Failure to Recover

If an individual fails to recover within the maximum duration expectancy period, the reader may wish to reference the following questions to assist in better understanding the specifics of an individual's medical case.

Regarding diagnosis:

- Does individual have a history of aspiration pneumonia or obstruction of airway by a foreign body?
- Is individual at greater risk due to impaired consciousness, seizure disorders, alcohol intoxication, or because of poor control of swallowing?
- Does individual have a history of tooth decay or periodontal disease?
- Are immune system deficiencies (immunocompromised), chronic obstructive pulmonary disease (COPD), or lung tumor(s) present?
- Does individual complain of fever, a vague feeling of illness (malaise), cough, weight loss, a foul taste in the mouth, or increased sputum production that is foul smelling or possibly bloody? Shortness of breath, diminished appetite (anorexia), night sweats, and chest pains near the ribs?
- Were chest x-rays taken and a bronchoscopy done?
- Were sputum culture and culture of fluid from the trachea (transtracheal aspiration) obtained?
- Were blood cultures or a culture of the pleural fluid required?
- Was blood drawn for measurement of arterial blood gases (ABGs)?
- Was the diagnosis of lung abscess confirmed?
- Does chest x-ray show abscess shrinkage?

Regarding treatment:

- Were antibiotics given intravenously for the first week then followed by oral antibiotics for 4 to 8 weeks?
- Was antibiotic specific to the organism causing the infection?
- Did individual complete taking the antibiotic, as prescribed?
- Is antibiotic resistance an issue?
- Was antibiotic therapy continued until individual's chest x-ray cleared?
- Was chest physical therapy given to promote drainage of the lung?
- Was surgical insertion of a tube (chest tube) between the lung and chest wall required to drain pus collected in the pleural cavity (empyema)?
- Did treatment include fever-reducing medication (antipyretics) and cough suppressants, increased fluid intake, rest, and a program to increase nutritional intake, as needed?
- Were dental and swallowing problems addressed?
- If the abscess was resistant to treatment (refractory) or hemorrhage occurred was surgery done to remove the segment or lobe of the lung involved (segmentectomy or lobectomy)? Was surgery successful?

Regarding prognosis:

- Was sufficient time given for the abscess to heal?
- Was individual absolutely compliant with the antibiotic regimen?
- Is length of recovery affected by the size of the abscess, a compromised immune system, or the need for surgical drainage?
- If the abscess has not been drained, should it be drained now to facilitate healing?
- Would individual benefit from consultation with a specialist (pulmonologist, infectious disease specialist)?
- Have complications occurred from the release of microorganisms into other areas of the lung causing damage to large blood vessels in the lungs or a bronchopleural fistula?
- Have microorganisms migrated to the lining of the brain, forming a brain abscess?
- How will complications be treated and what is expected outcome with treatment?

References

"Pneumonia with Lung Abscess." Medline Plus Health Information. 2000 05 Dec 2000 <http://medlineplus.adam.com/ency/article/000121.htm>.

Watchie, Joanne. Cardiopulmonary Physical Therapy. Philadelphia: W.B. Saunders Company, 1995.

Abscess, Palmar

Other names / synonyms: Cellulitis Palm of Hand, Palmar Abscess

682.4

Definition

A palmar abscess is an abscess located deep within the tissues of the palm of the hand. An abscess is a localized infection, usually bacterial, that has been walled off by a protective lining called a pyogenic membrane. The abscess is a defense mechanism designed to prevent the spread of the infecting organism to other parts of the body. It is made up of destroyed tissue cells, white blood cells (leukocytes) carried to the area to fight the infection, and microorganisms (dead and alive).

Palmar abscess usually occurs because of an injury that allowed microorganisms to enter deep tissues of the palm and multiply. Microorganisms enter through a deep puncture wound, injury from a high-pressure paint, staple, or grease gun (high-pressure injection injury), or spread of infection from a nearby structure (e.g., fingers). The infecting organism may also be transported through the bloodstream (hematogenous spread) to the hand. Calluses or blisters on the palm can allow microbes to penetrate to deeper tissues.

An abscess can form in any of the compartments formed by the complex array of bones, joints, tendons, and nerves that make up the hand. A finger web space abscess that involves both the palm and top of the hand is called a collar button abscess. An abscess on the palm near the little finger is called a mid-palmar space abscess, and one near the thumb is a thenar space abscess.

Palmar abscess is a rare but serious infection. Individuals working with their hands in a dirty environment (e.g., construction workers, landscapers, and mechanics) are at a higher risk for developing palmar abscess. Young males who are new to a job requiring the use of a paint, staple, or grease gun are at a higher risk of sustaining high-pressure injection injuries to the hand.

Diagnosis

History: There may be a recent history of injury to the hand. The individual may complain of pain and swelling of a palm. This pain is usually intense and throbbing.

Physical exam: The exam reveals tense swelling, redness (erythema), and tenderness. There may be evidence of injury to the hand or the presence of blisters or calluses. The individual has limited range of motion in the hand. Hand movement increases pain. Through pressing and manipulating the fingers, the hand is examined for Kanavel's four signs. These signs are finger(s) in a partially closed (flexed) position, pain on straightening (extension) the finger(s), swelling of the finger(s), and tenderness.

Tests: Samples of pus and possibly blood should be cultured to identify the causative organism(s). Antibiotic sensitivity tests may be performed to determine the optimal drugs for treatment. Plain x-rays and ultrasound exams may also be administered.

Treatment

The individual elevates the hand and motion is restricted (immobilization). The abscess is cut and drained (incision and drainage) and irrigated with an antibiotic solution. At the discretion of the surgeon, treatment may involve the temporary placement of a tube (catheter) into the palm incision and a wick into the incision at the top of the hand to allow for irrigation (closed suction irrigation) of the abscess space. This technique is used less frequently however because it is labor intensive, requires hospitalization, and causes discomfort.

Palmar abscess is treated with oral antibiotics. Hospitalization for observation and to administer intravenous antibiotics may be required for individuals with a suppressed immune system (those with AIDS or certain cancers), diabetes, a history of splenectomy (asplenia), an infection unresponsive to outpatient treatment, bloodstream infection (sepsis), or involvement of a joint, tendon, or bone. A tetanus vaccination may be administered. Finger amputation may be required for individuals with severe high-pressure paint injection injury originating at a finger.

Prognosis

Full resolution of the infection should result using standard treatment with oral antibiotics, incision and drainage with irrigation (with or without the closed suction drainage technique), elevation, and immobilization. The addition of intravenous antibiotics to the standard treatment can effectively resolve a palmar infection. Finger amputation can successfully treat high-pressure injection injury.

The hand should recover full function, however, there may be permanent disability if tissue death (necrosis) caused damage to muscles or nerves.

Differential Diagnosis

A foreign body, cellulitis, infection of the tendon sheath (tenosynovitis), cysts, or tumors may produce similar symptoms.

Specialists

- Hand Surgeon
- Orthopedic Surgeon

Rehabilitation

Individuals with palmar abscess may require rehabilitation to regain hand and wrist function. An occupational therapist or physical therapist that is also a certified hand therapist should see the individual.

Therapy first addresses pain control and the reduction of swelling. Individuals learn to position the hand so that it rests above the elbow on a pillow to decrease swelling in the hand. Therapists may also perform retrograde massage where swelling is manually drained from the hand by massaging from the hand toward the direction of the shoulder. Therapists perform scar massage to promote healing and scar mobility over the surgical site. Ice packs decrease pain and swelling after exercise.

Individuals may also need to perform desensitization exercises in which the area where the abscess was excised is rubbed with a variety of items such as cotton balls, ice cubes, and rough-textured towels. This is performed to prevent hypersensitivity to different stimuli.

Therapists teach stretching techniques to increase range of motion at the wrist and forearm. Therapists may passively stretch the wrist and the forearm to increase flexion and extension and increase rotation. Individuals learn to stretch the wrist by holding the elbow straight and using their other hand to help bend the wrist into flexion and extension. Individuals stretch the forearm by placing their other hand on the forearm and using it to help turn the forearm in the two rotational directions. Therapists may passively stretch the individual's fingers into flexion and extension. Individuals learn to stretch their fingers by making a fist and by extending the fingers and adding overpressure with their noninjured hand to increase these motions. Touching the thumb to each finger restores thumb and finger opposition.

Strengthening exercises are necessary to restore function. Individuals use light hand weights to strengthen wrist flexion and extension and forearm rotation. They place the forearm on a table for support for these exercises. Individuals squeeze therapy putty to restore hand strength. Pinching therapy putty between the fingers or by placing a rubber band around two fingers at a time and spreading them apart strengthen the muscles of the fingers. Individuals learn functional exercises such as turning a doorknob and grasping/turning a key and perform exercises that emphasize dexterity such as picking up pegs and placing them in a pegboard.

Work Restrictions / Accommodations

Individuals will be unable to lift and carry heavy or bulky objects, operate equipment, or perform other tasks that require use of both hands. Individuals who operate a telephone may need to use a headset. If the dominant hand is affected, the individual may be unable to write legibly or type well. This also affects fine motor skills such as those needed to work in a laboratory. Individuals whose dominant hand is affected may require a temporary or permanent reassignment of duties. Other restrictions and accommodations resulting from temporary or permanent limited use of one hand depend on specific job responsibilities.

Complementary and Alternative Therapies

Content is intended for awareness only. Treatments may or may not be effective. Scientific evidence may be lacking and some substances have potentially toxic effects. Dr. Presley Reed and the editors do not endorse the use of these therapies in the absence of consultation with a licensed medical professional.

Slippery elm - Used as an emollient, it may protect irritated skin in wounds and abscesses.

Comorbid Conditions

Diabetes, organ transplantation, and immunodeficiency diseases (AIDS and certain cancers) may increase the length of disability.

Complications

The presence of more than one infectious agent will complicate treatment. Tissue death (necrosis) can occur. The infection may spread locally and involve more of the hand. It may also spread into the bloodstream causing a generalized sepsis and the possible infection of other structures.

Factors Influencing Duration

The treatment required, any complications, extent of tissue damage, the individual's response to treatment, the extremity involved, and the nature of work performed affect the length of disability.

Length of Disability

Duration depends on job requirements and whether dominant or non-dominant extremity is involved. Disability may be permanent for individuals with permanent limited hand function who perform heavy work or work requiring full use of both hands.

Duration in Days

Job Classification	Minimum	Optimum	Maximum
Sedentary work	0	7	14
Light work	0	7	14
Medium work	1	10	21
Heavy work	3	10	21
Very Heavy work	3	10	21

Failure to Recover

If an individual fails to recover within the maximum duration expectancy period, the reader may wish to reference the following questions to assist in better understanding the specifics of an individual's medical case.

Regarding diagnosis:

- Does individual have any risk factors such as working with hands in a dirty environment or using a high-pressure paint or grease gun?
- Has individual reported a recent injury to the hand?
- Was there intense throbbing pain with swelling?
- Was there evidence of an injury or the presence of blisters or calluses?
- Was movement painful with limited range of motion? Was the area red and swollen?
- Was a culture and sensitivity of the affected area done? If necessary, were blood cultures performed?
- Were x-rays and ultrasound performed?
- Were conditions with similar symptoms ruled out?

Regarding treatment:

- Was incision and drainage done?

- Is individual on oral antibiotics? Did individual respond to treatment?
- Was hospitalization necessary?
- Was amputation necessary?
- Did individual receive a tetanus booster?
- Did other structures such as joints become involved? Was there any muscle or nerve damage?

Regarding prognosis:

- Is individual active in physical therapy? Does the therapist specialize in the treatment of the hand? Is a home exercise program in place?
- Can individual's employer accommodate any necessary restrictions?
- Is the affected hand dominant or nondominant?
- Does individual have any conditions that may affect ability to recover?
- Does individual have any complications such as multiple infecting organisms?
- Did individual develop sepsis or infections in other structures?

References

Beers, Mark, and Robert Berkow. The Merck Manual of Diagnosis and Therapy. Whitehouse Station, NJ: Merck & Co, 1999 28 Aug 2000 <http://www.merck.no/pubs/mmanual/section5/chapter61/61d.htm>.

Kisner, Carolyn, and Lynn Allen Colby. "The Wrist and Hand." Therapeutic Exercise: Foundations and Techniques, 2nd ed. Philadelphia: F.A. Davis Company, 1990. 289-315.

Abscess, Perirectal

Other names / synonyms: Intersphincteric Abscess, Ischiorectal Abscess, Perianal Abscess, Supralevator Abscess

566

Definition

Perirectal abscess is a condition in which an infection occurs in the tissues surrounding the rectum or anus. The infection results in the formation of a pus-filled pocket within the tissue. A channel (fistula) may also form leading from the abscess into other tissues, or into the rectum or anus. In some cases, the abscess can spread to both sides of the rectum or anus to form a horseshoe-shaped abscess.

There are 4 types of perirectal abscesses (perianal, ischiorectal, intersphincteric, supralevator) that are classified according to their location in the tissue. There are also 4 types of fistulas (intersphincteric, transsphincteric, extrasphincteric, suprasphincteric) that are classified according to their anatomic relationship to the muscles in the anus (anal sphincter). Notably, an intersphincteric abscess is always associated with a fistula.

Risk factors for perirectal abscess include diarrhea, physical trauma such as a hard stool or foreign body, injury such as a crack (fissure) in the anal tissue, Crohn's disease, an immune system that is not functioning well (immunocompromised), cancer (malignant neoplasm), hidradenitis suppurativa, tuberculosis, and pelvic infections such as diverticulitis or appendicitis. Other risk factors may include diabetes mellitus, blood disorders (dyscrasia), ulcerative colitis, chronic kidney (renal) failure, hemorrhoids, genitourinary infection, alcoholism, pregnancy, and a previous perirectal abscess or fistula.

Perirectal abscess can occur at any age; however, the average age of occurrence is 45 years. The condition is more common in males than females by a 2:1 ratio, although the frequency is approximately 14 times higher in HIV-positive, homosexual, and bisexual males than in the general male population. The most common type of perirectal abscess is perianal (43% of all cases), followed by ischiorectal (23%), intersphincteric (21%), supralevator (7%), and unclassified abscess (6%).

Fistula formation is most commonly associated with intersphincteric abscess (47% of cases), and less so with supralevator (43%), perianal (35%), and ischiorectal (25%). The condition occurs in white and black individuals at an approximately equal rate.

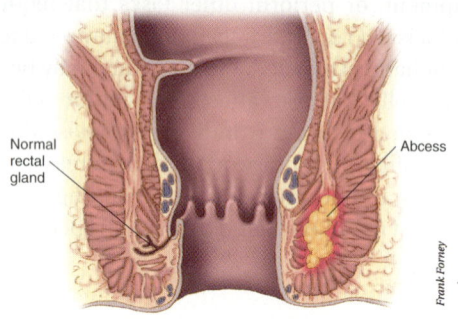

Diagnosis

History: Individuals will usually complain of pain and swelling in the area around the rectum (perirectal area), drainage of pus from the rectum or perirectum, fever, chills, constipation, and loss of appetite (anorexia). Other, less common, complaints may include weakness, dizziness, diarrhea, nausea and vomiting, difficult or painful urination (dysuria), a feeling of general discomfort (malaise), abdominal pain, itching around the perirectal area (perirectal pruritus), pain in the groin area (inguinal pain), sweating (diaphoresis), and sudden fainting (syncope).

Physical exam: External physical examination usually reveals localized tenderness, redness (erythema), or swelling of the perirectal area. Insertion of a gloved finger into the anus (digital rectal examination) may reveal extreme tenderness and tightening (guarding) of the anal sphincter in response to touch. Severe pain during examination may necessitate regional or general anesthesia during this procedure. Digital rectal exam may also reveal a fistula opening if one is present. Digital rectal examination should be avoided in individuals whose immune systems are compromised because this procedure may lead to unwanted contamination of the blood with bacteria (bacteremia). In females, a pelvic examination may be helpful in making the diagnosis.

Tests: Tests are not needed generally for the diagnosis. However, a complete blood count (CBC) with white blood cell differential may show an increase in the white blood cell count. A sample of pus from the abscess cavity may be tested for aerobic and anaerobic cultures. High-frequency sound waves (ultrasound) may be used to confirm and map out the extent of the abscess. Occasionally, insertion of a fiber-optic viewing microscope through the anus and into the rectum (proctosigmoidoscopy) may be helpful in diagnosis.

Treatment

Prompt surgical drainage under local or general anesthesia is the treatment for perirectal abscess. Drainage may be done by making an incision (radial stab incision). For abscesses that have spread to both sides of the perirectal area (horseshoe abscess), separate stab incisions may be made to allow complete drainage to occur. The wound may then be packed with medicated gauze, which can be removed 24 hours following the procedure. If a fistula is present, an incision (anal fistulotomy) may be made using an electrically-heated needle (electrocautery), which allows the fistula to heal.

Systemic, broad-spectrum antibiotics may be prescribed, although it has been suggested that they should not be used except in certain circumstances, such as for individuals with a biologic prosthesis (such as a hip prosthesis), pacemaker, or cardiac valve replacement; individuals who are immunocompromised (human immunodeficiency virus, or HIV; acquired immunodeficiency syndrome, or AIDS; and leukemia), or those who have received chemotherapy; individuals with an unusual degree of infection with the presence of gas-forming bacteria or inflamed connective tissue (cellulitis); and in individuals who are not able to receive immediate surgical drainage.

Prognosis

Perirectal abscess that is treated using drainage (and in some cases antibiotics) usually heals promptly in otherwise healthy individuals. Restoration of normal rectal function may be expected in 85-90% of cases. Antibiotics alone are generally not effective in treating perirectal abscess. Without prompt drainage treatment, there is a high risk of progression to a horseshoe abscess, and/or massive infection and tissue death (sepsis and necrosis). The mortality associated with sepsis can be as high as 40 percent. Recurrence rates of perirectal abscess following surgical drainage range from 35-95%; however, recent studies report recurrence rates as low as 30 percent. These same studies show that recurrence is generally high in individuals with diabetes mellitus (40%) or Crohn's disease (42%).

Three-fourths of individuals with recurrent perirectal abscess will also present with a persistent fistula. Uncontrollable intestinal gas (incontinence of flatus) occurs in individuals who have been treated for perirectal abscess approximately 5-10% of the time. Twenty percent of individuals who are treated for perirectal abscess will have incontinence of liquids and solids from the intestine. Finally, perirectal abscess in immunocompromised individuals is associated with mortality in 45-78% of cases.

Differential Diagnosis

Conditions that present with similar symptoms include periurethral abscess in the male or Bartholin's gland abscess in the female. Also, pilonidal sinus, hidradenitis suppurativa, colorectal cancer, diverticulitis, anal fistula, tubercular abscess, sebaceous cysts, actinomycosis, fissure-in-ano, folliculitis of the perianal skin, and rectocele.

Specialists

- Colorectal Surgeon
- Gastroenterologist
- General Surgeon

Work Restrictions / Accommodations

Prolonged sitting, standing, or walking may be particularly uncomfortable until complete healing has occurred. Heavy physical labor may have to be restricted until recovery is complete.

Comorbid Conditions

Existing conditions that may impact an individual's ability to recover and further lengthen their disability include blood disorders (dyscrasia), heart disease, chronic kidney (renal) failure, hemorrhoids, Crohn's disease, ulcerative colitis, diabetes, and previous treatment for perirectal abscess.

Complications

Complications of perirectal abscess include progression of the infection to the point where tissue death occurs (necrotizing infection), spreading of the microbes into the blood stream (bacteremia), and generalized infection of the blood and tissues (sepsis) that may lead to organ dysfunction (shock). Also, extensive anal and perianal skin infection (cellulitis) that is characterized by local heat, redness, pain, and swelling, and occasionally by fever, malaise, chills, and headache may occur. This may be accompanied by production of fetid gas just underneath the skin (crepitation), which is a surgical emergency. Perirectal abscess that is left untreated in immunocompromised individuals can be deadly.

Factors Influencing Duration

Factors that might influence the length of disability include the severity of the symptoms and extent of the infection, the individual's response to treatment, and older age. Complications of bacteremia or sepsis will also influence the length of disability. If the abscess is not drained adequately, there is an increased risk of recurrence and longer disability.

Length of Disability

There may be limitations on the amount of heavy physical labor an individual is able to perform until recovery is complete.

Surgical drainage.

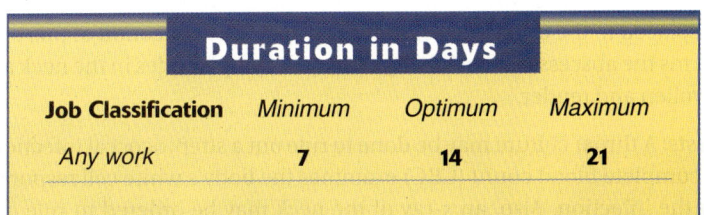

Duration in Days

Job Classification	Minimum	Optimum	Maximum
Any work	7	14	21

Abscess, Perirectal

Failure to Recover

If an individual fails to recover within the maximum duration expectancy period, the reader may wish to reference the following questions to assist in better understanding the specifics of an individual's medical case.

Regarding diagnosis:

- Does the individual have any risk factors for perirectal abscess such as diarrhea, rectal trauma anal fissures, Crohn's disease, or immune suppression?
- What type of abscess and/or fistula does the individual have?
- Was the diagnosis based on the findings in the physical exam?
- Were other conditions with similar symptoms (e.g., pilonidal sinus, hidradenitis suppurativa, colorectal cancer, diverticulitis, anal fistula, tubercular abscess, sebaceous cysts, actinomycosis, fissure-in-ano) considered in the differential diagnosis?

Regarding treatment:

- Was the abscess drained promptly as well as treating a fistula, if present?
- Was it necessary for the individual to be on antibiotic therapy?

Regarding prognosis:

- Based on the treatment required and the underlying health of the individual, what was the expected outcome? Has adequate time elapsed for recovery?
- Does the individual have existing conditions that could impact recovery and prognosis such as blood dyscrasia, heart disease, chronic renal failure, hemorrhoids, Crohn's disease, ulcerative colitis, diabetes, or previous treatment for perirectal abscess?
- Did the individual experience any infectious complications such as cellulitis, or systemic infection that could impact recovery? Were the complications addressed promptly?
- Have appropriate work accommodations been made so the individual can return to work safely?

References

Bevans, D.W., et al. "Perirectal abscess. A potentially fatal illness." The American Journal of Surgery 126 1973: 765-768.

Marcus, R.H., R.J. Stine, and M.A. Cohen. "Perirectal abscess." Annals of Emergency Medicine 25 5 1995: 597-603.

Abscess, Peritonsillar

Other names / synonyms: Abscess of Tonsil, Peritonsillar Abscess, Quinsy

475

Definition

A peritonsillar abscess is a collection of pus between a tonsil and the tissue at the back of the throat.

The abscess usually occurs as a complication of tonsillitis. It can significantly prolong recovery from tonsillitis.

The infection may begin with a simple tonsil infection that spreads within the soft tissues at the back of the throat before it actually forms an abscess. Thus, the total area of the infection can be quite extensive. Very often, this abscess is caused by streptococcal bacteria, but it can also be caused by other organisms.

Peritonsillar abscess occurs most frequently in young adults.

Diagnosis

History: Symptoms may include a sore throat (especially when swallowing) headache, high fever, impaired speech, and drooling.

Physical exam: Examination of the throat reveals redness with swelling of the tonsils and surrounding tissues. The uvula may be swollen and displaced to the unaffected side of the throat. The collection of pus that forms the abscess can be directly observed. Lymph nodes in the neck are swollen and tender.

Tests: A throat culture may be done to rule out a streptococcal infection. A complete blood count (CBC) examines the body's white cell response to the infection. Also, an x-ray of the neck may be ordered to rule out other diagnoses.

Treatment

The infection must be treated with antibiotics. The abscess itself usually requires surgical incision and drainage. Pain relievers (analgesics) may be given for the throat pain. Because peritonsillar abscesses tend to recur, a tonsillectomy is recommended when the infection is cleared, usually about 6 weeks after the abscess was treated. In some cases, immediate tonsillectomy is performed in order to both drain the abscess and prevent recurrence (Quinsy tonsillectomy).

Prognosis

An individual with uncomplicated peritonsillar abscess can expect full recovery in a relatively short period of time. However, because a peritonsillar abscess tends to recur, the tonsils are usually removed (tonsillectomy) after abscess healing is complete.

Differential Diagnosis

The early symptoms of peritonsillar abscess can mimic influenza, nasopharyngitis, pharyngitis, acute tonsillitis, or strep throat. Once the abscess is visible, the diagnosis is clear.

Specialists

- Otolaryngologist

Work Restrictions / Accommodations

Uncomplicated cases of peritonsillar abscess generally do not require work restrictions, although talking may be difficult until the swelling and pain subside.

Comorbid Conditions

Any condition that would impair an individual's response to infection would prolong recovery and lengthen disability. Examples include diabetes and immune disorders.

Complications

Complications include the spread of the underlying infection into spaces in the neck and chest, the lining of the lungs, or the heart. Pus may be aspirated into the lungs, causing pneumonia. If the infection or swelling pushes the tongue upward and backward in the throat, the individual's ability to breathe may be compromised.

Factors Influencing Duration

Factors include age of the individual, size and location of the abscess, extent of infection, length of time before treatment was sought, method and response to treatment, underlying chronic medical conditions, or the presence of complications.

Length of Disability

Medical treatment including aspiration.

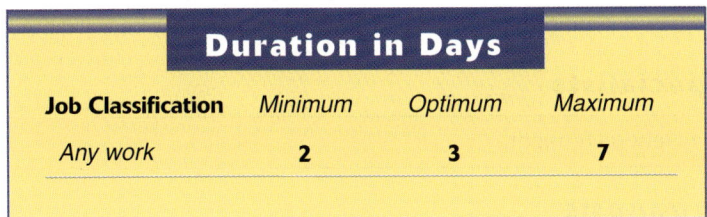

Job Classification	Minimum	Optimum	Maximum
Any work	2	3	7

Surgical drainage, with or without tonsillectomy.

Duration in Days

Job Classification	Minimum	Optimum	Maximum
Any work	7	14	21

Failure to Recover

If an individual fails to recover within the maximum duration expectancy period, the reader may wish to reference the following questions to assist in better understanding the specifics of an individual's medical case.

Regarding diagnosis:

- Did individual have an episode of tonsillitis?
- What organism has caused the abscess?
- On examination were the tonsils and surrounding tissues red and swollen?
- Was any pus observed?
- Were the lymph nodes in the neck swollen and tender?
- Were a throat culture and CBC done?
- Was an x-ray of the neck also done?

Regarding treatment:

- Was the abscess drained?
- Did individual have an immediate tonsillectomy?
- Did individual receive the appropriate antibiotics?

Regarding prognosis:

- Does individual have an underlying condition that may impair ability to heal or impair recovery from infection?
- Has individual had any complications?

References

Rowe, Lee, MD. "Otolaryngology." Current Surgical Diagnosis and Treatment. Way, Lawrence, ed. Norwalk: Appleton & Lange, 1991. 843-872.

Tierney, Lawrence, Stephen McPhee, and Maxine Papadakis. Current Medical Diagnosis and Treatment. New York: McGraw-Hill, 2000.

Abscess, Psoas

Other names / synonyms: Suppurative Peritonitis

567.2

Definition

Psoas abscess is an infection of the psoas muscle that runs from the middle-lower back region into the pelvis and thighs. The psoas muscle is the most powerful flexor of the thigh. It plays a prominent role in walking, running, kicking, and performing sit-ups. Inflammation, thickening, and retention of pus occur when the membranous sheath surrounding the muscle (psoas fascia) becomes infected with bacteria forming a psoas abscess. Psoas infection may occur on the left, right, or both (bilateral) sides (although bilateral incidence occurs in less than 3% of cases).

The two types of psoas abscesses are those that develop from infection of unknown origin (primary) and those that occur as a consequence of infection spreading from an adjacent organ (secondary). A certain type of bacterium (Staphylococcus aureus) is associated with primary psoas abscess 90% of the time, although other bacteria (Escherichia coli, Haemophilus influenza, Proteus mirabilis, Pasteurella multocida, and Salmonella newport) have also been reported.

Risk factors for primary psoas abscess are not known, however, trauma to the muscle may be an important factor in 18-20% of cases. Low socioeconomic class and poor nutrition have also been cited as possible predisposing factors. A major risk factor for secondary psoas abscess is gastrointestinal disease (inflammatory bowel disease, appendicitis, diverticulitis, bowel cancer, and Crohn's disease). The source of secondary psoas abscess is a gastrointestinal infection in 80% of individuals. Other risk factors include tuberculosis, kidney (renal) infection, chronic leukemia, Henoch Schönlein purpura, septic arthritis, pancreatitis, diabetic septicemia, and postoperative infection.

Psoas abscess is relatively uncommon with a worldwide incidence of approximately 4 cases a year. In the lesser-developed nations of Asia and Africa, 99% of all psoas abscesses are primary compared with 18% in Europe and 61% in US and Canada. Primary psoas abscess may occur at any age although 83% of cases are found in those under 30. The male to female ratio is 3 to 1, occurring equally on the right and left sides. Secondary psoas abscess is more common in adults and 78% of cases occur in individuals 50 years or younger. The male to female incidence ratio is equal in secondary psoas abscess and occurs more often on the right side (58-68% of cases). Secondary psoas abscess is usually associated with a mixture of different bacteria (Escherichia coli, bacteroides, staphylococcus, and streptococcus).

Diagnosis

History: Individuals complain of fever, chills, loss of appetite (anorexia), night sweats, vague weakness, discomfort, and weight loss. Pain in the abdomen, back, groin, hip, or knee may also be reported. With a more advanced condition, the individual may develop pain while walking.

Physical exam: A fever, increased heart rate (tachycardia), and a general wasted appearance may be evident. Tenderness may occur and in advanced cases, a mass can be felt (palpated) in the lower abdomen, back, or groin. Skin infection (cellulitis) characterized by local heat, redness, pain, and swelling may be evident. Manipulation of the hip on the side of the infection (ipsilateral) may cause some degree of pain. Individuals with advanced forms of psoas infection develop a limp on the affected side or lateral curvature (scoliosis) in the spine. A deformity while bending at the hip (flexion deformity) may eventually develop.

Tests: Tests may include a complete blood count (CBC) with differential, red blood cell (erythrocyte) sedimentation rate, and blood and urine cultures. Plain abdominal x-rays, x-rays with a barium enema or taken after injection of a radiopaque dye (intravenous pyelogram), and an upper gastrointestinal series may be useful in diagnosis. The abscess is usually visualized best using high-frequency sound waves (abdominal ultrasonography) or CT. Low-energy radio waves (MRI) may also be helpful.

Treatment

Conservative treatment includes broad-spectrum antibiotics (triple antibiotic therapy) followed by conversion to a single antistaphylococcal agent for abscesses infected with Staphylococcus aureus only. Aggressive treatment for primary psoas infection involves antibiotic treatment in combination with drainage of the abscess using a needle and syringe. Secondary psoas abscess is also treated with drainage and antibiotics. If there is gastrointestinal involvement, surgery to correct the bowel condition (removal of a bowel segment) may be warranted.

Specialists

- General Surgeon

Prognosis

Mortality from psoas abscess is nearly 100% if the condition is left untreated. Conservative treatment using antibiotics alone is usually only partially successful. The outcome is generally good with more aggressive therapy that combines drainage and antibiotics. Primary psoas abscess treated with antibiotics and drainage results in full recovery 97% of the time. However, even with treatment, the mortality rate for primary psoas abscess is approximately 2-3%. Secondary psoas abscess treated by drainage alone has a failure rate greater than 50%. Drainage combined with antibiotic therapy and surgery to treat the diseased bowel (if appropriate) carries a 69% success rate. Secondary psoas abscess has a 19% mortality rate.

Differential Diagnosis

Conditions that present with similar symptoms as psoas abscess include a variety of joint and spine (orthopedic) and infectious disorders of the skeleton such as joint sepsis or inflammatory arthritis of the hip. Other conditions include inflammation of the lower back (sacroiliitis); inflammation of the bone marrow and cartilage (osteomyelitis) in the spine, pelvis, or femur; trauma or cancerous cell growth (tumor) involving the spine, pelvis, or hip; and inflammation of the iliopsoas muscle (iliopsoas bursitis). Abdominal disorders such as renal abscess, abdominal or pelvic abscess (appendicitis, pelvic inflammatory disease), an abscess near the kidney (perinephric), and regional malignancies (i.e., colon cancer) are also a consideration.

Rehabilitation

Individual may perform light exercise under the supervision of a physician to stretch and strengthen muscles in the back, hips, and thighs. These exercises include straight leg raises, bridging exercises, and seated knee extensions. Initial activities may include limited walking, range of motion, and treadmill exercises.

Work Restrictions / Accommodations

Following drainage, the individual with psoas abscess continues medical therapy for approximately 3 weeks. Return to work in a limited capacity may be possible during this time if restrictions are made on heavy lifting, climbing, and walking long distances.

Comorbid Conditions

Existing conditions that may impact an individual's ability to recover and further lengthen disability include underlying infections such as tuberculosis, renal infection, or any infection following surgery. Systemic diseases such as leukemia, arthritis, pancreatitis, and diabetes may also have an effect.

Complications

Possible complications of psoas abscess include destruction of the psoas muscle and spread of the infection to other tissues. Delayed or inadequate therapy can result in general infection (sepsis) and death.

Factors Influencing Duration

The type of psoas abscess (primary or secondary) may influence the length of disability. Recovery time from secondary abscess may be more extensive because other tissues and organ systems (usually gastrointestinal) are involved. Older individuals may experience longer disability since their recovery time is usually longer. Type of bacteria causing the psoas infection can also be a factor. Certain microbes (e.g., enterococcus, Mycobacterium tuberculosis, Staphylococcus aureus, Streptococcus pneumoniae) have developed resistance to even the most potent antibiotics (e.g., vancomycin). Psoas infection caused by drug-resistant bacteria may influence the length of disability.

Length of Disability

The length of disability depends on the requirements of the job. Heavy physical labor, climbing, and extensive walking may be difficult until recovery is complete.

Surgical drainage.

Duration in Days

Job Classification	Minimum	Optimum	Maximum
Sedentary work	5	10	21
Light work	5	10	28
Medium work	5	14	42
Heavy work	5	28	42
Very Heavy work	5	28	42

Failure to Recover

If an individual fails to recover within the maximum duration expectancy period, the reader may wish to reference the following questions to assist in better understanding the specifics of an individual's medical case.

Regarding diagnosis:
- What type of psoas abscess does individual have? Primary or secondary?
- Was Staphylococcus aureus the primary cause of the abscess?
- Does individual have fever, chills, vague weakness or other symptoms?
- Was there tenderness or a mass in the lower abdomen, back, or groin?
- Does individual have a skin infection?
- Were other conditions with similar symptoms ruled out?

Regarding treatment:
- Did treatment include triple antibiotic therapy?
- Was abscess successfully drained?
- Was surgical intervention required?
- Did removal of bowel segment present additional problems?

Regarding prognosis:
- Would current therapy be enhanced if combined with antibiotics, drainage, or surgery?
- Would individual benefit from consultation with a specialist?
- Has the psoas infection spread into other vital organ systems? If so, how is this being addressed?
- Has individual experienced complications that may impact recovery?
- Does individual have an underlying condition that may impact recovery?

References

Desandre, A.R., F.J. Cottone, and M.L. Evers. "Isiopsoas Abscess: Etiology, Diagnosis, and Treatment." The American Surgeon 61 12 1995: 1087-1091.

Giladi, M., et al. "Pneumococcal Psoas Abscess: Report of a Case and Review of the World Literature." Israel Journal of Medical Science 32 1996: 771-774.

Gruenwald, I., J. Abrahamson, and O. Cohen. "Psoas Abscess: Case Report and Review of the Literature." The Journal of Urology 147 1992: 1624-1626.

Harrigan, R.A., F.H. Kauffman, and M.B. Love. "Tuberculous Psoas Abscess." The Journal of Emergency Medicine 13 4 1995: 493-498.

Kisner, Carolyn, and Lynn Allen Colby. Therapeutic Exercise: Foundations and Techniques, 2nd ed. Philadelphia: F.A. Davis Company, 1990.

LeMone, P., and K.M. Burke. Medical-Surgical Nursing. Upper Saddle River, NJ: Prentice Hall Health, 2000.

Abscess, Renal and Perinephric
Other names / synonyms: Kidney Abscess, Nephritic Abscess, Perirenal Abscess, Renal Carbuncle
590.2

Definition

A renal or perinephric abscess is a bacterial infection in or around the kidney (perirenal space).

The severity of the condition ranges from small, isolated abscesses to large, solid lesions that completely replace functioning kidney (renal) tissue. Perinephric abscess is an especially serious infection and requires immediate treatment. Perinephric abscesses are most often caused by bacteria (E. coli) that are found in the lower urinary tract. The bacteria may spread up from the tubes that transport urine from the kidneys to the bladder (ureters) or through the lymphatic system.

Risk factors for renal or perinephric abscess include polycystic kidney disease, hemodialysis treatment, spinal cord injury, a deficient (compromised) immune system, diabetes mellitus, urinary tract obstruction, renal or ureteral mineral deposits (calculi), abnormal growth (neoplasm) in the kidney, genitourinary tuberculosis, renal transplantation, surgical trauma to the kidney, steroid administration, and chronic or recurrent urinary tract infection.

The incidence of renal or perinephric abscess ranges from 1 to 10 cases per every 10,000 individuals. Most cases are a result of complications from a lower urinary tract infection. The condition affects men and women in equal proportion. Renal or perinephric abscesses usually occur singly and in only one kidney (unilateral). Sixty-three percent of the time it is the right kidney that is affected.

Diagnosis

History: Individuals may report flank pain on one side only, chills, pain during urination (dysuria), nausea, vomiting, weight loss, recent infection of the skin or urinary tract, night sweats, and loss of appetite (anorexia). Hip, thigh, or knee pain may also be reported.

Physical exam: The exam may reveal pain during manual examination (palpation) of the abdomen or flank, or abdominal lump (mass). Curvature (scoliosis) of the spine may be noted. Examination of the muscles and joints (musculoskeletal system) may reveal pain on bending toward the side opposite (contralateral) to the flank pain. Also, pain may be produced by active flexion of the thigh against resistance on the same (ipsilateral) side as the flank pain, or extension of the ipsilateral thigh while walking.

Tests: Urine and blood cultures, complete blood count (CBC) with white blood cell differential, electrolytes, creatinine, and urinalysis are required immediately to indicate the extent of infection. Urinalysis may show pus in the urine (pyuria), blood in the urine (hematuria), and/or protein in the urine (proteinuria). Gram stain and culture is done on samples of abscess fluid in order to identify the infectious bacterium. Other tests may include visualization of the kidney using high-frequency sound waves (renal ultrasound), computer-aided x-ray analysis (computerized tomography, or CT scan), low-energy radio waves (magnetic resonance imaging, or MRI), and assessment of renal inflammation by examining an image of the kidney on a screen following injection of a radioactive dye (gallium imaging). Accurate diagnosis in the early stages of infection is critical to the individual's survival.

Treatment

Treatment calls for immediate intravenous administration of broad-spectrum antibiotics followed by surgical drainage. Techniques used for abscess drainage are chosen based on the size and placement of the abscess. Draining the abscess with a needle inserted through the skin (percutaneous aspiration) is used for smaller, isolated lesions. For simple one-cavity (unilocular) abscesses within the kidney, drainage is done through a small tube (catheter drainage). Open surgery is required to drain a complex, multiple cavity (multilocular) abscesses. Urinary stones (calculi) found during diagnosis are also removed. Following drainage, specific antimicrobial therapy (based on gram stain and culture of the abscess fluid) is then administered intravenously until the individual has been without fever (afebrile) for 24 hours. Oral antibiotics are then provided. Severely ill individuals may also require feeding through an intravenous line (parenteral nutrition).

Removal of part or all of the kidney (partial or complete nephrectomy, respectively) may be necessary if tests indicate that the kidney is not functioning properly. An immediate nephrectomy is indicated when renal tissue is replaced by an infectious tumor (xanthogranulomatous pyelonephritis) or if the inflamed kidney becomes distended with gas (emphysematous pyelonephritis).

Prognosis

Accurate diagnosis in the early stages of infection is critical to the individual's survival. Full recovery occurs in the vast majority of cases with prompt abscess drainage and appropriate antibiotic treatment. Removal of part or all of a kidney may necessitate dialysis treatment on a routine basis if the other kidney is poorly functioning or absent. If left untreated, renal and perinephric abscesses are associated with a mortality rate ranging from 25%.

Differential Diagnosis

Conditions with similar symptoms include acute pyelonephritis and segmental bacterial nephritis.

Specialists

- General Surgeon
- Nephrologist
- Urologist

Rehabilitation

Intermittent positive pressure breathing exercises may be necessary to prevent pulmonary complications that can result from general anesthesia. Also, certain exercises may be performed to reduce postoperative pain and speed recovery, including progressive relaxation and deep breathing techniques. These may be performed several times per day until pain from inhalation/exhalation is less noticeable. Ankle flexes, knee bends, and crossed-leg muscle contractions (all while lying on the back) will help to increase circulation and make walking easier. These are especially valuable during the first 48 hours after surgery and should be performed 3-5 times per day during this time. Individuals may continue with these exercises for 4-6 weeks until recovery from surgery is complete and pain is no longer noticeable while walking or breathing.

An exercise rehabilitation program under the direction of a physician may benefit individuals who are receiving dialysis treatment. This may include 3 90-minute sessions per week on non-dialysis days. Each session should consist of a 10-minute warm-up period using an exercise bike or treadmill, followed by 50 minutes of intermittent aerobic exercise that incorporates calisthenics, step exercises, and/or flexibility exercises. This should be followed by a 10-minute cool down period. After 2 months of this regimen, an additional 10-minute stretching and low-resistance weight program may be added.

Work Restrictions / Accommodations

Extended sick leave may be required before the individual is able to return to work. Strenuous physical activity may need to be modified. If kidney dialysis is required, the individual may require an extended leave of absence or a switch to part-time or flex-time to accommodate their treatment schedule. Individuals who are receiving dialysis treatments should be assigned more sedentary duties.

Comorbid Conditions

Existing conditions that may impact an individual's ability to recover and further lengthen their disability include chronic or acute renal failure, diabetes mellitus, chronic obstructive pulmonary disease, or coronary artery disease.

Complications

Complications of renal or perinephric abscess may include development of a sub-diaphragmatic (subphrenic) abscess, empyema, nephrobronchial fistula, puncture (perforation) into the abdominal (peritoneal) cavity or the colon, psoas abscess, or flank abscess. Individuals with severe infection may develop renal failure and require the removal of a kidney (nephrectomy). Late-stage diagnosis may result in significant rates of death (mortality).

Factors Influencing Duration

Length of disability may be prolonged by serious complications such as pleural effusion, emphysema, or renal failure requiring nephrectomy. Elderly individuals may have a longer time of disability following surgery as they tend to have slower recovery times following this treatment.

Length of Disability

Disability relates to job requirements. Individuals who are receiving dialysis may need to be reassigned to sedentary duties on the days of treatment.

Nephrectomy, radical.

Duration in Days

Job Classification	Minimum	Optimum	Maximum
Sedentary work	14	28	42
Light work	14	28	56
Medium work	21	35	56
Heavy work	28	42	70
Very Heavy work	28	42	70

Nephrectomy, simple.

Duration in Days

Job Classification	Minimum	Optimum	Maximum
Sedentary work	7	21	35
Light work	7	28	35
Medium work	14	35	42
Heavy work	21	42	56
Very Heavy work	21	42	56

Surgical drainage.

Duration in Days

Job Classification	Minimum	Optimum	Maximum
Sedentary work	7	10	14
Light work	7	10	14
Medium work	10	14	21
Heavy work	15	21	28
Very Heavy work	15	21	28

Failure to Recover

If an individual fails to recover within the maximum duration expectancy period, the reader may wish to reference the following questions to assist in better understanding the specifics of an individual's medical case.

Regarding diagnosis:

- Does individual have a small abscess or is it large involving the entire kidney?
- Has individual had a recent bladder infection?
- Does individual have any risk factors such as polycystic renal disease, hemodialysis treatment, spinal cord injury, compromised immune system, diabetes, urinary tract obstruction or calculi, kidney neoplasm or tuberculosis, history of renal transplant, surgical trauma to the kidney, steroid administration, or chronic or recurrent urinary tract infection?
- Has individual had any flank pain, chills or night sweats, pain with urination, nausea, vomiting, weight loss or loss of appetite?
- Did individual have any lower extremity pain?
- On examination was an abdominal or flank mass palpable?
- Was curvature of the spine present?
- Were urine and blood cultures done?
- Did individual have a CBC, electrolytes, and kidney function tests?
- Was a urinalysis done?
- Did individual have renal ultrasound, CT scan, or MRI?
- Was gallium imaging done?
- Were similar conditions ruled out?

Regarding treatment:

- Was individual started early in treatment on broad-spectrum IV antibiotics? What technique was used to drain the abscess?
- Was specific antimicrobial therapy continued until individual was fever-free for 24 hours? Were oral antibiotics started at that time?
- Did it become necessary to do a partial or complete nephrectomy?
- Did it become necessary for individual to undergo dialysis?

Regarding prognosis:

- Does individual participate in a home exercise program as directed by their physician?
- Is individual's employer able to accommodate flextime or part-time work?
- Does individual have chronic or acute renal failure, diabetes mellitus, chronic obstructive pulmonary disease, or coronary artery disease?
- Did individual have any complications?

References

Dembry, L.M., and V.T. Andriole. "Renal and Perirenal Abscesses." Infectious Disease Clinics of North America 11 3 1997: 663-680.

LeMone, P., and K.M. Burke. Medical-Surgical Nursing. Upper Saddle River, NJ: Prentice Hall Health, 2000.

Abscess, Subdiaphragmatic

Other names / synonyms: Abdominopelvic Abscess, Intra-Abdominal Abscess, Mesenteric Abscess, Peritoneal Abscess, Retrocecal Abscess, Subphrenic Abscess, Suppurative Peritonitis

567.2

Definition

A subdiaphragmatic abscess is a localized accumulation of pus in the abdominal cavity just beneath the diaphragm. There may be more than one site of pus accumulation (multiple-space abscess) and this happens in 13% of cases.

Subdiaphragmatic abscess is classified into two groups, those for which no cause can be found (primary abscess), and those for which a cause is apparent (secondary abscess). Approximately 90% of subdiaphragmatic abscesses are secondary and the remainder are primary. Also, the abscess may be typed as one which develops slowly and persists for a long period of time (chronic), or one which begins abruptly and then tapers off after a short period of time (acute). Acute subdiaphragmatic abscess is far more common and it occurs in 91% of cases. Chronic subdiaphragmatic abscess tends to be generally devoid of symptoms and present for 6 months or longer. Subdiaphragmatic abscesses occur on the right side of the abdominal cavity 60% of the time, although in approximately 4% of cases they are found on both sides (bilateral).

Risk factors for primary subdiaphragmatic abscess are not known because this condition develops from unknown causes. Risk factors for secondary subdiaphragmatic abscess include ruptured appendix; biliary tract disease; liver infection; surgical operations on the stomach and duodenum; inflammation of the pancreas (pancreatitis); surgery to remove the gallbladder (cholecystectomy), part of the stomach (partial gastrectomy), or spleen (splenectomy); puncture (perforation) of the lower esophagus; and abnormal cell growth (neoplasia) in the gastrointestinal tract. Trauma that results in perforation of any abdominal organ or massive bleeding (hemorrhage) is also a major risk factor. Trauma is usually the result of a motor vehicle accident and injuries to the large intestine (colon), spleen, and kidney appear to carry the greatest risk for development of subdiaphragmatic abscess.

The over-all incidence of subdiaphragmatic abscess is difficult to estimate but it generally occurs in less than 1% of individuals who have had elective abdominal surgical procedures. The male to female incidence ratio is approximately equal in the United States, however, this may vary worldwide as Finland has reported a male-to-female predominance of 2:1. The peak incidence of subdiaphragmatic abscess occurs in individuals over 50 years of age.

Diagnosis

History: Symptoms of subdiaphragmatic abscess are varied and may be dependent upon the specific location of the abscess. Most individuals will complain of pain in the abdomen, chest, and/or shoulder. Nausea, vomiting, loss of appetite (anorexia), cough, difficult or rapid breathing (dyspnea or tachypnea, respectively), foul sputum, chills, sweating, and mental confusion may also be reported.

Physical exam: An exam often reveals fever, rapid heart rate (tachycardia), a cough that produces very little sputum (non-productive cough), decreased breath sounds, fluid accumulation in the skin (skin edema), tenderness over the 8th through 12th ribs (Krukow's sign), chronic hiccough, abdominal tenderness and swelling, absence of bowel sounds (hypoactive bowel sounds), yellowing of the skin (jaundice), fluid accumulation (edema) in the lower legs, and fluid accumulation in the abdomen (ascites). The individual usually appears apprehensive and confused.

Tests: Tests may include a complete blood count (CBC) with white cell differential, red blood cell (erythrocyte) sedimentation rate, and blood and urine cultures. Plain abdominal x-rays, x-rays with a barium enema, x-rays taken after injection of a radiopaque dye (intravenous pyelogram), or an upper gastrointestinal series may be useful in diagnosis. The abscess is usually visualized best using high-frequency sound waves (abdominal ultrasonography) or computer-aided x-ray analysis (computerized tomography or CT). Low-energy radio waves (magnetic resonance imaging or MRI) may also be helpful in this regard.

Treatment

Conservative treatment consists of nutritional support and broad-spectrum antibiotic therapy. Infection increases metabolic requirements, and nutritional support in the form of tube-feeding or administration of nutrients directly into a vein (parenteral nutrition) is usually important. Operative treatment for subdiaphragmatic abscess includes drainage using a needle and syringe (percutaneous drainage), or one of four different types of open surgical approaches (transpleural; extrapleural; extraperitoneal; transperitoneal). The type of surgical approach that is used depends largely upon the location of the abscess in the abdominal cavity. Antibiotic treatment can also be administered to individuals who are treated using surgery. Post-operative treatment includes adequate water and food intake, along with installation of an outlet (sump drain) that allows fluid to drain from the abscess cavity.

Prognosis

Mortality runs 85-100% in individuals with subdiaphragmatic abscess who are untreated. Conservative (non-surgical) treatment consisting of nutritional support and antibiotic therapy results in mortality approximately 30-50% of the time. Operative treatment with no antibiotics results in mortality 30-46% of the time, while using antibiotics in combination with surgery reduces mortality to as low as 8-11%.

Differential Diagnosis

Conditions that present with similar symptoms as subdiaphragmatic abscess include appendicitis, bowel obstruction, strangulated hernia, perforated gastric ulcer, Meckel's diverticulitis, ruptured spleen, acute cholecystitis, ruptured ectopic pregnancy or ovarian cyst, ruptured aortic aneurysm, and mesenteric thrombosis.

Specialists

- Gastroenterologist
- General Surgeon

Work Restrictions / Accommodations

Following surgical treatment, the individual with subdiaphragmatic abscess will continue medical therapy for approximately 3 weeks. There are restrictions on heavy lifting, climbing, and walking long distances. Return to work in a limited capacity may be possible during this time. If recovery does not occur and the individual's condition worsens, additional time away from work for further treatment may be required. If left untreated, the individual may become permanently disabled and mortality could result.

Comorbid Conditions

Existing conditions that may impact an individual's ability to recover and further lengthen disability include underlying infections such as tuberculosis, kidney infection, or any infection that occurs following surgery. Systemic diseases such as leukemia, pancreatitis, and diabetes may also have an effect.

Complications

Possible complications of subdiaphragmatic abscess may include systemic infection (septicemia); general ill health, malnutrition, weakness, and emaciation (cachexia); brain, lung, or liver abscess; creation of an open passage into the airway (bronchial fistula); puncture (perforation) of the diaphragm; inflammation of the tissue surrounding the heart (pericarditis); inflammation of tissues in the chest (mediastinitis); pneumonia; partial obstruction of a major vein (inferior vena cava) that returns blood to the heart; fluid accumulation of the lower limbs (pitting edema); blood vessel inflammation and clot formation (thrombophlebitis); blood clot formation in the lungs (pulmonary embolism); massive bleeding (hemorrhage); inflammation of the membranes covering the nerves and spinal cord (meningitis); and fluid in the lungs (pulmonary edema).

Factors Influencing Duration

The length of disability may be influenced by the type of drainage treatment (percutaneous or open surgery). Older individuals may experience longer disability as they usually require extended recovery time following treatment. Finally, the type of bacteria that caused the subdiaphragmatic infection can be a factor. Certain microbes (e.g., Enterococcus, Mycobacterium tuberculosis, Staphylococcus aureus, Streptococcus pneumoniae) have developed resistance to even the most potent antibiotics (e.g., vancomycin) and subdiaphragmatic abscess caused by drug-resistant bacteria may influence the length of disability.

Length of Disability

Heavy physical labor, climbing, and extensive walking may be difficult until recovery is complete. Disability may be permanent.

Open.

Duration in Days

Job Classification	Minimum	Optimum	Maximum
Sedentary work	14	21	28
Light work	14	21	28
Medium work	14	21	28
Heavy work	14	28	35
Very Heavy work	14	28	35

Percutaneous drainage.

Duration in Days

Job Classification	Minimum	Optimum	Maximum
Sedentary work	3	5	7
Light work	3	5	7
Medium work	3	5	7
Heavy work	5	7	14
Very Heavy work	5	7	14

Failure to Recover

If an individual fails to recover within the maximum duration expectancy period, the reader may wish to reference the following questions to assist in better understanding the specifics of an individual's medical case.

Regarding diagnosis:

- Does the individual have a primary or secondary abscess? Is it acute or chronic?
- Does the individual have any risk factors for secondary subdiaphragmatic abscess such as ruptured appendix; biliary tract disease; liver infection; surgical operations on the stomach and duodenum; pancreatitis; cholecystectomy, partial gastrectomy, or splenectomy; perforation of the lower esophagus; and neoplasia in the gastrointestinal tract?
- Has the individual had any trauma to any abdominal organs that resulted in perforation or hemorrhage?
- Does the individuals complain of pain in the abdomen, chest, and/or shoulder?
- Does the individual have nausea, vomiting, anorexia, cough, dyspnea or tachypnea, foul sputum, chills, sweating, and mental confusion?
- On physical exam were fever, tachycardia, a non-productive cough, decreased breath sounds, skin edema, tenderness over the 8th through 12th ribs (Krukow's sign), chronic hiccough, abdominal tenderness and swelling, hypoactive bowel sounds, jaundice, edema in the lower legs, or ascites?
- Does the individual appear apprehensive and confused?
- Has the individual had a CBC, ESR and blood and urine cultures?
- Has the individual had plain x-ray's, barium enema, IVP, Upper GI series, abdominal ultrasound, CT scan or MRI?
- Have conditions with similar symptoms been ruled out?

Regarding treatment:

- Is the individual being treated with broad-spectrum antibiotics and parenteral nutrition?
- Has the abscess been drained surgically?

Regarding prognosis:

- Is the individual's employer able to accommodate any necessary restrictions?
- Does the individual have any conditions that may affect their ability to recover?
- Does the individual have any complications such as septicemia, general ill health, malnutrition, weakness, and emaciation; brain, lung, or liver abscess; bronchial fistula; perforation of the diaphragm; pericarditis; mediastinitis; pneumonia; partial obstruction of the inferior vena cava; pitting edema; thrombophlebitis; pulmonary embolism; hemorrhage; meningitis; or pulmonary edema?

References

Ariel, I.M., and K.K. Kazarian. "Classification, diagnosis and treatment of subphrenic abscess." Review of Surgery 28 1 1971: 1-21.

Sanders, R.C. "The changing epidemiology of subphrenic abscess and its clinical and radiological consequences." British Journal of Surgery 57 6 1970: 449-55.

Achalasia

Other names / synonyms: Cardiospasm, Esophageal Achalasia, Esophageal Aperistalsis, Megaesophagus
530.0

Definition

Achalasia is an uncommon disorder of the esophagus that causes difficulty with swallowing. Moving food down the esophagus into the stomach requires an orderly wave of muscle contractions and relaxations (peristalsis). Achalasia is characterized by the failure of the muscles of the esophagus to move food down toward the stomach. Spasms also develop in the lower esophageal sphincter resulting in its failure to relax in response to swallowing, thus obstructing the passage of food from the esophagus into the stomach.

This condition is caused by a progressive loss of nerve cells that control the esophageal muscles. The cause of the damage and loss of nervous stimulation is unknown in the vast majority of cases. Achalasia can occasionally be caused by Chagas disease or parasitic infections, and has also been associated with Parkinson's disease, and other muscle/nerve (myoneural) disorders. This implies that achalasia may caused by hereditary factors or as the end result of a number of different underlying conditions. It develops gradually over a period of months or years.

The worldwide incidence of achalasia is estimated at 2 out of 100,000 persons per year. The age-specific incidence appears to have two peaks, the first at about 37 years of age and another at 50 years of age. The condition occurs equally among men and women. Studies in Singapore suggest an ethnic risk component, with Malays showing a significantly lower incidence than Chinese or Eastern Indians. In the US, however, the incidence occurs equally among whites and non-whites. The condition is more prevalent in the southern part of the US than in the Pacific and Great Lakes regions, suggesting that environmental factors, as yet unknown, may play a role in determining risk.

Diagnosis

History: The individual may complain of difficulty swallowing food and liquids (dysphagia) or regurgitation of undigested food, without symptoms of another illness. It might be described as "food not going down all the way" or "getting stuck halfway down." There may be a sense of fullness in the chest and weight loss. Sometimes the complaint is chest pain after eating, which can radiate to the back, neck, and arms. The individual may also experience coughing, especially at night, due to accidental inhalation of regurgitated material, drooling, and a heartburn sensation. The symptoms are usually slow in onset and progression.

Physical exam: There may be weight loss and signs of malnutrition, anemia, and vomiting blood. About a third of individuals experience nocturnal regurgitation, which can result in pneumonia.

Tests: A chest x-ray is usually done first. An x-ray of the esophagus (a barium swallow or esophagram), or upper GI series, can demonstrate the enlarged esophagus, lack of orderly muscular contractions and relaxations (peristalsis), and narrowing next to the stomach. Esophageal manometry is required for definitive diagnosis (a tube containing pressure sensors is inserted down the esophagus, and pressures are recorded during a swallow). It can demonstrate lack of peristalsis and abnormal sustained contractions (spasms) in the lower portion of the esophagus. An examination of the esophagus using a flexible fiber-optic tube (esophagoscopy) should reveal an enlarged esophagus but no obstruction.

Treatment

There are several types of drugs to help the smooth muscle of the esophagus relax. Long acting nitrates and calcium channel blockers can be used to lower the pressure at the lower esophagus sphincter and can be helpful in decreasing the severity of symptoms. Botulinum toxin can be injected directly into the spasming muscles, relaxing them for long periods and allowing food to pass. These injections, however, must be repeated at regular intervals varying from weeks to months.

The lower esophagus can be stretched open with a dilating instrument (forceful dilation) or by inflating a balloon passed halfway into the stomach (pneumatic dilation). If esophageal dilation is not effective, surgery can be performed to open the lower esophagus by cutting the muscles in spasm (myotomy). Finally, an incision may be made through the muscular coating of the lower part of the esophagus (esophagomyotomy) to reduce pressure in the lower sphincter.

Raising the head of the individual's bed can help to prevent pulmonary complications resulting from nocturnal aspiration of regurgitated food and liquid.

Prognosis

Achalasia is a chronic, progressive disorder. Medical and surgical treatments cannot cure the condition but they can control the symptoms and lessen complications, especially if a diagnosis is made early in this disease.

Esophageal dilation is effective in approximately 85% of individuals with achalasia, but may eventually need to be repeated. Medication may increase the time between repeat procedures. Complications of esophageal dilation, such as esophageal rupture, occur in fewer than 1% of cases.

Direct injection of the botulinum toxin yields improvement in 70-80% of individuals with achalasia, but this improvement may last only 6-12 months.

Myotomy has a success rate of approximately 85%; however, in 15% of individuals, the surgery is followed by symptomatic gastroesophageal reflux disease (GERD), the regurgitation of acid or food from the stomach into the esophagus.

Differential Diagnosis

Chest pain from achalasia may be indistinguishable from the pain of a heart attack. Achalasia may be confused with gallbladder or pancreas inflammation. Peptic ulcer disease or a peptic stricture should also be considered. Abnormalities of swallowing can result from emotional disorders (globus hystericus) or simply from aging (presbyesophagus). Esophageal cancer can result in mechanical obstruction of the esophagus. Regurgitation of food and stomach acid can result from a hiatal hernia or other causes of esophageal reflux. Scleroderma may cause difficulty with swallowing, as can Parkinson's disease. A pouch (diverticulum) can form off the side of the esophagus, trapping food and causing regurgitation of its contents or infection.

Specialists

- Gastroenterologist
- General Surgeon

Work Restrictions / Accommodations

Since frequent swallowing may provoke the spasms, meals should not be rushed and adequate time must be given for the individual to eat. If surgery is required, there may be temporary lifting restrictions.

Comorbid Conditions

Coexisting conditions that may impact recovery and lengthen disability include sleep apnea (with regurgitation of undigested food while sleeping), chronic lung problems such as asthma, and cancer of the esophagus.

Complications

Regurgitation may result in food spilling into the lungs, resulting in severe pneumonia (aspiration pneumonia), lung abscess, or the worsening of any pre-existing lung disease such as asthma. The inability to swallow food may result in malnutrition. The risk of esophageal cancer is believed to be higher in individuals with achalasia.

Factors Influencing Duration

The timeliness and effectiveness of treatment will determine the length of disability, as will the presence of any complications, especially pulmonary problems. If the diagnosis and subsequent treatment is delayed, disability will be prolonged. The method of treatment can also influence disability. Drug treatment usually does not involve any disability. Esophageal dilation is performed on an outpatient basis, and prompt return to work the following day may be expected. Open surgery has its own attendant disability period.

Length of Disability

The duration of disability depends upon whether the condition requires surgery, and on the individual's job requirements.

Medical treatment.

Duration in Days

Job Classification	Minimum	Optimum	Maximum
Any work	1	2	7

Dilation.

Duration in Days

Job Classification	Minimum	Optimum	Maximum
Any work	1	2	3

Failure to Recover

If an individual fails to recover within the maximum duration expectancy period, the reader may wish to reference the following questions to assist in better understanding the specifics of an individual's medical case.

Regarding diagnosis:

- Was diagnosis confirmed?
- Was esophageal manometry done?
- Was an x-ray of the esophagus performed to rule out the presence of a tumor or other mechanical disorder?
- Was endoscopy performed to rule out other conditions?
- Were new symptoms noted, such as vomiting of blood?

Regarding treatment:

- If individual is on drug therapy, are side effects creating a problem?
- Is individual maintaining the medication regimen despite side effects?
- If symptoms have not been significantly lessened with current treatment, have other treatment options been utilized or considered (drug therapy, Botulinum toxin injections, esophageal dilation, or surgical myotomy)?
- Is individual sleeping with the head of the bed elevated, to reduce the likelihood of aspiration?

Regarding prognosis:

- Has individual developed any associated complications, such as aspiration pneumonia or malnutrition?
- Are emotional factors impeding progress?
- Does individual have unrealistic expectations or does he/she understand that this condition is a progressive, lifelong disorder that must be continually dealt with?
- Would individual benefit from joining a support group?

References

Beers, Mark H., and Robert Berkow. The Merck Manual of Diagnosis and Therapy. Whitehouse Station, NJ: Merck & Co., Inc, 1999.

Podas, T., et al. "Achalasia: A Critical Review of Epidemiological Studies." American Journal of Gastroenterology 93 12 1998: 2345-2347.

Achilles Bursitis or Tendinitis

Other names / synonyms: Achilles Bursitis, Achilles Tendonitis, Achillobursitis, Tendocalcaneal Bursitis, Tendonitis of the Heel

726.71, 726.72

Definition

Achilles bursitis or tendinitis refers to a painful and inflammatory condition affecting the tendon that joins the heel bone to the calf muscle (Achilles tendon) or the small sacs (bursae) that surround that tendon. Tendons are fibrous tissues connecting muscles to bones or other structures. Bursae are small sacs or pouches found over most bony prominences. They provide cushioning and protect tendons and ligaments from wear by producing a lubricating synovial fluid that reduces the effects of friction and impact.

The Achilles tendon serves to raise and lower the heel during movement such as walking, running, and jumping. Repetitive forces on this tendon and its bursae from these types of activities can cause either of these inflammatory conditions. Changes in the tendon due to aging may also make the tendon more prone to inflammation. Individuals at a higher risk for developing this condition include manual laborers (those who perform certain repetitive tasks such as walking or going up and down steps) and athletes (who participate in running or jumping activities). Wearing ill-fitting shoes may also contribute to the development of tendonitis.

Other risk factors include those with a familial high cholesterol condition called familial hyperlipidemia type II. Some individuals with this type of cholesterol abnormality may develop fat-like deposits (xanthomas) in tendons that result in Achilles tendonitis.

The exact incidence and prevalence of Achilles bursitis or tendonitis is not reported, however, this condition is common in active middle-aged individuals.

Diagnosis

History: With either Achilles tendinitis or bursitis, individuals generally report heel or calf pain that is made worse by activity, although there may be pain while the individual is at rest. The area overlying the inflammation may be tender and swollen. Other reported signs include swelling around the joint and palpable grating (crepitus) when flexing and extending the foot. The individual may also report pain associated with occupational tasks and sports activities or a history of trauma to this area.

Physical exam: With tendinitis, physical examination usually reveals swelling and tenderness. Mobility (ankle extension - bending the foot up) may be limited because of pain. An examination of the individual's shoes may provide information with regard to the individual's gait or running pattern. Cases of Achilles bursitis usually involve swelling on both sides of the tendon with the individual experiencing pain upon extension of the ankle.

Tests: No diagnostic tests are usually required for Achilles tendinitis, although plain film x-rays of the joint and surrounding area may be taken. Diagnostic ultrasound may also be useful in examining the area particularly if the tendon is viewed during contraction. When the physician is not sure if the tendon is intact, MRI may be performed to identify tears, partial tears, inflammation, or tumors. In cases of suspected Achilles bursitis, joint or synovial fluid may be removed through aspiration and examined microscopically. This fluid will be cultured to help the physician diagnose whether bursitis is from infection or inflammation.

Treatment

The goal of treatment is to relieve pain, reduce inflammation, and rest the joint. Specific recommendations depend on the cause of the injury. Treatment may consist of a heel lift, applying ice, and protective pressure wraps to the area. The individuals should also decrease or modify the repetitive activity to allow the tendon to heal properly and prevent symptom recurrence. Nonsteroidal anti-inflammatory drugs (NSAIDs) are useful in relieving pain and inflammation. Severe cases of Achilles tendonitis may be treated by immobilizing the muscle and tendon using a brace, cane, or crutch and, in severe cases, casting of the foot and ankle. Following a recovery period, the individual may receive physical therapy and instruction in stretching exercises.

In cases of Achilles bursitis, the joint should be elevated and gentle compression applied, e.g., an elastic bandage. Some cases may require one or more injections of corticosteroids into the bursa to relieve inflammation, although most experts consider cortisone injection anywhere near the Achilles tendon as contraindicated since it may predispose Achilles tendon rupture.

In rare cases where tendonitis is persistent and unresponsive to nonsurgical treatment, debridement of the Achilles tendon may be suggested. This surgical procedure removes any unhealthy tissue (necrotic) around the Achilles tendon. The ankle is then placed in a cast until healing takes place (about 6 to 8 weeks). Once the cast is removed, physical therapy is performed to restore strength and mobility of the ankle and lower leg.

Prognosis

In general, Achilles tendonitis resolves completely following a period of rest, use of anti-inflammatory medications, and splinting or casting, when necessary. Acute bursitis may progress to chronic or long-term bursitis and result in limitations of ankle or foot range of motion.

Surgical debridement of the tendon generally has a good outcome but carries common surgical risks.

Differential Diagnosis

Differential diagnoses include rupture of the Achilles tendon, tearing of the tendon, arthritis, joint infection, fracture, or tumor of the bone or soft tissue.

Specialists

- Orthopedic Surgeon
- Podiatrist
- Rheumatologist

Rehabilitation

The initial goal of rehabilitation for Achilles bursitis or tendonitis is to decrease the inflammation and pain to the affected tendon or bursa. This allows the physical therapist to then focus on restoring flexibility and strength to the muscles of the foot and ankle. One of the initial steps in the rehabilitation process for this condition is to teach the individual to avoid pressure and stress on the inflamed bursa or tendon. This is accomplished through use of a pad around the inflamed bursa that prevents excess pressure when wearing footwear.

Another method to protect the Achilles tendon is a foam or gel cushion placed in the individual's shoe under the heel bone. This is to protect and reduce the stretch and stress on the involved Achilles tendon. Both techniques are utilized throughout the rehabilitation process until inflammation decreases.

Rehabilitation offers several possible treatments in controlling inflammation from bursitis or tendonitis. At the initial flare-up, the physical therapist may use cold treatments to control swelling and pain. Electrostimulation combined with a cold treatment is another technique used.

Once the initial pain and inflammation (acute stage of bursitis and tendonitis) improve, the use of heat is applied in the rehabilitation process. Heat treatments help relieve lower leg muscle and joint pain and stiffness. They also increase the blood flow that helps remove inflammation from the bursa or tendon. Moist heat packs are used over multiple layers of toweling to achieve a comfortable warming effect. Another form of heat treatment is ultrasound that uses high frequency sound waves to produce heat that penetrates deep into the involved bursa and surrounding joint and muscles.

When pain and swelling are greatly reduced, the physical therapist performs stretching exercises that help restore full motion to the affected ankle and ankle joints.

Once minimal discomfort is present with stretching, strengthening of this aspect of the lower leg begins with isotonic exercises. An example of this type of rehabilitation exercise is strengthening with weights and elastic bands. Strength training of this type also includes weight equipment/machines.

The physical therapist may need to modify the program for individuals with arthritis or other joint irritations and may depend on the extent of the Achilles bursitis or tendonitis. In severe cases, the individual may have the ankle immobilized in a walking cast or boot until inflammatory symptoms decrease. Occupational therapy becomes involved in the rehabilitation process if there is a need for foot inserts called orthotics. These shoe inserts address any malalignment issues of the foot and ankle that may contribute to the symptoms.

Work Restrictions / Accommodations

If casting is required, temporary transfer to sedentary duties may be necessary for individuals with jobs that require prolonged standing, walking, or lifting. Accommodations may need to be made during this usually short recovery period.

Individuals with chronic conditions should be permanently reassigned to jobs that do not require prolonged standing, walking, or lifting.

Complementary and Alternative Therapies

Content is intended for awareness only. Treatments may or may not be effective. Scientific evidence may be lacking and some substances have potentially toxic effects. Dr. Presley Reed and the editors do not endorse the use of these therapies in the absence of consultation with a licensed medical professional.

Shoes with flexible soles and inserts - May help to reduce tension on the tendon and stabilize the heel.

Warm or cool compresses - May help reduce pain and inflammation.

Heat treatment - Heat lamp, hot soaks, heating pads, liniments, ointments may increase circulation and help reduce inflammation.

Whirlpool - May improve circulation.

Arnica - Used externally, may aid in sprains and muscle aches.

Comorbid Conditions

Coexisting conditions that may impact recovery and lengthen disability include strain or sprain of the lower leg muscles and Achilles tendon or the presence of an infection introduced through broken skin at the time of injury. Rheumatoid arthritis can cause Achilles bursitis. Tendinitis also becomes more likely with repeated injury.

Complications

Possible complications include rupture of the tendon and symptom recurrence.

Factors Influencing Duration

Factors that may lengthen disability include the type, cause, and severity of the injury, type of treatment provided, individual's response to treatment, development of complications, and individual's compliance with treatment recommendations.

Length of Disability

Duration in Days

Job Classification	Minimum	Optimum	Maximum
Sedentary work	0	3	7
Light work	0	3	7
Medium work	0	7	14
Heavy work	7	14	21
Very Heavy work	7	14	21

Failure to Recover

If an individual fails to recover within the maximum duration expectancy period, the reader may wish to reference the following questions to assist in better understanding the specifics of an individual's medical case.

Regarding diagnosis:

- Was this a recurring injury?
- Was diagnosis confirmed with x-ray, diagnostic ultrasound, or MRI?
- Was synovial fluid aspirated and examined microscopically?
- Was the fluid cultured to differentiate between infection and inflammation?

Regarding treatment:

- If underlying infection was identified, how was it treated?
- Has infection resolved?
- Was immobilization required (pressure wraps, elastic bandages, brace, cast)?
- Was surgery indicated? Was surgery performed?
- Were anti-inflammatory drugs used to reduce inflammation?
- Did individual receive physical therapy and instruction on stretching exercises?
- Did individual use a cane or crutch?

Regarding prognosis:

- Did injury occur by a direct blow or is it due to a sprain or strain?
- Did individual return to work or activities too soon?
- Was individual adequately instructed in how to modify activities?
- Did individual wear protective strapping or adhesive bandage for several weeks after healing?
- Was individual instructed in prevention techniques (warm up before activity, proper moves and techniques for that activity, physical conditioning)?

References

Arnheim, Daniel D. Modern Principles of Athletic Training. St. Louis: Times Mirror/Mosby Publishing, 1989.

Braunwald, Eugene, et al. Harrison's Principles of Internal Medicine, 11th ed. New York: McGraw-Hill Book Company, 1987.

DerMarderosian, Ara, ed. The Review of Natural Products. St. Louis: Facts and Comparisons, 2000.

Griffith, H. Winter. Complete Guide to Sports Injuries. New York: The Berkley Publishing Group, 1986.

Kessler, R.M. Management of Common Musculoskeletal Disorders: Physical Therapy Principles and Methods. Philadelphia: J.B. Lippincott Co, 1990.

Medical Multimedia Group. "Achilles Tendonitis/Rupture." A Patient's Guide to Foot Problems. 22 May 2000 07 Dec 2000 <http://www.sechrest.com/mmg/reflib/foot/achilles/achilles.html>.

Achlorhydria and Hypochlorhydria

Other names / synonyms: Achylia, Achylosis, Gastric Achylia
536.0, 536.8

Definition

Hypochlorhydria and achlorhydria refer to decreased or nonexistent hydrochloric acid secretion in the stomach, respectively. Either condition may occur spontaneously as a result of a clinical disorder or from drug administration (iatrogenic).

Spontaneous hypochlorhydria or achlorhydria can occur from many different diseases including stomach (gastric) ulcer, stomach cancer (gastric carcinoma), various intestinal, immune and hormonal (endocrine) disorders, malnutrition, and kidney (renal) failure. Certain surgical procedures may also decrease or eliminate stomach acid production. The most common cause of spontaneous hypochlorhydria or achlorhydria is ongoing and lingering stomach inflammation (chronic atrophic gastritis).

Iatrogenic hypochlorhydria or achlorhydria caused by the administration of drugs may be either intermittent or persistent throughout the day depending on the drug taken. Intake of antacids or antihistamines rarely results in continuous decreased acid secretion throughout the 24-hour period. On the other hand, proton pump inhibitors (hydrogen-potassium ATPase inhibitors) may produce persistent hypochlorhydria or achlorhydria in some individuals.

The high gastric acid environment in the stomach has a normal protective function that inhibits bacterial growth within the stomach. Hypochlorhydria or achlorhydria decreases acidity and may permit bacterial growth in the stomach and upper small intestine (duodenum). The source of bacterial contamination is primarily from saliva and food and, possibly from the distal intestine.

Approximately 1 in 20 individuals may have achlorhydria without any symptoms. Hypochlorhydria or achlorhydria is equally common in males and females and has higher incidence in elderly individuals.

Diagnosis

History: Symptoms may include a desire to eat when not hungry, a sense of fullness after meals, and alternating constipation and diarrhea.

Physical exam: The exam is most likely normal and symptoms of the condition are not evident.

Tests: Acidity of gastric secretions can be measured in samples collected through a flexible tube inserted through the nose or mouth and into the stomach (naso- or orogastric tubes) while the individual is in a basal, fasted state. By measuring the acidity (pH) of these samples, achlorhydria can then be identified. A pH greater than 3.5 is commonly used to identify achlorhydria. Blood tests may also show elevated levels of a hormone (gastrin) that normally stimulates stomach acid secretion.

Bacterial overgrowth in the stomach is commonly associated with hypo- or achlorhydria. This can be diagnosed by culturing a gastric or upper intestinal aspirate to confirm the existence of a significant bacterial population. Two other methods are available to measure bacterial overgrowth. One is a breath test that monitors hydrogen production after ingestion of sugar or after ingestion of a radioactive sugar digested by the bacteria. In the second test, an individual exhales increased amounts of radioactivity if a large bacterial population is present in the stomach or duodenum.

Treatment

Insufficient hydrochloric acid secretion by the stomach is often the result of another disease process and treatment is usually directed to the underlying condition. The most common cause of hypo- or achlorhydria is chronic gastritis resulting from ingestion of irritating foods or anti-inflammatory medications. If anti-inflammatory medications must be taken, the individual may benefit by ingesting these with meals or milk. Antacids are usually discontinued if they result in hypo- or achlorhydria. Dietary counseling is often suggested. The primary treatment for bacterial overgrowth resulting from low gastric acid secretion is nutritional supplementation with fat and fat-soluble vitamins, injections of vitamin B_{12}, or administration of antibiotics.

Prognosis

The predicted outcome depends on the underlying cause of the hypo- or achlorhydric condition. Long-term consequences of hypo- or achlorhydria may include a tumor of the pancreas (gastrinoma) or overgrowth (hyperplasia) of hormone-secreting (endocrine) cells found in the inner lining (mucosa) of the stomach. Treatment for chronic atrophic gastritis (the most common cause of hypo- or achlorhydria) may be handled on an outpatient basis, and the predicted outcome is usually good if the causative factors for gastric irritation are eliminated. If the individual is taking acid-blocking drugs, cessation of this medication should return the stomach's acidity to normal. However, if the hypo- or achlorhydria is due to cancer or the result of a surgical procedure, the prognosis is more guarded.

Differential Diagnosis

Overuse or abuse of antacids may occasionally produce symptoms characteristic of hypo- or achlorhydria.

Specialists

- Gastroenterologist

Work Restrictions / Accommodations

Work restrictions or accommodations are dependent on the underlying cause of the condition and must be determined on an individual basis. For certain underlying causes of hypo- or achlorhydria, pain medication may be necessary to enable the individual to perform their full job responsibilities. Convenient access to bathroom facilities may be necessary if the individual experiences diarrhea.

Comorbid Conditions

Coexisting conditions that may impact recovery and lengthen disability from achlorhydria include pernicious anemia, gastric conditions requiring long-term acid-blocking therapy, stomach cancer (gastric carcinoma), HIV infection, or a history of surgical procedures to the stomach such as vagotomy, where the vagus nerve is cut to reduce production of digestive acid. Conditions that may be associated with hypochlorhydria include allergies, autoimmune diseases, thyroid disorders, diabetes, gallbladder disease, and chronic hepatitis.

Complications

Hypochlorhydria or achlorhydria may result in increased bacterial growth in the stomach and duodenum. This carries an increased risk for several infectious diseases as well as increased incidence and severity of cholera, salmonellosis, typhoid fever, shigellosis, colitis, brucellosis, and various parasitic infections. Stomach acid is important in liberating minerals from food thereby increasing the risk of individuals with hypo- or achlorhydria to develop calcium and zinc deficiencies. Loss of acid production may also alter the rate or extent of drug absorption.

Factors Influencing Duration

The length of disability may be influenced by the severity of the condition, the underlying cause of the condition and its response to treatment, or any complications.

Length of Disability

Vague diagnosis. Length of disability depends on the underlying cause of the condition. Duration will be minimal if chronic gastritis is the cause of low stomach acid secretion. Longer-term disability is expected if the underlying cause is gastric cancer.

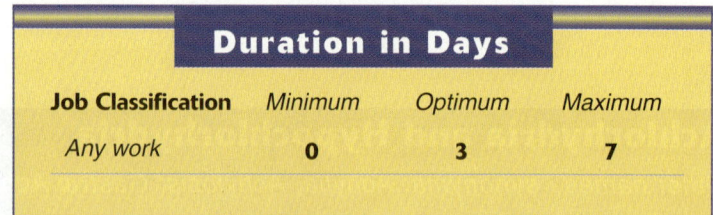

Duration in Days			
Job Classification	Minimum	Optimum	Maximum
Any work	0	3	7

Failure to Recover

If an individual fails to recover within the maximum duration expectancy period, the reader may wish to reference the following questions to assist in better understanding the specifics of an individual's medical case.

Regarding diagnosis:

- Does individual have a history of stomach ulcer or cancer, immune or hormonal disorders, malnutrition, or kidney failure?
- Does individual have chronic gastritis?
- Has individual undergone surgery recently?
- Has individual recently taken, or is individual currently taking antacids, antihistamines, or ATPase inhibitors?
- Does individual eat when not hungry and feel a sense of fullness after meals?
- Does individual experience alternating bouts of constipation and diarrhea?
- Was gastric acidity determined? Is the pH greater than 3.5 (achlorhydria)?
- Was gastrin measured? If so, is it elevated?
- Were cultures obtained or breath tests done to determine if significant bacterial growth is present?

Regarding treatment:

- Does individual have chronic gastritis?
- What foods or medications are being ingested that could be causing the gastritis?
- Are medications taken with meals or milk?
- Has individual discontinued taking antacids?
- Would individual benefit from counseling from a dietitian or nutritionist?
- Does individual have bacterial overgrowth in the stomach?
- Does individual take fat and fat-soluble vitamins, B$_{12}$ injections, or antibiotics? If so, is individual taking the medication as prescribed?

Regarding prognosis:

- What underlying condition caused the hypo- or achlorhydria? How is it being addressed?
- Has individual developed any infections? If so, how will they be treated and what is the expected outcome of treatment?
- Does individual have calcium or zinc deficiencies?
- If individual is on medication, how will this be affected by the hypo- or achlorhydria?
- Does individual have long-standing hypo- or achlorhydria? If so, has individual developed gastrinoma or an overgrowth of endocrine cells in the stomach lining? How will this be treated and what is expected outcome of treatment?

References

Davenport, Horace W. Physiology of the Digestive Tract. Chicago: Year Book Medical Publishers, Inc, 1982.

Peura, David A., and Richard L. Guerrant. "Achlorhydria and Enteric Bacterial Infections." Chronic Gastritis and Hypochlorhydria in the Elderly. Holt, Peter R., and Robert M. Russell, eds. Boca Raton: CRC Press, 1993. 127-141.

Acid Peel

Other names / synonyms: Chemexfoliation, Chemical Peel
86.24

Definition

Acid peels, also known as chemical peels, are applied to destroy the superficial layer of the skin and then remove (exfoliate) the dead skin cells (corneocytes). This allows a new skin layer to develop resulting in smoother facial skin. Acid peels that penetrate deeper into the outer layers of skin (epidermis) are often used to treat more subtle wrinkles (rhytid) than what a facelift (rhytidectomy) addresses, particularly around the eyes, mouth, and lips. It may also help remove the black/white heads of pimples, superficial scars, and superficial benign skin growths. An acid peel is usually an elective procedure.

Substances typically used for this procedure are found in nature such as alpha-hydroxy acids or glycolic acids (AHAs), and are associated with fruits, spoiled milk, or sugarcane. AHAs are generally used for mild skin scars and plugs of material within dilated hair follicles that frequently contain bacteria (comedones). Trichloroacetic acid and Jessner's peels are more toxic than AHA peels and cause destruction to the deeper layer of the skin. They are used to treat deep scars and skin growths but also permit the underlying new skin to resurface. The penetrating ability of the acid peel generally depends on the type or concentration of acid used.

The Plastic Surgery Information Service estimates that about 51,500 chemical peels were performed in the US in 1999.

Reason for Procedure

An acid peel stimulates the skin's natural rejuvenation processes. During the aging process, the skin thins and wrinkles, losing its elasticity. The acid peel removes (exfoliates) outer layers of dead skin while creating a healing response that both repairs and rejuvenates. Individuals seek treatment primarily to augment the results of a facelift and eliminate wrinkles that other cosmetic procedures fail to resolve. The treatment also addresses sun-damaged (photoaged) skin, precancerous skin lesions (actinic keratoses), skin growths (seborrheic keratoses), acne scars, patches of pigmented skin (lentigo), scaly skin (xerosis), dry skin disorder (ichthyosis), brown spots (melasma), and freckles.

Description

About two weeks prior to the procedure, individuals may be given lotion containing 3-10% AHA for applying once or twice daily to increase tolerance for the upcoming acid peel. Individuals may also be instructed to temporarily stop using certain products such as hair dyes that might irritate the skin. On the day of the procedure (done on an outpatient basis), the individual will be asked to refrain from wearing cosmetics or lotions. Residual debris or oils will also be cleansed from the face.

The individual's face is then coated with the acid peel agent. The more common, superficial peels (50-70% of cases) are done using an AHA where multiple treatments may be required. Trichloroacetic acid (TCA) is used in 15-50% of cases for deeper peels to remove scars. The deepest peels produce the smoothest skin and are done using substances such as phenol (carbolic acid, 88% in solution with water, oil or other substances). These are now used far less frequently however, because of potential complications.

As the acid penetrates the skin, an electric fan eliminates vapors that may otherwise linger. After applying an AHA, a burning sensation and reddening (erythema) of the skin usually begin to appear in a few minutes. This pinkish discoloration quickly returns to normal. If a TCA or Jessner's peel is used, the skin will turn white and then pink. After the skin changes color, the acid solution is diluted and rinsed from the face. Deeper peels take as long as an hour. The treatment may be followed by cool compresses applied to the face and a final cleansing. AHA peels occasionally result in slight flaking in a few localized areas for 1 to 2 days but the skin will not actually peel. After a TCA or Jessner's peel, the skin may turn brown, feel dry, flake, and peel for a few days.

The face may be washed as usual but only with gentle cleansers. A special emollient-type lotion is generally given for follow-up use at home. The individual will be told not to wear makeup until the skin returns to normal, usually in about a week. Sunscreens should be worn beginning the second day and direct sunlight must be avoided. The individual may experience sensations of stinging, itching, or burning during the healing period, but must refrain from peeling, pricking, scraping, or scratching the skin at all times. Depending on the type of acid peel used, follow-up treatments may be required at various intervals. The individual may also be required to apply low concentrations of AHA (3-10%) at home to maintain the skin's smoothness.

Prognosis

The results of an acid peel often depend on the type of agent used, the individual's skin type, physician expertise, and the individual's compliance with necessary follow-up measures such as home treatments. Since the peel tends to stimulate natural body processes, results are usually successful in terms of removing unwanted dry skin and improving appearance. Other outcomes may include an increased need to moisturize the skin and more thickened skin.

In order to maintain results from the procedure, the individual needs to continue to regularly apply a low concentration of AHAs to the face.

Specialists

- Dermatologist
- Plastic Surgeon

Work Restrictions / Accommodations

The individual will need to apply sunscreen and avoid direct exposure to the sun for at least a week after the procedure. If additional procedures are needed, time off from work may be required. The individual may need time during work to apply lotions to aid in the skin's recovery immediately after the procedure.

Comorbid Conditions

Individuals with darker skin may encounter problems with abnormal skin pigmentation resulting from the procedure.

Procedure Complications

Burning, stinging, and itching will result from treatment although these effects tend to resolve as healing progresses. Redness caused by dilation of the blood vessels (vasodilation) may linger in some cases. Some types of acid peel solutions may cause crusting or necrosis. Scarring and abnormal changes in skin pigment sometimes occur. Less potent acid peels rarely produce adverse effects.

Factors Influencing Duration

Acid peels are relatively mild procedures. Most individuals should be able to return to work within a day or two as long as exposure to direct sunlight is avoided. Complications may require additional medical treatment and time off from work.

Length of Disability

An individual working outside in direct sunlight may need time off work until healing is complete. If the individual must wear cosmetics or have a pleasing public appearance, time off may also be required until the skin completely heals.

Duration in Days

Job Classification	Minimum	Optimum	Maximum
Any work	1	3	7

References

American Society of Plastic Surgeons. "Plastic Surgery Information Service." Chemical Peel. 2000 27 Sept 2000 <http://www.plasticsurgery.org/surgery/chempeel.htm?ViewTemplate=stndviep%2Ehts&ServerKey=Primary&AdminImagePath=&Theme=&Company=ASPRS>.

Kneedler, Julia A., Sharon S. Sky, and Linda R. Sexton. "Understanding Alpha-Hydroxy Acids." Dermatology Nursing Aug 1998:13. Electric Library. 28 Sept 2000 <http://wwws.elibrary.com/search.cgi?id=>.

Acquired Immune Deficiency Syndrome

Other names / synonyms: AIDS
042, 042.9, 043.9

Definition

Acquired immune deficiency syndrome (AIDS) is a group of diseases or conditions consisting of the late or advanced stages of infection with the human immunodeficiency virus (HIV). Infection by HIV causes a severe weakening or breakdown of the body's immune system (immunosuppression). It infects all cells with the CD4+ molecule on their surface including a type of white cell called T lymphocytes (CD4+ T lymphocytes). CD4+ T lymphocytes normally help fight off infections caused by microorganisms invading the body. HIV-infected CD4+ T lymphocytes, however, will eventually be destroyed as a result of HIV replication within the cell. Consequently, after a period of time (latency period) when the HIV continues to replicate and CD4+ T lymphocyte numbers decrease, the immune system becomes compromised. Infections that are normally harmless become deadly (opportunistic infections), and these, along with various forms of cancer, are characteristic of AIDS. The time between initial HIV infection and the onset of AIDS is quite variable and may last from a few months to 10 or more years.

HIV does not survive outside the body. It is found in greater amounts in the blood, blood products, semen, and breast milk. Smaller amounts of virus are found in female genital secretions. In very rare cases, the virus is transmitted from one individual to another through contact with the skin.

HIV-infected individuals are diagnosed as having AIDS if their CD4+ T lymphocyte count is less than 200 cells per milliliter of blood (the normal range is 800 to 1,000) or if they have at least 1 of 25 qualifying opportunistic infections as defined by the Centers for Disease Control (CDC). A partial list of the HIV-related opportunistic diseases includes Pneumocystis carinii pneumonia (PCP), mycobacterium avium complex (MAC), cytomegalovirus (CMV), toxoplasmosis of the brain, recurrent pneumonia, shingles, HIV-related brain disease (encephalopathy), and a variety of different cancers such as Kaposi's sarcoma (KS), Burkitt's lymphoma, or lymphoma of the brain.

More than 600,000 cases of AIDS were reported to the CDC through 1998. Among adults, 84% of cases occurred in males, but the number of cases in females is rising. The total number of individuals living with AIDS increased in 1997, although the number of deaths decreased, probably because of the new drug therapies that are available. Densely populated metropolitan areas have the highest incidence rates for AIDS in the US; however, the disease is becoming more prevalent in southern rural areas.

Young adults form the largest percentage of individuals affected by HIV infection and AIDS, and the number of young adults contracting this infection during adolescence is increasing at a rapid rate. Only a small percentage of children or adolescents is affected with HIV; however, numbers among this group are also increasing. Hispanics and blacks in the US show a disproportionately high incidence of the disease and account for more than 50% of AIDS cases among all ethnic groups.

Diagnosis

History: Individuals with AIDS have invariably been infected with HIV. The individual may report short-term memory loss, difficulty concentrating, mood changes (usually depression, apathy, or suicidal ideation), altered mental status/dementia, cough and shortness of breath, night sweats, skin rashes or growths, easy bruising, unexpected nosebleeds, persistent fever, difficulty swallowing (dysphagia), vomiting, abdominal pain, headache, diarrhea, weight loss, chest pain, and visual changes including blurred vision or spots that interfere with vision (floaters).

Physical exam: Individuals with AIDS have symptoms of specific opportunistic infections or cancers. Those with full-blown AIDS may have a combination of skin (dermatologic), digestive (gastrointestinal), lung (pulmonary), brain and nerve (neurologic), eye (ophthalmologic), and/or muscle and bone (musculoskeletal) conditions. One type of growth (neoplasm) seen commonly in individuals with AIDS is Kaposi's sarcoma (KS). This appears as reddish-brown raised growths on the skin or in the mouth. Bleeding (hemorrhage) in the retina, yeast infections of the mouth (thrush) and vagina (candida), viral infections in the mouth, chronic herpes, and aggressive tooth or gum disease are also common. Weight loss and decreased physical vigor, appetite, and mental activity (wasting syndrome) may be present.

Tests: AIDS testing focuses initially upon verification of HIV infection using blood or urine tests, or with a home test.

Blood tests: HIV infection is determined by either direct detection of the virus itself or detection of the antibodies the individual produces in response to viral infection. Direct detection of the virus may be done following infection, but may be negative early in infection. The HIV polymerase chain reaction (PCR) or HIV culture tests are commonly used.

For antibody detection tests, however, there is a time delay before the immune system can mount a response against HIV, therefore a 6-month waiting period following infection is usually recommended in order to increase the reliability of the test. Note that HIV-infected individuals with AIDS symptoms are usually infected with the virus much longer than 6 months and HIV antibodies are almost always present in the bloodstream. The most common types of antibody tests for HIV diagnosis include the enzyme-linked immunoabsorbent assay (ELISA, with sensitivity and specificity more than 95% accurate), Western blot, immunofluorescence, radioimmune-precipitation, and hemagglutination.

Oral/Urine tests: The Food and Drug Administration (FDA) has currently approved one oral test. The Oral Fluid Vironostika HIV-1 MicroElisa System and the OraSure HIV-1 WB kit in combination with the OraSure Collection system are highly reliable in identifying HIV-infected individuals. A urine test approved by the FDA is the HIV-1 antibody ELISA. It has not been approved, however, as a stand-alone diagnostic test, and individuals with reactive urine specimens should be tested again using a blood test.

Home tests: The first FDA-approved at-home testing service called Confide was withdrawn from the market because of lack of consumer demand. Subsequently, the FDA approved the Home Access and Home Access Express tests currently available. The individual is provided a specimen collection device where a drop of the individual's blood is blotted onto a card. The specimen card is mailed to a central testing service and the individual is informed anonymously of the results by telephone. Post-test counseling is also provided.

The rate of progression of HIV and AIDS is directly related to the rate of increase in the number of viral particles (viral load) in the bloodstream or tissue of an infected individual. Viral load measurement can therefore serve as both an accurate predictor of HIV-related disease progression and an indicator of the effects of antiviral drug treatment. Viral load can be determined by measuring HIV ribonucleic acid (RNA) in plasma. The three types of assays commonly used to measure HIV RNA are the reverse transcription polymerase chain reaction (RT-PCR), the branched deoxyribonucleic acid (bDNA) test, and the nucleic acid sequence-based amplification (NASBA) test.

Other tests may be performed to monitor the extent of damage done to the immune system by the virus. Most important is a count of the number of CD4+ T-lymphocytes in the bloodstream using flow cytometry analysis. This test is also useful in monitoring the effectiveness of antiretroviral drug therapy, determining the risk for opportunistic diseases and the need for preventative (prophylactic) drug administration, and assessing the prognosis for the individual with AIDS.

Other tests may include a complete blood count (CBC) with a white blood cell differential count, blood urea nitrogen (BUN), creatinine and electrolytes, a blood culture, arterial blood gases (ABG), liver function tests, glucose and lipid profiles, stool culture, lumbar puncture and cerebrospinal fluid (CSF) analysis, a rapid plasma reagin (RPR) test or a Venereal Disease Research Laboratory (VDRL) test for syphilis, a hepatitis B core antibody test, hepatitis C and toxoplasmosis serology, a purified protein derivative (PPD) test for tuberculosis, and a pap smear in women. In some clinical settings, urinalysis, cytomegalovirus (CMV) serology, and a qualitative test for glucose-6-phosphate dehydrogenase (G6PD) may be advisable. A CT or MRI can be used to identify whether pneumonia or cancer is present.

Treatment

Important advances have been made regarding drug treatments that can slow the onset of AIDS following HIV infection. Initiation of drug treatment must be individualized and take into account the disease progression (viral load) and the degree of immunodeficiency as determined by the CD4+ T lymphocyte cell count and symptoms, functional impairment present in the individual. No study has specifically determined the best time to start drug treatment; however, it is believed that initiating highly active antiretroviral therapy (HAART) as early as possible offers the best chance at minimizing viral load and the development of opportunistic infections that characterize AIDS. Combination therapy using two nucleoside reverse transcriptase inhibitors (NRTIs) in conjunction with a protease inhibitor (PI) or a non-nucleoside reverse-transcriptase inhibitor (NNRTI) is recommended as the initial drug treatment in most individuals.

The drug regimen may be modified if the individual cannot tolerate one or more of the drugs or if there is a rising viral load, a declining CD4+ T lymphocyte count, or progression of clinical diseases characteristic of AIDS. Resistance to drug therapy is also a consideration because the high rate of HIV turnover may produce drug-resistant forms of the virus. Preventative (prophylactic) drug treatment for a common opportunistic disease such as pneumocystic carinii pneumonitis (PCP) is usually prescribed. The current drug of choice for PCP is trimethoprim-sulfamethoxazole (TMP-SMX).

Psychosocial issues are important at all stages following viral infection because adjustment/anxiety disorders, depression, and substance abuse are common in HIV-infected individuals. Neuropsychological testing, antidepressant therapy, and/or community support groups are important in the treatment of AIDS.

There has been tremendous effort to develop a vaccine that either prevents infection by HIV or boosts the immune system of an infected individual. Several vaccines have been partially successful in preventing HIV infection in nonhuman primates, however, these results have not been replicated in humans. Clinical trials with experimental vaccines began in 1987 and these experiments are ongoing. A few vaccines have moved into advanced (phase 3) clinical trials, although most have not gone beyond initial (phase 1) testing. Vaccine development has proven extraordinarily difficult because HIV mutates frequently. Consequently, scientists have had a hard time producing one or a combination of vaccines that overcome the mutated viruses that escape immune recognition.

Individuals with AIDS typically develop a variety of opportunistic infections, some rarely seen in humans before the advent of the AIDS epidemic. Many of these infections are caused by bacteria, parasites, viruses, and/or fungal organisms and are not curable, therefore treatment is aimed at controlling critical episodes of the diseases.

Single-celled (protozoan) parasites cause significant morbidity and mortality in individuals with AIDS. Some of these may respond to antimicrobial drugs but most do not have an effective treatment. Antiretroviral therapy that includes a protease inhibitor may result in improvement because of the individual's improved immunity. Antidiarrheal agents can be helpful in reducing stool volumes and immunomodulator (i.e., interleukin-2) in improving associated symptoms. To minimize parasitic infections, individuals with AIDS should avoid fecal contact; practice meticulous hand washing after handling pets, gardening, or before eating; and avoid ingesting river, lake, or swimming pool water, nonpasteurized juices or milks (cow, goat).

PCP is a single-celled organism previously considered a parasite but is now recognized as a fungus. PCP is the most common AIDS-defining illness in the US with lung inflammation (pneumonia) as the primary symptom. Antimicrobial treatment for PCP is typically administered prophylactically using TMP-SMZ. Unfortunately, there may be adverse reactions to TMP-SMZ such as rash, nausea, headache, depression, and kidney (renal) disease. Other fungal organisms may be treated with antifungal agents or antibiotics.

Some of the more common viruses seen in individuals with AIDS include cytomegalovirus (CMV), herpes simplex virus types 1 and 2 (HSV-1 and HSV-2), varicella-zoster virus (VZV), and Epstein-Barr virus (EBV). Antiviral drugs are typically prescribed for viral infections along with pain-reducing (analgesic) agents. Newer treatments may include vaccines against specific viruses or synthetic strands of deoxyribonucleic acid (DNA) that may prevent viral replication (antisense DNA).

Effective treatment for bacterial infection in individuals with AIDS is often difficult and may require a multidrug approach. Antibiotics are typically prescribed and vaccines are available to treat some strains of bacteria.

Various types of cancer (malignancies) are frequently seen in individuals with AIDS. These may include KS and various malignant lymphomas in the bone marrow, digestive tract, lungs, and central nervous system. Treatment for KS may include local injections of anticancer (antineoplastic) agents, localized radiation therapy, or surgical removal of skin lesions. Chemotherapy may also be used if multiple KS sites are found. Newer approaches include drugs that inhibit growth of blood vessels within the KS (angiogenesis inhibitors). Lymphomas are commonly treated with chemotherapy and/or radiation along with drugs that may inhibit cancerous growth.

Pain is a frequent symptom in individuals with AIDS and is often underestimated and undertreated. Concern about the addictive potential of medication and inadequate knowledge as to the best mechanisms of treatment have led to persistent pain for people with AIDS. Drug therapy may include opioids and anti-inflammatory agents on a routine basis to alleviate pain. Antidepressants may also be prescribed to enhance the individual's ability to cope with the disease.

Prognosis

The predicted longer-term outcome of AIDS is very poor. There is no recovery and the disease is inevitably fatal due to recurrent and progressive opportunistic infections. Nevertheless, the appearance of these infections and progression to full-blown AIDS may be delayed years or even decades with HAART drug therapy. Approximately two-thirds of HIV-positive individuals who start drug therapy have an undetectable viral load after 3 years of treatment. Other studies suggest that after 6 months of drug treatment, HIV replication is totally suppressed and 99.9% of the virus eliminated. Nevertheless, the virus is present, the individual is still infectious, and long-term drug therapy continues to be necessary.

Differential Diagnosis

Conditions that present with symptoms similar to the opportunistic infections characteristic of AIDS include infectious mononucleosis, EBV, toxoplasmosis, rubella, syphilis, viral hepatitis, disseminated gonococcal infection, HSV, typhus, Crohn's disease, candidiasis, cholecystitis, biliary colic, esophagitis, gastroenteritis, meningitis, ITP, pancreatitis, immunocompromised pneumonia, pneumothorax, septic shock, tuberculosis, or a number of other viral or spirochete infections.

Specialists

- Gastroenterologist
- Immunologist
- Infectious Disease Physician
- Internist
- Neurologist
- Oncologist
- Ophthalmologist
- Psychiatrist
- Pulmonologist

Rehabilitation

Individuals with AIDS suffer from a variety of opportunistic infections and diseases due to their compromised immune system. Individuals may require physical, occupational, speech, respiratory, and psychological therapy as well as consultation with a nutritionist depending on the AIDS-related illness. Psychological counseling may be necessary for most individuals.

Nutritional counseling may be necessary for a variety of reasons. Nutritionists assist individuals in making healthy food choices to maintain physical health thereby curtailing the amount of opportunistic infections an individual may contract. Consultation with a nutritionist can ensure that the necessary intake of vitamins and minerals is maintained when an individual presents with gastrointestinal distress or infections of the oral mucosa.

Individuals presenting with the muscle wasting inherent in AIDS should see a physical therapist. Individuals should adopt an exercise regimen that includes strengthening exercises such as walking and weight training that stabilize muscle strength. This exercise program reflects the individual's need and takes other AIDS-related illnesses into account. Physical therapists provide individuals with basic strengthening exercises for the arms and legs and instruct individuals in aerobic exercise such as treadmill walking. Individuals learn to monitor their pulse as well as their perceived exertion to ensure that exercise is performed within safe parameters.

Occupational therapy may be needed to address activities of daily living such as dressing and bathing techniques.

Respiratory therapy focuses on increasing lung capacity and decreasing the risk for the buildup of lung secretions. Respiratory therapists teach individuals pursed lip breathing that increases the airflow to the lungs. Individuals may also use a device that measures and displays the amount of air inspired (incentive spirometer) to help motivate them to take deeper breaths. Individuals learn to produce an effective cough through techniques such as huffing where air is breathed out forcefully while the mouth is open. Individuals also learn positions to relieve shortness of breath such as leaning forward while sitting with the arms resting on the thighs. Respiratory therapists may also perform chest percussion and utilize positioning techniques to promote the drainage of fluid/phlegm from the lungs.

Individuals with neurological impairments such as encephalopathy require physical, occupational, speech, and psychological therapy. Because individuals' neurological deficits may vary, the exact nature of physical and occupational therapy varies. Physical therapy addresses any muscle weakness, balance deficits, and ambulatory difficulties. Individuals learn to safely get in and out of bed, rise up from a chair, and enter and exit the bathtub. Individuals learn to walk with a cane or walker and how to propel a wheelchair. Speech therapists address difficulties with language construction. Individuals perform activities such as using contextual clues to complete sentences or identify pictures with the appropriate word.

Work Restrictions / Accommodations

In the workplace, HIV infection associated with AIDS is an important component of a comprehensive infectious disease policy. Universal precautions should be incorporated into all procedures regardless of the HIV status of employees. Ongoing education, engineering controls, and the use of safety devices can modify risk of exposure to blood-borne HIV. Universal precautions include washing hands, protection of intact skin, care and appropriate covering of damaged skin, proper handling and disposal of sharp objects, and careful handling of all blood and body fluids. Disposable latex or nitrile gloves should be worn during all medical procedures, emergency response, and industrial accidents. A plan for rapid evaluation and management should be in place in case HIV exposure or other exposure to high risk body fluids occurs.

AIDS is a progressive disease and work conditions may need to be adjusted for the individual as the condition worsens. Transfer to a job requiring less physical activity will eventually be a consideration. Extended sick leave for recovery and therapy for opportunistic infections is required. The individual with AIDS will ultimately become totally disabled and contingencies should be considered in advance.

Comorbid Conditions

Coexisting conditions that may impact recovery and lengthen disability include opportunistic diseases such as PCP, mycobacterium avium complex, cytomegalovirus, toxoplasmosis, hairy leukoplakia, shingles, progressive multifocal leukoencephalopathy, tuberculosis, cryptosporidium, and a variety of different cancers such as KS, non-Hodgkin lymphoma, CNS lymphoma, and cancers of the cervix and rectum. Other factors that may influence the length of disability include coexisting diseases that increase symptoms associated with various opportunistic infections. These include infectious diseases such as hepatitis B and tuberculosis as well as chronic infections or parasitic diseases such as malaria. Immunosuppressant drugs, pregnancy, malnutrition, genetic susceptibility, infection with other sexually transmitted diseases, and stress may also have effects. Chemical abuse can interfere with treatment and increase risk of further infections. Increased age appears to be a major determinant in the rapid progression of the disease.

Complications

Individuals may experience adverse side effects as a result of the drug therapy. These include nausea, severe headache, insomnia, anemia, depression, and renal disease.

Typical complications of AIDS include fatigue, dizziness, anorexia and weight loss, nausea and vomiting, diarrhea, cough, dysphagia, difficulty in breathing (dyspnea), pain, fever, itching (pruritus), sleep disturbances and night sweats, and psychological distress. Other complications may include skin diseases (dermatophytosis, psoriasis), inflammation of hair follicles (folliculitis), arthritis (Reiter's syndrome), decreased hemoglobin in the blood (anemia), bleeding into the skin or other organs (idiopathic thrombocytopenic purpura, or ITP), decreased white blood cell count (leukopenia), kidney disorders (nephropathy), mental disorders (dementia), a variety of cancerous tumors (Kaposi's sarcoma, Hodgkin's lymphoma, non-Hodgkin's lymphoma, and squamous cell carcinoma), mouth sores and lesions (oral hairy leukoplakia), and a variety of tooth and gum (periodontal) diseases (linear gingival erythema, necrotizing ulcerative gingivitis).

The type, number, and severity of these complications vary with the status of immune system functioning and progression of the AIDS disease. Most complications arise as a product of opportunistic infections when the immune system is in a compromised state.

Many of the diseases associated with HIV-infected individuals with full-blown AIDS arise from fungal infections (PCP, aspergillosis, candidiasis, cryptococcosis, histoplasmosis, coccidioidomycosis, penicilliosis), parasitic infections (cryptosporidiosis, isosporiasis, toxoplasmosis, microsporidiosis, Strongyloides stercoralis, Cyclospora cayetanensis), viral diseases (CMV, HSV-1, and HSV-2), VZV, EBV, poxvirus, parvovirus, human papillomavirus or HPV, hepatitis virus), and bacterial infections (mycobacteria, nocardiosis, Bartonella, Rhodococcus, haemophilus influenzae, pseudomonas aeruginosa, staphylococcus aureus, salmonella).

Factors Influencing Duration

Factors that may influence the length of disability include other diseases that increase symptoms associated with various opportunistic infections. These include infectious diseases such as hepatitis B and tuberculosis as well as chronic infections or parasitic diseases such as malaria. Immunosuppressant drugs, pregnancy, malnutrition, genetic susceptibility, infection with other sexually transmitted diseases, and stress may also have effects. Increased age appears to be a major determinant in the rapid progression of the disease.

Length of Disability

The duration of disability depends on the requirements of the job and the degree of disability experienced by the individual with AIDS. Progression of the disease is more rapid when there are higher viral loads and lower CD4+ T lymphocyte cell counts. Individuals with full-blown AIDS may be permanently disabled.

Failure to Recover

If an individual fails to recover within the maximum duration expectancy period, the reader may wish to reference the following questions to assist in better understanding the specifics of an individual's medical case.

Regarding diagnosis:

- Does individual have short-term memory loss, difficulty concentrating, mood changes (usually depression, apathy, or suicidal ideation), altered mental status/dementia, cough and shortness of breath, night sweats, skin rashes or growths, easy bruising, unexpected nosebleeds, persistent fever, difficulty swallowing (dysphagia), vomiting, abdominal pain, headache, diarrhea, weight loss, chest pain, and visual changes including blurred vision or spots that interfere with vision (floaters)?
- Are specific opportunistic infections or cancers present? Does individual have Kaposi's sarcoma (KS)?
- Were blood and urine tests performed? Was individual diagnosed as being HIV-positive or has illness progressed to the criteria of AIDS?

Regarding treatment:

- Is individual being treated with combination therapy?
- Is individual compliant with drug therapy? If not, what can be done to increase compliance?
- Is there evidence of antibiotic-resistant organisms?
- Are tests being done to monitor progression of the disease and evaluate the effectiveness of antiviral therapy?
- Is current treatment effective in preventing opportunistic infections? Are infections recurrent?
- Does treatment of these infections interfere with the action of antiviral drugs individual is using? If so, is there an alternative antiviral therapy available?
- Would another treatment modality result in longer lasting protection?
- Are malignancies present? Are they life threatening? Can they be treated surgically, chemically, or with radiation therapy?
- Has AIDS progressed to the point where palliative treatment of symptoms and individual's comfort are the primary considerations?
- What pain medications are in use? Are they sufficient? Should narcotic painkillers be implemented?
- Has individual been enrolled in a comprehensive therapy program based on his/her specific needs?
- Is HIV-wasting disease present? Is individual involved in muscle-strengthening exercises or weight training to maintain muscle strength?
- Can individual still perform activities required for own daily care?
- Is individual involved in neuropsychological testing, antidepressant therapy, and/or community support groups?
- Is gastrointestinal distress present?
- Is diarrhea and vomiting depleting individual of fluids and nutrients? Has fluid intake been increased?
- Is individual avoiding foods that create loose stools?
- Are nutritional supplements being incorporated into the diet?

Regarding prognosis:

- Does individual have coexisting conditions that may impact recovery?
- How advanced is the disease?
- Was treatment started before symptoms appeared?
- Is individual still capable of self-care and remaining in family home?
- Is hospice in place? Is hospitalization or 24-hour nursing care required?

References

Boss, Barbara J. "Alterations of Neurological Function." Pathophysiology. McCance, Kathryn L., and Sue E. Heuther, eds. St. Louis: Mosby, 1994. 527-586.

Kassler, W.J., P. Blanc, and R. Greenblatt. "The Use of Medicinal Herbs by Human Immunodeficiency Virus-infected Patients." Archives of Internal Medicine 151 11 1991: 2281-2288.

Actinomycosis

Other names / synonyms: Abdominal Actinomycosis, Actinomycotic Infection, Cervicofacial Actinomycosis, Lumpy Jaw, Thoracic Actinomycosis, Wooden Tongue

039, 039.0, 039.1, 039.2, 039.3, 039.4, 039.8, 039.9

Definition

Actinomycosis is an infection caused by actinomyces bacteria. Normally harmless inhabitants of the gums, teeth, and tonsils, these bacteria may help prevent tooth decay. They can become harmful, however, if they are moved into other body tissues through trauma, general surgery, dental surgery, or infection. Once inside the tissues, actinomyces can cause infection resulting in accumulations of white blood cells and breakdown products from dying tissues (pus). These localized collections of pus called abscesses can develop channels that allow the pus to drain through the skin or extend to other body spaces and internal organs.

The most common form of actinomycosis (about 60% of cases) occurs in the head and neck (cervicofacial actinomycosis). A less common form of actinomycosis, thoracic or pulmonary actinomycosis, starts in the lungs or is spread to the lungs from untreated actinomycosis in the head or neck. Abdominal actinomycosis is spread throughout the abdomen from a trauma such as placement of an intrauterine contraceptive device (IUD) or an injury to the anus. The infection can also spread through the bloodstream to other organs including the skin, liver, kidneys, ureters, ovaries, uterus, spinal vertebrae, and brain (generalized actinomycosis).

Affecting men slightly more often than women, actinomycosis usually occurs in the fourth through sixth decades of life. It is fairly rare, with approximately one new case seen each year at major institutions.

Diagnosis

History: The most common form of actinomycosis involves the head and neck (cervicofacial actinomycosis). History may include recent oral surgery or trauma, poor general health, poor oral hygiene, or alcoholism. Initial symptoms of actinomycosis may include pain at the site of infection and pus-filled lumps in the mouth, neck, or below the jaw. Pus draining to the skin's surface may contain yellow sulfur granules. Symptoms of thoracic actinomycosis also include cough with phlegm (sputum), shortness of breath, and chest pain. Abdominal actinomycosis is often associated with fever, abdominal pain, vomiting, diarrhea or constipation, and severe weight loss. Individual may use an IUD. Generalized actinomycosis infection symptoms may also include weight loss, weakness, fever, night sweats, and an overall feeling of illness (malaise).

Physical exam: With cervicofacial actinomycosis, the face or upper neck may reveal swelling, lumps, and oozing sores. The lump is hard, red to reddish-purple, and not particularly tender when touched. It is often located high in the neck near the angle of the jaw. The symptoms of thoracic actinomycosis include fever, chest pain, and a coughing up of phlegm and may not appear until the lungs are severely infected. In abdominal actinomycosis, hard masses in the abdomen can often be felt (palpated). Pus may drain through channels connecting the masses to the skin.

Tests: Using an ultrasound to locate the abscess, pus-filled fluid is drained (aspiration). This fluid is then grown (cultured) in the laboratory to determine if the infection was caused by actinomyces. Because therapy differs for this and similar infections, the culture for actinomycosis must be for microorganisms that can live without oxygen (anaerobic culture). Unfortunately, however, less than half of cultures grow the bacteria, so the abscess must sometimes be surgically removed (excised) and examined with a microscope to reveal the characteristic appearance of the bacteria and associated structures called sulfur granules. Although a CT of the neck usually shows the lump that may light up (enhance) around the rim when contrast dye is given, this appearance can also be seen in other conditions including tumors and cysts.

Treatment

When accessible, pus-filled lumps may be drained (debridement) or surgically removed (excision). Antibiotic therapy begins with injecting antibiotics directly into a vein for the first 1 to 2 months. After that, antibiotic tablets are taken by mouth for an additional several months to a year. This two-stage therapy approach is effective because injected antibiotics reach the invading bacteria more rapidly and at higher amounts. Followup with oral antibiotics protects against reoccurrence. In order to be effective, however, treatment must be continued for the entire recommended time period even after symptoms have completely disappeared. Duration of antibiotic treatment may extend 6 to 12 months in severe cases. When caught in the early stages, if surgery is not considered necessary, the individual may be treated entirely with antibiotics.

Respiratory therapy may be prescribed for individuals with pulmonary actinomycosis depending on the severity of the respiratory symptoms.

Prognosis

Although progress is slow and involves months of antibiotic therapy and possible surgery, most individuals do recover. Cervicofacial is the most easily treated. Prognosis is less encouraging for those with thoracic and abdominal actinomycosis or when the infection has spread (generalized) throughout the body. When the infection attacks the brain and spinal cord, more than 50% suffer neurologic damage and another 25% die.

If the underlying cause of infection is not removed, the individual is at risk for the disease to return in a more severe form. Untreated infection may cause extensive tissue injury or death.

Differential Diagnosis

Conditions that cause similar abscesses include cancer, tuberculosis, fungal, and other bacterial infections. Nocardia infections may have a similar history and symptoms as actinomycosis. Although tetanus can result in spasm of jaw muscles, it also involves other muscle groups and other neurologic signs. Pulmonary actinomycosis shares symptoms of tuberculosis and lung cancer including spitting up blood and masses in the lungs detected by radiology tests. Abdominal actinomycosis can be confused with Crohn's disease, amebiasis, appendicitis, adrenal gland cancer, colon cancer, and cancer of the pelvis or ovary that has extended into the urinary bladder, rectum, or uterus.

Specialists

- Dental Surgeon
- Dermatologist
- General Surgeon
- Gynecologist
- Infectious Disease Physician
- Internist
- Neurosurgeon
- Orthopedic Surgeon
- Pulmonologist

Work Restrictions / Accommodations

Work restrictions and accommodations depend on the location and extent of surgery. If breathing is difficult, walking may need to be limited or avoided for the individual with pulmonary actinomycosis.

Comorbid Conditions

Coexisting conditions that may impact recovery include diseases that affect the overall health of the individual such as alcoholism, diabetes, immune diseases or immunocompromised conditions, and cancer.

Complications

Actinomyces entering the bloodstream can spread widely throughout the body causing infection in the blood (sepsis), in the coverings of the brain and spinal cord (bacterial meningitis), or within the brain (brain abscess). Although rare, these complications are often rapidly fatal. Actinomyces involving the face or neck may spread to the gums (periodontal disease), jaw bone (osteomyelitis), or middle ear (otitis media). Pulmonary actinomycosis can spread down the bronchial tubes causing pneumonia.

Factors Influencing Duration

Length of disability may be influenced by severity of the infection, location of infection, progression of disease before diagnosis, delay of treatment, response to antibiotic treatment, need for extensive surgical intervention, and postoperative complications.

Length of Disability

Job Classification	Minimum	Optimum	Maximum
Sedentary work	0	2	14
Light work	0	2	14
Medium work	0	2	21
Heavy work	0	2	28
Very Heavy work	0	2	35

Duration in Days

Failure to Recover

If an individual fails to recover within the maximum duration expectancy period, the reader may wish to reference the following questions to assist in better understanding the specifics of an individual's medical case.

Regarding diagnosis:

- Does individual have history of recent oral surgery or trauma, poor general health, poor oral hygiene, or alcoholism?
- Are weight loss, weakness, fever, night sweats, and an overall feeling of illness (malaise) present?
- Does individual have pain at the site of infection and pus-filled lumps in the mouth, neck, or below the jaw? Does pus contain yellow sulfur granules?
- Is there cough with phlegm (sputum), shortness of breath, and chest pain?
- Does individual have fever, abdominal pain, vomiting, diarrhea or constipation, and severe weight loss?
- What type of culture was performed?
- How far has the infection spread?
- Were other conditions that cause similar abscesses ruled out?
- Was diagnosis of actinomycosis confirmed? What part of the body is it located?

Regarding treatment:

- Is infection responding to the antibiotics being given? If not, were bacteria grown (cultured) from the removed material tested to determine what antibiotics would be the most effective (culture and sensitivity)?
- Did individual receive antibiotics by injection prior to oral antibiotic therapy?
- Is individual capable of and committed to following treatment plan as prescribed?
- Did individual continue antibiotic therapy for entire prescribed time period?
- If not responding to antibiotic therapy, should abscess be removed surgically?

Regarding prognosis:

- Where was the infection located and treated?
- Does individual have a coexisting condition such as alcoholism, diabetes, immune diseases or immunocompromised conditions, and cancer that may impact recovery?

References

Bartkowski, S.B., et al. "Actinomycotic Osteomyelitis of the Mandible: Review of 15 Cases." Journal of Craniomaxillofacial Surgery 26 1 (1998): 63-67.

Belmont, M.J., P.M. Behar, and M.K. Wax. "Atypical Presentations of Actinomycosis." Head and Neck 21 3 1999: 264-268.

Chan, P.M., et al. "Splenic Actinomycosis." Journal of the Royal College of Surgeons of Edinburgh 44 5 (1999): 344-345.

Dweik, R.A., et al. "Actinomycosis and Plasma Cell Granuloma, Coincidence or Coexistence: Patient Report and Review of the Literature." Clinical Pediatrics (Philadelphia) 36 4 (1997): 229-233.

Hamid, D., et al. "Treatment Strategy for Pelvic Actinomycosis: Case Report and Review of the Literature." European Journal of Obstetrics and Gynecology and Reproductive Biology 89 2 (2000): 197-200.

Ossorio, M.A., et al. "Thoracic Actinomycosis and Human Immunodeficiency Virus Infection." Southern Medical Journal 90 11 (1997): 1136-1138.

Puzzilli, F., et al. "Intracranial Actinomycosis in Juvenile Patients. Case Report and Review of the Literature." Childs Nervous System 14 9 (1998): 463-466.

Quintero-Del-Rio, A.I., M. Trujillo, and C.W. Fink. "Actinomycotic Splenic Abscesses Presenting with Arthritis." Clinical and Experimental Rheumatology 15 4 (1997): 445-448.

Rice, D.H. "Chronic Inflammatory Disorders of the Salivary Glands." Otolaryngologic Clinics of North America 32 5 (1999): 813-818.

Sugano, S., et al. "Hepatic Actinomycosis: Case Report and Review of the Literature in Japan." Journal of Gastroenterology 32 5 (1997): 672-676.

Vazquez, A.M., et al. "Actinomycosis of the Tongue Associated with Human Immunodeficiency Virus Infection: Case Report." Journal of Oral and Maxillofacial Surgery 55 8 (1997): 879-881.

Warren, N.G. "Actinomycosis, Nocardiosis, and Actinomycetoma." Dermatologic Clinics 14 1 (1996): 85-95.

Yeung, M.K. "Molecular and Genetic Analyses of Actinomyces spp." Critical Reviews in Oral Biology and Medicine 10 2 (1999): 120-138.

Zitsch, R.P. III, and M. Bothwell. "Actinomycosis: A Potential Complication of Head and Neck Surgery." American Journal of Otolaryngology 20 4 (1999): 260-262.

Addictions, Mixed

Other names / synonyms: Polysubstance Abuse, Polysubstance Addiction

304.7, 304.8, 304.9

Definition

Mixed addictions are defined as the use of multiple substances in an addictive fashion. It has become increasingly rare for individuals to abuse a single substance in isolation. Because alcohol is legal and widely available, it was once common to find "pure" alcoholics who would never consider abusing other drugs, however, the use of multiple substances is currently the norm among addicts.

Polysubstance abuse is defined as repeated use of at least three groups of substances excluding caffeine and nicotine, with none of the three groups used predominantly over the others. There are four general patterns of mixed addictions: the indiscriminate use of any mood-altering substance either alone or in combination; the use of substances with opposing physiological properties such as alcohol and cocaine; the use of drugs with physiologically similar profiles such as tranquilizers and alcohol; and the substitution of one substance perceived as safer or less of a problem for another such as marijuana for alcohol.

Some mental health professionals consider compulsive gambling, compulsive sexual behaviors, workaholism, and eating disorders to be part of mixed addiction disorder and that adequate treatment should address all compulsive behaviors. An individual with polysubstance addiction continues to abuse multiple substances despite legal or work-related problems caused by substance abuse. For example, such an individual may engage in binge drinking on weekends, obtain codeine prescriptions in order to use more than the originally prescribed dose, snort cocaine several times a month, and smoke marijuana each time cocaine is used.

Diagnosis

History: Diagnosis is based on criteria listed in the DSM-IV-TR (Diagnostic and Statistical Manual of Mental Disorders, 4th Edition, Text Revision, published by the American Psychiatric Association). The individual gives a history of repeated use of multiple substances over the same 12-month period that caused a decline in interpersonal, occupational, and social functioning.

Diagnosis depends on the individual demonstrating at least three or more of the following criteria at any time in the same 12-month period: a need for markedly increased amounts of one or more substances to achieve the desired effect; diminished effects with continued use of the same amounts of a substance; symptoms of withdrawal including tremors, increased blood pressure, increased heart rate, cravings, sweating, diarrhea, muscle cramps, or fever when use of alcohol, opioids, sedatives, or hypnotics is interrupted; persistent unsuccessful attempts to quit or control substance use; a great deal of time spent in activities related to the use of or recovery from the use of various substances; social, occupational, recreational, or relational activities given up for the sake of substance use; and continued substance use despite knowledge of recurrent physical or psychological problems related to their use.

Physical exam: If the individual uses alcohol, physical evidence may include signs of withdrawal such as tremors, sweating, increased blood pressure, or increased heart rate. Examination by touch of the abdomen may reveal an enlarged liver (hepatomegaly) or a small hard liver and reddish discoloration of the palms (palmar erythema). Mental status exam may reveal confusion or disorientation. Neurological examination may reveal decreased sensation in the toes and fingers consistent with peripheral neuropathy, or problems with gait and coordination suggesting cerebellar dysfunction. If the individual is in withdrawal from opioids such as heroin, there may be muscle cramps, nausea and vomiting, diarrhea, increased blood pressure, and needle insertion marks on the arms or other body areas. Significant weight loss may accompany use of amphetamines, cocaine, or heroin.

Tests: Alcohol abuse leads to elevated blood levels of liver enzymes including glutamyl transferase, high blood lipids, and/or an anemia showing large red blood cells (macrocytic anemia). Urine drug screen may show the presence of cocaine, marijuana, opioids, codeine, or other substances if the test is performed after the individual recently used.

Treatment

Abstinence is the treatment goal. If the mixed addiction includes alcohol use, the individual may benefit from medications in the acute phase of alcohol withdrawal including benzodiazepines to decrease tremors and reduce or prevent increased blood pressure and heart rate. Other medications may be used for symptomatic treatment of diarrhea or muscle aches. Folic acid, thiamin, and vitamin B_{12} help counteract vitamin deficiencies.

Some individuals may be admitted to a hospital or a specialized alcohol detoxification unit for the first few days of treatment while others may be treated on an outpatient basis. Alcohol, sedative, hypnotic, anxiolytic, and, sometimes, opioid abuse may require hospitalization to facilitate safe withdrawal.

Other factors that may require inpatient substance abuse treatment are severe anxiety and/or depression or psychotic symptoms lasting beyond 1 to 3 days after abstinence or repeated outpatient failures. Hospitalization may be necessary if the individual is having severe withdrawal symptoms during detoxification or is violent toward self or others. A narcotic antagonist such as naltrexone diminishes the effects of alcohol. The drug Antabuse causes an individual to be intolerant of alcohol and can be used to help some individuals remain abstinent.

One approach to heroin treatment is called Ultra Rapid Opioid Detox (UROD) and involves the use of opiate antagonists and general anesthesia, allowing individuals to be safely detoxified within a few hours. This technique greatly shortens the time of detoxification, avoids the pain and other discomforts of withdrawal, allows earlier entry into the rehabilitation phase of a recovery program, minimizes time lost from work and family, and reduces the relatively high percentage of individuals who leave conventional detoxification programs prematurely. It is a high-risk procedure, however, that requires careful medical monitoring. Even though the success rate of this 1 to 2 day detoxification process is high, the actual measure of success is whether the individual remains abstinent over a period of time, usually after involvement with traditional outpatient addiction treatment programs.

Addiction recovery occurs in four phases. The acute phase focuses on alleviating symptoms of physiological withdrawal and typically lasts 3 to 5 days. The next phase consists of a one-month period of abstinence during which the individual focuses on changing behaviors. The early remission phase can last up to 12 months and the sustained remission phase lasts as long as the individual refrains from alcohol or substance use and no longer meets the criteria for substance dependence. Treatment for the one-month abstinence and early remission phases may include education on physical, emotional, and mental aspects of addiction and recovery, identification of stressors and stress management skills, training to improve coping skills, assertiveness training, and relaxation training.

Ongoing structured self-help programs such as Alcoholics Anonymous, Narcotics Anonymous, and Rational Recovery are recommended as an adjunct to treatment services. Regular but random drug screens may be part of the treatment process. It should also be understood that relapse may occur and even be part of the recovery process.

Prognosis

Some individuals respond to treatment and stay in remission from substance dependence for many years. However, some experience periods of relapse where they begin substance use after a period of remission and again meet the criteria for substance dependence. Other individuals can never abstain from substance use and do not experience any periods of remission.

Motivation to change is an important predictor of outcome. Chronic illness because of liver or gastrointestinal complications, neurological disability related to alcohol abuse, or death from overdose, suicide, or homicide may all result from mixed addictions.

Differential Diagnosis

In some instances, the substance-dependent individual may have a legitimate medical need that led to substance abuse. An example is the association between chronic pain disorder and narcotic dependence. Alcohol abuse may occasionally be confused with high blood sugar levels in diabetics (diabetic ketoacidosis) where the individual is frequently confused and disoriented and may have a fruity/acetonic breath odor. Other conditions with similar symptoms are low blood sugar (hypoglycemia), various dementias, liver failure, and other substance abuse.

Specialists

- Advanced Practice Registered Nurse
- Cardiologist
- Endocrinologist
- Gastroenterologist
- Neurologist
- Occupational Therapist
- Physical Therapist
- Psychiatrist
- Psychologist

Work Restrictions / Accommodations

Many employers have systems in place for individuals recovering from alcohol or substance dependence disorders that allow them to return to work under special contracts or conditions. These conditions usually include routine or random testing of blood and urine levels for identified substances and work performance and substance abuse treatment guidelines for the recovering individual.

Temporary work accommodations may include reducing or eliminating activities where the safety of self or others is contingent upon a constant and/or high level of alertness, such as driving motor vehicles, operating complex machinery, or handling dangerous chemicals; introducing the individual to new or stressful situations gradually under individually appropriate supervision; allowing some flexibility in scheduling to attend therapy appointments (which normally should occur during employee's personal time); promoting planned, proactive management of identified problem areas; and offering timely feedback on job performance issues. It will be helpful if accommodations are documented in a written plan designed to promote timely and safe transition back to full work productivity.

If the individual has chronic side effects of prolonged alcohol or substance use such as cardiac, liver, or nervous system damage, restriction to sedentary type activities may be necessary. Opportunities to obtain substances of abuse should be minimized, i.e., work in establishments serving liquor or in pharmacies where drugs are available.

Complementary and Alternative Therapies

Content is intended for awareness only. Treatments may or may not be effective. Scientific evidence may be lacking and some substances have potentially toxic effects. Dr. Presley Reed and the editors do not endorse the use of these therapies in the absence of consultation with a licensed medical professional.

St. John's wort - May decrease symptoms associated with mild to moderate depression.

Valerian - Said to act as an antianxiety.

Vitamin E - Said to act as an antioxidant.

Acupuncture - Said to relieve tension.

Acupressure - May help calm and balance emotion.

Biofeedback - May help reduce rapid heart rate, and rapid breathing associated with nervousness and raise awareness and control of physical processes in the body.

Visualization and Psychodrama - Said to provide insight into relationships and the addiction process.

Comorbid Conditions

Comorbid conditions that may impact recovery and lengthen disability include individuals with psychiatric illness as well as chemical dependency (dual diagnosis). These psychiatric illnesses include depression, bipolar affective disorder, schizophrenia and post-traumatic stress disorder. Other physical conditions are related to toxic effects of alcohol or the chemical substance on the brain and liver. For example, a liver damaged by alcohol is less capable of ridding the body of toxic substances. Medical conditions complicated by substance abuse include pregnancy, diabetes, hypertension, liver disease, infection with hepatitis B or C, or HIV infection.

Complications

Other psychiatric illnesses may complicate treatment of both the chemical dependency and the other illness (dual diagnosis). About half of those with bipolar mood (affective) disorder or schizophrenia may have drug or alcohol problems. Those with post-traumatic stress disorder may have substance abuse rates as high as 80%.

Drug abuse may cause psychiatric symptoms such as suspiciousness (paranoid psychoses) frequently seen with chronic amphetamine or cocaine abuse. Depression is commonly seen in alcohol, marijuana, or sedative dependency. Sudden withdrawal of alcohol in a habitual user can lead to tremors, anxiety, agitation, hallucinations, grand mal seizures, or death. Excessive prolonged use of alcohol can damage the stomach lining (gastritis), esophagus (esophageal varices), liver (liver failure, cirrhosis), pancreas (pancreatitis), and heart (cardiomyopathy), and increases risk of liver, gastrointestinal, and other cancers. Individuals who use intravenous drugs such as heroin are at increased risk for hepatitis and HIV.

Factors Influencing Duration

Length of disability is influenced by the duration and severity of the substance dependence, presence or absence of organ damage, any underlying mental illness, motivation to change, social support system, appropriateness of treatment choice, compliance with treatment, and adequacy of ongoing care.

Length of Disability

Maximum duration includes hospitalization. Duration varies from complete remission, to remission and then relapse, or no abstention or remission.

Uncomplicated drug abuse.

Duration in Days

Job Classification	Minimum	Optimum	Maximum
Any work	7	28	42

Failure to Recover

If an individual fails to recover within the maximum duration expectancy period, the reader may wish to reference the following questions to assist in better understanding the specifics of an individual's medical case.

Regarding diagnosis:

- Does individual display any one of the four general patterns for mixed addictions?
- Was a comprehensive assessment of this type completed on this individual? If not, what areas were omitted?
- Have all underlying medical and psychiatric disorders been identified?

Regarding treatment:

- What does individual's current treatment plan include?
- Would addition of other modalities be beneficial?
- What phase of recovery is individual currently experiencing? Have setbacks occurred?
- Was hospitalization required?

Regarding prognosis:

- Is individual currently involved in a support group?
- Does individual participate in a formal support group? What other support systems does individual have in place? Family? Friends? Social?
- Is individual receiving the needed tools, skills, and encouragement to move ahead with his/her life?

References

Duke, James A. The Green Pharmacy. Emmaus, PA: Rodale Press, Inc, 1997.

Frances, Allen. Diagnostic and Statistical Manual of Mental Disorders: 4th ed, text revision. Washington, DC: American Psychiatric Association, 2000.

Georgi, J.M. "The Spiritual Platform: Spirituality and Psychotherapy in Addiction Medicine." North Carolina Medical Journal 59 3 (1998): 168-171.

Healing with Vitamins. Feinstein, Alice, ed. Emmaus, PA: Rodale Press, Inc, 1996.

New Choices in Natural Healing. Gottlieb, Bill, ed. Emmaus, PA: Rodale Press, Inc, 1995.

Schwartz, M., et al. "The Value of Acupuncture Detoxification Programs in a Substance Abuse Treatment System." Journal of Substance Abuse Treatment 17 4 (1999): 305-312.

Addison's Disease

Other names / synonyms: Adrenal Insufficiency, Adrenocortical Insufficiency, Corticoadrenal Insufficiency, Primary Adrenal Gland Failure, Primary Adrenocortical Insufficiency, Waterhouse-Friderichsen Syndrome

255.4, 279.4

Definition

Addison's disease (adrenal insufficiency) occurs when the outer layer of the adrenal gland (cortex) is damaged causing it to produce insufficient amounts of certain corticosteroid hormones that are essential for life. The three types of corticosteroids are androgens and estrogens (affect sexual development and reproduction), glucocorticoid hormones such as cortisol (maintain glucose regulation, suppress immune responses, and provide stress responses), and mineralocorticoid hormones such as aldosterone (regulate sodium and potassium balance).

Adrenal insufficiency can occur for different reasons. In 70% of cases of primary adrenal insufficiency, the body's immune system attacks and slowly destroys the adrenal glands (autoimmune disease). Tuberculosis (once the most common cause of Addison's disease) is responsible for only about 20% of cases of primary adrenal insufficiency. Since the appearance of acquired immunodeficiency syndrome (AIDS), tuberculosis is on the rise and a corresponding increase in Addison's disease caused by tuberculosis is expected. Less common causes of primary adrenal insufficiency include chronic infections particularly fungal infections, amyloidosis, viral infections (cytomegalovirus or CMV) also associated with AIDS, hemorrhage of the adrenal glands, and surgical removal of both adrenal glands.

In secondary adrenal insufficiency, the adrenal glands are healthy but the body fails to stimulate them to release hormones. This occurs when the pituitary gland located at the base of the brain fails to secrete the hormone called adrenocorticotropin or ACTH. Causes of secondary adrenal insufficiency include long-term use of steroids such as prednisone and surgical removal of pituitary tumors (either cancerous or noncancerous). Less common causes are loss of blood flow to the pituitary gland or the surgical removal of either part of the pituitary gland or the area of the brain called the hypothalamus.

Addison's disease tends to run in families. Individuals who take steroids over a long period of time and then develop a severe infection, injury, or undergo a surgical procedure are at increased risk of developing Addison's disease. Other risk factors include the diseases of diabetes mellitus, hypoparathyroidism, hypopituitarism, pernicious anemia, testicular dysfunction, Graves' disease, chronic thyroiditis, and myasthenia gravis.

Approximately 8 in 100,000 individuals are affected with Addison's disease. It occurs almost equally in both men and women and can appear at any age but more often appears between the ages of 30 and 60.

Diagnosis

History: In most cases, symptoms appear gradually. Individuals often complain of progressively increasing weakness and fatigue, loss of appetite (anorexia), and unintentional weight loss. Many report dizziness or light-headedness especially when rising from a seated position. Abdominal pain, decreased tolerance to cold, hair loss (alopecia) particularly in women, and cravings for salty foods may also be reported. Nausea, vomiting, and chronic diarrhea occur in about 50% of cases. Women may report that their menstrual cycles have become irregular (dysmenorrhea) or stopped altogether (amenorrhea). In advanced cases, the individual may experience what is known as an Addisonian crisis and is characterized by sudden, penetrating pain to the lower back, abdomen, and/or legs; severe vomiting and diarrhea; and loss of consciousness. Moodiness, irritability, or depression may be evident.

Physical exam: Findings usually include low blood pressure (hypotension) that may worsen when the individual stands after sitting or lying down (orthostatic hypotension). The individual may be dehydrated. Skin changes are also commonly noted and include freckling and darkening of the skin. The skin darkening may resemble a deep tan but will be present even on parts of the body not exposed to the sun. The skin darkening may also be more visible on scars, pressure points (such as elbows, knees, and toes), lips, mucus membranes, and in skin folds.

Tests: The most specific test for Addison's disease is called the ACTH stimulation test. For this test, blood and/or urine samples are collected before and after a synthetic form of ACTH is given by injection. In a healthy individual, the cortisol levels are higher after the injection of ACTH; in individuals with Addison's disease, little or no change in cortisol levels is seen. If an abnormal result is obtained, a variation of this test where ACTH is given over a 2- to 3-day period may be conducted. Blood and/or urine samples are collected before and during a 2- to 3-day period. In this longer ACTH stimulation test, the cause of adrenal insufficiency can be determined. Primary adrenal insufficiency results in little or no cortisol production for the entire 72-hour period; secondary adrenal insufficiency shows an adequate response by the second or third day. High am ACTH levels confirm primary adrenal cause.

Other tests may also be conducted either to help confirm the diagnosis or help rule out other conditions. An insulin-induced hypoglycemia test evaluates the functioning of the pituitary gland and the hypothalamus. In this test, blood sugar (glucose) and cortisol levels are measured and fast-acting insulin is then given. The normal response is for glucose to fall and cortisol to rise and indicates a normal pituitary gland and hypothalamus.

Routine blood analysis generally shows low sodium and cortisol levels. On the other hand, potassium, calcium, blood urea nitrogen (BUN), and creatinine levels are high. If the individual has not eaten prior to the blood test, hypoglycemia may be noted and ACTH levels are high, and certain blood levels are higher than normal.

With an autoimmune disease, adrenal antibodies are present in the blood. An abdominal or chest x-ray may help determine if the adrenal glands have calcium deposits, which is a sign of tuberculosis infection. An abdominal CT may be performed to determine if the adrenal glands are smaller or larger than normal. Small adrenal glands are a sign of autoimmune adrenal disease and larger than normal adrenal glands are an indication of hemorrhage or infiltrative disease. A biopsy of the adrenal gland can rule out cancer.

Treatment

In the rare instances of Addisonian crisis, potentially life-threatening low blood pressure (hypotension), low blood sugar (hypoglycemia), and high levels of potassium (hyperkalemia) may occur. Individuals experiencing Addisonian crisis require immediate hospitalization. Treatment for Addisonian crisis includes immediate intravenous (IV) or intramuscular (IM) injections of steroids along with saltwater (saline) fluid replacements and sugar (glucose). Oral steroid medications may also be given.

Most cases of Addison's disease do not require inpatient treatment. The goal of therapy is to replace the hormones the body is not producing. Oral steroid medications are usually a combination of glucocorticoids and mineral corticoids and are taken for the remainder of the individual's life. The individual is counseled to avoid dehydration by drinking plenty of fluids. An identification and medical instruction bracelet is often advised and individuals are urged to carry injectable steroid medication for use in an emergency if medical care is not available.

Individuals with Addison's disease need to be made aware of the consequences of not following their medical regimen closely. Any stress such as illness, fever, hot and humid weather, profuse sweating, and even emotional stress can precipitate a sudden worsening of the condition and must be met with an increase in replacement hormones. Most individuals with Addison's disease are taught to give themselves an emergency injection of hydrocortisone in times of stress.

If an underlying disease is responsible such as tuberculosis, treatment of the underlying disease is important for recovery or resolution of symptoms.

Prognosis

With careful management, an individual with Addison's disease can live a full, relatively active life. However, illness, stress, and even general anesthesia for surgery can bring on an adrenal crisis necessitating special care and adjustments in replacement hormone dosages.

Untreated, Addison's disease is a progressive condition that can gradually result in severe abdominal pain, extremely low blood pressure, and kidney failure. All cases of untreated Addison's disease result in death. Addisonian crisis must be treated immediately or coma and death can occur.

Differential Diagnosis

Many of the symptoms of Addison's disease are common to a variety of other conditions such as hypoglycemia, gastrointestinal disorders, myopathies, syndrome of inappropriate antidiuretic hormone (SIADH), heavy metal poisoning, anorexia nervosa, nutritional disorders, hyperparathyroidism, Sprue syndrome, neurofibromatosis, Peutz-Jeghers syndrome, porphyria cutanea tarda, salt-losing nephritis, bronchogenic carcinoma, depression, and autoimmune polyglandular syndromes. Other associated conditions include diabetes mellitus, Graves' disease, Hashimoto's thyroiditis, hypoparathyroidism, hypercalcemia, ovarian failure, pernicious anemia, myasthenia gravis, vitiligo, chronic moniliasis, sarcoidosis, Sjögren's syndrome, chronic active hepatitis, Schmidt's syndrome, and adrenoleukodystrophy.

Specialists

- Endocrinologist

Work Restrictions / Accommodations

In most cases, work accommodations or restrictions are not necessary for individuals with Addison's disease. Taxing physical labor such as working in hot humid environments or work that carries a great deal of stress is unsuitable for an individual with Addison's disease. The particulars of the necessary accommodations vary significantly depending on the individual, severity of symptoms, individual's response to treatment, and job requirements.

Complementary and Alternative Therapies

Content is intended for awareness only. Treatments may or may not be effective. Scientific evidence may be lacking and some substances have potentially toxic effects. Dr. Presley Reed and the editors do not endorse the use of these therapies in the absence of consultation with a licensed medical professional.

Diet modification - Added table salt during periods of excessive exercise with sweating, during extremely hot weather, or episodes of vomiting or diarrhea may ease symptoms.

Comorbid Conditions

Conditions that may impact recovery and lengthen disability include autoimmune disorders, chronic candida infections, chronic active hepatitis, pernicious anemia, tuberculosis, and pregnancy.

Complications

Illness, injury, or any type of stress can result in a potentially life-threatening condition (Addisonian crisis) to be handled with an increase of the hydrocortisone dose.

Other possible complications include extremely high fever (hyperpyrexia), psychotic reactions, accidental overdose of steroid medications and, rarely, a temporary paralysis due to low levels of potassium.

Additional complications related to the individual's underlying disease might also occur and vary depending on the particulars of that disease.

Factors Influencing Duration

Individuals must be knowledgeable about their disease in order to avoid factors and environments that may cause an acute adrenal crisis. Those who are careless with their medication regimen or do not avoid stressful situations will have a longer disability and a higher incidence of complications.

Length of Disability

For those with particularly stressful or physically demanding jobs, disability may be permanent. If untreated, Addison's disease is fatal.

Duration in Days

Job Classification	Minimum	Optimum	Maximum
Sedentary work	0	3	7
Light work	0	7	14
Medium work	3	7	14
Heavy work	7	9	14
Very Heavy work	7	9	14

Failure to Recover

If an individual fails to recover within the maximum duration expectancy period, the reader may wish to reference the following questions to assist in better understanding the specifics of an individual's medical case.

Regarding diagnosis:

- Was diagnosis of Addison's disease confirmed through an ACTH stimulation test?
- Was the cause of the adrenocortical insufficiency identified (autoimmune disorder, infection, tumor, or hemorrhage in the adrenal glands)?
- Were causes also addressed?

Regarding treatment:

- Is individual on oral cortisol and fludrocortisone?
- Does current method of treatment appear to be effective?
- Has individual continued to experience any symptoms of adrenal crisis such as vomiting, diarrhea, fever, confusion, low blood pressure, or dehydration?
- If current treatment is not effective, is individual a candidate for surgery or radiation therapy?
- Is individual on and able to maintain a diet high in fluids, carbohydrates, and protein?
- Would individual benefit from instruction in stress management techniques?
- Does individual wear an identification/medical instruction bracelet?
- Does individual carry injectable steroid medication for use in an emergency if medical care is not available?

Regarding prognosis:

- Were underlying causes (autoimmune disorder, infection, tumor, TB) resolved or under control?
- Does individual realize that Addison's disease is a lifelong disorder that requires careful management including avoiding stress and infection?
- Is individual able to adhere to oral therapy and dietary recommendations?
- Does individual receive regular follow-up visits with physician?
- Has individual experienced any complications related to the Addison's disease?
- Does individual have an underlying condition that may impact recovery?

References

Kellerman, Rick, and Mark Gerstberger. "Addison's Disease." Griffith's 5-minute Clinical Consult. Dambro, Mark, ed. Philadelphia: Lippincott, Williams & Wilkins, 2000. 14-15.

Marguiles, Paul, MD. Addison's Disease: The Facts You Need to Know. National Adrenal Disease Foundation 16 Nov 2000 <http://medhelp.org/nadf/nadf3.htm>.

Tierney L.M., S.J. McPhee, and M.A. Papadakis. Current Medical Diagnosis and Treatment. Stamford: Appleton & Lange, 1997.

Addison's Disease. Wellness Web 05 May 2000 06 Jun 2000 <http://www.wellweb.com/INDEX/qaddison.htm>.

Adhesive Capsulitis of Shoulder

Other names / synonyms: Frozen Shoulder, Periarthritis

726.0

Definition

Often called "frozen shoulder," adhesive capsulitis is a condition of unknown cause characterized by significant limitation of both active and passive motions of the shoulder. Initially there is inflammation of, or at least increased blood flow in, the shoulder joint capsule, usually accompanied by insidious onset of pain. Later the capsule undergoes fibrosis (scarring) and gradually shrinks, thereby progressively restricting joint motion. Adhesive capsulitis should be distinguished from a stiff shoulder of known cause, e.g., arthritis, or prolonged immobilization following a proximal humerus fracture, rotator cuff repair, or other shoulder girdle injury/surgery. Theorized causes for adhesive capsulitis include autonomic dysfunction, genetic predisposition, and forgotten or unrecognized trauma. The incidence of adhesive capsulitis is also 5 times higher in diabetics. Other associated conditions include autoimmune, cerebrovascular, coronary artery, and cervical disc disease, as well as depression, hypothyroidism, and Parkinson's disease.

Adhesive capsulitis undergoes 3 phases of variable duration. The first (painful) phase lasts 2-9 months. The second (adhesive, stiffening or freezing) phase lasts 4-12 months. The third (recovery or thawing) phase is of variable duration and may take from several months to 2 years.

Adhesive capsulitis usually occurs between the ages of 40 and 60, and is more common in women (70% of cases) than men. The nondominant shoulder is more often involved; but it is bilateral in anywhere from 6-50% of individuals, and in a minority of these individuals, simultaneously bilateral. It occurs more frequently in sedentary individuals, and according to one study, more often in whites than blacks.

Diagnosis

History: Symptoms are of gradual onset, often beginning with pain followed by slowly worsening stiffness. However, sometimes motion loss is the first complaint. The discomfort is often vague but worse at night and with shoulder motions, prompting the individual to immobilize the joint, sometimes worsening the stiffness. Eventually the pain subsides.

Physical exam: Passive, as well as active, shoulder motions are decreased, often with pain at the extremes. Usually abduction and external rotation are most severely affected. Diagnostic criteria include loss of 30° of external rotation and less than 130° of flexion (both actively and passively). Tenderness is usually noted about the rotator cuff, often generalized rather than localized, but like the pain decreases over time.

Tests: The diagnosis is often made by history and physical exam alone. Plain x-rays of the shoulder should be taken initially to rule out fracture, arthritis, tumor, or calcium deposits in the rotator cuff tendons. However, in adhesive capsulitis x-rays are (by definition) normal. X-rays of cervical spine and/or electromyography (EMG) may be needed a nerve problem in the neck is suspected as a cause of the shoulder pain and stiffness. Blood tests may be ordered if there is suspicion of diabetes, infection, or an inflammatory condition like arthritis. If the diagnosis is in doubt, or there is lack of progress after approximately 3 months of treatment, more sophisticated testing may be performed. An arthrogram will demonstrate diminished shoulder capsule volume, a bone scan increased uptake, and an MRI scan increased blood flow in adhesive capsulitis.

Treatment

Treatment for adhesive capsulitis is usually nonoperative and begins with education regarding the condition, and reassurance regarding the favorable long term prognosis. Nonsteroidal anti-inflammatory drugs (NSAIDs) are often helpful for relief of pain and inflammation (when present). Non-narcotic analgesics may be used for persons intolerant of NSAIDs. However, the mainstay of treatment is physical therapy, initiated promptly upon diagnosis, and focusing on stretching then strengthening exercises. The exercises are initially supervised by a therapist but later can be performed on a self-directed basis, with periodic therapist and/or physician monitoring. Modalities such as ice, heat, and ultrasound may also be employed. If pain limits participations in therapy, local anesthetic-corticosteroid injections can be performed into the shoulder joint, the former providing short term pain relief, and the latter longer term reduction of inflammation and any associated discomfort. If performed, it is advisable to inject a relatively large volume, in an attempt to distend the contracted capsule. The combined effects of such injection will hopefully permit more aggressive therapy. Use of slings or other types of immobilization should be avoided.

If the individual is unable to regain motion after approximately 6-12 weeks of therapy, manipulation of the joint under general or regional anesthesia may be beneficial. Adhesive capsulitis can also be treated surgically, by cutting the capsule (capsular release). This is most commonly done through an arthroscope, although arthroscopy is difficult in adhesive capsulitis due to the contracted capsule and small joint volume. Open capsular release can also be performed, although this is rarely indicated since the natural history of adhesive capsulitis is one of progressive improvement. Diabetics are often not benefitted by manipulation, and more commonly require surgery if therapy fails.

Prognosis

Most individuals recover completely or almost so within 1-2 years. However, during this time most affected individuals are significantly limited in shoulder activities; and 7-42% of individuals are left with some permanent loss of shoulder motion, usually terminal rotation. Residual stiffness is 13 times more common in men that women. Diabetics are particularly predisposed to slow and incomplete recovery.

Differential Diagnosis

Subacromial bursitis, rotator cuff tendonitis or tear, impingement syndrome and/or fracture of proximal humerus may have symptoms and signs similar to adhesive capsulitis. However, barring prolonged immobilization, there should be no significant loss of passive shoulder motion with these conditions. Monoarticular (single joint) arthritis is another diagnosis to consider, but would be uncommon absent a prior history of arthritis and with normal x-rays.

Neurological problems that cause referral of pain into and/or muscle weakness about the shoulder girdle, e.g., a cervical disc herniation or brachial neuritis, can also mimic adhesive capsulitis. Additionally, tumors of bone or soft tissue may cause similar symptoms (especially tumors in the lung apex).

Specialists

- Orthopedic Surgeon
- Physiatrist
- Rheumatologist
- Sports Medicine Physician

Rehabilitation

Individuals with adhesive capsulitis may require outpatient physical therapy. However the key to recovery is compliance with daily home exercises. Individuals should also be encouraged to use the involved extremity, particularly for activities requiring shoulder motions.

Goals of therapy include reduction of pain and regaining shoulder motion and strength. Hot packs applied to the shoulder may diminish pain and relax muscles, facilitating stretching exercises. Ultrasound uses sound waves to produce deeper heating and may increase flexibility of the deeper muscles about the shoulder capsule. Ice packs often reduce pain and swelling (if any) about the shoulder after exercise. More specific means to restore shoulder motion include joint mobilization and passive stretching performed by a therapist. Individuals themselves can also perform active and passive range of motion exercises. The latter include wand exercises where a stick is grasped by both hands and the uninvolved extremity used to push or pull on the stick and move the involved shoulder through abduction, extension, flexion, and external rotation. Adduction stretching is performed by using the uninvolved hand to pull the involved elbow across the chest. Internal rotation stretching is accomplished by placing the involved hand behind the back and grasping a towel, which is then pulled upward by the uninvolved hand.

Strengthening exercises are commonly performed by moving the shoulder in the above directions against the resistance of rubber tubing, one end of which is held in the hand, with the other end attached to a stationary object. Individuals may also perform push-ups against a wall in a standing position and shoulder blade pinches to strengthen shoulder girdle muscles.

Work Restrictions / Accommodations

Limitations in lifting, carrying, and reaching overhead depend on the shoulder motion, strength, and pain someone has. Arm function can be classified as lost when individuals exhibit very limited shoulder motion, however, they usually retain use of their hand.

Time must be allowed for thrice weekly therapy sessions early in treatment. Individuals often need breaks during the workday to perform range-of-motion exercises, and access to ice packs after exercising. Occasionally, pain medications or muscle relaxants may have to be taken during work hours, and some might require modification of drug testing policies.

Complementary and Alternative Therapies

Content is intended for awareness only. Treatments may or may not be effective. Scientific evidence may be lacking and some substances have potentially toxic effects. Dr. Presley Reed and the editors do not endorse the use of these therapies in the absence of consultation with a licensed medical professional.

Heating pad or ice pack - May help reduce shoulder pain.

Chiropractic manipulation - Manipulation may worsen some types of stiff shoulder, hence correct diagnosis is important. Those treated by prolonged pulley traction and transcutaneous nerve stimulation may show much greater improvement than those treated with heating modalities followed by therapeutic exercises and gentle rhythmic stabilization manipulation.

Comorbid Conditions

Comorbid conditions that slow full recovery include rheumatoid and other types of arthritis, cancer, obesity, cardiovascular disease, impingement syndrome, rotator cuff tears, pain in the upper spine, and diabetes.

Complications

Impingement on or tears of rotator cuff may require surgery. Inflammatory conditions such as rheumatoid arthritis, lupus, or gout require management. Cervical nerve root impingement (pinched nerve in the neck) or brachial neuritis can cause weakness and pain around the shoulder. This not only confuses diagnosis but also causes the individual to avoid using the shoulder normally, which can lead to further stiffness. Disuse may cause loss of bone (osteoporosis) about the shoulder. The weaker bones, especially proximal humerus, may fracture should the individual fall or undergo manipulation under anesthesia. NSAIDs can cause stomach, liver, or kidney damage.

Factors Influencing Duration

Adhesive capsulitis takes anywhere from several months to 2 years to resolve. The presence of comorbid conditions usually prolongs disease and disability duration. Improper or delayed treatment also contributes to delayed recovery. Work absence will likely be greater if the dominant shoulder is affected and/or the occupation requires lifting, carrying, and overhead work. If the nondominant side is involved or the individual employed in sedentary or light work, earlier resumption of employment would be anticipated. If surgery is required for adhesive capsulitis or a comorbid condition, additional therapy will be necessary, perhaps 6-12 weeks in duration, further delaying return to work and other functions.

Length of Disability

Duration of disability depends on whether one or both shoulders is affected, if the dominant or nondominant shoulder is involved, whether the individual can be assigned a job where full shoulder motion is not needed, and if the job can be performed adequately while the individual takes pain medication.

Duration in Days

Job Classification	Minimum	Optimum	Maximum
Sedentary work	0	7	21
Light work	7	14	42
Medium work	42	84	112
Heavy work	56	140	Indefinite
Very Heavy work	56	140	Indefinite

Duration Trend from Normative Data*

Cases	Mean	Min	Max	No Lost Time	Over 6 Months
641	72	0	635	0.16%	4.68%

Percentile:	5th	25th	Median	75th	95th
Days:	12	26	49	90	165

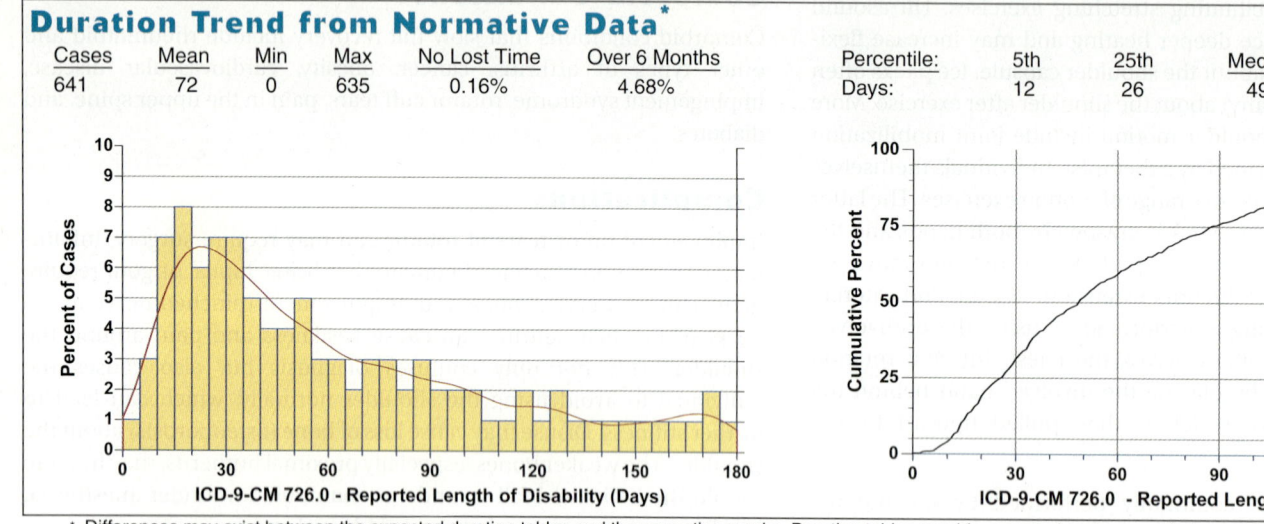

ICD-9-CM 726.0 - Reported Length of Disability (Days)

* Differences may exist between the expected duration tables and the normative graphs. Duration tables provide expected recovery periods based on the type of work performed by the individual. The normative graphs reflect the actual observed experience of many individuals across the spectrum of physical conditions, in a variety of industries, and with varying levels of case management.

Failure to Recover

If an individual fails to recover within the maximum duration expectancy period, the reader may wish to reference the following questions to assist in better understanding the specifics of an individual's medical case.

Regarding diagnosis:

- Was diagnosis of adhesive capsulitis confirmed?
- Did x-rays reveal any bony abnormalities?
- Was shoulder arthrogram or MRI done?
- Were there other comorbid conditions or complications accounting for the delayed recovery?
- Was a complete neurological exam done?

Regarding treatment:

- Was physical therapy prescribed to address function, not just to relieve pain?
- Did individual complete the recommended course of therapy?
- Did individual improve or worsen during physical therapy?
- Would he or she benefit from additional or a change in therapy?
- Has individual's need to continue self-directed therapy been accommodated at work?
- Has he or she been compliant with the treatment plan including recommended activity restrictions?
- Are comorbid conditions also being addressed in overall treatment plan?
- If a surgical procedure was required, were there any resulting complications?
- If recovery from this procedure is not progressing as expected, are there extenuating circumstances?

Regarding prognosis:

- How long after symptom onset was treatment sought?
- Did individual receive adequate education in prevention of future overuse problems?

References

Kisner, Carolyn, and Lynn Allen Colby. "The Shoulder and Shoulder Girdle." <u>Therapeutic Exercise: Foundations and Techniques</u>, 2nd ed. Philadelphia: F.A. Davis Company, 1990. 241-272.

Rizk, T.E., R.P. Christopher, and R.S. Inals. "Adhesive Capsulitis (Frozen Shoulder): A New Approach to its Management." <u>Archives of Physical and Medical Rehabilitation</u> 64 1 (1983): 29-33.

Adjustment Disorder with Depressed Mood

Other names / synonyms: Adjustment Reaction, Adjustment Reaction with Depressed Mood, Depressive Reaction (Brief and Chronic), Depressive Reaction (Brief), Depressive Reaction (Chronic), Grief Reaction

309, 309.0, 309.1, 309.2, 309.28

Definition

In an adjustment disorder, a psychological response occurs to an identifiable stressor or life event that results in significant emotional or behavioral symptoms. These symptoms usually result in decreased performance at work or school and temporary changes in social relationships.

The life stressor may be a single event such as termination of a relationship, a recurrent situation such as seasonal business crises, a continuous source of stress such as living in a crime-ridden neighborhood, a prolonged difficulty such as a chronic, debilitating medical condition, or multiple circumstances such as business difficulties plus marital problems.

In adjustment disorder with depressed mood, the main symptoms include depressed mood, tearfulness, or feelings of hopelessness.

Adjustment disorders are fairly common, depending on the population studied. They occur in up to 12% of general hospitalized individuals referred for a mental health consultation, in 10-30% of those in mental health outpatient settings, and as high as 50% of those who experience a specific stressor such as cardiac surgery.

Diagnosis

History: Diagnosis is based on criteria listed in the DSM-IV-TR (Diagnostic and Statistical Manual of Mental Disorders, 4th Edition, Text Revision, published by the American Psychiatric Association). The symptoms should occur within 3 months of the recognizable stressful event and should not last longer than 6 months after resolution of the stressful event or its consequences unless symptoms are in response to a chronic stressor.

The symptoms or behaviors are identified as either a marked distress in excess of what would be expected or a significant impairment in social or occupational functioning. The stress-related disturbance cannot be diagnosed as another specific psychiatric disorder or be merely an exacerbation of a pre-existing psychiatric disorder. The symptoms cannot be related to bereavement. However, adjustment disorder may be diagnosed in the presence of another psychiatric disorder if the latter does not account for the pattern of symptoms occurring in response to the stressor.

Physical exam: The exam is generally not helpful in diagnosing adjustment disorders. Observation of the individual's orientation, dress, mannerisms, behavior, and content of speech provide essential signs to help diagnose the illness. For example, individual may show poor attention to grooming or give statements inconsistent with emotional state (affect) such as saying "I feel fine" while clenching the jaw and frowning. Depressed mood may be associated with low volume and output of speech, blank or sad expression, and decreased or slowed spontaneous movement (psychomotor retardation).

Tests: Psychological testing can be helpful as an adjunct to diagnosing adjustment disorders. This may include the Minnesota Multiphasic Personality Inventory or other tests.

Treatment

Psychotherapy is the treatment of choice for adjustment disorders along with resolving the stressful situation or removing the individual from the situation. Group therapy can be effective especially when individuals in the group have experienced similar stressors. Individual psychotherapy helps explore the meaning of the stressor to the individual so that earlier traumas can be explored. Brief psychotherapy when utilized in a crisis intervention can help resolve the situation quickly using supportive techniques, suggestion, reassurance, environmental modification, and even hospitalization, if necessary. Pharmacotherapy utilizes antianxiety agents and antidepressants to reduce symptoms of anxiety and depression. These should be used judiciously and for brief periods.

Specialists

- Advanced Practice Registered Nurse
- Licensed Clinical Social Worker
- Occupational Therapist
- Psychiatrist
- Psychologist

Prognosis

The overall prognosis of adjustment disorder is favorable with appropriate treatment. Adjustment disorders generally occur within a short period of time following the stressor and, by definition, should last no longer than 6 months after the stressor or its consequences have ended. Individuals generally return to normal functioning within a few months.

Differential Diagnosis

Adjustment disorder with depressed mood must be differentiated from anxiety disorders where a specific stressor need not be identified, personality disorders exacerbated by stress, post-traumatic stress disorder where the stressor is extreme, psychological factors affecting medical condition, bereavement, and mood disorders.

Work Restrictions / Accommodations

Work restrictions or accommodations are necessary only infrequently, for the most serious cases. In these instances, time-limited restrictions and work accommodations should be individually determined based on the characteristics of the individual's response to the disorder, the functional requirements of the job and work environment, and the flexibility of the job and work site. The purpose of the restrictions/accommodation is to help maintain the worker's capacity to remain at the workplace without a work disruption or to promote timely and safe transition back to full work productivity.

Complementary and Alternative Therapies

Content is intended for awareness only. Treatments may or may not be effective. Scientific evidence may be lacking and some substances have potentially toxic effects. Dr. Presley Reed and the editors do not endorse the use of these therapies in the absence of consultation with a licensed medical professional.

St. John's wort -	May improve anxiety, depression, low self-esteem, and sleep problems.
Kava kava -	May act as an antianxiety.
Acupressure -	May help provide calm and emotional balance.
Creative therapy -	Individual can safely express/release painful experiences through art, dance, drama, music, or journal writing.
Guided imagery -	Visualizing scenes that boost self esteem may lift depression.
Hypnotherapy -	May reduce stimuli to areas of the brain linked to autonomic nervous system.
Meditation -	May decrease blood level of lactic acid.
Yoga -	May relieve stress by promoting relaxation.

Comorbid Conditions

Coexisting conditions that may affect recovery and lengthen disability include mixed anxiety and depressive disorders, the presence of other personality disorders, or current alcohol abuse or drug use.

Complications

Adjustment disorders may be associated with excessive substance abuse or use, somatic complaints and suicide attempts or, occasionally, suicide. If an individual with a pre-existing mental or medical illness is also diagnosed with an adjustment disorder, the course of that illness may be complicated or prolonged by decreased compliance with recommended treatment or increased hospital length of stay.

Factors Influencing Duration

In adjustment disorders, continued exposure to the stressor often leads to continuing maladaptive behavior and symptoms. The apparent severity of the stressor is not always predictive of the severity of symptoms, which depends on the degree, quantity, duration, and reversibility of the stressor; the work and home environment and support structure; and personal context or the significance of the stressor to the individual. The context of the individual's cultural setting should also be considered in determining whether the reaction to stress is in excess of what is expected.

Length of Disability

Duration of disability depends on response to psychotherapy and pharmacotherapy.

Duration in Days

Job Classification	Minimum	Optimum	Maximum
Any work	1	7	42

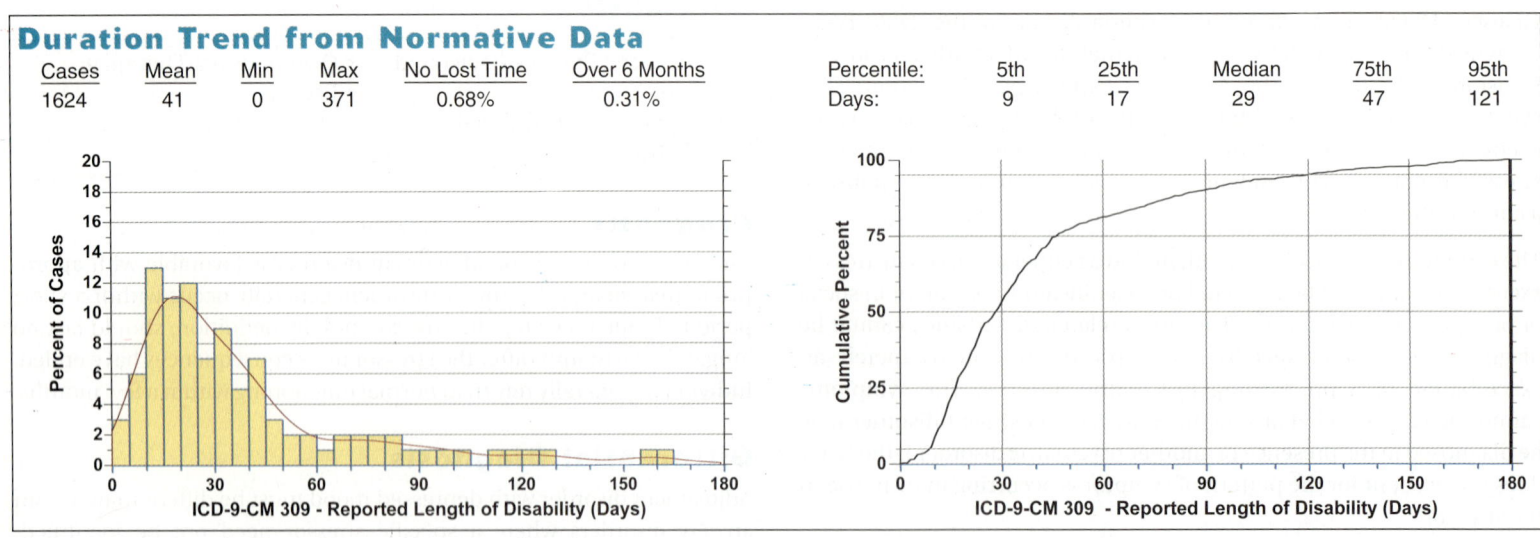

Duration Trend from Normative Data

Cases	Mean	Min	Max	No Lost Time	Over 6 Months
1624	41	0	371	0.68%	0.31%

Percentile:	5th	25th	Median	75th	95th
Days:	9	17	29	47	121

ICD-9-CM 309 - Reported Length of Disability (Days)

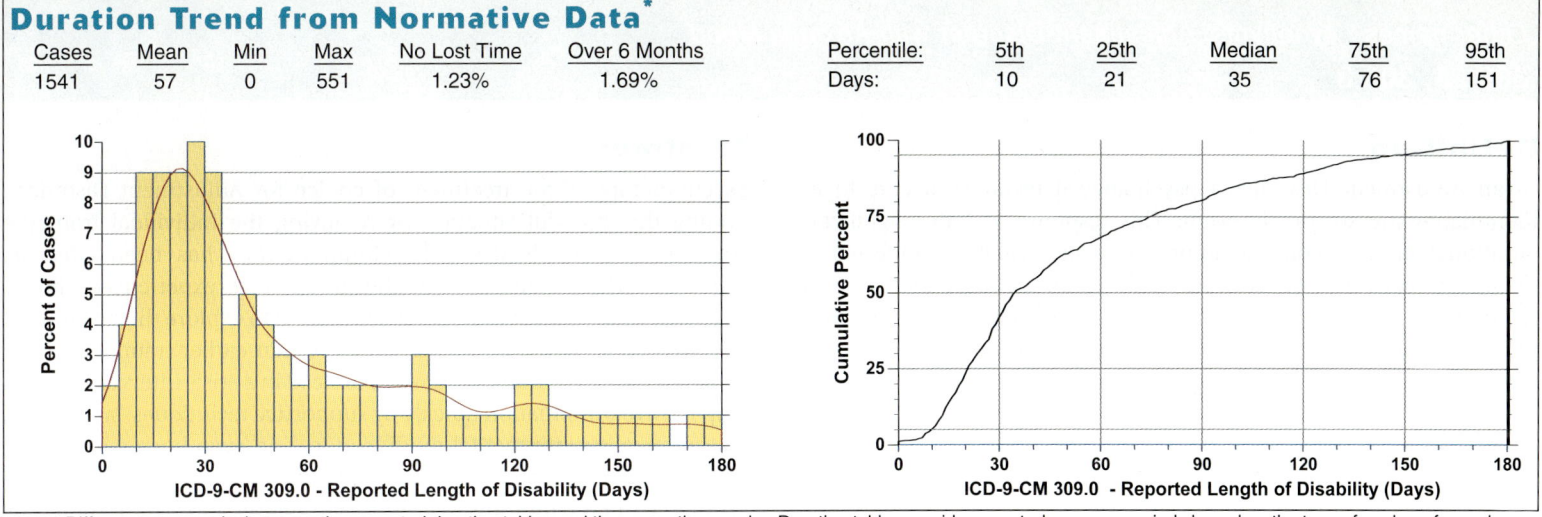

Failure to Recover

If an individual fails to recover within the maximum duration expectancy period, the reader may wish to reference the following questions to assist in better understanding the specifics of an individual's medical case.

Regarding diagnosis:

- Was diagnosis confirmed?
- Were similar disorders considered and ruled out such as major depression, bipolar affective disorder, mood disorders due directly to medical disorders or substance abuse, dysthymic disorders, acute stress disorder, post-traumatic stress disorder, or bereavement?
- Was there a history of depression or other psychological problem contributing to the current condition?
- What was the previous level of functioning?
- Was there significant reduction in functioning and if so, in what ways?
- If there is concurrent drug or alcohol abuse, to what extent were these conditions causing additional problems?

Regarding treatment:

- Was the stressful situation resolved?
- Was individual removed from it?
- If suicidal tendencies are present, is environmental modification being considered?
- If utilized, were antidepressants or tranquilizers effective?
- Would a longer trial be warranted?
- Are social supports adequate?
- Is additional supportive group or individual therapy needed?
- Has psychotherapy been added to the pharmacotherapy regimen for more effective results?

Regarding prognosis:

- How are current stresses being dealt with?
- How were major stresses dealt with in the past?
- If healthy and adaptive methods were used in the past, are they being used currently?
- If maladaptive (drug or alcohol abuse), to what extent are these conditions causing additional problems?
- What are the social supports? Family? Friends? Church or other community affiliations? Are these being utilized?
- Did symptoms resolve within 6 months?
- What is happening outside of work that may be contributing to or worsening the problems experienced at work?
- Are there incentives not to improve such as ongoing litigation, social security, or disability insurance?
- Did individual enjoy working previously?

References

Duke, James A. The Green Pharmacy. Emmaus, PA: Rodale Press, Inc, 1997.

Frances, Allen. Diagnostic and Statistical Manual of Mental Disorders: 4th ed, text revision. Washington, DC: American Psychiatric Association, 2000.

Hall, Laura Lee. "Making the ADA Work for People with Psychiatric Disabilities." Mental Disorder, Work Disability, and the Law. Bonnie, Richard J., and John Monahan, eds. Chicago: The University of Chicago Press, 1997. 241-280.

Healing with Vitamins. Feinstein, Alice, ed. Emmaus, PA: Rodale Press, Inc, 1996.

Jones R., et al. "Outcome for Adjustment Disorder with Depressed Mood: Comparison with Other Mood Disorders." Journal of Affective Disorders 55 1 (1999): 55-61.

New Choices in Natural Healing. Gottlieb, Bill, ed. Emmaus, PA: Rodale Press, Inc, 1995.

Adjustment Reaction with Anxious Mood

Other names / synonyms: Adjustment Disorder with Anxious Mood

309.24, 309.3

Definition

In an Adjustment Disorder, a psychological response occurs to an identifiable stressor or life event. This response includes significant emotional or behavioral symptoms that are usually manifested as decreased performance at work and temporary changes in social relationships. The life stressor may be a single event such as termination of a relationship; a recurrent situation, such as seasonal business crises; a continuous stressor, such as living in a crime-ridden neighborhood; a prolonged circumstance, such as a chronic, debilitating medical condition; or multiple events, such as business difficulties plus marital problems. In Adjustment Disorder with Anxiety, the symptoms include nervousness, worry, or jitteriness.

Adjustment Disorders are fairly common, depending upon the population studied. They occur in up to 12% of general hospital patients who are referred for a mental health consultation, in 10-30% of those in mental health outpatient settings, and in as many as 50% of those who experience a specific stressor, such as cardiac surgery.

Diagnosis

History: Diagnosis is based on criteria listed in the DSM-IV-TR (Diagnostic and Statistical Manual of Mental Disorders, 4th Edition, Text Revision, published by the American Psychiatric Association).

The symptoms should occur within 3 months of the recognizable stressful condition, and not persist longer than 6 months after the stressful situation or its consequences is resolved, unless the symptoms are in response to a chronic stressor. The symptoms or behaviors are identified as either a marked distress that is in excess of what would be expected, or a significant impairment in social or occupational functioning. The stress-related disturbance cannot be diagnosed as another specific psychiatric disorder or be merely an exacerbation of a pre-existing psychiatric disorder, and the symptoms cannot be related to bereavement. However, Adjustment Disorder may be diagnosed in the presence of another psychiatric disorder if the latter does not account for the pattern of symptoms that have occurred in response to the stressor.

Physical exam: The exam is generally not helpful in diagnosing Adjustment Disorders. Observation of the individual's orientation, dress, mannerisms, behavior, and content of speech provide essential signs to help diagnose the illness. For example, there may be poor attention to grooming, or verbalizations inconsistent with emotional state (affect), such as saying "I feel fine" while clenching the jaw and frowning. Physical manifestations of anxiety may include sweaty palms, rapid pulse, pale or flushed skin, frequent sighing, and restless behavior such as pacing or fidgeting.

Tests: Psychological testing, such as the Minnesota Multiphasic Personality Inventory, can be helpful as an adjunct to diagnosing Adjustment Disorders and anxiety states.

Treatment

Psychotherapy is the treatment of choice for Adjustment Disorders. Ending the stressful situation or removing the individual from the stressful situation is desirable. Group therapy has been effective, especially when individuals in the group have experienced similar stressors. Individual psychotherapy is helpful to explore the meaning of the stressful situation to the individual so that earlier traumas may be explored. Brief psychotherapy, when utilized in a crisis intervention, can help resolve the situation quickly by supportive techniques, suggestion, reassurance, environmental modification, and even hospitalization, if necessary. Pharmacotherapy utilizes antianxiety agents and antidepressants to reduce symptoms of anxiety and depression. These should be used judiciously and for brief periods.

Prognosis

The overall prognosis of Adjustment Disorder is favorable with appropriate treatment. Adjustment Disorders generally occur within a short period of time following the stress and, by definition, should last no longer than 6 months after the stressor or its consequences have ended. Individuals generally return to normal functioning within a few months.

Differential Diagnosis

Adjustment Disorder with Anxiety must be differentiated from Anxiety Disorders, in which a specific stressor need not be identified, Personality Disorders exacerbated by stress, Post-traumatic Stress Disorder, in which the stressor is extreme, Psychological Factors Affecting Medical Condition, Bereavement, and Mood Disorders.

Specialists

- Advanced Practice Registered Nurse
- Licensed Clinical Social Worker
- Occupational Therapist
- Psychiatrist
- Psychologist

Work Restrictions / Accommodations

Work restrictions or accommodations are necessary only infrequently, for the most serious cases. In these instances, time-limited restrictions and work accommodations should be individually determined based on the characteristics of the individual's response to the disorder, the functional requirements of the job and work environment, and the flexibility of the job and work site. The purpose of the restrictions/accommodation is to help maintain the worker's capacity to remain at the workplace without a work disruption or to promote timely and safe transition back to full work productivity.

Complementary and Alternative Therapies

Content is intended for awareness only. Treatments may or may not be effective. Scientific evidence may be lacking and some substances have potentially toxic effects. Dr. Presley Reed and the editors do not endorse the use of these therapies in the absence of consultation with a licensed medical professional.

Biofeedback -	May help individual to be aware of and learn to control response to stress.
Hypnotherapy -	May reduce stimuli to areas of the brain linked to autonomic nervous system.
Massage -	May reduce anxiety.
Relaxation therapy -	May reduce anxiety.
Yoga -	May relieve stress by promoting relaxation.

Comorbid Conditions

Alcohol abuse, drug use, and the presence of a personality disorder or chronic medical condition may lengthen disability.

Complications

Adjustment Disorders may be associated with excessive substance use or abuse, physical (somatic) complaints, and, occasionally, suicide attempts or suicide. If an individual with a pre-existing mental or medical illness is also diagnosed with an Adjustment Disorder, the course of that illness may be complicated or prolonged, such as by decreased compliance with recommended treatment or increased hospital length of stay.

Factors Influencing Duration

Continued exposure to the stressor will often lead to continuing maladaptive behavior and symptoms in adjustment disorders. The severity of the stressor is not always predictive of the severity of Adjustment Disorder. The severity of the condition depends on degree, quantity, duration, and reversibility of the stressor; the overall environment and social support structure; and personal context in terms of what the stressor means to the individual. The context of the individual's cultural setting should also be taken into account in determining whether the reaction to stress is in excess of what would be expected.

Length of Disability

Duration depends upon response to psychotherapy and pharmacotherapy.

Duration in Days

Job Classification	Minimum	Optimum	Maximum
Any work	1	7	42

Failure to Recover

If an individual fails to recover within the maximum duration expectancy period, the reader may wish to reference the following questions to assist in better understanding the specifics of an individual's medical case.

Regarding diagnosis:

- Was diagnosis confirmed?
- Did symptoms and behaviors match the criteria needed for diagnosis?
- Was stressor identified?
- What was individual's previous level of functioning?
- Was there a significant reduction in functioning?
- In what ways was individual's level of functioning impaired?
- Did individual have symptoms of other psychiatric disorders, such as Personality Disorders, Post-traumatic Stress Disorder, Acute Stress Disorder, Psychological Factors Affecting Medical Condition, Attention-Deficit/Hyperactivity Disorder, or Bereavement?
- Does the Adjustment Disorder represent the early stages of a more severe psychiatric disorder that has not yet been diagnosed?
- Was there a history of depression or other psychological problem that may be contributing to the current condition?
- If there is concurrent drug or alcohol abuse, to what extent are these conditions causing additional problems?

Regarding treatment:

- Has stressor been identified?
- Has stressor been resolved?
- Does individual need more frequent therapeutic encounters or the addition of another type of therapy or therapist?
- If group psychotherapy is being used, have individuals in the group experienced similar stressors? If not, is a more appropriate group environment available?
- Have antianxiety agents and antidepressants been given to reduce symptoms of anxiety or depression?
- Are side effects preventing optimal treatment response?
- Has psychotherapy been added to the pharmacotherapy regimen for the most effective results?

Regarding prognosis:

- If symptoms persist despite treatment, is environmental modification or hospitalization being considered?
- Does diagnosis need to be revisited?
- How are current stresses being dealt with?
- How were major stresses dealt with in the past?
- If healthy and adaptive methods were used in the past, are they being used currently?
- If maladaptive, such as drug or alcohol abuse, to what extent are these conditions causing additional problems?
- Does individual have a functional support system? Family? Friends? Church or other community affiliations? Are these being utilized effectively?
- Did individual enjoy previous work?

References

Dufel, Susan. The Merck Manual of Diagnosis and Therapy. Emmaus, PA: Rodale Press, Inc, 1997.

Frances, Allen. Diagnostic and Statistical Manual of Mental Disorders: 4th ed, text revision. Washington, DC: American Psychiatric Association, 2000.

Gottlieb, Bill, ed. New Choices in Natural Healing. Emmaus, PA: Rodale Press, Inc, 1995.

Hall, Laura Lee. "Making the ADA Work for People with Psychiatric Disabilities." Mental Disorder, Work Disability, and the Law. Bonnie, Richard J., and John Monahan, eds. Chicago: The University of Chicago Press, 1997. 241-280.

Adjustment Reaction with Predominant Disturbance of Conduct
Other names / synonyms: Adjustment Disorder with Conduct Disturbance, Predominant Disturbance of Conduct
309.3

Definition

An adjustment disorder is characterized by a psychological response to an identifiable stressor or life event that results in significant emotional or behavioral symptoms. In adjustment disorder with disturbance of conduct, the main feature is abnormal conduct violating the rights of others or going against societal norms. Examples include truancy, vandalism, reckless driving, fighting, or defaulting on legal responsibilities.

Life stressors that cause adjustment disorders may be single events such as the termination of a job, continuously stressful circumstances such as living in a crime-ridden neighborhood, prolonged circumstances such as a chronic and debilitating medical condition, or multiple simultaneous events such as business difficulties in addition to marital problems.

Adjustment disorder is fairly common depending on the population studied. It occurs in up to 12% of hospitalized individuals referred for a mental health consultation, in 10-30% of mental health outpatients, and in 50% of those who experience a specific stressor such as cardiac surgery.

Diagnosis

History: Diagnosis is based on criteria listed in the DSM-IV-TR. Symptoms should occur within 3 months of the identifiable stressful event and not last longer than 6 months after resolution of the stressor or its consequences unless the symptoms are in response to a chronic stressor.

The symptoms or behaviors are identified as either a marked distress in excess of what would be expected or a significant impairment in social or occupational functioning. The stress-related disturbance cannot be diagnosed as another specific psychiatric disorder or merely an exacerbation of a pre-existing psychiatric disorder. Symptoms cannot be related to bereavement. However, adjustment disorder may be diagnosed in the presence of another psychiatric disorder if the latter does not account for the pattern of symptoms occurring in response to the stressor.

Physical exam: The exam is generally not helpful in diagnosing adjustment disorders. Observation of the individual's orientation, dress, mannerisms, behavior, and content of speech provide essential signs to help diagnose the illness. For example, there may be poor attention to grooming or statements inconsistent with emotional state (affect) such as saying "I feel fine" while clenching the jaw and frowning.

Tests: Psychological testing can be helpful as an adjunct to diagnosing adjustment disorders and may include the Minnesota Multiphasic Personality Inventory or other personality tests.

Specialists

- Advanced Practice Registered Nurse
- Licensed Clinical Social Worker
- Occupational Therapist
- Psychiatrist
- Psychologist

Treatment

Psychotherapy is the treatment of choice for adjustment disorders along with resolution of the stressful situation or removal of the individual from it. Group therapy is effective especially when individuals in the group have experienced similar stressors. Individual psychotherapy is helpful to explore the meaning of the stressor to the individual so that earlier traumas may be explored. Brief psychotherapy when utilized in crisis intervention can help resolve the situation quickly using supportive techniques, suggestion, reassurance, environmental modification, and even hospitalization, if necessary. Pharmacotherapy utilizes antianxiety agents and antidepressants to reduce symptoms of anxiety and depression. These should be used judiciously and for brief periods.

Prognosis

Overall outcome of adjustment disorder is favorable with appropriate treatment. Adjustment disorders generally occur within a short period of time following the stress and should last no longer than 6 months after the stressor or its consequences have ended. Individuals generally return to normal functioning within a few months.

Differential Diagnosis

Adjustment disorder with anxiety must be differentiated from other anxiety disorders where a specific stressor does not need to be identified. These include personality disorders exacerbated by stress, post-traumatic stress disorder where the stressor is extreme, psychological factors that affect the medical condition, bereavement, mood disorders, and conduct disorders.

Work Restrictions / Accommodations

Work restrictions or accommodations are necessary only infrequently, for the most serious cases. In these instances, time-limited restrictions and work accommodations should be individually determined based on the characteristics of the individual's response to the disorder, the functional requirements of the job and work environment, and the flexibility of the job and work site. The purpose of the restrictions/accommodation is to help maintain the worker's capacity to remain at the workplace without a work disruption or to promote timely and safe transition back to full work productivity.

Complementary and Alternative Therapies

Content is intended for awareness only. Treatments may or may not be effective. Scientific evidence may be lacking and some substances have potentially toxic effects. Dr. Presley Reed and the editors do not endorse the use of these therapies in the absence of consultation with a licensed medical professional.

St. John's wort - May improve depression. Physician should be consulted before use however, as St. John's wort can cause significant herbal-drug interaction with other medication the individual may currently be taking.

Creative therapy - Individual can safely express/release painful experiences.

Diet modification - Alcohol, caffeine, and concentrated sugars should be avoided, as they tend to increase anxiety.

Exercise program - Regular exercise may help relieve depression.

Guided imagery - Visualizing scenes that boost self-esteem may help lift depression.

Hypnotherapy - Thought to reduce stimuli to areas of the brain linked to autonomic nervous system.

Yoga - May relieve stress by promoting relaxation.

Comorbid Conditions

Alcohol abuse, drug use/abuse, or the presence of a personality disorder or chronic medical condition may lengthen disability.

Complications

Adjustment disorders may be associated with excessive substance use or abuse, physical symptoms, or, occasionally, suicide attempts or suicide. If an individual with a pre-existing mental or medical illness is also diagnosed with an adjustment disorder, the course of that illness may be complicated or prolonged through decreased compliance with recommended treatment or increased hospital length of stay.

Factors Influencing Duration

Continued exposure to the stressor can often lead to continuing maladaptive behavior and symptoms. The severity of the stressor is not always predictive of the severity of symptoms. This depends on degree, quantity, duration, and reversibility of the stressor, work and home environment and social supports, and personal context in terms of significance of the stressor to the individual. The context of the individual's cultural setting should also be taken into account in determining whether the reaction to stress is in excess of what would be expected.

Length of Disability

Duration of disability depends on response to psychotherapy and pharmacotherapy.

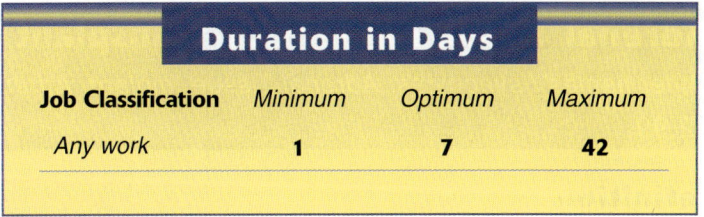

Duration in Days

Job Classification	Minimum	Optimum	Maximum
Any work	1	7	42

Failure to Recover

If an individual fails to recover within the maximum duration expectancy period, the reader may wish to reference the following questions to assist in better understanding the specifics of an individual's medical case.

Regarding diagnosis:

- Does individual exhibit significant emotional or behavioral symptoms as a result of a stressor or life event?
- Was diagnosis confirmed? Were other disorders ruled out?

Regarding treatment:

- Was stressful situation eliminated? Would environmental modification or hospitalization be beneficial?
- Were antianxiety agents or antidepressants effective?
- Are social supports adequate?
- Is additional or extended use of group or individual therapy warranted?

Regarding prognosis:

- How are current stresses being dealt with?
- How were major stresses dealt with in the past? If methods of coping are maladaptive (i.e., drug or alcohol abuse), to what extent are these conditions causing additional problems?
- Who are individual's social supports? Family? Friends? Church or other community affiliations? Are these being utilized?
- What is happening outside of work that may be contributing to or worsening the problems experienced at work?
- Are there incentives not to improve such as ongoing litigation, social security, or disability insurance?
- Does individual have an underlying condition that may impact recovery?
- Does individual have symptoms of other disorders that may be affecting recovery?
- Does a stressor exist that has not been identified?

References

Duke, James A. The Green Pharmacy. Emmaus, PA: Rodale Press, Inc, 1996.

Frances, Allen. Diagnostic and Statistical Manual of Mental Disorders: 4th Edition: Text Revision. Washington, DC: American Psychiatric Association, 2000.

Hall, Laura Lee. "Making the ADA work for people with psychiatric disabilities." Mental Disorder, Work Disability, and the Law. Bonnie, Richard J., and John Monahan, eds. Chicago: The University of Chicago Press, 1997. 241-280.

New Choices in Natural Healing. Gottlieb, Bill, ed. Englewood: Rodale Press, Inc, 1995.

Adrenal Tissue Implant or Transplant to Brain

Other names / synonyms: Adrenal Tissue Implant, Adrenal Tissue Transplant
02.99

Definition

An adrenal tissue implant is a surgical procedure where tissue is removed from the individual's adrenal gland (located above the kidney) and implanted into the brain (autotransplantation). More specifically, chromaffin tissue from the inner core (medulla) of the adrenal gland is removed and implanted in the area of the brain that controls the large involuntary movements of the skeletal muscles (the ventral mesencephalon). Chromaffin tissue is associated with the production of the catecholamines, and epinephrine and norepinephrine, the neurotransmitters similar to dopamine. Dopamine is the neurotransmitter that becomes deficient in the brains of individuals with Parkinson's disease.

Besides autotransplantation of the adrenal medulla, transplants of fetal brain tissue (ventral mesencephalon) and fetal adrenal medulla are currently being tested as therapeutic alternatives for individuals with Parkinson's disease.

Reason for Procedure

The adrenal tissue transplant procedure is used to treat the symptoms of Parkinson's disease and other diseases associated with tremors (palsy), rigidity, an absence of automatic movements such as writing legibly or speaking clearly, and instability. Parkinson's disease is the original (archetypal) disease treated using neurotransplantation. Researchers expect that lessons learned in treating Parkinson's disease will likely guide future therapies for other disease entities.

Parkinson's disease involves the gradual deterioration of nerve centers within the brain that coordinate movement through the action of two neurotransmitters, dopamine and acetylcholine. Because the medulla of the adrenal gland produces epinephrine and norepinephrine (similar to dopamine), many researchers believe that the transplanted tissue corrects this dopamine deficiency by either producing dopamine or somehow stimulating the degenerated areas of the brain to produce it. Following the adrenal transplant procedure, individuals tend to need less medication and experience less frequent incapacitation.

Description

There are two parts to the adrenal tissue implant procedure. Donor tissue (containing chromaffin cells) is first harvested from the adrenal medulla via abdominal surgery (using a transperitoneal surgical approach). The donor tissue is then implanted via stereotactic surgery, or sometimes via craniotomy, into the mesencephalon. Stereotactic brain surgery is minimally invasive and accurate unlike conventional, invasive brain surgery (craniotomy) that requires extensive opening of the skull and destruction of normal brain areas lying above the target area.

Stereotactic brain surgery uses computers to create 3-D images of the brain that guide surgeons allowing them to direct a needle or electrode precisely to the target. There are two types of stereotactic surgery, the frame-based version and the frameless version. In the frame-based version, a lightweight frame is attached to the head using local anesthesia. The head is imaged via CT, MRI, or angiography to identify the target in relation to the external frame. Any surgical tool the surgeon attaches to the head frame is calibrated to the 3-D coordinates of the target. In this way, the surgeon can approach the target with complete accuracy. In the newer frameless version, imaging markers are attached to the scalp to orient the surgeon in his approach. A new technique to identify the markers works with MRI and is called Magnetic Source Imaging.

Prognosis

A number of studies have shown that adrenal tissue implants can provide long-term improvement in the clinical symptomatology of individuals seriously disabled by Parkinson's disease and other diseases associated with palsy, rigidity, an absence of automatic movements such as writing legibly or speaking clearly, and instability. Other studies using similar techniques have failed to replicate these dramatic results.

Specialists

- Neurosurgeon

Work Restrictions / Accommodations

Individuals may need frequent breaks while at work. A designated place to rest for fatigue and a transfer to lighter duty work responsibilities are recommended. Activities that require lifting and carrying may also need to be restricted.

Comorbid Conditions

Pneumonia and injury from falls may lengthen disability.

Procedure Complications

Complications from the adrenal tissue transplant procedure include infection, inflammation of the pancreas (pancreatitis), profuse bleeding (hemorrhage), and postoperative high blood pressure (hypertension). The hypertension occurs because of the release of the hormone epinephrine from the adrenal glands during surgery. It has also been reported that individuals developed personality changes, altered sleep patterns, and delusions that may be due to altered levels of key brain neurotransmitters.

Factors Influencing Duration

Factors that may lengthen disability include the severity of the underlying Parkinson's disease, age of the individual, and trauma of the abdominal surgery itself in seriously affected Parkinsonian individuals.

Length of Disability

Duration of disability depends on severity of symptoms due to diagnosis (Parkinson's disease) and response to treatment.

Duration in Days

Job Classification	Minimum	Optimum	Maximum
Sedentary work	28	42	56
Light work	28	42	56
Medium work	42	63	84
Heavy work	70	84	Indefinite
Very Heavy work	70	84	Indefinite

References

Blackwell, David. Transplantation: A New Era in the Treatment of Parkinson's Disease. Indiana University School of Medicine: Terre Haute Center for Medical Education 05 Jan 2001 26 Feb 2001 <http://web.indstate.edu/thcme/anderson/Db.html>.

Popovic, J.R., and L.J. Kozak. National Hospital Discharge Survey: Annual Summary, 1998. National Center for Health Statistics 09 Sep 2000 23 Oct 2000 <http://www.cdc.gov/nchs/data/sr13_148.pdf>.

Adrenalectomy
Other names / synonyms: Adrenal Gland Removal
07.21, 07.3

Definition

An adrenalectomy is the complete or partial surgical removal of one or both adrenal glands. This procedure is done for pheochromocytoma or other tumors involving the adrenal glands, as well as for Cushing's syndrome.

The adrenal glands may be reached through several types of surgical approaches. Approaches include incision from the side (lateral approach), abdomen (abdominal approach), and back (posterior approach). An incision in the side of the body may be used when only one adrenal gland is to be removed. An abdominal or back incision may be used when both adrenal glands are being removed. This procedure involves hospitalization and general anesthesia. The adrenal glands can also be removed through a less invasive technique called laparoscopy. Through a small incision, fiber-optic cables are inserted so that the surgeon can see while specialized instruments are used to remove the tumor. This procedure is generally reserved for removal of benign (noncancerous) adrenal tumors.

The two adrenal glands, located on top of the kidneys, perform metabolic functions that are necessary for normal response to stress, trauma, and infections. The adrenal glands produce a variety of hormones. They produce cortisol, which helps to regulate metabolism of fats, carbohydrates, sodium, potassium, and protein. Cortisol is also used for anti-inflammatory purposes. Another hormone produced by the adrenal glands is aldosterone. Aldosterone causes sodium to be reabsorbed in the kidneys, which helps to regulate blood pressure, fluid volume, and blood chemistry through modulating levels of the electrolytes sodium and potassium. The other hormones produced by the adrenal glands are the androgen hormones, mainly testosterone and androstenedione (androsterone). As some of these hormones are vital, hormone replacement therapy may be necessary after adrenalectomy.

Reason for Procedure

An adrenalectomy may be performed for several reasons. This procedure is done to treat an over-secretion of adrenal hormones. The levels of the adrenal hormones must be maintained within a very small range for optimal health. Both underproduction and overproduction result in illness. Overproduction of adrenal hormones includes conditions known as primary hyperaldosteronism and Cushing's syndrome. Primary hyperaldosteronism is increased production of the hormone aldosterone, and Cushing's syndrome is increased production of the hormone cortisol. Abnormal production of these hormones may be due to a tumor. Adrenalectomy may also be performed to treat primary tumors arising in the adrenal glands, such as pheochromocytoma, which can also cause over-secretion of adrenal hormones. It may also be performed for treatment of tumors elsewhere in the body that are dependent on the adrenal hormones for growth, such as breast and prostate cancer.

Description

Before surgery, medications may be given to control output of adrenal gland hormones, and to control abnormal elevation in the blood pressure that may occur during surgical manipulation of the gland. Testing done before surgery usually includes blood and urine tests, kidney X-rays, and CT of the adrenal area.

Adrenalectomy may be performed in the hospital by a general surgeon by three different methods. General anesthesia is given by injection and inhalation, with an airway tube placed in the windpipe.

If the incision is to be made on the side of the body (lateral approach), the individual is positioned on the operating table lying with the operative side up. The site is cleansed with a surgical scrub solution and the individual is covered with surgical drapes. The incision is made between either the ninth and tenth ribs, tenth and eleventh ribs, or the eleventh and twelfth ribs, depending on the specific operative approach. The kidney and adrenal gland are exposed, and the adrenal gland is separated (dissected) from the kidney. The gland is removed after identification and clamping or clipping of the arterial and venous blood supplies. After removal of the gland, any bleeding is controlled (hemostasis) and the wound is closed.

For the abdominal approach, the individual is positioned lying on the back on the surgery table (supine). The abdomen is cleansed and surgical drapes are placed. An abdominal incision is made and the peritoneal cavity is opened. The adrenal glands are removed one at a time. Bleeding is again controlled, and the incision is closed.

For the posterior approach, the individual is positioned on the surgery table lying on the abdomen, with the surgical table slightly bent at the waist so that the person is in a "jackknife" position. The incision is made over the eleventh or twelfth rib. The kidney is exposed and positioned so that the adrenal gland can be approached. Blood vessels are identified and clipped for removal of the adrenal gland. Following removal of the gland and control of any bleeding, the incision is closed.

In all procedures, nearby organs are inspected to be certain that none were injured. At completion of the procedure, a dressing is applied. Tubes may be left in to allow drainage. Skin incisions are closed with stitches (sutures) or clips, which are usually removed in about 1 week.

Adrenalectomy for treatment of benign adrenal tumors, primary hyperaldosteronism, and Cushing's syndrome may also be performed using a laparoscopic procedure, in which the individual is positioned on their side. A series of small incisions, each about 1/4 to 3/4 of an inch, allows insertion of special instruments. One instrument instills air into the abdominal cavity so that the adrenal gland can be seen more easily with a fiber-optic camera. Long forceps and scissors are inserted through small incisions to dissect and remove adrenal tissue.

Prognosis

The outcome is generally good, with an average hospital stay of 7-10 days, and complete recovery from surgery in about 6 weeks, although it may be necessary to avoid vigorous exercise for about 3 months. The predicted outcome is reduction in output of the adrenal hormones. If both adrenal glands were removed, any production of adrenal hormones ceases, and life-long hormone replacement will be needed. Another predicted outcome of adrenalectomy is relief of hypertension that may have been due to increased production of adrenal hormones or an adrenal tumor. If the increase in adrenal hormones was due to the presence of an adrenal tumor, another outcome is complete absence of tumor.

Specialists

- Endocrinologist
- General Surgeon
- Internist
- Oncologist

Work Restrictions / Accommodations

Vigorous activity (heavy lifting or excessive pulling or stretching on the incision line) should be avoided for 3 months. Work restriction may be necessary if the job involves activities that would stress the incision, which might include occupations such as construction, heavy manufacturing, moving, or logging. Driving should be avoided for 1 week after surgery.

In the early postoperative period, heating pads or compresses may be helpful to relieve incisional pain, and the legs should be moved and elevated often to decrease the chance of blood clots (deep venous thrombosis). Daily activities, including work, should be resumed as soon as the individual is able.

Comorbid Conditions

Coexisting conditions that may affect recovery and lengthen disability include bilateral adrenal hyperplasia. Individuals with bilateral hyperplasia tend to have persistent disease even after the operation. Previous abdominal operations can make a laparoscopic adrenalectomy technically more difficult. Risk from surgery increases with age over 60, obesity, smoking, stress, poor nutrition, recent illness, alcoholism or other chronic illness, use of prescription medications or mind-altering drugs.

Procedure Complications

Complications that may occur during the procedure include potential life-threatening blood pressure abnormalities, including both blood pressure that is too high (hypertension) and blood pressure that is too low (hypotension). Postoperative wound infection, excessive bleeding, inadequate production of adrenal hormones, fluid retention, blood clots in the legs (deep venous thrombosis), and increased risk of life-threatening infections may also occur. Following the procedure, the blood sugar may drop abnormally low (hypoglycemia).

Factors Influencing Duration

Surgical complications and the type of work that the individual does may influence the length of disability. Following surgery, the individual is more likely to be disabled longer from strenuous work such as construction, heavy manufacturing, moving, or logging. Other factors include presurgical adrenal disease. If the procedure is performed for Cushing's syndrome, recovery can take months.

Length of Disability

Duration in Days			
Job Classification	Minimum	Optimum	Maximum
Sedentary work	21	28	42
Light work	21	35	42
Medium work	28	42	56
Heavy work	42	49	56
Very Heavy work	42	49	56

References

Fitzgerald, Paul A. "Endocrinology." Current Medical Diagnosis and Treatment, 39th ed. Tierney, Lawrence M., Stephen J. McPhee, and Maxine A. Papadakis, eds. New York: Lange Medical Books/McGraw-Hill, 2000. 1079-1151.

O'Connor, Daniel T. "Adrenal Medulla." Cecil Textbook of Medicine, 20th ed. Bennett, J. Claude, and Fred Plum, eds. Philadelphia: W.B. Saunders Company, 1996. 1253-1258.

Adult Respiratory Distress Syndrome

Other names / synonyms: Acute Respiratory Distress Syndrome, Congestive Atelectasis, Pump Lung, Shock Lung, Stiff Lung

518.5

Definition

Adult respiratory distress syndrome (ARDS) is the rapid onset of progressive respiratory failure caused by severe swelling in the lungs (pulmonary interstitial and alveolar edema), and diffuse alveolar damage, which usually develops within 2-4 days after an initiating trauma or illness. It is usually associated with other severe illnesses and the malfunction of other organs.

The condition is characterized by extensive lung inflammation and the abnormal accumulation of fluid in the lung tissue that is not associated with heart problems (noncardiogenic pulmonary edema), respiratory distress, pulmonary contusion, fat embolization, or inadequate oxygenation of the blood (hypoxemia).

ARDS may be precipitated by a variety of acute processes that either directly or indirectly injure the lung such as trauma, an infection in the blood (sepsis), bacterial or viral pneumonia, drug overdose, aspiration of gastric contents, acute hemorrhagic pancreatitis, inhalation of smoke or other toxic fumes, and shock which may be associated with extensive surgery and certain blood abnormalities.

The estimated incidence of ARDS in the US varies widely, ranging between 50,000 to 200,000 cases per year. ARDS has a fatality rate of about 50-60% despite supportive therapy including assisted respiration; fatality can vary based on pre-existing health, the age of the individual, and the severity of the condition causing the distress. It is a common problem in hospital intensive care units.

Specialists

- Critical Care Specialist
- Pulmonologist
- Infectious Disease Physician

Diagnosis

History: Individuals with ARDS complain of difficulty breathing (dyspnea). ARDS can follow a wide variety of pulmonary or nonpulmonary insults; other symptoms, if present, are usually related to the predisposing condition.

Physical exam: The exam findings are not disease-specific for ARDS, and include mottled or bluish complexion (cyanosis) due to decreased oxygen levels in the circulating blood, moist skin, labored breathing, excessively rapid shallow breathing (tachypnea), excessively rapid heartbeat (tachycardia), agitation, and lethargy followed by clouding of consciousness (obtundation). Listening with a stethoscope (auscultation) may detect crackles, rhonchi, or wheezes.

Tests: Lab studies will include sputum cultures and arterial blood gases (ABGs). Chest x-rays will be taken to check for the presence of infiltrates in both (bilateral) lungs. A pulmonary artery catheter may be placed. The classic series of tests to confirm a diagnosis of ARDS is a pulmonary arterial wedge pressure (PAWP), an alveolar oxygen pressure (PaO2), and fraction of inspired oxygen ratio (FiO2).

Treatment

Oxygenation must be maintained while the underlying cause of the lung injury is identified and corrected. Passing a tube (intubation) through the nose or mouth (endotracheal tube, or ETT) into the trachea is often required. Mechanical ventilation (respirator) or supportive breathing (positive end expiratory pressure, or PEEP) is usually necessary to support the damaged respiratory system. Medications (antibiotics, antivirals, antifungals) may be needed to treat infections. Management includes prevention of nutritional depletion, oxygen toxicity, superinfection, and renal failure.

Prognosis

The death rate for adult respiratory distress syndrome alone is approximately sixty percent. Non-survivors usually succumb to sepsis or multiple organ system failure. The death rate is proportionate to the number of failed organ systems. With four or more (including the lung), mortality is near one hundred percent. Except in severe cases, individuals who survive usually recover normal lung function with minimal, if any, persistent pulmonary symptoms; those who survive severe cases may suffer permanent pulmonary fibrosis and restrictive lung disease.

Differential Diagnosis

Other conditions that may present with similar symptoms include congestive heart failure, chronic obstructive pulmonary disease (COPD), aspiration pneumonia, bacterial pneumonia, immunocompromised pneumonia, viral pneumonia, hypervolemia, and smoke inhalation.

Work Restrictions / Accommodations

It is important to avoid smoke, fumes, dust, and any other irritant that could be inhaled while recovering from ARDS. Proper ventilation, masks, or respirators may be necessary. Inhaling extremely hot or extremely cold air can also trigger recurrence of symptoms. If the individual suffers from shortness of breath, a temporary or permanent reduction in the job's physical demands may be needed.

Comorbid Conditions

Existing conditions that may impact ability to recover and may further lengthen disability include cardiovascular problems, renal problems, and metastatic cancer.

Complications

Possible complications of this condition include tension pneumothorax, secondary bacterial superinfection of the lungs, and multiple organ system failure (especially renal failure).

Factors Influencing Duration

Factors that might influence the length of disability include the duration of disease prior to treatment, underlying cause of condition, type of treatment, response to treatment, and possible complications.

Length of Disability

Disability may be permanent.

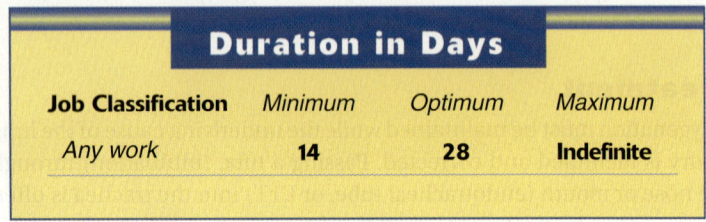

Job Classification	Minimum	Optimum	Maximum
Any work	14	28	Indefinite

Failure to Recover

If an individual fails to recover within the maximum duration expectancy period, the reader may wish to reference the following questions to assist in better understanding the specifics of an individual's medical case.

Regarding diagnosis:

- Does individual have difficulty breathing (dyspnea)?
- Although not disease-specific for ARDS, does individual have mottled or bluish complexion (cyanosis) due to decreased oxygen levels in the circulating blood, moist skin, labored breathing, excessively rapid shallow breathing (tachypnea), excessively rapid heartbeat (tachycardia), agitation, and lethargy followed by clouding of consciousness (obtundation)?
- Were sputum culture and arterial blood gases (ABGs) done? Chest x-ray? Were a pulmonary arterial wedge pressure (PAWP), an alveolar oxygen pressure (PaO2), and fraction of inspired oxygen ratio (FiO2) performed?
- Was diagnosis of adult respiratory distress syndrome confirmed?
- Were conditions with similar symptoms ruled out? Are sequelae (such as asthma) present?

Regarding treatment:

- Has underlying cause of the lung injury been identified? Is it responding to treatment?
- Were medications (antibiotics, antivirals, antifungals, corticosteroids) successful in resolving infection and reducing inflammation?
- Was culture and sensitivity done to identify the causative organism and determine the most effective medication?
- Were antibiotic-resistant organisms ruled out?
- If mechanical ventilation (respirator) or supportive breathing (positive end expiratory pressure, or PEEP) was necessary to support the damaged respiratory system, did complications occur when it was time to wean individual off the machine?

Regarding prognosis:

- Has normal lung function returned? Does individual have any residual pulmonary impairment?
- If condition was severe, was there permanent pulmonary fibrosis or restrictive lung disease? What impact does this have on individual's functional ability?
- Did complications develop such as tension pneumothorax, secondary bacterial superinfection of the lungs, or multiple organ system failure?

References

"Adult (Acute) Respiratory Distress Syndrome (ARDS)." American Lung Association 01 Jan 2001 20 Feb 2001 <http://www.lungusa.org/diseases/ards_factsheet.html>.

ARDS [adult respiratory distress syndrome]. HealthCentral.com 01 Jan 1998 A.D.A.M. Software, Inc. 01 Jan 2001 <http://www.healthcentral.com/mhc/top/000103.cfm>.

Afibrinogenemia

Other names / synonyms: Congenital Afibrinogenemia, Congenital Deficiency of Other Clotting Factors, Fibrinogen Deficiency

286.3

Definition

Afibrinogenemia is a rare, inherited bleeding disorder where blood cannot clot normally. Blood clotting depends on specific substances in the blood called clotting factors. Fibrinogen is a protein made by the liver and is one of these clotting factors. In afibrinogenemia, fibrinogen is absent in the blood due to a defect in its synthesis. Without fibrinogen, blood cannot clot normally when body tissue is injured.

Afibrinogenemia is an autosomal recessive disease. This means that an individual must inherit two genes (one from each parent) in order to be affected. Only 150 cases have been reported since the first case was documented in 1920. This disease equally affects men and women.

Diagnosis

History: Individuals may report a history of vomiting blood (hematemesis), blood in the stools (melena), prolonged menstrual bleeding, severe bleeding following trauma or surgery, and bleeding gums. In addition, there may be a history of spontaneous abortion and a general inability to carry a pregnancy full-term. Despite abnormal clotting, severe bleeding (hemorrhage) is less common than expected.

Physical exam: Gums may reveal evidence of bruising and bleeding. A small percentage of individuals have involvement of joints where bleeding occurs within the joint space (hemarthrosis). Poor wound healing may be observed. The individual may present with an episode of uncontrolled bleeding. A thorough history, including an accurate family history is essential for diagnosis.

Tests: Blood tests to check clotting (coagulation tests) are performed including prothrombin time (PT), partial thromboplastin time (PTT), and thrombin time (TT). A platelet count may show a mild reduction in the number of platelets. The most specific test for afibrinogenemia is a fibrinogen test, which measures the actual amount of fibrinogen in the blood. In this case, the test would reveal an absence of fibrinogen.

Treatment

Treatment involves replacing the missing fibrinogen with fibrinogen from transfused blood products. This is called fibrinogen replacement therapy (FRT). These blood products include plasma (the pale yellow liquid portion of whole blood) or cryoprecipitate (concentrate of clotting substances). FRT is given during times of acute bleeding, before surgery, or as a preventive measure during pregnancy. While receiving FRT, an individual's fibrinogen levels are monitored to check if they are adequate to prevent or stop bleeding.

As is the case for all individuals receiving blood products, individuals receiving FRT should also receive the complete series of hepatitis vaccinations as protection against the unlikely, but possible, transmission of hepatitis through blood products.

Prognosis

Afibrinogenemia is an incurable, lifelong condition. Individuals have a high incidence of hemorrhaging episodes. Bleeding, particularly intracranial bleeding is a common cause of death. With care and fibrinogen replacement therapy, however, life expectancy is normal.

Differential Diagnosis

Differential diagnoses include other fibrinogen abnormalities such as in liver disease or disseminated intravascular coagulation (DIC). Other bleeding disorders must be ruled out such as severe hypoprothrombinemia caused by a shortage of the clotting factor prothrombin, and Glanzmann thrombasthenia, an inherited bleeding disorder involving platelets.

Specialists

- Hematologist
- Internist

Work Restrictions / Accommodations

No work restrictions or accommodations are usually required with this condition. Care should be taken to ensure that the individual is working in a relatively safe environment. Where indicated, protective gear especially to the head should be worn. The employer should be aware of the condition so that the appropriate level of care can be obtained quickly in the event of an on-the-job injury.

Comorbid Conditions

Coexisting conditions that may impact recovery and lengthen disability include pregnancy and any other coagulation factor deficiencies.

Complications

Complications include unwanted blood clots in blood vessels.

Factors Influencing Duration

Surgery required for any condition increases the risk of severe or ongoing bleeding. Bodily injury particularly to the head can also precipitate a bleeding episode. Development of complications such as unwanted blood clots in blood vessels may prolong disability.

Length of Disability

No disability is expected unless bleeding occurs in response to surgery or trauma.

Failure to Recover

If an individual fails to recover within the maximum duration expectancy period, the reader may wish to reference the following questions to assist in better understanding the specifics of an individual's medical case.

Regarding diagnosis:

- Were differential diagnoses ruled out?
- Were coexisting conditions such as other coagulation factor deficiencies identified and addressed?
- Was diagnosis confirmed?
- If individual is pregnant, is physician working in conjunction with the OB-GYN specialist in regard to the treatment of afibrinogenemia and prevention of complications related to the pregnancy (bleeding during pregnancy, spontaneous abortion, general inability to carry the pregnancy to full-term)?

Regarding treatment:

- What type of replacement therapy is individual currently on? Normal plasma? Purified normal fibrinogen? Does it appear to be effective?
- Has individual continued to have bleeding episodes?
- Is change in therapy being considered?
- Was individual tested for antifibrinogen antibodies?
- What other treatment options can be considered?

Regarding prognosis:

- Does individual comprehend prognosis and is he/she able or willing to work with replacement therapy?
- Is individual aware of symptoms and diligent in reporting symptoms to physician?
- Can individual access appropriate level of care in case of emergency?

References

Kessler, Craig. "Coagulation Factor Deficiencies." Cecil Textbook of Medicine, 21st ed. Goldman, Lee, and J. Claude Bennett, eds. Philadelphia: W.B. Saunders Company, 2000. 1004-1012.

Ness, P.M., and H.A. Perkins. "Cryoprecipitate as a Reliable Source of Fibrinogen Replacement." Journal of the American Medical Association 241 16 (1979): 1690-1691.

Albuminuria

Other names / synonyms: Glomerular Proteinuria, Nephrotic Syndrome, Proteinuria
646.2, 791.0

Definition

Albuminuria is the presence of albumin in the urine and usually signifies a problem with kidney function. Albumin is a large protein found in the blood (serum albumin) and accounts for about 60% of the total protein. Hormones, drugs, and other substances can be carried throughout the bloodstream by attaching (binding) to albumin. The kidneys, in general, keep albumin and other proteins from seeping from the blood into the urine. When protein seeps into the urine (proteinuria), albumin accounts for about one-third of the total protein.

Albuminuria may occur in normal, healthy individuals standing and moving about (postural proteinuria), after strenuous exercise, during severe emotional stress, and after exposure to very cold temperatures such as a cold bath. It may also occur with high fever and dehydration.

The constant presence of a large amount of albumin is associated with kidney disease. It is also associated with complications of other diseases such as heart failure, diabetes mellitus, high blood pressure (hypertension), lupus (systemic lupus erythematosus), sickle cell disease, infection, preeclampsia, HIV, and rheumatoid arthritis.

Women may have trace amounts of albumin in the urine just before menstruation. Albuminuria may also occur immediately following delivery. In the US, approximately 4% of men and 7% of women will have a single positive test for albumin in their urine, but repeat testing shows a positive result in only 21% of the men and 7% of the women. Albuminuria that persists on repeat testing is more common with an increase in age partly because diseases causing albuminuria occur more frequently with aging.

Diagnosis

History: In general, individuals with albumin in the urine have no symptoms. Often, albuminuria is found when a urine test (urinalysis) is done as part of a routine physical examination. Some individuals have a history or symptoms of other medical conditions that increase the risk for albumin in the urine. These symptoms might include swelling (edema) of the feet, eyes, or genitals; cloudy, red, or frothy urine; joint discomfort; fever, night sweats, or weight loss.

Physical exam: The physical exam is typically normal, although there may be evidence of associated diseases with findings of heart disease, high blood pressure, swelling, rash, enlarged organs or lymph nodes, or joint deformities.

Tests: Albumin in the urine is determined either through a random routine urinalysis or a 24-hour urine test. A random routine urinalysis may be performed on a urine sample at any time. The three main components of a routine urinalysis are visual assessment of the appearance of the urine, testing with a special strip of paper (dipstick) dipped into the urine sample to determine the presence and amount of key urinary components, and microscopic examination of the urine. Albumin is identified with the dipstick (albumin is the only protein that can be identified with a dipstick). If there is more than a trace amount of albumin or if it is present on repeated testing, a 24-hour urine test may be performed by collecting all urine produced during a 24-hour period. This type of test allows measurement of various urine components including the amount of albumin. An ultrasound or biopsy of the kidneys may be done to identify problems in the kidney.

Other tests may be performed to identify possible conditions that are causing albumin in the urine. These conditions may be diabetes (glucose tolerance test, 2-hour postprandial glucose test, random blood glucose level), kidney disease (creatinine, blood urea nitrogen, x-rays called IVP of the urinary tract, kidney biopsy), or other medical diseases such as high blood pressure and heart failure.

Treatment

High blood pressure should be treated and brought to normal levels preferably less than 125/75. Angiotensin-converting enzyme inhibitors (ACE inhibitors) and angiotensin receptor antagonists reduce the amount of albumin in the urine independent of their effect on blood pressure. Any underlying or associated medical conditions should also be treated. Previous treatments considered such as albumin injected into the veins, treatment of high blood lipids or fats (hyperlipidemia) that can accompany albuminuria, and anticoagulation are now considered controversial and no longer recommended.

Prognosis

The outcome depends on the cause, duration, and severity of albuminuria. The presence of an occasional trace amount of albumin (microalbuminuria) is not associated with damage to the kidneys. In about half the individuals with albuminuria, the presence of albumin in the urine disappears in a few years without any damage to the kidneys. If albuminuria is due to an underlying disease, the kidneys may stop functioning adequately (kidney failure). Loss of kidney function occurs when there is kidney damage caused by an underlying disease such as diabetes or lupus. Individuals with high blood pressure and albuminuria have an increased risk of developing heart disease.

Differential Diagnosis

Albuminuria is a laboratory finding. Any condition associated with albuminuria must be included in the differential diagnosis. These conditions include kidney disease, diabetes, congestive heart failure, infection, lupus (systemic lupus erythematosus), multiple myeloma, sickle cell disease, HIV, rheumatoid arthritis, use of certain medications, and some types of cancer.

Specialists

• Internist	• Nephrologist

Work Restrictions / Accommodations

Work restrictions or accommodations are determined based on the underlying condition.

Comorbid Conditions

Albuminuria is a laboratory finding and may be the result of an underlying disease that causes damage to the kidneys. Recovery and disability are dependent on the severity and progression of the underlying disease.

Complementary and Alternative Therapies

Content is intended for awareness only. Treatments may or may not be effective. Scientific evidence may be lacking and some substances have potentially toxic effects. Dr. Presley Reed and the editors do not endorse the use of these therapies in the absence of consultation with a licensed medical professional.

Diet modification - Individuals with persistent albuminuria and fluid overload should be on a salt-restricted diet. Restriction of protein in the diet is controversial. While protein restriction may slow down deterioration of kidney function, it may also increase the risk of malnutrition. Most kidney specialists recommend either no restriction of protein in the diet or mild restriction to 0.8-1.0 g/kg/day.

Complications

There are no complications from occasional trace albuminuria (microalbuminuria). Any complications are due to persistent albuminuria or an underlying disease. Blood fats (lipids) may be elevated in individuals with albuminuria, and this condition (hyperlipidemia) does not tend to improve with dietary measures or specific medications. Hyperlipidemia, however, usually improves when the albuminuria is resolved.

Most individuals with albuminuria tend to leak the type of proteins into the urine that normally inhibit blood clotting and as a result, these individuals may have an increased risk for stroke, heart attack, or blood clots. Leakage into the urine of substances that normally fight infection (immunoglobulins) make individuals with albuminuria more vulnerable to bacterial infection. Loss of albumin into the urine makes it more likely that fluid will seep out of the blood vessels and into the body tissues. If this occurs in the lungs (pulmonary edema), there may be significant difficulty breathing and getting enough oxygen into the blood. Kidney failure and increased risk of heart disease are also possible complications of albuminuria.

Factors Influencing Duration

There are no factors that would influence length of disability.

Length of Disability

This is a vague diagnosis. Duration depends on the underlying condition.

Failure to Recover

If an individual fails to recover within the maximum duration expectancy period, the reader may wish to reference the following questions to assist in better understanding the specifics of an individual's medical case.

Regarding diagnosis:

- Is microalbuminuria or albuminuria due to an underlying disease that is impairing kidney function?
- Were blood fats elevated?
- Was a random routine urinalysis or a 24-hour urine test performed?

Regarding treatment:

- Can progression of the underlying disease be slowed with medical treatment such as adequate control of hyperglycemia and blood pressure in diabetics?

Regarding prognosis:

- Will the underlying medical condition result in renal failure necessitating dialysis or transplantation?
- Is blood pressure under control?
- Has individual experienced any complications?

References

Cutler, Ralph E. "Genitourinary Disorders." The Merck Manual, 17th ed. Beers, Mark H., and Robert Berkow, eds. Whitehouse Station, NJ: Merck Research Laboratories, 1999. 1803-1814.

Lieber, Joseph J. "Proteinuria." Saunders Manual of Medical Practice. Rakel, Robert E Philadelphia: W.B. Saunders Company, 2000. 690-693.

Alcohol and Drug Detoxification and Rehabilitation

Other names / synonyms: Alcohol or Substance Abuse Rehabilitation, Alcohol Withdrawal Protocol, Detox, Drug Treatment Program, Substance Abuse Detox Protocol, Substance Abuse Withdrawal Program

94.6, 94.61, 94.62, 94.63, 94.64, 94.65, 94.66

Definition

Alcohol and drug detoxification and rehabilitation is a medically supervised process of helping individuals through the withdrawal from an abused substance.

In situations where individuals have developed a physiological dependency on drugs of abuse such as alcohol, benzodiazepines, and opiates, a sudden withdrawal of the drug of abuse can lead to life-threatening symptoms. In these cases, medically supervised withdrawal is recommended. This process is sometimes referred to as a detoxification (or detox) program and can last for a few days (alcohol or heroin) to a few weeks (benzodiazepines). The individual does not need to be hospitalized or confined for the entire period, but does require some clinical supervision to monitor use of medications and possible side-effects from either the medications or the substance withdrawal. Some individuals may be admitted to a hospital or a specialized alcohol detoxification unit for the first few days of treatment, while others may be treated on an outpatient basis.

Treatment during the acute, or detoxification, phase requires close observation for at least 72-96 hours for the emergence of withdrawal symptoms. About one-third to one-half of individuals need medication therapy in the acute phase. This may include the use of benzodiazepines to decrease tremors and reduce or prevent increased blood pressure and heart rate, plus medications as needed for other symptoms, such as diarrhea or muscle aches. Folic acid, thiamin, and vitamin B_{12} are used to replace vitamin deficiencies.

Treatment for the one-month abstinence and early remission phases may include education on physical, emotional, and mental aspects of addiction and recovery, identification of stressors and stress management skills, improvement of coping skills, assertiveness training, and relaxation training. A narcotic antagonist such as naltrexone, which diminishes the effects of alcohol, or the drug Antabuse, which causes an individual to be intolerant of alcohol, can be used to help some individuals remain abstinent. In addition to professional treatment, many individuals are referred to self-help groups like Alcoholics Anonymous (AA) or Narcotics Anonymous (NA). The long-term support that self-help groups provide can be crucial in preventing relapse. An alternative to AA is Rational Recovery, a self-help group based on cognitive rather than spiritual principles.

Reason for Procedure

Sudden withdrawal of alcohol in an individual who has had excessive intake can lead to life-threatening symptoms (delirium tremens), and may require clinically supervised monitoring for safe withdrawal. A diagnosis of alcohol withdrawal is based on criteria listed in the DSM-IV-TR (Diagnostic and Statistical Manual of Mental Disorders, 4th Edition, Text Revision, published by the American Psychiatric Association). The criteria for alcohol withdrawal are that the individual has ceased using alcohol after heavy and prolonged use, has symptoms that cause clinically significant distress or impairment, and that the symptoms are not due to a general medical condition or other mental disorder. The individual should develop, within 4 to 72 hours of cessation of alcohol use, at least two of the following: evidence of autonomic hyperactivity such as sweating, fever, increased heart rate of greater than 100 beats per minute, or increased blood pressure; increased hand tremor; insomnia; gastrointestinal symptoms of nausea, vomiting, or diarrhea; transient episodes of seeing, feeling, or hearing things that aren't there (visual, tactile, or auditory hallucinations or illusions); psychomotor agitation; anxiety; and grand mal seizure.

Individuals undergoing benzodiazepine withdrawal are not quite as likely to develop sudden, life-threatening symptoms as those with alcohol withdrawal, but may still require clinical supervision for safe withdrawal. According to the DSM-IV-TR, criteria for benzodiazepine withdrawal are that the individual has ceased using benzodiazepines after heavy and prolonged use, has symptoms that cause clinically significant distress or impairment, and that the symptoms are not due to a general medical condition or other mental disorder. Benzodiazepine withdrawal symptoms are similar to alcohol withdrawal symptoms, with grand mal seizure a possibility in 20-30% of individuals undergoing untreated withdrawal. Individuals who have a dependence on benzodiazepines with longer-acting effects (half-life) may need several weeks before the acute withdrawal symptoms begin to abate.

The criteria for opiate withdrawal are that the individual has ceased using opiates, such as heroin or codeine, after heavy and prolonged use, has symptoms that cause clinically significant distress or impairment, and that the symptoms are not due to a general medical condition or other mental disorder. According to the DSM-IV-TR, individuals who suddenly cease use of opiates should meet three or more of the following criteria for withdrawal: depressed mood; nausea or vomiting; muscle aches; excessive tearing of the eyes or runny nose (lacrimation or rhinorrhea); enlarged (dilated) pupils, goosebumps (piloerection), or sweating; diarrhea; yawning; fever; and insomnia.

Many other drugs of abuse, such as cocaine, marijuana, or the amphetamines, do not require clinically supervised withdrawal protocols unless the individual has comorbid medical or psychiatric conditions.

Description

Recovery from alcohol dependence is described as occurring in four phases. The acute phase focuses on alleviating symptoms of physiological withdrawal, and typically lasts for 3 to 5 days. During the second phase, a one-month period of abstinence, the individual focuses on changing behaviors. The early remission phase can last up to 12 months, and the sustained remission phase lasts as long as the individual refrains from alcohol intake or from meeting the criteria for alcohol dependence.

The individual who meets the criteria for clinically supervised alcohol or drug detoxification can be monitored under several conditions. Some individuals are admitted to hospital medical, psychiatric, or chemical dependency units for observation and treatment, while others may be treated in detoxification facilities or on an outpatient basis. Nursing teams supported by a general medical practice may form an effective community-based detoxification program.

One effective method for inpatient treatment is to monitor the individual every two hours for developing symptoms of withdrawal, and to assign points for the severity of symptoms, based on a predetermined protocol. Points can be assigned for symptoms such as severity of hand tremor, fever, heart rate, elevated blood pressure, restlessness, sweatiness, nausea or vomiting, level of confusion, presence of auditory, visual, or tactile hallucinations, or seizure activity. Medication, usually one of the benzodiazepines, is given to about one-third to one-half of individuals based on severity of symptoms, and is gradually decreased as the symptoms decrease over a period of 72-96 hours. Supportive medications that may be used are antinausea medications, thiamine, and folic acid.

After the detoxification and alcohol withdrawal process has been completed, the individual can then be transitioned into a residential or outpatient substance abuse treatment program. A narcotic antagonist such as naltrexone, which diminishes the effects of alcohol, or the drug Antabuse, which causes an individual to be intolerant of alcohol, can be used to help some individuals remain abstinent. Medication therapy might include dopamine antagonists and/or antidepressants, as indicated by psychiatric or clinical evaluation.

Early remission treatment, which usually occurs in an outpatient setting, may include education on physical, emotional, and mental aspects of addiction and recovery, identification of stressors and stress management skills, improved coping skills, assertiveness training, relaxation training, or individual or family psychotherapy. Ongoing structured self-help programs such as Alcoholics Anonymous, Narcotics Anonymous, and Rational Recovery are recommended as an adjunct to treatment services. Regular but random drug screens may be part of the treatment process. It should also be understood that relapse may occur, and may even be part of the recovery process.

Prognosis

The outcome for most individuals who undergo clinically supervised alcohol or drug detoxification is marked improvement. Alcohol withdrawal symptoms usually subside within 4-7 days, although some symptoms, such as insomnia and anxiety, may persist for up to six months. In a study comparing short (less than 7 days) and long-term (15-28 days) residential rehabilitation, outcome was not significantly different in the two groups. If the individual remains abstinent, with or without further rehabilitation, the outlook for remission is positive.

However, if the individual relapses and continues with excessive, prolonged use of alcohol, benzodiazepines, or opiates such that the individual meets the criteria for substance dependence, any sudden cessation of the substance will require alcohol or drug detoxification again.

Most treated individuals can eventually stop their compulsive substance use and abstain from abused substances entirely, or experience only brief episodes of substance use that do not progress to abuse or dependence. Only 15-29% exhibit a pattern of chronic relapse requiring repeated intervention. Of those who remain abstinent for 2 years, almost 90% are substance-free at 10 years, and those who remain substance-free for 10 years have a very high likelihood (over 90%) of being substance-free at 20 years.

Individuals with lower levels of coexisting psychological disorders, who are able to develop new relationships, and who consistently make use of self-help groups are more likely to experience continued abstinence, accompanied by improvement in social and occupational functioning. Most experts agree that addicts need to do more than just "kick their habits." For lasting recovery, they need to think about rebuilding their lives, including finding meaning and motivation to move ahead.

Specialists

- Advanced Practice Registered Nurse
- Cardiologist
- Endocrinologist
- Gastroenterologist
- Neurologist
- Occupational Therapist
- Physical Therapist
- Psychiatrist
- Psychologist

Work Restrictions / Accommodations

Many employers have systems in place for individuals recovering from alcohol dependence disorders to return to work under special contracts or conditions. These conditions may provide guidelines for testing blood and urine levels of identified substances, for evaluating work performance, and for treating substance abuse in the recovering individual.

Temporary work accommodations may include reducing or eliminating activities where the safety of self or others is contingent upon a constant and/or high level of alertness, such as driving motor vehicles, operating complex machinery, or handling dangerous chemicals; introducing the individual to new or stressful situations gradually under individually appropriate supervision; allowing some flexibility in scheduling to attend therapy appointments (which normally should occur during employee's personal time); promoting planned, proactive management of identified problem areas; and offering timely feedback on job performance issues. It will be helpful if accommodations are documented in a written plan designed to promote timely and safe transition back to full work productivity.

Comorbid Conditions

Coexisting conditions that may affect recovery and lengthen disability include psychiatric illness as well as the chemical dependency (dual diagnosis). These psychiatric illnesses include depression, bipolar affective disorder, anxiety disorders, personality disorders, schizophrenia, and posttraumatic stress disorder. Other physical conditions are related to the toxic effects of alcohol or the chemical substance on the brain and liver. For instance, an alcohol-damaged liver is less able to rid the body of toxic substances. Other comorbid conditions include pregnancy, diabetes, hypertension, and liver disease.

Procedure Complications

In the acute phase of withdrawal, the individual may experience grand mal seizures, delirium tremens, hallucinations, adverse reaction to medications (sedatives or benzodiazepines) used to treat tremors and anxiety, potentially dangerous changes in heart rhythm and rate or in blood pressure, or dehydration from vomiting or diarrhea. Long-term effects of abstinence from a particular addictive substance, such as alcohol, may include increased use of other addictive substances, especially nicotine and coffee.

Factors Influencing Duration

Length of disability is influenced by the duration and severity of alcohol or drug dependence, presence or absence of organ damage, any underlying mental illness, other substance abuse, motivation of the individual to stay sober, the individual's social support system, appropriateness of treatment choice, compliance with treatment, and adequacy of ongoing care.

Length of Disability

Maximum duration includes hospitalization. Disability may be permanent. Some individuals are never able to abstain from alcohol intake and do not experience any periods of remission. Individuals with opiate dependence typically have a more difficult time maintaining prolonged periods of remission.

Duration in Days

Job Classification	Minimum	Optimum	Maximum
Any work	14	28	42

References

Aubin, H.J., et al. "Changes in Cigarette Smoking and Coffee Drinking After Alcohol Detoxification in Alcoholics." Addiction 94 3 (1999): 411-416.

Hall, Laura Lee. "Making the ADA Work for People with Psychiatric Disabilities." Mental Disorder, Work Disability, and the Law. Bonnie, Richard J., and John Monahan, eds. Chicago: The University of Chicago Press, 1997. 241-280.

Alcohol Intoxication, Acute

Other names / synonyms: Alcohol Overdose, Drunkenness, Inebriation

303.0, 305.0

Definition

Alcohol intoxication, or being drunk, is a reversible condition caused by recent ingestion of alcohol. It may or may not be associated with alcohol abuse or dependence. Behavioral symptoms such as belligerence, mood swings, forgetfulness, difficulty concentrating, and impaired judgment are due to the physiological effects of alcohol on the central nervous system. The severity and number of symptoms vary widely, depending upon the individual's tolerance for and experience with alcohol, the amount of alcohol used and how quickly it is consumed, the individual's expectations of the effects of alcohol, and even the environment in which alcohol is used. Short-term intoxication of a few hours may be associated with talkativeness, disinhibition, or a sense of feeling elated or "high" (euphoria). When intoxication persists for days or weeks, symptoms may include depression, inattention to personal hygiene, or impaired memory. In general, an individual is able to metabolize 1 drink per hour, defined as 12 ounces of beer or wine cooler, 5 ounces of non-fortified wine, or 1.5 ounces of distilled spirits. Signs and symptoms of intoxication are generally more severe when blood alcohol levels are rising rather than falling. Acute alcohol intoxication is accompanied in varying degrees by slurred speech, incoordination, unsteady gait, fast, jerky sideways movements of the eyeball (nystagmus), impaired attention or memory, stupor, coma, or death.

Alcohol use is common in the US, with about 70% of men and 60% of women having consumed alcohol during the previous year. The highest prevalence (77%) is in those aged 26-34 years, with only modest differences in racial groups. Lifetime risk of alcohol abuse or dependence in the US is between ten to fifteen percent. In the emergency room setting, as many as 50% of trauma patients are under the influence of alcohol and/or other drugs.

Alcohol is a central nervous system depressant that works by affecting the physical and chemical properties of nerve cell membranes. It enhances the action of GABA, a chemical that inhibits spread of nerve impulses and inhibits the action of glutamate, a chemical that causes excitation of nerves by enhancing spread of nerve impulses.

Females generally develop higher blood alcohol concentrations than males when consuming equal amounts of alcohol per kilogram of body weight because of their higher body fat content and lower levels of alcohol dehydrogenase in the mucosal lining of the stomach. Elderly individuals may develop more severe levels of alcohol intoxication because of an age-related increased brain susceptibility to alcohol, decreased rates of liver metabolism, and decreased percentages of body water. Up to 50% of Asian (Japanese, Chinese, Korean) individuals may have an enzyme deficiency that reduces their risk of developing an Alcohol Use Disorder. Young adults who are not dependent on alcohol, but who have a family history of alcoholism, have less response to a given dose of alcohol than similar individuals with no family history of alcoholism. Surprisingly, it appears that individuals who have an increased genetic risk of alcoholism can "handle their liquor" better, or drink more, than those at lower risk.

Diagnosis

Diagnosis is based on criteria listed in the DSM-IV-TR (Diagnostic and Statistical Manual of Mental Disorders, 4th Edition, Text Revision, published by the American Psychiatric Association). Diagnosis requires behavioral changes that are maladaptive, such as disinhibition of sexual or aggressive impulses, mood swings (lability), impaired judgment, or impaired social or occupational functioning. These symptoms must be associated with recent ingestion of alcohol in sufficient quantity to produce intoxication. At least 1 of the following signs must be present: slurred speech, incoordination, unsteady gait, nystagmus, or flushed face. An individual who shows mild behavioral effects of alcohol within a socially acceptable and physically innocuous range does not meet criteria for the diagnosis.

History: The individual, or family, friends, or others, typically give a history of recent ingestion of alcohol over a fairly short period of time. This may or may not be the first alcohol intoxication for this individual. The individual with a first-time or infrequent alcohol intoxication may present with a different history than the individual with chronic or repeated episodes of intoxication. Repeated episodes may be associated with the symptoms and behaviors of Alcohol Abuse or Dependence, while first-time or infrequent users are at higher risk for the life-threatening consequences of severe intoxication. A thorough history of frequency, amount, and most recent alcohol use can help determine the individual's risk.

Physical exam: Physical evidence of Alcohol Intoxication includes the smell of alcohol on the breath or body, slurred speech, lack of coordination, unsteady gait, rapid movement of the eyes to one side (nystagmus), impairment in attention or memory, stupor, or coma. If the individual is not seen soon after acute ingestion, signs of withdrawal may be present. These may include tremors, sweating, increased blood pressure and heart rate, or nausea or vomiting. Mental status exam may demonstrate that the individual is confused or disoriented.

Tests: An elevated blood alcohol concentration (BAC) above zero indicates some level of ingestion, although there is considerable individual variation of the effects of alcohol intoxication, so that some users may become intoxicated at much lower BAC. At BAC of 0.02-0.03, there is a slight feeling of being "high" (euphoria) and loss of shyness. At 0.04-0.06 BAC, the "high" feeling intensifies, with relaxation, lower inhibitions, a sensation of warmth, minor impairment of reasoning and memory, and lowered caution. At 0.07-0.09 BAC, there is slight impairment of balance, speech, vision, reaction time, and hearing. Judgment and self-control are reduced, and caution, reason, and memory are impaired. Many states identify levels of 80 (80 mg/dL - milligrams per deciliter; BAC 0.08) as being legally intoxicated. At 0.10-0.125 BAC, there is significant impairment of motor coordination and loss of judgment. Speech may be slurred, and balance, vision, reaction time, and hearing are impaired. At 0.13-0.15 BAC, there is gross motor impairment, lack of physical control, blurred vision, and major loss of balance. Mood changes from "high" or euphoric to dysphoric, with the perception that things are unpleasant. At 0.16-0.20 BAC, there may be anxiety, restlessness, and nausea, and the drinker takes on the appearance of a "sloppy drunk." At 0.25 BAC, the drinker needs assistance in walking, and experiences total mental confusion, dysphoria, nausea, and some vomiting. He or she may also fall asleep. At BAC of 0.3, there is loss of consciousness, followed by coma and possibly even death at 0.4 BAC due to respiratory arrest. Other blood tests can detect the effects of alcohol on the liver and bone marrow, with elevated liver enzymes, high blood lipids, and an anemia showing large red blood cells (macrocytic cells).

Treatment

Initially, treatment is aimed at protecting the intoxicated individual from harming him or herself or others, which may require physical restraints or the use of sedatives. Identifying and treating medical problems that require immediate attention associated with acute alcohol intoxication is a first priority. Treatment may be as simple as allowing the individual to "sleep it off," if the blood alcohol level is low and the individual has no symptoms of withdrawal, or as complicated as admission to an Intensive Care Unit, if the individual is experiencing respiratory arrest or coma. In severe intoxication, the airway must be protected, and respiratory and circulatory function must be monitored and supported. Use of other depressant drugs, disturbances in blood chemistry, infection, and head trauma must all be ruled out, or treated appropriately if discovered. Wernicke-Korsakoff syndrome may complicate acute alcohol intoxication, and should be treated aggressively with intravenous thiamine to prevent irreversible damage to the nervous system.

Once the individual has recovered from acute intoxication, he or she may be sent home with family or friends and referred to an outpatient alcoholism treatment program and Alcoholics Anonymous. The individual should not be allowed to drive while under the influence. If social supports are inadequate, referral to an inpatient alcoholism detoxification facility should be considered. Inpatient detoxification is recommended if there is a history of complicated withdrawal, such as seizures or delirium tremens. Psychiatric hospitalization is recommended for suicidal or homicidal thoughts, psychotic symptoms such as hallucinations, or worsening of any underlying psychiatric condition.

Prognosis

Prognosis is correlated with the presence of chronic alcoholism. Prognosis is positive, in most instances, unless irreversible physiological and/or psychological damage occurs through overdose or persistent episodes of intoxication.

Differential Diagnosis

High blood sugar levels in diabetics (diabetic ketoacidosis) may cause the individual to be confused and disoriented and to have a fruity/acetonic breath odor, and can therefore be misidentified as being due to alcohol intake. Other conditions with similar symptoms are low blood sugar (hypoglycemia), various dementias, liver failure, and other substance abuse disorders, such as inhalant abuse or prescription drug abuse. Psychiatric or behavioral symptoms associated with acute alcohol intoxication may be confused with those seen in other psychiatric disorders, and alcohol intoxication may actually unmask symptoms of an underlying psychiatric condition.

Specialists

- Advanced Practice Registered Nurse
- Cardiologist
- Neurologist
- Occupational Therapist
- Physical Therapist
- Psychiatrist
- Psychologist

Work Restrictions / Accommodations

The necessity of work restrictions and accommodations is rare unless a long lasting physiological impact or persistent episodes of intoxication occur. Depending on the occupational and/or business requirements, some employers have systems in place for individuals recovering from alcohol use disorders to return to work under special contracts or conditions. These conditions may provide guidelines for testing blood and urine levels of identified substances, and work performance and substance abuse treatment guidelines for the recovering individual. Individuals who are intoxicated should not be in the work place until after detoxification.

Comorbid Conditions

Coexisting conditions that may affect recovery and lengthen disability include psychiatric disorders such as depression, anxiety disorders, bipolar affective disorder, personality disorders, schizophrenia and posttraumatic stress disorder. Concurrent substance abuse and the physical conditions related to the toxic effects of alcohol or drugs on the brain and liver can also affect disability. For instance, an alcohol-damaged liver is less able to rid the body of toxic substances. Underlying medical conditions complicated by alcohol abuse include pregnancy, diabetes, hypertension and liver disease.

Complications

Alcohol intoxication, especially in an intolerant individual, can lead to seizures, respiratory arrest, coma, or death. Sudden withdrawal of alcohol in someone who has had an excessive intake can lead to tremors, anxiety, agitation, hallucinations, grand mal seizures, or death. Wernicke-Korsakoff syndrome is a neurological condition caused by an acute deficiency of the vitamin thiamine, often related to acute and chronic alcohol use. Symptoms include confusion, profound short-term memory loss, incoordination, and abnormalities of eye movement (gaze palsies).

Excessive prolonged use of alcohol can damage the stomach lining (gastritis), esophagus (esophageal varices), liver (liver failure, cirrhosis), pancreas (pancreatitis), and heart (cardiomyopathy). Poor nutrition contributes to anemias and vitamin deficiencies. Prolonged alcohol intake is toxic to the nervous system, and can damage the nerves in the hands, lower legs, and feet (peripheral neuropathy). Brain function may be chronically impaired and can lead to short- and long-term memory impairment, disturbances of balance and coordination, or the loss of higher brain functions such as judgment, abstract thinking, and language. Psychosocial consequences, such as loss of relationships and employment; legal consequences, such as arrests for "driving under the influence," motor vehicle accidents; violence; and suicide can be consequences of alcoholism. Heavy drinking during pregnancy can result in fetal alcohol syndrome.

Factors Influencing Duration

The amount of alcohol consumed, duration of consumption and the amount of time passed since the last ingestion can determine the course of alcohol metabolism, blood alcohol concentration, and resulting symptoms. Individuals vary considerably in their individual tolerance to the effects of alcohol. During the time the individual is intoxicated, there can be severe physiologic changes in the body. This can alter electrolytes, cardiac output, cerebral blood flow, and availability of oxygen to the brain. Cardiac arrhythmias may hasten myocardial infarction and cerebrovascular accidents. Long duration of intoxication (binge) can often lead to infections, pneumonia, and malnutrition.

Length of Disability

Duration table reflects recovery period from acute effects of alcohol. Length of disability is influenced by the duration and severity of alcohol use/abuse, presence or absence of organ damage, any underlying mental illness, other substance abuse, the individual's social support system, appropriateness of treatment choice, compliance with treatment, and adequacy of ongoing care. Unless there is a psychosis or severe physical illness present, there is no reason that an already employed individual should not be allowed to continue to work following recovery from acute intoxication provided no other physical affects are present. No one should be permitted to work under influence of alcohol.

Uncomplicated alcohol intoxication.

Duration in Days

Job Classification	Minimum	Optimum	Maximum
Any work	1	1	3

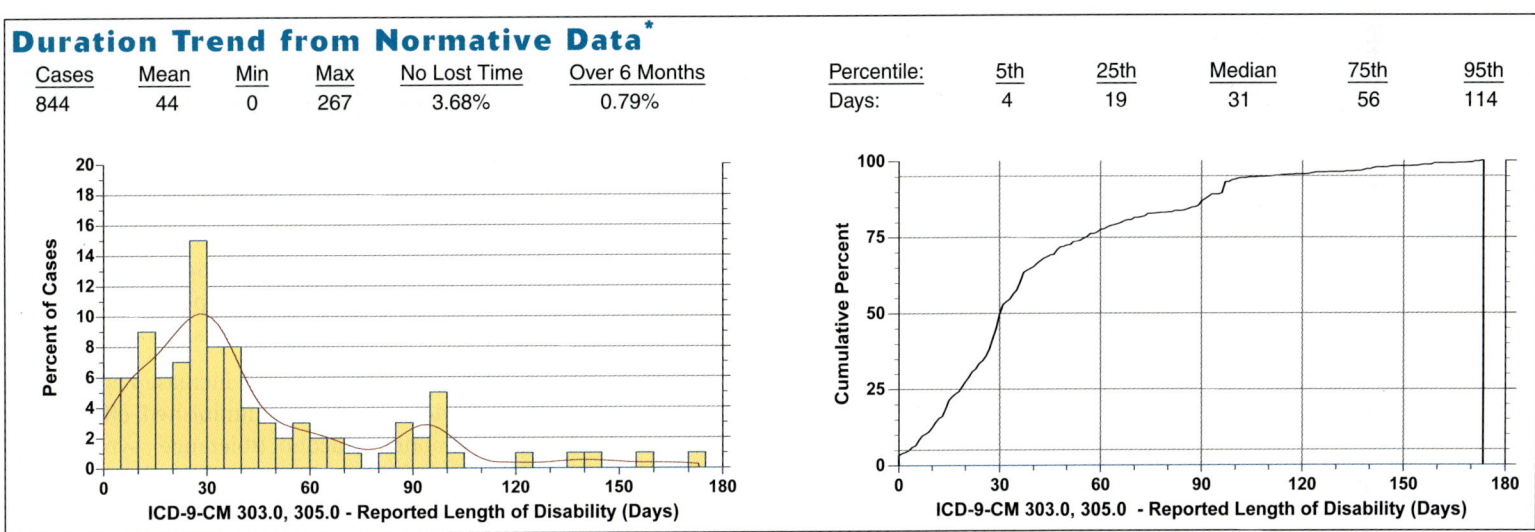

* Differences may exist between the expected duration tables and the normative graphs. Duration tables provide expected recovery periods based on the type of work performed by the individual. The normative graphs reflect the actual observed experience of many individuals across the spectrum of physical conditions, in a variety of industries, and with varying levels of case management.

Failure to Recover

If an individual fails to recover within the maximum duration expectancy period, the reader may wish to reference the following questions to assist in better understanding the specifics of an individual's medical case.

Regarding diagnosis:

- Was diagnosis of acute alcohol intoxication confirmed?
- Was this an isolated event or was there a history of alcohol intoxication?
- How frequently were the episodes occurring? For how long?
- Does each drinking episode result in intoxication?
- How much alcohol does individual estimate he or she consumes before becoming intoxicated?
- Did any medical complications result from the intoxication?
- Were any other chemical dependencies identified? Was each appropriately addressed?
- Were all underlying conditions, physical and psychiatric, identified? How do they affect treatment or prognosis?

Regarding treatment:

- Did individual make an uncomplicated recovery from the acute effects of alcohol?
- What further treatment is indicated?
- If complications occurred, how were they treated?
- Have they now been resolved?
- If concurrent chemical abuse was also identified, is appropriate treatment being applied to each issue?
- Are psychiatric illnesses complicating treatment?

Alcohol Intoxication, Acute

- Are these illnesses being addressed with regard to overall treatment?
- Is individual able to safely and consistently follow the treatment regimen?
- Is individual being treated on an inpatient or outpatient basis?
- Would individual benefit from a more supervised, structured treatment plan or an in-house treatment program?

Regarding prognosis:

- Did individual make appreciable progress within the treatment modality?
- Do any complications remain?
- What additional treatment(s) may be warranted?
- What are individual's social supports?
- Is there a functional support system in place? Family? Friends? Church or other community affiliations? Are these being utilized?
- Is individual involved in a local support group?
- If alcohol intoxication is an ongoing or frequent habit, how is it being addressed?
- How are current stresses being dealt with?
- How were major stresses dealt with in the past?
- If healthy and adaptive methods were used in the past, are they being used currently?
- What is happening outside of work that may be contributing to or worsening the problems experienced at work?
- What is being done to motivate individual towards rebuilding a functional, meaningful life?

References

Duke, James A. The Green Pharmacy. Emmaus, PA: Rodale Press, Inc, 1997.

Gottlieb, Bill, ed. New Choices in Natural Healing. Emmaus, PA: Rodale Press, Inc, 1995.

Alcoholism

Other names / synonyms: Alcohol Abuse, Alcohol Addiction, Alcohol Dependence, Alcohol Dependence Syndrome
303, 303.9, 303.90

Definition

Alcoholism or alcohol dependence occurs when an individual continues to use alcohol despite significant alcohol-related physical, emotional, relational, legal, or occupational problems. There is a strong need or compulsion to drink and it becomes difficult for the individual to stop drinking once begun. Repeated use results in the need for increased amounts over time in order to achieve intoxication (tolerance). Repeated heavy use also results in physiological and cognitive changes with decreasing blood and brain tissue concentration of alcohol known as withdrawal. Failure to abstain from using alcohol despite having difficulty associated with its use is referred to as compulsivity.

It is estimated that about 50% of the risk for alcohol dependence can be explained by genetic factors with the risk being 3 to 4 times higher in close relatives of individuals with alcoholism. The genetic predisposition may involve physical differences in liver enzymes or in chemicals within the nervous system that carry messages between nerve cells. Other risk factors may include cultural attitudes toward drinking and intoxication, the availability of alcohol, acquired personal experiences, and stress. Some cultures such as the Asian population show low prevalence rates. This may be related to a deficiency of an enzyme used in the metabolism of alcohol. In the US, whites and blacks have similar rates of alcohol dependency.

In the US, between 75-90% of the adult population have consumed alcohol at some time in their lives with alcoholism occurring in about 5% of the population. Nearly 14 million Americans or 1 in every 13 adults abuses alcohol or is an alcoholic. An additional 10 million are problem drinkers who may develop alcoholism. Most individuals who develop alcohol dependence do so by their late thirties. Between one-third to one-half of all alcoholics are women.

Diagnosis

History: The diagnosis is based on criteria listed in the DSM-IV-TR (Diagnostic and Statistical Manual of Mental Disorders, 4th Edition, Text Revision published by the American Psychiatric Association). There is a history of regular, often daily, alcohol intake over a period of time with withdrawal symptoms occurring within 4 to 12 hours of the last drink.

Diagnostic criteria include: a need for markedly increased amounts of alcohol to achieve intoxication (tolerance); diminished effects with continued use of the same amount of alcohol (tolerance); symptoms of withdrawal such as tremors, increased blood pressure or heart rate, cravings, sweating, diarrhea, or fever; persistent unsuccessful attempts to quit or control alcohol intake; a great deal of time spent in activities related to the use of or recovery from the use of alcohol; social, occupational, recreational, or relational activities given up for the sake of alcohol use; and continued alcohol use despite knowledge of recurrent physical or psychological problems related to its use

Diagnosis depends on the individual demonstrating at least 3 or more of these criteria at any time in the same 12-month period. Other symptoms noted on the history may include disturbing memory lapses (blackouts), poor appetite, heartburn, nausea, gas, decreased sex drive, and insomnia.

Physical exam: The exam may reveal signs of withdrawal such as tremors, sweating, increased blood pressure, or increased heart rate. Examination by gently pressing on the abdomen (palpation) may detect an enlarged liver or a small hard liver. The palms may be red (palmar erythema). Mental status exam may demonstrate that the individual is confused or disoriented. Neurological examination may show impaired gait and balance (cerebellar ataxia) or decreased vibration sense in the hands and feet (peripheral neuropathy).

Tests: An elevated blood glutamyl transferase is a good indicator for alcoholism. An elevated blood alcohol level without signs of intoxication indicates alcohol tolerance. Other blood tests can detect the effects of alcohol on the liver and bone marrow with elevated liver enzymes, high blood lipids, and anemia with large red blood cells (macrocytosis). Psychological testing may also be done as it can offer useful insights into underlying comorbid psychopathology in the individual.

Treatment

Recovery from alcoholism occurs in four phases. The first phase is an acute, detoxification phase that focuses on alleviating symptoms of physiological withdrawal and typically lasts for 3 to 5 days. The second phase is a 1-month period of abstinence during which the individual focuses on changing behaviors. The third phase is an early remission phase that can last up to 12 months. The fourth phase is a sustained remission phase that lasts as long as the individual abstains from alcohol intake or from meeting the criteria for alcoholism.

Treatment during the acute phase requires close observation for at least 72 to 96 hours for the emergence of withdrawal symptoms. Medication therapy in the acute phase includes the use of benzodiazepines to decrease tremors and reduce or prevent increased blood pressure and heart rate in addition to medications for other symptoms (e.g., diarrhea or muscle aches). Folic acid, thiamin, and vitamin B_{12} are used to replace vitamin deficiencies. Some individuals may be admitted to a hospital or a specialized alcohol detoxification unit for the first few days of treatment while others may be treated on an outpatient basis.

Treatment for the 1-month abstinence and early remission phases may include education on physical, emotional, and mental aspects of addiction and recovery, identification of stressors and stress management skills, improved coping skills, assertiveness training, and relaxation training. A narcotic antagonist such as naltrexone that diminishes the effects of alcohol or the drug Antabuse that causes an individual to be intolerant of alcohol can be used to help some individuals remain abstinent. In addition to professional treatment, many individuals are referred to self-help groups like Alcoholics Anonymous (AA). The long-term support that self-help groups provide can be crucial in preventing relapse.

An alternative to AA is Rational Recovery, a self-help group based on cognitive rather than spiritual principles. Because rehabilitated alcoholics are in danger of relapsing from even a single drink, successful rehabilitation requires total abstinence that is usually accomplished "one day at a time." Marital counseling and family support are often needed for long-term stability and resolution of codependency problems.

Prognosis

There are a significant number of individuals who respond to treatment and stay in remission from alcohol dependence for many years. However, there are individuals who experience periods of relapse where they begin alcohol intake after a period of remission and again meet the criteria for alcohol dependence. Other individuals are never able to abstain from alcohol intake and do not experience any periods of remission. The complications of alcoholism are serious, life-threatening, and potentially fatal especially if untreated.

Outcome is improved if the individual seeks treatment early in the disease process and has adequate social support systems in place. However, a significant number of individuals experience at least one relapse after treatment and some individuals (50%) never seek treatment.

Differential Diagnosis

High blood sugar levels in diabetics (diabetic ketoacidosis) where the individual may be confused and disoriented and have a fruity/acetonic breath odor can be misdiagnosed as alcohol intoxication. Other conditions with similar symptoms are low blood sugar (hypoglycemia), various dementias, liver failure, and other substance abuse disorders such as inhalant abuse or prescription drug abuse.

Specialists

- Advanced Practice Registered Nurse
- Cardiologist
- Endocrinologist
- Gastroenterologist
- Neurologist
- Occupational Therapist
- Physical Therapist
- Psychiatrist
- Psychologist

Rehabilitation

Once acute withdrawal is over and the individual has successfully completed alcohol detoxification, rehabilitation begins during hospitalization or with frequent outpatient visits. It involves ongoing medical monitoring, nutritional therapy, moderate physical exercise, education about alcoholism, and introduction to a 12-step self-help support group.

In addition to substance abuse treatment and support groups, physical therapy may be helpful if the individual has chronic problems with gait and balance or has become deconditioned due to inactivity during the period of addiction and early recovery. Occupational therapy assists the individual in developing communication skills, identifying and matching personal skills and work habits to the work place, and learning how nonalcohol-related participation in leisure activities contributes to overall health and well being. Supportive therapies include expressive therapies (art, music, or dance therapy), relaxation techniques, or breath therapy and may be helpful to decrease stress levels that can increase risk of relapse.

Complementary and Alternative Therapies

Content is intended for awareness only. Treatments may or may not be effective. Scientific evidence may be lacking and some substances have potentially toxic effects. Dr. Presley Reed and the editors do not endorse the use of these therapies in the absence of consultation with a licensed medical professional.

Acupuncture - May help to decrease cravings, reduce withdrawal symptoms, relieve tension, and help in relaxation.

Biofeedback - May increase awareness and control of physical processes in the body.

Visualization and psychodrama - Said to facilitate insight into the addiction.

Work Restrictions / Accommodations

Many employers have systems in place for individuals recovering from alcohol dependence disorders to return to work under special contracts or conditions. These conditions may provide guidelines for random testing of blood and urine levels of identified substances and provide work performance and substance abuse treatment guidelines for the recovering individual.

Temporary work accommodations may include reducing or eliminating activities where the safety of self or others is contingent upon a constant and/or high level of alertness, such as driving motor vehicles, operating complex machinery, or handling dangerous chemicals; introducing the individual to new or stressful situations gradually under individually appropriate supervision; allowing some flexibility in scheduling to attend therapy appointments (which normally should occur during employee's personal time); promoting planned, proactive management of identified problem areas; and offering timely feedback on job performance issues. It will be helpful if accommodations are documented in a written plan designed to promote timely and safe transition back to full work productivity.

If individuals have chronic side effects of prolonged alcohol intake such as cardiac, liver, or nervous system damage, they may need restriction to sedentary type activities. Certain jobs such as a bartender, hostess, or entertainer may involve exposure to alcohol and increase the risk of relapse.

Comorbid Conditions

Coexisting conditions that may affect recovery and lengthen disability include psychiatric disorders such as depression, anxiety disorders, bipolar affective disorder, personality disorders, schizophrenia, and posttraumatic stress disorder. Coexisting conditions may also include other chemical substance abuse disorders and the physical conditions related to the toxic effects of alcohol or the chemical substance on the brain and liver. For example, an alcohol-damaged liver is less able to rid the body of toxic substances. Medical conditions that are complicated by alcohol abuse include pregnancy, diabetes, hypertension, and liver disease.

Complications

Sudden withdrawal of alcohol in someone who has had excessive, regular intake can lead to tremors, anxiety, agitation, hallucinations, grand mal seizures, or death. Excessive prolonged use of alcohol can damage the stomach lining (gastritis), esophagus (esophageal varices), liver (liver failure, cirrhosis), pancreas (pancreatitis), and heart (cardiomyopathy). Poor nutrition contributes to anemias and vitamin deficiencies. Alcoholism leads to increased risk of certain cancers involving the liver, esophagus, throat, and voice box (larynx). Prolonged alcohol intake is toxic to the nervous system, and can damage the nerves in the hands, lower legs, and feet (peripheral neuropathy). Brain function may be chronically impaired and can lead to short and long-term memory impairment, disturbances of balance and coordination, or the loss of higher brain functions such as judgment, abstract thinking, and language.

The B vitamin thiamin is depleted in alcoholics. This deficiency can lead to a neurological disorder characterized by abnormalities in eye movements and loss of short-term memory (Wernicke-Korsakoff syndrome). Psychosocial consequences such as loss of relationships and employment, legal consequences such as arrests for "driving under the influence," motor vehicle accidents, violence, and suicide can be consequences of alcoholism. Job performance and child-care or household responsibilities may decline or be neglected. Anxiety related to drinking or to withdrawal may lead to abuse of anxiolytic medications or other mind-altering drugs. Heavy drinking during pregnancy can result in fetal alcohol syndrome, an incurable condition in the baby characterized by stunted growth, physical abnormalities, and mental retardation.

Factors Influencing Duration

Length of disability is influenced by the duration and severity of alcohol dependence, presence or absence of organ damage, any comorbid mental illness, other substance abuse, the individual's social support system, appropriateness of treatment choice, compliance with treatment, and adequacy of ongoing care.

Length of Disability

No one should be permitted to work under influence of alcohol. Maximum duration includes hospitalization.

Uncomplicated alcoholism.

Duration in Days

Job Classification	Minimum	Optimum	Maximum
Any work	7	28	42

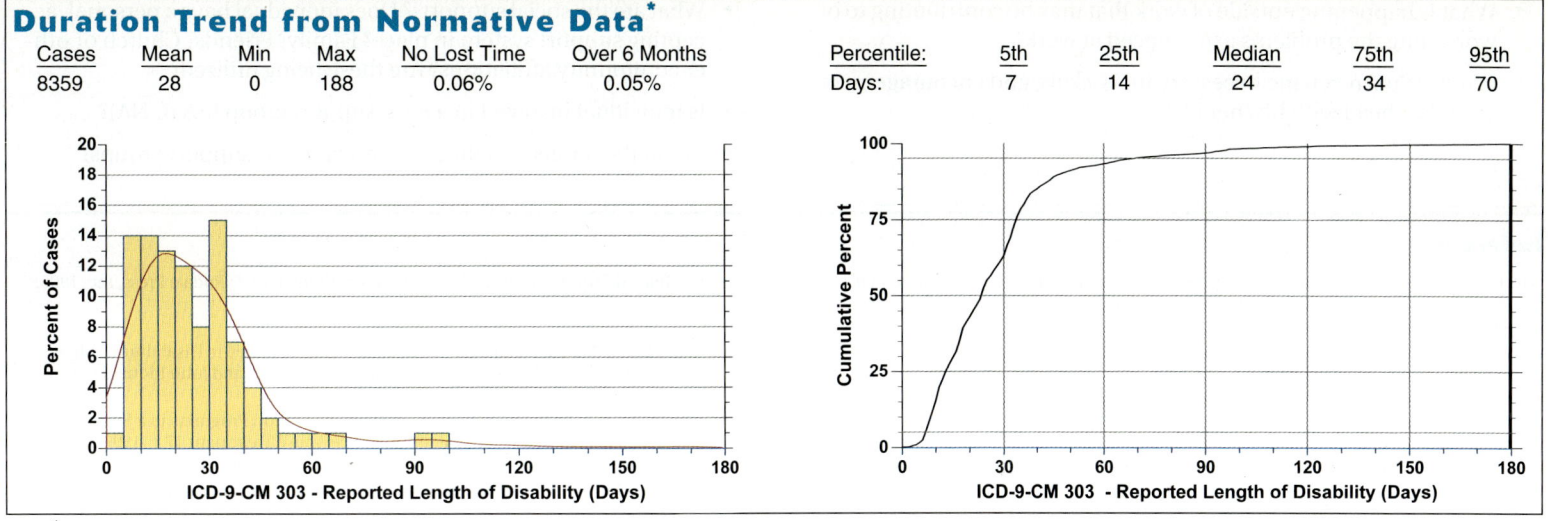

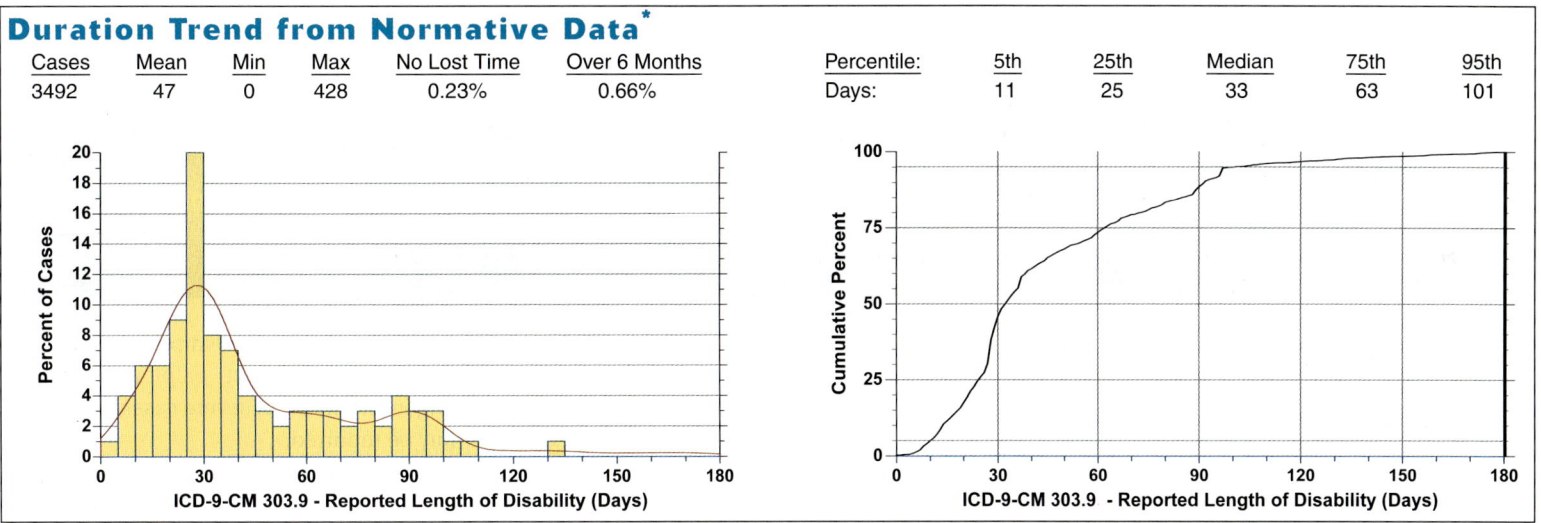

* Differences may exist between the expected duration tables and the normative graphs. Duration tables provide expected recovery periods based on the type of work performed by the individual. The normative graphs reflect the actual observed experience of many individuals across the spectrum of physical conditions, in a variety of industries, and with varying levels of case management.

Failure to Recover

If an individual fails to recover within the maximum duration expectancy period, the reader may wish to reference the following questions to assist in better understanding the specifics of an individual's medical case.

Regarding diagnosis:

- Was diagnosis of alcoholism confirmed? Alcohol abuse? Alcohol dependence?
- What is individual's drinking pattern?
- What medical complications resulted?
- Were any other chemical dependencies identified?
- Was each one appropriately addressed?
- Were all underlying conditions, physical and psychiatric, identified?
- How do they impact treatment or prognosis?

Regarding treatment:

- Was alcohol detoxification considered successful?
- Have other medical complications and nutritional deficiencies received treatment?
- If concurrent chemical abuse was also identified, is appropriate treatment being applied to each issue?
- Are psychiatric illnesses complicating treatment? Are these illnesses being addressed in regard to overall treatment?
- Is individual able to safely and consistently follow treatment regime?
- Is individual receiving treatment on an inpatient or outpatient basis?
- Would individual benefit from a more supervised, structured treatment plan or an in-house treatment program?

Regarding prognosis:

- Does individual appear to be making appreciable progress within current treatment modality?
- How are current stresses being dealt with?
- How were major stresses dealt with in the past?
- If healthy and adaptive methods were used in the past, are they being used currently?

Alcoholism

- What is happening outside of work that may be contributing to or worsening the problems experienced at work?
- Is individual receiving necessary tools, skills, and encouragement to move ahead with his/her life?
- What are the social supports? Does individual have a personal, accepting support system in place? Family? Friends? Church or other community affiliations? Are these being utilized?
- Is individual involved in a local support group (AA or NA)?
- Could the family benefit from education or support groups?

References

Doria, John, et al. "From Genes to Geography: The Cutting Edge of Alcohol Research." Alcohol Alert 48 (2000): 6. 03 Jan 2001 <http://silk.nih.gov/silk/niaaa1/publication/aa48.htm>.

Duke, James A. The Green Pharmacy. Emmaus, PA: Rodale Press, Inc, 1997.

Feinstein, Alice, ed. Healing with Vitamins. Emmaus, PA: Rodale Press, Inc, 1996.

Frances, Allen. Diagnostic and Statistical Manual of Mental Disorders: 4th ed, text revision. Washington, DC: American Psychiatric Association, 2000.

Georgi, J.M. "The Spiritual Platform: Spirituality and Psychotherapy in Addiction Medicine." North Carolina Medical Journal 59 3 (1998): 168-171.

Gottlieb, Bill, ed. New Choices in Natural Healing. Emmaus, PA: Rodale Press, Inc, 1995.

Hall, Laura Lee. "Making the ADA work for People with Psychiatric Disabilities." Mental Disorder, Work Disability, and the Law. Bonnie, Richard J., and John Monahan, eds. Chicago: The University of Chicago Press, 1996. 241-280.

Schwartz M., et al. "The Value of Acupuncture Detoxification Programs in a Substance Abuse Treatment System." Journal of Substance Abuse Treatment 17 4 (1999): 305-312.

Trudeau, D.L. "The Treatment of Addictive Disorders by Brain Wave Biofeedback: A Review and Suggestions for Future Research." Clinical Electroencephalography 31 1 (2000): 13-22.

Yelin, Edward H., and Mirium G. Cisternan. "Employment Patterns Among Persons With and Without Mental Conditions." Mental Disorder, Work Disability, and the Law. Bonnie, Richard J., and John Monahan, eds. Chicago: The University of Chicago Press, 1997. 25-52.

Aldosteronism

Other names / synonyms: Conn's Disease, Conn's Syndrome, Hyperaldosteronism, Idiopathic Aldosteronism, Primary Aldosteronism, Secondary Aldosteronism

255.1

Definition

Aldosteronism is a disorder caused by excessive production of the hormone aldosterone. Aldosterone is produced by the adrenal gland and is essential for normal kidney function. Oversecretion of aldosterone causes excess sodium to be retained while the kidneys excrete too much potassium.

The two types of aldosteronism are primary and secondary. Primary aldosteronism is caused by a tumor (usually noncancerous) of the adrenal gland (Conn's syndrome). Secondary aldosteronism occurs as a complication of other diseases, trauma, burns, or stress. Disorders such as heart failure and certain liver disease (e.g., cirrhosis) can reduce blood flow through the kidney and lead to excessive aldosterone production. High blood pressure (hypertension) is a sign of aldosteronism and can prompt the adrenal gland to secrete excess aldosterone, creating a self-perpetuating cycle.

Aldosteronism affects approximately 5-10% of individuals with hypertension. It can occur at any age but is more common between the ages of 30 and 60. Primary aldosteronism occurs most frequently in women between ages 30 and 50.

Diagnosis

History: Aldosteronism may not cause symptoms that prompt an individual to see a physician. When symptoms are present, they relate directly to the actions of aldosterone. Too much potassium excreted in the urine causes tiredness, weakness, muscle cramps, muscle spasms, and headaches. A low potassium level can cause overproduction of urine (polyuria) that results in excessive thirst (polydipsia) due to fluid loss. Some individuals may experience heart palpitations, often described as a fluttering feeling in the chest. In severe cases, periods of paralysis or mood changes may be reported.

Physical exam: Physical findings usually include hypertension. If the potassium level is severely low (hypokalemia), muscle weakness and decreased tendon reflexes can occur. In rare cases, high sodium levels may cause tissues to retain excessive amounts of fluid (edema).

Tests: Diagnosis is suggested by the combination of hypertension and a blood test that indicates a low potassium level. Renin and aldosterone are checked. Additional tests may include a 24-hour urine collection to measure aldosterone, free cortisol, and creatinine. If aldosterone levels are high, the diagnosis of aldosteronism can be confirmed by prescribing a medication (spironolactone), which blocks the activity of this hormone and checks if levels normalize. A CT or MRI of the adrenal glands may reveal a tumor.

Treatment

Treatment depends on the cause of the disease. Primary aldosteronism due to a tumor is often treated with surgical removal of the tumor. In some cases, part or all of one adrenal gland may be removed (adrenalectomy). Only in rare cases is it necessary to remove both adrenal glands. If the individual is unwilling or unable to undergo surgery, treatment then includes lifelong drug therapy with radiation therapy as an option, if the tumor is thought to be cancerous.

In cases where surgery is not completely effective or in cases of secondary aldosteronism or bilateral hyperplasia, restriction of salt in the diet and use of medication (a potassium-sparing diuretic) may be necessary. Maintaining a healthy weight, regular exercise, and avoidance of tobacco may also be helpful. When aldosteronism is secondary to another disorder, treating the underlying disease may help resolve the aldosteronism.

Specialists

- Cardiologist
- Endocrinologist
- General Surgeon
- Nephrologist

Prognosis

Prognosis is generally excellent with early diagnosis and treatment. Surgical removal of an adrenal tumor or an adrenalectomy results in complete resolution of symptoms and return to normal blood pressure in about 70% of cases. However, return to normal blood pressure often does not occur immediately following surgery but rather occurs gradually over 1 to 4 months. When a tumor is not responsible for the disease, in cases where it cannot be removed, or where both adrenals are involved, prognosis remains excellent with treatment. Medication and/or radiation therapy is effective for individuals with a tumor that cannot be treated surgically.

Maintaining a healthy, low salt (sodium) diet, getting regular exercise, not smoking, and taking prescribed medications are also highly effective treatments for this condition. When aldosteronism is secondary to another disease, treatment of that disease is important for a good outcome. Overall, the majority of cases will experience a complete recovery from all symptoms if the diagnosis of aldosteronism is made early in the progression of the disease, the cause of the condition is readily identified, and the symptoms and/or underlying disease are treated promptly.

If aldosteronism is untreated or if treatment is delayed, irreversible damage to the heart and/or kidneys can occur. Depending on the extent of such damage, the prognosis may be less optimistic.

Differential Diagnosis

Several other conditions may produce symptoms similar to those of aldosteronism and include excessive use of diuretics, renovascular hypertension, pheochromocytoma, renin-secreting tumors, malignant hypertension, congenital adrenal hyperplasia, deoxycorticosterone-producing tumors, exogenous mineralocorticoid, high dose glucocorticoid therapy, and Liddle's syndrome. In addition, a chemical found in licorice can cause a condition that mimics the symptoms of aldosteronism. This condition is called apparent mineralocorticoid excess syndrome and should be considered in individuals who eat significant amounts of candy with real licorice flavoring.

Work Restrictions / Accommodations

In many cases, work restrictions and/or accommodations are not necessary. Those with severe hypertension and whose jobs require strenuous activity may require temporary reassignment to a less physically demanding position. Individuals treated with radiation may require extended leave from work for external beam radiation as this causes prolonged fatigue.

Complementary and Alternative Therapies

Content is intended for awareness only. Treatments may or may not be effective. Scientific evidence may be lacking and some substances have potentially toxic effects. Dr. Presley Reed and the editors do not endorse the use of these therapies in the absence of consultation with a licensed medical professional.

Acupuncture - This may result in a hyperaldosteronemic effect, which is said to show a statistically significant correlation with a decrease in blood pressure.

Comorbid Conditions

Comorbid conditions that may impact recovery and lengthen disability in cases of primary aldosteronism include bilateral adrenal hyperplasia and renal vascular disease. In secondary aldosteronism, comorbid conditions include the underlying conditions or diseases that lead to the excessive aldosterone production such as pregnancy, heart failure, cirrhosis of the liver, trauma, burns, or stress.

Complications

In about one-third of the cases, hypertension is a common complication that persists or returns in spite of surgery. Hypertension can lead to irreversible kidney and heart disease. Severely low levels of potassium can cause irregular heartbeat (cardiac arrhythmia) that can be life-threatening. If treatment involves surgical removal of an adrenal tumor, some individuals may experience symptoms of low adrenal gland function especially low blood pressure (hypotension) for up to a year. Two percent of aldosterone-secreting tumors are cancerous (malignant).

Factors Influencing Duration

Length of disability may be influenced by the severity of symptoms, stage of tumor, the amount of damage to the organ systems caused by the disease prior to treatment, type of treatment, and response to treatment.

Length of Disability

The majority of individuals can expect complete recovery from all symptoms. If aldosteronism is untreated or if treatment is delayed, kidney and/or heart damage may be permanent. Depending on the extent of such damage, disability may also be permanent.

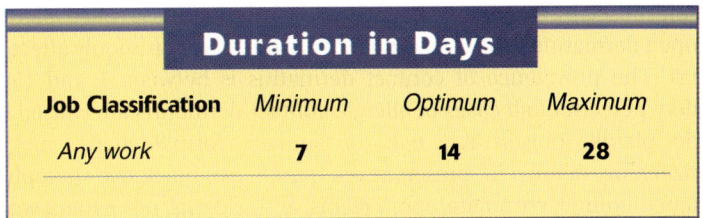

Duration in Days

Job Classification	Minimum	Optimum	Maximum
Any work	7	14	28

Failure to Recover

If an individual fails to recover within the maximum duration expectancy period, the reader may wish to reference the following questions to assist in better understanding the specifics of an individual's medical case.

Regarding diagnosis:

- Was individual tired, weak or experienced muscle cramps, spasms, or headaches?
- Does individual have polyuria and polydipsia?
- Did individual experience heart palpitations? Periods of paralysis? Mood changes?
- Does individual have hypertension?
- Were blood tests including sodium and potassium levels, performed? Was a 24-hour urine test done? CT or MRI of the adrenals?
- Was diagnosis confirmed by prescribing spironolactone?
- Were conditions with similar symptoms ruled out?

Regarding treatment:

- Is individual's aldosteronism primary or secondary?
- Did individual have surgery? Was it successful?
- Did individual opt for drug therapy? Radiation therapy?
- Has the underlying condition been treated?
- If overweight or a smoker, has individual addressed these correctable factors?
- Does individual exercise regularly?
- Did individual seek medical attention during early stages of the condition?
- Has individual been compliant with treatment program?

Regarding prognosis:

- Can individual's employer accommodate any necessary restrictions?
- Does individual have any conditions that may affect ability to recover?
- Did any complications arise such as hypertension? Hypotension?
- Has individual experienced any cardiac arrhythmias?

References

Anshelevich, I.V., M.A. Merson, and G.A. Afanas'eva. "Serum Aldosterone Level in Patients with Hypertension During Treatment by Acupuncture." Ter Arkh 57 10 (1985): 42-45.

Young, William. "Primary Aldosteronism." Griffith's 5-minute Clinical Consult. Dambro, Mark, ed. Philadelphia: Lippincott, Williams & Wilkins, 2000. 20-21.

Allergic Dermatitis

Other names / synonyms: Allergic Contact Dermatitis, Atopic Dermatitis, Drug Rash
693, 693.0

Definition

Allergic dermatitis refers to skin inflammation caused by an allergic (hypersensitivity) reaction to a substance. Allergies are mediated by immune cells, not antibodies. Allergic reactions occur when an individual's immune system becomes sensitized to a substance (sensitization phase) and then reacts when again exposed to that substance (elicitation phase). In the case of allergic dermatitis, this immune response occurs in the skin and causes a rash.

When caused by a topical substance, allergic dermatitis is called allergic contact dermatitis. The hands and face are the most commonly affected areas. The prevalence of contact dermatitis is between 1 and 15%. Ninety percent of all cases of allergic contact dermatitis are caused by toxic plants (poison ivy, oak, or sumac), formaldehyde, nickel, benzocaine, neomycin, preservatives (parabens), black dye (paraphenylenediamine), chromate, epoxy resins, antioxidants, permanent wave solutions, and fragrances. Allergic contact dermatitis accounts for 25% of all cases of contact dermatitis at the workplace.

Latex hypersensitivity is an emerging health problem. Latex is a natural product and is processed in a manner that retains protein allergens and leaves residual chemicals on latex gloves. Several studies have shown an average prevalence of about 10% in selected populations of dental professionals.

Allergic dermatitis may arise from contact with airborne allergens. Topical drug application causes dermatitis more often than other routes of drug administration. The most common drug allergens are penicillin, sulfonamides, aspirin, local anesthetics (benzocaine), and topical antibiotics (neomycin and bacitracin).

Although uncommon, individuals who become sensitized to a substance by skin contact may have a generalized skin reaction to the substance when it is taken internally (contact dermatitis).

Susceptibility to skin irritation seems to be influenced by age, race, and genetic background, whereas sex-related differences do not seem to exist.

Diagnosis

History: Within minutes, hours, or days following exposure to the allergenic substance, skin eruption develops with or without itching. Swelling or other symptoms such as fever and joint pain (arthralgia) may be present. A life-threatening generalized hypersensitivity reaction (anaphylaxis) characterized by hives, itching, angioedema, and breathing difficulties can occur. Individuals with a chronic condition complain of skin thickening (lichenification), scaling, fissures, and red, fluid-filled bumps (papulovesicles). The individual may report a recent change in detergent, soap, cosmetics, jewelry, or topical medication. The individual with poison oak, sumac, or ivy dermatitis often reports working or recreating outdoors.

Physical exam: Skin eruptions vary but rash is most often seen. Hives and angioedema are also common. Allergic contact dermatitis appears as red, hardened (indurated) skin, and blisters. The pattern, shape, and location of the rash help identify the causative substance. Less common, potentially life-threatening forms of allergic dermatitis also have blistering (bullous) eruptions with peeling layers of skin (exfoliative dermatitis) or large blisters (erythema multiforme).

Tests: Skin patch tests, provocative challenges, and some immunological testing may be required. Elevated total IgE suggests underlying allergy.

Treatment

The causative allergen is removed and avoided in the future. Mild itching is treated with wet dressings and astringent lotion. Topical corticosteroids, antihistamines, and tricyclic antidepressants can relieve moderate to severe itching. Oral steroids are reserved for individuals with extensive rash or rash that involves the face or genitals. Angioedema can be treated with topical corticosteroids or with oral steroids if necessary. Anaphylaxis is a life-threatening situation necessitating care in an emergency room and injectable steroids are indicated for this condition.

Prognosis

Symptoms usually subside within 10 to 20 days after removal of the offending substance. If the offending substance is not removed, the dermatitis may worsen and become chronic. Dermatitis may persist for years even with allergen avoidance.

Anaphylaxis and angioedema can occur upon exposure to the allergen, and are potentially fatal conditions for hypersensitive individuals.

Differential Diagnosis

Herpes infection, pityriasis rosea, irritant contact dermatitis, syphilis, seborrheic dermatitis, atopic dermatitis, nummular dermatitis, sweating disorders (dyshidrosis), psoriasis, and fungal infection can present similar symptoms.

Specialists

- Allergist
- Dermatologist

Work Restrictions / Accommodations

Because allergens may share common structural properties, the individual must avoid not only the known allergen, but also cross-reacting allergens (i.e., allergy to the anesthetic procaine may also include allergy to hair or textile dyes). Contact dermatitis may be avoided by removal (or replacement) of the allergenic substance or by wearing personal protective equipment (cotton-lined rubber gloves, aprons, sleeves, or face shield) and using barrier creams. Adequate ventilation is necessary if the allergen is airborne. Good housekeeping and personal hygiene practices are required. Personnel need to be educated in the safe handling of chemicals. Changes to the individual's position or duties may be required.

Comorbid Conditions

Coexisting conditions that may impact recovery and lengthen disability include all cross-reacting drugs. For instance, an allergy to penicillin or sulfonamides will often encompass allergies to their derivatives. An individual especially sensitive to penicillin can even react to penicillin in milk products. Drug allergies are unpredictable since reactions can occur even after an individual has been previously exposed to the drug without any allergic reactions.

Complications

Anaphylaxis, angioedema, secondary infection, inflammation of blood vessels (vasculitis), and involvement of other organs may complicate allergic dermatitis.

Factors Influencing Duration

Severity and extent of the allergic response and any complications affect the length of disability.

Length of Disability

Duration depends on job requirements, workplace exposure to allergen, and whether or not substitute, nonallergenic chemicals or substances may be used.

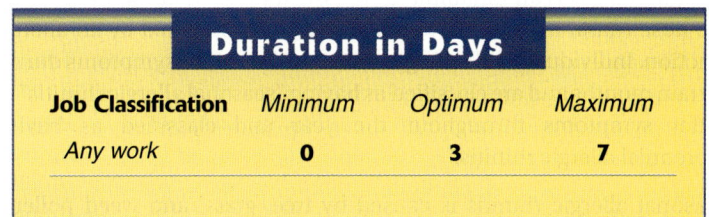

Job Classification	Minimum	Optimum	Maximum
Any work	0	3	7

Failure to Recover

If an individual fails to recover within the maximum duration expectancy period, the reader may wish to reference the following questions to assist in better understanding the specifics of an individual's medical case.

Regarding diagnosis:

- Does individual have symptoms of allergic dermatitis? Was there swelling, rash, itching, hives, or redness on the skin?
- Was an exposure history and complete skin examination performed?
- Was diagnosis confirmed with skin patch testing, provocative challenges, or immunological testing?
- If the diagnosis is uncertain, were other conditions with similar symptoms ruled out?
- Would individual benefit by consulting with a dermatologist or allergist?

Regarding treatment:

- Has the causative agent been identified?
- Have all possible causes of allergic dermatitis (both in the workplace and at home) been considered?
- Does the dermatitis improve over weekends or while individual is on vacation?

- Does individual work with or handle any known allergy-producing agents? If so, does individual use appropriate protective clothing?
- If the rash has failed to resolve or has worsened, is it possible that individual is reacting to the medication used to treat the rash?
- Have additional treatments such as topical or oral corticosteroids relieved itching?

Regarding prognosis:
- Was the offending agent identified?
- Has individual been compliant in avoiding the offending agent?
- Does individual have other skin conditions that may influence length of disability?
- Did individual suffer any complications that may impact ability to recover?

References

Anderson, Philip, and Kristin Malaker. "Most Common Skin Disorders." Managing Skin Diseases. Hiscock, Tim, ed. Baltimore: Williams & Wilkins, 1999. 50-53.

McCracken, S. "Latex Glove Hypersensitivity and Irritation: A Literature Review." Probe 33 1 (1999): 13-15.

Allergic Rhinitis

Other names / synonyms: Hay Fever, Hayfever, PAR, Paroxysmal Rhinorrhea, Perennial Allergic Rhinitis, SAR, Seasonal Allergic Rhinitis, Seasonal Rhinitis

477, 477.0, 477.8, 477.9

Definition

Allergic rhinitis is an inflammation of the mucous membrane lining of the nose (nasal mucosa). The inflammation is triggered by an allergic reaction. Individuals with allergic rhinitis either suffer symptoms during certain months and are classified as having "seasonal allergic rhinitis" or suffer symptoms throughout the year and classified as having "perennial allergic rhinitis."

Seasonal allergic rhinitis is caused by tree, grass, and weed pollens. Since trees, grasses, and weeds have well-defined pollinating periods, their pollens are airborne only during certain seasons. Perennial allergic rhinitis is usually caused by one of four common indoor allergens, i.e., animal dander, dust mites, cockroaches, and mold spores.

Allergic rhinitis is a very common disease and affects an estimated 25 to 30 million individuals in the US. The disease accounts for approximately 32 million doctor's office visits annually. It is more common in individuals with other allergies such as asthma or eczema, and tends to run in families. Although it can occur at any age, allergic rhinitis has its peak occurrence in the years of early adulthood, and affects women more than men.

Diagnosis

History: Individuals may report symptoms that occur at a certain time of day or in a certain season. Individuals may report an exposure to a specific substance such as cat dander, ragweed, or dust, or they may be unaware of what precipitated the episode. Symptoms can include sneezing, itching of the nose, eyes, mouth, throat, or skin, runny nose, stuffy nose, coughing, and headache.

Physical exam: The exam usually reveals reddened nose, swollen and either pale or red nasal membranes, and watery and reddened eyes (occasionally with dark circles underneath). Examination of the throat may reveal redness with postnasal drip. The lungs will be clear on examination.

Tests: Tests are not required to diagnose allergic rhinitis. Allergy testing is advised however, if the individual develops rhinitis on a frequent or chronic basis. Allergy skin tests help identify the specific allergens responsible so that exposure can be avoided or kept to a minimum.

Treatment

Treatment of allergic rhinitis begins with the identification of the agent(s) causing the allergic reaction. The four steps in treating allergic rhinitis are education, allergen avoidance, drug therapy, and allergy shots (specific allergen immunotherapy or desensitization).

Avoidance is key to successful treatment. All sources of an allergen at home or work should be removed. While avoidance is the best treatment, complete avoidance of a specific allergen may not be possible, in which case exposure should be minimized.

Drug therapy can include antihistamines, decongestants to reduce nasal congestion, and topical cromolyn sodium and corticosteroids to reduce the immune response.

Allergy shots (immunotherapy or desensitization) are occasionally recommended. Desensitization includes regular injections of the allergen(s) given in increasing doses to desensitize the body to the allergen.

Clinical trials have indicated that immunotherapy is expensive and of limited benefit. Nasal steroids are recommended as the first-line treatment for rhinitis.

Prognosis

While treatment can effectively reduce most symptoms of allergic rhinitis, treatment only affects the current exposure. Future exposures will cause another allergic reaction. Allergy identification through testing with attempts to avoid allergen exposure can reduce the number of future occurrences.

On occasion, an individual may outgrow an allergy as their immune system becomes less sensitive to the specific allergen(s). However, once a specific allergen has caused a reaction, it will generally continue to do so.

Desensitization often requires years of treatment and is effective in only about two-thirds of the individuals.

Differential Diagnosis

Conditions that mimic allergic rhinitis have either contrasting histories or additional or missing symptoms. Some of these conditions include viral upper respiratory tract infections (URTI) with symptoms of acute onset lasting only a few days plus fever, myalgia, and arthralgia; vasomotor rhinitis; rhinitis medicamentosa, characterized by nasal congestion secondary to overuse of vasoconstrictor nasal sprays. On occasion, individuals with upper airway foreign bodies or neoplasms may develop symptoms of chronic rhinitis.

Specialists

- Allergist
- Otolaryngologist

Work Restrictions / Accommodations

Workplace accommodations include the avoidance of inhaled irritants to which the individual is allergic. If complete avoidance is not possible at work, goggles and/or masks may need to be worn. Some over-the-counter and prescription drugs to treat allergic rhinitis require that the individual avoid driving or operating heavy equipment while taking the medication.

Comorbid Conditions

Compromised immunity, asthma, or a deviated nasal septum may lengthen treatment time and disability.

Complications

Complications associated with allergic rhinitis are few and generally minor. Most involve a superimposed viral or bacterial infection in the region of the nose and throat. Prolonged nasal congestion can precede a cold (nasopharyngitis) or can lead to obstruction of sinus drainage resulting in sinusitis. Continuous postnasal drip can cause inflammation of the throat (pharyngitis), tonsils (tonsillitis), or voice box (laryngitis). Although temporary use of a decongestant spray or drops may reduce symptoms, continued use can eventually make them worse. With immunotherapy, there is always the danger of a life-threatening allergic reaction (anaphylaxis) shortly after an allergy injection is given.

Factors Influencing Duration

Length of disability can be influenced by the severity of the individual's symptoms, effectiveness of symptom-relieving medication, ability to avoid the offending allergens, underlying chronic medical conditions involving the immune system or the respiratory tract, and any complication(s).

Length of Disability

This condition is seldom disabling.

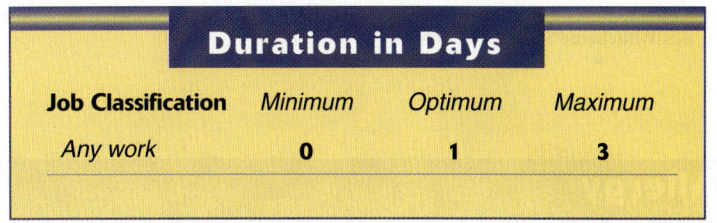

Job Classification	Minimum	Optimum	Maximum
Any work	0	1	3

Failure to Recover

If an individual fails to recover within the maximum duration expectancy period, the reader may wish to reference the following questions to assist in better understanding the specifics of an individual's medical case.

Regarding diagnosis:

- Does individual have seasonal allergies to trees, grasses, and weed pollens? Do the symptoms occur at a specific time of the day or year?
- Is individual at home when most symptomatic? Is individual allergic to indoor allergens such as animal dander, dust, cockroaches, or mold?
- Do symptoms include sneezing, itchy eyes, nose, mouth, throat, or skin? Does individual have a runny or stuffy nose? Cough or headache?
- On physical exam, were the affected areas reddened and swollen? Pale? Was postnasal drip present? Were the lungs clear?
- Has individual undergone allergy testing?
- Have conditions with similar symptoms been ruled out?

Regarding treatment:

- Has the agent(s) causing the allergic reaction been identified? Does individual attempt to avoid the offending agents?
- Has individual responded favorably to drug therapy? If not, have other drugs been tried?
- Has individual undergone specific allergy desensitization?
- Is individual compliant with the treatment regime?

Regarding prognosis:

- Can individual's employer accommodate any necessary restrictions?
- Can individual avoid the allergens or use personal protective equipment such as masks, goggles, or gloves? Does individual follow these restrictions while at home and play?
- Does individual have any conditions such as asthma or a compromised immune system that may delay recovery?
- Does individual have any complications such as a superimposed viral or bacterial infection in the nose or throat? Does individual have sinusitis?
- Is there irritation from the postnasal drip?
- Have decongestant sprays or drops been used for an extended period of time?

Allergic Rhinitis

References

Merck Manual of Diagnosis and Therapy, 17th ed. Beers, Mark H., and Robert Berkow, MD, eds. Whitehouse Station, NJ: Merck & Co., Inc., 1999.

Nash, D.B., S.D. Sullivan, and J. Mackowiak. "Optimizing Quality of Care and Cost Effectiveness in Treating Allergic Rhinitis in a Managed Care Setting." American Journal of Managed Care 6 1 Suppl (2000): S3-15.

Allergy
Other names / synonyms: Allergic Reaction, Atopic Disease, Hypersensitivity Reaction
995.3

Definition

Allergy is a condition occurring when an individual's immune system is hypersensitive or over-reactive. Ordinarily, the human immune system has a fine-tuned ability to distinguish between harmless substances in the environment such as dust, and potentially harmful agents such as viruses and bacteria. For an individual with allergies, however, the immune system reacts quickly, intensely, and inappropriately to one or more foreign substances that are ordinarily harmless.

The foreign substance that triggers an allergic reaction is called an allergen or antigen. When individuals with an allergy eat, touch, or inhale the particular foreign substance or allergen, their immune system mistakenly launches an attack against it. Allergic individuals produce immunoglobulin G (IgG) as well as a large amount of another antibody called immunoglobulin E (IgE). IgE is responsible for generating a full-scale reaction with symptoms such as swelling, skin rashes, or constant sneezing or coughing each and every time the individual is exposed to the offending substance (allergen).

In addition to heredity or genetic traits, certain environmental exposures (tobacco smoke), emotional factors, and conditions of physiological stress (puberty, pregnancy, or illness) may predispose individuals to allergic symptoms. Food, drugs, mold, pollen, insect bites, infection, physical agents (heat, cold, sun, pressure, or exercise), polyurethane plastics, paints, varnish, and latex or rubber products may trigger allergic reactions. Recently, there have been growing reports of allergic reactions to water-soluble proteins in latex products (e.g., rubber gloves, dental dams, condoms, and medical devices) particularly among medical personnel and individuals receiving medical care. Other common occupational allergens include animal dander that typically affects farmers, veterinarians, groomers, and laboratory workers. Hospital workers, photographers, and food service workers most commonly encounter chemicals such as formalin, hexachlorophene, ethylene diamine, and metabisulfite. Dust from flour, grains and wood can affect mill workers, carpenters, bakers, and lumberjacks.

Allergic reactions can be relatively localized to one or more body systems. Examples are hay fever (allergic rhinitis) that causes a running nose and sneezing; allergic conjunctivitis, characterized by itching and red eyes; and bronchial asthma that causes narrowing of airways. Ocular allergies describe several different allergic reactions in the eyes. These eye allergies produce symptoms of itching, redness, and tearing of the eyes following exposure to allergens in the air or substances coming in contact with the eye. Allergic conjunctivitis is the most common ocular allergy and occurs in the spring and fall months in conjunction with hay fever.

On rare occasions, an allergic reaction can result in a whole body response (anaphylaxis). This sudden, life-threatening allergic reaction can trigger a swollen throat and a constriction of the airways, rapid pulse, loss of consciousness, and a sudden drop in blood pressure (shock).

Researchers believe the tendency to develop allergies is primarily inherited. Children of parents with allergies have a much greater chance of developing them than children with nonallergic parents. A child who has one parent with allergies has a 1 in 4 chance of developing allergies. If both parents have allergies, the odds are further increased.

Approximately 1 out of 6 Americans has one or more significant allergies and suffers from a wide array of symptoms. Each year, Americans lose 3.5 million workdays because of allergies. Nearly half the individuals with allergies have hay fever (allergic rhinitis). This reaction to outdoor airborne allergens, usually tree and grass pollen, occurs on a seasonal basis. A second type of airborne allergy called perennial allergic rhinitis occurs year-round and is more likely due to indoor allergens such as pet dander or dust mites.

Approximately 6 to 10 million Americans are allergic to animal dander and about 2 million have allergic reactions to insect stings. Although food allergies are common in children, only about 1-2% of adults suffer from allergies to food. Approximately 15 million Americans have asthma caused by allergies.

Diagnosis

History: Depending on the system involved, the individual may complain of itching, rash, swelling, sneezing, runny nose, tearing, earache, sore throat, cough, breathing difficulties, and gastrointestinal symptoms like diarrhea. Individuals may describe certain conditions that trigger their symptoms. For example, they may report that the symptoms arise every time they are around animals or worsen in the spring and disappear during winter.

Common symptoms associated with reactions to latex are skin rashes, eye irritation (conjunctivitis), runny nose (rhinitis), narrowing of airways (bronchospasm), and even anaphylaxis.

Physical exam: The lungs, heart, and all other body areas affected by the allergic symptoms are examined. In mild cases of allergic rhinitis, the exam may reveal swelling, inflammation of the nasal passages, and nasal discharge. Swelling, redness, and tearing of the eyes are common in allergic conjunctivitis. Additional findings of redness and swelling in the ear canal and throat are not uncommon.

100   *The Medical Disability Advisor–Fourth Edition*

Large, irregular, red bumps on the skin (hives) may be present with food allergies, drug allergies, or allergic reaction to insect stings. Gastrointestinal symptoms are most common with food, food preservatives, and food additive allergies.

Wheezing or absent lung sounds and a rapid respiratory rate may be present in asthma or anaphylaxis. Cool, moist, and pale skin in conjunction with a rapid pulse and low blood pressure may be signs of shock due to anaphylaxis.

Tests: In addition to a physical exam, one or more diagnostic tests may be done. These tests help determine what triggers the allergy and evaluate the severity of the allergic reactions. A spirometer measures the amount of air entering and leaving the lungs (spirometry). It is useful in identifying lung disorders such as asthma that may cause narrowing of the airways.

In a scratch test, small amounts of the suspected allergen (dust, dander, or food) are placed on the skin surface. Development of a small, raised bump on the skin indicates an allergic response to that particular substance. In intradermal tests, small quantities of the suspected allergen are injected under the skin. A reaction of redness or swelling at the injection site indicates an allergic response. The radioallergosorbent test (RAST test) or blood test is used in individuals with disorders that may interfere with skin testing.

The patch test involves applying adhesive patches with allergens to the skin. Localized redness and swelling at the application site indicate positive reaction. In a challenge test, the suspected foods or medications are eliminated for a period of time and then, under medical observation, small amounts are reintroduced to see if they trigger an allergic reaction.

Treatment

The treatment of allergies often requires a combination of several approaches and therapies. The goals of treatment are to minimize the frequency and severity of reactions, maintain good health, and prevent complications. Current medical approaches to achieve these goals include allergen avoidance, medication to control or relieve symptoms, and allergy shots.

Antihistamines, decongestants, topical nasal steroids, eye drops, and inhalers are among the drugs used for short-term relief of some common allergy symptoms. For long-term management of severe allergy symptoms, a series of allergy shots (immunotherapy) may be effective. With immunotherapy, the allergy sufferer receives a series of shots with increasing doses of the offending allergen. When effective, the sensitivity to the allergen will gradually diminish until symptoms disappear. Other aids to managing symptoms include stress reduction and relaxation techniques. The specific treatment plan depends on the type and severity of the condition as well as lifestyle and environmental factors.

Prognosis

The duration of a single allergic episode may vary from a few minutes to several days. With no complications, an allergic reaction often has a good outcome but the condition may be chronic. However, with proper medical management and compliance with avoidance procedures and medication regimens, allergy symptoms can be well controlled. Immunotherapy has shown to be an effective and safe treatment for severe cases of asthma, allergic rhinitis, and insect venom allergy unresponsive to other therapies.

Differential Diagnosis

Other possibilities include bronchitis, the common cold, and gastrointestinal illness. In chronic cases, the allergic reaction may be a symptom of an infection, cancer, or a hormone or connective tissue disorder.

Specialists

- Allergist
- Dermatologist
- Internist

Work Restrictions / Accommodations

Allergic individuals need to avoid exposure to potential allergens. Work environments are generally safe for most individuals. However, there are substances in certain work environments that may present problems for some individuals with allergies. Occupations at most risk and that need special accommodations include farmers, veterinarians, groomers (reaction to animal dander), laboratory workers, hospital workers, photographers, food service workers (reaction to chemicals and food), mill workers, carpenters, bakers, and lumberjacks (reactions to wood, dust, grains, and flours). Avoiding the areas at work where the offending triggers are located can often minimize symptoms. In a few cases, asthma and allergy symptoms may be so severe that a change in occupation is the best solution.

Those treated with sedating antihistamines may suffer side effects of drowsiness and dizziness that can interfere with safe operation of machinery and equipment. Newer, less sedating antihistamines are available.

The National Institute for Occupational Safety and Health (NIOSH) published recommendations regarding prevention of latex-related allergies. These recommendations include providing nonlatex gloves when workers are not handling infectious materials, and using low-protein, powder-free gloves to protect workers handling infectious materials. In addition, NIOSH has several publications on guidelines for chemical safety in the workplace.

Complementary and Alternative Therapies

Content is intended for awareness only. Treatments may or may not be effective. Scientific evidence may be lacking and some substances have potentially toxic effects. Dr. Presley Reed and the editors do not endorse the use of these therapies in the absence of consultation with a licensed medical professional.

Acupuncture -	May reduce symptoms.
Chiropractic therapy -	Uses relationship between musculoskeletal structures and the nervous system in the restoration and maintenance of health.
Dietary management -	Certain foods can trigger allergies or exacerbate symptoms, e.g., dairy products can contribute to mucus production.
Exercise -	Can improve circulation, reduce stress, and boost immune system.
Smoking Cessation -	Smoking may exacerbate allergic reactions.

Comorbid Conditions

Comorbid conditions of chronic pulmonary disease or congestive heart failure may impact the individual's ability to recover and further lengthen disability.

Complications

Some individuals develop one or more associated medical problems that include nasal polyps, sinusitis, ear infections, bronchitis, eczema, and asthma.

Severe cases can occur within seconds and trigger a swollen throat and constriction of the airways (allergic asthma) rapid pulse, loss of consciousness, sudden drop in blood pressure, weakness, and cardiac collapse (anaphylactic shock) that require immediate medical treatment. Anaphylaxis usually results from allergic reactions to insect venom, vaccinations, medications, injections of x-ray contrast, and foods like peanuts and shellfish.

Factors Influencing Duration

Factors such as advanced age, cigarette use, and severity of symptoms can influence the length of disability. With industrial or chemical allergies, workplace accommodations influence the individual's ability to return to work.

Length of Disability

Duration depends on nature and severity of manifestations.

Localized allergic reaction.

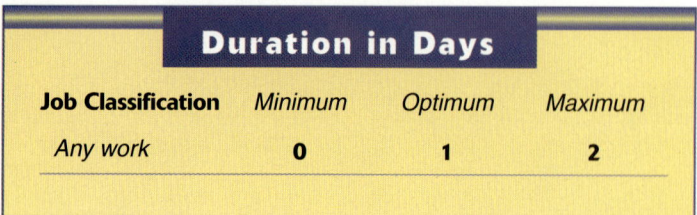

Duration in Days

Job Classification	Minimum	Optimum	Maximum
Any work	0	1	2

Failure to Recover

If an individual fails to recover within the maximum duration expectancy period, the reader may wish to reference the following questions to assist in better understanding the specifics of an individual's medical case.

Regarding diagnosis:

- Did the physical exam reveal findings of hives, rash, gastrointestinal distress, bronchospasm, conjunctivitis, or rhinitis? Anaphylactic shock? If so, was individual promptly referred to an emergency physician or allergist for treatment?
- Was allergen(s) positively identified? Was there more than one allergen in play?
- How was allergen(s) identified? Skin test? Direct allergen challenge?
- Was the offending allergen a substance exposed to in the work environment (latex, industrial material)?
- Was the allergen airborne or seasonal (i.e., pollen, dust, smoke)?
- Was the allergen present in the home environment (mold, dust mites, animal dander)?
- Were other conditions with similar symptoms ruled out?
- Was an elimination diet used to identify common foods that can trigger allergies?

Regarding treatment:

- Did individual receive prompt and appropriate control of the immediate allergy symptoms?
- Was anaphylaxis present? If so, was emergency intervention and support received?
- Is individual compliant with allergen avoidance recommendations? If not, are there barriers to compliance (such as lack of understanding, employment concerns)?
- Did individual receive treatment specific for the symptoms displayed?
- Were symptoms effectively relieved? If not, were more aggressive interventions considered?
- Is immunotherapy indicated?
- If a food allergy, was a nutritionist consulted to help individual restructure diet and increase awareness of ingredient combinations found in common foods?

Regarding prognosis:

- Are the frequency and severity of the allergy symptoms well controlled with the present therapy? If not, were other treatments tried?
- Were additional diagnostic tests done to determine if there are other possible allergens involved or if there is an associated complication such as a secondary infection (sinusitis, bronchitis)?
- Is individual compliant with the treatment recommendations? If not, why?
- If individual has had adverse reactions (dry mouth, palpitations, insomnia) to the medications, were other medications substituted?

- Was individual provided a smoke-free work environment? A pollution-free work environment? Improved ventilation or air filters? Protective masks or clothing? If not, could individual be moved to a different work site? A different type of work?
- Has immunotherapy been considered?
- Are there comorbid conditions or complications that may have impacted ability to recover?

References

Cyberdiet. "About Allergies and Asthma." Understanding Allergy and Asthma. Version 1 01 Apr 2000 03 Oct 2000 <http://www.cyberdiet.com/modules/aa/under/definitions/allergy.html>.

Patient and Public Resource Center: Facts About Allergies and Asthma. American Academy of Allergies, Asthma and Immunology. 1999 03 Oct 2000 <http://www.aaaai.org/public/default.stm>.

The Natural Pharmacist. "Allergies." Conditions. 03 Oct 2000 03 Oct 2000 <http://www.tnp.com/topic.asp?ID=329#top>.

Tierney, Lawrence M., Stephen J. McPhee, and Maxine Papadakis, eds. Current Medical Diagnosis and Treatment, 39th ed. New York: Lange Medical Books/McGraw-Hill, 2000.

Alopecia Areata

Other names / synonyms: Alopecia, Baldness, Patchy Hair Loss
704.01

Definition

Alopecia areata is a condition where hair is lost in patches. Hair loss most commonly occurs on the scalp but can also involve facial or body hair. The skin in these bald areas looks and feels normal. Hair loss may suddenly slow or stop and then just as suddenly increase in severity. As much as 60% of individuals with alopecia areata also have accompanying nail changes (i.e., pitting, ridging, and rough thick nails).

Alopecia areata usually refers to varying amounts of patchy hair loss to larger areas of little or no hair. This kind of hair loss generally takes place on the scalp but any hair-bearing surface can be affected. In alopecia totalis, all the scalp hair on the scalp is lost and the surface of the scalp becomes totally smooth. Alopecia universalis means loss of all hair on the head and body including eyelashes, eyebrows, underarm hair, and pubic hair.

Although the cause of alopecia areata is unknown, evidence points to an autoimmune disease where the body's immune system forms antibodies against itself. A genetic component may also be involved. Alopecia areata may be associated with an underlying condition such as pernicious anemia, Down's syndrome, an underactive thyroid gland, a skin disease with milk-white patches (vitiligo), or an inherited tendency to develop allergies (atopy).

Onset of alopecia areata tends to coincide with times of particular stress. White hairs are less affected than pigmented ones, so some individuals have reported that patches of hair appeared to "turn gray overnight."

Alopecia areata is not uncommon but is under-reported. Because hairless patches on the scalp may be small and covered by the hair growing from surrounding areas, a hairdresser is often the first to notice the condition.

The overall incidence of alopecia areata is 20.2 per 100,000 person-years. Rates are similar in men and women and occur in all age groups.

Diagnosis

History: Symptoms include patchy hair loss and sometimes pitted or deformed nails. There may be a history of alopecia areata in other family members.

Physical exam: Individuals will present with sharply defined round or oval patches of hair loss with no scarring of the underlying skin. If there is some hair left in the bald patches, it may be fine or broken and easily removed. Patches of alopecia may be seen in the eyebrows, eyelashes, beard, or body hair as well as on the scalp.

Tests: A complete blood count should be performed to rule out immune system disorders.

Treatment

Treatment focuses on relieving symptoms since the cause of alopecia areata is still unknown. The most common treatment involves injecting the bald patches with corticosteroids. Injections should not be repeated in the same site for at least 3 months.

Treatment is based on the extent of the disease and age. Individuals are divided into two groups, those with less than 50% scalp hair loss and those with more than 50% scalp hair loss.

Individuals with less than 50% hair loss may do nothing (there is a possibility that the hair will grow in on its own), inject the bald patches with corticosteroids (injections should not be repeated in the same site for at least 3 months) or minoxidil solution, or use a combination of these treatments.

Individuals with more than 50% hair loss may try topical immunotherapy using diphencyprone, PUVA, minoxidil, and cortisone cream, minoxidil and anthralin cream, or systemic steroids. Topical immunotherapy has a 50% chance of producing cosmetically acceptable regrowth.

Prognosis

The disease is highly variable with periods of spontaneous recovery and/or relapse. Individuals with alopecia areata can usually expect regrowth of lost hair within a few months to a few years. Treatment with steroids usually reduces this time to 4 to 6 weeks. If the individual has a history of atopic dermatitis or asthma, regrowth of lost hair is less likely. When the hair first grows back, it is usually fine and sometimes unpigmented, but normal hair eventually replaces it.

Differential Diagnosis

Other conditions that present with similar symptoms are androgenetic alopecia (male pattern baldness, female diffuse baldness) with genetic and hormonal causes, lichen planopilaris, discoid lupus erythematosus, folliculitis decalvans, fungal infection, and alopecia due to radiation or other skin damage.

Specialists

- Dermatologist
- Psychologist
- Psychiatrist

Work Restrictions / Accommodations

Usually no work restrictions or accommodations are required. The individual may be more comfortable if dress code restrictions are relaxed to allow the wearing of a hat.

Complementary and Alternative Therapies

Content is intended for awareness only. Treatments may or may not be effective. Scientific evidence may be lacking and some substances have potentially toxic effects. Dr. Presley Reed and the editors do not endorse the use of these therapies in the absence of consultation with a licensed medical professional.

Aromatherapy - May promote relaxation and relieve stress.

Biofeedback - May help individual learn to control responses to stress.

Hypnotherapy - May help individual cope with stressful situations.

Massage - Promotes relaxation and may help relieve stress.

Comorbid Conditions

Comorbid conditions include autoimmune disorders, hormone imbalance, skin conditions such as eczema and vitiligo, psychiatric disorders, or excessive stress.

Complications

Practical problems of alopecia universalis include perspiration trickling into the eyes (from lack of eyebrows), little protection from dust and glare (without eyelashes), and no protection in the nostrils or sinuses from foreign particles in the air (without nasal hairs).

Because of the cosmetic effects of the condition, it can have disturbing psychological consequences. The unpredictable course of the disease can be confusing and discouraging to the individual. One in four adults diagnosed with alopecia areata develop alopecia totalis where all scalp hair is lost.

Factors Influencing Duration

Although there is no physical disability associated with this disorder, it can result in an adjustment reaction with associated short-term disability.

Length of Disability

Disability is not associated with this condition.

Failure to Recover

If an individual fails to recover within the maximum duration expectancy period, the reader may wish to reference the following questions to assist in better understanding the specifics of an individual's medical case.

Regarding diagnosis:

- Was diagnosis of alopecia areata confirmed?
- Does individual have an underlying condition that may impact recovery? Are underlying conditions being appropriately addressed?

Regarding treatment:

- Has individual received treatment appropriate for extent of hair loss?
- What other options can now be tried?
- Would individual benefit from consultation with a dermatologist?
- Have areas of excessive stress been addressed?
- Has individual been educated in stress-reduction techniques?
- Would individual benefit from psychological counseling or enrollment in a support group?

Regarding prognosis:

- If individual has been doing watchful waiting, is he/she now ready to try a treatment option?
- Is individual aware that certain underlying conditions may impact hair regrowth?
- Would individual benefit from psychological counseling or enrollment in a support group?

References

Bertolino, A.P. "Alopecia Areata: A Clinical Overview." Postgraduate Medicine 107 7 (2000): 81-85, 89-90.

Lebwohl, Mark. "New Treatments for Alopecia Areata." Lancet 349 (1997): 9047.

Alzheimer's Disease

Other names / synonyms: Alzheimer's Sclerosis, Presenile Dementia, Senile Dementia

331.0

Definition

Alzheimer's disease is a progressive, irreversible, degenerative organic brain disorder (dementia) characterized by loss of memory (subtle deterioration progressing to profound memory loss), loss of mental powers (the ability to think, understand, reason, learn, and solve problems), personality changes, and an increasing inability to carry out the activities of daily living (eating, bathing, grooming, dressing, and toileting).

The cause of the disease remains unclear. Acetylcholine, a neurotransmitter thought to be involved in learning and memory, is severely diminished in the brains of individuals with Alzheimer's disease. The reason for this condition is unknown. In the past, it was believed that excessive levels of aluminum contributed to the development of Alzheimer's disease, but today there is no conclusive evidence to show that individuals with aluminum toxicity have a greater incidence of the disease.

Age is the most significant risk factor for the onset of Alzheimer's disease. Scientists believe individuals who develop signs of Alzheimer's before age 65 (early onset) have a variation of the disease that is genetically transmitted across multiple generations of the same family. Children who inherit any one of three genes (APP, Presenlin-1, and Presenlin-2) will develop the disease before age 65 and as early as their late twenties. A fourth gene (Apoe4) is a risk factor for early onset Alzheimer's, but not everyone who inherits this gene develops the disease later in life. The genetic variation of Alzheimer's, however, accounts for less than 10% of all reported cases.

Researchers are looking for a connection between Down's syndrome and Alzheimer's disease. Individuals with Down's syndrome exhibit symptoms of Alzheimer's at a much younger age than the general population (late forties or early fifties), and nearly all individuals with Down's syndrome who live past the age of 60 develop the disease. At autopsy, the degenerative changes in the brains of individuals with Down's syndrome are almost identical to the changes seen in the brains of individuals with Alzheimer's disease. Previous head trauma or central nervous system infection may also predispose an individual to develop Alzheimer's later in life.

Alzheimer's disease is the fourth leading cause of death in American adults following heart disease, cancer, and stroke. It is now recognized as a major health problem in the US, particularly in individuals over the age of 65 (late onset). Men and women are affected almost equally. The number of individuals diagnosed with Alzheimer's disease will increase dramatically in the next 10 to 20 years as the population born after the end of World War II begins to reach the age of 65.

Diagnosis

History: Because individuals with Alzheimer's are often unaware of changes in their mental powers or behavior, their families and friends become key factors in relating histories during the diagnostic process. Cognitive symptoms of Alzheimer's disease are memory loss (inability to recall recent events or new information), disorientation, confusion, and problems with reasoning and thinking. Behavioral symptoms are agitation, anxiety, delusions, depression, hallucinations, insomnia, and wandering.

The Alzheimer's Association (a nationally recognized clearinghouse of information on the disease) recognizes ten signs that may mark individuals with Alzheimer's: (1) memory loss that affects job skills, (2) difficulty performing familiar tasks, (3) problems with language, (4) disorientation to time and place, (5) poor or decreased judgment, (6) problems with abstract thinking, (7) misplacing things, (8) changes in mood or behavior, (9) changes in personality, and (10) loss of initiative.

In individuals with Down's syndrome, behavioral symptoms are sometimes more accurate warning signs of Alzheimer's disease than cognitive symptoms. The most easily detected symptoms in individuals with Down's syndrome are a sudden change in the ability to complete the activities of daily living, withdrawal from daily and social routines, aggression, frustration, and lack of interest in regular activities.

Physical exam: The diagnosis of Alzheimer's can only be confirmed by postmortem examination of brain tissue. The brain afflicted with Alzheimer's exhibits significant atrophy, the presence of sticky protein plaques outside of the nerve cells, and tangles (neurofibrillary tangles). For purposes of treatment, ruling out all other possible conditions that can cause mental impairment must be done before diagnosing for Alzheimer's disease. In addition to a complete physical exam, psychological and neurological exams may also be performed. Depending on how advanced the disease is, physical examination can confirm some of the reported symptoms.

Tests: There are no definitive tests to positively diagnose Alzheimer's. CT and MRI scans are usually performed and might reveal shrinkage of the brain (cerebral atrophy) and enlarged cavities (ventricles), but these signs are also found in other forms of dementia. Single photon emission computed tomography (SPECT) is used to measure the rate of brain cell metabolism. Neuropsychological testing is performed to determine the extent of cognitive dysfunction. Additional tests that may be performed to rule out other diseases include blood tests, a chest x-ray, and thyroid function tests.

Treatment

The pharmaceutical treatment of Alzheimer's disease is aimed at improving and controlling the decline in mental powers (cognition) and the undesirable behavioral symptoms that the individual may exhibit. Several anticholinesterase inhibitors have shown to slow the decline in cognitive function during the early or middle stages of Alzheimer's. Other helpful drugs are on the horizon, however, some of these drugs are toxic to the liver and require frequent laboratory monitoring of liver function.

Unfortunately, no pharmaceutical treatments are available for the disease's late stages. Studies have shown that estrogen may help protect against development of Alzheimer's and may slow progression in those who already have the disease. Depression that may accompany Alzheimer's can be treated with antidepressants, particularly the newer selective-serotonin re-uptake inhibitors. Other treatment, (supportive rather than therapeutic) is intended to maintain functional ability for as long as possible, meet personal care needs, and maintain a safe environment with a minimum of injuries.

Current research is focused on early diagnosis and treatment. A vaccine that may significantly delay the onset of Alzheimer's is in its first human trials. Individuals treated for other diseases with nonsteroidal anti-inflammatory drugs (NSAIDs) seem to have a lower risk of developing Alzheimer's. Researchers are interested in the role these drugs could play in reducing the risk of developing Alzheimer's disease.

Prognosis

The general course of Alzheimer's disease from the mild stages to death, averages 8 to 10 years. The three stages that individuals with Alzheimer's predictably move through are mild, moderate, and severe. During the mild stage, the individual may seem normal to the casual observer but is beginning to have a decline in memory and mental powers. In the middle stage, the individual is obviously impaired and requires a caregiver's supervision during the performance of daily activities. Delusions, agitation, pacing, and wandering often develop during this stage. In the severe stage, the individual is unable to communicate, cannot recognize family members, has bowel and bladder incontinence, and is unable to perform the activities of daily living. Death usually occurs as a result of other disease or injury brought on by the individual's weakened condition.

Differential Diagnosis

Differential diagnoses may include vitamin deficiency (particularly B_{12}), hypothyroidism, depression, alcoholic dementia, drug overdose, adverse drug reaction or interaction, syphilis, viral infections, chronic subdural hematoma, brain tumors, or hydrocephalus. The dementia associated with Alzheimer's must also be differentiated from dementia associated with other diseases (Parkinson's, Pick's, Creutzfeldt-Jakob's, and Huntington's) as well as dementia caused by multiple strokes in the brain.

Specialists

- Neurologist
- Physiatrist
- Psychiatrist

Rehabilitation

Individuals with Alzheimer's disease may require occupational therapy to help compensate for cognitive deficits. Occupational therapy focuses on maintaining realistic caregiver goals and maximizing safety in the home. Individuals and their caregivers learn to structure the individual's environment to allow for greater independence. Individuals can perform daily tasks better if the environment is held constant and the tasks are performed in the same daily routine rather than in changing daily tasks constantly. For example, keeping a washcloth, towel, and soap at the bedside every morning aid in cueing the individual to shower rather than relying on the individual to remember to shower as well as where the shower supplies are kept.

Individuals aware of their memory loss can compensate for forgetfulness by writing notes to remember daily tasks, labeling rooms to prevent getting lost, and providing themselves with other visual cues. Caregivers also learn to provide time cues such as a calendar and a clock in a highly visible area to keep the individuals oriented. Occupational therapy does not ordinarily focus on teaching new skills to individuals with Alzheimer's disease as this disease decreases problem-solving ability.

Individuals aware of their memory loss may require psychological counseling to help treat depression that often accompanies this disease. Group counseling may be necessary for individuals and their families to address the anger and aggressiveness that individuals with Alzheimer's disease often exhibit. Support groups can address individuals' concerns about their prognosis.

Work Restrictions / Accommodations

Very early in the course of the disease, limited work activities may be possible depending on the nature of the work and the individual's degree of deficiency in areas critical to the performance of a particular job. In most cases, however, a plan for retirement may need to be arranged fairly soon after the diagnosis of Alzheimer's disease.

Comorbid Conditions

Comorbid conditions influencing the length of disability for individuals with Alzheimer's disease include pre-existing chronic disease, conditions such as obesity and smoking, and disabilities.

Complications

Individuals with Alzheimer's disease are susceptible to all the acute and chronic diseases and conditions common to the elderly and physically disabled population. These include cancer, heart and vascular disease, stroke, blood clots, choking and aspiration, infectious disease, diabetes, respiratory disease, and neuromuscular complications associated with decreased mobility. Since these individuals are often unable to communicate health symptoms, caregivers must be responsible for alerting the individual's physician to changes in behavior, movement, consciousness, and bodily functions.

Individuals with Alzheimer's are also at increased risk for injury associated with impaired judgment, violence directed at others (as a result of neurologic changes, sensory overload, lack of appropriate coping mechanisms, and an unfamiliar environment), gait instability, muscle weakness, and sensory and perceptual changes. Recurrent falls are commonly seen in later stages. If surgical intervention is required for any of these conditions, the individual is subject to the usual surgical complications (infection, adverse reaction to the anesthetic, pneumonia, and poor wound closure). The tendency to wander away from caretakers and familiar surroundings puts these individuals at risk for traumatic injury, drowning, victimization, and death from unnatural causes.

Factors Influencing Duration

Factors that may influence the length of disability include the general health and fitness of the individual before being diagnosed with Alzheimer's disease, evidence of pre-existing diseases affecting any of the major body systems (e.g., diabetes, chronic obstructive lung disease, and chronic heart disease), diagnosis of an acute disease or condition that requires surgery, the individual's mental and emotional stability, access to rehabilitation facilities and home health care, and the strength of the individual's support system.

Length of Disability

Individuals diagnosed with Alzheimer's disease have permanent, progressive disability. In most cases, they do not noticeably improve but rather gradually deteriorate as they lose their mental and physical capacities. The goal of treatment and rehabilitation is to support the individual in performing daily activities and to forestall further deterioration in memory and mental powers for as long as possible. For those individuals who are sufficiently aware of their situation, early diagnosis offers an opportunity to plan retirement from work, arrange for management of their finances, and discuss the management of future medical problems while they are still competent. Skilled, supportive care can improve the quality of the individual's life.

Failure to Recover

If an individual fails to recover within the maximum duration expectancy period, the reader may wish to reference the following questions to assist in better understanding the specifics of an individual's medical case.

Regarding diagnosis:
- Was a presumptive diagnosis of Alzheimer's made?
- Were underlying medical and psychological conditions identified or ruled out?
- Is caregiver diligent in alerting individual's physician to changes in behavior, movement, consciousness, and bodily functions?
- Has individual experienced health-related complications?
- How are coexisting conditions being addressed?

Regarding treatment:
- To what extent is individual impaired?
- Can individual and/or family members still adequately care for needs? Would family benefit from social services in making long-range plans? Has family accessed appropriate services to care for individual?

Regarding prognosis:
- Are individual and family realistic in planning for the future?
- Will family be able to care for individual in home?
- Were other options investigated?

References

"Treating Behavioral Symptoms." The National Alzheimer's Disease Association. 08 Jun 2000 02 Feb 2001 <http://www.alz.org/hc/treatment/behavior.htm>.

Schunk, Carol. "Cognitive Impairment." Geriatric Physical Therapy. Guccione, Andrew A., ed. St. Louis: Mosby-Year Book, 1993. 139-148.

Amblyopia, Toxic
Other names / synonyms: Lazy Eye, Nutritional Amblyopia, Toxic Optic Neuropathy
368.00, 368.01, 377.34

Definition

Amblyopia is a Greek word that refers to dimness or dullness of vision that develops gradually or suddenly. Toxic amblyopia may be caused by cigarette smoke, medications such as chloramphenicol, ethambutol and digitalis, and toxic chemicals including lead and methanol.

The painless vision loss that occurs in both eyes (bilateral) is the result of a central defect (centrocecal scotoma) in the eye. The retina is the layer of the eyeball that generates and conveys nerve impulses back along the optic nerve to the brain. As the nerves in the eye degenerate over days or weeks, the defect slowly enlarges, creating a blind spot that progressively interferes with central vision. The defect may become large enough to cause total blindness. While amblyopia can exist in adults because of eye muscle problems experienced as children, toxic amblyopia usually develops later in life.

Incidence and prevalence statistics for toxic amblyopia are unavailable. Approximately, 10 million Americans as alcohol-dependents are at increased risk.

Diagnosis

History: The individual with toxic amblyopia may report a history of painless blurred vision slowly developing over a period of days or weeks. Although it starts as a small area, the vision loss can progress to total blindness. History may include malnutrition, chronic alcoholism, or exposure to toxic chemicals.

Physical exam: Although ophthalmoscopic exam may reveal little or no change, a slight swelling of the optic disk may be evident. Vision may be decreased in both eyes, and visual field studies may reveal a central defect (centrocecal scotoma) in the retina.

Central nervous system involvement indicates exposure to toxic chemicals. Symptoms and signs of chronic alcoholism may also be present such as muscle tenderness and numbness (peripheral neuropathy) in the legs, hand tremors, and dementia. Examiner should be alert to these non-ophthalmological symptoms and signs because they lead to important clues to the cause of an optic neuropathy.

Tests: Blood studies evaluate the level of vitamin B-complex and rule out vision loss caused by toxic chemicals or metabolic diseases such as diabetes. An image study of the visual pathway is always justified and is almost always indicated in individuals with situational neurogenic visual loss.

Treatment

Treatment involves avoiding tobacco, the medicines responsible for the condition, and toxic chemicals. Chelating drugs can help remove lead from the body.

Prognosis

If treated before the retina is permanently damaged, improvement usually occurs after avoiding toxic substances. If the condition is longstanding, however, improvement will be minimal. The individual may be severely and permanently visually impaired.

Differential Diagnosis

Other conditions with eye changes similar to those found in toxic amblyopia include pernicious anemia, methanol poisoning, retrobulbar neuritis, macular degeneration, diabetes mellitus, hypertension, temporal arteritis, brain injury, muscular dystrophy, and malnutrition.

Specialists

- Internist
- Medical Toxicologist
- Neurologist
- Ophthalmologist

Work Restrictions / Accommodations

Large computer screens and Braille keyboards may be useful tools in the early stages of toxic amblyopia. Once blind spots expand to block all central vision, major work restrictions and accommodations or a classification of permanent disability may be required. Work restrictions and accommodations focus on providing a safe environment and avoiding moving equipment and other obstacles hazardous to an individual with vision loss.

If permanent blindness occurs, the individual requires a wide range of rehabilitation and supportive interventions to prepare for a life without vision including grief counseling, physical therapy, occupational therapy, and various types of instruction and training (reading Braille, using a cane or seeing eye dog, using a voice-activated or Braille computer). In most instances, the individual will require at least some degree of employment retraining.

Comorbid Conditions

Comorbid conditions that may influence the length of disability include peripheral neuropathy.

Complications

Complications may include blindness and non-ophthalmological symptoms and signs.

Factors Influencing Duration

Factors influencing the length of disability include the individual's general health, mental and emotional stability, severity of symptoms, promptness and compliance with treatment, response to treatment, and scope of disability.

Length of Disability

Duration may depend on underlying cause.

Acute episode.

Duration in Days

Job Classification	Minimum	Optimum	Maximum
Any work	3	7	14

Failure to Recover

If an individual fails to recover within the maximum duration expectancy period, the reader may wish to reference the following questions to assist in better understanding the specifics of an individual's medical case.

Regarding diagnosis:

- Does individual have a history of alcoholism?
- Is individual suffering from malnutrition?
- Does individual smoke cigarettes?
- Does individual take chloramphenicol, ethambutol, or digitalis?
- Was individual exposed to lead or methanol?
- Does individual report blurred vision and sensitivity to light (photophobia) slowly developing over a period of days or weeks?
- Has individual's vision continued to worsen?
- Did eye examination, including visual field, studies indicate extent of disease?
- Were blood studies done to evaluate the level of vitamin B-complex and to rule out exposure to toxic chemicals or metabolic diseases?
- Were electromyography, myelography, CT, or MRI obtained to rule out diseases in the central nervous system that can cause blindness?
- Was the diagnosis of toxic amblyopia confirmed?

Regarding treatment:

- Was exposure to toxic substances stopped?
- Does individual require chelation therapy to remove lead from the body?
- Is individual able to avoid cigarette smoke? If a smoker, is individual enrolled (or willing to enroll) in a smoking-cessation program?
- Were offending medications stopped and replaced by alternate medication/treatment?
- Is individual abstaining from alcohol? Is individual enrolled (or willing to enroll) in a substance abuse program (Alcoholics Anonymous)?
- If malnutrition is a factor, is individual receiving instruction/support from a nutritionist? Has individual increased the intake of foods rich in vitamin B-complex?
- Has individual been compliant with taking the full course of vitamin B-complex injections?

Regarding prognosis:
- Was retina damaged permanently?
- Did treatment begin prior to retinal damage?
- How long has individual had this disorder?
- Is individual avoiding the toxic substances causing or contributing to condition (alcohol, cigarette smoke, certain medications, toxic substances)?
- If unable to maintain nutritional status, what can be done to ensure an adequate nutritional intake? Supervision? Halfway house?
- Since treatment, has individual developed crossing of the eyes (strabismus)?
- Has vision in the unaffected eye been damaged by injury or disease, resulting in increased visual impairment or blindness?

References

Tierney, Lawrence, Stephen McPhee, and Maxine Papadakis, eds. Current Medical Diagnosis and Treatment. New York: McGraw-Hill, 2000.

Weiner, William, and Christopher Goetz. Neurology for the Non-neurologist. Philadelphia: Lippincott Williams & Wilkins, 1999.

Amebiasis
Other names / synonyms: Colitis, Dysentery
006, 006.0, 006.1, 006.2, 006.3, 006.4, 006.5, 006.6, 006.8, 006.9

Definition

Amebiasis is an infection of the colon by a protozoan parasite called Entamoeba histolytica that can contaminate food or water. Transmission of the disease is through ingestion of contaminated water or food. The ameba then travels and settles in the large intestine where it multiplies. The disease can cause diarrhea and inflammation of the intestines (dysentery). Because most strains of amebas are noninvasive, however, most cases of amebiasis produce no symptoms or only a mild infection that remains undiagnosed. Amebiasis can range in severity from no symptoms with spontaneous healing to ulceration of the intestines with possible spreading to other tissues of the body including the liver, lungs, and brain. Untreated, the most severe forms may result in death, but this is very uncommon. The most common site for infection outside the intestines is the liver where it can form abscesses.

Because amebiasis is most prevalent in the tropics and subtropics, it is a potential concern to travelers. It also occurs, however, in temperate climates such as the US. Carried in the feces of infected individuals, the disease is typically transmitted by fecal contamination of water or food. This can occur through insects such as flies, the use of human excrement as fertilizer, handling food with contaminated hands, or individual-to-individual contact. Improved sanitary measures can control the disease. Thorough handwashing is essential in preventing transmission of the parasite.

Diagnosis

History: Individuals may have a history of travel to developing countries or oral-anal contact with an infected person. Symptoms of amebiasis can vary widely depending on the site and severity of the lesions caused by the parasite. In the great majority of cases, the individual has no symptoms. When present, symptoms include crampy abdominal pain and diarrhea. Progression may lead to blood and mucus in the diarrhea (amebic dysentery). Individuals with more severe amebiasis may also experience fever, weakness, nausea, vomiting, abdominal bloating, and severe abdominal pain.

Although symptoms of mild amebiasis usually begin 2 to 4 weeks after exposure, symptoms can develop as early as 4 days after exposure or up to a year later. If a liver abscess develops, individual may experience a sudden onset of upper abdominal pain accompanied by fever, loss of appetite, weight loss, and a general feeling of ill health (malaise).

Physical exam: If severe diarrhea is present, the lips, mouth, and skin may be dry from dehydration. Extreme dehydration can cause cardiac rhythmic disturbances. The abdomen may be tender especially if the abdominal cavity becomes infected (peritonitis). Chills, fever, and profuse perspiration usually accompany abdominal infections. When a liver abscess is present, the liver may be enlarged (hepatomegaly). The skin may turn pale and cold if shock develops.

Tests: Several stool samples (usually 3) are examined for the presence of parasites. Because they have various growth states, the protozoa can be difficult to visualize and stool samples may not be adequate for diagnosis. In this case, blood samples (serology) are examined for antiamebic antibodies. Blood cell counts may indicate high numbers of white blood cells. Liver enzymes may also be high. Colonoscopy may be used to visualize the intestinal lining to rule out other disorders that can mimic or occur in conjunction with amebiasis. For those cases more difficult to diagnosis, sigmoidoscopy can also retrieve tissue samples to be examined for amebas. For disease that has progressed to a liver abscess, abdominal ultrasound, CT, MRI, or radioisotope scanning may be used.

Treatment

Amebiasis can be successfully treated with a number of antiparasitic drugs such as metronidazole that specifically target protozoan pathogens (amebicides). Treatment typically lasts 10 days. Additional drugs may be needed to kill amebas living in the lining of the intestines. Replacement of fluids (rehydration therapy), electrolytes, and blood may be required. If vomiting is present, medication can be given intravenously. A liver abscess may need further treatment including drainage by needle aspiration or surgery.

There is no preventive medication regimen for amebiasis, therefore prevention consists of precautionary behaviors such as drinking treated water, eating thoroughly cooked foods, and washing fruits and vegetables carefully in treated water prior to eating them.

Prognosis

With proper treatment, the infection can be controlled usually without long-term effects. Most individuals recover fully within 2 to 4 weeks after beginning treatment. Without treatment, however, mortality can be high. Serious medical complications can develop into life-threatening conditions. Although rare, lung or brain infection can result in chronic disease.

Differential Diagnosis

Amebiasis may resemble any other cause of diarrhea as well as appendicitis, inflammatory bowel disease, cholecystitis, intestinal obstruction, or diverticulitis. Symptoms of chronic amebiasis may be similar to those of ulcerative colitis. An amebic liver abscess must be distinguished from a pyogenic abscess, echinococcal cyst, and hepatocellular carcinoma.

Specialists

- Cardiologist
- Gastroenterologist
- General Surgeon
- Infectious Disease Physician

Work Restrictions / Accommodations

The individual should not return to work while diarrhea is present unless constant, immediate access to a bathroom is assured. Abdominal discomfort and weakness may make physical exertion difficult. Frequent breaks and access to bathrooms may be needed. Co-workers may also be uncomfortable due to flatulence and odors from the infected individual. It may be preferable for the affected individual to work away from others until symptoms subside.

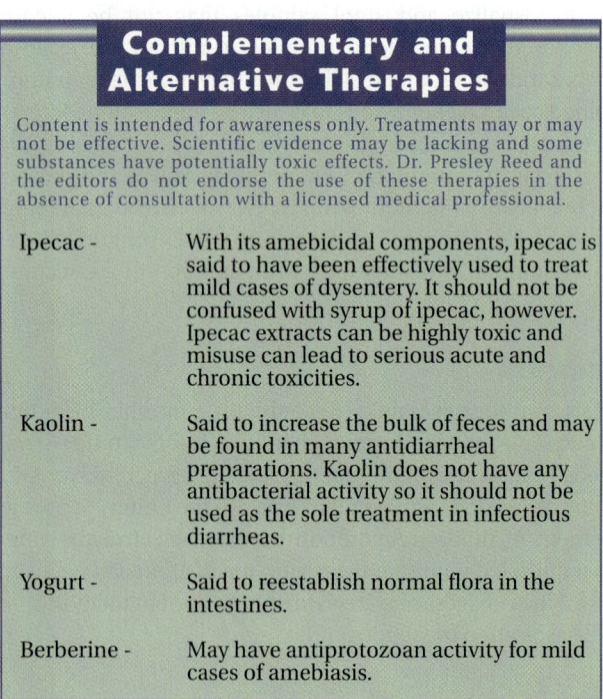

Complementary and Alternative Therapies

Content is intended for awareness only. Treatments may or may not be effective. Scientific evidence may be lacking and some substances have potentially toxic effects. Dr. Presley Reed and the editors do not endorse the use of these therapies in the absence of consultation with a licensed medical professional.

Ipecac -	With its amebicidal components, ipecac is said to have been effectively used to treat mild cases of dysentery. It should not be confused with syrup of ipecac, however. Ipecac extracts can be highly toxic and misuse can lead to serious acute and chronic toxicities.
Kaolin -	Said to increase the bulk of feces and may be found in many antidiarrheal preparations. Kaolin does not have any antibacterial activity so it should not be used as the sole treatment in infectious diarrheas.
Yogurt -	Said to reestablish normal flora in the intestines.
Berberine -	May have antiprotozoan activity for mild cases of amebiasis.

Comorbid Conditions

Coexisting conditions that may impact recovery include alcoholism, malnutrition, and the general health of the bowel. For example, inflammatory bowel disease may make it easier for the ameba to cause ulceration of the intestines. Immunosuppression can make an individual more prone to the disease and lengthen the course of it.

Complications

Extreme dehydration from persistent diarrhea may result in cardiac arrhythmia or a loss of body temperature control. Liver abscesses may develop and rupture into the abdominal cavity or tissues surrounding the lungs or heart. Although rare, the amebas may enter the bloodstream and infect the spleen, lungs, or brain. Ulceration of the bowel may occur.

Factors Influencing Duration

The length of disability is influenced by the severity of symptoms, extent of the disease (involvement of other organs such as the liver, lungs, or brain), and the individual's response to treatment. Surgery to drain liver abscesses may lengthen disability.

Length of Disability

Acute amebic dysentery (severe colitis).

Duration in Days

Job Classification	Minimum	Optimum	Maximum
Any work	3	7	14

Acute or chronic amebic colitis without abscess. Mild to moderate.

Duration in Days

Job Classification	Minimum	Optimum	Maximum
Any work	0	3	7

Failure to Recover

If an individual fails to recover within the maximum duration expectancy period, the reader may wish to reference the following questions to assist in better understanding the specifics of an individual's medical case.

Regarding diagnosis:

- Does individual have a history of recent travel in developing countries, or had intimate contact with an infected individual?
- Did individual present with any symptoms? If so, did individual experience crampy abdominal pain, diarrhea, bloody or mucus diarrhea and fever?
- Was diagnosis confirmed with stool and/or serological tests?
- Was there evidence of elevated liver enzymes? Were additional diagnostic tests done to rule out the possibility of associated liver abscesses or other organ involvement?

- If the diagnosis was unconfirmed, were other causes of diarrhea, such as parasitic, bacterial or viral infection, ruled out?
- Were other conditions with similar symptoms such as appendicitis, inflammatory bowel disease, cholecystitis, intestinal obstruction, or diverticulitis, ruled out?

Regarding treatment:

- Was the condition treated appropriately with antiparasitic medications, hydration and administration of antiemetic medications?
- If the symptoms persisted, were additional or alternative antiparasitic medications tried?
- Was drainage of a liver abscess indicated?
- Was individual instructed regarding ongoing food and fluid precautions (i.e., drinking water, washing produce, cooking meats)?

Regarding prognosis:

- Did individual receive prompt treatment?
- Did adequate time elapse for complete recovery (2 to 4 weeks)?
- Were additional stool and serological cultures done to rule out the possibility of a secondary bacterial infection?
- Did individual experience any associated complications (liver, lung or brain infections or severe fluid and electrolyte imbalance) that could impact recovery and prognosis?
- Does individual have any underlying condition (immune suppression, inflammatory bowel disease, malnutrition, alcoholism) that could impact ability to recover? If so, have these conditions been addressed in the treatment plan?

References

Di Stasi, L.C. "Amoebicidal Compounds From Medicinal Plants." Parassitologia 37 1 (1995): 29-39.

Ghoshal, S., B.N. Prasad, and V. Lakshmi. "Antiamoebic Activity of Piper Longum Fruits Against Entamoeba Histolytica in vitro and in vivo." Journal of Ethnopharmacology 50 3 (1996): 167-170.

Istre, G.R., K. Kreiss, and R.S. Hopkins. "An Outbreak of Amebiasis Spread by Colonic Irrigation at a Chiropractic Clinic." New England Journal of Medicine 307 6 (1982): 339-342.

Tierney, Lawrence, Stephen McPhee, and Maxine Papadakis. Current Medical Diagnosis and Treatment, 37th ed. Stamford: Appleton & Lange, 1998.

Amnesia
Other names / synonyms: Memory Loss
780.9

Definition

The term amnesia refers to partial or total inability to recall past experiences. Retrograde amnesia is memory loss for events that occurred before a head injury, prior to the onset of a specific illness, or from severe emotional trauma. Anterograde amnesia is the inability to remember events after a specific illness or injury. Transient amnesia is the brief or fleeting loss of memory, particularly after brain injury or seizures. Progressive amnesia is memory loss that worsens over time associated with dementias. Memory disturbances related to alcohol abuse and head trauma are the two most common causes of amnesia.

Amnesia generally results from damage to the areas on both sides of the brain that are involved in memory. Amnesia can result from systemic medical conditions (thiamine deficiency associated with alcohol abuse, malnourishment) infections of the brain (encephalitis), seizures, brain tumors, head injury, lack of oxygen to the brain, carbon monoxide poisoning, electroconvulsive therapy used to treat psychological problems, multiple sclerosis, or temporal lobe brain surgery. Amnesia can occur from altered blood flow to the brain (cerebrovascular disease) such as stroke or transient ischemic attack (TIA), or from drugs, alcohol, or exposure to toxins.

The exact prevalence and incidence of the amnesia disorders is unknown.

Diagnosis

History: The individual (or individual's family members) may report problems with memory. Onset may be sudden or occur slowly over time. Individual may report a recent precipitating event such as a fall, blow to the head, or other traumatic occurrence. The individual may complain of associated symptoms such as headache, vision problems, dizziness, confusion and disorientation, poor concentration, or sleepiness.

Physical exam: Because amnesia can result from a variety of underlying pathologies, a complete physical exam must be done to assure an accurate diagnosis. A detailed neurological status and function examination is required. Recent, intermediate, and long-term memory is tested. If a traumatic event precipitated the amnesia, this is used as a reference point to evaluate memory prior to the event (to rule out retrograde amnesia) and memory after the event (to rule out antegrade amnesia). Visual acuity, eye movement and pupil reaction, motor strength, coordination, sensory function, and reflex testing may help distinguish between widespread brain dysfunction (in infectious or metabolic process) and focal disorder (seen with brain tumors or brain hemorrhage). The individual may be evaluated for other high-level brain functions such as judgment, complex thought processes, and speech.

Tests: CT and MRI of the brain may be used to diagnose brain lesions or general atrophy. Lumbar puncture can be helpful in ruling out infectious origins of amnesia. An electroencephalogram (EEG) can determine seizure disorders. Blood work including a chemistry panel, drug screen, and liver function studies rule out toxic or metabolic abnormalities. Cerebral angiography detects defects in the blood vessels of the brain such as obstruction (thrombus) or blood clots (emboli).

Treatment

The primary goal in the management of amnesia is to treat the underlying cause. Those with amnesia related to brain injury or tumor usually require supportive medical care and possibly surgery to remove collections of blood (craniotomy with evacuation of hematoma) or the tumor (craniotomy with resection of tumor). A regimen of anticancer drugs (chemotherapy) along with radiation treatments (radiation therapy) may be indicated for individuals with cancerous brain tumors.

Avoidance of alcohol, thiamine supplementation, and restoration of a stable nutritional status is recommended for those with amnesia secondary to thiamine deficiencies. Individuals with amnesia secondary to brain infections require supportive medical care and antibiotic or antiviral medications. Seizure disorders are usually treated with antiseizure medications that are effective in preventing the recurrence of seizures but have little effect on restoring memory.

Those with age-associated memory impairment may need to be taught simple memory aids and techniques such as making lists and writing notes. A class of drugs called acetylcholinesterase inhibitors may be used to enhance memory function in individuals with Alzheimer's disease.

Because some cases of amnesia are associated with serious psychological states psychiatric counseling is often part of the treatment plan.

Prognosis

Most individuals with acute amnesia secondary to brain injury improve spontaneously over weeks to months. In adults, recovery after severe head injury most often occurs within the first 6 months with smaller improvements continuing for perhaps as long as 2 years. Patterns of recovery vary according to the degree of injury. Individuals with severe head injury may have persistent amnesia.

Outcomes for individuals with amnesia due to an underlying condition, such as cancerous (metastatic) brain tumors, depend upon said condition. Small, slow-growing tumors discovered early respond well to treatment with good outcome and little or no residual side effects or memory impairment.

Progressive or permanent memory loss is possible in individuals with amnesia due to infectious or degenerative brain disorders.

It is unclear to what extent psychiatric counseling affects the outcome of amnesia due to alcohol or drug abuse disorders. If the brain damage is significant, the risk of permanent brain dysfunction and associated amnesia increases.

Differential Diagnosis

Delirium or dementia have similar symptoms to amnesia and need to be part of the differential diagnosis.

Specialists

- Neurologist

Work Restrictions / Accommodations

Resumption of regular duties is appropriate once the individual regains full recall. Individuals with permanent or progressive amnesia may need reassignment and/or retraining or permanent disability.

Comorbid Conditions

Comorbid conditions that may impact ability to recover and lengthen disability are Alzheimer's disease, degenerative brain disorders, brain ischemia, infiltrating brain cancers, and mental illness.

Complications

Anxiety, depression, and associated intellectual or cognitive impairment may complicate amnestic disorders.

Factors Influencing Duration

The nature and degree of the underlying cause of amnesia and advanced age are factors that may influence disability.

Length of Disability

Duration depends on etiology. Contact physician for more information.

Failure to Recover

If an individual fails to recover within the maximum duration expectancy period, the reader may wish to reference the following questions to assist in better understanding the specifics of an individual's medical case.

Regarding diagnosis:

- Does individual have any systemic medical conditions such as thiamine deficiency associated with alcohol abuse, malnourished states, or encephalitis?
- Does individual have seizures, brain tumors, head injury, lack of oxygen to the brain, carbon monoxide poisoning, electroconvulsive therapy, multiple sclerosis, or temporal lobe brain surgery?
- Does individual have any conditions such as stroke or transient ischemic attack (TIA), or hardening of the arteries?
- Was individual exposed to toxins, drugs or alcohol?
- Does individual or family report memory problems? Was onset sudden or gradual?
- Does individual have a recent history of head trauma?
- Does individual complain of headache, vision problems, dizziness, confusion and disorientation, poor concentration, or sleepiness?
- Was individual given a complete physical examination? Neurological exam?
- Was individual evaluated for judgment, complex thought processes, and speech?
- Was CT, MRI, EEG, or lumbar puncture performed? Cerebral angiography?
- Were complete blood chemistry panel, and drug and alcohol screen performed?

112 The Medical Disability Advisor—Fourth Edition

- Were conditions with similar symptoms ruled out?

Regarding treatment:

- What is the underlying condition? Is it being treated?
- Was surgery indicated?
- Were antibiotics or antiviral drugs indicated?
- Was chemotherapy and/or radiation therapy indicated?
- Was individual given instruction regarding avoidance of alcohol, thiamine supplementation, and restoration of a stable nutritional status?
- If necessary, was individual taught to use memory aids?
- Are acetylcholinesterase inhibitors indicated?
- Is individual active in therapy with an appropriate mental health professional?

Regarding prognosis:

- Is individual's employer able to accommodate any necessary restrictions?
- Does individual have any conditions that may affect their ability to recover?
- Does individual have any complications such as anxiety, depression, and associated intellectual or cognitive impairment?

References

Beers, Mark H., and Robert Berkow, eds. The Merck Manual of Diagnosis and Therapy, 17th edition. Whitehouse Station: Merck & Co., Inc, 1999 23 Aug 2000 <http://www.merck.com/pubs/mmanual/section14/sec14.htm>.

Clochesy, John M., et al. Critical Care Nursing, Second edition. Philadelphia: W.B. Saunders Company, 1996.

Mahan, Kathleen L., and Sylvia Escott-Stump, eds. Krause's Food, Nutrition, and Diet Therapy, 10th edition. Philadelphia: W.B. Saunders Company, 2000.

Tierney, Lawrence M., Stephen J. McPhee, and Maxine A. Papadakis, eds. Current Medical Diagnosis and Treatment, 39th Edition. New York: Lange Medical Books/McGraw-Hill, 2000.

Amphetamine Dependence/Abuse

Other names / synonyms: Addiction to Dexedrine, Addiction to Preludin, Addiction to Ritalin, Amphetamine Addiction, Chalk Addiction, Crystal Addiction, Glass Addiction, Ice Addiction, Meth Addiction, Methamphetamine Addiction, Speed Addiction

304.4, 305.7

Definition

Amphetamines are potent central nervous system stimulants and include drugs such as amphetamine, dextroamphetamine, methamphetamine (speed), and various appetite suppressants and decongestants.

Amphetamine use releases the brain chemical dopamine, which stimulates brain cells, enhancing mood and movement. It may also damage brain cells that contain dopamine and another nerve chemical (neurotransmitter) called serotonin. Over time, levels of dopamine decrease. This may cause stiffness, tremor, and other symptoms similar to those in Parkinson's disease.

As with any addiction process, abuse and dependence are defined generally by continued use in the face of negative consequences. These consequences may fall into one or more of the following areas: physical and psychological health, occupational functioning, legal problems, interpersonal relationships, and financial affairs. A generally useful definition of dependence is loss of control over when and how much of the substance is used. For abuse to be present, all that is required is recurrent use in spite of any adverse consequences. A diagnosis is based on criteria listed in the DSM-IV-TR (Diagnostic and Statistical Manual of Mental Disorders, 4th Edition, Text Revision, published by the American Psychiatric Association).

Amphetamine dependence/abuse occurs when an individual uses one or more of the amphetamine substances in a maladaptive way resulting in at least three of the following symptoms: a need for increased amounts of amphetamines to achieve the desired effect (tolerance); withdrawal symptoms such as depression, fatigue, insomnia or hypersomnia, increased appetite, or agitation; using amphetamines in larger amounts or for longer than intended; a persistent, unsuccessful attempt to control use of the substance; much time spent using or obtaining amphetamines; giving up important activities in order to use amphetamines; and continued amphetamine use despite related physical, emotional, occupational, legal, or relational difficulties.

These substances can be taken orally, inhaled through the nose, smoked, or injected intravenously. The effects may appear in 30 to 40 minutes and last for 4 to 8 hours. Amphetamine use may result in feelings of being high or elated (euphoria), talkativeness, hyperactivity, restlessness, heightened awareness of threatening or other stimuli (hypervigilance), anxiety, tension, grandiosity, anger, and impaired judgment. Other effects may include decreased appetite, more rapid breathing, increased heart rate and blood pressure, fever (hyperthermia), confusion, tremors, seizures, suspiciousness (paranoia), and aggressive behavior. Fever and seizures can cause death.

Many individuals begin use of amphetamines to lose weight while others use illegal substances for recreational purposes. Smoked or injected amphetamine more commonly leads to dependence than does the oral form. Individuals who have used daily for 8 to 10 years tend to decrease or stop use because of adverse side effects such as depression, sleep disturbances, malnutrition, or cardiovascular complications including chronic chest pain or irregular heart rate.

As methamphetamine can be easily manufactured illegally from store-bought materials, it is the most prevalent synthetic drug manufactured in the US. Approximately 5% of adults acknowledge having used stimulant drugs to get high with 1% acknowledging use in the previous year. Amphetamine use is most prevalent from ages 18 to 30 (16% in one survey). Intravenous use is more common in lower socio-economic groups and is 3 to 4 times more common in men than women. Approximately equal numbers of men and women use amphetamines by other routes. In 1997, there were more than 50,000 hospital admissions in the US for treatment of methamphetamine abuse or its complications, accounting for almost 4% of all treatment admissions.

Diagnosis

History: Since there may be no dramatic physical effects seen when the drug is withdrawn, the history is very important in establishing this diagnosis. The DSM-IV-TR focuses on the use pattern during the past 12 months; in particular, use causing a decline in interpersonal, occupational, and social functioning. A noticeable drop in performance in work, school, or the home is considered sufficient, as is recurrent use of the substance in hazardous situations such as driving. Recurrent substance-related legal problems qualify for abuse as does persistent interpersonal or social problems either caused or worsened by use of the substance such as arguments with a spouse.

The difference between abuse and dependence is usually one of degree. In dependence, use of the substance becomes so compelling that it begins to shut out all other interests and pursuits. Depending on the particular substance, tolerance and withdrawal phenomenon may be present. Unsuccessful efforts have usually been made to cut down but use continues despite harmful physical or psychological effects. Amphetamine users may show a marked tolerance for the drug's effects. Withdrawal usually consists of utter physical and mental exhaustion in the wake of sustained use (runs or binges of use may last for days to weeks during which time the user sleeps infrequently, if at all).

Physical exam: Besides the psychological effects mentioned, the acute effects of amphetamines include a pronounced increase in heart rate and blood pressure, dilated pupils, elevated or lowered blood pressure, perspiration, nausea or vomiting, psychomotor agitation or retardation, muscular weakness, respiratory depression, chest pain, confusion, seizures, or coma. A common indicator of recent use is an excess of energy that expresses itself through constant movement. The user seems wired and hyperactive and may be extremely fidgety and restless or may repeat nonpurposeful movements. Over time, these drugs may take a major toll on physical health. One of the more obvious signs is weight loss. If the drugs are used intravenously, needle tracks may be visible. Use of these agents is also associated with an increased risk of heart attack, irregular heart rhythms, and stroke.

Psychosis may be evident in association with prolonged and severe abuse. This is often a paranoid form of psychosis that in some cases may be virtually indistinguishable from paranoid schizophrenia. This is usually temporary and reverses within hours to days as the effects of the drug wear off. In rare cases, however, the symptoms may persist for months to years.

Tests: Amphetamines are rapidly metabolized and eliminated therefore, urine tests remain positive for only 1 to 3 days. If there are abnormalities of heart rhythm or rate, electrocardiogram (ECG) may be warranted. Electroencephalogram (EEG) should be done if there is evidence of seizures or convulsions.

Treatment

Abstinence is the treatment goal. Fatigue, restlessness, and depression may occur several days after quitting the drug. Although antidepressant medications can be helpful in combating the depressive symptoms, severely depressed individuals may become suicidal. For this reason, chronic users may need to be hospitalized during drug withdrawal. For individuals who experience delusions or hallucinations, antipsychotic medications such as haloperidol or chlorpromazine may be given to calm and relieve distress. Individuals in this condition often benefit from psychiatric hospitalization.

In general, amphetamine recovery occurs in four phases. The acute phase focuses on alleviating symptoms of physiological withdrawal and typically lasts 3 to 5 days. The next phase is a 1-month period of abstinence during which the individual focuses on changing his or her behaviors. The early remission phase can last up to 12 months. The sustained remission phase lasts as long as the individual abstains from amphetamine use.

The most effective treatments for amphetamine dependence are cognitive behavioral therapy and addiction education and support groups. These interventions are designed to help modify the individual's thinking, expectancies, and behaviors and to increase coping skills for various life stressors. Early treatment usually occurs in an outpatient setting and may include education on physical, emotional, and mental aspects of addiction and recovery, identification of stressors and stress management skills, improved coping skills, assertiveness training, relaxation training, and individual or family psychotherapy. Ongoing structured self-help programs such as Alcoholics Anonymous, Narcotics Anonymous, and Rational Recovery are recommended as an adjunct to treatment services. Regular but random drug screens may be part of the treatment process.

Individual should understand that relapse may occur and is often even part of the recovery process. Medication therapy may include dopamine antagonists and/or antidepressants as indicated by psychiatric or clinical evaluation. Inpatient substance abuse treatment is needed for severe depression or psychotic symptoms lasting beyond 1 to 3 days after abstinence, for repeated outpatient failures, or if the individual is violent toward others, suicidal, or has severe withdrawal symptoms during detoxification.

Prognosis

Some individuals respond to treatment and stay in remission from substance abuse for many years. However, some individuals experience periods of relapse where they begin using amphetamines after a period of remission and again meet the criteria for substance abuse. Other individuals are never able to abstain from substance use/abuse and do not experience any periods of remission. Individuals who develop new relationships and consistently make use of self-help groups are more likely to experience continued abstinence and achieve improvement in social and occupational functioning. Most experts agree that addicts need to do more than just kick their habits. They need to make life changes and find meaning and motivation to move ahead.

Specific outcomes associated with amphetamine abuse may include weight loss and malnutrition, paranoid psychosis, brain damage, seizures, and heart disease. In 1997, methamphetamine was ranked ninth among all drug-related deaths, with about 500 deaths accounting for approximately 5% of total drug-related deaths.

Differential Diagnosis

Three clinical settings where amphetamines continue to be used include the treatment of attention deficit hyperactive disorder (ADHD), narcolepsy, and depression. ADHD is more common in children but may persist into adulthood and may be treated with amphetamines in certain situations. In this circumstance, the user may have had a legitimate medical requirement that led to the substance abuse. However, a more common situation is when the amphetamine user tries to fabricate a history to justify the addiction or legally obtain the drug. Even large amounts of certain decongestants can produce an amphetamine-like effect and be abused. A legitimate use of amphetamines is the occasional treatment of depression usually in the elderly or terminally ill.

Other stimulant abuse disorders such as cocaine or phencyclidine abuse may appear similar to amphetamine abuse. The individual may also abuse several substances, which makes it difficult to pinpoint behaviors specific to one substance. Psychiatric disorders (bipolar disorder, major depressive disorder, schizophrenia) or personality disorders (antisocial personality disorder, conduct disorder) can also present with similar behaviors.

Specialists

- Advanced Practice Registered Nurse
- Cardiologist
- Neurologist
- Occupational Therapist
- Physical Therapist
- Psychiatrist
- Psychologist

Work Restrictions / Accommodations

Many employers have systems in place for individuals recovering from substance abuse disorders that allow them to return to work under special contracts or conditions. These conditions usually include routine or random testing of blood and urine levels for identified substances and work performance and substance abuse treatment guidelines for the recovering individual. Individuals should not work at all if intoxicated.

Temporary work accommodations may include reducing or eliminating activities where the safety of self or others is contingent upon a constant and/or high level of alertness, such as driving motor vehicles, operating complex machinery, or handling dangerous chemicals; introducing the individual to new or stressful situations gradually under individually appropriate supervision; allowing some flexibility in scheduling to attend therapy appointments (which normally should occur during employee's personal time); promoting planned, proactive management of identified problem areas; and offering timely feedback on job performance issues. It will be helpful if accommodations are documented in a written plan designed to promote timely and safe transition back to full work productivity.

After detoxification, if the individual has chronic side effects of prolonged substance abuse such as cardiac, liver, or nervous system damage, restriction to sedentary type activities may be necessary. Access to addictive substances should be limited such as restricting work in pharmacies or establishments that serve liquor.

Comorbid Conditions

Comorbid conditions that may affect recovery and lengthen disability include the abuse of or dependence on alcohol or other substances, other psychiatric illnesses, infection with hepatitis B or C, and HIV infection. Individuals with chronic use of stimulants can sometimes become sensitized to any future use of stimulants. When this happens, small amounts of even mild stimulants such as caffeine can cause symptoms of paranoia and auditory hallucinations. The combination of a psychiatric illness with substance abuse (dual diagnosis) can complicate the treatment of both the chemical dependency as well as the psychiatric illness. Approximately one-third of those hospitalized for psychiatric disorders have coexisting non-nicotine substance use disorders.

Complications

Other psychiatric illnesses may be present and complicate treatment of both the amphetamine dependence and the other illness (dual diagnosis). About half of those with bipolar mood (affective) disorder or schizophrenia may have drug or alcohol problems. Those with post-traumatic stress disorder may have substance abuse rates as high as 80%. The individual with prolonged use may experience depression, weight loss with malnutrition, or impaired personal hygiene. Intravenous use may lead to skin infections, bacterial endocarditis, HIV, or hepatitis. Complications of amphetamine abuse may include weight loss and malnutrition, heart disease, or seizures. Brain damage from methamphetamine use can be similar to that caused by Alzheimer's disease, Parkinson's disease, stroke, or epilepsy.

Factors Influencing Duration

Length of disability is influenced by the duration and severity of amphetamine abuse, presence or absence of organ damage, any underlying mental illness, other substance abuse, motivation to change, the individual's social support system, appropriateness of treatment choice, compliance with treatment, and adequacy of ongoing care.

Length of Disability

Maximum duration includes hospitalization. After an initial detoxification period of a few days that does not usually require hospitalization, the individual is ready to return to work as long as accommodations are made for continued participation in a treatment program.

Detoxification and counseling.

Duration in Days

Job Classification	Minimum	Optimum	Maximum
Any work	7	14	42

Failure to Recover

If an individual fails to recover within the maximum duration expectancy period, the reader may wish to reference the following questions to assist in better understanding the specifics of an individual's medical case.

Regarding diagnosis:

- Does individual continue to use amphetamines despite the consequences?
- Does individual exhibit at least three psychological symptoms of amphetamine dependence or abuse?
- Does individual display any physical symptoms of amphetamine use?
- Were conditions with similar symptoms ruled out?
- Were all underlying medical and psychiatric disorders identified?

Regarding treatment:

- Is individual involved in a cognitive behavioral therapy program that helps modify individual's thinking, expectancies, and behaviors? Does this therapy program help increase individual's coping skills for various life stressors?
- Is individual participating in a substance recovery support group?
- If individual exhibits severe depression or suicidal tendencies, would he/she benefit from antidepressant medication or hospitalization until stabilized?
- If individual is experiencing psychotic symptoms, such as delusions or hallucinations, would individual benefit from antipsychotic drug therapy or psychiatric hospitalization?

Regarding prognosis:

- At what point of treatment is individual currently?
- Is he or she experiencing relapses? Are relapses decreasing in frequency?
- Would individual benefit from more frequent, more intense, or longer treatment?
- Does individual require external support and motivation to continue in treatment beyond the initial stage of detoxification?
- Does individual participate in a formal support group?
- What other support systems does individual have in place?
- Is individual able to develop new relationships?
- Is improvement evident in social and occupational functioning?
- Is individual receiving the necessary tools, skills, and encouragement to move ahead with his/her life?

References

Duke, James A. The Green Pharmacy. Emmaus, PA: Rodale Press, Inc, 1997.

Frances, Allen. Diagnostic and Statistical Manual of Mental Disorders: 4th ed, text revision. Washington, DC: American Psychiatric Association, 2000.

Healing with Vitamins. Feinstein, Alice, ed. Englewood: Rodale Press, Inc, 1996.

Methamphetamine. Infofax. 29 Mar 2000 08 Jan 2001 <http://www.nida.nih.gov/Infofax/methamphetamine.html>.

Methamphetamine. Office of National Drug Control Policy. 01 Jan 2000 09 Jan 2001 <http://www.whitehousedrugpolicy.gov/drugfact/methamphetamine/index.html>.

New Choices in Natural Healing. Gottlieb, Bill, ed. Emmaus, PA: Rodale Press, Inc, 1997.

Amputation
84.91

Definition

Amputation is a surgical procedure to remove all or part of a diseased or injured arm or leg (limb), or finger or toe (digit). Amputations may be performed at any level in the upper extremities, hands, fingers, lower extremities, feet, or toes. They should be performed at the level where healing is most likely to be complete while permitting the most efficient use of the limb following rehabilitation. Levels of amputation are referred to by site as upper extremity (UE), above elbow (AE), below elbow (BE), lower extremity (LE), above the knee (AK), below the knee (BK), or through the knee (TK).

The procedure is usually performed under a general anesthetic, although a local anesthetic is sometimes used for finger or toe amputations.

About 30,000 amputations are performed in the US every year, and the LE type accounts for 85%. About 75% of amputations are performed on men due to higher rate of causative injury and higher rate of smoking. Most amputations are done on individuals between the ages of 50 and 75, primarily because of the increased incidence of diabetes and peripheral vascular disease in this age group. Amputations in younger age groups are mostly performed as a result of severe injuries.

Reason for Procedure

The majority of amputations are performed as a result of a combination of disease of the arteries that impairs blood flow (atherosclerosis) and a blood clot (thrombosis) that blocks the blood supply to a limb and causes tissue death (gangrene). Amputation is also performed when a limb is severely affected by trauma or infection. The procedure may also be done to prevent the spread of bone cancer or skin cancer (malignant melanoma). The immediate aims of amputation are to remove diseased tissue and relieve pain. The surgery should be performed in a manner that will permit primary healing of the wound, construction of a stump, and the provision of prosthesis for useful function.

Description

Many surgical procedures are available for amputations of all levels. Most of these, however, have the same components. During the surgical procedure, the skin is cut (incised) and the muscles and other soft tissues are either cut through or pulled aside (retracted). The bone is then severed with a saw or the joint is severed through all of its soft tissue attachments (disarticulation). Large blood vessels are tied off (ligated) and smaller ones are sealed off with an electric needle (cauterization). Nerves are severed well above the stump to prevent irritation from the prosthesis. Sometimes the severed nerve will be implanted into a muscle area to prevent scarring of the severed nerve end (neuroma formation). Muscles and tendons are cut (resected) at the level of the amputation, and additional muscle tissue is removed (debulking) as necessary for prosthetic fitting. The bony stump is then remodeled and smoothed as necessary. A generous length of skin and muscle tissue left beyond the point of bone resection is used to create a flap which is then placed over the end of the stump and sewn (sutured) to the adjacent skin.

A drain may be inserted and is left protruding from between the sutures to allow fluid to escape from the surgical site. This drain is removed in 24 to 72 hours. In emergency amputations or in dirty or infected wounds, the wound may be left open to drain and is later closed (delayed closure). The area must be protected until healing is complete at which time prosthetic fitting, if appropriate, can be done.

Prognosis

Amputations are generally successful in arresting the spread of infection or cancer. However, loss of part or all of an extremity always produces some permanent disability. In lower extremity amputations, fitting with prosthesis will often permit some ambulation. Some upper extremity prostheses will also provide some regaining of function. Amputations of fingers, especially the thumb, can result in considerable reduction of ability to perform tasks involving manual dexterity.

Specialists

- General Surgeon
- Orthopedic Surgeon
- Physiatrist
- Vascular Surgeon

Rehabilitation

Rehabilitation after amputation varies greatly depending on what part of the body was amputated. In the early stages of rehabilitation for an amputation, controlling pain, and swelling and avoiding infection is very important. Cold treatments after extremity trauma or surgery associated with amputation cause blood vessels to become smaller, helping to control excess bleeding and swelling of soft tissues. This is accomplished using cold packs with or without compression. Physical therapists use various cold treatments often in conjunction with electrical stimulation. However, if extremity pain is severe and persists for extended periods of time, transcutaneous electrical nerve stimulation (T.E.N.S.) may be helpful, which is a form of electrostimulation. An electrical impulse predetermined by the physical therapist, produces a high frequency tingling sensation, which blocks the transmission and awareness of pain. Methods of electrical stimulation used in physical therapy decrease pain by producing an electrical response in the muscles around the region that was traumatized.

Once pain and swelling has subsided, rehabilitation then focuses on returning range of motion and strength to the remaining joints of the extremity (or residual limb) following amputation. Flexibility of specific muscles is important in order to return to as normal functioning as possible. For example, if the amputation is below the knee, keeping the hamstrings flexible is very critical. If the amputation is above the knee, the focus is on the hip muscles both in front and in back of the thigh. To address the front hip/thigh muscles, the therapist instructs the individual to lie on his or her stomach supporting the upper trunk on the elbows.

Strengthening of the residual upper or lower limb begins early in rehabilitation. Regarding lower extremity amputations, walking exercises (gait training) with the use of a temporary prosthesis often indicated and started when appropriate. A temporary prosthesis allows a predetermined amount of weight to be placed on the involved limb and enables the individual to progress with exercises while the size of the residual limb stabilizes, allowing a permanent prosthesis to be fitted.

The upper or lower extremity amputee depends heavily upon muscles to control the prosthesis. For example, the below the knee amputee depends on the muscles on the front of thigh for ambulating. Strong muscles on the side of the hips are also necessary to maintain stability of the pelvis. Ankle weights are also used for resistance as the muscles strengthen. Upper extremity amputation demands good arm muscle tone as well as control for finer movements requiring skill. All strengthening exercises are performed in three sets of ten repetitions, twice daily.

Exercises called functional training are important in rehabilitation focusing on the individual's physical demands at home and in the preparation to return to work. These activities, such as ascending and descending stairs or repeatedly practicing going from sitting to standing, should last for up to at least three minutes to complete. Upper extremities activities include dressing and other self-cares requiring reaching, pulling, and grasping. Such activities more closely match normal requirements of activities of daily living (ADLs).

A home exercise program is started at the time of the physical therapy evaluation with gradual progression in difficulty up to the date of discharge. The final step is to incorporate activities that will help the individual return home and to the work environment. This includes exercises that resemble work requirements and patient education regarding placement and removal of the prosthesis. Modifications may need to be made by the physical therapist for those individuals who have experienced traumatic extremity amputation. Variations in rehabilitation will depend on the location of the amputation and whether surgery and prosthesis is required.

Work Restrictions / Accommodations

Work restrictions or accommodations vary according to the site of the amputation. The individual may require wheelchair accessibility or retraining for a new job. Standing may be limited due to lower extremity amputations. Manipulation of objects may be limited if upper extremity amputations were performed.

Comorbid Conditions

The most common comorbid condition in nontraumatic amputations is diabetes mellitus and accounts for over 80% of such amputations. These individuals often have peripheral vascular disease, another major risk factor for amputations and coronary and/or cerebrovascular disease.

Procedure Complications

Complications from an amputation include infection, hematoma, necrosis, contractures, neuromas, and phantom limb pain.

Factors Influencing Duration

The underlying disease, complications, the particular limb or digit amputated and whether it is dominant, the individual's psychological status, whether or not prosthesis will be used, and the individual's job requirements may influence length of disability.

Length of Disability

Length of disability depends on the affected limb, level of amputation, number of amputations, ability to use a prosthesis, and comorbid conditions. The US Social Security Administration criteria for permanent total disability are loss of both hands or both feet, or loss of one hand and one foot.

References

Kessler, R.M. Management of Common Musculoskeletal Disorders: Physical Therapy Principles and Methods. Philadelphia: J.B. Lippincott Co, 1990

Tooms, Robert E. "General Principles of Amputations." Campbell's Operative Orthopedics, 9th ed, volume 1. Canale, S. Terry, ed. St. Louis: Mosby, 1998. 521-531.

Amputation (Traumatic), Foot
896, 896.0, 896.1, 896.2, 896.3

Definition

Traumatic amputation of the foot refers to a complete severing of the foot from the leg as a result of a traumatic incident.

Traumatic incidents that may cause traumatic foot amputations include car or motorcycle accidents, heavy machinery accidents as in farming equipment, or explosions such as a combat injury.

Diagnosis

History: The individual may report a history of a recent traumatic event resulting in severe injury to the foot. Individual may complain of pain, dizziness, and nausea. Individuals typically report they are unable to ambulate or bear weight on the extremity.

Physical exam: A prompt physical exam of vital signs, level of consciousness, opening of airway, and degree of blood loss is needed to evaluate the physical stability of the individual. Traumatic injuries may result in severe blood loss and shock. A quick assessment of the entire body is done to detect any other injuries that may be life-threatening or require immediate attention. Once stable, the individual's injury is thoroughly evaluated to determine the extent of injury and damage to adjacent bones and tissues.

The decision to attempt reattachment of the foot hinges on the condition of the severed foot and the reattachment site such as the degree of damage to bone, skin, muscles, nerves, and blood vessels. The extent of ankle damage also factors into the decision.

Tests: Arteriography (x-ray of arteries after injection of dye) or ultrasound scanning (duplex Doppler imaging) can assess the degree of blood vessel (vascular) injury at the amputation site. Plain x-rays of amputated part and stump are done to assess for fractures and status of adjacent joints. Laboratory studies such as complete blood count (CBC) and coagulation studies help monitor degree of blood loss and detect evidence of bleeding disorders.

Treatment

Initial field and emergency treatment of traumatic amputations of limbs focuses on controlling the bleeding and treating shock. Bleeding may be controlled initially by applying pressure to the site. Sometimes a carefully placed tourniquet is used to control bleeding but it must be snug enough to slow bleeding but not so tight that it impairs circulation to viable tissue. In the emergency department, surgical clamps or stitches (sutures) may be used as needed to stop bleeding from severed vessels.

Low blood pressure and rapid pulse are signs of shock most likely the result of excess blood loss. Intravenous fluids and possibly blood are administered for this condition through large intravenous lines.

The amputated foot is then carefully managed by placing it in a waterproof plastic bag and kept cool, usually in an ice container. It's important to not freeze the part. Prompt careful management of the amputated part reduces the damage to tissue from lack of circulation and increases the chances of successful reattachment (replantation).

Surgical treatment is always necessary following any traumatic amputation. Based on the condition of the amputated part and the stump, either surgical removal (amputation) or replantation is done.

Other factors that may influence treatment include the age of the individual, smoking status, any circulatory disorders, pre-existing psychosocial problems, work and recreational activities of the individual, and the desires and realistic expectations of the individual and family.

If the foot is mangled with extensive damage to the arteries, veins, nerves, muscles, joints and bones and was reattached, it would be functionally useless. Consequently, primary amputation is the better alternative. In traumatic amputations, the wound is usually left open to drain and closed later. At the time of wound closure, the bone end is cut clean and a generous length of skin and muscle tissue is left beyond the point of the bone amputation. Blood vessels are tied, nerves severed, and the skin flaps and muscles are stitched over the bone end to form a smooth, rounded stump.

If the entire foot has been amputated at the ankle (Syme's amputation), the tough heel skin is retained to cover the stump. The individual can then bear weight on the stump without necessarily having to use prosthesis. In partial foot amputations (where a portion of the foot is salvageable), the stump can be fashioned to interface with "shoe filler" in a manner that provides the most comfort and function. In replantation, reconnecting the blood vessels, nerves, muscles, and bones usually restores the severed limb. Multiple operations for reconstruction and skin grafts are usually necessary.

Reattachment of the amputated part is ideally performed within 4 to 6 hours after injury, but success has been reported up to 24 hours after the injury if the amputated part was cooled. Proper care of the amputated part is vital to successful replantation and usually involves packing the amputated part in cool water or ice.

In replantation surgery, the bone ends are shortened to eliminate tension on the repaired vessels. The bone is stabilized with wires. Tendon repairs are done next. Digital nerves and vessels are repaired with microsurgical instruments. Skin grafts or flaps may be required. The skin is then closed.

Prognosis

The long-term outcome for amputees has improved as a result of improved early emergency and critical care management, new surgical techniques, early rehabilitation, prosthesis fitting, and new prosthesis design. New limb replantation techniques have been moderately successful, but incomplete nerve regeneration remains a major limiting factor.

After losing a foot, an individual's mobility depends on several factors including age, attitude, general health, location of the amputation, and a properly fitted prosthesis. The individual's mental attitude is important. Most individuals adapt to the loss of a foot and remain physically active. Early vocational rehabilitation facilitates recovery and improves prognosis.

Specialists

- Orthopedic Surgeon
- Physiatrist
- Podiatrist
- Psychiatrist

Rehabilitation

In the early stages of rehabilitation for traumatic foot amputation, the primary focus is to control pain and swelling and avoid infection. Physical therapists use various cold treatments often in conjunction with electrical stimulation. Methods of electrical stimulation used in physical therapy decrease pain by producing an electrical response in the muscles around the traumatized region.

Cold treatments (cold packs with or without compression) after trauma or surgery make blood vessels smaller and help control excess bleeding and swelling of soft tissues. However, if foot pain is severe and persists for extended periods of time, transcutaneous electrical nerve stimulation (T.E.N.S.) may be helpful. T.E.N.S. is a form of electrostimulation. An electrical impulse, predetermined by the physical therapist, produces a high frequency tingling sensation that blocks the transmission and awareness of pain.

Once pain and swelling subside, rehabilitation progresses and focuses on returning range of motion and strength to the remaining joints of the foot and the ankle joint (if still intact). Flexibility of specific muscles is important to help the individual return to as normal a gait pattern as possible. Range-of-motion exercises begin and progress from passive exercises to exercises to active assist range of motion exercises. As the individual improves with increased motion of the foot and ankle, active range of motion begins. The individual performs all this motion independently.

If the ankle joint is intact, stretching of the calf muscles located in the back of the lower leg is important to prevent the foot from dropping down and catching on the ground when brought forward during walking. One effective stretch instructed by the physical therapist begins with the individual standing facing a wall and placing the involved foot behind the uninvolved foot. Keeping the back foot flat on the floor, the body weight is then shifted forward onto the front foot while sliding the hands up the wall. The knee of the back leg is kept straight and the heel remains on the floor. When an individual achieves full range of motion with minimal swelling, and can perform simple tasks such as ambulating with or without an assistive device (e.g., cane) without pain, a strengthening program is initiated.

The calf muscles on the back of the lower leg are strengthened through use of an elastic band wrapped around the forefoot with the opposite end held in the opposite hand. The individual brings the forefoot downward and inward in a diagonal pattern against the resistance of the elastic band. Resistance progresses to a heavier band as tolerated under the supervision of a physical therapist. Strengthening of the front muscle of the lower leg is accomplished with the elastic band wrapped around the forefoot. The opposite end is attached to a fixed object located in front of the foot while the individual sits on a flat surface with both knees straight. The foot is brought from a position of being flexed downward to an upward motion with the foot and toes moving toward the rest of the leg.

Training and exercises related to walking (gait training) are an important component in rehabilitation of the traumatic foot amputation. An artificial foot or prosthesis may be used by the individual and requires additional training.

Work Restrictions / Accommodations

Following either replantation or amputation, sensory and physical impairments of the stump or reimplanted foot limit the individual's ability to perform tasks that require prolonged standing or walking. Likewise, the limb may be more sensitive and susceptible to cold and cold injuries. Jobs that can be performed while sitting should be considered.

Comorbid Conditions

Smoking or pre-existing vascular insufficiency can greatly reduce the likelihood of success of replantation of the foot. Advanced age, diabetes mellitus, obesity, cardiovascular disease, pulmonary disease, and bleeding disorders may slow recovery from the injury or surgery.

Complications

Reattachment does not guarantee a useful foot. In spite of repeated, lengthy, and elaborate reconstructive surgeries, functional limitations may be severe. There may also be pain, loss of sensation in the sole of the foot, persistent bone infections (chronic osteomyelitis), stiff joints, deformity, and cold intolerance on the affected foot. The body may also reject the replanted foot. Bleeding, swelling, and infection are the usual complications of amputation.

A less common complication of reattachment occurs if the tissue suffers damage and death (necrosis). This dead tissue can produce large amounts of tissue byproducts that tax the kidneys and ultimately cause kidney dysfunction.

In those with surgical amputations rather than replantation, bleeding, swelling, and infection are also complications. In addition, a painful, noncancerous tumor of nerve tissue (neuroma) sometimes develops in the stump.

Factors Influencing Duration

Advanced age contributes to slow wound healing and physical recovery of trauma and surgery. Psychological adaptation to the injury and altered body function is important for good recovery. Depression may slow recovery and rehabilitation. Neuroma and spur formation at the amputated end of the bone may cause pain that can interfere with physical rehabilitation. Lack of vocational rehabilitation will likely prolong disability.

Concomitant injuries such as head trauma or internal injuries may contribute to a slower recovery and longer disability.

Length of Disability

Disability may be permanent.

Duration in Days

Job Classification	Minimum	Optimum	Maximum
Sedentary work	42	70	84
Light work	84	112	168
Medium work	112	168	Indefinite
Heavy work	112	168	Indefinite
Very Heavy work	112	168	Indefinite

Failure to Recover

If an individual fails to recover within the maximum duration expectancy period, the reader may wish to reference the following questions to assist in better understanding the specifics of an individual's medical case.

Regarding diagnosis:

- Did the diagnostic work up determine important factors such as the length of time between injury and treatment and condition of the amputated foot?
- Were appropriate diagnostic tests done (i.e., x-rays, nerve and muscle studies, vascular studies) to determine the degree of damage to bone, skin, muscles, nerves, and blood vessels?

Regarding treatment:

- Did individual receive emergency care that involved controlling bleeding, administering intravenous fluids, and supporting blood pressure, as needed?
- Was the amputated foot cared for properly by placing it in a plastic bag and cooling it in ice water?
- Was individual promptly evaluated by appropriate specialists (i.e., plastic surgeon experienced in replantation or orthopedic surgeon)?
- Was the treatment appropriate for the type of injury present?
- Were multiple surgeries necessary to repair structural damage?
- Was a prosthesis or artificial foot required?

Regarding prognosis:

- Considering the general health of individual and the type of surgery required, what was the expected outcome?
- Has adequate time elapsed for recovery?
- Did individual receive early rehabilitation? Has individual participated in appropriate physical and occupational rehabilitation programs? If not, what can be done to facilitate participation (transportation, psychological counseling)?
- Are signs evident of a poorly fitting prosthesis such as blisters, redness, or swelling of the limb? Has the fit been reevaluated?
- Did individual experience any surgical complications such as bleeding, bone or tissue infection, sensory loss, or development of neuroma that may influence length of disability and outcome?
- Does individual smoke or have a pre-existing vascular insufficiency? Does individual have any other conditions (i.e., advanced age, diabetes mellitus, obesity, cardiovascular disease, pulmonary disease, bleeding disorders) that may slow recovery?
- Does individual have feelings of hopelessness, a poor appetite, or other signs of mental depression? If so, has individual received behavioral or psychological interventions to address the mental depression?
- Does individual participate in a support group for amputees? Does individual have other support systems (family or friends)?

References

"Rehabilitation for Some Specific Problems." Merck Manual of Diagnosis and Therapy, 17th ed. Beers, Mark H., and Robert Berkow, MD, eds. Whitehouse Station, NJ: Merck & Co. Inc, 1999 14 July 2000 <http://www.merck.com/pubs/mmanual/section21/chapter291/291e.htm>.

Clochesy, John M., et al. Critical Care Nursing, 2nd ed. Philadelphia: W.B. Saunders Company, 1996.

Langdorf, Mark. Replantation. EMedicine.com Online 28 Jun 2000 14 Jul 2000 <http://www.emedicine.com/emerg/topic502.htm>.

Scully, Rosemary M., and Marylou R. Barnes. Physical Therapy. Philadelphia: J.B. Lippincott Company, 1989.

Amputation (Traumatic), Lower Extremity
897, 897.0, 897.1, 897.2, 897.3, 897.4, 897.5, 897.6, 897.7

Definition

A traumatic amputation of the lower extremity refers to losing a leg through injury. The leg may be severed in a car or motorcycle accident, as the result of a heavy machinery accident (as in farming equipment), or by an explosion (such as in a combat injury).

In the past, there was no alternative but to create skin flaps which, with remaining muscle, were stitched over the severed end of the bone to form a smooth and rounded stump. Newer techniques for shaping the stump have made fitting a prosthesis easier. Prostheses can now be attached by suction rather than by straps, making them easier to put on and take off. Recent advances in microsurgery have made reattachment (replantation) of severed limbs possible. This involves meticulous rejoining of the severed blood vessels and nerves. The immediate concern following a traumatic amputation of the leg is prevention of hemorrhage, edema, and infection. However, with the possibility of reattachment, an immediate decision is necessary. Whether or not a lower limb is salvageable is usually judged using a scoring system based on the individual, the condition of the injured limb, and the health care available. If it cannot be salvaged, the procedure and follow-up treatment is similar to that of amputation done because of disease processes.

Although 23,000 lower extremity amputations are performed annually in the US, the majority (80%) are for diseased limbs due to diabetes mellitus, peripheral vascular disease (gangrene), or cancer rather than for trauma. Of the approximately 4,600 lower extremity amputations performed for trauma, the majority of individuals are under the age of 50 years, and most (75%) are males. The prevalence of lower extremity amputations for all causes is about 1 million in the US, or about 1 to 300 individuals.

Diagnosis

History: It is important to know the circumstances of the injury and the time interval between the accident and first treatment. If 6-8 hours have elapsed since the leg was severed, tissue damage from absent circulation would prohibit reattachment. Other important factors include the age of the individual, smoking status, any underlying or previous diseases, pre-existing psychosocial problems, work and recreational activities of the individual, and the desires and realistic expectations of the individual and family.

Physical exam: The decision of whether or not to attempt reattachment of the leg is based on the condition of the severed leg and the reattachment site such as the degree of damage to bone, skin, muscles, nerves, and blood vessels. The mechanism of the injury and the location of the injury (above or below the knee joint) also factor into the decision. The individual is examined for multi-system, life-threatening injuries including shock, disseminated intravascular coagulation (DIC), and adult respiratory distress syndrome (ARDS).

Tests: Arteriography (x-ray of arteries after injection of dye) or ultrasound scanning (duplex Doppler imaging) are used to assess the degree of blood vessel (vascular) injury at the amputation site. The vascular status of the injured limb is the primary criterion that the physician would consider in deciding to amputate. If the arteriogram shows that adequate blood flow could be re-established with surgical repair or replantation, then these procedures wouldbe done instead of amputation. If adequate blood flow could not be re-established, if the injured leg is grossly contaminated, if it is mangled beyond reconstruction, or if there is already tissue death (necrosis) as evidenced by the muscle tissue not contracting when stimulated, then amputation is necessary.

Treatment

In a case where the extremity is mangled with extensive damage to the arteries, veins, nerves, muscles, joints and bones, even if the limb were reattached, it would be functionally useless. In this case, primary amputation is the better alternative. In traumatic amputations, the wound is usually left open to drain and is closed later. At the time of wound closure, the bone end is cut clean and a generous length of skin and muscle tissue is left beyond the point of the bone amputation. Blood vessels are tied, nerves severed, and the skin flaps and muscles are stitched over the bone end to form a smooth, rounded stump. Prosthesis can then be fitted. In reattachment, reconnecting the blood vessels, nerves, muscles, and bones usually restores the severed limb. Multiple operations for reconstruction and skin grafts are usually necessary.

Prognosis

After losing a leg, an individual's mobility depends on several factors including age, attitude, general health, the location of the amputation, and a properly fitted prosthesis. The individual's mental attitude is important. Some individuals remain physically active; others choose a life of confinement to wheelchairs. Young, healthy individuals usually adapt well to their prostheses and lead active lives, even returning to work and sports, while the outcome for older or debilitated individuals may be of a more sedentary nature. Physical therapy is important in the long-term outcome of amputees, as is a close relationship with the prosthetist. Many individuals have some degree of phantom pain that may require treatment. Most individuals have depression and other psychological problems dealing with the amputation, particularly initially. Appropriate counseling and joining a support group are helpful in dealing with these problems.

Specialists

- General Surgeon
- Orthopedic Surgeon
- Physiatrist
- Vascular Surgeon

Rehabilitation

In the early stages of rehabilitation for traumatic lower extremity amputation, monitoring circulation, controlling pain and swelling and avoiding infection is very important. Physical therapists use various cold treatments often in conjunction with electrical stimulation. Methods of electrical stimulation used in physical therapy decrease pain by producing an electrical response in the muscles around the traumatized region.

Cold treatments after lower extremity trauma or surgery cause blood vessels to become smaller and help to control excess bleeding and swelling of soft tissues. This is accomplished using cold packs with or without compression. However, if lower extremity pain is severe and persists for extended periods of time, transcutaneous electrical nerve stimulation (T.E.N.S.) may be helpful. T.E.N.S. is a form of electrostimulation. An electrical impulse predetermined by the physical therapist produces a high frequency tingling sensation, which blocks the transmission and awareness of pain.

Once pain and swelling have subsided, rehabilitation then focuses on returning range of motion and strength to the remaining joints of the lower extremity (or residual limb). Flexibility of specific muscles is important to help the individual return to as normal a gait pattern as is possible. If the amputation is below the knee, keeping the back thigh muscles (hamstrings) flexible is very critical. Prolonged stretching exercises (static stretching) specific for the hamstring muscles begins with the individual placing the knee joint in a gentle stretch by keeping the knee as straight as possible. This can be accomplished while the individual is lying on his or her back or sitting in a chair with the involved leg supported on a stool, keeping the knee straight.

If the amputation is above the knee, the focus is on the hip muscles both in front and in back of the thigh. To address the front hip/thigh muscles, the therapist instructs the individual to lie on his or her stomach supporting the upper trunk on the elbows. Strengthening of the residual limb begins early in rehabilitation along with walking exercises (gait training) with the use of a temporary prosthesis if indicated. A temporary prosthesis allows a predetermined amount of weight to be placed on the involved limb and enables the individual to progress with exercises while the size of the residual limb stabilizes, allowing a permanent prosthesis to be fitted.

The above-the-knee amputee depends heavily upon the rear hip muscles to control the prosthesis. The below-the-knee amputee depends on the muscles on the front of the thigh for ambulating. For example, performing leg raises help muscles that assist in straightening the knee as well as bringing the hip forward during walking. Ankle weights may used over the residual limb for resistance as the muscles strengthen. Hamstring curls may be performed with the individual on his/her stomach, bending and straightening the affected knee and using ankle weights for resistance around the residual limb.

Strong muscles on the side of the hips are also necessary to maintain stability of the pelvis. One exercise to help strengthen this area of the hip begins with the individual lying on the noninvolved side while raising the involved leg upward. Ankle weights are also used for resistance as the muscles strengthen. Functional training exercises are important in rehabilitation and focus on the individual's physical demands at home and in the preparation for the return to work such as ascending and descending stairs or repeatedly practicing going from sitting to standing. Such activities more closely match normal requirements of activities of daily living (ADLs). A home exercise program is started at the time of the physical therapy evaluation with gradual progression in difficulty up to the date of discharge.

The final step is to incorporate activities that help the individual return home and to the previous work environment. This includes exercises that resemble work requirements and patient education regarding placement and removal of the prosthesis. Modifications may need to be made by the physical therapist for those individuals who have traumatic lower extremity amputation. Variations in rehabilitation will depend on the location of the amputation and whether surgery and prosthesis is required.

Work Restrictions / Accommodations

The individual may no longer be able to perform duties that require sustained standing or walking. Work responsibilities may have to be modified to fit specific capabilities. A properly fitted prosthetic device may permit the individual to do some standing or walking.

Comorbid Conditions

Pre-existing conditions that could delay healing of the amputation site include diabetes mellitus, immunosuppressive therapy (for cancer or AIDS), coagulation disorders, and peripheral vascular disease.

Complications

Reattachment does not guarantee a useful limb. In spite of repeated, lengthy, and elaborate reconstructive operations, functional limitations may be severe. There may also be pain, loss of sensation in the sole of the foot, persistent bone infections (chronic osteomyelitis), stiff joints, and deformity. The body may also reject the reattached limb. Hemorrhage, edema, and infection are the usual complications of amputation. Noncancerous scarring of nerve tissue (neuroma) sometimes develops in the stump. Phantom limb pain is common, affecting up to 59% of individuals.

Factors Influencing Duration

Any other unrelated injuries, such as head and internal injuries sustained in a motor vehicle accident, would contribute to the length of disability.

Length of Disability

Disability may be permanent.

Duration in Days

Job Classification	Minimum	Optimum	Maximum
Sedentary work	42	70	84
Light work	84	112	168
Medium work	112	168	Indefinite
Heavy work	112	168	Indefinite
Very Heavy work	112	168	Indefinite

Failure to Recover

If an individual fails to recover within the maximum duration expectancy period, the reader may wish to reference the following questions to assist in better understanding the specifics of an individual's medical case.

Regarding diagnosis:

- Did the diagnostic work up determine important factors such as the length of time between injury and treatment and condition of the amputated extremity?
- Were appropriate diagnostic tests done (i.e., x-rays, nerve and muscle studies, vascular studies) to determine the degree of damage to bone, skin, muscles, nerves, and blood vessels?

Regarding treatment:

- Did individual receive emergency care that involved controlling bleeding, administering intravenous fluids, and supporting blood pressure as needed?
- Was the amputated limb cared for properly by placing it in a plastic bag and cooling it in ice water?
- Was individual promptly evaluated by appropriate specialists (i.e., trauma surgeon, plastic surgeon experienced in replantation, orthopedic surgeon)?
- Was the treatment appropriate for the type of injury present?
- Was there significant tissue destruction, vascular injury, or bone injury?
- Was replantation indicated?
- Were multiple surgeries necessary to repair structural damage?
- Was a prosthesis or artificial limb required?
- Did amputation site fail to heal? Was culture performed on any drainage present? Was infection treated by incision, drainage, and antibiotic therapy?

Regarding prognosis:

- Considering the general health of individual and the type of surgery required, what was the expected outcome?
- Has adequate time elapsed for recovery?
- Is there evidence of physical deformity that impairs ambulation?
- Did individual receive early rehabilitation? Has individual participated in appropriate physical and occupational rehabilitation programs? If not, what can be done to facilitate participation (transportation, psychological counseling)?
- Are signs evident of a poorly fitting prosthesis such as blisters, redness, or swelling of the limb? Was the fit reevaluated?
- Did individual experience any surgical complications such as bleeding, bone or tissue infection, sensory loss, or development of neuroma that may influence length of disability and outcome?
- Does individual smoke or have a pre-existing vascular insufficiency? Does individual have any other conditions (advanced age, diabetes mellitus, obesity, cardiovascular disease, immune suppression, pulmonary disease, bleeding disorders) that may slow recovery?
- Does individual have feelings of hopelessness, a poor appetite, or other signs of mental depression? If so, has individual received behavioral or psychological interventions to address the mental depression?
- Has infection spread beyond the level of the leg? Were follow-up x-rays and bone scans done to determine if additional bone removal (resection) is necessary?

References

Scully, Rosemary M., and Marylou R. Barnes. Physical Therapy. Philadelphia: J.B. Lippincott Company, 1989.

Tooms, Robert E. "Amputations of Lower Extremity." Campbell's Operative Orthopedics, 9th ed, volume 1. Canale, S. Terry, ed. St. Louis: Mosby, 1998. 532-541.

Amputation, Finger or Thumb
84.01, 84.02

Definition

Amputation of part or all of a finger or thumb (digit) usually results from trauma. It may be necessary to complete a partial traumatic amputation with a surgical procedure. Injury and disease may also functionally amputate a digit by crushing, mangling, stiffening, necrosing or otherwise destroying all or part it beyond hope of useful recovery. In such cases, salvage may be impossible and surgical amputation of the affected digit justified to improve the overall hand function. The decision at what anatomic level to amputate a digit is crucial. Maintaining as much length and function as possible is important. Every effort should be made to preserve or salvage the thumb, the most important digit from a functional standpoint. Causes of severe damage to fingers and thumb necessitating amputation include peripheral vascular disease, injury, infection, tumors, nerve injuries, and congenital abnormalities.

Reason for Procedure

Irreversible loss of the blood supply (ischemia) is the only absolute indication for amputation. The other major indication is when not amputating the digit or part of it will impair the overall hand function, such as a severe and irreparable damage due to injury, infection, peripheral vascular disease, tumor, nerve injury, or congenital abnormality. Further damage to any part of the affected hand from repetitive injury caused by lack of sensation, motion, or function of an already injured digit might necessitate amputation.

Description

Many procedures have been described for amputations of fingers and the thumb at various anatomic levels. Many of these involve advancement of flaps of skin and soft tissue for better wound coverage and functional result. Such hand surgery is complex and should be performed by a well trained and experienced hand surgeon. Although many procedures have been described for finger amputations, they all are performed in a similar manner. First, a skin incision is made, often in a flap fashion. All blood vessels are then identified, clamped, and tied off (ligated). The tendons are then identified and are severed. In some cases, they are allowed to retract, while in others they are sewn (sutured) to other tendons to maintain stability of the stump. A cut is then made through the bone (osteotomy) or through the joint (disarticulation), and the amputated segment is then detached and sent to the pathology department for examination. A flap of skin and soft tissue is then advanced into position to cover the cut bone or joint surface, and sutured to the adjacent skin. In infected cases, a drain is inserted into the wound and is removed in 24-48 hours. Sometimes, in severely infected wounds, the wound is left open to fill in (granulate) by the healing process known as secondary intention. In some cases of complete thumb amputation, the index finger is repositioned or the big toe is attached to the thumb stump to allow grasp and pinch to be restored.

Prognosis

Even after amputation the outcome can be positive if the thumb is spared. However, results tend to be poor with loss of the thumb or amputation of multiple digits. Results are better if enough length of the fingers is preserved to allow some grasping function. If amputation does not arrest the progression of an infection, further infection of the hand, wrist, and arm may occur, and even gangrene. This would necessitate another amputation farther up the hand or arm (proximal amputation). The same outcome could be seen in case of bone cancer affecting an amputated finger if the cancer has spread into the hand.

Specialists

- Hand Surgeon
- Hand Therapist
- Orthopedic Surgeon
- Plastic Surgeon
- Vascular Surgeon

Rehabilitation

Individuals who sustain amputation of a finger or thumb often begin rehabilitation at the hospital following surgery. Inpatient physical and occupational therapy focuses on maintaining motion of the remaining fingers and/or thumb, enhancing proper wound healing to minimize scarring, and decreasing swelling so the hand and digits can remain functional. To accomplish the latter, the hand is typically positioned above the elbow on a pillow or elevated above heart level in a sling.

Therapy may be performed by an occupational or physical therapist, and a certified hand therapist. Pain control, reduction of swelling, and maintenance or restoration of motion are the primary objectives of therapy. Hot packs provide heat to relieve pain and relax the hand musculature at the outset of each treatment. Therapists may perform cross-friction or other scar massage to improve healing at the amputation site.

Therapists and individuals themselves may passively stretch thumb and finger joints to decrease the risk of a contracture. Individuals also perform active range of motion exercises such as touching the thumb to each finger.

Strengthening exercises are crucial to restore hand function. Individuals squeeze and pinch therapy putty or place a rubber band around 2 fingers at a time and spreading them apart. Resistive exercises using light hand weights will strengthen wrist flexion and extension. Ice packs may be applied to the fingers and thumb after exercise.

Continued use of the uninjured digits and more proximal portions of the extremity is encouraged. Individuals re-learn how to button shirts, tie shoes, and grasp objects. They are also instructed in exercises emphasizing dexterity such as picking up pegs and placing them in a pegboard, and functional activities such as turning a doorknob and pinching then turning a key.

A prosthetist can make a finger or thumb tip that will attach on a remaining digit stump. However, the prosthesis is cosmetic (for appearance) and will not increase function, which is the primary goal of rehabilitation.

Work Restrictions / Accommodations

Depending on the digit(s) amputated, individuals may need to be retrained to a new job. Loss of the thumb produces the most disability, as it is crucially important in grasp and pinch (opposition). While individuals who have lost thumbs will not be able to effectively grasp tools, they may still be able to do tasks that only involve the fingers (such as typing). Loss of one or two fingers is not as devastating as that of the thumb, as most individuals can still use their hands for most tasks. However, amputation of multiple fingers produces more functional loss.

Comorbid Conditions

Healing of the amputation site may be delayed in individuals with diabetes mellitus, peripheral vascular disease, or infection. Rehabilitation may be delayed in individuals with arthritis of the remaining fingers, particularly those with rheumatoid arthritis. Nerve damage to any part of the hand will slow rehabilitation and return to optimum function.

Procedure Complications

Complications of amputations of finger or thumb include infection, hematoma, necrosis, joint contractures, neuromas, and phantom sensations.

Factors Influencing Duration

The underlying disease process or reason for the amputation, the particular digit affected, whether the dominant or non-dominant hand is affected, the individual's job requirements, and complications may all influence the length of disability. Because most human skills are hampered by partial or total loss of the thumb, preservation, reattachment, reconstruction, or replacement of a thumb has great functional merit.

Length of Disability

Finger Amputation

Job Classification	Duration in Days		
	Minimum	Optimum	Maximum
Sedentary work	7	14	42
Light work	7	14	42
Medium work	14	28	49
Heavy work	14	42	63
Very Heavy work	21	42	91

Thumb Amputation.

Job Classification	Duration in Days		
	Minimum	Optimum	Maximum
Sedentary work	14	35	63
Light work	21	42	63
Medium work	21	63	77
Heavy work	35	63	Indefinite
Very Heavy work	35	77	Indefinite

References

Calandruccio, James H. "Amputations." Campbell's Operative Orthopedics, 9th ed, volume 4. Canale, S. Terry, ed. St. Louis: Mosby, 1998. 3517-3547.

Louis, Dean S. "Amputations." Operative Hand Surgery, 3rd ed, volume 1. Green, David P., ed. New York: Churchill Livingstone, 1993. 53-99.

Amyotrophic Lateral Sclerosis
Other names / synonyms: ALS, Lou Gehrig's Disease, Motor Neuron Disease
335.20

Definition

Amyotrophic lateral sclerosis (ALS) is a rare, progressive neurological disorder in which nerves that control the body's muscle activity deteriorate (degenerate). ALS affects the nerves (motor neurons) located in the brain (medulla and cortex) and the spinal cord. Because of the neuron degeneration, electrical and chemical messages (impulses) originating in the brain do not reach the muscles they are meant to activate. The result is progressive weakness and wasting (atrophy) of the muscles.

The cause of ALS is not known. Some theoretical causes are genetic or inherited factors, environmental poisons (toxins), viral infections, or dysfunction of the body's defense system (immunological factors). Researchers are focusing their work on finding out why neurons die. Possible causes are overexposure to glutamate (a naturally occurring brain chemical), attacks by highly charged destructive molecules called free radicals, the presence of abnormal clumps of proteins possibly toxic to the nerve cells, and an abnormal tangling of the filaments that carry nutrients to the ends of the neurons.

The onset of ALS occurs between the ages of 40 and 70. One or two cases per 100,000 individuals are diagnosed each year in the US. Twice as many men as women are affected with the disease, and about 10% of ALS cases run in families (familial).

Diagnosis

History: The first symptoms of ALS are usually weakness of the hands and arms. Occasionally, the weakness may start in the legs but both arms and legs (extremities) are eventually involved. Limbs appear thin and wasted. Small areas of the muscle may quiver or twitch involuntarily (fasciculate). Individuals may complain of difficulty swallowing (dysphagia) and a tendency to choke on food or liquid. The mechanics of speech may be impaired if these muscles are involved (dysarthria). Other symptoms may include muscle cramping and stiffness making it difficult for the individual to hold objects and perform tasks that require fine hand movements. In the later stages, the muscles controlling respiration are impaired.

Physical exam: The physical exam is focused on assessing the individual's general state of health as well as the ability to walk and manipulate objects, swallow, and use the muscles controlling respiration. The existence of musculoskeletal pain should also be determined. As with any serious illness, individuals presenting with the symptoms of ALS may be anxious or depressed.

Tests: An electromyography (EMG) study of the muscles may reveal abnormal nerve activity. A diagnosis of ALS, however, should not be confirmed unless nerve degeneration (denervation) is present in three extremities. To rule out other diseases, additional testing may include biopsy of a wasted muscle, blood studies (serum creatine kinase may be elevated), x-ray study of the spinal cord after injected with dye (myelography), CT or MRI, and examination of the cerebrospinal fluid.

Treatment

The drug riluzole was approved in 1997, and its objective is to slow the progression of ALS by decreasing the amount of glutamate in the brain. In clinical trials, this drug has shown to delay death by a few months. Pharmaceutical research is underway to find a multidrug "cocktail" for treating neurodegenerative diseases based on the model used in the treatment of AIDS and cancer. Antidepressants can treat accompanying depression. Antibiotics are used to treat respiratory and urinary tract infections that can result from being immobile. Medication can also be prescribed to relieve musculoskeletal pain.

Other treatment is supportive rather than therapeutic and is intended to keep the individual as comfortable as possible. It may include grief therapy, physical therapy, occupational therapy, skin and mouth care, bowel and bladder care, nutrition support by feeding the individual directly through a surgically placed stomach tube, tracheostomy and mechanical ventilation for breathing problems. Caregivers need to be especially attentive with regard to the maintenance of bowel and bladder function, oral hygiene, protective eye care, and careful positioning so as to decrease the likelihood of pressure sores.

Prognosis

The progress of ALS is especially devastating because individuals with the disease retain their mental powers (cognition) while their bodies gradually waste away. Individuals in the end stages of ALS are totally paralyzed, unable to speak, move, or breathe on their own. While death from ALS usually occurs 2 to 6 years after the onset of the disease, some individuals have lived more than 20 years after diagnosis.

Differential Diagnosis

Differential diagnoses may include progressive bulbar palsy, pseudobulbar palsy, progressive spinal muscular atrophy, primary lateral sclerosis, spinal cord compression by tumor or cerebral spondylosis, chronic inflammatory disease of the spinal cord and meninges, and progressive weakness from intrinsic diseases of the muscles.

Specialists

- Neurologist
- Physiatrist

Rehabilitation

Rehabilitation can help individuals with ALS live in a more comfortable manner. The physical therapist addresses two major concerns, muscle cramping and weakness.

The physical therapist uses various techniques to provide relief from muscle cramps and progressive weakness. Muscle cramps are treated with the use of moist heat on the involved area followed by massage techniques emphasizing muscle relaxation. Electrostimulation combined with heat or cold treatment is another technique used in physical therapy to relax muscles. Gentle passive stretching of the involved muscle group treats muscle cramps and joint stiffness caused by ALS. In this exercise, the physical therapist improves motion by moving the limb through pain-free limits without effort from the individual.

Muscle weakness is treated with mild strengthening exercises to help the individual remain as functional as possible. If significant weakness is present, active assist exercises may be required (the individual performs some of the effort along with the help of the therapist). If improvement is noted and the exercises are tolerated well, the active range-of-motion exercises are introduced where the individual performs all the motion independently. Resistance is then added to each exercise using an elastic band or light weights.

Balance exercises like side stepping and walking with the eyes closed with and without assistance are beneficial when early signs of frequent stumbling and clumsiness are evident. Respiratory muscles can also become progressively weaker as the disease advances, therefore exercises to strengthen the muscles that assist in breathing become part of the rehabilitation program. An example of an exercise to strengthen the respiratory muscles is shoulder shrugs using light dumbbells. At each side, the individual holds a dumbbell weight in each hand, keeping the elbows straight. While in this position, the individual shrugs the shoulders, holds for 5 seconds, and returns to the starting position. The rehabilitation program varies between individuals with ALS. The intensity and progression of the exercise depend on the stage of the individual's disease and overall health.

Work Restrictions / Accommodations

Work is often therapeutic and the individual may strive to continue working as long as possible. Work activities may be limited depending on the nature of the work and the individual's degree of muscular weakness. The individual's workspace may need to be changed to accommodate a wheelchair and provide a safe environment. Safety issues and accommodations revolve around the individual's weakness and physical instability and the tendency to choke easily.

Comorbid Conditions

Comorbid conditions influencing the length of disability for individuals with ALS include pre-existing chronic disease, conditions such as obesity and smoking, and any disabilities.

Complications

Individuals with ALS are susceptible to all the acute and chronic diseases and conditions common to other chronically ill and weakened individuals with impaired mobility. These include cancer, heart and vascular disease, stroke, blood clots, choking and aspiration, infectious disease, gastrointestinal disorders, diabetes, respiratory disease, and pressure sores. If surgical intervention is required for any of these conditions, the individual is subject to the usual surgical complications (infection, adverse reaction to the anesthetic, pneumonia, and poor wound closure).

Factors Influencing Duration

Factors influencing the length of disability may include the general health and fitness of the individual before the diagnosis of ALS; evidence of pre-existing diseases (such as diabetes, chronic obstructive lung disease, and chronic heart disease) affecting any of the major body systems; diagnosis of an acute disease or condition requiring surgery; the individual's mental and emotional stability; access to rehabilitation facilities and home health care; and the strength of the individual's support system. Disability eventually will become permanent.

Length of Disability

As there is no known cure or effective treatment to slow the nerve deterioration, individuals diagnosed with ALS have permanent, progressive disability. The goal of treatment and rehabilitation is to support the individual in performing daily activities and to forestall further deterioration for as long as possible. Early diagnosis offers an opportunity to plan retirement from work, arrange for financial management, discuss the management of future medical problems, and make informed end-of-life decisions in advance (advanced directives).

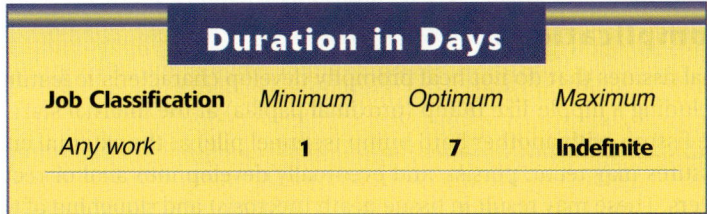

Duration in Days

Job Classification	Minimum	Optimum	Maximum
Any work	1	7	Indefinite

Failure to Recover

If an individual fails to recover within the maximum duration expectancy period, the reader may wish to reference the following questions to assist in better understanding the specifics of an individual's medical case.

Regarding diagnosis:

- Does individual complain of weakness of the hands, arms, or legs?
- Do small areas of the muscle quiver or twitch involuntarily (fasciculate)?
- Does individual complain of difficulty swallowing (dysphagia) and a tendency to choke on food or liquid?
- Does individual complain of impaired speech (dysarthria) or of muscle cramping and stiffness making it difficult to hold objects and perform tasks that require fine hand movements?
- Is breathing impaired?
- Does individual appear depressed or anxious?
- Was diagnosis of ALS confirmed?
- Were other tests such as a biopsy of a wasted muscle, blood studies (serum creatine kinase may be elevated), x-ray study of the spinal cord after injected with dye (myelography), CT or MRI, and examination of the cerebrospinal fluid, done to rule out other diseases?

Regarding treatment:

- Has riluzole been administered? Are any other medications available at this time?
- Would individual benefit from an antidepressant?
- Does individual require medication to relieve pain?
- Is individual receiving appropriate supportive care such as physical therapy, occupational therapy, home care or nutrition support?
- Do individual and/or family have realistic views about future care needs?
- Would social services be beneficial in helping create a long-range plan?
- Would family counseling be beneficial to help family members understand and cope with increasing demands?

Regarding prognosis:

- What stage of the disease is individual currently experiencing?
- Has family contacted, or are they willing to contact hospice, for end-stage care and support?
- Has individual developed any conditions (i.e., infections, malnutrition, vascular disease) associated with being chronically ill or weakened?

References

Amyotrophic Lateral Sclerosis Association. 2000 07 Jul 2000 <http://www.alsa.org>.

The ALS Newsletter. The Muscular Dystrophy Association. 2000 07 Jul 2000 <http://www.mdausa.org/publications/als/index.html>.

Anal Fissure and/or Rectal Ulcer

Other names / synonyms: Fissure in Ano, Rectal Ulcer
565.0, 569.41

Definition

Anal fissures and rectal ulcers are painful tears or cracks (linear ulceration or laceration) in the mucous membrane that extends from the anal sphincter upward into the anal canal.

Primary fissures are those that develop as a result of direct trauma to the anal canal. Secondary fissures are those that develop as a result of an underlying disease state. Ninety percent of the time, anal fissures are located in the back (posterior) midline of the rectum. Front (anterior) fissures are more common in women, usually as a result of childbirth. In women, up to 10% of fissures will be found anteriorly, whereas in men only 1% occur in this location.

Risk factors for developing primary fissures include passage of a large hard stool, constipation, rectal intercourse, or insertion of a foreign object through the anus into the rectum. Diseases that are risk factors for development of secondary anal fissures include inflammatory bowel disease (Crohn's disease, ulcerative colitis), leukemia, cancer (carcinoma), and rarely, syphilis or tuberculosis. Anal fissures occur in approximately 2% of the population, and they are found equally often in males and females. The average age at diagnosis is 35 years, although they may occur in individuals of any age.

Diagnosis

History: Individuals usually report a sharp burning, tearing, or throbbing pain during and soon after a bowel movement. Scant traces of bright red blood may be found on the toilet paper or in the toilet bowl.

Physical exam: Anal fissure is best identified by visual inspection. If the fissure is not visible, an examination done by inserting a gloved finger into the anus (digital rectal exam) may be necessary. This examination procedure may require a topical anesthetic because touching the fissure is often painful. The anal canal may spasm in response to the pain caused by digital rectal examination.

Tests: A flexible fiber-optic microscope (endoscope) may be used to visually exam the anus and lower rectum (anoscopy) in order to confirm the diagnosis of fissure. Other associated conditions, such as hemorrhoids or inflammatory bowel disease, may also be identified during this procedure.

Treatment

Fissures can be treated with ointments, warm sitz baths, high-fiber diet, increased fluid intake, and stool softeners (if constipation is present). Recently developed treatments include topical application of ointment that increases the blood flow (nitroglycerin) or injection of a drug (botulism toxin) into the anal tissue that causes relaxation of the anal sphincter. If these treatments are not effective, or if fissures are recurring and ulcerated, a procedure to enlarge the anus (anal dilatation) may be used. A more common procedure is surgical cutting of the sphincter muscle (lateral internal sphincterotomy). This surgery may be performed using local or general anesthesia.

Specialists

- Gastroenterologist
- General Surgeon
- Proctologist

Prognosis

Symptoms associated with anal fissure are generally relieved using warm sitz baths and high-fiber diet treatments. Topical application of nitroglycerin results in significant reduction in anal pain, and within 8 weeks of treatment 77% of individuals with anal fissures and 54% of individuals with rectal ulcers will show significant healing. Transient headache may result from this treatment in 35% of individuals. Injection of botulism toxin into the anal tissue produces a healing rate of approximately 80%, although 7% of individuals report fecal incontinence using this treatment. Anal dilation produces variable results although there is a relatively high incidence of gas (flatus) and incontinence along with anal swelling associated with this procedure. Lateral internal sphincterotomy results in a very high rate of healing in 70-100% of cases. Long-term complications of this procedure (such as incontinence, pain, and bleeding) usually have an incidence of less than 10 percent.

Differential Diagnosis

Conditions that present with similar symptoms include intersphincteric abscess, Crohn's disease, syphilis (primary chancre), AIDS, herpes simplex, leukemia, carcinoma, and malignant melanoma.

Work Restrictions / Accommodations

Uncomplicated cases require no work restrictions or special accommodations. Individuals recovering from surgery may need to avoid prolonged sitting and heavy physical labor until healing is complete.

Comorbid Conditions

Conditions that may impact an individual's ability to recover and further lengthen disability include pregnancy, chronic constipation, and low blood flow (ischemia) to the anal region.

Complications

Anal fissures that do not heal promptly develop characteristic features including a nipple-like bump (proximal papilla) at the internal start of the fissure, with another hard bump (sentinel pile) at the external end. Fissures may recur, persist, and eventually develop into anal or rectal ulcers. These may result in tissue death (necrosis) and sloughing of the anal tissue. A deep fissure involving the internal anal sphincter may result in scarring and anal narrowing (stenosis) of the anus if the condition is persistent.

Factors Influencing Duration

Length of disability may be influenced by the underlying cause of the condition, the extent and severity of the fissure, the method and response to treatment, or the presence of complications following treatment.

Length of Disability

Conservative treatment.

Duration in Days

Job Classification	Minimum	Optimum	Maximum
Any work	0	3	7

Surgical treatment.

Duration in Days

Job Classification	Minimum	Optimum	Maximum
Any work	7	14	21

Failure to Recover

If an individual fails to recover within the maximum duration expectancy period, the reader may wish to reference the following questions to assist in better understanding the specifics of an individual's medical case.

Regarding diagnosis:

- Does individual have constipation? Passage of a large hard stool?
- Does individual have rectal intercourse?
- Has individual inserted a foreign object through the anus into the rectum?

- Does individual have Crohn's disease or ulcerative colitis?
- Does individual have leukemia or cancer? Syphilis? Tuberculosis?
- On exam was the fissure identified by visual inspection?
- Was endoscopy done?
- Were conditions with similar symptoms ruled out?

Regarding treatment:

- Were conservative treatments such as ointments, sitz baths, high fiber diet, and increased fluid intake tried? Were they effective? Were stool softeners needed?
- Was it necessary to do injections, dilation, or surgery?

Regarding prognosis:

- Is individual's employer able to accommodate restrictions if needed?
- Does individual have any conditions that may affect ability to recover?
- Has individual had recurrent fissures?
- Did individual develop anal or rectal ulcers? Stenosis of the anus?

References

Bleday, R. "Hemorrhoids and Other Anorectal Disorders." Therapy of Digestive Disorders. Wolfe, M.M., ed. Philadelphia: W.B. Saunders Company, 2000. 701-707.

Chen, J., M. Michowitz, and J.B. Bawnik. "Solcoderm as Alternative Conservative Treatment for Acute anal Fissure: A Controlled Clinical Study." American Surgeon 58 11 (1992): 705-709.

Jost, W.H. "Incidence of Anal Fissure in Nonselected Neurological Patients." Diseases of the Colon and Rectum 42 6 (1999): 828.

LeMone, P., and K.M. Burke. Medical-Surgical Nursing. Upper Saddle River, NJ: Prentice Hall Health, 2000.

Anaphylactic Shock

Other names / synonyms: Anaphylaxis, Serum Sickness
995.0, 999.4

Definition

Anaphylactic shock is a sudden, circulatory collapse that results from a severe allergic reaction. It occurs when the immune system reacts to a foreign substance (allergen). In anaphylactic shock, the immune system releases many chemical substances including histamine and serotonin. These chemicals cause narrowing of the breathing passages and relaxation of blood vessels. The result may be life-threatening respiratory and circulatory failure otherwise known as anaphylactic shock.

Substances (allergens) that trigger allergic reactions are carried in foods, medications, and insect stings and eventually circulate in the bloodstream. Anaphylaxis can occur in response to any allergen. Although the initial exposure to an allergen does not usually cause severe symptoms, the potential to develop more severe symptoms of anaphylaxis increases with each subsequent exposure.

Common causes include insect bites or stings, horse serum (used in some vaccines), food allergies, and drug allergies. Pollens and other inhaled allergens rarely cause anaphylaxis. Some individuals have an anaphylactic reaction with no identifiable cause.

The true incidence of anaphylaxis is not known. However, there are fewer than 100 deaths per year from anaphylactic drug reactions or anaphylactic reactions to insect stings. Anaphylaxis can occur in anyone regardless of age, sex, or race. Those that have had a prior history of any type of allergic reaction are at increased risk of developing anaphylactic shock.

Diagnosis

History: If individuals are alert and coherent, they may report a history of an allergic reaction. They describe a sudden onset of symptoms such as restlessness, anxiety, nausea, swelling of lips, tongue, or other areas. They may report feeling lightheaded or dizzy and may have chest tightness or difficulty breathing. Most individuals report development of some sort of skin rash that usually itches.

Physical exam: The exam of individuals with anaphylactic shock is dependent on the organ systems affected and the severity of the attack. Vital signs may be abnormal with low blood pressure, rapid respirations, and rapid heart rate. Decreased level of consciousness, altered neurological status, and seizures may result due to inadequate circulation to the brain. Shortness of breath, coughing, and hoarseness are present when the anaphylaxis causes narrowing of airways or upper airway swelling. Swollen lips and tongue are common and may result in upper airway obstruction. Inadequate oxygenation and low blood pressure may cause weakness, dizziness, or decreased level of consciousness.

Chest pain may occur due to narrowing airways or inadequate blood flow to the heart (cardiac ischemia). More than 90% of individuals with anaphylactic shock have some combination of skin symptoms such as hives, swelling, rash, or itching. The skin may be cool, moist, and pale. In extreme or advanced stages, complete cardiopulmonary arrest may occur.

Tests: No immediate tests are required to establish the diagnosis. Skin tests are done later to identify the allergen.

Treatment

Anaphylactic shock is an emergency condition requiring immediate professional medical attention. CPR and other lifesaving measures may be required. This may include placing a tube through the nose or mouth into the airway (endotracheal intubation) or emergency surgery to place a tube directly into the trachea (tracheostomy). Epinephrine is given by injection and/or inhalation. This opens the airways and raises the blood pressure by constricting blood vessels.

Treatment for shock includes intravenous fluids and medications that support the actions of the heart and circulatory system. Antihistamines and corticosteroids may be given to further reduce symptoms after lifesaving measures and epinephrine are administered.

Prognosis

Anaphylaxis is a severe disorder with a guarded prognosis. Symptoms may resolve with prompt treatment. However, brain damage or death may occur even with treatment.

Differential Diagnosis

Other possibilities include epiglottitis, heart attack, pulmonary embolism, asthma attack, hereditary angioedema, seizure disorder, or a transfusion reaction.

Specialists

- Allergist
- Critical Care Specialist
- Emergency Medicine
- Internist

Work Restrictions / Accommodations

Those who have recovered without any physical impairments will only need to avoid exposure to known allergens. Those who have occupational allergies (i.e., exposure to latex, dust, or formaldehyde) may require appropriate work reassignments. Individuals with a history of anaphylactic shock or severe allergic reactions must have access to an emergency allergy kit that contains a preloaded dose of epinephrine for self-administration in case of subsequent exposure to the allergen. Specific accommodations may be needed for those with physical impairments following recovery from anaphylactic shock. The individual's physician should be consulted for guidance.

Comorbid Conditions

Asthma or cardiovascular system disorders may lengthen disability.

Complications

Complications include brain damage, obstructed airway, and heart attack. Medical disorders of the respiratory or cardiovascular systems can worsen due to the anaphylactic reaction.

Factors Influencing Duration

The severity of the reaction and response to treatment influence the length of disability.

Length of Disability

Duration depends on severity of reaction, workplace assignment, job demands. Disability may be permanent.

Duration in Days

Job Classification	Minimum	Optimum	Maximum
Any work	1	3	Indefinite

Failure to Recover

If an individual fails to recover within the maximum duration expectancy period, the reader may wish to reference the following questions to assist in better understanding the specifics of an individual's medical case.

Regarding diagnosis:

- Was diagnosis of anaphylactic shock made based on the presenting symptoms such as sudden onset of circulatory collapse, particularly in an individual with known allergies?
- Were other conditions such as epiglottitis, heart attack, pulmonary embolism, seizure disorder, transfusion reaction, asthma, or hereditary angioedema ruled out?
- Was responsible allergen identified (i.e., food, medication, insect sting) so future encounters can be anticipated or avoided?

Regarding treatment:

- Did individual receive prompt emergency care and life support interventions (airway, intravenous fluids, epinephrine administration) as indicated? Did individual respond to the emergency treatment?
- Were endotracheal intubation or tracheostomy required?
- After resuscitation, did individual show any signs of neurological impairment or heart damage? If so, was individual evaluated by appropriate specialists (i.e., neurologist or cardiologist) for ongoing care?

Regarding prognosis:

- Was individual referred to an allergist?
- Was allergy testing done to determine the offending allergen?
- Was individual instructed about allergen avoidance?
- Was individual instructed regarding emergency self-care in the case of unintended exposure (epinephrine injection)?
- If occupation puts individual at increased risk of allergen encounter such as insect stings is individual provided with appropriate protection?
- Have any complications developed associated with the anaphylactic reaction such as neurological impairment or heart attack? If so, what is expected outcome?
- Has individual received appropriate care and rehabilitation for the associated physical impairments?

References

Clochesy, John M., et al. Critical Care Nursing, 2nd ed. Philadelphia: W.B. Saunders Company, 1996.

Anaphylactic Shock, Food Reaction
995.6, 995.60, 995.61, 995.62, 995.63, 995.64, 995.65, 995.66, 995.67, 995.68, 995.69

Definition

Anaphylactic shock is an acute, life-threatening reaction to an allergen, and in this case, food is the allergen. Foods most likely to cause allergic reaction are nuts, legumes, seed, fish, and shellfish. Other foods that commonly cause allergies are milk, eggs, wheat, peanuts, soybeans, chocolate, and all products containing these foods as ingredients.

The individual may have previously been exposed to the offending food and then developed antibodies to it. The next time the food is encountered, a full-blown reaction occurs. A small trace of the food may cause an explosive reaction especially if the individual exercises after eating. On occasion, skin contact or inhalation of a food (such as flour) are all that is needed to cause a reaction.

Anaphylaxis is a rare but potentially fatal condition in which several different parts of the body experience allergic reactions. When anaphylactic shock occurs, the smooth muscles in the lungs and digestive tissue contract causing airway narrowing and stomach upset. The blood vessels of the body dilate or open up, and the plasma in the blood seeps out into tissues causing hives and fluid in the lungs (pulmonary edema). This causes the amount of circulating blood to decrease and shock begins. During the reaction, upper airway obstruction occurs from laryngeal edema or constriction of the air passages of the lung (bronchospasm).

The true incidence of anaphylaxis is not known partly because there is no precise definition of the syndrome. Some doctors reserve the term for the full-blown syndrome while others use it to describe milder cases. Fatal anaphylactic shock is rare but milder forms occur more frequently.

Diagnosis

History: Within 1 to 15 minutes after ingestion of the food, individual may experience an uneasy feeling that progresses to full agitation and panic. The individual may complain of rapid chest pulsation (palpitations) and a pins-and-needles feeling in the arms or legs (paresthesia). There may be itching (pruritus), throbbing in the ears, coughing, sneezing, difficulty breathing (dyspnea), nausea, vomiting, and abdominal pain.

Physical exam: Individuals may present with a flushed face, hives, and deep tissue swelling (angioedema) of the face, eyes, tongue, throat, and extremities. Individuals may cough, sneeze, and have difficulty breathing. Pulmonary edema and significant respiratory distress with blue color (cyanosis) and wheezing may be present. In the next 1 to 2 minutes, signs of shock with incontinence, seizures, and unconsciousness may occur. Breathing and heartbeat may stop soon after.

Tests: Blood is taken during or shortly after the individual is treated. A complete blood count (CBC), electrolytes, blood glucose, clotting profile, serum immunoglobulins, blood urea nitrogen, and creatinine are performed. Full allergy testing may or may not be done after recovery is complete.

Treatment

Immediate treatment is needed to preserve life. Mild reactions consisting of itching, hives, swelling of the skin and its subcutaneous layers (angioedema), mild wheezing, and nausea and vomiting may be treated by applying heart and vital sign monitors, giving epinephrine intramuscularly or intravenously once and possibly twice followed with an antihistamine by mouth for the next 24 hours.

More severe symptoms such as massive deep tissue swelling without blood pressure and heart reactions may be treated with an antihistamine first, then epinephrine, and followed by an antihistamine by mouth for 24 hours. A glucocorticoid may be given to suppress late-occurring symptoms.

Extreme symptoms with heart rhythm abnormalities, low blood pressure, and signs of shock may be treated with intravenous fluids, epinephrine, oxygen, intubation, tracheotomy (cricothyrotomy), and possibly vasopressor drugs to raise the blood pressure. Central venous pressure monitoring may begin as well as measurements of the arterial pressure on the left side of the heart. Full resuscitation with further medications, CPR, and electric shock defibrillation may be performed if heartbeat or breathing stops.

Once the individual stabilizes, observation should continue for late reaction symptoms for at least 24 hours after a severe or extreme reaction. Hot showers, baths, and alcohol must be avoided for at least 24 hours to prevent a recurrence of low blood pressure.

A medic alert bracelet should be worn. Individuals should be cautioned after an episode of anaphylaxis to avoid exposure to an inciting agent. When no inciting agent is identified, the individual should be referred to an allergist to identify the cause of anaphylaxis. Caution should also be given regarding eating in restaurants where the composition of dishes cannot be guaranteed.

Prognosis

Full recovery within 1 to 2 days is possible when the reaction is treated promptly and thoroughly. An individual in severe or extreme anaphylactic shock may die if treatment is not given quickly since the body cannot recover on its own. Death is usually a result of spasm of the muscles of the tiny air passages (bronchioles) in the lungs. Permanent brain, kidney, or heart damage may be present due to lack of oxygen (hypoxia) if shock was prolonged.

Differential Diagnosis

Similar symptoms may occur with an allergic reaction to other allergens besides food such as when one food is eaten to excess and a toxic level produces a one-time reaction. Choking on food, cardiogenic or hypovolemic shock, internal bleeding, blood poisoning with sepsis, coronary artery disease, myocardial infarction, severe heart failure, pulmonary edema, acute inflammation of the sac surrounding the heart and great blood vessels (pericarditis), or a severe asthma attack may also present with similar signs and symptoms.

Specialists

- Allergist
- Critical Care Specialist
- Emergency Medicine

Work Restrictions / Accommodations

The offending food should be avoided. The individual's employer or supervisor should be made aware of the allergy. The individual may need to carry an anaphylaxis treatment kit with injectable epinephrine to allow enough time to get to a hospital if another anaphylactic reaction occurs in the future. A co-worker or company nurse should be trained in its use in case another reaction occurs. The individual may need to wear a respirator or protective clothing and gloves to avoid inhalation and contact with the offending food (such as flour when working in a bakery).

Comorbid Conditions

Presence of cardiovascular disease or asthma may lengthen disability. Pulmonary insufficiency and gastrointestinal disease and disorder also worsen the effects of food allergy reactions.

Complications

Exercise after ingestion of the food allergen or use of beta-adrenergic medications can result in a more severe reaction. Heart damage, myocardial infarction, arrhythmias, cardiogenic shock, kidney failure or damage, edema of the brain (cerebral edema), and brain damage can occur if the reaction included decreased oxygen intake for a prolonged period. This will complicate treatment and delay recovery.

Factors Influencing Duration

The severity of a food-induced anaphylactic reaction and subsequent length of disability depends on the individual's age, sensitivity, target organ, and other medical conditions as well as the type and amount of food, method of exposure, timing of onset, exposure site, response to treatment, and other factors.

Length of Disability

Duration depends on the severity of the reaction. Disability may be permanent.

Duration in Days

Job Classification	Minimum	Optimum	Maximum
Any work	1	3	14

Failure to Recover

If an individual fails to recover within the maximum duration expectancy period, the reader may wish to reference the following questions to assist in better understanding the specifics of an individual's medical case.

Regarding diagnosis:

- Did individual receive a prompt evaluation by an emergency physician? By an allergist?
- Do the whole blood and urine analyses indicate an exposure to offending food materials?
- Is there a positive history of food allergies?
- Was source of allergic reaction identified?

Regarding treatment:

- Did individual receive prompt emergency care and life support interventions (airway, intravenous fluids, epinephrine administration) as indicated?
- Did individual respond to the emergency treatment?
- Were endotracheal intubation or tracheostomy required?
- Were glucocorticoids administered to suppress late-occurring symptoms?
- After resuscitation, did individual show any signs of neurological impairment or heart damage? If so, was individual evaluated by appropriate specialists (i.e., neurologist or cardiologist) for ongoing care?

Regarding prognosis:

- Was there any residual impairment?
- Did individual suffer any complications associated with the anaphylactic reaction such as neurological impairment or heart attack? If so, what is the expected outcome?
- Has individual received appropriate care and rehabilitation for the associated physical impairments?
- Was individual referred to an allergist? Was allergy testing to determine the offending allergen? Has individual been instructed about allergen avoidance?
- Was individual instructed regarding emergency self-care in the case of unintended exposure (epinephrine injection)?

References

Kim, H.M., and D.J. Yang. "Effect of Kumhwang-San on Anaphylactic Reaction in a Murine Model." Immunopharmacology and Immunotoxicology 21 1 (1999): 163-174.

Singh, J., and M. Clark. "Food Allergy." AAEM Emergency Medical and Family Health Guide - Immune. Plantz, Scott H., ed. 2000 01 Sep 2000 <http://emedicine.com/aaem/topic207.htm>.

Anemia

Other names / synonyms: Aplastic Anemia, Essential Anemia, Hemolytic Anemia, Hereditary Spherocytosis, Idiopathic Anemia, Iron Deficiency Anemia, Megaloblastic Anemia, Pernicious Anemia, Profound Anemia, Sickle Cell Anemia, Sideroblastic Anemia

281, 285.1, 285.9

Definition

Anemia is defined as an abnormally low number of red blood cells, an abnormally low amount of protein inside each red blood cell capable of carrying oxygen (hemoglobin), or an abnormally low measure of red cell mass (hematocrit). In each of these three deficiencies, the oxygen-carrying capacity of the blood is decreased, resulting in less oxygen for body tissues (hypoxia).

Anemia is not a disease but rather a symptom of many conditions or diseases. Causes are grouped into three categories: blood loss, red blood cell destruction, and impaired red blood cell production.

Blood loss can be sudden and acute such as following a traumatic penetrating injury, or it may be slow and chronic such as occurring in chronic gastrointestinal bleeding. Blood clotting disorders like hemophilia also cause excessive bleeding that may lead to anemia. Blood loss due to prolonged, heavy, or frequent menstrual bleeding is another cause of anemia.

Red blood cells may be destroyed or removed from circulation faster than they can be replaced by new cells produced in the bone marrow. This occurs when there are defects within the red blood cell (i.e., in sickle cell anemia or hereditary spherocytosis) or when antibodies attack and destroy otherwise healthy red blood cells (i.e., transfusion reaction or autoimmune disease). A general term for this type of anemia is hemolytic anemia.

Impaired red blood cell production is a broad category that includes conditions and diseases affecting either the number of red blood cells produced or how they are produced. Red blood cells are produced in the bone marrow in response to the action of a specific hormone (erythropoietin or EPO) made in the kidney. Kidney disease, chronic infection or inflammation, or cancer can decrease the production of EPO or interfere with its activity. Without active EPO, the bone marrow does not produce an adequate number of red blood cells.

Problems inside the bone marrow also interfere with production. Sometimes the marrow stops producing red blood cells that results in a very serious form of anemia called aplastic anemia. This can occur in response to a toxic drug or chemical or infection with certain viruses. Often, however, there is no known reason for the condition (idiopathic aplastic anemia). A decrease in red blood cell production (hypoplasia) is found with malnutrition particularly in the eating disorder called anorexia nervosa. Myelodysplasia refers to a condition where early red blood cells do not develop properly and die before being released into the circulatory system.

Red blood cell production is impaired if there is a problem with the synthesis of deoxyribonucleic acid (DNA) needed within the cell. This results in an anemia called megaloblastic anemia. Megaloblastic anemia is most often caused by a deficiency of either folate or vitamin B_{12} (pernicious anemia). Some cases of megaloblastic anemia are caused by certain drugs such as chemotherapeutic cancer drugs.

A problem with the synthesis of hemoglobin can also interfere with normal red blood cell production within the marrow. Because hemoglobin requires iron, a deficiency of iron creates a deficiency of functional hemoglobin. Iron deficiency anemia may result from an insufficient amount of iron in the diet. More often, however, it occurs because either blood loss or increased demand has triggered the marrow to increase production in an effort to replace lost red blood cells. Eventually, the marrow's supply of iron becomes depleted.

Chronic disease is another cause of anemia related to iron. Chronic disease interferes with the normal integration of iron into the red blood cell. Sideroblastic anemia is another type of anemia where iron is not utilized properly. Thalassemia occurs when there is an abnormal production of the proteins needed to make normal hemoglobin and results in anemia.

Some forms of anemia are inherited such as some types of hemolytic anemia and most blood clotting disorders. Disorders of hemoglobin such as sickle cell anemia and thalassemia are also inherited.

Approximately 4.1 million individuals in the US have anemia. Over half of these are under the age of 45. Anemia is more common in women than in men. It is present in 10-20% of menstruating women and 20-60% of pregnant women.

Iron deficiency anemia is the most common type of anemia and is closely associated with menstruating or pregnant women. It is rare in men but present is associated with gastrointestinal bleeding. Pernicious anemia is also more common in women, particularly blacks. It is less common in other racial or ethnic groups. Folate deficiency is associated with pregnancy, malnutrition, and alcoholism. Sickle cell anemia is the most common hemoglobinopathy and is found primarily in blacks. Thalassemia is associated with individuals of Mediterranean, Southeast Asian, and Middle Eastern or African descent.

Diagnosis

History: Symptoms depend on the suddenness of onset, severity of the condition, and individual's age and general state of health. Mild anemia and anemia with a gradual onset often have no symptoms. A healthy individual's bone marrow, heart, and lungs can usually compensate for mild anemia. Symptoms typically develop slowly. Sudden onset of anemia such as in severe bleeding (hemorrhage) brings immediate symptoms.

Individuals with general symptoms of anemia report fatigue, weight loss, headache, ringing in the ears (tinnitus), inability to concentrate, heart palpitations, and light-headedness when standing up. Some individuals may have abdominal discomfort, loss of appetite, nausea, diarrhea, or constipation. Individuals with iron deficiency anemia may also complain of a pins-and-needles feeling in the arms or legs and a burning sensation of the tongue. In severe anemia, exercise or exertion may cause breathing difficulties, dizziness, and chest pain.

Physical exam: Physical findings may include paleness (pallor) of the skin and creases in the palm of the hand and the mucous membrane (conjunctiva) that lines the eye. The heart rate may increase (tachycardia) and blood pressure may be low when standing up (orthostatic hypotension). If the anemia is severe, a heart murmur may be detected. Breathing rate may also be increased (tachypnea). The liver or spleen may be enlarged. In individuals with pernicious anemia, nerve function may be impaired (peripheral neuritis, neuropathy). Psychiatric symptoms such as depression or confusion may also be present. Individuals with anemia due to chronic disease may have evidence of infection, inflammation, or abnormal tissue growth. Iron deficiency anemia may cause inflammation of the lips (cheilitis) or tongue (glossitis). Fingernails may be fragile or spoon-shaped (koilonychia). Individuals with severe anemia have a decreased urinary output.

Tests: A complete blood count (CBC) reveals a low number of red blood cells, low hemoglobin, and/or a low hematocrit. A CBC also reveals the average size of the red blood cells (mean corpuscular volume, or MCV). Physical appearance of the red blood cells can be studied through microscopic examination of a peripheral blood smear. The CBC results plus the information related to the size and appearance of the red blood cells provide clues as to what the cause of anemia may be and what tests to perform next.

A reticulocyte count helps differentiate anemia caused by decreased red blood cell production from that caused by blood loss or increased destruction. Reticulocytes are immature red blood cells, newly released from the bone marrow. A normal number of reticulocytes in the blood indicates that the bone marrow is producing red blood cells. A low number of reticulocytes indicates that the anemia is due to a problem in the bone marrow.

Tests for iron include ferritin, serum iron, and total iron-binding capacity (TIBC). These tests differentiate iron deficiency anemia from other types of anemia involving iron such as sideroblastic anemia and anemia due to chronic disease.

Blood tests for folate and vitamin B_{12} differentiate between folate deficiency anemia and vitamin B_{12} deficiency anemia (pernicious anemia). In some cases, a Schilling's test is needed to further study vitamin B_{12} deficiency. Disorders of hemoglobin (i.e., thalassemia or sickle cell anemia) are confirmed with hemoglobin electrophoresis. This blood test identifies and measures abnormal forms of hemoglobin. Levels of methylmalonic acid and homocysteine can confirm B_{12} deficiency.

Sometimes a condition is diagnosed by a therapeutic trial. Iron replacement therapy is given for a suspected case of iron deficiency anemia. Vitamin B_{12} is given to detect vitamin B_{12} deficiency, and folate for folate deficiency anemia. The diagnosis is made if improvement is seen after therapy.

If the individual's symptoms and initial test results are indicative of a more serious form of anemia, a bone marrow aspiration and biopsy (a sample of bone marrow is removed for microscopic examination) may be necessary to see whether normal red blood cells are being produced at a normal rate. In rare equivocal cases, bone marrow examination may also be necessary to confirm iron deficiency anemia or megaloblastic changes caused by folate or vitamin B_{12} deficiency.

Other potential underlying causes can be ruled out by further tests such as kidney function tests, blood clotting tests, and fecal occult blood.

Treatment

The underlying condition or disease causing the anemia should be identified before beginning any treatment except when individual is unstable due to significant blood loss. In this case, a blood transfusion may be required in order to replace lost blood before a diagnosis can be made.

Treatment is directed toward the underlying cause of the anemia. Iron deficiency anemia due to low iron in the diet or increased demand (such as during pregnancy) is treated with oral iron supplements. Iron deficiency anemia caused by chronic bleeding is treated by finding the cause of the bleeding and treating that condition. Gastrointestinal bleeding is a common cause of iron deficiency anemia and may be treated with a medication such as a histamine (H2) antagonist to stop the bleeding.

Folate deficiency anemia is treated with oral folate supplements. Hormone erythropoietin (EPO) is the hormone that stimulates the bone marrow to produce red blood cells. Injections of EPO are given to replace the EPO deficiency caused by kidney disease. Anemia involving the immune system (immune hemolytic anemia) may be treated with steroids or other immunosuppressive drugs. Some types of anemia require removal of the spleen (splenectomy). More serious forms of anemia may require blood transfusions of red cells, exchange transfusions of whole blood, or a bone marrow transplant from a compatible donor.

Treatments are continued until the problem is corrected. Lifelong conditions require lifelong treatment. Most forms of pernicious anemia require lifelong vitamin B_{12} injections. Individuals with blood clotting disorders will need periodic replacement of the missing clotting factors for the rest of their lives.

Specialists

- Emergency Medicine
- Hematologist
- Internist
- Primary Care Provider

Prognosis

Outcome of anemia due to blood loss depends on the severity of the loss and response to treatment. If the source of bleeding is identified and corrected, acute anemia due to massive blood loss is successfully treated with transfused blood. Chronic anemia due to a small but chronic blood loss such as in gastrointestinal bleeding also responds to correction of the bleeding but without the need for transfusion.

Anemias caused by deficiencies can usually be corrected by replacement therapy. Iron deficiency anemia typically begins to respond to iron replacement therapy within one month and is resolved within two months. Megaloblastic anemia caused by a deficiency of either folate or vitamin B_{12} (pernicious anemia) shows evidence of correction within the bone marrow as quickly as 12 to 24 hours after replacement therapy begins. Blood measurements are back to normal within 2 months. Neuropsychiatric symptoms caused by pernicious anemia may take up to 12 to 18 months to show improvement. The symptoms may not go away completely but with ongoing treatment typically do not progress.

Individuals with severe lifelong anemia such as sickle cell anemia or thalassemia, have a shortened life expectancy. Without a bone marrow transplant, severe forms of some anemia are often fatal.

Differential Diagnosis

Individuals with chronic disease or malignancy may present with similar symptoms of fatigue. Heart failure produces many of the signs and symptoms associated with anemia.

Work Restrictions / Accommodations

Individuals with mild anemia do not typically require work accommodations or restrictions. Individuals with moderate anemia may experience fatigue, breathlessness, or dizziness with exertion. These individuals require a reduction in the physical requirements of work. This reduction may be temporary or permanent depending on the availability of and response to treatment. Individuals with severe anemia will likely need time off for more intensive treatment or surgery such as bone marrow transplant or splenectomy.

Comorbid Conditions

Individuals with anemia may have more than one disease process causing the anemia. For example, folate deficiency and vitamin B_{12} deficiency commonly occur at the same time. Individuals may have anemia due to a chronic immune condition such as rheumatoid arthritis then later develop a more severe anemia due to an autoimmune reaction against their own red blood cells. An individual with mild anemia may develop an infection with a certain virus such as parvovirus B_{19} that can attack the bone marrow. The bone marrow then stops or slows production of red blood cells and is no longer able to compensate for the mild anemia.

Individuals with cardiovascular or pulmonary disease have a more difficult time compensating for mild anemia. In these individuals, mild anemia will cause symptoms ordinarily brought on by more significant anemia. Lack of oxygen to tissues has a more profound affect on organs that have already been damaged due to some other disease process such as prior heart disease, coronary artery disease, cerebrovascular disease, and peripheral arterial disease.

Complications

Body organs, particularly the heart, may be damaged by hypoxia. Heart failure and death can occur in severe anemia.

Complementary and Alternative Therapies

Content is intended for awareness only. Treatments may or may not be effective. Scientific evidence may be lacking and some substances have potentially toxic effects. Dr. Presley Reed and the editors do not endorse the use of these therapies in the absence of consultation with a licensed medical professional.

Heme iron - For iron deficiency anemia, a diet that includes good sources of heme iron such as liver, red meats, and poultry may help with symptoms. Other sources of iron include cereals and breads.

Vitamin C - May help to increase iron absorption.

Cast-iron cookware - Cooking acidic foods in cast-iron cookware may leach small amounts of iron from the cookware and add to diet.

Raw leafy vegetables - Contains folic acid and may help individuals with folic acid deficiency anemia.

Factors Influencing Duration

Length of disability may be influenced by the type of anemia, rapidity of onset, severity of symptoms, the individual's age and overall general health, alcohol use, method of treatment, and individual's compliance with and response to treatment.

Length of Disability

Length of disability may be influenced by the type of anemia, severity of symptoms, treatment required, compliance with and response to treatment, and extent of fatigue or other complications.

Medical treatment.

Duration in Days

Job Classification	Minimum	Optimum	Maximum
Any work	3	7	14

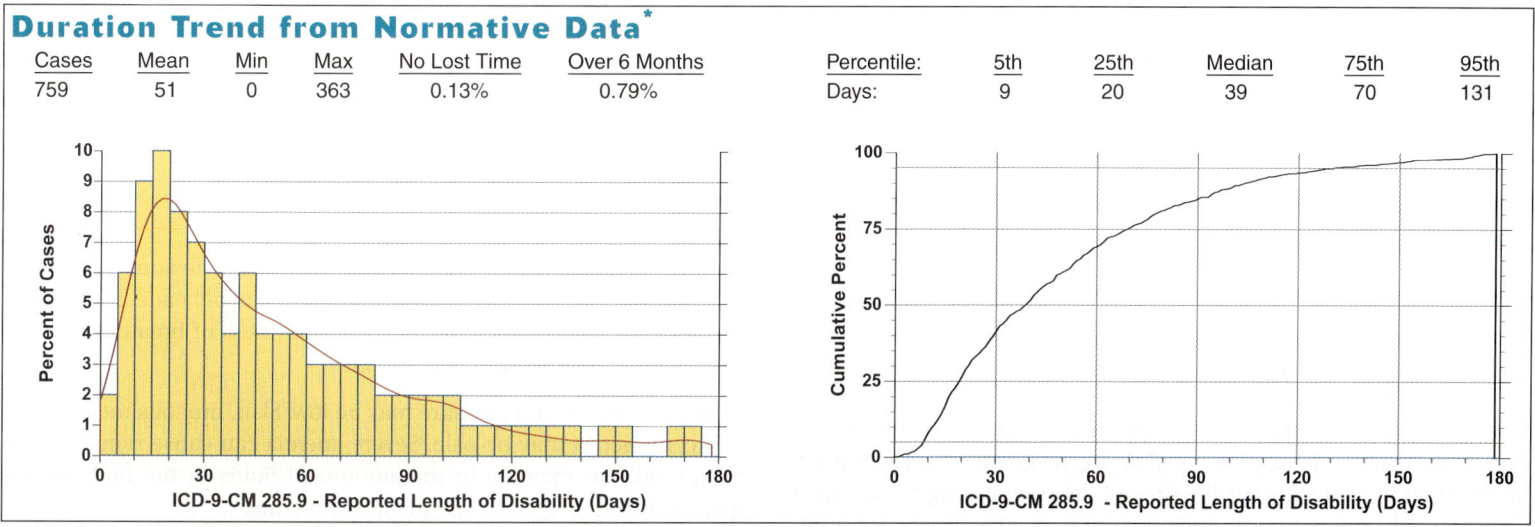

Duration Trend from Normative Data*

Cases	Mean	Min	Max	No Lost Time	Over 6 Months
759	51	0	363	0.13%	0.79%

Percentile:	5th	25th	Median	75th	95th
Days:	9	20	39	70	131

* Differences may exist between the expected duration tables and the normative graphs. Duration tables provide expected recovery periods based on the type of work performed by the individual. The normative graphs reflect the actual observed experience of many individuals across the spectrum of physical conditions, in a variety of industries, and with varying levels of case management.

Failure to Recover

If an individual fails to recover within the maximum duration expectancy period, the reader may wish to reference the following questions to assist in better understanding the specifics of an individual's medical case.

Regarding diagnosis:

- Does individual have underlying conditions creating risk of developing anemia such as recent blood loss, malignancy, or renal failure?
- Was diagnosis of anemia confirmed with a complete blood count?
- Were additional serological tests (e.g., total iron binding capacity) performed to determine type of anemia present?
- Was a diagnostic work up performed?

Regarding treatment:

- Has individual received the appropriate intervention to address the underlying cause of the anemia?
- Is individual complying with prescribed treatment?
- Is lifelong treatment necessary?
- Will individual require a splenectomy or bone marrow transplant?

Regarding prognosis:

- Has underlying cause of the anemia been identified and successfully treated?
- Is success of treatment being monitored by subsequent blood tests? Does individual have access to needed medical care?
- Does individual have an adequate diet? Would individual benefit from nutrition counseling?
- If anemia is related to alcohol abuse, has individual stopped using alcohol?
- Does individual have an underlying condition such as cardiac, pulmonary, kidney, or liver disease that may impact recovery?

References

Abrahamian, Fredrick, and Eric Wilke. Anemia, Chronic. eMedicine.com 11 Jul 2000 22 Aug 2000 <http://www.emedicine.com/emerg/topic808.htm>.

Allen, Robert. "Megaloblastic Anemias." Cecil Textbook of Medicine, 21st ed. Goldman, Lee, and J. Claude Bennett, eds. Philadelphia: W.B. Saunders Company, 2000. 859-867.

Berkow, Robert MD, ed. The Merck Manual of Medical Information: Home Edition. Whitehouse Station, NJ: Merck Research Laboratories, 1997.

Bogdonoff, Morton D., MD. Home Health Handbook. Perryville: International Masters Publishers, 2000.

Duffy, Thomas. "Microcytic and Hypochromic Anemias." Cecil Textbook of Medicine, 21st ed. Goldman, Lee, and J. Claude Bennett, eds. Philadelphia: W.B. Saunders Company, 2000. 855-859.

Duffy, Thomas. "Normochromic, Normocytic Anemias." Cecil Textbook of Medicine, 21st ed. Goldman, Lee, and J. Claude Bennett, eds. Philadelphia: W.B. Saunders Company, 2000. 853-855.

FASTATS A to Z: Anemia. National Center for Health Statistics. 26 Apr 1999 23 Aug 2000 <http://www.cdc.gov/nchs/fastats/anemia.htm>.

Goroll, Allan, Lawrence May, and Albert Mulley. Primary Care Medicine, 3rd ed. Philadelphia: Lippincott-Raven, 1995.

Kahsai, Daniel, and Craig Van Roekens. Anemia, Acute. eMedicine.com 18 Aug 2000 22 Aug 2000 <http://www.emedicine.com/emerg/topic808.htm>.

Zuckerman, Kenneth. "Approach to the Anemias." Cecil Textbook of Medicine, 21st ed. Goldman, Lee, and J. Claude Bennett, eds. Philadelphia: W.B. Saunders Company, 2000. 840-847.

Anemia Complicating Pregnancy

Other names / synonyms: Folic Acid Deficiency Anemia, Iron Deficiency Anemia, Macrocytic Anemia, Sickle Cell Anemia
648.2

Definition

Anemia during pregnancy occurs when there is less than the normal amount of red blood cells circulating in the mother's blood. Although most women experience anemia to some degree during pregnancy, it isn't usually harmful. Anemias resulting from hereditary abnormalities in hemoglobin, however, increase the risk of illness in the mother, and illness and death in the newborn.

The most common anemia of pregnancy is dilutional anemia due to relatively large increases in extracellular fluid volume than the increase in red cell manufacture. Iron deficiency accounts for approximately 95% of other forms of anemia associated with pregnancy. Because the mother must produce enough red blood cells to supply the fetus as well as herself, more iron is needed during pregnancy. Although iron deficiency anemia is usually caused by a nutritional deficiency during pregnancy, it can also be the result of a pre-existing iron deficiency, iron lost during menstrual periods, or a previous pregnancy. Unless nutritional intake of iron is supplemented during pregnancy, the woman will be deficient in iron stores at the time of delivery placing her at risk if postpartum bleeding occurs. Anemia during pregnancy can also result from a diet deficient in folic acid, the B vitamin needed to produce red blood cells.

Iron deficiency anemia is the most common blood (hematologic) disorder in pregnancy. Women at highest risk are those who have had several babies in quick succession, women carrying more than one fetus, and vomiting or not eating appropriately for any reason. Socio-economically deprived women with poor general nutrition are at greatest risk for anemia during pregnancy.

Diagnosis

History: A mild anemic condition may have no obvious symptoms. Individuals with moderate anemia may complain of headaches, fatigue, and lethargy. Severe anemia can cause shortness of breath, dizziness, chest pain, or palpitations with exercise.

Physical exam: Blood pressure may be low. Skin, mucous membranes, and conjunctiva may be pale. Severe anemia can cause signs of heart failure with an increase in the amount of fluids in the body tissues (peripheral edema) and a rise in blood pressure.

Tests: A complete blood count (CBC) with a hematocrit below 33, hemoglobin below 10, and MCV below 79 indicates anemia. Serum iron below 60 may signify the need to measure the iron-binding capacity. Vitamin B_{12} and folate levels may be measured to detect any deficiencies.

Treatment

During pregnancy, iron deficiency anemia is treated with oral iron preparations such as ferrous gluconate, given twice daily. A prenatal vitamin is prescribed at bedtime. In addition, a high iron diet is advised. Although rare, a women who fails to ingest or absorb adequate iron may require intravenous or injectable iron preparations. Folic acid or vitamin B_{12} may also be given by mouth or injection. In severe cases, blood transfusions may be needed especially if labor and delivery are imminent. Any underlying cause for the anemia should be treated.

Prognosis

Untreated, anemia during pregnancy can weaken the woman and make her less able to cope with physical or emotional stress. She will be more vulnerable to infection and may have premature delivery or an infant with impaired growth.

Prenatal iron and folic acid supplementation usually corrects maternal iron deficiency anemia prior to delivery. Depending on the cause of the anemia, iron supplementation may be needed by the mother indefinitely. Unless nutritional intake of iron is supplemented during pregnancy, the woman will be deficient in iron stores at the time of delivery, placing her at risk if postpartum bleeding occurs.

The newborn infant usually has a normal hemoglobin and hematocrit despite maternal anemia. Iron stores at birth may be low requiring iron supplementation in the infant's formula.

Differential Diagnosis

Other diagnoses may include hemolytic complications of pregnancy, chronic granulomatous bowel disease, alcohol or phenytoin ingestion, abnormal hemoglobin disorders (hemoglobinopathies), leukemia, gastrointestinal bleeding, cancer, and bowel disease.

Specialists

- Hematologist
- Obstetrician

Work Restrictions / Accommodations

Individual may need frequent meals and restroom breaks. If activity is restricted or more frequent, rest periods may be required and a temporary transfer to a more sedentary position may be necessary.

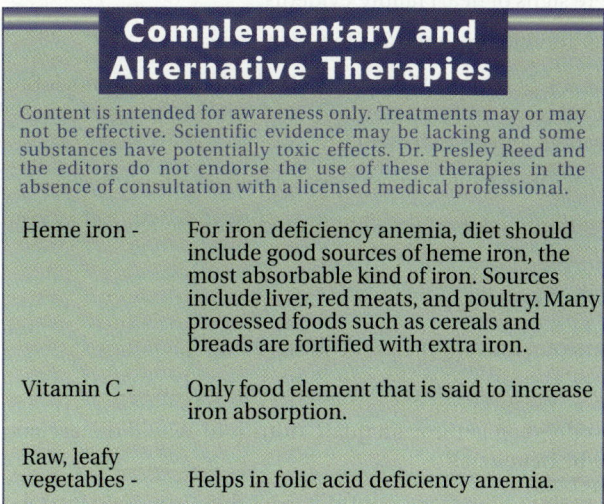

Comorbid Conditions

Diabetes mellitus, deep vein thrombosis, high risk pregnancy, or prior cesarean section may lengthen disability.

Complications

The side effects of gastric upset or constipation may make treatment unpleasant and decrease compliance. Megaloblastic (pernicious) anemia combined with folic acid deficiency is more difficult to treat. Folic acid deficiency can cause a reduction in white blood cells and platelets. A very low blood count can be life-threatening.

Factors Influencing Duration

Length of disability may be influenced by the type of anemia, severity of symptoms, treatment required, compliance with and response to treatment, and extent of fatigue or other complications.

Length of Disability

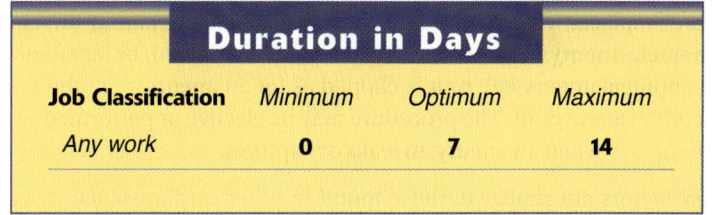

Job Classification	Minimum	Optimum	Maximum
Any work	0	7	14

Failure to Recover

If an individual fails to recover within the maximum duration expectancy period, the reader may wish to reference the following questions to assist in better understanding the specifics of an individual's medical case.

Regarding diagnosis:

- Does individual complain of headaches, fatigue, and lethargy?
- Is there shortness of breath, dizziness (vertigo), chest pain, or palpitations with exercise?
- Do symptoms include fatigue, frequent illness, and episodes of pain in the muscle, joints, chest, or abdomen?
- On exam, was blood pressure low? Skin, mucous membranes, and conjunctiva pale (pallor)?

- Were signs of heart failure evident?
- Was anemia present prior to pregnancy?
- Was a CBC done? What were the hematocrit, hemoglobin, and MCV levels? Were vitamin B$_{12}$ and folate levels measured? Were any deficiencies detected?
- Was a blood smear done? Hemoglobin electrophoresis?
- Was the type of anemia confirmed? Iron deficiency or folic acid deficiency?

Regarding treatment:

- Were oral iron supplements prescribed?
- Can individual comply with treatment regimen?
- Is individual getting adequate nutrition? Would dietary counseling be beneficial?
- Is anemia effectively controlled by diet, iron, and/or folic acid supplementation?
- Were intravenous or injectable iron preparations considered?

- Is blood count monitored frequently to determine effectiveness of treatment?
- Is individual compliant with scheduled prenatal checkups? If not, what can be done to increase compliance?
- Does individual have transportation to medical appointments? Does individual need baby-sitting or childcare in order to attend medical appointments?

Regarding prognosis:

- Was underlying cause of anemia resolved?
- Has anemia responded to treatment? Is individual compliant with treatment plan? If not, what can be done to increase compliance?
- Does individual have an underlying condition such as megaloblastic anemia that may complicate treatment and prognosis?
- Have any complications developed associated with the anemia (i.e., hypertension, heart failure)?
- Does individual have an underlying condition that may impact pregnancy or delivery?

References

Snow, C.F. "Laboratory Diagnosis of Vitamin B$_{12}$ and Folate Deficiency." Archives of Internal Medicine 159 12 (1999): 1289-1298.

Aneurysmectomy

Other names / synonyms: Abdominal Aortic Aneurysm Repair, Aneurysm Resection

38.3, 38.30, 38.31, 38.32, 38.33, 38.34, 38.35, 38.36, 38.37, 38.38, 38.39, 38.4, 38.41, 38.42, 38.43, 38.44, 38.45, 38.46, 38.47, 38.48, 38.49, 38.60

Definition

Aneurysmectomy is a surgical procedure where a dilated, weakened section of an artery (aneurysm) is removed (resected). The artery is either replaced with a synthetic graft as for an aneurysm in the chest (thoracic aneurysm), abdomen (abdominal aneurysm), or leg (femoral or popliteal aneurysm); or it is clipped as for an aneurysm in the brain (cerebral aneurysm). The procedure may be elective or performed as an emergency when an aneurysm leaks or ruptures.

Risk factors are similar to those found in other cardiovascular disease such as older age, smoking, high blood pressure (hypertension), atherosclerosis, and connective tissue disorders (Marfan's syndrome and Ehlers-Danlos syndrome).

The incidence of abdominal aortic aneurysms is about 2% of the elderly population. The male to female ratio is about 9 to 1. Aneurysms of the arteries in the leg are rare, but of these, the artery behind the knee (popliteal) is most affected. Thoracic aortic aneurysms are also rare and more frequently associated with connective tissue disorders or infections.

Reason for Procedure

Reasons for elective aneurysmectomy include an expanding aneurysm on neighboring structures and the size of the aneurysm even when symptoms are absent. The critical size of a symptomatic aneurysm warranting surgery varies according to the location, i.e., thoracic aneurysms and abdominal aneurysms greater than 6 cm carry a risk of possible fatal rupture. Cerebral aneurysms of much smaller size are frequently clipped rather than resected even when no symptoms occur.

Depending on its site, an aneurysm may be felt (palpated) or seen by noninvasive techniques including ultrasound, CT, and MRI. Alternatively, an invasive procedure involving the injection of a contrast medium (dye) to visualize the interior of an artery (arteriography) may be used. Any of these techniques can determine the size of the aneurysm.

Description

The specific surgical procedure varies according to the site of the aneurysm and the need for maintaining circulation to parts of the body beyond the aneurysm. All these procedures are performed in the operating room under general anesthesia.

Aneurysms that involve the upper (ascending) or horizontal (transverse) portion of the large artery in the chest (aorta) are resected and repaired while the individual is on the heart-lung machine (cardiopulmonary bypass). The individual's body temperature is profoundly lowered while on the heart-lung machine to protect the brain and heart. An incision is made through the midline of the chest and the sternum is split. The affected portion of the artery is then resected. Synthetic materials such as Dacron then replace the resected portion of the aorta. The sternum is held closed with wires and the skin stitched closed. Aneurysms in the lower (descending) thoracic aorta are resected and replaced and the individual's circulation maintained by something less complicated than total cardiopulmonary bypass. The techniques are under the general category of partial cardiopulmonary bypass or various shunts. The goal of these methods is to prevent damage to the spinal cord during the surgery.

Aneurysmectomy involving the lower abdominal aorta does not require that circulation be maintained to the lower portion of the body beyond the aneurysm since no vital organs (heart and brain) are in jeopardy and adequate natural pathways (collaterals) exist for the blood to reach the lower abdomen and legs. The abdomen is opened with a midline incision and the aorta is clamped. The affected portion of the aorta is then resected and replaced with a synthetic graft. The abdomen is closed with stitches.

Aneurysms in the legs are treated in much the same way as abdominal aortic aneurysms. The aneurysm is exposed, clamped, resected, and replaced and the skin stitched closed.

Aneurysmectomy involving an artery in the brain is done through clipping rather than resecting the aneurysm. During this procedure, the body is maintained at normal or somewhat lower temperatures. Under general anesthesia, the skull is opened and the brain exposed. The aneurysm is located and clipped. The skull is then closed usually with a metal plate or plates and screws. The skin is then stitched closed.

Prognosis

The outcome following aneurysmectomy depends on the site of the aneurysm and whether the procedure is elective or done as a result of an emergency. The operative mortality for elective thoracic aneurysmectomy is 5-10% with a survival rate after 5 years of 60%. The operative mortality for elective abdominal aneurysmectomy is 2-5%. The operative mortality for both emergency thoracic (approaching 80%) and abdominal aneurysmectomy (50%) is significantly higher than for elective surgery.

Specialists

- General Surgeon
- Neurosurgeon
- Thoracic Surgeon
- Vascular Surgeon

Work Restrictions / Accommodations

Individuals may require transfer to a less physically strenuous job for a period of time. In general, lifting more than 10 pounds for the first 6 weeks and no more than 50 pounds even after 6 months should be avoided. Individuals can often return to their preoperative activities after 6 months.

Comorbid Conditions

Conditions that impair proper healing such as diabetes can lengthen recovery time.

Procedure Complications

Complications common to aneurysmectomy irrespective of the procedure site include bleeding, infection, and complications from anesthetic use. Additional complications related to upper and transverse aorta aneurysmectomy and the heart-lung machine include stroke, heart attack (myocardial infarction), excess fluid in lung (pulmonary edema), shock, kidney (renal) failure, liver (hepatic) failure, destruction of red blood cells (hemolytic anemia), and death. Aneurysmectomy involving the lower thoracic aorta can result in paralysis of the lower half of the body. Major complications following aneurysmectomy involving the lower abdominal aorta are renal failure and vascular and neurological problems that affect the lower abdomen (i.e., impotence) and the legs (i.e., paralysis and loss of extremity). Stroke is the major complication of aneurysmectomy of aneurysms of the brain.

Factors Influencing Duration

The individual's age, pre-existing conditions (especially coronary heart disease and chronic lung disease), and complications of the procedure may affect the length of disability.

Length of Disability

Duration of the disability depends on type and location of aneurysm, whether or not it was ruptured, and job requirements. Disability may be permanent if the individual performs heavy work.

Aortic.

Duration in Days

Job Classification	Minimum	Optimum	Maximum
Sedentary work	56	70	112
Light work	56	84	Indefinite
Medium work	56	105	Indefinite
Heavy work	84	140	Indefinite
Very Heavy work	84	140	Indefinite

Cerebral.

Duration in Days

Job Classification	Minimum	Optimum	Maximum
Sedentary work	42	56	Indefinite
Light work	42	56	Indefinite
Medium work	56	70	Indefinite
Heavy work	70	84	Indefinite
Very Heavy work	70	84	Indefinite

References

Clochesy, John M., et al. Critical Care Nursing, 2nd ed. Philadelphia: W.B. Saunders Company, 1996.

Schwartz, Seymour, MD. Principles of Surgery. New York: McGraw-Hill, 1999.

Angina Decubitus

Other names / synonyms: Unstable Angina
413.0

Definition

Angina decubitus is an old(er) term not currently used. It refers to cardiac pain (angina) that occurs in the supine position. The terms rest angina and unstable angina are now used for the condition formerly called angina decubitus. In this edition, unstable angina is the term employed.

Angina Pectoris

Other names / synonyms: Angina, Angina Attack, Angina Syndrome, Cardiac Angina, Exertion Angina, Stable Angina, Vasomotor Angina
413, 413.9

Definition

Angina pectoris is discomfort in the chest or adjacent area because of low blood flow to the heart (myocardial ischemia) that limits delivery of oxygen to the heart muscle during exertion.

Usually, blood flow is decreased because of blockage within one or more of the coronary arteries supplying the heart muscle (coronary artery disease). This blockage is usually caused by gradual clogging of the artery with fatty buildup (atherosclerosis). However, sudden tightening or narrowing of the coronary artery (vasospasm) or severe narrowing of the aortic valve (aortic stenosis) may also interfere with coronary blood flow and cause angina.

Tobacco use, sedentary lifestyle, obesity, high blood pressure (hypertension), high cholesterol and lipids in the bloodstream (hyperlipidemia), low blood levels of high density lipoprotein, advancing age, diabetes mellitus, and a positive family history of heart disease are major risk factors associated with coronary artery disease that may lead to angina. Other risk factors may include low red blood cell count (anemia), irregular heartbeat (arrhythmia), or overactive thyroid gland (hyperthyroidism).

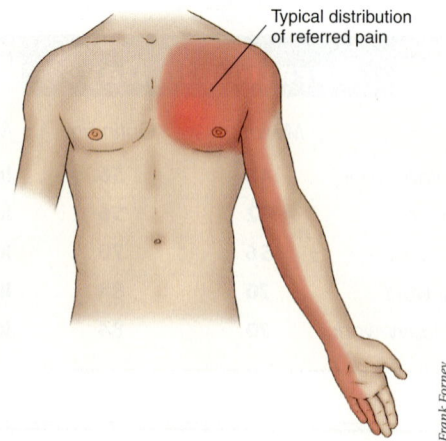

Typical distribution of referred pain

Frank Forney

Diagnosis

History: Angina is typically described as discomfort beneath the breastbone with pressure, heaviness, or a weight-like sensation that may travel (radiate) across the chest into one or both arms and extend into the fingers. It occasionally radiates to the back, between the shoulder blades, upper abdomen, neck, earlobes, or jaw. Individuals with angina sometimes complain of a pressure sensation, tightness, or squeezing in the chest. Angina is a generalized sensation and rarely can individuals point to the location of their discomfort.

Angina can be associated with shortness of breath, heavy sweating (diaphoresis), nausea, and vomiting. It can be brought on by exercise, stress, eating a heavy meal, or exposure to cold and wind. It usually occurs in the morning rather than at the end of the day. Anginal pain usually lasts at least 30 seconds but not longer than 15 minutes and is often relieved with rest or nitroglycerin medication.

Physical exam: The exam is usually normal in individuals with angina but it may reveal findings associated with risk factors for angina such as high blood pressure, irregular heartbeat, or abnormalities seen with an overactive thyroid. Listening to the heart (auscultation) may reveal extra sounds associated with valve dysfunction or heart failure. Auscultation of the carotid arteries in the neck may identify abnormal sounds (bruits) suggesting atherosclerosis. Baldness in men, especially at the top of the head rather than at the hairline, may indicate that the individual is at risk for heart disease.

Tests: Tests include the resting electrocardiogram (ECG) that looks at the electrical activity of the heart and detects old heart attack (myocardial infarction) or acute changes indicating the heart muscle is not getting enough blood flow. The graded exercise stress test looks at the ECG and the individual's symptoms during exercise, and is therefore more sensitive to detecting low blood flow to the heart than the routine ECG. Ambulatory Holter monitoring uses a cassette tape recorder to observe the ECG for a 24-hour period while the individual goes about usual activities. This test is therefore more sensitive to low blood flow conditions during stress or exercise, and to irregularities of heart rhythm that may occur only occasionally.

More sophisticated tests to look at the structure and function of the heart, its arteries, and valves include perfusion scintigraphy, radionuclide angiography, and two-dimensional echocardiography. Selective coronary angiography is the most definitive diagnostic test for examining the coronary arteries, but it is also invasive.

Treatment

To relieve the immediate pain of angina, individuals are advised to sit down as soon as the discomfort begins and remain quiet until the pain stops. A short-acting nitrate (nitroglycerin) can be placed under the tongue (sublingually). This usually relieves the pain within several minutes by enlarging the diameter (vasodilating) of the coronary arteries. The individual suffering from angina should keep nitroglycerin on hand at all times. If pain is not relieved by a repeat dose, emergency medical attention is needed.

For ongoing treatment, long-acting nitrates are often given in combination with beta-blocking agents to decrease the number and severity of angina attacks. Long-acting nitrates can be taken orally or administered as a skin patch or paste (topically). Calcium-channel blockers may also be prescribed to complement the antianginal action of vasodilators and beta-blockers. Other medical treatments that may be beneficial include enteric-coated aspirin to inhibit blood clotting, angiotensin-converting enzyme inhibitors to reduce long-term risk of developing unstable angina, and estrogen therapy to reduce low-density lipoprotein and increase high-density lipoprotein.

Lifestyle changes such as limiting dietary fat intake, getting adequate exercise, and ceasing to smoke can minimize progression of coronary artery disease and decrease the frequency and severity of angina. Individuals who are anxious and nervous may be advised to seek counseling, and a mild tranquilizer may be prescribed. Overweight individuals should be encouraged to reduce weight, avoid high-calorie and high-cholesterol diets, abstain from gas-forming foods, and rest for short periods following meals. A high-fiber diet may lower serum cholesterol and triglyceride levels, decrease hypertension, and decrease the number and severity of anginal attacks. A regular program of daily exercise and immediate abstinence from smoking should be encouraged. Individuals should avoid "passive smoking" (being with a smoker or in a smoke-filled room) in order to reduce the risk of angina.

Invasive procedures designed to increase coronary blood flow and ease the symptoms of angina include inflation of a balloon in the artery at the site of obstruction (percutaneous transluminal coronary angioplasty or PTCA), placement of a self-expanding device into the vessel at the site of obstruction (coronary stent), and a coronary artery bypass graft (CABG) where the obstructed part of the artery is surgically bypassed

Prognosis

Individuals with angina pectoris may remain stable for varying lengths of time, develop worsening symptoms (unstable angina), or progress to myocardial infarction or death. The prognosis for individuals treated only with medication depends on the severity and extent of ischemia, the presence or absence of complex cardiac arrhythmia, the site of vascular obstruction, the number of coronary vessels involved, how well the heart is functioning, and the extent that risk factors can be modified.

Individuals who undergo PTCA and/or implantation of a self-expanding device into the vessel at the site of occlusion (coronary stent) have a very low mortality rate associated with the procedure (1-3%). Many individuals show marked improvement and no longer experience angina a year later. However, in a significant number of individuals (~30%), the PTCA/stent-treated vessel will become blocked again (restenosis) and these individuals may need the procedure repeated. Alternatively, they may undergo a CABG. This procedure has a mortality rate of less than 3% and is highly effective in alleviating anginal pain. However, different institutions vary widely in their complication rate depending on the expertise of the surgeons. Without risk factor modification such as ceasing to smoke, correcting high blood pressure and hyperlipidemia, and weight reduction, the vessel may again become blocked after CABG.

Differential Diagnosis

Angina pectoris can be confused with several gastrointestinal disorders including gas or indigestion resulting from acid reflux into the esophagus (gastroesophageal reflux disease or GERD), peptic ulcer, and chronic gallbladder disease (cholecystitis). Abdominal pain secondary to involvement of blood vessels supplying the intestines (celiac and mesenteric vascular disease), musculoskeletal pain in the chest and shoulder, cervical disc disease, and viral infection or other inflammation of the heart coverings (pericarditis) may also be mistaken for angina.

Specialists

- Cardiologist

Rehabilitation

Cardiac rehabilitation can be very helpful for individuals with angina pectoris and may prevent future progression of the disease. With a specifically designed exercise program, an individual with angina pectoris can decrease his or her chest pain and substantially improve fitness levels.

Therapy often begins with low levels of exercise to prevent excessive stress and overexertion and promote overall mobility of the body. Exercise may begin in the coronary care unit of a hospital starting with low-level exercise with the individual on the back (supine position). The individual progresses with exercises to sitting and eventually to standing. Progressive walking (ambulating) and eventual stair climbing are an important part of individual's exercise program while hospitalized.

After the individual is discharged from the hospital, therapy to improve functional capacity by increasing physical endurance and promoting return to activity begins. Individuals not hospitalized because of angina pectoris usually begin at this phase. Individuals are typically attached to an ECG monitor, a device used to record the continuous electrical activity of the heart muscle. A physical therapist keeps a daily log of the individual's blood pressure, heart rate, and cardiac rhythm.

The next phase in therapy incorporates higher levels of exercise with the addition of recreational activities, as tolerated. Depending on the individual's condition, this phase may last for several months. Light jogging at approximately 5 miles per hour (mph) and cycling at approximately 12 mph is appropriate as long as the individual tolerates the rehabilitation program well. Moderate-intensity activity (walking, jogging, cycling, or other aerobic activity) is suggested. This should be supplemented by an increase in daily lifestyle activities such as walking breaks at work, using stairs, gardening, and household work.

Work Restrictions / Accommodations

Return to work may initially involve restriction to a lighter workload or part-time duty. Individuals with residual ischemia or impaired function of the heart muscle could require permanent restrictions. The individual with an active, hectic life at work may have to adjust to a lower activity level to avoid bringing on anginal attacks. Brief rest periods throughout the work day may be helpful in avoiding attacks.

Complementary and Alternative Therapies

Content is intended for awareness only. Treatments may or may not be effective. Scientific evidence may be lacking and some substances have potentially toxic effects. Dr. Presley Reed and the editors do not endorse the use of these therapies in the absence of consultation with a licensed medical professional.

Vitamin E -	Acts as an antioxidant and may protect against atherosclerosis.
Hawthorne -	May offer pain relief by improving blood flow to the heart muscle.
Gingko -	May offer pain relief by improving blood flow to the heart muscle.
Fish oils -	May increase "good cholesterol" (HDL cholesterol).
Garlic -	May reduce blood lipids and blood pressure and act as a blood thinner.
CoQ10 -	May improve heart muscle function.
Acupuncture -	Application of needles to specific points on the body may relieve pain.

Comorbid Conditions

Pre-existing conditions that may adversely affect recovery and lengthen disability include diabetes, heart failure, obesity, anemia, hyperthyroidism (thyrotoxicosis), renal failure, and infection.

Complications

If the coronary artery blockage causing angina is not reversed and blood flow is not restored either spontaneously or with treatment, the vessel may become permanently blocked and the heart muscle supplied by that artery may die, resulting in a heart attack (acute myocardial infarction). Decreased blood flow to the heart muscle can also cause irregular heartbeat (arrhythmia) that can prevent the heart muscle from pumping blood effectively. Complications following acute heart attack can include shock, heart failure, fluid in the lungs (pulmonary edema), blood clot in the lungs (pulmonary embolism), and recurrent myocardial infarction.

Factors Influencing Duration

The ability to return to work depends on the type and outcome of treatment, complications from treatment, severity of any residual symptoms, any other medical conditions, and demands of the individual's occupation. The individual's willingness to address correctable risk factors such as smoking, sedentary lifestyle, and obesity will influence the length of disability. For some individuals, cardiac rehabilitation may facilitate return to optimal function.

Length of Disability

The length of disability may depend on the physical and emotional requirements of the job. Disability may be permanent for physically demanding work

Angioplasty.

Duration in Days

Job Classification	Minimum	Optimum	Maximum
Sedentary work	3	7	14
Light work	3	7	14
Medium work	7	14	28
Heavy work	14	14	28
Very Heavy work	14	21	35

Coronary bypass.

Duration in Days

Job Classification	Minimum	Optimum	Maximum
Sedentary work	42	56	112
Light work	42	56	112
Medium work	56	70	140
Heavy work	56	84	140
Very Heavy work	56	112	168

Stable. Medical treatment.

Duration in Days

Job Classification	Minimum	Optimum	Maximum
Sedentary work	1	7	28
Light work	3	14	42
Medium work	21	28	56
Heavy work	21	42	84
Very Heavy work	21	42	84

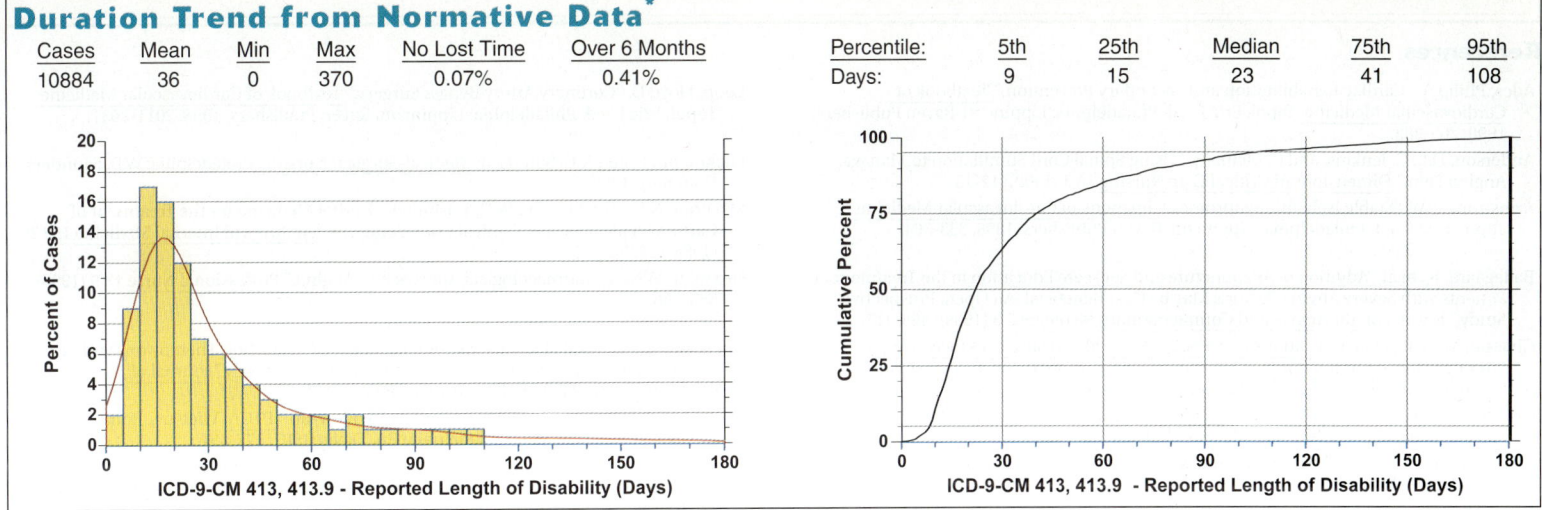

Failure to Recover

If an individual fails to recover within the maximum duration expectancy period, the reader may wish to reference the following questions to assist in better understanding the specifics of an individual's medical case.

Regarding diagnosis:

- Does individual have a history of coronary artery disease? Other risk factors for angina? Is there a family history of heart disease?
- Does individual describe pressure, heaviness, or a weight-like sensation in the area beneath the sternum? Does the pain radiate? If so, is it radiating across the chest, down one or both arms, and extending to the fingers? Does it radiate to the back, between the shoulder blades, upper abdomen, neck, earlobes, or jaw?
- Does individual experience shortness of breath, heavy sweating (diaphoresis), nausea, or vomiting?
- Was pain initiated by exercise, stress, eating a heavy meal, or exposure to cold and wind? Did it last 30 seconds to 15 minutes but no longer?
- Does individual take nitroglycerine? If so, was pain relieved after nitroglycerine was taken?
- Was a resting electrocardiogram (ECG) done? Did it reveal any abnormalities or changes?
- Was a graded exercise stress test done? Was individual able to complete the test? Were abnormalities or changes noted on the stress test ECG?
- Has individual worn an ambulatory Holter monitor to record the ECG for a 24-hour period?
- Have perfusion scintigraphy, radionuclide angiography, or two-dimensional echocardiography been performed?
- Was selective coronary angiography required to confirm the diagnosis?
- Was the diagnosis of angina pectoris confirmed?

Regarding treatment:

- Does individual sit down as soon as discomfort begins and remains quiet until pain stops?
- Does nitroglycerin placed under the tongue (sublingually) relieve pain within several minutes? Does individual keep nitroglycerin on hand at all times?
- Does individual know that if pain is not relieved by a repeat dose, emergency medical attention is needed?
- Does individual take long-acting nitrates, beta-blocking agents, and/or calcium-channel blockers? What about enteric-coated aspirin, angiotensin-converting enzyme inhibitors, or estrogen therapy?
- Is individual compliant with all medication regimens? Would a change in medication be helpful?
- Has individual made required lifestyle and diet changes?
- Could individual benefit from a less demanding job situation, either physically or emotionally? Would individual benefit from participation in a cardiac rehabilitation program?

Regarding prognosis:

- Has individual developed worsening symptoms (unstable angina)?
- How severe is the ischemia and how many vessels are involved?
- Does the individual have a complex cardiac arrhythmia?
- How well is the heart functioning?
- Has individual modified risk factors? Does individual understand the consequences of not modifying risk factors?
- Did individual undergo PTCA and/or implantation of a self-expanding device into the vessel at the site of occlusion (coronary stent)? To what extent has individual improved?
- Have the vessels become blocked again (restenosis)? Will PTCA or coronary stent reopen the vessels or will individual require coronary artery bypass graft (CABG) surgery?
- Have any complications occurred such as heart attack or arrhythmia?

References

Ades, Philip A. "Cardiac Rehabilitation and Secondary Prevention." Textbook of Cardiovascular Medicine. Topol, Eric J., ed. Philadelphia: Lippincott-Raven Publishers, 1998. 263-282.

Anderson, D.J., C. Jenkins, and C. McInally. "Using Spinal Cord Stimulation to Manage Angina Pain." Dimensions of Critical Care Nursing 18 3 (1999): 12-13.

Armstrong, P.W. "Stable Ischemic Syndromes." Textbook of Cardiovascular Medicine. Topol, Eric J., ed. Philadelphia: Lippincott-Raven Publishers, 1998. 333-364.

Ballegaard, S., et al. "Addition of Acupuncture and Self-care Education in the Treatment of Patients with Severe Angina Pectoris May be Cost Beneficial: An Open, Prospective Study." Journal of Alternative and Complementary Medicine 5 5 (1999): 405-413.

Chassin, Mark R., et al. Indications for Selected Medical and Surgical Procedures: A Literature Review and Ratings of Appropriateness. Coronary Artery Bypass Graft Surgery. Santa Monica: The Rand Corporation, 1986.

Crowley, Stephen T. "Angina." Cardiology Secrets. Adair, Olivia Vynn, and Edward P. Havranek, eds. Philadelphia: Hanley & Belfus, Inc, 1995. 76-80.

Kisner, C., and L. Colby. Therapeutic Exercise Foundations and Techniques. Philadelphia: F.A. Davis, 1990.

Loop, Floyd D. "Coronary Artery Bypass Surgery." Textbook of Cardiovascular Medicine. Topol, Eric J., ed. Philadelphia: Lippincott-Raven Publishers, 1998. 2011-2031.

Luckmann, J., and K.C. Sorensen. Medical-Surgical Nursing. Philadelphia: W.B. Saunders Company, 1987.

Mashour, N.H., G.I. Lin, and W.H. Frishman. "Herbal Medicine for the Treatment of Cardiovascular Disease: Clinical Considerations." Archives of Internal Medicine 158 20 (1998): 2225-2234.

Orwin, R. "A Non-pharmacological Approach to Angina." Professional Nurse 13 9 (1998): 583-586.

van Dixhoorn, J.J., and H.J. Duivenvoorden. "Effect of Relaxation Therapy on Cardiac Events After Myocardial Infarction: A 5-year Follow-up Study." Journal of Cardiopulmonary Rehabilitation 19 3 (1999): 178-185.

Vlietstra, Ronald E., and David R. Holmes, Jr. "Follow-up." PTCA. Vlietstra, Ronald E., and David R. Holmes, Jr., eds. Philadelphia: F.A. Davis, 1987. 177-187.

Zamarra, J.W., et al. "Usefulness of the Transcendental Meditation Program in the Treatment of Patients with Coronary Artery Disease." American Journal of Cardiology 77 10 (1996): 867-870.

Angina, Unstable

Other names / synonyms: Accelerating Angina, Acute Coronary Insufficiency, Crescendo Angina, Intermediate Coronary Syndrome, New-Onset Effort Angina, Preinfarction Angina, Preinfarction Syndrome, Progressive Angina, Rest Angina

411.1

Definition

Unstable angina may be defined as the new onset of chest pain with exertion (effort angina) within the past two months, the increasing frequency or longer duration of pre-existing effort angina, or the precipitation of pre-existing effort angina with less exertion than previously used. Alternatively, it may be defined as angina occurring at rest, usually longer than 20 minutes within the past week.

This condition represents a severity of hardening of the coronary arteries (coronary atherosclerosis) between stable effort angina and a heart attack (myocardial infarction). Unstable angina is caused by temporarily inadequate oxygen delivery to a portion of the heart muscle (myocardial ischemia) due to either increased oxygen demand (as during exercise) or decreased oxygen supply (as during spasm). Myocardial infarction involves a permanent loss of a portion of the heart's muscle cells. Not all individuals with unstable angina go on to infarction, although when infarction does occur, it is considered a serious development.

Since unstable angina is an expression of coronary atherosclerosis, in general, risk factors for unstable angina are the same as those for atherosclerosis.

Diagnosis

History: Pain in the center of the chest under the breast bone occurring at rest or with minimal exertion is typical. The individual reports a dull, heavy or burning sensation, not a sharp one. Pain may radiate to the arms, neck, back, or shoulders and occur in only one of these regions without involving the chest.

Physical exam: The exam during an episode of rest angina may reveal a change in the individual's blood pressure (higher or lower), disordered heart rhythm (gallop), a transient heart murmur, or skipped beats. Often, no abnormalities are present on physical exam.

Tests: A 12-lead electrocardiogram (ECG) during pain at rest may show characteristic changes of the ST-T segments (ST segment elevation or depression, inverted T waves), but may occasionally be normal. A stress test such as a treadmill or a dobutamine study may be done if the chest pain does not recur or occurs infrequently during hospitalization. Coronary angiography is often indicated to define anatomy and refine the prognosis. Blood tests to measure the release of cardiac enzymes from damaged heart tissue may help confirm or exclude the diagnosis. Blood enzyme tests usually remain normal with unstable angina since actual damage to the heart is absent or minimal. These enzyme blood tests include CK-MB, troponin-T, troponin-I, CK-MB isoforms, and myoglobin.

Treatment

Medical treatment for unstable angina includes nitroglycerin (NTG) given under the tongue (sublingually), orally or, more often in a vein (intravenously). NTG preparations improve blood flow through the arteries nourishing the heart. NTG preparations also dilate arteries and veins in the arms, legs, and stomach (peripheral arteries and veins), thereby reducing the oxygen consumption of the heart. Medications that control high blood pressure (i.e., calcium-channel blockers), lower the heart rate (i.e., beta-blockers), and control arrhythmias (i.e., digitalis, lidocaine, and quinidine) are also very useful.

Aspirin therapy or other antiplatelet agents are often prescribed to retard or prevent the formation of a blood clot (thrombus) in the coronary artery and thereby reduce the chances of heart attack. Similarly, intravenous heparin is often initially employed to prevent thrombus formation and reduce the immediate chances of heart attack. Aspirin or other antiplatelet drugs are continued indefinitely.

Initial treatment and management are based on the individual's risk of a heart attack or death while in the hospital. The risk is assessed at the time of admission. Individuals of low risk include those with rest pain lasting less than 20 minutes. Individuals at intermediate risk include those with chest pain at rest lasting longer than 20 minutes but relieved by sublingual NTG and individuals with effort angina of less than 2 months duration or more than 2 months duration occurring with distinctly less provocation. Individuals at high risk for heart attack include those with pain lasting more than 20 minutes unrelieved by NTG, marked ST-T wave changes during pain, and those with cardiovascular instability such as congestive heart failure and/or low blood pressure.

Individuals with low risk unstable angina may be treated as outpatients. Individuals with new onset chest pain with effort are given a trial of antianginal medication starting with a sublingual nitrate for use during anginal attacks and an oral beta-blocker for ongoing use. If this does not control the symptoms, a long-acting nitrate may be added, either by mouth or as a skin patch or paste (topically). Calcium-channel blockers are indicated for suspected coronary artery spasm (Prinzmetal's variant angina). An antiplatelet drug such as aspirin should be given to help reduce the possibility of a heart attack by inhibiting the development of a thrombus within the coronary artery.

Individuals with intermediate risk unstable angina who manifest with increasing angina are usually already taking antianginal medications. These medications should be adjusted, as necessary, until the symptoms are controlled or until higher doses are not tolerated.

Individuals with new onset effort angina should have a cardiac stress test performed to define the risk of future cardiac events more accurately and plan further treatment. In most cases, a cardiac stress test is performed when the heart rate and blood pressure have been appropriately reduced with medication(s). A resting heart rate of 50 beats per minute or less, and blood pressure of 120/80 or less are the usual goals. A treadmill study with or without a radioisotope (thallium) or a stress echo study using a drug called dobutamine are the two stress tests performed most often.

If a stress test shows ischemia despite the administration of medication(s), coronary arteriography is performed. This will indicate whether the blocked arteries can be successfully treated by a coronary revascularization procedure. Current revascularization procedures include balloon angioplasty, cleaning out the atherosclerotic material using a "roto-rooter" device (rotational atherectomy), laser removal of atherosclerotic material, insertion of a device to mechanically "prop open" the coronary artery (intracoronary stent), and coronary artery bypass grafting (CABG) using veins from the legs.

Individuals with intermediate risk unstable angina are usually hospitalized and treated the same as low risk individuals with unstable angina once they are pain-free. Individuals with ongoing pain at rest despite medication generally have coronary angiography performed to guide further therapy (i.e., more medication or a revascularization procedure). Those individuals who become pain-free with medical therapy alone usually have a cardiac stress test performed after being pain-free for 48 hours. The results are used to further assess risk and plan future treatment.

If the stress test does not produce angina or reveal ECG evidence of inadequate oxygen delivery to the heart muscle (myocardial ischemia), the individual is reclassified as low risk. Medical management is usually sufficient and the individual may be discharged from the hospital 1 to 2 days after the stress test.

Individuals at high risk usually have coronary angiography performed soon after admission followed by a revascularization procedure. Individuals with ongoing symptoms and/or ischemia indicated by ECG are hospitalized and admitted to either a coronary care unit (CCU) or a monitored bed in a less intensive setting. An oral beta-blocker may also be prescribed. A cardiac stress test is performed after the individual has been pain-free for 48 hours. The results are used to reassess risk and plan further treatment. If the stress test does not reveal ischemia, the individual is reclassified as low risk. Medical management is usually sufficient and the individual may be discharged from the hospital in 1 to 2 days.

If the stress test shows ischemia only during high levels of activity and if there is no evidence of left heart dysfunction (i.e., hypotension, difficulty breathing, or excessive fatigue), further diagnostic testing is required either by an alternative type of stress test or a coronary arteriography. If the stress test shows ischemia at low activity levels, or if there is evidence of left heart dysfunction, the individual is reclassified as high risk. Coronary arteriography may be indicated followed by revascularization.

High-risk unstable angina requires hospitalization and continuous ECG monitoring in a CCU. Initial treatment includes bed rest, oxygen, antiplatelet drugs, heparin, and antianginal medications. Sublingual nitrates are usually given first in addition to a beta-blocker. If the individual still has ischemia, a calcium-channel blocker may be added if coronary artery spasm is suspected. In severe cases, narcotics may be necessary to relieve pain.

Symptoms continuing after an hour or more of medical treatment are an indication for immediate coronary arteriography followed by coronary bypass surgery or angioplasty. This treatment improves revascularization. If the individual's heart is failing seriously, intra-aortic balloon counterpulsation may be needed to support circulation until coronary bypass or angioplasty can be performed. However, most individuals can be stabilized with medical treatment. The individual is allowed to walk at increasing intervals if pain-free and stabilized for 24 hours. When symptoms are clearly under control, the individual is moved to a regular bed.

Further medical evaluation is the next step. Revascularization improves the prognosis in high-risk individuals so coronary arteriography is performed usually within 24 hours to determine whether these procedures are feasible. After revascularization, ongoing treatment includes antiplatelet drugs and modification of risk factors. Anti-anginal drugs are not required unless residual ischemia occurs.

High-risk individuals who do not receive revascularization may require prolonged hospitalization. Individuals diagnosed with unstable angina receive the same ongoing treatment as prescribed for stable angina. These treatments include anti-anginal drugs, antiplatelet drugs, and modification of risk factors.

Prognosis

The outcome of unstable angina depends on several factors. One is the severity of the underlying coronary artery disease and if it involves one, two, or all three of the coronary arteries. Prognosis also depends on the risk assessment of an AMI on admission and on the type of treatment subsequently given. In many cases, revascularization by angioplasty, directional atherectomy, stenting, or CABG improves the prognosis. Unstable angina will either resume a stable course spontaneously or with therapy or progress to a heart attack. The unstable phase usually resolves within 8 weeks. If the individual survives the unstable phase, the prognosis becomes that of either stable angina pectoris or a myocardial infarction.

Differential Diagnosis

An actual myocardial infarction or chest pain due to coronary spasm (Prinzmetal's variant angina) are other possible diagnoses that may initially be confused with unstable angina. A heart attack can be excluded or confirmed by serial cardiac enzyme tests. Variant angina can be confirmed by an ECG obtained during pain showing marked ST segment elevation or by the administration during coronary angiography of a drug that can cause spasm (ergonovine). Noncardiac causes of chest pain that may mimic unstable angina include musculoskeletal conditions affecting the chest wall such as costochondritis, lung problems such as pulmonary embolism, or inflammation of the tissue covering the heart or lungs (pericarditis or pleuritis).

Specialists

- Cardiologist

Rehabilitation

The goal of rehabilitation for unstable angina is to design a physical conditioning program for the individual that increases the amount of activity yet limits the onset of symptoms of this form of angina. Individuals must first be able to identify and communicate the symptoms as true angina pain. The physical therapist and/or other healthcare personnel knowledgeable in treating various forms of angina use a scale to rank anginal symptoms and determine the amount and intensity of exercise prescribed. Scaling unstable angina becomes a beneficial tool for individuals to grade and communicate their angina symptoms during exercise to the physical therapist.

The exercise session for individuals with angina begins with a prolonged warm up period. Proper breathing while exercising is critical. The principles of mild aerobic conditioning in a physical therapy setting have been commonly used in developing a program for individuals with various forms of angina including unstable angina. Rehabilitation for this condition follows the same progression in related cardiac diseases with emphasis on avoiding fast bursts of activity and avoiding exertion while in a position of lying on one's back (supine).

Treatment of unstable angina begins with monitoring of symptoms throughout low demand aerobic activities. In a hospital or cardiac rehabilitation setting, individuals are monitored for heart rate, rhythm, blood pressure, and chest pain. Initial exercises focus on the individual in positions other than lying down that aggravate the condition. These activities include self-care activities such as sitting up in bed and moving from the bed to a chair. Calisthenics while sitting or standing are instructed of varying intensity. Walking (ambulating) with continuous monitoring of chest pain (angina pectoralis) is also part of this rehabilitation.

As endurance improves without symptoms of unstable angina, the use of a stationary bicycle beginning at very light resistance for 3 minutes is performed under supervision. This time is eventually increased. Exercises progress with time and intensity that vary from individual to individual. With improvement, work-type activities are incorporated into the rehabilitation regimen to address endurance needed for return to work.

This related increase in endurance also translates into a generally more active lifestyle. Endurance or aerobic routines such as running, brisk walking, cycling, or swimming are the ultimate goal to thereby increase the strength and efficiency of the heart. Because of the various degrees and effects each individual experiences with unstable angina and other forms of angina, modifications may need to be made for those individuals taking various medications or who are experiencing other conditions with resulting angina.

Work Restrictions / Accommodations

Activity is significantly limited during unstable angina. Restriction to no work or lighter and/or part-time work may be required after unstable angina has resolved depending on the individual's functional classification following a treadmill or other stress test. Return to work for individuals who have an AMI or go on to CABG is based on the time needed to recover from the AMI or surgery.

Comorbid Conditions

Other common medical conditions that may hinder recovery include obesity, hypertension, diabetes mellitus, lung disease, heart valve disease, peripheral atherosclerosis (atherosclerosis involving the carotid or lower extremity arteries), disease of the heart muscle (cardiomyopathy), and alcoholism.

Complications

The major complication of unstable angina is a myocardial infarction. Sudden death from a ventricular arrhythmia may occur but is infrequent. Additional complications arising from a myocardial infarction may develop.

Factors Influencing Duration

Factors influencing the length of disability include response to therapy, the presence or absence of complications of unstable angina (especially the presence or absence of heart attack), and the availability of lighter or part-time work on either a temporary or permanent basis. A cardiac rehabilitation program may facilitate recovery and shorten the period of disability.

Length of Disability

The expected length of disability depends on the individual's response to treatment, complications, and comorbid conditions. It may be brief if the individual responds to pharmacologic therapy or a revascularization procedure (PTCA, laser, stent, CABG). Disability may be more prolonged or permanent if a complication of unstable angina such as a heart attack occurs. Following coronary bypass, disability may be permanent. However, unstable angina itself does not cause a permanent disability.

Coronary balloon angioplasty.

Duration in Days

Job Classification	Minimum	Optimum	Maximum
Sedentary work	5	7	14
Light work	7	7	14
Medium work	14	21	28
Heavy work	14	21	28
Very Heavy work	21	28	35

Medical treatment

Duration in Days

Job Classification	Minimum	Optimum	Maximum
Sedentary work	5	7	14
Light work	5	7	14
Medium work	14	21	28
Heavy work	28	42	56
Very Heavy work	42	56	70

Coronary bypass.

Duration in Days

Job Classification	Minimum	Optimum	Maximum
Sedentary work	42	56	112
Light work	42	56	112
Medium work	56	70	140
Heavy work	56	84	140
Very Heavy work	56	112	168

Duration Trend from Normative Data*

Cases	Mean	Min	Max	No Lost Time	Over 6 Months
1425	53	0	554	0.21%	1.62%

Percentile:	5th	25th	Median	75th	95th
Days:	8	18	34	72	138

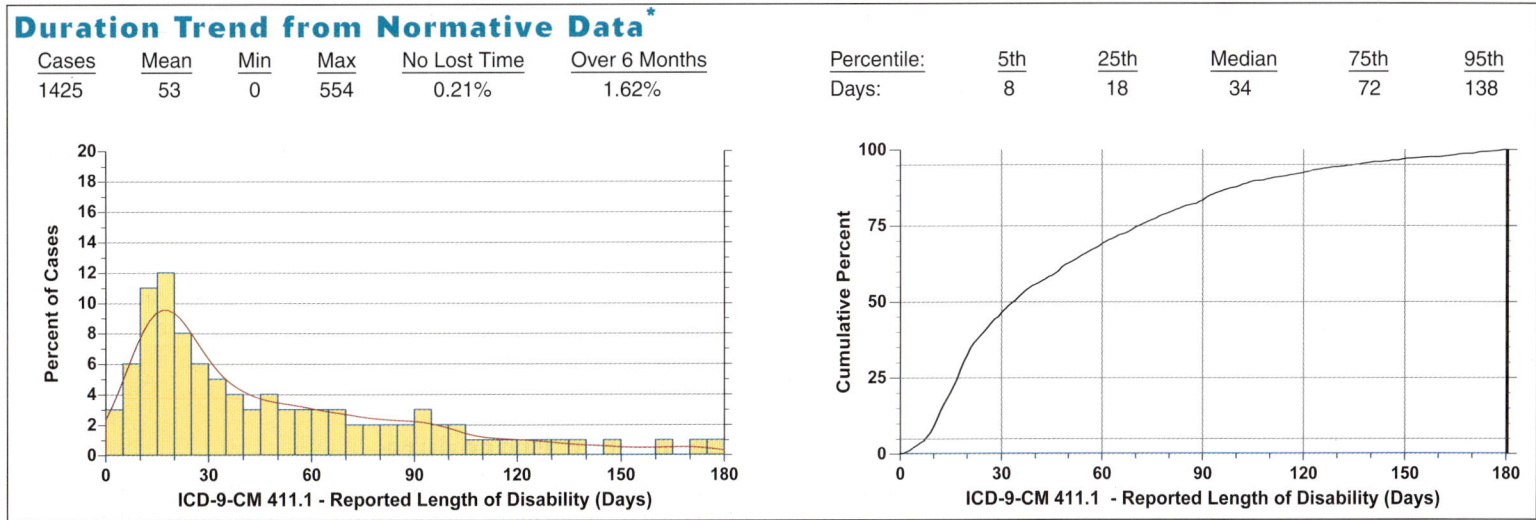

* Differences may exist between the expected duration tables and the normative graphs. Duration tables provide expected recovery periods based on the type of work performed by the individual. The normative graphs reflect the actual observed experience of many individuals across the spectrum of physical conditions, in a variety of industries, and with varying levels of case management.

Angina, Unstable

Failure to Recover

If an individual fails to recover within the maximum duration expectancy period, the reader may wish to reference the following questions to assist in better understanding the specifics of an individual's medical case.

Regarding diagnosis:

- Did individual present with any one of the clinical scenarios consistent with the diagnosis of unstable angina (new onset effort angina within the past two months, increasing frequency or longer duration of pre-existing effort angina, or precipitation of pre-existing effort angina with less exertion than previously used)?
- Did individual complain of dull, heavy, or burning pain in the chest that radiated to the arms, neck, back, or shoulders?
- Were there any abnormalities upon examination? Altered blood pressure, abnormal heart rhythm, or a heart murmur?
- Was a 12-lead ECG done? Did the findings indicate unstable angina?
- Was a coronary angiography performed and did results support the diagnosis?
- Were blood tests taken to measure cardiac enzymes? Did results confirm or exclude diagnosis?
- If the diagnosis was uncertain, were other conditions with similar findings ruled out, i.e., coronary artery spasm, costochondritis, pulmonary embolism, pericarditis, or pleurisy?

Regarding treatment:

- Based on individual's risk for pending heart attack, was treatment prompt and appropriate? Was individual hospitalized?
- Was individual categorized as low, intermediate, or high risk? Was pain relieved by sublingual NTG?
- Were anticoagulants, antiplatelets, or thrombolytic medications given? Was NTG prescribed? Were beta-blockers or calcium-channel blockers necessary to slow the heart rate?
- Did individual's symptoms (chest pain) resolve within 1 to 2 hours after medical intervention? If not, was arteriography and angioplasty or coronary artery bypass done?
- Was the unstable angina associated with heart failure? If so, was intra-aortic balloon counterpulsation attempted to support the blood pressure and improve cardiac performance?

Regarding prognosis:

- Did the angina stabilize following medical interventions?
- Was angiographic or surgical revascularization done? If so, what was the expected outcome?
- Did individual participate in a cardiac rehabilitation program, as recommended? If not, are barriers present that prevent compliance with rehabilitation recommendations, i.e., insurance limitations, lack of transportation, or lack of motivation?
- Was the unstable angina complicated by a myocardial infarction?
- Does individual have any medical conditions that may impact ability to recover or influence prognosis (obesity, hypertension, diabetes mellitus, lung disease, heart valve disease, peripheral atherosclerosis, cardiomyopathy, or alcoholism)?

References

Baum, Seth, J., MD. The Total Guide to a Healthy Heart. New York: Kensington Books, 1999.

Unstable Angina. Healthcentral.com. 1998. 02 Feb 2001 <http://www.healthcentral.com/mhc/top/000201.cfm>.

Angiocardiography
88.5, 88.50, 88.51, 88.52, 88.53, 88.54

Definition

Angiocardiography is x-ray examination of the blood vessels or chambers of the heart. It is made by tracing the course of a special fluid called contrast or dye visible by x-ray that has been injected into the bloodstream. The x-ray pictures are called angiograms. The left ventricle, aorta, and pulmonary arteries are the structures most often examined with this technique.

This technique is used to evaluate individuals for surgery on the heart and associated blood vessels. Although it is a valuable tool in assessing some of the more complicated aspects of heart function, it is also one of the most hazardous of all diagnostic procedures. Angiocardiography is performed in a hospital setting under strict controls since it is an invasive procedure.

The most frequently used angiocardiographic methods are biplane angiocardiography and cineangiocardiography. In the first method, large x-ray films are exposed in two planes at right angles to each other, which permits the simultaneous recording of two different views. In cineangiocardiography, the x-ray images are brightened several thousand times and photographed on motion-picture films. When projected, the passage of the opaque blood may be viewed in slow motion.

There are no accurate records as to the number of procedures performed but it is done in most major hospitals in the US on a daily basis.

Reason for Procedure

Angiocardiography can provide both structural (anatomic) and functional (hemodynamic) information about the heart and its vessels. It may reveal anatomical abnormalities such as aneurysms, narrowed or obstructed vessels, or heart chamber enlargement. Angiocardiography can also demonstrate abnormal blood flows or the failure of a valve to close that results in a back flush of blood.

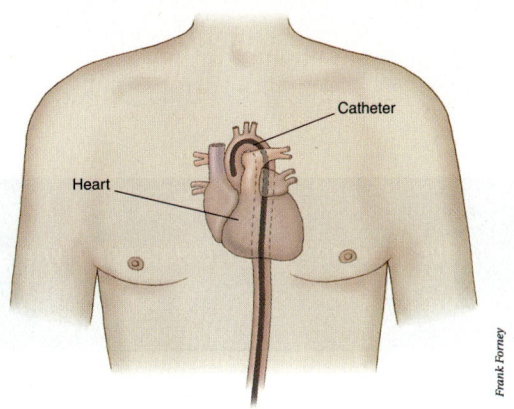

X-ray imaging of the ventricle evaluates the heart's performance. Another more accurate measurement of how the heart is functioning is the ejection fraction. This measurement correlates well with the individual's prognosis and is widely used as an index of ventricular performance. In normal adults, the ejection fraction is generally in the range of 50-70%. As it drops below 40%, the prognosis worsens significantly.

In addition to determining the heart's overall pumping capacity, detailed studies of ventricular wall motion may be done. This may reveal localized areas where wall motion is diminished, absent, or opposite in direction from normal motion. Wall motion analysis is especially useful in the evaluation of coronary artery disease. Areas of insufficient blood supply or tissue death (infarction) of the ventricle can be identified even when overall heart performance appears normal. Ventricular function can also be assessed by echocardiography, but angiocardiography provides more accurate information.

The arteries and veins of the lungs can be examined by injecting contrast medium into the pulmonary artery. The main purpose of pulmonary angiocardiography is to confirm a diagnosis of a suspected pulmonary plug. This plug is composed of a detached blood clot (thrombus) or other foreign body (embolus). Pulmonary angiocardiography is indicated when noninvasive test results are uncertain or when detailed anatomical information is needed to plan for surgical removal of a pulmonary embolus. Other pulmonary vascular disorders are also diagnosed with this procedure.

Description

The procedure is performed by inserting a long tube into a blood vessel (cardiac catheter) usually in the groin or arm and then advanced toward the heart. The catheter is placed into a vein to visualize the right side of the heart and the pulmonary arteries or into an artery to examine the aorta, coronary arteries, and left side of the heart. The size of the ventricle is measured when it is filled and after it has ejected blood. The difference between these two is the amount of blood pumped with each heartbeat.

After the catheter tip has been guided into the appropriate chamber or vessel, contrast medium is injected through the catheter. The contrast mixes with the blood and moves through the circulation with the movement observed by x-ray fluoroscopy. The fluoroscopic image is filmed or videotaped (cineangiocardiography) and can be replayed for later study and diagnosis.

Prognosis

The outcome from the procedure itself is expected to be uneventful. The test, in general, gives good indications of heart structure and damages. However, the procedure varies with the state of the disease in the individual and any adverse reactions to the dye. Major complications of the procedure are rare.

Specialists

- Cardiologist

Work Restrictions / Accommodations

The underlying condition for which the angiocardiography was performed may require adjustments in work requirements. In terms of the procedure itself, nonstrenuous work may resume within a few days to a week following the procedure. Strenuous physical activity or exercise should be temporarily avoided. Some individuals may experience nausea, vomiting, and coughing as a result of the procedure.

Comorbid Conditions

Blood diseases and disorders, hemophilia, liver disease, kidney disease, and respiratory disorders and diseases may interfere with the successful use of this procedure.

Procedure Complications

Serious reactions to the iodine-containing compounds used including radiopaque media not transparent to x-rays (radiopaque) may occur despite continued efforts to develop less harmful materials.

Major complications such as cardiac arrest, bleeding, infection, clot in vessel, muscle contractions and capillary dilation (anaphylactic reactions), shock, convulsions, blue skin (cyanosis), and kidney (renal) toxicity are rare. Should a blood clot become loosened, it could damage other parts of the body and result in very serious disability or in rare cases, death.

Allergic reactions may include hives (urticaria) and inflammation of eye and eyelid tissues (conjunctivitis). Lung spasms (bronchospasm), swelling of the throat (laryngeal edema), and difficulty breathing (dyspnea) are rare reactions. Abnormal ventricular rhythms (arrhythmias) are common if the catheter tip contacts the wall of the ventricle.

Factors Influencing Duration

Disability may be influenced by factors such as the site of insertion of the catheter, the setting, (inpatient or outpatient), and any complications. In most cases, duration of disability is due to the underlying disease.

Length of Disability

Duration in Days

Job Classification	Minimum	Optimum	Maximum
Any work	1	2	3

References

Beers, Mark H., MD, and Robert Berkow, MD. The Merck Manual of Diagnosis and Therapy, 17th ed. Beers, Rahway: Merck & Co., Inc, 1999. 11 Nov 2000 <http://www.merck.com/>.

Angioedema

Other names / synonyms: Allergic Angioedema, Angioedema, Angioneurotic Edema, Giant Urticaria, Hypersensitivity Angioedema, Quincke's Disease, Quincke's Edema

995.1

Definition

Angioedema (angioneurotic edema) is the development of large welts (urticaria, hives) or swelling below the surface of the skin especially around the throat and lips, as well as face, ears, hands, and feet. Angioedema can occur with or without hives. Angioedema is classified as allergic, hereditary, or idiopathic according to the underlying cause. Angioneurotic edema generally refers to swelling or hives in response to an emotional stimulus.

Allergic angioedema is an allergic immune reaction that is triggered by an allergen such as medications, shellfish, nuts, milk, insect stings, animal dander, and pollen.

Hereditary angioedema is characterized by recurrent but self-limited attacks of swelling involving the skin, subcutaneous tissue, upper respiratory tract, or gastrointestinal (GI) tract. Attacks may last from hours to days and may be precipitated by local trauma (e.g., dental procedures or tonsillectomy).

Angioedema may also occur following certain illnesses or infections such as autoimmune disorders or leukemia, or after exposure to certain compounds, x-ray contrast, opiates, dextran, aspirin, or other nonsteroidal anti-inflammatory drugs. When the cause is unknown, it is called idiopathic angioedema.

In the US, approximately 15% of the general population is affected by recurrent episodes of angioedema. It occurs with equal frequency in all races. Women tend to have more occurrences than men. The attacks increase in frequency after adolescence with the peak incidence occurring in the third decade of life.

Diagnosis

History: The individual may complain of swelling with or without itching, hoarseness, difficulty breathing and in rare cases, abdominal pain. These individuals often report a personal or family history of allergies, asthma, and eczema.

Physical exam: Individuals usually present with a sudden onset of swelling of the lips, tongue and throat, or welts on the eyes and ears. The extremities genitalia are occasionally affected. There may be abdominal distention and diminished bowels sounds may occur with massive swelling of the subcutaneous tissue in the abdominal region. There may be a crowing sound when inhaling (stridor) if the throat is affected.

Tests: If an allergic angioedema is suspected, allergy testing may be performed to identify the offending allergen. Immune assays may help determine if the angioedema is hereditary in nature.

Treatment

Most individuals with mild acute angioedema may be treated in the same manner as those with an allergic reaction through use of oral antihistamines.

More severe symptoms that do not respond to antihistamines may require the addition of subcutaneous epinephrine injections or steroids and medications that block histamine release sites (H-1 or H-2 antagonists). If the tongue or throat is involved, this may require inserting an artificial airway (endotracheal tube) through the mouth or nose and into the trachea to prevent airway obstruction. Hereditary angioedema tends to be resistant to the use of subcutaneous epinephrine, antihistamines, and steroids. In these cases, an anabolic steroid may be needed. Some clinicians report that prophylactic treatment with aminocaproic acid (usually used to prevent blood clot breakdown) is effective in reducing the incidence of recurrences in hereditary angioedema.

Prognosis

Mild cases of angioedema are generally harmless and resolve in a few days even without treatment. Those cases having severe symptoms such as a swelling of the throat or those complicated by anaphylactic shock usually respond promptly to steroids or medications that prevent histamine release (H-1 antagonist or H-2 antagonists) and have good outcomes. Hereditary angioedema may recur.

Differential Diagnosis

Asthma, inflammatory skin conditions such as cellulitis or dermatitis, infections of the epiglottis (epiglottitis), or abscesses of the tonsils or throat (pharynx) may have similar symptoms and should be included in the differential diagnosis.

Specialists

- Allergist
- Dermatologist
- Emergency Medicine

Work Restrictions / Accommodations

Allergic individuals should avoid contact with causative agents. Caution should be exercised during chronic therapy with antihistamines because of side effects of drowsiness or dizziness. Individuals on these medications should avoid work on ladders, scaffolds, and should not operate heavy machinery or drive vehicles. Non-sedating antihistamines are recommended.

Comorbid Conditions

Comorbid conditions of asthma or allergies may impact ability to recover and further lengthen disability.

Complications

Angioedema of the tongue or throat may be complicated by respiratory distress or complete airway obstruction. Angioedema resulting from an allergic reaction may be complicated by anaphylactic shock.

Factors Influencing Duration

The severity of the reaction, response to treatment, and whether an allergen can be identified may influence the length of disability.

Length of Disability

Duration in Days

Job Classification	Minimum	Optimum	Maximum
Any work	0	3	5

Failure to Recover

If an individual fails to recover within the maximum duration expectancy period, the reader may wish to reference the following questions to assist in better understanding the specifics of an individual's medical case.

Regarding diagnosis:

- Does individual have allergic, hereditary, or idiopathic angioedema?
- Does individual have urticaria around the face, eyes and ears? Hands? Feet? Throat? Genitalia?
- Is there swelling without urticaria?
- Does individual have hoarseness or difficulty breathing? Abdominal pain?
- Is there a personal or family history of allergies, asthma, and eczema? Stridor?
- Was allergy testing done? Immune assays?
- Were conditions with similar symptoms ruled out?

Regarding treatment:

- Was individual given an oral antihistamine?
- Was it necessary to insert an endotracheal tube?
- Was individual given epinephrine or steroids? H-1 or H-2 antagonists? Anabolic steroids?

Regarding prognosis:

- Can individual's employer accommodate any necessary restrictions?
- Does individual have any conditions that may affect ability to recover?
- Have any complications developed such as anaphylaxis?

References

Harrison's Principles of Internal Medicine, 11th ed. Braunwald, Eugene, ed. New York: McGraw-Hill Book Co, 1987.

Ankylosing Spondylitis

Other names / synonyms: Bechterew Syndrome, Marie Struempel Disease, Marie Strumpell Spondylitis, Poker Spine, Spondyloarthritis, Von Bechterew-Struempel Syndrome, Von Bechterew-Strumpell Syndrome

720.0, 721.6

Definition

Ankylosing spondylitis is a chronic, progressive inflammatory disorder that usually begins during early to mid-adulthood. The condition is characterized by inflammation (arthritis) of the joints of the spine (vertebral joints) and the joints of the hipbones and sacrum (sacroiliac joints). This inflammation results in pain, swelling, and stiffness of the affected joints and may potentially result in spinal immobility (ankylosis).

The underlying cause of ankylosing spondylitis is unknown but genetic factors may play a role. Between 90% and 95% of individuals with the disorder have a particular, genetically determined human leukocyte antigen (HLA) known as HLA-B27. The possible role of HLA-B27 in genetically predisposing individuals to ankylosing spondylitis remains undetermined.

Ankylosing spondylitis is a rare disorder affecting approximately 1.4% of the general population. The condition is more prevalent in males than females by about 3 to 1. The condition also occurs more frequently in whites than blacks. Blacks typically experience milder symptoms.

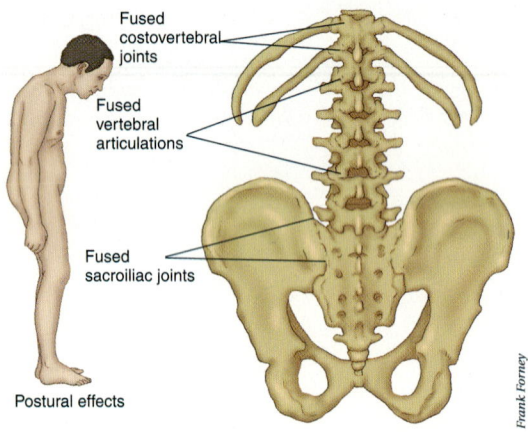

Diagnosis

History: Individuals typically complain of a gradual onset of low back pain over a period of a few months. The pain is usually worse in the morning and improves during the day. The pain follows a gradual ascending pattern from the sacral region to the lumbar to the thoracic and finally to the cervical spine. Individuals may also present with pain and stiffness of the rib cage.

Physical exam: The exam may reveal tenderness over the sacroiliac joints. An abnormal anterior convex curvature of the spine (lumbar lordosis) may be present and lumbar range of motion may be decreased. A purplish discoloration may be noted over severely affected joints. Normal chest expansion is decreased.

Tests: Routine lab tests are normal with the exception of low-grade anemia, erythrocyte sedimentation rate (ESR) that may be mildly elevated with active inflammation, and elevated serum alkaline phosphatase when active joint fusion occurs. The disease may be suspected if HLA-B27 is positive. X-rays of the pelvis will show characteristic inflammation of the sacroiliac joints (sacroiliitis) or fusion of sacroiliac joints. Lumbar x-rays may reveal fusion of the facet joints and, ultimately, the vertebral bodies may fuse together.

Treatment

The primary objective of treatment is to relieve pain. Nonsteroidal anti-inflammatory drugs (NSAIDs) (e.g., aspirin) are used to reduce pain and inflammation. Use of these medications should allow the individual to participate in exercise programs that improve posture and breathing. Physical therapy is used to maintain range of motion and strength as long as possible, and to teach proper posture and positioning so that joint fusions occur in "good position."

Surgical intervention may be necessary for some individuals. Surgical care may include surgical fusion (for stabilization), reduction and stabilization of spinal fractures (which are a potential complication), decompression of cervical or lumbar stenosis (if neurological deficits are present), and possible replacement of weight-bearing joints (e.g., hip). If spontaneous fusion of the spine has occurred in poor position, surgical correction of the spinal deformity by osteotomy of the spine can be done, usually at the cervicothoracic junction or in the lumbar spine.

Lifestyle modifications (exercises to improve posture and breathing) are essential to help preserve mobility and limit further disability. Smoking is discouraged since the disorder can eventually limit air exchange.

Prognosis

The goals of treatment are to relieve pain and enable exercise and postural training. Pharmacological treatment (anti-inflammatory drugs and immunosuppressants), exercise therapy (stretching, pool therapy, and deep breathing, and thoracic extension exercises), and surgical treatments (surgical fusion, reduction and stabilization, decompression, and replacement of weight-bearing joints) all leave individuals with some (lessened) symptoms of pain and stiffness. Outcome varies greatly with the individual. Most individuals with a job that is classified as sedentary or light remain employed and comparatively few develop severe functional disability. In recent studies, only 10-20% became significantly disabled over a period of 20 to 40 years. Disability correlates with duration of disease, disease activity, fixed spinal deformity, and spinal mobility. Severe hip involvement also results in greater impairment. A pattern of disease progression usually emerges after the first 10 years.

Differential Diagnosis

Other disorders that present with similar symptoms include cervical disk syndromes, spinal cord hemorrhage, spinal cord infarction, spinal epidural abscess, amyloidosis, rheumatoid arthritis, Reiter's syndrome, psoriatic arthritis, infective arthritis, and osteoarthritis.

Specialists

- Ophthalmologist
- Orthopedic Surgeon
- Physiatrist
- Rheumatologist

Rehabilitation

Physical therapy can be useful in decreasing pain and stiffness of the intervertebral joint as a result of ankylosing spondylitis. Treatments that utilize warm techniques can help provide relief and also increase joint mobility thereby improving motion of the lumbar spine. A form of heat treatment includes moist heat found in hot packs or ultrasound. Ultrasound uses high frequency sound waves that produce heat to penetrate deep into the involved muscles.

Physical therapy addressing exercises such as spine extension and breathing are performed to strengthen muscles and prevent poor posture. Teaching the individual to frequently rest in the prone (full extension) position helps prevent fusion in flexion (bent over deformity). One effective technique for the lumbar spine is called the press-up. The individual begins in a position on the stomach while supported on the elbows. The individual then raises the upper body upward, maintains this position and returns to the starting position. This exercise may be progressed by straightening the elbows and then eventually supporting the upper body solely on the hands. Exercises to strengthen the lower back and abdominal muscles are key in preventing excess stress and forces on the lumbar spine. Sit-ups performed help strengthen the abdominal muscles. Pelvic tilts are effective to help strengthen the lumbar spine.

Because of the nature of ankylosing spondylitis during a flare-up, many individuals experience stiff joints even with bed rest. For this reason, people with ankylosing spondylitis are encouraged to stretch their spine gently and remain active. Swimming is a good exercise for rehabilitating and conditioning the spine affected by ankylosing spondylitis, as it addresses both range of motion and strengthening.

Modifications may need to be made in rehabilitation for those with disc disease or other additional joint irritations of the spine. Education for proper lifting of heavy objects becomes very important in the rehabilitation process to help prepare the individual for return to work. Many individuals with significant ankylosing spondylitis are unable to do medium work, and few, if any, do heavy work. Lumbar supports are usually not advised for individuals with ankylosing spondylitis as they may increase the stiffness.

Work Restrictions / Accommodations

The stage and severity of the disease will determine the need for modifications in the work environment. For most individuals, early stage symptoms are manageable and few, if any, restrictions are required. The individual may need to take a few breaks during the day (from prolonged sitting or standing) to practice postural and breathing exercises. If there is significant hip involvement, heavy lifting and prolonged standing or walking may need to be decreased or eliminated.

Comorbid Conditions

Spinal fractures, herniated intervertebral discs, and obesity are conditions that could impact the individual's ability to recover and further lengthen disability.

Complications

Possible complications of ankylosing spondylitis include heart valve disease (e.g., aortic valve stenosis), aortitis, inflammations of the eyes (e.g., uveitis and iridocyclitis), formation of fibrous tissue in the lungs (pulmonary fibrosis), and bowel and bladder dysfunction. In addition, fractures of the spine can occur without any injury.

Factors Influencing Duration

Duration of disease, disease activity, spinal mobility, and peripheral joint involvement are all factors that might influence the length of disability.

Length of Disability

Disability may be permanent. Individuals with this diagnosis are not usually able to perform medium work, and are rarely capable of heavy work.

The US Social Security Administration's criteria for permanent and total disability due to ankylosing spondylitis are x-ray proof of diagnosis (fusion of sacroiliac joints and calcification of anterior and lateral ligaments) with "ankylosis or fixation of the cervical or dorsolumbar spine at 30 degrees or more of flexion."

Medical treatment.

Duration in Days

Job Classification	Minimum	Optimum	Maximum
Sedentary work	0	7	28
Light work	0	14	42
Medium work	0	112	Indefinite
Heavy work	0	168	Indefinite
Very Heavy work	0	168	Indefinite

Failure to Recover

If an individual fails to recover within the maximum duration expectancy period, the reader may wish to reference the following questions to assist in better understanding the specifics of an individual's medical case.

Regarding diagnosis:

- Was diagnosis of ankylosing spondylitis confirmed by x-ray or CT or by a rheumatologist?
- Were there any complications related to the ankylosing spondylitis?
- Does individual have an underlying condition that may impact recovery?

Regarding treatment:

- Has individual adhered to medication regimen?
- Has surgical intervention become necessary? Was procedure effective?
- If unable to quit smoking, would individual benefit from enrollment in a community cease-smoking program?

Regarding prognosis:
- Has individual been compliant with lifestyle modifications and exercise therapy? What can be done to increase compliance?
- What impact do symptoms have upon individual's ability to function?
- With workplace accommodations, will individual be able to continue in occupational duties?

References

Ankylosing Spondylitis. drkoop.com. 2000 26 Oct 2000 <http://www.drkoop.com/conditions/ency/article/000420.htm>.

Schaffert, A. Ankylosing Spondylitis from Neurology/Inflammatory and Demyelinating Diseases. eMedicine.com 2000. 26 Oct 2000 <http://emedicine.com/neuro/topic15.htm>.

Anorectal Fistula

Other names / synonyms: Anal Fistula, Fistula-in-Ano

565.1

Definition

An anorectal fistula is an abnormal tunnel or channel that has one opening in the anal canal (primary or internal opening) and the other opening in the skin surrounding the outside of the anus (secondary or external opening). Only one fistula usually occurs but on occasion, multiple fistulae may arise.

In most cases, anorectal fistula is caused from an abscess in the anal wall that discharges pus both into the anus and out onto the surrounding skin. Risk factors for development of anorectal fistula include inflammatory bowel disease (Crohn's disease or ulcerative colitis); anal fissures; physical trauma to the anal region resulting from a surgical drainage procedure, puncture wound, injection treatment for hemorrhoids or injury from an enema tip; cancer in the anal region; radiation therapy; and chlamydial infections.

Anorectal fistulas occur in men and women at an equal rate with the average age of incidence being about 40. Approximately 3% of the anorectal fistulas occurring each year are recurrent because of internal openings that were missed during initial treatment. One to two percent of recurrences are due to missed secondary openings.

Diagnosis

History: Individuals with anorectal fistula usually complain of drainage or discharge from the external opening onto the skin around the anus that may contain pus (purulent). Itching, tenderness, or pain during or after bowel movements may also be reported.

Physical exam: One or more external (secondary) openings on the skin around the anus (perianal) appear as raised, reddish skin lesions (papules) less than 1 cm in diameter. If they are open (patent), the external opening(s) may express a drop of pus upon manipulation with a gloved finger (palpation). Alternatively, the openings may be sealed. The channel may feel like a hardened, long, rounded structure (indurated cord). Examination with a gloved finger (digital rectal exam) can help determine how the channel lies within the tissue.

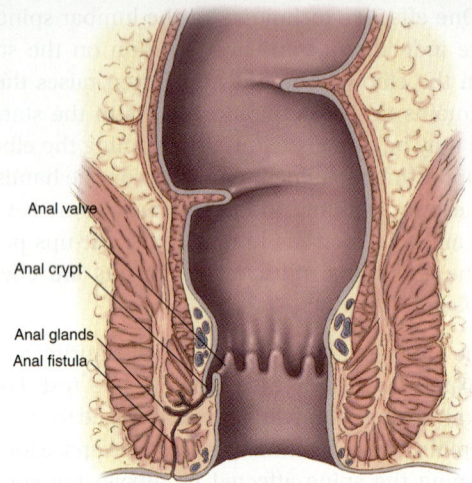

Frank Forney

Tests: Examination of the rectum (anoscopy or sigmoidoscopy) using a flexible, fiber-optic viewing instrument is required to locate the internal (primary) opening of the fistula channel. Injection of a contrast medium such as barium into the rectum and taking x-rays may also help identify the primary opening. X-rays of the upper gastrointestinal tract following ingestion of a radiopaque contrast medium (upper gastrointestinal series), CT, and high-frequency sound waves (ultrasonography) may be required in certain complex situations.

Treatment

Anorectal fistulas rarely heal spontaneously and are usually removed with minor surgery (fistulectomy or fistulotomy) under local anesthesia. Occasionally, a general anesthetic is required. During fistulectomy, the channel is opened, the fistulous lining removed, and the abscess drained. During fistulotomy, the whole channel is completely cut open and allowed to heal. In either case, broad-spectrum antibiotics may be prescribed before and after surgery. After surgery, management consists of warm sitz baths, frequent wound inspection, and attention to stool consistency. Stool softeners may aid in preventing constipation.

Prognosis

Following surgery, healing of an anorectal fistula proceeds without complications in the vast majority of cases. In individuals with more complicated fistulae, extensive surgical treatment may interfere with the ability to control defecation (continence) and lead to additional rectal surgery. Individuals with Crohn's disease, ulcerative colitis, diabetes, AIDS, chronic diarrhea, or other underlying conditions may experience recurring fistulas or wounds that heal improperly.

Differential Diagnosis

Conditions that present with similar symptoms as anorectal fistula include inflammation of the rectum and anus caused by infection, trauma, drugs, allergy, or radiation injury (proctitis). A condition that causes itching and an uncomfortable sensation around the anus (pruritus ani) or the symptoms of certain sexually transmitted diseases may also resemble anorectal fistula.

Specialists

- Gastroenterologist
- Proctologist
- Surgeon

Work Restrictions / Accommodations

Individuals recovering from surgery for anorectal fistula may need to avoid prolonged sitting and heavy physical labor until healing is complete.

Comorbid Conditions

Existing conditions that may impact the ability to recover and further lengthen disability include diabetes, AIDS, and chronic diarrhea.

Complications

Skin bridges may enclose an area within the channel and allow an infected area (abscess) to develop. Untreated fistulas may cause systemic infection. Rare examples of cancer (carcinoma) arising in anorectal fistulas have been reported.

Minor degrees of soiling or incontinence may occur after surgical treatment of a fistula.

Factors Influencing Duration

The duration of disability may depend on the type of anesthesia and extent of surgical intervention utilized for treatment.

Length of Disability

Duration may be longer for individuals with jobs that require long periods of sitting.

Surgical treatment.

Duration in Days

Job Classification	Minimum	Optimum	Maximum
Sedentary work	7	14	28
Light work	7	14	28
Medium work	14	21	42
Heavy work	14	21	42
Very Heavy work	14	21	42

Failure to Recover

If an individual fails to recover within the maximum duration expectancy period, the reader may wish to reference the following questions to assist in better understanding the specifics of an individual's medical case.

Regarding diagnosis:

- Does individual have inflammatory bowel disease or anal fissures?
- Was there any physical trauma to the anal region? Hemorrhoid treatment?
- Has individual had cancer or radiation treatment in the anal area?
- Is there a history of chlamydial infections?
- Was there an injury from an enema tip?
- Does individual complain of purulent drainage around the anus? Is there itching, tenderness, or pain? After a bowel movement?
- Did the physician find openings on the skin around the anus? Was pus expressed? Using a digital exam, was the channel palpable?
- Were anoscopy, sigmoidoscopy, or barium enema done? Were upper GI series, CT, and ultrasound performed?
- Were conditions with similar symptoms ruled out?

Regarding treatment:

- Did individual have surgery?
- Were broad-spectrum antibiotics prescribed before and after surgery?
- Is individual compliant with warm sitz baths and frequent wound inspection?

Regarding prognosis:

- Does individual have continence problems?
- Does individual have any conditions that may affect recovery?
- Has individual had recurrent fistulas?
- Can individual's employer accommodate restrictions?

References

LeMone, P., and K.M. Burke. Medical-Surgical Nursing. Upper Saddle River, NJ: Prentice Hall Health, 2000.

Schrock, T.R. "Examination of Anorectum and Diseases of Anorectum." Gastrointestinal Disease. Pathophysiology, Diagnosis, Management. Sleisenger, M.H., and J.S. Fordtran, eds. Philadelphia: W.B. Saunders Company, 1993. 1494-1516.

Antisocial Personality Disorder

Other names / synonyms: Amoral Personality Disorder, Dyssocial Personality Disorder, Psychopathic Personality Disorder, Psychopathy, Sociopathic Personality Disorder, Sociopathy

301.7

Definition

Antisocial personality disorder is characterized by a pervasive pattern of disregard for and violation of the rights of others. This pattern of behavior tends to be inflexible, maladaptive, and persistent, beginning in childhood or early adolescence and continuing into adulthood. Key features include ambition, persistence, goal-directed behavior, apparent need to control the environment, and unwillingness to trust the abilities of others. The antisocial personality performs antisocial or criminal acts, but the condition is not synonymous with criminality. As there is an inability to conform to social standards, it is also termed the dyssocial personality disorder.

As seen through the eyes of others, behavior appears as a spectrum from fearless in milder forms to reckless in the more severe forms of the disorder. Individuals with the disorder tend to be impulsive, forceful, aggressive, irresponsible, and seldom inhibited by danger or fear of punishment. Risk-taking behavior often provides a feeling of exhilaration. Individuals tend to have an inherent lack of consideration for the rights of others. In more severe cases, there is reckless disregard for the rights and welfare of self and others. There may be little remorse in using others to achieve their own desired goals. Individuals have difficulty developing and maintaining close interpersonal relationships that may stem from their fear that others will harm them in some way. They may also be argumentative, abusive, cruel, belligerent, or vindictive.

Individuals with antisocial personality disorder may repeatedly lie, manipulate others for personal power or gain, exhibit irresponsible sexual, parenting or work behaviors, default on debts, and fail to make amends for their behavior. They may blame their victims for being foolish, helpless, or deserving of mistreatment using rationalizations such as "losers deserve to lose," or "he had it coming anyway." These individuals usually display an inflated and arrogant self-appraisal, lack of empathy, and superficial charm.

The prevalence of this disorder is 3% in men and 1% in women. Onset is before the age of 15 with a higher prevalence in the lower socioeconomic class in urban areas. Prevalence in the prison population may be as high as 75%. It is five times more common among first-degree relatives of males with the disorder than among controls.

Diagnosis

History: A diagnosis is based on criteria listed in the DSM-IV-TR (Diagnostic and Statistical Manual of Mental Disorders, 4th Edition, Text Revision, published by the American Psychiatric Association). The individual must be at least 18 with a history of some symptoms of conduct disorder prior to age 15. Because deceit and manipulation are features of this disorder, it is helpful to obtain and integrate information from both the individual and collateral sources such as family, school, and community contacts, if possible. Specific behaviors characteristic of conduct disorder are aggression to people and animals, destruction of property, deceitfulness or theft, and serious violation of rules. If there is no history of conduct disorder, then the individual may be assessed for another mental disorder.

A diagnosis of antisocial personality disorder can be made if three or more of the following criteria are met: failure to conform to social norms of lawful behavior by repeatedly performing acts that could lead to arrest; repeated lying, use of aliases, or conning others for personal profit or pleasure; impulsivity or failure to plan ahead; irritability and aggressiveness with repeated physical fights or assaults; reckless disregard for the safety of self or others; repeated failure to sustain consistent work behavior or honor financial obligations; and lack of remorse for behavior. The diagnosis cannot be made if the behavior occurs exclusively during the course of a schizophrenia or manic episode.

Physical exam: The exam is not helpful in diagnosing this disorder.

Tests: An EEG (electroencephalogram) and a thorough neurological exam should be performed. Individuals with this disorder may show abnormal EEG results and neurological signs suggestive of minimal brain damage in childhood.

Treatment

Group and individual psychotherapy is most commonly utilized for antisocial personality disorder. Outpatient treatment is especially difficult and unlikely to provide long-lasting benefit. Once these individuals are among peers and in a therapeutic setting, they may become cooperative with treatment as motivation to change increases. Self-help groups have also been used in addition to family education and counseling.

Medications do not cure the disorder, but may be used to control the incapacitating symptoms of anxiety, depression, and physical violence. As there is a high incidence of substance abuse in this disorder, caution must be used in selecting and prescribing drug therapy. Some individuals with antisocial personality disorder may also have attention-deficit/hyperactivity disorder (ADHD) and may require a central nervous system stimulant to control the associated symptoms.

When hospitalization is required, definitive treatment is best carried out in a specialized unit. Inability to trust, fantasize, feel or learn should be specifically addressed. Firm limits are needed in addition to defining acceptable alternatives for deviant behaviors.

Prognosis

Antisocial personality disorder is considered a life-long disorder with a chronic course once it begins in late adolescence. Some studies report a decrease in symptoms especially criminal behavior by the fourth decade of life. Symptoms of anxiety and depression frequently improve with medications.

Differential Diagnosis

Antisocial behavior in adults can be exhibited in those with substance-related disorders or during the course of schizophrenia or a manic episode. Narcissistic personality disorder shares some qualities with antisocial personality disorder such as being tough-minded, superficial, exploitative, and not empathetic, however individuals with antisocial personality disorder show additional behaviors such as impulsiveness, aggressiveness, and deceitfulness. Other possible conditions include histrionic, borderline, or paranoid personality disorder.

Specialists

- Psychiatrist
- Psychologist

Work Restrictions / Accommodations

Work accommodations may include providing written job instructions; clear communications, expectations, and boundaries; providing conflict-resolution mechanisms; providing guidelines for feedback on problem areas and proactive management of problem areas.

The disrespect the this individual likely holds for authority figures and disregard for others' rights can create problems in management positions. The propensity for illegal acts prevents job duties requiring financial dealings or security.

Comorbid Conditions

Alcohol abuse, drug use, or the presence of depression or another psychiatric illness may lengthen disability. Individuals with antisocial personality disorder may also experience dysphoria, anxiety disorders, and other disorders of impulse control such as pathological gambling.

Complications

Real or perceived control by authority figures or institutions may lead to resistance and aggressive behavior. Alcohol or other substance abuse is commonly associated with this disorder and can produce significant complications. Violent deaths such as suicide, accidents, and homicides are more likely in individuals with antisocial personality disorder than in the general population. Depression may complicate this disorder especially once therapy begins. Illegal activities may lead to arrest, incarceration, or other legal ramifications. Irresponsibility and disregard for the welfare and rights of others often lead to problems at the workplace and in personal relationships.

Factors Influencing Duration

Factors influencing outcome include substance abuse and its associated complications, reluctance to undergo treatment, the individual's support system, and his or her financial and legal status.

Length of Disability

This condition represents a life-long pattern of behavior. In most cases, no disability is expected.

Failure to Recover

If an individual fails to recover within the maximum duration expectancy period, the reader may wish to reference the following questions to assist in better understanding the specifics of an individual's medical case.

Regarding diagnosis:

- Does individual fit criteria for antisocial personality disorder?
- Was the diagnosis confirmed?
- Was formal psychological testing performed?

Regarding treatment:

- Although psychotherapy is usually the treatment of choice for antisocial personality disorder, are medications being used to help stabilize mood swings or treat specific coexisting psychiatric disorders?
- If treatment difficulties are present, are they related to the health professional's misunderstanding of antisocial personality disorder?
- Because individual doesn't show a lack of remorse, is he/she assumed not to have any "real" feelings?
- Has individual been able to establish an effective trust-relationship with therapist? If not, what can be done to foster this connection?
- Is therapy following the approach that staying on "safe ground" is not likely to be as effective as discovering and labeling appropriate emotional states?
- Is individual learning to face up to the consequences of his/her behavior?
- Since the therapist should avoid using negative motivation, what does individual see as his/her motive for seeking therapy?
- Is individual involved in a group therapy situation devoted exclusively to antisocial personality disorder? Is it proving to be beneficial or counterproductive to therapy goals?
- Are individual and family involved in family therapy? Is the family participating in family therapy even if individual refuses to go?

Regarding prognosis:

- Does individual continue with behavior that may be a threat to self or others?
- Would individual benefit from extended treatment?
- Would a change in therapy or therapist be more beneficial?

References

Frances, Allen. Diagnostic and Statistical Manual of Mental Disorders: 4th ed, text revision. Washington, DC: American Psychiatric Association, 2000.

Grohol, John. Antisocial Personality Disorder. Psych Central. 01 Nov 1999 07 Aug 2000 <http://www.grohol.com/disorders/sx7.htm>.

Hall, Laura Lee. "Making the ADA Work for People with Psychiatric Disabilities." Mental Disorder, Work Disability, and the Law. Bonnie, Richard J., and John Monahan, eds. Chicago: The University of Chicago Press, 1997. 241-280.

Long, Philip. Antisocial Personality Disorder. Internet Mental Health. 01 Jan 2000 08 Dec 2000 <http://www.mentalhealth.com/dis1/p21-pe04.html>.

Anxiety Disorder, Generalized
Other names / synonyms: Generalized Anxiety Disorder, Overanxious Disorder of Childhood
300.02

Definition

Generalized anxiety disorder is characterized by chronic, excessive worry and fear about many aspects of life including competence at work or school, finances, or house repairs. Worry may extend to family members' health or life difficulties. The individual often notices anxiety immediately upon awakening. The anxiety is so severe that it impairs the person's ability to function in social relationships or at work.

This disorder is seen approximately twice as often in females than males. Onset in half of cases is in childhood or adolescence (overanxious disorder of childhood). It also commonly arises after age 20.

Diagnosis

History: Individuals report a high level of apprehension and fear that has been present for at least 6 months. Individuals cannot control their worrying. In addition to anxiety, at least three of the following are reported: restlessness, becoming easily fatigued, difficulty with concentration, irritability, muscle tension, and disturbed sleep. At least some of these symptoms have occurred numerous times in the past 6 months. Many individuals say they have felt nervous all their lives.

The diagnosis of generalized anxiety disorder is made only after other more specific diagnoses are eliminated such as panic disorder, major depression, excessive caffeine intake, or a medical condition. The disorder is not caused by substance abuse. If drug or alcohol abuse is present, it is usually an attempt by the individual to self-treat the anxiety. Generalized anxiety disorder is not diagnosed if symptoms occur only during another mood disorder or a psychotic episode.

Physical exam: Physical symptoms may include trembling, cold and sweaty hands, pale or flushed skin, or an elevated heart rate, rapid breathing, and/or high blood pressure.

Tests: Tests are not necessary to establish this diagnosis, although personality tests such as the Minnesota Multiphasic Personality Inventory may be helpful in determining whether or not there is an associated personality disorder. Self-rated scales such as the Beck Anxiety Scale may be useful in monitoring response to therapy.

Treatment

Treatment can include psychotherapy, relaxation training, biofeedback, and drug therapy. While the benzodiazepines can be used to treat anxiety, buspirone can relieve generalized anxiety without being habit-forming or addictive. Selective serotonin-reuptake inhibitors (SSRIs) are more helpful than the tricyclic antidepressants in treating generalized anxiety disorder.

Prognosis

Generalized anxiety is a chronic illness with the focus of anxiety changing from one concern to another. Although it frequently worsens when an acute life stress arises, the condition itself tends to become less intense as the individual ages.

Differential Diagnosis

Other anxiety disorders share similarities with this condition but have a more specific focus on the anxiety. These are panic disorder, social phobia, obsessive-compulsive disorder, anorexia nervosa, hypochondriasis or somatization disorder, post-traumatic stress disorder, anxiety caused by a prescription medicine, major depression, substance abuse, or medical condition (hyperthyroidism, pheochromocytoma), or anxiety occurring only during a mood or psychotic disorder.

Specialists

- Psychiatrist
- Psychologist

Work Restrictions / Accommodations

Work restrictions or accommodations are necessary only infrequently, for the most serious cases. In these instances, time-limited restrictions and work accommodations should be individually determined based on the characteristics of the individual's response to the disorder, the functional requirements of the job and work environment, and the flexibility of the job and work site. The purpose of the restrictions/accommodation is to help maintain the worker's capacity to remain at the workplace without a work disruption or to promote timely and safe transition back to full work productivity.

Complementary and Alternative Therapies

Content is intended for awareness only. Treatments may or may not be effective. Scientific evidence may be lacking and some substances have potentially toxic effects. Dr. Presley Reed and the editors do not endorse the use of these therapies in the absence of consultation with a licensed medical professional.

Relaxation techniques -	May help to reduce stress.
Biofeedback -	May help control muscle tension.
Diaphragmatic breathing -	May reduce anxiety and help the individual avoid hyperventilating.

Comorbid Conditions

Coexisting conditions that may impact recovery and lengthen disability include depression, substance abuse (especially alcohol dependency), panic disorder, social phobia, other anxiety disorders, and depression. Other conditions often associated with anxiety disorders include irritable bowel syndrome, insomnia, and headaches.

Complications

Depression can result from emotional exhaustion. Stress-related illnesses such as headaches or irritable bowel syndrome can occur. Individual may abuse or become dependent on antianxiety drugs, sleep medicines, or alcohol. Extreme anxiety may lead to a suicide attempt.

Factors Influencing Duration

The severity of the symptoms, response to treatment, coexistence of substance abuse (especially alcohol dependence), other psychological disorders, ego strength of the individual, and the individual's social support system can affect the length of disability.

Length of Disability

The condition may be chronic and if symptoms are severe, may be permanently disabling. If an individual responds to treatment and obtains symptom relief from medication, he/she will be able to return to work.

Duration in Days

Job Classification	Minimum	Optimum	Maximum
Any work	1	7	28

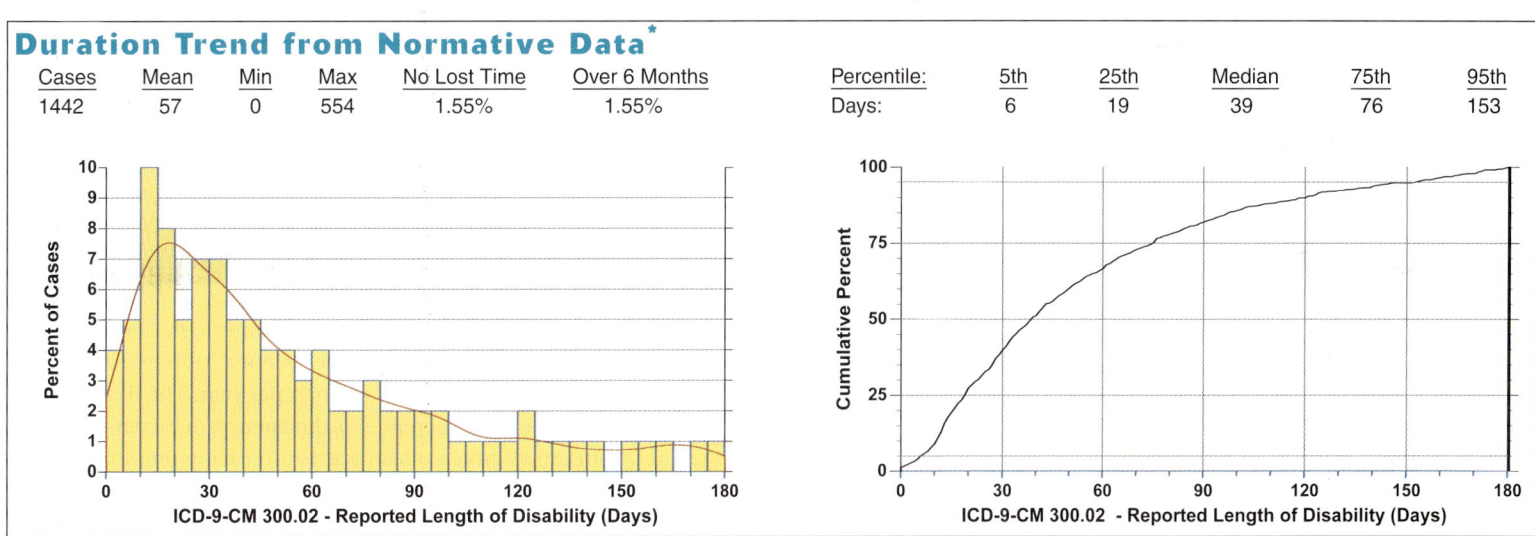

Duration Trend from Normative Data*

Cases	Mean	Min	Max	No Lost Time	Over 6 Months
1442	57	0	554	1.55%	1.55%

Percentile:	5th	25th	Median	75th	95th
Days:	6	19	39	76	153

ICD-9-CM 300.02 - Reported Length of Disability (Days)

* Differences may exist between the expected duration tables and the normative graphs. Duration tables provide expected recovery periods based on the type of work performed by the individual. The normative graphs reflect the actual observed experience of many individuals across the spectrum of physical conditions, in a variety of industries, and with varying levels of case management.

Anxiety Disorder, Generalized

Failure to Recover

If an individual fails to recover within the maximum duration expectancy period, the reader may wish to reference the following questions to assist in better understanding the specifics of an individual's medical case.

Regarding diagnosis:

- Was diagnosis confirmed?
- Does individual fit the criteria of at least 6 months of chronic exaggerated worry and tension that is unfounded or much more severe than the normal anxiety most individuals experience?
- Because generalized anxiety disorder symptoms must not be part of another mental disorder, have other psychological disorders been excluded?
- Were direct physiological effects of a substance, medication, or a general medical condition ruled out as the cause of the generalized anxiety symptoms?
- Were symptoms severe enough to cause significant distress or impairment in social, occupational, educational, or other important areas of functioning?
- Was such functional impairment evident or self-reported by individual?

Regarding treatment:

- Has drug therapy been effective in relieving anxiety symptoms?
- What other medication options may now be appropriate?
- Is individual taking medication properly?
- As treatment nears its end and physician gradually tapers the dosage, is individual able to understand directions and comply with a graduated dose schedule? If not, is there another available individual who can supervise the medication regimen?
- Is individual currently involved in a cognitive-behavioral type therapy that teaches individual to react differently to situations and physical sensations that trigger panic attacks or other anxiety symptoms? If not, would addition of this type of therapy be appropriate in the overall treatment plan?
- Would individual benefit from involvement in a therapy group that discusses progress, exchanges encouragement, and receives guidance from a therapist?
- What other forms of personal support are available for individual?

Regarding prognosis:

- Is an acute life stress interfering with individual's recovery?
- What type of coping skills does individual have or need to learn?
- Would individual benefit from additional counseling?

References

Etiology of Anxiety Disorders. Mental Health: A Report of the Surgeon General 2000 30 Sept 2000 <http://www.surgeongeneral.gov/library/mentalhealth/chapter4/sec2_1.html>.

What is Generalized Anxiety Disorder?. Anxiety Disorders Association of America. 2000 17 July 2000 <http://www.adaa.org/aboutanxietydisorders/gad/index.cfm>.

Aortic Aneurysm

Other names / synonyms: Descending Aneurysm, Fusiform Aneurysm, Saccular Aneurysm
441, 441.3, 441.4, 441.5, 441.9

Definition

An aortic aneurysm refers to an abnormal, localized blood vessel wall weakness and bulging or ballooning (dilation) in a segment of the aorta. The aorta is the largest artery in the body, beginning above the left chamber (ventricle) of the heart (ascending aorta), curving down (aortic arch), descending to the chest (descending thoracic aorta) and into the abdomen (abdominal aorta). Depending on the location of the aneurysm, it may be termed a thoracic aortic aneurysm or an abdominal aortic aneurysm.

Abdominal aortic aneurysms are more common than thoracic aortic aneurysms and account for approximately 75% of all aortic aneurysms. Abdominal aneurysms usually occur in the segment of the aorta between the kidneys and the arteries that go to the pelvis and legs (iliac arteries). Thoracic aneurysms occur in the ascending, transverse, or descending segments of the aorta.

Most aneurysms are approximately pea-sized, although they can be as small as a pinhead or as large as an orange. Aneurysms tend to grow at a rate of one-eighth to one-quarter of an inch per year. The likelihood of rupture, which may be fatal, increases as the aneurysm increases in size. As the aneurysm grows larger, it also exerts increasing pressure against neighboring organs and tissues that may result in potentially lethal complications.

The two primary causes of aneurysms are the build-up of fat cells and debris in the artery wall (atherosclerotic plaque) and high blood pressure (hypertension). Other causes include infection, trauma, inflammation of the arteries (arteritis), inherited conditions such as Marfan's syndrome, or untreated syphilis. There may also be an association between the abdominal aneurysm and connective tissue diseases such as systemic lupus erythematosus.

Risk factors for aortic aneurysms include increasing age, cigarette smoking, and a family tendency to aneurysms. Risk factors for abdominal aortic aneurysms included age 65 and older, smoking history longer than 40 years, systolic blood pressure greater than 160 mmHg, diastolic blood pressure greater than 100 mmHg, and high serum total cholesterol. High levels of high-density lipoprotein cholesterol and high-energy intake are associated with lower risk of abdominal aortic aneurysm.

Aortic aneurysms are 4 to 5 more times likely to occur in men than women. Men over age 55 and women over 70 have an increased incidence of aortic aneurysm; 3% of individuals over age 50 will experience an aortic aneurysm. About 9% of men who are in their 80s have an abdominal aortic aneurysm.

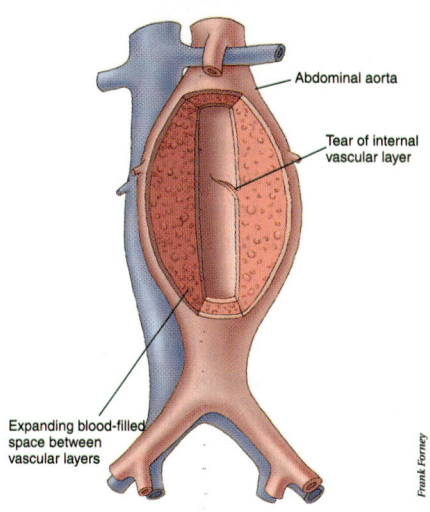

Diagnosis

History: Symptoms vary depending on the location and size of the aneurysm, whether aneurysm rupture has occurred, and whether there are associated effects due to increased pressure or blood leakage into surrounding organs and tissue. An individual with a thoracic aortic aneurysm may complain of sudden severe chest pain, shortness of breath, fainting, pallor, sweating, a bluish tinge around the mouth and on the nail beds (cyanosis), increased pulse rate, leg weakness, or transient paralysis. Individuals may also experience difficulty breathing, a brassy cough, or wheezing. Compression of the esophagus may cause hoarseness or loss of voice.

With an abdominal aortic aneurysm, individuals may be without symptoms (asymptomatic) and unaware of the condition. Some individuals may complain of an abnormal, pulsating feeling in the abdomen. Constant pain in the lower back region as a result of pressure on the lumbar nerves may be present.

Individuals experiencing severe, persistent chest, back, or abdominal pain may have an aneurysm that has already ruptured. Additional symptoms indicating that rupture has occurred include low blood pressure, weakness, sweating, and a fast heart rate (tachycardia).

Physical exam: With a thoracic aortic aneurysm, the physician may note an increased pulse rate or a bluish tinge around the mouth and fingernails (cyanosis). Listening to the heart with a stethoscope (auscultation) may reveal an abnormal sound between beats when the heart is at rest (diastolic murmur). An abrupt loss of the pulse at the wrist (radial) and the pulse inside the upper thigh (femoral), or wide variations in pulses or blood pressure between the arms and legs may be noted. The individual may appear to be in shock, usually associated with low blood pressure, but the upper number of the blood pressure (systolic) is normal or even elevated.

With an abdominal aortic aneurysm in non-obese individuals, a pulsating mass may be felt when applying light pressure with the fingertips (palpation). Swelling around the navel (umbilicus) may be evident. A soft, blowing sound (bruit) may be heard with a stethoscope placed over the aneurysm (auscultation). This condition rarely causes a diminished peripheral pulse.

Tests: Blood tests may show decreased hemoglobin levels that indicate blood loss from a leaking or ruptured aneurysm.

Thoracic aortic aneurysms may be diagnosed accidentally when a chest x-ray is ordered for an unrelated reason.

Abdominal ultrasound can determine the size and extent of an aneurysm. It is a noninvasive, cost-effective test that is nearly 100% accurate. Other tests may include CT or MRI. If there is concern that the aneurysm is located above the renal arteries, which occurs in approximately 10% of cases, aortography may be done. In this procedure, contrast medium is inserted into a vessel through the arm or leg and the flow of the medium monitored on x-ray. This reveals the precise size and location of the aneurysm. Electrocardiography (ECG) and echocardiography may help identify a dissecting aneurysm of the aortic root.

In a study of 198 individuals with abdominal aortic aneurysms, 48% were discovered by history and physical examination, 37% during an imaging or x-ray procedure, and 15% at surgery (laparotomy). Of those detected during an imaging or x-ray procedure, subsequent examination showed that 38% could be felt (palpated) in the abdomen although missed on initial examination. Thorough clinical examination is therefore extremely important in diagnosing this condition.

Treatment

Rupture or potential rupture of an abdominal aortic aneurysm or the presence of a dissecting thoracic aortic aneurysm constitutes a medical emergency. Emergency surgery must be performed. Additional stabilizing measures may also be necessary and can include the administration of antihypertensive medications, medications to decrease the force of vessel contractions, oxygen for respiratory distress, narcotic analgesics for pain relief, intravenous administration of fluids, and whole blood transfusions.

Although surgery is the only cure for an aortic aneurysm, the timing of surgical repair is based on the risk of surgery compared to the risk of rupture. The risk of rupture is determined by aneurysm location and size, rate of recent growth of the aneurysm, and onset of symptoms such as chest pain associated with the aneurysm. If surgery is to be delayed, the individual is treated medically with diet, exercise, and medication to reduce blood pressure, hoping to stabilize the damaged section of blood vessel and prevent further weakening of the vessel wall. High-risk cardiac individuals are considered poor surgical risks. Coronary artery problems must be addressed before surgery.

Surgery is recommended for aortic aneurysms 5 cm or larger in individuals without other medical complications. Nonemergency (elective) repair is often considered for aneurysms between 4 and 6 cm. The surgical repair of the aneurysm consists of removing the aneurysm (resection) and restoring blood flow using a synthetic or composite graft replacement. The damaged section of aorta may be replaced with a flexible Dacron tube graft.

Prognosis

Reducing the risk of rupture by surgical intervention generally allows the individual a good outcome (prognosis). Nonemergency (elective) surgery carries the risk of death in 4-6%, but the rate can be as low as 2% for those in good general health. If a rupture is imminent or has occurred, as many as half of individuals may die during surgery.

Differential Diagnosis

Differential diagnoses for a thoracic aortic aneurysm include unstable angina, pain related to acute chest trauma, blood in the chest cavity (hemothorax), air in the chest cavity causing a lung to collapse (pneumothorax), arterial embolism, heart attack (myocardial infarction), and ischemic heart disease. Those associated with an abdominal aortic aneurysm include unstable angina, acute myocardial infarction, pain related to acute chest or abdominal trauma, decreased blood flow to the intestines (intestinal ischemia), appendicitis, peptic ulcer, or intestinal obstruction.

Specialists

- Cardiologist
- Pulmonologist
- Vascular Surgeon

Rehabilitation

While individuals are awaiting nonemergency surgery and after the surgery, cardiac rehabilitation programs may be helpful in educating individuals in light exercise that strengthens the heart and lowers blood pressure while avoiding sudden physical strains that can momentarily increase blood pressure.

Outpatient physical and occupational therapy at a clinic specializing in cardiac rehabilitation may be warranted for individuals with aortic aneurysm. Cardiac rehabilitation centers offer ECG monitoring of all participants during the exercise sessions. Individuals learn to self-monitor their pulse and rate the amount of energy they expend by utilizing a rating of perceived exertion scale. This is a numbered scale that rates exercises from very, very light to very, very hard. Individuals use this scale and their pulse to stay within safe exercise parameters predetermined by their physicians. Individuals attend physical therapy to learn basic conditioning and stretching exercises.

Aerobic exercise is also performed such as treadmill walking or stationary bicycling. Initial activities may include limited walking, range of motion, and treadmill exercises. Eventually, more frequent walks, walk-jog, biking, and arm ergometer exercises are encouraged. Exercise may become more strenuous as permitted by the individual's physician with a goal of attaining 75-85% maximum intensity while walking, jogging, biking, swimming, performing calisthenics, and/or weight training. Eventually, individuals exercise independently of rehabilitation.

Occupational therapy addresses any fatigue or shortness of breath that may occur during activities of daily living. Individuals learn to utilize equipment such as a shower chair to decrease the energy expended during bathing, or a long-handled sponge to decrease the amount arm activity necessary. (Excessive arm activity is more taxing on the heart and can lead to fatigue). Occupational therapists teach energy conservation techniques where activities of daily living such as meal preparation are broken into smaller components that make tasks more manageable.

Work Restrictions / Accommodations

Strenuous physical activities need to be eliminated, possibly requiring transfer of the individual to a sedentary position. In some cases, disability may be permanent.

Comorbid Conditions

Atherosclerosis, hypertension, obesity, arterial inflammation (arteritis), or connective tissue disease such as Marfan's syndrome are underlying conditions that may influence length of disability.

Complications

Complications include rupture of the aneurysm that can result in significant deficits or even death from blood loss. Complications of surgical repair include death, stroke, heart attack (myocardial infarction), paralysis (paraplegia) related to decreased blood flow (ischemia) to the spinal cord, and kidney (renal) failure related to decreased blood flow through the renal arteries supplying the kidneys.

Factors Influencing Duration

Factors that may influence the length of disability associated with an aortic aneurysm include age of the individual, extent of surgical repair necessary, whether the aneurysm ruptures, and presence of postoperative complications such as heart attack (myocardial infarction) or kidney (renal) failure.

Length of Disability

Disability may be permanent for individuals who perform strenuous physical work or have serious postoperative complications.

Surgical treatment. Aneurysmectomy.

Duration in Days

Job Classification	Minimum	Optimum	Maximum
Sedentary work	56	70	112
Light work	56	84	Indefinite
Medium work	56	105	Indefinite
Heavy work	84	140	Indefinitie
Very Heavy work	84	140	Indefinite

Failure to Recover

If an individual fails to recover within the maximum duration expectancy period, the reader may wish to reference the following questions to assist in better understanding the specifics of an individual's medical case.

Regarding diagnosis:

- Does individual complain of sudden, severe chest pain, shortness of breath, fainting, a bluish tinge around mouth and nail beds (cyanosis), increased pulse rate, leg weakness, or transient paralysis, suggesting thoracic aortic aneurysm (TAA)?
- Does individual complain of an abnormal pulsating feeling in the abdomen or constant pain in the lower back region, suggesting abdominal aortic aneurysm (AAA)?

- Does individual have severe persistent chest, back, or abdominal pain?
- Was aneurysm ruptured?
- Were clinical findings consistent with the diagnosis of a thoracic or abdominal aneurysm?
- What abnormalities did the physician note when individual was examined? Did individual experience shock?
- Did blood tests show decreased hemoglobin levels, indicating blood loss? Did a chest x-ray show evidence of a thoracic aortic aneurysm? Did abdominal ultrasound reveal an AAA? Was CT or MRI required?
- Did individual receive prompt evaluation by a general or vascular surgeon?

Regarding treatment:

- Has rupture or imminent rupture necessitated emergency surgery? Did surgery result in any complications such as bleeding? If so, were these addressed and treated?
- If rupture is not imminent, should elective surgery be done urgently or should it be delayed to allow stabilization of heart and blood vessel disease?
- Is medical management optimal or should second opinion be obtained from appropriate specialists (cardiologist, cardiac surgeon, pulmonologist)?

Regarding prognosis:

- Was the surgery uncomplicated?
- Considering the severity of symptoms and the health status of individual, what was the expected outcome?
- Did the aneurysm rupture prior to surgery? If so, did individual experience any complications associated with the rupture and surgical repair such as stroke, heart attack, paralysis, or renal failure?
- Were these complications addressed in the treatment plan?
- Has individual received medical consultation by the appropriate specialists (cardiologist, neurologist, nephrologist)?
- Have the complications contributed to any permanent disabilities?

References

Abdominal Aortic Aneurysm. Bandolier. 01 Jan 2000 10 Feb 2001 <http://www.jr2.ox.ac.uk/Bandolier/band27/b27-3.html>.

Feinstein, Alice, ed. Healing with Vitamins. Emmaus, PA: Rodale Press, Inc, 1996.

Aortic Dissection
Other names / synonyms: Dissecting Aneurysm, Dissecting Hematoma
441.0

Definition

An aortic dissection is a tear in the inner layer of the aorta (intima) that causes bleeding into and along the wall of the aorta. It can also cause abnormal widening or ballooning of the aorta (aneurysm).

The aorta is the main artery in the body, beginning above the left chamber (ventricle) of the heart (ascending aorta), curving down (aortic arch) and descending to the chest (descending thoracic aorta) and into the abdomen (abdominal aorta). The artery is composed of an inner layer (intima), middle layer (media), and outer layer (adventitia).

A dissection of the aorta can occur anywhere along the artery; however, the most frequent sites for dissection are the ascending aorta (proximal or Type A dissection) and the descending thoracic aorta (distal, or Type B dissection). A tear in the intima results in blood surging into the media that causes the media to be torn from the adventitia. A false path for blood flow is then formed within the aorta, diminishing the blood flow to any artery fed by the aorta and resulting in failure of the aortic valve to function. Death frequently follows rupture of the aorta due to hemorrhaging into the area around the heart (pericardial cavity) or around the left lung (pleural space).

Risk factors for aortic dissection include hereditary disorders such as Marfan's syndrome, Ehlers-Danlos syndrome, and pseudoxanthoma elastoma. Other risk factors are cardiac or vascular abnormalities at birth (congenital anomalies), aortic valve disease, high blood pressure (hypertension), smoking, pregnancy, atherosclerosis, arteriosclerosis, inflammation of arteries (arteritis), abdominal aortic aneurysm, and traumatic injury, particularly blunt trauma to the chest (e.g., when the chest hits the steering wheel during a motor vehicle collision). There is also a risk for aortic dissection during cardiovascular surgery.

Aortic dissection occurs most commonly in males between the ages of 40 and 70; 35% of individuals die within 24 hours after the dissection occurs. During 1998, the estimated number of new cases of aortic dissection was greater than 10,000. Occurrence rate is 2 in 10,000 individuals.

Diagnosis

History: The main symptom associated with an aortic dissection is the sudden onset of very severe sharp, stabbing, tearing pain often in the chest, between the shoulder blades or in the back. The pain may travel to the head, neck, shoulders, arms, jaw, abdomen, hips, and legs as the dissection travels along the aorta. Individuals may also report shortness of breath (dyspnea) and marked difficulty breathing, dizziness and/or fainting, or rapid pulse (heart) rate. The individual may report complete or partial inability to move one side of the body (hemiplegia), particularly the lower part of the body, accompanied by decreased sensation.

When rupture or hemorrhaging occurs, effects associated with increased pressure on the surrounding structures such as the lungs, trachea, larynx, esophagus, and spinal nerves may be evident. Hoarseness or loss of voice may be related to compression of the esophagus. Other symptoms can include confusion, disorientation, problems concentrating, anxiety, dry mouth, or nausea and vomiting.

Physical exam: The physician may note profuse sweating, pallor, clammy skin, and an increased pulse rate. Using a stethoscope, a "blowing" sound may be heard in the chest or abdomen and a murmur during rests between heartbeats (diastolic murmur). There may also be intermittent loss of the pulses at the wrist (radial), groin (femoral), inner elbow (brachial), and ankle (pedal). Decreased blood pressure (hypotension) is generally associated with Type A dissection while hypertension is often noted with Type B dissection.

Tests: An electrocardiogram (ECG) or echocardiogram can determine if an individual is experiencing or has experienced a heart attack. A chest x-ray is taken to note the size of the aorta, determine if fluid has collected in the space around the lungs (pleural effusion), or see if there has been mediastinal widening. A catheter inserted into the aorta from an artery in the arm or leg (aortography) shows where the dissection originated, extent of the dissection, and extent of damage done to arteries fed by the aorta.

A procedure for diagnosing aortic dissection that causes no discomfort to the individual uses sound waves to visualize the inside the chest (transthoracic ultrasonography) or the esophagus (transesophageal ultrasonography). These tests help identify the sections of the aorta that will need surgery. CT and MRI of the chest are also useful diagnostic tests. Blood tests are performed to determine if individual has decreased hemoglobin levels that may indicate blood loss from the aorta. An enzyme analysis is also done to determine if the individual is having a heart attack (creatine kinase).

Treatment

Emergency surgery is typically performed on individuals with an aortic dissection. Goals are to stabilize the individual prior to surgery and prevent complications. Stabilization includes intravenous (IV) administration of fluids and medications to lower an elevated blood pressure (antihypertensive) or to maintain blood pressure in a low-to-normal range. Medication is also administered to decrease the force of vessel contractions, keep the heart rate slow, and relieve pain (narcotic analgesics). Oxygen is administered for breathing problems and, if necessary, blood transfusions may also be required. Cardiac beta-blocking medications may help reduce some symptoms.

Surgical repair of a Type A (proximal) dissection is done as quickly as possible. The surgery involves repairing or removing the damaged part of the aorta (aortic resection) and restoring blood flow using a replacement synthetic graft. If there is aortic valve insufficiency, treatment also includes valve repair (commissurotomy) or replacement with a mechanical (prosthesis) or human valve. Valve repair or replacement surgery is similar in magnitude to open-heart surgery. Most individuals with a Type A dissection will also need their coronary arteries reimplanted.

A Type B (distal) dissection also requires surgery (aortic resection) with synthetic graft replacement if it poses life-threatening complications such as lack of blood flow to the kidneys (causing renal failure), the arms or legs (limb ischemia), or other organs of the body, particularly the abdomen (visceral ischemia). Type B also requires aortic resection surgery if the dissection causes blood to leak out of the aorta or if the individual has symptoms of a "ballooning" of the aorta (aneurysm) that could rupture.

Prognosis

The mortality rate for aortic dissection is very high with 35% of individuals dying within the first 24 hours after dissection begins. This rate increases to 50% after 48 hours, 70% within 1 week, and 80% within 2 weeks. Surgical mortality is approximately 15% for Type A dissections and slightly higher than 15% for Type B dissections.

Individuals who survive surgery and take medications as prescribed have a survival rate of 35% at 10 years and some individuals may live as long as 25 years.

Differential Diagnosis

Differential diagnoses include uncontrollable chest pain (unstable angina), heart attack (myocardial infarction), pain related to acute chest trauma, blood in the cavity surrounding the lungs (hemothorax), or air in the cavity surrounding the lungs that results in a collapsed lung (pneumothorax).

Specialists

- Cardiologist
- Pulmonologist
- Vascular Surgeon

Rehabilitation

A gradual increase in physical activity may be accomplished through a hospital-based cardiac rehabilitation program. Exercises are performed on a treadmill or stationary bicycle while the individual is monitored by a health care professional. The amount and type of exercise the individual can tolerate is determined by the doctor. The cardiac rehabilitation specialist then designs a program geared toward the individual's abilities. As the individual progresses, monitoring decreases until the exercise regimen can be completed at home. The individual is instructed to inform the doctor if any change in ability to exercise is noticed.

Work Restrictions / Accommodations

Individual tolerance for physical exercise after surgery will dictate the level of physical activity possible. Underlying conditions, effects of surgical repair, or use of postoperative medications may require individual to be reassigned to a position that is not physically demanding.

Comorbid Conditions

Comorbid conditions may include obesity, hypertension, smoking, coronary artery disease, aortic valve disorder, and postsurgical complications such as myocardial infarction or stroke.

Complications

Possible complications include stroke, partial or complete paralysis, bleeding into the pericardium that causes compression of the heart due to increased pressure in the chest cavity (cardiac tamponade), redissection, aneurysm because of weakened walls, and worsening of aortic valve insufficiency.

Factors Influencing Duration

Age of individual, extent of surgical repair necessary, coupled with individual's response to surgery, individual's response to prescribed medications, and type and severity of any symptoms that may not have significantly improved with surgery can influence length of disability.

Length of Disability

Disability may be permanent.

Surgical treatment.

Duration in Days

Job Classification	Minimum	Optimum	Maximum
Sedentary work	56	84	Indefinite
Light work	56	84	Indefinite
Medium work	56	Indefinite	Indefinite
Heavy work	84	Indefinite	Indefinite
Very Heavy work	84	Indefinite	Indefinite

Failure to Recover

If an individual fails to recover within the maximum duration expectancy period, the reader may wish to reference the following questions to assist in better understanding the specifics of an individual's medical case.

Regarding diagnosis:

- Does individual have a Type A or B Dissection?
- Did individual have sudden onset of very severe sharp, stabbing, tearing pain in the chest, between the shoulder blades or in the back?
- Was individual's mental state altered?
- Does individual have a dry mouth? Nausea and vomiting?
- Did individual notice hoarseness?
- Does individual feel anxious?
- Was ECG or echocardiogram performed? Chest x-ray? Blood tests?
- Were transthoracic or transesophageal ultrasound, CT, or MRI performed?
- Does individual have any conditions that may affect ability to recover?

Regarding treatment:

- Did individual have emergency surgery?
- Was aortic valve insufficiency found? Was it repaired?
- Is individual on permanent medication therapy?

Regarding prognosis:

- Is individual active in rehabilitation?
- Is individual's employer able to accommodate any necessary restrictions?
- Does individual have any conditions that could affect ability to recover?
- Did individual have any postoperative complications such as heart attack, stroke, pericardial bleeding, or re-dissection?

References

"Diseases of the Aorta and Its Branches." Merck Manual of Diagnosis and Therapy, 17th ed. Beers, Mark H., and Robert Berkow, MD, eds. Whitehouse Station, NJ: Merck & Co. Inc, 1999. 05 Dec 2000 <http://www.merck.com/mmanual/section16/chapter211/211b.htm>.

DeBakey, Michael, and Antonio Gotto. The New Living Heart. Holbrook: Adams Media Services, 1997.

Aortic Insufficiency

Other names / synonyms: Acute Aortic Insufficiency, Aortic Incompetence, Aortic Regurgitation, Chronic Aortic Insufficiency, Chronic/Acute Aortic Insufficiency

395.1, 396.3, 424.1, 746.4

Definition

Aortic insufficiency (AI) is a condition characterized by the reverse flow of blood from the main artery of the body (aorta) into the major pumping chamber of the heart (left ventricle). This results in enlargement of the left ventricle due to the increased volume of blood it must pump.

AI may occur acutely or chronically with the former being due to acute rheumatic fever in children and bacterial endocarditis, trauma, and tearing (dissection) of the aorta in adults. Its more common causes include high blood pressure (hypertension), rheumatic heart disease in adults, and syphilis.

Some form of cardiovascular disease (CVD) is present in more than 59 million Americans that result in 2,600 deaths a day or 1 death every 33 seconds.

Diagnosis

History: History of possible causes should be noted. It is also important to note the first occurrence of the murmur, keeping in mind that the murmur is sometimes overlooked because of its soft, high-pitched quality.

Individuals with mild AI often have no symptoms. Those with more severe AI may report shortness of breath with activity (dyspnea with exertion) or fatigue.

Physical exam: The blood pressure often has a wide range of measurement. The characteristic murmur is confined to the filling phase of the cardiac cycle (diastole). Other murmurs may be present due to associated mitral valve disease and/or aortic valve narrowing (stenosis).

Tests: A chest x-ray and echocardiogram with Doppler flow velocity measurements are usually done initially and periodically afterwards in individuals with chronic AI, the frequency depending on the severity of the AI. These tests assess the size of the heart and the severity of the AI. The chest x-ray and echocardiogram also infer the presence or absence of heart failure. Cardiac catheterization and aortic angiography are usually done before repair of the valves. Echocardiography is a simple and sensitive way to diagnose one of the acute causes of AI-aortic dissecting aneurysm. Nuclear studies and/or echocardiography are useful to monitor an individual with aortic insufficiency, looking for new ventricular dilatation.

Treatment

Mild cases require no treatment. More severe cases are often treated with medications to strengthen the contraction of the left ventricle (digitalis preparations), medications to remove excess fluid (diuretics), and medications to reduce the work of the heart (vasodilators or unloading agents).

Elective surgical repair or replacement of the valve is usually indicated in symptomatic individuals with chronic AI. Emergent repair or replacement is done for acute, severe AI due to aortic valve endocarditis or a dissecting aneurysm of the aorta. Whenever possible, repair of the valve is performed. However, unlike mitral valve insufficiency where repair is often possible, this procedure is limited for individuals with AI because of the high diastolic pressure in the aorta.

Prognosis

Longevity in individuals with mild degrees of AI is often not affected. Those with more severe degrees of AI however require properly timed surgery. The overall operative mortality is about 5-7%. In low-risk individuals, it is only 1-2%. Age, associated coronary atherosclerosis, and impaired overall function of the left ventricle are associated with increased risk. Long-term survival is approximately 80% after 5 years. Among survivors, heart size often decreases dramatically following surgery and is associated with significant symptomatic improvement.

Differential Diagnosis

Other cardiac conditions causing a heart murmur may be mistaken for AI. However, appropriate tests usually clarify the cause. Multiple murmurs due to disorders of other heart valves may be present and require careful clinical evaluation.

Specialists

- Cardiologist
- Cardiothoracic Surgeon

Work Restrictions / Accommodations

No work restrictions or accommodations are necessary for individuals without symptoms. For those experiencing dyspnea with exertion and/or fatigue, reassignment to a less strenuous position may be necessary. For those who have had timely surgery, work restrictions may be fewer than preoperatively. Individuals receiving mechanical prosthetic valves may need reassignment if their job involves significant risk of injury due to the need to take blood thinners.

Comorbid Conditions

Diabetes, chronic lung disease, connective tissue disorders, obesity, coronary artery disease, or hypertension may lengthen disability.

Complications

The primary complication of AI is heart failure. As with aortic stenosis and other valvular problems, acute or subacute bacterial endocarditis is a possible complication of dental work and other medical procedures that allow bacteria to enter the bloodstream. Usually it is easily preventable by administrating appropriate antibiotics orally or intravenously just before dental work or when certain endoscopic procedures are performed.

Factors Influencing Duration

Disability varies with severity of disease at initial diagnosis, contributing underlying heart disease, whether the individual undergoes surgery, complications after surgery, age of the individual, and response to treatment.

Length of Disability

Following heart valve replacement, disability may be permanent.

Medical treatment.

Duration in Days

Job Classification	Minimum	Optimum	Maximum
Sedentary work	7	14	21
Light work	7	14	21
Medium work	7	14	21
Heavy work	7	21	28
Very Heavy work	7	21	28

Surgical treatment. Heart valve replacement.

Duration in Days

Job Classification	Minimum	Optimum	Maximum
Sedentary work	28	42	56
Light work	28	42	56
Medium work	56	70	84
Heavy work	Indefinite	Indefinite	Indefinite
Very Heavy work	Indefinite	Indefinite	Indefinite

Failure to Recover

If an individual fails to recover within the maximum duration expectancy period, the reader may wish to reference the following questions to assist in better understanding the specifics of an individual's medical case.

Regarding diagnosis:

- Did individual have rheumatic fever as a child? Does individual have rheumatic heart disease?
- Has individual experienced recent trauma?
- Does individual have hypertension or syphilis?
- Does individual complain of shortness of breath, weakness, fatigue, swollen ankles, palpitations, sweating during the night, or chest pain (angina)?
- Is fever present?
- Is there a significant difference between the systolic and diastolic numbers of the blood pressure? Is diastolic murmur present? Other murmurs?
- Was a chest x-ray or ECG performed since the initial diagnosis or after surgery?
- Do the physical exam results and clinical picture coincide or is aortography needed to confirm a diagnosis?

Regarding treatment:

- Has individual been taking medications as prescribed, participating in cardiac rehabilitation (if required), limiting activity, working on lifestyle changes, and participating in any other treatments prescribed?
- Would individual benefit from surgical repair or replacement of the valve?

Regarding prognosis:

- Have symptoms of AI worsened? How much do they interfere with daily activities?
- Is there worsening of an underlying disease or infection?
- What type of surgery is recommended? Repair or replacement of the valve? Is individual in a high- or low-risk surgical group?
- Has individual developed heart failure?
- Has individual undergone recent dental or medical procedures? If so, did individual take prophylactic antibiotics prior to the procedure?
- Does individual have endocarditis?

References

About Cardiovascular Disease. Center for Disease Control. 28 July 2000 15 Nov 2000 <http://www.cdc.gov/nccdphp/cvd/aboutcardio.htm>.

The Merck Manual of Diagnosis and Therapy. Beers, Mark, and Robert Berkow, eds. Medical Services, USMEDSA, USHH, 1999. 15 Nov 2000 <http://www.merck.com/pubs/mmanual/section16/chapter207/207b.htm>.

Aortic Valve Stenosis

Other names / synonyms: Rheumatic Aortic Stenosis
395.0, 396.0, 424.1, 746.3

Definition

Aortic valve stenosis occurs when the aortic valve fails to open completely, preventing the normal flow of blood out of the left lower chamber of the heart (ventricle) and impeding the flow of oxygenated blood to the body. The aortic valve is the door-like structure between the main pumping chamber of the heart (left ventricle) and the major artery carrying blood to the body (aorta). The increased work imposed on the left ventricle by the stenotic valve causes the ventricle to enlarge (hypertrophy) and over time, it may fail and lead to congestive heart failure.

Aortic stenosis is a congenital (50%) or acquired (50%) disorder of the aortic valve. Acquired narrowing (stenosis) of the valve may be caused by rheumatic fever or degenerative "wear and tear" related to high blood pressure, high blood cholesterol (hypercholesterolemia), and diabetes mellitus.

Men are affected more often than women. Currently, aortic stenosis is the most common reason for valve replacement in individuals over age 50.

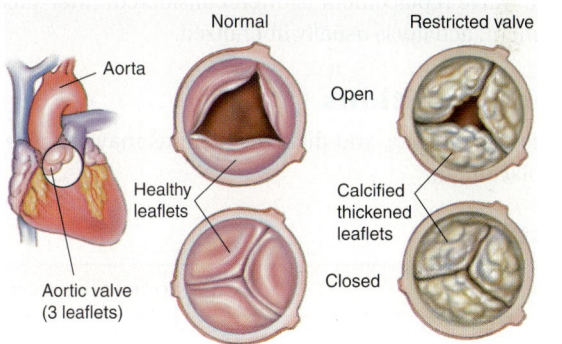

Diagnosis

History: The three principal symptoms of aortic stenosis are chest pain with exertion (angina pectoris), shortness of breath with exertion due to failure of the left ventricle (congestive heart failure), and sudden loss of consciousness (syncope). Symptoms usually do not develop until after age 50, but individuals may have had a heart murmur at an earlier age. Sometimes dizzy spells precede syncope. Similarly, mild shortness of breath with exertion often precedes congestive heart failure.

Physical exam: The blood pressure is usually normal and the heart rhythm regular. A heart murmur is audible with a stethoscope. A murmur due to associated leakage of the aortic valve (aortic insufficiency) and/or mitral valve disease may also be present.

Tests: An electrocardiogram (ECG) often shows enlargement of the left ventricle. A chest x-ray may show evidence of congestive heart failure. An ultrasound of the heart (echocardiogram) and Doppler flow study allow precise evaluation of the severity of the stenosis. The ECG, chest x-ray, and echocardiogram are repeated at varying intervals to follow the progress of the problem. A heart catheterization is done before valve surgery.

Treatment

No treatment is necessary for aortic stenosis in the absence of symptoms except prophylactic treatment to prevent bacterial endocarditis.

Treatment is initiated if and when any of the three symptoms occurs. In most instances, valve replacement is performed at that time.

Prognosis

Individual with mild aortic stenosis may have a normal life expectancy. However, symptoms often develop with moderate or severe aortic stenosis after age 50. Survival after symptom onset is (on average) 2 years in individuals with heart failure, 3 years with syncope, and 5 years with angina pectoris.

Differential Diagnosis

A heart murmur simulating aortic stenosis may be caused by mitral valve insufficiency.

Work Restrictions / Accommodations

No work restrictions or accommodations are necessary in the absence of symptoms. Individuals with aortic stenosis with symptoms often need to limit activity and transfer to modified duty may be necessary. At the same time, valve replacement is often considered. After successful valve replacement, activity is usually liberalized.

Comorbid Conditions

Pulmonary disease, obesity, and diabetes mellitus may affect recovery after valve replacement.

Specialists

- Cardiologist
- Cardiothoracic Surgeon

Complications

Angina, congestive heart failure, and syncope may complicate aortic stenosis and necessitate surgery.

Individuals with aortic stenosis are at increased risk of acquiring a bacterial infection called acute or subacute bacterial endocarditis on the valve. This potentially devastating complication is due to bacteria in the mouth or gastrointestinal (GI) tract entering the bloodstream during dental work or an endoscopic procedure. It is easily preventable by taking appropriate antibiotics before the procedure.

Factors Influencing Duration

Age, physical fitness, and motivation are factors that may influence disability in individuals undergoing surgery.

Length of Disability

Disability may be permanent.

Surgical Treatment. Heart valve replacement.

Duration in Days

Job Classification	Minimum	Optimum	Maximum
Sedentary work	28	42	56
Light work	28	42	56
Medium work	56	70	84
Heavy work	Indefinite	Indefinite	Indefinite
Very Heavy work	Indefinite	Indefinite	Indefinite

Failure to Recover

If an individual fails to recover within the maximum duration expectancy period, the reader may wish to reference the following questions to assist in better understanding the specifics of an individual's medical case.

Regarding diagnosis:

- Does individual exhibit early symptoms such as dizziness and mild shortness of breath?
- Were symptoms of a developing stenosis evident such as angina pectoris or syncope?
- Was echocardiogram performed? Was diagnosis confirmed?
- Is the aortic stenosis a congenital or acquired disorder?
- Did individual have rheumatic fever?
- Would individual benefit from consultation with a specialist (cardiologist, cardiac surgeon)?

Regarding treatment:

- Were prophylactic antibiotics given prior to dental work or endoscopic procedures to prevent a bacterial infection?
- Was surgical valve replacement indicated? If so, were appropriate medical interventions done to stabilize clinical symptoms prior to surgery?

Regarding prognosis:

- Were there any complications or comorbid conditions such as obesity, pulmonary disease, or diabetes mellitus? How severe was the stenosis?
- Did individual take antibiotic prophylaxis as recommended? Did bacterial endocarditis develop?
- Was surgical valve replacement done? Did individual experience any complications associated with the surgery, such as bleeding, rhythm disturbances or heart failure?
- What was the expected outcome?

References

About Cardiovascular Disease. Center for Disease Control. 28 July 2000 15 Nov 2000 <http://www.cdc.gov/nccdphp/cvd/aboutcardio.htm>.

Comprehensive Risk Reduction for Patients with Cardiovascular and Other Vascular Disease. American Heart Association. 1999 15 Nov 2000 <http://www.Americanheart.org/scientific/statements/1995/hguide2.html>.

Aphasia

Other names / synonyms: Alexia, Anomia, Dysarthria, Expressive Aphasia, Motor Aphasia, Receptive Aphasia, Sensory Aphasia

438.11, 784.3

Definition

Aphasia is a disorder of language involving inability to communicate through spoken or heard speech or written language. The two general types of aphasia are expressive (motor or Broca's aphasia) and receptive (sensory or Wernicke's) aphasia. Aphasia refers to complete impairment of language function whereas dysphasia refers to incomplete impairment with some function preserved.

Isolated expressive or receptive aphasia is called partial aphasia. Total (global) aphasia refers to a severe language impairment in which all modes of language (verbal, comprehension, reading, and writing) are impaired.

In expressive aphasia, the individual has difficulty producing spoken or written speech or may be totally unable to communicate verbally or in writing. Anomia is a less severe form of expressive aphasia where individuals have difficulty in naming objects. Alexia refers to the inability to read, whereas agraphia refers to the inability to write. In receptive aphasia, the ability to understand spoken or written language is either partially or totally lost.

Aphasia occurs when damages has occurred to one or more areas of the brain (speech centers) that control processes of speech or written language. These speech centers are in the dominant brain hemisphere, usually the left side in right-handed individuals and sometimes in left-handed individuals. Expressive aphasia involves part of the frontal lobe (Broca's area). Receptive aphasia involves a speech center further back in the brain (Wernicke's area in the temporal and parietal lobes). If nerve fibers connecting these areas are interrupted, more specific language deficits can occur (disconnection syndromes) such as alexia without agraphia, an unusual condition where the individual can write but cannot read what he or she has written.

Most aphasias are due to vascular disorders in the brain such as stroke involving the middle cerebral artery of the dominant hemisphere. Approximately 40% of stroke victims may have aphasia. Other common causes of aphasia include brain tumors, traumatic brain injury, and brain degenerative processes such as Alzheimer's disease and other dementias.

Diagnosis

History: The individual is typically unable to provide a good history, which must be obtained from the family or other sources. Individual may have experienced a recent accident, fall, loss of consciousness, or blow to the head. The problem may be with communicating or understanding speech or understanding written words. The individual may have trouble finding the right words, hesitate when speaking, or speak incomprehensible gibberish (word salad).

Physical exam: Attempting to communicate with the individual often reveals the language dysfunction. In expressive aphasia, speech is described as telegraphic, as there is very little verbal output and it is produced only with great difficulty and anguish. Connecting words, adjectives, and pronouns are often missing. However, ability to follow spoken or written commands is well-preserved.

Receptive aphasia is sometimes called fluent aphasia because there is increased speech output and the individual appears to be unaware that he or she is not making much sense. In receptive aphasia, nonspecific words like "something" or "somebody" replace specific words, and the individual has difficulty following written or spoken commands. A complete neurological evaluation is warranted to help determine associated impairments, which can help locate the source of dysfunction and help determine if it is secondary to a stroke, tumor, trauma, or degenerative disease. Associated problems may include difficulty carrying out complex tasks (apraxia), one-sided weakness (hemiparesis), numbness on one side (hemisensory deficit), and blindness on one side of individual's visual field. These deficits are usually on the right side if the individual is left hemisphere-dominant.

Tests: More formal tests for diagnosing aphasia such as the Boston Diagnostic Aphasia Examination may be done to gather more specific information about the area(s) of the brain that are most likely involved. X-rays studies such as a CT of the brain, MRI of the brain, and vascular studies (cerebral arteriogram, carotid artery Doppler) may help determine the cause and location of the aphasia. Electroencephalogram (EEG) may help determine if the language disturbance is related to seizure activity. Functional tests such as SPECT scan, brain mapping, PET scan, and regional cerebral blood flow testing help pinpoint the area(s) of brain dysfunction, but may not be necessary and more typically useful in research studies. Chemistry panel and liver function studies may be ordered to rule out a metabolic origin to the aphasia. Other blood work and electrocardiogram may be needed to rule out heart attack (myocardial infarction) accompanying stroke.

Treatment

Treatment varies according to the underlying cause of the aphasia. Supportive medical care is warranted for all disorders associated with aphasia. For example, if a brain tumor is present, surgical removal of the tumor (craniotomy with resection of tumor) may be needed. Treatment of stroke may include medication to break up the blood clot (thrombolysis) if the stroke is diagnosed early enough, blood thinners, and treatment of risk factors such as high blood pressure.

Speech therapy may be indicated. Therapy usually begins a few days after onset of aphasia when it is clear that the aphasia is long lasting. In cases of mild, partial aphasia, speech therapy may be initiated as soon as the individual's general condition is stable. However, those with complete (global) aphasia may do better when speech therapy is delayed until there is spontaneous return of some language function.

Prognosis

Outcome depends on the underlying disease and magnitude of the damage within the speech areas of the brain. As a rule, comprehension of language (receptive aphasia) improves more than the language function (expressive aphasia). Mild, partial aphasia may disappear spontaneously in hours or days or it may persist. Some improvement may continue for up to two years. Prognosis is poor for complete (global) aphasias lasting more than a week or two. Young individuals usually have better return of language function than the elderly.

Differential Diagnosis

Disturbances in hearing may prevent the individual from understanding spoken speech. Slurred speech (dysarthria) refers to problems with the mechanical production of speech rather than with the underlying language function. The individual with dementia or delirium may not be able to communicate and other deficits in higher thought processes (cognition) and level of consciousness may be present. Reversible episodes of speech arrest where the individual stops speaking may occur with seizures, TIAs, or migraine.

Specialists

- Neurologist

Rehabilitation

A speech rehabilitation program with a speech therapist or speech pathologist is usually recommended to help restore effective communication.

As weakness, sensory impairment, and visual impairment frequently accompany aphasia related to stroke or other cause, physical and occupational therapy may be needed to address these impairments. If severe expressive aphasia is accompanied by inability to use the muscles involved in speech, swallowing may also be impaired and may require its own evaluation and rehabilitation.

Work Restrictions / Accommodations

Restrictions and accommodations depend on job requirements. When responsibilities involve verbal or written communication, the individual may need to be reassigned. As effective or at least basic communication is needed for competitive employment of any type, disability may be permanent regardless of specific job duties.

Comorbid Conditions

Coexisting conditions that may affect recovery and disability include mental illness or impairment, other neurological conditions, and other organ system dysfunction or injury. Depending on the cause of aphasia, specific comorbid conditions such as high blood pressure and heart disease associated with stroke may occur.

Complications

Speech and language dysfunction may be permanent. Those with aphasia often experience anxiety, frustration, and temporary episodes of depression. Poor communication skills affect employment, social activities and relationships, and hinder medical care if the individual is unable to describe what is wrong or follow medical instructions.

Factors Influencing Duration

Size and location of any underlying brain lesions, degree of language impairment, foreign language, age, mental health, and education level may influence disability.

Length of Disability

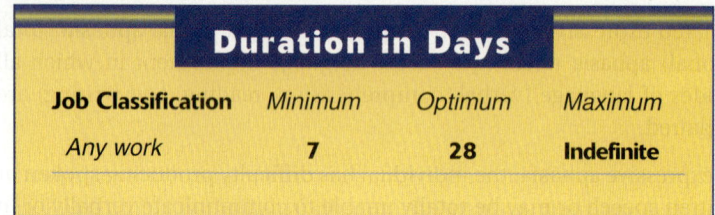

Job Classification	Minimum	Optimum	Maximum
Any work	7	28	Indefinite

Duration in Days

Failure to Recover

If an individual fails to recover within the maximum duration expectancy period, the reader may wish to reference the following questions to assist in better understanding the specifics of an individual's medical case.

Regarding diagnosis:

- Did individual experience a recent accident, fall, loss of consciousness, or blow to the head?
- Does individual have a problem communicating or understanding speech or understanding written words? Have trouble finding the right words, hesitate when speaking, or speak incomprehensible gibberish (word salad)?
- Were appropriate studies of the brain such as CT, MRI, or cerebral arteriograms ordered to determine the location and extension of brain lesion?
- Is the aphasia expressive or receptive? Is it partial or global?
- Was the underlying cause of aphasia identified?
- Is the aphasia transient or caused by permanent damage?

Regarding treatment:

- Was individual evaluated by a speech therapist or speech pathologist?
- Would individual benefit if therapy were postponed until clinical condition has stabilized?
- Does speech therapy appear to be effective?
- Is additional therapy warranted?

Regarding prognosis:

- Has individual regained any language function?
- Does individual display symptoms of depression such as withdrawn behavior, feelings of hopelessness or severe fatigue? Would individual benefit from mental health intervention?
- Is individual elderly?
- Is the underlying cause of the aphasia one from which individual may recover or stay the same such as stroke or head injury, or one that is likely to worsen such as malignant brain tumor?

References

Bates, E., et al. "Linguistic and Nonlinguistic Priming in Aphasia." Brain Language 76 1 (2001): 62-69.

Clochesy, John M., et al. Critical Care Nursing, 2nd ed. Philadelphia: W.B. Saunders Company, 1996.

Goldman, Lee, and J. Claude Bennett. Cecil Textbook of Medicine, 21st ed. Philadelphia: W.B. Saunders Company, 2000.

Grawemeyer, B., R. Cox, and C. Lum. "AUDIX: A Knowledge-based System for Speech-therapeutic Auditory Discrimination Exercises." Studies in Health and Technology Information 77 1 (2000): 568-572.

Heart and Stroke Guide. American Heart Association. 2000 22 Aug 2000 <http://:// www.americanheart.org/Heart_and_Stroke_A_Z_Guide/aphasia.html>.

Langdon, D., and E.K. Warrington. "The Role of the Left Hemisphere in Verbal and Spatial Reasoning Tasks." Cortex 36 5 (2000): 691-702.

Rosen, H.J., et al. "Neural Correlates of Recovery from Aphasia After Damage to Left Inferior Frontal Cortex." Neurology 55 12 (2000): 1883-1894.

Saffran, E.M. "Aphasia and the Relationship of Language and Brain." Seminars in Neurology 20 4 (2000): 409-418.

Sakai, K.L., R. Hashimoto, and F. Homae. "Sentence Processing in the Cerebral Cortex." Neuroscience Research 39 1 (2001): 1-10.

Tierney, Lawrence M., Stephen J. McPhee, and Maxine A. Papadakis, eds. Current Medical Diagnosis and Treatment, 39th ed. New York: Lange Medical Books/McGraw-Hill, 2000.

Aplastic Anemia
Other names / synonyms: Anemia Gravis, Ehrlich's Anemia, Hypoplastic Anemia, Refractory Anemia
284, 284.0, 284.8, 284.9

Definition

Aplastic anemia is the failure of the bone marrow to produce blood cells (red blood cells, white blood cells, and platelets) because the stem cells have been damaged. Stem cells are precursor cells from which all blood cell lines develop. As fewer new blood cells are produced, the old blood cells at the end of their lifespans are not replaced. This results in a decrease in the number of all blood cell types within the circulating blood (pancytopenia). Without red blood cells, anemia develops and oxygen cannot be distributed throughout the body. Without white blood cells, infections cannot be fought. Without platelets, blood does not clot normally.

Aplastic anemia may be acquired, inherited (congenital), or self-originating (idiopathic). The congenital form is called Fanconi anemia and is an autosomal recessive disease, therefore, in order for individuals to be affected, they must inherit one gene from each parent. Congenital aplastic anemia (Fanconi) develops before the ages of 30 to 40 in predisposed individuals. In addition to pancytopenia, individuals with Fanconi anemia often have other physical anomalies involving the skin, heart, genitourinary tract, skeletal system, central nervous system, growth, and mental capacity. It is estimated that 1 individual in 100 to 600 have the gene for this disease (are carriers) although they themselves are not affected.

Acquired aplastic anemia is more common. Damage to the stem cells may be caused by a variety of external agents such as ionizing radiation, the chemical benzene and its derivatives, chemotherapeutic cancer drugs, certain antibiotics, and other toxic chemicals like inorganic arsenic. Other agents only occasionally associated with aplastic anemia include a wide variety of drugs and chemicals such as some antibiotics, analgesics, and insecticides. Certain infections are also associated with aplastic anemia and include non-A, non-B, and non-C hepatitis; Epstein Barr virus; HIV; and parvovirus B_{19}. Acquired aplastic anemia may also result from an immune reaction where an individual's own immune system attacks the stem cells. Aplastic anemia can develop during pregnancy and may be associated with the accompanying rise in the female hormone estrogen. In more than half the cases of acquired or idiopathic aplastic anemia, the cause is never determined.

Each year in the US, approximately 3 to 9 individuals per million are diagnosed with aplastic anemia. In Europe and Israel, the incidence is 2 individuals per million and in some parts of Asia, the incidence is 4 individuals per million. Males and females develop the disease at equal rates with an average age at diagnosis of 25.

Diagnosis

History: Symptoms may begin weeks or months after exposure if due to a causative agent. Individual may report bleeding from the gums or other mucous membranes, bleeding under the skin, heavy menstrual flow, and easy bruising because of a low number of platelets. Individuals may feel weak and fatigued and have pallor due to anemia (low hemoglobin). Initially, individuals usually present with few, if any, systemic complaints. They may have ulcers of the mouth and tongue, fever, or a sore throat. There may be history of infection because of a low number of white blood cells (neutropenia). The individual may be pregnant, have a family history of Fanconi anemia, or a history of exposure to radiation, infection, chemicals, or drugs known to be associated with aplastic anemia.

Physical exam: Small capillary hemorrhages (bleeding) under the skin (petechiae) or larger areas of bruising under the skin (ecchymoses) may be seen. There may also be evidence of bleeding in the eye (retinal hemorrhage). If anemia is severe, a heart murmur may be detected. With Fanconi anemia, conditions such as skeletal anomalies, skin discoloration, mental retardation, or learning disabilities may be detected, but often not present.

Tests: A complete blood count (CBC) will show significant pancytopenia. A reticulocyte count shows a low number of immature red blood cells (reticulocytes). Diagnosis is generally confirmed by a bone marrow biopsy with an assessment of cellularity. The marrow is evaluated for the degree of maturation of all cell lines and has a low number of cells (hypocellular marrow). Abnormal cells are not found. Additional tests may be performed to identify the cause of the aplastic anemia. These tests may include serological tests to check for infection. If Fanconi anemia is suspected, a peripheral chromosome analysis (cytogenetic breakage study) is performed.

Treatment

Individuals with mild or moderate aplastic anemia generally do not require immediate treatment. They should, however, be monitored for any decline in their blood counts. When aplastic anemia is diagnosed, all drugs or medications should be stopped, if possible. Some drugs such as chemotherapeutic drugs and some forms of radiation may be medically necessary as a treatment for another serious condition such as cancer. In these cases, the benefit of the drug or radiation as opposed to its risks must be weighed before making the decision to continue or discontinue its use. If a toxic agent is determined as the cause of the aplastic anemia, it should be removed immediately.

In many cases, removal of the toxic agent allows the bone marrow to regenerate. During this time, only temporary supportive treatment may be necessary such as transfusions of red blood cells and platelets to keep blood counts adequate, and antibiotics to prevent infection. During this time, menstruation should also be suppressed.

In cases of severe aplastic anemia, a bone marrow transplant is the treatment of choice. The marrow must come from a matched donor, preferably a sibling. The risk of rejection increases with age, so bone marrow transplant is usually limited to individuals in good health under age 55. Blood transfusion should be avoided, if possible, in individuals who are candidates for a bone marrow transplant. The risk of graft rejection increases significantly with prior transfusion. When the bone marrow transplant is successful, no additional transfusions or transplants will be required.

If the individual is not a candidate for transplant or if a donor is not available, immunosuppressive therapy is the next best option. One or a combination of immunosuppressive drugs is taken. Male hormones (androgens) may successfully raise blood counts in some individuals where standard immunosuppression doesn't work. During immunosuppression or androgen therapy, transfusion of red blood cells and platelets are usually needed on an ongoing or temporary basis depending on the individual's response to therapy. After approximately 50 transfusions, an iron chelator drug should be given to remove excess iron introduced into the body by the transfused blood. Antibiotics should be given prophylactically to prevent infections. More recent therapy techniques subcutaneously or intravenously attempt to administer bioengineered molecules that increase the production of blood cell elements.

Individuals with Fanconi anemia are treated with androgens or bone marrow transplantation. Approximately half these individuals have increased production of red blood cells and platelets following androgen therapy, and some may have increased production of white blood cells. This type of therapy can continue for years but usually becomes ineffective over time, ultimately requiring bone marrow transplant to obtain a cure.

Prognosis

Left untreated, severe aplastic anemia has a median survival of only 3 months and only 20% of untreated individuals live for as long as a year. Death is usually a result of infection or hemorrhage. Bone marrow transplant that uses marrow from a matched sibling donor has a 70-80% cure rate in individuals with no previous blood transfusion. Previous transfusions increase the risk of rejection and decrease the cure rate.

Approximately 60% of individuals receiving immunosuppression therapy respond within 4 to 12 weeks. Recovery is usually not complete but the blood count rises to a level high enough where transfusion is no longer necessary. Response may be long-term, but many individuals will suffer relapse after immunosuppression therapy is discontinued. If relapse does occur, treatment is resumed and the prognosis is not affected.

Aplastic anemia brought on by pregnancy typically resolves following delivery or spontaneous or induced abortion.

Differential Diagnosis

Aplastic anemia must be differentiated from other causes of pancytopenia such as myelodysplasia, acute leukemia, hairy cell leukemia, thrombocytopenia, myelofibrosis, marrow-invading tumors, and tissue growth (myelophthisic anemia).

Specialists

- Hematologist
- Infectious Disease Physician
- Medical Toxicologist
- Psychologist
- Rheumatologist

Work Restrictions / Accommodations

As anemia advances, physical exertion must be reduced. Exposure to toxic chemicals must be limited. Time off for immunosuppressive therapy and blood transfusions must be allotted along with extended time off for bone marrow transplant and recovery.

Individuals with significantly decreased platelet counts need a safe work environment where they can avoid the risk of trauma or injury that could trigger acute bleeding. Where indicated, protective gear especially head protection should be worn. Office work or sedentary work is more appropriate than strenuous work involving heavy lifting or other physical exertion. The employer should be made aware of the condition so that the appropriate level of care can be obtained quickly in the event of an on-the-job injury.

Comorbid Conditions

Comorbid conditions include gastrointestinal bleeding, urologic disease, and high blood pressure. All are additional risk factors for bleeding.

Complications

Bone marrow transplant has the risk of infection, rejection, and the adverse effects associated with preparing for bone marrow transplant. Drugs used for immunosuppression also have adverse effects such as kidney toxicity, high blood pressure, seizures, opportunistic infections, and severe allergic (anaphylactic) reaction. Years later, approximately 25% of individuals treated with immunosuppression therapy develop other blood disorders such as paroxysmal nocturnal hemoglobinuria or myelodysplasia. Individuals with Fanconi anemia have a significantly higher risk of later developing leukemia. Infection is always a significant complication because of the individual's low number of white blood cells. Transfusion reactions can be severe and sometimes fatal in some individuals. If the individual's platelet counts drop to a dangerously low level, severe, even life-threatening bleeding can occur particularly within the brain (intracranial hemorrhage).

Factors Influencing Duration

The individual's age is a significant factor in determining if he or she is a candidate for bone marrow transplant as the risk of graft rejection increases with age. Other factors include previous blood transfusions, availability of a matched sibling donor, presence of infection, severity of pancytopenia, availability of appropriate drugs for treatment, and rejection following transplant.

Length of Disability

Job Classification	Minimum	Optimum	Maximum
Sedentary work	14	21	28
Light work	14	21	28
Medium work	21	28	42
Heavy work	42	49	56
Very Heavy work	42	49	84

Duration in Days

Failure to Recover

If an individual fails to recover within the maximum duration expectancy period, the reader may wish to reference the following questions to assist in better understanding the specifics of an individual's medical case.

Regarding diagnosis:

- Did individual present with symptoms consistent with aplastic anemia such as unusual bleeding, bruising, weakness, fatigue, poor color, and perhaps shortness of breath?
- Was diagnosis confirmed with bone marrow biopsy? Was a CBC performed?
- Was a cytogenetic breakage study done to determine congenital aplastic anemia?
- Does individual have acquired, congenital, or idiopathic aplastic anemia?
- Was a thorough exposure history investigated to detect an underlying cause?

Regarding treatment:

- Were all possible causative agents eliminated?
- Was a bone marrow transplant indicated (for those with severe symptoms and under age 55)?
- Was individual treated with immunosuppressive medications, antibiotics, and transfusions, because of age (greater than 55)?
- If individual has Fanconi anemia, was androgen therapy effective or was a bone marrow transplant necessary?

Regarding prognosis:

- Did anemia resolve as expected? For example, in acquired anemia, did symptoms resolve upon removal of the toxic substance? In pregnancy related aplastic anemia, did anemia resolve following delivery?
- Was a bone marrow transplant successful in resolving anemia?
- Does individual have any comorbid conditions (cancer, heart disease, liver or kidney failure) that may impact ability to recover?
- Did individual suffer any complications (hemorrhage, heart failure or infection) that would influence length of disability?

References

Ferri, Fred. Ferri's Clinical Advisor. St. Louis: Mosby, 2000.

Ravel, Richard. Clinical Laboratory Medicine, 6th ed. St. Louis: Mosby, 1995.

Appendectomy

Other names / synonyms: Excision of Appendix, Removal of the Appendix

47.0

Definition

Appendectomy is the medical term for surgical removal of the appendix.

The vermiform appendix is a small, finger-shaped projection of the first part of the large intestine (cecum) located near the juncture of the large and small intestines in the lower right abdomen. While the appendix is generally considered an unessential organ, and can therefore be removed without significant loss of body function, it produces a small amount of mucus that normally flows into the large intestine, and it contains lymphatic tissue, which is part of the immune system.

Appendectomy is performed when the appendix is inflamed (appendicitis). It is performed under general anesthesia, and individuals usually remain in the hospital for 1-3 days following the procedure. Because appendicitis is usually an acute condition, appendectomy is often performed as an emergency surgery.

Appendicitis occurs most often in young adults (15-25 years), and more often in men than women.

Reason for Procedure

Appendectomy is performed as treatment for inflammation of the appendix (appendicitis). Due to the nature of the signs and symptoms of acute appendicitis, the diagnosis is never certain until the appendix is inspected during open or laparoscopic surgery. In 25% of cases of suspected appendicitis, the appendix is removed even though it is free of disease at the time of the operation. A healthy appendix may be removed in the course of other abdominal surgery so that it does not become inflamed later, thus possibly sparing the individual additional emergency surgery later.

Description

Appendectomy is done by a general surgeon as an inpatient surgery under general anesthesia. Before surgery, blood and urine tests, x-rays, ultrasound, and/or CT of the abdomen may be needed.

During a conventional appendectomy, a small incision (McBurney incision) is made in the abdominal wall. The incision is placed in the lower right side of the abdomen, in the area over the appendix, and the muscles over it are split or cut. The surgeon then locates the appendix and inspects it. If there are no complications involving the surrounding tissues, the surgeon cuts the appendix away from the abdomen and/or large intestine. If a pocket of infection (abscess) has formed, it will be drained with a rubber tube that may be left in place after the surgery. The incisions are then closed, and the procedure is complete.

In about half of cases, surgeons may choose a newer technique for removing the appendix. This newer technique is called laparoscopic appendectomy, and it involves the use of a tiny video camera (laparoscope) that is inserted into the abdomen through a very small incision. During the laparoscopic procedure, the surgeon uses the video camera to view the abdominal cavity and its contents. As all regions of the abdomen can be seen easily, this technique is especially useful when the diagnosis of appendicitis is unclear. Specialized surgical tools that can also be inserted through tiny incisions are used to remove the appendix in the same manner as for the conventional open surgical procedure. The benefits of laparoscopic surgery include less postoperative discomfort and quicker recovery time.

Prognosis

Following an uncomplicated appendectomy, most individuals are discharged from the hospital within 1-3 days after the surgery. Activity will be limited for 1-3 weeks, but full recovery should be expected shortly thereafter. Individuals with complications can also expect full recovery, although the recovery period may be prolonged. Death following an uncomplicated appendectomy is rare.

In a retrospective study of 734 individuals, 5 of 45 (11%) who presented with severe infection of the abdominal cavity due to ruptured appendix (peritonitis) died.

Specialists

- General Surgeon

Work Restrictions / Accommodations

Extended sick leave may be required while the individual recovers. Driving should be avoided after surgery, and vigorous exercise or heavy lifting (not greater than 25 pounds for six weeks) should also be avoided.

Comorbid Conditions

The presence of other infections or inflammatory diseases, particularly of the gastrointestinal system, may delay recovery. Individuals with compromised immunity may experience a higher incidence of complications (such as infection) and may have a longer recovery period. Surgical risk increases with alcoholism, obesity, smoking, chronic disease of the heart, lungs, liver, or kidneys, or use of illegal drugs, laxatives, or prescription medications including those used for high blood pressure (antihypertensives), muscle relaxants, tranquilizers, sleep inducers (hypnotics), insulin, sedatives, beta-blockers, or steroids.

Procedure Complications

Potential complications of appendectomy include infection of the surgical incision, abscess, bleeding, and blockage of the intestines (bowel obstruction). Instruments used to cut the appendix away from the intestine could perforate the intestine or ureter. Appendectomy may lead to premature delivery if the individual being treated is pregnant.

In a study of 734 individuals who had appendectomy for acute appendicitis, 2% of those having laparoscopic appendectomy and 18% of those having open operation developed wound infection. However, it is difficult to compare the 2 groups, as those with rupture were more likely to be treated with open operation. In an analysis of multiple surgical series, rate of wound infection was 2.9% for laparoscopic appendectomy and 7.4% for open appendectomy, but localized infection within the abdomen (intra-abdominal abscess) occurred after surgery in 1.9% of laparoscopic appendectomies, compared with 0.8% of open procedures.

Factors Influencing Duration

The type of surgery, the skill of the surgeon, the presence of surgical complications, the condition of the appendix (intact, abscessed, or ruptured), and the individual's job requirements will influence the length of disability.

Length of Disability

Individuals who perform heavy work may require a longer recovery period.

Without complications. Open or laparoscopic.

Job Classification	Duration in Days Minimum	Optimum	Maximum
Sedentary work	1	3	7
Light work	1	3	7
Medium work	3	10	14
Heavy work	14	21	28
Very Heavy work	21	28	42

Ruptured.

Job Classification	Duration in Days Minimum	Optimum	Maximum
Sedentary work	10	21	28
Light work	10	21	28
Medium work	14	28	42
Heavy work	21	28	49
Very Heavy work	28	42	63

References

Ho, Hung S. Appendectomy. American College of Surgeons: Scientific American Surgery. 01 Jan 2000. 09 Feb 2001 <http://www.facs.org/sas/appendec.html>.

Shiel, William, MD, FACP, ed. "Appendectomy." MedicineNet.com. 01 Jan 2000. 04 Jan 2001 <http://www.medicinenet.com/script/main/Art.asp?li=MNI&ArticleKey=7990>.

Appendicitis
Other names / synonyms: Inflammation of the Vermiform Appendix
540, 540.0, 540.1, 540.9, 541, 542

Definition

Appendicitis refers to inflammation of the appendix (vermiform appendix), a small, narrow, tube-like pouch attached to and branching off from the first part of the large intestine (cecum).

The appendix is located in the lower right side of the abdomen (right iliac region) in an area designated as McBurney's point. The function of the appendix is not fully understood although it regularly fills and empties with digested food.

Approximately two-thirds of all cases of appendicitis result from the opening of the appendix becoming blocked (obstructed). There are no known predisposing factors to developing appendicitis, however, individuals may be at higher risk if they have other disorders that can lead to obstruction of the appendix. These include the presence of a foreign body, calculus, or stone in the intestine; an intestinal tumor; intestinal parasites such as pinworms; or fluid accumulation (edema) in the lymphoid tissue. Intestinal feces can also block the appendix.

Appendicitis is slightly more prevalent among men than women. Incidence peaks in the late teens and early twenties but older individuals (50 or older) who develop the condition generally have more complications and longer hospital stays. Appendicitis usually presents as an acute event. For some it may be recurrent or chronic. Among adults, appendicitis occurs at a rate of 1 to 2 per 1,000 individuals. Approximately 200,000 cases of appendicitis are treated surgically in the US each year.

Diagnosis

History: The classic initial symptom of appendicitis is crampy or colicky pain around the navel (periumbilical) and loss of appetite (anorexia). As the symptoms from the appendix move downward into the right lower abdominal area (right lower quadrant), the pain becomes localized above the appendix at what is known as McBurney's Point. Fever develops within several hours. Other symptoms may include nausea, vomiting, constipation, rectal tenderness, chills, and shaking. Moving, walking, or coughing may aggravate the pain. Individuals with appendicitis generally report being in good health before the onset of the condition.

Physical exam: Manipulation of the abdomen (palpation) reveals extreme tenderness at McBurney's Point. The individual frequently tightens (guards) the stomach muscles of the abdomen in response to palpating in this region. When the abdomen is depressed on the left side and held momentarily before being quickly released, the individual may experience a momentary increase in pain (rebound). This suggests inflammation has spread into the membrane lining the abdominopelvic walls (peritoneum). If the individual is pregnant, the enlarging fetus may alter the location of the appendix so the tenderness may be higher in the abdomen.

If the appendix has ruptured, the pain may disappear for a short period during which the individual feels better. However, within a short period, infection of the peritoneum (peritonitis) sets in. The pain then returns as the individual becomes progressively more ill. The entire abdomen becomes extremely tender and tight. A mild fever (less than 100 degrees F) may initially be present and increases if the appendix ruptures. In women, a rectal exam or a pelvic exam may help distinguish appendicitis from other conditions that produce abdominal pain.

Tests: Laboratory tests may include a complete blood count (CBC) that reveals an increase in white blood cell (WBC) count if an infection is present. A urinalysis helps identify any urological causes for the reported symptoms. Diagnostic tests may include high frequency sound waves (abdominal ultrasound) and x-rays taken following injection of a radiopaque dye (intravenous pyelogram). Abdominal x-rays may not always identify appendicitis. CT scan may also be helpful. For a definitive diagnosis, the abdomen may be examined with a fiber-optic microscope (laparoscopy) or visualized during an exploratory laparotomy. A pregnancy test is needed in sexually mature women to check for an abnormal (ectopic) pregnancy.

Treatment

The treatment of choice for an uncomplicated appendicitis is surgical removal of the appendix (appendectomy) as soon as possible. Surgery to remove the appendix is always done soon after diagnosis.

Appendectomy may be done through a surgical opening into the abdomen (laparotomy). Alternatively, a much smaller incision using a fiber-optic microscope (laparoscope) may be the preferred surgical method (laparotomy). If an abscess is suspected, surgery may be delayed until intravenous fluids and antibiotic medications are administered to reduce the potential for infection. The antibiotics are given during surgery and continued for at least 48 hours postoperatively. The consequences of missing the diagnosis are severe and may include death and generally the result of untreated or inadequately treated peritonitis.

Prognosis

The predicted outcome is generally good if complications do not develop. Mortality following surgical removal of the appendix (appendectomy) is less than 1% in cases without complications. The mortality rate rises to 5% if the appendix has ruptured (perforated) prior to surgery. As a result of misdiagnosis, 25% of appendixes surgically removed are normal. However, this is widely accepted as the price of avoiding the potentially serious complications of appendicitis.

Appendectomy may lead to premature delivery if the individual is pregnant.

Differential Diagnosis

Conditions that present with similar symptoms as appendicitis include gastroenteritis, irritable bowel syndrome, regional enteritis (Crohn's disease), kidney stone, urinary tract infection (UTI), constipation, inflammation of the gallbladder (acute cholecystitis), mesenteric infarction, abdominal cancer, ectopic pregnancy, pelvic inflammatory disease (PID), tubo-ovarian abscess, ruptured ovarian cyst, or pneumonia in the right lower lung.

Specialists

- General Surgeon

Work Restrictions / Accommodations

Individuals suffering from appendicitis are generally unable to work. After surgery, temporary restrictions on lifting (not greater than 25 pounds for six weeks) and heavy manual labor may be necessary until recovery is complete.

Comorbid Conditions

Existing conditions that may impact the ability to recover and further lengthen disability include gastroenteritis, irritable bowel syndrome, Crohn's disease, constipation, low blood flow to the abdominal tissues (mesenteric infarction), or gastrointestinal cancer.

Complications

Possible complications of appendicitis include rupture (perforation) of the appendix, general inflammation of the abdominal cavity (peritonitis), development of infection (abscess) within the appendix, perforation of the intestines, intestinal tissue death (gangrene), and inflammation of a part of the circulatory system (portal venous system) with pus formation (pylephlebitis). The latter condition is a rare but highly lethal complication of appendicitis characterized by chills, high fever, liver enlargement (hepatomegaly), and yellow discoloration (jaundice) of the skin.

Factors Influencing Duration

Factors that may influence disability include the individual's age, response to surgical treatment, and any complications associated with the condition such as rupture (perforation) of the appendix, general inflammation of the abdominal cavity (peritonitis), development of infection (abscess) within the appendix, and inflammation of a part of the circulatory system (portal venous system) with pus formation (pylephlebitis).

Length of Disability

Duration may be longer for individuals who perform heavy or very heavy work (lifting or physical labor). The length of disability from laparotomy is longer than from laparoscopy.

Without complications. Open or laparoscopic.

Duration in Days

Job Classification	Minimum	Optimum	Maximum
Sedentary work	1	3	7
Light work	1	3	7
Medium work	3	10	14
Heavy work	14	21	28
Very Heavy work	21	28	42

Ruptured.

Duration in Days

Job Classification	Minimum	Optimum	Maximum
Sedentary work	10	21	28
Light work	10	21	28
Medium work	14	28	42
Heavy work	21	28	49
Very Heavy work	28	42	63

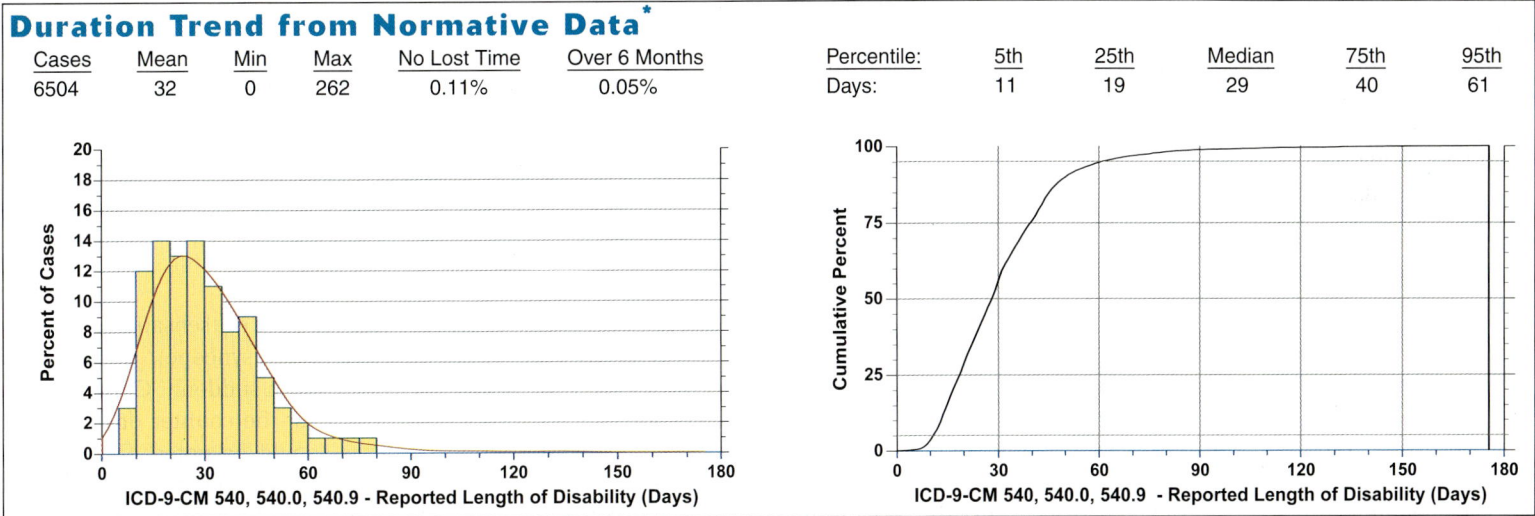

Duration Trend from Normative Data*

Cases	Mean	Min	Max	No Lost Time	Over 6 Months
6504	32	0	262	0.11%	0.05%

Percentile:	5th	25th	Median	75th	95th
Days:	11	19	29	40	61

ICD-9-CM 540, 540.0, 540.9 - Reported Length of Disability (Days)

* Differences may exist between the expected duration tables and the normative graphs. Duration tables provide expected recovery periods based on the type of work performed by the individual. The normative graphs reflect the actual observed experience of many individuals across the spectrum of physical conditions, in a variety of industries, and with varying levels of case management.

Failure to Recover

If an individual fails to recover within the maximum duration expectancy period, the reader may wish to reference the following questions to assist in better understanding the specifics of an individual's medical case.

Regarding diagnosis:

- Did individual complain of a crampy or colicky feeling around the navel?
- Did the pain then move down to McBurney's point?
- Was there loss of appetite?
- Was fever present? Chills or shaking?
- Did individual have nausea and vomiting? Constipation? Rectal pain?
- Did walking or moving aggravate their pain?
- On exam, was individual exquisitely tender at McBurney's point?
- Did individual have guarding when the abdomen was examined?
- Was individual pain free for a short time? Did the pain then worsen?
- If individual is female, was a pelvic and/or a rectal exam done?
- Was CBC with WBC done?
- Was an abdominal ultrasound done? IVP? CT?
- Was it necessary to do a laparoscopy?
- Were conditions with similar symptoms ruled out?

Regarding treatment:

- Did individual have an appendectomy?
- Did they have peritonitis?
- Is individual pregnant?

Appendicitis

Regarding prognosis:

- Did individual have a laparoscopic appendectomy? Laparotomy?
- Does individual have any conditions that may affect ability to recover?
- Did individual develop any complications such as perforation or peritonitis? Intestinal gangrene? Inflammation of the portal venous system?

References

"Acute Appendicitis." Yahoo! Health. 2001. 24 Jan 2001 <http://health.yahoo.com/health/diseases_and_conditions/disease_feed_data/acute_appendicitis/>.

LeMone, P., and K.M. Burke. Medical-Surgical Nursing. Upper Saddle River, NJ: Prentice Hall Health, 2000.

Vermeulen, M.I., T.J. van Vroonhoven, and P. Leguit. "Acute Appendicitis: A Serious Disease in the Elderly." Nederlands Tijdschrift voor Geneeskunde 139 32 (1995): 1635-1663.

Zheng, X.L., C. Chen, and X.Z. Wu. "Acupuncture Therapy in Acute Abdomen." American Journal of Chinese Medicine 13 1-4 (1985): 127-131.

Arrhythmia

Other names / synonyms: Cardiac Arrhythmia, Cardiac Dysrhythmia, Dysrhythmia, Heart Arrhythmia

427, 427.2, 427.8, 427.9

Definition

An arrhythmia may be defined as a disturbance of the heart's rhythm. An arrhythmia may result in a fast (tachycardia) or slow (bradycardia) heartbeat and produce an even (regular) or uneven (irregular) rhythm. An arrhythmia may occur suddenly (paroxysmal) or be long-standing (chronic). It may arise from the upper chambers (atria) or the lower chambers (ventricles) of the heart.

A common arrhythmia is caused by "skipped beats," which are early (premature) beats and result in a compensatory pause to allow the next beat to occur on time. But because they make it feel like the heart missed a beat, they are widely referred to as "skipped beats."

Premature beats arising from the atria are called premature atrial contractions (PACs) while premature beats arising from the ventricles are called premature ventricular contractions (PVCs). PACs and PVCs do not necessarily indicate heart disease. Many normal, healthy individuals have PACs or PVCs especially at rest or during sleep. They vanish when individuals are awake and active because the faster heart rate when awake and the activity "suppresses" the early beats. PACs and PVCs at rest are common in athletes because they have a slower resting heart rate from being physically fit.

PVCs may however, attest to the presence of underlying heart disease that may be serious. They may also indicate a narrowing of the coronary arteries secondary to cholesterol deposits commonly called hardening of the arteries (atherosclerosis). This condition leads to insufficient oxygen reaching the heart muscle (myocardial ischemia).

PVCs are classified as simple or complex. Simple PVCs are defined as single, early beats that occur amidst normal, regular beats. Complex PVCs are defined as two or more PVCs in a row that arise from more then one site (focus) within the heart (multifocal). Complex PVCs are more likely to be associated with underlying heart disease than simple PVCs. If a number of PVCs occur in a row, the resulting arrhythmia is known as ventricular tachycardia. This can be a life-threatening arrhythmia.

Two common arrhythmias arising from the atria are paroxysmal atrial tachycardia (PAT) and atrial fibrillation (AF). PAT often occurs in young, healthy individuals without heart disease. The heart beats at a rate of 150 to 250 beats per minute (BPM) rather than the normal 60 to 100 BPM. Despite the fast beating, individuals usually feel fine because they are young and healthy.

AF is also known as tachycardia and may occur in otherwise healthy individuals and those with significant heart disease. In healthy individuals, excess caffeine or alcohol, fatigue, some street drugs, and diet pills may cause AF. In other individuals, atherosclerosis, an overactive thyroid gland, rheumatic heart disease, lung disease, and inflammation of the surface of the heart (pericarditis) following open-heart surgery can cause AF. In older individuals, rapid AF may alternate with a slow heart rate rhythm. The arrhythmia is called the sick sinus syndrome or the tachycardia-bradycardia syndrome.

Diagnosis

History: Individuals may report chest pain and the sensation of a heavy or irregular heartbeat, dizziness, fainting (syncope), anxiety, and shortness of breath. Symptoms usually begin suddenly. Current use of medications such as prescriptions or over-the-counter drugs, herbal products, diet pills, and illegal drugs should be noted. Other useful information includes any stress the individual may be under, intake of food and drink that contain caffeine, or if and how much the individual smokes.

Physical exam: A rapid, slow, or irregular heart rate can be felt in the pulse or by listening to the heart. Blood pressure may be low. Signs of heart failure such as difficulty breathing (dyspnea), wheezing, cough, pallor or blue tinged skin or nails (cyanosis), abdominal distension, fainting, and swelling of the feet and ankles (edema) may be present. The feet may appear swollen due to circulation complications. The exam may also reveal a heartbeat that does not match the pulse at the wrist (apical radial heartbeat). If the arrhythmia is not present at the time, the physical exam may be completely normal.

Tests: An electrocardiogram (ECG) records the heart's electrical activity and is used to diagnose most arrhythmias. If the arrhythmia is not captured on an ECG, some individuals may be required to wear a portable monitor to record heart activity for 24 hours to document an intermittent arrhythmia. Blood chemistry may help find any chemical imbalance that may be causing the arrhythmias. A special (esophageal) ECG is occasionally needed for diagnosis. A stress ECG taken while the individual is performing an exercise such as rapid walking may be done in the evaluation of an arrhythmia.

Since ECGs are done while at rest and lying down, arrhythmias are frequently seen on such ECGs. However, when the individual is exercising, the early beats often go away.

Treatment

Simple PVCs are usually not treated whereas complex PVCs may or may not be treated. Complex PVCs may not be treated because often the medications used for treatment can have significant side effects that are not acceptable to the individual. Some medications have been known to actually make the arrhythmia worse (pro-arrhythmia effect). Even though many antiarrhythmia drugs are available, many PVCs are not treated because of the high incidence of side effects from these drugs.

PAT is often treated with having the individual hold his or her breath and strain down as if attempting to lift a heavy object. This is called a Valsalva maneuver. Rubbing on the side of the neck with the index finger (carotid sinus massage) can also stop PAT. Long-term treatments to prevent recurrences include medications like digitalis and beta-blockers. Long-term therapy is not used as often if an individual's bouts of PAT are infrequent and easily terminated by a Valsalva maneuver or carotid sinus massage.

PAF or chronic AF is more apt to be treated. In the case of PAF, treatment includes avoiding those stimulants that can cause the arrhythmia such as excess caffeine or alcohol and diet pills. Digitalis, quinidine, and other similar drugs may be used if necessary. Chronic AF is treated with digitalis or beta-blockers to keep the ventricles from beating too fast even though the atria continue to beat fast and irregularly (fibrillate). Anticoagulants are often used to decrease the chances of an embolus somewhere in the body.

Bradycardias that are due to a condition where the ventricles do not beat fast enough (heart block) are often treated with installation of a permanent pacemaker. Although pacemakers have a small incidence of associated technical problems and require that the battery be changed every 5 to 10 years, they are very effective in the treatment of bradycardias.

Prognosis

The predicted outcome of arrhythmias varies widely depending on the type of arrhythmia. Simple PVCs and PAT usually have a good outcome. Longevity is not affected in the majority of individuals with PAT or simple PVCs. Complex PVCs may result in no significant effect on survival if they are eradicated or well controlled by drugs. However, the underlying heart problem may affect survival. The drugs used for treatment of complex PVCs may be ineffective, cause significant side effects, or worsen the arrhythmia.

Chronic AF may be associated with complications such as a stroke or an embolus that affect survival. In addition, survival rates vary widely with chronic AF depending on the presence or absence of underlying heart disease. In individuals without any underlying heart disease (lone AF), longevity is not affected. In individuals with underlying heart disease, complications increase and survival decreases. The incidence of each complication depends on the type of underlying heart disease and the presence or absence of associated conditions such as congestive heart failure.

Differential Diagnosis

Panic and other anxiety disorders can have rapid heartbeat as a prominent symptom. Underlying diseases including thyroid problems, heart disease, and electrolyte imbalances may also be problematic. Excessive stress, caffeine intake, substance abuse, prescription and nonprescription drugs (e.g., cold medications), alcohol intake, and smoking may also result in symptoms similar to arrhythmia.

Specialists

- Cardiologist

Work Restrictions / Accommodations

If the arrhythmia involves temporary disturbances in consciousness, chest pain, or dizziness, a restriction of hazardous work or environments such as dangerous machinery or exposed heights may be required.

Comorbid Conditions

Conditions that may influence the length of disability include obesity, heart disease, thyroid disease, electrolyte imbalances, substance abuse, smoking, drinking alcohol, excessive caffeine intake, and stress.

Complications

A rapid arrhythmia can result in chest pain (angina) or a heart attack if there is underlying coronary artery disease. A very slow arrhythmia can result in loss of consciousness and associated injury. AF can lead to blood clot formation in the atria. The clots can break loose (embolize) and cause a stroke or other serious illness. Ventricular arrhythmias may actually cause the heart to beat wildly so that emergency medical intervention is required to save the individual's life.

Medications used to treat arrhythmia may cause more arrhythmias or make them worse.

Factors Influencing Duration

Disability varies with the specific arrhythmia, its severity, underlying disease, lifestyle habits, stress, obesity, age, severity of symptoms, and response to treatment.

Length of Disability

Length of disability depends on type of arrhythmia and on job requirements. If the individual performs physical labor and operates dangerous machinery, he/she may be unable to perform duties if symptoms include fainting, chest pain, shortness of breath, and dizziness. The individual's response to treatment and severity of symptoms will influence the length of disability.

Failure to Recover

If an individual fails to recover within the maximum duration expectancy period, the reader may wish to reference the following questions to assist in better understanding the specifics of an individual's medical case.

Regarding diagnosis:

- Did individual exhibit symptoms of an arrhythmia such as palpitations, dizziness, shortness of breath, and chest pain?
- Does individual smoke or use prescription or nonprescription medicines?
- Does individual have history of excessive fatigue, caffeine intake, or coronary artery disease?
- Was heart rate rapid, slow, or irregular during examination? Was blood pressure low?
- Did individual show signs of heart failure such as dyspnea, wheezing, cough, cyanosis, edema of the feet and ankles, abdominal distension, or fainting?
- Was the presence and type of arrhythmia confirmed with an ECG or Holter monitoring?
- Did individual feel like his or her heart misses a beat?
- Was the arrhythmia a PAC or PVC?
- What was individual's overall state of health?
- Was individual an athlete?
- Did individual have simple or complex PVCs? Have a number of PVCs occurred in row indicating ventricular tachycardia?

Regarding treatment:

- Was there an underlying cause for which individual was treated?
- Were contributory factors such as smoking or alcohol use eliminated?
- Were antiarrhythmias prescribed? Did individual experience any side effects?
- Were long-term treatment medications (i.e., digitalis and beta-blockers) necessary?
- Was a pacemaker necessary?
- Did individual have a rapid atrial or ventricular arrhythmia that did not response to medications so necessitated the use of electrical cardioversion?
- Was surgical ablation performed?

Regarding prognosis:

- Did individual suffer an arrhythmia considered life threatening?
- Was the arrhythmia associated with a myocardial infarction or cardiac arrest?
- Does individual have any underlying conditions (cardiac disease, pulmonary disease, thyroid disorders, obesity, smoking, alcohol, or substance abuse) that may impact ability to recover?

References

Facts About Arrhythmias. drkoop.com 01 Feb 1999. 28 Jul 2000 <http://www.drkoop.com/conditions/fainting/page_76_399.asp>.

Maleskey, Gale. Nature's Medicines. Emmaus, PA: Rodale Press, 1999.

Arterial Embolism and Thrombosis
Other names / synonyms: Air Emboli, Blood Clot, Fat Emboli, Thromboembolism, Thrombus
411.81, 444, 444.0, 444.1, 444.2, 444.8, 444.9, 453.9

Definition

Arterial thrombosis occurs when a blood clot (thrombus) adheres to the wall of a vessel (artery) and blocks the flow of blood. A blood clot that dislodges from the vessel wall and moves throughout the circulatory system is known as a thromboembolus. The occlusion of blood flow by a foreign particle (embolus) other than a blood clot within the vessel is known as an embolism.

An embolus may be any material that has formed a rounded mass (bolus) and moves through the circulatory system such as an air bubble, bacteria, fat, or cancer cells. Regardless of its composition, an embolus (or thromboembolus) eventually becomes lodged in an artery that is too small to accommodate its passage. The result is partial or complete blockage (occlusion) of blood through the artery. Tissues supplied with blood by the vessel may become starved for oxygen and nutrients. Individuals with arterial thrombosis or embolism often develop alternative (collateral) circulation to provide blood flow to the tissue to compensate for the loss of arterial flow. However, because it takes time for sufficient collateral circulation to develop, the loss of blood flow threatens the survival of tissues in the involved area of the body. Depending on the area of involvement, arterial embolism or thrombus may create serious conditions that can result in permanent damage to tissues and organs. When arterial flow is interrupted, tissue death (necrosis) and decay (gangrene) are possible, and in some cases, individuals may be at risk of losing their life.

Important risk factors for arterial embolism and thrombosis may include advanced age, cigarette smoking, high blood pressure (hypertension), obesity, blood serum fat (lipid) abnormalities (high serum levels of cholesterol, triglycerides, lipoprotein (a), or apolipoprotein B; low serum levels of high-density lipoprotein cholesterol), diabetes mellitus, abnormal blood coagulation factors, and low levels of physical exercise. A combination of two or more of these risk factors may produce more than an additive increase in risk for developing arterial embolism and thrombosis.

The incidence of arterial embolism and thrombosis in the heart (coronary) arteries, brain (cerebral) arteries, and arteries in the trunk, arms, and legs (periphery) is of epidemic proportions in western industrialized countries. In many industrialized nations including the US, complications of arterial embolism and thrombosis (particularly as they relate to ischemic or coronary heart disease) are the leading causes of death. Approximately 550,000 Americans die each year from heart-related arterial embolism and thrombosis and about 250,000 of these individuals are female. Approximately 100,000 of all these deaths are considered premature, i.e., prior to the average life expectancy. Although the incidence of arterial embolism and thrombosis is declining in some countries, in others such as Eastern Europe, incidence rates are increasing.

Diagnosis

History: Individuals with arterial embolism or thrombosis may complain of pain in the region of the affected vessel; numbness, coldness, tingling or pain in an extremity such as an arm or leg; muscle weakness, spasms, and/or paralysis; lack of a pulse (pulselessness) in the artery beyond the site of blockage; and paleness (pallor) or discoloration (mottling) of the skin in the affected extremity. The individual may report a recent surgery, a blood clotting disorder, stroke or cardiovascular disease, or a history of long-term intravenous therapy.

Physical exam: A pulse cannot usually be felt (palpated) in the artery beyond (distal to) the site of blockage. Coldness or mottling of the affected extremity is common and muscular effects such as weakness, spasms, or paralysis may be noted. There is often a distinct (demarcation) line at the blockage with pallor or bluish color (cyanosis) distal to the occlusion. Tissue death (necrosis) and decay (gangrene) may be observed in the affected tissue.

Tests: Laboratory and diagnostic tests are conducted to determine any underlying cause for thrombosis or embolism and to confirm presence of the obstruction. Tests may include measurement of cardiac enzymes in the blood (cardiac-specific troponin T or I, myoglobins, and creatine kinase isoenzymes). Blood cultures may be done to identify the organism responsible for an infection. Diagnostic tests include recording the electrical activity in the heart (electrocardiogram or ECG), visualization of the blood vessels using low-energy radio waves (MRI) or x-rays following injection of a radiopaque contrast material (arteriography), or studying the structure and motion of the heart with ultrasonic waves (echocardiography). Computer-enhanced arteriography (digital subtraction arteriography) is useful in individuals where the volume of radiopaque contrast material must be kept to a minimum. A flexible fiber-optic catheter inserted directly into an artery helps visualize its interior (fiberoptic angioscopy).

Treatment

Therapy may include administration of drugs that relax the blood vessels (vasodilators), enhance accessory (collateral) blood flow (serotonin antagonist, ketanserin), or reduce or prevent blood clots (antithrombotic therapy). Invasive treatments include removal of the obstruction (embolectomy) using either a flexible catheter inserted into the blood vessel or open surgery, direct administration of antithrombotic agents onto the clot in the vessel using a flexible catheter (intra-arterial thrombolysis), and cutting the nerves that stimulate blood vessels causing them to relax (lumbar sympathectomy). If tissue death (necrosis) and decay (gangrene) has set in an arm or leg, the limb may be removed (amputated) surgically.

Prognosis

The outcome varies depending on the location of the embolism and the extent that it affects blood supply to the area. Arterial embolism can be serious if not treated promptly and it may be life-threatening with a 25-30% death rate. The affected area can be permanently damaged with up to approximately 25% of cases requiring amputation of an affected extremity. Arterial emboli may recur even after successful treatment.

Drug treatments produce removal (lysis) of the obstruction in 50-80% of all cases. Removal of the obstruction using a flexible catheter or open surgery reduces mortality by nearly 50% and the need for limb amputation by approximately 35%. Intra-arterial thrombolysis reduces the blockage produced by a blood clot by 95% in 50% of cases. Restoration of adequate blood flow occurs in 50-80% of cases using this technique. Lumbar sympathectomy is usually used only in desperate cases, however, up to 50% reported a favorable response to this treatment. Limb amputation carries considerable (~50%) mortality primarily because of the severity of the diseases associated with this procedure. Limb amputation itself is usually remarkably well-tolerated.

Complementary and Alternative Therapies

Content is intended for awareness only. Treatments may or may not be effective. Scientific evidence may be lacking and some substances have potentially toxic effects. Dr. Presley Reed and the editors do not endorse the use of these therapies in the absence of consultation with a licensed medical professional.

Acupuncture - Insertion of needles into certain points on the body may alter circulation and coagulation characteristics of the blood.

Mechanical massage - Intermittent pressure on the extremities may reduce complications brought on by arterial embolism or thrombosis.

Differential Diagnosis

Conditions with similar symptoms as arterial embolism/thrombosis in the arms or legs include muscle cramps or spasm due to dehydration, calcium deficiency, or lactic acid build-up with excessive exercise. Conditions that produce symptoms characteristic of coronary artery blockage include protrusion of a portion of the stomach upward through the diaphragm (hiatal hernia), gastrointestinal disorders including gas or indigestion resulting from acid reflux into the esophagus (gastroesophageal reflux disease or GERD), perforated stomach ulcer, acute inflammation of the gallbladder or pancreas, or acute pericarditis. Thickening and calcification (arteriosclerosis) of the arterial walls can also cause reduce blood flow and produce symptoms associated with arterial embolism or thrombosis.

Specialists

- Cardiologist
- Invasive Radiologist
- Neurologist
- Radiologist
- Surgeon

Rehabilitation

Rehabilitation programs are individualized under the supervision of a physician. Each training period should consist of a 5-minute warm-up, intermittent exercise on a treadmill, and a 5-minute cool-down. Individuals may be encouraged to walk independently outside the supervised program.

Rehabilitation begins in the first few days postoperatively for individuals who have had a limb surgically amputated. Partial weight bearing may begin in the first week postoperatively after the first surgical dressing change has confirmed the integrity of the wound. Following dismissal from the hospital, individuals with any type of amputation should try to become as independent as possible with crutches or other aids. In the case of below-knee amputation, quadriceps-setting exercises should be encouraged. Individuals with above-knee amputations may require the use of a walker on a permanent basis.

Work Restrictions / Accommodations

Anxiety level is often increased in individuals who have experienced arterial embolism or thrombosis and a less stressful job situation may be required. Individuals may also require certain measures that promote blood circulation in affected tissues such as positional changes of the extremities on a routine basis; ankle, knee, wrist, or arm flexion exercises every few hours; and a warm environment. The individual may experience impaired physical mobility and strength following thromboembolism and strenuous or sustained physical activity may need to be restricted.

Comorbid Conditions

Existing conditions that may impact an individual's ability to recover and further lengthen disability include obesity, older age, existence of a prior heart attack (myocardial infarction or MI), high blood pressure (hypertension), diabetes mellitus, pregnancy, blood lipid disorders (hyperlipidemia), heart failure, anemia, hyperthyroidism (thyrotoxicosis), renal failure, and infection.

Complications

Possible complications of arterial embolism and thrombosis depend on the site of the obstruction. In all cases, there is reduced blood flow (ischemia) to the tissues supplied by the artery. If the obstruction is in a coronary vessel, death of the heart muscle (infarction) can occur and possibly result in heart failure and death. Blockage of an artery that supplies blood to the brain may result in a stroke. Blockage of arteries that supply other organs, arms, or legs may result in tissue death (necrosis) and decay (gangrene). In all cases, survival is questionable if left untreated.

Factors Influencing Duration

Length of disability may depend on the type of treatment, presence or absence of complications, and availability of lighter or part-time work on either a temporary or permanent basis. The individual's willingness to address correctable risk factors (i.e., smoking, sedentary lifestyle, or obesity) is fundamental in determining length of disability.

Length of Disability

Disability may be permanent for physically demanding work. A functional rehabilitation program may facilitate recovery and shorten the period of disability.

Failure to Recover

If an individual fails to recover within the maximum duration expectancy period, the reader may wish to reference the following questions to assist in better understanding the specifics of an individual's medical case.

Regarding diagnosis:

- Does individual have a history of cigarette smoking, high blood pressure (hypertension), obesity, diabetes mellitus, abnormal blood coagulation factors, and low levels of physical exercise?
- Does individual also have a history of blood serum fat (lipid) abnormalities such as high levels of cholesterol, triglycerides, lipoprotein (a), or apolipoprotein B?
- Has individual had recent surgery or stroke or undergone long-term intravenous therapy?
- Were cardiac enzymes in the blood (cardiac-specific troponin T or I, myoglobins, and creatine kinase isoenzymes) measured?
- Were blood cultures done to identify the organism responsible for an infection?
- Was electrocardiogram (ECG), echocardiogram, MRI, arteriography, or fiberoptic angioscopy done?
- Did tests reveal the underlying cause for and presence of the obstruction? Was the blockage partial or complete?

Regarding treatment:

- Was individual given medication to relax the blood vessels (vasodilators), enhance accessory (collateral) blood flow (serotonin antagonist, ketanserin), or reduce or prevent blood clots (antithrombotic therapy)?
- Was medication sufficient to resolve the thrombus/embolus?
- Did individual require removal of the obstruction (embolectomy) using either a flexible catheter inserted into the blood vessel or open surgery?
- Was administration of antithrombotic agents onto the clot in the vessel using a flexible catheter (intra-arterial thrombolysis) required?
- Did the individual have the nerves cut that stimulate blood vessels causing them to relax (lumbar sympathectomy)?
- Has tissue death (necrosis) and decay (gangrene) occurred in an arm or leg? Did the limb require surgical removal (amputated)?
- Did any complications arise after required surgery?

Regarding prognosis:

- What was the location of the embolism and to what extent was blood supply to the area affected?
- Was treatment received promptly?
- Was any permanent damage done to the affected area as a result of the blockage?
- Is individual compliant with all medication regimens?
- Was surgical intervention required? What type of surgery was done?
- Would individual benefit from any other surgical options?
- Were arteries that supply the heart and brain affected? If so, did individual experience heart attack (myocardial infarction) or stroke?
- Did tissue death (necrosis) and decay (gangrene) occur?
- Was amputation required? If so, would individual benefit from counseling to cope with the physical and emotional aspects of amputation?

References

Hull, R., and G.F. Pineo. <u>Disorders of Thrombosis.</u> Philadelphia: W.B. Saunders Company, 1996.

Ott, G.H., and N. Grunewald. "Intermittent Mechanical Massage for the Prevention of Thromboembolism." <u>Langenbecks Archiv fur Chirurgie</u> 369 (1986): 467-471.

Arterial Graft

Other names / synonyms: Blood Vessel Graft, Bypass Grafting, Revascularization

39.56, 39.57, 39.58

Definition

Arterial grafting is a surgical procedure performed to repair a blocked or damaged artery. Graft material may be veins or arteries from the individual's own vascular system (autograft), from blood vessels removed from cadavers, or prosthetic material (polyester or polytetrafluoroethylene). Arterial grafting procedures may be performed on the arteries of the heart (coronary arterial bypass graft, or CABG), aorta, legs, kidney, or intestine.

Arterial diseases due to atherosclerosis, such as peripheral vascular disease and aneurysm, are conditions that lead to this procedure.

Atherosclerosis is a slowly progressive disease. With atherosclerosis, arteries slowly become blocked due to accumulation of atherosclerotic plaques. Ultimately, blood flow becomes diminished because of the atherosclerosis, resulting in pain caused by lack of oxygen (ischemia) to tissue supplied by the blocked artery. The aorta may be affected by atherosclerosis, leading to aneurysm. Atherosclerosis of the arteries of the legs (iliac, superficial femoral, tibial) is known as peripheral vascular disease. Atherosclerosis in arteries of the intestinal tract and kidneys may also occur.

Arterial grafting is an extremely common surgical procedure, although exact statistics on the prevalence and incidence of this procedure are not available. Coronary artery bypass grafting is said to be one of the most commonly performed operations worldwide. Approximately 0.5% of individuals over age 50 suffer from peripheral arterial disease, and about 25% of these require surgery.

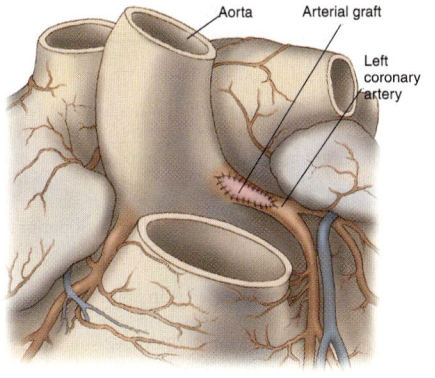

Reason for Procedure

This procedure is performed to repair blocked or damaged arteries and to restore adequate blood flow. Arterial diseases due to atherosclerosis, such as peripheral vascular disease and aneurysm, are common reasons for performing this surgery.

Arterial grafting is also done to repair weakened or ruptured sections of arteries (aneurysms). An aortic aneurysm (abdominal aortic aneurysm) may become life threatening if it becomes too large and ruptures. Grafting is often done to repair this type of aneurysm.

Arteries severely damaged by trauma may also be repaired with grafting.

Description

Arterial bypass grafting is performed by a vascular surgeon in the operating room. General anesthesia is used more often than spinal (epidural) anesthesia. The location of the incision depends on the location of the diseased artery. Arterial grafting in the legs may be performed through incisions in the groin area or in the legs, abdominal aortic aneurysm is repaired through an abdominal incision, and coronary arteries are repaired through an abdominal incision. During the surgery, x-rays using contrast medium (arteriograms) help visualize blood flow through the artery being repaired. Surgery may take several hours, depending on severity of the disease and difficulty of repair.

In coronary artery bypass grafting, the surgeon re-routes the blood flow through a "new" section of blood vessel to bypass the blocked section of coronary artery. In most cases, the individual's own internal mammary artery is used for the graft, although the saphenous vein in the leg may also be used. The individual does not suffer from removal of these blood vessels as other blood vessels can take over areas ordinarily supplied by these vessels. After the blood vessel to be used for the graft is removed (harvested), the chest is opened and the individual is put on a heart-lung machine (cardiopulmonary bypass) that takes over the function of the heart and lungs. This allows the individual to survive while the heart stops beating so that the surgeon can operate on the heart while it is still. The coronary artery is cut below the blocked area, and the downstream (distal) end of the harvested blood vessel (graft) is sewn to the coronary artery with a stitch (suture) finer than a human hair. If necessary, a side cut (incision) is made in the graft, and a sequential attachment (anastomosis) can be made to an additional section of the heart. The graft is measured to provide enough length to reach the ascending aorta, the large artery leaving the heart and delivering blood to the body, both when the heart is contracting and expanding. The graft is cut to the appropriate length, and the upstream (proximal) end is connected to the aorta. Additional bypass grafts are performed as needed by following the same procedure.

In peripheral artery bypass graft, the saphenous vein may be left in place, the valves inside the vein removed, and branches of the vein tied off. Both ends of the vein are then attached (anastomosed) to the blocked artery on either side of the blockage. When the vein is diseased or otherwise unsuitable, a synthetic bypass graft made of Gore-Tex or Dacron may be used.

Prognosis

Arterial grafting procedures improve blood flow to organs and to the limbs. At 5 years after arterial grafting with saphenous vein grafts, 60-80% are still patent, allowing blood to flow through them. Following planned (elective) abdominal aortic aneurysm repair, 60% of operated individuals are still alive 5 years following surgery. A study of free arterial grafts versus saphenous vein grafts for coronary bypass surgery showed that both types of grafts had similar outcomes, although some researchers feel that arterial grafts are superior.

Specialists

- Vascular Surgeon

Work Restrictions / Accommodations

Work accommodations following arterial grafting depend on the type of surgery performed and the physical location of the damaged vessel. Restrictions and accommodations also depend on the presence of other medical conditions, such as diabetes, coronary atherosclerosis, and arterial disease in other locations. Many individuals who have had arterial bypass procedures are older, and may require longer recovery time as a result of their age. Arterial bypass grafting may require several weeks for recovery. Recovery from an abdominal aortic aneurysm generally takes several weeks to months.

Comorbid Conditions

Several medical conditions may increase length of disability, including diabetes mellitus, coronary artery disease, peripheral vascular disease, cerebral vascular disease, and kidney disease.

Procedure Complications

Surgical complications of arterial grafting procedures in the legs may include bleeding (hematoma), clot formation, infection, development of an abnormal pathway between 2 organs (fistula), and dilation and bending of the artery resembling an aneurysm (pseudoaneurysm). If the revascularization procedure is unsuccessful, and ischemia is severe, amputation may be necessary.

Additional complications of abdominal aortic aneurysm repair include heart attack (myocardial infarction), kidney failure, decreased oxygen to the intestines (colonic or intestinal ischemia), respiratory problems, inadequate oxygen to the legs (limb ischemia), leg paralysis caused by decreased blood flow to the spinal cord, and stroke. Leakage around the graft (perigraft leakage) may be assessed with CT angiography, which is superior to conventional angiography. Long-term complications can also include development of an abnormal pathway between 2 organs (fistula) and development of another aneurysm.

In coronary artery bypass grafting, grafts may suddenly narrow, or go into spasm, blocking blood flow. This effect may be prevented by use of certain medications.

With time, arterial grafts may become blocked (no longer patent). Patency of peripheral artery grafts in the legs can be assessed with contrast-enhanced 3-dimensional MR angiography.

Factors Influencing Duration

The length of disability depends on the disorder or disease being treated with a graft implant and any complications encountered with the surgery.

Length of Disability

Duration depends on the underlying condition and the site and type of graft (bypass, patch, replacement). Length of disability may be affected by complications (infection, graft problems, embolism), continued ischemia to the limb, or amputation. Age and other medical conditions also will have an impact on length of disability.

Duration in Days

Job Classification	Minimum	Optimum	Maximum
Sedentary work	28	42	112
Light work	42	56	112
Medium work	42	56	112
Heavy work	56	70	Indefinite
Very Heavy work	56	84	Indefinite

References

Armerding, M.D., et al. "Aortic Aneurysmal Disease: Assessment of Stent-graft Treatment." Radiology 215 1 (2000): 138-146.

Coronary Artery Bypass Graft. MASA. 01 Jan 2000. 22 Feb 2001 <http://www.heartsurgeons.com/cabg2.htm>.

Gobel, F.L., M.R. Mooney, and K.J. Graham. "Coronary Artery Bypass Graft Degenerative Disease." Current Treatment Options in Cardiovascular Medicine 3 1 (2001): 47-54.

Hall, T.S., et al. "Comparison of the Flow Capacity of Free Arterial Grafts and Saphenous Vein Grafts for Coronary Bypass Surgery." Cardiovascular Surgery 9 1 (2001): 27-32.

Kidd, Jenifer F. Surveillance of Infrainguinal Grafts. Australasian Society for Ultrasound In Medicine. 01 Jan 2000. 24 Feb 2001 <http://www.medeserv.com.au/asum/open/papers/kidd.htm>.

Liu, M.H., et al. "Inhibition of Vasoconstriction by Angiotensin Receptor Antagonist GR117289C in Arterial Grafts." Annual of Thoracic Surgery 70 6 (2000): 2064-2069.

McKinsey, James F., Alan Graham, and Bruce Gewertz. "Diseases of the Vascular System." Essentials of General Surgery, 3rd ed. Lawrence, Peter F., ed. Philadelphia: Lippincott Williams & Wilkins, 2000. 435-463.

Muiesan, P., M. Rela, and N.D. Heaton. "Use of Cadaveric Superior Mesenteric Artery as Interpositional Vascular Graft in Orthoptic Liver Transplantation." British Journal of Surgery 88 1 (2001): 70-72.

Ouriel, K., and R.M. Green. "Arterial Disease." Principles of Surgery, Companion Handbook, 7th ed. Schwartz, Seymour I., ed. New York: McGraw-Hill, 1999. 517-524.

Tierney, Lawrence M., and Louis M. Messina. "Blood Vessels and Lymphatics." Current Medical Diagnosis and Treatment. Tierney, Lawrence M., Stephen J. McPhee, and Maxine Papadakis, eds. New York: Lange Medical Books/McGraw-Hill, 2000. 467-498.

Arteriography

Other names / synonyms: Angiography
88.4, 88.40, 88.41, 88.42, 88.43, 88.44, 88.45, 88.46, 88.47, 88.48, 88.49

Definition

Arteriography is a type of angiographic procedure. It is the x-ray examination of arteries using a contrast medium as opposed to venography, which is the x-ray examination of veins using a contrast medium. A contrast medium is a liquid, radio-opaque dye that is injected into an artery or vein to allow visualization (imaging) by x-ray.

Digital subtraction arteriography (DSA) uses computer techniques to process arteriographic images. In DSA, images of bone are removed (subtracted) from the x-ray image leaving only the image of the artery for study. This gives enhanced details useful for diagnostic and therapeutic purposes. Use of DSA is especially helpful for arteriography of the carotid and cerebral arteries of the head since these are adjacent to or surrounded by bone.

Arteriography is performed after an anesthetic is injected under the skin (local anesthetic). The procedure can take as little as a few minutes or up to 2 to 3 hours. An alternative to arteriography is the use of Doppler ultrasound.

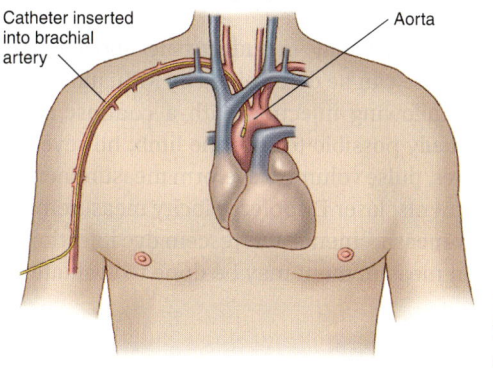

Reason for Procedure

Arteriography is done before operating on an artery to "see" its interior. This helps a physician decide if surgery is necessary and provides a road map for the surgeon to know exactly where to operate and how extensive an operation is necessary. Arteriography is performed before heart bypass surgery, aortic aneurysm repair, and other types of arterial surgery.

Arteriography can be used for diagnosis as well as for certain treatments that may eliminate the need for surgery such as percutaneous transluminal angioplasty (PTA). PTA consists of an inflatable balloon being guided into a plugged artery where it is inflated in order to compress and push fatty plaque formations to the side within the artery. Other therapeutic uses of arteriography include placement of stents to keep arteries from becoming plugged (occluded), therapeutic embolism (injection of a foreign substance into an artery to reduce or shut off the blood supply to a tumor), delivery of a medication to control bleeding directly into the bleeding vessel, and treating tumors by infusing medication directly into the artery supplying the organ containing the tumor.

Description

Arteriography is performed in a radiology or diagnostic-imaging department such as the heart catheterization laboratory. It can also be performed in the operating room during actual surgery. A local anesthetic is used. The procedure is done on an artery in the groin, arm, or neck but the groin artery is most often used. A long, slender, hollow tube (catheter) is inserted into the artery through a very small incision. The contrast medium is then injected through the catheter into the appropriate artery. Once the x-ray images have been made the catheter is removed. Pressure is applied to the skin over the entry site to stop any bleeding. Stitches are usually unnecessary. The individual is observed in the recovery room or hospital room for 6 to 8 hours. The individual is then discharged the same day or the next morning. Ordinary walking and a return to work the same day are usually allowed. If work involves lifting more than 20 pounds, 2 or 3 days off work is recommended to reduce the chance of rebleeding from the entry site.

Prognosis

The individual should return to performing all usual activities within 1 to 3 days after arteriography. If a complication of the procedure occurs, therapy will be required and the individual may be delayed in returning to work.

Specialists

- Cardiologist
- Radiologist
- Vascular Surgeon

Work Restrictions / Accommodations

Bending of the groin or elbow at whatever site was used for performance of the arteriography should be avoided for 1 day. Most individuals can return to work the day following arteriography if work does not involve bending of the groin or elbow or lifting more than 20 pounds. A longer restriction of activity may be required if an individual sustained a complication from the procedure.

Comorbid Conditions

Diabetes and dehydration may increase the risk of kidney complications from the dye because of the reduced blood flow to the kidney. If an individual has impaired kidney function before arteriography, the risk of worsening kidney functioning afterward increases.

Procedure Complications

The most common complication of arteriography is formation of a blood clot (thrombus) in the artery at the entry site. Other complications include an allergic reaction to the dye, bleeding from the puncture site, dislodgment of plaque from the inside of the artery (embolization), separation of the wall of the artery (dissection), infection, stroke, and kidney failure. Individuals taking certain medications for diabetes may develop low blood sugar (hypoglycemia). Entry site complications are more frequent if there is hardening of the arteries (atherosclerosis) at the entry site. If arteriography is done during surgery (intraoperatively), complications may arise due to the general anesthetic used.

Factors Influencing Duration
There is usually no disability after arteriography. If an entry site complication occurs, length of disability is related to treating the complication.

Length of Disability
Outpatient.

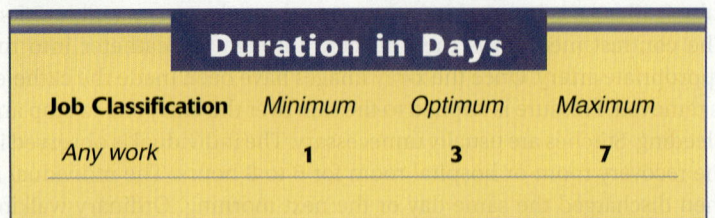

Job Classification	Minimum	Optimum	Maximum
Any work	1	3	7

References
Fischbach, Frances. "Ultrasound Studies." A Manual of Laboratory and Diagnostic Tests, 6th ed. Rader, Ilze, ed. Philadelphia: Lippincott, 2000. 900-947.

McQuaid, Kenneth R. "Alimentary Tract." Current Medical Diagnosis and Treatment, 39th ed. Tierney, Lawrence M., Stephen J. McPhee, and Maxine A. Papadakis, eds. New York: Lange Medical Books/McGraw-Hill, 2000. 553-655.

Arteriosclerotic Gangrene
Other names / synonyms: Dry Gangrene, Native Artery Gangrene, Pott's Gangrene, Senile Gangrene
440.24

Definition
Arteriosclerotic gangrene or dry gangrene is a condition that results when one or more arteries become obstructed.

Gangrene is a term used to describe the decay or death of tissue caused by a lack of blood supply. It is usually a complication of infectious or inflammatory processes, vascular disease, diabetes mellitus, injury or trauma, or degenerative changes secondary to chronic diseases. There are 3 major types of gangrene: dry, moist, and gas (a form of moist).

In arteriosclerotic gangrene, the tissue dies slowly due to lack of blood supply; it does not involve an infection. The affected area becomes black and cold, begins to dry out and whither, and eventually sloughs off over a period of a few weeks to a few months. Dry gangrene is most common in individuals with advanced blockages of the arteries (arteriosclerosis) resulting from diabetes. Hence, the term arteriosclerotic gangrene.

Arteriosclerosis is a common disorder affecting mainly men over 50 years old, and occurring in about 6 out of 1,000 individual. Individuals who have a personal or family history of coronary artery or cerebrovascular disease, diabetes mellitus, hypertension, kidney disease involving hemodialysis, smoking, or obesity are at higher risk.

Diagnosis
History: The individual will complain of pain, numbness, and tingling in the affected area. The affected area, typically the forefoot and toes, may also appear dry and wrinkly.

Physical exam: Upon touch (palpation), the area is extremely painful. Distinct color changes may be obvious; most often the skin will be black. Ulcers, decreased pulses, cold and dry skin, or dead (necrotic) tissue may be noted. The ulcers and dead tissue may emit a foul smell.

Tests: Laboratory tests may include tissue and blood cultures. The extent of the disease can be determined by MRI, ultrasound, and x-rays of the arteries following injection with a contrast medium (arteriograms). It is usually possible to save the limb; however, Doppler ankle systolic pressures, pulse volume waveform measurements, skin temperature measurements, laser Doppler velocity measurements, senon-133 skin blood flow measurements, fluorescein dye injections, and transcutaneous oxygen measurement may be done to evaluate the integrity of the limb.

Treatment
In early stages, this condition is often accompanied by pain and fever. Analgesics may be administered to treat these symptoms. Efforts will focus on improving circulation to the impaired area. Anticoagulants may be given to prevent blood clotting.

Bed rest must be maintained until the gangrene stops progressing and healing begins. Exercise must be balanced with rest; walking or other exercise to the point of pain is often alternated with rest periods. Over time, circulation improves because of the development of new, small (collateral) blood vessels. Smokers are advised to stop smoking as it constricts arteries, decreases the blood's ability to carry oxygen, and increases the risk of forming clots (thrombi and emboli).

Foot care, including wearing shoes that fit properly, is particularly important if diabetes mellitus is also present. Any cuts, scrapes, or injuries should be appropriately treated. Tissues heal more slowly when there is decreased circulation, making them more prone to infection.

Dry gangrene is rarely life threatening. In latter stages of the disease, regular monitoring of the disease progression is often all that is required. Ultimately, the area of dead tissue will disintegrate (become autolytic) and healing will take place at the demarcation line between the dead and healthy tissues.

Prognosis

In the absence of infection, the prognosis for dry gangrene is very good. It is generally not life threatening because healing usually takes place naturally at the junction between the living and dead tissue. The prognosis worsens if bacteria invade the necrotic tissue; systemic antibiotics will then be required as deeper tissues are likely to become infected.

Differential Diagnosis

Other conditions that present with similar symptoms include cellulitis, necrotizing fasciitis, deep venous thrombosis, and thrombophlebitis.

Specialists

- General Surgeon
- Internist
- Vascular Surgeon

Work Restrictions / Accommodations

Work restrictions may include extended work leave or temporary transfer to sedentary responsibilities. Work accommodations are highly variable and depend upon the extent of the area affected and the type of work the individual performs. As the forefoot and toes are the most commonly affected areas, prolonged standing, walking, and stair climbing may need to be reduced or eliminated.

Comorbid Conditions

Existing conditions that could impact ability to recover and further lengthen disability include obesity, diabetes mellitus, and systemic infection.

Complications

If the tissue becomes infected by bacteria, arteriosclerotic gangrene can develop into a more serious form of gangrene, known as wet gangrene. Infection in the underlying bone (osteomyelitis) is another possible complication.

Factors Influencing Duration

Length of disability may be influenced by the severity, extent, and location of the gangrene, method of treatment, and the development of complications.

Length of Disability

Duration depends upon severity and the limb or organ system involved. Contact physician to determine disability duration.

Failure to Recover

If an individual fails to recover within the maximum duration expectancy period, the reader may wish to reference the following questions to assist in better understanding the specifics of an individual's medical case.

Regarding diagnosis:

- Does individual have a history of chronic disease? History of smoking tobacco and/or obesity?
- Has individual experienced recent injury or trauma?
- Does individual complain of pain, numbness, and tingling in the forefoot and toes? Do the toes and forefoot appear to be dry and wrinkled?
- Are skin color changes noted?
- Are skin ulcerations present? Is there a foul smell emitted from the affected area?
- Were tissue and blood cultures taken?
- Did MRI, ultrasound, or arteriograms determine the extent of the disease?
- Does the integrity of the limb need evaluation with Doppler ankle systolic pressures, pulse volume waveform measurements, skin temperature measurements, laser Doppler velocity measurements, senon-133 skin blood flow measurements, fluorescein dye injections, or transcutaneous oxygen measurement?
- Was diagnosis confirmed?

Regarding treatment:

- Are pain and fever controlled with analgesics and antipyretics, respectively?
- Does individual require anticoagulants for prevention of blood clots (thrombi)?
- Did individual maintain bed rest until the gangrene stopped progressing?
- Has exercise been balanced with rest?
- If individual is a smoker, does individual understand the importance of not smoking?
- Does individual or caregiver understand the principles of appropriate foot care and infection prevention?

Regarding prognosis:

- Has individual developed an infection in the necrotic tissue? If so, was a culture taken to determine the most effective antibiotic and rule out antibiotic-resistant organisms?
- Was individual compliant with taking antibiotic(s)?
- Has individual quit smoking? If not, would individual benefit from enrollment in a smoking cessation program?
- Has individual participated with the prescribed exercise regimen?
- Have any complications developed such as wet gangrene or a bone infection (osteomyelitis)? If so, how will these be treated and what is the expected outcome with treatment?

References

New Zealand Chelation Clinic: Centre for Advanced Medicine, Ltd. Centre for Advanced Medicine, Ltd. 01 Jan 2000. 18 Jan 2001 <http://www.camltd.com/fact4.htm>.

The James Vincent Duhig Museum of Pathology. University of Queensland. 17 Mar 1997. 01 Jan 2001 <http://gsm.herston.uq.edu.au/pathology/museum/Demo_Museum/790.html>.

Arteriovenous Aneurysm

Other names / synonyms: Arteriovenous Fistula, Arteriovenous Malformation

747.6, 747.60

Definition

An aneurysm is a ballooning-out of the wall of an artery, vein, or the heart due to weakening of the wall by disease, injury, or an abnormality present at birth (congenital abnormality). In an arteriovenous aneurysm, the weakness in the artery results in abnormal communication between an artery and a vein. In this condition, blood flows from an artery directly into the neighboring vein or is carried into the vein by a connecting sac.

Arteriovenous aneurysms are usually the result of arteriosclerosis. Less common causes include trauma, inflammation of an artery (arteritis), and infection.

Some of the most common arteriovenous aneurysms occur in the popliteal arteries (the arteries located behind the knee joint). Aneurysms at this site, particularly when bilateral, are associated with abdominal aortic aneurysms. Aneurysms at this location do not often rupture but may be the site of blood clotting (thrombosis) and blood vessel obstruction (occlusion), damaging the affected limb.

According to reports issued by the Centers for Disease Control and Prevention (CDC) in 1998, 8,000 cases of arteriovenous aneurysm were diagnosed in the US.

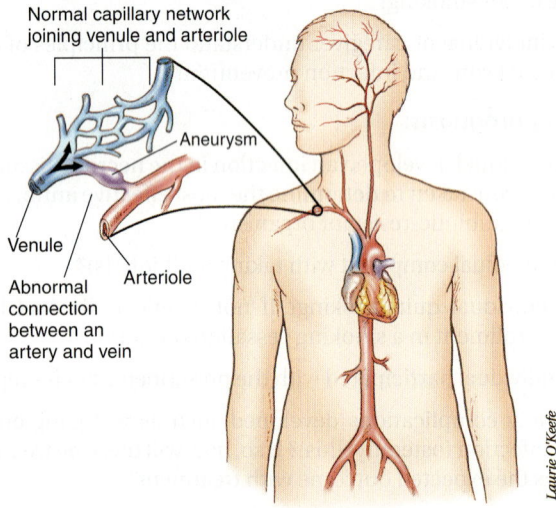

Diagnosis

History: Individuals may complain of pain and swelling of blood vessels. A history of high blood pressure (hypertension), tobacco use, inflammation of an artery (arteritis), hardening of arteries (arteriosclerosis), and some sexually transmitted diseases (e.g., syphilis) have been associated with vessel weakness.

Physical exam: If the aneurysm is located near the surface of the skin, a mass can be felt and the affected part is usually enlarged and warm with distended and often pulsating superficial veins. The altered movements involved in the circulation of blood may cause heart failure if a significant portion of the cardiac output is diverted through an experimentally created passage (fistula). Altered pulse sounds and aneurysmal swishing-like sounds (bruits) can be heard over the enlarged mass that may also be visibly pulsating. Symptoms sometimes occur from pressure on contiguous parts, high-pressure arterial flow within the involved veins, swelling at distant points (peripheral edema), abnormalities in the veins of the calf and thigh (venous varicosities), and skin color changes (stasis pigmentation).

Tests: Ultrasound, MRI, CT, and perfusion studies are conducted to correlate the symptoms reported by the individual (i.e., pain and swelling of blood vessels and a history of hypertension) and the findings from the physical exam (i.e., an enlarged mass under the skin, swishing-like sounds over the enlarged area, swelling at distant points, and skin color changes).

Treatment

Surgical removal of the aneurysm (aneurysm resection) and restoration of blood vessel continuity with graft replacement of the excised segment is the advised treatment. Drug therapy may be indicated for less serious cases. Treatment or control of underlying cardiovascular disease prevents or diminishes the possibility of additional degenerative vascular changes. Antibiotics are used at sites of localized bacterial or fungal infections.

Prognosis

Size and location of the aneurysm and rupture of the aneurysm before surgery greatly affect outcome after surgery. Overall, surgical removal of the aneurysm (aneurysm resection) and restoration of blood vessel continuity with graft replacement of the surgically removed (excised) segment lead to favorable outcome especially in cases where the individual is diagnosed early and treatment begins in the initial stages of the disease.

Differential Diagnosis

Other conditions with similar symptoms include intermittent leg pain with limping or lameness (claudication), varicose veins, vein inflammation association with the formation of a clot (thrombophlebitis), spasms of arteries in fingers and toes (Raynaud's disease), and progressive occlusive disease of the veins and arteries (Buerger's disease).

Specialists

- Cardiovascular Surgeon

Work Restrictions / Accommodations

Work accommodations are typically not associated with this disorder.

Comorbid Conditions

Comorbid conditions that may influence length of disability include obesity and chronic diseases such as diabetes, hypertension, and heart disease.

Complications

If the individual is over age 70 when surgery is performed, the surgery is a higher risk. Rupture prior to surgical repair or other cardiovascular or pulmonary diseases also makes the individual a poor surgical risk. Postsurgical hemorrhage may complicate treatment.

Factors Influencing Duration

Factors that may influence length of disability include the size and location of the aneurysm, extent of damage caused by the aneurysm such as rupture of the aneurysm before surgery, and late (rather than early) diagnosis and treatment. In rare cases, hemorrhage from aneurysms in the brain can cause temporary or permanent loss of one or more of the senses (i.e., loss of eyesight, speech) and ability to move and walk (ambulation).

Length of Disability

Duration of disability depends on site, size, and type of the aneurysm.

Failure to Recover

If an individual fails to recover within the maximum duration expectancy period, the reader may wish to reference the following questions to assist in better understanding the specifics of an individual's medical case.

Regarding diagnosis:

- Does individual have vascular or circulatory changes in the leg (popliteal region) or abdomen? History of arteriosclerosis?
- Does individual have symptoms and clinical history consistent with the diagnosis of arteriovenous aneurysm (i.e., bruits or palpable mass)? Were the symptoms associated with an extremity aneurysm or cerebral aneurysm?
- Was the diagnosis confirmed with diagnostic x-ray studies?
- Was the underlying cause determined (i.e., congenital or acquired)?
- Was any underlying infection or inflammation detected?
- If the diagnosis was uncertain, were other conditions with similar symptoms ruled out?
- Would individual benefit from consultation with a specialist (neurosurgeon, vascular surgeon, infectious disease specialist, internist, cardiologist)?

Regarding treatment:

- Were appropriate medications (antibiotics, antifungal agents, antihypertensives) administered for the given symptoms? Did the symptoms subside or stabilize?
- Was surgical resection considered?

Regarding prognosis:

- Based on the size and location of the aneurysm and severity of symptoms, what is expected outcome?
- Does individual have pre-existing conditions that increase operative risk or risk of complications (i.e., cardiac disease, chronic pulmonary disease, renal failure, liver failure, immune suppression, bleeding disorder)?
- Have any complications developed such as bleeding or infection that may influence length of disability?
- In cases of cerebral arteriovenous malformations, did any associated neurological deficits occur? If so, was neurological rehabilitation recommended?

References

Aneurysm. American Heart Association. 01 Jan 2000. 21 Jan 2001 <http://www.americanheart.org/Heart_and_Stroke_A_Z_Guide/aneurysm.html>.

Schwartz, Seymour, MD. Principles of Surgery. New York: McGraw-Hill, 1999.

Arthralgia

Other names / synonyms: Joint Pain

719.4, 719.40, 719.41, 719.42, 719.43, 719.44, 719.45, 719.46, 719.47, 719.49

Definition

Arthralgia means joint pain. The symptom may be used as a diagnosis until the true cause of the joint pain is determined, or indefinitely if examination and testing are inconclusive but the pain persists. Joint pain is a symptom of many different conditions that may be either localized or involve the whole body (systemic). Arthralgia may affect just one or multiple joints (polyarthralgia). In general, involvement of only one joint suggests localized disease, and multiple joints systemic disease.

Localized causes of arthralgia include infectious arthritis, inflammation of a bursa (bursitis), avascular necrosis, tumor, inflammation of a tendon (tendonitis) or tendon sheath (tenosynovitis), or trauma. Systemic causes of arthralgia include osteoarthritis, fibromyalgia, crystal-induced arthritis (gout or pseudogout), systemic lupus erythematosus, rheumatic fever, sickle cell disease, or rheumatoid arthritis. Lyme disease, influenza, and many other systemic bacterial and viral infections can also cause joint pain.

Arthralgia is a common symptom that affects virtually everyone at some point during life, and women more often than men. The prevalence of arthralgia increases with age.

Diagnosis

History: The individual may complain of pain in one or multiple joints. Helpful information about the pain includes time of day it occurs, what makes it worse or better, and any other symptoms like fever, sore throat, fatigue, joint swelling, or a general feeling of poor health (malaise).

Physical exam: The exam helps determine if the pain is from the joint itself, or referred, e.g., from nerve root impingement in the spine, nerve entrapment in the limb, or other pathology in the same extremity. For example, a hip problem may be manifested in knee pain. If from the joint itself, there may be joint tenderness, warmth, swelling, or redness. Joint motions are measured, with attention to whether the movement is painful or not, and smooth or accompanied by a crackling sound (crepitus) or catch. The individual may appear acutely or chronically ill.

Tests: Laboratory tests include erythrocyte sedimentation rate (ESR or sed rate), rheumatoid factor (RF), hemoglobin or hematocrit, white blood cell (WBC) count, uric acid levels, and antinuclear antibodies. Joint fluid may be analyzed for the presence of crystals, bacteria, blood, and inflammatory cells. X-rays of affected joints may detect fracture, tumor, joint space narrowing, pockets of fluid in the bone just under the cartilage (subchondral cysts), joint surface erosions, soft tissue calcifications, bone spurs at joint edges (marginal osteophytes), or other abnormalities. MRI or CT scans, ultrasound, arthrography or arthroscopy, synovial biopsy, bone scanning, bone biopsy may also be indicated. Electrodiagnostic testing such as electromyography or nerve conduction studies may be warranted if referred pain is suspected.

Treatment

Treatment depends on the underlying cause. Anti-inflammatory drugs and other analgesics may be used. Surgery may be indicated. For example, joint injury could be repaired by using a scope and long, narrow instruments inserted through small incisions (arthroscopy) or a single large incision (arthrotomy). Severely degenerated joints may be replaced with prostheses (arthroplasty).

Prognosis

The outcome varies greatly depending on the underlying cause. Surgery, if required, has a variable success rate depending on the nature and severity of the condition, and procedure performed. Joint replacement can be very successful in treating arthralgia caused by severe arthritis of the hip and knee.

Differential Diagnosis

Joint pain may be caused by a nearby fracture or soft tissue (muscle, tendon, or ligament) injury, or referred from the spine or more proximal portions of the same limb.

Specialists

- Internist
- Orthopedic Surgeon
- Pain Specialist
- Rheumatologist
- Surgeon

Rehabilitation

The goals of rehabilitation for arthralgia are to decrease the pain and increase the motion and strength of the involved joint(s). While the type of treatment depends on the underlying cause, rehabilitation often includes occupational or physical therapy. Decreasing pain associated with arthralgia allows the physical therapist to emphasize restoring strength to the muscles involved with that particular joint(s). Elevation of the affected joint will reduce swelling, and thereby pain. A therapist may also educate the individual on how to avoid pressure or stress on an inflamed joint by using an orthotic (splint), brace, soft foam pad, or walking aid (cane, crutch, or walker) until the pain and swelling diminish.

Ice packs or other cold treatments (cryotherapy) may also be used to control swelling and pain from acute inflammation. Electrical stimulation is another technique to decrease pain and relax muscles. Iontophoresis uses a small electric current to drive anti-inflammatory medication of the same electrical charge into the inflamed joint tissues.

Once the initial pain, swelling, and other symptoms and signs of acute joint inflammation improve, heat is often applied to further relieve pain and stiffness. The therapist may apply moist hot packs over one or more layers of toweling on the joint. Another form of heat treatment is ultrasound that uses high frequency sound waves to produce heat deeper in the soft tissues. However, this modality should not be used in the presence of infection or tumor, or over a prosthetic joint. Electrical stimulation may again be used at this stage of arthralgia to diminish pain and relax muscles.

Therapy usually also includes stretching exercises to restore motion to an affected joint. Passive range of motion exercises consist of the therapist moving the affected joint with no effort initiated by the individual.

Once motion returns to the joint, strengthening begins with gentle isometric exercises. Isometric resistance not only strengthens muscles around the joint but also improves joint stability while placing minimal stress on the joint. Isometrics are performed by trying to push, pull, or lift a fixed object. While the muscle contracts, it doesn't shorten, and there is no accompanying joint motion. Strengthening of the joint muscles is then progressed with the use of resistance throughout the range of motion (isotonic exercise), usually via instruction and supervision by a physical or occupational therapist, and employing devices such as free weights, elastic bands, and weight machines/equipment, as tolerated.

The physical therapist may need to modify treatment depending on the cause and severity of the arthralgia, which joint is affected joint, and whether surgery of the joint was required.

Work Restrictions / Accommodations

Work restrictions and accommodations vary depending on location of the affected joint, severity of symptoms and signs, underlying cause, and treatment required.

Comorbid Conditions

Systemic diseases such as AIDS, cancer, or diabetes may lengthen disability.

Complications

Complications are specific to the disease or condition causing the arthralgia. Anti-inflammatory drugs can cause stomach, liver, or kidney problems.

Factors Influencing Duration

The length of disability is determined by the underlying cause, severity of symptoms and findings, joint(s) involved, treatment used, results of therapy, and job demands.

Length of Disability

Disability duration depends on the cause and severity of the arthralgia, the joint(s) involved, and physical demands of the occupation.

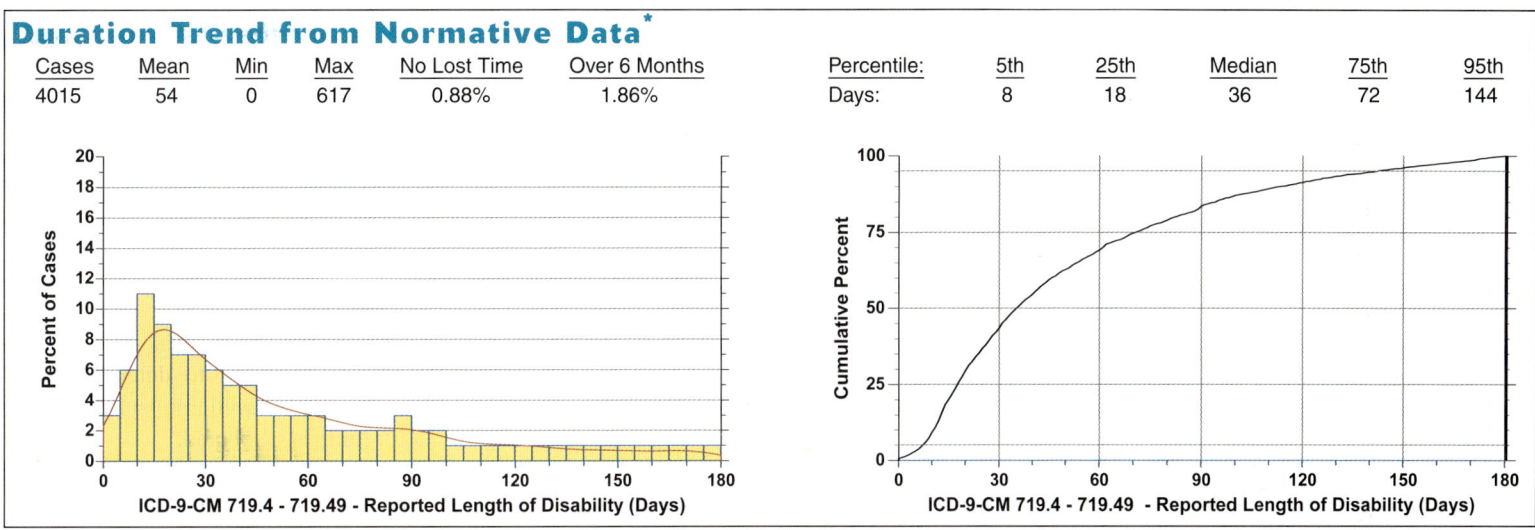

* Differences may exist between the expected duration tables and the normative graphs. Duration tables provide expected recovery periods based on the type of work performed by the individual. The normative graphs reflect the actual observed experience of many individuals across the spectrum of physical conditions, in a variety of industries, and with varying levels of case management.

Failure to Recover

If an individual fails to recover within the maximum duration expectancy period, the reader may wish to reference the following questions to assist in better understanding the specifics of an individual's medical case.

Regarding diagnosis:

- Does individual have any systemic causes of arthralgia such as osteoarthritis, fibromyalgia, gout, systemic lupus erythematosus, rheumatic fever, sickle cell disease, or rheumatoid arthritis?
- Does individual have Lyme disease, influenza, or other systemic bacterial and viral infections?
- Does individual have any localized causes of arthralgia such as infectious arthritis, bursitis, crystal-induced arthritis, avascular necrosis, tumor, trauma, tendinitis, or tenosynovitis?
- Does individual complain of pain in multiple joints or one joint? What time of day does it occur? What makes the pain worse or better?
- Does individual have fever, sore throat, fatigue, or malaise?
- On exam was there joint tenderness, warmth, swelling, or redness?
- Does the joint move smoothly or does it catch? Does movement cause pain?
- Was range of motion restricted?
- Were erythrocyte sedimentation rate, rheumatoid factor, hemoglobin or hematocrit, uric acid levels, and antinuclear factors done?
- Was joint fluid analyzed for crystals, microbes, blood, and inflammatory cells?
- Were x-rays, MRI, CT, ultrasound or arthroscopy performed?
- Were synovial biopsy, bone scanning, bone biopsy, electromyography, and thermography indicated?
- Were conditions with similar symptoms ruled out?

Regarding treatment:

- Did individual receive analgesics and anti-inflammatory drugs?
- Was surgery indicated?

Regarding prognosis:

- Is individual active in rehabilitation?

- Is individual's employer able to accommodate any necessary restrictions?
- Does individual have any conditions that may affect the ability to recover?

References

Beers, Mark, and Robert Berkow. The Merck Manual of Diagnosis and Therapy, 17th ed. Whitehouse Station, NJ: Merck & Co, 1999. 10 July 2000 <http://www.merck.com/pubs/mmanual>.

Kessler, R.M. Management of Common Musculoskeletal Disorders: Physical Therapy Principles and Methods. Philadelphia: J.B. Lippincott Co, 1990.

Arthritis, Infectious

Other names / synonyms: Gonococcal Infectious Arthritis, Non-Gonococcal Infectious Arthritis
711.0, 711.9

Definition

Infectious arthritis is an inflammation of one or more joints (principally the wrists, knees, or hips) that is caused by infection. Bacterial, viral or fungal infections usually are the source of infectious arthritis.

The bloodstream typically carries infection from diseases into the joints. Infection also can result from a wound, surgery, or injection involving the affected joint.

Infectious arthritis occurs in individuals of all ages, but, in adults, there may also be a history of osteoarthritis or rheumatoid arthritis. Infectious arthritis is linked to bacterial sources including gonorrhea, staphylococcus, tuberculosis, and Lyme disease. Viral sources of the condition include German measles, mononucleosis, mumps, hepatitis B and C, and HIV. Fungi are the least common sources of infectious arthritis, but can be found in soil, certain plants and bird droppings. Farmers are at greater risk than urban residents of acquiring fungal sources of infectious arthritis.

Gonococcal and non-gonococcal arthritis are the two principal types of the disease. Gonorrhea bacteria, transmitted through sexual contact, cause gonococcal arthritis that is four times more prevalent in women than in men. Young women are at highest risk of obtaining this form of infectious arthritis, which is common in urban areas. About one-third of individuals with gonorrhea complain of joint pain, although not all such cases are related to infectious arthritis. Individuals who obtain prompt treatment for gonococcal arthritis have a much better chance of full recovery than those affected by other forms of infectious arthritis (non-gonococcal). Annual incidence of non-gonococcal arthritis varies from 2 to 10 cases per 100,000 in the United States. Incidence of all cases of infectious arthritis is about 200 per 100,000 in the United States, and is lower in European countries (5 in 100,000 in Sweden). Africa, Latin America and Asia report much higher rates of infectious arthritis than the US.

Diagnosis

History: Depending on the underlying cause, individuals may complain of chills and fever, pain, heat, weakness and swelling in the joint. After several days, other joints may also be involved. The individual may also report red sores on the palms and soles, a rash, and pain in the wrists and ankles. The individual may have had an injury or undergone surgery prior to experiencing the condition.

Physical exam: Swelling in the joint may be noted, along with evidence of inflamed tendons. Fever and reduced range-of-motion in the involved joint are usually present.

Tests: Blood tests (serology) will be ordered, and a needle may be inserted to extract fluid from the joint (needle aspiration test) that will be placed in a special medium (culture) for microscopic examination indicating possible infection. Throat, urethral and rectal cultures may be needed as well. X-rays also may be needed to detect possible presence of joint injury. Joint tissue may be removed (biopsy) for examination if presence of tuberculosis or fungi is suspected.

Treatment

Prompt treatment of the condition is essential to prevent permanent joint damage. Gonococcal infectious arthritis usually responds well to oral antibiotic therapy. The initial treatment usually must begin in the hospital since some strains of gonococci are resistant to penicillin. Infectious arthritis caused by viral sources usually resolves on its own or has no specific treatment. For non-gonococcal arthritis related to bacterial and fungal infections, hospitalization may be necessary (up to a week), during which time the individual is given bedrest, intravenous fluids and oral or intravenous antibiotics. Needles may be used frequently to drain fluids from the affected joint (arthrocentesis). In some cases, the joint may be drained surgically (arthrotomy, arthroscopy). Splints may be used to limit movement of the joints and promote healing. Following discharge, most individuals are given oral antibiotics, which must be taken for one to four weeks. In some cases, antibiotic therapy may be needed for several months. Pain-relievers (analgesics) and anti-inflammatory drugs may also be prescribed. Anti-fungal medication may be required for infectious arthritis caused by fungi. After the condition is resolved, exercises that emphasize strength building and range-of-motion may be recommended.

Prognosis

Treatment for gonococcal arthritis is almost always successful, particularly if the condition is addressed promptly. Improvement usually takes place within 48 hours, and recovery is typically complete within two weeks. The outlook for individuals with non-gonococcal arthritis is less favorable, with a mortality rate of ten to fifteen percent. The mortality rate is higher when individuals develop respiratory problems or have the infection in several joints. At least some destruction of joints occurs in from 25-50% of non-gonococcal arthritis. When the condition is due to Lyme disease, symptoms may recur. Permanent joint damage typically results when medical intervention is delayed. Only about 60% of individuals with non-gonococcal arthritis recover completely.

Studies indicate that treatment involving drainage of the affected joint (when appropriate) results in a good outcome with minimal residual pain in 57-66% of cases, depending on the type of procedure used.

Differential Diagnosis

Non-gonococcal arthritis may initially be mistaken for gout, calcium pyrophosphate deposition disease, acute rheumatic fever, rheumatoid arthritis, viral arthritis, and Still's disease (juvenile rheumatoid arthritis). Gonococcal arthritis may be mistaken for Reiter's syndrome, Lyme disease, rheumatic fever and infective endocarditis.

Specialists

- Infectious Disease Physician
- Internist
- Orthopedic Surgeon
- Osteopath
- Rheumatologist

Work Restrictions / Accommodations

Depending on the infection's source, the individual may require several weeks or longer time off from work to recover from infectious arthritis. If the individual has had surgery for the condition, accommodations may be needed such as temporary assignment to tasks that require only mild physical activity. If significant damage has occurred in a weight bearing joint, certain tasks requiring extensive physical activity or heavy lifting may no longer be appropriate.

Comorbid Conditions

Individuals undergoing therapy to suppress immune reactions (corticosteroids) likely will have more difficulty recovering from infection. Individuals who have infections related to artificial limbs (prosthetics) are likely to require long-term treatment.

Complications

Complications primarily involving non-gonococcal infectious arthritis may include sudden onset (acute) respiratory distress. Permanent damage of the affected joint may also occur. Multiple joints are more likely to be involved if other joint disease is present such as rheumatoid arthritis or if the individual has diabetes mellitus. Individuals may have difficulty recovering from underlying infection if they have pre-existing conditions that compromise immune responses including rheumatoid arthritis, AIDS, sickle cell anemia, diabetes mellitus and cancer. Some types of infectious arthritis may produce red, tender bumps primarily on the lower legs (erythema nodosum). Viruses such as HIV and hepatitis B and C may cause infectious arthritis to be ongoing (chronic).

Factors Influencing Duration

The underlying cause of infectious arthritis, promptness and type of therapy, necessity for surgery and the individual's response to treatment will influence length of disability.

Length of Disability

Duration depends on site. If the individual has experienced permanent damage to a weight-bearing joint, tasks requiring heavy lifting or other intense physical activity may need to be reassigned. Some types of infectious arthritis go through cycles of relapse and recurrence. In some cases, individuals may experience permanent loss of full function of the affected joint.

With aspiration and antibiotics.

Duration in Days

Job Classification	Minimum	Optimum	Maximum
Sedentary work	3	7	14
Light work	3	7	14
Medium work	7	9	14
Heavy work	14	16	21
Very Heavy work	14	16	21

With surgical drainage.

Duration in Days

Job Classification	Minimum	Optimum	Maximum
Sedentary work	7	14	21
Light work	7	14	21
Medium work	14	21	28
Heavy work	14	21	42
Very Heavy work	14	21	42

Failure to Recover

If an individual fails to recover within the maximum duration expectancy period, the reader may wish to reference the following questions to assist in better understanding the specifics of an individual's medical case.

Regarding diagnosis:

- Has individual recently had an injury, surgery, or injection to the affected joint?
- Does individual have osteoarthritis or rheumatoid arthritis?
- Was there recent exposure to bacteria, viruses, or fungi?
- Does individual complain of fever, chills, pain, heat, weakness, or swelling in the joint?
- Were joints involved?
- Does individual also report red sores on the palms and soles, a rash, and pain in the wrists and ankles?
- On physical exam, did individual have swelling in the joint with inflamed tendons?

- Does individual have fever and reduced range of motion in the joint?
- Was serology testing done? Was a needle aspiration performed for culture and microscopic examination? Were throat, urethral, or rectal cultures done?
- Was x-ray or biopsy performed?
- Were conditions with similar symptoms ruled out?

Regarding treatment:

- Is individual being treated with antibiotics or antifungal medications?
- Was hospitalization necessary?
- Was individual's joint drained by arthrocentesis, arthrotomy, or arthroscopy?
- Is individual continuing drug therapy for up to 4 weeks?
- Is individual also being treated with analgesics and/or NSAIDs? Splints?
- Was physical therapy recommended?

Regarding prognosis:

- Is individual active in physical therapy? Is a home exercise program in place?
- Can individual's employer accommodate any necessary restrictions?
- Does individual have any conditions that may affect ability to recover?
- Have any complications developed such as acute respiratory distress, permanent damage of the affected joint, multiple joint involvement, erythema nodosum, or chronic infectious arthritis?

References

"Septic Arthritis." Dale, D.C., and Daniel D. Federman, MD New York: WebMD Corporation, 2000 Scientific American Medicine. 01 Feb 2001 <http://www.samed.com/sam/forms/index.htm>.

Arthritis and Other Rheumatic Diseases: Infectious Arthritis. Spartanburg Regional Healthcare System. 2000. 08 Jan 2001 <http://www.srhs.com/clinical/arthritis/infect.html>.

Dwyer, Edward. Non-gonococcal Infectious Arthritis. eMedicine.com. 05 Oct 2000. 08 Jan 2001 <http://emedicine.com/med/topic2935_1.htm>.

Schmid, Frank R., and Frederick Matsen III, eds. "Infectious Arthritis." University of Washington Department of Orthopaedics. 2000. 08 Jan 2001 <http://www.orthop.washington.edu/BoneJoint/zxtzzzzz1_1.html>.

Arthrodesis

Other names / synonyms: Artificial Ankylosis, Joint Fusion
81, 81.11, 81.20, 81.21, 81.22, 81.23, 81.26

Definition

The term arthrodesis describes the surgical fusion of a joint so that it is no longer capable of movement. Basically, the arthrodesis procedure is an artificially induced fusion of bones across a joint (ankylosis) performed to relieve pain or provide support in a diseased (such as in osteoarthritis) or injured joint.

Arthrodesis has been used to create fusions that ultimately relieve pain and provide stability in the ankle, wrist, knee, shoulder, hip, and other joints. By the time afflicted individuals present for surgery, they usually have little motion left in their arthritic joints and have adapted to living without the motion. Most of them are, therefore, grateful for the pain relief. As artificial joint replacement technique and implants for any joint improve, fewer arthrodeses but more joint replacements of that joint are performed.

According to reports issued by the Centers for Disease Control and Prevention (CDC) in 1998, over 1 million arthrodesis procedures were performed in the US; 468,000 on men; 625,000 on women. These statistics, which lumped together different kinds of arthrodeses, showed that the number of procedures was higher in the older age groups, with 550,000 procedures reported in the 65-years-and-over age group. From a geographic perspective, most of the procedures (356,000) were performed in the south region of the US while the numbers of procedures performed in the northeast, midwest, and west regions were considerable fewer but fairly equal among themselves.

Reason for Procedure

Arthrodesis is performed to control pain, to slow disease progression, to provide stability to a joint that has been damaged by arthritis or muscle weakness, and to correct deformity. Arthrodesis is also performed in individuals afflicted with poliomyelitis to reduce the number of joints the weakened or paralyzed muscles must control, and to treat progressive spinal deformity that does not respond to nonoperative treatment. Finally, arthrodesis is performed to enable individuals to return to productivity after the initial healing period is over.

Description

The technique of the arthrodesis procedure varies according to the type of arthrodesis (wrist, ankle, knee, hip, and shoulder joints) to be performed, but what the surgeon needs to achieve for the procedure to be successful is basically the same in most arthrodesis procedures. In general, arthrodeses are performed with the individual under general anesthesia and in a position that is conducive to the kind of arthrodesis being performed. There are two different techniques by which the bones in the joint are fused. For both techniques, the individual is deeply asleep and pain-free (general anesthesia). The surgeon makes an incision over the area to be treated and removes the joint surface on the bones on both sides of the joint (debridement). The purpose of the debridement of the bony surfaces is to increase surface contact area. For the first technique, the joint is then held stiff with a cast or metal hardware until the debride bone ends grow together (intra-articular arthrodesis).

For the second technique, fusion of the bone ends is achieved by implanting bone grafts along the side of the joint (extra-articular arthrodesis). For both techniques, the joint is required to be immobile and to rest for a defined period of time to allow for the fusion and healing to take place in and around the previous joint.

Prognosis

For most arthrodesis procedures, outcome after surgery tends to be quite successful.

According to The Journal of Foot and Ankle Surgery, it is generally accepted that the nonunion rate for a primary ankle arthrodesis is 10-20% and that, in spite of more advanced techniques and better appreciation of blood supply preservation, a certain number of individuals will require additional surgery.

In a recent study of 21 individuals who had undergone arthrodesis of part of the wrist joints, results were good for wrist strength (grip strength averaged 70% of the uninvolved wrist). Results were not so good for wrist motion. Range of motion averaged 35 degrees of extension, 30 degrees of flexion, 10 degrees of radial deviation, and 20 degrees of ulnar deviation. Most joints have no motion after an arthrodesis. Partial retained wrist motion occurs after a partial arthrodesis in that motion can still occur through the wrist joints not involved by fusion surgery. Results for pain reduction were good (eighty percent).

The studies that surveyed individuals who had undergone knee arthrodesis showed that the knee arthrodesis procedure provided a potential, stable base of support, at the expense of knee motion.

For individuals who had undergone shoulder arthrodesis, fusion rates of more than 90% have been consistently documented in the literature.

Individuals who have undergone hip arthrodesis are generally satisfied with the results of their hip fusion. Several long-term follow-up studies have documented patient satisfaction of approximately 70% at 30 years despite evidence of degenerative changes in the lumbar spine and adjacent joints of the lower extremities that typically manifest at 15 to 25 years after hip arthrodesis.

Specialists

- Hand Surgeon
- Orthopedic Surgeon
- Physiatrist
- Plastic Surgeon
- Podiatrist

Rehabilitation

The hand, wrist, and ankle are more commonly seen for rehabilitation following an arthrodesis; however, it is important to initially control postoperative pain and swelling for any joint fusion. This is followed by rehabilitating the individual to regain function of the body part involved. The physical therapist will use various methods to address postoperative symptoms.

Once solid fusion has occurred, strengthening of the muscles around the fused joint is important in regaining function of the associated limb. For example, the individual who has undergone an arthrodesis of the hip would benefit from strengthening exercises for the muscles that cross or are associated with the hip joint. This is because there are additional forces required of the muscles that compensate for the loss of the joint movement. This strengthening is important to the individual in returning to as normal walking patterns (gait) as possible. Instruction in the use of an assistive device such as a cane may be required shortly after surgery with progression to independent walking. Strengthening exercises are equally important for any arthrodesis performed on the upper extremities.

Modifications may need to be made by the physical therapist for those who have arthritis or other conditions near the joint that underwent arthrodesis. Rehabilitation will also vary depending upon the body part and joint(s) involved.

Work Restrictions / Accommodations

Work restrictions after arthrodesis depend on the kind of arthrodesis performed (i.e., ankle, wrist, knee, shoulder, and hip). In general, restrictions include limited or no use of joint and extremity during recovery. Use of assistive devices may be necessary, such as braces, crutches, and splints. Frequent rest periods that include elevation of the extremity are conducive to earlier return to full-time work.

The main accommodation is a review of drug policies at work, since the individual will have been prescribed medication for pain control and inflammation.

Comorbid Conditions

Obesity and cigarette smoking may lengthen disability. Osteoarthritis and nerve and muscle damage may also lengthen disability.

Procedure Complications

Complications of ankle arthrodesis include incomplete healing of the arthrodesis (nonunion, malunion).

Complications of wrist arthrodesis include loss of motion in wrist. For this reason, the procedure is relatively contraindicated in young, active individuals. Results from a recent study revealed mild degenerative changes in the radiocarpal joint in 2 of 21 individuals after a follow-up of 28 months.

Complications of knee arthrodesis include incomplete healing of the fusion (pseudoarthrosis or nonunion), the most frequent complication of knee arthrodesis. Indications from research are that the intramedullary nail may be the most reliable technique for achieving union. However, a recent study testing the nail reported nail breakage, nail migration, or bone fracture in 40-55% of cases studied.

Individuals who have undergone shoulder arthrodesis report loss of elbow motion, but this usually is temporary. Later postoperative complications include incomplete healing of the fusion (nonunion, malunion), painful hardware, and secondary onset of degenerative arthritis of the acromioclavicular joint. These complications are infrequent, as fusion rates of more than 90% have been consistently documented in the literature.

Complications of hip arthrodesis include increases in stress in the lumbar spine, contralateral hip, and ipsilateral knee; these increases require greater energy expenditure for walking and moving about (ambulation). It is important to point out that the extent of these complications is considerably greater for older, less than healthy individuals.

Factors Influencing Duration

Factors that might influence length of disability include the joint involved, tolerance of the resulting stiffness, underlying disease process and ability to modify work requirements after disability. The time to complete healing or fusion is variable, and at least some degree of disability will be present until the fusion is solidly healed.

Length of Disability

Duration of disability depends on underlying cause of the condition and the joint involved. In some cases, disability may be permanent.

References

Bonner, Felix, and Richard Worrell. Orthopaedics: Principles of Basic and Clinical Science. New York: CRC Press, 1999.

Canale, S. Terry, Kay S. Daugherty, and Linda Jones, eds. Campbell's Operative Orthopaedics, 9th ed. Carlsbad, CA: Mosby, Inc, 1998. 20 Feb 2001 <http://home.mdconsult.com/ >.

Koopman, William J. Arthritis and Allied Conditions, 13th ed. Philadelphia: Williams & Wilkins, 1997. 20 Feb 2001 <http://home.mdconsult.com/ >.

Popovic, J.R., and L.J. Kozak. National Hospital Discharge Survey: Annual Summary, 1998. National Center for Health Statistics. 01 Sep 2000. 15 Dec 2000 <http://www.cdc.gov/nchs/data/sr13_148.pdf>.

Scully, Rosemary M., and Marylou R. Barnes. Physical Therapy. Philadelphia : J.B. Lippincott Company, 1989.

Pell, R.F., MD. "Clinical Outcome After Primary Triple Arthrodesis." Wheeless' Textbook of Orthopaedics. 82-A 01 Jan 2000. 23 Oct 2000 <http://www.medmedia.com/oo3/170.htm>.

Arthrography

Other names / synonyms: Arthrogram
88.32

Definition

Arthrography is the use of dye (contrast material) injected into joints that allows the visualization of anatomical structures that do not normally appear on x-ray. When the contrast material is injected into the joint capsule, it floats around, over and under soft tissue, and casts a shadow on the x-ray film. The x-ray shows an outline of the structure. Arthrograms are interpreted by comparison with normal anatomy outlines. Abnormal changes such as ligament tears, ruptured bursal sacs, cartilage (meniscus) tears, and decreased joint space are then noted.

The use of CT and MRI have almost entirely replaced the arthrogram, although arthrograms are ordered most frequently for studies of the wrist. Some individuals cannot undergo MRI scanning because of cardiac pacemakers, metallic clips on intracranial arteries, or severe claustrophobia. Arthrography may be used instead of MRI in those individuals.

Reason for Procedure

Arthrography is a diagnostic procedure used to evaluate joint anatomy; specifically, soft tissue integrity.

Description

In this procedure, dye (contrast material) is injected directly into the joint space using a needle. X-rays are then taken. A radiologist or orthopedic surgeon then reads the x-rays to confirm the diagnosis. This procedure can be performed as an outpatient, and usually requires no anesthetic.

Prognosis

This is a diagnostic procedure. As such, the outcome of the procedure should be the gaining of additional information about the condition.

Specialists

- Orthopedic Surgeon
- Radiologist

Work Restrictions / Accommodations

Limited use of the extremity involved until pain and swelling have resolved may be necessary.

Comorbid Conditions

Bleeding disorders, such as hemophilia or Von Willebrand's disease, may lead to excessive bleeding into the joint from this procedure, and would lengthen disability.

Procedure Complications

Infection of the joint and bleeding from the needle puncture are the main complications that may result from this procedure.

Factors Influencing Duration

The underlying diagnosis would determine need for any extended disability. Complications will prolong disability periods.

Length of Disability

No disability is expected for a normal arthrogram. Duration may depend upon the cause (underlying condition) of abnormal arthrogram.

References

Day, Lorraine, MD, et al. "Orthopedics." Current Surgical Diagnosis and Treatment. Way, Lawrence Norwalk: Appleton & Lange, 1991. 986-1103.

Fongemie, Allen E., et al. "Management of Shoulder Impingement Syndrome and Rotator Cuff Tears." American Family Physician 5 6 (1998): 12. 24 Jan 2001 <http://www.aafp.org/afp/980215ap/fongemie.html>.

Arthroplasty, Elbow
Other names / synonyms: Elbow Replacement
81.84, 81.85

Definition

An elbow arthroplasty is a surgical procedure designed to either restructure the elbow joint or replace a diseased or seriously injured elbow joint with a prosthetic device made of metal and polyurethane.

The two types of arthroplasty are resection and total replacement. Resection arthroplasty corrects the elbow defect by surgically modifying the elbow. The four procedures that fall under the descriptive name of resection arthroplasty include limited, complete, functional, and interpositional arthroplasty. These procedures differ with regard to the extent of surgery and method for elbow reconstruction.

Total replacement arthroplasty replaces both sides of the elbow joint with artificial devices (prosthesis). Individuals with osteoarthritis, rheumatoid arthritis, and those who previously sustained an elbow injury are the most likely individuals to require elbow arthroplasty at some point. Elbow arthroplasty is therefore more commonly performed on the elderly than the young.

Reason for Procedure

Although the primary indications for elbow arthroplasty are pain, joint instability, and limited range of motion, pain relief is the primary goal. These procedures are performed to relieve pain and stiffness associated with degenerative osteoarthritis, rheumatoid arthritis, or post-traumatic arthritis that has failed to respond to medical treatment. It is occasionally used to treat severely fractured elbows.

Limited resection arthroplasty is performed on individuals with minimal damage to the elbow. Although rarely used, complete resection arthroplasty and functional resection arthroplasty are reserved for individuals with more extensive joint damage or severe joint infection. Interpositional arthroplasty is used to treat individuals with chronic pain who have failed to achieve adequate range of motion and where there is damage to more than 50% of the joint (articular) surface. Total replacement arthroplasty is used to treat individuals with severe pain and weakness caused by joint instability or those who have elbow immobility (ankylosis).

Limited and interpositional arthroplasties are less traumatic to the joint and the individual, and may be preferred over a total replacement arthroplasty. In some cases, resection arthroplasty may be tried first and then, if not successful, a total replacement arthroplasty may be performed. In general, resection arthroplasty is reserved for the younger individual and total replacement arthroplasty for the older individual.

Description

All arthroplasty procedures are performed under general anesthesia. The individual is usually lying on the back with the target arm lying across the chest. The affected joint is exposed and care is taken to avoid damage to the ulnar nerve. A limited resection arthroplasty involves minimal surgery such as the removal of the joint membrane (synovial membrane) or tip of the outer forearm bone (radius).

Complete resection arthroplasty removes the entire elbow joint leaving it essentially nonfunctional. For functional arthroplasty, the segment of the upper arm bone (humerus) at the elbow is fashioned into a sort of wedge that allows some forearm motion. Interpositional arthroplasty attempts to preserve the functional stability of the joint and reduce the likelihood of joint immobility or stiffness (re-ankylosis) by placing a membranous tissue (e.g., muscle, fat, skin, or tendon) between the bones that make up the joint. Before placing the interpositional membrane in place, the joint surface may require reconstruction to smooth out abnormal bone elements, insert screws or bone grafts, or relocate the ulnar nerve to avoid later nerve entrapment, pain, and weakness.

Once complete, a distraction device involving a threaded pin placed through the elbow joint may be useful during the first 3 to 4 weeks following the procedure to aid in preserving the range of motion achieved on the operating table.

In total replacement arthroplasty, the joint end of the humerus and inner forearm bone (ulna) are removed and channels are drilled into the center of the bones. The prosthetic devices are then cemented into the channels forming a new joint. Several types of joint prostheses are available. They are designed to provide full mobility (unconstrained), some mobility restrictions (semiconstrained), or no mobility (constrained). The choice of device depends on the extent of the disease process, what condition or disease is present (trauma, osteoarthritis, or rheumatoid arthritis), specific needs of the individual, and the experience of the surgeon. Following any type of arthroplasty, the elbow is immobilized in a straight (extended) or bent (flexed) position for a few days. Antibiotics and analgesics are provided, as needed.

Prognosis

Elbow arthroplasty has a good outcome. Total replacement arthroplasty has a more favorable outcome than any of the resection arthroplasty procedures. Of the resection arthroplasties, interposition arthroplasty has the best outcome with a 70% success rate. Between 90-95% of individuals undergoing total replacement arthroplasty experience relief of joint pain and improved elbow function. Although up to 25% of individuals undergoing elbow arthroplasty experience ulnar nerve damage, in most cases the effect is temporary.

Specialists

- Neurosurgeon
- Occupational Therapist
- Orthopedic Surgeon
- Physical Therapist
- Rheumatologist

Rehabilitation

Individuals who experienced total elbow arthroplasty require inpatient physical therapy for the days immediately following surgery. Swelling in the hand and forearm may decrease if the individual wears a sling or elevates the hand on a pillow. Therapists should also encourage movement of the shoulder, wrist, and hand to decrease swelling since the elbow is immobilized.

Outpatient therapy may occurs once an individual is discharged from the hospital. The first goal of therapy is to reduce pain and swelling. Hot packs are applied to the elbow prior to therapy for pain control and muscle relaxation. Ice packs are applied to the elbow after therapy, as needed, to decrease pain and swelling.

The second goal of therapy is to increase range of motion of the elbow and forearm. Individuals perform active-assisted elbow flexion with the forearm in neutral, pronated, and supinated positions. Therapists also passively straighten the elbow to help increase elbow extension. Individuals perform active forearm pronation and supination with the elbow bent to 90 degrees.

The final goal of therapy is to increase strength in the elbow and forearm. After 4 weeks, individuals may begin elbow extension against gravity and after 6 weeks, resistance exercises may begin. Individuals perform elbow flexion with the forearm in neutral, pronated, and supinated positions. Elbow extension exercises may be performed in addition to forearm pronation and supination with either manual or weighted resistance.

Work Restrictions / Accommodations

Individuals with jobs that require heavy lifting or strenuous activities involving the arm will need temporary reassignment to sedentary duties. The elbow may be immobilized during the recovery period temporarily making the individual unable to operate equipment or perform other tasks that require use of both hands. If the dominant arm was affected, the individual may be unable to write legibly, type well, or perform activities that require fine motor skills such as those needed to work in a laboratory or on an assembly line. Following the immobilization period, individuals may be advised to not lift more than 5 pounds for 3 months. The individual may be advised to never again lift more than 10 pounds with the affected arm. For individuals with positions that require heavy work and those who received a semiconstrained or constrained prosthetic joint, disability may be permanent necessitating a change in occupational responsibilities.

Comorbid Conditions

The condition for which elbow arthroplasty was performed (e.g., osteoarthritis, osteoporosis, or cancer), bleeding disorders (e.g., hemophilia), and if applicable, other injuries (e.g., fractures, lacerations, or damage to ligaments or cartilage) sustained during the traumatic event may influence the length of disability.

Procedure Complications

Complications associated with any elbow arthroplasty procedure include superficial or deep infection, dislocation, fracture, joint instability, bone spurs (exostosis), triceps muscle weakness or rupture, collection of serum (seroma) or blood (hematoma) in the tissues, and long-term failure (i.e., pain, joint stiffening, and joint instability). Damage to the ulnar nerve can lead to arm weakness and temporary burning or prickling sensations (paresthesia) in the arm. Loosening, breakage, or failure of the prosthesis are additional complications associated with total replacement procedures.

Factors Influencing Duration

Factors include the type of operation performed, the underlying disease for which the procedure was performed, development of complications, individual's compliance with therapy and rehabilitation recommendations, individual's job requirements, and whether the dominant or nondominant arm was involved.

Length of Disability

Duration depends on job requirements and may be permanent if heavy lifting is involved. If total elbow replacement is performed, individuals may be permanently restricted to sedentary work and/or modified duty.

Resection of radial head.

Duration in Days

Job Classification	Minimum	Optimum	Maximum
Sedentary work	14	28	56
Light work	14	28	56
Medium work	21	42	70
Heavy work	28	42	84
Very Heavy work	28	56	112

References

Cooney, William. "Elbow Arthroplasty: Historical Perspectives and Current Concepts." The Elbow and Its Disorders. Morrey, Bernard, ed. Philadelphia: W.B. Saunders Company, 2000. 583-601.

Kisner, Carolyn, and Lynn Allen Colby. "The Elbow and Forearm Complex." Therapeutic Exercise: Foundations and Techniques, 2nd ed. Philadelphia: F.A. Davis, 1990. 273-288.

Morrey, Bernard. "Complications of Elbow Replacement Surgery." The Elbow and Its Disorders. Philadelphia: W.B. Saunders Company, 2000. 667-677.

Nestor, Bryan, and Mark Figgie. "Elbow Arthritis: Surgical Treatment." Clinical Orthopaedics. Craig, Edward, ed. Philadelphia: Lippincott, Williams & Wilkins, 1999. 260-273.

Arthroscopy

Other names / synonyms: Joint Endoscopy, Scope

80.2, 80.20, 80.21, 80.22, 80.23, 80.24, 80.25, 80.26, 80.27, 80.28, 80.29

Definition

Arthroscopy literally means looking into a joint. The procedure involves inserting a small tube with lenses at each end, much like a periscope, attached to a fiberoptic light system into the joint space to visualize the interior of the joint. Either the surgeon can look directly through the lenses (the arthroscope) into the joint, or, more commonly, the picture is transmitted through a small video camera to a TV monitor.

A common misconception is that the arthroscope is a tool used to perform surgery. The "scope" is only used for visualization, and other small instruments are inserted into the joint to actually perform the surgery. Some fluid or gas (irrigation) must be infused into the joint to expand the space and help clear debris. Special solutions or gases are used depending on the joint being examined and the associated procedure planned. The result is 2 or more small incisions to insert the arthroscope, the irrigation fluid, and the surgical instruments. In very small joints, a special tube (cannula) is used to accommodate all the equipment necessary to perform the arthroscopy and associated surgical procedure.

Any joint can be examined using the arthroscope, most commonly the knee and shoulder. Other joints include the elbow, wrist, hip, ankle, temporomandibular (TMJ) and spine. Procedures that follow the arthroscopy range from removal of loose floating cartilage material (removal of loose bodies) to major reconstructive procedures.

Another common misconception is that if a procedure is done arthroscopically, it is a minor procedure with limited disability. While, in general, recovery is quicker for surgery done arthroscopically as opposed to "open" surgery, it is important to understand that using the arthroscope sometimes makes the procedure technically more difficult, and the associated procedure may be just as disabling as one done through larger incisions.

Using arthroscopic-assisted techniques for many surgical procedures by various surgical physician specialists has gained wide acceptance both by patients and physicians. The decision to use this technique will be based on surgeon training, availability of specialized equipment with well trained staff and agreement between physician and individual. Injuries, diseases or conditions affecting joints of the body could be appropriate choices for arthroscopic examination and arthroscopically assisted surgical procedures.

Reason for Procedure

The procedure is used for diagnostic reasons as well as to assist with or perform surgical techniques. Using the arthroscope to assist the surgeon may allow for less soft tissue damage than an open procedure, decreased postoperative pain and shorter hospital stay. Under direct visualization structures can be palpated, probed, removed, irrigated, repaired, débrided, or abraded. Associated procedures are often scheduled as diagnostic arthroscopy with a "possible (named) procedure" to follow. The "possible procedure" scheduled to follow the diagnostic arthroscopy would be based on clinical examination and test results before surgery.

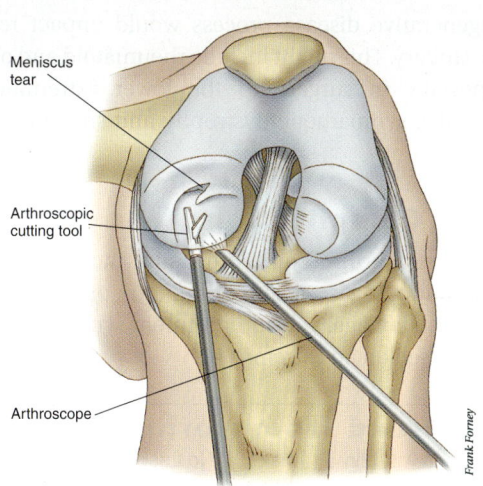

Description

Through small skin incisions, the arthroscope is introduced into the joint capsule and then, most commonly, attached to a video monitor. The joint capsule is first expanded with either fluid or gas, passed into and out of the joint capsule via small tubes. The fluid pressure is maintained either by pumps or gravity. Draining the fluid clears the visual field of blood and debris created during surgery. Surgical instruments used to cut, scrape, or remove tissue are inserted through another hole (portal) in the skin. Depending upon the procedure, tissue may be repaired, removed, or altered in some way. Orthopedic hardware may be inserted or removed, holes drilled and fixation verified as well. The arthroscope is used only to look into the joint, the actual surgical procedure is done with other instruments. The surgical procedure may require many small incisions (portals) through which various instruments are passed.

Arthroscopy may be performed under local, regional, or general anesthesia. The procedure is done in physician offices, ambulatory surgical centers, hospital outpatient facilities, and as inpatient stays. The type of anesthesia and location of the surgery is dependent on surgeon, anesthesiologist, and individual preference, physical condition of the individual, and expected associated procedures.

Prognosis

Problems being treated during an arthroscopic procedure dictate the possible outcome and vary tremendously. Anticipated results will vary from complete cure, to relief of pain either permanently or temporarily, to allowing for the staging or timing of multiple procedures. It is important for both the individual and physician to accept and agree on the expected outcome.

Specialists

- Dentist
- Hand Surgeon
- Neurosurgeon
- Oral Surgeon
- Orthopedic Surgeon
- Rheumatologist
- Thoracic Surgeon

Work Restrictions / Accommodations

Restrictions and accommodations depend on the underlying diagnosis, treatment, and outcome.

Comorbid Conditions

Ongoing degenerative disease process would impact recovery from arthroscopic surgery. This might include rheumatoid and osteoarthritis. Obesity, especially in surgery to the lower extremities, diabetes, neuropathy, reflex sympathetic dystrophy and smoking could impact recovery.

Procedure Complications

Complications from arthroscopic procedure include infection, nerve damage, absorption of gases used for inflation of the joint, collapse of lung, blood vessel damage, and compartment syndrome (especially if a tourniquet was used on an extremity).

Factors Influencing Duration

The associated procedure, underlying diagnosis, amount of joint swelling and postoperative pain affect the disability period. Any complication would add disability time. Some procedures associated with arthroscopy require extensive rehabilitation for recovery. Functional activities and weight bearing may also be restricted for several weeks after surgery, especially in procedures to the lower extremities and shoulders.

Length of Disability

The length of disability depends on the underlying diagnosis, site (joint), whether scope is used for diagnostic purposes or whether a surgical procedure is also performed.

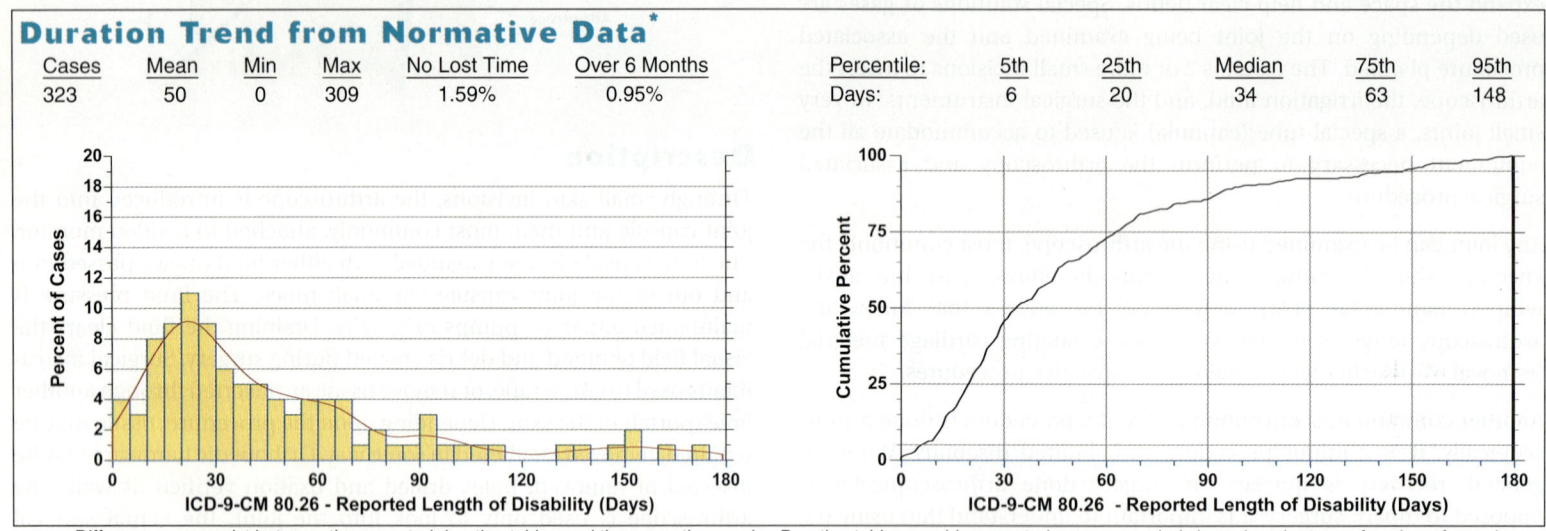

Duration Trend from Normative Data*

Cases	Mean	Min	Max	No Lost Time	Over 6 Months
323	50	0	309	1.59%	0.95%

Percentile:	5th	25th	Median	75th	95th
Days:	6	20	34	63	148

ICD-9-CM 80.26 - Reported Length of Disability (Days)

* Differences may exist between the expected duration tables and the normative graphs. Duration tables provide expected recovery periods based on the type of work performed by the individual. The normative graphs reflect the actual observed experience of many individuals across the spectrum of physical conditions, in a variety of industries, and with varying levels of case management.

References

DeLee, Jesse MD, and David M. Drez Jr., MD. Orthopedic Sports Medicine, Principles and Practice, Vol.1. Philadelphia: W.B. Saunders Company, 1994.

Asbestosis

Other names / synonyms: Asbestos Pneumoconiosis
501, 989.81

Definition

Asbestosis is a chronic lung condition caused by inhalation of asbestos particles (also called asbestosis dust). Asbestos is a commercial product derived from a naturally occurring group of minerals that form strong, flexible, and heat- and acid-resistant fibers. When asbestos particles are inhaled, they irritate the lung tissue. This irritation results in inflammation as the body tries to rid itself of the irritating particles. Prolonged inflammation leads to scarring of the lung tissue (pulmonary fibrosis) and eventually results in decreased lung capacity.

Asbestosis is associated with an increased risk of lung cancer. Studies have shown that the combination of smoking and asbestos exposure is particularly hazardous. A smoker exposed to asbestos fibers is at least 50 times more likely to develop lung cancer than a nonsmoker exposed to asbestos.

The risk to workers increases with heavier exposure and longer exposure time. The most at-risk occupations include miners and millers of asbestos, plumbers, pipefitters, steamfitters, electricians, insulation workers, carpenters, laborers (except construction), supervisors of precision production occupations, boilermakers, welders and cutters, and janitors and cleaners. Workers who may not have worked directly with asbestos but whose jobs were located near contaminated areas may also develop asbestosis. However, not all workers exposed to asbestos will develop the disease.

There tends to be a long gap between exposure to asbestosis dust and the onset of symptoms of asbestosis. In fact, it is common for 20 years or more to pass before symptoms are noted. Although fewer than ten new cases of asbestosis are diagnosed per 100,000 individuals in the US each year, it is estimated that more than one million individuals have been exposed to significant levels of asbestos fibers in the US. There were 876 deaths in the US attributed to asbestosis between 1979 and 1992. Production of asbestosis products peaked in the 1970s and, given the long latency period, the incidence of asbestosis is likely to increase over the next several years.

Men are more commonly affected than women since their occupations have a higher risk of asbestos exposure. The disease tends to occur predominantly between the ages of 40 to 75.

Diagnosis

History: The individual may describe a history of exposure to asbestos. However, symptoms may occur long after exposure and the individual may not link the two together. Symptoms may include shortness of breath, a cough or change in cough pattern, blood in the fluid coughed up from the lungs (sputum), pain in the chest or abdomen, difficulty in swallowing, prolonged hoarseness, or significant weight loss. Some individuals will not have any symptoms. In these cases, the diagnosis is usually made following routine chest x-ray, physical examination and/or test results.

Physical exam: Listening through a stethoscope (auscultation) may reveal changes in breath sounds (crackling) that indicate inflammatory lung disease. Slight swelling and discoloration of the nail beds (clubbing) may be noted. The skin may appear bluish gray (cyanosis) and signs of right-sided heart failure (prominence of the veins in the neck and swelling of the feet and ankles) may be noted.

Tests: Chest x-rays may reveal changes in the lungs. If x-ray films reveal any shadows on the lungs suggestive of early asbestosis, the individual is advised to stop working with asbestos even if no symptoms are present. A high resolution CT scan of the lungs is the best, non-invasive method for diagnosis may be ordered. Tests to evaluate lung capacity and function (pulmonary function tests) can assist in the diagnosis. These studies include spirometry and lung volume measurements (to detect any restriction of normal lung expansion or obstruction of air flow), blood gases (to assess the efficiency of gas exchange in the lungs), and diffusing capacity (to assess the efficiency of oxygen transportation from the lungs into the blood).

Treatment

Once asbestosis has developed, there is no effective cure. Damage to lung tissue is permanent and is often progressive. There is no treatment for asbestosis. Oxygen therapy may help minimize symptoms and/or cor pulmonale. Exposure to asbestos should be eliminated or minimized by using protective measures. Influenza and pneumococcal vaccines are often administered to reduce the risk of these infections. If the individual is a smoker, smoking should be stopped. The individual should also be informed of the risks and associated signs and symptoms of lung cancer and tuberculosis. In severe or advanced cases, lung transplant may be indicated.

Prognosis

The outcome of asbestosis is dependent on the combination of exposure duration, the degree to which the ability of the lungs to take up oxygen is impaired, and the presence or absence of complications. Individuals with a history of significant asbestos exposure over an extended period of time are more likely to experience more severe disease. Lung damage is permanent and usually results in some degree of disability. Death is a possibility. If a lung transplant is performed, the individual may experience a resolution of symptoms. Lung cancer is also more common among individuals with asbestosis.

Differential Diagnosis

Conditions with similar symptoms include lung diseases from exposure to other inorganic, fibrogenic dusts. Examples of these types of lung diseases include siderosis (inhalation of iron particles), stannosis (inhalation of tin oxide), baritosis (inhalation of barium dust), coal worker's pneumoconiosis, silicosis (inhalation of silica dust), talcosis (inhalation of talc), and Shaver's disease (a pneumoconiosis due to inhalation of bauxite).

Specialists

- Occupational Medicine Physician
- Pulmonologist

Work Restrictions / Accommodations

The individual should be removed from contact with asbestos dust. Prolonged sick leave may be required in severe cases particularly if a lung transplant is performed. Individuals whose jobs require strenuous or prolonged exercise or activity may need to be reassigned to a more sedentary position depending on their lung capacity and oxygenation status, especially when tested during or after exercise. If oxygen therapy is required, the individual should not work with certain flammable materials.

Comorbid Conditions

Pre-existing lung infections or comorbid lung disease can lengthen the period of disability.

Complications

Individuals with asbestosis are at an increased risk for pneumonia, lung cancer, and possibly colon cancer.

Factors Influencing Duration

Length of disability may be influenced from severity of symptoms, individual's overall health, history of smoking, or any complications.

Length of Disability

Duration of disability depends on severity, degree of fibrosis, and the individual's job requirements. Disability may also be permanent depending on the extent of damage to lung tissue and resultant impaired pulmonary function.

Duration in Days

Job Classification	Minimum	Optimum	Maximum
Sedentary work	0	7	14
Light work	0	7	14
Medium work	0	14	Indefinite
Heavy work	0	84	Indefinite
Very Heavy work	0	84	Indefinite

Failure to Recover

If an individual fails to recover within the maximum duration expectancy period, the reader may wish to reference the following questions to assist in better understanding the specifics of an individual's medical case.

Regarding diagnosis:

- Does individual with asbestosis have a history (either recent or long ago) of exposure to asbestos, particularly in the workplace?
- Does individual smoke or have a history of smoking?
- Does individual complain of shortness of breath, a cough or change in cough pattern, blood in the fluid coughed up from the lungs (sputum), pain in the chest or abdomen, difficulty swallowing, prolonged hoarseness, or significant weight loss?
- Did the physician hear changes in breath sounds (crackling) when listening to the lung with a stethoscope (auscultation)?
- Does individual exhibit slight swelling and discoloration of the nail beds (clubbing)?
- Does skin appear bluish gray?
- Was a chest x-ray taken and pulmonary function tests done? What were the results?
- Were arterial blood gases (ABGs) drawn to assess the efficiency of gas exchange in the lungs?
- Was the diagnosis of asbestosis confirmed?

Regarding treatment:

- Has further exposure to asbestos been eliminated or minimized by using protective measures?
- Has medication to open the airways (bronchodilators) been given? Is individual compliant with the medication regimen?
- Is home oxygen therapy required, based on the severity of symptoms and the blood oxygen level?
- Has individual been counseled about smoking cessation, if appropriate?

Regarding prognosis:

- How long was/has individual been exposed to asbestos?
- How severely impaired are the lungs? If very severe, is individual a candidate for lung transplant?
- Would individual be willing to participate in a smoking cessation program, if appropriate?
- Does individual have underlying illnesses that could be preventing improvement?
- Has individual developed pneumonia, tuberculosis, or lung cancer? If any of these complications have occurred, how will they be treated? What is expected outcome of the complication with treatment?

References

Asbestosis and Silicosis Surveillance. Texas Department of Health. 09 Oct 2000. <http://www.tdh.state.tx.us/epidemiology/assp.html>.

Silicosis and Asbestosis. Professional Health and Safety Consultants, Ltd. 09 Oct 2000. <http://www.healthandsafety.co.uk/silasb.htm>.

Ascites

Other names / synonyms: Hydroperitoneum

789.5

Definition

The term ascites refers to abnormal fluid accumulation in the abdominal cavity (peritoneal cavity).

The most common cause of ascites is elevated pressure in the liver circulation (portal hypertension) and accounts for over 80% of ascites cases. The elevated pressure causes leakage of fluid from the vessels in and around the liver into the abdominal cavity. By a similar process, severe congestive heart failure causes elevated pressure in the venous system that may also cause ascites. Ascites secondary to congestive heart failure however, is infrequent.

In the absence of portal hypertension, ascites can be associated with disorders involving the inner lining of the abdomen (peritoneum). The role of the peritoneum is to filter fluid moving through the abdominal cavity. Damage to this membrane often results in accumulation of fluid (ascites). Abdominal tumors, particularly ovarian tumors, can spread to the peritoneum and cause ascites. Tuberculosis can infect the peritoneum and result in ascites.

Chronic renal failure (nephrotic syndrome, chronic glomerulonephritis) can also be associated with ascites. Individuals on dialysis (hemodialysis) can have ascites. Inflammation of the pancreas or gallbladder with leakage of their secretions and contents into the abdomen can result in ascites.

Less frequent causes are diseases of the small intestine where protein is chronically lost from the body. In rare cases, severe underactivity of the thyroid gland (hypothyroidism) may cause ascites. An accumulation of fluid from the lymph system can occur when the lymph circulation becomes blocked by a tumor, thereby creating an ascites called chylous ascites.

Healthy men have little or no fluid in the peritoneal cavity, while women may have small amounts of fluid near the time of their menstrual cycle. With the exception of ascites from ovarian cancer in women, the exact prevalence of each disorder causing ascites is difficult to ascertain.

Diagnosis

History: Individuals may report that their belts or clothes are becoming tight around the waist or they experience a sudden weight gain. The individual may complain of generalized, constant, abdominal discomfort or pain. They may reveal a history of chronic illness such as hepatitis, alcoholic liver disease, congestive heart failure, or kidney failure. If the abdomen is severely distended, the individual may have difficulty breathing, especially when lying down.

Physical exam: The exam reveals mild to marked distention of the abdomen. The abdomen may feel firm or produce a wavelike action when touched (fluid wave). If there is pre-existing liver disease, the abdominal wall veins may be distended and clearly visible. In addition, the skin may appear yellow (jaundice); small veins may be visible on the nose, cheeks and upper chest (spider angiomata); and the palms may appear red or liver-colored.

The individual may look pale with thin extremities and may have rapid respirations. The neck veins may be distended, an indication of congestive heart failure. Generalized swelling (anasarca) may be present in congestive heart failure or renal failure. A fever may be present if the ascites is due to an infectious process. Firm lymph nodes near the left clavicle or around the umbilicus suggest abdominal cancer.

Tests: Ultrasound imaging of the abdomen can confirm the presence of ascites. Both ultrasound and CT scanning of the abdomen can be useful in identifying the cause of ascites. Withdrawing some of the ascites fluid with a needle through the abdominal wall (paracentesis) to evaluate the composition of the fluid is also useful in identifying the cause of ascites. A complete blood count may be done to determine if infection is present. Liver enzymes can confirm liver dysfunction. Elevated blood amylase levels may indicate inflammation of the pancreas. Blood urea nitrogen (BUN) and blood creatinine levels may be elevated in kidney failure.

Treatment

In addition to managing the underlying cause, treatment is directed at eliminating the excess fluid and preventing its reoccurrence. Initial treatment usually involves the use of diuretics. Withdrawing large amounts of the fluid through a needle (therapeutic paracentesis) can be done for those who do not respond to diuretic therapy. Those with ascites secondary to chronic liver failure may require surgical intervention to shunt ascites fluid into a large vein (peritoneovenous shunting). Another procedure done with x-ray guidance uses a catheter in the vein to place a shunt. This procedure (transjugular intrahepatic portosystemic shunt [TIPS]) has been proposed as a nonsurgical alternative to the peritoneovenous shunt in treating refractory ascites. Liver transplantation remains the most definitive therapy for liver disease and underlying ascites.

Prognosis

The predicted outcome depends on the underlying disease process. Since ascites is usually caused by a chronic, progressive disease process, the outlook is not good unless something can be done to correct the underlying disease. Of those with ascites secondary to liver failure, 50% will die within 2 years regardless of therapeutic intervention.

Therapeutic paracentesis is safe and effective in removing small to moderate amounts of ascitic fluid. Because this procedure carries the risk of abdominal infection and can cause low blood pressure or shock, it may not be appropriate for those with severe or refractory ascites. Peritoneovenous shunting is effective in reducing the ascites but carries an operative mortality rate of up to 30%. While relatively new, the TIPS procedure effectively reduces ascites in over 50% of the cases without the risk of surgery. However, following the TIPS procedure, over 30% developed shunt failure due to occlusion, and over 20% developed metabolic brain dysfunction (encephalopathy).

Outcome and survival vary following liver transplantation. The 6-month survival after liver transplantation in clinically stable individuals with chronic liver failure is as high as 90%. Critically ill individuals at the time of transplantation have a 6-month survival of only 65%.

Differential Diagnosis

Other possibilities are obesity, abdominal tumor, bowel obstruction, a dilated, distended colon (megacolon), or inflammatory bowel disease.

Specialists

- Gastroenterologist
- Hepatologist
- Internist

Work Restrictions / Accommodations

If an individual with ascites is able to work, they will most likely be restricted to sedentary work. Access to a restroom is needed for those receiving diuretic therapy. Most will require close medical follow-up with frequent trips to the doctor. Deteriorating physical and mental capacity is a potential problem in those with liver failure. Job assignments may need to be adjusted accordingly (i.e., eliminate operation of machinery). The treating physician(s) must determine further restrictions and accommodations related to the underlying cause of the ascites.

Complementary and Alternative Therapies

Content is intended for awareness only. Treatments may or may not be effective. Scientific evidence may be lacking and some substances have potentially toxic effects. Dr. Presley Reed and the editors do not endorse the use of these therapies in the absence of consultation with a licensed medical professional.

Milk thistle - Purported to have protective effects on the liver. It is available in the US and was approved for use by European councils and for the treatment of inflammatory liver diseases including alcoholic cirrhosis. Although it is not clear whether this therapy has any potential effect on ascites, individuals with ascites secondary to liver dysfunction may find it useful.

Comorbid Conditions

Comorbid conditions of liver, heart, kidney, and respiratory failure or cancer would impact the individual's ability to recover and thereby lengthen disability.

Complications

A serious complication is spontaneous bacterial peritonitis where the ascitic fluid may become infected without any identifiable cause or reason. Another complication of ascites is the movement of ascitic fluid into the lungs (hydrothorax) which can compromise breathing and cause respiratory failure especially in those with pre-existing lung disease. A weakening and outpouching of the abdominal wall (abdominal wall hernia) may also be a complication of ascites.

Factors Influencing Duration

The underlying disease process is the key factor in determining the course and length of disability.

Length of Disability

Duration depends on underlying cause. Contact physician for more information.

Failure to Recover

If an individual fails to recover within the maximum duration expectancy period, the reader may wish to reference the following questions to assist in better understanding the specifics of an individual's medical case.

Regarding diagnosis:

- Was there evidence of portal hypertension?
- Does individual have an abdominal or ovarian tumor?
- Does individual have tuberculosis that has infected the peritoneum?
- Was individual on dialysis? Have nephrotic syndrome? Chronic glomerulonephritis?
- Was there inflammation of the pancreas or gallbladder?
- Does individual have severe hypothyroidism?
- Was there sudden weight gain? Belt or clothes suddenly too tight?
- Does individual complain of generalized, constant, abdominal discomfort or pain?
- Was there a history of chronic illness such as hepatitis, alcoholic liver disease, congestive heart failure, or kidney failure?
- Does individual have difficulty breathing especially when lying down?
- On exam, was individual's abdomen distended? Firm? Was a fluid wave present?
- Are the veins of the abdominal wall distended? Is jaundice present? Spider angiomata?
- Do individual's palms appear red or liver-colored?
- Does individual look pale? Have thin extremities? Rapid respirations? Were the neck veins distended? Was there fever? Enlarged lymph nodes?
- Was generalized swelling (anasarca) present?
- Was abdominal ultrasound performed? CT? Was a paracentesis done and fluid analyzed? Was blood work, including CBC, liver enzymes, amylase, BUN, and blood creatinine, done?
- Were conditions with similar symptoms ruled out?

Regarding treatment:

- What is the underlying cause of the ascites? Is it being treated?
- Were diuretics used in an attempt to drain the fluid? Was a therapeutic paracentesis done?
- Has peritoneovenous shunting been considered? A transjugular intrahepatic portosystemic shunt [TIPS])?
- Is individual a candidate for a liver transplant?

Regarding prognosis:

- Can individual's employer accommodate any necessary restrictions?
- Does individual have any conditions that may affect ability to recover?
- Have any complications developed such as bacterial peritonitis, hydrothorax, or abdominal wall hernia?

References

Tierney, Lawrence M., Stephen J. McPhee, and Maxine A. Papadakis. Current Medical Diagnosis and Treatment, 39th ed. New York: Lange Medical Books/McGraw-Hill, 2000.

Aseptic Meningitis
Other names / synonyms: Serous Meningitis
047.9

Definition

Aseptic meningitis refers to a disease where the covering of the brain and spinal cord (meninges) becomes inflamed and is not the result of an acute bacterial infection. Because no bacterial organisms are found in the fluid surrounding the spinal cord and brain (cerebrospinal fluid or CSF), this type of meningitis is called aseptic.

About half of all cases of aseptic meningitis are caused by the viral subgroup enterovirus that includes the Coxsackie, echovirus, herpes type 1 and 2, rabies, and mumps viruses. Transmission is primarily fecal-oral with infection occurring across mucous membranes. After the virus has replicated within the gastrointestinal tract, the disease becomes established within the bloodstream. This is followed by viral crossover at the blood-brain barrier, allowing white blood cells and other inflammatory components into the cerebrospinal fluid (CSF).

Noninfective cases result from exposure to certain drugs, lead poisoning, reactions to vaccines, diseases of the meninges (e.g., brain tumors, stroke, multiple sclerosis, sarcoidosis, and leukemia), and infections from other nonbacterial microbes. Other forms of viral meningitis are epidemic and some are mosquito-borne (arboviruses such as St. Louis encephalitis). Meningitis may also occur as an immunologic complication of other viral infections such as chickenpox and measles.

This condition is a relatively rare syndrome usually seen from July through September. Only 1,000 to 2,000 new cases are reported yearly in the US. There is no racial or gender predilection, but populations that may be more susceptible include children or elderly individuals who interact or live in group settings. Causative viruses are only identified in about 11% of cases.

Diagnosis

History: The onset of symptoms may be acute (less than 24 hours) or subacute (occurring between 1 to 7 days). When an individual presents with acute meningitis, treatment must be initiated immediately with a more specific diagnosis made later. Individuals may relate a history of other viral infections occurring prior to showing symptoms of aseptic meningitis. They may have had exposure to mosquitoes or ticks, a systemic illness, exposure to tuberculosis, or traveled out of the country. Individuals may have used one of the medications that can cause the drug-induced form of the disease and includes certain anticancer drugs.

A headache and stiffness of the back and neck are the predominant initial symptoms. Other early symptoms may be vague and include fever and general discomfort and uneasiness (malaise). Additional symptoms associated with this disease are nausea and vomiting, muscle pain, hallucinations, decreased consciousness, confusion, and abnormal sensitivity to light (photophobia). If the condition progresses to encephalitis, cerebral dysfunction such as seizures, weakness, changes in consciousness or personality, and cranial nerve abnormalities may be reported.

Physical exam: Affected individuals generally have a headache, fever, and a stiff painful neck. Varying degrees of abnormal mental status may be evident and a full neurologic examination should be done. Although swelling of the optic disc (papilledema) is rare, a funduscopic examination should be done to look for this condition.

Tests: It is virtually impossible to clinically distinguish between bacterial and aseptic meningitis, therefore, the definitive diagnosis of aseptic meningitis is based on analysis of the CSF. CSF is withdrawn for examination during a procedure called a spinal tap. This fluid is studied for CSF cell count and component evaluation and for lactate levels. Diagnostic findings include normal glucose levels, mild elevation of protein, presence of a virus, and absence of bacteria upon culture.

Treatment

The most important aspect of treating aseptic meningitis is a fast and accurate diagnosis. Because there is no specific treatment for this condition, supportive therapy is aimed at reducing fever, rehydrating the individual, and correcting blood mineral levels (electrolytes). It also consists of managing any complications of encephalitis. Should encephalitis develop, the definitive therapy is slow, intravenous (IV) administration of antiviral drugs. The drugs should be started before the individual lapses into a coma and continued for at least 10 days. In severe cases, examination of the CSF removed during a spinal tap should be done immediately. While awaiting the results of the CSF analysis, therapy with broad-spectrum antibiotics (empiric antibiotic therapy) should be initiated.

Prognosis

Although severe cases can result in coma and death, complete recovery often occurs even in seriously ill individuals. Individuals with aseptic meningitis from other causes often recover spontaneously.

Differential Diagnosis

Acute bacterial meningitis can clinically resemble acute aseptic meningitis. However, bacteria will be identified in the CSF of individuals with bacterial meningitis.

Specialists

- Infectious Disease Physician
- Neurologist

Rehabilitation

Because individuals with aseptic meningitis suffer from mild influenza symptoms, no specific rehabilitation is usually necessary. Individuals may receive an evaluation from a physical therapist prior to discharge from the hospital. This is performed to determine if the individual has the strength and endurance necessary to safely walk and negotiate stairs without assistance.

Individuals with persistent neurological impairments such as poor coordination or decreased muscle tone may require physical and occupational therapy. Because individuals' neurological deficits may vary, the exact nature of physical and occupational therapy will vary. Physical therapy addresses any muscle weakness, balance deficits, and ambulatory difficulties that may arise. Individuals learn to safely get in and out of bed, rise from a chair, and get in and out of the bathtub. Individuals may learn to walk with a cane or walker if their balance remains unstable.

Occupational therapy addresses self-care strategies. Individuals learn to dress, bathe, and prepare meals in ways that adapt to their neurological impairment. For example, individuals with poor, fine motor coordination may begin to wear clothing with Velcro closures rather than buttons. Individuals may need to use a bathtub transfer bench and grab bars to safely use the bathtub. Individuals may need to prepare meals while sitting if their balance is impaired. Occupational therapists also teach cognitive strategies for individuals with impaired concentration. Individuals relearn vital tasks like making change, writing checks, and self-cueing to increase memory (e.g., making a list of tasks to be performed).

Work Restrictions / Accommodations

No accommodations are necessary as the individual will not work during this acute illness. If the individual has residual cerebral damage, work restrictions and accommodations are based on the type of damage and its severity.

Comorbid Conditions

Immunosuppressed individuals such as those on chemotherapy for cancer or those with AIDS are more susceptible to aseptic meningitis.

Complications

The development of cerebral dysfunction as a result of inadequate treatment or severe infection may complicate the disease. These cerebral dysfunction abnormalities include personality changes, alteration of consciousness, seizures, hearing loss, cranial nerve abnormalities, and neuromuscular impairments.

Factors Influencing Duration

The length of disability is influenced by the etiology of the meningitis, severity of the infection, age and health status of the individual, and any cerebral complications.

Length of Disability

Duration in Days

Job Classification	Minimum	Optimum	Maximum
Any work	14	21	42

Failure to Recover

If an individual fails to recover within the maximum duration expectancy period, the reader may wish to reference the following questions to assist in better understanding the specifics of an individual's medical case.

Regarding diagnosis:

- Does individual have a history of a recent viral infection?
- Was individual exposed to mosquitoes or ticks, a systemic illness, exposure to tuberculosis, or traveled out of the country?
- Was individual prescribed medications that can cause the drug-induced form of the disease?
- Does individual complain of a headache and stiffness of the back and neck?
- Does individual complain of fever and general discomfort and malaise?
- Does individual also have nausea and vomiting, muscle pain, hallucinations, decreased consciousness, confusion, and photophobia?
- Were seizures, weakness, changes in personality, or cranial nerve abnormalities noted?
- On exam, does individual have a fever and stiff painful neck?
- Was mental status altered? Was papilledema present?
- Was spinal tap with examination of the CSF performed?
- Were conditions with similar symptoms ruled out?

Regarding treatment:

- Is individual receiving supportive therapy while the diagnosis is being established?
- Has empiric antibiotic therapy been started?
- Is individual receiving anti-viral medication?

Regarding prognosis:

- If necessary, is individual active in rehabilitation?
- Does individual have any conditions that may affect ability to recover?
- Does individual have any complications such as personality changes, alteration of consciousness, seizures, hearing loss, cranial nerve abnormalities, or neuromuscular impairments?

References

Boss, Barbara J. "Alterations of Neurologic Function." Pathophysiology. McCance, Kathryn L., and Sue E. Heuther, eds. St. Louis: Mosby, 1994. 527-586.

Coyle, P.K. "Overview of acute and chronic meningitis." Neurology Clinics 17 4 (1999): 691-710.

O'Sullivan, Susan B. "Strategies to Improve Motor Control and Motor Learning." Physical Rehabilitation: Assessment and Treatment. O'Sullivan, Susan B., and Thomas J. Schmitz, eds. Philadelphia: F. A. Davis Company, 1994. 225-250.

Tunkel, Allan R., and W. Michael Scheld. "Acute Meningitis." Principles and Practice of Infectious Diseases, Fourth Edition, Volume 1. Mandell, Gerald L., John E. Bennett, and Raphael Dolin, eds. New York: Churchill Livingstone, 1995. 831-865.

Aspiration

Other names / synonyms: Arthrocentesis, Culdocentesis, Diagnostic Peritoneal Lavage, Fine Needle Aspiration, Lumbar Puncture, Paracentesis, Pericardiocentesis, Spinal Tap, Thoracentesis

ICD-9 Depends on Site

Definition

Aspiration is a procedure where fluid is suctioned out of a body cavity with a device called an aspirator. The aspirator is often a needle and syringe but can also be a siphon, rubber tubing, rubber bulb, or pump.

An abnormal amount of fluid can sometimes collect in a place where it should not such as the chest cavity. Abnormal fluid collection often signals an underlying illness. Part of the treatment for the underlying illness may include removal of the collected fluid (aspiration). Depending on the location of the fluid, aspiration has different names. For example, removal of fluid from the chest cavity is called thoracentesis and removal from the joints is called arthrocentesis.

Aspiration may also be used to diagnose an illness. For example, several diseases (e.g., meningitis, encephalitis, bleeding in the brain [brain hemorrhage], or poliomyelitis) can result in changes in the normal composition of the fluid within the spinal column (cerebrospinal fluid). If the doctor suspects one of these diseases, aspiration of the cerebrospinal fluid (commonly referred to as spinal tap) may be performed and the fluid analyzed in the laboratory. Aspiration of fluid is commonly performed to check for the presence of bacteria that signals an underlying infection.

Reason for Procedure

Aspiration is performed to remove an abnormal collection of fluid in treating a condition or to remove a sample of fluid or tissue for examination.

Accumulations of fluid in the chest cavity, abdominal cavity, joint spaces, or soft tissues are commonly aspirated for diagnosis or treatment. This fluid may be an excess of normal fluid or an abnormal fluid (pus, inflammatory fluid, blood) that needs to be removed.

In some cases, normally present fluid such as spinal fluid or tissue such as bone marrow is aspirated so a sample can be collected for evaluation and is often done when attempting to diagnose an illness.

Description

The specifics of the procedure vary depending on the site of aspiration. In general, the skin over the site of aspiration is sterilized usually with a liquid iodine solution. The skin is then numbed (anesthetized). The suctioning device (aspirator) is inserted into the fluid or tissue being collected. Using suction, the aspirator removes the desired amount of fluid or tissue that is collected in a sterile receptacle. The aspirator is removed and a bandage or other sterile dressing placed over the entry site.

Aspiration is usually an outpatient procedure unless the underlying condition is severe enough to warrant hospitalization.

Prognosis

Aspiration is a very effective method for obtaining fluid samples and/or draining abnormally collected fluid from a body cavity. Full recovery following this procedure is expected however the underlying condition necessitating the procedure may not be associated with a good prognosis.

Specialists

- Emergency Medicine
- General Surgeon

Work Restrictions / Accommodations

Restrictions and accommodations are not associated with this procedure.

Comorbid Conditions

Individuals with diabetes or compromised immune systems may heal more slowly.

Procedure Complications

Complications may vary depending on the site of aspiration but in general include bruising at the insertion point, bleeding, and infection. Aspirations of the chest cavity can be associated with a collapsed lung. Aspirations of the abdominal cavity rarely result in injury to the intestines or other organs.

Factors Influencing Duration

Aspiration is not associated with a period of disability. If complications arise, the period of disability is related to the type of complication, severity of symptoms, and individual's response to treatment.

Length of Disability

No disability is expected for the procedure itself.

References

"Joint Aspiration (Arthrocentesis)." MedicineNet.com. 17 July 2000. 09 Jan 2001 <http://www.medicinenet.com/Script/Main/Art.asp?li=MNI&d=144&cu=16583&w=0&ArticleKey=7084>.

Honig, Eric, and Roland Ingram. "Respiratory Medicine: Functional Assessment of the Lung: Diagnostic Techniques." Scientific American® Medicine Online Dale, D.C., and D.D. Federman, eds. New York: WebMD Corporation, 2000 Scientific American Medicine. 17 Jan 2001 <http://www.samed.com/sam/forms/index.htm>.

Aspiration Curettage of the Uterus
69.5, 69.51, 69.52, 69.59

Definition

Aspiration curettage is an office based surgical procedure that uses suction to remove samples of tissue from the lining of the cervix (endocervical canal) or the lining of the uterus (endometrium).

The aspiration curettage procedure is similar to the dilation and curettage (D & C) procedure used to evaluate and abnormal uterine bleeding, to obtain uterine tissue for testing and diagnosis of cancer of the uterus, and to remove contents of an incomplete miscarriage. In both procedures, the opening to a woman's uterus (cervix) is enlarged (dilated) and the lining of the endometrium scraped with a special instrument (curette). The aspiration curettage procedure uses a special curette to scrape endometrial tissue that is then removed it by suction.

Reports issued by Centers for Disease Control and Prevention (CDC) for 1998 revealed that 24,000 aspiration curettage procedures were performed on women inpatients in non-Federal, short-stay hospitals in the US. Almost all the procedures (23,000) were performed on women between the ages of 15 and 44. Figures for geographic distribution of prevalence indicated that essentially equal numbers of aspiration curettage procedures were performed in the South, West, and Northeast regions of the US, and that relatively few procedures were performed in the Midwest.

Reason for Procedure

Aspiration curettage is used to obtain tissue for microscopic evaluation in cases of abnormal uterine bleeding that includes heavy periods (menorrhagia), bleeding between periods, and bleeding during or after intercourse.

Description

The aspiration curettage is performed with the individual in the same position as that for a pelvic examination. The woman lies on an examination table with legs separated and supported in stirrups. With the individual anesthetized (usually with local anesthesia), the gynecologist begins by inserting a thin rod called a sound into the uterus to measure its depth. Next, a dilator is inserted and as the cervix stretches open (dilates), the gynecologist inserts larger and larger dilators of increasing thickness until an opening is large enough to begin the second phase of the surgery.

In the second phase of the procedure, a spoon-shaped surgical scraping instrument (aspirating curette) attached to a suction catheter is inserted into the endocervical canal or up into the uterus. The tissue to be sampled is scraped off and then removed by suction through the catheter connected to a vacuum pump. The entire endometrium can then be scraped with the curette to remove any remaining tissue.

Prognosis

Predicted outcome after an aspiration curettage procedure is good. Complications are usually minimal. A few individuals may experience some bleeding and mild period-like cramping during the procedure and for a day or so following it. Most individuals recover with no problems associated with the anesthesia or the procedure.

Specialists

- Gynecologist
- Primary Care Provider

Work Restrictions / Accommodations

Work restrictions or accommodations are generally not required. One day of sick leave is usually all that is required followed by a gradual return to strenuous job activities.

Comorbid Conditions

Comorbid conditions that may influence length of disability after an aspiration curettage procedure include heart, kidney, liver, or lung disorders, insulin dependent diabetes (IDDM), and any other diseases that may place limits on the procedure or the results of the procedure.

Procedure Complications

Complications include infection, perforation of the uterus, excessive bleeding, (hemorrhage), trauma to abdominal organs (such as rupture of the bowel or urinary bladder), and injury to the cervix. A rare result of injury to the cervix may be the inability of the cervix to retain the fetus within the uterus (cervical incompetence) resulting in spontaneous abortion (miscarriage) or premature birth.

Factors Influencing Duration

Length of disability may be influenced by the underlying reason for the procedure (menorrhagia, incomplete abortion, miscarriage, or testing and diagnosis) and the development of complications.

Length of Disability

Most individuals who undergo the procedure are able to return to work or resume previous activities within a day or so with only minor (immediate) restrictions such as refraining from strenuous exercise or driving on the day of the procedure.

Duration in Days

Job Classification	Minimum	Optimum	Maximum
Any work	1	3	7

References

Curran, Timothy. "Chapter 87 - Dilation and Curettage." Procedures for Primary Care Physicians, 1st ed. Pfenninger, John L., MD, and Grant C. Fowler, MD, eds. New York: Mosby Year Book, Inc, 1994. 672-677.

Asthma

Other names / synonyms: Allergic Asthma, Asthmatic Bronchitis, Bronchial Asthma, Catarrhal Asthma, Chronic Desquamating Eosinophilic Bronchitis, COPD, Reactive Airway Disease

493, 493.0, 493.00, 493.1, 493.2, 493.9

Definition

Asthma is either an acute or chronic lung disease in which airflow in and out of the lungs may be blocked by bronchial muscle squeezing and swelling, and excess mucus. Asthma is characterized by episodes of obstructed breathing, which occur due to narrowing of the breathing passages, making it difficult to inhale but even more difficult to exhale. With mild asthma, the airways are relatively normal between attacks. In more severe asthma, there is some degree of constant airway constriction, with additional narrowing that occurs during an acute attack.

Individuals with asthma may respond to certain factors (triggers) in the environment, which do not affect non-asthmatics. In response to a trigger, an asthmatic's airways become narrowed and inflamed, resulting in wheezing and/or coughing.

Asthma symptoms can be triggered by several factors including allergens or irritants, viral or sinus infections, stomach acid flowing back up the esophagus (reflux disease), medications or foods, emotional anxiety, and exercise. Allergic rhinitis (hay fever) is considered a risk factor in developing allergic asthma; up to 78% of individuals with allergic asthma also have allergic rhinitis. Symptoms of asthma and allergic rhinitis can be triggered by seasonal or year-round allergens - any substance that triggers allergies. These can include airborne pollens and molds, animal dander (dead skin flakes), house dust mite and cockroach droppings, and indoor molds.

Occupational asthma is generally defined as a respiratory disorder directly related to inhaling fumes, gases, dust, enzymes, metals, animal proteins, fungi, pollens, pharmaceutical agents, or other potentially harmful substances while "on the job." With occupational asthma, symptoms of asthma may develop for the first time in a previously healthy worker, or pre-existing asthma may be aggravated by exposures within the work place. Occupational asthma has become the most prevalent work-related lung disease in developed countries. However, the exact proportion of newly diagnosed cases of asthma in adults due to occupational exposure is unknown.

Between 12-15 million individuals in the US (approximately 5%) have asthma, and 15% of those may have job-related factors; the incidence appears to be rising in the industrialized world. Susceptibility to allergic asthma appears to be an inherited trait. Most cases begin before the age of 25, but asthma can begin at any age. Being born prematurely increases the risk of developing asthma later.

Diagnosis

History: Asthma attacks are typically episodic. Intervals between attacks can be days, months, or years; for some people asthma can become a daily problem. The symptoms of asthma vary, and are related to the severity of airway obstruction. Common symptoms during attacks include wheezing, coughing, chest tightness, and shortness of breath. They may only be able to speak in 1-2 word sentences. If severe airway obstruction interferes with the delivery of oxygen to the brain, individuals can become restless and confused; these symptoms are often worse at night, disturbing sleep. Exercise may precipitate asthma. Between attacks, symptoms are absent or greatly reduced. The individual will typically have a history of previous asthmatic attacks. Any information about events preceding an attack can be useful to determine a possible trigger for the asthma, but in some cases of very reactive airways, it can be difficult to isolate the cause(s).

Symptoms of occupational asthma include wheezing, chest tightness, and cough. Other associated symptoms may include runny nose, nasal congestion, and eye irritation. The cause may be allergic or non-allergic in nature, and the disease may persist for a lengthy period in some workers, even if they have discontinued exposure to the irritants that triggered their symptoms. Commonly, symptoms worsen through the work week, improve on the weekend, and recur when the worker returns to the job.

Physical exam: During an acute attack, listening to the chest will reveal wheezing on exhaling; in more advanced disease, there may be wheezes during inhalation as well. Other signs in acute asthma may include rapid breathing (tachypnea), a rapid heart rate (tachycardia), using the accessory muscles in the neck to help breathe, a bluish tinge to the skin (cyanosis), and an exaggerated fall in systolic blood pressure during inhalation. The examination of an asthmatic may be normal between attacks.

Tests: Chest x-ray and pulmonary function tests (PFTs) may appear normal between asthma attacks. During an acute asthmatic attack, airflow measurements (spirometry) will show a diminished lung capacity and flow rate on expiration. If symptoms and physical signs respond positively to the administration of bronchodilators, partially reversing the airflow measurements, this will confirm a diagnosis of asthma. Pulse oximetry will quickly measure the oxygen level in the blood. A complete blood count (CBC) may show an increased eosinophil count in allergic asthma. A microscopic exam of sputum may be done if an infection is suspected. Arterial blood gases and an EKG are indicated if the attack is severe and/or prolonged. Most allergic asthmatics have an elevated specialized protein (IgE) level in their blood.

Methacholine challenge tests can be used to diagnose hyper-reactive airways when pulmonary function tests are normal. If asthma is present only on the job, it may be necessary to measure airflow in the work place with a portable peak flow meter. Qualitative and quantitative tests for possible air and gas triggers may also be performed.

Treatment

Acute asthma is treated with bronchodilator inhalants and oxygen. Intravenous (IV) muscle relaxants and steroids may also be needed. If the attack is severe and prolonged, the individual will be admitted to the hospital for intensive treatment because respiratory failure can be a serious possible development. Inpatient treatment might require a positive-pressure oxygen mask or mechanical intermittent ventilation (respirator). Treatment of chronic asthma includes inhaled bronchodi-

A lators (sympathomimetics and parasympatholytics), anti-inflammatory medications (inhaled or systemic steroids, inhaled cromolyns, and leukotriene modifiers), theophyllines, and decreased exposure to causative agents.

Several medications are useful in treating the persons with frequent and/or severe asthma attacks. These include antihistamines, which relieve or prevent the symptoms of allergic rhinitis (hay fever) and other allergies. Decongestants are used to treat nasal congestion and other symptoms by shrinking blood vessels, thereby decreasing the amount of fluid that leaks out and reducing nasal congestion. Anti-inflammatory agents such as the nonsteroidal cromolyn and corticosteroids reduce asthma symptoms. Many of the cells that cause airway inflammation are known to produce potent chemicals within the body called leukotrienes. Leukotrienes are responsible for the contraction of the smooth muscles of the airway, for increasing fluid leakage from blood vessels in the lung, and promoting inflammation by attracting other inflammatory cells into the airways. Recently, oral anti-leukotriene medications have been introduced to fight the inflammatory response; they are also used to treat chronic asthma. Bronchodilators are generally used as asthma "rescue medications" to relieve coughing, wheezing, shortness of breath, and difficulty in breathing.

Aggressive treatment of pulmonary infections is recommended, along with immunization against influenza and pneumococcal pneumonia.

Complementary and Alternative Therapies

Content is intended for awareness only. Treatments may or may not be effective. Scientific evidence may be lacking and some substances have potentially toxic effects. Dr. Presley Reed and the editors do not endorse the use of these therapies in the absence of consultation with a licensed medical professional.

Biofeedback - Teaches individuals how to relieve tension and anxiety and loosen the muscles of the upper body.

Breathing exercises - Helps individuals to relax and emphasizes breathing through the nose rather than through the mouth.

Guided Imagery and Creative Visualization - Enables individuals to picture the airways widening, allowing air to flow easily in and out of the lungs, and to envision the weakening of allergens, so they can no longer trigger an attack.

Hypnotherapy - May help regulate breathing.

Meditation - Clears the mind to relieve emotional upset that may contribute to an asthma attack.

Yoga - Said to regulate and slow breathing and calms the mind.

Prognosis

The outcome in asthma is quite variable. Nearly 20% of individuals with asthma have some limitation in their daily lives due to the disease. A mild asthmatic attack may be treated easily with an extra dose of inhaled bronchodilator. A severe asthmatic attack developing over weeks might lead to severe, prolonged asthma, hospitalization, and multiple complications. If the individual's airways remain chronically inflamed, permanent disability may be seen.

Differential Diagnosis

Other causes of wheezing or abnormal breath sounds include left-sided heart failure, inhalation of a foreign body, acute or chronic bronchitis, and acute bronchiolitis. Narrowing of the trachea by an enlarged thyroid gland, a tumor, vocal cord dysfunction, narrowing of the bronchial tube (stenosis) may present with similar symptoms. Cystic fibrosis, pulmonary mucus plug, pulmonary fibrosis, panic disorder, pneumothorax, and toxic inhalation are also possibilities.

Specialists

- Allergist
- Pulmonologist

Work Restrictions / Accommodations

Avoiding fumes, gases, dusts, extreme temperatures, and any other airway irritants known to trigger an attack is essential. Masks and/or respirators should be used when required. When asthma is triggered by exercise or exertion, the individual may need to be reassigned to less strenuous duties and given the opportunity to use preventive medication.

Comorbid Conditions

Cardiac disease may lengthen disability. Gastrointestinal esophageal reflux disease (GERD) may lead to asthma attacks and worsen their effects. Smoking decreases effectiveness of medications and worsens the overall asthmatic condition.

Complications

Free air or gas within the pleural cavity (pneumothorax) or the abnormal presence of air in tissues that separate parts of the lung cavity (pneumomediastinum) can develop during severe asthma attacks, especially if the individual requires mechanical ventilation. In a severe asthma attack that does not respond to treatment, severe prolonged contraction (bronchospasm) of smooth muscles can result (status asthmaticus). This may be followed by respiratory failure and death. Individuals who have chronic pulmonary disease in addition to asthma will often have more severe and debilitating episodes of asthma.

Long-term steroid use by asthmatics can lead to blood chemistry disturbances, cataracts, osteoporosis, immunosuppression, and adrenal suppression. Over-treatment of asthma may precipitate cardiac arrhythmia.

Factors Influencing Duration

The factors most likely to influence disability are severity of the attack, development of complications, whether episodes are acute or part of a chronic condition, any underlying chronic medical conditions, and the individual's type of work.

Overall, the chronic, well-managed, mild to moderately severe asthmatic may experience very few days lost from work due to the disease.

Length of Disability

Acute attack.

Duration in Days			
Job Classification	Minimum	Optimum	Maximum
Any work	0	3	7

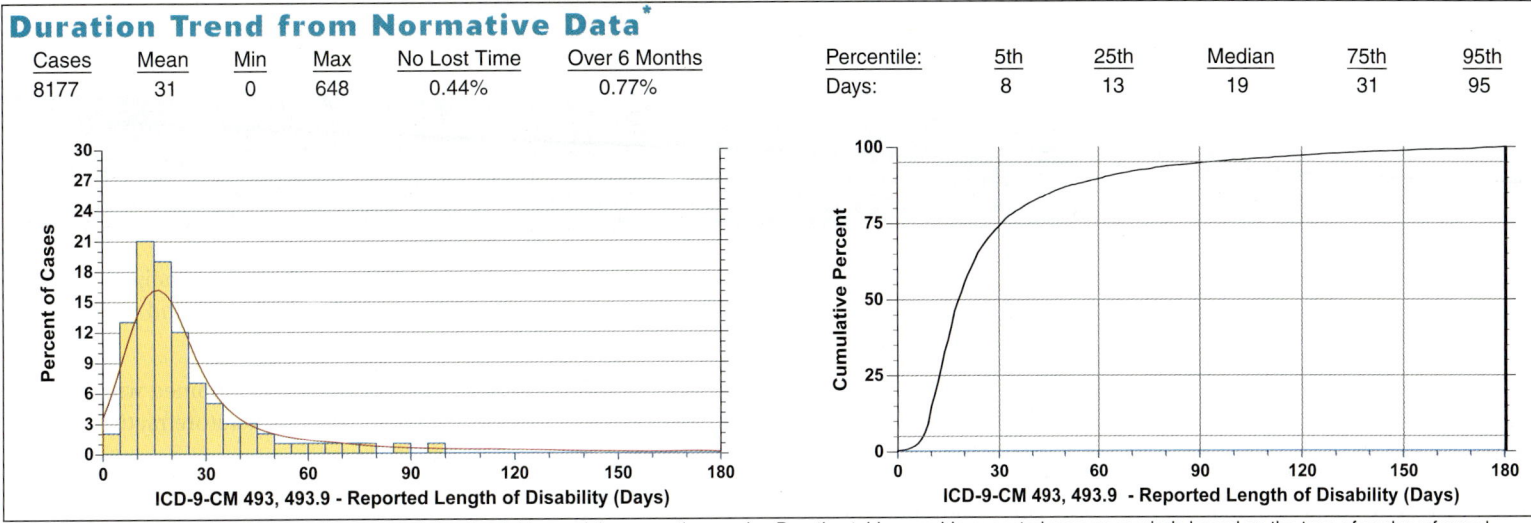

Duration Trend from Normative Data*

Cases	Mean	Min	Max	No Lost Time	Over 6 Months
8177	31	0	648	0.44%	0.77%

Percentile:	5th	25th	Median	75th	95th
Days:	8	13	19	31	95

ICD-9-CM 493, 493.9 - Reported Length of Disability (Days)

* Differences may exist between the expected duration tables and the normative graphs. Duration tables provide expected recovery periods based on the type of work performed by the individual. The normative graphs reflect the actual observed experience of many individuals across the spectrum of physical conditions, in a variety of industries, and with varying levels of case management.

Failure to Recover

If an individual fails to recover within the maximum duration expectancy period, the reader may wish to reference the following questions to assist in better understanding the specifics of an individual's medical case.

Regarding diagnosis:

- Does individual have allergies, URI, allergic rhinitis, or sinusitis?
- Does individual have any emotional anxiety?
- Does individual exercise?
- Was individual born prematurely?
- Are the asthma attacks episodic?
- Does individual complain of wheezing, coughing, chest tightness, and shortness of breath?
- Is individual only able to speak in 1-2 word sentences.
- Is individual restless and confused, especially at night?
- Is individual asymptomatic between attacks?
- Were symptoms worse through the workweek, improved on the weekend, and recurring when the worker returns to the job?
- Does individual have occupational asthma?
- Was there wheezing on exhalation and inhalation?
- Were other conditions present such as tachypnea, tachycardia, using the accessory muscles in the neck to help breathing, cyanosis, or an exaggerated fall in systolic blood pressure during inhalation?
- Were chest x-ray, pulmonary function tests, spirometry, pulse oximetry, and CBC done?
- Did symptoms and physical signs respond positively to the administration of bronchodilators?
- Was a microscopic exam of sputum done?
- Were arterial blood gases and an EKG done?
- Does individual have an elevated IgE?
- Was a methacholine challenge test done?
- Is asthma is present only on the job?
- Were qualitative and quantitative tests for possible air and gas triggers done?
- Were conditions with similar symptoms ruled out?

Regarding treatment:

- Was individual treated with bronchodilator inhalants and oxygen? Was it necessary to use IV muscle relaxants and steroids?
- Was individual admitted to the hospital?
- Was a respirator necessary?
- Has individual been immunized against influenza and pneumococcal pneumonia?

Regarding prognosis:

- Is individual's employer able to accommodate any necessary restrictions?
- Is individual able to avoid fumes, gases, dusts, extreme temperatures, and any other airway irritants known to trigger an attack?

Asthma

- Does individual use masks or respirators when required?
- Is asthma triggered by exercise or exertion? Does individual need sedentary work?
- Does individual have any conditions that may affect the ability to recover?
- Does individual have any complications such as pneumothorax, bronchospasm or status asthmaticus, or other chronic respiratory conditions?
- Has individual been on long term steroid use?

References

Sciammarella, M.D. J. "Asthma from AAEM Emergency Medical and Family Health Guide/ Lung And Airway." Emergency Medicine Online. eMedicine.com. Oct 2000. 10 Nov 2000 <http://emedicine.com/aaem/topic28.htm>.

Staton, Jr., G.W., and R.H. Ingram, Jr. "Asthma." Scientific American® Medicine Online Dale, D.C., and D.D. Federman, eds. New York: WebMD Corporation, 2000 Scientific American Medicine. 01 Feb 2001 <http://www.samed.com/sam/forms/index/htm>.

Astigmatism
Other names / synonyms: Refraction Error
367.2, 367.20

Definition

Astigmatism is a common condition where the light rays entering the eye fail to focus together at one point on the retina. The cornea is shaped like a football with two different curvatures. Moderate to severe visual distortion occurs in astigmatism where objects both near and far seem blurry or ghost-like. Astigmatism may be caused by an uneven curvature of the cornea (corneal astigmatism), irregularities of the crystalline lens (lenticular or residual astigmatism), or both. This condition tends to occur in individuals with nearsightedness (myopia) or farsightedness (hyperopia). It may also develop in one (unilateral) or both eyes (bilateral).

The condition is usually inherited. Severe degrees of astigmatism are often the result of some type of eye surgery such as corneal transplants, cataract surgery, or repair of a corneal laceration.

As high as 95% of individuals have some astigmatism, the degree measured in diopters (the refractive power of the eye). About 15% of adults have astigmatism greater than one diopter and an additional 2% have more severe astigmatism greater than three diopters.

Diagnosis

History: The individual reports blurry or distorted vision. An inconsistent ability to focus on objects either near or far may also be obvious.

Physical exam: The individual may or may not squint when trying to see objects.

Tests: A visual acuity test and a standard ophthalmic examination with refraction are done to determine what lens will best correct the individual's vision.

Treatment

Astigmatism may be corrected with eyeglasses that have partly concave or convex lenses or with hard contact lenses. Astigmatic (or incisional) keratotomy surgery may be an option for those who cannot tolerate glasses or contact lenses or for those where glasses or contact lenses do not satisfactorily correct vision. This procedure involves making small incisions across the axis of greatest corneal curve to flatten its shape.

Laser procedures may also be performed to correct astigmatism and include excimer laser photorefractive keratectomy and laser in situ keratomileusis (LASIK).

Surgical procedures for astigmatism are often combined with those to correct nearsightedness (myopia) and include keratorefractive surgery.

Prognosis

In most cases, the predicted outcome is good and the astigmatism is corrected although some types do not correct. Astigmatism due to scarring and some disorders that affect the cornea may not improve with eyeglasses but will correct with rigid contact lenses.

Astigmatic keratotomy or incisional keratotomy can have a variable outcome although with newer techniques, the outcome is generally good and results in a significant reduction in the degree of astigmatism.

The outcome of LASIK is good. Most individuals have very little discomfort. Some may experience only a foreign body sensation in the eye. LASIK can also be used to treat more severe cases of refractive errors.

Differential Diagnosis

Other errors of refraction (myopia, hyperopia, or presbyopia) are identified to determine how much they impair vision. Astigmatism may be a complication of surgery done to correct refractory errors. Excision of a cataract may also cause astigmatism.

Specialists

- Ophthalmologist

Work Restrictions / Accommodations

The individual's vision needs to be tested if keen visual acuity is an important aspect of the job. If eye protection is required while on the job, some individuals may need prescription eye protection including safety glasses or goggles for correction of the astigmatism. Those who wear contact lenses may be more sensitive to dust and fumes. When astigmatic keratotomy is performed, vigorous exercise should be restricted for 30 days and the individual must protect the eye(s) for 3 months.

Comorbid Conditions

Comorbid conditions affecting the outcome of astigmatic keratotomy include age and wound healing.

Complications

More than one angle of light may need adjustment in the same eye. This may make it more difficult or impossible to correct vision completely. Complications associated with wearing contact lenses include the risk of developing corneal abrasions.

Factors Influencing Duration

Individual tolerance and adjustment to glasses or contact lenses, the practitioner's skill in prescribing a corrective lens, and the quality of the glasses or lenses affect length of disability. If astigmatic keratotomy is performed, it will take several days to achieve maximum visual correction and glasses or contact lenses may still be required afterwards. Individual response to the procedure may also vary.

Length of Disability

In most cases, there is no disability associated with this condition.

Duration in Days

Job Classification	Minimum	Optimum	Maximum
Any work	1	1	1

Failure to Recover

If an individual fails to recover within the maximum duration expectancy period, the reader may wish to reference the following questions to assist in better understanding the specifics of an individual's medical case.

Regarding diagnosis:

- Did individual report distortion of vision or other visual disturbances?
- Was a visual acuity test done? Was an examination for refractory errors performed?
- Was diagnosis of astigmatism confirmed?

Regarding treatment:

- Were corrective glasses or contact lenses effective in correcting the astigmatism?
- If correction was not satisfactorily achieved with contact lenses or glasses, is individual a candidate for astigmatic keratotomy?

Regarding prognosis:

- Are there occupational or other circumstances that prevent individual from wearing contact lenses or prescription glasses? If so, have alternative treatments such as keratotomy or LASIK been considered?
- Following keratotomy or LASIK, was the correction less than optimal? Is it further correctable with addition of contact lenses or glasses?
- Does individual have a severe or uncorrectable astigmatism? Does individual have conditions such as advanced age or poor wound healing that would impact the recovery and outcome from keratotomy?
- Did any complications associated with keratotomy occur such as corneal abrasions that would impact recovery?
- How much does it impact individual's ability to function in present occupation?
- Have work accommodations been made to allow individual to return to work safely?

References

Abad, Juan Carlos, and Dimitri T. Azar. "Introduction to Refractive Surgery." Ophthalmology. Yanoff, Myron, and Jay S. Duker, eds. London: Mosby, 1999. 3.1.1-3.1.12.

Assil, Kerry K. "Radial and Astigmatic Keratotomy." Ophthalmology. Yanoff, Myron, and Jay S. Duker, eds. London: Mosby, 1999. 3.3.1-3.3.16.

Hardten, David R. "Excimer Laser Photorefractive Keratectomy." Ophthalmology. Yanoff, Myron, and Jay S. Duker, eds. London: Mosby, 1999. 3.4.1-3.4.18.

Miller, David. "Epidemiology of Refractive Errors." Ophthalmology. Yanoff, Myron, and Jay S. Duker, eds. London: Mosby, 1999. 2.8.1-2.8.2.

Slade, Stephen G., and John R. Doane. "LASIK - Laser in situ Keratomileusis." Ophthalmology. Yanoff, Myron, and Jay S. Duker, eds. London: Mosby, 1999. 3.6.1-3.6.8.

Solley, Wayne A., and Geoffrey Broocker. "General Eye Exam." Ophthalmology for the Primary Care Physician. Palay, David A., and Jay H. Krachmer, eds. St. Louis: Mosby, 1997. 1-21.

Wachler, Brian, S. Boxer, and Ronald R. Krueger. "Refractive Aspects of Cataract Surgery." Ophthalmology. Yanoff, Myron, and Jay S. Duker, eds. London: Mosby, 1999. 3.8.1-3.8.10.

Zabriskie, Norman A., and Randall J. Olson. "Occupational Eye Disorders." Environmental and Occupational Medicine, 3rd ed. Rom, William N., ed. Philadelphia: Lippincott-Raven, 1998. 743-754.

Astrocytoma

Other names / synonyms: Adult Noninfiltrating Astrocytoma, Anaplastic Astrocytoma, Glioblastoma, Glioblastoma Multiforme, Low Grade Astrocytoma, Pilocytic Astrocytoma

191.9, 192, 192.9, M9400/3

Definition

Astrocytoma is a malignant brain tumor composed of astrocytes. Astrocytes are the cells surrounding the nerve cells that form the support tissue for the brain and spinal cord.

Although all types of astrocytomas are very serious, they are classified in order of increasing malignancy. Astrocytomas are graded according to how invasive (or malignant) they are on a scale of one to four. Grade 1, a slow-growing tumor, may spread widely throughout the brain and be present for many years before causing any symptoms. A grade 4 astrocytoma, on the other hand, is a very fast-growing tumor, rapidly causing disabling symptoms. Grades 1 and 2 are considered "low-grade." A highly malignant variety of astrocytoma is known as glioblastoma multiforme.

Astrocytomas can occur anywhere in the central nervous system, including the cerebrum, cerebellum, brainstem, spinal cord, and optic nerve. The cause is unknown. However, individuals with neurofibromatosis and tuberous sclerosis are at higher risk for developing low-grade astrocytomas.

Astrocytomas are the most common type of tumor arising from supporting cells within the nervous system (glioma). Gliomas make up about 60% of all primary brain tumors, which are tumors that originated in the brain itself rather than spread from elsewhere in the body. Two to four new cases of glioma per 100,000 people are diagnosed each year in the US. Astrocytomas are slightly more common in whites than blacks, and in males than females.

Diagnosis

History: The individual may complain of headache, nausea, vomiting, a vague feeling of discomfort or illness (malaise), vision problems, personality or emotional changes, seizures, or lack of coordination on one side of the body.

Physical exam: Examination may reveal muscle weakness, lack of muscle coordination (ataxia), visual or other sensory disturbances, rapid movements of the pupils (nystagmus), or swelling of the optic disk (papilledema). Increased pressure inside the skull (increased intracranial pressure) may also be present.

Tests: CT scan and/or MRI are used to detect a mass and may also define its location, shape and size. Positron emission tomography (PET) scanning produces three-dimensional images that reflect the metabolic activity of the tissue being studied. Angiography (x-ray study of blood vessels after they have been injected with a contrast medium) may show stretching or displacement of normal cerebral vessels by the tumor. Angiography can also detect the presence of tumor vascularity (system of blood vessels), which may be necessary to distinguish a tumor mass from an arterial aneurysm (abnormal enlargement of a blood vessel). An electroencephalogram (EEG) records the electrical activity of the brain, and provides supporting information as to whether the tumor is causing a focal (limited) or widespread disturbance. A biopsy is performed whenever possible to confirm the exact type of tumor.

Treatment

With few exceptions, astrocytomas are not curable. Treatment is aimed at lengthening survival time and reducing symptoms. The type of treatment depends on the site of the tumor and the condition of the individual. By the time it is diagnosed, total surgical removal of an astrocytoma is usually impossible. At least minor surgery (biopsy), however, is usually performed to permit the diagnosis to be verified. Even though it may not be possible to remove all of the tumor, removing part of it can help reduce intracranial pressure and relieve symptoms (craniotomy with internal decompression or stereotactic volumetric reduction). Surgery may be followed by radiation therapy, depending on the specific location of the tumor. Astrocytomas, however, are not always responsive to radiation therapy. Chemotherapy is frequently used in association with surgery and/or radiation. Glucocorticoids are given to reduce brain swelling and decrease symptoms. A shunt may be inserted to drain excess cerebrospinal fluid in individuals with increased intracranial pressure.

Prognosis

Outcome depends on the extent of the disease. Individuals with low-grade astrocytomas (grades 1 and 2) have a median survival time of 7.5 years; however, individuals with very slow growing tumors in which complete surgical removal (stereotactic volumetric reduction) is possible may actually experience total remission. Individuals with grade 2 astrocytoma have a 5-year survival rate of about 34% without treatment, and about 70% with radiation therapy, and a median survival time of 4 years. Individuals with grade 3 astrocytoma have a median survival time of 18 months with treatment (radiation plus chemotherapy). Individuals with grade 4 astrocytoma have a median survival time of 17 weeks without treatment, 30 weeks with radiation, and 37 weeks with surgical removal of most of the tumor plus radiation.

Differential Diagnosis

Conditions with similar symptoms include benign or other type of malignant brain tumor, hydrocephalus, hematoma, brain abscess, aneurysm, ependymoma, cavernous sinus syndrome, cluster headache, head injury, intracranial hemorrhage, multiple sclerosis, subdural empyema, Tolosa-Hunt syndrome, and stroke.

Specialists

- Neurologist
- Neurosurgeon
- Oncologist
- Radiologist

Work Restrictions / Accommodations

Work ability will depend upon the neurological changes or deficits that accompany the tumor. For example, the presence of seizures would prevent the individual from driving and operating heavy equipment. Decreased motor coordination will interfere with any job requiring manual dexterity. Vision problems could result in any number of possible work restrictions.

Comorbid Conditions

Radiation necrosis may lengthen disability.

Complications

Complications are determined by the site of the tumor and extent of invasion of normal brain tissue, and can include blindness and endocrine disturbances. Up to 30% of individuals with malignant brain tumors develop blood clots (deep venous thrombosis). They are also prone to seizures and infections of the lung and urinary tract. In spite of treatment, tumor recurrence usually occurs within 6 to 12 months.

Factors Influencing Duration

The length of disability will be influenced by the specific location of the tumor, the grade of the tumor at the time of diagnosis, the method of treatment (surgery, radiation), age (older individuals have shorter survival times), and performance status (individuals who are neurologically normal live longer than those with a neurological deficit).

Length of Disability

For medical or surgical treatment, duration depends on size, site, and stage. Disability may be permanent.

Medical or surgical treatment.

Duration in Days

Job Classification	Minimum	Optimum	Maximum
Any work	42	182	Indefinite

Failure to Recover

If an individual fails to recover within the maximum duration expectancy period, the reader may wish to reference the following questions to assist in better understanding the specifics of an individual's medical case.

Regarding diagnosis:

- Did individual present with a new-onset of seizures or other symptoms suggestive of a brain tumor?
- Did the neurological exam reveal nervous system disorders that are consistent with the diagnosis of a brain tumor?
- Would individual benefit from consultation with a specialist (neurologist, neurosurgeon, neuroradiologist, neurooncologist)?
- Was the presence of a tumor visualized on an MRI, CT or PET?
- Was a tissue biopsy performed to distinguish the tumor type and aid in staging the malignancy?
- If the diagnosis was uncertain, were other conditions with similar symptoms ruled out?

Regarding treatment:

- Was surgical resection of the tumor performed?
- Did neurological symptoms persist or worsen? If so, were other measures done to relieve symptoms, such as administration of glucocorticoids to reduce swelling or insertion of shunts to relieve hydrocephalus?
- Were additional tumor suppressing interventions such as radiation therapy and or chemotherapy done?
- Was individual compliant with treatment recommendations (i.e., surgery, chemotherapy, radiation therapy)?
- Would individual and their family members benefit from additional counseling or brain tumor support groups?

Regarding prognosis:

- Based on the size, location and stage of the tumor, what was the expected outcome?
- Did individual experience any complications that may have impacted recovery and prognosis?

Complementary and Alternative Therapies

Content is intended for awareness only. Treatments may or may not be effective. Scientific evidence may be lacking and some substances have potentially toxic effects. Dr. Presley Reed and the editors do not endorse the use of these therapies in the absence of consultation with a licensed medical professional.

Cartilage - Shark and bovine cartilage is said to kill cancer cells directly, stimulate the immune system, and block formation of new blood vessels (angiogenesis) that tumors need for unrestricted growth

Hydrazine sulfate - Has been used as an antitumor agent and said to act as a treatment for body wasting (cachexia) associated with advanced cancer.

Coenzyme Q10 - Analogs of this substance may suppress cancer growth directly.

Cancell/Entelev - Said to slow or inhibit cancer cell formation.

References

Benardete, E. A., and George I. Jallo, MD. Low Grade Astrocytoma. eMedicine.com. 2000. 02 Jan 2001 <http://www.emedicine.com/neuro/topic190_pr.htm>.

Brain Tumor Classification. New York University Medical Center. 27 Jan 1996. 02 Jan 2001 <http://mcns10.med.nyu.edu/intro/tumors.html>.

Cancell/Entelev. National Cancer Institute. 01 Dec 2000. 02 Jan 2001 <http://cancernet.nci.nih.gov/cam/cancell.htm>.

Cartilage (Bovine and Shark). National Cancer Institute. 01 Dec 2000. 02 Jan 2001 <http://cancernet.nci.nih.gov/cam/cartilage.htm>.

Coenzyme Q10. National Cancer Institute. 01 Dec 2000. 02 Jan 2001 <http://cancernet.nci.nih.gov/cam/Q10.htm>.

Hydrazine Sulfate. National Cancer Institute. 01 Dec 2000. 02 Jan 2001 <http://cancernet.nci.nih.gov/cam/hydrazine.htm>.

Kelly, P. Astrocytomas. New York University Medical Center. 26 Jun 1995. 02 Jan 2001 <http://mcns10.med.nyu.edu/tumors/astro.html>.

Slevin, Maurice, MD, FRCP, ed. Astrocytoma. CancerBACUP. 01 Nov 1999. 02 Jan 2001 <http://www.cancerbacup.org.uk/info/factsheet/astrocy.htm>.

Atherosclerosis and Arteriosclerosis

Other names / synonyms: Arteriosclerotic Disease, Arteriosclerotic Obliterans, Endarteritis Deformans, Hardening of the Arteries, Occlusive Arteriosclerosis

440, 440.0, 440.1, 440.2, 440.20, 440.21, 440.22, 440.23, 440.29, 440.8, 440.9

Definition

Arteriosclerosis is an abnormal condition associated with thickening and loss of elasticity in the walls of arteries. It is a generic term and also widely referred to as hardening of the arteries. Atherosclerosis is a type of arteriosclerosis associated with fatty (lipid) deposition in the walls of arteries. This is uncharacteristic of other forms of arteriosclerosis such as arteriolosclerosis seen with high blood pressure (hypertension) and the rare Monckeberg's sclerosis. Atherosclerosis is the most prevalent and most important of the several types of arteriosclerosis.

Atherosclerosis affects arteries throughout the body, i.e., arteries in the heart, brain, kidneys, and extremities. Atherosclerosis causes more deaths in the US than the second and third leading causes of death (cancer and accidents) combined. It is the leading cause of morbidity and mortality worldwide in most other industrialized countries.

Risk factors for atherosclerosis are well known and include increased plasma cholesterol, cigarette smoking, hypertension, diabetes, obesity, age, male gender, and heredity. The three most important predictors of risk are plasma cholesterol concentration, cigarette smoking, and elevated blood pressure.

Men are affected 4 to 5 times more often than women, although heart disease from atherosclerosis is the leading cause of death in women as well as men. Through menopause, women are protected because of hormones. After this time, however, the number of heart attacks and strokes increases in women who are not undergoing estrogen replacement therapy, although there is a 10- to 15-year lag time.

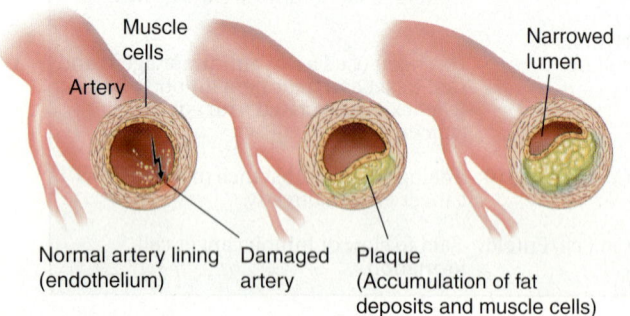

Diagnosis

History: Individuals with atherosclerosis may have symptoms referable to reduced arterial blood flow and oxygen delivery to one or more organs (tissues). Symptoms caused by inadequate oxygenation of living (viable) tissues are due to ischemia. If ischemia is prolonged, it may result in death (necrosis) of cells. The resultant irreversible death of tissue is referred to as infarction. Ischemia may be acute or chronic, whereas infarction is only acute.

Physical exam: Many signs of atherosclerosis are related to its specific clinical expressions. Physical exam may reveal a whistling sound (bruit) heard with a stethoscope placed directly over a narrowed but not completely closed artery. A diminished pulse may be felt in an artery beyond a narrowed segment of the vessel.

Examination of the small blood vessels (arterioles) in the retina of the eye with an ophthalmoscope is valuable for diagnosis. Atherosclerotic arterioles reflect light (emitted by the ophthalmoscope), giving them a "silver wire" appearance.

Tests: Test done on individuals with suspected or known atherosclerosis include measurement of the total blood cholesterol and the ratio of high-density lipoproteins (HDL) to low-density lipoproteins (LDL).

Plain x-rays may show calcium deposits in the walls of affected blood vessels that infer a diagnosis of atherosclerosis. X-rays with contrast material (angiography) allow visualization of the interior of arteries and permit both a definitive diagnosis of the disease and an assessment of its severity.

Doppler ultrasound, CT, and MRI are other (noninvasive) methods used to diagnose and assess the extent of atherosclerosis.

Treatment

Fundamental to the treatment of atherosclerosis and its consequences is risk factor modification. Cessation of cigarette smoking, lowering (high) blood pressure, controlling diabetes mellitus, exercise, attaining an optimal weight, and lowering plasma cholesterol to a normal level (less than 200 mg/dl) are lifestyle changes that can retard or reverse the progression of atherosclerosis. Six to eighteen months of such lifestyle changes are necessary to assess if the risk factor modification program is effective.

The three major sources of dietary cholesterol are egg yolks, animal fat, and red meats. In addition to reduction of dietary cholesterol intake, a cholesterol and LDL lowering drug belonging to a class of drugs known as statins is often prescribed if an individual has an LDL (bad cholesterol) level above 130 mg/dl. Many individuals with atherosclerosis also have a low HDL (good cholesterol) level. Niacin is commonly given to these individuals.

In addition to the above therapeutic measures, postmenopausal women often receive oral estrogen therapy to reduce the risk of atherosclerosis.

A small dose of aspirin (one-half adult aspirin or less daily) may also be given to individuals with atherosclerosis. The American Heart Association recommends that men 40 and over with 2 or more risk factors for atherosclerosis should take a low dose of aspirin daily.

Among individuals with atherosclerosis with localized obstructions that are potentially or actually causing ischemia, the obstruction may be removed surgically (endarterectomy), bypassed with another blood vessel (bypass surgery), displaced into the wall of the artery (angioplasty), vaporized with laser, drilled with a "roto-rooter" (atherectomy), or widened with a stent serving as a brace to keep the artery open.

Prognosis

Atherosclerosis is a progressive disease. It is frequently associated with and complicated by one or more of the clinical problems from ischemia or infarction. It carries a high morbidity and mortality with coronary heart disease being the most frequent cause. However, some individuals may have regression of atherosclerosis related to lipid lowering associated with dietary changes or pharmacologic therapy. Several studies have shown that progression can be slowed through use of lipid lowering drugs with 18 months of therapy, which reduces morbidity and mortality.

Differential Diagnosis

Other forms of arteriosclerosis (Monckeberg's sclerosis, arteriosclerosis) may cause similar clinical problems. Other conditions that can mimic atherosclerosis include Periarteritis nodosa (an inflammatory condition) and several other noninfectious causes of arterial inflammation known as Takayasu's arteritis and Kawasaki's disease seen in individuals of Japanese origin.

Specialists

- Cardiologist
- Cardiovascular Surgeon
- Internist
- Neurologist
- Vascular Surgeon

Work Restrictions / Accommodations

Work restrictions are not necessary for atherosclerosis itself but are often required for one of its complications. In addition, restrictions and accommodations may be needed for varying periods of time following a procedure to treat an atherosclerotic obstruction.

Comorbid Conditions

Diabetes mellitus, hypertension, elevated cholesterol levels in the blood (hypercholesterolemia), and obesity are all possible causes and comorbid conditions that may lengthen disability.

Complications

There are a number of possible complications of atherosclerosis due primarily to ischemia or infarction of one or more organs nourished by atherosclerotic arteries. These complications include stroke, heart attack (myocardial infarction), narrowing (stenosis) of a kidney (renal) artery causing hypertension and pain in the legs when walking (claudication), and expression (dilation) of an artery (aneurysm) especially of the abdominal aorta.

Factors Influencing Duration

Factors include the age of the individual, severity and extent of disease, individual's response to treatment, and any complications.

Length of Disability

There is usually no disability with atherosclerosis itself; however, since atherosclerosis often leads to ischemia or infarction of the heart, brain, kidneys, or legs, these complications may lead to disability.

Failure to Recover

If an individual fails to recover within the maximum duration expectancy period, the reader may wish to reference the following questions to assist in better understanding the specifics of an individual's medical case.

Regarding diagnosis:

- Does individual have increased plasma cholesterol?
- Is individual a smoker?
- Does individual have elevated blood pressure?
- Does individual have diabetes or obesity?
- How old is individual? Gender?
- What is family history for similar diseases?
- Were there symptoms of ischemia? Resulting in an infarction?
- On exam, was a bruit detected? Were any diminished pulses detected?
- Were there any changes in the retina of the eye?
- Was blood tested for cholesterol? Were both HDL and LDL testing done?
- Were plain x-rays taken? Angiography? Doppler ultrasound, CT, or MRI?
- Were conditions with similar symptoms ruled out?

Regarding treatment:

- Has individual addressed correctable risk factors suck as cessation of cigarette smoking, lowering high blood pressure, controlling diabetes, attaining an optimal weight, lowering plasma cholesterol, and a regular exercise program?
- Has individual made the lifestyle changes for 6 to 18 months?
- Is individual on medication to lower cholesterol and LDL?
- If individual is postmenopausal, is she taking estrogen replacement?
- Is individual taking a small dose of aspirin daily?
- Has individual required any surgical procedures to keep any arteries open?
- Has individual had any other procedures to keep the arteries open?

Regarding prognosis:

- Does individual have any conditions that may affect ability to recover?
- Has individual had any complications such as a myocardial infarction?
- Are there complaints of transient ischemic attacks or any problems with movement, sight, or body weakness that may suggest a stroke?
- Does individual have intermittent claudication?
- Is individual's blood pressure normal or elevated?

References

"Arteriosclerosis." Merck Manual of Diagnosis and Therapy, 17th ed. Beers, Mark H., and Robert Berkow, MD, eds. Whitehouse Station, NJ: Merck & Co., Inc, 1999. 05 Dec 2000 <http://www.merck.com/mmanual/section16/chapter201/201b.htm>.

Cardiovascular Disease Statistics. American Heart Association. 01 Jan 2000. 01 Jan 2001 <http://www.americanheart.org/statistics/biostats/biolc.htm>.

Cardiovascular Diseases. American Heart Association. 01 Jan 2000. 01 Jan 2001 <http://www.americanheart.org/Heart_and_Stroke_A_Z_Guide/cvds.html>.

DeBakey, Michael, and Antonio Gotto. The New Living Heart. Holbrook: Adams Media Services, 1997.

Atopic Dermatitis
Other names / synonyms: Asthmatic Dermatitis, Eczema
691.8

Definition

Atopic dermatitis is a chronic skin disorder beginning most commonly during infancy, childhood, or adolescence. Moist skin, dry skin, or psychological stressors irritate nerve endings in the skin and trigger the itch/scratch cycle.

The most common itch triggers are allergies, heat and high humidity, perspiration, cold weather, low humidity (leads to dryness), emotional stress, alcohol, and the common cold. Egg, milk, peanut, soy, wheat, dust mites, animal dander, wool, airborne allergens including pollens and certain chemicals (e.g., solvents, soaps, detergents, fragrances, or smoke), and molds are common allergens associated with atopic dermatitis. Itching occurs on apparently healthy skin and scratching makes the rash worse. Almost anything can be irritating to the skin when the rash is severe. The rash can be found on regions of the body that are damp (groin, buttocks, soles of feet, or cheeks) and dry (hands, tops of feet, or lower legs).

Atopic dermatitis is often associated with a personal or family history of other atopic conditions such as allergic rhinitis, allergic conjunctivitis, asthma, dermatographism, dry skin (xerosis), or keratosis pilaris.

The prevalence rate for atopic dermatitis is 10-15%. The exact cause of atopic dermatitis is unknown, but immunologic, genetic, physiologic, and pharmacologic factors play a role. Respiratory disorders (asthma) occur in 40-60% of atopic individuals.

Diagnosis

History: The individual reports frequent and persistent itching (pruritus). Scratching can be so severe that sleep and qualify of life are affected. The individual may also have allergic rhinitis and asthma.

Physical exam: Skin changes can take many forms including scratches and abrasions (excoriations); raised bumps (papules); thickened, scaly, red, or gray skin (lichenification); red, fluid-filled bumps (vesicles); and crusted lesions. Extensive cracks (fissures), weeping, and crusting may be present in advanced cases. Individuals with atopic dermatitis often have xerosis. Eye examination may reveal eye changes related to atopic dermatitis. Skin infections may occur more frequently than normal for people with atopic dermatitis because infectious skin organisms are often present in higher than normal numbers.

Tests: Immunologic and skin testing may be required. Elevated total immunoglobulin (IgE) suggests allergic cause. Prick skin or patch testing and a food challenge test may be performed if a food or airborne allergen is a suspected trigger.

Treatment

No known therapy is curative. Individuals should keep their nails short and clean to prevent bacterial infection. If dryness is a problem, the best way to get water into the skin is to soak in a bath or shower followed by immediate application of a thick layer of moisturizer to seal the water into the skin. If symptoms are caused by heat and sweating, bathing should be limited to once a day (for no more than 5 to 10 minutes) using only warm water and very mild soap.

Treatment consists of removing or reducing irritating factors using topical corticosteroids, applying moisturizers, and reducing stress. Severe itching is treated with antihistamines or tricyclic antidepressants. Cases that do not respond to conventional treatments may be treated with occlusion, leukotriene inhibitors, oral steroids, tar preparations, or psoralen plus UVA light (PUVA) therapy. Skin infections caused by bacteria (impetigo, staphylococcal, or streptococcal), fungus (athlete's foot), and viruses (herpes) are treated with antibiotics, antifungal, or antiviral medications either taken orally or applied directly to the skin.

Prognosis

The outcome of atopic dermatitis is difficult to predict. Outbreaks can be prevented if the individual follows preventive measures (i.e., using moisturizers or avoiding moist or dry skin conditions). The condition usually improves in the summer and worsens in the winter. Periods of remission appear more frequently as an individual grows older and spontaneous resolution occurs. Atopic dermatitis is rarely seen in individuals over 50 however associated symptoms such as dry skin remain for life. Early onset of disease correlates with greater severity.

Allergic rhinitis, asthma, a family history of atopic dermatitis, egg sensitivity, and widespread disease during infancy are associated with a poor prognosis.

Differential Diagnosis

The symptoms associated with atopic dermatitis can resemble impetigo, seborrheic dermatitis, psoriasis, contact dermatitis, mite infestation (scabies), immunodeficiency disorder, psychologically induced itching rash (neurodermatitis), and bacterial, viral or fungal infection. Cancer, thyroid disorders, and liver or kidney failure can cause itching and excoriations.

Specialists

- Allergist
- Dermatologist

Work Restrictions / Accommodations

Allergens, low or high humidity, excessive sweating, and chemical or airborne irritants may make itching and scratching worse. Individuals may need to be removed from environments that trigger dermatitis outbreaks.

Complementary and Alternative Therapies

Content is intended for awareness only. Treatments may or may not be effective. Scientific evidence may be lacking and some substances have potentially toxic effects. Dr. Presley Reed and the editors do not endorse the use of these therapies in the absence of consultation with a licensed medical professional.

Evening primrose oil -	May soothe itching.
Burdock root -	May reduce inflammation and reduce symptoms.
Vitamin B complex -	Said to promote healthy skin.

Comorbid Conditions

Immune system-suppressing diseases such as AIDS or certain cancers can increase the length of disability by making the individual more prone to skin infection. Respiratory disorders (e.g., asthma) occur in 40-60% of atopic individuals.

Complications

Bacterial, viral, and fungal infections are common because of poor skin barrier function and reduced immune functioning. In severe cases, the skin may become reddened and fall off in layers (exfoliative erythroderma). Cataracts may develop in the eyes.

Factors Influencing Duration

The severity of symptoms, location, extent of lesions, response to treatment, job requirements, and workplace environment influence the length of disability.

Length of Disability

Duration depends on job requirements. Disability may be of a sporadic or more chronic nature corresponding with dermatitis outbreaks. In most cases, no disability is expected.

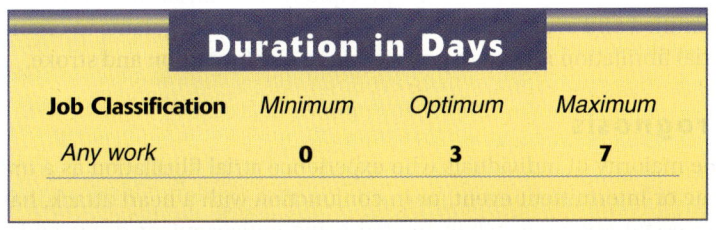

Duration in Days

Job Classification	Minimum	Optimum	Maximum
Any work	0	3	7

Failure to Recover

If an individual fails to recover within the maximum duration expectancy period, the reader may wish to reference the following questions to assist in better understanding the specifics of an individual's medical case.

Regarding diagnosis:

- Were symptoms present such as severe persistent itching and skin irritation (raised bumps, flaking, weeping, fissures, and crusting) characteristic of atopic dermatitis?
- Was immunologic and skin testing done to confirm the diagnosis?
- Does the rash appear where individual has had contact with a particular substance?
- Was individual a young child when the disease began?
- If the diagnosis was uncertain, were other conditions with similar symptoms such as impetigo, seborrheic dermatitis, psoriasis, contact dermatitis, and mite infestation neurodermatitis ruled out?
- Are the skin lesions greasy and scaly? Are lesions on the scalp, buttocks, and exterior surfaces? Is only one patch of skin affected and located in an area that is easy to scratch?
- Does the rash have an irregular edge with central clearing such as in a fungal infection? Were skin scrapings examined to identify rash caused by fungal infection or mite infestation?

Regarding treatment:

- Was individual compliant in following prescribed treatment of avoiding irritating factors and using topical corticosteroids or moisturizers?
- Did symptoms persist following conservative treatment? If so, were stress management techniques such as relaxation exercises tried?
- Have additional medications (leukotriene inhibitors, oral steroids) been used?
- Did individual suffer from associated skin infections? If so, were the infections treated with antibiotic, antifungal, or antiviral medications?

Regarding prognosis:

- Has individual consistently followed preventive measures? Have symptoms subsided as expected?
- Did individual suffer any complications such as bacterial, viral or fungal infections that may influence length of disability?
- Does individual have any pre-existing conditions such as allergic rhinitis, asthma, egg sensitivity, or widespread disease during infancy that may impact prognosis?

References

Anderson, Philip, and Kristin Malaker. "Most Common Skin Disorders." Managing Skin Diseases. Hiscock, Tim, ed. Baltimore: Williams & Wilkins, 1999. 56-58.

Beltrani, Vincent. "The Clinical Spectrum of Atopic Dermatitis." The Journal of Allergy and Clinical Immunology 104 (1999): S87-98.

Correale, Christine, et al. "Atopic Dermatitis: A Review of Diagnosis and Treatment." American Family Physician 60 4 (1999): 1191-1110.

Leung, Donald. "Atopic Dermatitis: New Insights and Opportunities for Therapeutic Intervention." The Journal of Allergy and Clinical Immunology 105 (2000): 860-876.

The Alternative Advisor. Somerville, Robert, et al., eds. Alexandria: Time Life Inc, 1997.

Wuthrich, Brunello. "Clinical Aspects, Epidemiology, and Prognosis of Atopic Dermatitis." Annals of Allergy, Asthma and Immunology 83 (1999): 464-470.

Atrial Fibrillation

Other names / synonyms: Atrial Flutter, Paroxysmal Atrial Fibrillation

427.3, 427.31

Definition

Atrial fibrillation is an abnormal heart rhythm (arrhythmia) in which the upper chambers of the heart (atria) beat irregularly, ineffectively, and very rapidly (up to 500 beats per minute). Only a portion of the electrical impulses that are generated by these atrial beats will pass through the specialized heart tissue (atrioventricular node) that normally acts as the impulse carrier to the lower chambers of the heart (ventricles). As a result, the ventricular beat is also rapid and irregular (80 to 160 beats per minute) which results in inefficient pumping action of the heart and reduced output of blood into the circulation. Another common problem with atrial fibrillation is the formation of blood clots (thromboemboli) in the atria that can enter the bloodstream and become lodged in an artery (embolism). This is particularly serious if it cuts off the blood supply leading to the brain, which results in a stroke.

Notably, atrial fibrillation may be found in individuals with no obvious heart disease or other likely precipitating cause (lone atrial fibrillation). Risk factors for atrial fibrillation include excessive alcohol, nicotine, or caffeine consumption. Other risk factors may include stress, fatigue, surgery, or certain prescription drugs. Atrial fibrillation is the most common type of heart arrhythmia and it accounts for 35% of all rhythmic disorders. The incidence of atrial fibrillation increases with age. For example, in the United States, 0.5% of the general population between the ages of 50-59 years has this condition, while 8.8% of those 80-89 years of age have it. The incidence is slightly higher in men than women and the male to female ratio is 1.3:1.

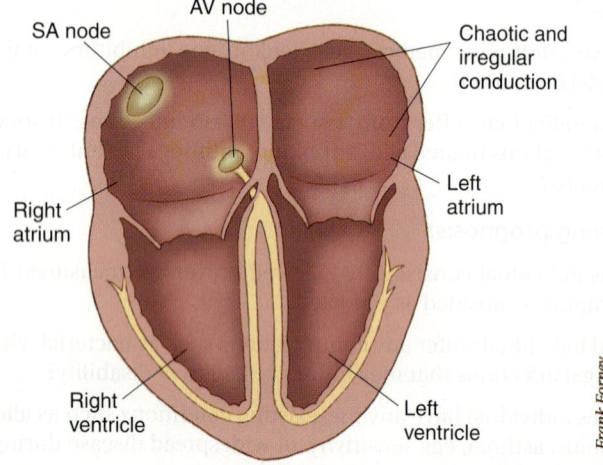

Diagnosis

History: Individuals may complain of fast or irregular heart beats, skipped beats, or occasional strong beats. Anxiety, fatigue, weakness, shortness of breath (dyspnea), light-headedness, or chest pain (angina pectoris) may also be reported. The arrhythmic symptoms may occur as sudden and temporary episodes (paroxysmally) before becoming the established rhythm.

Physical exam: Physical findings may include an irregular pulse or heart sounds, or high blood pressure (hypertension). The pulse rate that is felt in the individual's wrist may be slower than their chest heart rate (pulse deficit). This occurs when the pulse fails to reach the wrist because the heart, which is only partly filled, contracts prematurely.

Tests: Diagnosis is confirmed by recording the electrical activity of the heart (electrocardiogram or ECG). If the heart rhythm disturbance is intermittent, a portable electrocardiograph machine (Holter monitor) or event recorder may be used to monitor the individual's heart rate over a 24-hour period. Other tests that may be performed include blood tests to determine if oxygen is low in the blood (hypoxia), to determine if the pH is normal (acid-base balance), or to determine if certain dissolved substances in the blood are at abnormal levels (electrolyte imbalance). High frequency sound waves (ultrasound) may be used to visualize the heart (echocardiogram). Blood vessels in the heart may be visualized after injecting a contrast dye into the coronary arteries and then taking a series of x-rays (angiocardiography).

Treatment

Treatment involves restoration of the normal heart rate (or at least to slow the ventricular response) and prevention of blood clots. The heart rate usually can be made normal by giving anti-arrhythmic drugs. If the fibrillation persists, a short electrical shock applied to the heart (emergency defibrillation) may be necessary to restore the normal heart beat pattern. Anticoagulant drug therapy may be given to reduce the risk of blood clot formation (embolism). If the atrial fibrillation is of recent onset, treatment is usually directed at remedying the underlying disorder.

If the fibrillation is persistent, chronic, or combined with severe heart disease, antiarrhythmic drug therapy should be continued to control the heart rate. Surgery may be necessary if the cause of the fibrillation is found to be due to a narrowing of the valve between the atrium and the ventricle (mitral stenosis). If the underlying cause of the atrial fibrillation is not apparent, treatment usually consists of drugs (sedatives; digitalis) that keep the individual calm and that allow the heart to beat stronger. Contributing factors such as caffeine, alcohol, nicotine, or prescription drugs that may precipitate the atrial fibrillation are identified and avoided. The long-term use of anticoagulants in chronic atrial fibrillation is used to prevent blood clot formation and stroke.

Prognosis

The majority of individuals who experience atrial fibrillation as a one-time or intermittent event, or in conjunction with a heart attack, have successful outcomes when treated using anticoagulant drugs and/or antiarrhythmic drugs. The individual may require several weeks of follow-up drug therapy because it often takes four to six weeks before atrial function returns to normal.

For those individuals who require emergency defibrillation, 33% will have recurrence of atrial fibrillation within a week and 100% will experience recurrence within a year. Nevertheless, most individuals with chronic or persistent fibrillation do well with drug therapy although their need for it may be life-long. The likelihood of eliminating atrial fibrillation is small if it is persistent, chronic or combined with severe heart disease. Individuals who require surgery to replace the valve between the atrium and ventricle (mitral valve) may expect generally good results, although complications from this procedure may occur. These include blood clot (thromboembolism) in 9.5% of cases, bleeding (hemorrhage) as a result of anti-blood clotting medication (7.0% of cases), and valve leakage (6.5% of cases).

Differential Diagnosis

Conditions that present with similar symptoms as atrial fibrillation include other heart conditions such as abnormal functioning of the mitral valve that lies between the atrium and ventricle (Wolff-Parkinson-White syndrome), atrial flutter with heart block, shifting pacemaker that is associated with multifocal atrial ectopic beats, and paroxysmal atrial tachycardia. A toxic condition of the thyroid gland (thyrotoxicosis) may also present with symptoms similar to atrial fibrillation.

Specialists

- Cardiologist

Rehabilitation

Early incorporation of a physical rehabilitation program following treatment for atrial fibrillation may increase stability of the cardiac rhythm. As the individual gains strength, sitting for brief periods on the side of the bed and dangling the feet may be allowed. Self-care should be encouraged at this time and brief supervised walks in the hall may be allowed if there are no signs of complications. The length and duration of these walks should progressively increase according to the individual's endurance. Other activities may include range-of-motion and treadmill exercises.

Following hospital discharge or for individuals who receive treatments other than surgery, frequent walks, walk-jog, biking, and arm ergometer exercises are encouraged. The walking program aims toward a goal of two miles in less than 60 minutes. Eventually, exercise may become more strenuous with a goal of attaining 75-85% maximum intensity while walking, jogging, biking, swimming, performing calisthenics, and/or weight training.

Work Restrictions / Accommodations

Extended work leave may be needed if surgery or prolonged drug treatment is required. Individuals with jobs that involve strenuous physical activity or high levels of stress who are treated with anticoagulant drugs prior to treatment with defibrillation may require temporary transfer to sedentary activity. Restrictions from dangerous machinery, work at dangerous heights, or hazardous work may be necessary, especially if chronic anticoagulation therapy is prescribed.

Complementary and Alternative Therapies

Content is intended for awareness only. Treatments may or may not be effective. Scientific evidence may be lacking and some substances have potentially toxic effects. Dr. Presley Reed and the editors do not endorse the use of these therapies in the absence of consultation with a licensed medical professional.

Massage - Back massage may be useful in restoring cardiac rhythm in individuals with atrial fibrillation.

Acupuncture - Needles inserted into specific points on the body may help alleviate atrial fibrillation by reducing stress-related arrhythmias.

Comorbid Conditions

Existing conditions that may impact an individual's ability to recover and further lengthen their disability include underlying heart disease, rheumatic heart disease, disease of the heart muscle (cardiomyopathy), inflammation of the membrane that covers the heart (pericarditis), deformity of a heart valve causing it to leak (mitral valve prolapse), high blood pressure (hypertension), overactive thyroid (hyperthyroidism), toxic condition resulting from hyperthyroidism (thyrotoxicosis), pneumonia, atherosclerotic heart disease, and defects in the tissue that separates the right and left atria in the heart (atrial septal defect).

Complications

Possible complications of atrial fibrillation include formation of a blood clot (embolus) that can block blood flow to the brain, which results in a stroke. Other complications may include chest pain (angina pectoris), failure of the heart to pump blood adequately (heart failure), and life-threatening organ dysfunction (shock).

Factors Influencing Duration

The length of disability may be influenced by whether the atrial fibrillation is of recent onset or if it has been a chronic condition. Other factors may include the presence of any underlying heart disease, the method and response to treatment, the presence of complications, job requirements, and the age of the individual.

Length of Disability

Disability duration and its relationship to work depends on the stability of the rhythm. The length of disability may depend upon the physical and emotional requirements of the job. Disability may be permanent for physically demanding work.

Medical treatment.

Duration in Days

Job Classification	Minimum	Optimum	Maximum
Sedentary work	1	3	7
Light work	1	3	7
Medium work	1	7	14
Heavy work	7	14	21
Very Heavy work	7	14	21

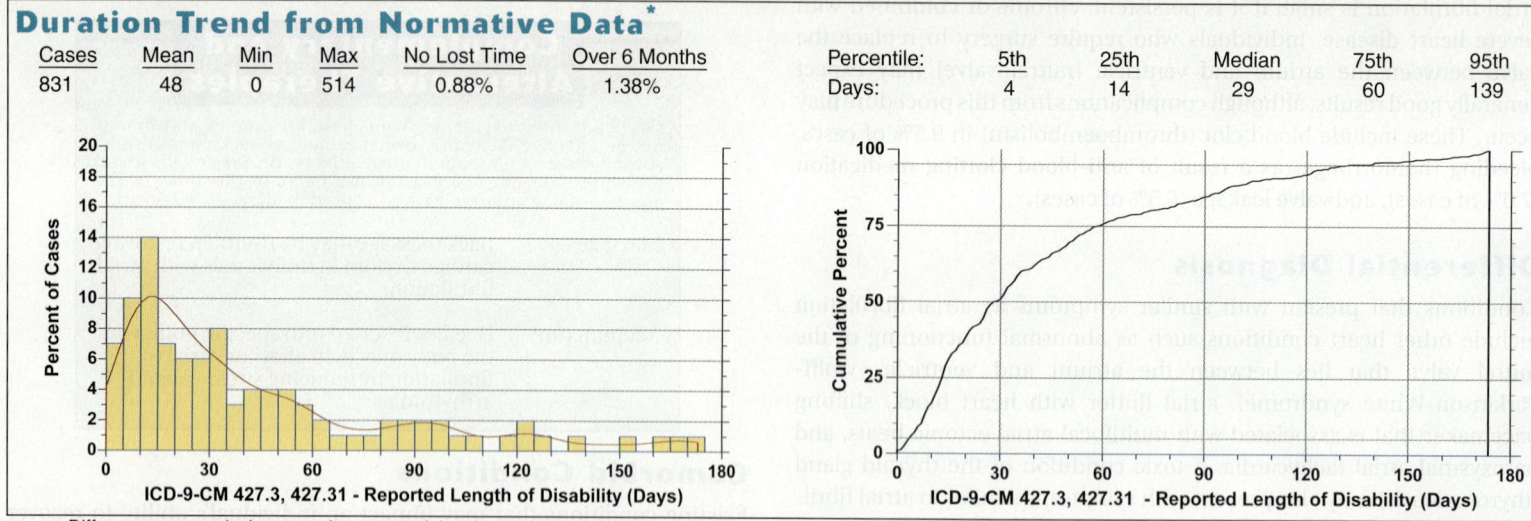

Failure to Recover

If an individual fails to recover within the maximum duration expectancy period, the reader may wish to reference the following questions to assist in better understanding the specifics of an individual's medical case.

Regarding diagnosis:

- What was individual's heart rate?
- Does individual use excessive nicotine, caffeine or alcohol?
- Does individual take medications that could have an adverse side effect?
- How does individual describe what the heartbeat feels like? Are the episodes of the abnormal beats paroxysmal?
- Does individual have anxiety, fatigue weakness, dyspnea or light-headedness?
- Was there complaint of chest pain?
- On exam was the pulse irregular? Were there abnormal heart sounds? Pulse deficit?
- Did individual have hypertension?
- Was an ECG performed? Was a Holter monitor used?
- Was complete blood testing done?
- Was an echocardiogram done? Angiography?
- Were conditions with similar symptoms ruled out?

Regarding treatment:

- Has individual responded to the anti-arrhythmic drugs?
- If not, was an emergency defibrillation necessary to restore normal heart rhythm?
- Is individual on anticoagulant drug therapy?
- Does individual have mitral valve stenosis? Is surgery to correct it indicated?

Regarding prognosis:

- Is individual actively participating in a home exercise program as recommended by the physician?
- Does individual have any conditions that may affect ability to recover?
- Has individual had any complications such as a stroke? Angina pectoris? Heart failure?

References

Curtis, M. "The Use of Massage in Restoring Cardiac Rhythm." Nursing Times 90 38 (1994): 36-37.

Prystowsky, E.N., and A. Katz. "Atrial Fibrillation." Textbook of Cardiovascular Medicine. Topol, E.J., eds. Philadelphia: Lippincott-Raven, 1998. 1661-1693.

Atrioventricular Block Incomplete (Second-Degree)

Other names / synonyms: 2:1 Atrioventricular Response Block, Atrioventricular Response Block, Mobitz Type I, Second-Degree AV Block, Second-Degree Incomplete AV Block

426.12, 426.13

Definition

Second-degree atrioventricular (AV) block refers to a delayed conduction of heartbeats (impulses) from the upper chambers (atria) to the lower chambers of the heart (ventricles). Not all impulses are conducted therefore the ventricles beat slower than the atria to some degree. Incomplete or second-degree block is divided into two types, Mobitz type I and Mobitz type II. Both are characterized by "dropped beats."

In Mobitz type I (also called Wenckebach block), the AV conduction time (reflected by the P-R interval) progressively increases over several heartbeats until an impulse is blocked. This blockage is usually due to a conduction problem in the AV node itself. Mobitz type I AV block may occur during a heart attack (acute myocardial infarction or AMI) involving the lower (inferior) surface of the heart. It is associated with various degenerative or infiltrative diseases of the heart such as amyloidosis and sarcoidosis and from certain cardiac drugs such as digitalis, beta-blockers, and some calcium-channel blockers. It may also result from acute rheumatic fever in children and can occur in well-trained athletes.

Mobitz type II is more serious and a much less common disorder. Individuals at risk for second-degree AV block, Mobitz type II are those who experienced a heart attack that damaged the front wall of the heart (anterior wall myocardial infarction). Other possible causes include pre-existing heart disease, inflammatory diseases (i.e., rheumatoid arthritis), infections, interrupted conduction pathways due to surgery, and scarring. Mobitz type II may also be caused by medications used to regulate the heart such as beta-blockers, calcium-channel blockers, and digitalis in addition to metabolic imbalances in the body.

Diagnosis

History: Symptoms may not be present with Mobitz type I or Mobitz type II block. However, individual may report light-headedness or weakness with Mobitz type I block and shortness of breath, chest pain, or palpitations with Mobitz type II block.

Physical exam: The exam reveals an irregular rhythm at a rate of 50 to 100 beats per minute with Mobitz type I. Mobitz type II AV block may present with a regular rhythm at a rate of 30 to 50 beats per minute.

Tests: The electrocardiogram (ECG) confirms second-degree AV block of both types. A portable ECG recorder (Holler recorder) with a 24-hour memory is often used document the arrhythmia.

Treatment

Mobitz type I AV block usually requires no specific treatment. If this type of block is drug-induced, withholding the medication leads to resolution of the AV block. If due to an AMI, the AV block usually resolves spontaneously as the AMI heals.

Treatment is required for a Mobitz type II AV block. A temporary or permanent pacemaker is inserted. Drugs therapy is either infective or unreliable.

Prognosis

Mobitz type I block is usually short-lived. When due to a drug or an inferior AMI, it generally resolves with time (days). However, sometimes it does progress to third-degree AV block (complete heart block). A pacemaker is infrequently necessary because the block is high enough that even if complete heart block occurred, the ventricles continue to beat at a rate of 45 beats per minute or more.

Mobitz type II is usually not short-lived and frequently progresses to complete heart block. A permanent pacemaker is then implanted because the block is lower and the ventricles beat at a rate of less than 45 beats per minute. Individuals can lead normal lives after pacemaker insertion.

Differential Diagnosis

Heart arrhythmias of many types can produce similar symptoms (atrial fibrillation, ventricular arrhythmias). ECG remains the best way to differentiate these arrhythmias.

Conditions that produce ECG changes similar to Mobitz type I block include intermittent sinoatrial exit block and frequent blocked atrial premature complexes.

Specialists

- Cardiologist

Work Restrictions / Accommodations

Individuals with Mobitz type I block (not due to an AMI) do not usually require work restrictions or accommodations. Individuals with Mobitz type II block do not usually require any significant work restrictions or accommodations for the conduction problem itself, since a permanent pacemaker was installed.

Comorbid Conditions

Comorbid conditions include underlying cardiovascular disease, hypertension, obesity, smoking, and diabetes mellitus.

Complications

Both Mobitz I and Mobitz II second-degree AV block may progress to third-degree AV block (complete heart block).

Factors Influencing Duration

Length of disability may be influenced by the underlying medical condition (e.g., heart attack), method of treatment required, and individual's job requirements.

Length of Disability

Job Classification	Duration in Days		
	Minimum	Optimum	Maximum
Sedentary work	14	42	Indefinite
Light work	14	42	Indefinite
Medium work	21	56	Indefinite
Heavy work	28	84	Indefinite
Very Heavy work	56	112	Indefinite

Failure to Recover

If an individual fails to recover within the maximum duration expectancy period, the reader may wish to reference the following questions to assist in better understanding the specifics of an individual's medical case.

Regarding diagnosis:

- Does individual complain of symptoms such as light-headedness, weakness, shortness of breath, chest pain, or palpitations?
- Were slow heart rhythm (bradycardia), dropped beats, variation in the first heart sounds, or an abnormal heart rhythm (gallop) heard?
- Was a recent electrocardiogram (ECG) done especially while symptoms are occurring?

Regarding treatment:

- Has individual taken medication as prescribed?
- Did individual undergo implantation of a cardioverter/defibrillator of catheter ablation therapy?

Regarding prognosis:

- How severe and frequent are the symptoms?
- Do symptoms interfere with daily activities?

References

About Cardiovascular Disease. Center for Disease Control. 28 July 2000. 15 Nov 2000 <http://www.cdc.gov/hccdphp/cvd/aboutcardio.htm>.

Comprehensive Risk Reduction for Patients with Coronary and Other Vascular Disease. American Heart Association. 1999. 14 Nov 2000 <http://www.Americanheart.org/scientific/statements/1995/hguide2.html>.

DeBakey, Michael, and Antonio Gotto. The New Living Heart. Holbrook: Adams Media Corporation, 1997.

McGoon, Michael. Mayo Clinic Heart Book. New York: William Morrow & Company, Inc, 1993.

Atrioventricular Block, Complete (Third-Degree)

Other names / synonyms: Atrioventricular Block, Complete Atrioventricular Block, Third-Degree Atrioventricular Block, Third-Degree AV Block, Third-Degree Heart Block

426.0

Definition

A complete heart block (third-degree atrioventricular-AV- block) occurs when no electrical impulses reach from the upper heart chambers (atria) to the lower heart chambers (ventricles). When this occurs, the ventricles use their back-up system of firing their own impulses (subsidiary pacemaker), but they fire too slowly, resulting in a serious drop in heart rate. This, in turn, results in less blood flow to the brain, which can result in loss of consciousness and even death.

The site of blockage of electrical impulses can be in the AV node, with rhythm maintained by pacemakers in the AV junction. On ECG (electrocardiogram), the portion of the heart tracing called the QRS complex is narrow, and heart rate is about 40-80 beats per minute. If the site of blockage is lower, in the bundle branches that normally carry electrical impulses to the ventricles, the subsidiary pacemaker is in the so-called Purkinje fibers. In this situation, QRS complexes are wide, and heart rate is slower, about 20-40 beats per minute.

Complete heart block most often occurs in individuals with pre-existing heart conditions including valvular disease, heart attack (myocardial infarction), insufficient blood supply to the heart muscle (ischemic heart disease), or drug toxicity.

Some form of cardiovascular disease (CVD) is present in more than 59 million Americans, resulting in 2600 deaths per day, or one death every 33 seconds.

Diagnosis

History: Individuals may report sudden loss of consciousness (syncope) or near syncope. When this occurs without warning, it is called a "drop attack" (Stokes-Adams attack). Heartbeats that are strong enough to make the person aware of them (palpitations), weakness, easy fatigability, decreased exercise capacity, shortness of breath, and chest pain are also reported.

Physical exam: Most notable is the slow, regular pulse rate (below 50 beats per minute) that does not accelerate during exercise.

Tests: Diagnosis is confirmed by an electrocardiogram (ECG).

Treatment

Treatment of the underlying medical problem is of critical importance. If heart block is due to drug toxicity, the drug needs to be discontinued immediately and a temporary ventricular demand pacemaker may be required. If, however, the block appears to be permanent (due to conduction system disease) or if it might recur, a permanent pacemaker needs to be promptly implanted. Accompanying heart attack (myocardial infarction) should be treated aggressively with monitoring, cardiovascular support, medications, and other measures as needed.

Drugs that cause increased contractility and heart rate may be used as a temporary measure until an artificial pacemaker can be installed. These include atropine, catecholamines (dopamine or epinephrine), and theophylline.

Prognosis

Most individuals recover after the installation of a pacemaker. Individuals with complete atrioventricular block following a myocardial infarction (heart attack) have a greater risk of death.

Differential Diagnosis

Conditions with similar symptoms originating from the heart include pulsus alternans, sinus bradycardia, sinus standstill with an escape rhythm, second-degree atrioventricular block of either Mobitz type I or II, and frequent premature atrial or ventricular contractions (PACs or PVCs) accompanied by full compensatory pauses.

Specialists

- Cardiologist

Rehabilitation

Individuals who have undergone placement of a pacemaker may attend a hospital-based cardiac rehabilitation program. These programs assist with lifestyle changes and exercise regimens appropriate for the condition and individual requirements. Individuals should attend outpatient physical and occupational therapy at a clinic that specializes in cardiac rehabilitation.

EKG-monitored exercise is required for 30-60 minutes, three to four times per week, and may last for several weeks until the individual is stable. Individuals learn to self-monitor their pulse and to rate the amount of energy they expend by utilizing a rating of perceived exertion scale. This is a numbered scale that rates exercises from very, very light to very, very hard. Individuals use this scale and their pulse to stay within safe exercise parameters that have been predetermined by their physicians. Individuals may attend physical therapy to learn basic conditioning and stretching exercises. Individuals also perform aerobic exercise such as treadmill walking or stationary bicycling. Initial activities may include limited walking, range-of-motion, and treadmill exercises. Eventually, more frequent walks, walk-jog, biking, and arm ergometer exercises may be encouraged. Exercise may become more strenuous as permitted by the physician with a goal of attaining 75-85% maximum intensity while walking, jogging, biking, swimming, performing calisthenics, and/or weight training.

Occupational therapy addresses any fatigue or shortness of breath that may occur during activities of daily living. Individuals learn to utilize equipment such as a shower chair to decrease the energy expended during bathing, or a long-handled sponge to decrease the amount arm activity necessary for bathing. (Excessive arm activity is more taxing on the heart and can lead to fatigue). Occupational therapists may teach energy conservation techniques, in which activities of daily living such as meal preparation are broken up into smaller components thereby making tasks more manageable.

Work Restrictions / Accommodations

Extended work leave may be required. If this condition is associated with other significant medical problems, temporary transfer to sedentary duties may be required while treatment is being performed.

Comorbid Conditions

Comorbid conditions that might influence length of disability include first degree atrioventricular block, second degree atrioventricular block, circulation disorders, obesity, and smoking. Heart attack (acute myocardial infarction) may be seen in up to half of individuals receiving emergency treatment for third degree AV block.

Complications

Possible complications include stroke, congestive heart failure, low blood pressure (circulatory shock), other forms of cardiovascular disease, diabetes mellitus, and other conditions associated with impaired circulation.

Factors Influencing Duration

Length of disability may be influenced by the age of the individual, the severity of symptoms and of underlying conditions, and the response to treatment.

Length of Disability

Duration in Days

Job Classification	Minimum	Optimum	Maximum
Sedentary work	14	21	42
Light work	14	21	42
Medium work	28	28	56
Heavy work	28	28	84
Very Heavy work	56	56	84

Failure to Recover

If an individual fails to recover within the maximum duration expectancy period, the reader may wish to reference the following questions to assist in better understanding the specifics of an individual's medical case.

Regarding diagnosis:

- What was individual's heart rate?
- Does individual have a history of a myocardial infarction, valvular disease, ischemic heart disease or drug toxicity?
- Has individual had a syncopal or near-syncopal episode?
- Does individual have palpitations? Decreased exercise capacity? Shortness of breath? Chest pain?
- Does individual fatigue easily?
- On exam, was individual's heart rate below 50 beats per minute?
- Was diagnosis confirmed with ECG?
- Were conditions with similar symptoms ruled out?

Regarding treatment:

- If the heart block is due to drug toxicity, has the drug been discontinued?
- Is individual being treated with atropine, dopamine, epinephrine or theophylline?
- Was a pacemaker implanted?

Regarding prognosis:

- Is individual active in cardiac rehabilitation?
- Is individual's employer able to accommodate any necessary restrictions?
- Does individual have any conditions that may affect their ability to recover?
- Does individual have any complications such as stroke, congestive heart failure, low blood pressure (circulatory shock) or other forms of cardiovascular disease?

References

"About Cardiovascular Disease." Cardiovascular Health. 28 July 2000. 14 Nov 2000 <http://www.cdc.gov/nccdphp/cvd/aboutcardio.htm>.

Feinstein, Alice, ed. Healing with Vitamins. Emmaus, PA: Rodale Press, Inc, 1996.

Atrioventricular Block, Incomplete (First-Degree)
Other names / synonyms: First-Degree AV Block, First-Degree Incomplete AV Block
426.11

Definition

First-degree atrioventricular (AV) block refers to abnormally slow conduction of heartbeats (impulses) from the upper chambers (atria) to the lower chambers (ventricles) of the heart. All impulses are conducted but the delay between the contraction of the atria and ventricles is slightly longer than normal. This results in a prolonged P-R interval on the electrocardiogram (ECG), the P wave reflecting atrial contraction and the R wave reflecting ventricular contraction. Consequently, while the atria beat normally, the ventricles lag slightly behind.

The causes of first-degree AV block include a heart attack (acute myocardial infarction), acute rheumatic fever as a child, scarring (fibrosis) of the pathway between the atria and ventricles in adults, a number of inflammatory or degenerative diseases, and certain drugs (most notably digitalis, beta-blockers, and some calcium-channel blockers). Importantly, first-degree AV block may also occur in trained athletes often in conjunction with a slow resting heart rate (bradycardia).

Diagnosis

History: There are no symptoms associated with first-degree AV block.

Physical exam: A decrease of the loudness of the first heart sound may be evident.

Tests: Diagnosis of first-degree AV block is confirmed by the prolonged P-R interval on the ECG.

Treatment

First-degree AV block requires no specific therapy. Treatment of the underlying cause usually results in its disappearance. Some individuals may progress to second-degree AV block. Those with underlying medical conditions are treated for the underlying condition rather than for the AV block.

Prognosis

First-degree AV block is not a life-threatening condition. Treatment of the underlying condition usually results in correction of first-degree AV block.

Differential Diagnosis

Premature atrial contractions (PACs) and premature ventricular contractions (PVCs) are conditions similar to first-degree AV block.

Specialists

- Cardiologist

Work Restrictions / Accommodations

Work restrictions and accommodations are not usually associated with first-degree AV block; however, an underlying medical condition such as rheumatoid arthritis, rheumatic heart disease, or an infection may necessitate work restrictions or accommodations. For those with underlying medical conditions, a decrease in activity may be necessary particularly if the job requires strenuous physical exertion.

Comorbid Conditions

Conditions that may influence length of disability include irregular heartbeats (arrhythmias).

Complications

There are usually no complications of first-degree AV block with the exception of possible progression to second-degree heart block.

Factors Influencing Duration

Length of disability may depend on job requirements and whether the individual has underlying medical conditions such as rheumatoid arthritis, infection, or rheumatic heart disease.

Length of Disability

Disability is not expected.

Failure to Recover

If an individual fails to recover within the maximum duration expectancy period, the reader may wish to reference the following questions to assist in better understanding the specifics of an individual's medical case.

Regarding diagnosis:

- Does individual have a history of an acute myocardial infarction, acute rheumatic fever as a child, fibrosis of the pathway between the atria and ventricles in adults, inflammatory or degenerative diseases?
- Is individual taking digitalis, beta-blockers, or calcium-channel blockers?
- Is individual a trained athlete with bradycardia?
- On physical exam, was a decrease of the loudness of the first heart sound evident?
- Was an ECG performed?

Regarding treatment:

- As first-degree AV block requires no specific therapy, is the underlying condition being treated?

Regarding prognosis:

- Is individual's employer able to accommodate any necessary restrictions?
- Does individual have any conditions that may affect ability to recover?
- Does individual have any complications such as progression to second-degree heart block?

References

"About Cardiovascular Disease." Centers for Disease Control. 28 July 2000. 14 Nov 2000 <http://www.cdc.gov/nccdphp/cvd/aboutcardio.htm>.

"Preventing Heart Attack and Death in Patients With Coronary Disease." American Heart Association. 1999. 14 Nov 2000 <http://www.americanheart.org/Scientific/statements/1995/hguide2.html>.

DeBakey, Michael, and Antonio Gotto. The New Living Heart. Holbrook, MA: Adams Media Corporation, 1997.

McGoon, Michael. Mayo Clinic Heart Book. New York: William Morrow & Company, Inc, 1993.

Atrophy, Muscular

Other names / synonyms: Atrophy of the Muscles, Muscle Atrophy, Muscle Wasting, Wasting

356.1, 359, 728.2

Definition

Muscle atrophy is the wasting or loss of muscle tissue resulting from either disease or lack of use.

In the general population, most muscular atrophy results from disuse. Sedentary jobs and decreased activity with aging can cause loss of muscle tone and significant atrophy. A study in 1990 showed that 21 days of physical immobilization of able-bodied individuals produced changes in the following areas: urinary function, calcium metabolism, blood chemistry and blood volume, gastric function, blood flow, blood structure with higher potential for lower extremity clogging, and skin integrity.

Muscle atrophy resulting from disease can be divided into two types: diseases affecting the nerves that supply the muscles (e.g., poliomyelitis and amyotrophic lateral sclerosis) and diseases of the muscle itself (e.g., muscular dystrophy and myotonic dystrophy).

The nerve supply to the muscle can be interrupted by becoming compressed or severed or by a disease within the nerve cells themselves. The site of the interruption can occur in the brain, spinal cord, or a peripheral nerve. Compression can occur by a herniated disc either within the spinal cord or where the nerve exits and becomes a nerve root. A nerve may also be trapped and compressed within certain tight anatomical spots such as with carpal tunnel or thoracic outlet syndromes. The nerve can be compressed by tissue swelling (a compartment syndrome) following a crushing injury, fracture, or a too-tight cast. A disease may exist within the nerve cells themselves with the nerve becoming temporarily or permanently nonfunctional. Examples include multiple sclerosis, Lou Gehrig's disease (amyotrophic lateral sclerosis), a stroke, or a viral infection of the nerve cells.

A muscle disease can be intrinsic to muscle tissue as in muscular dystrophy or myotonia. It can also be a response to a systemic disease such as a seriously underactive or overactive thyroid or adrenal gland, severe diabetes, or autoimmune illnesses like rheumatoid arthritis or dermatomyositis. It can be drug-induced from alcohol or opiate abuse or from prolonged use of steroids. Generalized muscle wasting (cachexia) can occur with advanced cancer or AIDS. Disuse atrophy can result from immobilization in a cast or sling. A reduced use of a muscle due to pain in a joint can occur such as limping after a knee or ankle injury. Disuse atrophy may also occur at the same time as a nerve supply interruption, as seen in ankylosing spondylitis.

Atrophy caused by lack of use is reversible with exercise.

Diagnosis

History: Individuals usually report loss of strength and muscle fatigue. Complaints may vary according to the muscles affected (e.g., atrophy of the chest muscles may cause breathing difficulty). It is important to elicit from the individual a time pattern and location of the symptoms.

Physical exam: The extent of atrophy is determined by general observation (lack of muscle tone, weakness of the specific muscles) and limb circumference measurements. Sensation and reflexes may or may not be abnormal.

Tests: Electromyography (EMG) can be helpful in unclear cases. Blood tests are generally not helpful. A muscle biopsy is sometimes done if polymyositis is suspected.

Treatment

The most common treatment for muscular atrophy is regular exercise often in a physical therapy program. The physical therapist works with the individual's physician to develop a specific program of exercises to help strengthen the muscle and restore as much normal activity as possible. Electrical stimulation can sometimes facilitate the return of muscle strength via application of a very weak current to the area that painlessly stimulates the muscle. In cases of atrophy caused by some whole-body diseases (autoimmune disorders), the physician may elect to use intramuscular injections of anabolic steroids. For some cases of severe atrophy where the muscle is in danger of shrinking so much that it can get short enough to contract a joint and cause further problems, a brace may be applied to the affected area.

Prognosis

Outcome depends on the causative disease. Most uncomplicated types of atrophy caused by a simple lack of use of a muscle or muscles can be treated with exercise with a full or nearly full recovery. If the individual has a more complicated medical problem (e.g., amyotrophic lateral sclerosis, muscular dystrophy), then atrophy is progressive through the remainder of the individual's life.

Differential Diagnosis

Other conditions that may present with similar symptoms include multiple sclerosis, acquired immune deficiency syndrome, Lyme disease, toxoplasmosis, rheumatoid arthritis, systemic lupus erythematosus, thyroid disease, diabetes, lymphoma and other carcinomas, and depression.

Specialists

- Neurologist
- Physiatrist

Rehabilitation

Physical therapy for muscular atrophy depends on the etiology (cause), extent, and location of the atrophy. For example, if the individual sustained an injury that severed the nerves enervating muscles of the foot, a different protocol is warranted than for someone experiencing a progressive muscular disease (e.g., muscular dystrophy). Muscular atrophy may also be due to immobility of the affected area from casting or other form of fixation. The latter form of muscular atrophy is the easiest and most straightforward to treat. Overlapping therapeutic strategies occur in all three cases but have common goals. These include maintaining range of motion for all joints, increasing or maintaining overall muscle integrity and strength, improving muscular efficiency (decreasing muscular effort when performing daily living tasks), and educating the individual on injury prevention. These goals are met through a progressive exercise routine that may include the assistance of an occupational therapist or a vocational specialist.

After an injury requiring limb fixation, therapy may consist of range-of-motion exercises for the noninjured areas of the body. Exercises such as arm raises or heel slides are done.

Neuromuscular stimulation may also be used for intact motor nerves to maintain range of motion and start the reeducation process for the muscle. This type of muscle stimulation can be used while performing movements that pattern appropriate biomechanics for that limb. Low voltage electromuscular stimulation (EMS) helps stimulate denervated muscles where peripheral nerve damage has occurred. These forms of muscle stimulation fall under the heading of transcutaneous electrical nerve stimulation (T.E.N.S.). T.E.N.S. is also effective as a sensory modality for decreasing intracellular fluid within the joint thus reducing pain. By changing the intensity, frequency, and pulse of the current, a sensory effect (decreased pain) or muscular effect (maximal recruitment of muscle fibers) can be noninvasively elicited in the individual.

As the individual gains more range of motion and fatigue is not an impeding factor, more challenging exercises involving resistance may be added. The time course for including resistive exercises depends on the type of injury. For example, muscular atrophy is addressed secondarily to a healing fracture. Regardless of injury type, different methods of hydrotherapy (aquatic rehabilitation) facilitate increased range of motion and weight bearing without maximal forces of gravity. For those individuals who cannot participate in a pool environment, a whirlpool is effective. Once the individual can tolerate his/her full weight, the routine can be split between aquatic and standard exercises.

Depending on the injury, core strength exercises help improve muscle efficiency and stabilization. An example of a core strength task is to sit or stand on an unstable surface while reaching for an object. These exercises are performed on a fitness ball or balance board. If paralysis is involved, recreational therapy using games such as balloon volleyball or billiards help build functional balance and manual dexterity.

An occupational therapist may evaluate the individual's home and work environment since some individuals may still be fatigued when performing repetitive or labor intensive tasks such as hammering. Additional support from a vocational rehabilitation specialist may be needed if paralysis or other permanent and debilitating injury is involved.

Work Restrictions / Accommodations

Work restrictions and accommodations are determined on an individual basis depending on the underlying cause of the muscular atrophy, the muscles affected, and severity of the atrophy. An individual with mild atrophy (caused by lack of use) may be able to continue working but in a limited capacity until an exercise program builds and tones the affected muscles. Individuals with atrophy caused by a progressive disease may need to reduce the physical workload periodically.

Complementary and Alternative Therapies

Content is intended for awareness only. Treatments may or may not be effective. Scientific evidence may be lacking and some substances have potentially toxic effects. Dr. Presley Reed and the editors do not endorse the use of these therapies in the absence of consultation with a licensed medical professional.

Massage therapy -	May reduce muscle atrophy by improving muscle tone and circulation.
Creatine -	Used by bodybuilders and other athletes; said to increase strength and muscle mass. Creatine is a naturally occurring compound made of the three amino acids arginine, glycine, and methionine.

Comorbid Conditions

Conditions that can impact ability to recover and further lengthen disability include obesity, osteoarthritis, diabetes, muscular dystrophy, multiple sclerosis, systemic lupus erythematosus, and myasthenia gravis.

Complications

Complications of muscle atrophy are highly dependent on the underlying cause of the atrophy. Muscle atrophy can result in mechanical strain on other muscles and joints, accelerating wear and fatigue.

Factors Influencing Duration

The severity of muscle atrophy, the muscle(s) affected, and underlying cause of the atrophy influence the disability period. The individual's ability and willingness to participate in rehabilitation will also be a factor in the length of disability.

Length of Disability

Disability may be permanent. The expected length of disability varies depending on the cause and the severity of the atrophy.

Failure to Recover

If an individual fails to recover within the maximum duration expectancy period, the reader may wish to reference the following questions to assist in better understanding the specifics of an individual's medical case.

Regarding diagnosis:

- Has individual become inactive? Do they have a sedentary job?
- Does individual have any diseases that affect the nerves that supply the muscles?
- Do they have diseases of the muscle itself?
- Does individual have a systemic disease?
- Was individual taking drugs such as opiates, steroids or alcohol?
- Was individual in a cast or other immobilization?
- Does individual complain of loss of strength and muscle fatigue?
- What muscles are affected? Is there a pattern to their symptoms?
- On exam was lack of muscle tone and weakness noted?
- Were limb circumference measurements done?
- Were sensation and reflexes diminished? Normal?
- Was an EMG and muscle biopsy done?
- Were conditions with similar symptoms ruled out?

Regarding treatment:

- Is individual exercising regularly? In a physical therapy program?
- Was electrical stimulation used?
- Was bracing necessary?
- Were anabolic steroids used if appropriate?

Regarding prognosis:

- Is individual's employer able to accommodate the necessary restrictions?
- Does individual have any conditions that may affect their ability to recover?
- Does individual have mechanical strain that is affecting other muscles or joints?

References

Hunter-Griffin, Letha. Athletic Training and Sports Medicine, 2nd ed. Rosemont: American Academy of Orthopedic Surgeons, 1991.

Muscle Atrophy. drkoop.com 2000. 09 Nov 2000 <http://www.drkoop.com/conditions/ency/article/003188.htm>.

Atrophy, Muscular (Progressive)

Other names / synonyms: Familial Muscular Atrophy, Hereditary Muscular Atrophy, Motor Neuron Disease, Pure Progressive Muscular Atrophy

335.21

Definition

Progressive muscular atrophy is an inherited disorder affecting the nerves that control muscle activity in the body (motor neuron disease). In progressive muscular atrophy, deterioration (degeneration) occurs in the anterior horn cells of the spinal cord, the motor nuclei of the lower cranial nerves, and the corticospinal and corticobulbar pathways. This condition is a progressively debilitating disease. As the nerves deteriorate, the weakened muscles of the hands, arms, and legs waste (atrophy), stiffen, and may twitch involuntarily (fasciculate). Muscles controlling swallowing, chewing, coughing, breathing, and speech may be affected to varying degrees, but those controlling the bowels and bladder are usually spared.

The five varieties of progressive muscular atrophy are progressive bulbar palsy, pseudobulbar palsy, progressive spinal muscular atrophy, primary lateral sclerosis, and amyotrophic lateral sclerosis.

Onset of the disease is usually between the ages of 30 and 60. More than one individual in a family may be affected.

Diagnosis

History: As the spinal cord nerves degenerate, individuals typically present with muscle weakness and wasting in the hands, arms, and legs. This may be accompanied by involuntary muscle twitching (fasciculation). In some forms of the disease, the face and tongue muscles are especially affected by twitching. Over time, the individual experiences increased difficulty speaking (dysarthria), swallowing (dysphagia), and breathing. Because awareness and intellect remain unchanged, this disease can be especially distressing for the individual and family.

Physical exam: The exam reveals progressive muscle weakness and wasting. Although individuals may have vague sensory complaints, the senses (hearing, sight, smell, taste, and touch) show no objective changes.

Tests: Diagnosis is confirmed through electromyography (EMG). Measurement of muscle electrical activity can show changes in chronic partial denervation. A muscle biopsy can also indicate nerve changes. To rule out other diseases, additional testing may include blood studies, myelography (x-ray study of the spinal cord that has been injected with contrast dye), CT, or MRI.

Treatment

At this time, there is no known effective treatment or means of slowing the nerve deterioration. Treatment, therefore, is designed to relieve specific symptoms and provide needed support. Anticholinergic drugs that decrease the amount of saliva produced by the salivary glands can be prescribed if drooling is troublesome. Benzodiazepine tranquilizers and muscle relaxants may decrease muscular spasticity.

Physical therapy and occupational therapy maintain joint mobility, prevent shortening of muscle tissue (contractures), and maintain strength in those muscles that are still functioning. Braces and walkers can provide stability and improve mobility. Independence is maintained as long as possible by the use of wheelchairs, walkers, and other aids.

In later stages, feeding by means of a tube inserted either through the nose and into the stomach (nasogastric tube) or through a surgical opening directly into the stomach (gastrostomy) may be necessary because of choking and difficulty swallowing. An opening in the windpipe (tracheostomy) may be necessary if respiratory muscles are severely affected.

Prognosis

The progress of progressive muscular atrophy is especially devastating because individuals with the disease retain their mental powers (cognition) while their bodies gradually waste away. Individuals in the end stages may be totally paralyzed and unable to speak, move, or breathe on their own. Death generally occurs 3 to 6 years after the onset of the disease, usually as a result of pulmonary infections.

Differential Diagnosis

Differential diagnoses include progressive bulbar palsy, pseudobulbar palsy, progressive spinal muscular atrophy, primary lateral sclerosis, amyotrophic lateral sclerosis, spinal cord compression by tumor, chronic inflammatory disease of the spinal cord and meninges, and progressive weakness for intrinsic diseases of muscles.

Specialists

- Internist
- Neurologist
- Occupational Therapist
- Physical Therapist
- Psychiatrist

Rehabilitation

The goal of rehabilitation for progressive muscular atrophy is to maintain function and enhance mobility for as long as possible. In the early stage of the disease, active range-of-motion physical therapy can help maintain flexibility and strength and relieve the musculoskeletal pain associated with muscular weakness, paralysis, and immobility. In active range-of-motion exercises, the individual performs all the motion independently with or without resistance from an outside force. Resistance is provided through use of an elastic band or light weights (isotonic exercise). Weights are often used by the therapist. As the weight is lifted throughout the range of motion, the muscle shortens and lengthens. In later stages, passive range of motion is preferable to avoid overexertion or possible damage to the muscles. In passive range-of-motion exercises the therapist moves the involved limb without effort from the individual.

Because of muscle weakness to the legs, balance exercises are beneficial and include side stepping and walking with the eyes closed with and without assistance. Respiratory muscles can also become progressively weak as the disease advances so exercises to strengthen muscles that assist in breathing become part of the program. For example, shoulder shrugs with light dumbbells are performed with the individual holding a dumbbell weight in each hand at the side, elbows straight. While keeping the elbows straight, the individual shrugs the shoulders, holds this position for 5 seconds, and then returns to the starting position. This exercise is performed twice a day and repeated 10 times in 2 to 3 sets.

Learning how to avoid injury is another important intervention in the rehabilitation of progressive muscular atrophy. Occupational therapy helps individuals arrange their homes and organize their lives in ways that support their physical and mental well being. Activities are also provided to relieve the mental boredom of inactivity. Devices and techniques that help the individual communicate are invaluable in maintaining peace of mind.

Counseling and support groups can help individuals and caregivers cope with the devastating physical aspects of the disease. The rehabilitation program varies between individuals with progressive muscular atrophy as the intensity and progression of the exercise depends on the stage of the disease and the individual's overall health.

Work Restrictions / Accommodations

Because work is often therapeutic, the individual may strive to continue working as long as possible. Limited work activities may be possible depending on the nature of the work and the individual's degree of muscular weakness. The individual's workspace may need to be changed to accommodate a wheelchair and provide a safe environment. Safety issues and accommodations revolve around the individual's weakness, physical instability, and tendency to choke.

Comorbid Conditions

Comorbid conditions that may impact recovery and lengthen disability include obesity, smoking, and pre-existing diseases that affect any of the major body systems such as diabetes, chronic obstructive lung disease, or chronic heart disease.

Complications

Individuals with progressive muscular atrophy are susceptible to all the diseases and conditions common to other chronically ill, weakened individuals with impaired mobility. These conditions include vascular disease, stroke, blood clots, choking and aspiration, infectious disease, gastrointestinal disorders, diabetes, respiratory complications, and pressure sores. If surgical intervention is required for any of these conditions, the individual is subject to the usual surgical complications such as infection, adverse reaction to the anesthetic, pneumonia, or poor wound closure.

Factors Influencing Duration

Length of disability may be influenced by the individual's general health and mental and emotional stability. The severity and progression of symptoms will ultimately determine how long the individual is able to continue working. Disability eventually becomes permanent.

Length of Disability

Disability may be permanent.

Failure to Recover

If an individual fails to recover within the maximum duration expectancy period, the reader may wish to reference the following questions to assist in better understanding the specifics of an individual's medical case.

Regarding diagnosis:

- Which of the five varieties of progressive muscular atrophy does individual have? Progressive bulbar palsy? Pseudobulbar palsy? Progressive spinal muscular atrophy? Primary lateral sclerosis or amyotrophic lateral sclerosis?
- Does individual have muscle weakness and wasting in the hand, arms, and legs? Does any involuntary muscle twitching (fasciculation) occur?
- Does individual have increased difficulty speaking, swallowing, and breathing? Was individual's awareness and intellect unchanged?
- Does individual have vague sensory complaints? Are hearing, sight, smell, taste, and touch unchanged?
- Was an EMG, muscle biopsy, blood tests, myelography, CT, or MRI done?
- Were conditions with similar symptoms ruled out?

Regarding treatment:

- Is individual receiving symptomatic treatment with support?
- Were anticholinergic drugs prescribed? Muscle relaxants?
- Is physical therapy involved in treatment?
- Was a feeding tube necessary? Tracheostomy?
- How long ago was the diagnosis made?

Regarding prognosis:

- Can individual's employer accommodate any necessary restrictions?
- Is individual active in rehabilitation? Does individual have a home exercise program?
- Are individual and caregivers involved in support groups? Counseling?
- Does individual have any conditions that may affect the disease process?
- Are there any complications such as vascular disease, stroke, blood clots, choking and aspiration, infectious disease, gastrointestinal disorders, diabetes, respiratory complications, or pressure sores?

References

Eberstein, A, and S. Eberstein. "Electrical Stimulation of Denervated Muscle: Is It Worthwhile?" Medicine and Science in Sports and Exercise 28 12 (1996): 1463-1469.

Hunsballe, J.M., and F.V. Mortensen. "Alternative Treatment Forms Used by Patients with Muscular Atrophy. A Questionnaire Study of the Use of Alternative Treatment by 345 Patients with Muscular Atrophy." Ugeskr Laeger 152 18 (1990): 1293-1296.

Scully, Rosemary M., and Marylou Barnes. Physical Therapy. Philadelphia: J.B. Lippincott Company, 1989.

Tierney, Lawrence M., Stephen J. McPhee, and Maxine Papadakis. Current Medical Diagnosis and Treatment. New York: McGraw-Hill, 2000.

Attention Deficit Disorder in Adults
Other names / synonyms: ADD, Attention-Deficit/Hyperactivity Disorder
314.0, 314.00, 314.01

Definition

Attention-deficit/hyperactivity disorder (ADHD) is a persistent pattern of inattention and/or hyperactivity-impulsivity more frequently displayed and more severe than typically observed in other individuals.

Symptoms occur most often in situations that demand sustained attention or are boring and difficult. They are more noticeable in a group environment than one-on-one situations. Impairment from symptoms should be displayed in at least two settings such as home and work.

Individuals may have a low frustration tolerance, fail to attend details of work, and make frequent careless mistakes. Individuals may also have difficulty sustaining attention to tasks or completing tasks or have difficulty organizing tasks and activities with work materials often scattered, lost, or carelessly handled. Individuals frequently shift from one uncompleted activity to another and fail to follow through on requests. They are easily distracted by irrelevant stimuli, fidget with hands or feet, or squirm while seated and have difficulty remaining seated in situations when it is expected. Other symptoms include difficulty engaging quietly in leisure activities, appearing to always be on the go, talking excessively, interrupting others during conversations, failing to listen to instructions, and feelings of restlessness and impatience.

The three subtypes of this disorder are ADHD combined type, ADHD predominantly inattentive type, and ADHD predominantly hyperactive-impulsive type. Individuals with ADHD may be labeled by others as bossy, lazy, or irresponsible when, in fact, problems with attention, concentration, and lack of follow-through occur with this disorder. ADHD begins in childhood and persists into adulthood for 15-70% of individuals. The symptoms may be more subtle and difficult to diagnose in an adult particularly if hyperactivity is absent. Adults with attention deficit disorder have developed more self-restraint and a better attention. By adulthood, the disorder is usually seen in its incomplete form. In adults, the symptoms of ADHD may be obscured by problems with relationships or work as well as mood disorders, substance abuse, or other psychological difficulties.

ADHD occurs more often in males than females. ADHD is more common in first-degree biological relatives of children diagnosed with ADHD. Brain pathways using the chemical dopamine may be affected in this disorder, as medications affecting dopamine levels are helpful in treating ADHD. Adults with ADHD are shown to have an abnormality of the dopamine D4 receptor gene.

Diagnosis

History: History involves any combination of failure to pay attention to details, difficulty maintaining attention to a task (especially an uninteresting one), not seeming to listen when spoken to, not following through on instructions, difficulty organizing tasks, avoidance of tasks requiring sustained mental attention, losing things, being easily distracted by surrounding stimuli, or forgetful in daily life.

Individual may also show symptoms of hyperactivity and impulsivity such as having difficulty sitting still or being quiet, talking excessively, difficulty waiting, or feelings of restlessness. These symptoms result in a significant limitation of social, occupational, and academic functioning. The individual may have a history of work or family conflicts related to difficulties with the ability to complete tasks. The individual should display symptoms in at least two settings although it is unusual for the individual to display the same level of dysfunction in all settings (work, school, family, or social). Symptoms are usually worse in settings that require sustained attention or lack novelty such as working on monotonous tasks.

Comprehensive clinical interview should include past and present ADHD symptoms, developmental and medical history, school and work history, psychiatric history, and medications history.

Physical exam: The exam is not helpful in this diagnosis although it may be observed that the individual is restless or fidgets. Minor physical anomalies such as low-set ears or a highly arched palate may occur at a higher rate in those with ADHD than in the general population.

Tests: Tests are not sufficient for diagnosis but may demonstrate a cognitive impairment such as inattention, disorganization, short-term memory, or executive functions (the ability to make themselves do something they dislike or are not interested in).

Treatment

Pharmacotherapy is the treatment of choice and usually includes one of the amphetamines or methylphenidate (Ritalin). Side effects from the medication can include insomnia, anorexia, irritability, weight loss, stomach pain, or headaches but these side effects may decrease in severity over a period of time or be managed by changing the dose strength and schedule.

Cognitive therapy may help the individual identify effective ways to reduce anxiety and view difficult situations in a different manner. Relaxation training, progressive muscle relaxation, and respiratory control training may help control restless behavior. Many therapists include homework and specific readings (bibliotherapy) for the individual to do between sessions. Since the individual may only spend a few sessions in one-on-one contact with a therapist, this method allows individuals to continue to work on their own with the aid of a printed manual. Psychodynamic treatment is another talk therapy where the therapist and individual work together to uncover underlying emotional conflicts and may be a helpful addition to the overall treatment plan.

Prognosis

Drug treatment usually improves the individual's functioning by improving attention span, concentration, memory, motor coordination, mood, and on-task behavior while decreasing daydreaming, hyperactivity, anger, and immature behavior. In an adult study of low-dose Adderall (mixed amphetamine salt), more than half of individuals improved although the drug tended to bring on anxiety symptoms in those with comorbid anxiety disorder.

Differential Diagnosis

Other conditions with similar symptoms are caffeine intoxication or side effects from bronchodilators or anticonvulsants, substance abuse (especially amphetamine-like substances), bipolar disorder, depression, generalized anxiety disorder, living in a chaotic environment, schizophrenia, or personality disorders such as avoidant, antisocial, borderline, or histrionic. Mild brain injury from head trauma, infections, or lack of oxygen may also have similar symptoms.

Specialists

- Advanced Practice Registered Nurse
- Occupational Therapist
- Psychiatrist
- Psychologist

Rehabilitation

Occupational therapy could assist the individual to develop communication skills or to identify and match personal skills and work habits to the work place.

Work Restrictions / Accommodations

An individual with ADHD generally performs better when engaged in personally stimulating activities, or in a one-to-one situation. Work restrictions or accommodations are necessary only infrequently, for the most serious cases. In these instances, time-limited restrictions and work accommodations should be individually determined based on the characteristics of the individual's response to the disorder, the functional requirements of the job and work environment, and the flexibility of the job and work site. The purpose of the restrictions/accommodation is to help maintain the worker's capacity to remain at the workplace without a work disruption or to promote timely and safe transition back to full work productivity.

Comorbid Conditions

Alcohol abuse or drug use may lengthen disability, as may the coexistence of other psychiatric disorders (depression, bipolar, or other mood disorder, dissociative disorder, personality disorder) or mental retardation. Neurological disorders such as traumatic brain injury may also lengthen disability.

Complications

Tourette's syndrome or tics can accompany ADHD. Anxiety disorders or depression can occur in reaction to the effects ADHD has on relationships, education and worth. Alcohol, cocaine, or amphetamine abuse may develop perhaps as an attempt to self-medicate for the condition. A higher rate of accidents and injuries may result from inattentiveness or impulsiveness. An antisocial personality disorder may emerge, leading to trouble with the law. ADHD can result in social isolation and difficult personal relationships. Educational achievement may suffer due to the disorder, and learning disabilities may affect reading, writing, or math. There may also be difficulty with learning strategies, memory, or problem solving. Poor work performance may lead to being fired and subsequent unemployment.

Factors Influencing Duration

The individual's specific impairments and strengths influence disability as well as the match between personal strengths and job duties. Length of disability is influenced by the duration and severity of ADHD, any underlying mental illness, other substance abuse, the individual's social support system, appropriateness of treatment choice, response to medications, compliance with treatment, and adequacy of ongoing care.

Length of Disability

Although symptoms of childhood ADHD may decrease in adulthood, some individuals may continue to have symptoms that interfere with work, family, or social life. Duration depends on severity of manifestations and exacerbating factors. In most cases, no disability is expected.

Failure to Recover

If an individual fails to recover within the maximum duration expectancy period, the reader may wish to reference the following questions to assist in better understanding the specifics of an individual's medical case.

Regarding diagnosis:

- Is there a family history of ADHD?
- Does individual take any medications? If so, for what conditions?
- Does individual report being unable to pay attention to details, not seeming to listen when spoken to, not following through on instructions, losing things, being easily distracted by surrounding stimuli, or forgetful in daily life?
- Does individual report difficulty maintaining attention to a task, difficulty organizing tasks, and avoidance of tasks requiring sustained mental attention?
- Does individual note work, family, or social conflicts related to difficulties completing tasks?
- Does individual have difficulty sitting still or waiting for anything?
- Does individual note that these symptoms are more noticeable in a group environment than one-on-one situations?
- Were tests, though not sufficient for diagnosis, done to demonstrate cognitive impairment such as inattention, disorganization, short-term memory, or executive functions (the ability to make oneself do something in which there is no interest)?
- Were other conditions identified or ruled out?
- Was diagnosis of ADHD confirmed?

Regarding treatment:

- Is individual taking medication for this disorder?
- Is the medication an amphetamines or methylphenidate (Ritalin)?
- If individual is not responding effectively to medication, would a dosage change be helpful or is a change of medication required?
- Does individual understand the importance of taking medications as prescribed?
- Is individual involved in a cognitive or psychodynamic therapy program?
- Is individual benefiting from therapy?
- Would individual benefit from attending a support group?

Regarding prognosis:

- Is the medication regimen adequately improving individual's functioning?
- Does individual have a positive relationship with the psychiatrist and/or therapist?
- Has individual been involved in the current form of treatment for over 6 weeks without a noticeable effect?
- Has the treatment plan been reassessed? What direction will the new treatment plan take?
- Does individual suffer from Tourette's syndrome or tics, which can accompany ADHD?
- Has individual developed anxiety disorders or depression from feeling impaired?
- Does individual abuse alcohol, cocaine, or amphetamines as an attempt to self-medicate for the condition?

References

Duke, James A. The Green Pharmacy. Emmaus, PA: Rodale Press, Inc, 1997.

Frances, Allen. Diagnostic and Statistical Manual of Mental Disorders: 4th ed., text revision. Washington, DC: American Psychiatric Association, 2000.

Horrigan, J.P., and L.J. Barnhill. "Low-dose Amphetamine Salts and Adult Attention-deficit/Hyperactivity Disorder." Journal of Clinical Psychiatry 61 6 (2000): 414-417.

Mandelkorn, Theodore D. Thoughts on the Medical Treatment of ADD/ADHD: A Physician's Perspective. ADDult Support of Washington for Adults with ADD. 01 Jan 2000. 17 Jan 2001 <http://www.addult.org/thoughts.htm>.

Muglia, P., et al. "Adult Attention Deficit Hyperactivity Disorder and the Dopamine D4 Receptor Gene." American Journal of Medical Genetics 96 3 (2000): 273-277.

New Choices in Natural Healing. Gottlieb, Bill, ed. Emmaus, PA: Rodale Press, Inc, 1995.

Smalley, S.L., et al. "Familial Clustering of Symptoms and Disruptive Behaviors in Multiplex Families with Attention-Deficit/Hyperactivity Disorder." Journal of the American Academy of Child and Adolescent Psychiatry 39 9 (2000): 1135-1143.

Weiss, M., L. Hechtman, and G. Weiss. "ADHD in Parents." Journal of the American Academy of Child and Adolescent Psychiatry 39 8 (2000): 1059-1061.

Avascular Necrosis

Other names / synonyms: Aseptic Necrosis, AVN, Osteonecrosis
733, 733.4, 733.40, 733.42

Definition

Avascular necrosis is a condition that results from poor blood supply to a particular area of bone, causing bone death.

Avascular necrosis can result from trauma and damage to the blood vessels that supply oxygen to the bone. Other causes of poor blood circulation to the bone include an obstruction (embolism) of air or fat that blocks the blood flow through the blood vessels, abnormally thick blood (hypercoagulable state), and inflammation of the blood vessel walls (vasculitis).

Avascular necrosis represents the final common pathway of several disease conditions. Conditions associated with avascular necrosis include pancreatitis, Cushing's syndrome, Gaucher disease, sickle cell disease, systemic lupus erythematosus, alcoholism, steroid usage, and radiation exposure. Many of these conditions result in impaired blood supply to the bone tissue that ultimately causes death (necrosis) of the bone.

The most common areas affected by avascular necrosis are the hip (femoral head), wrist (carpal scaphoid, navicular, lunate), ankle (talus), shoulder, and in segmental fractures. The femoral head is the most common site especially in men ages 40 to 59, and is often bilateral.

Epidemiological estimates suggest that 15,000 cases of avascular necrosis are reported each year in the US. The condition is most common in young males. The male-female ratio is 8 to 1. The afflicted individual is usually younger than 50.

Diagnosis

History: Symptomatic individuals may report pain after healing of a fracture, stiffness, or joint pain without associated trauma. Pain may be worse at night and after activity.

Physical exam: Pain is evident with active and passive motion. Individual typically has limited range of motion, muscle disuse atrophy, and weakness around the joint.

Tests: Routine joint x-rays reveal bony changes in later stages of the disease. Bone scans and MRI are used to locate and evaluate early signs of avascular necrosis.

Treatment

The treatment of avascular necrosis is critically dependent on the stage of the condition at diagnosis and on which joint is involved. Early avascular necrosis (before x-ray changes are evident) can be treated with a surgical procedure called core decompression. The procedure involves removing a core of bone from the involved area and sometimes grafting new bone into the area. The purpose of the bone graft is to promote formation of new blood supply that preserves the bone.

Later stages of avascular necrosis (when x-ray changes have occurred) inevitably lead to seriously damaged bone and joints that require joint replacement surgery.

Prognosis

Overall, early diagnosis and treatment of avascular necrosis may lead to a favorable outcome. The amount of bone involved and the presence or absence of joint surface collapse greatly affect outcome.

The core depression procedure is usually successful (improvement in blood supply and prevention of progressive bone destruction) in the very early stages of the disease, but for more advanced stages, the outcome is much less predictable.

Joint replacement surgery is successful in a high percentage of cases.

Differential Diagnosis

Other possibilities with similar symptoms include osteoporosis, osteoarthritis, Paget's disease of the bone, and stress fracture.

Specialists

- Endocrinologist
- Orthopedic Surgeon

Work Restrictions / Accommodations

Individuals may have limited use of the affected extremity. In avascular necrosis of the hip, for instance, crutches, a brace, walker, or wheelchair may be required. Frequent rest periods and modification of tasks to relieve stress to affected joints is an important component of the treatment of avascular necrosis.

Comorbid Conditions

Comorbid conditions that may influence length of disability include obesity, other complications of oral steroid use, and chronic diseases such as diabetes, high blood pressure, heart disease, osteoporosis, and alcoholism.

Complications

The underlying cause of avascular necrosis (i.e., trauma, damage to blood vessels, poor circulation, abnormally thick blood, and inflammation of blood vessel walls) can complicate treatment. Avascular necrosis can also cause fracture and osteoarthritis. A late stage complication of the disorder is a flattening of (collapse) the femoral head, the upper part of the thighbone (femur) that forms the ball portion of the hip joint. Collapse of the femoral head is followed by narrowed joint space and osteoarthritic changes in the opposing bones of the joint.

Factors Influencing Duration

Factors that may influence length of disability include underlying cause, location (ankle, wrist, elbow, shoulder), job requirements, response to treatment, treatment intervention, and compliance with treatment.

Length of Disability

Total hip replacement is not compatible with heavy or very heavy work. Disability may be permanent.

Total hip replacement.

Duration in Days

Job Classification	Minimum	Optimum	Maximum
Sedentary work	28	63	84
Light work	42	112	140
Medium work	84	112	182
Heavy work	Indefinite	Indefinite	Indefinite
Very Heavy work	Indefinite	Indefinite	Indefinite

Failure to Recover

If an individual fails to recover within the maximum duration expectancy period, the reader may wish to reference the following questions to assist in better understanding the specifics of an individual's medical case.

Regarding diagnosis:

- If symptomatic, does individual have pain after healing of a fracture, stiffness, or joint pain without associated trauma?
- Is the pain worse at night and after activity?
- Is pain evident with active and passive motion? Does individual have limited range of motion, muscle disuse atrophy, and weakness around the joint?
- Were signs of avascular necrosis seen on a bone scan or MRI?
- If the diagnosis is uncertain, were other conditions with similar symptoms such as osteoporosis, osteoarthritis, Paget's disease of the bone, and stress fracture ruled out?
- Would individual benefit from consultation with a specialist (orthopedic surgeon)?

Regarding treatment:

- Was the treatment appropriate for the stage of the avascular necrosis (core decompression, bone graft or joint replacement)? Was joint replacement required?
- Was physical rehabilitation recommended? Was individual compliant with the rehabilitation recommendations? If not, are there barriers to participation that could be addressed (insurance limits, transportation, lack of motivation)?
- If a systemic disease such as SLE or pancreatitis is associated with the development of avascular necrosis, was it addressed in the treatment plan?
- Was treatment initiated in the early or advanced stage of avascular necrosis?
- What type of surgical intervention was performed? Has adequate time elapsed for recovery from the surgical procedure?

Regarding prognosis:

- Was avascular necrosis diagnosed and treated early?
- If surgery was necessary, was it successful?
- Did individual have any other conditions (circulatory disturbances, immune suppression) or complications (fractures, bone compression, or osteoarthritis) that may have impacted recovery?

References

Aseptic Necrosis (Avascular Necrosis or Osteonecrosis). MedicineNet, Inc. 07 Sep 2000. 22 Jan 2001 <http://www.medicinenet.com/script/main/art.asp?li=MNI&ArticleKey=288>.

Canale, Terry S. Campbell's Operative Orthopaedics, 9th ed. Carlsbad, CA: Mosby, Inc, 1997. 03 Feb 2001 <http://home.mdconsult.com/das/book/view/868?sid=32544562>.

Quintana, J.M., et al. "Evaluation of the Appropriateness of Hip Joint Replacement Techniques." International Journal of Technology Assessment in Health Care 16 1 (2000). 02 Feb 2001 <http://home.mdconsult.com/das/journal/view/N/11358025?sid=32553120&source=HS,MI>.

Rosen, Peter, MD. Emergency Medicine: Concepts and Clinical Practice, 4th ed. St. Louis: Mosby-Year Book, Inc, 1998. 21 Jan 2001 <http://home.mdconsult.com/>.

Avoidant Personality Disorder
301.82

Definition

Avoidant personality disorder is characterized by a pervasive pattern of social inhibition, feelings of inadequacy, and being overly sensitive to negative evaluation. It represents a "detached" personality pattern. Detached individuals are typically introverted, aloof and seclusive, tend to avoid social activities, and are usually quite uncomfortable when forced to participate in such activities. They are extremely sensitive to rejection that may lead to social isolation and a withdrawn life. They tend to be shy, apprehensive, awkward, and uncomfortable with face-to-face contact, and may appear timid, withdrawn, evasive, and sometimes strange. Their speech is slow and constrained with frequent hesitations and fragmented thought sequences.

Individuals with this disorder fear placing their welfare and feelings in the hands of others and hesitate to trust or confide in others. They tend to be extremely introspective and self-conscious. They often perceive themselves as different from others and tend to be unsure of their identity and self-worth, lacking overall self-esteem. They often devaluate their own achievements, seeing themselves as isolated, discontent, and empty.

This personality disorder typically begins by early adulthood.

Diagnosis

History: The psychiatric interview and mental status exam are the primary methods utilized by the practitioner. In a clinical interview, the most striking aspect is the individual's anxiety about talking with the interviewer. The physician looks for symptoms of a pervasive pattern of social inhibition, feelings of inadequacy, and extreme sensitivity to negative evaluation.

According to the DSM-IV, beginning by early adulthood, individuals with avoidant personality disorder display four (or more) of the following: avoids occupational activities involving significant interpersonal contact because of fears of criticism, disapproval, or rejection; unwilling to get involved with others unless certain of being liked; shows restraint within intimate relationships because of the fear of being shamed or ridiculed; preoccupied with being criticized or rejected in social situations; inhibited in new interpersonal situations because of feelings of inadequacy; views self as socially inept, personally unappealing, or inferior to others; or unusually reluctant to take personal risks or engage in any new activities as they may prove embarrassing.

Physical exam: The exam is not helpful in diagnosing this disorder.

Tests: There are a variety of psychological tests that help identify and classify personality disorders when used in conjunction with the history.

Treatment

Treatment for avoidant personality disorder depends on establishing an alliance (based on trust) between the therapist and individual. Psychotherapeutic modalities include group, behavioral (assertiveness training), and individual therapy. One goal of therapy is to encourage the individual to move out into the world and take what are perceived as great risks of humiliation, rejection, and failure. The therapist should be cautious, however, when suggesting that the individual exercise new social skills outside of therapy because failure may reinforce feelings of poor self-esteem. Group therapy may help the individual cope with the exaggerated threat of rejection.

Pharmacotherapy has been used to deal with depression and anxiety, the most common features associated with avoidant personality disorder. Antianxiety agents may be useful in treating high levels of anxiety associated with this disorder.

Prognosis

Many individuals with avoidant personality disorder can function in society provided they are in a protected environment. A stable support system and a positive network of family and friends usually ensures a good outcome.

Differential Diagnosis

The personality traits found in the avoidant personality are similar to those of a schizoid personality who also tends to remain isolated and withdrawn. Other disorders that may be confused with avoidant personality disorder include histrionic, borderline, and passive-aggressive personality disorders, anxiety disorders, mood disorders, substance abuse, personality changes due to a general medical condition, and schizophrenic disorders.

Specialists

- Psychiatrist
- Psychologist

Work Restrictions / Accommodations

High profile positions with frequent contact on a one-to-one basis are uncomfortable and may even be intolerable for the individual with avoidant personality disorder. A work environment involving a small group of people is recommended. Contact with a large or unfamiliar group should be avoided.

Comorbid Conditions

Alcohol abuse or drug use, or the presence of another psychiatric illness may lengthen disability.

Complications

Any type of rejection in the life of the avoidant personality may lead to increasing social withdrawal. Criticism in any form is usually devastating and intensifies the dysfunction. Other complicating factors are the presence of anxiety, depression, or other coexistent psychiatric disorders including substance abuse. At work or home, any type of rejection or perceived rejection usually leads to withdrawal.

Factors Influencing Duration

The progress and effectiveness of the psychotherapy and the individual's level of functioning are all factors in the length of disability. Should their support system fail, these individuals are subject to symptoms of depression and anxiety that may lengthen disability.

Length of Disability

This condition represents a life-long pattern of behavior. In most cases, no disability is expected.

Failure to Recover

If an individual fails to recover within the maximum duration expectancy period, the reader may wish to reference the following questions to assist in better understanding the specifics of an individual's medical case.

Regarding diagnosis:

- Was diagnosis of avoidant personality disorder confirmed? Does individual's behavior fit criteria?

- Because individual may deem important life history, medical information or himself/herself too unimportant to mention, was physician able to get a comprehensive, realistic history? Do nonverbal clues give an indication of important information that may have been omitted?

- Were conditions with similar symptoms ruled out?

Regarding treatment:

- Is psychotherapy focused toward finding solutions to specific life problems?

- Has individual been able to establish and maintain a good working rapport with therapist? If not, what can be done to help facilitate rapport?

- If individual is taking medication, is it short-term and for a specific coexisting psychiatric condition? Could medication actually be interfering with effectiveness of the overall treatment?

Regarding prognosis:

- Since avoidant personality disorder may require long-term therapy, would group therapy be a good adjunct after termination of current individual therapy?

- Does individual have a stable, understanding support system?

References

Grohol, John. Avoidant Personality Disorder. Psych Central. 01 Nov 1999. 07 Aug 2000 <http://www.grohol.com/disorders>.

Long, Philip W., MD. Avoidant Personality Disorder. Internet Mental Health. 01 Jan 2000. 17 Oct 2000 <http://www.mentalhealth.com/dis1/p21-pe08.html>.

Back Pain

Other names / synonyms: Backache

724, 724.5

Definition

Backache or back pain is a symptom and not a specific disease that can have many causes. In individuals under age 50, identified causes include damaged vertebral discs (discogenic pain), strain, and muscle or tissue inflammation (myofascial pain). Older individuals may have a narrowing of the spinal canal or an underlying disease of the vertebrae.

Perhaps as many as 50% of all individuals with backache may never have a clear diagnosis of the underlying cause of the pain. With diagnostic injections, we are learning more about how different sources of pain behave and, therefore, this percentage is decreasing. For the other 50%, there is a clear diagnosis of the cause of the pain. Spinal complaints are usually "from the spine" and are of benign mechanical origins. However, spinal complaints may also involve disease such as tumor (rare), may be referred from the shoulder, hip, or internal organ, and, lastly, may represent physical manifestations of emotional disorder.

See Low Back Pain.

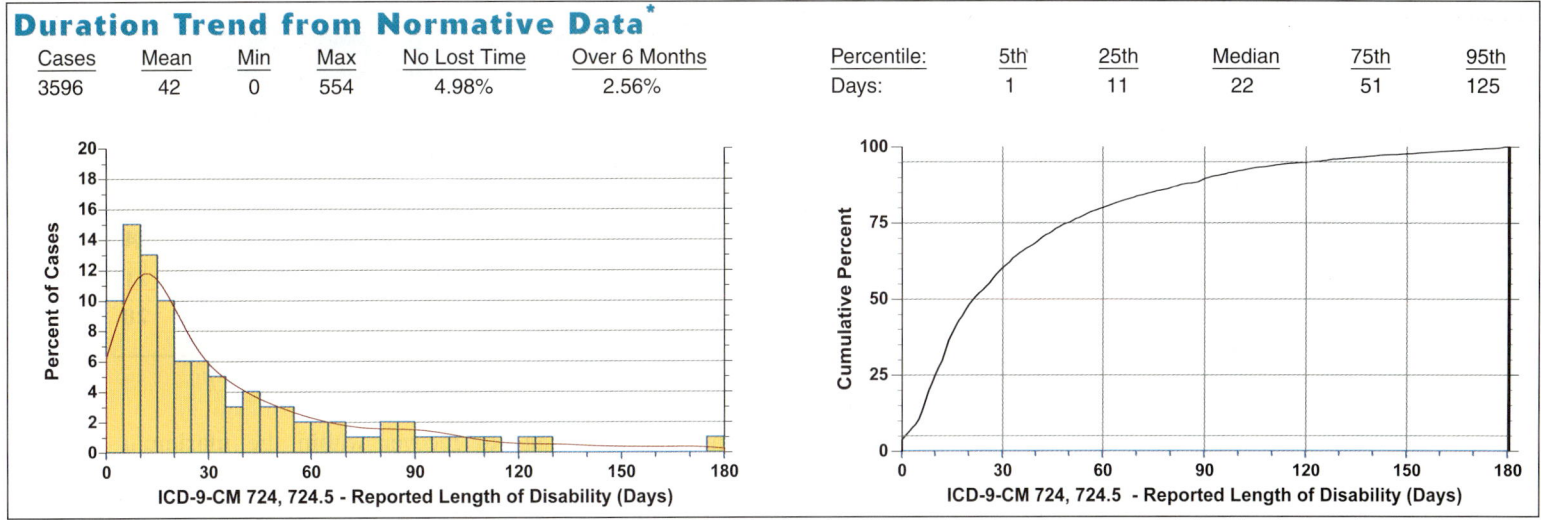

Duration Trend from Normative Data*

Cases	Mean	Min	Max	No Lost Time	Over 6 Months
3596	42	0	554	4.98%	2.56%

Percentile:	5th	25th	Median	75th	95th
Days:	1	11	22	51	125

* Differences may exist between the expected duration tables and the normative graphs. Duration tables provide expected recovery periods based on the type of work performed by the individual. The normative graphs reflect the actual observed experience of many individuals across the spectrum of physical conditions, in a variety of industries, and with varying levels of case management.

Baker's Cyst

Other names / synonyms: Popliteal Cyst

727, 727.51

Definition

A Baker's cyst is a swelling of one of the two fluid-filled sacs (anatomic bursae) located behind the knee (popliteal space). These two bursae communicate with the knee joint, such that increased synovial fluid in the knee (resulting from inflammation) can cause the bursae to enlarge and form a Baker's cyst. The Baker's cyst usually affects only one knee.

Of the 50% of Baker's cysts found in adults, 50% of these are associated with knee joint damage, particularly torn cartilage (meniscus). Other risk factors for Baker's cysts include rheumatoid arthritis and thrombophlebitis.

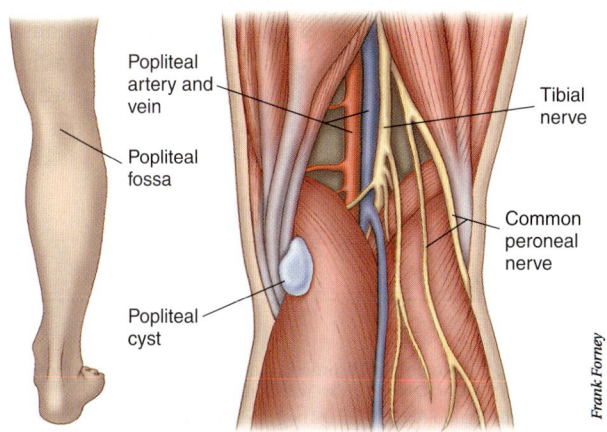

Diagnosis

History: Individuals may report knee pain on the back (posterior) side of the knee. Swelling may be present. Most individuals have no history of knee injury.

Physical exam: The exam may reveal a swelling behind the knee. This swollen area is often painful to the touch (palpation).

Tests: X-rays of the joint may show some soft tissue swelling. An MRI is very useful in evaluating the cyst, as well as intra articular pathology, like a torn meniscus, that may be the primary cause of the cyst.

Treatment

Conservative treatment with rest is often all that is necessary. Injection of the cyst or the knee with corticosteroid medication is often effective in reducing the size of the cyst as well as reducing symptoms. Surgery is indicated in cases unresponsive to injection.

Surgical treatment of associated joint pathology such as meniscectomy for a torn meniscus may relieve the symptoms without cyst removal. If the cyst is secondary to intra articular pathology, removing just the cyst without treatment of the underlying joint pathology often results in recurrence.

Two surgical procedures are commonly used to remove (excise) Baker's cysts. These are the Hughston, Baker, and Mello procedure and the Meyerding and Van Demark procedure. They are similar procedures that differ primarily in the position of the incision. Both procedures allow joint exposure for additional repairs.

Prognosis

Some individuals may be cured with injection alone. The cyst is usually secondary to intraarticular pathology. The prognosis is determined by the type and severity of injury or disease in the knee joint. Surgical repair with either the Hughston, Baker and Mello procedure or the Meyerding and Van Demark procedure provides good results with complete recovery.

Differential Diagnosis

Other possibilities include lipomas, xanthomas, vascular tumors, popliteal artery aneurysms, fibrosarcomas, and abscess.

Specialists

- Orthopedic Surgeon
- Rheumatologist

Work Restrictions / Accommodations

Individuals with severe knee pain and swelling and whose job requires prolonged standing may need temporary transfer to nonstanding duties. Squatting, kneeling, and crawling may need to be limited. If surgery is necessary, the individual needs to be off weight-bearing until healing is complete. The individual may need to use crutches postoperatively.

Comorbid Conditions

Comorbid conditions include torn meniscus, obesity, and arthritis of the knee joint.

Complications

A Baker's cyst may be complicated by thrombophlebitis and associated knee joint pathology such as a torn meniscus.

Factors Influencing Duration

Surgical complications, type of treatment given, and an individual's job requirements may influence length of disability.

Length of Disability

Medical treatment (including injection).

Duration in Days

Job Classification	Minimum	Optimum	Maximum
Sedentary work	0	3	7
Light work	0	3	7
Medium work	0	7	14
Heavy work	0	7	21
Very Heavy work	0	7	28

Failure to Recover

If an individual fails to recover within the maximum duration expectancy period, the reader may wish to reference the following questions to assist in better understanding the specifics of an individual's medical case.

Regarding diagnosis:

- Does individual have any risk factors for a Baker's cyst?
- Does individual have knee pain or swelling?
- Has individual received adequate diagnostic testing to establish the diagnosis?
- Were conditions with similar symptoms ruled out?

Regarding treatment:

- Did individual respond favorably to conservative treatment? Were injections effective?
- Was surgery necessary?

Regarding prognosis:

- Does individual have any conditions that may impact recovery?
- Have any complications developed?

References

Crenshaw, Andrew H. "Nontraumatic Disorders." Campbell's Operative Orthopedics, 9th ed. Canale, S. Terry, ed. St. Louis: Mosby-Year Book, Inc, 1998. 769-787.

Hertling, Darlene, and Randolf M. Kessler. "The Knee." Management of Common Musculoskeletal Disorders. Philadelphia: J.B. Lippincott Company, 1990. 298-358.

Kisner, Carolyn, and Lynn Allen Colby. Therapeutic Exercise: Foundations and Techniques, 2nd ed. Philadelphia: F.A. Davis Company, 1990.

Magee, David J. "Knee." Orthopedic Physical Assessment. Biblis, Margaret M., ed. Philadelphia: W.B. Saunders Company, 1992. 372-447.

Barotitis Media

Other names / synonyms: Aerotitis Media, Barotrauma, Ear Popping, Eustachian Tube Dysfunction, Pressure-Related Ear Pain

993, 993.0, 993.1

Definition

Barotitis media (barotrauma) is an inflammation of the middle ear caused by sudden changes in barometric pressure.

Proper function of the ear requires that the air pressure within the middle ear is equal to that of the surrounding atmosphere. Sudden changes in pressure can either put an outward push (traction) on the eardrum or cause it to collapse. In either case, the result can be pain and diminished or muffled hearing. Allergic or infectious upper respiratory tract conditions can block the venting function of the eustachian tube, making barotrauma during these activities more likely. Damage can range from painful pushing or pulling (traction) to bleeding and rupture of the eardrum. Tiny blood vessels can rupture in the walls of the middle ears, or in the membranes lining the inside of the sinuses. Displacement and stretching of the eardrum (tympanic membrane) may be accompanied by redness, swelling (edema), and bruising of the mucous membrane of the middle ear.

Barotrauma commonly occurs with altitude changes, such as with flying, scuba diving, or driving in the mountains. Barotitis media may also occur in any condition in which there is injury to the eustachian tube.

Barotrauma is common. Where there is a congested nose from allergies, colds, or upper respiratory infection, barotrauma is more likely.

Diagnosis

History: Symptoms may include a temporary ringing in the ear (tinnitus). Ears may feel full, and hearing may be impaired. A plugged feeling in the ear, mild-to-severe pain in the ears or over the cheekbones and forehead, and dizziness (vertigo) may also occur.

Physical exam: The exam may reveal a perforated eardrum (tympanic membrane) with fluid accumulation, or the membrane may have a purplish hue. An ear inspection may show a slight outward bulge or inward retraction of the eardrum.

Tests: There are no laboratory or other tests required to establish this diagnosis.

Treatment

The goal of treatment is relief of symptoms. In most cases, symptoms wear off within hours or days without treatment. Individuals are advised to keep soapy and dirty water out of the ear. If symptoms persist, medications may include decongestant nasal sprays, oral decongestants, or oral antihistamines. These medications may relieve nasal congestion and allow the eustachian tube to open. Antibiotics may be used to prevent ear infection if barotrauma is severe.

When a perforated eardrum (tympanic membrane) does not heal within 3 months, a paper patch may be used to cover the hole. If the patch fails, the membrane may need to be surgically repaired (tympanoplasty). If the tube will not open with other treatments, surgery may be necessary. An incision is made in the eardrum to allow pressure to equalize and fluid to drain (myringotomy). However, surgery is rarely necessary. Occasionally, tubes will be surgically placed in the eardrum if frequent altitude changes are unavoidable or if the individual is susceptible to barotrauma.

Attempts to open the eustachian tube and relieve pressure should be made first, including sucking on candy, chewing gum, or yawning. Inhaling and then gently exhaling while holding the nostrils closed and the mouth shut may open the tube.

To prevent barotrauma, individuals should not sleep during the descent when flying.

Prognosis

This is a self-limited condition. Both the pain and hearing loss usually resolve with time. Barotrauma is usually benign and responsive to self-care. Hearing loss is almost always temporary.

Differential Diagnosis

Conditions with similar symptoms include acute inflammation of the middle ear (otitis media) secondary to a bacterial infection and inner ear decompression sickness.

Specialists

- Otolaryngologist

Work Restrictions / Accommodations

In severe cases, temporary reassignment to non-diving or non-flying duties may be required until the condition is resolved. If possible, the individual should not fly or engage in scuba diving when suffering from allergic or infectious upper respiratory conditions. If flying must be done, the conditions should be resolved by chewing gum, swallowing, yawning, or using a nasal decongestant (spray is preferable to oral form) an hour before takeoff. The decongestant should be used again before landing when on an overseas flight.

Comorbid Conditions

Other pre-existing conditions of the eustachian tube can lengthen disability. Respiratory allergies may contribute to the severity of barotrauma (barotitis media).

Complications

Although the pressure changes experienced during ordinary airline flights are unlikely to rupture or perforate the eardrum, it can happen to high altitude pilots and scuba divers. Complications can also include infection. Loss of hearing in the ear(s) may also occur.

Factors Influencing Duration

Physical condition, general health, and presence of respiratory disease will influence the level of disability that may occur.

Complementary and Alternative Therapies

Content is intended for awareness only. Treatments may or may not be effective. Scientific evidence may be lacking and some substances have potentially toxic effects. Dr. Presley Reed and the editors do not endorse the use of these therapies in the absence of consultation with a licensed medical professional.

Sucking on candy -	May help open the eustachian tube and relieve pressure.
Gum chewing -	May help open the eustachian tube and relieve pressure.
Swallowing with mouth open -	May help open the eustachian tube and relieve pressure.
Hold nose and exhale -	May help open eustachian tube and relieve pressure.

Length of Disability

Duration depends on the severity.

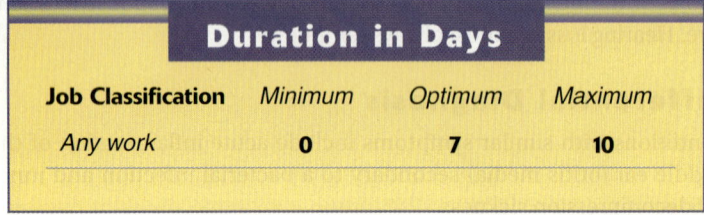

Duration in Days

Job Classification	Minimum	Optimum	Maximum
Any work	0	7	10

Failure to Recover

If an individual fails to recover within the maximum duration expectancy period, the reader may wish to reference the following questions to assist in better understanding the specifics of an individual's medical case.

Regarding diagnosis:

- Was diagnosis of barotitis media confirmed?
- Is the clinical illness, including the history, physical examination, and laboratory findings, consistent with other case descriptions?
- Were there complications? Were complications effectively addressed?
- Does individual have an underlying condition that may impact recovery?

Regarding treatment:

- Have symptoms persisted despite medications?
- Would individual benefit from surgical intervention?
- If individual sustained a perforated tympanic membrane, was healing delayed?
- What does current treatment plan entail?

Regarding prognosis:

- Has individual experienced this condition more than once?
- Are there special attributes of the particular individual that make it more or less likely that he or she would be so affected?
- Is there a positive history of changes in pressure in the workplace?
- Could changes in pressure be occurring outside the workplace, i.e., in the home, in the community, or in recreational activities?
- What can be done to avoid future occurrences?

References

Ear Barotrauma. National Institutes of Health, National Library of Medicine. 24 Aug 2000. 01 Jan 2001 <http://medlineplus.adam.com/ency/article/001064.htm>.

Tinnitus. InteliHealth, Inc. 18 Jan 2001. 01 Feb 2001 < http://www.intelihealth.com/IH/ihtIH?t=25660&p=~br,IHW|~st,24479|~r,WSIHW000|~b,*| >.

Bartholin's Gland Cyst

Other names / synonyms: Bartholinitis
616.2, 616.3

Definition

Bartholin's glands are two small glands located on both sides of the vaginal opening. A cyst can develop from one of the glands or the ducts. It can be chronically inflamed and painful.

Bartholin glands cysts develop from dilation of the duct following blockage of the duct opening. The glands are normally the size of a pea and drain into a duct that exits near a fold between the mucous membrane (hymen) and the outer lips of the vagina (labia). The gland's secretions provide some moisture for the vulva but are not needed for sexual lubrication. Therefore, removal of a Bartholin gland does not seem to compromise sexual function. Bartholin gland cysts tend to grow slowly and noninfected cysts are usually sterile.

Bartholin gland cysts are common problems in women of reproductive age. Although the cysts are usually asymptomatic, they may become enlarged or infected and cause significant pain. If the cyst becomes infected, the abscess can grow rapidly and become increasingly painful. Approximately 2% of all women worldwide develop Bartholin gland cysts or abscesses.

Diagnosis

History: Bartholin gland cysts are generally painless. When symptoms do occur, the individual may report vulvar pain, painful intercourse (dyspareunia), inability to engage in sports, and pain during walking or sitting. The individual may also notice a bulge in the labium majus or be found during a routine gynecologic examination.

Physical exam: The exam reveals a small mass on the side of the vaginal opening. The cysts normally cannot be felt (palpated). The Bartholin duct and surrounding tissue may be swollen due to the blocked duct. Infected cysts that develop abscesses show a large tender mass in the Bartholin gland area accompanied by a red, swollen, and inflamed vulva. The abscess may rupture and drain 4 to 5 days after onset.

Tests: Aspiration of an infected cyst for bacterial culture may be done to identify the causative microorganism and specifically treat the infection.

Treatment

Asymptomatic Bartholin gland cysts in individuals under the age of 40 may not require treatment. Some physicians advocate removal (excision) of all Bartholin gland cysts in individuals over 40 due to the possibility of cancer. If the cyst ruptures spontaneously, all that may be required is for the individual to take hot baths and sit in a tub of water so only the affected area is covered (sitz bath). If an infection develops, a broad-spectrum antibiotic is indicated until bacterial culture results are obtained and more specific antibiotics can be administered to treat the causative microorganism(s). Pain medications may also be used.

Incision and drainage should be avoided since many cysts and most abscesses can recur if treated only by incision. Definitive methods of treatment include placing a catheter (Word catheter) inside the cyst to provide drainage. The catheter is left in place for up to 4 weeks. The individual is asked to undergo pelvic rest until removal of the catheter and abstain from sexual intercourse. Over time, the resulting opening created by the catheter decreases in size and becomes unnoticeable. Another procedure (marsupialization) can be performed if the cyst recurs despite treatment with a Word catheter. In this procedure, an incision is made in the lining of the vulva and an oval of skin removed. This is followed by an incision in the cyst wall to drain the cyst or abscess. The new tract slowly shrinks over time and a new duct opening forms.

Other techniques such as a "window operation" involve making a larger incision where a large oval piece of the cyst wall is removed. The cyst wall is sewn to the skin as in marsupialization. Other techniques involve incision of Bartholin gland abscesses followed by curettage of the abscess cavity and application of silver nitrate to the cyst or abscess cavity. A carbon dioxide laser can also be used to excise the cyst. The laser does not offer any advantage over the less expensive and technically difficult procedures. Excision of the cyst may be required if it has recurred several times. Individuals with recurring cysts should be referred to a gynecologist experienced with excision procedures.

Prognosis

Lancing a Bartholin gland cyst may result in recurrence and should not be routinely performed. More effective treatments such as use of the Word catheter and marsupialization are the preferred methods and both can be performed in the office. The recurrence rate after marsupialization is about 10%. The window operation is a variation of the marsupialization procedure and has no known treatment failures or complications. It is theorized that the larger opening prevents blockage of the newly formed opening and may make the window operation more advantageous than the marsupialization procedure. The carbon dioxide laser is also an effective method of excision but does not offer any advantage over the other procedures. Full recovery is expected if the symptomatic cyst is treated with one of these procedures and infection is treated with a course of oral broad-spectrum antibiotics.

Differential Diagnosis

Conditions with similar symptoms include a number of vulvar and vaginal lesions that can mimic Bartholin gland cysts or abscesses. Sebaceous cysts of the vulva are common, often asymptomatic, and can become infected. Dysontogenetic cysts are benign mucus-containing cysts located on the outer lips of the vagina and are also asymptomatic. Bruises (hematomas) of the vulva caused by saddle injuries, sporting injuries, or other trauma should also be considered. Other tumors such as benign solid tumors of the vulva (i.e., fibromas, lipomas, and hidradenomas on the labia) should be biopsied if they bleed or removed if asymptomatic. Other rare vulvar masses include syringomas, leiomyomas, and neural sheath tumors, which occur in the area of the Bartholin gland.

Specialists

- General Surgeon
- Gynecologist

Work Restrictions / Accommodations

If the Bartholin gland is infected or develops an abscess, it can be so painful that the individual becomes incapacitated. Difficulty walking or sitting for long periods of time may limit work capacity. Adequate breaks with the opportunity to move around should be allowed.

Comorbid Conditions

Vaginal infections such as chlamydia or gonorrhea can cause the disability to lengthen since specific antibiotic treatment is indicated. Diabetes is also a comorbid condition that affects disability.

Complications

If the cyst becomes infected and is not treated initially with a broad-spectrum antibiotic, an abscess may form on the gland. If the abscess is not treated early with sitz baths until the abscess comes to a point, incision and treatment may be more difficult. A secondary infection may develop called bartholinitis, which is an inflammatory condition of one or both Bartholin's glands caused by bacterial infection.

Factors Influencing Duration

Surgical excision procedures can be performed in the office under local anesthesia and should not cause a long disability. If the cyst is painful and infected, then disability may be longer but should not exceed 2 weeks.

Length of Disability

Uncomplicated incision and drainage.

Duration in Days

Job Classification	Minimum	Optimum	Maximum
Any work	1	3	7

Failure to Recover

If an individual fails to recover within the maximum duration expectancy period, the reader may wish to reference the following questions to assist in better understanding the specifics of an individual's medical case.

Regarding diagnosis:

- If symptoms are present, does individual have vulvar pain, painful intercourse (dyspareunia), inability to engage in sports, and pain during walking or sitting? Does individual notice a bulge in the labium majus?
- Did physical exam reveal a small mass on the side of the vaginal opening? Was the Bartholin duct and surrounding tissue swollen?
- Was diagnosis confirmed through a gynecologic exam?
- Were conditions with similar symptoms such as sebaceous cysts, dysontogenetic cysts, bruises (hematomas) of the vulva, benign solid tumors, or rare vulva masses ruled out?

Regarding treatment:

- Given individual's age and diagnosis, was the treatment appropriate?
- Was a culture and sensitivity done to identify the causative organisms and determine the most effective antibiotic?
- Was surgery required?
- If the cyst was recurrent, was placement of a Word catheter or marsupialization done? Window operation or carbon dioxide laser?

Regarding prognosis:

- Does individual have any comorbid conditions that may impact ability to recover? If so, were these conditions addressed in the treatment plan?
- Did individual suffer any secondary infection?
- Did adequate time elapse for complete recovery?
- Would individual benefit from consultation with a specialist (gynecologist)?

References

Hill, D., Lense Ashley, and J. Jorge. "Office Management of Bartholin Gland Cysts and Abscesses." American Family Physician 5 6 (1998): 1-9.

Behçet's Syndrome
Other names / synonyms: Behçet's Disease
136, 136.1

Definition

Behçet's syndrome is a little-understood inflammatory disease that attacks various systems of the body in many different ways.

The condition usually begins with ulcers in the mouth; this can be found in combination with other symptoms. These symptoms include ulcers in the genital areas (apthous ulcers), eye inflammation (uveitis), or skin abnormalities. Optic disk damage (glaucoma) may cause blindness. Behçet's syndrome may also create irritation in the gastrointestinal tract or lungs. Inflammation may cause blood vessels to protrude, leading to possible clotting (thrombosis) responsible for strokes or heart disease. Afflicted individuals may also experience arthritis primarily in the knee, ankle, wrist, and elbow joints. In susceptible people, this disease can be triggered by a trauma or series of traumas including recurrent infections.

The disease generally is chronic with outbreaks typically lasting several weeks, followed by periods of remission and relapse. Infections or environmental factors may cause onset of the disease.

Heredity contributes to development of Behçet's syndrome, which occurs in about 1 in 10,000 individuals in populations of the Far East, Middle East and the Mediterranean area. The disease is rare in the US, occurring in about 1 in 500,000 individuals. Males are almost twice as likely to contract the disease.

Diagnosis

History: Weight loss or headaches may precede onset of the disease. Some of the first symptoms individuals may report include painful, recurrent sores in the mouth followed by genital lesions. Eye inflammation also is common, and can cause blurry vision. Individuals may also complain of ulcerated sores that may appear anywhere on the skin, most especially on the legs and upper torso. Varying symptoms may develop over a period of weeks or years, and could include abdominal discomfort, uncontrolled eye movements, joint pain, joint stiffness and swelling, and convulsions.

Physical exam: The exam may reveal pus-filled blisters often in the mouth or genital areas. Painful nodes may form in response to minor injuries. Inflammation of the iris (iritis), uvea (uveitis), or cornea (keratitis) of the eye may be seen, along with pus in the anterior chamber. The optic nerve may become inflamed, resulting in blindness. Blood vessels may protrude from inflammation (aneurysms) causing blockages (thrombophlebitis) or rupture.

Tests: For some individuals, placing a sterile or saline-filled needle in the skin will cause a positive reaction that looks like a rash or reddish circle surrounding the prick (pathergy test) indicating hypersensitivity. Laboratory tests may show elevated white blood cell counts, sedimentation rates, and antibody levels, but will not specifically identify Behçet's syndrome.

Treatment

Behçet's syndrome is treated according to the symptoms manifested, since there is no known cure for the disease. Mouth rinses can be used to treat oral sores. Topical drugs (corticosteroids) may reduce inflammation created by the disease in areas such as the skin, eyes, and joints. High doses of oral corticosteroids may alleviate central nervous system symptoms and uveitis, which sometimes result from Behçet's syndrome. Immunosuppressive drugs help control the overactive immune system and thus reduce inflammation; they have serious side effects that require regular monitoring. Other drugs that attack and destroy certain types of cells (cytotoxic) may also be used for uveitis. Drugs that disperse blood clots (anticoagulants) may be given for thrombosis, another possible manifestation of the disease. Surgery may be required for extreme conditions such as intestinal perforations that may result from Behçet's syndrome.

Prognosis

Behçet's disease is chronic and incurable. Because of the many manifestations of the disease, it's difficult to characterize the ultimate outcome. Outbreaks usually last several weeks, occurring more frequently in early stages of the disease. Cumulative effects through the years may have serious consequences, the most common of which is eye damage and possible blindness. Individuals of Japanese descent are more likely to develop blindness. Men tend to be more severely affected by Behçet's syndrome.

Differential Diagnosis

Behçet's syndrome is similar to lupus (systemic lupus erythematosus), Crohn's disease, meningitis, ulcerative colitis, ankylosing spondylosis, and herpes simplex.

Specialists

- Cardiologist
- Dermatologist
- Gastroenterologist
- Gynecologist
- Immunologist
- Neurologist
- Ophthalmologist
- Rheumatologist
- Urologist

Rehabilitation

Individuals with joint pain and stiffness might benefit from rehabilitation therapy recommended for those afflicted with arthritis.

Work Restrictions / Accommodations

Individuals should avoid heat, humid conditions, and chemicals, which may irritate the skin and eyes. Depending on the severity and type of symptoms, larger computer screens might assist those with visual impairment. For individuals with joint pain or stiffness, easy accessibility to work stations may be needed. Keyboards and seating may need to be positioned to ease discomfort. Moderate exertion and rest periods may be necessary.

Comorbid Conditions

Pregnancy tends to create more severe symptoms. Pre-existing diseases in the various bodily systems affected are likely to prolong or increase the severity of outbreaks.

Complications

Possible severe complications include paralysis, blindness, strokes, heart trouble, and destruction of protective tissue surrounding the brain (aseptic meningitis).

Factors Influencing Duration

Severity of symptoms, response to treatment, and development of complications such as secondary infection may influence the individual's ability to recover.

Length of Disability

There is no disability during early phases of disease process. Behçet's syndrome is chronic with periods of outbreaks, followed by remission. Complete recovery is unlikely.

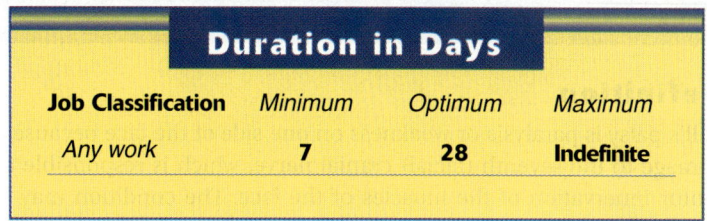

Duration in Days

Job Classification	Minimum	Optimum	Maximum
Any work	7	28	Indefinite

Failure to Recover

If an individual fails to recover within the maximum duration expectancy period, the reader may wish to reference the following questions to assist in better understanding the specifics of an individual's medical case.

Regarding diagnosis:

- Does individual have mouth ulcers?
- Has individual had recent weight loss or headaches?
- Has individual developed genital lesions?
- Does individual have eye inflammation? Blurry vision?
- Have blood vessels developed aneurysms from the inflammation?
- Are ulcerated sores present on the upper torso and legs?
- Is abdominal discomfort present? Swelling? Uncontrolled eye movement?
- Does individual have joint pain or stiffness?
- Does individual have convulsions?
- Were blood tests done? Pathergy test?
- Were conditions with similar symptoms ruled out?

Regarding treatment:

- Was individual able to control symptoms?
- Were corticosteroids helpful? Were cytotoxic drugs used?
- Were anticoagulants necessary?
- Was it necessary for individual to have surgery?
- How long does an outbreak last? How frequent?

Regarding prognosis:

- Can individual's employer accommodate any necessary restrictions?
- Does individual have any conditions such as heart trouble or aseptic meningitis that may affect ability to recover?
- Have any complications developed such as paralysis, blindness, or stroke?

References

Behçet's Disease. The John Hopkins Vasculitis Center. 1998. 01 Jan 2001 <http://vasculitis.med.jhu.edu/behcet's.htm>.

Malouf, David. "The Kyolgle Line." The Oxford Book of Travel Studies. Craig, Patricia, ed. Oxford: Oxford UP, 1996. 390-396.

Bell's Palsy

Other names / synonyms: Bell's Paralysis, Cranial Mononeuropathy VII, Idiopathic Facial Palsy, Idiopathic Facial Paralysis, Peripheral Facial Palsy, Unilateral Facial Paralysis

344, 351, 351.0

Definition

Bell's palsy is paralysis or weakness on one side of the face because of damage to the seventh (facial) cranial nerve, which is responsible for motor innervation of the muscles of the face. The condition may be accompanied by pain or discomfort, and usually begins suddenly and worsens over a 3- to 5-day period. The paralysis may be partial or complete.

The cause is usually unknown, but may be due to an inflammatory reaction or herpes simplex reactivation.

Between 40,000 and 65,000 new cases of Bell's palsy are diagnosed each year. There is a rising incidence of Bell's palsy in the second and third decade of life, then a leveling off in the 40s and 50s with an increase again after age 60. The incidence of Bell's palsy is similar in men and women. There is increased incidence in pregnant individuals and those with diabetes, influenza, a cold, or some other upper respiratory infection.

Diagnosis

History: The most obvious symptom of Bell's palsy is an unexplained episode of unilateral facial weakness or paralysis. The symptoms begin suddenly and usually peak within 3 to 5 days. Individuals may report other symptoms including a headache, tearing, drooling, difficulty eating and drinking, change in facial appearance, impairment of taste, and hearing loss. Some individuals report a mild cold, influenza, or other upper respiratory tract infection within a week prior to the onset of Bell's palsy.

Physical exam: The exam reveals facial asymmetry, drooling, increased distance between the top and bottom eyelids (palpebral fissure width), a smooth forehead, a flattened crease between the nose and the upper lip (nasolabial fold), and loss of sensation to the affected area of the face.

Tests: A careful cranial nerve examination should be performed including a tuning fork examination to test hearing and testing for corneal sensation. A skull x-ray or MRI may be performed to rule out tumor or infection. Nerve excitability testing may also be performed through the use of electromyography (EMG) for assessing facial paralysis by measuring voluntary motor activity, and electroneuronography for determining the extent of nerve fiber degeneration. EMG is not reliable sooner than 10 days after onset of the paralysis.

Treatment

There is no specific treatment available for Bell's palsy, although corticosteroids are commonly prescribed. In many cases, no treatment is recommended. When treatment is necessary, the goal is to relieve the symptoms. If an individual is unable to close the affected eye, lubricating eye drops may be used during the day, and lubricating ointment, an eye patch, or moist chamber lenses at night. Corticosteroids may reduce swelling and relieve pressure and inflammation on the facial nerve. Analgesics may be used for pain. Fifteen percent of individuals with an acute episode of Bell's palsy will be left with debilitating facial dysfunction. Some success in treatment has been achieved using electromyographic rehabilitation (EMGR), botulinum toxin injections, or surgical reanimation.

Surgical procedures to decompress the facial nerve may be attempted. The goal of facial nerve decompression surgery is to relieve pressure on the swollen facial nerve in its bony canal. This reduction in pressure allows blood vessels to supply the nerve with oxygen and nutrients, however, these procedures are not proven to benefit most individuals with Bell's palsy.

Prognosis

Approximately 60-80% of individuals with Bell's palsy experience a complete resolution of symptoms within a few weeks to a few months after onset. Some cases result in residual side effects and some in permanent changes. Surgical procedures to decompress the facial nerve have not been shown to routinely benefit individuals with Bell's palsy. Bell's palsy is not life threatening.

Differential Diagnosis

A stroke, tumor (i.e., acoustic neuroma, neurofibromatosis, or cholesteatoma), lyme disease, temporal bone fracture, diabetic neuropathy, bacterial infections of the ear, and viral infections (i.e., Epstein-Barr virus, herpes zoster, and HIV) may cause symptoms similar to Bell's palsy.

Specialists

- Neurologist
- Ophthalmologist
- Primary Care Provider

Rehabilitation

The priorities of rehabilitation in Bell's palsy are pain control, preservation of vision, improved facial function, and outward appearance (esthetic) restoration. When addressing pain from Bell's palsy, the physical therapist may utilize electrostimulation combined with heat or cold treatment to relax painful facial muscles affected by the condition. One popular associated technique is transcutaneous electrical nerve stimulation (T.E.N.S.) An electrical impulse predetermined by the physical therapist produces a high frequency tingling sensation blocking pain at that region.

Iontophoresis is another treatment in the rehabilitation of Bell's palsy. This technique uses a small electric current to drive anti-inflammatory medication of the same electrical charge into the painful muscle tissues. Electrical stimulation of affected muscles helps maintain tone until reinnervation occurs. Biofeedback is another technique that utilizes a special machine to teach the individual how to control certain body responses that reduce pain.

Once pain is brought under control, focus is then placed on reeducation of the facial muscles affected by the condition. Direct electrical stimulation of muscles innervated by the facial nerve is a common technique used in rehabilitation of Bell's palsy. Electrodes are placed over affected muscles that provide electrical impulses set to promote muscle contraction. This form of treatment can be advanced to what is called functional electrical stimulation. This consists of the physical therapist instructing the individual to contract specific facial muscles with the aid of the electrical stimulation unit.

Modifications may need to be made in the rehabilitation program depending on the extent of the muscle paralysis and whether surgical techniques were required to restore function to the face.

Work Restrictions / Accommodations

Individuals with jobs that require them to be exposed to harsh lighting, wind, or dust may require glasses, goggles, or lubricants to protect the eye.

Complementary and Alternative Therapies

Content is intended for awareness only. Treatments may or may not be effective. Scientific evidence may be lacking and some substances have potentially toxic effects. Dr. Presley Reed and the editors do not endorse the use of these therapies in the absence of consultation with a licensed medical professional.

Antivirals - Addition of acyclovir to a prednisone regimen may promote recovery of voluntary muscle motion.

Massage - Massaging the weakened muscles may help prevent facial muscles from tightening.

Comorbid Conditions

Corneal abrasion, corneal ulceration, or conjunctivitis may lengthen disability.

Complications

Complications of Bell's palsy include disfigurement from loss of facial movement, eye damage (corneal ulcers and infections), chronic spasm of facial muscles and/or eyelids, and chronic taste abnormalities.

Factors Influencing Duration

Factors that may influence the length of disability include severity of symptoms, duration of symptoms, and the need for surgery.

Length of Disability

Medical treatment.

Duration in Days

Job Classification	Minimum	Optimum	Maximum
Any work	3	10	21

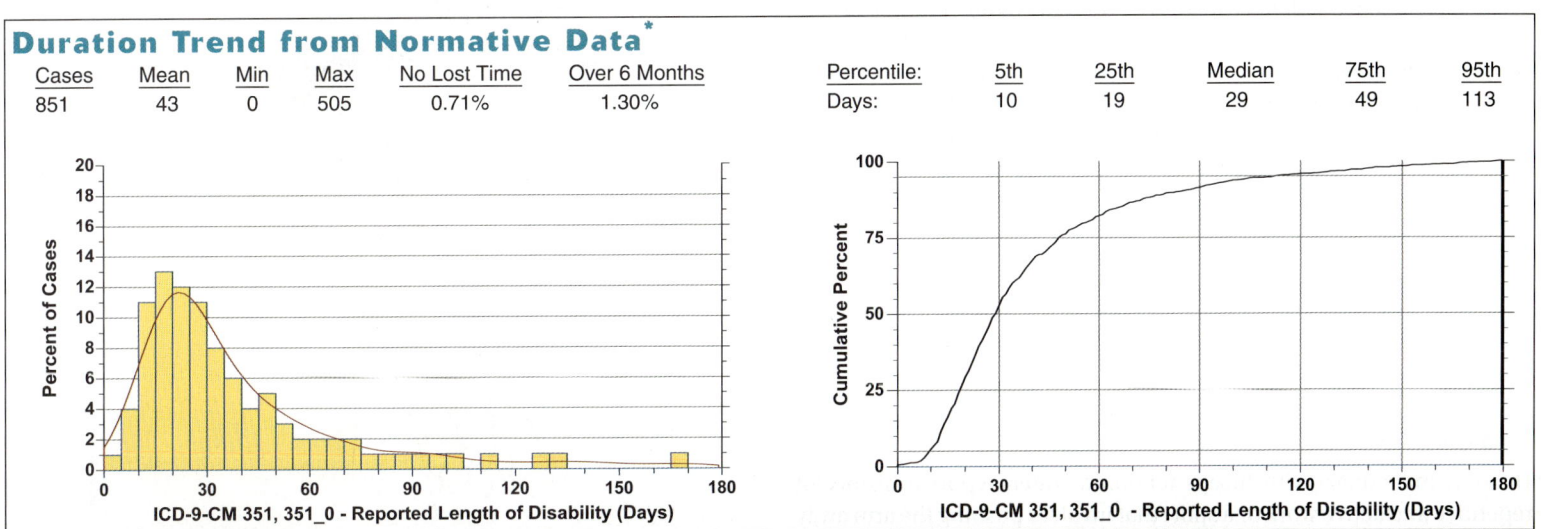

Duration Trend from Normative Data*

Cases	Mean	Min	Max	No Lost Time	Over 6 Months
851	43	0	505	0.71%	1.30%

Percentile:	5th	25th	Median	75th	95th
Days:	10	19	29	49	113

ICD-9-CM 351, 351_0 - Reported Length of Disability (Days)

* Differences may exist between the expected duration tables and the normative graphs. Duration tables provide expected recovery periods based on the type of work performed by the individual. The normative graphs reflect the actual observed experience of many individuals across the spectrum of physical conditions, in a variety of industries, and with varying levels of case management.

Bell's Palsy 247

Failure to Recover

If an individual fails to recover within the maximum duration expectancy period, the reader may wish to reference the following questions to assist in better understanding the specifics of an individual's medical case.

Regarding diagnosis:

- Does individual have an unexplained episode of unilateral facial weakness or paralysis?
- Does individual have a headache, tearing, drooling, difficulty eating and drinking, change in facial appearance, impairment of taste or hearing loss?
- Did individual report a mild cold, influenza, or other upper respiratory tract infection within a week prior to the onset of Bell's palsy?
- Does individual have diabetes?
- Is individual pregnant?
- Did the physical exam reveal facial asymmetry, drooling, increased distance between the top and bottom eyelids, a smooth forehead, a flattened crease between the nose and the upper lip, and loss of sensation to the affected area of the face?
- Was a thorough cranial nerve examination performed? Skull x-ray, EMG, or ENG?

Regarding treatment:

- Is individual receiving symptomatic treatment such as lubrication for the eyes? Corticosteroids? Analgesics?
- Does individual have residual debilitating facial dysfunction?
- Were EMGR, botulinum toxin injections, or surgical reanimation considered?

Regarding prognosis:

- Is individual active in physical therapy? Is a home exercise program in place?
- Can individual's employer accommodate any necessary restrictions?
- Does individual have any conditions that may affect ability to recover?
- Have any complications developed such as disfigurement from loss of facial movement, corneal ulcers and infections, chronic spasm of facial muscles and/or eyelids, or chronic taste abnormalities?

References

Bell's Palsy. drkoop.com. 23 Jun 2000. 23 Jun 2000 <http://www.drkoop.com/conditions/ency/article/000773.htm>.

Nervous System Disorders - Bell's Palsy. Methodist Health Care System. 2000. 22 Jun 2000 <http://methodisthealth.com/health/nervsystem/bells.htm>.

Biceps Tendonitis

Other names / synonyms: Biceps Tendinitis, Biceps Tendon Strain, Biceps Tendonitis, Flexor Muscle Tendinitis, Inflammation of the Biceps Tendon

726.12, 727.62

Definition

Biceps tendonitis is an inflammation of the biceps tendon, the fibrous structure that joins the muscle to the shoulder joint. Biceps tendonitis is often seen in active athletes such as swimmers, tennis players, javelin throwers, manual workers such as carpenters, and in anyone who constantly and vigorously throws their arms away from their bodies. These constant and repetitive actions irritate the biceps tendon. Other causes of biceps tendonitis are injury, gout, rheumatoid arthritis, or loss of elasticity as the tendon ages.

Work-related upper limb disorders including biceps tendonitis are among the most commonly reported occupational illnesses. In England, biceps tendonitis is reported to be an epidemic. Biceps tendonitis is among the five most common work-related skeletomuscular disorders among individuals attending the New York State Occupational Health Clinics network.

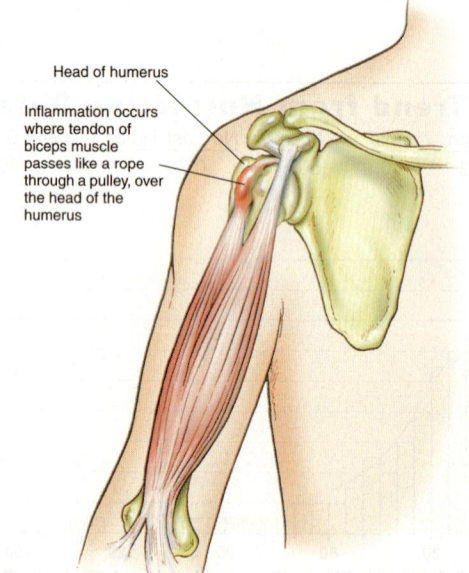

Diagnosis

History: Individuals with biceps tendonitis often report a history of repetitive and active work or a sport that involves pushing the arm away from the body or overhead. They report pain along the top of the shoulder, down inside the biceps muscle, or near the elbow. This pain is often worse at night and increases with rotation of the wrist.

Physical exam: The individual may have difficulty raising the affected arm due to pain. Pressing down on the shoulder for abnormalities (palpation) causes pain where the biceps sits along the bone. The neck is examined to rule out other causes for the symptoms. Biceps tendonitis frequently develops when other there are other conditions in the shoulder such as rotator cuff tear and impingement syndrome. If the tendon has ruptured, the biceps muscle is pulled down into the upper arm making the individual's arm look like "Popeye's" arm.

Tests: Routine shoulder x-rays are done to evaluate bony anatomy. MRI rules out a partial or complete tear of the tendon and determines damage in the rotator cuff. Ultrasound examination rules out other disorders.

Treatment

Athletes, carpenters, and other manual workers with biceps tendonitis are first told to stop the physical activities that brought on the condition. Additional treatment for mild biceps tendonitis includes cold therapy, oral nonsteroidal anti-inflammatory medications, and physical therapy to decrease inflammation and pain and maintain shoulder mobility. Corticosteroids may be injected into the shoulder if an individual does not respond to the above treatments. Biceps tendonitis is not treated surgically.

Prognosis

The predicted outcome is full recovery for otherwise healthy adults who restrict their activity as advised. Individuals with mild-to-moderate cases of biceps tendonitis will recover faster than those with severe cases. More severe cases also have the potential for a successful outcome, but recovery takes longer.

Differential Diagnosis

Other disorders that share some symptoms with biceps tendonitis include supraspinatus tendonitis, subacromial bursitis, impingement syndrome, rotator cuff tendonitis or tear, and cervical nerve root disorders.

Specialists

- Neurologist
- Occupational Therapist
- Orthopedic Surgeon
- Physical Therapist
- Rheumatologist

Rehabilitation

Individuals with bicipital tendonitis may be seen in outpatient physical therapy 2 times a week for 4 weeks.

The first goal of physical therapy is to decrease pain and inflammation. Individuals learn to apply ice packs to the area of tenderness as needed. Physical therapists may also perform cross-friction massage to promote the healing of the injured tendon. Individuals learn to rest the injured arm and identify possible activities that may have precipitated the condition.

The second goal of physical therapy is to increase range of motion. Bicipital tendonitis is often caused by a muscle imbalance in the shoulder musculature so any area of tightness should be identified and stretched. Therapists teach stretches such as the corner stretch where an individual stands in a corner, places one arm on each wall, and leans in to stretch the chest muscles. Individuals may also need to stretch the biceps muscle by using the noninjured arm to straighten the elbow of the injured arm.

The final goal of physical therapy is strengthening any weakened structures. Individuals perform isometric elbow flexion exercises where the noninjured arm resists the elbow bending of the injured arm. This exercise is progressed to biceps curls with light hand weights as tolerated by the individual. Individuals also learn to strengthen any weak musculature of the shoulder complex. Exercises such as shoulder blade squeezes where the shoulder blades are pinched together and shoulder external rotation may be necessary to restore muscle strength. Elastic tubing can be utilized to increase resistance.

Work Restrictions / Accommodations

Individuals should not use the affected arm for several days to weeks. Overhead work, repetitive arm motion, and limited lifting and carrying should be eliminated from work responsibilities.

Comorbid Conditions

Comorbid conditions influencing the length of disability include autoimmune diseases, cancer, diabetes, and obesity. Disability will be longer if biceps tendonitis developed with other injuries such as repetitive motion injuries.

Complications

The inflammation may become severe enough to weaken the tendon and lead to a tear of tendon fibers or complete rupture of the tendon. Other complications of biceps tendonitis that can prolong recovery are shoulder instability, impingement syndrome, supraspinatus tendonitis, calcium deposits inside the tendon, bursitis, inflammatory diseases, and inability to modify activities. Adhesive capsulitis may result from chronic inflammation in the shoulder.

Factors Influencing Duration

If individual's work requires the continued repetitive motion that caused the biceps tendonitis, duties may have to be altered to promote full recovery. If the tendonitis developed from a nonwork related activity, the individual can return to work provided he/she stops the activity or modifies the physical motions.

Length of Disability

Duration depends on severity, job requirements, and perhaps, whether dominant or non-dominant extremity is involved.

Medical Treatment.

Duration in Days

Job Classification	Minimum	Optimum	Maximum
Sedentary work	1	3	7
Light work	1	3	14
Medium work	3	14	28
Heavy work	3	14	28
Very Heavy work	3	21	42

Arthroscopic Surgery.

Duration in Days

Job Classification	Minimum	Optimum	Maximum
Sedentary work	7	14	21
Light work	7	14	21
Medium work	28	42	56
Heavy work	56	70	84
Very Heavy work	56	70	84

Failure to Recover

If an individual fails to recover within the maximum duration expectancy period, the reader may wish to reference the following questions to assist in better understanding the specifics of an individual's medical case.

Regarding diagnosis:

- Is individual an active athlete? Manual worker?
- Does individual have an injury, gout, rheumatoid arthritis, or loss of elasticity?
- Does individual report pain on top of the shoulder, in the biceps muscle, or elbow? Is the pain worse at night? Does it increase with rotation of the wrist?
- Does individual have difficulty raising the affected arm?
- On exam, was the shoulder tender to touch? Was the neck also examined?
- Does individual have a torn rotator cuff or impingement syndrome?
- Were x-rays, MRI, and ultrasound done?
- Were conditions with similar symptoms ruled out?

Regarding treatment:

- Has individual stopped the activity that brought on the condition?
- Did individual have a corticosteroid injection?

Regarding prognosis:

- Is individual active in physical therapy? Is a home exercise program in place?
- Can individual's employer accommodate necessary restrictions?
- Does individual have any conditions that may affect ability to recover?
- Has individual had a tear or rupture of the tendon?
- Have any other complications developed such as bursitis or shoulder instability?

References

Farin, P.U. "Sonography of the Biceps Tendon of the Shoulder: Normal and Pathologic Findings." Journal of Clinical Ultrasound 24 6 (1996): 309-316.

Kisner, Carolyn, and Lynn Allen Colby. "The Shoulder and Shoulder Girdle." Therapeutic Exercise: Foundations and Techniques, 2nd ed. Kisner, Carolyn, and Lynn Allen Colby, eds. Philadelphia: F.A. Davis Company, 1990. 241-271.

Sethi, N., R. Wright, and K. Yamaguchi. "Disorders of the Long Head of the Biceps Tendon." Journal of Shoulder and Elbow Surgery 8 6 (1999): 644-654.

Tsur, A., and S. Gillson. "Brachial Biceps Tendon Injuries in Young Female High-level Tennis Players." Croatian Medical Journal 41 2 (2000): 184-185.

Biofeedback

Other names / synonyms: Neurofeedback
94.39

Definition

Biofeedback is a noninvasive, interactive technique that allows individuals to gain control over physiological reactions that are thought to be unconscious and automatic.

Feelings of relaxation and increased ability to focus attention are the result of successful biofeedback techniques. Biofeedback requires the individual's participation to learn to control normally involuntary (autonomic) functions such as heart rate, blood pressure, brain waves, skin temperature, muscle tension, breathing, and digestion. Research indicates that approximately 80% of individuals are able to benefit from biofeedback.

During the procedure, measurements are made of either the individual's skin temperature, muscle tension, sweat production, or brain waves using electrodes that are placed on specific parts of the body. For example, if an individual is plagued by chronic headaches, electrodes will most likely be placed on the head. These biological measurements are then relayed back to the individual, usually in the form of a variable auditory tone. With this awareness, the individual can learn to change skin temperature, muscle tension, and other symptoms, thereby improving health concerns or breaking unwanted habits such as smoking or overeating. Although most physiological responses were previously thought to be involuntary, research has shown that biofeedback can control many of them, including heart rate, skin temperature and blood pressure.

The procedure usually takes a minimum of 10 sessions to see measurable improvement, but many individuals begin to notice improvement before 10 visits.

Reason for Procedure

Biofeedback can help improve a number of health and medical concerns. These include migraine headaches, tension headaches, neck pain, back pain, tooth grinding (bruxism), jaw joint pain (temporomandibular joint syndrome), other chronic pain, and high blood pressure (hypertension). Stress incontinence of the bladder or rectal incontinence can be improved by learning to increase tension in specific muscles. Attention Deficit Hyperactivity Disorder (ADHD) can be helped by changing the person's brain wave patterns, and therefore, improve the ability to concentrate. In Raynaud's disease, a circulatory disorder causing uncomfortably cold hands, biofeedback can increase circulation to the fingers.

New techniques and applications for biofeedback are constantly being developed by mental health professionals and researchers. These include repetitive stress injuries, and carpal tunnel, thoracic outlet, and irritable bowel syndromes or other disorders of gastrointestinal motility. Biofeedback can be used for stress-related disorders in general, by teaching the individual how to deepen powers of relaxation. It can also be incorporated into psychotherapy, to reveal physical signs of tension over a certain situation immediately, even if the individual is unaware of feeling a conflict about it.

Research shows that biofeedback is used successfully to help individuals stop smoking, lose weight, and conquer certain phobias. Many individuals prefer biofeedback over other treatments since it is noninvasive and does not involve medications or pain.

Description

Psychologists and therapists use a variety of instruments during biofeedback. Electromyographs (EMGs) measure the individual's muscle tension. Two sensors (electrodes) are placed on the skin over the muscle to be monitored, such as the forehead muscle (frontalis) in headaches, or the muscles that shrug the shoulders (trapezius) in stress-related conditions. The EMG amplifies the electrical sound made by muscle contraction, and allows the individual to hear it so that they can increase it or decrease it, depending on the condition being treated. Therapists use the EMG to relieve muscle stiffness, treat incontinence, and recondition injured or strained muscles.

Skin Temperature Gauges show changes in the amount of heat given off by the skin, a measurement that indicates any changes in blood flow. These gauges are used in the treatment of Raynaud's disease, high blood pressure, anxiety, and migraines. Galvanic Skin Response Sensors (GSRs) use the amount of sweat produced by an individual while under stress to measure the conductivity of the skin. They are often used to reduce anxiety or fears. Electroencephalographs (EEGs) measure brainwave activity. Conditions that may benefit from training on these machines include attention deficit hyperactivity disorder (ADHD), tooth grinding, head injuries, and depression (including bipolar depression and seasonal affective disorder). Electrocardiographs (ECGs) monitor the individual's heart rate and may be useful in relieving an overly rapid heartbeat and controlling high blood pressure. Respiration feedback devices concentrate on measuring the rate, rhythm, and type of breathing to help the individual lessen symptoms of asthma, anxiety, and hyperventilation, and to promote relaxation.

Biofeedback sessions usually last 30 to 60 minutes, and should not exceed 15 sessions.

Prognosis

The outcome is good when biofeedback is used as a treatment intervention to address a problem or symptom for which it is appropriate and if the individual completes the recommended course of biofeedback. The prognosis also depends on the individual's specific mental health diagnosis and any underlying physical problems.

Specialists

- Internist
- Licensed Clinical Social Worker
- Physiatrist
- Psychiatrist
- Psychologist

Work Restrictions / Accommodations

No restrictions are required; however, a flexible work schedule may be helpful if the individual must occasionally attend biofeedback sessions during work hours.

Comorbid Conditions

Comorbid conditions are not relevant to biofeedback.

Procedure Complications

Biofeedback is a safe and effective procedure and there are no known physical or emotional complications. It should be avoided in certain endocrine disorders such as diabetes, as it can change the need for insulin and other medications. It is not recommended in psychotic disorders, psychopathic personality disorder, or in extremely decompensated individuals.

Factors Influencing Duration

The individual's commitment to the biofeedback process, home practice, and response to treatment might influence the length of disability.

Length of Disability

No disability is expected for recovery from the procedure itself.

References

Biofeedback. AAPB. 1999. 15 Jan 2001 <http://www.aapb.org/public/AAPBpbiofeedback.html>.

Biofeedback.net. Biofeedback.net. 30 Dec 2000. 30 Dec 2000 <http://biofeedback.net>.

Duke, James A. The Green Pharmacy. Emmaus, PA: Rodale Press, Inc, 1996.

Gottlieb, Bill, ed. New Choices in Natural Healing. Emmaus, PA: Rodale Press, Inc, 1995.

Biopsy

Other names / synonyms: Tissue Sample, Tissue Sampling

ICD-9 Depends on Site

Definition

A biopsy is a procedure that is done to obtain a small sample of tissue (cells) for examination in a laboratory. In most cases, a biopsy is obtained to assist the physician in making a diagnosis.

For instance, a sample of a tumor can be examined to determine if it is cancerous (malignant) or noncancerous (benign). A biopsy can also be used to evaluate the severity or extent of a disease (for example, a biopsy of the liver or kidney). Biopsy of nerve or muscle may help diagnose certain neurological conditions, such as different types of neuropathies or myopathies. Biopsy of skin or other tissue containing blood vessels may help diagnose inflammation of the arteries (arteritis) seen in connective tissue diseases such as lupus or temporal arteritis. Bone marrow biopsy can help explain certain hematological conditions affecting the blood, such as anemia or leukemia. Biopsy of tissue lining a joint space (synovium) is helpful in diagnosing arthritis. Another common use of biopsy is to assess the effectiveness of certain medical treatments. For example, after chemotherapy for cancer, the physician may biopsy the affected tissues to see if the cancer has been destroyed.

There are several ways of approaching a biopsy sample: fine needle (a small core needle is inserted through the skin into the tissue in question), core needle (a larger core needle is inserted through the skin into the tissue in question to acquire a piece of tissue larger than could be acquired through a fine needle), or open excisional (in which an incision in made through the skin and the surgeon removes samples of the tissue in question). The type of approach used in acquiring the biopsy sample depends on the diagnosis being considered, and on whether there is concern over tumor cells spreading along the needle tract. A biopsy usually can be done as an outpatient procedure, except for the open biopsy, which is done as part of a surgical operation, under general anesthesia.

Reason for Procedure

Biopsies are done to obtain samples of tissues for further evaluation in the laboratory. This is commonly done to help the physician make a diagnosis, to help determine the severity or extent of a disease, to evaluate the effectiveness of certain treatments, or to determine the cause of certain inflammations or infections. Examination of a sample of a tumor can determine if it is cancerous (malignant) or noncancerous (benign). Biopsy of nerve or muscle may help diagnose certain neurological conditions, such as different types of neuropathies or myopathies. Biopsy of skin or other tissue containing blood vessels may help diagnose inflammation of the arteries (arteritis) seen in connective tissue diseases such as lupus or temporal arteritis. Bone marrow biopsy can help explain certain hematological conditions affecting the blood, such as anemia or leukemia. Biopsy of tissue lining a joint space (synovium) is helpful in diagnosing arthritis.

Description

The details of the procedure vary depending on the tissue being biopsied. The general procedures are described as follows:

For a skin or muscle biopsy, the skin over the area being sampled is sterilized, usually with an iodine solution. The area is then numbed (anesthetized) with local anesthetic. A small piece of tissue is cut away with a sterile scalpel, and the small wound is stitched (sutured) closed.

For a needle biopsy, the skin over the area being sampled is sterilized and numbed (anesthetized). A sterile needle is inserted through the skin and into the tissue being sampled. The needle (containing the sample) is removed, and the wound is covered with a bandage.

An open biopsy is done under general anesthesia, as part of a surgical operation. A sample of the tissue is cut away during the surgery. The whole organ or lump may be removed (excisional biopsy), or only a portion of the lump may be removed (incisional biopsy). If the remainder of the procedure depends on what the biopsy reveals, as in the case of breast removal (mastectomy) for a malignant tumor, a frozen section of cells from the biopsy is examined immediately by a pathologist for a preliminary reading. Frozen section diagnosis is not as reliable as fixed tissue diagnosis, which takes longer as the cells are subjected to different staining procedures. Final diagnosis awaits examination of the fixed section.

Endoscopic biopsy is done through a fiber-optic instrument (endoscope) inserted into the gastrointestinal tract (gastrointestinal endoscopy), urinary bladder (cystoscopy), abdomen (laparoscopy), joint cavity (arthroscopy), midportion of the chest (mediastinoscopy), airway and windpipe (laryngoscopy and bronchoscopy), or womb (colposcopy).

Skin, muscle, and needle biopsies are generally done as outpatient procedures, under local anesthetic. Depending on the tissue being sampled, the procedures can be complete within minutes or an hour or so. Open biopsies take longer, as dictated by the surgical procedure.

Prognosis

Full recovery is expected following biopsy.

Specialists

- Dermatologist
- Surgeon

Work Restrictions / Accommodations

Restrictions and accommodations are not needed for this procedure.

Comorbid Conditions

Individuals with diabetes or compromised immune systems may heal more slowly than other individuals. Individuals with poor blood clotting may be at increased risk of bleeding from the biopsy procedure.

Procedure Complications

Biopsy is generally uncomplicated. As with all surgical techniques, the risk of infection, bleeding, scarring, and allergic reaction to anesthesia should be considered. Surgical disruption of a cancerous tumor or localized infection (abscess) may rarely cause spread of cancer cells or infectious organisms.

Factors Influencing Duration

Factors influencing disability include the presence of complications, the type of biopsy (open vs. needle, for example), and the type and severity of the underlying disease making biopsy necessary.

Length of Disability

Disability will be longer for an individual who performs heavy work, especially if that individual has an open biopsy.

Open, needle.

Duration in Days

Job Classification	Minimum	Optimum	Maximum
Any work	1	2	3

References

Patient Information Publications. National Institutes of Health. 01 Jan 1990. 26 Jan 2001 <http://www.cc.nih.gov/ccc/patient_education/pepubs/needle.html>.

Uthman, Edward O. The Biopsy Report: A Patient's Guide. CancerGuide. 17 July 1995. 12 Feb 2001 <http://www.cancerguide.org/pathology.html>.

Bipolar Affective Disorder

Other names / synonyms: Affective Bipolar Disorder, Bipolar Affective Disorder, Bipolar Mood Disorder, Depressed, Manic, Manic Depressive Illness

296.4, 296.5, 296.6, 296.7

Definition

Bipolar affective disorder is a disturbance of the brain characterized by severe mood swings. When severe, an individual may alternate between extreme highs (mania) and extreme lows (depression) several times a year (rapid cycling). These episodes may last between a few days to a few months.

In mania, the essential feature is brain overactivity. Thought processes are accelerated, mood is generally elevated, the need for sleep is greatly reduced or absent, and energy seems limitless. Unfortunately, thinking becomes less critical and often illogical. Insight into the condition may be missing entirely as is the ability to discriminate between sound and faulty thinking. Consequently, through impaired judgment, individuals tend to greatly overestimate their abilities, act impulsively, and may completely ignore social conventions and often behave in a grossly inappropriate or outlandish manner. Psychosis may be present with delusions of grandeur such as being the president or Jesus Christ. The periods of depression are also dangerous particularly when they occur in the wake of a manic episode. The frantic energy, racing thoughts, exuberance, and optimism characteristic of mania is suddenly replaced by morbid preoccupation, hopelessness, and apathy.

Bipolar illness presents in many variations both in terms of the severity of mood swings and the rate at which they change. The number of mood cycles may be just a few over the course of a lifetime or as many as several per year (rapid cycling). Some individuals with sustained periods of a milder form of mania known as hypomania may productively harness the abundance of energy and ideas in very creative ways. Many of our most celebrated geniuses in music, literature, theater, science, and politics were probably so "afflicted." Others may experience long and intense depressions with only fleeting episodes of a near-normal mood in between.

There is no single proven cause but it is thought to be a biochemical problem related to lack of stability in transmission of nerve impulses in the brain. This biochemical imbalance makes individuals with bipolar affective disorder more vulnerable to emotional or physical stress.

The illness usually begins in the 20s but the course is variable. Lifetime prevalence figures vary between one and three percent. In the US, more than 1% of the adult population (more than 2 million individuals) have bipolar affective disorder. Men and women are equally affected. Incidence is higher in relatives of individuals with bipolar disorders.

Diagnosis

History: The diagnosis can be made based on history or by psychiatric evaluation during a manic phase. During a depressive phase, observation must be augmented by history to differentiate between bipolar and major depressive disorders. Even with a careful history, the diagnosis may prove to be incorrect in two-thirds of individuals.

A good medical history is initially necessary to exclude the use of steroids, thyroid supplements, other prescription medications, or nonprescription "street" drugs such as amphetamines and cocaine.

The DSM-IV spells out specific criteria for the diagnosis of a manic episode. In general, the mood disturbance must cause "marked impairment" in social or occupational functioning and must not be due to a medical condition, effect of a medication, or drug intoxication. Three of the following symptoms must be present for a minimum of 1 week: inflated self-esteem, decreased need for sleep, more talkative than usual, racing thoughts, easily distracted, increased purposeful activity, and excessive involvement in risky endeavors with potential adverse consequences.

There may be a history of conflicts at work; legal, financial and family problems; spending sprees or extravagant purchases; business misadventures; extramarital affairs; impulsive travel; or turbulent social relations. Psychosis may be present with delusions of grandeur such as the individual thinking that he or she is the president or Jesus Christ.

In the depressive episodes, individual has feelings of sadness, hopelessness, and loss of interest in life activities or relationships. These symptoms are present for at least 2 weeks and make it difficult for the individual to function. They are associated with at least four of the following: thoughts of death or suicide, trouble sleeping or sleeping too much, poor appetite or overeating, difficulty concentrating and making decisions, feeling slowed down or too agitated to sit still, feeling worthless or guilty with very low self esteem, and loss of energy or feeling tired all the time. Hearing voices or seeing things that aren't there (hallucinations) or believing things that aren't true (delusions) may accompany severe depressive episodes.

Physical exam: When the illness is first noticed, a thorough exam should be performed to exclude physical causes such as hyperthyroidism or neurological disease. Observation of the individual's orientation, dress, mannerisms, behavior, and content of speech provide essential signs to diagnose the illness. A psychiatric evaluation should be done as soon as possible if a manic episode is suspected.

Tests: Psychological testing may aid in diagnosis if the evaluation is made while the individual is in a near-normal mood and the history is merely suggestive of bipolar illness. Laboratory tests should be done to rule out endocrine or metabolic disturbances, or to monitor compliance if medications are already being prescribed. As low blood levels of thyroid hormone are more common in individuals with rapid cycling than in other individuals, thyroid function tests should be done before and after treatment. Urine drug testing should be done to rule out drugs as the acute cause of mania.

Treatment

Medications are the mainstay of treatment, with psychotherapy a useful supportive tool. Medications consist primarily of mood stabilizers, such as lithium and valproate, that moderate the intensity of mood swings. Antipsychotic medications and tranquilizers are also regularly used, especially during the acute phase of a manic episode. Carbamazepine may sometimes be a useful alternative. Unfortunately, many individuals choose not to take the medications as directed and as a result relapse into mania. Noncompliance with medications is sometimes due to unpleasant side effects. In other cases, however, it is clearly a matter of preference. Many bipolar individuals enjoy the "high" feelings associated with the mania too much to give it up. Because these medications are potentially damaging and prescribed for life, periodic laboratory testing is necessary.

Occasionally, the medications prove to be ineffective in bringing a manic episode under control. In this instance, electroconvulsive therapy (ECT) may control the acute episode, and may also be continued on a regular basis as a preventive measure against future mood swings.

During manic episodes, there is a high risk of accidental death. Psychiatric hospitalization is frequently necessary to ensure the individual's safety. The periods of depression are also dangerous, particularly when they occur in the wake of a manic episode, and may also require hospitalization. When antidepressants must be used, they should be given with a mood stabilizer to prevent the individual from rebounding into hypomania. As with most psychiatric illnesses, there is no cure. Medication-assisted remissions are common, however, and result in a near normal life. Although psychotherapy may be helpful for individuals and families in dealing with stress, it is usually only used as an adjunct to medication.

Prognosis

Individual outcomes vary greatly. During manic episodes, there is a high risk of accidental death. Manic episodes can last anywhere from a few days to several months. With medications, the duration of manic episodes can be shortened significantly but may still involve a month or more of intensive therapy, often on an inpatient basis. Suicide attempts may complicate a depressive episode.

In general, bipolar disorder cannot be cured but the symptoms can usually be controlled. Individuals can lead very normal and productive lives. In less fortunate cases, the illness may be nearly impossible to arrest or control and result in permanent total or near-total disability. Early in the course of the disease, spontaneous remissions of up to several years duration are sometimes seen. This "honeymoon period" may delay diagnosis or convince the individual that the diagnosis was incorrect.

Up to 60% of individuals with bipolar disorder obtain some relief from lithium, but the response rate in those with rapid cycling is only twenty to forty percent. Left untreated, the illness becomes worse with time and may end up being very resistant to treatment, rendering the individual incapable of working or having normal relationships.

Differential Diagnosis

Conditions with similar symptoms include schizophrenia, schizoaffective disorder, personality disorders (especially borderline personality disorder), and substance abuse. Because these conditions may coexist with manic-depressive illness, they can be particularly difficult to tell apart.

Substance abuse especially of amphetamines, cocaine, and LSD may be nearly impossible to differentiate from an acute manic episode until the substances wear off. If evaluation is done on an outpatient basis alone, the chronic abuse of substances and/or alcohol can mimic bipolar illness to an extraordinary degree.

Hyperthyroidism or other physical illnesses and effects of medications such as steroids or antidepressants can be confused with bipolar illness. Such diverse conditions such as delirium, stroke, brain tumor, and infection also may resemble or even cause manic episodes.

Specialists

- Psychiatrist
- Psychologist

Work Restrictions / Accommodations

Accommodations depend on the type of work required. Stressful events and/or lack of sleep may increase risk of igniting a manic episode. Rotating shifts should be avoided. Regular daytime hours may be necessary for significant periods of time. High-pressure jobs or jobs with deadlines requiring the individual to work extremely long hours over extended time periods are also not recommended. Leave of absence may be necessary periodically.

Complementary and Alternative Therapies

Content is intended for awareness only. Treatments may or may not be effective. Scientific evidence may be lacking and some substances have potentially toxic effects. Dr. Presley Reed and the editors do not endorse the use of these therapies in the absence of consultation with a licensed medical professional.

Frankincense -	Said to have an antianxiety effect.
Hops -	Said to have a sedative effect.
Black cohosh -	Said to be a sedative and mood enhancer.
Chamomile -	Said to act as a tranquilizer and mood enhancer.
Purslane -	Contains magnesium, potassium, calcium, folate, and lithium that may help stabilize mood.
Tyrosine -	May improve mood and helpful in anxiety.
Vitamin B_{12} and B_6 -	May affect production of brain serotonin and norepinephrine and improve alertness and mood.
Acupressure -	May help calm and balance emotion.
Relaxation therapy -	May relieve tension.
Support groups -	Said to increase compliance and help avoid hospitalization. Individuals may benefit from the experiences of those who have "been there." Support groups provide a forum for mutual acceptance, understanding, and self-discovery.

Comorbid Conditions

Coexisting conditions that may affect recovery and lengthen disability include substance abuse, severe or persistent eating disorders, obsessive-compulsive disorder, panic disorder, and suicidal tendencies. Studies now suggest that individuals with bipolar affective disorder complicated by substance abuse have more hospitalizations, higher incidence of anxiety, and an earlier onset of mood problems.

Complications

Complications depend on the severity of the illness and the presence of impaired reality testing (psychosis). The most serious complication is accidental death or suicide. Other consequences of impaired judgment may include conflicts at work; legal, financial and family problems; spending sprees or extravagant purchases; business misadventures; extramarital affairs; impulsive travel; and turbulent social relations. Substance abuse affects up to 50% of bipolar individuals and may interfere with treatment.

Factors Influencing Duration

A history of episodes of relatively short duration, good response to medications, and long periods of normal mood predict the shortest period of disability. Substance abuse, noncompliance with medications, psychosis, and a history of lengthy hospitalizations tend to delay recovery. Serious episodes of mania may take 1 to 2 months and occasionally longer to be controlled sufficiently to allow return to work. Some individuals may be unable to maintain stable employment largely because of substance abuse or problems getting along with others.

Length of Disability

Maximum disability duration includes hospitalization.

Duration in Days

Job Classification	Minimum	Optimum	Maximum
Any work	7	28	56

Failure to Recover

If an individual fails to recover within the maximum duration expectancy period, the reader may wish to reference the following questions to assist in better understanding the specifics of an individual's medical case.

Regarding diagnosis:

- Was the diagnosis confirmed? Based on what criteria?
- Even if a clear history of bipolar illness is present, have the history, physical exam, and testing excluded other possible causes of symptoms?
- Does medication and drug history reveal use of steroids, thyroid supplements, other prescription medications, or street drugs that could cause similar symptoms?
- Is there evidence of rapid cycling (defined as four or more episodes of mania, excitement with moderate behavior change, or depression in any 12-month period)? Because it responds poorly to treatment, could failure to improve be linked to rapid cycling?
- Because low blood levels of thyroid hormone are more common in individuals with rapid cycling than in other bipolar individuals, were thyroid function tests performed before and during treatment?
- Is there a history or evidence of current substance abuse that makes an individual more prone to cycling with shorter episodes than usual?

Regarding treatment:

- Does individual fit criteria for rapid cycling?
- Is thyroid replacement therapy warranted based on thyroid function tests?
- Has use of antidepressants precipitated hypomania, warranting discontinuation or change in medications?
- Is there current evidence of substance abuse? How successfully is the substance abuse being addressed?
- What plan is in place to ensure compliance with medication regime?

Bipolar Affective Disorder

- If combinations of medications and psychotherapy have not provided adequate relief, is electroconvulsive therapy (ECT) warranted at this time?
- If self-harm or personal neglect put individual at risk, is psychiatric hospitalization warranted?

Regarding prognosis:

- Does individual display any tendency toward self-harm or suicide? What preventive safeguards are in place?
- Is illness interfering with self-esteem, friendships, social supports, and career goal achievements?
- Would individual benefit from one-on-one psychotherapy based on interpersonal, cognitive, or behavioral approaches?
- Is individual involved in a support group?
- If no improvement occurs after 6 to 8 weeks or if symptoms have worsened, is it time to try another treatment approach or another medication? Get a second opinion from another health care professional?

References

Baron, M. "Linkage Mapping of Bipolar Affective Disorder." *American Journal of Medical Genetics* 96 6 (2000): 881-883.

Perugi, G., et al. "The Clinical Impact of Bipolar and Unipolar Affective Comorbidity on Obsessive-compulsive Disorder." *Journal of Affective Disorders* 46 1 (1997): 15-23.

Bipolar Affective Disorder, Depressed

Other names / synonyms: Affective Bipolar Disorder, Bipolar I Disorder, Depressed Bipolar Disorder, Depressed Type, Manic-Depressive Illness Depressed Type

296.5

Definition

Bipolar affective disorder is a disturbance of the brain characterized by severe mood swings. When severe, an individual may alternate between extreme highs (mania) and extreme lows (depression) several times a year (rapid cycling). Episodes of depression last from a few days to a few months and are characterized by morbid preoccupation, hopelessness, and apathy.

There is no single proven cause but it is thought to be a biochemical problem related to lack of stability in transmission of nerve impulses in the brain. This biochemical imbalance makes individuals with bipolar affective disorder more vulnerable to emotional or physical stress.

The illness usually begins in the 20s but the course is variable. Lifetime prevalence figures vary between one and three percent. In the US, more than 1% of the adult population (more than 2 million individuals) have bipolar affective disorder. Men and women are equally affected. Incidence is higher in relatives of individuals with bipolar disorders.

Diagnosis

History: Although the history is of greatest importance in establishing the diagnosis, a physical exam and laboratory tests should be done in every new case of suspected bipolar or depressive illness. A thorough history is vital in making the diagnosis of bipolar mood disorder. The actual criteria for the depressed phase of bipolar illness are the same as for major (unipolar) depression. The only difference is a history of manic or near-manic episodes not attributable to medications, drug abuse, or physical illness.

For a DSM-IV diagnosis, certain criteria must be met. Feelings of sadness, hopelessness, and loss of interest in life activities or relationships must be present for at least 2 weeks making it difficult for the individual to function. Diagnosis must also be associated with at least four of the following: thoughts of death or suicide, trouble sleeping or sleeping too much, poor appetite or overeating, difficulty concentrating and making decisions, feeling slowed down or too agitated to sit still, feeling worthless or guilty with low self-esteem, and loss of energy or feeling tired all the time.

Whenever possible, corroborative history from friends, family members, or employers is useful as is any family history of mental illness or suicides. A careful, nonjudgmental inventory of substance abuse should be made in every case. Not only can bipolar illness be confused with substance abuse, but the abuse will require specific treatment measures of its own. Severe depressive episodes may be associated with seeing visions (hallucinations), hearing voices, or having false beliefs (delusions).

Physical exam: Even with a clear-cut history of bipolar illness, physical causes capable of producing symptoms of depression, such as hypothyroidism, cancer, or any chronic illness need to be excluded. Observation of the individual's orientation, dress, mannerisms, behavior, and content of speech provide essential signs to diagnose the illness.

Tests: Psychological testing used in establishing the diagnosis may also provide a means of assessing severity and response to treatment. Laboratory testing, including thyroid function tests, or brain imaging studies may be necessary to exclude causes other than mood cycling. MRI brain scans may help predict outcome, as a recent study showed that those individuals with abnormalities deep in the brain (subcortical white matter lesions) had a worse outcome than those individuals without these abnormalities.

Treatment

For all phases of bipolar illness, psychiatric medications are the mainstay of treatment. Mood stabilizers such as lithium salts and divalproex sodium are almost always used. During a depressed phase, however, they may not offer enough improvement so antidepressants may also be necessary. Some antidepressants are thought to be associated with a greater risk of overtreating the depression and causing mania to surface or making the long-term course of bipolar illness worse. Care must be exercised when choosing the type and duration of antidepressant therapy.

When present, psychotic symptoms such as paranoid delusions need to be targeted specifically with antipsychotic medication. Psychotherapy added to treatment during the depressed phase may ensure that the individual remains safe until improvement occurs and that family integrity is supported. In some instances, the risk of self-harm or personal neglect is so great that psychiatric hospitalization is warranted.

Some cases of depression are treatment-resistant. No combination of medications or psychotherapy seems to provide adequate relief. In this circumstance, electroconvulsive therapy (ECT) is the treatment of choice and is both safe and extremely effective.

Prognosis

Most episodes of depression in the context of bipolar illness get better within several weeks. Although improvement is accelerated by treatment with medications, most individuals take up to 4 to 6 weeks to respond clinically to antidepressants. Up to 60% of individuals with bipolar disorder obtain some relief from lithium, although the response rate among those with rapid cycling is only twenty to forty percent. As more new medications continue to become available, there is a greater chance of finding one that is effective for a given individual. The long-term course of the illness is highly variable. Left untreated, however, it may get worse with time and tend to become resistant to treatment, leading to permanent disability with poor social function.

Differential Diagnosis

Although a history of manic episodes generally confirms the diagnosis, it must be emphasized that depression has many causes. A history of bipolar illness does not exclude other causes such as bereavement or medical causes. Post-traumatic stress disorder may lead to a major depression. A major symptom of schizophrenia and other forms of psychosis may be a marked deficit in outward emotion and purposeful activity that may be virtually impossible to distinguish from bipolar depression complicated by psychosis. Schizoaffective disorder is another diagnosis that resembles bipolar illness. In severe cases of personality disorder, especially borderline personality disorder, bipolar illness may be misdiagnosed or in some cases coexist.

Specialists

- Psychiatrist
- Psychologist

Work Restrictions / Accommodations

Highly stressful situations should be avoided as well as those demanding high levels of concentration and alertness. Irritability and low frustration tolerance can be major problems and should be considered in the work environment.

Comorbid Conditions

Coexisting conditions that may impact recovery and lengthen disability include neurological and developmental disorders, substance abuse, severe, persistent eating disorders, and any other disorders such as obsessive-compulsive disorder, panic disorder, and suicidal tendencies. Studies now suggest that individuals with bipolar affective disorder complicated by substance abuse have more hospitalizations, higher incidence of anxiety, and an earlier onset of mood problems.

Complications

The same complications seen in unipolar depression may be present in bipolar depression. The most serious complication is suicide. Other complications include psychotic symptoms such as hearing voices (hallucinations) or having strange beliefs (delusions) that are usually paranoid in nature. These may put the individual at risk for accidents or lapses in judgment. Malnutrition may complicate prolonged depressive episodes when loss of appetite is prominent. The most common complication is substance abuse especially alcohol and affects about one-half of those with bipolar illness. Another dangerous complication is the presence of a mix of both manic and depressed symptoms. There is always the risk that an episode of mania may follow depression and/or emerge partly as a result of antidepressant therapy.

Factors Influencing Duration

As in unipolar depression, factors influencing length of disability include the severity of the illness, presence of complicating factors such as substance abuse or suicide attempts, type of occupation, and response to therapy. This may translate from almost no time lost from work to a major leave of absence. Only the most severe cases of bipolar illness result in total and permanent disability. Most individuals should be restored to near normal functioning within a few months. If appropriate allowances and monitoring are provided, individuals may return to work sooner. Substance abuse also complicates and delays response to treatment. If a manic episode results from therapy, recovery will be significantly slowed as this condition may be even more serious than the initial depression.

Length of Disability

Maximum disability duration includes hospitalization.

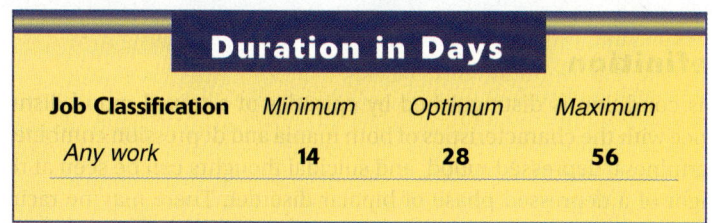

Duration in Days

Job Classification	Minimum	Optimum	Maximum
Any work	14	28	56

Failure to Recover

If an individual fails to recover within the maximum duration expectancy period, the reader may wish to reference the following questions to assist in better understanding the specifics of an individual's medical case.

Regarding diagnosis:

- Was diagnosis of bipolar affective disorder (depressed) confirmed?

- Because research indicates that diagnosis of any kind of affective disorder will prove to be incorrect in two-thirds of individuals, on what criteria is this individual's diagnosis based?
- Even if there is a clear history of bipolar illness, have the history, physical exam, and testing excluded other possible causes of symptoms?
- Does medication and drug history reveal use of beta-blockers, sedatives, or other prescription medications or street drugs that could cause symptoms resembling those seen in depression?
- Does brain MRI show deep white matter abnormalities associated with poor outcome?
- Does evidence exist of rapid cycling defined as four or more episodes of mania, excitement with moderate behavior change (hypomania), or depression in any 12-month period? Because it responds poorly to treatment, could failure to improve be linked to rapid cycling?
- Because low blood levels of thyroid hormone are more common in individuals with rapid cycling than in other bipolar individuals, were thyroid function tests performed before and during treatment?
- Is there a history or current evidence of substance abuse that may make an individual more prone to cycling with shorter episodes than usual?

Regarding treatment:

- Does individual fit criteria for rapid cycling? Is individual being treated with lithium even though the response rate among those with rapid cycling is considered only twenty to forty percent?
- Is thyroid replacement therapy warranted based on thyroid function tests?
- Has use of antidepressants precipitated hypomania, warranting discontinuation or change in medications?
- Does individual have substance abuse? Could it be responsible for limiting the effectiveness of lithium or reducing compliance with dosing regimen? How successfully is the substance abuse being addressed? In the meantime, what plan is in place to ensure compliance with medication regime?
- Although not officially a treatment for bipolar disorder, was carbamazepine considered as a supplement or alternative to divalproex sodium and lithium?
- If combinations of medications and psychotherapy have not provided adequate relief, is electroconvulsive therapy (ECT) warranted at this time?
- If self-harm or personal neglect puts individual at risk, is psychiatric hospitalization warranted?

Regarding prognosis:

- Considering that individuals with severe depression have a high suicide rate, does individual display any tendency toward self-harm or suicide? What preventive safeguards are in place?
- Is illness interfering with self-esteem, friendships, social supports, and career goal achievements?
- Would individual benefit from one-on-one psychotherapy based on interpersonal, cognitive, or behavioral approaches?
- Is individual involved in a support group?
- If no improvement occurs after 6 to 8 weeks or if symptoms worsen, is it time to try another treatment approach or another medication or get a second opinion from another healthcare professional?

References

Duke, James A. The Green Pharmacy. Emmaus, PA: Rodale Press, Inc, 1997.

Gottlieb, Bill, ed. New Choices in Natural Healing. Emmaus, PA: Rodale Press, Inc, 1995.

Bipolar Affective Disorder, Mixed

Other names / synonyms: Bipolar I Disorder

296.6

Definition

This condition is distinguished by episodes of a mixed mood disturbance with the characteristics of both mania and depression combined. Tearfulness, depressed mood, and suicidal thoughts can be seen at the height of a depressed phase of bipolar disorder. There may be racing thoughts in the manic phase. It is also called dysphoric mania, which is an uncomfortably excited mood experienced as unpleasant.

Other associated findings in a mixed episode are anger, panic attacks, agitation, anxiety, restlessness, suicidal thoughts, persecutory delusions, hallucinations, and confusion. This disorder is not a result of drug abuse, a side effect of a prescription medicine, or a medical disease such as hyperthyroidism. Mixed episodes can be experienced by one-third of those with bipolar disorder.

Women are more commonly affected than men.

Diagnosis

History: History reveals a combination of the features of mania and depression, with some symptoms present nearly every day for at least a week. This disturbance of mood causes a marked deterioration of relationships and work performance, requires hospitalization for safety reasons, or may be accompanied by psychotic features. In addition, the individual has had at least one occurrence of major depressive, manic, or mixed episode. This mood disorder is seen in the absence of other mental disturbances such as delusional disorder, schizoaffective disorder, schizophrenia, or other psychotic disorder. The individual may complain of depressed mood, loss of pleasure in normally pleasurable activities (anhedonia), guilt, suicidal thoughts, fatigue, and anxiety.

Physical exam: Physical exam is not helpful in making this diagnosis, although signs of chronic illness such as hypothyroidism or cancer may suggest a physical cause for the symptoms. Observation of the individual's orientation, dress, mannerisms, behavior, and content of speech provide essential signs to diagnose the illness.

Tests: Tests do not contribute to the diagnosis, although thyroid level and other blood tests may be necessary to exclude a physical basis for some symptoms.

Treatment

Short-term psychiatric hospitalization may be required for individual's safety. Drug therapy is needed. Lithium or anticonvulsants is the traditional treatment for mania, but lithium is less effective in individuals with mixed forms of bipolar disorder. A tranquilizer or an antipsychotic medication may be combined with lithium. Anticonvulsants and calcium-channel blockers are also used as mood stabilizers. Electroconvulsive therapy (ECT) is not common and may be less helpful than it is for individuals with pure bipolar depression or mania. Individual or group psychotherapy helps the individual investigate and cope with the psychological stresses that often trigger a manic episode.

Prognosis

Mixed bipolar disorder can have a more chronic course than the more common bipolar affective disorder. Suicidal tendencies are more common in individuals with mixed than those with manic bipolar disorder.

Differential Diagnosis

Other possibilities are schizoaffective disorder, schizophrenia, or a mood disorder due to drug abuse or medical disease.

Specialists

- Psychiatrist
- Psychologist

Work Restrictions / Accommodations

Individual restrictions and/or accommodations are dependent on the course of the disorder and the requirements of the job and work environment. The restrictions may be time-limited or ongoing, based on individual circumstances. Leave of absence may be necessary periodically. Close supervision of the individual's work may be useful due to the impaired judgment and insight that may occur with the onset of a manic episode.

Comorbid Conditions

Coexisting conditions that may impact recovery and lengthen disability include neurological and developmental disorders, substance abuse, severe or persistent eating disorders, obsessive-compulsive disorder, panic disorder, and suicidal tendencies. Studies now suggest that individuals with bipolar affective disorder complicated by substance abuse have more hospitalizations, higher incidence of anxiety, and an earlier onset of mood problems.

Complications

Suicide is a major risk but homicide is rare. Other complications may include ruined relationships, career, and finances; drug or alcohol abuse; disregard for nutrition and self-care; and exhaustion.

Complementary and Alternative Therapies

Content is intended for awareness only. Treatments may or may not be effective. Scientific evidence may be lacking and some substances have potentially toxic effects. Dr. Presley Reed and the editors do not endorse the use of these therapies in the absence of consultation with a licensed medical professional.

Frankincense -	Said to have an antianxiety effect.
Hops -	Said to have a sedative effect.
Black cohosh -	Said to be a sedative and mood enhancer.
Chamomile -	Said to act as a tranquilizer and mood enhancer.
Purslane -	Contains magnesium, potassium, calcium, folate, and lithium that may help stabilize mood.
Tyrosine -	May improve mood and helpful in anxiety.
Vitamin B_{12} and B_6 -	May affect production of brain serotonin and norepinephrine and improve alertness and mood.
Acupressure -	May help calm and balance emotion.
Relaxation therapy -	May relieve tension.
Support groups -	Said to increase compliance and help avoid hospitalization. Individuals may benefit from the experiences of those who have "been there." Support groups provide a forum for mutual acceptance, understanding, and self-discovery.

Factors Influencing Duration

Noncompliance with medical treatment can prolong disability. Coexisting psychiatric conditions can also prolong disability and complicate treatment.

Length of Disability

Maximum disability duration includes hospitalization.

Duration in Days

Job Classification	Minimum	Optimum	Maximum
Any work	14	28	56

Failure to Recover

If an individual fails to recover within the maximum duration expectancy period, the reader may wish to reference the following questions to assist in better understanding the specifics of an individual's medical case.

Regarding diagnosis:

- Was diagnosis of bipolar affective disorder (mixed) confirmed?
- Because research indicates that diagnosis of any kind of affective disorder will prove to be incorrect in two-thirds of individuals, on what criteria is this individual's diagnosis based?

- Even if a clear history of bipolar illness is present, have the history, physical exam, and testing excluded other possible causes of symptoms?
- Does medication and drug history reveal use of beta-blockers, sedatives, or other prescription medications or street drugs that could cause symptoms resembling those seen in depression?
- Does brain MRI show deep white matter abnormalities associated with poor outcome?
- Is evidence of rapid cycling present defined as four or more episodes of mania, excitement with moderate behavior change (hypomania), or depression in any 12-month period? Because it responds poorly to treatment, could failure to improve be linked to rapid cycling?
- Because low blood levels of thyroid hormone are more common in individuals with rapid cycling than in other bipolar individuals, were thyroid function tests performed before and during treatment?
- Is there a history or current evidence of substance abuse that may make an individual more prone to cycling with shorter episodes than usual?

Regarding treatment:

- Does individual fit criteria for rapid cycling?
- Is thyroid replacement therapy warranted based on thyroid function tests?
- Has use of antidepressants precipitated hypomania warranted discontinuation or change in medications?
- Is there current evidence of substance abuse?
- How successfully is the substance abuse being addressed?
- What plan is in place to ensure compliance with medication regime?
- If combinations of medications and psychotherapy have not provided adequate relief, is electroconvulsive therapy (ECT) warranted at this time?
- If self-harm or personal neglect put individual at risk, is psychiatric hospitalization warranted?

Regarding prognosis:

- Does individual display any tendency toward self-harm or suicide? What preventive safeguards are in place?
- Is illness interfering with self-esteem, friendships, social supports, and career goal achievements?
- Would individual benefit from one-on-one psychotherapy based on interpersonal, cognitive, or behavioral approaches? Is individual involved in a support group?
- If no improvement occurs after 6 to 8 weeks or if symptoms have worsened, is it time to try another treatment approach or another medication? Get a second opinion from another health care professional?

References

Bipolar Affective Disorder. National Depressive and Manic Depressive Association. 07 Jun 1999. 20 Jun 2000 <http://www.ndmda.org/rapid.htm>.

Cassidy, F., et al. "Diagnostic Depressive Symptoms of the Mixed Bipolar Episode." Psychological Medicine 30 2 (2000): 403-411.

Duke, James A. The Green Pharmacy. Emmaus, PA: Rodale Press, Inc, 1997.

Feinstein, Alice, ed. Healing with Vitamins. Emmaus, PA: Rodale Press, Inc, 1996.

Freeman, M.P., and S.L. McElroy. "Clinical Picture and Etiologic Models of Mixed States." Psychiatric Clinics of North America 22 3 (1999): 535-546.

Gottlieb, Bill, ed. New Choices in Natural Healing. Emmaus, PA: Rodale Press, Inc, 1997.

Koukopoulos, A. "Agitated Depression as a Mixed State and the Problem of Melancholia." Psychiatric Clinics of North America 22 3 (1999): 547-564.

Strakowski, S.M., et al. "Suicidality Among Patients with Mixed and Manic Bipolar Disorder." American Journal of Psychiatry 153 5 (1996): 674-676.

Bipolar Affective Disorder, Single Manic Episode

Other names / synonyms: Manic Disorder

296.0

Definition

A manic episode is characterized by an elevated or euphoric mood and inflated self-image. The episode usually has a rapid onset, building suddenly over a few days and lasting a few weeks to several months. The individual is filled with ideas and overflowing with energy. Behavior is dramatic, expansive, and usually overactive and may also be impulsive, intruding on other individuals or alienating friends, family, and coworkers. The individual may even become hostile if opposed. Because the individual has an inflated sense of self-worth (grandiosity), there is lack of insight into how harmful the mania is to relationships. Mood can be unstable or irritable and may be experienced as unpleasant. Mania may be associated with psychotic features such as seeing visions or hearing voices (hallucinations), or holding to untrue beliefs (delusions). Usually the psychotic features are in keeping with the individual's sense of extraordinary well-being.

This diagnosis is not considered if the symptoms of mania accompany a medical disorder such as hyperthyroidism, use of a prescription antidepressant, or drug abuse. Initial manic episodes can occur in individuals abstaining from alcohol after years of abuse.

The average age of onset is in the early 20s but the range is from adolescence to over age 50. The manic episode commonly appears after some psychologically stressful event.

Diagnosis

History: History reveals only one manic episode without any prior major depressive episodes, and is associated with a persistently elevated or irritable mood for at least a week. During the episode, the individual will exhibit at least three of the following symptoms: inflated opinion of self (grandiosity), needing drastically less sleep than normal, excessive talking, racing thoughts, distractibility, increased goal-directed activity, and indulging excessively in pleasurable activities that can result in undesirable consequences such as buying sprees or sexual binges. The manic episode leads to a marked impairment of relationships or work performance and may also endanger the individual or others.

Physical exam: The exam does not contribute to making this diagnosis. Observation of the individual's orientation, dress, mannerisms, behavior, and content of speech provide essential signs to diagnose the illness.

Tests: Tests do not establish the diagnosis. However, blood work may be helpful to rule out treatable causes of delirium that can cause similar symptoms.

Treatment

Psychiatric hospitalization may be required during an acute manic episode to stabilize medication and maintain the individual's safety. Lithium or Depakote is the traditional treatment for acute mania. As response may take a week or more, major or minor tranquilizers may be added. Anticonvulsants and calcium-channel blockers may also be useful as mood stabilizers. Electroconvulsive therapy (ECT) is rarely used.

Prognosis

Most manic episodes persist for a few weeks to several months and resolve without medical intervention. Most individuals will have recurrences of manic episodes. Classical bipolar affective disorder may emerge at a later time. Individuals who have their first manic episode younger than 21 are less likely to have a complete remission and more likely to develop bipolar affective disorder and substance abuse. After a single manic episode, sexual activity will more likely return to normal, but the individual may still have difficulties in the area of recreational enjoyment.

Differential Diagnosis

If the individual is over age 50 at the time of a first manic episode, medical disorders producing similar symptoms should be considered such as hyperthyroidism, Cushing's syndrome, brain tumor, or multiple sclerosis. A hypomanic episode is very similar to a manic episode with less impairment of social or occupational functioning. Drug abuse can cause behavior similar to mania as can side effects of an antidepressant medication or ECT. Major depressive episodes with irritable mood can also cause similar symptoms.

Specialists

- Psychiatrist
- Psychologist

Work Restrictions / Accommodations

Impairments in judgment and disruptive behavior generally prevent employment during a manic episode. After successful treatment, closer supervision of the individual's work may be useful particularly if safety issues are involved. Night shift or rotating shifts may increase the severity of this illness.

Complementary and Alternative Therapies

Content is intended for awareness only. Treatments may or may not be effective. Scientific evidence may be lacking and some substances have potentially toxic effects. Dr. Presley Reed and the editors do not endorse the use of these therapies in the absence of consultation with a licensed medical professional.

Frankincense -	Said to have an antianxiety effect.
Hops -	Said to have a sedative effect.
Black cohosh -	Said to be a sedative and mood enhancer.
Chamomile -	Said to act as a tranquilizer and mood enhancer.
Purslane -	Contains magnesium, potassium, calcium, folate, and lithium that may help stabilize mood.
Tyrosine -	May improve mood and helpful in anxiety.
Vitamin B_{12} and B_6 -	May affect production of brain serotonin and norepinephrine and improve alertness and mood.
Acupressure -	May help calm and balance emotion.
Relaxation therapy -	May relieve tension.
Support groups -	Said to increase compliance and help avoid hospitalization. Individuals may benefit from the experiences of those who have "been there." Support groups provide a forum for mutual acceptance, understanding, and self-discovery.

Comorbid Conditions

Current alcohol abuse or drug use or the presence of a personality disorder or other psychiatric condition may lengthen disability.

Complications

Complications may include accidental death or injury due to impaired judgment, divorce or other ruined relationships, exposure to sexually transmitted diseases because of promiscuity, financial ruin, drug or alcohol abuse, exhaustion, and disregard for self-care and nutrition.

Factors Influencing Duration

Poor compliance with medication and alcohol or drug abuse can increase the period of disability.

Length of Disability

Maximum disability duration includes hospitalization.

Duration in Days

Job Classification	Minimum	Optimum	Maximum
Any work	7	28	56

Failure to Recover

If an individual fails to recover within the maximum duration expectancy period, the reader may wish to reference the following questions to assist in better understanding the specifics of an individual's medical case.

Regarding diagnosis:

- Did individual exhibit signs of a manic episode?
- Was diagnosis confirmed?
- Were other conditions with similar symptoms ruled out?
- Based on the criteria that only one manic episode was experienced with no past major depressive episodes, was the diagnosis of bipolar affective disorder with single manic episode confirmed?

Regarding treatment:

- During the acute manic episode, was psychiatric hospitalization required to stabilize medication and maintain individual's safety?
- Is self-harm or personal neglect putting individual at risk?
- What medications were included in the drug therapy?
- Is individual taking medication as prescribed?
- If individual is not taking lithium or Depakote because of side effects, could alternate medication be used instead?
- Would psychotherapy help individual comply with therapy?
- Is illness interfering with self-esteem, friendships, social supports, and career goal achievements?
- Would individual benefit from one-on-one psychotherapy based on interpersonal, cognitive, or behavioral approaches?
- Is individual involved in a support group?

Regarding prognosis:

- Is individual younger than age 21 and thus less likely to have a complete remission while more likely to develop bipolar affective disorder and substance abuse?
- If symptoms have not completely resolved, is additional or extended therapy warranted?
- Does individual display any tendency toward self-harm or suicide? What preventive safeguards are in place?
- During the manic episode, did complications occur such as those due to impaired judgment that could impact recovery?
- Is an underlying personality disorder or other psychiatric condition impacting recovery?
- Does individual have a functional support system in place?
- Would group therapy be beneficial in helping individual and family understand the illness and better cope with it?
- Would individual and family benefit from enrollment in a support group?
- If no improvement occurs after 6 to 8 weeks or if symptoms have worsened, is it time to try another treatment approach or another medication? Get a second opinion from another health care professional?

References

Bipolar Treatment. Mental Help Net. 1996. 01 Feb 2001 <http://mentalhelp.net/disorders/sx20t.htm>.

Gottlieb, Bill, ed. New Choices in Natural Healing. Emmaus, PA: Rodale Press, Inc, 1995.

Bladder Fistulas

Other names / synonyms: Appendicovesical Fistula, Colovesical Fistula, Ileovesical Fistula, Rectovesical Fistula, Urethrovesical Fistula, Vesical Fistula, Vesicocutaneous Fistula, Vesicoenteric Fistula, Vesicovaginal Fistula

596.1, 596.2, 599

Definition

A bladder fistula (also called vesical fistula) is an abnormal channel between the interior of the urinary bladder and other organs or areas.

The channel (fistula) may form as a result of a birth (congenital) defect, damage done during surgery (surgical trauma), or as a result of certain diseases that can occur in the genital/urinary (genitourinary) system. There are a number of different types of bladder fistulas. These fistulas may form a connection between the bladder and the vagina (vesicovaginal), the skin of the abdomen (vesicocutaneous), the large intestine (colovesical, rectovesical), the small intestine (enterovesical), or the appendix (appendicovesical). Bladder fistulas that connect to any part of the large intestine or appendix are collectively referred to as vesicoenteric fistulas. The net result of any of these conditions is a free exchange of fluids between the bladder and the organ or area connected by the fistula.

Risk factors for vesicovaginal fistulas include gynecological procedures such as surgical removal of the uterus (hysterectomy), pelvic or uterine surgery, pelvic irradiation, or obstetric trauma. Other risk factors may include cancer (malignancy) in the pelvic region, prolonged labor, physical distortion of the bladder or uterus by an abnormal growth (mass) on the ovary, abnormal tissue growth in the pelvic region (endometriosis), low hemoglobin in the blood (anemia), lack of adequate nutrients in the diet (malnutrition), intake of steroids, tuberculosis, rape, or vigorous intercourse in young females.

Risk factors for colovesical, rectovesical, ileovesical, or appendicovesical fistulas include gastrointestinal inflammatory diseases (diverticulitis, Crohn's disease, ulcerative colitis, appendiceal/pelvic abscess, Meckel's diverticulum), diseases that produce abnormal growth in the gastrointestinal or urogenital tracts (colorectal cancer, lymphoma, AIDS, cervical cancer, leiomyosarcoma of the bladder), and trauma to organs within the pelvic region (gunshot wound, penetrating injury, pelvic fracture, open surgery).

Vesicocutaneous fistula is considered to be one of the less severe types of bladder fistulas. Risk factors for this type include obstruction of the urinary bladder or bladder cancer and trauma.

Bladder fistulas are rarely seen in daily clinical practice. In undeveloped countries, individuals with bladder fistula usually remain unknown to the medical establishment. It is estimated that approximately 500,000 untreated cases occur worldwide. In undeveloped countries, most vesicovaginal fistulas result from prolonged obstructed labor. This condition complicates 1 to 3 per 1,000 deliveries in West Africa. In developed countries, 50% of individuals with colon cancer, diverticulitis, bowel disease, or those who received radiation treatment in the pelvic region develop a vesicoenteric fistula. Colovesical fistula is the most common type of vesicoenteric fistula, affecting men three times as often as women, presumably because the uterus helps prevent fistula formation between the urinary bladder and large intestine.

Diagnosis

History: Individuals with a vesicovaginal fistula complain of an unpleasant ammonia odor coming from the vagina. Individuals with enterovesical fistulas may report pain in the lower abdomen, chills, fever, diarrhea, constipation, blood in the urine (hematuria), increased frequency and urgency of urination, and pain during urination (dysuria). They also may notice passage of urine through the rectum or the presence of mucus in their urine.

Physical exam: There are generally few physical findings with bladder fistula. An abdominal mass is felt (palpated) in a third of individuals. Abdominal tenderness and tightening of the abdominal muscles (guarding) in response to pressure are observed 30-50% of the time. In females, a pelvic examination may reveal inflammation and tenderness. Irritation of the abdominal skin may be observed in individuals with vesicocutaneous fistula.

Tests: Tests may include urinalysis, urine culture, and observation of the inside of the urinary bladder by insertion of a flexible fiber-optic microscope through the urethra and into the bladder (cytoscopy). Visualization of the bladder by filling it with a radionuclide and taking pictures with a fluoroscope (cystography) is useful for all types of bladder fistulas. The cystogram is the most effective method for diagnosis. CT may also help with diagnosis. For a vesicoenteric fistula, injection of a contrast medium into the large intestine and taking x-rays (barium enema) may be useful. During pregnancy when x-ray must be avoided, ultrasonography is a safe way to evaluate fistulas.

Treatment

In rare cases, a bladder fistula will close and heal spontaneously after insertion of a urinary catheter (conservative treatment). Bladder fistulas must usually be repaired surgically either as a single operation (single-stage) or multiple operation (multistage) procedure. A single-stage procedure is recommended for healthy individuals with good nutrition, no areas of infection (abscess) or severe inflammation, and without multiple organ involvement. Multistage procedures may be used for complicated bladder fistula.

A vesicovaginal fistula can be repaired surgically using a vaginal, abdominal, or combined approach. A vesicoenteric fistula is repaired surgically using a low abdominal incision and the diseased bowel and part of the bladder is removed (York-Mason procedure). For all surgical treatments of bladder fistula, an indwelling urethral catheter allowing urine to pass is necessary during the healing period.

Prognosis

Spontaneous closure of a bladder fistula after insertion of a bladder catheter occurs in approximately 2% of cases. Surgical treatment of bladder fistula corrects the condition in 85-95% of cases. In 6-15% of cases, the fistula recurs and can usually be managed conservatively with bladder catheterization and observation.

Differential Diagnosis

Conditions with similar symptoms include cancer in the pelvis or large intestine (colorectal cancer), diverticulitis, Crohn's disease, ulcerative colitis, Meckel's diverticulum, AIDS, ovarian cancer, endometriosis, any gastrointestinal inflammatory disease, and cervical cancer.

Specialists

- General Surgeon
- Gynecologist
- Urologist

Work Restrictions / Accommodations

Physical labor such as heavy lifting and climbing may need to be restricted following surgical treatment for bladder fistula. Bathroom facilities should be readily available for individuals with a bladder catheter. No work restrictions or special accommodations should be required after the individual makes a complete recovery.

Comorbid Conditions

Existing conditions that may impact an individual's ability to recover and further lengthen disability include any condition that causes an increase in urinary bladder distention and pressure such as bladder neck obstruction. Ongoing genitourinary infection and obesity may also lengthen disability time. Conditions predisposing to bladder fistula including pelvic, bladder, or intestinal tumors, or inflammatory disease of the intestines also lengthen disability.

Complications

Possible complications of bladder fistulas include spontaneous bleeding (hemorrhage), inflammation of tissues in the abdominal cavity (peritonitis), inflammation and infection of the genitourinary tract, and infection of the fistula itself.

Factors Influencing Duration

A bladder fistula is usually the result of an underlying disease state. The severity of this underlying condition influences the length of disability. Type of surgical treatment (i.e., single-stage or multistage procedure) also affects length of disability. Elderly individuals may have a longer disability time following surgery, as postoperative recovery times are usually slower.

Length of Disability

Duration of disability depends on job requirements and treatment. Heavy labor is restricted following surgery until recovery is complete. Remission of this condition without treatment occurs in approximately 10% of cases.

Surgical repair.

Duration in Days

Job Classification	Minimum	Optimum	Maximum
Sedentary work	42	49	56
Light work	42	49	56
Medium work	42	49	70
Heavy work	56	63	84
Very Heavy work	56	63	112

Failure to Recover

If an individual fails to recover within the maximum duration expectancy period, the reader may wish to reference the following questions to assist in better understanding the specifics of an individual's medical case.

Regarding diagnosis:

- Does individual have a history of bladder trauma, recent genitourinary surgery, or a genitourinary disease?
- Has individual had any symptoms characteristic of a bladder fistula such as vaginal odor, lower abdominal pain, chills, fever, diarrhea, constipation, dysuria, or hematuria?
- Was the diagnosis confirmed with one or more diagnostic tests such as cystoscopy, cystography, CT, or ultrasound?
- If the diagnosis was uncertain, were other conditions with similar symptoms ruled out (i.e., colorectal cancer, gynecological cancer, or inflammatory bowel disease)?

Regarding treatment:

- Did individual respond to conservative treatment (placement of a urinary catheter to allow for spontaneous healing)?
- Was it necessary for individual to have either single-stage or multistage surgery? Is an indwelling catheter in place?

Regarding prognosis:

- Were appropriate work accommodations (i.e., limiting physical labor and having bathroom facilities readily available) made so individual could return to work?
- Does individual have any existing conditions such as pelvic, bladder or intestinal tumors, or inflammatory bowel disease that may impact recovery and prognosis?
- Did individual suffer any associated complications such as hemorrhage or infection that could delay recovery or impact prognosis?

References

Adetilove, V.A., and F.O. Dare. "Obstetric Fistula: Evaluation with Ultrasonography." Journal of Ultrasound Medicine 19 4 (2000): 243-249.

Gonzalez-Serva, L. "Vesicoenteric Fistula." Glenn's Urologic Surgery. Graham, S.D., Jr, ed. Philadelphia: Lippincott-Raven Publishers, 1998. 227-233.

Lee, R.A., R.E. Symmonds, and T.J. Williams. "Current Status of Genitourinary Fistula." Obstetrics and Gynecology 72 3 (1988): 313-319.

LeMone, P., and K.M. Burke. Medical-Surgical Nursing. Upper Saddle River, NJ: Prentice Hall Health, 2000.

Bladder Polyps

Other names / synonyms: Benign Polyps with Prostatic-Type Epithelium, Benign Polyps with Prostatic-Type Epithelium (BPPE), Bladder Polyps, BPPE, Urinary Bladder Papilloma, Urinary Bladder Polyps

236.7, 239.4

Definition

A bladder polyp is a protruding growth from the mucous membrane within the urinary bladder that is a noncancerous (benign) tumor. It originates on the internal bladder wall and projects into the bladder cavity. A polyp with a broad base is called sessile; one with a long, narrow neck is called a pedunculated polyp. The surface of a polyp may be smooth, irregular, or multilobed. Urinary bladder polyps (also called urinary bladder papillomas) are uncommon tumors, and account for only 2% of all bladder tumors.

Generally, bladder polyps occur more frequently in men than in women, and affect those over 50. They have been associated with cigarette smoking and tend to occur in individuals who live in close proximity to dense, industrial areas, suggesting environmental and/or chemical causes.

Diagnosis

History: An individual with bladder polyps may report blood in the urine (hematuria) and, rarely, tenderness on the side (flank) of the body. Individuals with bladder papillomas will often report a history of smoking tobacco.

Physical exam: Individuals will appear normal upon physical examination.

Tests: Direct visual examination of the bladder using a fiber-optic device (cystoscopy) is used to visualize the polyps. A sample of tissue from the polyp (biopsy) may be taken and examined to determine if it is malignant. Cells from the polyp may also be obtained by flushing the bladder with fluid (bladder washing) and examining the returned fluid. To verify that the polyp is benign, bladder cancer tumor markers may be tested via blood or urine. These markers include carcinoembryonic antigen (CEA), polyamines, and fibrin degradation products. The individual may be asked to collect a midstream urine sample (clean catch) to analyze for blood in the urine (hematuria) and/or the presence of cancerous (malignant) cells.

A radiopaque solution may be injected into the bladder and then x-rayed to evaluate the size and location of the polyp or tumor (intravenous pyelogram or IVP). Computer-aided x-ray analysis (computerized axial tomography or CAT scan) may be performed to determine the degree of invasion of the polyp into the bladder wall.

Treatment

Bladder polyps are usually removed through a lighted, fiber-optic viewing device (cystoscope) that is inserted through the urinary canal (urethra) into the bladder (cystoscopy). In cases where bladder polyps recur or have become deadly (malignant), treatment may necessitate surgically removing all visible tumors (transurethral resection or TUR). Polyps may also be destroyed using electrical current (fulguration). If the polyps are cancerous and have invaded the muscle of the bladder, surgery to remove all or part of the bladder (cystectomy, partial cystectomy) may be necessary. This procedure can also require removing all anterior pelvic organs including the entire bladder (radical cystectomy), and usually includes creating a diversion to pass urine (cutaneous urinary diversion, continent catheterizing pouch, or orthoptic voiding diversion).

Prognosis

Urinary bladder papillomas are most often harmless (benign), so individuals usually have an excellent prognosis following their removal. However, recurrence is common; they reappear in nearly 70% of cases. Consequently, procedures to remove them may need to be done every 3 months. Approximately 5-7% of recurring polyps become deadly (malignant). If the surgery requires removing all anterior pelvic organs including the entire bladder (radical cystectomy), it may lead to significant morbidity and mortality in 50% of individuals who receive this treatment. Notably, techniques for creating urinary diversions may reduce mortality from radical cystectomy to fifteen to twenty percent.

Differential Diagnosis

Conditions that present with similar symptoms include bladder cancer, bladder inflammation (cystitis), kidney inflammation (pyelonephritis), or inflammation of the urethra (urethritis).

Specialists

- Pathologist
- Urologist

Work Restrictions / Accommodations

Time off for surgery and recuperation are usually necessary. Bathroom facilities should be readily available as the individual may have to urinate frequently. Fatigue may create the need for additional breaks during the recovery period. Otherwise, no work restrictions and accommodations are usually required.

Comorbid Conditions

Existing conditions that may impact an individual's ability to recover and further lengthen the disability of bladder polyps include inflammation of the prostate gland (prostatitis), cancer of the prostate gland, and cancer of the ureter.

Complications

Complications that may occur include the possibility of a tumor recurring or becoming deadly (malignant), and problems associated with urine flow and kidney function, including inflammation of the urethra (urethritis), bladder (cystitis), or kidney (pyelonephritis). If the polyps become malignant, they can spread (metastasize) into the lymph or other organ systems such as the lungs, the circulatory system, bone, and gastrointestinal system.

Factors Influencing Duration

Factors that may influence the length of disability include the development of complications and, in particular, the possibility of tumor recurrence or metastases into other areas or organs.

Length of Disability

Duration of disability will depend upon the requirements of the job. Heavy physical labor is usually restricted following surgery for bladder polyps until recovery is complete. For cystectomy, duration reflects recovery period for procedure only.

Endoscopic resection.

Duration in Days

Job Classification	Minimum	Optimum	Maximum
Sedentary work	7	14	28
Light work	7	14	28
Medium work	7	21	42
Heavy work	14	21	42
Very Heavy work	14	28	56

Cystectomy.

Duration in Days

Job Classification	Minimum	Optimum	Maximum
Sedentary work	42	49	42
Light work	42	49	42
Medium work	42	49	70
Heavy work	56	63	84
Very Heavy work	56	63	112

Failure to Recover

If an individual fails to recover within the maximum duration expectancy period, the reader may wish to reference the following questions to assist in better understanding the specifics of an individual's medical case.

Regarding diagnosis:

- Was blood found in the urine (hematuria)?
- Does individual smoke tobacco?
- Was bladder examined with a fiber-optic device (cystoscopy) to visualize the polyps? Was a biopsy taken and examined to determine if malignant? Was a radiopaque solution injected into the bladder then x-rayed?
- Was a CAT scan done to determine the degree of invasion into the bladder wall?
- Were conditions with similar symptoms ruled out?
- Was the diagnosis of bladder polyps confirmed?

Regarding treatment:

- Were polyps removed through cystoscopy, TUR (transurethral resection), or by fulguration? Were any complications associated with the procedure?
- Has polyp invaded the bladder wall?
- If the polyp was malignant, has it metastasized into other organ systems?
- Will treatment now include cystectomy or radical cystectomy?

Regarding prognosis:

- Have polyps recurred?
- Would individual benefit from consultation with a specialist (urologist)?
- Since 5-7% of recurring polyps become malignant, is individual being examined on a regular basis?
- Has individual experienced any complications such as urethritis, cystitis, or pyelonephritis as a result of the bladder polyps? Have complications received prompt, appropriate treatment?
- If radical cystectomy was necessary to remove all of the bladder and other pelvic organs, were any complications associated with the procedure? Have complications resolved with treatment?
- Does individual have an underlying condition that may impact recovery?

References

Anjum, M.I., et al. "Benign Polyps with Prostatic-type Epithelium of the Urethra and the Urinary Bladder." International Urology and Nephrology 29 3 (1997): 313-317.

LeMone, P., and K.M. Burke. Medical-Surgical Nursing. Upper Saddle River, NJ: Prentice Hall Health, 2000.

Remick, Jr., D.G., and N.B. Kumar. "Benign Polyps with Prostatic-type Epithelium of the Urethra and the Urinary Bladder." The American Journal of Surgical Pathology 8 11 (1984): 833-839.

Young, R.H. "Non-neoplastic Epithelial Abnormalities and Tumorlike Lesions." Pathology of the Urinary Bladder. Young, R.H., ed. New York: Churchill Livingstone, 1989. 1-64.

Blastomycosis

Other names / synonyms: Gilchrist's Disease, North American Blastomycosis

116, 116.0, 116.1, 116.2

Definition

Blastomycosis is an uncommon systemic fungal infection that affects primarily the lungs and skin, but may spread to other body sites, such as bones, genitourinary tract, and central nervous system. The infection is caused by the fungus Blastomyces dermatitidis, a fungus normally found in moist soil. When the soil is disturbed, fungal spores are released into the air where they can be inhaled.

Once inhaled, the spores enter the lungs and can cause asymptomatic infection, acute pneumonia, chronic pneumonia, or extrapulmonary disease. In some individuals, extrapulmonary involvement, such as skin lesions, may occur without accompanying lung involvement. The infection is rarely spread from individual to individual by direct contact with skin.

Blastomycosis is found primarily in the Central and Southeastern US along the Mississippi and Ohio River Valleys, the Midwestern states and portions of Canada that border the Great Lakes, and portions of New York and Canada along the St. Lawrence River. The states in which it is endemic are Mississippi, Arkansas, Kentucky, Tennessee, and Wisconsin. In endemic areas, the incidence is 1 to 2 cases per 100,000 individuals. It is more frequent in males than females, but this is likely due to the increased participation of males in high-risk vocations and recreational or occupational activities (farming, construction work, forestry, hunting, and camping). Blastomycosis is also infrequently found in some parts of Africa, India, Israel, and Saudi Arabia.

Diagnosis

History: Symptoms usually appear 30 to 45 days after exposure. Pulmonary symptoms include cough, chest pain, weight loss, weakness, and mild fever. Symptoms develop suddenly if the condition is acute. If the skin is involved, skin lesions are present. Bone or joint pain may be present if the infection has spread to these areas. The individual's occupational or recreational history usually includes exposure to moist soil.

Physical exam: The lungs may emit the abnormal breath sounds associated with pneumonia. Skin lesions, typically on the hands, arms, legs, or face, appear wart-like or as ulcers. Bone or joint infection will have local tenderness and swelling. Inflammation of the prostate and testicle may be present.

Tests: B. dermatitidis may be identified microscopically from sputum or skin lesions, or by fungal culture. Blood or skin tests are not accurate indicators of infection. Chest x-ray may reveal infiltrates and pneumonia. X-ray of a bone infection can show areas of bone destruction.

Treatment

Although some cases of acute pulmonary blastomycosis have spontaneously recovered without treatment, most cases require treatment. Blastomycosis is treated with antifungal drugs for up to 6 months. The choice of antifungal drug is made based on the severity of the disease, the site of involvement, the state of the individual's immune system, and whether or not the individual is pregnant.

Anti-inflammatory drugs may be used to decrease pain and inflammation. Follow-up exams for several years should be done to detect a recurrence of the disease. In some cases, treatment may be continued long term in order to prevent recurrence or progression.

Prognosis

The prognosis is good if treatment with antifungal drugs is begun early. Most infections will resolve with treatment, with cure rates of up to 100% reported. Left untreated, the disease eventually progresses and has a mortality rate of sixty percent. Advanced bone disease or brain involvement will lengthen disability and reduce the chance of complete recovery. Immunocompromised individuals, such as individuals who have had a transplant, or individuals with AIDS, have a less favorable cure rate. These individuals have a mortality rate of 30-40%, with most deaths occurring within the first few weeks of treatment. These individuals are also more prone to relapse.

Differential Diagnosis

Chronic skin lesions may resemble skin cancer, other fungal infections, and other skin conditions, such as bromoderma, pyoderma gangrenosum, Majocchi's granuloma, leishmaniasis, Mycobacterium marinum infection, and giant keratoacanthoma.

Pulmonary blastomycosis may resemble tuberculosis, other fungal lung infections, cancer, influenza, and bacterial pneumonia. Blastomycosis of the vertebrae may resemble tuberculosis.

Specialists

- Dermatologist
- Infectious Disease Physician
- Internist
- Occupational Medicine Physician
- Pulmonologist
- Urologist

Work Restrictions / Accommodations

Lung involvement may require temporary restrictions from heavy lifting and strenuous work. Frequent rest periods may be needed to accommodate workers who have difficulty with breathing. Severe respiratory disease or bony involvement may necessitate long-term accommodations for individuals involved in manual labor or those stand for extended periods.

Blastomycosis is not spread in the air from person to person. Transmission through direct contact with skin has been reported only rarely. Caution, however, should be used with clothing or other material contaminated with drainage from skin lesions.

Comorbid Conditions

Conditions that compromise the immune system will lengthen disability and complicate treatment. Individuals who are immunocompromised include those with AIDS, transplant recipients, and those who take medications that suppress the immune system.

Individuals taking medication to reduce stomach acid or individuals with genitourinary disease may not respond to certain medications. These individuals also may be more likely to relapse.

Complications

Scarring of lung tissues may lead to chronic respiratory insufficiencies. Some individuals may develop lung conditions (miliary disease or diffuse pneumonitis) that are often fatal. Infection in bones may destroy the bone if allowed to progress. If vertebrae or long bones are involved, the infection may result in loss of physical function. Untreated skin lesions may lead to the formation of extensively scarred tissue.

Approximately 5% of individuals develop central nervous system (CNS) manifestations, such as abscesses in the brain or spine, or meningitis. CNS involvement is primarily found in individuals with AIDS. Spread of the infection to multiple organs (liver, spleen, gastrointestinal tract, thyroid, pericardium, or adrenal glands) may develop. Individuals who are immunocompromised, such as those with AIDS, are more likely to develop respiratory failure or multiorgan involvement.

Factors Influencing Duration

Duration of disease before treatment, development of complications, effectiveness of treatment, and competence of the individual's immune system will influence the length of disability. Complications of bone, skin, lungs, or central nervous system will extend the disability.

Length of Disability

Duration in Days

Job Classification	Minimum	Optimum	Maximum
Sedentary work	3	14	21
Light work	3	14	21
Medium work	7	14	21
Heavy work	7	14	21
Very Heavy work	7	14	21

Failure to Recover

If an individual fails to recover within the maximum duration expectancy period, the reader may wish to reference the following questions to assist in better understanding the specifics of an individual's medical case.

Regarding diagnosis:

- Does individual have asymptomatic lung infections? Acute or chronic pneumonia? Extrapulmonary disease?
- Where does individual live?
- Has individual recently visited any of the known areas where blastomycosis is found?
- Were conditions with similar symptoms ruled out?

Regarding treatment:

- Did individual require treatment?
- Was individual treated with antifungal drugs? How long?
- Is individual being monitored for a recurrence?

Regarding prognosis:

- Was individual diagnosed and treated early in the disease process?
- Does individual have any conditions that could affect the ability to recover?
- Has individual developed miliary disease of diffuse pneumonitis?
- Does individual have any central nervous system manifestations?

References

Blastomycosis. Centers for Disease Control and Prevention, Division of Bacterial and Mycotic Diseases. 15 Sept 2000. 01 Jan 2001 <http://www.cdc.gov/ncidod/dbmd/diseaseinfo/blastomycosis_t.htm>.

Chapman, Stanley. "Blastomyces Dermatitidis." Principles and Practice of Infectious Diseases, 5th ed. Mandell, Gerald, et al., ed. Philadelphia: Churchill Livingstone, 2000. 2733-2744.

Blepharitis

Other names / synonyms: Nonulcerative Blepharitis

373, 373.00, 373.0, 373.01, 373.3, 373.32, 692.8

Definition

Allergies and infections are among many factors that may cause blepharitis, which is an inflammation of upper and lower eyelids. At the onset of the disease, overproductive oil glands may attract bacteria that irritate lid edges (margins), creating redness and scaling of skin. Secretions may cause eyelids to become crusted or "glued" together.

Occurring on both eyes (bilateral), blepharitis is a common condition that tends to recur though causes often are unknown. Blepharitis may manifest after exposure to dust, smoke, or irritating chemicals. Blepharitis also may occur as a reaction to certain types of eye makeup or eyedrops. The disease sometimes is associated with skin disorders or lice infestation in eyelashes.

Anterior blepharitis affects the outer or front portion of the eyelids. In an ulcerative form, the cause usually is related to a staphylococcal infection in the eyelash roots or follicles. In a non-ulcerative form, anterior blepharitis resembles dandruff and is frequently accompanied by scaling of the scalp, eyebrows, and ears (seborrhea).

When glands found in the inner portion of the eyelid (meibomian) are inflamed or blocked, posterior blepharitis may occur. These glands open onto the eyelid surface to produce an oily coating that helps protect the eye. Thicker-than-normal secretions or infection may obstruct the glands, causing inflammation and a painful burning sensation in the eyes.

Certain skin disorders such as seborrheic dermatitis, acne, and oily secretions from pores may be associated with blepharitis. Poor hygiene may also worsen the condition.

All adults have at least some irritation associated with blepharitis, but treatment is only required in more severe cases.

Diagnosis

History: Individuals may report irritation, itching, and burning at the edge of the eyelids, or the sensation of a foreign body in the eyes. Individuals may see scales or "granulations" clinging to both upper and lower eyelids. Individuals who have ulcerative blepharitis may report dry scales, red eyelids, and tiny ulcerations along the edge of the lids. Lashes also tend to fall out. Nonulcerative blepharitis produces greasy scales. In this form, individuals may only have slightly red eyelids. In a mixed infection, which is more common, both dry and greasy scales are present. Eyelid edges are red and may be ulcerated. With posterior blepharitis, there may be a history of repeated stye infections (hordeolum) or inflammation of the glands (chalazia).

Physical exam: The eyelid margins will be red, swollen, and may have dry and/or greasy scales. Eyelashes may be missing. The mucous membrane lining the eyelids (conjunctiva) may be irritated. In posterior blepharitis, meibomian glands at the edges of the lids may be swollen and produce an abnormal soft, cheesy substance when pressure is applied.

Tests: A culture of eye secretions may be done to rule out or identify infection. The individual may be tested for allergies.

Specialists

- Ophthalmologist

Treatment

Eyelid edges are cleansed several times daily with warm water and baby shampoo to remove scales. Scalp and eyebrows must also be kept clean. Medicated shampoo may be used to treat the scaly skin of seborrhea. Antibiotic ointment may be prescribed. Eyedrops that may have caused contact blepharitis are discontinued. Any underlying meibomian gland dysfunction of the inner eyelids may need to be treated with systemic antibiotics and topical steroids. Suspected allergens such as certain eye makeup might be eliminated as a possible source of the disease.

Prognosis

Blepharitis is very difficult to cure. It may become a chronic condition, needing repeated treatment. Scarring of the eyelids or permanent loss of lashes may occur. Contact blepharitis usually will resolve once the substance causing irritation is eliminated.

Differential Diagnosis

Conditions with similar symptoms include conjunctivitis and meibomian gland dysfunction.

Work Restrictions / Accommodations

Time may be needed several times daily for application of medicated ointment to the eyelids.

Comorbid Conditions

Blepharitis may be common among family members, indicating a genetic propensity for the condition. Individuals with Down's syndrome also are susceptible to the disease.

Complications

Nonulcerative blepharitis frequently causes conjunctivitis, which is inflammation of the inner lining of the eye. Ulcerative blepharitis can cause small sores along the lids. Eyelashes may fall out, and corneal ulcers may form. Red, swollen sores (styes) may form from an abscess. A firm mass of tissue (chalazion) may also accompany blepharitis.

Factors Influencing Duration

Factors that might influence disability include the underlying cause of the condition, severity of symptoms, response to and compliance with treatment, or the presence of complications.

Length of Disability

While unlikely to affect eyesight, the chronic and painful nature of the disease may be distracting for individuals engaged in tasks requiring extreme concentration.

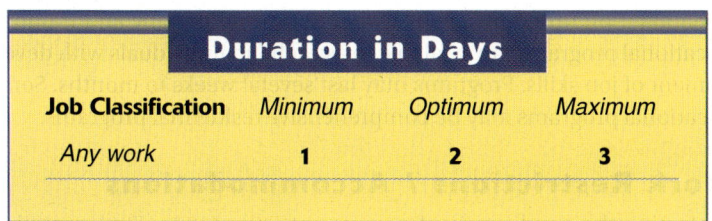

Duration in Days

Job Classification	Minimum	Optimum	Maximum
Any work	1	2	3

Failure to Recover

If an individual fails to recover within the maximum duration expectancy period, the reader may wish to reference the following questions to assist in better understanding the specifics of an individual's medical case.

Regarding diagnosis:

- Was individual exposed to dust, smoke, or irritating chemicals? Does individual use makeup or eye drops? Are there any skin disorders or lice infestation in eyelashes?
- What is individual's personal hygiene? Is it good?
- Does individual have irritation, itching, and burning at the edge of the eyelids or the sensation of a foreign body in the eyes?
- Does individual have dry scales, red eyelids, and tiny ulcerations along the edge of the lids?
- Do the eyelashes tend to fall out? Are greasy scales present?
- Does individual have both dry and greasy scales? Are the eyelid edges red and ulcerated? Are the eyelashes missing? Is the conjunctiva irritated?
- Are the meibomian glands swollen and produce an abnormal soft, cheesy substance when pressure is applied?
- Does individual have a history of repeated hordeolum or chalazia?
- Was a culture of eye secretions done?
- Was individual tested for allergies?
- Were conditions with similar symptoms ruled out?

Regarding treatment:

- Does individual cleanse the eyelid area several times a day with warm water and baby shampoo? Are the scalp and eyebrows kept clean?
- Has a medicated shampoo and antibiotic ointment been prescribed?
- Were eye drops or makeup that may have caused contact blepharitis discontinued?
- Have underlying meibomian gland dysfunction of the inner eyelids been treated with systemic antibiotics and topical steroids?
- Is individual compliant with treatment regimen?

Regarding prognosis:

- Can individual's employer accommodate any necessary restrictions?
- Does individual have any conditions that may affect ability to heal?
- Are any complications present such as conjunctivitis or corneal ulcers that may impact recovery?

References

Beers, Mark H., and Robert Berkow, MD, eds. Merck Manual of Diagnosis and Therapy, 17th ed. Whitehouse Station, NJ: Merck & Co., Inc, 1999.

Eye Facts. UIC Eye Center, University of Illinois. at Chicago 2000. 12 July 2000 <http://www.uic.edu/com/eye/patients/eyefacts/Blepharitis.htm>.

Blindness

Other names / synonyms: Legal Blindness

362.5, 362.8, 369, 369.00, 369.4, 377, 743, 950

Definition

Functional blindness is the permanent loss of vision sufficient to prevent one from being self-supporting, thus requiring dependence upon another person, agencies or devices in order to live. Legal blindness is defined as either the loss of central vision to the point that an individual with maximum corrective techniques can see only 20/200 or worse in the better eye, or constriction of the visual field in the better eye to less than 20 degrees of normal.

Blindness is caused by many diseases of the eyes and the body as well as by injury. It may be present at birth (congenital) or develop later in life (acquired). Blindness results from wasting (atrophy) of nerve and retinal cells.

Glaucoma is the leading preventable cause of blindness in the US even though incidence has decreased because of earlier detection, improved treatment, and a greater awareness of the disease. Senile macular degeneration is the leading cause of blindness in Western societies. It most common affects individuals over the age of 65. Of the 2 types of macular degeneration (exudative and atrophic), exudative ("wet") macular degeneration accounts for 90% of all macular degeneration blindness. New blood vessels grow behind the retina and it detaches, causing loss of central vision, but sparing peripheral and color vision.

Diabetic retinopathy is increasingly more common as a cause of blindness in the world. Both insulin and noninsulin dependent diabetics begin to show retinal changes 3-10 years after the disease begins. Macular swelling (edema), hemorrhages, and scarring (traction retinal detachment) of the inside of the eye causes blindness in this disease.

Between 500,000 and 1 million individuals are legally blind in the US. Half of these individuals are over 65 years of age.

Diagnosis

History: Individuals may report vision that has diminished suddenly or gradually over months or years.

Physical exam: Ophthalmoscopic exam may detect decreased pupil response to light, the presence of optic nerve swelling or wasting or changes in lens, cornea, vitreous, or retina. The blink response may be diminished. Eye movement may be abnormal.

Tests: Visual acuity and visual field tests help define the degree of vision loss. Special tests may be done if it is suspected that the individual is feigning symptoms of a disease or injury to obtain some desired outcome (malingering).

Treatment

Treatment depends on the underlying cause of loss of vision and blindness. Glaucoma is treated with eye drops and, sometimes, surgical procedures to reduce intraocular pressure. There are few treatments for macular degeneration. Some cases may be treated with laser eye procedures. Diabetic retinopathy is also treated with laser eye procedures.

Prognosis

Adaptation to visual loss varies. The best outcome results when referral is made for education before blindness is total. Some individuals are very independent with severe loss and others are incapacitated by minor sight restrictions.

Differential Diagnosis

Hysteria and malingering are other possibilities.

Specialists

- Ophthalmologist

Rehabilitation

Rehabilitation includes learning to adapt to the loss of vision and the use of visual aids. Visual aids such as telescopic lenses, high convex lenses, special reader magnifiers, and image intensifiers may be prescribed. The individual may be referred to agencies and schools for assistance with psychological and physical adaptation to the visual loss. Therapy programs are available that help the blind adjust to the loss of vision and restore a sense of psychological security. Individuals are taught how to rely on other senses in place of the eyes. Skills that help individuals remain independent are taught, including skills such as walking and traveling, the use of a cane, and keyboarding and other skills. Programs are available that teach the use of Braille.

Rehabilitation programs are available to provide therapy and training. Vocational programs are available to assist blind individuals with development of job skills. Programs may last several weeks to months. Some vocational programs may be comprehensive residential programs.

Work Restrictions / Accommodations

Protecting the good eye is of paramount importance. Eye protection may need to be worn, especially if one eye has been affected by trauma. In some cases, the good eye may be patched to encourage full recovery to an injured eye (to allow an injured lens to correct to the fullest possible degree), further decreasing visual ability while patching is in place. Visual aids may be needed at work such as telescopic lenses, high convex lenses, special reader magnifiers, and image intensifiers. The physical environment may need to be adjusted to accommodate the needs of an individual that is visually impaired. A guide dog may be needed, requiring accommodation to the workplace environment. Visually impaired workers need time to learn to move about the workplace with use of a cane or a guide dog. The individual may need various devices that can include computer aids or auditory cues. Keyboarding skills may need to be learned. Other skills may be necessary, such as the use of Braille and the technology necessary to print in Braille.

Comorbid Conditions

Type I diabetes and glaucoma may impair the ability to recover.

Complications

The eyeball is still susceptible to infection and injury and may deteriorate with time. The presence of hysteria or malingering may complicate diagnosis.

Factors Influencing Duration

The age at onset, individual temperament, educational level, economic resources, and whether visual loss was sudden or gradual all affect the degree of resultant disability.

Length of Disability

Physical disability may be limited, but, in general, blindness is permanent. Disability is determined on a case-by-case basis. For certain occupations, disability may be permanent.

Failure to Recover

If an individual fails to recover within the maximum duration expectancy period, the reader may wish to reference the following questions to assist in better understanding the specifics of an individual's medical case.

Regarding diagnosis:

- Was loss of vision confirmed through visual acuity and visual field testing?
- Does individual's vision loss qualify as functional or legal blindness?
- Does individual have an underlying condition that may impact recovery?
- Is malingering suspected?

Regarding treatment:

- Has the underlying cause of vision loss responded to treatment? Is there anything more that can be done?
- Has individual received assistance/training in regards to psychological and physical adaptation to the visual loss?
- Does individual have access to appropriate visual aids?

Regarding prognosis:

- What is the expectation for vision recovery?
- What is the degree of vision loss? Has progression of vision loss been arrested?
- How disabling is the vision loss?
- Does individual have occupational options or access to retraining?
- Can individual receive occupational re-training and visual adaption education before blindness is total?

References

Head, K.A. "Natural Therapies for Ocular Disorders, Part One: Diseases of the Retina." Alternative Medical Review 4 5 (1999): 342-359.

Itoh, Masayoshi. "Rehabilitation." The Merck Manual of Diagnosis and Therapy. Beers, Mark H., and Robert Berkow, eds. Whitehouse Station, NJ: Merck Research Laboratories, 1999. 2490-2497.

Palay, David A. "Ophthalmic Differential Diagnosis." Ophthalmology for the Primary Care Physician. Palay, David A., and Jay H. Krachmer, eds. St. Louis: Mosby, 1997. 23-35.

Rubsamen, Patrick E. "Posterior Segment Ocular Trauma." Ophthalmology. Yanoff, Myron, and Jay S. Duker, eds. London: Mosby, 1999. 8.43.1-8.43.6.

Bone Graft

Other names / synonyms: Bone Transplant

78.0

Definition

A bone graft is the placement of a piece of bone onto or into a damaged or defective bone to help repair it or replace a missing portion. Eventually most of the graft dies and is replaced by new bone. In the meantime, the graft provides a scaffold on which new bone will grow.

Some bone grafts are needed for structural support. A hard bone (cortical bone), such as the tibia or a rib, is used for this purpose. This type of bone can bear weight and will last a long time, even years, before it is replaced by new bone growth.

Some bone grafts are needed in order to grow new bone (osteogenesis). This type of graft requires a spongy bone (cancellous bone), such as the iliac crest. Although not as strong as cortical bone, cancellous bone triggers new bone growth more quickly. It does this either by supplying living cells or by triggering the growth of new cells by the host.

Sometimes bone is needed that already contains blood vessels (vascularized graft). This type of graft is needed in areas where blood supply is low or to repair large defects. Portions of the fibula (fibularis graft) and iliac crest are often used for vascularized bone grafts. These grafts remain and are not replaced by new bone growth.

Bone for the graft may be supplied from another site on the individual (autograft, or autogenic graft) or from another person or a cadaver (allograft, or allogenic graft). Bone grafts from other species (xenograft) have been attempted, but are not recommended due to poor outcomes.

Autograft is the best way in which to transplant living bone cells that will grow into new bone. The bones most commonly used for autografts are the tibia (used for cortical graft), the fibula (used for cancellous or whole bone transplant), and the iliac crest (used for cancellous graft).

An allograft is the best choice when more bone is needed than can be physically or safely removed from an individual. Allografts typically provide more structural support and less osteogenesis. They do, however, trigger the growth of new bone in the host, even though they don't provide living cells. Sometimes a graft that requires both structural support and osteogenesis will contain both autogenic and allogenic material.

Ceramic materials can be used as cancellous bone substitutes. Hydroxyapatite and tricalcium phosphate create scaffolding on which new bone can grow. Their structure allows easy access for blood vessels and bone-forming cells (osteogenic cells). They are used in areas where bulk, rather than strength, is needed. A mixture of hydroxyapatite/tricalcium phosphate, ceramic beads, fibrillar collagen, and added autogenous bone marrow elements has also been used as a substitute for cancellous grafts.

Approximately 45,000 bone graft procedures are performed each year.

Reason for Procedure

Bone grafts are used to promote healing (union) of fresh fractures, fill in areas left vacant after the removal of cysts or tumors, fuse joints (arthrodesis) such as in the spine (spinal fusion), repair major damage to a long bone, limit joint motion by placing a bone block (arthrorisis).

Description

Bone grafts are performed in a hospital under general or regional anesthesia. In an autograft, the bone is removed and implanted during the same surgery. In an allograft, the surgery includes only placing the bone graft.

The damaged portions of the bone are cut away and the graft is shaped to fit. The graft is either placed on top of the bone surface (overlay graft), as in a fracture repair, or inserted into an empty cavity within the bone (inlay graft), such as after a tumor or cyst has been removed.

Multiple cancellous chip grafts make use of pieces of cancellous bone. These pieces are packed into crevasses and holes created by the removal of a cyst or tumor. They are also packed around an artificial joint to stabilize it.

Hemicylindrical graft is an extensive surgical procedure in which a large hemicylindrical cortical graft is removed from the affected bone. This graft, plus additional cancellous bone from the iliac, is placed across the defect. This procedure is used to prevent amputation following the removal of certain bone tumors.

Whole bone transplant, using primarily the fibula, replaces large pieces of bone in the arms that have typically been damaged by removal of a large tumor or where other major bone loss has occurred.

Removing and implanting a vascularized graft is a type of microvascular surgery. It is more complicated than a nonvascularized graft.

Bone used in an allograft is obtained from a bone bank and is usually processed. If used fresh, it would, like other transplanted tissue, soon trigger an inflammatory reaction, undoing the repair process and endangering the life of the recipient. Processing (sterilization, followed by freezing or freeze-drying) reduces the graft's ability to trigger this reaction. Like any tissue donor, donors of bone grafts are screened for a number of conditions that would be hazardous to the recipient: bacterial, fungal, and viral (HIV, hepatitis B, and hepatitis C) infection; malignancy; collagen vascular disease; metabolic bone disease; and the presence of toxins.

A portion of an individual's own bone marrow (autologous bone marrow) is sometimes added to grafts to increase the potential of growing new bone. Biochemical substances, such as demineralized bone matrix (BMG), fibroblast growth factor (FGF), and platelet-derived growth factor (PDGF) are being studied for their ability to generate new bone growth in bone grafts. These studies show encouraging results.

Prognosis

The individual may feel weak or have difficulty with weight bearing for some time following the surgery. Although not all grafts generate the new bone growth or stability hoped for, both autogenic and allogenic bone grafts are typically successful.

Specialists

- Neurosurgeon
- Orthopedic Surgeon
- Plastic Surgeon

Rehabilitation

Individuals who undergo bone graft will most likely require physical therapy. The type and duration is related to the type and site of surgery (for example, hip replacement) and the site of autologous graft removal, if applicable. Individuals will learn range of motion and strengthening exercises for the muscles that surround the graft site and graft removal site (if applicable). Finally, individuals will learn mobility techniques for walking and transferring if the graft site is located on the low back or leg.

Work Restrictions / Accommodations

The surgical site must be protected until the physician deems it strong. The site in which an autograft was removed must be protected from injury such as fracture for up to 12 months. The type and site of surgery will dictate specific restrictions.

Comorbid Conditions

Disease that weakens bone tissue, such as metabolic bone disease, may prolong healing and lengthen disability.

Procedure Complications

In an autograft, the individual faces complications of both bone removal as well as bone placement. The surgery is longer and more complicated, with a greater risk of blood loss. The normal limb or iliac crest from which the graft is taken is at risk of damage and instability. Adjacent nerves and muscles are also at risk of damage. Recuperation is longer in order for both the donor and the recipient site to heal. The donor site is at risk of injury, such as fracture. After removal of a portion of the iliac crest, there is risk of hernia, nerve and arterial injury, and cosmetic deformity.

Despite screening, in an allograft there is the possibility of contracting a blood-borne disease from the donated tissue. And despite processing, the risk of an inflammatory reaction remains. This risk however is slight; no antirejection drugs are given in an allograft.

As in all surgeries, postsurgical infections are a risk in both allograft and autograft procedures. Anesthesia always carries the risks of breathing problems and reaction to the anesthetics used.

Factors Influencing Duration

Factors related to length of disability include the type of graft (auto- vs. allo-), site of graft (weight-bearing vs. nonweight-bearing), amount of blood loss, extent of graft, and subsequent infection.

Length of Disability

Duration depends on specific procedure and location of bone graft. Contact physician for more specific information.

References

Apley, A. Graham, and Louis Solomon. "Orthopaedic Procedures and Appliances." Concise System of Orthopaedics and Fractures. Apley, A. Graham, and Louis Solomon, eds. Oxford: Butterworth-Heinemann, Ltd, 1994. 96-107.

Canale, S. Terry, ed. Campbell's Operative Orthopaedics, 9th ed. St. Louis: Mosby, 1998.

National Center for Health Statistics. Detailed Diagnoses and Procedures, National Hospital Discharge Survey, 1997. Hyattsville: U.S. Department of Health and Human Services, 1997.

Rockwood, Charles, et al. Rockwood and Green's Fractures in Adults, 4th ed. Philadelphia: Lippincott-Raven, 1996.

Sandhu, Harvinder, Harpreet Grewal, and Hari Parvateneni. "Bone Grafting for Spinal Fusion." Orthopedic Clinics of North America 30 4 (1999): 685-698.

Stevenson, Sharon. "Biology of Bone Grafts." Orthopedic Clinics of North America 30 4 (1999): 543-552.

Bone Marrow Biopsy
Other names / synonyms: Biopsy of the Bone Marrow, Iliac Crest Tap, Sternal Tap
41.31

Definition

Both aspiration and/or biopsy of bone marrow for microscopic analysis are carried out under local anesthesia at the individual's bedside. For aspiration, a specialized hollow needle is advanced into the bone cavity (usually iliac crest). Approximately 0.4 mL liquid marrow and bone fragments are aspirated into a syringe then smeared onto a slide. Frequently, a bone marrow biopsy is performed as a complementary, but separate procedure (different equipment and site). A specialized biopsy needle (e.g., Jamshidi needle) is used to obtain a core of solid cortical bone. This technique preserves the normal marrow architecture of the biopsy sample and allows for formal histologic analysis.

Bone marrow is the soft, spongy material lining the insides of bones and is where blood cells are made.

The bone marrow aspiration and bone biopsy are usually performed concurrently. When bone marrow aspiration fails to provide an appropriate specimen, a bone marrow biopsy can be used to obtain bone marrow for laboratory analysis. The biopsied material can then be used to diagnose some types of cancer or anemia and other blood disorders or to identify the source of an unexplained fever. It can also be used to diagnose fibrosis of bone marrow and malignant tumors originating in the bone marrow (myelomas).

Reports issued by Centers for Disease Control and Prevention (CDC) for 1998 revealed 108,000 bone marrow biopsies performed on individuals in nonfederal, short-stay hospitals in the US. The bone marrow biopsy procedures, performed almost equally on males and females, were most prevalent in the South, least prevalent in the West, and equally prevalent in the Northeast and Midwest.

Reason for Procedure

Bone marrow biopsy is used in the diagnosis of a variety of disorders of the blood or blood-forming organs. The procedure may be used to evaluate iron shortage disorders and to diagnose or aid in the explanation of a decrease in the number of red blood cells (aplastic and macrocytic anemias) or a decrease in white blood cells (leukopenia) or platelets (thrombocytopenia). Bone marrow biopsy may be used in the diagnosis of primary hematological cancers (leukemias, lymphoma, or myeloma), to assess infiltration of the marrow by tumors originating in other areas of the body (i.e., breast and lung), and to follow the progress of therapy in anemias and leukemias. Additionally, a bone marrow biopsy may be indicated in cases that suggest replacement of normal bone marrow by fibrosis (myelofibrosis), to identify inflammations (parasitic, mycological, or bacterial) that may involve the marrow, or to diagnose lipid storage disease.

Description

After cleansing the skin, a local anesthetic is administered at the site of the biopsy (usually the back of the pelvic bone [iliac crest] or, less commonly, the breast bone [sternum]). The bone marrow aspiration involves insertion of a needle and the suction of marrow into a syringe. The bone biopsy procedure uses a special needle with a hollow core much like a leather punch. The needle is inserted into the bone, rotated to the right then to the left, withdrawn, and reinserted at a different angle. This sequence is repeated until a small, solid core of bone marrow tissue chip is separated from the bone marrow and drawn into the needle. After the needle is removed, a piece of fine wire threaded through its tip transfers the specimen onto sterile gauze. The individual may experience discomfort or pressure when the needle is inserted and a brief pulling sensation accompanied by momentary dull pain when the marrow is withdrawn. To conclude the procedure, pressure is applied to the biopsy site to stop bleeding and a bandage is used.

The specimen is then prepared for microscopic examination that may include freezing, chemically treating, slicing, and/or staining. A pathologist or hematologist examines the prepared specimen.

Prognosis

A normal bone marrow biopsy will show healthy adult bone marrow that contains yellow fat cells and connective tissue, and shows the blood cell producing red marrow.

In an abnormal biopsy, microscopic examination of the bone marrow may reveal a number of cancers such as granulomas, myelofibrosis, and lymphomas. Analyzing specimens help physicians diagnose iron, vitamin B_{12}, and folate deficiency as well as anemia and leukemia.

Specialists

- Hematologist
- Oncologist

Work Restrictions / Accommodations

Work restrictions and accommodations are not usually associated with this procedure.

Comorbid Conditions

Obesity can affect the ease with which the procedure is conducted. Results of the procedure may be affected if the individual has previously had radiation therapy at the biopsy site.

Procedure Complications

Complications may include bleeding at the biopsy site, infection, or a localized blood-filled swelling from a broken blood vessel (hematoma). In rare instances, the heart or a major blood vessel is pierced when marrow is extracted from the sternum. This can lead to severe, profuse bleeding (hemorrhage).

Factors Influencing Duration

Length of disability may be influenced by the underlying condition for which the biopsy was performed, the site of the biopsy, or the development of complications.

Length of Disability

Duration in Days

Job Classification	Minimum	Optimum	Maximum
Sedentary work	0	1	2
Light work	0	1	2
Medium work	0	1	2
Heavy work	1	2	2
Very Heavy work	2	3	3

References

Ableoff, Martin, D., James O. Armitage, and Allen S. Lichter. Clinical Oncology, 2nd ed. Philadelphia: Churchill Livingstone, Inc, 2000. 04 Feb 2001 <http://home.mdconsult.com/das/book/view/897?sid=32793168>.

Murphy, Gerald P., Lois B. Morris, and Dianne Lange. Informed Decisions: The Complete Book of Cancer Diagnosis, Treatment, and Recovery. New York: Viking, 1997.

Bone Marrow Transplant

Other names / synonyms: Allogeneic Bone Marrow Transplant, Allogeneic Bone Transplant, Auto Bone Marrow Transplant Without Purging, Autologous Bone Marrow Transplant, Syngeneic Bone Marrow Transplant, Unrelated Donor Bone Marrow Transplant

41.0, 41.00, 41.01, 41.03, 41.91

Definition

A bone marrow transplant is a medical procedure to transplant healthy bone marrow to individuals with deficient bone marrow function. The healthy bone marrow may be taken from the recipient individual (autograft) or from a donor individual (homograft).

Bone marrow is the soft, spongy tissue inside the cavities of the body's bones that manufactures the various cells of the blood and the immune system. These blood cells include white blood cells (leukocytes), which fight infection; red blood cells (erythrocytes), which carry oxygen to organs and tissues; and platelets, which enable the blood to clot. All blood cells develop from very immature cells called stem cells. Most stem cells are found in the bone marrow. Some cells called peripheral blood stem cells circulate in blood vessels throughout the body. Stem cells can be collected directly from the bone marrow or from the peripheral blood.

The four types of bone marrow transplants are autologous, syngeneic, allogeneic, and transplant from an unrelated donor. In an autologous transplant, the individual's own marrow is removed and returned to his or her body at an appropriate time.

In syngeneic transplant, the donor is an identical twin of the recipient individual. This is an attractive option since there is no graft rejection. Unfortunately, very few individuals have identical twins.

Allogeneic transplantation involves bone marrow donations from either a sibling or parent of the recipient individual. In order to avoid one of two complications, the potential donor individual is tested to determine whether six of his or her human lymphocyte antigen (HLA) proteins match those of the recipient individual. The first complication occurs when the donor individual's bone marrow does not genetically match the bone marrow of the recipient individual. This condition is referred to as graft-versus-host disease (GVHD) and can be life-threatening. The second complication is when the recipient individual's immune system destroys the donor individual's bone marrow in a process called graft rejection.

Should a match of HLA proteins not be found from a sibling or parent, bone marrow from an unrelated but HLA-matching donor may be used. HLA-matching donors can be sought through a national bone marrow donor program that lists more than 700,000 potential donors. As in allogeneic transplantation, the complications of GVHD and graft rejection are concerns.

Since 1968, bone marrow transplantation has been successfully used to treat diseases once thought incurable such as leukemia, aplastic anemia, lymphomas such as Hodgkin's disease, multiple myeloma, immune deficiency disorders, and solid tumors such as breast and ovarian cancers. In 1998, reports issued by the Centers for Disease Control and Prevention (CDC) revealed over 9,000 bone marrow transplants nationwide. Although bone marrow transplants now save thousands of lives each year, 70% of those needing a bone marrow transplant are unable to have one because a suitable marrow donor cannot be found.

Reason for Procedure

A bone marrow transplant can replace diseased or poorly functioning bone marrow with healthy marrow. A bone marrow transplant also enables a recipient to receive higher doses of cancer treatment. Chemotherapy or radiation therapy can kill abnormal cells but can also destroy normal cells found in the blood marrow. Through bone marrow transplant, cells lost to chemotherapy or radiation can be replaced with normal blood-forming cells.

Diseases treated with bone marrow transplantation include leukemia, lymphomas, multiple myeloma, solid tumors (especially breast tumors), and a range of blood disorders including thalassemia major, sickle cell anemia, and aplastic anemia. Syngeneic and allogeneic transplantation have been most effective in treating acute nonlymphocytic leukemia, severe aplastic anemia, and chronic myelogenous leukemia. Autologous transplants are most effective in treating Hodgkin and non-Hodgkin lymphomas.

Description

Regardless of whether the recipient individual or the donor individual provides the bone marrow used in the transplant, the procedure used to collect the marrow (bone marrow harvest) is the same. The bone marrow harvest takes place in a hospital operating room with the donor individual under general anesthesia. The procedure involves little risk and minimal discomfort.

While the donor individual (autologous or allogeneic) is under anesthesia, a needle is inserted into the cavity of the rear hipbone (iliac crest). Several skin punctures on each hip and multiple bone punctures are usually required to extract the requisite amount of bone marrow. There are no surgical incisions or stitches involved, only skin punctures where the needle was inserted.

The amount of bone marrow harvested depends on the size of the donor individual and the concentration of bone marrow in the donor individual's bones. Usually 1 to 2 quarts of marrow and blood are harvested. This may sound like a large quantity but only represents about 2% of an individual's bone marrow, an amount the body replaces in 4 weeks.

When the anesthesia wears off, the donor individual may feel some pain-like discomfort at the harvest site. The pain feels similar to the pain associated with a hard fall on ice and can usually be controlled with Tylenol. Donors who are not the bone marrow transplant individual (the recipient) are usually discharged after an overnight stay and can fully resume normal activities in a few days.

During the 2 to 4 weeks after the transplant while the individual waits for the transplanted bone marrow to migrate to the cavities of the large bones and engraft, the individual is very susceptible to infection and excessive bleeding and will feel very sick and weak. Extraordinary precautions are needed to minimize the individual's exposure to viruses and bacteria. Blood samples are taken daily to determine whether the engraftment has occurred and to monitor organ function. Multiple antibiotics and transfusions are administered to help prevent and fight infection.

Prognosis

An uneventful recovery is expected for the bone marrow donor. It will take about 4 weeks for the body to replace the amount of bone marrow donated.

Outcome for the recipient of a bone transplant procedure is good despite a somewhat lengthy period of recovery and rehabilitation. After 4 to 6 weeks in the hospital, the individual is discharged and recovery continued at home. Weakness may persist a few weeks longer. The individual will not be able to return to regular activities or full-time work for 6 months or more from the day of the transplant. During this time, visits to a hospital or clinic as an outpatient may be needed several times a week for monitoring, blood transfusions, and administration of other drugs, as needed.

The transplant recipient will eventually be strong enough to resume a normal routine and lead a productive, healthy life.

Specialists

- Hematologist
- Immunologist
- Oncologist

Work Restrictions / Accommodations

Individual may initially be restricted to work on a part-time basis with a gradual transition to full-time as strength and endurance increase. Work accommodations include time away from work for clinical and medical appointments and extended rest periods in a quiet place.

Comorbid Conditions

Comorbid conditions that may influence length of disability include obesity, insulin dependent diabetes (IDDM), and heart, kidney, liver, or lung disorders.

Procedure Complications

Two complications are directly related to the transplant. The first occurs when the donor individual's bone marrow does not genetically match the bone marrow of the recipient individual. This condition is referred to as GVHD and can be life-threatening as the attack on the recipient individual's organs and tissues impairs the ability to function. Approximately 50% of individuals undergoing allogeneic bone marrow transplant with a related HLA-matched donor develop some form of GVHD. Individuals who do develop GVHD, however, are less likely to have a relapse of their tumor. This condition is called the graft-versus-leukemia effect.

A second complication occurs when the recipient's immune system destroys the donor's bone marrow (GVHR).

Infections may become serious since it takes approximately 2 to 3 weeks for transplanted bone marrow to produce enough white blood cells to protect the body.

Other complications associated with a bone marrow transplant procedure include bleeding, post-transplant immunodeficiency, hypothyroidism, respiratory arrest, renal failure, pneumonia, allergic reactions, fever, anaphylactic shock, air embolism, and development of a second malignancy. Additional side effects may be associated with the immunosuppressive drugs given to help prevent graft rejection.

Factors Influencing Duration

Factors that may influence length of disability include the underlying reason for the bone marrow transplant, availability of a matching bone marrow donor, an individual's potential to reject the transplant, development of complications, time in remission preceding the bone marrow transplant, and use of maintenance chemotherapy.

Length of Disability

For the recipient individual, duration of disability may depend upon diagnosis, response to treatment, presence or absence of complications, autologous versus donor transplant, and job requirements.

For the donor individual, duration of disability may vary from 1 to 4 days, depending on job classification.

For the donor.

Duration in Days

Job Classification	Minimum	Optimum	Maximum
Sedentary work	0	2	2
Light work	0	2	2
Medium work	0	2	4
Heavy work	0	2	4
Very Heavy work	0	2	4

For the recipient.

Duration in Days

Job Classification	Minimum	Optimum	Maximum
Sedentary work	28	42	56
Light work	42	56	70
Medium work	56	70	84
Heavy work	70	84	112
Very Heavy work	70	98	112

References

Bone Marrow Transplant. The Nuts and Bolts of Bone Marrow Transplants. Columbia Presbyterian Medical Center. 01 Jan 2000. 25 Sept 2000 <http://cpmcnet.columbia.edu/dept/medicine/bonemarrow/bmtinfo.html>.

Bone Marrow Transplant. drkoop.com. 01 Sept 2000. 25 Sept 2000 <http://www.drkoop.com/conditions/ency/article/003009.htm>.

Bone Marrow Transplant. St. Jude Children's Research Hospital. 04 May 1999. 25 Sept 2000 <http://www.stjude.org/medical/bone.htm>.

Bone Marrow Transplant. The Lycos Network. 01 Dec 1999. 25 Sept 2000 <http://webmd.lycos.com/content/asset/adam_surgery_bone_marrow_transplant>.

Breast Cancer Center: Bone Marrow Transplant. OnHealth Network Company. 01 Sept 1999. 25 Sept 2000 <http://onhealth.webmd.com/conditions/condctr/breastcancer/item%2C100447.asp>.

Chapter 9: Graft Versus Host Disease. University of Pennsylvania. 01 Jan 2000. 27 Sept 2000 <http://www.oncolink.upenn.edu/specialty/med_onc/bmt/basics/bmt_9.html>.

Bone Scan
Other names / synonyms: Bone Scintigraphy, Nuclear Medicine Scan, Radionuclide Bone Scan, Scan-Bone
92.14

Definition

A bone scan is a diagnostic procedure used to evaluate abnormalities involving bones and joints. A radioactive substance (isotope) is injected intravenously, and the image of its distribution in the skeletal system is analyzed to detect certain diseases and conditions. The isotope, which poses no health risk, circulates throughout the body and collects (preferably) in bone tissue that is growing or is, for some reason, more active (tissue with a higher metabolism). Such metabolically active sites include areas of injury, infection, and bone cancer. A scanning device called a gamma camera is passed over the body to detect and record the metabolically active sites that are then imaged by a special computer.

Different isotopes are used to evaluate different problems. Scans are often ordered by the isotope name. For example, a technetium scan is ordered for studying problems with bone injury, a gallium scan for soft tissue and inflammation, an indium scan for infection, and a sulfur colloid scan for bone marrow.

The injection of a radioactive isotope is thought to be a safe procedure as the total dose of radiation absorbed is very small, similar to the amount of the radiation absorbed from one routine chest x-ray (0.13 rem). The radioactive isotope also has a short half-life (i.e., it decays rapidly into nonradioactive form), and is almost completely eliminated from the body within 24 hours via urination.

Reports issued by Centers for Disease Control and Prevention (CDC) for 1998, revealed that 43,000 bone scans were performed on inpatients in nonfederal, short-stay hospitals in the US. The bone scan procedures were almost equally divided between males and females and most prevalent in the Northwest. The level of prevalence was considerably lower in the Midwest, South, and West.

Reason for Procedure

Bone scans are frequently ordered to detect or rule out primary or metastatic bone cancer when x-rays reveal no abnormalities but when a malignancy is suspected. Bone scans also detect bone infection (osteomyelitis), determine the location of an abnormality before bone biopsy or surgery is performed, and diagnose stress fractures or other conditions that do not always appear on x-rays.

Bone scans are sensitive to the metabolism of a bone area as opposed to x-rays that are sensitive to the bone's structure. Therefore, bone scans can diagnose diseases and conditions not apparent on x-rays, e.g., bone scans can diagnose stress fractures and fractures of the carpal scaphoid in the wrist because they sense the increased metabolism of areas that are injured or healing, whereas x-rays cannot sense the minimal structural damage of such fractures.

Bone scans are also ordered to help diagnose early arthritic changes and monitor both the progression of the disease and the effectiveness of treatment, determine whether artificial joints have loosened or are infected, and evaluate the healing of bone grafts.

Description

A conventional bone scan is performed in a radiology facility, either in a hospital or an outpatient x-ray center. The individual sits in a chair or lies on a table while the radioactive substance is injected through a vein in the arm. There is then a 3 to 4 hour waiting period while the substance collects within the skeletal system. During this time, the individual is instructed to drink several glasses of water and to urinate frequently so as to ensure that the radioactive material is not concentrated in the urinary bladder (this concentration could obscure some of the pelvic bones during the procedure).

During the scan, the individual lies on the back on a table but may be repositioned to the stomach or side during the procedure. It is important that the individual not move during the procedure except when directed by the technologist. The radionuclide scanner sometimes called a gamma camera, is positioned over the body part to be examined. The camera, table, or both may change position during the study. In a total body bone scan, the individual is scanned from head to foot over a period of 30 to 60 minutes. The individual should experience no discomfort during this procedure.

Variations of the conventional bone scan procedure include the Single Photon Emission Computed Tomography (SPECT) scan and the 3-stage scan. The SPECT scan is added to the conventional bone scan procedure and can study a particular part of the body in more detail. The SPECT scan adds an additional 30 to 45 minutes to the procedure.

The 3-stage scan is similar to the conventional scan except the scanning takes place immediately after the radioactive substance is injected (approximately 20 minutes) and then again 2 to 4 hours later.

Prognosis

The scan is interpreted to be normal if there are no areas of increased or decreased metabolism. Areas of increased metabolism are called hot spots and areas of decreased metabolism are called cool spots. The normal appearance of the scan will vary according to the individual's age. In general, a normal scan shows a uniform concentration of the isotope uptake in all bones.

Abnormal results show a high concentration of the isotope in areas of increased bone activity. These areas appear brighter and are called hot spots. These hot spots may indicate healing fractures, tumor, infections, or other processes that trigger higher metabolism such as increased blood flow or new bone formation. Lower concentrations or cold spots, are indicators of decreased metabolism such as poor blood flow to an area of bone or bone destruction from a tumor.

Specialists

- Nuclear Medicine Physician
- Radiologist

Work Restrictions / Accommodations

Most individuals examined via a bone scan will require time away from work for two separate medical appointments, one with the radiologist or nuclear medicine physician for the procedure (several hours, at least a half day), and one with the physician ordering the test to discuss the results of the bone scan (1-hour appointment). Rarely, additional time off from work may be required after the procedure if the individual has an allergic reaction.

Comorbid Conditions

Comorbid conditions that might influence length of disability include obesity, diabetes, and AIDS.

Procedure Complications

The scanning portion of the exam is without risk. Use of the isotope is not recommended during pregnancy or for nursing mothers.

In individuals with poor kidney function, the bone may not absorb a sufficient amount of the isotope for a valid bone scan.

The rare individual who has an allergic reaction may develop a rash, swelling, or other side effects. These complications are typically short lived and easily treated with medication.

Factors Influencing Duration

Length of disability may be influenced by delayed diagnosis and treatment of an injury initially missed and belatedly diagnosed on the bone scan. In individuals with poor kidney function, the bone scan results may not be accurate or, in severe cases, enough of the isotope may not have been absorbed to perform the scan.

Length of Disability

Disability is not expected for individuals who undergo a bone scan. Barring side effects from the test, or discovery of a condition requiring urgent treatment, individuals are able to return to work or resume previous activities immediately after the scan.

References

Bone Scan. Adam.com. 01 Jan 1999. 16 Sept 2000 <http://www.adam.com/ency/article/003833ris.htm>.

Bone Scan. Blue Cross Blue Shield of Massachusetts, Inc. 2000. 17 Sept 2000 <http://www.ahealthyme.com/topic/bonescan>.

Breast Cancer Center: Bone Densitometry Test. The Cleveland Clinic. 2000. 22 Feb 2001 <http://onhealth.webmd.com/conditions/condctr/breastcancer/item%2C100439.asp>.

Canale, S. Terry, Kay Daugherty, and Linda Jones, eds. Campbell's Operative Orthopaedics, 9th ed. Wilmette, IL: Mosby, 1998. 25 Feb 2001 <http://home.mdconsult.com/das/book/view/868?sid=34717292>.

Health Information Library: Bone Scan Test Overview. Covenant Health - Health Information Library. 2000 19 Sept 2000 <http://12.31.13.107/Library/HealthGuide/MedicalTests/_showTopic.asp?topic_id=12480&pd_id=16915&sgml_id=hw200283>.

Popovic, J.R., and L.J. Kozak. National Hospital Discharge Survey: Annual Summary, 1998. National Center for Health Statistics. 09 Sept 2000. 30 Sept 2000 <http://www.cdc.gov/nchs/data/sr13_148.pdf>.

Bone Spur

Other names / synonyms: Osteophyte

726.91

Definition

A bone spur is an irregular projection or outgrowth of bone that appears most often on the spine and the heel, but appears as well in other body locations including the knee, elbow, hip, shoulder, nose, mouth, finger, toe, and neck.

Bone spurs are the results of changes to bones that occur over time or that are caused by repetitive stresses and inflammation. In the case of the spine, the fibrous cushions (disks) between vertebrae tend to toughen and shrink with age. Meanwhile, the tough, elastic cartilage at the ends of the bones progressively hardens. As the space between the vertebrae becomes narrower, the bone tends to compensate for the loss by growing knobby-like enlargements or bone spurs.

Unlike the rounded ends of bones in normal joints, bone spurs do not develop a layer of protective cartilage. In some cases, the new bony surfaces eventually smooth themselves through normal movement. But when they don't, bone spurs can rub against other bony surfaces, nerves or blood vessels, causing pain and inflammation.

In the case of the heel, bone spurs are thought to be caused by excessive pulling on and rubbing of the heel bone by tendons and the connective tissue attached to the bone (fascia). As the constant, abnormal pulling of the tendons and fascia irritates the heel bone; the body responds by producing a bone spur as a protective mechanism. At risk for heel spurs are individuals who are overweight, wear shoes with little cushion on hard floors, wear no arch supports in their shoes, lack flexibility in the calf muscles, and spend too much time on their feet. Also at risk are individuals with flat feet or high arches.

Bone spurs are often seen in older individuals who have disk problems, as well as in young individuals especially athletes, dancers, or laborers who have put unusual, repetitive stress on bones, ligaments, and tendons.

In the US, 11% of the population has bone spurs. Heel spur affects men and women equally.

Diagnosis

History: Most heel spurs, while visible on x-ray, are asymptomatic. Some individuals may report pain, numbness, pins-and-needles tingling, gross sensory loss, and muscular weakness, though this is not reported in the majority of cases. Individuals with spine spurs often report sudden, shooting pains that are not linked to an injury or particular physical activity. Individuals with heel spurs often report a sharp pain when putting weight on one or both feet.

Physical exam: When the physician touches the affected area (palpates), the individual with a bone spur may experience discomfort or pain.

Tests: The usual test to confirm bone spurs is an x-ray of the affected area. It is important, however, to point out why x-ray results should be viewed with caution. First, x-ray does not always detect very small bone spurs, and, second, many individuals who present with bone spurs on their x-ray never develop symptoms. Magnetic resonance imaging (MRI) or electromyography (EMG) is often used if symptoms suggest impairment of nerves or muscles. For individuals with indications of heel spur, the physician may also order a gait analysis.

Treatment

Treatment is aimed at relieving pain. Many physicians prescribe a combination of restricted movement, physical support for the affected area, and medication. Different combinations of these treatments help different individuals. Individuals often learn that they need to be an active force in their treatment.

For pain control, the physician usually prescribes aspirin, ibuprofen, or other anti-inflammatory painkillers. To restrict movement and take pressure off a pinched nerve (which is caused by irritation from the bone spur), the physician prescribes some type of orthopedic support, depending on the affected area. If the bone spur is located in the spine, the individual may be instructed to wear an orthopedic collar or a back brace. If the bone spur is located in the heel or foot, the individual may be instructed to wear supportive inserts (orthotics) in his or her shoes or to wrap the arch with padding. The purpose of the orthopedic support is to alleviate the stress of the irritation on the affected area.

Other helpful treatments for bone spurs are physical therapy, splints, ice packs, muscle stimulation, stretching exercises, massage, and ultrasound.

Only in severe cases (when conservative measures fail to relieve pain or when walking or other vital activities are impaired) is surgical removal of bone spurs considered, because most painful bone spurs have been shown to resolve without surgery.

Prognosis

In general, the predicted outcome for bone spurs is good in that the symptoms associated with many bone spurs can be resolved with conservative treatment measures. While the symptoms usually resolve, the spur persists and may gradually enlarge. With most types of bone spurs, permanent solutions can be achieved through prescribed physical therapy, traction, and structured home exercise regimens. In the case of spine spurs, regular, periodic use of braces or orthotic collars may also be prescribed. In the case of heel spurs, daily wearing of arch supports (orthotics) may be prescribed.

Surgical results (removal) for bone spurs are not predictable. Occasionally, pain persists even after surgery. And, surgical relief may be temporary because bone spurs can and do grow back.

Differential Diagnosis

Differential diagnosis regarding bone spurs on the spine might include back or neck pain from injury or strenuous physical activity, pain from a degenerated disk, and the pain of sciatica, which is caused by prolapse of an intervertebral disk.

Heel pain similar to the pain of a heel spur could also be the pain and swelling caused by an overproduction of uric acid (gout), by inflammation of ligament on the bottom of the foot that attaches to the heel (plantar fasciitis), by outward rotation of the heel and inward rotation of the ankle (pronation), by fracture of the heel bone (calcaneus), and by compression of the posterior tibial nerve (tarsal tunnel syndrome).

Specialists

- Orthopedic Surgeon
- Physiatrist
- Physical Therapist
- Podiatrist
- Sports Medicine Physician

Rehabilitation

Rehabilitation for bone spurs is dependent upon the location of the bone spur as well the extent of the condition. Individuals who undergo rehabilitation for bone spurs may require outpatient physical therapy to initially address pain and swelling. This is especially the case when surgery was required to remove the bone spur. However, this initial goal is the same for non-operative treatment of bone spurs as well. Electrical stimulation combined with a cold treatment is a technique used in physical therapy to relax muscles around the inflamed joint and help to decrease pain and inflammation.

Once the initial pain and inflammation have improved, the use of heat may be applied in the rehabilitation process. Moist heat in the form of hot packs is applied to the site to decrease pain and increase muscle flexibility prior to therapy. Ultrasound, a technique that uses sound waves to promote deep heating, or iontophoresis, a technique that uses electrical current to drive anti-inflammatory pain medication into a painful area, may also be utilized.

In some cases where the bone spur is easily felt by the therapist's fingers (palpable), deep friction massage techniques may be used to attempt to dissolve the bone spur. In this method the therapist moves his or her finger with the individual's skin back and forth over the region of the bone spur. This method is often used for spurs located near the surface of the skin such as on the heel of the foot. Rehabilitation of bone spurs also begins with the goals of reducing the pressure upon irritated tendon and/or tissues as a result of the bone spur. Treatment includes splints or orthotics fabricated by a physical or occupational therapist.

Modifications may need to be made by the physical therapist for those people who have other bone/joint irritations and depending on the extent of the bone spur and if surgical removal was necessary. Therapy progresses to a home program developed by the physical or occupational therapist.

Complementary and Alternative Therapies

Content is intended for awareness only. Treatments may or may not be effective. Scientific evidence may be lacking and some substances have potentially toxic effects. Dr. Presley Reed and the editors do not endorse the use of these therapies in the absence of consultation with a licensed medical professional.

Acupressure - May relieve pain.

Work Restrictions / Accommodations

The treatment and the condition itself may limit the individual's ability to return to previous work activities (temporarily in some cases). If a lower extremity is involved, use of an assistive device, such as a cane or walker, may be necessary to minimize weight and pressure on the area. If an upper extremity is involved, restrictions may include limited or no lifting and carrying. Use of medications for management of pain and inflammation may require review of drug policies. Safety issues may need to be evaluated.

Comorbid Conditions

Comorbid conditions that might influence the length of disability include obesity, chronic illnesses, such as heart disease and diabetes, and allergy to treatment medications.

Complications

Complications from bone spur arise when the stress and irritation of the nerves, muscles, and blood vessels occur over an extended period of time. In the case of spine spurs, the stress and irritation can lead to more serious conditions, such as degenerative arthritis (osteoarthritis), which can ultimately lead to spinal nerve damage. In the case of heel spurs, the stress and irritation can lead to the development of a fluid pocket (bursa) beneath the spur that becomes inflamed. The condition, called inferior calcaneal bursitis, usually adds a throbbing quality to the pain caused by the spur.

Factors Influencing Duration

Factors influencing the length of disability include the severity of pain associated with the bone spur, the method of treatment, the individual's response to treatment and adherence to recommendations, and the individual's job requirements and leisure activities.

Length of Disability

Conservative treatment.

Duration in Days

Job Classification	Minimum	Optimum	Maximum
Sedentary work	0	3	7
Light work	0	3	7
Medium work	3	7	10
Heavy work	3	10	14
Very Heavy work	3	10	14

Duration Trend from Normative Data*

Cases	Mean	Min	Max	No Lost Time	Over 6 Months
1265	48	0	345	0.24%	0.16%

Percentile:	5th	25th	Median	75th	95th
Days:	12	23	36	60	125

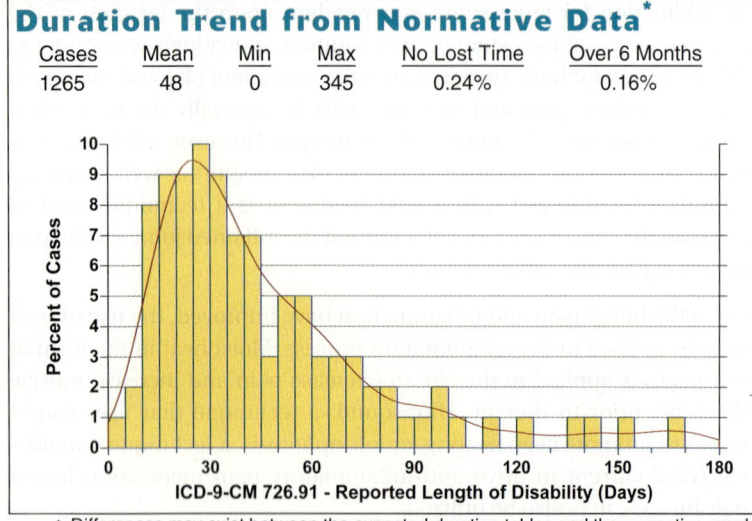
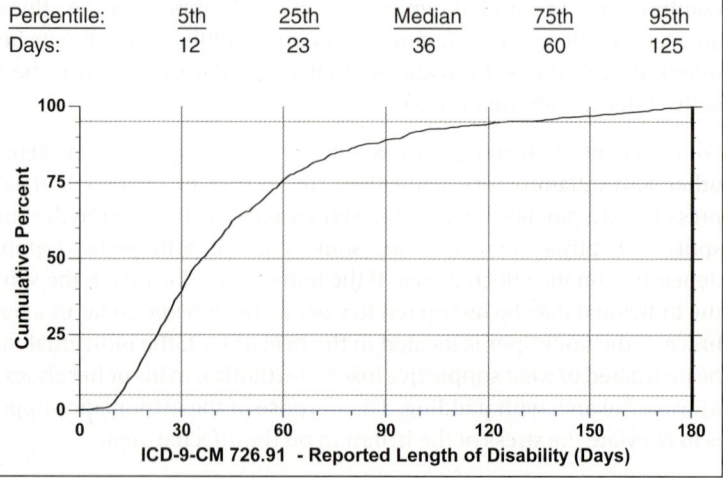

ICD-9-CM 726.91 - Reported Length of Disability (Days)

* Differences may exist between the expected duration tables and the normative graphs. Duration tables provide expected recovery periods based on the type of work performed by the individual. The normative graphs reflect the actual observed experience of many individuals across the spectrum of physical conditions, in a variety of industries, and with varying levels of case management.

Failure to Recover

If an individual fails to recover within the maximum duration expectancy period, the reader may wish to reference the following questions to assist in better understanding the specifics of an individual's medical case.

Regarding diagnosis:
- Where are the bone spurs located?
- Does individual have repeated stresses and irritation to the area?

- Is the bone spur rubbing against other bony surfaces? Nerves or blood vessels?
- Is individual overweight?
- Does individual wear shoes with little cushioning on hard floors? No arch supports in shoes?
- Does individual spend a great deal of time on feet?
- Do calf muscles lack flexibility?
- Does individual have flat feet? High arches?
- Is individual older with disc problems?
- Does individual put unusual repetitive stress on bones, ligaments, or tendons?
- Is pain present? Does numbness or pin-and-needles sensations occur? Does individual report sharp pain when putting weight on the feet?
- On physical exam, was the area tender to palpation?
- Was an x-ray done? MRI or EMG? Gait analysis?

- Were conditions with similar symptoms ruled out?

Regarding treatment:
- Are NSAIDs used for pain relief?
- Does individual have appropriate orthopedic support?
- Were physical therapy modalities used?
- Was surgery necessary?
- Does individual have a recurrent bone spur?

Regarding prognosis:
- Is individual active in rehabilitation?
- Can individual's employer accommodate any necessary restrictions?
- Does individual have any conditions that may affect ability to recover?
- Has individual developed osteoarthritis or inferior calcaneal bursitis?

References

"Foot Problems." Merck Manual of Medical Information - Home Edition. Beers, Mark H., and Robert Berkow, MD, eds. Whitehouse Station, NJ: Merck & Co. Inc, 2000. 07 Jan 2001 <http://www.merck.com/pubs/mmanual_home/sec5/56.htm>.

Kisner, C., and L. Colby. Therapeutic Exercise Foundations and Techniques. Philadelphia: F.A. Davis, 1990.

Bone Tumors
Other names / synonyms: Benign Bone Tumors, Malignant Neoplasm of Bone and Articular Cartilage, Osteoblastoma, Osteosarcoma

170, 170.0, 170.1, 170.2, 170.3, 170.4, 170.5, 170.6, 170.7, 170.8, 170.9, 198.5, 731.1

Definition

A bone tumor is an abnormal growth of cells within the bone that may be noncancerous (benign) or cancerous (malignant). Also, bone tumors may be primary (noncancerous or cancerous tumors that originate in the bone itself) or metastatic (cancers that originate elsewhere in the body, such as in the breast or prostate gland) and then spread to bone. In adults, most cancerous bone tumors are metastatic.

Benign bone tumors occur more frequently than malignant bone tumors. The most common benign bone tumors are osteochondromas. Some benign bone tumors regress on their own and do not require treatment.

Malignant bone tumors occur as a primary bone tumor or as cancer spread (metastasis) from another area of the body. Primary bone tumors are rare (less than 1% of all malignant tumors) and are more common in young men than in young women. Malignant bone tumors include osteosarcoma, fibrosarcoma, and chondrosarcoma, with osteosarcoma being the most common. Metastatic lesions to the bone usually arise from cancer of the breast, lung, prostate, kidney, and thyroid. These forms of cancer usually affect older individuals.

In the US, 2,000 cases of malignant bone tumors are diagnosed annually, with an estimated 1,300 deaths each year. Men are more likely to develop malignant bone tumors than women. Bone tumors occur most often in older adults (age 60 or older) with pre-existing bone disease or Paget's disease or in young adults (before age 30). A cause of bone tumors has not yet been found. Research is suggesting that individuals treated with certain kinds of anticancer drugs (alkylating agents) may be at increased risk.

Diagnosis

History: The most common symptom of all bone tumors is pain, especially pain that worsens at night. Other symptoms include swelling, stiffness, or tenderness, a mass that can be felt at the tumor site if the disease has advanced, or bone fractures. Individuals with Ewing's sarcoma (a rare, malignant tumor of the bone) often present with fever and weight loss. Some benign tumors have no symptoms.

Physical exam: The exam may reveal swelling, decreased mobility in an affected joint, muscle wasting, a limp, or a soft tissue mass. Individuals with rare bone tumors may also present with an enlarged liver or spleen.

Tests: Radiographic studies of the affected bone or joint may be performed. Bone biopsy or bone marrow aspiration may also be performed. If the results of the bone biopsy are consistent with malignancy, preoperative tests may include a chest x-ray, CT, and MRI. Angiography may be performed to view the positions of major blood vessels within a particular limb. Additionally, bone scan (scintigraphy) may be performed to evaluate whether a malignant tumor has spread to other areas (metastasized).

Treatment

Some benign bone tumors may not require treatment, but should be assessed periodically to check for progress or regression. Other benign bone tumors may require wide or radical surgery (resection). The resection of many benign bone tumors often leaves large deficits in the involved bone. Such deficits may be filled with bone grafted from the individual (autograft), with cadaveric bone (allograft) or with synthetic bone substitutes (e.g., coralline hydroxyapatite).

Dramatic advances have been made in the treatment of malignant bone tumors. The use of multiagent chemotherapy has made it possible to perform surgery that saves the limb from amputation (limb salvage surgery) with long-term satisfactory results. The individuals being treated are usually given a course of preoperative (neoadjuvant) chemotherapy. A response to chemotherapy that results in greater than 90% cell or tissue death (necrosis) is considered a good response. Ideally, individuals with a good response to chemotherapy are considered good candidates for limb salvage surgery. A poor response to chemotherapy will usually lead to amputation. Surgery is followed by a course of postoperative chemotherapy. In many instances, radiation is used in combination with chemotherapy for tumor control. Rehabilitation and physical therapy programs are often indicated after chemotherapy, radiation, or surgery.

Treatment for metastatic malignant tumors depends upon the primary tissue or organ involved. Though preoperative chemotherapy may be administered, the treatment of choice involves surgery to remove the diseased portion of the bone and reconstruction of the arm or leg. Surgery may involve a complete removal of the bone (resection) or amputation.

Prognosis

Most individuals with benign bone tumors are completely cured with treatment. The outcome for malignant tumors depends on the tumor grade, whether the tumor has invaded the center of the bone, and whether the cancerous cells have spread to other areas (metastasized). Low-grade malignant tumors have a good prognosis. The 2-year survival rate for osteosarcoma, the most common form of malignant bone tumor, is ten to twenty percent.

Differential Diagnosis

Differential diagnoses include osteomyelitis, glomus tumors involving bone, fracture callus, or metastatic neoplasm.

Specialists

- Hematologist
- Oncologist
- Orthopedic Surgeon
- Pathologist
- Radiation Oncologist
- Radiologist

Rehabilitation

Rehabilitation for bone tumors depends on the location of the tumor and whether the tumor is benign or malignant. In general, rehabilitation is aimed at restoring normal range of motion, flexibility, strength, and endurance. If surgical removal of the tumor was necessary, immobilization by use of a cast may be required for at least 6 weeks. Early passive and active range-of-motion exercises of the affected joint and muscles begin as soon as the cast is removed.

Range-of-motion exercises are generally initiated and performed as tolerated. In this early phase of strengthening, isometric exercises begin with muscles around the involved joint contracting yet no movement takes place at the joint. In this exercise, the individual pushes his or her outside of the foot into a wall or other immovable object.

The next phase of rehabilitation involves movement at the joint called isotonic exercise. An example of this type of rehabilitation exercise is strengthening with weights and elastic bands. As the resistance is lifted or pulled throughout the range of motion, the muscle shortens and lengthens. Strength training of this type will also include weight equipment/machines. The amount of resistance is determined by increasing the weight to a point where the individual's final repetition of each set is difficult but obtainable.

Pool rehabilitation is also used in the recovery of a bone tumor that may have required surgical removal. Specific exercises for the upper and lower extremities are performed in waist-deep water against resistance of the water. Because of the buoyancy affect, individuals often find it easier to place their weight on the limb that is being rehabilitated.

If the bone tumor affects the lower extremity, the physical therapist will also focus on training for proper ambulating (walking) at the appropriate time. This may initially begin with the use of an assistive device such as a walker and progress to a cane. Once the individual demonstrates independent and safe walking, the assistive device is generally discontinued.

Learning how to avoid injury is another important intervention in the rehabilitation for a bone tumor. Occupational therapy helps individuals arrange their homes and organize their lives in ways that support their physical and mental well being, and provide activities to relieve the mental boredom of inactivity. Devices and techniques that help the individual are invaluable in maintaining the individual's peace of mind.

Work Restrictions / Accommodations

Transfer to sedentary duties may be required for individuals who have undergone amputations. Extended work leave for surgery and postoperative therapy and rehabilitation may be required.

Complementary and Alternative Therapies

Content is intended for awareness only. Treatments may or may not be effective. Scientific evidence may be lacking and some substances have potentially toxic effects. Dr. Presley Reed and the editors do not endorse the use of these therapies in the absence of consultation with a licensed medical professional.

Vitamin C - May inhibit tumor growth.

Laetrile - Proponents claim cancer cure, cancer control, cancer prevention, relief from cancer pain, and facilitation of treatment with chemotherapy.

Antineoplaston therapy - Said to control tumor growth.

Oxygen therapy - Exposes cancer cells to high levels of oxygen (based on premise that cancer is caused by a deficiency of oxygen).

Shark cartilage - May prevent growth of new blood vessels that are essential to tumor growth.

Comorbid Conditions

Comorbid conditions that might influence the length of disability include obesity or excessive thinness, chronic illnesses, such as heart disease and diabetes, and allergy to treatment medications.

Complications

Some benign bone tumors may recur even after surgical removal (excision). Complications of malignant bone tumors include muscle wasting, pathological fractures, and the risk of developing a secondary malignancy.

Factors Influencing Duration

Factors influencing length of disability include the type and stage of disease at initial presentation, presence of concurrent infection and overall general health, type of treatment pursued, and any complications.

Length of Disability

Duration of disability depends on the specific site, size and type of tumor. Disability may be permanent.

Failure to Recover

If an individual fails to recover within the maximum duration expectancy period, the reader may wish to reference the following questions to assist in better understanding the specifics of an individual's medical case.

Regarding diagnosis:

- Is the tumor primary or metastatic?
- Does individual complain of pain? Does it worsen at night?
- Is swelling, stiffness, or tenderness present?
- Can individual feel a mass at the tumor site?
- Has individual had a bone fracture?
- On exam, were swelling, decreased mobility in a joint, or muscle wasting evident?
- Does individual limp?
- Was a soft tissue mass palpable?
- Does individual have an enlarged liver or spleen?
- Were x-rays, bone biopsy, and bone marrow testing done? Chest x-ray, CT, MRI, and bone scan?
- Were conditions with similar symptoms ruled out?

Regarding treatment:

- If treatment is not needed, does individual have regular check-ups?
- Was surgical resection necessary?
- Was a bone graft done?
- If necessary, has individual had pre- and postoperative chemotherapy? Radiation therapy?
- Was amputation necessary?

Regarding prognosis:

- Is individual active in rehabilitation?
- Can individual's employer accommodate necessary restrictions?
- Does individual have any conditions that may affect ability to recover?
- Has the tumor recurred?
- Has individual had any pathological fractures? Muscle wasting?
- Did a second malignancy develop?

References

"Tumors of Bones and Joints." Merck Manual of Diagnosis and Therapy, 17th ed. Beers, Mark H., and Robert Berkow, MD, eds. Whitehouse Station, NJ: Merck & Co., Inc, 1999. 14 Feb 2001 <http://www.merck.com/pubs/mmanual/section5/chapter56/56a.htm>.

Bone Tumors. adam.com. 01 Jan 2000. 05 Dec 2000 <http://thirdage.adam.com/ency/article/001230.htm>.

Bone Tumors. drkoop.com. 01 Jan 2000. 05 Dec 2000 <http://www.drkoop.com/conditions/ency/article/001230.htm>.

Dambro, Mark R., MD. Griffith's 5-minute Clinical Consult, 1999 ed. Philadelphia: Lippincott Williams & Wilkins, 1999. 14 Feb 2001 <http://home.mdconsult.com/das/book/view/846?sid=33670751>.

Kessler, R.M. Management of Common Musculoskeletal Disorders: Physical Therapy Principles and Methods. Philadelphia: J.B. Lippincott Co, 1990.

Kisner, C., and L. Colby. Therapeutic Exercise Foundations and Techniques. Philadelphia: F.A. Davis, 1990.

Borderline Personality Disorder
301.83, 309.21

Definition

The key feature of the borderline personality disorder is the individual's instability in several areas, including social behavior, mood, and self-image. Individuals with borderline personality disorder stand on the border between neurosis and psychosis, and are characterized by an extraordinarily unstable affect, mood, behavior, and self-image. They often appear anxious or impulsive, with abrupt, unexpected, and apparently spontaneous outbursts (psychotic episodes) that make their behavior seem unpredictable. Irregular sleep-wake cycles suggest some form of instability in regulated patterns of arousal. Borderline individuals tend to shift from experiencing a normal mood on one hand to inappropriately intense anger and rage, then to excitement or euphoria. In addition to their vacillating and unstable mood, they also seem to experience a chronic anxiety.

Borderlines may engage in self-damaging behaviors related to poor impulse control, and as a mechanism to deal with extreme anxiety brought on by feelings of guilt and self-loathing. These behaviors may include recurrent accidents, fights, self-mutilation, suicidal gestures, overeating, gambling, spending sprees, shoplifting, or promiscuous sexual behavior. They have difficulty tolerating normal levels of frustration, anxiety, rejection, and loss, and almost always appear to be in a state of crisis.

Separation anxiety is a prime motivator in the interpersonal behavior of borderline individuals, as they are exceedingly dependent on others. They usually form unstable and intense "love-hate" relationships, tending to view others simplistically as being all good or all bad. Identity disturbances are common, as they are uncertain about who they are and where they are headed in life.

This disorder occurs in about 1-2% of the general population, and is twice as common in women as in men. First-degree relatives of borderlines have an increased prevalence of major depressive disorder, alcohol use disorders, and substance abuse.

Diagnosis

History: Psychiatric interview and mental status exam are the primary methods of diagnosis. According to the DSM-IV, diagnosis of borderline personality disorder requires a pervasive pattern of instability of interpersonal relationships, self-image, and mood (affect), and marked impulsivity beginning by early adulthood and present in a variety of situations, with at least 5 of the following 9 criteria: frantic efforts to avoid real or imagined abandonment (not including suicidal or self-mutilating behavior); a pattern of unstable and intense interpersonal relationships alternating between seeing others as all good (idealization) or all bad (devaluation); identity disturbance with a markedly and persistently unstable self-image; impulsivity in at least two areas that are potentially self-damaging other than suicidal or self-mutilating behavior (spending, sex, substance abuse, reckless driving, or binge eating); recurrent suicidal behavior, gestures, or threats, or self-mutilating behavior; rapidly changing and extreme variation in mood (affective instability) such as intense episodic feelings of displeasure (dysphoria), irritability, or anxiety usually lasting a few hours and only rarely more than a few days; chronic feelings of emptiness; inappropriate, intense anger or difficulty controlling anger, such as frequent displays of temper, constant anger, or recurrent physical fights; or transient, stress-related paranoid ideas or severe feelings of being detached from reality (dissociative symptoms).

Physical exam: The exam is generally not helpful in the diagnosis of borderline personality disorder. Observation of the individual's orientation, dress, mannerisms, behavior, and content of speech may provide essential signs to help diagnose the illness.

Tests: Sleep studies may be helpful, as some individuals show shortened rapid eye movement (REM) latency and sleep continuity disturbances, abnormal dexamethasone-suppression test results, and abnormal thyrotropin-releasing hormone test results. These changes are also seen in some cases of depressive disorders.

Treatment

The primary treatment for borderline personality disorder is psychotherapy. As these individuals tend to form intense love-hate relationships, they may first cast their therapist as an idealized rescuer, then despise him as the villain when things go wrong. The therapist must avoid this struggle, and must be aware that the borderline personality tends to pit different caregivers against each other. At the same time, the therapist must tolerate the borderline's episodic angry outbursts to demonstrate that he need not fear abandonment.

Borderline patients are often hospitalized for their suicide attempts, but both admission and discharge are difficult because of power struggles with caregivers and family. In the hospital setting, intensive individual and group psychotherapy are both useful. A multidisciplinary approach is most successful, utilizing staff trained in recreational, occupational, and vocational therapy. Group therapy should be supportive rather than focused on analyzing motivations for the individual's behavior. Both in individual and group therapy, the therapist should help the individual set limits for their own behavior, respect limits set by other people, and solve problems using a reality-based approach. Ideally, individuals remain in the hospital until they show marked improvement, but long-term hospitalization can sometimes make the borderline worse due to increased acting-out and mimicking the behaviors of more disturbed individuals. After hospitalization, an outpatient therapist can stabilize the individual and help prevent future hospitalizations. Outpatient psychotherapy usually consists of 2 to 3 sessions weekly over a period of years. Family counseling may help families deal with the stress involved in relating to the borderline patient.

Behavior therapy and social skills training are utilized in an inpatient or outpatient setting. Research suggests that behavior therapy may be better than traditional psychotherapy in terms of decreasing suicidal behavior and anger, and improving social adjustment. Outpatient settings utilized for these individuals include halfway houses, day treatment programs, night hospitals and other support groups.

Antipsychotics may help control anger, hostility, and brief psychotic episodes. Mood-stabilizing medications including lithium or antiepileptic drugs may help with mood swings. Serotonergics and monoamine oxidase inhibitors (MAOIs) may help stabilize impulsive behavior and depressive symptoms. Benzodiazepines (anti-panic or anti-anxiety drugs) can help anxiety, but long-term use should be avoided due to addictive potential.

Prognosis

Without adequate treatment, borderline personality disorder may be lifelong, and may even end in suicide. Outcome is better as long as treatment is initiated and maintained. In this scenario, psychotherapy and pharmacotherapy may allow the individual to maintain relationships. In a study of 500 borderline patients over 20 years, 40% were clinically recovered, 75% were self-supporting and doing reasonably well, and 7% had committed suicide.

Differential Diagnosis

Borderline personality disorder may be thought of as an extreme extension of less severe personality disorders (dependent, histrionic, passive-aggressive, or schizotypical). Associated Axis I disorders include generalized anxiety disorder, panic disorder, brief reactive psychosis, major depression and schizo-affective disorder.

Specialists

- Psychiatrist
- Psychologist

Work Restrictions / Accommodations

The borderline individual functions best in a disciplined environment with consistent support from coworkers and supervisors. These individuals become bored easily, and should avoid jobs requiring repetitious acts, such as working on an assembly line. Due to the irregularity in their sleep-wake cycle, frequent shift changes are to be avoided. Some flexibility in scheduling may be needed to accommodate ongoing therapy (which normally should occur during the employee's personal time).

Comorbid Conditions

Coexisting conditions that may impact recovery and lengthen disability include substance abuse and the presence of mood disorders, eating disorders (particularly bulimia), post-traumatic stress disorder, attention-deficit/hyperactivity disorder, and other personality disorders.

Complications

The borderline personality tends to be in a constant state of turmoil. There appears to be a constant and intense quest for support, security, and love in relationships. Complications occur when there is separation from, abandonment by, or disapproval from another person. Coexisting substance abuse, eating disorders, and promiscuity can all lead to complications in the course of the disorder. Other psychiatric disorders associated with the disorder will complicate the course, prognosis, and outcome. Suicide is the most serious complication, and injury to self or others can also occur.

Factors Influencing Duration

Complications, severity of the condition, response to treatment, support systems, and job duties may influence the length of disability.

Length of Disability

This condition represents a life-long pattern of behavior. In most cases, no disability is expected.

Failure to Recover

If an individual fails to recover within the maximum duration expectancy period, the reader may wish to reference the following questions to assist in better understanding the specifics of an individual's medical case.

Regarding diagnosis:

- Does individual's behavior fit the criteria for borderline personality disorder?
- Was diagnosis confirmed?
- Were underlying medical conditions including substance abuse ruled out?

Regarding treatment:

- Can physician and therapist keep in mind that individual's behavior is caused by the disorder and not through a desire to be disruptive?
- Has individual displayed any suicidal tendencies? Is physician/therapist aware of these?
- Is this individual aware of what to do and who to contact when in crisis?
- If individual has difficulty with daily functioning, would he/she benefit from a more structured in-house treatment program?
- Because there is currently a controversy regarding appropriate use versus over-medication, are antidepressant and antianxiety medications used appropriately and only during appropriate times in treatment?
- How long has individual been taking this medication? Is medication used in combination with psychotherapy?
- Would individual benefit from a dialectical behavior approach to better control life and emotions?
- Is individual involved in a group therapy or support group that allows individual to share common experiences and feelings, expand coping skills, and develop new, healthier social relationships?

Regarding prognosis:

- Was goal of therapy toward independent functioning, not complete restructuring of individual's personality?
- Since treatment is likely to be lengthy, lasting at least a year, does individual have realistic goals?

References

Grohol, John. <u>Borderline Personality Disorder</u>. Psych Central. 01 Nov 1999. 07 Aug 2000 <http://www.grohol.com/disorders/sx10.htm>.

<u>Overview of Borderline Personality Disorder</u>. Personality Disorders Institute. 01 Jan 2000. 17 Oct 2000 <http://www.borderlinedisorders.com/public.htm>.

Botulism

Other names / synonyms: Food Poisoning

005, 005.1

Definition

Botulism is a rare type of food poisoning that causes progressive muscular paralysis and nervous system disturbances. Toxins produced by the bacteria Clostridium botulinum affect the transmission of nerve impulses. Muscles such as those in the throat and those that control breathing become paralyzed. Death may result from respiratory failure.

Botulism is usually caused by eating contaminated food. Even minute amounts can lead to severe poisoning. Because the bacteria, which can survive under adverse conditions, can only multiply in the absence of air (anaerobic), they thrive in improperly preserved or canned food. Foods most commonly infected with the toxin are spiced, smoked, vacuum-packed, or home-canned foods that are eaten without cooking. Boiling food for at least 20 minutes can destroy the toxin. One sign of contaminated food is a can with a bulging lid or sides; however, contaminated foods may look and taste normal. Botulism bacteria are also found in the soil. Botulism can occur if these organisms enter skin broken during an injury.

The main form of human botulism throughout the world is the classic food-borne. In the US, the geographic distribution of cases by toxin type parallels the distribution of organism types found in the environment. Type A predominates west of the Rocky Mountains; type B, although generally distributed, is more common in the East; and type E is found in the Pacific Northwest, Alaska, and the Great Lakes area. In the US, food-borne botulism has been associated primarily with home-canned food, particularly vegetables, fruit, and condiments, and less commonly with meat and fish.

Although wound botulism is very rare, most of the documented cases have been found in the US. On very rare occasions, botulism results from growth and toxin produced in humans. Botulism occurs in animals with much higher frequency.

Diagnosis

History: Symptoms usually appear between 8 to 36 hours after eating contaminated food. They may include difficulty swallowing or speaking, dry mouth, nausea, vomiting, abdominal cramps, diarrhea, and blurred or double vision. As paralysis of the nervous system progresses, symptoms include weakness of upper and lower extremities, dizziness, difficulty walking, and difficulty breathing.

Physical exam: The exam may reveal dilated, fixed pupils, drooping eyelids (ptosis), decreased gag reflex or tongue weakness, partial paralysis of face, weakness of upper and lower extremities, poor muscular coordination (ataxia), and decreased, absent or increased deep tendon reflexes. Pulse is rapid but weak.

Tests: Cultures or toxin analysis (assays) may be done on blood (serum), stool, wound, or on remnants of suspected food. Nerve studies may be done by recording the electrical activity in the muscles through electromyography (EMG) or by skin testing.

Treatment

Maintenance of airway and breathing is crucial. Respiratory paralysis may lead to death unless mechanical assistance (respirator) is provided. Botulinum antitoxin is given to adults. Although the antitoxin can't undo the damage, it may slow or stop further damage, allowing the body to heal itself over the next few months. Antitoxin is most effective if given within 72 hours of symptom onset. Drugs (purgatives) and wound débridement may be used to remove any unabsorbed toxin. Intravenous fluids may be given to prevent dehydration.

Prognosis

Botulism is a life-threatening condition. Suffocation due to paralysis of the respiratory muscles results in death in about 70% of untreated cases. Prompt treatment with an antitoxin reduces the risk of death to less than twenty-five percent.

Differential Diagnosis

Conditions with similar symptoms include myasthenia gravis, Lambert-Eaton syndrome, tick paralysis, acute inflammatory polyneuropathy, magnesium toxicity and Guillain-Barré syndrome.

Specialists

- General Surgeon
- Infectious Disease Physician
- Neurologist
- Physiatrist

Work Restrictions / Accommodations

Work accommodations may include a temporary transfer to sedentary duties and elimination of duties that require heavy lifting. The individual's work area may need to be relocated nearer to the entrance/exit in order to decrease the amount of walking required or the employer may need to support a worker's ability to get from parking lot to work area (e.g., avoid walking stairs).

Comorbid Conditions

Immune deficiency or any concurrent illness associated with dehydration, weakness, and anorexia may lengthen disability.

Complications

Complications include aspiration pneumonia, abscess formation, neurological impairment, and persistent psychological problems.

Factors Influencing Duration

Length of disability may be influenced by the severity of symptoms, the need for ventilatory support, the extent of residual impairment, or the presence of complications.

Length of Disability

Uncomplicated.

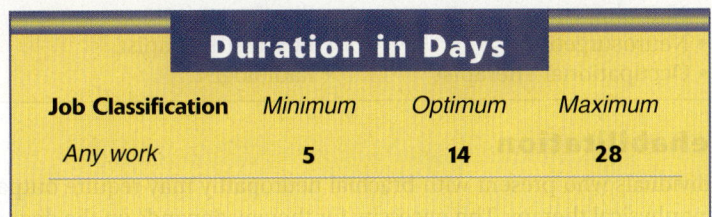

Job Classification	Minimum	Optimum	Maximum
Any work	5	14	28

Failure to Recover

If an individual fails to recover within the maximum duration expectancy period, the reader may wish to reference the following questions to assist in better understanding the specifics of an individual's medical case.

Regarding diagnosis:

- Has individual eaten any potentially contaminated food?
- Does individual have a cut that was exposed to soil?
- How long after exposure did the symptoms appear?
- Does individual have difficulty swallowing or speaking? Dry mouth? Does individual have symptoms of nausea, vomiting, diarrhea, or abdominal cramps? Is vision blurred or double? Does individual have dilated fixed pupils or ptosis? Is individual having trouble walking? Breathing?
- Is there a decreased gag reflex, tongue weakness, or partial paralysis of face? Does individual have weakness of the extremities and ataxia? Were deep tendon reflexes decreased, absent, or increased?
- Is the pulse rapid but weak?
- Were blood, stool, and wound tests performed? Was the suspected food tested? Were nerve conduction studies done?
- Have conditions with similar symptoms been ruled out?

Regarding treatment:

- Was a respirator necessary?
- Was the individual given botulinum antitoxin? Within 72 hours?
- Were purgatives used?
- Was the wound débrided?
- Were IV fluids needed?

Regarding prognosis:

- Can individual's employer accommodate any necessary restrictions?
- Does individual have any conditions that may affect ability to recover?
- Did complications arise such as aspiration pneumonia or abscess?
- Does individual have neurological impairment or persistent psychological problems?

References

Merck Manual of Diagnosis and Therapy, 17th ed. Beers, Mark H., and Robert Berkow, MD, eds. Whitehouse Station, NJ: Merck & Co., Inc, 1999

Puggiari, M., and M. Cherington. "Botulism and Guanidine. Ten Years Later." JAMA 240 21 (1978): 2276-2277.

Shapiro, R.L., C. Hatheway, and D.L. Swerdlow. "Botulism in the United States: A Clinical and Epidemiologic Review." Annals of Internal Medicine 129 3 (1998): 221-228.

Tierney, Lawrence, Stephen McPhee, and Maxine Papadakis. Current Medical Diagnosis and Treatment. Stamford: Appleton & Lange, 1998.

Brachial Neuropathy

Other names / synonyms: Brachial Neuritis, Brachial Plexopathy, Brachial Plexus Dysfunction, Brachial Plexus Neuropathy

353, 723.4, 953.4

Definition

Brachial neuritis or brachial neuropathy is an inflammation of the nerves (neuritis) in the shoulder area (brachial nerves).

A form of brachial neuropathy called idiopathic brachial neuropathy is rare and occurs in an apparently healthy individual. For no apparent reason, the individual suddenly experiences shoulder pain and loss of use of an arm.

A specific form of brachial neuropathy called acute brachial neuropathy (also known as acute brachial radiculitis and Parsonage-Turner syndrome) has been diagnosed in individuals with fever following an infection.

Brachial neuropathy can result from traumatic injury to the network of nerves in the shoulder (brachial plexus). Such traumas include falling off a ladder, jerking the arm, having a tumor press down on the nerves, radiation therapy for cancer, and gunshot and stab wounds. Brachial neuropathy rarely follows surgery (when the individual was in the prone position), viral infections, cervical nerve blocks, or injections of serum, vaccines, or antibiotics.

Brachial neuropathy affects adults of all ages, males slightly more than females, and heroin addicts considerably more than the general population. In heroin or other drug abusers, overdoses cause unconsciousness for hours during which sustained posturing with pressure on the brachial plexus (nerve) can cause the nerve damage.

Diagnosis

History: The history of the nontraumatic form of this condition is the sudden onset of a severe ache in the muscles of the shoulder and frequently the arm and neck. Pain is constant, not relieved by rest, worsens at night, and usually lasts less than a day. Individuals may think they twisted their neck or pulled a muscle. Whether or not the pain subsides, numbness and muscle weakness in the arm and shoulder usually follows within 3 to 10 days. The individual may have a recent history of infection, injections, or vaccinations. The individual may lose the use of that arm.

Physical exam: The affected arm may be hanging weakly or be held by the individual's other arm. The muscles of the shoulder and upper arm (deltoid, biceps, triceps, and serratus anterior muscles) may be partially or almost totally paralyzed. The arm muscles may have decreased reflexes and the arm and shoulder have decreased sensation. Very rarely, both shoulders and arms are affected.

Tests: Imaging studies and needle electromyography (EMG) are tests that confirm diagnosis. The time of onset of symptoms is very important since needle EMG evidence of denervation takes at least 10 days and, frequently, 21 days, to develop following nerve injury. Thus, a negative needle EMG examination done within 10 days of the onset of symptoms should be repeated later. A three-week interval is recommended in order to make certain that enough time has passed for needle EMG findings to be detectable. Brachial plexus neuropathy may have been diagnosed as an isolated inflamed nerve, suggesting local compression. EMG will determine whether this is correct or if the whole area is inflamed. Nerve conduction studies should be done to rule out peripheral neuropathy due to systemic diseases. Both needle EMG and nerve conduction studies are electrophysiological tests.

Treatment

Brachial neuropathy is treated conservatively. While the pain is still present, pain relievers (analgesics) are given. The pain may be severe enough for chronic narcotic therapy. A short course of high dose oral steroids may be given. If brachial neuropathy developed during rigorous exercise, the individual is told to stop exercising the affected arm. The individual is generally advised to avoid constantly supporting the arm in a sling because of the risk of a "frozen shoulder." If pain and arm numbness continues for some weeks, physical therapy with range-of-motion exercises is recommended.

Prognosis

Full functional recovery is expected in most individuals although recovery can be slow. Full recovery may take a year or longer. The muscle numbness and decreased sensation usually last from 6 to 12 weeks. Some individuals continue to have residual feelings of weakness, and others may continue to have winging of the shoulder blade (scapula) and poor shoulder muscle control.

Differential Diagnosis

Other possible diagnoses could include thoracic outlet syndrome, ruptured cervical disc, syringomyelia, spinal cord or brain tumor, rotator cuff syndrome, spondylosis, long thoracic nerve or suprascapular nerve compression, polymyalgia rheumatica, and reactions from a vaccine or serum.

Specialists

- Anesthesiologist
- Neurologist
- Neurosurgeon
- Occupational Therapist
- Orthopedic Surgeon
- Physiatrist
- Physical Therapist
- Radiologist

Rehabilitation

Individuals who present with brachial neuropathy may require outpatient physical therapy. The necessity for therapy depends on the degree of pain and weakness in the shoulder and upper arm.

The first goal of therapy is pain control. This is accomplished through the use of a sling to provide support to the shoulder. Individuals also learn to support the arm on a pillow when sitting in a chair. These techniques decrease the strain experienced by the inflamed nerves by decreasing the amount of traction forces to the shoulder that occur when the arm hangs in a dependent position. For individuals whose pain is not easily relieved, a transcutaneous electrical nerve stimulation (T.E.N.S.) unit may be provided. This technique utilizes a small device that emits intermittent electrical impulses through electrodes placed on the shoulder and/or neck. These impulses block the perception of pain by the brain.

The second goal of therapy is maintaining range of motion at the neck, shoulder, and elbow. Individuals perform gentle, active range-of-motion exercises for the neck, shoulder, and arm in a pain-free range. Individuals move the neck into forward bending, extension, side bending, and rotation. Individuals move the shoulder into the motion required to reach up overhead (forward flexion) and the motion required to reach out to the side (abduction). The shoulder stretches are performed by placing the hand on a therapy ball and rolling the ball forward and out to the side. Elbow stretches are performed by manually bending and straightening the elbow.

The third goal of therapy is the restoration of strength in the shoulder and elbow. Initially, isometric strengthening is conducted. The individual is progressed to resistance exercises using elastic tubing and light hand weights. Individuals are progressed to resistance exercises once the physician feels that further injury to the nerves will not be sustained.

For individuals with persistent shoulder or elbow weakness, neuromuscular electrical stimulation (N.M.E.S.) may be appropriate. This technique utilizes a small device that emits an electrical impulse through electrodes placed on the weakened muscles. The impulse is strong enough to produce a muscle contraction and minimize muscle atrophy.

Work Restrictions / Accommodations

The otherwise healthy individual will be limited by the pain, numbness, and weakness of his/her arm limiting lifting, carrying, and reaching overhead.

Comorbid Conditions

Comorbid conditions influencing the length of disability include autoimmune diseases, cancer, heroin, or other drug addiction, and obesity. Disability will be longer if brachial neuropathy developed after the individual suffered other injuries such as from a fall or a motor vehicle crash.

Complications

Pain may not disappear with the onset of muscle weakness suggesting that the pain may be caused by an underlying injury or disease. Obesity may make testing difficult to interpret and may prolong recovery.

Factors Influencing Duration

One factor influencing the length of disability is whether the individual's work requires full use of the involved arm. If the individual is not in pain and has enough residual function in the unaffected arm for normal duties, the length of disability can be short. Prolonged pain with shoulder or arm motion increases length of disability. Any residual muscle weakness can increase length of disability and make some tasks either impractical or unsafe depending on the form of work. If recovery continues slowly over 1 to 3 years, medium to very heavy work will not be possible. If nerve damage is significant and permanent, the individual may be permanently limited to modified duty.

Length of Disability

Disability may be permanent depending upon the severity of nerve damage.

Failure to Recover

If an individual fails to recover within the maximum duration expectancy period, the reader may wish to reference the following questions to assist in better understanding the specifics of an individual's medical case.

Regarding diagnosis

- What type of brachial neuropathy was diagnosed?
- Is there a proven cause of diagnosis or is the neuropathy considered idiopathic?
- Has individual had recent fever and infection?
- Has individual had any recent trauma to the arm or shoulder area? Radiation therapy? Gun shot or stab wound to the area?
- Has individual recently had surgery or injections in the area?
- Did individual have a sudden onset of severe aching in the shoulder? How long did it last?
- Has individual developed muscle weakness in the same shoulder and arm? Numbness in the arm?
- Are the reflexes decreased in the arm and/or shoulder? Paralysis in the shoulder or upper arm?
- Was an MRI or cervical spine and brachial plexus and needle EMG done? Nerve conduction study?
- Were any changes in abnormalities found in electrodiagnostic studies after onset as compared to later studies?
- Were conditions with similar symptoms ruled out?

Regarding treatment:

- Has individual responded to conservative therapy?
- Did individual have a short course of oral steroids?
- How long have symptoms persisted?
- Is individual in physical therapy?
- Was individual evaluated for appropriateness of treatment at a multidisciplinary pain and functional restoration center?

Regarding prognosis:

- Did individual have full functional recovery or experience residual feelings of weakness? Did individual have winging of the scapula and poor shoulder muscle control?

References

Nelson, Roger, and Dean P. Currier. Clinical Electrotherapy. Norwalk: Appleton & Lange, 1991.

Wong, L., and A.L. Dellon. "Brachial Neuritis Presenting as Anterior Interosseous Nerve Compression - Implications for Diagnosis and Treatment: A Case Report." Journal of Hand Surgery - American Volume 22 3 (1997): 536-539.

Brain Abscess
Other names / synonyms: Cerebral Abscess, Intracranial Abscess
324, 324.0

Definition

A brain abscess is an infected cavity, filled with pus, which forms within the brain tissue. The infecting organism can be fungus, protozoa, or bacteria.

About 40% of brain abscesses stem from infections of the middle ear (otitis media), the mastoid portion of one of the bones of the skull near the ear (mastoiditis), or the sinuses (sinusitis). Another 30% of brain abscesses result from an infection that spread from another part of the body, such as the lungs, skin, or heart valves. Of these, lung (pulmonary) infections have been cited as frequent sources, although dental infections are increasingly seen as primary sites. Penetrating head injury or neurosurgical procedure accounts for another 10% of cases.

Brain abscess is rare in the general population, but individuals whose immune systems do not work well (immunocompromised) or have other conditions that interfere with the body's healing process are particularly at-risk for developing a brain abscess. Examples of other individuals at risk include diabetics, AIDS or HIV infected individuals, individuals on immunosuppressing drugs after organ or tissue transplantation, heroin or alcohol abusers, individuals with artificial (prosthetic) or congenitally damaged heart valves, and those with certain cancers (lymphomas). Also at-risk are those individuals who do not seek medical help for infections, thus failing to receive the proper antibiotic therapy. Although brain abscess can occur at any age, it is most common in individuals ages 10 to 35, peaking in the third decade. Men develop brain abscesses twice as often as women.

Diagnosis

History: The location of the abscess may determine the type of symptoms, including headache, fever, drowsiness, inattention, confusion, nausea, vomiting, stiff neck, visual complaints, and seizures. A history of previous infection in another part of the body is often reported. Abscesses resulting from ear or sinus infections are typically located in the part of the brain nearest the source.

Physical exam: Abnormalities observed on physical examination vary depending on the site of the abscess, with specific neurological findings reflecting swelling (edema) around the abscess. Some common findings include low-grade fever, neck stiffness (nuchal rigidity) in about 25% of cases, seizures, inability to move the eyes, swelling of the optic nerve seen by looking into the eye with an ophthalmoscope (papilledema), and visual disturbances. Altered mental status may range from subtle personality changes, to drowsiness, or even deep coma. If the infection has spread from another site, evidence of the primary infection may also be present.

Tests: Lab (blood) tests are rarely helpful in establishing a definite diagnosis. The white blood cell count (WBC) is often slightly elevated and the erythrocyte sedimentation rate (ESR) may be elevated in up to 60% of individuals. CT scan may make a definitive diagnosis, although MRI is generally a more reliable diagnostic tool. Early in the course, abscesses show up as low-density, irregular zones that do not enhance on CT scan when a contrast dye is given. As the disease progresses, the distinctive ring enhancement becomes obvious as the abscess wall thickens. Examination of cerebrospinal fluid can help confirm infection, but lumbar puncture is too risky because the sudden release of pressure within the skull (increased intracranial pressure) can cause the brain to shift downward in the skull cavity, putting pressure on vital structures (cerebral herniation), which can lead to irreversible brain damage and death. Drainage of fluid or pus from the abscess can be guided by CT (stereotactic biopsy). Pus that is drained from the abscess can be examined under the microscope and cultured to identify the causative organism. Skull x-rays and radioisotope bone scan can help identify areas of bone destruction, and magnetic resonance imaging (MRI) is also useful in visualizing the abscess.

Treatment

Treatment consists of antibiotics to fight the underlying infection within the skull cavity (increased intracranial pressure, or ICP) and inflammation. When the abscess is smaller than 2 cm, administration of intravenous antibiotics is usually sufficient to eliminate the infection. However, the neurosurgeon should be notified right away to participate in the decision of whether surgery is needed.

If the abscess is larger than 2 cms, fails to shrink with antibiotic treatment, or if the individual's symptoms fail to improve, surgical removal of fluid (aspiration) or drainage of the abscess may be necessary. Other treatments during the acute phase of the problem include assisted breathing (mechanical ventilation) and the administration of intravenous fluids. When intracranial pressure is increased, assisted breathing at a rapid rate (hyperventilation) may help reduce pressure by decreasing brain swelling. Anticonvulsant medications may also be given to help prevent seizures.

Prognosis

Brain abscesses are medical emergencies that require rapid diagnosis and effective treatment. With early diagnosis and proper treatment, the infection is curable. Characteristics associated with an excellent prognosis include young age, absence of severe neurological defects, absence of neurological deterioration during initial assessment and treatment, and absence of other existing medical problems. Approximately 10% of individuals with brain abscess die from the condition. If there is evidence of brain swelling causing downward displacement of the brain within the skull (brain herniation) when the individual is first seen, mortality is higher than fifty percent. Seizures, permanent brain damage, coma, and death can occur without proper treatment.

Differential Diagnosis

Differential diagnoses may include primary or spreading (metastatic) brain tumor, extradural abscess, subdural effusion, cerebrovascular disease, stroke, subacute and chronic meningitis, and central nervous system degenerative disease.

Specialists

- Neurologist
- Neurosurgeon

Rehabilitation

Individuals with brain abscess may require a variety of rehabilitation services depending on the location and treatments required.

Physical therapy and occupational therapy may be required for a range of services including general conditioning exercises if the individual is weakened from the treatment required, to positioning and passive stretching if the individual is comatose. Physical therapy may be required for gait and transfer training if the individual's balance and coordination has been affected. Occupational therapy may be necessary to address activities of daily living such as dressing and bathing techniques. If an individual fatigues easily, energy conservation methods, such as allowing dishes to soak for a while to decrease the effort required to wash the dishes may also be taught in occupational therapy.

Work Restrictions / Accommodations

Due to the variable nature of the disease, work restrictions and accommodations require consideration on an individual, case-by-case basis. If physical and/or mental disabilities (such as difficulty walking, speaking, seeing, or hearing, or changes in personality) occur as a result of brain damage attributed to the brain abscess, environmental workplace adaptations may be necessary. Vocational retraining may also be needed. Time off from work to attend physical therapy, counseling, and/or doctors' appointments may be required.

Comorbid Conditions

Endocarditis, lung abscess, dental abscess, residual focal defect, increased incidence of seizure due to scar tissue in the brain, or neuropsychiatric changes may lengthen the disability. Individuals with underlying disease and/or compromised immune systems such as diabetes, AIDS, or cancer may be less likely to fully recover from a brain abscess.

Complications

Seizures and other neurological symptoms such as paralysis or speech problems vary depending on the location of the abscess and the effectiveness of treatment. Brain swelling (edema) associated with the abscess, or bleeding (hemorrhage) into the abscess may increase pressure inside the skull, forcing the upper brain (cerebrum) downward into the space normally occupied by the lower brain (brainstem). This process is called uncal or tonsillar herniation, and it often results in irreversible coma and death. If the individual remains unconscious (comatose) for an extended period of time, skin breakdown, pressure sores, and loss of joint mobility (contractures) may occur. Rupture of the abscess into the fluid-filled chambers within the brain (ventricles) is usually fatal. Individuals with underlying disease and/or compromised immune systems, such as diabetes, AIDS, or cancer may be less likely to recover fully from a brain abscess.

Factors Influencing Duration

Factors influencing the length of disability include the location and size of the abscess, type of causative microorganism, and response to treatment. When effective treatment is received early in the course, a previously healthy individual can expect to recover completely following discharge from the hospital. Some individuals, particularly those with underlying disease, may experience long-term or permanent disability. Such disability may be either physical or emotional or both.

Length of Disability

The length of disability will depend on comorbid conditions, residual effects, and any resulting brain damage. Disability status will also depend on work requirements and the availability of vocational retraining. Disability may be permanent.

Medical treatment.

Duration in Days

Job Classification	Minimum	Optimum	Maximum
Any work	28	35	Indefinite

Surgical treatment.

Duration in Days

Job Classification	Minimum	Optimum	Maximum
Any work	42	70	Indefinite

Failure to Recover

If an individual fails to recover within the maximum duration expectancy period, the reader may wish to reference the following questions to assist in better understanding the specifics of an individual's medical case.

Regarding diagnosis:

- Has individual recently had otitis media, mastoiditis, or sinusitis?
- Could the infection have spread from the lungs, heart, or skin?
- Has individual had a dental infection?
- Is individual immunocompromised? Diabetic?
- Does individual have an artificial heart valve?
- Is individual an IV drug or alcohol abuser?
- Does individual have cancer?
- Did neurological finding suggest swelling around the abscess?
- Is a low-grade fever present? Neck stiffness?
- Does the individual experience seizures?
- Does individual have inability to move the eyes? Papilledema? Visual disturbances?
- Is mental status altered?
- Is a primary infection site evident?
- Were a WBC and sedimentation rate done? Brain x-rays? CT? MRI? Skull x-rays and a bone scan?
- Was abscess drained? Was a culture and sensitivity done?
- Were conditions with similar symptoms ruled out?

Regarding treatment:

- Was the abscess diagnosed and treated early?
- Is individual on antibiotics? Anticonvulsants?
- Was it necessary for individual to be on a ventilator? Was hyperventilation tried?

Regarding prognosis:

- Is individual participating in a rehabilitation program?
- Are all the necessary team members involved?
- Can individual's employer accommodate any necessary restrictions?
- Does individual have any conditions that could affect ability to recover? Any physical or emotional complications?

References

Anderson, Kenneth N., revision ed. Mosby's Medical, Nursing, and Allied Health Dictionary, 5th ed. St. Louis: Mosby, 1998.

Harris, Susan R. "Functional Abilities in Context." Contemporary Management of Motor Control Problems. Lister, Marilyn J., ed. Fredericksburg: The Foundation for Physical Therapy, 1991. 253-259.

Brain Injury

Other names / synonyms: Brain Dysfunction, Encephalopathy, Head Injury, Head Trauma, Organic Brain Syndrome, TBI, Traumatic Brain Injury

435, 437, 850, 850.0, 850.1, 850.2, 850.3, 850.4, 850.5, 850.9, 853, 853.0, 853.00, 853.01, 853.02, 853.03, 853.04, 853.05, 853.06, 853.09, 853.1, 853.10, 853.11, 853.12, 853.13, 853.14, 853.15, 853.16, 853.19, 854, 854.0, 854.00, 854.01, 854.02, 854.03, 854.04, 854.05, 854.06, 854.09, 854.1, 854.10, 854.11, 854.12, 854.13, 854.14, 854.15, 854.16, 854.19

Definition

Brain injury occurs when the tissues of the brain suffer an acute injury that results in temporary, chronic, or permanent damage and/or dysfunction. The brain is a very sensitive organ subject to injury from a variety of insults. Some of the major causes of brain injury include traumatic injury, lack of oxygen (hypoxic/anoxic injury), lack of blood flow (ischemic), infection, and metabolic disorders.

Brain hypoxia/ischemia may result from traumatic brain injury, circulatory problems such as cerebral vessel spasm or stroke, and lack of oxygenation that may occur during cardiopulmonary arrest. Lack of adequate oxygen to the brain causes cell death that can be localized or widespread. The extent of brain cell death influences the degree of neurological impairment and disability.

Metabolic disorders that may contribute to brain injury include liver failure, low blood sugar (hypoglycemia), kidney (renal) failure, and toxic exposures to such substances as alcohol, drugs, sedatives, poisons, and some heavy metals. In general, brain injury associated with metabolic disorders is widespread and affects the entire brain.

Brain injury can result in loss of body movement (paralysis), weakness of muscles (paresis), abnormal muscle stiffness and movements (spasticity), memory loss (amnesia) or impairment, loss of consciousness, coma, personality changes, blindness, seizures, or disruption of various chemical processes of the body.

Each year approximately 5% of the population sustains brain injuries significant enough to result in lost time from normal activities including work. The major causes of traumatic brain injury are motor vehicle accidents, falls, and assaults. Motor vehicle accidents occur most frequently in the 15 to 24-year-old age group and account for nearly half of all traumatic brain injuries. Falls are most common among the elderly.

Diagnosis

History: History may reveal a motor vehicle accident or fall. The individual (or individual's family members) may report signs of confusion or disorientation or the individual may have been found unconscious. Other symptoms include headaches, nausea and vomiting, loss of muscle control, muscle weakness, paralysis, blurred vision, dizziness, impaired memory, anxiety, irritability, decreased concentration, insomnia, sleepiness, or seizures. Past medical history can reveal episodes of seizures, personality changes, frequent falls, or loss of control of normal movements. There may also be a history of alcohol or drug use.

Physical exam: The exam includes evaluation of level of consciousness, pupil response and vital signs, motor function, reflexes, and memory. The level of consciousness is the most sensitive indicator of neurological function. The Glasgow Coma Scale (GCS) is an internationally recognized tool for evaluating level of I the acute post injury period and has been used to predict outcome. A GCS score of 15 is normal although brain injury may still have occurred. A GCS score of 3 is the lowest possible score and represents a deep coma state. The lower the score, the worse the neurologic injury to the brain and the higher the morbidity and mortality.

The Rancho Los Amigos Scale is a brain injury assessment tool that may be used throughout brain injury care to monitor progress relative to providing a description of the individual's cognitive-behavioral status.

Vital signs are taken as a baseline and then monitored for changes throughout the recovery. A hallmark of severe brain injury or imminent crisis is a loss of the normal autoregulation of blood pressure and pulse called the Cushing's reflex. This generally results in a sudden rise in blood pressure and a slowing of the pulse.

Breathing rate and pattern is also evaluated and may provide clues to the area of brain injured. Irregularities in breathing patterns may indicate pressure or damage to the many respiratory centers scattered throughout the brain.

Pupils are normally equal in size, round, and briskly reactive to light. Brain injury and pressure on the nerves leading to the pupils can produce changes in pupil size, shape, and reaction to light and movement. These changes can be correlated with the severity and type of brain injury. A sudden enlargement (dilation) of one pupil (anisocoria) is an ominous sign that requires immediate intervention. This typically signals increased pressure on one side of the brain causing the brain to shift downward in the skull cavity (uncal or tonsillar herniation).

Drooping of one side of the face is a classic sign indicating damage to the nerve pathways that supply the muscles of the face. Reflexes may be overactive (hyperreflexia) and reflecting pressure on motor pathways that control movement. The head and neck may be bruised and swollen. There may be blood in the ear and behind the eardrum (Battle's sign) and the individual may show signs of hearing difficulty. Darkening under the eye (raccoon's eyes) may signify fracture of the base of the skull. Speech can be slurred or absent (mutism). Difficulties with expressive or receptive language may be seen (dysphasia or aphasia). The individual may show a lack of normal sense of smell (anosmia), which may reflect damage to the foremost part of the brain behind the forehead (frontal lobe). There may be signs of memory failure/loss.

A specialized part of the physical exam done on an individual in coma is called caloric testing. The physician uses a syringe to put ice water against the eardrum. The resulting pattern of movement of the eyes helps determine what nerves of the part of the brain are injured.

Tests: Since trauma to the head is often associated with fracture or other injury to the neck, the neck should be stabilized on a special board (cervical board) until neck fracture is ruled out by x-ray. Tests include x-rays of the skull or other areas where fracture is suspected, brain and neck CT, and MRI of the head and neck. Lab tests include blood chemistry tests. Drug and alcohol screens should be performed if the cause of brain injury is unclear. A brain wave test (electroencephalogram or EEG) may be useful in some cases where seizures are noted and or suspected.

Treatment

As in any acute emergency, the individual's airway, breathing, and circulation must be maintained. Depending on the nature and severity of the injury, this may require assisted breathing (intubation and mechanical ventilation), CPR (cardiopulmonary resuscitation), and/or administration of oxygen, intravenous fluids, or medications acting on the heart or blood vessels. Accompanying problems such as disturbances in blood chemistry or infections should be treated. When there is trauma to the head, neck fracture and spinal cord injury must be assumed until ruled out. More severe cases of brain trauma may require immediate surgical intervention (craniotomy) to relieve pressure on the brain from swelling and bleeding (e.g., subdural hematoma). Drugs that decrease brain swelling, control seizures, or lower blood pressure may also be used.

If loss of consciousness does not last more than 20-30 minutes or post-traumatic amnesia is less than 24 hours, if head CT or MRI shows no bleeding or damaged areas, and if neurological examination shows no focal abnormalities, these individuals can usually be released from the hospital and observed at home by a family member. More severe cases usually require close observation of the individual's vital signs such as pulse, respiration, and blood pressure. The pupils, reflexes, level of consciousness, and neurological function should be checked regularly.

Prognosis

Outcome is usually excellent with complete recovery expected in mild brain injury with loss or alteration in consciousness lasting less than 30 minutes, normal brain CT or MRI, and normal neurological examination. Chances for recovery depend on the severity of brain injury but tend to improve with prompt treatment. Outcome is usually better in younger individuals. Recognition and rapid surgical intervention to remove rapidly accumulating blood or blood clots (craniotomy with evacuation of hematoma) can be life-saving and is vital to improving the outcome of brain-injured individuals. A primary cause of death in those with brain injury is due to delay in surgical intervention. Causes of such delays may be failure to recognize the rate and significance of the bleeding and deterioration of neurological function or lack of access to surgical intervention.

Recovery may take weeks to months. In adults, most recovery after severe brain injury occurs within the first 6 months. However, recovery may continue for up to 2 years and longer in part based on the primary neuropathology of the injury. Possible outcomes include memory loss, seizures, intellectual impairment, muscular weakness in an arm or leg, depression, language problems, or slurred speech but patterns of recovery vary. The injury may be fatal in cases of damage to the vital centers that regulate breathing and blood flow.

Differential Diagnosis

Metabolic disorders such as diabetes or hypothyroidism, infectious diseases (i.e., meningitis or encephalitis), drug and alcohol abuse, brain tumor, stroke, or misuse of prescription drugs can have a similar presentation to brain injury.

Specialists

- Internist
- Neurologist
- Neurosurgeon
- Physiatrist
- Psychiatrist

Rehabilitation

Any brain injury that has caused physical and mental deficits may need rehabilitation in order to facilitate recovery. The overall objective for rehabilitation of individuals with traumatic brain injury is to return them as quickly and as fully as possible to the mainstream of their lives. This requires achieving functional recovery and assisting the individual in coping with disabilities that may remain.

Achieving goals is a common phrase used by the physical, occupational, and often the speech therapist in rehabilitation of a head injury resulting in brain injury. Goal setting is necessary for effective use of time and resources when treating severe symptoms that have resulted from trauma to the brain. An organized treatment approach from a team of healthcare professionals is necessary for a complete treatment. Rehabilitation varies for each individual because of the uniqueness of the problems after each particular brain injury. Treatment of the unconscious individual begins with passive range-of-motion exercises that consist of the therapist moving joints of the upper and lower extremities to prevent loss of mobility (contractures) or blood clots. Involvement in treatment of family members as well as the rehabilitation team can help motivate and support the individual. Sensory stimulation from a nearby radio or individuals talking may be helpful even when level of consciousness is decreased, however, there is no data showing efficacy in unconscious individuals (those in a coma or vegetative state).

A physiatrist can best assess the degree of mental and functional disability following brain injury. Rehabilitation is then recommended based on the degree of deficits. Most individuals with severe brain injury (e.g., initial Glasgow Coma scores less than or equal to 8) benefit from formal neurorehabilitation. Most individuals with moderate to severe brain injury and significant mental and functional deficits will be referred to an inpatient rehabilitation facility. Even after regaining consciousness, the individual may still be confused and easily distracted and will benefit from exercises to promote memory return. Instruction designed to help the individual carry out simple tasks can be as elementary as motivating individuals to receive an object in their hand or assisting them to go from a sitting position to a standing position.

Sequencing of activities from easy to more difficult is later emphasized in the rehabilitation of a head injury. For example, teaching the individual to rise from a chair is part of the rehabilitation program before instructing proper walking patterns. Once the individual regains his/her thinking processes, rehabilitation may turn to the needs of muscular strength, endurance, and flexibility. Muscle imbalance is corrected by traditional methods used in physical therapy with techniques to help make the muscle and nervous system work together. Group activities may take place in mat classes, wheelchair classes, or in other activities such as volleyball games.

When appropriate, the final phase of the rehabilitation following brain injury involves the individual's reinstatement to work. The exercises both physically and mentally are now directed toward the work requirements. Modifications may need to be made by the physical therapist for those with various levels of head trauma. Participants in the rehabilitation program can include physical, occupational, speech, and recreational therapists as well as social workers.

Work Restrictions / Accommodations

In mild or less severe cases, a worker may temporarily need shorter work hours or frequent breaks. Time off from work for ongoing rehabilitation and treatment may be necessary.

In severe cases, individuals may be left with permanent disabilities/handicaps that prevents them from doing previous duties. Such cases require adjustment in duties and expectations, vocational rehabilitation or training, and possibly a complete change in job assignment. Accommodations may need to be made so that the workplace is wheelchair-accessible for those with ambulation problems.

Comorbid Conditions

Pre-existing behavioral, social, cognitive, or neurological deficits (mental illness, drug abuse, mental impairment, or seizures) may lengthen disability.

Complications

Complications may include previously diagnosed or undiagnosed medical conditions such as bleeding disorders, high blood pressure, seizures, or drug or alcohol use. Persistent memory or thinking problems, depression, weakness, numbness, visual problems, and difficulties with speaking or understanding speech may complicate brain injury depending on the location of the injury and its severity.

Factors Influencing Duration

Factors that influence length of disability are age, severity of injury, and the individual's willingness and ability to follow a treatment plan.

Length of Disability

Disability may be much longer or permanent with severe concussion.

Mild concussion only.

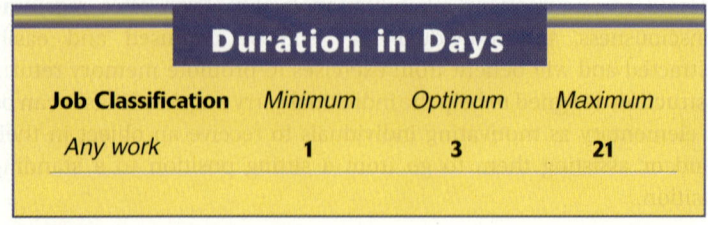

Duration in Days				
Job Classification	Minimum	Optimum	Maximum
Any work	1	3	21

Failure to Recover

If an individual fails to recover within the maximum duration expectancy period, the reader may wish to reference the following questions to assist in better understanding the specifics of an individual's medical case.

Regarding diagnosis:

- Has individual experienced a traumatic head injury?
- Does individual have circulatory problems such as cerebral vessel spasm or stroke?
- Did lack of oxygenation occur during cardiopulmonary arrest?
- Does individual have liver failure, hypoglycemia, or kidney failure?
- Was individual exposed to toxic substances such as alcohol, drugs, sedatives, poisons, and some heavy metals?
- On exam, what was level of consciousness, pupil response, vital signs, motor function, reflexes, and memory?
- What was individual's initial Glasgow Coma Score? Rancho Los Amigos Scale?
- What were individual's vital signs? Have they been stable or labile?
- Was pupil testing normal or abnormal? Does individual have raccoon eyes?
- Is there drooping on one side of the face? Are the reflexes overactive?
- Is there blood in the ear or behind the eardrum? Any hearing difficulty?
- Does individual have any speech abnormalities?
- What were the results of caloric testing on the individual?
- Was the neck stabilized until a fracture was ruled out?
- Has individual had skull x-rays? Brain and neck CT? MRI? EEG? Did individual have blood chemistry tests? Drug and alcohol screens?
- Were conditions with similar symptoms ruled out?

Regarding treatment:

- Was CPR necessary? Intubation and mechanical ventilation?
- Was it necessary to do a craniotomy?
- Was individual given drugs to reduce brain swelling? Control seizures and blood pressure, if needed?
- Was individual hospitalized or released to home care?

Regarding prognosis:

- Can individual's employer accommodate any necessary restrictions?
- Is individual actively participating in a brain injury rehab program? Is family involved in the rehabilitation?
- Is neurorehabilitation needed? If so, is individual in a program?
- Does individual have any conditions that may affect total recovery?
- Are there any complications such as persistent memory or thinking problems? Speech? Understanding speech? Depression? Weakness? Visual problems?

References

Clochesy, John M., et al. Critical Care Nursing, 2nd ed. Philadelphia: W.B. Saunders Company, 1996.

Umphred, Darcy A. Neurological Rehabilitation. St. Louis: C.V. Mosby Company, 1990.

Breast Biopsy

Other names / synonyms: Lumpectomy

85.11, 85.12, 85.21

Definition

A breast biopsy is a method of obtaining tissue from a lump or other abnormality within the breast.

There are essentially two types of breast biopsies performed: needle biopsy and open or surgical biopsy. Variations of these two types of breast biopsy are performed. An open biopsy involves removing either a sample of the lump (incisional biopsy) or the entire lump and some of the surrounding tissue (excisional biopsy). Needle biopsies use a needle to remove a sample of tissue from the center of the lump (core biopsy). Small lumps may be removed in their entirety by needle biopsy. Stereotactic core biopsy uses breast x-ray (mammography) equipment and an automated biopsy gun to perform a needle biopsy. A new development in the field of breast biopsy is the computer-driven breast biopsy system that can remove a large core of breast tissue.

Women who have a higher risk of developing breast cancer include those with a family history of breast cancer, genetic alterations that may make them prone to breast cancer, or noncancerous (benign) breast disease. Also at risk are women who are greater than 50 years old (especially if overweight), consume alcohol, began menstruating before 12 years of age, went through menopause after 55 years of age, had their first child after 30 years of age, or have no biological children. Men who have had radiation exposure and those who have Klinefelter's syndrome are at an increased risk of developing breast cancer. In the US, more than 180,000 individuals are diagnosed with breast cancer each year, fewer than 1,500 of which are men. The incidence of breast cancer varies for different age groups; for instance, approximately 150 per 100,000 women in their 40s will be diagnosed with breast cancer each year. In the US, between 0.5-1 million breast biopsies are performed each year.

Reason for Procedure

Breast biopsy is performed to collect tissue samples from a breast lump or other abnormality to determine if the lump is noncancerous (benign) or cancerous (malignant). Because about 30% of all lesions thought to be malignant are found to be benign upon biopsy, and about 15% thought to be benign are proven malignant, biopsy is the best way to test a breast lump so that treatment options can be explored.

Description

Breast biopsies may be performed in a hospital, a mammography suite, or an operating room. Most biopsies are performed under local (surface and deep) anesthesia on an outpatient basis. A sedative may be required if the individual is particularly anxious about the procedure.

For breast lumps that cannot be felt (nonpalpable), imaging-guided breast biopsy may be performed. For this procedure, a fine needle or wire is guided into the lump by mammography or ultrasound localization to serve as a marker for the surgeon. A dye injection technique may be used alone or in conjunction with a needle or wire guide to mark the lesion. The needle is placed into the lump and a dye is released as the needle is withdrawn thereby leaving a visible track. Needle biopsies are most frequently used to obtain samples of suspicious, nonpalpable lesions that were identified by mammography. Needle biopsy is performed with either a large cutting needle (core needle biopsy) or a fine needle that sucks (aspirates) cells from the lump (fine-needle aspiration). Ultrasound may be used in conjunction with needle biopsies in order to visualize the needle path and the lump. With fine needle biopsy, standard office needles and syringes are used and local anesthesia is not usually necessary. The needle penetrates the breast tissue and, while suction is applied, is moved back and forth to sample several sites within the lump. Once enough tissue has been obtained, the needle is removed and pressure is applied to the prick site to stop bleeding.

Core needle biopsy requires a small cut (incision) into which the biopsy needle is inserted. Slivers of breast tissue are obtained by applying suction with a syringe or vacuum-suction device.

Stereotactic core biopsy utilizes a mammography unit with the additional equipment necessary to perform a needle biopsy. For stereotactic core biopsy, the individual either sits upright or lies face down (prone) on a table so that the breast undergoing biopsy hangs down through a hole in the table. The breast is gently pressed between a plate (compression plate) and a platform (detector plate). The stereotactic equipment calculates the location of the lump and removes one or more samples using a needle or biopsy gun. Once a core biopsy needle is removed, pressure is applied to the wound to stop bleeding.

The computer-driven breast biopsy system is a lengthy procedure that has numerous disadvantages, which include the necessity for surgically-sterile conditions and creation of a large wound that must be stitched (sutured) closed.

Open biopsies are recommended for older individuals because the risk of developing breast cancer increases with age and a definitive diagnosis is essential.

Incisional biopsies are performed in cases of large masses, abnormalities that are consistent with inflammatory cancer, and other abnormalities for which conservation of the breast is not possible. Excisional biopsies can be performed on most breast lumps and have the advantage that, because the entire lump is removed, the diagnosis is definitive and the follow-up process is simplified (i.e., further treatment may not be necessary).

For open biopsies, the individual lies on his or her back and a scalpel is used to cut into the breast to remove some or the entire lump. Tissue from an open biopsy may be sent immediately to the pathologist so that, if indicated, additional tissue may be excised. Bleeding is controlled using electricity, a laser beam (cautery), or fine stitches (sutures). The incision is sutured closed with care so that scarring is minimal.

A cytologist or cytopathologist analyzes tissue obtained by fine needle aspiration. A pathologist analyzes other biopsy samples.

Prognosis

Most biopsy procedures successfully sample the breast lump. Up to 18% of needle biopsies must be repeated because of a disagreement between imaging studies and the biopsy findings, inadequate tissue sampling, or a need for a broader sample. However, needle biopsies are less invasive, less traumatic, and result in a quicker recovery than open biopsies. Eighty percent of breast biopsies are benign.

Following a needle biopsy, individuals can return to normal activities almost immediately.

Specialists

- General Surgeon

Work Restrictions / Accommodations

Strenuous activities (especially lifting or reaching overhead) may be restricted if an open excision is performed. For a few days following the biopsy, the individual may need to apply an ice pack to the breast several times a day, so may require more frequent rest breaks.

Comorbid Conditions

Obesity or enlarged or large breasts may make breast biopsy more difficult and cause more discomfort, which could lengthen disability.

Procedure Complications

Fine needle aspirations are rarely complicated. Core needle biopsies can cause bleeding (hemorrhage) and blood accumulation within breast tissue (hematoma). Complications associated with open breast biopsy include hemorrhage, hematoma, infection, black-and-blue marks beneath the skin (ecchymosis), numbness, and prickling or burning sensations (paresthesias). An interference with breast feeding can occur following breast biopsy near or beneath the nipple. Guide wires may break or be cut during surgery and can remain stable or migrate to other parts of the body.

Factors Influencing Duration

The method of biopsy including amount of tissue removed, size of incision, type of anesthesia used, the presence of complications, and the individual's response to the procedure will determine the length of disability. Individuals who have had an open biopsy will have a longer recovery time, depending on the extent of the surgery.

Length of Disability

Duration may be longer if strenuous activities are part of the job duties. For open or excisional biopsy, duration depends on amount of tissue removed, and size of incision.

Needle/aspiration.

Duration in Days

Job Classification	Minimum	Optimum	Maximum
Sedentary work	1	1	1
Light work	1	1	1
Medium work	1	1	2
Heavy work	1	2	3
Very Heavy work	1	2	3

Open/excisional.

Duration in Days

Job Classification	Minimum	Optimum	Maximum
Sedentary work	1	3	14
Light work	1	3	14
Medium work	1	3	14
Heavy work	3	7	21
Very Heavy work	3	7	21

References

Dershaw, D. David. "Equipment, Technique, Quality Assurance, and Accreditation for Imaging-guided Breast Biopsy Procedures." The Radiologic Clinics of North America: Breast Imaging. Feig, Stephen, ed. Philadelphia: W.B. Saunders Company, 2000. 773-789.

Kopans, Daniel. "Imaging-guided Needle Placement for Biopsy and the Preoperative Localization of Clinically Ocult Lesions." Breast Imaging. Kopans, Daniel, ed. Philadelphia: Lippincott-Raven, 1998. 637-720.

Liberman, Laura. "Clinical Management Issues in Percutaneous Core Breast Biopsy." The Radiologic Clinics of North America: Breast Imaging. Feig, Stephen, ed. Philadelphia: W.B. Saunders Company, 2000. 791-807.

Pennanen, Marie. "Breast Cancer Screening and Diagnosis." Surgery of the Breast: Principles and Art. Spear, Scott, ed. Philadelphia: Lippincott-Raven, 1998. 23-68.

Bronchiectasis

Other names / synonyms: Acquired Bronchiectasis, Bronchial Dilatation, Bronchiectasis, Congenital Bronchiectasis, Dry Bronchiectasis, Wet Bronchiectasis

494, 748.61

Definition

Bronchiectasis is a lung disease characterized by irreversible enlargement (dilatation) of the lower lung airways and destruction of lung tissue.

It is usually caused by repeated infections and inflammation, which can start a vicious cycle. Inflammation causes a partial obstruction of a part of the lung, causing secretions to collect, which sets the stage for infections to develop and persist, damaging the surrounding lung tissue.

Bronchiectasis is not an independent lung disease, but is a consequence of some other disease process. A lung infection may be from tuberculosis, a fungus, virus, or may result from obstruction by a tumor or an inhaled foreign object.

Bronchiectasis can also follow lung injury from inhaling corrosive gases or one's own stomach contents. Other causes are cystic fibrosis, and a syndrome of nonfunctioning motile extensions of a cell surface (cilia) in the airways, both of which allow the collection of secretions in the airways of the lung. There may be anatomical birth defects in the lung, such as cysts or softening of the airways, which can begin the cycle of obstruction, infection, and bronchiectasis. Immune deficiencies cause bronchiectasis due to recurrent infections.

In the US, where immunizations and antibiotics are readily available, bronchiectasis is uncommon except in older individuals, occurring in about 1 in 10,000 individuals. Incidence has declined over the past 20-30 years, associated with increased use of vaccines and antibiotics. In Native Americans in Alaska, there is a 4-fold higher incidence than in the general population. It is a major cause of morbidity in less-developed countries.

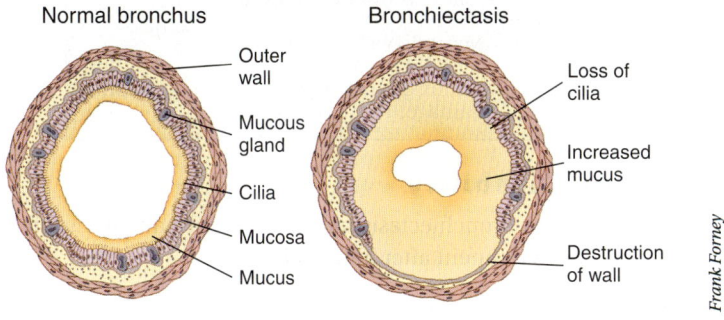

Diagnosis

History: The individual complains of cough, productive of variable amounts of mucus (sputum). The sputum is yellow-green and/or blood streaked. Cough and sputum production are increased at night. Wheezing is common. Cough may worsen when the individual lies on one side. There is a history of shortness of breath, which gets worse with exercise. With long-standing bronchiectasis, there may be loss of appetite, weight loss, fatigue, and frequent sinus infections. In the variant called "dry bronchiectasis," there is cough but only minimal sputum production. The skin or muscle may be enlarged around the fingernails (clubbing). The individual may complain of sensations of feeling the heart beat (palpitations).

Physical exam: The exam may reveal abnormal breath sounds indicating retained secretions in the lung. Wheezes may be heard. The skin may be discolored and bluish (cyanotic). The individual may be pale and may have a foul breath odor. The ankles, feet, and legs may be swollen. Heartbeat may be irregular.

Tests: Although the chest x-ray usually reveals markings in the lung indicative of bronchiectasis, chest x-ray can be normal early in the course. A computerized tomographic (CT) scan is a more accurate diagnostic method. Other tests include sputum culture and pulmonary function tests. An instrumental examination of the bronchial path (bronchoscopy) may be done for localized disease in which a foreign object or tumor is suspected. It is important to diagnose the underlying predisposing factors that lead to the bronchiectasis. A complete blood count (CBC) may reveal anemia. Pulmonary function testing including arterial blood gas helps document severity of lung and respiratory dysfunction. An immunoglobulin test may reveal an immunodeficiency.

Treatment

The goal of therapy is to improve symptoms, reduce complications, control exacerbations, and reduce morbidity and mortality. Early recognition is essential in bronchiectasis, and management of underlying conditions is essential to overall treatment. Treatment consists of antibiotic therapy. The choice of antibiotic is guided by microscopic examination of the sputum (Gram stain) and sputum culture. Physical therapy (chest percussion and postural drainage) is done to encourage drainage of secretions from the lung. Additional treatment can include bronchodilators, agents to loosen lung secretions (mucolytics), smoking cessation, supplemental oxygen, and vaccination against influenza and pneumococcal pneumonia. Anti-inflammatory medications including steroids may be helpful, especially in bronchiectasis related to cystic fibrosis or aspergillosis.

Surgical removal of the diseased part of the lung (pneumonectomy) is considered if the individual is unresponsive to medical therapy, is well localized, and is limited to one lung or less. On occasion, individuals with end-stage bronchiectasis may be considered for lung transplantation. Single and double lung transplantation has been used as treatment for severe bronchiectasis, predominantly when related to cystic fibrosis. In general, individuals with cystic fibrosis and bronchiectasis should be considered for lung transplant when forced expiratory volume in 1 second (FEV1) falls below 30% of predicted. Lung transplantation in females and younger individuals may need to be considered even sooner.

Treatment is also needed for the underlying cause of bronchiectasis, such as cystic fibrosis, an inherited disorder characterized by recurrent sinopulmonary infections in sinuses and airways (immotile cilia syndrome), foreign body aspiration, allergic bronchopulmonary aspergillosis (a disease characterized by colonization of the airways by a fungus, aspergillus, in an allergic asthmatic), or congenital absence or low levels of gamma globulin (hypogammaglobulinemia).

Prognosis

Overall the prognosis is good, but varies with the underlying disease or predisposing condition, as well as with the amount of lung tissue destroyed. The expected outcome gets worse with multiple successive pulmonary infections. Individuals who have had bronchiectasis from childhood usually have a shortened life expectancy. In general, individuals do well if they are compliant with all treatment regimens and practice routine preventive medical strategies. Lung transplantations have a reasonable chance of success provided the individual makes healthy lifestyle changes.

Differential Diagnosis

Other lung diseases with some similarities to bronchiectasis are pneumonia, chronic or acute bronchitis, loss of lung volume (atelectasis), and asthma. Cystic fibrosis may present with similar signs and symptoms.

Specialists

- Infectious Disease Physician
- Pulmonologist
- Thoracic Surgeon

Work Restrictions / Accommodations

In localized, early stage bronchiectasis, there may be no need for restriction of workload. If more severe lung damage has occurred, significant restriction of physical workload may be needed. In both instances, it is wise to wear proper respiratory protection and to avoid irritating dusts and gases.

Comorbid Conditions

Pre-existing asthma and allergies may worsen the effects of bronchiectasis, as does smoking. Cystic fibrosis increases the risk of bronchiectasis, and carries with it significant disability. Recurrent pulmonary infections adversely affect duration of disability.

Complications

The most common complication is pulmonary infection. If severe, pulmonary infection can lead to respiratory failure. Chronic infections can create a strain on the right side of the heart, causing enlargement of the right ventricle of the heart (cor pulmonale). Other complications are lung abscess, pus in a body cavity (empyema), bronchopleural fistula, and pneumothorax, all of which are more common in individuals with onset of bronchiectasis early in life.

Factors Influencing Duration

Disability is affected by any underlying medical conditions, age at onset of disease, current age, presence and type of infections, and individual compliance with treatment plans.

Complementary and Alternative Therapies

Content is intended for awareness only. Treatments may or may not be effective. Scientific evidence may be lacking and some substances have potentially toxic effects. Dr. Presley Reed and the editors do not endorse the use of these therapies in the absence of consultation with a licensed medical professional.

Vitamin C -	May reduce risk of bronchitis and wheezing and improve lung capacity.
Beta-carotene -	Antioxidant that may shield lungs against damage.
Cayenne pepper -	May help break up bronchial secretions.
Conchgrass -	May relieve bronchitis.
Echinacea -	Said to boost immune system function.
English plantain -	May act as a cough suppressant and an antibacterial and relieve bronchitis.
Eucalyptus oil -	May help loosen mucus when applied to chest.
Garlic -	May prevent bronchitis.
Horehound -	May relieve bronchial symptoms.
Knotgrass -	May relieve bronchial symptoms.
Magnesium -	May decrease risk of respiratory diseases.
Marsh mallow -	May relieve bronchial symptoms and bronchitis. May have an anti-inflammatory effect.
Mullein -	Said to act as an expectorant and antibacterial.
Primrose -	May act as an expectorant.
Selenium -	Antioxidant that may shield lung against damage.
Soapwort -	Contains saponins with anti-inflammatory properties, which may relieve bronchial symptoms.
Stinging nettle -	May relieve bronchitis.
Vitamin E -	Antioxidant that may shield lung against damage.

Length of Disability

Lifelong existence of bronchiectasis may lead to permanent disability. Disability may be permanent after lung excision.

Medical treatment of acute exacerbation.

Duration in Days

Job Classification	Minimum	Optimum	Maximum
Sedentary work	7	14	28
Light work	7	14	28
Medium work	7	14	28
Heavy work	7	21	28
Very Heavy work	7	21	28

Lung excision, partial (lobectomy).

Duration in Days

Job Classification	Minimum	Optimum	Maximum
Sedentary work	21	28	56
Light work	21	28	56
Medium work	28	42	70
Heavy work	42	56	84
Very Heavy work	42	Indefinite	Indefinite

Failure to Recover

If an individual fails to recover within the maximum duration expectancy period, the reader may wish to reference the following questions to assist in better understanding the specifics of an individual's medical case.

Regarding diagnosis:

- Has the individual had a history of repeated bronchial or lung infections or inflammation?
- Did the individual experience symptoms of a productive cough, purulent sputum, hemoptysis, dyspnea or wheezing?
- Did the physical exam reveal abnormal breath sounds, tachypnea, pale skin or cyanosis, and leg edema?
- Were diagnostic x-rays (chest x-ray or CT scan) done to confirm the diagnosis?
- Was the severity of the disease determined with additional tests such as pulmonary functions studies and/or arterial blood gases?
- Were other lung conditions (atelectasis, asthma, pneumonia, cystic fibrosis) ruled out?

Regarding treatment:

- Was the individual responsive to standard medical interventions such as oxygen and respiratory therapy, administration of bronchodilators or anti-inflammatories?
- Was the individual instructed to avoid bronchial irritants such as tobacco smoke?
- Did the individual receive prophylactic vaccination for influenza and pneumococcal pneumonia?
- Has the individual been compliant with the treatment regimen?
- Would the individual benefit from a smoking cessation program?
- Was surgical intervention indicated?

Regarding prognosis:

- Were appropriate work accommodations (reduced physical workload, protection from respiratory irritants) made to allow the individual to return to work safely?
- Based on the individual's clinical condition and treatment required, what was the expected outcome?
- Does the individual have a history of recurrent pulmonary infections or other underlying pulmonary disease that may impact recovery and prognosis?
- Did the individual suffer any associated complications such as cor pulmonale, lung abscesses, fistula or pneumothorax that could impact recovery and prognosis?

References

"Bronchiectasis." Adam.com. 2000. 05 Dec 2000 <http://medlineplus.adam.com/ency/article/000144.htm>.

Duke, James A. The Green Pharmacy. Emmaus, PA: Rodale Press, Inc, 1997.

Feinstein, Alice, ed. Healing with Vitamins. Emmaus, PA: Rodale Press, Inc, 1996.

Gompertz, S., et al. "Relationship Between Airway Inflammation and the Frequency of Exacerbations in Patients with Smoking Related COPD." Thorax 56 1 (2001): 36-41.

Gottlieb, Bill, ed. New Choices in Natural Healing. Emmaus, PA: Rodale Press, Inc, 1997.

Meyer, Keith C., MD. Pathogenesis, Diagnosis, and Treatment of Bronchiectasis. American College of Chest Physicians 29 Dec 2000. 22 Feb 2001 <http://www.chestnet.org/education/pccu/vol13/lesson21.html>.

Bronchitis, Acute

Other names / synonyms: Bronchitis, Bronchitis with Bronchospasm or Obstruction, Exudative Bronchitis, Membranous Bronchitis, Purulent Bronchitis, Septic Bronchitis

466, 466.0, 506.0

Definition

Acute bronchitis is an inflammation of the mucous membranes lining the air passages of the lungs (bronchi). Both large and small airways can be involved, with swelling and fluid leakage. The condition is acute and limited in duration.

The most common risk factor for developing acute bronchitis is a recent viral upper respiratory infection such as the common cold (caused by a rhinovirus). The viral infection produces bronchial inflammation, which in turn can cause bronchitis and secondary bacterial infection. Environmental factors such as gases, fumes, chemicals, dust, and smoke may also contribute to the development of acute bronchitis. These irritants may cause or prolong an episode of acute bronchitis.

On an annual basis, acute bronchitis occurs in 4 out of 100 individuals. Acute bronchitis occurs in individuals of all ages and occupations, and occurs with about equal frequency in men and women. However, the chances of contracting acute bronchitis are increased in smokers, the aged, the chronically ill, those with decreased immunity, and those who are occupationally exposed to respiratory irritants and do not wear respiratory protection.

Diagnosis

History: The individual may report a frequent cough, with or without production of sputum. The sputum might be reported as yellow or green. The individual may also complain of mild fever, loss of appetite, difficulty breathing, wheezing, malaise, and difficulty sleeping due to fits of coughing. The individual may report a recent history of head cold, sinus infection, or heavy exposure to an allergen or irritant.

Physical exam: The exam of the chest usually reveals course breath sounds. Wheezing might also be present.

Tests: There are no specific tests used to diagnose acute bronchitis. However, a chest x-ray may be performed to rule out pneumonia. A sputum culture may be done to determine if the inflammation is caused by a bacteria. If shortness of breath or wheezing is reported, additional tests to measure airway obstruction (spirometry) may be done to check for other lung problems.

Treatment

The goal of treatment is to relieve symptoms. Medications may include bronchodilators, which open up the bronchial passages. An expectorant may be recommended to help liquefy the mucus secretions, and may be supplemented with a cough suppressant. An antipyretic may be recommended for fever reduction. Because acute bronchitis is caused by a virus, antibiotics are not indicated. However, if a secondary bacterial infection has developed, as may be indicated by yellow or green sputum, antibiotics may also be prescribed. If the acute bronchitis is environmentally induced, the individual must first be removed from that environment, and the causative agent needs to be identified. The agent is either removed from the environment or the individual is provided respiratory protection from the agent.

Supportive treatment measures include rest, use of a cool mist vaporizer to soothe air passages, and increased fluid intake to maintain hydration and thin secretions. Smokers are advised to quit or at least refrain from smoking until the infection is cured.

Prognosis

The prognosis for the individual with uncomplicated acute bronchitis is excellent. The course of the disease is generally 3 to 5 days of acute symptoms with a gradual recovery over the next 7 to 10 days. If a bacterial infection is present, recovery time may be longer. It is not unusual for the cough to remain as much as 1 week after other symptoms have subsided and the individual has returned to work.

Environmentally induced acute bronchitis is often cured as soon as the offending toxin or allergen is removed from the individual's surroundings.

Differential Diagnosis

Other conditions that may present in a manner similar to acute bronchitis are pneumonia, chronic bronchitis, asthma, chronic obstructive pulmonary disease, emphysema, acute sinusitis, aspiration, bacterial tracheitis, bronchiectasis, cystic fibrosis, influenza, and reactive airway disease.

Specialists

- Internist
- Pulmonologist

Work Restrictions / Accommodations

It is important to avoid smoke, fumes, dust, and any other irritant that could be inhaled while recovering from acute bronchitis. Proper ventilation, masks, or respirators may be in order. The inhalation of extremely hot or extremely cold air can also trigger recurrence of coughing and wheezing. If an individual has had shortness of breath with the bronchitis, a temporary reduction of the job's physical demands may be needed.

Comorbid Conditions

Comorbid conditions that may influence length of disability include asthma, chronic obstructive pulmonary disease and other lung disorders, and any condition that weakens the individual's immune response (e.g., AIDS).

Complications

Bronchitis can progress to pneumonia and respiratory failure in the elderly, in those with chronic lung disease and/or other medical conditions, and those with decreased immunity. Less than 5% of individuals with acute bronchitis develop pneumonia.

Factors Influencing Duration

The length of time it takes for an individual to return to work is influenced by the severity of the symptoms, the individual's age, general health, pre-existing chronic medical illness (especially lung disease), cigarette smoking, and the presence of complications.

Length of Disability

Duration will be influenced by lung congestion from other conditions and whether or not the individual is a smoker.

Duration in Days

Job Classification	Minimum	Optimum	Maximum
Sedentary work	1	5	10
Light work	1	5	10
Medium work	1	5	10
Heavy work	1	7	10
Very Heavy work	1	7	10

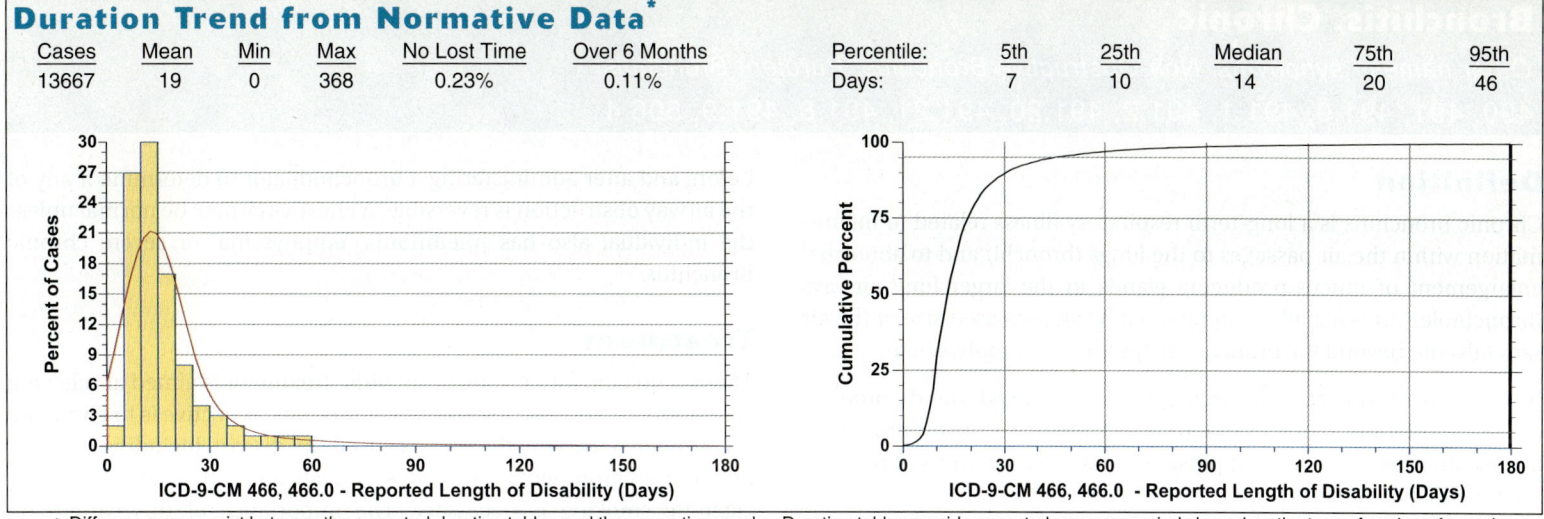

Duration Trend from Normative Data*

Cases	Mean	Min	Max	No Lost Time	Over 6 Months
13667	19	0	368	0.23%	0.11%

Percentile:	5th	25th	Median	75th	95th
Days:	7	10	14	20	46

* Differences may exist between the expected duration tables and the normative graphs. Duration tables provide expected recovery periods based on the type of work performed by the individual. The normative graphs reflect the actual observed experience of many individuals across the spectrum of physical conditions, in a variety of industries, and with varying levels of case management.

Failure to Recover

If an individual fails to recover within the maximum duration expectancy period, the reader may wish to reference the following questions to assist in better understanding the specifics of an individual's medical case.

Regarding diagnosis:

- Did the individual present with a clinical history and symptoms consistent with the diagnosis of acute bronchitis?
- Did the physical exam reveal abnormal breath sounds?
- If the diagnosis was uncertain, were additional diagnostic tests performed to rule out other conditions with similar symptoms?

Regarding treatment:

- Was the treatment appropriate for the symptoms manifested?
- Was the individual compliant with treatment recommendations (such as rest, smoking cessation, avoidance of other bronchial irritants)? If not, were there barriers that interfered with compliance (such as lack of understanding, lack of motivation)?

Regarding prognosis:

- Did adequate time elapse for full recovery?
- Did the individual have any comorbid conditions that may have influenced length of disability?
- Did the individual develop any complications that may have influenced prognosis?

References

Acute bronchitis. American Academy of Family Physicians. 1 Jan 2000. 01 Jan 2001 <http://familydoctor.org/handouts/229.html>.

Bronchitis, Chronic

Other names / synonyms: Non-Obstructive Bronchitis, Purulent Bronchitis

490, 491, 491.0, 491.1, 491.2, 491.20, 491.21, 491.8, 491.9, 506.4

Definition

Chronic bronchitis is a long-term respiratory illness related to inflammation within the air passages to the lungs (bronchi) and to abnormal enlargement of mucus-producing glands in the larger lung airways (bronchioles). It is usually accompanied by an increased size of the air sacs (alveoli) beyond the bronchioles (pulmonary emphysema).

In individuals with chronic bronchitis, the enlarged glands produce excessive amounts of mucus that triggers coughing. Chronic bronchitis is officially diagnosed when it persists for at least 3 months of the year for 2 consecutive years.

In addition to the basic diagnosis of chronic bronchitis, some doctors further subdivide this illness into more specific subtypes. If the cough produces thin and clear mucus, then the condition is called simple chronic bronchitis, but if the mucus is thick and discolored, it becomes chronic mucopurulent (mucus with pus present) bronchitis. If an individual develops significant airway obstruction in addition to the chronic cough, the condition is termed chronic bronchitis with obstruction. If episodes of asthmatic symptoms (wheezing and shortness of breath) occur, it is called chronic asthmatic bronchitis.

Risk factors for chronic bronchitis include tobacco smoking, air pollution, and working where exposure to airborne organic dusts or toxic gases occurs. This is especially prevalent in cotton mills and plastic manufacturing plants. Other risk factors include a history of frequent upper respiratory illnesses, infections, or allergies; pneumonia during childhood; a nonsmoker who shares living space with a smoker (exposure to second-hand smoke); or having an identical twin with chronic bronchitis. Among smokers, the severity of the disease relates to the amount and duration of smoking.

Bronchitis is nearly always self-limited in the otherwise healthy individual although it frequently results in absenteeism from work.

Currently, some form of chronic bronchitis affects about 3% of the American population, most commonly among males over age 40. Chronic bronchitis, emphysema, and asthma as a group of conditions are the fifth leading cause of death in the US.

Diagnosis

History: The individual may report a cough producing sputum that may or may not contain some blood on most days. An occupational history is important in determining if specific irritants play a role.

Physical exam: The individual's respiratory rate and chest expansion may appear normal in early simple bronchitis. The individual with chronic obstructive bronchitis may have an increased respiratory rate, labored respirations, barrel-shaped chest, and bluish color to the skin (cyanosis). Listening to the chest likely reveals coarse sounds (rhonchi) that clear with coughing and possibly wheezing or other abnormal breath sounds (rales).

Tests: The type and severity of chronic bronchitis is determined by pulmonary function testing. This may include simple airflow (spirometry), blood oxygen saturation (pulse oximetry), lung volume, and arterial blood gas measurements. The testing can be done both before and after administering a bronchodilator to determine if any of the airway obstruction is reversible. A chest x-ray may be normal unless the individual also has pneumonia, emphysema, or severe chronic bronchitis.

Treatment

There is no cure for chronic bronchitis. Treatment is aimed at relieving symptoms and preventing complications. First objective is to eliminate the bronchial irritants that have caused the disease including occupational or environmental exposures to dusts and fumes. Discontinuing cigarette smoking is necessary. The importance of this cannot be overemphasized. Using a humidifier, deep breathing, and effective coughing exercises and occasionally postural drainage and striking the back with short, sharp blows (percussion) can also help facilitate removal of thick mucus from airways and prevent the pooling of secretions that leads to infections.

Individuals with an asthmatic component to their chronic bronchitis are given bronchodilators. If the asthmatic component is severe, steroids may be used to break the cycle of airway reactivity. Antibiotics are given during an acute episode of bronchitis when sputum normally white in color changes to yellow or green. Individuals with long-standing chronic obstructive bronchitis and declining lung function may benefit from supplemental oxygen therapy.

Immunization against pneumococcal pneumonia and influenza is recommended for individuals with chronic bronchitis because of the increased risk of complications and prolonged recovery time if acute respiratory diseases develop.

Prognosis

Early recognition and treatment of chronic bronchitis combined with smoking cessation significantly improves the chances of a good outcome.

Individuals with chronic obstructive bronchitis usually become permanently disabled at some point even with treatment and smoking cessation. The frequency of complications including shortness of breath, declining lung function, and airflow obstruction gradually worsens. Ultimately individuals who are severely incapacitated may need a lung transplant. If a smoker with chronic bronchitis kicks the habit, even those with severe symptoms can slow the progression of lung deterioration.

Differential Diagnosis

Other diagnoses with similarities to chronic bronchitis are asthma, emphysema, acute bronchitis, bronchiectasis, acute sinusitis, cystic fibrosis, influenza, and pneumonia. Tuberculosis, lung cancer, pulmonary embolism, and the AIDS-related complex may also present with similar signs and symptoms.

Specialists

- Pulmonologist

Work Restrictions / Accommodations

Reduction of airway irritants in the environment and/or the use of respiratory protective masks can help reduce time lost from work. Avoiding very cold or hot air temperatures can also be helpful. Individuals with long-standing chronic bronchitis may have reduced capacity for physical work and any such duties may need to be temporarily or permanently restricted. Individuals who require supplemental oxygen at work may present a hazard in the workplace.

Comorbid Conditions

Underlying lung disease such as industrial dust disease may lengthen disability. Severe cases occasionally produce deterioration in those with significant underlying cardiopulmonary disease and weakened immune systems. A simple cold may easily progress to acute bronchitis or pneumonia.

Complications

The most common complication of chronic bronchitis is an episode of acute bronchitis, pneumonia, or emphysema. Chronic bronchitis compromises the defense mechanisms of the lung so infections that develop may be either mild or severe enough to require hospitalization. The most debilitating complications are right heart failure (cor pulmonale) and respiratory failure. An acute infection usually precedes an episode of respiratory failure.

Sometimes bronchial secretions collect in the lungs and thicken. If the individual cannot cough up these thick secretions, they may totally obstruct the flow of air into a part of the lung. The lung tissue behind the obstruction will then collapse (atelectasis).

Factors Influencing Duration

The severity of the disease, any complications, age, other underlying medical conditions, and compliance with the prescribed treatment can all influence disability.

Chronic bronchitis symptoms worsen when atmospheric concentrations of sulfur dioxide and other air pollutants (smog) increase. These symptoms are intensified when individuals also smoke. Any superimposed acute respiratory illness and exposure to colds and influenza either at home or in public can increase the period of disability. Surgery or any other physical stress can worsen symptoms.

Length of Disability

Disability is more likely to occur with acute exacerbations. Duration will be influenced by lung congestion from other conditions and whether or not the individual is a smoker. Disability may be permanent for individuals who work around respiratory irritants such as second-hand smoke, dust, pollens, and industrial or other air pollutants.

Acute exacerbations.

Duration in Days

Job Classification	Minimum	Optimum	Maximum
Any work	7	14	21

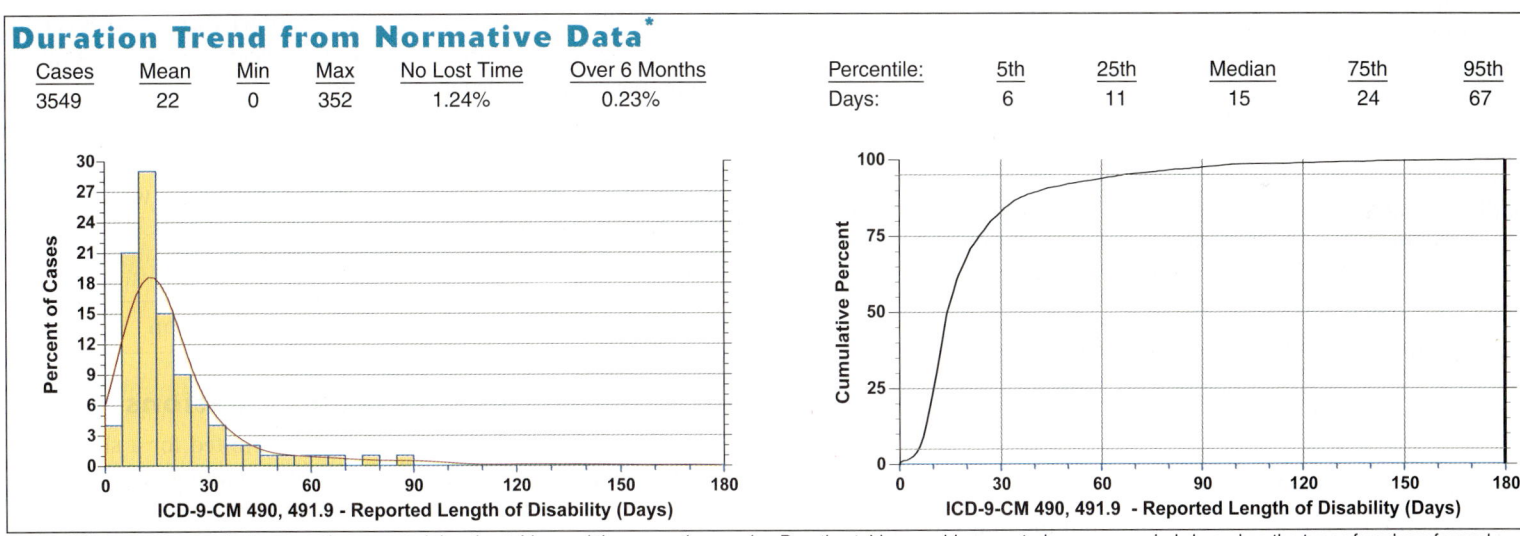

Duration Trend from Normative Data*

Cases	Mean	Min	Max	No Lost Time	Over 6 Months
3549	22	0	352	1.24%	0.23%

Percentile:	5th	25th	Median	75th	95th
Days:	6	11	15	24	67

ICD-9-CM 490, 491.9 - Reported Length of Disability (Days)

* Differences may exist between the expected duration tables and the normative graphs. Duration tables provide expected recovery periods based on the type of work performed by the individual. The normative graphs reflect the actual observed experience of many individuals across the spectrum of physical conditions, in a variety of industries, and with varying levels of case management.

Failure to Recover

If an individual fails to recover within the maximum duration expectancy period, the reader may wish to reference the following questions to assist in better understanding the specifics of an individual's medical case.

Regarding diagnosis:

- Does individual meet the chronic bronchitis criteria of having a persistent cough for at least 3 months a year for 2 years?

- Was lung condition evaluated through spirometry, pulse oximetry, lung volume and arterial blood gas measurements?
- Were conditions with similar symptoms ruled out?
- Does bronchitis have an asthmatic component?

Regarding treatment:

- Were bronchial irritants removed from the environment?

Bronchitis, Chronic 303

- Has individual quit smoking cigarettes? If unable to quit on his/her own, would individual benefit from enrollment in a community stop-smoking program?
- Is individual using a humidifier?
- Does individual participate in a home respiratory care program?
- If individual has an asthmatic component to chronic bronchitis, were steroids used effectively to break the cycle of airway reactivity?

Regarding prognosis:

- Does individual have an underlying lung or cardiopulmonary disease that may impact recovery?

- Have any complications occurred as a result of the bronchitis?
- Is individual a smoker or former smoker?
- Is individual exposed to second-hand smoke? What can be done to limit or eliminate exposure?
- Has individual had any occupational exposure to airborne organic dusts or toxic gases? What can be done to prevent further exposure?
- Does individual live where smog is a problem?

References

Chronic Bronchitis. American Lung Association. 2001. 21 Feb 2001 <http://www.lungusa.org/diseases/lungchronic.html>.

Chronic Obstructive Pulmonary Disease. InteliHealth Inc. 08 Feb 2001. 21 Feb 2001 <http://www.intelihealth.com/IH/ihtIH?t=9635&p=~br,IHW|~st,24479|~r,WSIHW000|~b,*|>.

Kleinschmidt, Paul MD. "Chronic Obstructive Pulmonary Disease and Emphysema." eMedicine.com 24 Jan 2001. 21 Feb 2001 <http://www.emedicine.com/emerg/topic99.htm>.

Staton, Gerald W. Jr., and Roland H. Ingram, Jr., MD. "Section 14. Chapter III. Chronic Obstructive Diseases of the Lung." Scientific American® Medicine Online Dale, D.C., and D.D. Federman New York: WebMD Corporation, 2000 Scientific American Medicine. 05 Dec 2000 <http://www.samed.com/sam/forms/index/htm>.

Bronchoscopic Biopsy

Other names / synonyms: Bronchial Biopsy, Bronchus Biopsy, Brush Biopsy, Endoscopic (Closed) Biopsy, Washing Biopsy

33.24

Definition

Bronchial biopsy is the removal of small tissue samples of the main airways of the lungs (bronchi) or alveolar tissue (transbronchoscopic biopsy) for analysis by use of a scope (bronchoscope).

Individuals with a history of smoking or exposure to harmful chemicals (e.g., asbestos, silicates), those who have lung disease (e.g., asthma, cystic fibrosis), and the elderly are at a higher risk of developing a lung condition that would necessitate a bronchial biopsy. This is usually done for detecting and diagnosing lung cancer (bronchial biopsy) or foreign bodies, or for diagnosing and determining causation in certain types of interstitial lung diseases.

Approximately half a million bronchoscopies are performed in the US each year. Often, these bronchoscopies involve removal of tissue samples.

Reason for Procedure

This procedure is used to obtain tissue from the lungs for laboratory evaluation of inflammation, infections, tumors, pneumonia, and any other lung disease or condition.

Description

Bronchial biopsy is usually an outpatient procedure. An intravenous line may be established. Vital signs, electrocardiogram (ECG) tracings, and blood oxygen saturation are checked throughout the procedure. The individual is sedated and the upper airways are numbed using a local anesthetic. The fiberoptic scope (bronchoscope) is inserted through a nostril or the mouth, past the voice box (larynx), through the windpipe (trachea), and into a bronchus. In addition, local anesthetic may be applied through the bronchoscope to the air passages to suppress cough. The lung passages are viewed on a monitor. Instruments such as forceps, brushes, small cutting devices, or needles can be passed through to the bronchoscope to collect the tissue samples. Multiple specimens are usually obtained.

Prognosis

Bronchial biopsy is a routine procedure that is generally well tolerated and rarely causes complications.

Specialists

- Pulmonologist
- Thoracic Surgeon

Work Restrictions / Accommodations

The vocal capacity of the individual may be limited for a short time following this procedure. Individuals whose job duties require use of their voice may need to be temporarily reassigned.

Comorbid Conditions

Asthma, AIDS, bleeding disorders (e.g., hemophilia), or chronic obstructive pulmonary disease may influence the length of disability.

Procedure Complications

Complications are rare but include cardiac arrhythmia, drug reactions, bleeding (hemorrhage), air accumulation in the membranes surrounding the lungs (pneumothorax), pneumonia, or worsening of lung disease.

Factors Influencing Duration

The overall health of the individual and the development of complications would influence the length of disability.

Length of Disability

Disability is not expected from this procedure. Duration depends on type of anesthesia (local or general); may be longer due to biopsy complications.

Duration in Days

Job Classification	Minimum	Optimum	Maximum
Any work	1	1	1

References

Thompson, Austin, and Stephen Rennard. "Diagnostic Procedures Not Involving the Pleura." *Textbook of Pulmonary Diseases.* Baum, Gerald, et al., eds. Philadelphia: Lippincott-Raven, 1998. 239-253.

Weinberger, Steven. "Evaluation of the Patient with Pulmonary Disease." *Principles of Pulmonary Medicine.* Weinberger, Steven, ed. Philadelphia: W.B. Saunders Company, 1998. 30-63.

Bronchoscopy

Other names / synonyms: Endoscopic Examination of the Bronchi

33.22

Definition

Bronchoscopy is the examination or treatment of the main airways of the lungs (bronchi) by means of a fiberoptic scope (bronchoscope). Bronchoscopies are primarily performed to evaluate the pathway of the airways (e.g., is obstruction present due to mucus, tumors, foreign bodies, etc.) or to obtain specimens (biopsy, infectious agents, analysis after lavage).

Approximately half a million bronchoscopies are performed in the US each year.

Reason for Procedure

Bronchoscopy is used in the diagnosis and treatment of lung disorders. In addition to inspecting the bronchi for abnormalities and disease, bronchoscopy can be used to collect mucus samples, obtain cells from distant airways, or to take small samples of lung tissue (bronchial biopsy) for microscopic analysis. Bronchoscopy can be used to remove foreign objects or to remove thick mucus secretions. Abnormal growths can be destroyed or damaged blood vessels sealed off by means of laser (laser cauterization), heat (heat cauterization, diathermy), or freezing (cryocauterization) performed using attachments on the bronchoscope.

Description

Bronchoscopy is usually an outpatient procedure. An intravenous line may be established. Vital signs, electrocardiogram (ECG) tracings, and blood oxygen saturation are checked throughout the procedure. The individual is sedated and the upper airways are numbed using a local anesthetic. In addition, local anesthetic may be applied through the bronchoscope to the air passages to suppress cough. The bronchoscope is inserted through a nostril or the mouth, past the voice box (larynx), through the windpipe (trachea), and into a bronchus. The lung passages are viewed on a monitor. Instruments can be inserted through the bronchoscope, including forceps, small cutting devices, brushes, needles, tiny tubes (catheters), and devices for performing cauterization. The bronchoscope can also be used in conjunction with an x-ray examination of the bronchi (bronchography).

Prognosis

In most cases, bronchoscopy is an effective tool in the diagnosis and treatment of lung disorders. Bronchoscopy is a routine procedure that is generally well tolerated and rarely causes complications.

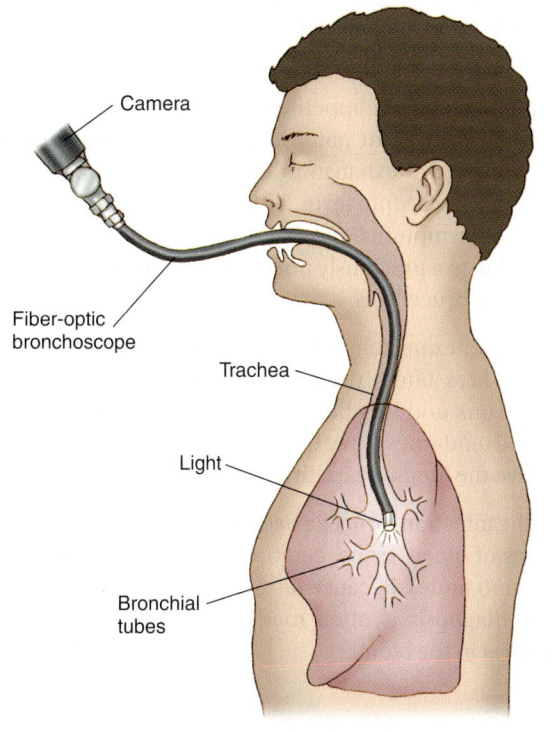

Frank Forney

Specialists

- Pulmonologist
- Thoracic Surgeon

Work Restrictions / Accommodations

The vocal capacity of the individual may be limited for a short time following this procedure. Individuals whose job duties require use of their voice may need to be temporarily reassigned.

Comorbid Conditions

Asthma, AIDS, bleeding disorders (e.g., hemophilia), smoking, chronic obstructive pulmonary disease, or any other lung diseases or conditions may influence the length of disability. The underlying cause for which the procedure was performed can significantly influence the length of disability.

Procedure Complications

Complications are rare but include cardiac arrhythmia, drug reactions, bleeding (hemorrhage), air accumulation in the membranes surrounding the lungs (pneumothorax), pneumonia, or worsening of lung disease.

Factors Influencing Duration

No disability is expected in most cases unless the individual had complications. The length of disability may be influenced by the underlying cause for which the procedure was done, type of treatment done, and the development of complications. Duration depends on type of anesthesia (local or general); may be longer if biopsy is done.

Length of Disability

Duration in Days

Job Classification	Minimum	Optimum	Maximum
Any work	1	1	1

References

Thompson, Austin, and Stephen Rennard. "Diagnostic Procedures Not Involving the Pleura." Textbook of Pulmonary Diseases. Baum, Gerald, et al., eds. Philadelphia: Lippincott-Raven, 1998. 239-253.

Weinberger, Steven. "Evaluation of the Patient with Pulmonary Disease." Principles of Pulmonary Medicine. Weinberger, Steven, ed. Philadelphia: W.B. Saunders Company, 1998. 30-63.

Brucellosis
Other names / synonyms: Bang's Disease, Malta Fever, Mediterranean Fever, Undulant Fever
023, 023.0, 023.1, 023.2, 023.3, 023.8, 023.9

Definition

Brucellosis is a systemic, fever-producing infection caused by any of four species of brucella bacteria: B. abortus, B. melitensis, B. suis, and B. canis. It is transmitted to humans from animals particularly by cattle, pigs, goats, and sheep. The bacteria can be passed when a break in the skin comes into direct contact with contaminated animal products (i.e., tissue, blood, or urine) or by consuming raw unpasteurized milk or contaminated dairy products. The bacteria can also be spread through the air and inhaled by individuals working in animal pens or stables, or in laboratories where the bacteria are grown.

Brucellosis is considered an occupational disease among animal workers. It occurs more often in men than women. The disease is found worldwide particularly in the Mediterranean, north and east Africa, the Middle East, India, central Asia, Mexico, and Central and South America. In the US, most cases are in the rural Midwest or in individuals who recently traveled abroad in an endemic area. On a worldwide basis, the disease is often unreported. In the US, less than 120 cases are reported each year.

Diagnosis

History: The disease can come on slowly (insidious) with headache, neck pain, and a mild sick feeling, or can start suddenly with chills, severe headache, weakness, and occasional diarrhea. Fever is the predominant symptom, and may be ongoing or follow a pattern of normal temperature in the morning accompanied by profuse sweating then a return of fever by evening. The fever usually lasts 1 to 5 days and is followed by a 2- to 14-day period with diminished or no symptoms (remission). The fever then returns after this period.

Symptoms may now include appetite loss, weight loss, severe constipation, abdominal pain, joint pain, insomnia, irritability, depression, emotional instability, and exhaustion after minimal activity. Although brucellosis can take a chronic form with periods of illness alternating with periods of no symptoms, persistent illness lasting longer than 2 months may be due to a previously unsuspected underlying disease or a complication of the brucellosis.

Physical exam: The exam may reveal enlarged lymph nodes and an enlarged spleen. Less often, the liver may be enlarged. A rash may develop on the trunk and legs but not the face. Joints may be swollen and tender. Spine tenderness may be noted. On rare occurrences, infections may involve the lungs, heart, brain, or liver.

Tests: Early in the infection, brucella bacteria can be identified in microbiologic cultures of blood, urine, cerebrospinal fluid, or tissue such as found in the lymph nodes. Because results from these cultures can take up to 4 weeks, diagnosis is often made on rising levels of brucella-specific antibodies in the blood.

306   The Medical Disability Advisor—Fourth Edition

Treatment

Instead of using any single drug, brucellosis is treated by using a combination of antibacterial drugs (antibiotics) taken over a 6-week period. Seriously ill individuals may need to take corticosteroids to suppress the immune system. Severe muscle pain may require a prescription pain reliever. Localized infection in the form of lesions may be a reservoir for bacteria untouched by drug therapy. These lesions may cause recurring infection and need to be drained in order to release harbored bacteria. Relapse can be as high as 50%. Approximately 5% of individuals may still have a relapse after treatment is completed. In these cases, treatment should be repeated.

Prognosis

With combination drug therapy, most individuals recover in 2 to 3 weeks. Even widespread infections may be cured. Untreated, however, the infection may progress and increase in severity and also affect new tissues. Although brucellosis can take a chronic form with periods of illness alternating with periods of no symptoms, persistent illness lasting longer than 2 months may be due to a previously unsuspected underlying disease or a complication of the brucellosis. With a mortality rate of less than 2%, the most likely cause of death is endocarditis caused by Brucella melitensis.

Differential Diagnosis

Similar acute, fever-producing illnesses include Q fever, influenza, mononucleosis, tularemia, and enteric fever. Chronic brucellosis may resemble Hodgkin disease, tuberculosis, HIV or AIDS infection, malaria, and disseminated fungal infections such as coccidioidomycosis and histoplasmosis.

Specialists

- Cardiologist
- Infectious Disease Physician
- Neurologist
- Orthopedist

Work Restrictions / Accommodations

Even with treatment, accommodations for periodic absences may be needed during relapses. Brucellosis is not spread between individuals, so interpersonal infection control measures are not required.

Comorbid Conditions

Pregnancy and renal insufficiency may limit the drugs or dosage used for treatment causing a delay in recovery.

Complications

The most frequent complications involve inflammation of the vertebrae (spondylitis), the heart (endocarditis), brain (meningoencephalitis), or the joints (arthritis). Less common complications include inflammation of the lungs (pneumonitis), liver (hepatitis), gallbladder (cholecystitis), the testes (orchitis), or the epididymis (epididymitis).

Factors Influencing Duration

Factors that might influence disability include the severity of symptoms, development of complications, effectiveness of drug therapy, and individual's compliance with the long treatment protocol. Infection of the heart, lungs, or central nervous system will require longer disability leaves than at the earlier stage of the disease.

Length of Disability

Duration in Days

Job Classification	Minimum	Optimum	Maximum
Any work	7	10	21

Failure to Recover

If an individual fails to recover within the maximum duration expectancy period, the reader may wish to reference the following questions to assist in better understanding the specifics of an individual's medical case.

Regarding diagnosis:

- Was diagnosis of brucellosis confirmed? Was diagnosis made on rising levels of brucella-specific antibodies in the blood, or through microbiologic cultures of blood, urine, cerebrospinal fluid, or tissue?
- Were conditions with similar symptoms been ruled out?
- Has individual experienced any complications related to the brucellosis?
- Does individual have a coexisting condition, such as pregnancy or renal insufficiency that may limit the drugs or dosage, complicate treatment, or impact recovery?

Regarding treatment:

- Is individual taking all medications as prescribed?
- If individual is unable to comply with treatment regimen, who else is available to administer medication?
- Because they may harbor bacteria, causing recurring infection, have localized infections been drained?
- If individual had a relapse of symptoms, was treatment repeated? With what results? Was initial infection ever completely resolved?

Regarding prognosis:

- Because drug therapy may take up to 6 weeks, did individual get tired of the prolonged treatment regimen and stop treatment? What can be done to enhance compliance?
- Have symptoms persisted despite treatment?
- Because illness lasting longer than 2 months may be due to a previously unsuspected underlying disease or a complication of the brucellosis, have underlying conditions been ruled out? Are more diagnostic tests warranted?
- Does diagnosis need to be revisited?
- Would individual benefit from evaluation by an infectious disease specialist?
- Is individual aware of the importance of seeking early treatment in the event of relapse?
- How is individual dealing with the psychological and emotional stress of the illness? Is individual realistic about illness?
- Would individual benefit from psychological counseling?

References

Chin, James. Control of Communicable Diseases, 17th ed. Washington, DC: American Public Health Association, 2000.

Liu, J.B., W.C. Zhou, and Q.Z. Wang. "Clinical and Experimental Studies of Supplemented Sini San in Treating Chronic Brucellosis." Chung Kuo Chung Hsi I Chieh Ho Tsa Chih 17 2 (1997): 470-472.

Buerger's Disease

Other names / synonyms: Thromboangiitis Obliterans
443, 443.1

Definition

Buerger's disease is a chronic condition in which acute inflammation occurs and blood clots (thromboses) form in the small- or medium-sized arteries of the hands, legs, and feet. The disease primarily affects medium-sized blood vessels.

Intense pain develops because of insufficient blood flow either during activities (claudication) or at rest because the thromboses formed in the lining of the arterial blood vessels decrease the blood flow. As they grow larger, blood flow may stop entirely and in the most serious cases, gangrene can develop.

Buerger's disease primarily affects heavy to moderate cigarette smokers but its exact cause is unknown. However, evidence suggests it may be the result of a genetically based hypersensitivity reaction to nicotine or that it may be caused by an autoimmune disorder where the body is tricked into attacking collagen, a blood vessel constituent.

The largest affected group is young men from age 20 to 40 who smoke heavily. Only approximately 5% of the cases occur in women. Buerger's disease is most common in Jewish men and is most prevalent in Asia, India, and the Middle East.

Diagnosis

History: Disease onset is gradual. Individuals may report tingling, numbness, burning, pain, inflammation, and swelling in the extremities and limbs (legs, feet, and hands) that may radiate to other more central areas of the body. These symptoms are aggravated by exercise and relieved with rest. Extremities exposed to cold may also appear bluish due to lack of oxygen (cyanotic). They may then turn red, become hot, and begin to tingle. Intermittent cramping usually occurs with exercise and may be reported in the affected extremity as a result of inadequate blood flow (claudication). In the later stages, other associated symptoms can include skin ulceration, muscle atrophy, and gangrene (especially in the fingers and toes).

Physical exam: The exam may reveal swelling (edema), ulcers, muscle atrophy, and gangrene in the digits. Color changes can be seen in the affected extremity due to diminished blood flow. New blood vessels (collateral circulation) may form around the clots and may be seen as twisted, superficial vessels. The pulse may be diminished or absent from the affected extremities and blood pressure may decrease.

Tests: The diagnosis can usually be made with an arteriogram of the upper and lower extremities. This reveals narrow (stenosis) or blocked (occluded) blood flow in multiple areas, vascular damage seen in the corkscrew appearance of the arteries, and evidence of developing collateral blood vessels.

Treatment

It is essential that individuals with Buerger's disease stop smoking immediately and completely. Secondary treatment focuses on preventing complications and providing relief from symptoms. Individuals are warned to avoid factors that could exacerbate problems that include trauma, exposure to extreme temperatures, and emotional stress. The individual must be instructed regarding proper foot care including correctly fitted shoes and cotton or wool socks, and regular inspection of the feet and hands for evidence of cuts, abrasions, redness, or sores (ulcers).

Antibiotics, corticosteroids, anticoagulants, and many vasodilators have proven ineffective against Buerger's disease. However, some success has occurred with pentoxifylline, calcium blockers, thromboxane inhibitors, prostaglandin E, and angiogenic growth factors. Bypass grafts are not generally appropriate because of the small size and large number of the vessels involved in the disorder.

Foot ulcers are generally treated with enforced bed rest and use of a specially designed padded footboard or bed cradle that eliminates pressure from bed linens. In severe cases where ulcers do not heal, gangrene develops accompanied by intractable pain. Amputation of the affected digit or limb may be necessary.

When ulcers, gangrene, and pain while at rest are resolved, the individual should begin to walk 15 to 30 minutes twice a day to help maintain circulation.

Prognosis

The outcome varies with the severity of the disease upon initial diagnosis, any underlying medical condition, and individual's level of compliance with the recommended treatment program. If the individual persists in smoking or cannot avoid breathing environmental (secondhand) smoke, the disease will progress and multiple limb amputations may result. If the condition is diagnosed early, a fair outcome including partial healing of the affected area and some restoration of blood flow can sometimes be achieved if the individual refrains from smoking.

Differential Diagnosis

Disorders with similar symptoms include muscle tears or cramps, a ruptured cyst, cellulitis, lymphangitis, functional peripheral vascular disorder, Raynaud's phenomenon, and occlusive arterial disease.

Specialists

- Cardiovascular Surgeon
- Orthopedic Surgeon
- Internist

Work Restrictions / Accommodations

The individual should not be exposed to environments where others are smoking. In extreme or acute cases, it may be necessary to minimize or eliminate strenuous physical activity. Individuals whose jobs require constant exposure to extreme cold temperatures may need to be reassigned.

Comorbid Conditions

Other conditions that impair circulation to the extremities may lengthen disability and include cardiovascular diseases, diabetes mellitus, trauma, or connective tissue disorders like scleroderma, rheumatoid arthritis, and systemic lupus erythematosus.

Complications

Possible complications include deep vein thrombosis, pulmonary embolism, venous stasis, limb ulceration, gangrene, and amputation.

Factors Influencing Duration

Factors that may influence length of disability include whether or not the individual continues to smoke, extent of tissue damage, treatment and progression of the acute stage, and development of complications.

The duration of disability also depends on whether the job is strenuous and/or stressful, whether it involves exposure to extremes of temperature, and whether secondhand smoke can be avoided

Length of Disability

If environmental factors are impossible to control within the context of the particular employment situation or the condition progresses to the extent that gangrene and amputation result, disability may be permanent.

Medical treatment.

Duration in Days

Job Classification	Minimum	Optimum	Maximum
Sedentary work	7	14	Indefinite
Light work	14	28	Indefinite
Medium work	28	42	Indefinite
Heavy work	42	56	Indefinite
Very Heavy work	42	56	Indefinite

Failure to Recover

If an individual fails to recover within the maximum duration expectancy period, the reader may wish to reference the following questions to assist in better understanding the specifics of an individual's medical case.

Regarding diagnosis:

- Has individual had intense pain in the hand, legs, or feet with activity?
- Does individual smoke? How much?
- What is individual's age? Ethnic background?
- Does individual have numbness, tingling, burning sensation, or pain in the hands, legs, or feet? Is there inflammation or swelling in the hands, legs, or feet? Do these radiate to other more central parts of the body?
- Has individual noticed that these extremities turn bluish when exposed to cold? Do they later turn red, become hot and tingle?
- Does individual have symptoms of advanced disease such as skin ulcerations, muscle atrophy, or gangrene?
- On physical exam, was edema, ulcers, muscle atrophy, or gangrene in the digits present?
- Were color changes seen in the affected extremity?
- Is there evidence of collateral circulation forming?
- Does individual have palpable pulses in the affected extremities?
- Has individual had an arteriogram?
- Were conditions with similar symptoms ruled out?

Regarding treatment:

- Has individual stopped smoking? Does individual avoid exposure to secondhand smoke, exposure to extreme temperatures, trauma, and emotional stress?
- Was individual instructed in proper foot care including wearing correctly fitted shoes and cotton or wool socks?
- Does individual regularly inspect the feet and hands for evidence of cuts, abrasions, redness, ulcers, or gangrene? Is this incorporated into daily hygiene routine?
- Was any medication helpful in treatment?
- Was amputation necessary?

Regarding prognosis:

- Can individual's employer accommodate any necessary restrictions?
- Does individual have any conditions that may affect recovery?
- Have any complications developed such as deep vein thrombosis, pulmonary embolism, venous stasis, limb ulceration, or gangrene?

References

"Buerger's Disease." The Johns Hopkins Vasculitis Center. 1998. 23 Jan 2001 <http://vasculitis.med.jhu.edu/buerger.htm>.

Jaff, M.R. "Thromboangiitis Obliterans (Buerger's Disease)." Current Treatment Options Cardiovascular Medicine 2 3 (2000): 205-212.

Bundle Branch Block

Other names / synonyms: Fascicular Block, Incomplete Bundle Branch Block, Intraventricular Conduction Disorder, LBBB, Left Bundle Branch Block, RBBB, Right Bundle Branch Block

426.2, 426.3, 426.4, 426.5

Definition

The term bundle branch block (BBB) refers to impaired transmission of electrical impulses through specialized conduction pathways (tissue) known as bundles. The bundles contain many small nerves, much like an electrical cord contains many fine wires. In the heart, the electrical impulses are the "messengers" that tell the two lower chambers (ventricles) to pump blood. If either of the two bundles is damaged, the transmission of the electrical impulses is blocked.

There are two bundles, one delivering electrical impulses to the left ventricle, the other to the right ventricle. Impaired conduction through each is termed left bundle branch block (LBBB) and right bundle branch block (RBBB), respectively. Although LBBB and RBBB separately produce no symptoms and are recognizable only by the electrocardiogram (ECG), their importance resides in their potential to occur simultaneously resulting in neither ventricle contracting (asystole).

RBBB is more common and less serious than LBBB. RBBB is present in 4% of routine ECGs. LBBB exists in 1% of ECGs. The causes of both include hardening of the arteries (atherosclerosis), high blood pressure (hypertension), enlargement (hypertrophy) of either ventricle, trauma, a variety of diseases in which normal heart muscle is replaced by abnormal tissue (i.e., amyloidosis, sarcoidosis and hemachromatosis), and scarring (fibrosis) of the bundles due to unknown (idiopathic) causes. LBBB may also be due to idiopathic fibrosis of the bundle branch.

The incidence of BBB is 0.6% of the total population. This value increases up to 2% after the age of 60. LBBB is not as common as RBBB but has been associated with heart disease and an increased mortality rate. Six percent of individuals with LBBB and an abnormal pattern of electrical activation of the heart (left axis deviation) progress to complete heart block.

Diagnosis

History: Since BBB alone produces no symptoms, the most important aspects of the history pertain to the duration of the conduction defect and whether conditions exist that can cause conduction defects such as trauma to the front of the chest or exertion (effort angina) that may reflect underlying coronary atherosclerosis.

Physical exam: No abnormalities are produced by BBB; however, abnormalities from the conditions that cause BBB may exist such as hypertension or a heart murmur associated with aortic valvular disease.

Tests: The ECG is the only test that confirms BBB. Other tests such as the chest x-ray and echocardiogram may disclose abnormalities due to related processes that cause BBB.

Treatment

There is no treatment for BBB. If there is alternating BBB or additional abnormalities of the conduction system, a permanent pacemaker may be implanted. Sometimes a temporary pacemaker is inserted prior to elective noncardiac surgery because of the possibility that the anesthetic may worsen the conduction problem.

Prognosis

The outcome of RBBB and LBBB depends, in part, on whether they are acute or chronic. Acute RBBB or LBBB in the setting of an acute myocardial infarction (AMI) may indicate the need for a temporary pacemaker. Chronic RBBB may be well tolerated for years and not affect longevity. Airline pilots with RBBB alone are allowed to continue working. LBBB, however, is more serious. It may be a forerunner (precursor) of an AMI or sudden death.

Differential Diagnosis

Wolf-Parkinson-White (WPW) syndrome mimics both RBBB and LBBB. In addition, hyperkalemia, certain other metabolic disorders, and some drugs such as procainamide can produce an ECG pattern resembling BBB. A so-called nonspecific intraventricular conduction defect can resemble BBB of both types.

Specialists

- Cardiologist

Work Restrictions / Accommodations

Restrictions of physical activity may be recommended with or without pacemaker insertion.

Individuals who experience dizziness or fainting (syncope) may need restrictions from hazardous work, dangerous machinery, or exposed heights.

Comorbid Conditions

Conditions that decrease blood flow to the bundle branches or AV junction such as myocardial infarction (MI) or chronic ischemia may impact the severity of BBB. Trauma to the AV node resulting from cardiac surgery may have a similar effect. Hyperkalemia, congenital heart disease, aortic and mitral valvular disease, diabetes mellitus, pulmonary insufficiency, and renal disease that requires dialysis can further lengthen disability. Less commonly, infiltrative and connective tissue diseases can have detrimental effects.

Complications

Either RBBB or LBBB may progress to complete heart block (CHB). CHB, in turn, may be associated with sudden loss of consciousness (syncope) and warrant a pacemaker. LBBB but not RBBB obscures the ECG recognition of both old and recent heart attacks (myocardial infarctions). In general, LBBB makes the ECG recognition of other electrocardiographic abnormalities difficult or impossible. Individuals with LBBB carry an increased risk of concomitant cardiovascular disease.

Factors Influencing Duration

The type of BBB, its cause, underlying conditions, treatment, and response to the particular treatment may affect the length of disability. Age may also be a factor because BBB and severe heart block is generally more common in the elderly.

Length of Disability

Disability may be minimal in individuals with less severe forms of BBB. Disability may be permanent if job requirements are physically demanding and BBB has progressed to complete heart block.

Failure to Recover

If an individual fails to recover within the maximum duration expectancy period, the reader may wish to reference the following questions to assist in better understanding the specifics of an individual's medical case.

Regarding diagnosis:

- Was diagnosis of bundle branch block (BBB) confirmed?
- Were conditions with similar symptoms ruled out?

Regarding treatment:

- Does individual have an underlying condition that may impact recovery?
- Do medications for underlying cardiac condition need to be changed or dosage adjusted?
- If abnormalities are present in the conduction system, would individual benefit from a temporary or permanent pacemaker?

Regarding prognosis:

- Since BBB may be caused by underlying conditions such as atherosclerosis, are underlying cardiac conditions being adequately addressed?
- If there is evidence of a progression towards complete heart block, what interventions can be done to slow or prevent this progression?

References

Deharo, J.C. "Left Bundle Branch Block. Electrocardiographic and Prognostic Aspects." Archives des Maladies du Coeur et des Vaisseaux 93 3 Spec No (2000): 31-37.

Kuo, C. "Successful Treatment of Complete Left Bundle Branch Block Complicating Acute Viral Myocarditis Employing Chinese Herbs." American Journal of Chinese Medicine 14 3-4 (1986): 124-130.

Luckmann, Joan, and Karen C. Sorensen. "Nursing People Experiencing Cardiac Arrhythmias." Medical-Surgical Nursing. Kay, Dudley Philadelphia: W.B. Saunders Company, 1987. 901-926.

Nicolai, P., et al. "Anomalies of the T-wave Following Treatment of Complete Chronic Left Branch Block by Massage of the Carotid Sinus or Injection of Adenosine Triphosphate." Archives des Maladies du Coeur et des Vaisseaux 77 7 (1984): 791-799.

Umphred, Darcy A. Neurological Rehabilitation. St. Louis: The C.V. Mosby Company, 1990.

Wolbrette, Deborah L., and Gerald V. Naccarelli. "Sinus Nodal Dysfunction and AV Conduction Disturbances." Textbook of Cardiovascular Medicine. Topol, Eric J., ed. Philadelphia: Lippincott-Raven Publishers, 1998. 1637-1660.

Bunion

Other names / synonyms: Hallux Abducto Valgus, Hallux Valgus

727.1, 735.0

Definition

A bunion is an enlargement of the medial side (medial eminence) of the first metatarsal, which is the foot bone that connects to the big toe.

The bunions that affect younger individuals usually result from a structural deformity of the first metatarsal called "metatarsus primus varus." This malposition of the metatarsal allows the portion of the metatarsal head by the base of the big toe to be irritated by shoe pressure. This part of the metatarsal is called the "medial eminence," and it enlarges over time. Sometimes a soft-tissue sac (bursa) forms between the skin and the enlarged bone, and this too becomes inflamed (bursitis). The big toe (hallux) drifts toward the second toe, sometimes underlapping or overlapping it. Arthritis of the big toe joint may develop (hallux limitus or hallux rigidus).

Bunions are thought to be hereditary, but tight-fitting shoes can accelerate the development of a bunion or can aggravate an existing bunion. Bunions may not be painful (asymptomatic), or may be painful on the medial eminence area with shoe wear. Bunions are two to four times more common in women than men. The incidence of bunions is 3% of the population in the 15- to 30-year age group, 9% in 31- to 60-year olds, and 16% of the population over age 60.

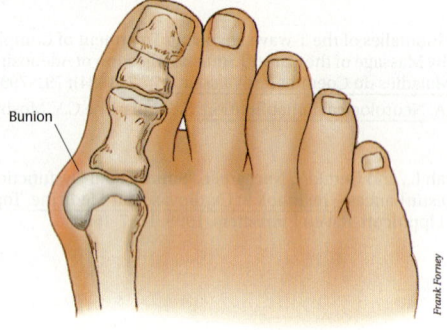

Diagnosis

History: Individuals may complain of a painful, bony enlargement on the inside edge (medial side) of the first metatarsal. The big toe may turn outward, growing over or under the second toe. The individual may relate a history of pain in this area when wearing shoes. The individual may relate that the bunion does not hurt.

Physical exam: The exam may reveal swelling and tenderness of the joint at the base of the big toe. The big toe turns outward, possible growing over or under the second toe. There may be pain when touching (palpation) the bunion, and there may be pain when the joint between the metatarsal and toe is moved.

Tests: X-rays reveal the size of the enlargement, extent of joint damage, and angular relationship between the first and second metatarsals (intermetatarsal angle). Blood tests rule out other diseases such as rheumatoid arthritis and gout.

Treatment

Nonpainful (asymptomatic) bunions require no treatment. Bunions that are small and only mildly painful are managed by wearing wider shoes and sometimes with foam padding devices to relieve pressure. The painful bursitis of bunions can be treated conservatively with corticosteroid injections.

In cases that do not respond to conservative treatment, surgery is indicated. Over 100 different surgical procedures have been described for bunions, and over a dozen are in common use today. These range from the simple removal of the enlarged bump (silver procedure) to procedures in which the bones of the big toe and metatarsal are cut (osteotomy) and repositioned. These osteotomy procedures may involve cutting and repositioning the big toe bone (proximal phalanx; Akin procedure) or the first metatarsal bone at the portion closest to the toe (distal portion or metatarsal head; Mitchell, Austin, Hohmann, Wilson procedures) or the portion closest to the midfoot (proximal portion or metatarsal base; Loison-Balascescu, Mau procedures). If arthritis of the metatarsophalangeal joint is present, removal of the joint (Keller procedure) or fusion of the joint (McKeever procedure) is necessary. Most osteotomy procedures require internal fixation and immobilization.

Prognosis

Early treatment of a small bunion with corticosteroid injection may relieve the symptoms and circumvent the surgery associated with more severe cases. Large bunions may need surgery to relieve symptoms, but this surgery is routinely successful with full recovery and relief of pain expected.

Differential Diagnosis

Gout, rheumatoid arthritis, and osteoarthritis can all cause pain and swelling of the first metatarsal head area, but are easily distinguished radiographically from bunion deformity.

Specialists

- Orthopedic Surgeon
- Podiatrist

Work Restrictions / Accommodations

With surgery, prolonged standing and walking are limited until the foot is completely healed. This can take 6 to 8 weeks. The individual will need to elevate the foot periodically throughout the day. The individual will not be able to drive until normal footwear is allowed. The individual may have to use a walker, crutches, or wheelchair. Because the individual will probably be taking pain medication, drug policies must be reviewed.

Comorbid Conditions

Poor blood supply (atherosclerosis) and peripheral neuropathy (such as diabetic neuropathy) may lengthen disability.

Complications

Untreated bunions may continue to worsen. Degenerative arthritis in the big toe metatarsophalangeal joint may develop and may cause pain and stiffness.

Factors Influencing Duration

Disability after surgery could be lengthened by advanced age, poor nutrition, or surgical complications.

Complementary and Alternative Therapies

Content is intended for awareness only. Treatments may or may not be effective. Scientific evidence may be lacking and some substances have potentially toxic effects. Dr. Presley Reed and the editors do not endorse the use of these therapies in the absence of consultation with a licensed medical professional.

Foot exercises - Foot exercises (particularly toe pick-ups, clenches, and crawls) can strengthen foot muscles and may help relieve symptoms in mild cases.

Length of Disability

For bunionectomy with osteotomy, medium to very heavy work should be suspended until healing is confirmed on follow-up x-ray.

Bunionectomy without osteotomy.

Duration in Days

Job Classification	Minimum	Optimum	Maximum
Sedentary work	7	14	21
Light work	7	21	21
Medium work	14	21	28
Heavy work	28	35	42
Very Heavy work	28	35	42

Bunionectomy with osteotomy.

Duration in Days

Job Classification	Minimum	Optimum	Maximum
Sedentary work	14	21	28
Light work	21	28	42
Medium work	28	42	84
Heavy work	42	84	168
Very Heavy work	42	84	168

Duration Trend from Normative Data*

Cases	Mean	Min	Max	No Lost Time	Over 6 Months
5124	61	0	426	0.22%	0.67%

Percentile:	5th	25th	Median	75th	95th
Days:	15	34	55	79	129

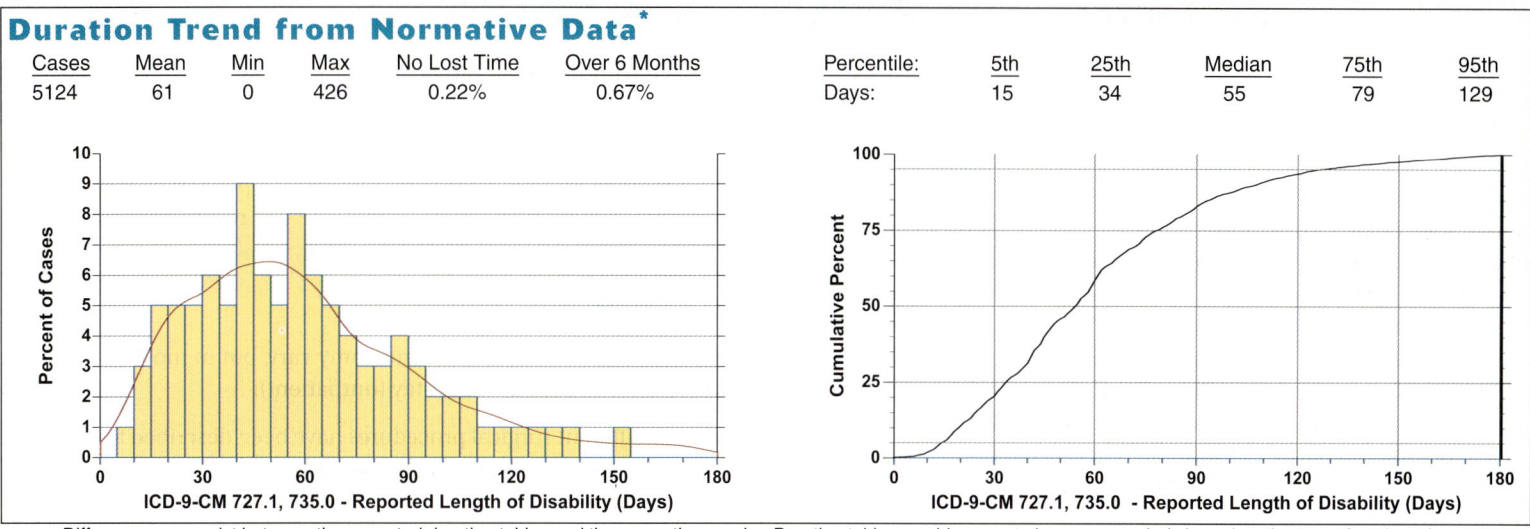

* Differences may exist between the expected duration tables and the normative graphs. Duration tables provide expected recovery periods based on the type of work performed by the individual. The normative graphs reflect the actual observed experience of many individuals across the spectrum of physical conditions, in a variety of industries, and with varying levels of case management.

Failure to Recover

If an individual fails to recover within the maximum duration expectancy period, the reader may wish to reference the following questions to assist in better understanding the specifics of an individual's medical case.

Regarding diagnosis:

- Did individual experience symptoms such as a painful bony enlargement on the inside edge of the big toe?
- Did the physical exam confirm the diagnosis of a bunion?
- Were x-rays done to determine the size of the bunion and extent of joint displacement or damage?
- Were additional diagnostic studies done to rule out other conditions such as arthritis or gout?

Regarding treatment:

- Were conservative measures such as selecting larger, more comfortable footwear or placement of taping and toe spacers effective at reducing discomfort?
- Did the condition warrant surgical intervention (severe deformity, worsening deformity, worsening pain)?
- Would individual benefit from removal of joint (Keller procedure) or fusion of the joint (McKeever procedure)?

Regarding prognosis:

- Based on the treatment required, what was the expected recovery?
- Did adequate time elapse for recovery? Did individual return to activity too soon?
- Have follow-up x-rays been taken to rule out complications of the bunion surgery including infection, osteomyelitis, nonunion, recurrence, avascular necrosis, and reflex sympathetic dystrophy?
- Does individual have any underlying conditions such as vascular disease, obesity, or diabetes that may impact recovery and prognosis?

References

Bogdonoff, Morton D., MD, ed. "Bunions." Home Health Handbook. Subak-Sharpe, Genell J., ed. Pittsburgh: Home Health Handbook, 2000. 6-13.

Schuberth, Jack M. Preferred Practice Guidelines: Hallux Valgus in the Healthy Adult. Park Ridge, IL: American College of Foot and Ankle Surgeons, 1998.

Bunionectomy

Other names / synonyms: Keller Operation, Mayo Operation, McBride Bunionectomy
77.5, 77.51, 77.53, 77.59

Definition

A bunionectomy is a procedure used to remove a painful bump (bunion) on the great toe.

Bunions typically form because of instability and misalignment of the bones and related structures in the feet. With these abnormalities, normal stresses applied to the foot are accompanied by improper distribution of weight. Misaligned and/or enlarged bones that cause the big toe (great toe) to push against the neighboring second toe create a painful bunion. The condition worsens as friction from shoe pressure creates swelling and inflammation of soft tissue (bursae) overlying the affected big toe joint (metatarsophalangeal joint). Improperly fitted shoes that are too narrow or have high heels commonly aggravate the condition, which is why women tend to require surgery more often than men.

More than 2 1/2 million US residents have bunions, with women three times more likely to have the condition. Not all bunions require surgery, however. There are dozens of different procedures and approaches for surgical correction of bunions, which may be classified as mild, moderate, severe, or arthritic.

Reason for Procedure

Nonoperative treatments such as wearing comfortable, well-fitting shoes with sufficient toe room or a special toe pad or corrective sock likely will be tried first. If these approaches are unsuccessful or if a bunion grows too large and/or painful, then surgical correction often is required. Without surgical intervention, large bunions often worsen and the condition becomes increasingly painful. Surgical correction also may be needed to keep the condition from recurring.

Because of the extended recovery time and the pain associated with the procedure, a bunionectomy is usually the last resort in treatment of a bunion.

Description

Methods of performing a bunionectomy vary, but in most cases do not involve an overnight hospital stay (outpatient).

Over 100 different surgical procedures have been described for bunions, and over a dozen are still in common use today. Common features of bunion surgery follow.

Usually, a regional (local) anesthetic is used, with sedation given as needed. In some cases, general anesthesia may be required. A tourniquet may be applied to the thigh or ankle to prevent bleeding during surgery. The leg and thigh are washed to prevent infection. An incision is made at the top of the big toe and first (metatarsal) joint or, in other methods, through the side of the foot. Part of exposed bone may be removed (osteotomy) and realigned. A portion of the pad-like sac (bursa), which reduces friction between tendon and joint, may also need to be removed. Tendons and other soft tissue also may be manipulated or lengthened to assist with realignment. Screws or wires may be required to help maintain the new alignment (internal fixation). Warm, sterile salt (saline) water then is used to irrigate the wound, and stitching (sutures) or adhesive strips will close the wound. A dressing is then applied. Pain relievers (analgesics) may be prescribed. Individuals usually are advised to keep the foot elevated for all but brief periods of time during the first 48 hours after surgery.

Prognosis

Most individuals undergoing a bunionectomy experience a full recovery and correction of the underlying condition. Success rates depend on the severity of the original condition and how much if any bone must be removed to correct alignment of the foot. The possibility of future complications could be alleviated if individuals wear shoes that do not constrict the foot and aggravate the condition.

Recovery time greatly depends on the severity of the condition and surgical method used for correction. During the healing process, individuals typically will be fitted with bandages and specially adapted, sandal-like footwear for at least several weeks before regular shoes can be worn.

Untreated, bunions may develop into related conditions such as calluses, misaligned toes (hammertoes), or wearing down of bone (osteoarthritis).

Specialists

- Orthopedic Surgeon
- Podiatrist

Work Restrictions / Accommodations

Individuals may be unable to walk or stand to attend to work tasks for several weeks following surgery. Temporary assignment to tasks that require sitting only may be needed.

Comorbid Conditions

Poor nutrition, recent illness and/or alcoholism could increase recovery time following a bunionectomy and lengthen disability. Individuals with diabetes and/or peripheral vascular disease heal from foot surgery more slowly.

Procedure Complications

Individuals who do not follow proper procedures for protecting the foot after surgery may experience re-injury or infection of the surgical wound. Excess bleeding or difficulty breathing could occur during surgery. The original condition may return despite surgery. The individual may also experience joint stiffness or bone death caused by an impaired blood supply (osteonecrosis). Other conditions that may accompany bunions such as nerve tumors (neuromas), bone deterioration (osteoarthritis), calluses, or misaligned toes (hammertoes) may require additional treatment.

Factors Influencing Duration

If both feet (bilateral) require surgical correction, the individual's period of disability will be lengthened. Any complications such as infection may also affect length of disability.

Individuals who perform tasks that involve sitting may be able to return to work within several days. Individuals who must stand may require several weeks or longer for recovery.

Length of Disability

The individual will require more time off from work if tasks involve standing or walking.

Bunionectomy without osteotomy.

Duration in Days

Job Classification	Minimum	Optimum	Maximum
Sedentary work	3	7	14
Light work	7	21	21
Medium work	14	21	28
Heavy work	28	35	42
Very Heavy work	28	35	42

With osteotomy.

Duration in Days

Job Classification	Minimum	Optimum	Maximum
Sedentary work	14	21	42
Light work	21	28	42
Medium work	28	42	84
Heavy work	42	84	168
Very Heavy work	42	84	168

References

Medstar Foot and Ankle Center. Bunion Information Page. Los Angeles Institute for Foot, Ankle and Bunion Surgery. 01 May 1999. 06 Jan 2001 <http://www.bunionman.com/BunIndex.html>.

Burn of Eye

Other names / synonyms: Eye Burn

692.71, 940, 940.0, 940.1, 940.2, 940.3, 940.4, 940.5, 940.9, 941.2

Definition

A burn of the eye refers to a burn of the cornea, lens, or retina of the eye. Burns to eye structures may be due to thermal injury, chemical exposure, ultraviolet radiation, or electrical injury. Causes of burns to the eyes and eyelids include heat (flames, scalding liquids, hot appliances such as curling irons, tobacco ash), chemicals (corrosive), ultraviolet radiation (welding, sunburn injury) or electricity (electricity, lightning).

Burns to the eyelid occur in about 20-30% of facial burns. Burns to the eye itself occur less commonly than burns of the eyelid because the blink reflex, rapid head movement, and use of the hands and arms to shield the eyes and protect them from injury.

Diagnosis

History: Information from the individual as to the type of exposure is important in guiding treatment for a burn to the eye. If the injury is due to chemical exposure, an individual usually reports the splashing of a chemical. An individual with injury from thermal exposure reports flames, steam, or exposure to a hot appliance. Individuals may also have other burn or accident injuries. An individual with injury to the eye from ultraviolet radiation reports exposure to a welding arc or sunlamp while not wearing appropriate eye protection. Individuals experiencing an electrical injury usually report exposure to electricity or lightning.

Physical exam: The findings may vary depending on the structures affected (eye, eyelid, or both) and the severity of the injury. The eyes and eyelids are examined for any remaining chemical material not completely flushed prior to physical exam. If discovered, this material will be removed or flushed once again. The eye is examined using an ophthalmoscope and slit-lamp, a specialized microscope that allows better visualization cornea and anterior eye structures. To evaluate the cornea and sclera, fluorescein dye eyedrops are instilled into the eye. Abnormal areas become "stained" with the fluorescein and an epithelial injury or corneal ulceration can be identified. Ultraviolet radiation injuries may also require fluorescein staining.

In mild corneal injury, physical exam may reveal redness and swelling (edema) of the cornea or the white part of the eye (sclera). In severe burns, the cornea may have an opaque appearance, and the sclera may appear very white due to loss of blood vessels. The eyelids may show signs of first, second- or third-degree burns (redness in first degree, blisters in second-degree burns; in third-degree burns, they appear dark and leathery).

Examination may include an evaluation of the pressure inside the eye (intraocular pressure). Intraocular pressure may be elevated in a chemical injury.

Tests: If a chemical burn has occurred, the acidity of the eye may be measured. This is done with pH paper.

Treatment

Treatment of thermal injury depends on severity of injury and may include topical antibiotics, patching, and cycloplegic eye drops. Treatment depends on the type of injury and severity. If the injury involves chemical exposure, initial treatment consists of a thorough flushing to remove any chemical that may remain in contact with the eyelids or eyes. Treatment of chemical burns to the eyes may also involve use of systemic or topical analgesics, or topical steroids and medications to reduce ocular pressure, if needed. Surgical treatment may include plastic surgery repair of the eyelid (blepharoplasty) or corneal surgery or grafting (keratoplasty). Ultraviolet radiation burns to the eye may be treated with antibiotic eye ointment, patching, cold compresses for comfort, rest, and oral analgesics. If patching is not tolerated, ophthalmic nonsteroidal anti-inflammatory drops may be used.

In individuals where only one eye has been injured, conjunctival transplantation from the opposite eye offers an alternative therapy that avoids both intraocular surgery and introduction of foreign tissue.

Prognosis

Topical steroids, analgesics, antibiotics, and medications used to reduce intraocular pressure (ophthalmic medications) are generally effective, but final outcome depends on cause of the burn, injury severity and development of complications.

Injury from an alkali burn may be severe due to the depth with which the chemical penetrates eye structures. Loss of vision may result. Injury from acidic chemicals may be limited to the cornea since acidic chemicals do not tend to penetrate through the cornea. Glaucoma may occur with chemical injury. Cataracts can result from electrical injury and may cause decreased vision. Injury from ultraviolet radiation usually heals without problems following treatment with ophthalmic ointment and patching.

Outcome of blepharoplasty depends on extent of surgery. The outcome may be excellent following small repairs of the eyelid. Larger repairs or repairs of full thickness injury may result in formation of thick, tight scar tissue (contracture). Skin grafting may be necessary for large injuries. The outcome of skin grafting may be excellent but can also result in scar and contracture formation. Contracture may result in lid retraction that may prevent the eye from closing completely (lagophthalmos).

Differential Diagnosis

History of the injury will identify whether the burn is a result of thermal, ultraviolet, chemical, or electrical exposure.

Specialists

- Burn Specialist
- Emergency Medicine
- Ophthalmologist
- Plastic Surgeon

Rehabilitation

Rehabilitation may be necessary if the burn results in loss of vision. Rehabilitation programs provide therapy and training to those who are visually impaired. Occupational therapists may be involved in low-vision programs that address many facets of vision. Individuals learn to increase the lighting in an area where they work or read to improve vision. Glare is reduced wherever possible at home and work through use of flat coat paint on walls, carpeting on floors, and sunglasses. Individuals use magnifying devices, large-print books, and bright detail on dark background (such as a computer monitor) to improve vision while reading and working.

Occupational therapists instruct individuals who have deficits in depth perception to use a cane for negotiating steps and curbs. Individuals are also retrained in activities of daily living such as feeding themselves. Occupational therapists make suggestions to increase safety in the home such as removing throw rugs and other tripping hazards and keeping necessary objects like house keys in the same place for easy retrieval. Visually impaired individuals may also use independent agencies that provide in-depth services such as training in the use of a guide dog, a cane for mobility, and Braille instruction.

Vocational programs are available to assist individuals in developing job skills if alternative employment becomes necessary. Programs may last several weeks to months. Some vocational programs may be comprehensive residential programs.

Work Restrictions / Accommodations

Time off from work may be necessary while recovering from thermal injury or following a chemical burn. If a major burn occurred, the individual may become disabled. Loss of vision may result. Visual aids may be needed depending on the degree of visual impairment. Eye patching may be necessary for a short time following ultraviolet radiation injury. Individuals with ultraviolet radiation injury may require time off work due to discomfort and use of analgesics during recovery. Individuals who develop cataracts following electrical injury may have decreased vision, and cataract excision may become necessary in some cases.

Comorbid Conditions

Comorbid conditions may include associated trauma and burn injuries.

Complications

Complications from chemical burn injury to the eye include chronic inflammation, adhesion formation, lid deformities, glaucoma, development of cataracts, and scarring of the cornea and conjunctiva. Thermal injury complications also involve formation of scars, both of the cornea and the eyelid. Complications from electrical or lightning injury may include cataract formation, retinal detachment, corneal burns, intraocular hemorrhage, and other ophthalmic complications.

Factors Influencing Duration

Factors that may influence disability include severity of the ophthalmic injury and development of ophthalmic complications.

Length of Disability

Duration depends on nature of the injury (unilateral or bilateral) and severity of the burn.

Unilateral.

Duration in Days

Job Classification	Minimum	Optimum	Maximum
Any work	3	7	Indefinite

Failure to Recover

If an individual fails to recover within the maximum duration expectancy period, the reader may wish to reference the following questions to assist in better understanding the specifics of an individual's medical case.

Regarding diagnosis:

- What type of burn did individual sustain (thermal, chemical, ultraviolet radiation, or electrical)?
- Were the eyes examined for corneal injury?
- Was fluorescein dye used to examine the eyes for epithelial injury?

Regarding treatment:

- Was individual treated for a chemical burn?
- Were the eyes immediately and thoroughly flushed?
- Was analgesic or topical steroid used?
- Was surgical intervention required?
- Was individual treated for a thermal or ultraviolet radiation injury?
- Was patching tolerated?
- If not, were ophthalmic nonsteroidal anti-inflammatory drops used?
- Does individual have only one injured eye?
- Was conjunctival transplantation performed? Did it work?

Regarding prognosis:

- Did the individual suffer any complications (chronic inflammation, adhesion formation, lid deformities, glaucoma, development of cataracts, scarring of the cornea and conjunctiva, retinal detachment, intraocular hemorrhage) or associated trauma or burn injuries that may impact ability to recover and lengthen disability?
- Did the individual suffer permanent visual impairment?
- Did the individual participate in vision rehabilitation?

References

Chinnis, Ann S., Janet M. Williams, and Kimberly N. Treat. "Electrical Injuries." Emergency Medicine, 5th edition. Tintinalli, Judith E., ed. New York: McGraw-Hill, 2000. 1292-1298.

Thoft, R.A. "Conjunctival transplantation as an alternative to keratoplasty." Ophthalmology 86 6 (1979): 1084-92.

Burn of Head and Neck (Includes Face)

Other names / synonyms: Facial Burn, Neck Burn

941, 941.0, 941.05, 941.06, 941.07, 941.08, 941.1, 941.2, 941.3, 941.4, 949.0, 949.1, 949.2, 949.3

Definition

A burn is an injury to body tissues resulting from heat, electricity, chemicals, radiation, steam, or heated gases. Burns involving the head and neck are often characterized as severe burns because of potential injury to the eyes, ears, respiratory passages, and lungs. Burns impair the ability of the skin to prevent heat and water loss and protect against infection.

Burns to the head, face, and neck are commonly due to heat (thermal) and chemical injury. Burns are often associated with smoking and alcohol use. Many burns occur in the home due to scalds from hot liquids or house fires. Flash and flame burns may result in inhalation injury.

Chemical burns account for about 10% of all burn injuries and occur as a result of exposure to acid or alkali chemicals or from the deployment of automobile airbags.

Electrical burns are the least common burn injury and result from exposure to electrical current. Injury is caused as the current enters the body, passes through it, and again as it exits the body. The head is a common site for an electrical entrance wound.

Industries that place individuals at increased risk of burns to the head, face, and neck may include any manufacturing occupation involving the use of hot machinery or liquids. Occupations involving gas, propane, or other flammable liquids may also increase the risk of burns to the face, head, and neck.

Burns are described in degrees. A first-degree burn only affects the topmost layer of the skin (epidermis) and causes redness without any blistering. A common first-degree burn is sunburn. A second-degree burn involves deeper layers of the skin and results in painful blisters. Superficial second-degree burns often occur from scalds or short flashes. They are very painful but generally heal in about 3 weeks without scarring. Deeper second-degree burns are often caused from flames, oil, or grease and result in scarring. Third-degree burns involve burns through the entire layer of skin and the layer of tissue below the skin (subcutaneous tissue). Third-degree burns often appear very pale and cause little pain since all nerve endings have been destroyed. These burns may be due to flames, scalds, and chemical and electrical injuries. There are significant scars from this type of burn with development of abnormal stiffening of those joints involved in the injury (contractures). Fourth-degree burns are extremely deep and cause injury to the muscle and bone.

The amount of skin surface injured, depth of the burn injury, and location determine the seriousness of burn injury. The skin of the eyelids is very thin (about 1 mm in thickness), allowing for increased severity. Severe burns also include inhalation injury, electrical burns, burns where other trauma has occurred, and burns in individuals at high risk for complications or death, particularly for those over age 65, and with prior medical problems.

Individuals with significant facial burns often experience burns to the ears and may result in loss of the entire external ear.

Diagnosis

History: The individual or family reports exposure to flames, chemicals, electricity, or ultraviolet radiation and will usually report significant pain. There may be little pain if it is a third-degree burn. With steam or fires, there may be inhalation injury. The individual may have a history of cigarette smoking or alcohol use.

Physical exam: In first-degree burn, redness without blistering occurs as in facial sunburn. Large blisters may be apparent on the face in second-degree burn. The skin of the face and head may be very pale in third-degree burn. In fourth-degree burn, injury may extend into bone or muscle or the ears may be lost. A combination of burn depths may occur. The individual may have breathing difficulties. Associated injury includes burns to the eyes. In an electrical injury, both the entrance and exit wounds are noted with signs of injury between the two wounds.

Tests: For minor or moderate burns, testing is generally not needed. For severe burns, tests may include determination of the amount of oxygen in the blood (arterial blood gases), electrolytes, carboxyhemoglobin, blood urea nitrogen, blood sugar, and a complete blood count (CBC).

Complementary and Alternative Therapies

Content is intended for awareness only. Treatments may or may not be effective. Scientific evidence may be lacking and some substances have potentially toxic effects. Dr. Presley Reed and the editors do not endorse the use of these therapies in the absence of consultation with a licensed medical professional.

Aloe -	May help soothe irritated skin.
Vitamin A -	May enhance or accelerate wound healing
Vitamin C -	May enhance wound healing and reduce wound inflammation.
Zinc -	May enhance wound healing especially in individuals deficient in this mineral.
Arnica -	Acts as a disinfectant for wounds when applied externally.
Calendula -	May be used as an antibacterial, antifungal, antiviral, and anti-inflammatory ointment.
Clove and Goldenseal -	May be used externally as an antiseptic to promote wound healing.
Comfrey -	May be used externally to promote wound healing.
Echinacea -	May stimulate immune system to promote healing.
Garlic -	Said to fight infection.
Gotu kola -	May stimulate regeneration of skin cells and underlying tissue.
Horse balm -	Used externally as an antiseptic to promote wound healing.
Iron -	Said to play a key role in collagen formation needed to repair skin and soft tissue wounds.
Ivy -	May fight secondary infection.
Teatree oil -	May be used externally as an antiseptic for burns, cuts, and abrasions.
Vitamin E -	May reduce inflammation and enhance wound healing and skin repair.
Vitamin K -	May enhance blood clotting and reduce bleeding associated with wounds.

Treatment

Serious burns to the eyes, ears, and face usually require specialized care in a burn center because of the risk of significant scarring and loss of function. Breathing is a primary concern during initial evaluation and emergency treatment. The extent and duration of treatment vary depending on the amount of body surface burned and any associated injuries.

Emergency treatment for first- and second-degree burns includes immersing the affected area in cool running water for 10 minutes or more until the burning feelings subside. If the victim is burnt through clothing, the clothing should be left on and immersed in water. Chemical burns require immediate and thorough flushing to remove any remaining chemical. If the victim is still connected to the electrical contact following an electrical burn, they should not be pulled off. The current should be switched off if possible or pushed away from the victim with a wooden stick or other item that does not conduct electricity. CPR and emergency treatment are needed if the victim has stopped breathing.

Treatment of first-degree burns requires no treatment. Treatment of second-degree burns includes cleansing, removal of large blisters (debridement), and application of an antibacterial burn ointment and nonstick occlusive dressings. If the burn is expected to take longer than 3 weeks to heal, it may be surgically removed (excised). Skin is taken from another area of the body and placed (grafted) on the burn to speed healing and minimize infection.

Third-degree burns require extensive treatment. The burn area is cleansed and dead tissue scraped off (débrided). Severely burned skin becomes tight and rigid and is known as eschar. Eschar that encircles the neck and chest may restrict the ability to breathe and compress blood flow to vital organs. To release the tightness and allow breathing, an incision (escharotomy) may be needed along the neck. Repeated debridement may be necessary to fully determine the depth of the burn injury. Excision and grafting are usually done to minimize the frequency of debridement and prevent infection. If the victim has insufficient healthy skin remaining for grafting, bioengineered skin may be used. Reconstruction of facial defects is very challenging. Full-thickness skin grafts are preserved but these may create problems at the donor site. Skin over the side of the chest is a good site for skin grafts because of its larger surface area, similar color, thickness, skin quality, and texture. Long-term treatment includes prevention of infection, excision and grafting, nutritional support, care of associated trauma and other medical conditions, plastic surgery to reconstruct facial structures if necessary, and rehabilitation.

Prognosis

Outcome is good for first-degree burns. First-degree burns to the head and neck heal in a few days without scarring. Outcome of superficial second-degree burns is good with healing in about 3 weeks without scarring or impairment of function when no infection occurs. If the burn is deeper or if infection occurs, healing may take 3 to 9 weeks with significant scar formation.

Outcome of third- and fourth-degree burns is poor with significant scarring of the face. Skin grafting replaces skin permanently lost in the burn injury. The appearance of grafted skin may vary. It sometimes blends into nearby healthy skin very well but sometimes a distinct mark is noticeable between the normal and grafted skin.

Reconstruction of the nose and other areas of destroyed tissue improves cosmetic outcome. Following severe burns to the face, however, the individual's appearance may never be the same. In addition to damage to the nose, the ears and hair may be lost. Loss of vision may result from severe damage to the eyes. Inhalation injury associated with burns or the development of an infection may result in death.

Differential Diagnosis

Diagnosis of burn injury is usually self-evident. Determination of the depth of the burn sometimes takes a few hours or days. Full extent of electrical injury may take a few days to determine.

Specialists

- Burn Specialist
- General Surgeon
- Plastic Surgeon

Rehabilitation

The need for rehabilitation depends on the severity of the burn and any associated injuries. Deep second-, third-and fourth-degree burns require weeks to months for treatment and healing. Physical therapists trained in burn rehabilitation are important in the overall treatment of individuals with burns to the head and neck. The primary focus is to control scar formation and regain any loss of motion and strength to joints of the neck and adjoining shoulder region affected by the burn.

Once the individual is stabilized, compressive dressings or masks are measured and fitted by the physical therapist. These dressings are worn up to several months depending on the amount of potential scar formation. Neck and shoulder regions are monitored closely for potential stiffening of the joint region (joint contractures). If neck/shoulder mobility is restricted from the burn, the physical therapist performs range-of-motion exercises to the neck and shoulder region to prevent potential stiffening of the joint.

Occupational therapy is important for individuals with loss of function related to face and neck burns by helping them adapt to daily living activities. Speech therapy is important in rehabilitation if the burn has affected speech and/or swallowing. Psychological and social services may also be part of the rehabilitative team when the individual returns to work.

Work Restrictions / Accommodations

Work restrictions and accommodations vary depending on severity of the burn. For minor burns of the face, neck, and head, no restrictions are needed. For severe burns, several months of time off for recovery and surgical procedures may be necessary. The individual may have frequent follow-up appointments. Further reconstructive and plastic surgery may be required.

An individual with severe burns to the neck and head may no longer be able to perform normal activities. The individual may not be able to wear clothes with high or tight necklines especially if compressive dressings are needed to control scar formation. Wigs may be necessary if the hair is lost. A speakerphone may be necessary if dressings to the ears make it difficult to hold a handset phone to the ears. Individuals with severe scarring or loss of function due to severe burns to the neck and head need counseling.

Comorbid Conditions

Immunosuppression or bleeding disorders may lead to higher rate of infection or bleeding complications and complicate skin grafting. Pre-existing liver or kidney disease or malnutrition may be aggravated by the metabolic demands of burn healing.

Complications

Complications include smoke and carbon monoxide inhalation, respiratory difficulty, eye injury, and any associated injuries. Burns to the ears may be complicated by inflammation of the ear cartilage (otochondritis). With a third-degree burn to the head, there may be permanent loss of the hair. Infection can worsen the depth of a burn injury, necessitate skin grafting, and prolong healing time. It can also destroy skin grafts and necessitate a second skin graft procedure. In severe and extensive burns, kidney, liver, respiratory, and heart failure and overwhelming infection (sepsis) may be fatal.

Factors Influencing Duration

Factors that may influence disability include injury to the eyes, inhalation injury, and associated injury or burns to other parts of the body. Development of infection prolongs recovery and healing time and may necessitate other treatments and procedures such as skin grafting or plastic reconstruction. Age, gender, pre-existing conditions, and specific job duties may all affect outcome and duration of disability.

Length of Disability

For small first, second, (less that fifteen percent of body surface) and third-degree burns (less than one percent of body surface), duration depends on site. The depth and severity of the burn influence the length of disability. Severe burns may lead to permanent disability or death.

Small first- and second-degree (less that fifteen percent of body surface), third-degree (less than one percent of body surface).

Duration in Days

Job Classification	Minimum	Optimum	Maximum
Sedentary work	1	7	28
Light work	1	7	28
Medium work	1	7	28
Heavy work	1	7	28
Very Heavy work	1	7	28

First- and second-degree (more than fifteen percent of body surface), third-degree (more than one percent of body surface), and/or inhalation burns.

Duration in Days

Job Classification	Minimum	Optimum	Maximum
Sedentary work	28	42	56
Light work	28	42	56
Medium work	42	56	84
Heavy work	56	84	112
Very Heavy work	56	84	112

Failure to Recover

If an individual fails to recover within the maximum duration expectancy period, the reader may wish to reference the following questions to assist in better understanding the specifics of an individual's medical case.

Regarding diagnosis:

- Was the burn injury thermal, chemical, electrical, or a result of ultraviolet radiation?
- Was the burn first-, second-, third-, or fourth-degree?

- What percentage of body surface area was burned?
- Was there smoke inhalation?
- Did the burn affect the eyes? What other associated burns occurred?
- What other associated injuries occurred?

Regarding treatment:

- Was individual's breathing impaired? Was an incision made into the burn (escharotomy) to relieve breathing?
- Has individual undergone repeated skin debridement?
- Was excision and grafting performed?
- Did infection occur?
- How severe is scar formation?
- What treatment was given for associated trauma such as burns to the eyes?

- Was plastic surgery required to reconstruct facial structures?
- Has individual started a physical rehabilitation program?
- Is individual in need of speech or respiratory therapy?

Regarding prognosis:

- Does individual have other conditions such as diabetes, heart disease, respiratory disease, immunosuppression or bleeding disorders, pre-existing liver or kidney disease, or malnutrition that may affect recovery?
- How severely was individual burned?
- What is age and gender of individual?
- Would individual benefit from psychological counseling for body image changes and/or to cope with pain?
- Have complications developed? If so, what are they and what is expected outcome with treatment?

References

Celikoz, B., et al. "Reconstruction of Facial Defects and Burn Scars Using Large Size Freehand Full-Thickness Skin Graft from Lateral Thoracic Region." Burns 27 2 (2001): 174-178.

Cioffi, W.G. "What's New in Burns and Metabolism." Journal of American College Surgery 192 2 (2001): 241-254.

Duke, James A. The Green Pharmacy. Emmaus: Rodale Press, Inc, 1997.

Emmett, Edward A. "Occupational Diseases of the Skin." Cecil Textbook of Medicine, 20th ed. Bennett, J. Claude, and Fred Plum, eds. Philadelphia: W.B. Saunders Company, 1996. 2220-2222.

Fauerbach, J.A., et al. "Barriers to Employment Among Working-Aged Patients with Major Burn Injury." Journal of Burn Care and Rehabilitation 22 1 (2001): 26-34.

Feinstein, Alice, ed. Healing With Vitamins. Emmaus: Rodale Press, Inc, 1996.

Goodwin, Cleon W. "Electrical Injury." Cecil Textbook of Medicine, 20th ed. Bennett, J. Claude, and Fred Plum, eds. Philadelphia: W.B. Saunders Company, 1996. 64-67.

Kao, C.C., and W.L.Garner. "Acute Burns." Plastic Reconstructive Surgery 101 7 (2000): 2482-2483.

Kisner, C., and L. Colby. Therapeutic Exercise Foundations and Techniques. Philadelphia: F.A. Davis, 1990.

O'Keefe, G.E., J.L. Hunt, and G.F. Purdue. "An Evaluation of Risk Factors for Mortality After Burn Trauma and the Identification of Gender-Dependent Differences in Outcomes." Journal of American College Surgery 192 2 (2001): 153-160.

Sohn, Augustine J. "Burns." Saunders Manual of Medical Practice, 2nd ed. Rakel, Robert E., ed. Philadelphia: W.B. Saunders Company, 2000. 1301-1303.

Talbot-Stern, Janet. "Burns." The Clinical Practice of Emergency Medicine, 2nd ed. Harwood-Nuss, Ann L., ed. Philadelphia: Lippincott-Raven, 1996. 561-565.

Urdaneta, Anne, and Michael Lucchesi. "Common Disorders of the External, Middle, and Inner Ear." Emergency Medicine, 5th ed. Tintinalli, Judith E., ed. New York: McGraw-Hill, 2000. 1501-1525.

Van Loey, N.E., A.W. Faber, and L.A. Taal. "Do Burn Patients Need Burn Specific Multidisciplinary Outpatient Aftercare: Research Results." Burns 27 2 (2001): 103-110.

Warden, G.D., and D.M. Heimbach. "Burns." Principles of Surgery, Companion Handbook, 7th ed. Schwartz, Seymour I New York: McGraw-Hill, 1999. 183-221.

Wiebelhaus, P., and S.L. Hansen. "What You Should Know About Managing Burn Emergencies." Nursing 31 1 (2000): 36-41.

Burn of Wrist and Hand

Other names / synonyms: Hand Burn
944, 944.01, 944.02, 944.05, 944.06, 944.07, 944.08

Definition

A burn is an injury to body tissues from exposure to heat (flames, hot liquids, steam, hot appliances), electricity (including lightning), chemicals (acidic or alkali, deployment of automobile airbags), and radiation (ultraviolet radiation, welding). Even though a burn to the hand only involves a small percentage of the total body surface area (about 1% for the palm and about 2% for the entire hand), any third-degree burn of the hand is considered severe. With burns of the wrist, there is potential for impaired circulation. The risk of disability is due to decreased function of the hand from contractures.

Burns impair the skin's ability to prevent heat and water loss and protect against infection. Burns to the wrist and hand can result from a wide variety of exposures. The most commonly reported burn injury is in the home while working in the kitchen. Thermal-type burns are the most common and are due to exposure to hot materials such as liquids (scalds), flames (house fires), or steam (car radiators). Chemical burns account for about 10% of all burn injuries and occur as a result of exposure to acid or alkali chemicals or the deployment of automobile airbags.

Electrical burns are least common and occur when the body is exposed to an electrical current. Injuries are sustained at points when the current enters, passes through, and exits the body. The most common sites of an electrical entrance wound are the hands and head. Fingers and hands may be destroyed by electrical injury.

Burns are described as described as first-, second-, third-, or fourth-degree. A first-degree burn only affects the topmost layer of the skin (epidermis) and causes redness without any blistering. A common first-degree burn is sunburn.

A second-degree burn involves deeper layers of the skin and results in painful blisters. Superficial second-degree burns often result from scalds or short flashes. These burns may be very painful but generally heal in about 3 weeks without scarring. Deeper second-degree burns often result from flames, oil, or grease.

Third-degree burns affect the entire layer of skin and the layer of tissue below the skin (subcutaneous tissue). Third-degree burns are often very pale and cause little pain at first since all nerve endings have been destroyed. These burns may result from flames, scalds, chemical, and electrical injuries. Individual will have significant scars and develop abnormal bending and stiffening (contractures) of those joints involved in the injury.

Fourth-degree burns are extremely severe and extend deep into muscle and bone and sometimes cause loss of hands or fingers.

Burn injuries are often a combination of burn depths. The seriousness of burn injury is determined by the amount of skin surface injured, depth of the burn injury, and location of the injury. Severe burns include serious burns to the hands.

Diagnosis

History: Except in a third-degree burn that destroys nerve endings, there is usually significant pain. Large blisters may form at the burn area. The individual may report other injuries.

Physical exam: In a first-degree burn, redness without blistering occurs as in sunburn. In a second-degree burn, there may be large blisters on the hands, wrist, or fingers. The skin may appear very pale in a third-degree burn. In a fourth-degree burn, injury may extend into bone or muscle or the fingers or hand may be lost. A combination of burn depths may be noted. In an electrical injury, signs of injury may be seen between the entrance and exit wounds.

Tests: For burns to the hand or wrist, testing is generally not needed.

Treatment

Emergency treatment for first- and second-degree burns includes immersing the affected area in cool running water for 10 minutes or more until the burning feelings subside. If the victim is burnt through clothing, the clothing should be left on and immersed in water. Chemical burns require immediate and thorough flushing to remove any remaining chemical. If the victim is still connected to the electrical contact following an electrical burn, they should not be pulled off. The current should be switched off if possible or pushed away from the victim with a wooden stick or other item that does not conduct electricity. CPR and emergency treatment are needed if the victim has stopped breathing.

Individuals with more than minor burns to the wrist and hand are admitted to burn centers. Treatment of second-degree burns may include cleansing, removal of large blisters (debridement), and application of an antibacterial burn ointment. If the burn is expected to take longer than 3 weeks to heal, it may be surgically removed (excised). Skin taken from another area of the body is then placed (grafted) on the burn to speed healing and minimize infection. Third-degree burns require extensive treatment. The burn area is cleansed and débrided. Repeated debridement may be necessary to fully determine the depth of the burn injury. Excision and grafting are usually done to minimize the frequency of debridement and prevent infection. Burns to the hands are also treated with splinting to prevent abnormal bending of the joints (contractures).

Emergency treatment for chemical burns includes prompt removal of chemicals from the skin in order to limit injury. All jewelry must be removed from the fingers and wrists to prevent constriction that may occur as swelling increases following a burn. If the burned tissue (eschar) impairs circulation to the hand or fingers, an incision is made through the burn to relieve the tightness (escharotomy) and allow adequate circulation. Amputation of the fingers or hand may be required for severe burn injuries where circulation is destroyed or when bone and tissue are destroyed.

Long-term treatment includes prevention of infection, excision and grafting, nutritional support, care of associated trauma, other medical conditions, and plastic surgery or orthopedic repair to improve functioning of the fingers and hands. Long-term rehabilitation may be needed.

Prognosis

The outcome varies depending on the severity of the burn. Loss of fingers or the hand is a possibility. Full function of the hands and fingers may be permanently lost.

First-degree burns begin to heal in a few days with no scarring. Superficial second-degree burns without infection heal spontaneously in about 3 weeks without scarring or impairment of function. With deeper burns, healing may take 3 to 9 weeks if no evidence of infection occurs. Scar formation is significant in deep burns. Third- and fourth-degree burns do not heal without skin grafting. Skin grafting improves the outcome by providing a permanent transplantation of skin from other parts of the body to replace skin permanently lost in the burn injury. The appearance of grafted skin may vary. It sometimes blends into nearby healthy skin very well or there may be a distinct mark between normal skin and the grafted skin.

Differential Diagnosis

Diagnosis of the burn injury is usually clear-cut. Determination of the depth of the burn may take a few hours or days. Full extent of electrical injury may take a few days to determine.

Specialists

• Burn Specialist	• Orthopedic Surgeon
• General Surgeon	• Plastic Surgeon

Rehabilitation

Burns of the wrist and hand may require a combined rehabilitative program of splinting and exercise (certified hand therapist). Splinting the hand and wrist in a specific position prevents further loss of motion from damage to tendons, joints, or skin grafts. However, if the hand or wrist receives only a superficial burn, no splint is necessary.

If the burn occurs on the top of the hand (dorsally), fingers may pull upward or downward and deform at the joints. If the burn occurs on the palm, the hand may deform in a cupped position. This loss may be permanent and lead to disfigurement. Hand and wrist rehabilitation depends on the severity of the burn. The initial goal is to decrease edema.

If the individual is responsive, the therapist may choose more active muscle exercises such as having the individual touch each finger to the tip of the thumb. If the individual remains unconscious, the therapist may have to manipulate the fingers or wrist (passive exercise). Exercises are usually performed several times a day as tolerated. There are some contraindications to exercise when the burn is located on the hand.

The therapist must evaluate the depth of burn and the potential for rupture of the extensor mechanism of the hand due to tissue weakness. If a high probability exists for damaging the muscle or tendons that extend the hand, repeated flexion and extension (opening and closing) of the hand is avoided. If the tendon is covered with viable tissue, only gentle flexion (curling the fingers toward the palm) is allowed until more healing occurs.

If the individual's fingernails are intact, a splint with the involved fingers placed in dynamic traction by an elastic thread attached from the fingernails to the outer splint may be worn. When the individual extends the fingers, light tension is achieved.

Once the surgical procedure is over, the grafted area becomes part of the rehabilitation program. It is important that the skin graft adheres to the graft surface. Excessive stress from movement or weight on the newly grafted tissue causes separation.

The individual usually performs active range-of-motion exercises for the first week after the graft to lessen the forces on it. Once complete range of motion of the wrist or fingers is restored, the individual may perform resistive exercises using a pressure glove. Two weeks after a skin graft, the graft or skin is usually healed enough to apply a pressure glove used to reduce disfiguring scar tissue formation. The pressure glove is measured before the hand or wrist graft fully heals. Because the glove is worn for many months depending on the extent of the burn, the therapist must be aware of any problems such as narrowing of the arches of the palm. Strengthening exercises involve gripping (squeezing a ball lightly) and wrist exercises that require the hand to turn with the thumb down (pronate) or up (supinate). These exercises may be done in a whirlpool using the massaging and resistive affects of the water.

Other modalities such as neuromuscular stimulation may also help restore wrist function. Wrist extension after a severe burn may be difficult to maintain especially after surgery. To help strengthen weak extensor muscles of the wrist, neuromuscular electrical stimulation may be used.

During later stages of therapy, the individual begins a more comprehensive home exercise routine that includes stretching and endurance exercise on the arm ergometer. By the end of the third month or when all wounds are closed, the individual may participate in a work-conditioning program to identify any potential problems on re-entering the work force. If the individual maintains his or her current occupation, an occupational therapist evaluates the different hand motions involved in the work performed and simulates them in the therapy environment.

Work Restrictions / Accommodations

Work restrictions and accommodations vary depending on the severity of the burn. Restrictions are not usually required for minor burns of the hands and wrists. For severe burns, several months of time off for recovery and surgical procedures may be needed. Compressive dressings may need to be worn for several months to prevent scar formation. The fingers and hands may be weak or stiff and full function of the hands and fingers may be permanently lost. If fingers or hands were amputated or if burns occurred to other parts of the body, job requirements and accommodations may be necessary. The individual may require frequent follow-up appointments.

Before the individual returns to work, skin irritation problems such as garment friction during repeated hand movements should be identified. Adaptive equipment may be needed such as thicker and built-up railing handles or arms of chairs to assist in gripping.

Complementary and Alternative Therapies

Content is intended for awareness only. Treatments may or may not be effective. Scientific evidence may be lacking and some substances have potentially toxic effects. Dr. Presley Reed and the editors do not endorse the use of these therapies in the absence of consultation with a licensed medical professional.

Aloe -	May help soothe irritated skin.
Vitamin A -	May enhance or accelerate wound healing
Vitamin C -	May enhance wound healing and reduce wound inflammation.
Zinc -	May enhance wound healing especially in individuals deficient in this mineral.
Arnica -	Acts as a disinfectant for wounds when applied externally.
Calendula -	May be used as an antibacterial, antifungal, antiviral, and anti-inflammatory ointment.
Clove and Goldenseal -	May be used externally as an antiseptic to promote wound healing.
Comfrey -	May be used externally to promote wound healing.
Echinacea -	May stimulate immune system to promote healing.
Garlic -	Said to fight infection.
Gotu kola -	May stimulate regeneration of skin cells and underlying tissue.
Horse balm -	Used externally as an antiseptic to promote wound healing.
Iron -	Said to play a key role in collagen formation needed to repair skin and soft tissue wounds.
Ivy -	May fight secondary infection.
Teatree oil -	May be used externally as an antiseptic for burns, cuts, and abrasions.
Vitamin E -	May reduce inflammation and enhance wound healing and skin repair.
Vitamin K -	May enhance blood clotting and reduce bleeding associated with wounds.

Comorbid Conditions

Immunosuppression or bleeding disorders may lead to higher rate of infection or bleeding complications and may complicate skin grafting. Pre-existing liver or kidney disease or malnutrition may be aggravated by the metabolic demands of burn healing.

Complications

In the first 72 hours after the burn, fluid accumulates in the compartments of the hand that decreases blood flow and increases pressure. Uncontrolled swelling (edema) is a dangerous condition that may require an emergency fasciotomy when incisions are made in the muscles of the hand to relieve pressure. Other complications are impaired blood circulation, decreased movement, and loss of fingers due to constriction by eschar.

Factors Influencing Duration

Factors that may influence disability include burns to other parts of the body. Development of infection prolongs recovery and healing time and may necessitate other treatments and procedures such as skin grafting or plastic reconstruction. Severity and extent of burn, response to treatment, associated injuries, age, and specific job duties may all affect duration of disability.

Length of Disability

Duration depends on the severity, type, and site of the burn. Loss of digits or function also affects length of disability. Third or fourth-degree burn of hands may be permanently disabling.

Small first- and second-degree (less that fifteen percent of body surface), third-degree (less than one percent of body surface).

Duration in Days

Job Classification	Minimum	Optimum	Maximum
Sedentary work	3	7	28
Light work	3	7	28
Medium work	3	7	28
Heavy work	3	7	28
Very Heavy work	3	7	28

First- and second-degree (more than fifteen percent of body surface), third-degree (more than one percent of body surface), and/or inhalation burns.

Duration in Days

Job Classification	Minimum	Optimum	Maximum
Sedentary work	28	42	56
Light work	28	42	56
Medium work	42	56	84
Heavy work	56	84	112
Very Heavy work	56	84	112

Failure to Recover

If an individual fails to recover within the maximum duration expectancy period, the reader may wish to reference the following questions to assist in better understanding the specifics of an individual's medical case.

Regarding diagnosis:

- Did the burn involve thermal, chemical, electrical, or ultraviolet radiation injury?
- Was the burn first, second-, third-, or fourth-degree?
- What percentage of body surface area was burned?
- Did individual complain of pain, redness, or blistering?
- What other associated burns or injuries occurred?
- Were pulses present in the fingers and wrist?

Regarding treatment:

- For minor burns, was the skin exposed to cold running water for 10 minutes?
- For more severe burns, was excision and grafting performed?
- Was repeated debridement of the burn area required?
- Was a program of splinting and exercise prescribed to prevent abnormal bending of joints (contractures)?
- Is individual compliant with rehabilitation?

Regarding prognosis:

- How severely was individual burned?
- Did infection develop? If so, was individual compliant with antibiotic treatment?
- Are underlying conditions present that could prevent healing and prolong recovery?
- How severe is scar formation or contracture?
- Did individual lose the fingers or hand? If so, how will this affect the daily activities of individual?
- Would individual benefit from psychological and occupational therapy?

References

Carrougher, Gretchen J. "Nursing Care of Clients with Burn Injury." Luckmann's Core Principles and Practice of Medical-Surgical Nursing. Polaski, Arlene L., and Suzanne E. Tatro, eds. Philadelphia: W.B. Saunders Company, 1996. 1365-1388.

Cioffi, W.G. "What's New in Burns and Metabolism." Journal of American College Surgery 192 2 (2001): 241-254.

Duke, James A. The Green Pharmacy. Emmaus: Rodale Press, Inc, 1997.

Fauerbach, J.A., et al. "Barriers to Employment Among Working-Aged Patients with Major Burn Injury." Journal of Burn Care and Rehabilitation 22 1 (2001): 26-34.

Matheson, J.D., J. Clayton, and M.J. Muller. "The Reduction of Itch During Burn Wound Healing." Journal of Burn Care and Rehabilitation 22 1 (2001): 76-81.

Richard, Reginald, and Marlys Staley. Burn Care and Rehabilitation: Principles and Practice. Philadelphia: F.A. Davis Company, 1994.

Sohn, Augustine J. "Burns." Saunders Manual of Medical Practice, 2nd ed. Rakel, Robert E., ed. Philadelphia: W.B. Saunders Company, 2000. 1301-1303.

Van Loey, N.E., A.E. Faber, and L.A. Taal. "Do Burn Patients Need Burn Specific Multidisciplinary Outpatient Aftercare: Research Results." 27 2 (2001): 103-110.

References (Continued)

Feinstein, Alice, ed. Healing with Vitamins. Emmaus: Rodale Press, Inc, 1996.

Kao, C.C., and W.L. Garner. "Acute Burns." Plastic Reconstructive Surgery 101 7 (2001): 2482-2493.

Warden, G.D., and D.M. Heimbach. "Burns." Principles of Surgery Companion Handbook, 7th ed. Schwartz, Seymour I., ed. New York: McGraw-Hill, 1999. 183-221.

Wiebelhaus, P., and S.L. Hansen. "What You Should Know About Managing Burn Emergencies." Nursing 31 1 (2000): 36-41.

Bursitis

Other names / synonyms: Carpet-Layer's Knee, Clergyman's Knee, Dialysis Elbow, Housemaid's Knee, Lunger's Elbow, Miner's Elbow, Student's Elbow, Weaver's Bottom

726, 727.3

Definition

Bursitis is the painful inflammation of a bursa. Bursae are fluid-filled sacs that cushion the movement between the bones, muscles, and tendons near the joints. While the number varies, most individuals have between 150 and 160 bursae throughout the body. Bursae are lined with synovial cells that secrete a fluid rich in collagen and proteins. The synovial fluid acts as a lubricant when body parts move. When this fluid becomes infected with bacteria or irritated because of excessive movement, the condition known as bursitis results.

Bursitis is most often caused by trauma especially prolonged or repetitive movements. Other causes of bursitis include infection (usually found in bursae close to the surface of the skin) and crystal deposits (due to gout, rheumatoid arthritis, or scleroderma).

The exact incidence of bursitis in athletes and nonathletes is not known because no published epidemiologic studies have been done.

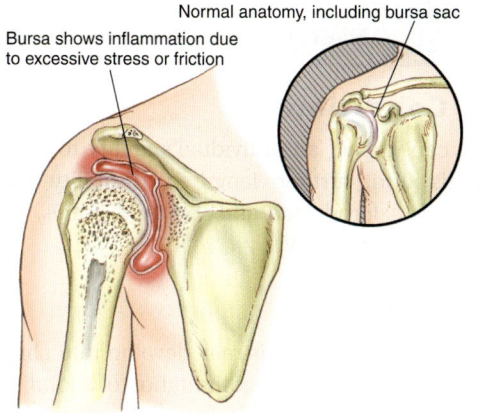

Bursa shows inflammation due to excessive stress or friction

Normal anatomy, including bursa sac

Laurie O'Keefe

Diagnosis

History: Individuals may report localized tenderness, warmth, swelling, redness of the skin, and loss of function (limited joint motion). If the bursa is infected, the individual may report systemic symptoms including fever and red streaks leading from the bursae. Limited motion of an extremity may be noted by the individual. Questions should be directed to a history of recent trauma directly over the bursae or to repetitive activity.

Physical exam: Visual inspection may reveal swelling. Skin should be inspected for breakdown and possible entry of a foreign object. Touching (palpation) the affected joint and bursae often reveals soft, boggy or tense tissue depending on the amount of fluid build up. The bursa is tender. Motion is limited by pain and swelling in acute cases. More chronic conditions may show decreased motion from adhesions and thickening of the tissue. Muscle weakness may develop from lack of use (disuse atrophy).

Tests: Plain x-rays of the joint and surrounding area are normal in acute cases unless calcium deposits have developed. It is important to look for changes in the bone from more chronic irritation and to rule out bone infection (osteomyelitis). The bursa fluid may be examined by aspiration to rule out gout and infection (synovial fluid analysis). If an infection is suspected, blood tests may be ordered (ESR, CBC).

Treatment

Initial treatment of bursitis involves protection of the affected bursa including padding for bursa close to the surface of the skin, resting the affected area, application of ice for 10 minutes at least twice a day to treat both inflammation and pain, compression (elastic bandage), elevation of the affected area above the level of the heart, and medication (e.g., aspirin, ibuprofen or other anti-inflammatory medications).

If the bursitis is not due to an infection and is not responding to the initial treatment, the physician may inject the affected bursa with a corticosteroid. The corticosteroid injection reduces inflammation immediately and may have a lasting effect.

Surgical excision of bursae (bursectomy) may be required if the condition is chronic or frequently recurrent. Surgery is generally performed if and only if conservative treatment fails. The operation varies according to the site of the affected bursa.

If the individual has infectious bursitis, antibiotics should be started as soon as blood cultures are drawn. Individuals with systemic symptoms (e.g., fever or chills) may require admission to the hospital and intravenous antibiotics administered. Staphylococcus aureus is the most common organism accounting for greater than 80% of infectious bursitis cases. Antibiotics should be administered in combination with repeated aspirations every 1 to 3 days.

Prognosis

In general, bursitis responds well to conservative treatment. Most individuals respond to therapy in 3 to 4 days. If the bursitis is due to infection, the area may need to be drained every 1 to 3 days until the infected fluid does not return. If the underlying cause of the condition is not corrected, chronic bursitis may develop.

Bursectomy usually yields a satisfactory outcome.

Differential Diagnosis

Rheumatoid arthritis, blunt injuries to the abdomen, tendonitis, tumors of the bone or soft tissue, cellulitis, and costochondritis (inflammation of the rib joints) can appear similar to bursitis. Unsuspected or hidden fractures may also have similar findings.

Specialists

- Orthopedic Surgeon
- Physiatrist
- Podiatrist
- Rheumatologist
- Sports Medicine Physician

Rehabilitation

The goal of rehabilitation for bursitis is to decrease the inflammation and pain to the inflamed bursa. This allows the physical therapist to then focus on restoring motion and strength to any associated joints involved. Early in the condition, the physical therapist instructs the individual to elevate the affected joint to help reduce swelling. The individual also learns how to avoid pressure from the inflamed bursa by applying an elastic bandage, sling, or soft foam pad to protect the involved area until the swelling goes down.

Rehabilitation offers several possible treatments in controlling inflammation as a result of bursitis. At the initial flare-up, the physical therapist uses cold treatments to control swelling and pain. Electrical stimulation combined with a cold treatment is another technique that relaxes muscles around the inflamed bursa and helps decrease pain and inflammation.

Once the initial pain and inflammation (acute stage of bursitis) improve, heat is applied in the rehabilitation process. Heat treatments help relieve muscle and joint pain and stiffness along with increasing the blood flow to help remove inflammation from the bursa. Moist heat packs are used over multiple layers of toweling to achieve a comfortable warming effect. Ultrasound is a technique that uses high frequency sound waves to produce heat that penetrates deep into the involved bursa and surrounding joint and muscles.

Once pain and swelling are greatly reduced, the physical therapist performs stretching exercises that help restore full motion to an affected joint and/or limb. Such passive range of motion exercises consist of the therapist moving the affected limb with no effort initiated by the individual. The physical therapist may need to modify the program depending on the location of the affected bursa, stage of the inflammation (i.e., recent flare up or ongoing pain), and whether surgery was required. However, it is rarely necessary to surgically remove an affected bursa.

Work Restrictions / Accommodations

If a certain activity (repetitive motion) caused the individual's bursitis, then the individual may need to limit the activity or use protective measures. For example, kneepads or some type of cushioning should be used for gardening or scrubbing the floor. Plumbers, roofers, and carpet layers should wear knee protection. Shoes with appropriate cushioning or ankle pads may need to be worn. Individual should perform exercises to strengthen the muscles and improve flexibility around the affected bursa.

Using heat or ice treatments after work to relieve any soreness that may occur helps to reduce the recurrence of bursitis.

Anti-inflammatory medications (e.g., aspirin or ibuprofen) can be used after working to relieve pain and inflammation.

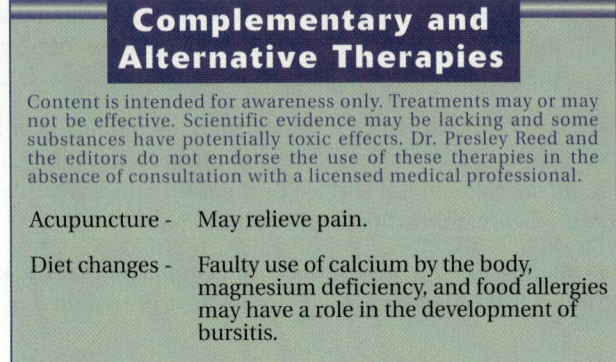

Complementary and Alternative Therapies

Content is intended for awareness only. Treatments may or may not be effective. Scientific evidence may be lacking and some substances have potentially toxic effects. Dr. Presley Reed and the editors do not endorse the use of these therapies in the absence of consultation with a licensed medical professional.

Acupuncture -	May relieve pain.
Diet changes -	Faulty use of calcium by the body, magnesium deficiency, and food allergies may have a role in the development of bursitis.
Magnetic field therapy -	May relieve pain.

Comorbid Conditions

Conditions that can impact an individual's ability to recover from all types of bursitis and further lengthen disability include gout, rheumatoid arthritis, scleroderma, and obesity, diabetes, and a compromised immune system (e.g., HIV).

Complications

Poorly treated or untreated bursitis may develop into chronic bursitis. Frozen joint syndrome or permanent limitation of a joint's mobility are other possible complications.

Factors Influencing Duration

Factors that may influence length of disability include the number of bursae affected, site, cause, activity, response to treatment, and individual understanding of the disease and treatment process. It is essential for the individual to understand that a restriction of the repetitive motion that caused the bursitis may be necessary.

Length of Disability

Duration depends on site and type of treatment.

Duration in Days

Job Classification	Minimum	Optimum	Maximum
Sedentary work	0	3	7
Light work	0	3	7
Medium work	0	3	7
Heavy work	3	7	14
Very Heavy work	3	7	14

Duration Trend from Normative Data*

Cases	Mean	Min	Max	No Lost Time	Over 6 Months
2611	38	0	438	0.27%	0.19%

Percentile:	5th	25th	Median	75th	95th
Days:	6	15	25	47	115

ICD-9-CM 727.3 - Reported Length of Disability (Days)

* Differences may exist between the expected duration tables and the normative graphs. Duration tables provide expected recovery periods based on the type of work performed by the individual. The normative graphs reflect the actual observed experience of many individuals across the spectrum of physical conditions, in a variety of industries, and with varying levels of case management.

Failure to Recover

If an individual fails to recover within the maximum duration expectancy period, the reader may wish to reference the following questions to assist in better understanding the specifics of an individual's medical case.

Regarding diagnosis:

- Was the diagnosis of bursitis confirmed?
- Did laboratory examination of synovial fluid aspiration reveal crystals or bacterial infection?
- Has individual experienced any complications?

Regarding treatment:

- If symptoms were not reduced by conservative methods, was the inflamed bursa injected with a corticosteroid?
- Have all conservative modalities failed?
- Is surgical intervention warranted?
- Was culture and sensitivity done to identify the infecting organism and determine most effective antibiotic? Were antibiotic-resistant organisms ruled out?
- Were aspirations done on a regular basis to monitor effectiveness of treatment?
- Has individual received appropriate physical therapy?

Regarding prognosis:

- Was joint function impaired?
- Would individual benefit from additional physical therapy to strengthen muscles and reestablish the joint's full range of motion?
- In infectious bursitis, was the area drained until the infectious fluid no longer returned? Could infection still be present?
- Would individual benefit from additional antibiotic therapy?
- Were comorbid conditions such as gout, rheumatoid arthritis, or chronic overuse appropriately addressed?

References

Griffith, H. Winter. Complete Guide to Sports Injuries. New York: The Berkley Publishing Group, 1997.

Kessler, R.M. Management of Common Musculoskeletal Disorders: Physical Therapy Principles and Methods. Philadelphia: J.B. Lippincott Co, 1990.

Byssinosis

Other names / synonyms: Brown Lung, Brown Lung Disease, Byssinosis Pneumonoconiosis, Cannabinosis, Cotton Dust Asthma, Cotton Worker's Disease, Cotton-Mill Fever, Monday Chest-Tightness, Monday Fever, Occupational Byssinosis, Pneumoconiosis

504

Definition

Byssinosis is a lung disease caused by an allergy to an unknown agent found in dust produced during the processing of organic fibers such as cotton, flax, hemp, or sisal that is inhaled.

Byssinosis is characterized by a feeling of tightness in the chest, coughing, wheezing, and shortness of breath. Byssinosis is usually found among individuals working with crude or unprocessed materials. Workers opening bales of raw cotton or who work with hemp, sisal, or flax, or are involved in the early stages of processing are at the highest risk for developing this disease. Smoking also increases the risk.

Byssinosis used to be prevalent in textile-producing nations worldwide. Preventive measures in the textile industry have lowered the incidence of the disease in the US and other developed nations, but is still common in developing countries where preventive measures are not in place. In the US, there are fewer than 10 deaths annually due to this disease. The majority of US cases are reported in North Carolina, followed by South Carolina, Georgia, and Vermont, and occur primarily in those over the age of 50. Other large cotton-producing countries include China, India, Pakistan, Uzbekistan, Brazil, Turkey, Australia, Turkmenistan, and Egypt.

Diagnosis

History: Symptoms include a history of exposure to dusts from textile manufacture, tightness in the chest, wheezing, coughing, and shortness of breath when exposed to the dust produced during processing of cotton, flax, hemp, or sisal. The symptoms usually lessen or go away when the worker goes home. Symptoms are more pronounced on the first day after returning to work following a weekend or vacation. They gradually lessen with repeated exposure throughout the week. In chronic byssinosis, symptoms persist even when the individual is away from work.

Physical exam: Listening to breath sounds through a stethoscope (auscultation) may reveal abnormally dry or moist respiratory sounds (rales).

Tests: Pulmonary function tests using spirometers and peak flow meters evaluate lung volume and capacity, and help identify and measure any obstructions or restrictions (or combination of both) in air flow through the lungs, thus confirming the presence of lung disease. Arterial blood gases (ABG) assess the efficiency of gas exchange in the lungs by showing its rate of absorption into the blood. Chest x-rays may be helpful in ruling out other lung disorders.

Treatment

Treatment is aimed at reducing symptoms, the most important being to limit exposure to the offending dust. This can be achieved by wearing protective clothing and a face mask, and implementing industrial dust control measures, if possible. Those who smoke should be encouraged to quit. Drugs may be used to widen or expand the channels within the airways of the lungs (bronchodilators). Severe cases may require medication to reduce inflammation in the lungs (corticosteroids). Chronic byssinosis may also require supplemental oxygen and breathing exercises.

Prognosis

In most individuals, symptoms are temporary and have no long-term effects. Most individuals fully recover after eliminating their exposure to the offending dust. Chronic exposure over a period of years however, may permanently impair lung function. Although rare, death due to byssinosis is possible.

Specialists

- Occupational Medicine Physician
- Pulmonologist

Differential Diagnosis

Conditions with similar symptoms include asthma and bronchitis. Other forms of pneumoconiosis (including asbestosis, silicosis, siderosis, stannosis) should also be eliminated as possibilities.

Work Restrictions / Accommodations

Protective clothing and/or facemasks should be provided to workers exposed to cotton dust or other unprocessed organic fibers. Particularly sensitive individuals or those with severe or advanced byssinosis may require reassignment to a position involving little or no contact with the offending dust. If lung damage becomes extensive, prolonged or strenuous activity may become impossible. If oxygen therapy is initiated, the individual will need to avoid certain flammable materials.

Comorbid Conditions

Other lung disease or other lung infections may prolong disability.

Complications

Byssinosis can lead to chronic bronchitis. Lung damage can become extensive and result in respiratory failure.

Factors Influencing Duration

Duration of disability may be influenced by severity of symptoms, the individual's overall health, or the presence of complications. An individual who smokes may lengthen disability by aggravating the symptoms.

Length of Disability

Disability will be longer for those with diminished lung capacity performing moderate-to-heavy work. If lung damage is extensive, disability may be permanent.

Acute exacerbations due to re-exposure.

Duration in Days

Job Classification	Minimum	Optimum	Maximum
Sedentary work	1	2	7
Light work	1	2	7
Medium work	2	3	7
Heavy work	2	4	10
Very Heavy work	3	5	10

Failure to Recover

If an individual fails to recover within the maximum duration expectancy period, the reader may wish to reference the following questions to assist in better understanding the specifics of an individual's medical case.

Regarding diagnosis:

- Does individual work in the textile industry?
- Is individual a smoker?
- Does individual have tightness in the chest? Wheezing? Coughing? Short of breath?
- Are the symptoms better when away from work? Are they more pronounced the first day back to work after a weekend or vacation? Do symptoms lessen as the workweek goes on?
- Were rales present on auscultation?
- Does individual have decreased breathing capacity?
- Has individual had a pulmonary function test? Chest x-ray? Arterial blood gasses?
- Have conditions with similar symptoms been ruled out?

Regarding treatment:

- Is individual being treated with corticosteroids? Bronchodilators? If so, are the medications being used according to the physician's instructions?
- Has exposure to the offending dust been minimized?
- Has individual quit smoking?
- Is supplemental oxygen necessary? Breathing exercises?

Regarding prognosis:

- Can individual's employer accommodate any necessary restrictions?
- Does individual have any conditions that could affect ability to recover?
- Have any complications occurred such as chronic bronchitis or respiratory failure?

References

Britannica.com. "Byssinosis." Encyclopedia Britannica. 2000. 01 Jan 2001 <http://www.britannica.com/seo/b/byssinosis/>.

Byssinosis (Cotton Dust). Thrive Online. 2000. 01 Jan 2001 <http://www.thriveonline.com/medical/library/article/001089.html>.

Caisson Disease

Other names / synonyms: Decompression Illness, Decompression Sickness, The Bends

993.3

Definition

Caisson disease got its name from the pressurized submerged structures, caissons, which were used to prepare river bottoms for the placement of supports for bridges. Caisson disease is more commonly called decompression sickness (DCS). Decompression sickness, usually manifesting as joint pain or neurological dysfunction, occurs after exiting the compressed air environment. The condition not only occurs in individuals who work in compressed air, but also in recreational and professional divers and aviators who fly at high altitude. After a reduction in ambient pressure, nitrogen in body tissues can become supersaturated, and form bubbles, which then damage tissue.

A rapid reduction in ambient pressure, after uptake of excessive amounts of nitrogen, may cause bubbles to form in those tissues and produce symptoms. Once bubbles have formed, they will increase in size as nitrogen diffuses into them from surrounding tissues.

Decompression sickness can occur after one breathes compressed gas at depths usually greater than 30 feet (a pressure equal to 13.3 pounds per square inch [psi] above sea level pressure). A diagnosis of DCS is made on recent history of scuba diving after excluding other illnesses and injuries. Adequate diagnosis requires a thorough neurological and physical exam.

Diagnosis

History: Symptoms of DCS can be mild, severe or even life threatening, depending on the location of the bubbles in the tissues. Paralysis, which occurs when bubble accumulate in the spinal cord, is one of the most serious symptoms of DCS. More commonly, individuals report fatigue, joint or muscle pain in the extremities and pins and needles (paresthesias) over any part of the body. Pain, usually localized in the joints, is another common initial symptom. Other associated symptoms may be headache, vertigo and general or specific weakness.

A dive history helps determine the likelihood of a decompression event. Relevant information includes the number of dives, depth and duration of dives.

Approximately 50% of all initial symptoms of DCS will begin within 2 hours after the diver surfaces.

Physical exam: Motor weakness, fatigue, headache, vertigo, numbness to sensation (hypesthesia), reflex asymmetry and altered mental status may be evident. Most symptoms occur within 24 hours after exposure; altitude exposure, including flying commercial aircraft, can sometimes provoke symptoms.

With the exception of injury to the inner ear, clinical evaluation at the bedside remains the best way to diagnose DCI.

Tests: To date, modern imaging techniques have not proven beneficial in assessing DCI, but they can be used to rule out other medical illness or injury. Similarly, clinical laboratory studies are not usually helpful except to exclude hypoglycemia or illicit drug use.

Individuals who present with vertigo, suggesting inner ear involvement, may require audiography and electronystagmography after recompression treatment. This will quantify the deficit and provide a baseline against which further assessments can be compared.

Treatment

Recompression therapy should not be delayed for additional testing. If recompression treatment is not immediately available, administration of intravenous or oral fluids to correct dehydration and 100% oxygen are recommended. If possible, 100% oxygen, should be dispensed through a tight-fitting non-rebreather mask or demand valve. Increased partial pressures of oxygen in the lungs and arterial blood help speed the elimination of nitrogen from body tissues and resolve symptoms.

Treatment of decompression illness is recompression in a hyperbaric chamber. The usual treatment in a multiplace chamber consists of a 285-minute pressure exposure called a Treatment Table 6, which uses 100% oxygen breathing mixed with intermittent periods of air breathing. By increasing ambient pressure, existing bubbles in the body are also reduced in size, facilitating an immediate resolution of symptoms. While most cases resolve after a single recompression, additional hyperbaric treatments may be necessary. More resistant cases of DCS may require up to 7 recompression treatments until symptoms either resolve or plateau. Depending on the severity of the injury, one may require hospitalization.

Prognosis

Complete recovery is expected if there is minimal pain or neurological symptoms after a dive, early application of 100% oxygen, early recompression in a hyperbaric chamber, and resolution of symptoms during the initial recompression therapy.

Conversely, divers who have severe spinal and cerebral symptoms - loss of consciousness and paralysis - may have residual neurological effects even after definitive treatment.

Mild cases of DCS, especially associated with altitude, often resolve spontaneously or after treatment with oxygen and fluids. However, symptoms can recur, and all individuals should be evaluated medically for treatment in a hyperbaric chamber.

Differential Diagnosis

Medical conditions such as hyperventilation, influenza, recent history of muscle and joint trauma, neck and spinal injury and various peripheral and nervous system disorders such as carpal tunnel syndrome or ruptured spinal discs can mimic DCS.

Arterial gas embolism (AGE), another condition that can occur in divers, results from breath holding or gas trapping due to disease during ascent; if the lungs cannot empty their excess gas, they will over-inflate, causing rupture and entry of gas into the bloodstream. DCS and AGE are commonly referred to as decompression illness (DCI). Although they differ in pathology, their treatment and outcome are largely the same.

Specialists

- Emergency Medicine

Rehabilitation

Individuals who have suffered DCS may experience recurrent symptoms if exposed to altitude. Therefore, it is usually recommended that following treatment and resolution of symptoms, 72 hours elapse before altitude exposure (e.g., commercial flight). Individuals experiencing more severe forms of DCS, especially spinal and cerebral symptoms, may require longer.

Anyone suffering from cerebral or spinal cord symptoms may require physical therapy. Rehabilitation for these individuals is the same as for stroke or spinal cord injury patients, although the outcome is usually better. Major improvement in motor function can occur over 6 to 12 months following treatment. Deep vein thrombosis can also occur, and therefore prophylaxis is appropriate. Physical therapy focuses on maintaining one's mobility and muscular strength, and relearning walking and balancing skills. Given time for functioning to return to normal, DCS individuals have a high rate of complete recovery.

Work Restrictions / Accommodations

In addition to restricting travel by aircraft or altitude exposures, individuals who have had DCI may be restricted from breathing compressed gas for one week to several months, depending on the severity of injury and response to recompression. As for when to return to diving, commercial or occupational cases of DCS may have a shorter convalescence period than aviators.

Comorbid Conditions

The presence of any disease that would impair the absorption or transport of oxygen may impair the effectiveness of treatment and recovery. Coexisting injuries such as a pneumothorax or a near drowning episode should be treated before a diver can undergo recompression in a hyperbaric chamber.

Complications

Possible complications of decompression sickness can range from mild arthritic-type joint pain, permanent loss of sensation in an extremity, bowel and bladder retention, difficulty with balance and walking and paralysis. Impairments can curtail normal daily activities such as work, recreational, self-care and sexual function.

Factors Influencing Duration

Disability factors include extent of decompression illness, timelines of oxygen and recompression therapy, if individual has spinal cord or cerebral symptoms.

Length of Disability

This condition can range from the very mild to the severe. Disability may be permanent. Contact physician to obtain specific case information.

Failure to Recover

If an individual fails to recover within the maximum duration expectancy period, the reader may wish to reference the following questions to assist in better understanding the specifics of an individual's medical case.

Regarding diagnosis:

- Does the individual's work or recreational environment involve breathing compressed air, such as scuba diving or flying at high altitudes?
- If the individual is a diver, how many dives has the individual recently done, at what depth, and for how long?
- Does the individual complain of fatigue, joint or muscle pain in the extremities, or the sensation of pins-and-needles (paresthesias) in any part of the body?
- Does the individual report headache, vertigo, or general or specific weakness?
- Does the individual report the inability to move (paralysis)?
- Have imaging tests been done to rule out other illness or injury?
- Have laboratory tests been done to rule out decreased blood sugar (hypoglycemia) or illicit drug use?
- Was the diagnosis of DCS confirmed?

Regarding treatment:

- Was recompression therapy administered immediately via a hyperbaric chamber?
- If not available, were intravenous or oral fluids and 100% oxygen administered immediately?
- Did recompression occur after one treatment or did the individual require additional treatments in the hyperbaric chamber?
- Was hospitalization required?
- Was 100% oxygen dispensed through a tight-fitting non-rebreather mask or demand valve?
- If the individual experienced vertigo, were audiography and electronystagmography done after recompression treatment to quantify the deficit and provide a baseline against which further assessments could be compared?
- Were symptoms completely resolved after recompression treatment?

Regarding prognosis:

- How severe were the symptoms?
- Did the individual receive early application of 100% oxygen or early recompression in a hyperbaric chamber?
- Did resolution of symptoms occur after the initial recompression therapy?
- Have symptoms recurred?
- If so, has the individual been evaluated for treatment in a hyperbaric chamber?
- Did spinal and cerebral symptoms occur?

- Does the individual have residual neurological effects such as permanent loss of sensation in extremities, stool and urine retention, difficulty with balance and walking, or paralysis?
- How will these affect the daily activities of the individual?
- Would the individual benefit from rehabilitation for neurological deficits?

References

Moon, R.E., and P.J. Sheffield. "Guidelines for Treatment of Decompression Illness." Aviation, Space, and Environmental Medicine 68 3 (1997): 234-243.

Vann, Richard, and Donna Uguccioni, eds. Report on Decompression Illness, Diving Fatalities and Project Dive Exploration. Durham: Divers Alert Network, 2001.

Calculus, Bladder

Other names / synonyms: Bladder Stones
594, 594.0, 594.1, 594.2

Definition

Bladder calculi are stone-like masses (composed of mineral salts) that form in the bladder. Normal urine contains predictable amounts of calcium, magnesium, uric acid, and other by-products of metabolism, which have passed into the bladder in solution form. However, under certain conditions the chemicals may crystalize and form stone-like particles. Once formed, continued crystallization is stimulated. Most bladder stones are struvite stones (infection stone) or composed of uric acid.

The primary risk factor for forming bladder stones is decreased flow of urine from the bladder (bladder stasis). This can be a result of urethral strictures or a neurogenic bladder. Other risk factors include radiation cystitis and bladder neck obstruction. Dietary factors may also be implicated. Other causes include bladder diverticula and foreign bodies.

Individuals in the Middle East and Southeast Asia are more at risk for bladder stones than individuals who live in the US.

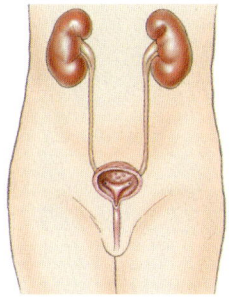 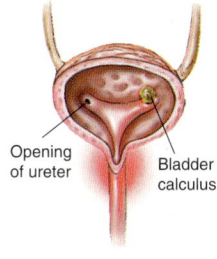

Opening of ureter — Bladder calculus

Laurie O'Keefe

Diagnosis

History: Symptoms may include urinary difficulty, frequency, and urgency, or interruption of the urinary stream. Individuals may complain of lower abdominal pain due to the obstruction of the passage from the bladder to the outside of the body (urethra) by the stone. There may be discomfort and an inability to find relief in any position. Blood in the urine is common.

Physical exam: Applying light pressure with fingertips (palpation) may reveal an enlarged and tender bladder (bladder distension).

Tests: The urine is examined (urinalysis) for red blood cells (hematuria), pus (pyuria), the presence of crystals, and the acidity or alkalinity (pH) of the urine. X-ray studies (abdominal films) can visualize most bladder stones. Excretory urograms can be performed to view the urinary tract to determine the presence of stones. CT scan can be used to view radiolucent stones. Cystoscopy will identify all bladder calculi.

Treatment

Pain relievers (analgesics) and drugs that destroy microorganisms (antimicrobials) may be prescribed until the stones can be removed.

Small stones may be removed through a tube that is passed through the urethra into the bladder (cystoscope, cystourethroscopy). Larger calculi may be broken up and removed using a laser probe passed through a telescopic tube scope into the bladder (laser lithotripsy).

Prior to 1986, when the lithotripsy came into routine use, open surgery was done to remove bladder stones (cysto-lithotomy); less than 5% now undergo this procedure. It is still done, however, if large stones do not respond to laser pulverizing, or laser use is contraindicated. This procedure requires the administration of general anesthesia, after which an incision is made through the abdomen into the neck of the bladder. Calculi are then removed and the bladder sutured. This surgery requires an indwelling catheter for about a week to prevent urine leaking from the scar, followed by bed rest for several weeks.

Prognosis

The outcome (prognosis) is excellent. Recurrent stones are uncommon if the obstruction and infection are treated.

Differential Diagnosis

Conditions with similar symptoms include an enlarged prostate, appendicitis, ectopic pregnancy, bladder infections, and other urinary tract stones.

Specialists

- Urologist

Work Restrictions / Accommodations

Restrictions or accommodations generally are not necessary following removal of stones.

Comorbid Conditions

Bladder infection (cystitis), and underlying metabolic disorders might influence length of disability.

Complications

Infection of the bladder and urethral obstruction may complicate bladder calculi.

Factors Influencing Duration

The individual's response to treatment may influence length of disability. Bladder infections will also prolong length of disability.

Length of Disability

Lithotripsy, Extracorpeal Shock Wave.

Duration in Days

Job Classification	Minimum	Optimum	Maximum
Sedentary work	1	2	7
Light work	1	2	7
Medium work	1	2	7
Heavy work	1	2	7
Very Heavy work	1	2	7

Cystoscopic removal (cystoscopy).

Duration in Days

Job Classification	Minimum	Optimum	Maximum
Sedentary work	3	7	14
Light work	3	7	14
Medium work	3	7	14
Heavy work	3	7	14
Very Heavy work	3	7	14

Open surgery.

Duration in Days

Job Classification	Minimum	Optimum	Maximum
Sedentary work	7	14	21
Light work	14	17	21
Medium work	21	25	28
Heavy work	28	35	42
Very Heavy work	28	35	42

Failure to Recover

If an individual fails to recover within the maximum duration expectancy period, the reader may wish to reference the following questions to assist in better understanding the specifics of an individual's medical case.

Regarding diagnosis:

- Did the individual present with symptoms of urinary urgency, frequency or hesitancy? Did they complain of lower abdominal pain?
- Did the physical exam reveal an enlarged bladder that was tender to palpation?
- Were bladder calculi detected with diagnostic x-rays (urography, CT scan) or cystoscopy?
- If the diagnosis was uncertain, were other conditions with similar symptoms (enlarged prostate, appendicitis, or ectopic pregnancy) ruled out?

Regarding treatment:

- Did conditions exist that warranted intervention with cystourethroscopy, lithotomy, or lithotripsy?

Regarding prognosis:

- If recovery is taking longer than expected, what are the extenuating circumstances?
- Does the individual have any conditions such as nephritis, cystitis, or underlying metabolic disorders that could impact recovery and prognosis?
- Did the individual suffer any complications associated with the urinary calculi or treatment procedures that could influence length of recovery?

References

Beers, Mark, and Robert Berkow, eds. The Merck Manual of Diagnosis and Therapy. Online: Medical Services, USMEDSA, USHH, 1999. 01 Jan 2001 <http://www.merck.com/pubs/mmanual>.

Williams, Richard, MD, and James Donovan, MD. "Urology." Current Surgical Diagnosis and Treatment. Way, Lawrence, MD, ed. Norwalk: Appleton & Lange, 1991. 886-949.

Calculus, Renal (Kidney and Ureter)

Other names / synonyms: Kidney Stone, Nephrolithiasis, Ureteral Stone, Urolithiasis

592, 592.0, 592.1, 592.9

Definition

Renal calculi (nephrolithiasis) are stone-like masses that have developed in the kidneys. The calculi are formed by the accumulation of minerals in the urine.

Most cases of renal calculi have no identifiable underlying cause, although some are formed as a result of an underlying metabolic disorder or an infection.

Normal urine contains predictable amounts of calcium, magnesium, uric acid, and other by-products of metabolism. They are normally in solution and pass into the bladder. Sometimes, the chemicals may crystalize and form a stone-like particle in the kidney. Once formed, it stimulates continued crystallization. Approximately 80% of kidney and ureteral stones are composed mainly of calcium oxalate, although some are also formed by calcium phosphate. Higher levels of oxalate in the urine may be the result of a diet high in oxalic acid (rhubarb, leafy vegetables, coffee). When combined with calcium, oxalate forms a salt that dissolves poorly, so an abnormally high level of oxalate in the urine encourages stone formation. Calcium stones may also be the first evidence of metabolic disturbances associated with overactive parathyroid glands (hyperparathyroidism). They may also be associated with renal tubular acidosis, sarcoidosis, vitamin D intoxication, and "idiopathic" hypercalciuria.

Five percent of renal stones are composed of uric acid. These stones may occur in individuals with gout, some forms of cancer, and in chronic fluid depletion (dehydration). Approximately 2% of calculi are formed from the amino acid cystine, and affect individuals with particular inherited metabolic disorders.

Approximately 13% of renal calculi are linked with chronic infections of the urinary tract. Bacterial action on a substance in urine (urea) results in urine with high alkaline and ammonium content. Called struvite stones, these stones are composed of a combination of calcium, magnesium, and ammonium phosphate. A struvite stone may fill the entire network of urine-collecting ducts within the kidney, as well as the top part of the ureter.

Each year in the US, approximately 1 individual per 1,000 is hospitalized with a renal calculus. Renal stones are more common in males than in females; they have a high rate of recurrence. Forty-fifty percent of men who have developed a renal stone will have a recurrence within 5 years, and 60-80% of males will have a recurrence within 10 years. Females have a recurrence rate of renal stones that is two thirds of that for males. The incidence of renal stones is highest in the summer months. This may occur because perspiration caused by the warmer weather concentrates the urine with precipitation of the dissolved minerals.

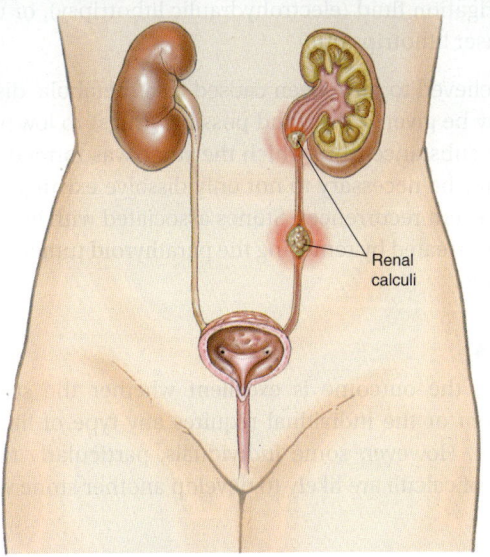

Renal calculi

Diagnosis

History: Symptoms vary according to the site and size of the stone. Small stones in the kidney may cause no symptoms until they start to pass down the tube that carries urine from the kidney to the bladder (ureter). The resulting pain (renal colic) is excruciating and intermittent. Individuals may report pain that starts on the far right or far left side of the back (flank), then moves toward the groin. The pain may be so severe that it causes nausea and vomiting, which can then result in significant fluid depletion (dehydration). Blood may be noted in the urine (hematuria). Fever, chills, and frequent urination may also be reported.

Physical exam: The individual may appear to be in severe pain; this may result in an elevated blood pressure. Tapping softly on the flank worsens the pain. Light pressure applied with the fingertips (palpation) to the lower abdomen may reveal an enlarged and tender bladder (bladder distension).

Tests: Microscopic examination of the urine may reveal large numbers of red blood cells (hematuria), pus (pyuria), and the presence of crystals. Urine cultures should be done to check for evidence of an infection. X-ray studies of the kidneys, ureters, and bladder (KUB) can confirm the presence of most renal calculi and show the site of the stone. The most definitive test is an x-ray of the kidneys taken after contrast medium is injected into the arm (intravenous urography; IVU). This test can confirm the site of the stone and indicate any obstruction of the urinary tract above the stone. Obstruction can also be monitored by ultrasound scanning and by computed tomography scanning (CT scan).

Treatment

The majority of small stones (less than 5 millimeters in diameter) are passed into the urine with relatively few problems. Fluid intake is increased to encourage the passage of the stone from the kidney, through the ureter, into the bladder, and out through the urethra. Walking is also encouraged as this facilitates stone passage.

Stones that cause obstruction and are accompanied by fever and/or infection require immediate treatment. The individual will be hospitalized and treated with intravenous (IV) antibiotics and bedrest; pain will be relieved with narcotic analgesics. Once the individual is stable and underlying conditions have been treated, the stones will be removed using one, or more, of several procedures. Extracorporeal shock wave lithotripsy (ESWL) focuses shock waves on small stones from outside the body and is used to disintegrate them. Removal of calculi in the ureter requires inserting a viewing tube (ureteroscope) into the ureter. If the calculus is easily viewed and not large, a device with a basket-like tip is inserted that grasps and removes it.

Large calculi often require disintegration prior to removal. The calculi can be crushed using sound waves (ultrasonic lithotripsy), using shock waves with irrigation fluid (electrohydraulic lithotripsy), or using laser technology (laser lithotripsy).

If a stone is believed to have been caused by a metabolic disorder, the individual may be given a diet (and possibly drugs) to lower the urine content of the substance from which the stone was formed. Increased fluid intake may be necessary to not only dissolve existing stones, but also to help prevent recurrences. Stones associated with hyperparathyroidism are also treated by removing the parathyroid tumor responsible for the condition.

Prognosis

In most cases, the outcome is excellent whether the stone passes without incident or the individual requires any type of lithotripsy or basket-removal. However, some individuals, particularly males, who have a history of calculi are likely to develop another stone within 5-10 years.

Differential Diagnosis

Conditions with similar symptoms include pyelonephritis, kidney tumor, back strain, cholecystitis, appendicitis, stomach ulcer (peptic ulcer), inflammation of the pancreas (pancreatitis), or ectopic pregnancy.

Specialists

- Nephrologist
- Urologist

Work Restrictions / Accommodations

Individuals who are in the midst of passing a kidney stone are unable to work, but may resume work once the stone passes. Those who have jobs in which the sudden and severe pain from a calculus could put them at risk (such as heavy-equipment operators, construction workers, or those who do heavy lifting) may need to stay home or be assigned less dangerous duties when experiencing kidney stone problems. Individuals with stones also may require restrictions on bending, stooping, and heavy lifting. All will require frequent access to fluids to aid in hydration. Those who are hospitalized will need from several days to weeks to recover, depending on what procedure was done while in the hospital.

Comorbid Conditions

Urinary tract infection, underlying metabolic disorders, overactive parathyroid glands (hyperparathyroidism), and obesity may influence length of disability.

Complications

Renal calculi may be associated with recurrent episodes of urinary tract infection. Any obstruction to urine flow may result in rapid kidney damage or severe kidney infection (pyelonephritis).

Complementary and Alternative Therapies

Content is intended for awareness only. Treatments may or may not be effective. Scientific evidence may be lacking and some substances have potentially toxic effects. Dr. Presley Reed and the editors do not endorse the use of these therapies in the absence of consultation with a licensed medical professional.

Naturopathy - If individual has a tendency to develop kidney stones, it is important to maintain body fluids by adequate fluid intake and avoidance of profuse sweating. Drinking 3-4 quarts of liquids daily, especially during the night, increases urination, dilutes urine, and makes it harder for substances to bind together, forming stones.

Vitamin therapy - Vitamin B6 supplements may reduce the body's production of oxalate.

Mineral therapy - Oxalate is a mineral salt that, when combined with calcium, may contribute to stone formation. Magnesium supplements may increase the solubility of calcium and oxalate, making it more difficult for these compounds to crystallize into stones.

Factors Influencing Duration

Length of disability may be influenced by the age of the individual, response to treatment, and whether complications develop.

Length of Disability

For extraction or disintegration of stones, duration depends on size, location, and type of calculus.

Medical treatment.

Duration in Days

Job Classification	Minimum	Optimum	Maximum
Any work	1	3	7

Lithotripsy, extracorporeal shock wave.

Duration in Days

Job Classification	Minimum	Optimum	Maximum
Any work	3	7	14

Ureteroscopic stone extraction/disintegration or percutaneous lithotripsy.

Duration in Days

Job Classification	Minimum	Optimum	Maximum
Any work	3	7	14

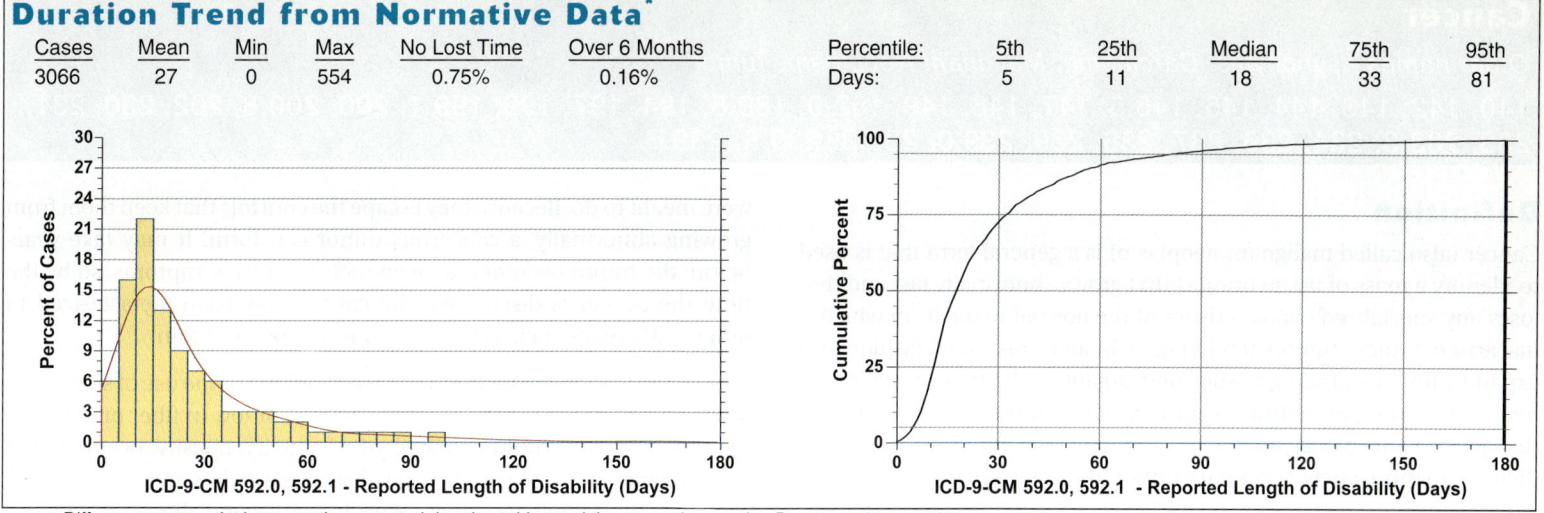

Failure to Recover

If an individual fails to recover within the maximum duration expectancy period, the reader may wish to reference the following questions to assist in better understanding the specifics of an individual's medical case.

Regarding diagnosis:

- Has diagnosis of renal calculus been confirmed through x-ray studies, ultrasound scanning, or CT scan of the abdomen?
- Has intravenous urography (IVU) been done to determine site of the stone and whether there is obstruction above the stone?
- Have urine cultures been done to determine if there is an infection?
- Has individual experienced any complications associated with the stones in the kidney or ureters?
- Does individual have an underlying condition, such as a metabolic disorder or hyperparathyroidism that may impact recovery?

Regarding treatment:

- Does discomfort persist despite the passage of small stones? Could additional, larger stones still be present?
- Was ESWL successful in disintegrating the stones into pieces small enough that they could be passed? If not, was ultrasonic lithotripsy, electrohydraulic lithotripsy, or laser lithotripsy utilized?
- If not successfully removed via ureteroscope, what procedure was used for removal of stone from ureter?
- Has individual been compliant with prescribed diet, drug therapy and increased fluid intake? Have stones recurred?
- If stones are associated with hyperparathyroidism, have one or more of the parathyroid glands been removed? Has this been effective in correcting the hyperparathyroidism condition?

Regarding prognosis:

- With larger stones, or if an infection or obstruction to the urinary flow is present, was surgical intervention required to prevent damage to kidney? What is the prognosis associated with that specific procedure?
- For what reason has disability persisted beyond expectations?
- Does individual have a history of renal calculi? What can be done to reduce risk factors for future recurrence?

References

"Urinary Calculi." Merck Manual of Diagnosis and Therapy, 17th ed. Beers, Mark H., and Robert Berkow, MD, eds. Whitehouse Station, NJ: Merck & Co., Inc., 1999. 05 Dec 2000 <http://www.merck.com/mmanual/section17/chapter221/221a.htm>.

Hanno, Phillip, and Alan Wein. Clinical Manual of Urology. New York: McGraw-Hill, 1994.

Cancer

Other names / synonyms: Carcinoma, Malignant Neoplasm, Tumor

140, 142, 143, 144, 145, 145.5, 147, 148, 149, 162.0, 189.8, 194, 197, 199, 199.1, 200, 200.8, 202, 230, 231, 233, 233.3, 234, 236, 237, 238, 239, 239.0, 239.3, 239.5, 239.7

Definition

Cancer (also called malignant neoplasm) is a general term that is used to identify a mass of tissue (tumor) that grows abnormally fast and that loses any specialized characteristics of the normal tissue from which it has arisen. Cancer tumors tend to grow in an unrestricted fashion and expand into surrounding tissues and organs. Cells from a malignant neoplasm can separate from the initial tumor, travel to a different site (usually via the blood stream or lymphatic system), and then start dividing to form a new, secondary tumor (metastasis).

Cancer usually develops in major organs such as the lungs, breasts, intestines, pancreas, lymphatic system (Hodgkin's and non-Hodgkin's lymphoma), the prostate gland in men, and the ovaries in women. Other sites of cancer formation include the urinary bladder, skin, mouth, lips, and throat, kidney, thyroid, esophagus, brain, adrenal gland, stomach, and in women, the uterus. Malignant neoplasms can also develop in the blood cell-forming tissues located in the bone marrow (leukemia).

It is usually not known what causes cancerous cells begin growing. One possible mechanism is that cancer-causing agents (carcinogens) may act on certain genes (oncogenes) within the cell to trigger mutations. The change in oncogenes is then passed on to all offspring cells, which divide more rapidly than the normal surrounding cells. Usually, the offspring cells show abnormal physical characteristics, including lack of differentiation, so they no longer perform the specialized task that they were meant to do. Because they escape the controls that keep them from growing abnormally, a cancerous tumor can form. It may take years before the tumor becomes large enough to cause symptoms, so by the time the cancer is discovered, the cancer may have metastasized to other vital organs such as the liver, lungs, bones, or brain.

Risk factors for cancer include cigarette smoking or the use of smokeless tobacco; a diet that is high in fat or calories, or low in fiber or calcium; high alcohol consumption; low physical activity; obesity; occupational carcinogens such as asbestos, pesticides, hair dressing compounds, soot, tar, formaldehyde, vinyl chloride, and wood dusts; in women, certain reproductive and sexual factors such as early age at first menstruation (menarche), late age at menopause, never having been pregnant (nulliparity) or not carrying a pregnancy beyond 6 months, late first pregnancy (35 years or older); multiple sexual partners; infection with certain viruses (hepatitis B and C, human papillomavirus, Epstein-Barr virus, human immunodeficiency virus or HIV) or other biological agent (Schistosoma, Helicobacter pylori); radiation; anti-cancer drugs; hormones (estrogen, androgenic steroids); advanced age; and low socioeconomic status. Gender may predispose some individuals to some types of cancer. There may also be a genetic tendency to certain types of cancers within family groups.

Cancer is second only to heart disease as the leading cause of death in the US.

References

LeMone, P., and K.M. Burke. Medical-Surgical Nursing. Upper Saddle River, NJ: Prentice Hall Health, 2000.

Reid, M. "Cancer Control and Epidemiology." Cancer Nursing Principles and Practice. Yarbro, C.H., et al., eds. Boston: Jones & Bartlett Publishers, 2000. 60-81.

Cancer, Bladder

Other names / synonyms: Bladder Cancer, Bladder Carcinoma, Cancer of the Bladder, Cancer of the Urinary Bladder, Carcinoma of the Bladder

188, 188.0, 188.1, 188.2, 188.3, 188.4, 188.5, 188.6, 188.7, 188.8, 188.9, 198.1, 233.7

Definition

Bladder cancer occurs when cancerous cells develop in the hollow sac (urinary bladder) that stores urine before it is eliminated. It is the most common cancer of the urinary tract and includes several different types. Most bladder cancers arise from a certain cell type (urothelial cells) in the bladder. These tumors are commonly called transitional cell carcinomas (TCC). Most bladder cancers (60-75%) are growths within the hollow part of the bladder (lumen), although these growths may infiltrate the bladder wall.

There is a 2- to 5-fold increased risk of bladder cancer in individuals who smoke cigarettes. Risk of bladder cancer increases with occupational exposure to chemicals called aromatic amines in industries involving aniline dyes, rubber, leather, paint, hair dyes, or textiles. Other possible risk factors include use of dietary sweeteners, chronic infections with certain parasites (Schistosoma hematobium), and previous treatment with the anticancer drug cyclophosphamide. There may also be a genetic predisposition to develop bladder cancer.

Bladder cancer is the fifth most common cancer and the twelfth leading cause of cancer death. It accounts for approximately 4% of all cancers in the US, with approximately 50,000 new cases annually and about 11,000 deaths each year. This accounts for 2.9% of all cancer deaths among men and 1.5% among women. These values are slightly higher in the United Kingdom, where bladder cancer accounts for 4.4% and 2.4% of cancer deaths among men and women, respectively. These are relatively high rates compared to Eastern Europe and several areas of Asia including Hong Kong, Japan, and China where the rate of occurrence is 10 to 20 per 100,000.

Bladder cancer is common in whites, with the incidence rate only 50% as prevalent in Hispanics and blacks. Bladder cancer is three times more common in men than women. The incidence of bladder cancer tends to increase sharply with age with approximately two-thirds of the cases occurring in individuals 65 and older.

Diagnosis

History: Individuals with bladder cancer often report blood in the urine (hematuria) that is usually painless until late in the course of the disease. Other symptoms may include increased frequency of urination accompanied by a painful, burning sensation in the genitalia. If the cancer has spread (metastasized) into other organ systems, the individual may report weakness, loss of energy (asthenia), loss of appetite (anorexia), and weight loss. They may also report difficulty in breathing or symptoms of chest pain if the cancer has spread to the lungs or bone pain if metastasized to the bones.

Physical exam: Individuals appear normal on physical examination unless the cancer has spread. In this case, there may be weight loss and decreased physical vigor, appetite, and mental activity.

Tests: Direct visual examination of the bladder using a fiber optic device (cystoscopy) may reveal a lesion in the bladder. A sample of tissue from the tumor (biopsy) may be taken during this examination to determine malignancy. Tumor cells may also be obtained by flushing the bladder with fluid (bladder washing) then examining the cells under the microscope. Tumor markers for bladder cancer may be in the blood or urine and include carcinoembryonic antigen (CEA), polyamines, and fibrin degradation products. An injection of radioisotopes taken up into bone and then detected (bone scan), CT, chest x-ray, and MRI may be used to determine if the cancer has spread to other areas. Intravenous pyelogram (IVP) is a specialized x-ray taken after intravenous administration of a contrast dye that is filtered out by the kidney, making it possible to visualize the entire urinary tract.

Treatment

The treatment for bladder cancer depends on the stage of the disease and the general health of the individual. Tumors confined to the layers of the bladder closest to the hollow portion (superficial) may be treated by surgically removing all visible tumors (transurethral resection or TUR). Bleeding is the most common complication of TUR but tearing (perforation) of the bladder can also occur. Approximately 75% of bladder tumors are superficial at the time of diagnosis. Additional therapy, including chemotherapy or treatment to increase the immune response (Bacille Calmette-Guerin or BCG), may be used to decrease recurrence and prevent tumor progression. These agents can be administered directly into the bladder through a catheter for 2 hours a week for 6 to 8 weeks.

Surgical removal of all or part of the bladder (cystectomy) is one method to treat cancer that has invaded the muscle of the bladder. Complete bladder removal leads to loss of bladder and sexual function. Cystectomy may include removal of all anterior pelvic organs including the bladder (radical cystectomy). This surgery usually includes creating a diversion to pass urine (cutaneous urinary diversion, continent catheterizing pouch, or orthoptic voiding diversion). A piece of small intestine may be used to transfer urine directly from the kidneys and ureters through a hole created in the skin that leads to an external collection bag (ileal conduit). A special form of continent urinary diversion creates a urinary reservoir attached to the urethra so the individual can urinate through the penis.

If the cancer has metastasized to local pelvic lymph nodes, treatment is usually cystectomy and removal of the lymph nodes (pelvic lymphadenectomy) combined with chemotherapy. For individuals who may not tolerate radical surgery, treatment with external radiation alone (radiotherapy) or in combination with chemotherapy (chemoradiotherapy) may be appropriate. Timing as to when chemotherapy should be given relative to bladder removal is somewhat controversial.

Novel therapeutic strategies may include the use of antibodies to carry high activity radiation to the bladder tumor (radioimmunotherapy or RIT) or administration of fat globules (liposomes) that contain anticancer drugs. Gene therapy is another new treatment approach based on correction of the specific molecular abnormality that gave rise to the disease.

Prognosis

The predicted outcome for treatment of bladder cancer depends on the extent of the disease at initial diagnosis and the choice of treatment. The majority of bladder cancers can be treated successfully by TUR with a mortality rate of 2% following this treatment. However, there is a considerable risk of recurrence (50-70%) of superficial bladder tumors following TUR, and 5-30% progress to invasive disease. Adjuvant chemotherapy or BCG treatment to enhance the immune response may decrease the incidence of recurrence to less than fifty percent. Individuals whose cancer has invaded the muscle of the bladder have a 5-year survival rate of only 25% or less despite receiving surgical treatment. Radical cystectomy to remove the entire bladder and other pelvic organs may lead to significant morbidity and mortality in 50% of individuals receiving this treatment. Mortality from cystectomy may decrease 15-20% if techniques for creating urinary diversions are used.

Virtually all individuals with bladder cancer that has metastasized into other organ systems succumb to the disease within 2 years of diagnosis despite chemotherapy and/or radiation therapy treatments. Radioimmunotherapy has not been found effective in delivery of lethal doses of radiation to bladder tumors. Liposomal treatment is still being tested and clinical trials have not yet been performed.

Differential Diagnosis

Conditions that present with similar symptoms to bladder cancer include inflammation or infection of the urinary bladder and ureters (cystitis) or, in males, inflammation of the prostate gland (prostatitis). Treatment with blood thinners or disorders of blood clotting can cause bleeding into the urine that may arouse suspicion of bladder cancer. Kidney stones also cause blood in the urine, but the severe, characteristic pain is usually not misdiagnosed as bladder cancer.

Specialists

- Oncologist
- Pathologist
- Radiologist
- Urologist

Rehabilitation

Several types of rehabilitation benefit individuals recovering from bladder cancer. Supportive rehabilitation allows individuals to gain some control over the ordinary activities of life and helps them cope emotionally. This may include group vocational rehabilitation to help the individual transition back into the workplace or a return to school and/or retraining if the individual cannot physically return to the previous workplace and career. Palliative rehabilitation addresses the pain an individual experiences, allows some level of physical comfort, and provides emotional support and assistance in day-to-day functioning.

Physical rehabilitation allows individuals to regain strength and stamina that were lost due to the disease process and during treatment. Individuals recovering from bladder cancer are usually very weak. Strengthening starts at a low level and progresses only as tolerated, especially if strengthening is attempted during the course of treatment. If surgery is required, breathing exercises after surgery may be useful to prevent postoperative pulmonary complications. Certain exercises may also be performed to reduce postoperative pain and speed recovery and include progressive relaxation and deep breathing techniques. The individual lies on the back and performs ankle pumps (flexing the ankle back and forth) and knee bends to help increase circulation and make walking easier.

Early in physical rehabilitation of this disease, the individual should perform range-of-motion exercises to help return mobility to joints and stretch key muscles that will enable the individual to return to activities of daily living.

When resistance is tolerated, the individual performs isotonic exercise using an elastic band or light weights that strengthen the muscles. As the individual lifts the weight throughout the range of motion, the muscle shortens and lengthens. Because muscle weakness to the legs is likely, balance exercises are beneficial and include sidestepping and walking with the eyes closed with and without assistance.

The frequency and duration of the rehabilitation program vary among individuals with bladder cancer. Intensity and progression of the exercises depend on the prognosis, whether surgery was performed, if the individual is receiving any current cancer treatment, the extent of the disease, and the individual's overall health.

Work Restrictions / Accommodations

Individuals whose bladder cancer is detected and successfully treated in the early stages usually have minimal work restrictions or accommodations following recovery and return to work. However, duties at work may be restricted and should not include heavy lifting or hard physical labor following surgery, chemotherapy, and/or radiation therapy until recovery is complete. Bathroom facilities should be readily available, as the individual may have to urinate frequently. Fatigue may create the need for additional breaks during this period of recovery. Metastatic cancer is generally associated with permanent disability.

Comorbid Conditions

Existing conditions that may affect an individual's ability to recover and further lengthen disability from bladder cancer include inflammation of the prostate gland (prostatitis), cancer of the prostate gland, and cancer of the ureter. Any conditions that weaken the immune system such as AIDS or alcoholism may impair the body's defenses against the tumor, and also complicate side effects of treatment. Smoking is a known risk factor for bladder cancer and continued smoking may increase the risk of recurrence or invasion and decrease the rate of remission.

Complications

Complications of bladder cancer may include infection, bleeding, and obstruction of urinary flow. Treatment can lead to loss of bladder and sexual function. Bladder cancer can metastasize into the lymph or other organ systems including the lungs, circulatory system, bone, and gastrointestinal system.

Factors Influencing Duration

Factors that might influence the length of disability include the extent of the disease at initial diagnosis, type of treatment, and complications of treatment. Age at the time of diagnosis may be a factor since older individuals require longer recovery times from treatment. The expected length of disability is increased when radiation and/or chemotherapy is used.

Length of Disability

Duration of disability depends on the requirements of the job. Heavy physical labor is usually restricted following surgery, chemotherapy, and/or radiation therapy treatments. Metastatic disease is generally associated with permanent disability.

For cystoscopy and cystectomy, duration depends on stage, grade, cell type, adjuvant chemotherapy, or radiation therapy. Duration reflects recovery period for procedure only. Disability may be permanent.

Transurethral resection.

Duration in Days

Job Classification	Minimum	Optimum	Maximum
Sedentary work	7	9	14
Light work	7	9	14
Medium work	14	16	21
Heavy work	21	24	28
Very Heavy work	21	24	28

Endoscopic resection (cystoscopy).

Duration in Days

Job Classification	Minimum	Optimum	Maximum
Sedentary work	7	14	28
Light work	7	14	28
Medium work	7	21	42
Heavy work	14	21	42
Very Heavy work	14	28	56

With cystectomy.

Duration in Days

Job Classification	Minimum	Optimum	Maximum
Sedentary work	42	49	56
Light work	42	49	56
Medium work	42	49	70
Heavy work	56	63	84
Very Heavy work	56	63	112

Failure to Recover

If an individual fails to recover within the maximum duration expectancy period, the reader may wish to reference the following questions to assist in better understanding the specifics of an individual's medical case.

Regarding diagnosis:

- Was the diagnosis of bladder cancer confirmed?
- Did the surgery remove all the cancerous tissue?
- Has the tumor metastasized into other organ systems?
- Were underlying conditions identified or ruled out? If present, are they being appropriately addressed?

Regarding treatment:

- Did individual receive chemotherapy or BCG in addition to surgery? Would it be a useful adjunct to treatment at this time?
- Because surgical removal of all or part of the bladder (cystectomy) can be physically and emotionally traumatic, would individual benefit from supportive counseling?
- If the cancer has metastasized to local pelvic lymph nodes, what treatment route has individual undergone (pelvic lymphadenectomy, chemotherapy, radiotherapy, chemoradiotherapy)? Is it now appropriate to add or change modalities?
- Is individual a candidate for one of the newer treatment strategies such as antibodies to carry high activity radiation to the bladder tumor (RIT), administration of liposomes that contain anticancer drugs, or gene therapy?

Regarding prognosis:

- Did recurrence of the bladder tumor occur?
- Because adjuvant chemotherapy or BCG treatment to enhance the immune response may decrease the incidence of recurrence to less than 50%, would this be a useful adjunct to treatment at this time?
- Does individual have a realistic concept of prognosis?
- Does individual have a supportive family or friends?
- Would counseling be beneficial?
- Because continued smoking may increase the risk of recurrence or invasion and decrease the rate of remission, was individual warned about the risk of continued smoking?

References

Diagnosis and Treatment of Bladder Cancer. Cancer News. 01 Jan 2000. 28 Oct 2000 <http://www.cancernews.com/bladder1.htm>.

Ayala, A.G., and J.Y. Ro. "Premalignant Lesions of the Urothelium and Transitional Cell Tumors." Pathology of the Urinary Bladder. Young, R.H., ed. New York: Churchill Livingstone, 1989. 65-102.

Brauers, A., and G. Jakse. "Epidemiology and Biology of Human Urinary Bladder Cancer." Journal of Cancer Research and Clinical Oncology 126 10 (2000): 575-583.

Collado, A., et al. "Early Complications of Endoscopic Treatment for Superficial Bladder Tumors." Journal of Urology 164 5 (2000): 1529-1532.

Kalble, T., and T. Otto. "Unconventional Therapeutic Methods in Superficial Bladder Cancer." Urologe-Ausgabe A 33 6 (1994): 553-556.

Kisner, C., and L. Colby. Therapeutic Exercise Foundations and Techniques. Philadelphia: F.A. Davis, 1990.

LeMone, P., and K.M. Burke. Medical-Surgical Nursing. Upper Saddle River, NJ: Prentice Hall Health, 2000.

Scully, Rosemary M., and Marylou R. Barnes. Physical Therapy. Philadelphia: J.B. Lippincott Company, 1989.

Cancer, Bone

Other names / synonyms: Chrondrosarcoma, Ewing's Sarcoma, Osteoscaroma

170

Definition

Bone cancer begins in bone, cartilage, or other bone tissue when abnormal cells develop, multiply, and spread to form tumors that damage and destroy bone, nerves, and tissues (including organs).

Cancer that originates in bone tissue is referred to as primary bone cancer. Secondary bone cancer occurs when malignant cells from a primary cancer site (such as the kidney, lung, prostate, breast, or thyroid) spread (metastasize) to the bones. Common sites of secondary bone cancer include the ribs, skull, pelvis, and vertebrae.

Primary bone cancers are called sarcomas. There are several types of sarcomas, each originating in a different type of bone tissue. Sarcomas can occur in any of the 206 bones of the body, but not much is known about their cause. Research has revealed that excessive exposure to radiation and inherited genetic risk factors may be associated with osteosarcoma. Other risk factors include bone disease that results in the replacement of normal bone marrow with fibrous, vascular tissue (Paget's disease), overactive parathyroid gland, long-term bone infection (osteomyelitis), radiation and chemotherapy treatments for other conditions, and bones that have been previously fractured.

Primary bone cancer is a rare disease with about 500 new cases reported each year in the US. The majority of cases are diagnosed during the second decade (during adolescence), but there is a second peak in the sixth decade.

Osteosarcoma accounts for nearly 60% of all primary bone cancers. Ewing's sarcoma originates in bone marrow and occurs most often in young adults. Chondrosarcoma originates in cartilage and tends to attack middle-aged adults. Other, less common types of bone cancer that occur in adults include fibrosarcoma, malignant giant cell tumor, and chordoma. More males than females are diagnosed. About 3 out of every 100,000 individuals will develop primary bone cancer. Malignant bone tumors are twice as common as benign bone tumors.

Diagnosis

History: Symptoms of bone cancer tend to develop slowly, depending on the type, location, and size of the tumor. Pain in the bones and joints is the most frequent symptom. The pain is often accompanied with swelling, is more intense at night, is not necessarily associated with movement, and may be dull and constant, or felt only when pressure is applied. Sometimes a firm, tender lump on the surface of the bone can be felt through the skin. The lump may or may not be painful. Individuals in the late stages of the disease may present with fever, weight loss, fatigue, impaired mobility, and spontaneous bone fractures (resulting from bones weakened by the disease).

Physical exam: The physician may find a swelling in the affected area by touch (palpation). Many individuals feel pain when the pressure is applied. In other individuals, the physical exam may reveal a tender lump on the surface of the bone that the physician can feel though the skin. The lump may or may not be painful when pressure is applied.

Tests: Based on the information obtained from the individual's medical history and physical exam, the physician may recommend a combination of the following: blood and urine tests, angiograms, bone biopsies, x-rays or a bone scan, and other imaging techniques such as CT or MRI to determine whether the cancer has spread to or from another part of the body.

Treatment

Treatment may include radiation to shrink the tumor, slow its growth, and relieve the pain. Tumor excision or resection may be performed to remove part or all of the diseased bone if the individual has been diagnosed with osteosarcoma, chondrosarcoma, or fibrosarcoma (sometimes this includes amputation).

Treatment may include a combination of radiation therapy and tumor excision or resection, along with anticancer drugs (chemotherapy). Antibiotics may be prescribed to treat infections that may occur from lowered resistance to various bacteria (a side effect from chemotherapy).

A metal prosthetic device or a bone graft from a cadaver may be inserted to strengthen a weakened bone segment. Growth of tumors may be slowed with estrogen or hypothalamic hormones (hormone therapy). Surgery to remove such hormone-producing organs as the ovaries, testes, or adrenals (oophorotomy, orchiectomy, or adrenalectomy) may be performed when there is risk of secondary cancer due to spread of a tumor from the breast or prostate.

Prognosis

Individuals with osteosarcoma who have bone metastases are rarely cured. Individuals with isolated (nonmetastatic) osteosarcoma at the time of presentation are cured 60-70% of the time with pre-reduction chemotherapy, complete surgical removal, and postsurgery chemotherapy. A small percentage of osteosarcomas involve only the surface of the bone and generally are of a low histologic grade. Individuals with low-grade osteosarcomas are frequently treated with surgery only and have a better survival rate than individuals with conventional high-grade osteosarcomas.

For Ewing's sarcoma, the most important prognosis variable at the time of diagnosis is whether the cancer has spread. Other prognostic factors include the size of the primary tumor and whether the tumor is situated in a central or peripheral location. The current expected cure rate (5-year disease-free survival) is 50-60% for nonmetastatic disease at the time of diagnosis. A less favorable cure rate (5-year disease-free survival) of approximately 40% is expected for individuals whose primary disease site is located in the pelvis.

For chondrosarcoma, prognostic variables include the presence of metastatic disease and a high histologic grade of the disease. Differentiated chondrosarcomas are cured in only 10% of cases. The pelvis as a primary site of disease also carries a worse prognosis than peripheral sites. Individuals with low-grade lesions have a 70-85% survival rate after complete resection.

Differential Diagnosis

Differential diagnosis for primary bone cancer might include various forms of secondary bone cancer, benign bone tumors, cancers that arise from cells produced in the bone marrow rather than the cells that make hard bone tissue (such as leukemia, multiple myeloma, and lymphoma), Paget's disease, and osteomyelitis.

Specialists

• Dietary Advisor	• Orthopedist
• Oncologist	• Psychologist
• Orthopedic Surgeon	• Radiation Oncologist

Rehabilitation

Several types of rehabilitation may benefit individuals recovering from bone cancer. Supportive rehabilitation allows the individual to gain some control over the ordinary activities of life and to cope emotionally. This may take the form of group vocational rehabilitation and may help with the individual's transition back into the work place. This may include returning to school and/or retraining when the individual is physically unable to return to his or her previous work place and career. Palliative rehabilitation allows individuals in advanced stages of the disease to achieve some level of physical comfort, and provides emotional support and assistance in day-to-day functioning.

In general, physical rehabilitation is aimed at restoring normal range of motion, flexibility, and strength of involved joints, and increasing overall endurance. If surgical removal of a malignant bone tumor is necessary, immobilization with a cast may be required for at least 6 weeks. Early passive and active range-of-motion exercises of the affected joint and muscles begin as soon as the cast is removed.

Physical rehabilitation for bone cancer may allow the individual to regain some strength and stamina lost due to the disease process and during treatment of the disease. Individuals recovering from bone cancer are usually very weak and strengthening is started at a low level and progressed only as tolerated. This is especially the case if strengthening is attempted during the course of treatment. If surgery is required, breathing exercises after surgery may be useful in preventing postoperative pulmonary complications. Also, certain exercises may be performed to reduce postoperative pain and speed recovery including progressive relaxation and deep breathing techniques. While the individual is lying on his or her back, ankle pumps (flexing the ankle back and forth) and knee bends help to increase circulation and make walking easier.

Also early on in the physical rehabilitation of this disease, range-of-motion exercises are started to return mobility to joints and stretch key muscles, helping the individual return to activities of daily living.

When resistance is tolerated, isotonic exercises may be introduced. These are typically performed with the use an elastic band or light weights. As the weight is lifted throughout the range of motion, the muscle shortens and lengthens.

If the bone tumor is located in the lower extremity, the physical therapist will also focus on training for proper ambulating (walking) at the appropriate time. This may initially begin with the use of an assistive device such as a walker and progress to a cane. Once the individual demonstrates independent and safe walking, the assistive device is generally discontinued.

Because muscle weakness to the legs is likely following bone cancer, balance exercises are beneficial. Learning how to avoid injury is another important intervention in the rehabilitation of a person with a bone tumor. Occupational therapy helps individuals arrange their homes and organize their lives in ways that support their physical and mental well being, and provides activities to relieve the mental boredom of inactivity. Devices and techniques that help the individual are invaluable in maintaining the individual's peace of mind.

The frequency and duration of the rehabilitation program will vary among individuals with bone cancer. Intensity and progression of the exercise will depend on the prognosis, the extent of the disease, whether any surgery was performed, whether the individual is receiving any current cancer treatment, and the individual's overall health.

Work Restrictions / Accommodations

The treatment and the disease itself may weaken the individual and severely limit his or her ability to return to previous work activities. The individual may be able to work a restricted number of hours per day or days per week. Work responsibilities may need to be largely sedentary. Additionally, the individual may need a place at work where he or she may periodically rest. Some individuals undergoing chemotherapy and/or radiation therapy may require additional leave from work.

In some cases, the rigors of the disease and treatment may preclude the individual from ever returning to work.

Comorbid Conditions

Comorbid conditions that might influence the length of disability include obesity or excessive thinness, chronic illnesses, such as heart disease and diabetes, and allergy to treatment medications.

Complications

Complications for primary bone cancer are related to the advance of the disease when the tumor spreads (metastasizes) to surrounding tissue, adjoining organs other bones, or to other parts of the body. For Ewing's sarcoma and osteosarcoma, the most common sites of metastases are other bones and the lungs.

A major complication is the tumor that encompasses an area that confounds or does not allow for its removal (for example, metastases to the lungs).

Complications related to treatment may include a temporary burn to the skin and fatigue from radiation therapy; nausea, vomiting, mouth sores, hair loss, and lowered resistance to infection from chemotherapy; and infection of the surgical site and possible blood clotting disturbances from the surgery. Many older individuals find it difficult to tolerate surgery, chemotherapy, and radiation therapy because their health status is often poor.

Factors Influencing Duration

Factors that might influence the length of disability include the stage of disease at initial presentation (presence of distant metastases or not), the location of the cancer, the effectiveness of the surgery, radiation, chemotherapy, and the presence or absence of complications of the cancer itself and of the treatments.

Length of Disability

This is a vague diagnosis. Duration depends on the type, whether primary or secondary, spread (metastasis) of the disease, and the amount of tissue that has been damaged. Disability associated with bone cancer may be permanent.

Failure to Recover

If an individual fails to recover within the maximum duration expectancy period, the reader may wish to reference the following questions to assist in better understanding the specifics of an individual's medical case.

Regarding diagnosis:

- Does individual have primary or secondary bone cancer?
- Is there a history of excessive exposure to radiation?
- Does individual have any inherited genetic risk factors? Additional risk factors for primary bone cancer such as Paget's disease, overactive parathyroid gland, long-term osteomyelitis, radiation and chemotherapy treatments for other conditions, or previously fractured bones? Does individual have any risk factors for secondary bone cancer such as cancer in the kidney, lung, prostate, breast, or thyroid?
- Does individual complain of pain in the bones and joints with swelling? Is the pain more intense at night? Not necessarily associated with movement? Is it dull and constant or felt only when pressure is applied? Does individual complain of fever, weight loss, fatigue, impaired mobility, or spontaneous bone fractures?
- Can individual feel a bump on the surface of the bone?
- On physical exam, was swelling or a lump in the affected area present? Was it painful?
- Were blood and urine tests done? Angiogram, bone biopsy, x-rays, bone scan, CT, or MRI?
- Were conditions with similar symptoms ruled out?

Regarding treatment:

- Is individual being treated with radiation, tumor excision or resection, chemotherapy, or a combination of all three treatments?
- Did individual receive antibiotics, if necessary?

- Was amputation necessary?
- If indicated, is individual receiving hormone therapy or removal of hormone-producing organs?

Regarding prognosis:

- Is individual active in rehabilitation?
- Can individual's employer accommodate any necessary restrictions?
- Does individual have any conditions that may affect ability to recover?
- Have any complications developed such as metastasis or the tumor encompassing an area that confounds or does not allow for its removal?
- Does individual have any treatment complications such as a temporary burn to the skin, fatigue, nausea, vomiting, mouth sores, hair loss, lowered resistance to infection, infection of the surgical site, or possible blood clotting disturbances from the surgery?

References

"Chapter 56: Tumors of Bones and Joints." Merck Manual of Diagnosis and Therapy, 17th ed. Beers, Mark H., and Robert Berkow, MD, eds. Whitehouse Station, NJ: Merck & Co., Inc, 1999. 14 Feb 2001 <http://www.merck.com/pubs/mmanual/section5/chapter56/56c.htm>.

NCI Fact Sheet: Questions and Answers About Bone Cancer. National Cancer Institute. 01 Jan 1999. 09 Jan 2001 <http://www.oncolink.com/pdq_html/6/engl/600626.html>.

Cancer, Brain

Other names / synonyms: Astrocytoma, Brain Cancer, Glioblastoma, Glioma, Malignant Brain Tumor, Malignant Neoplasm of the Brain

191, 191.0, 191.1, 191.2, 191.3, 191.4, 191.5, 191.6, 191.7, 191.8, 191.9, 198.3

Definition

Brain cancer is a malignant tumor (or tumors) that originates from any of the cells that make up the brain (primary brain cancer) or migrates to brain cells from other cancerous parts of the body (secondary or metastatic brain cancer).

Tumors that occur in the brain can be noncancerous (benign) as well as cancerous (malignant). Unlike malignant tumors, benign tumors do not invade other tissue. An important point about benign tumors is that they can be just as dangerous over time as malignant tumors when they begin to increase the amount of mass in the skull, compress vital structures, and cause serious symptoms and complications. Unlike lung, colon, and breast cancers, primary brain cancers rarely spread to other organs. Death usually occurs as a result of uncontrolled growth within the confines of the skull. As the tumor compresses vital brain centers controlling consciousness and bodily functions, the individual lapses into coma, and breathing ultimately stops.

Primary brain tumors are classified by cell type of origin and by how malignant the cells appear (histological grade). Location of the tumor and whether the tumor spreads throughout the cerebrospinal fluid bathing the brain also helps classify some brain tumors. Glial tumors originate from connecting and supporting brain cells called glia. These tumors include astrocytomas, ependymomas, oligodendroglioma, mixed tumors, medulloblastomas, and the highly malignant glioblastoma multiforme. Tumors derived from cells other than glia include pineal parenchymal tumors, germ cell tumors, craniopharyngiomas, meningiomas, and choroid plexus tumors.

Exposure to x-rays, chemicals such as vinyl chloride associated with rubber manufacturing, dye making, and other industries, rare genetic conditions such as neurofibromatosis, compromised immune systems related to use of immunosuppressant drugs following organ transplantation or acquired immune deficiency syndrome (AIDS) may all increase risk of brain cancer. Genetic factors may be involved, but the exact mechanism is unclear.

There are 15,000-18,000 cases of primary brain cancer reported every year in the US, causing about 10,000-14,000 deaths per year, and accounting for 2-3% of cancers reported each year in the US. Much more common is secondary brain cancer (brain metastasis) with at least 80,000 cases per year in the US. Since lung, breast, colon, and other cancers spread (metastasize) to the brain, and since the brain is a vital structure, secondary brain cancer accounts for about 20% of total cancer deaths each year.

Diagnosis

History: Individuals may complain of headache, nausea, and vomiting. Other general symptoms include drowsiness, lethargy, personality changes, impaired intellectual function, and seizures. Depending on the tumor location, individuals may complain of localized weakness, numbness, speech difficulty, or other neurological symptoms.

Physical exam: Examination with an instrument that examines the inside of the eye (ophthalmoscope) reveals a swelling of the optic nerve at the point where the nerve enters the eyeball (papilledema) in approximately one-half of individuals with brain tumors, reflecting increased pressure within the skull. Abnormalities are frequently seen on a neurological exam, depending on the location of the tumor. The neurological exam tests the senses (vision, smell, touch, taste, etc.), motor responses, muscle strength, coordination, reflex response, and autonomic responses (increase and decrease in pulse, breathing, sweating in response to stimuli). Abnormalities may be observed in the individual's vision if a cancerous tumor is present in the occipital lobe of the brain or in motor responses and coordination if a cancerous tumor is present in the cerebellum (a brain structure toward the back of the skull involved in coordination and movement). A neurological exam may be relatively normal when the tumor is located in the frontal lobes of the brain.

Tests: CT and/or MRI are essential for locating a tumor. Use of dye injected into the vein during these procedures makes the tumor more visible. A surgical biopsy is necessary to confirm the diagnosis and is usually performed at the time of surgery to remove the tumor. Before surgery, an arteriogram (angiogram) may be helpful to determine which blood vessels supply the tumor. In individuals with seizures, electroencephalogram (EEG) is usually indicated. Skull x-ray is rarely necessary except in tumors such as meningiomas that may invade or press against the bone.

Withdrawal of cerebrospinal fluid from the spinal canal for diagnostic purposes (lumbar puncture) may help to rule out an infectious process or tumor in the membranes that surround the brain (pia mater and arachnoid membranes). The tumor may also be evaluated by assaying tumor markers present in spinal fluid. However, spinal tap (lumbar puncture) usually cannot be done when the individual has a brain tumor, as withdrawal of cerebrospinal fluid from the spinal canal causes sudden lowering of pressure. If pressure within the skull is increased due to the brain tumor, the brain may drop downward (herniate) through the skull opening where the spinal cord emerges (foramen magnum). As herniation compresses vital brain structures against the bony skull, coma and death may follow.

If a tumor of the pituitary gland is suspected, a variety of hormones may be measured from a blood sample. Single photon emission tomography (SPECT) and positron emission tomography (PET) are being widely used to evaluate certain types of brain cancer.

Treatment

Treatment depends on factors related to the cancer, such as tissue type, location and size of the tumor, and the degree of cancer spread (metastasis). Treatment also depends on the individual's overall health and medical history, the individual's tolerance for specific medications, procedures, and therapies, and expectations for the course of the disease. Surgery is the first choice for treatment, and is usually followed by radiation and chemotherapy. Surgical techniques have been improved to allow access to deeply embedded tumors that were previously inaccessible. For example, stereotactic and frameless sterotactic surgery often allow more precise localization of the tumor. Chemotherapy may be given by mouth or by injection into the vein. To deliver chemotherapy more directly to the tumor, it has sometimes been given into an artery supplying the tumor, or more commonly into the cerebrospinal fluid through shunt tubing accessible from the skull (Ommaya reservoir). Recent trials are evaluating the safety and effectiveness of chemotherapy being applied directly to the tumor by placing a piece of plastic-like material coated with the drug against the tumor during surgery. Different methods of administering radiation therapy are also being evaluated (hyperfractionated irradiation, accelerated fraction radiation, stereotactic radiosurgery, radiosensitizers, hyperthermia, interstitial brachytherapy, intraoperative radiation therapy). Steroids (adrenal cortical hormones or glucocorticoids) are usually given to reduce brain swelling and reduce symptoms. Anticonvulsants may be needed in individuals with seizures, and are usually given around the time of surgery to prevent this complication.

Aggressive malignant tumors are often treated with a combination of surgery and radiation therapy, which slows their progress. However, this combined approach is not an option when the dosage needed to kill cancer cells risks damaging the sensitive brain tissues.

Aggressive malignant tumors are also treated with a combination of surgery and anticancer drugs (chemotherapy). Brain cancer is difficult to treat with chemotherapy for two reasons: the cancer cells in the cancerous central nervous system (CNS) tend to become resistant to the anticancer drugs as the tumor grows and controversy exists over whether anticancer drugs can penetrate the blood-brain barrier, the protective barrier that keeps certain substances from entering the brain.

Since there has been limited success with radiation and chemotherapy treatments, individuals may be asked to enroll in clinical trials for experimental treatments (e.g., immunotherapy, gene therapy).

Prognosis

The outcome for an individual with brain cancer depends on the cell type, how malignant the cells appear under the microscope (histological grade), how soon the cancerous tumor is detected, where the tumor is located in the brain, how much of the tumor can be removed by surgery, and the individual's response to treatment.

Response to radiation and chemotherapy has met with limited success because the dosage of radiation needed to kill cancer cells in the brain also damages sensitive brain tissues, and because cancer cells in the brain can become resistant to chemotherapy drugs.

Many malignant brain tumors tend to recur within 6 to 12 months after initial diagnosis. Overall, the 5-year survival rate for brain cancer is approximately twenty-five percent.

For individuals with brain cancer that is the result of cancer that has spread (metastasis) from another part of the body (secondary brain cancer), except when an isolated metastasis can be surgically removed, there is no cure, and the median survival period is less than 12 months.

Differential Diagnosis

Other masses within the brain include benign tumor of the brain, brain abscess, hemorrhage (hematoma or contusion), or blood vessel malformation (arteriovenous malformation or aneurysm). Other conditions that may have similar symptoms and findings include stroke, metabolic dysfunction, meningoencephalitis, benign intracranial hypertension, and degenerative processes such as Alzheimer's disease.

Specialists

- Neurologist
- Neurosurgeon
- Oncologist
- Radiation Oncologist
- Radiation Therapist

Rehabilitation

Individuals with the diagnosis of brain cancer require physical and occupational therapy on an inpatient basis, as well as possibly home care or outpatient therapy. Individuals may also require speech therapy. The extent and types of therapy necessary vary among individuals contingent upon the location of the tumor, how localized the tumor is, and the treatment required. Therapy focuses on the following areas: improving communication; maintaining range of motion; increasing strength; improving coordination; improving balance; and improving functional abilities such as gait.

To improve communication, speech therapists teach individuals specific lip, tongue, and facial muscle positions that result in clarifying speech. Individuals with the inability to communicate orally may learn to communicate through a variety of other methods.

Individuals may experience weakness and decreased function in their arms and/or legs. A comprehensive stretching program is critical to maintaining range of motion in the joints. Occupational and physical therapists instruct individuals and their family members how to safely stretch the arms and legs. For example, individuals learn to stretch the wrist and fingers into flexion and extension to preserve hand function. Individuals learn to stretch the hamstrings by lying on the back and bringing the leg up toward the ceiling to promote the sitting balance.

Individuals also learn a strengthening program in occupational and physical therapy for the arms and legs to maintain functional abilities. Individuals perform arm exercises such as elbow extension with light hand weights so that crutches or a walker could be used. Bridging exercises may be performed, in which the individual lies on the back with the knees bent and lifts the buttocks up from the bed. This promotes the ability to get up out of a chair.

Individuals may have impaired coordination. Individuals perform fine motor coordination exercises in occupational therapy such as picking up pegs and placing them in a pegboard or may work on practical coordination exercises such as fastening buttons or practicing their signatures. Individuals work on gross motor coordination in physical therapy such as kicking a soccer ball that is rolled toward them or throwing beanbags at a target.

Individuals work on sitting and standing balance in physical and occupational therapy. For example, occupational therapists may work on dynamic sitting balance to promote dressing and grooming abilities. Sitting balance can be improved by having an individual sit on a therapy ball while attempting to reach for objects placed at various distances from the individual. Physical therapists may focus on standing balance to preserve the ability to walk.

The main focus of physical and occupational therapy is to maximize functional capabilities. Occupational therapists teach individuals skills such as getting in and out of the shower, dressing, and meal preparation. Occupational therapists may order equipment such as a tub seat, a long-handled shoehorn, or kitchen utensils with thick handles to make these tasks easier. Physical therapists teach skills such as getting in and out of bed, walking, or using a wheelchair.

Individuals who are in the end stages of brain cancer may require palliative therapy, in which the primary focus is pain control.

Work Restrictions / Accommodations

Possible changes in intellect, coordination, strength, vision, and other neurologic functions may necessitate specific work restrictions and accommodations. Some job requirements may be impossible for individuals with brain cancer, and permanent disability is not unusual.

Comorbid Conditions

As the disease progresses, it destroys both cancer cells and healthy cells, causing a debilitation of stamina in the individual. Existing conditions such as obesity or excessive thinness, chronic illness (such as a heart condition or diabetes), and allergy to treatment medications often add to the debilitation from the disease and from the treatment. The effects of coexisting neurologic diseases, such as stroke or Alzheimer's disease, may be additive with those of the brain cancer. Certain neurologic conditions such as seizures may be aggravated by the brain cancer.

Complications

Possible complications of brain cancer include neurologic impairment (deficit) such as paralysis or language disturbance, seizures, increased risk of blood clots (thromboembolic complications), brain herniation, and coma. Complications of brain cancer treatment include damage to neighboring brain structures, infections, seizures, delayed deterioration following radiation therapy, and immunosuppression from chemotherapy.

Factors Influencing Duration

All of the factors that determine the type of treatment will also influence the length of disability because they determine the ultimate prognosis. Those factors include cell type and degree of malignancy, tissue involvement, location of the tumor, extent of cancer spread (metastasis), overall health and medical history, and the individual's tolerance for specific medications, procedures, and therapies. Some surgical treatments and radiation therapy may lead to destruction or impairment of other brain structures, causing additional complications.

Length of Disability

Duration depends on cell type, site, and type of treatment. Disability may be permanent.

Medical or surgical treatment.

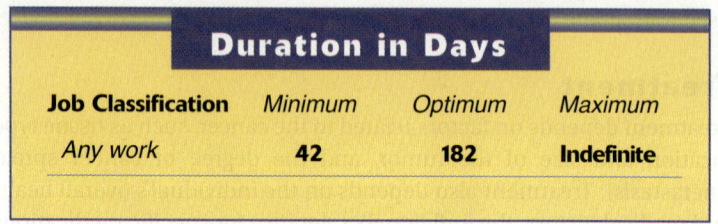

Job Classification	Minimum	Optimum	Maximum
Any work	42	182	Indefinite

Failure to Recover

If an individual fails to recover within the maximum duration expectancy period, the reader may wish to reference the following questions to assist in better understanding the specifics of an individual's medical case.

Regarding diagnosis:

- Does individual complain of headache, nausea, and vomiting? Notice drowsiness, personality changes, impaired intellectual function, and seizures?
- Have CT and/or MRI confirmed the existence and location of a brain mass?
- Before surgery, would an arteriogram help determine blood supply to the tumor, facilitating removal?
- Was the specific cell type and degree of malignancy confirmed from surgically removed tissue?
- Is the brain cancer primary or metastatic? If metastatic, was the tumor of origin treated?
- Is there suspicion that the tumor has invaded cerebrospinal fluid? Is it safe to remove cerebrospinal fluid by lumbar puncture to find out or would this cause brain herniation?

Regarding treatment:

- Can the entire tumor be removed without compromising neighboring structures or should surgery be limited to biopsy?
- Was radiation or chemotherapy given? If no improvement has occurred with these measures, is individual a candidate for experimental forms of radiation or chemotherapy?

- Does the appearance of new or worsening symptoms reflect tumor growth or complications from surgery, radiation, or chemotherapy?
- Are steroids being given to relieve symptoms from brain swelling?
- Are anticonvulsants being given to individuals with seizures? Has individual responded well to the medications?

Regarding prognosis:

- What type of brain cancer does individual have?
- How malignant are the cells? Was the entire tumor removed with surgery?
- Has individual undergone radiation and/or chemotherapy treatment? What is individual's response to surgery and other treatments?
- Did individual's brain cancer result from a metastasis? Was it possible to surgically remove the metastasis? If not, how long is individual expected to live?
- Has individual experienced complications from the cancer or from surgery or other treatments? What are they? How will these complications be treated and how will they affect the individual?
- Would counseling and rehabilitation assist with emotional and physical aspects of recovery?
- Should second opinion consultations be obtained regarding diagnosis and treatment?

References

Brain Cancer. University of Pennsylvania. 17 Feb 2001. 22 Feb 2001 <http://cancer.med.upenn.edu/disease/brain/>.

Boss, Barbara J. "Alterations of Neurologic Function." Pathophysiology. McCance, Kathryn L., and Sue E. Heuther, et. al. St. Louis : Mosby-Year Book, Inc, 1994. 527-586.

Brannon, Linda, and Jess Feist. "Living with Chronic Illness." Health Psychology. King, Kenneth Belmont: Wadsworth Publishing Company, 1992. 275-315.

Kisner, Carolyn, and Lynn Allen Colby. Therapeutic Exercise: Foundation and Techniques, 2nd ed. Philadelphia: F.A. Davis Company, 1990.

Mount Auburn Hospital. Health Information: Brain Cancer. CareGroup. 01 Jan 1999. 01 Jan 2001 <http://www.mtauburn.caregroup.org/htinfo/Cancer/brain.asp>.

Murphy, Gerald P., Lois B. Morris, and Dianne Lange. Informed Decisions: The Complete Book of Cancer Diagnosis, Treatment, and Recovery. New York: Viking, 1997.

Oncology Forum/Oncology Channel. Brain Cancer. Oncology World. 26 Feb 2001. 26 Feb 2001 <http://www.oncologychannel.com/braincancer/>.

OnHealth Network Company. Conditions A-Z: Brain Cancer. OnHealth Network Company. 01 July 1998. 01 Jan 2001 <http://onhealth.webmd.com/conditions/resource/conditions/item,238.asp>.

Saint Joseph's Hospital of Marshfield. Brain Cancers. Saint Joseph's Hospital of Marshfield, Inc. 01 Jan 1999. 01 Jan 2001 <http://www.stjosephs-marshfield.org/neurosciences/brain.htm>.

Stillwell, Jonathan. "Brain Cancer." Canceranswers.com. 01 Jan 1997. 01 Jan 2001 <http://www.canceranswers.com/Brain.Cancer.html>.

Cancer, Breast

Other names / synonyms: Breast Cancer, Breast Carcinoma, Breast Neoplasm
174.0, 174.1, 174.2, 174.3, 174.4, 174.5, 174.6, 174.8, 174.9, 175, 198.81, 233.0

Definition

Breast cancer is cancer of breast tissue cells. Like all cancerous cells, cancerous breast tissue cells multiply in an "out-of-control" manner. They may invade nearby breast tissue (invasive breast cancer) or may spread to other parts of the body (metastatic breast cancer).

Each breast is divided into sections called lobes and within each lobe are smaller lobules. Tubes (ducts) lead from each lobule out to the nipple. Breast cancer involves either cells of the lobules (lobular carcinoma) or cells of the ducts (ductal carcinoma).

When cancer cells enter the blood or lymph fluid, breast cancer can metastasize outside the breast. It often spreads to the lymph nodes located under the arm or may spread to more distant structures and organs.

The extent of an individual's breast cancer is described by its stage. There are 5 stages with stage 0 being the most contained and stage IV the most extensive. In stage 0, the cancer is confined to either the lobular or the ductal cells. It has not invaded nearby breast tissue. Stage 0 cancer in the lobule cells (lobular carcinoma in situ) seldom becomes invasive. It does, however, increase a woman's risk of later developing invasive breast cancer. Stage 0 cancer of the ductal cells (ductal carcinoma in situ) is more apt to become invasive.

Stage I and stage II are considered early stage cancers. In stage I, cancer has invaded nearby breast tissue but has not moved beyond the breast. Stage II differs from stage I in that either the mass of cancer cells (tumor) is larger or the cancer has spread to a lymph node under the arm.

Stage III is referred to as locally advanced cancer. The tumor is at least 2 inches across and a large amount has metastasized to the lymph nodes under the arm or to other nearby lymph nodes or tissue.

Stage IV is metastatic breast cancer where the cancer has spread to more distant structures and organs particularly the bones, lungs, liver, or brain.

Inflammatory breast cancer is a rare type of breast cancer where the breast appears inflamed and the tissue is red and warm. The skin may have pits or ridges. This type of cancer spreads quickly.

Other risk factors in addition to age include women who have already had breast cancer, those with one first-line relative (mother, daughter, or sister) or at least two second-line relatives (cousin or aunt) with breast cancer, breast tissue with previous precancerous changes, and a genetic predisposition toward breast cancer (i.e., BRCA1 or BRCA2).

Other risk factors are related to exposure to estrogen. This group includes women who menstruated before the age of 12, those who had their first child after age 30, women with no natural-born children, postmenopausal women, and those who have used hormone replacement therapy or birth control pills over a long period of time. Women with very dense breast tissue or who have had previous radiation to the breasts are also at an increased risk.

Although these risk factors have been identified, it is important to note that most women with breast cancer have none of these risk factors. Likewise, most women with these risk factors never develop breast cancer.

Following skin cancer, breast cancer is the most common type of cancer in women. As a woman ages, her risk of breast cancer increases. Although it can affect young women, it most often strikes women over the age of 50.

Diagnosis

History: Changes to the breast may be found during breast self-examination. The individual may report a lump or thickening of the breast or tissue under the arm. The breast may have changed shape or size or have a different skin texture. There may be a discharge from the nipple or the nipple may be turned inward. The skin on the breast or the nipple may be red, warm, or scaly.

Signs of breast cancer may not be evident or identified during self-examination.

Physical exam: During a breast examination, the physician uses his/her fingers to feel (palpate) and press on the breast and surrounding tissue. As in the breast self-examination, symptoms of breast cancer include a lump or thickening, change in breast shape or size, discharge from or change in a nipple, and/or a change in skin texture including inflammation.

Tests: Mammography is a screening test for breast cancer. It is also the first test performed to follow-up the physical signs of breast cancer. These x-ray films give more information about physical lumps, thickenings, and may reveal lumps not yet been discovered by physical examination. Mammography cannot confirm if a lump is cancerous. Further diagnostic tests are needed.

Ultrasound helps distinguish between a malignant or benign lump. Because benign lumps are typically fluid-filled sacs (cysts) and malignant lumps are solid masses, they show up differently on ultrasound. However, cancer cannot be confirmed or ruled out with certainty by ultrasound.

For a confirmed diagnosis, cells from the suspicious tissue must be removed and examined under a microscope (biopsy). The biopsy may be a fine needle aspiration, needle (core), or surgical biopsy. If the biopsied cells are cancerous, it is especially important to find out if there are cancer cells in the lymph nodes under the arm. These nodes are also biopsied.

Some but not all cancer cells need female hormones (estrogen or progesterone) in order to grow. Cells from the removed material are tested with estrogen (estrogen receptor assay) and progesterone (progesterone receptor assay). If a hormone receptor test is positive, the cancer cells will need the tested hormone in order to grow. If negative, the cells do not need the hormone. This test gives important information about what type of treatment may be effective against this particular cancer.

The Hercep test is also performed on a portion of the removed material. It identifies those cancer cells that make too much of a certain protein called HER2. Like the hormone receptor tests, this test gives important information about possible treatment.

Other tests are done on the bones, liver, or lungs to check if the cancer has metastasized.

Treatment

Treatment is based on the size and location of the cancer, stage of the cancer, and results of certain laboratory tests such as hormone receptor tests. The physician also considers the woman's age, menopausal status, health, and breast size. Treatment is based on whether the effects of the treatment are needed only in a very specific location (local treatment) or throughout the entire body (systemic treatment).

In general, the smaller and more contained the cancer, the more localized the treatment. Conversely, the larger the cancer and the more it has invaded nearby tissue or spread throughout the body, the more aggressive and systemic the treatment. The most common treatment for breast cancer includes both local and systemic treatments.

Surgery is the most common breast cancer treatment. A lumpectomy is the removal of only the cancerous lump and its surrounding tissue. While the cancer is removed, most of the breast tissue is spared. A segmental or partial mastectomy is another type of breast-sparing surgery. In this procedure, the lump and surrounding tissue are removed. A more extensive surgery may involve removal of the entire breast (modified radical mastectomy). The radical mastectomy removes the entire breast, all or most of the nearby lymph nodes, usually some of the lining over the breast, and some chest muscles (this is rarely performed). A woman can choose to have surgery to rebuild her breast (breast reconstruction) at the time of the initial surgery or at a later date.

Studies show improved survival rates when chemotherapy and/or radiation are used following surgery. Chemotherapy uses drugs or a combination of drugs to kill the cancer cells. The drugs are taken orally or by injection according to a cycle. The individual takes the chemotherapy for a limited amount of time, then has a break for a limited amount of time. The cycles repeat as often as prescribed. Radiation therapy uses radiation to kill cancer cells. The radiation may come from a machine (external radiation) or from radioactive material surgically implanted inside the individual.

Hormone therapy is used against cancer cells that need either estrogen or progesterone in order to grow (those that test positive for hormone receptors). Hormones can be made unavailable to these cells by chemically changing the hormones into an unusable form. Selective estrogen receptor modulators (SERMs) prevent breast tissue cells from using estrogen, thus slowing or stopping cancer cell growth. SERMs also reduce the frequency of breast cancer in women at high risk. Used following surgery, SERMs reduce the chances of the cancer returning or a new cancer forming in the other breast. Another method of hormone therapy is to eliminate the source of the hormones such as removing the ovaries (oophorectomy).

Chemotherapy, radiation, and hormone therapy can also be adjuvant therapy both before and after surgery. For example, radiation therapy may be used before surgery to shrink a tumor that makes removal easier. It can also be used after surgery to help kill any cancer cells that surgery missed. Radiation therapy can be combined with chemotherapy or hormone therapy.

The most aggressive treatments for breast cancer are autologous bone marrow transplants and peripheral stem cell transplants. Some cancers may only respond to very heavy doses of chemotherapy. These doses, however, destroy an individual's bone marrow, the source of the blood supply. These transplants are attempts to rescue an individual from the loss of bone marrow by providing cells that will regrow healthy bone marrow once chemotherapy is over.

Prognosis

The outcome depends primarily on the type of cancer and its stage. A woman's age, menopausal status, and general health also contribute to the outcome.

The best outcome is with small tumors that have not invaded nearby tissue or spread to any lymph nodes. For individuals with this scenario, 90% are disease-free after 10 years. If the cancer has spread to the underarm lymph nodes, disease-free survival at 10 years drops.

Systemic adjuvant therapy significantly increases the odds of a successful outcome.

Differential Diagnosis

Fibrocystic changes, fibroadenoma, hamartoma, lipoma, fat necrosis, and intraductal papilloma are noncancerous breast conditions that may resemble breast cancer.

Specialists

- General Surgeon
- Oncologist
- Physical Therapist
- Plastic Surgeon
- Psychologist
- Radiation Oncologist

Rehabilitation

Physical therapy may be needed after mastectomy to reduce postoperative swelling and to stretch and strengthen arm and shoulder muscles. Individuals rest their hand on a pillow so it is higher than the elbow. This decreases swelling in the fingers. Individuals may also squeeze therapy putty to promote the circulation of fluid from the hand. Individuals perform reverse shoulder rolls and shoulder blade squeezes to promote normalized posture. Individuals also perform range-of-motion exercises where both arms grasp a cane, and the nonaffected arm assists the other arm in reaching up overhead and reaching out to the side.

An important facet of physical therapy for postmastectomy is lymphedema education. Individuals learn to recognize the early symptoms of lymphedema such as increased heaviness in the arm, tightness of the skin, stiffness in the hand and fingers, and altered sensation in the arm. They also learn to avoid triggers of lymphedema such as wearing tight brassieres, cutting their cuticles, and exposure to cigarette smoke.

Individuals with lymphedema as a result of a mastectomy or radiation therapy may require additional physical or occupational therapy. The first goal of therapy is to reduce swelling. This can be done through positioning the arm, retrograde massage, and intermittent mechanical compression. This last technique utilizes a sleeve with separate chambers that sequentially fill with air to help push the swelling from the hand. Individuals also learn to perform light exercises such therapy putty squeezes and biceps curls to further pump fluid from the arm. Therapists may also fit the individual with an elastic support stocking. Individuals learn to avoid sources of overload on the lymphatic system such as prolonged arm activities and heat (including heating pads).

Work Restrictions / Accommodations

Reassignment of job duties may be needed if job requires upper body motion and strength. Following a mastectomy, a woman may lose muscle strength in her arms and shoulders. Her range of motion may also be reduced. These losses may be permanent or temporary.

Lymphedema in an arm may interfere with job duties requiring use of that arm. Because an injured arm is more at risk with lymphedema, protection of the affected arm while on the job may be prudent.

Women undergoing radiation therapy, chemotherapy, or hormone therapy may feel fatigued and require a private place to rest. While taking chemotherapy, accommodations may be needed for time off or for lenient breaks in order to handle side effects such as nausea and vomiting. Damage done to the skin by radiation may require that a woman wear loose clothing until the skin heals.

Bone marrow and peripheral stem cell transplants require a long preparation and recovery period during which the individual cannot work.

Comorbid Conditions

Pregnancy and breastfeeding (lactation) may worsen the prognosis and lengthen disability. These conditions make it more difficult to detect breast cancer early when it can be most successfully treated. Breast cancer also tends to progress more rapidly during pregnancy. In addition, treatment decisions may be altered.

Acute symptoms of menopause and depression may lengthen disability.

Complications

Side effects from treatment can be significant as healthy cells may be damaged along with the cancerous cells. Radiation causes fatigue and red tender skin. Chemotherapy increases the risk of infection and causes fatigue, nausea and vomiting, and hair loss. In some cases, it may weaken the heart or cause another type of cancer such as leukemia. Chemotherapy may also damage the ovaries leading to menopausal symptoms (hot flashes, vaginal discharge, and irregular periods).

Surgery results in pain and tenderness to the region with an increased risk of infection. Some women experience numbness that may be permanent. Surgery where the ovaries are removed results in menopausal symptoms.

Swelling in the arm due to the accumulation of lymph fluid (lymphedema) is a risk after the lymph nodes are removed from under the arms. It can happen immediately or anytime after surgery. An injured or infected arm is at particular risk.

Hormone therapy also can cause menopausal symptoms. In addition, some treating drugs can cause blood clots especially in the legs, and cancer of the uterine lining (endometrial cancer).

Metastasized cancer can cause a variety of symptoms depending on where it has spread, e.g., if spread to the bone, it can be very painful.

The psychological impact of this disease cannot be ignored. Most women report feeling a loss of self-esteem, decrease or total loss of sexuality, fears about dying, general feelings of anxiety, sadness, anger, irritability, difficulty with concentration, and changes in sleep and eating patterns. Depression is common.

Factors Influencing Duration

Length of disability varies significantly according to the type of treatment and extent of the cancer. The more extensive the cancer and aggressive the treatment, the longer the period of disability.

Length of Disability

For individuals with lumpectomy, segmental or partial mastectomy, duration depends on amount of tissue removed, size of incision, and type of anesthesia (local or general). For individuals with radical mastectomy, duration depends on whether dominant or nondominant arm is affected and extent of surgery. Older women and those in poor health usually experience a longer period of recovery. A woman's nutritional status also plays a part in length of disability. Women with metastatic disease that has spread to bone, brain, lungs, or liver are permanently disabled.

For all procedures, the duration reflects recovery from procedure only.

Lumpectomy, segmental, or partial mastectomy.

Duration in Days

Job Classification	Minimum	Optimum	Maximum
Sedentary work	1	3	14
Light work	1	3	14
Medium work	1	3	14
Heavy work	3	7	21
Very Heavy work	3	7	21

Radical or modified radical mastectomy.

Duration in Days

Job Classification	Minimum	Optimum	Maximum
Sedentary work	21	28	42
Light work	28	35	42
Medium work	42	49	56
Heavy work	56	63	84
Very Heavy work	56	63	84

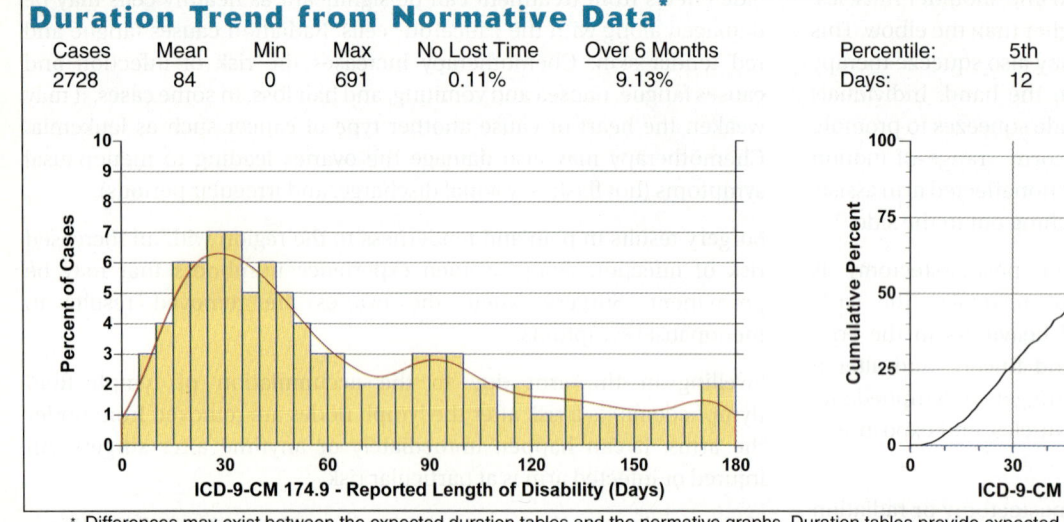
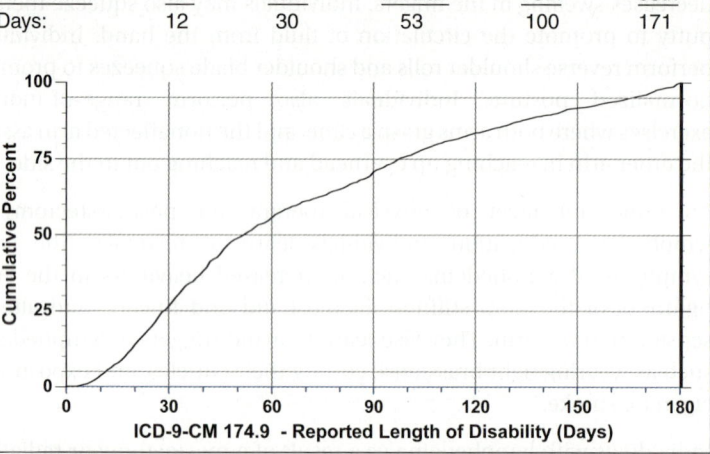

Duration Trend from Normative Data*

Cases	Mean	Min	Max	No Lost Time	Over 6 Months
2728	84	0	691	0.11%	9.13%

Percentile:	5th	25th	Median	75th	95th
Days:	12	30	53	100	171

* Differences may exist between the expected duration tables and the normative graphs. Duration tables provide expected recovery periods based on the type of work performed by the individual. The normative graphs reflect the actual observed experience of many individuals across the spectrum of physical conditions, in a variety of industries, and with varying levels of case management.

Failure to Recover

If an individual fails to recover within the maximum duration expectancy period, the reader may wish to reference the following questions to assist in better understanding the specifics of an individual's medical case.

Regarding diagnosis:

- Was diagnosis of breast cancer confirmed?
- Were conditions with similar symptoms ruled out?
- Does individual have an underlying condition such as pregnancy that may impact recovery?

Regarding treatment:

- Was treatment based on the size and location of the cancer, stage of the cancer, and results of certain laboratory tests such as hormone receptor tests?
- Did treatment also take into consideration the woman's age, menopausal status, health, and breast size?
- Since systemic adjuvant therapy significantly increases the odds of a successful outcome, was appropriate chemotherapy, radiation, and/or hormone therapy used as adjuvant therapy both before and after surgery?
- If aggressive treatment is warranted, is individual a candidate for a bone marrow transplant?

- Although unavoidable, are treatment side effects being effectively managed?
- If it was necessary to remove the lymph nodes, are appropriate efforts being made to prevent lymphedema?

Regarding prognosis:

- Is individual developing acute menopausal symptoms due to surgical removal of the ovaries? What can be done to relieve or minimize symptoms?
- If individual had a mastectomy, was breast reconstruction an option?
- Was reconstruction surgery performed? If not, what are the barriers to having that surgery?
- How is individual's nutritional status? Is individual getting enough rest?
- Because surgery and chemotherapy increase the risk of infection, is individual unnecessarily exposed to infection at home or on the job?
- Is the psychological impact of this disease being addressed? Was referral made for counseling?

References

Breast Cancer (PDQ®). National Cancer Institute. 1999. 27 Dec 1999 <http://cancernet.nci.nih.gov/cancer_types/breast_cancer.shtml>.

Giuliano, Armando. "Breast." Current Medical Diagnosis and Treatment. Tierney, Lawrence, Stephen McPhee, and Maxine Papadakis, eds. New York: Lange Medical Books/McGraw-Hill, 2000. 698-722.

Cancer, Cervix
Other names / synonyms: Cervical Neoplasia
180, 180.0, 180.1, 180.8, 180.9, 198.82, 233.1

Definition

Cervical cancer refers to cancer of the narrowed entry to the uterus (cervix). Cervical cancer is categorized into stages 0 through IV. Stage 0 refers to cancer limited to only the cells on the surface layer of the cervix (carcinoma in situ or preinvasive cancer). Stage IV refers to cancer that has spread beyond the pelvis and involves the bladder, rectum, or distant organs.

Cervical cancer is considered to be a sexually transmitted disease and has been associated with the human papillomavirus (HPV). The most commonly noted risk factors for cervical cancer include beginning sexual intercourse at 16 years or younger, history of multiple sexual partners, history of genital HPV infections or other sexually transmitted diseases, and a previous precancerous cervical lesion. Women who have had many children and those who are long-term users of oral contraceptives (5 or more years) are also at increased risk of developing cancer of the cervix. Older women (60 years or greater) are also considered at higher risk for developing invasive cervical cancer. Smoking and exposure to secondhand smoke also increase risks.

There are 15,000 new cases of cervical cancer each year in the US. The incidence among Hispanics is higher than in blacks, which is greater than in whites. The incidence is higher in developing countries than in the US. The rate of death due to cervical cancer has decreased 70% since the development of a screening test (Pap smear) for cervical cancer 50 years ago.

Diagnosis

History: Women often have no symptoms of cervical cancer. If the cancer has progressed, abdominal swelling (edema) may be present. Some women report a bloody discharge between menstrual periods or after sexual intercourse, or a vaginal discharge with or without odor.

Physical exam: Carcinoma in situ will not be seen on routine pelvic examination. Women with invasive cervical cancer may have an

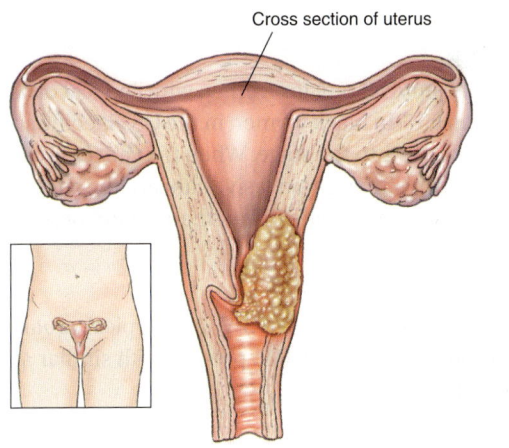

Cross section of uterus

Laurie O'Keefe

abnormal growth visible on the cervix that can be detected during a routine pelvic exam.

Tests: The Pap smear is the best method to detect cervical cancer particularly in its early stage. The Pap smear identifies all stages of cervical cancer. An abnormal Pap smear often requires a more detailed examination of the cervix using colposcopy. Colposcopy uses a magnifying instrument called a colposcope to examine the cervix and look for suspicious tissue. If suspicious tissue is seen, a piece of tissue may be removed (biopsy) and sent to the laboratory for examination. Endocervical curettage may also be performed. In this procedure, tissue is scraped from the inside of the cervix. Like a biopsy, it is sent to the laboratory for examination. A cone biopsy is the removal and examination of a larger piece of tissue, usually cone- or cylinder-shaped.

If there is evidence that the cancer has spread, x-rays, CT, or MRI may be needed. Examination of the bladder or rectum may be done with an endoscopy procedure where a thin tube with a camera on one end is inserted into the ureter or rectum.

Treatment

Early lesions may be removed by cone biopsy, laser vaporization or excision, cryosurgery, or simple hysterectomy where only the uterus with cervix is removed. Frequently, both diagnosis and treatment for stage 0, carcinoma in situ, can be achieved through the use of the loop electrosurgical excision procedure (LEEP).

Invasive cervical cancers are most often treated with a radical hysterectomy with removal of the uterus, ovaries, upper portion of the vagina and pelvic lymph nodes. Radiation therapy may also be used as the sole treatment for invasive cervical cancer or in combination with hysterectomy. Chemotherapy may be used in metastatic disease.

Risk of cervical cancer can be reduced by the use of barrier methods of contraception (condom, diaphragm) combined with spermicidal agents. In addition, diets that are high in beta-carotene and possibly vitamins C, E, and folate have been shown to reduce risk of developing cervical cancer.

Women who have regular Pap smears rarely present with advanced cervical cancer.

Current recommendations are that all women begin having Pap tests when they are 18 years of age or initiate sexual activity. A Pap test for 3 consecutive years is suggested. If findings are normal on each of these tests, women and their physicians can decide whether or not to reduce the frequency of testing to once every 3 years.

Prognosis

The overall 5-year survival rate for women with cervical cancer is 68% in white women and 55% in black women in the US. Specific survival rates, however, vary according to the stage. When the cancer is caught early in stage 0 (carcinoma in situ or preinvasive cancer), the survival rate is 99-100%. Stage IV has a survival rate of less than twenty percent.

Differential Diagnosis

Cervical polyps, cervical infection, HPV, and atypical squamous cells of undetermined significance (ASCUS) present with similar symptoms or Pap smear findings.

Specialists

- General Surgeon
- Gynecologist
- Oncologist
- Psychologist
- Radiation Oncologist

Work Restrictions / Accommodations

Women treated nonsurgically for stage 0 (carcinoma in situ) should not require special accommodations or work restrictions. Women treated surgically with either a simple or radical hysterectomy and those undergoing radiation therapy may benefit from having a place at the work site where they may periodically rest. Work responsibilities for these women may need to be primarily sedentary. Return to work may start with part-time hours with a slow transition to full-time. Women undergoing radiation therapy may require leave from work to complete their treatments.

Comorbid Conditions

The presence of other sexually transmitted diseases or pregnancy may complicate treatment and delay recovery.

Complications

Untreated cervical cancer may result in massive and acute vaginal bleeding. It also may spread to other body sites including the bladder, rectum, lymph nodes, and central nervous system.

Complications associated with the treatment of stage 0 (carcinoma in situ) are usually limited to bleeding after the surgical treatment. However, women who have been treated with one or more of the nonsurgical interventions may develop subsequent problems maintaining a full-term pregnancy due to the fact that the cervix has become incompetent or weakened and possibly scarred as a result of the treatments.

Radiation therapy for invasive cervical cancer may result in complications such as damage to the rectum, urinary incontinence, and scarring that can interfere with sexual intercourse. Psychological reactions such as depression, irritability, feelings of sexual inadequacy, and guilt can accompany this disease.

Factors Influencing Duration

Factors influencing the length of disability include the woman's age, type and stage of disease at initial presentation, presence of concurrent infection and overall general health, type of treatment pursued, and any complications. Younger women with stage 0 will recover most quickly and have the highest likelihood of long-term survival. In contrast, women with invasive disease requiring radical surgery and/or radiation therapy or those in poor health at the onset of treatment will be disabled for a longer period and least likely to survive their disease.

Length of Disability

For abdominal or radical hysterectomy, duration depends on stage, grade, cell type, adjuvant chemotherapy or radiation therapy. Disability may be permanent. For abdominal and radical hysterectomy, duration reflects recovery period for procedure only.

Cervical conization.

Duration in Days

Job Classification	Minimum	Optimum	Maximum
Sedentary work	2	3	7
Light work	2	3	7
Medium work	2	5	7
Heavy work	2	5	10
Very Heavy work	2	5	10

Abdominal hysterectomy.

Duration in Days

Job Classification	Minimum	Optimum	Maximum
Sedentary work	28	42	56
Light work	28	42	56
Medium work	42	56	70
Heavy work	42	70	84
Very Heavy work	42	84	98

Radical hysterectomy.

Duration in Days

Job Classification	Minimum	Optimum	Maximum
Sedentary work	42	49	56
Light work	56	63	70
Medium work	70	77	84
Heavy work	70	84	98
Very Heavy work	70	84	98

Failure to Recover

If an individual fails to recover within the maximum duration expectancy period, the reader may wish to reference the following questions to assist in better understanding the specifics of an individual's medical case.

Regarding diagnosis:

- Was diagnosis of cervical cancer confirmed?
- Were conditions with similar symptoms ruled out?
- Has individual experienced psychological reactions such as depression, irritability, feelings of sexual inadequacy, and guilt that can accompany this disease?

Regarding treatment:

- What stage is the cancer?
- With what procedure was it treated (cone biopsy, laser vaporization, excision, cryosurgery, or loop electrosurgical excision procedure)?
- Was all the cancerous tissue removed?
- Was a hysterectomy performed?
- Is radiation being used as sole treatment or in combination with hysterectomy?
- If advanced, to what body sites has the cancer spread?
- Were lymph nodes removed?
- Would individual also benefit from chemotherapy?

Regarding prognosis:

- At what stage was cancer diagnosed?
- Was initial treatment successful? Was additional treatment required?
- Does individual have an underlying condition such as pregnancy that may complicate treatment or delay recovery?
- Has individual experienced any complications as a result of the cancer or treatment for the cancer?
- Since treatment options such as the addition of radiation or chemotherapy may extend recovery time by several months, was adequate time allotted for recovery?
- If disability has extended past expected duration, what are the extenuating circumstances?

References

Study Reveals Nearly 40 Percent of American Women Risked Their Lives by Failing to Have a Pap Test This Year. CAP Today. 28 Oct 1997. 09 Oct 1998 <http://www.cap.org/html/public/gallup.html>.

MacKay, Trent H. "Gynecology." Current Medical Diagnosis and Treatment, 39th ed. Tierney, Lawrence, Stephen McPhee, and Maxine Papadakis, eds. New York: Lange Medical Books/McGraw-Hill, 2000. 723-757.

Cancer, Colon

Other names / synonyms: Bowel Cancer, Cancer of the Colon, Cancer of the Large Intestine, Colorectal Cancer
153, 153.0, 153.1, 153.2, 153.3, 153.4, 153.5, 153.6, 153.7, 153.8, 153.9, 197.5, 230.3

Definition

Colon cancer is the development of cancerous tumors in the large intestine (colon). The large intestine and the rectum are comparable tissues, and cancers affecting them tend to behave similarly. Thus, the term colorectal cancer is frequently used to refer to malignancies within these organs.

There are a number of factors that increase the risk of developing colon cancer. There is a higher incidence in economically advantaged populations that exhibit westernized lifestyle practices. Diet appears to be a major factor and colon cancer is up to 10 times more common in societies with food intake that is high in calories, red meat, and animal fat, and low in fiber. Other factors that are associated with an increased risk of colon cancer include smoking tobacco, drinking alcohol, and a sedentary lifestyle. The incidence of colon cancer rises sharply after age 40, and 90% of cases occur in individuals over the age of 50. A personal history of abnormal tissue masses (polyps) in the colon or a family history of colorectal cancer also increases the risk. Other risk factors include genetic predisposition (familial polyposis and hereditary nonpolyposis syndromes), the presence of other inflammatory diseases of the bowel (ulcerative colitis, Crohn's disease), and the presence of other cancers such as breast, ovarian, and endometrial cancer.

Individuals who are at-risk for developing colon cancer include those who have had ulcerative colitis or Crohn's disease for more than 7 years, a family history of inherited colorectal cancer (hereditary nonpolyposis or familial polyposis), individuals with family members who developed colon cancer before age 55, or those with two or more immediate relatives with colon cancer. The familial adenomatous polyposis (FAP) gene is rare but predisposes individuals to colorectal cancer.

Cancer of the colon and rectum accounts for about 10% of all cancer deaths and nearly 15% of all cancers that are diagnosed every year in the US. This makes colorectal cancer the second leading cause of cancer-related death among males and females in the US. Colon cancer is by far the most common type of intestinal cancer. Approximately 150,000 Americans develop colorectal cancer every year and 60,000 die of the disease annually. It is the third most commonly occurring malignancy in both women and men.

Diagnosis

History: Individuals with colon cancer may report rectal bleeding, changed bowel habits, abdominal pain that radiates toward the middle of the abdomen (umbilicus) or around the anus (perianal), loss of appetite (anorexia), nausea, and/or vomiting. These symptoms tend to vary depending upon the location of the tumor. In general, if the tumor is located in the segment of colon closest to the small intestine (right or ascending colon), individuals often report abdominal pain, nausea, and vomiting. Tumors in the segment of colon that is farthest from the small intestine and closest to the rectum (left or descending colon) are more likely to cause passage of blood or mucus, an alteration in bowel habits, and a feeling that the bowel is not empty after defecation. Regardless of the tumor's location, weakness and fatigue may be reported due to chronic blood loss, and constipation may alternate with increased frequency and loose stools. Occasionally, the individual will report no symptoms at all until the tumor grows so large that it causes a bowel obstruction or rupture of the intestine.

Physical exam: Examination with the hands (palpation) of the abdomen or examination with one gloved finger in the rectum and the other hand pressing on the abdomen (bimanual rectal exam) may reveal a colonic mass. Abdominal palpation may also reveal an enlarged liver which suggests that the cancer has spread from the colon to other nearby organs (metastasized).

Tests: A chemical test done on a stool sample (fecal occult blood test, or FOBT) can identify blood that may be hidden within the fecal material (occult blood). Twenty to forty percent of individuals who test positive for occult blood will be found to have colorectal cancer. A complete blood count (CBC) can be done to rule out anemia. Additional blood tests, including measurement of a molecule that is associated with cancer cells (carcinoembryonic antigen, or CEA test), a liver enzymes test, and a kidney function test may indicate the extent of disease spreading (metastasis) from the colon to other organs.

Diagnostic tests for colon cancer may include an x-ray procedure to visualize the colon (barium enema) or visualization of the entire colon (full colonoscopy) using a flexible viewing instrument (endoscope) that is inserted through the rectum. Colonoscopy also allows a small sample of tissue (biopsy) to be taken from the tumor, and this can then be examined microscopically to confirm that it is cancerous (pathological confirmation). Individuals who have suspicious abnormalities that were detected using barium enema but tissue biopsies that were negative for cancer will usually need surgery for a definitive diagnosis.

A chest x-ray may be used to look for evidence of metastasis into the lungs. The extent of cancer growth (staging) can be determined using harmless, low-energy radio waves (MRI) or computer analysis of x-ray data (CT). Ultrasound from within the colon (endoluminal ultrasound) can provide important information about the depth that colorectal cancers have invaded into or through the bowel wall.

The familial adenomatous polyposis (FAP) gene is rare but predisposes individuals to colorectal cancer. Individuals who are positive for this gene should be regularly screened for colon cancer beginning at 15 years of age.

Treatment

An evaluation of the degree to which the cancer has spread (staging) is important to determine the type of treatment that the individual should receive, and to estimate the individual's long-term survival possibilities. Surgery to remove the cancerous tissue and a small amount of the surrounding normal tissue (partial colectomy) is the primary treatment for colon cancer. After removal of the tumor, the cut ends of the bowel are sewn together to re-establish the intestinal channel. The individual may require an artificial opening (stoma) of the colon through the abdominal wall for the purpose of bowel elimination (colostomy). A colostomy may be temporary or permanent depending upon the portion of bowel that was surgically removed. However, a permanent colostomy is seldom needed by individuals who have been surgically treated for colon cancer.

Other (adjuvant) therapies may be performed in addition to surgery including radiation therapy, chemotherapy, and therapy to enhance the individual's immune response (immunotherapy). Radiation therapy administered before surgery may reduce tumor size and make it easier to remove the cancerous tissue. Also, radioisotopes implanted into the area of the tumor may minimize the possibility of recurrence. Ingestion of certain antibiotics appears to enhance the effects of radiation. Chemotherapeutic drugs administered after surgery also may be beneficial in preventing recurrence of the disease. Other drugs (analgesics) can be used for pain relief following surgery.

Prognosis

Overall 5-year survival rates from colon cancer have improved significantly in recent years, probably due to better therapy and early detection; early detection is associated closely with improved survival. The cure rate for colon cancer that is detected in its early stages is eighty to ninety percent. Racial differences in survival rates have been observed, and between 1983 and 1989, the 5-year survival rate was 61% in white males, 59% in white females, 48% in black males, and 49% in black females.

It is estimated that more than 40% of the 131,000 individuals with new cases of colon cancer diagnosed in 1996 will die of their disease within the next 5 years. The high fatality rate reflects the fact that many individuals have advanced, incurable colon cancer at the time of diagnosis.

The specific location of the cancer may affect the outcome. A temporary or permanent colostomy may produce psychological problems, and as a result, individuals may become anxious and depressed.

Differential Diagnosis

Conditions that present with similar symptoms include irritable bowel syndrome (IBS), diverticular disease, ischemic colitis, inflammatory bowel disease, infectious colitis, and hemorrhoids.

Specialists

- Colorectal Surgeon
- Gastroenterologist
- General Surgeon
- Oncologist
- Radiation Oncologist

Rehabilitation

A regular exercise routine may be useful in reducing the risk of recurrence of colon cancer. Exercise such as walking, jogging, or swimming (30 to 45 minutes per session) is usually beneficial.

Work Restrictions / Accommodations

In the absence of other medical complications, individuals who have had surgery for colon cancer should be able to return to their previous duties. However, those with colostomies may need frequent breaks and emotional support, and heavy or prolonged lifting should be avoided until recovery is complete. Some individuals may require more sedentary work for a period of time due to weakness and fatigue following surgery, radiation therapy, or chemotherapy.

Comorbid Conditions

Existing conditions that may impact an individual's ability to recover and further lengthen disability include any other diseases that affect the major organ systems of the body such as the liver, lungs, spleen, and pancreas. Other gastrointestinal abnormalities such as Crohn's disease, ulcerative colitis, or irritable bowel disease may also lengthen disability.

Complications

Possible complications of colon cancer are related to the stage the disease has reached by the time of diagnosis. Chronic blood loss at the site of the tumor may result in low concentrations of iron in the blood (iron deficiency anemia). In some cases, the tumor can grow so large that it causes bowel obstruction or rupture of the intestine. A certain type of colonic tumor may occur (carcinoid tumor) that is slow growing and usually symptomless. However, carcinoid tumors often secrete excessive amounts of compounds that activate blood vessels (vasoactive substances). They can metastasize widely and have effects on the circulatory system. Colonic tumors may enter the lymphatic tissue in the wall of the gut. This can damage the intestinal wall and nearby lymph nodes causing malabsorption of food. Further metastasis through the lymph system may allow the cancer to spread to neighboring tissues such as the liver and spleen.

Factors Influencing Duration

Factors that might influence the length of disability include the stage at which the cancer was detected, the length of colon that was removed during surgery, the presence of a temporary or permanent colostomy, the effectiveness of radiation, chemotherapy, or immunotherapy treatments, and the individual's response to these treatments. Advanced age may also be a factor as older individuals often require longer recovery times.

Length of Disability

Duration depends on extent of colectomy (partial vs. total) and whether a colostomy is required. Heavy physical labor will be restricted for 5 to 6 weeks following partial colectomy and possibly longer if postoperative chemotherapy or radiation therapy treatments are necessary. Disability may be permanent depending on the extent of the disease. Recurrence of colon cancer is common and occurs in approximately 30% of cases. Surgical treatment. Durations reflect recovery from procedure only.

Surgical treatment.

Duration in Days

Job Classification	Minimum	Optimum	Maximum
Sedentary work	28	42	70
Light work	28	49	70
Medium work	42	63	84
Heavy work	56	84	112
Very Heavy work	56	84	112

Failure to Recover

If an individual fails to recover within the maximum duration expectancy period, the reader may wish to reference the following questions to assist in better understanding the specifics of an individual's medical case.

Regarding diagnosis:

- Is individual anemic due to blood loss?
- Was there obstruction or rupture of the intestine?
- Has individual suffered from nutrition problems due to malabsorption of food?
- Were other conditions such as irritable bowel syndrome (IBS), diverticular disease, ischemic colitis, inflammatory bowel disease, infectious colitis, and hemorrhoids ruled out?
- Was the diagnosis of colon cancer confirmed?
- At what stage of the disease was diagnosis made?

Regarding treatment:

- Did colectomy remove all the cancerous tissue?
- Was colostomy performed? Temporary or permanent? If temporary, what is the time frame for reconstruction? Is individual capable of appropriate colostomy care?
- Assuming bowel resection was performed, are different postoperative drug or radiation therapy treatments needed?
- Are adjuvant therapies a part of the treatment plan?
- What options (radiation therapy, chemotherapy, immunotherapy, or implantation of radioisotopes) would now be appropriate to include?

Regarding prognosis:

- What was the location of the cancer?
- Was condition diagnosed in an early stage?
- Was treatment prompt and appropriate for that stage?
- Has the tumor metastasized into other organ systems?
- Did colonic tumor recur?
- Does individual have an underlying condition that may impact recovery?
- Has individual experienced any complications?
- Is individual depressed or anxious? If so, was a referral made for counseling?

References

Bresalier, R.S., and Y.S. Kim. "Malignant Neoplasms of the Large Intestine." Gastrointestinal Disease. Sleisenger, M.H., and J.S. Fordtran, eds. Philadelphia: W.B. Saunders Company, 1993. 1449-1493.

Ma, L., V. Iani, and J. Moan. "Combination Therapy: Photochemotherapy; Electric Current; and Ionizing Radiation. Different Combinations Studied in a WiDr Human Colon Adenocarcinoma Cell Line." Journal of Photochemistry and Photobiology. B-Biology 21 2-3 (1993): 149-154.

Schottenfeld, D. "Epidemiology." Cancer of the Colon, Rectum, and Anus. Cohen, A.M., and S.J. Winawer, eds. New York: McGraw-Hill, Inc, 1995. 11-24.

Schroy, P.C., III. "Polyps, Adenocarcinomas, and Other Intestinal Tumors." Therapy of Digestive Disorders. Wolfe, M.M., ed. Philadelphia: W.B. Saunders Company, 2000. 645-673.

Steele, R.J.C. "Outcomes in Colorectal Cancer - Is There a Case for Specialization?" Colorectal Cancer. Scholefield, J.H., ed. Malden, MA: Blackwell Science, Inc, 2000. 29-38.

Turler, A., et al. "Local Treatment of Hepatic Metastases with Low-level Direct Electric Current: Experimental Results." Scandinavian Journal of Gastroenterology 35 3 (2000): 322-328.

Cancer, Esophagus

Other names / synonyms: Cancer of the Esophagus, Esophageal Cancer

150, 150.0, 150.1, 150.2, 150.3, 150.4, 150.5, 150.8, 150.9, 197.8, 230.1

Definition

Cancer of the esophagus, the passageway from the throat to the stomach, arises from the cells lining the esophagus. The tumor can arise anywhere along the length of the esophagus, resulting in narrowing and obstruction of the passageway. The cause has been linked with prolonged tobacco and alcohol use.

Esophageal cancer occurs more frequently in men than women, at a ratio of approximately two to one. It occurs most frequently between age 50 and 60 and accounts for 1% of all cancers.

Diagnosis

History: The individual may complain of difficulty in swallowing (dysphagia) or pain during swallowing. Swallowing difficulty usually occurs with solid foods, but as the disease progresses, this problem may occur with swallowing liquids as well. There is usually rapid and progressive weight loss, poor appetite, fatigue, and often hoarseness.

Physical exam: The exam is rarely helpful in diagnosis of esophageal cancer. Enlarged lymph nodes in the neck or fluid collection in the chest or abdomen may be found late in the disease. Direct observation of the upper gastrointestinal tract using a flexible optical instrument (endoscope) may reveal a growth on the walls of the esophagus.

Tests: A complete blood count (CBC) may be done to determine if the individual has low hemoglobin in the blood (anemia). Liver function tests (SGOT, alkaline phosphatase, and bilirubin) may be performed to determine if the cancer has metastasized to the liver. The esophagus may be visualized by x-ray after swallowing an opaque dye (barium swallow x-ray) or by using an endoscope (endoscopy). Both of these tests may discern the location of the tumor and degree of obstruction within the esophagus. Also, during endoscopy, a biopsy of the tumor can be taken for microscopic examination to determine if it is cancerous. An endoscopic examination of the upper respiratory tract (bronchoscopy) may determine if the tumor is present in the upper airways. High-frequency sound waves (endoscopic ultrasound) may be used in the early stages of the disease to determine the extent of spread (metastasis) of the cancer to organs that lie near the esophagus. The degree of metastasis can also be determined using harmless, low-energy radio waves (MRI) or computer analysis of x-ray data (CT).

Treatment

Treatment may involve surgery to remove the affected part of the esophagus, radiation therapy before or after surgery, chemotherapy, or a combination of these methods. Aggressive surgical approaches are usually used in the early stages of the disease, and the esophagus along with part of the stomach may be completely removed (esophagogastrectomy). A portion of the individual's large intestine (left colon) is then used to reestablish the passageway between the throat and the remainder of the stomach. If surgery is not possible, radiation therapy and chemotherapy may be used to slow the growth and spread of esophageal cancer.

Prognosis

Generally, cancer of the esophagus has a poor prognosis and fewer than 10% of individuals who have this condition will survive 5 years after diagnosis. Only 50-60% of individuals with cancer of the esophagus are able to have their tumors removed surgically. Approximately 40% of tumors that are removed surgically will have been found to have metastasized into other organs, which drastically limits the possibility of a cure. Individuals who are long-term survivors of esophageal cancer usually have tumors that have not grown and metastasized to any great degree.

Differential Diagnosis

A harmless (benign) tightening (stricture) or benign tumor of the esophagus may also cause difficulty swallowing. Other large tumors in the chest may compress the esophagus and cause difficulty swallowing (dysphagia). Muscle contractions in the esophagus (esophageal spasm) may also cause dysphagia.

Specialists

- General Surgeon
- Oncologist
- Radiation Oncologist
- Thoracic Surgeon

Work Restrictions / Accommodations

Most individuals will require more sedentary work for a period of time due to weakness and fatigue following surgery, radiation therapy, and/or chemotherapy. Frequent breaks may be needed, and heavy or prolonged physical exertion may have to be avoided.

Comorbid Conditions

Conditions that may impact an individual's ability to recover and further lengthen the disability include malnutrition. Disability may also be lengthened if the individual has degenerative disease (cirrhosis) of the liver. Use of tobacco will influence length of disability.

Complications

Possible complications of esophageal cancer include complete obstruction of the esophagus leading to difficulty in swallowing (dysphagia) and eating. Also, this cancer may spread (metastasize) into the tube in the neck that conveys air to the lungs (trachea) or the upper airways of the lungs (bronchi). This can create an abnormal opening (fistula) into the lung that results in pneumonia or lung infection (abscess). Sudden and fatal bleeding (hemorrhage) is also a possibility. The tumor may metastasize to the lymph system or to the surface of the heart causing heartbeat disturbances (arrhythmia).

Factors Influencing Duration

Factors that might influence the length of disability from esophageal cancer include the age of the individual, access to adequate health care, size and location of the tumor, whether the tumor has metastasized into other organs, nutritional status, the type of treatment that is necessary, and the response of the individual to treatment. Continued use of alcohol and/or tobacco may cause recurrence of the disease.

Length of Disability

Duration depends on stage, grade, cell type, adjuvant chemotherapy or radiation therapy. The duration of disability may depend upon the requirements of the job. Heavy labor will be restricted post-treatment for a period of time until recovery is complete. Disability may be permanent. For esophagectomy, duration reflects recovery from procedure only.

Surgical treatment (esophagectomy).

Duration in Days

Job Classification	Minimum	Optimum	Maximum
Sedentary work	10	21	28
Light work	10	21	28
Medium work	10	28	42
Heavy work	10	28	42
Very Heavy work	10	28	42

Failure to Recover

If an individual fails to recover within the maximum duration expectancy period, the reader may wish to reference the following questions to assist in better understanding the specifics of an individual's medical case.

Regarding diagnosis:

- Does individual use tobacco in any form?
- Were such conditions as benign strictures, benign tumor of the esophagus, large tumors in the chest that compress the esophagus, and esophageal spasm ruled out?
- Was the diagnosis of esophageal cancer confirmed?

Regarding treatment:

- Was individual treated with surgery, radiation therapy, and/or chemotherapy?
- Was the treatment appropriate?
- Would individual benefit from additional radiation, surgery, or chemotherapy?

Regarding prognosis:

- Has the tumor metastasized into other organ systems?
- Is individual depressed? If so, was a referral made for counseling?
- Has individual experienced any complications such as complete obstruction of the esophagus, metastasis to trachea or bronchi, pneumonia, abscess, or hemorrhage?
- Have any underlying conditions developed that may impact recovery such as malnutrition or cirrhosis of the liver?

References

Given, B.A., and S.J. Simmons. <u>Gastroenterology in Clinical Nursing</u>. St. Louis: The C.V. Mosby Company, 1984.

Vinayek, R., and B. Levin. "Endoscopic Diagnosis." <u>Cancer of the Esophagus</u>. DeMeester, T.R., and B. Levin, eds. Orlando: Grune & Stratton, Inc, 1985. 43-56.

Cancer, Kidney

Other names / synonyms: Adenocarcinoma, Adenocarcinoma of the Kidney, Cancer of the Kidney, Hypernephroma, Kidney Cancer, Kidney Neoplasm, Renal Cancer, Renal Cell Carcinoma, Renal Neoplasm

189, 189.0, 189.1, 233.9, 236.90

Definition

Kidney cancer (renal cell carcinoma) occurs when a deadly (malignant) tumor grows in the kidney. This cancer is usually identified late in the course of the disease and half of kidney cancers are found incidentally while evaluating another condition such as a urinary infection. One-third of individuals with kidney cancer will present with a tumor that has already spread (metastasized) beyond the kidney.

The most significant risk factors for renal cell carcinoma appear to be tobacco and obesity. Other suspected risk factors include analgesic abuse, the chronic irritation associated with kidney stones (renal calculi), and exposure to cadmium and various petroleum products.

Renal cancer accounts for 5% of all adult cancers and most cases occur between the ages of 50 and 70. The condition is 2 to 3 times more prevalent in men than women. There are approximately 30,000 new cases of renal cell carcinoma each year in the US with approximately 12,000 deaths from kidney cancer occurring annually.

Diagnosis

History: Most individuals will not report any symptoms in the early stage of renal cell carcinoma. In the more advanced stage, individuals may report blood in the urine (hematuria), pain in the flank, weight loss, and/or shortness of breath.

Physical exam: A mass may be felt on the kidney using finger manipulation (palpation), however, in the vast majority of individuals, there are no remarkable findings on physical examination.

Tests: Urinalysis may reveal blood in the urine. A complete blood count (CBC) may be performed to determine the number of red blood cells in the blood and results may show a low red cell count (anemia). X-ray analysis of the kidney (intravenous pyelogram or IVP) can be used to accurately identify a renal tumor. High-frequency sound waves (renal ultrasonography) or a CT can provide additional information such as the size of the tumor, whether it is fluid-filled (cystic) or solid, and if the circulatory system and/or lymph nodes are involved. Visualization of the blood vessels following injection of a radiopaque dye (arteriography) may determine whether or not the cancer involves the arteries. MRI is another tool that may be used to assess involvement of the renal veins or inferior vena cava. A chest x-ray will determine if the cancer has spread to the lungs. There is no screening test to detect renal cell carcinoma in its early stages.

Treatment

Complete surgical removal of the kidney, regional lymph nodes, adrenal gland, and part of the ureter (radical nephrectomy) is the treatment of choice for localized renal carcinoma. If the tumor has spread (metastasized) to other organs, radical nephrectomy may be of little use unless the tumor mass is causing problems such as pain or bleeding (hemorrhage). In this case, radical nephrectomy may be performed for pain relief and to arrest bleeding rather than achieve a cure. Individuals with metastatic renal carcinoma are typically treated with chemotherapy or antibodies attached to cancer-fighting biological agents such as interferon-alpha (immunotherapy). Radiation therapy may be employed for renal cancer that has metastasized into the bones or lungs.

Prognosis

Spontaneous regression of renal tumors occurs in less than 1% of all cases. Otherwise, the predicted outcome of renal cancer depends on the stage of the tumor at the time of treatment. The 5-year survival rate is 65% for early-stage cancer treated surgically by radical nephrectomy. This figure drops to 40% for more advanced renal carcinoma. Ten-year survival rates are 40% and 35% for early and locally advanced cancers, respectively. The overall 5-year survival rate is less than 5% if the tumor has metastasized to other organs.

Differential Diagnosis

Conditions that present with symptoms similar to renal cancer may include a harmless (benign) renal cyst or tumor, an infected area containing pus (abscess) within the kidney, tuberculosis, or cancer of another small organ (adrenal gland) located near the kidney.

Specialists

- Oncologist
- Radiation Oncologist
- Urologist

Rehabilitation

Individuals recovering from kidney cancer would benefit from several types of rehabilitation. Supportive rehabilitation allows individuals to gain some control over ordinary activities of life and helps them cope emotionally. This may include group vocational rehabilitation to help the individual transition back into the workplace or a return to school and/or retraining if the individual cannot physically return to the previous workplace and career. Palliative rehabilitation addresses the pain an individual experiences, allows some level of physical comfort, and provides emotional support and assistance in day-to-day functioning.

Physical rehabilitation allows individuals to regain strength and stamina that were lost due to the disease process and during treatment. Individuals recovering from kidney cancer are usually very weak. Strengthening starts at a low level and progresses only as tolerated, especially if strengthening is attempted during the course of treatment. If surgery is required, breathing exercises after surgery may be useful to prevent postoperative pulmonary complications. Certain exercises may also be performed to reduce postoperative pain and speed recovery and include progressive relaxation and deep breathing techniques. The individual lies on the back and performs ankle pumps (flexing the ankle back and forth) and knee bends to help increase circulation and make walking easier.

Early in physical rehabilitation of this disease, the individual should perform range-of-motion exercises to help return mobility to joints and stretch key muscles that will enable the individual to return to activities of daily living. When resistance is tolerated, the individual performs isotonic exercise using an elastic band or light weights that strengthen the muscles. As the individual lifts the weight throughout the range of motion, the muscle shortens and lengthens. Because muscle weakness to the legs is likely, balance exercises are beneficial.

The frequency and duration of the rehabilitation program vary among individuals with kidney cancer. Intensity and progression of the exercises depend on the prognosis, whether surgery was performed, if the individual is receiving any current cancer treatment, extent of the disease, and individual's overall health.

Work Restrictions / Accommodations

Job restrictions may include extended work leave or accommodations. The incision used for nephrectomy is extensive and may cause significant discomfort. Muscular pain usually results from this surgery and accommodations should be made to alleviate this problem. Accommodations may include proper positioning, massage, heat, and analgesics. Bowel function may be altered and appropriate bathroom facilities should be made easily available. Less strenuous or stationary work should be considered until the individual recovers from surgical treatment, chemotherapy, and/or radiation therapy.

Comorbid Conditions

Existing conditions that may impact an individual's ability to recover and further lengthen the disability include obesity and continued exposure to tobacco smoke, cadmium, and various petroleum products.

Complications

Complications occur when the carcinoma has spread to other areas of the body including lungs, bone, lymph nodes, liver, and the central nervous system. A urinary fistula may develop. Metastasis into these other organs may produce bone pain, pneumonia, fatigue, and weight loss. Fracture of a long bone may occur from this cancer.

Factors Influencing Duration

Factors influencing the length of disability include the type and stage of the disease at initial presentation, the presence of concurrent infection and overall general health, type of treatment used, and complications such as infection, hemorrhage, or metastasis of the cancer.

Length of Disability

Duration depends on stage, grade, cell type, and adjuvant radiation therapy. The individual will spend at least a week in the hospital following nephrectomy. Extensive recovery time may be needed to allow full recovery from surgery, chemotherapy, and/or radiation therapy. The individual may not recover if the tumor has metastasized beyond the kidney into other organ systems. Disability may be permanent. Duration reflects recovery period for surgery only.

Surgical treatment (nephrectomy, radical).

Duration in Days

Job Classification	Minimum	Optimum	Maximum
Sedentary work	14	28	42
Light work	14	28	56
Medium work	21	35	56
Heavy work	28	42	70
Very Heavy work	28	42	70

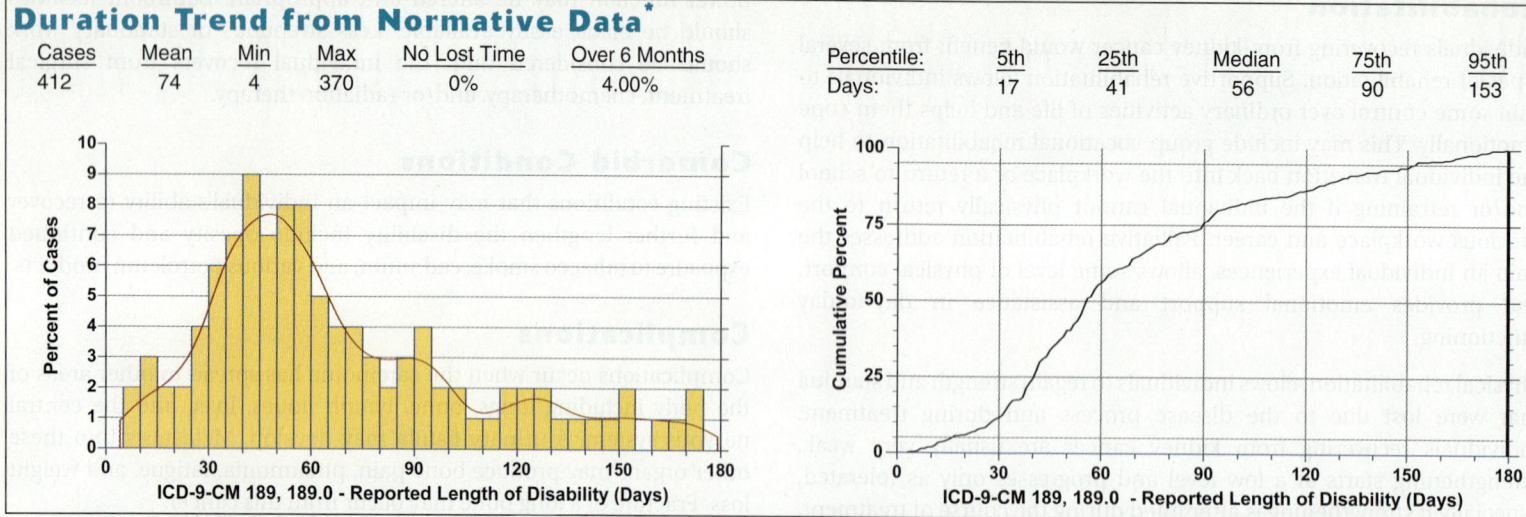

Duration Trend from Normative Data*

Cases	Mean	Min	Max	No Lost Time	Over 6 Months
412	74	4	370	0%	4.00%

Percentile:	5th	25th	Median	75th	95th
Days:	17	41	56	90	153

*Differences may exist between the expected duration tables and the normative graphs. Duration tables provide expected recovery periods based on the type of work performed by the individual. The normative graphs reflect the actual observed experience of many individuals across the spectrum of physical conditions, in a variety of industries, and with varying levels of case management.

Failure to Recover

If an individual fails to recover within the maximum duration expectancy period, the reader may wish to reference the following questions to assist in better understanding the specifics of an individual's medical case.

Regarding diagnosis:

- Does individual have a urinary fistula?
- Were other conditions such as benign renal cyst or tumor, kidney abscess, tuberculosis, or cancer of the adrenal gland ruled out?
- Was diagnosis of renal cancer confirmed?
- Has the carcinoma metastasized to other areas of the body including lungs, bone, lymph nodes, liver, and the central nervous system?

Regarding treatment:

- If not a cure, would surgery provide symptom relief?
- If symptoms are not relieved through current therapy, what other options are available?
- Would individual benefit from the addition of adjuvant therapies such as chemotherapy, immunotherapy, or radiation therapy?

Regarding prognosis:

- Has the tumor metastasized into other organ systems?
- Would surgery help relieve symptoms and improve the quality of life?
- Does individual have a functional support system in place?
- Would individual benefit from psychological counseling or enrollment in a support group?

References

Kisner, C., and L. Colby. Therapeutic Exercise Foundations and Techniques. Philadelphia: F.A. Davis, 1990.

LeMone, P., and K.M. Burke. Medical-Surgical Nursing. Upper Saddle River, NJ: Prentice Hall Health, 2000.

Rittenhouse, J.R., P.D. Lui, and B.H. Lau. "Chinese Medicinal Herbs Reverse Macrophage Suppression Induced by Urological Tumors." Journal of Urology 146 2 (1991): 486-490.

Scully, Rosemary M., and Marylou R. Barnes. Physical Therapy. Philadelphia: J.B. Lippincott Company, 1989.

Cancer, Liver

Other names / synonyms: Cancer of the Liver, Cholangiocarcinoma, Cholangiosarcoma, HCC, Hepatocarcinoma, Hepatocellular Carcinoma, Hepatocellular Carcinoma (HCC), Liver Cancer, Liver Cell Cancer, Liver Cell Carcinoma

155, 155.0, 155.1, 155.2, 197.7, 230.8

Definition

Liver cancer is the growth of a deadly (malignant) tumor in the liver, the largest organ in the body located in the upper right part of the abdominal cavity. The liver has many functions such as neutralizing poisons, metabolizing nutrients, producing blood clotting proteins and some hormones, producing bile, and storing vitamins in the body. The two common types of tumors that develop directly from liver cells (primary tumors) are cancer from hepatocytes (hepatocellular carcinoma or HCC) and cancer from epithelial cells in the bile ducts of the liver (cholangiosarcoma).

Risk factors for liver cancer include infection with certain viral infections (hepatitis B or hepatitis C), the most common cause of liver cancer worldwide. Men older than 50 who have both hepatitis B and C are especially at high risk in developing liver cancer.

Another common cause of liver cancer in some parts of the world is toxins (aflatoxins) generated by fungi (aspergillus flavus and aspergillus parasiticus) found on nuts and meal stored under hot, humid conditions. This type of cancer is also associated with chronic degenerative disease of the liver (cirrhosis) that may occur as a result of chronic alcohol abuse, nutritional deprivation, or exposure to chemicals such as pesticides, chlorinated hydrocarbons, aromatic amines, and chlorophenols. More than half to three-quarters of individuals with liver cancer have cirrhosis, and 5% of individuals with cirrhosis eventually develop liver cancer. Minor risk factors for liver cancer may include oral contraceptive steroids, cigarette smoking, glycogen storage disease, accumulation of copper in the liver due to a genetic disorder (Wilson's disease), and a hereditary metabolic disease that results in excessive iron deposition in the liver (hemochromatosis).

Liver cancer is relatively rare in the US but is becoming more common. It is the most common cancer in some countries. Countries considered high risk for liver cancer include sub-Saharan Africa, Southeast Asia, and China with annual incidence rates of more than 20 per 100,000 individuals. Japan and southern Europe are intermediate areas of risk (10 to 20 per 100,000 of the population per year), while England, North and South America, Scandinavia, India, and Australia are low areas of risk (5 per 100,000 per year). There are 2,500 new cases of liver cancer each year in the US, and it is up to four times more common in men than women.

Diagnosis

History: The individual may complain of upper abdominal pain often on the right side, weight loss, and loss of appetite (anorexia). A history of hepatitis and cirrhosis from alcohol or other causes could be significant.

Physical exam: There may be a yellow discoloration (jaundice) of the skin, whites (sclera) of the eyes, and mucous membranes. Examination of the abdomen using the hands or fingers (palpation) may reveal an enlarged, tender liver, a lump (mass) on the liver, and swelling as a result of fluid (ascites).

Tests: Levels of blood cholesterol, liver enzymes in the bloodstream (alkaline phosphatase or ALP and serum gamma glutamyl transpeptidase or GGTP), serum bilirubin, and urine bilirubin are often elevated. Complete blood count (CBC) may show an abnormally low number of red blood cells (anemia). A biological marker called alpha-fetoprotein (AFP) is elevated in 50-70% of Americans with liver cancer, but may also be elevated in other types of tumors. Screening tests for hepatitis B and C viruses may also be done. A CT of the abdomen and a sample of the liver tissue using CT-guided liver biopsy are the techniques for definitive diagnosis of primary liver cancer.

Visualization of the liver following injection of radiopaque dye (arteriography) and an MRI may be used to determine if the individual would benefit from surgery. Looking at the abdominal organs through a fiber optic device inserted through a small cut in the abdominal wall (laparoscopy) may also help determine whether surgery is necessary.

Treatment

The only treatment that may cure liver cancer is either surgery to remove the diseased portion of the liver (liver resection) or replacement of the liver (liver transplantation). The types of liver resection are based on the portion of the organ to be removed (i.e., right or left hepatectomy, right or left lobectomy, extended left hepatectomy). Whenever possible, resection is the treatment of choice for liver cancer. Only 9-27% of individuals, however, are suitable for this treatment due to the size of the lesion or the degree to which it has spread (metastasized).

Nonsurgical treatments designed to relieve discomfort (palliative) should be considered including chemotherapy, radiation therapy, treatment using antibodies or biological response modifiers (monoclonal antibodies), injection of alcohol directly into the liver to kill diseased tissue (direct intralesional treatment), or partial elimination of blood flow to the diseased tissue. Chemotherapy may be used in conjunction with surgery to minimize the possibility of further spread of the disease. Radiation therapy may be applied from an external source (external beam irradiation) or internally by injecting radiolabeled antibodies that seek out the tumor (internal irradiation with radioimmunoglobulin).

Prognosis

In general, the disease-free 5-year survival rate ranges from 29-58% if the tumor is detected early and the individual undergoes surgical resection. The 5-year survival rate for individuals receiving a liver transplant ranges from twenty to thirty-six percent. The average survival rate for individuals who are not candidates for surgery and receive palliative treatment is only 3 to 4 months. Liver cancer is rapidly fatal in more advanced cases. Alpha-fetoprotein levels may help determine outcome, as survival is significantly longer when this biological marker of liver cancer is absent. Other factors associated with a more favorable outcome include better health, ability to perform daily activities when the diagnosis is first made, and normal levels of liver enzymes.

Differential Diagnosis

Conditions that present with symptoms similar to liver cancer include other harmless (benign) and malignant liver tumors. Benign tumors may include a closed sac containing fluid or semisolid material (cyst), a mass of blood vessels (hemangioma), or a small, firm, rounded mass (nodule). Cancer that has spread from other organs (metastatic cancer) to produce a secondary tumor in the liver will have characteristics similar to primary liver cancer.

Specialists

- Gastroenterologist
- General Surgeon
- Oncologist
- Radiation Oncologist

Work Restrictions / Accommodations

Individuals may require more sedentary work for a period of time due to weakness and fatigue following surgery. Medium- to heavy-duty responsibilities should be postponed. If chemotherapy is used in conjunction with surgery, the individual may need extended recovery time from this treatment. Individuals who receive palliative treatment only will generally not return to work even in a limited capacity.

Comorbid Conditions

Prior liver disease or exposure to environmental toxins or alcohol that cause cirrhosis may affect an individual's ability to recover from liver cancer. Malnutrition may also lengthen the disability. Bleeding disorders may make the individual more vulnerable to lack of blood clotting factors ordinarily produced by the liver.

Complications

Complications of liver cancer are related to the stage of the disease. The condition has a tendency to invade the blood vessels and lymph glands of the liver producing circulatory problems within the organ. The individual may also have bleeding (hemorrhage) problems because the damaged liver may not adequately produce the proteins normally required for blood clotting. The liver is located close to several vital organs including the lung and spleen. Liver tumors may metastasize into these organs directly or indirectly via the lymphatic or vascular systems and lead to widespread cancer throughout the body.

Factors Influencing Duration

Factors influencing the length of disability include the type and stage of the disease at initial presentation, the presence of concurrent infection and overall general health, type of treatment pursued, response to treatment, and any underlying complications. Disability due to liver cancer may be permanent in advanced cases where surgery or transplantation is not an option.

Length of Disability

The duration of disability may depend on the requirements of the job. Heavy physical labor is restricted for 5 to 6 weeks following liver resection or transplantation and possibly longer if postoperative chemotherapy treatment is necessary. Advanced liver cancer precludes return to work. Disability may be permanent.

Hepatocarcinoma. Medical or surgical treatment.

Duration in Days

Job Classification	Minimum	Optimum	Maximum
Any work	42	91	Indefinite

Failure to Recover

If an individual fails to recover within the maximum duration expectancy period, the reader may wish to reference the following questions to assist in better understanding the specifics of an individual's medical case.

Regarding diagnosis:

- Does individual complain of upper abdominal pain often on the right side, weight loss, and loss of appetite (anorexia)?
- Does individual have history of hepatitis and cirrhosis from alcohol or other causes?
- Is yellow discoloration (jaundice) present of the skin, whites (sclera) of the eyes, and mucous membranes?
- Did examination of the abdomen using the hands or fingers (palpation) reveal an enlarged, tender liver, a lump (mass) on the liver, and swelling as a result of fluid (ascites)?
- Were tests show elevated levels of blood cholesterol, liver enzymes in the blood stream (alkaline phosphatase or ALP and serum gamma glutamyl transpeptidase or GGTP), serum bilirubin, and urine bilirubin?
- Were other conditions with similar symptoms including benign tumors or cysts, hemangioma, nodules, or secondary tumors ruled out?
- Was diagnosis of liver cancer confirmed?

Regarding treatment:

- If resection is not an option, is individual a candidate for liver transplantation?
- Is individual on local or national transplant lists?
- Would individual benefit from either chemotherapy to minimize further spread of the disease or radiation therapy (external or internal)?
- Were nonsurgical treatments designed to relieve discomfort such as, chemotherapy, radiation therapy, treatment using antibodies or biological response modifiers, direct intralesional treatment, or partial elimination of blood flow to the diseased tissue considered?
- If symptoms are not relieved through current therapy, what other options are available?

Regarding prognosis:

- At what stage was cancer detected?
- Was surgery performed?
- Has individual experienced any complications such as hemorrhage or other circulatory problems that may impact recovery?
- Does individual have underlying conditions (prior liver disease, malnutrition, exposure to environmental toxins or alcohol resulting in cirrhosis, or increased vulnerability to bleeding disorders due to lack of blood clotting factors) that may impact recovery?
- What is the prognosis for individual?
- Does individual have a functional support system in place?
- Would individual benefit from psychological counseling or enrollment in a support group?

References

Adult Primary Liver Cancer. National Cancer Institute. 01 Jan 2000. 31 Oct 2000 <http://www.meb.uni-bonn.de/cancernet/101195.html>.

LeMone, P., and K.M. Burke. Medical-Surgical Nursing. Upper Saddle River, NJ: Prentice Hall Health, 2000.

Cancer, Lung

Other names / synonyms: Bronchogenic Carcinoma, Carcinoma of the Lung, Lung Cancer, Lung Carcinoma, Malignant Neoplasm of Bronchus, Malignant Neoplasm of the Trachea, Non-Small Lung Cell Carcinoma, NSLCC, SCLC, Small-Cell Lung Carcinoma

162.2, 162.3, 162.4, 162.5, 162.8, 162.9, 197.0, 231.2

Definition

Lung cancer is also called carcinoma of the lung and refers to an abnormal growth within the lung tissue and the airways of the lungs (trachea and bronchi or tracheobronchial tree). Most lung cancers arise from the bronchial tree and are referred to as bronchogenic carcinoma. Lung cancer is classified into two major types according to the type of cell present in the tumor. These are small cell lung carcinoma (SCLC) and nonsmall cell lung carcinoma (NSCLC). It is important to note that these are different types of cancer and have key differences in incidence, potential to spread, treatment options, and outcome.

NSCLC can be further grouped into three types of cancer that are large-cell carcinoma, squamous cell carcinoma, and adenocarcinoma. SCLC is the most rapidly increasing type of lung cancer especially in women and accounts for about 25% of all new lung cancer cases. It is characterized by rapid growth, early spread into nearby tissues and organs (metastasis), and rapid recurrence. Typically, SCLC metastasizes into the brain, bone, bone marrow, liver, and/or lymph nodes.

The greatest risk factor for lung cancer is tobacco smoke. Only about 2% of lung cancers occur in nonsmokers. Other risk factors include exposure to certain industrial agents such as asbestos, arsenic, ionizing radiation, nickel, and aromatic hydrocarbons and indoor air pollutants such as radon gas and secondhand smoke.

Lung cancer is increasing worldwide at a rate of 0.5% per year. In all countries, rates are higher in urban than rural areas, and 2 to 6 times higher in males than females. In European countries, it is the leading cause of cancer incidence and mortality and accounts for about 21% of all cancer cases in men. The US ranks fifth (men) and first (women) in mortality rates from lung cancer when compared to other industrialized nations. In the US, lung cancer is the leading cause of cancer mortality in men and women with approximately 170,000 new cases with about 157,400 deaths a year. The age-adjusted mortality rate per 100,000 in the US is 70.9 for men and 33.8 for women. Although the mortality rate in American men decreased by about 1.4% per year between 1990 and 1994, this rate increased in American women by about 1.7% per year.

Diagnosis

History: Individuals may report (in order of frequency) persistent cough, coughing up blood (hemoptysis), shortness of breath (dyspnea), chest pain, weight loss, hoarseness, and localized bone pain. The bone pain can be anywhere because of the ability of the lung cancer to spread. Lung cancer is sometimes not discovered until the affected individual is treated for another condition such as pneumonia. Individuals may have a history of smoking or exposure to industrial carcinogens. In the vast majority of cases, the lung tumor will have metastasized into adjacent tissues and organs when it is first diagnosed. Only 15% of individuals with lung cancer have no signs or symptoms (asymptomatic).

Physical exam: Findings may be variable and depend on the stage of the disease and the extent of local, regional, or distant spread of the cancer. Physical examination of the chest and lungs may be normal. Wheezes or the absence of breath sounds in part of the lungs can indicate partial or total obstruction of the airways. An enlargement of the lymph nodes around the neck and collarbones or localized chest tenderness may indicate spread of the cancer to these areas (metastatic cancer).

Tests: Blood tests to measure electrolytes, serum calcium, liver function tests, kidney function, and complete blood count (CBC) are routine. A chest x-ray is the primary tool for diagnosing lung cancer and is especially helpful if previous chest x-rays are available for comparison. The sputum may be examined microscopically for cancer cells (sputum cytology). If cancer cells are not found, the area of a suspected tumor is directly viewed through a flexible tube (bronchoscopy) and a tissue sample (biopsy) taken for examination under a microscope. A needle biopsy may be performed if the tumor is beyond reach of the bronchoscopy procedure.

A biopsy may be taken on occasion through a tube passed by a chest surgeon into a portion of the chest (mediastinum) using a procedure called mediastinoscopy. CT of the chest, abdomen, and brain allow further evaluation of general x-ray findings. CT may also help identify the position of the tumor more precisely and whether the cancer has metastasized. MRI may also be used to make these evaluations. A radioactive substance can be injected and pictures taken (bone scintigraphy) to determine if the cancer has metastasized to the bone.

Treatment

Individuals with NSCLC that has not metastasized out of the lung are candidates for surgical removal of the diseased lobe (lobectomy) or the entire lung (pneumonectomy) and the surrounding lymph nodes (lymphadenectomy). A smaller segment of the lung may be removed if the individual cannot tolerate a lobectomy, however, complete removal of all tumorous tissue is usually the goal of surgery. High-energy, radioactive particles (radiation therapy) may be used for treatment of NSCLC when surgery is not an option. If the cancer has spread to other organs, treatment with one or more anticancer drugs (combination chemotherapy) may be used in addition to radiation and/or surgical treatment.

Combination chemotherapy is usually the treatment of choice for individuals with SCLC because of rapid growth, tendency to metastasize, and sensitivity to chemotherapeutic drugs. Most individuals with SCLC have cancer that has spread extensively by the time of diagnosis and are not candidates for surgery. Chemotherapy and radiation therapy may also be used to relieve disease symptoms (palliative treatment) in individuals with SCLC.

Other medications for individuals with either NSCLC or SCLC include drugs to reduce airway obstruction (bronchodilators) and antibiotics to treat infection. Pain relief (analgesic) therapy may be necessary following surgery and for advanced lung cancers.

Prognosis

SCLC may be classified as either limited stage disease or extensive stage disease. In limited stage disease (30% of cases), the tumor is regional and confined to one area within the lung. The 5-year survival rate is 10-15% following surgery and chemotherapy treatments. SCLC tumors are classified as extensive stage if they have spread to other organs beyond the lungs. Note that extensive stage disease is not the same as end stage disease (when death is imminent). The 2-year survival rate is less than 10% for extensive stage disease.

The 5-year survival rate is 50-60% for individuals with NSCLC that is limited to the lungs who receive surgery as treatment. Alternatively, these individuals sometimes respond well to chemotherapy and occasional cures may be seen. The 5-year survival rate decreases to 30-40% for more advanced NSCLC that must be treated with surgery or radiation in combination with chemotherapy. Chemotherapy may add to the duration of survival, however, it rarely enhances the cure rate.

Differential Diagnosis

Conditions with similar symptoms as lung cancer include bronchitis, tuberculosis, pneumonia, fungal infections of the lung, lung abscess, harmless (benign) tumors of the lung, and metastatic cancer that has spread to the lung from another organ.

Specialists

- General Surgeon
- Oncologist
- Pulmonologist
- Radiation Oncologist
- Thoracic Surgeon

Work Restrictions / Accommodations

Individuals who have surgery and do not need chemotherapy may resume their previous duties after an appropriate amount of time to recuperate. Individuals on chemotherapy and/or radiation treatment will have periods of absence from the workplace.

Comorbid Conditions

Conditions that may impact an individual's ability to recover and further lengthen disability include chronic lung disease (emphysema) and decreased lung function as a result of surgery or radiation therapy.

Complications

Complications are usually related to the amount of metastasis. Lung cancer often invades surrounding tissue including the ribs, major blood vessels, and/or major nerves that can cause additional problems. Lung inflammation or infection (pneumonia) is a common complication and wheezing and shortness of breath may occur as a result of airway obstruction. Confusion, disturbances of gait and balance, headache, and personality changes may occur if the tumor has metastasized into the brain. Spread of the tumor into bone can result in bone pain, fractures, and spinal cord injury. Bone marrow invasion may result in an abnormally small number of platelets (thrombocytopenia) and red blood cells (anemia) in the bloodstream. Large tumors may cause obstruction of a major vein that returns blood to the heart (vena caval obstruction) and this can result in swelling (edema) of the head and neck, headache, dizziness, vision disturbances, and sudden loss of consciousness (syncope).

Factors Influencing Duration

Factors that may influence length of disability include the type and stage of the disease at initial presentation, any concurrent infections, overall general health, type of treatment, and any complications that may result from treatment. In general, chemotherapy and radiation therapy treatments extend the length of disability.

Length of Disability

A large percentage of individuals will not recovery from lung cancer. Individuals who can return to work may be able to perform in only a limited capacity if they are undergoing continued radiation and/or chemotherapy treatments. Chemotherapy is usually administered on an inpatient basis every 3 to 4 weeks for 4 to 6 months. Each time chemotherapy is administered, time off will be necessary. Heavy physical labor and extended hours may not be possible until recovery is complete. Disability may be permanent.

For individuals with non-small cell lung carcinoma and pneumonectomy, disability may be permanent for heavy and very heavy work.

Chemotherapy. Small cell lung carcinoma.

Job Classification	Minimum	Optimum	Maximum
Sedentary work	42	84	Indefinite
Light work	42	84	Indefinite
Medium work	42	84	Indefinite
Heavy work	42	84	Indefinite
Very Heavy work	42	84	Indefinite

Non-small cell lung carcinoma. Lung excision, partial (lobectomy).

Job Classification	Minimum	Optimum	Maximum
Sedentary work	21	28	Indefinite
Light work	21	28	Indefinite
Medium work	28	42	Indefinite
Heavy work	42	56	Indefinite
Very Heavy work	42	Indefinite	Indefinite

Non-small cell lung carcinoma. Pneumonectomy.

Job Classification	Minimum	Optimum	Maximum
Sedentary work	56	70	Indefinite
Light work	56	70	Indefinite
Medium work	70	70	Indefinite
Heavy work	70	Indefinite	Indefinite
Very Heavy work	Indefinite	Indefinite	Indefinite

Duration Trend from Normative Data*

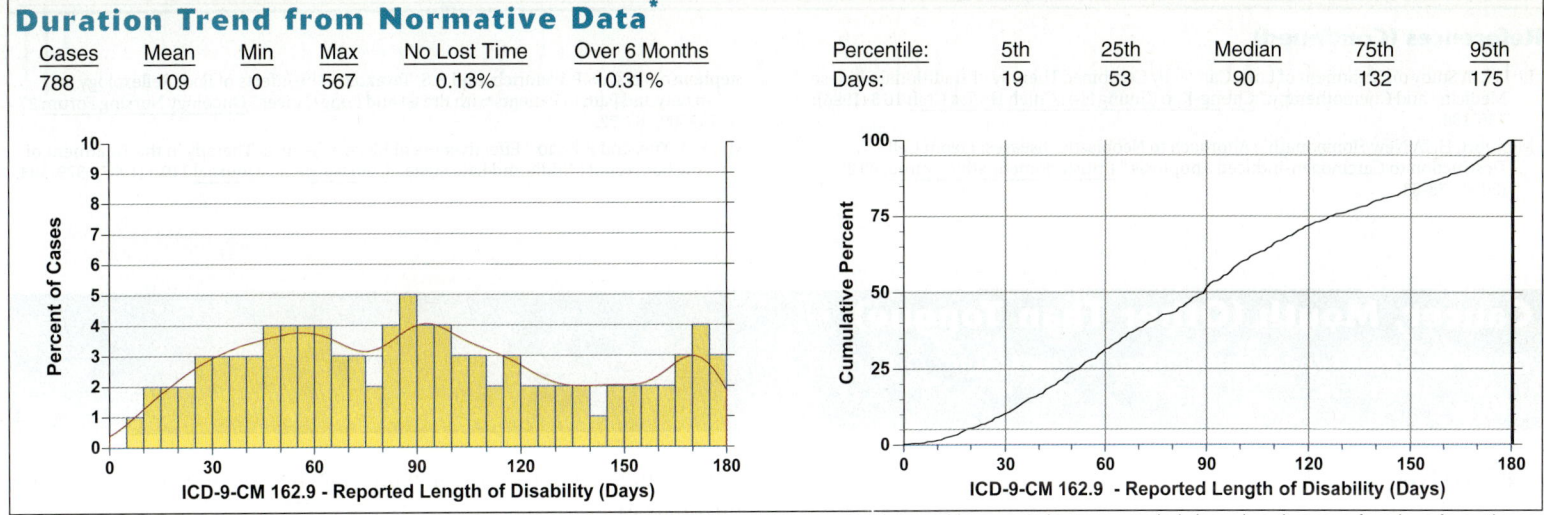

Cases	Mean	Min	Max	No Lost Time	Over 6 Months	Percentile:	5th	25th	Median	75th	95th
788	109	0	567	0.13%	10.31%	Days:	19	53	90	132	175

*Differences may exist between the expected duration tables and the normative graphs. Duration tables provide expected recovery periods based on the type of work performed by the individual. The normative graphs reflect the actual observed experience of many individuals across the spectrum of physical conditions, in a variety of industries, and with varying levels of case management.

Failure to Recover

If an individual fails to recover within the maximum duration expectancy period, the reader may wish to reference the following questions to assist in better understanding the specifics of an individual's medical case.

Regarding diagnosis:

- Does individual present with symptoms (persistent cough, coughing up blood (hemoptysis), shortness of breath (dyspnea), chest pain, weight loss, hoarseness, and localized bone pain) of lung cancer?
- Were diagnostic tests performed?
- Were conditions (bronchitis, tuberculosis, pneumonia, fungal infections of the lung, lung abscess, benign neoplasms of the lung, and metastatic cancer that has spread to the lung from another organ) with similar symptoms ruled out?
- Was the diagnosis of lung cancer confirmed?
- What type does individual have, small cell lung carcinoma (SCLC) or non-small cell lung carcinoma (NSCLC)?

Regarding treatment:

- If surgical treatment was utilized, was the tumor completely removed?
- Has the tumor metastasized into other organ systems?
- If not already being used, would chemotherapy and/or radiation treatments be beneficial?
- Is treatment goal considered curative or palliative at this point?
- How effective are current treatments in achieving their goals?
- What more can be done?
- Are medications being utilized, as appropriate?
- Are pain relief efforts effective?
- What more can be done to make individual comfortable?

Regarding prognosis:

- Has the cancer metastasized?
- Has individual contracted pneumonia, resulting in airway obstruction?
- Does individual exhibit confusion, disturbances of gait and balance, headache, and personality changes?
- Is individual experiencing bone pain, fractures, spinal cord injury, anemia, headache, dizziness, syncope, or vision disturbances?
- Has individual experienced any other complications?
- Does individual have an underlying condition that may impact recovery such as emphysema or decreased lung function as a result of surgery or radiation therapy?
- Was individual's condition classified as limited stage or extensive stage disease?
- Would additional surgery or addition of combination chemotherapy be beneficial at this stage in the disease?
- Would chemotherapy add to the duration of survival?
- Does individual (or individual's family) need assistance in caring for individual? Would individual/family benefit from social services evaluation?
- Was individual/family introduced to the services hospice provides?

References

DeVore, R.F., and D.H. Johnson. "Chemotherapy for Small Cell Lung Cancer." Lung Cancer. Pass, H.I., et al., eds. Philadelphia: Lippincott Williams & Wilkins, 2000. 923-939.

LeMone, P., and K.M. Burke. Medical-Surgical Nursing. Upper Saddle River, NJ: Prentice Hall Health, 2000.

Schiller, J.H. "Chemotherapy for Advanced Non-small Cell Lung Cancer." Lung Cancer. Pass, H.I., et al., eds. Philadelphia: Lippincott Williams & Wilkins, 2000. 889-902.

Schottenfeld, D. "Etiology and Epidemiology of Lung Cancer." Lung Cancer. Pass, H.I., et al., eds. Philadelphia: Lippincott Williams & Wilkins, 2000. 367-388.

References (Continued)

Li, J.H. "A Study on Treatment of Lung Cancer by Combined Therapy of Traditional Chinese Medicine and Chemotherapy." Chung-Kuo Chuing Hsi i Chieh Ho Tsa Chih 16 3 (1996): 136-138.

Montfort, H. "A New Homeopathic Approach to Neoplastic Diseases: Freom Cell Destruction to Carcinogen-induced Apoptosis." British Homeopathic Journal 89 2 (2000): 78-83.

Stephenson, N.L., S.P. Weinrich, and A.S. Tavakoli. "The Effects of Foot Reflexology on Anxiety and Pain in Patients with Breast and Lung Cancer." Oncology Nursing Forum 27 1 (2000): 67-72.

Xin, Y., F. Xue, and F. Zhao. "Effectiveness of Electrochemical Therapy in the Treatment of Lung Cancers of Middle and Late Stage." Chinese Medical Journal 110 5 (1997): 379-383.

Cancer, Mouth (Other Than Tongue)
Other names / synonyms: Cancer of the Mouth, Oral Cancer
145.9

Definition

Mouth cancer is the development of cancerous tumors on the lips, gums (gingiva), inside the cheek (buccal), roof of the mouth (hard palate), floor of the mouth, or in the throat (oropharynx) but does not include the tongue. Mouth cancers most commonly occur on the lips or the floor of the mouth. While there are a number of different cancers that can be found in the oral cavity, the most common is squamous cell carcinoma.

Risk factors for mouth cancer almost always include smoking tobacco in any form, using smokeless tobacco or snuff, and consuming alcohol. Other causes may be poor oral hygiene with bacterial irritation, persistent physical trauma in the mouth such as from jagged teeth or improperly fitting dentures, consuming spicy food or drink, malnutrition, syphilis, or chronic degenerative disease (cirrhosis) of the liver. Infection with the human immunodeficiency virus (HIV) and development of acquired immune deficiency syndrome (AIDS) have implications for the occurrence of mouth cancer because malignancies associated with HIV infection often appear in the mouth.

Mouth cancer is generally found in older individuals with approximately 95% of cases occurring in individuals over 40. The average age at the time of diagnosis is about 60 years. Cancer of the lip is related to exposure to the sun, wind, and the elements and is often found among farmers, ranchers, field workers, telephone linemen, and others working or recreating outdoors. Mouth cancer occurs more frequently in men than women with a ratio of approximately 2 to 1. Mouth cancer (other than tongue cancer) accounts for over 6,000 deaths every year in the US, about 1.2% of all cancer-related deaths. The relative survival rate for blacks with mouth cancer is lower than for whites.

Diagnosis

History: Mouth cancer is often painless in its early stage. Individuals may complain of irritation in the mouth or throat and usually report pain only when the cancer develops into a crater-like (ulcerated) lesion. Individuals may also report a lump in the neck that represents spread (metastasis) of the cancer from the mouth into the lymph nodes.

Physical exam: Sometimes a noncancerous but nonhealing raw area is persistent for many months before an actual cancer forms. Early stage mouth cancer may appear as small, apparently harmless areas of abnormal hardness (induration) or ulcerations. As the disease progresses, there is destruction (erosion) of the inner lining of the mouth, redness or inflammation (erythema) of mucus membranes in the mouth, an induration in normally soft mouth tissues, mouth sores that do not heal (chronicity), hardening or enlargement of the lymph nodes (lymphadenopathy), or white patches on the mouth mucosa (leukoplakia).

Tests: Individual cells may be scraped from the mouth lesion and examined microscopically to determine if they are cancerous (exfoliate cytology). It may be necessary to perform this test more than once because it is not always conclusive. If exfoliate cytology indicates that the cells are cancerous or if the lesion looks suspiciously like cancer, a small piece of tissue should be taken from the lesion (incisional biopsy) and examined under the microscope to determine if it is malignant.

The lymph nodes may be biopsied if it is still unclear whether the primary mouth lesion is cancerous. In this case, the entire lymph node should be removed (excisional biopsy) and tested. A fine-needle aspiration biopsy is an accurate technique for identifying mouth lesions that have spread to the lymph nodes. The fine-needle biopsy may also be used to sample tumors in salivary glands. After a mouth tumor is identified as cancer, computer-aided x-ray analysis (computerized axial tomography or CAT scan) or low-energy radio waves (MRI) can be used to determine the extent of tumor growth.

Treatment

The primary forms of treatment useful in managing mouth cancers are surgery and/or radiation therapy. Treatment depends on the stage and site of the malignancy. In general, surgery is the treatment of choice for tumors of the lower lip, tumors not sensitive to radiation, recurrent tumors in areas previously irradiated, in areas where side effects of radiation may be more severe than the defects produced by surgery, and for tumors involving bone, lymph nodes, and salivary glands. Surgical treatment frequently involves removal (local excision or resection) of the tumor along with associated lymph nodes (lymphectomy). Portions of the lower jaw may be removed surgically (mandibulectomy) when the cancer occurs on the floor of the mouth or the lower jaw. This surgery is often carried out in conjunction with removal of part of the neck and throat (radical neck dissection).

Surgical treatment has the disadvantage of sacrificing cosmetically and functionally important structures such as the lip(s), lower jaw (mandible), and in some special cases, the eye. Artificial body parts (prostheses) are often used to reconstruct the face and mouth during surgery. The amount of tissue that can be removed surgically may be restricted because the inner mouth (intraoral) location of most tumors reduces the probability of removing all cancerous tissue.

Radiation therapy is often used by itself for treatment of small and superficial tumors that have not produced an abundance of dying tissue. Alternatively, large tumors on the floor of the mouth or the cheek (buccal mucosa) may be amenable to radiation therapy. Radiation is preferable in many cases if surgical removal of the cancer will result in severe morbidity. However, radiotherapy in the mouth area can also be debilitating as it may result in decreased salivary function and taste sensation, making it difficult for the individual to maintain weight and general condition.

Combination treatment using radiation therapy and surgery may be used if the cancerous lesion is large, deeply invasive, and if bone is involved. Combination treatment is often advantageous if the tumor has entered the lymph nodes since a greater number of cancerous lymphatic structures can be treated.

Chemotherapy by itself has not been successful in treating mouth cancers. However, when used in combination with surgery or irradiation as an accessory treatment, it can moderate the intensity of the disease (palliative treatment).

Some individuals treated for mouth cancer may fail to return to work. They experience feelings of shame, worthlessness, and dejection because of the physical deformity that may result from surgery and may become socially isolated. A support system that includes the family, psychologist or psychiatrist, speech therapist, occupational therapist, physical therapist, and perhaps a vocational rehabilitation counselor may be beneficial until recovery is complete.

Prognosis

The predicted outcome of mouth cancer varies depending on the stage and site of the lesion and the adequacy of initial treatment. Early detection and prompt treatment are very important to improve chances of survival. The individual's general health, tobacco and alcohol use, and coping abilities are important secondary factors. Recurrence of mouth cancer is common.

In general, the overall survival rate for individuals with mouth cancer is poor and less than half survive the disease. Five-year survival rates for individuals who undergo surgery (local excision or resection) to remove localized tumors detected in early stages (prior to metastasis) range from 40-90% depending on the site of the tumor. Five-year survival rates following surgery for localized tumors on the roof of the mouth (hard palate) range from 40-90% while those on the soft palate, the inner cheek (buccal mucosa), and the floor of the mouth range from 40-70%. Survival rates following surgery on gingiva tumors range from 50-60%. Overall, 5-year survival rates drop to between 5-50% for individuals with mouth tumors that have metastasized or are in an advanced stage of growth.

Differential Diagnosis

Conditions that present with symptoms similar to mouth cancer include a multitude of ill-defined, variable appearing, harmless (benign) lesions that are found in the oral cavity. These may include various herpes viruses that produce cold sores in the mouth. Growth of harmless connective tissue (fibroma), fat cells (lipoma), or nerve cells (neurofibroma), or blood vessel swelling (hemangioma) can produce lesions similar to mouth cancer. Chronic irritation of oral tissue by physical, heat (thermal), or chemical factors may cause lesions (leukoplakia) that appear cancerous. Leukoplakia may also occur from other systemic factors such as poor nutrition or syphilis.

Specialists

- Dentist
- General Surgeon
- Occupational Therapist
- Oncologist
- Oral Surgeon
- Otolaryngologist
- Physical Therapist
- Psychiatrist
- Psychologist
- Radiation Oncologist
- Speech Pathologist

Rehabilitation

If surgery is required for the removal of a tumor, rehabilitation following excision is often prescribed as the individual may experience voice and swallowing dysfunction. Speech, swallowing, control of saliva, and chewing (mastication) can be adversely affected by both surgical and radiation treatment. Rehabilitation for mouth cancer requires a team approach to include a clinical social worker and vocational rehabilitation counselor.

Occupational and physical therapists treat individuals with muscle dysfunction by retraining altered facial muscles affected by the disease and/or treatment. Therapists instruct various facial positions and expressions that help re-educate the specific facial muscles. In some cases, the therapist may utilize a form of electrical stimulation that focuses on muscle re-education in conjunction with exercises. Electrical stimulation involves the use of a unit with two pads called electrodes placed in the region of the affected muscle. Exercises are conducted with the aid of electrical current to contract each muscle.

Speech pathologists are important in the rehabilitation process. They are trained to adapt the individual's speech mechanism to a new prosthesis, if needed. The speech pathologist will also help the individual regain speech function from altered vocal abilities.

Dental professionals may also be involved with individuals with mouth cancer. These healthcare professionals help instruct individuals on plaque control and the avoidance of severe dental disease. Interaction with dental professionals should be ongoing until the individual fully adapts to the condition.

The rehabilitation program may need modifications based on the various degrees of mouth cancer. Modifications are also made when surgery is required. The extent of surgery affects the nature and the progression of the rehabilitation.

Work Restrictions / Accommodations

Most individuals require more sedentary work for a period of time due to weakness and fatigue following surgery, radiation therapy, or chemotherapy. Frequent breaks may be needed, and heavy or prolonged physical exertion may have to be avoided until recovery is complete. Individuals who have undergone disfiguring surgery may have difficulty returning to the normal workplace. However, in the absence of other medical or emotional complications, individuals treated for mouth cancer should be able to return to their previous duties after a period of recovery. Time off may be necessary for psychiatric or psychological counseling or follow-up medical appointments.

Comorbid Conditions

Infection with HIV and subsequent development of AIDS usually leaves an individual susceptible to development of mouth cancer. Diabetes and high blood pressure (hypertension) are associated with erosive oral lichen planus (OLP) that may be precancerous in nature. Cervical cancer is another possible comorbid condition.

Complications

Complications of mouth cancer may include infection in the bloodstream (sepsis), bleeding, general systemic infections (septicemia or pneumonia), dental disease, loss of appetite (anorexia), weight loss (cachexia), facial paralysis, loss of chewing (masticatory) ability, abnormal enlargement of jaw and facial features due to tumor growth, and low hemoglobin content in the blood (anemia). Severe bleeding (hemorrhage) may also occur as the tumor destroys blood vessels that lie in close proximity.

Factors Influencing Duration

Factors that may influence the length of disability include the location of the cancer in or on the mouth and the degree of metastases into other areas, the individual's age, use of tobacco and alcohol, socioeconomic status, stage of the disease upon detection, access to adequate health care, type and extent of treatment for the disease, and mental health of the individual during treatment and recovery. The individual's willingness to adapt to a different lifestyle by abstaining from tobacco and alcohol (if a consideration), and ability to reintegrate themselves into society and the workplace following treatment will have a major impact on the length of disability. Some cancers of the mouth require follow-up surgery to restore function and plastic or restorative surgery to assist with disfigurement.

Length of Disability

Duration depends on the site and extent of surgery. Heavy labor is restricted post-treatment and for a period of time until recovery is complete. Recurrence of mouth cancer is common. For surgical treatment, duration reflects recovery from procedure only. Disability may be permanent.

Surgical treatment.

Duration in Days

Job Classification	Minimum	Optimum	Maximum
Sedentary work	21	42	Indefinite
Light work	21	42	Indefinite
Medium work	28	42	Indefinite
Heavy work	42	56	Indefinite
Very Heavy work	42	56	Indefinite

Failure to Recover

If an individual fails to recover within the maximum duration expectancy period, the reader may wish to reference the following questions to assist in better understanding the specifics of an individual's medical case.

Regarding diagnosis:

- Does individual have diabetes or hypertension also associated with erosive OLP that may be precancerous in nature?
- Has cancer metastasized into the lymph system?
- Were other conditions such as fibroma, lipoma, neurofibroma, hemangioma, and various herpes viruses that produce cold sores in the mouth ruled out?
- Was the diagnosis of mouth cancer confirmed?

Regarding treatment:

- What is the stage and site of the malignancy?
- Is the treatment choice surgery and/or radiation therapy?
- What was the rationale for individual's surgery?
- Were prostheses required? Incorporated as part of the surgery? Will additional surgeries be required for prostheses?
- Was surgeon able to remove entire tumor? Most of it?
- Was individual treated with radiation therapy alone?
- Has individual experienced debilitating effects from radiation such as weight loss due to decreased salivary function and taste sensation?
- Did individual receive both surgery and radiation therapy?
- If cancer has metastasized, would addition of radiation now be warranted?
- Would chemotherapy in combination with surgery or irradiation help ease painful or uncomfortable symptoms?

Regarding prognosis:

- How do secondary factors such as individual's general health, coping abilities, and tobacco and alcohol use impact individual's case?
- Does individual have an underlying condition that may impact recovery such as HIV, AIDS, or other immune system disorder?
- Has individual developed complications such as oral infections or bleeding, general infections (septicemia or pneumonia), dental disease, loss of appetite, weight loss, facial paralysis, loss of chewing ability, anemia or abnormal enlargement of jaw and facial features due to tumor growth?
- Is individual realistic about prognosis?
- Would individual benefit from psychological or vocational counseling?

References

Beumer, J., III, I. Zlotolow, and T.A. Curtis. "Rehabilitation." Oral Cancer. Silverman, S., Jr., ed. Atlanta: The American Cancer Society, 1990. 127-148.

Fu, K., and S. Silverman, Jr. "Spread of Tumor." Oral Cancer. Silverman, S. Jr., ed. Atlanta: The American Cancer Society, 1990. 61-64.

Fu, K., and S. Silverman, Jr. "Prognosis." Oral Cancer. Silverman, S., Jr., ed. Atlanta: The American Cancer Society, 1990. 91-93.

Galante, M., et al. "Treatment." Oral Cancer. Silverman, S., Jr., ed. Atlanta: The American Cancer Society, 1990. 65-80.

Omura, S., et al. "In Vivo Antitumor Effects of Electrochemotherapy in a Tongue Cancer Model." Journal of Oral and Maxillofacial Surgery 57 8 (1999): 965-972.

Sallay, K., G. Kovesi, and F. Dori. "Circulating Immune Complex Studies on Patients with Oral Lichen Planus." Oral Surgery, Oral Medicine, Oral Pathology 68 5 (1989): 567-570.

Silverman, S., Jr. "Epidemiology." Oral Cancer. Silverman, S., Jr., ed. Atlanta: The American Cancer Society, 1990. 1-6.

Silverman, S., Jr., and E.J. Shillitoe. "Etiology and Predisposing Factors." Oral Cancer. Silverman, S., Jr., ed. Atlanta: The American Cancer Society, 1990. 7-39.

References (Continued)

Kisner, C., and L. Colby. Therapeutic Exercise Foundations and Techniques. Philadelphia: F.A. Davis Company, 1990.

Langdon, J.D. "Natural History, Response to Treatment and Prognosis." Malignant Tumours of the Oral Cavity. Henk, J.M., and J.D. Langdon, eds. London: Edward Arnold Ltd, 1985. 53-70.

Luckmann, J., and K.C. Sorensen. Medical-Surgical Nursing. Philadelphia: W.B. Saunders Company, 1987.

Silverman, S., Jr., and M. Schubert. "Leukemia and Lymphoma." Oral Cancer. Silverman, S., Jr., ed. Atlanta: The American Cancer Society, 1990. 95-109.

Silverman, S., Jr., and W.P. Dillon. "Diagnosis." Oral Cancer. Silverman, S., Jr., ed. Atlanta: The American Cancer Society, 1990. 41-60.

Spitz, M.R., et al. "Association Between Malignancies of the Upper Aerodigestive Tract and Uterine Cervix." Head and Neck 14 5 (1992): 347-351.

Cancer, Oropharynx

Other names / synonyms: Cancer of the Oropharynx, Oropharyngeal Cancer, Throat Cancer

146, 146.0, 146.1, 146.2, 146.3, 146.4, 146.5, 146.6, 146.7, 146.8, 146.9, 230.0, 235.1

Definition

Oropharyngeal cancer is the development of cancerous tumors in the back part of the mouth or upper region of the throat. Cancers in this region tend to develop open sores (ulcerative) and may spread (metastasize) locally or throughout the body.

Risk factors for oropharyngeal cancer include tobacco use in any form, alcohol consumption, exposure to occupational health hazards (including man-made mineral vitreous or wool fibers, mustard gas, vinyl chloride polymers, isopropyl alcohol, hexavalent chromium, tannin extract, and azo dyes), viral infections such as human papilloma virus, genetic predisposition, and exposure to aryl hydrocarbon hydroxylase.

Oropharyngeal cancer is generally found in older individuals with approximately 95% of cases occurring in individuals over 40. The average age at the time of diagnosis is about 61. Oropharyngeal cancer occurs more frequently in men than women at a ratio of approximately 2 to 1. Cancer of the oropharynx accounts for approximately 27% of all mouth cancers and approximately 2,500 individuals die of this condition each year in the US. Survival rates for blacks with cancer of the oropharynx are lower than for whites. Worldwide, the highest rates of oropharyngeal cancer are found in China and the Far East (11.8 deaths per 100,000 population) and in France (9.5 deaths per 100,000).

Diagnosis

History: Cancer of the oropharynx is often painless in its early stage. Individuals may complain of irritation in the throat and usually only report pain when the cancer develops into a crater-like (ulcerated) lesion. Individuals may also report a lump in the neck that represents spread (metastasis) of the cancer from the oropharynx. Individuals may also report a change in their voice.

Physical exam: Early stage oropharyngeal cancer may appear as small, apparently harmless areas of hardness or ulceration. Areas of tissue hardness (also referred to as areas of induration) or areas of ulceration usually represent tissue that is being infiltrated by a tumor. As the disease progresses, destruction of the inner lining in the back of the mouth or throat (erosion), redness or inflammation (erythema) of mucus membranes in the oropharynx, induration in normally soft throat tissues, oropharyngeal sores that do not heal (chronicity), hardening or enlargement of the lymph nodes (lymphadenopathy), or white patches on the oropharyngeal mucosa (leukoplakia) are commonly observed. Eroded areas may appear ulcerated with irregular borders or raised edges. The individual may have enlarged, nontender lymph nodes in the neck. There may be evidence of metastasis of the cancer into other areas of the mouth or tongue.

Tests: Individual cells may be scraped from the lesion and observed microscopically to determine if they are cancerous (exfoliate cytology). It may be necessary however, to perform this test more than once, as it is not always conclusive. If exfoliate cytology indicates that the cells are cancerous or if the lesion looks suspiciously like cancer, a small piece of tissue should be taken from the lesion (incisional biopsy) and examined microscopically to determine malignancy. The lymph nodes may be biopsied if it is still unclear whether the primary oropharyngeal lesion is cancerous. In this case, the entire lymph node can be removed (excisional biopsy) and tested. Alternatively, a fine needle aspiration biopsy is an acceptable and accurate technique for identifying oropharyngeal lesions that have spread to the lymph nodes. After an oropharyngeal tumor is identified as cancer, CT or MRI can determine the extent of tumor growth.

Treatment

The primary forms of treatment useful in managing oropharyngeal cancer are surgery and/or radiation therapy. The treatment depends on the stage and site of the malignancy. In general, surgery is the treatment of choice for tumors not sensitive to radiation, recurrent tumors in the oropharynx previously irradiated, and in situations where the side effects of radiation are more severe than the defects produced by surgery.

Surgical treatment frequently involves removal (local excision or resection) of the tumor along with the associated lymph nodes (lymphectomy) that may contain cancer. If the tumor has spread to other areas of the mouth or jaw, these areas may also be removed. This surgery is often carried out in conjunction with removal of part of the neck and throat (radical neck dissection). Surgical treatment may have the disadvantage of sacrificing function of the vocal cords if the larynx is removed. If the cancer has spread to other areas of the mouth, cosmetically and functionally important structures such as the lip(s), lower jaw (mandible), and in some special cases, the eye may be removed. If this is the case, artificial body parts (prostheses) are often used to reconstruct the face and mouth during surgery.

Radiation therapy is often used by itself for treatment of small and superficial oropharyngeal tumors that have not produced an abundance of dying tissue. Radiation is preferable in many cases when surgical removal of the cancer will result in severe morbidity. However, radiotherapy in the mouth area can also be debilitating as it may result in decreased salivary function and taste sensation making it difficult for the individual to maintain weight and general condition.

Combination treatment using radiation therapy and surgery may be used if the cancerous lesion has metastasized, is large, deeply invasive, and if bone is involved. Combination treatment is often advantageous if the tumor has entered the lymph nodes since a greater number of cancerous lymphatic structures can be treated.

Chemotherapy by itself has not been successful in treating cancer of the oropharynx. However, when used in combination with surgery or irradiation as an accessory treatment, it can moderate the intensity of the disease (palliative treatment).

A support system consisting of a clinical social worker and a vocational rehabilitation counselor is usually necessary throughout the course of treatment until recovery is complete.

Prognosis

The predicted outcome of oropharyngeal cancer varies depending on the stage and size of the lesion and the adequacy of initial treatment. Early detection and prompt treatment are very important to improve the chances of survival. The individual's general health, coping abilities, and tobacco and alcohol use are important secondary factors. Recurrence of oropharyngeal cancer is common.

In general, the overall survival rate for individuals with oropharyngeal cancer is poor and less than half survive the disease. The 5-year survival rate for individuals who undergo surgery (local excision or resection) to remove localized tumors detected in early stages (prior to metastasis) is fifty-three percent. The 5-year survival rate drops to 30% for individuals with metastasized oropharyngeal tumors or that are in an advanced stage of growth.

Differential Diagnosis

Conditions that present with symptoms similar to cancer of the oropharynx include a multitude of ill-defined, variable appearing, harmless (benign) lesions found in the oral cavity. These may include various herpes viruses that produce cold sores in the mouth and throat. Growth of harmless connective tissue (fibroma), fat cells (lipoma), or nerve cell (neurofibroma) or blood vessel swelling (hemangioma) can produce lesions similar to oropharyngeal cancer. Chronic irritation of oral tissue by physical, heat (thermal), or chemical factors may cause lesions (leukoplakia) that appear cancerous. Leukoplakia may also occur from other systemic factors such as poor nutrition or syphilis.

Specialists

- General Surgeon
- Oncologist
- Otolaryngologist
- Plastic Surgeon
- Radiation Oncologist

Rehabilitation

If surgery is required for the removal of a tumor, rehabilitation following excision is often prescribed as the individual may experience voice and swallowing dysfunction. Speech, swallowing, control of saliva, and chewing (mastication) can be adversely affected by both surgical and radiation treatment. Radiation treatment may produce the need for healthcare individuals to help manage abnormal tissue(s). Rehabilitation for oropharynx cancer requires a team approach to include a clinical social worker and a vocational rehabilitation counselor.

Occupational and physical therapists treat individuals with muscle dysfunction by retraining altered facial muscles affected by the disease and/or treatment. Therapists instruct various facial positions and expressions that help re-educate the specific facial muscles. In some cases, the therapist may utilize a form of electrical stimulation that focuses on muscle re-education in conjunction with exercises. Electrical stimulation involves the use of a unit with two pads called electrodes placed in the region of the affected muscle. Exercises are conducted with the aid of electrical current to contract each muscle.

Speech pathologists are important in the rehabilitation process. They are trained to adapt the individual's speech mechanism to a new prosthesis, if needed. The speech pathologist will also help the individual regain speech function from altered vocal abilities.

Dental professionals may also be involved with individuals with oropharynx cancer. These healthcare professionals help instruct individuals on plaque control and the avoidance of severe dental disease. Interaction with dental professionals should be ongoing until the individual fully adapts to the condition.

The rehabilitation program may need modifications based on the various degrees of oropharynx cancer. Modifications are also made when surgery is required. The extent of surgery affects the nature and the progression of the rehabilitation.

Work Restrictions / Accommodations

Most individuals require more sedentary work for a period of time due to weakness and fatigue following surgery, radiation therapy, or chemotherapy. Frequent breaks may be needed, and heavy or prolonged physical exertion may have to be avoided until recovery is complete. Accommodations may have to be made for individuals with restricted vocal capabilities following treatment and who must use their voice in the workplace. Accommodations may also be necessary for individuals with swallowing difficulties following surgical treatment. In the absence of other medical complications and with these accommodations in effect, individuals treated for oropharyngeal cancer should be able to return to their previous duties after a period of recovery.

Comorbid Conditions

Infection with the human immunodeficiency virus (HIV) and subsequent development of acquired immune deficiency syndrome (AIDS) usually leaves an individual susceptible to development of cancers in the mouth and throat. Following removal of a cancerous lesion in the oropharynx, secondary lesions may occur to a higher extent in individuals infected with human papillomavirus (HPV) and women with cervical cancer. Diabetes and high blood pressure (hypertension) are associated with erosive oral lichen planus (OLP) that may be precancerous in nature.

Complications

Complications of oropharyngeal cancer may include local infections (sepsis) and bleeding, general infections (septicemia or pneumonia), loss of appetite (anorexia), weight loss (cachexia), low hemoglobin content in the blood (anemia), and abnormal enlargement of neck, jaw, and facial features due to tumor growth. Severe bleeding (hemorrhage) may also occur as a result of the tumor destroying blood vessels that lie in close proximity. The tumor can metastasize into the lymph system and Hodgkin disease, non-Hodgkin lymphoma, Burkitt's lymphoma, and multiple myeloma may develop.

Factors Influencing Duration

Factors that may influence the length of disability include the location of the cancer in or on the mouth, degree of metastases into other areas, individual's age, use of tobacco and alcohol, socioeconomic status, stage of the disease upon detection, access to adequate health care, type and extent of treatment for the disease, and mental health of the individual during treatment and recovery. The individual's willingness to adapt to a different lifestyle by abstaining from tobacco and alcohol and the ability to reintegrate into society and the workplace following treatment will have a major impact on the length of disability.

Length of Disability

Duration for individuals with surgery depends on site and extent of surgery. The duration of disability may depend on the requirements of the job. Heavy labor is restricted post-treatment and for a period of time until recovery is complete. Recurrence of oropharyngeal cancer is common. Disability may be permanent. For individuals with surgical treatment, duration reflects recovery from procedure only.

Medical treatment with radiation therapy.

Duration in Days

Job Classification	Minimum	Optimum	Maximum
Sedentary work	7	9	14
Light work	7	9	14
Medium work	7	9	14
Heavy work	7	14	21
Very Heavy work	7	14	21

Surgical treatment.

Duration in Days

Job Classification	Minimum	Optimum	Maximum
Sedentary work	21	42	Indefinite
Light work	21	42	Indefinite
Medium work	28	42	Indefinite
Heavy work	42	56	Indefinite
Very Heavy work	42	56	Indefinite

Failure to Recover

If an individual fails to recover within the maximum duration expectancy period, the reader may wish to reference the following questions to assist in better understanding the specifics of an individual's medical case.

Regarding diagnosis:

- Was diagnosis of oropharyngeal cancer confirmed through exfoliate cytology, incisional biopsy, and/or lymph node biopsy?
- After an oropharyngeal tumor is identified as cancer, was CT or MRI performed to determine the extent of tumor growth?
- Has the tumor metastasized into the lymph system?
- Does individual have HIV/AIDS?
- Does individual have cervical cancer or infected with human papillomavirus (HPV)?

Regarding treatment:

- Was surgery the treatment of choice? If so, were prostheses used to reconstruct the face and mouth during surgery? Is additional reconstruction anticipated?
- Would individual benefit from the addition of radiation therapy to current treatment plan?
- If radiation therapy was the treatment, what is being done to counteract the side effects of decreasing salivary function and taste sensation making if difficult for individual to maintain weight and general condition?
- Is a support system in place consisting of a clinical social worker and a vocational rehabilitation counselor? Has individual taken advantage of these services?

Regarding prognosis:

- At what stage was the cancer detected?
- Was treatment started promptly?
- Has the cancer recurred?
- How are individual's general health, coping abilities, and tobacco and alcohol use?
- What has individual done to modify risk factors?
- Does individual have another underlying condition such as diabetes or hypertension that may impact recovery?
- Have complications developed such as local infections and bleeding, general infections (septicemia or pneumonia), anorexia, weight loss, anemia, and abnormal enlargement of neck, jaw, and facial features due to tumor growth?
- Has individual experienced any other complications as a result of the oropharyngeal cancer?
- Would individual benefit from additional psychological or vocational counseling?

References

Berger, T., and S. Silverman, Jr. "Oral and Cutaneous Manifestations of Gastrointestinal Disease." Gastrointestinal Disease. Pathophysiology, Diagnosis, Management. Sleisenger, M.H., and J.S. Fordtran, eds. Philadelphia: W.B. Saunders Company, 1993. 268-285.

LeMone, P., and K.M. Burke. Medical-Surgical Nursing. Upper Saddle River, NJ: Prentice Hall Health, 2000.

Cancer, Ovary

Other names / synonyms: Cancer of the Ovary, Epithelial Carcinoma of the Ovary, Malignant Neoplasm of the Ovary, Ovarian Cancer, Ovarian Epithelial Cancer

183, 183.0, 198.6, 236.2

Definition

Ovarian cancer is a life-threatening (malignant) tumor that develops in one or both ovaries. There are normally two ovaries, one on each side of the womb (uterus).

Risk factors for the development of ovarian cancer include family history, age, frequency of egg release from the ovary (ovulation), and ethnic and dietary factors. Although positive family history of ovarian, breast, or uterine cancer in first-degree relatives (mother, sister, or daughter) is the most significant risk factor, it is found in only 5-10% of cases. Feminine powders or deodorant sprays may be associated with increased risk.

Women whose number of ovulations is decreased by pregnancies, irregular periods, birth control pills, or breast feeding may be less likely to develop ovarian cancer. Tubal ligation and hysterectomy have also been associated with a reduced risk of ovarian cancer, but the evidence is less conclusive.

Incidence of ovarian cancer increases with age from approximately 20 per 100,000 for women age 30 to 50, to 40 per 100,000 for women age 50 to 75. Although ovarian cancer occurs most commonly after menopause (average age is 63), it may occur at any age.

Ovarian cancer is the fifth leading cause of new cancer cases, and accounts for 4% of all cancers in women. According to the American Cancer Society, approximately 25,000 new cases of ovarian cancer are diagnosed each year with about 14,500 deaths.

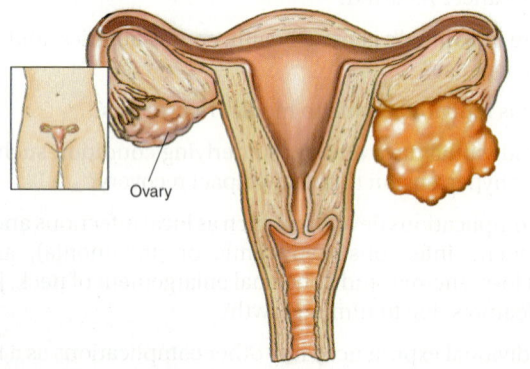

Diagnosis

History: History is nonspecific in that symptoms are vague and resemble those of menopausal ailments and intestinal illnesses. Individuals may report indigestion, gas, nausea, vomiting, loss of appetite, a feeling of fullness after small meals, pelvic or abdominal pain, swelling or fullness, increased frequency or urgency of urination, unexplained change in bowel habits, unexplained weight gain or loss, pain during intercourse, ongoing fatigue, lower back pain, shortness of breath, and, in rare cases, postmenopausal vaginal bleeding. These symptoms do not usually become apparent until the later stages of the disease when the cancer mass is large enough to interfere with pelvic organs such as the bladder or rectum, or has spread to the abdominal cavity.

Physical exam: There is not yet a physical exam or screening test to detect ovarian cancer in its early stages. Unfortunately, because ovarian cancer often has no symptoms in its earliest stages, over 70% of women are in an advanced stage of the disease when diagnosed.

Annual gynecologic exams (pelvic exams) can reveal the presence of the disease, usually in its later stages. During the pelvic exam, which also includes a Pap smear, the physician examines the vagina, rectum, and lower abdomen for indications of ovarian cancer such as ovarian and abdominal enlargement and fluid in the abdominal cavity (ascites).

Tests: At the present time, there is no definitive screening test for detection of ovarian cancer in its early stages comparable to mammography for early detection of breast cancer. Surgery performed to confirm the presence of cancer suspected from physical exam (laparotomy) is the only definitive way to diagnose ovarian cancer. During laparotomy, the tumor is removed for laboratory evaluation and fluid from the abdominal cavity is assessed for presence of cancer cells.

Noninvasive tests such as ultrasound performed with a small instrument in the vagina (transvaginal ultrasound), CT and MRI, and the CA-125 blood test may help distinguish between benign and cancerous tumors. X-ray tests (barium enema or intravenous pyelogram) are used if involvement of the colon or urinary system is suspected. The CA-125 blood test measures a protein secreted by ovarian cancer cells that is elevated in over 80% of individuals with ovarian cancer. However, the test is not perfect. Normal levels of CA-125 are somewhat ambiguous, as the protein is also secreted by other cancerous and precancerous conditions. Furthermore, approximately 50% of women with early ovarian cancer do not show elevated CA-125 levels.

Treatment

Ovarian cancer treatment usually involves a combination of surgery to remove (excise) the tumor, chemotherapy that uses drugs to kill the cancer cells, and radiation (high energy x-rays) to kill cancer cells.

The initial treatment for ovarian cancer is surgery. Complete surgical intervention includes surgical staging and debulking. Surgical staging is the examination of tissues and organs in the pelvic cavity to accurately assess the disease. Debulking is removal of as much of the cancerous tissue as possible. The ovaries, fallopian tubes, uterus, the fold of fatty tissue covering and padding the organs in the abdomen (omentum), and affected lymph nodes or surrounding tissues are usually removed.

After surgery, most individuals are treated with chemotherapy. Chemotherapy becomes the mainstay of the treatment process if the cancer recurs. New combinations of chemotherapy drugs have demonstrated improved survival rates in recent years. It is usually administered intravenously on an outpatient basis within a few weeks after surgery. The treatment is repeated every 3 weeks for a total of 6 times. Each 3-week interval is referred to as a "cycle" of chemotherapy. Chemotherapy can also be given by injecting it directly into the fluid inside the abdominal and pelvic cavity (intraperitoneally).

Radiation therapy is not administered as often as chemotherapy because of its toxicity; however, it is used when afflicted areas are painful and not responding to chemotherapy, or when the disease has spread to the brain, bones, or lungs. Radiation is usually given by aiming radiation beams at the abdomen. Radioactive phosphorus can also be injected intraperitoneally.

Treatment with surgery and chemotherapy is tailored to the 4 stages of the disease. In Stage I (cancer confined to the ovary), surgery is performed for staging and debulking. In Stage II (cancer spread outside of the ovary but confined to the pelvis), both surgery and chemotherapy are used. In Stage III (cancer spread to the abdomen), surgery and chemotherapy are used and sometimes they are followed by a second operation (second-look laparotomy). In Stage IV (cancer spread to liver or beyond the abdomen), chemotherapy alone is used. Removal of the tumor in this advanced stage has questionable value.

Ovarian cancer patients are urged to seek the expertise of a qualified gynecologic oncologist rather than a gynecologist, oncologist, or surgeon for their final diagnosis and treatment. In a study involving 291 women with ovarian cancer, researchers from George Washington University found that surgical staging was properly performed by gynecologic oncologists in 97% of cases, 52% when performed by gynecologists and obstetricians, and 35% when performed by general surgeons.

Prognosis

The most significant predictor of outcome is the stage of the cancer at the time of diagnosis. Ovarian cancers are staged (Stages I-IV) according to whether they are localized (remain in the ovary) or have spread beyond the ovary. The 5-year survival rates for the four stages are Stage I, 90%; Stage II, 70%; Stage III, 25%; and Stage IV, 10 percent.

Outcome is also contingent on the cell type and grade of the cancer at the time of diagnosis and other factors. About 80% of ovarian cancers fall into 1 of 4 major cell subtypes based on their origin and shape as viewed under a microscope. These subtypes are serous, endometrioid, mucinous, and clear cell. Clear cell carcinomas are the most difficult to treat even when the cancer is confined to the ovary. Ovarian tumors are graded on a scale of 1, 2, or 3, according to how well or poorly organized they are. Grade 3 indicates very abnormal, poorly defined tissue.

Researchers are in disagreement over other factors such as age (younger women have a better prognosis) and presence of BRCA1 (women who carry the BRCA1 genetic mutation may have a better prognosis).

Overall, past research indicates that 33% of all individuals with ovarian cancer will be alive 5 years following diagnosis. This low survival rate is due to the fact that the disease is rarely detected early. The best survival rates are in women where the disease has not spread beyond the ovary (90% of women diagnosed with Stage I disease will survive for 5 years). Outcome also depends on what is discovered during a second exploratory surgery (laparotomy) performed after the individual is treated.

Differential Diagnosis

A benign ovarian cyst or tumor, multiple cysts of the ovary, and ovarian infection are other possibilities. In some women, benign cysts are normal parts of the menstrual cycle. Because these cysts are typically reabsorbed, no treatment is required. One type of benign tumor (dermoid tumor) can easily be removed by surgery. Another type (borderline ovarian tumor) resembles both benign and malignant tumors but, unlike malignant tumors, borderline tumors rarely spread (metastasize) or cause death. Secondary ovarian cancer occurs when cancers originating in the breast, colon, stomach, or uterus spread to the ovaries.

Specialists

- General Surgeon
- Gynecologist
- Oncologist
- Radiation Oncologist

Rehabilitation

Women diagnosed with ovarian cancer require physical and occupational therapy prior to discharge from the hospital. Additional home care therapy to address weakness and decreased endurance due to chemotherapy and/or radiation may be necessary. Following surgery to remove cancerous ovaries (and usually the fallopian tubes and uterus), intermittent positive pressure breathing exercises may be necessary to prevent pulmonary complications. Also, certain exercises may be performed to reduce postoperative pain and speed recovery, including progressive relaxation and deep breathing techniques. These may be performed several times per day until pain from inhalation/exhalation is less noticeable. Physical therapists instruct women to hold a pillow to the abdomen when walking, coughing, or laughing. The pillow acts as a splint in place of the weakened abdominal muscles, and decreases the amount of perceived pain during these activities. Women learn to perform pelvic tilts, in which the low back is flattened against the bed and forward bending of the neck, both of which are performed while the woman lies on her back. These exercises strengthen the abdominal muscles. Ankle flexes, knee bends, and crossed-leg muscle contractions (all while lying on the back) will help to increase circulation and make walking easier.

Some women may have temporary balance deficits due to fatigue from cancer treatments. Physical therapists instruct these individuals in walking with a cane or walker to help improve safety during ambulation. Occupational therapists also address energy conservation techniques, such as keeping frequently needed objects such as the telephone closer at hand to reduce the amount of walking the woman needs to do.

Women with the diagnosis of cancer may find it beneficial to undergo psychological counseling either on an individual basis or in a support group setting.

Work Restrictions / Accommodations

Work restrictions and accommodations include restricting the number of hours worked per day and number of days per week. Work responsibilities may need to be largely sedentary. Because of fatigue and weakness from the surgery and extended chemotherapy (and radiation therapy if it is a part of the treatment program), a woman may need a place at the work site where she can periodically rest. Women undergoing chemotherapy and/or radiation may need additional leave from work.

Comorbid Conditions

Comorbid conditions influencing the length of disability include obesity or excessive thinness, medical history of other significant illnesses or conditions, and allergy to treatment medications.

Complications

Complications of ovarian cancer are caused by spread of the cancer to other organs with progressive loss of function in those organs. Examples of complications include bowel obstruction, urinary obstruction, fluid collection in the chest (pleural effusions), and ascites. Bowel and urinary obstructions can result in loss of the use of the bowel and urinary tract. Pleural effusions cause shortness of breath and difficulty breathing and sometimes a mild, nonproductive cough. The symptoms of abdominal ascites increase with the increasing amount of fluid and include abdominal enlargement (distention), loss of appetite, shortness of breath, abdominal pain, low blood pressure, weakness, and fatigue.

Factors Influencing Duration

Factors influencing the length of disability include age, type, and stage of disease at initial presentation, concurrent infection and overall general health, and presence or absence of complications from the cancer itself or treatment. Younger women with an earlier stage of the disease have the best chance for long-term recovery. Older women and women with poorer general health or more advanced disease may have a longer disability due to medical or surgical complications. Most women undergo a second exploratory surgery to determine if the disease has been eliminated, and this requires an additional disability period. Chemotherapy and radiation therapy may extend the recovery period. Disability may be permanent.

Length of Disability

Duration depends on stage, grade, cell type, adjuvant chemotherapy or radiation therapy. Disability may be permanent. For all procedures, duration reflects recovery period from procedure only.

Salpingo-oophorectomy or abdominal hysterectomy.

Duration in Days

Job Classification	Minimum	Optimum	Maximum
Sedentary work	28	42	56
Light work	28	42	56
Medium work	42	56	70
Heavy work	42	70	84
Very Heavy work	42	84	98

Radical hysterectomy.

Duration in Days

Job Classification	Minimum	Optimum	Maximum
Sedentary work	42	49	56
Light work	56	63	70
Medium work	70	77	84
Heavy work	70	84	98
Very Heavy work	70	84	98

Failure to Recover

If an individual fails to recover within the maximum duration expectancy period, the reader may wish to reference the following questions to assist in better understanding the specifics of an individual's medical case.

Regarding diagnosis:

- Does individual complain of indigestion, gas, nausea, vomiting, loss of appetite, or a feeling of fullness after small meals?
- Is there pelvic or abdominal pain, increased frequency or urgency of urination, unexplained change in bowel habits, unexplained weight gain or loss, pain during intercourse, ongoing fatigue, lower back pain, or shortness of breath?
- Did the physician note ovarian and abdominal enlargement and fluid in the abdominal cavity (ascites) during a pelvic exam?
- Does the physician believe the ovaries to be the primary site for the cancer or could the tumor be a secondary breast, lung, or other type of cancer that has spread to the ovaries?

Regarding treatment:

- Did surgery successfully remove all evidence of cancer cells?
- Has individual undergone chemotherapy and/or radiation therapy?
- Did individual tolerate and complete those therapies? If not, would individual benefit from experimental treatments?
- Did individual receive treatment from a gynecologic oncologist?

Regarding prognosis:

- What stage of ovarian cancer does individual have?
- Were all treatment options explored?
- Would individual benefit from second opinion consultations?
- Would individual benefit from counseling for psychological and emotional effects from the disease?
- What, if any, complications have developed? How can these be treated? What is expected outcome of the complication with treatment? How do these complications affect the activities of daily living for individual?

References

Questions and Answers About Complementary and Alternative Medicine in Cancer Treatment. CancerNet. 13 Dec 2000. 01 Jan 2001 <http://cis.nci.nih.gov/fact/9_14.htm>.

Brannon, Linda, and Jess Feist. "Living with Chronic Illness." Health Psychology. King, Kenneth, ed. Belmont: Wadsworth Publishing Company, 1992. 275-315.

Kisner, Carolyn, and Lynn Allen Colby. Therapeutic Exercise: Foundations and Techniques, 2nd ed. Philadelphia: F.A. Davis Company, 1990.

Murphy, Gerald, Lois Morris, and Dianne Lange. Informed Decisions: The Complete Book of Cancer Diagnosis, Treatment, and Recovery. New York: Viking, 1997.

Piver, Steven, and Gene Wilder. Gilda's Disease. New York: Broadway Books, 1996.

Tirgan, M. Hossein, MD. Malignant Ascites. Tirgan Oncology Associates. 01 Jan 2000. 01 Jan 2001 <http://www.tirgan.com/ascites.htm>.

Cancer, Pancreas

Other names / synonyms: Cancer of the Pancreas, Carcinoma of the Pancreas, Pancreatic Cancer
157, 157.0, 157.1, 157.2, 157.3, 157.4, 157.8, 157.9

Definition

Cancer of the pancreas refers to uncontrolled growth of new cells within the pancreas, an elongated gland attached to the first portion of the small intestine (duodenum). The pancreas is located behind the stomach and extends across and toward the back of the abdominal cavity. Because it lies behind many of the other abdominal organs, it is often difficult to access. The pancreas is subdivided into three anatomic regions (the head, body, and tail) and serves two major functions (digestion and the regulation of blood sugars). It produces secretions (enzymes) that empty into the small intestine and aid in the digestion of food as it passes through the intestines. It also releases hormones (insulin, glucagon) directly into the circulatory system that help regulate the concentration of sugar in the bloodstream.

The cause of pancreatic cancer is unknown but there may be a relationship between inflammation of the pancreas (chronic pancreatitis), diabetes and pancreatic cancer. Other risk factors may include age (most frequently diagnosed between 45 to 85 years), gender (it occurs in men twice as often as women), cigarette smoking, high fat or high caloric intake, coffee drinking, and exposure to industrial chemical carcinogens such as gasoline, beta naphthylamine, benzidine, dry-cleaning solvents, and substances used in the chemical coke and metal industries. Alcohol consumption has not been conclusively associated with pancreatic cancer.

The estimated mortality from pancreatic cancer in the US is 27,000 individuals a year. It is the fourth most common cancer death for men and the fifth most common for women. The incidence among blacks is 14.9 per 100,000 compared to 8.7 per 100,000 among whites. High-risk countries for pancreatic cancer include the US, England, the Scandinavian countries, and Israel. France appears to be at midlevel risk while Southern Europe and Southeast Asian countries are at low risk.

Diagnosis

History: The individual usually reports a vague pain in the upper region of the abdominal cavity that sometimes spreads around or through the back. Other symptoms can include rapid and marked weight loss; a yellow discoloration (jaundice) of the skin, whites of the eyes (sclera), and mucous membranes; persistent back pain that worsens while eating or lying down; weakness and loss of energy (asthenia); signs of low blood sugar (hypoglycemia) such as fatigue, shakiness, chills, headaches, and anxious feelings; loss of appetite (anorexia); nausea and/or vomiting; constipation; light-colored stool; and dark-colored urine.

Physical exam: Examination of the abdomen may reveal abdominal extension due to an enlarged liver, upper abdominal mass, or enlarged gallbladder.

Tests: There is no single specific test for detection of pancreatic cancer and diagnosis is most often determined by multiple tests. Computer-aided x-ray analysis (computerized axial tomography or CAT scan) is usually the first step and may be complemented by other tests using low-energy radio waves (MRI) or high-frequency sound waves (endoluminal ultrasonography or ultrasound) to visualize the tumor.

The pancreatic and bile ducts may also be visualized to determine if they are narrowed or obstructed by the tumor. This is done with a fiberoptic device (endoscope) passed through the mouth in ever-narrowing tubing (cannula) into the stomach, through the duodenum, and into the small intestine (endoscopic retrograde cholangiopancreatography or ERCP). This procedure serves two purposes: (1) the pancreatic cells floating in digestive juices can be removed for microscopic inspection and examined for their ability to secrete digestive juices (pancreatic function test), and (2) an opaque dye can be injected through the cannula into the pancreatic duct or bile duct (transhepatic cholangiography) allowing x-rays to show whether or not ducts have narrowed or are blocked. The pancreatic duct may also be visualized by injecting a contrast dye directly into a vein (intravenous cholangiography) and viewed radiographically.

A pancreatic tissue biopsy (percutaneous needle biopsy) may be taken with the aid of an x-ray device to examine deep structures (fluoroscope) and microscopically look for signs of cancer cells. Low levels of the digestive enzyme trypsin in pancreatic juice may indicate cancer of the pancreas. Blood tests for pancreatic cancer include those for carcinoembryonic antigen (CEA), pancreatic oncofetal antigen (POA), and carbohydrate antigen 19-9 (CA 19-9).

Treatment

Treatment of pancreatic cancer usually requires an integrated approach involving surgery, radiation therapy, and chemotherapy. In general, surgery to cure the cancer is only possible in individuals whose tumor is localized to the head of the pancreas. This occurs in only 10% of cases. Removal of the tumor and head of the pancreas, duodenum, part of the stomach, common bile duct, and surrounding lymph nodes (cephaliopancreaticoduodenal resection or Whipple's procedure) may be done if the cancer has not spread into other organs (metastasis).

Pancreatic cancer in the tail or body of the organ usually presents as more advanced disease than cancer of the head of the pancreas. Surgery on these tumors is designed to reduce the discomfort of the disease but not to produce a cure (palliative treatment). Partial or complete removal of the pancreas (pancreatectomy) along with various surgical bypass procedures that allow continued secretion of digestive juices into the intestine (cholecystoenterostomy or pancreaticojejunostomy) could be performed. These individuals will need insulin and/or a pancreatic enzyme supplementation depending on how much of the pancreas remains following surgery.

Radiation therapy may be used in addition to surgery or as the primary treatment for tumors that cannot be surgically treated. When radiation therapy is the primary treatment, it is most often used to relieve painful symptoms and make individuals comfortable. In these cases, surgery may be necessary, however, to alleviate any liver complications causing jaundice or bowel obstructions that may have developed. Most clinical studies indicate that chemotherapy has little impact on survival or quality of life in individuals with pancreatic cancer. The compound gemcitabine (2',2'-difluorodeoxycytidine) however, improves pain control, weight gain, and survival times. This compound is now the drug of choice for treatment of advanced pancreatic cancer because it is tolerated well by most individuals.

Prognosis

The predicted outcome for individuals with pancreatic cancer is very poor with a 5-year cure rate of only 1% following diagnosis and after surgical treatment using the Whipple procedure. Individuals without surgery can only hope for a very short survival. Partial or total pancreatectomy causes digestive disorders such as poor absorption of fats (steatorrhea) and deficiency of various dietary nutrients (dietary deficiency syndrome). These conditions are usually compensated for with administration of pancreatic extracts. Weight loss is common. Pancreatectomy may also lead to diabetes that requires ongoing treatment with insulin and serious alteration of the individual's quality of life.

Chemotherapy or radiation treatment used in addition to surgery also diminishes the quality of survival. Numerous follow-up medical examinations are required for individuals surviving pancreatic cancer for any length of time.

Differential Diagnosis

Conditions that present with symptoms similar to pancreatic cancer include harmless (benign) growth of the pancreas, inflammation of the pancreas (pancreatitis), cancer of the bile duct, or cancer of another organ that has metastasized to the pancreas.

Specialists

- Endocrinologist
- Gastroenterologist
- General Surgeon
- Oncologist
- Radiation Oncologist

Rehabilitation

Long-term rehabilitation is not a consideration for most individuals with pancreatic cancer as the condition is quickly fatal. For those individuals who have had Whipple's procedure, intermittent positive pressure breathing exercises may be useful in preventing postoperative pulmonary complications. Certain exercises may also be performed to reduce postoperative pain and speed recovery including progressive relaxation and deep breathing techniques. While lying on the back, the individual performs ankle pumps (flexing the ankle back and forth) and knee bends to help increase circulation and make walking easier.

Work Restrictions / Accommodations

With few exceptions, individuals with pancreatic cancer will not return to work in any capacity. The rare individual who is cured of pancreatic cancer may require more sedentary work for a period of time because of weakness and fatigue following surgery, radiation therapy, or chemotherapy.

Comorbid Conditions

Existing conditions that may impact the ability to recover and further lengthen disability include prolonged malnutrition, digestive disorders such as Crohn's disease or colitis, and systemic diseases such as diabetes.

Complications

The pancreas is located close to a number of vital organs in the abdominal cavity including the liver, stomach, duodenum, small intestine, spleen, kidney, large intestine (colon), and lymph nodes. A pancreatic tumor often metastasizes into these organs directly or indirectly via the lymphatic or vascular systems, particularly if it continues to develop undetected and untreated. This usually leads to widespread cancer throughout the abdominal cavity and accumulation of fluid within the abdomen (ascites). If the cancer spreads via the vascular system, the most commonly affected organ is the liver followed by the lung and (less frequently) bone and brain.

Factors Influencing Duration

Factors that may influence the length of disability include the site and stage of the tumor at initial diagnosis. Disability may be permanent.

Length of Disability

Disability is permanent for most individuals and usually there is no recovery. The few individuals who are cured may require more sedentary work until recovery from surgery, chemotherapy, and radiation treatment is complete. For individuals with pancreaticoduodenectomy or Whipple procedure, duration depends on extent of resection. Durations reflect recovery from procedure only. Disability may be permanent.

Pancreatectomy (total).

Duration in Days

Job Classification	Minimum	Optimum	Maximum
Sedentary work	42	56	Indefinite
Light work	42	56	Indefinite
Medium work	56	70	Indefinite
Heavy work	70	84	Indefinite
Very Heavy work	70	84	Indefinite

Pancreaticoduodenectomy or Whipple procedure.

Job Classification	Duration in Days		
	Minimum	Optimum	Maximum
Sedentary work	42	56	Indefinite
Light work	42	56	Indefinite
Medium work	56	70	Indefinite
Heavy work	70	84	Indefinite
Very Heavy work	70	84	Indefinite

Failure to Recover

If an individual fails to recover within the maximum duration expectancy period, the reader may wish to reference the following questions to assist in better understanding the specifics of an individual's medical case.

Regarding diagnosis:

- How old is individual? Gender?
- Does individual have risk factors such as cigarette smoking, high fat or high caloric intake, and coffee drinking? Chronic pancreatitis or diabetes?
- Does individual have a history of exposure to industrial chemical carcinogens such as gasoline, beta naphthylamine, benzidine, dry-cleaning solvents, or substances used in the chemical coke and metal industries?
- Does individual report vague pain in the upper abdomen that sometimes spreads around or through the back?
- Has individual had recent, rapid and marked weight loss?
- Does individual have jaundice of the skin, sclera, and mucous membranes? Persistent back pain that worsens while eating or lying down? Does individual have weakness and loss of energy? Anorexia, nausea and/or vomiting, constipation, light-colored stool, and dark-colored urine?
- Are signs of hypoglycemia present such as fatigue, shakiness, chills, headaches, and anxious feelings?
- On exam, does individual have abdominal distension? Liver or any masses palpable?
- Was CT, MRI, ultrasound, or endoscopy done? Transhepatic cholangiography or intravenous cholangiography? Pancreatic tissue biopsy?
- Does individual have low levels of the digestive enzyme trypsin in the pancreatic juice? Was individual's blood tested for carcinoembryonic antigen (CEA), pancreatic oncofetal antigen (POA), and carbohydrate antigen 19-9 (CA 19-9)?
- Were conditions with similar symptoms ruled out?

Regarding treatment:

- Has individual had surgery, radiation therapy, and chemotherapy?
- Has the cancer metastasized? Was palliative surgery done?
- Is it necessary to treat individual with insulin and/or pancreatic enzymes?

Regarding prognosis:

- If individual returns to work, can employer accommodate any necessary restrictions?
- Does individual have any conditions that may affect ability to recover?
- Have any complications developed such ascites or metastasis?

References

Cello, J.P. "Carcinoma of the Pancreas." Gastrointestinal Disease. Pathophysiology, Diagnosis, Management. Sleiosenger, M.H., and J.S. Fordtran, eds. Philadelphia: W.B. Saunders Company, 1993. 1682-1694.

LeMone, P., and K.M. Burke. Medical-Surgical Nursing. Upper Saddle River, NJ: Prentice Hall Health, 2000.

Cancer, Pleura

Other names / synonyms: Benign Local Pleural Fibroma, Celothelioma, Localized Fibrous Tumor of the Pleura, Mesothelioma, Pleural Cancer

163, 163.0, 163.1, 163.8, 163.9, 197.2, 235.8

Definition

Pleural cancer (mesothelioma) refers to an abnormal growth in the tissue that lines the chest wall and envelops the lungs (pleura). Mesothelioma begins with numerous small lumps (nodules) covering the pleura. Eventually these nodules form a sheet-like thickening that encases and compresses the lungs. Mesothelioma may spread (metastasize) very quickly into lymph nodes, lungs, brain, adrenal glands, liver, and bone marrow. The major risk factor for this type of cancer is exposure to asbestos fibers. Onset of mesothelioma however, does not usually occur until 20 years after asbestos exposure. It is interesting to note that smoking does not increase the risk for those working with asbestos.

Other risk factors may include chronic inflammation of the pleura and a history of exposure to ionizing radiation.

Localized mesothelioma is more rare than mesothelioma and is often harmless (benign). Localized mesothelioma may arise from tumors originating in the abdominal (visceral) pleura that project into the pleural cavity surrounding the lungs. Only 30% of these tumors are malignant, but they may cause fluid to escape from blood vessels into the pleural cavity because of rupture or seepage (effusion). Localized mesothelioma has no association with asbestos. There may be, however, a relationship to several metabolic disorders that include low blood sugar (hypoglycemia) and abnormal expansion of the ends of the long bones of the body (hypertrophic osteoarthropathy).

Average age at onset for mesothelioma is about 60. Mesothelioma affects men more than women with a male to female ratio of about 3 to 1. In the US, the average age-adjusted incidence per 100,000 is 1.6 among white males and 0.4 among white females. In the US, there are approximately 2,000 new cases every year. Areas of elevated incidence of mesothelioma worldwide include England, Wales, Japan, and South Africa. Occurrences may be high in these areas due to environmental or job-related hazards such as shipbuilding, mining, and asbestos manufacturing.

Diagnosis

History: Individuals may report chest pain, shortness of breath (dyspnea), loss of appetite (anorexia), weight loss, fatigue, cough, or fever. Bone and joint pain, swelling, and arthritis may also be reported. The individual may report a past history of asbestos exposure (20 to 30 years).

Physical exam: Physical findings may include diminished breath sounds and other physical findings indicating fluid in the chest cavity. Some individuals may have broadening and thickening of the ends of the fingers (clubbing) that is associated with lung (pulmonary) disease. There may be associated metabolic abnormalities including hypoglycemia and low blood sodium (hyponatremia).

Tests: The presence of fluid in the chest cavity (pleural effusion) or a tumor mass may be seen by chest x-ray. CT and MRI are also useful in determining the extent of the disease. Tissue samples (biopsy) may be taken by means of needle aspiration or surgical excision to evaluate the tissue under a microscope.

Treatment

Localized mesothelioma tumors are treated by removal (excision) of the diseased portion of lung (pneumonectomy). Surgical treatment of mesothelioma may involve pneumonectomy along with removal of one or more ribs (pleurectomy) and/or part of the diaphragm (extrapleural pneumonectomy with resection of the diaphragm). One or more anticancer drugs (combination chemotherapy) or exposure of the tumor to ionizing radiation (external radiation therapy) may be used in combination with surgery. Radioactive particles (colloidal gold or chromic phosphate) may also be used to deliver high doses of radiation. Certain individuals with mesothelioma may be treated with radiation to relieve pain, dyspnea, and inability to eat (dysphagia).

Prognosis

Localized mesothelioma treated with surgery has a good prognosis and most individuals are cured with this treatment. In approximately 4% of cases, however, recurrence of the tumor may occur after several years.

Mesothelioma is usually a fatal disease. Average survival time from the onset of symptoms ranges from 5 months in extensive disease to 16 months when the disease is more limited. About 75% of individuals die within one year after diagnosis and those treated surgically have a 5-year survival rate of about nine percent. Certain chemotherapy treatments may cause partial remission in approximately 7% of individuals. External radiation therapy following surgery results in a slight increase in average survival time (14 to 16 months). If radiotherapy is used in combination with surgery and chemotherapy, average time of survival may increase up to 20 to 30 months.

Differential Diagnosis

Conditions that present with similar symptoms as mesothelioma include inflammation of the pleura (pleurisy), harmless (benign) seepage of fluid into the pleural space (pleural effusion), and growth of connective tissue within the pleural space (pleural fibrosis).

Specialists

- General Surgeon
- Oncologist
- Pulmonologist
- Radiation Oncologist
- Thoracic Surgeon

Work Restrictions / Accommodations

After surgery for localized mesothelioma, the individual may gradually return to normal job-related activities following a period of recovery. Mesothelioma is invariably fatal and individuals with this disease have a low probability of returning to work.

Comorbid Conditions

Conditions that may impact an individual's ability to recover and further lengthen disability include chronic lung disease (emphysema) and decreased lung function as a result of surgery or radiation therapy.

Complications

Spread (metastasis) of mesothelioma can lead to tumor growth into lymph nodes, liver, spleen, heart, and the nervous system. A localized mesothelioma tumor may grow large enough to cause dyspnea, dysphagia, and decreased flow in a major vein that returns blood to the heart (vena caval obstruction). If the localized mesothelioma metastasized from another organ, the primary tumor will have its own complications and therapeutic considerations.

Factors Influencing Duration

Factors that may influence the length of disability include stage of the disease at initial presentation, presence of concurrent infection, overall general health, type of treatment, and other complications.

Length of Disability

Disability may be permanent. Durations reflect recovery from the open pleural biopsy procedure only. Contact physician for additional information.

Pleural biopsy (open).

Duration in Days

Job Classification	Minimum	Optimum	Maximum
Sedentary work	21	28	35
Light work	21	28	35
Medium work	21	28	35
Heavy work	28	35	42
Very Heavy work	28	35	42

Failure to Recover

If an individual fails to recover within the maximum duration expectancy period, the reader may wish to reference the following questions to assist in better understanding the specifics of an individual's medical case.

Regarding diagnosis:

- Does individual have a history of exposure to asbestos fibers?
- Are other risk factors present such as chronic inflammation of the pleura and a history of exposure to ionizing radiation?
- Does individual have hypoglycemia or hypertrophic osteoarthropathy?
- How old is individual? Gender?
- Does the individual report chest pain, dyspnea, anorexia, weight loss, fatigue, cough, fever, bone and joint pain, swelling, and arthritis?
- Did physical exam reveal diminished or abnormal breath sounds?
- Does individual have clubbing of the fingers?
- Were a chest x-ray, CT, MRI, or biopsy done?
- Were conditions with similar symptoms ruled out?

Regarding treatment:

- Has individual had surgery, combination chemotherapy, or external radiation therapy?
- Was it necessary to use radioactive particles?

Regarding prognosis:

- If necessary, is individual active in rehabilitation?
- Can individual's employer accommodate any necessary restrictions?
- Does individual have any condition that may affect ability to recover?
- Have any complications developed such as metastasis, dyspnea, dysphagia, and vena cava obstruction?

References

Kittle, C.F. Mesothelioma Diagnosis and Management. Chicago: Yearbook Medical Publishers Inc, 1987.

Stephenson, N.L., S.P. Weinrich, and A.S. Tavakoli. "The Effects of Foot Reflexology on Anxiety and Pain in Patients with Breast and Lung Cancer." Oncology Nursing Forum 27 1 (2000): 67-72.

Notes

Cancer, Prostate

Other names / synonyms: Adenocarcinoma of the Prostate, Cancer of the Prostate, Malignant Neoplasm of the Prostate Gland, Prostate Cancer, Prostatic Adenocarcinoma, Prostatic Cancer

185, 198.89, 233.4, 236.5

Definition

Prostate cancer is a tumor found within a secretory gland (prostate) located within the male reproductive system. The prostate gland is about the size of a chestnut and surrounds the neck of the urinary bladder and the tube that carries urine away from the bladder (urethra). The prostate secretes fluid into the semen during ejaculation. Malignancy of the prostate is the most commonly diagnosed cancer in American males (other than skin cancer) and is the second leading cause of cancer deaths among men. The cancer is usually slow growing and commonly discovered during routine screening. Prostate cancer is often an incidental finding at autopsy after death from other causes.

Prostate cancer is rare before age 50, but increases substantially with each decade of life. Ninety-five percent of prostate cancer cases are diagnosed in men between the ages of 45 and 89, with a median age of 72. Race may also be a factor as the probability of a black male developing prostate cancer is 9.6% compared with 5.2% for a white male. Other risk factors include a family history of prostate cancer, certain occupational exposures such as cadmium and tire or rubber manufacturing, and a high-fat diet.

Approximately 179,300 new cases of prostate cancer were diagnosed in 1999 in the US, constituting 29% of all new male cancer cases. It is projected that approximately 37,000 American males will die as a result of this disease each year. Clinically diagnosed prostate cancer has the lowest incidence in Asian countries and the highest in Scandinavian countries. There is a 120-fold difference in incidence rates of prostate cancer when comparing Chinese men living in Shanghai and black men living in San Francisco. Mortality rates show similar disparity and the number of deaths from prostate cancer in Asian countries is remarkably lower than that in the US or Scandinavian countries.

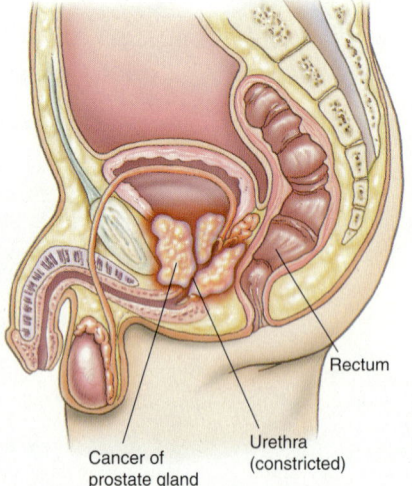

Cancer of prostate gland
Urethra (constricted)
Rectum
Laurie O'Keefe

Diagnosis

History: Early prostate cancer may not exhibit any symptoms and only be detected on screening examination. The individual may report frequent urination, a weak or interrupted urine stream, straining to urinate, difficulty starting urination or holding back urine, and pain or burning during urination. Bone pain is a common symptom of advanced prostate cancer as a result of spread (metastasis) of the tumor to bones such as the spine, pelvic bones, and ribs. Pain in the lower back, pelvis, or thighs may be reported if the tumor has metastasized into the pelvic nerves. Stool changes and painful defecation are common if the tumor has grown large enough to cause rectal obstruction. The individual may also report painful ejaculation and blood in the urine or semen.

Physical exam: Annual screening for prostate cancer is done by inserting a gloved finger into the rectum and feeling the prostate gland for signs of a tumor (digital rectal examination). Ten to twenty percent of prostatic tumors are too small to be detected by rectal examination however a hard nodule in the prostate of any man over 50 has about a 50% chance of being malignant. Biochemical screening using prostate-specific antigen (PSA) is combined with digital rectal exam for men over 50.

Tests: Detection and screening of prostate cancer may be done with various techniques that allow visualization of the tumor within the gland. These tests include high-frequency sound waves (transrectal ultrasound or TRUS), CT, and MRI. Intravenous pyelogram (IVP) is an x-ray study of the urinary tract after intravenous injection of a dye that concentrates in the urine. Cystoscopy allows the doctor to look into the urethra and bladder through a thin, lighted tube. CT may also be used in combination with radioactively labeled antibodies that bind to the prostate and allow better visualization of the tumor (radioimmunoscintigraphy).

Measurement of certain indicators of prostate cancer (tumor markers) in the bloodstream may also help in diagnosis. These include tests for the prostate specific antigen (PSA), prostatic acid phosphatase (PAP), and acid phosphatase. A definitive diagnosis can be made by taking a sample of tissue from the tumor within the prostate (needle biopsy) to determine if it is cancerous. Bone x-rays, bone scan, or chest x-ray may reveal spread of tumor to the bones or lungs. All these tests are used for staging or to determine whether the cancer has spread and where.

Treatment

Treatment for prostate cancer depends on the grade and stage of the disease, individual's age, general health, and treatment preference. No treatment (watchful waiting) is appropriate for individuals with localized tumors that have a very low progression rate and a high disease-specific survival rate. This usually includes men in their 60s or 70s and individuals with less than a 10-year life expectancy due to comorbid conditions. Men who should not take this treatment approach include those at high risk for the disease, have moderate to high-grade tumors, and younger men in their 40s and 50s with a life expectancy of more than 10 years.

Surgical removal of the prostate, seminal vesicles, and part of the vas deferens (radical prostatectomy) is a common treatment for early stage tumors found in younger individuals in excellent general health and who are expected to live at least 15 more years. For very early disease in older men, only the prostate tissue may be removed (simple prostatectomy). These surgeries are often curative for cancer that has not metastasized into other organs. Individuals with more advanced tumors are usually not candidates for this type of surgery, however, in some cases surgical removal of the tumor (transurethral resection of the prostate or TURP) may be useful to relieve urinary obstruction or other symptoms. A different surgical option for localized tumors is destruction of the tumor by insertion of a probe that alternately freezes and thaws the tissue (cryosurgery). At present, there is not enough information regarding the outcome of this treatment to compare it with established techniques.

Radiation therapy is an alternative primary treatment to surgery. Radiation can be delivered from an external x-ray machine (external beam radiotherapy) and/or by surgical implantation of radioactive pellets into and around the prostatic tumor (brachytherapy). Brachytherapy has advantages over external beam therapy in that it allows delivery of a high, localized dose to the tumor while minimizing the dose to surrounding normal tissue. The use of brachytherapy depends on accessibility of the tumor, the ability to accurately place the radioactive sources, and types of sources available. In some individuals, brachytherapy may be used in combination with other treatments such as external beam radiation and/or androgen deprivation therapy.

Individuals with advanced prostate cancer are most often treated by blocking the effects of the male sex hormone (testosterone) or by decreasing the amount of testosterone in the body (both treatments are termed androgen deprivation therapy). Androgen deprivation therapy is used for individuals with cancer that has spread beyond the prostate, as it relieves symptoms and slows the progress of the disease. Surgery to remove the testicles (orchiectomy) is one approach to removing testosterone.

Drugs that block the binding site (receptor) for testosterone decrease the growth-promoting effects that the male sex hormone has on prostatic tumors. The amount of testosterone in an individual's body can be decreased using drug therapy with either female sex hormone (estrogen) or luteinizing hormone releasing hormone (LHRH) agonists. Both of these inhibit testosterone secretion. Drug therapy using estrogen is usually not employed because of side effects such as breast enlargement and increased risk of heart failure.

Multiple chemotherapeutic agents have been tested for their effectiveness in treating prostate cancer that has metastasized into other organs. Chemotherapy response rates in clinical trials are greater than 50% for several treatments. More extensive trials are now underway and may demonstrate that these therapies actually increase survival rates.

Prognosis

The predicted outcome for individuals with prostate cancer depends on the stage, size, and grade of the tumor when diagnosed. In general, early stage and small tumors have the best prognosis. If the cancer is localized to the prostate, it can often be eradicated completely. Elimination of advanced tumors is more difficult. These cancers often recur locally and metastasize into the lymph system or adjacent organs.

Individuals treated by watchful waiting have a 10-year survival rate ranging from forty-five to ninety-three percent. Approximately 19% of individuals proceeding with watchful waiting will need a more invasive type of treatment later on.

Radical prostatectomy is the most effective treatment for localized prostate cancer. Clinical studies indicate that more individuals will be alive and free of cancer 15 years after diagnosis if this treatment is selected over other ones. Fifteen-year survival rates range from 71-93% following radical prostatectomy.

Initial survival results using cryosurgery compare favorably with other treatments, however approximately 41% of these individuals eventually have recurrence of the disease. Side effects from this technique include shedding of tissue from the urethra.

Radiation therapy treatment shows 5-, 10-, and 15-year survival rates of 85%, 65%, and 45%, respectively. However, recurrence of cancer is higher with external radiation therapy than after radical prostatectomy. Brachytherapy has an overall survival rate between 83% and 92% during the 3 to 7 years following treatment. Approximately half the individuals with metastatic prostate cancer treated with androgen deprivation therapy die of the disease within 3 years, however, the extent of the metastasis produces variable survival rates. If the cancer has spread extensively, there is a 36-month survival rate with complete androgen blockade, while individuals with minimal disease metastasis have a 42-month survival using this treatment.

Differential Diagnosis

Conditions that present with symptoms similar to prostate cancer include benign prostatic hypertrophy, chronic prostatitis, and prostatic abscess.

Specialists

- Oncologist
- Radiation Oncologist
- Urologist

Rehabilitation

Appropriate therapy for individuals with prostate cancer includes nutritional support, effective pain management, relevant palliative care, and social support. Following surgery for prostate cancer, intermittent positive pressure breathing exercises may help prevent postoperative pulmonary complications. Certain exercises may reduce postoperative pain and speed recovery including progressive relaxation and deep breathing techniques.

Physical therapy improves ventilation through breathing exercises that are localized to the area of involvement and then followed by a gradual strengthening program. Leg exercises may be started the first day following surgery to minimize the chance of blood clot (thromboemboli) formation. When resistance is tolerated, isotonic exercise begins using an elastic band or light weights. For example, as the individual lifts the weight throughout the range of motion, the muscle shortens and lengthens.

Physical therapy or consultation with a continence specialist may be needed following surgery to promote bladder control. Pelvic muscle exercises (Kegel exercises) performed on a routine basis for as long as a year following surgery can often eliminate or improve incontinence.

The frequency and duration of the rehabilitation program will vary among individuals with prostate cancer. Intensity and progression of exercise depend on the prognosis, if surgery was performed, if individual is receiving any current cancer treatment, the extent of the disease, and individual's overall health.

Work Restrictions / Accommodations

Return to work may be facilitated by temporary restrictions and/or accommodations depending on the extent of the cancer and type of treatment. For example, incontinent individuals may need to take frequent bathroom breaks. Individuals with advanced, symptomatic disease may be work-restricted due to pain, fatigue, and general debilitation. Some individuals may require more sedentary work for a period of time due to weakness and fatigue following surgery, radiation therapy, or chemotherapy.

Comorbid Conditions

Existing conditions that may affect individual's ability to recover and further lengthen disability include chronic systemic conditions such as heart disease, kidney disease, or diabetes.

Complications

Complications of early prostate cancer are often related to diagnostic procedures and/or treatment. Needle biopsy is a minimally invasive procedure but carries a slight risk of bleeding and infection. Radical prostatectomy often results in decreased sexual ability (impotence) and/or inability to control urination (urinary incontinence). Both of these conditions may be either temporary or permanent. Radiation therapy may also result in a gradual loss of sexual function as well as acute or chronic diarrhea, fatigue, skin changes, and hair loss in the irradiated area. Hormone therapy can cause loss of sexual desire and function and hot flashes. Depending on the drugs used, chemotherapy may cause susceptibility to infections, immune system compromise, fatigue, vomiting, bleeding tendencies, or hair loss.

Complications of advanced prostate cancer may occur as a direct result of the disease. Enlargement of the primary tumor may obstruct the urinary tract that can lead to urinary tract infections. The tumor may cause neurological dysfunction and/or pain if it grows large enough to press on nerves lying in or near the prostate. If the tumor is large enough to block the lymphatic system (lymphatic obstruction), the lower extremities may swell (lymphedema). If the tumor has metastasized, other complications may occur depending on the organs involved. Spread of the tumor into the spinal column can lead to compression fractures of the vertebrae or spinal cord compression with paralysis. Prostatic tumors may enter the lymphatic system resulting in a neoplasm of lymphoid tissue (lymphoma).

Factors Influencing Duration

Factors that may influence the length of disability from prostate cancer include the type and stage of the disease at initial presentation, concurrent infection, overall general health, type of treatment used, and response to treatment. Treatment of advanced prostate cancer can produce complications including adverse effects of hormonal therapy such as impotence, breast enlargement, nausea, hot flashes, adrenal insufficiency, liver toxicity, and blood clotting (thromboembolism). Orchiectomy may result in permanent impotence and sterility. Adverse effects of chemotherapy include nausea and vomiting, hair loss, and depressed immunity due to bone marrow toxicity.

Length of Disability

Duration depends on stage, grade, size, type of treatment, and adjuvant radiation or chemotherapy. Disability may be permanent. For procedures, durations reflect recovery period for procedure only.

Medical treatment (including radiation therapy).

Duration in Days

Job Classification	Minimum	Optimum	Maximum
Sedentary work	1	7	14
Light work	1	7	14
Medium work	1	7	14
Heavy work	1	7	14
Very Heavy work	1	7	14

Hormonal drug treatment.

Duration in Days

Job Classification	Minimum	Optimum	Maximum
Sedentary work	3	10	21
Light work	3	10	21
Medium work	3	10	21
Heavy work	7	14	42
Very Heavy work	7	14	42

Prostatectomy (transurethral).

Duration in Days

Job Classification	Minimum	Optimum	Maximum
Sedentary work	7	9	14
Light work	7	9	14
Medium work	14	16	21
Heavy work	21	24	28
Very Heavy work	21	24	28

Prostatectomy (retropubic, suprapubic, and perineal approach).

Duration in Days

Job Classification	Minimum	Optimum	Maximum
Sedentary work	14	21	28
Light work	14	21	28
Medium work	21	35	42
Heavy work	28	42	56
Very Heavy work	28	42	56

Prostatectomy, radical.

Job Classification	Duration in Days		
	Minimum	Optimum	Maximum
Sedentary work	21	42	84
Light work	21	42	84
Medium work	42	63	105
Heavy work	42	84	126
Very Heavy work	42	84	126

Chemotherapy.

Job Classification	Duration in Days		
	Minimum	Optimum	Maximum
Sedentary work	28	42	Indefinite
Light work	28	42	Indefinite
Medium work	28	42	Indefinite
Heavy work	42	56	Indefinite
Very Heavy work	42	56	Indefinite

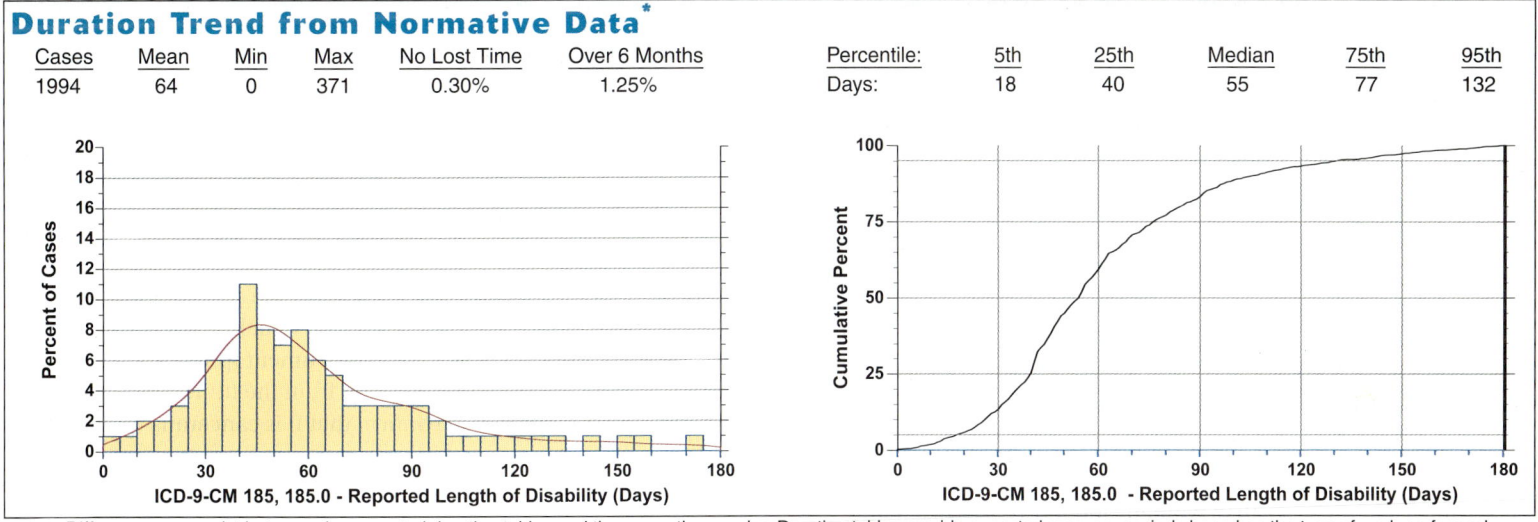

Duration Trend from Normative Data*

Cases	Mean	Min	Max	No Lost Time	Over 6 Months
1994	64	0	371	0.30%	1.25%

Percentile:	5th	25th	Median	75th	95th
Days:	18	40	55	77	132

ICD-9-CM 185, 185.0 - Reported Length of Disability (Days)

* Differences may exist between the expected duration tables and the normative graphs. Duration tables provide expected recovery periods based on the type of work performed by the individual. The normative graphs reflect the actual observed experience of many individuals across the spectrum of physical conditions, in a variety of industries, and with varying levels of case management.

Failure to Recover

If an individual fails to recover within the maximum duration expectancy period, the reader may wish to reference the following questions to assist in better understanding the specifics of an individual's medical case.

Regarding diagnosis:

- How old is individual? Ethnic background?
- Does individual have a family history of prostate cancer? History of exposure to cadmium and tire or rubber manufacturing?
- Does individual have high-fat diet?
- Does individual report frequent urination, a weak or interrupted urine stream, straining to urinate, difficulty starting urination or holding back urine, and pain or burning during urination? Stool changes? Painful defecation? Painful ejaculation? Blood in the urine or semen?
- Does individual report bone pain in the spine, pelvic bones, or ribs?
- Has individual had a digital rectal examination?
- Was ultrasound, CT, MRI, IVP, or cystoscopy done? Radioimmunoscintigraphy? Biopsy? Were bone x-rays, bone scan, or chest x-ray for staging done?
- Were conditions with similar symptoms ruled out?

Regarding treatment:

- Does individual's treatment consist of watchful waiting?
- Has individual had a simple or radical prostatectomy done?
- Did individual have external radiation therapy? Radioactive pellets?
- Was androgen deprivation therapy done? Chemotherapy?

Regarding prognosis:

- Can individual's employer accommodate any necessary restrictions?
- Does individual have any conditions that may affect ability to recover?
- Have any complications developed such as impotence, urinary incontinence, acute or chronic diarrhea, fatigue, skin changes, hot flashes, susceptibility to infections, immune system compromise, fatigue, vomiting, bleeding tendencies, or hair loss? Does individual have lymphedema or metastasis?

References

Prostate Cancer. National Cancer Institute. 2000. 31 Oct 2000 <http://cancernet.nci.nih.gov/wyntk_pubs/prostate.htm>.

Kirk, D. "A Rational Approach to Prostate Cancer." Practitioner 244 1614 (2000): 754-756,758.

Kisner, C., and L. Colby. Therapeutic Exercise Foundations and Techniques. Philadelphia: F.A. Davis, 1990.

LeMone, P., and K.M. Burke. Medical-Surgical Nursing. Upper Saddle River, NJ: Prentice Hall Health, 2000.

Cancer, Rectum

Other names / synonyms: Cancer of the Rectum, Colorectal Cancer, Malignant Neoplasm of Rectosigmoid Junction, Malignant Neoplasm of the Rectum, Rectal Cancer

154, 154.0, 154.1, 154.2, 154.3, 154.8, 197.5, 230.4

Definition

Rectal cancer is a tumor of the cells (mucosa) lining the rectum. Cancer of the rectum and large intestine (colon) are grouped together and referred to as colorectal cancer.

Rectal cancer may be both hereditary and related to diet. Experimental studies and dietary histories indicate that diets high in fat and red meat may be related to the incidence of colorectal cancer. Alcohol consumption has been implicated as well. Other diseases of the colon such as familial polyposis, inflammatory bowel disease, chronic ulcerative colitis, villous adenoma, Crohn's disease, and prior large bowel cancers increase the risk of colorectal cancer.

Cancer that occurs only in the rectum accounts for about 30% of the 133,500 colorectal cancer cases that occur annually. Men are affected by rectal cancer slightly more than women, and most cases occur after age 50. Colorectal cancer is the second most common visceral cancer in the US, and approximately 55,000 individuals die from this disease each year. The incidence of the disease among Americans is approximately 5%, and the long-term survival rate is only about 35%. The American Cancer Society recommends fecal occult blood testing on an annual basis, and flexible sigmoidoscopy every 5 years after age 50 for average individuals.

Diagnosis

History: Individuals may report a change in bowel habits, blood in the stool, loss of appetite (anorexia), nausea and/or vomiting, and a steady, gnawing rectal and abdominal pain. There may be symptoms of bleeding and obstruction. Weakness and fatigue may be reported due to chronic blood loss, and constipation may alternate with increased frequency and loose stools. Occasionally, the individual will report no symptoms at all until the tumor grows so large that it causes a bowel obstruction or rupture of the intestine.

Physical exam: Examination with the hands (palpation) of the abdomen or examination with one gloved finger in the rectum and the other hand pressing on the abdomen (bimanual rectal exam) may reveal a mass in the rectum. Seventy-five percent of cases of rectal cancer have a mass that is detected with a rectal exam. Abdominal palpation may also reveal an enlarged liver, which suggests that the cancer has spread from the rectum to other organs (metastasized). In advanced cases, rectal cancer that has spread can cause enlarged lymph glands near the collarbone (supraclavicular adenopathy) or other areas.

Tests: A chemical test done on a stool sample (fecal occult blood test, or FOBT) can identify blood that may be hidden within the fecal material (occult blood). Twenty to forty percent of individuals who test positive for occult blood will be found to have colorectal cancer. A complete blood count (CBC) can be done to rule out anemia. Additional blood tests, including measurement of a molecule that is associated with cancer cells (carcinoembryonic antigen, or CEA test), a liver enzymes test, and a kidney function test may indicate the extent of disease spreading (metastasis) from the rectum to other organs.

Diagnostic tests for rectal cancer may include an x-ray procedure to visualize the rectum (barium enema) or visualization of the rectum (proctoscopy) using a special optical instrument (proctoscope). A small sample of tissue (biopsy) may be taken from the tumor and this can be examined microscopically to confirm that it is cancerous (pathological confirmation).

A chest x-ray may be used to look for evidence of metastasis into the lungs. The extent of cancer growth (staging) can be determined using harmless, low-energy radio waves (MRI), or computer analysis of x-ray data (CT). Ultrasound from within the rectum (endoluminal ultrasound) can provide important information about the depth that the rectal cancer has invaded into or through the bowel wall.

Treatment

Surgical removal of the tumor and adjacent large intestine (colectomy), and lymph nodes (lymphectomy) that lie in close proximity is the treatment of choice for most rectal cancer. If the tumor is located high in the rectum, anterior resection is the preferred surgical approach because the circular muscles that comprise the anus (anal sphincter) can be left intact. If the tumor is located further down, and the anal sphincter must be removed during surgery, the individual may require an artificial opening (stoma) of the colon through the abdominal wall (colostomy) for the purpose of bowel elimination.

Small tumors in the rectum can be destroyed using the heat generated by a laser beam (laser photocoagulation). This procedure is performed endoscopically and is useful for individuals who are unable to tolerate major surgery. Other surgical options for small, localized rectal tumors include removal by local excision or destruction of the tissue using electric sparks (fulguration). Treatment using fulguration may be used to reduce the size of some large tumors for individuals who are poor surgical risks. This procedure may need to be repeated several times to be effective.

Radiation therapy may be used in addition to surgery for treating rectal tumors because it is not effective by itself as treatment for this type of cancer. Rectal cancer has a high rate of recurrence following surgical removal and pre- or postoperative radiation therapy may be useful in reducing the recurrence rate. Radiation treatment is used preoperatively to shrink large rectal tumors so they may be removed surgically.

Chemotherapy may be used pre- or postoperatively as a supplemental (adjunctive) therapy for rectal cancer. When combined with radiation therapy, chemotherapy improves local control and survival for individuals with rectal tumors.

Prognosis

Overall 5-year survival rates from rectal cancer have improved in recent years, probably due to better therapy and early detection. Local recurrence of rectal cancer occurs in up to 54% of cases, and the overall 5-year survival rate is approximately fifty percent. Fulguration or laser photocoagulation do not appear to improve the survival rate significantly because these procedures are associated with high rates of recurrence and other complicating factors. However, 5-year recurrence-free survival rates may be as high as 90% following excision of rectal tumors that are localized and show no metastasis.

Recent studies indicate that preoperative radiation often allows tumors to be removed surgically and individuals who receive this treatment in conjunction with surgery may have significantly better survival rates. It has been reported that individuals treated with radiation during surgery may have a 5-year survival rate of seventy-nine percent.

Following surgical treatment, a colostomy may produce psychological problems, and as a result, individuals may become anxious and depressed. Individuals with a colostomy usually should avoid odor- and gas-forming foods, and they must learn proper colostomy irrigation technique. Good skin and stoma care are important in preventing infection of the colostomy.

Differential Diagnosis

Conditions that may present with similar symptoms include harmless (benign) rectal polyps, cancer of the prostate gland, an enlarged prostate, fecal impactions (constipation), and bleeding from internal hemorrhoids.

Specialists

- Colorectal Surgeon
- Gastroenterologist
- General Surgeon
- Oncologist
- Radiation Oncologist

Rehabilitation

A regular exercise routine may be useful in reducing the risk of recurrence of rectal cancer. Exercise such as walking, jogging, or swimming (30 to 45 minutes per session) is usually beneficial.

Work Restrictions / Accommodations

Individuals whose rectal cancer is detected and treated in its early stages usually have no special work restrictions or accommodations following recovery and return to work. However, duties at work may be restricted and should not include heavy lifting or hard physical labor following surgery, chemotherapy, and/or radiation therapy until recovery is complete. Fatigue may create the need for additional breaks during this period of recovery.

Comorbid Conditions

Existing conditions that may impact an individual's ability to recover and further lengthen disability include any other diseases that affect the major organ systems of the body such as the liver, lungs, spleen, and pancreas. Other gastrointestinal abnormalities such as Crohn's disease, ulcerative colitis, or irritable bowel disease may also lengthen disability.

Complications

Complications of rectal cancer are related to the stage the disease has reached by the time of diagnosis. Chronic blood loss at the site of the tumor may result in low concentrations of iron in the blood (iron deficiency anemia). In some cases, the tumor can grow so large that it causes bowel obstruction or rupture of the intestine. Rectal tumors may enter the lymphatic tissue in the wall of the gut resulting in a neoplasm of lymphoid tissue (lymphoma). This can damage the intestinal wall and nearby lymph nodes. Further metastasis through the lymph system may allow the cancer to spread to neighboring tissues such as the liver and spleen.

Factors Influencing Duration

Factors that might influence the length of disability include the stage at which the cancer was detected, the amount of rectal tissue that was removed during surgery, the presence of a colostomy, the effectiveness of radiation or chemotherapy treatments, and the individual's response to these treatments. Advanced age may also be a factor, as older individuals often require longer recovery times.

Length of Disability

The duration of disability may depend upon the requirements of the job. Heavy physical labor will be restricted for 5 to 6 weeks following rectal surgery, and possibly longer if postoperative chemotherapy or radiation therapy treatments are necessary. Disability may be permanent. For abdominoperineal resection of rectum, durations reflect recovery from procedure only.

Surgical treatment (abdominoperineal resection of rectum).

Duration in Days

Job Classification	Minimum	Optimum	Maximum
Sedentary work	28	35	42
Light work	28	35	42
Medium work	42	49	56
Heavy work	56	70	84
Very Heavy work	56	70	84

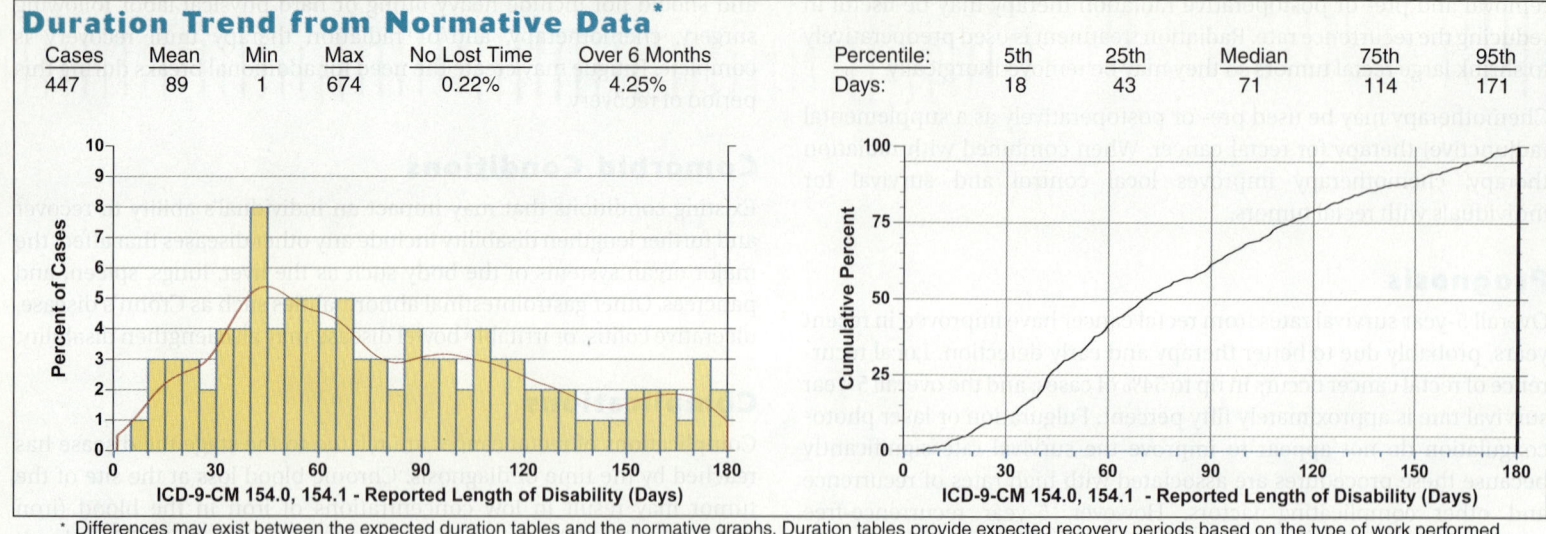

Failure to Recover

If an individual fails to recover within the maximum duration expectancy period, the reader may wish to reference the following questions to assist in better understanding the specifics of an individual's medical case.

Regarding diagnosis:

- Does individual have any other colon diseases?
- Does individual have a family history of colorectal cancer?
- What type of diet is individual accustomed to?
- Have bowel habits changed? Does blood appear in the stool?
- Does individual have a loss of appetite? Nausea or vomiting?
- Is gnawing rectal or abdominal pain present?
- Does individual have any weakness or fatigue?
- Was a fecal occult blood test done? CBC? CEA?
- Were liver enzymes and kidney function tests done?
- Has individual had a barium enema? Biopsy? MRI? CT? Ultrasound? Chest x-ray?
- Were conditions with similar symptoms ruled out?

Regarding treatment:

- Did individual have a small tumor?
- Was the tumor treated endoscopically with laser photocoagulation?
- Was excision or fulguration used?
- Was a colectomy with lymphectomy done?
- Did individual have a colostomy? Any associated psychological problems?
- Was radiation used? Chemotherapy?
- Was individual instructed in colostomy care and diet prior to discharge?

Regarding prognosis:

- Can individual's employer accommodate individual's restrictions?
- Does individual have any conditions that could affect ability to recover?
- What stage was the cancer when detected?
- Does individual have any metastatic disease?

References

Bressalier, R.S., and Y.S. Kim. "Malignant Neoplasms of the Large Intestine." Gastrointestinal Disease. Sleisenger, M.H., and J.S. Fordtran, eds. Philadelphia: W.B. Saunders Company, 1993. 1449-1493.

LeMone, P., and K.M. Burke. Medical-Surgical Nursing. Upper Saddle River, NJ: Prentice Hall Health, 2000.

Cancer, Skin

Other names / synonyms: Basal Cell Carcinoma, BCC, Malignant Melanoma, Melanoma, SCC, Skin Cancer, Squamous Cell Carcinoma

172, 172.0, 172.1, 172.2, 172.3, 172.4, 172.5, 172.6, 172.7, 172.8, 172.9, 173, 173.0, 173.1, 173.2, 173.3, 173.4, 173.5, 173.6, 173.7, 173.8, 173.9, 198.2, 232, 232.0, 232.1, 232.2, 232.3, 232.4, 232.5, 232.6, 232.7, 232.8, 232.9, 238.2, M8090/3, M8720/3

Definition

Skin cancer is a cancerous growth of any of the three types of skin cells: squamous cells (squamous cell carcinoma), basal cells (basal cell carcinoma), and melanocytes (melanoma or malignant melanoma). Skin cancer is linked to ultraviolet (UV) rays found in sunlight. Exposure to UV rays does not need to be direct. The UV light may be reflected off of water or snow. Even an umbrella doesn't completely shield someone from exposure to the sun's UV rays. UV rays are also present in the light in tanning beds, sun lamps, and sterilizers.

Risk factors for skin cancer include fair skin, increased exposure to the sun or other sources of UV rays, personal or family history of skin cancer, history of irradiation, increased age, and a weakened immune system.

Basal cell carcinoma is the most common type of skin cancer. Approximately 85% of tumors are found on the head and neck and 30% on the nose. The cancer originates in the lower layers of the skin. It grows slowly by encroaching on surrounding tissue. Basal cell carcinoma does not spread to other parts of the body.

Squamous cell carcinoma is the second most common type of skin cancer. This cancer affects the outermost layer of skin. Tumors are found primarily on the scalp, back of hands, lips, and nostrils. Squamous cell carcinoma can spread (metastasize) to other parts of the body, particularly the lymph nodes.

Malignant melanoma represents only 3% of all skin cancers but accounts for the greatest number of skin cancer deaths. It is a cancer of the pigmented cells (melanocytes) and often arises from a mole that has changed appearance (dysplastic nevus). It is commonly found on the back or lower extremities. It can metastasize to regional lymph nodes and internal organs. White Americans have a 1 in 90 lifetime risk of developing this type of skin cancer.

In the US, approximately 1 million individuals develop skin cancer each year. Approximately 75% of cases are basal cell, 20% squamous, and 4% malignant melanoma. The remaining 1% consists of less common types of skin cancer including Kaposi's sarcoma, a previously rare skin cancer now seen in about one-third of all individuals with AIDS. Men are at a greater risk. Dark-skinned individuals rarely develop basal and squamous cell carcinoma but can develop malignant melanoma particularly on the palms of the hands, soles of the feet, under nails, or in the mouth.

Diagnosis

History: Individuals report a skin growth or ulceration that has become enlarged and/or changed appearance. It may bleed and crust over.

Physical exam: Basal cell carcinoma presents as a small, pearly nodule on the skin that gradually increases in size. It may be ulcerated. Squamous cell carcinoma commonly appears as an ulcerated nodule, superficial erosion, or verrucous papule on the skin. Malignant melanoma presents as a flat or raised lesion with irregular borders. Exam may show varying colors including red, white black, and bluish. The lesions are typically asymmetrical with an irregular border and have a diameter of greater than 6 mm.

Tests: The skin tumor is removed (biopsy) and examined under the microscope to establish the diagnosis.

Treatment

Treatment of skin cancer requires surgical removal of the cancerous area. In some instances, a second surgery may be done that covers a wider area than the first to remove cancer tissue that may have spread to adjacent tissue.

For small basal cell and squamous cell cancers, the lesion may be scraped off (curettage) and some of the underlying tissue destroyed using an electric instrument (electrodesiccation). Cryosurgery may also be used to freeze off small lesions with well-defined borders. Larger lesions with well-defined borders and some of the surrounding tissue may be removed by excision surgery. Lesions in high-risk areas such as the nose and eyelids or lesions with poorly defined borders may be removed by Moh's micrographic surgery. With this procedure, very little healthy tissue needs to be removed. Cancerous tissue is shaved off in single thin layers. After each layer is removed, a microscopic examination is performed to check if the cancer is still present in that layer. Layers are removed until there is no more cancer present. Radiation is an option if prior surgery has failed, if the individual is not a candidate for surgery, or if the site of the lesion would make surgery difficult.

For malignant melanoma, the extent of surgery depends on the stage of the disease and usually involves a wide excision. After the lesion is examined microscopically, a second surgery may be necessary to remove a deeper border around the site. Removal of local lymph nodes may be done particularly if lymph nodes are enlarged. Chemotherapy is not generally useful in this disease. Immunotherapy is being increasingly employed as an adjunct to surgery. Radiation therapy may be used in certain individuals especially those with cancerous lesions on the nose, ears, and around the eyes or in older individuals not willing to undergo a surgical procedure. Radiation may also help symptoms of melanoma that has spread to the brain.

Individuals diagnosed with skin cancer should be monitored for new lesions or recurrences. Individuals with malignant melanoma should be examined at least every 6 months.

Prognosis

Both basal cell and squamous cell cancers have extremely high cure rates with treatment. Basal cell cancer after excision has a cure rate of 98% while squamous cell cancer has a cure rate in excess of ninety-five percent. Larger lesions and those on the scalp, forehead, ears, nose, lip, and eyelids are more likely to recur. Survival rate for malignant melanoma is based on size and depth of invasion and ranges from 98-

100% for shallow cancers to 44% for the deep cancers. If the cancer has spread to another body location, the 5-year survival is ten percent.

Differential Diagnosis

Other possibilities are benign moles (nevi) or birthmarks, skin tags, a benign fatty tumor (lipoma), benign accumulation of blood vessels under the skin (angioma), warts, keratoacanthoma, age spots (seborrheic keratoses), sunspots (actinic keratoses), xeroderma pigmentosa, basal cell nevus syndrome, molluscum contagiosum, sebaceous hyperplasia, psoriasis, and localized scleroderma.

Specialists

- Dermatologist
- General Surgeon
- Oncologist
- Plastic Surgeon
- Radiation Oncologist

Work Restrictions / Accommodations

Additional medical leave from work may be required for individuals with malignant melanoma undergoing chemotherapy, radiation therapy, or immunotherapy. All individuals with skin cancers must limit their subsequent exposure to sunlight or other sources of UV light.

Curettage and electrodesiccation, some excision, and some Moh's surgeries may be performed as outpatient surgery and require only the day of the procedure as a day of disability. Extensive Moh's surgeries may require 2 to 5 days (or more) of disability depending on the extent and location of the surgery.

Comorbid Conditions

Disability may be prolonged by conditions of immunosuppression such as post-transplantation. Prior radiation may cause the tumors in irradiated areas to be more aggressive.

Complications

Complications can result when skin cancers spread into the underlying tissues or structures such as erosion of the cartilage of the nose. Squamous and malignant melanoma may spread to lymphocytes and other body sites.

Factors Influencing Duration

Factors influencing the length of disability include the type and stage of cancer at initial presentation, size and location of the skin cancer, border definition of the lesion, depth of invasion, presence of metastases, individual's immune status and overall general health, type of treatment pursued, and any complications. Most complications are related to treatment. Simple surgical removal or Moh's surgery may lead to usual postsurgery problems such as infection. Drugs to alter the immune system (immunotherapy) may cause low blood pressure, fever, chills, diarrhea, nausea, vomiting, itchy skin, and infections. Radiation therapy may cause fatigue, mild to moderate redness of the skin, inflammation of the lining of the mouth, and possibly baldness. If the individual is receiving chemotherapy, radiotherapy, or immunotherapy, side effects of those therapies may be disabling for the entire length of treatment.

Length of Disability

For individuals with basal cell or squamous cell without metastases, duration depends on site, size of lesion, and cell type. For individuals with melanoma and excision with skin graft, duration depends on site and extent. For individuals with melanoma, duration depends on site. For all types, disability may be permanent.

Basal cell or squamous cell, no metastases.

Duration in Days

Job Classification	Minimum	Optimum	Maximum
Sedentary work	1	2	3
Light work	1	2	3
Medium work	1	2	4
Heavy work	2	3	7
Very Heavy work	2	3	7

Melanoma. Excision.

Duration in Days

Job Classification	Minimum	Optimum	Maximum
Sedentary work	1	2	7
Light work	1	2	7
Medium work	1	3	7
Heavy work	1	7	14
Very Heavy work	1	7	14

Melanoma. Excision with skin graft.

Duration in Days

Job Classification	Minimum	Optimum	Maximum
Sedentary work	7	7	14
Light work	7	7	14
Medium work	21	28	42
Heavy work	28	42	56
Very Heavy work	28	42	56

Failure to Recover

If an individual fails to recover within the maximum duration expectancy period, the reader may wish to reference the following questions to assist in better understanding the specifics of an individual's medical case.

Regarding diagnosis:

- Does individual have a history of increased ultraviolet exposure?
- Does individual have fair skin, personal or family history of skin cancer, history of irradiation, increased age, or a weakened immune system?
- Does individual have squamous cell carcinoma, basal cell carcinoma or melanoma, or malignant melanoma?

- Does individual report a skin growth or ulceration that has become enlarged and/or changed appearance? Does it bleed and crust over?
- On exam, does individual have a small, pearly nodule on the skin? Is it ulcerated?
- Does individual have an ulcerated nodule, superficial erosion, or verrucous papule? A flat or raised lesion with irregular borders? Is it red, white, black, or bluish? Asymmetrical and have a diameter of greater than 6 mm?
- Was a biopsy done?
- Were conditions with similar symptoms ruled out?

Regarding treatment:

- Was the skin cancer removed? Was it necessary to have a second surgery?
- Was it necessary for individual to have radiation therapy? Immunotherapy?
- Does individual see physician frequently to monitor the condition?
- Does individual practice self-exam for new tumors?

Regarding prognosis:

- Can individual's employer accommodate any necessary restrictions?
- Does individual have any condition that may affect ability to recover?
- Have any complications developed such as erosion of the cartilage of the nose or metastasis?

References

Ferri, Fred. Ferri's Clinical Advisor. St. Louis: Mosby, 2000.

Heller, R., M.J. Jaroszeski, and D.S. Reintgen. "Treatment of Cutaneous and Subcutaneous Tumors with Electrochemotherapy Using Intralesional Bleomycin." Cancer 83 1 (1998): 148-157.

Kisner, C., and L. Colby. Therapeutic Exercise Foundations and Techniques. Philadelphia: F.A. Davis, 1990.

Scully, Rosemary M., and Marylou R. Barnes. Physical Therapy. Philadelphia: J.B. Lippincott Company, 1989.

Cancer, Small Intestine (Including Duodenum)

Other names / synonyms: Adenoma of the Small Bowel, Adenoma, Benign, Cancer of the Duodenum, Cancer of the Small Intestine, Duodenal Cancer, Small Intestinal Cancer

152, 152.0, 152.1, 152.2, 152.8, 152.9, 197.4, 230.7

Definition

Small intestinal cancer is the development of cancerous tumors in the small bowel of the gastrointestinal tract. The small intestine is located in the upper portion of the intestinal tract and food from the stomach passes directly into it. Small bowel tumors may occur in the first part (duodenum), the middle section (jejunum), or the last segment (ileum) of the small intestine. There are four types of tumors associated with the small intestine (adenocarcinoma, carcinoid, lymphoma, and sarcoma), and they are identified by the type of tissue that is involved. Adenocarcinoma and carcinoid tumors are the most common types of small intestinal cancer.

Although the cause of small intestinal cancer is unknown, high dietary fat intake may increase the risk for developing the disease. Also, individuals with Crohn's or celiac disease may be at increased risk. Cancer of the small intestine can occur as a result of spread (metastasis) of a cancerous tumor from another organ in the body. Most individuals with small intestine tumors are over the age of 70, and there are approximately 4,600 new cases of small intestinal cancer per year in the US.

Diagnosis

History: Individual with small intestinal cancer may complain of abdominal pain, weight loss, blood in the stool, watery diarrhea, or sudden redness (flushing) of the head and neck.

Physical exam: Pressing down on the abdomen with the hands (palpation) may reveal a mass.

Tests: X-ray studies using barium as a contrast medium to outline the small intestine (upper GI series) can be used to visually identify a tumor. Additional diagnostic tests may include computerized analysis of x-ray data (CT) or a flexible viewing instrument (endoscope) that is inserted through the mouth to view the inside of the small intestine (endoscopy). Definitive diagnosis of small intestinal cancer requires taking a small piece of tissue from the tumor (biopsy) during endoscopy.

Treatment

Surgery to remove the cancer from the small bowel is the only treatment that may cure this condition. Most small intestinal cancers grow in the upper section of the small intestine (duodenum), and when located in this area it is usually necessary to remove part of the pancreas along with the tumor and a portion of the duodenum (pancreaticoduodenectomy). Removal of the tumor, along with a portion of the bowel, is the treatment of choice for cancer located in the jejunum and ileum as well. Removal of part of the small intestine may necessitate an opening through the abdominal wall for the evacuation of fecal material (ileostomy).

Prognosis

The overall 5-year survival rates for duodenal cancer following surgery to remove the tumor is poor and ranges from 20-35%. However, the predicted outcome depends upon the size of the tumor, how deep the tumor has spread into the bowel wall, and the extent of spread (metastasis) into other organs. If surgery completely removes the neoplasm and there is no metastasis into the lymph nodes or liver, the 5-year survival rate may be as high as 70-80%. For individuals diagnosed with adenocarcinoma, the 5-year survival rate decreases to 20-35%.

Neither chemotherapy nor radiation therapy is effective in improving survival in individuals with small intestinal cancer in its advanced stages.

Differential Diagnosis

Conditions that present with symptoms similar to small intestinal cancer include inflammatory bowel disease, Crohn's disease, and harmless (benign) tumors of the small intestine.

Specialists

- Gastroenterologist
- General Surgeon

Work Restrictions / Accommodations

In the absence of other medical complications, individuals who have had surgery for small intestinal cancer should be able to return to their previous duties. However, those with an ileostomy may need frequent breaks and emotional support, and heavy or prolonged lifting should be avoided until recovery is complete. Some individuals may require more sedentary work for a period of time due to weakness and fatigue following surgery, radiation therapy, or chemotherapy.

Comorbid Conditions

Existing conditions that may impact an individual's ability to recover and further lengthen disability include any other diseases that affect the major organ systems of the body such as the liver, lungs, spleen, and pancreas. Other gastrointestinal abnormalities such as Crohn's disease, ulcerative colitis, or irritable bowel disease may also lengthen disability.

Complications

Possible complications of small intestinal cancer include bowel obstruction and inadequate blood supply to the small intestine (bowel ischemia) with resulting tissue death (infarction). Spread of the cancer (metastasis) may occur, and when this happens it usually enters the liver. Metastasis to other organs such as the pancreas, stomach, and spleen may follow.

Factors Influencing Duration

Factors that might influence the length of disability include the stage at which the cancer was detected, the length of small intestine that was removed during surgery, the presence of an ileostomy, and the individual's response to surgical treatment. Advanced age may also be a factor as older individuals often require longer recovery times.

Length of Disability

The duration depends on recurrence. Heavy physical labor will be restricted for 5 to 6 weeks following partial removal of the small intestine, and possibly longer if postoperative chemotherapy or radiation therapy treatments are administered. Disability may be permanent. Durations reflect recovery from procedure only.

Surgical treatment.

Duration in Days

Job Classification	Minimum	Optimum	Maximum
Sedentary work	28	42	56
Light work	28	42	56
Medium work	28	42	56
Heavy work	42	56	84
Very Heavy work	42	56	84

Failure to Recover

If an individual fails to recover within the maximum duration expectancy period, the reader may wish to reference the following questions to assist in better understanding the specifics of an individual's medical case.

Regarding diagnosis:

- Does individual eat a high fat diet?
- Does individual have Crohn's or celiac disease?
- Is cancer present elsewhere in the body?
- Does individual complain of abdominal pain or weight loss? Noticed blood in the stool? Watery diarrhea?
- Has individual had sudden flushing of the head and neck?
- Was upper GI series done? CT? Endoscopy with biopsy?
- Were conditions with similar symptoms ruled out?

Regarding treatment:

- Did individual have surgery? How extensive was it?
- Does individual have an ileostomy?

Regarding prognosis:

- Can individual's employer accommodate these restrictions?
- Does individual have any conditions that could affect ability to recover?
- Has individual had a bowel obstruction or ischemia with infarction?
- Does individual have any metastasis?
- What stage was the cancer in when detected?

References

Boland, C.R., and Y.S. Kim. "Gastrointestinal Polyposis Syndromes." Gastrointestinal Disease. Sleisenger, M.H., and J.S. Fordtran, eds. Philadelphia: W.B. Saunders Company, 1993. 1430-1448.

Schroy, P.C., III. "Polyps, Adenocarcinomas, and Other Intestinal Tumors." Therapy of Digestive Diseases. Wolfe, M.M., eds. Philadelphia: W.B. Saunders Company, 2000. 645-673.

Cancer, Stomach

Other names / synonyms: Gastric Cancer, Gastric Carcinoma, Malignant Neoplasm of the Stomach, Stomach Cancer
151, 151.0, 151.1, 151.2, 151.3, 151.4, 151.5, 151.6, 151.8, 151.9, 197.8, 230.2, 235.2

Definition

Stomach cancer (also called gastric cancer) occurs when cancerous cells develop in any part of the stomach. About 90% of stomach cancers originate in the inner or mucosal layers of the stomach, and nearly half of these cancers, called adenocarcinomas, form in the lower third of the stomach. Other much less common cancers of the stomach are lymphomas, leiomyosarcomas, and adenoacanthomas. Stomach cancer can rarely be the result of cancerous cells spreading (metastasizing) from cancer in another part of the body.

Researchers have learned that some individuals are more at risk for developing stomach cancer than others. The disease has been found most often in individuals over age 55, it affects twice as many men as women, and is found more often among blacks than whites. Stomach cancer is more common in other parts of the world than the US such as Japan, Korea, parts of Eastern Europe, and Latin America. Researchers believe that the diets in these areas, which include foods that are eaten pickled, or preserved by drying, salting, or smoking, could play a role in the development of stomach cancer. Additional risk factors include prior stomach surgery, stomach inflammation, ulcers, or any condition that reduces the digestive juices (thus lowering acidity) in the stomach, such as pernicious anemia, achlorhydria, and atrophic gastritis. Exposure to certain dusts and fumes in the workplace and smoking has been linked to higher than average risk of stomach cancer. The incidence and mortality rate for stomach cancer has been on a worldwide decline for the past 60 years, possibly because of improved methods of food handling and preservation, especially freezing. Increased intake of vitamin C is also being considered a factor in the disease's decline.

Diagnosis

History: Stomach cancer may be hard to detect early because often early signs are nonexistent, nonspecific, or mimic other digestive conditions, such as an ulcer. The most common early symptoms are indigestion or heartburn, abdominal pain or discomfort, nausea, vomiting, constipation or diarrhea, occasional belching, a feeling of fullness even after a small meal, loss of appetite, weakness and fatigue. Less common symptoms are anemia and weight loss. Symptoms of advanced cancer include acute upper abdominal pain, blood in the stool or the vomitus, extreme weight loss, a palpable abdominal mass, accumulation of fluid in the abdomen (ascites), yellowish appearance of the skin (jaundice), and extreme malnutrition (cachexia).

Physical exam: With his or her hands, the physician palpates to feel for enlarged masses in the abdominal area as well as for enlarged lymph nodes. Enlarged lymph nodes, especially in the area of the left collar bone and left armpit, may represent a sign of spreading cancer (metastasis). A rectal exam to test for masses or other abnormal formations in the lower colon may be done to check for spread into the pelvis.

Tests: Tests consist of x-rays, fecal occult blood test, and endoscopy. X-rays are taken of the upper gastrointestinal (or GI) tract after the individual has ingested a barium solution (upper GI series). The barium solution outlines the stomach on the x-rays, making it easier for the doctor to detect tumors or other abnormal areas. The fecal occult blood test is a laboratory check for hidden or occult blood in the stool. An endoscopy is the direct examination of the esophagus and stomach using a thin, lighted tube (gastroscope) that is inserted through the mouth. Tissue biopsies are taken during the endoscopy for microscopic examination. A CT or ultrasound test is used to determine if, or how far, the cancer has spread.

Treatment

Treatment for stomach cancer depends upon the size, location, and extent of the tumor, staging of the disease, and a person's general health. The most common treatment is surgical removal of part or all of the stomach (subtotal, partial, or total gastrectomy). During a subtotal or partial gastrectomy, part of the stomach is removed and the remaining stomach portion is connected to the esophagus or the small intestine. Total gastrectomy is when the entire stomach, along with some of the tissue around the stomach and the lymph nodes near the tumor, are removed. After a total gastrectomy, the surgeon connects the esophagus directly to the small intestine.

Anticancer drugs (chemotherapy) are referred to as systemic therapy because the drugs--taken orally, by injection, or intravenously (via IV)-- enter the bloodstream and travel throughout the body. In cases of advanced stomach cancer, chemotherapy is used in combination with surgery to provide temporary relief by slowing tumor growth. It is also used as adjuvant therapy to enhance the effect of surgery by destroying remaining cancer cells. There is, as yet, no strong evidence that this combination prolongs life. Researchers are exploring the benefits of administering chemotherapy before surgery to slow tumor growth. A new method of chemotherapy, intraperitoneal chemotherapy, involves putting the anticancer drugs directly into the abdomen. Chemotherapy is also being studied as a primary treatment for cancer that has already spread and as a way to relieve symptoms of the disease. Chemotherapy is given in cycles such that a treatment period is followed by a recovery period, then another treatment, and so on.

Radiation therapy is the use of high-energy x-rays to damage cancer cells and thereby to retard their growth. Local radiation therapy affects only the cancer cells in the area treated. Researchers are conducting trials to determine whether the administration of radiation during surgery (intraoperative radiation therapy) will be beneficial. Radiation therapy may also be used to relieve pain or blockage and to treat cancers that cause chronic bleeding.

Immunotherapy (biological therapy) is a form of treatment that helps the body's immune system attack and destroy cancer cells, and may also help the body recover from some of the side effects of treatment. Another type of immunotherapy involves giving the person colony-stimulating factors after chemotherapy to help restore blood cell levels. Treatment is given to eradicate H. pylori infection, if present.

Treatment with surgery is tailored to Stages 0-III of the disease. The stages of stomach cancer are:

Stage 0: Cancer confined to the inner lining of the stomach (mucosa); no lymph node involvement and no metastasis.

Stage I: Cancer spread to but not through the membrane that lines the abdominal cavity.

Stage II: Cancer has penetrated the membrane that lines the abdominal cavity but has not spread to adjacent organs.

Stage III: Cancer involves nearby organs and possibly spreads to lymph nodes.

Stage IV: Cancer metastasized to distant organs, tissues, or lymph nodes.

The extent of the gastrectomy is contingent on the stage of the disease. In general, stages 0 through III cancers are considered operable for cure but stage IV cancers generally are not. Unfortunately, in more than 60% of individuals with stomach cancer who undergo surgery, metastasis makes total complete surgical removal of the stomach (total gastrectomy) impractical because the cancer has already spread to other parts of the body. Nevertheless, the surgeon may remove a large part of the tumor to relieve pain and prevent blockage. In some cases, a total gastrectomy serves as a palliative measure because it is performed to relieve symptoms rather than to cure the condition.

The stress, shock, and uncertainty surrounding the diagnosis of stomach cancer may require psychological or psychiatric intervention for some period of time.

Prognosis

The most significant predictors of outcome are the stage of the cancer at the time of diagnosis, the location of the tumor, and the type of surgery that can be performed. Because stomach cancer usually goes undetected in its early stages, the prognosis for more than 60% of individuals (Stages II-IV) presenting with symptoms is not good. In these individuals, surgery is usually performed to relieve symptoms rather than to act as a cure. Complete recovery is not anticipated. For about 30% of individuals (Stages 0 and I), surgery is performed to cure, and complete recovery is anticipated. It is important to remember that in Stages 0 and I, the cancer has not spread through the abdominal membrane; there is no metastasis or lymph node involvement. Many of the individuals in Stages 0 and I who are treated with surgery can basically expect to return to their normal lives; however, they will need to alter the size, content, and frequency of meals.

Differential Diagnosis

Differential diagnosis might include benign gastric ulcers, gastric polyps, or atopic gastritis; some of these may progress to cancer. Differential diagnosis might also include lymphoma and metastatic melanoma, which are two types of malignant cancers.

Specialists

- Dietary Advisor
- Gastroenterologist
- General Surgeon
- Oncologist
- Psychiatrist
- Psychologist
- Radiation Oncologist

Work Restrictions / Accommodations

The treatment and the disease itself may weaken the individual and severely limit his or her ability to return to previous work activities. The individual may be able to work a limited number of hours per day, or days per week, and their duties may need to be largely sedentary. Because of the rigors of the disease and treatment, the individual may need a place at work where he or she may periodically rest. Some individuals undergoing chemotherapy and/or radiation may require additional leave from work. Because of diminished stomach capacity, provisions will have to be made (at least temporarily) for the individual to eat several small meals during work hours (rather than simply one lunch break).

Comorbid Conditions

Comorbid conditions that might the length of disability include obesity or excessive thinness, personal medical history, and allergy to treatment medications.

As the disease progresses, it destroys both cancer cells and healthy cells, causing a debilitation of stamina in the individual. Existing conditions, such as obesity or excessive thinness, chronic illness (such as a heart condition or diabetes), and allergy to treatment medications often add to the debilitation from the disease and from the treatment.

Complications

Complications arise when the tumor spreads to surrounding tissue or adjoining organs. In two-thirds of individuals with stomach cancer, the most common route of spread (metastasis) is through the lymphatic system. The cancer extends to regional nodes around the stomach and/or to distant ones, such as those near the base of the neck. The tumor may also penetrate the stomach wall and invade the serous membrane that lines the abdominal cavity, spreading to adjoining organs of the digestive tract. Organs frequently affected are the pancreas, spleen, esophagus, intestines, and liver. Cancer cells may also spread to more distant sites via the bloodstream.

Factors Influencing Duration

Factors influencing the length of disability include the stage of disease at initial presentation (degree of metastases), the location of the cancer, whether the gastrectomy is total, partial, or subtotal, the presence of concurrent infection, overall general health, the presence or absence of complications of the cancer itself, and side effects of treatments. Stress and shock are also natural reactions to a diagnosis of stomach cancer.

Length of Disability

Length of disability depends on treatment. If the treatment is a subtotal, partial, or total gastrectomy, length of disability will depend on the individual's adjustment to a different regimen of eating. If treatment also includes chemotherapy or radiation therapy, the length of disability will depend on the individual's ability to recover from the rigors of these treatment regimes. Disability may be permanent.

Durations reflect recovery from procedure only.

Surgical treatment (gastrectomy)

Duration in Days

Job Classification	Minimum	Optimum	Maximum
Sedentary work	28	42	56
Light work	28	42	56
Medium work	42	56	70
Heavy work	42	56	70
Very Heavy work	42	56	70

Failure to Recover

If an individual fails to recover within the maximum duration expectancy period, the reader may wish to reference the following questions to assist in better understanding the specifics of an individual's medical case.

Regarding diagnosis:

- Has individual had previous stomach surgery?
- Did individual have previous stomach irritation or ulcers caused by Helicobacter pylori infections? Any conditions that reduce stomach acidity?
- Does individual take vitamin C?
- Is cancer present elsewhere in the body?
- Does individual have heartburn? Nausea? Vomiting? Belching? Constipation or diarrhea? Blood in the stool?
- Does individual have abdominal pain or discomfort? Loss of appetite? A feeling of fullness even after a small meal?
- Was there an unexplained weight loss?
- Did physical exam reveal a palpable abdominal mass? Ascites? Jaundice?
- Does individual appear malnourished?
- Were x-rays, fecal occult blood test, endoscopy, and an upper GI series done? Biopsy with the endoscopy? CT or ultrasound?
- Were conditions with similar symptoms ruled out?

Regarding treatment:

- Was individual's cancer operable?
- Was a subtotal, partial, or total gastrectomy done? A palliative total gastrectomy?
- Is individual on chemotherapy? Radiation therapy?
- Secondary to the stress, shock, and uncertainty of the disease, is individual seeing a mental health specialist?

Regarding prognosis:

- Can individual's employer accommodate any necessary restrictions?
- Does individual have any conditions that could affect recovery?
- What stage was the cancer in when diagnosed?
- Does individual have metastatic disease?

References

Diseases We Treat. The University of Chicago Hospitals and Health System. 2000. 01 Jan 2001 <http://gi.bsd.uchicago.edu/diseases/colorectandother/stomach/stomach.html>.

What You Need to Know About Stomach Cancer. CancerlinksUSA.com. 1999. 01 Jan 2001 <http://www.cancerlinksUSA.com/stomach/wynk.htm>.

Cancer Group. Stomach Cancer. Cancer Group. 1995. 01 Jan 2001 <http://www.cancergroup.com/em6.html>.

Fung, Man C., MD. Outline Summary of Stomach Cancer. University of Pennsylvania Cancer Center. 26 Aug 1999. 01 Jan 2001 <http://www.oncolink.upenn.edu/disease/gastric/gastric_review.html>.

Murphy, Gerald P., Lois B. Morris, and Dianne Lange. Informed Decisions: The Complete Book of Cancer Diagnosis, Treatment, and Recovery. New York: Penguin Books USA Inc, 1997.

Scully, Rosemary M., and Marylou Barnes. Physical Therapy. Philadelphia: J.B. Lippincott Company, 1989.

Cancer, Testicle(s)

Other names / synonyms: Malignant Tumor of the Testicle, Testicular Cancer, Testicular Choriocarcinoma, Testicular Embryonal Carcinoma, Testicular Seminoma, Testicular Yolk Sac Tumor

186, 186.9, 198.82, 233.6, 236.4

Definition

Testicular cancer is a malignant tumor of the testes. While the cause is unknown, factors that are acquired and factors that are present at birth (congenital) are associated with development of testicular tumor. Approximately 5% of testicular tumors develop in individuals who were born with an undescended testicle (cryptorchidism). This risk remains even after surgery to relocate the testes to the scrotum. Other acquired factors associated with testicular cancer include trauma and infection-related wasting or reduction in the size of the testicles (testicular atrophy).

The most common types of testicular cancers are seminomas and nonseminomas (teratoma, choriocarcinoma, embryonal carcinoma, or yolk sac tumor). Each type grows, spreads, and is treated differently. Seminomas are made up of just one type of cell, and probably develop from the cells that produce sperm. Nonseminomas consist of a mixture of different types of cells. Tumors that develop from testicular tissue or from lymphatic tissue are extremely rare.

Testicular tumors account for 1-2% of all cancerous tumors in men, and are four times more common in white men than black men. Except for leukemia, it is the most common malignancy in men between the ages of 15 and 35. Approximately 6,900 new cases of testicular cancer are diagnosed in the US each year, resulting in a mortality rate of 300 per year.

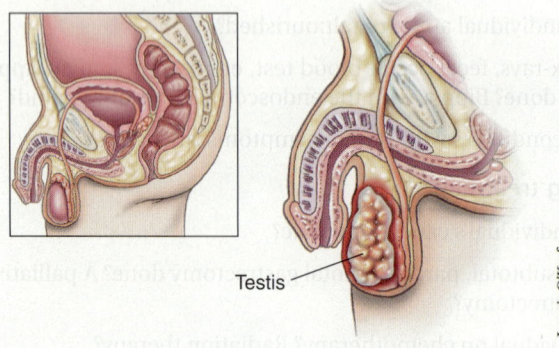

Testis

Laurie O'Keefe

Diagnosis

History: The most common symptom that individuals report is a firm swelling or lump in one testicle that may or may not be painful. The lump usually is about the size of a pea, but it could be as large as a marble or even an egg. Other abnormalities that are occasionally present include an enlarged testicle, a feeling of heaviness or sudden collection of fluid in the scrotum (hydrocele), pain and discomfort in a testicle or the scrotum, a dull ache in the lower abdomen, or enlarged or tender breast tissue (gynecomastia).

Most men discover testicular cancer themselves either unintentionally or during a self-examination. Self-examination during or directly after a shower or bath, when the skin of the scrotum is relaxed, increases the chances of finding testicular cancer early. Only regular testicular self-examination can detect a tumor early enough to provide assurance of a cure.

Physical exam: The physical exam usually reveals a mass or lump in the testicle or swollen scrotal skin. Occasionally breast enlargement is seen.

Tests: Definite diagnosis of testicular cancer can only be confirmed by the surgical removal of the testis (orchiectomy) and microscopic examination of the testicular tissue. This not only confirms the presence of cancer, but also identifies the type of cancer, and is an important part of treatment. Biopsy of the tumor without removal of the testicle is rarely done, but if it is, a special clamp should be used to avoid possible spillage and the resulting spread of cells if they prove to be cancerous. Ultrasound of the testis is useful to exclude other causes of scrotal masses. A chest x-ray is mandatory, as the lung is an area to which the cancer commonly spreads (metastasizes). Blood tests (human chorionic gonadotropin, alpha-fetoprotein, and LDH levels) and CT of the abdomen and pelvic region are important in diagnosis and treatment, and in detecting any evidence of spread of cancer to other parts of the body (metastasis), which helps determine the stage of the tumor. In Stage 1, cancer is confined to the testicle. In stage 2, cancer has spread to the lymph nodes located in the rear of the body below the diaphragm (retroperitoneal lymph nodes). In stage 3, cancer has spread beyond the lymph nodes to other organs. Lymphangiography may also help visualize the lymph nodes on an x-ray. If these appear to be involved, they may need to be removed surgically and examined under the microscope.

Treatment

No one treatment works for all testicular cancers. Each type responds differently to radiation and has different patterns of spread (metastases). Surgery to remove the testis (orchiectomy) may cure testicular cancer in its early stage. The testicle is usually removed through the groin to avoid the risk of spreading the cancer through contact with the loose skin of the scrotum. Since only 2% of men with testicular cancer develop a new tumor on the other side, the testicle without the tumor is usually left intact. Surgery may be followed by either radiation therapy or the administration of anticancer drugs (chemotherapy) or both, depending upon the type of cancer and its stage. Sometimes doctors recommend waiting to see if there is a relapse after surgery before starting any additional treatment. In this case, it is crucial for the individual to keep all follow-up appointments and to perform regular self-examination. Regional lymph node removal (lymphadenectomy) may also be necessary and should be followed by monthly monitoring and chest x-rays for the first year. Radiation therapy on the remaining testis and lymph glands is usually done in seminomas even when there is no indication that the disease has spread. Use of radiation therapy and/or chemotherapy is largely responsible for today's high cure rate for these cancers.

Prognosis

Prognosis varies according to the type of cancer and how far advanced it was when discovered. Most individuals recover completely. Of 6,000 cases seen annually, only about 300 deaths are reported. The cure rate for early stage testicular cancer is 95%. Cure rate for advanced disease is approximately 70%. Radiation therapy and chemotherapy may temporarily cause infertility or damage to the remaining testis, so birth control may be recommended for about 12 to 18 months after the therapy ends.

Differential Diagnosis

Epididymitis, testicular torsion, orchitis, spermatocele, hydrocele, or benign tumors of the testes are other possible causes of testicular lumps.

Specialists

- Oncologist
- Psychiatrist
- Radiation Oncologist
- Urologist

Work Restrictions / Accommodations

Work leave for treatment and recuperation will be required. Cancer drugs (chemotherapy) can cause nausea, vomiting, dehydration, loss of appetite, fatigue, lowered resistance to infections, and hair loss. Individuals who undergo radiation therapy may experience fatigue, lowered blood counts, and lowered resistance to infections. All the side effects associated with treatment may require work restrictions and accommodations.

Comorbid Conditions

Individuals with testicular trauma or torsion may be more prone to develop testicular cancer. Diseases that compromise the immune system, such as AIDS, may make individuals with testicular cancer more vulnerable to infection and delayed healing following surgery. Use of chemotherapy and radiation may also be limited in these individuals.

Complications

Testicular cancer can metastasize to other parts of the body, most commonly the lungs, liver, or the intestines. Treatment for testicular cancer may be associated with complications. Surgery to remove retroperitoneal lymph nodes may impair sexual function. Chemotherapy can cause increased risk of infection, nausea or vomiting, and hair loss in some individuals. Some drugs may cause infertility, but fertility is usually restored 2 to 3 years after therapy ends. Radiation can cause fatigue or lowered blood counts.

Factors Influencing Duration

Length of disability may be influenced by the type of tumor, the size of the tumor, the stage of disease (evidence of metastasis to other parts of the body), and the method of treatment.

Length of Disability

Duration depends on stage, grade, cell type, and adjuvant chemotherapy or radiation therapy. Remission is very common with different procedures and treatments. Length of disability also depends on the individual's response. Some individuals may not be able to perform very heavy work for some time after surgery. Disability may be permanent. Duration reflects recovery from procedure only.

Surgical treatment (orchiectomy).

Duration in Days

Job Classification	Minimum	Optimum	Maximum
Sedentary work	3	7	14
Light work	3	7	21
Medium work	7	14	21
Heavy work	7	14	21
Very Heavy work	7	14	21

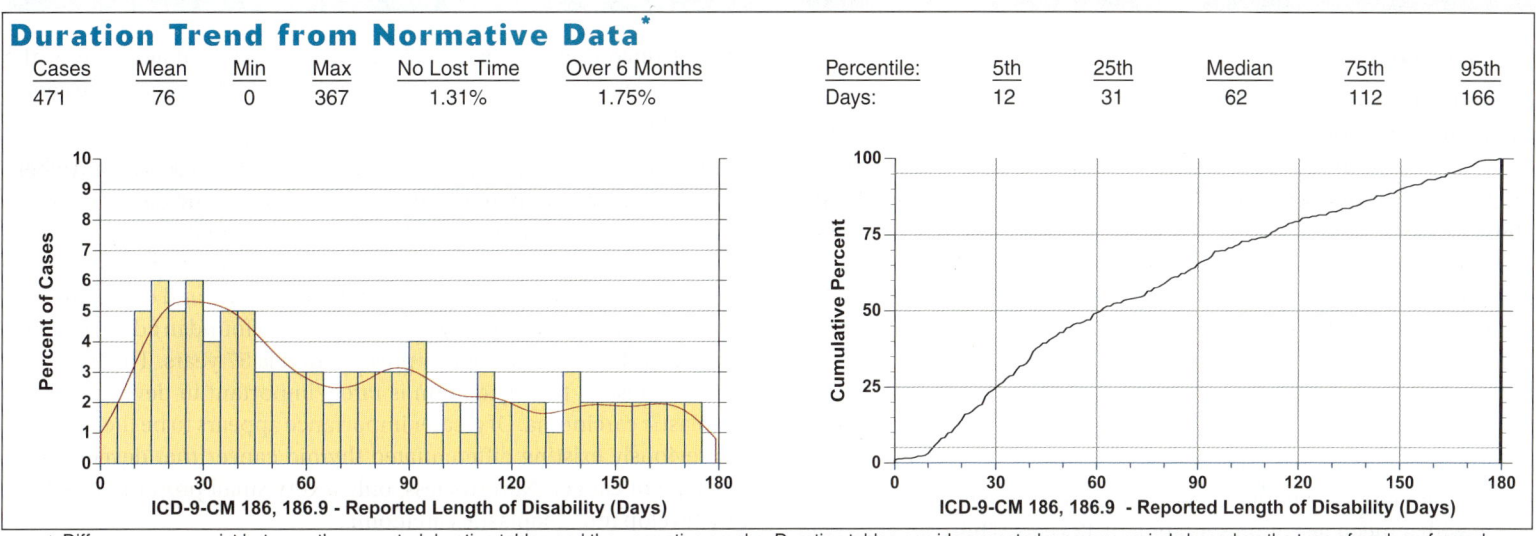

Duration Trend from Normative Data*

Cases	Mean	Min	Max	No Lost Time	Over 6 Months
471	76	0	367	1.31%	1.75%

Percentile:	5th	25th	Median	75th	95th
Days:	12	31	62	112	166

* Differences may exist between the expected duration tables and the normative graphs. Duration tables provide expected recovery periods based on the type of work performed by the individual. The normative graphs reflect the actual observed experience of many individuals across the spectrum of physical conditions, in a variety of industries, and with varying levels of case management.

Failure to Recover

If an individual fails to recover within the maximum duration expectancy period, the reader may wish to reference the following questions to assist in better understanding the specifics of an individual's medical case.

Regarding diagnosis:

- Does individual report a firm swelling or painful or nonpainful lump in one testicle?
- Does individual feel heaviness or sudden collection of fluid in the scrotum (hydrocele)?
- Is there pain and discomfort in a testicle or the scrotum?
- Does individual note a dull ache in the lower abdomen or enlarged or tender breast tissue (gynecomastia)?
- Was diagnosis confirmed by the surgical removal of the testis (orchiectomy) and microscopic examination of the tissue?
- Was the tumor surgically removed?
- Was ultrasound done to exclude other causes of scrotal masses?
- Were chest x-ray, blood tests, and CT of the abdomen and pelvic region done to detect evidence of spread of cancer to other parts of the body (metastasis)?

Regarding treatment:

- Is additional treatment such as radiation and/or chemotherapy required or has the doctor elected to postpone these treatments until individual has a recurrence?
- If no additional treatment is given, is individual being monitored closely, keeping all follow-up appointments and doing regular testicular self-examination?
- Was regional lymph node removal required?
- If individual does not respond to treatment, would individual benefit from experimental treatment?

Cancer, Testicle(s)

Regarding prognosis:
- Did individual have early stage testicular cancer or was the disease advanced?
- Did individual undergo orchiectomy? Was the surgery successful in removing the tumor?
- Did individual require lymphadenectomy? Does the physician believe all affected lymph nodes were removed?
- Has the cancer spread to other parts of the body and if so, what parts are involved?
- Does individual have effects from radiation therapy or chemotherapy? If so, what are they and how will they be treated?
- Would individual benefit from psychological counseling because of the disease or treatments for the disease?

References

"Chapter 233. Genitourinary Cancer." Merck Manual of Diagnosis and Therapy, 17th ed. Beers, Mark H., and Robert Berkow, MD, eds. Whitehouse Station, NJ: Merck & Co., Inc., 1999. 21 July 2000 <http://www.merck.com/pubs/mmanual/section17/chapter233/233i.htm>.

Med News. Testicular Cancer. National Cancer Institute. 2000. 01 Jan 2001 <http://imsdd.meb.uni-bonn.de/cancernet/101121.html>.

Cancer, Thyroid Gland

Other names / synonyms: Anaplastic Carcinoma, Cancer of the Thyroid, Follicular Carcinoma, Malignant Lymphoma of the Thyroid, Medullary Carcinoma, Papillary Carcinoma, Thyroid Cancer

193, 198.89

Definition

Thyroid cancer is a tumor that develops in the tissue of the thyroid gland, an organ located at the base of the neck that regulates body metabolism. Most thyroid cancers present as a small mass of regular or irregular shape (nodule) and there may be either single or multiple nodules. There are four main types of thyroid cancer that are classified according to their cell of origin and these are papillary, follicular, medullary, and anaplastic thyroid carcinomas. Papillary and follicular carcinomas (together referred to as differentiated thyroid cancer or DTC) comprise 80-90% of all thyroid cancers.

Papillary carcinoma may occur in any part of the thyroid gland, and these tumors vary in size from microscopic to several centimeters in diameter. These are slow growing cancers that may spread (metastasize). Papillary carcinoma occurs within a wide age range (5 to 85 years) with a mean age at presentation of 42 years. This type of thyroid cancer occurs more often in females than males at a ratio of 2.4 to 1. External radiation is of considerable importance with respect to causation of this type of cancer.

Follicular carcinoma is less common than papillary carcinoma with a mean age at presentation of 50 years. This cancer may occur in any part of the thyroid and in a wide variety of sizes. These tumors are well-defined when small, but as they enlarge, they may invade both the vessels and outer covering (capsule) of the thyroid. Follicular cancer has more of a tendency to metastasize via the bloodstream to the bones, lungs, liver and brain than does papillary carcinoma. However, unlike papillary cancer, there is only a minor association between follicular carcinoma and radiation. Rather, there appears to be a relationship between follicular carcinoma and dietary iodide. The highest incidence of follicular cancer has been reported from populations that often show an enlargement of the thyroid gland resulting from low intake of iodide (goiter).

Medullary carcinoma accounts for 3-10% of all thyroid carcinomas. It occurs in individuals of all ages with a mean age of 49. The female to male ratio is 1.3 to 1. The growth rate of medullary carcinomas varies widely; some tumors progress very slowly and survivals of 20 to 30 years are not uncommon. Inheritance appears to play a major role in the development of medullary cancer and up to 20% of cases may be genetically mediated.

Clinical reports indicate that anaplastic carcinoma makes up anywhere from 5-30% of all thyroid cancers. This broad incidence range is probably not accurate and is explained by the fact that in the past, many other deadly (malignant) cancers have been mistakenly included under this heading. In reality, anaplastic carcinoma is rare and comprises less than 5% of all thyroid carcinomas. It is not often found in adults younger than 40 and the average age at presentation is 57 years. The female to male ratio is 1.3 to 1. Radiation is rarely important in development of anaplastic carcinoma. Of greater importance appears to be the presence of previously existing differentiated thyroid cancer that develops into this type of cancer. Nevertheless, only a very small proportion of DTC will develop into anaplastic carcinoma.

Thyroid cancer constitutes about 1% of all malignant tumors and it is the most common endocrine malignancy. Each year, approximately 14,000 new cases occur in the United States with approximately 1,000 deaths reported annually. Generally, 5-year survival rates for individuals with thyroid cancer are better than ninety percent. For 5-year survivors, the relative survival rate for years 5 to 10 is in the range of 99%. Survival rates have improved over the past several decades due to earlier detection and, possibly, because of more effective treatment.

Diagnosis

History: Individuals with thyroid cancer usually report a single, firm, nontender lump (nodule) at the base of the neck. If the tumor is pressing on other structures in the neck, symptoms may include hoarseness or loss of voice from pressure on nerves in the vocal chord (larynx), and difficulty swallowing or breathing due to pressure on the throat (esophagus) or wind pipe (trachea), respectively. If the tumor has spread (metastasized), the individual may report respiratory difficulties, cough, blood in the sputum (hemoptysis), chest pain, and musculoskeletal problems such as bone pain.

Physical exam: Manipulation with the fingers (palpation) may reveal a single, firm, nontender, symmetric or asymmetric mass (nodule) at the base of the neck. Occasionally, the thyroid will appear perfectly normal despite the presence of a cancerous growth. More advanced thyroid tumors may be larger in size or they may have many nodules (multinodular). Often, these are firmly attached to adjacent structures in the neck and enlarged lymph nodes may be present if the tumor is advanced. Metastasis of the tumor may result in weight loss.

Tests: Thyroid nodules can be visualized by injecting or swallowing a radioisotope (131I or 99Tcm Pertechnetate) and recording images of the thyroid on a specialized (gamma) camera. The radioisotope is taken up only by the thyroid tissue and these results will allow determination of the size of the tumor and whether it has spread to other parts of the body. Other tests may include high-frequency sound waves (ultrasound) to visualize the tumor and measuring thyroid hormones (calcitonin and thyroxin) in response to stimulation of the thyroid gland (thyroid function tests). However, definitive diagnosis for thyroid cancer can only be made by obtaining a tissue sample (biopsy) from the nodule. Biopsies are obtained by aspirating cells through a needle inserted into the suspicious mass (fine needle aspiration biopsy or FNAB). Biopsy tissue is then used to determine if the nodule is cancerous.

Treatment

Surgery to remove part or all of the thyroid gland (partial or total thyroidectomy, respectively) is the most common treatment. If the cancer has spread into the lymphatic system, some lymph nodes may need to be removed (lymphadenectomy). Following surgery, radioactive iodine can be administered orally or by injection to destroy any residual cancer that may be left behind (131I radiotherapy). Alternatively, x-rays from an external source (external beam radiotherapy) may be used to treat larger, well-defined residual tumors. Radiation treatments may need to be repeated at one to five year intervals if residual cancer remains in the thyroid. Also, the loss of thyroid tissue after surgery or radiation treatment may result in decreased production of thyroid hormones (thyroxin and calcitonin), and hormonal supplements may be needed for lifetime maintenance. Finally, in early reports, certain chemotherapeutic agents (doxorubicin; cis-platinum) alone or in combination have been shown to be effective in treating thyroid cancer in some individuals.

Prognosis

The predicted outcome is dependent upon the type of thyroid cancer that is being discussed. Also, age of the individual at diagnosis is an important factor in all types of thyroid cancers and younger people have a much better prognosis than do the elderly. Papillary tumors grow slowly but may eventually invade local structures outside of the thyroid including lymph nodes. Papillary carcinoma has a cure rate of 90-95% if it is diagnosed and treated at an early stage by surgery, radiation, and/or chemotherapy. The risk of death increases with the size of the primary tumor and mortality almost never occurs if the primary lesion is less than 2 cm in diameter. Recurrences following treatment may occur in 20% of individuals. The outcome for individuals with follicular carcinoma depends upon their age and the degree of metastasis. Follicular tumors can be carried via the bloodstream and may spread (metastasize) to other body sites including the lungs, bone, liver, and brain. Advanced follicular cancer in older individuals has survival rates of 47% and 8% at 5 years and 20 years (respectively) following thyroidectomy and radiation treatment. Younger individuals with less advanced cancer have survival rates of 99% at 5 years and 86% at 20 years. The outcome for medullary carcinoma depends upon the stage of the tumor at diagnosis. Small medullary tumors are usually cured by thyroidectomy while more advanced tumors that are growing rapidly have a survival rate of less than 5% at 5 years following treatment with thyroidectomy, radiation, and/or chemotherapy. The prognosis for anaplastic carcinomas is poor and 5-year survival rates may range anywhere from 20-35% following treatment.

Differential Diagnosis

Conditions that present with similar symptoms as thyroid cancer include harmless (benign) thyroid nodules or cysts, chronic inflammation of the thyroid (Hashimoto's thyroiditis), enlargement of the thyroid gland (simple or multinodular goiter), or cancer that has spread from other organs into the thyroid gland (metastatic carcinoma).

Specialists

- Endocrinologist
- General Surgeon
- Oncologist
- Otolaryngologist
- Radiation Oncologist

Rehabilitation

If treatment for thyroid cancer requires a thyroidectomy, the individual will not be allowed to participate in an exercise program until swelling in the area of the incision is significantly lessened.

If the surgery requires full removal of the thyroid, damage to the recurrent nerve that enervates the vocal chords is highly probable. The individual usually experiences hoarseness or weakness in voice. The individual will undergo an assessment of vocal production such as speaking pitch, loudness, and voice quality. A typical program may include muscle relaxation techniques for upper thoracic muscles. The individual will be taught how to coordinate breathing and speaking for maximal vocal production. The individual may participate in vocal therapy. Depending on vocal production impairment, vocal rehabilitation can last up to 8 weeks. Speech therapy may also be necessary if the thyroid cancer metastasized and part of the tongue or lower jaw was surgically removed.

Work Restrictions / Accommodations

Extended work leave for surgery, therapy, and recuperation from these treatments is usually required. Some individuals may require a more sedentary position with minimal physical labor upon return to the workplace until recovery is complete.

Comorbid Conditions

Existing conditions that may impact an individual's ability to recover and further lengthen their disability from thyroid cancer include enlargement of the thyroid (goiter), inflammation of the thyroid (thyroiditis), and an over-active thyroid (Graves disease).

Complications

Medullary carcinomas can produce high concentrations of various humoral secretions (serotonin; prostaglandins; calcitonin; histamine; vasoactive peptide) that affect the circulatory system. Typically, an individual will exhibit flushing and diarrhea in response to these factors. Also, tumors of the adrenal gland (pheochromocytoma) commonly occur in individuals with medullary thyroid cancer. Anaplastic cancer grows very rapidly and can lead to difficulty in swallowing (dysphagia), breathing (dyspnea), and speaking (dysphonia). Metastasis into lymph nodes occurs in 80% of cases and into distant organs 50% of the time. Anaplastic cancer tumors may become large enough to obstruct one of the major vessels (superior vena cava) that returns blood to the heart.

Factors Influencing Duration

Age of the individual with thyroid cancer may impact disability. Generally, older individuals do not recover from this condition as easily as do younger individuals. Length of disability may also be influenced by the type of thyroid cancer, the stage of the disease, the presence of metastasis of the thyroid tumor, and the method of treatment. If radiation is used, a longer period of disability may be expected. Some individuals may have permanent disability.

Length of Disability

Duration depends on site, size, and stage of cancer. For thyroidectomy, duration also depends on partial versus total. Those treated by surgery, radiation, and chemotherapy will have limited capacity to perform heavy labor upon return to work. Recurrence of thyroid cancer following treatment is not uncommon. Disability may be permanent. Durations reflect recovery from surgery only.

Surgical removal (thyroidectomy).

Job Classification	Duration in Days		
	Minimum	Optimum	Maximum
Sedentary work	3	7	14
Light work	3	7	14
Medium work	7	14	21
Heavy work	7	28	42
Very Heavy work	7	28	42

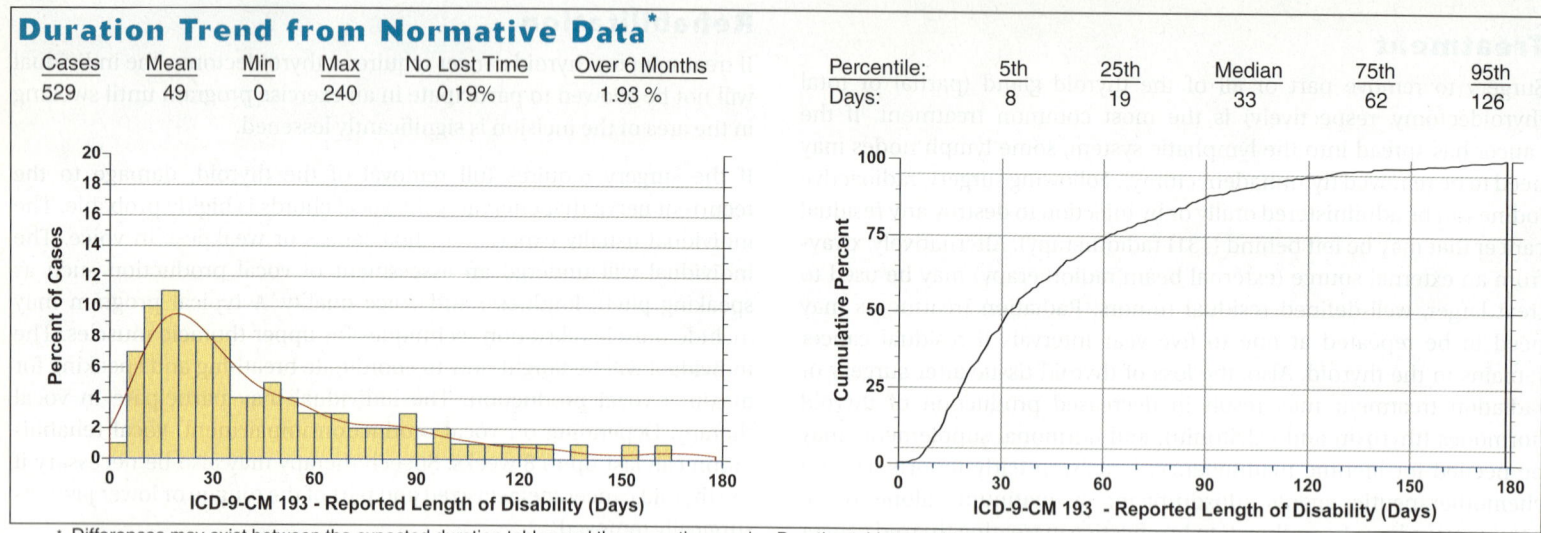

* Differences may exist between the expected duration tables and the normative graphs. Duration tables provide expected recovery periods based on the type of work performed by the individual. The normative graphs reflect the actual observed experience of many individuals across the spectrum of physical conditions, in a variety of industries, and with varying levels of case management.

Failure to Recover

If an individual fails to recover within the maximum duration expectancy period, the reader may wish to reference the following questions to assist in better understanding the specifics of an individual's medical case.

Regarding diagnosis:

- Does individual have family history of thyroid cancer?
- Was individual repeatedly exposed to external radiation?
- Does individual have low intake of dietary iodide, resulting in goiter?
- Is a single, firm, nontender lump (nodule) present at the base of the neck?
- Does individual complain of hoarseness or loss of voice or difficulty swallowing or breathing? Respiratory difficulties, cough, blood in the sputum (hemoptysis), chest pain, or bone pain, suggesting metastasis?
- Was the thyroid visualized on a gamma camera after injecting or swallowing a radioisotope? Was ultrasound done?
- Was a tissue sample (biopsy) from the thyroid obtained to confirm the diagnosis?
- Was a diagnosis of papillary, follicular, medullary, or anaplastic thyroid carcinoma confirmed?
- Has the thyroid cancer spread (metastasized) into other organ systems?

Regarding treatment:

- Was surgery done to remove part or all of the thyroid gland (partial or total thyroidectomy, respectively)?
- Did the cancer spread to the lymph nodes? If so, were they removed (lymphadenectomy)?
- Did individual receive radioactive iodine to destroy any residual cancer?

- Will individual require radiation treatments at 1- to 5-year intervals?
- Does individual require lifetime thyroid hormone (thyroxin and calcitonin) supplements?
- Would individual benefit from chemotherapy (doxorubicin; cis-platinum)?

Regarding prognosis:

- What type of thyroid cancer does individual have?
- Did treatment begin at an early stage of the cancer?
- Is this a recurrence?
- Has the cancer spread (metastasized)?
- Has individual developed flushing and diarrhea due to high concentrations of humoral secretions (serotonin, prostaglandins, calcitonin, histamine, vasoactive peptide) that affect the circulatory system?
- If individual has medullary cancer, has an adrenal gland tumor (pheochromocytoma) developed?
- If individual has anaplastic cancer, what is the expected survival time?

References

Audeh, M.W., L. Memsic, and A. Silberman. "Anaplastic Carcinoma, Lymphoma, Unusual Malignancies, and Chemotherapy for Thyroid Cancer." Thyroid Disease. Falk, S.A., ed. Philadelphia: Lippincott-Raven, 1997. 645-656.

Rosen, Clark, Deborah Anderson, and Thomas Murry. "Evaluating Hoarseness: Keeping Your Patient's Voice Healthy." American Family Physician June (1998): 13. 14 Jan 2001 <http://www.aafp.org/afp/980600ap/rosen.html>.

Cancer, Tongue

Other names / synonyms: Cancer of the Tongue, Lingual Cancer, Tongue Cancer
141, 141.0, 141.1, 141.2, 141.3, 141.4, 141.5, 141.6, 141.8, 141.9, 198.89, 230.0

Definition

Cancer of the tongue is a progressive and uncontrolled growth of cells of the tongue.

The most common type of tongue cancer is squamous cell carcinoma; other types are statistically uncommon. The tongue is divided into two separate anatomical areas: the oral tongue (the part that can be "stuck out," which extends back to a v-shaped group of lumps on the back of the tongue that are specialized taste buds), and the base of the tongue (behind these taste buds).

Most tongue cancers are found on the middle third of the side (lateral margin) of the oral tongue, and these often extend onto the bottom (ventral aspect) of the oral tongue. Approximately 20% occur on the front (anterior) third of the lateral margin, and only about 4% of occur on the top surface (dorsum) or the tip of the oral tongue. The tongue has an extensive circulatory and lymphatic supply and, consequently, the prognosis for individuals with tongue cancer is poor.

Risk factors for tongue cancer include poor oral hygiene with bacterial irritation; persistent physical trauma to the tongue such as from jagged teeth or improperly fitting dentures; smoking tobacco in any form or using smokeless tobacco or snuff; or syphilis. Infection with the human immunodeficiency virus (HIV) and development of acquired immune deficiency syndrome (AIDS) have implications for the occurrence of tongue cancer because the malignancies associated with HIV infection often appear in the mouth.

Tongue cancer occurs more frequently in men than women at a ratio of approximately 2 to 1, and is generally found in older men in their 60s and 70s. Cancer of the tongue accounts for about 25% of all oral cancers, and there are about 4,900 new cancer cases each year in the US. This incidence rate is exceeded in several other countries, including India, where the rate may be as high as 21 per 100,000 individuals.

Diagnosis

History: The individual usually reports an abnormal, outwardly growing (exophytic) lesion on the tongue that contains areas of open sores (ulceration). A few tongue cancers are without any symptoms (asymptomatic) in the early stages.

Cancer of the base of the tongue is usually larger when diagnosed because in the early stages it cannot be seen and creates few, if any, symptoms. In some cases, the cancer will spread quickly into the lymphatic system, and the individual may report only a lump in the neck. Later in the course of the disease, an ulcerated lesion that is several centimeters in diameter may be found. The individual usually complains of increasing pain, a sense of fullness, changes in what the voice sounds like, and speech and swallowing difficulty. The pain can be severe and constant, and may radiate to the neck and ears. There may be a history of cancer on the lips, inside the cheeks, on the roof of the mouth, or in the upper throat area.

Physical exam: A grayish lesion (ulcer) in the bottom of a furrow (fissure) or on the surface of the oral tongue may be evident. Patchy areas (lesions) that can be white or pink to red in color (leukoplakic) may or may not be associated with the ulcer. Later in the course of the disease, the ulcer may be hard in consistency with heaped-up (everted) edges. The floor of the ulcer may be grainy (granular), hardened (indurated), and may bleed easily. There are often other areas of dying tissue (necrosis) on the tongue. Infiltration (metastasis) of the cancer into the lymphatic system is common in later stages and many individuals will have enlarged lymph nodes that are detectable by touch (palpable).

Tests: Individual cells may be scraped from the tongue lesion and observed microscopically to determine if they are cancerous (exfoliate cytology). However, it may be necessary to perform this test more than once because it is not always conclusive. If exfoliate cytology indicates that the cells are cancerous or if the lesion looks suspiciously like cancer, a small piece of tissue may be taken from the lesion (incisional biopsy) and examined microscopically to determine if it is malignant. The lymph nodes may be biopsied if it is still unclear whether the primary tongue lesion is cancerous. In this case, the entire lymph node should be removed (excisional biopsy) and tested. Alternatively, a fine needle aspiration biopsy is an acceptable and accurate technique for identifying tongue lesions that have spread to the lymph nodes. After a tongue lesion has been identified as cancer, computer-aided x-ray analysis (computerized axial tomography, or CAT scan) or low-energy radio waves (magnetic resonance imaging, or MRI) can be used to determine the extent of tumor growth.

Treatment

Very small superficial lesions that have not spread can be treated by surgically removing (excision) part of the tongue (hemiglossectomy). The surgery should include removing at least 1 cm of healthy tissue around the lesion to ensure complete removal. Surgery on small oral tongue cancers has the advantage of rapid treatment, and still permits the use of radiation therapy as a treatment option should recurrence later develop (metastasize) into a different area of the oral cavity.

Treatment with x-rays to damage or destroy cancer cells (radiation therapy) is often used initially for intermediate stage tumors of oral or base of tongue cancers that may, if excised surgically, result in deformity or disability. Radiation treatment is usually performed by inserting radioactive substances into the tongue (interstitial irradiation). In some instances, radiation therapy will be used in combination with surgery. If radiation treatment fails or if the cancer has metastasized, more radical surgery is usually required, and the entire tongue may be removed (glossectomy). For advanced tumors, it is likely that metastases have spread into the lymphatic system or the bone, and surgical treatment frequently involves glossectomy along with removal of associated lymph nodes (lymphectomy). Portions of the lower jaw (mandible) may be removed (mandibulectomy) if the cancer has spread into this structure. Mandibulectomy is often carried out in conjunction with removal of part of the neck and throat (radical neck dissection). There may sometimes be the need to perform plastic surgery and/or reconstruction following tumor removal; radiation may need to be given after such surgery to minimize the possibility of recurrence.

Chemotherapy by itself has not been used successfully to treat tongue cancer. However, it has been used in combination with surgery or radiation therapy as an accessory treatment to moderate the intensity of the disease (palliative treatment). Results of clinical trials using chemotherapy in combination with surgery and/or radiation therapy to eliminate tongue cancer have so far been negative.

A support system, consisting of a clinical social worker and a vocational rehabilitation counselor, is usually necessary throughout the course of treatment until recovery is complete.

Prognosis

The predicted outcome of tongue cancer varies depending upon the stage of the lesion and the adequacy of the initial treatment. Early detection and prompt treatment is crucial to improving chances of survival, and the prognosis for early stage tumors is better with oral tongue cancer than with base of tongue cancer. The cancer may be completely cured by surgical intervention and/or radiation therapy. The individual's general health and coping abilities are important secondary factors. Local recurrence of early lesions after surgery is rare; however, the possibility of disease reappearance is enhanced considerably in individuals who smoke or chew tobacco. In more advanced tumors, recurrence may happen in 39% of cases. The outcome for more advanced tumors is not good if the cancer involves large areas of the tongue or if there has been metastases into the lymphatic system or other tissues.

Recent data indicates that the overall 5-year and 10-year survival rates are 65% and 53%, respectively, for individuals with oral tongue cancer. The 5-year survival rate for early stage tongue tumors that are treated with radiation only is better than eighty-five percent. Survival drops to 45-65% if both surgery and radiation therapy are needed for treatment of more advanced tumors. Individuals with very advanced tumors that have metastasized into the lymph or other tissues, and who are treated with a combination of surgery (if possible), radiation, and chemotherapy show a survival rate of close to 0% after 5 years.

Differential Diagnosis

Conditions that present with symptoms similar to tongue cancer include a multitude of ill-defined, variably appearing, harmless (benign) lesions that are found in the oral cavity. These may include various herpes viruses that produce cold sores on the tongue. Also, growth of harmless connective tissue (fibroma), fat cells (lipoma), nerve cells (neurofibroma), or blood vessel swelling (hemangioma) can produce lesions that look similar to tongue cancer. Chronic irritation of the tongue by physical, heat (thermal), or chemical factors may cause lesions (leukoplakia) that appear cancerous. Leukoplakia may also occur from other systemic factors such as poor nutrition or syphilis.

Specialists

- Dentist
- General Surgeon
- Occupational Therapist
- Oncologist
- Oral Surgeon
- Otolaryngologist
- Physical Therapist
- Psychiatrist
- Psychologist
- Radiation Oncologist
- Speech Pathologist
- Speech Therapist

Work Restrictions / Accommodations

Work accommodations may be required if the job requires verbal communication. Most individuals will need more sedentary work for a period of time due to weakness and fatigue following surgery, radiation therapy, or chemotherapy. Frequent breaks may be needed, and heavy or prolonged physical exertion may have to be avoided until recovery is complete. Individuals who have had disfiguring surgery may have difficulty returning to the normal work place, and sensitivity to this should be a consideration. However, in the absence of other physical disabilities, medical complications, or emotional problems, individuals who have had treatment for tongue cancer should be able to return to their previous duties after a period of recovery. Time off may be necessary for psychiatric or psychological counseling, or follow-up medical appointments.

Comorbid Conditions

Infection with the human immunodeficiency virus (HIV) and subsequent development of acquired immune deficiency syndrome (AIDS) usually leaves an individual susceptible to development of tongue cancer. Following removal of a cancerous lesion from the tongue, secondary lesions have occurred to a higher extent in individuals infected with human papillomavirus (HPV) and women who have cervical cancer. Diabetes and high blood pressure (hypertension) have been associated with erosive oral lichen planus (OLP), which may be precancerous in nature.

Complications

Cancer of the tongue may be complicated if it spreads to other areas of the mouth and throat because large tumors may impair tongue function by creating rigidity in tongue muscles.

Other complications may include infections in the blood stream (sepsis), bleeding, general systemic infections (septicemia or pneumonia), dental disease, loss of appetite (anorexia) and weight loss (cachexia), facial paralysis, loss of chewing (masticatory) ability, abnormal enlargement of jaw and facial features due to tumor growth, and low hemoglobin content in the blood (anemia). Severe bleeding (hemorrhage) may occur as the tumor destroys blood vessels that lie in close proximity to the tongue and mouth. Other cancers may develop if a tongue cancer tumor spreads (metastasizes) into the lymph system. Hodgkin's disease, non-Hodgkin's lymphoma, Burkitt's lymphoma, and multiple myeloma may develop; weight loss, itching (pruritus), fatigue, and mortality are also associated with these diseases.

Factors Influencing Duration

The length of disability will be influenced by the location of the cancer in the tongue and by the degree of metastasis into the mouth or throat. Other factors that might influence the length of disability include age, the use of tobacco and alcohol, socioeconomic status, stage of the disease upon detection, access to adequate health care, type and extent of treatment for the disease, and mental health of the individual during treatment and recovery. The individual's willingness to adapt to a different lifestyle by abstaining from tobacco and alcohol (if a consideration), and their ability to re-integrate themselves into society and the workplace following treatment, will have a major impact on the length of disability. Some tongue cancers may require follow-up surgery to restore function, and plastic or restorative surgery to assist with disfigurement.

Length of Disability

The duration of disability may depend on the location and size of cancer, treatment, and requirements of the job. Disability may be permanent.

Failure to Recover

If an individual fails to recover within the maximum duration expectancy period, the reader may wish to reference the following questions to assist in better understanding the specifics of an individual's medical case.

Regarding diagnosis:

- Does individual have poor oral hygiene?
- Has individual had persistent physical trauma to the tongue?
- Does individual use tobacco in any form? Alcohol or spicy food?
- Does individual have syphilis? Cirrhosis of the liver? AIDS?
- Is an abnormal ulcerated lesion on the tongue present?
- Does individual have pain or a sense of fullness?
- Did individual's voice change? Is speech difficult?
- Has individual experienced trouble swallowing?
- Does individual have severe and constant pain? Does it radiate?
- Does individual have a history of cancer anywhere near the tongue?
- Was exfoliate cytology done? Biopsy? Lymph node biopsy? Were CT or MRI performed?
- Were conditions with similar symptoms ruled out?

Regarding treatment:

- Was the tumor detected and treated early?
- Was the lesion small and superficial? Did individual have a hemiglossectomy done?
- Was the tumor more advanced? Was a glossectomy and lymphectomy done?
- Did individual have radiation therapy?
- Was it necessary to do a mandibulectomy with radical neck resections?
- Was plastic or reconstructive surgery needed?
- Was chemotherapy used with surgery and radiation? As palliative treatment?

Regarding prognosis:

- Is individual active in a rehabilitation program?
- Can individual's employer accommodate any necessary restrictions?
- At what stage was the tumor when diagnosed and treated?
- Has individual stopped the use of all forms of tobacco?

References

Beumer, J., III, I. Zlotolow, and T.A. Curtis. "Rehabilitation." Oral Cancer. Silverman, S., Jr., ed. Atlanta: The American Cancer Society, 1990. 127-148.

LeMone, P., and K.M. Burke. Medical-Surgical Nursing. Upper Saddle River, NJ: Prentice Hall Health, 2000.

Cancer, Uterus

Other names / synonyms: Cancer of the Uterus, Endometrial Cancer, Endometrial Carcinoma, Uterine Cancer, Uterine Sarcoma

179, 182, 182.0, 182.1, 182.8, 233.2, 236.0

Definition

Uterine cancer occurs when cancerous cells develop in the uterus. When the cancer arises from the lining of the uterus (endometrium), it is referred to as endometrial carcinoma. When the cancer arises in the muscle or other supporting tissues of the uterus, it is referred to as uterine sarcoma.

The cause of uterine cancer remains unknown. The disease has been shown to be more common in women who have experienced prolonged periods of estrogen exposure without progesterone to balance its effects. Risk factors, which are similar to those of breast cancer, are found in women who have had few or no children (pregnancy produces a flow of progesterone), who have experienced early menstruation and/or late menopause (after age 52), who have taken estrogen replacement therapy (ERT) without supplemental progestin (progestin is a hormone that prepares the uterus for egg implantation and pregnancy), who have a history of pelvic radiation therapy, those who have had tamoxifen therapy (tamoxifen is a drug used in breast cancer treatment and/or its prevention). Other risks include obesity, a history of diabetes and high blood pressure, a history of other cancers, an abnormal increase in the number of cells that line the uterus (a benign condition called endometrial hyperplasia that is considered a precancerous condition), lack of menstruation for extended periods of time, as sometimes occurs in obese or extremely thin women. There is preliminary evidence suggesting that women who eat a diet high in fat increase their risk of developing uterine cancer. White women have a higher incidence of uterine cancer than do black women.

Factors associated with lower risk of uterine cancer include having multiple children, use of oral contraceptives that combine both estrogen and progestin, and taking ERT combined with progesterone during menopause.

Endometrial carcinoma is the most common female genital cancer, accounting for 13% of all cancers in women. Uterine sarcoma accounts for less than 1% of gynecological malignancies. Uterine cancer, the third most common cancer in women, is rarely seen in women under the age of 50, and the risk rises sharply for women in their late 40s to mid-60s.

Diagnosis

History: Most women with uterine cancer do not experience symptoms. A small number report abnormal (such as postmenopausal) uterine bleeding, ranging from minor watery blood-tinged discharge or spotting that gradually increases in amount to heavy hemorrhage; painful or difficult urination or pain during intercourse may also be experienced. Women with late-stage disease may experience pain, weight loss, general weakness, changes in bowel and bladder habits, and pain in the pelvic area, back, or legs.

Physical exam: The doctor performs a pelvic exam where he or she checks the vagina, uterus, ovaries, bladder, and rectum for lumps or changes in shape or size. Also performed during the pelvic exam is the Pap test in which a sampling of cells is collected from the cervix and upper vagina and sent to a medical laboratory to be evaluated for cancer cells, abnormal cells (hyperplasia), or other abnormalities.

Tests: The doctor performs a battery of tests that include transvaginal ultrasound, blood tests of liver and kidney function, CT and MRI scans of the pelvis and abdomen, and tests to determine possible cancer spread beyond the uterus (metastasis) such as intravenous pyelogram (IVP), chest and skeletal x-rays, barium enema, cystoscopy, sigmoidoscopy, and lymphangiography. In addition to an endometrial biopsy where a sample of tissue is removed from inner and outer layers in the uterus, some women require a procedure where tissue is scraped from the lining of the uterus (D & C, or dilation and curettage). At this time, there are no standard tests to screen for early-stage uterine cancer. The Pap test, which is highly effective in detecting precancerous and cancerous (premalignant and malignant) changes in the cervix, is of limited use in diagnosing uterine cancer because it examines only cells from the inside of the cervix. The pelvic exam, on the other hand, can be helpful in the diagnosis.

Treatment

The choice of treatment depends on the size of the tumor, the stage of the disease, whether female hormones affect tumor growth, and tumor grade. (The tumor grade tells how closely the cancer resembles normal cells, and suggests how fast the cancer is likely to grow). Other factors considered when planning treatment are the woman's age and her general health.

Most women with uterine cancer are treated with surgery whereby the cancerous tumors are removed. Three types of surgery are: removal of the uterus (partial hysterectomy), removal of the fallopian tubes and ovaries (bilateral salpingo-oophorectomy), or removal of the uterus, along with the cervix, the upper vagina, and most of the tissue around the cervix (total hysterectomy). Lymph nodes near the tumor will also be removed and examined to see if they are cancerous. After examination of the surgically removed tumor and other affected organs and tissues, surgical staging is done to determine whether the cancer has spread and, if it has, to determine what other parts of the body are affected. If pathology tests show the cancer has not spread (metastasis) beyond the mucous lining of the uterus (endometrium), surgery may be the only treatment needed for an effective cure.

After surgery, many women whose cancer has spread are treated with high energy x-rays that have the potential to kill cancer cells (radiation therapy) in the affected area. In some cases, radiation is used before surgery to shrink the tumor. And, for a small number of women who cannot have surgery, radiation therapy is the mainstay of the treatment process.

Some are treated with anticancer drugs (chemotherapy) that kill the cancer cells. Chemotherapeutic drugs are most often administered intravenously (IV), and less frequently by mouth or by injection. A smaller number of women are given hormone therapy, such as progesterone-based therapy. Progesterone, given orally, prevents cancer cells from obtaining the hormones they need to grow. It is prepared from natural or synthetic progesterone, a hormone that is produced by the corpus luteum of the ovary and by the placenta. Both chemotherapy and hormone therapy are referred to as systemic treatments because the therapy agent travels through the body via the blood stream.

The type of treatment given is tailored to the five stages of the disease:

Stage 0 (Endometrial carcinoma confined to surface layer of endometrium): For women past child bearing age, some doctors recommend a procedure where the inside of the uterus is scraped (D & C, or dilation and curettage); this is followed by hormone treatment with progestins, one of several steroid hormones that prepares the uterus for egg implantation and pregnancy.

Stage I (Endometrial cancer confined to the uterus). Surgery: a total hysterectomy is done unless preoperative radiation reduces the size of tumor; then only a partial hysterectomy will be performed.

Stage II (Endometrial carcinoma spread to the cervix). Surgery: a total hysterectomy is done unless preoperative radiation reduces the size of tumor, then only a partial hysterectomy will be performed.

Stage III (Endometrial carcinoma spread outside uterus but remains within pelvis). Inoperable: radiation therapy is the treatment of choice.

Stage IV (Endometrial carcinoma spread to bladder, rectum, and other parts of the body including regional lymph nodes). Inoperable: radiation therapy is done if the cancer spread is limited to pelvis; distant metastases are treated with hormone therapy (progesterone) or radiation therapy.

Most stages of uterine sarcoma are treated with total hysterectomy with or without removal of the fallopian tubes and ovaries (depending on the woman's age and extent of the disease) along with removal of local lymph nodes. Some oncologists suggest supplemental (adjuvant) therapy, such as chemotherapy or radiation administered postoperatively, because risk of recurrence is high for uterine sarcoma.

Psychiatric or psychological counseling or intervention may be required because of the severity and life-threatening nature of this disease when it is generally diagnosed.

Prognosis

The most significant predictor of outcome is the stage of the cancer at the time of diagnosis. Uterine cancers are staged (Stages 0-IV) according to whether they are still localized (remaining in the uterus) or have spread beyond the uterus. The 5-year survival rates for the stages of endometrial cancer are:

Stage 0 (Cancer confined to uterine lining): nearly 100%

Stage I (Cancer confined to uterus): 75-100%

Stage II (Cancer spread to cervix): 60%

Stage III (Cancer spread outside uterus but remains in cervix): 30%

Stage IV (Cancer spread to other parts of the body including regional lymph nodes): 5%

The predicted outcome in Stages 0 and I, when the uterus has been surgically removed (hysterectomy) and the cancer confined to the uterus, is good and full recovery is anticipated.

The predicted outcome for treating stages of uterine cancer that has spread outside the uterus (Stages II - IV) with a hysterectomy is not as good and generally not done. Even when adjuvant therapies, such as chemotherapy and radiation are used, full recovery is not usually expected.

Uterine sarcoma is not as amenable to successful therapy. The 5-year survival rates are: Stage I: 50%; Stage II: 20%; Stage III: 10%; and Stage IV: 5% survival rate.

Surgical removal of the uterus, with or without removal of the ovaries and fallopian tubes, is used to treat most stages of uterine sarcoma. Even with adjuvant therapies such as chemotherapy and radiation, the outcome of surgical treatment of uterine sarcomas is not as good as that of uterine carcinoma. Optimism for full recovery from uterine sarcoma, especially when the disease has progressed to Stages II-IV, is low.

When uterine carcinoma and uterine sarcoma are considered together, survival rates for uterine cancer are generally quite high, especially if the disease is detected in an early stage. Overall 5-year survival rate, regardless of stage at detection, is 83%. This rate increases to 94% for disease that is detected and treated when the cancer is confined to the uterus. Survival for disease that has spread beyond the uterus drops to 67%.

Differential Diagnosis

Differential diagnosis might include uterine polyps, fibroid tumors, infection, ovarian cysts, or abnormal or irregular postmenopausal bleeding.

Specialists

• General Surgeon	• Oncologist
• Gynecologist	• Radiation Oncologist

Work Restrictions / Accommodations

Women recovering from surgery, or undergoing chemotherapy or radiation therapy, may require a place to rest periodically at the work site. Workplace responsibilities should initially be mostly sedentary. Accommodations for women undergoing chemotherapy and/or radiation therapy may include leave time from work to receive necessary treatments, as well as additional leave to permit adequate recovery time following treatment.

Comorbid Conditions

Comorbid conditions that might influence the length of disability may include obesity or excessive thinness, diabetes, personal medical history, and allergy to treatment medications.

Existing conditions such as obesity or excessive thinness, chronic illness (i.e., heart condition or diabetes), and allergy to treatment medications, often add to the debilitation from the disease and from the treatment.

Complications

Complications of uterine cancer are caused by the spread of the cancer to other organs and progressive functional loss of the affected organs. Some complications include bowel obstruction, urinary obstruction, and fluid collection in the abdominal area (ascites). Bowel and urinary obstructions could result in the surgical removal of the bowel and urinary tract. The symptoms of abdominal ascites depend on the amount of fluid in the space; the symptoms will increase as more fluid accumulates. Among the most common manifestations of uterine cancer are abdominal enlargement (distention), loss of appetite, shortness of breath, abdominal pain, low blood pressure, weakness and fatigue.

In addition, surgical complications include infection of the surgical site, blood clotting disruption, increased risk of blood clots (thrombosis) involving major veins in the pelvis and lower extremities, and damage to the urethra. Radiation therapy may cause urinary incontinence, bowel problems, and damage to some of the organs surrounding the uterus. Complications of chemotherapy include loss of appetite, weight loss, hair loss, nausea, vomiting, dehydration, electrolyte imbalance, extreme fatigue, and general feelings of ill health. In addition, there may be psychological complications such as loss of self-esteem, depression, loss of a woman's sense of sexuality, fear of pain, and fear of dying. Early detection and treatment of uterine cancer minimizes complications. However, women with advanced stage disease and/or generally poor health prior to treatment are likely to experience more serious complications.

Factors Influencing Duration

Factors influencing the length of disability include the woman's age, the type and stage of disease at initial presentation, the presence of concurrent infection, overall general health, side effects of treatment modalities, and the presence of complications. Older women, women in poor health, and women with disease that has spread outside the uterus, will require the longest period of time for recovery and may become permanently disabled. Chemotherapy and radiation therapy will extend the period of disability as much as 6 additional months. Resulting disability may be permanent.

Length of Disability

Duration depends on stage, grade, cell type, adjuvant chemotherapy or radiation therapy. Disability may be permanent. Durations reflect recovery period for procedures only.

Abdominal hysterectomy.

Duration in Days

Job Classification	Minimum	Optimum	Maximum
Sedentary work	28	42	56
Light work	28	42	56
Medium work	42	56	70
Heavy work	42	70	84
Very Heavy work	42	84	98

Radical hysterectomy.

Duration in Days

Job Classification	Minimum	Optimum	Maximum
Sedentary work	42	49	56
Light work	56	63	70
Medium work	70	77	84
Heavy work	70	84	98
Very Heavy work	70	84	98

Failure to Recover

If an individual fails to recover within the maximum duration expectancy period, the reader may wish to reference the following questions to assist in better understanding the specifics of an individual's medical case.

Regarding diagnosis:

- Does individual have a history of early menstruation and/or late menopause? History of pelvic radiation therapy or tamoxifen therapy? Diabetes, high blood pressure, other cancers, or no menstruation for extended periods of time (amenorrhea)?
- Does individual have few or no children?
- Has individual taken estrogen replacement therapy (ERT) without supplemental progestin?
- Does individual report abnormal (i.e., postmenopausal) uterine bleeding ranging from minor watery blood-tinged discharge or spotting to heavy hemorrhage?
- Does individual complain of painful or difficult urination or pain during intercourse? Weight loss, general weakness, changes in bowel and bladder habits, or pain in the pelvic area, back, or legs?
- Was a transvaginal ultrasound done? Were blood tests for liver and kidney function taken? Were CT and MRI of the pelvis and abdomen done? Did individual require tests to determine possible cancer spread (metastasis) such as intravenous pyelogram (IVP), chest and skeletal x-rays, barium enema, cystoscopy, sigmoidoscopy, and lymphangiography? Was an endometrial biopsy obtained or did individual have a dilation and curettage (D & C)?

Regarding treatment:

- What type of surgery did individual undergo? Removal of the uterus (partial hysterectomy), removal of fallopian tubes and ovaries (bilateral salpingo-oophorectomy), or removal of the uterus, cervix, upper vagina, and most of the tissue around the cervix (total hysterectomy)?
- Has the cancer spread (metastasized)? If so, how extensive is the metastasis?
- Does individual require treatment with high energy x-rays (radiation therapy)?
- Does individual require treatment with anticancer drugs (chemotherapy) or hormone therapy such as progesterone-based therapy?
- Does individual require psychological counseling or intervention to understand and cope with the nature of this disease?

Regarding prognosis:

- Of stages 0-IV for uterine cancer, what stage is individual's cancer classified (according to whether cancer cells are localized or have spread beyond the uterus)?
- Have complications occurred as a result of surgery, chemotherapy, or radiation therapy? As a result of the cancer metastasizing? Psychological complications?
- What is the treatment plan for complications? How will complications affect individual's activities of daily living?

References

Cancer of the Uterus. National Institute of Health - National Cancer Institute. 28 Oct 1998. 01 Jul 2000 <http://cancernet.nci.nih.gov/wyntk_pubs/uterus.htm>.

Understanding Hysterectomy. Berlex Laboratories. 22 Apr 1999. 03 Jul 2000 <http://www.womenslifestages.com/j_hysterectomy.html>.

Brannon, Linda, and Jess Feist. "Living with Chronic Illness." Health Psychology. King, Kenneth, ed. Belmont: Wadsworth, 1992. 275-315.

Guccione, Andrew. "Functional Assessment." Physical Rehabilitation: Assessment and Treatment. O'Sullivan, Susan B., and Thomas J. Schmitz, eds. Philadelphia: F.A. Davis Company, 1994. 193-208.

McCance, Kathryn L., and Lee K. Roberts. "Tumor Biology." Pathophysiology. McCance, Kathryn L., and Sue E. Heuther, eds. St. Louis: Mosby, 1994. 321-365.

Murphy, Gerald P., Lois B. Morris, and Dianne Lange. The American Cancer Society's Informed Decisions; The Complete Book of Cancer Diagnosis, Treatment, and Recovery. New York: Viking, 1997.

Candidiasis

Other names / synonyms: Candidosis, Moniliasis, Thrush, Yeast Infection
112, 112.0, 112.1, 112.2, 112.3, 112.5, 112.8, 112.9

Definition

Candidiasis is a general term to describe a variety of yeast infections typically caused by Candida albicans. Other Candida species, however, can also cause candidiasis. This yeast is normally present in the mouth, vagina, and feces, but the amount of yeast is kept in balance by the presence of normal bacteria in those areas.

Under certain abnormal conditions, the yeast can overgrow and cause infection of the outer layers of the skin and mucous membranes. A common condition leading to yeast overgrowth and infection is when the normal bacterial population is decreased by the use of antibiotics. Other conditions promote the growth of yeast without involving the bacterial population. These conditions include pregnancy, use of corticosteroids, HIV infection, and some metabolic infections such as diabetes or thyroid disorders.

Yeast overgrowth and infection may occur in the mouth (oral thrush), in the vagina or penis (genital candidiasis), between folds and surfaces of skin (intertrigo), and in and around the nails (paronychia and onychomycosis). Infection may also cause lesions in the esophagus, stomach, or intestine.

In some cases, the yeast enters the bloodstream and causes invasive disease affecting internal body organs, such as the kidney, spleen, lung, liver, eye, meninges, brain, and heart valves. This is called systemic or deep candidiasis. Individuals at risk for this type of infection include those who have a weakened immune system (such as individuals with AIDS, transplant recipients, or those who take immunosuppressive medication), those who have an indwelling intravenous catheter, low numbers of infection-fighting white blood cells (neutropenia), or malignancies of the blood. Individuals who have recently undergone surgery are also at an increased risk. Candidiasis of the urinary tract is a complication of urinary catheterization.

Individuals who develop infections typically develop them from infections from the yeast organisms carried inside their bodies. Some individuals, however, develop infection from Candida species that live outside the human body, in the environment or on inanimate objects. Candida yeast may also be passed from individual to individual through intimate contact.

Genital candidiasis in women (vulvovaginitis) is the second most common cause of vaginitis in women. Approximately 75% of women have had at least one episode. It is most common in women who are in their third trimester of pregnancy, have diabetes, or have recently taken antibiotics, birth-control pills, or corticosteroid medication. In adults, oral thrush is typically seen as an opportunistic infection in individuals with weakened immune systems. Up to 80% of HIV-infected individuals experience candidiasis of the mouth or throat. It also is seen in individuals who wear dentures, or who have a chronic, dry mouth caused by atrophy of the saliva glands (xerostomia). Candidiasis in the bloodstream (candidemia) occurs in 8 of every 100,000 individuals per year. It is the fourth most common cause of blood infection among hospitalized individuals in the US.

Diagnosis

History: Symptoms vary based on the location of the infection. Oral thrush causes a white coating to cover the tongue. In the esophagus (esophagitis), candidiasis may cause chest pain or difficulty swallowing. Genital candidiasis in women (vulvovaginitis) results in a white vaginal discharge, and swelling, redness, itching, and irritation of the genital area. Symptoms are typically more intense the week preceding the onset of menstrual bleeding. Genital candidiasis in men (balanitis) may produce a discharge from the penis. Candidiasis in the bloodstream produces fever and chills, and characteristic lesions on the trunk, arms, and legs.

Physical exam: Thrush appears as white or yellow curd-like patches in the mouth, usually starting with the tongue or inside the cheeks. When the patches are scraped off, the membranes are raw and bleed. The corners of the mouth may be inflamed. It may spread to the rest of the mouth as well as the tonsils, throat, larynx, esophagus, and respiratory system.

Vulvovaginitis is indicated by white cheese-like vaginal discharge, presence of pustular lesions in the vaginal area, and redness and swelling. The cervix typically appears normal. In men, the glans penis may be reddish with small blisters or ulcers. In more severe cases, the foreskin may be swollen, causing it to tighten over the penis (phimosis).

Skin infections appear as red, slightly swollen patches that may itch and ooze. Small red blisters may surround the patches. Skin infections are most commonly located in the skin folds, such as the armpits, navel, groin, buttocks, between the toes and fingers, or beneath the breasts. It may also affect the scalp and fingernails.

Fingernail infections start with painful red inflammation that may develop pus, or it may be located beneath the fingernail, causing the fingernail to loosen to expose a noticeably white or yellow color underneath it.

Other physical findings are related to involvement of other organs. For example, involvement of the eye is evidenced by specific findings from an eye examination.

Tests: Discharge from the vagina or penis, and scrapings from a thrush-coated tongue or from a superficial skin or nail lesion can be examined under a microscope to identify the yeast. A tissue biopsy of a lesion may also be examined microscopically for Candida. The diagnosis is confirmed by culture of the scrapings or discharge. Blood or tissue cultures are performed to rule out invasive candidiasis. Blood cultures, however, are negative in 50% of individuals with invasive infection. In these cases, tissue culture is necessary.

Treatment

Candidiasis is treated with either a topical or systemic antifungal medication, depending on the type of infection. If candidiasis is associated with another disorder such as diabetes mellitus or a blood malignancy, the underlying disease must be treated. If the infection is associated with use of antibiotics, medication should be stopped, if possible. If the infection was introduced through an indwelling catheter, the catheter should be removed or changed. If an artificial heart valve is infected, it must be removed as well.

Thrush is treated with antifungal mouth rinses. Antifungal powder may be used on dentures. Antifungal drugs are used for skin and fingernail infections. The skin needs to be kept dry and exposed to the air as much as possible. If the fingernail infection is persistent and has caused the nail to be deformed, the nail may need to be removed.

In women, genital candidiasis is treated with an antifungal ointment or suppository placed in the vagina. Gentian violet solution or boric acid tablets may also be effective. Other predisposing factors, such as using oral contraceptives, may need to be reevaluated. Some women may have recurrent episodes of vulvovaginitis that are difficult to treat. In men, an antifungal ointment may be used. If reinfection occurs, an individual's sexual partner may need to be treated.

For systemic infections, intravenous or oral antifungal drugs are used.

Prognosis

Prognosis may depend on the condition that precipitated candidiasis: its severity, chronicity, and treatability. Genital candidiasis typically responds to treatment within several days. Oral candidiasis (thrush) is often difficult to treat, particularly in individuals with AIDS, who often have an incomplete recovery following treatment. Outcome of invasive disease depends on extent of and site of infection. Dissemination is more likely and the outcome more serious when the individual has a progressive fatal underlying disease. Infection in the bloodstream (candidemia) has a high mortality rate, forty to sixty percent. Mortality rate is lower if the infection is introduced through an indwelling catheter rather than attributed to underlying disease.

Differential Diagnosis

Candidiasis of the skin must be differentiated from other skin infections, such as seborrhea dermatitis, tinea cruris (jock itch), psoriasis, and erythrasma. In men and women, genital candidiasis may resemble a urinary tract infection. In women, it shares symptoms with bacterial vaginosis or trichomoniasis.

Specialists

- Dermatologist
- Gynecologist
- Internist

Work Restrictions / Accommodations

Individuals should avoid hot, humid atmospheres and chemical exposures that can be secondarily irritating to the skin. Individuals with candidiasis affecting the nails should avoid keeping their hands in water for long periods of time.

Candida yeast can be passed from person to person through hand contact in medical settings. Infection control precautions should be practiced when cross-contamination between individuals is a possibility.

Comorbid Conditions

Conditions that weaken the immune system (AIDS, taking immunosuppressive drugs, organ transplant), conditions that require indwelling catheters or artificial heart valves, malignancy, and diabetes or other metabolic disorders lengthen disability.

Complications

Complications usually occur in those who are severely debilitated or whose immune systems are either deficient (AIDS) or suppressed (taking drugs to prevent rejection of an organ transplant). In such individuals, candidiasis may spread to the lungs, bladder, bone, esophagus, and other internal organs.

Factors Influencing Duration

Presence of serious underlying disease, candidiasis in the blood, and rapidity of treatment if infection is in the blood are factors that influence length of disability.

Length of Disability

Duration depends on site.

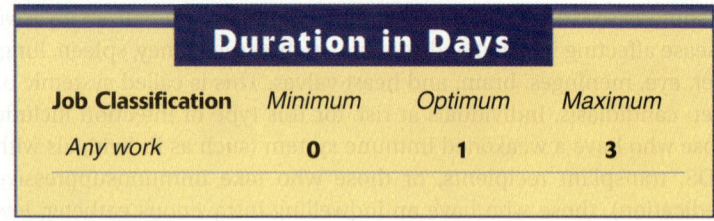

Job Classification	Minimum	Optimum	Maximum
Any work	0	1	3

Failure to Recover

If an individual fails to recover within the maximum duration expectancy period, the reader may wish to reference the following questions to assist in better understanding the specifics of an individual's medical case.

Regarding diagnosis:

- Does individual have a weakened immune system?
- Does individual have an indwelling IV catheter? Artificial heart valve?
- Does individual have neutropenia? Malignancies of the blood?
- Has individual recently had surgery?

- Is individual in the third trimester of pregnancy? Diabetic?
- Has individual recently taken antibiotics? Birth control pills? Corticosteroids?
- Does individual have a white coating covering the tongue?
- Does individual have chest pain or difficulty swallowing?
- Does individual have a white vaginal discharge? Swelling? Redness? Itching? Irritation?
- Is there discharge from the penis?
- Does individual have fever and chills?
- Do lesions occur on the trunk, arms, and legs?
- Was the discharge or skin scraping examined microscopically?
- Did individual have cultures of the scrapings or discharge? Blood?
- Were conditions with similar symptoms ruled out?

Regarding treatment:

- Was individual treated with either a topical or systemic antifungal medication?
- If individual has an underlying disease, is it being treated?
- If individual was on antibiotics, were they stopped?
- Was an indwelling catheter removed or changed?
- Was the artificial heart valve removed?

Regarding prognosis:

- Can individual's employer accommodate any necessary restrictions?
- Does individual have any conditions that could affect ability to recover?
- Has the candidiasis spread to other parts of the body?

References

Candidiasis. Centers for Disease Control and Prevention, Division of Bacterial and Mycotic Diseases. 06 Apr 2000. 01 Jan 2001 <http://www.cdc.gov/ncidod/dbmd/diseaseinfo/candidiasis_t.htm>.

Chin, James. Control of Communicable Diseases Manual, 17th ed. Washington, DC: American Public Health Association, 2000.

Dismukes, William. "Candidiasis." Cecil Textbook of Medicine, 21st ed. Goldman, Lee, and J. Claude Bennett, eds. Philadelphia: W.B. Saunders Company, 2000. 1871-1875.

Fotos, Pete, and Jeffrey Lilly. "Clinical Management of Oral and Perioral Candidosis." Dermatologic Clinics 14 2 (1996): 273-280.

Noyer, Charles, and Douglas Simon. "Oral and Esophageal Disorders." Gastroenterology Clinics 26 2 (1997): 241-257.

Nyirjesy, P., et al. "Over-the-counter and Alternative Medicines in the Treatment of Chronic Vaginal Symptoms." Obstetrical Gynecology 90 1 (1997): 50-53.

Carbuncle
680, 680.1, 680.2, 680.5, 680.9

Definition

A carbuncle is a cluster of boils (furuncles) that are interconnected under the skin. Boils are pus-filled hair follicles caused by infection by bacteria, usually Staphylococcus aureus. If a boil is neglected or mishandled (picked or squeezed), the infection can spread throughout the skin and cause a carbuncle.

Carbuncles commonly appear on the nape of the neck, upper back, and buttocks. Carbuncles are less common than single boils. They develop slowly and may not reach the skin's surface on their own to drain. The infecting bacteria can spread to other parts of the body, producing a potentially serious condition.

Men are more prone than women to get carbuncles. Individuals who are at risk for developing carbuncles include those who have acne, dermatitis, Job's syndrome, diabetes mellitus, pernicious anemia, a lowered resistance to infection (immunodeficient), and those who are elderly, malnourished, or obese. Carbuncles are also more likely to occur under conditions of poor hygiene, friction by clothing, or moist skin (maceration).

Although the exact incidence of carbuncles is unknown, they are not common.

Diagnosis

History: The individual may complain of a very large and extremely painful lump that may or may not be draining pus. The individual may report episodes of fever and extreme exhaustion (prostration).

Physical exam: The diagnosis is usually made by visual inspection of the affected area. A carbuncle initially presents as a painful lump (nodule), at first covered by tight, reddened skin that later becomes thin and develops holes (perforates), discharging a foul-smelling pus from several openings.

Tests: Occasionally, laboratory culture of the pus is necessary to identify the causative bacteria and determine antibiotic sensitivities. Routine blood tests may show an increase in the number of leukocytes in the blood (leukocytosis). Further tests of the blood and urine may be necessary if the physician suspects an underlying disorder (diabetes or immunodeficiency disease).

Treatment

Carbuncles may be treated with oral antibiotics, especially those that persist or are located on the face or spine. Hot compresses (cotton soaked in hot salty water) or plasters may be used to cause the pus-filled heads to burst, relieving the pain. If drainage and healing does not occur, surgical drainage (with removal of the core of the carbuncle) and possibly packing may be necessary. Continued spread of the infection would require intravenous antibiotics.

Prognosis

Although complete recovery is likely, outcome is dependent on the severity of the infection, response to treatment, and the individual's ability to resist infection. Any carbuncle that persists longer than 2 weeks might spread the infection to the bloodstream (septicemia) and internal organs. Internal Staphylococcal infections are life threatening.

Recurrence is possible and may affect individuals for months or years. A carbuncle can lead to permanent scarring.

Differential Diagnosis

Conditions with similar skin lesions include inflamed epidermal inclusion cyst, tinea profunda, conglobate acne, hidradenitis suppurativa, deep fungal infection, and botfly infestation.

Specialists

- Dermatologist
- General Surgeon
- Infectious Disease Physician

Work Restrictions / Accommodations

Depending on the location of the carbuncle, excessive sitting or walking may need to be restricted, and the use of personal protective equipment (respirator) may be affected.

Complementary and Alternative Therapies

Content is intended for awareness only. Treatments may or may not be effective. Scientific evidence may be lacking and some substances have potentially toxic effects. Dr. Presley Reed and the editors do not endorse the use of these therapies in the absence of consultation with a licensed medical professional.

Lu-Shen-Wan - A Chinese herbal medicine, which contains 6 ingredients, is sometimes applied topically to treat boils, carbuncles, and other skin infections. One ingredient, Venenum Bufonis, has caused contact dermatitis. When the concentration of this ingredient is reduced, this problem resolves.

Comorbid Conditions

Diabetes, obesity, and immunodeficiency diseases (e.g., AIDS and certain cancers) may increase the length of disability.

Complications

Carbuncles can progress to cellulitis, kidney (perinephric) abscess, bone inflammation (osteomyelitis), or leg vein inflammation associated with clot formation (thrombophlebitis). A carbuncle on or near the nose, cheeks, forehead, or spine can spread even more rapidly and form a brain or spinal abscess.

Factors Influencing Duration

The location and size of the carbuncle, severity of pain, spreading of the infection, and response to treatment may influence length of disability.

Length of Disability

Duration of disability depends upon site of carbuncle and job requirements. Disability may be longer for individuals whose jobs require a great deal of concentration (carbuncle causes extreme pain, which can be distracting).

Duration in Days

Job Classification	Minimum	Optimum	Maximum
Any work	0	1	3

Failure to Recover

If an individual fails to recover within the maximum duration expectancy period, the reader may wish to reference the following questions to assist in better understanding the specifics of an individual's medical case.

Regarding diagnosis:

- Was a boil neglected, picked, or squeezed?
- Does the individual have acne, dermatitis, Job's syndrome, diabetes mellitus, pernicious anemia, or immunodeficiency disorders?
- Is the individual elderly, malnourished, or obese?
- Does the individual have poor hygiene or maceration of the skin?
- Does the individual complain of a very large and extremely painful lump that may or may not be draining pus?
- Does the individual report episodes of fever and extreme exhaustion?
- Did the carbuncle initially present as a nodule, at first covered by tight, reddened skin that later perforates, discharging foul-smelling pus from several openings?
- Was a culture and sensitivity of the pus done?
- Were routine blood tests done?
- Were further tests to rule out an underlying disorder?
- Have conditions with similar symptoms been ruled out?

Regarding treatment:

- Has the individual been treated with oral antibiotics?
- Did the individual respond favorably to hot compresses?
- Was surgical drainage with removal of the core of the carbuncle necessary?

Regarding prognosis:

- Is the individual's employer able to accommodate any necessary restrictions?
- Does the individual have any conditions that may affect their ability to recover?
- Does the individual have any complications such as cellulitis, perinephric abscess, osteomyelitis, or thrombophlebitis?
- Was the carbuncle on or near the nose, cheeks, forehead, or spine?

References

Aly, Raza. "Staphylococcal Infections." Atlas of Infections of the Skin. Aly, Raza, and Howard Maibach, eds. New York: Churchill Livingstone, 1999. 115-122.

Hall, John. "Dermatologic Bacteriology." Sauer's Manual of Skin Diseases. Hall, John, ed. Philadelphia: Lippincott Williams & Wilkins, 2000. 150-151.

Lee, T.Y., and T.H. Lam. "Irritant Contact Dermatitis Due to a Chinese Herbal Medicine Lu-shen-wan." Contact Dermatitis 18 4 (1988): 213-218.

Pray, W. Steven. "Bacterial Infections of the Hair Follicles." U.S. Pharmacist 25 4 (2000): 01 Jan 2001 <http://www.medscape.com/jobson/USPharmacist/2000/v25.n04/usp2504.01/pnt-usp2504.01.html>.

Cardiac Arrest
427.5

Definition

Cardiac arrest is an abrupt halt in the pumping action of the heart. When the heart stops pumping, blood flow and breathing (respiration) also stop, resulting in a complete lack of oxygen delivery to vital organs. Cardiac arrest is a medical emergency that takes precedence over all other conditions, with the exception of an obstructed airway or massive bleeding (hemorrhaging); it results in swift death if not immediately controlled. Oxygenation through cardiopulmonary resuscitation (CPR) is necessary immediately in order to prevent permanent damage to the brain, liver, lungs, and kidneys, and to prevent death.

Cardiac arrest is caused by electrical dysfunction (80%) including ventricular fibrillation, ventricular tachycardia, and asystole, and mechanical failure (20%) such as cardiac rupture, acute myocardial infarction, acute tamponade, an obstructing tumor or thrombus, or chronic heart failure. Additional causes are circulatory shock caused by conditions such as hypovolemia secondary to massive internally or externally originating blood loss (hemorrhage), massive fluid loss such as occurs with burns, and hypothermia; ventilation abnormalities also lead to respiratory acidosis and cardiopulmonary arrest.

Other causes of cardiac arrest include the sudden cessation of breathing (respiratory arrest), a dislodged blood clot (embolus), an electrical injury (electrocution), drug overdose, or a severe allergic reaction (anaphylaxis). Myocardial infarction (heart attack) results in the sudden death of part of the heart tissue. It is usually caused by the blockage (occlusion) of one or more of the coronary arteries in the heart.

Factors that put an individual at a higher risk of experiencing a cardiac arrest include a history of arterial narrowing or a disease of the arteries that supply blood to the heart muscle (coronary artery disease), abnormal heart rhythm (arrhythmia), chest pain caused by lack of oxygen to the heart muscle (angina), and failure of the heart to maintain its pumping action and to deliver blood to the lungs and rest of the body (congestive heart failure). Other risk factors include advancing age, diabetes mellitus, metabolic disorders characterized by high levels of lipids in the blood (cholesterol, triglycerides, lipoproteins), high blood pressure (hypertension), tobacco smoking, fatty diet, stress, obesity, lack of regular exercise, and drug or alcohol abuse. Also at higher risk are individuals with a family history of heart disease. Individuals who have survived one episode of cardiac arrest are at an increased risk for recurrence.

Annually, 350,000 individuals die from cardiac arrest; the survival rate is 5%, but in cities with traffic congestion and slow elevators, the survival rate falls to one percent.

Each year, approximately 1.5 million individuals in the US experience an acute myocardial infarction; 500,000 will die, making it one of the leading medical emergencies in the US.

Diagnosis

History: The majority of sudden cardiac arrests manifest as abnormal (chaotic) heart rhythms, and are identifiable by an immediate loss of pulse, blood pressure, and consciousness. An individual who is having a myocardial infarction (MI or heart attack) may complain of pressure, tightness, or heaviness in the chest that usually lasts for 30 minutes or more. This sensation may travel (radiate) to the arms, particularly the left arm, or to the jaw. Complaints of shortness of breath (dyspnea) may be made and is often the main complaint for elderly individuals who are having a heart attack. Individuals may complain of sweating, nausea, or vomiting as well. Some individuals may say they have fainted (syncope), or may complain of dizziness.

Physical exam: The individual will appear to be in acute distress. The breathing rate (respiratory rate) may be increased due to anxiety, or due to lack of oxygenation. In those with an MI, listening to the heart with a stethoscope (auscultation) may reveal an increased heart rate (tachycardia), abnormal heart sounds (third and fourth heart sounds), and an abnormal sound that is heard between beats when the heart is at rest (diastolic murmur), much like the murmur heard in mitral insufficiency. An elevated or lowered blood pressure may be noted (hypertension or hypertension, respectively). The pulse rate also may be increased or decreased, depending on whether an irregular heartbeat (arrhythmia) is present. Listening to the lungs with a stethoscope (auscultation) generally will reveal no abnormalities.

Tests: An electrocardiogram (ECG) is done quickly to measure the electrical activity of the heart. The electrical activity changes seen identify the part of the heart involved as the infarction is occurring. Damaged heart muscle cells release enzymes into the bloodstream; a blood test measures cardiac enzymes (creatine kinase, or CK and CK-MB), and gives an indication as to the extent of heart muscle damage. After the individual's condition is stable, other tests may be done to assess how much damage has been done to the heart. These tests include inserting a catheter into the arm or groin to access the heart through a blood vessel (cardiac catheterization), injecting dye into blood vessels, and viewing them on x-ray (angiography), or using sound waves (ultrasound) to look at how the heart is functioning (echocardiography).

Treatment

Cardiopulmonary resuscitation (CPR) is required within the first 4 to 6 minutes in order to maintain oxygenation of the blood and prevent permanent tissue damage. Although CPR may restore a heartbeat, electrical shock (defibrillation) may be necessary to restore a normal heart rhythm. It is imperative that the individual be treated by a paramedic within the first 8 minutes and then taken to an emergency room as quickly as possible.

Once in the emergency room, an intravenous (IV) line will be started to administer drugs for pain relief and to assist the heart and vessels to function properly. If the heart fails to attain a normal rhythm, and that rhythm could be fatal, it is corrected by administering an electric shock to the heart (defibrillation). Once the individual is resuscitated, antiarrhythmic drugs are used to prevent future episodes of ventricular fibrillation. An electrocardiogram (ECG) is done right away; follow-up cardiac monitoring will be continuous. The individual will be given oxygen, aspirin, and nitroglycerin. Individuals deemed at high-risk for a recurrence may need to be fitted with an internal device that monitors the heart rhythm, delivering a shock at the first sign of ventricular fibrillation.

Asystole is the complete absence of heart muscle activity and is more difficult to reverse. It may respond to IV administration of epinephrine and calcium. In extreme cases, epinephrine may be injected directly into the heart. Once stabilized, a pacemaker, which monitors the cardiac rhythm and stimulates the heart if it fails to beat, may need to be installed.

In all cases of cardiac arrest, there is a disturbance in the blood's chemical constituents, making the blood more acidic. Sodium bicarbonate, given IV, usually corrects this imbalance. Other drugs such as lidocaine may also need to be given to stabilize the heart muscle.

Drugs that help to restore normal blood flow by opening the obstructed artery (thrombolytics) are often given if less than 12 hours have elapsed since the chest pain began.

The individual often will be transferred to a cardiac care unit (CCU) once stable for further treatment and continuous monitoring.

Prognosis

The outcome (prognosis) depends on the extent to which the heart is damaged and the age of the individual. If the individual receives resuscitation quickly and little damage was done, the outcome is excellent. For those who do not receive prompt medical treatment, the outcome may be poor. With CPR, defibrillation, and paramedic intervention within 8 minutes, the survival rate is about forty-three percent. If no CPR or defibrillation occurs with in the first 8 minutes, the survival rates plunges to two to eight percent. For those individuals who survive the initial onset and are treated in a hospital, many die within 3 months to 1 year after discharge from the hospital.

Differential Diagnosis

Conditions with similar symptoms include deflation of the lung (pneumothorax), a blood clot in the lung (pulmonary embolism), inflammation of the sac around the heart (pericarditis), inflammation of the gallbladder (cholecystitis), or aortic dissection.

Specialists

- Cardiologist
- Cardiothoracic Surgeon
- Critical Care Specialist
- Emergency Medicine

Rehabilitation

A physician often recommends that the individual participate in a hospital-based cardiac rehabilitation program. The goal of the program is to assist individuals who have had a heart attack to acquire and maintain a healthy lifestyle and to return to normal activities. These programs offer personally designed exercise programs in which the individual comes to the hospital 3 to 4 times per week for approximately 30 to 60 minutes each time for several weeks. The program also offers assistance with diet and weight improvement, and assists the individual in maintaining the exercise program and lifestyle changes well after the program ends.

Work Restrictions / Accommodations

Physical exertion and emotional stress should not exceed the individual's capabilities. Extended work leave may be required for recuperation and cardiac rehabilitation. Once individuals recover from cardiac arrest, they should not be allowed to return to strenuous physical labor.

Comorbid Conditions

Comorbid conditions include diabetes mellitus, obesity, smoking, high blood pressure (hypertension), increased cholesterol blood levels (hypercholesterolemia), and cardiac (heart) or vascular (blood vessels) disease.

Complications

Complications of cardiac arrest can include several types of irregular heartbeats, including ventricular fibrillation, ventricular tachycardia, and atrial fibrillation. Other complications include stroke, rupture of the heart, second- or third-degree heart block, right ventricular infarction, cardiogenic shock, and death.

Factors Influencing Duration

Severity of damage to the heart, the individual's age, and response to treatment and cardiac rehabilitation may influence disability.

Length of Disability

Disability may be permanent.

Duration in Days

Job Classification	Minimum	Optimum	Maximum
Sedentary work	16	42	Indefinite
Light work	21	42	Indefinite
Medium work	28	56	Indefinite
Heavy work	42	70	Indefinite
Very Heavy work	42	84	Indefinite

Failure to Recover

If an individual fails to recover within the maximum duration expectancy period, the reader may wish to reference the following questions to assist in better understanding the specifics of an individual's medical case.

Regarding diagnosis:

- Has individual experienced a recent heart attack (myocardial infarction)?
- Does individual have a history of heart disease? Is there a family history of heart disease?
- Does individual have a history of diabetes mellitus, increased lipids in the blood (cholesterol, triglycerides, lipoproteins), high blood pressure (hypertension), tobacco smoking, unhealthy diet, stress, obesity, lack of regular exercise, and/or drug or alcohol use?
- Does individual complain of pressure, tightness, or heaviness in the chest that usually lasts for 30 minutes or more? Does that sensation travel (radiate) to the arms, particularly the left arm or the jaw?
- Does individual complain of shortness of breath (dyspnea)? Is there sweating, nausea, or vomiting?
- Was an electrocardiogram (ECG) done quickly to measure the electrical activity of the heart? Were blood tests done to measure cardiac enzymes (creatine kinase-CK and CK-MB) to determine the extent of heart muscle damage? Was cardiac catheterization, ultrasound, or echocardiography performed?
- Was the diagnosis of cardiac arrest confirmed?

Regarding treatment:

- Did individual receive cardiopulmonary resuscitation (CPR) within the first 4 to 6 minutes of the cardiac arrest occurrence and then taken to a hospital?
- Was electrical shock (defibrillation) necessary to restore a normal heart rhythm?
- Once in the hospital and resuscitated, did individual receive anti-arrhythmic drugs, oxygen, aspirin, and nitroglycerin?
- If individual is at high risk for a recurrence, is an internal device required to deliver a shock at the first sign of ventricular fibrillation?
- Did individual experience complete absence of heart muscle activity (asystole) requiring administration of epinephrine and calcium? Did the epinephrine have to be injected directly into the heart?
- If less than 12 hours elapsed since the chest pain began, were thrombolytic drugs administered?
- How well did individual respond to treatment?

Regarding prognosis:

- How severely was the heart damaged? How old is individual?
- How quickly did individual receive medical care?
- Is this the first cardiac arrest experienced?
- Have complications developed such as ventricular fibrillation, ventricular tachycardia, and atrial fibrillation?
- Has stroke, rupture of the heart, second- or third-degree heart block, right ventricular infarction, or cardiogenic shock occurred?
- If complications developed, how will they be treated and what is expected outcome with treatment?

References

"Cardiac and Respiratory Arrest and Cardiopulmonary Resuscitation." Merck Manual of Diagnosis and Therapy, 17th ed. Beers, Mark H., and Robert Berkow, MD, eds. Whitehouse Station, NJ: Merck & Co., Inc, 1999 05 Dec 2000 <http://www.merck.com/pubs/mmanual/section16/chapter206/s06a.htm>.

Langberg, J.J., and D.B. Delurgio. "Ventricular Arrhythmias." Cardiovascular Medicine. Scientific American® Medicine Online Dale, D.C., and D.D. Federman New York: WebMD Corporation, 2000 Scientific American Medicine. 05 Dec 2000 <http://www.samed.com/sam/forms/index/htm>.

Cardiac Catheterization

Other names / synonyms: Right Heart Catheterization
37.21, 37.22, 37.23

Definition

Cardiac catheterization is an invasive diagnostic procedure that provides information about the heart's chambers and valves, coronary arteries, and the great vessels (aorta, pulmonary artery, pulmonary vein, and vena cava).

During the procedure, various pressures can be taken within the heart, opening and closing of the heart valves can be observed, pumping quality of the heart can be assessed, flow of blood into and through the heart chambers can be checked, and any narrowing or blockage of the coronary arteries can be measured. Either one or both sides of the heart may be catheterized. Right heart catheterization provides information about the right chambers of the heart (right atrium and ventricle), pulmonary artery, and right coronary arteries. Left heart catheterization provides information about the left chambers of the heart (left atrium and ventricle), aorta, and left coronary arteries.

Cardiac catheterizations are generally performed on ambulatory individuals in an outpatient or short-stay setting generally in a radiology or cardiac diagnostics lab. They may also be performed on individuals admitted through the emergency room with cardiac symptoms and other inpatients whose cardiac conditions have deteriorated. In either setting, an operating room and surgical team is usually available in case emergency heart surgery becomes necessary.

Cardiac catheterization is an extremely common procedure because of the large number of Americans with one or more types of cardiovascular disease (about 59,700,000). Coronary heart disease accounts for 12,200,000 of this number causing approximately 450,000 deaths annually. The odds for men developing some type of major cardiovascular disease before the age of 60 are 1 in 3; the odds for women are 1 in 10.

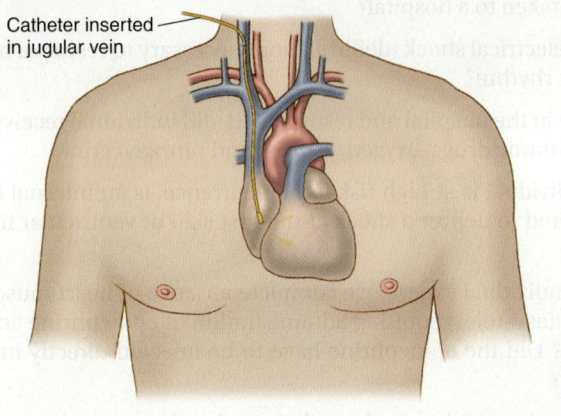

Catheter inserted in jugular vein

Frank Forney

Reason for Procedure

Cardiac catheterization may be indicated to confirm a diagnosis, determine the severity of the condition, plan treatment, and evaluate the response to treatment when noninvasive tests have failed to find a cause for an individual's suspected cardiac symptoms. Some of these noninvasive tests include electrocardiogram (ECG), echocardiography, cardiac stress test, and cardiac scanning.

A number of heart disorders may be diagnosed and evaluated by cardiac catheterization including heart attack (myocardial infarction), an enlarged area of the heart (ventricular hypertrophy), blockage in the pulmonary artery or one of its branches (pulmonary embolism), narrowed or blocked coronary arteries (with or without chest pain), narrowed or weakened heart valves (stenosis or regurgitation), congenital defects in the valves or chambers of the heart, inflammation of the heart (myocarditis), disease of the heart muscle (cardiomyopathy), and some heart rhythm disturbances (arrhythmias). The procedure may also be used to obtain blood samples within the heart or tissue samples (biopsies) of the heart muscle, measure the pumping ability of the heart muscle, and evaluate the success of surgical procedures on the heart.

Several disease-treating (therapeutic) procedures can be performed during a cardiac catheterization. These include the injection of clot-dissolving (thrombolytic) agents directly into a blocked coronary artery, dilation of a narrowed coronary artery with a balloon-tipped catheter (coronary balloon angioplasty), dilation of a narrowed (stenotic) heart valve with a balloon-tipped catheter (valvuloplasty), and radio wave destruction of abnormal electrical pathways that are causing heart irregularities (radiofrequency ablation).

How Procedure Is Performed

The operative area (arm, neck, or groin) is shaved and washed (prepped) with an antibacterial solution. The area is covered with a sterile drape, leaving the surgical field exposed. A mild sedative is first given to calm the individual and then a local anesthetic is injected over the blood vessel used as the entry point for the catheter. Access to the vein or artery may be obtained either by surgical exposure of the blood vessel (cutdown) followed by puncture of the vessel with a needle, or by a needle puncture directly through the skin and underlying tissue into the vessel (percutaneous). A guide wire is then inserted through the needle.

The catheter is passed over the guide wire and into the artery after the needle has been removed.

Guided by x-ray vision of deep tissue structures (fluoroscopy) in a darkened room, the physician advances the wire and catheter into various parts of the heart. After specific pressure readings are taken, a special liquid (dye or contrast medium) is injected through the catheter into the heart chambers and coronary arteries. The working heart can then be viewed on a video screen. When all scheduled therapeutic procedures are completed (i.e., valvuloplasty or balloon angioplasty), the catheter is removed with one smooth movement. If an incision has been made over the vessel, it is closed with sutures.

Prognosis

The immediate outcome for uncomplicated cardiac catheterization used for diagnostic purposes is excellent although outcomes after therapeutic procedures vary. Within the first 6 months after coronary balloon angioplasty, 30-40% of the treated coronary arteries close down again. The outcome after using thrombolytic agents to reopen a blocked coronary artery depends on how soon treatment began after the first symptoms of chest pain. If initiated within the first 1 to 3 hours, the mortality rate is reduced by 50% or more. However, if treatment does not begin until 12 or more hours after the onset of pain, the mortality rate is reduced by only ten percent.

Prognosis following balloon valvuloplasty is excellent in 80-90% of individuals with mitral valve stenosis who do not have regurgitation. Symptoms of congestive heart failure are relieved including pulmonary edema, shortness of breath, limitation of activity, and recurrent blood clots (in spite of treatment with blood thinners). The rate of recurrence of stenosis within the first 5 years is low with a mortality rate of approximately one to three percent.

The immediate outcome for those who have a balloon valvuloplasty because of pulmonary valve stenosis is also excellent. Symptoms are relieved including shortness of breath with exertion, fainting, chest pain, and right heart failure. The recurrence rate is very low with a mortality rate of approximately two to four percent.

Outcomes for treatment of less severe congenital aortic stenosis in young adults are good with balloon valvuloplasty. The individual usually gains long-term relief of symptoms with few complications. Outcomes for balloon valvuloplasty in older adults with severe aortic stenosis as a result of calcification are poor. Symptoms of heart failure may be relieved temporarily but the valve may quickly narrow again.

Specialists

- Cardiologist
- Cardiothoracic Surgeon

Rehabilitation

If cardiac catheterization leads to a diagnosis of cardiovascular disease, cardiac rehabilitation may be recommended. Sessions focus on improving the individual's capacity for activity and endurance and generally begin in an outpatient facility. The rehabilitation program for cardiac catheterization is planned in four phases that follow the same progression in other related cardiac diseases.

Phase one begins with low demand aerobic activities using large muscle groups such as the lower extremities. In a hospital or cardiac rehabilitation setting, individuals are monitored for heart rate and rhythm and blood pressure. Initial exercises include self-care activities such as sitting up in bed and moving from the bed to a chair. Calisthenics of varying intensity are performed such as marching in place and raising both arms overhead. Walking (ambulating) with continuous monitoring an initial 2 to 5 minutes progressing to 15 to 20 minutes is also part of this phase. The use of a stationary bicycle set at 50 revolutions per minute (RPM) for 3 minutes is performed under supervision.

Phase two consists of similar exercises with progression of time and intensity that varies from individual to individual.

Phase three is supervised in a rehabilitation center. A physical therapist experienced in cardiac rehabilitation keeps a daily log of the individual's blood pressure, heart rate, and cardiac rhythm. Individuals are typically attached to an ECG for testing, which is a device used to record the continuous electrical activity of the heart muscle. Higher levels of exercises comprise this phase with the addition of recreational activities such as swimming and outdoor hiking. Light jogging at approximately 5 miles per hour (mph) and cycling at approximately 12 mph is appropriate as long as the individual tolerates the rehabilitation program well.

Phase four of cardiac rehabilitation for cardiovascular heart disease occurs after discharge from the hospital. Long-term maintenance of performance levels reached during phases two and three are concerns at this time. Aerobic exercises that increase cardiovascular fitness are emphasized and described as walking briskly, running, jogging, swimming, climbing stairs, or bicycling. The American Heart Association recommends 30 to 60 minutes of aerobic activity 3 or 4 times a week to help keep high blood pressure under control. Throughout all phases, it is important to allow the heart rate to slowly return to normal after the exercises.

Family members are encouraged to participate in the rehabilitation program as it also provides education about lifestyle changes and reduces fear and anxiety about increasing activity and exercise. Education includes a review of medications, lifestyle changes and goal setting, nutrition counseling (a low-fat, no added salt diet), stress management, and instruction about the safe performance of activities such as sexual activity, work, and recreational activities.

Work Restrictions / Accommodations

Activity following cardiac catheterization is restricted for several days to prevent bleeding from the operative site. These restrictions include no driving, no heavy lifting, limited walking, and no climbing stairs. Individuals who have had a cardiac catheterization without experiencing serious complications or disabilities may be able to return to work in 1 to 2 weeks.

Individuals with residual chronic heart disease or chronic chest pain may require work restrictions and accommodations that conserve their energy and reduce strain on their hearts. Work hours may initially need to be limited and gradually increased over several weeks until the individual is working a full day. Other medical problems or permanent disabilities because of underlying medical conditions (i.e., diabetes, chronic obstructive lung disease, and chronic renal failure requiring dialysis) or postoperative complications (i.e., partial paralysis or speech impairment because of stroke) may also require work restrictions and accommodations.

Comorbid Conditions

Comorbid conditions that may influence length of disability for individuals who have had a cardiac catheterization include previous cardiac surgery and pre-existing diseases affecting any of the major body systems such as high blood pressure, chronic kidney (renal) disease, bleeding disorders, diabetes mellitus, chronic obstructive lung disease, chronic heart disease, and immunosuppressive diseases. Risk factors also include a history of smoking, alcoholism or other substance abuse, and obesity.

Procedure Complications

Complications of cardiac catheterization include bleeding or infection at the point the catheter entered the blood vessel; inflammation and clot formation (thrombophlebitis) within the blood vessel used; allergic reaction to the dye or contrast medium used to view the heart under fluoroscopy; dislodging a blood clot within a heart valve, coronary artery, or from the catheter tip that travels to the heart or brain causing a heart attack or stroke; serious heart irregularity (arrhythmia) as a result of the catheter's movement through sensitive parts of the heart; systemic infection; decreased blood pressure (hypotension); hemorrhage; and puncture of the heart wall that results in blood collecting in the sac around the heart and restricting its ability to beat (cardiac tamponade).

Factors Influencing Duration

Factors influencing the length of disability following cardiac catheterization include the underlying reason for the catheterization, number and severity of procedure complications, amount of blood loss if complications arise, number of blood transfusions required, success of any therapeutic procedures performed, individual's nutritional status, individual's mental and emotional stability, access to rehabilitation facilities, and strength of the individual's support system.

Length of Disability

Disability from the procedure itself is brief. Individual is observed for at least 2 hours after walking begins. The individual may go home after outpatient catheterization.

Duration in Days

Job Classification	Minimum	Optimum	Maximum
Any work	1	3	7

References

Cavanaugh, Bonita Morrow. Nurse's Manual of Laboratory and Diagnostic Tests. Philadelphia: F.A. Davis, 1999.

Meeker, Margaret, and Jane Rothrock. Alexander's Care of the Patient in Surgery. St. Louis: Mosby, 1999.

Cardiac Pacemaker Insertion

Other names / synonyms: Atrial Overdrive Pacing, Demand Pacemaker, Fixed Rate Pacemaker, Permanent Pacemaker, Temporary Pacemaker, Transvenous Pacemaker

37.80, 37.82, 37.83, 37.86, 37.87

Definition

Cardiac pacemaker insertion is the surgical implantation of a cardiac pacemaker, a device that supplies electrical impulses to the heart in order to maintain the heartbeat at a regular rate. A pacemaker stimulates the heart muscle with precisely timed discharges of electricity causing the heart to beat in a manner that mimics a naturally occurring heart rhythm.

Pacemakers consist of two main parts, the pulse generator and the pacing lead(s). The pulse generator controls the pacing system. It contains a small battery and electronic circuitry that produces the electrical impulses sent to the heart. It also interprets the signals it receives back from the beating heart. A typical pulse generator is often less than 2 inches wide and a quarter-inch thick, weighing about an ounce or less. The pacing leads are thin, specially insulated wires that carry electrical impulses to the heart and return signals from the heart to the pulse generator's "brain."

The two main types of pacemakers are fixed-rate and demand. A fixed-rate pacemaker discharges impulses at a fixed, steady rate, irrespective of the heart's activity. A demand pacemaker only discharges impulses when the heart rate slows or a beat is missed. A normal heartbeat and heart rate suppresses the pacemaker. In some cases, an external programmer can adjust the rate. More advanced types allow the heart rate to increase during exercise.

Since modern microelectronic circuits require little power and lithium batteries have a long life, a pacemaker usually runs satisfactorily for several years. Battery replacement involves only a minor operation.

Individuals who are in need of temporary or permanent pacemaker insertion include those with sick sinus syndrome, which is a cardiac conduction defect that causes the normal pacemaker of the heart (sinus node) to stop, slow down inappropriately, or pause for long durations. Other conditions that can lead to pacemaker insertion include incomplete heart block (second-degree heart block, type I and type II), complete heart block (third degree heart block), abnormal tachycardias (tachydysrhythmia), and hypersensitive carotid sinus syndrome. Individuals who have had heart surgery may need a temporary or permanent pacemaker. Generally, these heart rhythm disturbances are caused by coronary artery disease, heart chamber enlargement (hypertrophy or cardiomyopathy), congenital heart conduction disturbances, and heart muscle injury either from heart attack or cardiac surgery.

Implantation of a cardiac pacemaker is one of the most common operations involving the heart. Each year, between 100,000 to 175,000 permanent pacemakers are implanted in the US. While the procedure is occasionally done in children or young adults, it is more commonly performed in older individuals. In fact, nearly 80% of all pacemakers are implanted in individuals over the age of 65.

Reason for Procedure

A cardiac pacemaker is inserted in order to restore proper heart rhythm. Depending on the severity of the heart rhythm disturbance, the pacemaker insertion may be a nonurgent, elective procedure or it may be a life-saving, emergency procedure.

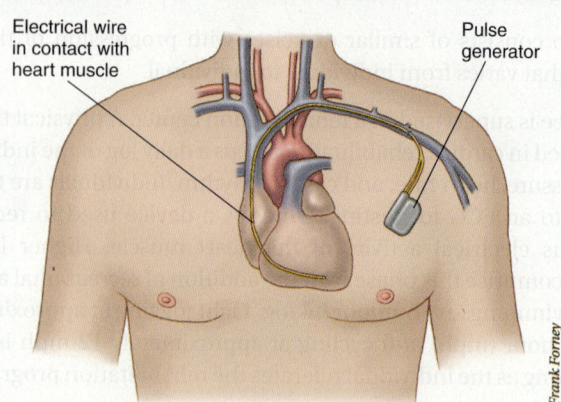

The beating of the heart is normally controlled by electrical signals that originate from a nerve bundle located in the right atrium of the heart (sinoatrial node or SA node). These signals pass on to the powerful ventricle muscles of the heart through another nerve bundle or node (atrioventricular, or AV node) and nerve distribution system (left and right bundle branches). This coordination of the atria and ventricles results in the normal heart rhythm.

Sometimes the SA node stops working properly, either speeding up or slowing down the rate of electrical impulses to the right atrium. If the rate is too slow, the heart does not supply enough blood to the body. Likewise, an extremely rapid heart rate reduces the pumping action of the heart, causing a low blood pressure and inadequate tissue oxygenation (ischemia). Problems may also occur with the electrical pathway between the atria and the ventricles (AV node). Poor timing between the contractions of the atria and the ventricles (asynchrony) may occur, or the signal to the ventricles may be blocked completely (heart block). The symptoms associated with these heart rhythm disturbances can range from dizziness and fatigue to complete loss of consciousness or cardiac arrest. When this occurs, a pacemaker implant may be required to establish a normal rhythm.

How Procedure Is Performed

Cardiac pacemaker implantation is a very common procedure done most often in an operating room or in a cardiac catheterization laboratory. The procedure lasts 1 to 2 hours, and usually requires only local anesthetic. In transvenous endocardial implantation, leads inserted through a vein are guided down into the heart. The tips of the leads are secured in position in either the right atrium or the right ventricle, or in both positions, depending on the part of the heart muscle to be stimulated and the condition being treated. Once the leads are in place, they are connected to the pulse generator and the pacemaker is adjusted to the appropriate stimulating and sensing thresholds. The pulse generator is fitted into a pocket created under the skin of the upper chest near the collarbone.

Sometimes, depending on the heart condition, the pacing lead is placed on the outside of the heart muscle (epicardial approach) instead. This procedure is done under general anesthesia, usually at the time of other heart surgery. The lead is attached to the outer surface of the part of the heart muscle to be stimulated. The pulse generator is fitted into a pocket constructed underneath the skin of the abdomen.

Occasionally, a temporary transvenous pacemaker is inserted to temporarily pace the heart. The temporary pacemaker may be used on individuals who only need the assistance of a pacemaker temporarily (i.e., those whose heart rhythm is likely to return to normal). Occasionally, in emergency situations (i.e., complete heart block) a temporary pacemaker is inserted in the emergency department or in the intensive care ward. The procedure for the temporary pacemaker insertion is similar to the transvenous endocardial implantation described above, except the pulse generator is strapped to the individual's arm rather than surgically implanted. Because the end of the pacemaker leads and the pulse generator lie outside the body and can be subject to damage, these temporary pacemakers are generally used for just a short time (2 to 3 days).

Prognosis

Outcome is generally good for both permanent and temporary pacemaker insertion. Temporary pacemakers placed under emergency settings have a higher risk of complications, particularly infection or thrombophlebitis.

Specialists

- Cardiologist
- Cardiovascular Surgeon
- Emergency Medicine

Work Restrictions / Accommodations

Strenuous activity will be temporarily restricted, including lifting, pulling, pushing objects over 10 pounds, reaching or stretching above the head, and sudden, jerky arm movements. Other restrictions apply to workplace use of powerful electromagnetic pulses that might interfere with the operation of the pacemaker. Sources include strong magnetic fields, electrical cables carrying over 10,000 amperes of current, alternating welding currents, powerful radio, TV and radar transmitters, power tools and assembly line robots, induction furnaces, and electric generating plants or substations. In addition, evidence has been reported that the latest generation of digital cell phones may interfere with pacemakers. Until further tests have been conducted, individuals with pacemakers should turn off cell phones when they are in a breast pocket, hold the phone at least 10 to 12 inches from the pacemaker when using it, and use the phone on the ear opposite to the implant. When in doubt, employers should consult with the individual's doctor regarding appropriate work restrictions and accommodations.

Comorbid Conditions

Recent heart attack, congestive heart failure, chronic lung disease, or bleeding disorders are comorbid conditions that may impact ability to recovery and further lengthen disability.

Procedure Complications

Complications of a pacemaker insertion procedure include infection, air embolism, collapse of the lung (pneumothorax), perforation of the heart wall (myocardial perforation), vascular or nerve damage, thrombophlebitis, bleeding, and abnormal atrial or ventricular heartbeats (premature atrial contractions, atrial tachycardia, premature ventricular contractions, ventricular tachycardia). These complications are infrequent when a permanent pacemaker is inserted in the operating room or cardiac catheterization laboratory. The complications are more common with temporary pacemaker insertions, particularly when the pacemaker is inserted under emergency circumstances.

These complications generally respond well to medical intervention (antibiotics or anti-inflammatory medications) once the temporary pacemaker is removed or replaced.

Factors Influencing Duration

The individual's age, type of surgical procedure, and incidence of complications may influence length of disability. In some cases, pacemaker implantation is done on an outpatient basis and requires only a few days of recovery. If the pacemaker was inserted to treat heart rhythm disturbances secondary to a heart attack or open heart surgery, the length of recovery will be longer.

Length of Disability

The procedure itself should relieve the symptoms of the previous disability to a great extent. No significant additional disability is expected from this procedure.

Duration in Days

Job Classification	Minimum	Optimum	Maximum
Sedentary work	3	4	7
Light work	3	4	7
Medium work	7	14	21
Heavy work	14	21	28
Very Heavy work	14	21	28

References

Alspach, JoAnn Grif, ed. Core Curriculum for Critical Care Nursing, 4th ed. Philadelphia: W.B. Saunders Company, 1991.

Xie, Baiyan, et al. "Permanent Cardiac Pacing." Emergency Medical Clinics of North America 16 2 (1998): 419-462.

Cardiac Stress Test

Other names / synonyms: Echo Stress Testing, Electrocardiograph Stress Testing, Exercise Stress Test, Exercise Testing, Exercise Tolerance Test, Nuclear Stress Testing, Pharmacologic Stress Test, Stress Testing

89.4, 89.41, 89.42, 89.43, 89.44

Definition

A cardiac stress test evaluates heart function during exertion. During exertion, the heart's demand for oxygen is increased. Testing the heart's reaction to this increased demand provides information necessary for the diagnosis of cardiac disease or abnormalities.

The heart's reaction to the exertion is usually measured by electrocardiography (ECG). ECG is a test that uses 12 sensors placed at specific locations on the individual's body. Through these sensors, the heart's electrical activity is measured. Additional methods of measuring the heart's reaction during a stress test include echocardiography, which uses ultrasound to visualize the heart structures, and a myocardial perfusion scan, an imaging procedure that uses a radioactive compound.

The cardiac stress test is a widely used test, among healthy and symptomatic populations, for screening and evaluation for heart disease. Coronary heart disease is a major cause of morbidity and death. In the US alone, more than 12 million individuals have a history of heart attack (myocardial infarction), chest pain (angina pectoris), or both.

Reason for Procedure

A cardiac stress test is performed to screen for coronary artery disease in asymptomatic individuals, to evaluate chest pain and its cause, to diagnose or rule out coronary artery disease, to identify arrhythmias that develop during exercise, to determine the functioning capacity of the heart after surgery or myocardial infarction, and to evaluate the effectiveness of therapy for cardiac arrhythmias or ischemic disorders.

How Procedure Is Performed

The individual undergoing cardiac stress testing is instructed to abstain from eating, drinking, or smoking within 2 to 4 hours prior to testing. A resting (baseline) ECG is obtained before beginning the test.

The exertion is typically induced by exercise, such as pedaling a stationary bicycle or walking on a treadmill. After an initial warm-up phase on the selected mode of exercise, the workload is gradually increased by small increments. At each exercise level (or after each minute of exercise, depending on the protocol), an ECG is recorded. ECGs are also recorded periodically for at least 6 to 10 minutes after exercise is stopped. If insufficient blood supply to the heart muscle (myocardial ischemia) develops during exercise, characteristic ECG changes will appear. Blood pressure is also checked at frequent intervals, and the individual is asked to report any symptoms experienced. For those who cannot perform the exercises, the cardiac effects of exercise may be simulated with certain medications that dilate the blood vessels (adrenergic or coronary vasodilators).

If echocardiography is done in conjunction with the stress test, a baseline echocardiogram is obtained prior to exercise. Another is done immediately after exercise. From these images, motion of the heart wall can be analyzed. If myocardial ischemia develops during exercise, abnormal wall motion will appear. If myocardial perfusion scan is performed, a radioactive compound is injected into a vein. The compound circulates throughout the heart and is taken up by the heart muscle (myocardium). The radioactivity is detected by special cameras that produce an image of the heart, revealing areas of oxygen deficiency (ischemia). The scan is obtained immediately after stopping exercise; a second scan is done several hours later after resting.

When an individual is unable to exercise, a pharmacologic perfusion study may be done.

Prognosis

The cardiac stress test is an effective and widely used procedure the provides information about an individual's heart and how it responds to exertion. This information is invaluable in screening for and evaluating heart disease.

Specialists

- Cardiologist

Work Restrictions / Accommodations

There are no restrictions or accommodations associated with a cardiac stress test.

Comorbid Conditions

Testing should be avoided in those with the following conditions: severe (acute) myocardial infarction, unstable angina pectoris, severe heart block, rapid arrhythmias, severe aortic stenosis, overt congestive heart failure, acute myocarditis, or other acute illnesses such as infections, severe anemia, hyperthyroidism, a history of transient ischemic attacks.

Individuals with any lung condition that prevents them from exercising should not participate in an exercise stress test, although a pharmacologic stress test may be approved by the physician.

Procedure Complications

The following complications may occur and necessitate termination of testing: irregular heart action (arrhythmias), a drop in blood pressure below baseline, chest pain (angina), difficulty breathing (dyspnea), dizziness or fainting, uncontrolled hypertension, excessive fatigue, or other significant symptoms. The possibility of fatal cardiac arrhythmias or myocardial infarction exists. Other reasons for terminating the test include reaching maximum capacity (target heart rate), or the person requests to stop testing.

Factors Influencing Duration

The length of disability is usually that of the underlying diagnosis. Unless complications occur, the procedure itself is not associated with disability.

Length of Disability

In most cases, no disability is associated with the procedure itself. Absence from work for administration of the test may be necessary.

References

Goldman, Lee, and J. Claude Bennett. Cecil Textbook of Medicine, 21st ed. Philadelphia: W.B. Saunders Company, 2000.

Pagana, Kathleen, and Timothy Pagana. Mosby's Manual of Diagnostic and Laboratory Tests. St. Louis: Mosby, 1998.

Cardiogenic Shock
Other names / synonyms: Heart Failure
785.51

Definition

Cardiogenic shock is a serious condition characterized by a low blood pressure (hypotension) associated with inadequate oxygenation of tissues (hypoperfusion). It may be caused by a heart attack (acute myocardial infarction) or a large blood clot in the lungs (pulmonary embolus). Shock due to blood loss (hypovolemic shock) and infection (septic shock) are not expressions of cardiogenic shock.

Blood is the carrier of oxygen to the tissues. Irrespective of whether the cause of cardiogenic shock is an acute myocardial infarction (AMI) or a pulmonary embolus, the result is insufficient blood reaching all organs of the body.

Cardiogenic shock does not occur alone. It is always secondary to another condition so prevalence and incidence depends on the condition causing it; i.e., AMI or pulmonary embolism. Incidence of cardiogenic shock appears in 1% of all AMIs and 1-2% of all cases of pulmonary emboli.

Diagnosis

History: Individuals with cardiogenic shock may describe severe chest pain related to the underlying AMI or pulmonary embolism. Shock in itself does not usually produce symptoms clearly recognizable by the individual.

Physical exam: The exam reveals hypotension, usually less than 80 mm Hg systolic. The heart rate is generally increased and the skin is cool and discolored (cyanotic and mottled). The individual may be confused, disoriented, or sometimes unconscious (comatose). There may be "crackles" (rales) in the lungs that are audible with a stethoscope.

Tests: An electrocardiogram (ECG) often shows an AMI if a heart attack is the cause of cardiogenic shock. If a pulmonary embolism is the cause, the ECG may show inferential changes of the embolism. These changes include a fast heart rate (tachycardia) and evidence of enlargement or strain of the right side of the heart.

Blood tests (cardiac enzymes) are abnormal if an AMI is the cause. Special x-ray tests of the lungs (lung scan and a pulmonary angiogram) are abnormal if a pulmonary embolism is the cause.

Treatment

Cardiogenic shock is treated with intravenous (IV) drugs that increase the blood pressure. Dopamine and dobutamine are usually used. When cardiogenic shock complicates open-heart surgery, a drug called amrinone that increases the strength of cardiac contraction is often also used.

A temporary mechanical device known as an intra-aortic balloon pump (IABP) is frequently used to treat cardiogenic shock due to an AMI or cardiogenic shock following open-heart surgery.

Measures to improve blood flow to the damaged heart muscle are sometimes performed in individuals with cardiogenic shock due to an AMI. These measures include the administration of IV drugs to dissolve the blood clot in the coronary artery causing the AMI (thrombolytic therapy), percutaneous transluminal coronary angioplasty (PTCA), and coronary artery bypass surgery (CABG). When a specific mechanical complication of an AMI is the primary reason for cardiogenic shock, surgery to repair the complication is performed. These mechanical complications of AMI include rupture of a heart valve, rupture of the wall between the 2 sides of the heart, and rupture of the free wall of the heart.

If a pulmonary embolism is the cause of cardiogenic shock, measures to dissolve the embolus with an IV drug specifically designed for that purpose (thrombolysis) or removal of the embolus by a surgical technique (embolectomy) might be utilized.

Prognosis

The prognosis of cardiogenic shock is not good. Cardiogenic shock is not a condition from which many individuals recover. Dopamine and dobutamine therapy elevates the blood pressure but does not decrease mortality because the underlying cause (AMI or pulmonary embolism) has not been addressed. In the case of AMI, only early revascularization procedures (thrombolytic therapy, PTCA, and CABG) appear to reduce mortality.

Differential Diagnosis

The 2 conditions that most often mimic cardiogenic shock are right ventricular infarction and pericardial tamponade. Hypovolemic and septic shock also result in hypotension. They can usually be differentiated from cardiogenic shock by appropriate laboratory tests.

Specialists

- Cardiologist
- Critical Care Specialist

Work Restrictions / Accommodations

There will be few, if any, work restrictions for individuals who recover and whose work is relatively sedentary and primarily cognitive in nature. Individuals performing more strenuous work may need to be reassigned to other duties.

Some individuals will never regain functional capacity following cardiogenic shock and will be permanently disabled.

Comorbid Conditions

Comorbid conditions of obesity, diabetes, peripheral vascular disease, chronic pulmonary disease, or liver or kidney failure may impact ability to recover and further lengthen disability.

Complications

Cardiogenic shock is itself a major complication of the condition that caused it (AMI or pulmonary embolism). Cardiogenic shock may have serious consequences as opposed to complications due to the underperfusion with oxygenated blood of various organs. This may result in a stroke, "shock" lung, and liver or kidney failure.

Factors Influencing Duration

If an individual survives cardiogenic shock, the subsequent length of disability is dictated by the overall function of the various organs that received inadequate blood flow when shock occurred.

Length of Disability

In some cases, disability may be permanent. Disability duration will depend upon recovery from underlying condition and cardiac function.

Failure to Recover

If an individual fails to recover within the maximum duration expectancy period, the reader may wish to reference the following questions to assist in better understanding the specifics of an individual's medical case.

Regarding diagnosis:

- Does the individual complain of severe chest pain?
- Is the individual hypotensive?
- Is the heart rate elevated?
- Is the skin cyanotic?
- Does the individual appear to be confused or disoriented?
- Are there abnormal lung sounds?
- Does an ECG reveal evidence of an AMI?
- Does the ECG show changes indicative of a PE?
- Are cardiac enzymes normal?
- Are a lung scan and/or pulmonary angiogram normal?

Regarding treatment:

- Did IV drug therapy successfully increase the blood pressure?
- Did the individual require placement of an IABP? Is the pump functioning properly?
- Did the individual require thrombolytic therapy? Was this treatment successful?
- Did the individual require PTCA or CABG? How successful was PTCA or CABG in improving blood flow to the heart?
- Did the individual require surgery to repair a mechanical complication of AMI? If so, was surgery successful? What is the recovery period for the surgery?
- Did the individual require thrombolytic therapy? Did therapy dissolve the embolus?
- Did the individual require an embolectomy? Was surgery successful? What is the recovery period for this surgery?

Regarding prognosis:

- What was the cause of the cardiogenic shock?
- If AMI, were early revascularization procedures successful?
- Have complications developed?
- Is the individual expected to recover?

References

Clochesy, John M., et al. Critical Care Nursing, 2nd ed. Philadelphia: W.B. Saunders Company, 1996.

Hostetler, Mark A., MD. "Cardiogenic Shock." eMedicine.com 01 Feb 2001. 13 March 2001 <http://www.emedicine.com/cgi-bin/foxweb.exe/showsection@d:/em/ga?book=emerg&sct=CARDIOVASCULAR>.

Cardiomyopathy

Other names / synonyms: Congestive Cardiomyopathy, Constrictive Cardiomyopathy, Familial Cardiomyopathy, Hypertrophic Nonobstructive Cardiomyopathy, Hypertrophic Obstructive Cardiomyopathy, Idiopathic Cardiomyopathy, Myocardiopathy, Primary Cardiomyopathy, Restrictive Cardiomyopathy

425, 425.1, 425.4, 425.9, 674.8

Definition

The term cardiomyopathy refers to a group of diseases characterized by primary involvement of the heart muscle itself. This is in distinction to a number of other groups of diseases including hypertensive, congenital, valvular, and arteriosclerotic heart disease where the heart muscle is secondarily involved.

The causes of dilated cardiomyopathy can be unknown (idiopathic). Secondary causes are infections, toxins (commonly alcohol and cocaine), endocrine problems (such as diabetes and thyroid disease), nutritional deficiencies, neuromuscular diseases (such as muscular dystrophy), genetic/familial disease, or as a complication of pregnancy or childbirth (peripartum cardiomyopathy).

In hypertrophic cardiomyopathy, the heart is enlarged but the heart findings are reversed. The muscular walls are extremely thick, creating less room inside the ventricular cavities. This condition often has a negative effect on the mitral valve and the wall between the 2 ventricles (septum).

Restrictive cardiomyopathy, the least common form of this disease, is typically a complication of a disorder associated with cancers of the blood (amyloidosis). It can be difficult to distinguish restrictive cardiomyopathy from constrictive pericarditis, which is curable with surgery.

Unlike many heart diseases that are typically associated with aging, cardiomyopathy strikes individuals of all ages. Dilated cardiomyopathy is found most often in middle-aged men. It is also seen in females following pregnancy. Hypertrophic cardiomyopathy is inherited in about 50% of cases and found mostly in individuals between the ages of 20 and 40.

Diagnosis

History: Symptoms that may occur with most cardiomyopathies irrespective of cause include those referable to the overall function of the heart as a pump. These symptoms are due to insufficient blood being pumped out of the heart leading to accumulation of excess fluid in the lungs, legs, and/or abdomen resulting in congestive heart failure (CHF). Individuals with CHF may have shortness of breath (dyspnea) with ordinary activities such as walking or climbing stairs or when lying down to sleep (orthopnea). Fatigue and weakness are other common symptoms.

Individuals with dilated cardiomyopathy may report shortness of breath (dyspnea) on exertion, orthopnea, difficulty breathing while sleeping (paroxysmal nocturnal dyspnea), fatigue, and occasionally rapid heart beats (palpitations).

Dyspnea on exertion and fatigue are the most prominent symptoms of restrictive cardiomyopathy. Other symptoms include an increased abdominal girth, swelling of the feet and ankles, and upper abdominal discomfort due to swelling of the liver. In individuals with restrictive cardiomyopathy secondary to infiltrative diseases such as amyloidosis and sarcoidosis, fainting (syncope) or near syncope and sudden death may occur.

Physical exam: Physical abnormalities relating to the specific cause of a cardiomyopathy may be noticed by the individual. Abnormalities not related to cause but reflecting CHF include prominence of the neck veins, sounds in the lungs audible with a stethoscope (rales), a heart murmur, an extra heart sound called a gallop, and swelling of the lower legs, ankles, and/or abdomen.

The individual with dilated cardiomyopathy often appears breathless and pale and has difficulty with breathing while lying down (recumbent). Fast heart rate (tachycardia) and abnormal beats (ectopic beats) while listening to the heart are common. There may be wheezing and other chest findings consistent with heart failure.

The only finding on physical exam in individuals with hypertrophic cardiomyopathy may be a systolic heart murmur that changes in character with different physical tests such as squatting or forcible exhalation (Valsalva maneuver), and stressing the heart with drugs such as amyl nitrate or nitroglycerin.

Common physical findings with restrictive cardiomyopathy are swelling of the ankles and feet, fluid in the abdomen (ascites), and an enlarged tender liver. The heart sounds are distant with extra sounds (gallops).

Tests: Laboratory tests are obtained to identify abnormalities related to specific causes. For example, thyroid function tests identify a possible thyroid disorder and cultures of various fluids help identify bacterial, viral, and fungal diseases.

In addition, an electrocardiogram (ECG), chest x-rays, and echocardiogram are usually obtained regardless of the possible cause to evaluate overall function of the heart. One or more of these tests will almost always be abnormal in an individual with a cardiomyopathy. Cardiac catheterization is often done and more specialized tests such as a CT or biopsy of the heart may be obtained.

Treatment

Treatment varies widely because of the many causes. In general, treatment of the CHF common to most cardiomyopathies usually includes combinations of medications to remove excess fluid from the body (diuretics), medications to strengthen the heart (digitalis preparations), and medications to reduce the work of the heart (vasodilators).

In some individuals, the mitral valve on the left side of the heart becomes leaky (incompetent, insufficient) allowing blood to travel in a reverse direction across it. This compounds CHF and may require heart surgery. Surgery consists of reconstructing the mitral valve (valvuloplasty) or replacing it with an artificial valve.

In other individuals where mitral valve surgery is not appropriate, cardiac transplantation or wrapping a muscle from the back (latissimus dorsi muscle) around the heart to strengthen it may be an alternative.

Cardiomyopathies attributable to infections are treated with the appropriate antimicrobials. Treatment may include anticoagulants to reduce the risk of blood clots. Some individuals may not respond to drug therapy. A heart transplant is indicated in the most serious case, if all the other criteria for transplantation surgery are met.

The drug regimen for hypertrophic cardiomyopathy often adds beta-receptor and calcium-channel blockers to assist the heart in functioning properly. If the treatment is not successful, the individual may benefit from implantation of a defibrillator device. Some individuals may require surgery to remove excess myocardial tissue in the intraventricular septum (septal myomectomy). In rare cases, a heart transplant is recommended. In individuals with restrictive cardiomyopathy, drug therapy is usually attempted but is often unsuccessful.

In addition to the specific therapies outlined above, individuals with all types of cardiomyopathy are usually urged to make lifestyle changes. Restriction of salt and abstention from alcohol are important dietary changes. Obesity must be addressed. Cessation of smoking reduces the workload on the heart.

Prognosis

Morbidity and mortality vary widely and are related to the cause of a given cardiomyopathy. Regardless of its cause, the natural history of a cardiomyopathy may be short with death occurring within months to 2 years. The clinical course may be relatively stable and surprisingly long. Overall, about 50% of individuals die within a 3- to 6-year period after the diagnosis is made.

Young individuals with a recent onset of dilated cardiomyopathy generally have a good outcome either because of successful drug therapy or spontaneous reversal of the cardiomyopathy. It is possible, however, that some individuals, particularly those who are older, may not respond to the medication with the most serious cases requiring a heart transplant.

Those with hypertrophic cardiomyopathy often have a poor prognosis since drug treatment is generally unsuccessful unless surgery is performed to remove excess myocardial tissue in the intraventricular septum (septal myomectomy). Although 5% of individuals do not survive the surgery, those who do experience great improvement and a good prognosis.

Restrictive cardiomyopathy does not often respond to treatment and the outcome is poor. Individuals with heart failure usually die within a year.

Differential Diagnosis

Other diseases causing CHF may mimic a cardiomyopathy including a number of pericardia-, valvular-, and arteriosclerotic-related causes of heart failure. Among individuals with restrictive cardiomyopathy, the condition often mimics constrictive pericarditis.

Specialists

- Cardiologist
- Cardiothoracic Surgeon

Rehabilitation

Physical therapy used in the rehabilitation of cardiomyopathy may be beneficial by providing a supervised exercise program to maintain strength and efficiency of the heart muscle. Individually designed exercise programs for cardiomyopathy are progressed on an as tolerated basis considered safe for each individual.

If rehabilitation begins in a hospital setting, low levels of exercise are prescribed to prevent the hazards of bed rest and reduce episodes of low blood pressure when changing positions (orthostatic hypotension). Exercise at this stage also maintains overall mobility of the body. Strengthening activities start at a low level with the individual on the back (supine position). The individual then progresses with exercises to sitting and eventually standing. Later in the program, progressive walking (ambulating) and eventually stair climbing are an important part of the individual's exercise program while still hospitalized.

When discharged from a hospital setting to an outpatient setting such as a rehabilitation center, individuals are typically attached to an ECG monitor during the exercise session. An ECG is a device used to record the continuous electrical activity of the heart muscle. A physical therapist keeps a daily log of the individual's blood pressure, heart rate, and cardiac rhythm. Individuals may stay involved with an outpatient program for up to a year to accomplish all their goals while still at modified work duty, if tolerated. If tolerated, higher levels of exercise begin with the addition of recreational activities. Modifications may need to be made because of the severity of the disease and if various prescribed medications alter the response to exercise.

Work Restrictions / Accommodations

Work restrictions are related to the severity of the CHF secondary to a cardiomyopathy. Few individuals will be able to perform strenuous work, some can perform moderately strenuous activities, and many can perform jobs that require primarily cognitive functioning. Accommodations may be needed for frequent medical appointments. Cardiopulmonary exercise tests are helpful in determining functional capacity.

Comorbid Conditions

Infections caused by varied microorganisms, the presence of coronary artery disease, and hypertension may lengthen disability.

Complications

Irregular, rapid heart beating (atrial fibrillation) may occur. A small blood clot (thrombus) may form within the heart and an even smaller piece can be dislodged (embolus) and carried by the bloodstream to any organ of the body with serious consequences. For example, an embolus to the brain can cause a stroke, while an embolus to the eye can cause blindness.

Factors Influencing Duration

Factors that influence disability include age of individual, onset of disease, and response to therapy.

Length of Disability

The length of disability depends on form, clinical presentation, underlying cause, job requirements and if, or how well, the individual responds to treatment. Disability may be permanent.

Medical treatment.

Duration in Days

Job Classification	Minimum	Optimum	Maximum
Sedentary work	7	28	Indefinite
Light work	7	28	Indefinite
Medium work	21	42	Indefinite
Heavy work	28	56	Indefinite
Very Heavy work	28	56	Indefinite

Duration Trend from Normative Data*

Cases	Mean	Min	Max	No Lost Time	Over 6 Months
505	72	4	399	0%	4.09%

Percentile:	5th	25th	Median	75th	95th
Days:	11	26	55	91	170

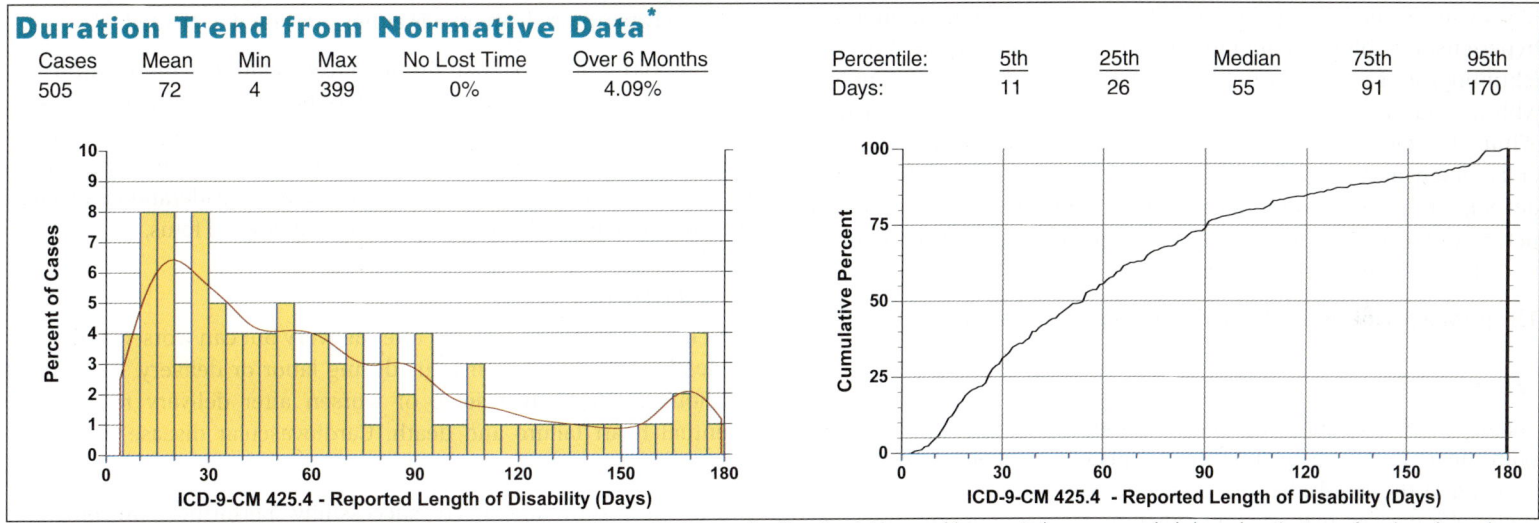

ICD-9-CM 425.4 - Reported Length of Disability (Days)

* Differences may exist between the expected duration tables and the normative graphs. Duration tables provide expected recovery periods based on the type of work performed by the individual. The normative graphs reflect the actual observed experience of many individuals across the spectrum of physical conditions, in a variety of industries, and with varying levels of case management.

Failure to Recover

If an individual fails to recover within the maximum duration expectancy period, the reader may wish to reference the following questions to assist in better understanding the specifics of an individual's medical case.

Regarding diagnosis:

- Does individual have shortness of breath (dyspnea) with ordinary activities or when lying down to sleep? On exertion?
- Is fatigue and weakness evident? Is there increased abdominal girth, swelling of the feet and ankles, and upper abdominal discomfort due to swelling of the liver?
- Are other abnormalities present such as prominent neck veins, sounds in the lungs audible with stethoscope, heart murmur, swelling of lower legs, ankles, and/or abdomen?
- Was an echocardiogram done to confirm the diagnosis and rule out other possible heart conditions?
- Was a myocardial biopsy done?
- Was diagnosis of cardiomyopathy confirmed? What type?

Regarding treatment:

- Were clinical symptoms addressed and treated appropriately?
- Is individual taking medications, as prescribed?
- Did the symptoms persist or worsen?
- Were corresponding adjustments made in specific drug therapy (additions, increased, or decreased dosage)?
- Is individual participating fully in the cardiac rehabilitation program including making lifestyle changes? If not, are there barriers that prevent compliance with the rehabilitation and treatment recommendations such as insurance limitations, lack of motivation, excess fatigue, or psychosocial stress?

Regarding prognosis:

- Does individual have any concurrent illnesses or conditions that may influence ability to recover?
- Has individual suffered from any complications that may impact recovery?
- Would individual benefit by consultation with a cardiac surgeon? Was heart surgery considered?

Cardiomyopathy

References

Beers, Mark, and Robert Berkow, eds. "Cardiomyopathy." The Merck Manual of Diagnosis and Therapy. Medical Services, USMEDSA, USHH, 1999. 01 Jan 2001 <http://www.merck.com/pubs/mmanual/section16/chapter203/203b.htm>.

Kisner, C., and L. Colby. Therapeutic Exercise Foundations and Techniques. Philadelphia: F.A. Davis, 1990.

Cardiovascular Disease in Pregnancy
648.6

Definition

Heart (cardiovascular) diseases may develop or worsen during pregnancy when there are changes in heart rate, blood pressure, blood volume, and the amount of blood pumped with each heartbeat.

In pregnant women, heart disease is most severe when there is valve narrowing (stenosis), high blood pressure in the lungs (pulmonary hypertension), blood detoured from right to left within the heart (shunting), and congestive heart failure. High blood pressure combined with a syndrome where the heart beats too rapidly (Wolff Parkinson White syndrome) can be deadly during pregnancy. Rarely, heart enlargement and congestive heart failure (peripartum cardiomyopathy) develop in the final month of pregnancy or after delivery. The cause of peripartum cardiomyopathy may be from viruses or a reaction of the body to infection (immune reaction).

The prevalence of "heart disease" among pregnant women is 0.5-2%.

Diagnosis

History: The individual may complain about shortness of breath, chest pain, heart fluttering (palpitations), episodic weakness, sweating, or swelling of the hands, legs, or feet. A past history of rheumatic fever, metabolic disease (e.g., diabetes mellitus), or serious infection (e.g., syphilis) could indicate possible predisposition to cardiovascular disease in pregnancy.

Physical exam: Blood pressure is carefully monitored. The heart is examined by listening with a stethoscope (auscultation). During pregnancy, a third heart sound and a systolic functional murmur can be normal. The heart rate normally increases. Upon physical examination, the individual may present with blue skin (cyanosis), swollen (distended) veins, fluid in the lungs, cough, breathing difficulty, and swelling of hands, legs, or feet.

Tests: An electrocardiogram (ECG) may be done to look for changes in heart rhythm and an echocardiogram to examine the heart walls and internal structures of the heart. A chest x-ray is taken to check for fluid in the lungs and measure heart size. Lab tests also include CBC, coagulation studies, and chemistry panel. Fetal ultrasound may be done to measure growth and fetal weight.

Treatment

Treatment for heart disease is best if initiated prior to pregnancy. When it is not discovered until pregnancy occurs, however, treatment aims for optimal health of the mother and fetus. Preventive treatment is vital in pregnant individuals with heart disease. To help prevent cardiac decompensation, the individual must avoid exposures and over-exertion. The physician and individual should devise a specific daily rest regimen (e.g., 10 hours/night in bed, scheduled morning and afternoon rest periods). After 20 weeks gestation, strenuous activities should be avoided. Antihypertensives, beta-blockers, or immunosuppressive drugs may be required to address symptoms. Anticoagulants may be used to prevent blood clots. Blood pressure, weight, and kidney function are closely monitored. Anemia is either prevented or treated.

If surgery is required to repair the heart (e.g., dilation of the left atrioventricular valve [mitral valvotomy]), it is best done during the last 3 months (trimester) of pregnancy. In severe cases that threaten the woman's life, a therapeutic abortion or premature delivery by cesarean section may be considered. In all cases, careful consideration is given to the preferred method of delivery for the woman and fetus.

Prognosis

Mild heart disease may resolve after delivery but can worsen and result in death of the woman or fetus during labor or delivery. Peripartum cardiomyopathy may resolve or worsen after delivery resulting in eventual heart failure and death. Cardiovascular disease may recur during future pregnancies.

Mitral valvotomy has been successfully performed on pregnant individuals, however there is a high risk of hypoxic damage to the fetus and placenta and a risk (<3%) of maternal operative mortality.

Differential Diagnosis

Preeclampsia, eclampsia, hemolysis, elevated liver enzymes, low platelets, HELLP syndrome, renal artery stenosis, coarctation of the aorta, Cushing's syndrome, systemic lupus erythematosus, and pheochromocytoma are differential diagnoses that must be ruled out.

Specialists

- Cardiologist
- Cardiovascular Surgeon
- Industrial Hygienist
- Neonatologist
- Obstetrician
- Perinatologist
- Pulmonologist
- Thoracic Surgeon

Work Restrictions / Accommodations

There may be mild to moderate restrictions on activity due to fatigue and anxiety. Work restrictions may include transfer to a sedentary job, elimination of strenuous work (especially heavy lifting), and an increased number of rest periods. The individual should avoid fumes, radiation, and chemical exposure. In certain cases, pregnancies complicated by heart disease will require complete work cessation.

Comorbid Conditions

Comorbid conditions that could impact the length or duration of disability include obesity, diabetes mellitus, kidney disease, and systemic infection.

Complications

Blood clots can form and lodge in the veins, lungs, heart, or brain. The brain, heart muscle, liver, or kidneys may be damaged resulting in hypertensive encephalopathy, stroke (cardiovascular accident), eclampsia, or kidney or heart failure. The lungs may fill with fluid (pulmonary edema). The main blood vessel in the abdomen or vessels supplying the heart may burst (dissecting aneurysm). Infection of the heart covering (pericarditis) can also occur. Drugs or other treatments can adversely affect the fetus and must be chosen with extreme care.

Factors Influencing Duration

Disability factors that will influence length of disability are the individual's age, type and severity of cardiovascular disease, treatment, complications, and the response of the woman and fetus.

Length of Disability

Duration depends on type and severity of cardiovascular disease. Contact physician for additional information.

Failure to Recover

If an individual fails to recover within the maximum duration expectancy period, the reader may wish to reference the following questions to assist in better understanding the specifics of an individual's medical case.

Regarding diagnosis:

- Was cardiovascular disease present prior to pregnancy? If not, at what stage of pregnancy did symptoms first appear?
- Does current disease involve stenosis, pulmonary hypertension, shunting, or congestive heart failure?
- Is the condition the most severe when these are present?
- Have conditions that could impact cardiovascular disease been identified or ruled out? If present, are they effectively under control?

Regarding treatment:

- Was the individual placed on bed rest?
- Were blood pressure, weight, and kidney function closely monitored?
- Did treatment include antihypertensives, beta-blockers, or immunosuppressive drugs to address symptoms?
- Were anticoagulants given to prevent blood clots?
- Was anemia prevented or treated?
- Was surgery required?
- Were there any complications to mother or child?
- Was therapeutic abortion or premature delivery by cesarean section performed?

Regarding prognosis:

- Has the individual responded to treatment?
- Was it a full term pregnancy?
- Did complications arise during labor or delivery?
- Has peripartum cardiomyopathy resolved?
- Is mother being monitored for cardiovascular complications that may yet occur?
- Has mother been informed that cardiovascular disease may recur during future pregnancies?
- Does mother comprehend the implied risk?

References

General Aspects of Heart Disease in Pregnancy. University of Washington. 1992. 25 Aug 2000 <http://faculty.washington.edu/momus/PB/generala.htm>.

Martin, Leonide L., Luigin Mastroianni, Jr., and Sharon J. Reeder. Maternity Nursing. Philadelphia: J.B. Lippincott, 1980.

Carotid Artery Occlusion
Other names / synonyms: Carotid Insufficiency
433.1

Definition

A carotid artery occlusion is a narrow, partially obstructed area in one of the carotid arteries of the neck, that prevents crucial blood flow to the brain. If blood flow to the brain continues to be blocked, a stroke, brain damage, and death can occur.

The occlusion is commonly caused by the deposit of fat cells within arterial walls (atherosclerosis), hardening and thickening of arterial walls (arteriosclerosis), or a tumor-like mass of plaque (atheroma). The blood clots (thrombi) that form as a result of these conditions can dislodge (emboli) and travel down throughout the arteries in the body, causing potentially devastating consequences. Carotid artery occlusion can be also compounded by the extension of cholesterol and calcium deposits into branches of the carotid arteries.

Other causes of carotid artery occlusion include inflammation of arteries (arteritis) or rheumatic heart disease. Thrombi and emboli from a bacterial infection of the heart (endocarditis), and an irregular beat of the upper chamber (atrium) of the heart (atrial fibrillation) or from a heart attack (myocardial infarction) can also cause occlusion. It is possible for cocaine and amphetamines to cause carotid artery occlusion.

Individuals at risk for carotid artery occlusion include those with atherosclerosis, arteriosclerosis, atheroma, hypertension, and diabetes mellitus. Most stroke-related illness and deaths occur in older adults: 74% of hospitalizations and 87% of deaths occur in individuals 65 years or older. Other risk factors include smoking, obesity, being black, and being a male. Stroke is the third leading cause of death in the US and the primary cause of disability.

Diagnosis

History: An individual may complain of fainting (syncope), dizziness, lightheadedness, confusion, headache, or nausea. The individual may also complain of numbness, weakness (hemiparesis), or temporary or permanent paralysis on one side of the body (hemiplegia). Complaints of blurred vision, difficulty with speech (aphasia), or decreased consciousness may be noted.

Physical exam: Applying light pressure with the fingertips (palpation) and listening with a stethoscope (auscultation) to the carotid arteries often reveals a soft, abnormal sound (bruit) indicating a decrease in blood flow. Blood pressure may be increased (hypertension).

Tests: Blood tests should be done to determine if the iron content in the red blood cells (hemoglobin) is low (anemia), and if the white blood cell count is elevated (leukocytosis) due to infection. Blood tests should also be done to determine if the blood clots too easily (hypercoagulable) and to determine the levels of fats in the blood (plasma lipids). A test that uses sound waves (ultrasonography) to determine if the blood flow is impaired in the carotid artery will be done. A chest x-ray should be taken to search for a primary lung tumor and cardiovascular disorders; an electrocardiogram (ECG) should be done to determine if the individual is having a heart attack or other heart problems. CT or MRI of the brain helps differentiate between lack of blood flow (ischemia), internal bleeding (hemorrhage), or a tumor. Because of its invasive nature, an x-ray view of the artery after injection of contrast medium (arteriography) may also be performed, but usually only when the diagnosis is not definite.

Treatment

Artery occlusion greater than 70% requires a surgical procedure in which an incision is made into the neck, the artery exposed, and obstruction removed (carotid endarterectomy). Closure of the artery may involve the use of a synthetic patch or graft. Chronic hypertension must be successfully treated before surgery. Active coronary artery disease may put the individual at too great risk thus eliminating surgery as a possible treatment choice. Individuals who are considered to be a surgical risk are treated with medications that inhibit clotting and prevent arterial build up.

Arteries less than 30% occluded are best managed by medically treating underlying causes, in much the same way treatment is given to those who are at surgical risk. This often includes medications for increased blood pressure (hypertension), coronary artery disease, and diabetes (oral hypoglycemics or insulin). Drugs that decrease blood clotting, such as aspirin or anticoagulants, may also be given.

Prognosis

The outcome for individuals depends on the site and size of the occlusion. If blood flow to the brain is impeded for very long clots will form; if they break free stroke, brain damage, and/or death can occur. The tissues of the brain will recover, however, if the interruption in blood flow lasts less than one hour.

Individuals who require only medical treatment for the occlusion often have a good prognosis; for those who have undergone surgical removal of the obstruction (carotid endarterectomy) the outcome is variable.

The prognosis for individuals whose disease has progressed to a stroke is difficult to predict and depends mainly on the type of brain damage sustained, however, complete recovery seldom occurs.

Differential Diagnosis

Differential diagnoses include brain tumor or abscess, seizure disorder, inflammation of the blood vessels (vasculitis), migraine headaches, and increased reaction to glucose (hyperinsulinism) in diabetics.

Specialists

- Cardiologist
- Internist
- Neurologist
- Vascular Surgeon

Work Restrictions / Accommodations

Depending upon the extent of the disease and treatment required, whether medical or surgical, the individual may need to refrain from strenuous physical activity. Transfer to a modified duty or sedentary job may be required. If the physician has ordered a rehabilitation program, individuals will require time off to participate. Individuals who have suffered a stroke may require either extended time off or permanent disability.

Comorbid Conditions

Hypertension, diabetes mellitus, obesity, and other cardiovascular diseases may lengthen disability.

Complications

Possible complications include small stroke-like attacks (transient ischemic attack--TIA), stroke, clot formation (thrombi), or bleeding (hemorrhage).

Factors Influencing Duration

Age and response to treatment, whether medical or surgical, may influence length of disability. Additionally, many individuals with coronary artery occlusion suffer a stroke, which would significantly affect length of disability.

Length of Disability

Duration depends on extent of disease, surgical procedure, and job demands.

Carotid endarterectomy.

Duration in Days

Job Classification	Minimum	Optimum	Maximum
Sedentary work	14	21	28
Light work	21	28	35
Medium work	28	35	42
Heavy work	42	49	56
Very Heavy work	42	49	56

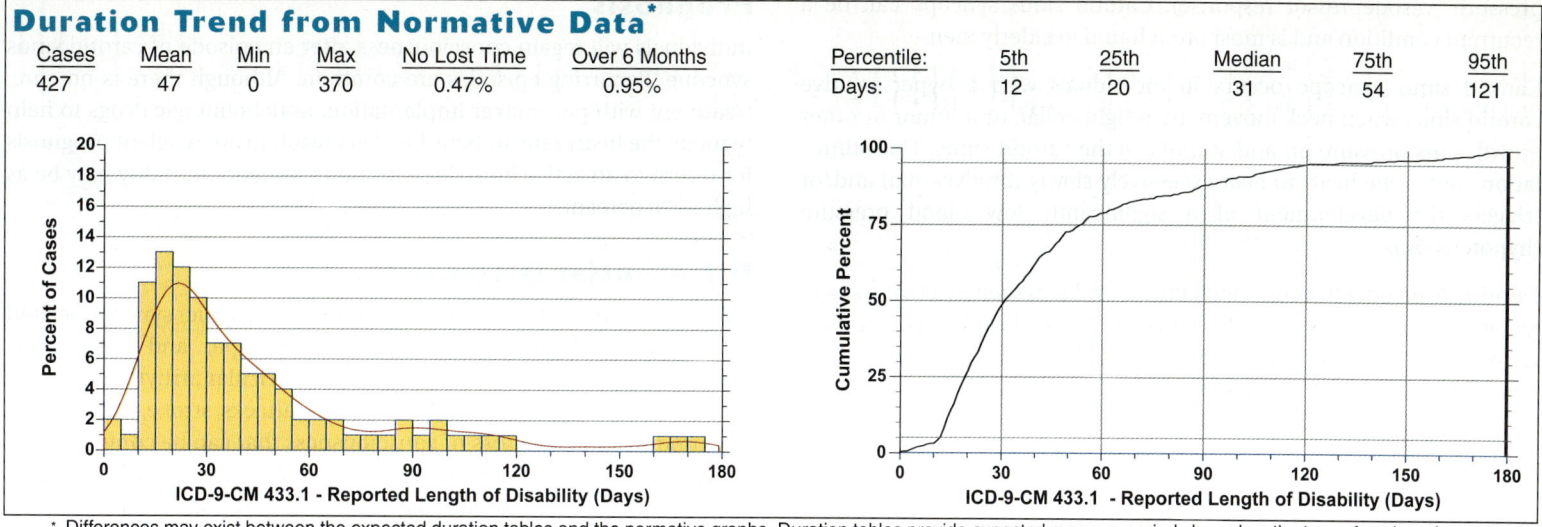

* Differences may exist between the expected duration tables and the normative graphs. Duration tables provide expected recovery periods based on the type of work performed by the individual. The normative graphs reflect the actual observed experience of many individuals across the spectrum of physical conditions, in a variety of industries, and with varying levels of case management.

Failure to Recover

If an individual fails to recover within the maximum duration expectancy period, the reader may wish to reference the following questions to assist in better understanding the specifics of an individual's medical case.

Regarding diagnosis:

- Has ultrasonography been done to evaluate blood flow in the carotid artery? Has diagnosis of carotid artery occlusion been confirmed? If diagnosis is doubtful, has arteriography been performed?
- Have conditions with similar symptoms been ruled out?
- Have coexisting conditions that may impact recovery such as hypertension, diabetes mellitus, obesity, and other cardiovascular diseases been identified or ruled out? If present, are these conditions responding to treatment?

Regarding treatment:

- If artery occlusion is greater than 70%, is individual a candidate for carotid endarterectomy? Has individual been experiencing stroke-like symptoms?
- If active coronary artery disease has put the individual at too great a risk for surgery, what are the treatment alternatives? Is individual suitable for surgical intervention at a later date?
- If artery occlusion is less than 30%, has medical treatment been successful? If not, what additional therapy is being considered?

Regarding prognosis:

- Depending on the site and size of the occlusion, what is the present prognosis for this individual if treated medically? Is individual now or ever a candidate for surgical intervention?
- If treated by endarterectomy, how successful was procedure?
- If disease has progressed to a stroke, what type of brain damage was sustained? To what extent is recovery expected?

References

Cardiovascular Diseases. American Heart Association. 2000. 05 Dec 2000 <http://www.americanheart.org/statistics/03cardio.html>.

Beers, Mark, and Robert Berkow, eds. The Merck Manual of Diagnosis and Therapy. Medical Services, USMEDSA, USHH, 1999. 05 Dec 2000 <http://www.merck.com/pubs/mmanual/section14/chapter174/174a.htm>.

Kisner, C., and L. Colby. Therapeutic Exercise Foundations and Techniques. Philadelphia: F.A. Davis, 1990.

Morgenstern, Lewis, and Scott Kasner. "Cerebrovascular Disorders. Neurology." Scientific American® Medicine Online Dale, D.C., and D.D. Federman, eds. New York: WebMD Corporation, 2000 Scientific American Medicine. 05 Dec 2000 <http://www.samed.com/sam/forms/index/htm>.

Carotid Sinus Syncope

Other names / synonyms: Carotid Sinus Hypersensitivity, Carotid Sinus Syndrome
337.0

Definition

Carotid sinus syncope is a temporary loss of consciousness or fainting (syncope) caused by overactivity or overstimulation of the carotid sinus, a receptor located in the large carotid arteries of the neck. Normally, the carotid sinus measures the blood pressure in the carotid artery and controls the heart so that the blood pressure remains constant. In carotid sinus syncope, hypersensitivity of the carotid sinus, caused by overactivity of the vagus nerve, sends a signal to the central nervous system, which initiates a reflex slowing of the heart and fall in blood pressure. The most common response is for electrical impulses triggering the heartbeat to stop (sinus node arrest), but a hypersensitive carotid sinus may also produce syncope by decreasing the blood pressure (vasodepressor response). Carotid sinus syncope can be a recurrent condition and is most often found in elderly men.

Carotid sinus syncope occurs in individuals with a hypersensitive carotid sinus when neck movement, a tight collar, or a tumor or other growth puts pressure on and stimulates the carotid sinus. This stimulation causes the heart to beat excessively slowly (bradycardia) and/or triggers the development of a significantly low blood pressure (hypotension).

Fainting (syncope) is a common clinical problem seen in 3% of visits to the emergency room, and accounts for 6% of hospital admissions. Carotid sinus syncope is more common in the elderly, especially elderly men. It is estimated that the prevalence of carotid sinus syncope might be over 40% in those individuals seeking medical assistance due to a fainting problem.

Diagnosis

History: The individual reports one or more episodes of unexplained fainting. Individuals may report turning the neck, shaving the neck, taking a shower with water hitting the neck forcefully, or wearing a tight collar before fainting. Other individuals may report having taken medication (including prescription, over-the-counter, vitamins, and herbal products), or experiencing hunger, fatigue, fear, or stress just before fainting. If other persons were present when the individual fainted, they should be asked to describe what happened immediately before, during, and immediately following the faint, and how long it took for the individual to regain consciousness.

Physical exam: A careful, gentle massage of the carotid sinus performed on one side of the neck may reveal an abnormally slow heart rate (bradycardia) and/or a significantly low blood pressure (hypotension). This should be done only by an experienced examiner and resuscitation equipment and medications should be available if needed, as the heart may stop (asystole) or a stroke could occur if a blood clot breaks off from the carotid artery. The examiner listens to the heartbeat for irregularities. A stethoscope placed over the carotid artery on both sides of the neck may reveal a murmur (carotid bruit). Such a murmur may indicate narrowing of the carotid artery.

Tests: An electrocardiogram (ECG) ay be done. Blood tests to check for possible electrolyte imbalances or anemia may also be performed. Other work-ups for other causes of syncope may also be indicated.

Treatment

A cardiac pacemaker permanently implanted into the chest wall is highly effective in treating carotid sinus syncope by electrically stimulating the heart to increase its rate when it is beating dangerously slowly. Medications may be prescribed to help regulate the heart rate. These include anticholinergic drugs (which inhibit transmission of excessive impulses from the carotid sinus) or beta-blockers (which interfere with the transmission of excessive stimuli from the carotid sinus). Individuals with carotid sinus syncope should be instructed not to wear tight collars, to use a razor rather than electric shaver, to avoid massage or pulsating showers on the neck, and to drink plenty of liquids to avoid dehydration, which may trigger syncope.

Prognosis

Individuals will regain consciousness after an episode of carotid sinus syncope. Recurring episodes are common. Although there is no cure, treatment with pacemaker implantation, anticholinergic drugs to help regulate the heart rate, or beta-blockers result in an excellent prognosis for return to an active lifestyle. Without treatment, mortality may be as high as 20 percent.

Differential Diagnosis

Other causes of syncope include postural (orthostatic) syncope related to orthostatic hypotension, vasovagal syncope, and cardiogenic syncope caused by sick sinus syndrome, ventricular arrhythmias, heart block, or aortic stenosis. Transient ischemic attacks, stroke, and epilepsy can produce transient loss of consciousness that can be confused with syncope. Intoxication with drugs or alcohol, endocrine disturbances such as hypoglycemia or adrenal failure, or infections such as urinary infection or pneumonia can also cause fainting.

Specialists

- Cardiologist

Work Restrictions / Accommodations

Without treatment, fainting (syncope) episodes will reoccur. Individuals who perform hazardous work or operate dangerous machinery may need to be reassigned to less hazardous duties. With treatment, the individual may need to assume duties gradually, especially if duties involve physical labor or the operation of dangerous equipment. Time off may be needed to attend cardiac rehabilitation programs if recommended by the individual's physician. Finally, depending on response to treatment, responsibilities involving strenuous physical labor may need to be changed if there is underlying cardiovascular disease or if the physician places limitations on physical activities. This is individualized, however, and will need to be assessed on a person-to-person basis.

Comorbid Conditions

Comorbid conditions that would affect recovery and further lengthen disability include obesity, cardiovascular disease, cerebrovascular disease, and other vascular conditions.

Complications

Complications such as injuries from falls and accidents occurring during the fainting episode may harm the individual, as well as others if the individual is driving a car or performing hazardous work.

Factors Influencing Duration

Severity of condition, frequency of syncopal episodes, response to treatment, age, general state of health, and specific job duties may influence length of disability.

Length of Disability

The length of disability will vary depending on the individual's response to treatment and the types of duties he/she performs. If physical labor is the main component of job requirements, return to work will be influenced by the effectiveness of treatment, complications of underlying disease, any continuing episodes of fainting (syncope), and the need for and response to cardiac rehabilitation.

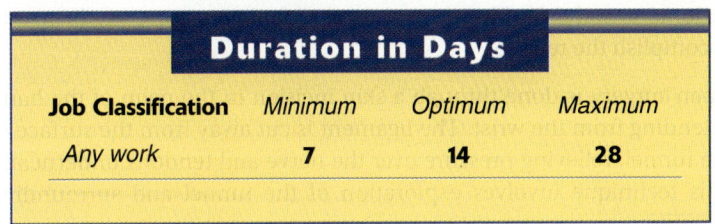

Duration in Days				
Job Classification	Minimum	Optimum	Maximum
Any work	7	14	28

Failure to Recover

If an individual fails to recover within the maximum duration expectancy period, the reader may wish to reference the following questions to assist in better understanding the specifics of an individual's medical case.

Regarding diagnosis:

- Has individual reported one or more episodes of unexplained fainting?
- Did individual have a tight collar on before fainting?
- Have they fainted while shaving the neck?
- Has individual fainted after taking medication?
- Do they report hunger, fatigue, fear, or stress just before fainting?
- Is individual elderly? Male?
- On exam did massage of the carotid sinus reveal bradycardia or hypotension?
- Did auscultation of the heart reveal any irregularities?
- Did auscultation of the carotid artery reveal any bruits?
- Has individual had an ECG? CBC? Electrolytes?
- Have other conditions with similar symptoms been ruled out?

Regarding treatment:

- Was a cardiac pacemaker permanently implanted?
- Is individual on medication to regulate the heart rate?
- Has prevention been discussed with individual?

Regarding prognosis:

- Is individual's employer able to accommodate any necessary restrictions?
- Does individual have any conditions that may affect their ability to recover?

References

Anderson, Kenneth, N., revision ed. Mosby's Medical, Nursing, and Allied Health Dictionary. St. Louis: Mosby, 1998.

Fleming, Thomas, RPh, chief ed. PDR for Herbal Medicines. Montvale: Medical Economics Company, Inc, 2000.

Leftheriotis, G., J.M. Dupuis, and J. Victor. "Cerebral Hemodynamics in Carotid Sinus Syndrome and Atrioventricular Block." American Journal of Cardiology 86 5 Pt. B (2000): 504-508.

Morag, Rumm, and Barry Brenner, MD. Syncope. eMedicine.com. 26 Jan 2001. 03 Mar 2001 <http://www.emedicine.com/emerg/topic876.htm>.

Carpal Tunnel Release

Other names / synonyms: CTR

04.43

Definition

Carpal tunnel release (CTR) is surgical treatment for carpal tunnel syndrome in the wrist. Treatment is aimed at creating more space for the median nerve and tendons that bend (flex) the fingers. Releasing or cutting the ligament that passes over the tunnel area created by the wrist bones creates more space for the compressed nerve and tendons.

Techniques for the procedure include an open release, endoscopic (arthroscopic) assisted release, and a mini-open release. All these techniques are considered outpatient procedures.

Involvement of other structures in the hand, surgeon' preference, and training influence the choice of technique used.

Elderly individuals, those with severe preoperative symptoms, and individuals involved with heavy manual labor especially if working with vibrating tools have longer, slower recovery from the procedure.

Approximately 260,000 carpal tunnel release operations are performed each year and 47% of these are related to work.

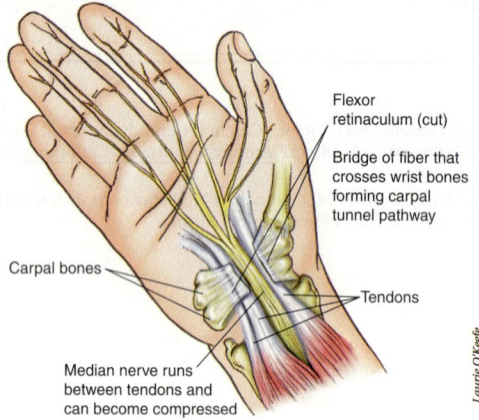

Reason for Procedure

The operation is done for carpal tunnel syndrome to relieve compression of the median nerve that supplies sensation to the thumb, index, long, and half of the ring finger. Carpal tunnel syndrome is a condition where the median nerve malfunctions resulting in numbness in these fingers, pins-and-needles (paresthesias) or pain in the fingers, and weakness in the thumb. If pressure on the median nerve is unrelieved, permanent nerve damage may occur. The goal of surgery is to alleviate symptoms of pain, tingling, and decreased strength.

The carpal tunnel is narrow and rigid and cannot expand to accommodate any swelling of the tendons or nerve. Swelling and subsequent nerve compression can result from normal wear and tear of aging, repetitive movements of the hand, dislocation or fracture of the wrist, rheumatoid arthritis, hypothyroidism, diabetes, or fluid retention (edema) in carpal tunnel (i.e., during pregnancy).

Carpal tunnel syndrome is most common in women although surgery is not always necessary. Pregnant woman for example most often recover completely after delivery.

How Procedure Is Performed

CTR is performed as an outpatient or in-office procedure under local or regional anesthesia. There are several techniques currently in use to accomplish the release.

Open surgery is done through a skin incision in the palm of the hand extending from the wrist. The ligament is cut away from the surface of the tunnel, relieving pressure over the nerve and tendons underneath. This technique involves exploration of the tunnel and surrounding structures.

Endoscopic-assisted carpal tunnel release utilizes standard arthroscopic technique with specially designed, smaller instruments. This procedure allows exploration of the tunnel with less tissue damage and release of the tendon while looking upward from below the ligament itself (as opposed to the open- and mini-open technique where the ligament is cut from above). However, the surgeon does not have the same view of other parts of the hand as seen during open procedures. Arthroscopic or endoscopic technique results in less scarring and a shorter disability time according to some research studies.

Choice of technique used by the surgeon depends on his/her training, the severity of symptoms, and availability of equipment.

Percutaneous balloon carpal tunnelplasty is an experimental technique where a small balloon-tipped catheter is inserted into the tunnel through skin incision and then inflated to stretch the ligament.

Prognosis

Release of the pressure on the nerve usually provides immediate relief from pain. Changes in sensation however may take a few weeks to resolve and regaining strength of the hand could take several weeks to months.

Although carpal tunnel surgery is one of the most common procedures in the US, there are few long-term outcome studies. Results of one study did show that 87% of individuals felt their recovery to be good to excellent along with 70% in another study reporting improvement of at least one symptom (pain, numbness, and tingling). Of these individuals, over 90% had improvement in grip strength.

Specialists

- Hand Surgeon
- Orthopedic Surgeon
- Plastic Surgeon

Rehabilitation

Individuals who undergo carpal tunnel release surgery may require outpatient therapy. Individuals should receive therapy from an occupational therapist or a physical therapist who is a certified hand therapist.

The first objective of therapy is to control pain and swelling. Individuals may use heat prior to therapy to increase muscle flexibility and decrease pain. Individuals may utilize ice packs after therapy to decrease pain and swelling. Individuals learn to perform scar massage to decrease the risk of forming painful adhesions. In addition, individuals may be provided with resting splints that place the wrist and hand in a less stressful position.

The second objective of therapy is to restore any lost range of motion at the wrist and hand. Therapists may passively stretch the wrist into flexion and extension within a pain-free range. Individuals may also stretch the wrist into these motions by adding overpressure with the other hand to increase the stretch. Individuals may perform active range-of-motion movements for wrist flexion and extension as well as thumb opposition to the other fingers.

The third objective of therapy is to restore strength at the wrist and hand. Individuals may use light hand weights to resist wrist flexion and extension. Individuals manually resist thumb flexion, extension, abduction, and opposition in order to increase thumb strength. Squeezing therapy putty also restores power grip. Squeezing resistive putty between the thumb and the first two fingers restores pinching strength.

The final objective of therapy is to discover if any factors in the individual's environment either at work or at home contributed to the carpal tunnel syndrome. For example, an individual may need to lower the height of the computer desk or use an ergonomic keyboard so the hands can be held in a more neutral position when typing.

Work Restrictions / Accommodations

If the carpal tunnel syndrome resulted from job-related activity, the individual may need to limit or remove the aggravating activity. The individual should take periodic rest periods, alternate activities, and/or wear a specially tailored splint. Correction of posture, avoiding prolonged exposure to vibration, and reconditioning of the hand are important.

During recovery from surgery, restrictions may include no use of the involved hand, no heavy lifting, and twisting of the hand or repetitive activity such as work on a conveyer belt.

Comorbid Conditions

Coexisting conditions that may impact recovery and lengthen disability include those that increase pressure on the nerve such as diabetes, rheumatoid arthritis, hypothyroidism, renal failure, obesity, high blood pressure, injury to the wrist or hand, and inflammation around the tendons (tenosynovitis). Damage to the median nerve from carpal tunnel syndrome may be permanent and therefore not relieved by surgery.

Other conditions of the upper extremity areas such as thoracic outlet syndrome and cervical radiculopathy from a herniated disc or cervical spondylosis particularly at C7 can mimic carpal tunnel syndrome and would not be relieved by carpal tunnel surgery.

Because of hormone changes that can cause fluid retention with tissue swelling, use of birth control pills, pregnancy, premenstrual syndrome, and menopause are also associated with carpal tunnel syndrome and influence recovery from CTR.

Procedure Complications

Tenosynovitis of the adjacent tendons may continue to cause pain after surgery. Infection is not common but can occur. Contracture of the skin and soft tissues can complicate recovery. Damage to the nerve during surgery is a risk in any of the techniques described. Reflex sympathetic dystopy is an uncommon complication. Scarring, pain, and stiffness may result. Risks involved with any of the techniques include damage to the median nerve or flexor tendons, increased inflammation, infection, skin contractures, and scarring. Some individuals may experience temporary loss of sensation on their fingers or return of preoperative symptoms.

Factors Influencing Duration

Factors include severity of the carpal tunnel syndrome and the duration of symptoms before CTR was performed. The longer the median nerve was compressed, the longer it may take for the nerve to recover. Recovery times are variable. Any postoperative complications will increase length of disability. Length of disability relates to hand activity (repetitive motion, awkward posture, grip force used) and may not directly relate to the amount of weight lifted.

Older individuals, those with severe preoperative symptoms, and individuals involved with heavy manual labor especially if working with vibrating tools have longer, slower recovery from the procedure.

Length of Disability

Because of some expected loss of wrist strength after surgery, up to 30% of individuals may not be able to return to a job that requires high amounts of force to the hand and wrist. Return to work following surgery is variable and may take longer with open procedure by up to 50%. Studies indicate that between 10-15% of individuals change jobs after surgery.

Open or endoscopic surgery.

Duration in Days

Job Classification	Minimum	Optimum	Maximum
Sedentary work	7	14	42
Light work	14	28	42
Medium work	14	35	56
Heavy work	28	42	84
Very Heavy work	28	56	84

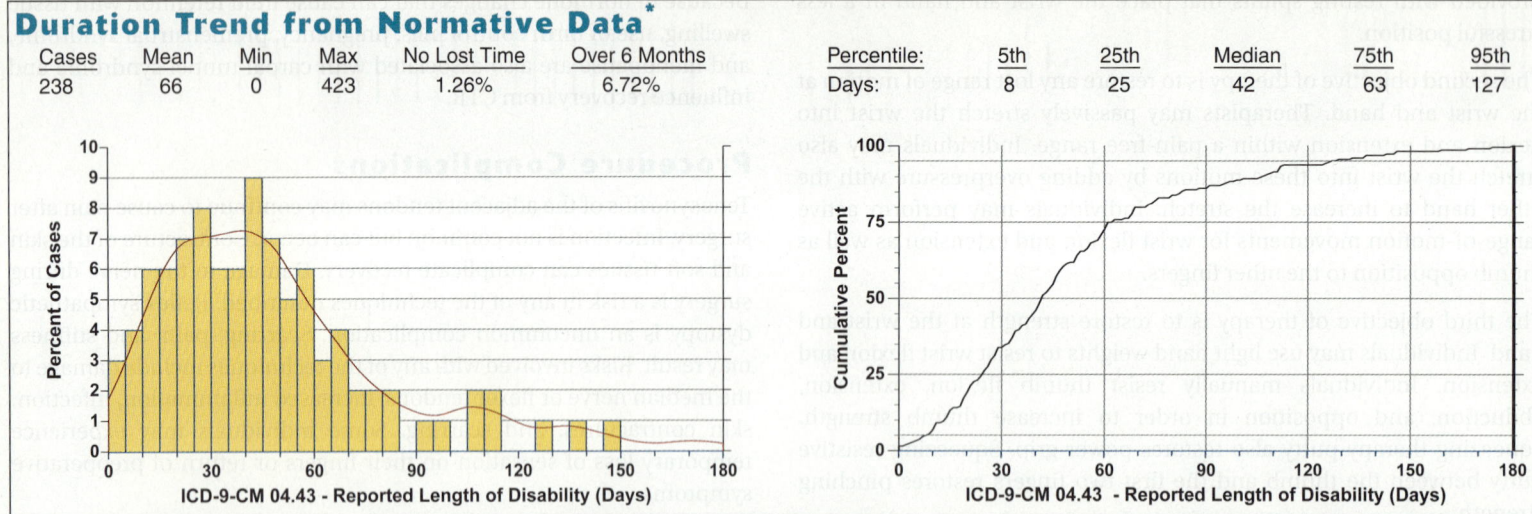

Duration Trend from Normative Data*

Cases	Mean	Min	Max	No Lost Time	Over 6 Months
238	66	0	423	1.26%	6.72%

Percentile:	5th	25th	Median	75th	95th
Days:	8	25	42	63	127

* Differences may exist between the expected duration tables and the normative graphs. Duration tables provide expected recovery periods based on the type of work performed by the individual. The normative graphs reflect the actual observed experience of many individuals across the spectrum of physical conditions, in a variety of industries, and with varying levels of case management.

References

Carpal Tunnel Syndrome. The Center for Orthopaedics and Sports Medicine. 03 Jun 1999. 16 Jun 2000 <http://www.arthroscopy.com/sp04004.htm>.

Magee, David J. "Forearm, Wrist, and Hand." Orthopedic Physical Assessment. Biblis, Margaret M., ed. Philadelphia: W.B. Saunders Company, 1992. 168-215.

Carpal Tunnel Syndrome

Other names / synonyms: CTS, Median Nerve Compression

354, 354.0

Definition

Considerable controversy continues to surround the cause (etiology), definition, diagnosis and treatment of persons with this disorder.

Carpal tunnel syndrome (CTS) refers to a condition where pain, prickling or tingling (paresthesias), or numbness radiates from the wrist into the palm of the hand and then down into the thumb, index, middle, and the thumb-side of the ring fingers. It is caused by an unusual pressure on the median nerve.

The main (median) nerve and its branches enter the hand through an internal opening (carpal tunnel) formed by the wrist bones (carpal bones) and the tough membrane that holds the bones together (transverse carpal ligaments). The median nerve supplies sensation to the palm of the hand, thumb, and first three fingers. Because this passageway is rigid, inflammation, swelling, or increased fluid retention may compress the nerve (nerve entrapment), causing pain and changes in sensation along the pathways where the nerve runs. Pain may eventually extend to the arm, shoulder, or neck.

Common causes of CTS are activities involving highly repetitive wrist motion, holding the wrist in awkward positions for sustained periods of time, and work-task stresses. Conditions that may lead to CTS include pregnancy, rheumatoid arthritis, renal failure, diabetes mellitus, acromegaly, multiple myeloma, amyloidosis, obesity, recent tuberculosis, fungal infection, and high blood pressure (hypertension).

Trauma or injury such as a wrist fracture or swelling of membranes surrounding the tendons in affected areas (tenosynovitis) may cause CTS. It may also occur in some individuals with degenerative neck conditions (cervical spondylosis). There is an increased frequency of CTS in alcoholics. In many cases, no source for the condition is readily apparent.

CTS is more common in women between the ages of 30 and 60. While women are three times more likely to have the condition than men, some studies indicate that incidence may also be strongly related to tasks performed. One study shows that men and women performing the same tasks have the same risk factors. Young men and women who perform highly repetitive tasks in the workplace are now emerging as a high-risk group. Repeated use of vibrating tools or tools requiring continual, firm gripping may lead to CTS.

Studies indicate that about 25% of workers in meatpacking industries in both the US and Europe develop CTS. Estimates of prevalence in the US vary from as low as 0.1% in the general population to 16% in workers in high-stress industries. A study from Great Britain indicated that up to 16% of the population develops CTS. In Sweden, a study found that about 4% of the general population had clinically proven CTS.

Diagnosis

History: Individuals may describe pain, tingling, numbness, or feeling of weakness in the wrist, hand, or fingers. In mild cases, pain is intermittent and often worsens at night or when individual first arises in the morning. The individual may complain of dropping items more frequently than usual. The fingers may at times feel "locked" and there may be problems pinching or grasping objects. On occasion, pain may radiate into the forearm, shoulder, neck, or chest. Hands or lower arms

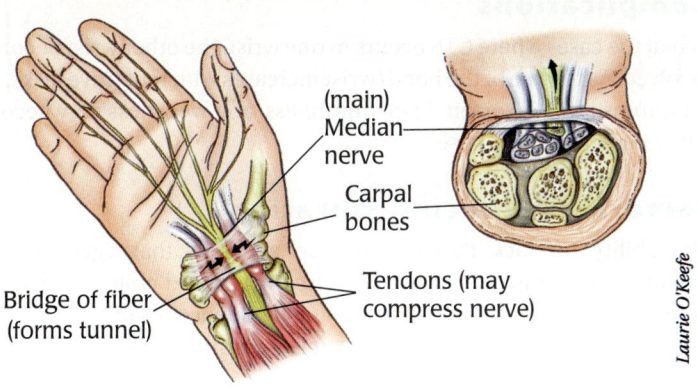

feel weak in the morning. Individuals with CTS may have problems performing detailed tasks such as writing or tying shoes, or tasks that require strength. Symptoms may be relieved by shaking the hand.

Physical exam: Changes in sensation are noted along the median nerve in the palm of the hand, thumb, and the first three fingers. There may be localized swelling in the wrist as well as tender spots where touched or squeezed (palpation). In chronic or severe cases, the palm may appear to be wasting away near the thumb (thenar eminence). The individual may be shown a diagram of the hand and wrist to indicate where pain or other sensations are present. An unaffected little finger generally indicates CTS.

Tapping on the median nerve near the front of the wrist typically reproduces the tingling feeling in the hand or forearm (positive Tinel's Sign). Flexing the individual's wrist against resistance and maintaining the position for between 15 seconds to 4 minutes may reproduce the pain and tingling (positive Phalen's Sign). These methods have a high rate of both false positive and false negative findings. Hand grip test may be weak.

Tests: Nerve conduction studies are performed to evaluate the nerve function (nerve conduction velocity, electromyography) and are the only objective tests that confirm the diagnosis. Blood tests (serology) for detection of rheumatoid arthritis, diabetes, and thyroid disease are frequently performed. Internal imaging of the wrist and hand (MRI) may be required in extreme cases to detect possible injuries. Plain film x-rays of the wrist are used to rule out bony abnormalities.

Treatment

Conservative treatment may include eliminating or greatly reducing movements or tasks that seem to cause or exacerbate the condition such as repetitive motion of the wrist and fingers or wrist-bending extremes (flexion and extension). Other treatment may include taking anti-inflammatory medication, wearing protective splints while at work and/or sleeping, stretching exercises, diuretics if appropriate, and possible corticosteroid injections into the carpal tunnel. An electrical current may be used to move medication through the skin into the area requiring treatment (iontophoresis).

In chronic or severe cases not related to pregnancy, surgery may be required. The procedure (open carpal tunnel release) involves cutting the ligament (roof of the carpal tunnel) and removing inflamed tissue around the tendons to relieve the pressure on the nerve. This is generally done on an outpatient basis with local anesthesia. Newer techniques involve inserting a fiberoptic scope through a small incision (endoscopic carpal tunnel release) to observe the inside of wrist structures during the procedure while incising the carpal ligament.

Prognosis

Symptoms may resolve with conservative management including reducing or abstaining from the aggravating activities. If pain and tingling increase or if weakness persists, surgery may be necessary. More than 80% of individuals experience permanent relief of symptoms after carpal tunnel release surgery. Endoscopic surgical methods are believed to have an even higher success rate because they require smaller incisions and shorter recovery time. Activity-related hand pain if due to CTS usually resolves in 1 to 2 months. Tingling and numbness may last a few weeks or months. Grip strength returns to normal, gradually over 1 to 2 years.

Differential Diagnosis

Other possible diagnoses include tendinitis of the wrist, rheumatoid arthritis, a tumor, diabetes, or hypothyroidism. A pinched nerve in the neck or elbow, cervical disc disorder, or thoracic outlet syndrome may mimic the symptoms of CTS.

Specialists

- Anesthesiologist
- Hand Therapist
- Neurologist
- Neurosurgeon
- Orthopedic Surgeon
- Physiatrist

Rehabilitation

Individuals with carpal tunnel syndrome may require outpatient therapy. Individuals should receive therapy from an occupational therapist or a physical therapist who is a certified hand therapist.

The first objective of therapy is pain control. Individuals may use heat prior to therapy to increase muscle flexibility and decrease pain. Individuals may use ice packs after therapy to decrease pain and swelling. In addition, splints may be provided that place the wrist and hand in a less stressful position.

The second objective of therapy is to restore any range of motion lost at the wrist and hand. Therapists may passively stretch the wrist into flexion and extension within a pain-free range. Individuals may also stretch the wrist into these motions by adding overpressure with the other hand to increase the stretch. Individuals engage in active range of motion for wrist flexion and extension as well as thumb opposition to the other fingers.

The third objective of therapy is the restoration of strength at the wrist and hand. Individuals may use light hand weights to resist wrist flexion and extension. Individuals use manual resistance with thumb flexion, extension, abduction, and opposition to increase thumb strength. Power grip is also restored by squeezing therapy putty. Pinching strength is restored by squeezing resistive putty between the thumb and the first two fingers.

The final objective of therapy is to discover if any factors in the individual's environment, either at work or home contributed to the CTS. For example, an individual may need to lower the height of the computer desk or may need an ergonomic keyboard that allows the hands to be held in a more neutral position when typing.

Complementary and Alternative Therapies

Content is intended for awareness only. Treatments may or may not be effective. Scientific evidence may be lacking and some substances have potentially toxic effects. Dr. Presley Reed and the editors do not endorse the use of these therapies in the absence of consultation with a licensed medical professional.

Acupressure -	Pressure applied to specific points may relieve pain.
Acupuncture -	May help relieve discomfort.
Bodywork -	Gentle wrist exercises and neck stretches can ease the pain of CTS and may help release the pinched nerve.
Hydrotherapy -	Cold compresses or alternating hot and cold compresses may provide relief.
Neural therapy -	Injections of anesthetics may treat the pain of chronic CTS.
Vitamin B6 -	May help relieve discomfort, but is not a cure. May work as a diuretic, reducing the swelling that often contributes to CTS.
Bromelain supplements -	May ease discomfort.
Arnica -	Applied externally, it may help relieve swelling and soreness.
Hypericum -	Applied externally, it may soothe inflammation.
Riboflavin and Biotin -	May enhance vitamin B6 effectiveness.

Work Restrictions / Accommodations

The individual may need to avoid tasks requiring repetitive wrist motion and extremes of wrist bending (flexion, extension) until the condition is resolved. Additionally, protective wrist splints may be used during work and sleep to maintain neutral wrist positions. Accommodation may be required at workstations such as ergonomically designed computer keyboards to provide support for the individual's hand and wrist. If the individual has had surgery, time off from work may be needed for several weeks for recovery. The individual may be required to avoid heavy lifting and repetitive motion for up to 2 months after surgery.

Comorbid Conditions

Diabetes mellitus or obesity may lengthen disability.

Complications

In half the cases where CTS occurs in one wrist, the other wrist becomes involved. As the use of the hand/wrist increases with repetitive tasks, the symptoms of CTS worsen. Pain, numbness, and weakness may become constant in advanced cases.

Factors Influencing Duration

The ability (or lack thereof) to stop activities that aggravate the condition, response to conservative treatment, and ability to perform tasks while wearing adaptive splints may influence disability time. The endoscopic form of carpal tunnel release surgery involving smaller incisions has a shorter recovery period.

Length of Disability

In a small percentage of cases, individuals may experience chronic problems because of nerve damage that may result from carpal tunnel syndrome. Recovery time for surgical treatment is variable and may take longer with open procedure by up to 50%.

Medical treatment (including injection).

Duration in Days

Job Classification	Minimum	Optimum	Maximum
Sedentary work	0	7	21
Light work	0	7	21
Medium work	0	14	28
Heavy work	0	21	42
Very Heavy work	0	28	63

Open or endoscopic surgery.

Duration in Days

Job Classification	Minimum	Optimum	Maximum
Sedentary work	7	14	42
Light work	14	28	42
Medium work	14	35	56
Heavy work	28	42	84
Very Heavy work	28	56	84

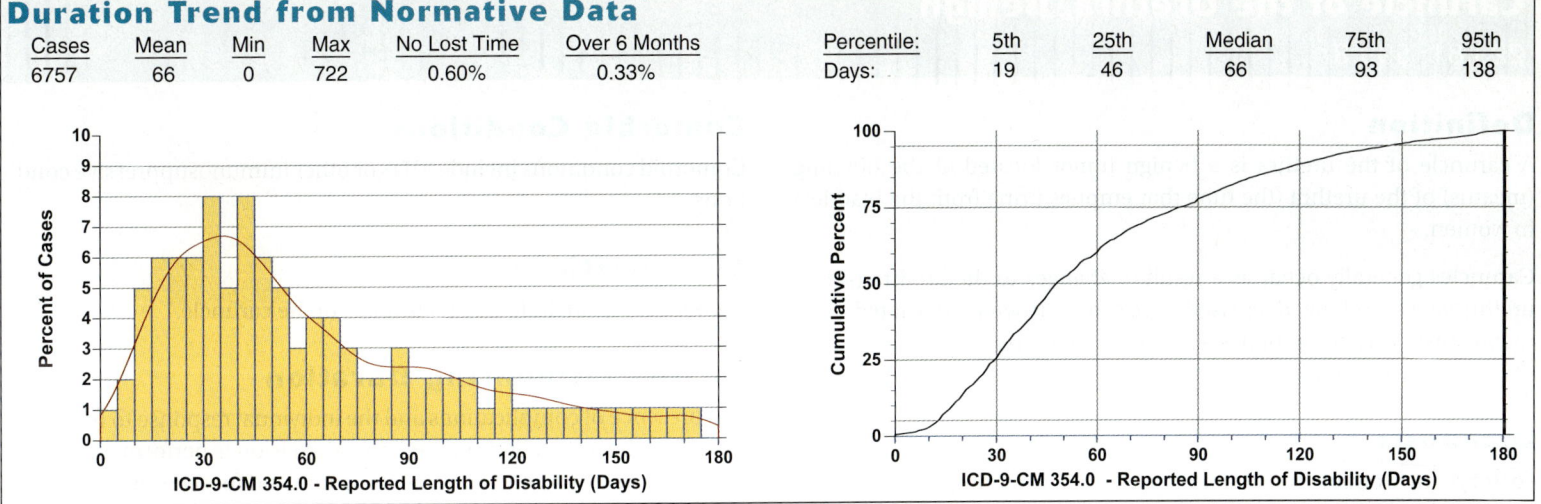

Failure to Recover

If an individual fails to recover within the maximum duration expectancy period, the reader may wish to reference the following questions to assist in better understanding the specifics of an individual's medical case.

Regarding diagnosis:

- Does individual have pain, tingling, numbness, or feeling of weakness in the wrist, hand, or fingers? Is pain intermittent, often worsening at night or when individual first gets up in the morning?
- Does individual complain of dropping items more frequently than usual?
- Do fingers feel "locked" at times? Does individual have problems pinching or grasping objects?
- Does physical exam reveal changes in sensation along the median nerve in the palm of the hand, thumb, and the first three fingers? Is localized swelling seen in the wrist as well as tender spots where touched or squeezed (palpation)?
- Does palm appear to be wasting away near the thumb (thenar eminence)?
- Does individual have a positive Tinel's or Phalen's sign?
- Were nerve conduction studies performed to evaluate the nerve function (nerve conduction velocity, electromyography)?
- Was diagnosis of carpal tunnel syndrome confirmed?
- Were conditions with similar symptoms ruled out?

Regarding treatment:

- If conservative methods have failed to relieve symptoms, is individual a candidate for carpal tunnel release?
- Did individual undergo open or endoscopic carpal tunnel release?
- Did individual experience any complications from the surgical procedure itself?
- Does individual continue to experience symptoms even after surgical intervention?
- What further treatment options are being considered?

Regarding prognosis:

- Does pain persist even after 2 months have passed since treatment?
- Does individual perform repetitive tasks such as gripping a tool for prolonged periods of time?
- Can individual refrain from activities that may aggravate the condition for as long as pain or other symptoms persist?
- Until symptoms resolve, should individual be transferred temporarily to a position that does not require repetitive motion?
- Is individual's computer keyboard ergonomically designed to provide support for the hand and wrist?
- Was individual given a splint to provide support for the wrist and hand? If so, is it being utilized as instructed?
- Does individual have a coexisting condition such as diabetes or pregnancy that may impact recovery?

References

A Patient's Guide to Cumulative Trauma Disorders: Carpal Tunnel Syndrome. Medical Multimedia Group. 22 May 2000. 25 Oct 2000 <http://www.sechrest.com/mmg/reflib/ctd/cts/cts.html>.

Kisner, Carolyn, and Lynn Allen Colby. "The Wrist and Hand." Therapeutic Exercise: Foundations and Techniques, 2nd ed. Philadelphia: F.A. Davis Company, 1990. 289-315.

Caruncle of the Urethra, Benign
223.81, 599.3

Definition
A caruncle of the urethra is a benign tumor located at the opening (meatus) of the urethra (the tube that empties urine from the bladder) in women.

Caruncles generally occur as a result of changes to the urethra (senile urethritis) caused by decreased levels of estrogen associated with menopause. It is commonly seen after menopause, and is only rarely seen prior to menopause.

Diagnosis
History: The woman is postmenopause. She may report pain with intercourse and after urinating. She may report bloody spotting with very mild trauma, and she may observe blood on the toilet paper after urinating.

Physical exam: On pelvic examination, a red, tender mass that bleeds easily is noted. It may have a broad base (sessile), or it may appear to be attached to the underlying tissue by a stem-like band (pedicle). It is observed at the backside (posterior) of the urethral meatus.

Tests: Biopsy of the mass may be required for definitive diagnosis.

Specialists
- Gynecologist
- Urologist

Treatment
Treatment of a urethral caruncle depends on severity of symptoms. No treatment is necessary for mild symptoms. Local removal (excision) of the caruncle may be performed if symptoms are troublesome to the woman. If senile urethritis is present, treatment with hormonal vaginal suppositories may be recommended. If the lesion is urethral cancer, definitive resection is the recommended treatment. The extent of treatment depends on size of lesion.

Prognosis
The outcome of mild symptoms is usually good. Surgical removal is only rarely indicated. Surgical removal of the caruncle is usually successful in treating the problem. The predicted outcome of treatment of urethral cancer that has not spread is good. However, if the cancer has spread the outcome is poor.

Differential Diagnosis
A urethral caruncle may be mistaken for several other conditions, including urethral cancer, senile urethritis, and thrombosis of the urethral vein.

Work Restrictions / Accommodations
Lifting and activity may be restricted for a short period during recovery from excision.

Comorbid Conditions
Comorbid conditions include AIDS or other immunosuppressive conditions.

Complications
Complications include rare recurrence of the caruncle.

Factors Influencing Duration
The presence of complications and the individual response to treatment will affect the length of disability. If local excision is performed, time off from work will be needed for the procedure and for recovery.

Length of Disability
Excision.

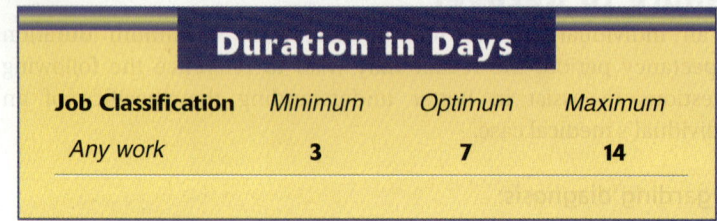

Duration in Days

Job Classification	Minimum	Optimum	Maximum
Any work	3	7	14

Failure to Recover
If an individual fails to recover within the maximum duration expectancy period, the reader may wish to reference the following questions to assist in better understanding the specifics of an individual's medical case.

Regarding diagnosis:
- Is woman past menopause?
- Does pain occur with intercourse and after urinating? Has bloody spotting with very mild trauma occurred? Blood on toilet paper after urinating?
- On pelvic exam, was a red tender mass that bleeds easily noted? Does it have a broad base (sessile) or is it attached to the underlying tissue by a stem-like band (pedicle)? Is it located at the backside (posterior) of the urethral meatus?
- Was a biopsy done to rule out cancer of the urethra?
- Would individual benefit from consultation with a gynecologist or urologist?
- Were other conditions such as urethral cancer, senile urethritis, and thrombosis of the urethral vein ruled out?

Regarding treatment:
- Were the symptoms severe enough to warrant treatment?
- Is surgical intervention necessary?
- If the caruncle was associated with senile urethritis, did treatment include hormonal vaginal suppositories?

Regarding prognosis:
- Did symptoms persist despite treatment?
- Has adequate time elapsed for complete recovery?
- Could this be a recurrence rather than lack of resolution?
- Does individual have a coexisting condition such as an immune suppressive disorder that may complicate treatment or impact recovery?

References

Doherty, Mark G., Larry J. Copeland, and Matthew A. Powell. "Clinical Anatomy of the Pelvis." Textbook of Gynecology, 2nd ed. Copeland, Larry J Philadelphia: W.B. Saunders Company, 2000. 17-57.

Morrow, C. Paul, and John P. Curtin. "Tumors of the Vulva." Synopsis of Gynecologic Oncology, 5th ed. Morrow, C. Paul, and John P. Curtin, eds. New York: Churchill Livingstone, 1998. 61-87.

Nagle, Gratia M. "Genitourinary Surgery." Alexander's Care of the Patient in Surgery. Meeker, Margaret H., and Jane C. Rothrock, eds. St. Louis: Mosby, 1999. 501-598.

Tanagho, Emil A. "Disorders of the Female Urethra." Smith's General Urology, 15th ed. Tanagho, Emil A., and Jack W. McAninch, eds. New York: Lange Medical Books/ McGraw-Hill, 2000. 676-683.

Cat Scratch Disease
Other names / synonyms: Cat Scratch Bartonellosis, CSD
078.3

Definition

Cat scratch disease is an infection transmitted to humans from cats by a scratch or other injury. It is caused by the bacterium Bartonella henselae.

Usually the cat is a kitten or young cat. The cat will have no evidence of illness. Rarely, the individual affected will not have exposure to cats, but will become infected from scratches from a dog, monkey, or from a thorn puncture. The condition occurs worldwide, and in temperate climates has a seasonal predominance between August and January.

Individuals who have HIV infection or are undergoing immunosuppressive therapy may develop a disseminated form of the disease. However, neither form of the infection is life threatening.

Approximately 43% of infected individuals are female. Family outbreaks have been reported in households with cats.

Diagnosis

History: Most individuals relate a history of exposure to cats and 75% relate a specific episode of a scratch or bite. Usually a primary lesion will develop within a few days at the site of the scratch. One to three weeks later, symptoms of a generalized infection will appear and the regional lymph nodes become enlarged. Fever and severe systemic symptoms may last for weeks.

Physical exam: The exam may reveal an infected, scabbed ulcer or a small, circular, solid elevation of the skin with a central pus-filled region. The lymph nodes are swollen, become filled with pus, occasionally draining spontaneously. Rashes of variable appearance may be seen.

Tests: Microscopic examination with special staining of a smear from the infection will reveal the organism. Skin testing is usually positive. Lymph node biopsy, which is rarely indicated, would show characteristic lesions called granulomas, which are masses of capillary buds and fibroblasts.

Treatment

Cat scratch disease usually resolves without therapy. The more severe disseminated form is treated with antibiotics. If a swollen lymph node fails to subside spontaneously after a few months and is painful, needle aspiration can be done to relieve pain and hasten recovery.

Prognosis

The prognosis for this infection is excellent. Although some individuals develop fever and severe systemic symptoms that may last for weeks, full recovery is expected, even in immunosuppressed individuals.

Differential Diagnosis

Lymphoma and other malignancies, tuberculosis, lymphogranuloma venereum, and acute bacterial infection may mimic the lymph node involvement. Cat scratch fever may be differentiated on the basis of nodal biopsy.

Specialists

- Infectious Disease Physician
- Internist

Work Restrictions / Accommodations

Work accommodations may be required while fever or severe systemic symptoms persist. These consist of permitting the individual to have decreased work duties and frequent rest breaks if fever, malaise, or fatigue occurs.

Complementary and Alternative Therapies

Content is intended for awareness only. Treatments may or may not be effective. Scientific evidence may be lacking and some substances have potentially toxic effects. Dr. Presley Reed and the editors do not endorse the use of these therapies in the absence of consultation with a licensed medical professional.

Heat therapy - Heat applied to painful lymph node may help relieve inflammation and discomfort.

Comorbid Conditions

Individuals who have HIV infection or are undergoing immunosuppressive therapy may develop a disseminated form of the disease. The infection, however, is not life threatening.

Complications

In rare instances, encephalitis may occur.

Factors Influencing Duration

Age and immune status will influence the length of disability. Immunocompromised individuals may develop complications that respond well to antibiotic treatment.

Length of Disability

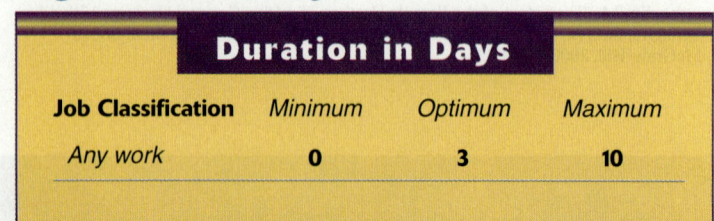

Job Classification	Minimum	Optimum	Maximum
Any work	0	3	10

Failure to Recover

If an individual fails to recover within the maximum duration expectancy period, the reader may wish to reference the following questions to assist in better understanding the specifics of an individual's medical case.

Regarding diagnosis:

- Does individual have a history of exposure to cats?
- Was individual recently scratched or bitten by a cat?
- On exam, was an infected, scabbed ulcer or a small, circular, solid elevation of the skin with a central pus-filled region present? Are lymph nodes swollen, filled with pus, and occasionally drain spontaneously? Are rashes of variable appearance seen?
- Was microscope examination with special staining of a smear from infection done?
- Was the diagnosis confirmed?
- In uncertain cases, was a blood test for antibodies or a lymph node biopsy used to confirm the diagnosis?

Regarding treatment:

- If symptoms are not resolving, if the infection is widespread, or if individual is immunosuppressed, is antibiotic therapy warranted?
- If a painful, swollen lymph node fails to subside after a few months, would needle aspiration drainage of the node help relieve pain and hasten recovery?

Regarding prognosis:

- Do symptoms persist beyond expected duration?
- Does diagnosis need to be revisited?
- Has individual experienced complications related to the illness such as eye problems with visual changes or brain swelling accompanied by headache or stupor?
- Does individual have an underlying condition that may impact recovery?
- Would individual benefit from evaluation by an infectious disease specialist?

References

Berkow, Robert, Mark H. Beers, and Andrew J. Fletcher, eds. The Merck Manual of Medical Information - Home Edition. Whitehouse Station, NJ: Merck & Co, Inc, 1997.

Maguina, C., and E. Gotuzzo. "Bartonellosis: Old and New." Infectious Disease Clinics of North America 14 1 (2000): 1-22.

Cataract
366, 366.1, 366.2, 366.4, 366.8, 366.9, 743.3

Definition

A cataract is a cloudy (opaque) area in the normally clear crystalline lens of the eye. Vision deteriorates when cloudiness obstructs light as it travels through the lens to the retina where focusing occurs. Cataracts spread over the entire lens or manifest as small, scattered cloudy areas. They are generally painless and occur over a period of a few months to several years.

An early stage of cataract development can produce increased hardness and density at the center of the lens (nuclear sclerosis). In an advanced stage, a cataract may appear brownish rather than the typical gray or white. Cataracts in adults can occur in the outer covering around the lens (capsule), the center (nucleus), or the area around the center (cortex). Cataracts may stop developing in the early stages and cause only minor vision decrease. If growth continues, vision will worsen and treatment will be needed.

Cataracts due to aging (senile) are the most common. Other causes include injury (trauma), infection, exposure to x-rays or sunlight (ultraviolet B radiation), drugs such as corticosteroids, diuretics or thiazines, and diseases such as diabetes mellitus. Smoking and alcohol use have been found to increase cataract occurrence. High levels of uric acid and low levels of riboflavin, vitamin E, iron, and protein are also thought to contribute to cataract formation. Cataracts are the leading cause of blindness in the world and the third leading cause of preventable blindness in the US. More than half of people aged 65 or older have cataracts. Cataract removal is the most common surgery for this age group.

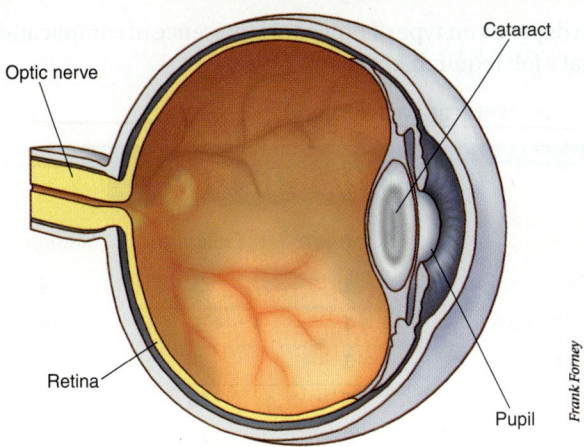

Diagnosis

History: Blurred or cloudy vision and the inability to see properly at night are among symptoms of cataracts. Individuals also may have difficulty perceiving light sources, which can produce glare or halos. Indistinct or double vision (diplopia) may occur continually or sporadically. An individual may report a new though temporary ability to read without glasses. Vision may lack subtle variations in shading. Pain typically is absent unless the cataract swells and causes increased pressure in the eyes (secondary glaucoma). Vision loss can be sudden or gradual.

Physical exam: A physical exam using an ophthalmoscope and slit lamp will reveal a cataract in a dilated pupil. Visual acuity is measured at a distance using high and low lighting with the Snellen visual acuity chart. Impairment of ability to see letters or shapes at a distance may be detected.

Tests: An examination using various lenses is performed to see if glasses or contact lenses can improve vision. Eyedrops dilate the pupil to enable thorough examination. A type and grade then are assigned to the cataract. Cataracts are commonly classified according to the color and severity of the cloudiness. A central (nuclear) cataract is graded according to the percentage of area affected. In cases of cataracts found in peripheral (cortical) or outer covering (posterior subcapsular), grades range from one (least affected) to four (most affected). The pressure inside the eye (intraocular pressure) can be measured to rule out glaucoma (tonography). Tests that measure the ability to see different color shading (contrast sensitivity testing) and glare may be performed. Dye may be injected into a hand vein to circulate into the eye and allow blood vessels there to be photographed and evaluated (fluorescein angiography). In certain cases, tests are done to predict the increase in vision that is expected to occur after cataract removal (potential acuity meter or laser interferometer testing). When an artificial lens insertion is planned, the length of the eye is measured and the curvature of the surface covering of the eye is evaluated. The entire area of vision may be tested to detect any darkened or distorted areas (visual field testing).

Treatment

When glasses or lenses no longer improve impaired vision, surgery is considered. The cataract is usually removed by techniques of phacoemulsification or extracapsular cataract extraction that allow the outer covering (capsule) of the lens to remain in place. The most common procedure involves inserting a small probe and using ultrasound vibration to break apart the cataract, which is suctioned out of the eye (phacoemulsification). The cataract and natural lens also may be removed manually through the extracapsular cataract extraction technique. An artificial lens may then be inserted (intraocular lens implantation). The lens more commonly is inserted behind the colored portion of the eye (iris), but also may be placed in front of the iris. Eyedrops and oral medication may be used before, during, and after surgery to reduce eye pressure (antiglaucoma). Antibiotics may be used to prevent infection. Anti-inflammatory agents also might be administered to prevent further damage caused by the eye tissue's reaction to injury. The eye may then be covered with a shield. If an artificial lens is not inserted, thick glasses (aphakic) or contact lenses will be needed and are prescribed when the eye is fully recovered. Glasses or contact lenses may be needed even if an artificial lens was inserted. Newly developed implantable lenses now offer options for correcting certain types of pre-existing vision deficiencies such as focusing problems (astigmatism).

Prognosis

Cataracts usually continue to develop over time causing vision to worsen. Surgical removal with artificial lens insertion will lead to improved vision in the majority of individuals. This usually results in improved quality of life and mental status. In some cases, additional treatment will be required if a secondary cataract forms, or a common complication causing cloudiness (posterior capsular opacification) occurs. In rare cases, retinal detachment or other serious complications of surgery may cause blindness.

Differential Diagnosis

Other causes of vision problems include head injury, medications that affect the central nervous system, eye injury, and other eye conditions such as glaucoma, retinal detachment or disease, optic nerve disease, corneal disease, pupil defects, refractive shift, eye tumors, or macular disease.

Specialists

- Internist
- Ophthalmologist

Work Restrictions / Accommodations

Lighting may need adjustment, or a hat or visor may be required to reduce glare. Tasks requiring reading, color recognition, distance determination, driving, or operation of machinery may be problematic depending on the extent of vision affected. The individual may need to wear glasses, filtered glasses, or contact lenses. Contact lens wearers may be more sensitive to fumes, dust, or other eye irritants. Eyestrain may result in the need to close the eyes during rest breaks. Sunshine and strong light may need to be avoided. Physical activity, lifting, and bending may be restricted for a period of time following surgery.

Comorbid Conditions

The individual's age may be a factor in the severity of the condition. Results may not be optimal if other diseases or injuries have damaged the retina or optic nerve.

Complications

Cataracts may be present in only one eye or may develop at different rates in both eyes. Attempts to improve vision with glasses or contact lenses may result in objects being seen as larger or smaller than actual size. The eyes may resist working together to gauge distance. Close-up vision may be blurred or double. Different lens prescriptions may need to be used for each eye and finely tuned until the best possible vision is obtained. Problems during surgery or the pre-existence of other eye diseases may rule out insertion of an intraocular lens. Following surgery, a secondary cataract (after-cataract) may form. A laser procedure then might be required to penetrate and clear up cloudiness (YAG laser capsulotomy).

Factors Influencing Duration

Factors influencing length of disability include age, mental status, and degree of vision affected. Additional factors include the possibility of other eye diseases and general physical health.

Length of Disability

Duration depends on type of procedure, presence of complications, and individual's job requirements.

Surgical treatment (cataract surgery).

Duration in Days

Job Classification	Minimum	Optimum	Maximum
Sedentary work	1	3	14
Light work	1	3	14
Medium work	3	7	14
Heavy work	7	14	28
Very Heavy work	7	21	35

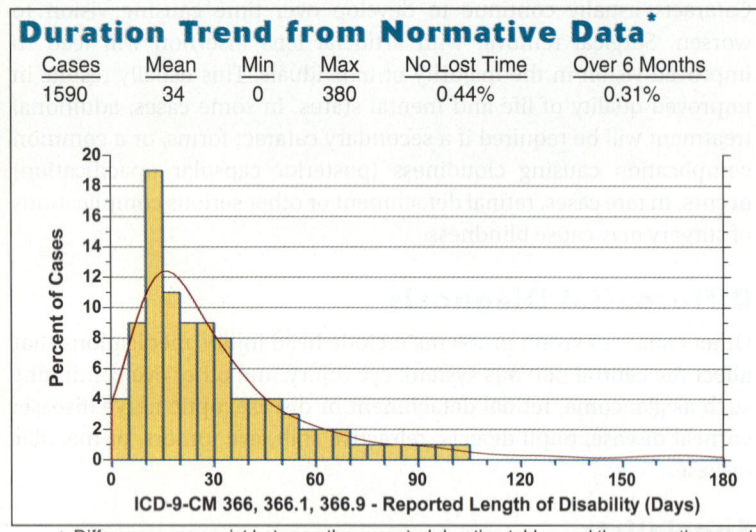
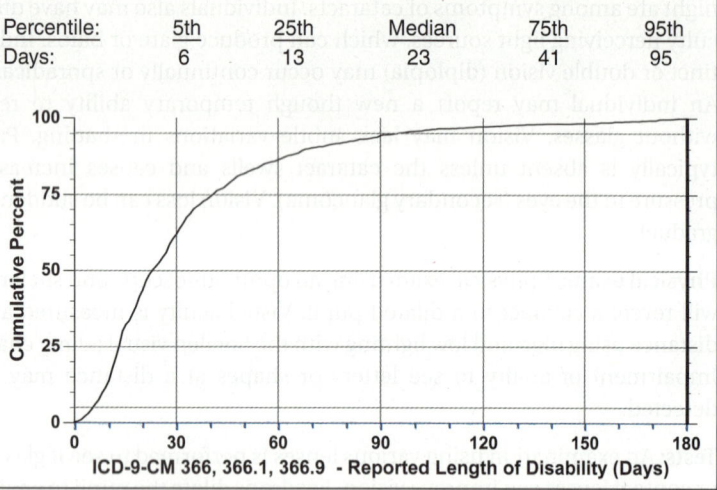

* Differences may exist between the expected duration tables and the normative graphs. Duration tables provide expected recovery periods based on the type of work performed by the individual. The normative graphs reflect the actual observed experience of many individuals across the spectrum of physical conditions, in a variety of industries, and with varying levels of case management.

Failure to Recover

If an individual fails to recover within the maximum duration expectancy period, the reader may wish to reference the following questions to assist in better understanding the specifics of an individual's medical case.

Regarding diagnosis:

- Has individual been properly tested to confirm cataract diagnosis and rule out the possibility of an eye injury or other diseases?
- Have appropriate methods and tests been applied to determine the extent of the cataract condition?
- Has individual experienced complications, related to either the cataract or its treatment, that may impact recovery?

Regarding treatment:

- Was artificial lens properly positioned?

- Is healing taking place as expected or has the process been complicated by an infection or injury?
- Has individual achieved optimal visual results following cataract removal?
- Have prescriptive lenses been finely tuned until the best possible vision is obtained?

Regarding prognosis:

- If vision was not significantly improved with the cataract removal, can vision be further corrected with prescription glasses or contact lenses?
- Has posterior capsular opacification occurred?
- Are further corrective procedures warranted?
- Has individual been instructed in lifestyle modifications that may help decrease cataract reoccurrence?

References

Mariotti, J.M., and A. Amza. "Traditional Treatment of Cataract in Niger. Apropos of 22 Cases." Journal of French Ophthalmology 16 3 (1993): 170-177.

National Eye Institute. Information for Patients: Cataract. National Institutes of Health. 01 Apr 2000. 24 Jun 2000 <http://www.nei.nih.gov/publications/cataracts.htm>.

Cataract Surgery
13.1, 13.2, 13.3, 13.4, 13.5, 13.6, 13.7

Definition

Surgery is the only option for correcting cataracts that occur when the natural lens behind the iris or colored portion of the eye becomes cloudy and obstructs vision. In most procedures, the eye's natural lens is removed and replaced with an artificial intraocular lens (IOL). In rare cases when an artificial lens is not implanted, the individual may need to wear thick glasses or contact lenses (aphakic) to replace natural lens functions.

The type of procedure used for cataract removal depends on individual needs, condition of the eye, and type of vision correction planned after removal of the eye's natural lens. Phacoemulsification is by far the most common procedure. With this method, high frequency sound waves (ultrasound) are transmitted into the eye through a probe in order to break the cataract and natural lens into pieces for removal. Extracapsular cataract extraction requires larger incisions to allow the surgeon using a microscopic instrument to manually remove the cataract and natural lens. In both procedures, the capsule holding the natural lens is left in place. An older and now rarely used procedure called intracapsular extraction involves manual removal of the cataract, natural lens, and entire capsule. Individuals undergoing this process must wear thick glasses or contact lenses (aphakic) to replace vision lost with removal of the natural lens.

Aging is considered the main reason for development of cataracts although injury or condition at birth (congenital) may also be contributing factors. Heredity, diabetes, and metabolic disorders also may contribute to formation of cataracts. About half of individuals from age 65 to 74 have cataracts. In populations age 75 or older, about 70% have the condition.

Reason for Procedure

Cataracts are removed when they are cloudy enough to interfere with vision during daily activities. While mild cataracts may require only glasses for vision correction, surgical removal is needed when the condition becomes so severe that daily activities are hampered.

How Procedure Is Performed

A physical exam prior to the procedure will ascertain health risks. A measurement of the eye determines the type and power of the intraocular lens needed to replace the individual's natural lens where the cataract is located. Procedures are usually performed on an outpatient basis in a clinic or surgical center. A sedative may be administered. Anesthesia is applied topically or injected into the eye.

In the most common procedure called phacoemulsification, the surgeon uses an operating microscope and precision instruments to cut a small incision into the cornea or front covering of the eye. A probe attached to a phacoemulsification machine is then inserted to administer high frequency ultrasonic vibrations that will shatter the cataract and natural lens of the eye. The phaco machine also sends liquid through the probe for suctioning and irrigating to remove fragments and clean the wound. If the surgeon uses the extracapsular cataract extraction technique, the cataract and natural lens will be removed manually in one piece through a larger incision.

An artificial lens then is inserted into the now empty capsular bag that once surrounded the natural lens. No incisions are usually needed to close the wound unless the extracapsular cataract extraction method is used. A shield is taped over the eye for protection. Surgery is performed on only one eye at a time. Eyedrops and over-the-counter pain medication may be prescribed. Most procedures take no longer than 30 minutes depending on the severity of the cataract.

Prognosis

Recent refinements in cataract surgical techniques now mean a 98% success rate as reported by the American Society of Cataract and Refractive Surgery. Most complications are also successfully treated. In many cases, individuals experience improvement in previous vision because of implantations of newly developed intraocular lenses designed to correct refractive errors. Healing should be complete within several months although glasses may be required to correct residual vision deficiencies such as inadequate near vision caused by aging (presbyopia).

Specialists

- Ophthalmologist

Work Restrictions / Accommodations

Depending on the procedure, the individual may need to move cautiously and avoid heavy lifting and straining for one month. An eye shield or glasses should be worn to protect the eyes. Eyesight testing may be needed to determine the individual's ability to perform tasks requiring visual acuity.

Comorbid Conditions

Surgical results may not be optimal if the individual has macular degeneration causing deterioration of the retina (where images are formed), glaucoma, high pressure in the eye, or diabetes mellitus.

Procedure Complications

A common complication of cataract surgery may occur days, months, or years later when the back portion of the lens capsule clouds over (posterior capsular opacification). The condition is usually easily and painlessly treated with a laser that penetrates the membrane, allowing the cloudiness to clear away (YAG capsulotomy). Cataract surgery may cause light sensitivity accompanied by halos or glare. Rare complications include infection, corneal swelling or cloudiness, excessive bleeding in the eye, retinal detachment, glaucoma (damage to optic nerves), or high eye pressure. If the artificial lens implanted becomes dislocated, retreatment may be needed. Extremely rare complications may include blindness or loss of the treated eye.

Factors Influencing Duration

The method of cataract removal used, any complications, and the individual's response affect length of disability.

Length of Disability

Duration depends on type of procedure, presence of complications, and individual's job requirements. The individual must refrain from heavy work and in some cases activities such as bending immediately after the procedure should be avoided so as not to cause damage the eye.

Duration in Days

Job Classification	Minimum	Optimum	Maximum
Sedentary work	1	3	14
Light work	1	3	14
Medium work	3	7	14
Heavy work	7	14	28
Very Heavy work	7	21	35

References

American Society of Cataract and Refractive Surgery. White Paper on Cataract Surgery. American Academy of Ophthalmology. 01 Apr 1996. 22 Jul 2000 <http://www.ascrs.org/eye/white.html>.

Cauda Equina Syndrome
225.3, 344.6, 344.60, 344.61, 952.4

Definition

Cauda equina syndrome is a dull aching pain of the perineum, bladder, and sacrum due to compression of the multiple spinal nerve roots in the spinal canal. The collection of spinal roots that descend from the lower part of the spinal cord and occupy the vertebral canal of the lumbar region, sacrum and coccyx is called the cauda equina. The appearance resembles the tail of a horse. This compression of the lumbar, sacral, and coccygeal nerve roots results in pain radiating along the sciatic nerve down both legs. In progressive cauda equina syndrome, the spinal cord is tethered and there may be involvement of nerves supplying the bladder, rectum, and/or external genitalia.

Pressure on these nerves may result in the development of a lesion in the nervous system causing weakness in bladder control (neurogenic bladder) and loss of bowel control from a loose rectal sphincter. Sexual function may also be impaired; males may be unable to have an erection (impotence). An acute cauda equina syndrome may occur following some unusual activity (e.g., rowing or falling), a herniated lumbar disc, spinal fracture or dislocation, or a tumor. Cauda equina syndrome may also be a complication of other conditions such as lyme disease, rheumatoid arthritic conditions like ankylosing spondylitis, or in individuals with spinal cord abnormalities such as spina bifida or narrowing of the vertebral or nerve root canal (spinal stenosis). Use of continuous spinal anesthesia during surgical procedures also increases the risk of cauda equina syndrome.

The incidence is approximately 5 in 1,000 and occurs equally in Europe and the US.

Diagnosis

History: Individuals may report loss of bladder and/or bowel control, abnormal touch sensations (paresthesias) such as burning, prickling, or skin crawling feeling (formication) where the individual feels as though tiny insects are crawling over the skin, and a loss of sexual function (impotence). Pain in the back, rectal area, or both lower legs may also be reported. Leg symptoms may be reported on both sides, however, one side may be more affected. Numbness in the perineum may also occur. If the condition is due to a tumor, there may be paralysis, leg muscle loss (atrophy), and inability to flex the foot upward (foot drop).

Physical exam: The exam may reveal precipitating conditions such as herniation, spondylitis, or arthritis. Localization of the pain to a specific area and alterations of motor, reflex, or sensory function in the legs provide clues to the diagnosis. Neurological examination may show muscle weakness and absence of deep tendon reflexes in the lower extremities with accompanying numbness that extends to the genital and anal (perineum) area (areflexia paralysis). There may be a loss of anal sphincter tone (sphincteric disorder) noted on rectal examination.

Tests: Tests may include CT, MRI, or myelogram. Other x-rays or a bone scan may be obtained to diagnose the underlying cause. Measurement of the pressure exerted at varying degrees of capacity of the urinary bladder (cystometrogram) may reveal weakness of bladder control and disturbances of bladder function that produces urgency and incontinence.

Treatment

Surgery is the treatment of choice for this condition. In most cases, emergency decompression surgery relieves pressure on the nerves and prevents permanent nerve damage. The timing of surgical decompression is controversial, but most surgeons recommend emergent decompression preferably within 48 hours after onset of cauda equina syndrome over delayed surgery. Medication for pre- and postoperative pain may be necessary.

Prognosis

Outcome depends on prompt diagnosis and surgical treatment. Bladder and rectal dysfunction are associated with a delay in surgery. Significant improvement in sensory and motor deficits and urinary and rectal function occurs with emergent decompression within 48 hours. Preoperative conditions like back pain are associated with urinary and rectal dysfunction and preoperative rectal dysfunction is associated with worsened outcome in urinary incontinence. In addition, increasing age is associated with poorer postoperative sexual function.

Differential Diagnosis

Neurogenic bladder may be caused by other diseases such as multiple sclerosis, tabes dorsalis, pernicious anemia, or lesions in portions of the spinal cord other than the cauda equina.

Specialists

- Neurologist
- Neurosurgeon
- Orthopedic Surgeon
- Physiatrist

Rehabilitation

The team caring for an individual with a spinal cord injury may include a social worker, vocational specialist, and/or occupational therapist. Rehabilitation protocol depends on the severity of spinal cord injury not the cauda equina syndrome. However, it is imperative that the cauda equina syndrome be alleviated before a rehabilitative plan is set.

If left unattended, severe and permanent damage to bladder and bowel organs may result compounding the individual's recovery from the spinal injury. Catheterization may be necessary during initial stages of exercise to assist with bladder control. As healing from the cauda equina injury occurs, normal or close to normal bladder and bowel function may resume. However, partial catheterization may continue up to 2 years or longer depending on the extent of damage.

Once decompression surgery is performed, the only therapy is rest until bladder and bowel function can be assessed. The individual receives catheterization every 4 to 6 hours daily. Bowel contents may be removed manually every day or every other day. Bowel movements are assisted through gravity and exercise. Since the individual loses voluntary control of bowel function initially, accidents may occur during exercise sessions that require walking movements. Full recovery of bladder and bowel function may take up to 2 years.

Concomitant with neurogenic (originating from nerves) dysfunction of the bladder and bowel, there is also muscle weakness or paralysis in the lower extremities. Muscle weakness and paralysis are addressed based on the extent and severity of injury.

An occupational therapist may assist with wheelchair and daily living skills training. If the individual returns to work, vocational rehabilitation may also be necessary. In some cases, the work environment must be adapted to accommodate not only the individual's physical disabilities but also the problems of bowel and bladder functioning. Therapeutic outcomes for individuals with spinal cord injury with cauda equina syndrome are variable and may include full or partial paralysis with bladder and bowel dysfunction.

Work Restrictions / Accommodations

Work restrictions and accommodations depend on the extent of damage to the nerves, degree of postoperative pain, and impairment of bladder and rectal functions. Persisting sensory and motor deficits may impact the individual's ability to perform work even at a limited capacity.

Comorbid Conditions

Tumors or lesions of the spinal cord and any other degenerative diseases such as ankylosing spondylitis may further lengthen disability.

Complications

Preoperative back pain and bladder or bowel dysfunction may require urgent surgery and complicate the surgical outcome.

Factors Influencing Duration

Factors that may affect the length of disability depend on the underlying cause of the condition, extent of functional loss that persists after surgery, severity of pain, and other symptoms associated with the condition.

Length of Disability

Resolution of the condition with surgery is common. However, persisting conditions after surgery such as loss of bowel and bladder function may impact the length of disability and the individual's ability to perform job requirements. Disability may be permanent.

Surgical treatment.

Duration in Days

Job Classification	Minimum	Optimum	Maximum
Sedentary work	28	42	Indefinite
Light work	28	42	Indefinite
Medium work	42	91	Indefinite
Heavy work	Indefinite	Indefinite	Indefinite
Very Heavy work	Indefinite	Indefinite	Indefinite

Failure to Recover

If an individual fails to recover within the maximum duration expectancy period, the reader may wish to reference the following questions to assist in better understanding the specifics of an individual's medical case.

Regarding diagnosis:

- Was diagnosis of cauda equina syndrome confirmed?
- If cauda equina syndrome was suspected, was a radiographic examination required to confirm the diagnosis?
- Was a CT, MRI, x-ray, or a bone scan obtained to diagnose the underlying cause?
- Do difficulties with bladder control warrant further testing?

Regarding treatment:

- Was individual adequately medicated for pre- and postoperative pain?
- Was the surgery successful in decompressing the spinal nerve roots?

Regarding prognosis:

- Do bladder and rectal dysfunction persist?
- Were complications associated with the surgical procedure? If so, what were they and what further treatment will they require?
- What additional pain relief and/or function recovery is still expected?

References

Adams, Raymond D., Maurice Victor, and Allan H. Ropeer. Principles of Neurology. New York: McGraw Hill, 1997.

Rowland, Louis P., MD, ed. Merritt's Textbook of Neurology. Philadelphia: Lea & Febiger, 1989.

Celiac Plexus Block

Other names / synonyms: Celiac Plexus Nerve Block, Celiac Plexus Neurolytic Block, Solar Plexus Block
05.35

Definition

Celiac plexus block is a treatment for chronic abdominal pain. In this procedure, either local anesthetic is injected for a temporary (diagnostic) block or alcohol or phenol (lytic agent) is injected into nerves to destroy the passage of pain signals.

The nerves comprising the celiac or solar plexus are located behind the stomach and in front of the aorta. These nerves serve the pancreas, stomach, spleen, kidney, and small intestine.

Conditions that may require the use of this procedure to alleviate pain are pancreatic cancer and other abdominal cancers.

Pain accounts for approximately 40 million visits per year to a physician's office. Fifty percent of individuals with cancer describe their pain as moderate in severity, but 46% of individuals with cancer have pain that cannot be alleviated with medications.

Reason for Procedure

This procedure is used to treat pain associated with cancer of the pancreas and pain associated with other cancerous tumors within the abdomen. Celiac plexus block in association with intercostal nerve block may also be used in surgical procedures of the upper abdomen.

How Procedure Is Performed

Once local anesthesia is given to the individual, alcohol or phenol guided by ultrasound, CT, or x-ray (radiography) is injected into the celiac plexus destroying the ability of the nerves to transmit pain signals. Once the procedure is completed, the individual may experience numbness and have difficulty moving the body at the site of the injection. Generally, this procedure may be done on an outpatient basis; however, if the individual experiences any adverse effects from the procedure, admission to the hospital may be recommended.

Prognosis

Celiac plexus block provides temporary relief of pain in approximately 75% of cases and pain relief may last for several months. However, the underlying reason for the procedure such as pancreatic tumor often has a fatal outcome.

Specialists

- Anesthesiologist

Rehabilitation

Individuals who undergo a celiac plexus block may require physical therapy depending on the underlying diagnosis. Individuals who have a celiac plexus block in conjunction with abdominal surgery may require abdominal strengthening exercises such as sit-ups. In addition, individuals may want to hold a pillow against the abdomen as a splint during coughing, laughing, and walking to decrease the pain associated with abdominal surgery.

Individuals who undergo a celiac plexus block in conjunction with more serious diagnoses such as pancreatitis or pancreatic cancer may require more intensive physical and occupational therapy for strengthening and conditioning. If the prognosis is poor, individuals may benefit from hospice therapy. Hospice therapists focus on the control of pain through such means as positioning and massage.

Some individuals may require more comprehensive pain management through a pain clinic, particularly if the response to pain is disproportionate to the painful stimulus. Individuals receive physical therapy for pain control. Physical therapists may use body massage or trigger point massage to decrease muscle spasms. Individuals use biofeedback to help decrease any muscle tension and thereby decrease pain. Individuals may also use a T.E.N.S. unit that delivers low frequency electrical stimuli via surface electrodes to interrupt the perception of pain.

Occupational therapists teach energy and joint conservation techniques where activities of daily living such as meal preparation are broken into smaller components that make tasks more manageable.

Work Restrictions / Accommodations

Restrictions or accommodations associated with the procedure itself are not usually necessary but may be required because of the underlying condition for the procedure. Restrictions may include no heavy lifting or strenuous physical labor.

Comorbid Conditions

Underlying conditions that may influence length of disability are nonabdominal cancers, AIDS, multiple sclerosis, and sickle cell anemia.

Procedure Complications

Complications of celiac plexus block can include infection at the site of the injection or an adverse reaction to the agent used to block the nerve impulses.

Factors Influencing Duration

Length of disability is influenced by the effectiveness of the procedure in blocking pain, age of the individual, and whether the underlying cause for the nerve block is a terminal disease.

Length of Disability

Disability is not associated with recovery from the procedure. Disability may be associated with the underlying cause.

Duration in Days

Job Classification	Minimum	Optimum	Maximum
Sedentary work	3	4	7
Light work	3	9	7
Medium work	7	9	14
Heavy work	7	14	21
Very Heavy work	7	21	35

References

Headley, Barbara J. "Chronic Pain Management." Physical Rehabilitation: Assessment and Treatment. O'Sullivan, Susan B, and Thomas J. Schmitz, eds. Philadelphia: F.A. Davis Company, 1994. 577-602.

Payne R., and R.R. Allen. "Pain." Neurology. Scientific American® Medicine Online Dale, D.C., and D.D. Federman, eds. New York: WebMD Corporation, 2000 Scientific American Medicine. 05 Dec 2000 <http://www.samed.com/sam/forms/index/htm>.

Cellulitis
681, 682.1, 682.2, 682.3, 682.9

Definition

Cellulitis is a diffuse, spreading inflammation of deep skin (dermis) and possibly the underlying muscle, commonly caused by streptococcus or staphylococcus bacteria.

The bacteria enter the dermis through a break in the skin caused by trauma, surgery, burns, dermatitis, or bites (insect or animal). However, there may be no apparent site of entry. The face, neck, and legs are the areas most often affected by cellulitis. Cellulitis of the eye socket (orbital cellulitis) can spread from facial, oral, or sinus infections, or occur following trauma to the eyelid. Cellulitis can also occur after childbirth and spread from the uterus to other pelvic organs.

Individuals with a history of coronary artery bypass surgery are at risk of developing recurrent cellulitis at the site where the donor leg (saphenous) vein was removed. Individuals with a deficient immune system (organ transplant recipients or individuals with AIDS), accumulation of lymph fluid (lymphedema), venous insufficiency, diabetes, and those who are intravenous drug abusers are at a greater risk of developing cellulitis. In adults, cellulitis of the face more commonly affects those over the age of 50.

Individuals frequently develop minor skin infections, but the immune system and the inhospitable nature of the outer skin readily eliminate the invading bacteria. Cellulitis can occur if the skin break is deep, fails to heal naturally, and a large number of infecting bacteria are present. The incidence of cellulitis is unknown and orbital cellulitis is rare.

Diagnosis

History: The individual complains of an area of skin that is red, hot, swollen, and tender. Symptoms may also include fever or chills. The individual may report a recent history of a skin breach at the affected site. The individual who complains of redness and swelling of the eyelid may also report pain, impaired eye mobility, fever, and a feeling of discomfort and fatigue (malaise).

Physical exam: The infected area usually develops red, ill-defined borders and may resemble the texture of orange skin (peau d'orange). Neighboring lymph nodes may be inflamed and swollen. The infected area may contain a red streak characteristic of an inflamed lymphatic vessel (lymphangitis). Individuals with eye socket cellulitis undergo a thorough examination of the skin, teeth, mouth, and nasopharynx to isolate the source of infection.

Tests: Needle aspirations and cultures of pus and/or blood may be performed to identify the causative organism, however, the causative agent is often never found. Antibiotic sensitivity tests may be performed. Individuals with eye socket cellulitis may require plain x-rays or a CT of the sinuses to isolate the source of infection.

Treatment

Cellulitis is treated with rest, elevation of infected part, cold compresses, analgesics, and antibiotics. If antibiotic therapy is ineffective, the infected area may have to be cut open (incised) and drained. Complicated cellulitis may require hospitalization and intravenous antibiotics.

Prognosis

Antibiotic therapy usually provides prompt and complete resolution of cellulitis. A good outcome can be expected following an incision and drainage procedure. If left untreated, cellulitis can occasionally kill the tissue (gangrene) and/or the bacteria may enter the bloodstream (bacteremia) and multiply (sepsis) causing a serious, life-threatening condition.

Differential Diagnosis

Superficial skin infection (erysipelas), deep vein clots (thrombosis), yeast (Candida) infection of apposed skin surfaces (intertrigo), psoriasis, herpetic whitlow, and pinworm infection can present with similar signs and symptoms.

Specialists

- Dermatologist
- Internist
- Infectious Disease Physician

Work Restrictions / Accommodations

If infection is located on fingers or hand, certain work responsibilities (i.e., working with food, children, elderly, or direct personal health care) may need to be restricted until the infection is completely cleared. If lower extremities are involved, sedentary work and the ability to elevate the legs may be necessary. Depending on the location of infection, the use of personal protective equipment (respirator) may be needed.

Comorbid Conditions

Coronary artery bypass, diabetes, AIDS, organ transplantation, cancer, disorders of lymph nodes, or diseases causing impaired circulation (e.g., arteriosclerosis) can affect the length of disability.

Complications

Cellulitis can progress to lymphangitis or abscess. Infection by additional bacteria (superinfection) may occur. Cellulitis of the scalp may cause scarring and hair loss (alopecia). Orbital cellulitis may progress to blindness, cavernous sinus clots (thrombosis), inflammation of all tissues of the eye (panophthalmitis), or spread of the infection to the brain or tissues lining the brain and spinal cord (meninges). Older individuals may develop leg vein inflammation associated with a blood clot (thrombophlebitis).

Factors Influencing Duration

Severity of infection, location of infection, whether the infected area needs to be drained, and if hospitalization is required can influence the length of disability.

Length of Disability

Duration depends on site, type, severity of infection, and job requirements.

Duration in Days

Job Classification	Minimum	Optimum	Maximum
Sedentary work	1	1	7
Light work	1	1	7
Medium work	1	2	7
Heavy work	1	3	7
Very Heavy work	1	3	7

Duration Trend from Normative Data*

Cases	Mean	Min	Max	No Lost Time	Over 6 Months
10198	26	0	349	0.06%	0.07%

Percentile:	5th	25th	Median	75th	95th
Days:	8	12	17	29	87

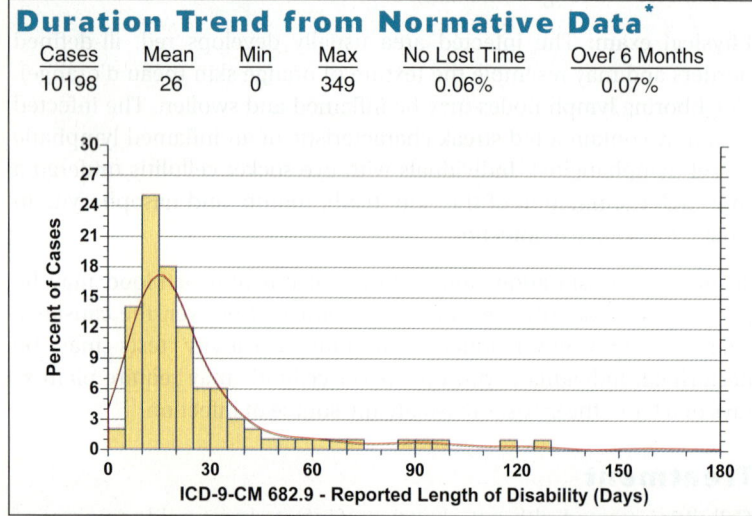
ICD-9-CM 682.9 - Reported Length of Disability (Days)

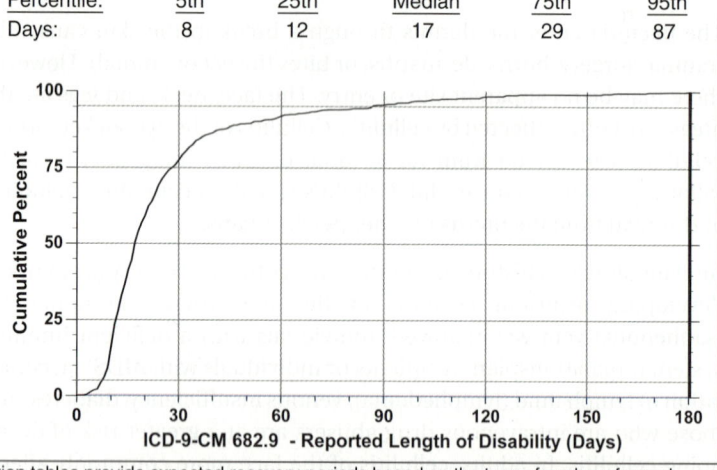
ICD-9-CM 682.9 - Reported Length of Disability (Days)

* Differences may exist between the expected duration tables and the normative graphs. Duration tables provide expected recovery periods based on the type of work performed by the individual. The normative graphs reflect the actual observed experience of many individuals across the spectrum of physical conditions, in a variety of industries, and with varying levels of case management.

Failure to Recover

If an individual fails to recover within the maximum duration expectancy period, the reader may wish to reference the following questions to assist in better understanding the specifics of an individual's medical case.

Regarding diagnosis:

- Has individual experienced any trauma, surgery, burns, dermatitis, insect or animal bites, or other infections?
- Does individual have a history of coronary artery bypass surgery?
- Does individuals have a deficient immune system, lymphedema, venous insufficiency, or diabetes? Is individual an intravenous drug abuser?
- Does individual complain of an area of skin that is red, hot, swollen, and tender? Are fever or chills present? Is there redness and swelling of the eyelid with pain, impaired eye mobility, fever, and malaise?
- On exam, is the area red with ill-defined borders? Does it resemble the texture of orange skin? Are neighboring lymph nodes inflamed and swollen?

- Were a culture and sensitivity done? Has individual with eye socket cellulitis had x-rays or CT?
- Were conditions with similar symptoms ruled out?

Regarding treatment:

- Is individual being treated with rest, elevation of the infected part, cold compresses, analgesics, and antibiotics?
- Was it necessary to do an incision and drainage?
- Was individual hospitalized and given IV antibiotics?

Regarding prognosis:

- Can individual's employer accommodate any necessary restrictions?
- Does individual have any conditions that may affect ability to recover?
- Have any complications developed such as lymphangitis, abscess, superinfection, alopecia, blindness, cavernous sinus clots, panophthalmitis, or spread of the infection to the meninges? Has individual developed thrombophlebitis?

References

Aly, Raza. "Streptococcal Infections." Atlas of Infections of the Skin. Aly, Raza, and Howard Maibach, eds. New York: Churchill Livingstone, 1999. 123-131.

Stevens, Dennis. "Cellulitis and Abscesses." Clinical Infectious Diseases: A Practical Approach. Root, Richard, et al., eds. New York: Oxford University Press, 1999. 501-503.

Cerebral Aneurysm (Non-Ruptured)

Other names / synonyms: Acquired Brain Aneurysm, Arteriosclerotic Brain Aneurysm, Berry Aneurysm, Brain Aneurysm
437.3

Definition

A cerebral aneurysm refers to a localized weakness in the wall of a vein or artery in the brain. The weakness results in a ballooning (dilation) of the vessel; it resembles a sack of blood attached to one side of the blood vessel by a narrow neck. The most common form is a small aneurysm called a berry aneurysm. Clusters of berry aneurysms are often noted in the large arteries at the base of the brain, but can occur in any area of the brain. Other types of cerebral aneurysms may involve dilation of the entire circumference of the blood vessel in an area, or may appear as a ballooning out of part of a blood vessel. These cerebral aneurysms can occur in any part of the brain.

Most aneurysms are about the size of a pea, although they can be as small as a pinhead or as large as an orange. Aneurysms tend to grow at a rate of one-eighth to one-quarter inch per year; the likelihood of rupture increases as the aneurysm increases in size. As the aneurysm grows, increased pressure is exerted against neighboring organs and tissue, and can result in potentially lethal complications.

Cerebral aneurysms develop from either a vessel wall weakness at birth (congenital defect), from a degenerative process, or a combination of the two. For example, should an individual have a congenitally weak arterial wall and later develop a build-up of fatty cells within the arteries (atherosclerosis), the resulting high blood pressure (hypertension) could cause an aneurysm to develop that may later rupture. Other causes of cerebral aneurysm are head trauma or a tumor. Individuals who may be more at risk for developing cerebral aneurysm are those with a history of hypertension, smoking, cerebrovascular disease, cardiovascular disease, or diabetes mellitus. Berry aneurysm is also associated with polycystic kidney disease and malformation of the aorta that causes narrowing of that vessel (coarctation).

Cerebral aneurysms more commonly occur in women than in men, but some type of aneurysm occurs in approximately 5% of the population. New cases of cerebral aneurysms that have ruptured occur in approximately 4 of 100,000 individuals yearly. Most aneurysms remain asymptomatic throughout life.

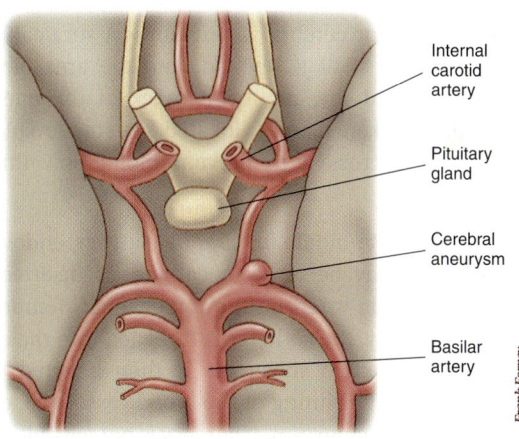

Diagnosis

History: It is possible that the individual will have no symptoms (asymptomatic) until the aneurysm ruptures and complications develop. Bleeding is the most common cause of symptoms, and subarachnoid hemorrhage is the most usual type of bleed. Those who witness the individual with a rupture might describe behavioral changes, changes in ability to speak or move, mental "fogginess," or sudden loss of consciousness. Weakness, numbness, or other nerve function loss may develop because of pressure from the aneurysm on adjacent brain tissue, or because arterial spasm has caused reduced blood flow to other blood vessels near a ruptured aneurysm.

The individual may report a history or head trauma, or an extremely severe headache that came on suddenly accompanied by nausea and vomiting, visual changes, eyelid drooping, stiff neck, a feeling of lethargy or sleepiness, irritability, or impaired speech.

Physical exam: Blood pressure may be elevated (hypertension). Brain function (neurological) examination may reveal inappropriate answers to questions, weakness in muscle tone and decreased ability to move, and the inability of the pupils of the eye to dilate and constrict equally or react normally to light. Eyes may not move appropriately and the eyelids may appear droopy. Swelling of the optic nerve (papilledema) may also be seen.

Tests: MRA (magnetic resonance angiography), in which a catheter is inserted into an artery, contrast medium injected, and the unruptured aneurysm visualized via x-ray, is often the test of choice to diagnose an aneurysm. CT of the head indicates if bleeding (hemorrhage) has occurred, but does not always locate the aneurysm. If the CT does not show any bleeding but bleeding is suspected, a lumbar puncture may be done to check for blood in the cerebrospinal fluid (CSF) to determine whether pressure inside the skull (intracranial pressure) has increased. A complete blood count (CBC) to determine if there is internal bleeding, measuring arterial blood gases to determine if the blood is being sufficiently oxygenated, and coagulation studies to determine if the blood is clotting appropriately will also be done. A special MRI such as magnetic resonance angiography may be used.

Treatment

Prior to rupture, treatment focuses on reducing the risk of rupture. Symptoms of a cerebral aneurysm generally do not appear until it has begun to bleed (hemorrhage); at that point it is a medical emergency. Treatment then focuses on controlling symptoms to prevent further bleeding or the development of potentially serious complications.

The primary treatment for cerebral aneurysm is a surgical procedure known as clipping. The skull is opened, and the area between the normal blood vessel and the aneurysm (neck of the aneurysm) is identified. Once this weakened area is located, the surgeon places a clip (or clamp or suture) across it to prevent blood flow through the aneurysm.

If the individual is not a candidate for clipping surgery, endovascular or embolization surgery may be done. A catheter is inserted into the cerebral artery through an artery in the upper thigh (femoral artery); while it is viewed on x-ray, the catheter is threaded into the aneurysm. Small coils or a silicone-like substance is then injected to fill the aneurysm, sealing it off. The lining of the blood vessel will, eventually, grow over the neck of the aneurysm. If surgery is not feasible because of either the location or size of the aneurysm, or the individual's medical condition, treatment consists of conservative measures. This includes complete bedrest in a quiet, darkened room with limited visitors. A sedative may be prescribed to minimize stress, a narcotic analgesic for pain relief, and, if necessary, a medication to prevent seizures (antiepileptic). The individual is advised to avoid aspirin, coffee, and stimulants.

If the individual is hypertensive, they may be given an antihypertensive drug to lower blood pressure. A calcium-channel blocker medication may be given to control blood vessel spasms that could precipitate a rupture. Corticosteroids may be administered and fluid intake restricted to reduce swelling (edema). The individual will be positioned at a 45-degree angle and an ice bag may be applied to relieve headaches. Cooling measures may also be instituted to diminish blood flow to the brain and reduce the risk of aneurysm rupture.

Prognosis

Outcome is related to location and size of aneurysm. Small aneurysms that never rupture may go undetected with the consequence that the individual may never have any symptoms. As an aneurysm enlarges, the risk of rupture, a life-threatening, neurological emergency increases significantly. When an aneurysm ruptures, 25% of individuals die within 24 hours, and an additional 25% will die within 3 months. More than 50% of the remaining individuals will most likely have some type of permanent neurological impairment.

With early detection, the individual generally will have a very good outcome after surgical aneurysm clipping. Individuals who cannot undergo surgical clipping and require endovascular surgery also have a very good outcome, depending on the underlying reason(s) why surgical clipping of the aneurysm posed a risk.

Differential Diagnosis

Differential diagnoses include migraine headache, a congenital arteriovenous malformation in the brain, a tumor (neoplasm), seizure disorder, cerebral hemorrhage, and cerebrovascular accident (CVA).

Specialists

- Cardiovascular Surgeon
- Neurosurgeon
- Neurologist

Work Restrictions / Accommodations

Strenuous physical activity puts an individual at greater risk for rupture of an aneurysm, so permanent reassignment may be required for those who do heavy physical labor. A sedentary environment that is not stressful may be warranted.

Comorbid Conditions

Hypertension and cardiovascular disease may lengthen disability.

Complications

Factors that may complicate a cerebral aneurysm include subarachnoid hemorrhage, neurological defects such as partial paralysis, loss of sensation, speech loss or impairment, visual problems, seizures, stroke, additional bleeding, an abnormal accumulation of cerebral spinal fluid within the cranial cavity (hydrocephalus), and death.

Factors Influencing Duration

Factors that may influence length of disability include age of the individual, location and size of the aneurysm, the point at which diagnosis is made, type of surgical procedure used to repair the aneurysm, individual's response to treatment, and whether the aneurysm ruptures.

Length of Disability

Length of disability depends on job requirements and extent of neurological damage, if any. Disability may be permanent.

Non-ruptured.

Duration in Days

Job Classification	Minimum	Optimum	Maximum
Sedentary work	5	14	21
Light work	5	14	21
Medium work	5	14	Indefinite
Heavy work	5	14	Indefinite
Very Heavy work	5	14	Indefinite

Failure to Recover

If an individual fails to recover within the maximum duration expectancy period, the reader may wish to reference the following questions to assist in better understanding the specifics of an individual's medical case.

Regarding diagnosis:

- What is the size of individual's aneurysm?
- Was individual's "rupture" witnessed? If so, what did the observer see?
- Does individual have a history of head injury?
- Was individual's brain function abnormal? If so, to what extent?
- Did individual have papilledema?
- Was an angiogram done? CT? What were the results?
- Was a lumbar puncture done?
- Did individual have a CBC and coagulation studies? What were the results?

Regarding treatment:

- Did individual have surgical clipping of the aneurysm?
- If individual was not a candidate for clipping, was endovascular or embolization surgery performed? If not, what is the response to conservative treatment?
- Is individual on medication to reduce stress? Prevent seizures? Lower blood pressure?
- Is individual on a calcium-channel blocker to control blood vessel spasms? Corticosteroids to reduce brain swelling?

Regarding prognosis:

- Have any complications developed? What were they?
- Does individual have hypertension or cardiovascular disease?

References

Beers, Mark, MD, and Robert Berkow, MD, eds. The Merck Manual of Diagnosis and Therapy. Medical Services, USMEDSA, USHH, 1999. 01 Jan 2001 <http://www.merck.com/pubs/mmanual>.

Cerebral Contusion, Closed

Other names / synonyms: Brain Bruise, Cerebral Bruise

851, 851.0, 851.00, 851.01, 851.02, 851.03, 851.04, 851.05, 851.06, 851.09, 851.4, 851.40, 851.41, 851.42, 851.43, 851.44, 851.45, 851.46, 851.49

Definition

A cerebral contusion is a bruising of the brain resulting from blunt impact to the head or acceleration/deceleration injury. The individual usually suffers prolonged unconsciousness that can be fatal. A closed cerebral contusion indicates that the individual's brain was not penetrated.

The most common causes of closed cerebral contusions are motor vehicle accidents and other accidents, both work-related and recreational.

Nearly 10 million individuals in the US sustain a brain injury each year. The most common cause is a motor vehicle accident. A study of motor vehicle crashes in Monroe County, New York determined that from 1983 to 1986, cranial injuries were the most likely cause of death in over 65% of individuals. This New York study further found that death from cerebral contusion was more likely in individuals not wearing seat belts (71%) compared with those wearing seatbelts (37%). A brain contusion is the most common fatal injury in adult cyclists and is related to not wearing helmets.

Diagnosis

History: The individual is possibly unconscious when examined by medical personnel. A common symptom is prolonged unconsciousness (coma). The conscious individual reports headache, dizziness, nausea, vomiting, weakness of the extremities (paresis), and make inappropriate responses to questions.

Physical exam: Level of consciousness is disturbed. A neurological examination may not reveal any localizing signs. The individual with no other serious injuries other than cerebral contusion will not have a fractured skull or any signs of opening or penetration of the skull.

Tests: Skull x-rays check for a fracture. CT or MRI detect any bleeding in the skull. The Glasgow Coma Scale classifies the severity of brain injury with a score of 15 as normal and progressively lower scores indicating greater neurologic injury to the brain.

Treatment

The treatment of cerebral contusions is supportive. Breathing and circulation are supported, if needed, and often the individual is restrained during treatment. Frequent assessment of neurological status is important in case changes occur that indicate the need for further treatment (i.e., medication to reduce swelling in the brain). Brain swelling caused by the build up of fluids as a result of the contusion (cerebral edema) is reduced by continuous infusion of high protein fluids (oncotic therapy with 25% bovine serum albumin) with frequent measurement of oncotic pressure and adjustment of fluids and electrolytes. "Blossoming" hemorrhagic contusions may require surgical intervention.

Prognosis

Mortality from cerebral contusions ranges from 25-60%. Adults over age 50 do not recover as rapidly or as frequently as younger individuals. Individuals in a coma do not do as well and the longer the coma, the greater the probability of dying or permanent neurological damage. In general, individuals with oncotic therapy have a better chance of survival without permanent neurological damage.

Differential Diagnosis

Other possible diagnoses include a less severe cerebral concussion or brain injury from lack of oxygen to that region (ischemic brain injury also called stroke).

Specialists

- Neurologist
- Neuropsychologist
- Neurosurgeon

Rehabilitation

Individuals with closed cerebral contusion may present with a variety of behavioral, physical and cognitive disabilities depending on the severity and location of the injury. Individuals may need treatment by physical, occupational, speech therapists, neuropsychologists, vocational counselors, and social workers.

Individuals may present with motor control deficits. Physical and occupational therapists treat balance and coordination disorders that may be present. Individuals with impaired coordination perform fine motor coordination exercises in occupational therapy such as picking up pegs and placing them in a pegboard. They may also work on practical coordination exercises such as fastening buttons or practicing signatures. Individuals work on gross motor coordination in physical therapy such as kicking a soccer ball rolling toward them or throwing beanbags at a target.

Individuals with impaired balance engage in physical and occupational therapy. For example, occupational therapists may work on dynamic sitting balance to promote dressing and grooming abilities. Sitting balance can be improved by having an individual sit on a therapy ball and attempt to reach for objects placed at various distances. Physical therapists may focus on standing balance to preserve the ability to walk. Individuals may perform exercises in parallel bars such as walking heel-and-toe to help improve standing balance. Because individuals with motor control deficits may also have difficulty planning out movements (dyspraxia), therapists may need to provide cues for the sequence of common tasks like getting out of a chair.

The main focus of physical and occupational therapy in the area of motor control is to maximize functional capabilities. Occupational therapists teach individuals skills such as getting in and out of the shower, dressing, and meal preparation. Physical therapists teach skills such as getting in and out of bed, walking, or using a wheelchair.

Individuals with poor motor control of the facial muscles may require speech therapy for improved clarity of speech and increased safety in swallowing. Speech therapy can also strengthen the muscles of the face for improved speech and swallowing. Individuals with hearing loss may require speech therapy. Individuals may have difficulty speaking or understanding speech (aphasia) due to brain injury. Speech therapy focuses on skills such as word finding and sentence completion. Individuals may perform activities like identifying pictures with the appropriate word or using contextual cues in a sentence in order to complete it.

Individuals may also present with perceptual deficits. Occupational and physical therapists provide methods for increasing safety such as a cane to compensate for decreased balance from double vision. Individuals may require an occupational or physical therapist to assess their homes for tripping hazards such as throw rugs.

Physical therapy improves overall endurance by teaching stretching and strengthening exercises of the arms and legs. Individuals may also perform aerobic activity such as walking on a treadmill or riding a stationary bicycle to further increase endurance.

Individuals may present with cognitive deficits due to brain injury. Occupational therapists evaluate and treat any deficits. Individuals learn to compensate for cognitive deficits by writing down instructions they need to remember, practicing tasks such as making change, or writing notes to remind themselves of important tasks such as locking the door or turning off the oven.

A neuropsychologist may be necessary for individuals with more severe deficits. Vocational counselors work with occupational, physical, and speech therapists to replicate job task requirements in therapy. These counselors help individuals keep future career plans realistic and ease the transition back to work.

Work Restrictions / Accommodations

Individuals who fully recover should be able to return to work within 6 weeks and complete duties. The only accommodation may be follow-up physician visits. Individuals with permanent brain damage may be on permanent disability.

Comorbid Conditions

Comorbid conditions that slow full recovery include other brain injuries (i.e., skull fracture and hematoma), diabetes, stroke, heart disease, Alzheimer's disease, and dementia.

Complications

Possible complications include poor general health, inability to reduce the swelling of the brain (cerebral edema), skull fracture, large bleeding into the brain (large intracerebral hematoma), traumatic injuries to other parts of the body, low oxygen concentration in the blood (hypoxia), fever or low body temperature, and acute renal failure.

Factors Influencing Duration

Prolonged coma, residual disturbances of memory, dizziness, inability to concentrate, behavioral problems, other diseases or injuries, and poor response to psychotherapy increase the length of disability.

Length of Disability

The length of disability for the otherwise healthy individual is at least 2 to 3 months. Disability may be permanent.

Duration in Days

Job Classification	Minimum	Optimum	Maximum
Any work	91	119	Indefinite

Failure to Recover

If an individual fails to recover within the maximum duration expectancy period, the reader may wish to reference the following questions to assist in better understanding the specifics of an individual's medical case.

Regarding diagnosis:

- Was individual in a motor vehicle accident or other accident?
- Was individual conscious or unconscious when examined?
- Does individual report headache, dizziness, nausea, vomiting, weakness of the extremities, or make inappropriate responses to questions?
- Has individual had skull x-rays, CT or MRI? Has individual had controlled diagnostic blocks? What was individual's initial Glasgow Coma Scale score?
- Were conditions with similar symptoms ruled out?

Regarding treatment:

- Is individual receiving supportive treatment?
- Was a respirator necessary?
- Was individual treated with medication to reduce brain swelling?

Regarding prognosis:

- Is individual active in physical therapy? Is a home exercise program in place?
- Can individual's employer accommodate any necessary restrictions?
- Does individual have any complications such as poor general health, inability to reduce the cerebral edema, skull fracture, large intracerebral hematoma, traumatic injuries to other parts of the body, hypoxia, fever or low body temperature, or acute renal failure?

References

Boss, Barbara J. "Alterations of Neurologic Function." Pathophysiology. McCance, Kathryn L., and Sue E. Heuther, eds. St. Louis: Mosby, 1994. 527-586.

Leahy, Patricia. "Traumatic Head Injury." Physical Rehabilitation: Assessment and Treatment. O'Sullivan, Susan B., and Thomas J. Schmitz, eds. Philadelphia: F.A. Davis Company, 1994. 491-508.

Salazar, A.M., et al. "Cognitive Rehabilitation for Traumatic Brain Injury: A Randomized Trial. Defense and Veterans Head Injury Program (DVHIP) Study Group." Journal of the American Medical Association 283 23 (2000): 3075-3081.

Swiercinsky, Dennis P., PhD, et al. Traumatic Head Injury. Kansas City: The Brain Injury Association, Inc, 1995.

Swierzewski, M.J., et al. "Deaths from Motor Vehicle Crashes: Patterns of Injury in Restrained and Unrestrained Victims." Journal of Trauma 37 3 (1994): 404-407.

Teasdale, T.W., and A.W. Engberg. "Disability Pensions in Relation to Traumatic Brain Injury: A Population Study." Brain Injury 14 4 (2000): 363-372.

Cerebral Hemorrhage

Other names / synonyms: Apoplexy, Basilar Hemorrhage, Brain Hemorrhage, Bulbar Hemorrhage, Cephalic Hemorrhage, Cerebellar Hemorrhage, Cerebellum Hemorrhage, Cerebral Hemorrhage, Cerebral Parenchymal Hemorrhage, Cerebromeningeal Hemorrhage, Cerebrospinal Hemorrhage, Cerebrovascular Accident, Cerebrum Hemorrhage, Cortical Hemorrhage, Hemorrhagic Cerebrovascular Accident, Hemorrhagic Stroke, Intracerebral Hemorrhage, Stroke, Subcortical Hemorrhage

431, 803.3

Definition

Cerebral hemorrhage is bleeding within the brain (cerebrum). It is one form of stroke. A stroke is an acute neurological deficit due to a deprivation of cerebral blood flow. Cerebral blood flow may be acutely interrupted by a blood clot (thrombus) forming on a cholesterol deposit (plaque) in a cerebral artery, a blood clot forming in the neck or heart that breaks off and travels to the brain (cerebral embolus), or a bleed (hemorrhage) into the brain, i.e., a cerebral hemorrhage. Intracerebral hemorrhage refers to a hemorrhage within the brain and intracranial hemorrhage refers to a hemorrhage within the skull. Therefore, the term intracranial hemorrhage includes an intracerebral hemorrhage, but not vice versa.

The most frequent cause of cerebral hemorrhage is high blood pressure (hypertension). Other causes include aneurysm rupture, arteriovenous malformation rupture, cerebral amyloid angiopathy, bleeding disorders such as hemophilia, anticoagulant therapy with blood thinners, trauma, collagen vascular diseases such as systemic lupus erythematosus, brain tumors, and cocaine use.

Risk factors for hemorrhagic stroke include hypertension, elevated serum cholesterol, use of blood thinners (anticoagulants and antiplatelet agents), past history of transient ischemic attack, and drinking alcohol. Hypertensives are more than twice as likely to have hemorrhagic stroke as are individuals with normal blood pressure. Untreated hypertension is associated with greater risk of hemorrhagic stroke than hypertension that is well controlled with medications. In 80% of cases, cerebral hemorrhage caused by high blood pressure is found in deep brain structures (basal ganglia or thalamus) or in the white matter. High blood pressure and smoking are thought to cause changes in the walls of small arteries that makes them more likely to rupture.

Cerebral amyloid angiopathy, caused by build-up of amyloid protein in blood vessels supplying the brain and its coatings, causes both large hemorrhages into a single brain lobe (lobar hemorrhage) and small hemorrhages near the brain surface (cortical hemorrhages). Blood disorders such as leukemia may cause many small hemorrhages scattered throughout the brain tissue, or larger hemorrhages.

Strokes in general and cerebral hemorrhages specifically are more frequent in individuals between ages 50 and 90, with a peak incidence above age 80. Smokers, diabetics, and hypertensives have a higher incidence of stroke. Stroke is also more prevalent in Scandinavian countries than in the Mediterranean. It occurs more often in blacks than whites, partly because hypertension is more frequent in blacks.

Diagnosis

History: Hallmark symptoms of cerebral hemorrhage are headache and vomiting that help to distinguish hemorrhage from other causes of stroke. Other symptoms include visual disturbances, difficulty talking (aphasia), arm or leg weakness (paresis), and impaired consciousness ranging from drowsiness to coma.

Physical exam: Blood pressure is usually elevated. The individual may be alert, drowsy or unconscious. Neurological examination helps determine the location of the hemorrhage through focal abnormalities such as weakness, sensory disturbances, abnormalities in language or other higher processes, or impairments in the nerves supplying the head and neck (cranial nerves).

Tests: Brain CT demonstrates hemorrhages of 1 cm or more in diameter. Smaller hemorrhages may be undetectable. MRI is more sensitive in identifying hemorrhage in some areas of the brain. Injection of dye (contrast medium) into the carotid artery (arteriography) is sometimes done, especially if ruptured aneurysm or arteriovenous malformation is suspected as the cause of hemorrhage. Spinal tap (lumbar puncture) is generally avoided if cerebral hemorrhage is documented on CT or MRI because of risk associated with the procedure when pressure within the skull is increased. Removing spinal fluid from the spinal canal may cause a drop in pressure below the brain, allowing the brain to move downward (herniate) into the spinal canal. Brain herniation can lead to compression of vital structures, coma, and death.

Treatment

If the individual is awake or drowsy, treatment usually consists of measures to reduce the brain swelling around hemorrhage. Fluid restriction and medications to remove excess fluid (diuretics) are employed. If the individual is less alert or comatose, surgical removal (evacuation) of the hemorrhage may be done. If the bleeding came from a ruptured aneurysm, surgery may be needed to clip the aneurysm to avoid rebleeding. If additional aneurysms are associated, they may also be removed.

Other supportive measures include medications to reduce blood pressure, treat heart rhythm disturbances (arrhythmias), treat seizures, and relieve arterial narrowing (vasospasm), which occurs when blood spreads from brain tissue into the cerebrospinal fluid bathing the brain. Assisted breathing (tracheostomy with intubation and mechanical ventilation) may be needed if the individual is in coma. More frequent, deeper breaths (hyperventilation) may help reduce pressure within the brain by decreasing levels of carbon dioxide. Transcranial Doppler or intraventricular pressure monitoring may be needed to help optimize treatment.

Prognosis

In approximately half of cerebral hemorrhage cases, extensive bleeding causes increased pressure on the brain and results in death. Half of the individuals with cerebral hemorrhages caused by hypertension die in the first 48 hours. Factors that predict death within the first month following cerebral hemorrhage include level of consciousness when the individual is first seen, rupture of the hemorrhage into the ventricular system channeling cerebrospinal fluid (intraventricular hemorrhage), size of hemorrhage, and age and sex (males over age 70 have the worst outcome). Hypertensive hemorrhages are more than five times as likely to be fatal as those not associated with hypertension.

Some individuals may recover completely or sustain some degree of brain damage. Recovery and rehabilitation depend upon the location and extent of bleeding and the degree of tissue damage sustained as a result of the hemorrhage or treatment procedures. The extent of brain damage can be reduced by minimizing the length of time between the onset of symptoms and start of treatment.

Differential Diagnosis

Neurological diagnoses that can be associated with similar symptoms include concussion, migraine headache, encephalopathy, tumor, and seizure.

Specialists

- Neurologist
- Neurosurgeon

Rehabilitation

The type and length of rehabilitation depend on the location of the hemorrhage and any residual damage as a result of the hemorrhage. Types of therapy that may be necessary include physical therapy to help regain strength and the ability to walk, occupational therapy to perform household and daily living skills such as bathing and dressing, speech therapy to learn to speak and understand verbal and written communication, and vocational counseling if new job skills are required.

Work Restrictions / Accommodations

The type and extent of work accommodations that may be required depend upon the degree of permanent brain damage sustained. Certain functions may be relearned by using and retraining other areas of the brain through rehabilitative therapy. Adaptive devices and architectural modifications may be necessary to accommodate the individual upon return to work.

Comorbid Conditions

Hypertension, hypercholesterolemia, smoking, cerebral amyloid angiopathy, bleeding disorders, aneurysm, arteriovenous malformation and cocaine use may be associated with cerebral hemorrhage, and each is associated with its own morbidity that could lengthen disability.

Complications

Possible complications of cerebral hemorrhage include inhalation of mouth or stomach contents into the lungs (aspiration pneumonia), heart attack (acute myocardial infarction), brain arterial narrowing (vasospasm) causing secondary brain damage, seizures, and downward movement of the brain into the spinal canal (herniation) which compresses vital brain structures, leading to coma or death. Depending on the location of the hemorrhage, complications may include weakness or paralysis on one side (hemiparesis or hemiplegia), language disturbance (aphasia), or other neurological impairments.

Factors Influencing Duration

The location, type of vessel involved, and cause of the cerebral hemorrhage, coupled with the length of time between the onset of symptoms and start of treatment, affects the extent and length of disability. Individuals may have ongoing difficulties with speech and understanding language. Others may have diminished mental function and permanent physical limitations.

Length of Disability

For craniotomy or craniectomy, duration depends on site, severity, and underlying cause. Residual impairments in survivors may be severe, precluding employment. Disability may be permanent. Duration reflects recovery from procedure only.

Craniotomy or craniectomy.

Duration in Days

Job Classification	Minimum	Optimum	Maximum
Sedentary work	21	42	Indefinite
Light work	28	42	Indefinite
Medium work	35	56	Indefinite
Heavy work	42	56	Indefinite
Very Heavy work	42	56	Indefinite

Cerebral aneurysmectomy.

Duration in Days

Job Classification	Minimum	Optimum	Maximum
Sedentary work	42	56	Indefinite
Light work	42	56	Indefinite
Medium work	56	70	Indefinite
Heavy work	70	84	Indefinite
Very Heavy work	70	84	Indefinite

Failure to Recover

If an individual fails to recover within the maximum duration expectancy period, the reader may wish to reference the following questions to assist in better understanding the specifics of an individual's medical case.

Regarding diagnosis:

- Does individual have a history of high blood pressure (hypertension)? History of bleeding disorders such as hemophilia or collagen vascular diseases such as systemic lupus erythematosus (SLE)?
- Does individual have a history of having a small stroke (transient ischemic attack)?
- Does individual take blood thinners (anticoagulants or antiplatelet agents)?
- Did a recent trauma to the head occur?
- Does individual use cocaine?
- Does individual complain of headache and vomiting?
- Are visual disturbances, difficulty talking (aphasia), arm or leg weakness (paresis), or impaired consciousness ranging from drowsiness to coma present?
- Was brain CT done to reveal hemorrhages of 1 cm or more? MRI?
- Was arteriography of the carotid artery performed?
- Was the diagnosis of cerebral hemorrhage confirmed?
- Was the cause of the hemorrhage identified?

Regarding treatment:

- If individual is fairly alert, were medications to remove excess fluid (diuretics) given and fluid restriction maintained to reduce brain swelling?
- If individual is not alert or is comatose, was surgical removal (evacuation) of the hemorrhage done?
- If the bleeding was from ruptured aneurysm, was surgery done to clip the aneurysm?
- Is individual taking medication to lower blood pressure, treat heart rhythm disturbances (arrhythmias), treat seizures, and relieve arterial narrowing (vasospasm)?
- Is individual responding to the medications?
- If individual is in a coma, is transcranial Doppler or intraventricular pressure monitoring required to optimize treatment?

Regarding prognosis:

- What was the level of consciousness when first seen?
- Did the hemorrhage rupture into the ventricular system channeling cerebrospinal fluid (CSF)?
- How large was the hemorrhage?
- What is the age and sex of individual?
- Was this hemorrhage associated with hypertension?
- Did individual sustain brain damage? If so, how much recovery can be expected with rehabilitation?
- Has individual experienced complications such as aspiration pneumonia, heart attack (myocardial infarction), brain artery narrowing (vasospasm), seizures, and downward movement of the brain into the spinal canal (herniation)?
- What type of neurological damage was done? Would rehabilitation return individual to reasonable functioning on a daily basis?
- Is individual in a coma? What are the possibilities that individual will come out of the coma?

References

Cerebral Aneurysm. drkoop.com. 1998. 20 Jul 2000 <http://www.drkoop.com/conditions/ency/article/001414.htm>.

Naff, N.J., et al. "Treatment of Intraventricular Hemorrhage with Urokinase: Effects on 30 Day Survival." Stroke 31 4 (2000): 841-847.

Cerebral Palsy

Other names / synonyms: Dyskinetic Cerebral Palsy, Spastic Cerebral Palsy

333.7, 343, 343.9

Definition

Cerebral palsy refers to a group of chronic disorders impairing motor function (control of movement) due to brain injury occurring before, during, or shortly after birth. The disorder is nonprogressive (static) and generally does not worsen over time. The manifestations of the illness are the same from childhood to adulthood. The cause is not fully known but it is believed that cerebral palsy can be caused by abnormalities resulting from abnormal implantation of the ovum or fetus, maternal diseases, external toxins, or metabolic disorders. The most frequent risk factor associated with cerebral palsy is birth weight below 2,500 grams, which may occur in premature delivery, small-for-gestational-age infants, or multiple births.

The most common causes are brain hemorrhage and ischemic brain damage. Other conditions that may predispose an individual to cerebral palsy include complications of childbirth such as abruptio placentae, prolapsed umbilical cord, and breech birth, which can lead to intracranial bleeding and reduced oxygen supply to the tissues (hypoxia), causing brain injury.

There are three major types of cerebral palsy: spastic, dyskinetic, and ataxic. Combinations of two types or, rarely, all three types may occur. Nearly half of all cerebral palsy cases are spastic cerebral palsy, the most common and less severe form of the disease. Individuals in this group display varying degrees of paralysis of the limbs on one side of the body (hemiparesis), paralysis of all four limbs and trunk (tetraparesis), or all four limbs but with the legs and feet more severely affected than the arms and hands (diparesis). Dyskinetic cerebral palsy is characterized by abnormal involuntary movements, especially slow, twisting, writhing movements (athetosis), which are seen in young children and adults. Ataxic cerebral palsy occurs in less than 5% of individuals with cerebral palsy and is characterized by tremors, unsteadiness, lack of coordination, and quick, jerky, dance-like (choreic) movements.

Individuals born with low birth weights are at higher risk for developmental problems. In the US, about 85% of low birth weight babies survive, and of these, 5-15% have cerebral palsy, and about 25-30% are mentally impaired at school age. Because the illness does not develop in adulthood, the incidence of cerebral palsy is the same for adults as for children, which is estimated at 1.6 per 1,000 neonatal survivors. Some individuals with cerebral palsy are also affected by other disorders, including seizures and mental impairment, but cerebral palsy does not always cause a profound handicap, and the severity of the disorder can vary.

Diagnosis

History: Cerebral palsy is difficult to recognize and diagnose in early infancy but is easy to recognize in children and adults. Early signs of cerebral palsy usually appear before the age of three. A careful history of possible prenatal, perinatal or postnatal injuries to the developing nervous system should be obtained from the family. Symptoms include difficulty with fine motor skills, such as writing, difficulty with balance and walking, and involuntary movements.

Physical exam: Motor abnormalities that have their onset early in life and continue through adulthood are numerous and diverse. The individual usually has slow motor development, hyperreflexia, and altered muscle tone. Individuals with hemiparesis have increased tone in the limbs and develop a characteristic gait and posture. Walking may seem normal but the abnormality is apparent when the individual runs. Tendon reflexes are increased on the affected side, spasticity and clonus may be present. In tetraparesis, both cerebral hemispheres are involved and speech impairment, drooling, and difficulty swallowing (dysphagia) develop. Fine motor skills, including rapid hand movements and asymmetric forearm function, and reflexes should be tested. In dyskinetic cerebral palsy there is enlargement (hypertrophy) of the continually moving muscles, especially of the neck and shoulders.

Tests: CT, MRI and electroencephalography (EEG) are often utilized in the diagnosis. Laboratory testing of blood and cerebrospinal fluid are also conducted to test for meningitis and metabolic disorders causing similar symptoms.

Treatment

The goals of therapy are to improve function, control seizures, and help the individual establish an emotional life that approaches normal. Drugs to control seizures and muscle spasms and special braces that compensate for muscle imbalance may be used. Other treatments that can be employed include physical, occupational, speech, and behavioral therapy. Orthopedic surgery (if appropriate) and mechanical devices that help correct, support, align, or prevent deformities (orthoses) can improve function of the legs. Counseling for emotional and psychological needs may also be utilized. Therapy should be tailored to individual needs at a particular time and age.

Prognosis

Cerebral palsy cannot be cured; however, function can be improved in almost all cases, especially with early treatment and management of neurological problems such as seizures. Although cerebral palsy is not progressive, most individuals will develop some form of motor abnormality or seizures (epilepsy), and most will reach adult years.

The severity of cerebral palsy varies depending on the degree of damage to the nervous system. In some cases, an individual may exhibit normal intelligence despite motor abnormalities. Individuals with less severe impairment can lead productive lives and are able to perform light work. In severe forms of the disease, special care may be required, and the individual may be limited in work capacity. For example, if the individual requires a wheelchair and also has mental impairment, then even light work may not be possible.

Differential Diagnosis

Differential diagnosis includes other diseases or injuries of the brain such as hereditary (congenital) ataxia, spinal cord injury and malformation, spina bifida, subdural hematoma, brain tumor, hemiparesis, Tay-Sachs disease, and metachromatic leukodystrophy. Metabolic disorders such as phenylketonuria, glutaric aciduria, and mucopolysaccharidosis must also be distinguished from cerebral palsy.

Specialists

- Audiologist
- Neonatologist
- Neurologist
- Neuropsychologist
- Neurosurgeon
- Occupational Therapist
- Orthopedic Surgeon
- Physiatrist
- Physical Therapist
- Psychiatrist
- Psychologist

Rehabilitation

Because cerebral palsy is a diagnosis that incorporates a variety of different symptoms, individuals with this diagnosis will have varied rehabilitation needs. Physical, occupational, and speech therapists all may play a role in the care of an individual with cerebral palsy, with the frequency and duration of rehabilitation dependent upon the needs of the individual. Individuals typically require therapy in the following areas: communication, range of motion, strength, balance, coordination, and functional activities such as mobility.

Individuals with cerebral palsy may have speech that is unclear. Speech therapists teach individuals specific lip, tongue, and facial muscle positions that result in clarifying speech.

Individuals with cerebral palsy typically have spasticity, which is characterized by having so much muscle tone in one or more muscle groups that the muscles do not function properly due to stiffness. This can create imbalances in strength, which impacts on balance and functional mobility. Physical and occupational therapists address increased muscle tone by aggressively stretching any affected muscle groups. Individuals and their caregivers learn to carry out these stretching techniques to further improve range of motion. Physical and occupational therapists may consult with an orthotist, who custom-fits braces and splints, to provide splints that produce a sustained stretch to specific joints.

Individuals also learn to strengthen any weak muscles to maximize their functional abilities in both occupational and physical therapy. For example, if an individual has weak ankles, standing heel and toe raises can be performed to increase strength. Physical and occupational therapists may consult with an orthotist to provide braces for the arms or legs for individuals with persistent muscle weakness.

Individuals who have balance deficits require occupational and physical therapy. Physical therapists may work with an individual in a set of parallel bars. Individuals perform activities such as walking heel to toe or walking sideways while using the bars for support as needed. Individuals may also walk in a figure-8 pattern to emphasize balance when changing directions. Occupational therapists may focus on an individual's sitting balance through activities such as putting on shoes or preparing a meal.

Individuals with impaired coordination also require physical and/or occupational therapy. Individuals may perform activities with the physical therapist such as standing and kicking a ball that is rolled toward them at different speeds and from different directions. Individuals may perform activities such as tossing bean-bags at a specific target or picking up pegs and placing them into a pegboard in occupational therapy.

Individuals with cerebral palsy also may require physical and occupational therapy to increase their functional mobility. Both occupational and physical therapists instruct individuals in safe mobility. Individuals learn to get out of bed, up from a chair, and in and out of the bathtub. Individuals may learn to use adaptive equipment such as a bath bench or bed rail to accomplish these tasks.

Work Restrictions / Accommodations

Work restrictions and accommodations depend upon the type of cerebral palsy the individual has and the severity of motor abnormalities, seizures (epilepsy), and mental impairment. Each case would require individual evaluation to determine work limitations. For example, if an individual's neurological problems and difficulty with motor functions are addressed, then performance of work in a limited capacity such as from a wheelchair or with the use of mechanical walking devices or braces may be possible, in the absence of severe mental impairment.

Comorbid Conditions

Obesity could affect walking ability in individuals. The individual with seizures (epilepsy) that are uncontrolled may lose mental ability and become functionally worse. Individuals with the spastic form of cerebral palsy may develop fixed deformities of the limbs due to non-use of the muscles and joints if not treated early.

Complications

Although cerebral palsy is not progressive, individuals may develop other neurological problems including seizures (epilepsy), mental retardation, attention deficit disorder, hyperactivity, visual impairment, difficulty swallowing, speech impairment (dysarthria), and hearing loss. Some individuals who are walking may become unable to walk if they gain too much weight. Other potential problems that affect the muscles and joints include scoliosis, hip dislocation, muscle and joint stiffness, and unequal leg length.

Factors Influencing Duration

Factors affecting disability include the type and severity of cerebral palsy. The emotional state of the individual is also important in adjusting to the disability. Availability of work accommodations for individuals with cerebral palsy is another factor influencing the ability to work in a supportive environment.

Length of Disability

Cerebral palsy is a lifelong disease and there is no cure. In less severe cases, most adults may work if the job accommodates their disability.

Failure to Recover

If an individual fails to recover within the maximum duration expectancy period, the reader may wish to reference the following questions to assist in better understanding the specifics of an individual's medical case.

Regarding diagnosis:

- Was individual's birth weight below 2,500 grams?
- Does individual have spastic, dyskinetic, or ataxic cerebral palsy?
- Does individual have trouble with fine motor skills? Difficulty with walking or balance?
- At what age did the symptoms appear?
- Were CT, MRI, and EEG done? Blood tests? Lumbar puncture?
- Were conditions with similar symptoms ruled out?

Regarding treatment:

- Does individual have seizures? Are they controlled?
- Is individual on medications for muscle spasms?
- Was individual fitted with orthoses?
- Was orthopedic surgery necessary?

Regarding prognosis:

- Is individual active in a rehabilitation program?
- If obese, is individual in a weight management program?
- Can individual's employer accommodate any necessary restrictions?

References

Adams, Raymond D., Maurice Victor, and Allan H. Ropper. Principles of Neurology, 6th ed. New York: McGraw Hill, 1997.

Fetters, Linda. "Cerebral Palsy: Contemporary Treatment Concepts." Contemporary Management of Motor Control Problems. Lister, Marilyn J., ed. Fredericksburg: The Foundation for Physical Therapy, 1991. 219-224.

O'Sullivan, Susan B. "Strategies to Improve Motor Control and Motor Learning." Physical Rehabilitation: Assessment and Treatment. O'Sullivan, Susan B., and Thomas J. Schmitz, eds. Philadelphia: F.A. Davis Company, 1994. 225-249.

Rowland, Lewis P. Merritt's Textbook of Neurology, 8th ed. Philadelphia: Lea & Febiger, 1989.

Sarno, Martha Taylor. "Neurogenic Disorders of Speech and Language." Physical Rehabilitation: Assessment and Treatment. O'Sullivan, Susan B., and Thomas J. Schmitz, eds. Philadelphia: F.A. Davis Company, 1994. 633-653.

Toner, L.V., K. Cook, and G.C. Elder. "Improved Ankle Function in Children After Computer-assisted Motor Learning." Developmental Medicine and Child Neurology 40 12 (1998): 829-835.

Cerebrovascular Accident

Other names / synonyms: Acute Cerebrovascular Disease, Brain Attack, Cerebral Infarction, Cerebral Seizure, Cerebrovascular Accident, Craniovascular Accident, CVA, Stroke

436

Definition

A cerebrovascular accident is commonly known as a stroke or "brain attack." A stroke involves sudden, localized damage in the brain due to lack of blood flow (ischemic stroke) or abnormal bleeding in the brain (hemorrhagic stroke).

The two main causes of ischemic stroke are clots within the arteries that feed the brain (cerebral thrombosis), and particles that move through the bloodstream resulting in a blockage (cerebral embolism). Bleeding from a ruptured blood vessel causes hemorrhagic stroke. The blood vessel may rupture because of high blood pressure (hypertension), increased tendency toward bleeding (clotting disorder), abnormally weakened blood vessel (aneurysm), or abnormal communication between arteries and veins (arteriovenous malformation).

Modifiable risk factors for stroke are hypertension, diabetes mellitus, cigarette smoking, previous reversible stroke-like episodes (transient ischemic attacks or TIAs), high cholesterol, heart disease, congestive heart failure, cocaine use, obesity, and heavy alcohol consumption. Risk factors that cannot be modified are gender, age, race, prior stroke, and family history.

Stroke ranks as the second or third cause of death in developed nations and the third cause of death in the US, killing about 160,000 individuals a year. It is also one of the leading causes of adult disability. Approximately 730,000 individuals in the US have a new or recurrent stroke each year. Two-thirds of all strokes occur in adults over the age of 65 with the risk of stroke doubling with each decade after age 55. Blacks experience stroke almost twice as much as whites. This is due to a higher incidence rate and risk factors for stroke that include hypertension, diabetes, obesity, smoking, and sickle cell anemia. The stroke risk for younger women who smoke and take the pill (high estrogen oral contraceptive) is 22 times higher than the average.

Diagnosis

History: Onset of hemorrhagic stroke is usually sudden with maximal symptoms at onset. There may be sudden, severe headache and/or sudden lapse into unconsciousness (coma). Past history may be positive for seizures or headaches. In ischemic stroke, symptoms usually develop more gradually over minutes to hours, although the stroke may occur during sleep so that the individual may awaken with what appears to be a sudden deficit.

Symptoms vary depending on the blood vessel affected by the stroke. Recognizing the pattern of symptoms can help diagnose whether the stroke involves the front of the brain (anterior circulation) or back of the brain including the cerebellum or brain stem (posterior circulation). Symptoms may include numbness (paresthesia) or weakness (paresis) in the face, arm, or leg, usually on one side of the body (hemianesthesia or hemiparesis); difficulty in speaking or understanding speech (expressive or receptive aphasia); vision loss affecting one or both eyes (visual field cut); double vision (diplopia); slurred speech (dysarthria); difficulty swallowing (dysphagia); difficulty walking (gait ataxia and/or dyspraxia); dizziness (vertigo); or loss of balance or coordination.

Physical exam: Physical findings vary depending on the location of the stroke. Other findings may include increased or decreased muscle tone (hypertonia or hypotonia) or reflex changes. If the stroke affects the brain stem, there may be difficulty with temperature and blood pressure regulation and breathing.

Tests: Brain CT and MRI determine the area affected by the stroke and the presence or absence of bleeding. An arteriogram may be performed to determine if a hemorrhagic stroke is due to a congenital malformation in the brain (arteriovenous malformation) or aneurysm, or to determine whether surgery is needed to bypass a blocked (occluded) artery. Tests for heart attack (myocardial infarction), which is common in stroke, include electrocardiogram (ECG) and heart enzymes. In embolic stroke, tests to determine the source of clots (emboli) include a carotid Doppler to examine the neck arteries and an echocardiogram to examine the heart valves.

Treatment

Suspected stroke victims must be brought to the hospital immediately, as drugs are now available that can help dissolve clots in ischemic strokes and improve outcome provided the drug is given within 3 hours of symptom onset. Brain CT is done immediately to rule out bleeding. If the individual meets other criteria such as the absence of high blood pressure, tissue plasminogen activator (tPA) may be given according to strict protocol. Some individuals who do not meet criteria for tPA may be given heparin, aspirin, or other blood thinners to prevent additional strokes or a worsening of the stroke. However, heparin may cause bleeding in an ischemic stroke (e.g., nonhemorrhagic). For this reason, brain CT is always done to rule out bleeding. Other medications may be indicated to control high blood pressure, high blood lipids, or severe muscle spasms, or to control complications such as heart attack.

Surgery (carotid endarterectomy) may be performed to either scrape out fatty deposits that may cause further blockages in arteries or to bypass blocked areas. In hemorrhagic strokes, surgery may be indicated to stop further bleeding by tying off (clipping) ruptured aneurysms or some of the blood vessels feeding an arteriovenous malformation. If pressure inside the brain is increased because of bleeding into the chambers (ventricles) within the brain, placing a shunt into the ventricles may help drain some of the excess blood and cerebrospinal fluid. Blood pressure, oxygenation, and blood chemistries must be carefully regulated to minimize the amount of brain damage resulting from the stroke.

Prognosis

Recovery rates vary depending on stroke severity and the control of risk factors such as cocaine/tobacco usage, high blood pressure, and diet. Stroke has an overall mortality rate of 26.4 per 100,000 individuals, with higher mortality in brain stem stroke or hemorrhagic stroke where loss of consciousness (coma) occurred. About 10-18% of stroke survivors have a second stroke within a year. Of the 4 million people living with stroke, one-third experience mild disability, one-third moderate disability, and one-third severe disability.

Differential Diagnosis

Since stroke is a medical emergency and immediate treatment offers the best chance for recovery, stroke must be presumed in individuals with symptoms until stroke is definitely ruled out. A transient ischemic attack (TIA) resembles a stroke, but symptoms resolve completely within 24 hours, usually within 20 minutes. Other conditions that may resemble stroke in presenting symptoms include migraine headaches, seizure disorders, brain tumors, and subdural hematomas.

Specialists

- Cardiologist
- Cognitive Rehabilitation Specialist
- Internist
- Neurologist
- Occupational Therapist
- Orthotist
- Physiatrist
- Physical Therapist
- Psychiatrist
- Speech Therapist

Rehabilitation

Individuals who experience a stroke may require various rehabilitation services including physical therapy, occupational therapy, speech therapy, and orthotic management. Therapy should begin as soon as the individual is medically stable, usually within 72 hours.

The focus of occupational therapy is to regain the individual's ability to perform activities of daily living. Occupational therapists teach individuals to perform activities such as washing dishes and doing the laundry while maintaining their balance. Individuals learn to either perform such tasks while sitting down on a kitchen stool or by holding an equal stance through each leg to maintain a standing position. Individuals also learn bathing and dressing techniques. Occupational therapists may order equipment such as a tub transfer bench to assist individuals in utilizing the bathtub or elastic shoelaces to promote ease of dressing.

Occupational therapists promote the return of upper extremity and hand function through a variety of activities. Often the upper arm separates (subluxation) from the shoulder girdle due to the loss of muscle tone. Neuromuscular electrical stimulation (NMES) uses electrodes that provide external stimulation to the muscles to counteract this symptom. More frequently, individuals use a hemi-sling that helps support the arm to prevent subluxation. Occupational therapists may stretch the upper extremity and teach self-stretching techniques so the arm can regain maximum potential. Individuals perform strengthening exercises such as shoulder shrugs, biceps curls, and hand grasps.

Physical therapy focuses on stretching and strengthening any weakness. Therapists may passively stretch any affected joints. Physical therapy also focuses on improving mobility skills including transfer training. The physical therapist teaches individuals to roll in bed, transfer from lying to sitting, and from sitting to standing. Therapy teaches the individual to roll to both sides and bear weight evenly when sitting and standing. Individuals also learn mobility techniques such as walking and climbing stairs utilizing a pyramid cane or four-pronged cane. Orthotic management may also be required for individuals to regain function. A night splint may be made that places the hand in a more functional position. An orthotist may make an individual a leg splint to promote better control of the ankle and knee during ambulation.

Speech therapy may be required to strengthen the muscles of the face for improved speech and swallowing. Individuals may need counseling by a psychologist or psychiatrist to help adjust to their altered functional abilities and body image.

Work Restrictions / Accommodations

When returning to the workplace, an individual who has suffered a stroke will have varying needs. If a cane, walker, or wheelchair is necessary, the work environment should be free of barriers that limit mobility. Individuals may need a less stimulating work environment to improve concentration if cognition was affected by the stroke. Individuals may need adaptive equipment such as pens and pencils with built-up shafts that allow better gripping. Individuals may need to change job positions if the original job required heavy lifting or prolonged standing.

Complementary and Alternative Therapies

Content is intended for awareness only. Treatments may or may not be effective. Scientific evidence may be lacking and some substances have potentially toxic effects. Dr. Presley Reed and the editors do not endorse the use of these therapies in the absence of consultation with a licensed medical professional.

Acupuncture -	May help restore the body's balance.
Anger management -	Angry outbursts may increase the risk of stroke because they cause sharp increases in blood pressure.
Antioxidants -	Vitamins C and E and other antioxidants may repair damaged tissue by decreasing free radical damage.
Fish oil -	Fish oil is high in the omega-3 fatty acids that help prevent strokes and may assist the body in building new cells.
Ginkgo -	May aid stroke rehabilitation by improving blood flow through the brain.
Garlic -	Garlic reduces blood pressure and cholesterol and may help prevent the internal blood clots that trigger most strokes.

Comorbid Conditions

High blood pressure is the primary predictor of a stroke. Coronary artery disease, heart valve defects, irregular heartbeat, and enlargement of one of the heart's chambers can create clots that may break loose and cause another stroke. A history of TIA also predicts future strokes and about 35% of all thrombotic strokes are preceded by TIA. High cholesterol causes buildup of fatty plaques in blood vessels that can lead to future ischemic strokes. Diabetes mellitus causes damaged blood vessels throughout the body. Other comorbid conditions include obesity and accompanying poor diet.

Complications

Complications vary with the severity and location of the stroke, and the amount of time between the onset of stroke and treatment. Individuals with stroke are at increased risk for having another stroke or myocardial infarction. Heart monitors should be used following stroke, as 30-50% of these individuals will have abnormal or irregular heart rhythms (cardiac arrhythmia). Because of decreased muscle activity, there is a risk of blood clots (deep vein thrombosis). These blood clots can travel to the lungs (pulmonary embolism) and cause serious respiratory problems or even death.

Difficulty swallowing and decreased alertness can allow food or saliva to enter the lungs (aspiration) and cause sudden death due to choking or lung infection (aspiration pneumonia). Seizures occur in 10-20% of individuals with ischemic stroke, and 50% of individuals with hemorrhagic stroke affecting the cortex or gray matter that covers the front part of the brain. Urinary incontinence and poor bladder function may result in urinary tract infection or kidney problems. Depression affects more than half of individuals with stroke, especially when the stroke affects the left side of the brain. Individuals with stroke are at increased risk of falls due to factors such as poor judgment, poor balance and coordination, and weakness. Uncontrolled muscle spasm can lead to joint stiffness and immobility (contractures). Shoulder injury can result due to decreased muscle tone. Bedsores (decubitus ulcers) may occur if the individual does not make frequent position changes and may be a source of infection that enters the bloodstream (sepsis).

Factors Influencing Duration

Delay in treatment of stroke influences recovery. Age at onset also affects recovery, with older adults experiencing longer lasting effects than those with onset before age 45. Blacks are twice as likely to die from a stroke than whites and experience greater physical disability and longer lasting disability from stroke than any other racial group in the US. Women are more likely to die from stroke than men, and with their increased life expectancy, a stroke at advanced age is more of a possibility. Disability varies with location and size of stroke and response to treatment.

Length of Disability

The duration of disability depends on the location and severity of the stroke and response to treatment. Job requirements may also affect length of disability. Disability may be permanent for individuals with jobs that require long periods of standing, heavy lifting, or the use of both hands.

Duration in Days

Job Classification	Minimum	Optimum	Maximum
Sedentary work	28	63	Indefinite
Light work	28	63	Indefinite
Medium work	28	70	Indefinite
Heavy work	28	91	Indefinite
Very Heavy work	28	91	Indefinite

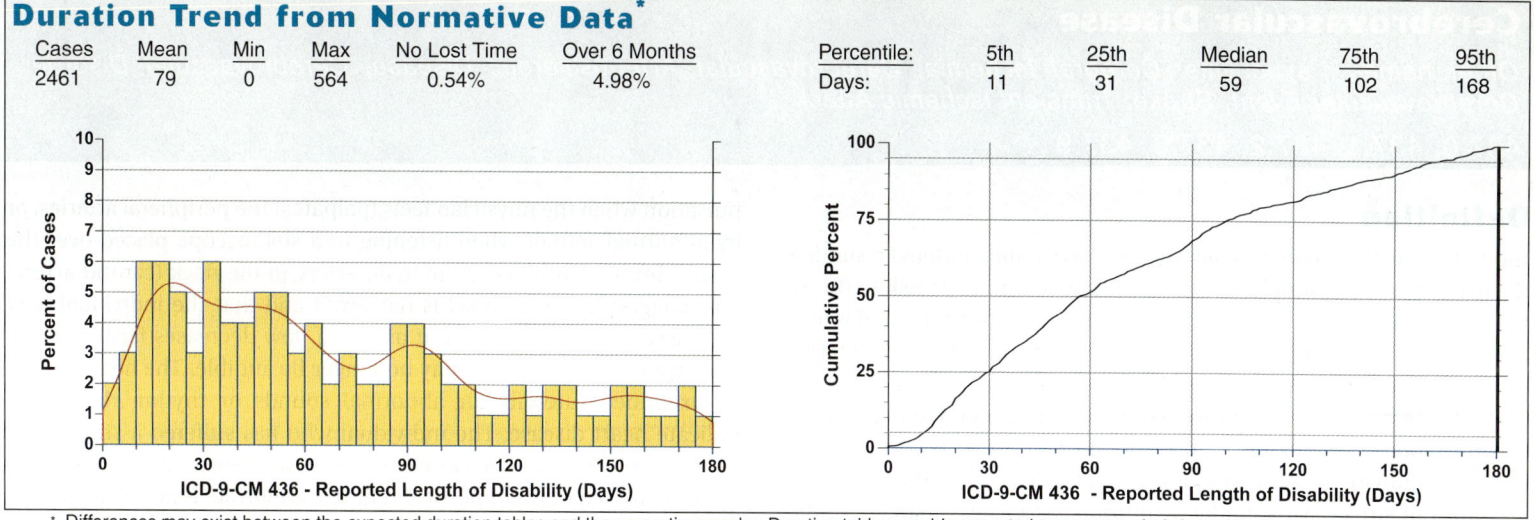

Failure to Recover

If an individual fails to recover within the maximum duration expectancy period, the reader may wish to reference the following questions to assist in better understanding the specifics of an individual's medical case.

Regarding diagnosis:

- Does individual have any risk factors such as hypertension, clotting disorder, aneurysm, or arteriovenous malformation? Prior stroke?
- What is individual's age? Gender? Ethnic background? Family history?
- Does individual have diabetes mellitus, TIAs, high cholesterol, heart disease, or congestive heart failure? Does individual smoke, use cocaine, or abuse alcohol? Is individual obese?
- Did individual experience a sudden, severe headache and/or sudden coma?
- Has paresthesia or paresis in the face, arm, or leg occurred, usually on one side of the body? Was expressive or receptive aphasia, visual field cut, diplopia, dysarthria, dysphagia, gait ataxia, vertigo or loss of balance or coordination reported?
- On physical exam, was increased or decreased muscle tone or reflex changes observed?
- Does individual have difficulty with temperature and blood pressure regulation and breathing?
- Were a brain CT, MRI, or arteriogram done? ECG and heart enzymes performed? Doppler or echocardiogram?
- Were conditions with similar symptoms ruled out?

Regarding treatment:

- Was individual taken to the hospital immediately?
- Was the TPA protocol administered?
- Is individual being treated with heparin, aspirin, or other blood thinners?
- Is it necessary to administer other medications to control high blood pressure, high blood lipids, severe muscle spasms, or complications such as heart attack?
- Was carotid endarterectomy performed? Clipping? Shunt?

Regarding prognosis:

- Has individual addressed any correctable risk factors?
- Is individual active in rehabilitation? Is a home exercise program in place?
- Does individual have any complications such as another stroke, myocardial infarction, cardiac arrhythmia, deep vein thrombosis, pulmonary embolism, or aspiration pneumonia?
- Does individual have seizures, urinary tract infection or kidney problems, other injuries from falls, contractures, bedsores, or sepsis? Is individual depressed?

References

American Association of Naturopathic MedicineHome Page. American Association of Naturopathic Medicine. 14 Apr 2000. 25 May 2000 <http://www.naturopathic.org/Library/articles.lay/EK.stroke.html>.

National Stroke Association Home Page. National Stroke Association. 1999. 19 May 2000 <http://www.stroke.org>.

Boss, Barbara, Peter Sunderland, and Joleen Heath. "Alterations of Neurologic Function." Pathophysiology: The Biologic Basis for Disease in Adults and Children. McCance, Kathryn, and Sue Heuther, eds. St. Louis: Mosby, 1994. 527-586.

Gresham, G., Pamela Duncan, and William Stason. Clinical Practice Guideline: Quick Reference Guide for Clinicians. Rockville: U.S. Department of Health and Human Services, 1995.

Henkel, John. "New Success Against Stroke." FDA Home Page. 03 Jan 1998. 19 May 2000 <http://www.fda.gov/fdac/features/1998/298_stroke.html>.

O'Sullivan, Susan B. "Stroke." Physical Rehabilitation: Assessment and Treatment. O'Sullivan, Susan B., and Thomas J. Schmitz, eds. Philadelphia: F.A. Davis Company, 1994. 327-360.

Cerebrovascular Disease

Other names / synonyms: Cerebral Ischemia, Cerebrovascular Arteriosclerotic Disease, Cerebrovascular Disorder, Cerebrovascular Event, Stroke, Transient Ischemic Attack

437.0, 437.1, 437.2, 437.3, 437.9

Definition

Individuals with cerebrovascular disease have either suffered a sudden decrease in oxygen supply to the brain (stroke) or are at risk to do so. Cerebrovascular disease is the most frequent cause of stroke, and is also a common cause of progressive memory loss and intellectual deterioration due to decreased blood flow and oxygen supply to the brain (vascular dementia). Cerebrovascular disease is a general term meaning that the blood vessels in the brain are not normal. Stroke is often the first sign that individuals have cerebrovascular disease, but there may be warnings of stroke, with similar symptoms lasting less than 24 hours, which then return to normal.

A stroke occurs when the constant supply of oxygen and nutrients to the individual's brain is cut off because the blood vessel either is blocked or starts to leak, causing bleeding into the brain. That part of the brain that is cut off from its blood supply can rapidly deteriorate due to death of nerve cells.

Cerebrovascular disease is the most common cause of neurologic disability in industrialized countries. Risk factors include cardiovascular disease, cigarette smoking, increased age, obesity, diabetes, diet lacking in fruits and vegetables, and lack of regular exercise. Nearly 70% of individuals who suffer stroke have high blood pressure (hypertension). Risk of a first or subsequent stroke is lowered in individuals taking blood pressure lowering drugs (antihypertensives) and blood cholesterol lowering drugs (including the statins).

In the US, up to half of women die of heart disease or stroke. About 600,000 Americans each year have a stroke, and about 160,000 of them die. In both men and women, stroke is the third leading cause of death, and cerebrovascular disease is a major cause of disability in both men and women. Individuals with cardiovascular disease and diabetes are at higher risk for cerebrovascular disease. Individuals with predominantly Hispanic, black, or Native American ancestry have higher risk for cerebrovascular disease and stroke than those with predominantly European or Asian ancestry.

Diagnosis

History: Individuals may report episodes of fainting (syncope), dizziness, confusion, headache, nausea, numbness, weakness, paralysis of one side of the body, visual symptoms, difficulty in speaking or in understanding speech, trouble walking, and loss of balance or coordination. When an individual reports suffering the worst headache of his/her life, this should raise a red flag for the diagnosis of bleeding into the brain (subarachnoid hemorrhage). Their medical history may include reports of risk factors such as high blood pressure (hypertension), heart disease, high blood lipids or cholesterol (hyperlipidemia or hypercholesterolemia), smoking, inflammation of the medium-sized arteries supplying the head and eyes (arteritis), trauma, increased red blood cells (polycythemia), and sickle cell disease.

Physical exam: An individual with cerebrovascular disease who is at risk for stroke may be obese or have high blood pressure (hypertension). Clogged arteries (atherosclerosis) may be detected by decreased pulsation when the physician feels (palpates) the peripheral arteries, or by abnormal sounds when listening to a stethoscope placed over the artery (bruit). A bruit over the main artery in the neck (carotid artery) may suggest that the vessel is narrowed and that the individual is at increased risk for a stroke, but as blood flow decreases farther in the narrowed artery, the bruit may no longer be audible. The heart should be examined carefully for abnormal sounds or rhythm that could indicate heart disease. The individual who has suffered a stroke may have neurologic signs such as weakness or numbness on one side of the body, increased or asymmetrical reflexes, abnormal reflexes suggesting involvement of motor pathways, visual field cut, abnormal eye movements or reflexes, decreased or asymmetrical gag reflex, droop of one side of the face, difficulty speaking or understanding spoken speech, slurred speech, coordination or balance difficulties. The pattern of neurologic abnormalities helps the physician determine the location of the stroke.

Tests: CT and MRI are radiology tests that give pictures of the brain structure. Carotid ultrasound or transcranial ultrasound (blood flow tests) help to find any blocks in the passage of blood to and through the brain. A more detailed look at the arteries requires angiography, in which a catheter is inserted into a large leg artery (femoral artery) and threaded back toward the neck. Arteries supplying the brain can then be visualized by x-rays when a special dye is injected through the catheter. Blood samples are also used to diagnose diabetes, high blood cholesterol, or any other condition that raises blood lipid concentrations (hyperlipidemia). ECG (electrocardiogram) helps to determine whether the individual has suffered a heart attack, which frequently accompanies stroke. Electroencephalogram (EEG) may help diagnose stroke through the pattern of brain wave activity, and should be done if the individual is thought to be suffering seizures after a stroke. Spinal tap (lumbar puncture) may be needed to diagnose bleeding into the brain (subarachnoid hemorrhage), although blood is usually obvious on brain CT, and a spinal tap is then unnecessary and should be avoided.

Treatment

Suspected stroke, also called a "brain attack" to emphasize its similarities to heart attack, is a true medical emergency. At the first appearance of warning signs of a stroke, 911 should be called and the individual should go immediately to the hospital by ambulance, preferably to a stroke center skilled in the TPA (tissue plasminogen activator) protocol. This drug can break up blood clots in brain arteries and reverse or minimize damage to the brain, but it must be given within 3 hours of onset of stroke symptoms. For this reason, it is critical that no time be wasted in getting to the hospital, in being seen by the stroke team, and in having the brain CT and other tests needed before the drug can be given.

Treatment for an individual with cerebrovascular disease is aimed at preventing a first or subsequent stroke, including drugs that prevent blood clots from forming (anticoagulants and thrombolytics), drugs that lower blood pressure (ACE inhibitors, diuretics, calcium channel blockers, antihypertensives, and beta-blockers), and drugs for lowering blood cholesterol, such as the statins. Smoking must be stopped, and other lifestyle measures that may be helpful include a low-fat diet rich in fruits and vegetables (according to the recommendations of the American Dietetic Association) and a regular exercise program.

Surgery (carotid endarterectomy) is sometimes also performed to unclog a neck artery (carotid artery) so that blood can flow freely to the brain and a stroke may be prevented.

Prognosis

Outcome varies with the extent of disease and brain damage at the time of treatment and other chronic underlying medical complications. The individual who was healthy and had no neurologic symptoms before suffering a mild stroke may completely recover and lead a normal life after following the prescribed treatment. The individual who has suffered a massive stroke may be permanently paralyzed on one side of the body and no longer be able to speak. The individual who has suffered more than one stroke may be completely paralyzed and may have his or her life shortened considerably. Recovery of any movement or speech may be very limited. Of the 600,000 Americans having a stroke each year, approximately 160,000 die from it.

If carotid endarterectomy is performed, the individual may avoid a stroke. Recovery from this surgery should be complete within 6 weeks, and the individual may be able to return to his/her normal activities including work.

Differential Diagnosis

A brain tumor, aneurysm, or arteriovenous malformation may present with neurological impairments resembling those of a completed stroke. Seizures followed by paralysis may be confused with impending or acute stroke. Alzheimer's disease may resemble multi-infarct or vascular dementia. Cerebral vasculitis associated with collagen-vascular diseases such as lupus may be confused with cerebrovascular disease related to atherosclerosis. If an individual falls during an unwitnessed stroke, it may be difficult to determine which impairments are due to the stroke and which to the fall. Especially in the elderly, even a minor blow to the head or seemingly insignificant fall can give rise to bleeding between the skull and the brain (subdural hematoma) which may be confused with an evolving stroke. A blow to the neck can cause one of the major arteries supplying the brain (carotid or vertebral artery) to weaken and balloon out (traumatic aneurysm), which may give rise to stroke-like symptoms.

Specialists

- Cardiologist
- Infectious Disease Physician
- Internist
- Neurologist
- Neurosurgeon
- Physiatrist
- Psychiatrist
- Pulmonologist
- Radiologist

Rehabilitation

Rehabilitation includes a determined effort to decrease stroke risk, which may include drugs to lower blood lipids and high blood pressure, and a program of healthy diet, regular exercise, no smoking, and moderate alcohol use. When a stroke causes persistent weakness, numbness, or coordination difficulties, physical and occupational therapy are indicated to prevent joint immobility (contractures) and to allow maximal independence in walking and in activities of daily living.

The length of therapy depends on the severity of the stroke. Speech therapy may be indicated if the individual suffers from difficulty in speaking, understanding speech, or swallowing. Respiratory therapy may be indicated if the individual is bedridden and has trouble breathing or clearing secretions, or if pneumonia is present. Vocational rehabilitation may be needed to facilitate return to work. Support groups and counseling may help individuals and families adjust to their disability and lifestyle changes. Social work intervention may be needed to facilitate proper placement, home care, or home modifications.

Work Restrictions / Accommodations

To prevent a stroke, an individual needs to incorporate into his/her daily life frequent exercise and a healthy diet including plenty of fruits and vegetables. Work should include frequent walking and light lifting. Once an individual has had a stroke, restrictions and accommodations depend on the extent and nature of the disability, if the individual is able to return to work at all. For example, the work place may need to be wheelchair-accessible, and individuals with slurred speech may no longer be able to answer telephones.

Comorbid Conditions

Comorbid conditions that slow full recovery include obesity, diabetes, heart disease, other chronic medical conditions, or other neurologic disease.

Complications

Individuals with cerebrovascular disease are at significant risk for stroke. The individual who is obese and/or diabetic, smokes cigarettes, has high blood pressure, and has high blood lipid concentrations has the greatest risk for stroke. Neurologic complications of stroke include permanent brain damage, with possible impairments of weakness, paralysis, numbness, difficulties speaking (expressive aphasia), difficulty understanding speech (receptive aphasia), vision problems, difficulty swallowing, slurred speech (dysarthria), seizures, and problems with walking or coordination. Perhaps because of these deficits or because of involvement of certain brain pathways, the individual who has suffered a stroke frequently becomes depressed, especially if the stroke involves the left half (hemisphere) of the brain. A single large stroke or many small strokes can cause progressive deterioration in memory, intellect, and personality (vascular or multi-infarct dementia). Strokes can be fatal if vital brain centers controlling the heart or respiration are involved, or if the individual suffers a heart attack along with the stroke. If swallowing or gag reflex is affected, the individual may choke on secretions that then enter the lungs, where they can give rise to pneumonia (aspiration pneumonia). Immobility and increased clotting factors present in the blood following a stroke increase the risk of blood clots in the legs (deep venous thrombosis) that can then travel to the lungs (pulmonary embolus). Individuals who are paralyzed from a stroke may develop immobility of joints (contractures) or bedsores (pressure ulcers or decubitus ulcers), especially if physical therapy or nursing care is inadequate.

Factors Influencing Duration

Factors influencing the length of disability include the individual's age and response to treatment, job duties, whether the individual suffers a stroke as a result of cerebrovascular disease, and the severity and complications of the stroke.

Cerebrovascular Disease

Length of Disability

Duration of disability depends on whether the individual suffers a stroke, and the severity of the resulting impairments. If the individual does suffer a stroke, disability may be permanent. Contact physician for additional information.

Failure to Recover

If an individual fails to recover within the maximum duration expectancy period, the reader may wish to reference the following questions to assist in better understanding the specifics of an individual's medical case.

Regarding diagnosis:

- Has individual had warning sings of a stroke? Has individual had a stroke?
- Does individual have hypertension, heart disease, or smoke cigarettes?
- Is individual obese? Have high blood lipids?
- Does individual have arteritis, trauma, polycythemia, or sickle cell disease?
- Has individual had a CT and MRI? Angiography? Blood tests? ECG? EEG?
- Were conditions with similar symptoms ruled out?

Regarding treatment:

- Was individual taken by ambulance to the hospital at the first sign of stroke?
- Did individual receive TPA?
- Is individual on medication to lower blood pressure? Lower cholesterol? To prevent blood clots?
- Has smoking cessation and a low-fat diet been into lifestyle? Does individual exercise regularly?
- Was surgery necessary to unclog the artery?

Regarding prognosis:

- Does individual actively participate in a rehabilitation program that includes physical and occupational therapy as well as education in diet?
- Does individual actively participate in a home exercise program?
- If needed, is individual enrolled in vocational rehabilitation?
- Has individual (and family, if needed) attended support groups or sought counseling?
- Does individual have any conditions that may affect ability to recover?
- What was the severity of individual's stroke and complications?

References

Albers, G.W., and J.G. Tijssen. "Antiplatelet Therapy: New Foundations for Optimal Treatment Decisions." Neurology 53 7 Suppl 4 (1999): S25-31.

Kuehnen, J., et al. "Cranial Nerve Syndrome in Thrombosis of the Transverse/Sigmoid Sinuses." Brain 121 Pt 2 (1998): 381-388.

Cervical Biopsy
67.11, E870

Definition

A cervical biopsy is a procedure in which tissue samples are taken from the opening of the uterus (cervix). A cervical biopsy is done when there are indications of cervical abnormalities that are detected by Pap smears or by direct visualization during a gynecological exam. It is primarily a diagnostic procedure; however, it can also be a treatment when small abnormal tissue patches (lesions) are removed in their entirety. Women who had their first sexual activity at an early age, and those who have had multiple sexual partners, are at an increased risk for having abnormal Pap smears and, thus, the potential need for a cervical biopsy.

In the US, there are 2.5 million new cases of abnormal cell growth (dysplasia) on the cervix (cervical intraepithelial neoplasia), and 13,500 cases of invasive cervical cancer diagnosed each year.

Reason for Procedure

A cervical biopsy is typically performed after a woman has had abnormal results (i.e., signs of precancerous or cancerous cells) from a Pap smear or has visible lesions on her vagina, labia, or cervix. It is also performed to monitor the status of women who have been treated for cervical dysplasia or cancer. The tissue removed in this procedure will be carefully examined for signs of human papilloma virus (HPV), which is associated with cancer, and for cells that indicate a precancerous (dysplastic) or cancerous state.

How Procedure Is Performed

The cervical biopsy is an outpatient procedure routinely performed in the physician's office. The woman lies on the exam table with her legs in the stirrups (lithotomy position). An instrument (speculum) is inserted into the vagina to hold it open so the cervix can be visualized. The cervix is then cleansed using a vaginal swab that is soaked in a salt solution (saline). Using a lighted magnifying instrument (colposcope), the vagina and cervix are carefully examined for signs of inflammation or abnormal surface tissue patterns. To allow visualization of abnormal surfaces, a solution of acetic acid is applied to the cervix. The acetic acid removes the mucus and turns precancerous and cancerous regions of the cervix white (acetowhitening). A topical anesthetic may be applied a few minutes before taking the biopsy. Tissue samples will be taken from any abnormal-appearing regions of the cervix using sharp, grasping instruments (biopsy forceps) or a large bore needle (punch biopsy). Bleeding is stopped by applying pressure with a vaginal swab or by applying a chemical (chemical cauterization). The tissue samples are sent to the laboratory for microscopic analysis.

Prognosis

Cervical biopsy is a routine, simple procedure that causes no ill effects to the woman. Most cervical samples are found to be benign.

Specialists

- Gynecologist

Work Restrictions / Accommodations

No restrictions or accommodations are necessary following routine cervical biopsy.

Comorbid Conditions

Cervicitis, bleeding disorders (e.g., hemophilia) and pelvic inflammatory disease (PID) can influence the length of disability.

Procedure Complications

Complications following cervical biopsy are rare; however, hemorrhage and infection can occur.

Factors Influencing Duration

Other than the short time required for the procedure, the only disability time required will be for possible follow-up procedures at 3- and 6-month intervals. Disability time may be necessary if complications occur. If results from the biopsy indicate cancer, the individual can be expected to require substantial time off for treatment.

Length of Disability

Cervical biopsy.

Duration in Days

Job Classification	Minimum	Optimum	Maximum
Sedentary work	1	1	1
Light work	1	1	1
Medium work	1	1	3
Heavy work	1	2	3
Very Heavy work	1	2	3

Cone biopsy.

Duration in Days

Job Classification	Minimum	Optimum	Maximum
Sedentary work	2	3	7
Light work	2	3	7
Medium work	2	5	7
Heavy work	2	5	10
Very Heavy work	2	5	10

References

Brewer, Molly, Alma Sbach, and Judy Sandella. "Abnormal Papanicolaou Smears and Human Papilloma Virus." Glass's Office Gynecology. Curtis, Michele, and Michael Hopkins, eds. Baltimore: Williams & Wilkins, 1999. 219-40.

Krebs, Hans. "Premalignant Lesions of the Cervix." Textbook of Gynecology. Copeland, Larry, and John Jarrell, eds. Philadelphia: W.B. Saunders Company, 2000. 1225-1259.

Cervical Cauterization

Other names / synonyms: Cervical Electrocoagulation, Cryotherapy

67.32

Definition

Cervical cauterization is a procedure that is used to destroy abnormal (noncancerous or precancerous) cells on the opening to the womb (cervix).

Cauterization is carried out through the use of heat, electricity, cold, corrosive chemicals, or laser. The most common methods involve high frequency electric current (electrocoagulation) or freezing (cryocautery, cryotherapy, cryosurgery).

Although infection by human papilloma virus (HPV) is a common cause of cervical lesions, the cause in most cases is unknown. Women who have had their first sexual activity at an early age and those who have had multiple sexual partners are at an increased risk of developing abnormal cells on the cervix and other cervix conditions that would require cauterization. Cervical cauterization is a very common procedure.

In the US, there are 2.5 million new cases of abnormal cell growth (dysplasia) of the cervix (cervical intraepithelial neoplasia) and 13,500 cases of invasive cervical cancer each year.

Reason for Procedure

Cervical cauterization is commonly used to treat inflammation of the cervix (cervicitis), liquid-filled sacs (cysts), noncancerous erosions of the cervix, and small areas of abnormal tissue (cervical dysplasia). Cauterization is used to treat cervical lesions caused by human papilloma virus (HPV) as 20% of such lesions progress to cancer. It may also be used to stop bleeding that is occurring either spontaneously or following a cervical procedure such as cervical biopsy, cervical polypectomy, or cervical conization. (Cervical cancer is not treated with cauterization but by more aggressive means including surgery and radiation therapy.)

How Procedure Is Performed

Cauterization is an outpatient procedure that is routinely performed in the physician's office. It is also performed in outpatient surgery centers and the hospital. The woman lies on the exam table with her legs in the stirrups (lithotomy position). An instrument (speculum) is inserted into the vagina to hold it open to allow visualization of the cervix. The cervix is cleansed using a vaginal swab that is soaked in a salt solution (saline). Using a lighted, magnifying instrument (colposcope), the vagina and cervix are carefully examined for signs of inflammation or abnormal surface patterns. To allow visualization of abnormal surfaces, a solution of acetic acid is applied to the cervix. The acetic acid turns precancerous and cancerous regions of the cervix white (acetowhitening). A surface anesthetic or cervical nerve block may be administered a few minutes prior to cauterization. Cauterization is performed on any abnormal appearing regions of the cervix. The method chosen depends on the experience of the physician, availability of necessary equipment, and extent of the lesion.

Hot cautery is the oldest method used to treat cervical dysplasia. A device similar to a soldering iron is heated to a dull red color and touched to the cervical lesion.

Electrocoagulation diathermy uses electric current to destroy tissue. The current is delivered to the tissue through needle or ball electrodes. Electrocoagulation diathermy of deep cervical tissue requires general anesthesia.

Cryocautery is performed on small low risk lesions (i.e., when there is little concern of cancer) that are confined to the outer cervix (ectocervix) and is one of the least invasive treatment methods. For cryocautery, a metal probe is chilled through expansion of a compressed gas (nitrous oxide or carbon dioxide) to a temperature well below freezing. The probe is coated with a jelly and touched to the cervical lesion where it causes rapid freezing and destruction of the tissue. Small mild lesions are usually frozen once, whereas large, moderate-to-severe lesions may be frozen twice.

Chemical cautery is used to treat cervical cysts, noncancerous erosions of the cervix, and cervicitis. The area to be cauterized must be dried using a cotton swab to prevent the chemical from trickling onto normal tissue. A cotton swab that has been moistened with the chemical cauterant (e.g., bichloracetic acid) is touched to the cervical lesion. Cervical cysts would be punctured before application of the cauterant. After a few minutes the cauterized area is wiped with a dry swab to remove any residual chemical. Laser cautery (laser vaporization) is an effective treatment for all cervical dysplasias including those that are too large for cryocautery and those that slightly extend into the cervical canal (endocervix). Because of the expense of laser cautery equipment, most laser cauterizations are performed in outpatient surgery centers and hospitals and frequently involve general anesthesia. Laser cauterization is carried out by aiming a carbon dioxide laser beam at the cervical dysplasia. Because of the fine degree of control over the depth and width of tissue destruction, the laser can precisely vaporize the dysplasia while leaving adjacent normal tissue intact. A smoke evacuator is utilized to remove smoke from the vagina. Antibiotics and analgesics are prescribed as needed.

Prognosis

Historically, hot cautery is not very effective because regions of dysplastic cells can be missed. Electrocoagulation has a high success rate and is associated with a recurrence rate of 3-14%. Cryocautery successfully removes 82-92% of cervical dysplasias and is associated with a low recurrence rate for mild cervical dysplasia. The recurrence rate is 10-40% when cryocautery is used to treat moderate-to-severe cervical dysplasia. Chemical cauterization has a high success rate for mild dysplasias. Laser cautery has a high success rate and a recurrence rate of 4-23%.

Specialists

- Gynecologist
- Primary Care Provider

Work Restrictions / Accommodations

Work restrictions and accommodations are not usually associated with this procedure.

Comorbid Conditions

Cervicitis, bleeding disorders (such as hemophilia), and pelvic inflammatory disease can influence the length of disability.

Procedure Complications

Complications associated with cervical cauterization include uterine cramping, lightheadedness, hot flashes, and headaches (vasomotor reactions), profuse watery vaginal discharge, bleeding (hemorrhage), upwardly spreading (ascending) infection, and narrowing (stenosis) of the cervical canal.

Factors Influencing Duration

Disability is not usually associated with cervical cauterization; however, the type and extent of the diseased tissue to be cauterized or the presence of complications may cause disability.

Length of Disability

Duration in Days

Job Classification	Minimum	Optimum	Maximum
Sedentary work	1	1	2
Light work	1	1	2
Medium work	1	1	2
Heavy work	1	2	3
Very Heavy work	1	2	3

References

Brewer, Molly, Alma Sbach, and Judy Sandella. "Abnormal Papanicolaou Smears and Human Papilloma Virus." Glass's Office Gynecology. Curtis, Michele, and Hopkins, Michael, eds. Baltimore: Williams & Wilkins, 1999. 219-240.

Krebs, Hans. "Premalignant Lesions of the Cervix." Textbook of Gynecology. Copeland, Larry, and John Jarrell, eds. Philadelphia: W.B. Saunders Company, 2000. 1225-1259.

Cervical Conization

Other names / synonyms: Biopsy - Cone, Cone Biopsy

67.2

Definition

Cervical conization (cone biopsy) is a surgical procedure where a wedge- or cone-shaped tissue sample is excised from the central portion of the neck of the womb (cervix) for diagnostic and treatment purposes. As a diagnostic tool, the procedure is used to check cervical cells for cancer especially when magnified visual inspection (colposcopy) and cervical biopsy procedures have not provided adequate evidence to confirm or rule out diagnosis. As a treatment tool, cervical conization is used to remove cells that are undergoing changes that could be precancerous (abnormal cells).

After the procedure, the biopsied tissue is examined in the laboratory for abnormal or precancerous cells (cervical dysplasia) and for cancerous cells. If the tissue tests positive for cervical dysplasia, further tests and treatment are scheduled. If the tissue tests negative for cancer, no other treatment is necessary. If the tissue tests positive for cancer, additional treatment such as further surgery or radiation are scheduled.

Approximately 50,000 cervical conizations are performed in the US every year.

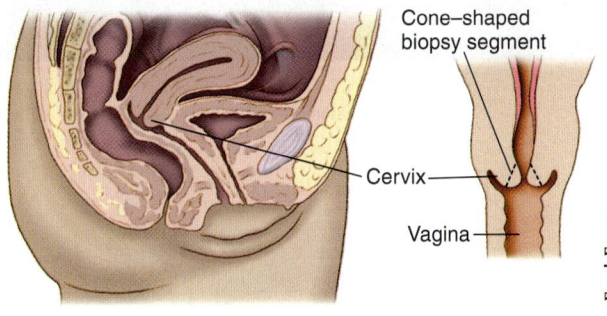

Reason for Procedure

A cone biopsy is usually performed when a Pap smear or series of smears is abnormal but a magnified visual inspection of the cervix (colposcopy) fails to reveal the exact area of the abnormality. Cone biopsy helps diagnose invasive cervical cancer (carcinoma) or precancerous conditions in the endocervical canal inside the cervix (cervical dysplasia). Cone biopsy is also used for further evaluation when a significant difference exists between Pap smear and tissue sample (cervical biopsy) laboratory results. A cone biopsy may also be performed to treat localized, well-defined areas of disease or growths on the cervix.

How Procedure Is Performed

With the individual under general anesthesia, the surgeon begins the procedure by bathing the cervix with a solution and putting two stitches into the cervix to help control bleeding. A scalpel is used to remove a cone-shaped (or wedge-shaped) tissue sample from the central portion of the cervix. The base of the cone is taken from the opening of the cervix. The middle and tip of the cone are taken from the cervical canal so that the cone-shaped piece of tissue removed has the opening of the uterus running through its center. If the purpose of the procedure is diagnostic, the cut edges of the cervix are sutured. If the purpose of the procedure is therapeutic, laser, heat (cauterization), or freezing (cryotherapy) techniques may be used instead since sutures are not required.

Prognosis

Barring significant complications, satisfactory outcome is likely in both diagnostic and treatment situations because a large tissue sample is obtained (larger than obtained by a colposcopy or cervical biopsy).

Normal lab results from cervical conization point to a negative cancer diagnosis. Abnormal lab results indicate an area of precancerous or cancerous cells.

After a cervical conization procedure, most individuals are advised to avoid strenuous exercise for up to 2 weeks. Oral pain medications are prescribed to manage pain. Sexual intercourse, tampons, and douching should be avoided until the incision is completely healed, usually in 5 to 6 weeks.

Specialists

- Gynecologist

Work Restrictions / Accommodations

Strenuous physical activities may need to be temporarily modified.

Comorbid Conditions

There is almost no disability. Obesity, previous abdominal surgeries, heart and lung conditions, and allergy to anesthesia drugs and pain medications are comorbid conditions that may influence recovery and length of disability.

Procedure Complications

Complications from the procedure include heavy bleeding and in rare circumstances, a perforation or infection of the uterus. Individual may experience a miscarriage due to incompetent cervix. Possible infertility may also occur. Scar tissue can interfere with vaginal childbirth or menstrual flow. Although rare, these complications are considered significant. Individuals are urged to ask their physician whether colposcopy or cervical biopsy could be performed instead.

As with any procedure performed under general anesthesia, the possibility exists of reaction to the anesthesia drugs or associated breathing problems.

Factors Influencing Duration

Disability is not usually associated with this procedure.

Length of Disability

Most individuals can return to work or resume previous activities within a few days with minor restrictions such as refraining from strenuous exercise or heavy lifting for up to two weeks.

Job Classification	Duration in Days		
	Minimum	Optimum	Maximum
Sedentary work	2	3	7
Light work	2	3	7
Medium work	2	5	7
Heavy work	2	5	10
Very Heavy work	2	5	10

References

Lynch, C. Cervical Conization. Folsom Obstetrics & Gynecology Medical Group, Inc. 30 May 2000. 15 Jul 2000 <http://folsomobgyn.com/cervical_conization.htm>.

Cervical Disc Disorder with Myelopathy

Other names / synonyms: Cervical Radiculopathy, Cervical Spondylosis, Cervical Spondylotic Myelopathy

722.71

Definition

This diagnosis describes a herniated disc in the neck (the cervical region of the spine) with compression and dysfunction of the spinal cord (myelopathy). The spinal cord can become compressed by a herniated disc alone, or in combination with degenerative changes (cervical spondylosis), or a developmentally narrow spinal canal (spinal stenosis). This disorder is less common than cervical disc herniation without myelopathy. While both disorders cause neck pain and disturbance in arm sensation and strength, myelopathy involves additional neurological disturbances in the legs and possibly bowel or bladder control impairment.

Individuals with cervical disc disorders including myelopathy show signs and symptoms of dysfunction in the nerves of the spinal cord, called myelopathy, or, in a nerve root, called radiculopathy.

The normal degenerative process in cervical intervertebral discs begins by the third decade of life. By the fifth decade of life, most individuals exhibit some degenerative changes. Men tend to have a higher incidence of degeneration than women, and the changes are more severe. By the age of 65, 95% of men and 70% of women show degenerative changes in the cervical spine. Nevertheless, many individuals have no symptoms. These degenerative changes can slowly narrow the spinal canal until spinal cord compression (myelopathy) occurs. Myelopathy can also begin suddenly if due to a massive cervical disc rupture. Cervical spondylotic myelopathy is the most common type of spinal cord dysfunction in individuals older than 55.

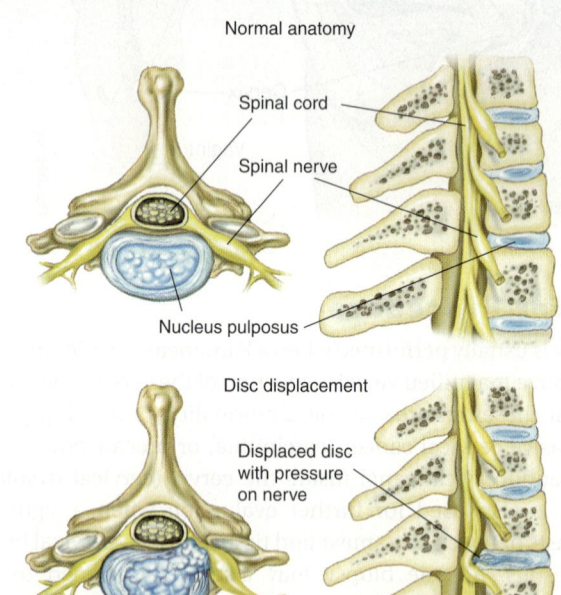

Diagnosis

History: History is of neck and arm pain, and pins-and-needles sensations (paresthesias) may be reported. Individuals may report clumsiness or difficulty using the hands and legs. Subtle disturbances in gait may be reported, with gradual deterioration. Bowel or bladder control problems may be reported, as well as sexual dysfunction. The symptoms may present in different ways. There may be a central spinal cord syndrome, and individuals may have weakness in the arms, even greater weakness in the legs, and arm reflexes that are depressed corresponding to the level of compression.

Physical exam: The exam with a herniated disc may reveal loss of sensation in the distribution of a cervical nerve, most commonly at the sixth or seventh cervical roots. There is muscle weakness and loss of reflexes corresponding to the nerve being compressed. Spasticity of the leg muscles may be noted. This results in a gait disturbance. Sensory and motor changes are usually present, but may appear separately. Pain may be aggravated by bending the head backward or rotating to the affected side. With spondylosis, physical signs may be more diffuse, because spondylosis usually occurs at more than one level in the cervical spine. There may be some restriction in neck motion from spondylosis. Muscle atrophy in the forearms can be seen in long-standing cases. Loss of sensory and motor function below the level of spinal cord compression may be evident (anterior spinal artery syndrome - blockage of the artery by a centrally herniated disc).

Tests: Plain x-rays of the cervical spine are taken, including flexion and extension films to detect instability in the spine. MRI detects spinal cord compression. A CT myelogram may also be done. These last two techniques can also detect narrowing of the spinal canal.

Treatment

The majority of individuals can be treated without surgery. The goals of treatment are to decrease pain, improve function, and prevent recurrence. Conservative treatment can be done if the disease is not progressive. A short period of bed rest (2 days) may be helpful in reducing the intensity of the pain; bedrest must then be followed by mobilization. A soft cervical collar is often used at this time to limit neck movement and relieve pain and spasm in the neck.

The next phase of treatment involves physical therapy (primarily active exercise). Medication may be prescribed to relieve pain and may include anti-inflammatory medication (such as aspirin), narcotics, and muscle relaxants. Cervical epidural steroid injection(s) are often helpful for the symptoms of associated radiculopathy (arm pain and weakness).

Surgery is necessary if symptoms and signs progress or if the individual fails to improve. In cases of cervical disc herniation, surgery is aimed at decompressing the spinal cord. Surgical treatment of cervical myelopathy most commonly entails anterior cervical discectomy and fusion (ACDF); this procedure involves removal of the herniated disc and fusion of the vertebrae to increase stability. If spondylosis is present, a cervical spinal fusion may also be done.

Prognosis

Conservative treatment may stop the progression of nerve damage, but there is less likelihood that it will improve the individual's condition. Results are best if the history is short, less than a few months. Most surgical procedures are successful. Satisfactory results are obtained in over 90% of individuals who undergo anterior cervical discectomy and fusion (ACDF).

If surgery is performed, 50% of individuals may return to full employment, 40% to light employment, and 10% remain disabled, even though improved.

Differential Diagnosis

A tumor in the spinal canal, an epidural abscess, or hematoma can also produce symptoms of spinal cord compression, as can a transverse myelitis or degenerative disease of the spinal cord. Other possible diagnoses include neurologic disease (such as cerebrovascular accident, multiple sclerosis, amyotrophic lateral sclerosis, Guillain-Barré), and upper extremity nerve entrapment syndromes (such as thoracic outlet syndrome, carpal tunnel syndrome, and idiopathic brachial neuritis).

Specialists

- Anesthesiologist
- Neurologist
- Neurosurgeon
- Orthopedic Surgeon
- Physiatrist

Rehabilitation

Rehabilitation is an important aspect in regaining mobility in the neck (cervical) region as well as regaining strength to muscles that may have been affected by a resulting myelopathy. Initially, physical therapy may be needed to decrease pain originating from the disorder. Treatments involving cold or heat control muscle pain and spasm in the cervical muscles. Forms of heat treatment include ultrasound, which uses high frequency sound waves that produce heat and penetrate deep into the involved muscles.

Electrostimulation combined with heat or cold treatment is another technique used in physical therapy to relax muscles. Transcutaneous electrical nerve stimulation (T.E.N.S.) is a form of electrostimulation consisting of a small, battery powered device that emits electrical impulses through electrodes placed on the skin. These electrical impulses, predetermined by the physical therapist, produce a high frequency tingling sensation blocking pain at that level of the spine.

Traction is another popular form of rehabilitation for the displaced cervical disc. Whether the therapist applies it mechanically or manually, traction produces a separation of joint surfaces of the cervical spine to help reduce the disc displacement and decompress any structures causing associated pain. This device is attached to the head and distracts the cervical spine helping to relieve tight muscles and possibly decreases the pressure on any irritated and compressed nerve. The therapist may also give instructions in the use of a home traction unit. This device, using a pulley system and weights, also attaches to the head, pulling it upward as the individual sits in a chair. It is usually applied a few times a day and can be used while sitting or lying in bed.

Soft tissue mobilization and joint mobilization techniques are used by a physical therapist experienced in manual therapy to help improve mobility. This is a hands-on approach providing the effects of increased elasticity of the muscles, thereby improving flexibility. Joint mobilization becomes important to increase the movement at each spinal level resulting in overall cervical spine motion.

Range of motion for the neck normally includes forward and side bending. Rotation and extension are taught with caution at the appropriate time by the therapist or physician.

Once the cervical disorder has been stabilized and there is no longer a concern of increasing pressure against the involved nerve and spinal cord, strengthening of the neck and upper extremities become important in the rehabilitation process. Isometric resistance helps strengthen the muscles of the neck without moving the neck through the range of motion. These exercises are helpful to improve stability.

Strengthening of the cervical muscles with exercises that use resistance throughout the range of motion. This is accomplished with devices such as wall pulleys, and universal and nautilus-type equipment as tolerated and under the supervision and instruction of a physical therapist.

Examples of muscles potentially affected from a cervical disorder are those located between the neck and shoulder (trapezius), the shoulder muscles (deltoid), and virtually any of the other muscles of the arm, hands, and fingers. This is because these nerves to these muscles are responsible for sending messages to and from the brain. They pass through the spinal column at the neck region.

Strengthening of the upper extremities begins slowly by addressing endurance with low resistance and high repetitions and then progresses to more focus on strengthening by fewer repetitions and heavier resistance.

Modifications may need to be made by the physical therapist for those individuals who have other joint irritations of the cervical spine. Because of the various degrees of myelopathy affecting the involved cervical and/or upper extremity muscles, some restrictions may be placed on the progression of the range of motion and strengthening.

Work Restrictions / Accommodations

Work may need to be modified to allow for weakness in the arms and/or legs, decreased dexterity, and an abnormal gait. Overhead work (neck extension) should be avoided. Driving may be difficult or impossible due to limitations on range of movement and discomfort produced by the vibration of the vehicle. Hard physical labor may be severely limited or impossible. Work modifications may be temporary or permanent depending on the individual's response to treatment.

Complementary and Alternative Therapies

Content is intended for awareness only. Treatments may or may not be effective. Scientific evidence may be lacking and some substances have potentially toxic effects. Dr. Presley Reed and the editors do not endorse the use of these therapies in the absence of consultation with a licensed medical professional.

Manipulation, cervical spine - Said to re-establish "nerve energy" flow throughout the nervous system by correcting slight misalignments of the spine.

Comorbid Conditions

Conditions that could lengthen recovery include obesity, pregnancy, and any condition that significantly limits mobility. Individuals with significant cervical spondylosis with myelopathy frequently have similar spondylosis in the lumbar spine, which further limits function.

Complications

Permanent nerve damage can occur, which may be so severe as to cause paralysis of the affected limbs. Chronic-pain-induced depression may occur in some individuals.

Factors Influencing Duration

The length of disability will depend on the severity and duration of spinal cord compression, severity of sensory and motor symptoms, whether surgery was performed, whether nonsurgical treatment regimens are followed, age of the individual, and the response to treatment.

Length of Disability

Duration depends on position of neck (when extended) at work and job requirements for use of arms elevated over shoulder level. Even with improvement after treatment, myelopathy is usually incompatible with heavy work.

For individuals with fusion, disability may be permanent.

Myelopathy, even successfully treated with laminectomy, is not compatible with return to heavy work. Disability may be permanent.

Medical treatment.

Duration in Days

Job Classification	Minimum	Optimum	Maximum
Sedentary work	21	28	35
Light work	21	28	42
Medium work	28	42	84
Heavy work	Indefinite	Indefinite	Indefinite
Very Heavy work	Indefinite	Indefinite	Indefinite

Surgical treatment. Fusion.

Duration in Days

Job Classification	Minimum	Optimum	Maximum
Sedentary work	42	49	84
Light work	56	63	84
Medium work	70	119	182
Heavy work	Indefinite	Indefinite	Indefinite
Very Heavy work	Indefinite	Indefinite	Indefinite

Surgical treatment. Laminectomy.

Duration in Days

Job Classification	Minimum	Optimum	Maximum
Sedentary work	21	35	91
Light work	28	42	119
Medium work	42	84	182
Heavy work	Indefinite	Indefinite	Indefinite
Very Heavy work	Indefinite	Indefinite	Indefinite

Failure to Recover

If an individual fails to recover within the maximum duration expectancy period, the reader may wish to reference the following questions to assist in better understanding the specifics of an individual's medical case.

Regarding diagnosis:

- Does individual have accompanying sensory and motor impairments?
- Is the gait abnormal?
- Are individual's reflexes abnormal?
- Is more than one cervical level involved?
- In the case of disc herniation, did a precipitating event occur?
- Was the onset of symptoms prolonged with no periods of recovery?
- Was diagnosis of cervical disc disorder with myelopathy confirmed?
- Were MRI or myelography and CT done to confirm the diagnosis?

Regarding treatment:

- Did individual's condition respond to conservative treatment?
- Were medications (anti-inflammatory, narcotics, muscle relaxants) prescribed and effective in relieving pain?
- Did individual receive physical therapy?
- Did individual adhere to a regimen of bed rest followed by isometric exercise, aerobic training, and resistance training?
- Is individual a candidate for surgery? Which procedure? Based on what criteria?
- Would individual benefit from psychological counseling or enrollment in a chronic pain program?

Regarding prognosis:

- What are individual's physical limitations? How severely do they impact function?
- What is individual's history?
- How soon after onset of symptoms did individual seek treatment?
- What type of surgical procedure did individual undergo? Were multiple cervical levels involved?
- Has individual experienced complications?
- Does individual have an underlying condition that may impact recovery such as obesity, pregnancy, or any condition that significantly limits mobility?

References

Brower, Richard. "Cervical Disc Disease." The Spine. Herkowitz, H.N., et al., ed. Philadelphia: W.B. Saunders Company, 1999. 455-496.

Kessler, R.M. Management of Common Musculoskeletal Disorders: Physical Therapy Principles and Methods. Philadelphia: J.B. Lippincott Company, 1990.

Scully, Rosemary M., and Marylou Barnes. Physical Therapy. Philadelphia: J.B. Lippincott Company, 1989.

Sidhu, Kanwaldeep, et al. "Surgical Management of Cervical Disc Disease." The Spine. Herkowitz, H.N., et al, eds. Philadelphia: W.B. Saunders Company, 1999. 497-529.

Cervical Dysplasia
Other names / synonyms: Cervical Anaplasia
622.1

Definition

Cervical dysplasia is the development of abnormal cells (cellular deviations) in the lining of the uterine cervix. The cells may multiply or increase in number and progress toward abnormal cellular changes (atypical epithelium) with a loss of the ability of cells to distinguish between one another (cell differentiation), and may slowly lead to cervical cancer (carcinoma).

Risk factors that may be associated with the development of abnormal cervical cells include intercourse at an early age, sexual relations with many partners, genital herpesvirus infection, such as HPV (human papilloma virus), multiple births (multiparity), hormones, poor obstetric and gynecologic care, and smoking. Cervical dysplasia can occur in women at any age, depending on extent of exposure to risk factors. It has been estimated that about 25% of HPV positive women less than 25 years old develop cervical cancer within 15 years after the onset of viral infection. However, women less than 30 years old have a high rate of HPV with normal PAP (Papanicolaou) smear findings.

Cervical dysplasia may regress, persist, or progress to clinical disease. However, cervical dysplasia is considered to be the precursor of cervical cancer.

Diagnosis

History: Early cervical dysplasia is usually asymptomatic, but there may be light vaginal discharge or spotting of blood. Advanced lesions may cause heavier vaginal discharge, leakage from the bladder, or rectal fistulas (abnormal openings on the surface of the anus), anorexia, weight loss, and back and leg pains. Previous infection with HPV should be noted since there is a high incidence of HPV in women with cervical cancer.

Physical exam: The presence of genital warts caused by HPV infection may be revealed during a routine pelvic examination.

Tests: The Papanicolaou (PAP) test, a microscopic examination of the cells of the cervix, can detect cervical cancer and is very important in screening; however, definitive diagnosis is based on examination with an instrument used to examine the vagina and cervix (coloscope) and biopsy of cervical tissue. Cervicography, a relatively new diagnostic method in which a photograph of the cervix is taken, can be examined for evidence of dysplastic changes.

Treatment

Infection and sexually transmitted disease should be appropriately treated and repeat Pap tests obtained. The area of dysplasia should be removed. Procedures used to remove the dysplasia include excision or the use of subfreezing temperature to destroy tissue (cryosurgery).

More advanced tumors may be treated with radiation therapy or removal of the uterus (hysterectomy). A small number of cases may result in hyperplasia of the lining of the uterus (endometrium), in which case the tissue may be removed by a widening of the cervix and scraping of the uterus with a curette (dilation and curettage, or D&C).

Prognosis

If detected early and properly treated, cervical dysplasia can regress and not progress to clinical disease. However, the condition can recur after being effectively treated. If treatment is delayed, then the risk of developing cervical cancer can increase.

The outcome of cryosurgery and removal of the dysplasia is relatively poor, with some reported treatment failure rates of 6.2 percent. Chemotherapy and radiotherapy in addition to hysterectomy has been shown to be of benefit in the treatment of recurrent cervical cancer.

Differential Diagnosis

Cervical tumors such as squamous cell carcinomas, adenocarcinomas, and other mixtures of these kinds, or, in rare cases, sarcomas, are other possible diagnoses.

Specialists

- Gynecologist

Rehabilitation

In general, rehabilitation of the cervical dysplasia depends greatly on whether the condition regresses, persists, or progresses to a clinical disease. Rehabilitation may be necessary if the area of cervical dysplasia was removed and complications later developed such as low back pain, abdominal and general muscle weakness. Physical therapy allows individuals to regain strength and stamina lost due to the disease process, treatment, and recuperation from cervical dysplasia. Individuals recovering from corrective surgery are usually very weak so low-level strengthening begins, then progresses as tolerated by the individual. This is especially the case if strengthening is attempted during the course of treatment. To help clear the lungs after surgery, a respiratory or physical therapist instructs the individual in breathing exercises to help regain normal respiration and encourage coughing.

Early in physical rehabilitation, range-of-motion exercises may help return mobility to the affected joints and key muscles and enable the individual to return to the activities of daily living. The physical therapist first accomplishes this by moving the limb with no assistance by the individual. The next step is active range of motion in which the individual performs all the motion independently with or without resistance from an outside force. When resistance is tolerated, the individual may proceed to isotonic exercise using an elastic band or light weights that provide resistance.

The frequency and duration of the rehabilitation program vary among individuals with cervical dysplasia. Intensity and progression of the exercise depend on the extent of treatment, if surgery was required, and the individual's overall health.

The physical therapist may need to make modifications for those individuals with cervical dysplasia. If the individual has significant muscle weakness of the abdomen and pelvic region, the healing response may initially take longer, with more stretching and strengthening before return to work. In some advanced cases, tumors may be treated with radiation therapy or removal of the uterus (hysterectomy). Therapy for those individuals is modified according to the course of primary treatment.

Once the individual is allowed to return to work, it is important to initially minimize excessive bending, lifting, and twisting of the trunk.

Work Restrictions / Accommodations

Work restrictions and accommodations are not usually associated with this diagnosis. However, if symptoms of pain are present, they may have an impact on ability to perform heavy work.

Complementary and Alternative Therapies

Content is intended for awareness only. Treatments may or may not be effective. Scientific evidence may be lacking and some substances have potentially toxic effects. Dr. Presley Reed and the editors do not endorse the use of these therapies in the absence of consultation with a licensed medical professional.

Escharotic Treatment - A naturopathic treatment where special herbs and enzymes are applied to the cervix and left on for some time, and then a vaginal suppository called a vaginal depletion pack is inserted into the vagina and left in for 24 hours. This treatment is repeated several times, depending on the degree of dysplasia.

Comorbid Conditions

Endometriosis may impact recovery.

Complications

Cervical dysplasia may regress, persist, or progress into cervical cancer. Cervical cancer invades tissues of nearby organs and may spread through the lymphatic system to other areas of the body such as the lungs, brain, bone, and liver. Possible complications of treatment include hemorrhage and infection.

Factors Influencing Duration

The degree of dysplasia and necessary diagnostic testing and treatment procedures may influence the length of the disability.

Length of Disability

Duration depends on degree of dysplasia and associated tests and treatment options selected.

Loop electrosurgical excision or laser.

Duration in Days

Job Classification	Minimum	Optimum	Maximum
Sedentary work	1	2	3
Light work	1	2	3
Medium work	1	2	3
Heavy work	1	3	3
Very Heavy work	1	3	3

Cervical conization.

Duration in Days

Job Classification	Minimum	Optimum	Maximum
Sedentary work	2	3	7
Light work	2	3	7
Medium work	2	5	7
Heavy work	2	5	10
Very Heavy work	2	5	10

Failure to Recover

If an individual fails to recover within the maximum duration expectancy period, the reader may wish to reference the following questions to assist in better understanding the specifics of an individual's medical case.

Regarding diagnosis:

- Did the individual have intercourse at an early age or sexual relations with many partners?
- Does the individual have genital herpes virus infection, human papilloma virus, multiple births, poor obstetric and gynecologic care, or smoking?
- Has the individual had any abnormal vaginal discharge?
- Does the individual have any fistulas?
- On physical exam were genital warts (HPV) present?
- Has the individual had a PAP test?
- Has the individual had a biopsy of the cervical tissue?
- Did the individual have a cervicography done?
- Have other conditions with similar symptoms been ruled out?

Regarding treatment:

- Were any infections and sexually transmitted diseases appropriately treated?
- Did the individual have a repeat Pap test?
- Was the area of dysplasia removed?
- Was a D&C necessary?
- Was radiation therapy or hysterectomy indicated?

Regarding prognosis:

- Is the individual's employer able to accommodate any necessary restrictions?
- Does the individual have any conditions that may affect their ability to recover?
- Does the individual have any complications, such as the cervical dysplasia progressing into cervical cancer? Did the individual have a hemorrhage or infection?

References

Apgar, B.S., and G. Brotzman. "HPV Testing in the Evaluation of the Minimally Abnormal Papanicolaou Smear." American Family Physician 59 10 (1999): 2794-2801.

Kobelin, M.H., et al. "Incidence and Predictors of Cervical Dysplasia in Patients with Minimally Abnormal Papanicolaou Smears." Obstetrical Gynecology 92 (1998): 356-359.

Scully, Rosemary M., and Marylou R. Barnes. Physical Therapy. Philadelphia: J.B. Lippincott Company, 1989.

Soule, Deb. The Roots of Healing. Secaucus: Carol Publishing Group, 1996.

Cervical Polypectomy

Other names / synonyms: Excision of Cervical Polyps
67.39

Definition

Cervical polypectomy is the removal of a small tumor (polyp), often growing on a stalk, from the opening of the womb (cervix). The polyps are generally noncancerous (benign), and can also be located inside the cervical canal (endocervix).

Cervical polyps are caused by an overgrowth of normal tissue. They are relatively common and most do not cause symptoms. They occur in approximately 4% of women, most often women who are in menopause (perimenopausal), past menopause (postmenopausal), or who have had several pregnancies (multigravida). Women who have had a cone-shaped section of cervical tissue removed by a laser beam (laser conization) are at an increased risk of developing cervical polyps.

Reason for Procedure

Cervical polyps usually cause no symptoms aside from some light bleeding or spotting caused by irritation from a tampon or sexual intercourse (postcoital bleeding). Polyps are generally removed because of this bleeding, or to prevent additional future irritation and bleeding. Although most polyps are benign, all should be removed and examined because cancerous (malignant) changes may develop; some cervical cancers first appear as polyps.

How Procedure Is Performed

Polypectomy is usually an outpatient procedure performed in the physician's office. It is generally painless, so no anesthesia is required. The woman lies on the exam table with her legs in the stirrups (lithotomy position); an instrument (speculum) is then inserted into the vagina to hold it open to visualize the cervix. The cervix is cleansed using a vaginal swab soaked in an antiseptic solution. The polyp is grasped with a surgical clamp (hemostat), twisted several times, and pulled until it is freed. The polyp is sent for microscopic examination (pathology) to rule out cancer. The base of the polyp is then removed by scraping it off with a sharp surgical instrument (curettage), or by using heat, cold, or chemicals to destroy the tissue (cauterization).

If the polyp is large, or if it is attached by a broad base rather than a stalk, it may need to be cut off and the wound stitched (sutured) closed. This procedure may be done under local anesthesia in the hospital because of the possible risk of excessive bleeding (hemorrhage).

If the cervix is soft, distended, or partially opened, and the polyp is large or not clearly visible, dilation and curettage (D&C) will be done. The cervical opening will also be widened (dilated) so that the cervical canal and womb (uterus) may be examined for other polyps. All removed polyps will be biopsied for evidence of cancer.

Prognosis

Regardless of the method used, cervical polypectomy is a routine procedure that has an excellent outcome without ill effect on the woman. More than 99% of all cervical polyps are benign.

Specialists

- Gynecologist

Work Restrictions / Accommodations

Other than time off for the procedure, work restrictions or accommodations are not usually required.

Comorbid Conditions

Cervicitis, bleeding disorders (e.g., hemophilia), and pelvic inflammatory disease can influence the length of disability.

Procedure Complications

Complications following cervical polypectomy are rare; however, hemorrhage and infection can occur.

Factors Influencing Duration

The development of complications may require disability time.

Length of Disability

Simple excision.

Duration in Days

Job Classification	Minimum	Optimum	Maximum
Any work	1	3	7

References

Adelson, Mark, and Katherine Adelson. "Miscellaneous Benign Disorders of the Upper Genital Tract." Textbook of Gynecology. Copeland, Larry, and John Jarrell, eds. Philadelphia: W.B. Saunders Company, 2000. 723-739.

Scott, Pamela. "Performing Cervical Polypectomy." Journal of the American Association of Physician Assistants 12 6 (1999): 81-82.

Cervical Polyps

Other names / synonyms: Mucous Polyp of Cervix
622.7

Definition

A cervical polyp is an elongated or projectile growth arising from the mucosal surface of the lower end of the uterus (cervix) or the endocervical canal. These small, fragile growths hang from a stalk and protrude through the cervical opening (os). These growths are typically non-cancerous (benign), but are usually removed because they can become infected, may become cancerous (in 1% or less of women), and causes irregular bleeding and/or bleeding after sexual intercourse. Cervical polyps may be associated with chronic inflammation, can be an abnormal response to increased levels of estrogen, or result from local congestion of cervical blood vessels.

The development of cervical polyps rarely occurs before the onset of menstrual periods (menarche), but is commonly found in women over 20 or who have had several children. In most cases, only a single polyp is present, but sometimes two or more polyps are found.

Diagnosis

History: Women may complain of spotty vaginal bleeding in the form of a pink discharge containing mucous or pus, or a white or yellow colored mucous discharge (leukorrhea). The spotting may occur between periods or after sexual intercourse; women who have gone through menopause may report bleeding.

Douching or straining to have a bowel movement may also produce spotting. Some women may experience abnormally heavy periods (menorrhagia), while others do not experience any symptoms.

Physical exam: Cervical polyps are usually felt during a routine pelvic examination and often appear as smooth, red or purple, finger-like projections protruding from the cervical canal.

Tests: A Pap smear test is performed during the physical exam to detect any precancerous changes in the surface layer of the cervical cells (dysplasia). A cervical biopsy is usually done and it typically reveals mildly abnormal cells and signs of infection.

Treatment

Removal of most cervical polyps is usually done as a simple outpatient procedure. Gentle, manual twisting of a cervical polyp is typically enough to remove it; however, a polyp is often removed by tying a surgical thread around its base and cutting it off. Removing the base can be done either by electrocautery or laser surgery; there may be some light bleeding after this procedure. If the polyp is large or if the cervix is dilated or soft, the cervix may be dilated more and the polyp scraped off (dilatation and curettage, or D&C); the uterus is then also explored for signs of more polyps. Once removed, polyp regrowth is uncommon.

Although most cervical polyps are benign, the removed tissue is sent to a pathologist for microscopic examination. Because many polyps are infected, antibiotic medication is often given either as a preventative (prophylactically) or with any sign of infection.

Prognosis

Complete recovery is expected from uncomplicated polyp removal. If the polyp is not removed, there is a 1% chance that cancer will later develop.

Differential Diagnosis

Other possible conditions include cancerous growths, cervical irritations or infections, and cervical warts. Growths from the uterus (myomas, endometrial polyps) can occasionally extend outside of the cervix.

Specialists

- Gynecologist

Work Restrictions / Accommodations

Depending on the symptoms and method of treatment, work responsibilities may need to be adjusted for a short time and should include avoiding heavy lifting and extended periods of standing.

Comorbid Conditions

A diagnosis of anemia may impact the individual's ability to recover, particularly if blood loss is significant.

Complications

Complications are directly related to the number of polyps and the method of treatment. Cervical polyps are generally considered to be infected and, after their removal, the infection can spread to the uterus. If a D&C is required, complications from that procedure include damage and scarring of the cervix and uterus, and, rarely, perforation of the uterus. Occasionally a cervical polyp will be located high in the cervix, making it hard to see; polyps in this location have been known to cause infertility. Some types of cervical cancers may first appear as a small polyp.

Factors Influencing Duration

The severity of symptoms, number of polyps, and method of treatment influence length of disability. Finding a malignant neoplasm would also influence the length of disability.

Length of Disability

Simple excision in office.

Duration in Days

Job Classification	Minimum	Optimum	Maximum
Sedentary work	1	3	7
Light work	1	3	7
Medium work	1	3	7
Heavy work	1	3	7
Very Heavy work	1	3	7

With D&C.

Duration in Days

Job Classification	Minimum	Optimum	Maximum
Sedentary work	2	3	7
Light work	2	3	7
Medium work	3	4	7
Heavy work	3	4	7
Very Heavy work	3	4	7

Failure to Recover

If an individual fails to recover within the maximum duration expectancy period, the reader may wish to reference the following questions to assist in better understanding the specifics of an individual's medical case.

Regarding diagnosis:

- Does individual have chronic cervical inflammation, increased levels of estrogen, or local congestion of cervical blood vessels?
- How many children does individual have?
- Does individual complain of spotty vaginal bleeding in the form of a pink discharge containing mucous or pus, or a white or yellow colored mucous discharge (leukorrhea)?
- Does individual's spotting occur between periods? After sexual intercourse? Does individual report spotting after douching or straining to have a bowel movement? Does individual experience abnormally heavy periods (menorrhagia)?
- Was a pelvic examination done? Were smooth, red or purple, finger-like projections protruding from the cervical canal present?
- Has individual had a Pap smear? A cervical biopsy?
- Were conditions with similar symptoms ruled out?

Regarding treatment:

- Was individual's cervical polyp removed? Was it sent to the pathologist?
- Is individual being treated with antibiotics?

Regarding prognosis:

- Can individual's employer accommodate any necessary restrictions?
- Does individual have any conditions that may affect ability to recover?

- Have any complications developed such as uterine infection, damage and scarring of the cervix and uterus, perforation of the uterus, infertility, or cervical cancer?

References

Rosenthal, Sara M. The Gynecological Sourcebook. New York: NTC/Contemporary, 1999.

Cervicitis

Other names / synonyms: Cervicitis, Infection of the Cervix, Inflammation of the Cervix, Inflammatory Disease of Cervix
616.0

Definition

Cervicitis is an inflammation of the cervix (the neck and outlet of the womb, or uterus). It can be caused by a vaginal infection, by a sexually transmitted disease such as gonorrhea, chlamydia, or genital herpes; or by injuries to the cervix from childbirth, abortion, miscarriage, or surgery on the uterus. Cervicitis can also result from the use of certain medications, from hormonal changes, or from the insertion of an intrauterine device (IUD). It can also be a sign of pregnancy. Cervicitis can be an acute or chronic condition.

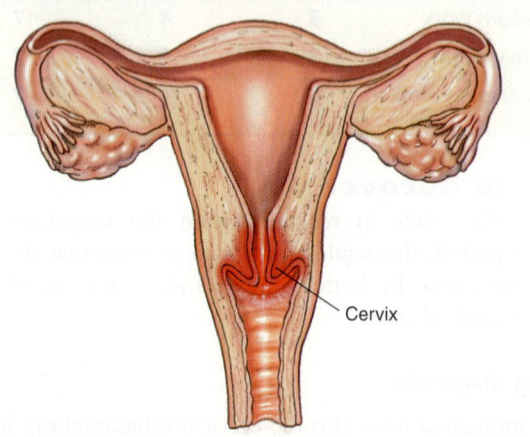

Cervix

Laurie O'Keefe

Diagnosis

History: Acute cervicitis often is not associated with any symptoms and may be an incidental finding during a routine pelvic exam. Chronic cervicitis may be associated with the following symptoms: abnormal blood-streaked vaginal discharge, pain during sexual intercourse (dyspareunia), vaginal bleeding after intercourse, painful menstrual periods, spotting between periods, lower abdominal pain, backache, fever, painful urination (dysuria), and change in urinary frequency, or urgency. A yellowish discharge may indicate a chlamydia infection.

Physical exam: With the pelvic examination, the cervix is found to be inflamed and there may be a discharge. Genital herpes (HSV) may be evident as blisters or open sores on the cervix. Examination may also reveal red, granular, irregular lesions on the external area of the cervix.

Tests: Swabs are taken of any discharge and analyzed to identify the microorganism responsible for the inflammation. Although the most accurate tests involve growing the culture in the laboratory, test results are then delayed for up to 3 days. Several rapid tests have been developed using dye to detect bacterial or viral proteins (chlamydia or herpes), and a gram stain is a quick test for gonorrhea. These tests allow the doctor to have results at the time of the office visit. Chlamydia, however, is easily confused with gonorrhea because their symptoms are so similar and they often occur together. Therefore, many doctors prefer to use both culture and rapid test methods to increase accuracy of the diagnosis.

Treatment

For bacterial causes of infection, treatment is with antibiotics. Herpes infections are treated with an antiviral medication (acyclovir) that controls, but does not cure, the infection and gives symptomatic relief. Since chlamydia and gonorrhea are sexually transmitted, the individual's sexual partner(s) also need to be treated. If symptoms persist, the infected tissue on the cervix is destroyed with heat (cauterization), freezing (cryotherapy), or laser therapy. Minor injuries to the cervix, such as a tear in the sidewall that may occur during childbirth, are repaired, usually immediately after delivery.

Prognosis

With appropriate treatment (medication, cryotherapy, cauterization, laser therapy), full recovery is expected. If proper treatment is delayed or does not occur, injuries to the cervix or other cervical complications may result. In some cases, cervicitis can become chronic.

Differential Diagnosis

Other conditions causing similar symptoms include pelvic inflammatory disease, vaginitis, cervical cancer, sexually transmitted diseases, or urinary tract infection.

Specialists

- Gynecologist

Work Restrictions / Accommodations

Symptoms and treatment received will dictate any specific restrictions or accommodations. Restrictions are not usually required when treatment is with antibiotic medication. If treated with cryotherapy, cauterization, or laser therapy, long periods of sitting should be limited.

Comorbid Conditions

Other conditions independently associated with inflammatory cervical smears include bacterial vaginosis, chlamydia, herpes simplex virus, HIV, cytomegalovirus infections, and human papillomavirus (HPV). A progression of inflammatory cervical smears to squamous intraepithelial lesions (SIL) has been associated with HPV infection.

Complications

If untreated, a cervicitis infection can spread to the lining of the uterus (endometritis) or the fallopian tubes (salpingitis) and may cause pelvic inflammatory disease (PID). These conditions increase the risk of infertility, tubal pregnancy, and the development of chronic pelvic pain. A pregnant woman with untreated cervicitis may infect her baby during delivery. Eye infections in the newborn (neonatal ophthalmia) can lead to blindness. Chlamydia may also cause infant pneumonia.

Factors Influencing Duration

The length of disability may be influenced by the underlying cause of the cervicitis, the severity of symptoms, any complications, and the type of treatment.

Length of Disability

Medical treatment.

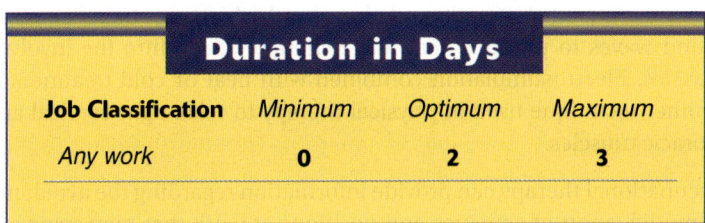

Failure to Recover

If an individual fails to recover within the maximum duration expectancy period, the reader may wish to reference the following questions to assist in better understanding the specifics of an individual's medical case.

Regarding diagnosis:

- Does the individual complain of blood-streaked vaginal discharge, pain during sexual intercourse (dyspareunia), vaginal bleeding after intercourse, painful menstrual periods, or spotting between periods?
- Does she complain of lower abdominal pain, backache, fever, painful urination (dysuria), change in urinary frequency, or urgency?
- Did the physician find the cervix to be inflamed on pelvic exam?
- Were blisters or open sores on the cervix present, suggesting genital herpes (HSV)?
- Has any underlying cause been identified and addressed?
- Were cultures of vaginal discharge taken? If not, were rapid tests for chlamydia, herpes, and gonorrhea done?
- Has the organism causing the cervicitis been identified?
- Is the organism a bacterium or a virus?

Regarding treatment:

- Was the organism causing the infection positively identified?
- Did the individual receive antibiotics or antiviral medication?
- Was she 100% compliant with the medication regimen?
- Has the individual been retested after completion of treatment to determine if the infection completely resolved?
- Do the symptoms continue?
- Will the individual require cauterization, cryotherapy, or laser therapy?

Regarding prognosis:

- Is the cervicitis an acute or chronic condition?
- If chronic, what treatment has the individual received in the past?
- Should another culture be taken to positively identify the causative organism? What other coexisting conditions may be making the individual susceptible to frequent infections?
- Has the sexual partner(s) been tested and treated?
- Did the individual follow the treatment plan exactly as prescribed?
- Could the individual be reinfected by her sexual partner(s)?
- Was treatment obtained in a timely fashion?
- Has the infection spread to other organs in the reproductive system?
- Was the woman pregnant?
- Was she infected at the time she gave birth?

References

Cervicitis. rxmed.com. 15 Jun 2000. 01 Jan 2001 <http://www.rxmed.com/illnesses/cervicitis.html >.

Miller. K.E., and J.C. Graves. "Update on the Prevention and Treatment of Sexually Transmitted Diseases." American Family Physician 61 2 (2000): 379-386.

Cervicobrachial Syndrome

Other names / synonyms: Cervicobrachial Neuralgia, Cervicobrachialgia

723.3

Definition

Cervicobrachial syndrome is a chronic pain disorder where individuals report pain, abnormal sensations such as burning, tickling, pricking, or tingling (paresthesia), and cramps in the neck, shoulders, and along the arms. No objective pathology is present to permit a specific diagnosis. US health professionals refer to this condition as "neck pain" and/or "shoulder pain." Acupuncturists and chiropractors in the US and health professionals outside the US refer to this condition as cervicobrachial syndrome.

Diagnosis

History: Individuals may have a history of office work in unchanging postures or manual work with repetitive tasks and constant use such as typing on computers, writing with ballpoint pens, or moving objects onto conveyor belts. Individuals may complain of pain and fatigue of the wrist, forearm, shoulders, and neck; a swelling sensation of the hands; pins and needles; and numbness of the upper extremity. Pain is increased by activity and relieved by rest, however it may also increase at night. Individuals may have the sensation of wearing gloves when they are not.

Physical exam: The arms, shoulders, and neck appear normal but are painful to touch and the neck may be stiff. Individuals may have poor posture with head and neck stooped forward and shoulders rounded.

Tests: Radiographic tests are needed in order to rule out other objectively verifiable causes for the symptoms. Psychological testing and evaluation are helpful to understand psychosocial stressors. Electrodiagnostic tests may be given to rule out nerve damage.

Treatment

Treatment is symptomatic. Pain and sleep disorders are relieved with medications. A cervical collar or wrist splints may be used briefly to support the muscles. Physical therapy may decrease symptoms and improve function. Individuals are told to increase their exercise activity, especially stretching exercises of the neck and shoulder.

Physical therapy and/or splints may be useful in preventing a condition in which shortened muscles around joints cause abnormal and sometimes painful positioning of the joints (contractures).

Prognosis

Recovery from cervicobrachial syndrome may be complete, partial, or very limited.

Differential Diagnosis

The individual diagnosed with cervicobrachial syndrome may have fibromyalgia, rheumatoid arthritis, diabetic peripheral neuropathy, tendinitis, myofascial pain, or degeneration of a cervical disc. Until the past few years, it was assumed that individuals suffering pain and weakness in the cervicobrachial region were malingering or hysterical. Careful physical and psychological examination will rule out individuals faking symptoms.

Specialists

- Neurologist
- Occupational Therapist
- Orthopedic Surgeon
- Physiatrist
- Physical Therapist
- Psychiatrist
- Psychologist
- Rheumatologist

Rehabilitation

Rehabilitation for cervicobrachial syndrome focuses on decreasing the pain, numbness, tingling, and perceived weakness of the arm and hand. Tight muscles in the neck are stretched passively and by active range of motion exercises. The individual can use resistance while strengthening these muscles with elastic cords or free weights and flexing forward at the waist.

The physical therapist instructs the individual regarding good posture. For example, the individual stands straight and moves the shoulders back.

Stretching of muscles associated with cervicobrachial syndrome often begin with heat treatments that are beneficial for increasing tissue temperature and circulation and promoting flexibility. Forms of heat treatment include hot packs and ultrasound, which uses high frequency sound waves to produce heat that penetrates deep into the involved muscles. Electrostimulation combined with heat or cold treatment is another technique used in physical therapy to relax tight cervical and thoracic muscles.

Occupational therapy can provide information regarding the avoidance or modification of activities and positions at work that may aggravate the symptoms. An occupational therapy visit to the work setting may be helpful for the individual returning to the same line of work that caused the disorder.

The frequency and duration of the rehabilitation program vary for cervicobrachial syndrome depending on the extent of the syndrome, and the progress made from the treatment. In some cases, psychotherapy may be needed to develop coping skills when there are significant changes or stress in the work and family environments.

Work Restrictions / Accommodations

Ergonomic changes at the work place may permit the individual to work more comfortably. This can be as simple as changing the size of a ballpoint pen, providing a chair that takes the weight off the forearms, or talking into a telephone headset. Retraining or training in a new job may be helpful for cases that don't respond to treatment.

> **Complementary and Alternative Therapies**
>
> Content is intended for awareness only. Treatments may or may not be effective. Scientific evidence may be lacking and some substances have potentially toxic effects. Dr. Presley Reed and the editors do not endorse the use of these therapies in the absence of consultation with a licensed medical professional.
>
> Acupuncture - May provide pain relief.
>
> Chiropractic therapy - Spinal adjustment may provide symptom relief.

Comorbid Conditions

Comorbid conditions influencing the length of disability include neck pain, autoimmune diseases, cancer, and obesity. Psychiatric comorbidity will be the most prevalent condition associated with failure to respond to treatment.

Complications

There are no specific complications. With time, some individuals initially diagnosed as cervicobrachial syndrome are later recognized to actually have fibromyalgia, rheumatoid arthritis, and other conditions.

Factors Influencing Duration

Factors influencing length of disability include the individual's job requirements, development of psychological problems associated with the disability, and lack of adequate coping skills. Some individuals may have persistent pain for years.

Length of Disability

Disability should be brief and temporary. Work ability is determined entirely by psychosocial tolerance of symptoms and not by risk of complications or lack of capacity.

Duration in Days

Job Classification	Minimum	Optimum	Maximum
Sedentary work	0	3	7
Light work	0	5	14
Medium work	0	7	21
Heavy work	0	14	28
Very Heavy work	0	21	42

Failure to Recover

If an individual fails to recover within the maximum duration expectancy period, the reader may wish to reference the following questions to assist in better understanding the specifics of an individual's medical case.

Regarding diagnosis:

- Does individual have history of office work in unchanging postures or manual work with repetitive tasks and constant?
- Does individual have pain and fatigue of the wrist, forearm, shoulders, and neck; a swelling sensation of the hands; pins and needles; and numbness of the upper extremity? Is pain increased by activity and relieved by rest? Does it increase at night?
- Are the arms, shoulders, and neck painful to touch? Is the neck stiff?
- Were electrodiagnostic tests given to rule out nerve damage?
- Was diagnosis of cervicobrachial syndrome confirmed by diagnostic tests and consultations?
- Were other conditions with similar symptoms ruled out?

Regarding treatment:

- Has individual changed the repetitive activity associated with the symptoms? What other repetitive activity may individual still be doing?
- Has individual completed the recommended course of physical therapy?
- If not already involved in this form of rehabilitation, would individual benefit from occupational therapy?
- Was psychological evaluation obtained?

Regarding prognosis:

- Did individual show any improvement during physical therapy?
- If outcome was not as expected, what are the extenuating circumstances?
- To what extent do symptoms impair function?
- Does individual need retraining?
- Does individual have an underlying condition that may impact recovery?
- Would individual benefit from psychotherapy or psychological counseling?

References

Cohen, M.L. "In Search of the Pathogenesis of Refractory Cervicobrachial Pain Syndrome: A Deconstruction of the RSI Phenomenon." Medical Journal of Australia 156 6 (1992): 432-436.

Kisner, C., and L. Colby. Therapeutic Exercise Foundations and Techniques. Philadelphia: F.A. Davis, 1990.

Cesarean Delivery

Other names / synonyms: Cesarean, Cesarean Birth, Cesarean Section, C-Section

669.7, 74, 74.0, 74.1, 74.4, 74.9, 74.99

Definition

A cesarean delivery is the surgical delivery of an infant by way of an incision through the mother's abdominal wall (laparotomy) and into the uterus (hysterotomy). A cesarean delivery can be a planned or an emergency procedure.

There are approximately 1 million cesarean deliveries in the US each year making it the most frequently performed major surgical procedure. Recently an effort has been made to reduce the number of cesarean deliveries and repeat cesarean deliveries. The frequency of cesarean delivery varies between the different regions and states in the US and between different hospitals and physicians. Cesarean delivery rates are slightly higher in the northeastern and southern states. After reaching a high point in the 1980s, the frequency of cesarean deliveries has steadily decreased in the 1990s, and now equals approximately 10-20% of live births in the US. The frequency of vaginal birth after cesarean (VBAC) delivery has increased in the 1990s to 28% of live births. Between 60-80% of VBACs are successful.

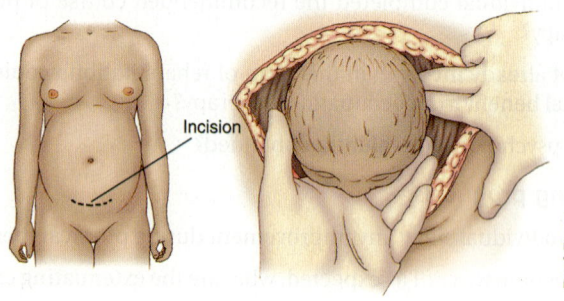

Reason for Procedure

A cesarean is indicated in any situation where labor and/or vaginal delivery pose significant risks to the mother, baby, or both. The decision to perform a cesarean depends on the context of the overall situation. In each case, the relative risks to both the mother and fetus associated with cesarean versus vaginal delivery must be taken into consideration. In some cases, the choice is clear; in others, opinions may differ.

Situations when cesarean delivery is indicated include fetal distress, which is an indication that the baby's circulation and well being are compromised in some way. This can be evident by abnormalities in fetal heart rate or if the amniotic fluid contains fetal waste (meconium). Abnormalities of labor (dystocia) where the baby does not make progress toward being born can include a head too large to pass through the mother's pelvis (cephalopelvic disproportion), a very large baby (macrosomia), and/or dysfunction in uterine contractions. Prolonged labor usually poses greater risks to the fetus than the mother. Dystocia accounts for approximately 30% of all cesarean deliveries, making it the most significant contributing factor to cesarean delivery in the US.

An abnormal position of the fetus such as the baby lying with its buttocks down (breech presentation), sideways (transverse presentation), or with a brow/posterior face position in the uterus can make vaginal delivery impossible or risky and requires a cesarean section to prevent fetal trauma. About 10% of all cesarean deliveries are because of the breech presentation.

If there are two or more fetuses (multiple gestation), a cesarean section may be performed for the safety of the multiple babies. Congenital abnormalities of the fetus may also require a cesarean to reduce fetal risk or trauma from a vaginal delivery.

A premature infant may have to be delivered by cesarean section due to fetal or maternal complications. Unless labor begins spontaneously, the alternatives are to induce labor or to do a cesarean delivery. In many such cases, cesarean is preferable in order to reduce fetal risk.

In some cases, the umbilical cord drops out through the cervix (prolapses) before the fetus is delivered. This can result in compression of the cord and interruption of the baby's blood supply, and generally requires an emergency cesarean.

A malpositioned placenta that totally or partially covers the opening of the cervix (placenta previa) is associated with maternal hemorrhage and increased fetal risk. This usually requires a cesarean depending on the degree of cervical blocking. Total previa where the placenta completely covers the cervix always requires a cesarean.

Premature separation of the placenta from the uterine wall before delivery (abruptio placentae) can result in loss of fetal blood supply as well as severe maternal hemorrhage. Unless vaginal delivery can be accomplished rapidly, cesarean section is indicated. Stable abruptions do not usually require a cesarean.

Certain maternal infections such as genital herpes active at the time of delivery can be an indication for a cesarean because passing the fetus through an infected birth canal can result in a life-threatening infection in the newborn.

Pregnancy-induced hypertension (preeclampsia or eclampsia, also called toxemia of pregnancy) may endanger both the mother and fetus. The decision to perform a cesarean depends on the severity of the condition and on how soon vaginal delivery can reasonably be accomplished.

Idiopathic thrombocytopenic purpura is an autoimmune disorder in the mother that can also affect the baby's platelets and result in a blood-clotting defect. A cesarean may be performed in the presence of ITP as the trauma of a vaginal birth may cause bleeding into the infant's brain (intracranial bleeding).

A mother with pregnancy complicated by diabetes mellitus may pose significant fetal risk. In some cases, a cesarean section may be performed to remove the fetus as soon as possible from a dangerous intrauterine environment.

Erythroblastosis fetalis can result from a blood type (Rh) incompatibility between mother and fetus and cause anemia in the fetus. If the fetus is severely affected or if fetal distress occurs, a cesarean is performed.

Sometimes the mother has a condition where the muscles of the cervix are weak (incompetent cervix), which results in repeated spontaneous abortions (miscarriages). In these circumstances, the cervix is sewn closed in a surgical procedure called cervical cerclage. This allows the pregnancy to continue to term. In cases where the stitches are left in place permanently, the baby is delivered by cesarean section.

Advanced invasive cervical cancer may be a reason to avoid labor because dilation of the cervix could promote spread of the cancer. However, localized cervical cancer (carcinoma in situ) is not an indication for cesarean.

A woman who has had a previous cesarean section may require a repeat cesarean depending on the type of uterine incision previously used and the circumstances of her first cesarean section. If the uterine incision was a horizontal (transverse) lower segment incision, it may be safe to proceed with vaginal delivery in a subsequent pregnancy. However, a vertical uterine incision (classical or upper segment) heals less strongly so a cesarean is recommended for subsequent deliveries to avoid the risk of the uterus breaking open (rupture). Cesarean is also performed if the previous incision type is unknown or undocumented or if the primary cesarean section was complicated by postpartum infection.

Cerebral aneurysm or history of cerebral hemorrhage in the mother can be indications for cesarean because bearing down during labor puts the mother at risk for a stroke. Serious heart disease such as mitral stenosis is another indication for cesarean in order to reduce the demands of labor and vaginal delivery on a compromised heart.

Other indicators for cesarean delivery include a narrow vaginal opening (vaginal atresia), failed medical induction, or pelvic tumors.

How Procedure Is Performed

Cesarean delivery is performed under general or regional (spinal or epidural) anesthesia. Antibiotics are frequently administered preoperatively (prophylaxis) and a tube to drain urine (urinary catheter) is inserted into the bladder. A transverse, lower uterine incision is the most common method used. An incision is first made into the abdomen and then the layers (e.g., skin, muscle) are opened one at a time. The bladder is held out of the way to gain access to the lower uterus. If the fetus is very large, very small, or in an abnormal position, a vertical uterine incision may be necessary to provide a larger opening.

Once the uterus has been opened, the sac holding the fetus (amniotic sac) is ruptured and the fetus is delivered. The umbilical cord is clamped and cut and the placenta delivered. The inside of the uterus is checked to ensure that no abnormalities or residual material of pregnancy remains. Any excess blood or amniotic fluid is suctioned out of the uterus and abdominal cavity. Then the uterus and layers of the abdomen are stitched (sutured) together one layer at a time. The woman is monitored for signs of infection, excessive bleeding, or other complications. Discharge from the hospital usually occurs within 4 days postcesarean delivery.

Prognosis

Most cesarean deliveries are successful and without complications for the mother or infant.

Specialists

- Obstetrician
- Perinatologist

Work Restrictions / Accommodations

Stair climbing, lifting, and driving may be temporarily restricted after cesarean section usually for less than a week. Accommodations may also include less strenuous or slower-paced work, part-time work, and/or frequent rest periods. Flexible hours, job sharing, or on-site childcare is useful for many new mothers. Mothers who are breastfeeding may require additional break time and a private room in which to breastfeed their infant or pump (express) breast milk. The vast majority of women who have uncomplicated pregnancy and cesarean delivery recover to full sedentary-modified duty work capacity by 6 weeks postpartum.

Comorbid Conditions

High blood pressure (hypertension), diabetes, depression, deep vein clots (thrombosis), and high-risk pregnancy can increase the length of disability.

Procedure Complications

Maternal complications can include fever, infection of the uterus (endometritis), infection of the incision, urinary tract infection, excessive bleeding (hemorrhage), shock secondary to hemorrhage, blockage of an artery to the lung by a blood clot (lung embolism), high blood pressure (hypertension), and inflammation of a vein due to clot formation (thrombophlebitis). On occasion, removal of the uterus (hysterectomy) must be performed if there is uncontrolled bleeding, uterine infection, or cancer. With general anesthesia comes the risk of inhalation of stomach contents (aspiration) that can cause inflammation of the lungs (pneumonitis). Fewer than 1 in 1,000 cesarean deliveries result in maternal death. Many of these deaths result from an underlying illness or complications associated with anesthesia. Depression may develop following childbirth.

Long-term complications may include scar tissue (adhesions) that can cause intestinal blockage (obstruction), incisions that open (dehiscence) in the uterus during a subsequent pregnancy, and uterine rupture during subsequent labor. The incidence of uterine rupture during vaginal birth after cesarean is as high as 8% depending on the type of uterine incision. Uterine rupture can be life threatening for both the mother and the fetus.

Fetal complications include an increased incidence of respiratory distress syndrome and incomplete lung expansion (atelectasis).

Factors Influencing Duration

Recovery may be prolonged if the mother's general health is poor or if medical or psychological complications develop.

Length of Disability

Disability duration depends on job requirements. Disability may be longer for jobs that require lifting, driving, or prolonged physical activity.

Duration in Days

Job Classification	Minimum	Optimum	Maximum
Sedentary work	28	42	42
Light work	28	42	42
Medium work	28	42	42
Heavy work	42	49	56
Very Heavy work	42	49	56

Notes

Duration Trend from Normative Data*

Cases	Mean	Min	Max	No Lost Time	Over 6 Months
2818	65	0	409	0.04%	0.89%

Percentile:	5th	25th	Median	75th	95th
Days:	41	55	57	72	109

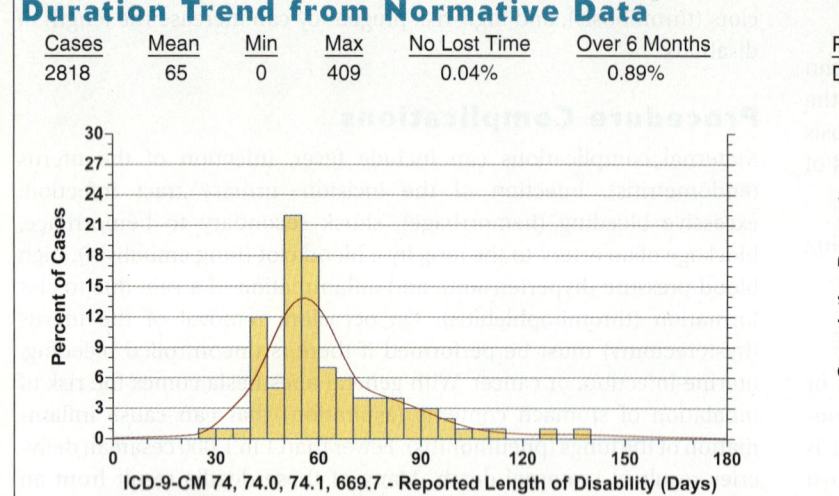

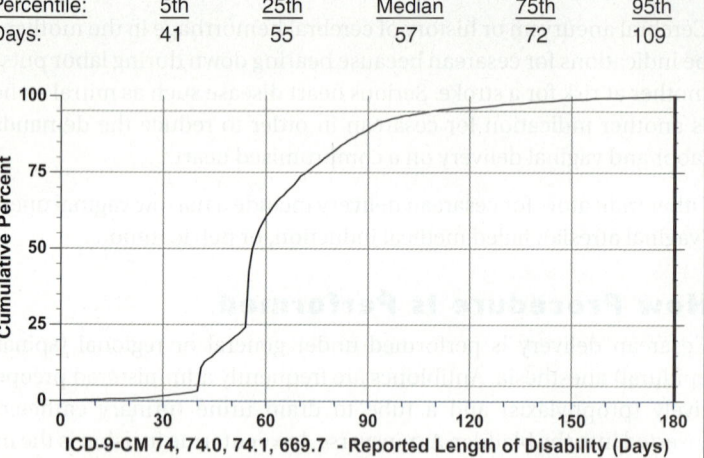

ICD-9-CM 74, 74.0, 74.1, 669.7 - Reported Length of Disability (Days)

* Differences may exist between the expected duration tables and the normative graphs. Duration tables provide expected recovery periods based on the type of work performed by the individual. The normative graphs reflect the actual observed experience of many individuals across the spectrum of physical conditions, in a variety of industries, and with varying levels of case management.

References

Flamm, Bruce, and Edward Quilligan. Cesarean Section: Guidelines for Appropriate Utilization. New York: Springer-Verlag, 1995.

Kisner, Caroline, and Lynn Allen Colby. "Principles of Exercise for the Obstetric Patient." Therapeutic Exercise: Foundations and Techniques. Philadelphia: F.A. Davis, 1990. 547-576.

Menard, Kathryn M. "Cesarean Delivery Rates in the United States." Obstetric and Gynecology Clinics of North America 26 2 (1999): 275-286.

Scott, James. "Cesarean Delivery." Danforth's Obstetrics and Gynecology. Scott, James, et al., eds. Philadelphia: Lippincott Williams & Wilkins, 1999. 457-470.

Chagas' Disease

Other names / synonyms: American Trypanosomiasis, South American Trypanosomiasis

086, 086.0, 086.1, 086.2, 086.3, 086.4, 086.5, 086.9

Definition

Chagas' disease is an infection caused by the parasite Trypanosoma cruzi. The infection is spread through contact with the reduviid bug or by blood transfusions or organ transplants from infected individuals. It is spread to humans when an infected bug deposits feces on an individual's skin usually at night while sleeping. The individual accidentally rubs the feces into the bite wound, an open cut, the eyes, or mouth. It can also be passed from infected mothers to their babies during pregnancy, at delivery, while breastfeeding, or by eating uncooked food contaminated with infective feces from the bugs.

The trypanosomes first reproduce at the point of entry into the skin. They then enter the blood and spread to the entire body especially the heart, skeletal muscle, and brain. A boil-like skin lesion called a chagoma may form at the site of the bite and in other areas. This is the acute phase of Chagas' disease.

Approximately one-third of individuals who get the infection may develop chronic Chagas' disease months, years, or even decades after becoming infected. For those who develop chronic symptoms, life expectancy decreases by an average of 9 years. The heart is most commonly involved and complications may include arrhythmias or congestive heart failure. Congestive heart failure brought on by Chagas' disease is usually rapidly fatal.

The disease is most common in South America, Central America, northern Mexico, and rarely, the southwestern US. These are the geographic areas where the parasite is found. The disease is seen more frequently among individuals in rural areas who dwell in poorly constructed homes (particularly those made of mud, adobe, or thatch) especially those with dirt floors or cracks in the walls (a favorite dwelling place for the reduviid bugs). Travelers to endemic areas rarely become infected.

Although the reduviid bug inhabits the southwestern US, less than 10 cases of the disease were reported from this area. However, many individuals from countries where the disease is endemic have immigrated to the US with 50,000 to 100,000 of these immigrants having the disease at a rate of 1 in 500 to 1,000 individuals. Worldwide, 16 to 18 million individuals are infected and 50,000 die each year from this disease. The overall death rate is 1% of the infected population.

Diagnosis

History: History may include travel to South or Central America, northern Mexico, or the southwestern US. There is usually a history of an insect bite at night most commonly on the face and followed by development of a red lump. Some individuals may be infected and never develop symptoms.

The three stages of infection are acute, indeterminate, and chronic, each with different symptoms. Acute symptoms occur only in about 1% of cases and include swelling of the eye on one side of the face usually at the bite wound or where the feces were rubbed into the eye. Other symptoms include weakness and fatigue, a generalized ill feeling (malaise), prolonged fever, enlarged liver or spleen, and swollen lymph glands. Occasionally a rash, loss of appetite, and diarrhea and vomiting are reported. These symptoms generally last 4 to 8 weeks and then go away even without treatment.

During the indeterminate stage occurring 8 to 10 weeks after infection, individuals move into an asymptomatic state. In the final chronic stage usually between 10 to 20 years after initial infection, the most serious symptoms appear. Not everyone, however, develops the chronic symptoms of Chagas' disease. These symptoms include heart problems such as chest pain, enlarged heart (cardiomegaly), altered heart rate or rhythm (arrhythmias), and heart failure or cardiac arrest. This disease can also lead to digestive and intestinal tract enlargement. An enlarged esophagus (megaesophagus) can result in problems swallowing (dysphagia) and symptoms of acid reflux. Stomach problems can bring on pain and regurgitation and an enlarged colon (megacolon) can result in abdominal pain and severe or chronic constipation. Individuals with a compromised immune system such as HIV or AIDS generally experience more severe symptoms.

Physical exam: The exam reveals one-sided swelling of the eyelids of one eye (Romana sign) and reddening due to infection of the outer covering of the eye (conjunctivitis). Lymph node enlargement and tenderness may be present. Boil-like lesions (chagomas) on the skin may be evident. Enlargement of the liver and spleen and rapid pulse may be noted.

Tests: Trypanosomes may be isolated in the blood in most acute infections. In chronic cases, trypanosomes can be detected by blood culture or inoculation into laboratory mice or rats. Blood tests for trypanosome-specific antibodies are available but not particularly accurate.

Treatment

Symptoms of Chagas' disease usually resolve after several weeks with or without treatment. Antibiotic drugs may be used to treat acute infections and may help reduce the duration of acute symptoms but does not necessarily prevent development or progression of the chronic stage of the disease.

Treatment of heart arrhythmias often requires a device that uses electrical impulses to stimulate heart muscle contraction at a regular rate (pacemaker). Congestive heart failure associated with Chagas' disease is treated with the same medications used for congestive heart failure from other causes. Megaesophagus is usually managed with dietary measures and a megacolon can be treated with laxatives and a high fiber diet.

Spraying insecticides on the walls, patching cracks in walls, cementing dirt floors, and using bed nets in mud, adobe, or thatch houses may prevent Chagas' disease.

Prognosis

Prognosis depends on the stage of infection at diagnosis. Acute infections have a fair prognosis. Many individuals recover without treatment and if antibiotics are used, only 50% of individuals obtain a parasitologic cure. The chronic form of the disease can appear years or even decades after exposure. Individuals with chronic Chagas' disease usually develop arrhythmias, congestive heart failure, and possibly a megacolon and megaesophagus. These chronic complications can all lead to disability and death.

Differential Diagnosis

Other noninfectious causes of heart disease may resemble Chagas' disease. Several species of trypanosomes may be present in the bloodstream but do not cause disease.

Specialists

- Cardiologist
- Gastroenterologist
- Infectious Disease Physician
- Internist

Work Restrictions / Accommodations

Individuals with advanced chronic disease may require restrictions from strenuous activities or accommodations for extra rest periods. Neurological side effects of drug therapy may require temporary accommodations if tremors or peripheral neuropathy are observed.

Comorbid Conditions

Immunosuppressed individuals such as those on chemotherapy for cancer or AIDS may have more severe infections.

Complications

Arrhythmias and heart block are the primary complications. Some individuals develop megaesophagus and in only rare cases does it result in death, and then primarily because of anorexia. Some individuals develop a megacolon. In rare, severe cases, colon obstruction can result in perforation, septicemia, and death. Both a megaesophagus and a megacolon can interfere with normal digestive action. If the brain becomes infected, seizures can develop and significantly increase mortality rates. Treatment can have its own complications since the most effective drugs create significant side effects in most individuals.

Factors Influencing Duration

Length of disability depends on the stage and severity of disease at time of diagnosis. Chronic heart disease or severe acute disease will lengthen the time of disability.

Length of Disability

Disability may be stage dependent.

Duration in Days

Job Classification	Minimum	Optimum	Maximum
Any work	3	7	21

Failure to Recover

If an individual fails to recover within the maximum duration expectancy period, the reader may wish to reference the following questions to assist in better understanding the specifics of an individual's medical case.

Regarding diagnosis:

- Where does individual live? In a poorly constructed house with a dirt floor?
- Did individual emigrate from a country where the disease is endemic? Has individual traveled to areas where the disease is endemic?
- Did an insect bite individual at night? Did a red lump develop? Eye irritation?
- Does individual have weakness and fatigue, malaise, prolonged fever, enlarged liver or spleen, or swollen lymph glands? Has a rash developed? Does individual have loss of appetite or diarrhea and vomiting? How long did these symptoms last?
- Is there chest pain, cardiomegaly, arrhythmias, heart failure, or cardiac arrest?
- On exam, did individual have one-sided swelling of the eyelids and conjunctivitis? Were individual's lymph nodes enlarged and tender? Were chagomas evident on the skin? Liver and spleen enlarged? Rapid pulse?
- Does individual have megaesophagus? Dysphagia?
- Is pain and regurgitation present? Megacolon?
- Does individual have a compromised immune system?
- Were trypanosomes isolated in the blood? Was it necessary to do a blood culture or inoculation into laboratory mice or rats?
- Were conditions with similar symptoms ruled out?

Regarding treatment:

- Was individual treated with antibiotics in the acute phase?
- Is any congestive heart failure being treated traditionally?
- Is individual following any dietary measures necessary for megaesophagus?
- If present, is megacolon being treated with laxatives and a high-fiber diet?
- Were measures taken to prevent future bug bites?

Regarding prognosis:

- Can individual's employer accommodate any necessary restrictions?
- Does individual have any conditions that may affect ability to recover?
- Have any complications developed such as arrhythmias, anorexia, colon obstruction, perforation, septicemia, or death?
- Has individual's brain become infected? Does individual have side effects from the treatment?

References

Harry, M., F. Lema, and C.A. Romana. "Chagas Disease Challenge." Lancet 355 (2000): 236.

Kirchhoff, Louis V. "Trypanosoma Species." Principles and Practice of Infectious Diseases, 4th ed, vol 2. Mandell, Gerald L., John E. Bennett, and Raphael Dolin, eds. New York: Churchill Livingstone, 1995. 2442-2450.

Chancroid

Other names / synonyms: Simple Chancre, Soft Chancre, Venereal Sore
099, 099.0, 099.8, 099.9

Definition

Chancroid is a sexually transmitted bacterial infection caused by the bacterium Hemophiles ducreyi and is characterized by painful genital ulcers. The bacteria are transmitted from an individual with open chancroid sores to another through sexual contact. They enter the skin through an opening such as a scratch or cut.

Because several sexually transmitted diseases can be transmitted at the same time, those infected with chancroid should also be checked for syphilis, herpes, and HIV infection. Chancroid may be a risk factor for contracting the HIV virus.

Chancroid disease is most common among drug users, prostitutes, and men who frequent prostitutes. It is more common in men than in women. Men have three times a greater risk for contracting the disease from an infected partner.

Chancroid occurs all over the world but tends to be more common in developing and Third World countries particularly tropical countries such as sub-Saharan Africa. Chancroid occurs in some areas of the US including the southern and eastern portions but typically occurs periodically in discrete outbreaks. The majority of individuals in the US diagnosed with chancroid have traveled in endemic areas outside the country. The number of cases in the US reached a high in 1987 with 5,000 reported cases, but this has now decreased to about 700 cases per year.

Diagnosis

History: Chancroid begins with a small bump (papule) that first appears 4 to 7 days after exposure to an infected individual. It becomes ulcerated within 1 day and is painful. It ranges in size from 1/8 to 2 inches. It has sharply defined, irregular borders and an easily bleeding base covered with grayish material (exudate). Individuals usually report recent sexual activity. In more serious cases, fever, chills, tiredness, and a general feeling of illness (malaise) may be reported.

Physical exam: The exam may reveal swollen and painful lymph nodes in the groin (inguinal) area. The most common locations of ulcers in men are on or around the foreskin, penis, and scrotum. In women, the most common locations are on opposing surfaces of the labia majora and the perianal or inner thigh areas.

Tests: A definitive diagnosis of chancroid requires the culture of the bacterium Hemophiles ducreyi from within the ulcer. However, this is not always practical as the bacterium is difficult to culture. Alternatively, microscopic examination of ulcerated tissue is done.

Because several sexually transmitted diseases can be transmitted at the same time, those infected with chancroid should also be checked for syphilis, herpes, and HIV infection.

Treatment

Chancroids can resolve spontaneously but some individuals may experience months of painful ulceration and draining. It is generally treated with oral and/or intramuscular injections of antibiotics that usually result in rapid clearing of the lesions with a minimum of scarring. The individual should be reexamined after 3 months to be sure the infection is gone. If the lymph nodes are filled with pus, they may be drained by needle aspiration. Chances of contracting chancroid can be reduced by limiting the number of sexual partners, using condoms, and practicing good personal hygiene.

Prognosis

Skin sores usually heal within 2 weeks with antibiotic treatment. If lymph nodes are drained, soreness may persist for a few weeks. Once an individual has had chancroid infection, they do not have immunity. The disease can reoccur if reexposure occurs.

Differential Diagnosis

Syphilis or herpes are other possible diagnoses although the sores of syphilis are usually painless.

Specialists

- Gynecologist
- Infectious Disease Physician
- Internist
- Urologist

Work Restrictions / Accommodations

Work restrictions or accommodations are usually unnecessary.

Complementary and Alternative Therapies

Content is intended for awareness only. Treatments may or may not be effective. Scientific evidence may be lacking and some substances have potentially toxic effects. Dr. Presley Reed and the editors do not endorse the use of these therapies in the absence of consultation with a licensed medical professional.

Goldenseal -	Poultice applied several times a day may help relieve symptoms.
Oregon grape root -	Poultice applied several times a day may help relieve symptoms.
Hydrotherapy -	Warm sitz baths infused with tea tree oil may help relieve symptoms.

Comorbid Conditions

A suppression of the immune system can increase disability, as can the presence of other sexually transmitted diseases.

Complications

Complications for men consist of persistent sores on the genitals, inflammation of the head of the penis (balanitis), tight foreskin, and scars on the foreskin of uncircumcised males (phimosis). Both men and women can develop urethral fistulas.

Factors Influencing Duration

If the disease has caused infection of the nearby lymph nodes and requires aspiration, disability duration may be somewhat increased.

Length of Disability

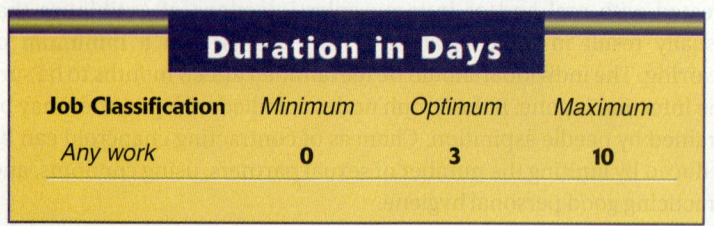

Job Classification	Minimum	Optimum	Maximum
Any work	0	3	10

Failure to Recover

If an individual fails to recover within the maximum duration expectancy period, the reader may wish to reference the following questions to assist in better understanding the specifics of an individual's medical case.

Regarding diagnosis:

- Has individual traveled to an area where chancroid is endemic? Did individual have sexual contact with an infected individual while there?
- Is individual a drug user, prostitute, or one who frequents prostitutes?
- Did individual first notice a small bump on the genitals? Did it ulcerate and become painful?
- Does the lesion have sharply defined, irregular borders? Does the base bleed easily? Is exudate present?
- Does individual have fever, chills, tiredness, and malaise? Are the inguinal lymph nodes swollen and painful?
- Has individual had a culture or microscopic examination of the ulceration?
- Was individual tested for other STDs as well?
- Were conditions with similar symptoms ruled out?

Regarding treatment:

- Is individual being treated with oral and/or intramuscular injections of antibiotics?
- Was individual scheduled for reexamination in 3 months?
- Was it necessary to aspirate any lymph nodes?

Regarding prognosis:

- Has individual addressed correctable lifestyle risk factors?
- Does individual have any conditions that may affect ability to recover?
- Have any complications developed such as persistent sores on the genitals, balanitis, tight foreskin, and phimosis? Does individual have urethral fistulas?

References

1998 Guidelines for Treatment of Sexually Transmitted Diseases. Centers for Disease Control and Prevention. 05 Apr 2000. 22 Aug 2000 <http://aepo-xdv-www.epo.cdc.gov/wonder/prevguid/p0000480/p0000480.asp>.

Brooks, G.F., J.S. Butel, and S.A. Morse. Medical Microbiology. Stamford: Appleton & Lange, 1998.

Chemonucleolysis of Inteveterbral Disc

Other names / synonyms: Intervertebral Chemonucleolysis, Intervertebral Disc Chemolysis
80.52

Definition

Chemonucleolysis is a procedure where the gelatinous center (the nucleus pulposus) of a symptomatic intervertebral disc is dissolved by the injection of the enzyme chymopapain. It is considered a less invasive alternative to the surgical removal of the intervertebral disc (discectomy). In the US, this procedure is performed only on lumbar vertebrae. In other parts of the world, it is performed on lumbar and cervical vertebrae.

Although the procedure has been in use for over 30 years, it remains controversial. Many experts consider it safe and effective while others believe it carries unacceptable risk for potential complications.

Reports between 1985 and 1993 of 7,335 individuals treated worldwide were analyzed. Chemonucleolysis is somewhat less effective than open discectomy but can successfully and safely be used in about 4 of 5 carefully selected individuals without the trauma, risks, and subsequent fibrosis associated with lumbar disc surgery.

Reason for Procedure

Chemonucleolysis is performed to treat nerve-related or sciatic (radicular) pain in the leg caused by a displaced or herniated, intervertebral disc. A displaced intervertebral disc is one where the nucleus pulposus has begun to bulge or herniate out of the perimeter of the disc. In this position, it impinges on adjacent spinal nerve(s), causing pain and possibly nerve deficit in the legs. Dissolving the nucleus reduces pressure inside the disc and subsequently reduces pressure and impingement on the affected nerve(s). This, in turn, alleviates the radicular pain and nerve deficit.

This procedure should be considered only after more conservative therapy has proven ineffective and should be performed only after objective evidence has confirmed that the disc in question is the cause of the radicular pain. This means that the vertebral level of suspected nerve root impingement must correlate with the individual's symptoms and/or physical exam evidence of neurologic deficit.

Chemonucleolysis is typically limited to only one disc level. Rarely is it performed on two disc levels, and then only with confirmation that both levels are involved. Chemonucleolysis is also limited by the extent of disc displacement. It can be performed only on a disc where the bulging or herniated portion of the nucleus pulposus is still connected with the remainder of the nucleus. If the portion has completely separated itself (a sequestered disc), chemonucleolysis should not be performed. It also should not be performed on a previously operated disc.

How Procedure Is Performed

This procedure is performed in the hospital, typically on an outpatient basis. It is performed under either general or local anesthesia, but local is preferred.

To reduce the chance of an allergic reaction to the chymopapain, the individual is given anti-histamine medication, usually both H. and H2 blockers, for 24-72 hours before the procedure. At the time of the procedure, the individual is well hydrated and has at least one open intravenous (IV) line placed in case emergency allergy treatment is needed.

With the individual correctly positioned on the procedure table, a needle is inserted through the skin into the center (the nucleus pulposus) of the identified intervertebral disc. The position of the needle is critical. Its placement in the center of the disc is visually confirmed with C-arm fluoroscopy (x-ray). Once the needle's placement is confirmed, the disc is tested (discography) to make sure that the correct disc has been penetrated. The disc is injected with saline or water. If the correct disc was injected, the injection should reproduce the individual's leg pain. Further confirmation of the disc disorder may be obtained from x-ray images taken after the injection of x-ray dye (discography). Sometimes a dye is injected instead of water or saline. Water or saline is preferred because of potential reactions to the dye.

Next, only a small test dose of chymopapain is injected, which is followed by a 10-15 minute waiting period. During this period the individual is observed for signs of an allergic reaction to the enzyme. If there is any sign of a reaction, the rest of the dose is withheld. Otherwise, the complete dose is then injected.

Prognosis

The rate of good to excellent results with chemonucleolysis is generally about 70%, while "open" surgical discectomy has an 80-90% rate of good to excellent results. In one study of 87 individuals followed for approximately 12 years after the procedure, 67% had an excellent response with continued normal activity, 4.5% had a moderate response with a return to less-than-normal activity, and 29% had no improvement.

Although many individuals experience immediate relief of pain, maximum improvement typically takes up to 6 weeks or may take several months. Individuals may have lower back spasms ("chemical discitis") lasting several days or pain and stiffness lasting several days, weeks, or even months. Once normal activities are resumed, it is common to have a temporary return of pain. Those who fail to improve with chemonucleolysis may be candidates for "open" disc surgery.

The mortality rate associated with chemonucleolysis is less that 0.002%.

Specialists

| • Anesthesiologist | • Spine Surgeon |

Rehabilitation

Physical therapy is important in the rehabilitation of individuals who have undergone the procedure of chemonucleolysis. Although the procedure is relatively noninvasive, some stiffness of the spine muscles can occur in addition to muscle weakness that may have developed prior to the procedure. The physical therapist can provide therapy immediately following the chemonucleolysis to help reduce pain. Electrostimulation combined with heat or cold treatments is a technique used in physical therapy to relax muscles of the spine in the affected region.

Once postoperative pain decreases, a flexibility program is one of the priorities in rehabilitation following chemonucleolysis. The individual may be instructed in several exercises.

Additional strengthening of the spine muscles is then progressed with the use of resistance throughout the range of motion. The physical therapist introduces this by using devices such as wall pulleys, universal, and nautilus type equipment. Aerobic exercise may be utilized in back rehabilitation. This type of exercise encourages the release of the body's own pain relievers (endorphins). Other activities instructed by the physical therapist that do not place excess stress on the back are walking short distances, using a stationary bike, and swimming. The physical therapist may also help improve posture for recovery and long-term protection of further disc problems. For example, specific stabilization exercises that can promote better spinal alignment by strengthening the shoulder blade (scapulae), mid back (thoracic), and lumbar region are instructed and are believed to help reduce excess stress on the vertebral discs.

Weight resistance exercises instructed by the physical therapist to increase strength of the lower extremities are included in the rehabilitation following the procedure of chemonucleolysis. Examples of these exercises are leg curls, leg presses, and bending both knees slightly while standing (half knee squats).

The final phase of the rehabilitation following chemonucleolysis involves the individual's reinstatement to work, or what may also be known as "work hardening." The exercises are now directed toward the work requirements and also include instruction of proper lifting to prevent further injury. Back schools are available in many rehabilitation programs focusing on managing back pain and preventing its recurrence. Education for proper lifting of heavy objects is important in the rehabilitation of the lumbar spine and to prepare the individual for returning to work.

Modifications may need to be made by the physical therapist for those who have arthritis or other spine conditions. This will vary depending on the level of the spine where the chemonucleolysis was performed.

Work Restrictions / Accommodations

Usually, restrictions will gradually decrease over the first 3 months, and full duty will be recommended by 3 months after the procedure.

Comorbid Conditions

Individuals with comorbid conditions that would adversely affect recovery would likely not be candidates for the procedure. In addition to those at risk for anaphylactic shock, individuals who have a severe spinal condition or neurologic deficit, such as cauda equina syndrome, severe spondylolisthesis, spinal cord tumor, or severe spinal stenosis, should not have the procedure. It is not advisable to perform chemonucleolysis on a disc that was previously operated upon. Pregnant women and individuals with infection or inflammation should also be excluded. Other conditions that could rule out an individual include hypertension, morbid obesity, history of stroke (personal or family), peripheral neuropathy, and cerebrovascular anomaly.

Procedure Complications

Anaphylactic shock, the most severe type of allergic reaction, is the complication of most concern. It is reported in approximately 0.5% of individuals having chemonucleolysis. Females are more likely than males to have this complication. Symptoms of anaphylactic shock may develop immediately or up to 2 hours after the enzyme is injected. Hypotension and/or bronchospasm are usually the first symptoms. If not treated immediately, these symptoms will be followed by swelling of the throat (laryngeal edema), irregular heartbeats, cardiac arrest, coma, and death.

The risk of anaphylactic shock can be reduced by taking certain measures. The precautions of taking anti-histamine medication for 72 hours before the procedure, over-hydration, and an open IV line significantly reduce risk of reaction and speeds up the treatment response time if a reaction does occur. Another measure to reduce the risk is to check for sensitivity to chymopapain before the procedure by performing blood or skin allergy tests.

In addition, anyone who has previously been injected with chymopapain or has a known sensitivity to chymopapain or papaya (from which the enzyme is derived) or papaya derivatives (found in some contact lens solutions or meat tenderizers) should not have the procedure. Individuals taking beta-blockers have a higher risk of severe anaphylactic shock and may be advised against the procedure (beta-blockers inhibit epinephrine, complicating treatment of shock should it develop). Finally, local anesthesia seems to have a lower risk (0.4%) of anaphylactic shock compared to general anesthesia (0.6%). This may be because an alert individual can detect and report beginning signs of an allergic reaction.

Other signs of less severe allergic reaction, such as itching (rash urticaria) should also be noted. These signs can take place immediately or up to 15 days after the procedure.

Neurologic complications, severe and mild, have been associated with chemonucleolysis. A severe condition affecting the spinal cord (acute transverse myelitis/acute transverse myelopathy (ATM)), has been reported in association with 1 in 18,000 cases of chemonucleolysis. A cause and effect relationship, however, has not been confirmed. Symptoms of paralysis (paraplegia) or weakness (paraparesis) in the legs begin 2-3 weeks after the procedure. The risk for ATM seems to be increased if more than one disc is injected.

Less severe neurologic complications include leg pain or weakness, foot drop, tingling in the leg, numbness of legs or toes, cramping in calves, pain in opposite leg, and decreased sensitivity to pain (hyperalgesia).

Spinal epidural hemorrhage and inflammation of the disc (discitis), due either to a bacterial infection or a chemical reaction, have also been associated with chemonucleolysis. Some individuals have minor side effects, such as dizziness, urinary retention, and headaches for a short time after the procedure.

C-arm fluoroscopy carries the minimal risk of radiation exposure. When positioning the needle, there may be damage to nerve roots, dura, and blood vessels. If general anesthesia is used, there is risk for associated complications, such as breathing trouble and reaction to the anesthetics.

Factors Influencing Duration

Individual response to therapy, level of compliance with recovery orders, and complications influence length of disability.

Length of Disability

Chemonucleolysis may be incompatible with heavy or very heavy work.

Duration in Days

Job Classification	Minimum	Optimum	Maximum
Sedentary work	1	7	56
Light work	1	14	56
Medium work	42	42	84
Heavy work	42	42	91
Very Heavy work	42	42	91

References

Chymopapain (Chymodiactin®) Monograph. RxMED. 03 Jul 1998. 13 Jul 2000 <http://www.rxmed.com/monographs/bak/chymod.html>.

Alexander, A. Herbert, MD. "Chemonucleolysis for Lumbar Disc Herniation." The International Intradiscal Therapy Society. 19 Oct 1998. 13 Jul 2000 <http://www.iits.org>.

Hall, Hamilton. "Lower Back Pain: Surgery Indications and Options." Neurologic Clinic 17 1 (1999): 113-130.

Malone, Terry R., Thomas McPoil, and Arthur J. Nitz. Orthopedic and Sports Physical Therapy. St. Louis: Mosby, 1997.

Nordby, E.J., and P.H. Wright. "Efficacy of Chymopapain in Chemonucleolysis. A Review." Spine 19 22 (1994): 2578-2583.

Poynton, A., et al. "Chymopapain Chemonucleolysis: A Review of 105 Cases." Journal of the Royal College of Surgeons of Edinburgh 43 (1998): 407-709.

Chemotherapy

Other names / synonyms: Anticancer Drug Therapy, Cytotoxic Cancer Treatment, Injection

99.25

Definition

Chemotherapy is the administration of drugs (antineoplastic or cytotoxic agents) that destroy cancer cells.

Antineoplastic drugs interfere with cell division, which is the cell's method of reproduction. If the cell is unable to reproduce, it will eventually die without another cell to replace it. The net effect is a decrease in tumor cells. Increased knowledge of the molecular biology of tumor cells has led to the exploration of promising new cancer treatments, such as those using monoclonal antibodies, matrix metalloproteinase inhibitors, and gene transfer and alteration.

Cancer cell death can occur using several different methods, including damaging the cell's DNA (the molecular structure that dictates cell growth and function), changing the cell's ability to absorb or release fluid (osmotic stress), causing a mechanical attack via an anticancer drug, or interfering with the cancer cell's ability to develop its own blood supply.

Chemotherapy drugs are usually administered intravenously over a period of several weeks to several months. Three or four weeks between treatments are usually required for the body to recover from the effects of a single treatment. Multiple antineoplastic drugs may be used. When combined, they work in conjunction to destroy the cancer cells (synergism).

Reason for Procedure

Chemotherapy is used to destroy cancer cells that remain after other forms of cancer treatment, such as surgery or radiation treatments. Chemotherapy is also the only treatment for some types of malignancies. Since the leukemias and lymphomas are not localized like solid tumors, excision and irradiation are not feasible. Therefore, systemic treatment is needed. This is also the case when tumors have spread to multiple, distant sites in the body (metastatic cancer). Chemotherapy may also be used for palliative treatment of a tumor, which means that, even though the individual is not expected to recover, the comfort level can be significantly increased if the tumor or cancer can be abated.

How Procedure Is Performed

There are numerous different chemotherapeutic agents, most of which are administered by a slow intravenous injection. Chemotherapy is frequently done on an outpatient basis, with the individual having a series of treatments over a period of several weeks to months.

Although the process may vary, a typical approach would be for the individual to relax in a recliner while receiving the intravenous chemotherapy. Rather than requiring a new intravenous catheter placement for each chemotherapy session, many individuals have a catheter that stays in place for a prolonged period of time, up to several months, if necessary. This catheter is inserted, through a tiny incision on the chest, into the large vein entering the heart. The catheter then lies just beneath the skin. There is a small device beneath the skin at the end of the catheter that is used for insertion of the tubing that is used to deliver the chemotherapy agent. Depending upon the type of agent that is used, the individual may receive supportive medications or other treatments to decrease some of the unpleasant side effects of chemotherapy, such as nausea. The time required for each chemotherapy session usually takes several hours, depending upon preparation time and time required for monitoring after the procedure.

Prognosis

The outcome varies from full recovery to palliative treatment. The effect of the chemotherapy depends upon the stage of the underlying cancer, whether the cancer is localized or systemic, the general health of the individual, cytotoxic agents chosen, and any other medical conditions.

Specialists

- Hematologist
- Oncologist

Work Restrictions / Accommodations

Restrictions and accommodations will be determined based on the side effects of therapy and underlying disease. Periodic absences for treatment and recovery from treatment may be required.

Comorbid Conditions

The presence of other medical conditions, malnutrition, obesity, recent surgery or surgical complications, or depression may lengthen disability.

Procedure Complications

Chemotherapy can have many adverse effects, most of which resolve after treatment has been completed. Common side effects of chemotherapy include nausea and vomiting, anorexia, the loss of hair, or pain. Other complications include pain or inflammation of the injection site. The most serious, even life-threatening, complications of some types of chemotherapy are secondary leukemia and cardiac impairment, both of which are rare. Risk factors for cardiac toxicity include older age, pre-existing cardiac disease, higher cumulative dose of the cytotoxic agent, and irradiation of the heart. Women undergoing chemotherapy for breast cancer may experience permanent or prolonged menstrual dysfunction. Ovarian failure is common in women over age 40 who are receiving chemotherapy. Studies have shown that women who have been treated for breast cancer and then become pregnant do not have a worse outcome than women who have not been treated.

Factors Influencing Duration

The length of disability is highly variable, depending on the type of cancer being treated, the individual's general health, age, type of drug(s) being administered, dosage, side effects of the treatment itself, and schedule of administration.

Length of Disability

Length of disability depends upon the individual's response to treatment and underlying condition and can vary from a few days to permanent disability. Contact physician for additional information.

References

Bunn, P.A. Jr., et al. "New Therapeutic Strategies for Lung Cancer: Biology and Molecular Biology Come of Age." Chest 117(4 suppl1) (2000): 163S-168S.

Foley, K.M. "Advances in Cancer Pain." Archives of Neurology 56(4) (1999): 413-417.

Hartmann, J.T., et al. "Future Prospects in the Chemotherapy of Metastatic Nonseminomatous Testicular Germ-cell Cancer." World Journal of Urology 17(5) (1999): 324-333.

Hayes, A.J., Y.L. Li, and M.E. Lippman. "Science, Medicine, and the Future. Antivascular Therapy: A New Approach to Cancer Treatment." British Medical Journal 318 7187 (1999): 853-856.

Chest Pain
Other names / synonyms: Angina
786.5, 786.50

Definition

Chest pain is the sensation of "pressure," "stabbing," or "tightness" that can occur with disorders in the chest wall, chest cavity, back, or abdominal cavity.

Chest pain can be a symptom of many different disorders, ranging in significance from minor to life threatening. Since the nerve supply (and pain sensation) of the chest is integrated with many structures and organs in the chest cavity, any disorder in this broad region can cause chest pain. The pain can arise from various organs of the chest (heart, aorta, lungs, trachea, bronchi, or esophagus), linings of the chest cavity (pleura or pericardium), or from the chest wall (ribs, sternum, muscle, nerve, or other soft tissue, including the breasts). For example, intercostal neuritis, an inflammatory condition affecting the nerves around the ribs, causes chest pain. In addition, pain may be projected (referred) to the chest from other locations (abdomen, spine or shoulders). Finally, when chest pain of any cause is chronic or recurrent, psychological factors may play a role in it continuing indefinitely.

Some prominent causes of chest pain include angina pectoris, caused by the heart muscle receiving insufficient oxygenated blood. Angina pain is usually associated with exertion or emotional stress that places an added workload upon the heart muscle. Stable angina pectoris may be present for years. An inadequate blood supply to the heart that is severe or prolonged enough to cause damage to the heart muscle (myocardial infarction) produces pain in the same areas as angina, but the pain lasts longer and is more severe. Angina pectoris and myocardial infarction are usually caused by narrowing of the coronary arteries (coronary artery disease). Angina can also be caused by temporary coronary spasms (Prinzmetal's angina or variant angina), narrowing of the aortic valve (aortic stenosis), or a thickening of the heart wall (hypertrophic cardiomyopathy).

Pericarditis, an inflammation of the membrane (pericardium) surrounding the heart, causes sharp pain in the center of the chest. In some cases it is severe enough to mimic a heart attack. Mitral valve prolapse refers to a common, slight deformity of a valve situated in the left side of the heart. Although usually without symptoms, it occasionally produces chest pain. Diseases of the aorta, the main artery of the body, that may cause chest pain include aortic aneurysm (a weakening or ballooning of the wall of the aorta) and aortic dissection (separation of layers due to a tear in the inner layer of the aortic wall).

Chest pain may be caused by pleurisy, which is an inflammation of the membranes (pleurae) that surround the lungs and cover the inner surface of the chest wall. Pleurisy can be caused by many disorders, including viral and bacterial infections (such as pneumonia or bronchitis), pneumothorax, any lung disease that extends to the pleura, or from an injury (such as a fractured rib). Cancer of the lung may cause pain as it spreads to the pleura and ribs.

Pulmonary embolism occurs when a blood clot from the venous system becomes lodged in the lungs. A massive pulmonary embolism may produce chest pain similar to that of a heart attack. Other respiratory diseases that may cause chest pain include acute bacterial pneumonia, a lung abscess, or inflammation of the trachea and bronchi (tracheobronchitis).

Pain in the chest wall may be due to an inflammation of the muscles between ribs and diaphragm (pleurodynia). It can be caused by a variety of disorders, including viral infection, fibromyalgia, and an inflammation of the joints between the ribs and the breastbone (costochondritis). When warmth, redness, or swelling accompanies this inflammation, it is known as Tietze's syndrome.

Intercostal neuritis is an inflammation of the nerves that run alongside the ribs. Causes of intercostal neuritis include diabetes mellitus and shingles (herpes zoster).

Other causes of chest wall pain include injury (fracture of ribs or sternum) or strained muscles (soft tissue injury), intercostal muscle spasm, chest wall tumors, or breast disease.

Pressure on nerve roots attached to the spinal cord may result in a sharp pain that travels to the front of the chest. Pain may be caused by osteoarthritis, injury to vertebrae, a displaced or prolapsed disc, or other musculoskeletal disorders.

Abdominal disorders that can refer pain to the chest include inflammation of the gallbladder (cholecystitis), inflammation of the pancreas (pancreatitis), and peptic ulcers. Occasionally, this referred pain is severe enough to mimic angina pectoris.

The esophagus is a common source of chest pain. Pain may be the result of structural disorders (esophageal strictures, cancer), esophagitis, or functional abnormalities (esophageal spasms). Heartburn (gastroesophageal reflux) produces pain behind the breastbone. It is caused when acid from the stomach is regurgitated into the esophagus. Pain originating from the esophagus can easily be confused with angina pectoris because it mimics it in location, radiation, and quality, and can occur with exertion.

Chest pain without a specific diagnosis is referred to as nonspecific chest pain.

As the symptom of chest pain can arise from a variety of disorders, the exact prevalence of chest pain cannot be ascertained.

Diagnosis

History: Individuals may describe their chest discomfort with terms like sharp, dull, aching, boring, stabbing, crushing, squeezing, pressure, tearing, and burning. They may complain of pain that is localized in the middle of the chest, or pain that extends to their jaw, back, shoulders, arms, or abdomen. The individual may reveal that the pain is sudden or ongoing, and may describe things that precipitate the pain or relieve the pain. They may complain of other associated symptoms such as sweating, nausea, vomiting, a sensation of the heart beating rapidly or intensely (palpitations), dizziness, fainting, shortness of breath, cough, and difficulty swallowing. They may mention a past medical history of heart disease, lung disease, or chest injury.

Physical exam: As chest pain can arise from a variety of different causes, a thorough examination is often necessary to find a definite diagnosis. The characteristics of the pain may provide a helpful clue. The exam may reveal pain that increases in intensity when a deep breath is taken, which suggests that the lungs or chest wall are involved. Individuals may present with pain that arises with physical activity, which may be associated with heart conditions. An irregular pulse, change in blood pressure, or abnormal heart sounds may be present, and this may be associated with heart or lung conditions. Individuals who present with a rapid respiratory rate and abnormal lung sounds may have lung problems such as pneumonia, pleuritis, or pulmonary embolism. Areas that are tender on palpation may represent bruising, muscle tears, or fractures that could be the underlying cause of the pain. Masses (either cancerous or noncancerous) in the chest, back, or abdomen may put pressure on nerves in the chest cavity and result in chest pain.

Other symptoms may include swelling or pain in the legs, indicative of clots in the deep veins of the legs (deep vein thrombosis).

Tests: A wide variety of diagnostic tests and procedures may be employed in the evaluation of chest pain. Electrocardiography (EKG) to detect myocardial ischemia (deficient blood supply) and other cardiac abnormalities, an ultrasound exam (echocardiogram) to visualize the valves and internal structure of the heart, and a cardiac stress test (exercise tolerance test, treadmill test) are noninvasive and cost effective measures to exclude chest pain of cardiac origin. Myocardial perfusion scans use a radioactive chemical injected intravenously that passes through the coronary circulation, and is taken up by the heart muscle (myocardium). The radioactivity is detected by scintillation cameras, which produces an image of the heart, and detects areas of insufficient blood supply to the heart muscle.

Coronary arteriography (contrast x-ray of the coronary arteries, also called coronary angiography) can be used to confirm or rule out coronary artery disease (CAD). Because this procedure has significant risks, it is usually performed if results of the stress tests are inconclusive, or to differentiate coronary spasm from blockage of the coronary arteries.

Once cardiovascular disease has been ruled out with reasonable certainty, other causes should be systematically excluded. Endoscopy or an upper GI series (x-rays of the upper gastrointestinal tract) can be used to rule out peptic ulcer disease or structural abnormalities of the esophagus. Abdominal ultrasound exam can look for diseases of the gallbladder, pancreas, and liver. Gastroesophageal reflux can be checked by measuring esophageal pH. Esophageal spasm and other motility disorders can be diagnosed by means of esophageal manometry (pressure measurement).

Pain can result from an interaction of physical disorders and psychological factors. If emotional or behavioral symptoms are prominent, and no specific cause of chest pain can be identified, a psychological or psychiatric evaluation may be indicated.

Treatment

The treatment of chest pain depends on the specific diagnosis, and is directed at correcting the underlying cause to prevent the reoccurrence of pain and associated problems. In many cases, however, no specific diagnosis can be determined.

Treatment of chest pain of undetermined origin once serious disease has been ruled out (nonspecific chest pain) begins with reassurance that the pain is not a symptom of serious disease. It should be recognized that some individuals may go on to develop coronary artery disease (CAD), so teaching the lifestyle modification techniques (diet, and exercise) to reduce risk factors may be indicated. For pain relief, medical treatment is based on what works. Anti-anginal drugs may relieve symptoms in some individuals, even if there is no evidence of CAD or coronary spasm. When anti-anginal drugs are prescribed, it should be made clear to the individual that they are not being prescribed for any detectable heart disease.

Gastrointestinal drugs may also be used. Some individuals respond to a trial of antacids, histamine antagonists, and/or anti-reflux therapy. Anticholinergic drugs may also be helpful, perhaps because of their relaxing effect on the esophagus. Tricyclic antidepressants are thought to have a pain relieving effect independent of their antidepressant action. If depression is a contributing factor, that would be a further indication for these drugs. If anxiety is prominent, anti-anxiety drugs may be given. Relaxation techniques such as biofeedback may also be helpful. Psychotherapy or behavioral therapy may be considered, particularly in individuals who have been diagnosed with psychiatric disorders. Individuals without psychiatric disorders may also benefit from short-term psychological or behavioral therapy to help them understand and cope with their symptoms.

Prognosis

The prognosis of chest pain depends on the specific diagnosis. Individuals with nonspecific chest pain have a low incidence of heart problems. From that standpoint, the prognosis is excellent. However, most of these individuals continue to have recurrent pain. Nonspecific chest pain is statistically associated with an increased incidence of psychological disorders including depression, anxiety disorders, or symptoms for which no physical cause can be found (somatoform disorders). Many continue to worry about heart disease, despite reassurance. Whether the pain leads to psychological disturbance, or vice versa, is not always clear. Despite the absence of disease, the prognosis for return to work is often poor, particularly if a psychiatric disorder is present.

Differential Diagnosis

Many other conditions can present with similar symptoms. These may include angina pectoris, coronary artery disease (CAD), myocardial infarction, Prinzmetal's angina, variant angina, aortic stenosis, aortic dissection, pleurisy, bone or soft tissue inflammation, gallbladder inflammation (cholecystitis), inflammation of the pancreas (pancreatitis), or peptic ulcer disease.

Specialists

- Cardiologist
- Critical Care Specialist
- Emergency Medicine

Rehabilitation

Rehabilitation used for chest pain is dependent on the cause and origin of the symptoms. If the cause is from muscle spasm involving one or more of the chest muscles, a decrease in the present activity followed by stretching usually reduces the symptoms. The physical therapist often instructs individuals in various stretching techniques that do not involve machines or hands-on methods. An example of such a stretch for chest pain resulting from a muscle spasm involves the individual standing in a corner of a room with a hand on each adjoining wall at chest height. The individual then slowly leans into the corner until a stretch is felt in the chest area.

If the chest pain comes from the heart muscle (angina), the goal is to design a physical conditioning program for the individual that increases the amount of activity, yet limits the onset of symptoms from this form of chest pain. In this case, individuals must first identify and communicate the symptoms as true angina pain. The physical therapist or other healthcare personnel knowledgeable in treating various forms of angina uses a scale to rank angina symptoms that helps determine the amount and intensity of the prescribed exercise.

Once cleared of any serious cardiac conditions, and exercise is not a contraindication, exercise sessions begin with a prolonged warm-up period. Proper breathing while exercising is critical for all individuals whether the origin is a muscle spasm or cardiac in nature. The principles of mild aerobic conditioning in physical therapy were used to develop a program for individuals with various forms of chest pain that include angina.

Treatment of chest pain is monitored by the rehabilitation professional throughout low-demand aerobic activities. If treatment occurs in a hospital setting, individuals are monitored for heart rate, rhythm, blood pressure, and chest pain. Initial exercises for chest pain can begin in various positions depending on the type of chest pain. For example, some forms of chest pain or angina are irritated while lying down. Calisthenics may be performed with varying degrees of intensity while sitting or standing such as marching in place or raising both arms overhead. The individual may also be continuously monitored for chest pain while walking (ambulating).

As endurance improves without symptoms of chest pain, the individual may use a stationary bicycle under supervision beginning at very light resistance. Exercises progress with time and intensity and vary among individuals. With improvement, work-type activities are incorporated into the rehabilitation regimen to address endurance that may be needed upon return to work. This increase in endurance will also translate into a generally more active lifestyle. The ultimate goal is to increase the strength and efficiency of the heart using endurance or aerobic routines such as running, brisk walking, cycling, or swimming.

Because of the various degrees and effects each individual experiences with chest pain and other forms of angina, modifications may be needed for those individuals taking various medications or who experience other conditions that result in chest pain.

Work Restrictions / Accommodations

For nonspecific chest pain, heavy or strenuous activity may need to be restricted if it produces or aggravates symptoms.

Comorbid Conditions

Comorbid conditions include psychiatric disturbances, obesity, diabetes, chronic lung disease, congenital heart disease, chronic or progressive arthritic conditions, or renal or liver dysfunction.

Complications

Complications depend on the underlying condition. Individuals with nonspecific chest pain may continue to have recurrent pain. Many continue to worry about heart disease despite reassurance, which may lead to self-imposed activity restrictions and frequent emergency room visits.

Factors Influencing Duration

Length of disability is directly dependent upon diagnosis. For nonspecific chest pain, disability is influenced by the severity, frequency, and duration of pain episodes, the individual's understanding or interpretation of the symptoms, and the presence or absence of a psychiatric disorder. Disability may result not only from pain, but also from self-imposed restrictions on activities.

Length of Disability

Duration depends on cause. Contact physician for specific diagnosis. In some cases, disability may be permanent.

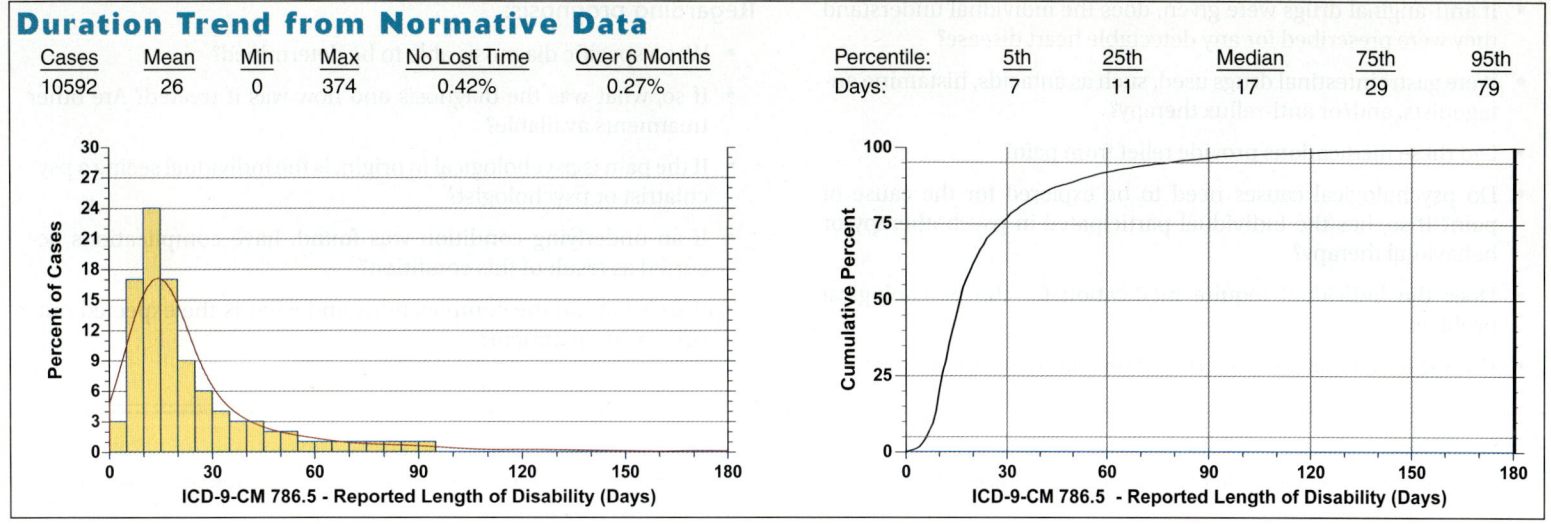

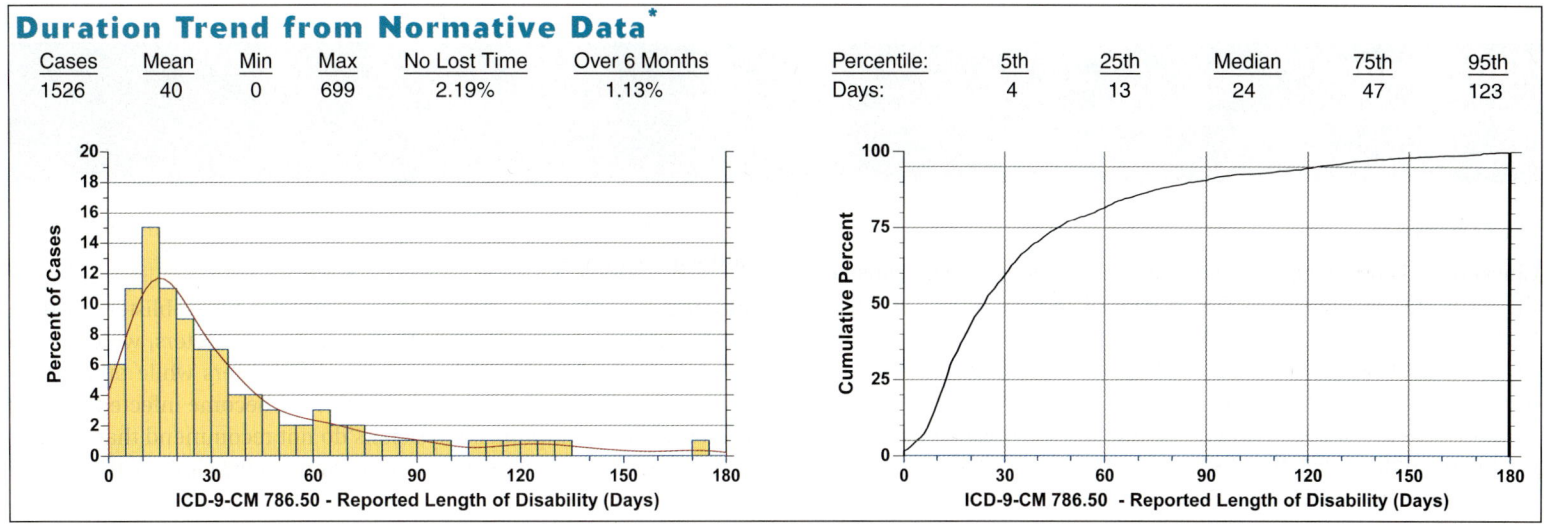

* Differences may exist between the expected duration tables and the normative graphs. Duration tables provide expected recovery periods based on the type of work performed by the individual. The normative graphs reflect the actual observed experience of many individuals across the spectrum of physical conditions, in a variety of industries, and with varying levels of case management.

Failure to Recover

If an individual fails to recover within the maximum duration expectancy period, the reader may wish to reference the following questions to assist in better understanding the specifics of an individual's medical case.

Regarding diagnosis:

- Does the individual have a history of angina pectoris?
- Does the individual have underlying lung, heart, esophageal, stomach, or inflammatory conditions?
- Has the individual had a recent bacterial or viral infection?
- Is the chest pain chronic or recurrent, suggesting involvement of psychological factors?
- Has the individual had a recent injury to the chest wall, such as fractured ribs or sternum, or strained muscles (soft tissue injury)?
- How is the pain described? Is it sharp, dull, aching, boring, stabbing, crushing, squeezing, pressure, tearing, or burning?
- Is the pain only in the chest or does it radiate to the jaw, back, shoulders, arms or abdomen?
- Is there anything that precipitates the pain or relieves the pain?
- Are other symptoms, such as sweating, nausea, vomiting, a sensation of the heart beating rapidly or intensely (palpitations), dizziness, fainting, shortness of breath, cough, or difficulty swallowing present? Were electrocardiogram (ECG), echocardiogram, or stress test (exercise tolerance test) done?
- Were invasive tests, such as myocardial perfusion scan or coronary arteriography, required?
- Was chest pain caused by a cardiac abnormality?
- If not, were other tests, such as an upper gastrointestinal tract x-rays, abdominal ultrasound, or esophageal manometry done to rule out other conditions?
- What a specific diagnosis able to be confirmed, or is this nonspecific chest pain?

Regarding treatment:

- What is the underlying cause of the chest pain?
- If the individual is at risk for development of coronary artery disease (CAD), have lifestyle modification techniques (diet and exercise) been given?
- What kind of pain medication was given? Has the pain effectively been relieved?

- If anti-anginal drugs were given, does the individual understand they were prescribed for any detectable heart disease?
- Were gastrointestinal drugs used, such as antacids, histamine antagonists, and/or anti-reflux therapy?
- Did these medications provide relief from pain?
- Do psychological causes need to be explored for the cause of pain? If so, has the individual participated in psychotherapy or behavioral therapy?
- Does the individual require medication for the psychological problem?
- Has the individual been instructed on relaxation techniques?

Regarding prognosis:
- Was a specific diagnosis able to be determined?
- If so, what was the diagnosis and how was it treated? Are other treatments available?
- If the pain is psychological in origin, is the individual seeing a psychiatrist or psychologist?
- If an underlying condition was found, have complications occurred as result of this condition?
- If so, what are the complications and what is the expected outcome with treatment?

References

Clochesy, John M., et al. Critical Care Nursing, 2nd ed. Philadelphia: W.B. Saunders Company, 1996.

Tierney, Lawrence M., Stephen McPhee, and Maxine A. Papadakis, eds. Current Medical Diagnosis and Treatment, 39th ed. New York: Lange Medical Books/McGraw-Hill, 2000.

Chickenpox
Other names / synonyms: Varicella
052, 052.0, 052.1, 052.7, 052.8, 052.9

Definition

Chickenpox is usually a mild, yet highly contagious disease caused by the virus varicella zoster (VZV), a type of herpes virus. The disease localizes on the skin causing a characteristic rash followed by bumps or the "pox." Chickenpox is spread from person to person by respiratory droplets or by contact with pus from the lesions, either through direct contact or by contact with articles contaminated by lesion discharge. It is also possible to get the disease from an individual infected with herpes zoster (shingles), because they are both herpes viruses.

After having chickenpox, an individual typically gains lifelong immunity to the disease. Although typically a harmless disease in children, adults with chickenpox are more likely to develop complications, as are those who are immunocompromised.

An estimated 4 million cases occur each year, the greatest number developing in the late winter and spring. Most children become infected by the time they are 10 years old. Since introduction of the chickenpox vaccine in 1995, it is rapidly being eliminated as a childhood disease. Statistics are not yet available regarding how many individuals now contract chickenpox.

Diagnosis

History: Individuals may report an initial fever, and generalized aching and weakness (malaise). This is followed by an itchy rash that occurs anywhere from 10 to 21 days after contact with an infected individual. It begins on the trunk and then moves to the face, scalp, mouth, limbs, and other parts of the body. A few small reddish bumps (papules) develop from the rash over 2 to 4 days and quickly fill with fluid to form blisters (vesicles); they typically appear first in small groupings. The blisters eventually burst or break, forming crusts or scabs over a 1- to 2-week period; the scabs generally fall off in 9 to 13 days. Additional blisters can develop at any time during this process. The itching from the blisters and scabs can be severe.

Physical exam: The exam may reveal fluid-filled blisters with a reddened base, ranging in size from 5 to 10 millimeters, which are in clusters. Some individuals have only a few blisters while others may have several hundred. Some individuals may become infected without presenting any symptoms. Physicians do not recommend that persons who believe they have the chickenpox come to the clinic as the disease is highly contagious.

Tests: Usually a history and physical exam will be sufficient to make the diagnosis. Blood tests for VZV-specific antibodies, or recovery of virus from early lesions, may confirm chickenpox infection.

Treatment

Because chickenpox is a self-limiting disease it is usually only treated symptomatically. There are anti-viral drugs that can be used in some cases. Oral antihistamines can be taken for itching; topical treatments can relieve itching and help dry out the sores. Cool water soaks or compresses, and bathing with baking soda in a tub of lukewarm water can also relieve itching. Aspirin must not be used with chickenpox as it has been associated with the risk of developing Reye's syndrome. Acetaminophen, however, can be taken as an analgesic and to reduce fever. Also, the skin should be kept clean and fingernails trimmed (to inhibit scratching) to prevent secondary bacterial infections. Acyclovir can be used to treat people more than 2-years old; it can help reduce the severity of symptoms if taken within 24 hours of the rash's first appearance. It may also be prescribed in severe cases or for people who are immunosuppressed.

Chickenpox can be prevented by vaccination, which was introduced in 1995. The long-term effects of this vaccine, however, are unknown; specifically how it affects the development of herpes zoster later in life.

Prognosis

Chickenpox usually heals in 2 weeks. More serious cases of chickenpox such as those that cause pneumonia in adults can have a mortality rate of 10% or higher.

Differential Diagnosis

The skin rash may appear similar to smallpox, generalized herpes simplex infection, and impetigo.

Specialists

- Dermatologist
- Infectious Disease Physician
- Internist
- Primary Care Provider

Work Restrictions / Accommodations

Individuals with chickenpox should stay home for a week after all blisters have broken and become scabbed over, to minimize the spread of disease, and especially to protect coworkers who are pregnant or have impaired immunity.

Complementary and Alternative Therapies

Content is intended for awareness only. Treatments may or may not be effective. Scientific evidence may be lacking and some substances have potentially toxic effects. Dr. Presley Reed and the editors do not endorse the use of these therapies in the absence of consultation with a licensed medical professional.

Hydrotherapy - Cool water soaks or compresses and bathing with baking soda or finely ground oatmeal in a tub of lukewarm water may relieve itching.

Comorbid Conditions

Individuals with a compromised immune system often suffer more serious complications.

Complications

Complications may include pneumonia, encephalitis, Reye's syndrome, and transient arthritis. Cerebellar ataxia, characterized by a very unsteady walk, may appear during convalescence or later. When blisters are scratched open, there is a chance that they can become infected by bacteria, most frequently with staphylococcus. Some secondary infections may become severe enough to require hospitalization. Chickenpox can cause small depression-type scarring, most often around the eyes. After chickenpox clears, the virus can become dormant in the body causing herpes zoster, also known as shingles, later in life. Women who acquire chickenpox early in pregnancy are at risk for fetal congenital malformations.

Factors Influencing Duration

Complications such as pneumonia, encephalitis, or bacterial infection can lengthen the disability.

Length of Disability

Duration in Days

Job Classification	Minimum	Optimum	Maximum
Any work	7	10	14

Duration Trend from Normative Data*

Cases	Mean	Min	Max	No Lost Time	Over 6 Months
2428	15	1	134	0.04%	0%

Percentile:	5th	25th	Median	75th	95th
Days:	9	12	14	17	25

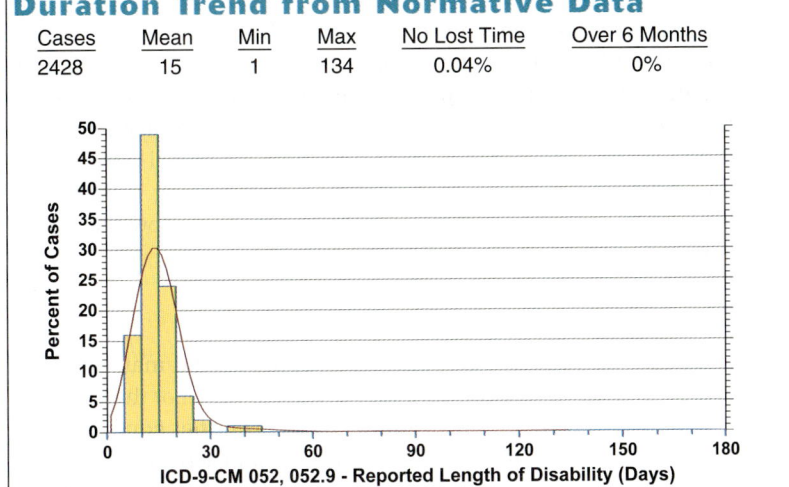

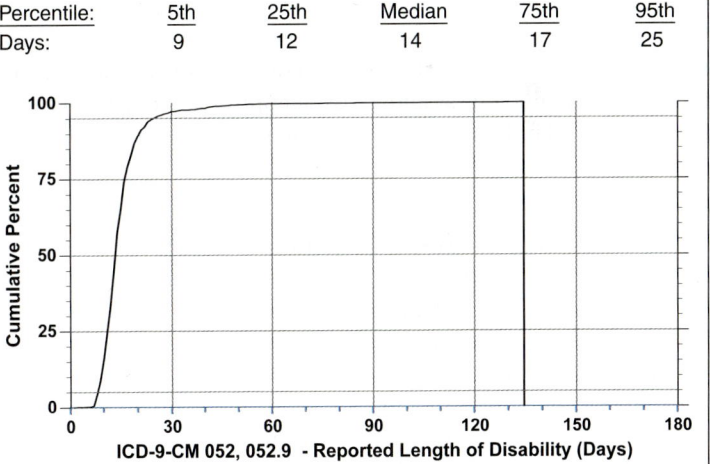

ICD-9-CM 052, 052.9 - Reported Length of Disability (Days)

* Differences may exist between the expected duration tables and the normative graphs. Duration tables provide expected recovery periods based on the type of work performed by the individual. The normative graphs reflect the actual observed experience of many individuals across the spectrum of physical conditions, in a variety of industries, and with varying levels of case management.

Failure to Recover

If an individual fails to recover within the maximum duration expectancy period, the reader may wish to reference the following questions to assist in better understanding the specifics of an individual's medical case.

Regarding diagnosis:

- Was individual exposed to someone with chickenpox or shingles in the past 10 to 21 days?
- Did individual initially report a fever, generalized aching, and weakness followed by an itchy rash beginning on the trunk and then spreading to the face, scalp, mouth, limbs, and other parts of the body?
- Did papules form in a few days and quickly form vesicles? Did they appear first in small groupings? Did vesicles break and form crusts or scabs over a 1- to 2-week period? Are they extremely itchy? Have new vesicles formed?
- Were conditions with similar symptoms ruled out?

Regarding treatment:

- Is individual being treated symptomatically?
- Is individual being treated with antiviral medication? Oral antihistamines?
- Was individual instructed to use acetaminophen rather than aspirin?
- Were individual's fingernails trimmed?

Regarding prognosis:

- Does individual have any conditions that may affect ability to recover?
- Have any complications developed such as pneumonia, encephalitis, Reye's syndrome, transient arthritis cerebellar ataxia, secondary infection, scarring, or herpes zoster? Is individual pregnant and possibly at risk for fetal congenital malformations?

References

Brooks, G.F., J.S. Butel, and S.A. Morse. Medical Microbiology. Stamford: Appleton & Lange, 1998.

Tierney, L.M., S.J. McPhee, and M.A. Papadakis. Current Medical Diagnosis and Treatment. Stamford: Appleton & Lange, 1998.

Chiropractic Adjustments and Manipulations
ICD-9 Depends on Procedure, 739.1, 739.2, 739.3, 739.4, 739.5, 739.6, 739.7

Definition

Chiropractic is a healthcare profession specializing in the use of manual and ancillary therapies especially spinal adjustments (manipulations) to treat various conditions. Chiropractors employ adjustments and other noninvasive procedures to treat the neuromusculoskeletal systems. The original founding belief of chiropractic was that health and disease are affected by anatomical osseous relations, which affect the function of the nervous system. Loss of appropriate mechanics results in ill health and inflammation with the remedy being the restoration of proper mechanics by means of an adjustment.

Chiropractic treatment is often used to treat vertebral subluxation syndrome or complex. The American Chiropractic Association Basic Procedural Manual (fourth edition) defines subluxation as "an abnormal physical relationship between adjacent anatomic structures whose contiguous tissues are eliciting neurological responses that may be clinically manifested as symptoms, signs, functional change, and morphologic alterations of a disease state, but less than the complete disruption of a dislocation or fracture." In other words, subluxations are believed to cause disease.

The existence of a subluxation is determined by physical examination and may include feeling with the hands (palpation) and orthopedic and neurologic tests. Some chiropractors use x-rays to rule out other spinal disorders. Subluxations usually involve the spine and are treated with adjustments.

On average, 10% of adults in the US (or 27 million) consult a chiropractor each year. One out of three individuals with low back pain seek treatment from a chiropractor. Eighty percent of the individuals consulting a chiropractor do so for neuromusculoskeletal problems; 65% of these individuals seek treatment for back pain.

Reason for Procedure

Chiropractic adjustments are performed with the intention of eliminating the direct and reflex effects resulting from compromised mechanics (subluxation) resulting from falls, accidents, stress, overexertion, tension, faulty posture, and other factors. Adjustments are performed to relieve pain, restore motion, remodel scar tissue (adhesions), relieve muscle spasms, and promote healing. Chiropractic adjustments and manipulations may be beneficial for low back pain, headache, and neck pain.

How Procedure Is Performed

There are many types of chiropractic adjustments and manipulations and just as many different techniques to decide which of these adjustments to use. Each chiropractor draws upon his or her education and experience to choose the optimal maneuver(s) for each individual from the more than 96 chiropractic maneuvers used. In general, adjustments incorporate a manual thrust in a definite direction with a specific force and at a particular point of the anatomy to correct a subluxation. The chiropractor must determine how much force to use to correct the subluxation. The placement and position of both the chiropractor and individual are also important. Adjustment techniques include short-lever and long-lever thrusts. Chiropractors may employ a variety of approaches and the diversity in practice may be great. Some chiropractors treat all ailments through spinal adjustments while other chiropractors may not employ adjustments at all.

Prognosis

More than 90% of all individuals who seek chiropractic care report a positive outcome from treatment.

Specialists

- Chiropractor
- Physical Therapist

Work Restrictions / Accommodations

Lifting, twisting, carrying, overhead work, standing, and walking may need to be restricted while treatments are in progress. Workstation ergonomics need to be addressed. Adjusting work table height, chair height, and use of foot rests are all beneficial for individuals with back or neck pain. An adjustable chair and proper height of the computer monitor allow for optimal posture and neck positioning. Individuals with neck pain who spend a great deal of time on the telephone would benefit from a head set. Individuals with back or neck pain may benefit from rest periods including an opportunity to lie down during such breaks. The individual may require additional time off for frequent treatment sessions.

Comorbid Conditions

Osteoporosis, obesity, spinal diseases and conditions (e.g., degenerative disc disease, and disc herniation), fibromyalgia, hypothyroidism, multiple sclerosis and psychosocial factors can influence the length of disability. An underlying condition or (if chiropractic care is sought following trauma) associated injuries can also influence length of disability.

Procedure Complications

Most adverse effects are from neck (cervical) manipulation. Serious complications from neck manipulation are rare and include brainstem or cerebellum infarction, locked-in syndrome, Wallenberg syndrome, spinal cord compression, tracheal rupture, vertebral fracture, internal carotid blood clot (hematoma), and diaphragm paralysis. Cauda equina syndrome is a severe complication associated with lower (lumbar) spine manipulation.

Factors Influencing Duration

No disability is expected with this procedure, however, the underlying condition for which chiropractic care is sought may cause disability.

Length of Disability

No disability is expected to result from this procedure. Disability may occur as a result of an underlying condition.

References

Research Demonstrates Effectiveness and Popularity of Chiropractic Care. American Chiropractic Association. 30 Oct 1998. 01 Oct 2000 <http://www.amerchiro.org/about_chiro/chiro_popularity.html>.

Kaptchuk, Ted, and David Eisenberg. "Chiropractic: Origins, Controversies, and Contributions." Archives of Internal Medicine 158 (1998): 2215-2224.

Cholangiography

Other names / synonyms: Endoscopic Retrograde Cholangiopancreatography, ERCP, Percutaneous Transhepatic Cholangiography, Postoperative Cholangiography, PTC

87.51, 87.53, 87.54

Definition

Cholangiography is a procedure that allows visualization of the ducts (i.e., common bile duct and cystic duct) that carry bile from the liver and gallbladder into the small intestine. Following injection of a radiopaque dye (iodipamide meglumine) into the ducts, x-ray pictures (cholangiograms) are taken of the abdominal area in which the ducts are located. If the dye is not seen in a section of the bile ducts, it provides evidence that the duct is obstructed.

There are 3 types of cholangiography that differ in how the dye is injected into the ductile system. Postoperative cholangiography is done by injecting the dye into a T-shaped rubber tube that is inserted into the common bile duct during surgery to remove the gallbladder (cholecystectomy) or common bile duct exploration. Percutaneous transhepatic cholangiography (PTC) involves injecting the dye into the ductile system in the liver via a long, slender needle. Endoscopic retrograde cholangiopancreatography (ERCP) involves passage of a flexible fiber-optic microscope (endoscope) through the mouth into the small intestine (duodenum). A tube (catheter) is then passed into the common bile duct (and possibly the pancreatic duct), and radiopaque dye is injected.

Bile duct obstruction usually results from stones (calculi) that have formed in the gallbladder and passed into the common bile duct. Other less common causes of bile duct obstruction may include abnormal tissue growth (malignant tumor) or harmless (benign) strictures within the duct. The presence of calculi in the bile ducts is referred to as choledocholithiasis. Risk factors for formation of calculi in the gallbladder (gallstones or cholelithiasis) that can lead to choledocholithiasis include female sex, obesity, increased age, North American Indian ethnicity, a high fat and calorie diet, and a family history of gallstones. In the US, 20% of individuals aged 65 or older have gallstones, and each year more than 500,000 people undergo treatment for this condition.

Reason for Procedure

Cholangiography is a procedure that allows the bile ducts to be visualized and a determination made as to whether they are narrowed or blocked. This procedure may be performed on individuals who have abdominal pain, yellow-tinted skin (jaundice), and fever or chills (Charcot's triad), or liver and spleen enlargement. All these symptoms are suggestive of obstruction and inflammation of the bile ducts (cholangitis). Cholangiography may also be performed on individuals suspected of having a tumor that is blocking the bile ducts or individuals who have an abnormal stricture of the ducts that is causing blockage. Symptoms of these conditions may include those seen with cholangitis.

How Procedure Is Performed

There are 3 types of cholangiography that differ in how the dye is injected into the ductile system: Postoperative cholangiography, percutaneous transhepatic cholangiography (PTC), and endoscopic retrograde cholangiopancreatography (ERCP).

Postoperative cholangiography is performed after surgery to remove the gallbladder (cholecystectomy) or common bile duct exploration. During the surgery, a T-shaped rubber tube will have been inserted into the common bile duct to facilitate drainage. Seven to ten days later, the cholangiography test will be performed. Food and drink will be withheld, and an enema may be administered about 1 hour prior to the test.

The individual will be asked to lay on his/her back (supine position) on a flat, hard (radiographic) table. The T-tube will be cleaned and approximately 5 ml of radiopaque contrast medium will be injected into the T-tube, and x-ray images will be taken. Additional contrast medium is usually injected (20-25 ml) and other x-rays will be taken in a variety of positions on the table. The individual is then assisted to a standing position for additional x-rays. The entire procedure, to this point, will have taken about 15 minutes. A final x-ray will be taken 15 minutes after the final injection of contrast medium to record the emptying of contrast-laden bile into the small intestine (duodenum). Postoperative cholangiography is not painful, although the individual may feel a bloating sensation in the upper right part of the abdomen (upper right quadrant) as the contrast medium is injected.

Percutaneous transhepatic cholangiography (PTC) is performed by injecting radiopaque contrast medium directly into the bile ductile system located in the liver. The individual will be instructed to fast for 8 hours before the test. Individuals will be secured on their back (supine position) onto a flat, hard table (tilting x-ray table) that rotates into vertical and horizontal positions during the procedure. A sedative may be administered before the procedure begins. The upper right part of the abdomen (upper right quadrant) will be cleansed, covered with a drape, and injected with a local anesthetic. The individual will be asked to hold his/her breath at the end of expiration while a long, thin needle is inserted through the abdominal wall and into the liver. The needle will be slowly withdrawn as contrast medium is injected. X-ray films will be taken with the individual in different positions (supine and lateral recumbent positions). After the necessary x-rays have been taken, the needle is removed and a sterile dressing will be applied to the puncture site. The entire procedure takes approximately 30 minutes and it is usually required that the individual rest for at least 6 hours after the procedure is completed.

Endoscopic retrograde cholangiopancreatography (ERCP) is performed by injecting radiopaque contrast medium directly into the bile ducts and pancreatic duct through a flexible tube (endoscope) that is inserted through the mouth and down into the digestive system. The individual will be instructed to fast after midnight prior to the day of the procedure. Just prior to the procedure, an intravenous (IV) line will be inserted into a blood vessel in order to administer drugs and fluids. A sedative will be given via the IV line and the individual will be relaxed but conscious. Also, a local anesthetic will be sprayed on the back of the throat to calm the gag reflex. The spray will have an unpleasant taste, and it will make the tongue and throat feel swollen. There may be difficulty in swallowing after administration of the local anesthetic. A mouth guard, which will not obstruct breathing in any way, may be inserted to protect the individual's teeth from the endoscope. The individual will lie on the left side (left lateral position) as the endoscope is threaded into the mouth, throat, stomach, and small intestine (duodenum). The individual will then be assisted to a position lying flat on the stomach (prone position). A small tube (cannula) is then inserted through the endoscope and into the bile and pancreatic ducts. A small amount (2-5 ml) of contrast medium is injected through the cannula to allow visualization of the pancreas by x-ray. The cannula is then repositioned and an additional 10-15 ml of contrast medium are injected to allow x-ray visualization of the bile ducts. The individual will be asked to remain in the prone position while the x-ray films are developed and reviewed. If necessary, additional films may be taken. If not, the cannula and endoscope will be removed and the procedure will be complete. Normally, ERCP takes 30-60 minutes. Food and fluids will be withheld until the throat anesthetic wears off and the gag reflex returns. Recovery time is generally 4-8 hours.

Prognosis

With cholangiography, the bile ducts will be visible on x-ray film. ERCP will show the pancreatic ducts as well. Obstruction within the bile duct system will be identified by the lack of radiopaque contrast medium in a segment of the duct. Also, if there is obstruction, the bile ducts usually appear to have a larger diameter (dilated) than normal. Non-obstructed ducts will be of normal size.

Specialists

- Gastroenterologist
- General Surgeon
- Internist

Work Restrictions / Accommodations

A full day will be required to complete the test and allow for recovery. There should not be any limitations at work following cholangiography unless unforeseen complications such as an allergic reaction occur during the test. In this case, additional recovery time at home may be required.

Comorbid Conditions

Existing conditions that may impact an individual's ability to recover following cholangiography include bleeding abnormalities; sepsis, peritonitis, or cellulitis of the abdominal wall; anemia; ascites; cancer; and acute pancreatitis.

Procedure Complications

Complications of any type of cholangiography may include an allergic reaction to the radiopaque contrast medium, nausea, vomiting, excessive salivation, flushing, skin eruptions (urticaria), and excessive sweating (diaphoresis). Additional complications of PTC may include increased heart rate (tachycardia); inflammation of the abdominal cavity (peritonitis); chills and fever; abdominal pain, tenderness, and distention; and infection of the abdominal cavity. Additional complications of ERCP may include slowed breathing rate (respiratory depression); cessation of breathing (apnea); low blood pressure (hypotension); low heart rate (bradycardia); throat spasm (laryngospasm); puncture (perforation) of the gut; inflammation of the bile ducts (cholangitis); and inflammation of the pancreas (pancreatitis).

Factors Influencing Duration

The underlying condition, the presence of complications and the individual's response to the procedure will determine the length of disability. Sensitivity to radiopaque contrast medium may also further lengthen disability.

Length of Disability

The duration of disability from cholangiography should ordinarily be no longer than 1 day unless unforeseen complications arise.

Duration in Days

Job Classification	Minimum	Optimum	Maximum
Any work	1	1	3

References

Bozymski, E.M. "Endoscopic Retrograde Cholangiopancreatography." Manual of Gastroenterologic Procedures. Drossman, D.A., ed. New York: Raven Press, 1993. 150-156.

Loeb, S. Illustrated Guide to Diagnostic Tests. Springhouse, PA: Springhouse Corporation, 1994.

Cholecystectomy

Other names / synonyms: Excision of Gallbladder, Lap Chole, Laparoscopic Cholecystectomy

51.2, 51.22, 51.23

Definition

Cholecystectomy is the surgical removal of the gallbladder.

The gallbladder may be removed through a laparoscopic procedure or as an open surgical procedure. The laparoscopic method is used in more than 90% of cholecystectomies. A thin viewing instrument (laparoscope) is inserted through a small abdominal incision. In an open surgical procedure, the abdomen is cut open to expose the gallbladder. Open surgical removal of the gallbladder is used most when complications are encountered during a laparoscopic procedure (2-5% of cases). X-ray studies of the bile ducts after they are injected with a contrast material (cholangiography) is frequently performed during a cholecystectomy to determine if there is any obstruction of the common bile duct by biliary stones (gallstones that form in the bile duct instead of the gallbladder). If stones are present, they are removed.

Cholecystectomy is most often performed for symptomatic gallbladder disease, usually stones in the gallbladder (cholelithiasis) or inflammation of the gallbladder (cholecystitis). These diseases are more common in females, and predominantly affect women in childbearing years; although any sex or age may be afflicted.

Gallstones, with resulting cholecystectomies, become progressively more common with age. In the US, approximately twenty percent of individuals over 65 have had symptoms of gallstones. Women have gallstones two to three times more often than men do. Other factors that increase the risk of gallstones include obesity, and a diet high in sugar and fat.

Reason for Procedure

Cholecystectomy is most often performed to relieve recurrent cramping pain caused by gallstones (biliary calculi) obstructing or passing through the cystic ducts. Cholecystectomy may be scheduled as an early but elective procedure during the first day or two of symptoms, or it may be planned at least six weeks later if there are no complications. The gallbladder is not usually removed if it contains stones that are not causing any symptoms. However, failure to remove the gallbladder when symptoms recur usually results in acute inflammation of the gallbladder (cholecystitis).

Occasionally, an emergency cholecystectomy is required for bursting (perforation) or pus formation (empyema) within the gallbladder. Rarely, cholecystectomy may be performed for cancer of the gallbladder, bile ducts, or pancreas.

How Procedure Is Performed

Cholecystectomy is performed in the operating room under general anesthesia. Laparoscopic cholecystectomy is the most commonly performed method of gallbladder removal. A small incision is made around the umbilicus and a camera is inserted. The abdominal cavity is inflated for better viewing (insufflation). Three smaller incisions are made on the abdomen to allow for insertion of the instruments. The artery to the gallbladder and the cystic duct (tubular canal carrying bile from the gallbladder) are tied off and cut. The gallbladder is freed from its surrounding tissue and removed. The incisions are stitched shut.

In an open cholecystectomy, the abdominal cavity is opened using a right or midline abdominal incision. The artery to the gallbladder and the cystic duct leading from it are tied off and cut, and the gallbladder is removed. Before closing the abdomen, drains are placed under the liver and in the bile duct. The drains, which are kept in place from four to ten days, are removed after x-ray studies show there are no more stones.

Recovery from a laparoscopic cholecystectomy is typically rapid. The individual usually leaves the hospital the next day. Soreness is minimal, and return to work is often in a couple of weeks. Open cholecystectomies usually necessitate a longer hospital stay, often up to five days. Once the pain has diminished and the individual is tolerating a regular diet, the individual is discharged home.

Prognosis

Cholecystectomy for gallstones or inflammation (cholecystitis) usually results in cure. There are no dietary restrictions after removal of the gallbladder and no long-term consequences. Occasionally, in about 2-4% of individuals, gallstones can form in the bile ducts, even after the removal of the gallbladder. This is usually treatable with an endoscopic procedure where a scope is inserted into the stomach and small intestine through the mouth (ERCP).

Cholecystectomy for cancer of the gallbladder, bile ducts, or pancreas is usually for comfort only. The prognosis for these types of cancer is dismal, with mortality rates approaching ninety-five to one hundred percent.

Specialists

- Gastroenterologist
- General Surgeon

Work Restrictions / Accommodations

Heavy lifting and strenuous activity may need to be modified following surgery. Aside from that, special work restrictions or accommodations are not usually associated with this procedure.

Comorbid Conditions

Diabetes would impair an individual's ability to recover from this procedure.

Procedure Complications

The most common complications of this procedure are bleeding or wound infection. Rarely, the duct that drains bile from the liver (common bile duct) can be injured during this procedure. If this were to occur, the duct would need to be repaired immediately with an open procedure. Fortunately, this complication occurs in only about 1% of operations. Sometimes, an unnoticed injury to one of the bile ducts can result in a bile leak into the abdomen. These are usually self-limited, but sometimes a separate procedure is necessary to repair the injury. Retained gallstones in the bile ducts can also occur. These can be removed with a separate procedure using a scope.

Factors Influencing Duration

Factors include the type of procedure and the presence of complications or underlying disease(s).

Length of Disability

Laparoscopic.

Duration in Days

Job Classification	Minimum	Optimum	Maximum
Sedentary work	3	10	14
Light work	3	10	21
Medium work	10	14	28
Heavy work	14	21	42
Very Heavy work	14	21	42

Open.

Duration in Days

Job Classification	Minimum	Optimum	Maximum
Sedentary work	7	14	36
Light work	10	14	36
Medium work	14	21	42
Heavy work	21	28	56
Very Heavy work	28	42	56

Duration Trend from Normative Data*

Cases	Mean	Min	Max	No Lost Time	Over 6 Months
751	27	0	316	0.8%	0.54%

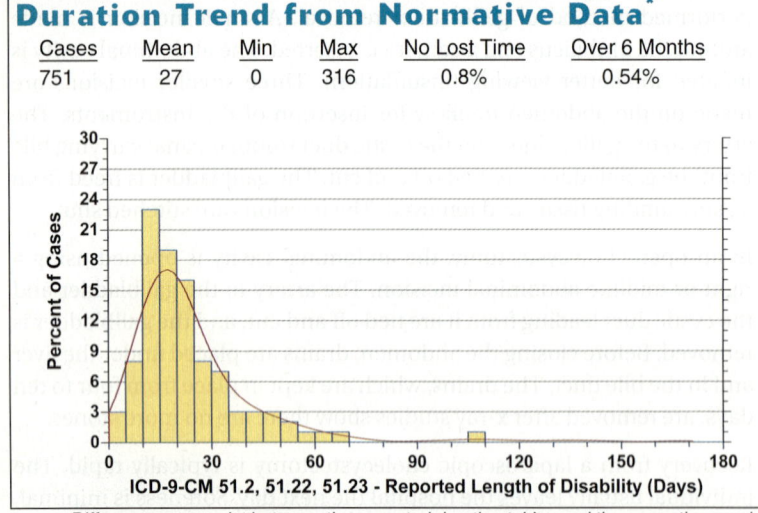

ICD-9-CM 51.2, 51.22, 51.23 - Reported Length of Disability (Days)

Percentile:	5th	25th	Median	75th	95th
Days:	8	14	19	29	60

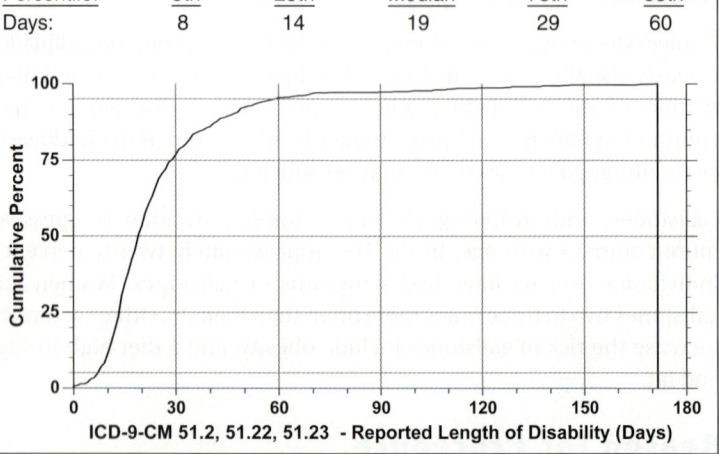

ICD-9-CM 51.2, 51.22, 51.23 - Reported Length of Disability (Days)

* Differences may exist between the expected duration tables and the normative graphs. Duration tables provide expected recovery periods based on the type of work performed by the individual. The normative graphs reflect the actual observed experience of many individuals across the spectrum of physical conditions, in a variety of industries, and with varying levels of case management.

References

Ahmed Aijaz, Ramsey C. Cheung, and Emmet B.Keeffe, MDs. "Managment of Gallstones and Their Complications." AAFP. 15 Mar 2000. 24 Jan 2001 <http://www.aafp.org/afp/20000315/1673.html>.

Schwartz, Seymour, MD. Principles of Surgery. New York: McGraw-Hill, 1999.

Cholecystitis

Other names / synonyms: Inflammation of the Gallbladder

575.0, 575.1, 575.2, 575.4, 575.8

Definition

Cholecystitis is an inflammation of the gallbladder, a small sack-like organ located in the upper right-hand side of the abdomen. In a healthy individual, the gallbladder temporarily stores bile, a substance produced by the liver that helps the body digest fat. After a meal, particularly a high-fat meal, bile passes from the gallbladder through the cystic and common bile ducts and into the small intestine where it helps process fats.

Cholecystitis is characterized by pain in the upper right-hand side of the abdomen, which increases in intensity over 2-3 minutes, and then levels off in intensity, persisting for 20 minutes or more. The pain (called biliary colic) may be intense and may radiate from the abdomen to the back and/or shoulder; it generally follows meals by 1-6 hours. Episodes generally come and go over a period of 2-3 days, and are almost always completely gone within one week.

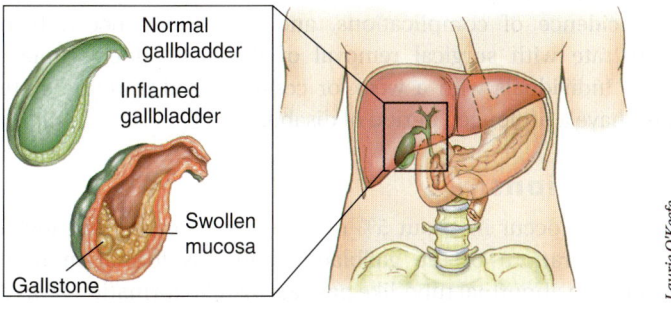

Laurie O'Keefe

Most cases (90-95%) of cholecystitis occur in individuals who have rock-like deposits (gallstones) in the gallbladder, a condition called cholelithiasis. If a gallstone passes from the gallbladder and blocks the cystic duct, bile becomes trapped in the gallbladder. The trapped bile irritates the walls of the gallbladder and also provides an ideal environment for infection-causing bacteria. As the body responds to irritation and/or infection, the gallbladder becomes inflamed resulting in what is known as acute cholecystitis. If mild cases of acute cholecystitis repeatedly flare-up and resolve over a long period of time, a condition known as chronic cholecystitis can result. In chronic cholecystitis, the walls of the gallbladder thicken gradually, and the gallbladder eventually becomes shrunken and useless.

In some individuals, particularly pregnant women, those who have rapidly lost weight, or those who are nourished through a feeding tube or intravenously, the bile may contain a thick, insoluble material known as gallbladder sludge. Gallbladder sludge can cause cholecystitis. Severely stressful situations such as multiple trauma, Salmonella poisoning, sepsis, or cardiac surgery can also cause cholecystitis (acalculous cholecystitis). This type of cholecystitis is serious and is associated with an increased risk of complications. Other causes include a growth (neoplasm) in the common bile duct, narrowing (stricture) of the common bile duct, or a loss of blood flow (ischemia) to the gallbladder wall. Ischemia is rare and is generally seen in diabetics. Cholecystitis can result when the gallbladder becomes twisted, although this is uncommon.

Cholecystitis is a relatively common condition. The risk for developing this disease increases steadily with age, with peak incidence in the fifties and sixties. Twice as many women as men are affected by this condition. Native Americans are at increased risk for this disease, with 30% affected by age 30 and 80% affected by age 60. In comparison, 30% of whites and 20% of blacks are diagnosed with cholecystitis by age sixty. Other risk factors include use of birth control pills (oral contraceptives), obesity, Asian ethnicity, fertility, diabetes, and chronic alcohol use.

Diagnosis

History: Individuals with acute cholecystitis complain of steady pain or discomfort (biliary colic) in the middle/upper abdomen. The discomfort may be located in the center or upper right-hand side of the abdomen in the area of the liver and gallbladder, or just under the breastbone. In some individuals, this abdominal discomfort spreads from the abdomen to the back and shoulder area. Often, discomfort is associated with nausea and vomiting. Upon questioning, the individual may relate that these symptoms tend to occur soon after meals and begin gradually, increasing in intensity over a period of 2-3 minutes. After reaching peak intensity, the symptoms level off and persist for 20 minutes or more before beginning to subside.

Individuals with chronic cholecystitis may complain of vague abdominal pain and mild indigestion (dyspepsia) following fatty meals. They may also complain of nausea and an increased frequency of belching.

Physical exam: The individual may have a mild-to-moderate fever. Pressing on (palpating) the abdomen in the area of the gallbladder and liver may reveal local tenderness. While palpating this area, the individual may be asked to take a deep breath. If inhalation stops when the area is pressed, this is known as a positive "Murphy's sign," and is characteristic of acute cholecystitis. In about 5% of cases, the gallbladder can be felt (palpated). One-fifth of individuals may have a yellowish discoloration of the skin and whites of the eyes (sclerae) known as jaundice.

Tests: In most cases, the doctor orders blood tests to evaluate liver function and check for signs of inflammation and/or infection. A test that uses sound waves (ultrasound) to create a video image of internal organs (in this case the gallbladder, liver, and sometimes the pancreas) is often used to determine the presence of gallstones. Ultrasound can also show thickening of the gallbladder wall, stretching (distention) of the gallbladder, and the presence of gallbladder sludge. If interpreted by an experienced observer, this test is 85-95% sensitive in diagnosing cholecystis. An x-ray or a computed tomography (CT) scan may also be obtained to help the physician confirm the diagnosis and rule out other conditions such as gallbladder cancer. An hepatobiliary scan visualizes the cystic duct to diagnose blockage (obstruction).

Treatment

Acute cholecystitis with mild symptoms can be treated with medication to reduce inflammation and relieve pain (nonsteroidal anti-inflammatories). If an infection is also present, antibiotics are also given. Medications to help break down gallstones may also be needed.

When the symptoms are moderate to severe, the individual is often admitted to the hospital for intravenous medication, fluids, and nutrition. Medication may include pain relievers (analgesics), anti-inflammatories, and antibiotics. The individual will not be allowed to eat, and a tube may be passed from the nose into the stomach to keep the stomach empty and prevent stimulation of the gallbladder. Surgical removal of the gallbladder is the appropriate treatment for symptomatic cholecystitis. The preferred technique is called laparoscopic cholecystectomy, and involves removal of the gallbladder through small tubes inserted through small cuts (incisions) in the abdomen. The surgeon uses a small camera (laparoscope), which is also inserted through a small incision. Laparoscopic cholecystectomy is the procedure used in about 90% of cholecystectomies. If laparoscopic cholecystectomy is not available or is not appropriate, a standard "open" surgical procedure can be used to remove the gallbladder through an incision in the abdominal wall. Open surgery is needed if the gallbladder is torn (perforated). In some cases, gallstones blocking the bile duct may be broken down by high-energy shock-waves (shock-wave lithotripsy).

Treatment of any underlying illness, such as gallstones or abnormal growths, is an important aspect of treatment. If an underlying illness would increase the risks of surgery, surgery can be delayed while that illness is treated.

Complicated cases may require immediate, emergency surgery.

Prognosis

The prognosis for cholecystitis is good. Removal of the gallbladder (cholecystectomy) is the treatment of choice if the individual is experiencing symptoms. Cholecystectomy (either laparoscopic or open surgery) is associated with a 0.1% mortality rate in individuals under 50 years of age; 0.8% in those over fifty. The laparoscopic procedure is associated with less pain, a shorter hospital stay, and a shorter recovery period than the open procedure. Cholecystectomy provides a complete resolution of symptoms in 75-90% of cases.

In cases where cholecystitis is treated with medication and not surgery, 25% of individuals will have another episode of acute cholecystitis within 1 year, and 60% will have another episode within 6 years.

After cholecystectomy, gallstones may occur in the bile ducts, a condition known as choledocholithiasis.

Complicated cases of cholecystitis may have a less favorable prognosis, depending on the specifics of the complication.

Differential Diagnosis

The signs and symptoms of cholecystitis are common to many other illnesses. The following conditions should be considered when making the diagnosis of cholecystitis: inflammation of the pancreas (pancreatitis), an ulcer of the stomach (peptic ulcer) or small intestine (duodenal ulcer), inflammation of a part of the intestinal tract (diverticulitis), inflammation of the appendix (appendicitis), an abscess or tumor of the liver (hepatic abscess, hepatic tumor), a condition called irritable bowel disease, cancer of the bile duct, and common indigestion.

Specialists

- Gastroenterologist
- General Surgeon

Work Restrictions / Accommodations

Individuals with cholecystitis can expect complete recovery following treatment, thus no work restrictions or special accommodations are generally required. Individuals undergoing open surgery may need to avoid heavy lifting and strenuous physical work for several weeks as they recover. Temporary assignment to a sedentary position may be helpful for individuals recovering from surgery, if their regular jobs are physically demanding.

Comorbid Conditions

Individuals with diabetes have a higher incidence of complications, and thus may have a longer period of disability. The elderly also have a higher incidence of complications, and they experience a higher mortality rate with surgical removal of the gallbladder (cholecystectomy). Individuals with a weak or compromised immune system may also have a prolonged period of disability.

Complications

Complications occur in about 5% of cholecystitis cases, and include tearing (perforation) of the gallbladder; abscess formation of the gallbladder; an abnormal tube-like passage (fistula) formation from the gallbladder to the intestine, colon, or skin; gangrene; pus in the abdominal cavity (empyema); inflammation of the bile ducts (cholangitis), liver (hepatitis), or pancreas (pancreatitis); intestinal obstruction (gallstone ileus); and cancer. Individuals treated without surgery are at higher risk for developing gallbladder perforation, which has a 25% mortality rate.

Factors Influencing Duration

The length of disability will be affected by the severity of the individual's symptoms, the presence of complications and whether surgery is required. If surgery is required, the method (laparoscopic or open) of surgery, the presence of surgical complications, and the individual's ability to heal will also affect the period of disability. Surgical removal of the gallbladder (cholecystectomy) is associated with a mortality rate of 0.1-0.8%, depending on the age of the individual. If surgery is not required, recovery may vary depending on the individual's response to prescribed medication.

Length of Disability

Episodes of acute cholecystitis rarely persist for more than 1 week. Most individuals will experience a complete resolution of symptoms. If surgery is required, the technique used will affect the period of disability. Laparoscopic surgery is associated with a shorter hospital stay, less postoperative pain, and a shorter recovery period than open surgery.

Laparoscopic cholecystectomy.

Duration in Days

Job Classification	Minimum	Optimum	Maximum
Sedentary work	3	10	14
Light work	3	10	21
Medium work	10	14	28
Heavy work	14	21	42
Very Heavy work	14	21	42

Medical treatment.

Duration in Days

Job Classification	Minimum	Optimum	Maximum
Sedentary work	3	7	14
Light work	3	7	14
Medium work	3	7	21
Heavy work	3	7	28
Very Heavy work	3	7	28

Open (conventional) cholecystectomy.

Duration in Days

Job Classification	Minimum	Optimum	Maximum
Sedentary work	7	14	36
Light work	10	14	36
Medium work	14	21	42
Heavy work	21	28	56
Very Heavy work	28	42	56

Duration Trend from Normative Data*

Cases	Mean	Min	Max	No Lost Time	Over 6 Months
2582	31	0	607	0.39%	0.23%

Percentile:	5th	25th	Median	75th	95th
Days:	10	16	23	37	69

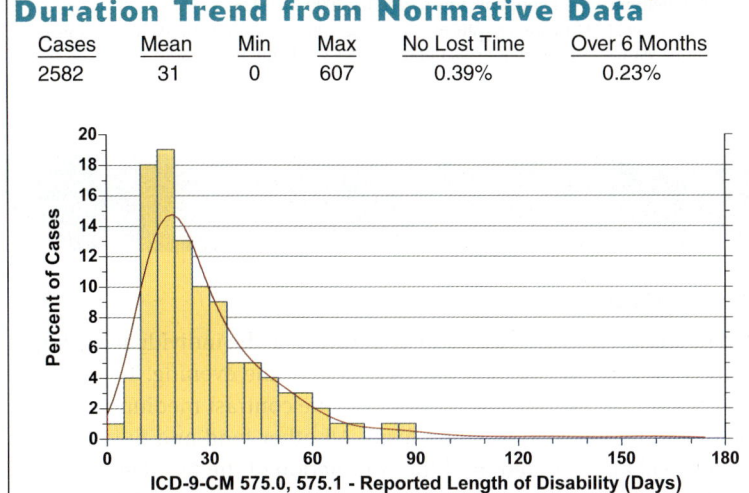
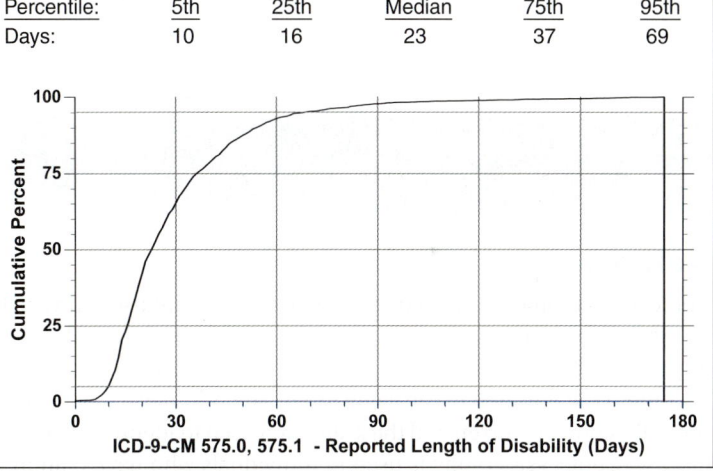

ICD-9-CM 575.0, 575.1 - Reported Length of Disability (Days)

* Differences may exist between the expected duration tables and the normative graphs. Duration tables provide expected recovery periods based on the type of work performed by the individual. The normative graphs reflect the actual observed experience of many individuals across the spectrum of physical conditions, in a variety of industries, and with varying levels of case management.

Failure to Recover

If an individual fails to recover within the maximum duration expectancy period, the reader may wish to reference the following questions to assist in better understanding the specifics of an individual's medical case.

Regarding diagnosis:

- Does individual have a history of severely stressful situations such as multiple trauma, Salmonella poisoning, sepsis, or cardiac surgery? Obesity, diabetes, or chronic alcohol use?
- Is individual pregnant? Has individual lost weight rapidly? Is individual nourished through a feeding tube or intravenously?
- Does individual use birth control pills (oral contraceptives)?
- Does individual complain of steady pain or discomfort (biliary colic) in the middle/upper abdomen?
- Does the pain spread from the abdomen to the back and shoulder area?
- Does individual report nausea and vomiting?
- Do the symptoms tend to occur soon after meals, and begin gradually, increasing in intensity over a period of 2 to 3 minutes?
- Do the symptoms level off and persist for approximately 20 minutes before beginning to subside?
- Were blood tests done to evaluate liver function and check for signs of inflammation and/or infection? Was ultrasound done to determine the presence of gallstones?

- Was an x-ray or a CT done to help the physician confirm the diagnosis and rule out other conditions such as gallbladder cancer?
- If a blockage of the cystic duct is suspected, was a hepatobiliary scan done?
- Was the diagnosis of cholecystitis confirmed?

Regarding treatment:

- If individual had mild symptoms, were nonsteroidal anti-inflammatories (NSAIDs) administered?
- Was any infection treated with antibiotics? Was individual compliant with the medication regimen?
- If individual has moderate to severe symptoms, was hospitalization required?
- Were gallstones able to be broken down by high-energy shock waves (shock-wave lithotripsy) or was surgery required?
- If surgery was necessary, was removal of the gallbladder (cholecystectomy) done via a laparoscope or was open surgery required?
- Did individual experience any complications after shock-wave lithotripsy, laparoscopic cholecystectomy, or open cholecystectomy?
- Is individual following diet and alcohol restrictions?

Regarding prognosis:

- Was individual treated with medication or surgery?
- If treatment was with medication, has another episode of cholecystitis occurred? Has perforation of the gallbladder occurred?
- If treatment was surgical, have gallstones developed in the bile ducts (choledocholithiasis)?
- Were there any postsurgical complications, such as bleeding or infection?
- Has individual developed any complications from this disorder, such as fistula formation from the gallbladder to the intestine, colon or skin; gangrene; empyema; cholangitis, hepatitis, or pancreatitis; intestinal obstruction; or cancer?
- How will complications be treated and what is the expected outcome with treatment?

References

Berkow, Robert, Mark Beers, and Andrew Fletcher, eds. The Merck Manual of Medical Information. New York: Pocket Books, 1997.

Duke, James A. The Green Pharmacy. Emmaus, PA: Rodale Press, Inc, 1997.

Feinstein, Alice, ed. Healing with Vitamins. Emmaus, PA: Rodale Press, Inc, 1997.

Gottlieb, Bill, ed. New Choices in Natural Healing. Englewood: Rodale Press, Inc, 1995.

Iber, Frank. "Cholecystitis." Griffith's 5-minute Clinical Consult. Dambro, Mark, ed. Philadelphia: Lippincott, Williams & Wilkins, 2000. 224-225.

Rosen, C.L., et al. "Ultrasonography by Emergency Physicians in Patients with Suspected Cholecystitis." American Journal of Emergency Medicine 19 1 (2001): 32-36.

Cholecystography
87.59

Definition

Cholecystography is a procedure in which x-rays are used to visualize the gallbladder following ingestion of a radiopaque dye. The dye is ingested with a high-fat meal at noon on the day before the test, and it becomes concentrated in the gallbladder. The next day, x-ray images of the gallbladder are taken and these are then used to identify biliary tract disease. Cholecystography is used in individuals who have pain in the upper right part of their abdomen (upper right epigastric pain), intolerance to fatty foods, yellow skin (jaundice), and gallstones.

Stones (calculi) that have formed in the gallbladder may pass into the common bile duct where they can obstruct the flow of bile into the small intestine (duodenum). The presence of calculi in the bile ducts is referred to as choledocholithiasis. Risk factors for formation of calculi in the gallbladder (gallstones or cholelithiasis) that can lead to choledocholithiasis include female sex, obesity, increased age, North American Indian ethnicity, a high fat and calorie diet, and a family history of gallstones. In the US, 20% of individuals aged 65 or older have gallstones, and each year more than 500,000 individuals undergo treatment for this condition.

Reason for Procedure

Cholecystography is performed in order to visualize the anatomy of the gallbladder. It is usually performed in individuals who have gallstones (cholelithiasis), gallbladder disease, or cystic duct disease.

How Procedure Is Performed

On the day before the procedure is performed, the individual will ingest a high-fat noon meal and a fat-free meal in the evening. Two to three hours after the evening meal, a radiopaque contrast medium (iopanoic acid) will be ingested in tablet form. All other food and fluids (except water) will be restricted until the completion of the test. On the day of the test, an enema may be administered. The individual will then lie face down (prone position) on a hard, flat (radiographic) table and x-ray films will be taken of the gallbladder. The individual will then lay on the left side (left lateral decubitus position), and then stand erect while more x-ray images are captured. The individual may then be given a high-fat meal or synthetic fat-containing agent to stimulate gallbladder emptying. X-rays will be taken 15 and 30 minutes following the fat stimulus in order visualize the bile duct. Films may also be taken at 60 minutes if the gallbladder empties slowly. Normal food intake can be resumed after the test is completed.

Prognosis

A normal gallbladder will appear pear-shaped with smooth, thin walls. Its size may be variable; however, the basic structure will be outlined clearly on x-ray film. Gallstones will show up on the film as negative shadows that can change position within the gallbladder. Other abnormalities (such as polyps or tumors) will be fixed in one position. If the gallbladder fails to light up on the x-ray, it may indicate a form of gallbladder inflammatory disease (cholecystitis). Cholecystitis or obstruction of the common bile duct may also be indicated by failure of the gallbladder to contract following stimulation by fat ingestion. Cholecystography may be repeated the next day if the x-ray films are inconclusive.

Specialists

- Gastroenterologist
- General Surgeon
- Internist
- Radiologist

Work Restrictions / Accommodations

There should not be any limitations at work following cholangiography unless unforeseen complications such as an allergic reaction occur during the test. In this case, additional recovery time at home may be required.

Comorbid Conditions

Existing conditions that may impact an individual's ability to recover and further lengthen their disability include severe kidney (renal) or liver (hepatic) damage, or hypersensitivity to iodine, seafood, or the radiopaque contrast medium used in the test.

Procedure Complications

A complication of cholecystography may include an allergic reaction to the radiopaque contrast medium. Other complications of contrast medium ingestion may include diarrhea, nausea, vomiting, abdominal cramps, and painful urination (dysuria).

Factors Influencing Duration

Allergic reaction or other side effects in response to ingestion of contrast medium might influence the length of disability. The underlying cause for the procedure may also be a factor. If gallstones, gallbladder disease, or cystic duct disease are discovered, further medical and/or surgical treatments may be necessary.

Length of Disability

The duration of disability from cholecystography should ordinarily be no longer than 1 day unless unforeseen complications arise. However, the results of the test may necessitate further treatment and, in this case, disability may be lengthened.

Duration in Days

Job Classification	Minimum	Optimum	Maximum
Any work	1	1	3

References

Donovan, J.M., and S.J. Shields. "Treatment of Gallstones." <u>Therapy of Digestive Disorders.</u> Wolfe, M.M., ed. Philadelphia: W.B. Saunders Company, 2000. 207-218.

Loeb, S. <u>Illustrated Guide to Diagnostic Tests.</u> Springhouse, PA: Springhouse Corporation, 1994.

Cholelithiasis

Other names / synonyms: Biliary Calculi, Choledocholithiasis, Gallstones
574, 574.0, 574.1, 574.10, 574.2, 574.3, 574.4, 574.5, 574.6, 574.8

Definition

Cholelithiasis is a condition in which crystals (gallstones, or biliary calculi) form and remain in the gallbladder. The major component of most gallstones is cholesterol; however, some are composed mainly of calcium salts, and others are composed mainly of crystallized bile pigments.

The gallbladder stores a substance called bile that aids in digestion. Normal bile contains high levels of cholesterol, which usually remains in liquid form. When the bile contains too much cholesterol it is said to be supersaturated with cholesterol. When this occurs, solid crystals of cholesterol (gallstones) form and settle out of the liquid bile. Other causes of cholelithiasis include production of bile that contains inadequate amounts of certain chemicals (phospholipids or bile acids) or blockage of the tubes carrying bile from the gallbladder to the intestine (biliary stasis). Why some people develop gallstones while others do not is unknown.

Cholelithiasis affects 8-10% of the population, or 10-20% of adults, with increased incidence in Native Americans, Asians, Hispanics, and fair-skinned people of northern European descent. Blacks are less likely to get gallstones, except for those with sickle cell disease (who get gallstones early in life). Every year 1-3% of people develop gallstones. Women are twice as likely as men to develop this condition. The risk of cholelithiasis increases with age, with individuals in their sixties most often affected. Other factors that increase the risk of gallstones include obesity, pregnancy, use of estrogen replacement therapy or birth control pills (oral contraceptives), a Western diet high in animal fats, and a family history of gallstones. Women who have more than one child are also at increased risk, as are individuals who have received long-term intravenous nutrition and those with artificial heart valves. Other medical conditions that may increase the risk of cholelithiasis include short gut syndrome, inflammatory bowel disease, cirrhosis of the liver, sickle cell anemia, hereditary spherocytosis, biliary parasites, or childhood cancer. Individuals with diabetes are at increased risk for complications from cholelithiasis.

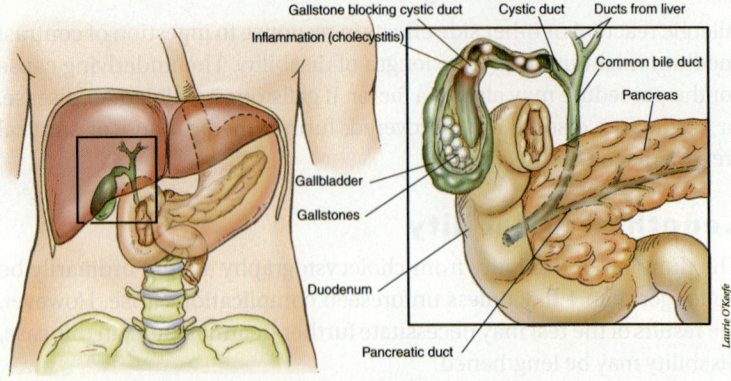

Diagnosis

History: In more than half of cases, the individual will not experience any symptoms that prompt a visit to the physician. In these individuals, the diagnosis is usually made following examination for some other reason. When symptoms do occur, the individual complains of pain (biliary colic) that begins abruptly and is often triggered by a large fatty meal. The pain is usually located in the right upper or middle abdomen, and may radiate to the shoulder or back. The pain is steady and can be quite intense, subsiding gradually over a period of minutes to several hours. The individual may describe the feeling as indigestion. It may be accompanied by nausea and/or vomiting. Other symptoms that are not specific to gallstones may include belching and bloating.

Physical exam: The exam is usually normal, except for possible tenderness in the right upper abdomen. Rarely, an enlarged gallbladder may be felt when pressing (palpating) the abdomen. Fever, rapid heart rate (tachycardia) and low blood pressure (hypotension) may suggest complications including infection of the biliary tree (cholangitis) or gallbladder (cholecystitis).

Tests: About 98% of gallstones can be detected with a test called ultrasonography which uses sound waves to create an image of the gallbladder on a video screen. In another test called cholecystography, the individual drinks a solution containing a substance that can be seen on an x-ray, showing a blockage in the gallbladder or the outline of a gallstone. In most cases, the physician uses both tests to confirm the diagnosis of cholelithiasis. Computed tomography (CT) scans are not helpful in most cases. Plain x-rays done for another reason may make the diagnosis of asymptomatic gallstones, as 10-30% of stones can be seen on x-rays.

Treatment

Many individuals with cholelithiasis have no symptoms (asymptomatic), and these cases do not require treatment of any kind. However, low-fat, low-cholesterol, low-sugar diet may help protect against subsequent gallstone formation. Diabetics and pregnant women with asymptomatic gallstones should be followed closely to see if they develop symptoms or complications. Other individuals at risk of complications from asymptomatic gallstones should be offered non-emergency (elective) removal of the gallbladder (cholecystectomy). These may include individuals with cirrhosis, portal hypertension, sickle cell disease, and transplant candidates. Individuals with calcium deposits outlining the wall of the gallbladder as seen on x-ray should consider non-emergency cholecystectomy, as one-quarter of these individuals may develop gallbladder cancer.

For individuals with bothersome symptoms, there are 2 nonsurgical methods of removing gallstones. In one method, the individual takes medication that dissolves small gallstones after 6-12 months of treatment, although gallstones recur in about half of cases. There is another procedure under investigation, called extracorporeal shock wave lithotripsy, in which sound waves are used to dissolve the gallstones. This procedure is not yet approved by the United States Food and Drug Administration. In both of these cases, the dissolved stones are then passed from the gallbladder and into the intestines, where they leave the body in the feces. These methods are not appropriate for all cases. Individuals may also be advised to take pain-relieving medication (analgesics) to provide immediate relief of symptoms. A low-fat diet may help prevent recurrence.

For individuals in whom the above procedures are not appropriate, the gallbladder may be removed surgically (cholecystectomy). When surgery is the best option, immediate surgery is preferred, as delay is associated with complications, increased operative time, and longer hospitalization.

Prognosis

Cholelithiasis is associated with an excellent prognosis for most individuals. In more than half of cases, individuals never experience symptoms. Small stones may pass into the intestine without difficulty and be eliminated in the stool.

Following non-emergency (elective) surgical removal of the gallbladder (cholecystectomy), 0.5% of individuals die, and 10% suffer complications. Emergency procedures have a slightly higher mortality rate of 3-5%, and a complication rate of 30-50 percent. Even after cholecystectomy, gallstones may recur in the bile ducts. Medical treatment to dissolve gallstones leads to recurrence in about half of cases, particularly if the diet is not modified to reduce the intake of animal fat.

Differential Diagnosis

Many other conditions share signs and symptoms with cholelithiasis and should be considered when making this diagnosis. These include common indigestion; stomach (peptic) ulcers; gallstones in the bile ducts (choledocholithiasis); gastroesophageal reflux disease (GERD); inflammation of the liver (hepatitis); inflammation of the pancreas (pancreatitis); inflammation of the appendix (appendicitis); coronary artery disease; pneumonia; cancer of the gallbladder; kidney (renal) stones; blood clots; narrowing (stricture) of the esophagus, bile ducts, or intestines; gallbladder polyps; or a condition called biliary sludge.

Specialists

- Gastroenterologist
- General Surgeon

Work Restrictions / Accommodations

Most individuals will not be bothered by symptoms and thus will not require any work restrictions or accommodations. Time off may be required after surgery to allow recovery from the procedure. This recovery period will vary considerably depending on the specifics of the procedure (open vs. laparoscopic), the presence of surgical complications, and the individual's response to treatment. Upon returning from work, heavy lifting and/or strenuous activity may be restricted temporarily while the individual regains strength and stamina.

Complementary and Alternative Therapies

Content is intended for awareness only. Treatments may or may not be effective. Scientific evidence may be lacking and some substances have potentially toxic effects. Dr. Presley Reed and the editors do not endorse the use of these therapies in the absence of consultation with a licensed medical professional.

Celandine -	Contains chelidonine, which may relax biliary tract muscles and may improve bile flow.
Milk thistle -	Contains silymarin, which increases bile solubility and may help prevent gallstones.
Calcium -	Said to lower cholesterol in gallbladder in men, helping to prevent gallstones, but may actually contribute to gallstone formation in women.
Spearmint -	Has been traditionally used to treat gallstones.
Cardamom -	Contains borneol, which may be helpful in treating gallstones.
Peppermint -	Has been traditionally used to treat gallstones.
Turmeric -	Contains curcumin, which reduced gallstones in a mouse study.
Reflexology -	Working points corresponding to liver and gallbladder may help relieve gallbladder problems.

Comorbid Conditions

Anemia or pancreatitis may lengthen disability. Individuals with diabetes are more prone to complications of gallstones such as infection of the bile ducts (cholangitis) or gallbladder (cholecystitis), and thus may experience prolonged disability. Illnesses predisposing to cholelithiasis may be associated with their own complications that affect disability. These include cirrhosis of the liver, sickle cell disease, other hemolytic diseases of the blood such as spherocytosis, extensive burns, and ileal disease.

Complications

Cholelithiasis can cause inflammation of the gallbladder (cholecystitis), or in 10-15% of cases stones may travel to the bile ducts (choledocholithiasis). Infection of the bile ducts (cholangitis) may result. In rare cases, a large gallstone may erode through the gallbladder wall into the intestine and cause intestinal blockage (gallstone ileus). Infection in the bile duct or gallbladder may lead to generalized infection (sepsis) or inflammation of the pancreas (pancreatitis).

Factors Influencing Duration

The presence of complications and the individual's response to treatment may affect the recovery period. In cases requiring surgical removal of the gallbladder (cholecystectomy), the disability period will be longer than in cases not requiring surgery. The period of disability will also depend on the type of surgical procedure (open vs. laparoscopic), the presence of surgical complications, and the individual's response to treatment.

Length of Disability

Most individuals will not experience symptoms, and thus will not experience a period of disability. Even in those who experience symptoms, complete recovery is expected for most. Heavy lifting and/or strenuous activity may be restricted temporarily. If surgery (cholecystectomy) is required, death is a rare complication.

Medical treatment or extracorporeal shock wave lithotripsy.

Duration in Days

Job Classification	Minimum	Optimum	Maximum
Sedentary work	3	7	14
Light work	3	7	14
Medium work	3	7	14
Heavy work	3	7	14
Very Heavy work	3	7	14

Laparoscopic cholecystectomy.

Duration in Days

Job Classification	Minimum	Optimum	Maximum
Sedentary work	3	10	14
Light work	3	10	21
Medium work	10	14	28
Heavy work	14	21	42
Very Heavy work	14	21	42

Open (conventional) cholecystectomy.

Duration in Days

Job Classification	Minimum	Optimum	Maximum
Sedentary work	7	14	36
Light work	10	14	36
Medium work	14	21	42
Heavy work	21	28	56
Very Heavy work	28	42	56

Duration Trend from Normative Data*

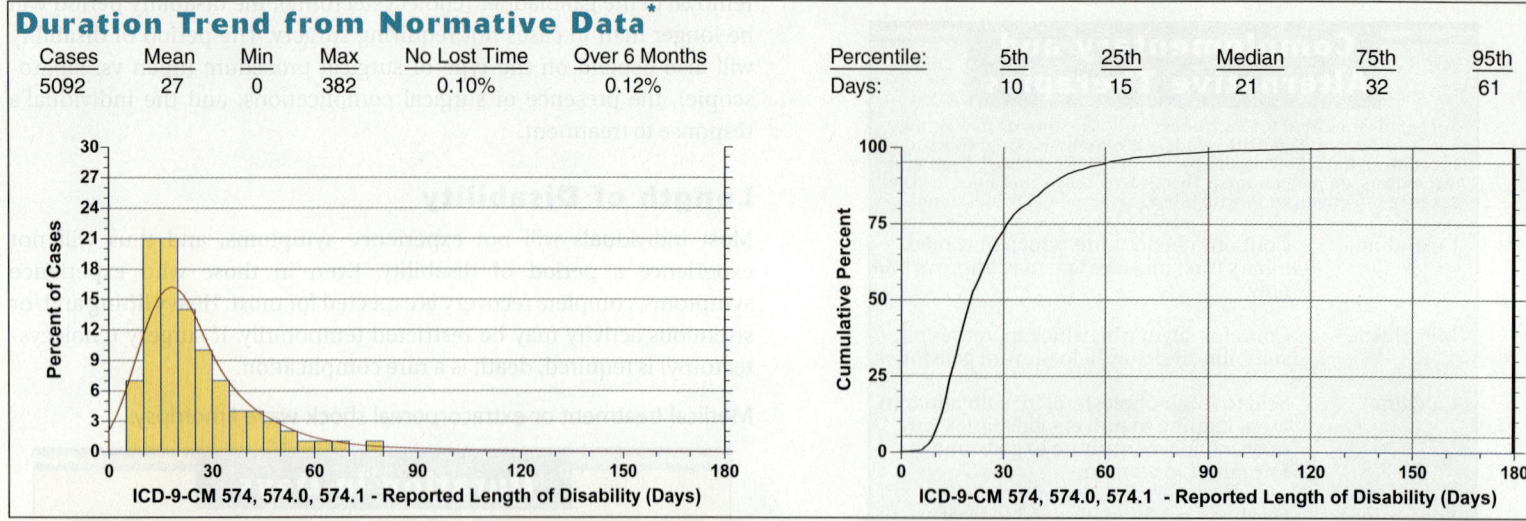

Cases	Mean	Min	Max	No Lost Time	Over 6 Months
5092	27	0	382	0.10%	0.12%

Percentile:	5th	25th	Median	75th	95th
Days:	10	15	21	32	61

* Differences may exist between the expected duration tables and the normative graphs. Duration tables provide expected recovery periods based on the type of work performed by the individual. The normative graphs reflect the actual observed experience of many individuals across the spectrum of physical conditions, in a variety of industries, and with varying levels of case management.

Failure to Recover

If an individual fails to recover within the maximum duration expectancy period, the reader may wish to reference the following questions to assist in better understanding the specifics of an individual's medical case.

Regarding diagnosis:

- Does the individual have obesity, pregnancy, use estrogen replacement therapy or oral contraceptives, a Western diet high in animal fats, a family history of gallstones, received long-term intravenous nutrition, or have artificial heart valves?
- Does the individual have short gut syndrome, inflammatory bowel disease, cirrhosis of the liver, sickle cell anemia, hereditary spherocytosis, biliary parasites, or childhood cancer?
- Did their pain begin abruptly after a large fatty meal?
- Was the pain in the right upper or middle abdomen? Did it radiate to the shoulder or back? Was it steady and intense, subsiding gradually over a period of time?
- Did the individual think it was indigestion?
- Did they have nausea and/or vomiting?
- Was the individual tender in the right upper abdomen?
- Was the gallbladder palpable?
- Did the individual have fever, tachycardia, or hypotension?
- Did the individual have an ultrasound and cholecystogram done?
- Have conditions with similar symptoms been ruled out?

Regarding treatment:

- Is the individual following a low-fat, low-cholesterol, and low-sugar diet?
- Is the individual at risk of complications from asymptomatic gallstones?
- Does the individual have calcium deposits outlining the wall of the gallbladder on x-ray?
- Has the individual had a cholecystectomy done?

Regarding prognosis:

- Did the individual have an open or laparoscopic procedure?
- Is the individual's employer able to accommodate any necessary restrictions?
- Does the individual have any conditions that could affect their recovery?
- Does the individual have any complications such as cholangitis?
- Do they have gallstone ileus?
- Do they have sepsis or pancreatitis?

References

Agarwal, M., et al. "An Ultrasonographic Evaluation of Gallbladder Emptying in Patients with Cholelithiasis." Journal of Clinical Gastroenterology 31 4 (2001): 309-313.

Berkow, Robert, Mark Beers, and Andrew Fletcher, eds. The Merck Manual of Medical Information. New York: Pocket Books, 1997.

Bruel, J. "Cholelithiasis and Choledocholithiasis: Diagnostic Imaging." Abdominal Imaging 26 1 (2001): 1-2.

Duke, James A. The Green Pharmacy. Emmaus, PA: Rodale Press, Inc, 1997.

Feinstein, Alice, ed. Healing with Vitamins. Emmaus, PA: Rodale Press, Inc, 1996.

Gottlieb, Bill, ed. New Choices in Natural Healing. Emmaus, PA: Rodale Press, Inc, 1995.

Millat, B., G. Decker, and A. Fingerhut. "Imaging of Cholelithiasis: What Does the Surgeon Need?" Abdominal Imaging 26 1 (2001): 3-6.

Rutledge, D., D. Jones, and R. Rege. "Consequences of Delay in Surgical Treatment of Biliary Disease." American Journal of Surgery 180 6 (2000): 466-469.

Santen, Sally, MD. Cholelithiasis. eMedicine.com. 12 Sep 2000. 24 Feb 2001 <http://www.emedicine.com/emerg/topic97.htm>.

Williams, Gary. "Cholelithiasis." Griffith's 5-minute Clinical Consult. Dambro, Mark, ed. Philadelphia: Lippincott, Williams & Wilkins, 2000. 228-229.

Choriocarcinoma

Other names / synonyms: Chorioblastoma, Chorioepithelioma, Chorionepithelioma, Invasive Hydatidiform Mole, Trophoblastic Tumor

181

Definition

Choriocarcinoma is a rare, rapidly growing, and potentially metastatic cancer that occurs when malignant cells develop from the chorion, a membrane that forms during pregnancy, which gives rise to the placenta.

Nearly 50% of all individuals who develop a choriocarcinoma have a previous history of a hydatidiform mole. A hydatidiform mole is a non-cancerous growth that results from an abnormal pregnancy in which grape-like cysts form instead of an embryo. Twenty-five percent of choriocarcinoma growths occur in the tissue that remains in the uterus after a full-term pregnancy, and 20-25% occur following an abortion (this includes spontaneous abortion, or miscarriage), a pregnancy that begins to develop in the fallopian tube (ectopic pregnancy), or genital tumor.

Other risk factors for choriocarcinoma include an incomplete abortion, maternal age beyond 40, low socioeconomic status, and a diet low in protein, folic acid, and/or carotene. In the US, choriocarcinoma occurs in one of every 40,000 pregnancies; the incidence is higher in Mexico and some Asian countries.

Diagnosis

History: The most common symptom is abnormal bleeding from the vagina, not associated with a menstrual period. The woman may have a history of previous hydatidiform mole, delivery of a normal pregnancy, an abortion, or termination of an ectopic pregnancy. If a woman is pregnant, and does not detect fetal movement at the expected gestational stage, choriocarcinoma should be considered.

Physical exam: During an internal (pelvic) examination, the uterus may exhibit bumps or an unusual size or shape. In pregnant women, the size from the top of the uterus (fundus) to the pubic bone is measured on every prenatal visit and compared to the average uterine size expected for the gestational age. If the physical examination shows the uterus to be significantly larger than would be expected for the age of the fetus, then multiple births, hydatidiform mole, choriocarcinoma, or other potential complications should be suspected. The woman may also show abnormal nipple discharge.

Tests: In a woman who is not pregnant, evidence of the hormone beta human chorionic gonadotropin (hCG) in the blood may be a sign of choriocarcinoma. The tumor may be seen by ultrasound imaging. A CT is done to detect potential metastatic tumor in other areas.

Treatment

Treatment depends on the stage of the disease at the time it is diagnosed. If surgical excision of the cancer is done, the entire uterus is generally removed (hysterectomy); this is followed by chemotherapy either alone or in conjunction with radiation therapy. Radiation therapy may also be done to other areas where the cancer has spread (metastasis). However, in early-stage cancer that has not spread (nonmetastatic), a woman of child-bearing age may consider chemotherapy alone in order to spare the uterus.

During treatment, serum levels of hCG are measured to evaluate the individual's response to treatment. In addition, liver and kidney functions are continuously monitored.

Prognosis

The prognosis for individuals with choriocarcinoma depends on the stage at which the condition is diagnosed. Prognosis is considered good if the associated pregnancy was recent, the blood level of the hormone beta hCG is low, and the disease has not spread to the liver or brain.

Since the condition is usually diagnosed early, the prognosis is generally favorable. Individuals whose disease has not spread (metastasized), and who are treated with chemotherapy, or a combination of chemotherapy and radiation therapy or surgery, can typically expect a 90% 5-year survival rate; the chance of relapse is rare. Eighty-seven percent of those individuals whose cancer has spread, and who are treated with chemotherapy and radiation can expect to achieve remission.

Differential Diagnosis

Other conditions with similar symptoms may include first trimester pregnancy, excess amniotic fluid (polyhydramnios), and other uterine malignancies.

Specialists

• Gynecologist	• Pathologist
• Obstetrician	• Radiation Oncologist
• Oncologist	

Work Restrictions / Accommodations

Chemotherapy can be debilitating, resulting in nausea, weakness, and fatigue. Extended time off may be required. When the individual returns, the work responsibilities may need to be primarily sedentary. Return to work may start with part-time hours, with slow transition to full-time. Women undergoing chemotherapy and/or radiation therapy may require leave from work to complete their treatments.

Comorbid Conditions

Comorbid conditions may include infection and immune system disorders.

Complications

Complications associated with choriocarcinoma are related to the possibility of the cancer spreading (metastasis). In individuals in whom the cancer has spread to the lungs, pneumonia is a common complication. The disease may also spread to the brain or other areas of the body.

Factors Influencing Duration

Factors influencing the length of disability include the woman's age, type and stage of disease at diagnosis, general condition of the individual, possibility of cancer recurrence, and development of complications.

Individuals who receive a combination of chemotherapy and radiation treatment will require a longer recuperation time.

Length of Disability

Duration depends on stage, grade, cell type, adjuvant chemotherapy or radiation therapy. Disability may be permanent.

Hysterectomy, radical (female).

Job Classification	Minimum	Optimum	Maximum
Sedentary work	42	49	56
Light work	56	63	70
Medium work	70	77	84
Heavy work	70	84	98
Very Heavy work	70	84	98

Duration in Days

Failure to Recover

If an individual fails to recover within the maximum duration expectancy period, the reader may wish to reference the following questions to assist in better understanding the specifics of an individual's medical case.

Regarding diagnosis:

- Does individual have abnormal bleeding from the vagina, not associated with a menstrual period?
- Does individual have a history of previous hydatidiform mole, delivery of a normal pregnancy, an abortion, or termination of an ectopic pregnancy?
- During an internal (pelvic) examination, did uterus exhibit bumps or an unusual size or shape?
- Was the hormone beta human chorionic gonadotropin (hCG) in the blood?
- Was diagnosis of choriocarcinoma confirmed through ultrasound imaging?
- Is there evidence of metastasis?
- What organs are involved?

Regarding treatment:

- If still an early-stage cancer that has not spread, has the woman considered chemotherapy alone in order to spare the uterus?
- Was a hysterectomy performed?
- Was chemotherapy effective?
- With metastatic disease, in addition to hysterectomy and chemotherapy, was radiation therapy applied to areas where the cancer has spread?

Regarding prognosis:

- At what stage was condition diagnosed?
- Although the prognosis is generally favorable if the condition is diagnosed early, how will treatment impact recovery and disability duration?
- Does individual have a coexisting condition that may complicate treatment or impact recovery?

References

OncoLink. University of Pennsylvania. 2000. 01 Jan 2001 <http://www.oncolink.upenn.edu/pdq/201163.html>.

National Library of Medicine. "Choriocarcinoma." MEDLINEplus. 2000. 01 Jan 2001 <http://medlineplus.adam.com/ency/article/001496.htm>.

Chorioretinitis

Other names / synonyms: Retinitis
363.20

Definition

Chorioretinitis is a general term often applied to inflammation of the light-sensitive layer on the back of the eye (retina) and the layer below that nourishes it (choroid). The disease may be associated with microorganisms causing general infection such as Toxoplasma gondii (toxoplasmosis). Chorioretinitis also may occur as a symptom of infections related to syphilis, cat scratch disease, histoplasmosis, tuberculosis, and other illnesses.

Chorioretinitis sometimes occurs in individuals susceptible to infections, including those with immune disorders or who take drugs that suppress immune responses after organ transplants. The disease may cause lesions, scarring, or damage to the retina resulting in a blind spot in the visual field (scotoma). In one study of individuals with AIDS, almost 3% were found to have chorioretinitis.

Diagnosis

History: Symptoms begin suddenly or gradually and may consist of blurred or decreased vision, sensitivity to light, and floating dark spots (floaters) in the visual field. Pain is usually absent or mild. If the untreated disease has progressed, blindness may result.

Physical exam: The exam may show a constricted or irregular pupil. Clouded regions in the gelatinous portions of the eyeball and light-colored patches may show evidence of lesions. If healing already has occurred, the lesions may manifest as scarred areas with abnormal pigmentation and possible blind spots in the visual field (scotoma).

Tests: Tests may include an examination through an illuminated instrument (ophthalmoscopy) that magnifies the eye's interior (fundus).

Treatment

Treatment varies according to the cause and may include antibiotic or antiviral drugs, corticosteroids, and use of a laser beam to destroy retinal hemorrhages (photocoagulation). If the vitreous becomes fibrous, suction or removal of affected tissue may be required (vitrectomy).

Prognosis

While treatment may cause the disease to regress, recurrences are possible. Permanent damage and accompanying vision loss could be significant if remissions continue. Useful vision tends to be retained in at least one eye, depending on the cause of the condition. The disease could last months or years. If the central portion of the retina (macula) is unaffected by the disease, complete visual recovery is probable. A serious complication such as retinal detachment, if untreatable, may cause total blindness.

Differential Diagnosis

Rubella, chloroquine toxicity, choroiditis, retinitis, uveitis, eye injury, retained intraocular foreign body, vascular occlusion, age-related macular degeneration, cataracts, pterygium, conjunctivitis, retinal detachment, and other eye infections may produce similar symptoms. Other diseases associated with chorioretinitis are tuberculosis, syphilis, immune disorders such as AIDS, Cushing's syndrome, Proteus syndrome, rheumatoid arthritis, toxoplasmosis, histoplasmosis, toxocariasis, sarcoidosis, pars planitis, sympathetic ophthalmia, and wrinkly skin syndrome.

Specialists

- Ophthalmologist

Work Restrictions / Accommodations

Vision will need to be evaluated periodically in relation to the individual's work requirements. The individual may be unable to drive, use machinery, or work at night. Sunlight and bright light may need to be avoided and frequent breaks may be required to give the individual the opportunity to close and rest the eyes. In some cases involving permanent damage, the individual may need magnification to aid vision.

Comorbid Conditions

Individuals with immune disorders such as AIDS or organ transplant recipients who are taking drugs that suppress the immune system may have difficulty recovering from chorioretinitis associated with infections.

Complications

Secondary glaucoma may occur. Swelling (edema) in the retina's central area (macula) along with retinal hemorrhages may cause retinal detachment. Viruses that might be the source of the disease may become resistant to antiviral medications. While corticosteroids may be needed to suppress the eye's inflammatory response and protect vision, these drugs also have been found to cause outbreaks of certain infections that may result in chorioretinitis.

Factors Influencing Duration

The underlying cause of the chorioretinitis, how fast the disease progresses, and the amount of possible permanent vision damage may affect recovery. Referrals to agencies for the visually impaired may be necessary to assist the individual experiencing disability.

Length of Disability

Individuals with permanent vision loss may be unable to perform certain tasks requiring visual acuity. Physical disability may be limited, but visual loss is permanent.

Duration in Days

Job Classification	Minimum	Optimum	Maximum
Sedentary work	7	10	14
Light work	7	10	14
Medium work	7	10	21
Heavy work	7	14	21
Very Heavy work	7	14	21

Failure to Recover

If an individual fails to recover within the maximum duration expectancy period, the reader may wish to reference the following questions to assist in better understanding the specifics of an individual's medical case.

Regarding diagnosis:

- Has individual had syphilis, cat scratch disease, histoplasmosis, tuberculosis, toxoplasmosis, or other illnesses?
- Is the individual immunocompromised?
- Has the individual noticed blurred or decreased vision? Photophobia? Floaters? Did it happen gradually or suddenly?
- Does individual have pain?
- Have conditions with similar symptoms been ruled out?
- Has the individual been tested for diseases associated with chorioretinitis?

Regarding treatment:

- Has the individual been treated with antibiotics? Antiviral drugs? Corticosteroids?
- Has the individual had laser photocoagulation?
- Was a vitrectomy necessary?
- Has the individual had a recurrence?
- Is the macula affected?
- Did retinal detachment occur?

Regarding prognosis:

- Can individual's employer accommodate any necessary restrictions?
- Does the individual have any conditions that may affect ability to recover?
- Has the individual developed glaucoma? Any other complications?
- If necessary, has the individual been referred to a low-vision specialist?

References

Parnell, Jeffrey R., and Lee M. Jampol. "Retinal Insider." *Review of Ophthalmology* May (1998): 6. 10 Oct 2000 <http://www.revophth.com>.

Poletti, J., A. Poletti, and S. Franzini. "Treatment by Acupuncture of Central Serous Chorioretinopathy." *Bulletin des Societies de Opthalmologie de France* 88 6-7 (1988): 917-919.

Chromoblastomycosis
Other names / synonyms: Chromomycosis, Dermatitis Verrucosa
117.2

Definition

Chromoblastomycosis is a chronic fungal infection (mycosis) of the skin.

Chromoblastomycosis is caused by a variety of darkly colored fungi found in wood, soil, and decaying vegetation. The infection is contracted when an individual is exposed to the fungi through a penetrating injury, such as stepping on a sliver of contaminated wood when barefooted. The infection typically affects the legs and feet, causing discomfort and disfigurement.

A disease of the tropics, chromoblastomycosis is found sporadically among agricultural workers in Central America, Caribbean Islands, South Pacific Islands, Australia, Japan, Madagascar, and Africa. Occasional cases have been reported in the southern US. Rare in women, the disease is most common in men between ages 30 and 50.

Diagnosis

History: Individuals may report a small pink papule or ulcer on the skin that becomes a spreading lesion. For some individuals and over a period of months to years, it may spread to surrounding tissues, becoming large, purplish, and wart-like. The lesion may eventually interfere with lymph circulation, causing an accumulation of fluid in the leg. This sometimes results in a massive enlargement of the leg (elephantiasis). Often the lesion will have been present for a long time until disfigurement, swelling, or a secondary bacteria infection prompts the individual to see a physician.

Physical exam: A large wart-like (verrucous) or irregular flat (annular) lesion is observed on the skin. The lesion may be tender to touch, but is usually painless. Satellite lesions may be seen surrounding the original lesion. Often the lesion will be draining pus (purulent material). Signs of secondary bacteria infection may be evident. The individual should be otherwise healthy.

Tests: Preliminary identification of the fungus can be made through microscopic examinations of skin scrapings, using potassium hydroxide (KOH) as the chemical reagent. A fungal culture of the skin scraping can also be performed to confirm the identification of the fungus responsible. Return of results from a culture may take 4 to 6 weeks.

Treatment

Surgical removal (excision) of a small early lesion is the best treatment choice. More advanced cases are treated with one or a combination of antifungal drugs taken for 4 to 6 weeks. Physical treatments have been used with some success and include heat, cold (cryotherapy), electric current (electrosurgery), and radiation therapy.

Elephantiasis may improve following drainage of accumulated fluid and the surgical removal of excess fatty and fibrous tissue (debulking surgery). Good hygiene is vital in the management of elephantiasis. The affected area should be washed twice daily with soap and water and raised at night. Shoes should be worn and nails kept clean and trimmed at all times. Small wounds, cuts, or scratches should be treated with antiseptic or antibiotic creams. Counseling may be needed to handle the psychological and social stresses associated with this condition.

Prognosis

Chromomycosis is a chronic infection very resistant to treatment. Only a little over half the individuals respond to treatment. The remainder continue to have long-term residual infection.

Lymphatic swelling, caught early, will resolve with treatment of the infection. Swelling that has advanced to elephantiasis may be irreversible. If the affected area is kept free of bacterial or fungal infection, other nearby lymph vessels can sometimes successfully reestablish lymph flow, decreasing the amount of tissue damage and disfigurement. Debulking surgery where excess tissue is removed may also be successful in reducing disfigurement.

Differential Diagnosis

Conditions with similar symptoms include blastomycosis, yaws, tertiary syphilis, tuberculosis verruca cutis, leishmaniasis, mycetoma, sporotrichosis, squamous cell carcinoma, and leprosy.

Specialists

- Dermatologist
- General Surgeon
- Infectious Disease Physician
- Plastic Surgeon

Work Restrictions / Accommodations

If the individual has severe lymphatic swelling in a leg (elephantiasis), transfer to a job that requires no standing or prolonged walking may be required. If surgical excision is performed, extended disability leave may be necessary for recovery.

The infection is not spread from individual to individual, so interpersonal on-the-job infection control measures are not required.

Comorbid Conditions

Any condition that prolongs wound healing or interferes with circulation in the lower extremities, such as diabetes or peripheral vascular disease, may delay healing and prolong disability.

Complications

Complications include secondary bacterial infection and massive swelling of an extremity due to blocked lymphatic vessels (elephantiasis). Rarely, the infection may spread to an internal organ, such as the pancreas, liver, bowel, or brain. Skin cancer may develop in longstanding lesions. The disfigurement associated with elephantiasis has profound psychological and social consequences.

Factors Influencing Duration

Factors include the extent and severity of the disease, treatment used, or presence of complications.

Length of Disability

Duration in Days

Job Classification	Minimum	Optimum	Maximum
Any work	3	7	14

Failure to Recover

If an individual fails to recover within the maximum duration expectancy period, the reader may wish to reference the following questions to assist in better understanding the specifics of an individual's medical case.

Regarding diagnosis:

- Where does individual live? Central America, Caribbean Islands, South Pacific Islands, Australia, Japan, Madagascar, Africa, or the US?
- Did individual have a lesion on the foot or leg that spread?
- Does individual have elephantiasis? Secondary bacterial infections?
- On physical exam, was a large wart-like lesion observed? Satellite lesions? Was the lesion purulent?
- Did individual have skin scrapings done? KOH prep? Culture?
- Were conditions with similar symptoms ruled out?

Regarding treatment:

- Was the lesion small? Was it surgically removed? Or was the lesion larger?
- Is individual on antifungal drugs? For how long?
- Have heat or cryotherapy been used? Electrosurgery? Radiation?
- Was debulking surgery done?
- Does individual understand the importance of good hygiene to manage the disease?
- If needed, is individual in counseling?

Regarding prognosis:

- Can individual's employer accommodate any necessary restrictions?
- Does individual have any conditions that may affect ability to recover?
- Has the infection spread to an internal organ?

References

Lymphedema: A Brief Overview. National Lymphedema Network. 2000. 18 Aug 2000 <http://www.lymphnet.org/whatis.html>.

Mandell, Gerald, John Bennett, and Raphael Dolin. Principles and Practice of Infectious Diseases, 5th ed. Philadelphia: Churchill Livingstone, 2000.

Chronic Fatigue Syndrome
780.71

Definition

Considerable controversy continues to surround the cause (etiology), definition, diagnosis and treatment of persons with this disorder.

Chronic Fatigue Syndrome (CFS) is a label applied to persons who report severe chronic fatigue out of proportion to their efforts. The label CFS implies that a major component is the symptom of chronic fatigue and not the fatigue associated with serious medical illness, sleep problems or life stresses. Only a small fraction of persons who report chronic fatigue symptoms meet the criteria for CFS.

There is no known cause for CFS. Based on available evidence to date, there is no convincing evidence that CFS is an infectious disorder, a neuroendocrine disorder or an immunologic disorder. The primary task for the physician is to exclude known and treatable conditions as the cause for the chronic fatigue symptoms. Chronic fatigue itself is not CFS.

Diagnosis

History: CFS implies that: 1) there is an unexplained persistent or relapsing post-exertional fatigue of at least 6 months duration, 2) the fatigue is of new or definite onset, 3) the fatigue is out of proportion to an ongoing exertional effort, 4) the fatigue is not substantially alleviated by rest, 5) it results in substantial reduction in previous levels of activities of daily living.

In addition, four or more of the following symptoms must begin after the onset of fatigue and be present concurrently with the period of fatigue: 1) self-reported difficulty with memory or concentration leading to self limitation in previous levels of activities of daily living, 2) sensation of sore throat, 3) tender lymph nodes, 4) widespread nonanatomic muscle pain, 5) multijoint pain without joint swelling or redness, 6) headache, 7) nonrestorative sleep, 8) post-exertional malaise lasting more than 24 hours.

Physical exam: The physical examination is normal.

Tests: There is no test(s) that confirms the diagnosis of CFS. Routing laboratory testing is reserved for ruling out other medical conditions.

The diagnosis based on the above criteria should only be established after there has been a complete history and physical examination with appropriate diagnostic studies to exclude other conditions that may be diagnosed to explain the symptoms. In the absence of other concurrent medical conditions suggested by history, physical examination or routine laboratory testing, the diagnosis of CFS is based on the person's self-report.

Treatment

There is no specific treatment for CFS.

Psychologic symptoms are often associated with CFS. Hence, cognitive and behavioral interventions may be useful in the treatment of CFS; for example, education, counseling and a structured plan to increase physical and social activity. Medication treatment is reserved for specific symptoms indicative of depression or anxiety.

The following therapies have not been validated through adequately designed controlled trials, may have unwanted side effects, may serve to reinforce counterproductive behaviors and are not recommended for the treatment of CFS: antifungal and antiviral agents, thyroid hormone supplement, intravenous immunoglobulins and low-dose steroid therapy.

Prognosis

The prognosis for individuals with this disorder is unknown because there are no scientifically valid outcome studies upon which to base an opinion regarding prognosis.

Differential Diagnosis

Other conditions that may be diagnosed to explain the symptoms of CFS include: eating disorders (anorexia nervosa, bulimia nervosa), major depressive disorder (MDD), neurally-mediated hypotension, preoccupation with physical discomfort (somatoform disorder), bipolar disorder, schizophrenia, delusional disorders, seasonal affective disorder (SAD), obsessive-compulsive disorder, Cushing syndrome, dementia, sleeping disorders (sleep apnea), breathing disorders (hypoxia, hypercapnia), myalgic encephalomyelitis, Lyme disease, Addison's disease, hypothyroidism, hyperthyroidism, diabetes mellitus, hepatitis B, hepatitis C, alcohol or substance abuse, AIDS, tuberculosis, anemia, endocarditis, rheumatoid arthritis, systemic lupus erythematosus, endocrine disorders, neuromuscular disorders, malignancy, metabolic/nutritional disorder, and immune or inflammatory disease.

Specialists

- Internist
- Primary Care Provider
- Psychiatrist
- Psychologist

Work Restrictions / Accommodations

Individuals with this disorder have no identifiable objective medical basis for their symptoms; that is, individuals with this disorder report symptoms but have normal physical examinations and normal findings on diagnostic testing. Consequently, there is no objective medical basis upon which to predicate work restrictions or accommodations.

Comorbid Conditions

Comorbid conditions include obesity and psychiatric disorders (affective or anxiety disorders, psychoses or somatoform disorders).

Complications

Complications can arise from treatment (i.e., unwanted side effects or reinforcement of counterproductive behaviors) or from the person's behavior (i.e., self-limitation of physical activities leading to deconditioning and increased fatigue with exertion).

Factors Influencing Duration

The factors influencing duration of disability are unknown because there are no scientifically valid studies that have determined the factors influencing duration of disability in this disorder.

Length of Disability

Although individuals with this disorder may self-limit their work and social activities, there may be no objective medical basis for disability. This is a controversial diagnosis. Contact physician for more information.

Failure to Recover

If an individual fails to recover within the maximum duration expectancy period, the reader may wish to reference the following questions to assist in better understanding the specifics of an individual's medical case.

Regarding diagnosis:

- Does individual have an unexplained persistent or relapsing post-exertional fatigue of at least 6 months duration? Is the fatigue of new or definite onset? Is fatigue out of proportion to an ongoing exertional effort? Does rest not substantially alleviate fatigue?

- Does fatigue result in substantial reduction in previous levels of activities of daily living?

- After onset of fatigue, does individual have difficulty with memory or concentration leading to self-limitation in previous levels of activities of daily living? Does individual have the sensation of sore throat? Tender lymph nodes? Is there widespread nonanatomic muscle pain? Multi-joint pain without joint swelling or redness? Headache? Non-restorative sleep? Post-exertional malaise lasting more than 24 hours?

- Have alternative diagnoses been investigated?

Regarding treatment:

- Have unproven treatments resulted in unwanted side effects?
- Have treatment methods reinforced counterproductive behaviors?

- Were cognitive and behavioral interventions employed?

Regarding prognosis:

- Were psychosocial factors such as family and workplace dynamics considered?

References

Ensalada, L.H. "The Importance of Illness Behavior in Disability Management." In Randolph, D.C., and M.I., eds. Occupational Medicine State of the Art Reviews: Risk and Disability Evaluation in the Workplace. Philadelphia: Hanley & Belfus, October/December 2000.

Farrar, D.J., S.E. Locke, and F.G. Kantrowitz. "Chronic Fatigue Syndrome 1: Etiology and Pathogenesis." Behav Med; 21 (1995):5-16.

Fukuda, K., et al. "The Chronic Fatigue Syndrome: A Comprehensive Approach to its Definition and Study." Ann Internal Med 121 12,15 (1994):953-9.

Hadler, N.M. "Fibromyalgia, Chronic Fatigue, and Other Iatrogenic Diagnostic Algorithms. Do Some Labels Escalate Illness in Vulnerable Patients?" Postgrad Med 102 2 (1997):171-2.

Position Paper: Chronic Fatigue Syndrome: Impairment and Disability Issues. American Academy of Disability Evaluating Physicians. May 1999.

The Facts about Chronic Fatigue Syndrome. Centers for Disease Control and Prevention. Atlanta, GA: National Center for Infectious Diseases., March 1995.

Chronic Obstructive Pulmonary Disease

Other names / synonyms: Asthma, CAO, Chronic Airway Obstruction, Chronic Bronchitis, COPD, Emphysema

496

Definition

Chronic obstructive pulmonary disease (COPD) is comprised primarily of two related diseases -- chronic bronchitis and emphysema. In both diseases, chronic obstruction of the flow of air through the airways and out of the lungs occurs and the obstruction is generally permanent and progressive over time. Asthma is also a pulmonary disease where obstruction to the flow of air out of the lungs occurs. Unlike chronic bronchitis and emphysema, however, the obstruction in asthma is usually reversible. Between attacks of asthma, the flow of air through the airways is usually good.

In some individuals with COPD, the obstruction can be partially reversed by medications that enlarge or dilate the airways (bronchodilators) as with asthma. Conversely, some individuals with asthma can develop permanent airway obstruction if chronic inflammation of the airways leads to scarring and narrowing of the airways. A frequent overlap among individuals with COPD also occurs. Individuals with emphysema may have some of the characteristics of chronic bronchitis. Similarly, individuals with chronic bronchitis may also have some of the characteristics of emphysema.

Since emphysema and chronic bronchitis often occur together and overlap, some experts prefer the name chronic obstructive pulmonary disease (COPD) rather than either chronic bronchitis or emphysema. Currently, COPD affects at least 16 million Americans with more than 100,000 deaths annually.

Smoking is responsible for 90% of COPD in the US. Although not all cigarette smokers develop COPD, an estimated 15% will. Current smokers with COPD have higher death rates than ex-smokers with COPD. More frequent respiratory symptoms such as coughing and shortness of breath occur and more deterioration is seen in lung function than for ex-smokers. Effects of passive smoking or second-hand smoke on the lungs are not well quantified.

Air pollution can cause problems for individuals with lung disease, but it is unclear whether air pollution contributes to the development of COPD. Some occupational pollutants such as cadmium and silica do increase the risk of COPD. Individuals at risk for this type of occupational pollution include coal miners, construction workers, metal workers, and cotton workers.

Another well-established cause of COPD is a deficiency of alpha-1 antitrypsin (AAT). AAT deficiency is a rare genetic (inherited) disorder that accounts for less than 1% of the COPD in the US. Normal function of the lung is dependent on elastic fibers surrounding the airways and in the alveolar walls. Elastic fibers are composed of a protein called elastin. An enzyme called elastase in the lungs (higher in cigarette smokers) can break down the elastin and damage the airways and alveoli. Another protein called alpha-1 antitrypsin (AAT) produced by the liver and released into the blood is present in normal lungs and can block the damaging effects of elastase on elastin.

In the US, approximately 8 million individuals have chronic bronchitis and 2 million have emphysema. COPD is the fourth leading cause of death in the US and affects 32 million adults. COPD occurs more predominantly in individuals older than 40.

Diagnosis

History: Individuals with COPD present with a combination of signs and symptoms of chronic bronchitis, emphysema, and asthma. Symptoms include worsening shortness of breath with exertion (dyspnea), cough, wheezing, and frequent colds.

Physical exam: The exam in emphysema usually reveals a chest permanently resembling the shape of a barrel (barrel chest), rapid and labored breathing, rapid heart rate (tachycardia), and normal skin color. Breath sounds are faint. Individuals with chronic bronchitis have less distressed breathing but the skin may appear blue. Unique breath sounds with a musical-type pitch indicate secretions or inflammation in the airways (rhonchi).

Tests: Chronic obstructive pulmonary disease is specifically diagnosed by pulmonary function tests (PFTs). Simple measurement of air flow (spirometry) can be done in the doctor's office to confirm COPD. The diagnosis, classification of severity, prognosis, and guidance of treatment is determined by a complete PFT done in a standardized PFT laboratory. Blood gas analysis is another indicator of severity of disease.

A chest x-ray can also provide information on the severity of COPD. Serum chemistry and a complete blood count (CBC) may also be done.

Treatment

The general treatment goals for COPD are to optimize lung function, slow down or stop disease progression, prevent acute flare-ups and complications, and maintain quality of life. Specific treatment includes smoking cessation, bronchodilators, antibiotics, supplemental oxygen, and occasionally corticosteroids. Certain treatments may be used chronically and others may be added during acute worsening or infections. A few individuals may be candidates for surgical removal (wedge resection) of large bubble-like structures (bullae) or for lung transplantation.

Prognosis

If smoking is stopped during the early stages of COPD, some of the damage in the small airways may return to normal. Individuals with mild COPD treated early may be free of disability. Individuals with severe COPD will continue to have progressively deteriorating lung function despite treatment and usually become permanently disabled.

The individual's age and postbronchodilator forced expiratory volume in one second (FEV1) are the most important predictors of prognosis. Young age and FEV1 greater than 50% have a predicted good prognosis. Older individuals and those with more severe lung disease do worse. Supplemental oxygen (when indicated) has been shown to increase survival. Smoking cessation improves prognosis. Increase in size (hypertrophy) of the right ventricle in the heart (cor pulmonale), abnormally increased arterial carbon dioxide tension (hypercapnia), rapid heartbeat (tachycardia), and malnutrition indicate a poor prognosis.

Differential Diagnosis

Other conditions with some similarities are pneumonia, a tumor of the throat or lungs, acute bronchitis, bronchiectasis, asthma, allergies, occupational lung disease, heart disease, cystic fibrosis, sarcoidosis, pulmonary fibrosis, pulmonary emboli, and pulmonary edema.

Specialists

- Internist
- Pulmonologist

Rehabilitation

Pulmonary rehabilitation combines exercise training and behavioral and educational programs designed to help individuals with COPD control symptoms and improve day-to-day activities. Individuals work closely with their doctors, nurses, psychologists, exercise specialists, dietitians, and respiratory, physical, and occupational therapists. Pulmonary rehabilitation helps reduce the number and length of hospital stays and increases the chances of living longer. Pulmonary rehabilitation involves exercise training of the lower body, upper body, and ventilatory muscle. It also includes psychosocial support and educational programs.

Since smoking is the primary risk factor for the onset and worsening of COPD, many pulmonary rehabilitation programs provide educational sessions and counseling to help individuals stop smoking.

Work Restrictions / Accommodations

Individuals with COPD should avoid inhaled irritants in the workplace such as gases, fumes, and dust. Very cold or hot air temperatures should also be avoided. Work at higher altitudes may be discouraged with moderate or severe COPD. Tolerance for physical exertion may be limited with COPD. If individuals with an asthmatic component to their COPD have an acute attack while working, they should be given time to take inhaled medication and rest, and then evaluated for ability to continue working.

Comorbid Conditions

Pre-existing heart disease, asthma, or allergies may lengthen disability.

Complications

The two most serious complications of COPD are right-sided heart failure (cor pulmonale) and respiratory failure. If the impairment is severe enough, the individual may succumb to respiratory failure. Most COPD individuals recover from their first few episodes of respiratory failure. However, episodes of respiratory failure that occur more frequently are signs of the last stages of this chronic disease. Some COPD individuals develop single or multiple large, irregular-shaped air spaces called bullae. These bullae can be large enough to compromise good portions of the lung by crowding and compressing them. They can also break, causing an accumulation of air in the chest cavity (pneumothorax) that further compromises pulmonary function. Increased blood pressure in the lung (pulmonary hypertension) and malnutrition are sometimes complications of COPD.

Factors Influencing Duration

Factors include type of COPD, severity of the disease when treatment began, current severity of COPD, individual's compliance with treatment protocols, age of the individual, existence of other chronic medical conditions or complications, frequency of acute flare-ups, and working and living environments. Exposure to secondhand smoke, occupational exposure to irritants, air pollution levels, and physical condition may all influence disability and the ability to recover.

Length of Disability

Disability duration will be determined by specific diagnosis. Disability is more likely to occur with acute exacerbations. Disability may be permanent.

Acute exacerbations.

Duration in Days

Job Classification	Minimum	Optimum	Maximum
Sedentary work	5	7	Indefinite
Light work	5	7	Indefinite
Medium work	5	10	Indefinite
Heavy work	5	14	Indefinite
Very Heavy work	5	14	Indefinite

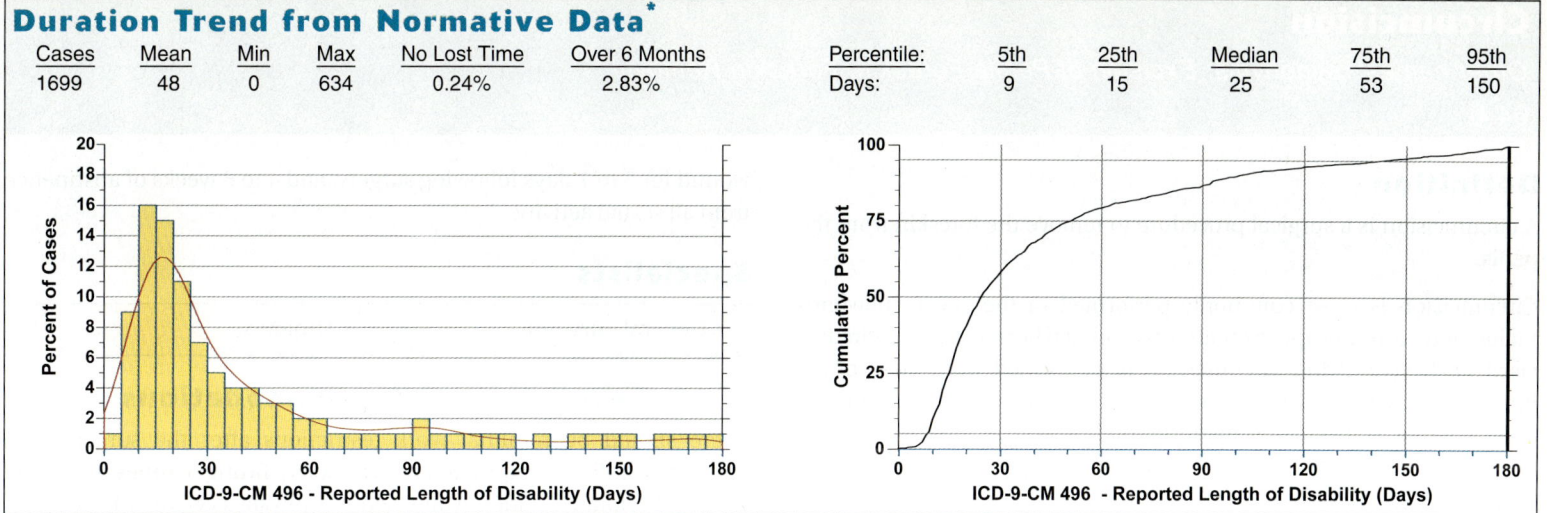

* Differences may exist between the expected duration tables and the normative graphs. Duration tables provide expected recovery periods based on the type of work performed by the individual. The normative graphs reflect the actual observed experience of many individuals across the spectrum of physical conditions, in a variety of industries, and with varying levels of case management.

Failure to Recover

If an individual fails to recover within the maximum duration expectancy period, the reader may wish to reference the following questions to assist in better understanding the specifics of an individual's medical case.

Regarding diagnosis:

- Does individual have a history of smoking? If so, how much has individual smoked and for how long?
- Was individual exposed to cadmium or silica including occupations such as coal mining, construction work, or metal or cotton work?
- Although rare, does individual have a deficiency of the protein alpha-1 antitrypsin (AAT)?
- Does individual complain of shortness of breath with exertion (dyspnea), progressive exercise limitation, or alteration in mental status? Is there coughing wheezing, excess body fluids (plethora), or frequent colds?
- Does individual have a barrel-shaped chest?
- Were pulmonary function tests (PFTs) and/or spirometry done? Were arterial blood gases (ABGs), blood chemistry, and a complete blood count (CBC) performed? Was a chest x-ray obtained? What did all test results reveal?
- Was the diagnosis of COPD confirmed?

Regarding treatment:

- Has individual completely stopped smoking? If not, was individual urged to participate in a smoking cessation program?
- Has individual participated in a pulmonary rehabilitation program?
- Were bronchodilators, antibiotics, supplemental oxygen, and corticosteroids administered, as needed?
- Is individual compliant with the medication regimen?
- Is individual a candidate for surgical removal (wedge resection) of large bubble-like structures (bullae)?
- Is individual a candidate for lung surgery or transplantation? Would individual benefit from consultation with a specialist (transplant surgeon)?

Regarding prognosis:

- How advanced is the disease?
- Has individual completely stopped smoking? Was smoking stopped and treatment begun during the early stages of COPD?
- Is individual's postbronchodilator forced expiratory volume in one second (FEV1) better, worse, or the same?
- Has individual developed right-sided heart failure (cor pulmonale), abnormally increased arterial carbon dioxide tension (hypercapnia), malnutrition, or respiratory failure?
- Is this the first episode of respiratory failure or is it a recurrence, suggesting late stage disease?
- Has pneumothorax occurred, further compromising pulmonary function? How severely is pulmonary function compromised? How will this affect the ability of individual to function?
- Has individual developed increased blood pressure in the lung (pulmonary hypertension)?

References

Around the Clock with COPD (Chronic Obstructive Pulmonary Disease). American Lung Association. 2000. 05 Dec 2000 <http://www.lungusa.org/diseases/copd_clock.html>.

Staton, J.R., and G.W. Ingram, Jr., RH. "Chronic Obstructive Diseases of the Lung." Scientific American® Medicine Online Dale, D.C., and D.D. Federman New York: WebMD Corporation, 2000 Scientific American Medicine. 05 Dec 2000 <http://www.samed.com/sam/forms/index/htm>.

Circumcision

Other names / synonyms: Excision of Penile Foreskin, Foreskin Removal

64.0

Definition

A circumcision is a surgical procedure to remove the foreskin from the penis.

Circumcision is most commonly performed in the US on newborn males, and currently approximately 60% of newborn males are circumcised each year. Adult circumcision is performed much less often; however, accurate incidence rates are not available. The reasons for adult circumcision include medical conditions (e.g., disorders of the foreskin) and nonmedical issues, including social, religious, or personal reasons.

Reason for Procedure

The most common medical reasons for adult circumcision are tightness of the foreskin that prevents its retraction over the head of the penis (phimosis) and the inability to position the foreskin back over the head of the penis after retraction (paraphimosis), which is a urologic emergency. Other medical reasons for adult circumcision include recurrent inflammation of the glans of the penis (balanitis) and of the foreskin (posthitis), cancer of the penis, tears in the fold of skin on the underside of the penis (frenulum), and genital warts (condylomata) on the foreskin. Common nonmedical reasons for elective circumcision include social, religious, or personal reasons.

How Procedure Is Performed

Adult circumcision is usually performed as an outpatient procedure under local anesthesia, which entails a dorsal penile nerve block, with or without a ring block. The individual may be administered an antianxiety drug (such as diazepam) as well. The foreskin is then surgically removed using a dorsal slit technique (most common in individuals with phimosis or paraphimosis), a ventral slit technique, or a sleeve technique (which is also used in children). The wound is then sutured, and a dressing of petroleum jelly or petroleum gauze and sterile white gauze may be applied over the sutures.

Prognosis

The outcome is very good to excellent in most cases, and full recovery can be expected. Full recovery generally requires daily cleaning of the wound for 5 to 7 days following surgery, and 4 to 6 weeks of abstinence from all sexual activity.

Specialists

- General Surgeon
- Urologist

Work Restrictions / Accommodations

There should be minimal work restrictions after the surgery. The individual will be required to wear loose-fitting clothes following surgery. Prolonged standing and vigorous physical activity may need to be temporarily avoided.

Comorbid Conditions

Individuals with diabetes have a higher risk of postoperative infection, which could prolong recovery time.

Procedure Complications

Possible complications of adult circumcision include bleeding, wound infection, collection of blood at the incisional site (hematoma), swelling, pain, poor cosmetic appearance, tearing of the sutures due to erection before complete healing, complications from the anesthetic, changes in sensation during intercourse, and urethral injury.

Factors Influencing Duration

Complications from the procedure such as hemorrhage, infection, and urethral damage may increase the length of disability.

Length of Disability

Most men are able to return to work the day after surgery.

Duration in Days

Job Classification	Minimum	Optimum	Maximum
Any work	1	3	7

References

Choe, Jong, and Hye Kim. Phimosis, Adult Circumcision and Buried Penis. eMedicine.com. 01 Jan 2000. 15 Jan 2001 < http://emedicine.com/med/topic2873.htm>.

Holman, J., and Keith Stuessi. Adult Circumcision. American Academy of Family Physicians. 15 Mar 1999. 15 Jan 2001 <http://www.aafp.org/afp/990315ap/1514.html>.

Cirrhosis of the Liver

Other names / synonyms: Cryptogenic Cirrhosis of Liver, Macronodular Cirrhosis, Portal Cirrhosis, Post-Hepatic Cirrhosis, Postnecrotic Cirrhosis

571.5, 571.6, 571.8, 571.9

Definition

Cirrhosis is a chronic liver disease characterized by the progressive and irreversible destruction of liver tissue.

When exposed to an infectious agent, alcohol, or other toxic substances, liver cells may be killed faster than they can be replaced. Connective tissue cells then replace the liver cells, causing the liver to initially increase in size to compensate for the loss of function. If the scar tissue formation continues, however, the liver is unable to compensate adequately and may shrink in size.

There are numerous forms of cirrhosis that are distinguished by the known or suspected cause, the tissue changes observed in liver biopsies, and the symptoms that an individual exhibits. Cirrhosis occurs as a result of viral infection, chronic exposure to alcohol, drugs, or toxic substance, or in association with another disease. Alcohol-induced cirrhosis is the most common type, occurring in nearly 15% of alcoholics. Cryptogenic or post-hepatic cirrhosis occurs following some cases of infection with the hepatitis B or hepatitis C virus. The cause of primary biliary cirrhosis, which involves the inflammation of tiny ducts that carry bile within the liver, is unknown. It tends to affect women between the ages of 35 and 60. Cirrhosis may also result from the accumulation of excessive amounts of either iron (hemochromatosis) or copper (Wilson's disease) within the liver or as a result of a congenital error of metabolism, as in alpha-1-antitrypsin enzyme deficiency.

At least 30,000 deaths per year in the US can be attributed to cirrhosis of the liver. Additionally, the liver cancer associated with some types of cirrhosis accounts for another 10,000 deaths annually. The overall incidence of cirrhosis in the US is 360 per 100,000 population, or approximately 900,000 total individuals.

Diagnosis

History: The different forms of cirrhosis share many clinical signs and symptoms. Individuals may report loss of appetite, abdominal pain, weight loss, yellowing of the skin (jaundice), water retention (edema, ascites), and spider veins. Other signs and symptoms are unique to the type of cirrhosis.

Males with alcoholic cirrhosis may report an increase in breast size (gynecomastia) and a decrease in testicular size (testicular atrophy). Females may report menstrual irregularities or the complete cessation of menstruation (amenorrhea).

Physical exam: In primary biliary cirrhosis, the physical examination may be completely normal early on in the course of the disease. However, as the disease progresses, physical examination may reveal findings common to cirrhosis of all causes. These include increased skin pigmentation, intense itching (pruritus), dark urine, soft yellow spots of fat accumulation on the eyelids (xanthelasmas and xanthomas), an enlarged liver and spleen, and increased tissue at the end of the fingers (clubbing). Up to 40% of individuals with cirrhosis have no symptoms (asymptomatic), and the cirrhosis is discovered on routine examination or autopsy.

Tests: In all cases, definitive diagnosis requires a liver biopsy in which a small piece of liver tissue is removed and examined microscopically for signs of inflammation, scarring, or infection. Other tests that may be performed include obtaining a complete blood count (CBC), measuring key liver enzymes, folate and vitamin B12 levels, serum chemistries, viral antibodies, serum immunoglobulin levels, and antibodies to DNA, smooth muscle, and mitochondria. Cholangiography (a procedure used to visualize the gallbladder duct and determine whether an obstruction is present) may be recommended for those individuals suspected of having primary biliary cirrhosis.

Treatment

Treatment is largely dependent upon the cause of the cirrhosis. Some methods of treating cirrhosis, regardless of the underlying cause, include dietary restrictions, such as placing an individual on a low-protein diet, supplementation with vitamins A, K, and D, and salt restrictions to reduce problems associated with fluid retention (ascites, edema). Individuals with alcoholic cirrhosis will be instructed to stop drinking alcohol. Individuals with primary biliary cirrhosis may be treated with antihistamines to relieve symptoms of itching and anti-inflammatory drugs, such as corticosteroids. In addition, liver transplants may be recommended for individuals with end-stage liver disease and ascites.

Prognosis

Although cirrhotic liver damage is permanent and irreversible, treatment is usually successful in prolonging life, decreasing morbidity, and preventing complications. Survival is a function of the severity of liver disease. Most individuals with cirrhosis will develop increasing jaundice, weakness, ascites, and portal hypertension within 5 years of diagnosis. Individuals with alcoholic cirrhosis who stop drinking have a 5-year survival rate of 60%, while those who continue to drink have a 5-year survival rate of only 40 percent. Individuals with advanced alcoholic cirrhosis typically die sooner.

Individuals with primary biliary cirrhosis die within 5-10 years of diagnosis. After 5 years, approximately 67% are still alive. Individuals not exhibiting symptoms generally survive longer.

Differential Diagnosis

Differential diagnoses include other causes of liver cell injury, idiopathic portal hypertension, schistosomiasis, and congenital hepatic fibrosis.

Specialists

- Gastroenterologist
- General Surgeon
- Hepatologist
- Internist

Work Restrictions / Accommodations

Extended work leave, transfer to sedentary work, and increased rest periods may be needed and will require consideration on an individual, case-by-case basis. Since the condition is progressive, these individuals may need increasingly longer periods of time off and may have frequent hospitalizations. Eventually, most individuals will need to be on permanent disability status and will be unable to work.

Complementary and Alternative Therapies

Content is intended for awareness only. Treatments may or may not be effective. Scientific evidence may be lacking and some substances have potentially toxic effects. Dr. Presley Reed and the editors do not endorse the use of these therapies in the absence of consultation with a licensed medical professional.

Silybum marianum - May exert antioxidative, anti lipid peroxidative, antifibrotic, anti-inflammatory, immunomodulating, and liver-regenerating effects.

Comorbid Conditions

Advanced age, debilitation, poor nutritional status, cardiac diseases, and renal diseases may lengthen disability.

Complications

Almost all forms of cirrhosis are associated with portal hypertension, esophageal bleeding, enlarged spleen, fluid retention (ascites and edema), and coma. Other complications may include portal vein thrombosis (blood clot formation), the development of liver tumors, altered drug metabolism, spontaneous bacterial peritonitis, in which fluid accumulating within the abdomen becomes infected, and hepatic encephalopathy, in which the brain is poisoned by high blood levels of certain metabolic byproducts.

Factors Influencing Duration

Factors include the severity and extent of disease at the time of diagnosis, the type of cirrhosis and underlying cause, the age and general health of the individual upon initial diagnosis, and the development of complications, such as bleeding, blood flow impairment through the portal vein, which serves the liver (portal hypertension), ascites, and inflammation of the pancreas (pancreatitis). Many of these individuals will be unable to work.

Length of Disability

Disability may be permanent.

Medical treatment.

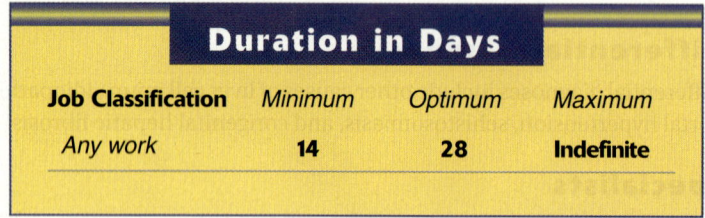

Duration in Days

Job Classification	Minimum	Optimum	Maximum
Any work	14	28	Indefinite

Failure to Recover

If an individual fails to recover within the maximum duration expectancy period, the reader may wish to reference the following questions to assist in better understanding the specifics of an individual's medical case.

Regarding diagnosis:

- Does individual report loss of appetite, abdominal pain, weight loss, yellowing of the skin (jaundice), water retention (edema, ascites), and spider veins?
- If male, has the breast size increased (gynecomastia) and the testicular size decreased (testicular atrophy)? If female, are there menstrual irregularities or the complete cessation of menstruation (amenorrhea)?
- Does individual have increased skin pigmentation, intense itching (pruritus), dark urine, soft yellow spots of fat accumulation on the eyelids (xanthelasmas and xanthomas), an enlarged liver and spleen, and increased tissue at the end of the fingers (clubbing)?
- Is individual asymptomatic?
- Was liver biopsy performed and examined microscopically for signs of inflammation, scarring, or infection? Were other tests done such as a complete blood count (CBC), measuring key liver enzymes, folate and vitamin B12 levels, serum chemistries, viral antibodies, serum immunoglobulin levels, and antibodies to DNA, smooth muscle, and mitochondria? Cholangiography?
- Was diagnosis of cirrhosis of the liver confirmed?
- If diagnosis is uncertain, were other conditions with similar symptoms ruled out?

Regarding treatment:

- Was treatment appropriate for the underlying cause of the cirrhosis? Was it effective?
- Was individual instructed in dietary restrictions including low-protein and salt?
- Did individual receive supplementation with vitamins A, K, and D?
- Were symptoms of biliary cirrhosis effectively relieved through drug therapy?
- Does individual with alcoholic cirrhosis understand the importance of not drinking alcoholic beverages?
- Can individual stop drinking? Was individual referred to a community support group such as AA?
- Is individual a candidate for a liver transplant? On a national transplant list?

Regarding prognosis:

- At what stage of the disease was cirrhosis diagnosed?
- What is the expected outcome for this type and severity of cirrhosis?
- Does individual have a coexisting condition such as advanced age, debilitation, poor nutritional status, cardiac or renal disease that may complicate treatment or impact recovery?
- Have any complications developed?
- If symptoms do not respond to treatment, does diagnosis need to be revisited?

References

Conn, Harold O., and Colin E. Atterbury. "Cirrhosis." Diseases of the Liver, 7th ed. Schiff, Leon, and Eugene R. Schiff, eds. Philadelphia: J.B. Lippincott, 1993. 875-934.

Luper, S. "A Review of Plants Used in the Treatment of Liver Disease: Part 1." Alternative Medical Review 3 6 (1998): 410-421.

Cluster Headache

Other names / synonyms: Bing-Horton's Neuralgia, Ciliary Neuralgia, Erythroprosopalgia, Histamine Cephalgia, Histamine Headache, Migrainous Neuralgia

346.2, 349

Definition

Cluster headaches are so named because they typically occur in clusters over a period of time, usually 1 to 2 months. This is followed by a headache-free period of several months until another cluster of headaches begins. The headache is usually severe, lasts a few minutes to less than an hour, and mostly affects the temple or the area around one eye. It is often associated with involvement of the autonomic nervous system that controls involuntary bodily functions with symptoms such as forehead sweating, tearing, and runny nose, all occurring on the same side as the headache.

No specific cause has been found for the disorder but it appears related to a release of histamine, serotonin, or similar substances from body tissues that cause painful widening (dilatation) of blood vessels. Heavy smoking, alcohol use, stress, or certain foods such as red wine, nuts, cheese, and seafood may trigger attacks.

Cluster headaches are fairly uncommon and occur more frequently in men, usually beginning between the ages of 15 and 40. In some individuals, episodes occur at regular intervals without let-up. This is referred to as chronic cluster headache and comprises 20% of individuals who suffer from cluster headaches.

Cluster headaches may represent a variation of migraine headache. In the US, the incidence of cluster headaches is estimated at 2-9% for migraine sufferers. The prevalence rate in males is 0.4-1%, and cluster headache is 6 times more common in men than women. In affected men, 80% are heavy smokers and 50% have a history of heavy alcohol use.

Diagnosis

History: Cluster headaches occur as severe, sudden headaches that begin without warning and commonly wake the individual from sleep. These headaches occur daily over many days or weeks and often at the same time every night or infrequently during the day. Once the cluster of headaches is over, individuals may be headache-free for periods of 2 months to 20 years. Episodes of pain come on suddenly, peak in about 10 to 15 minutes, and last 10 minutes to 3 hours. The headaches occur on one side of the head, usually centering around the eye and may be described as a boring pain as if the eye is being pushed out. Most cluster headaches involve the forehead or cheek region of the face but up to one-fifth may result in pain in other areas such as the back of the neck or along the artery on the side of the neck (carotid artery). Many individuals report that stress, glare, alcohol, heavy smoking, or specific foods (i.e., red wine, nuts, cheese, and seafood) trigger their headaches.

Physical exam: If the individual is examined while experiencing a headache, the exam may reveal a blocked or runny nose, eye redness, and tearing. The pupil on the same side as the pain may be smaller than in the other eye and the eyelid on the same side may be drooping (Horner's syndrome). There may also be nausea and sweating on the same side of the forehead. These findings suggest involvement of the autonomic nervous system that controls involuntary bodily functions. Tenderness may occur on the scalp, face, and carotid artery.

Tests: There is no known technical diagnostic test that will confirm a diagnosis of cluster headache. Diagnosis is based on history and presenting signs and symptoms.

Treatment

Medications that constrict blood vessels (vasoconstrictors) including ergot alkaloids given by inhalation may help relieve an acute episode. A new type of vasoconstrictor useful in the treatment of migraine headaches may also be effective for cluster headaches when given by mouth or injection under the skin (subcutaneous). Oxygen inhalation is also used. Antiemetics and sedatives may be useful in treating the accompanying nausea and agitation. For prevention, various drugs have been generally effective including ergot alkaloids, beta-blockers, tricyclic antidepressants, corticosteroids, lithium carbonate, and calcium-channel blockers. Surgery or radiowave-induced damage (radiofrequency thermocoagulation) that interrupts the nerve supplying sensation to the face (trigeminal nerve) or to the autonomic pathways may be considered if medications are ineffective and if the headache is always on the same side.

If the individual becomes dependent on or addicted to pain medication, he/she may need treatment for substance abuse. If smoking or drinking alcoholic beverages trigger an attack, the individual may need assistance to stop smoking and/or drinking.

To prevent cluster headaches from occurring or worsening, headache triggers such as alcohol or specific foods should be avoided. Insufficient sleep, strong emotions, and excessive physical activity may bring on attacks. Tobacco may interfere with medications used to treat cluster headache and narcotics may allow episodic cluster to become chronic cluster.

Prognosis

The outcome is variable and quite individualized. Headaches may be well managed medically or resist treatment. There are no known predictors of positive (or negative) outcomes. Remissions may be prolonged for 20 years or more. Episodic cluster headache may be transformed to chronic cluster headache.

Differential Diagnosis

Migraine headache, rebound headache, seasonal or other allergic reactions, disorders of the eye such as acute optic neuritis or acute glaucoma, and temporal arteritis or other connective tissue disorders are other possibilities.

Internal carotid artery dissection, leaking cerebral aneurysm, or cerebral venous thrombosis may have similar symptoms.

Specialists

- Neurologist
- Psychologist

Work Restrictions / Accommodations

The flexibility to go to a quiet, dark location at the onset of a headache may be useful. Depending on the type of medication taken and its effects, the individual may need to leave work or come in late the morning after an attack. Strenuous physical activity, glare, and undue stress may trigger attacks and should be avoided.

Complementary and Alternative Therapies

Content is intended for awareness only. Treatments may or may not be effective. Scientific evidence may be lacking and some substances have potentially toxic effects. Dr. Presley Reed and the editors do not endorse the use of these therapies in the absence of consultation with a licensed medical professional.

Coffee -	Contains caffeine that constricts blood vessels.
Relaxation therapy, massage, reflexology -	May relieve tension.
Fish oil and flaxseed oil -	May have anti-inflammatory action.
Magnesium -	Deficiency in magnesium can trigger headaches.
Riboflavin -	May help ward off attacks through effect on brain energy metabolism.
Evening primrose -	May help with pain, as it contains pain reliever phenylalanine.
Feverfew -	May relieve pain and act as a sedative.
Willow bark -	Contains Salicylates (active ingredient in aspirin), which may help relieve pain.

Comorbid Conditions

Comorbid conditions that can affect recovery include substance abuse, stress, and other types of headaches including migraine.

Complications

Overuse of pain medicines can result in their becoming ineffective and create a risk of drug addiction. Inability to avoid smoking, alcohol, stress, and foods that trigger the attack may also aggravate the condition. Impaired judgment because of severe pain during attacks may lead to self-injury or even suicide attempts.

Factors Influencing Duration

Duration of disability depends on the time of day attacks occur, duration and frequency of clusters, and response to treatment. The individual's ability to avoid triggering factors such as stress, smoking, red wine, and certain foods like cheese, nuts, and seafood may also influence the length of disability.

Length of Disability

Length of disability depends on job requirements. Disability varies depending on severity and frequency of attacks and the individual's ability to avoid triggers.

For each single episode.

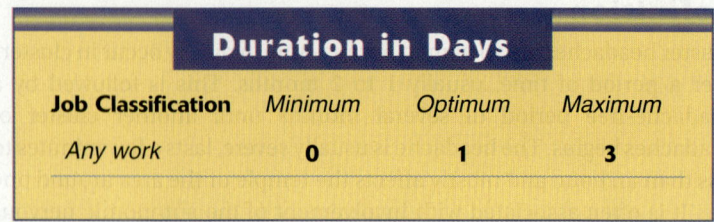

Job Classification	Minimum	Optimum	Maximum
Any work	0	1	3

Failure to Recover

If an individual fails to recover within the maximum duration expectancy period, the reader may wish to reference the following questions to assist in better understanding the specifics of an individual's medical case.

Regarding diagnosis:

- Did a severe, sudden headache develop without warning? Was headache on one side of the head? Did it center around the eye?
- While individual was experiencing a headache, did physical exam reveal a blocked or runny nose, eye redness, and tearing? Is pupil on the same side as the pain smaller than in the other eye? Does eyelid on same side droop (Horner's syndrome)?
- Does individual have nausea and sweating on the same side of the forehead?
- Was headache trigger such as smoking, alcohol, stress, or certain foods identified?
- Were conditions with similar symptoms ruled out?
- Was diagnosis of cluster headaches confirmed?

Regarding treatment:

- Is individual taking medication as prescribed? How long after onset of symptoms did individual wait to seek treatment?
- If medications are ineffective or if the headache is always on the same side, is individual a candidate for more aggressive treatment such as surgery or radiofrequency thermocoagulation?
- Does individual understand the concept of headache triggers? Is individual capable of and diligent in avoiding factors (alcohol, specific foods, insufficient sleep, strong emotions, excessive physical activity, tobacco) that might trigger an attack?
- Does individual understand that overuse of pain medicines can result in them becoming ineffective and creates a risk of drug addiction? Is individual showing evidence of addiction to pain medication?

Regarding prognosis:

- Is headache medically managed or does it resist treatment?
- Is individual aware of and able to avoid smoking, stress, alcohol, and foods that could trigger an attack?
- Are there factors at work such as strenuous physical activity, glare, or undue stress that may also trigger attacks?
- Has impaired judgment during attacks of severe pain lead to self-injury or suicide attempts?
- Do work accommodations allow individual to go to a quiet, dark location at the onset of a headache and leave work or come in late the morning after an attack? Would these accommodations help decrease disability and allow individual to remain in present occupational duties?
- Does individual have an underlying condition that may impact recovery such as substance abuse, stress, or other types of headaches including migraine?

References

"Cluster Headaches." National Library of Medicine. 03 May 2000. 01 Jul 2000 <http://medlineplus.adam.com/ency/article/000786.htm>.

Feinstein, Alice, ed. Healing with Vitamins. Emmaus, PA: Rodale Press, Inc, 1996.

Coarctation of the Aorta
747.1

Definition

Coarctation of the aorta is an area of localized narrowing or constriction (stenosis) of the major artery (aorta) leading blood away from the heart to the body. All other arteries branch from the aorta and continue branching into smaller and smaller vessels. The coarctation results in low blood pressure and low blood flow in blood vessels given off past the narrowing, and high blood pressure in blood vessels branching off before the area of coarctation.

In many instances, coarctation of the aorta occurs as a birth defect (congenital disorder). However, individuals with high blood pressure (hypertension), coronary artery disease, dilated portions of arteries (aneurysms), blood vessel obstructions or clots (embolisms), and premature narrowing of the arteries (atherosclerosis) may also develop the disorder.

The narrowing of the aorta may be caused by extra tissue inside the blood vessel that reduces the blood vessel's cross-sectional area. Alternatively, the narrowing may be caused by underdevelopment of a portion of the aorta itself, which causes a longer section of blood vessel with reduced diameter. The narrowing is most often seen in the portion of the aorta called the isthmus, which is the narrowest portion in normal aortas. The sequence of events that follows once the narrowing is apparent is that the blood flow across the narrow portion is obstructed. As a result, the pressure of the blood builds up in the arterial branches before (or proximal to) the coarctation. At the same time, blood flow is decreased in the part of the aorta beyond the area of the coarctation.

In its most common form, coarctation of the aorta causes high blood pressure in the upper body and arms and low blood pressure in the lower body and legs. The consequences of high blood pressure in the upper body include failure of the left side of the heart (left ventricle failure) from overwork, as the heart tries to pump blood past the narrowed area where there is great resistance to flow. This is associated with thickening and hardening (atherosclerosis) of arteries in the upper body, and increased risk of stroke (cerebrovascular accident) as the blood vessels in the brain may burst from high pressure.

Coarctation of the aorta, the fourth most common congenital heart defect, is found mostly in males and tends to occur in more than one member of the same family. It is not uncommon for the disorder to go undiagnosed until early adulthood. Coarctation of the aorta occurs in approximately 1 out of 10,000 individuals, most of whom are than 40 years old. Simple coarctation is not associated with other defects involving the heart or great vessels, and is the type most commonly seen in adults. In complex coarctation, which is usually detected in infancy, there are other birth defects involving the heart.

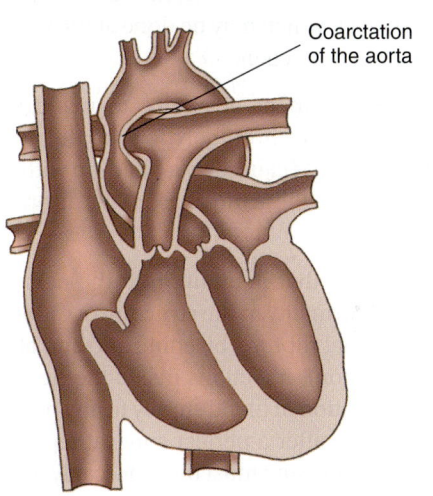

Frank Forney

Diagnosis

History: The most common symptoms of coarctation of the aorta are dizziness, pounding headache, fainting, fatigue, nosebleeds, cramps in the legs during exercise, cold legs or feet, and high blood pressure (hypertension).

Physical exam: Diminished or absent pulses are common in the arteries in the thigh and groin (femoral) area. Blood pressure may be elevated in the arms and decreased in the legs.

Tests: Tests that confirm the presence of coarctation of the aorta include x-ray viewing and examination of the aorta after injection of dye (coronary angiography), digital subtraction angiography, computed tomography (CT) of the chest, magnetic resonance imaging (MRI) of the chest, high-frequency sound waves that image the heart and surrounding tissues (echocardiography), chest x-ray, Doppler ultrasound of the aorta, electrocardiograms (ECG), and cardiac catheterization. Blood testing that screens for lipid abnormalities is also appropriate. Diagnosis is based on blood pressure changes in the upper and lower body, which may become more obvious with exercise stress testing, and on imaging procedures of the chest. After the age of 10, chest x-ray tests show notching of the ribs. All individuals should be screened for a hole in the heart muscle that forms a wall between the ventricles (ventricular septal defects, or VSD), for an inherited disorder in which numerous cysts on both kidneys gradually increase in size until most of the normal kidney tissue is destroyed (polycystic kidney disease), and for small saclike structures at the branch points of arteries (berry aneurysms). Berry aneurysms can easily be ruptured during periods of hypertension or stress.

Treatment

Surgery is usually advised to remove the area of obstruction. During surgery, the narrowed segment of the aorta is removed and then repaired by placing the 2 free ends of the aorta back together (anastomosis) if the gap is small, or larger gaps may be bridged with a synthetic material (Dacron graft). It is important to point out that surgical repair is performed even for minor defects because of possible complications if left untreated.

Two procedures, dilating the narrowed segment of the aorta with balloons (balloon angioplasty) and performing surgery to remove atherosclerotic plaque from the artery (endarterectomy), serve as alternatives to surgical removal of the area of obstruction. Individuals with associated narrowing (stenosis) of the aortic valve may also require surgery to correct this defect, which may be done at the same time as or separately from the coarctation repair.

Medication is often the treatment of choice to manage associated hypertension. More specifically, thrombolytic drug therapy is used in instances where the narrowing is caused by a build-up within the artery. Corticosteroids may be used in the acute phase of the disorder to rapidly diminish symptoms.

It is important to remember that in addition to the narrowing in the aorta, there may be an abnormality in the structure of the artery as well. Therefore, the risk for arterial rupture, bleeding into and along the wall of the aorta (aortic dissection), infections inside the heart and valves (endocarditis), and interruption of blood supply to any part of the brain (stroke), may continue even after a perfect surgical repair. To prevent these abnormalities, blood pressure must be impeccably monitored and controlled.

Prognosis

Mean survival of individuals with untreated coarctation is 35 years, with 75% of individuals dead by age fifty. Most develop high blood pressure during childhood, and failure of the left side of the heart (left ventricular failure) in their fifties. Death is usually caused by rupture or dissection of the aorta, bleeding into the brain (cerebral hemorrhage), infection involving the arteries (infective endarteritis) or the heart (infective endocarditis), heart failure, coronary artery disease, or coexisting disease of the aortic valve.

In some cases, coarctation of the aorta is curable with surgery, and rapid improvement of symptoms can be expected after the repair. High blood pressure resolves in about half of individuals. Death during the procedure occurs in less than one percent. Complications of the surgery may include paraplegia if blood flow to the spinal cord is interrupted, false aneurysm or dissection at the repair site, or leakage or rupture of an aneurysm.

In other cases, surgery does not "cure" all of the problems associated with the disorder. For instance, many individuals continue to have high blood pressure after the defect is surgically repaired. Although the high blood pressure resolves after a few weeks following surgery in some cases, close monitoring including exercise testing and medication are required to keep blood pressure at a safe level. Many individuals continue to have high blood pressure requiring medication to control it throughout their lifetime.

Overall, there is an earlier incidence of death among individuals with aortic repair than among the general public; however, repair leads to a marked increase in longevity over those individuals who do not opt for the repair. Today, diagnosis of a coarctation and the subsequent repair typically occur during infancy.

Differential Diagnosis

Other possibilities include aortic insufficiency, and a ballooning or widening of the aorta (aneurysm).

Specialists

• Cardiologist	• Cardiovascular Surgeon

Work Restrictions / Accommodations

Individuals returning to work after being treated for coarctation of the aorta may initially require lighter and/or part-time duty. Such restrictions need to be evaluated on a case-by-case basis and extended based on the maintenance of the individual's blood pressure at a safe level. Exercise may cause unsafe blood pressure increases even in individuals whose blood pressure is typically normal.

Serious cardiac conditions including coarctation and its complications may disqualify individuals from certain occupations. A worker with a job affecting public safety may not be able to continue in that position.

Comorbid Conditions

Comorbid conditions that might influence length of disability include alcoholism, severe viral infection, high blood pressure (hypertension), and pain or discomfort in the chest caused by insufficient blood flow to the heart muscle (coronary artery disease, or CAD). Abnormalities associated with coarctation may include a bicuspid aortic valve in up to 85% of cases, aneurysms of brain arteries (berry aneurysms of the Circle of Willis), ventricular septal defect, and aneurysms of the arteries traveling between the ribs (intercostal artery aneurysms). Coarctation is seen in about 35% of individuals with Turner's syndrome, a condition in females related to absence of one of the X-chromosomes.

Complications

Complications of coarctation of the aorta include abnormal ballooning or widening of the aorta (aortic aneurysm), bleeding into and along the wall of the aorta (aortic dissection), progressive narrowing of the aortic valve resulting in the obstructed passage of blood from the left ventricle into the aorta (aortic stenosis), enlargement of the left side of the heart (left ventricular hypertrophy), aortic rupture, severe high blood pressure (hypertension), inflammation or infection of the inside lining of the heart chambers and heart valves (endocarditis), bleeding within the brain (intracerebral hemorrhage), interruption of blood supply to any part of the brain (stroke), inability of the heart to pump blood efficiently (heart failure), irreversible injury to the heart muscle (heart attack or myocardial infarction), and pain or discomfort in the chest caused by insufficient blood flow to the heart muscle (coronary artery disease, or CAD).

In 25-50% of individuals with coarctation, a bicuspid aortic valve (rather than the normal tricuspid valve) is present. Individuals with bicuspid valves are at risk for life-threatening irregularities in the rhythm of their heart beat (arrhythmias), infections inside the heart and valves (endocarditis), and infections on the inside layers of an artery (endarteritis). Less commonly-occurring, associated heart defects include mitral valve abnormalities, a hole in the heart muscle that forms a wall between the ventricles (ventricular septal defects, or VSD), and left ventricular outflow tract obstruction. Noncardiac abnormalities of the arteries (such as aneurysm) are also associated with coarctation of the aorta.

Factors Influencing Duration

Factors that might influence length of disability include advanced age of individual at time of surgery, response to therapy, postoperative hypertension, associated complications, and narrowing of the aorta after treatment (re-stenosis).

Length of Disability

Disability varies and is contingent on the severity of the condition and on how successfully blood pressure is maintained at a safe level. Return to work depends on complications, recovery, and job demands.

Failure to Recover

If an individual fails to recover within the maximum duration expectancy period, the reader may wish to reference the following questions to assist in better understanding the specifics of an individual's medical case.

Regarding diagnosis:

- Does individual have a history of coarctation of the aorta at birth? History of aneurysms or emboli?
- Does individual have high blood pressure (hypertension) or other forms of coronary artery disease?
- Does individual complain of dizziness, pounding headache, fainting, fatigue, nosebleeds, cramps in the legs during exercise, and/or cold legs or feet?
- Do blood pressure measurements indicate an elevation in the arms and reduction in the legs?
- Were tests done to confirm the presence of coarctation of the aorta done such as coronary angiography, digital subtraction angiography, CT, MRI, echocardiography, chest x-ray, ultrasound, electrocardiogram (ECG), or cardiac catheterization?
- Was blood testing done to screen for lipid abnormalities?
- Was the diagnosis of coarctation of the aorta confirmed?
- Was the underlying cause identified?

Regarding treatment:

- Was surgery done to remove the area of obstruction?
- Was the area of obstruction small, allowing the two free ends of the aorta to be surgically joined (anastomosis)?
- Was the obstruction larger, requiring surgical bridging with a synthetic material (Dacron graft)?
- Were alternative procedures sufficient to correct the problem, i.e., balloon angioplasty or endarterectomy?
- What medication(s) is individual taking to control blood pressure?
- Is individual compliant with the drug regimen?

Regarding prognosis:

- Is blood pressure being adequately controlled?
- Does individual undergo periodic exercise stress testing as required?
- Would individual benefit from a cardiac rehabilitation program?
- Has individual developed any complications from surgical procedures such as hemorrhage or infection?
- Has individual developed complications of the disease such as aortic aneurysm, aortic dissection, aortic stenosis, left ventricular hypertrophy, aortic rupture, endocarditis, intracerebral hemorrhage, stroke, heart failure, or myocardial infarction?
- How severe are the complications and how will they be treated? What is the expected outcome for these complications with treatment?

References

"Coarctation of the Aorta." drkoop.com. 01 Jan 2000. 01 Jan 2001 <http://www.drkoop.com/conditions/ency/article/000191.htm>.

Mack, G., G.H. Burch, and D.J. Sahn. "Coarctation of the Aorta." Current Treatment Options in Cardiovascular Medicine 1 4 (1999): 347-354.

Cocaine Dependence/Abuse

Other names / synonyms: Cocaine Abuse, Cocaine Addiction, Crack Abuse

304.2, 305.6

Definition

Cocaine is a naturally occurring substance produced from the leaves of the coca plant. It belongs to a class of drugs known as stimulants, as it directly affects the brain.

While cocaine has a high potential for abuse, it may sometimes be prescribed for legitimate medical uses, such as a local anesthetic for some eye, ear, and throat surgery. Cocaine may be inhaled through the nose, smoked, chewed, or injected into the veins, producing almost immediate central nervous system effects. These effects include feelings of well-being, confidence, and euphoria.

Cocaine can come in many forms. Cocaine hydrochloride salt is a white powder that dissolves in water. Users can inject the resulting solution into a vein (intravenously) or inhale it into the nose. The freebase form of cocaine that has not been neutralized by an acid to make the hydrochloride salt, can be smoked. The white powder sold on the street is usually diluted with inert substances such as cornstarch or talcum powder, or with active drugs such as the local anesthetic procaine or with stimulants such as amphetamines.

Cocaine dependence usually begins with episodic use (abuse), which may involve using the drug 2 or 3 days a week, or bingeing. During binges, the user may consume a significant amount of cocaine in a short period, stopping only when exhausted or when the cocaine supply ends. Because cocaine's effects dissipate within about 30 to 50 minutes, there is a need for frequent dosing to maintain the desired effects, which can lead to dependence after only a few weeks or months of recreational use.

Based on data from a 1996 survey, approximately 10% of the population in the US report ever having used cocaine and 2% reported using crack cocaine. Individuals between ages 26 and 34 report the highest lifetime use, with 21% reporting cocaine use, and 4% reporting crack cocaine use. Adults age 18 to 25 have a higher rate of current cocaine use than those in any other age group. Men are one and a half times to twice as likely as women to abuse cocaine. In 1997, an estimated 1.5 million Americans, or 0.7% of those age 12 and older, were current cocaine users. Rates of current cocaine use were 1.4% of blacks, 0.8% of Hispanics, and 0.6% of whites. The number of chronic cocaine users may be as high as 3.6 million at present.

Diagnosis

History: The diagnosis is based on criteria listed in the DSM-IV-TR (Diagnostic and Statistical Manual of Mental Disorders, 4th Edition, Text Revision, published by the American Psychiatric Association). Users may report effects almost immediately after a single dose, which may disappear within a few minutes or hours. When cocaine is taken in small amounts up to 100 mg, these effects may include intense elation (euphoria), and feeling energetic, talkative, and mentally alert, with temporarily decreased need for food and sleep. Some users report that they can perform simple physical and mental tasks more quickly, while others report the opposite effect.

Individuals who have been using cocaine for a long period of time may suffer from restlessness, extreme excitability, and insomnia. Repeated use of high doses of cocaine in some individuals may lead to a toxic psychosis characterized by mounting anxiety, paranoia, and auditory, visual, and tactile hallucinations. Upon withdrawal of occasional cocaine use, physical symptoms will be minimal, if they occur at all, and may include abdominal cramps, nausea, diarrhea, fever, chills, and exhaustion. However, with chronic use, abrupt cessation will result in depression, sleep disturbances, sluggishness (lethargy), muscle aches, and a tremendous craving for the drug.

Physical exam: After a single dose of 100 mg or less, there may be enlarged (dilated) pupils, constricted blood vessels causing pale, cool skin and increased blood pressure, and increased temperature and heart rate. In long-term users, exam may reveal enlarged (dilated) reactive pupils, increased heart rate and blood pressure, rapid breathing, increased perspiration, and anxiety. The individual should be examined for a perforated nasal septum or decreased sense of smell from inhaling cocaine, or needle marks and abscesses indicating injection. With time, marked weight loss may be evident. A mental status examination may reveal signs of confusion, paranoia, hallucinations, impulsivity, agitation, and hyperactivity. Symptoms of a cocaine overdose include an elevated temperature, shallow respirations, and increased heart rate and blood pressure.

Tests: A polydrug blood or urine screen test can confirm cocaine use and the approximate amount used, if done within a few hours of use. Psychological testing may also be done as it can offer useful insights into underlying psychopathology in the individual dependent on cocaine. Electrocardiogram may reveal disturbances of heart rhythm.

Treatment

In the acute or chronic phases of cocaine intoxication, any medical complications must be treated promptly, including disturbances in the heart rhythm, or dangerous elevations of blood pressure. Loss of blood flow to the heart (heart attack or myocardial infarction) or intestine (ischemic colitis) must be treated appropriately. There is some debate over whether therapy to dissolve blood clots (thrombolytic therapy) should be used in heart attack related to cocaine abuse. Perforated nasal septum sometimes needs surgical repair, and abscesses for infected injection sites may need antibiotic treatment or surgical drainage.

Abstinence is the treatment goal. After the individual ceases using cocaine, it takes about a week to rid the body of the acute effects of cocaine withdrawal, including fatigue, unpleasant dreams, insomnia or hypersomnia, increased appetite, slowed thinking and physical reactions (psychomotor retardation), or agitation. Medication therapy may include dopamine antagonists, mixed dopamine agonists such as pergolide, and/or antidepressants. Because most individuals do not benefit from any currently available pharmacotherapy for withdrawal symptoms, drug therapy is not ordinarily indicated as an initial treatment. However, individuals with a more severe dependence or who fail to respond to psychosocial treatment should be considered for treatment with dopaminergic medications. Other common psychologic disorders common to cocaine addicts, depression and manic-depression, may require treatment with antidepressants or lithium.

Acupuncture has also been shown to reduce withdrawal symptoms as well as counteract the craving for cocaine.

Treatment services, which include individual psychotherapy, family therapy, drug education, acupuncture, and relaxation training, are usually conducted in an outpatient setting. The only clearly accepted factors indicating need for inpatient cocaine abuse treatment are severe depression or psychotic symptoms lasting beyond one to three days after abstinence or repeated outpatient failures. Therefore, hospitalization may be necessary if the individual is violent towards others, suicidal, or is having severe withdrawal symptoms during detoxification. Ongoing structured self-help programs such as Cocaine Anonymous and Rational Recovery are recommended as an adjunct to treatment services. Regular but random drug screens should be part of the treatment process. It should also be understood that relapse is often part of the recovery process.

The most effective treatment for cocaine use disorders is one of intensive (more than twice a week) outpatient treatment (during the initial stage of treatment) in which a variety of treatment modalities are used simultaneously, and in which the focus is abstinence. Cocaine intoxication can produce hypertension, tachycardia, seizures, and paranoid delusions. Usually self-limited and requiring only supportive care, acute agitations may benefit from sedation with benzodiazepines. The psychosocial treatments found to be most effective for individuals with cocaine use disorders are: cognitive-behavioral therapies, behavioral therapies, and psychodynamic-psychotherapy. Cognitive-behavioral therapy is a short-term focused approach. Assuming that learning processes play an important role in development and continuation of cocaine abuse/dependence, the same learning processes are used to help individuals reduce drug use. The individual is taught to recognize the situations in which they are most likely to use cocaine, avoid these situations when appropriate, and cope more effectively with a range of problems and behaviors associated with drug abuse.

A behavioral therapy component showing positive results is "contingency management." This approaches uses a voucher-based system to give positive rewards (contingent) for staying in treatment and remaining cocaine free. Based on drug-free urine tests, the individual earns points that can be exchanged for items that encourage healthy living such as joining a gym, or going to a movie and dinner. The treatment plan should consider all underlying psychiatric or general medical conditions, gender-related factors (including the possibility of pregnancy), social and living environment, cultural factors, and family characteristics. Withdrawing from long-term cocaine abuse requires close supervision because the individual may become depressed and suicidal.

Individuals with more severe problems, such as coexisting psychiatric disorders or criminal involvement, often benefit from therapeutic communities or residential programs with planned lengths of stay of 6 to 12 months. These programs focus on re-socialization of the individual to society and include on-site vocational rehabilitation and other supportive services. When combined with cognitive-behavioral therapy, recovery support groups (such as Narcotics Anonymous) also appear to be effective in long-term drug-free recovery. Duration of treatment should be tailored to the individual's needs, and may vary from a few months extended therapy lasting more than one year. Monitoring for substance use should be intensified during periods of high relapse risk, including the early stages of treatment, periods of transition to less intensive levels of care, and the first year after completion of active treatment.

Prognosis

There are a significant number of individuals who respond to treatment and stay in remission from cocaine dependence for many years. Only a minority of individuals (15-29%) exhibit a pattern of chronic relapse requiring repeated intervention. There are individuals who experience periods of relapse, in which they begin cocaine use after a period of remission, and again meet the criteria for substance dependence.

Of those who remain abstinent for 2 years, almost 90% are substance-free at 10 years, and those who remain substance-free for 10 years have a very high likelihood (over 90%) of being substance-free at 20 years.

There are other individuals who are never able to abstain from cocaine use and who do not experience any periods of remission.

Differential Diagnosis

The long-term effects of cocaine (such as restlessness, extreme excitability, insomnia, and paranoia) are often identical to amphetamine psychosis and very similar to paranoid schizophrenia. The individual using cocaine may be suffering from a psychiatric disorder along with the substance abuse disorder. If substance abuse predates the onset of affective symptoms, then primary substance abuse with a secondary mood disorder would be diagnosed.

Specialists

- Advanced Practice Registered Nurse
- Cardiologist
- Gastroenterologist
- General Surgeon
- Occupational Therapist
- Psychiatrist
- Psychologist

Work Restrictions / Accommodations

Many employers have systems in place for individuals recovering from substance dependence disorders to return to work under special contracts or conditions. These conditions may provide guidelines for testing blood and urine levels of identified substances and provide work performance and substance abuse treatment guidelines for the recovering individual. Cocaine should not be tolerated at the workplace, because employees who use cocaine on the job endanger their safety and that of their coworkers, and often create a negative work environment.

Temporary work accommodations may include reducing or eliminating activities where the safety of self or others is contingent upon a constant and/or high level of alertness, such as driving motor vehicles, operating complex machinery, or handling dangerous chemicals; introducing the individual to new or stressful situations gradually under individually appropriate supervision; allowing some flexibility in scheduling to attend therapy appointments (which normally should occur during employee's personal time); promoting planned, proactive management of identified problem areas; and offering timely feedback on job performance issues. It will be helpful if accommodations are documented in a written plan designed to promote timely and safe transition back to full work productivity.

Comorbid Conditions

Coexisting conditions that may affect recovery and lengthen disability include the presence of psychiatric disorders, infection with hepatitis B or C, HIV infection, and the abuse of or dependence on alcohol or other substances. Studies show the most common polydrug combination to be alcohol, cocaine, and marijuana. When cocaine and alcohol are taken together, the two drugs are converted by the body to cocaethylene, which has a longer duration of action in the brain and is more toxic than either drug alone. The mixture of cocaine and alcohol is the most common two-drug combination resulting in drug-related death.

Individuals who have chronically used stimulants can occasionally become sensitized (kindling) to any future use of stimulants. When this happens, small amounts of even mild stimulants, such as caffeine, can cause symptoms of paranoia and auditory hallucinations.

A pregnant women who uses cocaine also faces increased risk of prematurity, low infant birth weight, still birth, and sudden infant death syndrome (SIDS).

The combination of a psychiatric illness with substance abuse (dual diagnosis) can complicate the treatment of both the chemical dependency as well as the psychiatric illness. Up to 90% of the individuals diagnosed with a clinical psychiatric disorder also report a substance use disorder sometime in their lifetime. In addition, approximately one-third of hospitalized psychiatric patients manifest coexisting non-nicotine substance use disorders.

Complications

Complications of cocaine use may include sinusitis, runny nose (rhinitis), perforated nasal septum, nosebleeds, lung damage, and respiratory paralysis. Users who inject the drug risk not only overdose, but also infections from non-sterile needles, such as skin abscesses, inflammation of the membranes of the spinal cord or brain (meningitis) as well as hepatitis or acquired immune deficiency syndrome (AIDS) from sharing needles with others.

The most common cardiac complications of cocaine use are heart attack (myocardial infarction), irregular or abnormal heart rhythm (cardiac arrhythmias), stroke, and rupture of the ascending aorta and sudden cardiac death. Other complications include polydrug abuse. Narrowing of blood vessels supplying the intestine may cause ischemic colitis, a potentially life-threatening complication in which bowel tissue dies, giving way to massive infection. Because cocaine use decreases appetite and food intake, significant weight loss and malnutrition may result. Psychiatric complications include severe anxiety and depression.

Factors Influencing Duration

It has been demonstrated that the most reliable predictor of treatment outcome, regardless of treatment strategy, is the individual's readiness to change. The severity of the abuse/dependence, the success of the treatment program, appropriate individual-treatment matching, and any physical complications may influence the length of disability as well. A stable history of employment is also a major predictor of permanent abstinence.

Length of Disability

Maximum duration includes hospitalization. A significant number of individuals respond to treatment and maintain remission.

Detoxification and counseling.

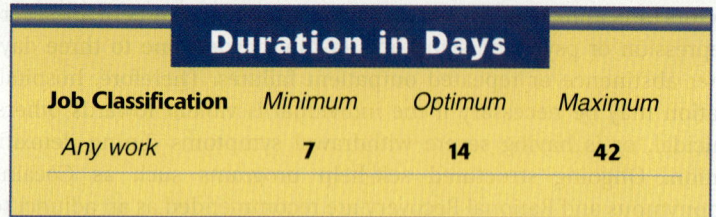

Job Classification	Minimum	Optimum	Maximum
Any work	7	14	42

Failure to Recover

If an individual fails to recover within the maximum duration expectancy period, the reader may wish to reference the following questions to assist in better understanding the specifics of an individual's medical case.

Regarding diagnosis:

- Was a comprehensive assessment completed on this individual?
- Were all underlying medical and psychiatric disorders identified?
- Were other conditions with similar long-term effects such as amphetamine psychosis and paranoid schizophrenia ruled out?

Regarding treatment:

- Does individual receive intensive (more than twice a week) outpatient treatment where a variety of treatment modalities are used simultaneously and that focuses on abstinence?
- Has individual experienced any withdrawal symptoms such as cravings and lack of pleasure in what is normally pleasurable?
- Has individual responded to psychosocial treatment? If not, would individual respond to dopaminergic medications?
- Would individual benefit from addition of drug therapy to the overall treatment plan?
- Is cognitive-behavioral therapy part of individual's current treatment plan?
- Would individual benefit from the contingency management approach?
- Does individual's current treatment plan take underlying psychiatric or general medical conditions into consideration? What changes could be made to better meet this individual's needs?
- Would individual benefit from involvement in a therapeutic community or residential program?
- Does individual participate in a recovery support group?
- Is individual currently in any of the higher risk periods such as periods of high relapse risk or periods of transition to less intensive levels of care? What monitoring system is in place?

Regarding prognosis:

- Where is individual in the treatment regime?
- Has individual experienced relapses? Are they decreasing in frequency?
- Would individual benefit from more frequent, more intense, or longer treatment duration?
- Is individual currently involved in a support group? Which one? Does individual participate in a formal support group? What other support systems does individual have in place?
- Is individual receiving necessary tools, skills, and encouragement to move ahead with his/her life?
- Does individual have an underlying condition that may impact recovery?
- Have any complications developed from cocaine intoxication such as hypertension, tachycardia, seizures, or paranoid delusions?

References

Cocaine Addiction. Narconon. 01 Jan 2000. 03 Jan 2001 <http://www.cocaineaddiction.com/cocaine_coke.html>.

Frances, Allen. Diagnostic and Statistical Manual of Mental Disorders: 4th ed, text revision. Washington, DC: American Psychiatric Association, 2000.

Coccidioidomycosis

Other names / synonyms: Coccidioidal Granuloma, Desert Fever, Desert Rheumatism, Posada's Disease, San Joaquin Fever, Valley Fever

114, 114.0, 114.1, 114.2, 114.3, 114.4, 114.5, 114.9

Definition

Coccidioidomycosis is a fungal infection caused by Coccidioides immitis, a fungus that lives in the soil and releases spores into the air where they can be inhaled. The infective spores can also remain in dust that covers or contaminates an inanimate object, and can be released at a later time even when the object is removed from the area.

One-half to two-thirds of all cases are either asymptomatic or mild and do not require medical attention. The remaining cases begin with a respiratory infection. This primary infection is typically nonprogressive and self-limiting. A small percentage of individuals (0.5%) develop a disseminated infection. Dissemination can occur within weeks of the primary infection or may develop slowly over a period of years. This infection may cause respiratory symptoms or spread to the skin, bone, joints, and central nervous system. In some cases, the infection spreads to the central nervous system and causes serious disease such as coccidioidal meningitis (inflammation of the membranes of the spinal cord or brain). Disseminated coccidioidomycosis is often fatal.

Individuals at greatest risk are those exposed to dust such as farmers, migrant workers, archeologists, or those who recently traveled in or relocated to endemic areas (area where disease is present). Coccidioidomycosis has emerged as an important opportunistic infection (infection that takes advantage of a weakened immune system). Approximately 25% of HIV-infected individuals living in an endemic area will contract coccidioidomycosis. Dissemination of the disease is more common in blacks, Filipinos, other Asians, pregnant women, and immunocompromised individuals, e.g., those with AIDS, taking immunosuppressant medications, or transplant recipients. Dissemination is more common in men than women.

Coccidioidomycosis is typically found in the arid and semiarid regions of the southwestern US, i.e., Arizona, California, and Texas, in addition to parts of Mexico and South America. Approximately 100,000 cases develop each year, although incidence varies from year to year and may be related to environmental conditions such as rainfall, dust storms, or earthquakes.

Diagnosis

History: Up to two-thirds of infected individuals are without symptoms (asymptomatic) or have symptoms mild enough to preclude medical attention. When symptoms are present, they typically develop within 1 to 4 weeks after exposure. Symptoms of primary infection may include cough, chest pain, shortness of breath, fever, night sweats, fatigue, weight loss, and headache. Some individuals develop joint pain or nodes and lesions on the legs (erythema nodosum). Individuals may have a history of residence or travel in endemic areas.

Physical exam: Individuals may present with a fine rash, fever, and migratory joint pain upon physical examination. There may also be evidence of pneumonia including a cough with increased sputum production. Abnormal lung sounds are indications of inflammation of the membrane surrounding the lung (pleurisy). Evidence of disseminated infection includes skin involvement, bone infection (particularly in the vertebrae and long bones), joint infection (particularly of the knee), enlarged lymph nodes, and contained areas of infection (abscesses). Altered mental status, headache, and vomiting are often present in individuals with meningitis.

Tests: Coccidioides immitis can be identified in culture or microscopic examination of sputum, pus, urine, cerebrospinal fluid (CSF), or tissue. A skin test is positive in more than 95% of individuals with primary coccidioidomycosis. A negative test, however, doesn't rule out the infection. It may take several days or weeks for an individual to present with a positive reaction. In an individual with a known coccidioidomycosis infection, a negative skin test indicates that the infection may be disseminated. Blood (serology) tests are useful both for diagnosis and prognosis, although these tests may be negative in immunocompromised individuals. Tests may include immunodiffusion test (CIE), tube precipitin test, and antibody titers. Lumbar puncture may be done to rule out meningitis. X-ray studies, MRI, or CT can indicate the spread of the disease.

Treatment

Primary infection is usually self-limiting and does not typically require treatment. For individuals requiring treatment, i.e., with pneumonia or disease that has spread to other areas (disseminated), antifungal drugs are given for up to 1 year or more. Immunocompromised individuals may need to continue antifungal treatment indefinitely.

Chest (thoracic) surgery is occasionally indicated for removal (resection) of giant, infected, or ruptured hollows carved in lung tissue by the disease process (cavities). Some individuals may need surgical removal of dead or diseased tissue (debridement) and drainage of abscesses and other infected sites. Bones weakened by infection may require stabilization.

Prognosis

Primary infection typically resolves without treatment within 6 to 8 weeks. Disseminated infection, however, may be fatal especially in HIV-infected individuals and those with meningitis. Neurologic affects of meningitis may be permanent. One-third of individuals with disseminated infection relapse even after long periods of treatment.

Differential Diagnosis

Primary infection has similar symptoms to the common cold, influenza, or other upper respiratory illness. Coccidioidomycosis resembles tuberculosis.

Specialists

- Infectious Disease Physician
- Neurologist
- Neurosurgeon
- Orthopedic Surgeon
- Pulmonologist
- Thoracic Surgeon

Rehabilitation

If the lungs are affected by coccidioidomycosis, physical and respiratory therapy in conjunction with medications can be important in the overall treatment for rehabilitation of the individual with this condition. When hospitalized with coccidioidomycosis, the physical or respiratory therapist helps the individual cough and mobilize secretions to clear the airway. The individual lies in a position that allows the most effective drainage of secretions, often in a side-lying position with the affected side upward and the head slightly lower than the chest. In addition to proper positioning, physical therapists perform percussion and vibration techniques to the affected areas to help "shake loose" mucus and secretions. The therapist performs chest percussion with the hands in a cupped position, mildly striking repeatedly over the area of the lung affected by coccidioidomycosis.

Physical therapy also improves ventilation through breathing exercises localized to the area of involvement. This is followed by a gradual strengthening program.

Once the symptoms of coccidioidomycosis subside and breathing becomes easier, focus is then placed on strength and endurance by incorporating aerobic-type activity into the rehabilitation program. By building endurance, the individual increases the ability to work and the resistance to fatigue. A physical therapist experienced in cardiac and pulmonary rehabilitation keeps a daily log of the individual's blood pressure, heart rate, and cardiac rhythm. As endurance increases without symptoms of shortness of breath, the individual begins active upper and lower extremity exercises using very light resistance in addition to light aerobic activities such as brisk walking and low-resistance biking.

Neurologic damage or bone and joint involvement may require physical or occupational therapy rehabilitation and depends on what nerves are affected by the disease. If coccidioidomycosis results in bone and joint involvement, the rehabilitation program begins once pain and other symptoms subside. This is followed by range-of-motion exercises to return joint mobility.

For individuals with coccidioidomycosis, the physical therapist may need to modify the program depending on what organs are involved. This is especially the case when symptoms include cough, weight loss, and fatigue.

Work Restrictions / Accommodations

Uncomplicated primary coccidioidomycosis does not require work restrictions or accommodations although some individuals may require time off for recovery. Accommodations may be needed for disseminated infection and will depend on the severity and sites of disease. For example, infection spreading to bone or joint may require work restrictions that put less demand on the affected bone or joint.

Coccidioidomycosis is not spread from individual to individual, however caution should be used with clothing or other material contaminated with drainage from skin lesions.

Comorbid Conditions

Immunocompromised conditions such as AIDS, immunosuppressive therapy, or organ transplant may lengthen disability. Diabetes may also lengthen disability.

Complications

Immunocompromised individuals are at greatest risk for complications. Coccidioidomycosis may develop into chronic lung (pulmonary) conditions including chronic pneumonia and the formation of nodules or cavities in the lung tissue. Individuals with diabetes may be more likely to develop thin-walled chronic cavities within the lung.

Once the disease spreads beyond the lungs, common sites of infection include the joints, skin, and cerebral nervous system (CNS). In the CNS, coccidioidomycosis can develop into meningitis, a possibly fatal condition.

Factors Influencing Duration

The presence and severity of dissemination, response to treatment, and development of complications determine the length of disability.

Length of Disability

Respiratory coccidioidomycosis.

Job Classification	Minimum	Optimum	Maximum
Any work	3	7	14

Duration in Days

Failure to Recover

If an individual fails to recover within the maximum duration expectancy period, the reader may wish to reference the following questions to assist in better understanding the specifics of an individual's medical case.

Regarding diagnosis:

- Did individual have an exposure history suggestive of coccidioidomycosis infection?
- Did individual present with symptoms consistent with the diagnosis?
- Does individual have a high risk of coccidioidomycosis infection (i.e., farm worker, archeologist, construction worker, or immune suppressed individual)?
- Was the diagnosis confirmed with coccidioidomycosis in skin testing or serological testing?
- If the diagnosis was uncertain, were other conditions with similar symptoms ruled out? Was there evidence of disseminated infection?
- Would individual benefit from consultation with a specialist (infectious disease specialist, pulmonologist, neurologist, orthopedic surgeon, neurosurgeon, thoracic surgeon)?

Regarding treatment:

- Was the treatment appropriate for the type of infectious involvement?
- Was surgery required?
- Was individual compliant with prescribed treatment?

Regarding prognosis:

- Has adequate time elapsed for recovery?
- Does individual have pre-existing conditions that may influence the length of disability?
- Have the symptoms persisted even with antifungal treatment?
- Has individual been reevaluated for disseminated infection?
- Does individual have associated neurological involvement (meningitis)?
- What is the expected outcome?

References

Coccidioidomycosis. Centers for Disease Control and Prevention, Division of Bacterial and Mycotic Diseases. 06 Apr 2000. 15 Sep 2000 <http://www.cdc.gov/ncidod/dbmd/diseaseinfo/coccidioidomycosis_t.htm>.

Chin, James. Control of Communicable Diseases Manual, 17th ed. Washington, DC: American Public Health Association, 2000.

Galgiani, John. "Coccidioidomycosis: A Regional Disease of National Importance." Annals of Internal Medicine 130 4 (1999): 293-300.

Galgiani, John. "Coccidioides Immitis." Principles and Practice of Infectious Diseases, 5th ed. Mandell, Gerald, John Bennett, and Raphael Dolin, eds. Philadelphia: Churchill Livingstone, 2000. 2746-2755.

Kirkland, Theo, and Joshua Fierer. "Coccidioidomycosis: A Reemerging Infectious Disease." Emerging Infectious Diseases 2 3 (1996): 192-199.

Kisner, C., and L. Colby. Therapeutic Exercise Foundations and Techniques. Philadelphia: F.A. Davis, 1990.

Coccygodynia

Other names / synonyms: Coccyalgia, Coccydynia, Tailbone Pain
724.79

Definition

Coccygodynia is a throbbing or aching pain in and around the area of the tailbone (coccyx).

Coccygodynia is sometimes caused by some traumatic injury to the coccyx such as a fall on the bottom in the sitting position. Another common cause in females is birth trauma that occurs during difficult child delivery (parturition). The L5-S1 disc may cause referred pain felt at the tailbone. However, in the vast majority of cases, there is no identifiable cause of the condition (idiopathic).

Risk factors for coccygodynia include prolonged sitting; any activity in which there are repeated blows to the coccyx such as riding a horse, motorcycle, bicycle, tractor, jeep, or snowmobile; poor sitting posture; and surgery that is performed with the individual laying on the back with knees flexed (lithotomy or dorsosacral position). Psychological problems (hysteria, depression) represent a high risk for the onset of coccygodynia. Coccygodynia occurs almost exclusively in women (97% of individuals with this condition).

Diagnosis

History: Individuals with coccygodynia will complain of pain in the tailbone (coccygeal) area. They may also report persistent rectal pain and fullness, pain on defecation, reduced anal sphincter control, and constipation.

Physical exam: A standard gynecological exam of the female pelvis should be done to detect any gynecological pathology. The individual may appear anxious or depressed during physical examination. The coccyx should be examined with one gloved finger in the individual's rectum and another gloved finger (on the other hand) on the skin (perineum) just underneath the tip of the coccyx (bimanual rectal examination). The coccyx is then palpated and manipulated, and the individual with coccygodynia will report a sharp pain in response to this maneuver.

Tests: X-rays of the sacrum coccyx should be taken. MRI of the lumbar spine may be indicated if L5-S1 disc pathology is suspected. Ultrasound may help identify any sort of gynecological pathology. The stool may be tested for occult blood (guaiac test). A behavioral assessment may be done to determine if there are any abnormal personality traits.

Treatment

Conservative treatment involves sitting in a hot sitz bath, use of a "doughnut" or coccyx pillow, chair modification, adjustable height, adjustable seat tilt, and increased cushion, instruction in sitting mechanics, and taking a nonsteroidal anti-inflammatory drug (NSAID).

Individuals with persistent cases of coccygodynia may be treated by physiotherapy, which consists of daily exposure of the coccyx to high-frequency sound waves (ultrasound) for 2 weeks followed by 2 weeks of therapeutic heat (short-wave diathermy) applied to the coccyx. Should these methods fail, anesthetic and steroidal drugs may be injected locally into the tissue surrounding the coccyx. This procedure may be repeated after one month, if necessary. If coccygodynia persists, the coccyx may be manipulated under general anesthesia and the coccygeal region injected again with anesthetic and steroidal drug.

Surgical removal of the coccyx (coccygectomy) may be considered in individuals who still experience pain following these treatments if it is believed that the cause is physical rather than psychological, but the results are frequently disappointing.

Prognosis

Conservative treatment (sitting in a hot sitz bath, use of a doughnut or coccyx pillow, chair modification, instruction in sitting mechanics, and taking a nonsteroidal anti-inflammatory drug) resolves the problem in most individuals within 6 months. Individuals who do not respond to conservative treatment and who are treated using local injection of anesthetic and steroidal drug are relieved of their symptoms almost 60% of the time. Recurrence of the condition happens within 1 year in approximately 21% of cases following this treatment. Coccygeal manipulation and injection is successful in 85% of cases and recurrence happens 28% of the time within a year.

Differential Diagnosis

Conditions that may present with similar symptoms as coccygodynia include pain referral from other nearby structures (uterus, ovaries, sacroiliac joint; lumbosacral area), hysteria, depression, pilonidal cyst, proctalgia fugax, and perirectal abscess.

Specialists

- Chiropractor
- Orthopedic Surgeon
- Physical Therapist
- Psychiatrist

Rehabilitation

Rehabilitation therapy may entail correction of sitting posture and restoration of lower back mobility under the direction of a physical therapist.

Work Restrictions / Accommodations

Work restrictions and accommodations usually include avoidance of prolonged sitting. This can be accomplished, for example, by permitting 5-minute standing breaks every hour. If sitting is required (e.g., professional drivers or pilots), the individual may have to use a doughnut- or U-shaped pillow to protect the coccyx from further trauma. Standing, walking, and carrying are generally not affected.

Complementary and Alternative Therapies

Content is intended for awareness only. Treatments may or may not be effective. Scientific evidence may be lacking and some substances have potentially toxic effects. Dr. Presley Reed and the editors do not endorse the use of these therapies in the absence of consultation with a licensed medical professional.

Massage - Gentle rubbing of the coccyx may help relieve pain symptoms.

Acupuncture - Insertion of needles into specific points on the body may alleviate pain associated with coccygodynia.

Comorbid Conditions

Existing conditions that may impact an individual's ability to recover and further lengthen their disability include pregnancy and psychiatric conditions.

Complications

Possible complications of coccygodynia include the inability to sit for extended periods of time. Also, the individual may be limited as to the type of physical labor he/she can perform.

Factors Influencing Duration

Factors that might influence disability include the severity of the coccygodynia and the individual's response to treatment for the condition. It has been suggested that psychological dysfunction may be a cause for onset and the individual's mental health status could play a role in the length of disability. Notably, a relationship between coccygodynia and anxiety, depression, or hysteria has never been proven.

Length of Disability

Duration in Days

Job Classification	Minimum	Optimum	Maximum
Sedentary work	0	3	5
Light work	0	3	5
Medium work	0	3	5
Heavy work	0	3	7
Very Heavy work	0	3	7

Failure to Recover

If an individual fails to recover within the maximum duration expectancy period, the reader may wish to reference the following questions to assist in better understanding the specifics of an individual's medical case.

Regarding diagnosis:

- Does individual complain of pain in the tailbone (coccygeal) area? Persistent rectal pain and fullness, pain on defecation, reduced anal sphincter control, and constipation?
- Did a bimanual rectal exam reveal pain in the coccygeal area?
- Were x-rays of the sacrum coccyx taken? MRI of the lumbar spine? Was stool tested for occult blood (guaiac test)?
- Were other conditions with similar symptoms ruled out?

Regarding treatment:

- Were conservative measures such as sitting in a hot sitz bath, use of a doughnut or coccyx pillow, chair modification, adjustable height, adjustable seat tilt, and increased cushion, instruction in sitting mechanics, and taking a nonsteroidal anti-inflammatory drug (NSAID) effective at relieving the symptoms? If not, was physiotherapy or injections of anesthetic or steroids tried?
- Was surgery considered?

Regarding prognosis:

- Did the symptoms persist or recur after conservative treatment?
- Was surgery indicated?
- Does individual have conditions that may impact ability to recover and lengthen disability?
- Were appropriate accommodations made regarding individual's work?

References

Finneson, B.E. Low Back Pain. Philadelphia: J.B. Lippincott Company, 1980.

Maigne, J.Y. "Lateral Dynamic X-rays in the Sitting Position and Coccygeal Discography in Common Coccydynia." Movement, Stability and Low Back Pain. Vleeming, A., et al., eds. New York: Churchill Livingstone, 1997. 385-391.

Cochlear Implant

Other names / synonyms: Artificial Ear, Electronic Ear
20.96

Definition

A cochlear implant is a small, complex electronic device that is surgically placed under the skin behind the ear. The implant can help to provide a sense of sound to a person who is profoundly deaf or severely hard of hearing.

An implant has 4 basic parts. The first is a microphone that picks up sound from the environment. The second is a speech processor that selects and arranges sounds picked up by the microphone. The third is a transmitter and receiver/stimulator that receives signals from the speech processor and converts them into electric impulses. The transmitter is an external part of the device and the receiver/stimulator is an internal portion that has the electrodes attached. The fourth part of the implant device is the electrodes that collect the impulses from the stimulator and sends them to the brain.

An implant does not restore or create normal hearing. Instead, under the appropriate conditions, it can give a deaf person a useful auditory understanding of the environment and help him or her to understand speech.

A cochlear implant is very different from a hearing aid. Hearing aids amplify sound. Cochlear implants compensate for damaged or non-working parts of the inner ear. When hearing is functioning normally, complicated parts of the inner ear convert sound waves in the air into electrical impulses. These impulses are then sent to the brain, where a hearing person recognizes them as sound. A cochlear implant works in a similar manner. It electronically finds useful sounds and then sends them to the brain. Hearing through an implant may sound different from normal hearing, but it allows many people to communicate fully with oral communication in person and over the phone.

There are approximately 18,000 individuals with cochlear implants worldwide. Most of these are in the US, Canada, and Australia. The implant users include both males and females ranging in age from 18 months to well into the later years.

Reason for Procedure

Treatment for severe deafness is one the primary reasons for the cochlear implant. The sensitive structures within the cochlea may have been damaged by trauma, toxic effect of drugs, or infection.

When the auditory nerve carrying sound signals to the brain is intact, but receives no stimulus, the implant provides signals that can be taken up by the auditory nerve.

How Procedure Is Performed

Cochlear implant surgery is performed under a general anesthetic in a sterile operating environment. It may be done either as an outpatient or in hospital.

An incision is made behind and slightly above the ear. The skin flap is laid back to expose the underlying tissue and bone. A burr-type instrument is used to drill a circular hole in the bone for preparation for implanting the internal coil. The mastoid bone in the ear is opened to gain access for the electrodes that will be led from the internal coil into the inner ear. The internal coil is then positioned in the prepared site and secured with stitches. The electrodes are inserted deep in the inner ear into the cochlea, which is the organ that transforms sound vibrations into nerve impulses for transmission to the brain. The incision is then closed and bandaged.

Once the surgical wound is healed, an external unit consisting of a stimulator with built-in microphone is provided for wearing behind the ear. It may be attached to eyeglasses or a headband or special magnets between the internal and external components.

Prognosis

Auditory performance with a cochlear implant varies among individuals. Available data indicate that performance is better in individuals who have a shorter duration of deafness, were implanted before age 6 years, and acquired language before their hearing loss occurred. Auditory performance is not affected by the reason for the hearing loss.

The individual should expect complete healing without complications. Stitches will be removed a few days after surgery. One or more follow up visits to the implant facility will be needed to program the implant. The hearing capability with the implant will vary from person to person and cannot be reliably predicted. A cochlear implant improves hearing but cannot restore normal hearing. The individual should be psychologically prepared to continue learning permanently.

Specialists

- Otolaryngologist

Work Restrictions / Accommodations

There are no special accommodations required for the individual who returns to his normal occupation and work. However, should the individual change jobs, the employer may need to provide listening and hearing assistive devices for use by the individual. Such devices may include special telephones and access to relay services, amplifiers, and signal lights.

Speech pathology programs and training will be needed for several weeks to introduce or re-introduce the individual to the hearing world. Continuous practice at identifying sounds and voices are needed.

Comorbid Conditions

Any medical condition that would create a problem during surgery (i.e., heart disease, pulmonary insufficiency, kidney disease, liver disease, allergies, and neurological disorders) may increase the risks of surgery. Any recent or chronic illness would be cause for delaying the surgery. Use of mind-altering drugs, including narcotics, psychedelics, hallucinogens, marijuana, sedatives, hypnotics, or cocaine would likely interfere with the recovery process and diminish the likelihood of successful use of the cochlear implant.

Procedure Complications

Major complications (those requiring revision surgery) include flap problems, device migration or extrusion, and device failure. Facial palsy is also considered a major complication but is distinctly uncommon and rarely permanent. No mortalities have been attributed to cochlear implantation.

Minor complications are those that resolve without surgical intervention. The most common is unwanted facial nerve stimulation with electrode activation, which is readily rectified by device reprogramming.

Long-term complications of implantation relate to flap breakdown, electrode migration and receiver/stimulator migration. Particularly in the child, the potential consequences of otitis media have been of concern, but as the implanted electrode becomes ensheathed in a fibrous envelope, it appears protected from the consequences of local infection.

Reimplantation is necessary in approximately 5% of cases because of improper electrode insertion or migration, device failure, serious flap complication, or loss of manufacturer support. Bleeding, vertigo, and surgical-wound infection may also occur.

Factors Influencing Duration

Age, physical condition, mental attitude, and ability to adapt to using the cochlear implant may impact the recovery.

Length of Disability

Duration in Days

Job Classification	Minimum	Optimum	Maximum
Any work	14	21	28

References

"Cochlear Implant." Healthgate.com 23 Feb 2000. 02 Jan 2001 <http://search1.healthgate.com/sym/surg42.shtml>.

Cochlear Implants. National Institute on Deafness and Other Communication Disorders. 01 Mar 2000. 2 Jan 2001 <http://www.nidcd.nih.gov/health/pubs_hb/coch.htm>.

Cognitive Therapy

Other names / synonyms: Cognitive Behavioral Therapy
94.33

Definition

Cognitive therapy is a widely used form of psychotherapy that focuses on changing thought patterns, styles and mechanisms in order to change behavior and emotional content. Cognitive therapy is based on the theory that individuals with depression, anxiety, and other emotional disorders have maladaptive or ineffective thought patterns and behavioral difficulties.

A primary goal of cognitive therapy is to identify negative or distorted "automatic" thoughts. Automatic thoughts occur when an individual is experiencing a particular situation or is recalling significant events from the past. Individuals with depression and anxiety have many more negative or fearful automatic thoughts than others, and these distorted thoughts usually cause painful emotional reactions. In addition, negative automatic thoughts can be associated with behaviors (i.e., helplessness, withdrawal, or avoidance) that worsen the problem.

Individuals with depression or anxiety disorders experience a circle of problematic thoughts, emotions, and behaviors.

Automatic thoughts are usually based on faulty logic or ineffective reasoning. Cognitive therapy helps individuals recognize and change these cognitive errors (sometimes called cognitive distortions). Some of the commonly described cognitive errors include: "all or nothing" thinking, personalization, and overgeneralization.

In cognitive therapy, individuals are taught how to detect cognitive errors and develop more effective thought patterns. For example, an individual may think, "I will never make friends because I'm so shy." Therapy would focus on changing this automatic thought to a more positive cognition such as, "Although I'm very shy, I can still make friends and meet new people." Another focus of cognitive therapy is on underlying "schemas." Schemas are the "basic rules" for interpreting information from daily living. Schemas (also called core beliefs) can be either adaptive or maladaptive. Cognitive therapists assist individuals in improving destructive schemas. Thus, cognitive intervention is more complex than changing automatic thoughts.

Cognitive therapy tends to be highly structured and logical, with both the therapist and the individual actively involved in the treatment. It can be used with individuals, couples, and families, and is conducted in outpatient and inpatient settings.

Reason for Procedure

Cognitive therapy is an effective treatment for a wide range of emotional problems including depression, anxiety, panic attacks, phobias such as social phobia or agoraphobia, relationship and marital problems, and stress-related disorders. It can be used for people with mania, anorexia nervosa, bulimia, chronic fatigue syndrome, cocaine abuse, and obsession with imagined physical ailments (hypochondriasis). Some mental health experts recommend the use of cognitive therapy for individuals that need help with procrastination, bereavement, and sexual problems. Cognitive therapy also helps to develop certain skills, such as assertiveness.

How Procedure Is Performed

Cognitive therapy uses various cognitive and behavioral techniques to treat anxiety disorders and milder forms of depression. It is usually a short-term treatment lasting for 10 to 20 sessions. In the early phase, the clinician establishes a good working relationship with the individual, and teaches him or her the basic principles of cognitive therapy. In the middle phase, dysfunctional patterns of information processing and behavior are recorded. The final phase of treatment reinforces skills learned earlier in therapy, and prepares individuals to manage problems on their own.

The main technique is known as "cognitive restructuring." This procedure attempts to alter the way a person thinks about certain circumstances that trigger fears or anxieties. Cognitive restructuring is intended to change the thought patterns that cause anxiety. Relaxation training and breathing exercises are often used to provide anxious individuals with a strategy to decrease their symptoms, especially in stressful situations. Exposure therapy may also be used for anxious individuals. In this procedure, individuals follow a gradual, systematic plan to learn to use anxiety management strategies to cope with irrational fears or phobic situations. Cognitive therapy also includes a number of behavioral interventions such as activity scheduling and graded task assignments. These procedures are used to improve behavioral problems and to influence cognitive functioning. Task assignments are also useful in measuring treatment goals and outcomes.

Prognosis

The outcome is good if the individual is committed to psychotherapy and the cognitive therapy process. The predicted outcome also depends on the individual's specific mental health diagnosis.

Specialists

• Licensed Clinical Social Worker	• Psychologist
	• Psychiatrist

Work Restrictions / Accommodations

A flexible work schedule is helpful when the individual must attend therapy during normal working hours. Other adjustments may be needed, depending on the specific mental health condition being treated.

Attendance at support groups, group therapy, or job coaching sessions may be recommended, depending on the individual's specific diagnosis and treatment goals.

Comorbid Conditions

In general, if the individual has been diagnosed with a personality disorder, this may lengthen the disability period. The presence of a substance abuse problem or active addiction may also impede recovery. If an individual is extremely depressed or suicidal, this could significantly lengthen disability.

Procedure Complications

Since cognitive therapy is a safe and effective form of psychotherapy, there are no known complications, particularly if conducted by licensed and qualified mental health professionals. However, if the individual is seriously depressed or suicidal, cognitive therapy may not be the treatment of choice. Depending upon the diagnosis, cognitive therapy should be used conjointly with psychopharmacology.

Factors Influencing Duration

If a psychiatric hospitalization is necessary, this is likely to affect the length of disability.

Length of Disability

No disability is expected to result from this therapy. Disability may occur as a result of an underlying condition.

References

Basics of Cognitive Therapy. MindStreet. 01 Jan 2000. 16 Jan 2001 <http://mindstreet.com/cbt.html>.

Wright, J.H., and A.T. Beck. "Cognitive Therapy." American Psychiatric Press Textbook of Psychiatry, 2nd ed. Hales, R.E., S.E. Yudofsky, and J.A. Talbott, eds. Washington, DC: American Psychiatric Press, 1995. 1083-1114.

Coin Lesion
793.1

Definition

Coin lesion is a term describing a round or nearly round lung mass (like a coin) found on a chest x-ray. Coin lesions have been associated with both non-cancerous (benign) and cancerous (malignant) tumors, tuberculosis infection, cysts, and fungal infections. The most common cause of a coin lesion, however, is a malignant tumor of the lung. On rare occasions, humans infected with the dog heart worm (Dirofilaria immitis), may also develop a coin lesion.

The finding of a coin lesion is more of a warning flag to the clinician than a diagnosis itself. While the coin lesion displaces normal lung tissue, it does not cause symptoms unless there is airway obstruction, pleural invasion, interference with respiratory mechanics, or involvement of blood vessels or nerves. Consequently, many coin lesions are discovered on routine chest x-rays in apparently healthy individuals.

Inflammatory lesions, such as those in tuberculosis infection or fungal infection, often double in volume in less than 5 weeks, while cancerous lesions may take between 1-18 months to double. Non-cancerous lesions grow very slowly or not at all. A solitary lesion that does not change in size over 2 years is generally deemed non-cancerous (benign).

The older the individual, the greater the chances that the lesion is malignant; the probability is less than 2% below age 30 and increases by 10-15% with each succeeding decade. A history of smoking greatly increases the probability that the lesion is malignant, as does concurrent weight loss, headache, or bone pain.

Diagnosis

History: The individuals may complain of chest pain or shortness of breath. However, in many cases the individual will have no specific physical complaints. They may report a history of cancer or may have had recent travel or exposure to tuberculosis.

Physical exam: Frequently, the physical reveals no abnormal findings. Those who have an underlying infection may have a fever, productive cough, and abnormal breath sounds. Shortness of breath, rapid respirations, and poor oxygenation may be associated with advanced infections or large lesions that extend into major airways or lung blood circulation. Weight loss may be a finding associated with tuberculosis or malignant lesions.

Tests: Coin lesions are discovered on a routine chest x-ray. This finding then prompts the need for additional tests to determine the cause of the lesion. CT of the chest may be done to better illustrate the characteristics of the coin lesion. Lab tests may include complete blood count (CBC), routine serum chemistries, and sputum cultures. Direct examination of the airways with a lighted scope (bronchoscopy) may be done. Surgical excision of the lesion (thoracotomy) may be needed to determine if the lesion is benign or malignant.

Treatment

Treatment depends on the cause of the lesion. Since tuberculosis is a potential community health hazard, all possible or proven cases of tuberculosis are reported to the local and state public health departments. Tuberculosis infections are treated (usually on an outpatient basis) with one of several antituberculosis medication regimens recommended by the Center for Disease Control and Prevention (CDC).

Antifungal medications are used to treat lesions of fungal origin. If the lesion does not appear to have an infectious origin, surgical biopsy of the mass (thoracotomy with biopsy of lung mass) may be done to determine if the lesion is malignant or benign. Malignant lesions may be completely removed (thoracotomy with excision of lung mass). Ongoing treatment may include cancer chemotherapy and or radiation therapy to arrest the growth of the cancer. Benign lesions are usually monitored closely to assess any change or growth.

Prognosis

The outcome will vary depending upon the cause. Benign coin lesions have positive outcomes. Underlying tuberculosis is usually cured following antibiotic therapy. However, underlying lung cancer has a 5-year survival rate ranging from 30-60%.

Differential Diagnosis

A coin lesion is a descriptive term of an x-ray finding that may result from lung infections, cysts, and a variety of non-cancerous and cancerous lung tumors.

Upon discovering a coin lesion, malignant tumors, tuberculosis infection, fungal infection, and benign cysts should all be included in the differential diagnosis.

Specialists

- Pulmonologist
- Thoracic Surgeon

Work Restrictions / Accommodations

Work restrictions and accommodations are dictated by the underlying cause, the required treatment, and the degree of associated disability. Those with benign coin lesions do not usually require any work restrictions or accommodations. Following treatment for tuberculosis infections or lung cancer, those with residual lung or organ dysfunction may need light-duty jobs to avoid overexertion.

Comorbid Conditions

Comorbid conditions such as obesity, immune system dysfunction, or chronic lung disease would impact ability to recover and further lengthen disability.

Complications

Complications associated with coin lesions depend on the underlying cause. Lesions from tuberculosis infection may be associated with complications due to failure of treatment, such as antibiotic resistance, that would prolong the therapy. Adverse side effects from the antibiotic treatment may include nausea, vomiting, yellowing of skin or eyes, fever, and abdominal pain. On occasion, tuberculosis can spread (disseminated TB) to the kidneys, spine, or liver.

Complications of coin lesions associated with lung cancer may include pneumonia, or spread (metastasis) to surrounding tissue, bone, brain, or liver.

Factors Influencing Duration

There are no factors influencing the length of disability.

Length of Disability

Duration depends on size, location, and type.

Failure to Recover

If an individual fails to recover within the maximum duration expectancy period, the reader may wish to reference the following questions to assist in better understanding the specifics of an individual's medical case.

Regarding diagnosis:

- Was the coin lesion found on a routine chest x-ray?
- Is individual being tested extensively to determine underlying cause of the coin lesion?
- Does individual report chest pain, shortness of breath, weight loss, headache, or bone pain?
- On exam, was there a fever, productive cough, or abnormal breath sounds?
- Does individual have rapid respirations or poor oxygenation?
- Does individual smoke? Have a history of cancer?
- Has individual traveled recently or been exposed to tuberculosis?
- Was CT of the chest done? Bronchoscopy? Thoracotomy? Were CBC, routine serum chemistries, and sputum cultures performed?
- Were conditions with similar symptoms ruled out?

Regarding treatment:

- What is the underlying condition? Is it being treated appropriately?
- If lesions were of fungal origin, were antifungal medications used? Was surgical biopsy of the mass done to determine if lesion is malignant or benign? If malignant, was lesion removed? Was cancer chemotherapy or radiation therapy tried?

Regarding prognosis:

- Can individual's employer accommodate any necessary restrictions?
- Does individual have any conditions that may affect ability to recover?
- Have any complication developed such as antibiotic resistance, adverse side effects of the antibiotics, or disseminated TB? Does individual have pneumonia, or metastasis?

References

Goldman, Lee, and J. Claude Bennett. Cecil Textbook of Medicine, 21st ed. Philadelphia: W B. Saunders Company, 2000.

Cold

Other names / synonyms: Common Cold, Coryza, Head Cold, Nasopharyngitis, Rhinitis, Upper Respiratory Tract Infection, URI

460

Definition

The common cold is an acute and self-limited illness caused by any of more than 250 viruses that invade the mucus cells of the nose and disrupt their normal functioning. Once infected with one of the 250 strains, the immune system develops antibodies to it, so any subsequent colds are the result of one of the other 249 strains. The illness is characterized by a runny nose (rhinorrhea), nasal congestion, sneezing, mild fatigue, mild fever, and sore throat, with or without a cough. Symptoms of this illness are confined to the upper respiratory tract and do not involve the lungs.

Although many individuals believe that exposure to cold weather can result in a cold, researchers have shown that exposure to cold temperatures has little or no effect on the development of a cold. Susceptibility to colds is also not thought to be related to factors such as diet, exercise, or enlarged tonsils, but rather to factors like psychological stress, allergic disorders (affecting the nose or throat), and menstrual cycles. Cold viruses are transmitted by direct contact through hands, by droplet contamination, or inhalation in the air (cough, sneeze). After exposure to a cold-causing virus, symptoms usually appear within 48 to 72 hours.

Normal healthy adults may average 2 to 4 colds per year, although the range varies greatly. In a single year in the US, individuals suffer an estimated 1 billion colds. Women (age 20 to 30) have more colds than men. Colds generally last from 5 to 7 days, with about 25% having symptoms that continue for up to 2 weeks. Colds are the most frequent cause of absenteeism from work.

Diagnosis

History: Common symptoms include dry, sore, or scratchy throat; runny or stuffy nose; cough; sneezing; headache; and body aches.

Physical exam: Mild fever (99-101 degrees F) may be present. Examination may reveal reddening of the throat or nose with swelling of these mucosal tissues. Lymph nodes in the neck may be enlarged and tender.

Tests: Diagnosis is based on clinical signs and symptoms; no laboratory tests or x-rays are necessary for diagnosis.

Treatment

The infected individual should be isolated as much as possible to avoid contaminating others. Without treatment, cold symptoms should disappear in about 7 to 10 days. Because no cure for the common cold exists, only symptomatic treatment is available: bed rest, increased fluid intake, gargling with warm salt water (to relieve inflammation, discomfort, and swelling of the throat), saline gel (for irritated nasal tissue), and analgesics (for headache and fever).

Nonprescription cold preparations (decongestants and cough suppressants) may relieve some cold symptoms, but will not cure or even shorten the duration of the illness.

Since antibiotics do not kill viruses, these drugs should not be used to treat routine colds. Antibiotics should be reserved for treating any bacterial complications of colds (sinusitis or ear infections).

Prognosis

The prognosis for the common cold is excellent. Individuals can expect symptoms to disappear in approximately 7 to 10 days and a complete recovery to pre-illness health. In individuals with chronic respiratory conditions, the decreased immunity caused by the cold may put these individuals at greater risk for developing secondary bacterial infections, such as sinusitis, bronchitis, or pneumonia. In these cases, a protracted recovery period may be expected.

Differential Diagnosis

When additional symptoms develop or if symptoms persist longer than a few weeks it may be a sign of a more serious condition. For example, flu (influenza) is usually signaled by severe headache, chills, and fever. Cold-like symptoms that last more than 2 weeks may be caused by an infection of the sinus cavities (bacterial sinusitis), which requires a physician's diagnosis and possibly antibiotic treatment.

Specialists

- Otolaryngologist
- Primary Care Provider

Work Restrictions / Accommodations

A day of bed rest may be necessary for a particularly bad cold. Usually, individuals may continue to work despite cold symptoms. Individuals with colds should be encouraged to take precautions not to infect other workers, including staying as isolated from others as possible, using tissues and discarding them properly after use, and washing hands frequently. As with other respiratory illnesses, exposure to inhaled irritants such a dust, gases, smoke, and cold air should be minimized or avoided.

Comorbid Conditions

Autoimmune disease, chronic lung disease, chronic respiratory conditions, and asthma may lengthen the duration of the cold or make the individual more susceptible to secondary bacterial infections.

Complications

The great majority of common colds run their course without complication. The most common complications of colds are secondary bacterial infections (sinusitis and ear infection). Individuals with pre-existing respiratory conditions (asthma or chronic lung disease) are more susceptible to secondary bacterial infections such as bronchitis or pneumonia.

Factors Influencing Duration

Severity of symptoms will determine the length of disability in a previously healthy person. If symptoms are mild, there may be no loss of time from work. If the symptoms are severe, or complications occur, disability may be longer.

Length of Disability

Duration depends on severity of symptoms, complications, and individual's job requirement.

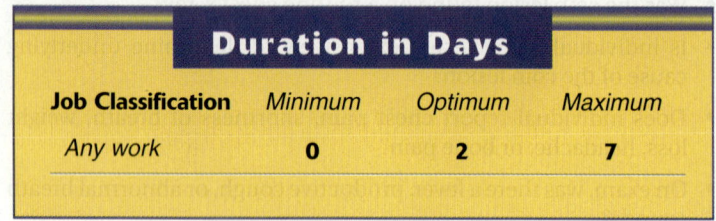

Duration in Days

Job Classification	Minimum	Optimum	Maximum
Any work	0	2	7

Failure to Recover

If an individual fails to recover within the maximum duration expectancy period, the reader may wish to reference the following questions to assist in better understanding the specifics of an individual's medical case.

Regarding diagnosis:

- Does individual have a runny nose? Congestion? Sneezing? Sore throat? Cough?
- Does individual have a mild fever or fatigue? Enlarged lymph nodes?
- Are the lungs involved?
- Does individual have additional symptoms? Have they lasted more than 2 weeks?

Regarding treatment:

- Was individual isolated as much as possible to prevent spread?
- Is individual following a proper treatment regimen (rest, increased fluids, analgesics)?
- Is individual a smoker?

Regarding prognosis:

- Can individual's employer accommodate any necessary restrictions?
- Does individual have any conditions that may affect ability to recover?
- Have any complications developed such as a secondary bacterial infection?

Colitis

Other names / synonyms: Enteritis, Gastroenteritis, IBD, Ileitis, Inflammatory Bowel Disease, Jejunitis
558, 558.1, 558.2, 558.9

Definition

Colitis refers to inflammation of the large intestine (colon). The inflammation may be due to infection caused by virus, ameba, or a bacterium (such as Campylobacter) producing toxins that irritate the lining of the intestine. Bacteria directly infecting the inner lining of the colon may also cause colitis.

If antibiotics are taken over a prolonged period of time, they may cause antibiotic-associated colitis. This occurs when bacteria normally living in the intestine are killed by extended antibiotic usage. Another type of bacterium (Clostridium difficile) may then proliferate and produce a toxin that irritates the colon. The antibiotic itself may also have an irritative effect that can cause colonic inflammation.

In the elderly, ischemic colitis may occur when narrowing of the blood vessels (atherosclerosis) impairs the blood supply to the intestinal wall. Ulcerative colitis is another serious intestinal disorder that usually begins in young adulthood and is of unknown origin. This condition is characterized by inflammation limited to the colon and rectum.

Colitis occurs at all ages but has a higher incidence among young adults and individuals of Jewish descent. Both sexes are affected equally by colitis.

Diagnosis

History: Individuals may report watery diarrhea containing mucus, pus, or blood; abdominal pain, tenderness, or spasm (colic); and intermittent or irregular fever.

Physical exam: A digital exam of the rectum with a gloved finger may be performed to detect irregularities. A stethoscope may be used to listen to bowel sounds (auscultation).

Tests: A sample of feces is examined for parasites, and a culture or stained smear is microscopically analyzed to identify bacteria. A flexible viewing scope (endoscope or sigmoidoscope) may be used to examine the inside of the rectum and colon for inflammation or ulceration of the lining (colonoscopy). Small samples (biopsies) of inflamed areas of the large intestine may be taken for examination with a microscope. A radiographic procedure to visualize the colon (barium enema) may help identify areas of narrowing or severe inflammation.

Treatment

Most infections that cause acute colitis resolve without treatment. However, infections caused by Campylobacter or clostridium may need to be treated with antibiotics. Individuals treated with antibiotics specific for only certain microorganisms run the risk of infection by nontargeted bacteria. Consequently, broad-spectrum antibiotics should be used to minimize the potential for secondary infection and development of tissue death and decay (gangrene) or infection (sepsis). Amebic infections are sometimes treated with antiamebic medication (amebicides).

When colitis is caused by low blood flow (ischemia), it may be treated by surgical removal of the diseased section of the colon (colectomy). Ulcerative colitis is treated with a combination of anti-inflammatory drugs (corticosteroids), a special diet, and vitamin supplements. If surgical intervention is necessary for ulcerative colitis, the entire colon and rectum are commonly removed (total proctocolectomy).

Following surgery, the individual may require an artificial opening (stoma) of the colon through the abdominal wall to enable bowel emptying (colostomy). A colostomy may be temporary or permanent depending on the portion of bowel surgically removed. If the entire colon and rectum are removed, the individual will require a permanent stoma of the lower small intestine (ileum) through the abdominal wall (ileostomy).

Prognosis

Colitis caused by infection may resolve without treatment. If treatment is necessary, however, the infection usually responds well to medication. Antibiotic-associated colitis normally clears up once the antibiotic therapy is discontinued. Ulcerative colitis is a chronic condition requiring long-term management. The predicted outcome for ischemic colitis may depend on the extent of damaged colon removed.

Differential Diagnosis

Conditions that present with similar symptoms include inflammation localized to a specific area of the gastrointestinal tract (Crohn's disease), inflammation of the rectum (proctitis), inflammation of a pouch formed abnormally in the colon (diverticular disease), or intestinal cancer (colon carcinoma). Irritable bowel syndrome (IBS) is a functional disorder and must also be considered.

Specialists

- Gastroenterologist
- General Surgeon

Rehabilitation

A regular exercise routine may be useful in reducing the risk of ischemic colitis. Aerobic exercise such as walking, jogging, or swimming (30 to 45 minutes per session) is usually beneficial. For individuals who do not engage in regular exercise, a consultation with a physical therapist may be useful. Individuals learn how to properly warm-up all muscle groups, stretch to prevent injury, and gradually increase the amount of exercise performed.

Work Restrictions / Accommodations

Work restrictions and accommodations are not usually associated with this condition although ready access to bathroom facilities may be necessary. Following a prolonged episode of colitis, the individual may need to limit strenuous activities until physical stamina returns. If treatment involves surgery, return to work will probably be delayed for several weeks and may then be limited to modified duty for a period of time until recovery is complete.

Complementary and Alternative Therapies

Content is intended for awareness only. Treatments may or may not be effective. Scientific evidence may be lacking and some substances have potentially toxic effects. Dr. Presley Reed and the editors do not endorse the use of these therapies in the absence of consultation with a licensed medical professional.

Acupuncture	May effectively decrease symptoms of colitis.
Biofeedback	Monitoring gastrointestinal activity may help in controlling symptoms of colitis.
Massage	May help relieve pain associated with colitis.

Comorbid Conditions

Any disease affecting circulation to the digestive tract may further lengthen disability caused by colitis.

Complications

Prolonged diarrhea may result in dehydration and electrolyte imbalance. In severe cases of colitis, intestinal bleeding (hemorrhage) and perforation of the colon can occur.

Factors Influencing Duration

In general, this disease does not disable individuals unless there is a complication that makes surgical intervention necessary. The severity of the symptoms, type of treatment, response to treatment, and the presence of complications may influence length of disability.

Length of Disability

A mild episode of colitis can be treated easily in 1 to 2 days. If the individual has moderate to severe ischemic colitis, hospitalization is usually required and a longer recovery period (1 week or more) will be needed. If abdominal surgery is required, 4 to 6 weeks may be needed before an individual can return to work.

Acute.

Duration in Days

Job Classification	Minimum	Optimum	Maximum
Sedentary work	0	3	7
Light work	0	3	7
Medium work	0	3	7
Heavy work	0	3	7
Very Heavy work	0	3	7

Colon resection, partial laparoscopic.

Duration in Days

Job Classification	Minimum	Optimum	Maximum
Sedentary work	10	14	21
Light work	10	14	21
Medium work	14	21	28
Heavy work	14	35	42
Very Heavy work	14	42	56

Colon resection, partial open.

Duration in Days

Job Classification	Minimum	Optimum	Maximum
Sedentary work	21	28	42
Light work	21	28	42
Medium work	28	35	56
Heavy work	35	42	56
Very Heavy work	42	42	56

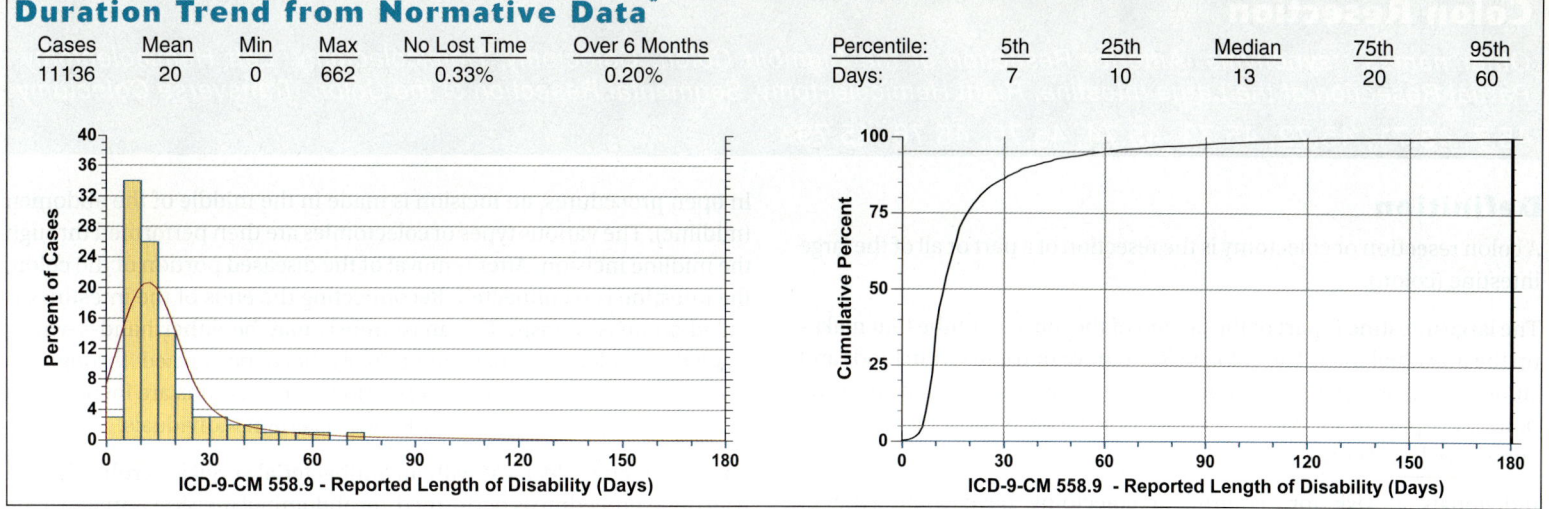

* Differences may exist between the expected duration tables and the normative graphs. Duration tables provide expected recovery periods based on the type of work performed by the individual. The normative graphs reflect the actual observed experience of many individuals across the spectrum of physical conditions, in a variety of industries, and with varying levels of case management.

Failure to Recover

If an individual fails to recover within the maximum duration expectancy period, the reader may wish to reference the following questions to assist in better understanding the specifics of an individual's medical case.

Regarding diagnosis:

- Has the individual been on long-term antibiotic therapy?
- Does the individual have atherosclerosis? Ulcerative colitis?
- What is the individual's ethnic background? Age?
- Does the individual report watery diarrhea containing mucus, pus, or blood; abdominal pain, tenderness, or spasm (colic); and intermittent or irregular fever?
- Did the individual have a digital examination of the rectum?
- Was auscultation of the abdomen done?
- Has the individual had comprehensive stool testing done?
- Has the individual had a sigmoidoscopy or colonoscopy? Biopsies?
- Has the individual had a barium enema?
- Have conditions with similar symptoms been ruled out?

Regarding treatment:

- Is the individual being treated with broad-spectrum antibiotics or amebicides?
- Is the individual being treated with corticosteroids, special diet and vitamin supplements?
- Was it necessary for the individual to have a colectomy or total proctocolectomy?
- Does the individual have a colostomy or ileostomy?

Regarding prognosis:

- Does the individual exercise regularly?
- Is the individual's employer able to accommodate any necessary restrictions?
- Does the individual have any conditions that may affect their ability to recover?
- Does the individual have any complications such as dehydration, electrolyte imbalance, intestinal hemorrhage or perforation of the colon?

References

Davenport, Horace W. Physiology of the Digestive Tract. Chicago: Year Book Medical Publishers, Inc, 1982.

Song, G.Q. "Clinical Analysis of 60 Cases of Ulcerative Colitis Treated with Chinese Traditional Medicinal Herbs." Chinese Journal of Modern Developments in Traditional Medicine 5 8 (1985): 474-475.

Colon Resection

Other names / synonyms: Anterior Resection of the Sigmoid Colon, Colectomy, Hemicolectomy, Left Hemicolectomy, Partial Resection of the Large Intestine, Right Hemicolectomy, Segmental Resection of the Colon, Transverse Colectomy

45.7, 45.71, 45.72, 45.73, 45.74, 45.75, 45.76, 45.79

Definition

A colon resection or colectomy is the resection of a part or all of the large intestine (colon).

The large intestine is part of the far end of the muscular tube that makes up the intestinal tract. The colon helps remove nutrients from foods and stores the waste material (stool or feces) until it is expelled from the body. This part of the intestinal tract is also called the large intestine, large bowel, and colon.

Individuals at risk for requiring a colectomy have some type of gastrointestinal disorder such as diverticulitis, cancer, Crohn's disease, ulcerative colitis, volvulus, obstruction, and trauma. With the exception of trauma, partial colectomy is performed equally on both sexes. Colectomy for trauma is three times more common in males.

About 15% of individuals with diverticulitis require colectomy. Colorectal cancer occurs in about 5% of Americans. Most of these individuals require surgical resection although very small tumors can be removed by procedures performed through the anus (transanal). About 60% individuals with Crohn's disease require a colectomy within 10 years of developing the disease and about 50% of individuals require a second surgery within 10 years for disease recurrence. About 20-25% of individuals with ulcerative colitis require colectomy. Colon resection is necessary for treatment of volvulus completed by gangrene or if the volvulus affects the transverse colon.

Reason for Procedure

Colectomy is used to treat a variety of gastrointestinal disorders. It is performed to treat small sacs on the walls of the colon that become inflamed (diverticulitis). Colectomies are performed to remove colon cancer. A colectomy can also treat inflammatory conditions of the bowel (Crohn's disease) or an intestinal obstruction that may develop due to cancer. A colectomy is also performed for an intestinal condition where the intestine twists and causes an obstruction (volvulus). When the intestinal tract is damaged due to trauma, a colectomy may be performed.

How Procedure Is Performed

A colon resection or colectomy is performed in the hospital as an inpatient procedure using general anesthesia.

There are several types of colectomies. The type to be performed depends on the location of the diseased portion of the intestine. If the right side of the colon is to be removed, it is called a right hemicolectomy. If the part of the colon on the individual's left side is to be removed, it is known as a left colectomy. A transverse colectomy is performed when the part of the colon that crosses from the right to the left side (transverse colon) is removed. In an anterior resection of the sigmoid colon, the part of the colon next to the rectum (sigmoid colon) is removed.

In open procedures, an incision is made in the middle of the abdomen (midline). The various types of colectomies are then performed through the midline incision. After removal of the diseased portion of the colon, the intestine is reconnected. Reconnecting the ends of the intestines is called an anastomosis. The anastomosis may be either hand-sewn or stapled. A colectomy has traditionally been performed through an abdominal incision (open surgery). However, surgeons are increasingly performing laparoscopic colectomies on certain individuals.

The abdomen is cleansed with an antibacterial surgical scrub solution. If an open procedure is performed, an abdominal incision is made. If the procedure is done laparoscopically, small puncture wounds are made in the abdomen and the laparoscopy equipment is gently inserted through the wounds. A very small abdominal incision is needed for performing the anastomosis during laparoscopic procedures. With either procedure, the surgeon works down through abdominal tissues to the segment of the colon to be removed. It is loosened from surrounding tissues (mobilized) and the blood supply to that part of the colon is identified. The blood supply to the diseased segment is divided from the vessels that supply the remaining segments of the colon, and the blood vessels supplying the diseased bowel segment are closed off to prevent bleeding. The diseased portion of the colon is removed. The ends of the colon that remain are usually reconnected (anastomosed). Sometimes the colon cannot be reconnected and a colostomy is required. Drain tubes may be placed to allow drainage of any secretions that accumulate. The incision is sutured closed. Dressings are placed over the incision.

Prognosis

Colectomy reduces the risk of recurrence of diverticular disease from 30% to 5-10%, risk of recurrence. In Crohn's disease, about half the individuals require a second surgery within 10 years of the initial surgery. Colectomy is generally curative for ulcerative colitis and for obstructions due to volvulus.

The outcome of colectomy performed for treatment of cancer varies depending on the stage and spread of the cancer at the time of diagnosis as well as individual's response to treatment. The outcome of individuals with colon cancer diagnosed in the early stage is good. About 90% of these individuals survive.

Specialists

- Colorectal Surgeon
- Gastroenterologist
- General Surgeon

Work Restrictions / Accommodations

Several weeks off of work may be needed for wound healing and recovery. Light work may be resumed. Heavy lifting should be avoided until approved by the surgeon. If treatment is necessary for cancer, time off from work may be necessary for treatment and recovery.

Comorbid Conditions

Comorbid conditions such as diabetes and obesity may impact wound-healing time and increase the risk of infection.

Procedure Complications

Complications due to colectomy may include wound infection, pelvic abscess, leakage at the sites where the intestines were sutured together (anastomosis sites), development of an abnormal tube-like passage (fistula), narrowing of the intestines where the intestines were sutured together, and a recurrence of disease.

Factors Influencing Duration

Factors that may influence the length of disability include number and severity of postoperative complications (i.e., wound infection, bleeding, abscess, or an adverse reaction to a general anesthetic), amount of blood loss during surgery and postoperatively, success of the surgery, individual's nutritional status and mental and emotional stability, and strength of the individual's support system.

Length of Disability

Duration depends on diagnosis for which the procedure is done and whether or not a colostomy is required.

Partial, laparoscopic.

Duration in Days

Job Classification	Minimum	Optimum	Maximum
Sedentary work	10	14	21
Light work	10	14	21
Medium work	14	21	28
Heavy work	14	35	42
Very Heavy work	14	42	56

Partial, open.

Duration in Days

Job Classification	Minimum	Optimum	Maximum
Sedentary work	21	28	42
Light work	21	28	42
Medium work	28	35	56
Heavy work	35	42	56
Very Heavy work	42	42	56

References

Bell, Richard M. "Surgical Procedures, Techniques, and Skills." Essentials of General Surgery, 3rd ed. Lawrence, Peter F., ed. Philadelphia: Lippincott Williams & Wilkins, 2000. 522-563.

McQuaid, Kenneth R. "Alimentary Tract." Current Medical Diagnosis and Treatment, 39th ed. Tierney, Lawrence, et al., eds. New York: Lange Medical Books/McGraw-Hill, 2000. 553-655.

O'Connell, Michael J. "Carcinoma of the Colon." Current Therapy in Cancer, 2nd ed. Foley, John F., Julie M. Vose, and James O. Armitage, eds. Philadelphia: W.B. Saunders Company, 1999. 97-99.

Petty, Lynda R. "Gastrointestinal Surgery." Alexander's Care of the Patient in Surgery, 11th ed. Meeker, Margaret H., and Jane Rothrock, eds. St. Louis: Mosby, 1999. 313-370.

Yamada, Tadataka. "Inflammatory Bowel Disease." Handbook of Gastroenterology. Yamada, Tadataka, ed. Philadelphia: Lippincott Williams & Wilkins, 1998. 402-418.

Yamada, Tadataka. "Structural Anomalies and Diverticular Disease of the Colon." Handbook of Gastroenterology. Yamada, Tadataka, ed. Philadelphia: Lippincott Williams & Wilkins, 1998. 375-382.

Colonoscopy

Other names / synonyms: Coloscopy, Endoscopy of Colon, Fiberoptic Colonoscopy, Flexible Colonoscopy

45.23

Definition

Colonoscopy is a procedure in which the lining of the entire large intestine (large bowel or colon) is examined using a colonoscope. The colonoscope is a flexible instrument about one-half inch in diameter and about 4 feet in length. It transmits light, allowing the physician to examine the lining of the colon from beginning (cecum) to end (anus); sometimes the last several inches of the small intestine can also be examined. To further facilitate the examination, the colon is inflated with air to widen the walls; this enables the physician to visualize inflamed tissue, abnormal growths, ulcers, bleeding, and spasms. Suction can be used to remove secretions.

Colonoscopy is recommended to evaluate conditions of altered bowel habit, unexplained diarrhea, constipation, abdominal pain, occult or frank blood in stools, colon polyps, cancer, or unexplained anemia.

Colonoscopy is generally not performed in cases of bowel perforation or tear, severe diverticulitis, colitis, inflammatory bowel disease, clinically unstable individuals, or those who have not followed the dietary restrictions and cleansing routine prescribed prior to the procedure.

Reason for Procedure

Colonoscopy is often prescribed a screening procedure to detect colorectal cancer, or abnormal growths (polyps) in the rectum and along the entire large intestine that may increase the risk of such cancer. Colonoscopy is also used to locate strictures, diagnose inflammatory bowel disease, and detect areas of hemorrhage that may be causing persistent bloody diarrhea, and abdominal pain, or iron deficiency anemia of unknown etiology. Minor operative procedures can be performed utilizing the colonoscope, including tissue biopsy, polypectomy, colon decompression, dilation of colonic strictures, electrocoagulation of bleeding sites, removal of foreign bodies, and electrocautery (fulguration) of tumors. A biopsy taken during the procedure can confirm other test findings, x-rays, or imaging studies. Colonoscopy can be used to diagnose Crohn's disease and ulcerative colitis.

How Procedure Is Performed

The colonoscopy is performed in a specialized endoscopy suite either in a clinic or as an outpatient procedure in a hospital. The individual is awake, but kept sedated with IV sedatives and analgesics.

After examining and lubricating the rectal opening, the physician inserts a long, flexible, lighted tube (colonoscope) into the individual's rectum, guides it through the lower GI tract, and up into the colon. The colonoscope transmits an image of the inside of the colon on a monitor so the physician can carefully examine it. Because the colonoscope is flexible, the physician can move it around the curves of the colon. As the examination progresses, the individual may be asked to change position occasionally to facilitate the scope's passage through the colon. To improve visualization, the physician may gently infuse air into the colon. This sometimes causes a painless sensation of abdominal fullness.

If the colonoscopy reveals any unusual conditions, such as inflammation, ulcer, tumor, or abnormal growth (polyp), the physician may photograph them so they can be part of the individual's permanent medical record and allow other physicians to evaluate the results. To better evaluate any areas of suspected abnormality, the physician will take a brushing or biopsy of the colon lining. Brushing involves passing a tiny nylon brush though the center of the colonoscope, rubbing it against the lining of the colon, and retrieving bits of tissue for later analysis. Tissue samples (biopsy) or stool samples are collected with tiny metal forceps or suction devices that are introduced through special channels in the colonoscope. Both of these procedures are painless for the individual. Should a small polyp be discovered during the procedure, it is usually immediately removed with electrocautery snares. This may prevent colon cancer from developing and eliminate the need for major surgery. Laser therapy can also be done through a colonoscope.

Prognosis

Colonoscopy generally provides reliable diagnostic information for diagnosis and treatment when performed periodically. Normal results reveal colon tissue that is healthy.

Abnormal results indicate the following possibilities: inflammatory bowel disease, diverticulitis, ulcerative colitis, tumor, lower GI bleeding (hemorrhage), or polyp. Through colonoscopy, the detection and removal of polyps provides early prevention of colon cancer.

Specialists

- Colorectal Surgeon
- Gastroenterologist
- Surgeon

Work Restrictions / Accommodations

After a colonoscopy, most individuals are advised to avoid driving or operating machinery for the remainder of the day, because judgment and reflexes are likely to be impaired by the sedation given before and during the procedure. Most individuals are ready to return to work the day following the procedure.

Comorbid Conditions

Comorbid conditions that may influence length of disability include diverticulitis, discovery of a tumor, bowel perforation, inflammatory bowel disease, colitis, allergic reaction to medications used in relation to the procedure, and chronic illnesses, such as heart disease, hypertension, and diabetes.

Procedure Complications

The principal complications of colonoscopy are a tear through the bowel wall (perforation of the colon) or bleeding (hemorrhage). Although perforation will require surgery, certain cases may be treated with antibiotics and intravenous fluids. Bleeding may occur at the site of either a biopsy or polyp removal. Typically minor in degree, such bleeding may stop on its own or be controlled by cauterization. Fortunately, both perforation of the colon and bleeding are quite rare, and occur in 0.14-1% of cases.

The individual should inform his or her physician of all allergies and medical conditions. In some individuals, the IV site may become inflamed and tender; this is generally short-lived and not serious, and can be successfully treated by applying warm compresses to the area. Occasionally an infection will develop, requiring antibiotics. Other complications can include either a reaction to the sedative medication given or over-sedation, causing respiratory depression or low blood pressure (hypotension), or dehydration because of the laxatives and enemas required for pre-procedure bowel cleansing.

Factors Influencing Duration

Factors that might influence length of disability include the underlying condition that prompted the procedure, and the development of complications (primarily due to the medications used with the colonoscopy).

Length of Disability

With or without biopsy.

Duration in Days

Job Classification	Minimum	Optimum	Maximum
Any work	0	2	3

References

Borland-Groover Procedures - Colonoscopy. Borland-Groover Clinic. 01 Jan 2000. 01 Jan 2001 <http://www.borland-groover.com/articles/colonoscopy.htm>.

Colonoscopy. National Digestive Diseases Information Clearinghouse. 07 Jul 1998. 01 Jan 2001 <http://www.niddk.nih.gov/health/digest/pubs/diagtest/colo.htm>.

Colonoscopy. Three Rivers Endoscopy Center. 01 Jan 1997. 01 Jan 2001 <http://www.gihealth.com/TREC2/scopes.colonoscopy.html>.

American Society for Gastrointestinal Endoscopy. Your Colonoscopy at Emory. Emory University School of Medicine. 30 Jan 2000. 01 Jan 2001 <http://www.emory.edu/WHSC/MED/GI/aboutcol.html>.

Popovic J.R., and L.J. Kozak. Vital and Health Statistics National Hospital Discharge Survey: Annual Summary, 1998, Series 13 No. 148. Centers for Disease Control and Prevention (CDC). 01 Sep 2000. 01 Jan 2001 <http://www.cdc.gov/nchs/data/sr13_148.pdf>.

Saltz, Richard K., MD. "Colonoscopy." Colonoscopy Diagnostic Center. 01 Jan 1998. 20 Feb 2001 <http://www.bellydoc.com/articles/article23.htm>.

Colorado Tick Fever

Other names / synonyms: Colorado Tick Virus, Mountain Fever
066.1

Definition

Colorado tick fever is a viral infection that is spread by the bite of ticks that have fed on the blood of infected animals such as rodents, birds, and some larger mammals. Fever, headaches, and muscle aches often accompany the onset of Colorado tick fever (CTF).

The disease is limited to mountainous regions (elevations above 4,000 feet) in the western US and Canada. CTF is prevalent during spring and early summer when ticks are most active. The disease tends to affect more males and young adults, although extended outdoor activity in pertinent areas likely is the major underlying risk factor. The disease is thought to be significantly unreported or misdiagnosed, with only a few hundred cases of CTF recorded annually.

Diagnosis

History: Symptoms include abrupt onset of fever, chills, headache, fatigue, joint pain, nausea, and vomiting. The individual may experience loss of appetite and unusual intolerance of light (photophobia). Occasionally, a faint rash develops. The fever is usually quite high and lasts 2 to 3 days. The fever lapses for a few days, then recurs in several bouts (biphasic). Fatigue sometimes lasting weeks may be reported. The individual may remember experiencing one or more tick bites during outdoor activity in pertinent mountainous areas.

Physical exam: Fever is usually present, although it may be in its remission phase. A few individuals have a faint rash. The spleen and liver may be enlarged (palpable).

Tests: A complete blood count (CBC) generally reveals an abnormal decrease in white blood cells (leukopenia). A decrease in platelets (thrombocytopenia) is characteristic. Certain antibodies possibly indicating presence of the disease may be detected through staining of the blood with a chemically treated dye (immunofluorescence).

Treatment

Since no specific treatment is available, medical intervention involves relieving symptoms. Fluids are recommended. Pain relievers (analgesics) and/or fever-reducing agents (antipyretics) also might be recommended.

Prognosis

The disease is usually self-limited, although it may be followed by a period of weakness (asthenia) lasting weeks or months. Most individuals recover completely with long-lasting immunity. In extremely rare cases, individuals may die if organs such as the heart or lungs are severely affected.

Differential Diagnosis

Conditions with similar symptoms include influenza, rheumatic fever, measles, rubella, typhoid fever, leptospirosis, Rocky Mountain spotted fever, tularemia, babesiosis, ehrlichiosis, Lyme disease, and other tick-borne illnesses.

Specialists

- Infectious Disease Physician
- Primary Care Provider

Work Restrictions / Accommodations

Strenuous activities may need to be modified until physical stamina returns.

Comorbid Conditions

Immune disorders and pre-existing lung, liver, or heart conditions may increase the severity of symptoms and lengthen recovery time.

Complications

Complications may include inflammation of the brain and its membrane coverings (meningoencephalitis), inflammation of the heart (myocarditis) or the membrane covering the heart (pericarditis), inflammation of the testicles (orchitis), or liver inflammation (hepatitis). If thrombocytopenia is severe, bleeding may occur. Symptoms resembling a heart attack (myocardial infarction) also have been reported.

Factors Influencing Duration

The individual's age, severity of disease, or the presence of complications may influence length of disability.

Length of Disability

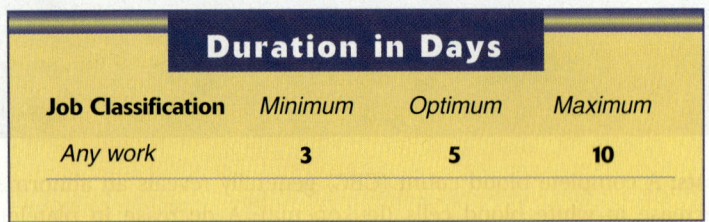

Job Classification	Minimum	Optimum	Maximum
Any work	3	5	10

Failure to Recover

If an individual fails to recover within the maximum duration expectancy period, the reader may wish to reference the following questions to assist in better understanding the specifics of an individual's medical case.

Regarding diagnosis:

- At what elevation does individual live, work, or play?
- Did individual have abrupt onset of fever, chills, headache, fatigue, joint pain, nausea, and vomiting? Does individual have a rash?
- Did individual experience loss of appetite or photophobia?
- Does individual have a high fever? Did it go away and then come back?
- Does individual complain of fatigue that has lasted for weeks?
- Does individual remember having a tick bite?
- On exam, were the liver and spleen enlarged? Was a rash evident? Fever?
- Has individual had a CBC? Immunofluorescence testing?
- Were conditions with similar symptoms ruled out?

Regarding treatment:

- Has individual responded favorably to symptomatic treatment such as administration of fluids, pain relievers (analgesics), and/or fever-reducing agents (antipyretics)?

Regarding prognosis:

- Can individual's employer accommodate any necessary restrictions?
- Does individual have any conditions that may affect ability to recover?
- Have any complications developed such as meningitis, myocarditis, pericarditis, orchitis, hepatitis, or thrombocytopenia?

References

Calisher, Charles H., and Robert B. Craven. "Colorado Tick Fever: Current Approaches to Diagnosis and Treatment." Infections in Medicine 15 8 (1998): 8. Medscape. 13 Aug 2000 <http://www.medscape.com/SCP/IIM/1998/v15.n08/m3198.cali/m3198.cali-01.html>.

Colostomy and Ileostomy

Other names / synonyms: Continent Ileostomy, Diverting Colostomy, Diverting Colostomy/Ileostomy, Diverting Ileostomy, Hendon Ileostomy, Intestinal Stoma, Ostomy, Permanent Ileostomy, Tangential Ileostomy, Temporary Colostomy, Temporary Ileostomy, Tube Ileostomy

46.1, 46.10, 46.11, 46.13, 46.20, 46.21, 46.22

Definition

Colostomy and ileostomy are surgical procedures that alter the normal route for elimination of feces. An opening (stoma) is created in the abdominal wall. The intestine (colon or ileum) is brought to the stoma to create an artificial outlet for the gastrointestinal tract. Because the stool is diverted from its normal course before reaching the anal sphincter, individuals with an ostomy are incontinent. The stool is eliminated into a pouch (appliance) worn securely over the opening.

Intestinal stomas may be permanent or temporary. Often, a temporary stoma is done to allow a part of the bowel to heal after injury or disease (for example, with diverticulitis, cancer, or Crohn's disease). After the area is healed, the stoma is closed and the bowel is reconnected so that the normal elimination process can continue.

When the procedure is done as part of the treatment for cancer, the size and site of the tumor determine the type of surgical procedure. An attempt is always made to preserve the anal sphincter if there is a chance that a permanent colostomy can be avoided. If there is severe involvement of the rectum, the anus and rectum are removed, and the anal area is closed (proctocolectomy).

Conditions most often treated with a colostomy or ileostomy include cancer, Crohn's disease, diverticulitis, ulcerative colitis, familial polyposis, and ischemic (dead) bowel.

About 15% of colorectal cancer patients require a permanent colostomy.

Reason for Procedure

There are numerous reasons for the placement of an ostomy. A colostomy or ileostomy is usually created to bypass an obstructed portion of bowel, or to divert the feces away from a segment of bowel that has had to be resected for some reason (cancer, disease, and dead bowel).

The most frequent reason for the placement of a colostomy is in the treatment of colon cancer, where a segment of bowel affected with the tumor has been removed. Often, the bowel can be put back together (anastomosis) during the cancer surgery if the bowel is cleaned out first. However, this is often not an option, and so a colostomy is placed to divert the feces until a later procedure can be performed to take down the ostomy. Sometimes the colostomy is permanent.

Other conditions treated with a colostomy or ileostomy include ulcerative colitis, familial polyposis, Crohn's disease, and ischemic (dead) bowel. Usually, ulcerative colitis and familial polyposis can avoid colostomy at the initial surgery. If not, the colostomy is often temporary. Ischemic bowel results in a dead part of intestine that must be removed. The location and type of ostomy varies according to the extent of dead bowel. Sometimes these ostomies are permanent.

How Procedure Is Performed

The individual is taken to the operating room and general anesthesia is administered. The surgeon makes an incision on the abdomen and locates the affected portion of bowel. After performing the necessary other procedures, depending on the individual's disease, the surgeon will find a good segment of intestine to use for the ostomy. A small incision is made in a different location on the abdomen, and the intestine is brought up and sutured to the abdominal wall.

Sometimes a loop of intestine is brought up so that there are two stomas at the same place. This is a loop ostomy, and this type is often used to decompress an obstructed bowel. If just the cut end of intestine is brought up to the skin, it is an end ostomy and only one stoma will be seen. This type of ostomy is known as a diverting ostomy, because all of the feces are diverted to the outside.

After the individual wakes from anesthesia, it usually takes a few days for the ostomy to start excreting feces. Once bowel function has returned, the individual can be started on a liquid diet, which is slowly advanced.

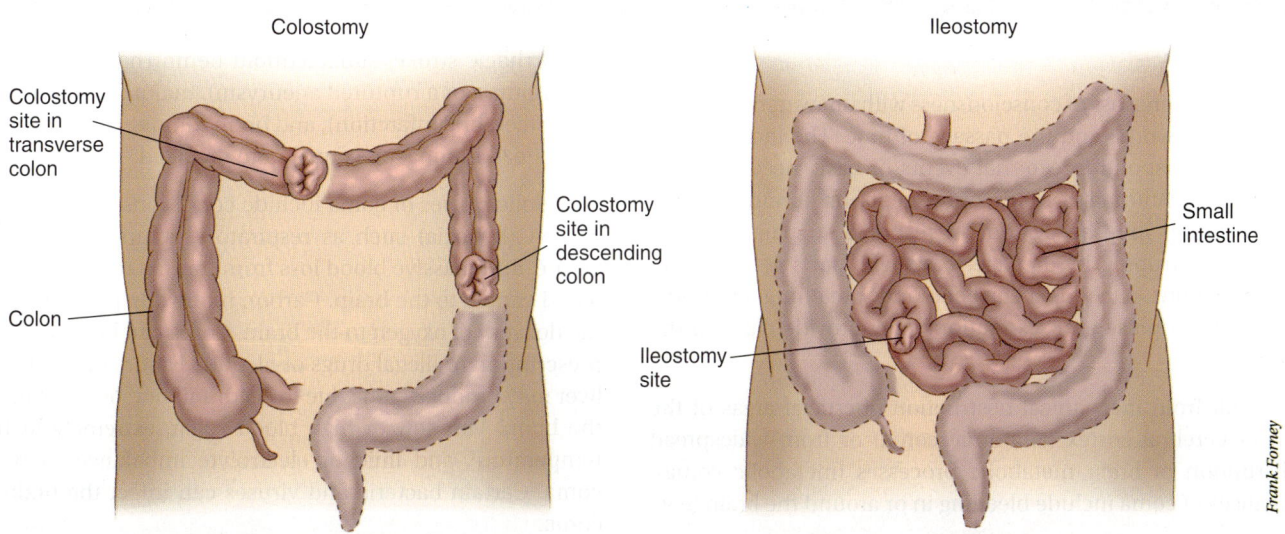

Prognosis

Colostomy and ileostomy are generally well tolerated, and most individuals make a full recovery. A period of adjustment to having an ostomy and learning to manage the appliances is necessary. In most cases, individuals can continue to lead a full and active life. Further outcome considerations depend on the underlying disease process.

Specialists

- Colorectal Surgeon
- General Surgeon

Work Restrictions / Accommodations

Individuals should avoid lifting, pushing, or pulling more than 5-10 pounds for at least 6 weeks immediately after the operation. The individual must learn how to apply the appliances and care for the ostomy.

Comorbid Conditions

The individual's ability to recover would be negatively affected by any immunosuppressive condition.

Procedure Complications

Complications of colostomy/ileostomy are similar for other bowel surgeries and include: wound infection, bowel injury, ileus, bleeding, or death. Sometimes the ostomy can die (necrosis) due to inadequate blood supply. If this were to happen, a second surgical procedure would be required to create a new ostomy.

Factors Influencing Duration

The disease that prompted the procedure, the extent of the resection, and the presence of complications will influence the length of disability.

There are significant psychological hurdles with these procedures that may contribute to the length of the disability.

Length of Disability

For ileostomy with bowel resection, duration depends on type and extent of bowel resection.

Colostomy.

Duration in Days

Job Classification	Minimum	Optimum	Maximum
Sedentary work	14	21	28
Light work	21	28	35
Medium work	28	42	56
Heavy work	42	49	63
Very Heavy work	42	56	70

Ileostomy. With bowel resection.

Duration in Days

Job Classification	Minimum	Optimum	Maximum
Sedentary work	28	42	70
Light work	28	56	70
Medium work	42	63	84
Heavy work	56	84	112
Very Heavy work	56	98	126

References

Schwartz, Seymour, MD. Principles of Surgery. New York: McGraw-Hill, 1999.

Coma

Other names / synonyms: Comatose, Loss of Consciousness
780.01, 780.03

Definition

Coma is a state involving loss of consciousness with unawareness of self, others, the external world, and the passage of time. The individual in coma is unable to respond to external events or basic needs such as eating or drinking. Automatic reflex movements or abnormal body positions (posturing) may be evident in response to pain or other stimuli. Unless interrupted by damage to specific parts of the brain, involuntary functions such as heartbeat and breathing continue, although changes in pulse and respirations may provide clues to the cause of coma.

Coma can result from mechanical destruction of crucial areas of the brain stem or cerebral cortex (anatomic coma) or from widespread (global) disruption of brain metabolic processes (metabolic coma). Structural causes of coma include bleeding in or around the brain (e.g., hemorrhagic stroke, subarachnoid hemorrhage, subdural or epidural hematomas, or a ruptured aneurysm), major stroke with death of brain tissue (cerebral infarction), and brain tumors. Coma can be the result of blunt head trauma, or a gunshot to the head.

Metabolic causes of coma include conditions that deprive the brain of oxygen (hypoxia) such as respiratory failure, asphyxiation, or heart failure, and massive blood loss from trauma resulting in an inadequate blood supply to the brain. Carbon monoxide poisoning interferes with the delivery of oxygen to the brain. Coma can be caused by overdose of prescription or illegal drugs or alcohol. Failure of the lungs, kidneys, or liver may produce coma due to accumulation of waste products toxic to the brain. Very low or high blood sugar, extremely high or low body temperature, and fluid or electrolyte imbalances may also produce coma. Certain bacteria and viruses can infect the brain and result in coma.

Head trauma, drug use, epilepsy, and brain infections are the most common causes of coma in individuals less than 40 years of age. Cardiovascular disease (especially stroke) and metabolic disorders (e.g., diabetes mellitus, hypoglycemia, coma from liver failure, electrolyte disorders, and uremia) are common causes in those over 40.

Diagnosis

History: Details of the individual's medical history and circumstances surrounding the onset of coma and subsequent events may be gathered from the individual's family members or emergency attendants. History reported may include head injury, convulsions, or drug use (legal or illegal). Symptoms reported may include fever or headache before the onset of coma if coma is related to brain infection. High blood pressure and the sudden development of severe headache and vomiting just before loss of consciousness may suggest intracranial hemorrhage. A medical history of diabetes, epilepsy, liver disease, kidney disease, or cancer may also suggest specific causes of coma.

Physical exam: A variety of breathing disturbances such as rapid, deep respirations (hyperventilation) or slow, irregular respirations (atactic breathing) may be evident. Different breathing patterns point to damage at different levels of the brain or brain stem. In response to painful stimuli, purposeful movement such as withdrawing a limb is a likely indication that the sensory and motor nervous pathways are intact. Abnormal body posturing (decorticate or decerebrate) in response to pain suggests more serious damage to the brain. No movement in response to painful stimuli suggests serious damage at the level of the brain stem. Asymmetry in movement or reflexes may indicate structural damage to one side of the brain.

The presence of a single, dilated pupil (anisocoria) is a serious sign and may indicate increased pressure within the skull (intracranial pressure) that causes the brain to swell (brain herniation). Tiny pupils that respond to light tend to occur in metabolic derangements. Some structural brain lesions such as blood clots or tumors can cause the eyes to be positioned to one side or in a downward gaze. Other examinations of eye movement include the "Doll's head" eye response where the individual's head is rotated from side to side. Under normal conditions, the eyes stay fixed and centered. With brain damage, the eyes move abnormally. Another test of eye movement involves irrigating an ear with cold water (cold water calorics). Individuals with an intact brain stem will produce a reflex (oculovestibular reflex) eye movement to one side. This reflex is absent or asymmetrical if there are brain stem lesions.

The vital signs are also important in the initial evaluation of coma. A low body core temperature (hypothermia) can produce coma and a slow pulse (bradycardia).

The Glasgow Coma Scale is a practical and standardized system for assessing the degree of coma. It also aids in predicting the duration and ultimate outcome, especially in individuals with head trauma. The three determinants of the system are the opening of the eyes, verbal response, and motor response. Each item has a numerical score and is the sum of the numeric values. A total score of 15 indicates minimal impairment, 7 indicates coma, and 3 signifies deep coma.

Tests: Blood tests should be done for metabolic causes of coma including low or high blood sugar, electrolyte disturbances, liver and kidney function, and drug blood levels. A CT or MRI is indicated for the diagnosis of anatomic causes of coma. A lumbar puncture (spinal tap) may be done if a CT or MRI shows no lesions or tumors. The cerebrospinal fluid obtained from the lumbar puncture can help diagnose an infection or hemorrhage in the brain. An electroencephalogram (EEG) may determine if an individual's coma is secondary to seizures. The pattern of electrical activity can sometimes suggest an infectious or vascular cause.

Treatment

The immediate goal in the management of coma is to prevent further brain damage. Any evidence of low blood pressure, inadequate oxygenation, low blood sugar, or low body temperature is treated promptly. If the cause is hypoglycemia, intravenous sugar is administered, as coma due to low blood sugar may improve rapidly when sugar is given. Thiamine is a B vitamin and may be given with the sugar in alcoholics or others in a malnourished state.

Low blood pressure (hypotension) is usually treated with fluids or with medications.

Insertion of an artificial airway and the use of mechanical ventilation may be needed in cases of inadequate ventilation. If intracranial pressure is increased, the reducing of carbon dioxide by raising the respiratory rate (hyperventilation) helps decrease intracranial pressure. In some cases, surgical insertion of an intracranial pressure monitor may be needed. If intracranial pressure is raised because of brain swelling, steroids or mannitol may help decrease it.

In cases of hypothermia, restoring normal body temperature may reverse coma.

The cause of the coma usually determines the therapy. Once a diagnosis is made, surgery (craniotomy) may be indicated to remove any masses, stop hemorrhage, or decrease pressure on the brain. Treatment of infectious or metabolic causes of coma is directed at correcting the underlying cause. The neurologic and medical status needs to be monitored continuously in intensive care situations.

Prognosis

The outcome from coma is dependent primarily on the cause. Mortality is high for severe head injury (40%), liver failure (60%), and anoxia (90% at one year if coma lasts more than 6 hours). Those individuals with coma secondary to drug ingestion generally have a good outcome if prompt, effective emergency care is received.

Differential Diagnosis

A mute state following brain damage called "locked-in syndrome" or "de-efferented state" produces symptoms similar to coma. However, in these cases, individuals are fully aware of their surroundings but physically unable to respond. Psychological withdrawal in catatonic schizophrenia can also show unresponsiveness to external stimuli, however, the absence of neurological signs help distinguish this condition from coma.

Specialists

- Critical Care Specialist
- Neurologist
- Neurosurgeon

Rehabilitation

Rehabilitation should begin almost immediately in acute coma with passive range of motion and frequent turning to avoid limb contractures and bedsores. Sensory stimulation may help recovery. Negative comments should never be made around individuals in coma as some who recover may report recollection of events while in the unresponsive state.

All individuals in coma longer than a week will most likely require some sort of long-term care and rehabilitation. The type of rehabilitation is based on the degree of functional impairment. Those with severe functional impairments will usually require admission to a rehabilitation or extended care facility. Such facilities can provide ongoing medical care, physical therapy, administer nutrition, and provide grooming. On occasion, physically stable individuals in coma can be cared for at home.

In some cases, there is good recovery from coma with only mild functional and intellectual impairments. In these circumstances, outpatient neurological rehabilitation may be appropriate. The type and frequency of therapy will be dictated by the type and degree of impairments and may include occupational, physical, and/or speech therapy.

Work Restrictions / Accommodations

The individual in coma is disabled and unable to work. Those who recover from coma may have persistent impairments of physical and intellectual function and so may necessitate appropriate reassignment of job responsibilities and possible job retraining.

Comorbid Conditions

Comorbid conditions that may affect the ability to recover and further lengthen disability are liver failure, cancer, advanced age, heart and lung disease, drug or alcohol abuse, brain tumor, or stroke.

Complications

Complications may include lung damage from prolonged artificial ventilation, urinary infection from prolonged use of urinary catheters, dehydration, overhydration, blood chemistry imbalance, vitamin deficiency, or malnutrition from prolonged dependence on intravenous solutions for nourishment. Skin damage or limb contractures can result from being immobile. Other complications such as seizures or paralysis are determined by the cause of the coma and the length of time the individual is comatose. Deep coma can become a permanent condition (persistent vegetative state).

Factors Influencing Duration

The underlying cause, the degree and location of injury (if any), and associated complications will all influence the length of disability. Some individuals are permanently disabled in one or more neurological functions. In general, the elderly have poorer outcomes than younger comatose individuals. The outcome is often not good for individuals in poor health before the coma.

Length of Disability

Duration depends on cause. Contact physician to obtain more information. Disability may be permanent or full recovery may ocur.

Failure to Recover

If an individual fails to recover within the maximum duration expectancy period, the reader may wish to reference the following questions to assist in better understanding the specifics of an individual's medical case.

Regarding diagnosis:

- Was a diagnosis of coma based on a thorough history and physical exam?
- Was the underlying cause of the coma determined with diagnostic tests?
- Would the individual benefit from consultation with specialists in the treatment of the underlying cause (neurologist, neurosurgeon, radiologist, internist, endocrinologist, critical care specialist, infectious disease specialist)?

Regarding treatment:

- Was there any extended delay between the onset of symptoms and treatment?
- Was necessary life-saving support (airway, breathing, cardiac compressions) provided as appropriate?
- Was the treatment appropriate for the underlying condition?
- Was surgery required?
- Was rehabilitation started promptly?
- Did the rehabilitation intervention include sensory stimulation?
- Would the individual benefit from consultation with a physiatrist or specialist in neurological rehabilitation?

Regarding prognosis:

- Considering the underlying cause and the presence of comorbid conditions, what was the expected outcome for the individual (full recovery, partial disability, persistent coma (persistent vegetative state)?
- Did the individual suffer any complications that may impact the length of disability?
- Has the individual been evaluated for long-term care and rehabilitation? If so, has the individual been receiving appropriate long-term care and rehabilitation?
- Are there barriers preventing access to care and rehabilitation (i.e., lack of insurance coverage, lack of local facilities)?
- Have all rehabilitation and long-term care options been explored?
- Is the family and significant others receiving appropriate support and guidance in coping with the individual's condition (i.e., social services, head injury support groups, behavioral counseling, financial counseling)?

References

Bone, Roger C., ed. Pulmonary and Critical Care Medicine. Philadelphia: Mosby-Year Book, Inc, 1998.

Tierney, Lawrence M., Stephen J. McPhee, and Maxine A. Papadakis, eds. Current Medical Diagnosis and Treatment, 39th ed. New York: Lange Medical Books/McGraw-Hill, 2000.

Compartment Syndrome

Other names / synonyms: Compartmental Syndrome
958.8

Definition

Acute compartment syndrome is a limb- and, sometimes, life-threatening condition of increased fluid pressure within a closed space (compartment) in the body. The increased pressure reduces blood flow that can lead to permanent nerve and muscle damage. It most commonly occurs in the arm or leg but may also occur in the buttock and abdomen. Untreated, severe compartment syndrome can lead to kidney (renal) failure and death.

Acute compartment syndrome may be caused by a tight cast or dressing; tight closure of the inelastic membrane surrounding muscles and organs (fascia); prolonged external pressure on a limb (e.g., during surgery or unconsciousness); swelling (edema) or bleeding (hemorrhage) from burns, trauma, frostbite, infection, or insect bites; edema after a return of blood flow (revascularization) following repair of blood vessel injury or blockage (obstruction); or edema resulting from the intravenous administration of fluids. Even vigorous exercise can cause an injury that progresses to compartment syndrome. The most common cause of acute compartment syndrome is fracture of the front bone of the lower leg (tibia).

Individuals may develop a long-term (chronic) form of compartment syndrome usually caused through overuse of an extremity by an endurance athlete (e.g., runner). Symptoms and the high compartment pressure dissipate when the offending activity is stopped. Abdominal compartment syndrome has a broad (systemic) effect on organ and physiologic functions. It is caused by abdominal trauma, an inflamed pancreas (pancreatitis), internal bleeding (hemorrhage), intestinal blockage (obstruction), liver transplantation, a ruptured aortic aneurysm, severe intra-abdominal infection, and the use of pneumatic antishock garments or military antishock trousers. Abdominal compartment syndrome is fatal if not diagnosed or treated promptly.

Acute compartment syndrome is a common occurrence following trauma to a limb. Three-quarters of all cases of compartment syndrome are caused by bone fractures and 4% of these occurred in individuals with tibial fractures. Individuals at risk for acute compartment syndrome are those suffering from high-velocity injuries, breaks (fractures) of a long bone, penetrating injuries (e.g., stabbings, gunshot wounds), crush injuries, and those involved in collisional sports such as football or hockey. Runners, cross-country skiers, soccer players, and walkers are also at risk for chronic compartment syndrome.

Diagnosis

History: The individual complains of pain, tightness, and decreased movement of the affected limb. Limb weakness, sensory deficits, and/or a burning sensation (paresthesia) may also be reported. There may be a history of a recent injury, surgery, or an intravenous line. Individuals with compartment syndrome of the buttock area may complain of referred pain to the legs. The athlete with chronic compartment syndrome may complain of leg pain while exercising that is relieved when at rest. This pain is experienced for weeks to months. The individual with abdominal compartment syndrome complains of bloating (abdominal distension) and breathing difficulties and may have a recent history of abdominal surgery or trauma.

Physical exam: The affected limb is compared to the unaffected limb. The affected limb is swollen with tenseness over the affected compartment. Muscle stretching causes pain or tingling. The pain is greater than expected for the particular injury. There may also be numbness (anesthesia). The pulse in the wrist or ankle is usually present. In an individual with abdominal compartment syndrome, abdominal distension, increased breathing rate, rapid heart rate (tachycardia), and decreased urine output may be evident.

Tests: The compartment pressure (intracompartmental tissue fluid pressures) is measured using a tonometer in which a fine tube (catheter) is inserted into the affected area to a point just below the fascia. Blood tests may include SMA-16, complete blood count (CBC), PT, and myoglobin. Urine tests for myoglobin may also be performed. Plain x-rays and ultrasound scanning may be performed. Bladder pressure monitoring uses a urinary catheter attached to either a fluid manometer or transducer to diagnose abdominal compartment syndrome.

Treatment

Any restricting dressings or casts are removed. The affected limb is maintained in a position level with the body. Oxygen may be provided to increase the amount of arterial oxygen and possibly delay tissue damage. Immediate surgical treatment is indicated if symptoms do not resolve quickly.

To relieve pressure, deep cuts (incisions) are made (fasciotomy) over the affected compartment. Fasciotomy of the hand usually requires four incisions, two on the back of the hand, one into the mound of tissue at the base of the thumb (thenar region), and one into the tissue at the base of the little finger (hypothenar region). Fasciotomy of the lower leg usually requires two incisions, one situated on the front to one side (anterolateral) and the other situated on the center back (posteromedial). Fasciotomy of the upper leg is usually performed with one incision into the side of the thigh. Fasciotomy of the foot involves incising the affected portion of the foot. The incisions are left open and sterile dressings applied. The incisions are closed with stitches (sutures) or skin grafts about 5 to 10 days later. Antibiotics and analgesics are provided, as needed.

In high-risk cases, fasciotomy may be performed as a preventive (prophylactic) measure. Factors indicative for fasciotomy include a lengthy delay between injury and surgery, an episode of low blood pressure (hypotension) prior to surgery, considerable preoperative swelling of the injured limb, a crushed limb where both arteries and veins are injured, and if major venous repair (ligation) is required.

Chronic compartment syndrome may be treated conservatively with rest, ice, elevation, and analgesics, and the individual may gradually return to the activity that caused the syndrome. Fasciotomy may be necessary should conservative treatment be ineffective. Mild abdominal compartment syndrome is treated conservatively by elevating the head of the bed and encouraging the individual to cough and breathe deeply. Moderate to severe abdominal compartment syndrome is treated by cutting open the abdomen (laparotomy) to reduce the pressure (decompression) by removing the fluid causing the increased pressure. The abdominal incision may be left open for a few days in cases of trauma to prevent recurrence of compartment syndrome.

Prognosis

There may be a return of full function or permanent disability to the affected limb depending on how soon fasciotomy was performed. Return of full limb function is expected if fasciotomy was performed within 6 hours. If not treated within 12 hours, functional abnormality occurs in 80% and loss of limb (amputation) in as many as 40% of individuals. Fasciotomy results in long skin scars. Conservative treatments for chronic and abdominal compartment syndromes can be effective for mild cases. Surgical decompression for abdominal compartment syndrome has a good success rate.

Differential Diagnosis

Conditions with symptoms that can mimic compartment syndrome of a limb include skin inflammation (cellulitis), jellyfish stings, blood clots (deep venous thrombosis and thrombophlebitis), gas gangrene, necrotizing fasciitis, blood vessel injuries, and disintegration of muscle tissue. Stress fracture, shin splints, and tendon inflammation (tendinitis) can mimic chronic compartment syndrome. The initial injury may also have caused nerve or muscle damage.

Specialists

- Hand Surgeon
- Orthopedic Surgeon
- Physiatrist
- Plastic Surgeon
- Vascular Surgeon

Rehabilitation

Individuals with compartment syndrome may require physical or occupational therapy depending on the extent of the injury. The main goals of therapy are to reduce swelling and pain, increase strength and range of motion, and decrease nerve sensitivity.

Individuals with persistent swelling are instructed to elevate the affected body part. In the case of compartment syndrome of the forearm, the hand is elevated above the arm. Therapists may also perform retrograde massage to help push fluid away from the extremities. Individuals perform ankle pumps where the foot is moved up and down or hand squeezes. These exercises help prevent fluid from pooling in the foot or hand. Individuals who have undergone surgical fasciotomies to reduce pressure are instructed in the difference between surgical pains and pain due to infection. Once the incision from a fasciotomy heals, the therapist may instruct the individual to perform scar massage to help promote healing and decrease sensitivity over the scar tissue.

Therapists may passively stretch the affected joints to help increase range of motion. Individuals with contractures resulting from compartment syndrome may be fitted with an orthotic splint to position the affected joint in a more functional position.

Individuals with loss of strength in the wrist and hand may perform hand squeezes with therapy putty and wrist curls with light hand weights. Individuals with decreased foot and lower leg strength may perform standing heel and toe raises. Other exercises may be instructed depending on the location of the injury. Individuals also perform more functional strengthening exercises such as grasping a key or treadmill walking.

Individuals experiencing nerve damage as a result of compartment syndrome may benefit from desensitization. Desensitization is performed by rubbing areas of the body that experience heightened responses to pressure or temperature with a variety of stimuli such as ice cubes, soft cotton, burlap, and terry cloth. This helps the nerves modify their response.

Work Restrictions / Accommodations

Movement of the affected limb is restricted until the individual recovers. The individual with upper limb compartment syndrome is temporarily unable to lift and carry heavy or bulky objects, operate equipment, or perform other tasks requiring use of both hands. If the dominant arm or hand was affected, the individual may be unable to write legibly or type well. Likewise, compartment syndrome in the dominant hand affects fine motor skills such as those needed to work in a laboratory. These individuals may require a temporary or permanent reassignment of duties. Compartment syndrome in a lower limb may affect the individual's ability to stand or sit for extended periods of time. The effect of any permanent movement limitations as a result of limb compartment syndrome needs to be fully evaluated. Individuals recovering from abdominal surgery are temporarily unable to lift heavy objects or operate machinery.

Comorbid Conditions

Conditions such as cellulitis, gas gangrene, blood clots, and blood vessel injuries may influence the length of disability. The condition causing the abdominal compartment syndrome (e.g., abdominal trauma, internal bleeding, liver transplantation) may increase the length of disability.

Complications

Muscle and nerve cell death will occur if the pressure within the compartment is not relieved within 6 to 8 hours. This may lead to pain, deformity, loss of movement (paralysis), permanent muscle contraction (Volkmann's contracture), or loss of limb. Other complications include infection and kidney (renal) failure. Complications associated with abdominal compartment syndrome include heart and blood (cardiovascular) function abnormalities, renal failure, changes in lung (pulmonary) function, and increased pressure in the brain. Unrecognized and/or untreated abdominal or limb compartment syndromes can be fatal.

Factors Influencing Duration

Factors that may influence the length of disability include promptness of treatment, extent of treatment, any complications, and the response of the individual. For compartment syndrome of the hand, duration depends on whether the dominant or nondominant hand was affected.

Length of Disability

Duration depends on job requirements and location of the compartment syndrome.

Forearm.

Duration in Days

Job Classification	Minimum	Optimum	Maximum
Sedentary work	14	28	56
Light work	21	42	72
Medium work	42	42	Indefinite
Heavy work	70	91	Indefinite
Very Heavy work	91	119	Indefinite

Leg.

Duration in Days

Job Classification	Minimum	Optimum	Maximum
Sedentary work	14	42	63
Light work	21	63	91
Medium work	42	91	Indefinite
Heavy work	63	119	Indefinite
Very Heavy work	63	182	Indefinite

Failure to Recover

If an individual fails to recover within the maximum duration expectancy period, the reader may wish to reference the following questions to assist in better understanding the specifics of an individual's medical case.

Regarding diagnosis:

- Was compartment syndrome confirmed by measuring the actual compartment pressure with a tonometer?
- Were conditions with similar symptoms of compartment syndrome ruled out in the initial diagnosis?
- Was there a delay in the diagnosis of compartment syndrome?
- Was compartment syndrome not detected until after a lengthy surgery to repair trauma injuries?
- Did the individual also suffer from fractured bones?
- Did the individual suffer from a brain (intracranial) or spinal cord injury?
- Did individual ingest drugs?

Regarding treatment:

- Was fasciotomy performed promptly?
- If a conservative approach has failed to relieve symptoms, has surgical intervention (fasciotomy) been considered?

Regarding prognosis:

- Was there a delay in the diagnosis?
- Was treatment provided within 6 hours of occurrence?
- Has the individual followed prescribed physical and occupational therapy on a regular basis?
- Has adequate time elapsed to allow for complete recovery and return of strength and coordination of the dominant hand?
- Were appropriate work accommodations made to allow for the recovery?
- Have there been any complications?
- Would individual benefit from consultation with an appropriate specialist (physiatrist, nephrologist, cardiologist, pulmonologist, neurologist)?
- Are there any comorbid conditions that may impact ability to recover? If so, have these conditions been addressed in the treatment plan?

References

Apley, A. Graham, and Louis Solomon. "Complications of Fractures." Concise System of Orthopaedics and Fractures. Apley, A. Graham, and Louis Solomon, eds. Oxford: Butterworth-Heinemann Ltd, 1994. 256-262.

Shackford, Steven, and Norman Rich. "Peripheral Vascular Injury." Trauma. Mattox, Kenneth, David Feliciano, and Earnest Moore, eds. New York: McGraw-Hill, 2000. 1011-1044.

Complex Regional Pain Syndrome

Other names / synonyms: Algodystrophy, Causalgia, CRPS, CRPS I, CRPS II, Neurodystrophy, Reflex Sympathetic Dystrophy Syndrome, RSD, RSDS, Shoulder-Hand Syndrome, Sudek's Atrophy, Sympathalgia

337.2

Definition

Considerable controversy continues to surround the cause (etiology), definition, diagnosis and treatment of persons with these disorders.

There is no single term or universally accepted case definition for persons with these disorders. These disorders are characterized by pain that is present without stimulation or movement, which occurs beyond the territory of a single peripheral nerve and which is disproportionate to the inciting event. The pain is associated with specific objective findings, including swelling, skin color changes, sweating changes, temperature changes, reduced passive range of motion and alteration of skin texture.

The cause of Complex Regional Pain Syndrome (CRPS) is unknown. Sympathetic nervous system dysfunction was thought to be involved in the generation of the symptoms and signs; hence, the term reflex sympathetic dystrophy (RSD). Causalgia was considered similar to RSD except, unlike RSD, it followed a lesion of a peripheral nerve, either of a major mixed motor and sensory nerve in the proximal extremity (major causalgia) or of a purely sensory branch more distally (minor causalgia). A recent reconsideration of these syndromes has generated new terminology and ideas concerning the underlying pathophysiology. The International Association for the Study of Pain has proposed the term complex regional pain syndrome, which has replaced the term RSD with CRPS I and causalgia with CRPS II. Consistent with the earlier terminology, CRPS II follows a nerve injury but CRPS I does not. CRPS I and CRPS II are similar in all other respects.

CRPS differs from earlier views of RSD and causalgia. First, CRPS is diagnosed by history and clinical findings. Second, regional sympathetic blockade has no role in the diagnosis of CRPS. Third, sympathetic dysfunction is not assumed to be the basic pathophysiologic mechanism; rather, sympathetic dysfunction is associated with a group of pain disorders that responds positively to sympathetic block but that may be independent of CRPS. Fourth, sympathetically maintained pain (SMP) may be present in a variety of painful conditions including or independent of CRPS. Fifth, neither staging nor grading is seen as useful from a descriptive, diagnostic or therapeutic standpoint. Sixth, even simple designations of mild, moderate or severe forms are beyond current knowledge levels.

Diagnosis

History: The individual with CRPS reports pain that is present without stimulation or movement, which occurs beyond the territory of a single peripheral nerve and which is disproportionate to the inciting event.

Physical exam: The individual with CRPS can exhibit swelling, local skin color change of red or purple, local sweating changes, local temperature changes, reduced passive range of motion and local alteration of skin texture of smooth or shiny in the affected extremity.

Tests: The individual with CRPS can exhibit periarticular demineralization on plain x-rays and increased uptake in the entire affected extremity during the early phase, but increased periarticular uptake during the third phase, on 3-phase bone scan. Based on evidence to date, the following tests have no role in diagnosing CRPS: quantitative sudomotor axon reflex test (Q-SART), thermography, electrodiagnostic studies, radiographic bone density, sympathetic blockade, peripheral nerve block, epidural or spinal block.

The approach to the diagnosis of CRPS should be conservative and based on objective signs. Signs are objective evidence of disease, i.e., such evidence which is perceptible to the examining physician as opposed to the subjective sensations (symptoms) of the individual. The objective diagnostic criteria for CRPS are comprised of eight criteria, six clinical signs and two radiographic signs. The six clinical signs are: swelling, local skin color change of red or purple, local sweating changes, local temperature changes, reduced passive range of motion in contiguous or contained joints, local alteration of skin texture of smooth or shiny. The two radiographic signs are demineralization of underlying bony structures on plain x-rays and increased uptake in the entire affected extremity during the early phase, but increased periarticular uptake during the third phase, on 3-phase bone scan. If five or more of the eight clinical and radiographic signs are present, then a diagnosis of probable CRPS is warranted. If less than five of the signs are present, there is no CRPS.

The following caveats must be considered when using the above criteria to diagnose CRPS. First, the required clinical and radiographic signs must be present concurrently. Second, the criteria are not based on the person's self-report, but are based upon objective findings which can be identified during a standard examination and which can be demonstrated by standard clinical and radiologic techniques. For example, a person who reports swelling but who has no objectively documented swelling does not meet the diagnostic criterion for swelling. Third, the required clinical and radiographic signs do not come and go. For example, the objective signs are not present one day, absent the next day and then present the day after.

Treatment

Reported therapies for CRPS have not been confirmed by defined, prospective, controlled, double-blind randomized trials with long-term quantitative assessment of outcome. Reported, but nonverified therapies include: sympathetic block (stellate ganglion, lumbar, continuous, chemical, thermocoagulation), surgical sympathectomy, intravenous regional medication (bretylium, corticosteroids, guanethidine, reserpine), epidural block, spinal block, dorsal column nerve stimulation, peripheral nerve stimulation, acupuncture, medications (anticonvulsants, antidepressants, benzodiazepines, corticosteroids, phenoxybenzamine, nifedipine, prazosin, propanolol), psychotherapy, physical therapy.

Although there is no proven treatment for CRPS, the single most important intervention appears to be appropriate, aggressive, active and passive physical therapy. Other modalities may be used to facilitate such therapy. However, there are no properly defined, properly controlled, double-blind studies with adequate long-term outcome measures to enable categorical statements about treatment efficacy.

Prognosis

The prognosis for persons with CRPS is unknown because there are no scientifically valid outcome studies upon which to base categorical statements about prognosis.

Differential Diagnosis

The differential diagnosis is comprised of other conditions which would account for the symptoms and signs including: infection (cellulitis, osteomyelitis, and septic arthritis), malignancy, neurological disorders (nerve entrapment syndromes, peripheral neuropathies, and central pain syndromes), psychiatric disorders (conversion disorder, factitious disorder, and pain disorder), rheumatological disorders (adhesive capsulitis, Dupuytren's contracture, gouty arthritis, rheumatoid arthritis, scleroderma, systemic lupus erythematosus, and tenosynovitis), and vascular disorders (arterial insufficiency, thrombophlebitis, and lymphedema).

Specialists

- Neurologist
- Pain Specialist
- Physiatrist
- Psychiatrist
- Psychologist

Work Restrictions / Accommodations

Categorical statements regarding work restrictions/accommodations are not possible due to the wide range of clinical presentations of persons with CRPS. Work restrictions/accommodations are based upon the interaction between a person's medical impairment (if any) and his/her job requirements.

Comorbid Conditions

Comorbid conditions which could influence the duration of disability include: infection (cellulitis, osteomyelitis, and septic arthritis), malignancy, neurological disorders (nerve entrapment syndromes, peripheral neuropathies, and central pain syndromes), psychiatric disorders (conversion disorder, factitious disorder, and pain disorder), rheumatological disorders (adhesive capsulitis, Dupuytren's contracture, gouty arthritis, rheumatoid arthritis, scleroderma, systemic lupus erythematosus, and tenosynovitis), and vascular disorders (arterial insufficiency, thrombophlebitis, and lymphedema).

Complications

Complications are related to the inciting event (i.e., fracture, infection, crush injury), to treatment (i.e., undesirable side effects or reinforcement of counterproductive behaviors) or to the person's behavior (i.e., self-limitation of activities of daily living).

Factors Influencing Duration

There are no scientifically valid studies that have determined the factors influencing duration of disability in CRPS; however, the duration of disability is likely influenced by the severity of the condition, comorbid conditions and complications.

Length of Disability

Length of disability is based upon the interaction between an individual's medical impairment and his/her job requirements. Categorical statements about length of disability are not possible due to the wide range of clinical presentations of individuals with CRPS. For sympathectomy, duration depends on site (cervical, lumbar, etc.), severity, response to treatment, and duration of symptoms. Late diagnosis and inadequate treatment may result in permanent disability. This is a controversial diagnosis. Contact physician for more information.

Sympathectomy (ganglionectomy).

Job Classification	Minimum	Optimum	Maximum
Sedentary work	7	14	21
Light work	7	14	21
Medium work	14	21	28
Heavy work	14	21	28
Very Heavy work	14	21	28

Duration in Days

Failure to Recover

If an individual fails to recover within the maximum duration expectancy period, the reader may wish to reference the following questions to assist in better understanding the specifics of an individual's medical case.

Regarding diagnosis:

- Were alternative diagnoses investigated?
- Were concurrent or comorbid diagnoses investigated?
- Was diagnosis based solely on the individual's self-report?
- Was diagnosis based on objective diagnostic criteria identified during a standard examination and by standard clinical and radiologic techniques?

Regarding treatment:

- Was appropriate, aggressive, active, and passive physical therapy performed?
- Have unproven treatments resulted in unwanted side effects?
- Have treatment methods reinforced counterproductive behaviors?

Regarding prognosis:

- Were psychosocial factors such as family and workplace dynamics considered?
- Were mental and behavioral disorders (depression, somatoform disorders, factitious disorders) considered?
- Were inappropriate illness behaviors (symptom exaggeration, malingering) considered?

References

Ensalada, L.H. "Reflex Sympathetic Dystrophy (RSD)/Complex Regional Pain Syndrome I (CRPS I)." *The Guides* Casebook: Cases to Accompany Guides to the Evaluation of Permanent Impairment, 4th Edition. Brigham, C.R., ed. Washington DC: American Medical Association, 1999.

Ensalada, L.H. "The Importance of Illness Behavior in Disability Management." Occupational Medicine State of the Art Reviews: Risk and Disability Evaluation in the Workplace. Randolph, D.C., and M.I. Ranavaya, eds. Philadelphia: Hanley & Belfus, October/December 2000.

Janig, W., and M. Stanton-Hicks, eds. Reflex Sympathetic Dystrophy: A Reappraisal. Progress in Pain Research and Management Volume 6. Seattle:IASP Press, 1996.

Stanton-Hicks, M. ed. Pain and the Sympathetic Nervous System. Boston: Kluwer Academic Publishers, 1990.

Computerized Axial Tomography
Other names / synonyms: CAT Scan, Computed Tomography, CT Scan
ICD-9 Code Depends on Site

Definition

Computed tomography (CT), formerly referred to as computerized axial tomography, is a noninvasive diagnostic form of x-ray that uses x-ray radiation to make cross-sectional images (slices), in different planes, of the interior of the body. Unlike the flat films of conventional radiography, the CT scanner circles the body measuring the transmission of x-rays as they pass through body structures, and taking multiple x-rays as it repeats this measurement (called a projection) in many different directions through the same section or slice of the body. When a sufficient number of projections in different directions are measured, the resulting data can create a single, unique arrangement in 2 dimensions of the intervening body structure. Adjacent 2-dimensional slices can then be reconstructed to produce 3-dimensional structures for visualization of abnormalities, or for surgical planning.

A dye-like material (contrast medium) may be injected intravenously to make blood vessels, organs, or abnormalities show up more clearly. Compared to other diagnostic methods (angiography, ventriculography), CT scanning is simple, quick, and, because it uses an ultra-thin low-dose x-ray beam, it provides less exposure to radiation; it gives highly detailed visualization of the internal organs and soft tissues, providing a view of an entire area of interest with a single exposure. Spiral CT is advantageous for trauma victims because it minimizes time spent performing the scan.

CT scanning is used for the diagnosis and treatment of head injury or body trauma or to detect tumors or other abnormalities.

Reason for Procedure

CT scans are indicated to detect or confirm the characteristics, size, and involvement of abnormal structural changes. Wherever the location, a tumor can be evaluated before definitive treatment is begun. A head CT can provide direct information about bruises (contusions) or blood clots (hematomas) within or outside (epidural or subdural hematomas) the brain. CT of the spine is indicated in cases of suspected disc herniation, spinal infection, trauma, or intraspinal tumor. A face or neck CT is indicated for inflammation or infection, fractures of the facial structures, or for assessing foreign bodies within the eye socket (orbit). Chest CTs are most commonly used to detect suspected cancers (malignancies) and to determine the extent to which the cancer has spread (metastasis). CT is used to define the presence and extent of the ballooning of a blood vessel due to weakness of the vessel wall (traumatic aneurysms) and the splitting of an aortic vessel wall (aortic dissections). High-resolution CT can help evaluate lung diseases and, when used with dye (intravenous contrast), can be used to confirm an inflammation of the pancreas (acute pancreatitis).

CT may also be useful in differentiating a kidney tumor from a faintly calcified stone that may not be visible on plain x-ray. It can also classify kidney injuries by defining the extent of lacerations, hematomas, or urine leaking into the abdominal cavity. In the pelvis, CT can provide information regarding the extent of tumors in the lymphatic system and their relationship to normal structures. While bone fractures are usually evaluated by standard x-ray, CT scan provides more precise information about the presence, location, orientation, and relationship of fracture fragments in complex anatomic regions such as the pelvis, shoulder, foot, and ankle. CT can provide precise locations and help guide the needle to sample of cells withdrawn through a needle for microscopic examination (aspiration biopsies), to withdraw a core of tissue withdrawn through a large-bore needle, for microscopic examination (core biopsy), for through the skin (percutaneous),drainage of abdominal abscesses, or for other fluid collections. CT can also be used to guide the placement of various catheters or surgical instruments. The CT may not be diagnostically helpful for people who cannot lie still (due to some neurological diseases), for those who have a fear of being surrounded by or contained within a machine, for the extremely obese, or for those who have a pacemaker or intracranial metallic object.

How Procedure Is Performed

The individual being scanned must lie still on a padded metal couch that is encircled by the CT scanner. The individual is positioned in the scanner so that the correct part of the body is located in the center of the scanner. Scans are painless, and most take between 10 to 30 minutes. If an intravenous contrast medium is required, a temporary catheter or needle is placed into a vein for injection of that medium. There is usually no need for specific pre-procedure preparation, although some abdominal scans may require that the individual fast for a short period of time. Scans that focus on the bladder will need the bladder to be full prior to scanning.

Prognosis

CT scanning provides highly detailed information, as well as a view of an entire area of interest with a single exposure.

Specialists

- General Surgeon
- Internist
- Oncologist
- Orthopedist
- Radiologist

Work Restrictions / Accommodations

No work restrictions and accommodations are expected with this procedure.

Comorbid Conditions

There are no comorbid conditions associated with this procedure.

Procedure Complications

There is minimal risk of complication from radiation. If a contrast medium is used, there is a risk of allergy to the medium. Because some contrast mediums use an iodine base, individuals who are allergic to iodine or shellfish, which also contain high levels of iodine, need to inform their healthcare providers of this allergy. Because x-rays can be harmful to a developing fetus, pregnant women need to inform their healthcare provider of this condition.

Factors Influencing Duration

No disability is expected with this procedure.

Length of Disability

No disability is expected to result from this therapy. Disability may occur as a result of an underlying condition.

References

"Computerized Axial Tomography of the Head or Brain, Face, Neck, or Spine." American College of Radiology. 05 Nov 1999. 20 Feb 2001 <http://www.acr.org/departments/econ/members_only/cac/axialtopgo.html>.

Bushong, Stewart C., ed. Radiologic Science for Technologists. St. Louis: Mosby, Inc, 1997.

Campbell, Robert J. Psychiatric Dictionary. New York: The Guilford Press, 1996.

Profit, Rex E. "Computed Radiography." Merrill's Atlas of Radiographic Positions and Radiologic Procedures. Ballinger, Philip W., and Eugene D. Frank, eds. St. Louis: Mosby, Inc, 1999. 307-322.

Concussion, Cerebral

Other names / synonyms: Head Injury
850.0, 850.1, 850.2, 850.3, 850.4, 850.5, 850.9

Definition

A cerebral concussion describes a brief loss of consciousness after head injury, with no immediate or delayed evidence of structural brain damage.

Consciousness may be lost for a few seconds in a mild injury or for hours or days after a more severe injury. The loss of consciousness is the result of a blow to the head and can be mild with transient loss of consciousness and possible impairment of the higher mental functions, such as loss of memory (retrograde amnesia) and emotional instability (lability). In severe concussion, there is prolonged unconsciousness with impairment of the function of the brain stem, such as transient loss of respiratory reflex, blood vessel (vasomotor) activity, and dilation of the pupils. Concussion is different from contusion in that in the former, the injury is functional, whereas in the latter it is organic. If unconsciousness lasts for more than 6 hours, there is presumed to have been brain tissue injury.

Diagnosis

History: The individual may have history of an injury to the head followed by loss of consciousness. Loss of consciousness or brief loss of contact with the environment is the characteristic feature of simple concussion. Loss of consciousness may be prolonged when there is swelling, hemorrhage, or diffuse nerve (axonal) injury (DAI), or contusion or laceration of the outer brain (cortex). On recovering, severity of the symptoms is related to the degree of brain damage.

Individuals with a concussion may be slightly dazed for a few minutes and complain of headaches for 12 hours or longer. Mental confusion may be prolonged. Surgical shock may be present, especially if there is injury to other areas of the body. Headaches and dizziness may be present after head injury.

Physical exam: The exam may reveal inadequate oxygen to the cells (hypoxia) characterized by rapid heartbeat, high blood pressure, dizziness, mental confusion, and peripheral constriction of blood vessels, shock, and multiple injuries. A neurologic evaluation is done to diagnose coma in the absence of external trauma. The examiner may also test for abnormal eye movements (tonic deviations of the eyes) and rhythmic movements of the eyes (nystagmus), and pupillary reflex abnormalities. One-sided paralysis (hemiplegia), impairment of language function (aphasia), and cranial nerve paralysis (palsy) are neurologic signs that may be seen depending on the extent and site of the brain damage.

Tests: The Glasgow Coma Scale has been used as a semiquantitative measure of the severity of brain injury and provides a guide to outcome. CT evaluates the head injury itself if there has been any alteration of consciousness or if there are signs of brain damage. MRI and PET studies may be important in the evaluation of late stages of recovery from head injury but are not important in acute care. Lumbar puncture may be done to examine the cerebrospinal fluid (CSF) if there is question of infection. Electroencephalogram (EEG) is not an emergency test but it is taken later to aid in outcome.

Treatment

Treatment of individuals with cerebral concussion is either operative or nonoperative. Nonoperative therapy consists of general care of the individual and control of intracranial pressure.

Severely injured individuals are typically treated in an intensive care unit and observed for multiple injuries, pulmonary function and infection, bladder function, nutrition, and skin care. The individual should be examined frequently to evaluate state of awareness and the presence or absence of signs of injury to the nerves. If the individual remains comatose for more than 12 hours, nutrition can be administered by nasal tube or parenterally. The administration of sedative drugs should be avoided in acute injury. Anticonvulsant drugs can be used if seizures develop. Care should be taken to make sure the individual is not dehydrated by ensuring adequate fluid intake by injection, if necessary.

Prognosis

The outcome for the individual with head injury is related to the site and severity of the injury. With mild concussion or minor degrees of cerebral swelling, individuals fully recover from loss of consciousness with no residual effects. The mortality rate is zero in individuals with simple concussion and is less than 2% when there is a mild degree of cerebral swelling. The mortality rate increases when the cortex is contused (5%) or lacerated (41%). Death may result immediately after the injury or from complications.

Differential Diagnosis

A cerebral contusion can have similar symptoms and signs.

Specialists

- Neurologist
- Neurosurgeon
- Psychiatrist

Rehabilitation

Individuals who sustain a concussion may present with a variety of physical and cognitive disabilities, depending on the severity of the injury. Individuals with mild concussions require no specific therapy and are able to return to their prior level of function after a period of rest. Individuals with moderate or severe concussion may need to be treated by physical, occupational, and speech therapists, as well as neuropsychologists, vocational counselors, and social workers.

Individuals with severe concussions may lapse into a period of sustained unconsciousness (coma). Individuals in the early stages of coma are unresponsive and would require a general program of stretching, developed by physical and occupational therapists, which would be taught to caregivers. Caregivers also learn how to position individuals to decrease the risk for bedsores. Individuals who are unresponsive may respond to sensory stimulation.

Individuals may present with motor control deficits. Physical and occupational therapists treat balance and coordination disorders that may be present. Individuals with impaired coordination perform fine-motor coordination exercises in occupational therapy such as picking up pegs and placing them in a pegboard, or may work on practical coordination exercises such as fastening buttons or practicing their signatures. Individuals work on gross motor coordination in physical therapy such as kicking a soccer ball that is rolled toward them or throwing beanbags at a target.

Individuals with impaired balance engage in physical and occupational therapy. For example, occupational therapists may work on dynamic sitting balance to promote dressing and grooming abilities. Sitting balance can be improved by having an individual sit on a therapy ball while attempting to reach for objects placed at various distances from the individual. Physical therapists may focus on standing balance to preserve the ability to walk. Individuals may perform exercises in a set of parallel bars, such as walking heel-to-toe to help improve standing balance.

The main focus of physical and occupational therapy in the area of motor control is to maximize functional capabilities. Individuals with poor motor control of the facial muscles may require speech therapy for improved clarity of speech and increased safety in swallowing. Speech therapy can also strengthen the muscles of the face for improved speech and swallowing. Individuals with hearing loss may require speech therapy.

Individuals may also present with perceptual deficits. Occupational and physical therapists provide methods to increase safety, such as a cane to compensate for decreased balance due to double vision. Individuals may require an occupational or physical therapist to assess their homes to remove tripping hazards such as throw rugs. Individuals may present with persistent fatigue due to deficits in the regulatory centers of the brain. Occupational therapists may teach energy conservation techniques, in which activities of daily living such as meal preparation are broken up into smaller components, thereby making tasks more manageable.

Physical therapy addresses decreased endurance by teaching stretching, strengthening, and exercises. Individuals may also perform aerobic activity such as walking on a treadmill or riding a stationary bicycle to further increase endurance.

Individuals may present with cognitive deficits due to brain injury. Occupational therapists evaluate and treat any deficits that are present. Individuals may present with difficulty speaking or understanding speech (aphasia) due to brain injury. Speech therapy may focus on skills such as word finding and sentence completion.

A neuropsychologist may be necessary for individuals with more severe deficits. Vocational counselors work with occupational, physical, and speech therapists to replicate job task requirements in therapy.

Work Restrictions / Accommodations

Individuals with simple concussion are usually allowed to return to their usual activities after 24 hours of observation and an additional 24 to 48 hours. The period of bed rest and convalescence for individuals with more severe head injuries is determined by the response to treatment. Return to active work should be deferred for 2 to 3 months after hospital discharge if there has been a severe degree of brain injury.

Comorbid Conditions

Other neurological conditions such as seizure disorder (epilepsy) may further lengthen disability.

Complications

Complications of head injuries include bleeding in the skull (subarachnoid, extradural, subdural, or intracerebral hemorrhage). Some leaking of blood into the spaces in the skull is expected in any individual with an injury to the head. Leaking of blood may be a warning sign to the physician that the brain has been injured and serious damage to the brain or its coverings may have occurred. A rare complication caused by distortion of the brain by an extradural or subdural hemorrhage is injury to the wall of the carotid or other arteries followed by thrombosis of these blood vessels (cerebral thrombosis). Thrombosis of the cerebral arteries may develop several days or weeks after head injury in elderly individuals with cerebral hardening of the arteries (arteriosclerosis). Head trauma can also cause arteriovenous fistulas formed as laceration of the internal carotid artery in the brain. Infections within the intracranial cavity following injury to the head may occur as meningitis or brain abscess.

A rare complication of brain injuries is the formation of a cyst in the intracranial space. This complication may develop in fractures of the skull. Brain lesions are less common in simple concussion. The most common symptoms of brain damage are paralysis of one side of the body (hemiplegia) and speech disturbances. Seizure disorder (epilepsy) as convulsive seizures is an infrequent symptom of acute phase of the head injury. Seizures may occur immediately after or within the first few days of the injury. The seizures are related to the acute brain damage or to the presence of intracerebral hemorrhage or infection. In most individuals, seizures do not develop until months after the injury occurred. Psychosis and mental disorders are usually transient and some impairment of mental faculties is common after injury to the head. Long-term psychotic episodes are rare. Serious mental problems are found only in cases of severe injury. Post-traumatic syndrome occurs in approximately 35-40% of individuals who sustain minor or severe injuries to the head and consists of a group of symptoms including headache, dizziness, insomnia, irritability, restlessness, excessive perspiration (hyperhidrosis), inability to concentrate, depression, and other personality changes.

Factors Influencing Duration

The severity of the head injury and any complications such as brain damage, post-traumatic syndrome symptoms, and mental impairment may also affect the length of disability.

Length of Disability

Duration depends on the severity of the injury and on job requirements (level of concentration required)

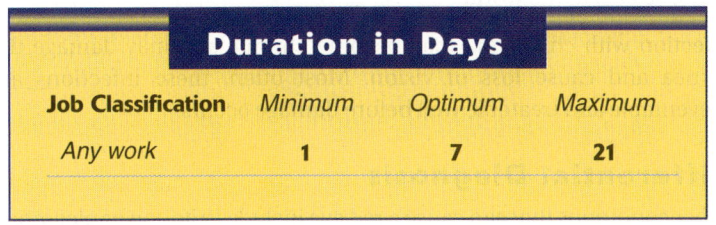

Failure to Recover

If an individual fails to recover within the maximum duration expectancy period, the reader may wish to reference the following questions to assist in better understanding the specifics of an individual's medical case.

Regarding diagnosis:

- Does the individual have history of a head injury followed by loss of consciousness?
- How long was the individual unconscious?
- Does the individual complain of a headache or dizziness?
- On exam did the individual have a rapid heartbeat, high blood pressure, dizziness, mental confusion, and peripheral constriction of blood vessels, and shock? Were there other injuries?
- Was a complete neurological examination done? Did the individual have tonic deviations of the eyes, nystagmus, or pupillary reflex abnormalities? Was hemiplegia, aphasia, or palsy present?
- What was the individual's initial Glasgow Coma Scale score?
- Has the individual had a CT scan, MRI or PET? Was a lumbar puncture done? Did the individual have an EEG later?
- Have conditions with similar symptoms been ruled out?

Regarding treatment:

- Did the individual's treatment consist of observation and discharge?
- Was surgery necessary? Did the individual then receive the appropriate supportive care in intensive care?

Regarding prognosis:

- Is the individual active in rehabilitation?
- Does the individual have a home exercise program?
- Is the individual's employer able to accommodate any necessary restrictions?
- Does the individual have any conditions that may affect their ability to recover?
- Does the individual have any complications such as subarachnoid, extradural, subdural, or intracerebral hemorrhage? Did the individual have a cerebral thrombosis? Did the individual develop any arteriovenous fistulas? Did the individual develop meningitis or brain abscess? Has a cyst formed in the intracranial space? Does the individual have a seizure disorder? Does the individual have post-traumatic syndrome?

References

Boss, Barbara J. "Alterations of Neurologic Function." Pathophysiology. McCance, Kathryn L., and Sue E. Heuther, eds. St. Louis: Mosby, 1994. 527-586.

Harmon, Kimberly G. "Assessment and Management of Concussion in Sports." American Academy of Family Physicians. 01 Sep 1999. 24 Jan 2001 <http://www.aafp.org/990901ap/887.html>.

Leahy, Patricia. "Traumatic Head Injury." Physical Rehabilitation: Assessment and Treatment. O'Sullivan, Susan B., and Thomas J. Schmitz, eds. Philadelphia: F.A. Davis, 1994. 491-508.

Swiercinsky, Dennis P., PhD, et al. Traumatic Head Injury. Kansas City: The Brain Injury Association, Inc, 1995.

Conjunctivitis

Other names / synonyms: Pink Eye

077.99, 372, 372.0, 372.00, 372.1, 372.10, 372.30, 372.39

Definition

Conjunctivitis (or "pink eye") is inflammation of the lining of the eyeball and inner surface of the eyelids.

It is the most common eye disease. Bacterial conjunctivitis occurs much less commonly than viral conjunctivitis, especially in the US, but bacterial conjunctivitis and some forms of viral conjunctivitis may occur in epidemic numbers. Viral conjunctivitis is the more common type of conjunctivitis, and it is one of the most common reasons for visiting an emergency room or a doctor's office.

Inflammation may occur as a result of a variety of causes including infection due to bacteria or viruses, allergies, airborne particles, or chemicals. Often, within about one week of infection of the first eye, the second eye becomes infected. Two types of viruses that can cause viral conjunctivitis are the adenovirus and the herpes simplex virus.

As mentioned previously, bacterial conjunctivitis is much less common. The incidence of bacterial conjunctivitis varies in the US and the world, depending on the bacteria responsible for the infection. In the US, infection is often due to the bacteria haemophilus influenzae, and it occurs in southern rural areas from Georgia to California during the summer and early autumn months. Another bacteria commonly responsible for conjunctivitis, in the US and throughout the world, is the bacteria staphylococcus aureus. Bacterial conjunctivitis is more likely to occur if there is an abnormality on the surface of the eye or the eyelid. Systemic immunosuppression also increases the risk of bacterial conjunctivitis. Chlamydia and gonorrhea bacteria can also cause conjunctivitis. About 1 out of every 300 adults who has a genital chlamydia infection develops an ophthalmic chlamydia infection. Conjunctivitis due to gonorrhea infection most commonly affects sexually active young adults. In underdeveloped parts of the world where infection may not be treated, conjunctivitis due to chlamydia and gonorrhea can result in destruction of eye structures and blindness.

Allergic conjunctivitis is most common in early adulthood. It may occur seasonally, or it may be perennial.

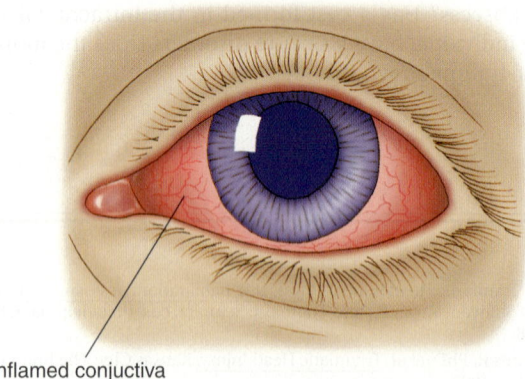

Inflamed conjuctiva

Frank Forney

Diagnosis

History: Symptoms include redness, itching, and burning of the eye(s), and a watery discharge. Some individuals may report the eyelids being stuck together in the morning. Usually these symptoms begin in one eye and appear in the other eye a few days later.

There may have been exposure to conjunctivitis or its causative agents in the recent past. If itching is the primary symptom, it may suggest an allergic conjunctivitis. If family members have had conjunctivitis recently, an infectious cause is likely. The individual may report having a cold just prior to the onset of conjunctivitis.

Physical exam: One or both eyes appear red, often with a swollen eyelid from rubbing the eye. The cornea is not affected. In the uncommon cases caused by gonorrhea or chlamydia, there will be signs of genital infection as well.

Tests: If a mucus discharge is present, it can be cultured for bacterial or viral organisms.

Treatment

Treatment depends on the cause of the inflammation. Bacterial infections are treated with antibiotic eyedrops, and some viral infections are treated with antiviral agents. In certain circumstances, the ophthalmologist may prescribe corticosteroid eye drops to relieve the symptoms. In many cases, conjunctivitis may resolve without medication.

Prognosis

Most cases of viral and many cases of bacterial conjunctivitis resolve without treatment (self-limiting). When treatment is prescribed, most individuals respond to appropriate treatment with no adverse effects. Corneal irritation, poor vision and light sensitivity may persist for several weeks following an initial viral infection. Bacterial infections respond well to antibiotic eye drops, and, when indicated, to systemic antibiotics (given either orally or as an injection).

Untreated infection with the gonococcal bacteria can affect the cornea, resulting in blindness. Blindness as a result of corneal damage by bacteria (including gonorrhea) is a leading cause of blindness (involving only one eye) in the world.

Infection with chlamydia may become chronic and may damage the cornea and cause loss of vision. Most often, these infections are preventable and treatable well before damage occurs.

Differential Diagnosis

Other conditions that can cause a red eye include irritation or ulceration of the cornea from a contact lens or foreign body, inflammation of the iris, corneal herpes simplex infection, and acute angle-closure glaucoma. However, these are usually associated with more severe pain and decreased visual acuity.

Specialists

- Ophthalmologist

Work Restrictions / Accommodations

Some infections may be spread easily between employees if poor hygiene is practiced. Hands must be washed after touching an infected eye. Towels should never be shared or reused. Some healthcare employees may be restricted from work until symptoms improve to prevent spread to at-risk individuals.

Complementary and Alternative Therapies

Content is intended for awareness only. Treatments may or may not be effective. Scientific evidence may be lacking and some substances have potentially toxic effects. Dr. Presley Reed and the editors do not endorse the use of these therapies in the absence of consultation with a licensed medical professional.

Hydrotherapy - A compress placed over closed eyes may be soothing. Cold compresses may be used if the conjunctivitis is allergy-related; warm for everything else. See physician immediately if there is a change in vision, pain in eyes, or yellow or green discharge from eyes.

Comorbid Conditions

Bacterial conjunctivitis is more likely to occur if there has been trauma to the surface of the eye (which may happen with contact lens use), preceding infection (such as with herpes simplex infection), or if the individual is immunosuppressed.

Complications

Herpes simplex viral infections can cause ulceration of the cornea if left untreated. Infection with gonococcal bacteria may cause corneal ulceration, abscess, perforation, destruction of the eye, and blindness. In underdeveloped countries, infection with chlamydia can result in scarring and damage to the cornea, which may result in blindness. Scarring and damage to the cornea due to chlamydia is known as trachoma. In developed countries, chlamydial conjunctivitis usually does not cause corneal scarring and damage.

Factors Influencing Duration

The underlying cause, treatment, and response to treatment may influence length of disability. If the conjunctivitis does not respond to initial treatment, other treatments may have to be explored. Untreated gonococcal conjunctivitis may result in destruction of the affected eye(s) resulting in blindness.

Length of Disability

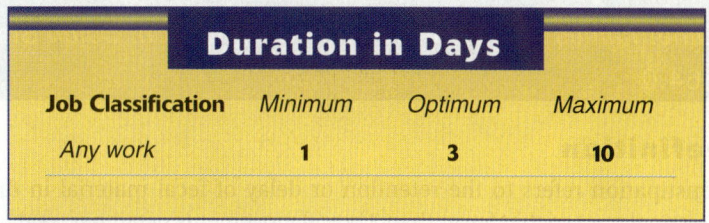

Job Classification	Minimum	Optimum	Maximum
Any work	1	3	10

Duration in Days

Failure to Recover

If an individual fails to recover within the maximum duration expectancy period, the reader may wish to reference the following questions to assist in better understanding the specifics of an individual's medical case.

Regarding diagnosis:

- Has diagnosis of conjunctivitis been confirmed by physical examination?
- If present, was mucus cultured for bacterial or viral organisms?
- Was there exposure to someone who had conjunctivitis or to its causative agents in the recent past?

Regarding treatment:

- Were appropriate antibiotic eye drops or systemic antibiotics prescribed?
- Did symptoms resolve with antibiotic treatment?
- Were symptoms resolved with antiviral agents? Were symptoms resolved with corticosteroid eye drops?

Regarding prognosis:

- To what extent are decreased vision and light sensitivity impacting function?
- How much longer are these symptoms expected to persist?
- If infection is not responding to treatment, has a culture and sensitivity been done to determine the most effective antibiotic to use and to rule out antibiotic-resistant organisms?
- Has individual experienced any complications (corneal ulceration, abscess, perforation, destruction of the eye, and blindness) as a result of the conjunctivitis?
- Does individual have any underlying conditions (i.e., immune suppression) that may impact recovery?

References

Benenson, Abram S. "Acute Bacterial Conjunctivitis." Control of Communicable Diseases, 16th ed. Benenson, Abram S., ed. Washington, DC: American Public Health Association, 1995. 106-109.

Rubenstein, Jonathan B. "Disorders of the Conjunctiva and Limbus." Ophthalmology. Yanoff, Myron, and Jay S. Duker, eds. London: Mosby, 1999. 5.1.1-5.1.22.

Constipation

Other names / synonyms: Atonia Constipation, Colon Stasis, Fecalith, Inactive Colon, Lazy Colon, Obstipation

564.0

Definition

Constipation refers to the retention or delay of fecal material in the intestinal tract so that fewer than 3 bowel movements occur per week. It is usually a symptom of another disease state such as inflammation of the bowel (irritable bowel syndrome, or IBS), enlarged toxic colon (Hirschsprung's disease), low thyroid function (hypothyroidism), diminished inhalation/exhalation capacity of the lungs (chronic obstructive pulmonary disease, or COPD), stroke, paralysis affecting the lower spine, Parkinson's disease, colon cancer, tuberculosis, infection of the colon (diverticulitis), or loss of neural innervation to the colon (neurogenic disease).

Constipation is also common in pregnant women and individuals who have taken narcotic drugs. Constipation may be complicated by high consumption of coffee or tea and low caloric intake.

Constipation is the most common digestive complaint in the US. It increases markedly after age 60 and one-third of all elderly individuals report constipation. Also, it is more prevalent in families with low income and less education.

Diagnosis

History: Individuals will report problems having bowel movements or complain of hard, dry stools. Sensations of fullness or pressure in the rectum and a frequent urge to defecate are also common. After prolonged constipation, there may be a sense of stomach (epigastric) fullness along with nausea, belching, stomach distention, return of stomach contents into the mouth (regurgitation), or abdominal discomfort. Long-term, untreated constipation may produce headache, dizziness (vertigo), general weakness and discomfort (malaise), loss of appetite (anorexia), or a bad taste in the mouth.

Physical exam: The exam may reveal increased anal canal muscle tone and crack-like lesions on the anus (anal fissures). The individual may also have a distended abdomen and there could be an accumulation (impaction) of hardened, dry (inspissated) feces that can be felt in the area of the lower bowel (rectum, or sigmoid/transverse colon).

Tests: Tests are not ordinarily needed to ascertain that an individual has constipation because the history and physical exam will provide adequate information. However, in some cases, tests may be performed to ascertain the cause of constipation. Thyroid and parathyroid function tests may be performed along with a test for urinary tract infection. The interior of the colon can be inspected by inserting a flexible optic instrument (endoscope) through the rectal opening and up into the colon (colonoscopy). The colon can also be visualized externally using a radiographic procedure (barium enema). Functional tests may include measurement of transit time through the colon (colorectal transit time) using radiopaque markers (colonic scintigraphy) or recording abnormal electrical activity of the colon by colonoscopy. Anorectal morphology and dynamics can be studied during defecation using a barium paste that reproduces stool consistency (defecography).

Treatment

Individuals are advised to increase intake of fluids and dietary fiber, and to increase physical activity as much as possible. Dietary fiber intake may be increased by consuming more raw fruits and vegetables, whole grain cereals, and breads. In some cases, individuals may be given laxatives or gastrointestinal motility drugs. However, dependence on laxatives is a possibility and their use should be monitored closely. If there is an underlying cause for the constipation such as low thyroid levels or colon cancer, the primary disease is treated appropriately with medication or surgery (colectomy).

Prognosis

Most individuals can expect a full recovery and a return to normal bowel function. However, more severe gastrointestinal symptoms may appear if problems with constipation continue. If surgery is required to remove a cancerous portion of bowel, the individual may require an artificial opening (stoma) of the colon through the abdominal wall for the purpose of bowel elimination (colostomy). A colostomy may be temporary or permanent depending upon the portion of bowel that was surgically removed.

Differential Diagnosis

Conditions that may present with similar symptoms include irritable bowel syndrome (IBS), toxic inflamed colon (Hirschsprung's disease), colon cancer, and low thyroid function (hypothyroidism).

Specialists

- Gastroenterologist
- General Surgeon
- Primary Care Provider

Work Restrictions / Accommodations

Most individuals will have no work restrictions or accommodations while being treated for constipation. However, restriction to light or sedentary work for 4-6 weeks may be required when an individual returns to the job after recovery from surgery.

> **Complementary and Alternative Therapies**
>
> Content is intended for awareness only. Treatments may or may not be effective. Scientific evidence may be lacking and some substances have potentially toxic effects. Dr. Presley Reed and the editors do not endorse the use of these therapies in the absence of consultation with a licensed medical professional.
>
> Biofeedback - Visual and auditory feedback of anal sphincter pressures may enhance anorectal relaxation ability.
>
> Acupuncture - Insertion of needles at certain points on the body may improve bowel function.
>
> Colonic massage - Propulsive abdominal wall massage may decrease transit time through the colon.
>
> Baduanjin - Ancient Chinese exercises may be effective for constipation.
>
> Colon cleansing - Enemas administered into the rectum may relieve constipation.

Comorbid Conditions

Individuals with hemorrhoids, fissures, or other anorectal lesions often experience pain when passing feces. Consequently, they ignore the urge to defecate for fear of the associated pain and constipation may be the result. Also, constipation occurs more frequently in obese individuals. There are numerous disease states that can affect an individual's ability to recover from constipation including diabetes, low thyroid function (hypothyroidism), various neurogenic disorders such as Hirschsprung's and Parkinson's disease, and many diseases of the large bowel including colon tumors and diverticulitis.

Complications

Urinary tract infections and urinary stones (bladder calculi) are commonly associated with constipation. Usually, chronic constipation is a symptom of an underlying disease state or condition.

Factors Influencing Duration

Disability is determinate on the underlying condition.

Length of Disability

No disability is expected to result from this symptom. Disability may occur as a result of an underlying condition. Contact physician to obtain additional information.

Failure to Recover

If an individual fails to recover within the maximum duration expectancy period, the reader may wish to reference the following questions to assist in better understanding the specifics of an individual's medical case.

Regarding diagnosis:

- Does individual fit the criteria for constipation?
- What is the underlying cause of constipation?
- Does individual have an underlying medical condition that may complicate treatment or impact recovery?

Regarding treatment:

- If there is an underlying cause for the constipation, such as low thyroid levels or colon cancer, was the primary disease is appropriately? Is treatment for the underlying disorder effective? Will the individual require surgery to correct the underlying disorder?
- Is the individual compliant with modification of dietary fiber and fluid intake?
- Does individual exercise routinely?
- If individual is taking laxatives or gastric motility drugs, has he/she become dependent on these drugs to have a bowel movement? How can individual be effectively weaned off medication?

Regarding prognosis:

- Has constipation resolved or become less frequent?
- Has individual been compliant with treatment regimen? If not, what can be done to enhance compliance?
- Has underlying condition responded to treatment?
- If constipation was due to bowel cancer, was a colostomy required? Will it be temporary or permanent?
- Have complications occurred as a result of the underlying disease or condition that caused the constipation? Are complications responding to treatment?

References

Chia, Y.W., et al. "Microchip Implants on the Anterior Sacral Roots in Patients with Spinal Trauma: Does It Improve Bowel Function?" Diseases of the Colon and Rectum 39 6 (1996): 690-694.

Davenport, Horace W. Physiology of the Digestive Tract. Chicago: Year Book Medical Publishers, Inc, 1982.

Devroede, Ghislain. "Constipation." Gastrointestinal Disease. Pathophysiology/Diagnosis/Management. Sleisenger, Marvin H., and John S. Fordtran, eds. Philadelphia: W.B. Saunders Company, 1993. 837-887.

Klauser, A.G., et al. "Abdominal Wall Massage: Effect on Colonic Function in Healthy Volunteers and in Patients with Chronic Constipation." Zeitschrift fur Gastroenterologie 30 4 (1992): 247-251.

Klauser, A.G., et al. "Body Acupuncture: Effect on Colonic Function in Chronic Constipation." Zeitschrift fur Gastroenterologie 31 10 (1993): 605-608.

Koh, T.C. "Baduanjin - An Ancient Chinese Exercise." American Journal of Chinese Medicine 10 1-4 (1982): 14-21.

Krogh, K., et al. "Treatment of Anal Incontinence and Constipation with Transanal Irrigation." Ugeskrift for Laeger 161 3 (1999): 253-256.

McKee, R.F., et al. "Identification of Patients Likely to Benefit From Biofeedback for Outlet Obstruction Constipation." British Journal of Surgery 86 3 (1999): 355-359.

Morse, Theresa. "Large Intestine." Gastroenterology Nursing. A Core Curriculum. Domkowski, Kathleen G., and Nancy S. Schlossberg, eds. St. Louis: Mosby, 1998. 139-153.

Nair, P., and J.F. Mayberry. "Vegetarianism, Dietary Fibre and Gastro-intestinal Disease." Digestive Diseases 12 3 (1994): 177-185.

Sandler, R.S., M.C. Jordan, and B.J. Shelton. "Demographic and Dietary Determinants of Constipation in the US Population." American Journal of Public Health 80 2 (1990): 185-189.

Towers, A.L., et al. "Constipation in the Elderly: Influence of Dietary, Psychological, and Physiological Factors." Journal of the American Geriatrics Society 42 7 (1994): 701-706.

Contact Dermatitis

Other names / synonyms: Irritant Contact Dermatitis

692, 692.0, 692.1, 692.2, 692.3, 692.4, 692.81, 692.82, 692.9

Definition

Contact dermatitis is a skin inflammation that comes in two forms, irritant and allergic, and occurs when the skin comes in direct contact with an irritating or allergenic substance, respectively.

Irritant contact dermatitis can cause overly dry (xerosis) or moist (maceration) skin conditions. Common irritants are detergents, nickel (found in jewelry and the fastenings of underclothes), certain chemicals, rubber gloves, condoms, certain cosmetics, and medications used on the skin (topical). Contact dermatitis caused by an irritant develops within minutes or hours after exposure. Irritant contact dermatitis occurs more often in individuals whose work brings them into frequent contact with irritants such as soaps, detergents, chemicals, and abrasives. Individuals in certain outdoor and manufacturing occupations are at higher risk for exposure to allergens and irritants that may cause dermatitis. These substances can either erode the protective oily barriers of the skin or physically injure its surface. The irritant form accounts for 80% of all cases of contact dermatitis.

Allergic reactions occur when an individual's immune system becomes sensitized to a substance (sensitization phase) and then reacts again when it is exposed to the same substance (elicitation phase). In the case of allergic contact dermatitis, this immune response occurs on the skin resulting in the appearance of a rash. Causes for 90% of all allergic contact dermatitis cases are toxic plants (poison ivy, oak, or sumac), formaldehyde, nickel, benzocaine, neomycin, preservatives (parabens), black dye (paraphenylenediamine), chromate, epoxy resins, antioxidants, permanent wave solutions, and fragrances. Allergic contact dermatitis accounts for 25% of all cases of contact dermatitis at the workplace and usually occurs within 24 to 48 hours after contact. Continued exposure may result in a chronic dermatitis.

The prevalence of contact dermatitis is between 1% and 10% and accounts for 90% of all occupational skin disease.

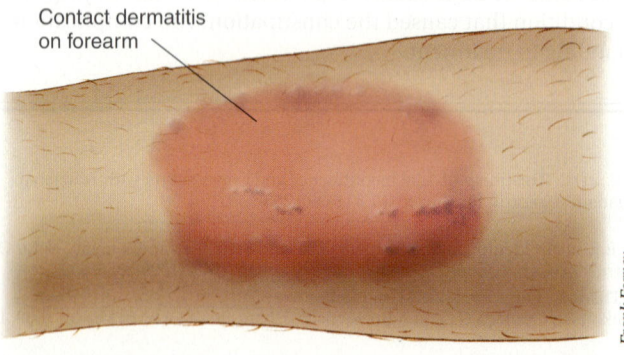

Contact dermatitis on forearm

Frank Forney

Diagnosis

History: In the early stages, irritant contact dermatitis is likely to produce stinging or burning while allergic contact dermatitis causes itching. The individual will complain of red, swollen, itchy areas on the skin. Blisters, weeping, and crusting may also be present. The individual may report a previous reaction to a suspected substance or a recent change in detergent, soap, cosmetics, jewelry, topical medication or the use of new chemicals at the workplace. The individual with poison oak or ivy dermatitis often reports working or recreating outdoors.

Physical exam: A total skin examination is performed. The early stages of contact dermatitis are characterized by areas of reddened (erythematous) and swollen (edematous) skin followed by development of small and large blisters (vesicles and bullae, respectively). The blisters may ooze and then crust over with scab formation. Chronic contact dermatitis appears as red, thickened (lichenification) skin with cracks (fissures).

The pattern, shape, and location of the rash help identify the causative substance. For example, poison ivy or oak allergic dermatitis is commonly seen as a streak or line of blisters on the arms or legs. Causes of irritant contact dermatitis on the scalp may be hair tints, sprays, or tonics, and on the face may be cosmetics, soaps, or shaving materials.

Tests: Skin patch tests, provocative challenges, and some immunological testing may be required. Elevated total IgE suggests an allergic reaction.

Treatment

Primary treatment consists of identifying the offending agent and avoiding it. Topical corticosteroids, oral antihistamines, or astringent lotions may be used. Oral corticosteroids may be required for severe cases or for those involving the genitals or face. Dry (xerosis) irritant contact dermatitis is treated by lubrication with cream. Treatment for moist (macerated) irritant contact dermatitis is to avoid wet skin conditions.

Prognosis

If the agent causing contact dermatitis can be identified and avoided, the skin inflammation will usually resolve within a few weeks for allergic contact dermatitis and a few days for irritant contact dermatitis. Occupational contact dermatitis clears in 25% of individuals, shows 50% improvement with periodic recurrence, and is persistent and severe in 25% of affected individuals. Allergic contact dermatitis may persist for years even with allergen avoidance.

Generalized hypersensitivity reaction (anaphylaxis and angioedema) by extremely hypersensitive individuals is potentially fatal and can occur upon exposure to the allergen.

Differential Diagnosis

Impetigo, scabies, dermatophytid, atopic dermatitis, photodermatitis, psoriasis, fungal infection, and pompholyx can have similar skin lesions.

Specialists

- Allergist
- Dermatologist

Work Restrictions / Accommodations

Contact dermatitis may be avoided by removal (or replacement) of the offending substance or by wearing personal protective equipment (e.g., cotton-lined rubber gloves) and using barrier creams. A change in occupational responsibilities may be necessary if contact with the irritating or allergenic industrial substance is unavoidable.

Comorbid Conditions

Atopic dermatitis, psoriasis, acne, and stasis dermatitis can predispose an individual to contact dermatitis. Immune system-suppressing diseases such as AIDS or certain cancers can increase the length of disability by making the individual more prone to skin infection.

Complications

Secondary infection is a common complication of contact dermatitis. Inflammation of blood vessels (vasculitis) and involvement of other organs may complicate allergic contact dermatitis. A life-threatening generalized hypersensitivity reaction (anaphylaxis) characterized by hives (urticaria), itching, welts or swelling below the surface of the skin (angioedema), and breathing difficulties can occur in individuals with allergic contact dermatitis. Less common, potentially life-threatening forms of allergic contact dermatitis have blistering (bullous) eruptions with peeling layers of skin (exfoliative erythroderma) or large blisters (erythema multiforme).

Factors Influencing Duration

Length of disability may be influenced by the underlying cause, site, severity and extent of the dermatitis, the development of a secondary bacterial infection, the individual's job requirements, and response to treatment.

Length of Disability

In most cases, no disability is expected. The length of disability depends on job requirements.

Duration in Days

Job Classification	Minimum	Optimum	Maximum
Any work	0	3	7

Failure to Recover

If an individual fails to recover within the maximum duration expectancy period, the reader may wish to reference the following questions to assist in better understanding the specifics of an individual's medical case.

Regarding diagnosis:

- Does individual have irritant or allergic contact dermatitis?
- Does individual report overly dry or moist skin?
- Does stinging and burning or itching occur?
- Are there red, swollen, itchy areas on the skin?
- Does individual also have blisters, weeping, and crusting?
- Is the skin red and thickened with cracks?
- Does individual report a previous reaction to a suspected substance?
- Has individual had contact with detergents, nickel, certain chemicals, rubber gloves, condoms, certain cosmetics, or topical medications?
- Has individual recently made a change in detergent, soap, cosmetics, jewelry, topical medication, or the use of new chemicals at the workplace?
- Does individual report working or recreating outdoors?
- Has individual had skin patch tests, provocative challenges, or immunological testing?
- Were conditions with similar symptoms ruled out?

Regarding treatment:

- Was the offending agent identified? Does individual attempt to avoid it?
- Was individual treated with topical corticosteroids, oral antihistamines, or astringent lotions?
- Did it become necessary to use oral corticosteroids?
- Is dry irritant contact dermatitis being treated by lubrication with cream?
- Does individual with moist irritant contact dermatitis avoid wet skin conditions?

Regarding prognosis:

- Can individual's employer accommodate any necessary restrictions?
- Does individual have any conditions that may affect ability to recover?
- Have any complications developed such as secondary infection, vasculitis, anaphylaxis, angioedema, or breathing difficulties?
- Does individual have exfoliative erythroderma or erythema multiforme?

References

Anderson, Philip, and Kristin Malaker. "Most Common Skin Disorders." Managing Skin Diseases. Hiscock, Tim, ed. Baltimore: Williams & Wilkins, 1999. 50-55.

Rietschel, Robert. "Occupational Contact Dermatitis." The Lancet 349 (1997): 1093-1095.

Contusion

Other names / synonyms: Black-and-Blue Mark, Bruise, Ecchymosis

924.8, 924.9

Definition

A contusion is an injury to any organ of the body that does not involve a break in the skin. Contusions result when small blood vessels (capillaries) are broken. A collection of blood (hematoma) results when there is a hole or small break in a vein. A superficial contusion has bleeding into the skin or just below the skin (subcutaneous tissue) that is initially visible as a black-and-blue mark. This mark changes colors in a few days to brown, green, and yellow and then fades.

Contusions are usually caused by a fall or direct blow from a blunt object. They are classified as mild, moderate, or severe. If the contusion is superficial, it involves only the skin and subcutaneous tissue. If deep, the muscle and bone may also be involved. Blood can accumulate and form a hematoma within the muscle.

Muscle and bone contusions can result from trauma such as a car accident. Major trauma can result in contusions of internal organs such as the kidneys, lungs, heart, or brain. Deep contusions are tender and cannot be seen unless superficial contusions accompany them.

Individuals at risk for contusions are involved in specific sports, have a bleeding disorder (e.g., hemophilia), vitamin deficiency, are obese, and take aspirin or anticoagulants.

Contusions are very common and 5% of the population sustains a contusion in any year. Every year approximately 165,000 work-related contusion injuries lead to time away from work. The most common diagnoses in individuals taken to emergency rooms after the Oklahoma City bombing in 1995 were lacerations/contusions. A Dutch study of the clinical records of 19,593 individuals admitted to a hospital emergency room for accidental falls from 1990 to 1997 found that 64% were between the ages of 10 and 59 and that contusion was the major injury in 20% of these individuals. Females 50 and older are more likely to be injured than males.

Diagnosis

History: The individual may have a history of a recent injury, usually a blow or a fall. In general, the individual with a contusion complains of skin discoloration, swelling, and pain. Depending on the location of the contusion, restricted movement or stiffness is a possibility.

Physical exam: The contusion may appear dark blue or red, or yellow-green depending on how soon the physical exam was performed after the injury. The site feels firm and tender to the touch. Swelling is usually apparent around the bruise. There may be evidence of limited range of motion and/or loss of function of the nearby joint. The extent of the contusion may not be visible for 2 to 3 days.

Tests: Tests are usually not needed for this diagnosis. Plain x-rays may be taken for moderate to severe contusions to determine the extent of injury and to rule out bone fracture. MRI and CT are used to diagnose deep organ contusions such as in the heart and lung. If the individual has a history of contusions caused by very minor trauma, blood-clotting factors may be tested.

Treatment

Superficial contusions usually do not require medical attention and are seldom disabling. Ice should be immediately applied to the injury for the first day. This may stop the bleeding and limit the size of the contusion. After 24 to 48 hours, application of heat may help speed resorption of the blood and can be applied in the form of hot soaks, hot showers, heating pads, heat lamps, heat liniments or ointments, or a hot whirlpool bath. Painkillers (analgesics) are administered for pain.

Deeper contusions involving muscle or bone are treated optimally with rest, ice, compression, and elevation. A compression bandage may be worn for 3 days. Vigorous physical activity should be avoided for the first 48 hours. Crutches may be prescribed for individuals with a contusion to the hip, pelvis, buttocks, or lower extremities. A sling may be prescribed for individuals with a clavicle, scapula, or upper extremity contusion. Contusions of internal organs may require hospitalization for observation or supportive treatment. For example, individuals with lung contusions may need oxygen and possibly mechanical ventilation. A contusion of the heart is treated as a heart attack (myocardial infarction).

Prognosis

Most contusions resolve without disability. Healing times vary with the severity of the injury. Superficial contusions disappear in a week or two after the individual is treated conservatively, as described. Contusions involving internal organs can also disappear after hospitalization and supportive treatment. Internal contusions are potentially serious and without treatment can result in permanent disability or death.

Differential Diagnosis

If a tender mass is evident with or without skin discoloration, the condition may be a hematoma. A bone fracture may present as a contusion. A contusion could possibly be a sign of bleeding in deeper organs.

Specialists

- Emergency Medicine
- General Surgeon
- Orthopedic Surgeon
- Primary Care Provider

Rehabilitation

Since contusions can occur in various parts of the body (i.e., elbow, forearm, hand, or thigh), treatment protocols may vary due to body location. Body part location also determines possible severity of contusion. In general, superficial contusions do not need rehabilitation. Physical therapy may be required for severe contusions. Myositis ossificans usually begins within the first or second week after a severe contusion. Rest and ultrasound are usually the only prescription in these cases until further clearance by the primary physician. It should be noted that ultrasound is not initially prescribed for the contusion as it may cause further inflammatory reaction to the area.

Beginning rehabilitation for contusions to the upper or lower body are similar in that the affected limb may be immobilized for the first 48 hours either by a sling or a compression bandage. Depending on the severity of the contusion, ice therapy may continue after the injury. Active range-of-motion exercises may be initiated when pain tolerance allows and include pointing and flexing the feet. Duration of exercise sessions depends on the pain level of the individual and the presence or absence of myositis ossificans.

If myositis ossificans is not present, strengthening exercises are added to the individual's routine. Once range of motion and flexibility is restored, the individual may engage in a progressive resistance program.

During this latter stage of contusion rehabilitation, heat, ultrasound, and massage may be beneficial in hastening recovery. The main goal for the individual is to increase strength and endurance in the affected limb. The individual may continue to engage in a structured therapy program or a home routine. The individual may also return to modified duty at the workplace.

Occupational therapy is usually not needed unless the contusion was severe enough to cause permanent muscular damage. This is especially true of pulmonary (lung) contusions and heart contusions that may require respiratory therapy and physical therapy. Cerebral contusions may also cause partial paralysis. Return to work for individuals with these extreme contusions is dependent on their level of recovery.

Work Restrictions / Accommodations

Restrictions and accommodations are determined based on the location and severity of the contusion and if it interferes with job responsibilities. Depending on work duties, the individual may need to be temporarily reassigned. Pain and swelling may interfere with performance of the job. If a standing position causes increased pain, a sitting job may be needed for the first week if an individual sustains a superficial contusion. A deep organ contusion may result from a serious underlying illness or serious injury. Accommodations at the workplace are needed according to the illness or injury.

Comorbid Conditions

Bleeding disorders (e.g., hemophilia) can lead to a more severe contusion that may increase the length of disability. Fibromyalgia, poor nutrition, osteoporosis, other injuries such as fractures and lacerations, arthritis, diabetes, heart disease, cancer and lung diseases may slow full recovery.

Complications

Skin breaks (lacerations) may be prone to infection. Inflammation (cellulitis) can occur surrounding a break in the skin. Hematomas within the muscle prolong the recovery time and delay return of function. Pressure on the local blood vessels from swelling or bleeding can result in compartment syndrome that can cause permanent muscle and nerve damage. Bleeding within the muscle can lead to loss of hip function. On occasion, damaged muscle can convert into a bony substance (ossification), a condition known as myositis ossificans. This may cause disfigurement and impaired muscle function. Infections may occur following surgery. Repeat injury to a joint can cause instability or arthritis. Fatal soft-tissue infection (necrotizing fasciitis) can result from a simple contusion.

Factors Influencing Duration

Most contusions are not disabling. Hematomas, any complications, and the individual's response to treatment influence the length of disability. The main factors influencing disability include whether the individual sustained more serious injuries than the contusion, if the contusion is potentially life-threatening such as in the heart or lung, and if the individual has any serious illnesses.

Length of Disability

For small and/or superficial contusions, no disability is usually expected. For extensive and/or deep contusions, length of disability depends on site and severity. Disability may be permanent if the contusion is life-threatening and/or the individual has other serious disease or illnesses.

Duration in Days

Job Classification	Minimum	Optimum	Maximum
Sedentary work	0	1	3
Light work	0	1	3
Medium work	0	1	7
Heavy work	0	1	7
Very Heavy work	0	1	7

Failure to Recover

If an individual fails to recover within the maximum duration expectancy period, the reader may wish to reference the following questions to assist in better understanding the specifics of an individual's medical case.

Regarding diagnosis:

- Does individual have a history of a recent injury such as a fall, direct blow, motor vehicle accident, or sports injury?
- Does individual have a bleeding disorder? Vitamin deficiency? Obesity? Take aspirin or anticoagulants?
- On exam, what color is the contusion? Is the site firm and tender to palpation? Is swelling apparent around the bruise? Is there restricted movement or stiffness?
- Did individual have an x-ray? MRI or CT? Blood-clotting factors?
- Were conditions with similar symptoms ruled out?

Regarding treatment:

- Was individual treated with ice for the first 24 to 28 hours? Was heat then applied?
- Was individual given analgesics?
- Were deeper contusions involving muscle or bone treated with rest, ice, compression, and elevation?
- Was it necessary for individual to use crutches? A sling?
- Did individual have internal contusions? Was individual hospitalized?

Regarding prognosis:

- If necessary, is individual active in physical therapy? Is a home exercise program in place?
- Can individual's employer accommodate any necessary restrictions?
- Does individual have any conditions that may affect ability to recover?
- Have any complications developed such as infection, cellulitis, compartment syndrome, myositis ossificans, or necrotizing fasciitis? Does individual have joint instability or arthritis?

References

Bealle, D., and D.L. Johnson. "Subchondral Contusion of the Knee Caused by Axial Loading From Dashboard Impact Detection by Magnetic Resonance Imaging." Journal of the Southern Orthopaedic Association 9 1 (2000): 13-18.

Bernau, A., and G. Kruppa. "Low Frequency Electro-stimulation and Ultrasonic Therapy." Z Orthop Ihre Grenzgeb 119 1 (1981): 126-137.

Kingma, J., and H.J. Ten Duis. "Severity of Injuries Due to Accidental Fall Across the Life Span: A Retrospective Hospital-based Study." Perceptual and Motor Skills 90 1 (2000): 62-72.

Tyburski, J.G., et al. "Pulmonary Contusions: Quantifying the Lesions on Chest X-ray Films and the Factors Affecting Prognosis." The Journal of Trauma 5 5 (1999): 833-888.

Contusion, Eye

Other names / synonyms: Black Eye, Lid Contusion

921.0, 921.1, 921.2, 921.3, 921.9

Definition

A contusion is a bruise, which is a soft tissue injury that does not involve a break in the skin. The eyes are particularly prone to contusions because the skin lies close to the underlying bone. Eye contusions involve the eye, eyelid, eye socket, and associated muscles. Eye contusions are usually the result of a blunt injury to the eye. The injury may be incurred during a vehicular accident or a fight. Blood seeps out of damaged small blood vessels and into the surrounding tissue forming black-and blue marks beneath the skin (ecchymosis).

Individuals at risk for eye contusions are those who are in locations where fights are known to occur or around individuals prone to fighting; work in occupations that are prone to causing eye injury, such as construction work or carpentry; work around or with individuals who are combative (law enforcement, fire fighting, health care settings, mental institutions, nursing homes) participate in certain sports such as basketball, hockey, boxing, football, racquetball; use a rotary-style lawn mower; or use a slingshot or BB gun. Other risk factors include a medical history of a bleeding disorder (hemophilia), vitamin deficiency, and use of medications that promote bleeding (aspirin, anticoagulants).

Contusions are very common, and 5% of the population sustains a contusion in any year. Approximately 165,000 work-related contusion injuries each year lead to time away from work.

Diagnosis

History: History is of a recent injury to the eye. The individual may complain of pain, swelling, and discoloration of the eyelid and surrounding area. Visual disturbances (e.g., blurred vision, double vision) may be reported.

Physical exam: The exam may reveal bleeding, swelling, and tenderness in the eyelids and skin around the eye. The extent of the contusion may not be visible for 2-3 days. A thorough eye examination may be performed to determine the extent of the eye injury and may include vision testing, range of eye motion, determination of the depth of the front chamber (anterior chamber) of the eye, visualization of any cuts (lacerations) or foreign bodies in the eye or eyelid, and presence of any bleeding (hemorrhage) within the eye.

Tests: If a fracture of the eye socket or surrounding facial bone is suspected, plain x-rays will be taken.

Treatment

The eyelid and area surrounding the eye is gently washed using a mild soap and water. In the first 24 hours, ice packs are placed on the eyelid to reduce swelling and decrease internal bleeding. After the first day, hot compresses may be used to aid in absorption of the blood. Sunglasses may be worn to protect the eyes from bright light. The individual's head should be elevated during sleep. Possible medications include analgesics, antibiotics, and/or drops to dilate the eye pupil (to rest the eye muscles).

Prognosis

Uncomplicated contusions of the eye completely resolve within 2 weeks.

Differential Diagnosis

Fracture of facial bones, eye socket, or the skull bone near the eye are other possible diagnoses.

Specialists

- Emergency Medicine
- Ophthalmologist

Work Restrictions / Accommodations

If visual disturbances are present, a temporary change from work duties that require detailed vision or depth perception may be necessary. The individual may be temporarily unable to wear protective goggles and/or a respirator.

Comorbid Conditions

Bleeding disorders (e.g., hemophilia) can lead to a more severe contusion. Other injuries (e.g., fractures, lacerations) sustained during the traumatic event can influence the length of disability.

Complications

Bleeding may occur beneath the membrane that covers the eyeball (conjunctiva). The injury also could cause swelling or rupture of the cornea, bleeding within the front chamber of the eye (hyphema), damage to the iris, bleeding in the back chamber of the eye (vitreous hemorrhage), bleeding and swelling of the retina, retinal detachment, fracture of the eye socket, optic nerve injury, cataract, infection, or permanent loss of vision. Occasionally, damaged muscle can convert into a bony substance (ossification), which may cause disfigurement.

Although most of these injuries are immediately noticeable, some may not be evident for days or weeks. Ongoing bleeding inside the front chamber of the eye can result in glaucoma.

Factors Influencing Duration

Black eyes are rarely disabling. But any complications or associated injuries might influence the length of disability, especially if surgery is required.

Length of Disability

Duration depends on severity.

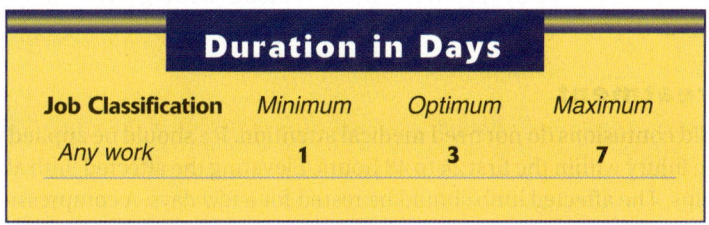

Job Classification	Minimum	Optimum	Maximum
Any work	1	3	7

Failure to Recover

If an individual fails to recover within the maximum duration expectancy period, the reader may wish to reference the following questions to assist in better understanding the specifics of an individual's medical case.

Regarding diagnosis:

- Does the individual's work or play put them at higher risk for a blunt injury to the eye?
- Does the individual have a bleeding disorder or vitamin deficiency?
- Is the individual on anticoagulant therapy?
- Does the individual complain of pain, swelling, discoloration of the eyelid and blurred or double vision?
- On exam what was the extent of the injury?
- Is there bleeding in the eye?
- Did the individual have visual acuity and range of eye motion testing?
- Did the individual have an x-ray?
- Have conditions with similar symptoms been ruled out?

Regarding treatment:

- Was the individual treated by cleansing the area and applying an ice pack?
- Did the individual switch to hot compresses after 24 hours of ice?
- Is the individual sleeping with the head elevated? Wearing sunglasses?
- Did it become necessary to add analgesics, antibiotics or dilate the pupil?

Regarding prognosis:

- Is the individual's employer able to accommodate any necessary restrictions?
- Does the individual have any condition that may affect their ability to recover?
- Does the individual have any complications such as subconjunctival hemorrhage, hyphema, glaucoma, damage to the iris, vitreous hemorrhage, bleeding and swelling of the retina, retinal detachment, fracture of the eye socket, optic nerve injury, cataract, infection, or permanent loss of vision?
- Does the individual have any ossification?

References

Mayer, Thom, and Errikos Constant. "Trauma to the Face." <u>Principles and Practice of Emergency Medicine.</u> Schwartz, George, ed. Baltimore: Williams and Wilkins, 1999. 273-292.

# Contusion, Lower Limb

Other names / synonyms: Bruise of the Leg(s), Bruised Leg
924, 924.0, 924.00, 924.01, 924.1, 924.10, 924.11, 924.2, 924.20, 924.21, 924.3, 924.4, 924.5, 924.8, 924.9

Definition

Contusions are bruises that are injuries not involving a break in the skin but that cause damage to the skin and underlying tissues. Blood seeps out of damaged small blood vessels and into the surrounding tissue forming black-and-blue marks beneath the skin (ecchymosis). After injury, gravity may pull the blood downward so the ecchymosis may be far from the contusion site. A direct blow from a blunt object usually causes a contusion.

Contusions are classified as mild, moderate, or severe. If the contusion is superficial, it involves only the skin and tissue immediately below the skin (subcutaneous tissue). If deep, the muscle and bone may also be involved. Blood can accumulate forming a hematoma within the muscle. Individuals at risk for contusions of the lower limbs may have a bleeding disorder (e.g., hemophilia) or a vitamin deficiency, be involved in specific sports, or take aspirin or anticoagulants.

Contusions of the thigh are common injuries sustained by athletes. Individuals at risk for thigh contusions are those in collision sports such as football, soccer, ice hockey, and field hockey.

The knee is highly prone to contusions. It is a common injury sustained by contact with the dashboard during a motor vehicle accident. Individuals at risk for knee contusions include those who participate in contact sports (e.g., football, hockey), running sports (e.g., track and field, cross-country), or riding sports (e.g., bicycling, motorcycling), especially if they do not wear protective equipment. The lower leg is prone to contusions because it is often exposed to direct blows.

Contusions directly over the shinbone (tibia) are more likely to be severe. Individuals at risk for suffering from lower leg contusions are those participating in contact sports such as football and hockey. Ankle contusions are common but not usually serious. Individuals at risk for ankle contusions include those who participate in contact sports such as ice hockey, field hockey, and soccer especially when protective equipment is not worn. Contusions of the foot may be caused from a direct blow to the foot, by wearing an athletic shoe with faulty spikes or cleats, or wearing a wrinkled sock. Individuals at risk for foot contusions are those participating in contact sports such as football, basketball, or baseball especially if protective footwear is not worn. Contusions of the toenail result from the impact of a dropped object and from kicking sports such as football and soccer. Because the toenail limits the ability of the tissues to swell, these contusions may be very painful. If the injury is severe, the nail itself may lift off the nail bed or may no longer be intact.

Contusions are very common and 5% of the population sustains a contusion in any year. Approximately 165,000 work-related contusion injuries every year lead to time away from work.

Diagnosis

History: The individual may have a history of a recent injury usually a blow or fall. In general, the individual with a contusion of the lower limb may complain of skin discoloration, swelling, pain, and possibly restricted limb movement. The individual with a knee contusion may complain of restricted movement of the knee. Cuts (lacerations) are commonly associated with knee contusions. The individual with a contusion to the lower leg may complain of pain, limited leg function, and may report the feeling of an electric shock at the time of injury followed by loss of function. Contusions of the toenail appear as blackened areas beneath the nail.

Physical exam: The contusion may appear dark blue or red, or yellow-green depending on how soon the physical exam was performed after the injury. The site feels firm and tender to the touch. Swelling is usually apparent around the bruise. There may be evidence of limited range of motion and/or loss of function of the affected limb. The extent of the contusion may not be visible for 2 to 3 days. Individuals with a lower leg contusion may have signs of paralysis (a "dropped foot").

Tests: Tests are usually not needed for this diagnosis. Plain x-rays may be taken for moderate to severe contusions to determine the extent of injury and to rule out bone fracture. If the individual has a history of contusions caused by very minor trauma, blood-clotting factors may be tested.

Treatment

Mild contusions do not need medical attention. Ice should be applied to the injury within the first 24 to 48 hours. Elevating the affected limb also helps. The affected limb should be rested for a few days. A compression bandage may be worn for 3 days. Heat may be applied after the first 24 to 48 hours in the form of hot soaks, hot showers, heating pads, heat lamps, heat liniments or ointments, or a hot whirlpool bath. Analgesics may be taken to relieve pain. For foot contusions, local anesthetics and corticosteroids may be injected directly into the contusion.

Prognosis

Most contusions resolve without disability. Healing times vary with the severity of the injury. Knee contusions heal within 2 to 6 weeks, lower leg contusions in 1 to 2 weeks. Ankle contusions generally heal in 2 to 4 days, foot contusions in 1 to 2 weeks. Toenail contusions should heal within 1 to 2 weeks although it takes several months for the toenail to grow out.

Differential Diagnosis

If a tender mass is evident with or without skin discoloration, the condition may be a hematoma. Bone fractures may present with similar symptoms and should be included in the differential diagnosis.

Specialists

- General Surgeon
- Orthopedic Surgeon
- Physiatrist
- Physical Therapist
- Podiatrist

Rehabilitation

Physical therapy may be required for serious contusions. Rehabilitation varies depending on the area of the contusion. In general, rehabilitation focuses on restoring normal range of motion, flexibility, strength, and endurance, and reducing pain. In the case of a thigh contusion, hot packs may be applied to the thigh to reduce pain and promote flexibility of the muscles. In addition, the therapist may perform deep tissue massage to reduce any persistent muscle spasm. The individual engages in quadriceps and hamstring stretches to address the muscles in the front and back of the thigh, respectively. Strengthening exercises such as straight leg raises, knee extensions, and minisquats are also performed. Individuals engage in endurance activities such as treadmill walking or stationary cycling. Cold packs are then applied to the contusion to reduce pain and swelling associated with exercise.

Work Restrictions / Accommodations

Contusions in a lower limb may affect the individual's ability to walk, stand, or sit for extended periods of time necessitating the need for temporary accommodations. Movement of the affected limb is restricted until the individual recovers. Operation of a car or other vehicle may temporarily be affected. Crutches or a cane may need to be used or a brace worn over the affected limb. Depending on work duties, the individual may need to be on temporary active duty or have present job duties modified.

Comorbid Conditions

Bleeding disorders such as hemophilia can lead to a more severe contusion that may increase the length of disability. Fibromyalgia, poor nutrition, osteoporosis, diabetes, and injuries (e.g., fractures, lacerations) sustained during the traumatic event may also influence the length of disability.

Complications

Skin breaks of the lower leg, especially in the ankle, may be prone to infection. Skin inflammation (cellulitis) can occur surrounding a break in the skin. Injuries that cause a lower leg contusion can damage the peroneal nerve and result in nerve inflammation (neuritis) or a temporary loss of function (paralysis). A hematoma within the muscle prolongs recovery time and delays return of function. Pressure on the muscle from swelling or bleeding especially in the lower leg can result in compartment syndrome that can cause permanent muscle and nerve damage. On occasion, damaged muscle can convert into a bony substance (ossification), a condition known as myositis ossificans. This may cause disfigurement and impaired muscle function.

Factors Influencing Duration

The part of the limb, type of treatment needed, hematomas, any complications, and the individual's response to treatment influence the length of disability.

Length of Disability

Duration depends on severity and job requirements.

Duration in Days

Job Classification	Minimum	Optimum	Maximum
Sedentary work	0	1	3
Light work	0	1	3
Medium work	0	1	7
Heavy work	0	1	7
Very Heavy work	0	1	7

Duration Trend from Normative Data*

Cases	Mean	Min	Max	No Lost Time	Over 6 Months
1420	37	0	251	2.18%	0.21%

Percentile:	5th	25th	Median	75th	95th
Days:	6	14	25	49	104

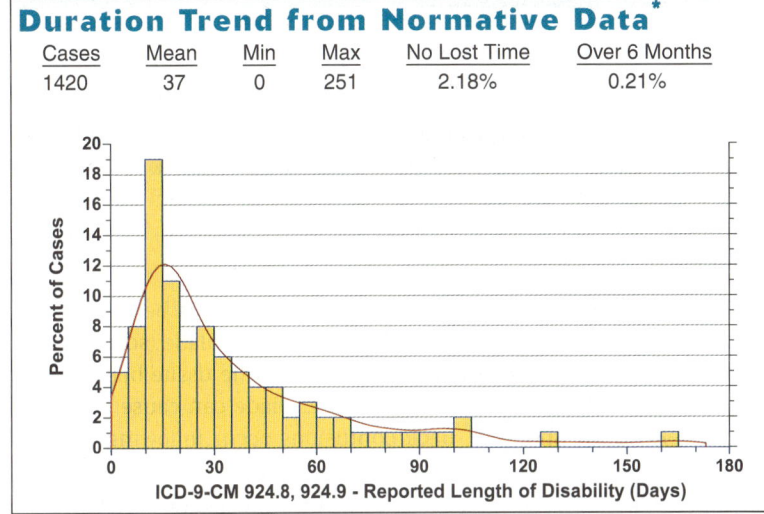
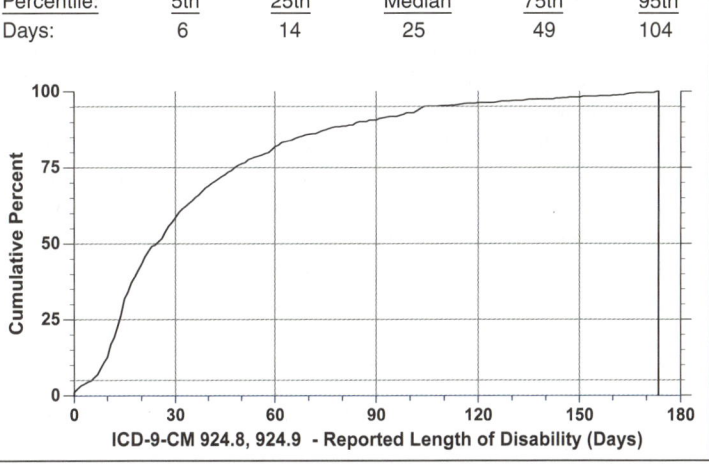

ICD-9-CM 924.8, 924.9 - Reported Length of Disability (Days)

* Differences may exist between the expected duration tables and the normative graphs. Duration tables provide expected recovery periods based on the type of work performed by the individual. The normative graphs reflect the actual observed experience of many individuals across the spectrum of physical conditions, in a variety of industries, and with varying levels of case management.

Failure to Recover

If an individual fails to recover within the maximum duration expectancy period, the reader may wish to reference the following questions to assist in better understanding the specifics of an individual's medical case.

Regarding diagnosis:
- Does the individual's work or play put them at risk for a blunt injury to the lower extremities?
- Is the individual's contusion mild, moderate or severe?
- Does the individual have a bleeding disorder? Vitamin deficiency?
- Is the individual on anticoagulant therapy?
- Does the individual complain of skin discoloration, swelling, pain, and restricted limb movement? Any lacerations?

Contusion, Lower Limb

- Did the individual report the feeling of an electric shock at the time of injury followed by loss of function?
- On physical exam, what color was the contusion?
- Was the site firm and tender to palpation? Was it swollen? Limited range of motion?
- Does the individual have any sign of paralysis?
- Did the individual have an x-ray? Blood clotting factor's tested?
- Have conditions with similar symptoms been ruled out?

Regarding treatment:

- Did the individual use ice packs for 24-48 hours? Elevate the limb?
- Was a compression bandage used?
- Did the individual switch to hot compresses after the first 48 hours?
- Did the individual use analgesics?
- Was it necessary to inject a foot contusion with local anesthetics and corticosteroids?

Regarding prognosis:

- Is the individual active in physical therapy?
- Does the individual have a home exercise program?
- Is the individual's employer able to accommodate any necessary restrictions?
- Does the individual have any conditions that may affect their ability to recover?
- Does the individual have any complications such as infection, cellulitis, peroneal nerve injury with neuritis or temporary paralysis, hematoma, compartment syndrome, or myositis ossificans?

References

Bonfiglio, Richard, Anita L. Cone, and Francis Lagattuta. "Pathophysiology of Soft Tissue Injuries." Soft Tissue Injuries: Diagnosis and Treatment. Windsor, Robert, and Dennis Lox, eds. Philadelphia: Hanley & Belfus, Inc, 1998. 1-11.

Garrett, William, and Donald Kirkendall. "The Structure and Function of Skeletal Muscle." Principles of Orthopaedic Practice. Dee, Roger, et al., eds. New York: McGraw-Hill, 1997. 119-128.

Kisner, Carolyn, and Lynn Allen Colby. Therapeutic Exercise: Foundations and Technique, 2nd ed. Philadelphia: F.A. Davis, 1990.

Magee, David J. "Lower Leg, Ankle, and Foot." Orthopedic Physical Assessment. Biblis, Margaret M., ed. Philadelphia: W.B. Saunders Company, 1992. 448-515.

Mooar, Pekka. "The Thigh, Knee, and Patella." Musculoskeletal Primary Care. Gates, Sharon, and Pekka Mooar, eds. Philadelphia: Lippincott Williams & Wilkins, 1999. 217-249.

Nixon, James. "The Lower Leg, Ankle, and Foot." Musculoskeletal Primary Care. Gates, Sharon, and Pekka Mooar, eds. Philadelphia: Lippincott Williams & Wilkins, 1999. 250-287.

Contusion, Trunk

Other names / synonyms: Body Bruise
922, 922.0, 922.1, 922.2, 922.3, 922.4, 922.8, 922.9

Definition

Contusions of the trunk may involve the breast, chest wall, abdominal wall, back, hip, buttocks, pelvis, genitals, or pelvic floor (perineum). A contusion is an injury that does not involve a break in the skin but causes damage to the skin and underlying tissues. It is usually caused by a fall or direct blow from a blunt object. Blood seeps out of damaged small blood vessels and into the surrounding tissue forming black-and-blue marks beneath the skin (ecchymosis). After injury, gravity may pull the blood downward so the ecchymosis can be far from the contusion site.

Contusions are classified as mild, moderate, or severe. If the contusion is superficial, it involves only the skin and tissue immediately below the skin (subcutaneous tissue). If deep, the muscle and bone may also be involved. Blood can accumulate forming a hematoma within the muscle.

Individuals at risk for contusions of the trunk include those involved in specific sports, have a bleeding disorder (e.g., hemophilia), a vitamin deficiency, are obese, and who take aspirin or anticoagulants.

The chest wall is particularly vulnerable to contusions because of the proximity of bone to the skin surface. Collarbone (clavicle) contusions are usually associated with an injury to the breastbone (sternum) or shoulder joint and can cause restricted movement of the chest and shoulder. Individuals at risk for sustaining chest wall or abdominal wall contusions include those who participate in contact sports such as boxing, football, ice hockey, wrestling, and basketball.

A breast contusion involves the breast, nipple, and underlying tissues and can occur in both men and women. Individuals at risk of sustaining breast contusions are those who participate in contact sports (e.g., wrestling, softball, baseball, and boxing), especially if protective equipment is not worn.

The back is also particularly vulnerable to contusions because of the proximity of bone to the skin surface. The shoulder blade (scapula) is at risk because it protrudes slightly and there is little tissue between the bone and skin. Contusions to the shoulder blade can cause restricted movement of the shoulder. Back contusions occur following a fall or blow by a blunt object. Individuals at risk for back contusions are those who participate in contact sports such as football, ice hockey, or soccer.

Areas of the hip and pelvis with a greater risk for sustaining particularly painful contusions are the upper tip of the pelvic bone (iliac crest); the lower, front region of the pubic bone (pubic ramus); the upper, outer corner of the thigh bone (greater trochanter); and the lower, rear region of the pelvic bone (ischial tuberosity). A contusion at the iliac crest with formation of a hematoma within the connective tissue covering the bone (periosteum) is called a "hip pointer." Individuals who fall onto the buttocks may incur a contusion at the ischial tuberosity; those who fall on the side or receive a blow from a blunt object may have a contusion at the greater trochanter. Individuals falling forward or receiving a blow from a blunt object may incur a contusion at the iliac crest. Contusions at the pubic ramus may occur if an individual falls across a bar (e.g., gymnastics). Injuries to the buttocks can affect the sciatic nerve.

Contusions are one of the most common hip and pelvis injuries sustained by athletes. Individuals with a higher risk of sustaining buttock contusions are those participating in contact sports especially football, basketball, ice hockey, and baseball (e.g., sliding), and sports with the potential for falling from a height such as pole-vaulting, high-jumping, gymnastics, or skating. Perineal contusions are caused by a fall or a direct blow to the floor of the pelvis and are often associated with genital contusions. Individuals at an increased risk of sustaining perineal and/or genital contusions are those participating in ice-skating, cycling, gymnastics, and horseback riding.

Contusions are very common and 5% of the population sustains a contusion in any year. Every year approximately 165,000 work-related contusion injuries lead to time away from work.

Diagnosis

History: The individual may have a history of a recent injury, usually a blow or a fall. In general, the individual with a contusion of the trunk complains of skin discoloration, swelling, and pain. Depending on the location of the contusion, restricted movement or stiffness is possible. Individuals with a contusion at the clavicle or scapula may complain of shoulder pain and limited shoulder mobility. The individual with a contusion at the greater trochanter complains of pain with hip movement. Those with a contusion at the ischial tuberosity report pain when raising the leg. The individual with a contusion at the iliac crest complains of difficulty walking and standing upright.

Physical exam: The contusion may appear dark blue or red, or yellow-green depending on how soon the physical exam was performed after the injury. The site feels firm and tender to the touch. Swelling is usually apparent around the bruise. There may be evidence of limited range of motion and/or loss of function of the nearby joint. The extent of the contusion may not be visible for 2 to 3 days. Individuals with a breast contusion may have a firm, tender region surrounding the nipple.

Tests: Tests are usually not needed for this diagnosis. Plain x-rays may be taken for moderate to severe contusions to determine the extent of injury and to rule out bone fracture. Ultrasound scanning may be performed on individuals with testicular contusions to assess the extent of injury. If the individual has a history of contusions caused by very minor trauma, blood-clotting factors may be tested.

Treatment

Mild contusions do not need medical attention. The affected muscle and associated joint should be rested for a few days. Ice should be applied to the injury within the first 24 to 48 hours. A compression bandage may be worn for 3 days. Vigorous physical activity should be avoided for the first 48 hours. Heat may be applied after the first 24 to 48 hours in the form of hot soaks, hot showers, heating pads, heat lamps, heat liniments or ointments, or a hot whirlpool bath. Severe testicular contusions may require surgery (orchiotomy) to drain accumulated blood and repair damage sustained during the injury. Crutches may be prescribed for individuals with a contusion to the hip, pelvis, or buttocks. A sling may be prescribed for individuals with a clavicle or scapula contusion. Analgesics may be taken to relieve pain.

Prognosis

Most contusions resolve without disability. Healing times vary with the severity of the injury. Chest and abdominal contusions generally heal within 2 weeks. Breast contusions usually heal within 2 to 6 weeks, back contusions in 2 weeks. Contusions in the pelvis and hip region usually heal in 1 to 4 weeks and genital contusions in 2 weeks. Orchiotomy has a good outcome.

Differential Diagnosis

If a tender mass is evident with or without skin discoloration, the condition may be a hematoma. A bone fracture may present as a contusion. A contusion could possibly be a sign of bleeding in deeper organs.

Specialists

- General Surgeon
- Gynecologist
- Physiatrist
- Urologist

Rehabilitation

Basic goals in the rehabilitation of a contusion of the trunk region are to decrease pain and swelling and allow the individual to regain full motion, flexibility, strength, and endurance of the muscle/soft tissues involved. The final result is aimed at returning the individual to full function for work and recreational activities with minimal risk of reinjury. The physical therapist determines the method for rehabilitation based on the severity of the trunk contusion and whether any joints are causing difficulty with movement and function.

If the trunk contusion produces severe pain and hematoma formation, initial ice with an elastic wrap compress is often used. After this period, heat treatments are helpful to reduce inflammation and pain and are beneficial to stretch the affected muscles. Forms of heat treatment include ultrasound. This method uses high frequency sound waves to produce heat that penetrates deep into the involved muscles. Electrical stimulation combined with heat or cold treatment is another technique used to relax irritated muscles that may be in spasm.

Gentle passive stretching of the trunk region affected by the contusion is initiated. Another technique is called the cat stretch. William's flexion exercises are also helpful in returning motion to the trunk and low back region associated with the trunk.

Once full range of motion is restored, rehabilitation then focuses on returning general strength to the trunk region. Sit-ups help strengthen the abdominal muscles. Calisthenics such as push-ups strengthen the muscles in the front upper portion of the trunk. Cross-crunch sit-ups help strengthen the side muscles of the trunk. Another strengthening exercise for this region is to have the individual lie on the back and perform circles with the legs as if riding a bicycle.

Swimming is a good exercise for conditioning the trunk as it incorporates all trunk motions against the mild resistance of the water.

If the individual has significant soft tissue damage to skin, muscle, and/or ligaments, the healing response may initially take longer with more stretching and strengthening required before returning to work. This is especially the case if the rib cage region is involved and breathing is difficult and painful because of the need to expand the chest/rib cage when breathing in (inhalation). Once the individual returns to work, it is important to initially minimize excessive bending, lifting, and twisting of the trunk. Rehabilitation of the contusion depends greatly on the degree of the tissue injury.

Work Restrictions / Accommodations

Restrictions and accommodations are determined based on the location and severity of the contusion and if it interferes with job responsibilities. Depending on work duties, the individual can either be returned to previous duties with accommodations or be temporarily reassigned. Contusions in hip, pelvis, buttocks, perineum, or genitals may affect the individual's ability to walk, stand, or sit for extended periods of time so temporary accommodations may be necessary. Individuals with contusions at the scapula or clavicle may have some restricted mobility of the shoulder that could affect lifting and overhead work.

Comorbid Conditions

Bleeding disorders (e.g., hemophilia) can lead to a more severe contusion that may increase the length of disability. Fibromyalgia, poor nutrition, osteoporosis, and other injuries (e.g., fractures and lacerations) may also influence the length of disability.

Complications

Skin breaks (laceration) may be prone to infection. Inflammation (cellulitis) can occur surrounding a break in the skin. Hematomas within the muscle prolong the recovery time and delay return of function. Pressure on the local blood vessels from swelling or bleeding can result in compartment syndrome that can cause permanent muscle and nerve damage. Bleeding within the muscle can lead to loss of hip function. On occasion, damaged muscle can convert into a bony substance (ossification), a condition known as myositis ossificans. This may cause disfigurement and impaired muscle function.

Infections may occur following surgery. Repeat injury to a joint can cause instability or arthritis. Pelvic bone fracture and injury to the sciatic nerve are common complications of buttock contusions. In women, severe perineal contusions can cause scarring and narrowing of the birth canal (vagina). In men, severe genital contusions may lead to loss of a testicle.

Factors Influencing Duration

Most contusions are not disabling. Hematomas, any complications, and the individual's response to treatment influence the length of disability.

Length of Disability

Duration of disability depends on severity and job requirements.

Duration in Days

Job Classification	Minimum	Optimum	Maximum
Sedentary work	0	1	3
Light work	0	1	3
Medium work	0	1	7
Heavy work	0	1	7
Very Heavy work	0	1	7

Duration Trend from Normative Data*

Cases	Mean	Min	Max	No Lost Time	Over 6 Months
2170	41	0	440	1.48%	1.91%

Percentile:	5th	25th	Median	75th	95th
Days:	6	15	26	47	103

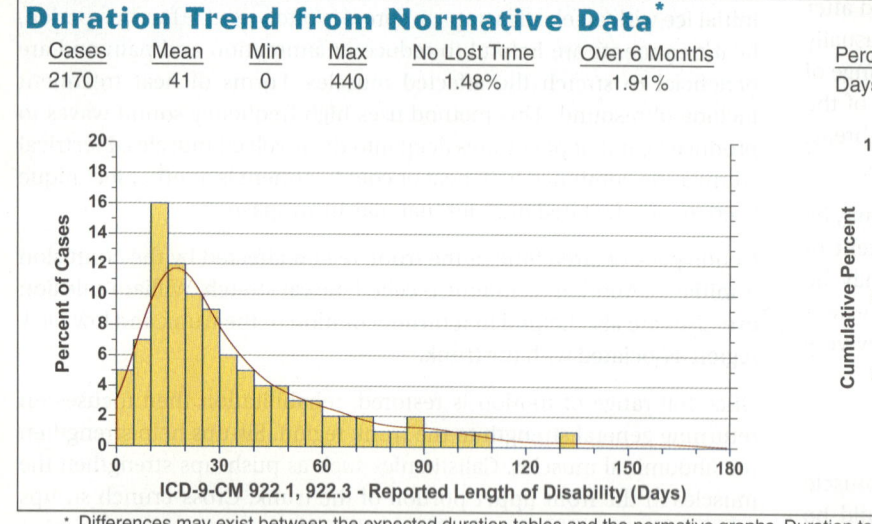
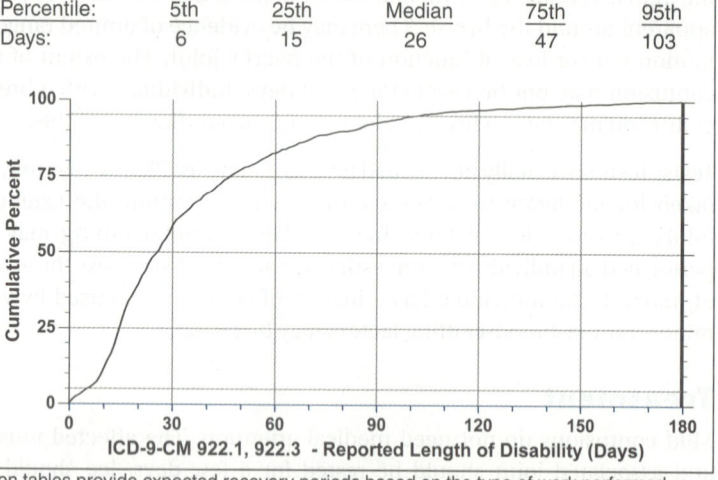

ICD-9-CM 922.1, 922.3 - Reported Length of Disability (Days)

* Differences may exist between the expected duration tables and the normative graphs. Duration tables provide expected recovery periods based on the type of work performed by the individual. The normative graphs reflect the actual observed experience of many individuals across the spectrum of physical conditions, in a variety of industries, and with varying levels of case management.

Failure to Recover

If an individual fails to recover within the maximum duration expectancy period, the reader may wish to reference the following questions to assist in better understanding the specifics of an individual's medical case.

Regarding diagnosis:

- Was there evidence of a severe contusion, such as swelling, pain, loss of function, noted in the initial physical exam?

- Was the contusion re-examined 2 to 3 days after the initial injury to confirm the severity of the contusion?

- Have plain x-rays been taken to rule out the possibility of fractures?

- Has a CT scan or MRI been done to rule out bleeding or damage into underlying organs (lungs, liver, kidney, etc)?

Regarding treatment:

- Have symptoms persisted despite treatment with conservative measures?

- Have more aggressive interventions been considered?
- Have physical aides (such as crutches, walkers or slings) been tried as an aid to recovery?

Regarding prognosis:

- Has adequate time elapsed for complete healing?
- Did the individual resume normal activities too soon after a severe contusion?
- Has physical therapy been implemented?
- Does the individual have signs suggestive of an infection, such as a break in the skin, persistent swelling, redness or fever? If so, have appropriate interventions been implemented (such as wound cultures, antibiotic therapy, wound cleansing)?
- Does the individual have persistent swelling, loss of sensation or loss of function that may be indicative of one of these complications?
- Does the individual with a buttock contusion complain of pain that radiates down the leg? If so, have these complications been considered by the health care provider and addressed in the treatment plan?
- Has temporary reassignment of job duties been considered?
- Did the individual suffer a contusion to the testicle that required surgical intervention? If so, has adequate time elapsed for full recovery from the procedure?
- Does the individual have any pre-existing conditions that may impact ability to recover and further lengthen disability?

References

Bonfiglio, Richard, L. Anita Cone, and Francis Lagattuta. "Pathophysiology of Soft Tissue Injuries." Soft Tissue Injuries: Diagnosis and Treatment. Windsor, Robert, and Dennis Lox, eds. Philadelphia: Hanley & Belfus, Inc, 1998. 1-11.

Garrett, William, and David Kirkendall. "The Structure and Function of Skeletal Muscle." Principles of Orthopaedic Practice. Dee, Roger, et al., eds. New York: McGraw-Hill, 1997. 119-128.

Kisner, C., and L. Colby. Therapeutic Exercise Foundations and Techniques. Philadelphia: F.A. Davis, 1990.

Mooar, Pekka. "The Hip and Pelvis." Musculoskeletal Primary Care. Gates, Sharon, and Pekka Mooar, eds. Philadelphia: Lippincott Williams & Wilkins, 1999. 196-216.

Contusion, Upper Limb

Other names / synonyms: Bruise of the Arm(s), Bruised Arm

923, 923.0, 923.00, 923.01, 923.02, 923.03, 923.09, 923.1, 923.10, 923.11, 923.2, 923.20, 923.21, 923.3, 923.8, 923.9

Definition

A contusion of the upper limb is a bruise to the upper arm, forearm and wrist, and fingers. It is an injury that does not involve a break in the skin but causes damage to the skin and underlying tissues. A contusion is usually caused by a fall or direct blow from a blunt object. Blood seeps out of damaged small blood vessels and into the surrounding tissue forming black-and-blue marks beneath the skin (ecchymosis). After injury, gravity may pull the blood downward so the ecchymosis can be far from the contusion site.

Contusions are classified as mild, moderate, or severe. If the contusion is superficial, it involves only the skin and tissue immediately below the skin (subcutaneous tissue). If deep, the muscle and bone may also be involved. Blood can accumulate forming a hematoma within the muscle.

Upper arm contusions primarily affect the muscles, particularly the triceps and biceps. Contusions located in the upper arm near the elbow may affect the radial nerve causing a tingling sensation, numbness, and a dropped wrist. Falling down and hitting the elbow can cause a radial nerve contusion. Individuals at increased risk for upper arm contusions are those who participate in contact sports (e.g., football, baseball, or ice hockey), especially if the upper arm and elbow are not adequately protected.

A direct blow from a blunt object to the forearm and wrist causes a contusion. Individuals at risk for forearm or wrist contusions include those who participate in violent contact sports (e.g., football or ice hockey), especially if protective equipment is not worn. The hand is particularly vulnerable to contusions because of its use in all sports and daily activities. Certain contact sports such as ice hockey, handball, and karate place the athlete at a high risk for sustaining a hand contusion, especially if protective hand gear is not worn.

Fingernail contusions can occur during sporting activities (e.g., ice hockey) when protective equipment is not worn. This can occur when an object is dropped on the fingers or the fingers get caught in something (e.g., a door). Fingernail contusions may be very painful because the fingernail limits the ability of the tissues to swell. If the blunt trauma is severe, the nail itself may lift off the nail bed or may no longer be intact.

Individuals involved in specific sports, have a bleeding disorder (e.g., hemophilia) or a vitamin deficiency, and those who take aspirin or anticoagulants are at risk for contusions of the upper limbs.

Contusions are very common, and 5% of the population sustains a contusion in any year. Approximately 165,000 work-related contusion injuries every year lead to time away from work.

Diagnosis

History: In general, the individual with a contusion of the upper limb may complain of skin discoloration, swelling, pain, and possibly restricted limb movement. Individuals with contusions of the upper arm near the elbow may report a shocking or tingling feeling, numbness in the wrist and hand, partial loss of movement in the thumb, and a dropped wrist. Contusions of the fingernail appear as blackened areas beneath the nail.

Physical exam: The contusion may appear dark blue or red, or yellow-green depending on how soon the physical exam was performed after the injury. The site feels firm and tender to the touch. Swelling is usually apparent around the bruise. There may be evidence of limited range of motion and/or loss of function of the affected limb. The extent of the contusion may not be visible for 2 to 3 days. Contusions in the vicinity of the radial nerve can produce a dropped wrist with partial loss of movement of the fingers.

Tests: Tests are usually not needed for this diagnosis. Plain x-rays may be taken for moderate-to-severe contusions to determine the extent of injury and to rule out bone fracture. If the individual has a history of contusions caused by very minor trauma, blood-clotting factors may be tested.

Treatment

Mild contusions do not need medical attention. Ice should be applied to the injury within the first 24 to 48 hours. Elevating the affected limb also helps. The affected limb should be rested for a few days and immobilized with a sling. A compression bandage may be worn for 3 days. Heat may be applied after the first 24 to 48 hours in the form of hot soaks, hot showers, heating pads, heat lamps, heat liniments or ointments, or a hot whirlpool bath. Analgesics may be taken to relieve pain. Injuries to the radial nerve may require surgery to stitch (suture) the nerve into muscle tissue (Rouhier's technique).

Prognosis

Most contusions resolve without disability. Healing times vary with the severity of the injury. Upper arm contusions usually heal in 1 to 2 weeks. Healing of a radial nerve contusion usually takes 2 months; however, in a few cases full recovery is never realized. Surgery to transfer the radial nerve to muscle tissue (Rouhier's technique) has a good outcome, provided permanent nerve damage did not previously occur. Forearm contusions usually heal in 2 to 3 weeks, and wrist contusions in 2 weeks. Contusions of the hand usually heal in 1 to 3 weeks. Fingernail contusions should heal within 1 to 2 weeks, although it takes several months for the nail to grow out.

Differential Diagnosis

If a tender mass is evident with or without skin discoloration, the condition may be a hematoma. Fracture of an upper limb bone is also a possibility.

Specialists

- General Surgeon
- Hand Surgeon
- Neurosurgeon
- Orthopedic Surgeon
- Physiatrist
- Physical Therapist

Rehabilitation

Basic goals in the rehabilitation of a contusion of the upper limb are to decrease pain and swelling and allow the individual to regain full motion, flexibility, strength, and endurance of the muscle/joint structures involved. The final result is aimed at returning the individual to full function for work and recreational activities with minimal risk of reinjury. The physical therapist determines the method for rehabilitation based on the severity of the contusion and whether any joints of the upper limb are causing difficulty with movement and function.

Heat treatments are helpful to reduce inflammation and pain and are beneficial to stretch the affected muscles. Electrical stimulation combined with heat or cold treatment is another technique used to relax irritated muscles that may be in spasm.

Rehabilitation usually progresses to range of motion of the upper limb. Individuals begin with passive range-of-motion exercises and then progress to active assist range of motion exercises. As the individual improves with increased motion of the upper limb, the next step is active range of motion. If the shoulder joint is affected, the individual uses a cane or wand to perform these exercises with a physical therapist or independently. When the movement is pain-free, the individual may progress to a towel stretch sequence with the arms raised overhead and stretching behind the back.

The instruction of isometric strengthening exercises begins early in the strengthening phase of rehabilitation. Isometric exercise involves the contraction of muscles around the affected joint yet no movement takes place at the joint. Once both range-of-motion and isometric exercises are tolerated, the individual progresses to isotonic strengthening that involves movement at and around the joint. An example of this type of rehabilitation exercise is strengthening with weights using weight equipment/machines and elastic bands.

Work Restrictions / Accommodations

Depending on work duties, the individual may need to be temporarily reassigned. Movement of the affected limb will be restricted until the individual recovers. The individual with an upper limb contusion may be temporarily unable to lift and carry heavy or bulky objects, operate equipment, or perform other tasks requiring use of both hands. Individuals whose dominant arm or hand is affected may require a temporary reassignment of duties.

Comorbid Conditions

Bleeding disorders (e.g., hemophilia) can lead to a more severe contusion that may increase the length of disability. Fibromyalgia, poor nutrition, and osteoporosis sustained during the traumatic event may also influence the length of disability.

Complications

Skin breaks (lacerations) may be prone to infection. Inflammation (cellulitis) can occur surrounding a break in the skin. Hematomas within the muscle prolong the recovery time and delay return of function. Pressure on the local blood vessels from swelling or bleeding can result in compartment syndrome, which can cause permanent muscle and nerve damage. On occasion, damaged muscle can convert into a bony substance (ossification), a condition known as myositis ossificans. This may cause disfigurement and impaired muscle function. Contusions in the upper arm near the elbow can cause permanent damage to the radial nerve resulting in forearm and hand disability. Contusions of the hand can be complicated by infection of the tendon sheaths (tenosynovitis) or rupture of tendons.

Factors Influencing Duration

The part of the limb, type of treatment needed, hematomas, any complications, and the individual's response to treatment influence the length of disability.

Length of Disability

Duration depends on severity, whether the dominant or non-dominant extremity is involved, and job requirements.

Duration in Days

Job Classification	Minimum	Optimum	Maximum
Sedentary work	0	1	3
Light work	0	1	3
Medium work	0	1	7
Heavy work	0	1	7
Very Heavy work	0	1	7

Failure to Recover

If an individual fails to recover within the maximum duration expectancy period, the reader may wish to reference the following questions to assist in better understanding the specifics of an individual's medical case.

Regarding diagnosis:

- Was there evidence of a severe contusion (such as swelling, pain, loss of function) noted in the initial physical exam?
- Was the contusion re-examined 2 to 3 days after the initial injury to confirm the severity of the contusion?
- Were x-rays done to rule out other injuries (such as fractures) that may present with similar symptoms?

Regarding treatment:

- Have symptoms persisted despite treatment with conservative measures?
- Has the individual been compliant with prescribed therapy (ice, elevation, rest)?
- Have analgesics been tried to reduce pain and aid to recovery?
- Has a diagnosis of radial nerve injury been made? If so, has surgery been considered in the treatment plan?
- Has physical therapy been implemented?
- Did the individual resume normal activities too soon after a severe contusion?

Regarding prognosis:

- Has the individual been reevaluated for the possibility of a more serious injury (i.e., radial nerve damage) or an associated complication?
- Does the individual have signs suggestive of an infection, such as a break in the skin, persistent swelling, redness, fever, or loss of function? If so, have appropriate interventions been implemented (such as wound cultures, antibiotic therapy, wound cleansing, or surgical intervention)?
- Does the individual have persistent swelling, loss of sensation, or loss of function that may be indicative of one of these complications?
- If so, have these complications been considered by the healthcare provider and addressed in the treatment plan?
- Did the individual suffer complications associated with the contusion that required surgical intervention? If so, has adequate time elapsed for full recovery from the procedure?
- Has temporary reassignment of job duties been considered?
- Does the individual have any pre-existing conditions that may impact ability to recover and further lengthen disability?

References

Bonfiglio, Richard, L. Anita Cone, and Francis Lagattuta. "Pathophysiology of Soft Tissue Injuries." Soft Tissue Injuries: Diagnosis and Treatment. Windsor, Robert, and Dennis Lox, eds. Philadelphia: Hanley & Belfus, Inc., 1998. 1-11.

Garrett, William, and Donald Kirkendall. "The Structure and Function of Skeletal Muscle." Principles of Orthopaedic Practice. Dee, Roger, et al., eds. New York: McGraw-Hill, 1997. 119-128.

Kessler, R.M. Management of Common Musculoskeletal Disorders: Physical Therapy Principles and Methods. Philadelphia: J.B. Lippincott Co, 1990.

Kisner, C., and L. Colby. Therapeutic Exercise Foundations and Techniques. Philadelphia: F.A. Davis, 1990.

Conversion Disorder

Other names / synonyms: Briquet's Syndrome, Conversion Disorder, Hysteria, Hysterical Blindness, Hysterical Deafness, Hysterical Paralysis, Somatoform Disorder

300.11

Definition

Conversion disorder is a condition that presents as an impairment or loss of a physical function suggestive of a physical disorder but is actually the expression of an underlying psychological conflict or need. Unexplainable physical symptoms seen in conversion disorder may include a disturbance of sensation, muscle strength, convulsions, involuntary movement, or some combination of these. Symptoms develop in the presence of unconscious psychological conflict and stress that become converted into a physical ailment. The physical complaint can serve to reduce anxiety and prevent conscious recognition of the underlying psychological conflict.

The individual may also benefit from the symptoms in other ways (secondary gain) such as gaining attention or support from family and friends, a reward of some kind, or avoidance of unwanted responsibilities. Although most individuals appear unconcerned emotionally about their illness and are unaware of any psychological conflicts, some experience anguish over their new symptoms. The symptoms are not intentionally or consciously faked but there is no known medical condition to account for the findings. Instead of corresponding to any known anatomic or neurological patterns typical of illness having a physical basis, the symptoms may instead correspond to the individual's concept of a disease.

Conversion disorder is diagnosed only after a thorough medical examination fails to find a physical explanation for the symptoms. Some diseases take years for diagnosis so conversion disorder should be considered a tentative, working diagnosis. Even when a known disease is present, conversion disorder can still exist if the symptoms cannot be explained by the medical illness. Up to two-thirds of those with conversion disorder also have a neurological condition.

Symptoms more commonly involve the left side, especially in women. It is not drug-related or part of a culturally approved ritual or behavior. Conversion disorder is not diagnosed if symptoms are limited to pain or sexual dysfunction. These have separate diagnoses.

The prevalence of conversion disorder varies widely ranging from 1 to 30 per 10,000 individuals. One study reported that conversion disorder accounted for 1-12% of psychiatric consultations for hospitalized medical and surgical inpatients. Onset is usually between ages 10 and 35. It is more frequent in women (anywhere from 2 to 10 times more prevalent than in men), and in rural settings, lower socioeconomic groups, and military personnel exposed to combat.

Diagnosis

History: Individual has history of a sensory disturbance (i.e., numbness, double vision, blindness, deafness, or hallucinations), muscle disturbance (localized weakness or paralysis, incoordination, difficulty swallowing, or a "lump in the throat"), convulsions, or some combination of these. The disturbance closely follows a major psychological stress or conflict but the symptoms are not faked or intentionally produced. Symptoms cannot be fully explained by a general medical condition, the direct effects of a drug or other substance such as alcohol, or as a culturally typical behavior or experience. Significant distress, alteration in interpersonal relationships, or decrease in occupational functioning must be present. The symptoms are not limited to pain or sexual dysfunction and are not better explained by another mental disorder.

Physical exam: The exam shows findings inconsistent with medical knowledge. Numbness is often in a pattern resembling a glove or stocking, not the pattern of the known nerve supply. A paralyzed body part may not perform according to known nerve and muscle anatomy. Muscle strength may be normal in muscles opposite the "paralyzed" ones and reflexes are normal. Various specialized examination maneuvers can help the doctor differentiate complaints related to physical causes from those that are conversion symptoms.

Tests: Neurological tests are normal. Electromyogram (EMG) and nerve conduction velocity testing are normal in "paralyzed" muscles. Somatosensory evoked potential testing is normal in limbs with no sensation. Electroencephalogram (EEG) is normal in conversion seizures. Psychological tests such as the Minnesota Multiphasic Personality Inventory (MMPI or MMPI-2) may show a profile characteristic of conversion disorder.

Treatment

Psychotherapy can be helpful to resolve the intrapsychic conflict. Because individuals may be resistant to the idea that symptoms are the result of a psychological problem, therapy may have to be couched in terms of stress reduction and coping skills for a chronic illness. Therapy should avoid reinforcing the sick role as a solution to the problem. Group therapy is best and provides social support and interaction that can reduce anxiety. Hypnotherapy can be useful. Drug therapy is used only if there is a coexisting anxiety or depressive disorder. As physically based (organic) illness and conversion disorder may coexist, all individuals with conversion symptoms should be treated as if they have an organic illness.

Prognosis

Recovery rates range from 15-74%. Conversion symptoms are generally self-limited and may resolve within 2 weeks if hospitalization is part of the treatment. While psychotherapy may lead to dramatic recovery in some individuals, recurrence of symptoms is seen in one-fourth of individuals within 1 year of the first episode. Factors associated with good outcome include being male, sudden onset of symptoms, occurrence of symptoms following a stressful event, good health before appearance of conversion symptoms, and lack of accompanying physical or psychiatric disorder. Symptoms of paralysis and blindness have a good prognosis while seizures and tremor have a worse outlook. The longer the individual has been in the sick role and regressed, the more difficult treatment can be. If the individual has other psychopathology or a chaotic social situation, disability can be prolonged. A documented neurological disease may also determine disability.

Differential Diagnosis

Malingering is a possibility especially in men if there is a financial reward such as settlement following a lawsuit or avoidance of work or military duty. Psychological conditions with similar conditions include major depression, catatonic schizophrenia, histrionic personality disorder, post-traumatic stress disorder, pain disorder, somatization disorder, hypochondriasis, schizophrenia, and dissociative disorders. In their early stages, medical conditions such as multiple sclerosis, myasthenia gravis, amyotrophic lateral sclerosis, brain stem tumor, and dystonias can be misdiagnosed as a conversion disorder. Periodic paralysis, optic neuritis, vocal cord paralysis, and early AIDS are other medical possibilities.

Specialists

- Internist
- Neurologist
- Psychiatrist
- Psychologist

Work Restrictions / Accommodations

Work restrictions or accommodations are necessary only infrequently, for the most serious cases. In these instances, time-limited restrictions and work accommodations should be individually determined based on the characteristics of the individual's response to the disorder, the functional requirements of the job and work environment, and the flexibility of the job and work site. The purpose of the restrictions/accommodation is to help maintain the worker's capacity to remain at the workplace without a work disruption or to promote timely and safe transition back to full work productivity.

Complementary and Alternative Therapies

Content is intended for awareness only. Treatments may or may not be effective. Scientific evidence may be lacking and some substances have potentially toxic effects. Dr. Presley Reed and the editors do not endorse the use of these therapies in the absence of consultation with a licensed medical professional.

Hypnosis — May be helpful in psychological conflict resolution.

Comorbid Conditions

Coexisting conditions that may affect recovery and lengthen disability include substance abuse, somatization disorder, or personality disorders. Many individuals with conversion disorder also suffer from a bipolar affective disorder.

Complications

Loss of muscle tone or bulk related to not using the affected limb is a rare complication. Individuals may hurt themselves when falling, convulsing, or as a result of "blindness." Conversion disorder may lead to a vicious cycle in which "sick" behavior is reinforced through increased attention, avoidance of responsibility, or other secondary gain. This in turn may lead to worsening of conversion symptoms or development of new ones.

Factors Influencing Duration

Factors that may influence the length of disability include acute onset of symptoms, type of symptoms presenting, a known source of psychological distress, and prompt treatment.

Length of Disability

Duration in Days

Job Classification	Minimum	Optimum	Maximum
Any work	7	14	28

Failure to Recover

If an individual fails to recover within the maximum duration expectancy period, the reader may wish to reference the following questions to assist in better understanding the specifics of an individual's medical case.

Regarding diagnosis:

- Has an extensive medical examination ruled out any underlying medical explanation or other cause of the symptoms?
- Was clinically significant distress or impairment in social, occupational, or other important areas of functioning evident or reported by the individual?
- Was diagnosis of conversion disorder confirmed?

Regarding treatment:

- Because a trusting relationship with the physician is essential to treatment, has individual established a good doctor-patient relationship? If not, what can be done to build or restore this relationship?
- If anxiety or depressive disorders are present, are these disorders being effectively addressed with drug therapy?
- If individual is resistant to the idea that symptoms are a result of a psychological problem, would individual be more accepting if behavioral therapy was presented as stress reduction or coping skills for a chronic illness?
- Would individual benefit from a group therapy environment where social support and interaction are used to reduce anxiety?

Regarding prognosis:

- Since a strong positive correlation exists between duration of conversion symptoms and the time required to resolve them, what was the interval between onset of symptoms and start of treatment?
- Has the individual experienced any recurrences that may predict future episodes?

References

Dufel, Susan. Conversion Disorder. eMedicine.com 01 Jan 2000. 30 Sept 2000 <http://www.emedicine.com/emerg/topic112.htm>.

First, Michael B., ed. Diagnostic and Statistical Manual of Mental Disorders. Washington, DC: American Psychiatric Association, 1994.

Cor Pulmonale, Acute and Chronic

Other names / synonyms: Right Heart Failure

415.0, 416.0, 416.1, 416.8, 416.9

Definition

Cor pulmonale refers to enlargement of the pumping chamber on the right side of the heart (right ventricle) secondary to diseases of the lungs. Cor pulmonale often leads to failure of the right ventricle. Cor pulmonale and right ventricular failure may occur quickly (acutely) or slowly (chronically).

Significant causes of chronic cor pulmonale include the so-called restrictive lung diseases due to a variety of conditions such as pneumoconiosis, sarcoidoses, collagen vascular diseases, bronchiectases, and cystic fibrosis. Another frequent cause of chronic cor pulmonale is occlusion of the blood vessels carrying blood to the lungs (pulmonary arteries) by blood clots (emboli) originating in the legs from thrombophlebitis. About 50,000 individuals die each year in the US from pulmonary emboli. Most of these cases have repeated pulmonary emboli that lead to chronic cor pulmonale but some have one or two large pulmonary emboli that cause acute cor pulmonale.

Chronic cor pulmonale is far more frequent than acute cor pulmonale and constitutes about 5% of all heart disease in the US and approximately 10% of all hospital admissions for heart failure. The most common cause of chronic cor pulmonale in the US is chronic obstructive pulmonary disease (COPD) due to cigarette smoking. Since more men than women smoke in the US, the prevalence of COPD and cor pulmonale is greater in men than in women. COPD exists in about 15 million Americans and contributes to or causes about 200,000 deaths per year. Cor pulmonale is an important factor in at least 20% of these deaths.

Diagnosis

History: Symptoms of cor pulmonale are often similar to the symptoms of the underlying lung disorder. It is therefore necessary to first determine the type and severity of lung disease and then look for signs of cor pulmonale. In general, the individual may report breathlessness, easy fatigability, and cough.

Physical exam: Signs of cor pulmonale include bluish discoloration of the fingertips (cyanosis), a loud second heart sound, and distended neck veins. Swelling (edema) of the feet and ankles may also be present if there is associated right heart failure.

Tests: A chest x-ray, electrocardiogram (ECG), and measurement of blood gases (amounts of oxygen and carbon dioxide in the blood) are abnormal in nearly all individuals with cor pulmonale. Breathing tests (pulmonary function studies) are often done to determine if the underlying lung disease is COPD or restrictive lung disease. A lung scan or pulmonary arteriogram may help ascertain if pulmonary emboli are causing cor pulmonale. An echocardiogram and/or right heart catheterization are useful techniques in assessing the severity of cor pulmonale.

Treatment

Fundamental to the treatment of cor pulmonale is medical treatment of the underlying lung disease. If the lung disease improves, the signs and symptoms of cor pulmonale are relieved.

Therapy applicable to cor pulmonale due to any cause includes long-term oxygen and medications to remove excess fluid from the body (diuretics). If the blood count (hematocrit) exceeds 55%, periodic removal of a unit of blood by phlebotomy may be performed. This reduces the chances of complications such as a heart attack or stroke related to thick blood (polycythemia) in such individuals.

There is no surgical treatment for most causes of cor pulmonale. Removal of pulmonary emboli is sometimes done for acute and on occasion for chronic cor pulmonale. Lung transplantation may be advised for some younger individuals with cor pulmonale due to cystic fibrosis or primary pulmonary hypertension.

Prognosis

The outcome depends more on the treatment and control of the underlying lung disease than on cor pulmonale itself. If cor pulmonale is associated with right heart failure, the prognosis is not as good. The average life expectancy after prognosis is 3 to 4 years but survival of 8 to 10 years is possible.

Differential Diagnosis

Conditions with similar symptoms may include left-sided heart failure, congestive heart failure, pneumonia, viral or bacterial infection, and pulmonary fibrosis.

Specialists

- Cardiologist
- Critical Care Specialist
- Pulmonologist

Rehabilitation

Because acute and chronic cor pulmonale often occurs from pulmonary high blood pressure (hypertension) originating from lung disorders, reducing the demand for oxygen is the cornerstone in the rehabilitation process. Strategies for reduction of the individual's oxygen demand include decreasing the work of breathing through breathing exercises, postural alterations, reduction of accessory breathing movements, and relaxation exercises. To allow the individual to slowly accommodate to the increase in oxygen demand, the exercise session begins with prolonged warm-up.

An exercise to promote both relaxation and a postural alteration for the muscles that aid in breathing has the individual assuming a relaxed sitting position while leaning forward resting the forearms on the thighs or a pillow in the lap.

A physical therapist experienced in cardiac and pulmonary rehabilitation keeps a daily log of the individual's blood pressure, heart rate, and cardiac rhythm. As the individual progresses with relaxation techniques, active assist range-of-motion exercises to the upper and lower extremities begin. In these exercises, the individual performs some of the motion/effort along with the help of the therapist. As the individual improves with increased endurance, the individual performs active range-of-motion exercises independently. As endurance continues to increase without symptoms of shortness of breath, active upper and lower extremity exercises begin with very light resistance. Individuals also begin light aerobic activities (brisk walking and low-resistance biking).

The exercise program/rehabilitation for individuals with cor pulmonale may be a lengthy process in order to obtain maximum benefit of increasing pulmonary stamina. Because most individuals with pulmonary disorders are managed with medication, it is important that the therapist has a medication history for each individual since many of these drugs alter the acute and chronic response to exercise.

Work Restrictions / Accommodations

Work restrictions and accommodations may allow the individual to continue gainful employment. Part-time or less strenuous work may be within the physical limitations of some individuals with cor pulmonale.

Comorbid Conditions

Smoking, obesity, pulmonary or respiratory infection, congenital heart disease, or living at high altitudes can influence length of disability.

Complications

Cor pulmonale is often associated with right heart failure and as such may be considered more a consequence than a complication. An irregular heartbeat from atrial fibrillation and a heart attack (acute myocardial infarction) or stroke due to polycythemia may occur.

Factors Influencing Duration

The age of the individual, severity of symptoms, high altitudes, and response to treatment can influence length of disability.

Length of Disability

Duration depends on cardiac function. Disability may be permanent.

Acute.

Duration in Days

Job Classification	Minimum	Optimum	Maximum
Sedentary work	7	7	14
Light work	7	7	14
Medium work	7	14	28
Heavy work	14	14	35
Very Heavy work	14	28	35

Chronic.

Duration in Days

Job Classification	Minimum	Optimum	Maximum
Sedentary work	35	42	Indefinite
Light work	35	42	Indefinite
Medium work	42	42	Indefinite
Heavy work	42	112	Indefinite
Very Heavy work	84	112	Indefinite

Failure to Recover

If an individual fails to recover within the maximum duration expectancy period, the reader may wish to reference the following questions to assist in better understanding the specifics of an individual's medical case.

Regarding diagnosis:

- Does individual have acute or chronic cor pulmonale?
- Does individual have pneumoconiosis, sarcoidoses, collagen vascular diseases, bronchiectases, or cystic fibrosis? COPD?
- Does individual smoke?
- Does individual have a pulmonary embolus?
- Does individual report breathlessness, easy fatigability, and cough?
- On exam, were individual's fingertips cyanotic?
- Did individual have a loud second heart sound, distended neck veins, and edema of the feet and ankles?
- Were a chest x-ray, ECG, and arterial blood gasses done?
- Were pulmonary function studies, lung scan, pulmonary arteriogram, echocardiogram and/or right heart catheterization performed?
- Were conditions with similar symptoms ruled out?

Regarding treatment:

- What is the underlying condition? Is it being treated?
- Is individual being treated with oxygen and diuretics?
- Does individual have polycythemia? Was a phlebotomy done?
- Was it necessary to remove pulmonary emboli?
- Is individual a candidate for a lung transplant?

Regarding prognosis:

- Is individual active in rehabilitation?
- Can individual's employer accommodate any necessary restrictions?
- Have any complications developed such as right heart failure, atrial fibrillation, acute myocardial infarction, or stroke?

References

About Cardiovascular Disease. Center for Disease Control. 28 Jul 2000. 14 Nov 2000 <http://www.cdc.gov/nccdphp/cvd/aboutcardio.htm>.

Comprehensive Risk Reduction for Patients with Coronary and Other Vascular Disease. American Heart Association. 1999. 14 Nov 2000 <http://www.americanheart.org/scientific/>.

DeBakey, Michael, and Antonio Gotto. The New Living Heart. Holbrook: Adams Media Corporation, 1997.

Kisne, Carolyn MS, PT, and Lynn Allen Colby, MS, PT. Therapeutic Exercise: Foundations and Techniques. Philadelphia: F.A. Davis, 1990.

Corn and Callus, Infected

Other names / synonyms: Callositas, Callosity, Clavus, Heloma, Tyloma

700

Definition

Both corns (clavus or heloma) and calluses (callosity, callositas, tyloma) are areas of thickened skin resulting from repeated rubbing or pressure.

Calluses can form anywhere on the body but usually appear over bony areas such as fingers, feet, elbows, or in any place where the skin is subject to repeated rubbing or pressure (e.g., the jaw of a violinist). They usually appear as oval or elongated, gray or brown in color, and slightly elevated with a smooth surface. They are generally not painful.

Corns appear on the feet and typically result when poorly fitting shoes cause pressure and/or friction to the feet. In addition, shoes that are too small or too pointed (common in women's shoes) cause the toes to press together. This pressure can also produce corns. Corns are usually ring-shaped. Hard corns occur most commonly over the top and side part of the fifth toe (the little or baby toe) while soft corns arise between toes, typically between the fourth and fifth toes. Unlike calluses, corns tend to be quite painful.

Calluses are equally common in men and women but corns occur more frequently in women than in men. This is likely due to the fact that women's shoes are generally designed in ways that put excessive pressure on the toes and ball of the foot. Historically, social pressure to wear small shoe sizes has caused some women to wear shoes that are too small.

Diagnosis

History: Calluses do not generally cause symptoms that would prompt an individual to seek medical attention. Individuals with corns usually complain of pain that worsens with direct pressure. If infected, both corns and calluses will be tender.

Physical exam: The physical exam is the most important single factor in the diagnosis of corns and calluses and reveals a thickening of the skin. Calluses are generally oval or elongated, gray or brown in color, slightly elevated, and generally painless. Calluses can occur on any part of the body but are usually found on the fingers, elbows, feet, or other areas exposed to repeated pressure and/or friction. Corns tend to be ring-shaped and painful. Corns occur on the feet, usually on the toes.

If corns or calluses are infected, the area is tender. The surrounding skin may be red and warm to the touch. In some cases, pus is present. The individual may have a low-grade fever.

Tests: Tests are not normally required. Physical examination and history are generally sufficient to make a diagnosis. However, in some cases, weight-bearing x-rays may be helpful in determining the cause of the problem.

Treatment

Calluses do not normally interfere with an individual's daily life so treatment is not required. In fact, calluses can provide a protective cushion and are best left untreated. Examples of this include calluses on the fingers of guitar players and on the hands of manual workers or athletes. However, if the callus is bothersome, it can be removed either by scraping or shaving. Similarly, the individual can soak the callus in warm water such as while bathing and rub it with a pumice stone to gradually remove it. Development of new calluses can be prevented through avoidance of repetitive friction or pressure. Protective padding as sold at most pharmacies can be helpful. If the calluses are on the feet, properly fitting shoes may help prevent recurrence.

Corns generally require treatment since they are associated with pain. The most effective treatment involves the selection of proper shoes. Shoes should be flat or low-heeled and made of soft leather. The toe box should be rounded or squared in shape with adequate room for the toes, and the shoe should be wide and long enough to accommodate the foot comfortably. Shock absorbing padding may be helpful in relieving pressure on the feet. Medications are available to apply to the corn itself. These are generally effective although the process may be slow. Faster results can be obtained by having the nurse or physician scrape or shave the lesion.

Infection is treated with antibiotics that can be taken by mouth or applied directly to the skin. Sometimes both types of antibiotics are used.

Prognosis

Corns and calluses are associated with an excellent prognosis and are generally responsive to treatment.

Differential Diagnosis

Calluses and corns are usually readily diagnosed based on the individual's history and physical examination. In some cases, corns can be confused with plantar warts.

Specialists

- Dermatologist
- Podiatrist
- Primary Care Provider

Work Restrictions / Accommodations

For most individuals, work restrictions or accommodations are not necessary. In some cases, individuals with corns may need to avoid prolonged standing or walking until the condition resolves. In situations where job requirements dictate a certain type of footwear, individuals with corns may benefit from reassignment to a position where comfortable footwear can be worn.

Comorbid Conditions

Individuals with poor circulation or diabetes mellitus are at increased risk for complications and may have more severe symptoms and a longer recovery period.

Complications

Corns and calluses are generally uncomplicated. Advanced or untreated infections can lead to ulceration of the skin or infection of the blood (sepsis). Sepsis can progress to coma and death. Infection is much more common in individuals not able to care for themselves or who have poor circulation or diabetes.

Factors Influencing Duration

The location of the callus or corn, extent of the infection, presence (and severity) of pain, response to treatment, and individual's job requirements influence the length of disability.

Length of Disability

Conservative treatment.

Duration in Days

Job Classification	Minimum	Optimum	Maximum
Sedentary work	0	1	3
Light work	0	1	3
Medium work	0	1	5
Heavy work	0	1	5
Very Heavy work	0	1	5

Failure to Recover

If an individual fails to recover within the maximum duration expectancy period, the reader may wish to reference the following questions to assist in better understanding the specifics of an individual's medical case.

Regarding diagnosis:

- Does the individual have thickening of the skin as a result of repeated rubbing or pressure? Where is it located? The fingers, feet, or elbows?
- Is the corn or callus infected?
- Was the skin red and warm to the touch?
- Was pus present?
- Does individual have a low-grade fever?
- Was the causative organism identified with a wound culture?
- Have other conditions such as plantar warts, bursitis, and misalignment of the joints been ruled out?

Regarding treatment:

- If callus was bothersome, was it removed either by scraping or shaving?
- Did individual soak callus in warm water and rub with a pumice stone?
- Were the sources of rubbing or pressure eliminated?
- Did individual with a corn switch to comfortable flat or low-heeled shoes made of soft leather with adequate room for the toes? Do the shoes have sufficient padding that relieves pressure?
- Was the area kept clean?
- Were topical or oral antibiotics administered?
- Did symptoms persist? If so, was a repeat culture done?

Regarding prognosis:

- Does the individual have any conditions such as poor circulation or diabetes mellitus that may impact severity of symptoms and lengthen recovery?
- Was the infection advanced or untreated? If so, did ulceration or infection of the blood (sepsis) result?

References

"Superficial Skin Disorders." The Merck Manual of Medical Information. Berkow, Robert, Mark Beers, Mark, and Andrew Fletcher, eds. New York: Pocket Books, 1997. 1044-1048.

Corneal Abrasion
918.1

Definition

Corneal abrasions result from damage to the cornea. The cornea is the clear outer surface of the eye. It has 2 major functions: to refract light, thus helping to focus images on the retina, and to act as a protective barrier to keep organisms from entering into the eye.

Corneal abrasions typically occur as the result of blunt trauma, sharp projectile injury, intrusion of a foreign body, contact lens wear, or the wearing away of the corneal surface (recurrent corneal erosion). Recurrent corneal erosion is caused by incomplete healing, genetic factors, and/or underlying metabolic disease (corneal dystrophy). When only the top layer of cells (epithelium) is affected, a superficial wound occurs. Deeper, more serious wounds result from penetrating the thicker, inner layer of the cornea (stroma).

A corneal abrasion may also be caused by external forces such as a contact lens or scratch from a fingernail. Because of the large number of contact wearers, estimated at about 25 million in the US, abrasions related to their wear are common, particularly when they are worn for extended periods or overnight.

Corneal abrasions are also caused by direct injury, dust particles, and debris. During activities such as welding or exposure to sunlamps, unprotected eyes can be injured by ultraviolet burns. Researchers also have identified modern sources of corneal abrasion such as exposure to pepper spray and being struck by air bags that spontaneously inflate following a motor vehicle accident. Individuals undergoing surgery are considered at risk of developing corneal abrasions when eyes are left partially open during recovery from anesthesia. Abrasions are one of the most common sports-related eye injuries seen.

About 10% of the visits to emergency eye care centers are related to corneal abrasions. Corneal abrasions are more common among younger, physically active individuals. Almost all individuals will experience at least a minor form of corneal abrasion during their lifetimes.

Diagnosis

History: As with any eye trauma, immediate medical evaluation and appropriate treatment are necessary to optimize the outcome. Complaints may include significant pain that worsens with eye or eyelid movement. Uncontrollable blinking or lid squeezing may occur (blepharospasm); severe light sensitivity (photophobia) may develop. Visual acuity may be decreased, vision may be blurred, and excessive tearing may be evident. The individual may also complain of a foreign body sensation. A recent injury or incident involving the eye may be reported. The individual also might have experienced a prior eye injury months or even years earlier, followed by repeated episodes of pain and/or other symptoms.

Physical exam: Reddened conjunctiva, eyelid swelling, foreign body, masses, iritis, or other abnormalities may be seen.

Tests: Fluorescein dye (Seidel test) will be instilled to highlight affected areas; the eye will then be examined using a penlight, slit lamp, or microscope (biomicroscopy). Visual acuity will also be assessed (visual acuity test). Other visual imaging of the eye's outer or internal structures may be needed including ultrasound, magnetic resonance imaging (MRI), x-rays, or CT scan. Fluid from the eye may be microscopically examined (cultured) for evidence of an infection.

Treatment

A tetanus vaccination may be given to prevent potentially serious infection by bacteria that typically invade the body through a scratch or wound.

Treatment will vary depending on the nature of the wound. Antispasmodic eyedrops (cycloplegic) may be applied to relieve discomfort caused by involuntary eye muscle movements. Medication may be applied to dilate the pupil (mydriatics), after which a topical antibiotic ointment or eyedrop will be applied to superficial wounds. Ointments are not used to treat penetrating wounds because it is possible for them to damage inner eye structures. Any foreign body in the eye will be removed by thorough washing with fluids (irrigation) or by using a surgical instrument (excision).

Medical personnel have recently questioned the traditional use of pressure dressings over injured eyes, because of increasing evidence that this impedes the healing response. However, recurring symptoms may require application of a 24-hour pressure dressing. Artificial tears also may be needed for lubrication. In general contact lens wearing should be avoided; however, soft contact lenses, used as therapeutic bandages, may be worn in certain cases to promote healing.

The eye will be examined and treated daily until healing is evident, generally within 48-72 hours. In cases where complications create extreme scarring, a relatively new laser procedure may be needed to smooth out the scars and restore a smooth surface to the cornea to improve vision (phototherapeutic keratectomy). Lacerations may need to be surgically repaired.

Prognosis

Typical corneal abrasions that do not involve a foreign body usually heal completely in 1-3 days, unless complications develop. The time it takes to heal from using a laser to treat scarring (phototherapeutic keratectomy) depends upon the severity of the condition. As a fairly new procedure, outcomes are not widely known, but most individuals who participated in phototherapeutic keratectomy studies experienced significant visual improvement within several months to years.

If a corneal ulcer and related complications develop, including severe scarring, a corneal transplant will be necessary to restore vision. Depending on the severity of the condition, vision usually is restored within a year following a corneal transplant.

Differential Diagnosis

Conditions with similar symptoms include keratitis, corneal ulcer, corneal laceration, anterior uveitis, iritis, conjunctivitis, acute glaucoma, foreign body, hordeolum, chalazion, abscessed tooth, sinusitis, temporal arteritis, tumor, and other eye injuries.

Specialists

- Emergency Medicine
- Ophthalmologist

Work Restrictions / Accommodations

Depending on the severity of symptoms, one or more days off from work may be needed to recover from most superficial corneal abrasions. Safety glasses may need to be worn if there is a possibility of reinjuring the eye. If lingering symptoms hamper vision, and necessary tasks ordinarily require keen visual acuity, the individual may need temporary reassignment. If the individual does not heal completely from the corneal abrasion, symptoms may recur over a period of years. In this case, an individual who must rely on constant, keen visual acuity may require permanent reassignment to other tasks. Complications could result in permanent or partial vision loss, possibly requiring workstation accommodations such as ample illumination, magnification, or large print.

Complementary and Alternative Therapies

Content is intended for awareness only. Treatments may or may not be effective. Scientific evidence may be lacking and some substances have potentially toxic effects. Dr. Presley Reed and the editors do not endorse the use of these therapies in the absence of consultation with a licensed medical professional.

Artificial Tears - Thick Artificial Tears can provide lubrication and comfort. Before using, consult physician to ensure use does not interfere with prescribed treatment.

Comorbid Conditions

Individuals with immune disorders, diabetes, or who take corticosteroids, which hamper immune responses for other conditions, may experience delayed healing responses.

Complications

Abrasions can create an opening for infection to invade the cornea or other eye structures. Abrasions can also hide tiny penetrating wounds of the eye, causing them to be missed during the exam. Delays in seeking treatment enhance the potential for infection or other serious complications, such as scarring or infected corneal ulcer, to develop. This can cause permanent visual impairment or total loss. If the individual is taking corticosteroids to reduce inflammation because of other conditions, healing responses can be significantly hampered. The incomplete healing of serious corneal abrasions may cause symptoms to periodically recur (recurrent corneal erosion) over a period of months or years.

Individuals who wear contact lenses overnight, or for a period of days without removing them (extended wear), and who do not properly clean contact lenses risk experiencing repeated incidents of corneal abrasion. Improper contact lens hygiene can also lead to infection accompanying the abrasion, extending recovery time.

Factors Influencing Duration

The individual's response to treatment, type of treatment, the development of any complications, and possible involvement of both eyes could influence length of disability.

Length of Disability

Duration depends on whether one or both eyes are involved. If complications cause short-term or permanent vision loss, the individual may be unable to perform tasks requiring keen visual acuity.

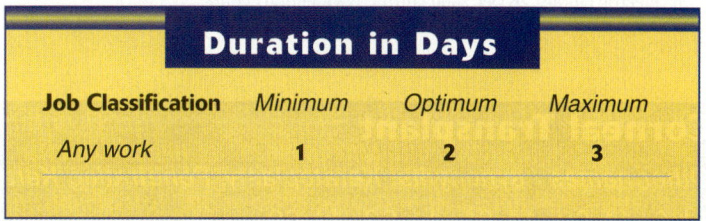

Job Classification	Minimum	Optimum	Maximum
Any work	1	2	3

Duration in Days

Failure to Recover

If an individual fails to recover within the maximum duration expectancy period, the reader may wish to reference the following questions to assist in better understanding the specifics of an individual's medical case.

Regarding diagnosis:

- Has the individual had any blunt trauma, sharp projectile injury, intrusion of a foreign body, or contact lens wear?
- Does the individual have corneal dystrophy?
- Does the individual complain of significant pain with eye or eyelid movement?
- Does the individual have blepharospasm or photophobia?
- Does the individual have any visual disturbances? Is there excessive tearing?
- Does the individual state it feels like there is a foreign body in the eye?
- On exam, were reddened conjunctiva, eyelid swelling, foreign body, masses, iritis, or other abnormalities seen?
- Did the individual have a fluorescein stain done? Visual acuity test?
- Did the individual have an ultrasound, MRI, x-rays, CT scan, or culture of eye fluid?
- Have conditions with similar symptoms been ruled out?

Regarding treatment:

- If needed, was a tetanus booster given?
- Was a foreign body removed by irrigation or excision?
- Was the individual treated with anti-spasmodic eye drops, pupil dilation, and topical antibiotic ointment or eye drops? Artificial tears?
- Was it necessary to use a pressure dressing?
- Has the individual temporarily discontinued wearing contact lenses?
- Was a laceration present? Was it repaired surgically?
- Is the individual seeing their physician daily until healing is complete?

Corneal Abrasion

Regarding prognosis:

- Is the individual's employer able to accommodate any necessary restrictions?
- Does the individual have any conditions that may affect their ability to recover?
- Does the individual have any complications such as infection, a hidden tiny penetrating wound, scarring or infected corneal ulcer, visual impairment or loss, slow healing secondary to corticosteroid treatment, or recurrent corneal erosion?
- Does the individual wear contact lenses overnight or have improper contact lens hygiene?

References

Wingate, Sue. "Treating Corneal Abrasions." The Nurse Practitioner 24 01 Jan 1999: 53-54, 57. Electric Library. 26 Dec 2000 <http://www.elibrary.com>.

Corneal Transplant
Other names / synonyms: Keratoplasty, Penetrating Keratoplasty, PK
11.6, 11.60, 11.61, 11.63, 11.69

Definition

Corneal transplant, also known as penetrating keratoplasty (PK), is a surgical procedure performed in an outpatient setting under local anesthesia. Corneal transplant involves replacing the individual's diseased or scarred clear outer covering of the eye (cornea) with a piece of donor cornea (allograft). The success rate for this type of transplant surgery varies depending on the underlying disease, but is generally very high. Rejection of the transplanted tissue is rare, occurring in only 20% of cases.

Corneal transplant becomes necessary when an individual's cornea becomes cloudy, scarred or distorted, preventing light from reaching the part of the eye called the retina. Inherited degenerative diseases, infections, ulcers, and physical trauma (i.e., burns, scratches, foreign objects such as metal chips or splinters, fireworks, chemicals, etc.) can all cause corneal damage. While inherited diseases and infections or ulcers are difficult or even impossible to avoid, the use of protective eyewear can substantially reduce the risk of corneal injury.

Approximately 46,000 corneal transplants are performed each year.

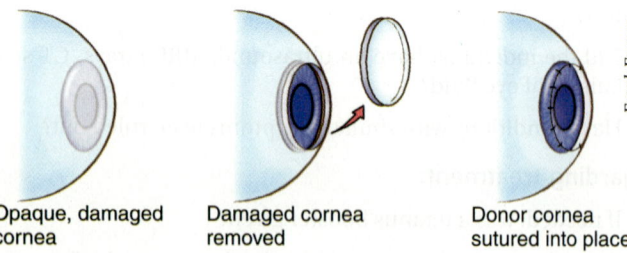

Opaque, damaged cornea | Damaged cornea removed | Donor cornea sutured into place

Frank Forney

Reason for Procedure

The purpose of a corneal transplant is to replace a diseased/scarred/distorted cornea with a healthy one. A corneal transplant will be considered when the individual's eyesight is diminished due to a diseased, scarred, swollen, or otherwise distorted cornea. Corneal transplant is generally performed when other measures (medication) to repair the cornea have failed.

Several conditions are treated with corneal transplant, including ocular herpes virus infections, corneal dystrophies such as Fuch's dystropy, keratoconus lattice dystrophy, map-dot-fingerprint dystrophy, and iridocorneal endothelial syndrome. Corneal scarring may also result from trauma or injury, or it could be a complication of another surgical procedure.

How Procedure Is Performed

Corneal transplant surgery is performed in an outpatient setting. Individuals may be given a sedative if they are anxious about the procedure. Shortly before the procedure, the surgeon or nursing staff will administer a local anesthetic to numb the eye and to control eye movement. Operating with the aid of a surgical microscope, the surgeon will remove a circle of tissue from the center of the cornea. The circle of tissue is approximately 8 mm in diameter, and is removed with an instrument called a trephine, which acts like a cookie cutter. Once the damaged cornea has been removed, the surgeon will remove a matching piece of tissue from the donor cornea, and stitch it into place in the recipient's eye. The stitches are very fine, barely visible and largely nonirritating. The stitches will remain in place until the wound heals properly (anywhere from 2 months to over 1 year).

Following corneal transplant, the individual's vision will be blurred, but will gradually clear over time. It may take up to 6 months for vision to return to normal. Glasses may be prescribed to help improve vision in the meantime. The individual will generally experience very little discomfort.

Eyedrop medication will be prescribed by the surgeon to promote healing and prevent infection. These medications will be needed for several months.

Prognosis

The success rate for corneal transplant surgery will vary depending on the underlying disease, but is generally very high. Rejection of the transplanted tissue is rare, occurring in only 20% of cases.

Most individuals will recover completely. Rarely, individuals may experience a complication (rejection, severe infection) resulting in permanent damage. If the procedure was required as treatment for an underlying disease such as corneal dystrophy, that disease could recur, affecting the new cornea, and possibly requiring a second procedure.

Specialists

- Ophthalmologist

Work Restrictions / Accommodations

Vision should be evaluated when it is critical to the individual's work assignment. As the cornea heals slowly, the individual may require an alternative assignment until vision returns to normal. Those who require the use of safety glasses may need to obtain a pair with a corrective prescription. Some individuals may be fit with a therapeutic contact lens, and will be more sensitive to eye irritants, fumes, and dust. Larger computer screens may be helpful as the individual's vision returns to normal. Eye drops may be needed for a prolonged period of time after surgery, and accommodations for frequent breaks may be required. There may be limitations on strenuous activities, lifting, and bending following surgery.

Comorbid Conditions

A history of previous transplants may influence disability. Immunosuppressive conditions may influence length of disability.

Procedure Complications

The primary risk associated with corneal transplantation is rejection of the transplant. Fortunately, this risk is low--less than 10% for most conditions requiring transplantation, and about 20% when all conditions (including the risky ones) are considered. Rejection does not occur within the first 2 months following the procedure, but can occur at any time after. Signs of impending rejection are redness, sensitivity to light, sudden change in vision, and increased eye pain. If any of these signs are noted by the individual, the surgeon should be contacted immediately.

Prompt treatment (usually with a corticosteroid such as cortisone eye drops) is effective in stabilizing the cornea and reversing the rejection. Delayed treatment, or a particularly severe rejection could cloud the cornea, necessitating another procedure. Recent research suggests that matching the donor and recipient blood types may be more important for preventing rejection than matching their tissue types. Young individuals and those having repeated transplants have an increased risk of rejection.

Due to the slow healing rate of the corneal wound, infection is another potential complication. It should also be noted that the condition necessitating the transplant in the first place may return and require a second transplant at a later date.

Factors Influencing Duration

The individual may be physically able to return to work in a matter of weeks, although vision may be impaired for several months. Complications such as infection or rejection could lengthen the period of disability. However, rejection tends to have a latency period of about 2 months, and will not normally occur before the individual returns to work. Younger individuals and those who have had repeated procedures are at an increased risk for complications, and thus may be more likely to experience a prolonged disability.

Length of Disability

The length of disability will depend on the individual's job requirements and may be incompatible with return to very heavy work. Heavy lifting, strenuous work, and repeated or prolonged bending should be avoided after surgery.

Duration in Days

Job Classification	Minimum	Optimum	Maximum
Sedentary work	14	21	28
Light work	14	21	28
Medium work	28	35	42
Heavy work	42	56	Indefinite
Very Heavy work	42	56	Indefinite

References

Cornea and Corneal Disease. National Eye Institute. 01 Apr 2000. 20 Jul 2000 <http://www.nei.nih.gov/publications/cornea.htm>.

Did You Know?. Eye Bank Association of America. 1999. 07 Aug 2000 <http://www.restoresight.org>.

Corneal Ulcer
370.0, 370.00

Definition

A corneal ulcer is a break, erosion, or open sore in the clear front layer of the eye (cornea). Although usually superficial, ulcers can sometimes extend into the underlying middle layer (stroma) of the cornea where microorganisms may penetrate to cause potentially serious infections. Because the body's natural healing responses tend to be less effective in this area of the eye, corneal ulcers are the most common cause of impaired vision and blindness in the world.

Corneal ulcers typically are caused by abrasions or scratches or result from improper or extended wearing of contact lenses. When the cornea is deprived of oxygen due to extended use of contact lenses, infection is more likely. Microorganisms causing infection also may attach to soft contact lenses that are not properly cleaned and disinfected. The annual incidence of corneal ulcers in contact lens users is .04% for daily wear and .21% for extended wear. About 25 million people wear contact lenses in the US.

Other causes may include viral infections particularly associated with herpes simplex or herpes zoster viruses and bacterial infections linked to contaminated eye drops. Eyes also may be damaged by exposure to soil or fungi. Vitamin A deficiency or protein malnutrition may also cause the condition. Other factors in development of corneal ulcers include use of corticosteroid eye drops, chemical damage, excessive exposure to air or ultraviolet light, or corneal attack by the body's own immune system (autoimmunity).

Eye conditions that may make a corneal ulcer more likely include "dry eye" (keratoconjunctivitis sicca), eyelid deformities (entropion, ectropion), diminished sensation in the cornea that may lead to injury, and an increased susceptibility to infection due to a lowered immune system (immunosuppressed state). In rare cases, laser or surgical vision correction procedures (LASIK, PRK, RK) have produced corneal ulcers. Individuals dealing with shellfish, such as oyster shuckers, have been found to be susceptible to corneal ulcers because of the presence of specific strains of microorganisms that may infect the eye.

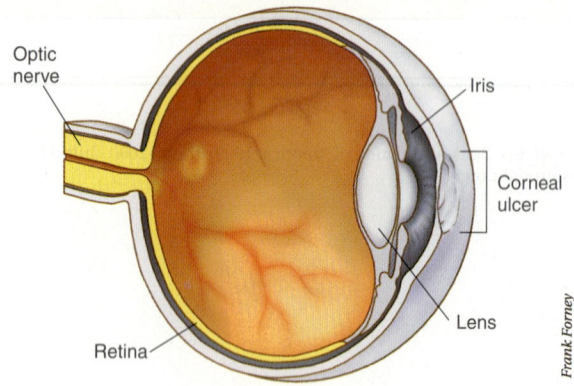

Diagnosis

History: Symptoms may include eye pain that is worse with eye or lid movement, severe sensitivity to light (photophobia), blurred or cloudy vision, tearing, and occasionally yellow drainage (pus). There may be a history of eye injury or recent eye disease. The pain may be most obvious when the eyes first open after a period of sleep. Although corneal ulcers are very painful, chronic ones may become less so. Redness may appear in the white of the eye. The cornea may start to whiten. In extreme cases, vision may worsen.

Physical exam: An anesthetic eyedrop may need to be given to make the eye exam tolerable. If there is pus collecting behind the cornea, a dull gray circle will be present on the cornea (hypopyon).

Tests: Visual acuity testing will be done to determine the sharpness and discrimination of the vision. A fluorescein dye, instilled into the eye, fills the ulcer (fluorescein staining) and reflects back green light when a fluorescent light is shown on it. The cornea also may be examined by an illuminated microscope or slit lamp (biomicroscopy). If an infection is suspected, material from the ulcer may be removed by swab and observed to identify responsible microorganisms that grow in nutritive substances (culture). A new laboratory method may directly identify specific genes or DNA sequences of microorganisms responsible for infections (polymerase chain reaction).

Treatment

A topical antibiotic ointment may be applied to prevent infection. Protective patches may be needed in cases of deeper perforations, but generally are avoided since oxygen must be allowed to the area to promote healing. A topical anesthetic may be needed to ease pain. Treatment for ulcers caused by infection must begin as soon as possible. Antibiotic medication is typically given by mouth, by eyedrops, and/or by injection into a vein (intravenously) for 4-5 days. Underlying conditions that may have caused the ulcer need to be corrected. Noninfectious ulcers that fail to heal may respond to a "bandage" contact lens that protects the area, or to a temporary joining of the eyelids (tarsorrhaphy). A saline solution (artificial tears) may also be needed for moistening.

Prognosis

Superficial, noninfectious ulcers caused by mechanical injury usually heal quickly. Most uncomplicated cases of corneal ulcers usually resolve completely within several weeks. More severe corneal ulcers can cause minimal to severe scarring that decreases vision enough to warrant a corneal transplant to restore sight. Depending on the cause, corneal ulcers can recur. In extreme cases, the damaged eye may need to be removed (enucleation).

Differential Diagnosis

Conditions with similar symptoms include uveitis, keratitis, corneal abrasion, foreign body, conjunctivitis, hordeolum, chalazion, abscessed tooth, sinusitis, temporal arteritis, tumor, and glaucoma.

Specialists

- Ophthalmologist

Work Restrictions / Accommodations

Visual acuity should be tested if it is important to the individual's job. Sunlight and ultraviolet light may need to be avoided during the healing process. If the individual experiences permanent vision loss, work station accommodations may be needed such as magnified and high contrast print. Extra illumination may also be required.

Complementary and Alternative Therapies

Content is intended for awareness only. Treatments may or may not be effective. Scientific evidence may be lacking and some substances have potentially toxic effects. Dr. Presley Reed and the editors do not endorse the use of these therapies in the absence of consultation with a licensed medical professional.

Hydrotherapy - A cool or warm cloth applied to the closed eye may help relieve pain and discomfort.

Comorbid Conditions

Eyelid deformities such as those that prevent the individual from fully blinking may both prevent healing and create recurrences of corneal ulcers. Improper hygiene or extended wear contacts may cause infections in contact lens wearers who develop corneal ulcers.

Complications

An infected ulcer can cause softening and perforation of the cornea, infection of the entire eye (panophthalmitis), and partial or total loss of vision. Healing may be slow if the individual is immunosuppressed because of an underlying disease such as rheumatoid arthritis or diabetes mellitus. Corticosteroids used to control inflammation for this or other conditions may decrease healing responses. If the underlying cause is not corrected, ulcers can recur.

Factors Influencing Duration

Length of disability may be influenced by the underlying cause and severity of the ulcer, the type of treatment, the individual's response to treatment, or the presence of complications. If the individual did not seek prompt treatment for the condition, an infection or other complications could result in permanent vision loss.

Length of Disability

Duration depends on severity of ulcer, its cause, and complications due to scarring such as depth perception problem. Physical disability may be limited, but visual loss may be persistent or permanent.

One eye.

Duration in Days

Job Classification	Minimum	Optimum	Maximum
Any work	1	5	14

Failure to Recover

If an individual fails to recover within the maximum duration expectancy period, the reader may wish to reference the following questions to assist in better understanding the specifics of an individual's medical case.

Regarding diagnosis:
- Does the individual have a corneal abrasion? Wear contact lenses?
- Does the individual use eye drops? Might they be contaminated?
- Has the individual had any chemical damage, excessive exposure to air or ultraviolet light, or corneal attack by the body's own immune system (autoimmunity)?
- Does the individual have dry eye syndrome? Entropion or ectropion?
- Does the individual's job put them at higher risk?
- Does the individual have diminished sensation in the cornea?
- Has the individual had a laser or surgical vision correction procedures?
- Does the individual complain of eye pain that is worse with eye or lid movement, photophobia, blurred or cloudy vision, tearing, or pus?
- Is there redness in the white of the eye? Has the cornea started to whiten?
- Was it necessary to use an anesthetic eye drop to make the eye exam tolerable?
- Is a dull gray circle present on the cornea (hypopyon)?
- Has the individual had a fluorescein stain done? Visual acuity? Culture?
- Have conditions with similar symptoms been ruled out?

Regarding treatment:
- Is the individual being treated with antibiotics?
- Have underlying conditions been corrected?
- Was it necessary to use a protective patch? Artificial tears?
- Was a "bandage" contact lens used?
- Was it necessary to temporarily join eyelids (tarsorrhaphy)?

Regarding prognosis:
- Is the individual's employer able to accommodate any necessary restrictions?
- Does the individual have any conditions that may affect their ability to recover?
- Does the individual have any complications such as softening and perforation of the cornea, infection of the entire eye, and partial or total loss of vision? Does the individual have slow healing secondary to immunosuppression?

References

Wingate, Sue. "Treating Corneal Abrasions." The Nurse Practitioner 24 01 Jun 1999: 53-54, 57. Electric Library. 27 Oct 2000 <http://www.elibrary.com>.

Coronary Arteriography

Other names / synonyms: Coronary Angiography

88.55, 88.56, 88.57

Definition

Coronary arteriography is an x-ray procedure involving the injection of dye (contrast medium) into the three coronary arteries of the heart to allow visualization of their interior.

More than 1 million coronary arteriographies are done each year in the US. It is the most frequently performed arteriographic procedure.

Reason for Procedure

Coronary arteriographies are done to determine the presence or absence of narrowing (obstruction) of the coronary arteries by cholesterol build-ups (plaques) or by a small blood clot (thrombus) in the case of a heart attack.

Cholesterol plaques are due to widespread (diffuse) disease of arteries called atherosclerosis. Coronary arteriography allows the extent of the disease to be evaluated. Accordingly, it is routinely done before therapeutic procedures such as angioplasty, bypass surgery, and insertion of a stent.

Diseases for which coronary arteriography is done include effort angina, unstable angina, and acute myocardial infarction. It is also often performed after a therapeutic procedure to assess the effect of the procedure and if symptoms recurred. This can help decide between a repeat procedure and an alternative one. A coronary arteriography may be done preoperatively in individuals undergoing noncardiac surgery to evaluate the risk of such surgery. It is frequently done in individuals without known heart diseases but who experience chest pain of uncertain cause. This helps establish if chest pain is due to coronary atherosclerosis.

How Procedure Is Performed

Coronary arteriography may be done on an inpatient or outpatient basis. Individuals with mild or stable symptoms due to effort angina often have coronary arteriography as outpatient. Outpatient procedures are done with smaller diameter catheters to reduce the possibility of delayed bleeding from the access site in the groin. It is performed as an inpatient procedure on those individuals with unstable angina or heart attack. In most instances, the procedure is done under local anesthetic in a specially equipped cardiac catheterization laboratory.

A variety of long, slender tubes (catheters) may be used to enter the coronary arteries. Dye is injected through the catheter into the coronary artery as x-rays are taken. Multiple pictures (images) are obtained at various angles to ensure no narrowing is overlooked. In contrast to the static images of most x-rays, coronary arteriography images are recorded in motion to allow the visualization of the interior of the vessel during the flow of blood while the heart is beating.

Prognosis

The outcome of the procedure is generally good. Stroke can occur during the procedure or in the first few hours after it's over in individuals with cerebrovascular disease. A transient sense of warmth especially in the head and face may be experienced after injection. Cardiovascular responses may include rapid heartbeat (tachycardia). Nausea, vomiting, and coughing are minor side effects.

Specialists

- Cardiologist

Work Restrictions / Accommodations

Most individuals undergoing uncomplicated coronary arteriography can return to work the following day. Work that involves lifting more than 10 pounds or bending or squatting should be avoided for 3 days to prevent delayed bleeding from the entry site in the groin area.

Comorbid Conditions

Individuals with cerebrovascular disease may react adversely to the test. It could worsen the effects of their disease, lengthen disability, and extend recovery time.

Procedure Complications

Complications of coronary arteriography are divided into those occurring at the artery site (the femoral artery in the groin) and those affecting the heart or other organs. Entry site complications include damage to the artery requiring repair (0.6%) and delayed bleeding requiring transfusion (0.3%). Cardiac complications include death (0.8%), acute myocardial infarction (1.5%), arrhythmias requiring electrical cardio version (2%), and dissection of the heart (<1%). Noncardiac, nonaccess site complications include stroke (0.5%), serious allergic reaction to dye (1%), renal failure (1%) and a blood clot dislodged from the catheter tip or from within the heart to a distant organ (embolus) (<0.1%)

Factors Influencing Duration

Individuals undergoing uncomplicated coronary arteriography should have no permanent disability related to the procedure.

Length of Disability

No disability is expected for this procedure. Disability may occur as a result of an underlying condition.

Duration in Days

Job Classification	Minimum	Optimum	Maximum
Any work	1	3	7

References

Arteriography. Med Help International. 1996. 15 Nov 2000 <http://www.medhelp.org/glossary/new/gls_0470.htm>.

Balentine, J., and A. Eisenhart. "Aortic Stenosis from Emergency Medicine/Cardiovascular." Emergency Medicine Online 20 Oct 2000. 10 Nov 2000 <http://www.emedicine.com/emerg/topic40.htm>.

Coronary Atherosclerosis

Other names / synonyms: Arteriosclerotic Heart Disease, ASHD, CAD, Chronic Ischemic Heart Disease, Coronary Artery Disease

414, 414.0, 414.8, 414.9

Definition

Coronary atherosclerosis is the accumulation of fatty deposits along the inside walls of the coronary arteries supplying the heart muscle. As the fatty deposits (atheromas or plaques) slowly increase in size over the years, the artery becomes narrow in places (stenosis) and blood flow to the heart is reduced. The stenosis may become so significant that blood supply is inadequate to meet the needs of the heart (myocardial ischemia). Myocardial ischemia typically results in chest pain (angina pectoris), but may also be without symptoms (silent ischemia). Total blockage of a coronary artery results in a heart attack (myocardial infarction).

Risk factors for coronary atherosclerosis include male gender, age, family history of atherosclerosis, particularly before age 50, high blood pressure, diabetes, high blood cholesterol, smoking, obesity, poor physical fitness, elevated homocysteine levels, and low estrogen levels (in women). Emotional stress also may play a role. The risk associated with high blood cholesterol is actually created by the high levels of a specific type of cholesterol, low-density lipoprotein cholesterol. In contrast, high levels of another type of cholesterol (high-density lipoprotein cholesterol) decreases the risk. Risk factors play the greatest role in disease of young or middle-aged adults. In later life, disease occurs more often irrespective of risk factors.

Approximately 7 million individuals have coronary atherosclerosis in the US. It is the most common type of heart disease and the leading cause of death. More than 500,000 individuals die each year from myocardial infarction caused by coronary atherosclerosis. Men have coronary atherosclerosis at 4 times the rates of women. The condition peaks in occurrence for men between the ages of 50 and 60. In women, it peaks between 60 and 70.

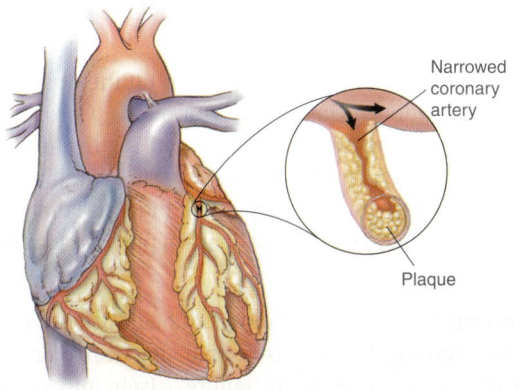
Narrowed coronary artery
Plaque
Laurie O'Keefe

Diagnosis

History: In the early stages of coronary atherosclerosis, the individual may have no symptoms. In later stages, the individual may have chest pain or pressure with exertion that is relieved by rest (angina), or history of heart attack (myocardial infarction).

Physical exam: The exam is usually not directly helpful in this diagnosis but may reveal risk factors such as high blood pressure or obesity.

Tests: Blood cholesterol testing, including total cholesterol and low- and high-density lipoproteins (LDL and HDL), demonstrates increased total cholesterol and increased low-density lipoproteins. An electrocardiogram (ECG) at rest looks for electrical abnormalities of the heart. An ECG during physical exertion (exercise stress test) can detect heart abnormalities induced by lack of blood flow, and subsequent lack of oxygen, to the heart muscle. If an individual can't exercise to the degree needed for the stress test, a drug can be given to simulate the effect of exercise on the heart (physiologic stress test).

Nuclear scanning during a stress test (radionuclide stress test) involves injecting a radioactive isotope into a vein before the test. During the test, the examiner can watch the flow of blood through the heart and can identify areas in which blood flow is decreased. Ultrasound can also be applied during a stress test (stress echocardiography) to watch blood flow and the heart as it pumps during exercise.

The most definitive test is the coronary angiogram. A thin catheter is inserted into a vein in the arm or groin. It is guided up into the opening of the coronary arteries. Once it is in place, radioactive dye is injected through the catheter into the coronary arteries. A x-ray captures the movement of the dye through the heart in a picture called an angiogram. In this procedure, the exact location and degree of blockage can be identified.

Treatment

Risk factors should be treated whether symptoms are present or not. This helps prevent progression of coronary artery disease and, to some extent, can actually reverse it. Many of the risk factors are potentially treatable. Cessation of smoking is essential. Hypertension may be controlled by salt restriction, exercise, stress management, and medication. Diabetes can be managed by diet, exercise, and medication if necessary. Diet and exercise are also helpful in normalizing cholesterol levels. If this is not successful, cholesterol-lowering drugs can be added. A small daily dose of an anti-platelet drug helps inhibit blood clotting. For women, estrogen replacement may be recommended after menopause.

Severe coronary atherosclerosis may require a procedure to remove areas of stenosis. Coronary angioplasty uses a catheter inserted into the coronary arteries to the place of blockage. On the end of the catheter is a deflated balloon. Once the catheter is in place, the balloon is inflated, widening the artery. If this is not successful, coronary artery bypass surgery may be needed. The blocked portion of coronary artery is removed and replaced with a healthy portion of vessel removed from the leg, chest, or arm.

Prognosis

Once coronary atherosclerosis develops, it must be managed for life. The risk of subsequent cardiac events or disruption of general circulation depends on control of the disease through medication and lifestyle changes. Medication and lifestyle changes can prevent the disease's progression by reducing future fatty deposits. They also can bring about a small reduction in fatty deposits already present. Medication has the additional effect of softening of the fatty deposits, making them less likely to break away from the cell wall and cause vessel blockage within the heart. There appears to be no reduction in mortality from all causes, however, among individuals who take lipid-lowering medication.

Surgical procedures, such as coronary angioplasty or bypass surgery, successfully remove diseased portions of blood vessels, but the risk remains of future blockage due to ongoing fatty deposits.

Differential Diagnosis

Other sources of chest pain include angina pectoris, spasm of the esophagus, chest wall pain, acute inflammation of the gallbladder, hiatal hernia, and panic attack.

Specialists

- Cardiologist
- Cardiovascular Surgeon

Rehabilitation

Rehabilitation for coronary atherosclerosis follows similar phases as other cardiac conditions in which surgery is performed.

Therapy may begins in the hospital with low levels of exercise to prevent some of the negative effects of bed rest (mainly muscle weakness and joint stiffness). Mild exercise can also help reduce episodes of low blood pressure when changing positions (orthostatic hypotension) and maintain overall mobility of the body. Individuals will perform low-level exercises lying on the back (supine position). The individual progresses with exercises while sitting and eventually while standing. Progressive walking (ambulating) and eventually stair climbing are an important part of the individual's exercise program while hospitalized. Intensity is gradually increased until the individual is discharged from the hospital.

Therapy focuses next on improving functional capacity by increasing the physical endurance and promoting return to activity. An electrocardiograph, attached to the individual, is used to record the continuous electrical activity of the heart muscle. A physical therapist keeps a daily log of the individual's blood pressure, heart rate, and cardiac rhythm.

Depending on the individual's condition, they may stay involved with an outpatient program for up to a year to accomplish all of the their goals while still at modified work duty. Eventually, individuals will perform higher levels of exercise with the addition of recreational activities such as swimming and outdoor hiking. Light jogging and cycling is appropriate as long as the individual is tolerating the rehabilitation program well. Because of the various degrees of coronary atherosclerosis, modifications may need to be made for those individuals who suffered a heart attack and/or underwent surgery.

Work Restrictions / Accommodations

In early stages, there are typically no restrictions. Although exercise is recommended, this activity can typically be accomplished during off-work hours. During periods of intense rehabilitation, time off may be required for visits to the physical therapist or participation in a rehabilitation program.

As the condition progresses and arteries become more lined with fatty deposits, physical capacity is likely to decrease due to decreased coronary blood flow and oxygenation of the heart. At this point, restrictions will be based on stress test results and response to treatment. Individuals with strenuous physical job requirements may need a more sedentary job assignment. If angioplasty or bypass surgery is required, accommodations will be needed during recovery period.

Complementary and Alternative Therapies

Content is intended for awareness only. Treatments may or may not be effective. Scientific evidence may be lacking and some substances have potentially toxic effects. Dr. Presley Reed and the editors do not endorse the use of these therapies in the absence of consultation with a licensed medical professional.

Niacin -	High doses may lower cholesterol.
Vitamin E -	May raise levels of high-density lipoproteins.
Diet -	Studies show that vegetarians may have lower levels of blood cholesterol and lower blood pressure than meat eaters.
Acupuncture -	May help in breaking smoking habits (a risk factor in atherosclerosis).
Garlic -	Said to have lipid-lowering properties.

Comorbid Conditions

Diabetes mellitus, severe stress reaction, nicotine abuse, hyperlipidemia, or obesity may lengthen disability.

Complications

Angina may remain stable for long periods. With progression of the disease, the anginal episodes may increase in severity and duration, become less responsive to medication, and/or be precipitated by less exertion. A worsening or less predictable pattern of angina is referred to as unstable angina.

A heart attack (myocardial infarction) can result if the obstruction in a coronary artery suddenly becomes complete. Coronary artery obstruction may be triggered by blood clotting (thrombosis) in a narrowed artery. It may also be triggered by a clot that separates (embolism) and is carried downstream until it blocks a smaller artery. A heart attack then results and may cause death of part of the heart muscle due to lack of oxygen.

Individuals who survive massive or repeated heart attacks may be left with so little functioning heart muscle that the heart can no longer pump effectively (congestive heart failure). Ischemic or damaged myocardium may also result in disturbances of heart rhythm (arrhythmias) such as atrial fibrillation or ventricular fibrillation. Atherosclerosis may also occur in other arteries throughout the body, such as the legs, causing impaired circulation.

Factors Influencing Duration

Ability to work depends on the outcome of treatment (relief of symptoms, improved ventricular function) and the severity of any residual symptoms, the presence or absence of other medical conditions, and the individual's occupation.

Length of Disability

Duration depends on location, severity, and which arteries are involved. Contact physician for additional information.

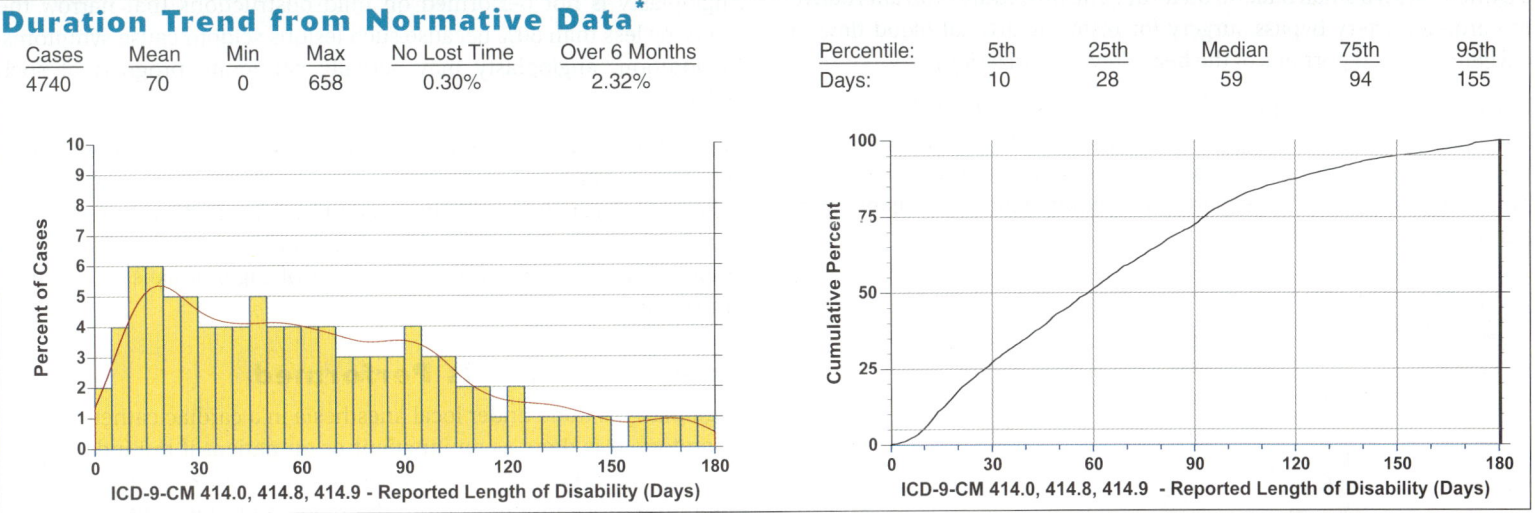

* Differences may exist between the expected duration tables and the normative graphs. Duration tables provide expected recovery periods based on the type of work performed by the individual. The normative graphs reflect the actual observed experience of many individuals across the spectrum of physical conditions, in a variety of industries, and with varying levels of case management.

Failure to Recover

If an individual fails to recover within the maximum duration expectancy period, the reader may wish to reference the following questions to assist in better understanding the specifics of an individual's medical case.

Regarding diagnosis:

- Does individual have risk factors such as male gender, age, family history of atherosclerosis, particularly before age 50, high blood pressure, diabetes, high blood cholesterol, smoking, obesity, poor physical fitness, elevated homocysteine levels, low estrogen levels (in women), or emotional stress?
- Does individual have angina or a history of myocardial infarction?
- On physical exam, were high blood pressure or obesity present?
- Has individual had complete blood lipid testing, ECG at rest and exercise?
- Was a radionuclide stress test done? Stress echocardiography? Coronary angiogram?
- Were conditions with similar symptoms ruled out?

Regarding treatment:

- Was coronary angioplasty done?
- Was it necessary to do coronary bypass surgery?

Regarding prognosis:

- Is individual active in rehabilitation?
- Can individual's employer accommodate any necessary restrictions?
- Does individual have any conditions that may affect ability to recover?
- Have any complications developed such as unstable angina, myocardial infarction, congestive heart failure, and arrhythmias such as atrial fibrillation or ventricular fibrillation?
- Does individual have atherosclerosis in other arteries throughout the body causing impaired circulation?

References

Atherosclerosis. MedicineNet.com. 1998. 14 Oct 2000 <http://www.4woman.gov/faq/atheroscle.htm>.

Facts About Coronary Heart Disease. National Heart, Lung, and Blood Institute. 1993. 14 Oct 2000 <http://www.nhlbi.nih.gov/health/public/heart/other/chdfacts.htm>.

Cheng, W. "Clinical and Experimental Study of Garlic in Preventing and Treating Cardiovascular Diseases." Chung Hsi I Chieh Ho Tsa Chih 10 10 (1990): 635-637, 640.

Fu, G.Q. "Experimental Study on Effect of Lipid-lowering and Treating Coronary Atherosclerosis with Chinese Herbal Prescription." Chung Hsi I Chieh Ho Tsa Chih 10 12 (1990): 740-741, 710.

Goldman, Lee, and J. Claude Bennett. Cecil Textbook of Medicine, 21st ed. Philadelphia: W.B. Saunders Company, 2000.

Goroll, Allan, Lawrence May, and Albert Mulley. Primary Care Medicine, 3rd ed. Philadelphia: Lippincott-Raven, 1995.

He, G. "Effect of the Prevention and Treatment of Atherosclerosis of a Mixture of Hawthorn and Motherworn." Chung Hsi I Chieh Ho Tsa Chih 10 6 (1990): 361, 326.

Massie, Barry, and Thomas Amidon. "Heart." Current Medical Diagnosis and Treatment, 39th ed. Tierney, Lawrence, Stephen McPhee, and Maxine Papadakis, eds. New York: Lange Medical Books/McGraw-Hill, 2000. 351-443.

McArdle, William, Frank Katch, and Victor Katch. Exercise Physiology. Energy, Nutrition, and Human Performance. Philadelphia: Lea & Febiger, 1991.

Scully, Rosemary M., and Marylou R. Barnes. Physical Therapy. Philadelphia: J.B. Lippincott Company, 1989.

Coronary Balloon Angioplasty

Other names / synonyms: Percutaneous Transluminal Coronary Angioplasty

36.01, 36.02, 36.05

Definition

Coronary balloon angioplasty is a procedure designed to widen segments of coronary arteries narrowed by atherosclerosis plaque using a catheter with a small balloon on its tip. The procedure is an alternative to coronary artery bypass surgery for restoring arterial blood flow to oxygen-deprived portions of the heart (revascularization).

Coronary balloon angioplasty is routinely done in university hospitals and many other institutions with a bed capacity greater than 250. Nationwide, however, it is performed in less than half of all hospitals. This is because it requires expertise and equipment not available in or affordable by smaller hospitals.

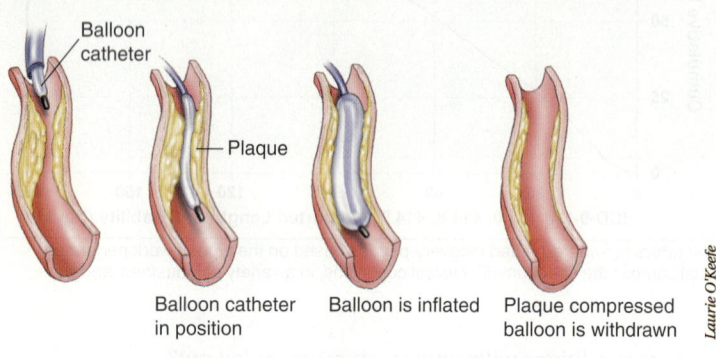

Reason for Procedure

Initially, this procedure was performed on individuals with predictable chronic pain in the chest during exertion (effort angina). Now, however, it is used for various acute coronary syndromes (unstable angina), heart attack (acute myocardial infarction), and on individuals who have survived a cardiac arrest outside of the hospital.

Angioplasty may be done to relieve obstructions in one, two, or all three of the coronary arteries. It is usually performed for single-vessel disease and in some cases of double-vessel disease. Individuals with three-vessel disease often have bypass surgery performed rather than angioplasty because it is safer. Those with disease of the most important coronary artery (left main coronary artery) almost always have bypass surgery.

The ideal situation for angioplasty is a narrowing (stenosis) located in a straight segment of the first part of a coronary artery without angulations or branching. The narrowing is preferably short (less than 1 cm in length), not total (incomplete occlusion), and symmetrical without calcium or a fresh blood clot (thrombus). The extent and severity of the coronary narrowing are determined beforehand by a coronary angiogram. Recent technological advances have been made such as "steerable" guide wires and balloons that can be inflated even when narrowing is less than ideal.

Angioplasty can also be performed on bypass grafts that have become blocked. This is only done during the first year after bypass surgery since occlusion during the first year is usually due to thickening of the dilated artery. If angioplasty is attempted on older vein grafts, heart damage may occur since occlusion of these older grafts is often a result of build up of atherosclerotic material that can be dislodged into the more distant portion of the coronary artery.

Angioplasty is not performed on mild obstructions that narrow the artery by less than 50% because such lesions seldom cause symptoms. In addition, angioplasty may actually accelerate progress of such lesions.

Contraindications to angioplasty include lesions that are more than 2 cm long, twisted (tortuous) vessels, certain branching configuration (where there is risk of occluding one branch while dilating the other), total occlusions older than 3 months, and old vein grafts (risk of embolization). In these situations, the risk of angioplasty is greater and/or the results are poorer.

How Procedure Is Performed

Angioplasty is done under local anesthesia in a cardiac catheterization laboratory. It is done as an inpatient or outpatient if the individual is discharged within 24 hours after admission. Aspirin is usually taken before the procedure to thin out the blood and reduce the risk of the formation of an acute blood clot at the angioplasty site.

A balloon-tipped catheter is inserted through the skin (percutaneously) into the aorta and advanced under a fluoroscope to the mouth of the coronary artery to be dilated. It is then further advanced into the vessel to the point narrowing where it is inflated to a specific pressure with a small amount of fluid for 30 to 60 seconds. Repeat x-rays of the artery are taken to ascertain if it has been adequately opened. The procedure usually requires repeat balloon inflations since it is unusual to obtain a completely satisfactory opening with only one inflation.

Prognosis

The majority (95%) of individuals who have angioplasty done for stable effort angina have either immediate complete resolution or a significant improvement of their symptoms. For those with the procedure done for unstable angina, relief of symptoms is almost as high (ninety percent). However, a recurrence of angina occurs in about 30% of individuals with stable angina within 6 months of the procedure due to a recurrence of the narrowing (restenosis) that led to the angioplasty. This requires a repeat angioplasty. Several repeat angioplasties are sometimes performed.

After 7 to 10 years, nearly 90% of individuals with effort angina are free of angina or have minimal symptoms. The annual infarction rate is about 3% and survival rate at 10 years is eighty percent.

Despite a significant reduction of symptoms and enhancement of life quality and participation in leisure activities, only about 60% of individuals return to work.

Specialists

- Cardiologist
- Cardiovascular Surgeon

Work Restrictions / Accommodations

Within the first week after angioplasty, individuals should avoid lifting more than 10 to 15 pounds and avoid bending as much as possible to reduce the chances of late bleeding from the entry site in the groin. If an acute myocardial infarction or urgent bypass surgery is necessary, other work restrictions may be needed.

Comorbid Conditions

Comorbid conditions include diabetes, obesity, lung disease, peripheral vascular disease, and kidney disease.

Procedure Complications

The most common serious nonfatal complication of angioplasty is abrupt closure of the coronary at the site of balloon inflation. This occurs in about 3% of individuals and requires emergency bypass surgery to avert heart damage (acute myocardial infarction) and/or death. About half the individuals have a major nonfatal acute myocardial infarction and another quarter have a smaller nonfatal AMI. About 2% of individuals undergoing emergency bypass surgery do not survive.

Less serious complications of angioplasty include a ventricular arrhythmia requiring electrical cardioversion (2%), emergency recatheterization because of a delayed occlusion (1%), femoral artery damage that requires repair (0.6%), blood loss requiring transfusion (0.3%), perforation of the coronary artery (0.1%), and stroke (0.03%).

Factors Influencing Duration

Age, procedural complications, job requirements, and coexistence of vascular disease elsewhere may affect the duration of disability.

Length of Disability

No disability is expected for recovery from this procedure. Duration depends on underlying condition and presence of complications.

Duration in Days

Job Classification	Minimum	Optimum	Maximum
Sedentary work	3	7	14
Light work	3	7	14
Medium work	7	14	28
Heavy work	14	14	28
Very Heavy work	14	21	35

References

Meeker, Margaret, and Jane Rothrock. Alexander's Care of the Patient in Surgery. St. Louis: Mosby, 1999.

Coronary Bypass

Other names / synonyms: Cabbage, CABG, Coronary Artery Bypass Graft
36.1, 36.10, 36.11, 36.12, 36.13, 36.14, 36.15, 36.16, 36.19

Definition

Coronary bypass surgery refers to either of two operative procedures that go around (bypass) cholesterol-laden deposits (atherosclerotic plaques) in coronary arteries. One technique utilizes veins taken from the legs (saphenous veins) as the bypass channel (conduit) while the other technique makes use of an artery taken from the inside of the chest wall (internal mammary artery) to bypass atherosclerotic plaques.

Risk factors for coronary bypass surgery include a family history of coronary heart disease (CHD), advancing age, male gender, abnormalities in the blood levels of fats and fatty acids (lipids), high blood pressure (hypertension), physical inactivity, cigarette smoking, diabetes mellitus, elevated blood levels of homocysteine, and low levels of estrogen in women. Before age 60, men are more likely to have coronary artery disease (women's hearts are protected by estrogen until menopause) but after that age the incidence equalizes between men and women.

Approximately 300,000 coronary bypass operations are done each year in the US making it one of the most frequently performed operations in the country. About 1 in every 1,000 individuals over age 35 has the operation done each year with men having the operation more than women.

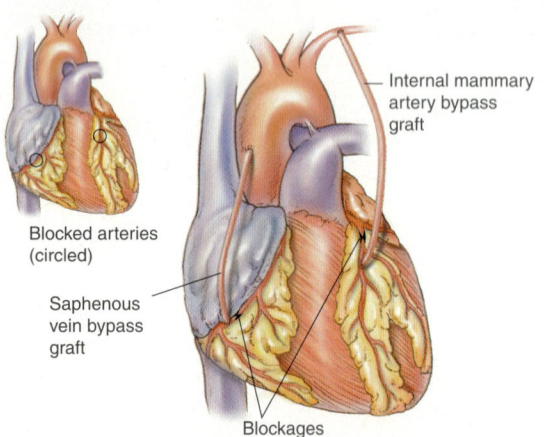

Reason for Procedure

The principal reason for bypass surgery is to relieve discomfort in the chest associated with activity (effort angina) experienced by individuals with cholesterol plaques in their coronary arteries. The plaques limit or impede the flow of blood through the vessels. The delivery of oxygen to the heart muscle (myocardium) is reduced as a result. The condition of cholesterol-laden plaques is often referred to as "hardening of the arteries" or arteriosclerosis. This is a partial misnomer however because it is only in older individuals with more advanced plaques containing as much calcium as cholesterol that the arteries actually become hardened. If cholesterol (lipid) deposits prevail, the term atherosclerosis is applied.

A secondary reason for coronary bypass surgery is to prolong life in (some) individuals with coronary atherosclerosis.

How Procedure Is Performed

The procedure is done utilizing the heart-lung machine also known as cardiopulmonary bypass. The individual's blood is supplemented by donors' blood to provide an adequate volume of oxygen-carrying red blood cells to circulate through the heart-lung machine. The heart-lung machine then oxygenates the blood and pumps it back into the individual's body while the is not beating. The motionless state of the heart allows the surgery to be done under conditions conducive to the best technical result.

The saphenous vein is removed from one or both legs and used to bypass narrowed areas of the coronary arteries identified preoperatively by the coronary angiogram. One and sometimes both internal mammary arteries (IMAs) may be used in addition to the saphenous veins.

After bypassing the narrowed coronary arteries, the individual is gradually weaned from the heart-lung machine. Sometimes a device known as an intra-aortic balloon pump is used to assist smooth weaning from the heart-lung machine. The balloon pump is then gradually discontinued over one to several days.

Prognosis

Relief of effort angina is the major reason for bypass surgery and is achieved in more than 90% of individuals for up to one year after surgery. Angina however recurs in a number of individuals underscoring the fact that bypass surgery is not a cure. Between 2 and 5 years following surgery, effort angina reappears in 25% of cases. Between 6 and 10 years after surgery, angina recurs in nearly half the individuals. Ten years after the initial operation, 50% of individuals will have a return of symptoms. Fewer individuals will have recurrent angina if they made major risk factor modifications and took two antiplatelet medications (aspirin and dipyridamole) to thin out the blood postoperatively. The medications must be taken indefinitely.

Recurrence of angina is due to partial narrowing or complete occlusion of the vein bypass due to atherosclerosis. Atherosclerosis is the disease process leading to surgery that originally narrowed (obstructed) the coronary arteries and led to bypass surgery. Therefore, the rate of vein bypass occlusion is similar to the rate of recurrent angina. After one year, 10% of bypasses are occluded and after 10 years only 50% remain open. Vein bypass occlusion occurs more often in older individuals, diabetics, and those who continue to smoke cigarettes and/or do not reduce their cholesterol intake and blood level. The vein bypass occlusion rate like the recurrent angina rate is also higher in those who do not take aspirin and dipyridamole.

The left IMA may be used as a bypass channel (conduit) instead of or in addition to one of the saphenous veins. A saphenous vein can be divided into a number of sections to bypass multiple obstructed vessels. The IMA, however, can only be used once. Since the IMA is an artery similar

592   The Medical Disability Advisor—Fourth Edition

in size and thickness to one of the arteries being bypassed and the saphenous vein is a vein, the IMA is a better conduit.

Advantages of an IMA bypass are that it remains open (patent) in 90% of individuals after 10 years as opposed to 50% of saphenous vein bypasses, and that survival at 10 years in individuals where IMA was used to bypass one of several obstructed coronary arteries is equal to the survival rate in the general population. The disadvantages of the IMA are that it can only be used to bypass one narrowed coronary artery and that the operative time is significantly prolonged. The advantages outweigh the disadvantages therefore the IMA is usually used to bypass one vessel and the saphenous vein used for all others.

Specialists

- Cardiologist
- Cardiovascular Surgeon

Work Restrictions / Accommodations

Among individuals performing minimally strenuous work such as accountants and teachers work may be resumed 2 to 4 weeks after surgery. Among individuals performing more strenuous work, 6 to 12 weeks may be required before work is resumed. Most individuals can return to the job they performed before surgery.

Comorbid Conditions

Comorbid conditions include diseases that affect any of the major body systems such as high blood pressure, chronic renal disease, bleeding disorders, diabetes mellitus, chronic obstructive lung disease, chronic heart disease, and immunosuppressive diseases. A history of smoking, alcoholism or other substance abuse, and obesity are also comorbid conditions.

Procedure Complications

Heart bypass surgery may be accompanied by complications due to the anesthetic, heart-lung machine, or the surgery itself. The most serious complications are a heart attack (in about 10% of individuals), stroke (1-5%) and death (one to two percent). Other complications include bleeding requiring reoperation (2-5%), wound infection (1%), arrhythmias (40%), and worsened hypertension (thirty-three percent).

A number of other complications may develop during the early postoperative (perioperative) period and include endocarditis, kidney (renal) failure, hemolytic anemia, pericarditis, gastrointestinal (GI) bleeding, and respiratory failure. Each of these complications occurs in 5% or less of cases.

Factors Influencing Duration

Individuals with an IMA used as a bypass conduit may require a longer time off work if work involves lifting more than 10 pounds or repeatedly reaching above their head. Those who are older and overweight may also be disabled longer.

Length of Disability

Duration depends on underlying condition and presence of complications. Disability may be permanent.

Duration in Days

Job Classification	Minimum	Optimum	Maximum
Sedentary work	42	56	112
Light work	42	56	112
Medium work	56	70	140
Heavy work	56	84	140
Very Heavy work	56	112	168

References

Lewis, Sharon, Margaret Heitkemper, and Shannon Dirksen. Medical-Surgical Nursing. St. Louis: Mosby, 2000.

Meeker, Margaret, and Jane Rothrock. Alexander's Care of the Patient in Surgery. St. Louis: Mosby, 1999.

Coronary Thrombolysis
Other names / synonyms: Cardiac Thrombolytic Therapy, Intracoronary Artery Thrombolytic Infusion
36.04

Definition

Coronary thrombolysis is a drug therapy given to restore blood flow to the heart following a heart attack (acute myocardial infarction). In acute myocardial infarction (AMI), blood flow in the blood vessels of the heart (coronary arteries) is blocked by a blood clot (thrombi, thrombotic occlusion). A drug that dissolves the clot (thrombolytic drug) is injected into an intravenous (IV) line inserted near the clot. Either one drug or a combination of thrombolytic drugs is used.

First used in the 1970s, thrombolytic therapy is credited for reducing in-hospital mortality rates by up to 50%. Not everyone who could benefit from this therapy, however, receives it. In the US, there are over one million new or repeat AMIs per year. Approximately half the individuals suffering these AMIs do not arrive at the hospital in time for the therapy to be effective. Others do not receive the therapy because of medical reasons or because it is not offered. Preliminary results from an ongoing major study indicate that only half of the individuals with AMI seen in a hospital actually receive thrombolytic therapy. Other studies reveal that men receive thrombolytic therapy more often than women.

Reason for Procedure

If blood flow to the heart is not restored following a heart attack, the heart is deprived of oxygen and the individual dies. Thrombolysis under appropriate circumstances quickly restores blood flow to the heart.

The therapy should be given to individuals with classic symptoms of heart attack or electrocardiography (ECG) evidence of AMI and who have had pain for less than 6 hours. ECG tests heart function and can detect AMI by checking the heart's electrical impulses. Although benefits are diminished, therapy may be given up to 12 hours after the onset of pain. There is some flexibility in this time frame if the onset of pain was sudden and constant or intermittent.

How Procedure Is Performed

The thrombolytic drug is typically administered in the emergency room preferably within 30 minutes after the individual arrives. The drug is injected directly into a blood vessel through an intravenous (IV) line. Anesthesia is not needed.

Anticlotting medication is usually given at the same time (through an IV or injected through the skin) and continued for 3 to 5 days. It is usually discontinued at least 24 hours before discharge. Aspirin also helps counteract blood clots and should be given as soon as a heart attack is diagnosed. Aspirin should be continued indefinitely.

Prognosis

Coronary blood flow is restored within 90 minutes in 33-60% of individuals after they begin thrombolytic therapy. When therapy is given to individuals with a specific ECG finding within 6 hours from onset of chest pain, mortality drops by twenty-nine percent. The ECG analyzes heart function by checking the heart's electrical impulses by placing electrodes at various sites on the body. The specific finding is called ST segment elevation that is an abnormal electrical impulse strongly suggesting AMI. The benefit of the therapy lasts for years. Individuals who have had this therapy are at low risk for another heart attack or death from heart attack.

Studies indicate that individuals with no ECG evidence of heart attack are not helped by thrombolysis, and may even be made worse.

When aspirin is added to thrombolytic therapy, the benefit is nearly doubled. Aspirin continued indefinitely is associated with a 25% reduction in death, reinfarction, and stroke.

Specialists

- Cardiologist
- Cardiovascular Surgeon

Rehabilitation

Thrombolysis requires no follow-up rehabilitation, however, rehabilitation specific to AMI is needed. Individuals who experience AMI should attend outpatient physical and occupational therapy at a clinic specializing in cardiac rehabilitation. Cardiac rehabilitation speeds recovery by strengthening the heart muscle and thus increasing the amount of activity an individual can tolerate. Cardiac rehabilitation centers offer ECG monitoring of all participants during the exercise sessions.

Work Restrictions / Accommodations

Thrombolysis itself does not require subsequent work restrictions and accommodations. Recovery from a heart attack, however, will likely require adjustments. Tests (such as exercise testing) performed before individual is discharged from the hospital help assess what normal activities can be restarted and where caution is needed.

Comorbid Conditions

Conditions that increase the risk of bleeding or the risk of intracerebral hemorrhage increase the likelihood of these complications occurring. These complications increase the length of disability.

Procedure Complications

Because coronary thrombolysis increases the risk of bleeding, it must be administered with caution to individuals with conditions that may increase their tendency to bleed.

This caution applies to conditions such as bleeding disorders, gastrointestinal bleeding, and recent surgery. Bleeding inside the skull (intracerebral hemorrhage) is the most severe possible complication. Individuals with high blood pressure, low body weight, history of stroke, and those on warfarin therapy are at increased risk for intracerebral hemorrhage.

Individuals recently receiving streptokinase (one of the most common thrombolytic drugs) may have an allergic reaction to it when given again. To reduce this risk, streptokinase should not be given within 2 years of a previous dose.

Factors Influencing Duration

Age and general health prior to the heart attack influence disability. In general, younger and healthier individuals recover more quickly. The extent of cardiac tissue damage before blood flow was restored significantly influences the rate of recovery.

Length of Disability

No disability is expected to result from this therapy. Duration depends on the underlying condition for which the procedure is performed.

References

Heart Attack and Angina Statistics. American Heart Association. 01 May 2000. 05 Aug 2000 <http://www.americanheart.org/Heart_and_Stroke_A_Z_Guide/has.html>.

Tavazzi, Luigi. "Clinical Epidemiology of Acute Myocardial Infarction." American Heart Journal 138 2 (1999): 48-54.

Costochondritis
733.6

Definition

Costochondritis occurs when connective tissue (cartilage) of the rib cage becomes inflamed.

The affected location typically is where cartilage is found between the inner ribs and sternum (costochondral junction). While the individual may experience discomfort, effects are usually benign. Medical definitions vary regarding the condition, which also may be described as a symptom of repeated minor trauma or underlying disease such as rheumatoid arthritis. Bacterial or fungal infections also have been proposed as possible causes. Some researchers believe that certain types of costochondritis may be inherited.

In one study involving individuals who visited emergency medical facilities, the condition was diagnosed more frequently in women and Hispanics. The condition also occurs more frequently in individuals age 40 or older. One study reported that chest pains occur in about 10% of the general population, with about 30% of these cases diagnosed as costochondritis.

Diagnosis

History: Individuals may complain of mild or severe chest pain, which may radiate to the shoulder or arms. The pain is aggravated by chest wall movement related to deep breathing, coughing or sneezing. If the individual is quiet and restricts movement, symptoms typically improve. The symptoms may vary in intensity.

Physical exam: The exam almost always reveals tenderness or pain when pressure is applied (palpation) to the affected area. With costochondritis, no swelling (edema) will be noted when pressure is applied. The diagnosis might be confirmed if pain relief occurs after injection of a local anesthetic in the affected area.

Tests: A chest x-ray, electrocardiogram (ECG), and blood tests (serology) may be needed to rule out heart disease or any possible underlying conditions. A bone (gallium) scan may also be used.

Treatment

Treatment may include rest, avoidance of activities that may aggravate the pain, pain relievers (analgesics), nonsteroidal anti-inflammatory drugs (NSAIDs), application of heat and/or ice, topical spray (ethyl chloride) that has a cooling effect, and local injection of an anesthetic. In some cases, a stronger anti-inflammatory agent (corticosteroid) may be used. Emergency attention may be required to rule out the possibility of a heart attack.

Prognosis

While causes of costochondritis are not well understood, studies have shown that most cases seemingly unrelated to other conditions resolve on their own within one year. With treatment, improvement in associated pain usually occurs within two months. This type of costochondritis typically heals completely, though it is possible that the condition will recur. Outcomes will vary greatly when the condition is a symptom of underlying injuries or diseases, each with a different prognosis. Costochondritis that is related to hereditary factors may be ongoing (chronic).

Differential Diagnosis

Other possibilities include myocardial infarction, Tietze's syndrome, osteoarthritis, fibrositis, fibromyalgia, lymphoma, rheumatoid arthritis, and other rheumatological disease (disorders involving inflammation, muscle/joint pain). Symptoms also may be similar to various injuries, abdominal trauma, anxiety, gout, herpes zoster, and lung neoplasm.

Specialists

- Internist
- Orthopedist
- Rheumatologist

Work Restrictions / Accommodations

Restrictions will depend on the degree of inflammation and pain involved. Activities that aggravate pain, such as lifting or other strenuous activities, should be temporarily eliminated from responsibilities until the individual has recovered.

Complementary and Alternative Therapies

Content is intended for awareness only. Treatments may or may not be effective. Scientific evidence may be lacking and some substances have potentially toxic effects. Dr. Presley Reed and the editors do not endorse the use of these therapies in the absence of consultation with a licensed medical professional.

Biofeedback - This method may be used to control pain and involves use of recording instruments measuring biological responses. The individual controls physical responses through behavior or mental (cognitive) processes.

Comorbid Conditions

Individuals with gastroesophageal disorders such as gastroesophageal reflux or irritable esophagus may experience ongoing (chronic) symptoms creating non-specific chest pain, which may influence the length of disability.

Complications

Costochondritis can be a symptom of other diseases, which may need to be treated independently. These conditions can include inflammatory bowel disease, fibromyalgia, psoriatic arthritis, Reiter's disease and ankylosing spondylitis. Individuals with a possible inherited tendency for costochondritis may experience ongoing (chronic) symptoms.

Factors Influencing Duration

Since costochondritis is benign in its effects, the individual may experience continuing discomfort but no accompanying disability.

Length of Disability

The expected length of disability is variable while tests are done to rule out serious diseases. Once this diagnosis is established, there should be no disability.

Duration in Days

Job Classification	Minimum	Optimum	Maximum
Sedentary work	0	1	3
Light work	0	1	3
Medium work	0	1	3
Heavy work	1	1	3
Very Heavy work	1	1	3

Failure to Recover

If an individual fails to recover within the maximum duration expectancy period, the reader may wish to reference the following questions to assist in better understanding the specifics of an individual's medical case.

Regarding diagnosis:

- Does individual complain of mild or severe chest pain that may radiate to the shoulder or arms? Does the pain become worse with chest wall movement related to deep breathing, coughing, or sneezing?
- If individual is quiet and restricts movement, is the pain relieved?
- Does the physician note tenderness or pain when pressure is applied (palpation) to the area?
- Did the physician inject a local anesthetic in the affected area, relieving pain and confirming the diagnosis?
- Were underlying conditions ruled out with a chest x-ray, electrocardiogram (ECG), and blood tests (serology)?
- Does a bone (gallium) scan need to be done?

Regarding treatment:

- Have medications such as pain relievers and/or anti-inflammatory drugs provided relief from symptoms? Have other measures provided relief?
- Was individual compliant with medications and treatments?
- Does individual need a corticosteroid?

Regarding prognosis:

- Did individual require treatment or did the condition resolve on its own?
- Was this caused by an injury or underlying disorder? Were these conditions addressed?
- Does individual have inherited costochondritis?
- Does individual have an underlying disorder that is causing costochondritis-like pain? Is individual being treated for the underlying disorder? Was treatment for the disorder successful?

References

Flowers, Lynn K., and Brian D. Wippermann, MD. Costochondritis. eMedicine.com 20 Nov 2000. 07 Jan 2001 <http://www.emedicine.com/emerg/topic116.htm>.

Scanlon, Patrick, MD, et al. "ACC/AHA Guidelines for Coronary Angiography." American College of Cardiology 33 6 1999: 30. Jan 2001 <http://www.acc.org/clinical/guidelines/coronary/jac6292fla4.htm>.

Craniectomy

Other names / synonyms: Brain Surgery
01.25

Definition

Craniectomy is the surgical removal of a portion of skull (cranium) in order to provide adequate exposure to the surface of the brain. This exposure provides the surgeon with access to treat bleeding caused by head trauma or to drain brain abscesses. A craniectomy also allows surgical treatment of diseases that affect the cranial nerves supplying sensation and movement to the structures of the head and neck. The procedure is classified as an emergency when pressure within the skull (usually from bleeding within the brain or its coverings) increases to a dangerous level (increased intracranial pressure).

A craniectomy is performed in a major operating room under general anesthesia. Craniectomy procedures vary in length depending on the difficulty involved in locating the bleeding (hematoma) or abscess or in dissecting around the involved cranial nerve.

Reason for Procedure

Craniectomy is most commonly performed to remove (evacuation) a collection of blood and blood clots (hematomas) from beneath the skull. Hematomas beneath the skull take up space, compress the brain, and decrease the flow of blood and oxygen to brain tissue. If not removed promptly, hematomas often cause permanent brain damage. When found between the skull and outer covering of the brain (dura mater), hematomas are called epidural hematomas. Those found between the outer and middle coverings of the brain are called subdural hematomas.

Craniectomy performed at the base of the skull is called suboccipital craniectomy. This approach allows exploration of the lower back portion of the brain (posterior fossa) and surgical treatment of diseases affecting certain cranial nerves. Through a suboccipital craniectomy, the fifth cranial nerve (trigeminal nerve) can be decompressed or deliberately cut in order to treat severe facial pain (trigeminal neuralgia). The ninth cranial nerve (glossopharyngeal nerve) can be cut to treat severe pain originating in the throat and spreading to the ear (glossopharyngeal neuralgia). This approach may also be used to remove tumors (acoustic neuromas) from the hearing (auditory) canal, or to cut a portion of the eighth cranial nerve (the vestibular branch of the vestibulocochlear nerve) when surgically treating Ménière's disease.

How Procedure Is Performed

Craniectomy is done in the operating room under general anesthesia. An incision is made in the scalp above the location of the hematoma, abscess, or other condition to be treated while the tissues are held open with small retractors. A bone flap is not turned. Instead, one or more small holes (burr holes) are drilled into the skull with a special drill. The edges of the burr holes are chipped away (rongeuer) to enlarge the opening. If a larger opening is needed, a circular saw or a router blade craniotome may be used to connect the burr holes. The circular piece of bone is then removed, exposing a larger work surface for the surgeon.

The collection of blood, clots, or bloody fluid is suctioned out. To control vascular bleeding, the blood vessel is burned (cauterized) the blood vessel or clamped with clips. The brain is irrigated with saline irrigating solution until the return runs clear. A drain may be placed under the skull or dura mater and brought to the outside through a puncture hole in the scalp. The bone is not replaced, although under some circumstances, the long gap is filled with an acrylic material molded in the shape of the skull. The incision is closed and the wound is covered with a sterile dressing.

Prognosis

Predicted outcome after a craniectomy depends upon the underlying condition, the success of the surgical procedure performed through this approach, and the number and severity of postoperative complications. Individuals who suffer permanent brain damage from bleeding, infection, or increased intracranial pressure may have decreased cognitive ability. They may not be able to perform tasks they could before surgery. In some cases, the impairment can be severe enough and requires permanent disability. Individuals with acoustic neuromas removed through a suboccipital craniectomy may experience permanent hearing loss and incapacitating balance problems.

Specialists

- Neurosurgeon

Rehabilitation

Rehabilitative therapy for individuals who have undergone a craniectomy is aimed at restoring the functions required for activities of daily living. Therapy may range in intensity from minimal to long-term chronic rehabilitative care depending on the nature and severity of the injury or disease requiring treatment through a craniectomy approach. For example, an individual with a craniectomy for an epidural hematoma following head trauma may require physical, occupational, speech, and cognitive therapy in an inpatient rehabilitative center for several months.

Individuals undergoing craniectomy to treat disorders of the cranial nerves have outpatient rehabilitation plans geared toward the effects of injury to the cranial nerves such as difficulties in hearing, swallowing, maintaining balance, and using the muscles of facial expression. Such therapy continues until maximum restoration of function or adjustment to loss of function is attained and could take several weeks to several months.

Work Restrictions / Accommodations

Individuals who have undergone a craniectomy have portions of their brains unprotected by bone. These individuals risk severe injury if assigned to work in an environment that contains moving equipment, falling objects, or similar hazards.

Those who have undergone surgery on their cranial nerves may have decreased sensation and movement in their mouths and the structures of the face and require certain restrictions and accommodations. For example, individuals with decreased sensation of the facial skin may have difficulty judging the severity of temperatures and be at risk for frostbite or severe sunburn if working outdoors. Individuals experiencing chronic pain as a result of damage to the cranial nerves during neurological surgery may have difficulty maintaining the level of concentration required of their presurgery assignment. Individuals with damage to the facial nerve during removal of an acoustic neuroma may not be able to completely close their eyes on the affected side and would be ill suited for environments that involve dust and other irritating particles or fumes. Individuals left with balance problems after surgical removal of an acoustic neuroma may require transfer to a sedentary job.

Individuals with surgery on the glossopharyngeal nerve may have a decreased gag reflex and difficulty swallowing (dysphagia). This situation requires a well-developed safety program with an emphasis on emergency care for a choking individual. Individuals may also have trouble making certain sounds and being easily understood over the telephone.

Comorbid Conditions

When a craniectomy is performed because of head trauma, the individual often has other major internal and orthopedic injuries. Other comorbid conditions include underlying medical conditions that put the individual at a higher risk for surgical procedures include diabetes, heart disease, and pulmonary disease.

Procedure Complications

Complications of surgery performed through a craniectomy approach include bleeding, swelling of brain tissue resulting in nerve cell damage, wound infection, cranial nerve damage, leakage of the fluid covering the brain (cerebrospinal fluid), and headache (postoperative headache). Air that enters a vein (venous air embolism) can form an air bubble, block off a small vessel, and cause a stroke. Complications of general anesthesia include allergic reaction to the anesthetic agent (anaphylaxis), decreased respiratory rate or effort, airway obstruction, and partial or complete collapse of the lung (atelectasis). A rare but often fatal complication of general anesthesia is a rapid rise in body temperature (malignant hyperthermia).

Factors Influencing Duration

Factors influencing the length of disability include the reason for the craniectomy, success or lack of success in treating the condition, complications, coexisting diseases affecting any of the major body systems, the individual's mental and emotional stability, access to rehabilitation facilities, and the strength of the individual's support system.

Length of Disability

Disability may be permanent.

Duration in Days

Job Classification	Minimum	Optimum	Maximum
Sedentary work	21	42	Indefinite
Light work	28	42	Indefinite
Medium work	35	56	Indefinite
Heavy work	42	56	Indefinite
Very Heavy work	42	56	Indefinite

References

Meeker, Margaret H., and Jane C. Rothrock. Alexander's Care of the Patient in Surgery. St. Louis: Mosby, 1999.

Tierney, Lawrence M., Jr., Stephen J. McPhee, and Maxine A. Papadakis, eds. Current Medical Diagnosis and Treatment. New York: Lange Medical Books/McGraw-Hill, 2000.

Craniotomy

Other names / synonyms: Brain Surgery

01.24

Definition

Craniotomy refers to the removal of part of the skull bone (cranium) in order to perform an operation on the brain.

Conditions that may require surgical intervention include epilepsy; movement disorders, such as Parkinson's disease; tumors; psychiatric disorders that do not respond to medical treatment; and chronic pain, particularly when it affects the face, such as in trigeminal neuralgia.

Reason for Procedure

A craniotomy is done to reach the brain tissue in order to perform a biopsy, remove a tumor, drain an abscess, remove a blood clot, and to repair a weak blood vessel (cerebral aneurysm). This procedure is also done to stop bleeding after head trauma, to treat epilepsy, and to treat certain kinds of nerve pain in the face (trigeminal neuralgia and tic douloureux).

How Procedure Is Performed

Prior to the operation, the individual is given a general anesthetic and part, or all, of the scalp is shaved. The layers of skin, muscle, and membrane are cut away from the skull. A series of holes (burr holes) are bored into the skull. Using a router blade craniotome, the skull is cut between the burr holes. The piece of bone is then either lifted back (on a hinge of muscle) or removed completely. The outer membrane lining the brain (dura) is coagulated and opened. A small incision is made through the inner membranes to access the area of the brain that requires surgery. Once the brain tissue is revealed, the surgeon either removes, stimulates electrically, or disconnects or interrupts the area of the brain that has been identified as the cause of the problem.

After the operation, the piece of bone is replaced, and the membranes, muscle, and skin are sewn back into place.

Prognosis

Complete recovery from craniotomy, regardless of the reason for the surgery, may take up to 8 weeks. Generally, disorders such as epilepsy, movement disorder, tumor, or chronic pain respond very well to surgical intervention.

Specialists

- Neurosurgeon

Rehabilitation

Individuals who undergo craniotomy may require a variety of rehabilitation services depending on the location and treatments required. Physical therapy and occupational therapy may be required for a range of services including general conditioning exercises if the individual is weakened from the surgery to functional skills retraining, depending on which areas of the brain were affected.

Physical therapy focuses on stretching and strengthening any weakened muscles. Individuals and their family members learn to perform a stretching and strengthening program. Physical therapy may be required for gait and transfer training if the individual's balance and coordination has been affected. Physical therapists teach individuals to roll in bed, to transfer from lying to sitting, and to transfer from sitting to standing. Individuals also learn mobility techniques such as walking and climbing stairs. Therapists may need to teach individuals to walk with a cane or walker if balance remains impaired. For those individuals unable to walk, the physical therapist may order a wheelchair.

Speech therapy may be needed to promote clarity in speech, swallowing ability, and the understanding of speech if the areas of the brain that control these activities were affected. Speech therapy may be required to strengthen the muscles of the face for improved speech and swallowing.

Respiratory therapy may be required to decrease congestion in the lungs, particularly if an individual is bedridden for a period of time. Respiratory therapists may perform chest percussion and utilize positioning techniques to promote the drainage of fluid/phlegm from the lungs. The individual may learn coughing techniques to assist in clearing the lungs of phlegm.

Work Restrictions / Accommodations

Responsibilities, such as heavy lifting, strenuous physical duties, or use of fine motor skills and driving may need to be modified for an extended period of time. The individual may require time off to attend physical, occupational, or speech therapy sessions. Accommodations for walking difficulties, such as parking in a handicapped area and being allowed more time to get to designated locations, may be required. If the individual has difficulty with speech, telephone duties should be temporarily discontinued. If job skills need to be relearned, time should be allowed for this process. If the individual cannot relearn the job, other opportunities should be sought that the individual is able to do.

Comorbid Conditions

When a craniectomy is performed because of head trauma, the individual will often have other major internal and orthopedic injuries that will affect the length of disability. Other comorbid conditions include diabetes, heart disease, and pulmonary disease.

Procedure Complications

Complications of craniotomy may include infection, bleeding in the brain, and injury to brain tissue causing difficulty with speech or movement.

Factors Influencing Duration

The underlying reason for the craniotomy and the presence of complications may influence the length of disability.

Length of Disability

Duration of disability will depend on job requirements, but may be permanent for individuals who experience brain damage or for individuals with brain cancer.

Duration in Days

Job Classification	Minimum	Optimum	Maximum
Sedentary work	21	42	Indefinite
Light work	28	42	Indefinite
Medium work	35	56	Indefinite
Heavy work	42	56	Indefinite
Very Heavy work	42	56	Indefinite

References

Cosgrove, G. Rees. Functional and Stereotactic Neurosurgery. Massachusetts General Hospital - Harvard Medical School. 21 Jan 2001. 14 Feb 2001 <http://neurosurgery.mgh.harvard.edu/fnctnlhp.htm>.

Guccione, Andrew A. "Functional Assessment." Physical Rehabilitation: Assessment and Treatment. O'Sullivan, Susan B., and Thomas J. Schmitz, eds. Philadelphia: F.A. Davis Company, 1994. 193-208.

Kisner, Carolyn, and Lynn Allen Colby. Therapeutic Exercise: Foundations and Techniques. Philadelphia: F.A. Davis Company, 1990.

MedlinePlus Health Information. "Brain Surgery." Medical Encyclopedia. 2000 19 Jan 2001 <http://medlineplus.adam.com/ency/article/003018ris.htm>.

O'Sullivan, Susan B. "Strategies to Improve Motor Control and Motor Learning." Physical Rehabilitation: Assessment and Treatment. O'Sullivan, Susan B., and Thomas J. Schmitz, eds. Philadelphia: F.A. Davis Company, 1994. 225-250.

Schwartz, Seymour, MD. Principles of Surgery. New York: McGraw-Hill, 1999.

Crohn's Disease

Other names / synonyms: Enteritis, Ileitis, Regional Enteritis

555, 555.0, 555.1, 555.2, 555.9

Definition

Crohn's disease is a type of inflammatory bowel disease. It produces areas of patchy inflammation primarily in the small intestine, but can also produce inflammation in any part of the digestive tract, including the mouth, esophagus, stomach, and colon. Where inflammation exists, it extends into all the tissue layers. This results in abdominal pain, diarrhea, gastrointestinal bleeding, and poor absorption (malabsorption) of nutrients from food.

The disease affects men and women equally and typically develops before the age of 30 years. Although the disease is chronic, usually lasting a lifetime, it produces inflammation intermittently and can be in remission for long periods of time.

The cause of Crohn's disease is unknown, but an immune system abnormality may play a role. Because the disease seems to run in families, there may be a genetic element to its development. Crohn's disease is found in 0.1% of the population and is most common in white and Jewish individuals. Stress is believed to aggravate the disease.

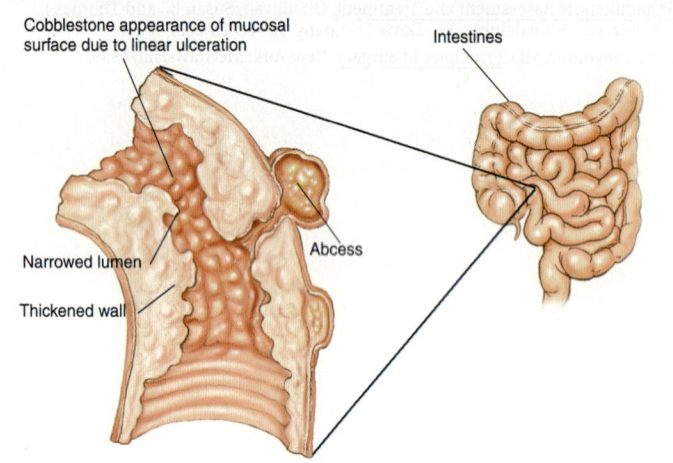

Diagnosis

History: Symptoms vary according to the severity of the disease, the location of the inflammation, and whether intestinal complications have developed. Typically an individual experiences intermittent periods of fever, diarrhea, pain in the lower right abdomen, fatigue, and weight loss.

Sometimes, symptoms develop outside of the digestive tract. Joint pain, swelling, and tenderness are common extraintestinal symptoms.

Physical exam: The exam may reveal tenderness, distention, or a mass when examining the lower right abdomen. During periods of partial obstruction or bloody diarrhea, excessive bowel sounds may be heard. Ulcers may be found in the mouth and abscesses or fistulas near the anus and rectum. The tongue may be inflamed (atrophic glossitis).

Joint involvement may be found, as well as enlargement of the liver and spleen. There may be areas of inflammation on the back of the legs (erythema nodosum).

Tests: Barium contrast x-rays taken of the intestine reveal patchy areas of inflammation ("cobblestone" appearance), ulcers, narrowing (strictures), or abnormal passageways due to erosion of the intestine (fistulas).

Endoscopy of the small intestine (esophagogastroduodenoscopy) or colon (colonoscopy) enables visualization of these intestinal abnormalities. Thick firm areas of inflammation (granulomas) may be discovered. Biopsy of these areas can confirm the diagnosis.

Laboratory tests measure and monitor the effects of inflammation, such as anemia, infection, and malabsorption. An increased erythrocyte sedimentation rate ("sed" rate) indicates active inflammation. An increased white blood cell count (WBC) indicates inflammation and possible infection. Microbiologic cultures may be needed to find the cause of a bacterial or parasitic infection.

Chronic bleeding may lead to anemia, and will cause the hematocrit and hemoglobin to be decreased. Chronic diarrhea results in low blood levels of potassium, magnesium, calcium, and albumin. Malabsorption results in low vitamin B12 and folate levels. Positive fecal occult blood test indicates blood in the stool.

Treatment

Crohn's disease cannot be cured, but its symptoms can be controlled through nutrition and diet modifications, medication, and sometimes surgery.

Nutrition is important in this disease, so a diet adequate in calories, vitamins, and protein is recommended. Diet modifications vary according to the symptoms of the disease. During periods of diarrhea, a low-fat, high-fiber diet should be followed. In contrast, early in the relapse of the disease or if symptoms of obstruction are present, a low-fiber diet is needed. During an acute stage of the disease, no food should be taken by mouth in order to rest the colon.

Sometimes, especially with advanced disease, nutritional supplementation is needed. Nutrients may be placed directly into the stomach or intestine through a tube (enteral therapy) or into the bloodstream intravenously (total parenteral nutrition, or TPN).

Anti-inflammatory drugs of the 5-amino salicylic acid group are given to reduce inflammation. Corticosteroids reduce inflammation during an acute attack, but are given for only a few months at a time because they may cause significant long-term adverse effects. Immunosuppressive drugs are given to help relieve symptoms in individuals with severe progressive disease who have not responded to other treatments.

Iron may be needed to treat anemia, and vitamin B12 injections may be needed due to malabsorption, particularly if there is advanced disease of the small intestine. When abscesses are present, antibiotics are given to fight the infection. Bile salt binding agents or other antidiarrheal medications may be helpful during episodes of diarrhea. These, however, should be used with caution.

Many individuals gain significant relief from surgery in which a portion of the intestine is removed (resection). In severe disease, the entire colon may be removed (colectomy). Depending on how much of the intestine is removed, a temporary or permanent passageway may need to be created through which waste materials can be emptied. Surgery may also be needed to remove a fistula (fistulectomy) or open an obstructed portion of intestine (stricturoplasty).

As with any chronic disease, living with Crohn's disease is challenging. Psychotherapy or participation in a support group may help an individual cope with the particular difficulties of Crohn's disease and the general difficulties of chronic disease.

Prognosis

With medical and surgical management, individuals with Crohn's disease can be fully functioning throughout a long life. The disease will have periods of exacerbation and periods of remission, but typically does not lead to death.

Drug treatment is effective, but may require a long period of time before results are seen for some complications. For example, drug treatment for fistulas may take 3-6 months. For many individuals, surgery brings symptomatic relief that lasts from 5-15 years.

Differential Diagnosis

Crohn's disease may be confused with other inflammatory bowel diseases, such as ulcerative colitis, irritable bowel syndrome, and diverticulitis. The symptoms of parasitic, fungal, or bacterial infections may mimic the symptoms of Crohn's disease, as can colon cancer, lymphoma, AIDS, and appendicitis.

Specialists

- Colorectal Surgeon
- Gastroenterologist
- General Surgeon

Work Restrictions / Accommodations

Flexible and private lavatory access may be needed, particularly during periods of exacerbation. Severe attacks may require a lighter work assignment or time off for recovery or hospitalization. If surgery is performed, individuals may need to be restricted from heavy lifting for a short period.

Complementary and Alternative Therapies

Content is intended for awareness only. Treatments may or may not be effective. Scientific evidence may be lacking and some substances have potentially toxic effects. Dr. Presley Reed and the editors do not endorse the use of these therapies in the absence of consultation with a licensed medical professional.

Enteric-coated fish oil -	Fish oil has anti-inflammatory properties.
Zinc -	May remove free radicals that may be responsible for inflammation; studies in progress.
Hypnosis -	May enable individual to handle stress and control autoimmune antibodies that may play a role in the disease.

Comorbid Conditions

Presence of psychiatric conditions may lengthen disability.

Complications

Inflammation can lead to narrowing (stricture) and blocking (obstruction) of the intestines; the development of abnormal passageways (fistulas) leading from the intestine to another part of the body such as the skin, bladder, vagina, or another portion of the intestine; and areas of infection (abscesses). Repeated excision of obstructed segments of intestine can lead to the short bowel syndrome, which exaggerates the symptoms of diarrhea, weight loss, and malnutrition.

Bleeding from inflamed areas may develop into severe hemorrhage, although this is uncommon. Inflammation and diarrhea make it difficult for nutrients to be absorbed through the wall of the small intestine. This may lead to a state of malnutrition. The colon may expand and develop into a condition known as toxic megacolon.

Individuals with Crohn's disease may develop other disorders outside of the gastrointestinal tract, such as arthritis, skin problems, eye and mouth inflammation, kidney stones, gallstones, and liver disease. Crohn's disease increases the risk of colon cancer, a development that significantly influences the severity of the disease.

Long-term use of corticosteroids may cause osteoporosis, cataracts, diabetes, hypertension, and aseptic necrosis of the hip.

Factors Influencing Duration

The length and frequency of disability will depend on several factors: the degree of inflammation, the amount of bleeding, the individual's nutritional state, and the extent to which an individual's disease can be controlled through diet and medication. If abscesses, obstruction, or fistulas are present, surgery may be needed. Although surgery results in immediate disability, the potential for greater symptomatic relief will typically decrease future disability.

Smoking has been found to increase the recurrence rate of Crohn's disease.

Length of Disability

Medical treatment.

Duration in Days

Job Classification	Minimum	Optimum	Maximum
Sedentary work	7	14	28
Light work	7	14	28
Medium work	7	14	28
Heavy work	7	14	28
Very Heavy work	7	14	28

Surgical treatment (ileostomy with bowel resection).

Duration in Days

Job Classification	Minimum	Optimum	Maximum
Sedentary work	28	42	70
Light work	28	56	70
Medium work	42	63	84
Heavy work	56	84	112
Very Heavy work	56	98	126

Duration Trend from Normative Data*

Cases	Mean	Min	Max	No Lost Time	Over 6 Months
733	57	0	594	1.91%	2.05%

Percentile:	5th	25th	Median	75th	95th
Days:	7	21	41	71	155

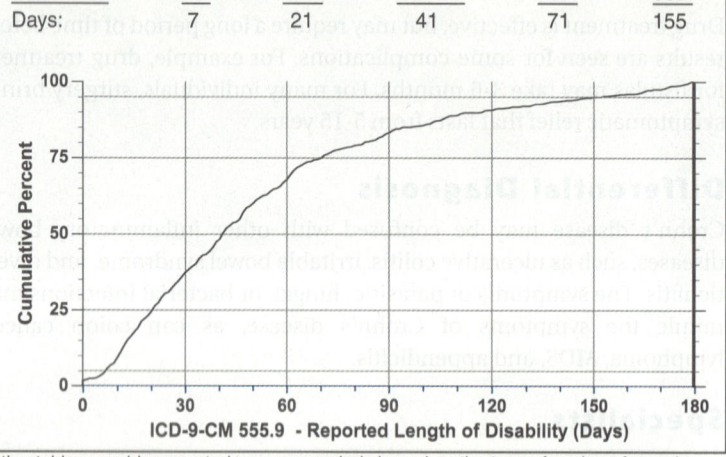

ICD-9-CM 555.9 - Reported Length of Disability (Days)

* Differences may exist between the expected duration tables and the normative graphs. Duration tables provide expected recovery periods based on the type of work performed by the individual. The normative graphs reflect the actual observed experience of many individuals across the spectrum of physical conditions, in a variety of industries, and with varying levels of case management.

Failure to Recover

If an individual fails to recover within the maximum duration expectancy period, the reader may wish to reference the following questions to assist in better understanding the specifics of an individual's medical case.

Regarding diagnosis:

- Does the individual, or the individual's family, have a history of Crohn's disease?
- Does the individual complain of intermittent periods of fever, diarrhea, pain in the lower right abdomen, fatigue, and/or weight loss?
- Has the individual experienced symptoms outside of the digestive tract (extraintestinal), such as pain, swelling, and tenderness in the joints?
- Does the individual complain of sores in the mouth and an inflamed tongue?
- Were barium contrast x-rays taken of the intestine?
- Was endoscopy of the small intestine (esophagogastroduodenoscopy) or colon (colonoscopy) done?
- Was a tissue sample (biopsy) of the intestine taken to confirm the diagnosis?
- Was a complete blood count (CBC) done to rule out anemia and infection?
- Was an erythrocyte sedimentation rate (ESR) done to verify an active inflammation?
- Were blood chemistries done to determine if electrolytes are low due to diarrhea?
- Were vitamin B12 and folate levels tested to determine if the individual has a malabsorption problem?
- Was a stool sample tested for unseen (occult) blood? Has the diagnosis been confirmed?

Regarding treatment:

- Is the individual on a diet that is adequate in calories, vitamins, and protein?
- Is the individual compliant with the diet and supplement regimens?
- If the disease is advanced, is the individual receiving nutritional supplementation, such as enteral therapy or total parenteral nutrition (TPN)?
- Is the individual taking anti-inflammatory medication? Has the individual responded to the medication?
- If the individual has not responded to anti-inflammatory drugs, does the individual require immunosuppressive drugs?

602 *The Medical Disability Advisor—Fourth Edition*

- If the individual is anemic or has pernicious anemia, are iron or vitamin B12 being taken, respectively?
- Does the individual require surgery to remove part or all of the colon (partial or total colectomy, respectively)?
- Was a temporary or permanent passageway surgically created through which waste materials can be emptied (colostomy)?
- Would the individual benefit from psychotherapy and/or participation in a support group to cope with the illness?

Regarding prognosis:

- Has the individual experienced short- or long-term adverse effects of the medication?
- Is the individual malnourished, prolonging recovery?
- Did the individual require surgery to alleviate symptoms of the disease? If so, what surgery was required? Were there any postsurgical complications?
- Has the individual experienced narrowing (stricture) or blocking (obstruction) of the intestines?
- Have abnormal passageways (fistulas) developed from the intestine to another part of the body such as the skin, bladder, vagina?

References

Crohn's Disease. National Digestive Diseases Information Clearinghouse. 01 Apr 2000. 26 Jun 2000 <http://www.niddk.nih.gov/health/digest/pubs/crohns/crohns.htm>.

Ferri, Fred. Ferri's Clinical Advisor. St. Louis: Mosby, 2000.

Crush Wounds

Other names / synonyms: Crush Injury

925, 925.1, 925.2, 926, 926.0, 926.1, 926.11, 926.12, 926.19, 926.8, 926.9, 927, 927.0, 927.00, 927.01, 927.02, 927.03, 927.09, 927.1, 927.10, 927.11, 927.2, 927.20, 927.21, 927.3, 927.8, 927.9, 928, 928.0, 928.00, 928.01, 928.1, 928.10, 928.11, 928.2, 928.20, 928.21, 928.3, 928.8, 928.9, 929, 929.0, 929.9

Definition

Crush wounds with severe trauma most commonly occur in multiple casualty disasters such as bombings, earthquakes, building collapse, train accidents, and mining accidents. They are the result of prolonged compression or pressure on various parts or all of the body. Crush injuries may result in fatal injury or severe metabolic abnormalities that can result in death. Careful monitoring of these individuals is essential.

A New Jersey study of 1,575 individuals with work-related injuries found that 13.8% had crush injuries of the lower limb. In Japan, 6.1% of the 6,107 victims of a single earthquake were diagnosed retrospectively with crush syndrome and 13.4% subsequently died. The major sites of crush injury were in the lower extremities (74%), followed by the upper extremities (10%) and the trunk (9%).

Diagnosis

History: The individual's crush wounds may result from a fall, industrial or transportation accident, weapons, or explosives. Dangerous symptoms that could lead to death from crush syndrome are low fluid volume (extreme hypovolemic shock), high blood potassium concentrations (hyperkalemia), low blood calcium concentration (hypocalcemia), metabolic acidosis, acute myoglobinuric kidney (renal) failure, and compromised circulation and function of tissues within a compartment bounded by bone (compartment syndrome).

Physical exam: Vital signs (blood pressure, pulse, and respiration) are closely monitored. Injuries to the chest or abdomen may cause shallow, restricted breathing. Arrhythmias may be present. The number of injured extremities determines the severity of crush syndrome.

Tests: X-rays, MRI, and CT may identify internal injuries. Peak serum concentration of creatine kinase is measured to estimate the severity of crush syndrome.

Treatment

Treatment for individuals with multiple crush wounds consists of early administration of intravenous fluids preferably given at the site where trauma occurred, followed by an osmotic diuretic (mannitol) that prevents reabsorption of water by the kidney. This treatment can prevent shock and arrhythmias. With this regimen, survival of lives and limbs increases substantially as does prevention of acute myoglobinuric renal failure in individuals suffering from crush syndrome. Arrhythmia and other heart problems are treated with continuous oxygen at high pressure (hyperbaric oxygenation) and fluid and electrolyte replacement.

Crush injuries can be severe and devastating to the individual with long-term impairment and disability. Crush injuries not only result in damage to the overlying soft tissue envelope, but also result in damage to the neurovascular structures and the bony and ligamentous supportive structures. Treatment varies according to the nature of the crush wound. In an acute situation, it may be difficult to decide whether an attempt at a salvage procedure should be made or whether a primary amputation should be performed. There are situations when a primary amputation of an extremity is the treatment of choice.

Prognosis

Outcome varies with the extent of the crush wound. Outcome is excellent for otherwise healthy individuals who do not go into shock, with injuries that do not require mechanical ventilation or amputation, and if minor or no surgery is required.

A crush wound too badly torn to repair results in either amputation of the crushed limb or can become gangrenous. Recovery after amputation can be complete, however, the individual can die from other complications of crush syndrome.

Since the 1950s, mechanical lungs have been used to force breath into an individual with crush wounds to the chest (intermittent positive pressure ventilator). With this treatment, individuals will most likely survive if they have not suffered massive internal bleeding.

Differential Diagnosis

The diagnosis is evident.

Specialists

- Emergency Medicine
- General Surgeon
- Neurologist
- Neurosurgeon
- Orthopedic Surgeon
- Physiatrist

Rehabilitation

Crush wounds require a multilevel approach to rehabilitation since they involve damage to the muscle, bone, nerve, and tissue. Another complication with crush wounds is that they usually do not affect one body part. Although usually confined to a general area of the body, these types of wounds may involve both legs and the pelvis. Severe deformity and psychological trauma usually result from these types of injuries. In their mildest form, a crush wound may only affect a finger or toe. The rehabilitation processes is less acute and time consuming although complications from deadening of tissue or bone due to insufficient blood supply (necrosis) are always present. For more severe cases, the rehabilitation process is arduous and requires the combined effort of many healthcare professionals such as physical, occupational, and vocational therapists as well psychiatric and/or psychological professionals.

Exercise rehabilitation is progressed slowly in all cases. Therapy protocol varies greatly due to the wide range of possible outcomes. For example, if the crush injury effects the flexor mechanism of the hand, a splint with the involved fingers placed in dynamic traction by an elastic thread attached from the finger nails to the outer splint may be worn. This mechanism helps take pressure off the healing flexor structures while the hand is not in motion. Light tension is achieved, however, when the individual extends the fingers.

Early mobilization of the fingers within the cast also helps reduce the adhesion formation that can limit motion and slow progress of therapy. If the injury involves a fractured femur (long bone of the leg), the individual may perform muscle-sets involving isometric tightening of a set of muscles such as the quadriceps or gastrocnemius. These exercises can be initiated while the leg is still immobilized. In addition, electromuscular stimulation may be used for accessible leg muscles such as quadriceps, gastrocnemius, and tibialis anterior. The individual may undergo treatments for both upper and lower body simultaneously. All treatments are performed to pain tolerance.

If the limb must be amputated, the individual should begin education on prosthetics. Rehabilitation protocol should be redesigned to teach daily living skills and functioning given the absence of the limb. If rehabilitation progresses, the individual advances to exercises that include an active range of motion. For example, an active range-of-motion exercise for the hand consists of the hand in full extension. For lower body areas such as the knee, active exercises in the direction of the free range of motion are necessary to maintain that motion. Exercises such as leg extension in a short arc may be performed. Each exercise, however, must be based on the extent of injury and current level of function.

Another important aspect of rehabilitation is scar tissue care. If there is continued pain, ice massage or heat should be applied before and after any exercise treatment. The individual may also experience extreme sensitivity to the site of surgery. Activities that decrease hypersensitivity (desensitization) for the hand include materials with differing textures being rubbed, taped, or rolled over the sensitive area for either continuous or intermittent intervals.

Once any pins or rods are fully removed from the limb, more functional exercises such as gripping and turning a door handle are performed. It may take as long as 2 to 3 months for the individual to attempt actual weight bearing on lower extremities. The individual is taught to use a wheelchair. Other therapy during this time may include participating in an aqua or whirlpool routine. The warmth and massaging action of the water helps increase blood flow throughout the body and increases range of motion for the hips, legs, and arms. Initially, the individual may engage in deep water walking or bicycling using a flotation device. The exercise simulates normal movement and serves to improve aerobic conditioning. Individuals experiencing an amputated arm use the pool to regain body balance.

In combination with an exercise routine, an occupational therapist may start to evaluate remaining function. Occupational therapy is especially important for those individuals who have lost a limb. It is not uncommon for an individual with a crush wound to experience organ damage. Breathing may also be affected depending on the location of the wound. All these issues affect the individual's ability to return to work.

Work Restrictions / Accommodations

Possible work restrictions and special accommodations are determined on an individual basis. For example, an individual whose legs have been amputated may no longer be able to work in an occupation that requires use of both legs such as a construction worker, roofer, or beat policeman. An individual with a sedentary job may return to work. Vehicles may need to be modified to allow an amputee to drive and maintain a profession that requires driving.

Comorbid Conditions

Comorbid conditions that slow full recovery include cancer, diabetes, heart disease, obesity, osteoporosis, and previous limb injuries.

Complications

Severe systemic manifestation of trauma and ischemia involving soft tissues (primarily skeletal muscle) is due to prolonged severe crushing. This leads to increased permeability of the cell membrane and to release of potassium, enzymes, and myoglobin from within cells. Ischemic renal dysfunction secondary to hypotension and diminished renal perfusion results in acute tubular necrosis and uremia.

Other possible complications include increased clotting of blood (hypercoagulability) that results in deep vein thrombosis and pulmonary embolism, immune suppression that results in infection at the wound site or systemic, hemorrhagic shock, and fat embolism that results in lack of oxygen in the blood (acute hypoxia). Raised pressure within a closed compartment (acute compartment syndrome) is a serious complication of crush syndrome.

Factors Influencing Duration

Disability factors include loss of limb, age and overall health of the individual, and any complications.

Length of Disability

Length of disability depends on the location and severity of the injury, and job requirements. In some cases, disability will be permanent.

Failure to Recover

If an individual fails to recover within the maximum duration expectancy period, the reader may wish to reference the following questions to assist in better understanding the specifics of an individual's medical case.

Regarding diagnosis:

- Was individual involved in a multiple casualty accident?
- How long was the body part compressed?
- Has individual developed hypovolemic shock? Hyperkalemia or hypocalcemia?
- Does individual have metabolic acidosis? Renal failure? Compartment syndrome?
- Is individual's breathing shallow? Are cardiac arrhythmias present?
- Did individual have x-rays, MRI, and CT? Was peak serum concentration of creatine kinase done?

Regarding treatment:

- Did individual receive intravenous fluids at the trauma site?
- Were arrhythmias and other heart problems treated with hyperbaric oxygenation?
- Did individual receive fluid and electrolyte replacement?
- Was the limb salvaged? Was a primary amputation done?
- Was an amputation done later secondary to gangrene?

Regarding prognosis:

- Is individual in a rehabilitation program?
- Are the appropriate professionals on the rehabilitation team?
- Can individual's employer accommodate any necessary restrictions?
- Does individual have any conditions that may affect ability to recover?
- Are there any complications such as renal failure, deep vein thrombosis, or pulmonary embolism that may affect recovery?

References

Better, O.S. "Rescue and Salvage of Casualties Suffering from the Crush Syndrome After Mass Disasters." Mil Medicine 164 5 (1999): 366-369.

Miranda, Michael. "Management of Severe Lower Extremity Trauma: Early Care and Outcome Considerations." Complications in Orthopedics 12 01 (1997): 4. 14 Jan 2001 <http://www.medscape.com/SCP/CIO/1997/v12.n01/o650.miranda/o650.miranda.html>.

Cryotherapy, Genital Warts (Female)
71.3, 86.3

Definition

Cryotherapy (cryosurgery, cryocautery) of genital warts is a procedure used to destroy warts by freezing. In women, genital warts can involve the external genitalia (vulva), birth canal (vagina), opening to the uterus (cervix), and anus.

Genital warts are caused from the sexually transmitted human papilloma virus (HPV). Warts may occur singly but most often occur in large numbers. Women who have had their first sexual activity at an early age and those with multiple sexual partners are at an increased risk of developing genital warts. In the US, one million cases of genital warts are diagnosed each year.

Reason for Procedure

Cryotherapy is used to remove genital warts. Genital warts can be disfiguring, itchy, painful, and can bleed. Twenty percent of cervical warts progress to cancer so all cervical warts should be removed.

How Procedure Is Performed

Cryotherapy is an outpatient procedure routinely performed in the physician's office. It is also performed in outpatient surgery centers and the hospital. The individual lies on the exam table with legs in the stirrups (lithotomy position). For warts within the vagina or on the cervix, an instrument (speculum) is inserted into the vagina to hold it open to allow visualization of the cervix. A surface anesthetic or local nerve block may be administered a few minutes prior to cryotherapy. The two methods of cryotherapy are the cryogun and liquid nitrogen. Cryogun enables the physician to control the freeze time and size of the treated region. As a result, cryogun is frequently used for gynecologic cryotherapy. The cryogun uses a metal probe chilled through expansion of a compressed gas (nitrous oxide or carbon dioxide) to a temperature well below freezing. The probe is coated with a jelly and touched to the wart.

Alternatively, a liquid nitrogen-soaked cotton swab is touched to the wart or a liquid nitrogen spray applied. Both the cryogun and the liquid nitrogen method cause rapid freezing and destruction of the tissue. The freeze zone encompasses a small amount of healthy skin surrounding the wart. Small warts are usually frozen once whereas large warts may be frozen twice. More than one treatment may be necessary. Analgesics and antibiotics are prescribed, as needed.

Prognosis

Treated areas heal within 1 to 3 weeks. Cryotherapy has a cure rate of 60-70% for warts. Both the cryogun and liquid nitrogen can successfully destroy genital warts, but use of a cryogun is more precise and has fewer complications. Because cryotherapy does not always kill the virus that lives in skin cells, genital warts recur approximately 20% of the time.

Specialists

- Dermatologist
- Gynecologist
- Primary Care Provider
- Urologist

Work Restrictions / Accommodations

Other than time off for follow-up appointments and repeat treatments, no work restrictions or accommodations are required.

Comorbid Conditions

Pregnancy, conditions associated with decreased immune function (e.g., AIDS, cancer, organ transplant recipients), and other sexually transmitted diseases such as syphilis, herpes, or gonorrhea may influence the length of disability.

Procedure Complications

Complications associated with cryotherapy of genital warts include bleeding, blistering, swelling, decreased pigmentation (hypopigmentation), hair loss, infection, changes in sensation, and scarring. Cold-sensitive individuals may experience hives (urticaria) and fainting (syncope). Cryotherapy of the vagina or cervix can also cause intense cramping, watery discharge, and upwardly spreading (ascending) infection. Cryotherapy of the cervix can lead to narrowing (stenosis) of the cervical canal.

Factors Influencing Duration

The development of complications, severity of the warts, and number of warts may influence the length of disability.

Length of Disability

Cryotherapy does not generally cause disability.

Duration in Days

Job Classification	Minimum	Optimum	Maximum
Any work	0	1	2

References

Jackson, Arthur. "Cryosurgery: A Guide for GPs." The Practitioner 245 (1999): 131-136.

Wetmore, Stephen. "Cryosurgery for Common Skin Lesions." Canadian Family Physician 45 (1999): 964-974.

Cryotherapy, Genital Warts (Male)

Other names / synonyms: Liquid Nitrogen Treatment
64.2, 86.3

Definition

Cryotherapy is the application of chemical agents at extremely low temperatures to unwanted tissue, including male genital warts, resulting in localized tissue death and wart removal.

While a number of cryotherapy cooling agents have been used in the past, including a salt-ice mixture (-20 degrees centigrade) and carbon dioxide snow (-80 degrees centigrade), liquid nitrogen (-196 degrees centigrade) is most commonly used to treat male genital warts.

Male genital warts are a sexually transmitted disease that occurs as a result of infection with the human papillomavirus (HPV). HPV is the most prevalent sexually transmitted viral disease in the US; there are 70 known types of HPV. It is estimated that 2% of the sexually active population has visible genital warts; up to 10% of sexually active men are HPV carriers. Nearly 1 million men in the US have visible genital warts, and approximately 5 million men carry the HPV without visible lesions.

Reason for Procedure

Cryotherapy is done to remove male genital warts. It is performed on individuals with visible warts on their penis, scrotum, anus, or any other part of the genital area. Because genital warts are transmitted sexually and are associated with cervical cancer in females, the men are normally treated. The male sexual partners of females who have genital warts are usually referred to a urologist for examination and subsequent treatment.

How Procedure Is Performed

Cryotherapy is done as an outpatient procedure in a doctor's office or clinic. The individual disrobes and puts on a gown that gives the physician access to the genital area. No skin preparation is needed before cryotherapy treatment, and no pre-procedure sedatives or anesthetics are given. Liquid nitrogen is applied to the genital wart using a cotton bud, a spraying device (cryospray), or a metal probe (cryoprobe), and held there until an ice ball forms on the lesion. The ice ball is usually extended to include a few millimeters of normal skin around the wart. The ice ball is then allowed to thaw. This freeze-thaw cycle is repeated several times to achieve maximum destruction of the wart. For some there is a feeling of slight discomfort, for others the pain is moderately severe. It takes approximately 1-2 minutes to treat each wart. After treatment is completed, the area can be washed normally; dressings are not usually required. A skin cream (topical steroid) may be applied once or twice a day for a few days to decrease inflammation of the treated areas. Mild pain-relief medication, such as over-the-counter analgesics, may be needed by a few individuals. The procedure usually needs to be repeated every 2-3 weeks until the warts disappear.

Prognosis

Cryotherapy treatment usually eliminates small penile warts after 2-4 treatments. Clinical studies indicate that genital warts will clear after cryotherapy in 61-93% of cases. Ulceration of the treated area happens very rarely using cryotherapy. Notably, this treatment does not eliminate the HPV infection; even though the genital warts will have disappeared, the individual still carries the virus. Consequently, recurrence of genital warts following cryotherapy usually occurs within months to years, depending upon other medical treatment received.

Cryotherapy results in minimal residual tissue scarring compared with other treatments (electrocautery, surgical excision, laser therapy, topical chemical application) that have been used to treat genital warts.

Specialists

- Dermatologist
- Primary Care Provider
- Urologist

Work Restrictions / Accommodations

The individual may be at the doctor's office or clinic for several hours receiving treatment. No recovery time is needed following cryotherapy; no work restrictions or accommodations are required.

Comorbid Conditions

Individuals with diabetes or other circulatory problems may have longer recovery times if complications should occur following the procedure.

Procedure Complications

Complications of cryotherapy for male genital warts may include blistering, darkening (pigmentation), infection, ulceration, and pitting of the treated areas. Nerve damage may also result.

Factors Influencing Duration

Disability may be lengthened by complications following treatment such as infection, blistering, or ulceration. Genital warts usually need repeated cryotherapy treatment, requiring multiple visits to the physician's office or clinic.

Length of Disability

The individual may require several hours for a single cryotherapy treatment of genital warts. Multiple visits to the treatment center (spaced 2-3 weeks apart) are usually necessary.

Duration in Days

Job Classification	Minimum	Optimum	Maximum
Any work	0	1	2

References

Abdullah, A.N., M. Walzman, and A. Wade. "Treatment of External Genital Warts Comparing Cryotherapy (Liquid Nitrogen) and Trichloroacetic Acid." Sexually Transmitted Diseases 20 (1993): 344-345.

Damstra, R.J., and W.A. van Vloten. "Cryotherapy in the Treatment of Condylomata Acuminata: A Controlled Study of 64 Patients." Journal of Dermatologic Surgery and Oncology 17 3 (1991): 273-276.

Ferenczy, A. "Epidemiology and Clinical Pathophysiology of Condylomata Acuminata." American Journal of Obstetrics and Gynecology 172 4S (1995): 1331-1339.

Sodera, V.K. Minor Surgery in Practice. Cambridge: Cambridge University Press, 1994.

Cryptococcosis

Other names / synonyms: Busse-Buschke Disease, Torula
117.5

Definition

Cryptococcosis is a fungal infection caused by Cryptococcus neoformans. It is found in the soil, especially in areas associated with pigeon droppings. An individual becomes infected by inhaling the fungus when it is released from the soil into the air. In healthy individuals, the infection remains in the airways of the lungs, does not progress to serious disease, and seldom produces significant symptoms.

In individuals who have a weakened immune system (immunocompromised)--such as those with AIDS, transplant recipients, or those who take immunosuppressive medication--the infection frequently progresses into a serious lung infection and spreads throughout the body. Most commonly, the lungs and central nervous system (CNS) are affected. Infection in the CNS can lead to meningitis, the most common manifestation of cryptococcosis. In fact, cryptococcosis is the most common cause of fungal meningitis. Less frequently, infection spreads to the blood, skin, bones, and prostate.

Cryptococcosis is seen primarily in immunocompromised individuals, and is therefore considered an opportunistic infection. The incidence in the general population is 0.2 to 0.9 cases per 100,000 individuals. Among individuals with AIDS, the incidence is 2 to 4 cases per 1,000 individuals. In the US, 5-10% of individuals with AIDS develop cryptococcosis. In Africa, the rate is thirty percent. These reported numbers are believed to be underestimates of the actual occurrence.

Cryptococcosis is found worldwide and in equal numbers among races. More men than women develop the infection, but this is likely due to the higher incidence of HIV infection in men. When corrected for HIV infection, the incidence among men and women is equal.

Diagnosis

History: Healthy individuals seldom have symptoms. When they are present, they typically are nonspecific. Symptoms of lower respiratory tract involvement include fever, cough, shortness of breath, or chest pain. When the infection affects the central nervous system, symptoms may include headache, fever, nausea and vomiting, dizziness, irritability, drowsiness, or confusion.

Physical exam: Physical findings depend on the extent of the infection and the sites involved. If the infection has not progressed, the exam may be normal. Pulmonary involvement may be evidenced by abnormal lung sounds. Central nervous system involvement is associated with signs of neck rigidity and altered mental state (irritability, confusion, dizziness, depressed consciousness). When the skin is involved, small slightly elevated lesions (papules), lesions containing pus (pustules), or ulcers may be present. Joint and bone involvement are evidenced by signs of inflammation or infection (arthritis and osteomyelitis). Other physical findings may point to involvement of other body sites, such as the membrane surrounding the heart (pericardium), heart muscle (myocardium), liver, adrenal glands, kidneys, or prostate.

Tests: Cryptococcus may be identified in microscopic examination of tissue or cerebrospinal fluid (CSF). Serology tests may be performed on blood or CSF to detect the cryptococcal antigen. To rule out meningitis, cerebrospinal spinal fluid (CSF) is obtained through lumbar puncture. Analysis of the CFS reveals increased pressure, increased lymphocytes, fungal cells, increased protein, and decreased glucose. Sputum cultures are positive in only 20% of cases involving the lungs. Confirmation of pulmonary cryptococcosis requires antigen detection in lung (pleural) fluid or culture of lung tissue obtained by placement of a tube inside the bronchi, the thoracic cavity (bronchoscopy or thoracoscopy), or by open lung biopsy.

Treatment

Treatment decisions are based on the body sites involved and on the immune status of the individual. In a healthy individual, primary infection in the lung is often not treated. Symptomatic or progressive infection or any degree of infection in an immunocompromised individual is treated with antifungal drugs until all evidence of disease is gone. It is not uncommon for drugs to be continued for up to 3 years in some individuals. HIV-infected individuals may require a different drug regimen than noninfected individuals. In addition, their treatment is typically life long.

Repeated lumbar punctures or ventricular shunting may be used to relieve high cerebrospinal fluid pressures or increased cerebrospinal fluid within the ventricles of the brain (hydrocephalus). Surgical removal of diseased tissue (resection) may be needed with extensive lung involvement.

Prognosis

Approximately 5-25% of cryptococcosis cases are fatal, regardless of treatment. Most deaths occur within the first few weeks of treatment. Typically deaths involve individuals who are immunocompromised. Among individuals with AIDS, full recovery from cryptococcosis is not expected. Relapse occurs 50% of the time, requiring these individuals to be on lifelong treatment. Meningitis may lead to blindness and permanent neurologic damage.

Symptoms (such as fever, cough, or chest pain) in an immunocompetent individual typically disappear within days to weeks without treatment. Studies have shown that 86-93% of cases of more severe cryptococcal infection (excluding meningitis) in non-HIV-infected individuals are cured with antifungal drugs.

Differential Diagnosis

Conditions with similar symptoms include other types of infective pneumonia or meningitis, central nervous system lymphoma, and brain tumors.

Specialists

- Infectious Disease Physician
- Neurologist
- Neurosurgeon
- Orthopedic Surgeon
- Pulmonologist
- Thoracic Surgeon

Work Restrictions / Accommodations

Uncomplicated primary cryptococcosis does not require work restrictions or accommodations, although some individuals may require time off for recovery. Accommodations may be needed for progressive infection and will depend on the severity and sites of disease. Individuals with meningitis may require extensive time off and may suffer permanent disability.

Cryptococcosis is not spread from person to person. Caution, however, should be used with clothing or other material contaminated with drainage from skin lesions.

Comorbid Conditions

Immunocompromised conditions, such as AIDS, immunosuppressive therapy, organ transplant, and lymphoproliferative malignancy lengthen disability. Diabetes also may lengthen disability.

Complications

Complications are typically associated with cryptococcal meningitis. These include increased cerebrospinal fluid within the ventricles of the brain (hydrocephalus), inflammation of the brain (encephalitis), damage to the optic nerve, inflammation of the blood vessels in the brain stem (brain-stem vasculitis), and lesions on the brain and spinal cord.

Factors Influencing Duration

Length of disability is determined by the presence and severity of disease progression, response to treatment, and development of complications, particularly neurologic complications.

Length of Disability

Duration depends on the organ involved and whether there is central nervous system involvement. Disability may be permanent.

Duration in Days

Job Classification	Minimum	Optimum	Maximum
Sedentary work	3	28	63
Light work	3	28	63
Medium work	3	28	91
Heavy work	3	28	119
Very Heavy work	3	28	119

Failure to Recover

If an individual fails to recover within the maximum duration expectancy period, the reader may wish to reference the following questions to assist in better understanding the specifics of an individual's medical case.

Regarding diagnosis:

- Does individual have a history of AIDS, being a transplant recipient, or taking immunosuppressive medication?
- Does individual have a weakened immune system (immunocompromised) for any other reason?
- Does individual complain of fever, cough, shortness of breath, or chest pain? Headache, fever, nausea and vomiting, dizziness, irritability, drowsiness, or confusion?
- Were abnormal lung sounds heard on examination? Did exam reveal neck rigidity and altered mental state?
- Are other body sites involved such as the membrane surrounding the heart (pericardium), heart muscle (myocardium), liver, adrenal glands, kidneys, or prostate?
- Has microscopic exam of lung tissue identified Cryptococcus neoformans? Was cerebrospinal fluid (CSF) examined to detect the cryptococcal antigen and/or to rule out meningitis?
- Did culture or antigen testing confirm cryptococcosis?

Regarding treatment:

- If individual is healthy, is any treatment required at all?
- If individual is immunocompromised, did treatment include antifungal drugs?
- If individual is HIV-infected, what drug regimen is required? Will this regimen be taken for the rest of individual's life?
- Is individual compliant with drug therapy?
- Does individual have high CSF pressures or increased CSF within the ventricles of the brain (hydrocephalus)? If so, would individual benefit from lumbar puncture or ventricular shunting?
- Does individual have extensive lung involvement? If so, is surgical removal of diseased tissue (resection) required?
- Were there any postsurgical complications?

Regarding prognosis:

- Is individual healthy or immunocompromised?
- What type of immunocompromised condition does individual have?
- What is the percentage of recovery expected?
- Has relapse occurred?
- What is the extent of disease progression?
- Has meningitis developed? If so, how will meningitis be treated and what is expected outcome with treatment?

References

Cryptococcosis. Centers for Disease Control and Prevention, Division of Bacterial and Mycotic Diseases. 04 Apr 2000. 15 Sep 2000 <http://www.cdc.gov/ncidod/dbmd/diseaseinfo/cryptococcosis_t.htm>.

Nunez, Marina, James Peacock, and Robert Chin. "Pulmonary Cryptococcosis in the Immunocompetent Host. Therapy with Oral Fluconazole: A Report of Four Cases and a Review of the Literature." Chest 118 2 (2000): 527-534.

Culdoscopy
70.22

Definition

Culdoscopy is the visual examination of organs inside the female pelvic cavity using a specific type of endoscope (culdoscope), which is inserted through the back wall of the upper vagina (vaginal fornix). Culdoscopy is used to investigate infertility or hormonal (endocrine) problems, unexplained abdominal or pelvic pain, pregnancy that has developed outside the uterus (ectopic pregnancy), and to evaluate the condition in which the lining of the womb transplants to other organs (endometriosis). Culdoscopy can also be used to obtain eggs from an ovary and for sterilization.

Culdoscopy has been replaced by laparoscopy, in which a specific type of endoscope (laparoscope) is inserted through the abdomen to examine the pelvic organs. However, with the recent development of a small flexible culdoscope and procedures that use culdoscopy in combination with other surgical methods, culdoscopy may be making a comeback.

See Laparoscopy for additional information.

Curvature of the Spine, Acquired
Other names / synonyms: Abnormal Spine Curvature, Kyphosis, Lordosis
737, 737.10, 737.20, 737.30, 737.8, 737.9

Definition

Acquired curvature of the spine is the condition in which the spine develops abnormal curves.

The spine is naturally curved. When viewed from the side, the inward (concave posteriorly) curve of the neck (cervical spine) and lower back (lumbar spine) are called lordosis. If this is increased beyond normal, it is called increased (hyper) lordosis. The upper back (thoracic spine) normally has an outward curve (convex posteriorly) and increased curvature in this region is called kyphosis. Scoliosis is a side-to-side deviation in the normally straight vertical line of the spine when viewed from behind. It may or may not include rotation or deformity of the back bones (vertebrae).

Scoliosis is the most common type of abnormal spine curvature. Scoliosis may be combined with kyphosis (kyphoscoliosis) or increased lordosis (lordoscoliosis). Scoliosis in adults may be the progression of spine curvature that went undiagnosed during childhood or can be caused by degeneration of the discs that lie between the bones of the spine (intervertebral discs). Abnormal curvatures may progress, which is related to the age and gender of the individual, the underlying cause, and the degree of the curvature. The greatest progression tends to occur during the accelerated growth spurt of puberty. Although abnormal curvatures may be inborn (congenital) or acquired, most cases are acquired.

Scoliosis may be fixed or compensated. A fixed scoliosis is a change in the structure of the vertebrae that results in a C-shaped or S-shaped spine. Fixed scoliosis is further classified as to the cause (congenital, neuromuscular, and idiopathic) and deformity present. A compensated scoliosis has a flexible segment above or below the major curve and tends to maintain normal body alignment. Neuromuscular and idiopathic scoliosis are the acquired curvatures of the spine.

Idiopathic scoliosis is the most common type of scoliosis and refers to cases in which the cause is unknown. It may occur at any age but usually develops during middle or late childhood. Idiopathic scoliosis is classified according to age of onset (infantile, juvenile, adolescent, or adult). Idiopathic scoliosis tends to run in families.

Neuromuscular scoliosis results from muscular weakness, muscular imbalance, or neurologic dysfunction and paralysis. Diseases that cause neuromuscular scoliosis include muscular dystrophy, spina bifida, syringomyelia, Friedreich's ataxia, and cerebral palsy. Scheuermann's kyphosis or disease is an abnormal increase in the thoracic spine's kyphosis resulting from structural changes to the vertebra. The cause is unknown, but the deformity is localized and painless.

Abnormal curvatures may be associated with other diseases such as neurofibromatosis, Marfan's syndrome, and Ehlers-Danlos syndrome. Acquired kyphosis is usually caused by trauma with an associated spine fracture, but is also caused by osteoporosis, inflammation, disc degeneration, endocrine diseases, Paget's disease, polio, tuberculosis, infection, and cancer of the spine.

Approximately 2% of women and less than 0.5% of men have some amount of abnormal spine curvature. It can occur at any age, but is most often noted during adolescence. Individuals who have a family history of abnormal spine curvature and those who have one of the diseases mentioned above are at an increased risk of developing abnormal curvature.

Diagnosis

History: The individual may report the presence of excessive curvature of the spine and possibly related changes in shape to other parts of the torso (hips, shoulders, chest, and waistline). The individual may complain of back pain and fatigue. Individuals with severe curvatures may complain of breathing difficulties and weakness. There may be a family history of abnormal spine curvature.

Physical exam: Individuals with scoliosis may present with uneven (asymmetrical) hips and/or shoulders and an abnormal waistline tilt with pronounced indentation on one side. Signs of kyphosis may include a rounded back, while individuals with lordosis will display a sway back.

Spinal curvature may be apparent by the Adam's test, in which the individual bends forward with the legs straight and the arms extended. The skin overlying the spine may have light brown (cafe au lait) spots,

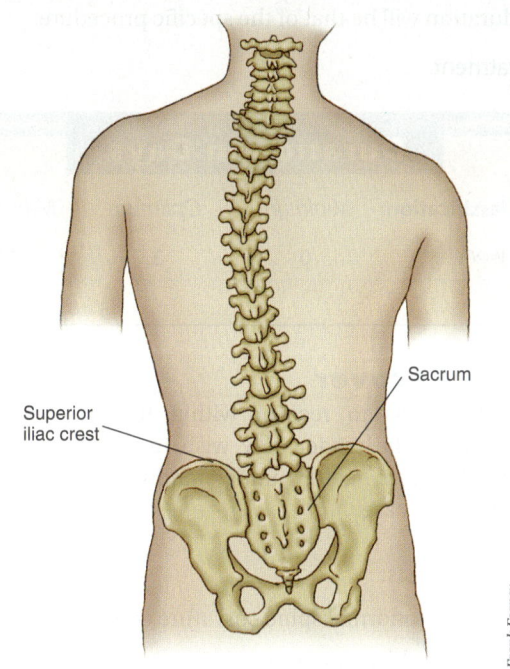

hairy patches, dimples, or skin tags. Armpit (axillary) freckles may be seen. The individual may have an abnormal walking style (gait) and asymmetrical limb lengths. Abnormal reflexes may be detected. Clubbing of the fingers would indicate cardiopulmonary impairment seen only with severe deformity.

Tests: Plain x-rays of the spine with the individual standing, bending, and lying down would be taken. MRI or myelogram with CT may be used in individuals with neurological abnormalities, unusual curve patterns, or rapidly progressive curvatures. Pulmonary and cardiac function tests are used for individuals with curvature greater than 60 degrees or with signs and symptoms consistent with respiratory problems. Preoperative CT myelopathy or MRI is usually performed. X-rays of the spine with measurement of the Cobb angle is used for kyphosis.

Treatment

Most individuals with scoliosis do not have a greater number or severity of spinal complaints compared to those without scoliosis. The presence of scoliosis does not necessarily mean the scoliosis is the source of spinal pain. If so, treatment will depend upon the extent and severity of the curvature, the age of the individual, and the underlying cause of the curvature. Several methods are available. Mild curvatures (those less than 10 degrees) in adults are often treated conservatively. Treatment may consist of observation only or it may include passive and active exercises. Conservative treatment may include NSAIDs as needed for pain relief.

More severe forms of spine curvature require either immobilization (bracing) or surgery. Surgery is indicated for individuals with progressive curvatures, curves greater than 40 degrees, neuromuscular scoliosis, severe pain, and other significant symptoms (cardiac or pulmonary problems). The type of surgery is dependent on the type, severity, and extent of the curvature, the age of the individual, and whether previous attempts at corrections have been made.

A common surgical method used to realign the spine is spinal fusion (arthrodesis) with fixation devices (e.g., rods, screws), which may be performed either from the back (posterior approach) or through the chest (anterior approach). Excision operations, such as removal of intervertebral discs (discectomy), and/or removal of vertebral body or bodies (corpectomy) are other surgical options. Fusion and excision procedures may be used in combination. Surgery requires hospitalization, but individuals are mobilized early and may be discharged by 5 days postoperatively.

Prognosis

Most cases of scoliosis or kyphosis with severe deformity can be corrected to mild deformity.

For milder cases, conservative measures are effective in reducing pain and, possibly, deformity in young adults and adults with minor curvature. In many instances, compensated scoliosis can be corrected by exercise. In most cases, arthrodesis and/or discectomy have a good outcome and can reduce pain and deformity. Individuals with a degenerative disease or whole body (systemic) disease have a poor prognosis.

Differential Diagnosis

There are no other possible diagnoses. The deformity is obvious.

Specialists

- Cardiologist
- Chiropractor
- Neurologist
- Orthopedic Surgeon
- Physical Therapist
- Pulmonologist
- Radiologist

Rehabilitation

Individuals with curvature of the spine may require physical therapy. Rehabilitation is aimed at restoring normal flexibility, strength, and breathing as well as reducing pain.

Individuals who experience pain as a result of tight muscles may use a heating pad prior to exercise or whenever needed for pain control. Individuals may also receive ultrasound treatments.

Individuals learn flexibility exercises of the neck, shoulders, back, and trunk to help promote normalized posture. In general, individuals perform active range-of-motion exercises of the neck in all directions. Individuals stretch the chest muscles by standing in a corner, placing one arm on each wall, and leaning the trunk in toward the corner. Individuals stretch the trunk muscles by facing a wall and reaching the arms up the wall until a stretch is felt. Individuals learn to stretch trunk muscles that are tight on one side as in the case of scoliosis by sitting on their heels and bending forward so that the hands are stretched out in front of them. The hands are then walked to the side opposite the side of tightness until a stretch is felt in the side. Individuals may also need to stretch the hamstring and quadriceps muscles if these muscle groups are tight.

Individuals learn strengthening exercises to help correct any postural abnormalities that may be caused by weakened muscle groups. Individuals with forward curvature of the spine as in the case of kyphosis may need to do exercises such as chin tucks where the neck is retracted and the chin is flattened against the neck. Exercises to strengthen the upper back include shoulder blade pinches where the shoulder blades are squeezed together.

Individuals with a lateral curve as in the case of scoliosis learn to strengthen the muscles opposite the side of the spine where the muscles are tight. This is performed by lying on the side of muscle tightness and then lifting the upper trunk from the exercise mat.

All individuals learn to strengthen the lower back with pelvic tilts and trunk extension. Pelvic tilts are performed by flattening the lower back against an exercise mat while contacting the abdominal muscles. Extension exercises are performed by lying on the stomach and lifting the upper body or both the upper body and legs from the exercise mat.

Lung function can be compromised with severe curvature of the spine due to the ribcage pressing inward and preventing full lung expansion. Because of this, individuals learn to perform deep breathing exercises to enhance lung function. Exercises such as diaphragmatic breathing are performed with the individual lying on the back and resting the hands on the abdomen. The individual then breathes in and the abdomen expands upward causing the hands to rise. This exercise should be performed at frequent intervals throughout the day.

Work Restrictions / Accommodations

Individuals may need extended time off for surgery, recuperation, and physical therapy. Work restrictions and special accommodations need to be established on an individual basis. Activities involving lifting and carrying may need to be limited. Workstation modification to permit good posture may be helpful. To reduce the risk of complications, individuals who are treated surgically may not be allowed to work during the early recovery period.

Comorbid Conditions

Obesity, cardiopulmonary conditions, and general debility may influence the length of disability.

Complications

Complications include progressive curvature, postural and neuromuscular problems, pain, difficulty walking, pronounced deformity, loss of height, and heart and lung problems.

Factors Influencing Duration

Factors include type and severity of the spine curvature, development of complications, type of treatment, and individual's job or lifestyle requirements.

Length of Disability

Duration depends on cause, severity, and type of curvature. If surgery is indicated, duration will be that of the specific procedure.

Medical treatment.

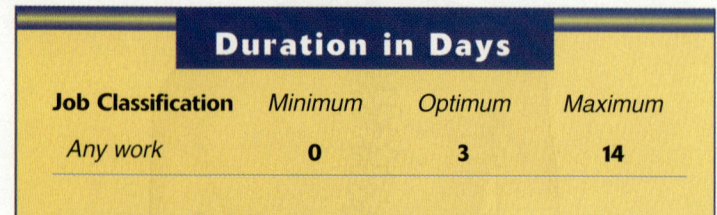

Job Classification	Minimum	Optimum	Maximum
Any work	0	3	14

Failure to Recover

If an individual fails to recover within the maximum duration expectancy period, the reader may wish to reference the following questions to assist in better understanding the specifics of an individual's medical case.

Regarding diagnosis:

- Is individual's abnormal spine curvature congenital or acquired?
- Is there a family history of scoliosis?
- What kind of scoliosis does individual have?
- Does individual complain of back pain and fatigue? Breathing difficulties and weakness?
- Was curvature apparent on physical exam?
- Were plain x-rays performed? MRI or myelogram with CT?
- Does individual have any risk factors?
- Does individual show signs of neurologic involvement?

Regarding treatment:

- Has individual responded favorable to conservative treatment?
- Was surgery necessary?

Regarding prognosis:

- Is individual active in physical therapy? Is a home exercise program in place?
- Can individual's employer accommodate necessary restrictions?
- Is individual obese?
- Does individual have a pre-existing cardiopulmonary condition?
- Have any complications developed such as progressive curvature, postural and neuromuscular problems, pain, difficulty walking, pronounced deformity, loss of height, and heart and lung problems?

References

In Depth Review of Scoliosis: Introduction. Scoliosis Research Society. 1999. 01 Jan 2001 <http://srs.org/htm/library/review/review01.htm>.

Kisner, Carolyn, and Lynn Allen Colby. "Scoliosis." Therapeutic Exercise: Foundations and Techniques, 2nd ed. Philadelphia: F.A. Davis Company, 1990. 519-543.

Pinto, Waldermar, MD, et al. "Common Sense in the Management of Adolescent Idiopathic Scoliosis." Orthopedic Clinics of North America 25 2 (1994): 215-223.

Saunders, H. Duane, and Robin Saunders. Evaluation, Treatment, and Prevention of Musculoskeletal Disorders, Volume 1. Chaska: The Saunders Group, 1993.

Cushing's Syndrome

Other names / synonyms: Cushing's Disease, Hypercortisolism

255.0

Definition

Cushing's syndrome is a condition caused by excess corticosteroids in an individual's body. These steroids can be produced by the body itself, or can result from high doses of medical steroids being administered to the individual. Cushing's syndrome is characterized by a large, round face and a thick torso with comparatively thin arms and legs. Muscle weakness, depression, hallucinations, thin skin that bruises easily and heals slowly, and purple streaks on the abdomen are also common signs and symptoms of this condition.

The adrenal glands located on top of the kidneys produce cortisol. Under normal conditions, the release of cortisol is controlled by the pituitary gland and the hypothalamus in the brain. The hypothalamus sends a hormone (corticotropin releasing hormone, CRH) to the pituitary gland. CRH causes the pituitary gland to secrete a hormone called ACTH (adrenocorticotropic hormone). ACTH is the signal for the adrenal gland to produce cortisol.

When a tumor (adenoma) of the pituitary gland produces excessive amounts of ACTH, there is a subsequent release of excess cortisol by the adrenal glands. This condition is called Cushing's disease (hypercortisolism), and it accounts for about 70% of the naturally occurring (endogenous) cases of Cushing's syndrome. Another 20-25% of the naturally occurring cases of Cushing's syndrome are caused by release of cortisol from non-cancerous (benign) or cancerous (malignant) tumors of the adrenal gland (adrenal adenoma and adrenal carcinoma). The remaining 5% of cases are caused by the production of ACTH by a tumor (either benign or malignant) located elsewhere in the body (ectopic ACTH syndrome).

Another common cause of Cushing's syndrome is due to the administration of glucocorticoid drugs (such as prednisone) or ACTH for various medical reasons. Examples of some medical conditions that might be treated with glucocorticoids or ACTH include rheumatoid arthritis, lupus, asthma or other chronic inflammatory diseases.

While Cushing's syndrome is not inherited, some people have an inherited predisposition to tumors of the hormone-secreting glands. This predisposition places these individuals at a higher risk for Cushing's syndrome than the general population.

Cushing's syndrome is relatively rare, affecting about 10 to 15 of every million individuals each year. It most commonly affects adults between the ages of 20 and 50, although it can strike at any age. Cushing's disease (due to pituitary adenomas) is five times more common in women than in men. Ectopic ACTH syndrome is caused by lung tumors (usually carcinoid) in 50% of cases. Other ACTH producing tumors include thymomas, pancreatic islet cell carcinomas, and medullary carcinomas of the thyroid. Ectopic ACTH syndrome affects men three times as often as women. Adrenal tumors are most often non-cancerous, and generally appear at age 40, in men and women equally.

Individuals with any disease requiring prolonged use of corticosteroid medications are at increased risk for developing Cushing's syndrome.

Diagnosis

History: Frequent complaints include weight gain, fatigue, muscle weakness (especially of the upper arms and thighs), easy bruising, poor wound healing, thinning scalp hair, abnormal growth of body hair and purple streaking (striae) of the breasts, buttocks, lower abdomen and thighs. Individuals may also complain of excessive thirst and frequent urination. Psychiatric symptoms include mood swings, depression, and personality changes (steroid psychosis). Women may notice changes in the menstrual flow (oligomenorrhea or amenorrhea), and men may complain of decreased sex drive (libido) and inability to achieve or maintain an erection (impotence). Often, individuals will report that routine bending, lifting or rising from a chair has become difficult or painful.

Physical exam: High blood pressure (hypertension) is seen in over 80% of cases. There are some striking physical changes in Cushing's syndrome. The face is round and unusually red. Acne may be present. Obesity is common, 50% of individuals gain weight in the abdomen and buttocks while the arms and legs are normal. Fat pads appear over the collarbones and upper spine.

Tests: If it has been determined from the history and physical exam that the individual is not showing the signs of Cushing's syndrome from prescribed medications, further testing is carried out at two levels. First, it must be determined whether the individual has elevated levels of cortisol. A 24-hour urine collection is taken and the amount of cortisol in the urine is measured. The cortisol level will be elevated in individuals with Cushing's syndrome. Another test is the overnight dexamethasone suppression test. Dexamethasone is a steroid medication that will suppress ACTH release and lower the early morning levels of blood cortisol in normal individuals, but have no effect in individuals with Cushing's syndrome.

The second level of testing is carried out once the diagnosis of Cushing's syndrome is established. The cause of the disease must be determined: is it a tumor of the pituitary gland, adrenal glands, or a tumor that is stimulating the adrenal glands through ectopic ACTH secretion. A test called the CRH stimulation test is often performed to help distinguish Cushing's syndrome due to pituitary adenomas from those with ectopic ACTH syndrome or cortisol-secreting adrenal tumors. In the CRH stimulation test, individuals are given an injection of CRH. Those with a pituitary adenoma usually experience a rise in blood levels of ACTH and cortisol. This response is rarely seen in people with ectopic ACTH syndrome and practically never in those with cortisol-secreting adrenal tumors. Routine chest x-rays are done and CT of the chest is done in cases of suspected cases of ectopic ACTH production. A CT of the adrenal glands can show an adrenal tumor, or in the case of a pituitary tumor that stimulates both glands, enlarged adrenal glands. MRI of the pituitary gland is done in cases of suspected pituitary tumors.

Blood tests may also show high levels of sugar (hyperglycemia), fat (hyperlipidemia), or potassium (hyperkalemia) and abnormal numbers of certain white blood cells (neutrophilia, lymphopenia).

Treatment

If the condition is caused by over medication, it is treated by reducing the dosage of glucocorticoids or changing the medication. When the underlying cause is a benign or malignant tumor of the adrenal gland, the tumor must be surgically removed.

The treatment of choice for tumors of the pituitary gland is surgical removal. Irradiation of the pituitary gland has a lower success rate, has a higher rate of complications, and notable improvement may not be noted for a year or more. Hormone replacement therapy usually follows surgery, and, in some cases, must be continued for life.

Medical treatment (chemotherapy) is usually not recommended as the primary treatment for Cushing's syndrome but is an alternative if surgery is not possible and may be used with radiation treatments to hasten better results. If the cause of Cushing's syndrome is from ectopic ACTH, treatment is directed at the underlying disease.

Prognosis

The effects of hypercortisolism secondary to a malignancy of the adrenal glands are usually detected in later stages of the disease after the cancer has spread to other organs such as the liver and lungs and has a poor prognosis.

Surgery to remove pituitary and adrenal adenomas is generally successful, but there is a recurrence rate of up to 20% over the next 10 years, and the individual may require hydrocortisone therapy from 6 months to 3 years until the normal hormone balance by the body is fully restored.

Individuals with pituitary tumors treated by irradiation rather than surgery have a recurrence in about 75% of cases. The greatest success rates are found in individuals whose condition has been caused by underlying adrenal tumors and who have had surgery without immediate complications.

Differential Diagnosis

Other conditions share signs and symptoms with Cushing's syndrome and should be considered when making this diagnosis. For example, obesity and depression can cause elevated cortisol levels; polycystic ovarian syndrome can cause menstrual irregularities; puberty can cause mood swings, irritability, depression, and weight gain; diabetes mellitus can cause hyperglycemia, weight gain and irritability; and weight gain, elevated fat in the blood, and high blood pressure are also associated with insulin resistance and diabetes (Metabolic Syndrome-X).

Specialists

- Endocrinologist
- Neurosurgeon
- Oncologist
- Radiologist
- Surgeon
- Urologist

Work Restrictions / Accommodations

No restrictions or accommodations should be necessary once the individual returns to work.

Comorbid Conditions

Pregnancy can exacerbate Cushing's syndrome and increase the period of disability.

Complications

Cushing's syndrome is complicated by high blood pressure, diabetes, infections, and emotional disturbances. The bones become fragile (osteoporosis), and compression fractures of the spine are common. Untreated, Cushing's disease has a 50% death rate within five years. Pituitary adenomas are only seen on 50% of the MRI tests, hence it is important that the biochemical testing is thorough before surgery. On the other hand, the smaller the pituitary tumor, the better the chances for a cure through surgery.

Factors Influencing Duration

Individuals who require surgery can be expected to spend several days in the hospital with additional recovery time at home. Untreated, Cushing's syndrome can be fatal.

Length of Disability

Disability may be permanent.

Adrenalectomy.

Duration in Days

Job Classification	Minimum	Optimum	Maximum
Sedentary work	21	28	42
Light work	21	35	42
Medium work	28	42	56
Heavy work	42	49	56
Very Heavy work	42	49	56

Resection of pituitary adenoma.

Duration in Days

Job Classification	Minimum	Optimum	Maximum
Sedentary work	21	28	56
Light work	21	28	56
Medium work	28	35	70
Heavy work	42	42	70
Very Heavy work	42	42	70

Failure to Recover

If an individual fails to recover within the maximum duration expectancy period, the reader may wish to reference the following questions to assist in better understanding the specifics of an individual's medical case.

Regarding diagnosis:

- Does individual have a large, round face and a thick torso with comparatively thin arms and legs?
- Does individual also have muscle weakness, thin skin that bruises easily and heals slowly, and purple streaks on the abdomen, breasts, buttocks and thighs?
- Does individual have a pituitary tumor, adrenal tumor, small cell lung cancer, thymomas, pancreatic islet cell carcinomas, or medullary carcinomas of the thyroid?

- Is individual being treated with glucocorticoid drugs for another condition?
- Does individual have a family history of tumors of the hormone-secreting glands?
- Does individual complain of weight gain, fatigue, thinning scalp hair, excessive body hair, excessive thirst, and frequent urination?
- Does individual have mood swings, depression, hallucinations, and personality changes?
- Does individual have oligomenorrhea or amenorrhea? Decreased libido? Impotence? Does individual report that routine bending, lifting, or rising from a chair is difficult or painful?
- On exam, are symptoms present such as hypertension, red round face, acne, and weight gain in the abdomen and buttocks or fat pads over the collarbones and upper spine?
- Were cortisol levels tested? Was individual tested for the presence of cortisol-secreting tumors?
- Was an overnight dexamethasone suppression test done? CT or MRI? Comprehensive blood testing? Was inferior petrosal sinus sampling done?
- Were conditions with similar symptoms ruled out?

Regarding treatment:

- Is the condition caused by overmedication? Is the dosage of glucocorticoids reduced or the medication changed?
- Is the condition caused by a tumor? Was it surgically removed? Is individual on hormone replacement therapy?

Regarding prognosis:

- Does individual have any conditions that may affect ability to recover?
- Have any complications developed such as high blood pressure, diabetes, infections, emotional disturbances, osteoporosis, and compression fractures of the spine?

References

Cushing's Syndrome. National Institute of Diabetes and Digestive and Kidney Diseases. 20 Feb 1998. 17 Nov 2000 <http://www.niddk.nih.gov/health/endo/pubs/cushings/cushings.htm>.

Young, William. "Cushing's Disease and Syndrome." Griffith's 5-minute Clinical Consult. Dambro, Mark, ed. Philadelphia: Lippincott, Williams & Wilkins, 2000. 278-279.

Cystectomy

Other names / synonyms: Excision of Bladder, Partial Cystectomy, Radical Cystectomy, Simple Cystectomy, Total Excision
57.6, 57.7, 57.71

Definition

Cystectomy is the surgical removal of the urinary bladder through an incision in the lower abdomen. The removal can be partial, complete (simple), or can involve surrounding structures as well (radical).

Simple cystectomy is performed for benign conditions of the bladder, such as intractable bleeding, severe cystitis, radiation cystitis, and contracted bladder. Partial cystectomy is not commonly performed for cancer because of the high recurrence rate of bladder tumors.

Radical cystectomy is the most common procedure. It is usually performed for treatment of invasive bladder cancer.

Approximately 45,000 new cases of bladder cancer are found per year. The peak age of incidence is 50 to 70 years old. About 2% of all cancer deaths are due to bladder cancer. Risk factors include exposure to industrial chemicals and smoking.

Reason for Procedure

Simple cystectomy is performed for benign conditions of the bladder, such as intractable bleeding, severe cystitis, radiation cystitis, and contracted bladder. Partial cystectomy is not commonly performed because of the high recurrence rate of bladder tumors. It is reserved for tumors located in the dome of the bladder of older individuals who are poor surgical risks for major operations. Radical cystectomy is the most common procedure. It is usually performed for treatment of invasive bladder cancer.

How Procedure Is Performed

Cystectomy is performed in the operating room under general anesthesia. It is an inpatient procedure.

The procedure can be performed as simple, partial, and radical. Simple cystectomy involves the removal of the bladder, but preserves the surrounding structure. Partial cystectomy involves the removal of only the diseased portions of the bladder. A urethral catheter is left in place for 7 days after surgery. Radical cystectomy involves the removal of the bladder with surrounding muscle, lymph nodes, and other structures. In men, it means that the prostate and seminal vesicles are removed, producing impotence. In women, it means the possible removal of the urethra, uterus, uterine tubes, ovaries, and a segment of the vaginal wall.

Both simple and radical cystectomy require permanent urinary diversion. This can be accomplished with either a standard ileal conduit or a bladder substitution. The ileal conduit is constructed from sections of ileum. The ureters are implanted into the one end of the conduit and the other end is brought through an opening in the abdominal wall (stoma). Bladder substitution is a more complex operation. A segment of bowel is isolated, with its blood supply, and fashioned into a pouch and connected to the urethra (if it is not removed), thus avoiding a stoma. Once proper functioning of the remaining bladder/urinary diversion conduit is confirmed, the individual is ready for discharge.

Prognosis

Recovery from a cystectomy can require several weeks. The outcome depends on the underlying condition. Partial cystectomies for benign conditions often result in cure, although recurrence is possible. If the procedure was performed for bladder cancer, the prognosis depends upon the stage of disease. Superficial tumors with no spread have a 90% 5-year survival rate. The survival drops significantly with deeper invasion or spread to other organs. Metastatic bladder cancer has a less than 5% 5-year survival rate.

Specialists

- General Surgeon
- Urologist

Work Restrictions / Accommodations

Work restrictions and special accommodations are determined on an individual basis. Individuals may need to be moved near restroom facilities.

Comorbid Conditions

Coronary artery disease, diabetes mellitus, or chronic obstructive pulmonary disease may lengthen disability.

Procedure Complications

The most common complications are bleeding or wound infection. The large or small intestine may be injured during the procedure, which may necessitate repair, an ostomy, or further surgery. Impotence can be a complication of partial or simple cystectomy; it is a certainty in radical cystectomy. Injury can occur to the uterus, fallopian tubes, ovaries, prostate, seminal vesicles, and nerves and blood vessels in the area.

Factors Influencing Duration

The extent and type of cystectomy performed, reason for the procedure, any ongoing treatments, complications, and the age and overall health of the individual may influence the length of disability.

Length of Disability

Bladder cancer may require chemotherapy and radiation therapy. Durations will increase by several weeks for continent diversion. Duration depends on partial versus total.

Duration in Days

Job Classification	Minimum	Optimum	Maximum
Sedentary work	42	49	56
Light work	42	49	56
Medium work	42	49	70
Heavy work	56	63	84
Very Heavy work	56	63	112

References

Schwartz, Seymour, MD. Principles of Surgery. New York: McGraw-Hill, 1999.

Cystitis, Acute

Other names / synonyms: Acute Cystitis, Bladder Infection, Cystitis, Urinary Tract Infection, UTI

595, 595.0

Definition

Acute cystitis is an inflammation of the lining of the urinary bladder (the mucosa) caused by a bacterial infection.

Most infections (80%) occur when bacteria that originates in either the small or large intestine (coliform bacteria) travel up the urethra into the bladder. Acute cystitis occurs mainly in adult women, because these bacteria inhabit the meatus to the vagina, and are easily introduced into area around the urethral entrance during intercourse or upon performing normal hygiene.

Other risk factors include diabetes, which results in a high-glucose urine that encourages bacterial growth; a diet low in fruit and protein, because these foods help make the urine more acidic and less hospitable to bacteria; and using an ill-fitting contraceptive diaphragm, which can prevent complete emptying of the bladder. Poor hygiene habits, such as cleaning from back to front after defecation, or wearing soiled underwear, are also risk factors. Other risk factors include urinary tract obstruction, neurogenic bladder dysfunction, vesicoureteral reflux, and pregnancy.

Twenty percent of all women experience this condition at some point in their lives. In men, the incidence of cystitis rises with age and occurs most often after age 50; it is usually caused by prostate enlargement, which results in incomplete emptying of the bladder.

Diagnosis

History: Onset is generally sudden; the most common complaints include a frequent, urgent need to urinate while passing only small amounts of urine, painful urination (dysuria), discomfort felt as pressure or mild to moderate pain in the lower abdomen (suprapubic) and back, loss of bladder control (incontinence), and blood in the urine (hematuria).

Physical exam: Fever is uncommon in cases of cystitis. The only physical signs may be tenderness in the lower abdomen and urethra as well as hematuria.

Tests: Tests include urinalysis. Precautions must be taken to avoid contamination of the specimen with bacteria from the external genitalia by first cleaning with a disinfectant and then obtaining a midstream specimen (clean catch); nitrites and leucocyte esterase will be present in the urine. The urine is cultured to identify the bacterial infection. In most cases of acute cystitis, the urinalysis also reveals pus in the urine (pyuria). About half the time, microscopic hematuria is indicated.

Treatment

Acute cystitis is generally treated with antibiotics for 3-10 days. Other drugs, such as a urinary tract pain reliever (analgesic) may be given for the first 1-2 days to reduce burning and discomfort.

616 The Medical Disability Advisor—Fourth Edition

The individual is encouraged to drink 2 or more quarts of water per day to encourage flushing of the bladder with dilute urine. Low-dose preventive (prophylactic) antibiotics may be given in cases of recurring cystitis.

Specialists

- Gynecologist
- Internist
- Primary Care Provider
- Urologist

Prognosis

Acute cystitis is usually cured by 1-2 courses of antibiotics. The condition may resolve without antibiotic therapy, and some women self-treat with fluid loading instead of seeing a physician. However, antibiotics provide symptomatic relief, lessen the length and severity of the disorder, and reduce the incidence of complications and recurrence.

Differential Diagnosis

Other diseases that may mimic symptoms of acute cystitis are infection of the ureters and kidneys (pyelonephritis), infections of the urethra from sexually transmitted diseases (urethritis), and other forms of cystitis (hemorrhagic, vesicular, or interstitial cystitis).

Work Restrictions / Accommodations

The employee may need to take more frequent restroom breaks. No other special needs are anticipated. However, in many cases the urgent need to urinate is so constant that work may be impractical for a day or two until the medication begins to take effect.

Comorbid Conditions

Comorbid conditions include urinary tract structural defects and immune system disorders.

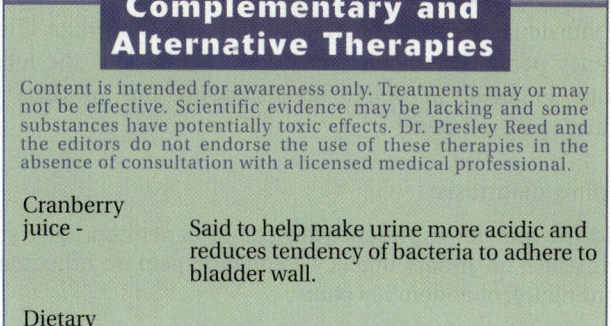

Complementary and Alternative Therapies

Content is intended for awareness only. Treatments may or may not be effective. Scientific evidence may be lacking and some substances have potentially toxic effects. Dr. Presley Reed and the editors do not endorse the use of these therapies in the absence of consultation with a licensed medical professional.

Cranberry juice - Said to help make urine more acidic and reduces tendency of bacteria to adhere to bladder wall.

Dietary modification - A diet adequate in fruit and protein may help make the urine more acidic and less hospitable to bacteria. Drinking 2 or more quarts of water per day encourages flushing of the bladder with dilute urine.

Complications

Possible complications include progression of the infection to the ureters and kidneys (pyelonephritis).

Factors Influencing Duration

Factors that might influence the length of disability include whether appropriate antibiotic treatment is administered, and the presence of comorbid conditions such as urinary tract abnormalities or immune system disorders.

Length of Disability

Duration in Days

Job Classification	Minimum	Optimum	Maximum
Any work	0	3	7

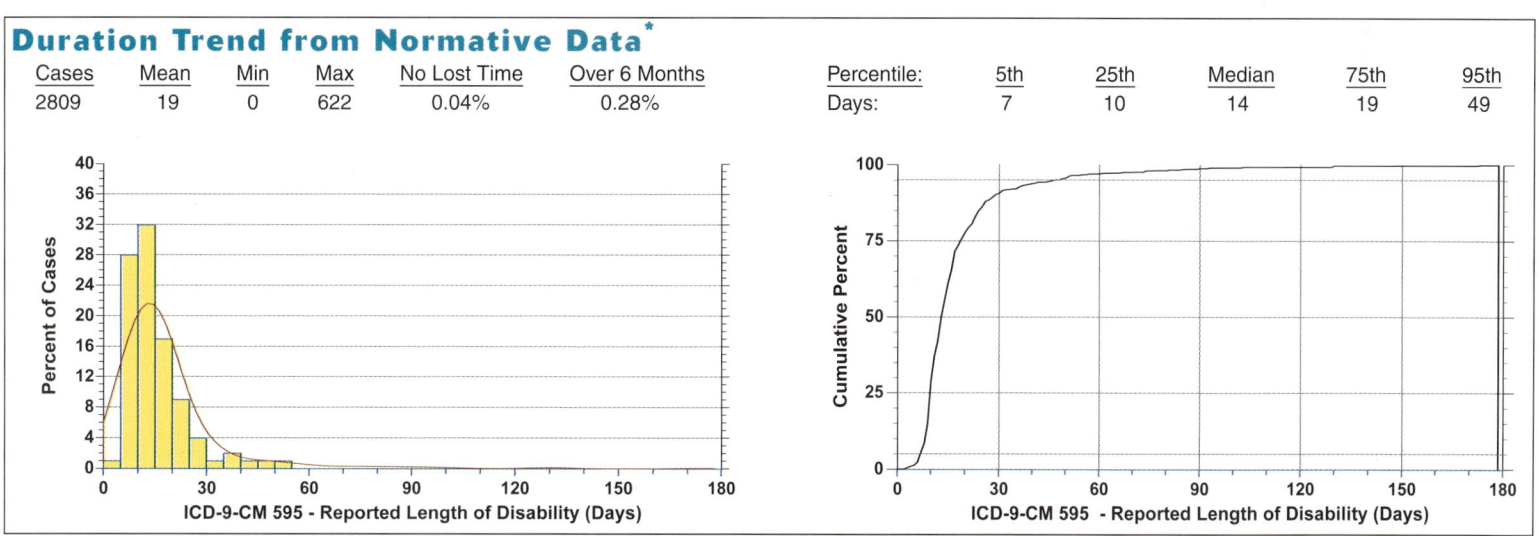

Duration Trend from Normative Data*

Cases	Mean	Min	Max	No Lost Time	Over 6 Months
2809	19	0	622	0.04%	0.28%

Percentile:	5th	25th	Median	75th	95th
Days:	7	10	14	19	49

ICD-9-CM 595 - Reported Length of Disability (Days)

* Differences may exist between the expected duration tables and the normative graphs. Duration tables provide expected recovery periods based on the type of work performed by the individual. The normative graphs reflect the actual observed experience of many individuals across the spectrum of physical conditions, in a variety of industries, and with varying levels of case management.

Failure to Recover

If an individual fails to recover within the maximum duration expectancy period, the reader may wish to reference the following questions to assist in better understanding the specifics of an individual's medical case.

Regarding diagnosis:

- Did the individual present with common genitourinary symptoms such as urinary urgency, frequency, pain on urination, incontinence, or abdominal pain?
- Does the individual have a history of recurrent cystitis?
- Has a urine culture confirmed the diagnosis of acute cystitis?
- Is the bacteria cultured resistant to the antibiotic used?
- Did the individual warrant further diagnostic studies to rule out an underlying urinary tract defect (stricture or prostatic hypertrophy)?

Regarding treatment:

- Was an antibiotic sensitivity done to determine the appropriate antibiotic treatment? Was the individual instructed to increase fluid intake to 2 quarts or more per day?
- Has the individual completed the full course of antibiotic therapy?
- If the cystitis is recurrent, would the individual benefit from prophylactic antibiotics?

Regarding prognosis:

- Did the symptoms persist? Was a repeat culture and sensitivity done to rule out the possibility of antibiotic resistance? Were appropriate adjustments in the antibiotic therapy made?
- Were additional studies done to determine if the infection progressed to the ureters or kidneys?
- Has the individual been examined for the possibility of other urinary tract disorders?
- Does the individual have any underlying conditions such as diabetes, immune system dysfunction, or structural abnormalities that may impact recovery and prognosis? Have these conditions been addressed in the treatment plan?
- Has the individual been instructed on hygiene and other practices, such as emptying the bladder immediately after sexual relations that help to prevent recurrence?

References

"Urinary Tract Infection." Family Practice Notebook. 16 Dec 2000. 24 Jan 2001 <http://www.fpnotebook.com/URO5.htm>.

Howes, David. Urinary Tract Infection, Male. eMedicine.com. 23 Oct 2000. 1 Jan 2001 <http://www.emedicine.com/emerg/topic625.htm>.

Cystitis, Interstitial

Other names / synonyms: Chronic Cystitis, IC, LC, Submucous Cystitis

595.1

Definition

Interstitial cystitis is an inflammation of the urinary bladder. Pinpoint areas of bleeding (hemorrhages) develop in the bladder wall resulting in scar tissue that causes the bladder to stiffen and contract, making it less able to expand, and reducing its capacity from 12 ounces to 2 ounces. Interstitial cystitis is much less common than cystitis caused from a bacterial urinary tract infection.

The exact cause of interstitial cystitis is unknown. Risk factors include previous urinary tract infections and immunological diseases. Possible causes include disorders in which the body's own immune system mistakenly attacks the bladder (autoimmune disorder), an allergic reaction, hormonal disturbances, defects in the mucous lining that normally protect the bladder, the presence of toxic substances in the urine, or an abnormality of the spine. Interstitial cystitis might also be related to scarring from a condition in which fragments of the uterine lining are found in other parts of the pelvic cavity (endometriosis) or from surgical removal of the uterus (hysterectomy), since both are common in women with interstitial cystitis.

Women account for about 90% of cases. Interstitial cystitis occurs in approximately 60 out of 100,000 women in the US; reported prevalence in Europe has been 3 times lower, but uncertainties in diagnosis probably contribute to this difference.

Diagnosis

History: Symptoms include pain, burning, or cramping with urination, frequent urination, and feeling pressure (urgency) to urinate. The pain increases as the bladder fills, causing an uncontrollable urge to urinate. In most cases, a course of antibiotics will have failed to resolve the symptoms. In severe cases, individuals may urinate more than 60 times a day, and up to 10 times during the night. Two-thirds of individuals report pain during sexual intercourse (dyspareunia); in women symptoms may increase during menses. Coffee, tea, carbonated drinks, alcohol, and spicy or acidic foods may aggravate the symptoms.

Physical exam: In women, a pelvic exam is done to rule out other conditions that could cause similar symptoms, such as vaginal infection or endometriosis. In men, the urethral opening is examined for evidence of a skin lesion, swelling, or discharge; the prostate and testes are examined for swelling and tenderness, and to rule out conditions such as urethritis, prostatitis, and orchitis.

Tests: Urinalysis and culture are performed to rule out urinary tract infection. In men, prostatic fluid is also analyzed. If the urine is sterile while symptoms continue over a period of weeks or months, interstitial cystitis is suspected. The definitive test for the condition is fiber-optic examination of the bladder (cytoscopy) under anesthesia, to look for pinpoint bleeding (glomerulation) caused by chronic irritation, and thickening and inflammation of the bladder wall. During the course of the cytoscopy, a tissue sample may be removed for biopsy. Microscopic examination can confirm the presence of inflammation and rule out bladder cancer.

Treatment

A cure is not yet known, so treatment is aimed at symptomatic relief. The oral medication pentosan polysulfate sodium (Elmiron), approved as a treatment for interstitial cystitis in 1996, improves symptoms in about 38% of cases. Elmiron is a synthetic oral highly sulfonated mucopolysaccharide intended to increase the protective layer of the bladder wall. Oral pain relievers such as aspirin, ibuprofen, or codeine may be helpful. Tricyclic antidepressants can also help reduce the chronic pain and the stress that accompanies interstitial cystitis. Another option involves delivering dimethyl sulfoxide or other medicated solutions directly into the bladder through a urethral catheter. Aimed at inhibiting painful inflammation, this technique involves at least 6-8 weeks of biweekly treatments. Some highly motivated individuals may be trained to catheterize themselves so that they can perform the treatments at home.

Stretching the bladder by filling it with fluid under pressure (hydrodistention) can bring temporary relief from symptoms. Surgery is possible to expand bladders that have shrunken due to the disease process. Dietary changes focus on avoiding irritating substances such as spicy foods, citrus fruits, tomatoes, coffee, tea, chocolate, alcohol, and tobacco. Rarely, if more conservative treatments are ineffective and symptoms are severe, surgery may be considered. Surgery includes burning off (fulguration) or cutting away (resection) ulcers using instruments inserted through the urethra using a cystoscope, surgical augmentation of the bladder using tissue from the individual's large intestine, or bladder removal (cystectomy). After a cystectomy, urine is usually collected in a bag attached to a stomal opening in the abdomen. Continent urinary diversions eliminating the need for a bag (appliance) can be offered to the individual.

Prognosis

Interstitial cystitis is a chronic disease. Individuals are helped by careful management of the condition and adjustment of treatments to provide maximum short-term relief. Bladder distention, for example, provides excellent short-term relief, but may need to be repeated after several months. Treatment with Elmiron should continue for at least 6 months before assessing whether it is helpful. Studies of entire patient populations have indicated that no currently available treatments have a significant long-term impact on symptoms. In many cases, symptoms disappear either spontaneously or in response to some particular treatment, but recur at a later time.

Differential Diagnosis

Conditions with similar symptoms include urinary tract infections (UTI), bladder wall spasms, kidney stones, sexually transmitted diseases, and bladder cancer. In women, vaginal infections and endometriosis are possibilities. In men, prostatitis must be ruled out.

Specialists

- Gynecologist
- Infectious Disease Physician
- Internist
- Urologist

Work Restrictions / Accommodations

Frequent and unscheduled breaks are usually necessary due to the constant urge to urinate. Employees might benefit from support groups to address the emotional aspect of dealing with a chronic disorder. There are support groups specifically for interstitial cystitis. The opportunity to perform gentle stretching exercises also seems to help many individuals with interstitial cystitis.

Complementary and Alternative Therapies

Content is intended for awareness only. Treatments may or may not be effective. Scientific evidence may be lacking and some substances have potentially toxic effects. Dr. Presley Reed and the editors do not endorse the use of these therapies in the absence of consultation with a licensed medical professional.

T.E.N.S. -	Said to block pain signals, strengthen pelvic muscles, and/or increase blood flow to the bladder.
Acupuncture -	May provide pain relief.
Massage -	May relax muscles.
Imagery -	May help to reduce stress.

Comorbid Conditions

Comorbid conditions include autoimmune disorders.

Complications

Complications include urine forcing its way backwards through the ureter into the kidney (urinary reflux) and chronic pelvic pain. Depression may result from decreased quality of life due to constant urinary symptoms and pain.

Factors Influencing Duration

Length of disability is influenced by the severity of symptoms, the type of treatment, and its effectiveness.

Length of Disability

If symptoms are severe, disability may be permanent, especially if individuals perform work that is not compatible with frequent unscheduled bathroom breaks.

Duration in Days

Job Classification	Minimum	Optimum	Maximum
Any work	1	5	7

Failure to Recover

If an individual fails to recover within the maximum duration expectancy period, the reader may wish to reference the following questions to assist in better understanding the specifics of an individual's medical case.

Regarding diagnosis:

- Has individual had previous urinary tract infections?
- Does individual have an autoimmune disorder? Hormonal disturbances? Endometriosis?
- Does individual have a toxic substance in their urine? Spine abnormality?
- Has individual had a hysterectomy?
- Does individual experience pain, burning, or cramping with urination?
- Does individual have urinary frequency and urgency?
- Does individual report that antibiotics have failed to resolve the problem?
- If female, does individual report the symptoms worsen during the menstrual period?
- Does individual have dyspareunia?
- Was a pelvic exam done?
- Were the prostate, testes, and urethral opening examined?
- Have a urinalysis and culture been done? Prostatic fluid examined?
- Has individual had a cystoscopy been done? Was a biopsy done?
- Have conditions with similar symptoms been ruled out?

Regarding treatment:

- Has the new drug, Elmiron, been tried? Oral pain relievers? Tricyclic antidepressants?
- Has individual tried dimethyl sulfoxide directly into the bladder through a catheter?
- Was hydrodistention tried?
- Has individual avoided spicy foods, citrus, tomatoes, coffee, tea, and chocolate in diet?
- Does individual avoid alcohol?
- Has individual quit smoking?
- Did a cystectomy become necessary?

Regarding prognosis:

- Is individual's employer able to accommodate any necessary restrictions?
- Does individual have any conditions that could affect their ability to recover?
- Does individual have urinary reflux or chronic pelvic pain?
- Is individual involved in a support group or counseling?

References

Beers, Mark H., and Robert Berkow. The Merck Manual of Diagnosis and Therapy. Whitehouse Station, NJ: Merck & Co., Inc, 1999.

Propert, K.J., et al. "A Prospective Study of Interstitial Cystitis: Results of Longitudinal Followup of the Interstitial Cystitis Data Base Cohort." Journal of Urology 163 5 (2000): 1434-1439.

Cystocele or Rectocele

Other names / synonyms: Cystic Hernia, Cystourethrocele, Female Urethrocele, Vaginal Prolapse

618.0, 618.2, 618.3, 618.4

Definition

A cystocele is a protrusion (herniation) of the urinary bladder against the front (anterior) vaginal wall. A rectocele is a herniation of the rectum against the back (posterior) wall of the vagina.

A cystocele occurs when the tissues separating the bladder and vagina weaken, cause a bulge, and allow the bladder to droop into the vagina. Other portions of the vaginal vault may also fall down (prolapse), but they may or may not cause symptoms to develop.

A rectocele occurs when the muscles between the rectum and the vagina become weak from childbearing, old age, or surgery, allowing the rectum to herniate, and cause a bulge of the posterior vagina. The condition may also reflect a weakness present in the wall since birth (congenital), and, in severe cases, will result in painful intercourse (dyspareunia) and difficulty defecating.

Cystocele and rectocele are typically seen in women who have had multiple vaginal births; they often develop together. Straining, whether due to giving birth, from heavy lifting, or from repeated straining during bowel movements, may also cause the bladder to prolapse. While some degree of cystocele may be present after childbirth, it can worsen at menopause due to the lack of female hormones (estrogen), which causes the muscles around the vagina and bladder to weaken. A mild cystocele (grade 1) is when the bladder droops only a short way into the vagina. A more severe type (grade 2) means that the bladder has drooped into the vagina far enough to reach the vaginal opening. The most advance cystocele (grade 3) is when the bladder bulges out through the vaginal opening.

The incidences of cystocele and rectocele are hard to specify since many of the studies have been done on varied populations. However, about 40% of postmenopausal women may experience cystocele or rectocele, and up to 50% of cases are estimated to occur among the elderly.

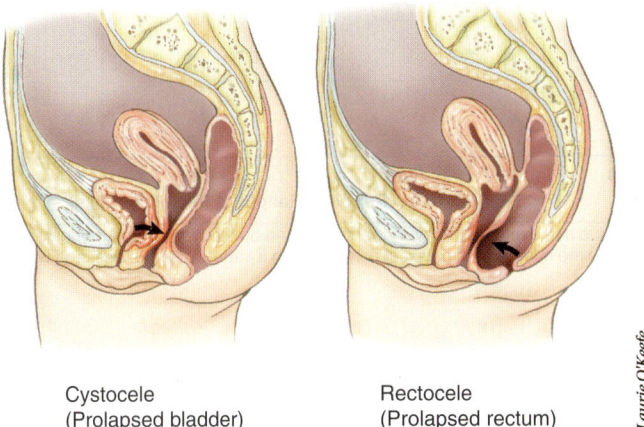

Cystocele (Prolapsed bladder)
Rectocele (Prolapsed rectum)

Laurie O'Keefe

Diagnosis

History: A cystocele or rectocele may or may not be symptomatic. The individual may report a sensation of vaginal fullness or pressure, the feeling that something is falling out, a feeling that the bladder does not completely empty, urinary frequency, the need to push the bladder up in order to urinate, or the feeling of a mass bulging into the vagina. Symptoms can be aggravated by physical activity, prolonged standing, coughing, sneezing, or straining. If the urethra has been pulled out of position, the individual may leak urine when coughing, laughing, or lifting a heavy object (stress incontinence). A rectocele may cause constipation because of interference with muscle contractions in the rectum. The individual may also report having to manually push in (reduce) the rectocele before defecating.

Physical exam: A doctor may be able to diagnose a grade 2 or grade 3 cystocele from a description of the symptoms and physical examination of the vagina. The fallen part of the bladder may be visible upon examination of the vagina; a smooth, bulging mass will be seen through the vaginal wall below the level of the cervix. Bearing down or straining moves the mass even farther into the vagina. Rectocele also reveals a bulging of the vagina and may also be visible upon visual examination.

Tests: A test that involves taking x-rays of the bladder during urination (voiding cystourethrogram) shows the shape of the bladder and reveals problems that might block the normal flow of urine. Other x-rays and tests may be needed to rule out other problems in the urinary system, including a fluoroscopic examination (cinefluorography) while voiding to exclude other bladder abnormalities. Cystometry measures bladder capacity and control. A uroflowmeter analyses the urine flow.

Treatment

Treatment options range from no treatment for a mild cystocele to surgery for a serious cystocele. A mild cystocele that may be bothersome can be treated with a device called a pessary. It is inserted into the vagina to support the vaginal walls, provide pelvic support, and hold the bladder in place. Pessaries come in a variety of shapes and sizes to allow for a comfortable fit. It can be a temporary management option, or in the case of older individuals who are not candidates for surgery, the treatment of choice. Pessaries must be removed regularly to avoid infection and prevent ulcers from developing.

Large cystoceles or rectoceles may require surgical repair to move the bladder back, suspending it into a more normal position (the Burch Colposuspension). Surgery permits better bladder control and allows for a more active lifestyle. Estrogen replacement therapy (ERT) may be recommended for postmenopausal women. This can help strengthen the muscles around the bladder and vagina, and can be used alone, with a pessary, or before and after surgery. The individual should be told of the advantages and risks of taking estrogen. Kegel muscle strengthening exercises will also be recommended.

Prognosis

Prognosis after surgery is excellent as long as the individual avoids conditions or activities that increase pressure in the pelvic and rectal area. If nonsurgical treatment with a pessary or other supportive device is chosen, the outcome is good, but may provide only temporary improvement in some cases.

Differential Diagnosis

Bladder infection mimicking the symptoms of cystocele, enlargement of the uterus by fibroids, bladder tumors, or a large urethral herniation may be other possibilities.

Specialists

- Gynecologist
- Urologist

Rehabilitation

Pelvic floor exercises (Kegel exercises) may help strengthen the muscles of the vagina and those between the rectum and vagina.

Work Restrictions / Accommodations

Heavy lifting or straining can cause the cystocele or rectocele to worsen, so must be avoided. The individual can return to work after treatment, but should continue to avoid heavy lifting or straining, and prolonged standing.

Comorbid Conditions

Obesity and constipation will affect the weight on the muscles and could worsen the condition.

Complications

A large cystocele can cause urine to leak when the individual sneezes, coughs, laughs, lifts, or does anything that puts pressure on the bladder (stress incontinence). It may also cause incomplete emptying of the bladder leading to recurrent urinary tract infections. The uterus can also drop from its normal position into the vagina (uterine prolapse), and is often associated with a cystocele because of the weakened vaginal tissue. Removal of the uterus (hysterectomy) may need to be done at the same time as the repair of a cystocele or rectocele. Sexual difficulties due to vaginal looseness may also occur.

Factors Influencing Duration

Disability will be lengthened if corrective surgery is performed, and its duration will depend on job requirements, especially if heavy work and lifting is a job requirement. Several days in the hospital and 4 to 6 weeks of recuperation should be expected for a full return to normal function. Age and overall physical health are also factors influencing recovery.

Length of Disability

Surgical treatment. Hernia repair.

Duration in Days

Job Classification	Minimum	Optimum	Maximum
Sedentary work	28	42	56
Light work	28	42	56
Medium work	42	42	56
Heavy work	42	56	70
Very Heavy work	42	56	70

Duration Trend from Normative Data*

Cases	Mean	Min	Max	No Lost Time	Over 6 Months
1301	51	0	182	0.23%	0.08%

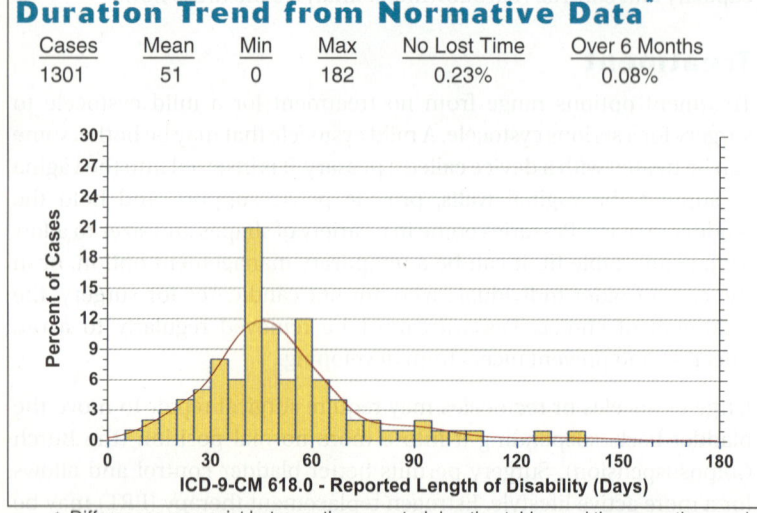

Percentile:	5th	25th	Median	75th	95th
Days:	20	39	46	59	96

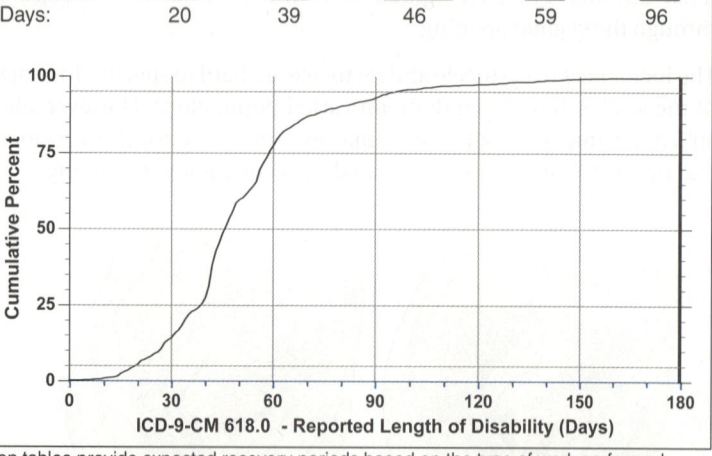

* Differences may exist between the expected duration tables and the normative graphs. Duration tables provide expected recovery periods based on the type of work performed by the individual. The normative graphs reflect the actual observed experience of many individuals across the spectrum of physical conditions, in a variety of industries, and with varying levels of case management.

Failure to Recover

If an individual fails to recover within the maximum duration expectancy period, the reader may wish to reference the following questions to assist in better understanding the specifics of an individual's medical case.

Regarding diagnosis:

- Was diagnosis of cystocele or rectocele confirmed?
- Were other bladder or uterine abnormalities considered in the differential diagnosis?
- Has individual experienced any complications associated with the cystocele or rectocele, such as stress incontinence, incomplete emptying of the bladder leading to recurrent urinary tract infections, or uterine prolapse due to weakened vaginal tissue?
- Does the individual have coexisting conditions, such as obesity and constipation that affect the weight on the muscles, and could worsen the condition?

Regarding treatment:

- If treatment was by pessary, was it chosen as a temporary management option, or because the individual was older and not a candidate for surgery? If for temporary management, what further treatment will be required?
- Was surgical repair successful in moving the bladder back into a more normal position? Was better bladder control achieved? Is further therapy anticipated?
- If postmenopausal, was estrogen replacement therapy (ERT) recommended to help strengthen muscles around the bladder and vagina? Was individual informed of the advantages and risks of taking estrogen?
- Has individual been compliant with recommended pelvic floor exercises (Kegel exercises) to help strengthen muscles of the vagina and those between the rectum and vagina?

Regarding prognosis:

- If treated nonsurgically with a pessary or other supportive device, does individual understand that although the outcome may be good, this may be only a temporary improvement?
- Following surgical correction, does individual understand that she must avoid conditions or activities that increase pressure in the pelvic and rectal area? Was individual instructed in proper ergonomics for lifting heavy objects?

References

National Institute of Diabetes and Digestive and Kidney Diseases (NIDDK). Cystocele (Fallen Bladder). NIDDK. 01 May 1999. 1 Jan 2001 <http://www.niddk.nih.gov/health/urolog/summary/cystocel/index.htm>.

Viera, Anthony J., and Margaret Larkins-Pettigrew. "Practical Use of the Pessary." American Family Physician 5 4 (2000): 15-20.

Cystoscopy, Transurethral

Other names / synonyms: Bladder Examination

57.32, 57.33

Definition

Transurethral cystoscopy is a method of direct visualization of the bladder and urethra. It is performed using a lighted fiber optic tube called a cystoscope.

The cystoscope has a self-contained optical lens system that provides a magnified, illuminated view of the urethra, the section of the urethra surrounded by the prostate gland (prostatic urethra), the bladder, and the openings of the ureters into the bladder (ureteral orifices). Small scopes can be passed through the cystoscope, allowing assessment of the tube that carries urine from the kidney to the bladder (ureter) and the inner area (pelvis) of the kidney. Contrast can be injected into the ureter visualizing both the ureter and renal pelvis (retrograde pyelogram). Cystoscopes are either rigid or flexible. Rigid cystoscopes are long, straight, and stiff instruments. Flexible cystoscopes are also long, but they can be gently bent and curved. Flexible cystoscopes cause less discomfort to the individual, and they can be used at the bedside and in an office setting, as well as in an operating room. Flexible cystoscopes are also used when the individual cannot be positioned with the legs up in stirrups (lithotomy position), but must be positioned flat on the back.

A variety of procedures may be performed through the cystoscope. The cystoscope permits the urologist to obtain a urine specimen from each kidney to evaluate its function. Cup forceps can be inserted through the cystoscope in order to remove a small sample of the tissue for microscopic analysis (biopsy), or for removal of kidney stones (renal calculi). Flushing (irrigation) and suction are also performed through the cystoscope. Cystoscopes may be attached to video camera equipment for recording and to allow the individual the opportunity to view abnormalities.

A cystoscopy may be performed for diagnosis or treatment of several conditions. Conditions include blood of unknown origin in the urine (hematuria), urinary incontinence, abnormal urine collection in the bladder (urinary retention), abnormal urine collection in the kidney due to an obstruction (hydronephrosis), an enlarged prostate gland (benign prostatic hypertrophy), suspected cancer (urethra, prostate, ureter or renal pelvis), urinary tract stones, abnormal narrowing or constriction (strictures), obstruction at the point where the ureter joins the kidney (ureteropelvic junction), bladder inflammation with abnormal bleeding (hemorrhagic cystitis), infection, abnormal tracts between the urethra and nearby structures (fistula), or chronic inflammation within the walls of the bladder (interstitial cystitis).

Reason for Procedure

A cystoscopy is a diagnostic procedure performed for diagnosis of a number of abnormalities of the urinary tract. It may be performed for urinary tract symptoms such as when there is blood of unknown origin in the urine (hematuria) and when there is urinary incontinence. It may be performed for evaluation and diagnosis of conditions such as abnormal urine collection in the bladder (urinary retention), abnormal urine collection in the kidney due to an obstruction (hydronephrosis), an enlarged prostate gland (benign prostatic hypertrophy), suspected cancer (urethra, prostate, ureter or renal pelvis), urinary tract stones, abnormal narrowing or constriction (strictures), obstruction at the point where the ureter joins the kidney (ureteropelvic junction), bladder inflammation with abnormal bleeding (hemorrhagic cystitis), infection, abnormal tracts between the urethra and nearby structures (fistula), or chronic inflammation within the walls of the bladder (interstitial cystitis).

While cystoscopy is generally a diagnostic procedure, it may also be performed for therapeutic purposes. Using additional instruments that are passed through the cystoscope, stones (calculi) in the bladder, ureter, or urethra may be removed, bleeding sites may be controlled through electrocautery, strictures may be opened (dilated), and small tumors in the bladder may be removed (tumor resection).

How Procedure Is Performed

Transurethral cystoscopy is most often performed under sedation. Alternatively, spinal or general anesthesia may be used. The opening of the urethra (meatus) is cleansed with a surgical scrub solution, or if therapeutic procedures are planned, the perineal area may be also cleansed. A local topical anesthetic is instilled into the urethra by the urologist before the cystoscope is inserted (also called a cystourethroscope) into the urethra. An irrigation system is attached to the cystoscope, and the scope is passed up through the urethra to the bladder. If the ureters are to be examined, ureteral catheters are passed through the cystoscope. Examination includes visualization of the interior of the urethra, the bladder, and the ureteral openings. In males, the prostate, bladder neck, and the area containing the ejaculatory duct (verumontanum) are also examined. In females, the urethra, bladder neck and bladder are examined.

Urine may be obtained for culture or to be sent to the pathologist to identify abnormal or cancerous cells (cytology).

Prognosis

The predicted outcome is accurate diagnosis of conditions affecting the urinary tract. Diagnosis may include the cause of hematuria and urinary incontinence. Conditions that may be diagnosed during cystoscopy include abnormal urine collection in the bladder (urinary retention), abnormal urine collection in the kidney due to an obstruction (hydronephrosis), an enlarged prostate gland (benign prostatic hypertrophy), cancer (urethra, prostate, ureter or renal pelvis), urinary tract stones, abnormal narrowing or constriction (strictures), obstruction at the point where the ureter joins the kidney (ureteropelvic junction), bladder inflammation with abnormal bleeding (hemorrhagic cystitis), infection, abnormal tracts between the urethra and nearby structures (fistula), or chronic inflammation within the walls of the bladder (interstitial cystitis).

The outcome of therapeutic procedures performed with cystoscopy (removal of stones, electrocautery of bleeding sites, opening of strictures, and removal of small tumors) is generally good.

Specialists

- Urologist

Work Restrictions / Accommodations

Work restrictions or accommodations are not usually associated with this procedure.

Comorbid Conditions

The presence of a bleeding disorder may impact recovery.

Procedure Complications

Complications may include injury or perforation to the urethra or bladder and infection. Bleeding may occur from sites that are biopsied.

Factors Influencing Duration

Length of disability may be influenced by the underlying condition for which the procedure was performed or by any complications.

Length of Disability

No disability is expected for this procedure. Disability may occur as a result of an underlying condition.

For bladder biopsy.

Duration in Days

Job Classification	Minimum	Optimum	Maximum
Any work	1	3	4

References

Cunningham, F. Gary, et al. "Renal and Urinary Tract Disorders." Williams Obstetrics, 20th ed. Cunningham, F. Gary, et al., eds. New York: McGraw-Hill, 1997. 1125-1144.

Stoller, Marshall L. "Retrograde Instrumentation of the Urinary Tract." Smith's General Urology, 15th ed. Tanagho, Emil A., and Jack W. McAninch, eds. New York: Lange Medical Books/McGraw-Hill, 2000. 196-207.

Cystourethroplasty of Bladder Neck

Other names / synonyms: Anterior Y-Plasty of Vesical Neck, Bladder Neck Reconstruction, Cystoplasty, Plastic Operation on Bladder and/or Vesical Neck, Vesical Fundus Resection, Young-Dees-Leadbetter Bladder Neck Reconstruction

57.85

Definition

This procedure involves reconstruction of the junction between the bladder and urethra. Cystourethroplasty refers to various procedures. Cysto is a term referring to the bladder and urethroplasty is the repair or reconstruction (plastic surgery) of the urethra. The bladder neck (also referred to as the vesical neck) is the lower part of the bladder that connects to the urethra. A series of surgeries may be done 3 to 6 months apart, if needed. Grafting of skin or tissues may be involved.

Cystourethroplasty procedures are performed to repair congenital abnormalities, complications following prostatectomy, and traumatic injury.

Congenital abnormalities repaired with bladder neck reconstruction procedures include bladder exstrophy (where the bladder protrudes through the skin) and when the ureter connects into the prostatic urethra (in males) or the urethra (in females). The incidence of bladder exstrophy is between one in 10,000 to 50,000 births. Males are more commonly affected with a ratio of about 2.3 to 1.

In adults, bladder neck reconstruction may be performed to repair abnormalities associated with prior prostate surgery in men and pelvic surgery performed to treat urinary incontinence in women. In men, incontinence occurs most often following a radical prostatectomy beginning about 3% and up to 87%. The incidence of incontinence is low after transurethral prostatectomy. Estimates of the failure rate of surgeries performed in women to correct incontinence vary from 5-60%. Repair of the bladder, bladder neck, and urethra may be necessary following traumatic injury. In men, urethral injury may be located in the part of the urethra from the bladder neck to just below the prostate known as the posterior urethra. Ninety-one percent of cases of posterior urethral injury occur as a result of pelvic fracture. Rupture of the bladder occurs in 10-29% of cases of urethral injury.

Reason for Procedure

Cystourethroplasty may be performed to repair abnormalities of the bladder, relieve a narrow urethra (stricture), or repair an obstructed urethra involving the portion near the bladder. Most commonly, bladder neck reconstruction procedures are performed to repair abnormalities present at birth (congenital). Because repair of congenital abnormalities may require a series of reconstruction procedures, it may also be performed in young men with previous surgeries for repair of congenital abnormalities.

How Procedure Is Performed

This surgery is done in an operating room usually under general anesthesia. An incision is made over the pubic bone. The actual reconstruction procedure depends on the underlying cause and specific procedure to be performed. A urinary catheter may be placed in the urethra or through the skin of the abdomen into the bladder for a period of time to aid in healing.

Repair of congenital abnormalities is complex and often involves more than one procedure in order to complete all repairs. In addition to closing the bladder and abdomen, pelvic bones may be surgically altered (osteotomy), bladder neck must be repaired, ureters require reimplantation, and urethra may require correction especially if the meatus is abnormally located (epispadias). Grafting may be necessary.

For repair of urethral rupture, general anesthesia is used and the individual placed in the lithotomy position. An abdominal incision is made. Any blood in the pelvic area (hematoma) is drained. The urethral injury and any bladder lacerations are repaired. In some repairs, a catheter (Foley catheter) may be placed through the urethra during the healing process. In other cases, a catheter may be placed through the skin directly into the bladder (cystostomy tube).

Prognosis

The outcome of repair of congenital abnormalities is relief of urinary symptoms such as incontinence. About 75-87% of individuals regain control of urination (continence) following bladder neck reconstruction performed for repair of bladder exstrophy.

Specialists

- Urologist

Work Restrictions / Accommodations

Time off from work is necessary during recovery from surgery. Recovery time is longer when open procedures are used. Time off from work may also be longer if fractures to pelvic bones occurred. Development of complications such as an infection may prolong the recovery time. Clothes need to be loose fitting if a urinary catheter is in place. Time during the workday may be needed to care for a catheter. Lifting and activity can be restricted after surgery.

Comorbid Conditions

Comorbid conditions may include those that increase the risk of infection or prolonged healing such as diabetes and AIDS.

Procedure Complications

Complications may include those possible with any surgical procedure such as wound infection and bleeding. Some complications are specific to the procedure performed and the underlying condition. Complications associated with repair of bladder exstrophy include incontinence, infection, wound separation (dehiscence), obstruction, and urinary stones. Complications of repair of urethral rupture may include incontinence, impotence, and urethral strictures.

Factors Influencing Duration

The need for a series of surgeries, the underlying problem, associated injuries such as a pelvic fracture, and any complications affect the length of disability.

Length of Disability

Duration in Days

Job Classification	Minimum	Optimum	Maximum
Sedentary work	42	49	56
Light work	42	49	56
Medium work	42	49	70
Heavy work	56	63	84
Very Heavy work	56	63	112

References

Carr, Michael C., and Michael E. Mitchell. "Anatomic Incontinence." Urinary Incontinence. O'Donnell, Pat D St. Louis: Mosby, 1997. 163-171.

Munarriz, Ricardo M., and Gennaro A. Carpinito. "Urethral Injury." Operative Urology. Krane, Robert J., Mike B. Siroky, and John M. Fitzpatrick, eds. New York: Churchill Livingstone, 2000. 209214.

Dacryocystitis

Other names / synonyms: Lacrimal Sac Infection, Nasolacrimal Duct Obstruction, Tear Duct Obstruction, Tear Sac Infection

375.30, 375.32, 375.42

Definition

Dacryocystitis is an inflammation and infection of the tear sac (lacrimal) located between the inside corner of the eyelid and the nose. It usually affects only one eye. When the tear drainage system (nasolacrimal duct) is blocked (obstructed) due to scarring, injury, chronic sinus infection, or other factors, bacteria may grow in the trapped fluid. Congenital dacryocystitis occurs when tear ducts fail to develop properly during infancy. Unusually positioned (ectopic) teeth may also compress and obstruct tear ducts. Dacryocystitis is more common in the elderly, and four times more common in women than in men.

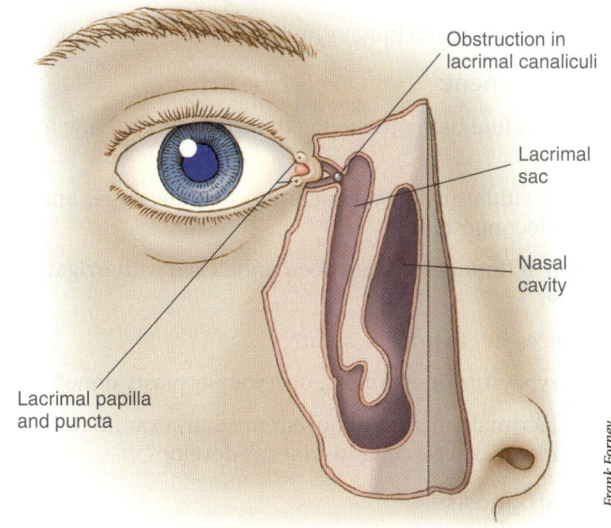

Diagnosis

History: Symptoms include recurring pain, redness, and swelling in the area between the inner corner of the eyelid and the nose. Pus may occasionally discharge from the inner corner (canthus). Before infection, blockage of the nasolacrimal duct may have caused a watery eye or excess tearing. Dacryocystitis may follow a history of injury to the area or recent nasal infection.

Physical exam: The exam may reveal redness, swelling, and tenderness over the involved lacrimal gland, extending to the cheek in extreme cases. Pressure over the lacrimal sac may produce mucus or pus. In chronic cases, the only sign might be slight swelling over the lacrimal sac.

Tests: X-rays of the nose and facial bones may rule out a fracture or structural deformity. Fluid expressed from the lacrimal gland can be cultured or stained for identification of infectious organisms. X-ray studies of dye injected into the tear drainage system might pinpoint the site of the obstruction (dacryocystography).

Treatment

Acute and chronic forms of dacryocystitis may respond to antibiotic ointment or drops, although systemic antibiotics (oral, intravenous, or injection) may be needed. Warm compresses, massage, and analgesics provide some pain relief, and oral decongestants may promote opening of the tear drainage system. Unblocking the tear drainage system generally is the only permanent cure for severe or recurrent infections. Irrigation sometimes clears the blockage. A fluid composed of the same solution as tears (saline solution) is flushed through a narrow tube (cannula), which is inserted into a drainage opening in the tear duct.

If irrigation and antibiotics fail to clear symptoms, the nose is examined to ensure adequate drainage space. A silicone tube (stent) can be inserted into the nasolacrimal duct for 3-6 months. A laser probe inserted in the duct could remove the obstruction, or surgery (dacryocystorhinostomy) may create a permanent drain between the tear sac and the nose. Balloon catheters have been used to clear partial blockages (dacryocystoplasty). If medical and surgical treatments described above fail, the lacrimal sac itself may be surgically removed. Until the condition is resolved, daily examinations are crucial to prevent complications such as spread of infection into surrounding eye tissue (orbital cellulitis).

Prognosis

Dacryocystitis tends to recur until the nasolacrimal duct blockage is removed.

Differential Diagnosis

Conditions with similar symptoms include nasal injury, deviated septum, excessive inflammation of nasal passages (hypertrophic rhinitis), nasal polyps, excessive bone development in the nose (hypertrophied inferior turbinate), frontal sinusitis, less severe lacrimal sac obstructions, and inadequate or unformed tear duct openings present at birth (residual congenital dacryostenosis). Excessive tearing and abnormal discharges also are associated with "pink eye" or eye infections (conjunctivitis), atypical positioning of the tear duct, and corneal problems such as "dry eye" or abrasions. Another similar condition, canaliculitis, results from swelling and pain in the inner corner of eyelid (canthus).

Specialists

- Ophthalmologist
- Otolaryngologist

Work Restrictions / Accommodations

Work restrictions and accommodations are not usually required with this condition, other than avoidance of dusty or dirty work areas or exposure to fumes that might further irritate the eye.

Comorbid Conditions

Chronic sinusitis with accompanying recurring infections might complicate or increase length of time needed for treatment of dacryocystitis.

Complications

An abscess may form and rupture, causing drainage through a new opening (fistula). Bacterial (Pneumococcal) dacryocystitis may traumatize the cornea, creating an open sore (corneal ulcer). Recurring acute infections may result in a red, brawny, hardened area (induration) over the lacrimal sac. Chronic dacryocystitis increases the risk of infection that spreads into surrounding eye tissue (orbital cellulitis).

Factors Influencing Duration

Length of disability may be influenced by severity of symptoms, method of treatment, response to treatment, or complications. Careless personal hygiene is known to spread infection linked to recurrences of dacryocystitis. As an example, frequent eye rubbing can cause bacterial contamination.

Length of Disability

Duration of any disability associated with dacryocystitis depends on severity and possible complications. The condition could be ongoing or recurrent until blockages within the tear drainage system are resolved.

Surgical treatment.

Duration in Days

Job Classification	Minimum	Optimum	Maximum
Sedentary work	2	5	10
Light work	2	5	10
Medium work	3	5	14
Heavy work	3	5	14
Very Heavy work	3	5	14

Failure to Recover

If an individual fails to recover within the maximum duration expectancy period, the reader may wish to reference the following questions to assist in better understanding the specifics of an individual's medical case.

Regarding diagnosis:

- Does the individual have a chronic sinus infection? Scarring or injury of the nasolacrimal duct? Did the tear ducts develop improperly during infancy?
- Does the individual complain of recurring pain, redness, and swelling in the area between the inner corner of the eyelid and the nose? Has pus been present in the inner canthus?
- Has the individual had a watery eye or excessive tearing?
- On exam is there redness, swelling, and tenderness over the involved lacrimal gland, extending to the cheek in extreme cases? Only slight swelling over the lacrimal sac?
- Does pressure over the lacrimal sac produce mucus or pus?
- Has the individual had an x-ray of the nose and facial bones?
- Was the fluid expressed from the lacrimal gland cultured or stained?
- Did the individual have dacryocystography?
- Have conditions with similar symptoms been ruled out?

Regarding treatment:

- Is the individual being treated with topical or systemic antibiotics?
- Is the individual using warm compresses, massage, analgesics, and oral decongestants?
- Has the tear drainage system been unblocked with irrigation? Laser probe?
- Was it necessary to put in a stent?
- Was dacryocystorhinostomy or dacryocystoplasty done?
- Was the lacrimal sac itself removed? Are daily examinations being done to insure orbital cellulitis doesn't develop?

Regarding prognosis:

- Is the individual's employer able to accommodate any necessary restrictions?
- Does the individual have any conditions that may affect their ability to heal?
- Does the individual have any complications such as a fistula, corneal ulcer, induration over the lacrimal sac, or orbital cellulitis?

References

Beaty, Laura, and Robert L. Herting. "Ophthalmology: Orbit, Eyelids, and Lacrimal Apparatus." The University of Iowa Family Practice Handbook, 3rd ed Graber, Mark A., Peter P. Toth, and Robert L. Herting, eds. Iowa City: University of Iowa College of Medicine, 1997 672. Virtual Hospital. 23 May 2000 <http://www.vh.org/Providers/ClinRef/FPHandbook/Chapter12/04-12.html>.

Beers, Mark H., and Robert Berkow, eds. The Merck Manual of Diagnosis and Therapy, 17th ed. Whitehouse Station, NJ: Merck & Co., Inc, 1999.

Dacryostenosis
Other names / synonyms: Nasolacrimal Duct Obstruction
375.56

Definition

Dacryostenosis is a condition in which the tear duct (nasolacrimal duct) is partially or totally closed due to scarring, blockage, or narrowing of the tear duct.

In adults, tear duct blockages are usually caused by chronic nasal infection, or severe or chronic inflammation of the membrane covering the eyeball and lining of the eyelid (conjunctivitis). Inherited abnormality resulting in blockage usually appears in infancy; infection of the tear duct occurs in all ages but is most common among children. Injuries including fractures of the nose, facial bones, or eye also may create the condition; another cause is nasal polyps.

Acquired dacryostenosis is more common in individuals 50 years or older. Middle-aged women have a higher incidence of the disease because their tear ducts are narrow and more prone to blockage. In one study, the condition was found in about 15% of individuals with cleft lip and palate disorders. The condition also is associated with long-term cocaine inhalation.

Diagnosis

History: Symptoms include excessive tearing that runs down the cheeks (epiphora) from either one or both eyes. The individual may also complain of chronic sinus infections, pink eye (conjunctivitis), or a previous injury to the affected area. The eyelids may be crusted together. Pain and swelling in the inner corner of the eyelids may be reported.

Physical exam: Pressure applied over the nasolacrimal duct may release a large amount of mucus or pus from the blocked duct. Swelling and redness in the area of the tear duct or in the white of the eye surrounding the tear duct may be detected. A bluish swelling below the inside lower eyelid may indicate a blockage of the tear duct.

Tests: Microscopic examination of tear duct fluid that has been cultured may identify the bacteria causing the infection. The duct may be irrigated with material that provides contrast for x-ray studies (contrast medium) to help identify an injury or site of an obstruction. A local anesthetic may be applied, followed by injection of a fluid with the same composition as tears (saline solution) that contains a special dye (fluorescein eye stain), to pinpoint the site of an obstruction. Some researchers recommend biopsies of the nasolacrimal duct obstruction in order to rule out tumors.

Treatment

Often the condition requires no more treatment than manual massage of the area to remove clogging contents. Simple infections are usually treated with either oral or topical antibiotics. In mild cases, or where a partial blockage is suspected, probing may be done under local anesthetic to unblock the tear duct. A saline solution may be flushed through the duct, possibly followed by probing with increasingly larger instruments, to fully open (dilate) the passage. This is often done in the doctor's office with local anesthesia. After dilation, the tear duct system is again irrigated with saline. Hospitalization and intravenous (IV) antibiotics to resolve the infection may be indicated in some severe or recurrent cases. A newer procedure to clear partial or mild obstructions involves inserting and dilating balloon-like material (balloon dacryoplasty) to open the duct. In more severe cases, a tube (stent) made of silicone or other materials may be inserted into the nasolacrimal duct for 3-6 months to treat the obstruction. Surgery (dacryocystorhinostomy) to create a permanent drain between the tear duct and the nasal passage may be needed. Surgical implantation of an artificial tear duct (Jones glass tube) is necessary in some cases.

Prognosis

Although blockages in milder cases may be cleared by irrigation, probing, or other methods, the obstruction may recur along with continuing infections. Where appropriate, dilating the duct with balloon-like material (balloon dacryoplasty) has about an 85% reported success rate. Treatment with stents or the surgical creation of permanent drainage between the tear duct and nasal passage (dacryocystorhinostomy) have about a 90% success rate. Depending on the extent of infection or other complications, individuals treated in an office environment will likely recover within several days. Surgical intervention requiring hospitalization may need several weeks of recovery time.

Without treatment, permanent scarring of the tear duct may occur.

Differential Diagnosis

Conditions with similar symptoms include contact with physical or chemical irritants, tumors (neoplasm), inflammation of the gland that secretes tears (lacrimal gland), facial cellulitis, sinusitis, uveitis, blepharitis, thyroiditis, and infection of the tear duct or tear gland (dacryocystitis). Conditions with similar symptoms that also may lead to dacryostenosis include chronic rhinitis, conjunctivitis, mucosal polyps, structural abnormalities, or injuries.

Specialists

- Ophthalmologist

Work Restrictions / Accommodations

If complications such as tearing or infections recur or become chronic, the individual may be unable to perform tasks requiring keen visual acuity or concentration. Strenuous activities must be reduced during treatment for infection. Time off from work may be needed until the condition has resolved.

Comorbid Conditions

Chronic sinus infections may lead to recurrences of dacryostenosis. Individuals who have engaged in long-term inhalation of cocaine may have severely or permanently damaged their tear duct system.

Complications

Prolonged blockage of the nasolacrimal duct can lead to recurrent infections (dacryocystitis), which also may spread into the tissue surrounding the eye (orbital cellulitis). Surgical intervention might create scarring.

Factors Influencing Duration

If the individual requires hospitalization and surgical intervention, recovery time may take several weeks. Complications such as recurrent infections may also lengthen disability

Length of Disability

Complications such as eye infections or excessive tearing may lengthen disability for individuals whose tasks require keen visual acuity and concentration.

Surgical treatment.

Duration in Days

Job Classification	Minimum	Optimum	Maximum
Sedentary work	2	5	10
Light work	2	5	10
Medium work	3	5	14
Heavy work	3	5	14
Very Heavy work	3	5	14

Failure to Recover

If an individual fails to recover within the maximum duration expectancy period, the reader may wish to reference the following questions to assist in better understanding the specifics of an individual's medical case.

Regarding diagnosis:

- Does the individual have chronic nasal or conjunctival infection?
- Did the individual's tear ducts develop improperly in infancy?
- Has the individual had fractures of the nose, facial bones, or eye?
- Does the individual have nasal polyps? Cleft lip and palate disorders?
- Has the individual inhaled cocaine on a long term basis?
- Does the individual complain of excessive tearing, eyelids crusted together or pain and swelling in the inner corner of the eyelids?
- On exam does pressure over the nasolacrimal duct release a large amount of mucus or pus? Is swelling or redness present? Is there bluish swelling below the inside lower lid?
- Has the fluid expressed from the duct been cultured?
- Has the individual had contrast x-ray studies of the duct? Was a biopsy done?
- Have conditions with similar symptoms been ruled out?

Regarding treatment:

- Has manual massage of the area been done?
- Has the individual been treated with topical or oral antibiotics?
- Has the blockage been removed using a probe or irrigation? Was the duct dilated?
- Was it necessary to hospitalize the individual for IV antibiotics?
- Was a balloon dacryoplasty done? Was a stent inserted?
- Was it necessary to perform a dacryocystorhinostomy?
- Was surgical implantation of an artificial tear duct (Jones glass tube) necessary?

Regarding prognosis:

- Is the individual's employer able to accommodate any necessary restrictions?
- Does the individual have any conditions that may affect their ability to recover?
- Does the individual have any complication such as dacryocystitis, orbital cellulitis or scarring from surgery?

References

HealthCentral. "Blocked Tear Duct." <u>General Health Encyclopedia</u>. 1998 Adam.com. 11 Oct 2000 <http://www.healthcentral.com/mhc/top/001016.cfm>.

De Quervain's Release
82.01

Definition

De Quervain's release is a surgical procedure to relieve pressure caused by inflamed covering of the tendons (sheath, retinaculum) in the area of the thumb (abductor pollicis longus and extensor pollicis brevis). This condition is known as stenosing radial tenosynovitis or De Quervain's disease.

Stenosing tenosynovitis of the extensor pollicis brevis and abductor pollicis longus tendons is a condition where the tendon and its covering (tenosynovioma or tendon sheath) become inflamed usually as a result of repetitive motion. The involved tendons are usually normal, only the covering is inflamed. Because the area within the wrist is confined, any inflammation reduces available space for the tendon-pulley mechanism to function. Pain and increased inflammation are caused when the tendon and its swollen sheath is pulled through the tighter space. It becomes difficult for the tendon to move and consequently begins to catch and rub, producing jerky movements and causing more pain and inflammation.

In De Quervain's syndrome, the tenosynovitis affects two specific tendons of the wrist, the abductor pollicis longus and the extensor pollicis brevis. This surgery does not affect the conditions that originally led to the development of the inflamed tendon sheath such as repetitive motion. However, it does affect disease progression because it removes the conditions that perpetuate and increase the pain and inflammation.

The procedure is done through a small incision along the thumb side of the wrist on an outpatient basis under local or regional anesthesia.

The precise cause of De Quervain's syndrome is unknown. Excessive friction from overuse may precipitate onset as incidence seems to be increased in individuals with repeated activity involved in combined forceful gripping and hard twisting of the wrist. Work activities at risk include those individuals doing buffing, grinding, punch press operators, sewing, cutting, packing, housekeeping, cooking, meat packing or butchering, and operating room personnel.

Reason for Procedure

De Quervain's release is used to relieve pain and inflammation associated with constriction (stenosing tenosynovitis) of the tendons of the thumb that has not responded to conservative treatment. However, if one or more local anesthetic-corticosteroid injections have failed to provide at least temporary pain relief, and the physician is reasonably certain the appropriate place (first extensor compartment) was injected, surgery should be deferred and consideration given to another diagnosis. The goal of the surgery is to relieve the entrapment of the tendons caused by inflammation and compression under the tendon sheath (retinaculum). The incision through the tendon sheath and the removal (excision) of swollen tendon covering (tenosynovioma) decreases pressure on the tendons, allowing them to glide more easily.

Description

De Quervain's release is accomplished through a skin incision exposing the tendon sheath (retinaculum) along the thumb (radial) side of the wrist. The sheath is cut (released) and inflamed material (tenosynovioma) is removed from around the tendons. The release is done using regional or local anesthesia in an outpatient setting.

Prognosis

Relief of symptoms is the optimum outcome. Surgery is generally performed only after conservative measures over several months, including one or more local anesthetic-corticosteroid injections, have failed. Such cases may have developed more severe constriction about the tendon sheath, complicating complete recovery. If aggravating activities such as repetitive gripping and lifting are not altered, remission may occur.

Specialists

- Occupational Therapist
- Orthopedic Surgeon
- Physiatrist
- Physical Therapist
- Rheumatologist

Rehabilitation

After De Quervain's release procedures, the thumb is dressed with an antiseptic dressing and splinted so that the wrist and thumb remain in neutral position and the fingers are free to move. Once the dressing is removed, therapy is initiated.

The goal of the first week of therapy is to prevent scar tissue formation around the incision, to reduce swelling (edema), and increase range of motion. Pain is also controlled using modalities such as ice massage and T.E.N.S. (Transcutaneous Electrical Nerve Stimulation) if the pain is extreme. The individual may also be taught to perform retrograde massage by massaging the forearm and then progressively moving to the hand, avoiding the surgical site. To prevent scar tissue build up (adhesions), active range-of-motion exercises for the wrist and thumb of the affected hand may be performed.

The individual may also experience extreme sensitivity to the site of surgery. Activities that decrease hypersensitivity (desensitization) should start immediately if sensitization occurs. These activities include materials with differing textures being rubbed, taped, or rolled over the sensitive area for either continuous or intermittent intervals.

The splint is removed when performing exercises. The individual is taught how to protect the thumb by eliminating forceful thumb flexion or holding the hand in a pinch position for prolonged periods of time. An occupational therapist may assess the individual's daily work and home routines to make suggestions on how to eliminate repetitive strain on the thumb during these activities. Both hands should be monitored for strength, flexibility, and endurance as the dominant hand may be injured.

Gripping exercises such as squeezing a tennis ball or putty and more functional exercises such a picking up objects are added to the routine. As therapy progresses, exercises should be reflective of the work environment. The individual should be reintroduced to tools used at work (i.e., a hammer. The individual must work to improve hand endurance. The work environment must be reassessed in preparation for the individual's return to work. Changes in job environment may include wearing a splint while performing tasks that require continuous wrist motion or rotating tasks that may induce repetitive strain to the thumb.

Work Restrictions / Accommodations

Individuals whose work involves lifting or heavy hand and wrist usage while grip is maintained will require temporary reassignment to more sedentary work duties. Light, normal usage of the fingers is encouraged after surgical release. In cases of wrist tendon releases, normal hand usage is encouraged with limited wrist movement. During the early rehabilitative stages, a splint may be used on the affected hand that limits dexterity. Work safety issues need to be addressed.

Comorbid Conditions

Any underlying inflammatory or neurovascular disease can impact the outcome of the procedure as well as the progression of the condition postoperatively. Wound healing can be adversely affected by smoking. Tendency to form stiff, large scars (keloids) may slow progress.

Procedure Complications

Complications may include infection, damage to blood vessels or nerves, increased inflammation and pain, and reflex sympathetic dystrophy. Specifically during surgery, care must be taken to avoid cutting a sensory branch of the radial nerve as this will result in loss of feeling and, perhaps, a neuroma just as painful and debilitating as the original condition.

Factors Influencing Duration

Factors include the extent of disease progression, whether the dominant or nondominant hand is involved, severity of symptoms, development of complications, and individual's job requirements.

Length of Disability

Job Classification	Duration in Days		
	Minimum	Optimum	Maximum
Sedentary work	1	7	21
Light work	3	14	21
Medium work	7	21	42
Heavy work	21	28	56
Very Heavy work	21	28	56

Notes

References

deQuervain's Tenosynovitis Postoperative. eHand.com. 01 Mar 2000. 06 Jul 2000 <http://www.eatonhand.com/thr/thr061.htm>.

Blue, Carolyn, and Pamela Levin. "Ergonomics." Orthopaedic Nursing, 2nd ed. Maher, Ann, Susan Salmond, and Teresa Pellino, eds. Philadelphia: W.B. Saunders Company, 1998. 65-76.

Browne, P.S. Basic Facts in Orthopaedics, 2nd ed. Palo Alto, CA: Mosby-Year Book, Inc, 1985.

Mercier, L.R. Practical Orthopedics, 4th ed. St. Louis: Mosby-Year Book, Inc, 1995.

Totten, Patricia. "Therapist's Management of deQuervain's Disease." Rehabilitation of the Hand: Surgery and Therapy, 3rd ed. Hunter, James, et al., eds. St. Louis: The C.V. Mosby Company, 1990. 308-317.

Turek's Orthopaedics, Principles and Their Application, 5th ed. Weinstein, S.L. and J.A. Buckwalter, eds. Philadelphia: Lippincott-Raven, 1994.

Decubitus Ulcer

Other names / synonyms: Bedsore, Decubitus, Pressure Sore, Pressure Ulcer

707.0, 707.9

Definition

Decubitus ulcers (decubiti) are skin erosions (ulcers) of various thicknesses that develop from prolonged pressure of skin and underlying tissue against bony prominences.

The underlying origin of decubiti is tissue death from pressure (pressure necrosis). Local factors such as denervated skin, skin with poor circulation, and loss of fat cushioning can predispose to skin breakdown. The ulcer may be of various sizes, shapes, and depth. Sometimes, a small skin ulcer will have a much larger area of destruction below the skin surface.

Decubiti are classified by size, depth, shape, infection, and type and amount of drainage. Five systems of decubitus classification have been described. These are the Sessing Scale; Wound Healing Scale; Sussman Wound Healing Scale; Pressure Sore Status Tool; and Pressure Ulcer Scale for Healing. These systems are useful in categorizing the wounds to plan treatment.

It is estimated that 1 million Americans develop decubiti annually. The incidence is higher among individuals in acute care settings. Over 90% of decubitus ulcers occur in elderly, bedridden individuals who have chronic, debilitating disease or who are unable to change position. Decubitus ulcers occur in paraplegics who have diminished or absent sensation in the pressure area. and in individuals who develop a pressure point from a cast or appliance, or from prolonged bedrest recovering from another condition. It is estimated that 7.4% of individuals with spinal cord injuries develop decubiti.

Diagnosis

History: Individuals will have a decreased ambulatory ability. Individuals may report the appearance of a wound that may or may not be painful. If the wound is infected, the individual will complain of fever and a feeling of uneasiness (malaise).

Physical exam: The exam reveals skin ulceration with a red surrounding area. Further exploration will determine whether underlying tissues are affected. Deeper tissues will be eroded, often with exposure of muscle, tendon, or bone.

Tests: Culture of the wound material is necessary to determine the specific bacteria causing infection (if any). A wound biopsy may be performed to rule out vasculitis and skin cancers. Since decubiti usually form over bony pressure points, an x-ray may be used to evaluate underlying bone to rule out deep bone infection (osteomyelitis). If the x-ray findings are questionable (equivocal), a bone scan (scintigram) may help to evaluate the bony changes.

Treatment

Decubitus ulcers are serious lesions that require prompt attention at the earliest stage of the skin redness. With proper bodily turning and relief of pressure, decubitus ulcers are usually preventable. If the ulcer is small and noninfected, topical drying agents and removal of pressure may be sufficient therapy. Infected wounds and bigger sores require use of systemic antibiotics, surgical excision, plastic surgery, and sometimes hyperbaric oxygen therapy (HBO).

A comprehensive wound care program is usually necessary for these ulcers. This can involve physical therapy (range of motion exercises and hydrotherapy), frequent removal of dead tissue (debridement), wound cleansing, topical medications, and dressing changes with various specialized dressing materials. After healing, special devices to relieve pressure to prevent recurrence are necessary.

Prognosis

Noninfected, small pressure sores may heal, leaving a scar. The outcome of infected, bigger sores is difficult to predict. Recurrence is a problem, since the situation that caused the lesion usually persists. Many of these individuals are elderly and debilitated, and may never heal. Healing in such individuals is slow and difficult. Younger, healthier individuals with postinjury decubiti heal more quickly.

Differential Diagnosis

Diabetic ulcerations, vasculitis, or gangrene are other diagnostic possibilities.

Specialists

- General Surgeon
- Orthopedic Surgeon
- Plastic Surgeon
- Vascular Surgeon
- Wound Care Specialist

Work Restrictions / Accommodations

The individual cannot work until healing has occurred. Once healing has occurred, pressure to the area of the previous decubitus must be avoided. For example, if the wound was on the buttocks area (sacrum), the individual may need to sit on a cushion to reduce pressure.

Complementary and Alternative Therapies

Content is intended for awareness only. Treatments may or may not be effective. Scientific evidence may be lacking and some substances have potentially toxic effects. Dr. Presley Reed and the editors do not endorse the use of these therapies in the absence of consultation with a licensed medical professional.

Electrical stimulation - Said to increase the rate of healing by more than 50% by increasing blood flow and pressure distribution.

Comorbid Conditions

Comorbid conditions that delay healing include diabetes mellitus, peripheral vascular disease, decreased mobility, limb contractures, stroke (cerebral vascular accident, or CVA), obesity, and thinning (atrophy) of skin.

Complications

Complications include recurrence, infection, abscess, and slow healing. Formation of basal cell or squamous cell carcinomas or skin cancers (malignant transformation) can occur in 1% of longstanding ulcers.

Factors Influencing Duration

The underlying condition, location and size of the ulceration, presence of infection, and response to treatment may influence the length of disability.

Length of Disability

Duration depends on underlying condition and job demands.

Failure to Recover

If an individual fails to recover within the maximum duration expectancy period, the reader may wish to reference the following questions to assist in better understanding the specifics of an individual's medical case.

Regarding diagnosis:

- Does the individual have denervated skin or skin with poor circulation?
- Does the individual have loss of fat cushioning?
- Does the individual have decreased ability to ambulate?
- Have underlying tissues been affected?
- Is there deep tissue erosion exposure of muscle, tendon, or bone?
- Has the wound been cultured? Was a wound biopsy done?
- Was an x-ray and bone scan done?
- Have conditions with similar symptoms been ruled out?

Regarding treatment:

- Is the individual's decubitus small?
- Did they respond to drying agents and removal of any pressure?
- Is the individual's decubitus large? Is it infected?
- Was surgical excision needed? Was plastic surgery necessary?
- Was hyperbaric oxygen therapy needed?

Regarding prognosis:

- Is the individual's employer able to accommodate any necessary restrictions?
- Does the individual have any conditions that may affect their ability to recover?
- Has the individual had a recurrence? Is it infected?

References

Bates-Jensen, Barbara M. "Chronic Wound Assessment." Nursing Clinics of North America 34 4 (1999): 799-839.

Cohen, Philip R., and Janet H. Prystowsky. "Traumatic and Neurotrophic Ulcers." Principles and Practice of Dermatology, 2nd ed. Sams, W. Mitchell, and Peter J. Lynch, eds. New York: Churchill Livingstone, Inc, 1996. 923-929.

Degeneration, Cervical Intervertebral Disc

Other names / synonyms: Cervical Disc Disease, Degenerative Disc Disease, Degenerative Disorder of the Cervical Spine

722.4, 722.7

Definition

A cervical disc is a semirigid structure that separates and cushions the vertebral bodies in the neck (cervical spine). A degenerating cervical intervertebral disc loses some of its thickness and becomes rigid allowing the vertebrae in the neck to come closer together. Bone spurs (osteophytes) may form about the disc. Disc protrusions and extrusions (herniations) may occur. Degenerative changes to the cervical spine can occur following moderate or severe trauma or repetitive minor trauma.

Disc degeneration is a normal process of aging. The water content of intervertebral discs decreases with age causing the discs to become rigid. Ten percent of individuals in their mid-twenties and nearly 95% of individuals at age 65 have signs of cervical disc degeneration.

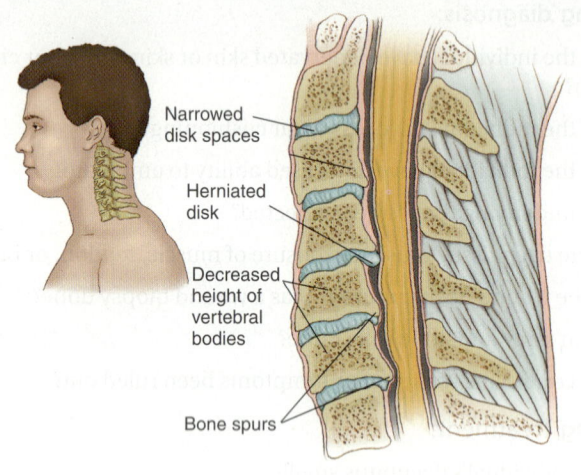

Diagnosis

History: Individuals may complain of pain aggravated by neck movement, particularly by tilting the head backward (neck extension) and rotating or tilting the head to either side. The pain is relieved by rest and changing neck position. Muscle spasm, neck stiffness, and headache may also be present. Pain may extend into the shoulders, arms, chest, and/or face. Some individuals complain of worsening pain in the morning or with nighttime awakening. Unusual symptoms include a ringing or buzzing sound in the ears (tinnitus), dizziness, periodic blurred vision, and pain behind the eyes (retroocular).

Physical exam: The exam may reveal localized or diffuse tenderness. Abnormality of certain reflexes, motor weakness, and sensory changes may indicate nerve involvement. Alternatively, physical exam may be unremarkable.

Tests: Plain x-rays show narrowing of the disc space and osteophyte formation, if present. Other radiologic testing that may be performed include CT, MRI, cervical myelography, and cervical angiography. Laboratory blood analysis may include ESR, WBC analysis, thyroid and parathyroid studies, and liver function studies.

Treatment

The goals of treatment are to relieve pain and minimize progression of the degenerative process. Medications frequently used include nonsteroidal anti-inflammatory drugs (NSAIDs), muscle relaxants, narcotics, and antidepressants. When symptoms are acute, rest and immobilization are the mainstay of treatment. Activity is adjusted to tolerance and complete bed rest for 1 to 2 days is seldom necessary. A cervical collar may be worn for a few days to provide support and limit neck motion. Traction may be indicated, especially if a herniated disc is compressing a nerve root.

Manipulation of the cervical spine is a very common procedure. It is not used specifically for disc degeneration but may be helpful in pain reduction and improved mobility in the first 1 to 2 months of symptoms. As symptoms subside, activity is gradually increased. This may include physical therapy and/or a home exercise program to mobilize and strengthen the neck and shoulders.

Postural strain such as the position of shoulder depression and a protruding chin (cervical extension) are common to sedentary workers and may produce pain or increase existing symptoms. Attention to spinal alignment, use of the backrest of a chair, and tucking the chin in position while sitting to work will reduce strain on the neck. Frequent changes of position also assist in relieving or preventing symptoms. A neck pillow may help nocturnal problems.

Techniques for reducing muscle tension such as relaxation training and biofeedback may also be helpful. Good posture and frequent changes of position help prevent fatigue. Preventive and maintenance measures (exercise, stress management techniques, or proper body mechanics) should be continued indefinitely.

Individuals whose pain is not relieved by conservative measures may benefit from a pain clinic or rehabilitation program. If pain does not subside within several weeks, further evaluation is necessary. It is not clear why some cervical discs become painful and benefit from excision and fusion.

Prognosis

Cervical disc degeneration is a chronic, irreversible condition not predictive of symptoms.

Differential Diagnosis

Mechanical instability may be a cause of recurrent pain. In some cases, persistent pain may be due to arthritis of the facet joints. Infection, fracture, tumor (intraspinal or extraspinal), fibromyalgia, myofascitis, anterior interosseous syndrome (entrapment of the deep branch of the median nerve in the proximal forearm), carpal tunnel syndrome, cubital tunnel syndrome, thoracic outlet syndrome, brachial plexus disorders, or radial nerve compression may present with similar symptoms. Thyroid or parotid disease may rarely cause neck pain. Neck pain may also have a psychological origin (psychogenic).

Specialists

- Anesthesiologist
- Chiropractor
- Neurologist
- Neurosurgeon
- Occupational Therapist
- Orthopedic Surgeon
- Pain Specialist
- Physiatrist
- Physical Therapist
- Rheumatologist

Rehabilitation

Individuals with degenerative disc disease in the cervical spine may benefit from therapy. The first objective of therapy is to control pain. Hot packs and ultrasound provide deep heating of the neck musculature. Therapists may massage the neck to further reduce muscle spasm. Mechanical or manual traction of the cervical spine may be warranted to decrease persistent muscle spasm. These techniques increase space between the vertebral bodies and provide indirect relief.

The second objective of therapy is to restore range of motion at the neck, trunk, and shoulder girdle. Physical therapists and chiropractors passively stretch the neck into rotation, side bending, flexion, and rotation. Individuals learn to actively move the neck in each of these directions to further increase motion. Individuals can increase the stretch of the neck by applying manual overpressure as the neck is moved in each of these directions. Individuals also stretch tight chest muscles that can promote poor posture.

The third goal of therapy is to increase strength. Strengthening exercises increase muscular support of the cervical spine. Individuals may perform gentle isometric exercises. In these exercises, one hand is used for light resistance while the neck is moved into each available direction. Chin tucks also strengthen the neck musculature. This exercise lengthens the spine by bringing the head straight back so that the chin is tucked into the neck. Postural muscles may also require strengthening after a prolonged period of neck immobilization. Rolling the shoulders backward and pinching the shoulder blades together are examples of postural exercises.

The final goal of therapy is to reeducate the individual in proper posture and ergonomics. Individuals are taught to sit and stand with the ears aligned over the shoulders. An evaluation of frequent work and home postures should be performed. For example, if the individual works at a computer frequently, the height of the monitor may need to be adjusted so that it is at eye level and directly in front of the individual. A chair with a lumbar support may also be helpful to promote correct sitting posture. Individuals should sleep on no more than one pillow and avoid sleeping on their stomachs. Individuals may require a cervical pillow with a built-in neck roll to attain correct spinal alignment during sleep.

Work Restrictions / Accommodations

Activities involving lifting and carrying may need to be limited. Workstation modification to permit good posture may be helpful. Overhead work (neck extension) should be avoided. Use of pain medications and muscle relaxants can affect dexterity and alertness.

Comorbid Conditions

Arthritis of the facet joints and depression may increase the length of disability.

Complications

Cervical disc protrusions or extrusions (herniation) or cervical nerve compression by bone spurs (radiculopathy) are complications of degenerating cervical discs.

Complementary and Alternative Therapies

Content is intended for awareness only. Treatments may or may not be effective. Scientific evidence may be lacking and some substances have potentially toxic effects. Dr. Presley Reed and the editors do not endorse the use of these therapies in the absence of consultation with a licensed medical professional.

Chiropractic -	Spinal manipulation may ease pain.
Ice or heat treatments -	May help control muscle pain.
Massage -	May increase circulation, relax tight muscles, and relieve pain.
Therapeutic ultrasound or diathermy -	Used to project heat deep into the tissues of the spine, which may increase mobility.

Factors Influencing Duration

Length of disability depends on the location and number of the affected discs, severity of the disc disease, severity of osteophytes, nature of any neurological involvement, presence or absence of objective sensory loss and/or muscle weakness, duration of these neurological deficits (acute or chronic), other sources of pain such as facet joint arthritis or mechanical instability, and type of treatment. Psychosocial factors may affect length of disability.

Length of Disability

Duration depends on job requirements and extent of disease progression. Disability may be permanent.

Medical treatment.

Duration in Days

Job Classification	Minimum	Optimum	Maximum
Sedentary work	1	14	21
Light work	1	14	28
Medium work	1	28	42
Heavy work	1	42	84
Very Heavy work	1	42	84

Fusion.

Duration in Days

Job Classification	Minimum	Optimum	Maximum
Sedentary work	42	49	84
Light work	56	63	84
Medium work	70	119	182
Heavy work	Indefinite	Indefinite	Indefinite
Very Heavy work	Indefinite	Indefinite	Indefinite

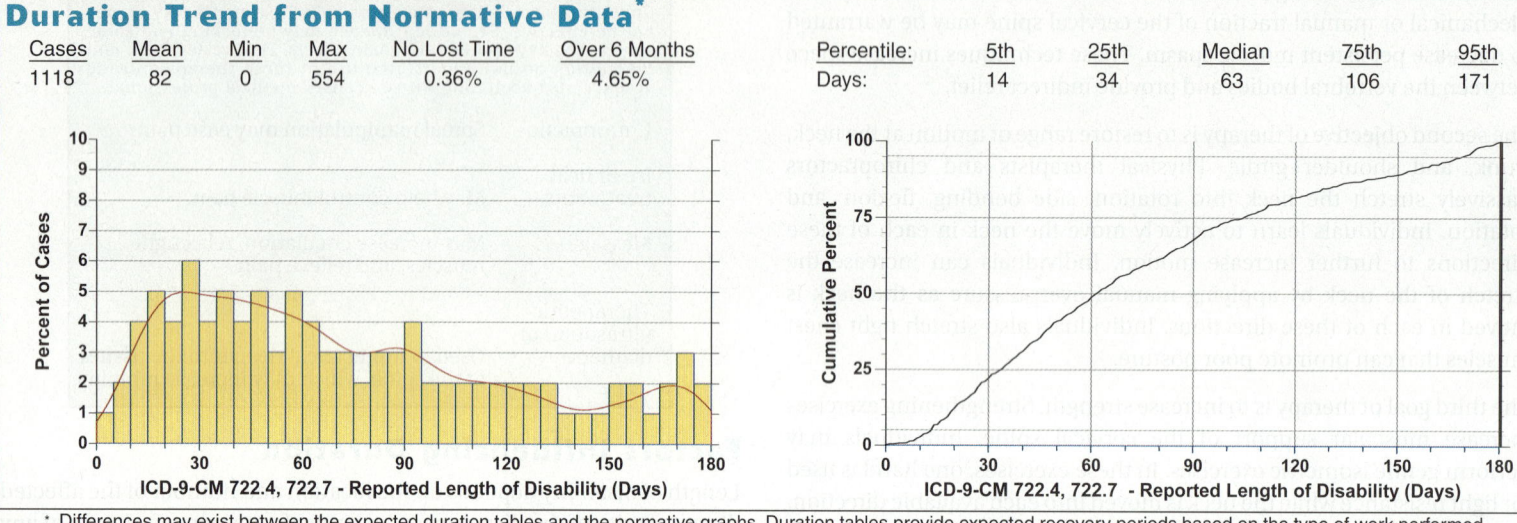

Duration Trend from Normative Data*

Cases	Mean	Min	Max	No Lost Time	Over 6 Months
1118	82	0	554	0.36%	4.65%

Percentile:	5th	25th	Median	75th	95th
Days:	14	34	63	106	171

ICD-9-CM 722.4, 722.7 - Reported Length of Disability (Days)

* Differences may exist between the expected duration tables and the normative graphs. Duration tables provide expected recovery periods based on the type of work performed by the individual. The normative graphs reflect the actual observed experience of many individuals across the spectrum of physical conditions, in a variety of industries, and with varying levels of case management.

Failure to Recover

If an individual fails to recover within the maximum duration expectancy period, the reader may wish to reference the following questions to assist in better understanding the specifics of an individual's medical case.

Regarding diagnosis:

- Does individual complain of pain aggravated by neck movement, particularly by tilting the head backward (neck extension) and rotating or tilting the head to either side? Do rest and changing neck position relieve pain?
- Does individual have muscle spasm, neck stiffness, and headache?
- Does pain extend into the shoulders, arms, chest, and/or face? Does it worsen in the morning or with nighttime awakening?
- On exam, is localized or diffuse tenderness present? Abnormality of certain reflexes, motor weakness, and sensory changes?
- Were plain x-rays done? CT, contrast-enhanced CT, or MRI?
- Were blood tests performed including ESR, WBC analysis, thyroid and parathyroid studies, and liver function studies?
- Were other causes of neck and/or arm pain ruled out?

Regarding treatment:

- Was manipulation tried?
- What medications is individual taking? Are they helpful?
- Is individual using a cervical collar for more than a few days?
- Is individual in physical therapy?
- Does individual have a sedentary job? Taken measures to correct posture and change position frequently? Relaxation training or biofeedback?
- Has individual participated in a pain clinic or rehab program? Is surgery needed?

Regarding prognosis:

- Has the physical therapist instructed individual on how to exercise at home?
- Can individual's employer accommodate restrictions necessary restrictions?
- How severe are the symptoms?
- Has the disc degeneration progressed to a point where the symptoms are not changing, and, thus, recovery is unlikely?
- Have any complications developed such as cervical disc protrusions or extrusions (herniation) or cervical nerve compression by bone spurs (radiculopathy)?
- Could individual be exaggerating symptoms because of impending litigation or avoidance of work?

References

An, Howard. "Clinical Presentation of Discogenic Neck Pain, Radiculopathy, and Myelopathy." The Cervical Spine. Clark, Charles, ed. Philadelphia: Lippincott-Raven, 1998. 755-764.

Benner, Benjamin. "Etiology, Pathogenesis, and Natural History of Discogenic Neck Pain, Radiculopathy, and Myelopathy." The Cervical Spine. Clark, Charles, ed. Philadelphia: Lippincott-Raven, 1998. 735-740.

Davis, C.H.G. "Disc and Degenerative Disease: Stenosis, Spondylosis and Subluxation." Spinal Cord Disease: Basic Science, Diagnosis and Management. Critchley, Edmund, and Andrew Eisen, eds. London: Springer-Verlag, 1997. 251-259.

Hage, Michael, and Karen Hayes. "Mechanical Spinal Traction." Manual for Physical Agents. Hayes, Karen, ed. Norwalk: Appleton & Lange, 1993. 75-82.

Hamill, Christopher. "Degenerative Diseases and Disk Disorders of the Cervical Spine." Principles of Orthopaedic Practice. Dee, Roger, et al., eds. New York: McGraw-Hill, 1997. 1351-1372.

Kisner, Carolyn, and Lynn Allen Colby. "The Spine: Treatment of Acute Problems." Therapeutic Exercise: Foundations and Techniques, 2nd ed. Philadelphia: F.A. Davis Company, 1990. 473-499.

Kurz, Lawrence. "Nonoperative Treatment of Degenerative Disorders of the Cervical Spine." The Cervical Spine. Clark, Charles, ed. Philadelphia: Lippincott-Raven, 1998. 779-783.

Sachs, Barton. "Differential Diagnosis of Neck Pain, Arm Pain, and Myelopathy." The Cervical Spine. Clark, Charles, ed. Philadelphia: Lippincott-Raven, 1998. 741-753.

Saunders, H. Duane, and Robin Saunders. Evaluation, Treatment, and Prevention of Musculoskeletal Disorders, Vol. 1 Spine. Chaska: Saunders Group, 1995.

Schneider, W., and J. Dvorak. "Functional Treatment of Diseases and Injuries of the Cervical Spine." Orthopade 25 6 (1996): 519-523.

Degeneration, Lumbar Intervertebral Disc
Other names / synonyms: Degenerative Disc Disease, Low Back Pain, Lumbar Disc Disease
722.52

Definition

A lumbar disc is a semi-rigid structure that separates and cushions the vertebral bodies in the lumbar spine. Degeneration of a lumbar disc occurs when the space between the vertebrae narrows and bone spurs form (osteophytes). As in the cervical and thoracic spines, lumbar disc degeneration is part of normal aging. The disc is usually soft and gelatin-like in the center (nucleus pulposus) and surrounded by a tough cartilage ring (annulus). The gelatin center is soft because of its high water content. The water content decreases with age, which causes the disc to become more rigid.

Studies have shown that by the age of 35 years, 30% of all individuals have a degenerated disc at one or more levels in the lumbar spine. By the age of 60, that figure is over ninety percent. When the disc space narrows, it places stress on the other joints of the vertebrae (facet joints) and this degeneration of the joints and surrounding soft tissues may lead to chronic low back pain. Usually, the cause of back pain cannot be proven, but because pain and degeneration coexist, the pain may be attributed to the degenerative changes.

Low back pain due to lumbar disc degeneration tends to occur at a younger age in men than in women. The tendency to develop lumbar disc degeneration is genetic in some cases. Smoking has been shown to increase the risk of and rate of disc degeneration.

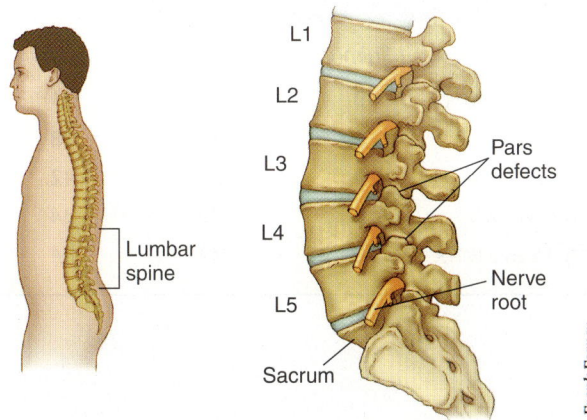

Diagnosis

History: Individuals may complain of pain in the lower back and buttocks. The pain is often brought on by activity and relieved with rest. The intermittent character of pain, but not unrelenting pain, is characteristic of disc degeneration. Over time, episodes of pain may become more frequent and intense. The individual may describe a sense of stiffness, weakness, or instability between acute episodes of pain.

Physical exam: The exam is often unremarkable. Limited range of motion is usually noted in both forward flexion and extension. Palpation of the lumbar spine may cause pain at the level of the symptomatic degenerative disc. The neuromuscular exam is directed at excluding any symptoms or signs of spinal nerve involvement.

Tests: Plain x-rays will show the narrowing of the disc space and some osteophyte formation on the vertebral bodies as aging changes. These changes are usually not the cause of the symptoms. Further testing is not indicated unless there are signs and symptoms of spinal nerve irritation or systemic disease. Discography is a very controversial test with no clear literature proof that it can reliably identify the source of back pain or lead to an effective treatment. Flexion extension plain x-rays are used to detect spinal instability, which is uncommon, and when seen, is almost always in elderly women.

Treatment

Conservative treatment with intermittent bed rest (usually for 2 days), medication such as nonsteroidal anti-inflammatory agents (NSAIDs), aspirin (if tolerated), and perhaps a lumbar support corset is usually all that is needed to relieve pain. It is important for the individual to understand the role of body mechanics in lumbar disc disease. Exercises to improve posture, mobility and strength and a few manipulative treatments to the back are sometimes helpful. Aerobic exercise is added to the treatment regimen, since decreased aerobic fitness is a risk factor for recurrence of symptoms.

Surgery is uncommon, but is indicated in cases of chronic disc degeneration with significant back pain and degeneration limited to 1 or 2 disc levels. In these cases, fusion of the affected vertebrae is sometimes tried, although literature proof of effectiveness is lacking.

Among individual with acute low back pain, the outcomes are similar whether they receive care from primary care practitioners, chiropractors, or orthopedic surgeons.

Prognosis

Normal aging or lumbar disc degeneration is chronic and irreversible. Acute episodes of pain and weakness resolve in a few weeks. Much of the outcome depends on the activity level of the individual. In general, individuals with heavy jobs have more difficulty functioning despite back pain than individuals with light jobs. The prognosis is very good following conservative treatment in a large majority of individuals. Individuals who do not follow a treatment regimen that includes strength-building exercises tend to have a poorer outcome with more frequent and prolonged recurrence of back pain.

Differential Diagnosis

Low back strain and sprains cause similar symptoms but are seen following trauma or injury. Tumors, infections, arthritis, fractures or a narrowing of the spinal canal (spinal stenosis) all could present similar symptoms.

Specialists

- Chiropractor
- Neurologist
- Neurosurgeon
- Occupational Medicine Physician
- Occupational Therapist
- Orthopedic Surgeon
- Physiatrist
- Physical Therapist
- Rheumatologist

Rehabilitation

Physical therapy may be needed in the rehabilitation of the symptoms due to lumbar disc degeneration. The physical therapist can provide noninvasive therapies, such as ultrasound or diathermy (to project heat deep into the tissues of the back), or administer manual therapy, if mobility of the spine is impaired. Methods of cold treatment include cold packs applied to the neck region before or after exercises.

Electrical stimulation combined with heat or cold treatment is another technique used in physical therapy to relax muscles of the lumbar spine affected by degeneration. Popular in the treatment of low back pain, transcutaneous electrical nerve stimulation (T.E.N.S.) produces a high frequency tingling sensation blocking pain at that level of the spine.

A flexibility program is one of the priorities in rehabilitation of the lumbar spine. Education for proper lifting of heavy objects is important in the rehabilitation of the lumbar spine and to prepare the individual for returning to work.

The therapist may help improve posture and develop an exercise program for recovery and long-term protection. Appropriate exercise can improve overall posture, strength, and flexibility.

Work Restrictions / Accommodations

Temporary work restrictions should include avoiding heavy lifting, twisting motions, prolonged sitting or standing, and activities that involve heavy vibration (such as driving large vehicles and use of construction equipment such as jackhammers). Individuals may benefit from rest periods, including an opportunity to lie down during such breaks. Use of pain medication and muscle relaxants can affect dexterity and alertness. Safety issues will need to be evaluated. Work-hardening programs and worksite evaluations are beneficial to many individuals and may allow for earlier return from disability.

Complementary and Alternative Therapies

Content is intended for awareness only. Treatments may or may not be effective. Scientific evidence may be lacking and some substances have potentially toxic effects. Dr. Presley Reed and the editors do not endorse the use of these therapies in the absence of consultation with a licensed medical professional.

Chiropractic -	Spinal manipulation may ease pain.
Ice or heat treatments -	May help control muscle pain.
Massage -	May increase circulation, relax tight muscles, and relieve pain.
Therapeutic ultrasound or diathermy -	Used to project heat deep into the tissues of the spine, which may increase mobility.

Comorbid Conditions

Severe scoliosis, a narrowed spinal canal, osteoarthritis, anxiety, and depression may prolong episodes of lower back pain associated with lumbar disc degeneration.

Complications

The condition may progress to a symptomatic lumbar disc herniation. Severe degeneration may cause compression of the motor fibers of the nerve root, and may result in weakness or paralysis of the affected muscle group, along with loss of tone and atrophy.

Factors Influencing Duration

Individual age, occupation, aerobic fitness level, and severity of symptoms are all related to the length of disability. Psychosocial factors may affect length of disability.

Length of Disability

Disability may be permanent.

Medical treatment.

Duration in Days

Job Classification	Minimum	Optimum	Maximum
Sedentary work	0	14	21
Light work	0	14	28
Medium work	0	28	42
Heavy work	0	42	84
Very Heavy work	0	42	84

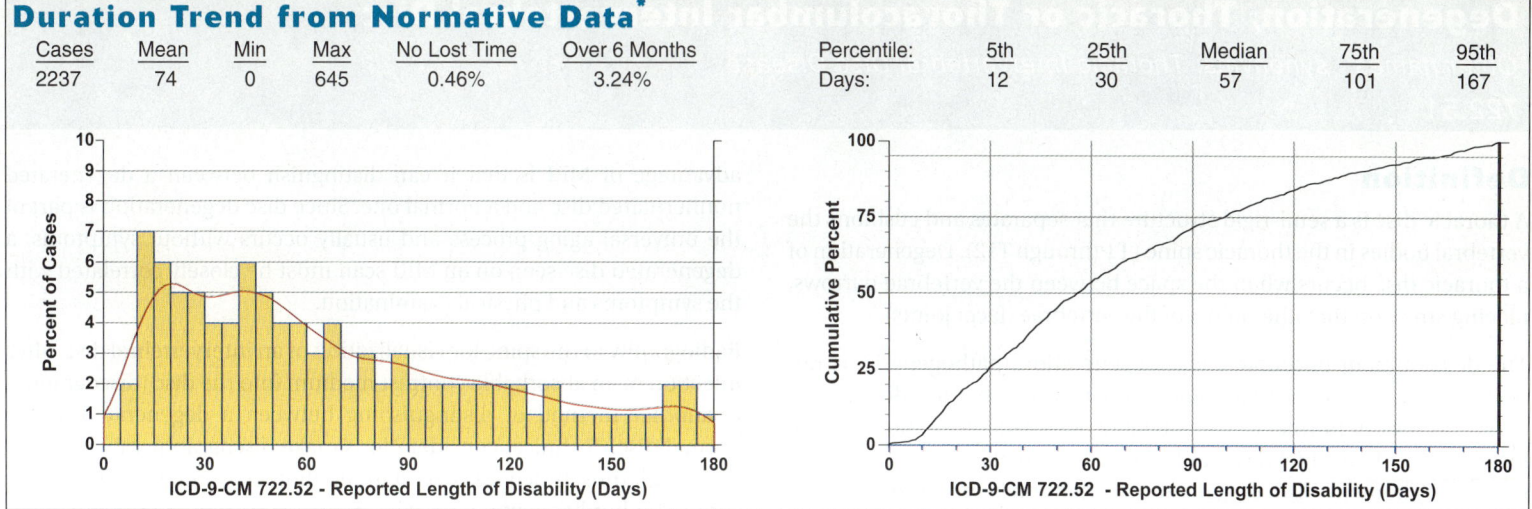

Failure to Recover

If an individual fails to recover within the maximum duration expectancy period, the reader may wish to reference the following questions to assist in better understanding the specifics of an individual's medical case.

Regarding diagnosis:

- Does individual complain of pain in the lower back and buttocks? Is it brought on by activity and relieved with rest? Is it episodic or unrelenting and progressive?
- What causes individual's pain?
- Were x-rays done? Was degeneration confirmed?
- Was MRI performed?
- Were conditions such as tumors, infections, arthritis, fractures, or a narrowing of the spinal canal (spinal stenosis) ruled out?

Regarding treatment:

- Did individual respond to conservative therapy?
- Does individual have a home-exercise program that includes some aerobic activity?
- How long has individual had intractable back pain?
- Is individual a candidate for surgery?

Regarding prognosis:

- Is individual active in physical therapy?
- Was individual trained in proper body mechanics and lifting?
- Has individual incorporated exercises that improve posture, flexibility, and strength into the home-exercise program?
- Are conditions such as severe scoliosis, a narrowed spinal canal, osteoporosis, or osteoarthritis present?
- Does individual report a change in symptoms?

References

Carey, T.S, J. Garrett, and A. Jackman. "The Outcomes and Costs of Care for Acute Low Back Pain Among Patients Seen by Primary Care Practitioners, Chiropractors, and Orthopedic Surgeons." New England Journal of Medicine 333 14 (1995): 913-917.

Hlavin, Mary, and Russell Hardy. "Clinical Diagnosis of Herniated Lumbar Disc." Lumbar Disc Disease. Hardy, Russell, ed. New York: Raven Press, 1993. 17-24.

Stephens, Susan, and Gordon Bell. "Natural History and Epidemiology of Lumbar Disc Degeneration." Lumbar Disc Disease. Hardy, Russell, ed. New York: Raven Press, 1993. 13-16.

Wisneski, Ronald, et al. "Lumbar Disc Disease." The Spine. Herkowitz, H.N., et al., eds. Philadelphia: W.B. Saunders Company, 1999. 613-673.

Degeneration, Thoracic or Thoracolumbar Intervertebral Disc

Other names / synonyms: Thoracic Intervertebral Disc Disease

722.51

Definition

A thoracic disc is a semi-rigid structure that separates and cushions the vertebral bodies in the thoracic spine (T1 through T12). Degeneration of a thoracic disc occurs when the space between the vertebrae narrows, placing stress on the other joints of the vertebrae (facet joints).

The development of thoracic disc degeneration (pathogenesis) is not well defined. As in the cervical and lumbar spines, thoracic disc degeneration is part of normal aging. An aging or degenerative thoracic disc loses some of its thickness and elasticity and its ability to absorb impacts. Thoracic disc degeneration often does not produce any symptoms, and symptoms are much less common than with disc degeneration in the neck (cervical spine) or low back (lumbar spine). This is because very little motion is associated with the thoracic spine, compared to the neck and low back. Disc degeneration most often affects the lower thoracic spine, between T9 and T12. Degenerated thoracic discs are frequently observed on an MRI, but may or may not cause back pain.

The incidence of thoracic disc degeneration increases with age, but because it is often asymptomatic, the true incidence is unknown. Symptomatic thoracic disc degeneration may occur when the degenerated disc slips from its normal position between the vertebrae (disc herniation or protrusion). Thoracic disc protrusions account for only 0.15-4% of all symptomatic disc protrusions. Thoracic herniated discs occur equally as often in men and women.

Diagnosis

History: Individuals may complain of back pain (by virtue of its frequency and often debilitating nature), decreases in sensation, and weakness of the extremities.

Physical exam: The physician will put pressure on (palpate) the spine, which may cause tenderness over the affected area. The individual may show limited and/or painful thoracic motion, especially rotation.

Tests: In the thoracic region, plain x-rays may show calcification of a thoracic disc. Other degenerative changes such as bony outgrowths (osteophytes) or disc space narrowing are also usually present. These may occur in asymptomatic individuals, and are not necessarily significant. In addition to degenerative changes, x-rays may show congenital or developmental deformities of the spine such as side-to-side curvature (scoliosis) or hunchback (kyphosis). Individuals who have such deformities may be predisposed to accelerated degeneration. If mechanical instability is suspected as a cause of recurrent pain, it can be documented by x-rays taken with the spine bent forward (flexion) or backward (extension). In the thoracic spine, this is extremely rare.

CT may be useful in ruling out some other spinal disorders such as fracture, tumor, or infection; however, in the thoracic region it cannot reliably rule out displacement of thoracic intervertebral discs unless it is done in combination with myelography. MRI can usually rule out disc displacement (herniation) as well as other spinal disorders. A further advantage of MRI is that it can distinguish between a degenerated nonherniated disc and a normal one. Since disc degeneration is part of the universal aging process and usually occurs without symptoms, a degenerated disc seen on an MRI scan must be closely correlated with the symptoms and physical examination.

Radiography of the spine for visualization of an intervertebral disc, after injection of an absorbable contrast medium into the disc (discography) is another method of distinguishing between a degenerated and a normal disc. Technical considerations make discography much harder to do and, thus, much less useful in the thoracic spine than it is in the cervical or lumbar spine.

Treatment

The goal of conservative treatment is to relieve pain. When symptoms are acute, short-term rest and immobilization of the spine are often needed, but activity is encouraged as soon as possible. If the individual is up and about, a back brace may be used. For relief of pain and inflammation, nonsteroidal anti-inflammatory drugs (NSAIDs) may be given. If pain is severe, a narcotic may be added. If anxiety and tension are prominent, anti depressants may be helpful. Muscle relaxants are frequently prescribed; however, their effectiveness is due to their sedative action. Narcotics, sedatives, and muscle relaxants are usually used only for brief periods of time. Ongoing use should be weighed against the potential for abuse. Other treatments such as ice, heat, massage, and ultrasound therapy may help relieve pain. Spinal manipulation is often performed and may be effective for some individuals.

As symptoms subside, activity is gradually increased and may include a home exercise program. Preventive and maintenance measures such as exercise and correct body mechanics should be continued indefinitely.

Prognosis

Normal aging or thoracic disc degeneration is chronic and irreversible. Acute episodes of pain and weakness may be self-limiting to a few weeks. Much of the outcome depends on the activity level of the individual and how much they are willing to follow the guidelines of exercise and maintenance of normal activity. The prognosis for relief of symptoms with conservative treatment is good.

Differential Diagnosis

Conditions that present with similar symptomatology include infection, osteoporotic fracture, rheumatoid arthritis of the spine, ankylosing spondylitis, Paget's disease, and tumor.

Specialists

- Anesthesiologist
- Chiropractor
- Occupational Medicine Physician
- Orthopedic Surgeon
- Physiatrist
- Physical Therapist
- Rheumatologist
- Sports Medicine Physician

Rehabilitation

Degeneration of the thoracic and thoracolumbar intervertebral disc may benefit from rehabilitation to decrease pain and regain mobility and strength to that particular region of the spine. Therapy to reduce followed by spinal exercises may be all that is required for mild cases. However, more involved rehabilitation is required for severe and progressive degeneration. Passive intervention should be time limited, with emphasis on active intervention.

The therapist provides noninvasive methods to decrease pain. Cold or heat treatments help control muscle pain of the thoracic spine. Methods of cold treatment include cold packs applied to the spine before or after activity. If mobility of the lumbar spine is impaired, therapies such as ultrasound or diathermy are used to project heat deep into the tissues of the spine. Manual therapy techniques are also administered.

Electrical stimulation combined with heat or cold treatment is another technique of physical therapy that relaxes the muscles of the thoracic and lumbar spine affected by degeneration. To help control pain throughout the rehabilitation process, the physical therapist may use transcutaneous electrical nerve stimulation (TENS). This consists of a battery-powered device attached to electrodes placed on the skin in the region of the pain. An electrical impulse, predetermined by the physical therapist, produces a high frequency tingling sensation that blocks pain at that level of the spine. The physical therapist often helps in the fitting and instruction of the use of a brace.

The late phase of the rehabilitation program involves the individual's reinstatement to work or "work hardening." Exercises are now directed toward work requirements, and also include instruction in proper lifting to prevent injury. Back schools are available in many rehabilitation programs and focus on managing spine disorders and preventing recurrence of symptoms.

The physical therapist may need to make modifications for those individuals with significant degeneration and arthritis or other conditions of the spine.

Work Restrictions / Accommodations

Temporary work restrictions may include avoidance of prolonged standing or sitting, lifting, carrying, bending, and twisting during episodes of acute pain. Individuals may benefit from brief rest periods including an opportunity to lie down and/or walk.

Complementary and Alternative Therapies

Content is intended for awareness only. Treatments may or may not be effective. Scientific evidence may be lacking and some substances have potentially toxic effects. Dr. Presley Reed and the editors do not endorse the use of these therapies in the absence of consultation with a licensed medical professional.

Chiropractic -	Spinal manipulation may ease pain.
Ice or heat treatments -	May help control muscle pain of the thoracic spine.
Massage -	May increase circulation, relax tight muscles, and relieve pain.
Therapeutic ultrasound or diathermy -	Used to project heat deep into the tissues of the spine, which may increase mobility.

Comorbid Conditions

Comorbid conditions that could affect the length of disability and recovery time include obesity and congenital diseases or anomalies of the spine and back.

Complications

The condition may rarely progress to a symptomatic thoracic disc herniation. Spinal stenosis, which results from an overall reduction of the spinal canal, lateral recesses, or neural foramina, is another possible complication. However, spinal stenosis is much more common in the lumbar and cervical regions.

Factors Influencing Duration

Length of disability depends on the location and number of the affected discs, the severity or phase of the disc disease (degeneration, bulging, or herniation), the severity of bone spurs (spondylosis), the nature of any neurological compression (nerve root, spinal cord, or cauda equina), the presence or absence of objective sensory loss and/or muscle weakness, the duration of such neurological deficits, whether they're acute or chronic, the presence of other sources of pain like facet joint arthritis or mechanical instability, and the type of treatment.

Length of Disability

Medical treatment.

Duration in Days

Job Classification	Minimum	Optimum	Maximum
Sedentary work	1	14	28
Light work	1	14	28
Medium work	1	21	42
Heavy work	1	28	56
Very Heavy work	1	28	56

Failure to Recover

If an individual fails to recover within the maximum duration expectancy period, the reader may wish to reference the following questions to assist in better understanding the specifics of an individual's medical case.

Regarding diagnosis:

- Does individual complain of back pain, decreases in sensation, and weakness of the extremities?
- Does palpating the spine cause tenderness over the affected area? Is thoracic motion limited and/or painful especially when in rotation?
- Was diagnosis of degeneration of thoracic or thoracolumbar intervertebral disc confirmed through x-ray or MRI?
- Did MRI rule out conditions such as spinal infection, tumor, fracture, and disc herniation?

Regarding treatment:

- Did symptoms respond to bed rest?
- Have conservative measures helped relieve pain?

- Was ongoing use of narcotics, sedatives, and muscle relaxants weighed against the potential for dependency?
- Was individual compliant with exercise program?

Regarding prognosis:

- Does individual participate in a rehabilitation program? Compliant with guidelines?
- To what extent does pain impact function? What modifications are needed?
- Were medications, exercises, manipulation, and bracing all tried?
- Does individual have an underlying condition that may impact recovery?
- Have any complications developed?

References

Currier, B.L., et al. "Thoracic Disc Disease." The Spine. Herkowitz, H.N., et al., eds. Philadelphia: W.B. Saunders Company, 1999. 581-595.

Kessler, R.M. Management of Common Musculoskeletal Disorders: Physical Therapy Principles and Methods. Philadelphia: J.B. Lippincott Company, 1990.

Kisner, C., and L. Colby. Therapeutic Exercise Foundations and Techniques. Philadelphia: F.A. Davis Company, 1990.

Stillerman C.B., and M.H. Weiss. "Management of Thoracic Disc Disease." Clinical Neurosurgery 38 (1992): 325-352.

Dehydration
Other names / synonyms: Fluid Loss, Water Loss
276.5

Definition

Dehydration occurs when water output exceeds water intake, leaving the body with less water than is needed to sustain life. This water deficit can be accompanied by an imbalance in the electrolytes sodium, potassium, and chloride, which must be maintained within narrow limits for proper body functioning.

The normal water content of the adult body is 40-65% of the total body weight. The volume and composition of body fluid is usually maintained by the kidneys in spite of wide fluctuation in dietary intake and metabolic activity. However, a lack of normal intake or an increase in normal output of water can upset this balance.

Intake of water may decrease when the individual is unconscious, delirious, or unable to take fluids due to nausea or injury to the mouth or gastrointestinal tract. Water loss may be increased when fever, profuse sweating, diarrhea, vomiting, or burns are present. Excess water may also be lost due to diuretic therapy, dialysis, tube feedings without adequate water replacement, or movement of water into tissues such as the skin or lungs. Fluid losses up to 5% are considered mild; up to 10% are considered moderate; and up to 15% are considered severe.

Diseases such as diabetes mellitus and insipidus, kidney failure, or adrenal insufficiency will also upset the normal fluid balance of the body.

Dehydration most often occurs in the very young and in the elderly.

Diagnosis

History: The history may include an injury or illness that prevents the normal intake of water. Unless unconscious, the individual will complain of weight loss within a short period, and dryness of the mouth and skin. A faint feeling accompanied by dizziness may be present, especially upon arising.

Physical exam: The individual will have dry mucous membranes and decreased skin elasticity. Upon arising from a lying or sitting position, the blood pressure will drop and the pulse will rise (orthostatic hypotension). Central venous pressure and intraocular pressures will be decreased and the pulse pressure will be narrowed.

Signs of electrolyte imbalance that may accompany dehydration include changes in mental status and personality, heart irregularities (arrhythmia), muscle rigidity, tremors, spasticity, seizures, or coma. The urine will be concentrated, darker and stronger smelling than usual.

Tests: The urinalysis will show an increased specific gravity (except in the case of diabetes insipidus), and decreased sodium and other electrolytes content. The hematocrit may be increased from the normal baseline. There may be a mild-to-moderate increase in the blood urea, nitrogen, and creatinine. Plasma concentration of a solution of substances (osmolality) will be elevated and the serum electrolytes may be abnormal. Other tests may be done to determine the specific cause of the dehydration (for example, a blood sugar to check for diabetes).

Treatment

Water will be replaced by mouth in mild dehydration and/or via intravenous fluid replacement. The type of intravenous fluid therapy depends on the electrolyte levels and the concentration of a solution of the substances (osmolality) of the individual's blood and may include saline (sodium chloride) with or without electrolytes added. Blood pressure, pulse, hematocrit, and central venous pressure may be monitored during fluid replacement therapy.

The speed of replacement will depend in part on the severity of the dehydration and kidney and heart functioning. Half of the fluid deficit may be replaced in the first 24 hours of treatment and the remainder given more slowly after that. The underlying cause of the dehydration will be treated as well.

Prognosis

Rapid recognition and treatment of dehydration will result in a successful outcome. In the absence of complications, fluid balance is usually restored. Severe dehydration can result in cardiovascular collapse and death if not treated quickly. Untreated severe dehydration may result in seizures, permanent brain damage, or death.

Differential Diagnosis

Blood volume depletion has similar symptoms. Cardiovascular disease and disorders may present with similar signs and symptoms.

Specialists

- Cardiologist
- Dietary Advisor
- Emergency Medicine
- Endocrinologist
- Hematologist
- Hepatologist
- Industrial Hygienist
- Nephrologist
- Physical Therapist
- Rheumatologist

Work Restrictions / Accommodations

Water intake will need to be maintained during working hours. The individual may need to be advised on the proper precautions to take to avoid excessive fluid loss and electrolyte imbalance. The individual may be in a weakened state from severe loss of fluids. The individual should avoid strenuous activities and activities that produce excessive sweating. Work in hot and humid environments should be avoided until fluid levels and electrolyte balances have been re-established.

Complementary and Alternative Therapies

Content is intended for awareness only. Treatments may or may not be effective. Scientific evidence may be lacking and some substances have potentially toxic effects. Dr. Presley Reed and the editors do not endorse the use of these therapies in the absence of consultation with a licensed medical professional.

Rehydration - If caught early, under normal circumstances, mild dehydration may be treated by simple rehydration. Oral fluids such as fresh lemonade with salt in it is a very effective method of maintaining salt balance with fluid intake. Sports drinks can also effectively restore body fluids and salt balance. It is always recommended, however, that individual still contact a physician to rule out underlying conditions and ensure a proper, complete recovery.

Comorbid Conditions

The presence of heart, kidney, or adrenal disease will worsen the effects of dehydration, complicate treatment, and lengthen the recovery period. Diabetes and liver disease may contribute to and worsen the secondary effects of dehydration.

Complications

The presence of electrolyte imbalances will complicate fluid replacement therapy requiring close calculation of content according to the individual's needs. Fluid loss that cannot be stopped will threaten the outcome.

Factors Influencing Duration

The underlying cause of the dehydration, required therapy, and individual's response to therapy will determine the length of disability. The recurrence of dehydration or the presence of complications may lengthen recovery time. Age, physical condition, and general health will influence the individual's ability to undergo and respond to successful re-hydration.

Length of Disability

Duration depends on cause and severity. Severe dehydration may be life threatening.

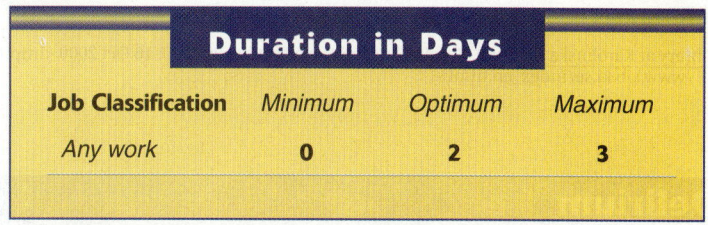

Duration in Days

Job Classification	Minimum	Optimum	Maximum
Any work	0	2	3

Failure to Recover

If an individual fails to recover within the maximum duration expectancy period, the reader may wish to reference the following questions to assist in better understanding the specifics of an individual's medical case.

Regarding diagnosis:

- Does individual have a fever or profuse sweating? Diarrhea or vomiting? Nausea?
- Did individual have a severe burn?
- Is individual on diuretic therapy, dialysis, or tube feedings?
- Has water moved into the skin or lungs?
- Does individual have diabetes? Kidney failure? Adrenal insufficiency?
- Is there an injury to the mouth or GI tract?
- On exam, does individual have dry mucous membranes? Decreased skin elasticity?
- Is there evidence of orthostatic hypotension?
- Are the central venous and intraocular pressures decreased?
- Is there a narrowed pulse pressure? Arrhythmias?
- Have any changes in mental status occurred?
- Does individual have any muscle rigidity, tremors, spasticity, seizures, or coma?
- Is the urine dark and concentrated?
- Were CBC and urinalysis performed? Electrolytes? Bun? Creatinine? Was an osmolality test done?
- Were conditions with similar symptoms ruled out?

Regarding treatment:

- Has individual had fluid replacement either orally or intravenously?
- Is underlying cause also being treated?
- Was the dehydration recognized and treated promptly?
- Were electrolytes monitored during replacement?

Regarding prognosis:

- Can individual's employer accommodate any necessary restrictions?
- Were individual, family, and/or caretaker educated in the early symptoms of dehydration and the necessary interventions? Are preventive measures being taken?

Dehydration 643

- Does individual have any conditions that may affect ability to recover?
- Is individual continuing to lose fluid? Has an electrolyte imbalance?

References

Library at Karolinska Institute. Karolinska Institute of Medicine. 2000. 16 Oct 2000 <http://www.kib.ki.se/index_en.html>.

Keller, V.E. "Management of Nausea and Vomiting in Children." Journal of Pediatry 10 5 (1995): 280-286.

Delirium

Other names / synonyms: Acute Encephalopathy, Acute Organic Brain Syndrome
ICD-9 Depends on Cause

Definition

Delirium is an acute disturbance in level of consciousness and thought processes (cognition) that develops over a short period of time, and is a significant change from previous functioning. Attention, concentration, speech, memory, or perceptions may be impaired.

This condition has several causes. General medical conditions causing delirium include low blood sugar (hypoglycemia) or other disturbances in blood chemistry, lack of oxygen (hypoxia), high fever (hyperthermia), infection of the brain or its coverings (encephalitis or meningitis), other massive infection (sepsis, endocarditis), liver or kidney failure, or head injury. Medications and drugs that may induce delirium include corticosteroids, pain medications, anti-asthma drugs, hallucinogens, cocaine, and alcohol withdrawal syndrome. Other causes may be disturbances in the sleep-wake cycle, or postoperative effects of anesthesia, blood loss, or other factors related to surgery. Delirium may have multiple causes or the cause(s) may be unknown.

Older individuals appear to be more susceptible to delirium, perhaps because of physiological differences or changes associated with aging. Rates of delirium increase from 0.4% from ages 18 to 55 years to 1.1% after age 55. In a study of nearly 500 individuals over age 65 seen in the emergency room, almost 10% were delirious, but delirium was recognized by the emergency room physician in only one-third of these individuals. Most individuals with delirium had neurologic or lung (pulmonary) diseases. Prevalence of delirium in the hospitalized medically ill ranges from 10-30%, with 25% of cancer patients, 30-40% of AIDS patients, and 80% of those with terminal illnesses developing delirium. It is not unusual for early symptoms such as restlessness, anxiety, disorientation, distractibility, or sleep disturbance to progress to delirium within 1 to 3 days. Delirium may lead to medical complications such as pneumonia or skin ulcers (decubiti), or to institutional placement. Delirium is also associated with an increased risk of dying during hospitalization, due to underlying illnesses and increased risk of complications.

Diagnosis

History: Diagnosis is based on criteria listed in the DSM-IV-TR (Diagnostic and Statistical Manual of Mental Disorders, 4th Edition, Text Revision, published by the American Psychiatric Association). History is usually given by the family or caregiver, as the individual is often too confused to give a reliable history. Symptoms develop over a period of a few hours to a few days, with symptoms that fluctuate throughout the day and are generally worse at night (sundowning), when there are fewer environmental cues and less stimulation available. The individual may alternate between decreased states of alertness and consciousness (lethargy), with sluggishness and apathy, and hyperactive states. During periods of heightened arousal, there may be episodes of seeing or hearing things that aren't there (visual or auditory hallucinations), misinterpreting perceptions (illusions), false but persistent beliefs (delusions), or agitation. Visual hallucinations are most common, but there may also be hallucinations involving the sense of hearing (auditory), touch (tactile), taste (gustatory), or smell (olfactory). Illusions may cause the individual to misinterpret environmental stimuli, such as mistaking a banging door as a gunshot. In a study of 227 individuals with delirium, 43% had psychotic symptoms, with 27% having visual hallucinations, 12% auditory hallucinations, 2.7% tactile hallucinations, and 26% delusions.

The individual is often unaware of his/her own altered state of consciousness, and may be confused and disoriented to person, place, or time. He or she may be unable to identify caregivers or family members, and may not know his or her location or the day, date, time, or year. Fear may cause the individual to attack caregivers because of perceived threats, or because of a delusion, such as, "They're trying to poison my food." Other emotional states may include anxiety, irritability, or euphoria. History may reveal a possible cause of delirium, such as a general medical condition such as low blood sugar (hypoglycemia) or other disturbance in blood chemistry, fever, infection, liver or kidney failure, head injury, alcohol withdrawal syndrome, terminal illness, AIDS, or recent use of a medication or drug (corticosteroids, pain medications, anti-asthma drugs, hallucinogens, cocaine).

Physical exam: In response to hallucinations or illusions, the individual may startle easily, talk to imagined voices, or pick at the air or bedclothes. They may be sleepy (lethargic) or overly alert and fearful (hypervigilant). They may be unable to focus on a conversational topic, be easily distracted, or continue to answer a previous question rather than shifting focus to a new topic (perseveration). Language may be disturbed, with slurred speech (dysarthria), inability to name objects (dysnomia), inability to write (dysgraphia), or exhibit rambling, irrelevant, or incoherent speech. General physical examination may reveal jaundice or enlarged liver (hepatomegaly) suggesting liver failure, bluish discoloration (cyanosis) or shortness of breath (dyspnea) suggesting lack of oxygen (hypoxia), fever suggesting infection, or other underlying cause of delirium. Neurological examination may reveal abnormal reflexes (frontal lobe release signs) suggesting diffuse brain involvement, or focal weakness suggesting dysfunction in a specific brain location, as might be seen with head trauma.

Tests: Verbal tests can be given to determine the individual's level of orientation, such as asking the names of family members or the time of day. Simple memory tests, such as asking the individual to recall items or count backwards, might be helpful. Caution should be used when using verbal or memory tests to ascertain levels of orientation, since education level and cultural background and differences could affect an individual's answers. There are no specific diagnostic lab tests except those that might better define an underlying general medical condition or intoxication. An electroencephalogram (EEG) typically shows abnormal, generalized slowing or, occasionally, fast activity (alcohol withdrawal delirium). Blood work is needed to determine specific imbalances in blood chemistry that might be contributing to delirium. Arterial blood gas tests, as well as a chest x-ray, and electrocardiogram, might be utilized if disease of the lungs or heart is suspected as the underlying cause. Cultures of blood and body fluids should be performed if systemic infection is suspected. Urine and blood drug screens or levels of specific medications are helpful is delirium is related to a specific substance.

Treatment

Identifying and treating the underlying medical condition is the first priority. If the delirium is related to use of a substance or medication, then the offending substance should be discontinued or changed. Alcohol withdrawal delirium requires medication management, usually with benzodiazepines, to prevent delirium, hallucinations, and seizures. An improvement in nutrition and in the general medical condition may decrease delirium symptoms. Treatment also includes strategies to protect the individual from wandering or self-injury, and reorientation activities. During the acute delirium phase, especially if the individual is hospitalized and attempting to pull out intravenous lines or breathing tubes, physical restraints or sedative medications might be required, but only as a last resort. Reorientation activities include environmental cues such as windows, large-faced clocks, calendars, and pictures of family members; speaking clearly and simply when communicating with the individual; and offering reassurances of safety. Antipsychotic medications may be needed for active hallucinations, but should be used sparingly, as any drugs may aggravate confusion and lethargy. Supportive and educational therapy for the family may also be helpful, and their presence may provide a calming and stabilizing effect. Preventive measures such as those used by the Hospital Elder Life Program may help identify individuals at risk for delirium, and ward off future episodes.

Prognosis

Many instances of delirium resolve within hours or days, especially if underlying conditions are treated. However, symptoms may persist in some individuals for months, or even until death. Most individuals who experience delirium recover fully, but delirium occasionally progresses to stupor, coma, seizures, or death, especially if the underlying cause is not recognized or treated. Up to 60% of elderly individuals may have persisting symptoms of delirium. Although delirium is a bad prognostic sign in hospitalized patients, delirium in psychotic patients may paradoxically be a good sign that psychotic and affective symptoms may improve or even resolve.

Differential Diagnosis

Delirium is commonly confused with dementia, a more chronic condition not associated with disturbances of consciousness. However, delirium can suddenly appear in the setting of a pre-existing dementia. Symptoms similar to those seen in delirium may also be seen with brief psychotic disorder, schizophrenia, or other psychotic disorders, mood disorder with psychotic features, or malingering. Sensory deprivation may also lead to confusion similar to that seen in delirium.

Specialists

- Cardiologist
- Internist
- Neurologist
- Occupational Therapist
- Physical Therapist
- Psychiatrist
- Pulmonologist

Work Restrictions / Accommodations

The individual actively experiencing delirium should not work. If the individual is recovering from an illness-related or substance-related delirium, temporary work accommodations may include reducing or eliminating activities where the safety of self or others is contingent upon a constant and/or high level of alertness, such as driving motor vehicles, operating complex machinery, or handling dangerous chemicals; introducing the individual to new or stressful situations gradually under individually appropriate supervision; allowing some flexibility in scheduling to attend therapy appointments (which normally should occur during employee's personal time); promoting planned, proactive management of identified problem areas; and offering timely feedback on job performance issues. It will be helpful if accommodations are documented in a written plan designed to promote timely and safe transition back to full work productivity. If the individual has chronic side effects of a prolonged general medical illness, such as cardiac, liver, or nervous system damage, work should be limited to sedentary activities.

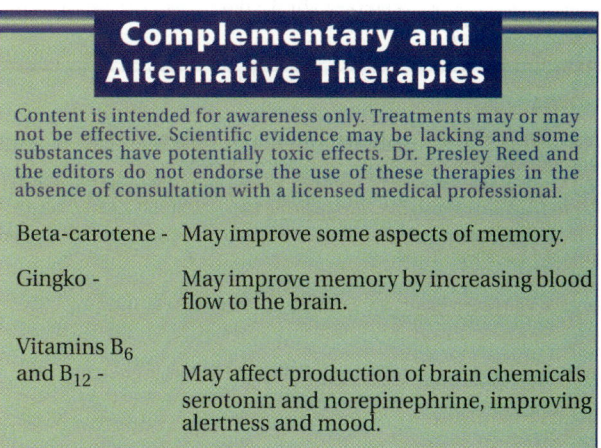

Complementary and Alternative Therapies

Content is intended for awareness only. Treatments may or may not be effective. Scientific evidence may be lacking and some substances have potentially toxic effects. Dr. Presley Reed and the editors do not endorse the use of these therapies in the absence of consultation with a licensed medical professional.

Beta-carotene - May improve some aspects of memory.

Gingko - May improve memory by increasing blood flow to the brain.

Vitamins B_6 and B_{12} - May affect production of brain chemicals serotonin and norepinephrine, improving alertness and mood.

Comorbid Conditions

Coexisting conditions that may affect recovery and lengthen disability include psychiatric disorders such as dementia or depression. Concurrent substance abuse and physical conditions related to the toxic effects of alcohol or drugs on the brain and liver can also affect disability. For instance, an alcohol-damaged liver is less able to rid the body of toxic substances. Underlying medical conditions may prolong disability.

Complications

Injury could result if the individual falls out of bed or gets entangled with intravenous lines or catheters. Medically ill individuals, especially the elderly, may have serious complications associated with delirium, including pneumonia and decubitus ulcers. These individuals may exhibit functional decline or the inability to attend to daily activities such as feeding, dressing, toileting, or hygiene, which may lead to institutional placement. Postoperative delirium is associated with increased risk for complications, longer postoperative recuperation, and increased risk of long-term disability. Older individuals who develop delirium during a hospitalization may have up to a 20-75% chance of dying during that hospitalization. Up to 25% of older individuals with delirium die within a 6-month period of discharge from the hospital.

Factors Influencing Duration

The nature and responsiveness to treatment of the underlying disorder greatly influence duration of disability. Individuals with terminal medical conditions, such as end-stage renal or liver disease, end-stage AIDS, or terminal cancer show long-lasting symptoms of delirium.

Length of Disability

If the delirium does not resolve in a few hours or days, symptoms may persist in some individuals for months, or even result in death. Disability may be permanent.

Failure to Recover

If an individual fails to recover within the maximum duration expectancy period, the reader may wish to reference the following questions to assist in better understanding the specifics of an individual's medical case.

Regarding diagnosis:

- Because a comprehensive psychiatric and medical evaluation is essential in developing a treatment plan, did evaluation include a detailed history of past and present substance or medication use, a general medical and psychiatric history and examination, history of all prior psychiatric treatments with outcomes, family and social history, screening of blood, breath or urine for abused substances, and laboratory tests to help confirm the presence or absence of general medical conditions often associated with delirium, such as hypoglycemia or other disturbance in blood chemistry, fever, infection, liver or kidney failure, hypoxia, head injury, AIDS, or end-stage cancer? If evaluation was not this comprehensive, what areas were omitted? Would this information affect the current treatment plan? What changes can now be made?

- Were other psychiatric disorders ruled out?

- Since delirium may have multiple causes, were underlying medical disorders identified, treated, or ruled out?

- Are any medications contributing to altered mental status?

Regarding treatment:

- If medications are contributing to altered mental status, can these be changed or discontinued?

- Is an improvement in nutrition or general medical condition decreasing delirium symptoms? Is underlying medical condition responding to treatment?

- Was hospitalization required?

- Did treatment include strategies to protect individual from wandering or self-injury?

- Did therapy include reorientation activities?

- Because supportive and educational therapy for the family may not only be helpful, but their presence may provide a calming and stabilizing effect, is family involved in the therapy process?

Regarding prognosis:

- Was underlying cause identified? Is underlying cause being effectively addressed through a comprehensive treatment plan?

- Is family actively involved in therapy process?

- Were preventive measures initiated to identify and help ward off future episodes?

References

Allen, Francis. Diagnostic and Statistical Manual of Mental Disorders, 4th ed, text revision. Washington, DC: American Psychiatric Association, 2000.

Bostwick, J.M. "The Many Faces of Confusion, Timing and Collateral History Often Hold the Key to Diagnosis." Postgraduate Medicine 108 6 (2000): 60-2,65-6,71-2.

Crippen, D. "Life-threatening Brain Failure and Agitation in the Intensive Care Unit." Critical Care 4 2 (2000): 81-90.

Duke, James A. The Green Pharmacy. Emmaus, PA: Rodale Press, Inc, 1997.

Feinstein, Alice, ed. Healing with Vitamins. Emmaus, PA: Rodale Press, Inc, 1996.

Gottlieb, Bill, ed. New Choices in Natural Healing. Emmaus, PA: Rodale Press, Inc, 1995.

House, R.M. "Delirium and Agitation." Current Treatment Options in Neurology 2 2 (2000): 141-150.

Inouye, S.K., et al. "The Hospital Elder-life Program: A Model of Care to Prevent Cognitive and Functional Decline in Older Hospitalized Patients." Journal of the American Geriatric Society 48 12 (2000): 1697-1706.

Lawlor, P.G., R.L. Fainsinger, and E.D. Bruera. "Delirium at the End of Life: Critical Issues in Clinical Practice and Research." Journal of the American Medical Association 284 19 (2000): 2427-2429.

Webster, R., and S. Holroyd. "Prevalence of Psychotic Symptoms in Delirium." Psychosomatics 41 6 (2000): 519-522.

Delivery, Spontaneous and/or Assisted Vaginal

Other names / synonyms: Childbirth, Vaginal Birth, Vaginal Delivery

73.59

Definition

Spontaneous vaginal delivery is the birth of a baby and delivery of the placenta from the uterus, through the cervix, and the birth canal (vagina). This process results from contractions of the uterus during labor. Most women deliver 38 to 40 weeks after becoming pregnant (conception). In some vaginal deliveries, additional assistance is employed to assist vaginal delivery using forceps or vacuum extraction applied to the baby's head.

The regular muscular contractions of the uterus in labor cause the cervix to soften, thin (efface), and open (dilate), so that the baby may travel from the uterus through the bony pelvis to the vaginal opening. The average labor lasts 12 to 14 hours for a woman having her first baby (nulliparous) and about 8 hours for subsequent babies.

Labor occurs in 3 stages. The first stage begins with regular contractions that effect cervical dilation and ends when the cervix dilates to 10 cms. The second stage ends with the baby's birth. The third stage ends with delivery of the placenta, which usually separates from the uterine wall within 5 minutes after delivery.

Of the 4 million births in the US each year, approximately 3.2 million are born vaginally.

Reason for Procedure

Vaginal delivery proceeds if the maternal pelvis can accommodate the baby's presenting part, usually the head. The pelvis ordinarily widens during labor to allow passage of the baby's head. The decision to proceed with a vaginal delivery may be influenced by the obstetrical history of previous labors, types of deliveries, and estimated infant weight and status of mother and baby.

Assistance using vacuum extraction or forceps delivery may be needed in certain conditions. If the baby appears to be in distress, it may need to be delivered more quickly using assistance. If pushing continues for a long time once the cervix is fully dilated to 10 cm, both mother and baby may become exhausted. If contractions fade away or if the baby is in an awkward position, such as with his spine against the mother's spine (posterior position), forceps assistance or vacuum extraction may be needed for delivery.

Description

Labor is allowed to progress naturally whenever possible. The mother is encouraged to assume whatever positions are the most comfortable for her during contractions. Vertical positions such as standing or kneeling may be preferable, if tolerated. Walking, showering, and soaking in a hot tub can ease labor pain and allow it to progress more rapidly. Pain medication administered locally, by injection (intravenous), or into the spine (epidural) may be given at the mother's request.

The baby usually presents head first, with its face rotated toward the mother's spine and crowns to spontaneously deliver vaginally with maternal pushing efforts that are coordinated with contractions. If the baby's head does not spontaneously rotate and descend, instruments such as forceps or a vacuum extractor may be used to gently turn or turn and assist with the final expulsion of the baby's head (assisted vaginal delivery). This type of assistance may also be used if the mother tires of pushing or contractions cease prior to delivery or in the instance of fetal or maternal distress for more rapid delivery.

For use of either forceps or vacuum extraction, the cervix must be completely dilated, the maternal bladder must be empty and the mother's feet/legs are placed in stirrups to maximally expose her perineum. An incision to enlarge the vaginal opening (episiotomy) may or may not be necessary. For a vacuum extraction, a soft or metal cup is applied to the crown of the baby's head and suction traction is applied to the cup while the mother pushes. The traction, combined with maternal pushing, propels the baby from the vagina. The cup is removed once the baby's head is entirely delivered. For forceps assistance, the metal forceps are applied to the sides of the baby's head and can be used to turn or tun and lift the baby's head from the vagina with the assistance of the mother's contractions/pushing efforts. Local or regional anesthesia (spinal or epidural) may be used for all types of vaginal deliveries and is more commonly used if assistance with forceps or a vacuum extractor is necessary.

Other techniques that can be used to assist with stimulation of labor include rupturing the bag of amniotic fluid surrounding the baby (amniotomy), induction (stimulation) of contractions, or enhancement of inefficient contractions using the hormone oxytocin. Oxytocin is also usually given after delivery of the baby and placenta to contract the uterus and reduce postpartum bleeding.

Prognosis

Most spontaneous or assisted vaginal deliveries are uncomplicated. Mother and infant are usually able to leave the hospital within 48 hours.

Because of hormonal and psychological changes associated with birth and delivery, some mothers may experience postpartum blues, usually beginning 2 to 3 days after delivery (postpartum). This usually resolves spontaneously, but may need treatment if prolonged. If prolonged, the postpartum blues may actually be an underlying depression and require further consultation and treatment.

Specialists

- Certified Nurse Midwife
- Obstetrician
- Perinatologist
- Primary Care Provider

Rehabilitation

A woman who has had a normal delivery without excessive tearing or pain can begin exercise and rehabilitation as soon as a month after the birth. The woman should be pain free and cleared by her physician before beginning a postnatal exercise regimen.

After checking for separation of the abdominal muscles (diastasis), the first focus of rehabilitation is restoring overall body strength and strengthening the pelvic floor muscles (urethra, vagina, and anus).

Core strength work can include bridging (lying supine with feet flat on floor and lifting hips upward and then slowly lowering back to floor), abdominal crunches, pelvic tilts (lying supine on the floor with the knees bent, consciously pulling the low back into the floor), heel slides (lying on back, knees bent, feet on floor close to buttocks, sliding one heel out while extending the leg fully, then slowly sliding the heel back to the beginning), gluteal toning such as hip extensions (while standing, lifting the leg to the back and squeezing gluteus and hamstring muscles), squats, and plies.

In addition to core work, the therapist may also initiate a cardiovascular routine. Walking or light running helps strengthen the core muscles and help the woman regain her pre-pregnant posture. After 2 weeks, women can begin to add more exercises to her workout.

If the woman is breastfeeding, it is important to note that some infants may dislike the taste of the milk after a workout. Lactic acid produced during the workout can affect the milk. The client may want to pump her breasts before an excessive workout.

Work Restrictions / Accommodations

Most women recover rapidly from an otherwise uncomplicated vaginal or assisted vaginal delivery. They may have a period of time of reduced physical activity immediately after post delivery due to vaginal bleeding and cramping or episiotomy pain as their uterus/perineum heals from the delivery. The vast majority of women with uncomplicated singleton pregnancies and vaginal or assisted vaginal delivery are physiologically stable to return to full time work within 4 to 6 weeks of delivery. Accommodations for women who are breastfeeding may include such things as additional breaks and privacy rooms in the workplace where they can breastfeed or pump the breasts. Breastfeeding in and of itself is not a disabling condition.

Comorbid Conditions

Disability may be lengthened by diabetes mellitus, high blood pressure (hypertension), deep vein clots (thrombosis), infection, hemorrhage, or postpartum depression.

Procedure Complications

Complications of assisted or spontaneous vaginal delivery affecting the mother include excessive bleeding (hemorrhage), inability to urinate (urine retention), loss of bladder control (urinary incontinence), bruising (hematoma) of the perineum, varying degrees of tearing (laceration) of the perineum, and infection. Pressure on the nerve supplying the genitalia (pudendal nerve) may lead to decreased sensation in this area and/or sexual dysfunction.

Complications affecting the infant may include scalp infection or bleeding, scalp hematoma from the vacuum cup, and/or facial laceration/trauma from forceps placement. In some circumstances, temporary or permanent nerve damage may occur to the baby following assisted vaginal deliveries.

Factors Influencing Duration

Length of disability may be influenced by a high-risk pregnancy, complications to mother or infant, or job requirements. Disability may be longer if heavy lifting is a part of the woman's responsibilities.

Length of Disability

Duration reflects accepted standard postdelivery recovery period, not medical recovery time.

Duration in Days

Job Classification	Minimum	Optimum	Maximum
Any work	28	42	42

References

Birth-assisted Delivery. Mother and Baby. 01 Jan 2000. 16 Jan 2001 <http://www.motherandbaby.co.uk/birth/article.htm?402>.

Putta, Lakshmidevi V., and Jeanne Spencer. "Assisted Vaginal Delivery Using the Vacuum Extractor." American Family Physician (15 Sep 2000): 1-8.

Delusional Disorder

Other names / synonyms: Capgras' Syndrome, Delusional Disorder, Delusions of Misidentification or Impersonation, Folie a Deux, Late-Onset Paraphrenia, Paranoid States, Paraphrenia

297, 297.9

Definition

Delusional disorder is an uncommon psychiatric condition characterized by the presence of one or more persistent delusions or false beliefs that usually involve a misinterpretation of perceptions or experiences. At face value, these delusions often seem entirely believable (nonbizarre) as they focus on experiences that could conceivably occur in real life.

Delusional disorders are divided into different types depending on the predominant delusion such as being followed (persecutory type), having a disease (somatic type), being loved at a distance (erotomanic type), having an unfaithful sexual partner (jealous type), or having inflated worth, power, identity, or knowledge (grandiose type). Individuals are usually unaware of the psychiatric nature of the condition and may seek out internists, lawyers, or the police rather than psychiatrists or psychologists. Delusional episodes have no known cause. Delusions of persecution (paranoid states) may be acute and short-lived or persistent as they develop into an elaborate system of fixed beliefs.

Although the number diagnosed with delusional disorder is low (24 to 30 individuals per 100,000), the condition is probably much more common since the delusions may remain hidden for years and are manifested only in nonmedical situations. Age at onset of symptoms is usually middle or late adulthood.

Diagnosis

History: History centers around fixed beliefs that the individual holds to be true. Persecutory or paranoid delusions involve the belief that others are conspiring against and persecuting the individual. Delusions of grandeur (grandiose delusions) involve the belief that the individual possesses extraordinary powers or talents. Associated symptoms may be more readily disclosed by the family rather than the individual and include anger, irritability, suspiciousness, grandiose behavior or gestures, lack of humor, and extreme level of alertness and always being on guard (hypervigilance).

Individuals may have extreme sensitivity to criticism or setbacks (hypersensitivity), obstinate behavior, and resentfulness. The individual may act defensively, seem guarded or hostile, pay extreme attention to details, file frequent legal complaints, or be reclusive, secretive, excessively critical, self-righteous, aggressive, or violent. The individual may hear voices that comment on his or her behavior, converse with one another, or make critical and abusive comments (auditory hallucinations). Hallucinations of sound, sight, smell, taste, or touch may also occur although auditory hallucinations are by far the most common.

According to the DSM-IV, diagnosis of delusional disorder requires at least one month's duration of the delusion; impact on functioning consistent with the delusion or its ramifications; generally normal appearance and behavior; and the exclusion of schizophrenia, mood disorder, substance-induced psychosis, and medical disease. Apart from the impact of the delusion, functioning is not markedly impaired and behavior is not obviously odd or bizarre. If disturbances of mood occur with the delusions, their total duration is brief relative to the duration of the delusional periods.

Physical exam: The exam does not contribute significantly to this diagnosis although observation of the individual's orientation, dress, mannerisms, behavior, and content of speech may help diagnose the condition.

Tests: Psychological testing does not establish the diagnosis but may be recommended by the attending psychiatrist or psychologist to obtain more information about the delusions or associated symptoms. For example, the Minnesota Multiphasic Personality Inventory or other personality testing may reveal paranoid or grandiose beliefs or concerns related to physical health.

Treatment

Individual psychotherapy may be helpful but is extremely difficult since the individual's distrust and lack of acceptance that they are mentally ill usually prevents contact with a therapist. Even if they do seek help, their fixed beliefs are resistant to therapy. Initially, it is more helpful to focus on associated depression or anxiety. With time, the therapist may gently challenge the beliefs by pointing out how they interfere with the individual's life. Therapy should be supportive and problem-oriented rather than insight-oriented because the individual's suspiciousness and hypersensitivity may lead to misinterpretation. Group therapy is not recommended due to the individual's mistrust.

Antipsychotic medication is recommended if individual has active psychosis, anxiety, agitation, or severe impairment. The antipsychotic medication pimozide has been linked to partial or full recovery in 80% of individuals, but no formal studies have been done to compare this medication to others for this condition. As individuals are usually suspicious of medication and neglect to take it, long-lasting injections may be preferable to taking medications by mouth. Regular medication management sessions are often necessary in case the individual has side effects or no improvement in symptoms. Electroconvulsive therapy has been tried but is not recommended.

Prognosis

Outcome is variable. Individuals with this disorder are frequently loyal, hard-working employees who require flexible and tolerant managers. Fixed beliefs may interfere with good judgment and lead to problems at work, in financial affairs, or personal relationships. Although a recent book by Munro suggests that 80% of individuals with delusional disorder have a partial or full recovery when given the antipsychotic drug pimozide, this response rate has not been confirmed in systematic studies.

Differential Diagnosis

The cluster of disorders with symptoms and features typical of delusional disorder includes paranoid personality disorder, paranoid schizophrenia, delusional disorder, mood disorder with psychotic features, substance-induced psychotic disorder, body dysmorphic disorder, and obsessive-compulsive disorder.

Specialists

- Licensed Clinical Social Worker
- Psychiatrist
- Psychologist

Work Restrictions / Accommodations

Work accommodations might include the use of a job coach to establish consistent, predictable work behaviors; the development of a structured, consistent set of work activities; limiting contact with coworkers and the general public; and flexibility in schedule to accommodate medical or psychiatric appointments.

Comorbid Conditions

Coexisting conditions that may affect recovery and lengthen disability include mood disorders, chronic post-traumatic stress disorder, alcohol or other substance abuse, body dysmorphic disorder, suicidal tendencies, and schizophrenia.

Complications

Violence to self or others could occur if the individual's delusions are of a persecutory or homicidal nature. Delusions seen in this disorder may overlap with mood disorders or schizophrenia.

Factors Influencing Duration

Disability depends on the degree and nature of reality distortion and whether it interferes with work. The intensity of emotional disturbance (fear and hostility) also influences disability. Disability is variable for this general category of mental disturbances.

Length of Disability

Duration depends on cause, job requirements, and the severity of the individual's delusional belief system. Maximum duration includes hospitalization. Disability may be permanent.

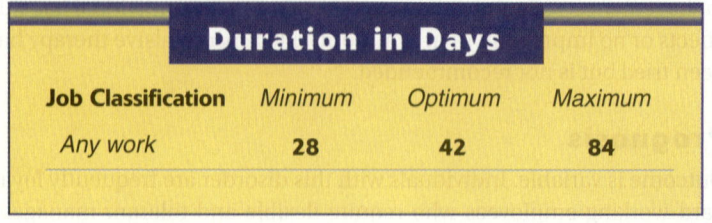

Job Classification	Minimum	Optimum	Maximum
Any work	28	42	84

Failure to Recover

If an individual fails to recover within the maximum duration expectancy period, the reader may wish to reference the following questions to assist in better understanding the specifics of an individual's medical case.

Regarding diagnosis:

- Does individual have one or more persistent delusions or false beliefs that usually involve a misinterpretation of perceptions or experiences?
- Does individual fit criteria set forth by the DSM-IV?
- What specific type of delusion disorder does individual have? Persecutory, somatic, erotomanic, jealous, or grandiose?
- Since other disorders may present with symptoms and features typical of delusional disorder, is there an overlap with another psychological condition such as paranoid personality disorder, paranoid schizophrenia, delusional disorder, mood disorder with psychotic features, substance-induced psychotic disorder, body dysmorphic disorder, and obsessive-compulsive disorder?
- Was diagnosis of delusional disorder confirmed?

Regarding treatment:

- What treatment modalities or types of therapy have been used so far? If not effective, what else is being considered?
- Would a treatment combination be more beneficial?
- If individual has active psychosis, anxiety, agitation, or severe impairment, were antipsychotic drugs used?
- If individual is suspicious of medication and neglects to take it, are long-lasting injections an option?
- Is individual compliant with regular medication management sessions? What can be done to enhance compliance?
- If individual's delusions are of a persecutory or homicidal nature, is the physician aware of this progression?
- Has physician assessed the extent to which individual is willing to act on delusions?
- Was individual hospitalized or is hospitalization being considered until individual is no longer a threat to self or others?

Regarding prognosis:

- Although delusional disorders do not generally lead to severe impairment or changes in personality, where on this continuum does individual appear to be? Is individual remaining static or progressing to an unhealthy level?
- Does individual have an underlying condition such as mood disorders, chronic post-traumatic stress disorder, alcohol or other substance abuse, body dysmorphic disorder, suicidal tendencies, or schizophrenia that may be complicating treatment or impacting recovery?

References

Diagnostic and Statistical Manual of Mental Disorders IV (Text Revision). American Psychiatric Association Washington, DC: American Psychiatric Association, 1999.

Hammer M.B., et al. "Psychotic Features in Chronic Posttraumatic Stress Disorder and Schizophrenia: Comparative Severity." Journal of Nervous and Mental Disease 188 4 (2000): 217-221.

Manschreck, T.C. "Delusional Disorder: The Recognition and Management of Paranoia." Journal of Clinical Psychiatry 57 Suppl. 3 (1996): 32-38.

Munro, Alistair. Delusional Disorder: Paranoia and Related Illnesses. New York: Cambridge University Press, 1999.

Dementia

Other names / synonyms: Alzheimer's-Type Dementia, Chronic Organic Brain Syndrome, Multiple Cognitive Deficits, Senile Dementia, Senile Dementia of the Alzheimer Type, Vascular Dementia

ICD-9 Depends on Cause

Definition

Dementia is a general term describing a group of disorders in which memory and thought processes (cognition) become impaired for a period of at least 6 months. Unlike mental retardation, dementia involves a change in thinking abilities relative to baseline.

Dementia can be caused by about 50 different disorders, but 50-70% of cases are caused by Alzheimer's disease, and 20-30% by vascular disease. In many forms of dementia, such as Alzheimer's disease and other neurodegenerative disorders, symptoms develop slowly, are relatively stable rather than fluctuating, and continue into a slow decline. However, other forms of dementia, such as vascular dementia associated with small strokes (multi-infarct dementia) may begin abruptly and worsen in stepwise fashion, with relative stability between each decline. In dementia secondary to head trauma or encephalitis, memory problems are worst at the outset, and remain relatively stable or may even improve with time.

Impaired memory is a prominent and early symptom of dementia. New skills and knowledge are difficult to learn, while old skills and knowledge are eventually lost. Valuables may be lost, such as a wallet or keys. The person may become lost, even in familiar surroundings. Late in dementia, individuals may forget their occupation, family members, or even their name. Other symptoms are difficulty naming objects or people (anomia), rambling speech, difficulty performing certain activities (apraxia), or failure to recognize certain objects (agnosia). Executive functions, such as thinking abstractly, planning, and initiating complex activities, can be impaired. Poor judgment and insight are common. The individual usually has little or no awareness of memory loss or other abnormalities. Individuals have an unrealistic view of their capabilities or their future. For example, they may talk of starting a business or driving. There can be mood and sleep disturbances. False beliefs (delusions) are common, especially paranoid delusions involving others stealing from them or conspiring against them. Individuals with dementia may have further deterioration of cognitive abilities with stress, either physical stress such as a viral illness or minor surgery, or psychological stress such as bereavement.

Alzheimer's disease is the most common cause of dementia, followed by stroke and Parkinson's disease. Other possibilities include Huntington's disease, brain injury, tumor, infection (AIDS, syphilis), autoimmune diseases such as lupus, hypothyroidism or other endocrine diseases, liver disease, a neurological disease such as multiple sclerosis, normal pressure hydrocephalus, or heavy metal poisoning with lead or mercury. Dementia could also be a long-lasting effect of drug or alcohol abuse.

The prevalence of dementia increases with age. The age of onset is usually late in life, with the highest prevalence above 85 years. An estimated 2-4% over age 65 have dementia of the Alzheimer's type. Prevalence ranges from about 1.5% for individuals age 65 to 69 up to 16-50% for those over 85. In a study of 252 elderly Canadians living in the community, 64% had undetected dementia.

Diagnosis

History: History should be obtained from or at least corroborated by the family or caregivers, as the individual often lacks judgment and is unaware that anything is wrong. The diagnosis of dementia involves a deterioration in memory from baseline. Depending on the underlying cause of dementia, memory and thinking may get worse gradually or in stepwise fashion, or may be worst at the outset, with stability or even gradual improvement with time. Other symptoms may include difficulty recognizing people or objects, performing skills, or organizing one's life. These impairments cause a decline in social or occupational functioning, including taking care of basic tasks of life such as bathing, dressing, and eating. Diagnosis requires the presence of memory impairment plus one or more of the following: language disturbance (aphasia); inability to carry out motor activities in spite of preserved motor function (apraxia), such as inability to use a toilet; inability to identify objects (agnosia); or inability to plan or organize activities (impaired executive functioning). History should also focus on alcohol or medication use that could be affecting cognitive function.

Physical exam: The exam could show signs of an underlying disease, such as vascular disorders or vitamin deficiencies. A lack of facial expression (flat affect) might be present. On neurological examination, abnormalities might include symmetrically abnormal reflexes (frontal lobe release signs). In dementia caused by vascular disease, multiple sclerosis, or autoimmune conditions, there might be multifocal findings reflecting abnormalities in several different brain structures. These might include asymmetrical reflexes, weakness on one side, or abnormalities in the cranial nerves supplying strength and sensation to the head and neck. In dementia caused by a brain tumor, single stroke, or head trauma, the neurological examination might show abnormalities restricted to a single location in the nervous system.

Tests: Tests include mental status examinations or more detailed neuropsychological testing to document cognitive impairment. Neuroimaging, such as computed tomography (CT) and magnetic resonance imaging (MRI), may reveal shrinking of brain substance (cerebral atrophy), strokes, tumors, or other abnormalities. Positron-emission tomography (PET) or single photon emission computed tomography (SPECT) scans, thought to be more of a research tool than CT and MRI, may show functional changes in parts of the brain involved in thought processing (frontal or parietal lobes). Blood work may show treatable endocrine, metabolic, autoimmune, or infectious causes, such as hypothyroidism, vitamin B_{12} or folate deficiency, syphilis, or lupus. Electroencephalogram (EEG) may be helpful in those forms of dementia with specific EEG patterns, such as Jakob-Creutzfeldt disease. Spinal tap (lumbar puncture) is usually unnecessary, but may help diagnose autoimmune or infectious forms of dementia. Research suggests that certain markers in spinal fluid may be elevated in Alzheimer's disease.

Treatment

Treatment is aimed at slowing the effects of any underlying cause. Vascular dementia, for example, can be treated with drugs that lower blood pressure and anticoagulants; preventive treatment for this condition includes diet, exercise, and control of diabetes. Approximately 20% of all cases of dementia are treatable.

Treatment for dementia of the Alzheimer's type has not yet been effective. Donepezil hydrochloride has been shown to extend the functional ability of some individuals with mild to moderate Alzheimer's disease. Newer medications, such as tacrine hydrochloride and rivastigmine, are being studied for their effectiveness in slowing the symptoms of dementia. A regular and consistent schedule of activities can help some individuals avoid emotional outbursts, while lithium, anticonvulsant medications, or antipsychotics may be needed in others. Teaching the caregiver strategies for coping with the physical, emotional, and legal burdens of dementia is a crucial part of the treatment plan. Educational materials, support groups, and social service intervention may help prevent caregivers from becoming depressed or anxious, which is a significant risk. Identifying individuals at risk for dementia, such as those with a strong family history, may allow earlier intervention with preventive medications such as statins or anti-inflammatory drugs. These might theoretically help prevent dementia in individuals at risk, based on epidemiologic studies showing decreased risk of dementia in individuals using these medications.

Prognosis

Dementia is usually irreversible and often progressive, although 20% of cases are treatable, demanding a thorough workup as soon as possible. Early diagnosis may allow symptoms to be decreased or delayed with treatment, but the underlying deterioration usually continues. Other benefits of early diagnosis include more effective planning by the family, and prevention of motor vehicle or other accidents due to driving while impaired.

Differential Diagnosis

Other disorders in which memory problems are prominent include delirium, which comes on suddenly, fluctuates, and is associated with an altered level of consciousness. Dementia may come on suddenly but is more often gradual in onset, is stable for longer periods, and is not usually associated with decreased level of consciousness. Mental retardation is associated with memory and thinking problems, but is present since birth, unlike dementia, which comes on later in life. Depression can be associated with pseudodementia in which thought processes are slowed and forgetfulness is common. These two conditions can be distinguished on neuropsychological testing, as depression is associated with poor performance on timed tasks, and with many answers of "I don't know," even though the individual may get the right answer if pressed. Other conditions that may be confused with dementia include amnestic disorder, substance abuse, schizophrenia, and malingering.

Specialists

- Advanced Practice Registered Nurse
- Internist
- Neurologist
- Occupational Therapist
- Physical Therapist
- Psychiatrist
- Psychologist

Rehabilitation

Physical therapy might be helpful if the individual has problems with gait and balance. Occupational therapy might help the individual to adapt to simpler communication or self-care skills. Relaxation techniques might be helpful in decreasing stress. However, demented individuals often are too impaired to allow carryover from one therapy session to the next, particularly in progressive dementia such as Alzheimer's disease. Rehabilitation is more appropriate in static forms of dementia such as those associated with head trauma, a single stroke, or encephalitis. Mildly to moderately demented individuals may benefit from "day groups" stressing orientation, social interaction, and reminiscence therapy, such as listening to music which was popular in their youth, or talking about work, parenting, or other experiences relating to earlier life.

Work Restrictions / Accommodations

Those in very early stages might function better with set routines, clear instructions, and well-learned tasks. Individuals in later stages of dementia are usually not employable.

Comorbid Conditions

Coexisting conditions that may affect recovery and lengthen disability include psychiatric disorders such as depression. Concurrent substance abuse, and physical conditions related to the toxic effects of alcohol or drugs on the brain, can also lengthen disability. Vascular disorders, infections, and other acute or chronic illnesses could also exacerbate dementia symptoms.

Complications

Individuals with dementia can become aggressive or violent toward others. Suicide is possible in the early stages when individuals are still capable of carrying out a plan. Falls, injuries, and other accidents are common because of impaired judgment and coordination. When demented individuals lose control of their bowels and bladder (become incontinent), they are more likely to get urinary infections and bedsores (decubitus ulcers), and to be institutionalized. Bedridden individuals with dementia are more likely to develop pneumonia, blood clots (thromboembolism), bedsores, and joint immobility (contractures). Vascular dementia is likely to be complicated by additional strokes and heart attack (myocardial infarction), which may be fatal. Poor appetite and difficulty manipulating utensils may lead to malnutrition or dehydration. Seizures may occur in vascular dementia or in dementias related to autoimmune disease, infection, or trauma.

Factors Influencing Duration

Diagnosis and treatment of a treatable dementia may lead to restored mental function. The severity of dementia and extent of available social supports can influence disability. Most forms of dementia are incompatible with gainful employment.

Length of Disability

If the underlying cause of the dementia is not treatable, the dementia may continue to progress. Disability may be permanent.

Failure to Recover

If an individual fails to recover within the maximum duration expectancy period, the reader may wish to reference the following questions to assist in better understanding the specifics of an individual's medical case.

Regarding diagnosis:

- Was a thorough workup done to identify and exclude all treatable causes of dementia?
- Has history focused on alcohol or medication use that could be affecting cognitive function?
- Does individual have difficulty recognizing people or objects, performing skills, or organizing daily activities of life?
- On neurological exam, were abnormalities present such as symmetrically abnormal reflexes (frontal lobe release signs)?
- Were conditions with similar symptoms ruled out?
- Was diagnosis of dementia confirmed?

Regarding treatment:

- Are underlying cause(s) responding to appropriate treatment? If not, should treatment plan be reevaluated?
- Has individual received a trial of medications now available that may help slow the development of cognitive deficits?
- Does individual have hallucinations, delusions, or agitation that may respond to appropriate medications?
- Was caregiver taught strategies for coping with the physical, emotional, and legal burdens of dementia?
- Are educational materials, support groups, and social service intervention being utilized to help prevent caregiver from becoming depressed or anxious?

Regarding prognosis:

- Did early diagnosis allow symptoms to be decreased or delayed with treatment?
- Did early intervention include treatment with preventive medications such as statins or anti-inflammatory drugs? If diagnosis is uncertain, is individual still at risk for dementia?
- Is individual a candidate for preventive medications?
- Was family able to effectively plan strategies for coping with the physical, emotional, and legal burdens of dementia?
- Would caregiver(s) benefit from social service intervention? Enrollment in a support group?
- Does individual have a coexisting condition that may impact recovery such as depression, concurrent substance abuse, or toxic effects of alcohol or drugs on the brain?
- Are vascular disorders, infections, and other acute or chronic illnesses present that could exacerbate dementia symptoms?

References

Dementia. Medline Plus. 2000. 31 Jan 2001 <http://www.nlm.nih.gov/medlineplus/dementia.html>.

Dementia. Neurology Channel. 03 Oct 2000. 31 Jan 2001 <http://neurologychannel.com/dementia/>.

Allen, Francis. Diagnostic and Statistical Manual of Mental Disorders, 4th ed, text revision. Washington, DC: American Psychiatric Association, 2000.

Daniel, D.G. "Antipsychotic Treatment of Psychosis and Agitation in the Elderly." Journal of Clinical Psychiatry 61 Suppl. 14 (2000): 49-52.

Duke, James A. The Green Pharmacy. Emmaus, PA: Rodale Press, Inc, 1997.

Feinstein, Alice, ed. Healing with Vitamins. Emmaus, PA: Rodale Press, Inc, 1996.

Gottlieb, Bill, ed. New Choices in Natural Healing. Emmaus, PA: Rodale Press, Inc, 1997.

Relkin, N. "Screening and Early Diagnosis of Dementia." American Journal of Managed Care 6 Suppl. 22 (2000): S1111-24.

Ritchie, K., S. Artero, and J. Touchon. "Classification Criteria for Mild Cognitive Impairment: A Population-based Validation Study." Neurology 56 1 (2001): 37-42.

Sternberg, S.A., C. Wolfson, and M. Baumgarten. "Undetected Dementia in Community-dwelling Older People: The Canadian Study of Health and Aging." Journal of the American Geriatric Society 48 11 (2000): 1430-1434.

Dementia, Alzheimer's Type, with Delusions (Late Onset)

Other names / synonyms: Alzheimer Disease with Delusions, Senile Dementia of Alzheimer's Type with Delusions, Senile Psychosis

290.2

Definition

Alzheimer's type dementia with delusions describes a loss of mental functions accompanied by psychotic, delusional features generally emerging after age 65. Memory becomes impaired, first with a reduced ability to learn new tasks or information and later with difficulty remembering even overlearned information acquired much earlier in life. Alzheimer's disease appears to be a metabolic disease of the brain that begins many years before symptoms of intellectual decline begin.

Other symptoms include difficulty in finding words, performing routine activities, recognizing familiar things or individuals, or planning and organizing life goals. Delusions are prominent where the individual holds firmly to a false belief that no one else can verify. A common delusion is that others are conspiring to hurt, steal, or abandon them. Sensory hallucinations may also be present especially those that relate to the delusion. For example, an individual who believes he or she is infested with bugs might "see" them, or if an individual believes others are conspiring against him, may "hear" them whispering. Other symptoms of dementia of the Alzheimer's type are disorientation to time and location, agitation and aggressive behavior in some cases, and loss of judgment and insight. The individual usually has no awareness of impairments and may make plans inconsistent with current disabilities.

Alzheimer's is diagnosed only after excluding other causes of progressive mental decline such as stroke, Parkinson's disease, Huntington's disease, fluid accumulation in the brain (hydrocephalus), or brain tumor. The exact cause of Alzheimer's disease is unknown, but different factors may interact in complex ways to predispose someone to the condition including genetic mutations of the amyloid precursor protein involved in formation of characteristic abnormalities within nerve cells (plaques), genes that increase susceptibility to the condition (including the apolipoprotein E4 allele), and environmental influences. Head trauma of moderate or severe intensity may predispose and individual to Alzheimer's disease.

Use of medications such as anti-inflammatory drugs may protect against it according to recent epidemiological studies. However, controlled clinical trials have not been done to confirm these theories.

The prevalence of Alzheimer's disease increases with age, with the highest prevalence over age 85. It is the most common cause of progressive loss of intellectual function (dementia) over age 55. It is more common in women than men, perhaps because women generally live longer. There are an estimated 3 to 4 million cases in the US.

Diagnosis

History: History is marked by progressive memory difficulties generally beginning after age 65. There is also impairment in at least one of the following areas: finding words (aphasia), performing usual activities of daily living, recognizing people or objects, and planning or organizing. Personality changes with increasing irritability are seen early in the disease. Diagnosis of Alzheimer's disease is unlikely if the onset of symptoms is sudden, if there are specific and focal neurological signs, or if there are seizures or trouble walking early in the illness.

History will have to be provided by family or others who know or have observed the individual. Observation of the individual's orientation, dress, mannerisms, behavior, and content of speech are helpful in diagnosing the illness. History should determine if there is any personal history of medical conditions or recent problems such as head trauma or alcohol abuse that could impair intellectual function. Family history may reveal relatives with impairment of memory or intellect. Detailed medication inventory may detect drugs that can cause memory difficulties, either alone or in combination.

Physical exam: The exam is generally normal until later in the disease when a disturbance of gait is observed and abnormal reflexes present that suggest abnormalities in the brain area located behind the forehead (frontal lobe release signs). Detailed neurological testing should be done to exclude other conditions such as Parkinson's disease, stroke, or brain tumor. General physical exam should also be thorough to rule out diseases of other organ systems such as thyroid or liver abnormalities that can also affect mental function.

Tests: Neuropsychological testing can document specific abnormalities of mental functions. CT or MRI usually shows a shrinking of the brain (cerebral atrophy) and should be done to rule out other conditions such as stroke, brain tumor, or bleeding under the skull (subdural hematoma). These tests can support the diagnosis but not prove it. Electroencephalogram (EEG) may show diffuse abnormalities and slowing but is not generally helpful and may not be needed unless specific diseases with characteristic EEG abnormalities are suspected such as Jakob-Creutzfeldt disease. Similarly, spinal tap (lumbar puncture) may not be needed unless chronic meningitis is suspected. Blood work rules out endocrine or biochemical derangements that can cloud intellectual function such as hypothyroidism or vitamin B_{12} deficiency.

Treatment

The disease is not yet directly treatable but antipsychotic drugs may be helpful in controlling the delusions, hallucinations, agitation, and wandering tendencies. If depression is present, antidepressant medications are useful. Elderly individuals in general and those with Alzheimer's disease in particular, tend to be very sensitive to the side effects of antipsychotic and antidepressant medications. These should be started at the lowest possible dose, monitoring the individuals carefully to be sure they are not getting worse. Memory-enhancing drugs that increase activity in the cholinergic system, such as donepezil (Aricept) may be temporarily helpful. The environment and amount of stimulation should be kept as familiar and constant as possible. Total custodial care may be required as the disease progresses.

While individuals lack the intellectual skills needed to participate in formal rehabilitation, they may benefit in the early stages from Alzheimer's groups where orientation is reinforced through calendars and other visual cues, and group activities and socialization are encouraged. Reminiscence therapy using old photographs or favorite songs or movies may help the individual retain their sense of identity. Caregivers often benefit from a support group and need education about safety measures and other strategies helpful in coping with individuals with Alzheimer's.

Prognosis

The progression of impairments is usually slow and there may be plateaus where nothing really changes for long periods of time. Late in the disease, the individual may become bedridden and unable to speak. The average time from onset of symptoms to death is 8 to 10 years. Death is often from unrelated causes such as heart attack, but there is a higher risk of fatal pneumonia, kidney infection, or infected bedsores related to being bedridden and having no control over bladder or bowel function (urinary and bowel incontinence).

Differential Diagnosis

Other possibilities are delirium, alcohol abuse, amnesia disorder, strokes (vascular dementia), dementia from medical conditions such as AIDS or Parkinson's disease, drug- or alcohol-induced dementia, schizophrenia, major depression, and malingering. Toxic exposures to carbon monoxide, pesticides, or gardening materials should be considered especially if neighbors or household members are similarly affected. Blood tests should be done to rule out hypothyroidism, vitamin B_{12} or thiamine deficiency, and liver or kidney failure.

Specialists

- Neurologist
- Psychiatrist
- Psychologist

Rehabilitation

Individuals with Alzheimer's disease may require occupational therapy to help compensate for cognitive deficits. Occupational therapy focuses on maintaining realistic caregiver goals and maximizing safety in the home. Individuals and their caregivers learn to structure the individual's environment to allow for greater independence.

Individuals can perform daily tasks better if the environment is held constant and the tasks are performed in the same daily routine. For example, keeping a washcloth, towel, and soap at the bedside every morning aids in cueing the individual to shower rather than relying on the individual to remember to shower as well as where the shower supplies are kept. Individuals who are aware of their memory loss can compensate for forgetfulness by writing notes to remember daily tasks, labeling rooms to prevent getting lost, and providing themselves with other visual cues. Caregivers also learn to provide time cues such as a calendar and a clock in a highly visible area to keep the individual oriented. Occupational therapy does not ordinarily focus on teaching new skills to individuals with Alzheimer's disease as this disease decreases problem-solving ability.

Individuals aware of their memory loss may require psychological counseling to help treat depression that often accompanies this disease. Group counseling may also be necessary for individuals and their families to address the anger and aggressiveness that individuals with Alzheimer's disease often exhibit. Support groups can address individuals' concerns about their prognosis.

Work Restrictions / Accommodations

Early in the course of the illness, the individual may continue to work at routine overlearned tasks. Eventually, as the disease progresses, the individual is unable to work.

Comorbid Conditions

Current alcohol abuse or drug use, or the presence of a personality disorder or other psychiatric condition may initially affect disability. Individuals with Alzheimer's disease may have further decline in mental function even with relatively mild medical illnesses such as urinary or respiratory infection. Vascular dementia secondary to heart disease and small strokes frequently accompany Alzheimer's disease as does Parkinson's disease, with outcome generally worse and rate of decline more rapid than in the isolated condition.

Complications

As the disease progresses, impaired judgment and decreased mobility may lead to falls or other accidents. Infections become increasingly likely if the individual is incontinent and bedridden. Electrolyte disturbances are possible because of dehydration or malnutrition. Seizures are eventually present in approximately 10% of those with Alzheimer's. Suicide is possible early in the disease as the individual comes to terms with the progressive intellectual decline that is likely to follow.

Factors Influencing Duration

Individuals may temporarily return to work after diagnosis. The severity of mental impairment and the availability of social support can influence the degree of disability. This is a progressive disease and eventually leads to total disability.

Length of Disability

This condition eventually results in total and permanent disability.

Failure to Recover

If an individual fails to recover within the maximum duration expectancy period, the reader may wish to reference the following questions to assist in better understanding the specifics of an individual's medical case.

Regarding diagnosis:

- Does individual have history marked by progressive memory difficulties generally beginning after age 65?
- Does individual have impairment finding words (aphasia), performing usual activities of daily living, recognizing people or objects, and planning or organizing?
- Are personality changes with increasing irritability seen?
- Was neuropsychological testing done? CT or MRI?
- Were conditions with similar symptoms ruled out?
- Was the diagnosis of dementia Alzheimer's type with delusions (late onset) confirmed?

Regarding treatment:

- Has drug therapy helped reduce symptoms?
- Were antidepressant medications effective against depression?
- Were antipsychotic drugs used to help control delusions, hallucinations, agitation, and wandering tendencies?
- If drug therapy is not effective in reducing symptoms, could dosage be safely increased?
- Would individual benefit from addition of memory-enhancing drugs to current treatment regimen?
- Since environment and amount of stimulation should be kept as familiar and constant as possible, can individual remain at home at the present time?
- Would individual benefit from companion or adult day-care environment?
- Does the present caregiver need additional outside help such as a home health aide?

Regarding prognosis:

- Were underlying conditions identified that may impact recovery such as urinary or respiratory infection, vascular dementia, and Parkinson's disease? If present, are underlying conditions being effectively addressed?
- Do individual and family have realistic expectations?
- Because total custodial care may be required as the disease progresses, has the family made long-term plans for individual's care?
- Would the family benefit from social worker input in making these decisions?

References

"Alzheimer Disease and the Dementias." Scientific American® Medicine Online. Dale D.C., and D.D. Federman, eds New York: WebMD Corporation, 2000. 26 Oct 2000 <http://www.samed.com/sam/forms/index.htm>.

Schunk, Carol. "Cognitive Impairment." Geriatric Physical Therapy. Guccione, Andrew A., ed. St. Louis: Mosby-Year Book, Inc, 1993. 139-148.

References (Continued)

Brannon, Linda, and Jess Feist. "Living with Chronic Disease." Health Psychology. King, Kenneth, ed. Belmont: Wadsworth Publishing Company, 1992. 275-315.

Cameron, I., et al. "Use of Donepezil for the Treatment of Mild-moderate Alzheimer's Disease: An Audit of the Assessment and Treatment of Patients in Routine Clinical Practice." International Journal of Geriatric Psychiatry 15 10 (2000): 887-891.

St. George-Hyslop, P. "Alzheimer's Disease." Neurobiology of Disease 7 5 Pt. B (2000): 546-548.

van Dongen, M.C., et al. "The Efficacy of Gingko for Elderly People with Dementia and Age-associated Memory Impairment: New Results of a Randomized Clinical Trial." Journal of the American Geriatrics Society 48 10 (2000): 1183-1194.

Dengue Fever
Other names / synonyms: Breakbone Fever
061

Definition

Dengue fever is a tropical disease caused by a virus (Flavivirus) and transmitted through the bite of the Aedes aegypti mosquito. Humans with the infection serve as the source. There are four varieties (serotypes) numbered one through four. Becoming infected with one serotype does not provide protection against becoming infected with any other serotypes. A second infection can have worse symptoms.

The virus, which may remain in the blood for several months, is spread when a mosquito bites an infected individual and then bites someone else. Dengue fever is often called "breakbone fever" because muscle and bone pain is very severe. Characteristic of dengue fever is a fever curve where the individual has a high fever that drops to normal and then suddenly recurs to its former degree ("biphasic fever curve").

Dengue fever occurs in tropical regions including Southeast Asia, Australia, the Pacific region, parts of Africa, South and Central America, and the Caribbean. Occasional outbreaks have occurred in Mexico, Puerto Rico, and the Virgin Islands. Individuals working outdoors in endemic areas are at greater risk for dengue fever, as are travelers to these areas.

Worldwide, there are over 100 million cases of dengue fever annually. In the US, 50 to 100 cases are recognized annually, but these cases are travelers from endemic areas rather than individuals who acquired the infection within the US. No locally acquired (autochthonous) cases have been reported in the US (including the Hawaiian islands) since 1986, when cases were reported in Texas.

Diagnosis

History: Symptoms appear 5 to 8 days after being bitten by an infected mosquito and usually include fever, chills, lethargy, nausea, vomiting, and severe aching of the back, extremities, muscles, and joints. The individual may also complain of severe headaches including pain behind the eye (retro-orbital), loss of appetite, sore throat, and change in taste. After about 3 days, the symptoms often subside, only to return a few days later. This second phase lasts 1 to 2 days, and is accompanied by a skin rash and similar but usually more forceful symptoms than in the first phase.

Physical exam: A skin rash or small, flat, purplish-red spots (petechiae) on the hands, feet, arms, legs, trunk, and neck, but not on the face, may be evident. Palpation (examination by pressing with hands) of the abdomen may reveal a slightly enlarged liver or spleen, and lymph nodes may be enlarged.

Tests: Viruses may be identified (isolated) in the blood during the acute phase of the illness. A complete blood count (CBC) characteristically reveals an abnormal decrease in white blood cells (leukopenia).

Treatment

There is no cure for dengue fever, so treatment is aimed at relieving symptoms (symptomatic). Individuals should get plenty of rest and drink lots of fluids. According to the Center for Disease Control, acetaminophen should be used as an analgesic (pain reliever), but aspirin should be avoided. Sedatives may provide relief from severe pain in muscles and joints. No vaccine against the disease is currently available.

Prognosis

The vast majority of individuals have a benign, uncomplicated course. Most individuals recover completely, although full recovery may take several weeks. Infection with one serotype of Dengue fever only confers immunity against that serotype but not against the other three serotypes. Subsequent infection with Dengue may lead to the extremely serious Dengue Hemorrhagic Fever.

Differential Diagnosis

Conditions with similar symptoms include measles, scarlet fever, typhoid, malaria, yellow fever, scrub typhus, Q fever, leptospirosis, influenza, roseola infantum, and tropical viral infections such as chikungunya and o'nyong-nyong.

Work Restrictions / Accommodations

Extended sick leave may be required due to slow convalescence. According to the Center for Disease Control, absent complications symptoms may last 10 days, with complete recovery taking 2 to 4 weeks. If an individual must return to work prior to full recovery, the individual should be permitted to work decreased hours and to have frequent rest periods.

Specialists

- Infectious Disease Physician
- Tropical Disease Specialist
- Internist

Comorbid Conditions

Immunosuppression from chemotherapy or AIDS would impair recovery and lengthen disability.

Complications

Serious complications are uncommon. Depression, pneumonia, bone marrow failure, and infections of the iris (iritis), testicles (orchitis), or ovaries (oophoritis) are rare complications. Development of Dengue hemorrhagic fever, in which bleeding develops in the gums, skin, and intestinal tract, and Dengue shock syndrome, characterized by rapidly plunging blood pressure are rare but have a poor prognosis and a 2-5% fatality rate.

Factors Influencing Duration

Length of disability may be influenced by the severity of disease or symptoms or by the presence of complications. Development of Dengue hemorrhagic fever or Dengue shock syndrome, the most severe complications, will significantly lengthen the disability period.

Length of Disability

Duration in Days

Job Classification	Minimum	Optimum	Maximum
Sedentary work	7	14	21
Light work	7	14	21
Medium work	14	21	28
Heavy work	21	28	42
Very Heavy work	21	28	42

Failure to Recover

If an individual fails to recover within the maximum duration expectancy period, the reader may wish to reference the following questions to assist in better understanding the specifics of an individual's medical case.

Regarding diagnosis:

- Does individual live in an area where the disease is endemic? Has individual traveled to an area where the disease is endemic?
- Did individual have a mosquito bite?
- Does individual have fever, chills, lethargy, nausea, vomiting, severe aching of the back, extremities, muscles, and joints, and severe headache behind the eyes?
- Does individual complain of loss of appetite, sore throat, and change in taste?
- Did the symptoms subside in about 3 days and then return in a few days?
- Does individual now have a skin rash and similar but more forceful symptoms than in the first phase?
- On exam, does individual have petechiae on the hands, feet, arms, legs, trunk, and neck, but not on the face?
- On palpation, is the liver or spleen enlarged? Are lymph nodes enlarged?
- Was CBC performed? Was the virus isolated in the blood?
- Were conditions with similar symptoms ruled out?

Regarding treatment:

- As there is no cure for dengue fever, has individual received symptomatic treatment?
- Is individual resting and drinking lots of fluids?
- Is individual using acetaminophen rather than aspirin as an analgesic?
- Was it necessary to prescribe sedatives for severe muscle and joint pain?

Regarding prognosis:

- Can individual's employer accommodate any necessary restrictions?
- Does individual have any conditions that may affect ability to recover?
- Have any complications developed such as depression, pneumonia, bone marrow failure, iritis orchitis, oophoritis, Dengue hemorrhagic fever, or Dengue shock syndrome?

References

Monath, Thomas P. "Flavaviruses." Principles and Practice of Infectious Diseases, 4th ed, vol. 2. Mandell, Gerald L., John E. Bennett, and Raphael Dolin, eds. New York: Churchill Livingstone, 1995. 1465-1473.

Shope, Robert E. "Introduction to Hemorrhagic Fever Viruses." Cecil Textbook of Medicine, 20th ed, vol. 2. Bennett, J. Claude, and Fred Plum, eds. Philadelphia: W.B. Saunders Company, 1996. 1797-1798.

Dental Disorders

Other names / synonyms: Abnormal Dentition, Dental Caries, Dental Cavities, Tooth Decay

520, 520.9, 521, 521.0, 521.7, 521.9

Definition

Dental disorders and tooth decay refer to conditions that result in damage to tooth structure. In mammals, all teeth consist of three layers. The outer layer called the enamel is the hardest tissue in the body. The middle layer called dentine is less hard than enamel and similar in composition to bone. The pulp is the innermost layer and provides nourishment to the tooth.

Tooth decay begins when bacteria that are normally present in the mouth between teeth and between teeth and gums combine with saliva and debris from sugary and starchy foods to form a sticky substance (plaque) that adheres to the teeth.

The plaque contains acids that destroy the tooth's enamel and dentine by removing calcium and other minerals from them. Tooth decay usually begins on the surface enamel and in pits and fissures between adjacent teeth, creating holes in the tooth. From the enamel, the process of decay spreads to the underlying dentine and may ultimately involve the tooth pulp. Cavities are usually painless until they grow very large in the dentine and the pulp layers of the tooth.

Other forms of dental disorders include tooth abscess, discoloration, faulty alignment, and wisdom teeth complications. Tooth abscess occurs when a cavity left untreated enables bacteria to infect the nerve tissue within the pulp of the tooth. Tooth discoloration can occur as a result of damage to the pulp layer of the tooth from extensive tooth decay or trauma. Faulty alignment entails an abnormality in the relationship between teeth in opposing jaws (malocclusion) or misalignment of one or more teeth. Wisdom teeth complications include crowding, gum disease, and poor positioning.

Dental disorders are more common in individuals whose personal behaviors (e.g., tobacco use, alcohol abuse, poor diet), medications, or coexisting medical illnesses (e.g., diabetes mellitus, human immunodeficiency virus infection) increase the risk of oral pathology. Individuals who practice poor oral hygiene (lack of regular brushing, flossing, and dental examination and cleaning), eat chewy, sticky foods between meals without brushing or at least rinsing afterwards, and constantly sip sugary drinks or frequently suck on candy or mints are at risk for dental disorders.

The average adult in the US has 10 to 17 decayed, missing, or filled permanent teeth.

Diagnosis

History: Symptomatic individuals with tooth decay present with sensitivity to cold or hot foods and liquids and tooth pain that manifests itself especially when individual is eating. Individuals with tooth decay in its early stages may have no symptoms.

Physical exam: The dentist performs a complete oral exam that may or may not reveal pits or holes (cavities) in the teeth. Most cavities are discovered in the early stages during routine checkups. The surface of the tooth may be soft when probed with a sharp instrument. Pain may not be present until the advanced stages of tooth decay.

Tests: Dental x-rays can show some cavities before they are visible to the eye. The most common x-ray procedure is a bite wing where a small piece of film is placed in the mouth behind a section of the teeth. The individual bites down on the paper tab around the film that holds the film in place. The x-ray machine is aimed at that section of teeth and a picture is taken. Most dental x-rays include four or more views of the teeth. Sinus x-rays may also be taken if disease of the sinuses is suspected.

Treatment

For tooth decay, the decayed material is removed by drilling and replaced with a restorative material such as sliver alloy, gold, porcelain, or plastic. Porcelain and plastic more closely match the natural tooth appearance and may be preferred for front teeth. Silver amalgam (alloy) and gold are stronger and are often used on back teeth.

For tooth abscess, root canal surgery may be recommended in an attempt to preserve the tooth. The center of the tooth including the nerve and vascular tissue (pulp) may be removed along with decayed portions of the tooth. The root and surface of the tooth remain in place. The cavity created in the core is filled and repaired and a crown may be placed over the tooth. In some cases, excision (surgical drainage) of the abscess or extraction of the affected tooth may be necessary.

Anesthetics (local, nitrous oxide gas, or other general anesthetic) may be required in some cases for drilling or other treatment of tooth decay or abscess.

Tooth discoloration may be corrected cosmetically through the use of opalescence bleaching gel dispensed in soft, thin plastic bleaching trays custom fitted for the individual's mouth.

For misaligned teeth, a dentist specializing in the treatment of misaligned teeth (orthodontist) prescribes and oversees the use of a retainer or braces.

Specialists

- Infectious Disease Physician
- Tropical Disease Specialist
- Internist

Prognosis

Outcome of tooth decay treated by a filling is usually positive. The effectiveness of root canal therapy will probably last a lifetime but occasionally an abscess persists even after root canal therapy is performed. In such an instance, another surgical procedure is required to remove the diseased tissue from the tip of the root and reseal it with another filling. Tooth discoloration is ongoing so the bleaching procedure will probably need to be repeated from time to time. Most of the time, misaligned teeth remain aligned if the individual closely follows the recommendations of his or her orthodontist with regard to the prescribed retainer or braces.

Differential Diagnosis

Differential diagnosis may include biting down too hard on a tooth (traumatic occlusion), sinus infection, root sensitivity, or fractured tooth (partial or complete).

Work Restrictions / Accommodations

The individual can usually return to work the same day if dental disorders are treated in the early stages. A day or so of sick leave may be required for more complicated treatments such as a root canal.

Complementary and Alternative Therapies

Content is intended for awareness only. Treatments may or may not be effective. Scientific evidence may be lacking and some substances have potentially toxic effects. Dr. Presley Reed and the editors do not endorse the use of these therapies in the absence of consultation with a licensed medical professional.

Antibacterial therapy - May help keep bacteria under control. Chewing gum containing xylitol may also help.

Diet modification - Individuals prone to dental cavities should avoid eating chewy, sticky foods between meals without brushing or at least rinsing afterwards; constantly sipping sugary drinks; and frequently sucking on candy or mints. Although drinking artificially sweetened soft drinks helps, diet colas often contain acid that can also lead to tooth decay.

Fluoride - Makes tooth enamel more resistant to the acid causing tooth decay. If drinking water is not currently fluoridated, use of toothpaste that contains fluoride is beneficial; sodium fluoride drops or tablets or fluoride directly applied to teeth are helpful in preventing tooth decay.

Glass ionomer - Tooth-colored filling that is said to release fluoride to individuals prone to decay at the gum line. It can also be used to restore areas damaged by overzealous brushing.

Plastic sealants - Said to protect hard-to-reach grooves on the back teeth and form an effective barrier against acid-producing bacteria.

Comorbid Conditions

Comorbid conditions that may influence length of disability include medically compromising conditions such as diabetes mellitus and human immunodeficiency virus (HIV) infection. Individuals taking medications that cause dry mouth are also at higher risk for bacterial infections.

Complications

Complications of tooth decay include abscess of the tooth/gums caused from bacterial infection of the tooth root or periodontal infection, chronic discomfort in the mouth, exposure of bone in the socket after a lower back tooth has been removed (dry socket), and fractured tooth. The restorative material used to fill a cavity may need to be replaced over time due to looseness and damage.

Factors Influencing Duration

Factors that may influence length of disability include infections and the necessity for surgery to extract teeth.

Length of Disability

Duration depends on the type of disorder and treatment. Dental caries are not associated with disability.

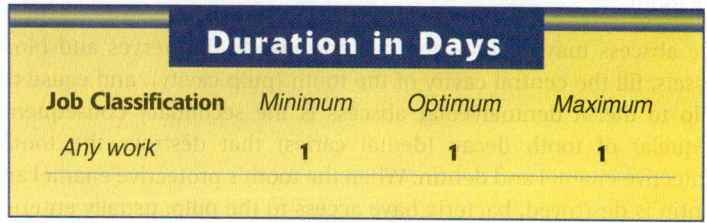

Duration in Days

Job Classification	Minimum	Optimum	Maximum
Any work	1	1	1

Failure to Recover

If an individual fails to recover within the maximum duration expectancy period, the reader may wish to reference the following questions to assist in better understanding the specifics of an individual's medical case.

Regarding diagnosis:

- Has type and origin of dental disorder been confirmed through thorough dental x-rays?
- Have similar conditions, such as sinus infection, been ruled out?
- Has individual experienced any complications?
- Is there an underlying condition that puts individual at increased risk for dental disorders?

Regarding treatment:

- Were dental procedures able to preserve the tooth?
- Did individual experience any complications related to the procedure?
- Would individual benefit from the use of a retainer or braces?
- How effective was the procedure?
- Did individual adhere to prescribed treatment plan?

Regarding prognosis:

- Did procedure accomplish the anticipated goal? If not, what further or additional treatments are now warranted?
- Is individual willing to modify these behaviors in return for better dental health?
- Would individual benefit from consultation with a nutritionist?
- Is individual willing to get regular dental check-ups in order to monitor or ward off further dental disorders?

References

"Chapter 94: Tooth Disorders." Merck Manual of Medical Information - Home Edition, Section 8, Chapter 94. Beers, Mark H., and Robert Berkow, MD, eds. Whitehouse Station, NJ: Merck & Co., Inc., 1999. 23 Feb 2001 <http://http://www.merck.com/pubs/mmanual_home/sec8/94.htm>.

Tooth Abscess. HealthCentral.com, Inc. 01 Dec 1999. 17 Jan 2001 <http://healthcentralsympatico.com/mhc/top/001060.cfm>.

Dental Disorders 659

Dentoalveolar Abscess

Other names / synonyms: Dental Abscess, Periapical Abscess

522, 522.5

Definition

A dentoalveolar abscess is a pus-filled sac in the tissue around the root of a tooth.

The abscess may occur when bacteria invade the nerves and blood vessels, fill the central cavity of the tooth (pulp cavity), and cause the pulp to die. A dentoalveolar abscess is the secondary consequence (sequela) of tooth decay (dental caries) that destroys the tooth's protective enamel and dentin. When the tooth's protective enamel and dentin is destroyed, bacteria have access to the pulp, usually entering directly through a fracture or along damaged blood vessels. Pus formed by this infection occasionally finds its way to the gumline of the tooth. More frequently, the pus is discharged into surrounding tissues, causing painful inflammation.

According to reports issued by the Centers for Disease Control and Prevention (CDC) in 1998, the number cases of dentoalveolar abscess diagnosed in the US was 9,000.

Diagnosis

History: Symptoms include toothache or painful throbbing, swelling, or reddening of the gums; extremely painful biting or chewing; and sensitivity to heat and cold. The individual may also complain of fever, headache, and general fatigue.

An untreated abscess eventually erodes a small channel (sinus) through the jawbone to the surface of the gum where a swelling (gumboil) may occur. The swelling may burst and discharge foul-tasting pus into the mouth.

Physical exam: Upon examination, the dentist may find swollen, reddened gums or swollen glands in the neck and side of the face. There may be an indication that the abscess has spread through surrounding tissues and bone such as pus on the gumline.

Tests: An x-ray helps confirm the diagnosis by determining the exact location of the abscess and whether the abscess has penetrated the structure supporting the teeth (periodontal structure).

Treatment

Treatment is aimed at saving the tooth. A root canal procedure drains the abscess by drilling down through the crown of the tooth and into the pulp cavity, allowing the pus to escape. After cleaning and disinfecting the pulp cavity, the cavity if filled with antibiotic paste and covered with a temporary filling. An antibiotic may be prescribed if the infection has spread beyond the tooth. After a week or so, the temporary filling is removed and the canal examined to ascertain that the infection has been checked. The canal is then filled with dental cement and the tooth fitted with an artificial crown.

If the tooth cannot be saved, it is pulled (extracted) and the abscess drained. Antibiotics are given to clear any residual infection.

Prognosis

Root canal therapy and antibiotic therapy are usually effective in saving the tooth. If the tooth cannot be saved, it must be pulled (extracted). Tooth extraction is a last resort.

Differential Diagnosis

Conditions with similar symptoms include acute gingivitis and periodontal abscess. A fractured tooth can have similar symptoms.

Specialists

- Dentist

Work Restrictions / Accommodations

Restrictions may be necessary for the individual whose duties involve telephone communication, giving in-house or sales presentations, conducting interviews, or any other work responsibilities where the individual is required to talk. Work responsibilities may need to be temporarily shifted to those that are less verbally demanding such as word processing and information systems and database management.

Comorbid Conditions

Comorbid conditions that may influence length of disability after treatment for gingivitis include medically compromising conditions such as diabetes mellitus and human immunodeficiency virus (HIV) infection. Individuals on medications that cause dry mouth are also at higher risk for bacterial infections.

Complications

In some cases, pus from a dentoalveolar abscess can drain through the alveolar bone into soft tissue below and cause inflammation or even infection of the blood (bacteremia). When this type of infection occurs in individuals with a history of rheumatic fever or artificial heart valves (chronic atrial fibrillation), these individuals are at risk for inflammation of the internal lining of the heart, especially the heart valves (endocarditis).

Factors Influencing Duration

Length of disability may be influenced by the method and effectiveness of treatment, recurrence of the abscess, or any complications. Most individuals require little recuperation time for root canal or tooth extraction.

Length of Disability

Duration depends on specific dental problem and/or procedure.

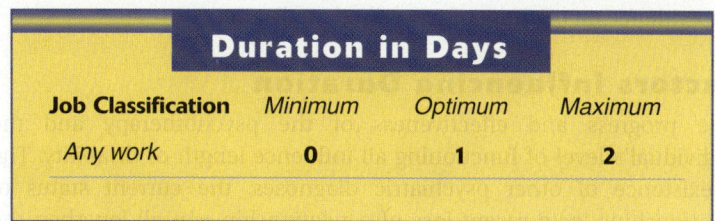

Failure to Recover

If an individual fails to recover within the maximum duration expectancy period, the reader may wish to reference the following questions to assist in better understanding the specifics of an individual's medical case.

Regarding diagnosis:

- Have the gums had injuries from aggressive tooth brushing, toothpick punctures or food that has been forced into the gumline?

- Did the abscess develop quickly or gradually?
- Was an x-ray done? What were the results?
- Were gingivitis and periodontal abscesses ruled out?

Regarding treatment:

- Was the pus drained from the abscess? Was the individual given antibiotics? Did it become necessary to remove the tooth because of severe damage?

Regarding prognosis:

- Does the individual's employer have work they can do on a temporary basis that involves minimal talking?
- Does the individual have any medically compromising conditions, such as diabetes mellitus and human immunodeficiency virus (HIV) infection, that might influence the length of disability after treatment for gingivitis?

References

"Chapter 106: Teeth and Periodontium." Merck Manual of Diagnosis and Therapy, 17th ed. Beers, Mark H., and Robert Berkow, MD Whitehouse Station, NJ: Merck & Co., Inc., 1999. 20 Jan 2001 <http://www.merck.com/pubs/mmanual/section9/chapter106/106e.htm>.

Oral Abscess. healthseva.com. 01 Jan 2000. 20 Jan 2001 <http://www.healthseva.com/content/dentistry/oralabcess_2.php3>.

Dependent Personality Disorder

Other names / synonyms: Inadequate Personality Disorder
301.6, 301.8

Definition

This disorder is characterized by a pervasive pattern of dependent and submissive behavior. Individuals with dependent personality disorder demonstrate helplessness, docility and search for support and reassurance. They appear to subordinate their own needs to those of others, and in a submissive way get others to assume responsibility for major areas of their lives. They are usually quite needy for attention, social contact, and encouragement from others. They appear self-deprecating, as they feel inferior and are willing to abdicate self-responsibility and self-control to others. They often tolerate intimidation and abuse in hopes of avoiding loneliness and abandonment. They may experience intense discomfort when left alone even for brief periods of time.

Individuals with this disorder tend to avoid positions of responsibility and have difficulty making decisions without an excessive amount of advice and reassurance from others. They become anxious if asked to assume leadership roles, as they prefer the submissive role. This disorder is more common in women than men. Individuals with chronic physical illness in childhood may be prone to this disorder.

Diagnosis

History: The psychiatric interview and mental status exam are the primary methods utilized by the practitioner. The physician looks for symptoms of a pervasive and excessive need to be taken care of that lead to submissive and clinging behavior and fears of separation, beginning by early adulthood and present in a variety of contexts.

According to the DSM-IV, 5 or more of the following 8 personality traits must be present to justify the diagnosis: difficulty making everyday decisions without an excessive amount of advice and reassurance from others; need for others to assume responsibility in most major areas of his or her life; difficulty expressing disagreement with others because of fear of loss of support or approval; difficulty initiating projects or doing things independently because of lack of self-confidence in judgment; excessive measures to obtain nurturance and support from others, even volunteering to do things that are unpleasant; discomfort or helplessness when alone because of exaggerated fears of inability to provide self-care; urgency in seeking another relationship as a source of care and support when a close relationship ends; or unrealistic preoccupation with fears of being left alone to care for himself or herself.

Physical exam: The exam is not helpful in diagnosing this disorder. Observation of the individual's orientation, dress, mannerisms, behavior, and content of speech provide essential signs to help diagnose the illness.

Tests: Various psychological tests can be performed to help identify and classify personality disorders, in conjunction with the history.

Treatment

Psychotherapy for individuals with dependent personality can be successful. With the support of a therapist, they learn the root cause of their dependent behaviors and develop effective coping strategies and self-reliant behavior. The therapist should reassure the individual about being available and accessible, within realistic limits. Insight-oriented, behavioral, assertiveness training, family therapy, and group therapy have all been used, with successful outcomes in many cases. Termination of therapy is often difficult, as the individual often feels dependent on the therapist.

Pharmacotherapy has been used to deal with depression and anxiety that commonly accompany dependent personality disorder. Anti-anxiety agents (benzodiazepines) and antidepressants have been useful in treating high levels of anxiety and panic attacks associated with this disorder. However, drugs should be avoided when possible in these individuals, as they are at high risk of drug dependence and abuse. Hospitalization is rarely needed, except in situations of severe loss or emotional crisis.

Prognosis

Dependent personality disorder is generally not as disabling as the other personality disorders. Treatment with one or more of the psychotherapies often leads to successful outcome. The most common problem areas involve work and relationships.

Differential Diagnosis

The personality traits found in the dependent personality are also found in many other psychiatric disorders, especially histrionic and borderline personality disorders. Dependent behavior is also seen in persons with fear of public places (agoraphobia), but can be differentiated from dependent personality disorder by their high levels of anxiety and even panic.

Specialists

- Psychiatrist
- Psychologist

Work Restrictions / Accommodations

Work accommodations may include the use of a job coach to establish consistent, predictable work behaviors; the development of a structured, consistent set of work activities; communication of clear expectations for work performance; and close supervision.

Comorbid Conditions

Alcohol abuse or drug use, or the presence of another psychiatric illness may lengthen disability.

Complications

Individuals with dependent personalities require a relationship to feel validated. Complications will most likely occur when difficulty arises in relating to other people at work or at home. Loss of the person upon whom they are dependent can lead to an episode of major depression, generalized anxiety, or panic.

At work, particular problems might arise if they are assigned to work independently or without close supervision.

A coexisting psychiatric disorder (major depression, panic attacks, and general anxiety) may intensify their already dysfunctional behavior, as can the use of illegal substances. These individuals are at higher risk of dependence on or abuse of prescribed medications.

Factors Influencing Duration

The progress and effectiveness of the psychotherapy and the individual's level of functioning all influence length of disability. The coexistence of other psychiatric diagnoses, the current status of relationships, or a recent loss of a relationship can all lengthen the course of rehabilitation.

Length of Disability

This condition represents a life-long pattern of behavior. In most cases, no disability is expected.

Failure to Recover

If an individual fails to recover within the maximum duration expectancy period, the reader may wish to reference the following questions to assist in better understanding the specifics of an individual's medical case.

Regarding diagnosis:

- Does individual display a submissive, clinging behavior with fear of separation? Does individual's behavior fit the criteria for dependent personality disorder?
- Did a comprehensive physical exam rule out any underlying physical conditions?
- Were other psychiatric disorders such as histrionic and borderline personality disorders ruled out?
- Was diagnosis confirmed?

Regarding treatment:

- Is individual currently involved in the type of psychotherapy that focuses on solutions to specific life problems individual is currently experiencing?
- Does individual also have a coexisting psychiatric condition? Is this condition being adequately addressed? Does the psychiatric condition interfere with treatment for the dependent personality disorder?
- What medications are being taken and for what purpose?
- What has individual been told about the medication he/she is taking? Is the medication purpose clear and valid?
- Does individual also take medication prescribed by any other health care provider?
- Has the primary physician/therapist reviewed all medication currently being taken to ensure that individual is not abusing it?
- Is individual involved in group therapy? Could individual be using the group to supplement existing or new dependent relationships? Is this the only therapy individual is involved in at this time?
- What can be added to balance the treatment plan?

Regarding prognosis:

- As the end of therapy approaches, is individual re-experiencing feelings of insecurity, lack of self-confidence, increased anxiety, and perhaps even depression?
- Has the therapist adequately prepared individual for therapy termination?
- Does individual appear to be realistically facing termination of therapy?
- Was individual seeking a solution to current conflicts rather than life-changing therapy?
- Was individual encouraged to explore newfound self-reliance?
- Does individual appear ready and able to move on with his/her life?

References

Long, Phillip. Dependent Personality Disorder. Internet Mental Health. 01 Jan 2000. 18 Oct 2000 <http://www.mentalhealth.com/rx/p23-pe09.html>.

Depersonalization Disorder
300.6

Definition

This disorder is characterized by persistent or recurrent episodes of feeling detached or removed from oneself, one's thoughts, feelings, or body. Individuals may feel as if they are watching themselves as outside observers, or may experience themselves as being in a dream or a movie, or feeling like a robot not in charge of their own actions.

It is not a psychosis, in that the person only feels like a robot and does not believe that he or she actually is a robot. The individuals are aware that their experience is abnormal, unlike a psychotic disorder. Depersonalization disorder causes marked distress to the individual and/or impaired social or occupational functioning.

An episode of depersonalization can last for just a few seconds to several years. Onset can be sudden if the person is in a life-threatening situation. The person with this disorder usually seeks treatment for some other symptom; however, anxiety and depression may be associated with this disorder, along with obsessive thinking or worries about bodily concerns. The person may find it difficult to describe the symptoms, either because it is hard to put into words or for fear of being considered crazy. The world, people, and objects could also be experienced as strange or distorted (derealization).

Experiences of depersonalization are quite common, usually provoked by severe stress, trauma, or traveling to a new place, but they are normally limited to a single episode. This symptom may coexist with major depression, hypochondriasis, substance-related disorders, or other mental disorders. Depersonalization disorder is diagnosed only when this is the individual's primary or only symptom. The disorder is usually first treated in adolescence or early adulthood, but may begin in childhood. It is seen equally in men and women. Women with depersonalization tend to have feelings of displeasure (dysphoria), whereas men with depersonalization tend to be intellectually obsessive. Although the syndrome is rare, the symptom of depersonalization is found in up to 80% of psychiatric populations, and in 50-70% of normal individuals at some time in their lives. As in obsessive-compulsive disorder, neurobiological studies have shown dysfunction in the left half (hemisphere) of the brain.

Diagnosis

History: History may reveal perceptions that the individual's body, physical being, or body parts are foreign, or that thoughts and behaviors seem alien and automatic.

Other symptoms may include a clouding or narrowing of consciousness, a distorted sense of time, preoccupation with physical symptoms or bodily function (hypochondriasis), and a tendency to be introspective.

DSM-IV criteria for diagnosis include persistent or recurrent feelings of being detached from one's own thoughts, feelings, or body. There may be the impression of observing oneself, or it may feel like being in a dream. There are no other symptoms of distorted reality, as it is not a psychotic disorder. The depersonalization results in significant distress, or impairment of relationships or work performance. Depersonalization is diagnosed only if it is experienced separately from other mental disorders, such as schizophrenia, panic disorder, or acute stress disorder, and if it is not caused by a drug, especially a hallucinogen, or medical illness such as temporal lobe epilepsy.

Physical exam: The exam does not contribute to this diagnosis, except for the appearance of a bland or flat emotional state (flat affect). Observation of the individual's orientation, dress, mannerisms, behavior, and content of speech provide essential signs to diagnose the illness.

Tests: The diagnosis is not established with specific tests, but electroencephalogram (EEG) should be done to rule out temporal lobe seizures.

Treatment

This condition is very difficult to treat with psychotherapy and/or medication. If depersonalization is clearly due to a psychological trauma, recovery of the unconscious traumatic memories and releasing the emotions surrounding them can be helpful. This might be done with hypnotherapy, since these individuals are good subjects for hypnosis. Some people benefit from knowing that depersonalization or derealization has happened to others, that they are not going crazy, and that they can survive it. Serotonin-reuptake blockers are sometimes helpful. Stress management techniques may help reduce anxiety, and hence need for escape from reality. However, meditation or other relaxation techniques are not recommended, as they could contribute to further depersonalization. Anti-anxiety drugs and alcohol should also be avoided. "Self-instruction training" may help individuals deal with stressful situations to avoid an episode of depersonalization. This involves attempts to change negative self-statements and to replace them with coping self-statements. In extreme cases, electroconvulsive shock therapy or brain surgery (prefrontal leucotomy) might be considered.

Prognosis

Approximately half of individuals with depersonalization disorder have a chronic course, either continuously or with relapses in response to an actual or perceived threat.

Differential Diagnosis

Depersonalization symptoms are common in schizophrenia or major depression, and could be a result of drug abuse, brain tumor, and temporal lobe epilepsy. Depersonalization disorder differs from the other dissociative disorders in that the perception of self is merely changed, not lost altogether. Hearing voices (hallucinations) and false beliefs (delusions) are present in schizophrenia, but not in depersonalization disorder.

Specialists

- Psychiatrist
- Psychologist

Work Restrictions / Accommodations

Work accommodations might include the use of a job coach to establish consistent, predictable work behaviors; the development of a structured, consistent set of work activities; limiting contact with coworkers and the general public; and flexibility in schedule to accommodate medical or psychiatric appointments.

Complementary and Alternative Therapies

Content is intended for awareness only. Treatments may or may not be effective. Scientific evidence may be lacking and some substances have potentially toxic effects. Dr. Presley Reed and the editors do not endorse the use of these therapies in the absence of consultation with a licensed medical professional.

Hypnosis - When depersonalization is clearly due to a psychological trauma, hypnosis may be helpful in the recovery of the unconscious traumatic memories and releasing the emotions surrounding them.

Comorbid Conditions

Alcohol abuse or drug use, or the presence of a personality disorder may lengthen disability.

Complications

Drug or alcohol abuse could result, as an attempt to self-medicate the underlying anxiety.

Factors Influencing Duration

The frequency and severity of symptoms, exacerbating factors, and associated disorders influence length of disability.

Length of Disability

In most cases, no disability is expected.

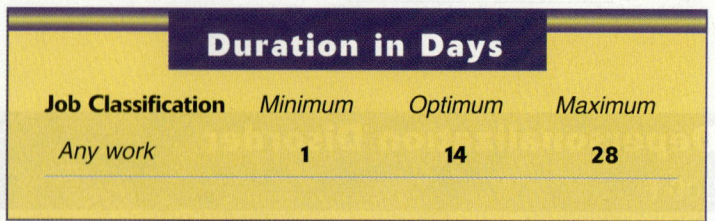

Job Classification	Minimum	Optimum	Maximum
Any work	1	14	28

Failure to Recover

If an individual fails to recover within the maximum duration expectancy period, the reader may wish to reference the following questions to assist in better understanding the specifics of an individual's medical case.

Regarding diagnosis:

- Does individual fit the criteria for depersonalization disorder? Was diagnosis confirmed?
- Are individual's depersonalization experiences a part of another mental disorder or a separate condition?
- Were other mental disorders with similar symptoms ruled out?
- Were physiological effects of a substance (abuse or medication) and general medical condition such as temporal lobe epilepsy ruled out as the cause of the symptoms?

Regarding treatment:

- What type of treatment (psychodynamic psychotherapy, behavior therapy, tranquilizers, antidepressants) did individual receive?
- What additional therapy options might now be warranted?
- Would hypnosis be beneficial in recovering unconscious traumatic memories and releasing the emotions surrounding them?
- Since stresses associated with the onset of the depersonalization episodes must be addressed, were these stresses identified? How are they being relieved?

Regarding prognosis:

- Is individual making any appreciable, even if gradual, progress?
- Have exacerbations occurred with actual or perceived stressful events?
- What progress was made to identify and relieve these stressors?

References

Abbas, S., C.S. Prabha, and M. Srivastava. "The Use of Fluoxetine and Buspirone for Treatment-refractory Depersonalization Disorder." Journal of Clinical Psychology 56 (1995): 484.

Noyes, R., and R. Kletti. "Depersonalization in Response to Life-threatening Danger." Comprehensive Psychology 18 (1997): 375-384.

Depression, Major

Other names / synonyms: Depressive Psychosis, Major Depressive Disorder, Psychotic Depression, Unipolar Depression

296.2, 296.20, 296.22, 296.23, 296.3, 296.32, 296.33, 311

Definition

Depression is a serious medical illness that negatively affects how an individual feels, thinks, and acts. Everyone experiences depressed moods as a result of a change, either in the form of a setback or a loss, or as Freud said, "everyday misery." The sadness and depressed feelings that accompany the changes and losses of life are usually appropriate, necessary, transitory, and can present an opportunity for personal growth. However, depression that persists and results in serious dysfunction in daily life could be an indication of a depressive disorder that may need to be treated as a medical problem. Severity, duration, and presence of other symptoms are factors that distinguish normal sadness from a depressive disorder.

Depression has been alluded to by a variety of terms in both medical and popular literature. "Melancholia" was the generic term used in early English texts for all emotional disorders, including depressive ones. Today, depression is referred to as a mood disorder. The three primary subtypes are major depression, chronic depression (dysthymia), and atypical depression. Major depression is severe depression in which the individual experiences a decline in general level of functioning. Dysthymia is a mild, chronic depression that lasts 2 years or longer. Atypical depression is characterized by increased appetite and sleeping more than usual.

Major depression is characterized by a general slowing down of physical and mental activity, including a lowering of mood. This may manifest as irritability, sadness, dejection, tearfulness, and a sense of hopelessness, anguish, and despair. Psychosomatic symptoms such as fatigue, loss of appetite, weight loss, sleep disturbance, and multiple forms of bodily discomfort may be present. Feelings of self-reproach, worthlessness, and guilt may be extreme.

Thought processes may also be affected, with impaired memory, and diminished ability to think, concentrate, or make decisions. Other symptoms may include extreme agitation, diminished interest or pleasure in day-to-day activities (anhedonia), and ruminations on death or suicide.

Major depression can afflict anyone, regardless of age, race, class, or gender. In the US, about 17 million Americans are estimated to develop depression each year. Major risk factors are female gender, age, family history, bereavement, and brain injury. Women suffer from the disorder at least twice as often as men in societies around the world. The peak age at onset is between 20 and 25 and 40 and 45 years. Although older individuals frequently seek treatment, there is no evidence that major depression is more common in older than in younger adults. Individuals who have parents or siblings with major depression have a 1.5 to 3 times greater risk of developing this disorder. Grief is a risk factor because it often turns into major depression, especially in bereaved spouses, who often meet the criteria for major depression. In the US, lifetime risk is 10-25% for women, and 5-12% for men. Major depression has also been shown to be influenced by cultural differences. A new international study (17 researchers, 38,000 individuals from 10 countries) revealed that the lifetime risk of depression ranged from 1.5% in Taiwan to 19% in Lebanon. Risks in other countries, in ascending order, were 2.9% in Korea, 4.3% in Puerto Rico, 5.2% in the US, 9.2% in Germany, 9.6% in Canada, 11.6% in New Zealand, and 16.4% in France.

The chances in a lifetime of experiencing a bout with major depression are about 17%, but only a third of depressed individuals receive proper treatment. Recently, a study showed that of bereaved spouses who meet major depression criteria, 83% received no antidepressant medication. One explanation for the low percentage of treatment of depressed individuals is that society has stigmatized mental illness for so long that people with depression, and sometimes their families, feel too ashamed to acknowledge the disease and to seek treatment.

Diagnosis

One of the difficulties in accurately diagnosing depression is distinguishing the normal sadness following a major disappointment or loss from clinical depression. All humans experience sadness periodically and, following episodes of loss or extreme stress, individuals may develop some symptoms of depression, yet still not be considered as suffering from a clinical depression.

According to the fourth edition of Diagnostic and Statistical Manual of Mental Disorders (DSM-IV), depression is diagnosed when an individual experiences persistent feelings of sadness or anxiety, with loss of interest or pleasure in usual activities (anhedonia). In addition, 5 or more of the following symptoms must be present for at least 2 consecutive weeks: changes in appetite that result in weight losses or gains not related to dieting; insomnia or oversleeping; loss of energy or increased fatigue; restlessness or irritability; feelings of worthlessness or inappropriate guilt; difficulty thinking, concentrating, or making decisions; and thoughts of death or suicide, or attempts at suicide.

Depression is diagnosed only if the above symptoms are not due to any other psychiatric conditions (such as bipolar disorder), medical conditions (such as neurological or hormonal problems), or physical illnesses (such as cancer or heart attack). Symptoms must not be due to unexpected side effects of medications or substance abuse. Although depression is not diagnosed in bereavement or substance abuse, both bereavement and substance-induced depression may lead to disability.

In addition to the above criteria, a thorough history, physical exam, and laboratory tests should be considered when diagnosing each new case of suspected depression.

History: A thorough history includes an account of current and previous symptoms, questions about mood, memory, and changes in relationships, and corroborative history from friends, family members, or employers. It is important to determine whether there is a family history of depression or of suicides. A careful, non-judgmental inventory of substance abuse should be made in every case, as this requires specific treatment measures of its own. A general history of psychological problems could predispose an individual to depression. Because physical conditions have been associated with depression, a thorough history should includes an account of diseases such as neurologic disorders (stroke, Parkinson's, and Alzheimer's disease, multiple sclerosis, epilepsy, encephalitis, brain tumors); endocrine disorders (diabetes mellitus, hypothyroidism, and hyperparathyroidism); and other disorders (coronary artery disease, cancer, and chronic fatigue syndrome). Conversely, individuals with major depression may see a medical doctor for physical complaints of headache, abdominal pain, body aches, low energy, feeling poorly, or problems with sexual function.

It is also important to obtain a complete history of medications the individual is taking because major depression has been shown to be a side effect of some medications, especially antihypertensive agents such as calcium channel blockers, beta blockers, analgesics, and some anti-migraine headache preparations.

Physical exam: Complete physical examination and medical work-up are indicated to rule out medical causes. Illnesses that frequently cause depression include hyperthyroidism and other glandular disturbances, cancer, stroke, and heart attack. As these illnesses are usually associated with dramatic symptoms, individuals are likely to have already sought medical attention. When the disease process is less acute and without many outward signs, however, depression may be the only complaint.

Tests: Besides routine laboratory tests, more specialized endocrine tests may be helpful in establishing the diagnosis. A CT may also be requested to test for relatively rare causes such as brain tumor or a clinically silent stroke. Psychological tests such as the Minnesota Multiphasic Personality Inventory may be helpful. Self-rated questionnaires such as the Beck Depression Inventory may be useful in establishing a baseline of reported symptoms and monitoring response to treatment.

Treatment

Treatment choice depends on the outcome of the evaluation (history, physical exam, and tests). Treatment usually consists of psychotherapy, medications, or both. Today, there are a number of effective antidepressant medications that work by correcting imbalances in the levels of brain chemicals (neurotransmitters). About two-thirds of individuals treated will respond to one or more medications. Generally, these medications take full effect 3 to 6 weeks after treatment has begun. Psychiatrists usually recommend that individuals continue to take the medication for 5 or more months after symptoms have improved.

Treatment of depression consists of three phases. Acute treatment, lasting 6 to 12 weeks, is aimed at remission of symptoms. Continuation treatment, lasting 4 to 9 months, is aimed at preventing relapse. During this phase, medication should be continued at full dosage. Psychotherapy may also be helpful. Maintenance treatment is aimed at preventing new episodes (recurrence) in individuals with prior episodes. Although only maintenance medication can prevent recurrence, maintenance psychotherapy may delay the next episode. Individuals and their families should be educated before treatment about the diagnosis, likely outcome, treatment options, costs, and side effects.

Psychotherapy or talk therapy may be used alone for treatment of mild depression. Antidepressant medications in combination with psychotherapy are used for moderate to major depression. Different types of psychotherapy include cognitive behavioral therapy, psychodynamic psychotherapy, interpersonal therapy, and supportive psychotherapy. In a major analysis of four randomized comparative studies, cognitive behavior therapy was shown to be as effective as antidepressants in treating severe or major depression, but not dysthymia. Much of the success of psychologic therapy, in any case, depends on the skill of the therapist.

Research indicates that using a combination of antidepressants and therapy is more effective than either treatment alone for most individuals, possibly because most individuals are more likely to take their medication regularly when they are also undergoing therapy.

For those for whom neither medications nor psychotherapy are effective, other techniques, such as shock therapy (electroconvulsive therapy or ECT), are safe and effective. Although ECT has received bad press since it was introduced in the 1930s, it has been refined over the years, and is now successful in treating more than 90% of individuals suffering from mood disorders.

Psychiatric hospitalization is warranted in instances when there is indication of personal neglect or high risk of self-harm.

Prognosis

Most individuals with a major depressive episode will get better. As the number of available antidepressant medications continues to grow, most individuals will respond to at least one of these. Individual may also benefit from psychotherapy. With time, recovery is usually complete, though risk of relapse increases with each episode. More than half of all individuals with one episode of major depression will have another, while those individuals with a history of three previous episodes have a 90% likelihood of having a fourth. Because of this high relapse rate, it is now recommended that individuals with a history of multiple depressive episodes receive medication for the rest of their lives.

Spontaneous recovery may take months. During that time the individual is at such a great risk of complications that it would be unthinkable not to intervene. Risk of recurrence is about 70% at 5 years, and at least 80% at 8 years. For individuals with severe major depression, 76% on antidepressants recover, whereas only 18% on sugar pills (placebo) or on psychotherapy without medication recover.

Poor outcome is associated with inadequate treatment, severe initial symptoms, early age of onset, greater number of previous episodes, only partial recovery after 1 year, having another severe mental or medical disorder, and family dysfunction.

Major depression causes more physical and social dysfunction than many chronic medical conditions.

Differential Diagnosis

Bipolar mood disorder often consists at least partly of recurrent episodes of mild to severe depression. Often, the initial mood swings that characterize this condition are one or more episodes of depression. Only later does a manic episode reveal the correct diagnosis. It should also be emphasized that depressive illness is part of a spectrum ranging from a less severe form of depression that sometimes presents with major depression symptoms (dysthymia) to a major depressive disorder.

Although dysthymia sometimes shares some of the features of major depression, dysthymia does not satisfy all of the major depression criteria. The most important being that it does not represent a marked departure from the individual's normal mood, without the adverse impact on social and occupational functioning seen in major depression. An adjustment disorder with depressed mood may come close to meeting criteria for major depression. Post-traumatic stress disorder (PTSD) may lead to a major depression, and other anxiety disorders may share features as well. A major symptom of schizophrenia and other psychoses may be a marked deficit in outward emotion and purposeful activity. This may be virtually impossible to distinguish from a psychotic depression at the time of presentation, especially in a younger individual with no psychiatric history. The same holds true for schizoaffective disorder, which represents a combination of simultaneous psychosis and mood change. Finally, it is important to recall that the diagnostic criteria for major depression insist that the following be ruled-out as the primary cause: substance abuse; the side effects of medications such as beta-blockers or benzodiazepines; illness causing an organic mental disorder (such as hypothyroidism); and normal bereavement following a tragic life event.

Specialists

- Licensed Professional Counselors (LPCS)
- Psychiatrist

Work Restrictions / Accommodations

Temporary work accommodations may include the avoidance of stressful situations and may include reducing or eliminating activities where the safety of self or others is contingent upon a constant and/or high level of alertness, such as driving motor vehicles, operating complex machinery, or handling dangerous chemicals; introducing the individual to new or stressful situations gradually under individually appropriate supervision; allowing some flexibility in scheduling to attend therapy appointments (which normally should occur during employee's personal time); promoting planned, proactive management of identified problem areas; and offering timely feedback on job performance issues. It will be helpful if accommodations are documented in a written plan designed to promote timely and safe transition back to full work productivity. Daytime work hours may be necessary for a period of time.

Complementary and Alternative Therapies

Content is intended for awareness only. Treatments may or may not be effective. Scientific evidence may be lacking and some substances have potentially toxic effects. Dr. Presley Reed and the editors do not endorse the use of these therapies in the absence of consultation with a licensed medical professional.

St. John's wort - Said to act as an antidepressant.

Comorbid Conditions

Coexisting conditions that may impact recovery and lengthen disability include traumatic medical illnesses (such as cancer, heart disease, stroke), physical disabilities, suicidal tendencies, anorexia nervosa and bulimia, substance abuse, history of childhood sexual abuse, panic disorder, anxiety disorders, and other personality or psychiatric disorders.

Major depression appears to increase disability in heart patients, perhaps because it can lead to a worsening of symptoms as well as to poor adherence to cardiac treatment regiments. In addition, heart attack survivors with major depression have a 3 to 4 times greater risk of dying within six months than those who do not suffer from depression. Clinical depression occurs in 10-27% of stroke survivors. Early diagnosis and treatment of coexisting depression are important because this second illness adds to the individual's suffering, interferes with rehabilitation and family relationships, and reduces quality of life.

Complications

Substance abuse, especially alcohol, frequently complicates a diagnosis for depression, although in some cases it may be difficult to determine which problem is primary. About 80-90% of individuals with major depression also have anxiety symptoms, such as anxiety, obsessive preoccupation, panic attacks, phobias, and excessive health concerns, and about one-third also have a full-blown anxiety disorder--usually panic disorder, obsessive-compulsive disorder, or social phobia. Anxiety symptoms may require special treatment, but frequently respond to antidepressant medications, reinforcing the view that the two disorders share common brain chemistry imbalances. Approximately 1 in 10 individuals who has experienced a major depressive episode will subsequently be diagnosed as having bipolar mood disorder, a chronic condition with episodes of both depression and mania, that may only partly respond to treatment. In some cases, an episode of bipolar mood disorder may emerge as the result of antidepressant medication use.

In extremely severe cases of major depression, psychotic symptoms may be present, such as hearing voices (auditory hallucinations) or having false beliefs (delusions).

Up to 15% of individuals with severe major depression die by suicide. Death rate is 4 times higher over age 55. Suicide attempt may paradoxically occur as the individual begins to respond to therapy because the extreme apathy sometimes seen in major depression before treatment may actually prevent them from committing suicide due to lack of motivation or energy.

Factors Influencing Duration

Length of duration might be influenced by the severity of the illness, the presence of complicating factors such as substance abuse or suicide attempts, response to therapy, and the occupation requirements. Only in the most severe and unusual cases should this result in permanent disability.

Substance abuse will complicate treatment and may significantly delay returning to work. Suicide attempts that lead to hospitalization will also be associated with longer periods of disability.

Length of Disability

Maximum disability duration includes hospitalization.

Duration in Days

Job Classification	Minimum	Optimum	Maximum
Any work	14	21	56

Duration Trend from Normative Data

Cases	Mean	Min	Max	No Lost Time	Over 6 Months	Percentile:	5th	25th	Median	75th	95th
14775	72	0	696	1.10%	3.59%	Days:	14	32	61	103	169

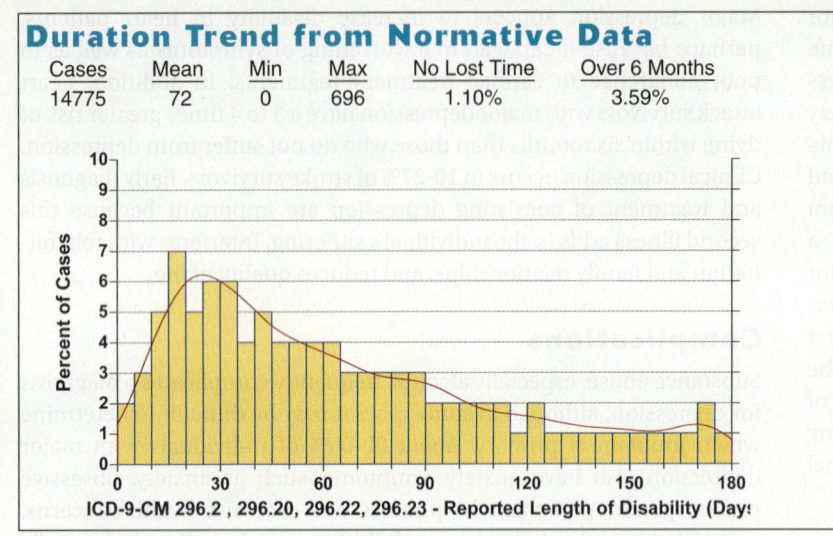
ICD-9-CM 296.2, 296.20, 296.22, 296.23 - Reported Length of Disability (Days)

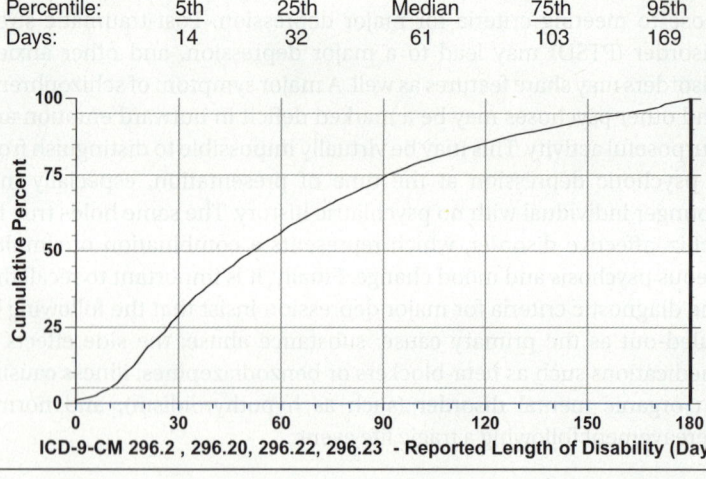
ICD-9-CM 296.2, 296.20, 296.22, 296.23 - Reported Length of Disability (Days)

Duration Trend from Normative Data

Cases	Mean	Min	Max	No Lost Time	Over 6 Months	Percentile:	5th	25th	Median	75th	95th
9726	79	0	519	0.18%	3.75%	Days:	14	32	61	103	169

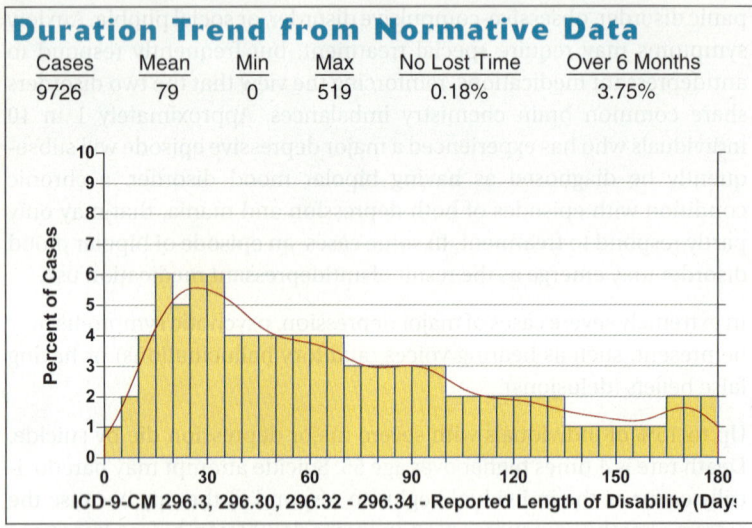
ICD-9-CM 296.3, 296.30, 296.32 - 296.34 - Reported Length of Disability (Days)

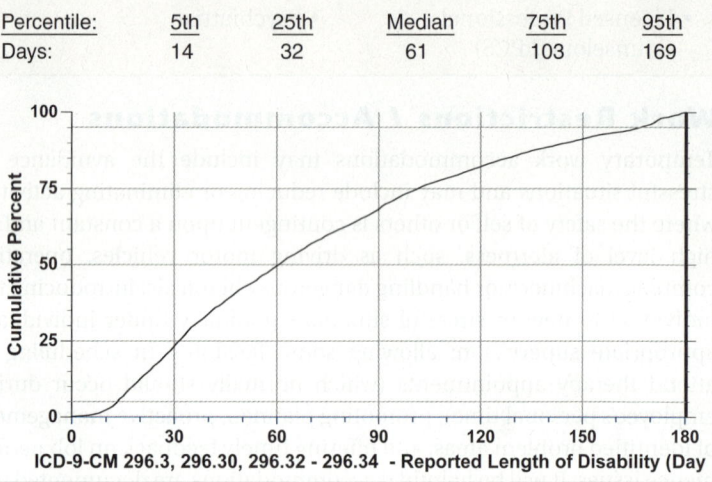
ICD-9-CM 296.3, 296.30, 296.32 - 296.34 - Reported Length of Disability (Days)

Duration Trend from Normative Data*

Cases	Mean	Min	Max	No Lost Time	Over 6 Months	Percentile:	5th	25th	Median	75th	95th
4526	58	0	473	1.15%	3.07%	Days:	7	21	39	74	138

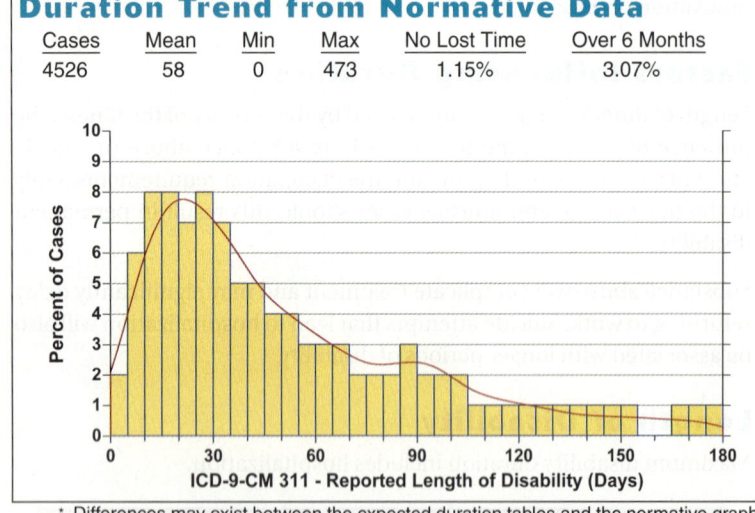
ICD-9-CM 311 - Reported Length of Disability (Days)

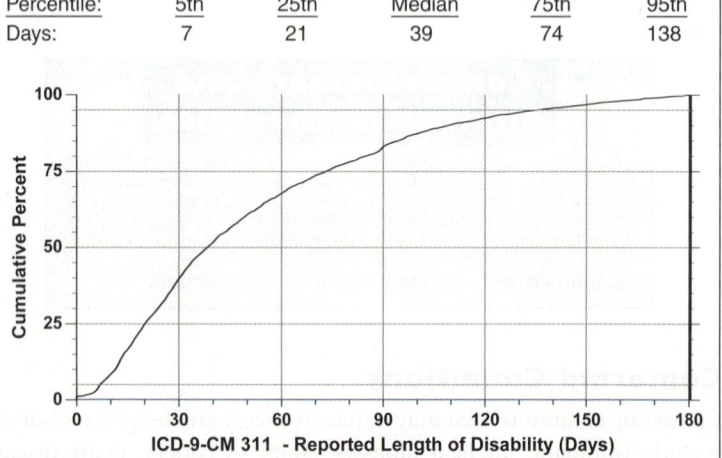
ICD-9-CM 311 - Reported Length of Disability (Days)

* Differences may exist between the expected duration tables and the normative graphs. Duration tables provide expected recovery periods based on the type of work performed by the individual. The normative graphs reflect the actual observed experience of many individuals across the spectrum of physical conditions, in a variety of industries, and with varying levels of case management.

Failure to Recover

If an individual fails to recover within the maximum duration expectancy period, the reader may wish to reference the following questions to assist in better understanding the specifics of an individual's medical case.

Regarding diagnosis:

- Was a thorough history obtained? Does family have history of depression or of suicides?
- Was substance abuse identified or ruled out?
- Does individual have history of psychological problems? Does individual have any physical conditions such as neurologic disorders (stroke, Parkinson's, epilepsy), endocrine disorders (diabetes mellitus, hypothyroidism, or hyperparathyroidism), or other disorders (cancer, coronary artery disease)?
- Were endocrine tests done?
- Is the physician an expert in diagnosis and biochemical therapy?
- Was diagnosis confirmed?
- Is it possible that individual was misdiagnosed?
- Would individual benefit from a second opinion?

Regarding treatment:

- Since major depression is the result of biochemical imbalances in the brain, is the physician adequately trained in biochemical therapy?
- Even though the right medication is prescribed, does the dosage need to be increased in order to achieve an adequate level of therapeutic benefit?
- Is individual beginning to feel any positive response from current medication(s)? Because responses differ and several trials of medicine may be needed before an effective treatment is found, is change of medication warranted at this time?
- If individual is experiencing side effects from current medication, is individual comfortable with and diligent in reporting side effects to doctor? If not, does individual trust family member or caregiver to share this information with physician?
- Is psychotherapy being used as part of individual's treatment regimen?
- Is individual learning to recognize and change behaviors, thoughts, or relationships that cause or maintain depression? Is therapy helping individual to develop more healthful and rewarding habits?
- Are underlying medical conditions that may complicate treatment or impact recovery being effectively addressed?
- If individual's depression is incapacitating, severe and life threatening, or if he/she cannot take or does not respond to antidepressant medications, is electroconvulsive therapy (ECT) being considered at this time?
- Is individual seriously contemplating suicide or previously attempted it? Does the threat of self-harm or personal neglect put individual at risk?
- Is individual frail because of weight loss or at risk for heart problems because of severe agitation?
- Would individual benefit from hospitalization until self-care is possible?

Regarding prognosis:

- Assuming diagnosis and treatment are accurate, can individual comprehend and follow medication treatment regimen including proper dose to be taking, what time of day to take medication, and how to increase dosage when ordered? If individual is not capable, is another responsible individual available to oversee treatment? If not, would individual benefit from hospitalization until self-care is possible?
- Was individual made aware of possible side effects and what to do if a side effect is experienced?
- Does individual have a good working rapport with his/her physician?
- Does individual know how often to see physician and is transportation available? Is individual diligent about keeping appointments?
- Has the physician informed individual as to what to do to improve response to treatment and which activities to avoid to increase the likelihood of improvement? Is individual engaged in psychotherapy?
- What other support is available to individual? Family? Friends? Church? Support group?

References

"Probing the Darkness: Diagnosis and Treatment of Major Depression." Adapted from the Agency for Health Care Policy and Research (AHCPR) Depression Guideline Vol 2 No 1 (1995): 03 Jul 2000 <http://www.ices.on.ca/docs/fb2190.htm>.

Long, Phillip, MD. Major Depressive Disorder. Agency for Health Care Policy and Research. 18 Nov 1994. 16 Oct 2000 <http://www.mentalhealth.com/bookah/p44-dq.html>.

Depressive Psychosis

Other names / synonyms: Major Depressive Episode with Psychotic Features, Psychotic Reactive Depression, Severe Depression with Psychotic Features

298.0

Definition

Depressive psychosis is an older term for what is now usually referred to as major depression with psychotic features. This disorder includes symptoms of both depression and psychosis in an individual without an underlying diagnosis of a psychotic disorder. A major depressive episode occurs when there is a period of at least two weeks during which there is either depressed mood, a loss of interest or pleasure in nearly all activities, and at least three other symptoms, including significant, unintended weight gain or loss; insomnia or sleeping excessively (hypersomnia); psychomotor agitation or retardation; fatigue or loss of energy; feelings of worthlessness or inappropriate guilt; lack of concentration; recurrent thoughts of death or suicidal ideation. In major depression with psychotic features, the individual reports or exhibits false beliefs (delusions) and/or sees or hears things that aren't there (visual or auditory hallucinations). The delusions or hallucinations usually refer to depressive themes (mood-congruent psychotic features), such as the belief that one is responsible for the death of a loved one or that one is being punished because of a moral transgression. Hallucinations are usually temporary, and may involve voices that berate the individual for perceived wrongs. Occasionally, the content of the delusions or hallucinations has no apparent relationship to depressive themes (mood-incongruent psychotic features) and may include delusions that one is being persecuted or that others can control one's thoughts. In general, mood-incongruent psychotic features are associated with a poorer prognosis than mood-congruent psychotic features.

It is not known why some individuals with major depression develop psychotic features, but it is most likely related to disturbances in brain chemistry (dysregulation of neurotransmitter systems). Involved brain chemicals may include serotonin, dopamine, norepinephrine, acetylcholine, and gamma-aminobutyric acid, as well as other hormones and enzyme systems. Psychotic symptoms are most likely to emerge in the three-month period following any major life event, such as bereavement or job loss.

Culture can influence the way in which an individual experiences and expresses a depressive psychosis. Somatic complaints of nerves or headaches in Latino cultures, weakness or imbalance in Asian cultures, heart problems in Middle Eastern cultures, or feelings of sadness and guilt in North American and Western European cultures may all be expressions of depression that combine features of depressive, anxiety, and somatoform disorders. An individual's culturally guided fear of being bewitched, or feeling of being visited by the dead must be distinguished from actual hallucinations or delusions. Women are twice as likely as men to develop a major depressive disorder and, in many cultures, are more encouraged to express their fears and feelings than are men. Approximately 10-25% of women and 5-12% of men are at a lifetime risk for developing a depressive disorder, with only a small percentage of those exhibiting psychotic features.

Diagnosis

A diagnosis is based on criteria listed in the DSM-IV-TR (Diagnostic and Statistical Manual of Mental Disorders, 4th Edition, Text Revision, published by the American Psychiatric Association). A major depressive episode occurs when there is a period of at least two weeks during which there is either depressed mood, a loss of interest or pleasure in nearly all activities, and at least three other symptoms, including significant, unintended weight gain or loss; insomnia or sleeping excessively (hypersomnia); psychomotor agitation or retardation; fatigue or loss of energy; feelings of worthlessness or inappropriate guilt; lack of concentration; recurrent thoughts of death or suicidal ideation. In major depression with psychotic features, the individual reports or exhibits false beliefs (delusions) and/or sees or hears things that aren't there (visual or auditory hallucinations). The delusions or hallucinations usually refer to depressive themes (mood-congruent psychotic features), such as the belief that one is responsible for the death of a loved one or that one is being punished because of a moral transgression. Hallucinations are usually temporary, and may involve voices that berate the individual for perceived wrongs. Occasionally, the content of the delusions or hallucinations has no apparent relationship to depressive themes (mood-incongruent psychotic features) and may include delusions that one is being persecuted or that others can control one's thoughts.

History: The individual and/or family/friends usually give a history of several weeks to months of depressed mood, feelings of sadness or hopelessness, poor appetite or overeating, difficulty sleeping (insomnia) or sleeping too much (hypersomnia), low energy and fatigue, low self-esteem, poor concentration, difficulty making decisions, thoughts of death, or suicide attempt. The individual may also give a history of problems at work, relationship and/or sexual problems, having the same unpleasant or worrisome thoughts over and over (obsessive rumination), anxiety, excessive worry over physical health, multiple somatic complaints (indigestion, headaches, fatigue, stomach pain, back pain), or alcohol/substance abuse.

Physical exam: The individual may be tearful or have a facial expression that is sad or lacking in animation. There may be restlessness and hyperactivity (psychomotor agitation) or slowed, decreased movement (psychomotor retardation), documented unintended weight gain or loss, wrist lacerations or other evidence of recent suicide attempts, listening or talking to people who are not there (hallucinations) or false, persistent beliefs (delusions).

Tests: There are no diagnostic laboratory tests for this disorder, but the electroencephalogram (EEG) may indicate sleep abnormalities. The Beck Depression Scale is a brief self-rating scale useful in monitoring changes in level of depression with treatment. The MMPI (Minnesota Multiphasic Personality Inventory) is a more extensive psychological profile that can provide information about the individual's mental and emotional status. Blood work should be done to rule out treatable causes of depression, such as hypothyroidism.

Treatment

The goal of treatment is for the individual to have an improved mood with diminished negative symptoms (anxiety, fatigue, insomnia or hypersomnia, lack of appetite, tearfulness, rumination, suicidal ideation), and to diminish or eliminate the psychotic features (delusions and hallucinations) of the depressive episode. Hospitalization may be needed if the physician or mental health professional believes that the individual is dangerous to self or others.

The first line of treatment is the use of antipsychotic and antidepressant medication. For proper diagnosis and administration of antidepressant medication, physicians who are expert in diagnosis and in pharmacotherapy must be consulted. Antipsychotic drugs can be effective in reducing or eliminating symptoms such as false beliefs (delusions), hearing or seeing things that aren't there (hallucinations), and disorganized thinking.

After the acute symptoms have cleared, the continued use of antipsychotic drugs substantially reduces the probability of future episodes, if the individual does not develop significant adverse effects such as sedation, muscle stiffness, tremors, weight gain, or abnormal muscle movements (tardive dyskinesia). Informed medical monitoring must be a mandatory part of all treatment. Most side effects can be eliminated or minimized by adjustment in dosage or type of medication. Psychotic symptoms should clear up within a few days or weeks of treatment, but depressive symptoms may take 3 to 12 weeks to diminish. Serotonin reuptake inhibitor (the SSRIs) antidepressants and the newer atypical antidepressants are the medications of choice because of their effectiveness and low level of side effects. Somatic symptoms, such as sleep, appetite, and psychomotor disturbances, usually respond first to medication, and then the cognitive symptoms, such as low self-esteem, guilt, pessimism, or suicidal ideation, diminish. It may be necessary to try more than one medication or a combination of medicines to achieve a good result. Because responses differ, several trials of medicine may be needed before an effective treatment is found.

For individuals whose depression is incapacitating, severe, or life-threatening, or for those who cannot take or do not respond to antidepressant medications, electroconvulsive therapy (ECT) is a safe and often effective treatment for severe depression.

Psychotherapy has also been shown to be an effective treatment in depression. Supportive psychotherapy generally provides a therapeutic explanation of the depressive symptoms, education and feedback about the progression of the depression, and may include identification of stressors and stress management skills, improved coping skills, assertiveness training, and relaxation training. The goals of therapy may include simple emotional support, insight into sources of thoughts, feelings, perceptions, or behaviors, relief of symptoms such as anxiety or depression, stress management, behavioral changes, or crisis intervention. These interventions are designed to help modify the individual's thinking, expectancies, and behaviors, and to increase coping skills for various life stressors.

Prognosis

An untreated episode may last four months or longer, with remission occurring in 20-30% of cases. Some individuals may have symptoms that persist for years, and may develop some disability due to these symptoms. About 60% of individuals who have one episode go on to have a second episode, while 90% of individuals who have had a third episode will develop a fourth. Those who receive treatment have significantly improved recovery rates. Depressive psychosis is a strong risk factor for suicide. In severe, untreated depression, suicide rate is as high as 15%. Only about one-third of those diagnosed with depression get proper treatment, and about two-thirds of those with any kind of affective disorder are misdiagnosed.

Differential Diagnosis

Major depressive disorder with psychotic features must be distinguished from a previously undiagnosed psychotic disorder, a mood disorder due to a general medical condition, a substance-induced mood disorder, dysthymic disorder, schizoaffective disorder, or dementia. Metabolic causes of depressed symptoms, such as hypothyroidism, should be ruled out.

Specialists

- Advanced Practice Registered Nurse
- Internist
- Occupational Therapist
- Physical Therapist
- Psychiatrist
- Psychologist

Work Restrictions / Accommodations

Temporary work accommodations may include reducing or eliminating activities where the safety of self or others is contingent upon a constant and/or high level of alertness, such as driving motor vehicles, operating complex machinery, or handling dangerous chemicals; introducing the individual to new or stressful situations gradually under individually appropriate supervision; allowing some flexibility in scheduling to attend therapy appointments (which normally should occur during employee's personal time); promoting planned, proactive management of identified problem areas; and offering timely feedback on job performance issues. It will be helpful if accommodations are documented in a written plan designed to promote timely and safe transition back to full work productivity.

Comorbid Conditions

Coexisting conditions that may affect recovery and lengthen disability include alcohol and other substance abuse disorders, major depression, schizophrenia, anxiety disorders, panic disorder, bipolar depression, depressive-mania, and pure-mania. About one-quarter of those with major depression are also substance abusers. If the individual has a comorbid medical condition, such as multiple sclerosis, stroke, hypothyroidism, or cardiac disease, both treatment and length of disability may be affected.

Complications

The most serious complication of depressive psychosis is death from suicide. Up to 15% of individuals with major depressive disorder commit suicide, and the risk is increased if the individual has an episode of major depression with psychotic features. Up to 20-25% of individuals with general medical conditions, such as diabetes, carcinoma, stroke, or myocardial infarction, may have a concurrent episode of depression, which complicates the length and treatment of both conditions. Those individuals who are severely depressed or whose psychosis prevents them from getting adequate food or sleep may suffer physical consequences of malnutrition or other health problems.

Factors Influencing Duration

Length of disability is influenced by the duration and severity of the depressive episode and psychotic features, any underlying mental illness, other substance abuse, the individual's social support system, appropriateness of treatment choice, response to medications, compliance with treatment, and adequacy of ongoing care.

Length of Disability

An untreated episode may last four months or longer and then go into remission. Individuals who receive treatment can generally expect a decrease in psychotic symptoms within a few days, and improved mood within 4 weeks. Most individuals are able to return to premorbid functioning, but some will have persistent low-level symptoms. Only 5-10% of individuals meet the full criteria for depressive disorder for 2 or more years.

Duration in Days

Job Classification	Minimum	Optimum	Maximum
Any work	14	28	56

Failure to Recover

If an individual fails to recover within the maximum duration expectancy period, the reader may wish to reference the following questions to assist in better understanding the specifics of an individual's medical case.

Regarding diagnosis:

- Was diagnosis of depressive psychosis confirmed through history, mental status examination, and psychological testing?
- Is the physician trained in psychological diagnosis?
- Was substance abuse identified or ruled out?
- Has physical exam or testing excluded hypothyroidism, multiple sclerosis, cancer, stroke, or other chronic medical illness?

Regarding treatment:

- If substance abuse was present, was it treated appropriately?
- Since depressive psychosis indicates that individual is no longer capable of discriminating fantasy from reality, does individual pose a threat to self or others?
- Was individual assessed for violent tendencies? Because violence may be used in retaliation for imagined persecution, has physician assessed the degree of danger posed by the delusions, particularly the extent to which the individuals is willing to act on delusions?
- Do delusions appear to be progressing to an unhealthy situation? Is physician aware of this progression?
- Because a suicide plan represents an emergency situation, was individual assessed for suicidal intent or attempt? Are proper precautions in place to prevent suicide attempt?
- Is current drug therapy appropriate for individual? Is the dosage high enough to be effective?
- Is the treating physician adequately trained in pharmacotherapy?
- Was an expert in diagnosis and biochemical therapy consulted?
- Has individual experienced a positive response from current antidepressant medication(s)?
- Since individual responses differ, were trials of several medicines or a combination of medicines done to find the most effective treatment? Is a change of antidepressant medication or dosage warranted at this time?
- Although antipsychotic drugs may have substantially reduced the probability of future episodes, has individual experienced significant adverse side effects?
- Since most side effects can be eliminated or minimized by adjustment in dosage or type of medication, is individual competent and diligent in reporting side effects to the doctor? If not, is there a family member or caregiver who could reliably report side effects?
- Should antipsychotic medications be adjusted, changed, or discontinued? Are additional medications needed to counteract the side effects?
- If depression is incapacitating, severe, or life threatening or if individual cannot take or does not respond to antidepressant medications, was electroconvulsive therapy (ECT) considered an option at this time?
- Was psychotherapy used to help individual recognize and change behaviors, thoughts, or relationships that cause or maintain depression?

Regarding prognosis:

- Do symptoms persist despite treatment?
- Does individual have a coexisting condition such as diabetes, carcinoma, stroke, myocardial infarction, major depression, schizophrenia, anxiety or panic disorder, bipolar depression, depressive-mania, pure-mania that could complicate treatment or impact recovery?
- Since it is estimated that only one-third of those diagnosed with depression get proper treatment, is physician a specialist in psychiatric disorders?
- Would individual benefit from a second opinion?

References

Bebbington, P., et al. "Life Events and Psychosis. Initial Results from the Camberwell Collaborative Psychosis Study." British Journal of Psychiatry 162 (1993): 72-79.

Frances, Allen. Diagnostic and Statistical Manual of Mental Disorders: 4th ed, text revision. Washington, DC: American Psychiatric Association, 2000.

Dercum's Disease

Other names / synonyms: Adiposis Dolorosa

272.7, 272.8, 272.9

Definition

Dercum's disease, or Adiposis dolorosa, is a rare, chronic disorder characterized by the accumulation of painful, benign fatty tumors (lipomas) beneath the skin (subcutaneous). The tumors are most often located on the trunk and limbs, sparing the face, hands, and feet. This disease tends to occur in obese individuals, although weight loss may occur as the disease progresses.

Dercum's disease has not been well characterized in the medical literature, and its cause is unknown at this time. Although the cause of the pain is unclear, it is believed to be due to insufficient blood supply (ischemia) due to obstruction from very small blood clots (microthrombi). This disease appears to run in families, and generally affects menopausal women who are about 40 to 50 years of age. It is 5 times more common in women than men.

Diagnosis

History: Symptoms include multiple painful fatty masses, generalized obesity, weakness, fatigue, and mental disturbances such as emotional instability, depression, mental confusion, and/or dementia.

Physical exam: The exam reveals painful fatty tissue immediately below the subcutaneous layer of the skin. Most individuals are obese.

Tests: Diagnostic tests are not usually necessary. An individual who has the symptoms described above is diagnosed as having Dercum's disease.

Treatment

There is no specific treatment for Dercum's disease. Pain may be relieved by steroids, analgesics, or intravenously administered anesthetic. Painful lipomas may be surgically suctioned out (liposuction) or surgically excised (lipectomy). This may be beneficial to some individuals, although surgery may not provide complete relief of symptoms and may not prevent recurrence of the fatty deposits. It has been suggested that weight loss may benefit these individuals, but weight loss is often noted in progression of this disease.

Prognosis

For the most part, this is a progressive disease. Some individuals may respond to surgical excision of the painful lipomas. A few individuals may experience spontaneous remission. However, the disease usually progresses due to the non-responsiveness of the tumors to treatment.

Differential Diagnosis

Conditions with similar symptoms include Fröhlich's syndrome (obesity with retarded development of the sex glands), adenolipomatosis (a condition in which glandular tissue is replaced by fatty tissue), lipodystrophia progressiva (a progressive disease in which abnormal fats are laid down in the skin), Cushing's syndrome (an adrenal gland disease), Weber-Christian disease (inflammation of the subcutaneous layer of skin), osteoarthritis (degeneration of the joints), and neurofibromatosis (a condition where there are abnormal skin growths noted all over the body). A condition called myasthenia gravis should also be excluded in obese individuals.

Specialists

- Dermatologist
- General Surgeon
- Plastic Surgeon
- Primary Care Provider

Work Restrictions / Accommodations

In the later stages of the disease, individuals may need to do sedentary work due to the location and pain of their numerous lipomas.

Comorbid Conditions

Obesity may contribute to the severity of the disease, but weight loss is often noted in progression of this disease.

Complications

Complications may occur if the fatty lipoma becomes infected with a bacteria normally found on the skin. The individual could then develop infection of the skin (cellulitis) or a small, localized abscess under the skin (carbuncle/furuncle).

Factors Influencing Duration

Length of disability may be influenced by the extent of the disease, method of treatment, and individual's response to treatment. Individuals who respond to IV treatment or surgical removal of the lipomas experience limited disability. As the disease progresses, others may find it too painful to work due to the location and size of their lipomas.

Length of Disability

Disability may be permanent for individuals who are unresponsive to treatment. Individuals who do respond to treatment may experience only limited disability.

Duration in Days

Job Classification	Minimum	Optimum	Maximum
Sedentary work	3	5	10
Light work	3	5	10
Medium work	7	10	14
Heavy work	7	14	28
Very Heavy work	10	14	28

Failure to Recover

If an individual fails to recover within the maximum duration expectancy period, the reader may wish to reference the following questions to assist in better understanding the specifics of an individual's medical case.

Regarding diagnosis:

- Does individual have painful subcutaneous lipomas located on the trunk and limbs?
- Is individual obese?
- Does individual have a family history of the disease?
- Does individual have weakness, fatigue, emotional instability, depression, mental confusion, and/or dementia?
- On exam, are painful lipomas present? Obesity? Weight loss?
- Were conditions with similar symptoms ruled out?

Regarding treatment:

- Were the painful lipomas removed?
- Was individual treated with steroids, analgesics, or IV anesthetic?

Regarding prognosis:

- Can individual's employer accommodate any necessary restrictions?
- Does individual have any conditions that may affect ability to recover?
- Have any complications developed such as cellulitis or carbuncle/furuncle?

References

Adiposis Dolorosa. National Institute of Health. 03 Nov 1994. 04 Jul 2000 <http://www.ncbi.nlm.nih.gov/htbin-post/Omim/dispmim?103200>.

Brodovsky S., et al. "Adiposis Dolorosa (Dercum's disease): 10-year Follow-up." Annals of Plastic Surgery 33 6 (1994): 664-668.

Dermatitis

Other names / synonyms: Atopic Dermatitis, Contact Dermatitis, Eczema, Photodermatitis, Seborrheic Dermatitis, Stasis Dermatitis

629.9, 692.83, 692.89, 692.9

Definition

Dermatitis is a general term for inflammation of the skin. Although it can be due to an allergic reaction, dermatitis often occurs without any known cause. The main forms of dermatitis are contact dermatitis, seborrheic dermatitis, photodermatitis, eczema (atopic dermatitis), and stasis dermatitis.

Contact dermatitis accounts for 90% of all occupational skin disease and occurs when skin comes in direct contact with an irritating or allergenic substance. Irritant contact dermatitis can cause overly dry (xerosis) or moist (maceration) skin changes. Common irritants include detergents, nickel (found in jewelry and underwear fastenings), certain chemicals, rubber gloves, condoms, certain cosmetics, and medications designed for use on the skin (topical). Dermatitis caused by an irritant develops within minutes or hours after exposure. Irritant contact dermatitis accounts for 80% of all cases of contact dermatitis.

Direct contact with plants such as poison oak and ivy (including inhalation of smoke from burning plants) can cause allergic contact dermatitis. Other common causes of allergic contact dermatitis include cosmetics, metal compounds, skin medications and creams, and chemicals used in the manufacture of clothing. Symptoms may range from a mild, temporary redness to severe swelling and blisters. Allergic contact dermatitis usually occurs within 24 to 48 hours after contact. Continued exposure can result in chronic dermatitis.

Dandruff, the most common seborrheic dermatitis, is characterized by dry or greasy scaling of the scalp. Sometimes itching occurs but without hair loss. The face and chest can also be affected. Although the exact cause is unknown, the rash often develops during times of stress.

Photodermatitis is the reaction of skin to photochemical activity such as sunlight, x-rays, or ultraviolet light. Certain oral medications can make the skin suddenly more sensitive to sunlight. Skin reactions include redness, peeling, rash (hives), blisters, and thickened, scaly patches.

Eczema (atopic dermatitis) refers to a chronic, itchy inflammation of the upper layers of skin that often occurs in individuals with many other allergic disorders. While usually appearing by two years of age, it may also occur for the first time quite late in life. Although the exact cause of atopic dermatitis is unknown, immunologic, genetic, physiologic, and pharmacologic factors play a role. There is a family history of the disease in about 70% of all cases. The hallmark symptom of atopic dermatitis is itching of apparently healthy skin. Emotional stress, changes in temperature or humidity, bacterial skin infections, and contact with irritating clothing (especially wool), can make itching worse. The resultant scratching causes a rash that can be found on either damp (groin, buttocks, soles of feet, cheeks) or dry (hands, tops of feet, lower legs) regions of the body.

Stasis dermatitis is caused by poor blood circulation and characterized by itchy, red, scaly patches on the lower legs. Over time, the skin turns dark brown. Increased swelling caused by the pooling blood can lead to severe skin damage including weeping, crusts, fissures, and scratches (excoriations).

Diagnosis

History: The hallmark sign of dermatitis is a rash that can vary considerably depending on the cause. Symptoms usually include itching, burning, and stinging. The individual may report a recent change in detergent, soap, cosmetics, jewelry, or topical medication. Individuals with poison oak or ivy dermatitis often report that they had been working or recreating outdoors. Symptoms of seborrheic dermatitis include a red, scaly, itchy rash that usually starts on the scalp and/or face (particularly the nose and eyebrows), chest, and back. Photodermatitis is characterized by sunburn that may blister or take on the appearance of contact dermatitis. The main symptoms of atopic dermatitis are itching and scratching. Stasis dermatitis is localized in the legs.

Physical exam: A total skin examination should be performed. The affected area may be red and irritated. Small blisters may be present, broken open, or crusted over. The appearance of irritant contact dermatitis depends on the cause. Individuals with atopic dermatitis may also have excoriations caused by scratching. Swelling (edema) is present in the lower legs and ankles of individuals with stasis dermatitis.

Tests: Skin patch tests may be performed, as needed, to identify the source of the irritation or allergic reaction. Suspect substances, kept in place with identifying tapes, are applied to the skin on the individual's back. The skin is inspected several days later to see if any of the substances caused a reaction. Photo patch tests in which treated patches of skin are exposed to ultraviolet light, may be performed in individuals with photodermatitis.

Treatment

Since treatment depends on the underlying cause of the inflammation, it must be tailored in each case.

If the agent causing contact dermatitis can be avoided, the skin inflammation will usually clear within a few weeks. Soaking in cool water can help relieve symptoms. Calamine lotion can dry lesions and help control the itching. Antihistamines help relieve itching, especially at night. For severe cases, topical or oral corticosteroids may be prescribed. An oral antibiotic may be needed for a brief period to control a secondary infection.

Seborrheic dermatitis of the scalp is treated with medicated shampoo.

To help prevent exacerbations of eczema (atopic dermatitis), the skin should be kept well-hydrated with moisturizing lotions and bathing should be infrequent.

The long-term goal for stasis dermatitis is to reduce the pooling of fluid (edema) in the legs. Treatment may include support hose or compression stockings. Ulcers are treated with zinc oxide paste and corticosteroid creams. Individuals may need treatment with an Unna boot (cast-like dressing containing a zinc paste). The boot protects the skin and the paste helps heal it.

Prognosis

The outcome of dermatitis depends on the underlying cause. If the agent causing contact dermatitis can be identified and avoided, the skin inflammation will usually resolve itself within a few weeks. Occupational contact dermatitis clears in 25% of individuals, improves with periodic recurrence in 50% of individuals, and is persistent and severe in 25% of individuals. Allergic photodermatitis may persist for weeks or years. Seborrheic dermatitis has periods of worsening and periods of remission. There is no cure for eczema (atopic dermatitis), but it can be controlled with treatment. Individuals with stasis dermatitis often have recurring problems, particularly if measures to counteract persistent edema and tissue changes are not conscientiously adhered to throughout life.

Differential Diagnosis

Hives (urticaria), erythema multiforme, lichen planus, pityriasis rosea, psoriasis, sweating disorders (dyshidrosis), and fungal infections can have similar symptoms. Stasis dermatitis may resemble other diabetic skin eruptions.

Specialists

- Dermatologist

Work Restrictions / Accommodations

Work restrictions or accommodations may be related to location of rash, type of work, or clothing that must be worn. If the rash is located on the fingers or hands, working with food or in direct contact with other individuals would not be appropriate. Work uniforms, gloves, or equipment made of certain fabrics can further irritate the rash. Contact dermatitis may be avoided by removal (or replacement) of the offending substance or by wearing personal protective equipment (cotton-lined rubber gloves) and using barrier creams. Individuals with photodermatitis need to avoid sun exposure. Changes to the individual's position or duties may be required. For individuals with stasis dermatitis, heavy lifting or prolonged standing may need to be limited. The individual would benefit from periods of leg elevation throughout the work day.

Complementary and Alternative Therapies

Content is intended for awareness only. Treatments may or may not be effective. Scientific evidence may be lacking and some substances have potentially toxic effects. Dr. Presley Reed and the editors do not endorse the use of these therapies in the absence of consultation with a licensed medical professional.

Ultraviolet light therapy -	May be effective for atopic dermatitis when used with oral doses of psoralen, a drug that intensifies the effects of ultraviolet light on the skin. Ultraviolet light therapy should not be used on children because of its potential long-term side effects, including skin cancer and cataracts.
Aloe -	Used topically, aloe appears to inhibit infection and promote healing.
Primrose oil -	Used topically, has been shown to be effective in providing relief, improving skin condition, and reducing reliance on corticosteroid medication.

Comorbid Conditions

Atopic dermatitis, psoriasis, acne, and stasis dermatitis can predispose the individual to contact dermatitis. Immune system-suppressing diseases such as AIDS or certain cancers can make the individual more prone to skin infection. Other coexisting conditions that may impact recovery and lengthen disability include secondary infections, mental or emotional problems, and poor general health.

Complications

Because of poor skin barrier function, bacterial (staphylococcal or streptococcal), viral, and fungal infections are common complications of dermatitis. In severe cases, the skin may become reddened and fall off in layers (exfoliative erythroderma). Poor hygiene and poor general health can also complicate dermatitis.

Factors Influencing Duration

The length of disability may be influenced by the cause of the dermatitis, severity of symptoms, location and extent of the lesions, response to treatment, job requirements, and the workplace environment (overly dry or humid conditions can make dermatitis worse).

Length of Disability

Disability duration depends on job requirements. In most cases, no disability is expected.

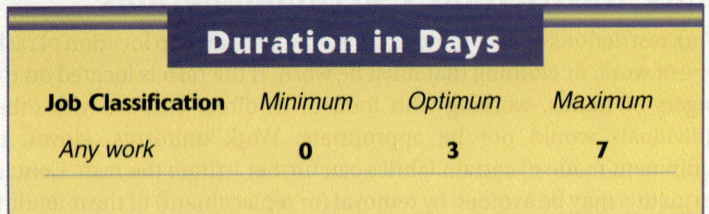

Job Classification	Minimum	Optimum	Maximum
Any work	0	3	7

Failure to Recover

If an individual fails to recover within the maximum duration expectancy period, the reader may wish to reference the following questions to assist in better understanding the specifics of an individual's medical case.

Regarding diagnosis:

- Does the individual have contact dermatitis, seborrheic dermatitis, photodermatitis, eczema (atopic dermatitis), or stasis dermatitis?
- Does the individual complain of overly dry or moist skin?
- Does the individual complain of redness of the skin, severe swelling, blisters, dry or greasy scales on the scalp, peeling skin, thickened scaly patches, itching of apparently healthy skin, or itchy, red, scaly patches on the lower legs?
- Does the individual complain of itching, burning and stinging?
- Does the individual report a recent change in detergent, soap, cosmetics, jewelry, or topical medication?
- Does the individual report that they had been working or recreating outdoors?
- Does the individual have a family history of atopic dermatitis?
- Did the individual have a total skin examination?
- Has the individual had skin patch testing? Photo patch tests?
- Have conditions with similar symptoms been ruled out?

Regarding treatment:

- Is the individual able to avoid the agent causing the inflammation?
- Has the individual tried soaking in cool water, Calamine lotion, antihistamines, topical or oral corticosteroids, or an oral antibiotic?
- Has the individual used a medicated shampoo when indicated?
- Does the individual keep the skin well hydrated?
- For stasis dermatitis, has the individual tried support hose, compression stockings, zinc oxide paste, corticosteroid creams or an Unna boot?

Regarding prognosis:

- Is the individual's employer able to accommodate any necessary restrictions?
- Does the individual have any conditions that may affect their ability to recover?
- Does the individual have any complications such as infections or exfoliative erythroderma?
- Does the individual have poor hygiene or poor general health?

References

Phototherapy. New Zealand Dermatological Society. 09 Nov 2000. 01 Feb 2001 <http://www.dermnet.org.nz/index.html>.

Anderson, Philip, and Kristin Malaker. "Most Common Skin Disorders." Managing Skin Diseases. Hiscock, Tim, ed. Baltimore: Williams & Wilkins, 1999. 35-120.

Kirby, A.J., and R.J. Schmidt. "The Antioxidant Activity of Chinese Herbs for Eczema and of Placebo Herbs - I." Journal of Ethnopharmacology 56 2 (1997): 103-108.

Marks, James, and Vincent DeLeo. Contact and Occupational Dermatology. St. Louis: Mosby, 1997.

Dermatomyositis
710.3

Definition

Dermatomyositis is a fairly rare connective tissue disease in which there is chronic inflammation of the skeletal muscles, generally accompanied by inflammation and degeneration of the skin.

Dermatomyositis may be triggered by viruses or immune system disorders. Some researchers also theorize that in some the condition could be caused by the immune system's efforts to fight off onset of cancer. Certain types of dermatomyositis also may be related to metabolic abnormalities.

Dermatomyositis is classified, along with other conditions causing inflammation in skeletal muscles, in a group called idiopathic inflammatory myopathies. They occur in 1 in 100,000 individuals; about 5.5 cases per 1 million individuals are diagnosed each year. Dermatomyositis most commonly occurs either in individuals age 50 to 60 or in children between 5 and 15, and is twice as likely to affect females. Childhood dermatomyositis usually is not associated with a malignancy.

Diagnosis

History: Muscle stiffness, soreness, and weakness are the primary complaints, usually noted first in the upper arms and legs. Dusky red inflamed rashes may also develop on the face, neck, upper chest, and joint surfaces such as elbows; a purplish swelling will be seen around the eyelids. Individuals often complain of the inability to climb stairs or raise their arms above their heads. Difficulty in swallowing (dysphagia) or breathing (dyspnea), including shortness of breath, may also be reported. Symptoms can develop gradually or suddenly; muscle pain is most often reported with sudden onset. Symptoms may have developed after a mild injury or an illness which was accompanied by fever or rash. In extreme cases of muscle weakness, the individual may require a wheelchair.

Physical exam: Weakness may be noted in the neck muscles (particularly at the front of the neck), thighs, and shoulders. The muscles are occasionally tender and swollen. The disease typically causes a scaly red rash found on skin of the face, knuckles, elbows, knees, or ankles. The fingers and nails may be warm and red. Swelling around the eye can be seen, along with a purplish discoloration of the eyelids. Nodules of calcium deposits under the skin (calcinosis) may be noted.

Tests: Blood tests (serology) may show elevated levels of muscle enzymes (creatine phosphokinase, aldolase, and LDH). Tests of the electrical activity of muscles (electromyography) may also be conducted to show patterns suggestive of the disease. Imaging internal structures may be required through high-powered magnets and computers (magnetic resonance imaging, or MRI), high frequency sound waves (ultrasonography), or low-dose x-rays (CT). An EKG may also be done.

Removing a sample of an affected muscle (biopsy), usually the quadriceps or deltoid, may be needed for a definitive diagnosis; microscopic examination may show a characteristic kind of inflammation. In older adults, evaluations and accompanying tests may be necessary to detect possible cancer.

Treatment

The initial treatment for dermatomyositis is an anti-inflammatory drug (corticosteroid), initially given in high doses then tapered once improvement begins. A maintenance dose is usually needed indefinitely. If there is no response to steroid treatment, other drugs to suppress the immune response such as intravenous immune globulin (IVIG) therapy may be necessary. Individuals with dermatomyositis also will be advised to wear sunscreen preparations and protective clothing to avoid potentially harmful sun exposure. Individuals who develop calcium deposits under the skin (calcinosis) may need surgery (excision) to remove nodules; medication also may be given to prevent calcinosis. A supportive splint may be needed to protect soft tissue and joints.

Prognosis

For those individuals who respond to therapy, the expected outcome is either reduced severity or the disappearance of symptoms (remission). If, or when, relapses occur, individuals will typically respond to therapy again. However, in those who fail to respond to therapy, as the muscle weakness progresses the disease may result in permanent disability. The mortality rate rises as the age of disease onset increases, due either to the disease or a developing cancer. Death may result from severe and prolonged muscle weakness, malnutrition, pneumonia, or respiratory failure.

Differential Diagnosis

Similar disorders causing muscle weakness are scleroderma, myalgia, polymyositis, discoid lupus erythematosus, systemic lupus erythematosus (SLE), osteoarthritis, and rheumatoid arthritis. Other disease possibilities are hyperthyroidism and hypothyroidism, chronic inflammatory polyneuropathy, multiple sclerosis, myasthenia gravis, Eaton-Lambert disease, and amyotrophic lateral sclerosis (ALS, or Lou Gehrig disease). Drugs and alcohol can also produce muscle weakness. The rash of dermatomyositis can be similar to lupus, psoriasis, lichen planus, and mycosis fungoides. Other conditions that mimic or cause muscle inflammation include trichinosis, tuberculous pyomyositis, Lyme myositis, influenza myositis, viral myositis, toxoplasma myositis, trypanosomiasis, osteomyelitis, neuromuscular complications accompanying AIDS, paraneoplastic neuropathy, cellulitis, deep vein thrombosis, wasting syndrome, and hematoma.

Work Restrictions / Accommodations

Accommodations may need to be considered based on the severity and type of muscle weakness, and response to therapy. Individuals with dermatomyositis should wear sunscreen and protective clothing to avoid potentially harmful sun exposure. Individuals with progressive or severe muscle weakness may be unable to perform tasks requiring physical strength, flexibility, and/or endurance. Individuals confined to a wheelchair will require accessible workstations.

Comorbid Conditions

Comorbid conditions that might influence disability include diabetes mellitus or osteoporosis.

Complications

Older individuals with dermatomyositis have an increased risk of developing cancer. The malignancy may be present along with the initial symptoms or may develop later. Steroids used to suppress the disease and improve muscle weakness can cause side effects in susceptible individuals, including additional muscle weakness, cataracts, and lowered resistance to infections. As part of the condition, some individuals develop calcium deposits under the skin (calcinosis) that may be painful and/or become infected.

Specialists

- Dermatologist
- Neurologist
- Oncologist
- Physiatrist
- Rheumatologist

Factors Influencing Duration

The individual's response to therapy is a primary factor in determining the length of the disability. Duration varies greatly depending on the individual's age, type, and severity of the muscle involvement, ability to swallow, and presence of cancer.

Length of Disability

Severe muscle weakness on initial examination indicates possible permanent damage and is an indicator of continuing disability. Disability may be permanent.

Duration in Days

Job Classification	Minimum	Optimum	Maximum
Sedentary work	1	14	42
Light work	1	21	91
Medium work	7	42	182
Heavy work	Indefinite	Indefinite	Indefinite
Very Heavy work	Indefinite	Indefinite	Indefinite

Failure to Recover

If an individual fails to recover within the maximum duration expectancy period, the reader may wish to reference the following questions to assist in better understanding the specifics of an individual's medical case.

Regarding diagnosis:

- Does individual have muscle stiffness, soreness, and weakness first noted in the upper arms and legs?
- Are dusky red inflamed rashes seen on the face, neck, upper chest, and joint surfaces such as elbows? A purplish swelling around the eyelids?
- Does individual have difficult swallowing (dysphagia) or breathing (dyspnea), including shortness of breath?
- Did individual recently have a mild injury or illness that was accompanies by fever or rash?
- On exam, was weakness noted in the neck muscles (particularly at the front of the neck), thighs, and shoulders? Are muscles tender and swollen?
- Was diagnosis of dermatomyositis confirmed?
- Were conditions with similar symptoms ruled out?

Regarding treatment:

- Were anti-inflammatory medications (corticosteroids) or other appropriate therapy given to suppress immune responses that are causing the condition? If these drugs were ineffective, was individual given intravenous gamma globulin?
- Did individual have severe muscle weakness and possible permanent damage before therapy began?
- Did individual receive physical therapy in order to build muscle strength?
- If medication failed to prevent calcinosis, is surgery indicated to remove nodules?
- Was individual diagnosed with an underlying cancer accompanying the condition?
- Did condition improve once the tumor was removed?

Regarding prognosis:

- If individual has not experienced a remission, was there at least a reduced severity of symptoms?
- Could another drug or combination of drugs be used more effectively?
- If this episode is a relapse, has individual again responded to therapy? If not, what other treatment options are available?
- If muscle weakness has progressed, to what extent does it impact function?
- If confined to a wheelchair, would an accessible workstation allow individual to continue in occupation?
- Has individual experienced any complications related to the dermatomyositis such as malignancy, calcinosis, acute renal failure, and cardiac, pulmonary, or abdominal problems?
- Does individual have any coexisting conditions such as cancer, diabetes mellitus, or osteoporosis that may impact recovery?

References

"Dermatomyositis." Adam.com. 01 Jan 2001. 13 Feb 2001 <http://health.yahoo.com/health/diseases_and_conditions/disease_feed_data/dermatomyositis>.

"Facts About Polymyositis and Dermatomyositis." Muscular Dystrophy Association. 2000. 20 Feb 2001 <http://www.mdausa.org/publications/fa-myosi.html>.

Deviated Nasal Septum

Definition

The nasal septum is the partition in the nose separating the two nostrils. Comprised of bone and cartilage, this partition is covered with a mucous membrane. The nasal septum is usually straight and reasonably centered. In some individuals, however, the septum is bent (deviated). The bending or deviation may partially or completely block the nasal passage. Blocking the nasal passage can interfere with sinus drainage that makes the individual prone to sinus inflammation (sinusitis). Because excess airflow through the unblocked passage can dry out the mucous membrane, the individual may also be prone to nosebleeds.

There are two main types of deviation. One occurs when the lower end of the septum becomes dislocated and pushed to one side, narrowing one of the nostrils. The other type results when the septum deforms into an S-shape causing a partial or complete blockage of both nostrils.

Although it can be caused by a birth defect, most cases of deviated nasal septum are the result of trauma. Deviated nasal septum occurs in approximately 26 out of every 1,000 men and 20 out of every 1,000 women.

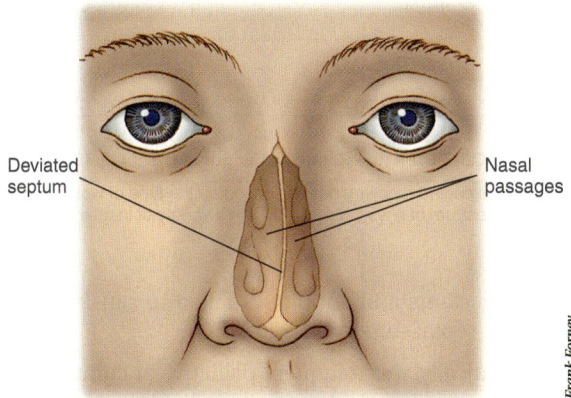

Diagnosis

History: Symptoms are not always associated with a deviated septum. Depending on the severity of the obstruction, individuals may report chronic nasal congestion, sinusitis, repeated ear infections, headache, or nosebleeds. Scuba divers with a deviated septum may have difficulty equalizing the pressure in their ears when they dive.

Physical exam: Visual inspection may reveal an inequality in the size of the nostrils and/or a deformity in the septum. A deformity of the external nose is sometimes also apparent.

Tests: Sinus x-rays may be taken to confirm the nasal septal deviation and to evaluate for sinus infection.

Treatment

Mild forms of nasal septum deviation require no medical intervention other than treatment of occasional nasal congestion or sinusitis. These are treated with decongestants or antibiotics, respectively. A general practitioner should monitor long-term use of decongestants as misuse can cause rebound symptoms.

When the deviation is more severe and obstructs breathing, surgical intervention is necessary. A surgical procedure called submucous resection is usually done under general anesthesia. During this procedure, the lining of the nose is peeled back from the septum. The cartilage and bone are removed from the deviated area and the lining replaced. The nose is packed for about 24 hours to maintain the septum in the correct position. Another surgical procedure called septoplasty removes less of the septum. In this procedure, the septum is straightened and centrally repositioned. The septum may be held in place with splints placed inside the nostrils.

Prognosis

Prognosis is usually good after either septoplasty or submucous resection. Most individuals are up and about within a few days and can return to sedentary work in about 1 week. Swelling may be present for a few months after surgery.

Differential Diagnosis

A deviated nasal septum usually occurs after traumatic injury to the nose. There is generally no question about the definitive diagnosis.

Specialists

- Otolaryngologist
- Plastic Surgeon

Work Restrictions / Accommodations

Individuals may need to avoid respiratory irritants (smoke and dust) for a short period.

Comorbid Conditions

Chronic nasal congestion and allergies may adversely affect the outcome of treatment. A severely deformed nose may require rhinoplasty in addition to septoplasty.

Complications

A deviated nasal septum can interfere with normal drainage from the sinuses and result in recurrent sinus infections. Drainage of mucus from the middle ear can also be hindered by a deviated nasal septum and result in repeated ear infections or a condition called "glue ear."

Factors Influencing Duration

Factors that may lengthen disability include severity of breathing difficulties, other deformities of the nose requiring additional correction, type of treatment or surgical repair, and response to treatment.

Length of Disability

Surgical treatment (septoplasty).

Duration in Days

Job Classification	Minimum	Optimum	Maximum
Sedentary work	3	10	14
Light work	3	10	14
Medium work	3	14	21
Heavy work	7	14	21
Very Heavy work	7	14	21

Notes

Duration Trend from Normative Data*

Cases	Mean	Min	Max	No Lost Time	Over 6 Months
2143	20	0	196	0.47%	0.05%

Percentile:	5th	25th	Median	75th	95th
Days:	8	13	17	24	46

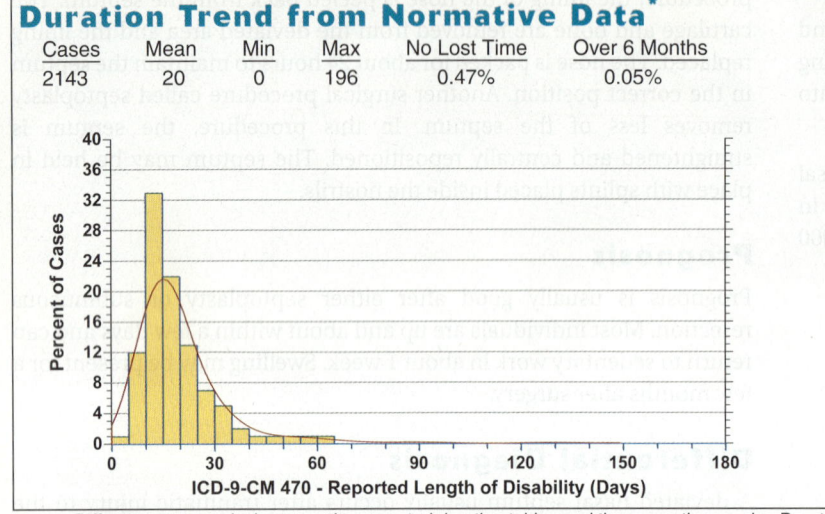
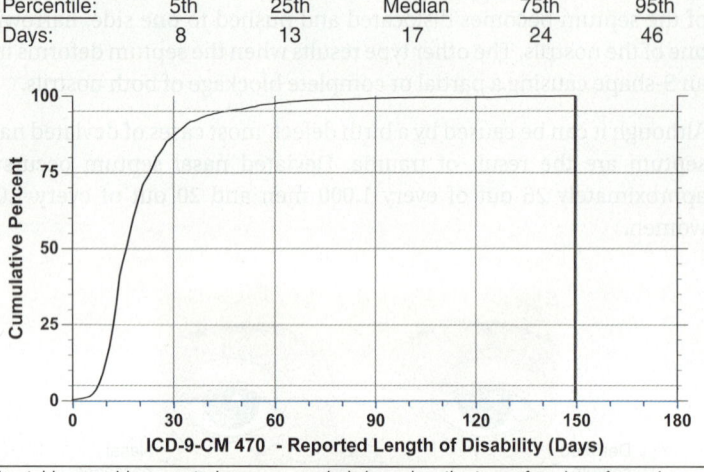

* Differences may exist between the expected duration tables and the normative graphs. Duration tables provide expected recovery periods based on the type of work performed by the individual. The normative graphs reflect the actual observed experience of many individuals across the spectrum of physical conditions, in a variety of industries, and with varying levels of case management.

Failure to Recover

If an individual fails to recover within the maximum duration expectancy period, the reader may wish to reference the following questions to assist in better understanding the specifics of an individual's medical case.

Regarding diagnosis:

- What is the cause of the deviated septum? Birth defect? Trauma?
- If trauma related, did additional injuries occur to the nose or surrounding area requiring additional treatment or correction? Rhinoplasty?

Regarding treatment:

- How long were symptoms present prior to correction? How severe?
- Have decongestants and antibiotics failed to satisfactorily treat individual? Is septal surgery warranted?
- If treated medically, was treatment palliative or curative? Will additional treatment (surgical correction) be necessary in the future?

Regarding prognosis:

- If surgical correction was required, what method was used? Submucous resection? Septoplasty?
- Was successful correction accomplished? If not, what is being considered as future treatment? Rhinoplasty?
- Do symptoms persist despite surgical correction?

References

Deviated Nasal Septum. PPP Healthcare International-Health at Hand. 2000. 12 July 2000 <http://www.ppphealthcare.co.uk/html/health/nasalsep.htm>.

Otolaryngology - Deviated Septum. Methodist Health Care System. 2000. 12 July 2000 <http://methodisthealth.com/otolaryn/deviated.htm>.

Otolaryngology - Ear, Nose, and Throat Disorders. Thomas Jefferson University Hospital. 2000. 12 July 2000 <http://www.jeffersonhospital.org/show.asp?durki=5106>.

Septum, Deviated. Rush-Presbyterian-St. Luke's Medical Center. 1998. 12 July 2000 <http://www.rush.edu/worldbook/articles/019000a/019000082.html>.

Diabetes Insipidus

Other names / synonyms: Nephrogenic Diabetes Insipidus, Posterior Pituitary Insufficiency

253.5

Definition

Diabetes insipidus is a rare disease characterized by excessive thirst (polydipsia) and the excretion of enormous quantities of dilute urine (polyuria). Vasopressin, also known as antidiuretic hormone (ADH), controls the amount of water passed by the kidneys into the urine in order to maintain a constant dilution of the blood. ADH is produced in an area of the brain called the hypothalamus and stored in a gland at the base of the brain (pituitary gland). Diabetes insipidus can occur if the hypothalamus fails to produce adequate amounts of ADH or if the pituitary gland fails to secrete adequate amounts of ADH into the bloodstream. Without ADH, water filtered by the kidneys (glomerular filtrate) is excreted in the urine rather than being reabsorbed by the kidneys. In rare instances, ADH levels are normal, but the kidneys do not respond to it (nephrogenic diabetes insipidus).

Causes of diabetes insipidus include head trauma, injury to the hypothalamus or pituitary gland during surgery, brain injury (particularly a fracture at the base of the skull), brain tumors, sarcoidosis, pituitary tumors, tuberculosis, some forms of meningitis or encephalitis, and vascular causes such as a stroke or aneurysm. Diabetes insipidus can be caused by a rare disease called histiocytosis X (Hand-Schuller-Christian disease). Although usually present at birth (congenital), nephrogenic diabetes insipidus may be caused by a kidney disease (pyelonephritis) and can be worsened by certain drugs. Diabetes insipidus can also be idiopathic.

Diabetes insipidus has no relationship with the more familiar diabetes mellitus, a disorder of carbohydrate metabolism. In rare cases, psychologic symptoms of excessive thirst can result in excessive fluid intake and urination. Although symptoms may resemble diabetes insipidus, the individual usually does not awaken during the night to urinate. Over time, excessive fluid intake can diminish responsiveness to antidiuretic hormone.

Diagnosis

History: The individual reports polydipsia, drinking large amounts of water, and excessive urination (polyuria), especially frequent urination at night (nocturia). When matched by similar intake of water, the individual may pass between 10 and 40 pints of urine every 24 hours. Other complaints may be fatigue, muscle weakness, dry skin, constipation, and dizziness. Without adequate water intake, dehydration can lead to confusion and coma.

Physical exam: When fluid intake has kept up with fluid loss, physical exam may be unremarkable. When fluid intake has been insufficient, early signs of dehydration may occur and include a slow return of skin to original shape when gently pinched and released (poor turgidity), dry mucous membranes, and a systolic blood pressure below 100 (hypotension). Other findings on exam may include a heart rate above 100 beats per minute (tachycardia), weak pulses in the arms and legs, cool and clammy skin, and shallow but rapid respirations.

Tests: Urine is tested for sugar to rule out diabetes mellitus. Urinalysis may also show a low specific gravity and osmolality. Urine may be almost colorless. Blood tests may reveal abnormal levels of many electrolytes.

The water deprivation test is widely regarded as the most reliable test for diabetes insipidus. Because this test deprives the individual of fluids, it must be conducted in a doctor's office or medical facility. During the test, urine production, blood electrolyte (sodium) levels, and weight are measured regularly for several hours. As soon as the blood pressure falls, the heart rate increases, or there is a 5% loss in body weight, the test is stopped and the individual is given an injection of antidiuretic hormone. The diagnosis is confirmed if excessive urination stops, the blood pressure rises, and the heart beats more normally.

Treatment

Whenever possible, the underlying cause of diabetes insipidus is treated. Modified forms of antidiuretic hormone taken by nasal spray several times a day can help maintain normal urine output. Taking too much of this drug, however, can cause fluid retention and sodium deficiency in the blood (hyponatremia), which can lead to seizures and death. Antidiuretic hormone can also be given by injection to unconscious individuals.

Drugs that stimulate antidiuretic hormone production (chlorpropamide, carbamazepine, clofibrate, or thiazides) can be used to control cases or partial and mild diabetes insipidus. Such agents, however, will not offer symptom relief in individuals with severe diabetes insipidus.

Drugs are ineffective in individuals with nephrogenic diabetes insipidus. These individuals are placed on a low-sodium diet and treated with a drug to slow the development of thirst symptoms.

Prognosis

The degree of recovery is largely dependent on the underlying cause of the disease. Complete resolution of symptoms may not be seen in individuals with severe disease. Chronic diabetes insipidus, although inconvenient, is not usually a dire medical condition. When properly treated, diabetes insipidus itself does not reduce life expectancy. The prognosis, therefore, depends on the underlying disease.

Differential Diagnosis

Other diagnoses may be diabetes mellitus, misuse of diuretics (water pills), or self-overhydration (psychogenic diabetes insipidus).

Specialists

- Endocrinologist
- Infectious Disease Physician
- Internist
- Neurologist
- Urologist

Work Restrictions / Accommodations

Working at heights, in an extremely warm work environment, or excessive prolonged physical exertion should be avoided. Accommodations for frequent breaks may be necessary and access to drinking water must always be available.

Comorbid Conditions

Any condition that might impact on the individual's compliance with the treatment regimen (i.e., depression or diminished mental capacity) could delay recovery or predispose the individual to relapse. Diabetes insipidus associated with preeclampsia or hepatic dysfunction may occur in the last trimester of pregnancy. Individuals with impaired thirst mechanism are very prone to excessive sodium in the blood (hypernatremia).

Complications

Dehydration is the most common complication of diabetes insipidus and can progress to low blood pressure (hypotension), dizziness, confusion, stupor, shock, or coma. Electrolyte imbalance and vascular collapse may also occur. If left untreated, death could result. Access to water is critical in prevention of dehydration.

Factors Influencing Duration

Length of disability might be influenced by the underlying cause of the diabetes insipidus, progression of the underlying cause, or resistance of the underlying cause to treatment. Complications such as dehydration, hypotension, shock, or coma can also lengthen the period of disability.

Length of Disability

With complications, disability may be permanent.

Acute episode without complications.

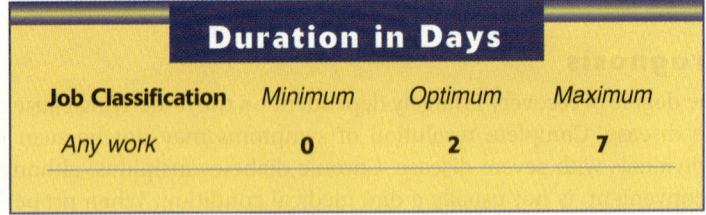

Duration in Days				
Job Classification	Minimum	Optimum	Maximum
Any work	0	2	7

Failure to Recover

If an individual fails to recover within the maximum duration expectancy period, the reader may wish to reference the following questions to assist in better understanding the specifics of an individual's medical case.

Regarding diagnosis:

- Does individual have a history of head trauma, injury to the hypothalamus or pituitary gland during surgery, brain injury (particularly a fracture at the base of the skull), brain tumors, sarcoidosis, tuberculosis, some forms of meningitis or encephalitis, or vascular causes such as a stroke or aneurysm?
- Does individual have histiocytosis X (Hand-Schuller-Christian disease)? Pyelonephritis?
- Does individual have psychological symptoms of excessive thirst?
- Does individual report polydipsia, drinking large amounts of water, and polyuria especially nocturia?
- Does individual complain of fatigue, muscle weakness, dry skin, and constipation?
- On exam, does individual have poor skin turgor, dry mucous membranes, hypotension, tachycardia, weak pulses in the arms and legs, cool and clammy skin, and shallow but rapid respirations?
- Was urinalysis and comprehensive blood testing done? Water deprivation test?
- Were conditions with similar symptoms ruled out?

Regarding treatment:

- If possible, was the underlying condition treated?
- Was individual treated with modified forms of antidiuretic hormone?
- Does individual watch for signs of edema?
- Was individual treated with chlorpropamide, carbamazepine, clofibrate, or thiazides to stimulate antidiuretic hormone production?
- As drugs are ineffective in individuals with nephrogenic diabetes insipidus, was individual treated with a low-sodium diet and a drug to slow the development of thirst symptoms?

Regarding prognosis:

- Can individual's employer accommodate any necessary restrictions?
- Does individual have any conditions that may affect ability to recover?
- Have any complications developed such as dehydration, hypotension, dizziness, confusion, stupor, shock, or coma? Does individual have electrolyte imbalance and vascular collapse? Did death ensue?

References

Klonoff, E.A., and D.J. Moore. "Compulsive Polydipsia Presenting as Diabetes Insipidus: A Behavioral Approach." Journal of Behavior Therapy and Experimental Psychiatry 15 4 (1984): 353-358.

Liu, James. "Pituitary Gland Disorders." Merck Manual of Medical Information. Berkow, Robert, ed. New York: Pocket Books, 1997. 764-772.

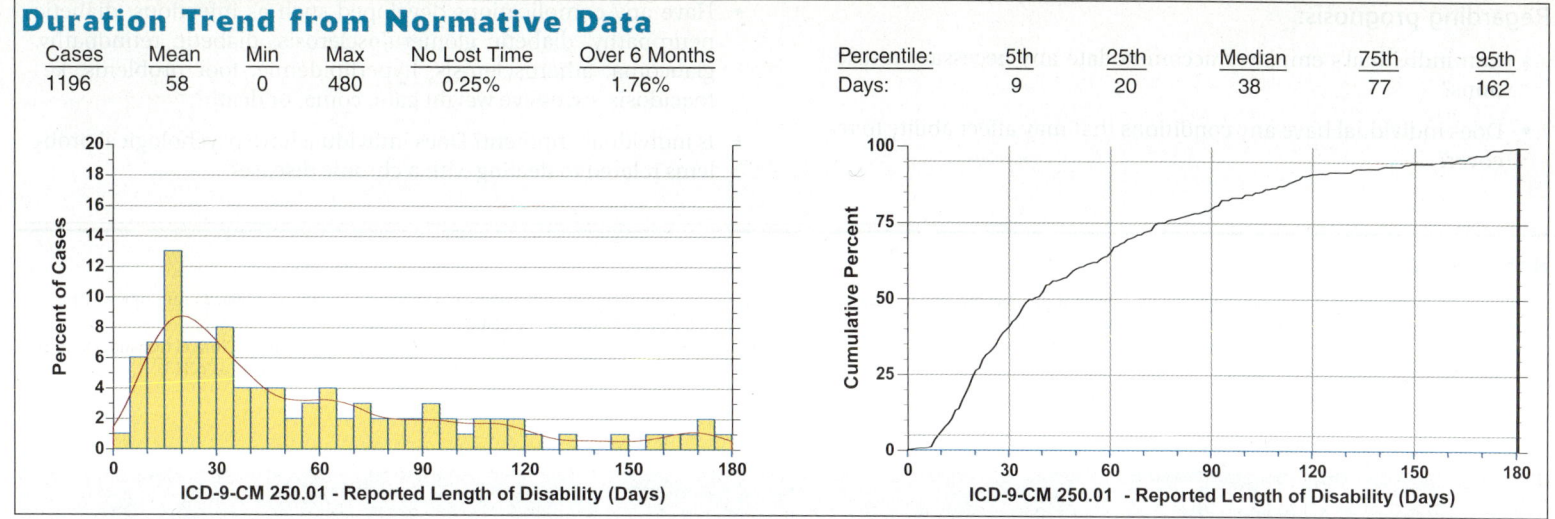

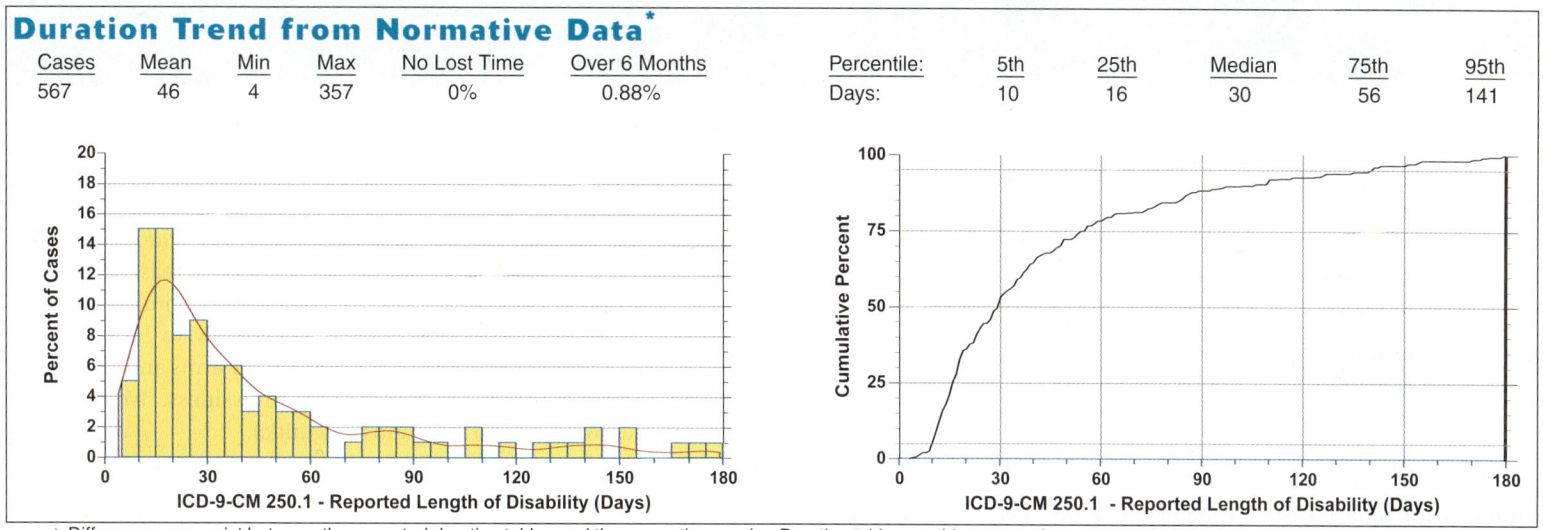

* Differences may exist between the expected duration tables and the normative graphs. Duration tables provide expected recovery periods based on the type of work performed by the individual. The normative graphs reflect the actual observed experience of many individuals across the spectrum of physical conditions, in a variety of industries, and with varying levels of case management.

Failure to Recover

If an individual fails to recover within the maximum duration expectancy period, the reader may wish to reference the following questions to assist in better understanding the specifics of an individual's medical case.

Regarding diagnosis:

- Does individual have a family history of diabetes?
- Does individual complain of polydipsia, polyuria, weight loss despite normal or increased food intake, fatigue, headaches, muscle wasting, muscle cramps, vision changes, visible weight loss from loss of body fluids, anxiety, nausea, vomiting, diarrhea and/or constipation? Does individual have polyphagia or anorexia?
- Did physical exam reveal hypotension, weak rapid pulse, or dry mucous membranes (especially the mouth)? Was breathing deep and rapid?
- At the time of diagnosis, was individual thin with little or no body fat?
- Does individual's breath have a fruity odor to it?
- Was urine testing done for glucose and ketones? Comprehensive blood sugar testing? Complete blood chemistry testing?
- Were conditions with similar symptoms ruled out?

Regarding treatment:

- Were injections of insulin given?
- Does individual self-monitor blood sugar?
- Has individual received training regarding diet, exercise, and stress reduction? Daily foot care? Early treatment of minor scratches or wounds?
- Was individual compliant with treatment regime?
- Is individual a candidate for an insulin pump?

Diabetes Mellitus Type I

Regarding prognosis:

- Can individual's employer accommodate any necessary restrictions?
- Does individual have any conditions that may affect ability to recover?
- Have any complications developed such as infections, diabetic neuropathy, diabetic glomerulosclerosis, diabetic retinopathy, glaucoma, atherosclerosis, hyperlipidemia, foot problems, ketoacidosis, excessive weight gain, coma, or death?
- Is individual impotent? Does individual have psychological problems related to dealing with a chronic disease?

References

"Diabetes Mellitus." The Merck Manual of Medical Information. Berkow, Robert, Mark Beers, and Andrew Fletcher, eds. New York: Pocket Books, 1997. 788-795.

About Type 1 Diabetes. American Diabetes Association. 2000. 24 Aug 2000 <http://www.diabetes.org/ada/Type1.asp>.

Diabetes Facts and Figures. American Diabetes Association. 2000. 24 Aug 2000 <http://www.diabetes.org/ada/facts.asp>.

Schultz, Robert. "Diabetes Mellitus, Type 1." Griffith's 5-minute Clinical Consult. Dambro, Mark, ed. Philadelphia: Lippincott, Williams & Wilkins, 2000. 312-313.

Diabetes Mellitus Type II

Other names / synonyms: Adult Onset Diabetes Mellitus, NIDDM, Non-Insulin Dependent Diabetes Mellitus, Nonketotic Diabetes Mellitus, Type 2 Diabetes, Type 2 Diabetes Mellitus

250, 250.00

Definition

Diabetes mellitus (diabetes) is a chronic disorder characterized by abnormally high levels of a simple sugar (glucose) in the blood (hyperglycemia). Type II diabetes (or non-insulin dependent diabetes mellitus) is an endocrine abnormality caused by a combination of insulin resistance and insufficient levels of insulin.

Insulin is a hormone produced in an organ near the stomach called the pancreas; it is required by the body to convert food into energy. In Type II diabetes, often the pancreas is unable to produce or secrete sufficient amounts of insulin; this inability varies considerably from person to person. Usually, the insulin is not functioning properly, so the glucose cannot be transported from the blood into body's cells and accumulates in the blood, causing hyperglycemia.

Risk factors include a family history of Type II diabetes, over age 40, lack of regular exercise, and poor diet. Obesity is strongly associated with Type II diabetes; approximately 90% are more than 20% over the ideal body weight, and the chance of a susceptible adult developing Type II diabetes doubles for every 20% increase in body weight. The incidence also increases with age and obesity because as individuals age, they tend to gain weight and develop central abdominal obesity. In addition, women who had pregnancy-related diabetes (gestational diabetes) or women who gave birth to a baby weighing over 9 pounds are at an increased risk of developing Type II diabetes. Other risk factors include the presence of hypertension, low HDL cholesterol and high triglycerides. Women with polycystic ovary syndrome are also at a higher risk. Blacks, Hispanics, and Native Americans have a significantly higher risk of developing Type II diabetes than the general population. Among whites, this disease occurs more frequently in women than men.

There are approximately 15 million Americans with Type II diabetes, and roughly one-third are unaware that they have the disease. Type II diabetes accounts for 80-95% of all cases of diabetes diagnosed.

Diagnosis

History: Individuals are usually asymptomatic and only occasionally display the classic symptoms of diabetes mellitus. Therefore it can go unrecognized for many years. Classic symptoms include increased urination (polyuria) and excessive thirst. There is increased fluid and food consumption (polydipsia and polyphagia). The individual may complain of frequent skin infections that are slow to heal, itching, blurred vision, tingling, numbness, and pain in the arms and legs. There may be a feeling of general fatigue and drowsiness. Women may experience chronic vaginal infections (vaginitis).

Physical exam: High blood pressure is present in half the cases, and obesity is a common finding. The feet and lower legs are examined carefully for signs of ulceration and gangrene. Diabetes affects the peripheral nerves (diabetic neuropathy) with decreased sensation to pain. There may be diminished pulses in the feet. An eye exam will reveal changes in the blood vessels, bleeding, and yellow or white patches in the retina (diabetic retinopathy), all characteristics of complications of Type II diabetes.

Tests: Urine dipstick tests and regular urinalysis measure the amount of sugar in the urine (glycosuria, always an abnormal finding). The absence of ketosis (abnormally elevated concentration of ketones) is a primary feature that distinguishes Type II from Type I diabetes. A chemistry profile can measure the serum creatinine to determine kidney function. Common tests for Type II diabetes include measuring blood sugar levels either as they exist normally (non-fasting blood glucose level), or after abstaining from food or fluids for 12 hours (fasting blood glucose level). The oral glucose tolerance test is frequently used to help confirm the diagnosis of diabetes. This test measures the glucose in the blood for 2 hours after drinking a set amount of glucose. Diabetics show an abnormal rise in the blood sugar (hyperglycemia).

Treatment

According to the American Diabetes Association, eating well-balanced, healthy meals, and regular aerobic exercise are the best treatment and preventive measures for those with diabetes or a family history of the disease. Both can significantly improve glucose tolerance, and decrease medication requirements. Therefore, individual education in weight control through diet and exercise can be a very effective combination in controlling Type II diabetes. Stress reduction techniques also assist in controlling Type II diabetes. Self-care education, aimed at providing early intervention for any injuries to the lower legs and feet (including small scratches), should include the daily inspection of feet and lower extremities, daily foot cleansing, moisturizing, and nail trimming. Wearing protective footwear can additionally guard against injury. If diet, exercise and stress reduction are not effective in controlling blood sugar levels, the physician may need to prescribe medication to lower it (oral hypoglycemics). Diabetes Mellitus Type II is a progressive disease so virtually all individuals with this disease will need medications to control it.

In some cases, oral medications may not be enough to control glucose levels, and insulin therapy is needed. Insulin may be administered alone or in combination with an oral medication. Insulin is self-injected and the individual will be trained by the physician or his staff in the proper method of injection. Insulin therapy might also be required if exercise and diet are particularly difficult for an individual (a peson with physical disabilities, non-obese individuals).

Treatment also includes monitoring blood glucose levels at regular intervals by the physician, and daily by the individual with a home-monitoring machine. Periodically testing the amount of glucose bound to a protein in the red blood cells called hemoglobin (glycosylated hemoglobin) is usually done. This test provides an indication of the glucose levels over the preceding 60 to 90 days. The individual should be educated on the symptoms of, and early response to, hyperglycemia and abnormally low glucose levels (hypoglycemia). The individual should also have regular physical and eye exams.

Prognosis

Exercise and weight loss makes the body more sensitive to the action of insulin and helps control the blood glucose levels. With good control of blood glucose levels and compliance with self-care, the outcome is favorable. The development of complications will adversely impact outcome. For instance, blindness and kidney disease can result in permanent disability. Nearly 200,000 individuals die from diabetes each year.

Differential Diagnosis

Differential diagnosis may be Type I diabetes. Gestational diabetes seen during pregnancy may be the first sign of developing Type II diabetes. Diseases of the endocrine system or pancreas, and reactions to certain drugs can have the same symptoms as diabetes.

Specialists

- Cardiologist
- Endocrinologist
- Nephrologist
- Neurologist
- Ophthalmologist
- Orthopedic Surgeon
- Podiatrist
- Psychologist
- Urologist

Work Restrictions / Accommodations

Individuals may need to change jobs if requirements include working in extreme temperatures, operating high-speed equipment, working with sharp objects, or working in high places. Individuals will need appropriate protective footwear (safety shoes). Individuals should refrain from strenuous or prolonged physical activity and working alone or in isolated areas. Frequent breaks and a private area for glucose monitoring may be necessary. The presence of complications may dictate other accommodations (e.g., foot problems may require a sedentary position).

Complementary and Alternative Therapies

Content is intended for awareness only. Treatments may or may not be effective. Scientific evidence may be lacking and some substances have potentially toxic effects. Dr. Presley Reed and the editors do not endorse the use of these therapies in the absence of consultation with a licensed medical professional.

Diet - A modified and/or controlled diet may help balance blood sugar and control weight.

Comorbid Conditions

Obesity, renal failure, obstructive sleep apnea, hypertension, peripheral vascular disease, cardiovascular disease, depression, and infectious disease may lengthen disability.

Complications

Complications of Type II diabetes mellitus include low blood sugar (hypoglycemia), infection, gangrene, amputation of a lower extremity, skin ulceration, eye disease (diabetic retinopathy, glaucoma), cataracts, impotence, joint disease (Charcot joints), nerve damage (diabetic neuropathy), disease of the heart and/or blood vessels (cardiovascular disease, atherosclerosis), heart attack, stroke, or kidney failure.

Diabetic coma and ketoacidosis, seen in Type I diabetes, are rare in this disease. Hyperosmolar, non-ketonic coma, however, is seen in newly diagnosed individuals and the elderly and has a very high associated mortality rate.

Factors Influencing Duration

Factors influencing the length of disability include the presence and progression of complications. Infections, loss of vision, amputation of foot or leg, or dialysis will greatly lengthen disability.

Length of Disability

Type II diabetes is a chronic condition, so true recovery may never occur. Length of disability depends upon the presence of complications, response to treatment, and the specific job requirements. Disability may be permanent.

Without complications.

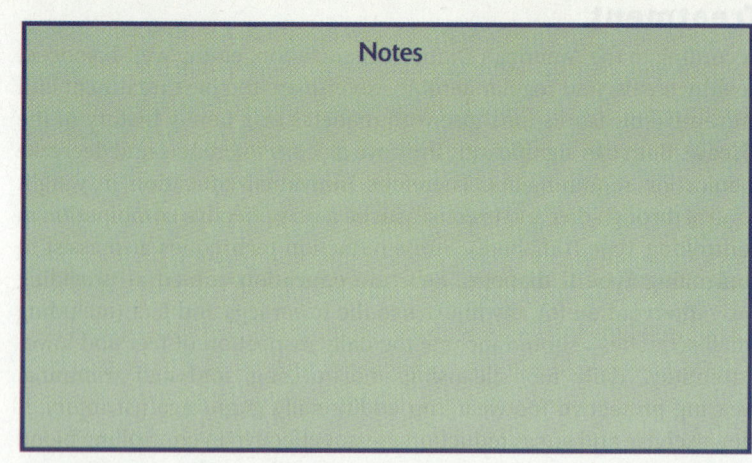

Duration in Days

Job Classification	Minimum	Optimum	Maximum
Any work	0	3	7

Duration Trend from Normative Data*

Cases	Mean	Min	Max	No Lost Time	Over 6 Months
2452	52	0	373	0.78%	0.65%

Percentile:	5th	25th	Median	75th	95th
Days:	10	18	35	68	152

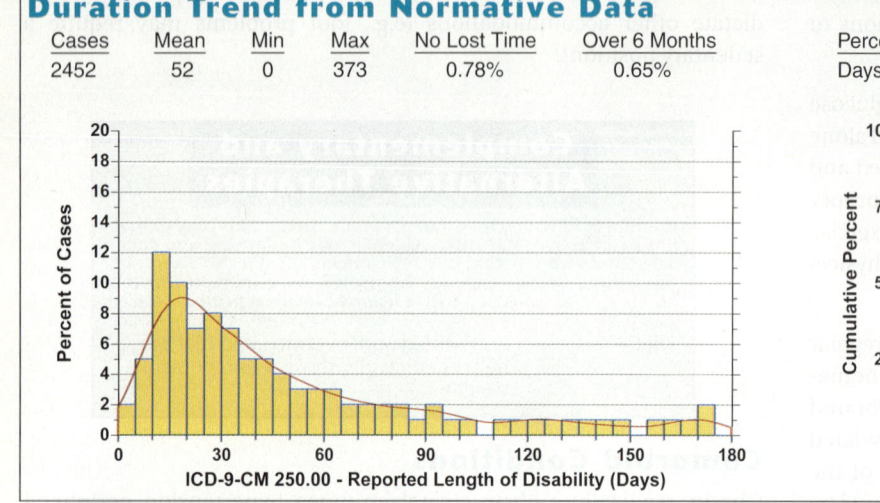
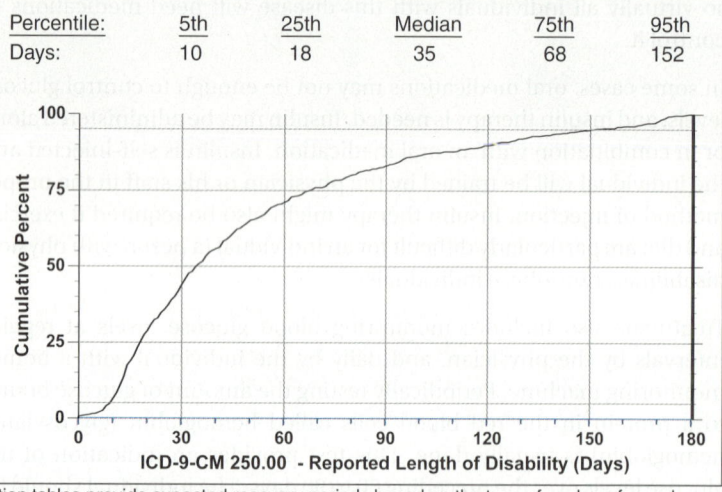

ICD-9-CM 250.00 - Reported Length of Disability (Days)

* Differences may exist between the expected duration tables and the normative graphs. Duration tables provide expected recovery periods based on the type of work performed by the individual. The normative graphs reflect the actual observed experience of many individuals across the spectrum of physical conditions, in a variety of industries, and with varying levels of case management.

Failure to Recover

If an individual fails to recover within the maximum duration expectancy period, the reader may wish to reference the following questions to assist in better understanding the specifics of an individual's medical case.

Regarding diagnosis:

- Does individual have a family history of diabetes?
- Is individual over 40, have a poor diet, and no regular exercise?
- Is individual obese? Did individual have gestational diabetes?
- Does individual have polydipsia, polyuria, and polyphagia?
- Does individual complain of frequent skin infections that are slow to heal, itching, blurred vision, tingling, numbness, pain in the arms and legs, general fatigue and drowsiness? If female, does individual have chronic vaginitis?
- On exam, did individual have hypertension, obesity, leg ulcers, diminished pulses in the feet, or changes in the eye?
- Were a urinalysis, comprehensive blood sugar testing, and complete chemistry panel done?
- Were conditions with similar symptom ruled out?

Regarding treatment:

- Does individual eat well-balanced, healthy meals and participate in regular aerobic exercise?
- Was individual trained in daily inspection and early intervention of injuries to the lower legs? Daily foot care?
- Were oral hypoglycemics given?
- Does individual monitor blood sugar regularly?
- Has it become necessary for individual to take insulin?
- Was individual compliant with treatment regime?

Regarding prognosis:

- Can individual's employer accommodate any necessary restrictions?
- Are blood pressure and cholesterol being controlled?
- Was smoking cessation advised?
- Does individual have any conditions that may affect ability to recover?
- Have any complications developed such as hypoglycemia, infection, gangrene, amputation of a lower extremity, skin ulceration, diabetic retinopathy, glaucoma, cataracts, impotence, joint disease, diabetic neuropathy, cardiovascular disease, atherosclerosis, heart attack, stroke, or kidney failure?

References

About Type 2 Diabetes. American Diabetes Association. 24 Aug 2000 <http://www.diabetes.org/ada/type2.asp>.

Diabetes Facts and Figures. American Diabetes Association. 24 Aug 2000 <http://www.diabetes.org/ada/facts.asp>.

HbA1c Measurement. Children with Diabetes. 31 May 2000. 05 Oct 2000 <http://www.childrenwithdiabetes.com/d_06_h00.htm>.

Gray, David. "Diabetes Mellitus, Type 2." Griffith's 5-minute Clinical Consult. Dambro, Mark, ed. Philadelphia: Lippincott, Williams & Wilkins, 2000. 314-315.

Diabetic Gangrene
250.7

Definition

Diabetic gangrene is tissue death (gangrene) that occurs in an individual with diabetes mellitus (diabetic). Gangrene is usually caused by obstruction of the blood and oxygen supply to an organ or a tissue followed by bacterial infection. The blood flow obstruction is generally caused by inflammation, injury, or is due to disease of the blood vessels (vascular disease) such as hardening of the arteries (arteriosclerosis). Subsequent infection with certain types of bacteria (anaerobic bacteria), including certain species of Streptococcus, Enterobacteriaceae, and Clostridia, results in gangrene.

Diabetes mellitus interferes with the function of many body systems, including the blood vessels and circulatory system. Disease of the blood vessels (vascular disease) results in poor circulation of blood, particularly to the lower extremities (legs and feet). As a result, diabetics tend to get wounds, including ulcers (particularly on the feet), and healing tends to be very slow. Because circulation is poor, these wounds can become infected by anaerobic bacteria, and the result is gangrene. Even without an open wound, anaerobic bacteria can infect tissue in which circulation is poor.

Diabetic gangrene occurs equally in men and women with diabetes. It can develop at any age, and risk factors include vascular disease, poor foot care, open wounds, traumatic injury, and malnutrition. This disease is serious and potentially life-threatening; death occurs in approximately 20% of cases. Untreated cases are fatal.

Diagnosis

History: Individuals who report symptoms are diabetics who have an infection, usually on their legs or feet. There may be pain; however, diabetics often have nerve damage and may not feel pain. The individual may say that the skin surrounding the infection has progressed from pale, to red or bronze, and eventually to greenish black. Often, the infection will have progressed rapidly. In some cases, the skin will be warm and swollen; blisters may also be present.

Physical exam: The exam will reveal tissue death (necrosis) around the area of the infection. Fever and a rapid pulse may also be noted. Blisters (bullae) may have a brownish, foul smelling discharge. In some cases, the bacteria will produce gas, resulting in an audible crackling sound and/or a crackle-like feeling of the skin.

Tests: An x-ray, CT scan, or MRI will show the amount of gas present beneath the surface of the skin. In addition, a CT scan or MRI can also help determine the extent of tissue damage to skin, muscle, and bone. Culturing the wound can identify the causative organism; however, because of the emergent nature of this condition, surgical amputation may need to be performed even before culture results are available.

Treatment

Diabetic gangrene is a serious and potentially life-threatening disease. The individual is generally admitted to the hospital for treatment and observation. Fluids, nutritional support, and antibiotics are given intravenously. The surgeon will remove the dead tissue (débridement), often under general anesthesia. If circulation to the affected area is poor, amputation may be required to prevent spread of the infection. Exposure to high pressure (hyperbaric) oxygen may help kill the responsible bacteria.

Prognosis

Diabetic gangrene is a serious and potentially fatal disease. When it is diagnosed promptly and the individual is admitted to the hospital for intravenous medication, exposure to high pressure oxygen, and surgical removal of dead tissue, the prognosis is fair. Amputation of the affected limb may be necessary, resulting in loss of function. Even with adequate treatment, death occurs in 20% of cases. Untreated diabetic gangrene is fatal.

Differential Diagnosis

Gangrene can occur in the absence of diabetes, and will have similar signs and symptoms as diabetic gangrene. The primary difference will be that the individual will not have a history of diabetes.

Specialists

- Endocrinologist
- Infectious Disease Physician
- Orthopedic Surgeon
- Psychiatrist
- Psychologist
- Vascular Surgeon

Work Restrictions / Accommodations

Prolonged sick leave may be required for inpatient therapy, surgical recovery, and/or rehabilitation in the case of amputation. Individuals who have had a limb amputated may need to be reassigned depending upon their job requirements and physical limitations. If the individual develops depression, time off may be needed for psychiatric or psychological counseling.

Comorbid Conditions

Individuals with a compromised immune system may have more severe disease and a longer recovery period. When amputation is required, obesity and depression may also impact the recovery period.

Complications

A possible complication of diabetic gangrene would be spread of the infection into the bloodstream (sepsis, or septicemia).

Factors Influencing Duration

Length of disability may be influenced by the severity of the disease, the extent of vascular/circulatory damage, the individual's response to treatment, the timeliness of treatment, and the development of complications.

Length of Disability

Duration depends on the individual's job requirements and the site of infection or amputation (e.g., a surgeon who loses an index finger, a dancer who loses a foot or leg). In some cases, disability may be permanent (death occurs in approximately 20% of cases; untreated cases are fatal).

Failure to Recover

If an individual fails to recover within the maximum duration expectancy period, the reader may wish to reference the following questions to assist in better understanding the specifics of an individual's medical case.

Regarding diagnosis:

- Does the individual have arteriosclerosis?
- Did the individual have pain at the wound site?
- Has the skin become discolored progressing to greenish black?
- Is necrosis present on exam? Any blisters? Is any crackling heard or felt?
- Has the individual had x-rays, CT scan, or MRI?
- Has the wound been cultured? Sensitivity done?
- Did it become necessary to do an emergency amputation?

Regarding treatment:

- Is the individual hospitalized for aggressive treatment?
- Did amputation become necessary?
- Was hyperbaric oxygen tried?

Regarding prognosis:

- If amputation was necessary is the individual active in a rehabilitation program?
- Have blood sugars been controlled during hospitalization?
- Is the individual's employer able to accommodate any necessary restrictions?
- Does the individual have any conditions that may affect ability to recover?
- Has the individual had any complications such as sepsis? If needed, is the individual in counseling with an appropriate mental health provider?

References

"Infections of the Skin and Underlying Tissues." The Merck Manual of Medical Information. Berkow, Robert, Mark Beers, and Andrew Fletcher, eds. New York: Pocket Books, 1997. 932-935.

Furste, Wesley, and Auausto Aauirre. "Anaerobic and Necrotizing Infections." Griffith's 5-minute Clinical Consult. Dambro, Mark, ed. Philadelphia: Lippincott, Williams & Wilkins, 2000. 38-39.

Diabetic Glomerulosclerosis
Other names / synonyms: Diabetic Kidney Disease, Diabetic Nephropathy
250.4

Definition

Diabetic glomerulosclerosis describes the scarring or hardening of tiny arteries in the kidney (glomeruli) seen in diabetics. The glomeruli normally filter the blood, allowing excess water and waste to pass into the urine while keeping nutrients in the blood. Diabetic glomerulosclerosis interferes with this filtering mechanism, allowing a protein (albumin) to spill into the urine (albuminuria). The loss of albumin in the urine results in decreased levels in the blood. The result is swelling due to fluid retention (edema).

The exact cause of diabetic glomerulosclerosis is unknown. This disease develops slowly, so it is more common in those who have had diabetes for many years. Other risk factors include poor control of blood glucose levels, sedentary lifestyle, excessive protein intake, poor diet, and high blood pressure (hypertension).

This disease affects about 4 out of every 10,000 individuals. About 40% of those with insulin-dependent diabetes (20% of for non-insulin-dependent diabetes) will develop diabetic glomerulosclerosis.

Diagnosis

History: The individual usually has a history of diabetes for 10 or more years. The individual may complain of swelling of the face, hands, and feet (edema); headaches, dizziness, fatigue, loss of appetite, nausea, vomiting, a general ill-feeling (malaise), frequent hiccups, generalized itching (pruritus), and/or shortness of breath. Individuals may also report a foamy appearance of the urine, unintentional weight gain (from fluid retention) or unintended weight loss (due to loss of body mass).

Physical exam: The exam may reveal high blood pressure (hypertension) and swelling; the earliest sign is high blood pressure. When listening to the lungs, the physician may hear a moist crackling sound indicating fluid in the lungs. An eye exam may show signs of a disease of the part back of the eye (retinopathy).

Tests: A urine test will reveal an increased protein level. The physician may order a blood chemistry panel, which measures the amount of albumin, urea, creatinine, and uric acid to determine kidney function. In some cases, a kidney biopsy may be indicated to confirm the diagnosis and identify the extent of damage. Other tests may include a lipid profile to measure the amount of triglycerides and cholesterol levels; 24-hour urinalysis to measure the amount of albumin, uric acid, urea, and creatinine excreted by the kidneys; a para-amino hippuric acid excretion test to measure the flow of plasma in the kidney; and a radionucleotide renal imaging test to view and assess the function and structural components of the kidneys.

Treatment

Diabetic glomerulosclerosis is a progressive disease. The goal of treatment is to slow progression and control complications. Treatment should include control of hypertension with antihypertensive medication, a low protein, low cholesterol and low fat diet, and strict control of blood glucose level. Advanced disease may require dialysis or transplant (kidney failure).

Prognosis

Diabetic glomerulosclerosis is a progressive disease. Because there are no symptoms for several years, kidney function is usually already impaired by the time the diagnosis is made. The individual's compliance with treatment may delay progression to kidney failure and the need for dialysis or transplant. If dialysis or transplant is necessary, death from complications of these procedures occurs twice as often in diabetics than in non-diabetic individuals undergoing the same procedures.

Differential Diagnosis

Differential diagnosis might include pyelonephritis, nephrosclerosis, nephropathy, or nephrotoxicity.

Specialists

- Endocrinologist
- Nephrologist
- Urologist

Work Restrictions / Accommodations

Those with physically demanding positions may require reassignment to a position requiring less physical activity. Individuals with severe fatigue may require a shorter work day and/or a shorter work week. Complicated cases may require flexible hours to accommodate dialysis.

Complementary and Alternative Therapies

Content is intended for awareness only. Treatments may or may not be effective. Scientific evidence may be lacking and some substances have potentially toxic effects. Dr. Presley Reed and the editors do not endorse the use of these therapies in the absence of consultation with a licensed medical professional.

Chinese herbal medicines - Jiawei Shenqi Dihuang Tang, Tang Shen Ning, and Tangshenkang may decrease protein in the urine (proteinuria) and improve kidney function.

Comorbid Conditions

Obesity and infectious disease may lengthen disability.

Complications

Complications include hypertension, hypoglycemia, stroke, infection, cardiac ischemia, and kidney failure. Peripheral edema can be debilitating, and may increase the risk of diabetic foot ulcers in individuals whose feet are already compromised.

Factors Influencing Duration

Factors include the individual's compliance with diabetic care, the level of kidney function at the time of diagnosis, or the presence of urinary tract infection.

Length of Disability

Early stages of diabetic glomerulosclerosis are not associated with disability. As the disease progresses, the period of disability will be extended. Disability may be permanent.

Duration in Days

Job Classification	Minimum	Optimum	Maximum
Sedentary work	3	14	21
Light work	3	14	21
Medium work	3	14	28
Heavy work	7	14	63
Very Heavy work	10	14	63

Failure to Recover

If an individual fails to recover within the maximum duration expectancy period, the reader may wish to reference the following questions to assist in better understanding the specifics of an individual's medical case.

Regarding diagnosis:

- Does the individual have inadequate control of their blood glucose levels?
- Do they have a sedentary lifestyle? Excessive protein intake? Poor diet?
- Does the individual have hypertension?
- How long has the individual had diabetes?
- Does the individual complain of edema of the face, hands, and feet?
- Do they have headaches, dizziness, fatigue, loss of appetite, nausea or vomiting?
- Do they complain of malaise, frequent hiccups, pruritus, and/or shortness of breath?
- Does the individual report a foamy appearance of the urine?
- Do they have unintentional weight gain or loss?
- On exam does the individual have hypertension? Edema? Fluid in the lungs? Retinopathy?
- Has the individual had complete blood chemistry testing and urinalysis? 24 hour urine?
- Was a kidney biopsy done? IVP? Para-amino hippuric acid excretion test?
- Have conditions with similar symptoms been ruled out?

Regarding treatment:

- Is the individual compliant with the physician's instructions, particularly with regard to control of blood pressure and control of blood sugar and diet?
- Is dialysis required? Has a transplant been considered?

Regarding prognosis:

- Is the individual's employer able to accommodate any necessary restrictions?
- Does the individual have any conditions That may affect their ability to recover?
- Does the individual have any complications such as hypertension, hypoglycemia, stroke, infection, cardiac ischemia or kidney failure?

References

Glomerular Diseases. National Kidney and Urologic Diseases Information Clearinghouse. 24 Jun 1999. 9 Nov 2000 <http://www.niddk.nih.gov/health/kidney/pubs/glomer/glomer.htm>.

Chen, Y., L. Wei, and M. Ma. "Effect of Jiawei Shenqi Dihuang Tang on the Content of Urinary Protein in Patients with Diabetic Nephropathy." Journal of Traditional Chinese Medicine 17 3 (1997): 184-186.

Gao, Y., R. Lu, R, and X. Wang. "A Clinical Trial of Tang Shen Ning for Treatment of Diabetic Nephropathy." Journal of Traditional Chinese Medicine 18 4 (1998): 247-252.

Sang, Y., X.B. Wang, and Q. Han. "Effects of Tangshenkang Capsule on Diabetic Nephropathy." Chung Kuo Chung Hsi I Chieh Ho Tsa Chih 16 7 (1996): 398-401.

Diabetic Neuropathy
Other names / synonyms: Diabetic Nerve Damage
250.6, 357.2

Definition

Diabetic neuropathy is a complication of the disease diabetes mellitus. Diabetic neuropathy is defined as nerve damage (neuropathy) resulting from decreased blood flow and elevated blood sugar levels as seen in diabetic individuals. There are two basic types of neuropathy, peripheral and autonomic, and are differentiated by the nerves affected.

Peripheral neuropathy affects the nerves of the head and spinal column as well as the nerves that branch out from the spinal column. This type of neuropathy tends to develop in stages. It begins with a tingling sensation that, over time, develops to pain and eventually to a loss of pain sensation.

Autonomic neuropathy involves nerves that control the involuntary movement of vital organs such as the heart, the digestive system, the glands, etc. Autonomic neuropathy is characterized by low blood pressure (hypotension), diarrhea, constipation, sexual impotence, vision problems, eye pain, and other symptoms.

Diabetic neuropathy affects approximately 6 out of every 10,000 individuals. It is more likely to develop in individuals with poorly controlled blood sugar levels. On average, diabetic neuropathy occurs 10-20 years after diabetes has been diagnosed, although some diabetics will never develop neuropathy, and others will develop this condition relatively early.

Diagnosis

History: The individual will have a history of diabetes mellitus, usually for over 10 years. Symptoms will vary depending on the nerves affected, and will develop gradually over a period of years. Common complaints include tingling, pain, decreased sensation or loss of sensation, particularly in the feet or hands. Drooping of the eyelid, mouth, or face may also occur as nerves to the facial muscles are damaged. If the autonomic nerves are affected, diarrhea, constipation, loss of bladder control (urinary incontinence), sexual impotence, and difficulty swallowing may be reported. Additional symptoms include vision changes, dizziness (particularly with position changes), weakness, speech impairment, and involuntary muscle contractions. Pain may also cause difficulty sleeping.

Physical exam: The exam may reveal a decreased skin temperature, a reddish-blue discoloration of the hands, lower legs, and feet with loss of skin color to the tissues when the arm or leg is elevated (vascular insufficiency). There may be a decrease or absence of ankle reflexes, and the individual may not be able to distinguish sharp from dull or hot from cold when applied to the skin (2-point discrimination). The most subtle finding is the decrease of light touch and pain sensation in the toes. The physician may also find a decrease or absence of pulses or a drop in blood pressure with positional changes from lying or sitting to standing (postural hypotension). The individual's nails may be very thick and have ridges with dryness and cracks in the skin.

Tests: A blood glucose test will confirm diabetic neuropathy typically, but a screen for other causes of neuropathy may be considered. Tests for delayed gastric emptying are sometimes useful. Anscore testing, which measures autonomic neuropathy of the heart, has recently been developed and is used to diagnose diabetic neuropathy.

Treatment

Diabetic neuropathy is a progressive disease. Treatment is aimed at alleviating symptoms. Control of the underlying diabetes is important. Medications may be prescribed (as needed) to control pain (analgesics, antidepressants and/or anticonvulsants), insomnia (sedatives, antidepressants), anxiety (sedatives, antidepressants), and muscle cramps (muscle relaxants).

Prognosis

The process of diabetic neuropathy is not well understood. The disease is progressive. If untreated or poorly treated (those who do not adequately control their blood sugar), the outcome is poor. If caught early and treated adequately, progression can be stopped or slowed, making for a better outcome. Treatment of pain and control of blood sugar levels are effective in stopping or slowing the progression. In some individuals, medication may restore some degree of nerve function; however, substantial reversal of nerve damage is rare.

Differential Diagnosis

Other possibilities could include atherosclerosis, phlebitis, diseases of immune system, nutritional abnormalities, B_{12} deficiency, thyroid disease, and systemic infectious diseases (such as Guillain Barré syndrome, infectious mononucleosis, and syphilis).

Specialists

- Neurologist
- Ophthalmologist
- Podiatrist

Work Restrictions / Accommodations

Individuals should avoid extreme temperature variations or moist/wet areas. Extended/prolonged standing could increase complications, so reassignment to a more sedentary position may be required. The use of gloves and appropriate footwear (safety shoes) may be necessary. Individual should also avoid direct skin exposure to chemicals. Individuals who have lost sensation to a particular body part may need to be reassigned depending on their job requirements. For example, a chef who could not feel pain in his hand would be prone to burns.

Complementary and Alternative Therapies

Content is intended for awareness only. Treatments may or may not be effective. Scientific evidence may be lacking and some substances have potentially toxic effects. Dr. Presley Reed and the editors do not endorse the use of these therapies in the absence of consultation with a licensed medical professional.

Acupuncture -	May reduce the need for pain relief medication (analgesics). Its mechanism of action remains speculative.
Goshajinkigan -	An herbal medicine that may relieve subjective symptoms and improve vibration sensation. Its mechanism of action is not known.
Intravenous alpha-lipoic acid -	Said to have a positive influence on impaired neurovascular reflex arc causing a decrease in pain symptoms.
Capsaicin -	The pungent ingredient in red peppers is believed to desensitize sensory neurons reducing the need for pain relief medication (analgesics).

Comorbid Conditions

Vascular disease may increase the risk of complications, particularly following injury.

Complications

Complications of diabetic neuropathy may include bladder infections or muscle wasting (diabetic amyotrophy). In addition, individuals with this condition are at increased risk of traumatic injury including burns, infection, or gangrene. Charcot joint disease is a complication resulting in fractures and collapsing bones in the feet, and occurs in individuals with good vascular supply and neuropathy.

Factors Influencing Duration

Factors include the severity of infection, the degree to which the diabetes is controlled, and if there is amputation of an arm or leg. Length of disability may be influenced by loss of muscular coordination, sensory loss, and accidental self-injury.

Length of Disability

Disability depends on the extent of nerve damage, the nerves affected, the presence of complications, and the individual's job requirements. Disability may be permanent. Contact physician for more specific information.

Failure to Recover

If an individual fails to recover within the maximum duration expectancy period, the reader may wish to reference the following questions to assist in better understanding the specifics of an individual's medical case.

Regarding diagnosis:

- How long has the individual had diabetes?
- Does the individual have peripheral or autonomic neuropathy?
- Does the individual complain of a tingling, pain, decreased sensation or loss of sensation, particularly in the feet or hands?
- Does the individual have hypotension, drooping of the eyelid, mouth, or face?
- Does the individual have diarrhea, constipation, urinary incontinence, sexual impotence, difficulty swallowing, vision changes, dizziness (particularly with position changes), weakness, speech impairment, and involuntary muscle contractions?
- Does pain cause difficulty sleeping?
- On exam does the individual have decreased skin temperature, a reddish-blue discoloration of the hands, lower legs, and feet with vascular insufficiency? Is there a decrease or absence of ankle reflexes? Is the individual able to distinguish sharp from dull or hot from cold? Is there an absence of pulses? Postural hypotension? Abnormal nails and skin?
- Have conditions with similar symptoms been ruled out?

Regarding treatment:

- Is the individual receiving treatment that is aimed at alleviating symptoms?
- Does the individual have control of the underlying diabetes?
- If needed have medications been prescribed to control pain, insomnia, anxiety, and muscle cramps?

Regarding prognosis:

- Is the individual's employer able to accommodate any necessary restrictions?
- Does the individual have any conditions that may affect their ability to recover?
- Does the individual have any complications such as bladder infections, diabetic amyotrophy, and individuals with this condition are at increased risk of traumatic injury including burns, infection, or gangrene?

References

Diabetic neuropathy. Thrive Online. 2000. 09 Nov 2000 <http://www.thriveonline.oxygen.com/medical/library/article/000693.html>.

Abuaisha, B.B., J.B. Costanzi, and A.J. Boulton. "Acupuncture for Treatment of Chronic Painful Peripheral Diabetic Neuropathy: A Long-term Study." Diabetes Research and Clinical Practice 39 2 (1998): 115-121.

Fusco, B.M., and M. Giacovazzo. "Peppers and Pain. The Promise of Capsaicin." Drugs 53 6 (1997): 909-914.

Haak, E.S., K.H. Usadel, and M. Kohleisen. "The Effect of Alpha-lipoic Acid on the Neurovascular Reflex Arc in Patients with Diabetic Neuropathy Assessed by Capillary Microscopy." Microvasc Res 58 1 (1999): 28-34.

Hamza, M.A., P.F. White, and W.F. Craig. "Percutaneous Electrical Stimulation: A Novel Analgesic Therapy for Diabetic Neuropathic Pain." Diabetes Care 23 3 (2000): 365-370.

Tawata, M., A. Kurihara, and K. Nitta. "The Effects of Goshajinkigan, a Herbal Medicine, on Subjective Symptoms and Vibratory Threshold in Patients with Diabetic Neuropathy." Diabetes Research and Clinical Practice 26 2 (1994): 121-128.

Diabetic Retinopathy

Other names / synonyms: Background Retinopathy, Malignant Retinopathy, Nonproliferative Retinopathy, Proliferative Retinopathy, Simple Retinopathy

250.5, 362.0

Definition

Diabetic retinopathy refers to progressive damage to the blood vessels in the back part of the eye (retina) caused by high blood sugar levels (hyperglycemia). The two types of diabetic retinopathy are nonproliferative and proliferative.

Nonproliferative or background retinopathy occurs early in the course of the disease. Small capillaries in the retina may weaken or break, leaking blood that then forms small, dot-like bleeding (hemorrhages). The leaking and fluid accumulation in the macular portion of the retina often causes swelling (macular edema) and may blur, decrease, or distort vision.

As diabetic retinopathy progresses, new blood vessels develop where they don't belong (neovascularization). This stage is called proliferative diabetic retinopathy. These new, weaker vessels hemorrhage more easily into the jelly-like substance that fills the eye (vitreous humor). They can also bleed into the colored part of the eye (iris) or the filtering mechanism of the eye (trabecular meshwork). The abnormal blood vessel growth may cause spots (floaters), scarring, retinal detachment, or glaucoma.

Diabetic retinopathy occurs most often in individuals with diabetes mellitus. The effects of hyperglycemia add up over time (cumulative). This puts individuals who have had diabetes mellitus for many years at a higher risk for developing diabetic retinopathy. In fact, about 80% of individuals who have had diabetes mellitus for at least 15 years have some damage to the retinal blood vessels. Poor blood sugar control (glycemia), pregnancy, kidney complications, high blood pressure (hypertension), and smoking all increase the risk of developing diabetic retinopathy.

Diabetic retinopathy is the leading cause of blindness in individuals from the ages of 20 to 74, with 12,000 to 24,000 Americans losing their sight each year.

Diagnosis

History: The individual has a history of diabetes. The individual may report areas of vision that are blocked (by floaters or flashes), blurred or cloudy vision, the inability to see fine details, or a sudden total loss of vision. Other possible symptoms include distorted vision or pain due to pressure behind the eyes. Individuals with nonproliferative diabetic retinopathy may report only a decrease in visual acuity. Early on, during the preventable stage, there may be no symptoms.

Physical exam: An eye exam using an instrument that allows the eye doctor to view the retina (ophthalmoscope) may reveal tiny ballooned-out areas of blood vessels (microaneurysms), dot hemorrhages, and/or white to yellow fat (lipid) deposits (hard exudates) on the retina. Swelling of the area of the retina that absorbs light and relates to color vision (macula) may be noted. In proliferative diabetic retinopathy, neovascularization, hemorrhage, scarring, and physical detachment of the retina from the eye wall may be noted. A standard vision test (reading letters from an eye chart) may reveal vision loss. In advanced cases, eye pressure may be elevated.

Tests: Tests may include ocular ultrasound (ultrasonography), rapid sequence of photographs that visualize the passage of a dye through the blood vessels of the eye (fluorescein angiography), and measuring eye pressure (glaucoma testing).

Treatment

Medication is not effective against diabetic retinopathy.

The standard treatment for proliferative diabetic retinopathy is laser surgery (laser pan retinal photocoagulation or PRP). While it can create blind spots in the peripheral vision, this procedure reduces the risk of severe vision loss by up to 90%. During PRP, the laser is used to seal retinal tears, seal off leaking blood vessels, or destroy oxygen-deprived retinal tissue outside the area of central vision. The laser can also be aimed along the sides of the retina to prevent growth of abnormal new vessels or seal the retina to the wall of the eye and prevent retinal detachment.

In some cases, a procedure called cryoretinopexy can be performed instead of laser photocoagulation. The purpose is the same but instead of a laser, extreme cold is used to freeze the areas of abnormal vessel growth.

Advanced cases of proliferative diabetic retinopathy may also be treated by a microsurgical procedure to remove the bloody, fibrous, vitreous humor (vitrectomy). In order to maintain the shape of the eyeball, the removed vitreous humor is then replaced with either a thick, gel-like substance similar to the natural vitreous humor or a clear salt solution (saline). If the retina has become detached, it can be surgically reattached to the back of the eye.

Prognosis

When diabetic retinopathy is diagnosed and monitored closely from the early stages, the outlook is good. Regular examination by an ophthalmologist increases the likelihood of catching complications early and treating them promptly, thereby improving the prognosis. The presence of white spots on the retina (cotton wool spots) is an ominous sign and usually indicates rapidly progressing retinopathy. If treatment is delayed, proliferative diabetic retinopathy can result in blindness.

Laser photocoagulation is approximately 90% effective in reducing the risk of serious vision loss. Cryoretinopexy is also effective but is associated with pain from the freezing process and has a higher incidence of complications such as inflammation.

Vitrectomy is generally reserved for advanced cases of proliferative diabetic retinopathy. The outcome depends on the extent of damage or vision loss prior to the procedure. If preoperative vision loss was due primarily to a cloudy vitreous, the procedure will be more successful than if significant damage to the retina has occurred.

Vision loss already occurring cannot always be restored.

Differential Diagnosis

Other conditions that produce symptoms similar to diabetic retinopathy include radiation retinopathy, hypertensive retinopathy, and retinal vitreous obstruction.

Specialists

- Ophthalmologist

Work Restrictions / Accommodations

Any restrictions or accommodations must be tailored to the degree of visual impairment. Larger computer screens may be helpful to individuals with only mild to moderately blurred vision. Individuals whose jobs require close work, fine detail, and driving or operating heavy machinery may require alternative work assignments.

Comorbid Conditions

Obesity, kidney (renal) failure, coronary artery disease, depression and other psychiatric disorders, and infectious disease may lengthen disability.

Complications

Complications include separation of the retina from the back of the eye (detached retina), glaucoma, and/or blindness.

Factors Influencing Duration

Regular eye exams with early detection and surgical intervention can slow or stop progression of diabetic retinopathy. Severity of the disease significantly impacts the duration of disability. If visual impairment occurs, disability may be permanent.

Length of Disability

Disability must be determined on a case-by-case basis. The length of disability varies with the individual's job requirements. For example, if the job requires driving and the individual cannot be reassigned to a non driving position, disability may be permanent. Conversely, individuals whose jobs do not require acute vision may have very short or no disability.

Failure to Recover

If an individual fails to recover within the maximum duration expectancy period, the reader may wish to reference the following questions to assist in better understanding the specifics of an individual's medical case.

Regarding diagnosis:

- How long has the individual had diabetes?
- Does the individual also have kidney complications, hypertension, or poor blood sugar control? Is the individual pregnant or a smoker?
- Does the individual report areas of vision that are blocked by floaters or flashes, blurred or cloudy vision, the inability to see fine details, or a sudden total loss of vision?
- Does the individual have pain behind the eyes?
- On exam did the eye doctor find microaneurysms, dot hemorrhages, and/or lipid deposits on the retina?
- Is there swelling of the macula?
- Did the physician find neovascularization, hemorrhage, scarring, or retinal detachment?
- Did the individual have a visual acuity test?
- Did the individual have an ultrasound, fluorescein angiography, and glaucoma testing?
- Have conditions with similar symptoms been ruled out?

Regarding treatment:

- Has the individual been treated with laser surgery? Cryoretinopexy?
- Did it become necessary to perform a vitrectomy? Surgically reattach the retina?

Regarding prognosis:

- Is the individual's employer able to accommodate any necessary restrictions?
- Does the individual have any conditions that may affect ability to recover?
- Has the individual had any complications such as detached retina, glaucoma, and/or blindness?

References

Diabetic Retinopathy. Harvard Medical School. 12 Jan 2001. 24 Feb 2001 <http://www.intelihealth.com/IH/ihtIH?d=dmtContent&c=233217&p=~br,IHW|~st,331|~r,WSIHW000|~b,*|>.

Allinson, Richard. "Diabetic Retinopathy." Griffith's 5-minute Clinical Consult. Dambro, Mark, ed. Philadelphia: Lippincott, Williams & Wilkins, 2000. 942-943.

Diarrhea

Other names / synonyms: Acute Diarrheal Illness, Acute Enteritis, Dysentery, Gastroenteritis, The Runs
558.9, 787.9

Definition

Diarrhea is an increase in the fluidity, frequency, and/or volume of bowel movements as compared to the usual pattern for a particular individual. Diarrhea is a symptom of an underlying condition and may be acute or chronic.

In normal bowel activity, the large intestine (colon) absorbs much of the water from the liquid food residues that pass through it, resulting in semisolid feces. Diarrhea results when the intestinal contents pass through the colon too quickly or when an inflamed small intestine secrets fluid back into the fecal material.

The cause of diarrhea in most cases is unknown. Many individuals contract diarrhea through infections (bacterial, parasitic, viral) that usually occur after the ingestion of contaminated food or water. Infections may also be transmitted individual-to-individual through contaminated hands or objects or in some cases through viral droplet infection. Diarrhea may also be caused by anxiety, failure to absorb certain foods, and drugs (including some antibiotics) that interfere with the harmless bacteria normally found in the intestines. Ingestion of magnesium laxatives or antacids, immune disorders such as Crohn's disease and ulcerative colitis, hormone abnormalities, and cancer of the large intestine may result in diarrhea. Diarrhea may accompany disease of small areas of the colon (diverticula), irritable bowel syndrome, fecal impaction, lack of blood and oxygen to portions of the intestines following radiation therapy, and with certain surgical procedures (stomach, small intestine segment). Diarrhea may also be associated with infectious processes outside the gastrointestinal tract such as pneumonia, urinary tract infection, and pelvic inflammatory disease.

Diarrhea is one of the most common illnesses in all age groups and is second only to the common cold as a cause of lost days of work. It is estimated that almost 100 million cases of acute diarrhea occur per year in adults in the US. Adults have about one bout with diarrhea a year. Less than 10% of cases of diarrhea are brought to the attention of a doctor because most individuals use home care effectively. Worldwide, diarrhea and dysentery (diarrhea that contains blood, pus, or mucus) are common disorders in third-world countries. In industrialized nations, the occurrence of diarrhea mirrors the US experience.

Diagnosis

History: Symptoms may include bowel movements that are increased in fluidity, frequency, or volume compared to the individual's usual pattern. Blood, secretions (mucus), or pus may be present in the stool when damage has occurred to the mucous lining of the intestinal tract. Other symptoms often associated with diarrhea include nausea, vomiting, and fever. Individuals may report family or friends with diarrhea or a history of recent travel.

Physical exam: The exam is usually normal although abdominal tenderness may be present. If diarrhea has occurred for a while, dehydration may be evident with signs of dry mouth, decreased blood pressure, weakness, lethargy, or confusion. Individual may have increased skin pigmentation or inflammation of the tongue (glossitis).

Tests: In most cases of acute diarrhea, laboratory investigation is unnecessary, unrevealing, and does not affect treatment or outcome. Microscopic examination of the stool for white blood cells (leukocytes) distinguishes noninflammatory from inflammatory diarrhea. If leukocytes are present, a stool culture is done to identify the infectious agent. If diarrhea persists for more than 10 days, examinations are done on three consecutive stools to look for eggs (ova) or parasites.

In cases of chronic diarrhea, additional tests may include 24-hour stool collection for weight and quantitative fecal fat to identify a malabsorption process, a stool laxative screen to rule out laxative abuse, and a stool osmolality to rule out lactase deficiency, laxative abuse, or malabsorption syndromes. Routine laboratory tests to rule out malabsorption, anemia, and inflammatory diseases include complete blood count (CBC), serum electrolytes, liver function tests, calcium, phosphorus, albumin, thyroid-stimulating hormone (TSH), total thyroxine (T4), beta-carotene, and prothrombin. In individuals with severe inflammation of the rectum or anus, direct visualization of the sigmoid colon and the entire colon via an instrument inserted into the rectum (sigmoidoscopy and colonoscopy) may be needed. Removal of a small sample of mucous membrane for microscopic analysis (biopsy) is warranted to distinguish infectious diarrhea from ulcerative colitis or ischemic colitis. X-ray studies of the digestive tract using barium to visualize the intestines are useful in detecting abnormal narrowing (strictures) or other anatomic abnormalities beyond the reach of the sigmoidoscope.

Specialists

- Gastroenterologist
- Internist
- Physiatrist

Treatment

Treatment is directed at the underlying cause of the diarrhea. Most cases of acute diarrhea do not require any treatment other than oral fluids (containing carbohydrates and electrolytes such as sports drinks) and temporary diet modification to exclude gluten or dairy products. Solid food should be avoided until diarrhea subsides. Antibiotic or antimicrobial therapy may be necessary when severe diarrhea is due to an infectious agent and to treat bacterial overgrowth. Antidiarrheal drugs may be used as a comfort measure. However, they should not be used in cases where diarrhea is caused by infection, as they may prolong the illness. In chronic diarrhea, hospitalization with intravenous fluid and electrolyte replacement may be required if dehydration is severe. Offending drugs should be discontinued, if possible.

Tumors are treated with surgery or chemotherapy. Pancreatic enzymes are used to treat pancreatic insufficiency. Bulk-forming agents are used in treating irritable bowel syndrome and disorders involving the anus or rectum. Fecal impaction may be resolved with the manual removal of the impaction. Antidiarrheal drugs should not be used when diarrhea is caused by an infection since they may prolong the illness.

Prognosis

In over 90% of cases, acute diarrhea is mild, self-limited, and responds within 5 days to rehydration therapy or antidiarrheal agents. Individuals with diarrhea caused by infectious agents recover with appropriate antibiotic therapy. Diarrhea resulting from other causes improves with treatment of the underlying condition. Individuals with diarrhea of probable immune cause may have chronic inflammation with bouts of diarrhea for years.

Most deaths from diarrhea occur in the elderly whose health may be put at risk from a moderate amount of dehydration.

Differential Diagnosis

No other conditions resemble diarrhea. A more advanced form of diarrhea is called dysentery and contains blood, pus, and mucus.

Work Restrictions / Accommodations

Leave of absence during the acute phase of the disease may be required.

Comorbid Conditions

Significant underlying medical conditions such as leukemia, lymphoma, sickle cell anemia, AIDS, or sepsis may lengthen disability. Inflammatory bowel disease contributes to the intensity of diarrhea, lengthens disability, and extends recovery.

Complications

The most common complications of diarrhea are dehydration and electrolyte imbalance.

Factors Influencing Duration

Length of disability may be influenced by the individual's age, severity of symptoms, and response to treatment.

Length of Disability

Duration depends on cause.

Duration in Days

Job Classification	Minimum	Optimum	Maximum
Any work	0	1	7

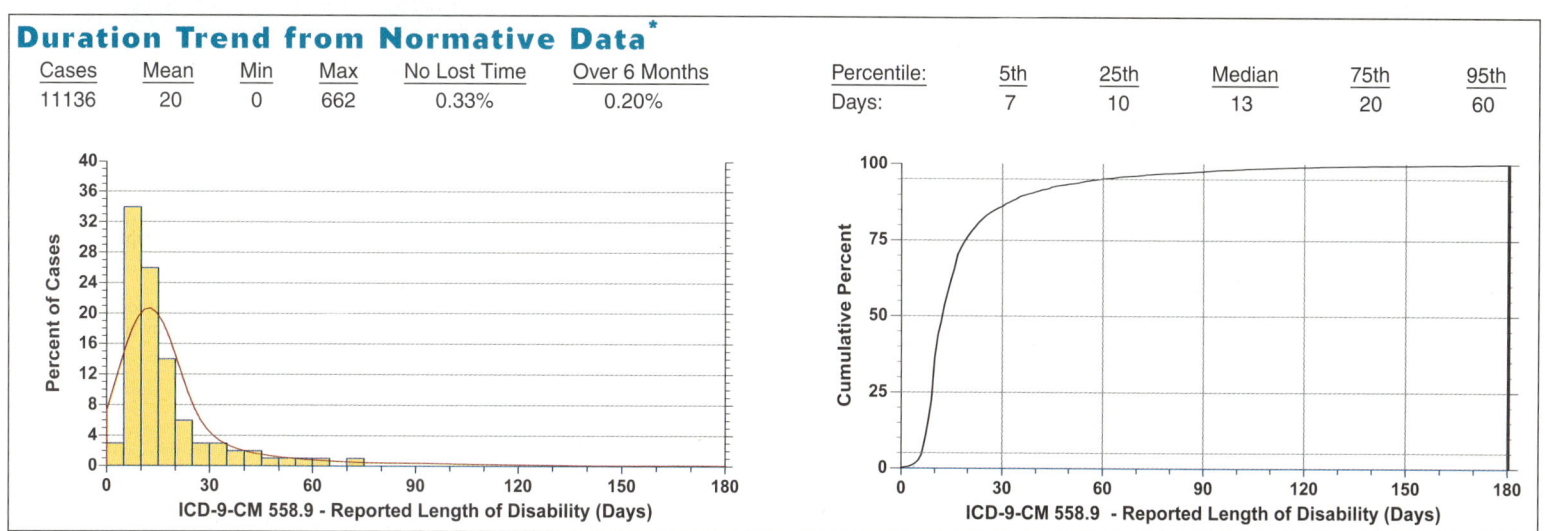

Duration Trend from Normative Data*

Cases	Mean	Min	Max	No Lost Time	Over 6 Months
11136	20	0	662	0.33%	0.20%

Percentile:	5th	25th	Median	75th	95th
Days:	7	10	13	20	60

ICD-9-CM 558.9 - Reported Length of Disability (Days)

* Differences may exist between the expected duration tables and the normative graphs. Duration tables provide expected recovery periods based on the type of work performed by the individual. The normative graphs reflect the actual observed experience of many individuals across the spectrum of physical conditions, in a variety of industries, and with varying levels of case management.

Failure to Recover

If an individual fails to recover within the maximum duration expectancy period, the reader may wish to reference the following questions to assist in better understanding the specifics of an individual's medical case.

Regarding diagnosis:

- Does individual complain of bowel movements that are increased in fluidity, frequency, or volume compared to usual pattern?
- Does blood, mucus, or pus occur in the stool? Does individual complain of nausea, vomiting, or fever?
- Do family or friends have diarrhea? Does individual have history of recent travel?
- Is individual anxious? Does individual fail to absorb certain foods? Taking drugs (including some antibiotics) that interfere with bacteria normally found in the intestines?
- Does individual use magnesium laxatives or antacids?
- Does individual have Crohn's disease, ulcerative colitis, hormone abnormalities, or cancer of the large intestine? Diverticula, irritable bowel syndrome, fecal impaction, lack of blood and oxygen to portions of the intestines following radiation therapy, or surgical procedures of the stomach or small intestine?
- Are infectious processes outside the gastrointestinal tract present such as pneumonia, urinary tract infection, or pelvic inflammatory disease?
- On exam, is the abdomen tender to palpation?
- Does individual have a dry mouth, decreased blood pressure, weakness, lethargy, or confusion, evidence of increased skin pigmentation, or glossitis?
- Was comprehensive stool testing done? CBC, serum electrolytes, liver function tests, calcium, phosphorus, albumin, TSH, T4, beta-carotene, and prothrombin testing?
- Was a sigmoidoscopy and/or colonoscopy performed? Biopsy? Barium enema?

Regarding treatment:

- What is the underlying condition? Is it being treated?
- Does individual use sports drinks to maintain hydration? Has individual modified diet?
- Are antidiarrheal drugs used?
- Was individual treated with antimicrobial therapy?
- Was hospitalization necessary?

Regarding prognosis:

- Can individual's employer accommodate any necessary restrictions?
- Does individual have any conditions that may affect ability to recover?
- Have any complications developed such as dehydration or electrolyte imbalance that may impact recovery?

Complementary and Alternative Therapies

Content is intended for awareness only. Treatments may or may not be effective. Scientific evidence may be lacking and some substances have potentially toxic effects. Dr. Presley Reed and the editors do not endorse the use of these therapies in the absence of consultation with a licensed medical professional.

Lactobacillus acidophilus -	May restore any beneficial intestinal bacteria lost during a bout with diarrhea.
Arsenium album -	May treat diarrhea from contaminated food (especially fruit) or water.
Chamomilla -	May relieve extreme irritability, peevishness, cramping, and sensitivity to pain that results from diarrhea.
Sulfur -	May treat form of diarrhea that drives the individual from bed in the early morning.
Aromatherapy -	May help treat diarrhea by massaging diluted essential oils (e.g., 1 part peppermint oil diluted with 20 parts almond oil) into the skin.
Meditation -	Reduces stress that may trigger diarrhea.
Nutritional therapy -	Nutritional therapy recognizes that diarrhea may be caused by eating too much of a particular food or by eating something the individual cannot tolerate.

References

Diarrhea. Knowledge Center. 2000. 17 Nov 2000 <http://www.knowledgecenters.versaware.com/notoc/getPage.asp?book=alternativemedicine&page=060000209.asp#060000210>.

Diarrhea. National Digestive Diseases Information Clearinghouse. 1999. 21 Nov 2000 <http://www.niddk.nih.gov/health/digest/pubs/diarrhea/diarrhea.htm>.

Karras, David, MD. "Diarrhea." eMedicine.com. 05 Nov 2000. 21 Nov 2000 <http://emedicine.com/aaem/topic155.htm>.

Toth, Peter P., MD, PhD. "Gastroenterology: Acute Diarrhea." University of Iowa Family Practice Handbook, 3rd ed. Iowa City: University of Iowa, 1999: 16. Nov 2000 <http://www.vh.org/Providers/ClinRef/FPHandbook/Chapter04/01-4.html>.

Dilation and Curettage

Other names / synonyms: D&C

69.0

Definition

Dilation and curettage (D&C) is a common minor surgical procedure in which the opening to a woman's uterus (cervix) is enlarged (dilated) and the lining of the uterus (endometrium) is scraped with a special instrument (curette). The scraping or removal of the endometrium causes no side effects, and the endometrium soon grows back to become a part of the normal menstrual cycle.

Reports issued by Centers for Disease Control and Prevention (CDC) for 1998 revealed 65,000 dilation curettage procedures performed on women inpatients in non-Federal, short-stay hospitals in the US. (It is important to point out that these reports excluded D&C procedures for termination of pregnancy, following delivery or abortion, or other D&C procedures.) Most of the 65,000 procedures (51,000) were performed on women between 15-44 years old. The procedure numbers (which were not statistically reliable) for the other groups showed that 7,000 were performed on women between 45-64 years old, and 7,000 on women 65 years old and older. Geographic distribution showed highest prevalence to be in the South region of the US (21,000) with the prevalence for the West, Midwest, and Northwest regions ranging between 14,000-15,000 procedures.

Reason for Procedure

The D&C is used to treat or evaluate dysfunctional uterine bleeding (DUB), which includes heavy periods (menorrhagia), bleeding between periods, bleeding during or after intercourse, or bleeding after menopause. By removing excessive uterine lining, D&C may prevent DUB, albeit sometimes only temporarily. D&C serves as a basis for testing and diagnosis of cancer of the uterus or other growths in the uterus, such as polyps and fibroid tumors. Testing procedures that may be employed with the D&C include ultrasonography, laparoscopy, and hysteroscopy.

D&C is used to remove the remaining tissue of an incomplete miscarriage, of an incomplete abortion, and of retained pregnancy tissue after a delivery, as well as to terminate a pregnancy (elective or therapeutic abortion).

Description

A D&C is performed with the individual in the same position that she assumes for a pelvic examination: lying on an examination table with legs apart and supported in stirrups. With the individual anesthetized (using local, general, or spinal anesthesia), the gynecologist begins the surgery by inserting a thin rod called a sound into the uterus to measure its depth. Next, a dilator is inserted and as the cervix stretches open (dilates), the gynecologist inserts larger and larger dilators of increasing thickness until an opening is large enough to begin the second phase of the surgery. In the second phase of the surgery, a spoon-shaped surgical scraping instrument (curette) is inserted into the uterus to scrape away the endometrium. The endometrium can also be removed by suction by inserting a hollow tube (catheter) that is connected to a vacuum pump through the cervix. Suction is applied to remove the retained tissue. The entire D&C procedure takes about 15 minutes. The individual is usually able to go home within 4-6 hours. However, if general or conscious sedation is used, she should arrange for someone to drive her home after the procedure.

Prognosis

The predicted outcome after a D&C procedure is good. After-effects are minimal. A few individuals may experience some bleeding and mild period-like cramping for a day or so following the procedure. Most individuals recover with no problems associated with the anesthesia or the procedure.

In general, D&Cs are successful in evaluating and treating abnormal uterine bleeding and in providing a diagnostic tool in addition to ultrasonography, hysteroscopy, and laparoscopy.

Specialists

- Gynecologist
- Primary Care Provider

Work Restrictions / Accommodations

Work restrictions or accommodations are generally not required following a D&C procedure. Usually, one day sick leave is all that is required, followed by a gradual return to strenuous job activities.

Comorbid Conditions

Comorbid conditions include heart, kidney, liver, or lung disorders, or medical complications.

Procedure Complications

As with any procedure performed under general anesthesia, possibilities exist for the individual to experience a reaction to the anesthesia and to have breathing problems. Other complications include perforation of the uterus, excessive bleeding (hemorrhage), infection, trauma to abdominal organs, and injury to the cervix. If the cervix is injured during the procedure, the cervix may not be able to retain a baby within the uterus (cervical incompetence) in future pregnancies, and may result in a spontaneous abortion (miscarriage) or premature birth.

Factors Influencing Duration

Length of disability may be influenced by the underlying reason for which the procedure was performed (e.g., menorrhagia, incomplete abortion, miscarriage, or testing and diagnosis) and the development of complications.

Length of Disability

There is almost never a disability period after a D&C procedure, unless complications develop. Most individuals who undergo a D&C are able to return to work or to resume previous activities within a day or so with only minor restrictions, such as refraining from strenuous exercise or driving on the day of the procedure.

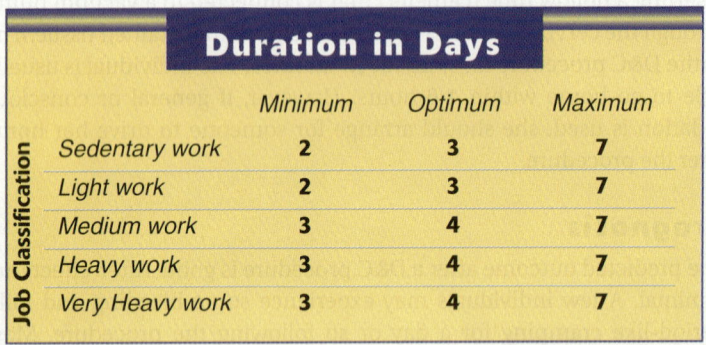

Job Classification	Minimum	Optimum	Maximum
Sedentary work	2	3	7
Light work	2	3	7
Medium work	3	4	7
Heavy work	3	4	7
Very Heavy work	3	4	7

Duration in Days

Notes

References

Dilation and Curettage (D & C). AudioHealth Library. 01 Jan 1996. 27 Sept 2000 <http://www.yourhealth.com/ahl/2156.html>.

Dilation and Curettage. Obstetrics and Gynecology Specialists, P.C. 01 Jan 2000. 27 Sept 2000 <http://www.obgyngroup.com/Medical%20Articles/surg_d100.htm>.

Menstrual Disorders. 1997-2000 Women's Health Interactive. 01 Jan 2000. 28 Sept 2000 <http://womens-health.com/health_center/gynecology/gyn_md_dc.html>.

National Hospital Discharge Survey: Annual Survey, 1998. U.S. Centers for Disease Control and Prevention. 01 Sep 2000. 30 Sept 2000 <http://www.cdc.gov/nchs/data/sr13_148.pdf>.

Owen, Philip. Dilation and Curettage (D & C). NetDoctor.co.uk . 01 Feb 2000. 26 Sept 2000 <http://www.netdoctor.co.uk/health_advice/facts/curettage.htm>.

Zaret, Barry L., MD, ed. Test Name - Dilation and Curettage (D & C). 27 Sept 2000 <http://webmd.lycos.com/content/asset/yale_lab_tests_test_name_dilation_and_curettage_d_amp_c.html>.

Dilation of Esophagus

Other names / synonyms: Bougie Dilation of Esophagus, Esophageal Expansion, Sound Dilation of Esophagus
42.92

Definition

Dilation of the esophagus is a procedure done to stretch the esophagus after it has become narrowed by disease. It involves the passage of a series of dilators down the esophagus, usually in several sessions.

The most common conditions treated with dilation include caustic injuries to the esophagus, narrowing of the esophagus due to esophageal cancer, difficulty swallowing (dysphagia), esophageal sphincter dysfunction, scleroderma, reflux esophagitis, and the inability of the muscles in the lower esophagus to relax (achalasia).

Other reasons for dilation include to remove thin membranes that typically occur in the mid or upper esophagus (esophageal webs), or to treat esophageal rings associated with a protrusion of the stomach upward into the chest cavity through the diaphragm (hiatal hernia).

Reason for Procedure

Esophageal dilation is used to stretch an esophagus when narrowing (strictures) caused by scar tissue, tumors, inflammation, or overactive musculature prevents normal swallowing.

In achalasia, the muscles in the lower esophagus are unable to relax. Dilation stretches and weakens these muscles so that normal swallowing can occur.

Esophageal cancer can compress the esophagus so that swallowing is difficult. Although esophageal cancer is usually treated with surgery, dilation may provide some relief.

Caustic injuries to the esophagus are the result of ingestion of corrosive substances (acids, lye, strong bases, industrial chemicals, etc.). Reflux esophagitis is a kind of caustic injury caused by the strong stomach acids coming up into the esophagus. After recovery from the initial injury, scar tissue often forms that can cause narrowing, or strictures, of the esophagus. Careful dilation can relieve this narrowing.

Some people have esophageal sphincter dysfunction, a tightening of the lower esophageal sphincter that does not allow the easy passage of food. This, too, can be treated with repeated dilations.

Scleroderma is a rare condition that affects almost all the tissues in the body, especially the skin. The esophagus can become narrowed in this condition due to thickening. Dilation is often used to open the esophagus in this condition.

Other reasons for dilation include the removal of thin membranes that typically occur in the mid or upper esophagus (esophageal webs), or the treatment of esophageal rings associated with a hiatal hernia (protrusion of the stomach upward into the chest cavity through the diaphragm).

Description

Esophageal dilation can be an outpatient procedure. The individual is usually given a sedative to decrease the discomfort of the procedure. Prior to the dilation, the individual must not eat for at least 8 hours. Under sedation, a fine, flexible viewing tube (endoscope) is passed through the mouth and down the esophagus, allowing visualization of the area to be stretched. Sometimes the individual swallows a length of thread that becomes anchored in the intestine. A metal guide is then passed down over the string.

Different types of dilators are available. The most common type involves the use of cylindrical rods with olive-shaped tips (bougies) of increasing size that are passed down over the guide wire, stretching the narrowed area. Another method involves the use of a fine tube with a balloon at the tip (balloon catheter). Instead of a guide wire, the tube may be used alongside the endoscope, passed through the scope, or used alone, guided by fluoroscopy. When it reaches the narrowed area of the esophagus, the balloon is inflated and kept in position for 3 minutes. It is then deflated and withdrawn. The procedure may then be repeated with a larger balloon.

Prognosis

In most conditions in which stricture or narrowing is the major component, such as achalasia, caustic injuries, scleroderma, or sphincter dysfunction, repeated dilations are necessary over the course of 6 months to a year. Overall, good-to-excellent results are obtained in 70-80% of individuals.

Esophageal cancer is an extremely morbid condition best treated with surgical resection. If resection is not possible, dilations can be used to relieve the difficulty of swallowing. In end-stage esophageal cancer treated with palliative dilations, death is the ultimate result, although dilation can keep the individual comfortable.

Esophageal webs and esophageal rings are frequently completely treated with only a few dilations.

Specialists

- Gastroenterologist
- General Surgeon
- Internist
- Thoracic Surgeon

Work Restrictions / Accommodations

Work restrictions or accommodations are not usually associated with this procedure.

Comorbid Conditions

Any disease that would impair an individual's ability to heal would lengthen recovery. An example would be diabetes or an immune disorder.

Procedure Complications

The complications associated with esophageal dilation are few and rare, but can be quite serious. Perforation of the esophagus during dilation can cause conditions such as infection of the surrounding tissues (mediastinitis), of the lung spaces (empyema), or abdominal cavity (peritonitis). The conditions are serious and must be treated with hospitalization and antibiotics. Sometimes surgery is necessary to repair the perforation. Death may be the result.

Factors Influencing Duration

Factors include severity of the symptoms or complications related to the procedure. Most conditions treated with esophageal dilations will require repeated sessions of dilation.

Length of Disability

Duration in Days

Job Classification	Minimum	Optimum	Maximum
Any work	0	2	3

References

Pellegrini, Carlos, and Lawrence Way. "Esophagus and Diaphragm." Current Surgical Diagnosis and Treatment. Way, Lawrence, ed. Norwalk: Appleton & Lange, 1991. 400-429.

Schwartz, Seymour, MD. Principles of Surgery. New York: McGraw-Hill, 1999.

Disc Calcification

Other names / synonyms: Intervertebral Chondrocalcinosis
722.9, 722.90, 722.91, 722.92, 722.93

Definition

Disc calcification occurs when the intervertebral discs between the bones of the spine develop calcium deposits in the gelatin-like center (nucleus pulposus), in the outer ring (annulus), or in the cartilage plate near the disc (chondrocalcinosis). The deposits are a sign of degenerative changes in the structure of the disc and usually cause no symptoms. However, the calcium deposits may enlarge and multiply, eventually leading to a rigid, calcified area. The deposits appear on x-ray and are frequently found coincidentally during an examination for another problem.

The thoracolumbar spine is the most frequent site of disc calcification. Disc calcification is found on routine radiographs in approximately 4-6% of individuals without disc herniation as compared to approximately 70% of individuals with disc herniation.

Intervertebral disc calcification usually occurs in individuals at least 55 or older. Disc calcification occurs with the same frequency in males and females.

Diagnosis

History: Calcification is usually a marker that degeneration at that disc level is old. Often there are no symptoms to go along with the x-ray findings. If there is pain, there is no way to reliably determine if the pain relates to the calcified disc.

Physical exam: There are few findings on the physical exam. A decreased range of motion with back maneuvers may be present. A complete neurological, vascular, and musculoskeletal exam should be performed to rule out any underlying diseases.

Tests: The diagnosis is made from plain x-ray exams. Further testing is not indicated unless other diseases are suspected.

Treatment

Disc calcification is a chronic, degenerative process. If pain is present, it is usually asymptomatic. It is treated with conservative back pain measures including rest from activities that aggravate the symptoms, ice or heat and general conditioning or physical therapy to decrease pain and increase strength. Medications to relieve pain and muscle spasm may be used. Surgery is rarely needed, but in cases where calcification leads to a disc herniation, the disc may need to be removed (discectomy). It is very rare for a calcified disc to cause nerve root impingement.

Prognosis

Based on absence of symptoms, "recovery" is usually "not applicable." Conservative treatment may be effective in relieving symptoms of unrelated back pain. However, like arthritis, disc calcification is a degenerative process not cured by these treatment modalities.

Differential Diagnosis

Calcification may have occurred secondary to infection, herniated or ruptured disc, spinal stenosis, chondrocalcinosis hemachromatosis, and a rare metabolic defect called ochronosis.

Specialists

- Infectious Disease Physician
- Neurosurgeon
- Orthopedist
- Radiologist
- Rheumatologist

Work Restrictions / Accommodations

During periods of acute symptoms, overhead work, repetitive bending, unassisted carrying and lifting, and prolonged sitting or standing may need to be restricted or eliminated. Depending on the progression of the disease and response to treatment, permanent reductions in physical workload may be required on an individual basis. Education for proper lifting of heavy objects is also important in the rehabilitation process to prepare the individual for returning to work.

Comorbid Conditions

Comorbid conditions that could affect recovery include obesity, herniated disc(s), and congenital diseases or anomalies of the spine and back. Chondrocalcinosis, if present, can affect multiple joints.

Complications

Although not common, the disc may eventually rupture (herniate) into the spinal canal causing pressure on the spinal cord or a nerve root. Spinal stenosis, infection, fractures, or inflammatory disease occurring at the same time require additional treatment.

Factors Influencing Duration

Length of disability may be influenced by the severity of the symptoms or if symptoms are aggravated by certain activities, the number of discs affected, the response to treatment, and any complications.

Length of Disability

Degenerative disc calcification may indicate that disc degeneration has progressed to the point that very heavy work is no longer reasonable.

Duration in Days

Job Classification	Minimum	Optimum	Maximum
Sedentary work	0	7	14
Light work	0	7	21
Medium work	0	14	42
Heavy work	0	42	84
Very Heavy work	0	56	91

Failure to Recover

If an individual fails to recover within the maximum duration expectancy period, the reader may wish to reference the following questions to assist in better understanding the specifics of an individual's medical case.

Regarding diagnosis:

- Has diagnosis of disc calcification been confirmed by x-ray?
- What are the symptoms experienced by the individual and how severe are they? Back stiffness or back pain? Decreased back motion, particularly rotation? Pain upon rotation?
- Has calcification led to disc herniation?

Regarding treatment:

- Were symptoms treated with conservative back pain measures?
- If disc herniation is present, does the disc need to be surgically removed (discectomy)?

Regarding prognosis:

- Is the individual experiencing residual pain or stiffness?
- What is the impact upon work requirements?
- Would referral to a chronic pain control program be beneficial?
- Is the individual aware the disc calcification is a chronic, degenerative process and is not cured by treatment?

References

Approaches to Differential Diagnosis in Musculoskeletal Imaging. University of Washington. 1994. 13 Oct 2000 <http://www.rad.washington.edu/mskbook/axialarthritis.html>.

Torticollis Caused by Intervertebral Disc Calcification. University of Delaware. 21 Feb 1996. 3 Oct 2000 <http://gait.aidi.udel.edu/res695/homepage/pd_ortho/educate/clincase/tort.htm>.

Bogduk, N., et al. Clinical Anatomy of the Lumbar Spine. Singapore: Longman Singapore Publishers, 1991.

Kessler, R.M. Management of Common Musculoskeletal Disorders: Physical Therapy Principles and Methods. Philadelphia: J.B. Lippincott Co, 1990.

Discectomy

Other names / synonyms: Excision of Intervertebral Disc
80.51, 80.59

Definition

A discectomy is the removal of herniated disc material in the spine, either by a direct incision over the affected vertebra and underlying disc, or by arthroscopic techniques. The surgery includes looking at the area around the disc and spinal canal, as well, evaluating for other possible causes of pain.

Individuals who have failed to respond to several months of conservative treatment often require surgical intervention. Individuals with acute symptoms of perineal numbness, loss of bowel or bladder control (cauda equina), decreased sensation and motor control of the lower extremities, or intractable pain are candidates for emergency surgical treatment.

Reason for Procedure

A discectomy is performed for two reasons. The first and most common reason is to decrease arm or leg pain caused by pressure on a spinal nerve root from a protruding (herniated) disc. If conservative treatment has failed to improve symptoms, surgery is an option. The usual indication is radicular pain present for at least 2-3 months.

The second indication for discectomy is as an emergency treatment for cauda equina syndrome. It is caused by massive mid-line protrusion of a lumbar disc that may produce varying degrees of permanent paralysis of the legs and loss of control of the bowels and bladder.

Description

Removal of the protruding disc material can be accomplished by an open technique using an incision along the spine under general anesthesia. Bone may need to be removed (laminotomy) to provide better visualization and to increase space for the nerve root (foraminotomy). Disc material that has extruded into the canal and is pressing on the nerve root is removed.

Arthroscopic assisted techniques utilize an arthroscope to visualize the involved disc. Through another small incision, instruments are inserted to remove the protruding disc material. The arthroscope may be inserted to the spine from the back of the individual (posterior approach) or through the chest cavity (video-assisted trans-thoracic surgery).

Enzymatic digestion of the disc material with chymopapain is another technique, sometimes done as an outpatient procedure.

Prognosis

Relief of symptoms is often obtained from discectomy. Lumbar discectomy yields good to excellent results in 80-90% of "non-compensation" individuals and 60% of workers' compensation individuals. When the indications for surgery are marginal, conservative treatment of symptoms of herniated disc may be as successful as surgical intervention.

Surgical results decrease when the radicular pain has been present for more than 6 months. Likewise, when individuals receive multiple back surgeries, success decreases with each additional operation.

Specialists

- Neurosurgeon
- Occupational Medicine Physician
- Orthopedic Surgeon
- Physiatrist

Rehabilitation

Rehabilitation following a discectomy at any level of the spine may be indicated for optimal recovery. Physical modalities may be used briefly to decrease pain and thus Fascioletta active exercise.

Stabilization exercises improve the balance of strength in the muscles around the spine without putting the spine in positions that may aggravate pain. These are typically introduced quite early in rehabilitation after a discectomy. If movement is painful, the first few days may be limited to isometric exercises. Isometric resistance helps strengthen the muscles of the spine without moving through the range of motion. These exercises are helpful to improve stability around the level of the discectomy.

A program of aerobic exercise becomes important for the individual who has undergone a discectomy. Walking, swimming, or biking are popular and do not expose the spine to bouncing forces or place the spine in positions of strain. Walking is often the exercise of choice following discectomy and can usually begin early in the rehabilitation phase. In addition to the aerobic benefits, walking promotes the balanced strengthening of the front and back muscles of the spine (flexors and extensors).

As with any postoperative rehabilitation, modifications may need to be made by the physical therapist for those who have arthritis or other spine conditions. This will vary depending on the level of the discectomy and type of surgery that was performed.

Work Restrictions / Accommodations

As in all conditions affecting the spine, overhead work, repetitive bending, unassisted carrying and lifting, and prolonged sitting may need to be restricted or eliminated in the early period following surgery.

Comorbid Conditions

Obesity, degenerative spine conditions, inflammatory disease, nerve root damage, and lack of physical conditioning could impact recovery from disc surgery. Surgical results are generally poorer in smokers.

Procedure Complications

Complications may include infection, nerve or vessel damage, spinal fluid fistula, failure to improve symptoms of nerve compression, or aggravation of symptoms.

Factors Influencing Duration

Recovery from disc surgery may be slowed by psychological factors including secondary gain from the condition. The underlying cause of disc disease may not have been affected by the surgery, and symptoms may progress at different levels in the spine. Any limits to physical training/conditioning would slow recovery, including age, access to rehabilitation, and motivation.

Length of Disability

Length of disability depends on the extent of the surgical procedure. The number of discs involved and any concurrent procedures such as laminectomy and spinal fusion may affect the length of disability. Surgical technique may also influence recovery time.

In contrast to historic practice, many spine surgeons now allow individuals, who have not had prior spine surgery, to return to "full duty" as quickly as possible after surgery. Several large recently reported series describe the average time to return to full duty as less than 8 weeks. Individuals with one or more prior back surgeries are usually given permanent restrictions preventing heavy or very heavy work.

Cervical or thoracic spine.

Duration in Days

Job Classification	Minimum	Optimum	Maximum
Sedentary work	14	42	56
Light work	21	42	56
Medium work	42	56	84
Heavy work	91	119	182
Very Heavy work	119	119	182

Lumbar spine.

Duration in Days

Job Classification	Minimum	Optimum	Maximum
Sedentary work	1	14	42
Light work	7	21	56
Medium work	14	42	84
Heavy work	91	119	182
Very Heavy work	119	147	182

References

"Disorders of the Spine." Orthopedic Nursing. Maher, Ann, Susan Salmond, and Teresa Pellino, eds. Philadelphia: Harcourt Brace & Company, 1998. 581-614.

Adams, John Crawford. Outline of Orthopaedics, 9th ed. New York: Churchill Livingstone, Inc, 1981.

Kessler, R.M. Management of Common Musculoskeletal Disorders: Physical Therapy Principles and Methods. Philadelphia: J.B. Lippincott Co, 1990.

Torg, Joseph S., Joseph J. Vegso, and Elizabeth Torg. Rehabilitation of Athletic Injuries. An Atlas of Therapeutic Exercise. Chicago: Year Book Medical Publishers, Inc, 1987.

Dislocation

Other names / synonyms: Joint Displacement, Joint Separation

830, 832, 833, 834, 835, 837, 839.8, 839.9

Definition

A dislocation is the displacement or separation of bones in a joint from their normal position.

Dislocations can occur in any joint. Joint dislocations are usually the result of a traumatic injury. The bones forming the joint can also be forced apart by an unusually strong muscle contraction during a seizure, or a dislocation may be present at birth (congenital dislocation). The surrounding support structures of the joint capsule (membrane encasing the joint), ligament, and tendons may be loose (lax) from an injury or disease allowing the joint to slip out of position. Complete or frank dislocation means that the joint surfaces have lost complete contact with each other.

Dislocation is usually accompanied by tearing of the joint ligaments and damage to the joint capsule. It is the tearing of these support structures that makes the injury so painful. A dislocation can also damage or compress nerves and blood vessels that pass near that point. Trauma severe enough to cause dislocation may also cause fracture of one or both of the bones involved.

When the surface of the joint remains in partial contact, like hanging on the edge of a cliff, it is called a subluxation or partial separation. When too much stress is applied to a joint, the support structures may be unable to maintain correct positions. This can also happen when heavy weight is combined with rotation. Swelling of a joint from an injury, infection, or other disease can also cause a subluxation. Recurrent subluxation, usually caused by loose connecting ligaments or joint capsule, can be the result of trauma, deterioration (degeneration), or a congenital abnormality of the joint and/or ligaments. While subluxation is unlikely to be associated with support tissue damage, recurrent subluxation may eventually result in chronic joint degeneration (osteoarthritis).

The incidence and risk of dislocation depend on the joint involved. Most limb dislocations (e.g., knee, ankle, elbow) are more commonly found in young males. Shoulder dislocations account for over one half of all major joint dislocations and occur in an estimated 17 of every 100,000 individuals.

Diagnosis

History: The individual usually reports a fall or serious trauma followed by excruciating pain in the affected area and/or inability to move the affected limb. The individual may report a sensation of something slipping or tearing. Symptoms of dislocation include pain, change in the shape of the joint (deformity), swelling, limitation of joint movement, bruise-like discoloration due to the rupture of small blood vessels (ecchymosis), and sometimes a change in the length of the extremity.

Physical exam: The joint may have an obvious change in shape (deformity) along with decreased function. Pressure applied to the affected joint (palpation) will reveal tenderness. If the displaced bones have slipped back into their normal position without treatment (spontaneous reduction), there may be no visual deformity, but abnormal motion (joint instability) may still be evident on physical examination. Limitation of joint movement, ecchymosis, and sometimes a change in the length of the extremity may be present. A complete nerve and vascular examination is essential.

Tests: Dislocations are confirmed with plain x-rays. Even if the bones have returned to their normal position, x-ray may reveal bone chips in the joint space, swelling in the joint space, or a fracture. Loose fragments that are composed entirely of cartilage cannot be seen on x-ray. If serious articular damage is suspected, the surrounding support structures can be evaluated by arthrography (joint x-ray with contrast dye), CT contrast studies, MRI, or arthroscopy. X-rays done while a physician gently pushes on the joint (stress x-ray) may be needed to determine joint looseness. A procedure that evaluates the electrical activity of the muscles (electromyography or EMG) may be necessary to study nerve function. Angiography may be required to detect blood vessel damage. For chronic, recurrent dislocations that spontaneously reduce, bone scans can help confirm the diagnosis.

Treatment

Under most circumstances, any joint dislocation should be treated as a medical emergency since nerve or blood vessel damage can result in permanent damage or limb loss if a dislocation is not treated promptly. Medical personnel will return the affected joint to its normal position (reduction of the affected joint) usually while the individual is under anesthesia. In general, the best results are obtained when reduction is done soon after injury. As time passes, muscles in the area tighten and hold the bones out of position, making relocation difficult. Sometimes an individual can relax enough that gentle pressure and correct manipulation will allow the bones to return to their normal position (closed reduction). If complete relaxation is not possible, gentle traction is applied to the joint, usually under sedation or anesthesia.

If part of the bone's surface inside the joint (articular surface) has been damaged or if soft tissue or bone fragments are trapped in the joint space, surgery will be needed before the joint can be repositioned and stability maintained. This can be accomplished through open surgery (open reduction) or arthroscopy.

If there is nerve or blood vessel damage, emergency surgery may be needed. Circulation impairment is an emergency. The tissues cannot tolerate loss of blood supply (ischemia) for longer than a few hours. If more than 8 hours elapse, there is a high likelihood that tissue death (gangrene) will develop and require amputation. Therefore, in cases of impaired circulation, immediate reduction is imperative followed by x-ray of the arteries (arteriography) to look for arterial damage. Any damage to major arteries is surgically repaired.

If a dislocation is treated by open reduction, torn ligaments may be repaired at the same time. If neurovascular damage is present, however, ligament repair is usually postponed to avoid further jeopardizing the limb. After reduction, the injured joint is immobilized. The method and duration of immobilization depends on the specific type of dislocation. Treatment then includes rest, ice, elevation of the limb, and pain medication. Anti-inflammatory medication may be used to reduce swelling.

Prognosis

Outcome depends on the joints involved and the severity of the dislocation. In general, traumatic, first-time dislocations without major damage to support structures or joint surfaces should return to normal in about 6 weeks. Complications, surgery, and noncompliance with treatment will delay recovery, sometimes for months. In some dislocations, surgery is indicated even when adequate reduction has been obtained. Surgery (open reduction or arthroscopy) can result in a more stable joint as in dislocations of the shoulder in young adults. Recurrent dislocations and subluxation are more difficult to treat and often result in some loss of normal joint function.

Differential Diagnosis

Fractures may appear to be joint dislocations or both conditions may occur at the same time. Acute bursitis may cause a deformity that is mistaken for a dislocation.

Specialists

- Neurologist
- Occupational Therapist
- Orthopedic Surgeon
- Physiatrist
- Physical Therapist
- Sports Medicine Physician
- Vascular Surgeon

Rehabilitation

A physical therapist may be needed for a rehabilitation program following a dislocation of any joint of the body to help individuals return to their previous activity level and prevent future dislocations. If the dislocation required surgical repair, physical therapy may begin as early as the first day after surgery or may begin after the joint has remained immobile for a length of time.

Initially in the rehabilitation process, the physical therapist may utilize various treatments to decrease pain and inflammation followed by stretching and strengthening of key muscles. Physical therapy involving cold or warm treatments can help control inflammation during the rehabilitation process by decreasing the amount of blood flow as well as offering relief of pain.

Once pain and swelling is controlled, exercise to the joint called range of motion is generally started and performed, as tolerated. This is often initiated in a warm whirlpool or in conjunction with another form of heat treatment and continued until all the movement is restored. The therapist may perform the range-of-motion exercises with the individual in a resting position such as sitting or lying down, depending on which joint is involved. This exercise progresses to active assist range of motion. As the individual improves with increased motion of the joint, the next step of progression is active range of motion. When an individual achieves full range of motion with minimal swelling and can perform simple tasks such as dressing and grooming using the involved joint without pain, a strengthening program is initiated.

In this early phase of strengthening, isometric exercises begin with muscles around the joint contracting yet no movement takes place at the joint. The next phase of rehabilitation involves movement at the joint (isotonic exercise). An example of this type of rehabilitation exercise is strengthening with weights. As the weight is lifted throughout the range of motion, the muscle shortens and lengthens. Strength training of this type also includes weight equipment/machines, elastic bands, or calisthenics where there is resistance against the muscles and involved joint.

Work Restrictions / Accommodations

Joints that are recovering from a dislocation must be protected from abnormal stress. The individual should avoid heavy weight bearing, twisting, and hyperextension. Any activity that produces or risks producing these types of stress must be eliminated. Protective equipment can be worn if the work environment is safe for such apparatus. The individual may require the opportunity to rest and elevate the affected limb and should have access to ice for cold therapy. Time off may be required for compliance with physical therapy appointments.

Comorbid Conditions

Any condition that restricts or impairs the individual's participation in an appropriate rehabilitation regimen could impact ability to recover and lengthen disability. Such conditions may include obesity or arthritis in the affected joint.

Complications

Dislocation of the spinal vertebrae as the result of a severe back injury can damage the spinal cord. Paralysis can occur below the point of injury. Dislocation of the shoulder or hip joint can damage major nerves in the arms or legs, resulting in paralysis. A dislocation can also cause blood vessel damage resulting in impaired circulation or, in the most serious cases, amputation of the limb. Occasionally, tissue around a dislocated joint becomes so weakened that even after treatment minimal pressure can cause another dislocation. Recurrent subluxation may eventually result in chronic joint degeneration (osteoarthritis). Associated fractures can sometimes be more common in postmenopausal women or in individuals with osteoporosis.

Factors Influencing Duration

Dominant extremity joint dislocation requires longer disability periods. The same is true for injuries complicated with nerve or vessel damage. Individuals who require surgery for either initial reduction or reconstruction will be disabled longer. There may, in fact, be separate disability periods. See also Sprains and Strains, Ankle.

Length of Disability

Duration may be longer for individuals who require surgery for either initial reduction or reconstruction. For ankle dislocation durations, sedentary and light work assumes duties may be performed in a sitting position. Disability duration for hand, finger or wrist dislocations depends on whether the dominant or non-dominant hand is involved. In hip dislocation, heavy work will not be possible if joint damage or avascular necrosis is present.

Hand or Finger (open).

Duration in Days

Job Classification	Minimum	Optimum	Maximum
Sedentary work	14	42	70
Light work	28	42	84
Medium work	42	56	84
Heavy work	42	56	84
Very Heavy work	42	56	84

Ankle. Open or closed.

Duration in Days

Job Classification	Minimum	Optimum	Maximum
Sedentary work	1	7	14
Light work	7	14	28
Medium work	21	42	70
Heavy work	70	77	84
Very Heavy work	84	98	112

Hip.

Duration in Days

Job Classification	Minimum	Optimum	Maximum
Sedentary work	21	25	28
Light work	21	25	28
Medium work	28	35	42
Heavy work	42	49	84
Very Heavy work	42	49	112

Elbow.

Duration in Days

Job Classification	Minimum	Optimum	Maximum
Sedentary work	7	10	14
Light work	7	14	28
Medium work	14	28	42
Heavy work	14	42	56
Very Heavy work	14	56	91

Jaw.

Duration in Days

Job Classification	Minimum	Optimum	Maximum
Sedentary work	1	3	7
Light work	1	3	7
Medium work	1	3	7
Heavy work	1	3	7
Very Heavy work	1	3	7

Hand or Finger (closed).

Duration in Days

Job Classification	Minimum	Optimum	Maximum
Sedentary work	1	3	7
Light work	1	3	7
Medium work	1	3	14
Heavy work	1	3	21
Very Heavy work	1	3	28

Wrist.

Duration in Days

Job Classification	Minimum	Optimum	Maximum
Sedentary work	1	28	63
Light work	1	35	63
Medium work	56	70	84
Heavy work	70	84	112
Very Heavy work	70	84	168

Failure to Recover

If an individual fails to recover within the maximum duration expectancy period, the reader may wish to reference the following questions to assist in better understanding the specifics of an individual's medical case.

Regarding diagnosis:

- Was there a gross deformity of the joint? Was the joint swollen? Is there pain?
- Is bruising present? Is there a change in the length of the extremity?
- Did individual suffer a major trauma to the affected joint?
- Has individual experienced loss of range of motion?
- Was there a fracture in addition to the dislocation?
- Is this injury a first time injury or a recurrent one?
- Was an arteriogram done? Has individual had an x-ray? Stress x-rays? CT or MRI? Arthroscopy? EMG? Angiography?
- Have conditions with similar symptoms been ruled out?

Regarding treatment:

- Was the dislocation reduced promptly? Was sedation or anesthesia needed?
- Was there any damage to the joint's articular surface? Was it surgically corrected?
- Were there any neurovascular injuries? Were they repaired? Delayed?
- Is the joint immobilized? Is individual using rest, ice, elevation, and pain medication?
- Has individual been given NSAIDs?

Regarding prognosis:

- Can individual's employer accommodate any necessary restrictions?
- Does individual have any conditions that may affect ability to recover?
- Did any complications occur such as paralysis, recurring dislocation, or osteoarthritis?

References

Arnheim, Daniel D. Modern Principles of Athletic Training. St. Louis: Mosby, 1989.

Newton, Edward, and Paul Carter, MDs. Dislocations, Hip. eMedicine.com. 13 Sep 2000. 01 Nov 2000 <http://www.emedicine.com/emerg/topic144.htm>.

Dislocation, Acromioclavicular Joint

Other names / synonyms: AC Separation, Shoulder Separation

831.04, 831.14

Definition

Acromioclavicular dislocation (more commonly AC separation) refers to an injury with separation of the collarbone (clavicle) from the shoulder blade (the scapula). This injury is often confused with a dislocation of the shoulder (glenohumeral dislocation), which is actually a separation of the bone of the upper arm (humerus) from the socket in the shoulder blade (glenoid cavity of the scapula).

The clavicle is attached to the scapula by two multipart ligaments, the acromioclavicular (AC) and the stronger coracoclavicular. These ligaments cross from the acromion to the clavicle and down from the clavicle to the coracoid process. Both the acromion and coracoid are parts of the scapula.

Injuries to this joint are graded from I to VI depending on the amount of ligament damage and the resulting separation of the joint. Grades I and II are more correctly called sprains and strains of the AC joint. Grade III injuries involve a tearing of all the ligaments, while Grades IV through VI include injury to the surrounding muscles. The clavicle can pierce the muscle around the shoulder (trapezius) when dislocated. Grades I and II are sometimes called an incomplete dislocation or subluxation. Grades III, IV, V, and VI constitute a true dislocation.

An AC dislocation disrupts shoulder function, limiting arm motion. The arm is directly attached to the boney skeleton at the AC joint only, where the scapula is attached to the clavicle.

AC dislocations occur 5 to 1 to 10 to 1 more often in men than women. In the general population, AC dislocations are most prevalent in the third decade of life. In the athletic population, AC separations are most frequent in 10- to 20-year-old males. Individuals who participate in aggressive sports, who are exposed to overhead objects or falls, and who do heavy, one-arm lifting are most at risk for this injury.

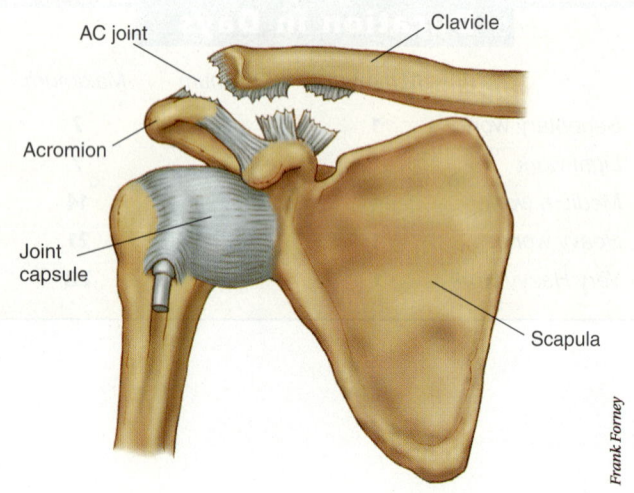

Frank Forney

Diagnosis

History: The individual most often reports a direct blow to the top of the shoulder area either from a fall or occasionally from a heavy object falling on the shoulder. An attempt to break a fall with an outstretched arm can also cause the dislocation. Individuals complain of tenderness and swelling on the top of the shoulder and loss of shoulder function. Individuals are aware of a bump on top of their shoulder and most often the skin has been scraped (abrasion.) In most cases, the individual holds the arm across the chest and applies upward pressure to the elbow.

Physical exam: The individual should be examined sitting up or standing. It may be too uncomfortable for the injured individual to sit and it is extremely difficult to lie down. Visual exam may reveal an asymmetry of the two shoulders with a noticeable bump on the affected side that increases with downward pull (traction) of the arm. There may be an abrasion across the shoulder joint. Considerable swelling may be present and discoloration (ecchymosis) may be evident over the injury.

There is a limited active range of motion and painful assisted range of motion of the joint. In grade III injuries, the high riding end of the clavicle may be rocked front to back (anterior-posterior) if examined shortly after the injury. Pain can be elicited over the coracoclavicular space. In grades IV through VI, the end of the clavicle may be depressed, aimed behind (posterior), above (superior), or below (inferior) the normal position. Comparison to the opposite shoulder is important when determining position. Pain is noted along the clavicle border as well as in the AC space and coracoclavicular space. The nerves to the arm and circulation to the extremity are examined by testing reflexes and sensation together with pulses and capillary filling.

Tests: X-rays of the AC joint confirm the diagnosis. The individual may be asked to hold a weight in the injured hand to pull the joint apart (stress test). This test can show the difference between complete dislocations and incomplete dislocations (subluxation). A nerve conduction and electromyogram study may be needed to assess nerve damage. In severe injuries, a CT or MRI may be needed to evaluate the position of the clavicle and injury to soft tissue structures about the shoulder.

Treatment

Treatment of a grade III dislocation ranges from closed reduction with application of a sling or harness (Kenny Howard Brace) to surgery.

Surgery (open reduction and internal fixation or ORIF) involves relocating the joint and repairing or replacing the torn coracoclavicular ligaments. A screw or some other type of fixation may be used to hold the joint in place while the repaired ligaments heal. The ligaments can be replaced with synthetic materials that eventually cover over with scar tissue. If a screw is inserted, it is often removed in approximately 6 to 8 weeks. During the healing phase, progressive, limited shoulder motion is allowed.

Grades IV-VI require surgery (ORIF) to reduce the dislocation and repair any damage to other structures. Implanted hardware may or may not be removed several weeks after surgery. These individuals will also wear a protective sling or harness and limited use of their arm and hand.

Prognosis

Grade III injuries treated without surgery may return to normal function and activity without restriction in approximately 6 to 8 weeks. Grade III separations however, may not respond to conservative therapy. If they do not respond, surgical treatment is almost always necessary. Where indicated, open reduction and internal fixation can be very successful in restoring shoulder function. Recovery from grade IV-VI is slower due to associated injuries to surrounding structures.

While the predicted treatment outcome is good, chronic pain and decreased joint function from degenerative arthritis does develop in a small percentage of individuals as they age. ORIF will leave a scar about 2 inches long over the AC joint.

Differential Diagnosis

Other conditions that may present with similar symptoms include acute traumatic bursitis, glenohumeral shoulder dislocation, and fractures of the clavicle.

Specialists

- Occupational Therapist
- Orthopedic Surgeon
- Physiatrist
- Physical Therapist
- Sports Medicine Physician

Rehabilitation

Rehabilitation of AC joint dislocation depends greatly on the severity of injury. The treatment of a minor AC separation may consist of a sling for comfort for several days. Even if the AC joint is not to be exercised, it becomes important to exercise the fingers, hands, and elbows to prevent stiffness.

The physical therapist may use cold or warm treatments throughout the period of rehabilitation to control inflammation and pain. Methods of cold treatment include cold packs. Forms of heat treatment used in the region of the AC joint include ultrasound. Electrical stimulation is another technique used in physical therapy to help decrease pain by mildly producing an electrical response in the muscle around the joint.

Rehabilitation of an AC dislocation begins with range-of-motion exercises to the shoulder in all pain-free movements. The individual using a cane or wand can perform these exercises independently or with a physical therapist. The individual may be progressed to a towel stretch sequence that involves raising the arms overhead and stretching behind the back.

Isometric strengthening exercises begin early in the strengthening phase. This exercise consists of the muscles around the joint contracting with no movement at the joint.

Once both range-of-motion and isometric exercises are tolerated, the individual progresses to isotonic strengthening involving movement at, and around, the AC joint. Strength training of this type may include weight equipment/machines and elastic bands. Some of the key areas emphasized are the trapezius muscles located between the shoulder and neck. The individual exercises the upper trapezius muscle by performing shoulder shrugs against light dumbbell resistance. In this particular exercise, the individual takes the shoulder from a forward position to upward and finally back to the starting position. The front shoulder muscles are also important in the strengthening process of the AC joint after dislocation. The individual performs a rowing motion with light resistance dumbbells while standing upright.

Heavy weight lifting activities should be avoided until the ligament heals. From this point, a gradual strengthening program advances, as tolerated. Overhead presses that also address the muscles on the front of the shoulder are a good example of strengthening at this phase, as are variations of dumbbell exercises to forward, backward, and sideways motions of the shoulder.

The physical therapist may need to modify this project for individuals with arthritis or other joint irritations. If the AC dislocation requires surgical repair, some restrictions may be placed on the progression of the range of motion and strengthening in certain movements. This varies depending on the degree of dislocation or type of surgery performed.

Work Restrictions / Accommodations

Individuals may be restricted by a sling or harness that limits manual dexterity. All treatments include avoidance of lifting, carrying, or overhead work for up to 2 months. Individuals who can use the nonoperative or injured side may need medication for pain control during the first few days of treatment. Such medications may alter mental alertness and require review of policies regarding medication use along with restrictions on driving and operating heavy machinery.

Comorbid Conditions

Conditions that may impact ability to recover and further lengthen disability include bursitis, osteoporosis, skin or wound infection, osteomyelitis, and smoking.

Complications

Skin abrasions are common with this injury and are watched during treatment to prevent infection. Careful attention must be given to the skin around the bump to observe stretching (tenting) over the high riding clavicle with the possibility of skin loss from blood supply (necrotizing) or the bone end cutting though the skin. Treatment may be necessary to prevent further damage to the skin and soft tissue around the deformity. As with other dislocation injuries, nerve and blood vessel damage are possible especially in grades IV through VI.

Factors Influencing Duration

Whether the injury occurred on the dominant versus nondominant side and the degree of dislocation are important factors. Work requirements for manual dexterity, lifting, or carrying increase the disability time. Surgical repair/reconstruction of either side increases disability time.

Length of Disability

Duration of disability is dependent on job requirements. Permanent disability from heavy lifting and overhead work may be necessary. For non-dominant injuries, individuals may return to work earlier if duties are one-handed. Dominant side injuries will require longer disability, as individuals are not able to use their hand above shoulder height in either sedentary or active jobs.

Duration in Days

Job Classification	Minimum	Optimum	Maximum
Sedentary work	1	7	21
Light work	14	21	28
Medium work	21	35	42
Heavy work	42	49	84
Very Heavy work	42	49	84

Duration Trend from Normative Data*

Cases	Mean	Min	Max	No Lost Time	Over 6 Months
1609	57	0	436	0.12%	1.12%

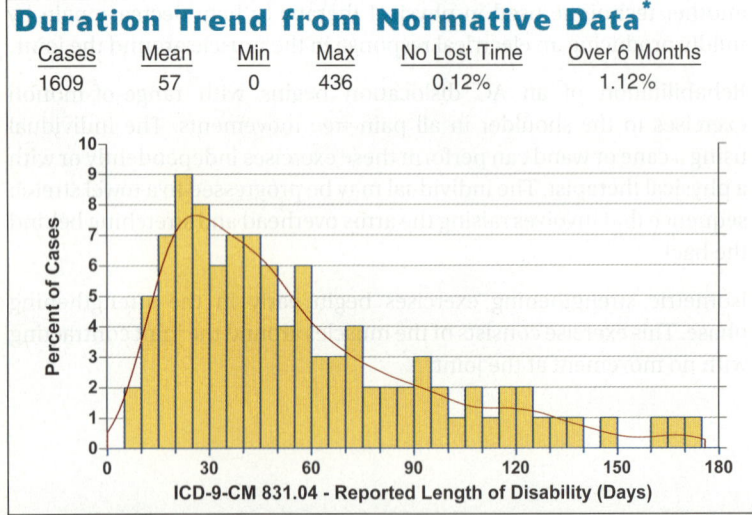

Percentile:	5th	25th	Median	75th	95th
Days:	14	27	44	73	130

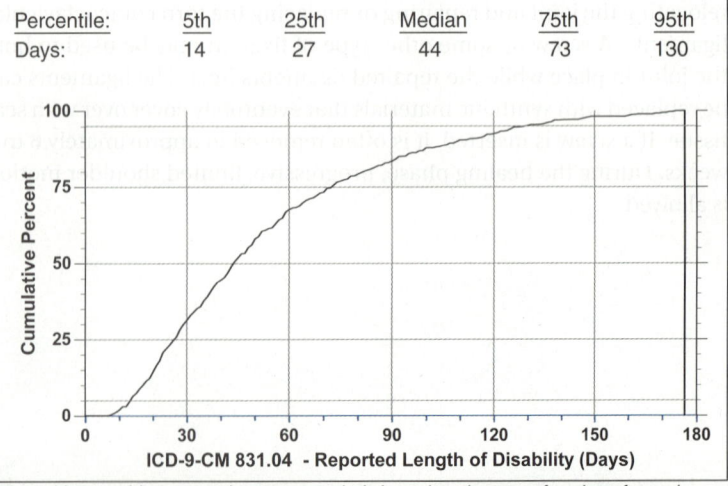

* Differences may exist between the expected duration tables and the normative graphs. Duration tables provide expected recovery periods based on the type of work performed by the individual. The normative graphs reflect the actual observed experience of many individuals across the spectrum of physical conditions, in a variety of industries, and with varying levels of case management.

Failure to Recover

If an individual fails to recover within the maximum duration expectancy period, the reader may wish to reference the following questions to assist in better understanding the specifics of an individual's medical case.

Regarding diagnosis:

- Has diagnosis of dislocation of AC joint been confirmed?
- Was joint deformity present?
- Did x-rays confirm a shoulder separation?
- Was there a fracture in addition to dislocation?
- Has individual experienced any complications?
- Does individual have a condition that may impact recovery?

Regarding treatment:

- Did conservative treatment fail?
- Has individual received comprehensive physical therapy?
- Was surgery performed? Open reduction or internal fixation?
- Did individual experience any complications from surgical procedure?

Regarding prognosis:

- Has pain resolved?
- Has function been restored? If not completely, to what degree?
- How does this impact the individual's ability to perform daily activities or job requirements?
- Would further rehabilitation increase functional ability?

References

Arnheim, Daniel. Modern Principles of Athletic Training. St. Louis: Mosby Publishing, 1989.

Malone, Terry R., Thomas McPoil, and Arthur J. Nitz. Orthopedic and Sports Physical Therapy. St. Louis: Mosby-Year Book Inc, 1997.

Dislocation, Cervical Vertebra
Other names / synonyms: Cervical Spine Dislocation
839.0, 839.08, 839.1, 839.40

Definition

Cervical vertebra dislocation refers to the displacement of a bone of the neck (cervical vertebra). Disruption of the supporting ligaments in the cervical spine allows one vertebra to shift position over the vertebrae below. This results in a partial dislocation (subluxation) or a complete dislocation of the cervical spine, with possible damage to the spinal cord.

The problem may be caused by injury or from degeneration. Cervical injuries occur as the result of trauma to the head (axial loading) or injury to the neck such as the head tipping too far backward (hyperextension) or forward (hyperflexion), or severe head rotation. Degenerative changes caused by disc disease or arthritis may also lead to more chronic subluxation/dislocation of the cervical spine. Fractures with dislocations are common, injuring and dislodging the vertebral segments, as well as affecting the overall alignment of the spine. Dislocations may be stable or unstable, depending on the extent of damage to the supporting ligaments and changes in the bone anatomy. Dislocations may also spontaneously realign (reduce), which may make diagnosis somewhat more challenging. The most devastating consequence of a traumatic dislocation of the cervical spine is injury to the spinal cord. While not all dislocations cause permanent spinal cord damage, careful screening and handling (transportation) of any individual with a neck injury cannot be over-emphasized. It is possible to have a cervical dislocation without spinal cord damage.

Dislocations are described by the vertebrae involved: upper cervical spine being C1 through C3, mid-cervical includes C3-C4, and lower cervical being C4 though C7.

Individuals who are at risk of cervical vertebra dislocation include those who participate in contact sports such as football, boxing, and hockey, and individuals with joint degenerative diseases (e.g., arthritis).

In one study, the overall incidence of cervical spine injuries was two percent. Subluxation without fractures accounted for 10.6% of these injuries.

Diagnosis

History: There may be a history of injury. Alternatively, there may be a history of a chronic back or joint condition. Individuals will report pain, commonly with a nodding motion, weakness in the shoulders and arms, and may describe a sensation of instability. Individuals may be apprehensive about moving their head. Temporary paralysis or general weakness, change in sensation (paresthesia), and flushing or feeling of warmth after the injury may be reported.

Physical exam: In any case of suspected neck injury, no examination for range of motion should be undertaken until screening x-rays are complete. Touching the back of the neck with the hands (palpation) may cause pain and there may be a decreased range of motion. Neurological findings of cervical spinal cord injury (e.g., breathing alteration, hand paralysis) may be noted.

Tests: Tests include screening x-ray films, including flexion, extension, and through the mouth (odontoid) views. Neurological studies, such as EMG and nerve conduction, may be performed if indicated. Special studies may also include CT scan and/or MRI. Myelogram or contrast MRI and CT scans may be required to evaluate injuries to the spinal cord.

Treatment

In acute traumatic injuries, the goals of treatment include protecting the cord from further injury, realignment (reduction) of the dislocation (and fracture if present), and obtaining and maintaining stability of the cervical spine. A closed reduction of the dislocation, in which traction is utilized to realign the vertebra, is nearly always attempted before an open, surgical reduction is utilized. Open reductions are used when closed reduction fails and for severe injuries, dislocations associated with fractures, and cases with spinal cord involvement. To maintain stability during healing, wires, screws, and/or plates (internal fixation) may be applied during open reduction or external traction may be used. In more chronic situations, stability may be obtained with spinal fusion and fixation (arthrodesis).

Prognosis

The outcome is favorable for dislocations without neurological complications that are reduced by either an open or closed method and in which stability is gained and maintained. There is a possibility of recurrent dislocation when there is extensive soft tissue damage and an associated fracture. Depending on the method employed, greater than 50% of the spinal fusions are successful. Those individuals who suffer neurological injury will have a less positive outcome. Injury to the cervical spinal cord can result in paralysis.

Differential Diagnosis

Fractures of the vertebrae, "burners or zingers," cervical radiculopathy, and spinal cord shock could present with similar findings.

Specialists

- Neurologist
- Neurosurgeon
- Occupational Therapist
- Orthopedic Surgeon
- Physiatrist
- Physical Therapist

Rehabilitation

Rehabilitation becomes an important aspect in regaining neck (cervical) stability following a cervical vertebra dislocation. Focus is placed upon decreasing pain and increasing range of motion, stability, strength, and endurance. Initially, physical therapy may be needed to decrease pain and inflammation originating from muscle spasms. Treatments involving cold or warm techniques can help provide relief during this process by controlling the amount of blood flow to the cervical muscles. Methods of cold treatment include cold packs A form of heat treatment includes ultrasound that uses high frequency sound waves, which produce heat that penetrates deep into the involved muscles.

Range of motion for the neck normally includes the individual sitting or standing, then bringing the head forward attempting to bring the chin to the chest. Lateral bending and rotation exercises are introduced to improve range of motion. Because of the amount of stress placed on the cervical region, positioning the head back with the neck into what is called "extension" is only performed when advised by the physician or physical therapist.

Isometric resistance helps strengthen the muscles of the neck without moving the neck through the range of motion. These exercises are performed with the individual placing the palm of one hand on the forehead and applying resistance with the hand while the individual tries to press the head forward without actually moving it.

Strengthening of the cervical muscles progresses with the use of resistance throughout the range of motion. Instruction with the supervision of a physical therapist usually accomplishes this with devices such as wall pulleys, and universal and nautilus-type equipment.

Work Restrictions / Accommodations

To reduce the risk of complications, the individual may not be allowed to work during the early recovery period. Limited use of arms and shoulders, restrictions on height of worktable, and limited sitting and standing are possible restrictions. Use of a soft or rigid cervical collar, upper body traction, or halo traction devices may be required for several weeks. These traction devices may severely limit dexterity and mobility. The individual may require frequent breaks. Temporarily working reduced hours may be necessary.

Comorbid Conditions

Arthritis, obesity, osteoporosis, other back disorders (disc degeneration, herniated disc), and other injuries (vertebral fractures, spinal cord injury, whiplash) sustained during the traumatic event may influence the length of disability.

Complications

Neurological deficits, including quadriplegia, are possible complications of the injury. Any underlying disease of the musculoskeletal system, especially those affecting ligamentous slackness, bone healing, and muscle strength would complicate treatment and recovery. Associated trauma to other structures would also complicate treatment and recovery. Dislocation resulting from an invasive injury (e.g., gunshot wound) can be complicated by infection of the blood (sepsis) or spinal fluid.

Factors Influencing Duration

Any complication of the injury or treatment would prolong disability. Associated injuries would also delay recovery. Inability to modify the work environment during recovery would add to the disability period. There may be permanent disability with any neurological complications.

Length of Disability

Duration depends on job requirements. Disability may be permanent.

Closed treatment without neurologic deficit.

Duration in Days

Job Classification	Minimum	Optimum	Maximum
Sedentary work	3	14	21
Light work	5	21	28
Medium work	28	56	91
Heavy work	42	91	119
Very Heavy work	42	119	182

Open treatment without neurologic deficit.

Duration in Days

Job Classification	Minimum	Optimum	Maximum
Sedentary work	21	35	56
Light work	42	49	56
Medium work	56	63	70
Heavy work	70	91	210
Very Heavy work	70	98	Indefinite

Failure to Recover

If an individual fails to recover within the maximum duration expectancy period, the reader may wish to reference the following questions to assist in better understanding the specifics of an individual's medical case.

Regarding diagnosis:

- Was diagnosis of dislocation of cervical vertebra confirmed?
- Have neurological studies, MRI, or CT scans been conducted to rule out a spinal cord injury?
- Did the individual sustain head injuries? Multiple injuries?
- Has individual experienced neurological deficits, including quadriplegia, or other complications?
- Does individual have any underlying condition that may impact recovery?

Regarding treatment:

- Was the closed reduction unsuccessful?
- Was an open reduction performed?
- Was the individual treated with external traction weights of greater than 50 pounds?
- Was he or she treated with traction for an extended period of time?
- If this is a chronic situation, would individual benefit from a spinal fusion and fixation?
- Is the individual wearing a cervical collar or traction device?

Regarding prognosis:

- Did delayed diagnosis delay reduction?
- Has malunion occurred?
- Was there damage to the ligaments?
- Would the individual benefit from spinal fusion?
- Did paralysis occur?
- How has injury impacted function?
- Has individual received comprehensive rehabilitation?

References

Arnheim, Daniel D. Modern Principles of Athletic Training. St. Louis: Times Mirror/Mosby Publishing, 1989.

Kessler, R.M. Management of Common Musculoskeletal Disorders: Physical Therapy Principles and Methods. Philadelphia: J.B. Lippincott Co, 1990.

Dislocation, Femorotibial (Knee) Joint

Other names / synonyms: Knee Dislocation, Tibia-Femur Dislocation

836, 836.0, 836.1, 836.2, 836.6, 836.60, 836.61, 836.62, 836.63, 836.64, 836.69

Definition

Femorotibial joint dislocation is the displacement of the thigh bone (femur) and the shin bone (tibia) from their normal positions at the knee joint.

There are 5 major types of knee dislocations that are classified according to the position of the tibia relative to the femur. An anterior dislocation is usually caused by severe knee hyperextension. A posterior dislocation occurs from a force on the tibia from front to back, such as from the dashboard of a vehicle during an accident. More than half of all dislocations are either anterior or posterior. The other 3 major types of knee dislocations are medial, lateral, and rotatory, in which the tibia is dislocated inwardly, outwardly, or in a twisted fashion, respectively. Femorotibial joint dislocation represents a major disruption of the knee's anatomy and can lead to loss of the limb if not given immediate emergency care.

Femorotibial joint dislocation is a relatively rare injury. The most common causes of femorotibial joint dislocation are motor vehicle collisions, pedestrians being struck by cars, industrial injuries, falls, and athletic injuries. Risk factors for knee dislocations include previous knee injuries, participation in contact sports (especially football or hockey), poor muscle conditioning, and congenital knee abnormalities.

Diagnosis

History: The individual will usually report a fall or serious trauma followed by excruciating pain and inability to bend the knee or bear any weight on it.

Physical exam: The exam may reveal gross deformity of the knee, swelling, and inability to move and/or bear weight on the knee. In some cases, the knee will have spontaneously relocated, in which case the joint must be examined for instability in full extension. By applying pressure (palpation) over the arteries of the leg, the physician may be able to detect possible vascular damage. The physician may also be able to determine whether nerve injury has occurred (peroneal nerve injury) by evaluating the individual's sensation between the great and second toe, as well as the ability of the individual to flex the foot.

Tests: Tests include x-rays to identify the dislocation as well as any associated fractures. A follow-up radiograph will also be done following relocation (reduction) of the knee. An arteriogram will be performed to assess damage to the arteries of the knee (popliteal artery injury).

Treatment

This condition is an orthopedic emergency. The dislocation must be reduced, if reduction has not occurred spontaneously. Reduction may be accomplished nonsurgically (closed reduction) by applying traction to the knee, usually under anesthesia (general anesthesia or spinal anesthesia). If closed reduction is unsuccessful due to damaged ligaments or menisci interposed between the joint surfaces, open reduction (surgery) is required. Following reduction, the knee will be immobilized in a splint or cast, usually for 6-8 weeks. Follow-up treatment includes rest, ice, compression, and elevation of the leg. In addition, the individual is given medicine to reduce pain and inflammation (e.g., analgesics, nonsteroidal anti-inflammatory drugs, and/or antianxiety drugs).

In cases involving vascular injury, immediate surgery (e.g., decompression or vessel reanastomosis) is necessary to restore normal blood circulation to the leg. Further surgery to repair damaged ligaments (e.g., ACL repair, PCL repair) may be required in severe cases.

Prognosis

When treated appropriately, 60-70% of individuals will return to having a painless, stable knee. Complete healing of the knee requires at least 6 weeks. Of the remaining 30-40% of individuals, approximately one half can expect to have a chronically unstable, painful knee. In femorotibial joint dislocations in which vascular damage has occurred, immediate surgery to repair the artery is of the utmost importance. Vascular repair (decompression or vessel reanastomosis) that is delayed for 8 hours or more following dislocation carries an amputation rate of more than 80%; however, if vascular repair surgery is done within 8 hours of the dislocation, an 80% success rate can be expected.

Differential Diagnosis

Fractures of the proximal tibia or distal femur can cause a similar deformity, but x-rays distinguish these injuries from femorotibial joint dislocation.

Specialists

- Orthopedic Surgeon
- Physiatrist
- Sports Medicine Physician
- Vascular Surgeon

Rehabilitation

Physical therapy may be recommended for successful recovery from a femorotibial joint dislocation. Because of the significant ligaments and cartilage structures within and around the knee, a physical therapist may be needed for a rehabilitation program following this dislocation to assist the individual to return to previous activity level and prevent future dislocations.

The therapist may need to use various methods to decrease pain and inflammation. Physical therapy involving cold or warm treatments can help control inflammation during this process by decreasing the amount of blood flow as well as offering relief of pain. Methods of cold treatment include cold packs. Forms of heat treatment include ultrasound, which uses high frequency sound waves producing heat that penetrates deep into the involved muscles.

Once pain and swelling is controlled and the physician has instructed the individual to begin movement of the knee, range of motion is started in rehabilitation and performed as tolerated. The individual begins with passive range-of-motion exercises and progresses to active assist range of motion and then to active range of motion. The primary goal is to maintain normal function and to prevent muscle atrophy without unwanted knee motion. Progression from phase one to another phase depends on tissue healing, pain, joint movement, and how stable the joint feels to the physician and individual.

A major goal is to achieve full and pain free motion of the knee joint along with strengthening of both the quadriceps and hamstring muscle groups. Leg raises are used to strengthen the quadriceps and are performed while the individual sits on the floor with the knees straight (also referred to as long sitting) with the uninvolved knee in a flexed or in a bent position while the involved leg is raised to the height of the opposite knee. Ankle weights are used for resistance as the muscles strengthen from this exercise. Hamstring curls may be introduced by the physical therapist. Stationary cycling initially using both legs and then progressing by using the affected leg only is also a goal.

In the intermediate stage of rehabilitation, the individual is encouraged to walk and may be allowed to return to modified work. For the individual who had reconstruction of any ligaments, this phase may not be reached for several months longer. More intense exercising is instructed in this phase with increased resistance cycling. Knee joint rehabilitation may also use isokinetic machines in which the speed of the knee motion is set by the physical therapist. An example of this type of exercise may begin with the individual sitting at a Cybex or similar machine with bending and straightening of the knee at 100 degrees per second and progressing to 300 degrees per second.

Individuals move on to resisted exercises (leg curls, leg press and half knee squats) with ankle weights or machines under supervision of the therapist. Stationary biking is increased to 20 minutes once a day; strengthening and addressing balance is also addressed.

Finally, exercise is directed toward work requirements. Rehabilitation of the dislocated femorotibial joint will vary depending on the degree of the dislocation or type of surgery that was performed.

Work Restrictions / Accommodations

Walking and standing need to be restricted. Use of crutches, a cane, or a walker is necessary during the first 6-8 weeks. The individual will be unable to participate in activities that require carrying, lifting, or more than minimal walking. If the individual's knee remains unstable, permanent avoidance of these types of activities may be required. The individual's ability to drive a vehicle may be temporarily restricted. The individual will need to elevate the leg as much as possible, and will need to be given the opportunity to apply ice to the knee. Pain medications may be sedating, and therefore the individual may be restricted from operating heavy machinery during treatment.

Comorbid Conditions

Any condition that restricts or impairs the individual's participation in an appropriate rehabilitation regiment could impact ability to recover and lengthen disability; such conditions may include obesity and arthritis in the knee joint.

Complications

The violent trauma required to dislocate the joint may also cause meniscus injury, fractures, and/or damage to the joint surfaces.

Factors Influencing Duration

Length of disability may be influenced by the severity of damage to the ligaments, menisci, articular surfaces, arteries and veins, and nerves. Disability may also be influenced by the severity of pain and swelling, and the individual's motivation to participate in a major rehabilitative effort.

Length of Disability

Residual neurovascular deficit (ankle foot orthosis), residual instability, and/or complications frequently preclude heavy or very heavy work.

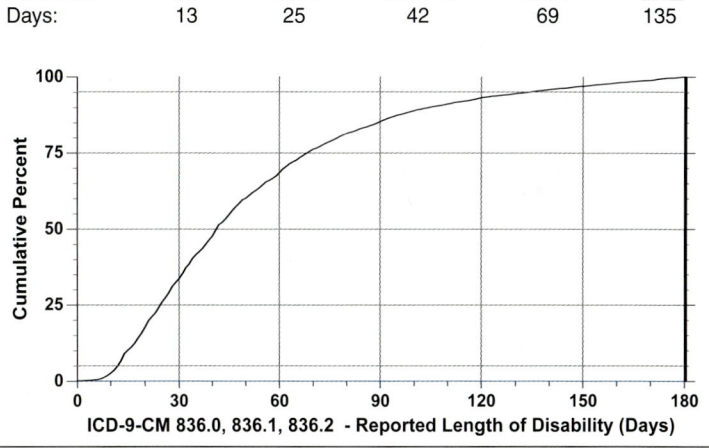

Duration in Days

Job Classification	Minimum	Optimum	Maximum
Sedentary work	7	14	28
Light work	14	21	42
Medium work	119	182	224
Heavy work	161	224	273
Very Heavy work	182	273	Indefinite

Duration Trend from Normative Data*

Cases	Mean	Min	Max	No Lost Time	Over 6 Months
15779	56	0	495	0.10%	1.62%

Percentile:	5th	25th	Median	75th	95th
Days:	13	25	42	69	135

ICD-9-CM 836.0, 836.1, 836.2 - Reported Length of Disability (Days)

* Differences may exist between the expected duration tables and the normative graphs. Duration tables provide expected recovery periods based on the type of work performed by the individual. The normative graphs reflect the actual observed experience of many individuals across the spectrum of physical conditions, in a variety of industries, and with varying levels of case management.

Failure to Recover

If an individual fails to recover within the maximum duration expectancy period, the reader may wish to reference the following questions to assist in better understanding the specifics of an individual's medical case.

Regarding diagnosis:

- Does the individual report a fall or serious trauma to the knee?
- Are they unable to bend the knee? Can they bear weight on it?
- On exam did the physician find gross deformity of the knee? Swelling?
- Was it locked? Could the individual walk on it?
- Is the joint stable or unstable?
- Was any vascular damage noted?
- Is there injury to the peroneal nerve?
- Has the individual had an x-ray? Was there a follow-up x-ray after reduction?
- Has the individual received appropriate diagnostic testing to establish the diagnosis?
- Have conditions with similar symptoms been ruled out?

Regarding treatment:

- Was the dislocation reduced on an emergency basis?
- Was the reduction done closed? Open?
- Is the knee immobilized?
- Were other injuries also repaired?
- Was the individual given medication to control pain and inflammation?

Regarding prognosis:

- Is the individual active in rehabilitation?
- Is the individual's employer able to accommodate any necessary restrictions?
- Does the individual have any conditions that may affect the ability to recover?
- Does the individual have meniscus injury, or damage to the joint surface or fracture?

Dislocation, Femorotibial (Knee) Joint

References

Knee Dislocation, Tibia-Femur. HealthGate.com. 23 Jun 1999. 1 Jan 2001 <http://www.healthgate.com/sport/sport47.shtml>.

Malone, Terry R., Thomas McPoil, and Arthur J. Nitz. Orthopedic and Sports Physical Therapy. St. Louis: Mosby, 1997.

Dislocation, Foot

Other names / synonyms: Disarticulation, Displacement, Interphalangeal Joint Dislocation, Luxation, Metatarsophalangeal Joint Dislocation

838, 838.0, 838.00, 838.01, 838.02, 838.03, 838.04, 838.05, 838.06, 838.09, 838.11, 838.12, 838.13, 838.14, 838.15, 838.16, 838.19

Definition

The foot can be divided into 3 sections. Within these sections (forefoot, midfoot, and hindfoot) are several joints supported by various ligaments. A severe injury (third-degree sprain) to any of these ligaments allows the joint(s) to dislocate. The direction of the force to the foot determines the direction of the dislocation(s). The injuries can be the result of a direct crushing force, from a twisting of the foot, impaction as in an auto accident, or from "stubbing" the toes. Landing in an abnormal position on the foot can also cause a dislocation(s). If the ligaments cannot absorb the stress, they tear, causing the joint to dislocate. Many of the dislocations are also accompanied by fractures.

Joint dislocations (luxations) result in the surface of the joint being completely separated with severe ligament and joint capsule damage. A partial dislocation (subluxation) is an incomplete dislocation. A portion of the joint surfaces remains intact and the supporting ligaments are stretched but not torn.

A common area for dislocation of the forefoot is the toe (interphalangeal joint). This can occur when the toe hits against a hard object or the toe is stubbed. The most common complete dislocation of the foot also occurs in the forefoot where the toes join the metatarsal bones (metatarsophalangeal joint). This dislocation requires immediate reduction.

The midfoot contains the navicular, cuboid, and cuneiform bones and involves the intertarsal joint. Dislocations in this area are caused by crushing blows to the top of the foot or when the individual experiences a fall. They are often difficult to diagnose and manage because of associated fractures, swelling, and subtle x-ray findings.

The joints of the hindfoot (talocalcaneal and subtalar joints, respectively) are susceptible to injuries from jumps, falls, and automobile accidents. These dislocations can also occur as a result of contact and kicking sports. As with dislocation of the intertarsal joint, dislocation of the hindfoot is often associated with fractures. Possible complications must be considered if the blood supply or nerve and tendon function are impaired.

Foot and ankle problems account for more than 4.8 million visits to physicians' offices each year. Ankle sprain is one of the most common injuries resulting in 1.2 million office visits a year, followed by ankle fractures that account for 675,000 visits every year.

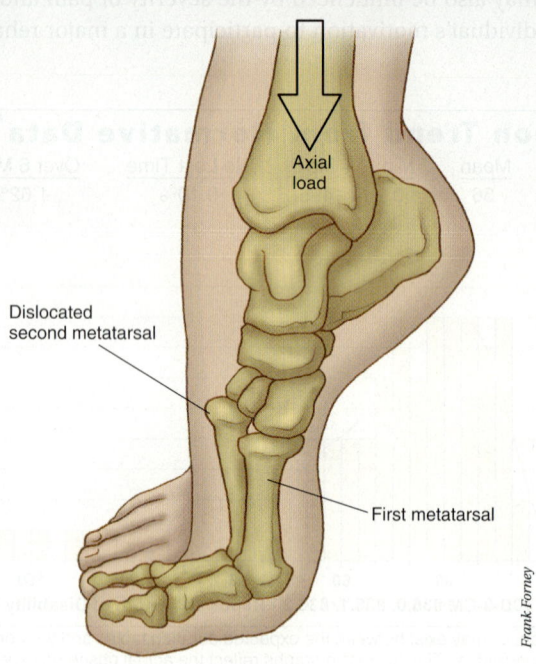

Diagnosis

History: The individual reports a history of recent traumatic injury and complains of pain, swelling, decreased activity, and/or difficulty with bearing weight on the foot. Depending on the severity and number of dislocations, the individual may be aware of a obvious change in appearance of the foot.

Physical exam: The exam may reveal localized pain when light pressure is applied with the fingers (palpation) over the joint(s) involved. Localized swelling and deformity of the area may also occur. Elevation and stretching (tenting) of the skin over the involved joint is often noted. If multiple joints or areas of the foot are involved, pain, swelling, and deformity may be more general over the foot. Decreased circulation and sensation (neurovascular compromise) may also be present.

Tests: The initial tests are x-rays in multiple angles followed by stress x-rays or CT, as required. Depending on the findings of the neurovascular examination, further studies of these systems may be required including Doppler venous testing and nerve conduction studies.

Treatment

Reduction of the dislocation under anesthesia (local, regional, or general) is required. This may be a closed reduction (nonsurgical) or open (surgical) procedure. There is some urgency to reduction in the hind and midfoot because of possible compromised circulation to the foot. Many of the dislocations are not stable after reduction and require internal fixation.

Dislocations of the hindfoot are often open or compound injuries that require management of the wounds as well. Dislocations with associated fractures most often require surgical reduction and fixation to regain joint stability.

Prognosis

Dislocations of the toe and forefoot should have a good outcome with proper management and compliance with treatment. Mid- and hindfoot dislocations have a much higher risk of complication and a less favorable outcome.

In individuals requiring surgical repair (stabilization) of the joint(s), the outcome is somewhat more guarded due to greater risk for complications. These individuals have often sustained more severe injuries.

Individuals who experience fracture with dislocation may require internal fixation of the fracture. The expected outcome is very good, but the treatment and recovery phases will be longer than in the above procedures. The possibility for infection and other complications increases with this procedure.

Differential Diagnosis

Fractures and chronic injuries not treated successfully could create similar symptoms. Individuals with inflammatory conditions such as rheumatoid arthritis may develop dislocations without trauma.

Specialists

- Orthopedic Surgeon
- Physiatrist
- Physical Therapist
- Podiatrist

Rehabilitation

Rehabilitation is important to regain joint stability following a foot dislocation and involves exercises for both strength and endurance. Focus is placed on the deep, innermost (intrinsic) muscles of the foot and the superficial (extrinsic) muscles. Muscles originating above the ankle with attachment at the foot are the anterior (front) and posterior (back) tibialis muscles. Both these muscles are important in maintaining the structure of the foot. Improving their function allows the individual with an unstable foot to stand and walk for longer periods before muscle fatigue sets in.

A towel gathering exercise where the toes pull and gather a towel positioned on a smooth surfaced floor in front of the foot can strengthen the intrinsic muscles of the foot.

The tibialis posterior muscle is strengthened with use of an elastic band wrapped around the forefoot with the opposite end held in the opposite hand. The individual brings the forefoot downward and inward in a diagonal pattern against the resistance of the elastic band. Strengthening of the tibialis anterior muscle is accomplished while the individual sits on the floor with the knees straight (also referred to as long sitting). The elastic band is wrapped around the forefoot with the opposite end attached to a fixed object located in front of the foot. The foot is brought from a position of being flexed downward to an upward motion, with the foot and toes moving toward the rest of the leg.

Balance exercises are very important when rehabilitating the dislocated foot as they train the joint to respond more effectively during activities that place strain on the previously dislocated joints of the foot. These exercises vary from fast walking and jogging in a figure-8 pattern to standing on the involved leg while catching a tossed ball and maintaining balance.

Work Restrictions / Accommodations

The location and treatment of the dislocation may require restrictions for a few weeks to months. The use of surgical shoes or casts in combination with crutches or canes is common; however, some activities may be limited (stair climbing, standing for long periods of time, and walking long distances). Use of hands while standing and manual dexterity can also be affected because of the crutches or canes, and lifting or carrying will not be possible. The foot will need to be elevated throughout the day to relieve pain and swelling.

Depending on the type of work, access to an elevator may be necessary. Modified duty, a temporary change of duties, a designated person to assist the individual as needed for certain job tasks, an area where the individual may rest and elevate the foot several times a day, and allowance for the individual to take prescribed medications may also be necessary. Time off from work for physical therapy treatments and doctors' visits may be needed.

Comorbid Conditions

Existing conditions that may impact ability to recover and further lengthen disability are chronic inflammatory or degenerative joint disease, diabetes mellitus, peripheral vascular disease, peripheral neuropathy, obesity, and any underlying condition affecting ligament laxity.

Complications

Trauma to the foot may exacerbate an underlying inflammatory condition such as rheumatoid arthritis osteoarthritis or gout. Individuals with diabetes mellitus are particularly at risk for foot complications. Degenerative diseases that affect the integrity of ligament tissue and the joint structure will complicate treatment.

Fractures, open wounds, and lacerations of tendons and blood vessels from the dislocation may complicate treatment. Infection, loss of blood supply to the bones (avascular necrosis), instability of the joint, damage to the skin, nerve injury, stiffness, degenerative arthritis, and loss of the arch are possible complications of the injury and/or treatment.

Factors Influencing Duration

Length of disability is influenced by the severity of symptoms, the presence or absence of a coexisting injury and/or underlying joint disease, type and outcome of treatment, and the job and life requirements of the individual.

Length of Disability

The duration of disability depends on job requirements. For dislocation of the tarsometatarsal joint, duration for sedentary and light work reflects work in a cast or brace.

Interphalangeal joint.

Duration in Days

Job Classification	Minimum	Optimum	Maximum
Sedentary work	1	2	3
Light work	1	2	3
Medium work	1	3	7
Heavy work	14	21	28
Very Heavy work	14	28	42

Metatarsophalangeal joint.

Duration in Days

Job Classification	Minimum	Optimum	Maximum
Sedentary work	1	2	3
Light work	1	2	3
Medium work	7	9	14
Heavy work	14	21	28
Very Heavy work	14	21	42

Midtarsal joint.

Duration in Days

Job Classification	Minimum	Optimum	Maximum
Sedentary work	1	3	7
Light work	7	9	14
Medium work	14	21	28
Heavy work	28	35	84
Very Heavy work	28	35	168

Subtalar joint.

Duration in Days

Job Classification	Minimum	Optimum	Maximum
Sedentary work	1	3	7
Light work	14	16	21
Medium work	28	35	84
Heavy work	42	49	154
Very Heavy work	42	49	175

Tarsometatarsal joint.

Duration in Days

Job Classification	Minimum	Optimum	Maximum
Sedentary work	1	10	21
Light work	14	42	70
Medium work	28	84	182
Heavy work	42	84	182
Very Heavy work	42	84	182

Failure to Recover

If an individual fails to recover within the maximum duration expectancy period, the reader may wish to reference the following questions to assist in better understanding the specifics of an individual's medical case.

Regarding diagnosis:

- Has the individual had an injury? What type?
- Does the individual complain of pain and swelling? Difficulty walking?
- Does the foot "look" different?
- Is there pain to the touch over the joint(s) involved?
- Is there tenting of the skin over the affected joint?
- Is there any neurovascular compromise?
- Has the individual had regular x-rays, stress x-rays and CT scan?
- Were Doppler venous tests done if necessary? Nerve conduction studies?
- Have conditions with similar symptoms been ruled out?

Regarding treatment:

- Was the dislocation reduced under anesthesia? Closed or open?
- Was internal fixation done?
- Were any additional injuries also treated?

Regarding prognosis:

- Is the individual active in physical therapy?
- Is the individual's employer able to accommodate the necessary restrictions?
- Does the individual have any conditions that may affect the ability to recover?
- Did the injury exacerbate an underlying inflammatory condition?
- Does the individual have diabetes?
- Does the individual have any degenerative diseases?
- Were any tendons or blood vessels lacerated?

References

The Foot and Ankle. American Academy of Orthopaedic Surgeons. 01 Mar 2000. 1 Jan 2001 <http://orthoinfo.aaos.org/fact/thr_report.cfm?Thread_ID=100&topcategory=Foot>.

Maher, Ann, Susan Salmond, and Teresa Pellino. Orthopaedic Nursing. Philadelphia: W.B. Saunders Co, 1994.

Dislocation, Glenohumeral

Other names / synonyms: Dislocated Shoulder, Shoulder Dislocation

831, 831.0, 831.00, 831.01, 831.02, 831.03

Definition

Glenohumeral dislocation is the separation of the upper arm bone (humerus) from the shoulder blade (scapula).

The glenohumeral joint is the most freely moving joint in the body that makes it prone to dislocation. The humeral head can dislocate forward (anterior dislocation), backward (posterior dislocation), downward (inferior dislocation; luxatio erecta), or upward (superior dislocation). Dislocations present for two days or less are called acute dislocations. Dislocations older than two days are called chronic or locked dislocations. Those occurring more than once are called recurrent dislocations. Approximately 95% of the glenohumeral dislocations are anterior dislocations and 4% are posterior dislocations. The other types of glenohumeral dislocations are rare.

Glenohumeral dislocations are usually caused by traumatic events. Acute anterior dislocation is usually caused by a forced outward rotation of the arm with the elbow away from the body (similar to the throwing motion) or, less commonly, by a fall on the hand or back of the shoulder. Acute posterior dislocations are most often the result of a direct blow to the shoulder or outstretched arm but can be caused by falling on the hand or front of the shoulder. Acute inferior or superior dislocations occur when a force or blow is directed downward or upward, respectively. Acute shoulder dislocations are a true emergency and require immediate attention. Chronic or recurrent dislocations are most common in individuals who were under the age of 30 when their first shoulder dislocation occurred. Chronic dislocations result from stretched supporting structures and changes in the bones that occur when the bones slip out of position.

Elderly women and young men who participate in sports are the two groups that most commonly sustain shoulder dislocations. Individuals at risk of sustaining a glenohumeral dislocation include those who have shoulder instability, a history of shoulder dislocation, or seizures (e.g., epilepsy). Alcoholics and athletes are also at a higher risk of dislocating a shoulder. Glenohumeral dislocation is common and accounts for greater than half of all joint dislocations in the US. An international estimate of the incidence of glenohumeral dislocation is 17 per 100,000 individuals.

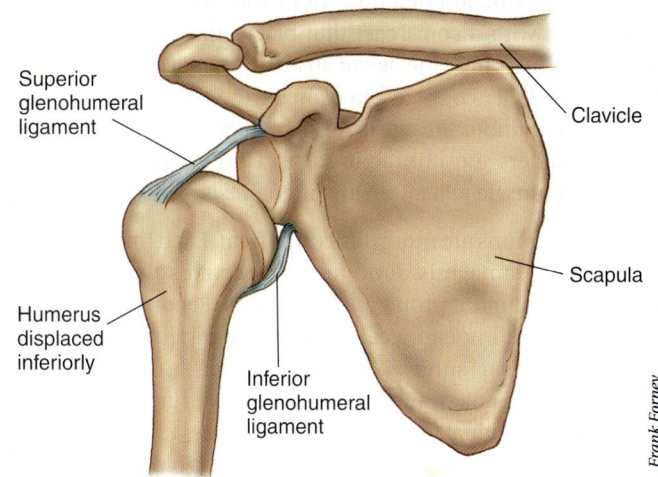

Diagnosis

History: The individual usually reports a traumatic event such as a fall, having the arm jerked backward, or trying to catch something heavy. Pain is extreme, immediate, and worsened by any motion. A sensation of slipping or tearing in the joint may be felt. Most commonly, individuals carry the arm with the elbow bent (abducted) and away (externally rotated) from the body. Less frequently, individuals carry their arm with the elbow abducted and held toward the body (internal rotation). If this is a repeat episode, the individual may have attempted to pop the shoulder back into place.

Physical exam: With a glenohumeral dislocation, a dimple in the skin occurs below the shoulder joint and the head of the humerus that can be felt with the hands (palpated). Attempting to move the arm through the throwing motion may demonstrate abnormal shoulder function and cause a high level of anxiety (positive apprehension sign) in the individual. Lower arm (distal) pulses may be faint and sensation altered.

Tests: Plain x-rays demonstrate the position of the humeral head that defines the direction of the dislocation. X-ray examination also shows any fractures in the bones that make up the shoulder. CT is performed if the diagnosis is unclear after viewing the plain films. MRI is indicated if a tear of the rotator cuff is suspected.

Specialists

- Home Health Care Specialist
- Occupational Therapist
- Orthopedic Surgeon
- Physiatrist
- Physical Therapist
- Sports Medicine Physician

Treatment

The need for realignment of the two bones (reduction) is urgent. Careful manipulation prevents possible nerve and blood vessel damage. Reductions are rarely attempted without an x-ray examination. Nonsurgical (closed) reduction is only possible when the muscles around the shoulder are relaxed. Medications for relief of pain and muscle relaxation are usually necessary. General anesthesia may be used to provide complete relaxation during the manipulation.

The method for reducing glenohumeral dislocations depends on the type of dislocation. A wide variety of different closed reduction methods exist. All utilize some form of traction to realign the two displaced bones. Pain relief is immediate and often quite dramatic with reduction. A sling or sling with waist strap (sling and swath) is worn to immobilize the joint. Following reduction of a posterior dislocation, the shoulder may be immobilized with a spica cast that places the arm in a gunslinger position. Individuals over the age of 40 are immobilized for 7 to 10 days and then gradually encouraged to exercise the shoulder as symptoms allow. Individuals under the age of 40 are at higher risk for redislocation and their shoulders are immobilized up to 6 weeks. Analgesics and medication for muscle relaxation are often prescribed.

Recurrent dislocations are more difficult to treat. Each time the shoulder dislocates, more damage is done to the structures that make up the shoulder making it more prone to dislocations. Recurrent dislocations, dislocations that fail nonsurgical reduction, and chronic dislocations are treated by open surgery (arthrotomy) or arthroscopy with a procedure called a Bankart repair. Reconstructive surgery may be done in young male individuals and high performance athletes who have a higher chance of recurrence. Chronic dislocations older than 6 months usually require joint replacement (arthroplasty).

Prognosis

Closed reduction is successful for 90% of the cases. Bankart repair has a 95% success rate, however, the arthroscopic approach is associated with a higher rate of redislocation than if performed by arthrotomy. Arthroplasty has a good outcome. Relief of pain and regaining a feeling of stability may come as early as 1 to 2 weeks. This is deceptive, as the stretched joint capsule takes about 6 weeks to heal and the shoulder muscles need about 4 weeks of strengthening to maintain stability. If there are no fractures or soft tissue damage, return to near normal activities may be anticipated. Individuals with recurring episodes of dislocation have a shorter recovery time after each episode but they are at greater risk for degenerative arthritis. Failure to rehabilitate the shoulder, with particular attention to scapular stability, decreases the overall stability of the joint and results in a poor outcome.

Differential Diagnosis

Fractures or dislocations of the acromioclavicular joint may give the same appearance. Fractures of the joint surface of the scapula (glenoid) or humeral head may mimic the pain of a dislocation or may have occurred when the shoulder dislocated and then spontaneously reduced. Muscle bruise and nerve palsy should be considered if the diagnosis is unclear.

Rehabilitation

Physical therapy is usually needed when an individual experiences a glenohumeral dislocation for the first time. Rehabilitation from surgery to rectify frequent dislocation of the humeral head can take up to 5 months for full recovery and may include occupational therapy. The key to establishing a successful progression of rehabilitation is to understand the direction of instability (e.g., anterior, posterior, or multidirectional). Initial and intermediate therapeutic protocol is essentially the same for any direction; however, when exercises become more functional, directional issues must be addressed.

Isometric exercises for the glenohumeral area and dynamic resistive exercises for the scapular region are initiated after 3 weeks of arm immobilization. Circumduction and pendulum swings are range-of-motion movements that may be part of the initial routine. Both exercises start with the individual leaning over a table with the uninvolved arm supporting the body. The involved arm is allowed to hang straight down in a relaxed position. The individual swings the arm in circles (counterclockwise and clockwise) while performing circumduction exercises with forward, backward, and side-to-side movements for the pendulum motion.

More challenging movements include active assisted exercises such as the rope-and-pulley. In this exercise, the individual performs front arm raises using an overhead pulley keeping the elbow straight and the palms facing down. The involved arm is raised as high as tolerated and held for 5 seconds. The uninvolved arm can assist as needed in raising the opposing arm. The motion of this exercise is not overhead. If the instability is posterior, the exercises are not taken above 90 degrees of flexion.

Once significant capsular healing has occurred (approximately 3 weeks), joint range-of-motion exercises for forward flexion and active resistive exercises for low ranges of internal/external rotation and the scapula begin. The active assisted exercises may include the use of a T-bar. By gripping the T-bar handle with the noninjured arm and placing the hand of the involved arm in different positions along the T end, the noninjured arm can assist the injured arm in performing external or internal rotation as well as abduction and adduction exercises. Thera-Band or 1- to 2-pound weights are used to start isotonic exercises. These exercises may involve other muscles such as the supraspinatus, deltoids, biceps, and triceps. Exercises can usually be brought into the overhead position after week five.

Restoration of full joint range is accomplished after two months. However, strength training is not enough to fully restore function to the injured shoulder. Functional exercises specific to the direction of instability are introduced toward the later phases of therapy. For example, an individual experiencing anterior dislocation must prove functionality in positions of abduction and external rotation, while those with posterior laxity must show stability in flexion, adduction, and internal rotation.

Those individuals with anterior laxity may benefit from the inertial exercise system where the individual performs a range of directional specific exercises with varying speed and position. Plyometric wall push-ups may benefit those individuals with posterior dislocation. A combination of strategies may benefit those with multidirectional joint laxity. During the functional phase of rehabilitation, all exercises should be performed to fatigue. Therapy is discontinued when individual reaches the highest level of functioning.

Work Restrictions / Accommodations

Access to ice for the control of pain and swelling allows earlier return to work for nondominant injuries. Use of a sling, sling and swath, or cast limit manual dexterity and may produce a hazard to the individual or others in the work environment. Lifting, carrying, and overhead work are restricted for several weeks or permanently. The individual may be temporarily unable to operate equipment, drive a motor vehicle, or perform other tasks that require use of both hands. If the dominant arm is affected, the individual may be unable to write legibly, type well, or perform activities that require fine motor skills such as needed to work in a laboratory or on an assembly line. An ergonometric evaluation of the workplace may be necessary. Change in job duties, sharing or alternating tasks, reduced work rate, more frequent rest breaks, and limiting the time and frequency of repetitive activities are important accommodations.

Some individuals never regain full range of motion or strength in the affected arm so may require a permanent reassignment of duties and necessitate retraining. Pain medication can affect mental alertness and may require alteration of drug use and testing policies by the employer. Individuals whose work environment places them at risk for recurrent episodes may be asked to wear a protective harness. Overhead use of the arm is restricted with this device.

Comorbid Conditions

Rotator cuff tear (and other arm injuries), impingement syndrome, tendonitis, osteoarthritis, rheumatoid arthritis, diabetes, gout, osteoporosis, and general debility can influence the length of disability.

Complications

Tears of the rotator cuff and a pulling away of its attachment to the arm (avulsion of the greater tuberosity) may occur. Damage to the axillary nerve controlling the shoulder muscle (deltoid), bone injury, blood vessel (vascular) injury, frozen shoulder (adhesive capsulitis), and joint disease (arthropathy) are other possible complications. Possible long-term complications include shoulder instability, persistent pain, decrease in range of motion, weakness, and glenohumeral degenerative arthritis.

Factors Influencing Duration

The need for surgery and any complications lengthen disability time. Individuals with recurrent episodes and who choose not to undergo surgery will recover from the acute stage of pain and swelling fairly quickly, sometimes in a few days. These individuals can return to normal activities when they are comfortable if they understand the risks of repeated dislocations. Job demands, such as overhead work, may influence disability duration.

Length of Disability

Duration depends on whether dominant or non-dominant extremity is involved. Disability may be longer for individuals whose job duties require full use of both arms. For those who have surgical treatment, duration depends on individual's age, open or arthroscopic, and whether dominant or non-dominant extremity is involved. Disability may be permanent for those required to do heavy lifting.

Medical treatment. Recurrent dislocation.

Job Classification	Minimum	Optimum	Maximum
Sedentary work	1	7	14
Light work	1	7	14
Medium work	7	14	21
Heavy work	7	21	28
Very Heavy work	7	21	28

Medical treatment. First-time dislocation.

Job Classification	Minimum	Optimum	Maximum
Sedentary work	7	14	28
Light work	21	28	56
Medium work	21	28	56
Heavy work	35	42	84
Very Heavy work	35	63	91

Surgical treatment. Anterior, posterior, inferior, or recurrent dislocation.

Job Classification	Minimum	Optimum	Maximum
Sedentary work	7	14	28
Light work	14	21	28
Medium work	42	56	84
Heavy work	70	84	140
Very Heavy work	70	84	140

Dislocation, Glenohumeral

Duration Trend from Normative Data*

Cases	Mean	Min	Max	No Lost Time	Over 6 Months
2476	69	0	492	0.36%	4.81%

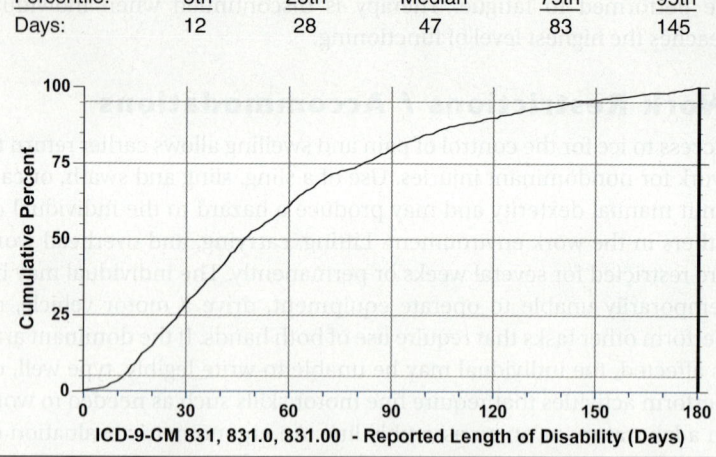

Percentile:	5th	25th	Median	75th	95th
Days:	12	28	47	83	145

ICD-9-CM 831, 831.0, 831.00 - Reported Length of Disability (Days)

* Differences may exist between the expected duration tables and the normative graphs. Duration tables provide expected recovery periods based on the type of work performed by the individual. The normative graphs reflect the actual observed experience of many individuals across the spectrum of physical conditions, in a variety of industries, and with varying levels of case management.

Failure to Recover

If an individual fails to recover within the maximum duration expectancy period, the reader may wish to reference the following questions to assist in better understanding the specifics of an individual's medical case.

Regarding diagnosis:

- Does the individual have shoulder instability, a history of shoulder dislocation, or seizures?
- Is the individual an alcoholic?
- Is the individual an athlete?
- Did a traumatic event occur?
- Is the pain extreme, immediate, and worsened by any motion?
- In what position does individual carry his/her arm?
- Is there a dimple in the skin below the shoulder joint and head of the humerus? What were the findings on physical exam?
- Has the individual received adequate diagnostic testing such as x-rays of the humeral head to establish the diagnosis?
- Were conditions with similar symptoms such as fracture or dislocation of the acromioclavicular joint, fracture of the glenoid or humeral head, muscle bruise, and nerve palsy ruled out?

Regarding treatment:

- Was reduction performed immediately?
- Is the individual over or under the age of 40?
- Were analgesics and muscle relaxants given?
- Has the individual received adequate treatment?

Regarding prognosis:

- Is the individual active in physical therapy?
- Is the individual involved in a home exercise program?
- Does the individual have any conditions such as rotator cuff tear, impingement syndrome, tendinitis, osteoarthritis, rheumatoid arthritis, diabetes, gout, osteoporosis, and general debility that could impact recovery?
- Does the individual have any complications such as avulsion of the greater tuberosity, damage to the axillary nerve, bone injury, vascular injury, adhesive capsulitis, and arthropathy that could lengthen disability?
- Is the individual under the age of 40?
- Is the individual at risk of sustaining repeat dislocations?

References

Boissonnault, William, and Steven Janos. "Dysfunction, Evaluation, and Treatment of the Shoulder." Orthopaedic Physical Therapy. Donatelli, Robert, and Michael Wooden, eds. New York: Churchill Livingstone, 1994. 169-232.

Reid, David. "Shoulder Region." Sports Injury Assessment and Rehabilitation. Reid, David, ed. New York: Churchill Livingstone, 1992. 895-998.

Dislocation, Patella (Kneecap)

Other names / synonyms: Dislocation of the Kneecap, Knee Injury, Kneecap Subluxation, Patellar Injury, Patello-femoral Dislocation

836.3, 836.4, 836.5

Definition

A patellar dislocation is a shifting of the kneecap out of its normal position.

The kneecap (patella) is a triangular-shaped bone imbedded in the tendons of the thigh muscle that normally slides in a groove of the femur (femoral groove) as the knee joint moves.

Changes in the shape of the patella or the femoral groove, or abnormal tension in the structures around the patella, can lead to a dislocation. The patella can dislocate or sublux (partially dislocate) following trauma, when it is pulled from the femoral groove by muscle force, or pushed by a direct blow. The first episode of patellar dislocation often occurs during adolescence. Episodes of repeated subluxation and dislocation are not uncommon, and will occur in approximately 1 in 6 individuals. With each episode, the restraining structures become more lax, compounding the problem.

Dislocation of the patella occurs more commonly in women, due to the wider shape of the female pelvis. The wider pelvis creates sharp angles for the muscle-tendon link between the hip and lower leg, creating a lateral pull on the patella. Patellar dislocation is also a risk of certain athletic activities; dislocation often results from a sudden change in direction while running, which puts the knee under stress. Patellar dislocation is also more common in individuals with "knock knee" (genu valgum), in which the knees are abnormally close together.

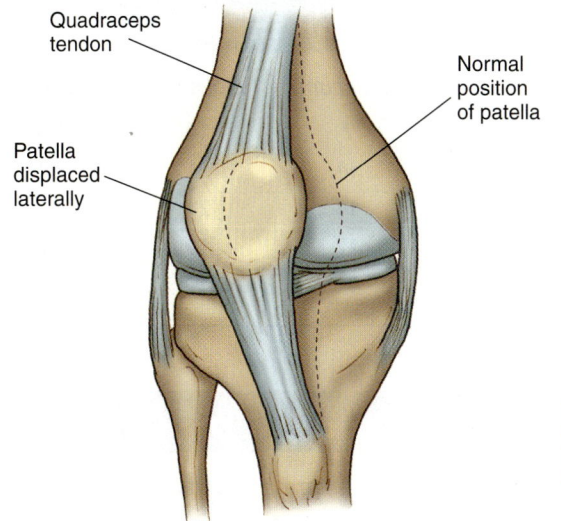

Frank Forney

Diagnosis

History: Individuals report knee pain and tenderness when the patella dislocates. The individual will usually report a traumatic event that causes the dislocation in the first episode. The individual presents with the knee bent (flexed) with a bulge on the outside edge, and cannot straighten his or her leg unless the patella is put back into its normal position (reduced).

Physical exam: If the patella has not been reduced, a deformity is noted along the proximal lateral knee. Swelling of the soft tissue is noted on both sides of the knee (medially and laterally). Tenderness is present along the medial aspect of the patella. Gentle pressure applied to the knee (palpation) will reveal an overly mobile (hypermobile) kneecap. The individual will have a positive apprehension test, in which the individual shows signs of apprehension when the patella is gently pushed laterally (this maneuver does not distress an individual with a normal patella). A positive apprehension test may be the main physical finding if the dislocation is recurrent and has already reduced.

Tests: Routine knee x-rays, including special patella views, are usually all that is needed to evaluate the patella position and rule out chondral fracture. In certain cases, MRI and CT scans may be done to further study the patella-femoral anatomy and patella motion (tracking) during knee flexion and extension. Bone scans may be ordered to rule out fractures and disease processes of the patella.

Treatment

Replacement of the patella to its normal position (reduction) is necessary immediately; sometimes, the dislocation may correct itself (spontaneous reduction) during transit to the emergency room. Reduction provides immediate pain relief. The physician will usually perform a closed reduction (i.e., without surgery) by gently flexing the hip and extending the knee and applying direct medial pressure to the patella. Following reduction, treatment entails immobilization of the knee with a brace or cast with the leg almost fully extended. The knee is typically kept immobilized for 3 weeks. Gentle active range of motion (ROM) exercises are then begun. Analgesics and anti-inflammatory agents may be used to treat pain and swelling.

In cases of recurrent patellar dislocations, surgical procedures designed to restore muscle balance around the patella may be indicated (e.g., proximal realignment or distal realignment). These procedures may be performed as open surgeries; occasionally, surgery may be done arthroscopically on an outpatient basis. If the patella has become lodged in the knee joint, open reduction (i.e., surgical reduction) may be necessary.

Prognosis

Conservative treatment (closed reduction, immobilization of the knee, gentle active range-of-motion exercises, and analgesics and anti-inflammatory agents) will often yield good results in first episodes if the offending activity is eliminated and patella femoral anatomy is normal. Approximately 50% of individuals may recover and have no further symptoms (asymptomatic). Approximately one third of individuals may have some minor residual symptoms, and 1 out of 6 may develop recurrent dislocation(s). Recurrent episodes usually go on to surgical treatment (proximal realignment or distal realignment) with long rehabilitation periods. One study has indicated that when treated nonoperatively, individuals with congenital abnormalities of the extensor mechanism of the knee have a lesser chance of a good or excellent outcome (approximately 50%) compared with individuals who do not have the abnormality (approximately 75%).

Differential Diagnosis

Knee ligament injuries, patella fracture, patella tendon rupture, quadriceps tendon rupture, osteochondritis dissecans, osteoarthritis, and rheumatoid arthritis may present with similar findings.

Specialists

- Occupational Therapist
- Orthopedic Surgeon
- Physiatrist
- Physical Therapist
- Sports Medicine Physician

Rehabilitation

Physical therapy may be recommended for successful recovery from a patellar dislocation. Modalities that use heat, cold, or electrical stimulation may be used to address any inflammation or pain.

During an immobilization period, isometric exercises are instructed for the knee joint that demand that the muscles around the knee joint contract yet no movement takes place at the joint. An example of an isometric exercise for the knee region is the quad set. In this exercise, the individual sits on the floor with his or her knees straight while pushing the back of the knee down onto the floor or other immovable surface.

After immobilization, the individual may be required to wear a horseshoe-shaped felt pad that is held in place around the patella by an elastic band or sleeve.

Quadriceps strengthening has been the cornerstone of patellar subluxation rehabilitation. The conventional program consists of leg raises involving an individual long sitting with the uninvolved knee in a flexed or bent position, while the involved leg is raised to the height of the opposite knee. Short-arc quad exercises are popular in the rehabilitation process and are described as the individual sitting on the floor with his or her knees straight (also referred to as long sitting). A bolster such as a coffee can or pillow is placed under the knee, positioning the knee joint to function in a 30-to-0 degree range. The individual is instructed to turn the foot outward before straightening the leg and then slowly lowering to the starting position

Stretching exercises are important in the rehabilitation program with emphasis placed upon improving the flexibility of the quadriceps, hamstrings, and calf muscles. Orthotics may need to be provided to address any foot dysfunction that can predispose an individual to patellar dislocation. This may be the case in the individual whose feet are flat and collapse inward (pronation).

Modifications may need to be made by the physical therapist for those who have arthritis or other joint irritations. If the joint dislocation required surgical repair, there may be some restriction on the progression of motion and strengthening of the knee. This varies depending on the degree of the patellar dislocation or type of surgery that was performed. A patellar-stabilizing brace may be required for a period of time when the individual has returned to work, especially if a considerable amount of ascending and descending stairs or knee bends beyond 90 degrees is necessary.

Work Restrictions / Accommodations

During early treatment and recovery, squatting, kneeling, climbing, and prolonged standing and walking should be restricted. Restrictions in these activities may become permanent. Use of knee braces, crutches, and cold therapy will be necessary. Frequent rest periods with leg elevation, along with medication for pain and swelling, are also usual recommendations.

Comorbid Conditions

Anatomical variances and looseness of structures that restrain the patella increase stress across the patella-femoral joint and may complicate treatment of patella subluxation or dislocation. Arthritis of the knee joint, obesity, and any condition that inhibits the individual's ability to perform rehabilitative exercise therapy would also impact ability to recover.

Complications

Complications of the dislocation include fracture of the patella or femoral condyle, loose body formation, chondromalacia of the patella and femoral groove, osteoarthritis, and recurrent episodes with accompanying muscle atrophy.

Factors Influencing Duration

Occupation, activity levels, treatment rendered, incidence of complications, individual compliance with exercise therapy, age, and frequency of recurrence will affect disability periods.

Length of Disability

Conservative treatment.

Duration in Days

Job Classification	Minimum	Optimum	Maximum
Sedentary work	7	14	28
Light work	14	21	42
Medium work	14	21	42
Heavy work	42	49	56
Very Heavy work	42	49	56

Surgical treatment.

Duration in Days

Job Classification	Minimum	Optimum	Maximum
Sedentary work	14	28	42
Light work	14	28	56
Medium work	21	42	84
Heavy work	42	84	168
Very Heavy work	42	112	168

Duration Trend from Normative Data*

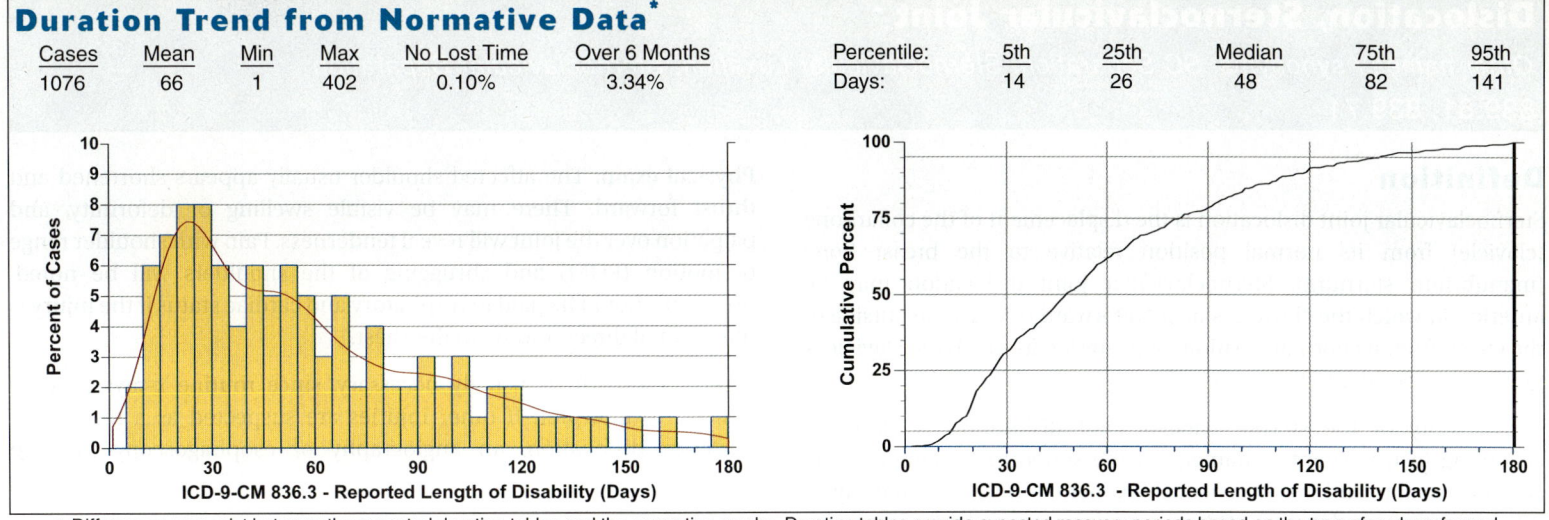

Cases	Mean	Min	Max	No Lost Time	Over 6 Months
1076	66	1	402	0.10%	3.34%

Percentile:	5th	25th	Median	75th	95th
Days:	14	26	48	82	141

* Differences may exist between the expected duration tables and the normative graphs. Duration tables provide expected recovery periods based on the type of work performed by the individual. The normative graphs reflect the actual observed experience of many individuals across the spectrum of physical conditions, in a variety of industries, and with varying levels of case management.

Failure to Recover

If an individual fails to recover within the maximum duration expectancy period, the reader may wish to reference the following questions to assist in better understanding the specifics of an individual's medical case.

Regarding diagnosis:

- Has the individual had trauma to the knee?
- Does the individual complain of knee pain, tenderness or a deformity?
- What is the individual's gender? Does the individual have "knock knees?"
- Did the individual present with the knee flexed?
- On exam, was there a deformity along the proximal lateral knee with soft tissue swelling?
- On palpation is tenderness and a hypermobile kneecap present?
- Does the individual have a positive apprehension test?
- Has the individual had an x-ray?
- Was it necessary to do a CT scan, MRI or bone scan?
- Have conditions with similar symptoms been ruled out?

Regarding treatment:

- Has the individual had patellar reduction done? Did it spontaneously reduce?
- Is the individual being treated with immobilization? Analgesics? NSAIDs?
- Is the individual's dislocation recurrent? Was it necessary to surgically correct it?

Regarding prognosis:

- Is the individual active in rehabilitation?
- Does the individual have a home exercise program?
- Is the individual's employer able to accommodate any necessary restrictions?
- Does the individual have any conditions that may affect the ability to recover?
- Does the individual have any complications such as fracture of the patella or femoral condyle, loose body formation, chondromalacia of the patella and femoral groove, osteoarthritis, or recurrent episodes with accompanying muscle atrophy?

References

The Knee - Part 5. Communications Mednet, Inc. 2000. 14 Nov 2000 <http://www.echo.uqam.ca/mednet/anglais/hermes_a/knee/part_5.html>.

Kessler, R.M. Management of Common Musculoskeletal Disorders: Physical Therapy Principles and Methods. Philadelphia: J.B. Lippincott Co, 1990.

Dislocation, Sternoclavicular Joint

Other names / synonyms: SC Separation, Sternoclavicular Luxation, Sternoclavicular Separation

839.61, 839.71

Definition

Sternoclavicular joint dislocation is the displacement of the collarbone (clavicle) from its normal position relative to the breast bone (manubrium sternum). Sternoclavicular joint dislocation may be anterior, in which the clavicle is pushed forward (toward the outside of the chest) from its normal position, or posterior, in which the clavicle is pushed backward into the chest.

The severity of the sternoclavicular joint dislocation is classified according to the extent of damage to the supporting ligaments (the sternoclavicular and costoclavicular ligaments). A first-degree injury involves an incomplete tear of the sternoclavicular and costoclavicular ligaments. A second-degree injury involves a complete tear of the sternoclavicular ligament and a partial tear of the costoclavicular ligament. A third-degree injury involves complete rupture of both ligaments and complete dislocation of the clavicle from the manubrium.

Sternoclavicular dislocations occur most often through the application of great force, such as that incurred during a severe, traumatic fall or motor vehicle accident, or from injury sustained during a contact sport such as football. Dislocation may also occur due to congenital, degenerative, or inflammatory processes. Only about 3-5% of all shoulder injuries involve sternoclavicular dislocation, and anterior dislocations outnumber posterior dislocations, which are rare, by anywhere from 9 to 1 to 20 to 1.

The overall incidence of sternoclavicular joint dislocations is highest in young males.

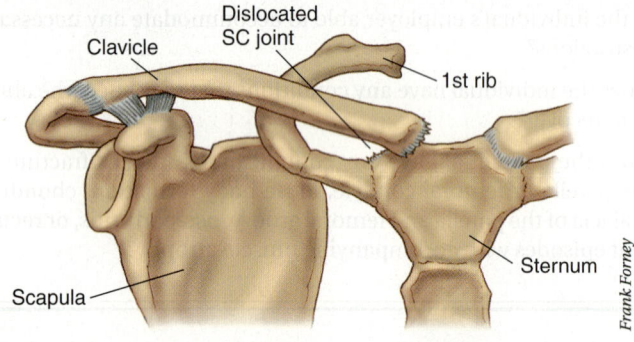

Diagnosis

History: The individual may report a specific event with trauma around the chest or shoulder area. The individual usually reports chest and shoulder pain that is increased by arm movement, especially elevation of the arm. The individual may also have weakness of the shoulder/arm on the affected side, and may report having heard or felt a "popping" at the time of the injury. Individuals with a posterior sternoclavicular dislocation may experience shortness of breath (dyspnea), difficulty swallowing (dysphagia), and tingling (paresthesia).

Physical exam: The affected shoulder usually appears shortened and thrust forward. There may be visible swelling or deformity, and palpation over the joint will reveal tenderness. Pain with shoulder range of motion (ROM) and shrugging of the shoulders will be noted. Attention should be paid to respiratory and cardiac status if the injury is the result of direct trauma to the chest.

Tests: CT or MRI is usually necessary, since routine x-rays may be difficult to interpret. If other injuries are suspected as a result of a posterior dislocation, an angiography or esophagoscopy may be indicated.

Treatment

Treatment of sternoclavicular joint dislocations depends upon the type of dislocation (anterior or posterior) and the severity of the injury (first, second, or third degree).

First-degree dislocations are treated conservatively with anti-inflammatory medications (to relieve pain and inflammation), rest of the affected arm and shoulder, ice (cold therapy), and placement of the affected arm in a sling.

With second-degree dislocations, a figure-8 harness is usually added to this regimen for 7 to 10 days. With a third degree injury, the joint must be replaced to its normal position, either manually or with surgery (a closed or open reduction). Reduction is usually done with the individual sedated or under general anesthesia. Following reduction, the treatment regimen for a second-degree injury is followed. In cases requiring reduction, longer periods of immobilization may be necessary. Posterior dislocations may require emergency treatment of associated injuries and/or complications.

Prognosis

First and second-degree dislocations are expected to have an excellent outcome following appropriate conservative treatment; prognosis for third degree dislocations may not be as good depending upon complications from associated injuries. Outcome with conservative treatment is good for anterior dislocations that do not require reduction or are easily reduced (closed reduction). Posterior dislocations usually require open reduction and may have a less positive outcome related to additional injuries sustained at the same time.

Differential Diagnosis

A fracture near the joint (clavicle, rib, scapular, or sternal fracture), arthritis of the joint, and tumor could present with similar findings.

Specialists

- Orthopedic Surgeon
- Thoracic Surgeon

Rehabilitation

Rehabilitation of a sternoclavicular joint dislocation depends greatly on the extent of the dislocation and associated tissue injury. If there is a significant amount of pain and loss of function, physical therapy may be necessary. The physical therapist may need to use cold or warm treatments throughout the period of rehabilitation to control inflammation and pain. Early on in the rehabilitation of a sternoclavicular joint dislocation, range-of-motion exercises are introduced to return normal motion to the shoulder complex. Some of these exercises include the pendulum exercise. Progression of this form of movement is achieved by the use of pulleys.

Isometric exercises are performed next that allow the muscles around the joint to contract without movement at the joint. An example of an isometric exercise for the shoulder complex is pushing the hand into the wall or other immovable object for a count of 10 seconds. As range of motion improves to the entire shoulder complex, and isometric exercises are tolerated with near maximum effort, gradual resistance with isotonic exercises is introduced. Muscles that are emphasized in the rehabilitation of a sternoclavicular joint dislocation are the front chest and shoulder muscles. Isotonic strengthening involves movement in the region of the sternoclavicular joint. An example of this type of rehabilitation exercise is strengthening with weights often used in rehabilitation. Strength training of this type will also include weight equipment/machines and elastic bands.

With the individual lying on his or her back, strengthening of the front chest muscles is accomplished with the use of gradual resistance during bench presses utilizing a grip narrower than the shoulder width. Exercises to strengthen the front of the shoulder are introduced as the individual performs a rowing motion with light resistance dumbbells while standing upright.

Similar to other shoulder complex dislocations, heavy weightlifting activities should be avoided for approximately 8 to 12 weeks until ligament has healed. From this point, a gradual strengthening program is advanced as tolerated. Overhead presses, which also address the muscles on the front of the shoulder, are a good example of strengthening at this phase as well as variations of dumbbell exercises.

Modifications may need to be made by the physical therapist for those who have arthritis or other joint irritations. If the sternoclavicular joint dislocation was severe enough to require surgical repair, some restrictions may be placed on the progression of the range of motion and strengthening in certain movements. This varies depending on the degree of dislocation or type of surgery that was performed.

Work Restrictions / Accommodations

Use of the affected arm and shoulder, including lifting and overhead work, should be restricted for 6 to 8 weeks, with a gradual increase in tolerance to load-bearing activities. Following successful rehabilitation, the majority of individuals are able to resume their full work load. Use of medications for pain control and swelling may require review of drug use policies.

Complementary and Alternative Therapies

Content is intended for awareness only. Treatments may or may not be effective. Scientific evidence may be lacking and some substances have potentially toxic effects. Dr. Presley Reed and the editors do not endorse the use of these therapies in the absence of consultation with a licensed medical professional.

Chiropractic joint manipulation - Specific joint manipulation may be successful in treating dislocation.

Comorbid Conditions

Existing conditions that could impact ability to recover and further lengthen disability include any condition that causes the ligaments to be weakened (e.g., torn or strained rotator cuff) and any condition that impairs the individual's ability to follow appropriate rehabilitative therapy (e.g., rheumatoid arthritis, bursitis, septic arthritis).

Complications

Anterior sternoclavicular joint dislocations usually do not cause serious complications, but may result in a permanent cosmetic deformity or decreased range of motion. Posterior sternoclavicular joint dislocations, however, have a 25% complication rate and may have life-threatening consequences if misdiagnosed. Such additional complications may involve tracheal, esophageal, or great vessel injury, including tracheal rupture, pneumothorax, laceration of the superior vena cava, occlusion of the subclavian artery and/or vein, and recurrent dislocations.

Factors Influencing Duration

Recognition of the injury, concomitant injuries, work activity expectations, weakened ligaments, and stability of the joint after healing may influence length of disability. Recovery could take 6-8 weeks for sternoclavicular dislocations without complications. Disability for dislocations with complications would also be dependent on concomitant conditions.

Length of Disability

Duration depends on whether dominant or non-dominant extremity is involved.

Duration in Days

Job Classification	Minimum	Optimum	Maximum
Sedentary work	3	7	21
Light work	3	21	35
Medium work	7	42	70
Heavy work	14	63	91
Very Heavy work	14	91	119

Failure to Recover

If an individual fails to recover within the maximum duration expectancy period, the reader may wish to reference the following questions to assist in better understanding the specifics of an individual's medical case.

Regarding diagnosis:

- Is individual's dislocation anterior or posterior?
- Was individual's dislocation first-, second-, or third-degree?
- What was the nature of the precipitating injury, a motor vehicle accident or sports injury?
- Did individual have a CT or MRI done? Was additional testing such as angiography or esophagoscopy necessary?
- Were conditions with similar symptoms ruled out?

Regarding treatment:

- Is individual following the prescribed conservative treatment regimen of NSAIDs, rest, and ice?
- Is individual wearing a figure-8 harness or sling as directed?
- Was a closed or open reduction done?

Regarding prognosis:

- Is individual active in physical therapy? Does individual participate in a home exercise program?
- Does individual do pendulum exercises several times a day?
- Can individual's employer accommodate any necessary restrictions?
- Does individual have any conditions that may affect the ability to recover?
- Does individual have any complications involving tracheal, esophageal, or great vessel injury including tracheal rupture, pneumothorax, laceration of the superior vena cava, occlusion of the subclavian artery and/or vein, and recurrent dislocations?

References

Sternoclavicular Joint Injury. eMedicine.com. 2000. 03 Nov 2000 <http://www.emedicine.com/emerg/topic783.htm>.

Arnheim, Daniel D. Modern Principles of Athletic Training. St. Louis: Mirror/Mosby, 1989.

Kaufman, R.L. "Manipulative Reduction and Management of Anterior Sternoclavicular Joint Dislocation." Journal of Manipulative Physiology and Therapy 20 5 (1997): 338-342.

Kessler, R.M. Management of Common Musculoskeletal Disorders: Physical Therapy Principles and Methods. Philadelphia: J.B. Lippincott Co, 1990.

Malone, Terry R., Thomas McPoil, and Arthur J. Nitz. Orthopedic and Sports Physical Therapy. St. Louis: Mosby, 1997.

Williams, Cyd C. "Posterior Sternoclavicular Joint Dislocation." The Physician and Sports Medicine 02 (1999): 6. 03 Nov 2000 <http://www.physsportsmed.com/issues/1999/02_99/williams.htm>.

Displacement, Cervical Intervertebral Disc Without Myelopathy

Other names / synonyms: Cervical Disc Herniation, Cervical Disc Prolapse, Cervical Disc Protrusion, Disc Herniation, Disc Protrusion, Disc Rupture, Herniated Disc, Herniated Nucleus Pulposis

722.0

Definition

Cervical disc displacement refers to abnormal protrusion or herniation of a disc that separates the cervical vertebrae in the neck region of the spine.

While there are 7 cervical vertebrae, the most common sites of disc displacement are between the fifth and sixth (C5-C6) or the sixth and seventh (C6-C7) cervical vertebrae. The displaced disc may press against nerves leaving the spinal cord, causing changes in sensory, motor, and reflex function (radiculopathy). Cervical disc displacement usually occurs as a result of a stress-induced defect in the cervical spine, and rarely as a result of a single traumatic event. Individuals at increased risk are those exposed to vibrational stress (such as professional drivers, jackhammer operators, etc.), heavy lifting, prolonged sedentary positions, or whiplash accidents.

In asymptomatic individuals, herniated cervical discs may be observed by MRI in 10% of adults younger than 40 years, and about 25% of those older than 40. Displaced cervical discs occur equally as often in men and women.

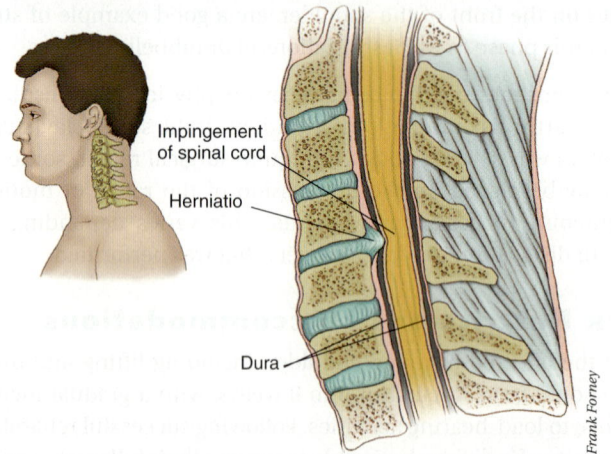

Diagnosis

History: History is of onset of neck pain, followed by radiation of the pain into in the shoulder, arm, forearm, or hand. Displacement of the C5-C6 disc usually results in pain that radiates from the base of neck, along the biceps muscle and lateral forearm, and into the back of the hand, the thumb, and the first two fingers. Displacement of the C6-C7 disc often results in pain or numbness in the middle finger, along with shoulder pain radiating into the triceps and forearm. The pain may have begun soon after an injury to the neck. Coughing or sneezing may be reported to make the pain worse. The individual may eventually notice weakness in the affected limb. Individuals may report being more comfortable sleeping in a reclining chair than in a bed.

Physical exam: The exam may show that pain is aggravated by neck movement, particularly when bending the head backward (hyperextension), and turning the head from side to side (rotation). Pain may also be increased by placing downward pressure on the top of the head (compression of the spine) and relieved by traction. These two maneuvers, applied manually during the physical exam, help to differentiate disc pain from other causes. Range-of-motion of the neck may be limited due to pain and muscle spasm. There may also be tenderness to firm pressure over the affected vertebra.

Tests: Plain x-rays are helpful primarily in ruling out other causes of pain such as tumor, infection, or fracture. The x-ray will usually show degenerative changes. These aging changes are also seen in asymptomatic individuals. In order to be considered significant, the x-ray findings must correlate closely with the symptoms and physical exam. If mechanical instability is suspected as a cause of recurrent pain, it can be documented by x-rays taken with the neck in flexion (forward bending) and hyperextension.

Myelography combined with CT has been considered the best way to diagnose a herniated cervical disc. Today, myelography can often be replaced by MRI. Electromyography (EMG) may be useful in distinguishing nerve root compression from a peripheral nerve problem such as carpal tunnel syndrome or ulnar nerve entrapment. However, a normal EMG does not rule out nerve root compression. As in the lumbar spine, asymptomatic herniations are frequently seen in normal volunteers. Disc herniations on imaging studies must correlate exactly with the nerve root deficit of symptoms on physical exam.

Treatment

Conservative treatment should always be tried first, except in cases of severe or progressive neurological compression. In the acute phase of a disc herniation, rest and immobilization are essential. If the individual is up and about, a cervical collar may be worn briefly to provide support and limit neck motion; however, strict bedrest may be prescribed in severe cases. Traction may be applied intermittently. (The individual may be taught to use intermittent traction at home.) For relief of pain and inflammation, nonsteroidal anti-inflammatory drugs (NSAIDs) or steroids may be given. If pain is severe, a narcotic may be added, or an anticonvulsant may be tried for its analgesic effect. If anxiety and tension are prominent, sedatives may be helpful. Muscle relaxants are frequently prescribed; however, their effectiveness probably is due to their sedative action. Narcotics, sedatives, and muscle relaxants are usually used only for brief periods of time. Ongoing use should be weighed against the potential for addiction or abuse. Other treatments such as ice, heat, massage, ultrasound therapy, and intermittent cervical traction may help relieve pain.

As symptoms subside, activity is gradually increased, including physical therapy and/or a home exercise program to strengthen and mobilize the neck and shoulder. Good posture and frequent changes in position help to prevent fatigue. Preventive and maintenance measures (exercise, stress management, proper body mechanics, etc.) should be continued indefinitely. If there is no improvement during the first 2 weeks, or if pain is still disabling after a maximum of 6 weeks, further evaluation is necessary.

Surgery is also indicated if the disc herniation is massive, thus compressing the spinal cord and causing bowel and/or bladder control impairment, or lower extremity weakness, sensory loss, or gait disturbance.

Recurrent pain may be due to mechanical instability; if this instability cannot be managed conservatively by muscle strengthening and good body mechanics, surgery may be indicated. Surgery involves removal of the protruding disc material (discectomy). Surgery may be considered if there is progressive or severe muscle weakness; severe arm pain with objective signs of nerve root compression, not improved by an adequate trial of conservative treatment; or recurrent pain due to mechanical instability that cannot be managed conservatively (an indication for fusion).

Prognosis

Therapy and bedrest may help symptoms, but do not change outcome. Most cervical disc herniations (an estimated 80-90%) improve without surgery. Surgery (discectomy) can have a high failure rate if individuals are not carefully selected. However, when properly indicated, discectomy with appropriate rehabilitation has a good outcome in 80-90% or noncompensation individuals.

Differential Diagnosis

Spondylosis, ligament injury, tumors of the spine, and certain neurological syndromes--including carpal tunnel syndrome, ulnar nerve entrapment, and thoracic outlet syndrome--present similarly to cervical disc displacement.

Specialists

- Neurologist
- Neurosurgeon
- Occupational Medicine Physician
- Orthopedic Surgeon
- Physiatrist
- Spine Surgeon
- Sports Medicine Physician

Rehabilitation

Rehabilitation is an important aspect in regaining mobility in the neck (cervical) region following an intervertebral disc displacement at that level of the spine. Focus is placed upon decreasing pain and increasing range of motion, stability, strength, and endurance.

Initially, physical therapy may be needed to decrease pain. Treatments involving cold or heat can help provide relief by controlling the amount of blood flow to the cervical muscles. Methods of cold treatment include cold packs applied to the neck region. Heat treatments become helpful to reduce pain and become beneficial prior to stretching of the neck muscles. Forms of heat treatment include ultrasound and diathermy that uses high frequency sound waves, producing heat that penetrates deep into the involved muscles.

Electrical stimulation combined with heat or cold treatment is another technique used in physical therapy to relax muscles. Traction is another popular form of rehabilitation for the displaced cervical disc. Whether the therapist applies it mechanically or manually, traction produces a separation of vertebra of the cervical spine to help reduce the pain.

Soft tissue mobilization and joint mobilization techniques are used by a physical therapist experienced in manual therapy to help improve mobility. This is a hands-on approach providing the effects of increased elasticity of the muscles, thereby improving flexibility. Joint mobilization becomes important to increase the movement at each spinal level resulting in overall cervical spine motion. A cervical epidural steroid injection may provide several weeks of significantly decreased pain.

Range of motion for the neck normally includes forward and side bending. Rotation and extension are introduced with caution at the appropriate time by the therapist or physician. Isometric resistance helps strengthen the muscles of the neck without moving the neck through the range of motion. These exercises are helpful to improve stability around the displaced cervical disc. Strengthening of the cervical muscles progresses with the use of resistance throughout the range of motion. The instruction and supervision of a physical therapist usually accomplishes this with devices such as wall pulleys and universal and nautilus type equipment as tolerated.

Modifications may need to be made by the physical therapist for those who have arthritis or other joint irritations of the cervical spine. If the cervical disc displacement required surgery, some restrictions may be placed on the progression of the range of motion and strengthening in certain movements. This varies depending on the degree of disc displacement or type surgery that was performed.

Work Restrictions / Accommodations

Individuals with displaced cervical discs usually are advised not to lift overhead or posture with the neck in extension. They cannot perform heavy lifting or repetitive twisting motions. Certain other duties that require extension of the neck (such as painting ceilings) may be unsuitable for individuals with limited range of motion of the head and neck.

Comorbid Conditions

Spondylosis, curvature of the spine (scoliosis), obesity, and psychological conditions such as depression may increase recovery time.

Complications

Worsening of the condition may cause pressure on the spinal cord as well as on the nerve roots. Functional disturbances and/or pathological changes in the spinal cord (myelopathy) may occur as a result of the displaced disk pressing on the spinal cord.

Factors Influencing Duration

Length of disability depends on the location and number of the affected discs, whether the individual also shows symptoms of degenerative disease (such as spondylosis), the nature of any neurological involvement, the presence or absence of neurological deficits (objective sensory loss and/or muscle weakness), the duration of neurological deficits (acute or chronic), the presence of other sources of pain (such as facet joint arthritis, mechanical instability), the individual's age, and the type of treatment (surgical versus nonsurgical).

Length of Disability

With medical treatment, duration depends on severity of symptoms. Persisting radicular pain from a cervical disc herniation, even without myelopathy, may not be compatible with heavy work. With discectomy and with no history of prior spine surgery, many individuals after a one level discectomy without fusion are now restricted to only "no overhead lifting" and thus can resume heavy work. Disability may be permanent following spinal fusion.

Medical treatment.

Duration in Days

Job Classification	Minimum	Optimum	Maximum
Sedentary work	0	7	21
Light work	0	14	28
Medium work	0	21	42
Heavy work	0	49	84
Very Heavy work	0	56	90

Discectomy.

Duration in Days

Job Classification	Minimum	Optimum	Maximum
Sedentary work	14	42	56
Light work	21	42	56
Medium work	42	56	84
Heavy work	91	119	182
Very Heavy work	91	119	182

Fusion.

Duration in Days

Job Classification	Minimum	Optimum	Maximum
Sedentary work	42	49	84
Light work	56	63	84
Medium work	70	119	182
Heavy work	Indefinite	Indefinite	Indefinite
Very Heavy work	Indefinite	Indefinite	Indefinite

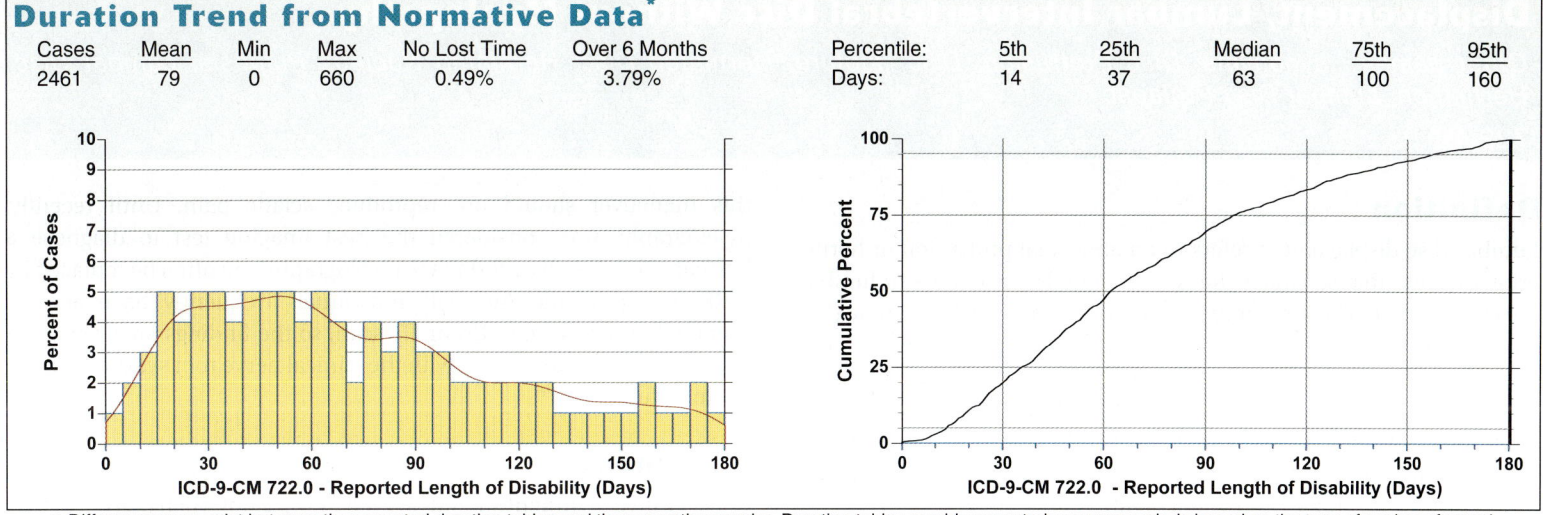

Duration Trend from Normative Data*

Cases	Mean	Min	Max	No Lost Time	Over 6 Months
2461	79	0	660	0.49%	3.79%

Percentile:	5th	25th	Median	75th	95th
Days:	14	37	63	100	160

* Differences may exist between the expected duration tables and the normative graphs. Duration tables provide expected recovery periods based on the type of work performed by the individual. The normative graphs reflect the actual observed experience of many individuals across the spectrum of physical conditions, in a variety of industries, and with varying levels of case management.

Failure to Recover

If an individual fails to recover within the maximum duration expectancy period, the reader may wish to reference the following questions to assist in better understanding the specifics of an individual's medical case.

Regarding diagnosis:

- What level is the displacement at?
- Has the individual been exposed to vibration stress? Heavy lifting?
- Is the individual sedentary?
- Has the individual had a whiplash injury?
- Does the neck pain radiate to the shoulder and down to the hand?
- Is there weakness in the extremity?
- Is the individual more comfortable sleeping in a recliner?
- On physical exam, is pain aggravated by neck movement?
- Is range of motion of the neck restricted?
- Is there tenderness to palpation over the affected vertebra?
- Have x-rays been done?
- Has the individual had a CT myelography or MRI?
- Has the individual had an EMG?
- Have conditions with similar symptoms been ruled out?

Regarding treatment:

- Did the individual respond favorably to conservative treatment?
- Was it necessary to use steroids? Narcotic pain relievers? Sedatives?
- Was ice, heat, massage, ultrasound therapy, and intermittent cervical traction used?
- Was surgery necessary?

Regarding prognosis:

- Is the individual active in rehabilitation? Do they have a home exercise program?
- Is the individual's employer able to accommodate the necessary restrictions?
- Does the individual have any conditions that may affect their ability to recover?
- Has the individual developed myelopathy?

References

Brower, Richard. "Cervical Disc Disease." The Spine. Herkowitz, H.N., et al Philadelphia: W.B. Saunders Company, 1999. 455-496.

Kessler, R.M. Management of Common Musculoskeletal Disorders: Physical Therapy Principles and Methods. Philadelphia: J.B. Lippincott Co, 1990.

Malone, Terry R., Thomas McPoil, and Arthur J. Nitz. Orthopedic and Sports Physical Therapy. St. Louis: Mosby, 1997.

Sidhu, Kanwaldeep, and Harry Herkowitz. "Surgical Management of Cervical Disc Disease." The Spine. Herkowitz, H.N., et al., eds. Philadelphia: W.B. Saunders Company, 1999. 497-529.

Displacement, Lumbar Intervertebral Disc Without Myelopathy

Other names / synonyms: Disc Protrusion, Disc Rupture, Herniated Disc, Herniated Nucleus Pulposis, Lumbar Disc Herniation, Lumbar Disc Prolapse

722.10

Definition

Lumbar disc displacement refers to an abnormal protrusion or herniation of a disc that separates the vertebrae in the lower back or lumbar area of the spine. The lumbar area of the spine contains 5 vertebrae (L1-L5), and the most common areas of disc herniation are between L4 and L5 and between L5 and the first sacral vertebrae (S1). When a lumbar disc is displaced, it may put pressure on the adjacent spinal nerve. Even without pressure on a nerve, the displaced lumbar disc may produce pain, although there is no reliable means to tell whether or not a given disc is responsible for an individual's pain.

Approximately 80-90% of individuals will experience low back pain in their lifetime, and disorders and degeneration of the lumbar intervertebral discs may account for the largest proportion of low back pain. Lumbar disc herniation occurs in men at a median age of 38 years and in women at a median age of 40 years. It is slightly more common in males than females (ratio: 1.45 to 1.10). There are no racial differences in the incidence of low back pain due to disc disease. A precipitating event, often a minor event or normal activity (i.e., trauma due to a fall or a strain due to lifting or even bending) is reported in a little over half of all cases of lumbar disc herniations.

Diagnosis

History: Trauma such as a fall, a blow to the spine, or a strain due to lifting (present in a little over half of the cases of lumbar disc herniation) may be reported. It may also occur without a history of trauma as part of the degenerative process. Back pain is common and often the earliest symptom of a herniated lumbar disc. It is almost always followed by radiation of the pain from the back or hip region down the back of the thigh and calf and frequently into the foot (sciatica). Pain from a herniated lumbar disc may be aggravated by sitting, standing, walking, or bending; it is relieved by lying down with the knees flexed and supported. Coughing or sneezing may also make the pain worse. In fewer than 50% of individuals, sensory loss (numbness) over the thigh, leg, or foot may be present. Some individuals report a pins and needles sensation. Rarely, some individuals report disturbances in bowel or bladder function.

Physical exam: The exam may reveal flattening of the normal curvature (lordosis) of the lumbar area of the back, slight hip and knee flexion, and a tendency for the individual to avoid putting weight on the affected leg when walking (antalgic gait). The physician will put pressure on the spine (palpation) and will tap on the affected area (percussion). Palpation may reveal tenderness and muscle spasm, and percussion of the involved vertebrae frequently causes pain. Reflex examination to test deep tendon reflexes will be performed. The ankle jerk reflex or the knee jerk reflex are diminished with lumbar disc herniations compressing the S1 nerve root or L4 nerve root, respectively.

Tests: The straight leg raising test (SLR, also called Lasegue's sign) is the most important test in the diagnosis of a herniated lumbar disc. With the individual in a reclining position, the affected leg is raised with the knee extended; this maneuver produces sciatic pain (below the knee) when herniation is present. The test is then repeated with the knee bent; this maneuver should not reproduce sciatic pain. Until recently, myelography was considered the best imaging test to diagnose a herniated lumbar disc. Today, CT myelography can often be replaced by MRI. Asymptomatic "normal" individuals frequently have asymptomatic herniations on MRI or CT scan, so the findings on an imaging study must correlate exactly with the clinical nerve root syndrome to be meaningful.

Treatment

Conservative treatment should be tried first, except when there are signs of severe or progressive nerve compression. Bedrest for a short period of time (usually 2 days) is recommended to decrease pain. The individual is instructed to avoid aggravating activities such as heavy lifting, bending, twisting, or prolonged sitting. A corset may be worn during the day to provide support. For relief of pain and inflammation, nonsteroidal anti-inflammatory drugs (NSAIDs) may be given. If pain is severe, a narcotic may be added or an anticonvulsant may be tried for its analgesic effects. Muscle relaxants are frequently prescribed, but their effectiveness is due to their sedative action. Other treatments such as ice, heat, massage, and ultrasound therapy may help relieve pain and muscle spasm.

As symptoms subside, activity is gradually increased, including physical therapy and/or a home exercise program to strengthen the low back and abdominal muscles and improve aerobic capacity (walking). The individual may attend "back school" to learn correct posture and body mechanics. Although some individuals may recover completely and permanently, recurrences are common. Therefore, preventive and maintenance measures (exercise, proper body mechanics, firm bed, etc.) should be continued indefinitely.

If there is little or no improvement after 4-6 weeks of treatment, further evaluation is necessary. Persisting pain may be due to a persisting herniation not being resorbed by the body. If this pain cannot be managed conservatively by muscle strengthening, good body mechanics, and/or bracing, it is an indication for surgery (discectomy).

If no other cause is found, individuals who have leg pain (radicular pain) as the predominant symptom may be relieved by an epidural corticosteroid injection. If this is unsuccessful, and MRI, and/or CT/myelography confirm a herniated disc at the appropriate level and compressing the nerve on the appropriate side to account for the symptoms, the individual is a candidate for surgery (discectomy). Midline or central disc herniations that do not cause nerve root compression rarely benefit from surgery. Individuals who have persistent back pain as the predominant symptom usually do not benefit from surgery; these individuals may benefit from a pain clinic or rehabilitation program.

The clearest indications for surgery are progressive muscle weakness (surgery should not be delayed); severe leg pain with objective signs of nerve root compression (nerve tension signs and/or loss of neurological function) not improved by an adequate trial of conservative treatment, with an imaging study that correlates with the nerve root suspected of compression by clinical exam; recurrent episodes of severe leg pain with objective signs of nerve root compression and a matching defect on imaging studies; and recurrent pain due to proven (flexion-extension x-rays) mechanical instability that cannot be managed conservatively (this is an indication for fusion). Bedrest for a few days may be a necessary concession to the pain.

Prognosis

An estimated 80-90% of lumbar disc herniations improve without surgery. As many as 20% of individuals recover completely, while another 60-70% are sufficiently improved to be able to live with their remaining pain. Sciatica improves within 10-30 days of onset in 75% of individuals. Most individuals recover in 6 months or less. Therapy and brief bedrest may help symptoms, but they do not change the outcome. Fewer than 20% of individuals become surgical candidates, and discectomy gives good or excellent results in 80-90% of non compensation individuals.

Differential Diagnosis

Disorders that may present similarly to lumber disc displacement include soft tissue low back strain, osteoarthritis, spinal cord tumor, multiple sclerosis, bone tumors or infections, pelvic infection/inflammation, pelvic fracture, peripheral nerve entrapment, spinal stenosis, diabetic mononeuritis multiplex, diabetic amyotrophy, and psychosocial stressors with somatization.

Specialists

- Anesthesiologist
- Occupational Medicine Physician
- Physiatrist
- Rheumatologist
- Spine Surgeon
- Sports Medicine Physician

Rehabilitation

Physical therapy may be needed in the rehabilitation of the displaced lumbar intervertebral disc. The physical therapist can provide noninvasive therapies, such as ultrasound, electrostimulation, diathermy or manual therapy. These modalities are used briefly at first to decrease pain and facilitate exercise program.

Traction can be used to try to decrease pressure on the disc, but in some individuals, it may increase the pain. Whether the therapist applies it mechanically, manually, or with the use of a home unit that utilizes the individual's body weight for the force needed, traction produces a separation of joint surfaces of the lumbar spine to help reduce the disc displacement and decompress any structures causing associated pain.

Modifications may need to be made by the physical therapist for those who have arthritis or other lumbar spine conditions. This will vary depending on the degree of disc displacement or type of surgery that may have been performed.

Work Restrictions / Accommodations

Early after a herniation occurs, modification may be necessary to avoid heavy lifting, prolonged exposure to vibration, or other activities that promote disc injury. Individuals may be required, at first, to wear a back support, brace, or corset (orthotic).

During the early postoperative stage, sitting may be restricted to no more than 45-60 minute intervals with frequent rest periods, which include walking and resting flat. Activities that require lifting, carrying, stooping, and twisting may need to be decreased, at first.

Comorbid Conditions

Obesity and depression may lengthen disability. Pregnancy is a common risk factor for displacement, and may increase recovery time.

Complications

Worsening of the condition may cause pressure on the spinal cord (L1-L2 disc) as well as on the nerve roots (lower discs), and may lead to degenerative radiculopathy. Large disc herniation may lead to cauda equina syndrome in 0.1% of individuals with a disc herniation.

Factors Influencing Duration

Length of disability depends on the location and number of the affected discs, the severity of the disc disease, the severity of concomitant bone spurs on the vertebrae (osteophytes, spondylosis), the nature of any neurological involvement, the presence or absence of objective sensory loss and/or muscle weakness, the duration of these neurological deficits (acute or chronic), the presence of other sources of pain (such as facet joint arthritis and mechanical instability), the type of treatment, and the individual's response to treatment.

Length of Disability

With medical treatment, duration depends on severity of symptoms. Persisting radicular pain from a lumbar disc herniation, even without myelopathy, may not be compatible with heavy work. Discectomy is not usually compatible with heavy and very heavy work. Disability may be permanent following spinal fusion.

Medical treatment.

Duration in Days

Job Classification	Minimum	Optimum	Maximum
Sedentary work	1	7	14
Light work	1	14	21
Medium work	1	21	42
Heavy work	1	56	91
Very Heavy work	1	91	168

Discectomy.

Duration in Days

Job Classification	Minimum	Optimum	Maximum
Sedentary work	1	14	42
Light work	7	21	56
Medium work	14	42	84
Heavy work	91	119	182
Very Heavy work	119	147	182

Displacement, Lumbar Intervertebral Disc Without Myelopathy

Fusion.

Duration in Days

Job Classification	Minimum	Optimum	Maximum
Sedentary work	42	49	84
Light work	56	63	84
Medium work	70	77	112
Heavy work	84	168	Indefinite
Very Heavy work	84	168	Indefinite

Duration Trend from Normative Data*

Cases	Mean	Min	Max	No Lost Time	Over 6 Months
9907	82	0	727	0.16%	3.50%

Percentile:	5th	25th	Median	75th	95th
Days:	16	36	66	108	170

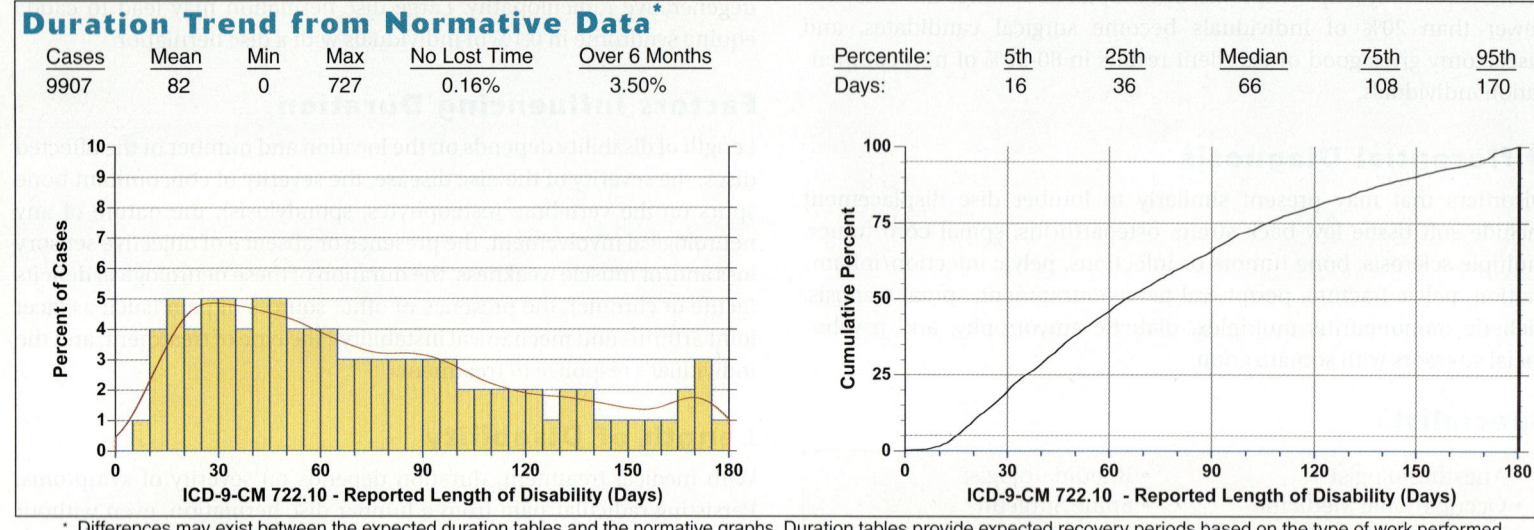

ICD-9-CM 722.10 - Reported Length of Disability (Days)

* Differences may exist between the expected duration tables and the normative graphs. Duration tables provide expected recovery periods based on the type of work performed by the individual. The normative graphs reflect the actual observed experience of many individuals across the spectrum of physical conditions, in a variety of industries, and with varying levels of case management.

Failure to Recover

If an individual fails to recover within the maximum duration expectancy period, the reader may wish to reference the following questions to assist in better understanding the specifics of an individual's medical case.

Regarding diagnosis:

- Did the individual report any trauma or strain to the back just prior to the onset of the pain?
- Does the individual have any pain into either leg?
- Does the individual have any numbness or pins and needles sensation? Where?
- Does the individual have any problems with bowel or bladder function?
- Did the exam reveal any abnormalities of the individual's normal curvature of the lumbar area of the back, slight hip or knee flexion?
- Does the individual have any gait abnormalities?
- Does the individual have diminished ankle and knee jerk reflexes?
- Was the individual's straight leg raising test positive?
- Did the individual have an MRI or CT myelography? What were the results?
- Have conditions with similar symptoms been ruled?

Regarding treatment:

- How did the individual respond to conservative treatment?
- Is the individual actively participating in physical therapy and a home exercise program?
- Has the individual been re-evaluated?
- Is discectomy indicated for the individual?
- Has the individual had an epidural corticosteroid injection? Was it successful?
- If not, is the individual a candidate for surgery? If not, has the individual been referred to a chronic pain clinic or rehabilitation program?

Regarding prognosis:

- Is pain the reason for failure to recover?
- Has a repeat MRI been performed?
- Have electrodiagnostic studies been performed?
- Are there psychological issues delaying recovery?
- Is the individual actively participating in physical therapy and a home exercise program?
- Is the individual obese or pregnant?

References

Golub, Benjamin, Richard Rovit, and Henry Mankin. "Cervical and Lumbar Disc Disease: A Review." Bulletin on the Rheumatic Diseases 21 (1971): 635-642.

Torg, Joseph S., Joseph J. Vegso, and Elizabeth Torg. Rehabilitation of Athletic Injuries. An Atlas of Therapeutic Exercise. Chicago: Year Book Medical Publishers, Inc, 1987.

Displacement, Thoracic Intervertebral Disc Without Myelopathy

Other names / synonyms: Disc Protrusion, Disc Rupture, Herniated Disc, Herniated Nucleus Pulposis, Thoracic Disc Herniation, Thoracic Disc Prolapse

722.11

Definition

This diagnosis describes a disc in the thoracic spine that has protruded (herniated) backward, perhaps putting pressure on a nerve but not causing spinal cord dysfunction. Symptomatic thoracic disc herniation is much less common than a symptomatic disc herniation in either the neck (cervical) or low back (lumbar). Historically, only about 0.15-4% of all symptomatic disc protrusions are in the thoracic spine. As in the cervical and lumbar spines, asymptomatic herniations in the thoracic spine are common incidental findings on MRI. Disc herniations can occur anywhere along the thoracic spine; however, approximately 75% of thoracic disc herniations occur in the lower part of the thoracic spine, between T8 and T12.

Thoracic disc protrusions occur with the same frequency in males and females. Most individuals experience thoracic disc protrusion during the fourth through sixth decades of life. Thoracic disc displacement is usually the result of the normal degenerative process, but approximately one-third of cases are the result of trauma.

Diagnosis

History: Individuals may present with complaints of acute, chronic, or recurrent mid-back pain. In some cases, the pain may begin abruptly after an injury; for example, a fall onto the buttocks or flat onto the feet. Pain may be aggravated by straining for a bowel movement, coughing, or sneezing. Other symptoms that individuals may experience include motor and sensory disturbances, and bowel or bladder dysfunction. Radicular pain and possibly sensory loss from nerve root compression follow the distribution of the intercostal nerve running below the rib at the level of the disc herniation. Thus, radicular thoracic pain goes to the front of the body (anterior midline).

Physical exam: Tenderness may be evident over the affected vertebra. Neurologic examination may reveal neurological deficits, chiefly decreased sensation along the course of a rib. If a thoracic disc causes spinal cord compression, the neurologic deficit will be in bowel and/or bladder control, or in lower extremity weakness or sensory alteration.

Tests: X-rays of the thoracic spine may be taken. X-rays help exclude tumor and infection. Calcification of a thoracic disc is usually at a different level from the symptomatic disc. In addition, the x-ray may show congenital or developmental deformities of the spine such as side-to-side curvature (scoliosis) or a hunchback (kyphosis). Individuals who have such deformities are predisposed to thoracic disc degeneration. The thoracic spine is slightly more difficult to image by myelography. Myelography is diagnostic in only about 56% of cases and has an 8% false-negative rate. An enhanced CT scan after myelography using a water-soluble contrast agent has been considered the diagnostic standard. MRI is also an effective test to confirm the diagnosis of thoracic disc herniation.

Treatment

Thoracic disc herniation with or without nerve root compression is almost always treated conservatively (nonsurgically). Rest and immobilization of the back is the mainstay of treatment. If the individual is up and about, a back brace may be worn to provide support and limit back motion. Strict bed rest may be prescribed in severe cases but only for a few days. Injection of local anesthetic around the spinal nerve (spinal nerve blocks) may be effective in relieving spinal nerve root (radicular) pain. As symptoms subside, activity is gradually increased. This may include physical therapy and/or a home exercise program. Preventive and maintenance measures (such as exercise, proper body mechanics) should be continued indefinitely. Job modification may be necessary to avoid aggravating activities.

Indications for surgery include lower extremity weakness or paralysis, and radicular pain refractive to conservative treatment measures. There are many surgical options. Laminectomy with disc excision, once the benchmark procedure, is rarely performed now because of the high risk of neurologic deterioration. Excision of the disc (discectomy) may be performed by first removing a piece of a rib along with a portion of the associated vertebra (costotransversectomy approach) through an opening in the wall of the chest (thoracotomy approach), or from an incision in the back, to one side of the midline (posterolateral approach). Fusion of the vertebral joint (arthrodesis) may be performed if surgery causes lateral instability.

Prognosis

While conservative treatment is the first line of therapy, outcome varies with the individual, depending upon the severity of symptoms. Results of thoracic disc surgery are not as good as the results of cervical or lumbar disc surgery. Approximately 14% of individuals undergoing surgical procedures for thoracic disc protrusion experience no relief from the surgery. There is a higher rate of permanent neurologic complication with surgery on the thoracic disc compared to cervical and lumbar discs, so the decision on surgical treatment should be deliberate. A second surgical opinion is strongly recommended.

Differential Diagnosis

Diseases and disorders that present with similar symptomatology include spinal tumors and infections, rheumatoid arthritis of the spine, ankylosing spondylitis, fractures, intercostal neuralgia, herpes zoster, and cervical and lumbar disc problems.

Specialists

- Anesthesiologist
- Neurosurgeon
- Occupational Medicine Physician
- Physiatrist
- Rheumatologist
- Spine Surgeon
- Sports Medicine Physician

Rehabilitation

The displaced thoracic intervertebral disc may need rehabilitation. Modalities such as ultrasound or diathermy may decrease pain. Both of these forms of treatment project heat deep into the tissues of the back. Electrostimulation combined with heat or cold treatment is another technique used in physical therapy to relax muscles of the thoracic spine affected by the displaced disc. T.E.N.S. (transcutaneous electrical nerve stimulation) is popular in the treatment of mid-back pain. An electrical impulse, predetermined by the physical therapist, produces a high frequency tingling sensation that blocks pain at that level of the spine.

Traction can be used to try to decrease pressure on the thoracic level of the spine. Whether the therapist applies it mechanically or manually, traction produces a separation of joint surfaces of the thoracic spine to help reduce the pain. A flexibility program is important in the rehabilitation of the thoracic spine. The individual may be instructed on several methods to stretch the midback. Swimming is a good exercise for conditioning the thoracic spine, as it will incorporate rotation against mild resistance of the water.

Strengthening of the thoracic muscles is accomplished with the use of resistance throughout range of motion exercises. The instruction and supervision of a physical therapist usually accomplishes this with devices such as wall pulleys, and universal and nautilus-type equipment as tolerated. Modifications may need to be made by the physical therapist for those who have arthritis or other joint irritations of the thoracic spine. If the thoracic disc displacement requires surgery, some restrictions may be placed on the progression of the range of motion and strengthening for certain movements. This varies depending on the degree of disc displacement or type of surgery that was performed. Education for proper lifting of heavy objects is important in the rehabilitation of the thoracic spine and to prepare the individual for returning to work.

Work Restrictions / Accommodations

Activities that require standing, sitting, lifting, carrying, bending, and twisting may need to be decreased or modified. Individuals may be required to wear a back brace (orthotic) to provide support and limit twisting motions. During the postoperative stage, the individual should be allowed frequent break periods that include walking and resting flat.

Comorbid Conditions

Comorbid conditions include obesity and congenital diseases or anomalies of the spine and back.

Complications

Progression is rare. The most common progression of symptoms is pain followed by sensory disturbance, weakness, and bowel and bladder dysfunction (loss of sphincter control and incontinence). Disc calcification is another possible outcome.

Factors Influencing Duration

Length of disability depends on the location and number of the affected discs, the severity of the disc disease, the severity of bone spurs (spondylosis), the nature of any neurological involvement, the presence or absence of objective sensory loss and/or muscle weakness, the duration of these neurological deficits (acute or chronic), the presence of other sources of pain (such as facet joint arthritis, mechanical instability), and the type of treatment.

Length of Disability

With medical treatment, duration depends on severity of symptoms. Persisting radicular pain from a thoracic disc herniation, even without myelopathy, may not be compatible with heavy work. Discectomy is usually not compatible with heavy and very heavy work. Disability may be permanent following spinal fusion.

Medical treatment.

Duration in Days

Job Classification	Minimum	Optimum	Maximum
Sedentary work	0	7	14
Light work	0	14	21
Medium work	0	21	42
Heavy work	0	56	91
Very Heavy work	0	91	168

Discectomy.

Duration in Days

Job Classification	Minimum	Optimum	Maximum
Sedentary work	14	42	56
Light work	21	42	56
Medium work	42	56	84
Heavy work	Indefinite	Indefinite	Indefinite
Very Heavy work	Indefinite	Indefinite	Indefinite

Fusion.

Duration in Days

Job Classification	Minimum	Optimum	Maximum
Sedentary work	42	49	84
Light work	56	63	84
Medium work	70	77	112
Heavy work	Indefinite	Indefinite	Indefinite
Very Heavy work	Indefinite	Indefinite	Indefinite

Failure to Recover

If an individual fails to recover within the maximum duration expectancy period, the reader may wish to reference the following questions to assist in better understanding the specifics of an individual's medical case.

Regarding diagnosis:

- Did the individual have an injury?
- Has the pain been chronic or recurrent?
- Is the pain aggravated by straining such as for a bowel movement, coughing, or sneezing?
- Has the individual had any problems with bowel or bladder function?
- What did the neurologic exams reveal?
- Has the individual had plain x-rays and either an enhanced CT after myelography or MRI? What was the result?
- Have conditions with similar symptoms been ruled out?

Regarding treatment:

- Did the individual respond to conservative treatment?
- Has the individual had a spinal nerve block done?
- Is the individual active in physical therapy?
- Does the individual have a home exercise program?
- Does the individual have lower extremity weakness or paralysis or bowel or bladder control impairment?
- Does the individual have radicular pain that has not responded to conservative treatment?
- Is the individual a surgical candidate?
- Has the individual had a second surgical opinion?

Regarding prognosis:

- Has the individual received instruction in proper body mechanics and lifting?
- Is the individual preparing to return to work?
- Is the individual obese of have a congenital disease or anomaly of the spine or back?
- Is the individual experiencing any progressive symptoms?
- Does the individual have more than one affected disc? Any other complications?

References

Currier B.L., et al. "Thoracic Disc Disease." The Spine. Herkowitz, H.N., et al., eds. Philadelphia: W.B. Saunders Company, 1999. 581-595.

Malone, Terry R., Thomas McPoil, and Arthur J. Nitz. Orthopedic and Sports Physical Therapy. St. Louis: Mosby, 1997.

Russell, T. "Thoracic Intervertebral Disc Protrusion: Experience of 67 Cases and Review of the Literature." British Journal of Neurosurgery 3 (1989): 153-160.

Scully, Rosemary M., and Marylou R. Barnes. Physical Therapy. Philadelphia: J.B. Lippincott Co, 1989.

Dissociative Personality Disorder

Other names / synonyms: Dissociative Identity Disorder, Dissociative Personality Disorder, MPD, Multiple Personality Disorder

300.14, 300.15

Definition

In this disorder, an individual demonstrates two or more distinct personalities, each appearing at different times. It is a serious, chronic, and potentially disabling or fatal condition.

The personalities or "alters" have their own characteristic ways of thinking, feeling, and perceiving. They each have different names, mannerisms, speech, mood, social preferences, age, race, habits, and memories. Each personality determines the individual's behavior and attitudes while it is dominant. One personality may appear normal, another hostile and aggressive, and yet another shy and withdrawn. Each personality is usually unaware of events that occurred when another personality was in charge. One personality, however, may have full knowledge of all the others. The other personalities may only have a sense of another individuals with a directing voice coming from inside and taking control of them. The average number of personalities is between five and ten but there may be as few as two or as many as a hundred.

Frequent memory gaps in personal history (dissociation) are a prominent feature of dissociative personality disorder. Dissociation is a psychological defense mechanism where the individual's identity, memories, ideas, feelings, or perceptions are separated from conscious awareness and can't be remembered or experienced voluntarily. The fragmentation into multiple personalities may be to protect the individual from unbearably painful events such as incest or physical abuse.

Substance abuse, significant stress, or pain (headache) can trigger a shift among personalities. This shift may occur suddenly in a matter of seconds or more gradually over hours or days. Sudden frightening memories (flashbacks) can intrude on any of the personalities.

Dissociative personality disorder is usually diagnosed around age 30 with symptoms often present for 6 or 7 years before diagnosis. It is 3 to 10 times more frequent in women than men. Dissociative personality disorder can be found in 3-4% of individuals hospitalized for other psychiatric problems.

Diagnosis

History: According to DSM-IV criteria, there must be two or more distinct identities or personalities that periodically take control of the individual's behavior. Memory gaps (amnesia) regarding important life events are too extensive to result from ordinary forgetfulness. In order to be diagnosed as dissociative personality disorder, the disturbance cannot be due to the direct physical effects of a substance such as alcohol intoxication or a general medical condition such as a seizure disorder.

There is nearly always a childhood history of severe physical, emotional, or sexual abuse. The individual may refer to himself or herself as "him," "her," "we," or "us." History may also reveal three or more previous psychiatric diagnoses with poor response to treatment. Various symptoms that may appear at different times include severe headaches, various types of physical pain, time distortions, and time lapses. Ability to function fluctuates from independence at work and home to disability. The individual may report feeling detached from self (depersonalization) or experience the surroundings as being unreal (derealization).

Physical exam: A dramatic change in appearance, mood, and behavior may occur when that personality (alter) is inquired about during a therapy session. Physical signs of self-mutilation may also be present.

Tests: Although tests are not usually useful in making this diagnosis, an electroencephalogram (EEG) may be done to check for partial complex seizures that can mimic the loss of memory seen with dissociation. Hypnosis or use of a sedative drug-facilitated interview may help reach alter personalities. Standardized tests can provide additional information critical to both diagnosis and adequate treatment planning. Such screening tools include the Dissociative Experience Scale, Dissociation Questionnaire, Questionnaire of Experiences of Dissociation, and informal office interviews.

Treatment

Individual psychotherapy is used to help integrate the fragmented personalities or at least to develop one dominant, more stable personality. Two or more weekly psychotherapy sessions may be needed for at least 3 to 6 years and followed by periodic visits thereafter. Hypnosis has been used to access the different personalities and retrieve memories. Drug therapy can treat symptoms of anxiety or depression when present in a specific personality. Treatment is often emotionally painful as previous crises are remembered and reprehensible actions committed by the alter personalities come to light. Several periods of psychiatric hospitalization may be needed to help the individual deal with this emotional trauma.

Prognosis

Dissociative personality disorder is a severe, chronic disorder that rarely resolves spontaneously. Psychotherapy is usually needed long-term with occasional hospitalizations for disruptive behavior or severe symptoms. Although a return to steady employment is possible, it is unlikely as recovery is usually incomplete. Suicide is thought to be more frequent than in any other psychiatric disorder.

Differential Diagnosis

Dissociative personality disorder can resemble schizophrenia especially if the individual hears voices or has feelings of being controlled by outside forces. Borderline personality disorder, dissociative amnesia, dissociative fugue states, and depersonalization disorder share some similar features with dissociative personality disorder. Anxiety or depressive disorders can be misdiagnosed when anxiety and/or depression are predominant symptoms. Other conditions with similar symptoms include drug or alcohol intoxication, complex partial seizures or temporal lobe epilepsy, rapidly cycling bipolar disorder, or post-traumatic stress disorder. Malingering is possible especially when criminal charges are pending. Individual may also have factitious disorder where there is a long pattern of seeking attention from the helping professions.

Specialists

- Psychiatrist
- Psychologist

Work Restrictions / Accommodations

Schedule may need to incorporate flex time, part-time or job-sharing positions, and a break time according to individual's needs rather than a fixed schedule. Restrictions and work accommodations should be individually determined based on the characteristics of the individual's response to the disorder, the functional requirements of the job and work environment, and the flexibility of the job and work site. The purpose of the restrictions/accommodations is to help maintain the worker's capacity to remain at the workplace without a work disruption or to promote timely and safe transition back to full work productivity.

Comorbid Conditions

Coexisting conditions that may impact recovery and lengthen disability include substance abuse, depression, anxiety, obsessive-compulsive disorder, eating disorders, and personality disorders. Headaches are extremely common as are hysterical conversion symptoms and symptoms of sexual dysfunction.

Complications

Complications may include psychosomatic conditions such as migraine headaches or irritable bowel syndrome. A depressive disorder or substance abuse can also complicate this condition. One of the personalities may commit a crime or an act of violence either against another individual or as self-mutilation. Impulsive behavior can lead to loss of important relationships and employment. Individuals with dissociative personality disorder may frequently attempt suicide and are thought to be more likely to commit suicide than individuals with any other psychiatric disorders.

Factors Influencing Duration

Length of disability may be influenced by the degree of personality fragmentation; the presence of disruptive, aggressive, or self-destructive behavior; response to treatment; and whether the individual remains involved with perpetrators of earlier abuse.

Length of Disability

Comorbid conditions may contribute to disability, which may be significant in some cases. This condition represents a lifelong pattern of behavior. Contact physician for more specific information.

Failure to Recover

If an individual fails to recover within the maximum duration expectancy period, the reader may wish to reference the following questions to assist in better understanding the specifics of an individual's medical case.

Regarding diagnosis:

- Does individual meet the criteria for dissociative personality disorder?
- Was there a history of childhood trauma particularly with continued and repeated sexual and/or physical abuse beginning in early childhood?
- Are there distinct personalities that have the capacity to take control of the body, each with its own unique behavior patterns and social relationships?
- Is the individual's inability to recall personal information too great to be explained by ordinary forgetfulness?
- Has the diagnosis been confirmed? On what basis?
- What diagnostic or screening procedures were utilized in the individual's diagnosis?
- Is there a history of earlier psychiatric diagnoses? Was individual previously misdiagnosed?
- Has substance abuse and/or the presence of underlying medical conditions been ruled out?

Regarding treatment:

- Has psychotherapy been effective in integrating the fragmented personalities into one personality?
- Would the individual benefit from in-patient therapy during the difficult time it takes to come to grips with particularly painful memories?
- If anxiety or depression is present in a specific personality, would the individual benefit from drug therapy?
- If individual is currently involved in electroconvulsive therapy, psychosurgery, or group therapy, and the therapy has not been effective, what therapy could be instituted?
- Since hypnosis may be useful in crisis management to help terminate spontaneous flashbacks or reorient the individual to external reality, does therapist feel that hypnosis would be useful in this case?

Regarding prognosis:

- What progress has been made toward integration of the alters?
- If the individual is still involved with the alleged abuser, is treatment aimed at reducing symptoms rather than achieving integration?
- If individual is still deeply involved with alleged abuser, what is being done to dissolve alliance or promote a more healthful relationship?
- Is individual aware of the risk of renewed dissociation if he/she does not practice or is capable of following through with new-found defenses and coping mechanisms?

References

"Chapter 90: Dissociative Disorders." Merck Manual of Diagnosis and Therapy, 17th ed. Beers, Mark H., and Robert Berkow, MD, eds. Whitehouse Station, NJ: Merck & Co., Inc, 1999. 09 Oct 2000 <http://www.merck.com/pubs/mmanual_home/sec7/90.htm>.

Guidelines for Treating Dissociative Identity Disorder in Adults. The International Society for the Study of Dissociation. 1997. 17 July 2000 <http://www.issd.org/indexpage/isdguide.htm>.

Diverticulosis and Diverticulitis of Colon

Other names / synonyms: Diverticular Inflammation
562, 562.0, 562.01, 562.1, 562.10, 562.11

Definition

Diverticulosis is a condition where the mucosal lining of the colon weakens and forms one or more narrow, sac-like projections (diverticula) through the muscular layer of the colon. Diverticulitis is a condition where one or more diverticula become infected, inflamed, and perforated. Diverticulitis may be described as the active condition of diverticulosis.

Ninety-five percent of the time that diverticulosis or diverticulitis are present, they affect the section of colon that lies immediately before the rectum (sigmoid colon).

Risk factors for diverticulosis and diverticulitis include a high fat and low fiber diet, decreased activity levels, advancing age, and postponement of defecation. Individuals in the US, Australia, United Kingdom, and France have high (and increasing) incidence rates of diverticulosis/diverticulitis. The disease is uncommon in Africa and Asia. Both sexes are equally affected. Five percent of individuals who are in their 40s have diverticulosis. Ten percent of individuals who are age 50 and older have diverticulosis while the condition affects 50-65% of those over 80. Although millions of individuals have diverticulosis, less than one-third ever develop symptoms associated with the condition. Ten to twenty percent of individuals with diverticulosis eventually develop diverticulitis.

Diagnosis

History: Individuals with diverticulosis are often asymptomatic. Only 20% of those with diverticulosis complain of colicky pain in the left side of the abdomen that is relieved by a bowel movement. Other symptoms may include diarrhea, constipation, gas pains, upset stomach, or painless rectal bleeding (hemorrhage). Individuals with diverticulitis complain of fever and acute pain (mild or severe) localized to the left

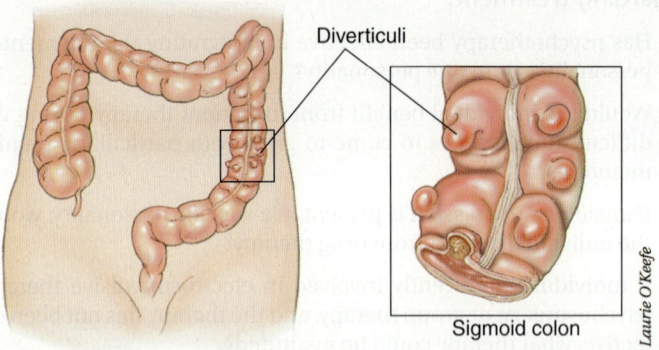

side of the abdomen. They may also report constipation or increased frequency of defecation. Other symptoms of diverticulitis include nausea, vomiting, painful urination, and/or increased urinary frequency.

Physical exam: Exploration of the abdomen with hands and fingers (palpation) may reveal a firm, tender section of colon that lies immediately before the rectum (sigmoid colon). Examination may also reveal a distended abdomen that is resonant or drum-like in tone (tympanic). With diverticulitis, palpation over the left lower quadrant of the abdomen produces pain. The individual may also respond to abdominal palpation by contracting (guarding) the abdominal muscles. The abdomen may be distended and tympanic. A tender mass in the abdomen and decreased bowel sounds may also occur in individuals with diverticulitis. The rectum may be tender on examination.

Tests: Tests for diverticulosis or diverticulitis include a complete blood count (CBC) with differential to determine the white blood cell (WBC) count, urinalysis and urine culture, guaiac testing of the stool to determine the presence of occult blood, and barium enema followed by x-rays to demonstrate the presence of either condition. Abdominal x-rays may reveal perforation of the diverticulum. CT may be useful in diagnosis. High frequency sound waves (ultrasound) may reveal diverticula that contain infection (abscess). A flexible, fiber-optic viewing scope is inserted through the anus and into the colon (sigmoidoscopy or colonoscopy) to assess for bleeding or strictures. X-rays are taken following injection of a radiopaque dye into a vein (intravenous pyelogram) to rule out the possibility of other conditions that produce symptoms similar to diverticulosis/diverticulitis (e.g., left ureter mass or colovesical fistula).

Treatment

Dietary modification is central to the management of either diverticulosis or diverticulitis and a high-residue diet with fiber is recommended. Individuals with mild symptoms are treated on an outpatient basis, advised to drink plenty of fluids, and given oral antibiotics. Those with more severe symptoms of diverticulitis may be hospitalized and treated using intravenous fluids and antibiotics. If individual has nausea and vomiting and bowel rest is prescribed, feeding may be done intravenously (total parenteral nutrition or TPN). Oral feeding may then be resumed gradually with clear liquids and gradual advancement to a soft, low-roughage diet. Stool-softeners and antispasmodic drugs may also be recommended.

Approximately 25% of individuals with diverticulitis require surgical intervention because of failure to respond to medical treatment or bleeding (hemorrhage) that cannot be controlled. The affected bowel segment is removed (bowel resection) and the cut ends of the bowel are then joined together (anastomosis). In some cases, a two-stage procedure is used (Hartmann procedure) whereby a temporary opening is created for emptying the bowel (colostomy) with anastomosis delayed until a later time. A second surgery is then performed 2 to 3 months later to create the anastomosis and close the temporary colostomy.

Prognosis

Approximately 85% of individuals can expect to have total relief from the diverticulitis and/or diverticulosis symptoms within 7 to 10 days following dietary modifications and medical therapy. Individuals with diverticulitis have recurrence of their condition about one-third of the time. Recurrence usually happens within the first year after the initial episode. Ninety percent of individuals develop recurrence within 5 years following medical treatment. Outcome for individuals treated surgically for diverticulitis using a single-step bowel resection and anastomosis or the Hartmann procedure is usually very good. The mortality rate following either type of surgery is less than 5%.

Differential Diagnosis

Conditions with similar symptoms as diverticulosis or diverticulitis include colon cancer, irritable bowel disease (IBD), inflammation of the small bowel (Crohn's disease), inflammation of the large colon (ulcerative colitis), lack of blood supply to the colon (ischemic colitis), tumor (adenoma) growth, uncontrolled cell growth (angiodysplasia), and milk (lactose) intolerance.

Specialists

- Gastroenterologist
- Surgeon

Work Restrictions / Accommodations

Work restrictions are usually necessary for individuals treated with surgery. They cannot lift heavy objects or perform hard manual labor for 4 to 6 weeks following return to work. Light sedentary duties should be prescribed during this time.

Comorbid Conditions

Existing conditions that may impact an individual's ability to recover and further lengthen disability include irritable bowel syndrome (IBS), colon cancer, Crohn's disease, ischemic colitis, ulcerative colitis, tumor (adenoma) growth, and angiodysplasia.

Complications

Complications of diverticulosis or diverticulitis include intra-abdominal abscess, colonic stricture, fistula formation, bowel obstruction, infection that has spread to the peritoneal lining of the abdomen, and rectal bleeding.

Factors Influencing Duration

Factors that can influence disability include severity of the symptoms and whether the individual receives surgical treatment. Age may also be a factor because older individuals usually require a longer period of recovery following surgery.

Length of Disability

The duration of disability depends on requirements of the job. Duration may be longer if heavy lifting or hard manual labor is involved.

Medical treatment.

Job Classification	Minimum	Optimum	Maximum
Any work	0	3	10

Duration in Days

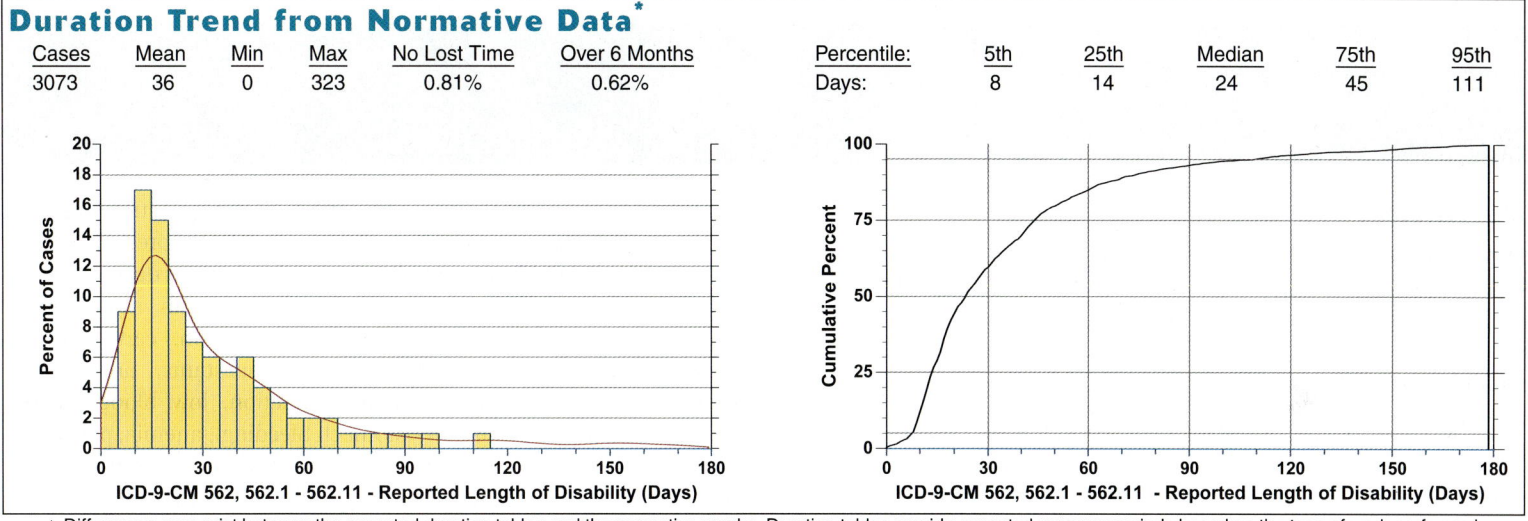

Duration Trend from Normative Data*

Cases	Mean	Min	Max	No Lost Time	Over 6 Months
3073	36	0	323	0.81%	0.62%

Percentile:	5th	25th	Median	75th	95th
Days:	8	14	24	45	111

ICD-9-CM 562, 562.1 - 562.11 - Reported Length of Disability (Days)

* Differences may exist between the expected duration tables and the normative graphs. Duration tables provide expected recovery periods based on the type of work performed by the individual. The normative graphs reflect the actual observed experience of many individuals across the spectrum of physical conditions, in a variety of industries, and with varying levels of case management.

Failure to Recover

If an individual fails to recover within the maximum duration expectancy period, the reader may wish to reference the following questions to assist in better understanding the specifics of an individual's medical case.

Regarding diagnosis:

- Is individual asymptomatic?
- Does individual report colicky pain in the left side of the abdomen that is relieved by a bowel movement?
- Does individual have diarrhea, constipation, gas pains, upset stomach, or painless rectal bleeding (hemorrhage)?
- Has fever occurred or acute pain (mild or severe) localized to the left side of the abdomen?
- Does individual experience frequency of defecation?
- Are symptoms such as vomiting, painful urination, and/or increased urinary frequency present?
- Does exploration of the abdomen with hands and fingers (palpation) reveal a firm, tender section of colon lying immediately before the rectum (sigmoid colon)?
- Is abdomen distended with a resonant or drum-like in tone (tympanic)?
- Has individual received adequate diagnostic testing to establish the diagnosis such as a complete blood count (CBC) with differential to determine the white blood cell (WBC) count, urinalysis and urine culture, guaiac testing of the stool to determine the presence of occult blood, and barium enema followed by x-rays to demonstrate the presence of either condition?
- Were abdominal x-rays done? CT or ultrasound?
- Does individual have diverticulosis or diverticulitis?
- If diagnosis is uncertain, were conditions with similar symptoms ruled out?

Regarding treatment:

- Since dietary modification is central to the management of either diverticulosis or diverticulitis, did individual comply with recommended diet?
- Did condition respond favorably to a high-residue diet with fiber?
- If symptoms were severe, was hospitalization and treatment with intravenous fluids and antibiotics required?
- Upon discharge, did individual follow instructions regarding clear liquids with gradual advancement to a soft, low-roughage diet?
- Were stool-softeners and antispasmodic drugs effective?
- If required, was surgery performed as a result of failure to respond to medical treatment or from hemorrhage that could not be controlled?
- If colostomy was necessary, was it temporary? Was date set for second procedure to create the anastomosis and close the temporary colostomy?

Diverticulosis and Diverticulitis of Colon

Regarding prognosis:

- Have symptoms persisted despite dietary modifications and medical therapy?
- Is this a recurrence of the condition?
- Does individual have a coexisting condition such as irritable bowel syndrome (IBS), colon cancer, Crohn's disease, ischemic colitis, ulcerative colitis, tumor, or angiodysplasia that may complicate treatment or impact recovery?
- Has individual experienced any complications related to the condition?

References

LeMone, P., and K.M. Burke. Medical-Surgical Nursing. Upper Saddle River, NJ: Prentice Hall Health, 2000.

Schmid-Ott, G., and F. Lamprecht. "Inpatient Treatment of a Patient with Large Duodenal Diverticulum and Psychogenic Vomiting - Somatic and Psychosomatic Approach." Versicherungsmedizin 49 5 (1997): 173-177.

Dizziness and Giddiness
Other names / synonyms: Faintness, Lightheadedness, Spinning, Vertigo
780.4

Definition

Dizziness is a term that is used to explain different sensations, such as lightheadedness and spinning (vertigo) accompanied by an involuntary, rapid, rhythmic eye movement (nystagmus), giddiness, and a feeling like one is going to faint (syncope). Without other symptoms, this condition is usually not serious.

There are many causes for dizziness and giddiness. Decrease in circulating blood and oxygen to the brain can cause dizziness and fainting. Sudden change in one's position from sitting or lying (postural hypotension) can also cause dizziness. It can result from medications to treat depression or high blood pressure (antihypertensives); from antihistamines or diuretics; with anemia due to blood loss; volume or fluid loss from sweating or other reasons; and from being frail and/or elderly.

Irregular heart rate or rhythm (dysrhythmia) can result in a sudden reduction in the amount of blood pumped to the brain and can cause dizziness. Temporary deficiency of blood in the brain secondary to narrowing of the arteries in the brain (cerebral transient ischemic attack, or TIA) can result in dizziness. When lightheaded dizziness leads to syncope or an actual loss of consciousness, problems with blood circulation (heart, blood vessels, and problems that affect their function) must be checked. It can also occur with diabetes mellitus and Parkinson's disease.

Disorders involving the balance organs in the ear such as resulting from infection or inflammation of the inner ear (labyrinthitis), inner ear fluid imbalance (Ménière's disease), viral infection of the vestibular nerve (vestibular neuronitis), and inner ear fluid leaking into the middle ear can cause individuals to feel dizzy or unsteady; ringing in the ears (tinnitus) can also develop. Dizziness can also be caused by general infections, head injury, blood circulation disorders, certain medications, and aging. Double vision (diplopia) is a more serious symptom that may indicate a disease affecting the brainstem, a warning of a serious stroke, or other disease processes. Slurred speech (dysarthria) that accompanies dizziness and vertigo points to a process affecting the brain itself.

Anxiety, stress, fatigue, fever, strenuous coughing, straining with defecation or urination, stomach flu, common cold, pressure on the neck (tight collar), spinning rapidly around in a circle (as during carnival rides), low blood pressure (hypotension), severe pain, injury, fright, standing rigidly at attention, alcohol intoxication, certain drugs, medications (including vasodilators, decongestants, and central nervous system depressants), hyperventilation, low blood glucose (hypoglycemia), blood loss (i.e., stomach bleeding), anemia, perforated ear drum (tympanic membrane), ear diseases (i.e., mastoiditis, otitis media, cholesteatoma, vestibular neuronitis), and hysterical seizures may also cause dizziness.

According to studies done by the National Institutes of Health, 42% of individuals will experience dizziness in their lifetime, and about 90 million Americans complain of dizziness to their doctors at least once in their lifetime.

Diagnosis

History: The individual is questioned in detail as to when dizziness occurs, the nature of the dizziness, how long the spells last, other concurrent symptoms, and for a history of any other disease processes. The individual may complain of lightheadedness, spinning (vertigo), fainting (syncope), unsteadiness, and the sense that surrounding noises are growing fainter and fainter. Sometimes other symptoms such as nausea, vomiting, visual blurring, sweating, generalized discomfort, and disorientation may follow dizziness.

Physical exam: Upon examination, the physician may detect problems with vision, sensitivity to noise or bright light (photophobia), ability to think (cognitive), or memory. The individual may be disoriented and sweat profusely. Blood pressure may be low (hypotension).

Tests: The underlying cause for dizziness may be determined by positional testing using Frenzel lenses. Vigorous head shaking in the horizontal plane for about 10 seconds may reveal the reason for dizziness. Other tests that may be used to rule out a balance disorder include a test of vestibular system (caloric test), a check for abnormal eye movements (electronystagmogram, or ENG), imaging studies of the head and neck (CT scan, MRI), and posturogram (where the individual stands on a platform and body sway is recorded in response to the movement of the platform), an audiogram to identify sensori-neural hearing loss resulting from nerve damage, carotid angiogram to identify narrowing or other abnormality in the carotid artery (main artery to the brain), carotid doppler studies, an EKG, chest x-ray, echocardiogram, wearing a Holter monitor to assess cardiac function, and psychological tests to evaluate stress and identify anxiety and panic disorders and their triggers.

Treatment

Treatment for dizziness is based on its underlying cause, and may consist of bed rest and taking medications such as antihistamines, centrally acting anticholinergics, antibiotics, or medications affecting the GABA (gamma-aminobutyric acid) receptors.

If medical management is not effective, surgery may be indicated. A variety of inner ear surgical procedures can be done for dizziness if the condition is due to a balance disorder. These include the removal of the interconnecting cavities/canals (labyrinth) that constitute the inner ear (labyrinthectomy), cutting the balance nerve (selective vestibular neurectomy), or placing a shunt within the labyrinth (endolymphatic shunt).

Postural hypotension is treated by educating individuals to be cautious about rising suddenly from bed, instructing them to exercise their legs and to sit at the edge of the bed (dangle) to make sure they do not feel lightheaded before standing.

Dietary changes and reducing alcohol, caffeine, and nicotine intake may be helpful in the treatment of dizziness. Regular exercise, moving slowly and deliberately, and taking good care of health are also important in treating this problem.

Prognosis

In most cases individuals recover fully. If dizziness is due to an underlying disease, prognosis will depend on that disease, its severity, and how well it can be treated. Attacks of dizziness are usually controlled in one-half to two-thirds of individuals who have the endolymphatic shunt. Recovery from this procedure is short compared to other procedures. Attacks of dizziness are permanently cured for a high percentage of people after selective vestibular neurectomy; labyrinthectomy also results in a high cure rate for dizziness.

Differential Diagnosis

Other conditions that present with similar symptoms may include vertigo, syncope, Ménière's disease, labyrinthitis, vestibular neuronitis, perilymph fistula, transient ischemic attack (TIA), and Stokes-Adams attacks.

Specialists

- Internist
- Neurologist
- Otolaryngologist

Work Restrictions / Accommodations

Work restrictions and accommodations may depend on the type of the job the individual performs. Operating machinery and handling hazardous objects pose a safety concern.

Comorbid Conditions

Comorbid conditions include low blood pressure, stress, and chronic dehydration.

Complications

Complications include trauma associated with falls that are due to fainting. An underlying disease process may have associated complications.

Factors Influencing Duration

Duration depends on the underlying cause of dizziness, the individual's response to treatment, and the nature of work performed.

Length of Disability

Duration depends on the underlying cause. Contact physician for additional information.

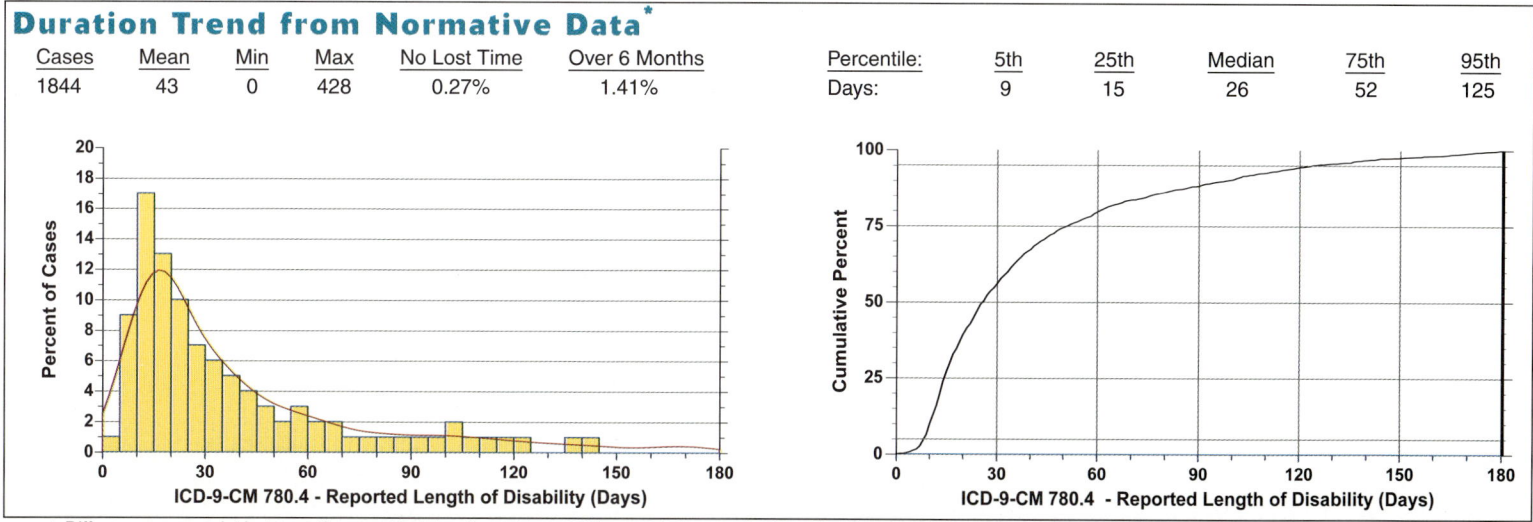

* Differences may exist between the expected duration tables and the normative graphs. Duration tables provide expected recovery periods based on the type of work performed by the individual. The normative graphs reflect the actual observed experience of many individuals across the spectrum of physical conditions, in a variety of industries, and with varying levels of case management.

Failure to Recover

If an individual fails to recover within the maximum duration expectancy period, the reader may wish to reference the following questions to assist in better understanding the specifics of an individual's medical case.

Regarding diagnosis:

- Does individual have postural hypotension? Does individual have an adverse side effect from prescription medications? Is there anemia or fluid loss? Does individual have an irregular heart rate or TIAs? Does individual any heart problems, diabetes, or Parkinson's disease? Are there any disorders of any part of the ear? Does individual have tinnitus?
- Has individual had a head injury?
- Is there double vision or slurred speech?
- Does individual exhibit anxiety, stress, fatigue, fever, or strenuous coughing?
- Has there been straining with defecation or urination, stomach flu, common cold, pressure on the neck (tight collar), or spinning rapidly around in a circle (as during carnival rides)? Does individual experience severe pain, injury, fright, or standing rigidly at attention?
- Are there signs of alcohol intoxication, hyperventilation, or hypoglycemia? Does individual have hysterical seizures?
- Were a caloric test, ENG, CT, MRI, and posturogram done? Was an audiogram, carotid angiogram, and Doppler studies performed? Has individual has an ECG, chest x-ray, echocardiogram, and Holter monitor?
- Was psychological testing done?
- Have conditions with similar symptoms been ruled out?

Regarding treatment:

- Has individual been on medications? Were they helpful? Is surgery indicated?
- Has individual made any necessary dietary changes such as reducing alcohol, caffeine, and nicotine intake?
- Does individual exercise regularly? Take good care of health?

Regarding prognosis:

- Has individual undergone vestibular rehabilitation with a trained professional?
- Can individual's employer accommodate any necessary restrictions?
- Does individual have any conditions that may affect ability to recover?
- Has individual experienced trauma associated with falls due to fainting?

References

"Dizziness." drkoop.com. 1999. 04 Feb 2001 <http://seniornet.drkoop.com/conditions/ency/article/003093.htm>.

Balance Disorders. National Institute of Health. 2000. 08 Feb 2001 <http://www.nidcd.nih.gov/health/pubs_hb/balance_disorders.htm>.

Beers, Mark, and Robert Berkow. The Merck Manual of Diagnosis and Therapy. Whitehouse Station, NJ: Merck Research Laboratories, 1999.

Yanofsky, Charles S., MD, et al. "Dizziness Explained." Pennsylvania Neurological Associates, Ltd. 18 April 1999. 04 Feb 2001 <http://www.pneuro.com/publications/dizzy/>.

Dry Eye Syndrome

Other names / synonyms: Keratitis Sicca, Keratoconjunctivitis Sicca

375.15, 375.5

Definition

Dry eye syndrome is caused by either quantity or quality deficiencies in one or more of the three different types of fluids that properly moisturize the eye. Improper lubrication causes the eyes to dry up (desiccation) and thus symptomatic complaints develop. On the surface of the eye, an oil film helps prevent evaporation of moisture while providing protection. A water (aqueous) layer below the oil film helps cleanse the eye. The inner layer of fluid (the mucin layer) coats the eye so it can retain moisture. When an individual ages, tear glands found on the eye's surface may cease to produce enough of these fluids.

Dry eyes may result from irregularities in the blink mechanism or excessive tear evaporation among those who fail to fully close their eyes when sleeping. Irregularities in the ocular surface may interfere with proper wetting of the transparent outer layer at the front of the eye that surrounds the pupil (cornea). Dry eye conditions also accompany collagen vascular disorders such as rheumatoid arthritis and autoimmune connective tissue disorders such as Sjögren's syndrome. Eyelid abnormalities or deficiencies in tear drainage systems are less common causes of dry eyes.

Dry eyes occur more often among older age groups particularly postmenopausal women. The syndrome affects about 20% of all adults and increases to more than 75% after age 65.

Diagnosis

History: Individuals may complain of dry eyes that feel gritty, scratchy, or sandy. Other symptoms are sensitivity to light and wind and irritation that accompanies eyelid movement. The individual may complain of a burning sensation or excessive tearing (epiphora) as the eyes attempt to compensate for rapid evaporation. Eyes may also redden, fail to produce tears, or feel sticky because of excessive mucus production. Symptoms are often exacerbated by poor air quality and low humidity and can be more prominent later in the day.

Physical exam: While eyes may appear normal upon simple observation, a slit lamp examination may show interrupted, minimal, or absent tear coverage over the eyes' surface. Tenacious yellowish mucus may be present in the lower part of the eye. The conjunctiva is a mucous membrane that covers most of the eye's surface and inner lining of the eyelids. It may lose its normal luster and appear thick, swollen, or red. Fluorescein stain applied to the eye may reveal the cells covering the cornea marked with dots or points (punctate epithelial keratopathy), conjunctival damage, or filaments floating across the corneal surface. Tear (lacrimal) gland enlargement may be seen with Sjögren's syndrome. In severe cases, the cornea and/or conjunctiva may stain with the rose bengal die.

Tests: Visual acuity is tested. A Schirmer test is performed where strips of filter paper are inserted between the eye and lower lid to measure wetness. Dry eye syndrome is confirmed when less than 15 milliliters of tears are produced in a 5-minute period. When a small amount of concentrated fluorescein is applied to the eye, the time it takes for the tear film to dissipate is measured and determines whether eyes are dry. Tiny dissolvable collagen plugs may be placed in tear channels (ducts) to create a buildup of moisture in the eye and determine whether symptoms are relieved without excessive tearing.

Treatment

Management is aimed at replenishing the eyes' moisture and/or delaying evaporation of the individual's natural tears. Dry eye syndrome cannot be cured so the focus of therapy is on controlling symptoms and reducing discomfort. Frequent applications of artificial tear solutions (ophthalmic lubricants) are necessary to keep eyes moist enough to prevent irritation, eye damage, and infection. Applications may be as frequent as every hour or more as needed, then tapered depending on response and symptomatic relief. Lubricating eye ointment may be applied at night to protect the eyes during sleep. Warm compresses also increase comfort. Keeping rooms humidified may be helpful.

Moisture chamber spectacles, swim goggles, or soft contact lenses help keep eyes moist. Agents that reduce mucous secretions in the eye may also be required (mucomimetic or mucolytic agents). Individual is first tested for improvement with a temporary block. When artificial tears fail to provide relief and the condition is severe, surgery is performed on the tear ducts. Tear duct openings may be closed through thermal heat cautery, silicone plugs, or laser heat energy. This allows tears to stay on the eye surface for a longer period of time. Artificial tears may still be needed but applied less frequently after surgery. In rare cases, the upper and lower eyelids may be stitched together (tarsorrhaphy) to help protect the eye and reduce loss of tears.

Prognosis

The condition is usually permanent and results in a lifetime use of artificial tears. In rare circumstances, dry eye syndrome can cause vision loss.

Differential Diagnosis

Conjunctivitis, blepharitis, eyelids that turn inwards, corneal erosions, ulcers, and iritis produce similar symptoms.

Specialists

- Ophthalmologist

Work Restrictions / Accommodations

Since the individual's vision may be blurred at times, eyesight must be assessed when important to the job. Time will be needed for application of artificial tears as often as necessary for comfort. The individual may need to avoid bright sunlight, windy conditions, smoke, and exceptionally dry environments.

> **Complementary and Alternative Therapies**
>
> Content is intended for awareness only. Treatments may or may not be effective. Scientific evidence may be lacking and some substances have potentially toxic effects. Dr. Presley Reed and the editors do not endorse the use of these therapies in the absence of consultation with a licensed medical professional.
>
> Optical aids - Moisture chamber spectacles, swim goggles, or soft contact lenses can help keep eyes moist.
>
> Ophthalmic lubricants - Artificial tear solutions keep eyes moist enough to prevent irritation, eye damage, and infection. Lubricating eye ointment can protect the eyes during sleep. Warm compresses and keeping rooms humidified may also increase comfort.

Comorbid Conditions

Dry eye syndrome may be associated with conditions causing lacrimal glands to malfunction such as complications of radiation therapy or diseases including Sjögren's syndrome. Dry eyes may result from Stevens-Johnson disease, which creates severe inflammation and sometimes adhesions in the conjunctiva. Familial autonomic dysfunction is a disorder of the nervous system that reduces tear production. Dry eye syndrome is linked to arthritis and abnormalities in tear drainage systems.

Complications

An individual with dry eyes is more susceptible to eye infections such as blepharitis, conjunctivitis, and filamentary or marginal keratitis that may lead to corneal ulcers. Certain medications such as antihistamines, antianxiety medications, oral contraceptions, and atropine derivatives are thought to contribute to the condition.

Factors Influencing Duration

Compliance with application of artificial tears, the presence or recurrence of complications, and response to treatment influence the length of disability. The need for surgery may also prolong disability. Severe cases may cause chronic vision disruption or loss of vision.

Length of Disability

Disability is usually not associated with this condition.

Duration in Days

Job Classification	Minimum	Optimum	Maximum
Any work	1	1	1

Failure to Recover

If an individual fails to recover within the maximum duration expectancy period, the reader may wish to reference the following questions to assist in better understanding the specifics of an individual's medical case.

Regarding diagnosis:

- Does the individual have irregularities in the blink mechanism?
- Does the individual fail to completely close their eyes while sleeping?
- Does the individual have irregularities in the ocular surface?
- Does the individual have collagen vascular disorders such as rheumatoid arthritis or autoimmune connective tissue disorders such as Sjögren's syndrome?
- Does the individual have eyelid abnormalities or deficiencies in tear drainage systems?
- Does the individual complain of dry eyes that feel gritty, scratchy, or sandy?
- Is the individual sensitive to light, wind or irritation that accompanies eyelid movement?
- Does the individual complain of a burning sensation or excessive tearing?
- Does the individual report that the eyes redden, fail to produce tears, or feel sticky?
- Does the individual report that the symptoms are worse with poor air quality, low humidity or late in the day?
- Did the individual have a slit lamp examination? Fluorescein stain? Rose bengal die?
- Did the individual have visual acuity testing? Schirmer test? Collagen plugs inserted?
- Have conditions with similar symptoms been ruled out?

Regarding treatment:

- Is the individual being treated with ophthalmic lubricants?
- Does the individual use lubricating ointment at night?
- Has the individual tried warm compresses? Humidification? Moisture chamber spectacles? Swim goggles? Soft contact lenses?
- Is the individual using mucomimetic or mucolytic agents?
- Has the individual been tested for improvement with a temporary block?
- Has the individual had surgery?
- Has it become necessary to perform tarsorrhaphy?
- Have conditions with similar conditions been ruled out?

Regarding prognosis:

- Is the individual's employer able to accommodate any necessary restrictions?
- Does the individual have any conditions that may affect their ability to recover?
- Does the individual have any complications such as blepharitis, conjunctivitis, and filamentary or marginal keratitis that may lead to corneal ulcers? Does the individual use medications such as antihistamines, antianxiety medications, oral contraceptions, or atropine derivatives?

References

"Keratoconjunctivitis Sicca." Merck Manual of Diagnosis and Therapy, 17th ed. Beers, Mark H., and Robert Berkow, MD, eds. Whitehouse Station, NJ: Merck & Co., Inc., 1999. 18 July 2000 <http://www.merck.com/pubs/mmanual/section8/chapter96/96e.htm>.

Dumping Syndrome

Other names / synonyms: Jejunal Syndrome, Post-Gastrectomy Syndrome, Post-Gastric Surgery Syndrome, Post-Vagotomy Syndrome

564.2

Definition

The dumping syndrome occurs when food passes too rapidly (dumps) from the stomach into the upper intestine (duodenum).

Symptoms of dumping syndrome that occur within 30 minutes of eating are called "early dumping." A meal, rich in carbohydrates, that is dumped too rapidly from the stomach can cause swelling in the upper intestine. At the same time, dumping causes an excess of certain intestinal hormones to be released into the bloodstream.

Symptoms associated with early dumping are thought to be caused by the combination of these hormones, the intestinal swelling, and changes in the blood circulation within the intestines (hypovolemia). "Late dumping" occurs 90-120 minutes after eating. Sugars absorbed from the intestine rapidly increase the blood glucose level, causing an excess amount of insulin to be released. Excess insulin then causes the blood glucose to drop below the normal level causing low blood sugar (hypoglycemia). The symptoms that are associated with late dumping are usually due to decreased levels of blood glucose and potassium.

Individuals who have had part of their stomach removed (partial gastrectomy) are at high risk for developing dumping syndrome because this procedure interferes with the normal mechanism that controls emptying of food from the stomach. Gastrectomy is a common treatment for individuals with acquired immune deficiency syndrome (AIDS) or otherwise healthy people who have developed stomach (gastric) cancer.

The incidence of dumping syndrome depends upon the type of gastric surgery that was performed. Generally, between 25-50% of all individuals who have undergone stomach surgery have some symptom of dumping syndrome; however, only 1-5% of these individuals have severely disabling symptoms. The incidence of significant dumping has been reported to occur in 6-14% of individuals after surgery that cuts the vagus nerve (truncal vagotomy) and in 14-20% of individuals after partial gastrectomy.

Diagnosis

History: Individuals usually complain of sweating and weakness after eating. They may also report skin flushing, faintness, a sensation of the heart beating rapidly or intensely (palpitations), bloating, feelings of fullness, abdominal pain, and diarrhea.

Physical exam: The examination may reveal an increased heart rate (tachycardia), profuse perspiration, abdominal distention or pain, and rumbling noises in the bowel (borborygmus). Weight loss and signs of malnutrition are commonly found in severe cases.

Tests: Diagnostic tests include taking x-rays after swallowing a contrast medium such as barium (upper gastrointestinal series). A flexible, fiber-optic microscope can be used to examine the stomach (upper endoscopy) to determine if the individual has a stomach ulcer, which can cause similar symptoms. Severity of the gastric dumping may be assessed by having the individual swallow glucose (oral glucose challenge) and then monitoring and scoring their symptoms (dumping provocation test). Also, rapid stomach emptying can be documented by having the individual swallow harmless radioactive markers with a meal and monitoring movement of these markers into the small intestine (scintigraphic assessment of gastric emptying time).

Treatment

Modification of the diet is the primary treatment method for dumping syndrome. Symptoms may be lessened or avoided by eating frequent, small meals. The best diet is low in refined sugar (simple carbohydrates) and high in protein. Liquids should be avoided during meals and then consumed an hour or more after eating. Symptoms may also be avoided by lying down after eating a large meal. Drug treatment (octreotide) can be given to inhibit insulin and intestinal hormone release, delay gastric emptying time, and inhibit food-induced blood circulatory changes. Surgical treatment may be considered for individuals who don't respond to medical therapies or for those who are unwilling to continue dietary modifications and drug treatment. These surgical procedures (including surgical narrowing of the gastrojejunal stoma, conversion of Billroth II anastomosis to Billroth I gastroduodenostomy, and jejunal interpositions) are usually reserved for individuals with truly severe symptoms of dumping syndrome.

Prognosis

The majority of individuals with dumping syndrome are treated adequately using dietary modifications alone. Drug (octreotide) treatment has been effective in the short-term and has been found to decrease the severity of symptoms 60-80 percent. It is not clear, at this point, whether drug treatment will be beneficial in long-term therapy. In one report, 80% of individuals with dumping syndrome reported lessening of symptoms after 15 months of drug treatment. Effectiveness of surgical treatments has been difficult to analyze because many of the procedures have good early results but long-term failures due to recurrence of the condition. At present, surgery is not used extensively for treatment of this condition.

Differential Diagnosis

Conditions with similar symptoms include low blood sugar (hypoglycemia), inflammation of the gallbladder (cholecystitis), and abnormal contractions of the bile duct (biliary tract spasms).

Specialists

- Gastroenterologist
- General Surgeon

Work Restrictions / Accommodations

Individuals may require a short recovery period and ready access to restroom facilities following a meal.

Complementary and Alternative Therapies

Content is intended for awareness only. Treatments may or may not be effective. Scientific evidence may be lacking and some substances have potentially toxic effects. Dr. Presley Reed and the editors do not endorse the use of these therapies in the absence of consultation with a licensed medical professional.

Dietary supplements -	Acarbose, guar gum, or Glucomannan may be added to meals to slow transit time from the stomach to the intestine. Intake of mineral water may also be helpful in this regard.
Acupuncture -	Inserting needles into certain points on the body may alleviate the symptoms associated with dumping syndrome.

Comorbid Conditions

Existing conditions that may impact an individual's ability to recover and further lengthen disability include acute or chronic gastroparesis, idiopathic cyclic nausea or vomiting, rumination syndrome, aerophagia syndrome, functional dyspepsia, or any other gastrointestinal motility disorder.

Complications

Possible complications of dumping syndrome include interference with food digestion, which results in decreased nutrient, vitamin, and mineral absorption into the body. Additionally, it is possible for the blood glucose to drop to levels low enough to cause mental confusion or incoherence following a meal. Individuals with severe dumping syndrome may lose weight (out of fear of eating meals) and eventually develop malnutrition.

Factors Influencing Duration

Length of disability may be influenced by the severity of the symptoms.

Length of Disability

Dumping syndrome is not usually disabling except in severe cases.

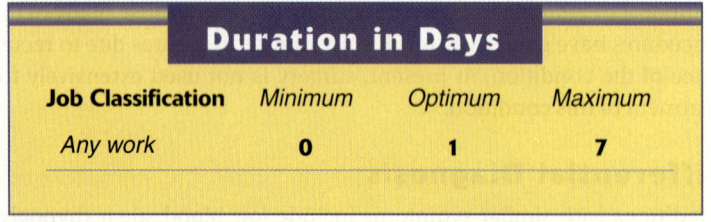

Duration in Days

Job Classification	Minimum	Optimum	Maximum
Any work	0	1	7

Failure to Recover

If an individual fails to recover within the maximum duration expectancy period, the reader may wish to reference the following questions to assist in better understanding the specifics of an individual's medical case.

Regarding diagnosis:

- Has the individual had a partial or complete gastrectomy? A vagotomy?
- Does the individual complain of sweating and weakness after eating?
- Does the individual report skin flushing, faintness, palpitations, bloating, feelings of fullness, abdominal pain, and diarrhea?
- On physical exam, does the individual have tachycardia, profuse perspiration, abdominal distention or pain, and rumbling noises in the bowel (borborygmus)?
- Does the individual have weight loss and signs of malnutrition?
- Has the individual had an Upper GI series, endoscopy, oral glucose challenge, dumping provocation test and scintigraphic assessment of gastric emptying time?
- Have conditions with similar symptoms been ruled out?

Regarding treatment:

- Has the individual modified their diet by eating frequent, small meals consisting of simple carbohydrates and high protein?
- Does the individual avoid consuming liquids during meals? Lying down after a meal?
- Is the individual being treated with octreotide?
- Has it become necessary for the individual to have surgery?

Regarding prognosis:

- Is the individual's employer able to accommodate any necessary restrictions?
- Does the individual have any conditions that may affect their ability to recover?
- Does the individual have any complications such as interference with food digestion which results in decreased nutrient, vitamin, and mineral absorption into the body? Does the individual have hypoglycemia with mental confusion or incoherence after a meal? Has the individual lost weight because of fear of eating meals and developed malnutrition?

References

Dumping Syndrome. HealthGateNetwork. 23 Feb 2000. 12 Jan 2001 <http://healthgate.com/choice/whs/cons/mdx-books/sym/sym133.shtml>.

Carvahal, S.H., and S.J. Mulvihill. "Postgastrectomy Syndromes: Dumping and Diarrhea." Gastroenterology Clinics of North America 23 2 (1994): 261-279.

Davenport, Horace W. Physiology of the Digestive Tract. Chicago: Year Book Medical Publishers, Inc, 1982.

Vaskivsky, M. "Experience with Acupuncture Treatment of Early Stages of Dumping Syndrome Within the Scope of Complex Spa Treatment." Fysiatrickay a Reumatologickay Vestniak 55 2 (1977): 85-92.

Vecht, J. Masclee, AAM, and C.B. Lamers. "The Dumping Syndrome. Current Insights into Pathophysiology, diagnosis and Treatment." Scandinavian Journal of Gastroenterology 32 Supplement 223 (1997): 21-27.

Vladimirov, V.I., et al. "The Correction of the Hormonal Response During the Treatment of the Dumping Syndrome with Potable Mineral Waters." Voprosy Kurortologii, Fizioterapii i Lechebnoi Fizicheskoi Kultury 2 (1999): 11-14.

Duodenitis

Other names / synonyms: Gastroduodenitis

535.6

Definition

Duodenitis is an inflammation of the inner (mucosal) lining of the upper segment of the small intestine (duodenum). The duodenum is connected directly to the stomach. Following a meal, partially digested food passes straight from the stomach into the duodenum where digestion continues.

Duodenitis rarely occurs by itself. It is usually associated with another gastrointestinal disorder such as stomach discomfort after eating (dyspepsia), viral infection (acute hepatitis), gallbladder inflammation (cholecystitis), stomach inflammation (gastritis), a lesion in the mucus membrane of the stomach or small intestine (ulcer disease), chronic infectious diarrhea, low blood flow to the intestine (ischemic bowel disease), chronic inflammatory bowel disease of unknown origin (Crohn's disease), or infection with a certain intestinal parasite (giardiasis). Infection with a bacterium (H. pylori) has also been associated with duodenitis.

The incidence of duodenitis appears unrelated to age and occurs as frequently in younger individuals as in the elderly. In the general population, duodenitis by itself occurs approximately 1% of the time. Individuals with dyspepsia have duodenitis in up to 41% of cases. Virtually 100% of all individuals with ulcer disease have accompanying duodenitis. While ulcers have a seasonal occurrence, duodenitis occurs throughout the year. Incidence of duodenitis in relatives of individuals with duodenal ulcer disease is higher than in relatives of individuals without duodenal ulcer.

Diagnosis

History: Individuals may complain of a sense of fullness after eating, excessive belching, heartburn, bloating, gas (flatulence), loss of appetite, nausea, vomiting, diarrhea, and vague abdominal discomfort or pain. These symptoms may occur more frequently in times of stress.

Physical exam: Abdominal distention and increased bowel sounds due to excessive gas in the stomach or intestine may be observed on physical examination. Signs of organic disease usually associated with duodenitis may include weight loss, enlarged abdominal organs, an abdominal mass, or blood in the stool.

Tests: To visualize the duodenum (upper gastrointestinal series), the individual swallows a radiopaque dye (barium) and then x-rays are taken of the gut. To visualize the inner lining (mucosa) of the duodenum (endoscopy), a fiberoptic microscope may be passed down the esophagus. Both these tests, however, provide only indirect evidence for duodenitis, and small samples of the duodenum should be obtained during endoscopy for definitive microscopic analysis (endoscopic biopsy). Sometimes larger samples of the duodenum are required for analysis. These can be obtained using a tube-like sampling device that allows a bigger piece of tissue to be secured (tube biopsy).

Treatment

Treatment for duodenitis usually involves therapy for the accompanying gastrointestinal disorder. Alcohol and caffeine intake should be modified, and medications that may irritate the gastrointestinal tract (such as nonsteroidal anti-inflammatory drugs or NSAIDs) should be curtailed or eliminated. Antacid drugs such as histamine receptor antagonists or proton pump inhibitors and treatments that protect the lining of the duodenum (sucralfate) may be beneficial.

H. Pylori or Giardia infections can be treated using appropriate antibiotic therapy.

Surgical intervention may include cutting the vagus nerve fibers that control digestive acid secretion (vagotomy), surgical removal of a portion of the stomach (gastrectomy), or opening the valve between the stomach and duodenum (pyloroplasty).

Prognosis

The predicted outcome depends on the effectiveness of the treatment for the underlying cause of the duodenitis. Most individuals with duodenitis with accompanying gastritis show at least some degree of recovery within 48 hours of treatment through use of antacids and modification of alcohol and caffeine intake. Bacterial or parasitic infections treated with antibiotics usually require a longer course of therapy and recovery may be expected within 10 to 14 days. If duodenitis is accompanied by gastric or duodenal ulcer, drug therapy can promote effective healing within 6 to 8 weeks in two-thirds of all cases. Longer-term drug therapy and surgical intervention will effectively reduce acid production in the vast majority of cases. Pyloroplasty is variably effective and reported to relieve pyloric stenosis 50-80% of the time.

Differential Diagnosis

Conditions that present with symptoms similar to duodenitis include various gastrointestinal tract abnormalities (irritable bowel syndrome, gastroesophageal reflux disease, food poisoning), pancreatic disease (pancreatic tumor, pancreatitis), diseases of the biliary tract, thyroid disease, and low blood flow to the heart (coronary ischemia). Pregnancy, the side effects of certain drugs, and excessive alcohol consumption may also produce symptoms similar to duodenitis.

Specialists

- Gastroenterologist
- Primary Care Provider

Rehabilitation

A regular exercise routine may be useful for the individual in reducing stress that can exacerbate duodenitis. Aerobic exercise such as walking, jogging, or swimming (30 to 45 minutes per session) is usually beneficial. If surgery was performed as a treatment intervention, intermittent positive pressure breathing exercises may be necessary to prevent pulmonary complications.

Work Restrictions / Accommodations

Work restrictions and accommodations are not usually associated with duodenitis however each case must be evaluated on an individual basis depending on the underlying cause for the condition. There are no work restrictions for individuals with duodenitis accompanied by mild ulcer disease or dyspepsia. Individuals with severe ulcer disease may need light or sedentary duty until recovery is complete. Individuals whose treatment includes surgery may need light to sedentary work with lifting restrictions for 2 to 4 weeks after a period of disability. Transfer to a less stressful position may be necessary if stress aggravates any of these conditions and compromises recovery.

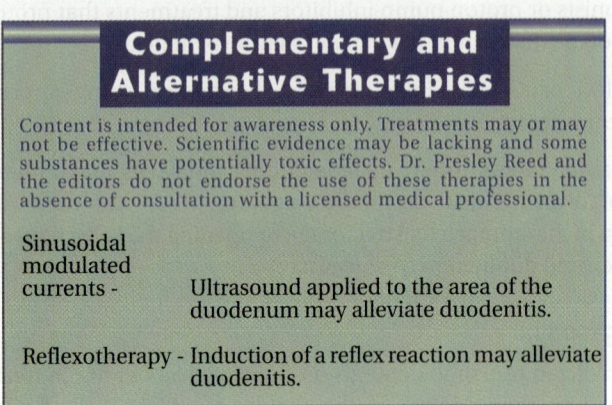

Complementary and Alternative Therapies

Content is intended for awareness only. Treatments may or may not be effective. Scientific evidence may be lacking and some substances have potentially toxic effects. Dr. Presley Reed and the editors do not endorse the use of these therapies in the absence of consultation with a licensed medical professional.

Sinusoidal modulated currents - Ultrasound applied to the area of the duodenum may alleviate duodenitis.

Reflexotherapy - Induction of a reflex reaction may alleviate duodenitis.

Comorbid Conditions

Existing conditions that may affect an individual's ability to recover from duodenitis and exacerbate the inflammation of the duodenum include pyloric ulcer disease, stomach cancer, and gastritis.

Complications

Duodenitis can be complicated by the underlying gastrointestinal condition. Inflammation may cause a lesion (ulcer) to form in the stomach or duodenum that can lead to bleeding (hemorrhage) and significant blood loss. If hemorrhage is chronic, it may lead to decreased iron content in the blood (iron deficiency anemia). Untreated ulcers may break through (perforate) the lining of the gastrointestinal tract. This allows blood, partially digested food, and hydrochloric acid into the abdominal cavity resulting in inflammation of the abdominal tissues (peritonitis). The individual will experience severe pain and may require emergency hospitalization and care.

Scarring of the outlet between the stomach and the duodenum (pylorus) may also occur in response to inflammation or ulceration. This can cause narrowing of the valve between these two organs (pyloric stenosis). Consequently, passage of food from the stomach into the duodenum may be restricted.

Factors Influencing Duration

The severity of the symptoms and response to treatment will influence the length of disability. Disability is prolonged if surgical intervention is required.

Length of Disability

Medical treatment.

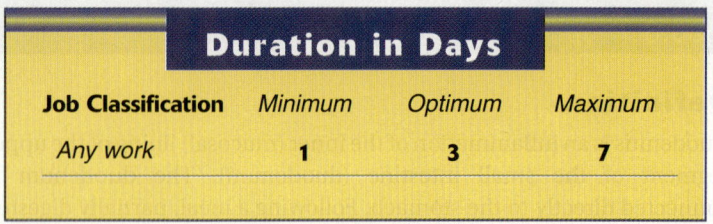

Duration in Days

Job Classification	Minimum	Optimum	Maximum
Any work	1	3	7

Failure to Recover

If an individual fails to recover within the maximum duration expectancy period, the reader may wish to reference the following questions to assist in better understanding the specifics of an individual's medical case.

Regarding diagnosis:

- Does the individual have dyspepsia, acute hepatitis, cholecystitis, gastritis, ulcer disease, chronic infectious diarrhea, ischemic bowel disease, Crohn's disease, giardiasis or H. pylori infection?
- Does the individual complain of a sense of fullness after eating, excessive belching, heartburn, bloating, flatulence, loss of appetite, nausea, vomiting, diarrhea, and vague abdominal discomfort or pain? Does stress seem to aggravate the symptoms?
- On physical exam were abdominal distention and increased bowel sounds present?
- Does the individual have weight loss, enlarged abdominal organs, an abdominal mass, or blood in the stool?
- Has the individual had an Upper GI series, endoscopy, and biopsy?
- Have conditions with similar symptoms been ruled out?

Regarding treatment:

- What is the individual's underlying condition? Is it being treated?
- Does the individual avoid alcohol, caffeine, and NSAIDs?
- Is the individual being treated with histamine receptor antagonists, proton pump inhibitors or sucralfate? Antibiotics if indicated?
- Has surgical intervention become necessary?

Regarding prognosis:

- Does the individual exercise regularly?
- Is the individual's employer able to accommodate any necessary restrictions?
- Does the individual have any conditions that may affect their ability to recover?
- Does the individual have any complications such as an ulcer, hemorrhage, iron deficiency anemia, perforation of the lining of the gastrointestinal tract, and peritonitis? Does the individual have scarring of the pylorus with pyloric stenosis?

References

Cheli, R., and H. Aste. Duodenitis. Acton, MA: Publishing Sciences Group, 1976.

LeMone, P., and K.M. Burke. Medical-Surgical Nursing. Upper Saddle River, NJ: Prentice Hall Health, 2000.

Dupuytren's Contracture

Other names / synonyms: Dupuytren's Disease

728.6

Definition

Dupuytren's contracture is an acquired condition in which the fibrous tissue band of the palm of the hand (palmar fascia) enlarges and forms nodules and cords of abnormal, thickened tissue (proliferative fibroplasia).

As the condition progresses, the skin adheres to the underlying fascia and causes contractures of the fingers toward the palm (flexor contractures). The fourth and fifth fingers are most commonly involved. The condition usually develops and progresses over several years, although some flexion contractures develop rapidly over a few weeks or months. In half of cases, both hands are affected.

The condition usually occurs in the fifth to seventh decades of life. The condition occurs 10 times more frequently in men than women. The cause is unknown but is thought to be hereditary. It is more common in people of Celtic or Scandinavian descent. The condition is uncommon in blacks and rare in Asians. The condition is more common and severe in individuals with epilepsy, diabetes mellitus, and alcoholism. Sometimes the condition will occur after trauma to the hand, although it is uncertain if this actually causes or merely precipitates the condition. In 5% of individuals, similar lesions also develop in the sole of one or both feet, and this condition is called "Ledderhose disease." In 3% of male individuals, a contracture of the penis called "Peyronie disease" occurs.

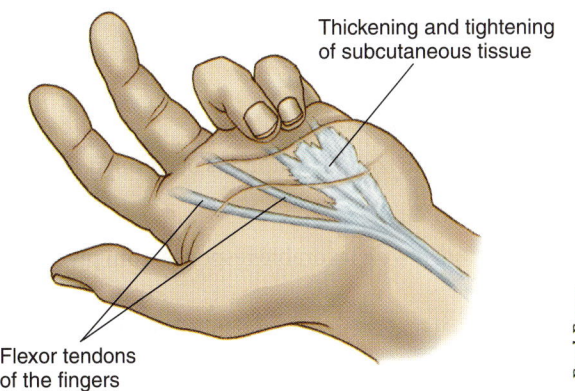

Thickening and tightening of subcutaneous tissue

Flexor tendons of the fingers

Frank Forney

Diagnosis

History: The disease itself is not painful, but individuals may complain of discomfort with the use of tools due to forceful gripping with the "lump" in the palm. The deformity and limited ability to open the hand to grasp large objects bring the individual to medical attention. The individual may complain that the fingers are contracted.

Physical exam: The skin puckers as the tissues in the palm of the hand thicken and become shorter. Small hard nodules form under the skin on the palm of the hand, spreading until it forms a hard band of tissue. Soft pads called "knuckle pads" are noticed on the tops of the middle joints of the involved fingers. In the tabletop test, the affected individual is not able to simultaneously place both the palm and fingers flat on a tabletop.

Tests: Although x-rays may show some contractures of the joints, no specific tests are necessary to make the diagnosis.

Treatment

In the early stages of Dupuytren's contracture, treatment includes physical therapy, corticosteroid injections into the growing nodules, splinting the fingers and hand, or a procedure in which the fibrous band (fascia) is divided into strips (needle fasciotomy). A surgical procedure called Dupuytren's release is usually necessary when the condition becomes so severe that it impedes hand function by limiting joint motion. A commonly cited threshold for this surgery is a positive tabletop test, in which the individual cannot simultaneously place both the palm and fingers flat on a tabletop. During the surgery, the bands of thickened, abnormal tissue under the skin are removed (fasciectomy), allowing better joint motion.

Prognosis

The disease is gradually progressive and the restriction in motion that increases with time will usually require surgery. The deformity and impairment are permanent without surgical intervention. Surgical correction removes the abnormal tissue, which restores movement. However, recurrences of this condition are common, even after surgery. The success of the surgery is determined the severity of the contractures (degree of fixation).

Differential Diagnosis

Scleroderma may present similarly. "Trigger finger" may cause similar contractures, and other types of nodules such as rheumatoid nodules and ganglia can resemble the nodule of Dupuytren's contracture.

Specialists

- Hand Surgeon
- Orthopedic Surgeon
- Plastic Surgeon

Rehabilitation

Rehabilitation of Dupuytren's contracture is difficult but may be an option for some individuals with increasingly fixed bending of their finger(s). Much of the treatment focuses around techniques to help stretch thickening tissues located on the palm of the hand called the palmar fascia, as well as stretching of fingers held in a flexed (bent) position or other associated deformities of the hand.

Heat-producing treatments may be used in rehabilitation by physical and occupational therapists to help increase the elasticity of tissue that has become abnormally thick. Superficial heat by way of hot packs is used to address tissue tightness as well as pain. In cases of significant pain, the physical therapist may use transcutaneous electrical nerve stimulation (T.E.N.S.).

Melted paraffin wax and mineral oil is used as a form of superficial heat and is especially useful when treating uneven body surfaces affected by the disease such as the fingers or hand. For example, if the hand is affected, the individual will dip the entire hand into a preheated container of paraffin wax, followed by covering the hand with a plastic bag and a towel for insulation.

Once the pain and swelling are under control, the physical therapist will begin addressing mobility and strength. Therapy may begin with passive range of motion exercises. This is progressed to active assist range of motion. As the individual improves with increased motion of the joint, active range of motion begins. This is often initiated in a warm whirlpool or in conjunction with another form of heat treatment and continued until as much motion as possible is restored.

The later phase of rehabilitation for Dupuytren's contracture involves the individual's reinstatement to work. Exercises are directed toward the work requirements with modifications made in the work environment as necessary. The fabricating of splints and other supportive structures may or may not become an option.

Modifications may need to be made by the physical and/or occupational therapist for those individuals who have Dupuytren's contracture. This will depend on whether surgical removal of the abnormal tissue was necessary or whether the condition was the result of stress or trauma, liver disease, diabetes, or the use of the anti-seizure medicine, which may also lead to the condition.

Work Restrictions / Accommodations

Depending on the nature of the work and the individual's job requirements, specific restrictions or accommodations may have to be made, especially if it is the dominant hand that is affected or if both hands are involved. The individual may have to change job functions that use the involved hand. After surgery, immobilization of the hand and postoperative rehabilitation will preclude using the involved hand until healing is complete.

Comorbid Conditions

Comorbid conditions include peripheral vascular disease and arthritis of the fingers.

Complications

Fixed contraction deformities of the hand may interfere with normal hand function.

Factors Influencing Duration

The extent of deformity, results of treatment, functional ability and job demand may impact the duration of disability.

Length of Disability

Duration depends on whether the dominant or nondominant hand is involved. Disability may be permanent.

Surgical treatment (Dupuytren's release).

Duration in Days

Job Classification	Minimum	Optimum	Maximum
Sedentary work	7	14	28
Light work	21	28	42
Medium work	28	42	84
Heavy work	35	56	112
Very Heavy work	42	56	112

Failure to Recover

If an individual fails to recover within the maximum duration expectancy period, the reader may wish to reference the following questions to assist in better understanding the specifics of an individual's medical case.

Regarding diagnosis:

- Does the individual have epilepsy, diabetes mellitus, or alcoholism?
- Did the individual seem medical attention secondary to difficulty using the hand?
- On exam were skin puckers found? Were small hard nodules found under the skin on the palm of the hand?
- Does the individual have soft pads called "knuckle pads" on the tops of the middle joints of the involved fingers?
- Was the tabletop test performed?
- Did the individual have x-rays?
- Have conditions with similar symptoms been ruled out?

Regarding treatment:

- Did the individual have a favorable response from physical therapy?
- Has the individual had corticosteroid injections into the nodules?
- Have the fingers and hand been splinted?
- Was it necessary to do a needle fasciotomy?
- Was a Dupuytren's release done?
- Has the individual had a recurrence?

Regarding prognosis:

- Is the individual active in physical therapy?
- Does the individual have a home exercise program?
- Is the individual's employer able to accommodate any necessary restrictions?
- Does the individual have any conditions that may affect the ability to recover?
- Does the individual have any fixed contraction deformities?

References

Calandruccio, James H. "Dupuytren's Contracture." Campbell's Operative Orthopedics, 9th ed, vol 4. Canale, S. Terry, ed. St. Louis: Mosby, 1998. 3675-3683.

Kessler, R.M. Management of Common Musculoskeletal Disorders: Physical Therapy Principles and Methods. Philadelphia: J.B. Lippincott Co, 1990.

Kisner, C., and L. Colby. Therapeutic Exercise Foundations and Techniques. Philadelphia: F.A. Davis, 1990.

McFarlane, Robert M. "Dupuytren's Contracture." Operative Hand Surgery, 3rd ed, vol 1. Green, David P., ed. New York: Churchill Livingstone, 1993. 563-590.

Dupuytren's Release

Other names / synonyms: Palmar Fasciectomy, Palmar Fasciotomy

82.35

Definition

Dupuytren's release is a surgical procedure (fasciotomy or fasciectomy) that involves making an incision in the palm of the hand to remove inflamed and contracted connective tissue (fascia) that covers, supports, and separates the tendons of the hand and fingers. The procedure is most often performed to treat Dupuytren's contracture disease in which the individual is unable to extend one or more fingers of the hand, causing significant functional impairment.

The extent of the operation is dependent upon whether the contracture affects one or several fingers. Dupuytren's contracture typically begins with the ring and little finger and, as the disease progresses, can involve all of the fingers. The timing of the operation is based on the rate of progression of the disease and, consequently, may be performed in stages.

There are five different methods to relieve a Dupuytren' contracture: subcutaneous fasciotomy, partial fasciectomy, complete fasciectomy, fasciectomy with skin grafting, and amputation. The partial fasciectomy is the most commonly used of these procedures. Various incisions may be used depending upon the location and extent of the condition. The extent of surgery is dependent upon the individual's history of previous surgical treatment, occupation, and the severity of contractures.

The incidence of Dupuytren's contracture, and therefore the need for the Dupuytren's operation, is greatest in those of Northern European or Celtic descent, is extremely low in non-whites, and increases steadily with age. Those individuals with diabetes mellitus, chronic alcoholism, chronic lung disease, epilepsy, or chronic tuberculosis appear to be at a higher risk of developing the disease and requiring treatment. The disease is most aggressive when onset is under age 40. In these individuals, involvement may be bilateral. Surgical treatment for these cases begins at an earlier age, but recurrence and spreading of the disease is common.

Reason for Procedure

This procedure is used to release the abnormal tightening (contracture) of the palmar fascia of the hand and fingers that cause pain and loss of hand function through contraction of the finger tendons and in the web space of the thumb. Surgery is recommended when the contractures hold flexion of the fingers at 30 degrees or more. Specifically, surgical treatment is aimed at relieving the fixed flexion deformities by removing the palmar fascia (fasciotomy) with preservation of the arteries and nerves, correction of the joint deformities, preservation of uninvolved skin, and maintenance of proper flexion and grip strength. The procedure is not designed to cure the disease, only to modify disease progression and improve hand function by removing obviously diseased tissue. It is indicated in individuals with a significant handicap who demonstrate a positive tabletop test in that they cannot simultaneously place both their palm and fingers flat on a tabletop.

Description

The techniques for surgery depend on the severity of the disease and extension to multiple tendons and the web space. All procedures are done under regional or general anesthesia and most often as an outpatient, depending on the individual's over all health.

The simplest procedure involves an incision in the skin and tissue just underneath the skin (subcutaneous) to reach the affected fascia. The fascia is then cut or released without removing it (fasciotomy) allowing the flexor tendons to slide their full length and, in turn, allowing the finger(s) to extend fully. This technique is used most in older or debilitated individuals or as a preliminary operation for a removal of the fascia (fasciectomy.) A partial fasciectomy is indicated when there is mild to moderate involvement of one or two fingers, while a fasciectomy with skin grafting is used most often in young people who have a poor prognosis because of severe hand contractures or who have a recurrence.

A more extensive fasciectomy is used when the contractures involve the entire palm and more than two fingers. An important aspect of the surgery is control of bleeding (hemostasis) to prevent complication from increased pressure post operatively and a site for infection to begin.

When the disease is severe and involves the joints in the fingers as well, the joints may be fused (arthrodesis.) If the problem is complicated with profound stiffness or decreases nerve function and circulation, amputation of the finger may also be considered.

After surgery, the fingers are placed in as much extension as can be gained under anesthesia and then bulky soft dressings are applied which act as an initial splint. Follow up care includes application of a custom splint to maintain the maximum amount of extension in the palm and fingers.

Prognosis

Because of some genetic predisposition to Dupuytren's disease and contractures, symptoms may reoccur or progress after treatment. This is most common in those individuals with onset before age 40. Between 50-80% of individuals treated surgically have good return of hand function and decreased pain for 10 years. Correction on the hand to finger joint (metacarpophalangeal joints) has the most successful long term outcome. Recurrence is most common in the first finger joint (proximal interphalangeal.) Long term use of extension splints at night are often recommended in this cases.

Specialists

- Hand Surgeon
- Occupational Therapist
- Orthopedic Surgeon
- Physical Therapist

Rehabilitation

The type of release and extent of incision are dependent on the amount of joint contracture. Once the operation is complete, a splint is created that holds the fingers in extension until healed. If the fingers are not in full extension postoperatively, the splint can help hold the fingers in extension by tightening or loosening the Velcro straps that adjust the splint. Splinting is gradually reduced to only nightwear.

The individual may be given a simple home program that includes flexion and extension exercises. The affected hand should be elevated during the initial weeks of healing to help control swelling (edema). Ice packs may also be used to control swelling. The splint is taken off and re-evaluated for fit during sessions with a physical therapist or occupational therapist.

Exercises are initially kept simple and are made part of the home routine, such as tendon gliding exercises. In the tendon gliding exercises, the hand starts in full extension, then the four fingers without the thumb are bent to form a table top, and then the fingers are bent at the finger joint to simulate a partial fist, and finally the thumb is closed to form a full fist. The individual is also instructed on breathing techniques to reduce anxiety and anticipation of pain that may cause co-contraction of muscles and increased muscle tension. Wrist and thumb exercises are added to the routine to continue to balance muscle groups.

When the incision is fully healed, the individual can engage in hydrotherapy where the water temperature can be heated to tolerance. The massaging action of the water further encourages blood flow through the hand. Different gripping exercises using objects of varying degrees of rigidity may be introduced to therapy. For example, the individual may start trying to squeeze a sponge or a cloth and then progressively move to squeezing a piece of Styrofoam.

To reduce the amount of contracture induced by the scar, scar management may be a daily part of the rehabilitation plan. Massaging a lanolin salve into the scar prior to each exercise session helps to keep the skin around the scar flexible. In addition to massage desensitization, exercises such as handling objects of differing textures are implemented until the incision area responds without irritation. The individual may work closely with an occupational therapist to ensure that functional exercises during the latter stages of therapy are matching the work environment. Therapy continues until maximal joint extension for all involved fingers is reached.

Work Restrictions / Accommodations

Extended work leave may be required. Individuals whose jobs require the use of the involved hand will require temporary transfer to other duties, if available. This change in job requirements may become permanent to prevent exacerbation of symptoms although specific work related aggravation is controversial. Some individuals may be able to retrain themselves to perform work duties with their unaffected hand. For others, a temporary leave of absence may be required. Occupational hand therapy is critical to recovery and may require work release time episodically through out the treatment phase for those workers able to return early.

Comorbid Conditions

Carpal tunnel syndrome, reflex sympathetic dystrophy, De Quervain's syndrome or any inflammatory disease or peripheral vascular disease could complicate treatment and recovery.

Procedure Complications

Bleeding into the soft tissues (hematoma), joint stiffness, mild sympathetic dystopy, nerve injury, skin slough, and recurrence of the disease may complicate recovery.

Factors Influencing Duration

Factors include whether the dominant hand was involved, the extent and severity of the condition, the extent of the surgery required to correct the condition, the development of complications, individual compliance with physical/occupational therapy requirements, the individual's age and general health, the presence of accompanying underlying conditions, and the individual's job requirements.

Length of Disability

Those workers with job requirements for manual dexterity may require job retraining. Duration depends on whether the dominant or non-dominant hand is involved. Disability may be permanent.

Duration in Days

Job Classification	Minimum	Optimum	Maximum
Sedentary work	7	14	28
Light work	21	21	42
Medium work	28	42	84
Heavy work	35	56	112
Very Heavy work	42	56	112

References

Bednar, Michael, and Terry Light. "Hand Surgery." Current Diagnosis and Treatment in Orthopedics. Skinner, Harry B Norwalk: Appleton & Lange, 1995. 483-485.

Hunter, James, et al. Rehabilitation of the Hand: Surgery and Therapy, 3rd ed. St. Louis: The C.V. Mosby Company, 1990.

Snider, Robert K., ed. Essentials of Musculoskeletal Care. Rosemont: American Academy of Orthopedic Surgeons, 1997.

Stanely, Barbara, and Susan Tribuzi. Concepts in Hand Rehabilitation. Philadelphia: F.A. Davis, 1992.

Dysentery

Other names / synonyms: Diarrhea, Gastroenteritis, Infectious Colitis, Traveler's Diarrhea

009

Definition

Dysentery is a general term used for inflammation of the intestines that results in severe or bloody diarrhea. The inflammation is generally caused by toxins produced by bacteria, viruses, protozoa, or worms, but can also be caused by chemical irritants. Dysentery is typically contracted through contaminated food or water but can also be transmitted individual-to-individual and via feces from infected individuals.

The two most common types of dysentery are bacillary dysentery and amebic dysentery. Bacillary dysentery, most often caused from infection by the bacterium Shigella, is also called shigellosis. This disease is most common in developing countries where it is present most of the time (endemic). Severe crowding and poor sanitation contribute to the spread of the disease. Worldwide, there are about 140 million cases of shigellosis per year. Bacillary dysenteries also occur each year in the US.

Amebic dysentery is most often caused from infection by the microscopic parasite Entamoeba histolytica, which can exist in two forms: either as free amoebae or as infective cysts. This infection is also more common in tropical, subtropical, and developing countries. It is estimated that about 10% of the world's population is infected with amoebae at any one time. In developed countries such as the US, amebic dysentery is most common in immigrants from countries where the disease is common, in homosexual men, and in residents of institutions including prisons, nursing homes, and institutions for the developmentally disabled. Ninety percent of carriers are asymptomatic.

Diagnosis

History: Those exposed may experience mild, severe, or no symptoms at all. Individuals may complain of abdominal pain, nausea, frequent watery (often foul smelling) diarrhea accompanied by blood and mucus, fever, and rectal pain. Vomiting, generalized muscle aches, and rapid weight loss can also accompany dysentery. Rarely, the amebic parasite will invade the body beyond the intestines and spread through the bloodstream, more seriously infecting other organs such as the liver, lungs, and brain.

Physical exam: The skin, mouth, and lips may appear dry due to dehydration. Lower abdominal tenderness may be present.

Tests: Cultures of stool samples are examined to identify the organism causing dysentery; often several samples must be obtained because the number of amoeba changes from day to day. Blood tests are used to measure abnormalities in the levels of essential minerals and salts (electrolytes).

Treatment

Treatment may not be necessary for mild cases of dysentery. For more severe cases, or cases caused by Shigella, cholera, Salmonella, C. difficile, Giardia, amebae, or sexually transmitted diseases, antibiotics are used to kill the responsible microorganisms. Identification of the organism that is causing the dysentery is important to determine the correct antibiotic. Antibiotics for shigellosis include the ampicillin, trimethoprim-sulfamethoxazole, tetracycline, or ciprofloxacin. Antibiotics used for amebiasis are nitroimidazole drugs such as metronidazole, which act upon the pathogenic microorganisms causing amebiasis but not shigellosis.

Symptoms such as dehydration are treated by fluid replacement either orally or intravenously.

Antidiarrheal medications such as diphenoxylate (Lomotil) and loperamide (Imodium) are not recommended because they can actually aggravate the diarrhea by prolonging contact of the pathogen with the lining of the intestines.

It is important for individuals with dysentery, as well as those having contact with that individual, to practice careful personal hygiene. Handwashing after defecation and before handling food is especially important.

Prognosis

With proper treatment, most cases of bacterial and amebic dysentery will subside within 10 days; most individuals recover fully within 2 to 4 weeks after beginning treatment. The prognosis for untreated disease varies with the immune status of the individual and the severity of disease. Extreme dehydration will prolong recovery and put the individual at greater risk for serious complications.

Differential Diagnosis

Many infectious agents can cause symptoms of mild dysentery. These include many species of bacteria, fungi, viruses, and amoebas.

Specialists

- Gastroenterologist
- Infectious Disease Physician
- Tropical Disease Specialist

Work Restrictions / Accommodations

The individual may require quarantine for up to one week. Food handlers need to be infection-free before they resume working. Accommodations and extended medical restrictions may be required for severe dehydration or untreated cases of severe disease.

Complementary and Alternative Therapies

Content is intended for awareness only. Treatments may or may not be effective. Scientific evidence may be lacking and some substances have potentially toxic effects. Dr. Presley Reed and the editors do not endorse the use of these therapies in the absence of consultation with a licensed medical professional.

Ipecac -	With its amebicidal components, ipecac has been effectively used to treat mild cases of dysentery. Should not be confused with syrup of ipecac, however. Ipecac extracts can be highly toxic and misuse can lead to serious acute and chronic toxicities.
Kaolin -	Because it increases the bulk of feces, it is used in many antidiarrheal preparations. It does not, however, have any antibacterial activity, so should not be used as the sole treatment in infectious diarrheas.
Yogurt -	May reestablish normal flora in the intestines.
Berberine -	Has antiprotozoan activity and may be used to treat mild cases of amebiasis.

Comorbid Conditions

Bacterial dysentery can be complicated by simultaneous infections with other infectious parasites or antibiotic-resistant strains of Shigella. The correct identification of other agents is sometimes elusive, making treatment difficult. Because the body's immune system aids in clearing bacterial infections, medical conditions that deplete or reduce immunity, or diminish the normal gastric acid barrier, may result in more severe cases of dysentery. The elderly suffer more severe cases of dysentery.

Complications

Dehydration is a common complication of diarrhea. Sepsis, seizures, kidney failure, and hemolytic uremia are rare complications of dysentery.

Factors Influencing Duration

Length of disability may be influenced by the severity of the disease at diagnosis, degree of dehydration at the initiation of treatment, whether or not causative organisms can be easily identified and symptoms treated, effectiveness of antibiotic treatment, presence of complications, immunosuppression, and the age of the individual (longer in the very young and the very old).

Length of Disability

Severity is highly variable due to dehydration, electrolyte loss. Disability may be up to one week when the infection is treated with antibiotics. For more severe infections, partial disability may last an additional four weeks.

Duration in Days

Job Classification	Minimum	Optimum	Maximum
Any work	3	7	10

Failure to Recover

If an individual fails to recover within the maximum duration expectancy period, the reader may wish to reference the following questions to assist in better understanding the specifics of an individual's medical case.

Regarding diagnosis:

- Has individual complained of abdominal pain, nausea, frequent watery (often foul-smelling) diarrhea accompanied by blood and mucus, fever, and rectal pain? Was there vomiting, generalized muscle aches, and rapid weight loss?
- Are skin, mouth, and lips dry? Is the abdomen tender?
- Were cultures of stool samples examined? Has the causative organism been positively identified? Were blood tests done to measure abnormalities in the levels of essential minerals and salts (electrolytes)?
- Has diagnosis of dysentery been confirmed?

Regarding treatment:

- Was culture and sensitivity done to determine the most effective antibiotic to use?
- Are the organisms causing dysentery resistant to the antimicrobial drugs used? Is a change in antibiotics warranted?
- Is individual experiencing a reaction to the current medication?
- Should diagnosis be revisited?
- If not able to replace fluid loss orally, has individual received intravenous rehydration?
- Is individual self-treating with over-the-counter antidiarrheal medication?

Regarding prognosis:

- Did individual delay seeking treatment?
- How much longer than expected have symptoms persisted?
- Does individual continue to be exposed to infective organisms or chemicals that may be causing the dysentery?
- Does individual have an underlying condition that may impact recovery?

References

Brooks, G.F., J.S. Butel, and S.A. Morse. Medical Microbiology. Stamford: Appleton & Lange, 1998.

World Health Organization. Fact Sheet N 108; Epidemic Dysentery. World Health Organization. 01 Oct 1996. 01 Jan 2001 <http://www.who.int/inf-fs/en/fact108.html>.

Dysfunctional Uterine Bleeding

Other names / synonyms: DUB, Dysfunctional Uterine Hemorrhage, Retained Menstruation, Suppression of Menstruation

626.2, 626.6, 626.8, 627, 627.0

Definition

Dysfunctional uterine bleeding is a nonspecific term for abnormal uterine bleeding caused by hormonal changes rather than injury, inflammation, tumor, or pregnancy. Endometrial cancer and endometrial lesions must be excluded before a diagnosis of dysfunctional bleeding is made. The female hormones estrogen and progesterone are normally produced in balance with each other through the interaction of the hypothalamus, pituitary glands, and the ovaries. Most cases of dysfunctional uterine bleeding result from menstrual cycles in which ovulation does not occur (anovulation). The remainder of the cases arise from problems associated with ovulation, such as a dysfunction of the corpus luteum.

Risk factors include obesity, polycystic ovary syndrome, endometriosis, and prolonged estrogen or progesterone use. Stress, crash diets, irregular sleep patterns, overwork, vigorous exercise, and drug or alcohol abuse can also disrupt normal hormone balance.

Dysfunctional uterine bleeding occurs most commonly at the beginning and end of the reproductive years. Twenty percent of cases occur in adolescent girls while women over age 45 years of age account for more than 50%.

Diagnosis

History: Bleeding described is outside the normal menstrual pattern. Bleeding may occur between menstrual periods. Periods may be excessively long and/or heavy. Pain may or may not be reported with the bleeding.

Pertinent history includes duration of bleeding, amount of flow, presence of clots, pain, relationship to last menstrual period, history of recent illnesses, and all medications taken in the previous several months.

Physical exam: A pelvic exam will be done with or without a general physical. Reproductive organs will be examined for problems, such as areas of bleeding, pregnancy, or tumors.

Tests: Diagnostic tests may include: cervical smear (Pap smear), complete blood count (CBC), sedimentation rate, blood glucose, coagulation tests, thyroid function, and pregnancy test. A pelvic ultrasound, hysterosalpingography, or MRI may be done to locate or rule out tumors. A biopsy, curettage, or aspiration of the uterus lining may be required for further tissue examination.

Treatment

Treatment is based on the woman's age, condition of the uterine lining, and plans regarding pregnancy. Treatment is separated into two groups: those with acute bleeding episodes and those with chronic repetitive bleeding problems. An acute bleeding episode is best controlled with high-dose estrogen. Treatment of chronic repetitive bleeding problems depends on the exact cause, and may consist of estrogen or progestin therapy. Oral contraceptives may help regulate the menstrual cycle. An intrauterine device (IUD) that releases a progestin has provided satisfactory treatment in some individuals. Nonsteroidal anti-inflammatory drugs may be required. Iron may be needed if the woman is anemic. The individual who presents with dysfunctional uterine bleeding and a history of menstrual cycle irregularity warrants an endometrial biopsy, regardless of age. Surgery may be needed if hormone therapy fails. Surgical options include dilation and curettage (D&C), laser or electrocautery, endometrial ablation, or hysterectomy. In order to rebuild the woman's hemoglobin count, medication may be necessary to stop the bleeding for up to 3 months prior to surgery.

Hormone imbalance may occur due to lifestyle issues, such as excessive stress, irregular sleep patterns, overwork, and drug or alcohol abuse. Corresponding lifestyle changes may correct the hormone imbalance.

Prognosis

With appropriate treatment, hormone balance can usually be achieved. If pregnancy is desired, infertility may need to be addressed with fertility drugs.

Corresponding lifestyle changes may correct hormonal imbalance due to lifestyle issues, such as excessive stress, irregular sleep patterns, overwork, and drug or alcohol abuse.

Differential Diagnosis

Other possible diagnoses include uterine fibroids, tumors of the reproductive organs, pelvic infection, endometriosis, endometrial polyps, von Willebrand's disease, uterine or ectopic pregnancy, and miscarriage.

Specialists

- Endocrinologist
- Gynecologist

Work Restrictions / Accommodations

Work restrictions, such as reduced workload or time off, may be needed if surgery is required or anemia is pronounced.

Comorbid Conditions

Women with obesity and polycystic ovary syndrome are prone to hormone imbalances, making treatment more difficult.

Complications

Prolonged and heavy bleeding can cause anemia. Continued hormonal imbalance may block ovulation, resulting in infertility.

Factors Influencing Duration

Length of disability is influenced by the severity of symptoms, method of treatment, and individual's response to treatment.

Length of Disability

With D&C.

Job Classification	Minimum	Optimum	Maximum
Sedentary work	2	3	7
Light work	2	3	7
Medium work	3	4	7
Heavy work	3	4	7
Very Heavy work	3	4	7

Duration Trend from Normative Data*

Cases	Mean	Min	Max	No Lost Time	Over 6 Months
6081	44	0	313	0.18%	0.08%

Percentile:	5th	25th	Median	75th	95th
Days:	10	30	43	56	78

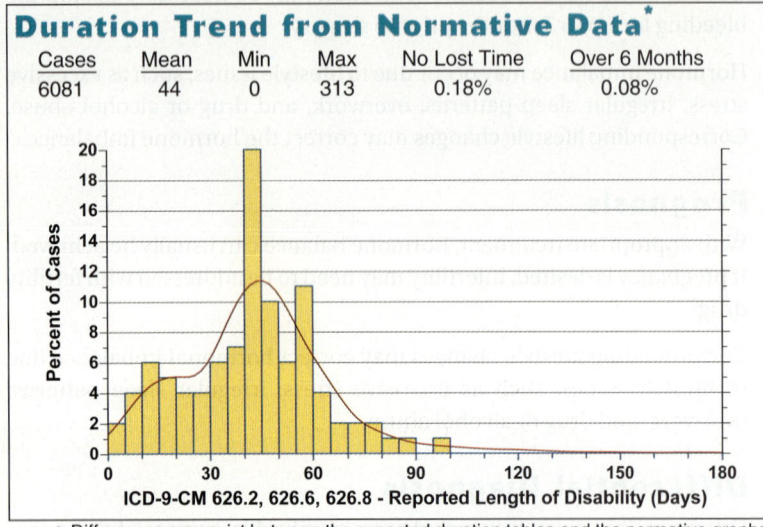
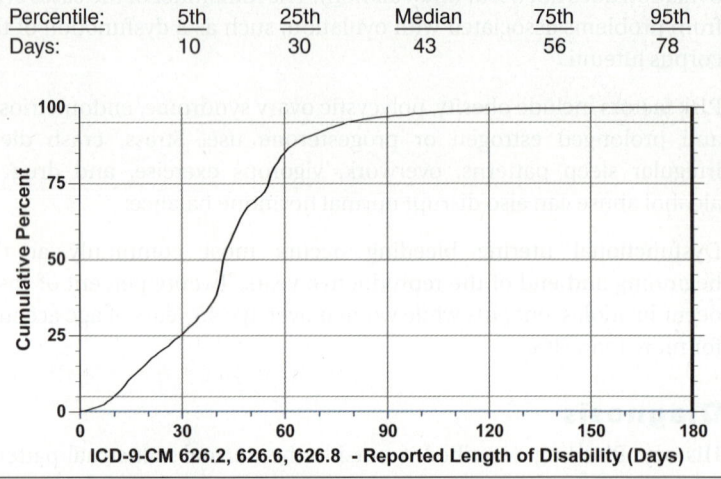

ICD-9-CM 626.2, 626.6, 626.8 - Reported Length of Disability (Days)

* Differences may exist between the expected duration tables and the normative graphs. Duration tables provide expected recovery periods based on the type of work performed by the individual. The normative graphs reflect the actual observed experience of many individuals across the spectrum of physical conditions, in a variety of industries, and with varying levels of case management.

Failure to Recover

If an individual fails to recover within the maximum duration expectancy period, the reader may wish to reference the following questions to assist in better understanding the specifics of an individual's medical case.

Regarding diagnosis:

- How old is the individual?
- Does individual have any risk factors such as obesity, polycystic ovary syndrome, endometriosis, and prolonged estrogen or progesterone use?
- Does individual have stress, use crash diets, have irregular sleep patterns, overwork, vigorous exercise, and drug or alcohol use?
- Has bleeding outside the normal menstrual cycle occurred? What is the duration of bleeding, amount of flow, presence of clots, pain, and relationship to last menstrual period?
- Has individual had any recent illnesses?
- What medications were taken in the previous several months?

- Was a pelvic exam done? Have a Pap smear, CBC, sedimentation rate, blood glucose, coagulation tests, thyroid function, and pregnancy test been performed? Has individual had a pelvic ultrasound, hysterosalpingography, or MRI? Was it necessary to do a uterine biopsy?
- Have conditions with similar symptoms been ruled out?

Regarding treatment:

- Is individual being treated with hormone therapy?
- Is individual on iron supplements, if needed?
- Was surgery necessary?
- Has individual addressed correctable lifestyle issues such as excessive stress, irregular sleep patterns, overwork, and drug or alcohol abuse?

Regarding prognosis:

- Can individual's employer accommodate any necessary restrictions?
- Does individual have any conditions that may affect ability to recover?
- Have any complications developed such as anemia or infertility?

References

Apgar, B.S. "Dysmenorrhea and Dysfunctional Uterine Bleeding." Primary Care 24 1 (1997): 161-178.

Ash, S.J., S.A. Farrell, and G. Flowerdew. "Endometrial Biopsy in DUB." Journal of Reproductive Medicine 41 12 (1996): 892-896.

Chuong, C.J., and P.F. Brenner. "Management of Abnormal Uterine Bleeding." American Journal of Obstetrical Gynecology 175 3 Pt 2 (1996): 787-792.

Crosignani, P.G., P. Vercellini, and P. Mosconi. "Levonorgestrel-Releasing Intrauterine Device Versus Hysteroscopic Endometrial Resection in the Treatment of Dysfunctional Uterine Bleeding." Obstetrical Gynecology 90 2 (1997): 257-263.

Ferri, Fred. Ferri's Clinical Advisor. St. Louis: Mosby, 2000.

MacKay, H. Trent. "Gynecology." Current Medical Diagnosis and Treatment. Tierney, Lawrence, Stephen McPhee, and Maxine Papadakis, eds. New York: Lange Medical Books/McGraw-Hill, 2000. 723-757.

Dyspepsia
Other names / synonyms: Indigestion, Nervous Indigestion
536.8

Definition

Dyspepsia is the medical term for indigestion. Dyspepsia often occurs as a symptom of an underlying disease or disorder.

Abdominal pain, discomfort or fullness, intestinal gas (flatulence), heartburn, and/or nausea are associated with dyspepsia. These symptoms may be brought on by eating too much, eating too quickly, or by eating foods that are very spicy, rich, or fatty. Symptoms are often increased during times of stress and dyspepsia may be referred to as nervous indigestion. Other causes of dyspepsia may include excessive intake of alcohol or caffeine, excess stomach acidity, reflux of stomach acid into the esophagus (gastroesophageal reflux), dysfunction of the stomach or intestines, abnormal quantity or quality of bile secretion, liver disease, parasitic infections, milk sugar (lactose) intolerance, pregnancy, pancreatic disease, cancer (malignancy) in the abdominal cavity, thyroid disease, and low blood flow to the heart (coronary ischemia). Dyspepsia may also occur with the use of certain drugs or dietary supplements including iron, nonsteroidal anti-inflammatory drugs (NSAIDs), antibiotics, diuretics, and cardiotonic glycosides. Persistent or recurrent dyspepsia is sometimes associated with a lesion in the stomach or small intestine (peptic ulcer), gallstones, or inflammation of the esophagus (esophagitis). However, in up to half of the individuals who seek treatment for dyspepsia, no underlying disease state or disorder is found for the reported symptoms.

Dyspepsia is extremely common throughout the US and Europe, and estimates of its prevalence range from 15-40% within the general population. Estimates vary because only a small proportion of individuals with dyspeptic symptoms seek medical advice. Dyspepsia accounts for approximately 5% of all general practitioner medical consultations and for 50% of all visits to gastroenterologists in the US. Neither sex nor social class appears to be a factor in the prevalence of this condition; however, the overall prevalence of dyspepsia decreases with age. Dyspepsia that is caused by another organic disease is usually found in males that are 40 years of age or older, and smokers tend to have a higher incidence of underlying organic disease associated with dyspepsia.

Diagnosis

History: Individuals may report a vague abdominal discomfort, a sense of fullness after eating, excessive belching, heartburn, bloating, gas (flatulence), and loss of appetite. Nausea and/or vomiting may also be reported. These symptoms can occur irregularly but they are usually increased during times of stress.

Physical exam: Abdominal distention and increased bowel sounds due to excessive gas in the stomach or intestine may be observed during physical examination. The site of the pain and pattern of symptoms can help to identify the underlying causes of dyspepsia. Weight loss, enlarged abdominal organs, abdominal mass, or blood in the stool are indicators of an underlying organic disease and point to the need for further investigation.

Tests: A chemical test done on a stool sample (fecal occult blood test or FOBT) should always be done and this can identify blood that may be hidden within the fecal material (occult blood). A complete blood count (CBC) and a test for liver function (liver chemistry panel) may also be done. A flexible fiber optic microscope can be used to examine the inside of the stomach (diagnostic gastroscopy) to identify stomach lesions (peptic ulcer disease), reflux of acid into the esophagus from the stomach (gastroesophageal reflux disease or GERD), and stomach cancer (gastric malignancy). Ultrasound (abdominal sonography) may be used to identify biliary or pancreatic disease.

Treatment

Treatment is directed at the underlying cause and alleviation of symptoms. Alcohol and caffeine intake should be curtailed and medications that exacerbate the problem (such as non-steroidal anti-inflammatory drugs or NSAIDs) should be eliminated. Self-medication with over-the-counter antacids may be helpful. Prescription medications that may be useful include histamine receptor antagonists, drugs that stimulate stomach emptying and decrease acid reflux into the esophagus (prokinetic agents), and drugs that prevent stomach acid secretion (proton pump inhibitors). In some cases, the individual may need to keep a record of food intake, symptoms, and daily events that may be stressful in order to reveal dietary or social factors that trigger the dyspepsia episodes.

Prognosis

Dyspepsia is not a disease in itself but is a symptom of other diseases or disorders. Consequently, the predicted outcome ultimately depends on the underlying cause of the dyspeptic symptoms. For acute treatment of dyspepsia, there is no evidence to suggest that antacid medications work better than an inert compound (placebo) in alleviating symptoms. Nevertheless, the effect of antacids to reduce dyspeptic symptoms may decrease the number of extensive and costly procedures such as endoscopy. Histamine receptor antagonists lead to a 50% reduction in acid output by the stomach, and this has been found to produce significant improvement in individuals who are experiencing pain and nausea. Prokinetic agents are found to be the most effective treatment for disorders of gastrointestinal motility. Drugs that inhibit acid secretion by the stomach (proton pump inhibitors) are usually the best treatment for acid reflux from the stomach into the esophagus (gastroesophageal reflux).

Differential Diagnosis

Dyspepsia is a symptom of many other diseases and disorders including gastrointestinal tract dysfunction, pancreatic disease, biliary tract disease, thyroid disease, coronary ischemia, pregnancy, side effects of certain drugs, and excessive alcohol consumption.

Specialists

- Gastroenterologist
- Primary Care Provider

Rehabilitation

Regular physical activity on a daily basis is recommended to relieve stress which may exacerbate dyspepsia. Aerobic exercise such as walking, jogging, or swimming (30-45 minutes per session) is usually beneficial.

Work Restrictions / Accommodations

Work restrictions and accommodations are not usually associated with dyspepsia. However, each case must be considered on an individual basis depending on the underlying cause for the condition. If stress is aggravating the dyspepsia, transfer to a less stressful position may be necessary.

Complementary and Alternative Therapies

Content is intended for awareness only. Treatments may or may not be effective. Scientific evidence may be lacking and some substances have potentially toxic effects. Dr. Presley Reed and the editors do not endorse the use of these therapies in the absence of consultation with a licensed medical professional.

Dietary modifications -	A bland diet may be beneficial in relieving the symptoms of dyspepsia.
Acupuncture -	Insertion of needles at specific body points may alleviate dyspepsia symptoms.
Chiropractic care -	Joint manipulation may relieve dyspepsia.
Baduanjin -	Ancient Chinese exercises may help dyspeptic symptoms.

Comorbid Conditions

Existing conditions that may impact an individual's ability to recover and further lengthen their disability include endocrine diseases that may have systemic effects such as diabetes mellitus, overactive parathyroid activity (hyperparathyroidism), and excess secretion by the thyroid gland (thyrotoxicosis).

Complications

Dyspepsia may be complicated by an underlying condition. Taking antacids or other prescription medications can mask a serious, underlying disease or disorder, and this may cause delay in diagnosis and treatment. Certain underlying diseases--including ulcer, cancer of the stomach or duodenum, and low blood flow to the heart (coronary ischemia)--may develop into life-threatening situations.

Factors Influencing Duration

The length of disability resulting from dyspepsia may be influenced by the severity of the symptoms, the underlying disease state that is causing the dyspeptic symptoms, and the response of the underlying disease to treatment.

Length of Disability

Duration depends on diagnosis. Typically, individuals with mild dyspepsia are not disabled for any extended period of time. However, if the underlying disease state is serious in nature, the length of disability could be extensive (e.g., ulcer, pancreatitis, biliary disease) or even permanent (stomach or duodenal cancer).

Duration in Days

Job Classification	Minimum	Optimum	Maximum
Any work	0	1	5

Failure to Recover

If an individual fails to recover within the maximum duration expectancy period, the reader may wish to reference the following questions to assist in better understanding the specifics of an individual's medical case.

Regarding diagnosis:

- Has any underlying cause of the dyspepsia, such as gastrointestinal tract dysfunction, pancreatic disease, biliary tract disease, thyroid disease, coronary ischemia, pregnancy, side effects of certain drugs, and excessive alcohol consumption been identified?
- Is individual receiving appropriate treatment for this condition?
- Have other underlying conditions (gastrointestinal ulcers, cancer or coronary ischemia) been ruled out?
- Does individual have a coexisting condition that may impact recovery, such as diabetes mellitus, hyperparathyroidism, or thyrotoxicosis?

Regarding treatment:

- Is the underlying condition serious enough to require more extensive treatment? Has the individual been evaluated by an appropriate specialist (gastroenterologist, endocrinologist, etc.)?

- Has the individual been compliant in eliminating substances that are known gastric irritants (alcohol, caffeine, NSAIDs, etc)?
- Have symptoms been relieved with over-the-counter antacids? If not, have prescription medications been tried?
- Has individual kept a record of daily food intake and events that may be stressful?
- Has individual been instructed in stress reduction techniques?

Regarding prognosis:

- Have any underlying conditions responded to treatment?
- Have symptoms persisted despite apparently successful treatment of underlying condition?
- Does diagnosis need to be revisited?
- Would individual benefit from any of the following: Stress reduction therapy? Dietary changes or counseling? Occupational change? Support group?

References

Bryner, P., and P.G. Staerker. "Indigestion and Heartburn: A Descriptive Study of Prevalence in Persons Seeking Care From Chiropractors." Journal of Manipulative and Physiological Therapeutics 19 5 (1996): 317-323.

LeMone, P., and K.M. Burke. Medical-Surgical Nursing. Upper Saddle River, NJ: Prentice Hall Health, 2000.

Dyspnea

Other names / synonyms: Breathlessness, Shortness of Breath

786.05, 786.06, 786.09

Definition

Dyspnea is the term for the sensation of abnormal or uncomfortable breathing in the context of what is normal for an individual. It manifests as breathlessness or increased respiratory effort. Dyspnea is experienced when the need for oxygen exceeds the actual or perceived capacity of the lungs to respond. This need results in an increased respiratory rate, thus increasing the physical effort needed for the individual to breathe.

The four general categories of dyspnea are cardiac, pulmonary, mixed cardiac or pulmonary, and noncardiac or nonpulmonary. Dyspnea can result from weakness or injury to the chest wall or chest muscles, decreased lung elasticity, obstruction of the airway, increased oxygen demand, or unrelated factors such as obesity.

Sudden onset of dyspnea (acute dyspnea) is most typically associated with narrowing of the airways or airflow obstruction (bronchospasm), blockage of one of the arteries of the lung (pulmonary embolism), acute heart failure or heart attack, pneumonia, or anxiety. Long-standing dyspnea (chronic dyspnea) is most often a manifestation of chronic or progressive diseases of the lung and/or heart such as chronic obstruction pulmonary disease (COPD). These diseases include chronic asthma, chronic bronchitis, emphysema, or congestive heart failure (CHF) where poor pumping action of the heart results in increased pressure and fluid in the lungs.

Dyspnea is a hallmark finding in asthma, a lung condition characterized by periodic inflammation and narrowing of the airways following exposure to airway irritants. It is a common condition occurring in about 5% of the population with equal frequency among men and women. Asthma tends to manifest before the age of 25. It may disappear spontaneously or become progressively worse and develop into a chronic condition.

Another cause of dyspnea is occupational lung disease (OLD), one of the ten leading causes of work-related health problems in the US. Risk factors for OLD include inhaling organic and inorganic dusts, irritant gases, and toxic fumes that adversely affect both the upper and lower respiratory tracts. Cigarette smokers have a greater risk of developing OLD. Dyspnea appears early in this disease process and becomes worse as the disease progresses.

COPD affects about 16 million Americans and is strongly associated with a history of cigarette smoking. CHF affects more than 3 million Americans, is more common in blacks than whites, and slightly more common in men than in women.

Diagnosis

History: Individual may complain of shortness of breath or "getting winded" when involved in their usual activities or at rest. Individuals may report shortness of breath occurring most commonly at night while lying flat in bed (orthopnea). Individuals may report the need to limit activities due to shortness of breath. They may describe other factors associated with the onset of dyspnea such as chest pain, anxiety, or exposure to smoke or other irritants. Individuals may have a history of heart or lung diseases, alcohol abuse, or smoking. They may report a recent respiratory infection, chest injury, surgery, or travel that required prolonged sitting.

Physical exam: The exam may reveal poor coloring or skin that is blue in color (cyanosis) and rapid respirations. Individuals may have a fever, wheeze, or cough. They may require a longer time than normal to exhale air (prolonged expiratory phase). The lungs may sound bubbly or crackling (rhonchi or rales) if they contain fluid. Lung sounds may be absent in cases of collapsed lung (pneumothorax) or pneumonia. Examination should be done for the presence of nasal polyps, septal deviation, postnasal discharge, jugular vein distention, decreased pulse, increased chest diameter, rapid heart rate (tachycardia), heart murmur, changes in the fingertips and toes (clubbing) that indicate severe hypoxia (reduced oxygen to the tissues), enlarged liver (hepatomegaly), or tissue swelling (edema).

Tests: Lab tests may include complete blood count (CBC), measure of arterial blood oxygen (arterial blood gases [ABG]), blood carbon monoxide levels, and renal function studies. Blood oxygen saturation may be measured using an infrared light sensor device on the finger (pulse oximeter). A chest x-ray and electrocardiogram (ECG) are typically done to determine the presence of any obvious lung or heart disorder. A radionuclide study of oxygen uptake and circulation in the lungs (ventilation-perfusion lung scan) may help rule out pulmonary embolus. Directly examining the small bronchial airways using a lighted scope (bronchoscopy) may be done in severe cases. Pulmonary function tests (PFT's) measure the degree to which an airway obstruction affects lung volumes and capacity. Other tests include an echocardiogram to detect heart valve abnormality, and cardiopulmonary exercise testing to quantify cardiac function and pulmonary ventilation.

Treatment

Initial efforts are aimed at ensuring and maintaining an open airway and providing assistive ventilation, if necessary. Supplemental oxygen therapy is usually given, at least initially, to all individuals suffering from dyspnea. Those unable to independently maintain an open airway (due to decreased level of alertness) may need an artificial airway established by inserting a tube through the mouth or nose and into the lungs (intubation).

Once the airway is open and breathing and oxygenation are stabilized, the main objective is to diagnose and treat the underlying cause. Asthma is managed by avoiding conditions that trigger the attacks and using a combination of oral and inhaled medications that open the airways (bronchodilators). COPD is treated with supplemental oxygen (as needed), bronchodilators, and antibiotics (if infection is present). OLD is managed with supplemental oxygen (as needed) and bronchodilators. For all the above conditions, avoidance of airway irritants such as cigarette smoke, wood smoke, toxic fumes and gases, air pollution, and workplace irritants is essential. Severe cases of asthma, COPD, and OLD can result in inadequate oxygenation (respiratory failure) that may require emergency respiratory support with intubation and initiation of mechanical breathing (ventilator).

Prognosis

Acute dyspnea often resolves with treatment of the underlying condition. This is not the case, however, in dyspnea associated with chronic conditions such as COPD or CHF. These conditions usually result in progressive dysfunction, severe disability, and eventual death.

Differential Diagnosis

Dyspnea may be associated with acute or chronic conditions of the heart or lungs. These conditions often present simultaneously and it may be difficult to determine if one or several of these underlying conditions are responsible for the symptom of dyspnea.

Specialists

- Cardiologist
- Emergency Medicine
- Internist
- Pulmonologist

Rehabilitation

Pulmonary rehabilitation may be recommended for those with dyspnea. The rehabilitation program usually consists of an aerobic exercise program. By building individuals' endurance through rehabilitation, they increase their ability to work and their resistance to fatigue. A physical therapist experienced in cardiac and pulmonary rehabilitation keeps a daily log of the individual's blood pressure, heart rate, and cardiac rhythm. As endurance increases without shortness of breath, the individual begins active upper and lower extremity exercises using very light resistance in addition to light aerobic activities that include brisk walking and low-resistance biking.

The principles of aerobic conditioning in physical therapy are commonly used to develop a program for individuals with pulmonary disorders. Low-demand aerobic activities using large muscle groups such as the lower extremities are initiated. Calisthenics are instructed of varying intensity like marching in place and raising both arms overhead.

Walking (ambulating) and the use of a stationary bicycle is added to therapy and should be initially performed under supervision. This form of aerobic exercise progresses with time and intensity and varies from individual to individual.

In some cases, individuals are attached to an electrocardiograph (ECG) monitor, a device used to record the continuous electrical activity of the heart muscle. Individuals move on to higher levels of exercise with the addition of recreational activities such as swimming and outdoor hiking. Light jogging at approximately 5 miles per hour (mph) and cycling at approximately 12 mph is appropriate as long as the individual tolerates the rehabilitation program well.

Finally, rehabilitation involves aerobic exercises that increase cardiovascular fitness. The individual with dyspnea is instructed in walking briskly, running, jogging, swimming, climbing stairs, or bicycling. The American Heart Association recommends 30 to 60 minutes of aerobic activity 3 or 4 times a week to help keep high blood pressure under control. Throughout all phases, it is important to allow the heart rate to slowly return to normal after exercise. Smoking cessation programs are recommended for all individuals who smoke.

Work Restrictions / Accommodations

Those who require continuous oxygen therapy must work in areas where there is no danger of igniting this gas. Work environment should be free of inhaled irritants or temperature extremes. Job responsibilities should not involve strenuous activity such as frequent stair climbing or heavy lifting. Frequent rest periods or shorter workdays may be needed if the individual is symptomatic.

Complementary and Alternative Therapies

Content is intended for awareness only. Treatments may or may not be effective. Scientific evidence may be lacking and some substances have potentially toxic effects. Dr. Presley Reed and the editors do not endorse the use of these therapies in the absence of consultation with a licensed medical professional.

Massage, meditation, and biofeedback - May help reduce stress and promote relaxation in anxiety-related dyspnea.

Comorbid Conditions

Pre-existing conditions of paraplegia or quadriplegia, neuromuscular disorders, heart failure, cancer, cigarette use, obesity, or obstructive lung disease may impact the ability to recover and further lengthen disability.

Complications

Complications of dyspnea secondary to lung or heart conditions include respiratory failure, heart failure, or spontaneous collapsed lung (pneumothorax).

Factors Influencing Duration

The severity of the underlying disease, age of the individual, compliance with treatment regimen, and any associated complications will influence disability.

Length of Disability

Duration depends on the underlying cause. Contact physician for more specific information.

Failure to Recover

If an individual fails to recover within the maximum duration expectancy period, the reader may wish to reference the following questions to assist in better understanding the specifics of an individual's medical case.

Regarding diagnosis:

- Does individual have weakness or injury to the chest wall or chest muscles, decreased lung elasticity, obstruction of the airway, increased oxygen demand, or unrelated factors such as obesity?
- Does individual have occupational lung disease (OLD)?
- Does individual complain of shortness of breath when involved in usual activities or at rest? Is it worse at night or when lying flat?
- Has individual experienced chest pain, anxiety, or exposure to smoke or other irritants? Does individual have a history of heart or lung diseases, alcohol abuse, or smoking? Does individual report a recent respiratory infection, chest injury, surgery, or travel that required prolonged sitting?
- On exam, is individual cyanotic and breathing rapidly?
- Does individual have a fever, wheeze, or cough? Abnormal lung sounds?
- Does individual have nasal polyps, septal deviation, postnasal discharge, jugular vein distention, decreased pulse, increased chest diameter, tachycardia, heart murmur, clubbing of the fingertips and toes, hepatomegaly, or edema?
- Has individual had a CBC, arterial blood gases, blood carbon monoxide levels, and renal function studies? Were chest x-ray, ECG, ventilation-perfusion lung scan, bronchoscopy, pulmonary function tests, echocardiogram, and cardiopulmonary exercise testing performed?
- Have conditions with similar symptoms been ruled out?

Regarding treatment:

- Did individual receive supplemental oxygen therapy? Was intubation necessary?
- What is the underlying cause of individual's dyspnea? Is it being treated?

Regarding prognosis:

- Is individual active in rehabilitation? Does individual have a home exercise program?
- Has individual addressed smoking cessation?
- Can individual's employer accommodate any necessary restrictions?
- Does individual have any conditions that may affect ability to recover?
- Did any complications arise such as respiratory failure, heart failure, or pneumothorax?

References

Kisner, C., and L. Colby. Therapeutic Exercise Foundations and Techniques. Philadelphia: F.A. Davis Company, 1990.

Tierney, Lawrence M., Stephen J. McPhee, and Maxine Papadakis, eds. Current Medical Diagnosis and Treatment, 39th ed. New York: Lange Medical Books/McGraw-Hill, 2000.

Dysthymic Disorder

Other names / synonyms: Dysthymia, Neurotic Depression, Reactive Depression

300.4

Definition

Dysthymic disorder is a chronic, low-grade depression. When the disorder begins in adulthood, it may be triggered by a major life transition such as the birth of a first child, bereavement, or job loss. Dysthymia can be related to personal stressors such as personality conflicts or relationship difficulties in some situations.

Individuals with dysthymia have persistent symptoms including a low mood, fatigue, hopelessness, difficulty concentrating, and problems with sleep and appetite. These symptoms persist most of the day and last over a period of two or more years. Individuals may have symptom-free periods but these seldom last longer than two consecutive months. The symptoms are generally milder but longer lasting than those of a major depressive episode.

If the symptoms are associated with another psychiatric impairment (major depression, schizophrenia, manic episodes, or organic psychosis), a diagnosis of dysthymia does not apply. Individuals diagnosed with dysthymic disorder must not have had a major depressive episode during the first two years of the syndrome.

In the course of their lifetime, about 5-6% of adults have dysthymic disorder, although the condition can begin in childhood in some cases. Women are 2 to 3 times more likely to develop dysthymia than men.

Diagnosis

History: A diagnosis of dysthymic disorder is based on standard criteria set forth in the DSM-IV-TR (Diagnostic and Statistical Manual of Mental Disorders, 4th Edition, Text Revision, published by the American Psychiatric Association). Persistent sadness, loss of pleasure (anhedonia), and withdrawal from usual activities over a period of two or more years are necessary to warrant this diagnosis.

The individual who suffers from dysthymic disorder must not have gone for more than two months without experiencing two or more of the following symptoms: poor appetite or overeating, insomnia or sleeping too much (hypersomnia), low energy or fatigue, low self-esteem, poor concentration or difficulty making decisions, or feelings of hopelessness.

Individual must not have had a major depressive episode during the first two years of the disturbance unless a full remission occurred without significant signs or symptoms for two months before development of the dysthymic disorder. Individual has never had a manic, mixed, or hypomanic episode and criteria have never been met for cyclothymic disorder. The disturbance must not occur exclusively during the course of a chronic psychotic disorder. The symptoms must not be due to the direct physiological effects of a medication or a general medical condition such as an underactive thyroid (hypothyroidism) and must cause clinically significant distress or impairment in social, occupational, or other important areas of functioning.

Physical exam: There are no typical abnormalities on physical examination. Facial expressions may reveal a depressed mood. Some individuals show uncharacteristic disregard for their appearance. Recent weight gain or loss or slowing of physical and mental processes (psychomotor retardation) may also be present. Observation of the individual's orientation, dress, mannerisms, behavior and content of speech may help diagnose the illness.

Tests: Dysthymia is not characterized by any abnormal laboratory tests. Psychological testing such as the Beck Depression Inventory or the Minnesota Multiphasic Personality Inventory may reveal evidence of depressed mood.

Treatment

Treatment usually consists of psychotherapy and antidepressant medications. Supportive counseling can address feelings of hopelessness. Cognitive therapy may help change the pessimistic ideas, unrealistic expectations, and overly critical self-evaluations that sustain the depressed mood, and can also help the individual distinguish between critical and minor life problems. Problem-solving therapy can help change stressful situations contributing to depression. Behavioral therapy can improve coping skills while interpersonal therapy may help resolve relationship conflicts. Family and friends may benefit from counseling or a support group to help them cope with the demands of the loved one's illness.

The treatment of choice for depressed mood is antidepressant medication, primarily serotonin-specific reuptake inhibitors (SSRIs). It begins with low dosage and continues for up to 3 months. If there is significant improvement in symptoms, therapy should continue for 2 to 3 years or for life. Approximately 62% of individuals with dysthymic disorder benefit from antidepressant medication. Guidelines for assessing potential of drug therapy include a positive family history and a past history of poor response to other forms of treatment. Hospitalization is generally not necessary unless there is a suicide plan or attempt.

Prognosis

Outcome is good with improvement in symptoms, well-being, and functioning after several months of drug treatment and psychotherapy. Since the disorder is chronic, long-term or recurrent treatment may be necessary depending on the severity of symptoms. Up to 80% of individuals have severe, long-term symptoms that cause problems with social and occupational functioning. Individuals often have trouble forming or sustaining relationships. Emotional distress can be serious with incidence of suicide ranging from 3-12%. Accompanying symptoms such as sleep disorder and chronic fatigue can be debilitating and lead dysthymic individuals to use health care services five times more often than unaffected individuals.

Differential Diagnosis

Many unrelated medical or personal stressors may present with symptoms of dysthymia. Dysthymic symptoms may be masking another problem such as a thyroid disorder or anemic condition or other organic mood syndromes such as those related to AIDS, Alzheimer's disease, multiple sclerosis, endocrine conditions, cancer, neurodegenerative diseases, or vitamin deficiencies. Psychiatric conditions resembling dysthymic disorder include mood disorders, psychotic disorders, and personality disorders. Numerous drugs and medications can cause some of the symptoms of dysthymia. The hallmark of the disorder is duration of at least two years.

Specialists

- Internist
- Psychiatrist
- Psychologist

Work Restrictions / Accommodations

Work restrictions or accommodations are necessary only infrequently, for the most serious cases. In these instances, time-limited restrictions and work accommodations should be individually determined based on the characteristics of the individual's response to the disorder, the functional requirements of the job and work environment, and the flexibility of the job and work site. The purpose of the restrictions/accommodation is to help maintain the worker's capacity to remain at the workplace without a work disruption or to promote timely and safe transition back to full work productivity.

Comorbid Conditions

Comorbid conditions that may impact recovery and lengthen disability include substance abuse, major depression, post-traumatic stress disorder, panic disorder, social phobia, generalized anxiety disorder, and personality disorders.

Complications

The most common complication is major depression (known as double depression) or an underlying personality disorder. Suicidal thoughts, plans, or gestures may also complicate dysthymia. If a suicide attempt is made, the individual must be reassessed by a mental health professional and treated for ongoing psychological needs. Medical needs such as wound care or other physical complaints must be addressed and a new psychiatric diagnosis formulated. If an individual has a personality disorder (an Axis II diagnosis), this can complicate treatment depending on the diagnosis. If the individual has adopted ineffective coping techniques as part of the underlying personality disorder, this can also impede or complicate treatment.

Factors Influencing Duration

Length of disability may be influenced by severity of symptoms (i.e., sleep disturbance) or the degree of psychomotor retardation (slowing of physical and mental processes). A suicide attempt may lengthen disability due to necessary medical treatment and the need for further psychological assessment.

Length of Disability

Dysthymia is seldom disabling. Remission and recurrence are common due to the chronic nature of dysthymia. Duration of disability also depends on job requirements. Emotionally stressful job duties may increase length of disability. Symptoms may interfere with optimal work performance.

Duration in Days

Job Classification	Minimum	Optimum	Maximum
Any work	1	14	28

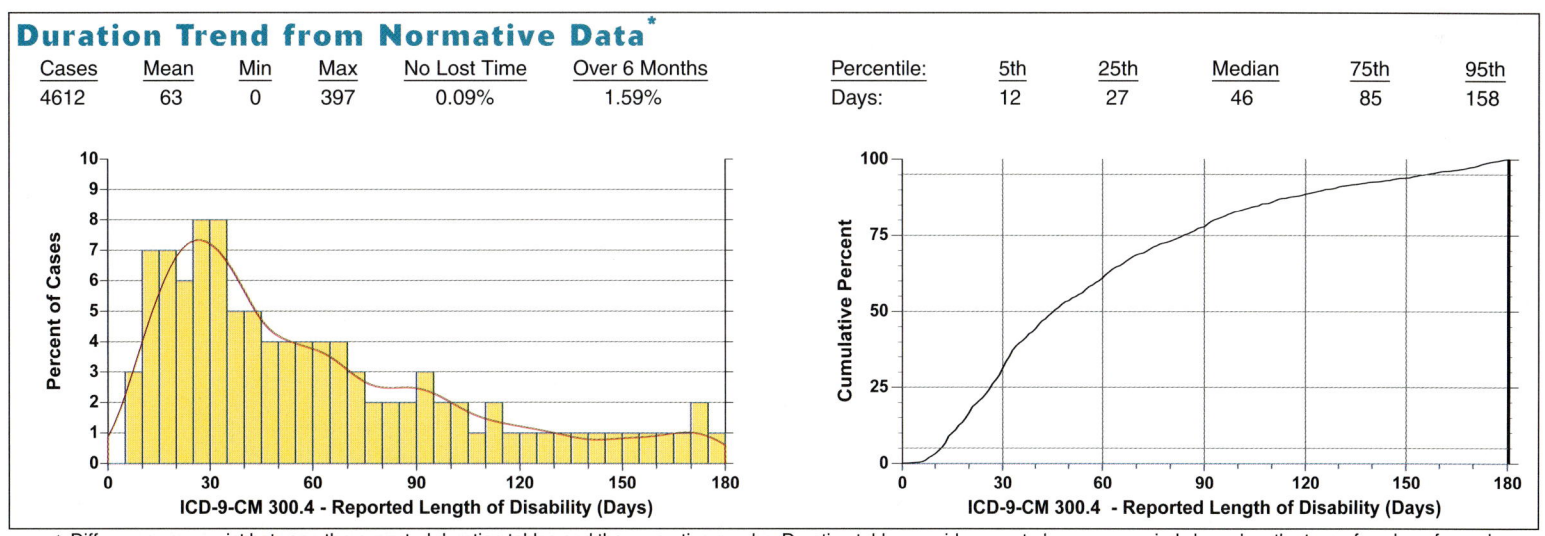

* Differences may exist between the expected duration tables and the normative graphs. Duration tables provide expected recovery periods based on the type of work performed by the individual. The normative graphs reflect the actual observed experience of many individuals across the spectrum of physical conditions, in a variety of industries, and with varying levels of case management.

Dysthymic Disorder

Failure to Recover

If an individual fails to recover within the maximum duration expectancy period, the reader may wish to reference the following questions to assist in better understanding the specifics of an individual's medical case.

Regarding diagnosis:

- Has diagnosis been confirmed?
- Is such functional impairment evident or reported by the individual?
- Does the individual meet the specific criteria for this diagnosis?
- Has substance abuse and/or the presence of underlying medical conditions been ruled out?

Regarding treatment:

- What is the focus of the therapy individual received or is currently involved in?
- Is the individual currently receiving drug therapy? If not, would the addition of drug therapy be beneficial to the current treatment plan?
- Does the individual's treatment plan include long-term use of amphetamines, barbiturates, and the benzodiazepines?
- Is the individual involved in a therapy group?
- Is the individual's family involved in therapy?
- What education or support has the family received?

Regarding prognosis:

- Is the individual aware that depression of this kind is often chronic with recurring episodes?
- Is the individual able to ask for help if symptoms return?

References

Dysthymic Disorder - Treatment. Internet Mental Health. 19 Aug 1997. 17 Jul 2000 <http://www.mentalhealth.com/fr00.html>.

Brown, David. Diagnostic and Statistical Manual, 4th revision. New York: American Psychiatric Press, 1999.

E. Coli

Other names / synonyms: Bacillary Dysentery, Diarrheogenic E. Coli, E. Coli Gastroenteritis, E. Coli O157:h7, EHEC, EIEC, Enterohemorrhagic E. Coli, Enteroinvasive E. Coli, Enterotoxigenic E. Coli, Enterovirulent E. Coli, Escherichia Coli, ETEC, Gastroenteritis, Hemorrhagic Colitis, Traveler's Diarrhea

008.0, 008.00, 008.09

Definition

Escherichia coli (E. coli) is a common type of bacteria with hundreds of strains. Typically harmless, most strains produce infection only under special circumstances such as when introduced into a body site that is normally sterile. Depending on the body site entered, E. coli can produce a variety of infections ranging from a routine infection of the urinary tract to a life-threatening infection of the blood (septicemia).

A number of E. coli strains are routinely harmful. They produce a mild to severe and sometimes fatal food-borne intestinal infection. Although E. coli is the most common type of bacteria in the intestine, when these harmful strains gain entrance they damage the intestinal wall either by releasing a toxin or by actually penetrating and invading the wall. The result is an intestinal infection (gastroenteritis) that causes diarrhea.

Six categories of E. coli produce diarrheal gastroenteritis. Three of these affect adults and are enterohemorrhagic E. coli (EHEC), enterotoxigenic E. coli (ETEC), and enteroinvasive E. coli (EIEC). Within each of these categories, there are a variety of E. coli strains.

EHEC is the one most often mentioned in the media today. It is referred to as E. coli O157:H7, although this is only one of a number of strains within this category. The toxin released by EHEC produces a type of bloody diarrhea known as hemorrhagic colitis. Serious and even fatal, complications can also develop. EHEC originates in animals particularly cattle and sometimes deer and passed to individuals through undercooked meat (particularly ground beef), water, and raw milk. It can also be transmitted through apple cider, fruits, and vegetables contaminated with feces from infected animals or other infected individuals.

ETEC is a common cause of traveler's diarrhea. Like EHEC, ETEC produces symptoms through the release of a toxin. The bacteria are passed from individual to individual through food or water contaminated with the infected individual's feces.

EIEC causes a type of gastroenteritis known as bacillary dysentery. It is also passed from individual to individual through contaminated food or water. Unlike EHEC and ETEC, EIEC does not produce a toxin but rather invades the intestinal wall. Primarily found in underdeveloped countries, only occasional cases have been reported in an industrialized country.

EHEC diarrhea occurs in North America, Europe, South Africa, Japan, and the southern portions of South America and Australia. In the US, EHEC produces approximately 73,000 cases of infection and causes 61 deaths each year.

In adults, ETEC typically occurs when an individual from an industrialized country visits a developing country. Up to 60% of North American visitors to Mexico develop ETEC traveler's diarrhea.

Diagnosis

History: Individuals with EHEC typically have bloody diarrhea and abdominal cramps. Usually no fever is present although sometimes an individual may report a mild fever. Symptoms begin 2 to 8 days after exposure to the bacteria and last 5 to 10 days.

Individuals with ETEC have large quantities of watery diarrhea. Some individuals also report abdominal cramps, vomiting, exhaustion, and diarrhea. Symptoms begin 10 to 72 hours after exposure and last fewer than 5 days.

EIEC produces symptoms that include watery diarrhea sometimes containing mucous, severe abdominal cramps, and fever. This diarrhea may become bloody.

Physical exam: The skin, mouth, and lips appear dry due to dehydration. Rapid breathing, drowsiness, or confusion may indicate acidosis, a condition where the acid-base balance is disturbed due to the prolonged diarrhea. Although the cause must be confirmed with testing, bloody or watery diarrhea alerts the physician to a diagnosis of diarrheal intestinal infection (gastroenteritis). Bloody diarrhea plus signs of kidney (renal) involvement may suggest EHEC.

Tests: EHEC may be grown and identified from a stool specimen with a special E. coli O157:H7 culture (not a routine bacterial stool culture). The organism may also be identified by a DNA probe test or by testing for the toxin it produces. Additional identifying information about the organism such as might be needed when studying an outbreak can be obtained from a serotyping test.

ETEC cannot be identified by a bacterial culture. It must be identified by a DNA probe test, a test for its toxin, or an immunoassay where one of its proteins is detected.

EIEC cannot be identified by bacterial culture. It is identified by a DNA probe test, an immunoassay where one of its proteins is detected, or a bioassay where its ability to invade tissue is detected. A clue to the presence of EIEC is the presence of white blood cells found during microscopic examination of a stool specimen.

Treatment

EHEC is primarily treated with fluid and electrolyte replacement. Whether or not antibiotics should be used is still a matter of debate. There is evidence to suggest that some antibiotics may precipitate the development of complications. Antidiarrheal drugs should not be used.

ETEC is also primarily treated with fluid and electrolyte replacement. If the diarrhea is severe, antibiotics may be prescribed. Antidiarrheal drugs may help alleviate the symptoms but can keep the bacteria in the system longer.

EIEC is treated with antibiotics.

Complications require hospitalization including intensive care treatment, renal dialysis, and blood transfusions.

Prognosis

Individuals with only the diarrhea phase of an E. coli intestinal infection usually have a complete recovery. ETEC and EIEC typically resolve without complications.

Of those with EHEC who develop the complication of HUS, one-third will continue to have long-term abnormal renal function. Some will require long-term renal dialysis. Approximately 8% will have long-term high blood pressure, seizures, blindness, and paralysis. With intensive care treatment, the death rate for HUS is 3-5%.

Differential Diagnosis

Diarrhea caused by E. coli should be differentiated from diarrhea or dysentery caused by other microorganisms such as the Shigella species. Cytomegalovirus can cause bloody diarrhea in immunocompromised individuals or individuals with HIV. EHEC may be confused with noninfectious conditions that also cause bloody diarrhea such as ischemic colitis, irritable bowel disease, and a condition where the bowel wraps around itself (intussusception).

Specialists

- Gastroenterologist
- Hematologist
- Infectious Disease Physician
- Internist
- Nephrologist

Work Restrictions / Accommodations

Individuals who work with food or provide care to children or other individuals should be relieved of these duties until diarrhea has stopped and they have been cleared to return to work. Elimination of the diarrhea-producing E. coli is verified by two negative stool cultures collected at least 24 hours apart. If antibiotics were taken, the cultures should be collected at least 48 hours after the last dose of antibiotics.

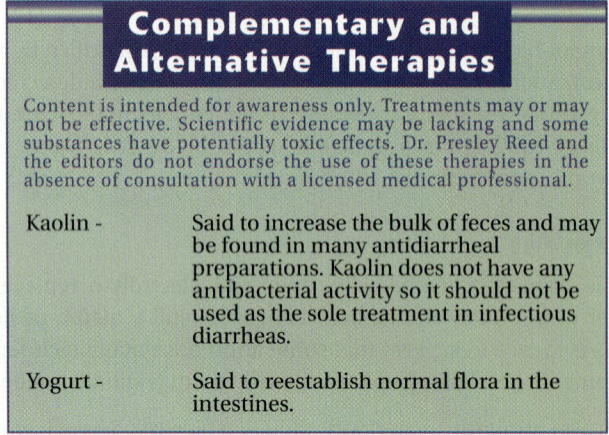

Complementary and Alternative Therapies

Content is intended for awareness only. Treatments may or may not be effective. Scientific evidence may be lacking and some substances have potentially toxic effects. Dr. Presley Reed and the editors do not endorse the use of these therapies in the absence of consultation with a licensed medical professional.

Kaolin - Said to increase the bulk of feces and may be found in many antidiarrheal preparations. Kaolin does not have any antibacterial activity so it should not be used as the sole treatment in infectious diarrheas.

Yogurt - Said to reestablish normal flora in the intestines.

Comorbid Conditions

Coexisting conditions that may impact recovery include compromised immune system, infection, or any concurrent illness associated with dehydration, anorexia, or weakness.

Complications

Up to 7% of individuals with EHEC develop a life-threatening condition called hemolytic uremic syndrome (HUS) in the second week following onset of diarrhea. In HUS, the absorbed bacterial toxin destroys red blood cells and causes renal failure. Some individuals with HUS need to have part of the their bowel removed (bowel resection). When absorbed into the bloodstream, E. coli toxins can also affect other organs such as the kidney. Prolonged or severe diarrhea can lead to severe dehydration and decreased blood pressure (hypovolemic shock).

Factors Influencing Duration

Factors that may lengthen disability include type of infection, severity of symptoms, degree to which dehydration and electrolyte imbalance is prevented or controlled, development of complications such as hemolytic uremic syndrome, age of the individual, and general health of the individual.

Length of Disability

Duration in Days

Job Classification	Minimum	Optimum	Maximum
Any work	3	5	10

Failure to Recover

If an individual fails to recover within the maximum duration expectancy period, the reader may wish to reference the following questions to assist in better understanding the specifics of an individual's medical case.

Regarding diagnosis:

- Does the individual have abdominal cramps, bloody or watery diarrhea and/or fever?
- Did the individual present with other systemic indications of infection (i.e., genitourinary symptoms, wound drainage, etc)? When did the symptoms begin?
- What did the individual have to eat or drink 2-8 days prior to the diarrhea?
- Has the individual traveled out of the country recently?
- Was there evidence of dehydration or electrolyte imbalance in the physical exam?
- Did the physical exam reveal findings indicative of genitourinary or systemic infection (i.e., fever, tachycardia, tachypnea, wound exudates, genitourinary symptoms)?
- Was the diagnosis of E. coli infection confirmed with appropriate cultures (i.e., stool cultures, urine cultures, blood cultures, wound cultures)?
- Was sensitivity testing done to identify the appropriate antibiotic therapy?

Regarding treatment:

- Have symptoms of dehydration or electrolyte imbalance been treated as needed with intravenous fluid replacement?
- Has the appropriate antibiotic therapy been administered?
- Have the fever and other symptoms resolved with the treatment? If not, were cultures repeated to rule out the possibility of antibiotic resistance or secondary infection?
- Were appropriate changes or additions made to the current antibiotic treatment?

Regarding prognosis:

- Did the individual receive prompt and appropriate supportive care and antibiotic treatment?
- Based on the underlying cause, severity of symptoms and general health of the individual, what was the expected outcome?
- Did the individual experience any associated complications (systemic infection, shock, etc) that could impact recovery and prognosis?
- Does the individual have any underlying conditions (i.e., chronic illness, immune suppression) that could impact ability to recover?

References

Escherichia coli O157:H7. Centers for Disease Control. 30 May 2000. 9 Aug 2000 <http://www.cdc.gov/ncidod/dbmd/diseaseinfo/escherichiacoli_g.htm>.

Mandell, Gerald, John Bennett, and Raphael Dolin. Principles and Practice of Infectious Diseases, 5th ed. Philadelphia: Churchill Livingstone, 2000.

Eating Disorders

Other names / synonyms: Anorexia Nervosa, Binge Eating Disorder, Bulimia Nervosa
306.4, 307.1, 307.5, 307.51

Definition

Eating disorders are psychological disturbances related to body image and eating habits. Anorexia nervosa and bulimia nervosa are two primary eating disorders recognized today. Both are serious, life-threatening conditions that are difficult to treat.

Anorexia nervosa, a potentially life-threatening condition, is characterized by obsessive concern over one's body weight, specifically the fear of appearing fat. As a result, individuals with this disorder rigidly restrict their dietary intake, are markedly underweight, and often suffer from malnutrition. Frequently the individual will abuse laxatives or deliberately cause vomiting in an effort to avoid what is regarded as excess calories. They may exercise excessively. Because their self-image is greatly distorted, they see themselves or parts of their body as grossly overweight even though they may appear emaciated to others. A major feature of this eating disorder is denial. While the problem is painfully evident to those around them, the afflicted individual is blind to it. Even when the condition is brought to their attention, there is little or no change in eating habits until failing health finally forces medical attention.

Bulimia nervosa, a closely related condition, is characterized by episodes of "binge" eating followed by desperate measures to avoid weight gain. Usual measures include dieting, purging (self-induced vomiting), laxative and/or diuretic abuse, and, in some cases, excessive exercise. Like anorexia, body image is distorted and there is a preoccupation with physical appearance. Unlike anorexia nervosa, however, most individuals with bulimia are of normal or near normal weight, or may even be somewhat overweight. Individuals with bulimia are at risk for a number of potentially serious health hazards including malnutrition, electrolyte imbalances, esophageal ulcers or rupture, and rampant dental decay.

While the cause of anorexia nervosa is unknown, social factors, especially the desire to be thin, appear to be important. Bulimia, on the other hand, stems from a combination of factors. Personality traits include impulsiveness, vulnerability, feelings of low self-esteem and helplessness, and the fear of becoming fat and unattractive. Although bulimia and other eating disorders are considered learned behavior, a suspected genetic link may also explain why they tend to run in families. Biochemical abnormalities may help to explain why some bulimic women cease to have their monthly menstrual period and also the relationship between eating disorders and depression, as evidenced by the unusually high suicide rate among bulimics.

Anorexia nervosa and bulimia nervosa predominantly afflict adolescent and younger-adult females, and are about 10 times more common in women than in men.

Binge eating disorder has recently been identified as an eating disorder. Unlike bulimia nervosa, binging is not followed by purging. Occurring most commonly in individuals who are already obese, excessive caloric intake leads to increasing body weight. Individuals with binge eating disorder tend to be older than those who have anorexia nervosa or bulimia nervosa, and nearly half of them are male.

Diagnosis

History: Because the individual may be trying to hide the disorder from others, laboratory and physical examination data may be used to support the diagnosis. Diagnostic criteria are published in the American Psychiatric Association's, Diagnostic and Statistical Manual of Mental Disorders, Fourth Edition (DSM-IV).

The critical elements under DSM-IV necessary to make the diagnosis of anorexia nervosa are: body weight less than 85% of what is normal for age, sex, and height; an intense fear of becoming fat or gaining weight; disturbed body image and/or denial of the problem; and, in women of childbearing age, loss of menstrual cycling due to malnutrition. Although half the individuals with anorexia nervosa binge and then purge (or similar compensatory measures), the other half simply restrict the amount of food that they will eat.

Individuals with bulimia nervosa rarely admit to their behavior. Behavior includes repeated episodes of excessive eating, while feeling a loss of control over what is consumed. Binges are followed by intense guilt and repeated efforts to prevent weight gain by purging, vigorous dieting, and excessive exercise. Although body weight actually tends to fluctuate around normal, self-esteem is overly dependent on their perceived body image. To be considered bulimia nervosa, the above must occur at least twice a week for 3 months, and these symptoms must present apart from episodes of anorexia nervosa.

An unspecified eating disorder refers to any condition similar to the above, but which fails to meet all of the criteria. Examples would include anorexia nervosa where menstrual cycling still occurs, or purging after even small meals. Binge eating disorder refers to a pattern of binge eating without purging. Although binge eating disorder does not result in the physical complications that can occur with bulimia nervosa, individuals with this disorder are distressed by it. Approximately 50% of binge eaters are depressed, compared to only about 5% of obese individuals who do not binge. Increased body weight leads to the medical complications associated with obesity.

Denial is a major feature of eating disorders. Although the problem is evident to those around them, the afflicted individual is blind to it. Even when the condition is brought to his or her attention, there is little or no change in eating habits until failing health finally forces medical attention.

Physical exam: Because individuals with eating disorders rarely admit to their behavior, the physician may be alerted to the condition by unexplained symptoms. Signs of anorexia include: emaciation, low blood pressure, low body temperature, skin dryness, fine downy hair covering the skin surface (lanugo), a severely slow heart rate (bradycardia), brittle nails, and thinning hair. Symptoms of bulimia include: loss of dental enamel on teeth and tooth decay, enlarged salivary glands, irritation of the esophagus, sores or calluses on the index finger or knuckle, and scars on the back of the dominant hand as a result of the hand rubbing against the teeth during forced vomiting episodes. Bulimia may not be evident until persistent vomiting causes a serious metabolic disturbance or internal bleeding. In some cases, attempted suicide is the first obvious indication. Symptoms associated with the excess body weight of binge eating disorder include: shortness of breath (dyspnea); fatigue; joint pains in the hips, knees, and ankles; and a general dissatisfaction with their state of health.

Tests: Laboratory testing is useful in making the diagnosis and monitoring for complications, such as blood salt imbalances, hormonal disturbances, heart problems, and dehydration. Another useful aspect of testing is to monitor compliance with treatment recommendations and to watch for relapse.

Treatment

Individual and family therapy are designed to address the physical, emotional, and behavioral elements involved in anorexia nervosa and bulimia nervosa. A variety of treatment approaches have been tried with moderate success. The more successful treatments involve multiple disciplines and include behavioral modification, psychotherapy, and careful medical attention. Individual therapy may be supplemented with an eating disorders group therapy.

When weight loss from anorexia has been rapid or severe (more than 25% below ideal body weight), restoring body weight is crucial. Because such weight loss can be life-threatening, the individual is usually hospitalized so that experienced staff members can firmly but gently encourage the individual to eat. If unsuccessful, the individual may have to be fed intravenously or through a tube inserted in the nose and passed into the stomach.

Anti-depressant medication has been found to be helpful for some individuals with bulimia, whether or not there is accompanying depression. In contrast, anti-depressant medication is typically not helpful for individuals with anorexia, unless it is used to treat accompanying depression.

Specific treatment for binge eating has been based on the treatment of bulimia nervosa. Although antidepressants and appetite suppressants are proving to be reasonably effective in controlling binge eating, psychotherapy appears to have longer-lasting effects.

Typically, treatment is carried out over months to years. In severe cases, inpatient treatment may be necessary. Medical complications may require hospitalization. Because eating disorders are potentially life threatening, good medical care, including frequent physical exams, is important.

Prognosis

Because eating disorders are usually quite complicated, it is difficult to predict the outcome. Generally, the younger the age at which the symptoms appear the poorer the prognosis. Over a 5-year span, approximately one third of individuals will have a complete or near complete remission of their symptoms, one third will show significant improvement, while the remaining one third either fail to improve or deteriorate. Death rate (mortality) is significant.

When an individual becomes malnourished, either from not eating or from constant purging, every major body system can be affected. The most dangerous are problems with the heart and fluid or electrolyte imbalances. As the heart gets weaker, less blood is pumped throughout the body. As the blood becomes more acidic (metabolic acidosis), potassium levels may decrease. Vomiting, laxatives, and diuretics worsen the situation. Resulting abnormal heart rhythms can lead to sudden death. Anorexia nervosa has a mortality rate of 4-5%, but some studies place it as high as 20 percent.

Differential Diagnosis

Two of the more common psychiatric syndromes that may be mistaken for eating disorders are major depressive disorder and schizophrenia. Obsessive-compulsive disorder and borderline personality disorder may have many of the same behaviors. A good history taken by a psychiatrist or licensed mental health professional is usually sufficient to exclude these other conditions. Physical causes such as brain tumors and other types of cancer, infections, hormone imbalances, and metabolic disorders need to be excluded through physical and laboratory tests. Obesity can be the result of hormonal disturbances or genetic conditions rather than the overeating associated with binge eating disorder.

Work Restrictions / Accommodations

Work restrictions or accommodations are necessary only infrequently for the most serious cases. When they are necessary, time-limited accommodations are based on individual need because of the variety of serious complications possible with eating disorders. Any job duty that heightens awareness of physical appearance such as modeling or dancing is apt to make these conditions worse. Highly stressful situations may worsen these illnesses or trigger a relapse.

Comorbid Conditions

Coexisting conditions that may lengthen disability include diabetes mellitus, and underlying diseases of the cardiovascular, pulmonary, or gastrointestinal systems. Because they share so many features in common, individuals with eating disorders may also abuse drugs or alcohol. Treatment is made more difficult as the individual "trades" addictions.

Other psychiatric disorders may coexist with eating disorders, complicating treatment and prolonging recovery. Major depressive disorder is common. One third to one half of individuals with bulimia nervosa have been found to have personality disorders, particularly borderline personality disorder. It is estimated that 50% of obese binge eaters suffer from depression.

Complications

Eating disorders can lead to serious medical problems, depression, and suicide. Complications associated with anorexia include absence of menstrual cycling, and other hormonal problems, and malnutrition. Severe imbalances in blood chemistry can cause irregular heartbeat, seizures, coma, and death. Muscle wasting, kidney failure, problems due to poor liver function and superior mesenteric artery syndrome are other possible complications. Weight can drop to less than 75% of normal, a very dangerous condition requiring hospitalization.

Individuals with bulimia also risk severe blood chemistry imbalances with associated complications, including rupture of the stomach or esophagus, and advanced dental decay. Depression, irritability, insomnia, and generally poor mental functioning are some of the more common psychological complications. Suicide is unusually high among bulimics.

Excessive accumulation of body fat (obesity) from binge eating disorder can lead to degenerative joint disease, arthritis, diabetes, and high blood pressure.

Factors Influencing Duration

Factors that might influence length of disability include severity and length of the disorder, mental health of the individual, response or resistance to treatment, and the presence of complications. Eating disorder complications range from relatively minor to life threatening.

Length of Disability

Maximum disability duration includes hospitalization. Length of disability is influenced by the severity of symptoms and the need for inpatient care.

Anorexia nervosa or bulimia nervosa. Medical treatment.

Duration in Days

Job Classification	Minimum	Optimum	Maximum
Any work	7	14	56

Specialists

- Internist
- Psychiatrist
- Psychologist

Failure to Recover

If an individual fails to recover within the maximum duration expectancy period, the reader may wish to reference the following questions to assist in better understanding the specifics of an individual's medical case.

Regarding diagnosis:

- Does individual's condition meet the criteria for an eating disorder? Has the diagnosis of anorexia nervosa or bulimia nervosa been confirmed?
- Have psychiatric disorders and underlying medical conditions with similar symptoms been ruled out?
- Does individual have an underlying condition that may impact recovery?
- If there is evidence of drug or alcohol abuse, how are these issues being addressed?

Regarding treatment:

- Is the individual being seen by a physician with training or experience in treating eating disorders? Does the individual feel comfortable with the physician?
- Does the therapist have special training and expertise in the treatment of eating disorders?
- Does the physician routinely monitor the individual for medical complications?
- What type of therapy is individual involved in? Is therapy individual or family oriented? Does the individual feel comfortable with the therapist? Does current therapy mode appear to be effective?
- Would individual benefit from being involved in a group therapy with other eating disorder individuals?
- Have medications such as antidepressants or appetite suppressants been effective in controlling binge eating?

Regarding prognosis:

- How motivated is individual to cooperate with his/her own health care?
- Do treatment goals need to be revisited? Are expectations realistic?
- Does the individual need assistance finding referrals, making appointments, and getting to appointments?
- Does the individual have support from family, friends, and co-workers?

References

American Psychiatric Association. Diagnostic and Statistical Manual of Mental Disorders: DSM-IV,. Washington, DC: American Psychiatric Association, 1994.

Ferri, Fred. Ferri's Clinical Advisor. St. Louis: Mosby, 2000.

Echinococcosis

Other names / synonyms: Alveolar Echinococcosis, Alveolar Hydatid Disease, Cystic Hydatid Disease, Hydatid Disease, Hydatidosis, Multilocular Echinococcosis

122, 122.0, 122.1, 122.2, 122.3, 122.4, 122.5, 122.6, 122.7, 122.8, 122.9

Definition

Echinococcosis is a parasitic infection primarily of the liver and lungs. The disease is caused from a tapeworm found in dogs or other canines. Two species of this tapeworm are the primary causes of infection, Echinococcus granulosus and Echinococcus multilocularis.

The adult form of E. granulosus is found primarily in dogs. The adult worm can be seen as a speck with the naked eye, but a microscope is needed to examine and identify the worm. The microscopic larval form is found in infected animals, primarily sheep, goats, cattle, pigs, or horses, or in infected people. In dogs, the adult worm is harmless. In people, the larval form causes a type of echinococcosis called cystic hydatid disease.

A dog first acquires the tapeworm infection by eating the raw meat of an animal infected with echinococcus larvae. In the dog's intestine, the larvae develop into adult tapeworms. The adult worms release their eggs through the dog's feces. People acquire the disease by ingesting these eggs via food, water, or an object contaminated with the feces. Inside the eggs are the young larval forms of the tapeworm that break through the stomach or intestinal wall and enter the blood or lymph vessels, then travel to the internal organs, primarily the liver. Although the liver is the most common destination for the larvae, they may also travel to the lungs, kidney, spleen, brain, or bone. Here they develop into a small cyst that slowly grows larger over a period of one or more years.

Cysts usually reach a diameter of several inches but may grow larger than 4 inches. The cyst contains fluid with millions of larvae. The cyst is surrounded by a thick wall of tissue produced by the individual's body as a kind of defense against the growing cyst. Eventually the cyst grows larger, despite the wall, and encroaches on surrounding tissue causing the onset of symptoms.

E. multilocularis causes a type of echinococcosis known as alveolar or multilocular echinococcosis. The adult worm is found primarily in wild canines, particularly foxes rather than dogs. The larval form is common in rodents. The cycle of infection follows the same pattern as E. granulosus, but differences develop once the eggs are inside the infected individual. Larval E. multilocularis migrate almost strictly to the liver and rarely to the lung. The cyst that forms does not trigger the building of a thick cyst wall by the infecting individual. This enables the cyst to spread more easily and invade surrounding tissue more extensively before eliciting symptoms. It is typical to have 5 to 15 years pass before symptoms are felt. By that time, considerable internal damage has been done. Consequently, alveolar echinococcosis is considered a more invasive and destructive disease than cystic hydatid disease.

E. granulosus, the most common of the two species, is found on every continent except Antarctica, predominately in areas where sheep and cattle are raised. It is particularly prevalent in China and Kenya. In the US, it is primarily found among immigrants or in the sheep-raising areas of Utah, Arizona, New Mexico, and California. Efforts to completely eliminate the infection were successful in Iceland where the tapeworm is no longer found. In Australia, New Zealand, and Cyprus, similar efforts have greatly reduced its incidence.

E. multilocularis is found in the Northern Hemisphere, particularly central Europe, the former Soviet Union, Siberia, northern Japan, Alaska, and Canada. It has been found, although rarely, in the north central US.

Diagnosis

History: An infected individual usually has a history of travel abroad or exposure to dogs or other canines associated with livestock. Symptoms vary according to the location, size, and number of cysts. Symptoms don't begin until the cyst either ruptures or becomes large enough to encroach on surrounding tissue. There may be a history of upper abdominal pain and nausea. If the cyst breaks open, fever, jaundice, and an itchy rash may be seen. Some individuals have a severe allergic reaction following such a rupture. If the cyst erodes into the lungs, there can be a chronic productive cough and chest pain.

Physical exam: Palpation may reveal a mass in the liver or other organ. If the cyst is in the liver, there may be evidence of jaundice, biliary colic-like symptoms, or other sign of liver involvement. In a lung, the cyst may cause blood or bile in the saliva (biliptysis or hemoptysis) or evidence of inflammation or blockage. Neurologic signs may be evident if the cyst is in the spine or brain.

Tests: Blood tests can detect antibodies to echinococcus, although these tests may be unreliable due to false-negative and false-positive results. In addition, many infected individuals don't produce antibodies against echinococcus. Therefore, the blood tests are not recommended.

The tests of choice are ultrasonography, CT scans, and x-ray, which may locate cysts and differentiate them from other types of growths. These imaging studies can also identify an inactive calcified cyst. The echinococcus larvae can be identified in microscopic examination of cyst fluid removed during surgery or a fine needle biopsy. Liver function tests may be abnormal if the cyst is in the liver.

Treatment

E. granulosus is treated most effectively by surgical removal of the cyst. In the liver, the procedure options include removal of the cyst (cystectomy), removal of the cyst plus part of the surrounding area (pericystectomy), or removal of a portion of the liver (hepatic resection). In the lung, the procedure options include extrusion of the cyst, pericystectomy, or removal of a lobe (lobectomy). To reduce the risk of recurrence, antiparasite drugs are given before and after surgical removal of the cyst.

If a cyst cannot be removed surgically, antiparasite drugs alone may be taken for up to 12 months. The protocol for and the effectiveness of drug therapy vary based on the location of the cyst. Antiparasite drugs are also given after rupture of cyst.

A newer alternative to surgery has shown some success. Guided by ultrasound imaging, a needle is inserted into the cyst. Fluid from inside the cyst is removed through the needle (percutaneous aspiration). An antiparasite solution is then injected back into the cyst. The solution is left in the cyst for up to 10 minutes, after which it is removed. Antiparasite drugs are given before and after the procedure. Lung cysts cannot be treated in this way.

Removal of an E. multilocularis cyst requires removal of a major portion (radical surgical resection) of the liver. Individuals then receive antiparasite drugs for 2 years after surgery and are monitored for at least 10 years. Some individuals have received liver transplants. Up to 40% of E. multilocularis cysts, however, are inoperable. In these cases, or when only part of the cyst can be surgically removed, long-term antiparasite drug therapy is usually administered.

Prognosis

The predicted outcome for echinococcosis depends on cyst location and the causative species. If the cyst has ruptured releasing its contents, or if secondary cysts have developed, the prognosis is poor.

For E. granulosus (cystic hydatid disease), most liver and lung cysts can be removed surgically with a cure rate of up to 90%. Up to 25% of individuals, however, will have a recurrence of the infection years after surgical removal. Mortality associated with surgery is 2% or less. When treated with chemotherapy, studies show that cysts will disappear in 30% of cases, significantly reduced in 30-50% of cases, and unaffected in 20-40% of cases. Bone cysts are particularly resistant to drug therapy. The success rate of percutaneous aspiration of cyst contents followed by injection of an antiparasite solution is similar to that of surgery. Left untreated, cystic hydatid disease is fatal for 15% of infected individuals.

The outcome for E. multilocularis (alveolar echinococcosis) infection is not as favorable. By the time it is detected, considerable damage has already been done. Cases that are operable carry a 0-5% mortality rate. Outcome for liver transplant treatment is still under question. Antiparasite drug treatment alone provides a 53-80% survival rate at 15 years. Infection may still recur in spite of radical surgical resection and antiparasite drug treatment. Left untreated, 90% of individuals will die within 10 years of onset of the infection, and 100% within 15 years.

Differential Diagnosis

The cyst may resemble a bacterial or amebic abscess, a malignant mass, liver cirrhosis, or a cyst present from birth (congenital cyst). Cysts in the lung must be differentiated from tuberculosis. Individuals with parasitic infections of other worms (helminths), cancer, and chronic immune disorders may have a false-positive echinococcus antibody test result.

Specialists

- Gastroenterologist
- Infectious Disease Physician
- Neurologist
- Orthopedist
- Pathologist
- Pulmonologist
- Surgeon

Work Restrictions / Accommodations

When cysts produce abdominal pressure, strenuous exertion that may rupture the cyst should be restricted. Rest periods or other accommodations may be required for individuals with cysts in the lungs, brain, or kidneys. Accommodations may increase over time with inoperable cysts. Recuperation will be required following surgery.

This infection is not spread between individuals, so interpersonal on-the-job infection control measures are not required.

Comorbid Conditions

Pregnant women should not take certain antiparasite drugs. Without these drugs, effective treatment may be delayed.

Complications

Echinococcosis may be complicated by the location of the cyst or by rupture of the cyst with release of fluid, either spontaneously, during surgery, or percutaneous aspiration. Spread of the cyst fluid will increase the risk of secondary cyst development in an inoperable or vital area. Infection can spread to the lungs, bile duct, and abdominal and pleural cavities. Sudden, rapid release of cyst contents may result in a severe allergic reaction (anaphylaxis) or death. Abnormal passageways from one body site to another caused by tissue erosion (fistulas) may develop in the biliary tract and lungs.

A cyst in the vertebrae may cause pressure on the spinal cord and paralysis. Cyst erosion in other bones may result in weakening and spontaneous fractures. Brain cysts may cause seizures and increased intracranial pressure. A secondary bacterial infection may develop within the cyst. Additional complications include gallstones, gastrointestinal bleeding, and hypertension in the portal vein of the liver (portal hypertension).

Factors Influencing Duration

Length of disability will be influenced by the location of the cyst(s) and the extent of secondary cyst development. When the cyst appears in an operable site, disability will be required to recover from the surgery. When the cyst is in an inoperable area, extended disability may result.

Length of Disability

Surgical treatment.

Duration in Days

Job Classification	Minimum	Optimum	Maximum
Any work	1	14	28

Failure to Recover

If an individual fails to recover within the maximum duration expectancy period, the reader may wish to reference the following questions to assist in better understanding the specifics of an individual's medical case.

Regarding diagnosis:

- Has echinococcosis been positively diagnosed through microscopic examination of cyst fluid contents?
- Has the species of echinococcus been determined? E. granulosus (cystic hydatid disease) or E. multilocularis (alveolar echinococcosis)?
- Where is the cyst located? Liver, lungs, brain? Vertebrae or bone?
- Is there evidence of secondary cysts? Where are they located?

Regarding treatment:

- Has the cyst been surgically removed?

- Has antiparasite drug therapy or percutaneous aspiration been used? If not, what type of treatment did individual receive?
- Was surgery or percutaneous aspiration accompanied by antiparasite drug therapy? If antiparasite drugs were prescribed, has the individual taken them?
- Has the cyst ruptured? If so, were antiparasite drugs prescribed and taken following the rupture?

Regarding prognosis:
- Was cyst due to E. granulosus or E. multilocularis?
- Was cyst surgically inaccessible?
- Was there evidence of spillage during surgical procedure?
- Are secondary cysts present?

References

Parasites and Health: Echinococcosis. Centers for Disease Control and Prevention, Division of Parasitic Diseases. 20 Apr 1998. 12 Aug 2000 <http://www.dpd.cdc.gov/DPDx/HTML/Echinococcosis.htm>.

Feldman, Mark, et al. Gastrointestinal and Liver Disease, 6th ed. Philadelphia: W.B. Saunders Company, 1998.

Echocardiography
Other names / synonyms: Echo, TEE, Trans-Esophageal Echocardiogram
88.72

Definition

Echocardiography is a noninvasive technique that uses high frequency sound waves to produce images of the heart's internal anatomy. A beam of ultrasonic waves is directed at the heart and partially reflected back by each tissue in its path. These reflected waves (echoes) are converted into electronic signals. The signals are displayed on a video screen, producing an image of the heart walls, chambers, and valves in motion.

Echocardiography is also performed using the esophagus that lies just behind the heart and employs ultrasound waves to make images of the heart chambers, valves and surrounding structures. However, esophageal echocardiography is not routinely done.

The echo images can be displayed in either one or two dimensions. In one-dimensional (M-mode) echocardiography, each structure in the beam's path appears as a wavy line. The waviness represents motion during the cardiac cycle: the opening and closing of valves and the movement of chamber walls as the heart contracts and expands. With two-dimensional (2-DE) echocardiography, a cross-sectional image of the heart is displayed on the screen and movement of the heart is seen live as it occurs.

Doppler echocardiography is a variation of M-mode that records echoes not from the heart itself but from blood moving through the heart. The frequency of the reflected sound waves depends on the speed at which the blood is moving. Doppler techniques can be used to measure the speed of blood flow as well as detect abnormal flow patterns.

Echocardiography is widely used in hospital and diagnostic laboratory settings in evaluating individuals of all ages suspected of having heart problems.

Reason for Procedure

Echocardiography is useful in the diagnosis of many types of cardiac disorders including valvular disease, heart muscle disease (cardiomyopathy), and coronary artery disease. It is also helpful in assessing the severity of these diseases and the prognosis. Since it is a noninvasive procedure, repeated examinations can be performed without risk in order to follow an individual's progress and assess the effectiveness of treatment.

One of the most important applications of echocardiography is in the assessment of valvular disease. Thickening or irregular shape of the valves can be detected and abnormal motion of the valves observed. In addition, Doppler techniques measure blood flow through a diseased valve.

Echocardiography is also used in a variety of disorders to assess the function of the heart muscle, especially the ventricles. Heart chamber volumes can be calculated. Wall thickness is measured and abnormalities of wall motion detected. Information on how well the heart is pumping can be obtained, however, this information is measured more accurately by cardiac catheterization.

Echocardiography is increasingly used with cardiac stress testing to evaluate individuals with chest pain. Echocardiograms are performed before and after exercise. If heart wall motion abnormalities appear after exercise but are absent at rest, this is a sensitive indicator of insufficient blood supply to the heart (myocardial ischemia).

Other uses of echocardiography include detection of masses inside the heart (tumors, blood clots), diagnosis of aortic disease (aortic aneurysm, aortic dissection), and detection of fluid around the heart (pericardial effusion as seen in pericarditis).

Description

The procedure is normally conducted in a hospital laboratory, clinical laboratory, or specialist's office on either an outpatient or inpatient basis. Echocardiography uses ultrasound (high-frequency sound waves) to produce an image of the internal structures of the heart.

An electronic device or transducer is placed on the surface of the chest. This converts electrical impulses into a narrow ultrasonic beam that penetrates body tissues but is reflected off surfaces where a change in tissue density occurs. The reflected sound waves are detected with a receiver also placed on the chest, transformed back into electrical impulses, and projected on the screen of a cathode-ray oscilloscope. Echoes from varied depths produce an image of the walls and valves of the heart and their motions. Such information can aid in diagnosing valve disease, congenital heart defects, and other cardiac abnormalities.

Transesophageal echocardiography (TEE) is a special type of imaging procedure. A tube with a transducer on the end of it is passed down an individual's throat and into the esophagus. The esophagus is close to the heart. Images from TEE can give very clear pictures of the heart and its structures.

There is little if any discomfort and hardly any time in the testing environment.

Prognosis

The outcome of the test depends on the skill of the operator. The individual should have no ill effects in undergoing the test. The test results are only for guidance and diagnosis of the underlying condition.

Information gained through echocardiography accurately reflects the condition under study. Coupled with other diagnostic techniques, the physician gains a clear picture of the scope and nature of heart actions and problems. This allows for a more informed and meaningful diagnosis.

Specialists

- Cardiologist

Work Restrictions / Accommodations

No restrictions are necessary for procedure itself, only for the underlying condition.

Comorbid Conditions

Any damaged skin may interfere with the utilization of echocardiography since it depends on close contact with the intact skin. Anxiety may also interfere with the conduct and interpretation of the test.

Procedure Complications

Because it is a noninvasive technique, there are few, if any, complications. However, complications from the underlying disease may be present.

Factors Influencing Duration

Disability is that of the underlying disease, unless a rare complication occurs.

Length of Disability

No disability is expected to result from this procedure. Disability may occur as a result of an underlying condition.

References

"Echocardiography." Medline Plus Health Information. 26 Sep 2000. 15 Nov 2000 <http://medlineplus.adam.com/ency/article/003869.htm>.

Heart Damage Detection. American Heart Association. 2000. 15 Nov 2000 <http://www.americanheart.org/Heart_and_Stroke_A_Z_Guide/hdam.html>.

Ectopic Pregnancy

Other names / synonyms: Abdominal Pregnancy, Ovarian Pregnancy, Tubal Pregnancy
633, 633.0, 633.1, 633.2, 633.8, 633.9

Definition

An ectopic pregnancy occurs when the fertilized egg implants/grows itself outside of the uterus. Almost all (more than 95%) ectopic pregnancies occur in a fallopian tube, which is how the term "tubal" pregnancy originated. On rare occasions, the egg may implant elsewhere such as in the abdomen, ovary, or cervix. Because the narrow fallopian tubes are not designed to hold a growing embryo, the fertilized egg in a tubal pregnancy cannot develop normally. Eventually, the thin walls of the fallopian tube stretch to the point of bursting (ruptures). If this happens, a woman is in danger of life-threatening blood loss (massive hemorrhage).

Most cases of ectopic pregnancy are caused by an inability of the fertilized egg to make its way through the fallopian tube into the uterus. This is often caused by an infection or inflammation of the tube that has caused it to become partially or entirely blocked. Scar tissue resulting from a previous infection or sexually transmitted disease such as chlamydia or gonorrhea may impede the egg's movement. Previous surgery in the pelvic area or on the fallopian tubes such as reversal of a tubal sterilization can also scar.

A condition where the tissue normally lining the uterus is found outside the uterus such as endometriosis can also cause blockage of a fallopian tube and predispose to ectopic. Another possible cause of ectopic pregnancy is an abnormality in the shape of the fallopian tube that may be due to abnormal growths or a birth (congenital) defect. There is also an increased risk of ectopic pregnancy in the fallopian tube if a woman uses an intrauterine device (IUD) for contraception.

Women with pelvic inflammatory disease (PID) are 6 to 10 times more likely to have an ectopic pregnancy. In a study of 745 women with PID who attempted to conceive, 6.4% had an ectopic pregnancy. The risk of ectopic pregnancy is also higher in women who have had a previous ectopic pregnancy, infertility procedures such as in vitro fertilization (IVF) or gamete intrafallopian tube transfer (GIFT), repeated induced abortions, or take medication to stimulate ovulation.

The rate of ectopic pregnancy has recently increased. It now occurs in about 7 of every 1,000 reported pregnancies in the US. Death from ectopic pregnancy is rare and occurs in fewer than 1 of every 2,500 cases. This is largely due to the existence of new techniques to detect ectopic pregnancy at an early stage when the risk to a pregnant woman is much lower.

Diagnosis

History: Symptoms may initially include lower abdominal pain (sharp, dull, or cramping). The pain may be constant or intermittent and is usually located on only one side of the abdomen. The woman may also

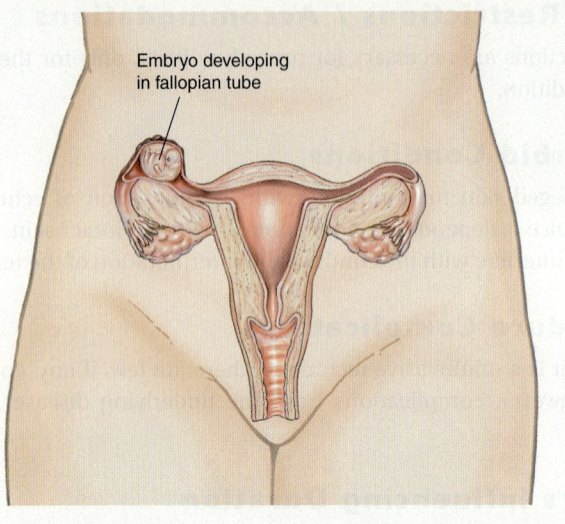

experience vaginal bleeding, nausea, vomiting, and frequent urination. After the fallopian tube has ruptured, lower abdominal pain becomes sharp and may spread (radiate) to the shoulders and neck. The woman may experience weakness and fainting spells. Ectopic pregnancy is usually discovered in the first two months of pregnancy when the woman may not even realize she is pregnant. Twenty percent of woman may not even have missed a menstrual period.

Physical exam: Prior to rupture, a tender mass may be felt in the area of one fallopian tube. After rupture, pain that has spread to the neck and shoulder area becomes severe when pressure is applied to the affected area or to the cervical area. Symptoms of internal bleeding or shock may occur including a weak, rapid pulse (tachycardia) and low blood pressure (hypotension).

Tests: A pregnancy test is usually done for any sexually active woman of childbearing age. Ultrasound or laparoscopy may also be performed in order to examine the abdominal cavity. These tests are considered diagnostic if motion of the fetus or the fetal heart is seen outside the uterus. This occurs in only 20% of ultrasound testing done in ectopic pregnancy. Blood tests for pregnancy hormone (HCG) or progesterone are often diagnostic of pregnancy but do not, in and of themselves, distinguish an intrauterine from an extrauterine pregnancy. A white blood count may be normal or increased. A culdocentesis may also be performed. In this procedure, a thin needle is inserted through the vaginal wall just below the uterus. A sample is taken of any fluid found in the space and the needle is then withdrawn. Finding free blood in the peritoneum (a positive culdocentesis) can be consistent with a ruptured or leaking ectopic.

Treatment

If rupture has occurred because of an ectopic pregnancy, internal bleeding and/or hemorrhage may lead to shock. Nearly 20% of ectopic pregnancies present in this manner. Initial treatment is to treat shock by keeping the woman warm, elevating her legs, and administering oxygen. A blood transfusion is performed and emergency care begins as soon as possible.

Surgical laparotomy is performed to stop the immediate loss of blood (where rupture has already occurred) or to confirm the diagnosis of ectopic pregnancy, remove the products of conception, and repair surrounding tissue damage. In nonemergency cases, minilaparotomy or laparoscopy may be alternative surgical methods. These methods have similar outcomes. They are less invasive and require minimal hospitalization or outpatient treatment. With prompt surgical treatment, a complete recovery is expected. Chances of conception may be slightly reduced but a normal pregnancy is still possible even if one fallopian tube has been removed. After surgery that spares at least one tube, chances of delivery are 55-60%, chances of additional ectopic pregnancy is 15%, and chances of infertility are 25-30%.

Nonsurgical (medical) management is being implemented by some hospitals for very early ectopic pregnancies that do not carry an immediate threat of rupture. In such cases, a drug that stops cell division (methotrexate) is administered and the woman is observed while various blood tests are obtained. This medical approach is relatively new but appears to be a promising treatment. When methotrexate is used, the woman's progress should be closely monitored for up to 4 to 6 weeks by her physician or healthcare provider since medication treatment is a relatively new option.

Prognosis

With prompt surgical treatment, a complete recovery is expected. Death occurs in less than 1 in 2,000 ectopic pregnancies or in about 40 to 50 women each year in the US. Chances of conception may be slightly reduced but a normal pregnancy is still possible even if one fallopian tube has been removed. Infertility occurs in about 25-50% and recurrent ectopic pregnancy is 15-30%

Differential Diagnosis

Conditions producing similar symptoms include appendicitis, a uterine pregnancy with complications, inflammation of a fallopian tube (acute salpingitis), a twisted ovarian cyst or fibroid tumor, or a ruptured ovarian cyst with hemorrhage.

Specialists

- Gynecologist
- Obstetrician
- Surgeon

Work Restrictions / Accommodations

Work responsibilities may need to be largely sedentary at first. Heavy work, especially that involving heavy lifting, may be temporarily restricted. Lifting and climbing may have to be limited initially after salpingectomy. Long periods of standing may need to be avoided. Work restrictions may also apply for several weeks after medical management of ectopic with methotrexate.

Comorbid Conditions

Removal of the fallopian tube (salpingectomy) or anemia due to excessive blood loss may further lengthen disability. Pre-existing conditions such as diabetes, heart disease, kidney or liver disease, cancer, AIDS or other immune system compromises, or obesity may lengthen disability.

Complications

If the site of the ectopic pregnancy ruptures, shock from the severe loss of blood is a serious complication. Delayed or absent treatment may result in death. Surrounding tissue structures may also be damaged by the developing pregnancy. After the fallopian tube is repaired, another tubal pregnancy may develop later. The tube may be damaged beyond repair and have to be removed (salpingectomy). Complications from surgery can include hemorrhage and infection.

Factors Influencing Duration

Expected length of disability depends on the type and extent of surgical treatment. Complications from surgery such as hemorrhage, infection, abdominal cramping and the individual's job requirements may influence the length of disability. The woman may also experience a normal grief reaction after the loss of a pregnancy. This may include an episode of depression that can lengthen disability.

Length of Disability

Duration of disability depends on job requirements and on whether surgery (laparotomy or salpingectomy) is necessary.

Laparoscopic surgery.

Duration in Days

Job Classification	Minimum	Optimum	Maximum
Sedentary work	3	7	21
Light work	3	7	21
Medium work	7	14	28
Heavy work	7	21	35
Very Heavy work	14	21	35

Open salpingectomy.

Duration in Days

Job Classification	Minimum	Optimum	Maximum
Sedentary work	28	42	56
Light work	28	42	56
Medium work	42	56	70
Heavy work	42	56	70
Very Heavy work	42	56	70

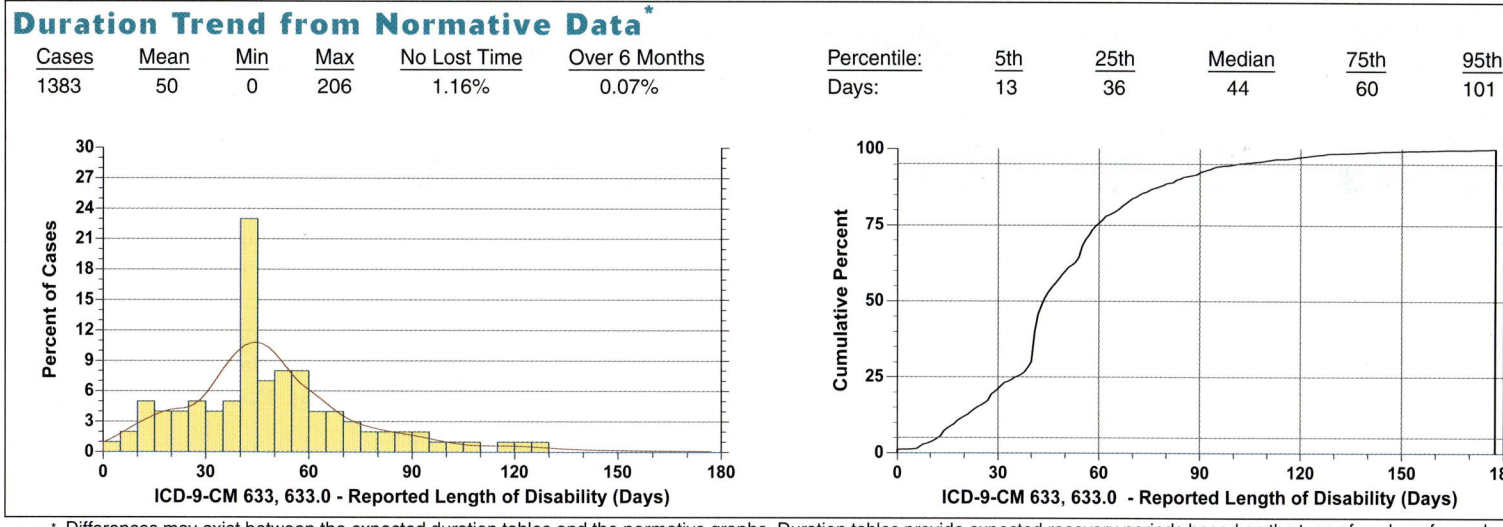

Duration Trend from Normative Data*

Cases	Mean	Min	Max	No Lost Time	Over 6 Months
1383	50	0	206	1.16%	0.07%

Percentile:	5th	25th	Median	75th	95th
Days:	13	36	44	60	101

ICD-9-CM 633, 633.0 - Reported Length of Disability (Days)

* Differences may exist between the expected duration tables and the normative graphs. Duration tables provide expected recovery periods based on the type of work performed by the individual. The normative graphs reflect the actual observed experience of many individuals across the spectrum of physical conditions, in a variety of industries, and with varying levels of case management.

Failure to Recover

If an individual fails to recover within the maximum duration expectancy period, the reader may wish to reference the following questions to assist in better understanding the specifics of an individual's medical case.

Regarding diagnosis:

- Has the individual experienced an infection or inflammation of the fallopian tubes?
- Does the individual have a history of ectopic pregnancy or of repeated, induced abortions?
- Does the individual use an IUD for contraception?
- Has the individual undergone in vitro fertilization (IVF) or gamete intrafallopian tube transfer (GIFT) for infertility?
- Does the individual take medication to stimulate ovulation?
- Does the individual have lower abdominal pain on one side only?
- Is there vaginal bleeding?

Ectopic Pregnancy 777

- Is nausea, vomiting, or frequent urination present?
- Is there a tender mass that can be felt in the area of one fallopian tube?
- Has a pregnancy test been done if the individual is a sexually active woman of childbearing age?
- Were ultrasound and laparoscopy done to determine if motion of the fetus or the fetal heart is seen outside the uterus?
- Were blood tests for pregnancy hormone (HCG) or progesterone done?
- Has a diagnosis of ectopic pregnancy been confirmed?

Regarding treatment:

- Was early ectopic pregnancy, without immediate threat of rupture, treated with an anticancer drug (methotrexate) while the individual was monitored and various blood tests were obtained (medical management)?
- Was medical management successful and without complications?
- If not, was minilaparotomy or laparoscopy required?
- Was the surgical procedure successful and without complications?
- If rupture occurred, was shock prevented?
- Was a blood transfusion required?
- Was surgical laparotomy performed to stop the immediate loss of blood?
- If so, was surgery successful and without complications?

Regarding prognosis:

- Is this a recurrent ectopic pregnancy?
- Did the individual obtain prompt medical and/or surgical treatment?
- Did the individual experience a complete recovery after treatment?
- Was the loss of blood significant enough to cause shock?
- Does the individual require removal of the fallopian tube (salpingectomy)?
- Did the individual experience significant blood loss and shock?
- Is there a recurrent ectopic pregnancy?
- Would the individual benefit from psychotherapy or counseling for grief or depression?
- Would the individual benefit from consultation with an infertility specialist?

References

Ectopic Pregnancy. Advanced Fertility. 01 Jan 2000. 11 July 2000 <http://www.advancedfertility.com/ectopic.htm>.

Ectopic Pregnancy. RxMed.com. 15 July 2000. 19 July 2000 <http://www.rxmed.com/illnesses/ectopic_pregnancy.html>.

Eczema

Other names / synonyms: Asteatotic Eczema, Atopic Dermatitis, Eczematous Dermatitis, Hand Eczema, Nummular Eczema, Stasis Dermatitis

692.9

Definition

Eczema is a general term describing a variety of skin disorders, all of them with inflamed patches of skin and scaling or tiny oozing blisters (vesicles). Eczema means "weeping" though drainage is usually seen only in the early stages of the various eczematous conditions. Eczematous disorders include irritant and allergic contact dermatitis, atopic dermatitis, seborrheic dermatitis, sunburn, scabies, stasis dermatitis, dyshidrotic eczema (pompholyx), and winter itch (xerotic or asteatotic eczema).

Eczema is a response to one or a combination of genetic factors and external triggers, however, it can also occur for no known reason. Causes of eczematous disorders can be irritants, allergens, trauma (e.g., scratching), mites (scabies), cold temperatures, and blood flow stoppage (stasis). Allergens that trigger eczema may be airborne (e.g., industrial substances), ingested (foods or drugs), or in contact with skin (e.g., poison ivy). Eczema may be associated with varicose veins and venous insufficiency in the lower extremities.

Eczema can affect individuals of any age or gender. Hand eczema is seen in individuals with frequent hand washing and exposure to moisture and soaps such as food handlers and healthcare workers. Eczema that forms characteristic coin-shaped or ringed lesions (nummular eczema) occurs most frequently in older men and young women. The cause of nummular eczema is unknown but may be related to dry skin and exposure to irritants. Individuals with poor circulation and varicose veins can develop a condition called stasis eczema or dermatitis. Xerotic or asteatotic eczema commonly occurs on the lower legs of elderly individuals during dry times of the year. Obese individuals are at increased risk to develop eczema.

Eczema is the most common skin problem for which people seek medical treatment. Almost 50% of occupational diseases are due to work-related skin injuries. Atopic dermatitis, the most common eczematous disorder, has a prevalence rate of 10-15%. The prevalence of contact dermatitis is between 1% and 10% and accounts for 90% of occupational skin disease.

Diagnosis

History: The most common complaint of eczema is itchiness (pruritus) associated with a scaly, wet, or dry rash. The rash may be a new problem or a chronic condition. The individual may relate a history of work or recreational activities where the skin is exposed to water, moisture, sun, or new personal care products.

Physical exam: In general, eczema presents with redness, warmth, swelling (edema), tenderness, weeping, crusting, scratches and cracks (excoriations), and thickened and scaling skin with a diffuse border.

Skin changes associated with atopic dermatitis are variable and include excoriations, raised bumps (papules); thickened, red, gray, or scaly skin (lichenification); red, fluid-filled bumps (vesicles); and crusted lesions.

Contact dermatitis presents as areas of reddened (erythematous) and swollen (edematous) skin followed by development of small and large blisters (vesicles and bullae, respectively). The pattern, shape, and location of the contact dermatitis rash help identify the causative substance. Hand eczema may present with dryness and cracking of the skin, with some redness and swelling. A variation of this condition, dyshidrotic eczema, has small, very itchy bumps along the fleshy parts of the palms and sides of the fingers. Nummular eczema has round scaly patches that look similar to ringworm and are found on the trunk, the back of the arms and hands, and the shins. Stasis dermatitis exhibits dark red discoloration of the skin on the lower leg, ankle, and top of the foot. Stasis dermatitis lesions can become irritated and inflamed and in many cases can result in skin ulcers.

Winter itch presents with fine cracks over the front surface of the thighs and shins and possibly a dry, shiny appearance. Scabies presents with the classic eczematous lesions found primarily on the ankles, webs of fingers and toes, scalp, wrists, bellybutton (umbilicus), genitals, or the nipples. Seborrheic dermatitis presents as red, itchy, scaly areas primarily on the face, scalp, groin, anogenital region, and/or below the breasts. Sunburn is characterized by a red, swollen, well-defined area of exposed skin. Lichen simplex chronicus is a late stage of eczema and consists of thickened, scaly skin due to chronic rubbing or scratching. Common areas for lichen simplex chronicus are the back of the neck, tops of feet, and ankles.

Tests: Though most of the eczemas are diagnosed through the history and physical exam, a scraping of the lesion should be examined under the microscope to rule out certain other skin disorders. Skin biopsy is done when persistent eczema is not responding to treatment. Skin patch tests, provocative challenges, and some immunological testing may be required. Elevated total IgE denotes underlying allergy.

Treatment

Antibiotics are an option for all cases of eczema since each type involves a degree of skin damage that leaves the individual susceptible to skin infections.

Treatment of atopic dermatitis consists of removal or reduction of irritating factors, use of topical corticosteroids, application of moisturizer, and reduction of stress. Severe itching is treated with antihistamines or tricyclic antidepressants.

Treatment of contact dermatitis consists primarily of identifying the offending agent and avoiding it. Topical corticosteroids, oral antihistamines, or astringent lotions may be used. Oral corticosteroids may be required for severe cases and those involving the genitals or face. Hand eczema may improve if vinyl gloves are worn at any time the hands come in contact with irritants. After washing, the hands should be thoroughly patted dry. Unscented hand cream should be applied throughout the day. Nummular eczema may be treated with corticosteroid ointment, antihistamines, antibiotics, and coal tar solution. Winter itch responds well to moisturizers or emollients, particularly those containing urea or alpha-hydroxy acids. Temporary relief from stasis eczema can be achieved with mild corticosteroid ointments. Swelling of the legs may be controlled through use of compression bandages or special stockings. Scabies is treated with a scabicide and an antihistamine. Sunburn is treated with cool baths or compresses, analgesics, and anesthetic sunburn spray. Seborrheic dermatitis is treated with persistent and frequent cleansing to remove scale and the possible application of a corticosteroid.

In general, irritating fabrics (wool, silk, and rough synthetics) should be avoided. Absorbent, nonirritating fabric (cotton) should be worn next to the skin. Soothing ointment should be applied to any affected area and covered with a dressing to prevent scratching.

Prognosis

Eczema is usually chronic with periods of remission. Episodes of eczema may be relieved by appropriate treatment. If the agent causing contact dermatitis can be identified and avoided, the skin inflammation will usually resolve within a few weeks for allergic contact dermatitis and a few days for irritant contact dermatitis. Occupational contact dermatitis clears in 25% of individuals, shows 50% improvement with periodic recurrence, and is persistent and severe in 25% of affected individuals. Scabies resolves in 1 to 2 weeks, sunburn symptoms in 3 to 5 days.

Differential Diagnosis

Tinea corporis, measles, scarlet fever, rubella, psoriasis, pityriasis rosea, and squamous cell carcinoma can mimic eczema.

Specialists

| • Allergist | • Dermatologist |

Work Restrictions / Accommodations

Work restrictions or accommodations depend on the location and extent of the eczema outbreak. Depending on the location of the eczema, the use of personal protective equipment (e.g., gloves or respirator) may be affected. Allergens, low humidity, excessive sweating, and irritants (wool, acrylic, soaps, and detergents) may make itching and scratching worse. Contact dermatitis may be avoided by removal (or replacement) of the offending substance or by wearing personal protective equipment (e.g., cotton-lined rubber gloves) and using barrier creams. A change in occupational responsibilities may be necessary if contact with the offending industrial substance is unavoidable.

Comorbid Conditions

Immune system-suppressing diseases such as AIDS or certain cancers can increase the length of disability by making the individual more prone to skin infection.

Complications

Infection by staphylococcus or streptococcus bacteria is very common. Eczema on the scalp can cause hair loss (alopecia). Chronic eczema may develop following a severe scabies infestation.

Factors Influencing Duration

The length of disability depends on the cause of eczema, site, extent, and effectiveness of treatment.

Length of Disability

Disability duration depends on job requirements. In most cases, no disability is expected.

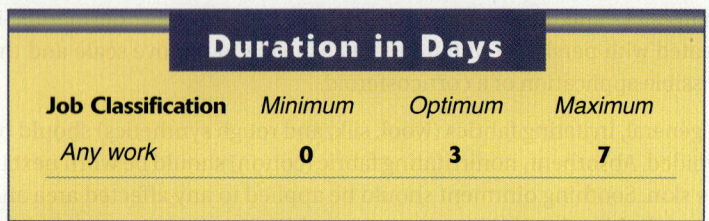

Job Classification	Minimum	Optimum	Maximum
Any work	0	3	7

Failure to Recover

If an individual fails to recover within the maximum duration expectancy period, the reader may wish to reference the following questions to assist in better understanding the specifics of an individual's medical case.

Regarding diagnosis:

- Did individual present with a scaly, itchy rash?
- Has a complete skin examination been performed? Were red scaly skin excoriations noted on the physical exam? Was there a particular pattern or location of the skin rash?
- Was a complete medical and personal history obtained?
- Is more than one individual at the workplace complaining of rash?
- Were skin scrapings and/or skin biopsy performed? Was individual tested for food allergy?
- Were other conditions with similar symptoms (tinea corporis, measles, scarlet fever, rubella, psoriasis, pityriasis rosea, and squamous cell carcinoma) ruled out?
- Was diagnosis of eczema confirmed?

Regarding treatment:

- Was individual instructed regarding avoiding skin irritants and stress reduction? Instructed to avoid irritating fabrics (wool, silk, and rough synthetics)?
- Were appropriate accommodations made at the workplace to limit exposure to skin irritants?
- Were topical corticosteroids and moisturizers effective in reducing the skin rash and itching? If not, were other medications such as antihistamines, antidepressants, or oral corticosteroids considered?
- Is there evidence of an associated skin infection? If so, were appropriate antibiotics prescribed?
- Is individual following the prescribed treatment plan? Were any other alternative treatments that could interfere with the effectiveness of the prescribed therapy tried?

Regarding prognosis:

- Have the symptoms persisted despite treatment?
- How severe are the symptoms? Are they incapacitating? Can individual perform the normal activities of daily life?
- What other treatment options are available?
- If individual cannot avoid irritant in the occupational environment, is a change of position or change of occupation warranted?
- Does individual have an underlying immune system-suppressing disease that could impact response to treatment?
- Has individual experienced any complications of eczema such as staphylococcus or streptococcus bacterial infection, or hair loss on the scalp (alopecia)?

References

Anderson, Philip, and Kristin Malaker. "Most Common Skin Disorders." Managing Skin Diseases. Hiscock, Tim, ed. Baltimore: Williams & Wilkins, 1999. 35-120.

Ruzicka, T. "Atopic Dermatitis Between Rationality and Irrationality." Archives of Dermatology 134 11 (1998): 1462-1469.

Electrocardiogram

Other names / synonyms: ECG, EKG
89.52

Definition

The electrocardiogram (ECG) is a recording of the electrical activity of the heart.

The ECG recording is made by placing small metal discs (electrodes) on the skin at several locations. These electrodes transmit electrical signals from the heart to the ECG machine, which then displays the recordings on a monitor as well as printing out a paper copy of the recording. Analysis and interpretation of these recordings indicate whether there are abnormal or life-threatening changes in the function of the heart. The ECG can be used for several different purposes, including the cardiac stress test and elective cardioversion.

A special use of the ECG, the cardiac stress test, measures heart activity while an individual is walking or running to determine whether there is current or potential heart disease. Analysis and interpretation of the ECG readings taken during the cardiac stress test can indicate, among other things, whether the individual has a blockage in the blood supply to the heart or an interference with the heart's ability to generate the correct sequence of electrical impulses needed for a normal heart rhythm.

The ECG is also essential for monitoring the status of an individual's heart rate during a procedure called elective cardioversion. Elective cardioversion is used to slow an abnormally fast heart rate (atrial fibrillation) that has not responded to medication used to slow the heart rate. During elective cardioversion the heart rate is slowed by pulsing an electric current, which is calibrated with the individual's ECG recording, through special electrodes placed on the individual's chest.

Many healthcare workers refer to the ECG as an "EKG" in order to prevent misunderstandings in the similarity of sound between ECG and EEG (electroencephalogram, a study of the brain).

Reason for Procedure

The ECG is essential in the diagnosis of various disease conditions of the heart, including coronary artery disease (angina and heart attack), disturbances in heart rhythm (arrhythmias), disturbances in electrical conduction (heart blocks), thickening of the heart muscle, or acute inflammation of the membrane that covers the heart (acute pericarditis). It can be used to determine whether a heart damage is due to a sudden heart attack (myocardial infarction) or to old damage.

Description

The individual receiving the ECG test lies on a bed or couch while small metal discs (electrodes) are placed on the skin at the wrists, ankles, and several locations across the chest. The skin needs to be clean and dry. The electrodes are connected by wires to a control unit that selects different combinations of electrodes to record. The resulting electrical signals are amplified and recorded on paper or displayed on a monitor screen. The test takes only a few minutes and is painless.

Prognosis

The electrocardiogram offers excellent diagnostic information about the electrical activity of the heart. It can be used in wellness and disease prevention as a part of an individual's routine health check-up or as an aid when diagnosing the reason for specific symptoms, such as chest pain.

Specialists

- Cardiologist

Work Restrictions / Accommodations

No work restrictions and accommodations are associated with this procedure.

Comorbid Conditions

The only conditions that affect ECG are those that prevent good contact between the electrodes and the skin, such as high levels of perspiration, physical defects such as an amputated limb, or individuals who are too agitated to cooperate with the test.

Procedure Complications

There is a slight risk of skin sensitivity to the electrodes.

Factors Influencing Duration

The underlying condition for which the ECG was used may influence the length of disability; however, there is no disability associated with the test itself.

Length of Disability

No disability is expected to result from this procedure. Disability may occur as a result of an underlying condition.

References

Beers, Mark H., and Berkow, Robert, eds. "Arrhythmias." The Merck Manual. Whitehouse Station, NJ: Merck Research Laboratories, 1999. 1710-1740.

Ellestad, Myrvin H. Stress Testing. Philadelphia: F.A. Davis Company, 1996.

Electroconvulsive Therapy

Other names / synonyms: ECT, Electroshock Therapy, Shock Therapy

94.27

Definition

Electroconvulsive therapy (ECT) is a treatment for certain mental disorders where a brief electrical stimulus is applied to the brain to induce a cerebral seizure under controlled conditions. The individual is first given a general anesthetic and a drug to block the muscular movements usually accompanying a seizure. The procedure is often performed 2 to 3 times a week for several weeks. It is primarily an inpatient therapy, but can also be done on an outpatient basis if the individual has a reliable caretaker at home. While ECT is an effective short-term therapy that creates some degree of improvement in 90% of individuals, the relapse rate may be relatively high, especially in the first 4 to 6 months. In order to reduce the likelihood of a relapse, ECT is used in combination with psychotherapy and antidepressant or antipsychotic drugs.

ECT is primarily for treatment of major depression, mania, and schizophrenia. Major depression is a persistent sad mood or loss of interest in activities that persists for at least 2 weeks in the absence of external precipitants. Mania is a mood disorder characterized by grandiose, hyperactive, irrational, and destructive behavior. Schizophrenia is a group of psychotic disorders characterized by withdrawal from reality, illogical patterns of thinking, delusions, and hallucinations, and is accompanied to varying degrees by other emotional, behavioral, or intellectual disturbances.

Most individuals receiving ECT are elderly, depressed, female inpatients in general or private psychiatric hospitals. Recent surveys revealed that ECT is used to treat almost 40,000 individuals in the US each year, however, most states do not require physicians to report administration of ECT so this annual estimate may not be accurate. Because of bad press, public complaints, and litigation regarding ECT, this procedure is on the decline. It is usually administered only after other treatment alternatives have been unsuccessful.

Reason for Procedure

ECT is used to treat individuals with severe or psychotic forms of mood disorders (major depression, mania, and schizophrenia) who have failed to respond to other therapies or who are considered at imminent risk for suicide. ECT becomes the treatment of choice when the afflicted individual cannot safely wait several weeks for antidepressants to become effective. For example, individuals with suicidal or homicidal thoughts, stupor, or extreme agitation may be candidates for ECT.

The procedure may also be used if drug therapy becomes intolerable due to side effects, or if the individual has a medical condition that precludes the use of certain antidepressants. ECT is chosen because it tends to make the individual accessible to productive effects of psychoactive medications and psychotherapy; reduces duration of episodes of mania, major depression, and schizophrenia; and, if used promptly, may shorten hospital stays of individuals with recurrent depression.

Description

ECT may be administered in a hospital or an outpatient clinic (less frequently). The individual is given a general anesthesia consisting of a short-acting barbiturate and a muscle relaxant. When the anesthesia takes effect, an electrode is placed above the temple of the nondominant side of the brain and a second in the middle of the forehead (unilateral ECT); or one electrode is placed above each temple (bilateral ECT). A very small current (one second or less duration) is passed through the brain to activate it, producing a seizure that lasts from 30 seconds to more than a minute. During the procedure, the anesthetized individual breathes pure oxygen and seizure and heart activity are monitored. Five to ten minutes after the procedure, the individual awakens and may experience symptoms such as confusion, headache, nausea, or muscle stiffness that resolve in 30 to 60 minutes.

The number of treatments required for an effective course of ECT varies substantially with individuals and medical conditions. For major depression, ECT usually consists of 6 to 12 treatments given 3 times a week. For mania and schizophrenia, the number of treatments may be substantially higher for a successful outcome.

Prognosis

Predicted outcome for treatment with ECT is contingent on the condition being treated and the seriousness of the condition. ECT has been shown to be life-saving and to produce dramatic results in cases of severe depression. ECT has a higher success rate as a treatment for major depression than any other form of treatment. A small number of methodologically sound studies have shown that ECT is superior in treatment efficacy relative to moderate doses of antidepressant drugs. Although ECT has been associated with some degree of improvement in 90% of individuals treated for depression, relapse rate is high, with the relapse usually occurring within the first 4 to 6 months following ECT.

Mania generally responds very well to ECT. The number of controlled studies documenting the effectiveness of ECT in mania is small, probably because this disorder usually responds well to pharmacological treatment.

Schizophrenia also responds well to ECT. Selected groups of schizophrenic individuals, particularly those with a brief duration of illness and/or prominent emotional (affective) symptoms, have been shown to respond as well to ECT as to neuroleptics. Data from methodologically sound studies indicate that ECT has a more limited role in the treatment of schizophrenia than in the treatment of mood disorders such as depression or mania. These data also suggest that the combination of ECT and neuroleptics is a more effective treatment than either ECT or neuroleptics alone.

Specialists

- Cardiologist
- Neurologist
- Psychiatrist
- Psychologist

Work Restrictions / Accommodations

Duties at work may need to be restricted based on memory impairment or incomplete response of the underlying condition to ECT. It is likely that the underlying condition will not allow the individual to perform employment duties until several weeks after the course of ECT treatments.

Comorbid Conditions

Comorbid conditions include previous psychiatric illnesses, sensitivity and allergy to psychoactive medications, and medical conditions precluding the use of psychoactive medications and ECT. Certain heart conditions or seizure disorders may preclude the use of ECT or increase the complication rate.

Procedure Complications

The major complications from ECT are cognitive side effects. Immediate side effects from ECT are rare except for headaches, muscle aches or soreness, nausea, and confusion that usually disappear during the first few hours following the procedure. During the course of ECT, there may be difficulty remembering newly learned information, or profound confusion and hallucinations (delirium). The learning difficulty and delirium usually disappear within weeks of completing the ECT course.

Some individuals also report a partial loss of memory for events that occurred during the days, weeks, and months preceding ECT. While most of these memories typically return over a period of days to months, some individuals have reported longer lasting problems. Conversely, other individuals report improved memory capability following ECT, possibly because of improvement in forgetfulness (amnesia) sometimes associated with major depression.

The severity of memory deficit is related to the number of treatments, type of electrode placement, and nature of electrical stimulus. Unilateral electrode placement is preferred over bilateral electrode placement by many psychiatrists because of fewer effects on cognition.

Physical complications such as spinal or other fractures reported in the early days of ECT are almost never reported in present practice because of administration of anesthesia and muscle relaxants in a controlled environment. Other physical complications such as a change in normal heart rhythm (arrhythmias) or increased seizure-like activity on EEG are still occasionally reported. Mortality from ECT is one-tenth of one percent, approximately the same as for general anesthesia.

Another possible complication is relapse of the psychiatric illness. As many as 20-50% of individuals who responded well to a course of ECT had a relapse within 6 months, therefore, some type of maintenance treatment (e.g., antidepressants, antipsychotic drugs [euroleptics]), or ECT administered monthly or at 6-week intervals) is often recommended to minimize relapse.

Factors Influencing Duration

Factors that might influence length of disability include memory problems, a relapse, or incomplete treatment response of the original condition.

Length of Disability

A short period of disability occurs after each ECT treatment. For 30 to 60 minutes after the treatment, the individual experiences significant confusion and disorientation. Longer-term disability involves memory. Factors influencing duration and intensity of disability following ECT include the type and severity of the underlying condition, the type of treatment (psychopharmacological or ECT or both), need for hospitalization, and response to treatment.

Table reflects durations of treatment and underlying medical condition. Maximum duration includes hospitalization.

Duration in Days

Job Classification	Minimum	Optimum	Maximum
Any work	7	28	56

References

Electroconvulsive therapy. NIH. 01 Jan 2000. 08 Nov 2000 <http://text.nlm.nih.gov/nih/cdc/www/51txt.html>.

Papolos, Demitri. All About ECT. www.schizophrenia.com. 01 Jan 1999. 19 Aug 2000 <http://www.schizophrenia.com/family/ect1.html>.

Electroencephalogram
Other names / synonyms: EEG
89.14

Definition

An electroencephalogram (EEG) is a graphic recording of the electric potential produced by brain cells, as detected by electrodes placed on the scalp. The resulting brain waves are called alpha, beta, delta, and theta rhythms according to the frequencies they produce.

The wave range frequency is from 2 to 12 cycles per second, with the dominant waves being 8 to 10 cycles per second at an amplitude from 10 to 100 microvolts. Variations in brain wave activity are correlated with different neurologic conditions such as seizure disorders (epilepsy), psychological states, and level of consciousness as in sleep versus awake states.

Electroencephalography is the process of recording brain wave activity. During neurosurgery, an electrode can be applied directly to the surface of the brain (intracranial electroencephalography) or placed within the brain tissue (depth electroencephalography) to detect brain tumors or lesions. A flat or isoelectric EEG is one in which no brain waves are recorded, indicating a complete lack of brain activity.

Reason for Procedure

The test is used to diagnose seizure disorders, brainstem disorders, local (focal) brain tumors or lesions, and impaired consciousness. EEGs are also done to investigate sleep disturbances such as narcolepsy. It can also help in the evaluation of coma, stroke, tremor, Alzheimer's disease, cerebrovascular disease, and brain death.

Description

Electrodes are attached to various areas of the individual's scalp with a jelly-like product (collodion). During the procedure, the individual remains quiet, with eyes closed, and refrains from talking or moving. In certain cases, prescribed activities such as breathing harder than usual (hyperventilation), adding flashing lights during the recording, or recording after a period of sleep deprivation may be requested.

Prognosis

The EEG is a noninvasive procedure that can be performed in the physician's office. The results of the EEG can be normal, abnormal, or abnormal but clinically insignificant.

Specialists

- Neurologist
- Neurophysiologist
- Neurosurgeon

Work Restrictions / Accommodations

An EEG can be performed on an outpatient basis. There are no work restrictions or special accommodations except for the individual who has the EEG to assess sleep disturbances. The individual will need to sleep after the procedure, which may require time away from work for a period of one day.

Procedure Complications

Recording of an EEG is a normally noninvasive procedure and usually has no associated complications.

Factors Influencing Duration

The underlying neurological or psychological condition for which the EEG is ordered may influence length of disability. If sleep deprivation is required, the individual must not sleep the night before the procedure, which may result in brief disability.

Length of Disability

No disability is expected to result from this procedure. Disability may occur as a result of an underlying condition.

References

Anderson K.N., L.E. Anderson, and W.D. Glanze. Mosby's Medical, Nursing, and Allied Health Dictionary, 5th ed. St. Louis: Mosby-Year Book, Inc, 1998.

Rowland, Lewis P. Merritt's Textbook of Neurology, 8th ed. Philadelphia: Lea & Febiger, 1989.

Electromyography

Other names / synonyms: Electrodiagnostic Study, EMG
93.08

Definition

Electromyography (EMG) is a neurophysiological test of muscle function. It involves recording the electrical activity of muscle groups during rest and contraction (tightening). Since muscle contraction ordinarily follows stimulation of a motor nerve, EMG also reflects motor (but not sensory) nerve function.

A motor nerve consists of a bundle of axons (fiber-like projections of neurons) whose cell bodies are located in the spinal cord. Each axon branches as it enters the muscle to end on a group of muscle cells (motor end plate). A motor neuron and the muscle cells that it stimulates are referred to as a motor unit. A muscle is made up of several units. When motor neurons are stimulated, electrical impulses travel along the axons. As a result, muscle cells are stimulated. Muscle contraction occurs when electrical impulses are produced in the muscle cells. During electromyography, testing needle electrodes are inserted into muscles to record their electrical activity. The electrical impulses display as waves on a device called an oscilloscope, and can also be heard through a loudspeaker.

After a peripheral nerve injury, regeneration of the nerve may occur. Before there is clinical improvement in muscle strength, signs of reinnervation (growth of living nerve back into the paralyzed muscle) can be detected on EMG. Repeat EMGs may be done to follow an individual's progress. Although an abnormal EMG is an indicator of disease, a normal EMG does not necessarily rule out disease. The EMG reflects motor function; it cannot detect damage to a sensory nerve.

EMGs are often avoided or done with great caution on individuals who are receiving anticoagulants. EMGs are generally not problematic for persons with pacemakers but nerve conduction studies requiring stimulation near pacemakers should be avoided.

Reason for Procedure

Electromyography is a useful diagnostic procedure for evaluating nerve and muscle disorders. It is typically performed on individuals who may have nerve root impingement within the vertebrae, due to disc herniation or bone spurs, or peripheral nerve injuries. Muscle recruitment patterns, specifically during maximal contraction, may be helpful in distinguishing between muscle and nerve disorders. EMG (usually in conjunction with nerve conduction studies) is helpful in determining the location of a nerve lesion.

Description

There are four phases to an EMG test. In the first phase, a group of skeletal muscles are chosen based on the nerve root and peripheral nerves that are suspected of dysfunction. The skin over the muscle is rubbed with isopropyl alcohol and a needle electrode is inserted into the muscle. The needle electrode records any action potentials and displays them on a screen that shows the wave formations of electrical current (oscilloscope). The oscilloscope is observed when the needle is first inserted into the muscle. A short burst of potentials will be seen when the needle is first inserted; however, injured muscle fibers produce increased insertional or injury potentials when the needle is moved around.

The second phase is the observation of the action potentials when a muscle is voluntarily contracted. The individual is asked to gently contract the muscle. When the needle electrode is near the motor endplate, where there is the highest concentration of motor neurons, a high frequency noise will be heard. The recorded action potential is studied to compare its duration (in milliseconds), its amplitude (in microvolts), and its waveform (or number of phases) against normal values for the particular muscle group being studied.

The third phase examines the sequence of action potentials generated when a muscle is contracted at a gradually increasing intensity. In a normally innervated muscle, the amplitude of the wave progressively increases as does the firing rate.

The fourth phase examines spontaneous activity when a muscle is at rest. Healthy muscle yields no action potentials in the absence of contraction. However, in a denervated muscle, action potentials are spontaneously discharged (fibrillation).

The data are collected and examined to ascertain the nature of the injury.

Prognosis

EMG, when correlated with clinical findings, is usually helpful in determining the diagnosis. It is generally a definitive procedure.

Abnormal electrical activity on EMG confirms the presence of neural involvement in muscular dysfunction. However, additional testing such as an MRI scan is often necessary to determine the location of the nerve injury. With positive test results, individuals are referred for rehabilitation specific to the nerve injury detected.

Individuals who have a negative EMG do not have the presence of nerve damage due to compression or lesion. These individuals may require other tests such as an MRI to rule out muscular dysfunction such as tendon rupture. These individuals then undergo rehabilitation appropriate for the diagnosis that is given once all diagnostic tests are performed.

Specialists

- Neurologist
- Physiatrist

Work Restrictions / Accommodations

No restrictions are necessary as a result of the test. If the EMG reveals nerve injury, appropriate accommodations may be necessary.

Comorbid Conditions

Primary muscle disease, motor neuron disease such as amyotrophic lateral sclerosis or polio, or multiple sclerosis may lengthen disability due to the impact these diseases have on muscle strength and nerve conduction.

Procedure Complications

Pain at the site of needle electrode insertion may occur during and after the EMG. The muscles may also experience pain and spasm after the EMG is completed. Bruising is rare, and with sterile, single use (disposable) needles infection is also unlikely.

Factors Influencing Duration

The underlying cause of the nerve dysfunction may impact recovery. Individuals with nerves that have been partially or completely severed or demyelinated may face longer recovery time than individuals who have decreased muscle strength due to herniated intervertebral discs.

Length of Disability

No disability is expected to result from this procedure. Disability may occur as a result of an underlying condition.

References

Nelson, Roger M., and David E. Nestor. "Electrophysiological Evaluation: An Overview." Clinical Electrotherapy. Nelson, Roger M., and Dean P. Currier, eds. Norwalk: Appleton & Lange, 1991. 331-360.

Embolectomy
38.0

Definition

Embolectomy is a surgical procedure that extracts a fragment of material (embolus) that is blocking blood flow through an artery.

The particle causing the blockage is usually a blood clot (thrombus), but it can also be a bubble of air or other gas, a piece of tissue or tumor, a clump of bacteria, bone marrow, cholesterol, fat, or any of other various substances. This obstruction is referred to as an embolism, which results when the particle arises from one part of the body (such as the heart), then breaks free and travels through the bloodstream until it lodges in an artery.

The exact incidence of arterial embolism is unclear. However, arterial embolism is usually a complication of heart disease. In most cases, coronary artery disease, with or without heart attack, is responsible for the development of emboli. A heart rhythm disturbance, in which the atria of the heart beat rapidly and irregularly (atrial fibrillation) is often present. Other forms of heart disease, such as rheumatic heart disease or bacterial endocarditis, are other causes of arterial embolism.

Coronary artery disease is more common in men than women and is most common in individuals over 40 years of age. Rheumatic heart disease, results from rheumatic fever infections, and causes deformities of the heart valves. Bacterial endocarditis is a disorder characterized by abnormal growths on the heart valves. Though it is relatively uncommon, it can develop in individuals with defective heart valves following invasive dental or surgical procedures or in association with intravenous drug use.

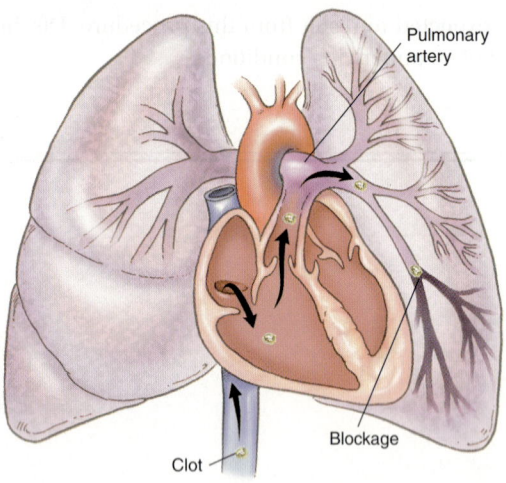

Reason for Procedure

An embolectomy is done to remove a fragment of material (emboli) that is obstructing the blood flow in an artery. Obstruction of blood flow prevents tissues from receiving adequate oxygen (ischemia), and may result in tissue death (necrosis). Embolism is a threat to body tissue and can be life threatening. Even in cases where there is obvious tissue death (necrosis or gangrene), an embolectomy may be done to limit the amount of tissue loss.

Description

The embolus is located either by an x-ray taken after injection of radio-paque dye into the blood vessel (arteriography) or imaging following injection of contrast medium (MRI angiography). In most cases, one or more emboli can be removed using a specially designed catheter with a small inflatable balloon at the tip (Fogarty catheter). A local anesthetic may be used if the embolus appears to be easily retrievable. If there are multiple emboli and the procedure is expected to be lengthy, a general anesthetic may be used. The catheter is inserted into a main artery and then passed beyond the embolus. The balloon is inflated. Then the catheter is withdrawn with the balloon inflated to pulling the embolus out. The artery is usually flushed with a solution to deter the formation of blood clots (usually heparin). The puncture or opening at the artery is then stitched closed.

Another approach may be used if the embolus is large or at a site that is difficult to reach with the Fogarty catheter. In this case, the artery is cut open (arteriotomy) at the site of the embolism, and the embolus is sucked out (aspirated). The Fogarty catheter may be used in conjunction with this approach to help remove distant emboli. After the procedure is completed, the artery is irrigated and stitched closed. Medications to deter formation of blood clots (anticoagulants) are continued for a few days following either of these approaches.

In cases when surgery is not possible, enzymes that dissolve blood clots (thrombolytic) and drugs to prevent further clot formation (anticoagulant) may be used instead.

Prognosis

The success of this procedure is dependent on the degree and extent of tissue damage from lack of blood flow (ischemia) at the time of the procedure. When the embolectomy is done promptly before there has been prolonged loss of blood flow and tissue death (necrosis), the outcome is usually good. Those cases that have significant tissue death (necrosis) require surgical removal of all the dead tissue. Depending on the area of the body affected, this may entail amputation of fingers, toes or legs.

Specialists

- General Surgeon
- Thoracic Surgeon
- Vascular Surgeon

Work Restrictions / Accommodations

Extended work leave may be required. The individual's job requirements will determine if any specific restrictions or accommodations are necessary. Restrictions may include no prolonged sitting and no heavy lifting during recovery period. Individuals on anticoagulants need to take protective measures to avoid cuts and bruises.

Comorbid Conditions

Comorbid conditions of diabetes, atherosclerosis, heart disease or bleeding disorders may impact ability to recover and further lengthen disability.

Procedure Complications

Complications include artery puncture or tearing, heart attack (from dislodged fragments that travel to the heart), bleeding, infection (rare) and swelling of an extremity after the blood flow is restored.

Factors Influencing Duration

Length of disability may be influenced by the site of the embolism, method and extent of the procedure, development of complications, or the individual's job requirements.

Length of Disability

Duration in Days

Job Classification	Minimum	Optimum	Maximum
Sedentary work	7	28	56
Light work	7	42	56
Medium work	14	42	84
Heavy work	21	64	112
Very Heavy work	21	64	112

References

Meeker, Margaret, and Jane Rothrock. Alexander's Care of the Patient in Surgery. St. Louis: Mosby, 1999.

Schwartz, Seymour, MD. Principles of Surgery. New York: McGraw-Hill, 1999.

Embolectomy, Pulmonary
Other names / synonyms: Pulmonary Embolectomy
38.05

Definition

Pulmonary embolectomy is a procedure to remove one or more large blood clots (embolus) from the lungs. It involves a large chest incision.

Emboli reach the lungs by traveling through the venous circulation after becoming detached from a stationary blood clot (thrombus) in the legs or pelvic region. The blood clots obstruct blood flow to the lungs. Clinically, the result is a low blood pressure (systemic hypotension) beyond the obstruction and a high pressure before it that leads to right heart failure.

Although pulmonary emboli are common, less than 5% of individuals with emboli develop hypotension or right heart failure requiring an embolectomy. Pulmonary embolectomy is not commonly performed and is reserved for those individuals with refractory systemic hypotension that has not responded to medical management.

Reason for Procedure

The reason for a pulmonary embolectomy is to extract life-threatening blood clots (emboli) from the pulmonary circulation. It is a life-saving emergency operation.

Most pulmonary embolectomies are done for acute massive pulmonary emboli. On occasion, the procedure is done for chronic emboli causing pulmonary high blood pressure (hypertension) and right heart failure.

Description

A large chest incision (thoracotomy) is required for performing a pulmonary embolectomy. It is done under general anesthesia in the operating room. The procedure is usually performed using the heart-lung machine (cardiopulmonary bypass) to support the individual's circulation while the emboli are removed. The emboli are removed with forceps or by suction. After removal, a filter is placed in the large vein that brings blood back to the heart from the pelvis and legs (inferior vena cava). The filter is designed to trap any further emboli before they can reach the lungs.

An alternative to pulmonary embolectomy by open-chest is removal of emboli using a special catheter inserted through the skin. This technique is called percutaneous pulmonary embolectomy. Emboli are sucked (aspirated) through the catheter and removed from the lungs. As with operative embolectomy, a filter is usually placed in the inferior vena cava at the end of the procedure to prevent recurrent emboli.

Prognosis

The mortality rate for pulmonary embolectomy is high at 30-50%. This is because the operation is performed on individuals who are extremely ill with profound hypotension and right heart failure. However, when the procedure is done electively on individuals with chronic heart failure and no systemic hypotension, the operation mortality is fifteen to twenty percent.

Specialists

- Cardiologist
- Cardiovascular Surgeon

Rehabilitation

Rehabilitation following a pulmonary embolectomy depends on the amount of damage as a result of the blood clot and the extent of the surgery required in removing the embolus. After the surgical removal of the embolus, the physical therapist and/or respiratory therapist help the postoperative individual cough to mobilize secretions and clear the airway. This is achieved with the individual lying in a position allowing the most effective drainage of secretions. The individual is often in a side lying position with the affected side upward and the head slightly lower than the chest.

Physical therapy improves ventilation with breathing exercises localized to the area of involvement. As with any surgical operation, rehabilitative exercises are critical in preventing further pulmonary emboli. Because blood clots in the leg veins are of a particular concern after an operation, early rehabilitation including activity such as walking is very important. If walking is not an option, leg exercises are instructed by the physical therapist or other rehabilitation professional to reduce the risk of clot formation. One example of this type of exercise is commonly referred to as ankle pumps. The individual elevates one or both legs above the heart while lying on the back and then pumps the foot and ankle up and down as if pumping the gas pedal of an automobile.

Rehabilitation then progresses to strengthening. A physical therapist experienced in cardiac and pulmonary rehabilitation keeps a daily log of the individual's blood pressure, heart rate, and cardiac rhythm throughout the exercise program. As the individual progresses with relaxation techniques, active assist range-of-motion exercises to the upper and lower extremities begin. The next step of progression is active range of motion and involves the individual performing all the motion independently. As endurance continues to increase without symptoms of shortness of breath, active upper and lower extremity exercises begin with very light resistance in addition to light aerobic activities such as brisk walking and low resistance biking.

The therapist informs the individual rehabilitating from a pulmonary embolectomy that the program can be a lengthy process in order to obtain maximum benefit of increasing pulmonary stamina and prevent future clotting. Because most individuals with pulmonary disorders are also managed with medication, it is important for each individual to inform the rehabilitation personnel as to what medications he or she is taking since many of these drugs alter the acute and chronic response to exercise.

Work Restrictions / Accommodations

Individuals may need to be temporarily reassigned to a less strenuous job. A combustion-free environment is necessary for those individuals on supplemental oxygen. Frequent breaks to ambulate even short distances may be needed to avoid prolonged stasis of blood in the legs and pelvis. Avoidance of work with a higher likelihood of trauma is advisable for those individuals on blood thinners (anticoagulants).

Comorbid Conditions

Any chronic heart or lung condition (congestive heart failure, COPD) will affect disability and individual's ability to recover.

Procedure Complications

In addition to wound infection and bleeding, complications include those related to use of the heart-lung machine such as destruction of red blood cells (hemolysis), hypotension requiring use of an intraaortic balloon pump, kidney (renal) failure, a variety of lung (pulmonary) problems, irregular heart beats (arrhythmias), a spectrum of neurologic conditions ranging from transient weakness to disabling stroke, and alteration of mental status (encephalopathy and delirium). The procedure also has a high mortality rate due to its emergent nature and the illness of the individual.

Factors Influencing Duration

Length of disability may be influenced by the number, size, and location of clots; extent of the procedure (transvenous versus surgery); development of complications; and requirements of the individual's job.

Length of Disability

Despite excellent therapeutic results with methods of conventional medicine using mostly drugs of natural origin such as glucocorticoids, individuals with eczema frequently use unproved complementary treatments. Duration depends on the method of treatment and the type of work or activities in which the individual is engaged. Individual is anticoagulated for three to six months.

Duration in Days

Job Classification	Minimum	Optimum	Maximum
Sedentary work	42	56	112
Light work	42	56	112
Medium work	56	70	Indefinite
Heavy work	56	84	Indefinite
Very Heavy work	56	112	Indefinite

References

Goldstone, Jerry, MD. "Veins and Lymphatics." Current Surgical Diagnosis and Treatment. Way, Lawrence Norwalk: Appleton & Lange, 1991. 768-792.

Schwartz, Seymour, MD. Principles of Surgery. New York: McGraw-Hill, 1999.

Embolism, Pulmonary

Other names / synonyms: Pulmonary Apoplexy, Pulmonary Thromboembolism, Pulmonary Thrombosis

415.1, 673, 673.0, 673.1, 673.2, 673.3, 673.8, 958.0, 958.1

Definition

A pulmonary embolism is blockage of the artery carrying blood from the heart to the lungs via the main circulatory unit of the lungs (pulmonary artery). The blockage usually arises from a blood clot originating in the veins of the legs that breaks loose, traveling to the heart and on to the pulmonary artery. However, many other substances are known to embolize the pulmonary circulation. These may include air (from a central vein catheter), amniotic fluid (dislodged in active labor), fat (arising from long bone fractures), foreign bodies (i.e., talc introduced during intravenous drug use), septic emboli (in acute endocarditis), or tumor cells.

In most cases, blockage is temporary. In others, the blockage can cause chest pain with shortness of breath, cough, and coughing of blood. A massive pulmonary embolism can put enormous stress on the right ventricle and halt the entire circulation system causing rapid death. With pulmonary embolism, there may also be death of lung tissue (pulmonary infarction).

Pulmonary embolism ranks as the third leading cause of death in hospitals with an estimated 50,000 deaths each year in the US. Risk factors for pulmonary embolism can include prolonged bed rest or inactivity, surgery, femur or pelvic trauma or surgery, central vein intravenous lines (central vein catheters), cancer, endocarditis, childbirth, stroke, congestive heart failure, frequent air travel, and obesity. Approximately 60% of individuals with blood clots in the deep veins of their upper legs (proximal deep vein thrombosis) develop pulmonary emboli.

Diagnosis

History: The individual usually experiences sudden chest pain that may radiate to the shoulder. This is often combined with a bluish pallor (cyanosis), a sudden shortness of breath, and very rapid breathing. In severe cases, the individual may faint or cough up blood and feel a keen sense of anxiety.

Physical exam: Typical findings include a rapid pulse, breathlessness, fainting, and collapse. Some individuals may present with a low-grade fever, cyanosis, abnormal lung sounds, and wheezing. Listening to the chest will reveal distinct patterns in heartbeat and blood flow. The individual will usually have a fever, high pulse rate and rapid breathing if the embolism resulted in an infarction. In cases of massive embolism, the individual will display signs of shock (cold, clammy skin, weak pulse, and low blood pressure).

Tests: Tests typically include chest x-ray, electrocardiogram, lung scan, and arterial blood gases. A pulmonary angiogram is the most definitive test to diagnose the presence of pulmonary emboli. A CT or MRI may be ordered on occasion as a noninvasive alternative for diagnosis.

Treatment

Treatment of pulmonary embolism initially focuses on relieving symptoms of the attack with a combination of oxygen, blood-thinning drugs (anticoagulant), morphine, and fluids. Anticoagulants can be used as a preventive measure but not a cure. They should not be used on individuals susceptible to bleeding due to other medical conditions such as esophageal varices, ulcers, and liver or kidney disease. If the individual remains in critical condition following the embolism and has not responded well to emergency measures, blood clot dissolving medications (thrombolytics) may be used.

Surgical removal of the embolus (pulmonary embolectomy) is an emergency procedure done as a last resort. Surgical ligation of the inferior vena cava (vena cava interruption) or insertion of an umbrella device into the inferior vena cava (blocks blood clots from traveling to the lungs) is considered when recurrence of the disease is life-threatening in cases where the individual cannot tolerate anticoagulant therapy or has septic thrombophlebitis of pelvic origin.

Prognosis

Prognosis depends on the underlying disease and proper diagnosis and treatment. The outcome for survival is good. After diagnosis and treatment, recurrence is unusual. Death from recurrent emboli occurs in less than 3% of the cases. Approximately 1% of individuals develop elevated circulatory pressure in the lungs secondary to persistent pulmonary emboli (chronic thromboembolic pulmonary hypertension). This can result in serious heart and lung problems or cause early death.

Comparative outcomes of pulmonary embolectomy and anticoagulation (with either thrombolytics or heparin) have not been extensively studied. Surgical interruption of the vena cava does not necessarily prevent subsequent embolism. Evidence of recurrent pulmonary embolism is reported in 20% of individuals after ligation. Insertion of an umbrella device effectively reduces the incidence of pulmonary emboli but is associated with increased risk of recurrent deep vein blood clots in the lower extremities. Thrombolytic therapy is associated with an increased risk of intracranial hemorrhage and hemorrhage at traumatic or surgical sites. The bleeding rate is 22% for individuals with thrombolysis compared to 9% for those treated with anticoagulation alone. Surgical embolectomy, which requires cardiopulmonary bypass, is associated with mortality rates as high as 37.5%. Mortality and morbidity are greatest in those with a history of cardiac arrest or pre-existing cardiovascular disease.

Differential Diagnosis

Other possibilities include pneumonia, pneumothorax, pleurisy, heart attack, or a rib fracture.

Specialists

- Cardiologist
- Cardiothoracic Surgeon
- Critical Care Specialist
- Internist
- Pulmonologist

Rehabilitation

The type of rehabilitation needed will depend on the underlying cause (i.e., surgery, trauma, or childbirth) of the pulmonary embolism.

Rehabilitation of a pulmonary embolism begins once the origin and reason for the blood clot is identified and the situation stabilized. The extent of rehabilitation will depend on the amount of damage resulting from the blood clot and whether surgery was required to remove the embolus. After a surgical operation, rehabilitative exercises are critical in preventing pulmonary emboli. Because blood clots in the leg veins are particularly common after an operation, early rehabilitation including activity such as walking is very important. If walking is not an option, the physical therapist or other rehabilitation professional will assign leg exercises to reduce the risk of clot formation.

Rehabilitation is more involved if the individual must regain strength following surgical removal of the pulmonary embolus. Early rehabilitation primarily focuses on preventing any breathing difficulties and regaining upper extremity range of motion that may have been lost due to surgery on the chest muscles. Early in the program while the individual is still hospitalized, strategies to reduce oxygen demand include decreasing the work of breathing through breathing exercises, postural alterations, reduction of accessory breathing movements, and relaxation exercises. To allow the individual to slowly adjust to the increase in oxygen demand, the exercise session begins with a prolonged warm-up.

An exercise that promotes both relaxation and a postural alteration for the muscles that aid in breathing begins with the individual assuming a relaxed sitting position while leaning forward and resting the forearms on the thighs or a pillow in the lap. A physical therapist experienced in cardiac and pulmonary rehabilitation keeps a daily log of the individual's blood pressure, heart rate, and cardiac rhythm. As the individual progresses with relaxation techniques, active assist range-of-motion exercises to the upper and lower extremities may be introduced. As the individual improves with increased endurance, the next step is active range of motion exercises. As endurance increases without shortness of breath, active upper and lower extremity exercises are initiated that use very light resistance in addition to light aerobic activities like brisk walking and low-resistance biking.

Rehabilitating from a pulmonary embolus can be a lengthy process in order to obtain the maximum benefit of increased pulmonary stamina and to prevent future clotting. Because most individuals with pulmonary disorders are managed with medication, it is important that rehabilitation personnel know what these medications are since many of these drugs alter the acute and chronic response to exercise. The major concern while on anticoagulation medication is the increased risk of bleeding, therefore, precautions should be taken to avoid tasks with a risk of physical trauma (heavy labor) that may precipitate bleeding.

Work Restrictions / Accommodations

Since pulmonary embolism is a result of a blood clot typically originating in the veins of the legs, it is vital for a predisposed individual to avoid sitting for prolonged periods of time. If long automobile or plane trips are a part of employment, the individual should take periodic breaks to restore circulation.

The major concern while on anticoagulation is the increased risk of bleeding; therefore, the individual should avoid high risk tasks such as heavy labor that may precipitate bleeding.

Complementary and Alternative Therapies

Content is intended for awareness only. Treatments may or may not be effective. Scientific evidence may be lacking and some substances have potentially toxic effects. Dr. Presley Reed and the editors do not endorse the use of these therapies in the absence of consultation with a licensed medical professional.

Qing Fei decoction - Used with heparin, may help treat pulmonary infarction.

Comorbid Conditions

Concomitant heart disease, postphlebitic syndrome, concomitant pulmonary disease, or residual clot may lengthen disability.

Complications

Complications include lung collapse (atelectasis), pulmonary hypertension, shock due to low cardiac output, cardiopulmonary arrest, infection, and lung infarction.

Factors Influencing Duration

Factors influencing the length of disability include advanced age, length of and response to anticoagulant therapy, underlying cause of the pulmonary embolus, and degree of pulmonary dysfunction.

Length of Disability

Despite excellent therapeutic results with methods of conventional medicine using mostly drugs of natural origin such as glucocorticoids, individuals with eczema frequently use unproved complementary treatments. Treatment with blood-thinning (anticoagulant) medications is usually continued for an average of 6 months following the episode. For surgical treatment (pulmonary embolectomy), durations reflect recovery from procedure only.

Medical treatment.

Duration in Days

Job Classification	Minimum	Optimum	Maximum
Sedentary work	7	14	28
Light work	7	14	28
Medium work	14	21	35
Heavy work	28	42	49
Very Heavy work	28	42	49

Surgical treatment. (Prophylaxis - vena cava interruption, intravascular, IVC umbrella).

Duration in Days

Job Classification	Minimum	Optimum	Maximum
Sedentary work	7	14	21
Light work	7	14	21
Medium work	14	21	Indefinite
Heavy work	84	112	Indefinite
Very Heavy work	84	112	Indefinite

Surgical treatment. (Prophylaxis - distal vein ligation).

Duration in Days

Job Classification	Minimum	Optimum	Maximum
Sedentary work	14	21	28
Light work	14	21	28
Medium work	28	35	Indefinite
Heavy work	84	112	Indefinite
Very Heavy work	84	112	Indefinite

Surgical treatment. (Prophylaxis - vena cava interruption, open surgery).

Duration in Days

Job Classification	Minimum	Optimum	Maximum
Sedentary work	28	35	42
Light work	28	35	42
Medium work	42	49	Indefinite
Heavy work	84	112	Indefinite
Very Heavy work	84	112	Indefinite

Surgical treatment (pulmonary embolectomy).

Duration in Days

Job Classification	Minimum	Optimum	Maximum
Sedentary work	42	56	112
Light work	42	56	112
Medium work	56	70	Indefinite
Heavy work	56	84	Indefinite
Very Heavy work	56	112	Indefinite

Failure to Recover

If an individual fails to recover within the maximum duration expectancy period, the reader may wish to reference the following questions to assist in better understanding the specifics of an individual's medical case.

Regarding diagnosis:

- Does the individual have chest pain with shortness of breath, cough, and coughing of blood? Is the individual cyanotic?
- Does the individual have risk factors such as prolonged bed rest or inactivity, surgery, femur or pelvic trauma, central vein catheters, cancer, endocarditis, childbirth, stroke, congestive heart failure, frequent air travel, or obesity?
- Does the individual have a proximal deep vein thrombosis?
- On exam did the individual have a rapid pulse, breathlessness, fainting and collapse?
- Did the individual have a low-grade fever, cyanosis, abnormal lung sounds, and wheezing? Does the individual have cold, clammy skin, weak pulse, and low blood pressure?
- Has the individual had a chest x-ray, electrocardiogram, lung scan, and arterial blood gases? Did the individual have a pulmonary angiogram, CT scan or MRI?
- Have conditions with similar symptoms been ruled out?

Regarding treatment:

- Is the individual being treated with oxygen, anticoagulants, morphine, and fluids?
- Was it necessary to use thrombolytics?
- Did it become necessary to perform surgery?

Regarding prognosis:

- Is the individual's employer able to accommodate any necessary restrictions?
- Does the individual have any conditions that may affect ability to recover?
- Does the individual have any complications such as atelectasis, pulmonary hypertension, shock due to low cardiac output, cardiopulmonary arrest, infection, or lung infarction?

References

Clochesy, John M., et al, eds. Critical Care Nursing, 2nd ed. Philadelphia: W.B. Saunders Company, 1996.

Tierney, Lawrence M., Stephen J. McPhee, and Maxine A. Papadkis, eds. Current Medical Diagnosis and Treatment 2000. New York: Lange Medical Books/McGraw-Hill, 2000.

Emphysema

Other names / synonyms: Chronic Obstructive Lung Disease, Pulmonary Emphysema

492, 492.0, 492.8

Definition

Emphysema is a type of chronic obstructive pulmonary disease (COPD) that primarily affects the air-exchanging spaces (alveoli) of the lungs. There is destruction of the walls of the alveoli leading to enlarged irregularly shaped air spaces that are very inefficient in exchanging and absorbing oxygen. The small airways also collapse on breathing out, resulting in airflow obstruction and with air becoming trapped in the lungs.

Emphysema is most often caused by chronic exposure to inhaled noxious gases. Cigarette smoking is the number one cause. Of course, not all smokers develop emphysema, but there is no test that can predict what smokers are most likely to develop the disease.

Individuals with emphysema usually also have some degree of chronic obstructive bronchitis or chronic asthmatic bronchitis. These three diseases combined represent the fourth leading cause of death in the US. Emphysema is generally diagnosed between the ages of 55 and 65.

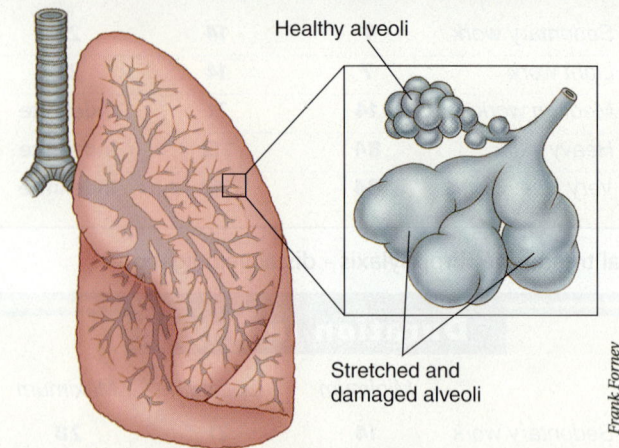

In addition to the majority of individuals whose emphysema is smoke-related, an estimated 100,000 Americans have an inherited form called alpha 1-antitryspin (AAT) deficiency-related emphysema. This type of emphysema is caused by an inherited gene mutation that results in a lack of the protective protein AAT. Under normal conditions, ATT shields the lungs from a natural enzyme called neutrophil elastase that helps fight bacteria and clean up dead lung tissue. Unless this enzyme is neutralized by AAT, it can also eventually damage lung tissue. Since individuals with inherited ATT deficiency lack sufficient ATT to neutralize neutrophil elastase, enzyme-related damage can rapidly lead to emphysema. In individuals with the inherited form of emphysema, lung damage can appear as early as age 30. This is decades sooner than the normal onset of emphysema in those whose illness is linked to smoking. Smoking is believed to cause emphysema in part because tobacco smoking inactivates AAT.

About 2 million Americans currently have emphysema. It is considered to be the most common cause of death from respiratory disease in the US. Most individuals (61%) with emphysema are cigarette-smoking males older than age 40 living in areas where pollution is a constant problem. However, the prevalence rate in women has recently increased by 11%.

Diagnosis

History: The individual complains of shortness of breath (dyspnea) that has worsened slowly over a long period of time, occurring with less and less exertion. In severe cases, it may be present even at rest. Chronic cough, wheezing, and recurrent lung infections may also be seen.

Physical exam: A physical examination shows decreased breath sounds with or without wheezing, abnormal breath sounds (rales), and prolonged exhalation (exhalation takes more than twice as long as inhalation). There may be an increased front-to-back diameter of the chest (barrel-shaped chest). There may be signs of chronic sleep deprivation or signs of chronically insufficient oxygen levels in the blood. Early in the disease, the chest may appear normal with only occasional wheezes or coarse breath sounds (rhonchi). As emphysema advances, the breath sounds become quite diminished. The individual may have labored breathing at rest or with minimal exertion.

Tests: Chest x-ray reveals an expanded chest and a decrease in the normal lung markings. Large air spaces (blebs or bullae) may also be identified in advanced stages. The most accurate diagnosis of emphysema is with pulmonary function tests (PFTs) that measure the severity of airflow obstruction. Blood tests may be done to measure the amount of oxygen and carbon dioxide in the blood. Other blood tests are used to check for low AAT levels, especially in a nonsmoker or young person who shows symptoms of emphysema. Measurement of blood oxygen content is nearly normal unless the individual is in respiratory failure. It is unusual for an individual to have pure emphysema without any clinical symptoms or pathology of asthma or bronchitis. A small amount of mucus may be collected and tested for respiratory infection. An exercise stress test may be done to determine a safe exercise level with or without the need for extra oxygen.

Treatment

No treatment can reverse or stop the course of emphysema but steps can be taken to relieve symptoms, treat complications, and minimize disability. The single critical factor for maintaining healthy lungs is the cessation of smoking. This is most effective at the early stages of emphysema but can also slow down the rate of decline of lung function in later stages.

Bronchodilators are prescribed if the airway obstruction is partially reversible, as demonstrated during pulmonary function testing. Steroids may also be prescribed if they are measurably helpful in decreasing airway obstruction. Supplemental oxygen therapy is used if the blood oxygen levels are below normal while at rest, or during exercise or sleep.

Vaccination against pneumococcal pneumonia and influenza is recommended due to the prolonged recovery time of individuals with emphysema from any type of lung infection. It is important that the individual be educated about the disease, how to conserve energy, how to avoid and recognize pulmonary infection, and how to breathe properly during exertion or severe dyspnea.

In certain individuals, surgical removal of large air spaces (bullae) may improve function of the remaining lung. Lung reduction surgery is a new treatment option. A lung transplant may be considered in severe cases. In individuals whose emphysema is caused by alpha 1-antitrypsin deficiency, intravenous administration of alpha-1 antitrypsin concentrate may slow down degeneration of lung function. Individuals with severe emphysema are cautioned to avoid high altitudes (over 4,000 feet) and to consider dry, pollution-free environments in which to live and work. They are also cautioned prior to air travel and special arrangements may be needed to determine and/or obtain oxygen during the flight.

Prognosis

Survival rates depend on the degree of airway obstruction. There is no cure for emphysema but this chronic condition can be treated and controlled. Individuals who follow treatment instructions and adopt good health habits can enjoy a fairly normal lifestyle for a long time. Even individuals whose emphysema is severe (those with a significant decrease in airflow rates and increased levels of carbon dioxide in the blood) have a good chance of surviving for 5 years or more. Unfortunately, in those individuals with emphysema who continue to smoke, research indicates that smoking dramatically increases the severity of the illness and may reduce life span by 10 years or more. Individuals with emphysema who live at high altitudes have a shorter survival.

When a lung transplant is successful, the individual is expected to regain normal life activities.

Differential Diagnosis

Asthma and chronic bronchitis can coexist with emphysema. Other disorders that cause shortness of breath are a lung tumor, pulmonary embolus, pneumonia, heart failure, and occupational lung diseases such as silicosis.

Specialists

- Internist
- Pulmonologist

Rehabilitation

Pulmonary rehabilitation combines exercise training and behavioral and educational programs designed to help individuals with emphysema control symptoms and improve day-to-day activities. It is a team approach. Individuals work closely with their doctors, nurses, psychologists, exercise specialists, dietitians, and respiratory, physical, and occupational therapists. The main goals of pulmonary rehabilitation are to help individuals improve their day-to-day lives and restore the ability to function independently. Pulmonary rehabilitation can help reduce the number and length of hospital stays and increases the chances of living longer.

Pulmonary rehabilitation involves exercise training of the lower body, upper body, and ventilatory muscle training. It also includes psychosocial support and educational programs.

Since smoking is known to be the primary risk factor for the onset of emphysema, many pulmonary rehabilitation programs provide educational sessions and counseling to help individuals stop smoking.

Work Restrictions / Accommodations

Individuals need to stay away from inhaled irritants and extremes of air temperatures in the work environment. The amount of physical work they can do depends on their lung function. Individuals wearing continuous oxygen must work in areas where there is no danger of explosion from the gas or open flames or sparks. Individuals must not work in areas that require respirator use.

The ideal work environment for individuals with emphysema is a dry atmosphere, free of pollution.

Comorbid Conditions

Pre-existing lung cancer, asthma, and allergies may worsen the effects of emphysema.

Complications

Enlargement and strain on the right side of the heart (cor pulmonale) may occur. Recurrent respiratory infections and pulmonary hypertension may be complications as well.

Factors Influencing Duration

The severity of the disease, age of the individual, presence and severity of complications, compliance with treatment, other chronic medical conditions (especially heart disease), and alpha-1 antitrypsin deficiency all affect the disability. Age, physical condition, and smoking influence progression of the disease and affect the likelihood of permanent disability.

Length of Disability

Disability may be permanent. Contact physician to obtain additional information.

Failure to Recover

If an individual fails to recover within the maximum duration expectancy period, the reader may wish to reference the following questions to assist in better understanding the specifics of an individual's medical case.

Regarding diagnosis:

- How old is individual?
- Is individual a smoker?
- Does individual have alpha 1-antitryspin (AAT) deficiency-related emphysema?
- Does individual have chronic obstructive bronchitis or chronic asthmatic bronchitis?
- Does individual complain of dyspnea that has worsened slowly over a long period of time and occurs with less and less exertion? Is it present at rest?
- Does individual report chronic cough, wheezing, and recurrent lung infections?
- On physical exam, does individual have decreased breath sounds, wheezing, rales, rhonchi, and prolonged exhalation? Does the chest appear enlarged on the right side? Does individual have a barrel-shaped chest?
- Does individual show signs of chronic sleep deprivation or insufficient oxygen levels?

- Has individual had a chest x-ray, pulmonary function testing, arterial blood gasses, AAT levels, cultures, and an exercise stress test?
- Were conditions with similar symptoms ruled out?

Regarding treatment:

- Is individual compliant with smoking cessation?
- Is individual being treated with bronchodilators, steroids, and oxygen therapy?
- If necessary, is individual receiving supplemental AAT?
- Has individual received vaccinations against pneumococcal pneumonia and influenza? Has individual been educated about the disease, how to conserve energy, how to avoid and recognize pulmonary infection, and how to breathe properly during exertion or severe dyspnea?
- Was surgery necessary?
- Does individual live and work in a dry, pollution free, low elevation environment?

Regarding prognosis:

- Is individual active in pulmonary rehabilitation? Is a home exercise program in place?
- Can individual's employer accommodate any necessary restrictions?
- Does individual have any conditions that may affect ability to recover?
- Have any complications developed such as cor pulmonale, recurrent respiratory infections, or pulmonary hypertension?

References

"Emphysema." Health Central, Inc. 07 Dec 2000 <http://www.healthcentral.com/mhc/top/000136.cfm>.

Kleinschmidt, Paul. "Chronic Obstructive Pulmonary Disease and Emphysema." eMedicine.com. 22 Feb 2001. 24 Feb 2001. <http://emedicine.com/emerg/topic99.htm>.

Empyema

Other names / synonyms: Pleural Abscess
510, 510.0, 510.9

Definition

Empyema is an accumulation of pus in the space between the lung and the membrane that surrounds it (pleural space). This pus contains white blood cells that fight infection (polymorphonuclear leukocytes) and blood proteins involved in clotting (fibrin). When pus builds up in the pleural space, it puts pressure on the lungs and results in shortness of breath and pain. As fibrin is laid down, it separates the pleural fluid into tiny pockets (loculation). Formation of scar tissue can entrap sections of lung and cause permanent lung damage.

Empyema is usually a complication of a lung infection (pneumonia) or a localized pocket of pus (abscess) in the lung. It may also result from an infection after chest surgery (postoperative infection), a traumatic penetrating chest injury, or a medical procedure that invades the chest such as thoracentesis or insertion of a chest tube. Pus from an abscess in the abdomen just beneath the lungs (subphrenic abscess) may also spread to the pleural space and result in empyema. Empyema can occur as a complication of many other conditions including septicemia, septic thrombophlebitis, spontaneous pneumothorax, mediastinitis, or esophageal rupture.

Risk factors for empyema include a recent history of pneumonia. Conditions that predispose to empyema include congestive heart failure, nephrotic syndrome, or cancer that invades the lymphatic drainage system of the chest.

Empyema tends to occur more frequently in the winter and the spring. It is found in 1 out of 10,000 individuals and is more common in the elderly than younger individuals. Men and women are equally affected and race is not a risk factor for this condition.

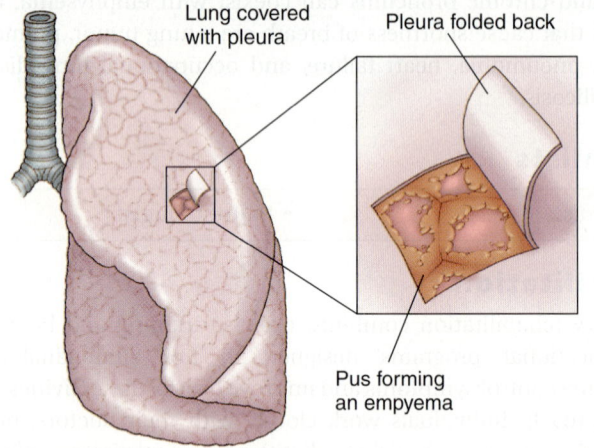

Diagnosis

History: In most cases, the individual reports a current or recent bout with pneumonia or a lung abscess. Chest pain is often reported and may be described as sharp pain that worsens when inhaling, coughing, or sneezing. Other common symptoms include cough, difficulty breathing (dyspnea), chills, night sweats, a general feeling of illness (malaise), loss of appetite (anorexia), and unintended weight loss.

Physical exam: Individual usually has a mild to moderate fever, rarely in excess of 102 degrees F. Rapid, shallow breathing may be noted when the individual tries to avoid deep breaths. Listening to the chest with a stethoscope reveals decreased breath sounds, wheezing, and a creaky sound in the chest. Asking the individual to speak while listening to the lungs may reveal a characteristic sound called egophony. Tenderness to pressure over the chest wall may occur. The breath may have a foul odor.

Tests: A standard chest x-ray may or may not be helpful and can appear normal if only a small volume of pus is present. X-ray taken with the individual lying on the side can detect a smaller effusion. Extensive pneumonia can obscure the empyema. It may be difficult to recognize a localized empyema.

A blood test often reveals an abnormally high level of white blood cells.

A definite diagnosis of empyema can only be made through obtaining a sample of pleural fluid, examining it microscopically, and culturing it. The fluid can be drawn out through a needle (thoracentesis) or during the insertion of a chest tube for drainage (thoracostomy). Ultrasonography and/or CT can also play a role in monitoring and treating empyema. If the amount of fluid seen on x-ray is small, the physician may elect to monitor the accumulation over time before undertaking an invasive diagnostic procedure.

Treatment

Empyema is usually treated on an inpatient basis with intravenous antibiotics for the underlying infection. Prompt drainage of the accumulated pus is important. While removal of pus with a needle (thoracentesis) can provide immediate relief, fluid usually reaccumulates quickly. Insertion of a chest tube (thoracostomy) allows continuous drainage of fluid. The individual's breathing (respiratory) status is monitored closely so respiratory assistance can be provided, as needed. Pain medication (analgesics) may be prescribed, if needed. If the pleural fluid collections are separated into smaller areas because of fibrin deposition (loculated), a medication to break up the fibrin such as urokinase may be instilled into the chest cavity.

An empyema may require many weeks to resolve. Once the underlying infection is controlled and the respiratory status is stable, individuals can be discharged from the hospital with a chest tube and drainage bag in place.

Prognosis

Outcome for empyema varies significantly depending on the underlying cause, promptness of treatment, and severity of individual's symptoms. In most cases, antibiotic therapy and prompt, continuous drainage of fluid provides complete recovery without permanent damage to the lungs. However, full recovery may require several weeks of hospitalization and several weeks of at-home recovery.

Elderly individuals are at an increased risk of developing complications. Complications are associated with a longer recovery and the possibility of a poor outcome. In rare, cases, death may occur.

Differential Diagnosis

The symptoms of empyema are often difficult to distinguish from those of the underlying infection. The pleural fluid may not be infected or it may be a collection of blood (hemothorax) or lymph (chylothorax). Many conditions can lead to an abnormal build-up of pleural fluid including cancer, rheumatoid arthritis, sarcoidosis, congestive heart failure, kidney failure, pulmonary embolism, or inflammatory disease.

Specialists

- General Surgeon
- Infectious Disease Physician
- Pulmonologist
- Thoracic Surgeon

Work Restrictions / Accommodations

Work restrictions are very individualized and affected by the individual's course of recovery and any complications. Prolonged sick leave is necessary for recovery. Upon return to work, flexibility in the work schedule may be needed to accommodate frequent check-up visits to the physician or rest breaks, as needed. Heavy lifting and physically demanding jobs may be limited. Frequent breaks may be necessary until lung function returns to normal.

Complementary and Alternative Therapies

Content is intended for awareness only. Treatments may or may not be effective. Scientific evidence may be lacking and some substances have potentially toxic effects. Dr. Presley Reed and the editors do not endorse the use of these therapies in the absence of consultation with a licensed medical professional.

Beta-carotene -	Antioxidant that may shield lung against damage.
Echinacea -	Said to boost immune system function.
English plantain -	May act as a cough suppressant and have an antibacterial effect.
Magnesium -	May help decrease risk of respiratory diseases.
Marsh mallow -	Said to have an anti-inflammatory effect.
Mullein -	Said to have an antibacterial effect.
Selenium -	May act as an antioxidant that shields lung against damage.
Soapwort -	Contains saponins, which may have anti-inflammatory properties.
Vitamin C -	May reduce the risk of wheezing and improve lung capacity.
Vitamin E -	May act as an antioxidant that shields lung against damage.

Comorbid Conditions

Individuals who smoke or are obese may take longer to recover. Suppressed or compromised immune system, chronic lung disease such as emphysema, or diabetes may lead to more severe symptoms and a longer recovery period.

Complications

Pus can become walled off into pockets (loculated), making it harder to treat. The empyema may be resistant to multiple antibiotics that make treatment more difficult and prolonged. Air can enter into the pleural space (pneumothorax) and scarring of the lungs (pulmonary fibrosis) can occur.

If left untreated, an erosion can occur between the breathing passages (bronchial tree) and the pleural space (bronchopleural fistula) or between the pleural space and the skin (empyema necessitatis). Respiratory failure and septic shock are extreme complications that can result in death.

Factors Influencing Duration

Factors influencing duration of disability include age, response to treatment, cause of empyema, presence of any complications, and type of work the individual is expected to perform. Individuals with sedentary positions usually have a shorter disability period. Conversely, individuals who perform heavy work or whose jobs are physically demanding have a longer period of disability.

Length of Disability

Disability is longer for those who perform heavy or physically demanding work. In rare cases, death can occur.

With drainage by thoracostomy tube.

Duration in Days

Job Classification	Minimum	Optimum	Maximum
Sedentary work	7	14	28
Light work	7	14	28
Medium work	7	21	42
Heavy work	14	21	42
Very Heavy work	14	21	42

Failure to Recover

If an individual fails to recover within the maximum duration expectancy period, the reader may wish to reference the following questions to assist in better understanding the specifics of an individual's medical case.

Regarding diagnosis:

- Has individual had recent pneumonia or a lung abscess?
- Has individual undergone recent chest surgery, insertion of a chest tube, or thoracentesis?
- Experienced recent trauma to the chest from a penetrating injury?
- Has individual had septicemia, mediastinitis, or esophageal rupture?
- Does individual report sharp chest pain that worsens on inhaling, coughing, or sneezing? Does individual have difficulty breathing (dyspnea), chills, night sweats, a general feeling of illness (malaise), loss of appetite (anorexia), and unintended weight loss?
- Was a sample of pleural fluid taken for exam and culture and for definitive diagnosis?
- Was a chest x-ray, ultrasound, and/or CT required?
- Was the diagnosis of empyema confirmed?
- What is the underlying cause of the infection?

Regarding treatment:

- Was individual hospitalized to receive intravenous antibiotics and for drainage of the accumulated pus?
- Was insertion of a chest tube (thoracostomy) done to allow for continuous drainage?
- If fibrin deposits are involved, did individual receive medication to dissolve the fibrin deposits (thrombolytics)?
- Did individual receive pain medication (analgesics)?
- Were chest tubes and drainage bags left in place when individual was discharged from the hospital?
- Was individual compliant with the treatment regimen including medications, at-home care, and follow-up examinations?

Regarding prognosis:

- Was the underlying cause promptly identified and treated?
- Was antibiotic therapy specific for the organism causing the infection?
- Was individual allowed several weeks of at-home recovery?
- Has individual complied with all medical instructions?
- Did individual develop a pneumothorax?
- Has lung scarring (pulmonary fibrosis) occurred?
- Have complications developed such as loculation, bronchopleural fistula, or sepsis that could lengthen disability?
- Does individual have underlying illnesses such as immune suppression or chronic lung disease that may affect recovery?

References

"Empyema." Adam.com. 1998. 12 Dec 2000 <http://www.healthcentral.com/mhc/top/000123.cfm>.

Staton, Gerald, and Roland Ingram. "Disorders of the Pleura, Hila and Mediastinum." Respiratory Medicine. Dale, D.C., and Daniel D. Federman, MD, eds. New York: WebMD Corporation, 2000 Scientific American Medicine. 14 Dec 2000 <http://www.samed.com/sam/forms/index.htm>.

Encephalitis

Other names / synonyms: Cerebritis, Encephalomyelitis, Equine Encephalitis

323, 323.5, 323.6, 323.8, 323.9

Definition

Encephalitis is an acute inflammatory disease of the brain usually caused by a mosquito-borne or, in some areas, a tick-borne virus. Other means of virus transmission include ingestion of infected goat's milk and accidental injection or inhalation of the virus.

In urban areas where mosquitoes are less prevalent, the disease is more commonly caused by a group of viruses called enteroviruses, i.e., those that multiply primarily in the intestinal tract. An increasing number of cases are caused by infection with the human immunodeficiency virus (HIV). Encephalitis can also occur as a secondary complication following viral infections such as measles, chickenpox, rubella, and mumps. Sporadic encephalitis is most commonly due to the herpes simplex virus.

Encephalitis can be a serious, life-threatening medical condition but can also be so mild that it is barely noticeable. Specific prevalence and incidence statistics are unknown, but the condition seems to occur more frequently in individuals with immune systems not functioning at optimum levels (immunosuppressed), and in areas where virus-carrying insects are prevalent.

Encephalitis is found throughout the Western Hemisphere, predominantly in the eastern regions of North, Central, and South America and throughout the US. It is impossible to determine true incidence, since reporting policies are not standardized or rigorously enforced. In the US, several thousand cases of viral encephalitis are reported yearly to the Centers for Disease Control (CDC). This is probably a fraction of the actual number. Herpes simplex encephalitis (HSE), the most common cause of sporadic encephalitis in western countries, is relatively rare, with an overall incidence of 0.2 per 100,000. Japanese virus encephalitis (JE), occurring principally in Japan, Southeast Asia, China, and India, is the most common viral encephalitis outside the US.

In 1999, a late summer outbreak of West Nile encephalitis, an arbovirus not previously found in the US, was implicated in several deaths in New York.

Diagnosis

History: The initial symptoms are a vague feeling of discomfort or illness (malaise), fever, headache, loss of appetite (anorexia), and nausea, and next progresses to a subtle change of personality and confusion. In later stages, mental disturbances become more apparent and there may be difficulty talking (dysphasia), weakness, seizures, severe disorientation, and coma. In secondary viral encephalitis, the disease may develop 5 to 10 days after onset of an initial viral infection such as mumps, measles, or chickenpox. The individual may be from or traveled to a region where mosquitoes and/or ticks were prevalent and had recently been bitten. Individuals may complain of a recent viral infection such as measles, mumps, or chickenpox. They may also complain of a back or neck ache.

Physical exam: There is evidence of fever, stiff neck and back, tremors, convulsions, seizures, paralysis of extremities, abnormal walk (gait), and abnormal reflex reactions. Deep loss of consciousness (coma) may occur and last for days or weeks.

Tests: A lumbar puncture collects spinal fluid for analysis and may reveal increased pressure of the cerebrospinal fluid as well as increased protein content and cell count (usually lymphocytes). A CT or MRI of the brain may detect lesions in the lobes of the brain near the temple and ear (temporal lobe lesions) caused by a herpes viral infection. Measuring the electrical activity of the brain by electroencephalography (EEG) is also useful to diagnose a herpes virus encephalitis, but a sample of brain tissue collected for microscopic examination (brain biopsy) is usually necessary to confirm this diagnosis and exclude other treatable diseases. Occasionally, taking a sample of the individual's blood during the disease and comparing it with a sample after the disease has resolved (acute and convalescent antibody titers) may be the only way of making a specific diagnosis of a viral infection.

Treatment

Treatment of all forms of encephalitis other than herpes encephalitis is entirely supportive. Supportive measures are used to maintain the individual's hydration, electrolyte balance, and nutritional needs. Supportive treatment includes fluids, nutrients, and electrolytes given intravenously. In otherwise stable individuals, elevating the head and monitoring the neurologic status are supportive measures. Medication may be needed to reduce fever (antipyretics), intracranial pressure, and inflammation (glucocorticoids), and to prevent seizures (anticonvulsants). Pain medication (analgesic) is given to reduce headache.

When more aggressive treatment is indicated, the use of diuresis may be recommended, provided that the circulatory volume is protected.

An antiviral medication (acyclovir) specific to treating herpes simplex viral infections is effective only against herpes encephalitis.

Prognosis

Overall, 10% of individuals with encephalitis die. In mild cases, full recovery occurs within 2 to 3 weeks. Encephalitis caused by eastern equine and herpes simplex viruses is associated with severe disease and high mortality rates. Severe cases usually require hospitalization and leave significant mental impairment including memory loss, the inability to speak coherently, lack of muscle coordination, paralysis, and hearing or vision defects. Individuals under the age of 30 and those only lethargic at the onset of treatment are more likely to survive than individuals who are older or comatose.

Differential Diagnosis

Conditions with similar symptoms include meningitis, cerebral abscess, septic emboli, cortical septic thrombophlebitis, toxic encephalopathies, subdural and subarachnoid hemorrhage, porphyria, and multiple sclerosis.

Specialists

- Infectious Disease Physician
- Neurologist

Rehabilitation

Individuals with encephalitis may require physical, occupational, and speech therapy depending on the impairments. Individuals with encephalitis may present with lack of muscle coordination, decreased balance, paralysis, hearing and vision deficits, and an inability to speak coherently. The frequency and duration should be determined by the severity of impairments.

Individuals may have impaired coordination with encephalitis. Individuals perform fine motor coordination exercises in occupational therapy such as picking up pegs and placing them in a pegboard, or they may work on practical coordination exercises such as fastening buttons or practicing their signatures. Individuals work on gross motor coordination in physical therapy such as kicking a soccer ball rolled toward them or throwing beanbags at a target.

Individuals practice sitting and standing balance in physical and occupational therapy. For example, occupational therapists may work on dynamic sitting balance to promote dressing and grooming abilities. Sitting balance can be improved by having an individual sit on a therapy ball and attempt to reach for objects placed at various distances. Physical therapists may focus on standing balance to preserve the ability to walk. Individuals may perform exercises in a set of parallel bars such as walking heel-to-toe to help improve standing balance.

Individuals who present with paralysis also require physical and occupational therapy. Both disciplines instruct caregivers about stretching programs for the arms and legs in order to maintain adequate flexibility. Occupational therapists instruct individuals in self-care strategies such as dressing and bathing, and may order adaptive equipment such as a tub seat to make tasks easier. Occupational therapists also instruct individuals in methods to make self-care easier. For example, individuals can wear clothing fastened with Velcro instead of buttons. Physical therapists instruct individuals in gross motor skills such as getting in and out of bed and transitioning from sitting to standing. Physical therapy also addresses walking, and individuals learn to walk using crutches or leg braces, where appropriate.

Individuals with decreased vision may require occupational or physical therapists to make a home safety assessment. Therapists can identify tripping hazards such as throw rugs or partially obstructed doorways, and can assist in rearranging the layout of rooms to increase safety. Physical therapists can instruct individuals on how to use a cane to help them negotiate stairs.

Individuals who present with the inability to speak coherently or with difficulty hearing may require speech therapy.

Work Restrictions / Accommodations

Restrictions or accommodations need consideration on an individual basis since the severity and complications of encephalitis are variable. If there are lingering speech and motor/coordination problems, job duties may need to be reassessed depending on the nature of the job. Responsibilities requiring significant amounts of public speaking may be in jeopardy if there is permanent speech impairment. Jobs requiring a great deal of mobility and physical labor may also need to be reassessed.

Comorbid Conditions

Coexisting infections may influence length of disability as well as AIDS and other immunosuppressed conditions.

Complications

Possible complications include seizures, brain damage that causes loss of sensation, coordination, and power in specific areas of the body, and/or speech difficulties, and death. The membranes that cover and enclose the brain (meninges) may also be involved, and these membranes may become inflamed (meningoencephalitis).

Factors Influencing Duration

The severity of the inflammation and symptoms, involvement of other nervous system structures, the individual's response to treatment, the presence of complications, and any permanent brain damage may influence length of disability.

Length of Disability

Length of disability will depend on job requirements, response to treatment, and presence and severity of any cognitive impairment. Disability may be permanent if mobility, coordination, and strength are affected and the individual's job requires significant manual labor. Job duties that require significant communication skills may be in jeopardy if speech is affected.

Failure to Recover

If an individual fails to recover within the maximum duration expectancy period, the reader may wish to reference the following questions to assist in better understanding the specifics of an individual's medical case.

Regarding diagnosis:

- Has individual recently been exposed to mosquitoes or ticks? Ingested goat's milk?
- Does individual have a history of intestinal tract infection (enterovirus)?
- Is individual human immunodeficiency virus (HIV)-positive? Immunosuppressed with any other condition?
- Has individual recently had measles, chickenpox, rubella, or mumps? Is individual infected with herpes simplex virus (HSV)?
- Is there a vague feeling of discomfort or illness (malaise), fever, headache, loss of appetite (anorexia), and nausea? Does individual report a stiff neck and back?
- Is there a change of personality and confusion? Does individual have more apparent mental disturbances, difficulty talking (dysphasia), weakness, seizures, or severe disorientation that suggests later stage disease?
- Was lumbar puncture done to collect spinal fluid? Were CT, MRI of the brain, or electroencephalography (EEG) performed? Was a brain biopsy required?
- Was a diagnosis of encephalitis confirmed?

Regarding treatment:

- For herpes encephalitis, did individual receive antiviral medication? Was the medication effective?
- For other forms of encephalitis, did individual receive supportive treatment including fluids, nutrients, and electrolytes given intravenously?

- Were medications administered to reduce fever (antipyretics), intracranial pressure, and inflammation (glucocorticoids)? To prevent seizures (anticonvulsants) and relieve pain (analgesics)?
- Did individual require aggressive treatment to eliminate excess fluid (diuresis)? If used, was diuresis effective?

Regarding prognosis:
- What was the cause and severity of the disease? If severe, did individual lose memory, ability to speak coherently, or muscle coordination?
- Is individual paralyzed?
- Are hearing or vision deficits present?
- Have seizures occurred?
- Have the membranes that enclose the brain (meninges) also been involved (meningoencephalitis)?
- How significantly is individual impaired? How will these impairments affect individual's daily activities?

References

Handbook of Diseases. Holmes, H., Nancy, ed Springhouse, NJ: Springhouse Corporation, 2000.

Lister, Marilyn J., ed. Contemporary Management of Motor Control Problems. Fairfax: Foundation for Physical Therapy, 1991.

Encephalopathy
348.3, 348.5

Definition

Encephalopathy refers to an abnormal condition of the structure or function of brain tissues (specifically degenerative conditions) that can result in inflammation and hemorrhaging. Encephalopathy may be caused by chronic conditions such as liver disease, viral or bacterial infections, high blood pressure, metabolic or nutritional diseases, and hereditary diseases. Some destructive conditions resulting in encephalopathy include long-term exposure to chemotherapeutic drugs or toxic chemicals and radiation therapy. It can be caused by repeated head trauma during boxing (boxer's encephalopathy) or develop during the final stage of a terminal illness.

The incidence of encephalopathy is difficult to assess due to its association with other conditions. Encephalopathy can occur at any age and may or may not be easily detected. It can resolve without treatment and without any lasting effects.

Diagnosis

History: Individuals may report associated symptoms of the various disease states associated with encephalopathy. If encephalopathy occurs independently of a pre-existing illness, symptoms may include seizures, decreased mental function, double vision, lack of muscular coordination, and tremors.

Physical exam: Findings include sensory impairment, loss of muscle tone, abnormal reflexes, failure of muscle coordination (ataxia), and involuntary movements.

Tests: Specific tests depend on the underlying condition causing inflammation of the brain (encephalitis). Blood tests and cultures can identify viral and bacterial infections, metabolic or nutritional deficiencies, and liver disease. CAT scan and MRI identify brain lesions, tumors, or other causes of brain dysfunction.

Treatment

Treatment depends on the cause of encephalopathy. If it is due to nutritional deficiency such as lack of a B vitamin (thiamine), then vitamin supplementation and an alteration in diet may be indicated. In the case of bacterial or viral infections, administering antibiotics may reduce toxins in the brain (cerebrotoxins). If encephalopathy is due to repeated head trauma (chronic or boxer's traumatic encephalopathy), no therapy is effective. In the presence of chronic disease such as associated with alcoholism (cirrhosis), treating the underlying illness and administering antibiotics will decrease the amount of cerebrotoxins and ammonia in the brain. A synthetic sugar (lactulose) can also be used in conjunction with antibiotics to enhance either the excretion or formation of ammonia.

Prognosis

In most cases, in the absence of a specific diagnosis, the outcome is unpredictable and related to the extent and progression or course of the underlying disease state. Serious encephalopathies may lead to necrosis of nerve cells in the brain causing retardation, cerebral palsy, or death. In advanced liver disease, hepatic encephalopathy may progress to deep coma (hepatic coma). Treating bacterial and viral infections with antibiotics can reduce cerebrotoxins and symptoms. In cases where treatment is started early, progression of the condition and damage to the brain may be minimized.

Differential Diagnosis

Encephalitis may be diagnosed alternatively in cases of an encephalopathy with inflammation.

Specialists

- Neurologist
- Neuropsychologist
- Occupational Therapist
- Physical Therapist
- Psychiatrist
- Psychologist
- Speech Therapist

Rehabilitation

If only minimal damage to the brain has occurred, the overall objective for rehabilitation is to quickly return the individual to normal activities. Rehabilitation may involve physical, occupational, and speech therapy, and/or cognitive retraining to help the individual achieve functional recovery and cope with any remaining disabilities.

Achieving goals is a common objective in rehabilitation of diseases affecting the brain. Goal setting is necessary for the effective use of time and resources when treating severe symptoms resulting from encephalopathy. An organized treatment approach from a team of healthcare professionals is necessary for a complete treatment program. Rehabilitation varies however, for each individual because of the uniqueness of the problems that result from the different areas of the brain affected.

If memory is affected, exercises are initiated that promote memory return and instruct the individual in carrying out simple tasks. This can be as simple as motivating individuals to receive an object in their hand or instructing them to move from a sitting to standing position.

The rehabilitation program sequences activities that progress from easy to more difficult such as teaching an individual how to get up from a chair to instruction in proper walking patterns. Once individuals regain their thinking processes, rehabilitation focuses on the needs of muscular strength, endurance, and flexibility. Muscle imbalance is corrected by using physical therapy techniques that help make the muscle and nervous system work together. Group activities may occur in mat classes, wheelchair classes, or in other activities such as volleyball games.

When appropriate, the final phase of rehabilitation following an episode of encephalopathy involves the individual's reinstatement to work. Both physical and mental exercises are directed toward work requirements. The physical therapist may need to modify the program for the various levels of encephalopathy.

Work Restrictions / Accommodations

If treatment of the underlying condition is successful and there is minimal brain damage from the encephalopathy, the individual may perform light work in a limited capacity if accommodations are made available. For example, an individual who recovers from a hepatic encephalopathy and has only mild mental dullness and confusion may be able to perform light work that requires simple mental ability. In these cases, the work environment should be quiet, safe, and accepting of individuals with a handicap.

Comorbid Conditions

Comorbid conditions include severe liver disease, viral and bacterial infections, metabolic brain disease, and severe hypoglycemia.

Complications

Complications are directly related to the disease causing the encephalopathy. Loss of nerve cells (neurons) in the brain can occur in some cases.

Factors Influencing Duration

The length of disability is influenced by the severity of the underlying disease and the residual outcome of the disease process.

Length of Disability

Return to modified duty may be possible in cases where prompt diagnosis is made and treatment is successful. Disability may be permanent.

Failure to Recover

If an individual fails to recover within the maximum duration expectancy period, the reader may wish to reference the following questions to assist in better understanding the specifics of an individual's medical case.

Regarding diagnosis:

- Does the individual have a history of liver disease, viral or bacterial infections, high blood pressure (hypertension), or metabolic or nutritional diseases?
- Has the individual had long-term exposure to chemotherapeutic drugs, toxic chemicals, or radiation therapy?
- Has the individual experienced repeated head trauma, such as with boxing?
- Is the individual in final stage of a terminal illness?
- Does the individual report symptoms associated with any of the above disease states?
- If not, does the individual complain of seizures, decreased mental function, double vision, lack of muscular coordination, and tremors?
- Were blood tests and cultures done to identify viral and bacterial infections, metabolic or nutritional deficiencies, or liver disease?
- Were computed tomography (CT scan) and magnetic resonance imaging (MRI) done to identify brain lesions, tumors, or other causes of brain dysfunction?
- Was the underlying disease diagnosed? If so, what is the underlying disease?
- Has the diagnosis of encephalopathy been confirmed?

Regarding treatment:

- If the disorder is caused by nutritional deficiency, were vitamin supplementation and an alteration in diet given?
- Was bacterial infection treated with antibiotics?
- Was drug treatment successful?
- Does the individual understand that if encephalopathy is due to repeated head trauma (chronic or boxer's traumatic encephalopathy) that no therapy is effective?
- If alcoholism with liver disease (cirrhosis) is present, were antibiotics administered to decrease the amount of cerebrotoxins and ammonia in the brain?
- Was lactulose also used in conjunction with antibiotics to enhance either the excretion or formation of ammonia?

Regarding prognosis:

- What is the extent of the underlying disease and how far has it progressed?
- Has the underlying condition responded to treatment? If not, what options are available?
- Was encephalopathy diagnosed and treated in its early stages?
- If antibiotics were used to treat infection, were they specific for the causative organism?
- Has serious encephalopathy led to necrosis of nerve cells in the brain causing retardation or cerebral palsy?
- Has hepatic encephalopathy progressed to deep coma (hepatic coma)?

References

Adams R.D., and Victor M. Ropper, AH. Principles of Neurology. New York: McGraw Hill, 1997.

Albers, J.W., et al. "Neurologic Evaluation of Workers Previously Diagnosed with Solvent-induced Toxic Encephalopathy." Journal of Occupational and Environmental Medicine 42 4 (2000): 410-423.

Rowland, Lewis P. Merritt's Textbook of Neurology, 8th ed. Philadelphia: Lea & Febiger, 1989.

Umphred, Darcy A. Neurological Rehabilitation. St. Louis: The C.V. Mosby Company, 1990.

Endarterectomy
38.1, 38.10, 38.16, 38.18

Definition

An endarterectomy is a surgical procedure performed to remove fatty deposits or plaque (secondary to atherosclerosis) from inside a blood vessel.

In atherosclerosis, fatty deposits (plaques) may accumulate within an artery and damage the arterial lining. Blood clots tend to form on the damaged lining and may eventually completely block (occlude) the vessel or break free and travel downstream or where until a smaller artery may become blocked.

These plaques often form within the arteries in the neck that provide blood flow to the brain, most frequently in the carotid artery (carotid artery stenosis). When a blood clot blocks the carotid artery, even temporarily, it interferes with blood flow and oxygen delivery (ischemia) to parts of the brain, causing brain tissue damage. At times the interruption of blood flow is temporary, causing fleeting neurological changes such as weakness, vision problems or fainting. The temporary interruption of blood flow to the brain is called a transient ischemic (without oxygen) attack (TIA).

Occasionally, similar plaque formations can cause sudden obstruction of blood flow in the artery under the clavicle (subclavian artery) or in the major artery of the upper thigh and groin (iliofemoral artery) causing ischemia to the arm or leg. An endarterectomy is sometimes used as an emergency measure to remove plaque from these arteries.

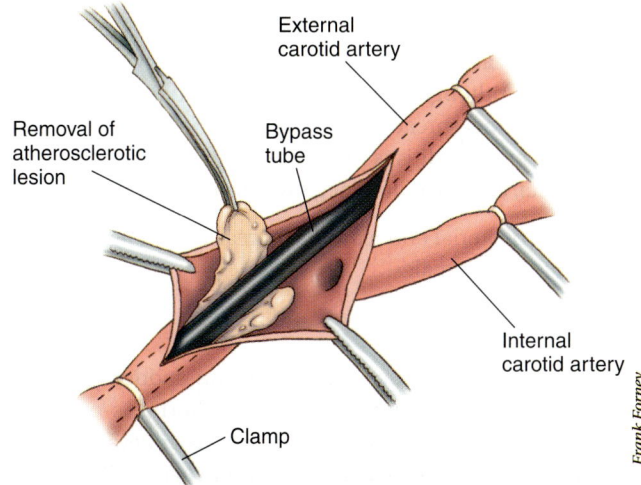

Reason for Procedure

This procedure is performed to improve blood flow to the brain. It is usually performed in individuals who have greater than 50% of their carotid artery blocked (stenosed) and are experiencing symptoms, such as transient weakness, vision problems or dizziness (transient ischemic attacks). By removing the plaque, normal blood flow to the brain is restored and the risk of a subsequent stroke is reduced. Occasionally, endarterectomy may be performed in the first few hours following a stroke. Once a stroke has completely evolved and brain ischemia is present, an endarterectomy is not recommended.

Though less common, an endarterectomy may be used to remove plaque and restore normal blood flow in other arteries such as the subclavian artery, femoral artery or the artery that supplies the gastrointestinal system (mesenteric artery).

Description

General anesthesia is used. The procedure begins with an incision in the neck to expose the carotid artery. Clamps are used to stop blood flow in that artery. The artery is opened and the plaque is lifted out. Any remaining fragments of plaque removed with a suction device. To minimize the risk of intraoperative stroke, electroencephalography (EEG) is used to monitor brain activity during the operation, allowing the physician to determine if circulation to the brain is adequate while the carotid artery is clamped. Artery closure may require patching with a synthetic material. Extreme caution must be used when restoring blood flow to prevent emboli.

The procedure is similar when done to remove plaque from other arteries, except there is no risk of stroke and therefore no need for electroencephalography monitoring.

Prognosis

When performed in good surgical candidates, the procedure is successful in removing the obstructing plaque and reduces the risk of stroke or death by as much as fifty percent. Usually, once the blood flow returns the neurological symptoms abate. The surgical mortality rate is low (less than 2%) and the risk of permanent neurological deficits (in carotid endarterectomies) is less than four percent.

Specialists

• Neurosurgeon	• Vascular Surgeon

Work Restrictions / Accommodations

Possible work restrictions and accommodations extended work leave for recuperation. Upon initial return to work individuals may need to temporarily avoid strenuous activities such as heavy lifting, pushing, or pulling. Employers may wish to consult with the individual's surgeon regarding appropriate timing for return to strenuous work.

Comorbid Conditions

Comorbid conditions of heart disease, chronic lung disease, bleeding disorders, or high blood pressure may impact ability to recover and further lengthen disability.

Procedure Complications

Due to careful continuous monitoring during the procedure, complications are minimized. However, any lengthy interruption of blood flow to the brain during the procedure may cause permanent brain damage (stroke). Other complications associated with endarterectomy include downstream occlusion of the artery by dislodged pieces of plaque (embolus), bleeding, high blood pressure (hypertension) or low blood pressure (hypotension).

Factors Influencing Duration

Factors that may influence the length of disability include the individual's age, the severity of the underlying disease, the location of the obstruction, whether a blood vessel graft is required, the presence of any pre-existing neurologic problems, and whether the individual has high blood pressure.

Length of Disability

Duration reflects recovery period for procedure only. Disability depends on underlying condition for which procedure is done, location of obstruction, and presence of complications.

Carotid artery.

Duration in Days

Job Classification	Minimum	Optimum	Maximum
Sedentary work	14	21	28
Light work	21	28	35
Medium work	28	35	42
Heavy work	42	49	56
Very Heavy work	42	49	56

References

Clochesy, John M., et al. Critical Care Nursing, 2nd ed. Philadelphia: W.B. Saunders Company, 1996.

Sabiston, David C., and H. Kim Lyerly. Textbook of Surgery, 15th ed. Philadelphia: W.B. Saunders Company, 1997.

Endocarditis, Bacterial

Other names / synonyms: Endocarditis, Infectious Endocarditis, SBE, Subacute Bacterial Endocarditis
421, 421.0, 421.9, 424.9

Definition

Bacterial endocarditis is an inflammation of the inner lining of the heart (endocardium) and particularly the heart valves due to infection. Infection may also occur at the site of a birth defect in which there is a hole between the left and right sides of the heart (septal defect), on the small tendons attached to the heart valves (chordae tendineae), or in the endocardium itself. Endocarditis may occur alone or as a complication of another disease. The infection can be caused by any number of microorganisms. It is classified as acute or sub-acute.

Bacterial endocarditis is seen most often when the endocardium has already been damaged by rheumatic heart disease, congenital heart disease, mitral valve prolapse, mitral valve insufficiency, or in individuals with prosthetic heart valves. Clots that have formed on the injured surfaces trap microorganisms entering the bloodstream. These microorganisms multiply rapidly, causing inflammation and further damage. Bacteria may enter the bloodstream during surgery, major dental treatment (especially tooth extraction), or exploratory procedures where a viewing tube is inserted into the body for diagnostic examination. Intravenous drug users are also at increased risk for bacterial endocarditis because of the possibility of introducing bacteria from a dirty syringe or unclean injection site directly into the blood stream.

Acute bacterial endocarditis refers to an inflammation with an abrupt onset. The infection progresses quickly and may destroy the heart valves, leading rapidly to progressive heart failure. In addition, clots attached to the damaged valves tend to break apart. These fragments of infected tissue are carried through the blood where they may block an artery (embolism) or spread infection to other parts of the body. Damage to valves and spread of the infection to other body areas occurs in a few days to several weeks. The staphylococci organism most often causes acute bacterial endocarditis. Sub-acute bacterial endocarditis refers to an inflammation that smolders undetected over several weeks to many months. Although it can cause serious damage to the heart valves, there is minimal spread to other areas of the body. The sub-acute form of bacterial endocarditis is most often caused by viridans streptococci, enterococci, and coagulase negative staphylococci organisms.

The incidence of bacterial endocarditis increases with age. Men have a higher incidence than females.

Diagnosis

History: Acute bacterial endocarditis comes on suddenly. Symptoms include high fever, severe chills, cough, and shortness of breath. In subacute bacterial endocarditis, the symptoms are general and nonspecific, such as fatigue, weakness, night sweats, or vague aches and pains. Fever may be low-grade, or absent in elderly and debilitated persons.

Physical exam: Fever, rapid or irregular heartbeat, and numerous small, flat, red to blue spots (petechiae) on the lining of the eye (conjunctiva), the arms and legs, and the mucous membranes of the mouth and throat may be evident upon exam. Dark, red, linear streaks (splinter hemorrhages) may be present in the nail beds, accompanied by small, raised, and tender blue or red areas in the pads of the fingers or toes (Osler's nodes). Exam may also reveal joint pain, muscle pain, and a heart murmur (new or changed).

Tests: Blood cultures are used both for diagnosis, sensitivity to antibiotics, and for following the response to therapy. Examination of tissue growth (vegetations) on the valves may also be done. Additional diagnostic laboratory tests include complete blood count (CBC), sedimentation rate, blood studies (serology), and urinalysis. Evaluation of the heart may include detecting abnormal valve function or heart disease with a procedure that uses sound waves to produce an image of the heart (echocardiogram), examining the electrical patterns of the heart through electrocardiogram (EKG), and via x-ray of blood vessels after injection with contrast medium (angiography).

Treatment

Treatment involves high doses of antibiotics given intravenously over a 4-6 week period. If infection has extensively damaged a heart valve, the valve may need to be surgically replaced with an artificial one (valve replacement). When an artificial heart valve that is already in place becomes infected, it must be replaced. Heart valve replacement often becomes an emergency procedure.

Prognosis

Most individuals recover completely. There is a mortality rate of 16-25%. The mortality rate increases with age, presence of underlying disease, development of congestive heart failure, or central nervous system complications. There is a 75-80% survival rate in individuals with prosthetic heart valves. Depending on the causative organism, relapses occur in 2-8% of individuals. Most relapses occur within 2 months after treatment.

Differential Diagnosis

Conditions with similar symptoms include acute rheumatic fever with carditis, periarteritis nodosa, poststreptococcal glomerulonephritis, and reaction to drugs.

Specialists

- Cardiologist
- Cardiovascular Surgeon
- Infectious Disease Physician
- Internist

Rehabilitation

Once the primary cause of bacterial endocarditis has been identified and treated, rehabilitation addresses weakness and functional deficits caused by the illness.

A physical therapist knowledgeable in cardiac rehabilitation will design an individualized exercise program considered safe for the individual's physical stamina; ECG monitoring of individuals is usually performed during the initial exercise sessions. Once the ECG demonstrates that the heart responds appropriately to exercise, individuals learn to self-monitor their pulse and to rate the amount of energy they expend by utilizing a rating of perceived exertion scale. This is a numbered scale that rates exercises from "very, very light" to "very, very hard." Individuals use this scale and their pulse to stay within safe exercise parameters that have been predetermined by their physicians.

Individuals perform aerobic exercise such as treadmill walking or stationary bicycling. The aerobic exercise helps the heart muscle improve its efficiency in the use of oxygen, which reduces the need for the heart to pump as much blood. This increased fitness level in turn reduces the total workload of the heart. The related increase in endurance enables individuals to resume their prior activity levels.

Occupational therapy addresses any fatigue or shortness of breath that may occur during activities of daily living. Individuals learn to utilize equipment such as a shower chair to decrease the energy expended during bathing, or a long-handled sponge to decrease the amount arm activity necessary for bathing (excessive arm activity is more taxing on the heart and can lead to fatigue). The physical and occupational therapists will also watch closely for any shortness of breath and rapid heartbeat, coughing up blood, and unexplained excessive weight loss. Because of the various degrees and effects resulting from of bacterial endocarditis, modifications are made for those individuals who are taking various medications or are experiencing other conditions resulting from the endocarditis.

When the individual has completely recovered from symptoms of bacterial endocarditis, individuals should participate in aerobic activity independently to promote continued cardiovascular endurance and strength.

Work Restrictions / Accommodations

Extended sick leave may be required. Individuals may need to be temporarily assigned to light or sedentary work until fully recovered.

Comorbid Conditions

Valvular disease, prosthetic valve replacement, previous bacterial endocarditis, complex congenital heart disease (i.e., transposition of the great vessels, tetralogy of Fallot), mitral valve prolapse, hypertrophic cardiomyopathy, drug addiction or any associated surgical procedures may lengthen disability.

Complications

Complications include blood vessels obstructed by fragments of tissue carried through the bloodstream (systemic emboli), tissue death in the spleen (splenic infarction), stroke, brain hemorrhage, valvular insufficiency, congestive heart failure, kidney failure, and thrombophlebitis. The emboli may also be infected, which can lead to overwhelming systemic infection (sepsis). Additionally, infection can extend into the heart muscle resulting in heart rhythm disturbances.

Factors Influencing Duration

Length of disability may be influenced by the site of infection, method of treatment, presence of significant underlying medical conditions, the particular organism causing the infection, the individual's response to treatment, presence of complications, and the individual's job requirements.

Length of Disability

Duration depends on cause. Infections caused by the organisms viridans streptococci, enterococci, or coagulase-negative staphylococci usually resolve on the average of 3-5 days of treatment. However, those infected by Staphylococcus Aureus or Pseudomonas Aeruginosa may have fevers and signs of infection that persist for 9-12 days. Fevers that persist beyond these ranges may be indicative of other superimposed infectious processes such as myocardial abscess or nosocomial infection. Relapses of bacterial endocarditis may occur within 1-2 months after completion of medical treatment.

If valve replacement surgery is required, the length of disability will be extended and may be permanent. Individual is anticoagulated.

Medical treatment.

Duration in Days

Job Classification	Minimum	Optimum	Maximum
Sedentary work	7	28	42
Light work	7	28	42
Medium work	14	42	56
Heavy work	21	56	70
Very Heavy work	21	56	70

Surgical treatment (heart valve replacement).

Duration in Days

Job Classification	Minimum	Optimum	Maximum
Sedentary work	28	42	56
Light work	28	42	56
Medium work	56	70	84
Heavy work	Indefinite	Indefinite	Indefinite
Very Heavy work	Indefinite	Indefinite	Indefinite

Surgical treatment (valvotomy).

Duration in Days

Job Classification	Minimum	Optimum	Maximum
Sedentary work	14	28	42
Light work	14	28	42
Medium work	28	49	70
Heavy work	42	70	Indefinite
Very Heavy work	42	70	Indefinite

Failure to Recover

If an individual fails to recover within the maximum duration expectancy period, the reader may wish to reference the following questions to assist in better understanding the specifics of an individual's medical case.

Regarding diagnosis:

- Does the individual have a history of rheumatic heart disease, congenital heart disease, mitral valve prolapse, mitral valve insufficiency, or a prosthetic heart valve?
- Has the individual recently had surgery, dental treatment, or exploratory procedures where a viewing tube is inserted into the body for diagnostic examination?
- Is the individual an intravenous drug user?
- Does the individual complain of high fever, severe chills, cough, and shortness of breath? Does the individual report fatigue, weakness, night sweats, vague aches and pains, low-grade or absent fever?
- On exam did the individual have fever, rapid or irregular heartbeat, and petechiae on the conjunctiva, the arms and legs, and the mucous membranes of the mouth and throat?
- Does the individual have splinter hemorrhages in the nail beds, accompanied by small, raised, and tender blue or red areas in the pads of the fingers or toes (Osler's nodes)?
- Does the exam also reveal joint pain, muscle pain, and a new or changed heart murmur?
- Has the individual had blood cultures and sensitivity, CBC, sedimentation rate, serology, urinalysis?
- Has the individual had an echocardiogram, EKG, and angiography?
- Have conditions with similar symptoms been ruled out?

Regarding treatment:

- Is the individual being treated with high dose IV antibiotics for 4-6 weeks?
- Was it necessary to surgically replace a damaged or infected heart valve?
- Was it necessary to do the surgery on an emergency basis?

Regarding prognosis:

- Is the individual active in rehabilitation?
- Is the individual's employer able to accommodate any necessary restrictions?
- Does the individual have any conditions that could affect ability to recover?
- Does the individual have any complications such as arrhythmias, systemic emboli, splenic infarction, stroke, brain hemorrhage, valvular insufficiency, congestive heart failure, kidney failure, or thrombophlebitis?
- Does the individual have sepsis?

References

Mate, I., et al. "Indications and Surgical Techniques in the Acute Phase of Infective Endocarditis." Rev Esp Cardiol 51 Suppl 2 (1998): 86-91.

McArdle, William, Frank Katch, and Victor Katch. Exercise Physiology. Energy, Nutrition, and Human Performance. Philadelphia: Lea & Febiger, 1991.

Tierney, Lawrence M., Stephen J. McPhee, and Maxine A. Papadakis, eds. Current Medical Diagnosis and Treatment, 39th ed. New York: Lange Medical Books/McGraw-Hill, 2000.

Watchie, Joanne. Cardiopulmonary Physical Therapy. Philadelphia: W.B. Saunders Company, 1995.

Endometriosis

Other names / synonyms: Ectopic Endometrium

617, 617.0, 617.1, 617.2, 617.3, 617.4, 617.5, 617.6, 617.8, 617.9

Definition

Endometriosis occurs when tissue that normally lines the uterus (endometrium) is found outside of the uterus. Common sites for endometriosis include the ovaries, fallopian tubes, external genitalia (vulva), and the ligaments supporting the uterus, intestine, bladder, cervix, and vagina. Although uncommon, endometriosis has been found outside the pelvis and abdomen including the lung area.

Endometriosis responds to hormones of the menstrual cycle. Each month endometrial implants grow and thicken as does the lining of the uterus. If pregnancy does not occur, the implants break down and bleed. But unlike the tissue in the uterus, endometrium has no way of leaving the body when it breaks down. Pain, inflammation, and the formation of scar tissue can result.

The cause of endometriosis is unclear but a common theory is "retrograde menstruation" where some menstrual blood flows backward out the fallopian tubes rather than exiting through the vagina. Endometrial cells in the menstrual flow may then attach themselves to various locations. Another theory suggests that endometrial cells may be passed through the lymph or blood circulations.

The exact incidence of endometriosis is unknown since surgery is required for a positive diagnosis. It is estimated that about 10% of all women develop some degree of endometriosis before reaching menopause. Until recently, a large percentage of individuals who complained of symptoms were dismissed as overly sensitive to pain. A recent study revealed that 27% of individuals diagnosed with endometriosis complained of symptoms for 6 years before a diagnosis was finally made.

Endometriosis most commonly occurs in childless women between the ages of 25 and 40, but can affect any woman (including those with children) at any time during childbearing years. When a woman becomes pregnant or menopausal, the endometriosis shrinks and much of the pain disappears. However, any scar tissue will remain and may continue to cause pain even though the menstrual cycle has ceased. Women are up to seven times more likely to have endometriosis if their mother, sister, or daughter has it than women with no affected relatives.

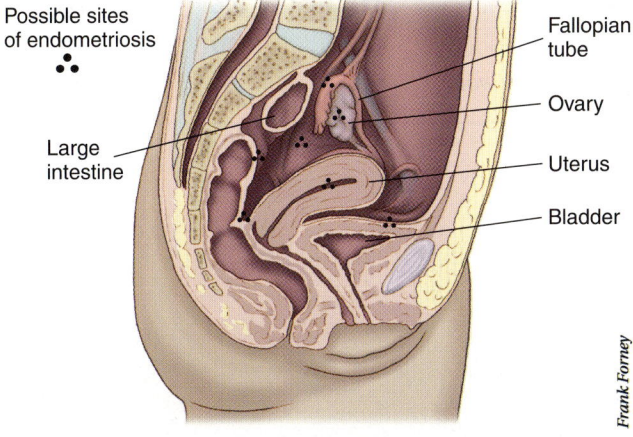

Diagnosis

History: Individuals report a variety of symptoms. Pelvic pain and abnormal or heavy menstrual bleeding are most commonly reported. There may be severe abdominal and/or lower back pain that begins prior to a menstrual period and becomes more severe toward the end of a period. Other possible symptoms are fatigue, pain with intercourse, diarrhea, constipation, painful bowel movements during the menstrual period, rectal bleeding or blood in the urine only during the menstrual period, and irregular bleeding or spotting between periods. Cramping lower abdominal pain may occur any time during the cycle.

A large endometrial growth can cause the sensation of pelvic pressure. Infertility is commonly reported, affecting about 30-40% of women with endometriosis. The amount of pain is not related to the extent of endometriosis. Some women with large or numerous growths have no pain while others with only minimal growths may experience severe pain. Many women with endometriosis report no symptoms.

Physical exam: A pelvic examination may detect the endometrial growths or tender areas when the uterus is palpated. Growths may also be seen if located in the upper vagina or on the cervix. However, many women have no abnormal findings on physical examination.

Tests: Laparoscopy is a surgical procedure that is the most common and accurate method to identify endometriosis. A small, lighted telescope is inserted into the abdomen and the pelvis and abdomen are inspected visually. Laparoscopy can reveal the location and size of endometrial growths and help in treatment decisions. Laparoscopic diagnosis should be confirmed by biopsy.

The amount of Ca125 (a protein found in the pelvic organs of individuals with endometriosis) may be monitored in women experiencing infertility and pain. Ca125 levels are higher in moderate-to-severe endometriosis and are used for both diagnosis and to follow the effects of therapy. A blood test to diagnose endometriosis may soon be available that would reveal elevated levels of Ca125. Additional tests may be necessary to explore other diagnoses with similar symptoms such as a pregnancy test for ectopic pregnancy, urinalysis for urinary infection, colonoscopy or barium enema to rule out bowel disease (such as diverticulitis), or ultrasound to rule out ovarian cancer.

Treatment

The approach to treatment is influenced by the severity of symptoms, extent of the disease, age of the woman, and her desire for future childbearing. Treatment can include careful observation, medical therapy, surgery, or a combination of treatment choices.

In women with no symptoms or only mild discomfort, careful observation may be all that is needed (there is no evidence that early treatment will prevent or lessen later symptoms). Pain relievers may be useful.

Hormone treatment for endometriosis includes birth control pills, high doses of another female hormone (progestins), or a male hormone derivative. Hormone therapy may help to halt the spread and reduce the pain of endometriosis by interrupting the menstrual cycle. Another treatment option is a synthetic hormone-like substance (GnRH analog) that temporarily interrupts the production of estrogen and produces a medical menopause. This treatment often shrinks the endometrial growths and provides significant relief from symptoms.

Conservative surgical treatment is to relieve painful symptoms of endometriosis while attempting to preserve the woman's childbearing ability. Endometrial implants and scar tissue can be cut or destroyed by an electrical current or laser (laparoscopy). If normal, the ovaries and fallopian tubes are untreated. Painful symptoms are relieved, but may return.

More extensive surgery is undertaken only when all other options have failed. This may involve removal of the uterus (hysterectomy) and both ovaries (oophorectomy), and perhaps the fallopian tubes (bilateral salpingo-oophorectomy). Although these methods may help prevent the recurrence of endometriosis, they also leave the woman unable to bear children and in a permanent state of menopause.

Prognosis

Most women obtain significant relief from pain and are still able to bear children. Current treatment offers relief from symptoms but not a cure. Endometriosis may even recur following surgery. The course of endometriosis in any individual cannot be predicted. Endometriosis can be reactivated if the woman takes estrogen replacement but usually does not recur in the majority of women.

Differential Diagnosis

Other possibilities include pelvic inflammatory disease, ovarian cysts or cancer, dysmenorrhea, a pelvic tumor, urinary tract infection, ectopic pregnancy, functional bowel disease, diverticulitis, and chronic appendicitis.

Specialists

- General Surgeon
- Gynecologist

Work Restrictions / Accommodations

If surgery is performed, work involving lifting, climbing, or physical exertion may need to be limited throughout the disability period. Work requiring prolonged standing may also need to be limited.

Comorbid Conditions

Anemia or another blood disorder may lengthen the disability.

Complications

Scar tissue (adhesions) can form and cause intestinal obstruction. Growths on or near the bladder can interfere with urinary function. Blood trapped inside the ovary can accumulate causing a noncancerous tumor (endometrioma). The disease can result in infertility. Recurring chronic pain or infertility may lead to depression and emotional issues. Side effects are frequent with hormonal treatment.

Factors Influencing Duration

Disability factors include severity of symptoms, location of growths, method of treatment, and any complications.

Length of Disability

Duration depends on job requirements.

Medical treatment.

Duration in Days

Job Classification	Minimum	Optimum	Maximum
Sedentary work	0	3	7
Light work	0	3	7
Medium work	0	3	7
Heavy work	0	3	7
Very Heavy work	0	3	7

Laparoscopic surgery.

Duration in Days

Job Classification	Minimum	Optimum	Maximum
Sedentary work	3	7	21
Light work	3	7	21
Medium work	7	14	28
Heavy work	7	21	35
Very Heavy work	14	21	35

Surgical treatment. Hysterectomy, abdominal.

Duration in Days

Job Classification	Minimum	Optimum	Maximum
Sedentary work	28	42	56
Light work	28	42	56
Medium work	42	56	70
Heavy work	42	70	84
Very Heavy work	42	84	98

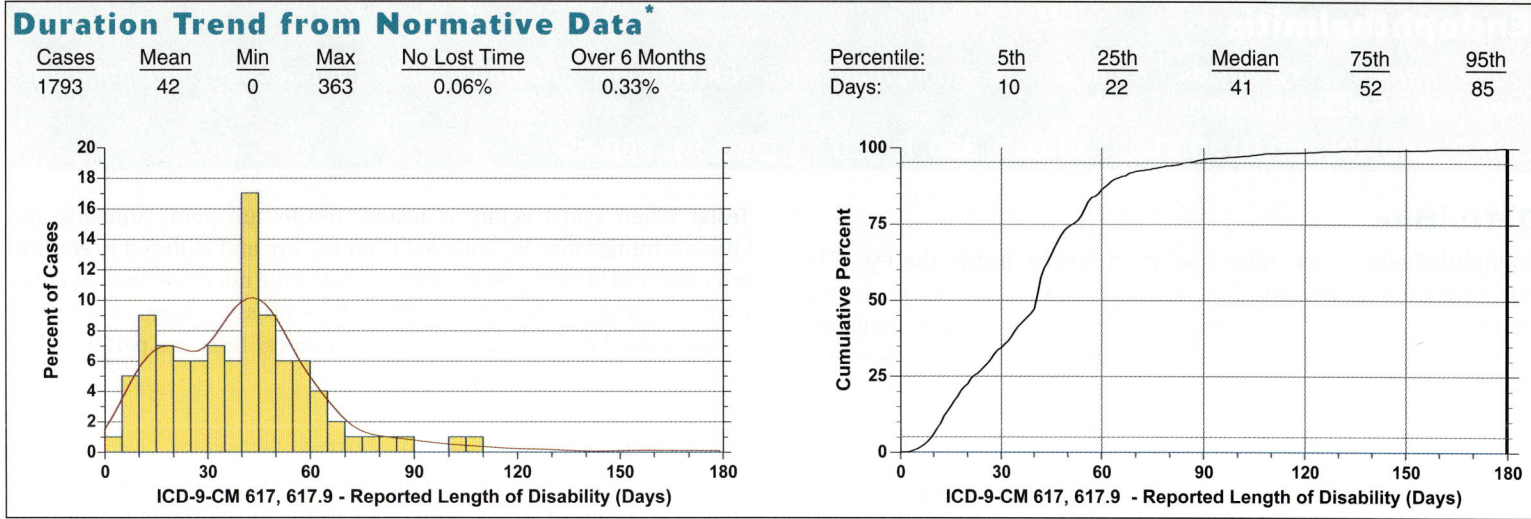

* Differences may exist between the expected duration tables and the normative graphs. Duration tables provide expected recovery periods based on the type of work performed by the individual. The normative graphs reflect the actual observed experience of many individuals across the spectrum of physical conditions, in a variety of industries, and with varying levels of case management.

Failure to Recover

If an individual fails to recover within the maximum duration expectancy period, the reader may wish to reference the following questions to assist in better understanding the specifics of an individual's medical case.

Regarding diagnosis:

- Does the individual have a family history of endometriosis?
- Does the individual report pelvic pain and abnormal or heavy menstrual bleeding?
- Does the individual report severe abdominal and/or lower back pain that begins prior to a menstrual period and becomes more severe toward the end of a period?
- Does the individual have fatigue, pain with intercourse, diarrhea, constipation, painful bowel movements during the menstrual period, rectal bleeding or blood in the urine only during the menstrual period, and irregular bleeding or spotting between periods?
- Does the individual report crampy lower abdominal pain that occurs any time during the cycle?
- On pelvic examination, were endometrial growths or tender areas present when the uterus is palpated?
- Were growths also present in the upper vagina or on the cervix?
- Has the individual had a laparoscopy with a biopsy, Ca125 levels, pregnancy test, urinalysis, colonoscopy or barium enema or ultrasound?
- Have conditions with similar symptoms been ruled out?

Regarding treatment:

- Is the individual being treated with careful observation, medical therapy, surgery, or a combination of treatment choices?
- Is the individual using pain relievers?
- Has the individual tried hormone treatment?
- Was it necessary for the individual to have surgery?

Regarding prognosis:

- Is the individual's employer able to accommodate any necessary restrictions?
- Does the individual have any conditions that may affect their ability to recover?
- Does the individual have any complications such as adhesions, intestinal obstruction, urinary dysfunction, endometrioma, infertility, depression or emotional issues?
- Does the individual have side effects of hormonal treatment?

References

Scialli, Anthony R., MD. Book of Women's Health. New York: William Morrow & Company, 1999.

Taylor, H, M. Guarnaccia, and D. Olive. "Alternative Medical Treatment for Endometriosis." Seminars in Reproductive Endocrinology 15 3 (1997): 285-290.

Endophthalmitis

Other names / synonyms: Endogenous Endophthalmitis, Exogenous Endophthalmitis, Intraocular Inflammation, Metastatic Endophthalmitis

360.0, 360.00, 360.01, 360.02, 360.03, 360.1, 360.11, 360.13, 360.19

Definition

Endophthalmitis is an inflammation of tissues inside the eye. The inflammation may be caused by bacteria (e.g., staphylococcus, streptococcus, gram-negative bacteria), fungi (e.g., candida, aspergillus), protozoa (e.g., acanthamoeba), and on rare occasions, viruses (e.g., Herpes simplex or Herpes zoster).

Endophthalmitis is classified as either exogenous or endogenous. Exogenous endophthalmitis can be a complication following eye surgery or a penetrating eye injury. Endogenous endophthalmitis is a complication of a blood-borne infection and extremely rare. Endophthalmitis can involve all layers of the eye, inner vitreous, and sclera.

The incidence of exogenous endophthalmitis varies with the cause. Incidence of endophthalmitis following extracapsular lens extraction and intraocular lens implantation is estimated between 0.07-0.12%.

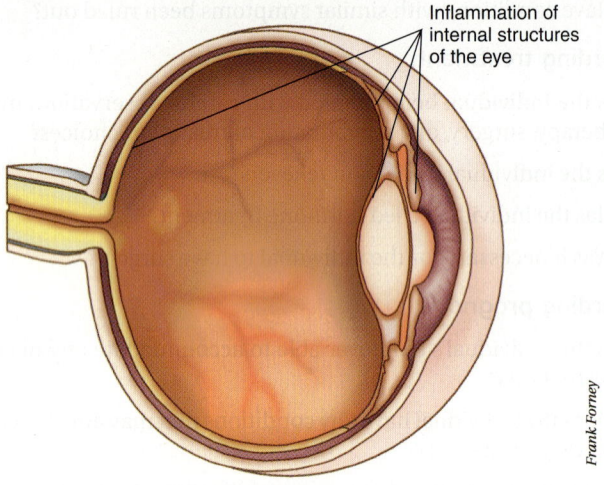

Inflammation of internal structures of the eye

Frank Forney

Diagnosis

History: Individuals report pain, decreased vision, and blurred vision. Redness and/or discharge may occur following eye surgery. If individuals report pain out of proportion to the amount of inflammation, it can be an early sign of endophthalmitis. Pain may not be present if infection is caused by a weak organism. Some cases may be totally asymptomatic.

Physical exam: Early clinical signs may include round, white retinal spots surrounded by hemorrhage (Roth's spots) and inflammation around the vessels of the retina (periphlebitis). A pus-like discharge may be present. The lids are swollen and the eye red, but these features may not be prominent. Later clinical signs may include swelling of the conjunctiva (chemosis), corneal edema, increased cells, flare, accumulation of pus in the anterior chamber (hypopyon), and abnormal protrusion of the eye (proptosis). The red reflex may be absent due to clouding of the fluid in the eye (vitreous humor). There may be opaque material suspended within the vitreous.

Tests: When visual acuity is tested, results are poor. Aqueous and vitreous humor may be removed from the eye and cultured to confirm infection and identify the organism causing the infection. In about one-fourth of all cases, the culture will not be successful. In cases of endogenous endophthalmitis, a number of medical tests are performed to identify the underlying systemic infection.

Treatment

Endophthalmitis is a medical emergency and must be treated immediately. The delay of a few hours can result in permanent blindness. Treatment may include removal of part of the vitreous fluid to dilute toxins produced by the bacteria and to decrease the numbers of bacteria in the eye (vitrectomy). Other treatment options are use of intraocular antibiotics, intraocular anti-inflammatory agents, and systemic antibiotics. Systemic antibiotics are not usually used for exogenous endophthalmitis but are considered important in treating endogenous endophthalmitis so to prevent the spread of the systemic infection.

Prognosis

Visual outcome varies widely. Early diagnosis and aggressive treatment of exogenous endophthalmitis are keys to a good outcome. The outcome of endogenous endophthalmitis when compared with exogenous endophthalmitis is often disappointing. Even with successful treatment, visual acuity is not expected to improve beyond the level at the start of treatment. The main factors contributing to a poor outcome are more virulent organisms, decreased immunity, and delay in diagnosis. Only about 40% of individuals with endogenous endophthalmitis retain useful vision.

Differential Diagnosis

Panophthalmitis, uveitis, ocular lymphoma, and sympathetic ophthalmia are other possible diagnoses.

Specialists

- Ophthalmologist

Work Restrictions / Accommodations

Vision needs to be evaluated if important to the individual's work. Because visual outcome varies widely, any number of special accommodations for individuals with visual impairment may be necessary (e.g., large print material or adequate lighting).

Comorbid Conditions

An important factor in the prognosis of endophthalmitis is the individual's immune status. The population at greatest risk includes immunocompromised individuals with leukemia, lymphoma, asplenia, and individuals taking immunosuppressive therapy. Individuals with chronic diseases such as diabetes mellitus, renal insufficiency, and malignancies are also at risk.

Complications

The vitreous humor may liquefy and form an abscess. Retinal detachment may occur.

Factors Influencing Duration

The particular organism causing the endophthalmitis, timeliness of treatment, complications, and individual's response to treatment all affect the length of disability.

Length of Disability

Duration in Days

Job Classification	Minimum	Optimum	Maximum
Sedentary work	7	14	28
Light work	7	14	28
Medium work	7	14	28
Heavy work	14	21	42
Very Heavy work	14	21	42

Failure to Recover

If an individual fails to recover within the maximum duration expectancy period, the reader may wish to reference the following questions to assist in better understanding the specifics of an individual's medical case.

Regarding diagnosis:

- Has diagnosis of endophthalmitis been confirmed?
- Have conditions with similar symptoms been ruled out?
- For exogenous endophthalmitis, have appropriate medical tests been performed to identify the underlying systemic infection?
- Has specific organism been identified?
- Has individual experienced any complications as a result of the endophthalmitis?
- Does individual have an underlying condition that may impact recovery?

Regarding treatment:

- Would dilution bacterial toxins through drainage of vitreous fluid be beneficial? Is individual a candidate for a vitrectomy or a partial vitrectomy?
- Was culture and sensitivity performed to identify causative organisms and determine the most effective antibiotic to use?
- Have antibiotic-resistant organisms been ruled out?
- Has the individual completed prescribed course of intraocular and/or systemic antibiotics? If not, what can be done to enhance compliance?

Regarding prognosis:

- To what extent has vision been impaired?
- Depending on occupational duties, would special accommodations for individuals with visual impairment allow individual to return to present position?
- Would individual benefit from a transfer or vocational re-training?

References

Eye Conditions. U-M Kellogg Eye Center, Department of Ophthalmology and Visual Sciences. 2000. 22 Jun 2000 <http://www.kellogg.umich.edu/conditions/neuro-opthy/endophthalmitis/html>.

Management of endophthalmitis. Royal College of Ophthalmologists. 1996. 23 Jun 2000 <http://www.rcophth.ac.uk/departments/focus1.html>.

Gimbel, H.V. "Endophthalmitis: Immediate Management Using Posterior Capsulorhexis and Anterior Vitrectomy Through Reopened Cataract Surgery Incision." Journal of Cataract and Refractive Surgery 23 1 (1997): 27-31.

Pflugfelder, S., and H. Flynn. "Infectious Endophthalmitis." Infectious Disease Clinics of North America 6 4 (1992): 859-873.

Romero, C., et al. "Endogenous Endophthalmitis: Case Report and Brief Review." American Family Physician 01 Aug 1999 23 Jun 2000 <http://www.aafp.org/afp/990800ap/510.html>.

Samson, C., and C. Foster. "Chronic Postoperative Endophthalmitis." International Ophthalmology Clinics 40 1 (2000): 57-67.

Endoscopy of Gastrointestinal Tract

Other names / synonyms: Colonoscopy, EGD, Esophagogastroduodenoscopy, Esophagoscopy, Gastroscopy, Sigmoidoscopy

42.23, 44.13

Definition

Flexible endoscopy of the gastrointestinal tract is a procedure in which a doctor uses a flexible endoscope to view the interior of the gastrointestinal tract. A flexible endoscope is a long, thin, fiber-optic viewing instrument. Endoscopy of the upper gastrointestinal tract is performed by inserting the device through the mouth and advancing it through the esophagus and, if necessary, into the stomach and the first part of the small intestine (the duodenum).

Endoscopy of the lower gastrointestinal tract (sigmoidoscopy and colonoscopy) is performed by insertion of the device through the anus into the sigmoid colon and colon.

Physicians may use sigmoidoscopy and colonoscopy to find the cause of diarrhea, abdominal pain, or constipation. They may also use the procedures to look for early signs of cancer in the colon and rectum. With sigmoidoscopy and colonoscopy, the physician can see bleeding, inflammation, abnormal growths, and ulcers.

Reason for Procedure

Endoscopy is chiefly a diagnostic procedure, but it has other uses as well. For example, with the endoscope the doctor can collect tissue specimens for later examination (biopsy), remove polyps, administer blood-clotting drugs at the site of bleeding, or tie off bleeding veins.

If an individual's symptoms suggest polyps, cancer, ulcers, esophageal varices, or other types of internal bleeding, endoscopy is a noninvasive and relatively uncomplicated way to confirm their presence. Endoscopy can also help a doctor detect problems that are not visible in x-rays. It is preferable to x-rays during pregnancy.

Total colonoscopy is becoming an accepted standard for physical examinations of individuals over age fifty.

Description

For esophagogastroduodenoscopy, the individual will be given a sedative or tranquilizer and a pain medication. A local anesthetic will be used in the mouth and back of the throat to lessen the reflex to cough or gag when the instrument is inserted.

The individual lies on his/her left side. When the anesthetics have taken effect, the tube (endoscope) is inserted and lowered through the esophagus, stomach, and into the upper part of the small intestine (duodenum). When the viewing is completed, and samples taken or medication applied, the tube will be removed. The individual may be asked to cough to force out any air or gas. No food or drink will be allowed for a short time following the procedure when the cough reflex has returned. Overall the test takes approximately 30 to 60 minutes.

For a sigmoidoscopy, individuals lie on their left side. The physician inserts the short, flexible, lighted tube called a sigmoidoscope into the rectum and advances it to examine the interior of the colon. Images are transmitted to a video display so that the physician can examine the inside carefully. Should anything unusual such as polyps or inflammation be found, the physician can take tissue samples (biopsy) through the sigmoidoscope. Sigmoidoscopy takes 10 to 20 minutes.

The main instrument that is used to look inside the colon is the colonoscope, which is a long, thin, flexible tube with a tiny video camera and a light on the end. Colonoscopy usually does not cause pain, although it may be uncomfortable. Individuals are given intravenous medication to relax and make them feel sleepy during the procedure. When the individual is fully relaxed, the physician does a rectal exam and inserts the lubricated colonoscope into the rectum. The scope is then advanced into the colon. Generally there is little or no discomfort. The physician may remove any polyps that are found, or he may take tissue samples (biopsy) for further examination. Other repairs may be considered during the examination as well.

Colonoscopy may be done in either a hospital or in an outpatient facility. The time needed for colonoscopy varies, but generally takes about 30 minutes. The individual will be cared for in a recovery area until the effects of the medication have worn off.

Prognosis

Endoscopy results indicate any disease state or the presence of abnormal growths and also provide the opportunity to take tissue samples (biopsy). In the majority of cases, the outcome of the endoscopic examination will add evidence to support a diagnosis.

The procedure itself has a good outcome when performed by a qualified doctor and staff. The reasons for carrying out the procedure and discoveries made during the procedure will govern the overall outcome of any disease process.

Specialists

- Colorectal Surgeon
- Gastroenterologist
- General Surgeon

Work Restrictions / Accommodations

No restrictions or accommodations should be necessary after recovery from the procedure.

Comorbid Conditions

Allergies and severe gastrointestinal diseases and disorders are comorbid conditions that might affect disability.

Procedure Complications

Complications of the procedure may include a tear or hole in the esophagus, stomach or upper part of the small intestine (duodenum) or other parts of the entire gastrointestinal tract. The individual may also have an adverse reaction to the anesthetic, any medications given or the sedative given before the procedure. Some of those adverse reactions may be difficulty breathing, lowered blood pressure (hypotension), stopped breathing (apnea), irregular heartbeat, or copious sweating. If a tissue sample has been taken (biopsy) there may be bleeding at the site.

Bleeding and puncture of the colon are possible complications of sigmoidoscopy and colonoscopy. A puncture of the colon walls requiring surgical repair is one of the complications of colonoscopy. However, such complications are uncommon.

Length of Disability

Duration reflects recovery from procedure only. Disability depends on the diagnosis and/or specific procedures performed.

Duration in Days

Job Classification	Minimum	Optimum	Maximum
Any work	1	1	2

References

"EGD (Esophagogastroduodenoscopy)." Health Central, Inc. 01 Oct 2000. 01 Jan 2001 <http://www.healthcentral.com/mhc/top/003338.cfm>.

"EGD (Esophagogastroduodenoscopy)." Medline Plus Health Information. 26 Sep 2000. 16 Jan 2001 <http://medlineplus.adam.com/ency/article/003888.htm>.

Enterostomy

Other names / synonyms: Delayed Opening Enterostomy, Duodenostomy, Duodenum Enterostomy, Enteral Feeding, Feeding Enterostomy, Gastrostomy, Jejunostomy, Percutaneous Enterostomy, Tube Feeding

46.3, 46.31, 46.32, 46.39

Definition

An enterostomy is the surgical creation of an opening through the abdominal wall into the stomach, duodenum, or jejunum for placement of a feeding tube.

Enterostomies are placed to provide a route for giving nutrition to individuals who are unable to take an adequate amount of oral nutrition and who require long-term nutritional support (more than 1 month). Many medications may also be given through an enterostomy tube.

The most common type of enterostomy is placement of an enterostomy tube into the stomach (gastrostomy). Gastrostomy is advantageous because feedings can be given at intervals in large volumes (bolus feeding). Enterostomies placed in the jejunum (jejunostomy) or into the duodenum (duodenostomy) require continuous infusion. A jejunostomy or duodenostomy is used when the individual is at risk of back-up of the feeding solution into the lungs (aspiration).

Enterostomy feeding can only be undertaken in individuals who have normal digestion and absorption. Many individuals live at home with an enterostomy tube.

Reason for Procedure

Enterostomies are placed in individuals who are unable to take an adequate amount of oral nutrition and who require long-term nutritional support (more than 1 month).

An enterostomy tube may be placed for many conditions. Enterostomy feedings may be recommended for conditions such as malnutrition (which can be due to cancer), eating disorders, severe chronic obstructive pulmonary disease (COPD), stroke, traumatic brain injury, metabolic disorders, encephalopathy, conditions of the mouth and esophagus, quadriplegia, major burns, or severe trauma to the upper body (torso).

A variety of nutritional solutions are available for administration through an enterostomy tube.

Description

Placement of a gastrostomy tube may be performed using a lighted fiber-optic tube (endoscope), with surgery, or using x-ray (radiology) to guide the insertion. Placement of a jejunostomy or duodenostomy tube also requires a surgical procedure.

General anesthesia or IV conscious sedation with analgesia may be used.

The traditional approach for placement of a gastrostomy is surgical with small abdominal incisions. A small incision is made through the abdominal wall. Two small sutures are placed in the wall of the stomach. The gastrostomy tube itself is inserted through a second small incision through the abdominal wall, and it is then inserted into the stomach between the two sutures. The stomach is tacked to the wall of the abdomen, and the incision is closed.

A fiberoptic tube (gastroscope) may be used for placement of the gastrostomy tube. This procedure is known as a percutaneous endoscopic gastrostomy (PEG). The gastroscope, which is a type of endoscope, is inserted through the mouth into the stomach. A large needle is used to puncture the outside wall of the abdomen into the stomach. A guidewire is inserted through the needle while visualized with the gastroscope. The gastroscope is removed and the gastrostomy tube is inserted into the stomach over the guidewire. A suture is placed to hold the tube in place.

Prognosis

The outcome of placement of an enterostomy is generally successful for the long-term delivery of nutritional fluids.

Specialists

- General Surgeon

Work Restrictions / Accommodations

Individuals should avoid lifting, pushing, or pulling more than 5-10 pounds for at least 6 weeks immediately after the operation. Many individuals who require enterostomy feeding are debilitated and weak. Prolonged time off from work or modified duty may be necessary until weight is regained and physical strength returns. In some individuals, there may be permanent disability as a result of the underlying condition.

Comorbid Conditions

Comorbid conditions include gastroesophageal reflux, diabetes, and physical debility and weakness.

Procedure Complications

Complications may include wound infection, incorrect placement of the tube, dislodgment of the tube, intestinal obstruction, and separation of the incision (dehiscence). With a gastrostomy, when the nutritional fluid is given, there is a chance that it will back-up from the stomach up into the esophagus (gastroesophageal reflux) or lungs (pulmonary aspiration). With jejunostomy or duodenostomy feedings, if a large volume of feeding solution is given at one time (bolus), a condition known as the dumping syndrome may occur.

Gastrointestinal complications may occur with the feeding itself. Other complications associated with feedings include diarrhea, malabsorption, abdominal cramping, nausea and vomiting, and abdominal distention. Gastrointestinal side-effects occur in about 10-20% of individuals receiving tube-feedings. Complications associated with abnormal metabolism may occur including fluid and electrolyte abnormalities, high blood sugar (hyperglycemia), and inadequate functioning of the kidneys (prerenal azotemia).

Factors Influencing Duration

The underlying reason necessitating the procedure and the presence of complications will influence the length of disability.

Length of Disability

Duration in Days

Job Classification	Minimum	Optimum	Maximum
Sedentary work	3	7	14
Light work	3	7	21
Medium work	3	14	28
Heavy work	3	14	35
Very Heavy work	3	21	42

References

Bell, Richard M. "Surgical Procedures, Techniques, and Skills." Essentials of General Surgery, 3rd ed. Lawrence, Peter F., ed. Philadelphia: Lippincott Williams & Wilkins, 2000. 522-563.

Petty, Lynda R. "Gastrointestinal Surgery." Alexander's Care of the Patient in Surgery, 11th ed. Meeker, Margaret H., and Jane C. Rothrock, eds. St. Louis: Mosby, 1999. 313-370.

Enthesopathy

Other names / synonyms: Enthesitis

726.3, 726.4, 726.5, 726.6, 726.64, 726.7, 726.8, 726.9

Definition

Enthesopathy is the result of an inflammatory process that involves the area where ligaments or tendons attach to bone (enthesis) by calcification or ossification.

Enthesopathy is a presenting symptom in many inflammatory conditions, but is not a disease in itself. Conditions in which enthesopathy is a symptom include the spondyloarthropathies, spinal arthritis, ankylosing spondylitis, reactive arthritis (formerly known as Reiter syndrome), psoriatic arthritis, enteropathic arthritis (accompanying ulcerative colitis and Crohn's disease), and such rare disorders as acne-associated arthritis, and Whipple disease. Enthesopathy is also seen as a complication of avulsion fractures and tendon tears (rarely).

When these inflammatory conditions occur, the enthesis can become irritated and painful, resulting in enthesopathy.

Diagnosis

History: Individuals will complain of pain, swelling and warmth over joints, which may be aggravated with activity. There is usually not a history of injury.

Physical exam: Touch will reveal tenderness over areas of tendon or ligament sites along with redness, and swelling of the joint (effusion) if the involved areas are superficial. Decreased range of motion may be noted in the involved joint.(The remainder of the exam would depend on the underlying condition being explored).

Tests: Blood laboratory studies such as: FANA, ANA, rheumatoid factor, HLAB27, ESR, Uric Acid, Urinalysis, CBC with differential are used to define underlying conditions. Joint fluid aspiration may be needed as well to define diseases such as gout and infection. X-rays are used to define changes in the bone.

Treatment

Treatment of the symptom of enthesopathy is dependent on the underlying condition. Nonsteroidal anti-inflammatory drugs (NSAIDs) are used in managing the conditions. In addition, exercise programs are essential to maintain range-of-motion, strength and mobility.

Prognosis

Recovery from enthesopathy is dependent on successful management of the underlying disease. Many of these diseases are prone to periods or remission and recurrence.

Differential Diagnosis

Any of the inflammatory diseases could have similar symptoms. Sprains, strains, synovitis, and tendonitis need to be ruled out.

Specialists

- Orthopedist
- Otolaryngologist
- Physiatrist
- Rheumatologist

Work Restrictions / Accommodations

Work restrictions and special accommodations are determined on an individual basis and are dependent on the severity of symptoms and job requirements.

Accommodations might include decreased work load, limited weight bearing activities, frequent rest periods, and change in tasks allowing for changes in body position.

Comorbid Conditions

Conditions affecting mobility such as obesity and neurological diseases would have a negative impact on individuals with enthesopathy.

Complications

Individuals with enthesopathy can have a severe and progressive disease resulting in incapacitating deformities. In addition, but rarely, individuals with ankylosing spondylitis might develop secondary amyloidosis.

Factors Influencing Duration

Severity of disease, the presence of complications, and job demands will influence the length of disability.

Length of Disability

Length of disability is dependent on management of the underlying disease and ability to modify job requirements. Contact physician for additional information.

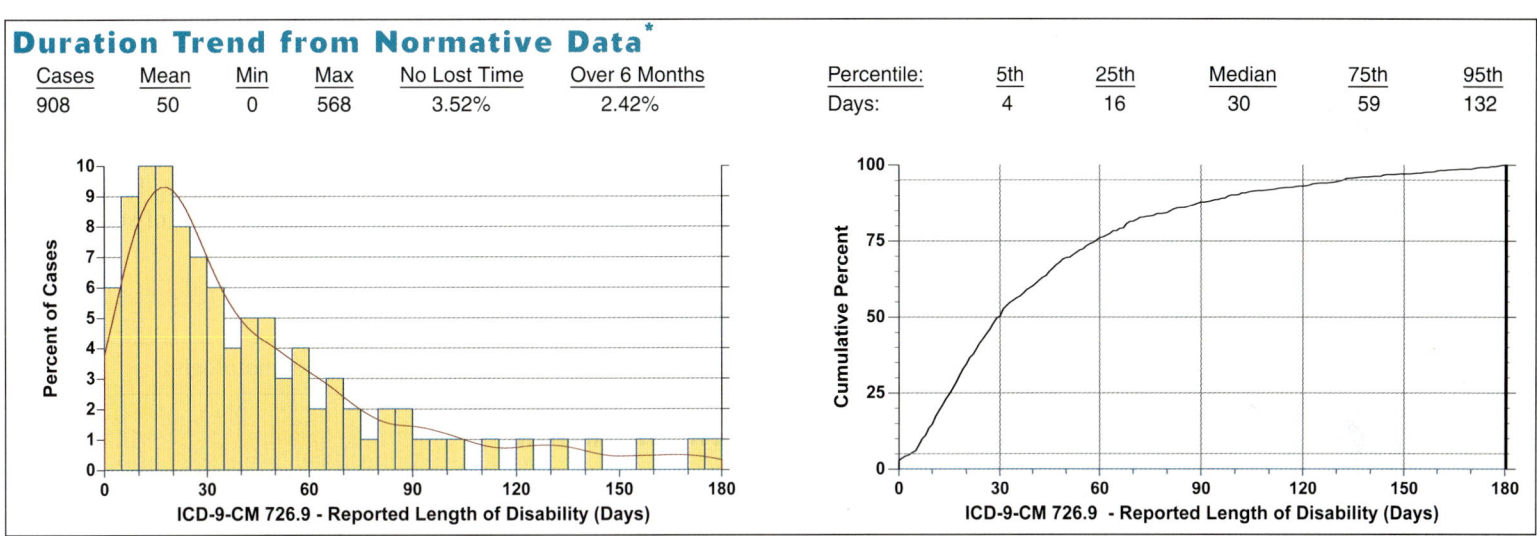

Duration Trend from Normative Data*

Cases	Mean	Min	Max	No Lost Time	Over 6 Months
908	50	0	568	3.52%	2.42%

Percentile:	5th	25th	Median	75th	95th
Days:	4	16	30	59	132

ICD-9-CM 726.9 - Reported Length of Disability (Days)

* Differences may exist between the expected duration tables and the normative graphs. Duration tables provide expected recovery periods based on the type of work performed by the individual. The normative graphs reflect the actual observed experience of many individuals across the spectrum of physical conditions, in a variety of industries, and with varying levels of case management.

Failure to Recover

If an individual fails to recover within the maximum duration expectancy period, the reader may wish to reference the following questions to assist in better understanding the specifics of an individual's medical case.

Regarding diagnosis:

- Does the individual complain of pain over joints?
- Is the pain aggravated with activity?
- Does the individual have a history of arthritis? What type of arthritis?
- Is the area over tendon and ligament tender to the touch, reddened, or swollen?
- Does the individual have decreased range of motion in the involved joint?
- Have blood tests for abnormalities related to arthritis-type conditions been obtained?
- Was the diagnosis confirmed?
- Have underlying conditions been identified and treated?
- Have x-rays been done to identify changes in the bone? Were changes identified?

Regarding treatment:

- Has the underlying condition been identified correctly?
- Is the individual taking NSAIDs and participating in an exercise program?
- Does the treatment appear to be relieving pain and improving mobility?

Regarding prognosis:

- Is the individual experiencing a recurrence of the underlying disease?
- Has the individual's underlying disease progressed?
- Does the individual have incapacitating joint deformities?
- How will this affect the individual's activities of daily living?

References

Anderson, Kenneth N., Lois E. Anderson, and Walter D. Glanze, eds. Mosby's Medical Dictionary. St. Louis: Mosby-Year Book, Inc, 1998.

Thompson, June M., et al. Mosby's Clinical Nursing, 4th ed. St. Louis: Mosby-Year Book, Inc, 1997.

Eosinophilic Fasciitis

Other names / synonyms: Diffuse Fasciitis with Eosinophilia, Shulman's Syndrome

728.0, 728.12, 728.81, 728.86, 728.89, 728.9

Definition

Eosinophilic fasciitis (EF) is a syndrome of painful swelling and stiffness of the extremities.

The symptoms are caused by inflammation of the muscles and surrounding tissue (fascia) but the exact cause of the inflammation is unknown. An infiltration of a certain type of white blood cells (eosinophils) is found in the fascia and muscle when biopsied.

In some cases, onset appears to follow unusual or excessive strenuous physical activity. EF affects all age groups, but highest incidence is ages between 30 and 60 years.

Diagnosis

History: The individual notices a gradual increase in pain, swelling, and inflammation of the skin of the extremities along with a gradual restriction of arm and leg movement along with muscle weakness. There may be symptoms of carpal tunnel syndrome - weakness with numbness and tingling, dry shiny skin, inability to make a fist. Fatigue and weight loss are common.

Physical exam: The skin is swollen and puckered giving it an orange-peel configuration over the arms and legs. Usually, the fingers and toes are not involved. The skin is taut and woody and restricted by the subcutaneous tissue. The face and trunk may also be involved. Other similar symptoms of scleroderma are not seen.

Tests: Blood tests show elevated eosinophils (type of blood cell), elevated sed rate and hyperglobulinemia, negative ANA and rheumatoid factor. The diagnosis is confirmed by biopsy of affected skin and fascia deep enough to include adjacent muscle fibers.

MRI demonstrates thickened fascia in the affected areas.

Treatment

Treatment is aimed at relieving the symptoms, not at curing the disease. Treatment includes high doses of corticosteroids initially. The dose is then lowered but may be required for two to five years. Other medications may include anti-ulcer medication, NSAIDs, and immunosuppressants.

Prognosis

The long-term outcome is unknown, however, in many individuals EF is self-limited and uncomplicated. Symptoms are usually successfully controlled with medication during active presentation of the syndrome. There have been some reports of spontaneous remissions.

Differential Diagnosis

Eosinophilic perimyositis and eosinophilic myositis have similar findings and symptoms. Symptoms of the early onset of scleroderma must also be ruled out.

Specialists

- Physiatrist
- Rheumatologist

Rehabilitation

Individuals with eosinophilic fasciitis may require physical or occupational therapy. Physical or occupational therapists address fatigue, pain, inflammation, and loss of range of motion in the affected body parts.

In general, occupational therapy addresses any fatigue that may occur during activities of daily living. Individuals learn to utilize equipment such as a shower chair to decrease the energy expended during bathing, or a long-handled sponge to decrease the amount of arm work an individual has to perform. Occupational therapists may teach energy conservation techniques.

Physical therapy addresses decreased endurance by teaching strengthening exercises of the arms and legs to improve overall endurance. Individuals may perform aerobic activity such as walking on a treadmill or riding a stationary bicycle to further increase endurance. Individuals learn to rate the amount of energy they expend by utilizing a rating of perceived exertion scale.

Range of motion is addressed in therapy to maintain function of the affected body parts. Therapists may passively stretch the area. Individuals learn to gently stretch the arms and legs. For example, if the individual is experiencing tightness in the ankle, the individual may stretch the ankle by placing a towel around the foot and pulling the toes toward himself or herself. This would preserve the ability to walk.

Individuals experiencing tightness in the fingers may perform exercises such as touching the thumb to each fingertip to maintain the ability to grasp a pen or a key. Individuals with persistent limitations in range of motion may require adaptive equipment for compensation. An individual may require a cane to compensate for gait abnormalities due to limitations in leg range of motion. An individual may require writing implements or kitchen utensils with wider shafts to compensate for decreased grasp.

Work Restrictions / Accommodations

These would be determined by the degree of incapacity and particular work activities required. The course of the disease is somewhat unpredictable requiring alteration in work activities based on symptoms at any given time.

When the upper extremities are most severely involved, dexterity and strength could be severely limited or only restricted to avoid repetitive motions.

Any activity that would increase swelling in the lower extremities such as long periods of standing, walking or sitting should be avoided. Again, restrictions on any job requirements could vary from day to day.

Comorbid Conditions

Chronic inflammatory or neurologic disease would make the course of EF more difficult.

Complications

Some individuals may develop thrombocytopenia, aplastic anemia, or paraneoplastic syndrome (rare).

Factors Influencing Duration

The response to treatment will influence the length of disability. The length of disability is highly variable based on location and severity.

Length of Disability

Return to work may be limited by residual muscle weakness and restriction of joint motion before successful rehabilitation is complete. Disability may be intermittent and/or prolonged depending upon the cause of the illness.

Duration in Days

Job Classification	Minimum	Optimum	Maximum
Sedentary work	0	7	21
Light work	0	7	21
Medium work	1	14	28
Heavy work	1	21	49
Very Heavy work	1	28	63

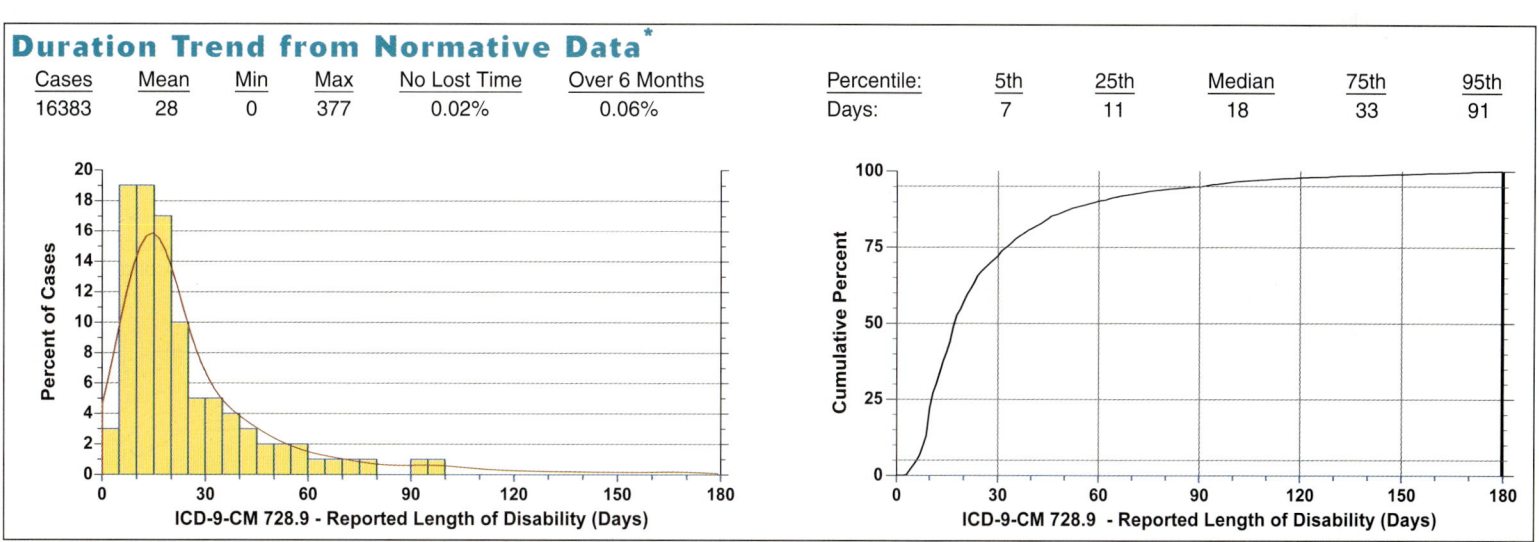

Duration Trend from Normative Data*

Cases	Mean	Min	Max	No Lost Time	Over 6 Months
16383	28	0	377	0.02%	0.06%

Percentile:	5th	25th	Median	75th	95th
Days:	7	11	18	33	91

* Differences may exist between the expected duration tables and the normative graphs. Duration tables provide expected recovery periods based on the type of work performed by the individual. The normative graphs reflect the actual observed experience of many individuals across the spectrum of physical conditions, in a variety of industries, and with varying levels of case management.

Failure to Recover

If an individual fails to recover within the maximum duration expectancy period, the reader may wish to reference the following questions to assist in better understanding the specifics of an individual's medical case.

Regarding diagnosis:

- Has the individual noticed a gradual increase in pain, swelling, and inflammation of the skin of the extremities along with a gradual restriction of arm and leg movement along with muscle weakness?
- Does the individual have symptoms of carpal tunnel syndrome, dry shiny skin, and the inability to make a fist?
- Does the individual have fatigue and weight loss?
- On exam does the skin over the arms and legs have an orange-peel configuration?
- Is the individual's skin taut and woody and restricted by the subcutaneous tissue?
- Are the face and trunk involved?
- Has the Individual had a CBC with differential, ESR, ANA and rheumatoid factor?
- Has the individual had a deep biopsy of affected skin and fascia? MRI?
- Have conditions with similar symptoms been ruled out?

Regarding treatment:

- Is the individual initially being treated with high doses of corticosteroids?
- Was the dose then lowered with plans to continue treatment up to 5 years if necessary?
- Is the individual on anti-ulcer medication, NSAIDs, or immunosuppressants?

Regarding prognosis:

- Is the individual active in physical therapy?

- Does the individual have a home exercise program?
- Is the individual's employer able to accommodate any necessary restrictions?
- Does the individual have any conditions that may affect the ability to recover?
- Does the individual have any complications such as thrombocytopenia, aplastic anemia, or paraneoplastic syndrome (rare)?

References

Guccione, Andrew A. "Functional Assessment." Physical Rehabilitation: Assessment and Treatment. O'Sullivan, Susan B., and Thomas J. Schmitz, ed. Philadelphia: F.A. Davis Company, 1994. 193-208.

Kisner, Carolyn, and Lynn Allen Colby. Therapeutic Exercise: Foundations and Applications, 2nd ed. Philadelphia: F.A. Davis Company, 1990.

Koopman, William. Arthritis and Allied Conditions, 13th ed. Baltimore: Williams & Wilkins, 1997. 08 Jan 2001 <http://home.mdconsult.com>.

Moxley, George, MD. "Scleroderma and Related Diseases." Scientific American® Medicine Online Dale, D.C., and D.D. Federman, eds. New York: WebMD Corporation, 2001 Scientific American Medicine. 11 Jan 2001 <http://www.samed.com/sam/forms/index/htm>.

Epicondylitis, Medial and Lateral

Other names / synonyms: Golfer's Elbow, Tennis Elbow
726.31, 726.32

Definition

Epicondylitis occurs when tendons in the elbow develop microscopic tears and inflammation.

The muscles and tendons responsible for wrist and finger movements attach in the elbow region to the upper arm bone (humerus). The areas of attachment are the round knobs just above the elbow joint (epicondyles). The tendons develop inflammation and, sometimes, microscopic tears. This process is known as epicondylitis either on the outside (lateral) or inside (medial) of the elbow. It is more commonly known as "tennis elbow" when on the lateral side and "golfer's elbow" when on the medial side.

Although the cause is unknown, epicondylitis may be a result of overuse or overexertion of the forearm and wrist muscles. Half of all tennis players have had symptoms of epicondylitis. Occupations that involve repetitive and/or stressful use of the forearm are associated with a higher incidence of epicondylitis and include cooks, utility workers, secretaries (and others spending a great deal of time on a keyboard), assembly line workers, cashiers, carpenters, plumbers, butchers, and politicians. Individuals participating in tennis, golf, baseball, swimming, racquetball, fly-fishing, weight lifting, and track and field sports are at an increased risk of developing epicondylitis.

Eighty percent of epicondylitis cases are caused by repetitive actions with the remainder caused by trauma. Epicondylitis typically afflicts individuals between the ages of thirty-five and fifty. Although men are twice as likely than women to develop medial epicondylitis, lateral epicondylitis afflicts men and women equally. Lateral epicondylitis is common and afflicts about 2% of the population of the US. It is 8 times more common than medial epicondylitis.

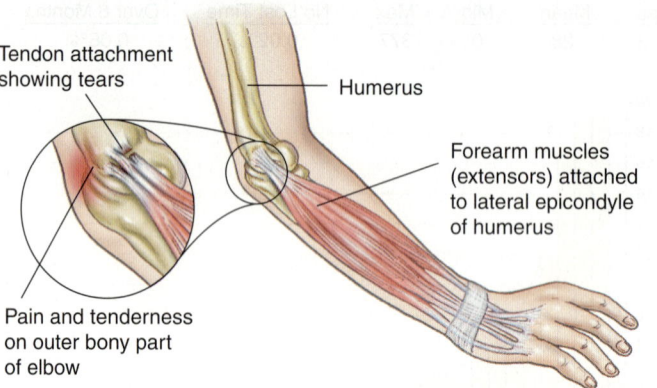

Diagnosis

History: The individual reports elbow pain and swelling and the inability to use the wrist of an arm, frequently the dominant arm. The symptoms may appear suddenly, but more often onset is gradual and progressive. Pain is localized to the elbow region initially, but may progress to involve the muscle mass of the forearm. Individuals may relate a change in activity or increase in size and weight of tools used immediately preceding the pain. Most cases, however, occur without an obvious cause. History of neck and shoulder injuries should be noted.

Physical exam: On physical examination, pain may be localized over either epicondyle and may increase with resisted wrist motion. Bending the wrist forward (flexion) causes pain for individuals with medial epicondylitis and bending the wrist backward (extension) causes pain for those with lateral epicondylitis. As the condition becomes more chronic, pain and weakness may involve the forearm as well, especially with resisted wrist and finger motion.

Tests: An injection test where a local anesthetic is injected into the most tender point of the elbow may confirm the diagnosis (pain caused by epicondylitis is relieved by the injection). When the diagnosis is in doubt or if an individual fails to respond to treatment x-rays are done to rule out bony abnormalities about the joint. MRI may show abnormal signals in the medial or lateral epicondyle but is usually unnecessary.

Treatment

Initial conservative treatment consists of rest from the precipitating or exacerbating activity, generally anti-inflammatory medication for pain and inflammation, and a band around the proximal forearm (forearm strap or counter-force brace). The forearm strap spreads the force of the muscle contraction over a greater area, and diminishes tensile stresses on the common extensor tendon. A wrist extension (cock-up) splint may be helpful in more severe cases. Ice often relieves pain after activity, with or without swelling. Massage may be beneficial. Stretching can be started immediately and strengthening exercises when the pain subsides.

Local anesthetic- corticosteroid injection may be used in individuals who do not improve after 6 to 8 weeks of treatment. The injection may not be fully effective for 5 to 7 days and can be repeated 3 times. Splints provide restriction of both the wrist and elbow and can be used in individuals not responding to other methods of treatment.

Surgery is rarely necessary, but may be performed on individuals with pain lasting longer than 6 months despite appropriate nonoperative treatment. Surgery usually involves open release of the tendon origin, excision of degenerated tendon and/or inflammatory tissue, and repair of any tendon gaps or tears. Any abnormalities in the elbow joint may be addressed concurrently.

Prognosis

Although recovery may be slow and tedious, most individuals have relief of all symptoms a year from onset. Conservative measures (i.e., nonsurgical) can relieve symptoms in more than 90% of the cases. Surgery relieves pain for 90-95% of the cases, although about 12% of individuals experience pain during aggressive activities. Ulnar nerve involvement is associated with a poor prognosis. Recurrence of epicondylitis later in life is common.

Differential Diagnosis

Irritation of the nerves around the elbow (e.g., nerve entrapment), fractures, loose bodies, ligament injuries, inflammatory disease, infection, joint (intraarticular) diseases, calcium deposits (calcification), compartment syndrome, neck (cervical spine) disorders, and pain traveling from another site (referred pain) may present with similar signs and symptoms as epicondylitis.

Specialists

- Hand Therapist
- Orthopedic Surgeon
- Physiatrist
- Rheumatologist
- Sports Medicine Physician

Rehabilitation

Individuals diagnosed with lateral or medial epicondylitis may attend outpatient physical therapy or occupational therapy. After initial therapy, transition should be made to a home exercise program.

Therapy addresses controlling pain and inflammation, restoring muscle flexibility, and increasing strength.

The control of pain and inflammation can be achieved through a variety of methods. Individuals apply hot packs to the elbow prior to exercise to reduce pain and increase muscle flexibility. The therapist may also use ultrasound, high frequency sound waves that heat deeper muscles and bone. Cross-friction massage is a technique used by therapists to promote healing of the injured tendons. Finally, individuals apply ice to the elbow after therapy or other activity.

Individuals increase the flexibility of the muscles extending from the elbow to the wrist through stretching. Therapists may passively stretch the wrist to increase flexion and extension and the forearm to increase rotation. Individuals learn to stretch the wrist by holding the elbow straight and using their other hand to help bend the wrist into flexion and extension.

Strengthening exercises are necessary to restore function and prevent reinjury. Individuals increase forearm strength through light resistive exercises. Light hand weights are used to strengthen wrist flexion and extension and forearm rotation. The forearm is placed on a table for support during these exercises. Individuals also squeeze therapy putty to further increase forearm strength. Functional exercises are performed such as wringing out a towel, turning a doorknob, or practicing the task that led to the injury (such as tennis or golf).

Work Restrictions / Accommodations

An ergonometric evaluation of the workplace may be necessary. The precipitating or exacerbating activity needs to be avoided until symptoms are relieved. Change in job duties, sharing or alternating tasks, and limiting time and frequency of repetitive activities are important accommodations. Use of vibrating tools such as impact wrenches or jackhammers should be minimized. Increasing or decreasing the size of tool grips so the wrist can be held in the "ideal" position is also helpful. Use of splints, straps, and casts affect dexterity and the individual may be temporarily unable to lift and carry heavy or bulky objects, operate equipment, or perform other tasks requiring the use of both hands. If the dominant arm was affected, the individual may be unable to write legibly, type well, or perform activities that require fine motor skills such as those in a laboratory or assembly line. Medications for pain and inflammation require evaluation of safety issues and drug policies.

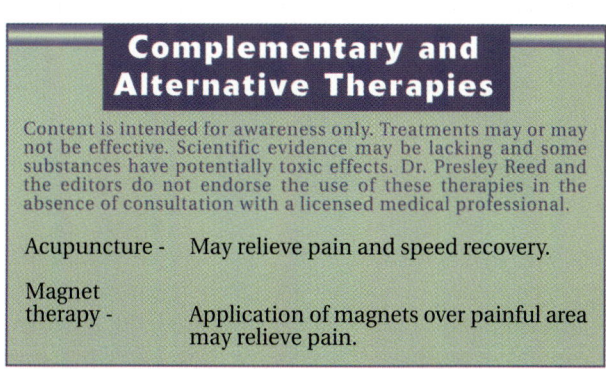

Complementary and Alternative Therapies

Content is intended for awareness only. Treatments may or may not be effective. Scientific evidence may be lacking and some substances have potentially toxic effects. Dr. Presley Reed and the editors do not endorse the use of these therapies in the absence of consultation with a licensed medical professional.

Acupuncture - May relieve pain and speed recovery.

Magnet therapy - Application of magnets over painful area may relieve pain.

Comorbid Conditions

Carpal tunnel syndrome, arthritis, cervical spine disease, and other injuries to the arm and shoulder may lengthen disability.

Complications

Radial neuropathy occurs in fewer than 5% of the cases of lateral epicondylitis. Ulnar neuropathy (cubital tunnel syndrome) occurs in 50% of the cases of medial epicondylitis. After local injections, there may be a 1- or 2-day increase in pain called postinjection flare.

Factors Influencing Duration

Dominant versus nondominant arm, work requirements, conservative versus surgical treatment, and compliance to rehabilitation program affect the length of disability.

Length of Disability

Duration of disability depends on job requirements, whether dominant or non-dominant extremity is involved, and work requirements (use of wrist, forearm). Disability may be longer for individuals with job duties that require intensive use of both arms or repetitive actions.

Duration in Days

Job Classification	Minimum	Optimum	Maximum
Sedentary work	0	7	28
Light work	1	10	28
Medium work	7	21	56
Heavy work	14	28	56
Very Heavy work	14	28	56

Failure to Recover

If an individual fails to recover within the maximum duration expectancy period, the reader may wish to reference the following questions to assist in better understanding the specifics of an individual's medical case.

Regarding diagnosis:

- Does the individual's occupation or hobby involve repetitive and/or stressful use of the forearm?
- Does the individual report elbow pain, swelling, and the inability to use the wrist and arm?
- Has the pain spread to the forearm?
- Is the affected elbow on the dominant or nondominant side?
- Does the individual have a history of neck or shoulder injuries?
- On physical examination, is the pain localized over either epicondyle?
- Does the pain increase with resisted wrist motion?
- Is there weakness noted in the forearm?
- Did the individual have an injection test done? X-ray? MRI?
- Have conditions with similar symptoms been ruled out?

Regarding treatment:

- Has the individual responded favorably to treatment consisting of rest from the aggravating activity, ice packs, NSAIDs, and a splint?
- Has the individual received a corticosteroid injection?
- Was surgery necessary?

Regarding prognosis:

- Is the individual active in physical therapy? Does the individual have a home exercise program?
- Is the individual's employer able to accommodate any necessary restrictions?
- Has the individual had an ergonomic evaluation of their work area?
- Does the individual have any conditions that may affect the ability to recover?
- Does the individual have any complications such as radial or ulnar neuropathy?
- Did the individual have a postinjection flare?

References

Gabel, Gerard, and Bernard Morrey. "Medial Epicondylitis." The Elbow and Its Disorders. Morrey, Bernard, ed. Philadelphia: W.B. Saunders Company, 2000. 537-542.

Magee, David J. "Forearm, Wrist, and Hand." Orthopedic Clinical Assessment. Biblis, Margaret M., ed. Philadelphia: W.B. Saunders Company, 1992. 168-215.

Epididymitis

Other names / synonyms: Inflammation of the Epididymis
098.13, 098.33, 604.9, 604.90

Definition

Epididymitis is inflammation of one or both of the tubules (epididymis) that are attached to each testicle. The epididymis act as conduits of sperm from the testes to the urethra. Epididymitis typically involves one testicle (unilateral) but may involve both testicles (bilateral).

The most common cause of epididymitis is bacterial infection. In sexually active men under 35, bacterial infections of chlamydia or gonorrhea are the most common causes of acute epididymitis. In nonsexually transmitted infections, gram-negative coliform bacteria (E. coli) is the most common infectious agent. In older men, epididymitis usually follows infections of the prostate gland (prostatitis) or urethra (urethritis). Direct trauma to the testicles or heavy lifting may precipitate acute epididymitis. It is infrequently caused by reflux of sterile urine.

Urinary tract infection or infections that can occur following diagnostic visualization of the lower urinary tract using fiberoptic equipment (cytoscopy) may also lead to epididymitis. Epididymitis caused by the tuberculosis virus occurs infrequently in the US, however, it is common in areas where tuberculosis is still a public health problem.

The prevalence of epididymitis in the general population is difficult to assess. The National Institutes of Health estimate that approximately 500,000 cases of epididymitis occur each year in the US. Others report an incidence rate of between 1 to 4 cases per 1,000 men each year. Epididymitis occurs worldwide, most commonly in men between the ages of 19 and 40. Approximately 15% of men will contract the condition during their lifetime.

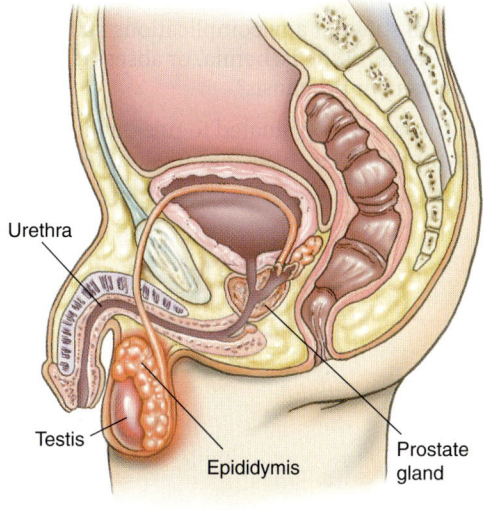

Diagnosis

History: Within 24 hours of onset, the initial symptoms are abdominal or flank pain because cellular inflammation typically begins in the vas deferens (testicular excretory duct). As the inflammation descends to the lower segment of the epididymis, the individual reports tenderness and pain in the scrotum, groin, and possibly the hip area. Pain is usually worse when standing or walking and may be relieved by elevating the legs. The individual may report frequent and painful urination (dysuria), nausea, fever, and chills. Older individuals may experience urinary retention. There may have been recent surgery or instrument examination of the urinary tract.

Physical exam: Fever may be present. The epididymis and scrotum are usually swollen, tender, and firmer than usual. The skin of the scrotum may appear reddened. If an abscess is present, the scrotum skin may be dry, flaky, and thinned. Elevating the scrotum usually diminishes the pain. There may be a discharge from the urethra.

Tests: Urine should be examined under the microscope for the presence of pus and bacteria (urinalysis). An attempt to grow the bacteria for further testing may be needed (urine culture and sensitivity). Discharge from the urethra can be similarly examined for signs of sexually transmitted diseases. A complete blood count (CBC) typically shows a marked increase in the number of white blood cells. Imaging studies may be used to differentiate epididymitis from other potential diagnoses such as testicular torsion (twisting of the spermatic cord and testicle).

Treatment

Antibiotics are given if a bacterial infection is causing the epididymitis. The type of antibiotic, how it is given, and the duration of the therapy depends on the bacterial strain causing the infection. Medication (analgesics) may be given for pain. Absolute bed rest is instituted for 3 to 4 days with the scrotum elevated and ice packs applied to relieve swelling. Occasionally, a local anesthetic is injected into the spermatic cord to relieve severe pain.

The treatment for nonbacterial epididymitis is identical except antibiotics are not administered. If the epididymitis occurred as a result of a sexually transmitted disease, then the individual's sexual partner(s) should also be treated with antibiotics. Strenuous exertion should be avoided for at least 2 weeks after the tenderness subsides. Surgical treatment (epididymectomy) to remove the section of inflamed epididymis is rarely necessary.

Prognosis

Prompt treatment using antibiotics and/or bed rest with scrotal elevation and ice application usually results in a favorable outcome. The individual's fertility may be reduced if the infection occurred in both the epididymis. Fertility may be at risk if there is resulting scarring from the epididymitis or if the individual requires surgery to remove a section of the inflamed epididymis (epididymectomy).

Differential Diagnosis

Conditions that present with similar symptoms include twisting of the spermatic cord and testicle (testicular torsion), collection of fluid within the scrotum (hydrocele), cysts within the epididymis that may contain spermatozoa (spermatocele), orchitis (inflammation of a testis), variocele (varicose vein in the scrotum), UTI (urinary tract infection), or testicular tumors.

Specialists

- Urologist

Work Restrictions / Accommodations

Strenuous physical strain at work should be avoided for a period of time (days to several weeks) determined by the treating physician.

Comorbid Conditions

Untreated sexually transmitted disease may cause recurrence of epididymitis and further lengthen the disability.

Complications

Prolonged, untreated swelling may decrease the blood supply to the scrotum (ischemia) with possible tissue damage. Although rare, spread of the infection to the testicles (epididymoorchitis) is another possible complication. An abscess may develop that would require an operation to drain the pocket of infection. Acute epididymitis may develop into chronic epididymitis if left untreated.

Factors Influencing Duration

Complications of epididymitis that require surgical treatment will increase the length of disability.

Length of Disability

Individual may need to avoid excessive lifting for 1 to 2 weeks.

Medical treatment. Non-septic.

Duration in Days

Job Classification	Minimum	Optimum	Maximum
Sedentary work	3	3	7
Light work	3	3	7
Medium work	3	3	7
Heavy work	3	7	14
Very Heavy work	3	7	14

Failure to Recover

If an individual fails to recover within the maximum duration expectancy period, the reader may wish to reference the following questions to assist in better understanding the specifics of an individual's medical case.

Regarding diagnosis:

- Is the individual sexually active? Do they have a history of prostatitis or urethritis?
- Did the individual have symptoms characteristic of epididymitis, such as abdominal or flank pain, scrotal, groin or hip pain and associated dysuria, nausea, or chills?
- Did the physical exam reveal a fever, inflamed scrotum or urethral discharge?
- Was there an elevated white blood cell count?
- Was a bacterial culture of the urethral discharge done? Was the culture positive? Was the organism a sexually transmitted organism?
- If the diagnosis was uncertain, were other conditions with similar symptoms (i.e., testicular torsion, hydrocele, spermatocele, orchitis, variocele, urinary tract infection or testicular tumor) considered in the differential diagnosis?

Regarding treatment:

- Have the appropriate antibiotics been prescribed?
- Has the individual been compliant with recommendations for bedrest and elevating the scrotum?
- If the bacterial is sexually transmitted, was antibiotic treatment prescribed for sexual partner(s)?
- Were analgesics, ice packs and bedrest effective in relieving pain? If not, was treatment with a local anesthetic injection considered?
- Was the inflammation significant enough to warrant surgical removal of the epididymis?

Regarding prognosis:

- Was the individual treated promptly with the appropriate antibiotics?
- Has a repeat culture and sensitivity been done to rule out recurrence or the presence of an antibiotic resistant bacteria?
- Has the individual adhered to the prescribed bed rest and avoidance of physical exertion for an appropriate period of time?
- Is surgery to remove the inflamed epididymis necessary?
- Has the individual suffered any complications such as spread of infection to the testis, tissue ischemia, or abscess formation that may impact recovery or prognosis?
- Has the individual been re-evaluated to rule out other conditions with similar symptoms (i.e., testicular torsion, testicular cancer, etc)?

References

Holtgrewe, H. Logan. "Transurethral Resection of the Prostate." Prostatic Diseases. Lepor, Herbert, ed. Philadelphia: W.B. Saunders Company, 2000. 232-245.

Nistal, M., and R. Paniagua. Testicular and Epididymal Pathology. New York: Thieme-Stratton Inc, 1984.

Epidural Hematoma

Other names / synonyms: Epidural Hemorrhage, Extradural Hematoma, Extradural Hemorrhage
432.0

Definition

An epidural hematoma is caused from bleeding between the skull and the outer membrane that covers the brain (dura mater). Rapid bleeding results in a localized accumulation of blood (hematoma) that presses on the brain tissue and leads to a rapid increase in pressure within the brain (increased intracranial pressure).

Ninety percent of all epidural hematomas are caused by head trauma due to car accidents, sports injuries, violent attacks, or falls and are associated with a skull fracture that crosses a portion of the middle meningeal artery or vein. In 60% of cases, the middle meningeal artery is the source of bleeding.

Epidural hematomas are not common and much less frequent than subdural hematomas. About 10% of brain injuries are classified as moderate to severe and thereby capable of causing bleeding within the skull. Only a small percentage results in an epidural hemorrhage.

Diagnosis

History: Usually after an epidural hematoma is sustained, it is usually followed by loss of consciousness, then an alert period, succeeded by deterioration and a return to an unconsciousness state. During the alert period, the individual usually complains of severe headache that may be accompanied by nausea or vomiting.

Physical exam: Enlarged or uneven pupils, weakness of an arm or a leg usually on the opposite side of the enlarged pupil, and localized exam abnormalities (focal neurologic deficits) related to pressure effects from the epidural hematoma may be evident upon exam.

Tests: CT of the brain usually confirms the diagnosis of an epidural hematoma, establishes its location, and often demonstrates an associated skull fracture.

Treatment

Epidural hematoma is treated surgically by evacuation of the hematoma. First, small holes are bored through the skull (burr holes) and then the clot is removed either manually or by suction (evacuation procedure).

Medications may be used as additional therapy and vary with the kind of symptoms and extent of brain damage. Anticonvulsants may be used to control or prevent seizures. Diuretics or corticosteroids can reduce swelling inside the skull. Antibiotics help control infection.

Prognosis

If the diagnosis is recognized immediately and surgery is performed, the outcome is generally good. If the individual is first seen during the lucid period, a CT may not be done because an epidural hematoma is not suspected. If the diagnosis and treatment of epidural hematoma are therefore delayed, incidence of death and/or long-term neurologic deficits increases.

Differential Diagnosis

Other conditions that may present with similar symptoms and/or signs include cerebral contusion, cerebral laceration, subdural hematoma, depressed fractures of the skull, and cranial concussion.

Specialists

- Internist
- Neurologist
- Neurosurgeon

Rehabilitation

If there is only minimal damage to the brain, the overall objective for rehabilitation of individuals with epidural hematoma injury is to return them as quickly and as fully as possible to the mainstream. Rehabilitation may involve physical, occupational, and speech therapy and/or cognitive retraining to help the individual achieve functional recovery and cope with disabilities that may remain.

Rehabilitation varies for each individual because of the uniqueness of the problems that result from different areas of the brain affected. Because of this, there is no specific process or technique for the rehabilitation program. Treatment guidelines for the individual who has lost voluntary motion of his or her limbs begin with passive range-of-motion exercises. If memory is affected by the epidural hematoma, exercises are initiated to promote memory return as well as instructing the individual to carry out simple tasks. This can be as elementary as motivating the individual to receive an object in his or her hand or instructing the individual to go from a sitting to standing position.

The rehabilitation program sequences activities that progress from easy to more difficult such as teaching the individual to rise from a chair to instructing proper walking patterns. Once the individual regains thinking processes, rehabilitation focuses on the needs of muscular strength, endurance, and flexibility. Muscle imbalance is corrected by using traditional physical therapy methods and techniques to help make the muscle and nervous system work together. Group activities may take place in mat classes, wheelchair classes, or in other activities such as volleyball games.

When appropriate, the final phase of rehabilitation following recovery from an epidural hematoma involves the individual's reinstatement to work. Physical and mental exercises are now directed toward the work requirements. Modifications may need to be made by the physical therapist for those individuals with various deficits after an epidural hematoma.

Work Restrictions / Accommodations

Work restrictions and accommodations after an epidural hematoma may vary from no restrictions and accommodations to marked restrictions and accommodations. This is a function of the degree of brain damage that may have occurred. The degree of brain damage, in turn, is a function of the size of the hematoma, rapidity with which surgery was performed, and the completeness of hematoma evacuation.

Comorbid Conditions

Lung disease, heart disease, diabetes, kidney disease, and peripheral vascular disease may affect an individual's ability to recover and/or extend the time of disability.

Complications

Without prompt surgical intervention, there is a high risk of death. Even with prompt surgical intervention, complications such as permanent brain damage and seizures may occur.

Factors Influencing Duration

Age, time delay before surgical intervention, success of the surgical procedure, and pre-existing conditions are factors that can influence the length of disability.

Length of Disability

Surgical treatment.

Duration in Days

Job Classification	Minimum	Optimum	Maximum
Sedentary work	21	42	Indefinite
Light work	28	42	Indefinite
Medium work	35	56	Indefinite
Heavy work	42	56	Indefinite
Very Heavy work	42	56	Indefinite

Failure to Recover

If an individual fails to recover within the maximum duration expectancy period, the reader may wish to reference the following questions to assist in better understanding the specifics of an individual's medical case.

Regarding diagnosis:

- Has the individual suffered a head injury?
- Did the individual lose consciousness and then have an alert period?
- Does the individual complain of a severe headache? Nausea or vomiting?
- Has the individual become unconscious again?
- On exam were the individual's pupils enlarged or unequal?
- Does the individual have weakness of an arm or leg?
- Has the individual had a CT scan?
- Have conditions with similar symptoms been ruled out?

Regarding treatment:

- Did the individual have surgery to evacuate the hematoma?
- Is the individual being treated with anticonvulsants, diuretics or corticosteroids?
- Is the individual receiving antibiotics?

Regarding prognosis:

- Is the individual active in rehabilitation?
- Is the individual's employer able to accommodate any necessary restrictions?
- Does the individual have any conditions that may affect ability to recover?
- Does the individual have any complications such as permanent brain damage, seizures, uncal hernia, or normal pressure hydrocephalus?

References

Cranial/Facial Trauma. Academic Press. 1998. 14 Aug 2000 <http://www.acapress.com/mono-12.htm>.

Neuroradiology Teaching File - Epidural Hematoma. Wayne State University. 2000. 14 Aug 2000 <http://www.med.wayne.edu/diagRadiology/TF/Neuro/Neuro6.htm>.

Epiglottitis

Other names / synonyms: Inflammation of the Epiglottis
464.3, 464.30, 464.31

Definition

Epiglottitis is a serious, life threatening bacterial infection of the epiglottis.

The epiglottis is the soft tissue flap in the throat that functions as a valve over the airway to the lungs (trachea). When swallowing, the epiglottis obstructs the trachea and prevents food, fluids, and secretions from entering the lungs. With epiglottitis, emergency medical intervention may be needed to prevent the swollen and inflamed epiglottis from causing total airway obstruction and death from asphyxia.

Most cases of epiglottitis are caused by the bacteria Haemophilus influenzae B (not to be confused with the influenza virus). Incidence has decreased since a vaccine against this pathogen was introduced. Incidence in adults is now approximately 1 out of 100,000 per year in the US. Epiglottitis is about three times more common in men than women with the average age about 45.

Diagnosis

History: The symptoms escalate quickly over 24 hours and include sore throat, coughing, drooling, lethargy, fever, and a muffled voice. This progresses to difficulty in breathing and swallowing. Usually epiglottitis does not follow an ordinary upper respiratory infection.

Physical exam: Individual may have swollen lymph nodes and respiratory distress may be evident. The individual appears ill and gentle pressure on the throat causes severe pain.

Tests: A swab of the epiglottis and a blood culture are usually done to identify the bacteria involved. In adults, direct fiber optic visualization of the epiglottis (nasopharyngoscopy) and x-ray evaluation may be appropriate to confirm the diagnosis. However, tests should be postponed in an emergency situation until the airway is secure.

Treatment

Individuals are admitted to the intensive care unit where they can be observed for signs of airway obstruction. It may be necessary to insert a breathing tube (intubation) until the swelling subsides. If the obstruction is too severe for intubation to be successful, a surgical procedure may be necessary where the epiglottis is bypassed and a breathing tube inserted into the airway through an incision in the neck (tracheostomy or cricothyrotomy). Intravenous antibiotics are given as well as analgesics to relieve pain.

Prognosis

With prompt and appropriate antibiotic treatment, there is usually complete resolution of the infection with no after effects. If intubation was necessary, the tube is usually removed within 48 hours after beginning treatment. However, the danger of sudden airway obstruction results in a mortality rate of approximately 7%.

Differential Diagnosis

Other conditions with similar symptoms may include anaphylaxis, anxiety attacks, ingestion of caustic substances, diphtheria, accidental inhalation of a foreign body into the trachea, mononucleosis, and bacterial infection of the pharynx (e.g., strep throat) or trachea.

Specialists

- Anesthesiologist
- General Surgeon
- Otolaryngologist

Work Restrictions / Accommodations

The individual cannot work at all until the acute condition with its threat of airway obstruction is resolved. Upon return, no work restrictions or special accommodations are required.

Comorbid Conditions

Comorbid conditions may include immune suppression.

Complications

The most common serious complication is a blocked airway that can lead to asphyxia and death. Other complications can include pneumonia, pulmonary edema, epiglottic abscess, cervical adenitis, pericarditis, meningitis, and septic shock.

Factors Influencing Duration

Factors that may influence the length of the disability include whether the individual needs to be intubated and if any complications occur.

Length of Disability

Duration in Days

Job Classification	Minimum	Optimum	Maximum
Any work	7	10	14

Failure to Recover

If an individual fails to recover within the maximum duration expectancy period, the reader may wish to reference the following questions to assist in better understanding the specifics of an individual's medical case.

Regarding diagnosis:

- Did symptoms escalate quickly over 24 hours and include sore throat, coughing, drooling, lethargy, fever, and a muffled voice? Did condition progress to difficulty in breathing and swallowing? What were the findings on physical exam? Swollen lymph nodes, respiratory distress, severe pain with gentle pressure applied to the throat?

- Has individual received adequate diagnostic testing to confirm the diagnosis such as a blood culture, nasopharyngoscopy, or x-ray evaluation?

- Were other conditions with similar symptoms such as anaphylaxis, anxiety attacks, ingestion of caustic substances, diphtheria, accidental inhalation of a foreign body into the trachea, mononucleosis, and bacterial infection of the pharynx or trachea ruled out?

Regarding treatment:

- Did individual receive prompt and appropriate antibiotic treatment?
- Were analgesics needed for pain?
- Was intubation done?
- Was tracheostomy or cricothyrotomy necessary?

Regarding prognosis:

- Does individual have immune suppression?
- Does individual have any complications such as a blocked airway, pneumonia, pulmonary edema, epiglottic abscess, cervical adenitis, pericarditis, meningitis, and septic shock that may impact recovery?

References

Bowman, Jeffrey Glenn. Epiglottitis, Adult. eMedicine.com 18 Aug 2000. 05 Jan 2001 <http://emedicine.com/emerg/topic169.htm>.

Tierney, Lawrence, Stephen McPhee, and Maxine Papadakis. Current Medical Diagnosis and Treatment. New York: McGraw-Hill, 2000.

Epilepsy

Other names / synonyms: Epileptic Convulsions, Epileptic Fits, Idiopathic Seizure Disorder, Recurrent Seizures, Seizure Disorder

345, 345.1, 345.2, 345.4, 345.7, 345.9, 445.8

Definition

Epilepsy is the term used to describe any seizure disorder with repeated episodes of seizures (of any type) with no known cause. Information is transmitted from one nerve cell to another through an electrochemical process (electrical activity). Seizures are caused by a chaotic and unregulated disruption of the normal electrical activity of the brain as measured by an electroencephalogram (EEG).

Epileptic seizures are generally classified into generalized and partial seizures. Generalized seizures affect all or most of the brain, affecting the whole body and causing loss of consciousness. Partial seizures affect only a portion of the brain and may not result in loss of consciousness. Although partial seizures begin in a limited area of the brain, the electrical disturbance can spread and affect the whole brain, possibly evolving into a generalized seizure.

The most recognized type of seizure is the convulsive or generalized motor seizure. It is characterized through abnormal and sometimes violent movements of the whole body or only parts of the body. It can start out as a partial seizure and evolve into a generalized seizure. An example of a generalized motor seizure is the grand mal seizure.

The cognitive or absence seizure occurs when the individual does not respond in a normal manner to his or her surroundings for a brief period of time. There is no loss of consciousness. Absence seizures may also be referred to as petit mal seizures.

Sensory seizures can result in a wide and strange variety of reported symptoms such as dizziness (vertigo) and tingling or numbness in a part of the body (paresthesias) or the perception of sounds, visions, and smells that do not really occur (auditory, visual, and olfactory hallucinations).

Seizures can be the result of various diseases or injuries. Epileptic seizures may be associated with birth trauma, head injury, central nervous system infections, brain tumor, stroke, ingestion of toxic substances, or metabolic imbalance. There may be an inherited tendency toward seizures.

Seizures with no apparent cause (idiopathic epilepsy) account for 75% of the cases in adults. These seizures may actually be due to microscopic brain lesions that occurred during birth or other trauma, or from unexplained metabolic disturbances. A single seizure or episode of seizures does not necessarily mean that the individual has epilepsy.

Epilepsy affects about 40 million individuals worldwide and about 2.5 million individuals in the US. It is equally common in men and women and affects all ages, with the highest incidence in children and the elderly.

Diagnosis

History: The type of symptoms and physical signs described by the individual or an observer depend on what part of the brain was affected. The history is very important in the diagnosis of epilepsy. A detailed description of the seizure from the individual themselves or an observer is noted. Since individuals often do not remember the event, information obtained from someone who has witnessed the seizure is a valuable part of the history. If the individual is conscious throughout the seizure, he or she may be able to recall symptoms or other details. Many individuals with epilepsy have no symptoms between seizures (the inter-ictal phase). Others may have an aura characterized by restlessness, irritability, or an uncomfortable feeling that precedes a seizure (pre-ictal state).

The documented seizures must be recurrent and chronic in order to make a diagnosis of epilepsy. An isolated seizure episode of any type is not an epileptic seizure. In fact, if there is no history of seizures, a single seizure or repeated seizures in a short period of time may be a sign of a serious underlying disease, chemical imbalance, drug or alcohol use, stroke, or a tumor.

Physical exam: The exam may be entirely normal. If the individual is examined immediately after the seizure, a complete neurological exam may be postponed if the individual lost consciousness or is not alert. The period after the seizure is called the post-ictal phase. Some types of seizures leave the individual fatigued or confused and unable to follow directions. It is important to focus on findings that may indicate a brain lesion.

Tests: The approach to testing depends on whether or not this was the individual's first seizure. If it was the first episode, extensive testing is necessary. Comprehensive blood tests look for a metabolic or chemical cause for the seizures. Routine tests include MRI, EEG, CT, and possibly a cerebral angiogram. The EEG is the most useful test in classifying seizures and can direct the best approach to therapy.

If the individual was previously seen for seizures and the diagnosis of a recurrent seizure disorder or epilepsy was established, then the testing is more limited. If the individual is on medication for seizures, measurement of blood drug levels can determine whether the individual has been taking the medications or if the dosage should be changed.

Treatment

Treatment of the underlying cause, if identified, may stop the occurrence of seizures. Such treatments may include medical or surgical interventions depending on the underlying cause.

Oral anticonvulsant medications help prevent or minimize the number and severity of future seizures. Response to treatment with oral anticonvulsants varies with different individuals. The medication or combination of medications and their dosages may be changed frequently until the optimal treatment regimen is found. These medications may have unpleasant side effects including drowsiness and impaired concentration that may lead to noncompliance. Follow-up ranges from monthly to annually depending on response to treatment. Monitoring of plasma drug levels is important for seizure control.

In approximately 15-25% of individuals with epilepsy, seizures cannot be controlled with medication and individuals may be evaluated for epilepsy surgery. The most common form of surgery involves the removal of the area of the temporal lobe where the seizures originate (temporal lobectomy). Resections of the frontal lobes can also be performed (extra-temporal resections).

Another treatment used when medications fail is vagal nerve stimulation (VNS). In this procedure, a generator is surgically implanted in the left chest wall. An electrode lead that is attached to the left vagus nerve is tunneled under the skin and connected to the generator. After implantation, the generator is programmed to deliver intermittent bursts of electricity to the vagus nerve.

Prognosis

Epilepsy (idiopathic seizure disorder) is a chronic, usually lifelong condition. Anticonvulsant therapies prevent or minimize the number of future seizures. Surgical removal of brain lesions may stop or lessen seizure activity. For some individuals, the need for medication may be reduced or eliminated over time (the milestone for this change in treatment is a seizure-free period of two years).

Death or permanent brain damage from epilepsy is rare but can occur with prolonged seizures or status epilepticus.

Differential Diagnosis

Seizures can be associated with many types of conditions including high fevers, syncope, hypoglycemia, confusional migraines, vertigo, cardiac arrhythmias, transient ischemic attacks, head injury, brain infections (e.g., encephalitis and meningitis), brain tumor, stroke, drug intoxication, and withdrawal from alcohol, narcotics, cocaine, tranquilizers, and sleeping pills.

Specialists

- Neurologist
- Neurosurgeon

Work Restrictions / Accommodations

An individual with epilepsy may be unable to perform jobs that require operating machinery, motor vehicles, or working from heights. Special precautions should be taken for those individuals at risk of recurrent seizures. These rules may be gradually relaxed if an individual remains seizure-free for a period of 1 year.

Individuals with epilepsy should wear a medical identification bracelet or carry an informational card to aid in obtaining proper medical treatment if a seizure occurs.

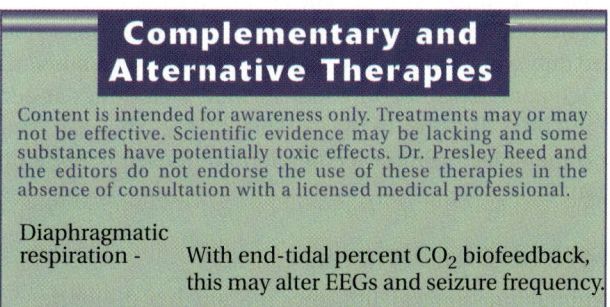

Complementary and Alternative Therapies

Content is intended for awareness only. Treatments may or may not be effective. Scientific evidence may be lacking and some substances have potentially toxic effects. Dr. Presley Reed and the editors do not endorse the use of these therapies in the absence of consultation with a licensed medical professional.

Diaphragmatic respiration - With end-tidal percent CO_2 biofeedback, this may alter EEGs and seizure frequency.

Comorbid Conditions

Individuals with epilepsy may have an underlying neurologic problem (e.g., congenital brain abnormalities, complications from kidney disease, liver disease, or brain injury) that may be causing the seizures.

Age-related physiologic changes may affect the pharmacokinetics of anticonvulsant therapies; therefore, careful, routine monitoring of anticonvulsant levels in older individuals is imperative.

Complications

Complications of epilepsy include prolonged seizures (status epilepticus), injury from falls, injuries from self-biting (during a seizure), injuries sustained while driving or operating machinery during a seizure, pneumonia secondary to foreign matter such as food particles in the lungs (aspiration pneumonia), stroke, brain damage, and learning disabilities.

Factors Influencing Duration

The frequency of seizures, response to treatment, and side effects of medications may influence disability. The work environment and duties of the individual may also be an influence, i.e., tasks such as driving that expose the individual or others to injury in the event of a seizure would not be acceptable for an individual with seizures that are not under control.

Length of Disability

There may be no disability with effective treatment and control of the seizures. The length of disability reflects time necessary to stabilize medications. Although seizure control is achieved in most individuals, disability may be permanent in those who do not respond to treatment.

Medical treatment.

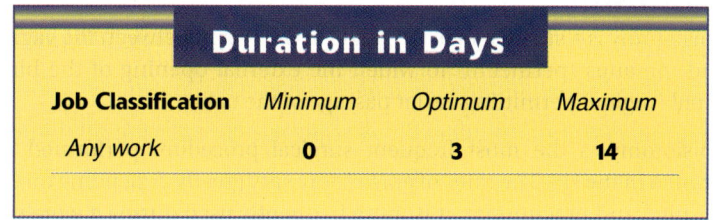

Duration in Days

Job Classification	Minimum	Optimum	Maximum
Any work	0	3	14

Failure to Recover

If an individual fails to recover within the maximum duration expectancy period, the reader may wish to reference the following questions to assist in better understanding the specifics of an individual's medical case.

Regarding diagnosis:

- What type of seizure does the individual have - generalized motor seizure (grand mal), partial seizure, cognitive or absence seizure (petit mal), or sensory seizure?
- Does the individual have idiopathic seizures?
- Does the individual have an aura?
- Has the individual had birth trauma, head injury, central nervous system infections, brain tumor, stroke, ingestion of toxic substances, or metabolic imbalance?
- Does the individual have a family history of seizures?
- Has the individual had a witnessed seizure?
- Are the individual's documented seizures recurrent and chronic?
- Has the individual had a single seizure or repeated seizures in a short period of time?
- Is it a sign of a serious underlying condition?

- Has the individual had comprehensive blood tests, skull x-rays, MRI, EEG, CT, and possibly a cerebral angiogram?
- If the individual has a diagnosis of epilepsy were drug levels done?
- Have conditions with similar symptoms been ruled out?

Regarding treatment:

- Has an underlying cause been identified?
- Is the individual on oral anticonvulsant drugs?
- Does the individual see their physician regularly for monitoring plasma drug levels?
- Is the individual a candidate for surgery?
- Has vagal nerve stimulation been considered?

Regarding prognosis:

- Is the individual's employer able to accommodate any necessary restrictions?
- Does the individual have any conditions that may affect their ability to recover?
- Does the individual have any complications such as status epilepticus, injury from falls, injuries from self-biting (during a seizure), injuries sustained while driving or operating machinery during a seizure, aspiration pneumonia, stroke, brain damage, and learning disabilities?

References

Epilepsy. drkoop.com. 2000. 22 Jun 2000 <http://www.drkoop.com/conditions/ency/article/000694.htm>.

Eisenschenk, Stephan, and Robin Gilmore. "Strategies for Successful Management of Older Patients with Seizures." Geriatrics 54 12 (1999): 31-46.

Fried, R., M.C. Fox, and R.M. Carlton. "Effect of Diaphragmatic Respiration with End-tidal CO2 Biofeedback on Respiration, EEG, and Seizure Frequency in Idiopathic Epilepsy." Annals of NY Academic Science 602 (1990): 67-96.

Lowenstein, D. "Status Epilepticus: An Overview of the Clinical Problem." Epilepsia 40 Suppl 1 (1999): S3-S8.

Niedermeyer, Ernst. The Epilepsies. Diagnosis and Management. Baltimore: Urban & Schwarzenberg, 1990.

Shafer, Patricia. "Epilepsy and Seizures." Nursing Clinics of North America 34 3 (1999): 743-758.

Episiotomy
73.6

Definition

Episiotomy is a surgical incision made in the region between the vagina and the anus (perineum) to widen the external opening of the birth canal (vagina) permitting easier passage of the baby.

Episiotomy is the most frequent surgical procedure performed on women in the US. The rates of episiotomy vary greatly depending on the hospital and practitioner. It is more frequently used during a woman's first delivery (nulliparas). Episiotomy is performed in 63% of deliveries in the US, 30% of those in Europe, and 56% in Denmark.

Reason for Procedure

An episiotomy is performed to prevent a tear of the perineum. An episiotomy is most often performed to facilitate the delivery of the baby. It allows for additional room in the vaginal opening needed by the instruments when an assisted delivery is necessary or when extra room is required because the baby is being in a compound or complex presentation. An episiotomy can also speed delivery in cases of fetal distress when the baby is not receiving enough oxygen during labor or when the pressure on the head of a premature baby needs to be reduced.

Description

A local anesthetic is used. Surgical scissors or a scalpel make a cut extending from the back wall of the vagina (through the perineal skin and muscles) to the side of the anus (mediolateral) or in a direct line with the anus (midline). Shortly after delivery, the cut tissues are stitched (sutured) together again. The stitches (sutures) dissolve after about 10 days.

Prognosis

In most cases, the episiotomy will heal without complication. Extensive tearing occurs between the vagina and the anus in up to 9% of women who have had a mediolateral episiotomy, and up to 24% with a midline episiotomy.

Specialists

- Obstetrician
- Primary Care Provider

Work Restrictions / Accommodations

Most women recover from an otherwise uncomplicated vaginal or assisted vaginal delivery within 4 to 6 weeks. They may have a period of time of reduced physical activity immediately after post delivery due to vaginal bleeding and cramping or episiotomy pain as their uterus/perineum heals from the delivery. The vast majority of women with uncomplicated singleton pregnancies and vaginal or assisted vaginal delivery are physiologically stable to return to full time sedentary or modified duty work within 4 to 6 weeks of delivery. Accommodations for women who are breast-feeding may include such things as additional breaks and privacy rooms in the workplace where they can breast-feed or pump the breasts. Breast-feeding in and of itself is not a disabling condition.

Comorbid Conditions

Postpartum depression can influence the length of disability.

Procedure Complications

Episiotomy can cause excessive pain, swelling, increased blood loss, bruising (hematoma), and lead to infection that may become walled off and form an abscess. Midline episiotomy can increase the rate of extensive (third- and fourth-degree) perineal tearing (laceration). Extensive tearing can damage the anal sphincter and lead to long-term incontinence of gas (flatus) and stool (feces) and formation of an abnormal passage (fistula) between the vagina and rectum (rectovaginal). Mediolateral episiotomy can cause excessive blood loss or painful and/or difficult sexual intercourse (dyspareunia).

Factors Influencing Duration

Disability beyond the normal time frame associated with vaginal delivery is not expected with this procedure.

Length of Disability

No disability is associated with this procedure. Duration of disability will be that of delivery.

References

Farrington, Pamela, and Kenneth Ward. "Normal Labor, Delivery, and Puerperium." Danforth's Obstetrics and Gynecology. Scott, James, et al., eds. Philadelphia: Lippincott, Williams & Wilkins, 1999. 91-109.

Myers-Helfgott, M. Gabrielle, and Andrew Helfgott. "Routine Use of Episiotomy in Modern Obstetrics. Should it be Performed?" Obstetrics and Gynecology Clinics of North America 26 2 (1999): 305-325.

Equine Encephalitis

Other names / synonyms: Equine Encephalomyelitis
062, 062.1, 062.2, 062.9, 064

Definition

Equine encephalitis is a viral infection that causes brain inflammation in humans. The equine form of the viral infection is primarily found in horses or mules although other mammals and birds may also be infected. Mosquitoes feeding on the blood of infected animals spread the disease to humans.

Occupational or recreational exposure to horses increases risk of infection. The disease is most prevalent during warmer months but may also occur year-round.

There are three major forms of equine encephalitis although various other isolated types of the infection also exist. Eastern equine encephalitis (EEE) is common during summer and fall when several varieties of mosquito carriers are active. Symptoms appear within several days after exposure. EEE infections can be extremely serious, leading to death in almost 50% of all cases however EEE is rare with only about 10 human cases reported annually. In the US, EEE is primarily found in the swamp areas of the Midwest and the eastern seaboard. It is also found in Central and South America and the Caribbean.

Western equine encephalitis (WEE) is primarily associated with one species of mosquito called Culex tarsalis that inhabits water sources such as irrigated agriculture fields in the western US and Canada. Symptoms usually appear about one week after exposure. An average of 10-20 cases of this form of encephalitis are reported annually. Mortality rate is about three percent. WEE frequently goes undiagnosed making occurrence probably much greater than reported.

Venezuelan equine encephalitis (VEE) is found primarily in Central and South America where widespread epidemics have occurred. The disease is carried by many different mosquito species. While much more common than other varieties of equine encephalitis, VEE is also far less severe. VEE usually manifests with flu-like symptoms that occur within several days of exposure. In one epidemic in the mid-1990s, more than 11,000 cases were documented. Records of VEE prevalence in this region, however, have not been kept on an ongoing basis. About 1% of all VEE cases result in death. While occurring naturally, VEE has also been developed as an agent of biological warfare.

Diagnosis

History: Early signs of the disease may include a sudden onset of fever, stiff neck, sore throat, headaches, and vomiting. Speech disturbances, light sensitivity (photophobia), lethargy, convulsions, or a coma may develop quickly. Personality changes may be present. If the central nervous system is affected in individuals with EEE, seizures and a coma may occur. While individuals with milder cases of WEE may only experience fever, drowsiness, or headaches, more severe illness may lead to confusion or weakness. Individuals with WEE may experience a sudden remission or complete recovery within only a few days. With VEE, the individual usually reports flu-like symptoms such as a vague onset of illness (malaise), cough, sore throat, nausea, and diarrhea. Possible occupational exposure to horses should be investigated.

Physical exam: The exam may reveal an individual who is excited, disoriented, stuporous, or in a coma. Abnormal reflexes or paralysis may be present.

Tests: Specific antibodies associated with EEE, WEE, or VEE may be identified through tests of the blood (serology) or cerebrospinal fluid. Analysis of antibody activity may be done through enzyme-linked immunosorbent assay (ELISA) or staining of the blood with a chemically treated dye (immunofluorescence). Deoxyribonucleic acid (DNA) analysis using polymerase chain reaction (PCR) tests may also be used to rapidly identify viral agents. Other indicators of the disease may be high cerebrospinal fluid (CSF) pressure and protein content. Brain or other damage may be detected through viewing the body's interior structures with magnet and radio waves (MRI). Measurements of brain wave activity through electroencephalography (EEG) may also be necessary.

Treatment

Although specific therapy for EEE or WEE infection is not available, symptom-relieving measures such as pain relievers (analgesics) may be used in uncomplicated cases. In more severe illness, supportive measures include reducing intracranial pressure with drugs, controlling convulsions, supporting respirations, and providing prolonged nutrition during coma. In addition, prevention or early treatment of bedsores (decubitus ulcers), pneumonia, and urinary tract infections is important. An individual confined to bed should be moved often to prevent both bedsores and pneumonia. If bedsores develop, treatment may range from applying dressings of gelatin material to skin transplants in severe cases. The individual should be urged to cough and practice deep breathing to help prevent pneumonia. If infections of the lungs or urinary tract develop, antibiotics may be required.

Since complications are potentially severe, individuals infected with equine encephalitis should be placed in facilities capable of intensive care support. Contact with mosquitoes or other insects capable of spreading infection should be avoided for at least 5 days after onset. Individuals should be monitored long-term for possible secondary effects of the disease (sequelae) such as impaired motor functions.

Since no antiviral agents exist to combat human forms of encephalitis, the best treatment is prevention through programs aimed at controlling mosquito populations. An early diagnosis may help prevent complications such as bacterial pneumonia.

Prognosis

Individuals with only a mild form of illness including those afflicted with VEE often recover completely. The prognosis for those infected with more severe forms of the illness can vary greatly. The mortality rate for EEE is about 50%. Many survivors suffer brain damage. Long-term problems such as impaired motor functions may develop even after an apparently successful recovery from EEE. The mortality rate for WEE is about 3%. Brain damage may occur in 13% of WEE cases.

Prevention of complications such as bedsores and pneumonia may shorten recovery time for an individual confined to bed with a severe form of equine encephalitis.

Differential Diagnosis

Mild forms of encephalitis may resemble meningitis. Severe forms may mimic a stroke, chemical intoxications, brain tumor, or brain abscess. Other forms of encephalitis include herpes simplex encephalitis (HSE), varicella-zoster encephalitis, or tick-borne encephalitis. Other conditions with similar symptoms include systemic lupus erythematosus, Lyme disease, Rocky Mountain Spotted Fever, Colorado tick fever, ehrlichiosis, Q fever, toxoplasmosis, hypoglycemia, tuberculosis, cat scratch disease, and leptospirosis.

Specialists

- Infectious Disease Physician
- Neurologist
- Respiratory Therapist

Rehabilitation

Rehabilitation may be helpful for individuals afflicted from the long-term effects of severe forms of equine encephalitis. These effects include lack of muscle coordination (deterioration of motor skills), loss of memory, inability to speak coherently, and hearing or vision defects.

If only minimal damage to the brain has occurred, the overall objective for rehabilitation is to quickly return the individual to normal activities Rehabilitation varies however, for each individual because of the uniqueness of the problems that result from the different areas of the brain affected.

Individuals who have lost voluntary motion of the limbs begin with passive range-of-motion exercises. If the condition initially produces a state of unconsciousness, rehabilitation often utilizes external sounds from a nearby radio or sounds of people passing in the hospital hallway to produce a stimulus that helps the individual recover and regain consciousness. When unconscious, individuals may progress from becoming less comatose or sleepy to more wakeful, however, they may still be confused and easily distracted. If memory is affected, exercises are initiated that promote memory return and instruct the individual in carrying out simple tasks. This can be as simple as motivating individuals to receive an object in their hand or instructing them to move from a sitting to standing position.

The rehabilitation program sequences activities that progress from easy to more difficult such as teaching an individual how to get up from a chair to instruction in proper walking patterns. Once individuals regain their thinking processes, rehabilitation focuses on the needs for muscular strength, endurance, and flexibility. Muscle imbalance is corrected by using physical therapy techniques that help make the muscle and nervous system work together. Group activities may occur in mat classes, wheelchair classes, or other activities such as volleyball games.

Because viruses that cause equine encephalitis don't respond to antibiotics, dietary professionals may also participate in the rehabilitation program. This discipline of treatment consists primarily of a healthy diet including plenty of liquids that allow the immune system to fight the virus. When appropriate, the final phase of rehabilitation following an episode of equine encephalitis involves the individual's reinstatement to work. Both physical and mental exercises are directed toward work requirements. The physical therapist may need to modify the program for the various levels of equine encephalitis infection.

Work Restrictions / Accommodations

Individuals with encephalitis should be restricted from working until treatment is finished. After treatment, accommodations may be required for conditions due to epilepsy, Parkinsonism, or intellectual or memory impairments. The individual's motor functions may be hampered, possibly requiring accommodation for access to work stations or use of equipment. The individual may be unable to perform tasks requiring physical strength or flexibility.

Comorbid Conditions

Impaired immune function worsens the individual's condition in all types of equine encephalitis.

Complications

Complications include bronchial pneumonia, urinary retention and infection, and decubitus ulcers. Late complications such as mental deterioration, Parkinsonism, and epilepsy may occur even after apparent recovery.

Factors Influencing Duration

Length of disability may be influenced by the severity of the brain infection, spread of infection to other parts of the central nervous system, and success of supportive therapies. If motor function is disrupted or brain activity impaired, the disability may be long-term and possibly permanent.

Length of Disability

Disability may be permanent.

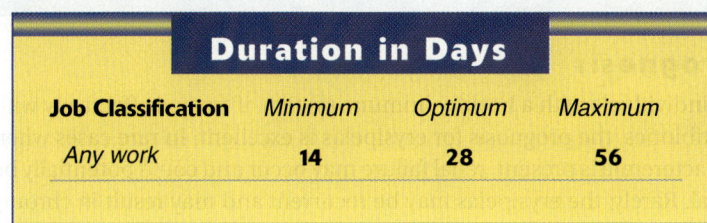

Job Classification	Minimum	Optimum	Maximum
Any work	14	28	56

Failure to Recover

If an individual fails to recover within the maximum duration expectancy period, the reader may wish to reference the following questions to assist in better understanding the specifics of an individual's medical case.

Regarding diagnosis:

- Does the individual have occupational or recreational exposure to horses?
- What time of year did symptoms occur?
- Did the individual have a sudden onset of fever, drowsiness, or weakness?
- Does the individual have a stiff neck, sore throat, headaches, and vomiting? Were flu-like symptoms reported?
- Does the individual have speech disturbances or photophobia?
- Has the individual become lethargic, had convulsions, or coma? Are there personality changes? Are reflexes abnormal? Is there paralysis?
- Did the individual experience a sudden remission?
- Has individual had antibody testing? A spinal tap? Were an MRI and EEG done?
- Have conditions with similar symptoms been ruled out?

Regarding treatment:

- Does the individual have mild or severe disease?
- Has the individual received medications to reduce ICP? Control convulsions?
- Was a respirator necessary?
- Has nutrition been maintained?
- Have measures been taken to prevent decubiti, pneumonia, and UTIs?

Regarding prognosis:

- Is individual active in rehabilitation?
- If necessary, can individual's employer accommodate restrictions?
- Does the individual have any conditions that may affect ability to recover?
- Did the individual develop any other infections?
- Is there mental deterioration, Parkinsonism, or epilepsy?

References

Viral Encephalitis. Mayo Clinic Health Oasis. 17 Aug 2000. 16 Sept 2000 <http://www.mayohealth.org/home?id=HQ01600>.

Umphred, Darcy A. Neurological Rehabilitation. St. Louis: The C.V. Mosby Company, 1990.

Erysipelas
035

Definition
Erysipelas is an acute, inflammatory infection of the skin caused by Group A streptococcal (rarely B, C, or G) beta-hemolytic streptococci.

The infection begins on the cheeks or face in about 5-20% of individuals. It affects the lower extremity in 70-80% of cases. It often begins by bacterial invasion through superficial breaks in the skin, or fungal infections between the toes (interdigital tinea pedis). These predisposing skin injuries include cuts, abrasions, skin ulcers, insect bites, eczema, existing skin rashes such as psoriasis, and occasionally follow trauma. Other parts of the body, such as the breast, can also be involved. The infection can penetrate the skin and form deep-seated abscesses. The infection also commonly involves the lymphatic vessels.

Erysipelas is seen more commonly in individuals with lymphatic obstruction or edema, circulatory insufficiency, diabetes, immunosuppression, and after such surgeries as saphenous vein grafting and radical mastectomy. Annual prevalence of erysipelas in the US is 27 in 100,000. It is primarily an adult disease and occurs slightly more often in women than in men.

Diagnosis
History: The individual will experience sudden onset of a fever and chills; muscle and joint pain, headache, and nausea may also be present. A painful rash begins 1-2 days later. The person may report prior injuries to the skin. If there is pre-existing immunodeficiency, erysipelas can affect apparently healthy skin.

Physical exam: The individual may appear well or toxic depending on the extent of the infection. They will present with a painful red spot, which increases in size daily and appears swollen; if it has affected areas of loose skin, such as eyelids, the swelling will be pronounced. Some persons may present when the spot has reached its maximum and has spread, forming a sharply-raised border with abrupt demarcation from surrounding, normal skin. The redness (erythema) is irregular with extensions that may follow lymphatic channels (lymphangitis). The lesions will also feel hot to the touch.

Tests: Group A hemolytic streptococci may be cultured from open wounds or cuts. The presence of antistreptococcal antibodies may be seen in the blood. A CBC (complete blood count) will also suggest evidence of infection; blood cultures can be used to rule out other more serious diagnoses.

Treatment
Erysipelas can sometimes resolve spontaneously, even without treatment. It is generally easily controlled with antibiotic treatment, usually administered orally. Abscesses or pustules may require surgical drainage. Swelling, headaches, and pain are treated with over-the-counter analgesics, or if severe, with physician-prescribed oral analgesic/narcotic combination medications. Bed rest with rehydration is recommended until the fever subsides. Cold compresses can be applied locally to hot lesions. If a co-existent fungal infection of the foot is present, it should be treated with topical and/or antifungal medications. For prolonged infections slow to respond to antibiotic treatment, careful drug sensitivities of the organism should be obtained.

Prognosis
In individuals with a healthy immune system, if treated effectively with antibiotics, the prognosis for erysipelas is excellent. In rare cases when a bacteremia is present, renal failure may occur and could potentially be fatal. Rarely, the erysipelas may be recurrent and may result in chronic swelling (lymphedema). Generally, the affected skin areas of erysipelas will heal without scarring.

Differential Diagnosis
Other bacterial and viral infections of the skin may result in rashes, fever, and/or skin blisters, but the expanding circle of inflammation with raised borders observed with erysipelas is definitive. Angioneurotic edema and contact dermatitis may also be mistaken for erysipelas. In cases of breast involvement, it may resemble inflammatory carcinoma of the breast. Other conditions that may resemble erysipelas include cellulitis, urticaria, herpes zoster, necrotizing fasciitis, dermatophytid, erysipeloid, polychondritis, scarlet fever, systemic lupus erythematous, and tuberculoid leprosy.

Specialists
- Dermatologist
- Infectious Disease Physician
- Plastic Surgeon

Work Restrictions / Accommodations
There should be no work restrictions or accommodations necessary once the condition resolves. Time off from work for a short period during the acute phase may be necessary.

Complementary and Alternative Therapies
Content is intended for awareness only. Treatments may or may not be effective. Scientific evidence may be lacking and some substances have potentially toxic effects. Dr. Presley Reed and the editors do not endorse the use of these therapies in the absence of consultation with a licensed medical professional.

Cold therapy - Cold compresses, applied locally to hot lesions, may help relieve pain.

Comorbid Conditions
Comorbid conditions include diabetes mellitus, peripheral vascular disease, and immunosuppression (individuals on chemotherapy or with AIDS).

Complications
If untreated, erysipelas may lead to systemic inflammatory disease and contribute to the development of chronic inflammation or swelling. Erysipelas may cause more severe disease in individuals with a compromised immune system. The presence of antibiotic-resistant strains of streptococcus will complicate treatment and may lengthen disability period. Other complications may include abscess, gangrene, pneumonia, scarlet fever, or meningitis. Lesions can become scarred. A bacteremia may develop in very young, elderly, or immunocompro-

mised individuals, and may lead to sepsis and renal failure. In treated cases of bacteremia, mortality is less than one percent.

Factors Influencing Duration

The length of disability will be influenced by extent of the infection at the time of diagnosis, the presence of other medical conditions that diminish an effective immune response to the infection, and the presence of an antibiotic-resistant strain of streptococcus.

Length of Disability

With treatment.

Duration in Days

Job Classification	Minimum	Optimum	Maximum
Any work	7	9	14

Failure to Recover

If an individual fails to recover within the maximum duration expectancy period, the reader may wish to reference the following questions to assist in better understanding the specifics of an individual's medical case.

Regarding diagnosis:

- Does the individual have any predisposing skin injuries?
- Does the individual have lymphatic obstruction or edema, circulatory insufficiency, diabetes, immunosuppression, or have such surgeries as saphenous vein grafting and radical mastectomy?
- Does the individual complain of sudden onset of fever and chills, muscle and joint pain, headache, and nausea? Did a painful rash begins 1-2 days later?
- On physical exam does the individual have a painful red spot, which increases in size daily and appears swollen? Has the spot reached its maximum and spread, forming a sharply-raised border with abrupt demarcation from surrounding, normal skin?
- Is lymphangitis present? Do the lesions also feel hot to the touch?
- Has the individual had a culture and sensitivity of the wound? Blood culture?
- Has the individual had a CBC and antistreptococcal antibodies?
- Have conditions with similar symptoms been ruled out?

Regarding treatment:

- Did the individual's erysipelas resolve spontaneously?
- Was the individual treated with oral antibiotics?
- Was the individual treated with analgesics, bed rest, re-hydration and cold compresses if necessary? Were any coexisting infections also treated?
- Did it become necessary to surgically drain any abscesses or pustules?

Regarding prognosis:

- Is the individual's employer able to accommodate any necessary restrictions?
- Does the individual have any conditions that may affect their ability to recover?
- Does the individual have any complication such as systemic inflammatory disease, the presence of antibiotic-resistant strains of streptococcus, abscess, gangrene, pneumonia, scarlet fever, or meningitis? Does the individual have sepsis? Have the lesions become scarred?

References

Hirschman, Jan V. "Bacterial Infections of the Skin." Principles and Practice of Dermatology, 2nd ed. Sams, W. Mitchell, and Peter J. Lynch, eds. New York: Churchill Livingstone, 1996. 79-90.

Swartz, Morton N. "Cellulitis and Subcutaneous Tissue Infections." Principles and Practice of Infectious Diseases, 4th ed, vol 1. Mandell, Gerald L., John E. Bennett, and Raphael Dolin, eds. New York: Churchill Livingstone, 1995. 909-929.

Erysipeloid

Other names / synonyms: Erysipelotrichosis, Fish Rose, Fish-Handler's Disease, Rosenbach's Disease, Rosenbach's Erysipeloid

027.1

Definition

Erysipeloid is a bacterial infection caused by Erysipelothrix rhusiopathiae. It is caused by skin contact with infected animals, and is usually an occupational disease of those who handle animal matter (infected carcasses, rendered products such as fertilizer and grease, bones, or shells). These individuals include meat-handlers, fishermen, slaughterhouse workers, and veterinarians.

The infection usually affects the fingers and hand. The bacteria gain entry via cuts or abrasions on the skin. A raised, purplish-red rash starts on the skin at the point of bacterial entry, and then spreads. Erysipeloid may lead to endocarditis and arthritis if not properly treated. The annual prevalence of erysipeloid in the US is 0.2 cases per 100,000 people.

Diagnosis

History: The individual usually relates an occupation requiring handling of unprocessed meat or fish. Symptoms include a reddish rash and swelling of the skin on the fingers or the back of the hand. The swelling may last for a few days, and may be severe enough to limit the use of the part. Individuals may also report burning and itching. The affected part may be painful up to 3 weeks. In individuals who develop infective arthritis, various joints may be painful with swelling (effusion). If endocarditis is present, the individual may complain of low-grade fever, night sweats, chills, fatigue, and weight loss. Low-grade fever occurs in 10% of individuals, while 20% report swelling of lymph nodes.

Physical exam: The exam shows an expanding red rash with a clear center, typically on the fingers, hands, or forearms. Fever is occasionally present. Individuals with joint involvement will have swelling of some joints. Individuals with endocarditis may have a heart murmur noted on examination.

Tests: The bacterium can often be cultured from drainage from the infected area. Sometimes, a full-thickness biopsy culture is needed to make the diagnosis. Isolation of the bacterium from joint fluid (synovial fluid) is necessary to diagnose the infectious arthritis. Isolation of the bacterium in the blood is necessary for the diagnosis of endocarditis.

Treatment

Antibiotic therapy for seven to ten days will usually clear the infection. In cases involving resistant strains, treatment with a second antibiotic may be required.

Intravenous administration of antibiotics is necessary to treat endocarditis or infective arthritis. It is often necessary to perform repeated needle aspiration drainage of infected joints even after a course of intravenous antibiotics.

Prognosis

The rash is usually self-limiting without lymph node involvement. Rarely, a blood infection (bacteremia) from the organism can occur and can result in infection of the heart (endocarditis) or joint (septic arthritis).

In individuals receiving appropriate antibiotic treatment, the prognosis for complete recovery is excellent. In those who are not treated adequately, endocarditis or arthritis may develop, but these are not usually severe and can be effectively treated. Needle aspiration of an infected joint, possibly on multiple occasions, will, in conjunction with antibiotic therapy, lead to resolution of the arthritis.

Differential Diagnosis

Several other infectious lesions may resemble erysipeloid. These include abscess, furuncle, cellulitis, and erysipelas. Noninfective conditions mimicking erysipeloid include ulcer, various insect or animal bites, and inflammatory rashes such as contact dermatitis.

Specialists

- Cardiologist
- Dermatologist
- Infectious Disease Physician

Work Restrictions / Accommodations

Individuals with erysipeloid should be restricted from handling meat or fish products until the infection is cured. They may need to avoid using their infected hand altogether until the infection has resolved and until the swelling and pain have disappeared.

Comorbid Conditions

Comorbid conditions include heart disease, diabetes mellitus, peripheral vascular disease, and immunosuppression (individuals on chemotherapy and those with AIDS).

Complications

Antibiotic-resistant strains will complicate therapy. Repeated infection may result in the development of allergic sensitivities. Reduced immunity may complicate the infection.

Factors Influencing Duration

The length of disability will be influenced by the severity of disease and the development of complications.

Length of Disability

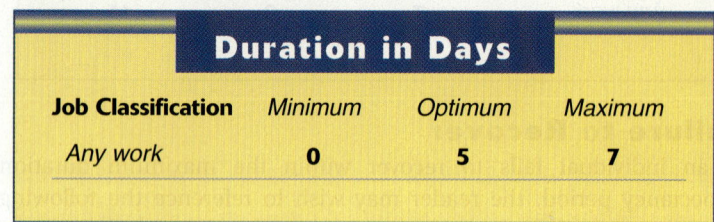

Job Classification	Minimum	Optimum	Maximum
Any work	0	5	7

Duration in Days

Failure to Recover

If an individual fails to recover within the maximum duration expectancy period, the reader may wish to reference the following questions to assist in better understanding the specifics of an individual's medical case.

Regarding diagnosis:

- Does the individual handle animal matter such as infected carcasses, rendered products such as fertilizer and grease, bones, or shells?
- Does the individual have a reddish rash and swelling of the skin on the fingers or the back of the hand?
- Was the swelling severe enough to limit the use of the part?
- Does the individual report burning and itching?
- Does the individual report several joints with pain and effusion?
- Does the individual also complain of low-grade fever, night sweats, chills, fatigue, and weight loss?
- On exam does the individual have an expanding red rash with a clear center on the fingers, hands, or forearms?
- Did the individual also have fever, joint swelling and a heart murmur?
- Has the individual had a culture and sensitivity on drainage from the affected area, synovial fluid or blood?
- Was a full thickness biopsy culture necessary?
- Have conditions with similar symptoms been ruled out?

Regarding treatment:

- Has the individual been treated with antibiotics for seven to ten days?
- Was treatment with a second antibiotic necessary?
- Does the individual also have infective arthritis and/or endocarditis?

- Was the individual treated with IV antibiotics?
- Was it necessary to perform repeated needle aspiration drainage of infected joints even after a course of intravenous antibiotics?

Regarding prognosis:

- Is the individual's employer able to accommodate any necessary restrictions?
- Does the individual have any conditions that may affect their ability to recover?
- Does the individual have any complications such as antibiotic-resistant strains or reduced immunity?

References

Reboli, Annette C. "Erysipeloid." Cecil Textbook of Medicine, 20th ed, vol. 2. Bennett, J. Claude, and Fred Plum, eds. Philadelphia: W.B. Saunders Company, 1996. 1673-1674.

Reboli, Annette C., and W. Edmund Farrar. "Erysipelothrix Rhusiopathiae." Principles and Practice of Infectious Diseases, 4th ed, vol. 2. Mandell, Gerald L., John E. Bennett, and Raphael Dolin, eds. New York: Churchill Livingstone, 1995. 1894-1896.

Erythema Multiforme
Other names / synonyms: Stevens-Johnson Disease
695.1, 695.9

Definition

Erythema multiforme (EM) is a skin rash producing redness or inflammation (erythema) and is characterized by skin lesions such as macules, papules, nodules, vesicles, bullae, and target lesions (bull's-eye-shaped lesions consisting of a central blemish with two or more concentric rings).

The three classifications of erythema multiforme are EM minor, EM major, and pure plaque toxic necrosis. EM minor is an acute form of the disease characterized by target lesions on the arms and legs. Symptoms are caused by an infection of herpes simplex.

EM major is also called Stevens Johnson syndrome and is characterized by the presence of target lesions, blisters, and detachment of the skin and mucous membranes. EM major also tends to follow herpes simplex virus infections.

Plaque toxic epidermal necrolysis may not be associated with target lesions but is associated with detachment of large areas of skin and is generally drug-induced.

Although some causes are known, up to 50% of cases have no known cause associated with the condition. It most often results from a drug reaction. Other causes include infectious diseases and radiation therapy.

Erythema multiforme is the most common eruptive rash characterized by distinctive macules or papules (maculopapular rash) and occurs more frequently in men than women. It most often affects individuals between age 20 and 30. The rash can be recurrent and is typically found on the palms, soles, knees, and elbows. In many individuals, the mucous membranes of the mouth and lips are involved.

Diagnosis

History: The individual may complain of a rash beginning on arms or legs and spreading to the face and rest of the body. Fever and extreme exhaustion (prostration) may be reported.

Physical exam: The rash may appear as a target or bull's-eye-shaped. It may progress toward raised, pale-centered hives (wheals) or blisters. In the severe form of Stevens Johnson syndrome, the mucous membranes of the mouth, lips, eyes, nasal passages, and genitals become inflamed and ulcerated. Lesions may also be found in the pharynx, larynx, and trachea.

Tests: Tests include skin biopsy with immunofluorescent examination and culture (rapid test) to rule out bacterial or viral infection.

Treatment

If the rash is caused by a reaction to medication, the medication should be discontinued and replaced. A bacterial infection is treated with antibiotics. Antiviral medications can lessen symptoms of viral infections. Anti-inflammatory medications such as corticosteroids can lessen inflammation and irritation. Protecting the skin and applying wet compresses for the oozing (exudative) lesions can be helpful. Severe forms of the illness may require pain medication, sedatives, and corticosteroids to reduce inflammation. It rare cases, plasma exchange may be indicated.

Prognosis

EM usually spontaneously resolves within 5 to 6 weeks from onset in most individuals. Treatment with pain medications, antibiotics in the presence of infection, and corticosteroids helps alleviate symptoms during the recovery process. Recurrent episodes of EM usually precede an outbreak of herpes simplex minor by several days. Individuals with recurrent episodes can have long periods without the illness.

Differential Diagnosis

Other possibilities include urticaria, erythema nodosum, rash of secondary syphilis, and potentially life-threatening infections such as meningococcemia, Rocky Mountain spotted fever, and dengue fever that may initially present with similar lesions as EM.

Specialists

- Dermatologist
- Internist

Work Restrictions / Accommodations

Leave for treatment and adequate time for resolution of the rash may be required for the severe forms of the illness. Once recovered, work restrictions or accommodations are not necessary.

Comorbid Conditions

Infectious diseases such as sarcoidosis that can cause similar rashes may complicate the diagnosis and further lengthen disability.

Complications

EM is rarely life threatening but can progress to necrotizing tracheobronchitis, meningitis, blindness, and kidney tube damage (renal tubular necrosis). Eating may be complicated by inflammation and cracking of the lips (cheilitis) and inflammation of the mouth (stomatitis). Individuals can have difficulty with urination due to inflammation of the glans penis (balanitis) or inflammation of the vulva (vulvitis). Eye problems such as inflammation of the conjunctiva (conjunctivitis) may be severe and can lead to inflammation of the cornea (keratitis) and ulceration.

Factors Influencing Duration

Factors influencing disability include severity of the EM, extent of treatment given, and any complicating illnesses.

Length of Disability

Duration in Days

Job Classification	Minimum	Optimum	Maximum
Any work	7	14	28

Failure to Recover

If an individual fails to recover within the maximum duration expectancy period, the reader may wish to reference the following questions to assist in better understanding the specifics of an individual's medical case.

Regarding diagnosis:

- Has individual had a recent herpes simplex infection? A drug reaction, infectious diseases, or radiation therapy?
- Does individual have erythema and skin lesions such as macules, papules, nodules, vesicles, bullae, and target lesions? A rash on the palms, soles, knees, elbows, and mucous membranes of the mouth and lips? Did it begin on the arms or legs and spread to the rest of the body?
- Does individual report fever and extreme exhaustion?
- Does exam reveal a rash that appears as a target and progresses toward raised, pale-centered hives or blisters?
- Are individual's mucous membranes of the mouth, lips, eyes, nasal passages, and genitals inflamed and ulcerated?
- Are lesions in the pharynx, larynx, and trachea present?
- Was a skin biopsy with immunofluorescent examination and culture done?
- Were conditions with similar symptoms ruled out?

Regarding treatment:

- Was individual's rash caused by a drug reaction? Was the drug discontinued?
- Was the rash caused by a bacterial or viral illness? Was individual treated with antibiotics or antiviral medications? Topical corticosteroid creams and wet compresses?
- Was it necessary to use pain medication, sedatives, and corticosteroids?
- Was plasma exchange indicated?

Regarding prognosis:

- Can individual's employer accommodate any necessary restrictions?
- Does individual have any conditions such as infectious diseases that may affect ability to recover?
- Have any complications developed such as cheilitis, stomatitis, balanitis, vulvitis, conjunctivitis, keratitis, necrotizing tracheobronchitis, meningitis, blindness, or renal tubular necrosis that could impact recovery?

References

McKinnon, Harry D. Jr., and Thomas Howard. "Evaluating the Febrile Patient with a Rash." American Family Physician 5 5 (2000): 19. 07 Dec 2000 <http://www.aafp.org/afp/20000815/804.html>.

Erythema Nodosum
695.2

Definition

Erythema nodosum is an acute inflammatory and immunologic condition involving the fatty tissue layer under the skin (panniculus adiposus). It is characterized by painful, red, tender swellings (nodules) on the lower legs, knees, and arms. The nodules usually last for several days or weeks.

In 40% of cases, the cause is unknown but may result from infectious causes such as beta-hemolytic streptococci and tuberculosis (mycobacterium species), medications, oral contraceptives, and other medical conditions such as systemic lupus erythematosus, sarcoidosis, ulcerative colitis, and pregnancy. It is more common in women than men and primarily affects young adults.

Diagnosis

History: Individuals report extremely painful nodules on the lower legs, knees, and arms. Other presenting features include fever, tiredness (malaise), and joint pain (arthralgias).

Physical exam: Bright-red nodules, 3 to 20 cm in diameter are scattered on both sides of the body, but not symmetrically. Most frequently the nodules appear on the lower legs and are also found on knees and arms but rarely on the face and neck. Lesions are often tender and hard.

Tests: Biopsy of the nodules for bacterial culture and causative factors is performed. Throat culture for group A beta-hemolytic streptococci is done to rule out beta strep infection. Tuberculin test helps rule out tuberculosis. A chest radiograph is done to rule out sarcoidosis.

Treatment

Appropriate treatment of underlying disease resolves the nodules. If caused by a reaction to a medication, the drug is usually stopped and replaced by an appropriate choice. Bed rest, pain medications, and anti-inflammatory medications (corticosteroids) may also be used in treatment. In the case of pregnancy, treatment of symptoms with bed rest and corticosteroids is recommended.

Prognosis

The course of erythema nodosum depends on the specific cause of the illness, but spontaneous resolution can be expected within 6 weeks. In cases where the individual is in poor health due to severity of the underlying illness, recovery may take longer.

Differential Diagnosis

Other possibilities include fungal infections that produce nodular lesions such as cryptococcosis, blastomycosis, coccidioidomycosis, histoplasmosis, and sporotrichosis. On rare occasions, bacteria may produce nodular lesions.

Specialists

- Dermatologist
- Internist

Work Restrictions / Accommodations

Prolonged standing with pressure on the lower legs may need to be restricted. Frequent rest breaks may also be necessary. In severe cases with fatigue and joint pain, several days of bed rest may be required.

Comorbid Conditions

Severe types of skin conditions that produce inflammation and skin lesions such as Stevens-Johnson syndrome can further lengthen disability.

Complications

In individuals with weakened immune systems, the underlying illness may not respond to treatment as in those with normal immune systems, and the condition may persist.

Factors Influencing Duration

Disability depends on response to treatment of the underlying condition. Individuals with weakened immune systems may have difficulty recovering from infectious illnesses that cause erythema nodosum.

Length of Disability

Duration may be that of the underlying cause.

Duration in Days

Job Classification	Minimum	Optimum	Maximum
Any work	7	14	28

Failure to Recover

If an individual fails to recover within the maximum duration expectancy period, the reader may wish to reference the following questions to assist in better understanding the specifics of an individual's medical case.

Regarding diagnosis:

- Does individual have painful red, nodules on the lower legs, knees, and arms that last for several days or weeks? Fever, malaise, or arthralgias?
- Has individual had beta-hemolytic streptococci or tuberculosis; used medications or oral contraceptives; or have systemic lupus erythematosus, sarcoidosis, ulcerative colitis, or pregnancy?
- On exam, were bright red nodules, 3 to 20 cm in diameter scattered asymmetrically on both sides of the body? Are the lesions tender and hard?
- Was a biopsy and culture of the nodules done? Throat culture? Tuberculin skin test or chest x-ray?
- Were conditions with similar symptoms ruled out?

Regarding treatment:

- What is individual's underlying condition? Is it being treated?
- Is individual pregnant? Was she treated with bed rest and corticosteroids?

Regarding prognosis:

- Can individual's employer accommodate any necessary restrictions?
- Does individual have any conditions that may affect ability to recover?
- Have any complications developed such as a weakened immune system that prevents individual from responding to treatment?

References

McKinnon, Harry D. Jr., and Thomas Howard. "Evaluating the Febrile Patient with a Rash." American Family Physician 5 6 (2000): 19. 12 Dec 2000 <http://www.aafp.org/afp/2000815/804.html>.

Esophageal Diverticula

Other names / synonyms: Acquired Diverticulum, Epiphrenic Diverticula, Epiphrenic Diverticulum, Hypopharyngeal Diverticula, Intramural Pseudodiverticulosis, Midesophageal Diverticula, Pharyngoesophageal Diverticula, Pulsion Diverticulum, Zenker's Diverticula, Zenker's Diverticulum

530.6, 750.4

Definition

Esophageal diverticula refer to sacs that protrude from the wall of the tube (esophagus) that leads from the throat to the stomach.

Esophageal diverticula can be classified in a number of different ways, but commonly they are placed into 1 of 4 different categories based upon their location in the esophagus. These locations are between the throat (pharynx) and the upper end of the esophagus (also called Zenker's or pharyngoesophageal diverticula); in the upper end or middle portion of the esophagus (hypopharyngeal or midesophageal diverticula); in the lower part of the esophagus near the diaphragm (epiphrenic diverticula); and all along the wall of the esophagus appearing as minute, flask-like outpouchings (intramural pseudodiverticulosis).

Pharyngoesophageal diverticula often occur when the circular muscle (upper esophageal sphincter or UES) at the entrance to the esophagus fails to relax during the act of swallowing. Instead, the sphincter resists the passage of food, and as the powerful throat muscles used for swallowing push against this resistance, part of the lining of the esophagus is forced back through the esophageal wall. The lining then bulges through the wall forming the diverticulum pouch. The diverticulum will gradually enlarge, and food can become trapped in it, causing irritation and swallowing difficulties. It has been suggested that risk factors for development of pharyngoesophageal diverticulum may include reflux of acid from the stomach into the esophagus (gastroesophageal reflux) or bulging of the stomach past the diaphragm into the chest cavity (hiatal hernia). However, there are no studies to date that prove an association between these conditions and development of pharyngoesophageal diverticula.

Midesophageal diverticula are the most common type of esophageal diverticula, and they may develop as a result of either pulling on the esophagus by connective tissue in the chest cavity (traction diverticulum) or by a force on the inside of the esophagus pushing out to form a pouch (pulsion diverticulum). Food accumulation in midesophageal diverticula is rare. Risk factors for this condition may include gastroesophageal reflux, although this is not yet proven.

In contrast, the major risk factor for epiphrenic diverticula is well-defined and it is when the muscles of the contractile ring that is located where the esophagus empties into the stomach (lower esophageal sphincter, or LES) fail to relax normally during swallowing. When the muscles of the LES (or any other part of the esophagus) do not relax (or contract) as they should normally, it is often referred to as a movement or motility disorder.

Major risk factors for intramural pseudodiverticulosis include chronic inflammation of the esophagus (esophagitis) and, possibly, esophageal motility disorders.

The incidence of esophageal diverticula is unknown and difficult to estimate because it is a relatively rare condition. Although esophageal diverticula may happen at any age, most (75%) occur in males between the ages of 41 and 70 years. The male to female ratio of esophageal diverticula is 3:1.

Diagnosis

History: Some individuals report no symptoms. Others may complain of a sensation of food sticking in the throat, or vague throat irritation, chest pain, intermittent cough, excessive salivation, vomiting after eating, difficulty swallowing (dysphagia), gurgling after swallowing, a sour metallic taste in the mouth, and bad breath (halitosis).

Physical exam: The exam may reveal no remarkable symptoms. In rare cases of pharyngoesophageal diverticula, the esophageal pouch may become so large that it produces a bulge on the side of the neck.

Tests: The diverticulum may be visualized by taking x-rays after swallowing a contrast medium such as barium (esophagram). Other tests to visualize the diverticulum may include insertion of a flexible fiber-optic microscope into the esophagus (endoscopy), use of high-frequency sound waves (ultrasound), or computer-aided x-ray analysis (computerized tomography, or CT).

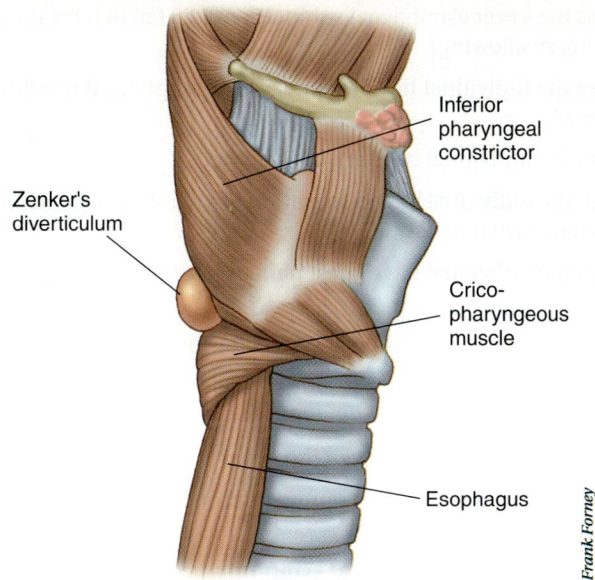

Treatment

Treatment is dependent on the type of diverticulum. Small pharyngoesophageal diverticula are usually not treated, while large diverticula of this type may require surgery (diverticulopexy, diverticulectomy, or cricopharyngeal myotomy). During these procedures, the sphincter muscle at the entrance of the esophagus may be partially cut to weaken it to help prevent recurrence of the condition. Recently, these surgeries have been performed using a flexible tube that is inserted into the esophagus (endoscopy) rather than as open surgery.

Treatment for midesophageal or epiphrenic diverticula is rarely needed. However, if treatment is necessary, it usually involves surgical removal of the diverticulum (diverticulectomy), and occasionally, separation of the esophageal muscle (myotomy). Intramural pseudodiverticulosis may be treated using a balloon to expand the esophagus (esophageal dilation).

Individuals are advised to avoid consumption of alcohol or irritating foods for a short period of time following surgical treatment for esophageal diverticula. Also, it is advisable that foods be liquid or softened until recovery is complete.

Prognosis

Surgical treatment (diverticulopexy, diverticulectomy, or cricopharyngeal myotomy) of large pharyngoesophageal diverticula usually produce excellent results greater than 96% of the time. Mortality from surgery is low at 1.2 percent. The rate of recurrence of the condition is 3.6 percent. If recurrence of the diverticulum requires that the surgery be repeated, complications can be expected and the mortality rate will rise to 3.2 percent. Individuals with midesophageal or epiphrenic diverticula who are treated surgically (diverticulectomy and/or myotomy) usually have good long-term results; however, mortality during the procedure may occur in up to 9% of cases, and leakage from the esophagus may happen 18% of the time. Intramural pseudodiverticulosis that is treated using esophageal dilation usually responds with relief of symptoms for a few years. Some individuals may require periodic dilations.

Differential Diagnosis

Conditions that present with similar symptoms as esophageal diverticula include esophageal fistula, esophageal cancer, esophageal spasm, esophageal web, hiatal hernia, and achalasia.

Specialists

| • Gastroenterologist | • General Surgeon |

Work Restrictions / Accommodations

Work restrictions and accommodations are not usually required for individuals with esophageal diverticula that are asymptomatic. Individuals who are treated using surgery may require a period of recovery at work where less physical labor (heavy lifting, climbing, etc.) is required.

Comorbid Conditions

Existing conditions that may impact an individual's ability to recover and further lengthen disability include pyloric ulcer disease, stomach cancer, and inflammation of the duodenum (duodenitis), any of which can increase gastric acid reflux into the esophagus (gastroesophageal reflux). Inflammation of the esophagus (esophagitis) may also lengthen recovery time.

Complications

Complications of esophageal diverticula are rare, but they may include formation of a lesion (ulceration) on the esophagus, uncontrolled coughing at night, and aspiration of stomach contents, which can result in fluid and/or abscess in the lungs (pneumonia). Formation of a hole (perforation), bleeding (hemorrhage), and compression of the esophagus may occur in pharyngoesophageal diverticulum.

Factors Influencing Duration

Length of disability may be influenced by the location and size of the diverticulum and the method of treatment. Disability will be longer for individuals who are treated using surgical techniques. Open surgery treatment for esophageal diverticula may require a longer recovery time than endoscopic surgery.

Length of Disability

Durations for open surgery depend on location and size of diverticula.

Medical treatment.

Duration in Days

Job Classification	Minimum	Optimum	Maximum
Sedentary work	0	1	2
Light work	0	1	2
Medium work	0	1	2
Heavy work	0	1	2
Very Heavy work	0	1	2

Endoscopic diverticulectomy.

Duration in Days

Job Classification	Minimum	Optimum	Maximum
Sedentary work	10	14	21
Light work	10	14	21
Medium work	10	14	21
Heavy work	10	21	28
Very Heavy work	10	21	28

Failure to Recover

If an individual fails to recover within the maximum duration expectancy period, the reader may wish to reference the following questions to assist in better understanding the specifics of an individual's medical case.

Regarding diagnosis:

- Does the individual have a problem with the esophageal sphincter relaxing?
- Does the lower esophageal sphincter or LES fail to relax normally during swallowing?
- Does the individual have esophagitis or esophageal motility disorders?
- Does the individual have any risk factors?
- Does the individual have a sensation of food sticking in the throat or vague throat irritation?
- Does the individual have chest pain or intermittent cough?
- Does the individual have excessive salivation, vomiting after eating, dysphagia, or gurgling after swallowing?
- Does the individual have a sour metallic taste in the mouth and halitosis?
- Is there a bulge on the side of the neck?
- Has the individual had an esophagram, endoscopy, ultrasound, or CT?
- Have conditions with similar symptoms been ruled out?

Regarding treatment:

- Has the individual had surgery?
- Has he/she had esophageal dilation done?
- Was he/she advised to avoid consumption of alcohol or irritating foods for a short time following surgery?

Regarding prognosis:

- Is the individual's employer able to accommodate any necessary restrictions?
- Does the individual have any conditions that could affect their recovery?
- Does the individual have complications such as ulceration on the esophagus or uncontrolled coughing at night?
- Has the individual aspirated stomach contents, causing pneumonia?
- Has he/she had perforation, hemorrhage, and compression of the esophagus?

References

Achkar, E. "Esophageal Diverticula." The Esophagus. Castell, D.O., and J.E. Richter, eds. Philadelphia: Lippincott Williams & Wilkins, 1999. 301-314.

LeMone, P., and K.M. Burke. Medical-Surgical Nursing. Upper Saddle River, NJ: Prentice Hall Health, 2000.

Esophageal Spasm

Other names / synonyms: Diffuse Esophageal Spasm, Esophageal Dyskinesia, Esophagospasm, Nonachalasia Motility Disorder, Nonspecific Esophageal Motility Disorder, Nutcracker Esophagus

530.5

Definition

Esophageal spasm refers to uncoordinated muscle contractions in the tube (esophagus) that leads from the throat to the stomach. It results in failure to effectively propel food down into the stomach after being swallowed. The contractions occur repeatedly and are abnormally powerful.

The exact cause of esophageal spasm is unknown, however, risk factors include irritation of the esophagus by acid that washes up from the stomach (reflux esophagitis), obstructions in the esophagus, emotional stress, or other conditions that may affect the normal function of the nervous system (e.g., diabetes or amyotrophic lateral sclerosis). Esophageal spasm may also be related to an inability of the muscles in the lower esophagus to relax (achalasia).

Esophageal spasms can occur in individuals of any age but are most common in those over 50. This condition occurs equally in both men and women. Esophageal spasm is uncommon and accounts for 3-10% of all gastrointestinal movement (motility) disorders.

Diagnosis

History: Individuals report pain in the chest or upper abdomen that can radiate to the back, neck, jaw, and/or arms. Difficulty swallowing (dysphagia) may also occur. Eating very hot or very cold foods or drinking carbonated beverages may trigger these symptoms. Individuals usually report intermittent symptoms that generally do not worsen.

Physical exam: Physical findings are usually normal.

Tests: Diagnostic tests may include motility studies of the esophagus (manometry), x-ray studies using barium as the contrast medium (esophagram), and a procedure where a fiber-optic viewing tube is passed down through the esophagus that allows visual examination of the inside of the esophagus (endoscopy).

Treatment

Esophageal spasm is generally a mild condition and is not life-threatening. Muscle spasms may be relieved with either anticholinergic or calcium-channel antagonist drugs. Cylinders of increasing size may be passed down the esophagus to relax or stretch the muscles (esophageal bougienage). Surgery to cut the esophageal muscle (esophagomyotomy) is rarely used in treating individuals with severe symptoms of esophageal spasm. Surgical treatment is reserved for individuals who have severe, lifestyle-compromising symptoms that cannot be improved using nonsurgical methods.

Nonpharmacologic treatment such as psychological counseling is directed at reassuring the individual and may be beneficial.

Prognosis

Esophageal spasm is harmless (benign) and does not worsen (nonprogressive). Reassurance may have significant positive effects. In some cases, psychological counseling has completely alleviated symptoms from the condition.

Anticholinergic drugs significantly decrease esophageal pressures in all individuals tested. However, the effects and usefulness of anticholinergic drugs on symptoms of esophageal spasm remain largely unstudied and unknown. Calcium-channel blockers are the most popular and effective drug treatment for esophageal spasm. In the vast majority of cases, these blockers decrease the force and duration of esophageal contractions and relieve certain associated symptoms such as chest pain. Cylinders of increasing size passed down the esophagus to relax or stretch the muscles (esophageal bougienage) produce only temporary (less than 4 weeks) improvement in most individuals. Clinical studies found this treatment has no effect on motility abnormalities of the esophagus.

Esophagomyotomy as a treatment for esophageal spasm is very limited, however, some studies indicate it to be an effective method for reducing symptoms.

Differential Diagnosis

Conditions that present with similar symptoms as esophageal spasm include achalasia and chest pain caused by insufficient blood supply to the heart muscles (angina pectoris).

Specialists

- Cardiologist
- Gastroenterologist
- General Surgeon

Work Restrictions / Accommodations

Work restrictions and accommodations are not usually required for esophageal spasm. However, if surgical correction is necessary, the individual may require extended work leave until recovery is complete.

Complementary and Alternative Therapies

Content is intended for awareness only. Treatments may or may not be effective. Scientific evidence may be lacking and some substances have potentially toxic effects. Dr. Presley Reed and the editors do not endorse the use of these therapies in the absence of consultation with a licensed medical professional.

Biofeedback - Relaxation techniques may be useful in alleviating symptoms of esophageal spasm.

Double swallowing - Swallowing twice (rather than once) when eating a bite of food may help relieve certain complications of esophageal spasm.

Comorbid Conditions

Existing conditions that may impact an individual's ability to recover and further lengthen disability include esophageal stricture, esophagitis, peptic ulcer disease, and esophageal diverticulum.

Complications

Possible complications of esophageal spasm include choking and aspiration pneumonia.

Factors Influencing Duration

Factors influencing length of disability include age, physical condition of the individual, or any medical conditions that aggravate the condition such as reflux esophagitis.

Length of Disability

Dilation.

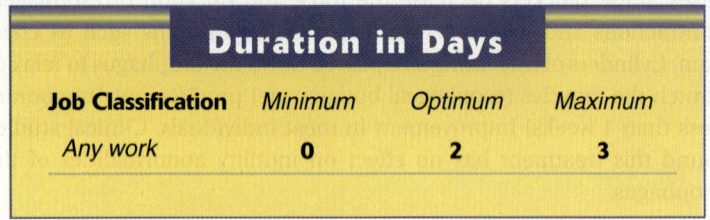

Job Classification	Minimum	Optimum	Maximum
Any work	0	2	3

Medical treatment.

Duration in Days

Job Classification	Minimum	Optimum	Maximum
Any work	1	3	14

Failure to Recover

If an individual fails to recover within the maximum duration expectancy period, the reader may wish to reference the following questions to assist in better understanding the specifics of an individual's medical case.

Regarding diagnosis:

- Does individual have reflux esophagitis or esophageal obstructions?
- Is individual experiencing emotional stress?
- Does individual have diabetes? Amyotrophic lateral sclerosis? Achalasia?
- Is there chest or upper abdomen pain? Dysphagia?
- Does eating hot or cold food or drinking carbonated beverages trigger symptoms? Do the symptoms stay the same?
- Has individual had manometry done? Esophagram? Endoscopy?
- Have conditions with similar symptoms been ruled out?

Regarding treatment:

- Has individual been treated with anticholinergic or calcium-channel antagonist drugs?
- Has esophageal bougienage been done?
- Did esophagomyotomy become necessary?
- Has psychological counseling been tried?

Regarding prognosis:

- Does individual have any conditions that may affect ability to recover?
- Does individual have problems with choking?
- Has individual ever had aspiration pneumonia?

References

Katz, P.O., and J.A. Castell. "Nonachalasia Motility Disorders." The Esophagus. Castell, D.O., and J.E. Richter, eds. Philadelphia: Lippincott Williams & Wilkins, 1999. 215-234.

LeMone, P., and K.M. Burke. Medical-Surgical Nursing. Upper Saddle River: Prentice Hall Health, 2000.

Esophageal Strictures

Other names / synonyms: Peptic Stricture
530.3, 530.9

Definition

Esophageal stricture is a narrowing of the tube (esophagus) that connects the throat to the stomach.

The narrowing may be due to abnormal tissue growth (cancer) or to conditions in which the normal surface tissue (mucosa) of the esophagus is replaced by scar tissue.

A major risk factor for the development of esophageal stricture is when stomach juices flow back up into the esophagus (reflux esophagitis), which causes constant irritation and swelling. Eventually, scar tissue (which can narrow the esophagus) will form and this happens in about 15% of individuals with reflux esophagitis. Other risk factors for development of esophageal stricture include prolonged use of nasal gastric feeding tubes or the accidental swallowing of strong acid or base. Esophageal strictures may also occur after surgery on the stomach or esophagus (gastroesophageal surgery), or after a procedure in which swollen veins at the bottom of the esophagus are obliterated by injection of an irritating solution (sclerotherapy for esophageal varices).

Esophageal stricture may happen at any age but it tends to occur more often in older individuals. The average age at diagnosis is 63 years. The condition occurs slightly more often in men than women with a 1.2:1 male:female ratio.

Diagnosis

History: Individuals may complain of painful or difficult swallowing (dysphagia), heartburn (dyspepsia), or of food coming back up into the mouth after swallowing (regurgitation).

Physical exam: The exam is usually normal except for apparent swallowing difficulties and, possibly, weight loss.

Tests: A procedure in which a flexible fiber-optic viewing tube is passed down the esophagus (endoscopy) allows for visual examination. At the same time, a small sample of tissue (biopsy) for microscopic analysis may be taken to rule out cancer. The esophagus may also be viewed using x-rays after swallowing a radiopaque contrast medium (barium esophagography). Muscle contraction studies (manometry) may be used.

Treatment

Lifestyle modifications are recommended for all individuals who have esophageal strictures. These include taking steps to decrease stomach acid reflux into the esophagus, such as to avoid eating before lying down and elevating the head of the bed. Other steps may be taken to avoid food impaction in the esophagus (e.g., chewing their food well; taking small bites).

In most cases of esophageal stricture, the narrowed area is widened by passing flexible cylindrical rods (bougies) of increasing size into the esophagus, which can stretch the narrowed area (esophageal bougienage). This is a nonsurgical procedure that is done on an outpatient basis. The narrowed area may also be widened using a tube with a balloon attached to its end (balloon catheter). This is another nonsurgical procedure in which the balloon is inserted into the narrowed area, inflated, and kept in position for several minutes. Individuals may also be given oral medication (proton pump inhibitors) to decrease stomach acid production and inhibit reflux esophagitis.

If these treatments are not helpful, surgery (fundoplication) to reduce gastric acid reflux into the esophagus may be performed. In rare cases, where severe strictures involve long segments of the esophagus (usually due to the swallowing of corrosives), the affected area may have to be surgically removed. A loop of colon or segment of stomach may be substituted for the removed esophageal segment. Another technique involves joining the ends of the shortened esophagus and bringing the stomach up into the chest to meet it. Individuals who are too old or frail for reconstructive surgery may be treated by inserting a soft, pliable feeding tube down through the esophageal stricture or by inserting a feeding tube into the stomach from the outside of the body by passing it through a surgical opening (gastrostomy).

Prognosis

Lifestyle modifications are sometimes helpful in treating individuals with esophageal stricture; however, they are usually never adequate as the sole treatment.

Stretching of the narrowed esophagus using cylindrical rods of increasing size (esophageal bougienage) or using a tube with a balloon attached to its end (balloon catheter) are used successfully to treat esophageal stricture 76-96% of the time.

Recurrence of esophageal stricture following dilation treatment is not uncommon, and is required in approximately 76% of cases. Treatment with proton pump inhibitors does not eliminate the need for dilation therapy; however, it has been found to decrease recurrence of the condition by inhibiting stomach acid production, and allowing the esophagus to heal. Surgery to reduce gastric acid reflux (fundoplication) shows good-to-excellent results in about 77% of cases. Up to 43% of individuals treated using fundoplication will require repeat esophageal dilation following antireflux surgery. Mortality resulting from this type of surgery is low at less than 1 percent. Other surgical procedures, such as substituting a segment of colon for the esophagus, or joining the ends of the shortened esophagus, are rarely performed. Generally, they are reserved for individuals who have an esophagus that is irreversibly damaged and who are not responsive to any other treatments. Insertion of a feeding tube through a surgical opening (gastrostomy) is usually reserved for older individuals who are unable to tolerate other treatments.

Differential Diagnosis

Conditions that present with similar symptoms as esophageal stricture include abnormal tissue growth in the esophagus (esophageal cancer) and an inability of the muscles in the lower esophagus to relax (achalasia).

Specialists

- Gastroenterologist
- General Surgeon

Rehabilitation

Regular physical activity on a daily basis is recommended to relieve stress that may exacerbate gastric acid reflux and esophageal irritation. Aerobic exercise such as walking, jogging, or swimming (30-45 minutes per session) is usually beneficial.

Work Restrictions / Accommodations

Work restrictions or accommodations are not usually associated with this condition unless surgery is performed. In this case, a period of recovery in which there is minimal physical labor and exertion may be required.

Comorbid Conditions

Existing conditions that may impact an individual's ability to recover and further lengthen disability include esophageal spasm, esophagitis, peptic ulcer disease, and esophageal diverticulum.

Complications

Complications from esophageal stricture may include bleeding or perforation of the esophagus, impaction of food in the esophagus, and aspiration of food into the lungs (pulmonary aspiration).

Factors Influencing Duration

Length of disability may be influenced by the age and physical condition of the individual, or the presence of other medical conditions that may aggravate the condition such as reflux esophagitis.

Length of Disability

The duration of disability should be minimal or nonexistent unless surgery was used as treatment. In this case, the individual may be expected to be disabled for several weeks until recovery is complete.

Dilation.

	Duration in Days		
Job Classification	Minimum	Optimum	Maximum
Sedentary work	0	2	3
Light work	0	2	3
Medium work	0	2	3
Heavy work	0	2	3
Very Heavy work	0	2	3

Surgical treatment. Open.

	Duration in Days		
Job Classification	Minimum	Optimum	Maximum
Sedentary work	42	49	56
Light work	42	49	56
Medium work	56	63	70
Heavy work	70	77	84
Very Heavy work	70	77	84

Failure to Recover

If an individual fails to recover within the maximum duration expectancy period, the reader may wish to reference the following questions to assist in better understanding the specifics of an individual's medical case.

Regarding diagnosis:

- Does the individual have reflux esophagitis?
- Has the individual had prolonged use of nasal gastric feeding tubes?
- Has the individual swallowed strong acid or base?
- Has the individual had gastroesophageal surgery or sclerotherapy for esophageal varices?
- Does the individual complain of dysphagia, dyspepsia, or regurgitation?
- Did the physician find apparent swallowing difficulties or weight loss?
- Were an endoscopy and biopsy done?
- Was an esophagography done?
- Did he/she have muscle contraction studies (manometry) done?
- Have conditions with similar symptoms been ruled out?

Regarding treatment:

- Is the individual on medications?
- Has he/she made the recommended lifestyle changes?
- Is he/she chewing food completely and taking small bites?
- Has the narrowed area of the esophagus been widened?
- Was it necessary to perform fundoplication?
- Was the affected area surgically removed?
- Was a feeding tube put down through the esophageal stricture or gastrostomy?

Regarding prognosis:

- Does the individual exercise regularly?
- If necessary, is the individual's employer able to accommodate restrictions?
- Does the individual have any conditions that may affect the ability to recover?
- Does the individual have any bleeding or perforation of the esophagus?
- Does he/she have impaction of food in the esophagus?
- Has he/she had pulmonary aspiration?

References

LeMone, P., and K.M. Burke. Medical-Surgical Nursing. Upper Saddle River, NJ: Prentice Hall Health, 2000.

O'Connor, J.B., and J.E. Richter. "Esophageal Strictures." The Esophagus. Castell, D.O., and J.E. Richter, eds. Philadelphia: Lippincott Williams & Wilkins, 1999. 473-483.

Tucker, L.E. "Esophageal Stricture: Results of Dilation of 300 Patients." Missouri Medicine 89 9 (1992): 668-670.

Wojcicki, M., et al. "Electrochemical Therapy in Palliative Treatment of Malignant Dysphagia: A Pilot Study." Hepato-Gastroenterology 46 25 (1999): 278-284.

Esophageal Varices

Other names / synonyms: Bleeding Esophageal Varix, Esophageal Varix
456.0, 456.1

Definition

Esophageal varices are fragile, swollen veins at the base of the muscular tube (esophagus) that serves as the conduit between the mouth and the stomach.

Although varices appear in the esophagus, they are caused by disease in the liver. A condition called portal hypertension develops over months or years as the liver becomes so severely scarred (usually from cirrhosis) that blood coursing from the abdominal organs can no longer filter through it. The blood must go somewhere, and over time, the body develops an abnormal bypass around the liver, varicose veins in the gastroesophageal junction, the point at which the stomach meets the esophagus. The pressure in these irregular veins is great. If they rupture, they may bleed profusely.

In the Western Hemisphere and Europe, the most common conditions that cause portal hypertension and lead to esophageal varices are cirrhosis of the liver and portal vein blockage (thrombosis). Cirrhosis accounts for 85% of the cases of portal hypertension in the US. The most common cause of cirrhosis is alcoholism. Roughly one-third of individuals with this condition develop serious, life-threatening bleeding when these varices rupture. About half of the individuals with massive bleeding from varices die. Almost two-thirds of the individuals who experience acute bleeding episodes die within 5 years. The incidence of esophageal varices is 1 out of 10,000 individuals.

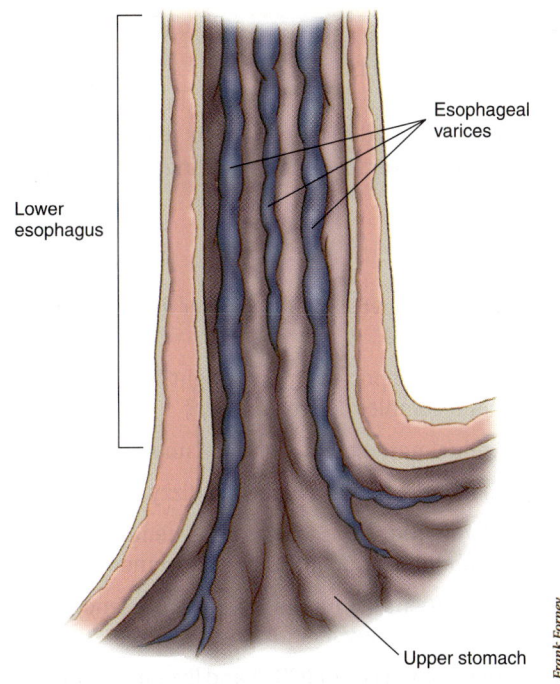

Diagnosis

History: Individuals with bleeding esophageal varices often vomit bright red blood or a brown substance that resembles coffee grounds. They may have bloody or tarry stools. They may feel dizzy and faint. A history of alcoholism can be significant. There are many other causes of gastrointestinal bleeding but profuse bleeding generally indicates ruptured varices.

Physical exam: An individual with nonbleeding varices may have signs that would raise suspicion of the presence of portal hypertension and cirrhosis. Distended veins over the surface of the abdomen and large swollen hemorrhoids are common. A shrunken, hard liver and an enlarged spleen can be felt. Some individuals have an inability to think clearly (encephalopathy); in conversation they may sound unclear or even incoherent. Signs of cirrhosis include abdominal fluid (ascites), endocrine changes and skin changes. In an individual who presents with active bleeding, low blood pressure (hypotension), fast pulse (tachycardia), and shock are common.

Tests: Lab tests include a complete blood count (CBC) and liver function tests. The level of protein in the blood (serum albumin) is determined. If an individual presents with active bleeding, blood must be typed and cross-matched for transfusions. Varices are visible on endoscopy or in an upper gastrointestinal series.

If the individual is not bleeding at the time of examination, magnified viewing of the troubled area with a lighted scope (an upper fiberoptic endoscopy) may be performed to assess the severity of the problem. Barium swallow x-rays may outline the varices.

Treatment

The individual is usually hospitalized in intensive care and may be given drugs intravenously to constrict the veins. A procedure to reduce blood flow to the varices may be performed (balloon tamponade). Sclerotherapy is a treatment involving the injection of a hardening (sclerosing) solution into vessels or tissues that are bleeding. Injection through an endoscope of a compound to irritate the tissue cells of the vein (endoscopic sclerotherapy) may be used on the problem veins and is often performed in two sessions. A newer method of endoscopic therapy is rubber band ligation of the varices (banding), which has fewer side effects than sclerotherapy.

When bleeding is severe, the individual must be treated immediately with fluids and blood transfusions. Individuals whose blood does not clot normally will require fresh-frozen plasma. If the bleeding cannot be controlled or if the individual requires more than 6 to 8 units of blood in the first 24 hours, surgery to create an artifical passageway (portal shunt) to redirect blood flow may be recommended. Nearly all types of treatment for esophageal varices have potentially serious side effects. The first step is to stabilize the blood volume by controlling blood pressure with drugs including vasopressin (given intravenously) and nitrates, or somatostatin, which decreases blood flow to the gastrointestinal tract. Drugs that lower blood pressure may also be given to reduce the risk of further bleeding. Some individuals avoid rebleeding by taking oral beta-blocking drugs, which offer the success rate of sclerotherapy without the side effects.

Prognosis

With successful surgical treatment (either a portal shunt or tying off the varix [banding], or sclerotherapy and strict adherence to abstinence from alcohol), the chances and severity of future bleeding episodes are reduced. Sclerotherapy stops immediate bleeding in 90% of cases. However, rebleeding is likely in most cases, usually within 6 weeks. When bleeding stops spontaneously without therapy, the individual may bleed again, usually within a week. Bleeding esophageal varices are a serious complication of liver disease and carry a poor prognosis.

Differential Diagnosis

Other conditions that may present with gastrointestinal bleeding include ulcers, gastrointestinal tumors, and arteriovenous malformations.

Specialists

- Alcohol Abuse Counselor
- Emergency Medicine
- Gastroenterologist
- Hepatologist
- Surgeon

Work Restrictions / Accommodations

The individual may need to be reassigned to less stressful work where conditions would not prevail that could lead to worsening of conditions that lead to esophageal varices. Individuals may need to have work scheduled such that they have time to visit physicians and therapists as necessary.

Comorbid Conditions

Substance abuse and dependence would interfere with the individual's ability to recover and worsen the effects of developing esophageal varices.

Complications

Rupture and bleeding of the varices is the most significant complication. Noncompliance with instructions to cease all drinking and practice better nutrition may cause complications. Recurrence of bleeding after treatment, reduced blood volume (hypovolemic shock), and esophageal narrowing (stricture) after surgery are complications as well.

Factors Influencing Duration

Continued alcohol consumption may lengthen disability and cause the condition to become permanent. Once esophageal varices have developed, the condition and its complications are permanent.

Length of Disability

Length of disability depends upon the state of alcohol consumption and a willingness to stop alcohol abuse. The likelihood of sudden bleeding episodes may lead to a state of permanent disability. Durations reflect recovery from procedures only.

Sclerotherapy of esophageal varices or ligation of esophageal varices.

Duration in Days

Job Classification	Minimum	Optimum	Maximum
Sedentary work	14	28	56
Light work	28	42	70
Medium work	42	63	84
Heavy work	56	70	112
Very Heavy work	56	70	112

Surgical treatment (portal systemic shunt).

Duration in Days

Job Classification	Minimum	Optimum	Maximum
Sedentary work	56	63	70
Light work	70	77	84
Medium work	84	98	112
Heavy work	112	126	182
Very Heavy work	112	126	182

Failure to Recover

If an individual fails to recover within the maximum duration expectancy period, the reader may wish to reference the following questions to assist in better understanding the specifics of an individual's medical case.

Regarding diagnosis:

- Does the individual have a history of liver disease resulting from alcoholism (cirrhosis)?
- Does the individual report vomiting bright red blood or a brown substance that resembles coffee grounds?
- Has the individual noted bloody or tarry stools?
- Does the individual complain of feeling dizzy or faint?
- Does the individual or physician note distended veins over the surface of the abdomen and large swollen hemorrhoids?
- Is it difficult for the individual to think clearly (encephalopathy) or to have a coherent conversation?
- Were a complete blood count (CBC) and liver function tests done?
- Was the level of protein in the blood (serum albumin) measured?
- Were varices visible on endoscopy or in an upper gastrointestinal x-ray (upper GI series)?
- Was an upper fiberoptic endoscopy performed to assess the severity of the problem?
- Was the diagnosis of esophageal varices confirmed?

Regarding treatment:

- Does the individual understand the importance of complete avoidance of alcohol?
- Was the individual hospitalized?
- Did the individual receive vasopressin (given intravenously) and nitrates, or somatostatin?
- Did the individual receive oral beta-blocking drugs?
- Was medication therapy successful?
- Was stopping blood flow to the varices (balloon tamponade) required?
- Was injection of a hardening (sclerosing) compound to irritate the tissue cells of the vein (endoscopic sclerotherapy) required?
- Was endoscopic rubber band ligation of the varices (banding) required?
- Do the varices continue to bleed, or was the procedure successful?
- If bleeding was severe and uncontrollable, was surgery to redirect blood flow via an artifical passageway (portal shunt) required?
- Was blood loss extensive?
- Did the individual experience any complications from severe bleeding or from surgery? Was the surgery successful?

Regarding prognosis:

- Is the individual absolutely compliant with abstinence from alcohol?
- If not, would the individual benefit from counseling regarding addictive behavior?
- Is this an initial episode of bleeding esophageal varices, or is this a rebleeding episode?
- How extensive is blood loss?
- What treatment plan is in place to address blood loss?
- If the individual had surgery, have any complications arisen post-operatively?
- What treatment will be given for the complications and what is the expected outcome with treatment?

References

"Bleeding Esophageal Varices." Medline Plus Health Information. 26 Sep 2000. 05 Dec 2000 <http://medlineplus.adam.com/ency/article/000268.htm>.

Keeffe, E.B. "Cirrhosis of the Liver." Scientific American® Medicine Online Dale, D.C., and D.D. Federman, eds. New York: WebMD Corporation, 2000 Scientific American Medicine. 05 Dec 2000 <http://www.samed.com/sam/forms/index/htm>.

Esophagectomy
Other names / synonyms: Esophageal Resection, Partial Excision of Esophagus
42.4

Definition

Esophagectomy is the partial or total removal of the tube-like structure that connects the throat to the stomach (esophagus).

The procedure is done to remove cancer of the esophagus. It is also done to remove areas of the esophagus that have been badly damaged following ingestion of caustic fluids (caustic esophageal injury) or to repair spontaneous ruptures of the esophagus.

The exact cause of esophageal cancer is unknown. However, chronic irritation of the esophagus from a wide range of sources is thought to be partially responsible for the cancer development. The most commonly reported irritants include tobacco, alcohol, dietary factors, lye, radiation, and refluxed gastric contents. In addition, there is a proven association of some esophageal cancers (adenocarcinoma) and Barrett's esophagus, a condition characterized by abnormal cell growth, strictures, and ulcerations of the esophagus. Within the US, the incidence of esophageal cancer is about 3 in 100,000 persons. Overall, the incidence is slowly increasing. Esophageal cancer is more common in blacks, Hawaiians, and Alaskan Natives.

Caustic esophageal injury occurs from accidental or deliberate ingestion of alkali (drain cleaners, etc.) or acid. These ingestions occur in adults with deliberate suicidal intentions.

Severe injuries to the esophagus that are associated with perforation of the esophagus, overwhelming infection, and shock can be treated with surgical esophagectomy. The most common causes of esophageal perforation are medical tubes and instruments, blunt trauma to the chest or neck, and forceful vomiting (Boerhaave's syndrome). Medical procedures such as rigid esophagoscopy, or upper endoscopy with biopsy, balloon dilation, or laser therapy procedures now cause over half of all perforations. Esophageal rupture from sudden forceful vomiting occurs infrequently, but often has catastrophic complications. It is reported to be associated with alcohol ingestion in more than 50% of the cases.

Reason for Procedure

Indications for esophagectomy include esophageal cancer, caustic injury to the esophagus, narrowed esophagus (stricture), and ruptured esophagus. In cases of esophageal cancer, the surgery is usually done to relieve problems with swallowing (dysphasia) rather than as a treatment for the cancer (palliative surgery).

Description

General anesthesia is used. An incision is made in the upper abdomen to reach the esophagus. The diseased section of the esophagus and any other adjacent areas involved are removed. Usually, the stomach is brought upwards into the chest cavity and joined directly to the remaining portion of the esophagus. If this is not possible, a section of bowel is removed and used to join the esophagus to the stomach. This is called a colonic interposition and requires an additional operation in the abdomen to obtain a piece of bowel. Sometimes a piece of tissue from somewhere else in the intestinal tract is used as a graft to join the esophagus to the stomach.

When there is extensive tissue damage in esophageal ruptures, the esophagus may be temporarily brought up and attached to an opening in the neck (cervical esophagostomy), to allow the tissue of the esophagus to heal before rejoining it to the stomach.

A tube is place in the chest cavity (chest tube) to drain any fluid that accumulates during or after the surgery. There will be a feeding tube placed in the intestinal tract, so that liquid food can be fed directly into the intestine, until the esophagus is healed. Intravenous feedings may be used as well to provide adequate nutrition until eating can be resumed.

Prognosis

Prompt treatment of esophageal ruptures or esophageal injury (from caustic ingestion) is associated with a cure rate of approximately 65%.

An esophagectomy usually relieves problems with swallowing in those with esophageal cancer. However, the cancer itself is associated with a 5-year survival of only 15%.

Specialists

- Gastroenterologist
- General Surgeon

Work Restrictions / Accommodations

Those being treated for esophageal cancer are generally not able to return to work due to progressive deterioration and ongoing treatments. Those who are able to return to work may require modified duty with frequent breaks until their strength and endurance is regained.

Comorbid Conditions

Comorbid conditions of immune suppression, heart disease, chronic lung disease, or alcoholic liver disease may impact ability to recover and further lengthen disability.

Procedure Complications

Complications that may result from this procedure include bleeding, infection, pneumonia, leaking of the incision line (anastomosis), and narrowing (stricture) of the anastomosis.

Factors Influencing Duration

Factors such as the underlying cause of the procedure, type of work performed, and the individual's general health and age may influence disability.

Length of Disability

Durations reflect recovery from procedure only. Additional disability may be associated with the underlying condition for which esophagectomy is performed. Due to ongoing treatments and progressive physical deterioration, disability may be permanent following esophagectomy in those with esophageal cancer.

Endoscopic esophagectomy.

Duration in Days

Job Classification	Minimum	Optimum	Maximum
Sedentary work	10	21	28
Light work	10	21	28
Medium work	10	28	42
Heavy work	10	28	42
Very Heavy work	10	28	42

References

Sabiston, David C., and H. Kim Lyerly. Textbook of Surgery, 15th ed. Philadelphia: W.B. Saunders Company, 1997.

Esophagitis

Other names / synonyms: Corrosive Esophagitis, Esophageal Inflammation, Infectious Esophagitis, Reflux Esophagitis
530.1, 530.10, 530.11, 530.19

Definition

Esophagitis refers to inflammation of the tube (esophagus) that leads from the back of the mouth or throat to the stomach.

There are 3 main types of esophagitis: reflux, infectious, and corrosive. Reflux esophagitis is a complication of backflow of stomach contents into the esophagus (gastroesophageal reflux). The stomach contents contain hydrochloric acid and a protein-digesting enzyme (pepsin). These can irritate and cause inflammation of the mucus membrane (mucosa) that lines the esophagus when it is exposed to these substances on a long-term basis. Risk factors for developing reflux esophagitis include gastroesophageal reflux disease (GERD), upset stomach (dyspepsia), or chronic ingestion of highly-seasoned foods or drugs that increase stomach acidity. It can also develop because of vomiting, surgery, or swallowing a sharp object.

Infectious esophagitis develops when fungus, yeasts (especially Candida), viruses (such as herpes or cytomegalovirus), or bacteria invade the esophagus causing it to become irritated and inflamed. Taking antibiotics is a risk factor for developing infectious esophagitis because they decrease the number of normal mouth and throat bacteria, while allowing other microscopic organisms to become dominant. Other risk factors for infectious esophagitis include diabetes mellitus, any condition that decreases the movement (motility) capacity of the esophagus, and the decreased responsiveness of the immune system, which can occur in individuals who receive organ transplants or who are infected with the human immunodeficiency virus (HIV).

Corrosive esophagitis will develop when the esophagus becomes burned, irritated, and inflamed in response to the accidental or deliberate ingestion of corrosive chemicals. The severity of the burn depends upon the type and concentration of the chemical, and the length of time the esophagus has been exposed to the chemical. As with other kinds of burns, esophageal burns are classified as first-, second-, or third-degree. First-degree burns of the esophagus involve only the outer (superficial) mucosa, while second-degree burns involve the entire thickness of the mucosa, and may extend into the muscular layer of the esophageal wall. Notably, ingestion of strong acids usually produces minor esophageal injury with severe stomach (gastric) burns. Risk factors for corrosive esophagitis include ingestion of strong acids (such as drain cleaners, vinegar, or aspirin) or bases (such as lye, oven cleaner, or ammonia).

The incidence of reflux esophagitis is estimated to be relatively low (less than 1%) in the general population; however, this figure increases to as high as 33% in individuals who have been treated for other gastrointestinal maladies such as hiatal hernia and gastritis. Infectious esophagitis occurs only occasionally in the general population (approximately 1%); however, it develops in 5-20% of individuals who have compromised immune systems. Ingestion of irritating materials that result in corrosive esophagitis happens usually among children. However, in all individuals, ingestion of household acids or bases results in corrosive esophagitis in approximately 46% of cases.

Diagnosis

History: Individuals may complain of pain underneath the breastbone (substernal), which is often described as burning. Reflux esophagitis (heartburn) may produce this pain 30-60 minutes after eating; it may be aggravated by lying down. The individual with infectious esophagitis may experience painful swallowing (odynophagia) or difficult swallowing (dysphagia). Symptoms of corrosive esophagitis include severe burning pain in the mouth and throat immediately after ingestion of the corrosive material, which increases with swallowing, followed by substernal chest pain.

Physical exam: The physical exam of an individual with reflux esophagitis may reveal abdominal distention and increased bowel sounds due to excessive gas in the stomach or intestines. Mouth sores (oral lesions) may be apparent with infectious esophagitis. A low-grade fever and enlarged lymph nodes may also be evident. Burns of the lining (mucosa) of the mouth and throat are usually seen with corrosive esophagitis. In some cases, the causative chemical may be identified by odor, and the individual may drool or gag.

Tests: The esophagus and stomach may be visualized by x-ray after swallowing a radiopaque contrast medium (upper GI series). A flexible fiber-optic microscope (endoscope) may be inserted into the esophagus to examine the inner (mucosal) lining and to obtain a tissue sample (biopsy) for microscopic analysis (endoscopy). Biopsy specimens may be cultured to identify bacteria or viruses. For corrosive esophagitis, endoscopy is done primarily to determine the extent and depth of esophageal burns.

Treatment

Left untreated, esophagitis can cause severe discomfort, swallowing difficulty severe enough to cause malnutrition or dehydration, and eventual esophageal scarring. Treatment for reflux esophagitis may be divided into 3 phases. Phase I involves general self-care measures that may decrease production of stomach acid. This includes taking over-the-counter antacids and reducing the intake of irritating and acid-producing foods. Phase II involves taking prescription medications such as histamine receptor antagonists, drugs that stimulate stomach emptying and decrease acid reflux into the esophagus (prokinetic agents), and drugs that prevent stomach acid secretion (proton pump inhibitors). Phase III includes surgical intervention, which may include severing the vagus nerve fibers that control the production of digestive acid (vagotomy), or surgically removing a portion of the stomach (subtotal gastrectomy).

Gastric acid reflux that causes esophagitis usually requires phase II or III treatment. Infectious esophagitis that is caused by a fungus usually requires oral antifungal medication. If this is ineffective, antifungal agents may be administered directly into a vein (intravenously). For viral esophagitis, antiviral agents may be given either orally or intravenously. Antibiotics are the best therapeutic option for bacterial esophagitis. Standard antituberculosis medication is recommended if microorganisms that cause tuberculosis (mycobacteria) are present.

Immediate supportive treatment is required for corrosive esophagitis. Fluids may be taken immediately after ingestion of the corrosive agent to help dilute the chemical. Vomiting should not be induced because this may result in further corrosive exposure and additional damage to the mucosa of the esophagus. Tubes inserted into the nose and down through the esophagus into the stomach (nasogastric, or NG tubes) should be avoided because they may perforate the damaged esophagus. Medications can be given for pain, and intravenous fluids may be administered to avoid the shut-down of vital organ systems (shock). Corticosteroids may be given to decrease inflammation, and antibiotics can be administered to prevent infection (prophylactically). Further treatment of corrosive esophagitis depends upon the extent and depth of the burn. First-degree burns usually heal without complications and do not require further treatment; the individual can be released from medical care after a period of observation. Second- or third-degree burns may be an indication that a surgical incision into the abdomen (laparotomy) for visualization of the external surface of the stomach and esophagus is necessary. A tissue sample (biopsy) may be taken to define the extent and depth of the burn. Second-degree and small, third-degree burns may be treated by placing a slender rod-like supportive device (stent) in the esophagus. While the esophagus heals, the individual is fed through a surgical opening (jejunostomy) in the second portion of the small intestine (jejunum). Extensive third-degree burns may be treated by removing (excising) part of the esophagus (esophagectomy); the esophagus can then be reconstructed 6-8 weeks later.

Prognosis

In most cases, reflux esophagitis is treated effectively using antacids to reduce stomach acidity. Histamine receptor antagonists or proton pump inhibitors lead to a 50% reduction in stomach acid output; this has produced significant relief of pain due to acid reflux (gastroesophageal reflux). There is usually some degree of postoperative morbidity if part of the stomach has been surgically removed (subtotal gastrectomy), including weight loss, cramping, or diarrhea. Subtotal gastrectomy used in combination with selective severing of the vagus nerve (highly selective vagotomy) is effective in decreasing stomach acid production and associated reflux esophagitis 95% of the time. Infectious esophagitis treated effectively with appropriate medications yields positive results in more than 90% of cases. Ongoing treatment of infectious esophagitis is necessary for those whose immune system is compromised to prevent recurrence. The outcome for corrosive esophagitis depends upon the type and amount of irritating agent that was consumed, and the effectiveness of treatment. Generally, esophageal burns from corrosive agents heal in a matter of days to weeks following appropriate treatment. If treatment included abdominal surgery (laparotomy) or esophageal reconstructive surgery, recovery may take weeks to months. However, most individuals may be expected to fully recover after these procedures.

Differential Diagnosis

Conditions that present with similar symptoms include Barrett's esophagus, Zollinger-Ellison syndrome, and scleroderma.

Specialists

- Gastroenterologist
- Otolaryngologist

Rehabilitation

Regular physical activity on a daily basis is recommended to relieve stress that may exacerbate gastric acid reflux and esophageal irritation. Aerobic exercise such as walking, jogging, or swimming (30-45 minutes per session) is usually beneficial.

Work Restrictions / Accommodations

Work restrictions and accommodations are not usually associated with esophagitis. However, each case must be evaluated on an individual basis taking into consideration the underlying cause for the condition. If stress is aggravating the esophagitis by increasing stomach acid reflux, transfer to a less stressful position may be necessary. Individuals with infectious esophagitis do not usually require work restrictions. However, if they have esophagitis because their immune system is compromised, they may require a less demanding work environment. Following initial treatment for corrosive esophagitis, most individuals may return to a full work load. If treatment included surgery, the individual may require a job with less demanding physical requirements until recovery is complete.

Complementary and Alternative Therapies

Content is intended for awareness only. Treatments may or may not be effective. Scientific evidence may be lacking and some substances have potentially toxic effects. Dr. Presley Reed and the editors do not endorse the use of these therapies in the absence of consultation with a licensed medical professional.

Biofeedback - Visual or auditory information about esophageal and gastric function may help reduce the symptoms of esophagitis.

Comorbid Conditions

Existing conditions that may impact an individual's ability to recovery and further lengthen their disability include pyloric ulcer disease, stomach cancer, and inflammation of the duodenum (duodenitis), any of which can exacerbate inflammation of the stomach and increase gastric acid reflux into the esophagus (gastroesophageal reflux). Individuals who are infected with the human immunodeficiency virus (HIV) will be susceptible to infectious esophagitis on a continual basis.

Complications

Complications of esophagitis may include narrowing of the esophagus (esophageal stricture) and the new growth of abnormal tissue (neoplasm) within the esophagus. Individuals with deep esophageal burns may occasionally develop an abnormal passageway (fistula) between the esophagus and an adjacent organ (trachea or aorta).

Factors Influencing Duration

Factors that might influence the length of an individual's disability include the cause of the esophageal inflammation, the extent of tissue damage, and the treatment used to alleviate the condition.

Length of Disability

Generally, the length of disability from esophagitis should be minimal except in extreme cases. Severe cases of corrosive esophagitis may require recovery time lasting days to weeks.

Reflux or infectious.

Duration in Days

Job Classification	Minimum	Optimum	Maximum
Any work	0	3	7

Corrosive.

Duration in Days

Job Classification	Minimum	Optimum	Maximum
Any work	14	21	28

Failure to Recover

If an individual fails to recover within the maximum duration expectancy period, the reader may wish to reference the following questions to assist in better understanding the specifics of an individual's medical case.

Regarding diagnosis:

- Does individual have reflux, infectious, or corrosive esophagitis?
- Does individual have gastroesophageal reflux disease (GERD), dyspepsia, or chronic ingestion of highly seasoned foods or drugs that increase stomach acidity?
- Has individual vomited, had surgery, or swallowed a sharp object?
- Were antibiotics recently taken?
- Does individual have diabetes or an immunocompromised condition?
- Were corrosive chemicals accidentally or intentionally ingested?
- Does individual complain of substernal pain or burning? Is it aggravated when lying down?
- Does individual complain of painful or difficult swallowing? Does severe burning pain occur in the mouth and throat immediately after ingestion of the corrosive material?
- On exam, does individual have abdominal distension? Increased bowel sounds? Are oral lesions present? Does individual have a fever? Positive lymph nodes? Is individual drooling or gagging?
- Has individual had an upper GI series? Endoscopy? Biopsy?
- Have conditions with similar symptoms been ruled out?

Regarding treatment:

- What is the underlying cause of the esophagitis? Is it being treated?
- Is individual on the appropriate medications? Was a vagotomy considered? Subtotal gastrectomy?
- Were fluids used to dilute the corrosive material?
- Was a laparotomy necessary? Was a biopsy done?
- Was it necessary to place a stent in the esophagus? Was a jejunostomy done?
- Was an esophagectomy necessary? Has it been reconstructed?

Regarding prognosis:

- Does individual exercise regularly?
- Can individual's employer accommodate any necessary restrictions?
- Does individual have any conditions that may affect ability to recover?
- Have any complications occurred such as esophageal stricture, neoplasm, or a fistula between the esophagus and the trachea or aorta?

References

Arcand, P., and A.J. Guerguerian. "Corrosive Esophagitis in Children." Chirurgie Pediatrique 23 1 (1982): 43-47.

Fraimow, H.S., and R.S. Klein. "Treatment of Esophageal Infections in the Immunocompromised Host." Therapy of Digestive Disorders. Wolfe, M.M., ed. Philadelphia: W.B. Saunders, 2000. 767-784.

Hajada, H., et al. "High Incidence of Reflux Esophagitis After Eradication Therapy for Helicobacter pylori: Impacts of Hiatal Hernia and Corpus Gastritis." Alimentary Pharmacology and Therapeutics 14 6 (2000): 729-735.

LeMone, P., and K.M. Burke. Medical-Surgical Nursing. Upper Saddle River, NJ: Prentice Hall Health, 2000.

Marzuk, P.M. "Biofeedback for Gastrointestinal Disorders: A Review of the Literature." Annals of Internal Medicine 103 2 (1985): 240-244.

Nikula, T.D., and V.A. Moiseenko. "The Microwave Resonance Therapy of Reflux Esophagitis." Vrachebnoe Delo 10 (1990): 97-99.

Esophagogastroduodenoscopy

Other names / synonyms: EGD, Panendoscopy, Upper Endoscopy, Upper GI Endoscopy

45.13

Definition

An esophagogastroduodenoscopy (EGD) is a procedure that enables the physician to examine the upper part of the gastrointestinal tract, i.e., the esophagus (swallowing tube), stomach, and duodenum (first portion of the small intestine) using a thin, flexible tube with its own lens and light source. Many conditions can be treated at the same time through the scope.

EGD is usually performed to identify the underlying reason for symptoms of persistent upper abdominal pain, nausea and vomiting (dyspepsia), or difficulty swallowing. It is also used to find sources of bleeding in the upper gastrointestinal tract.

A wide variety of disorders may cause dyspepsia such as reflux of the stomach contents (gastroesophageal reflux), peptic ulcer disease, inflammation or infection of the stomach (gastritis), slow gastric motility (gastroparesis), and cancer of the upper intestinal tract or biliary system (liver, gallbladder or pancreas). Esophageal narrowing (stricture), inflammation of the esophagus (esophagitis) and esophageal tumors can create painful or difficult swallowing. Upper gastrointestinal bleeding can arise from deep ulcers in the stomach or small intestinal (peptic ulcer disease), ruptured veins in the esophagus (ruptured esophageal varices) or from partial tears in the esophagus (Mallory-Weiss Syndrome).

Some factors are known to contribute these upper intestinal disturbances, including alcohol use, coffee or caffeine ingestion, chronic use of nonsteroidal anti-inflammatory agents, unsanitary food handling, and emotional stress. Often many of these factors are present in individuals with upper intestinal disturbances. However, sometimes the disturbances arise without any obvious underlying cause.

Reason for Procedure

EGD enables the physician to directly examine the gastrointestinal tract for inflammation, ulcers, or tumors of the esophagus, stomach, and duodenum. EGD can be useful in detecting early cancer and can be used to take tissue samples for laboratory examination (biopsy). EGD is also used to treat conditions present in the upper gastrointestinal tract. A variety of instruments can be passed through the endoscope that allows many abnormalities to be treated directly with little or no discomfort. For example, narrowed areas (strictures) can be enlarged with a balloon device. Small abnormal growths (polyps) or swallowed objects can be removed and upper gastrointestinal bleeding can be controlled. The EGD effectively controls bleeding and reduces the need for transfusions and surgery in many cases.

Description

Before the procedure, the individual's throat is numbed with a local anesthetic and a mild sedative may be administered. The individual is encouraged to swallow when gentle pressure from the endoscope is felt in the throat. The endoscope then enters the upper GI tract to begin examination. The endoscope is passed through the esophagus, stomach, and duodenum. Various devices may be passed through the endoscope to take tissue samples, administer solutions, or control bleeding as needed. The endoscope does not interfere with breathing during the procedure.

Prognosis

In general, the procedure is effective as a diagnostic tool and method of treatment for many disorders of the upper gastrointestinal tract. Since the procedure is done using a local anesthetic and is not as invasive as general surgery, the outcome is usually good.

Specialists

- Gastroenterologist

Work Restrictions / Accommodations

Work restrictions or special accommodations are not usually associated with this procedure.

Comorbid Conditions

Any underlying GI pathology such as esophageal ulcers, pancreatitis, or liver disease may lengthen disability.

Procedure Complications

Complications of the procedure, though rare, include bleeding, reaction to sedatives (i.e., drop in blood pressure, slow heart rate, or slow breathing), or a tear in the gastrointestinal tract (perforation). The risk is increased if the individual is taking aspirin or anticoagulants.

Factors Influencing Duration

Length of disability may be influenced by the type of procedure, the underlying disease, and the overall health of the individual. Recovery time for the procedure is variable.

Length of Disability

With or without biopsy.

Duration in Days

Job Classification	Minimum	Optimum	Maximum
Any work	1	1	2

References

Tierney, Lawrence M., Stephen J. McPhee, and Maxine A. Papadakis, eds. Current Medical Diagnosis and Treatment, 39th ed. New York: Lange Medical Books/McGraw-Hill, 2000.

Evoked Potentials

Other names / synonyms: BAEPs, Brain Stem Auditory Evoked Potentials, Cognitive Evoked Potentials, DEP, Dermatomal Evoked Potentials, EP, P300, SEP, Somatosensory Evoked Potentials, SSEP, VEP, Visual Evoked Potentials

ICD-9 Depends on Procedure

Definition

An evoked potential measures electrical activity in the brain that is produced (evoked) in response to an external sensory stimulus such as a flashing light, clicking noise, or light touch. Stimulation of a sensory nerve cell (neuron) results in an electrical discharge (depolarization) of the cell, generating an electrical impulse called an action potential; thus the name "evoked potential." These action potentials are called event-related potentials because they measure the brain's responses to some "event," such as a sensory stimulus (visual flash, light touch, or an auditory sound), a mental event (recognition of a specified target stimulus), or the omission of a stimulus (an increased time gap between stimuli). These tests are used to detect problems in the sensory functions of the nervous system, including vision, hearing, and touch.

The most commonly measured responses are brain stem/auditory, visual, and somatosensory. A Brainstem Auditory Evoked Potential (BAEP) checks the pathway from the ear to the brain and may help uncover the cause of hearing and balance problems or other symptoms. A Visual Evoked Potential (VEP) checks the pathway from the eyes to the brain and is used to help find the cause of certain vision problems and other conditions. It is often utilized to diagnose multiple sclerosis. A Somatosensory Evoked Potential (SEP) checks the pathway from the nerves in the arms or legs to the brain and is used to study the function of these nerves, the spinal cord, and brain. A Dermatomal Evoked Potential (DEP) is similar to an SEP, except that stimulation is done over areas thought to be more or less specific to a single nerve root, making it theoretically of greater use in disorders of spinal root function (radiculopathies). A cognitive evoked potential (P300) is a specialized auditory potential that detects response to a novel or unusual sound, making it a general measure of awareness and higher auditory processing.

Reason for Procedure

Evoked potential (EP) tests are used to evaluate nervous system functioning, detect nervous system abnormalities or lesions, monitor coma patients, monitor patients during surgical procedures, and test hearing or vision in infants and others whose hearing cannot be tested in standard ways. These studies can be used to determine a patient's baseline (usual) evoked response, and then be compared with information from EP tests conducted during or after surgery that might compromise function of a particular part of the nervous system. For example, dermatomal evoked potentials can monitor spinal nerve root function during anterior cervical fusion, posterior cervical fusion, spinal fusion, tumor removals, or surgeries to correct narrowing of the spinal column opening that contains the spinal cord (spinal stenosis) or curvature of the spine (scoliosis). Somatosensory EPs can monitor peripheral nerves that might be damaged by traction or manipulation during surgical procedures, such as carpal tunnel surgery, or orthopedic procedures involving traction that might damage the pudendal nerve supplying sensation to the genital area. While most EP studies track sensory pathways, motor EPs can be monitored during abdominal aneurysm surgery to prevent loss of blood flow (ischemia) to the spinal cord, which could result in paralysis of both legs (paraplegia). EP tests can also help diagnose multiple sclerosis or detect brain damage in head injury patients. EP tests can help predict outcome in coma, with greater accuracy than that of emergency room physicians looking only at clinical data. They can help localize an abnormality in function to a specific region of the nervous system, such as peripheral nerves, spinal cord, brain stem, or higher brain centers. Because EP tests are objective, and not subject to voluntary manipulation by the individual, they can be used to help distinguish organic disease of the nervous system from malingering. Cognitive EPs generally reflect degree of cognitive deterioration in Alzheimer's disease and other dementias.

Description

The action potentials evoked by stimuli during a test are detected by means of electrodes (thin metal discs) placed on the skin over the scalp, neck, arm, or leg. Signals from the electrodes during the testing process are detected by a computer, which amplifies, averages, and analyzes the responses, creating a print-out of the results, which are then interpreted by a physician. There are no pre-test preparations required, although individuals being tested should refrain from taking sedatives or other medications that could interfere with test results, and should not use hair spray or skin creams that could interfere with electrode function. Each evoked potential (EP) test usually lasts from 1-2 hours and is conducted with the individual lying comfortably on a couch. The tests may be performed singly or in various combinations, depending upon the symptoms being evaluated. During the brain stem auditory evoked potential (BAEP) test, electrodes are placed in several locations on the scalp and earlobes. Earphones are placed over the ears to deliver the stimulus (clicks or tones), usually into one ear at a time. The clicks or tones will sound many times per second during the test process. After one ear is tested, the other is usually tested as well. For the cognitive evoked potential, the individual is asked to count how many times he/she hears a tone that is different from the background tone. During the visual evoked potential (VEP) test, electrodes are attached to the individual's scalp in various locations. One eye is covered, and the individual is instructed to have a fixed gaze on a spot in the center of a video screen. A checkerboard pattern is displayed and then quickly reversed numerous times. The stimulus responses are then recorded and the procedure repeated for the other eye. During the somatosensory evoked potential (SEP) test, electrodes are attached to the skin over somatosensory pathways such as the wrist, knee, and ankle. Additional electrodes are placed above the clavicle (collarbone) and at the second cervical vertebrae (spinal column in the neck) for upper limb stimulation, and over the lower lumbar vertebrae in the back for lower limb stimulation. A painless electric shock is sent to the peripheral nerve through the stimulating electrode. The intensity of the shock is adjusted to produce a slight muscle response. Analysis is based on the measurement and averaging of the time it takes the current to reach the brain. The electrodes are repositioned, and the procedure is repeated on the other side of the body.

Prognosis

After the evoked potential test is performed, a neurologist or other physician will interpret the test results and give the individual being tested information about diagnosis, treatment, or the need for further tests. The outcome depends upon any underlying conditions, not on the evoked potential test itself.

Specialists

- Neurologist
- Neurosurgeon
- Otolaryngologist
- Physiatrist

Work Restrictions / Accommodations

Accommodations are based on any underlying disease or condition, not on the evoked potential test itself.

Comorbid Conditions

Local skin infections or conditions may momentarily appear worse after this procedure, if electrodes are positioned over affected areas. The individual may have a skin sensitivity to the paste used to attach the electrodes, or thin metal discs, to the skin. Severe limitations of hearing or vision may interfere with accurate test results. Visual and cognitive EPs require that the individual follow instructions, so these cannot be performed accurately if the individual is demented or comatose.

Procedure Complications

There are no side effects to evoked potential test procedures, other than possible skin sensitivity to the paste used to attach electrodes (thin metal discs) to the skin.

Factors Influencing Duration

Disability factors are related to underlying conditions rather than to the evoked potential test itself.

Length of Disability

No disability is expected to result from this procedure. Disability may occur as a result of an underlying condition.

References

Evoked Potentials. Hillcrest Health System. 01 Jan 1998. 12 Jan 2001 <http://www.hbmc.org/lev3.cfm/293>.

Madi, C., et al. "Improved Outcome Prediction in Unconscious Cardiac Arrest Survivors with Sensory Evoked Potentials Compared with Clinical Assessment." Critical Care Medicine 28 3 (2000): 721-726.

Excision of Bone Spur, Foot

Other names / synonyms: Bone Spur Resection, Exostectomy

77.68

Definition

Excision of a bone spur is the surgical removal of a bone spur (exostosis or osteophyte).

A bone spur is a benign bony growth that projects out of a bone. Bone spurs are caused by abnormal bone growth or imperfect bone remodeling. Bone spurs in the foot most frequently occur in the heel bone (calcaneus), in the ankle joint after a fracture, or on the top of the foot. A bone spur located under a toenail is called a subungual exostosis.

Bone spurs are fairly common conditions, although most do not cause symptoms. Individuals who are at an increased risk of suffering from symptomatic bone spurs include diabetics, athletes, and the obese. Men and women are equally affected.

Reason for Procedure

Foot pain is the primary indication for surgery. Pain may be caused by pressure on a nerve by the bone spur. There may be pain while wearing shoes. If the bone spur is on top of the foot, excision can be indicated if pain is not relieved by wearing modified shoes. A spur may also limit the range of motion of the ankle or bind ("catch") the joint during a certain movement. A bone spur that is causing a wound (ulceration) on the skin (as in a Charcot's foot) is usually excised. Bone spur excision is also used to treat heel spur syndrome (plantar fasciitis).

Description

Bone spur excision is usually performed on an outpatient basis. Because the foot is moist and carries a high number of bacteria, special care is taken to prepare for surgery. The foot and lower leg, with particular attention to the toe web spaces, is scrubbed for 8-10 minutes with an antibacterial soap. The foot and lower leg is then wrapped in sterile gauze until the individual is on the operating table. Immediately prior to surgery, the foot is washed with an antiseptic solution. Anesthesia may be regional or general. General anesthesia is used for cases in which regional anesthesia is undesirable (for diabetics) and for those in which regional anesthesia has failed. Regional anesthesia can be applied to the forefoot (forefoot or metatarsal block) for excisions in the front of the foot, or to the ankle (ankle block) for excisions in the back of the foot (hindfoot). A sedative is often used to relax the individual both prior to application of the regional anesthesia and during surgery. A tourniquet may be applied to the ankle and foot to reduce blood flow to the foot and allow for a clear work field.

During surgery, the foot is held firmly to prevent motion. At the ankle joint, a bone spur can be excised arthroscopically by use of a drill (burr). Bone spurs on the foot are removed via an open procedure by cutting (incising) into the foot, taking care to avoid damage to nerves and tendons. After the affected bone is exposed, a chisel-like knife (osteotome) is used to remove the spur and the site is smoothed using a coarse file (rasp). The incision is closed using stitches (sutures).

The individual usually wears post-operative shoes designed to accommodate swelling and bulky dressings. Antibiotics and analgesics are used as needed. The individual should rest and elevate the affected limb for 3-7 days following surgery.

Prognosis

In most cases, bone spur excision is successful and the individual experiences a complete recovery and a return to normal function. Bone spur excision to relieve the pain associated with plantar fasciitis has limited success.

Specialists

- Orthopedic Surgeon
- Physical Therapist
- Podiatrist

Work Restrictions / Accommodations

Prolonged standing or walking may be temporarily limited. Individuals whose work requires standing or walking may need temporary reassignment to a more sedentary position. Operation of a car or other motor vehicle may temporarily be affected. The individual may need to elevate the affected leg and possibly use a cane to walk. He or she may need a parking space closer to the work site.

Comorbid Conditions

Arthritis, obesity, diabetes, conditions causing impaired blood circulation (such as heart disease), and ankylosing spondylitis may lengthen disability.

Procedure Complications

Bone spur excision can weaken the bone, which could lead to a fracture.

Bone spurs can form again. Other complications include wound infection, scar tissue, damage to plantar nerves, accumulation of blood (hematoma), swelling (edema), splitting open of the incision site (dehiscence), deep venous blood clot (thrombus), and superficial vein inflammation caused by a thrombus (thrombophlebitis). Pressure on the local blood vessels from swelling or bleeding can result in compartment syndrome, which can cause permanent muscle and nerve damage.

Factors Influencing Duration

Factors that may influence the length of disability include number and severity of postoperative complications (i.e., wound infection, bleeding, chronic pain, or an adverse reaction to anesthetic), success of the surgery, individual's nutritional status and mental and emotional stability, and access to rehabilitation facilities.

Length of Disability

Duration depends on job requirements. Duration will be longer for individuals whose job duties require walking and standing.

Toe.

Duration in Days

Job Classification	Minimum	Optimum	Maximum
Sedentary work	1	3	7
Light work	1	3	7
Medium work	3	7	10
Heavy work	3	10	14
Very Heavy work	3	10	14

Heel.

Duration in Days

Job Classification	Minimum	Optimum	Maximum
Sedentary work	1	7	14
Light work	7	14	21
Medium work	14	21	28
Heavy work	21	28	42
Very Heavy work	21	28	42

References

Alvarez, Richard, and Saul Trevino. "Surgical Treatment of the Charcot Foot and Ankle." Operative Treatment of the Foot and Ankle. Kelikian, Armen, ed. Stamford: Appleton & Lange, 1999. 147-77.

Kisner, Carolyn, and Lynn Allen Colby. "The Ankle and Foot." Therapeutic Exercise: Foundations and Techniques, 2nd ed. Philadelphia: F.A. Davis, 1990. 385-408.

Excision of Lesion or Tissue of Skin and Subcutaneous Tissue
86.2

Definition

The skin is the tough layer of tissue that covers the body. It is the largest organ of the body and is divided into an outer layer of cells (epidermis) and a deeper layer containing blood and lymphatic vessels, nerves and hair follicles (dermis). The subcutaneous tissue lies beneath the skin and contains fat tissue, blood vessels, and nerves. A skin lesion is any visible abnormality of the skin including wounds, sores, rashes, boils, cysts, moles, vascular birthmarks, vascular, nerve or fat tumors, hypertrophic scars, and malignant tumors. They may be non-cancerous (benign), cancerous, large (gross), not directly visible (occult), or the originating point of growth (primary). Sometimes, there can be microscopic invasion of apparently healthy tissue by a lesion such as skin cancer. Excision of a lesion refers to the removal of a lesion and part of the surrounding, normal-appearing tissue.

Reason for Procedure

Excisions of a skin lesion or subcutaneous tissue are performed therapeutically, diagnostically (excisional biopsy), and/or cosmetically. Therapeutic excision of skin lesions is done to remove skin cancers or lesions suspected of being skin cancers. Therapeutic excisions may also be performed when the lesion is exposed to repeated rubbing or bumping, which may lead to bleeding and ulceration. Boils, cysts, moles, birthmarks, tumors, scars, and malignant tumors are all conditions that are treated with therapeutic excision.

Diagnostic excision is performed to determine the cause of a lesion. Causes can also include wounds, sores, rashes, cysts, moles, vascular birthmarks, vascular, nerve or fat tumors, hypertrophic scars, and malignant tumors such as squamous and basal cell cancers. Excision of malignant lesions is necessary for treatment and to prevent spreading to deeper or distant tissues (metastasis). Wide excision of malignancies ensures a better chance of eradication of the lesion. Excision of a benign lesion or tissue may be necessary if it is enlarging or spreading, if it is bothersome or painful, or if the appearance is unsightly. Cosmetic excision is done to remove moles, scars, cysts, and vascular birthmarks at the request of the individual in order to enhance appearance.

Description

The area of the lesion is thoroughly cleansed with an antibacterial solution. Local anesthetic is given. In some cases, general anesthesia may be used. Depending on the type of lesion and its size, different excision techniques may be used. The techniques for removal of benign and malignant lesions vary. An abscess may merely be opened and drained (incision and drainage). For an abscess or an infected cyst, a stab incision is made down to the pus-filled cavity. The small stab incision is then enlarged to allow full drainage of the abscess. The tip of the forceps is introduced into the cavity and then the jaws of the instrument are opened to improve drainage; additionally, the cavity should be explored by finger to break down all small spaces. Samples of the pus can be obtained for identification of the bacteria responsible for the infection (culture). The contents can also be aspirated (suction) by a tube passed through the incision. After completely draining, the cavity is thoroughly irrigated. The cavity may be packed with gauze containing an antibacterial medication. The exterior wound should be kept open until the cavity heals from within. A dressing is placed over the area.

Treatment with antibiotics is unnecessary unless there is evidence of spreading infection or unless the procedure was performed on the hand or face.

A cyst may be excised through incisions. For excision of a cyst, two slightly curved, intersecting, parallel incisions (elliptical) are made over the main portion of the cyst. Care is taken not to rupture the cyst. The incisions will be somewhat longer than the cyst, and the skin between the incisions will be removed intact with the cyst. The cyst and its covering skin can then be carefully lifted while gently cutting it away from the underlying tissue (dissecting). Any bleeding that occurred with removal is controlled (with pressure, cautery, or suturing). The skin is sutured together and a dressing is applied.

Warts and nevi may be removed by application of liquid nitrogen (cryotherapy), application of topical medications that remove the lesion, and by surgical methods (electrosurgery, CO_2 laser). Cryosurgery is performed by applying liquid nitrogen to the lesion, which causes freezing, until the area turns white. The area is allowed to thaw, and then the liquid nitrogen is reapplied. The wart will crust and fall off, usually in about a week. The procedure may be repeated if needed. Electrosurgery is performed by cleansing the area to be treated with a surgical scrub solution, injecting local anesthetic, and using electrosurgical equipment to apply heat to the lesion. Dressings are applied following the procedures. Many nevi require no treatment at all. Nevi with a potential for becoming malignant may be removed and biopsied. Lesions that may be malignant are removed. Skin lesions that are to be removed and biopsied may be removed by cutting the lesion above the skin line (shave biopsy), removing an oval core from the center of the lesion (punch biopsy), and by removing the entire lesion and its borders (excisional biopsy).

Prognosis

The predicted outcome may vary depending on the type and size of the lesion, and on whether the lesion is benign or malignant. Benign lesions should heal without problems. Malignant lesions found and treated in very early stages may also heal without problems. Depending on findings of biopsy and other indications, further treatment with chemotherapy or further surgery may be necessary. More advanced or spreading malignant lesions may require extensive surgery for removal, requiring grafting or reconstructive surgery. Other treatments and chemotherapy may be necessary.

Specialists

- Dermatologist
- General Surgeon
- Plastic Surgeon

Work Restrictions / Accommodations

Restrictions include hygienic care of the surrounding skin to prevent infection and avoidance of trauma until the wound is healed. Recovery from a skin excision may require time off from work or restricted activity may be necessary. If heavy lifting on the job is required, the individual may need to be reassigned in order to allow healing and prevent separation of the tissue at the incision. Heavy lifting places excessive stress and tension at incision sites on fingers and hands, the abdomen, knees, or any other area bearing weight or involved in movement.

Comorbid Conditions

Generally, there are no comorbid conditions. For extensive surgery, comorbid conditions may include underlying medical conditions that would place the individual at anesthetic or surgical risk (diabetes, heart disease, lung disease, etc).

Procedure Complications

Complications may include infection, bleeding, scarring, and spread of malignancy. Cryosurgery may cause permanent loss of skin color (depigmentation) in blacks and other individuals who have darkly pigmented skin.

Factors Influencing Duration

The underlying condition and presence of complications may influence the length of disability. The presence of malignancy, the extent of surgery and the need for other cancer treatments may also influence the length of disability.

Length of Disability

Duration depends on site, extent, and underlying condition. Malignancy and the presence of metastasis, as well as the need for extensive surgery, influence the length of disability.

Duration in Days

Job Classification	Minimum	Optimum	Maximum
Any work	1	2	3

References

Buffington, Sherry, and Clare Brabson. "Specimen Collection and Testing." Nursing Procedures, 3rd ed. Homes, H. Nancy, ed. Springhouse, PA: Springhouse Corporation, 2000. 132-165.

Robertson, Virginia E. "Warts and Nevi." Saunders Manual of Medical Practice, 2nd ed. Rakel, Robert E., ed. Philadelphia: W.B. Saunders Company, 2000. 1247-1250.

Excision of Morton's Neuroma
Other names / synonyms: Interdigital Neuroma, Plantar Neuroma
04.07

Definition

A Morton's neuroma is scar tissue that forms around and within a common digital nerve, which is located between the bases of 2 adjacent toes. Excision is the removal of the neuroma.

The cause of Morton's neuroma is unknown, but, because 88% of individuals with the condition are women, tight or pointed shoes have been suggested as possible causes or risk factors. It usually affects individuals over the age of 30 years. The nerve between the 3rd and 4th toes is involved in 65% of cases, and that between the 2nd and 3rd in 35%. The condition is effectively treated conservatively with corticosteroid injections in 75% of cases, but 25% eventually require surgical excision for relief of symptoms.

Reason for Procedure

Neuromas can cause pain in the foot and toes, especially when walking. Most cases of Morton's neuroma are effectively treated with conservative treatment. However, surgical removal of the neuroma is done to relieve symptoms in individuals who have not responded to conservative treatment.

Description

Anesthesia is administered, either general, intravenous sedation with local anesthetic injection in the foot or just with local anesthetic alone. The foot is then prepped and draped in the usual manner. Sometimes a tourniquet is used around the ankle to decrease bleeding during surgery. The skin is then cut (incision), usually on the top of the foot (dorsal surface) over the neuroma area. Some surgeons use an incision on the sole of the foot (plantar incision). The incision is then deepened, and the neuroma is visualized. It is then carefully cut out (excised) and is sent to the pathology laboratory for evaluation (pathological examination). The deep tissues and the skin are then sewn back together (suturing). A surgical dressing is applied, as well as a surgical shoe.

Prognosis

Complete relief of pain is achieved in the majority of individuals. Some will relate some residual postoperative numbness in the surgical site, but this is not usually troublesome. Recurrence of the neuroma is rare, much less than 1% of cases.

Specialists

- Orthopedic Surgeon
- Podiatrist

Rehabilitation

The individual will need to wear a surgical shoe for about 4 weeks and may need to wear a weight-relieving temporary orthosis (fracture brace) and/or shoe insert or metatarsal bar on the outside of the shoe.

Work Restrictions / Accommodations

The individual will need to wear a surgical shoe for about 4 weeks. Individuals will need to avoid prolonged standing or walking. Driving is not permitted with the affected foot. Due to the use of postoperative pain medications, drug policies should be reviewed.

Comorbid Conditions

Obesity, diabetic neuropathy, and peripheral vascular disease may lengthen disability.

Procedure Complications

Complications of the procedure include infection, wound edge separation (dehiscence), and recurrence of the neuroma.

Factors Influencing Duration

The occurrence of any complications will prolong disability. The surgical technique and postoperative treatment vary from surgeon to surgeon and will influence length of disability.

Length of Disability

Duration in Days

Job Classification	Minimum	Optimum	Maximum
Sedentary work	1	7	21
Light work	3	14	21
Medium work	3	21	28
Heavy work	7	28	35
Very Heavy work	7	28	42

References

Apley, A. Graham, and Louis Solomon. "The Ankle and Foot." Concise System of Orthopaedics and Fractures. Oxford: Butterworth-Heinemann Ltd, 1994. 209-223.

Kisner, Carolyn, and Lynn Allen Colby. "The Ankle and Foot." Therapeutic Exercise: Foundations and Techniques. Philadelphia: F.A. Davis Company, 1990. 385-408.

Magee, David J. "Lower Leg, Ankle, and Foot." Orthopedic Physical Assessment. Biblis, Margaret M., ed. Philadelphia: W.B. Saunders Company, 1992. 448-515.

Weiner, Jonathan P. Intermetatarsal Neuroma. Park Ridge, IL: American College of Foot and Ankle Surgeons, 1992.

Excision of Nail, Nail Bed, or Nail Fold
86.23

Definition

Excision of nail, nail bed, or nail fold is the partial or complete surgical removal of a fingernail or toenail, the nail bed, or the fold of skin covering the sides and base of the nail.

The nails (unguis) are the plates at the end of fingers and toes composed of the hard, fibrous protein keratin. The nail itself (nail plate) arises from specialized cells (matrix) and grows out over a specialized layer of skin (nail bed). The nail fold is the fold of skin that supports the nail plate on each of its sides. Nails are transparent and appear pink or dark pink in color due to the blood vessels that lie beneath the nail. It takes about 6 months for a nail to grow out.

Many signs of systemic illnesses can be observed in the nails. Nails are subject to injuries such as lacerations, crushing, and pulling away (avulsion). Blood may accumulate under the nail following trauma to the fingertip (subungual hematoma). The nails can be affected by skin diseases such as psoriasis, eczema, and by a chronic itchy skin disease (lichen planus). Nails are also subject to many bacterial, fungal, and viral infections. Onychomycosis is a fungal infection (tinea unguium or candida) of the nail. Paronychia is infection of the nail fold usually caused by candida. The nails may also be affected by both benign and malignant tumors.

Reason for Procedure

These procedures are generally performed for diagnosis and treatment of nail infections, tumors, a deformity of the nail (either from injury or a growth defect), and to relieve pain.

Fungal infections are unresponsive to ointments (topical treatment) and may not respond to oral (systemic) medications. A nail may need to be removed as a result of a chronic fungal infection unresponsive to treatment. A bacterial infection of the nail bed that doesn't respond quickly to antibiotics may be another reason for an excision.

Part of the nail fold may be removed as part of the surgery for an ingrown toenail, typically on the big toe.

Trauma to the nail may require its removal especially after a crushing injury. If the nail bed or nail folds have been disrupted by a large subungual hematoma, excision of the nail may be necessary. Excision of the nail may also be necessary to access the nail bed or the bone below in order to remove a bone growth (subungual exostosis).

The nail bed may be removed for cancers such as melanoma, squamous cell, or basal cell carcinoma in the nail bed. A nail fold biopsy may be done to evaluate connective tissue diseases such as lupus or scleroderma.

Description

The technique for repair of traumatic injuries depends on the type and severity of injury. The area is first cleansed with an antibacterial solution and a local anesthesia given for pain relief. Simple lacerations are repaired with sutures. Broken nails are gently removed from the nail bed with a small surgical instrument (hemostat). Removal (debridement) of foreign material or severely damaged tissue is performed. When possible, the excised nail is placed in a position over the repaired nail bed for use as a "splint" to allow proper growth, provide pain control, and to prevent gauze dressings from adhering to the nail bed.

An ingrown toenail is partially excised. A tourniquet is applied to control bleeding. The cuticle is freed from the area, and the part of the nail to be removed is freed from the nail bed. The nail for removal is cut from the nail to be left in place, and is then completely pulled away (avulsed) from the bed. Either a solution or electrocautery is used to prevent regrowth of the excised nail. The tourniquet is removed and antibiotic ointment and dressings applied.

Prognosis

Prognosis is favorable with excision in traumatic injury cases. If the excision is performed to remove or treat an infection, the outcome is generally good and the infection is satisfactorily treated. If the excision is performed to remove an ingrown toenail, the outcome is positive.

Specialists

- Emergency Medicine
- General Surgeon
- Hand Surgeon
- Orthopedic Surgeon
- Podiatrist

Work Restrictions / Accommodations

Time off from work may be necessary if pain medications are prescribed for recovery. Work restrictions may be needed if infection affects work activities. Prolonged standing or walking may need to be temporarily limited. Soft shoes may be temporarily required. If other injuries were sustained, restrictions and accommodations may be needed until recovery is complete.

Comorbid Conditions

Comorbid conditions may include diabetes mellitus, immunodeficient conditions, and circulatory disease.

Procedure Complications

Complications that may occur following traumatic injury to the nail may include nail deformity (split nail deformity), irregular nail surface, or failure of the nail to adhere to the nail bed. Complications of nail excision for ingrown toenails may include infection and regrowth of the excised nail.

Factors Influencing Duration

A circulatory impairment, diabetes, or arthritis in the last (distal interphalangeal) finger or toe joint will prolong disability. Infection may also influence the length of disability.

Length of Disability

Length of disability is affected by location, severity and extent of the injury, complications that may develop, job demands, and on whether dominant or non-dominant extremity is involved.

Uncomplicated.

Duration in Days

Job Classification	Minimum	Optimum	Maximum
Sedentary work	3	7	10
Light work	3	7	14
Medium work	7	14	21
Heavy work	7	14	21
Very Heavy work	7	14	28

References

Bass, Robert L. "Ingrown Toenail." Saunders Manual of Medical Practice, 2nd ed. Rakel, Robert E., ed. Philadelphia: W.B. Saunders Company, 2000. 1281-1283.

Desmond, Jeffrey S., and Carl R. Chudnofsky. "Hand Injuries." The Clinical Practice of Emergency Medicine, 2nd ed. Harwood-Nuss, Ann L., ed. Philadelphia: Lippincott-Raven, 1996. 493-508.

Haneke, Eckart. "Diseases of the Nails." Saunders Manual of Medical Practice, 2nd ed. Rakel, Robert E., ed. Philadelphia: W.B. Saunders Company, 2000. 1276-1280.

Parker, Frank. "Skin Diseases of General Importance." Cecil Textbook of Medicine, 20th ed. Bennett, J. Claude, and Fred Plum, eds. Philadelphia: W.B. Saunders Company, 2000. 2197-2220.

Excision or Destruction of Duodenal Lesion

Other names / synonyms: Endoscopic Excision of Duodenal Lesion, Open Destruction of Duodenal Lesion, Open Excision of Duodenal Lesion

45.3, 45.30, 45.31, 45.32

Definition

Excision or destruction of a duodenal lesion refers to the removal of a localized area of diseased or injured tissue in the first portion of the small intestine (duodenum). The procedure may be performed using a lighted instrument inserted through the mouth into the duodenum (endoscopy) or through an abdominal incision (open procedure).

Lesions of the duodenum are most often noncancerous (benign) tumors. Fifty to eighty percent of tumors of the small intestine (the duodenum is one part of the small intestine) are benign. Benign tumors in the duodenum can include polyps and other forms of tumors. Polyps are small tumors or flat growths in the mucous membrane that lines the duodenum. Tumors of the small intestine occur only very rarely. Polyps that originate from glandular epithelium (adenomatous) are the most common type of benign tumor found in the mucosa of the small intestine. The cause of polyps and benign tumors is not known, although some individuals may have a genetic tendency to develop polyps.

Reason for Procedure

The procedure is performed to remove polyps or tumors from the duodenum. It may also be performed to treat complications that develop as a result of the polyp or tumor, such as obstruction or bleeding.

Description

Duodenal lesions may be treated through open procedures in which an abdominal incision is made (laparotomy), or through procedures performed through fiber-optic instruments inserted through the abdominal wall (endoscopic). The type of procedure chosen depends on the underlying condition, exact location, and severity.

For open procedures, under general anesthesia, an incision is made through the abdominal wall. Once the lesion is located, it can be removed by excision (cutting it off), electrocautery (diseased tissue destroyed by electrical current), or by removing the section of tissue on which the lesion is located (resection).

For endoscopic procedures, a lighted instrument (endoscope) is passed through the mouth, into the stomach, and then into the duodenum. The endoscope consists of a thin, flexible fiber-optic viewing instrument with a controllable tip that enables it to be guided through the multiple bends of the gastrointestinal tract. The flexibility of the scope permits it to look forward, backward, and sideways, allowing the examiner to visually inspect the duodenum. Endoscopic tools such as forceps and cauterizing devices can be passed through a channel in the instrument. The instruments are used to remove or destroy any lesion detected.

Prognosis

The predicted outcome of excision or removal of duodenal lesions is generally good with successful removal of the polyp or tumor.

Specialists

- Gastroenterologist
- General Surgeon

Work Restrictions / Accommodations

Time off from work is necessary for the procedure and recovery period. Work place restrictions and special accommodations are not usually necessary after recovery from this procedure.

Comorbid Conditions

Comorbid conditions may include conditions that might delay wound healing in open procedures such as diabetes mellitus.

Procedure Complications

Complications from open procedures may include infection, bleeding, obstruction, and leakage at incision sites in the wall of the intestine. Complications from endoscopic procedures may include perforation and bleeding.

Factors Influencing Duration

Length of disability may be influenced by the type of procedure (endoscopic or laparotomy), type of lesion, location and extent of lesion, or presence of complications.

Length of Disability

Duration depends on type of procedure, cause and complications.

Local resection, open or endoscopic.

Duration in Days

Job Classification	Minimum	Optimum	Maximum
Sedentary work	14	21	28
Light work	14	28	35
Medium work	28	35	42
Heavy work	28	35	42
Very Heavy work	28	35	42

References

Ashley, S.W., D. Evoy, and J.M. Daly. "Stomach." Principles of Surgery Companion Handbook, 7th ed. Schwartz, Seymour I., ed. New York: McGraw-Hill, 1999. 603-618.

Markman, Maurie. "Small Bowel Cancers." Basic Cancer Medicine. Markman, Maurie, ed. Philadelphia: W.B. Saunders Company, 1997. 76-77.

Excision or Destruction of Plantar Warts
86.3

Definition

Excision of a plantar wart is the removal of a wart often found on the bottom (sole) of the foot.

Removal or excision typically involves use of chemicals such as acids or freezing agents, rather than extraction through a direct incision (surgical excision). Various methods of removing warts are through freezing with liquid nitrogen or other agents (cryotherapy, cryocautery), burning with a mild acid (chemical cautery), burning with an electric needle (electrocautery, electrodesiccation), treatment with a carbon dioxide laser (induced hyperthermia), and use of a surgical scooping technique in combination with acid (curettage). Topical chemical agents including corticosteroids also might be applied.

From 7-10% of US residents have plantar warts, which are caused by specific types of a common virus (Human Papilloma Virus) spread through direct contact with the skin or through bleeding from the affected area. The virus commonly is associated with warm, wet environments such as community pools.

Reason for Procedure

Untreated, plantar warts that do not resolve on their own may be associated over a period of years with lesions that can become precancerous. Plantar warts, which are caused by a virus, also are somewhat contagious. Leaving the condition untreated increases the possibility that plantar warts will spread to other individuals in locations such as public pools. The warts also can spread in clusters on the foot or, in some cases, to other parts of the body. Plantar warts can be very painful when pressure is applied to the foot through standing, walking or running.

858   The Medical Disability Advisor—Fourth Edition

Description

The procedure typically will be performed in a medical office on an outpatient basis. The area where the plantar warts are found will be cleaned, followed by possible cutting or shaving of some of the dead skin surrounding the area (debridement). Various procedures for removing the warts may be used alone or in combination with others.

When chemical cautery is used, acid may be placed on the warts either through direct application or through a plaster-like substance containing the acid that is cut in the shape of the wart and held onto the site by tape. Several applications left on the foot about eight hours daily may be required before the plantar warts and surrounding dead skin are ready to be filed or cut away. A doughnut-shaped pad may need to be worn over the wart during this form of treatment.

Cryotherapy or cryocautery involves use of cotton swabs or other applicators such as sprays to place a freezing agent, typically liquid nitrogen, directly on the affected site to destroy the warts. Additional applications may be needed at intervals of days or weeks. The warts should turn black and fall off when they are completely destroyed.

Deeper or multiple plantar warts may need to be excised by curettage that involves anesthetizing the involved area, identifying and marking appropriate margins, and scooping out the warts with a specialized instrument (dermal curette) possibly in combination with acid application.

With procedures called electrocautery or electrodissection, an electric needle is used to burn and remove the warts. Several treatments may be required before the warts are completely removed.

Various laser treatments are being explored for removal of plantar warts. A local anesthetic may be injected to numb the area prior to treatment. With a CO_2 laser, the light beam both cuts and vaporizes the plantar warts. Another method uses a pulsed dye laser to selectively destroy the wart. Laser treatments typically are not used because of the expense of the procedure.

Prognosis

Even without treatment, more than half of plantar warts eventually will resolve on their own. However, plantar warts often will reappear after or in weeks or months. About one-third of individuals with plantar warts have relapses. Treatments may need to be repeated several times or methods changed to completely destroy the virus that caused the original condition. New plantar warts also may appear following the initial treatment. In some cases, even repeated treatments will fail to resolve the condition. One study indicated an 83% success rate with no remission of plantar warts following a single cryotherapy treatment. The success rate was 92% when up to three cryotherapy treatments were used. Another study indicated a 100% success rate for laser therapy used to eliminate the underlying virus causing plantar warts.

Specialists

- Dermatologist
- Podiatrist

Work Restrictions / Accommodations

Individuals whose jobs require extensive standing may require temporary transfer to duties where they can remain seated while the excision heals.

Comorbid Conditions

Individuals with cardiovascular and circulatory disorders or diabetes mellitus may encounter greater difficulty with healing and recovery, including possible loss of sensation in the treated foot.

Procedure Complications

The initial treatment may fail to kill the virus causing the plantar warts, which may reappear. New plantar warts also might grow following initial treatment. Lesions might form in sites that have been treated. Direct surgical extraction (excision) can cause painful scarring and recurrence of the condition. A post-operative infection also might develop following a procedure. Bleeding from the wart can cause spreading of new warts to other parts of the body.

Factors Influencing Duration

While plantar warts without complications are benign, they can be extremely painful. Individuals who must stand or work on their feet for long hours may require time off from work until healing is complete. Individuals who perform tasks mostly while sitting should be able to return to work, but may require time off for procedures to be repeated as needed.

Length of Disability

Duration depends on rate of healing and weightbearing versus non-weightbearing location. If the condition cannot be resolved through excision or related procedures, certain individuals whose tasks require them to stand or stay on their feet for long periods of time may be adversely affected.

Duration in Days

Job Classification	Minimum	Optimum	Maximum
Sedentary work	1	3	7
Light work	1	7	14
Medium work	1	14	21
Heavy work	1	14	21
Very Heavy work	1	21	28

References

Cooper, Jeffrey. Warts, Plantar From Emergency Medicine/Dermatology. eMedicine.com. 13 Aug 2000. 8 Jan 2001 <http://www.emedicine.com/emerg/topic641.htm>.

Excision, Fusion, and Repair of Toes

Other names / synonyms: Amputation, Arthrodesis, Phalangectomy

77.58

Definition

Excision of a toe refers to the surgical removal of a toe or a portion of toe (e.g., distal phalanx). Fusion of a toe refers to the permanent fusing and immobilization of a joint or joints in a toe. Repair of a toe refers to the correcting or curing of a condition or disease in that toe.

Individuals with diabetes have 15-30 times greater risk of toe amputation than those without diabetes.

Reason for Procedure

The general indications for toe amputation are similar to those for any amputation (infection, arteriosclerosis with gangrene, etc.); however, specific indications for toe amputation exist as well. The fifth or baby toe is the most commonly amputated toe. It is usually removed for crowding (overriding on) the fourth toe. Other reasons for amputation include severe injury and tumor.

Fusion is indicated for great toe deformities (hallux valgus) plus second toe amputation, failed bunionectomy, advanced degenerative joint disease, rheumatoid arthritis, or severe deformity.

Repair procedures are performed for lesser toe deformities including hammertoe, mallet toe, claw toes, curly toes, or overlapping fifth toe.

Description

The excision or amputation procedure is performed as follows: The surgeon makes a cut in the toe and cuts through the muscles, bone, tendons, nerves, and blood vessels. The surgeon sews major blood vessels shut and may cauterize minor bleeding vessels, and sew the muscles over the remaining bone for padding. The soft tissue and skin will then be sewn closed to cover the muscles. A temporary drain may be left in the incision to allow blood and fluid to drain.

Arthrodesis or fusion is performed as follows: An incision is made over the joint, the capsule tissues are stripped both dorsally and plantarly so that the joint is widely exposed, bony growth from the surface of the bone (exostosis) is then excised (and saved as a source of bone graft), a large towel clip is used to help hold the joint steady, the cartilaginous and subchondral surfaces of the metatarsal and phalanx are removed, the metatarsal is shaped into a rounded cone, while the proximal phalangeal base is shaped into a symmetrically shaped rounded cup, wires and/or screws are placed to secure the joint, intra-operative radiographs (or fluoroscopy) are examined for areas of partial bone separation. Any areas of bone separation should be filled in with bone graft from the exostosis. The incision is then closed. The individual's foot will be placed in a non-weight bearing cast for 6 weeks, depending on radiographic results. Once the fusion mass has matured, the individual may find footwear somewhat limited, especially with regard to heel height. In some cases, individuals may prefer a rocker-bottom type of sole.

The procedures to repair toe deformities involve cutting or lengthening tendons, trimming or resection of a metatarsal head, soft tissue release, or a combination of these procedures. There are numerous repair procedures for various toe conditions; frequently used procedures to treat some of the more commonly occurring conditions are described here.

Hammer toes and claw toes can be treated with a procedure called a flexor-extensor transfer. Briefly, the individual is anesthetized with IV sedation and a local block. A small longitudinal incision is made over the plantar surface of the affected metacarpal head/neck region. The flexor digitorum longus (FDL) tendon is bluntly dissected out, elevated, and placed under tension. A short transverse incision is made just distal to the plantar distal interphalangeal (DIP) joint crease and with the FDL under tension, the tendon is transected from its insertion through the distal incision. The FDL is the pulled through the proximal incision and is longitudinally split down its median as far proximally as possible. A dorsal longitudinal incision is made over the proximal phalanx and the extensor tendon is bluntly exposed. Both sides of the tendon are bluntly dissected down to bone. Each arm of the FDL tendon is then passed into the dorsal wound on either side of the extensor tendon. With the toe in plantar flexion, the tendon is tightened down. The wounds are then closed and dressed.

An overlapping fifth toe can be treated with a procedure called Butler's Surgical Correction. Briefly, a dorsal incision is made over the little digit, centered over the EDL tendon (this will allow the toe to be derotated). A second incision is made on the plantar aspect of the original wound, which is brought laterally and proximally (this incision allows the toe to be moved laterally and plantarly). The contracted extensor tendon and the dorsal capsule are then released. For a positive surgical result, the toe must lie passively in a corrected position; forced correction may place tension on the digital vessels. Skin sutures will help keep the toe in a derotated position.

Prognosis

Toe amputation usually yields good results in the general population with a return to most normal activities. However, in the diabetic population, toe amputation can lead to future ulcerations.

Fusion or arthrodesis will alleviate pain but leave the individual with a joint that no longer moves. A rocker-sole shoe may be used to improve the gait following a fusion procedure.

The repair procedures described normally yield good results with a return to most normal activities.

Specialists

- Orthopedic Surgeon
- Podiatrist

Rehabilitation

Individuals who undergo excision, fusion, or repair of toes may require therapy. Heating pads may be applied to the toe and forefoot to decrease pain and increase muscle flexibility. Ice packs may be applied to the toes and forefoot as needed to decrease pain and swelling.

Increasing the flexibility of the toe, foot, and ankle is especially important for individuals who undergo joint fusion. Therapists may passively stretch the toe and forefoot into flexion and extension and may perform joint mobilizations on the toe joints. Individuals learn to manually stretch the toes and forefoot. Individuals stretch the ankle (into dorsiflexion) by placing a towel under the ball of the foot and using it to pull the foot toward them. Individuals also actively move the toe and the ankle. Strengthening the foot and ankle may be achieved by performing towel crunches in which individuals squeeze the toes around a towel placed on the floor. Individuals also engage in picking up small objects from the floor with the toes.

Therapists may manually resist the foot as an individual moves the ankle (into plantarflexion, dorsiflexion, inversion, and eversion). Elastic tubing with progressively increasing resistances can be used to strengthen the ankle in these motions as well. Standing heel and toe raises can be performed while standing on both feet, or while standing on the injured foot.

Individuals progress from walking with crutches or a cane to walking without assistance. Therapists focus on normalizing an individual's gait pattern once full-weight bearing through the foot is permitted; treadmill walking may be used to accomplish this.

Work Restrictions / Accommodations

Standing and walking may need to be temporarily limited. Crutches or a cane may need to be used for a short time postoperatively. Climbing, stooping, and squatting may need to be temporarily eliminated. Accommodation for the individual to keep the foot elevated might be needed.

Comorbid Conditions

Conditions that could impact ability to recover and further lengthen disability include obesity, diabetes, peripheral neuropathy, osteomyelitis, and osteoarthritis.

Procedure Complications

Complications of a toe excision (amputation) may include postoperative infection, blood clots, and gait changes. The individual's gait is usually normal with slow locomotion and impaired with rapid locomotion. Hallux valgus (deformity of the great toe) is a common complication of second toe amputations.

Complications of toe arthrodesis may include infection, blood clots, mal-union, non-union, and interphalangeal (IP) degenerative joint disease. If the arthrodesis results in excessive dorsiflexion, it may be complicated by the IP joint rubbing in the shoe, which may cause the toe to claw and restrict footwear. If the arthrodesis results in insufficient plantar flexion, it may be complicated by a lateral roll-off or vaulting gait.

All of the repair procedures may be complicated by postoperative infection and blood clots.

Factors Influencing Duration

The diagnosis, surgical technique, and any postoperative complications will influence the length of disability.

Length of Disability

Disability duration is based on specific procedure performed. Disability may be permanent for certain jobs.

Duration in Days

Job Classification	Minimum	Optimum	Maximum
Sedentary work	3	7	14
Light work	7	21	21
Medium work	14	21	28
Heavy work	28	35	42
Very Heavy work	28	35	42

References

Toe Amputation. Gentili.net. 2000. 26 Nov 2000 <http://www.gentili.net/amputations/toe_amputations.htm>.

Magee, David J. "Lower Leg, Ankle, and Foot." Orthopedic Physical Assessment. Biblis, Margaret M., ed. Philadelphia: W.B. Saunders Company, 1992. 448-515.

Explosive Personality Disorder

Other names / synonyms: Anger Attacks, Episodic Dyscontrol, Intermittent Explosive Disorder, Rage Attacks

301.1, 301.10, 301.13, 301.3, 301.5, 301.59, 301.9

Definition

Explosive personality disorder is characterized by episodes of aggressive, destructive behavior resulting in damage to an individual or property. The outburst can occur with little or no provocation, and the individual feels unable to resist the aggressive impulses. The feelings and behavior appear very suddenly and subside almost as quickly, often followed by regret or embarrassment over lack of self-control and the resulting damages. Between episodes, the individual may or may not appear generally impulsive or aggressive. The aggressive episodes typically last about 20 minutes and occur about 1 to 25 times a month.

This disorder is more common in men than women, although intermittent explosive symptoms can occur in premenstrual women, and usually begins in the teenage years or the twenties. It can appear quite suddenly. It is not due to schizophrenia, antisocial or borderline personality disorders, mania, attention deficit disorder, conduct disorder, medical causes such as a head injury or Alzheimer's disease, or abuse of drugs, alcohol, or prescribed medication. The DSM-IV classifies intermittent explosive disorder as being an impulse control disorder. Research suggests that this condition may be linked to bipolar disorder and that there may be abnormalities in a brain chemical called serotonin.

Diagnosis

History: Individual has a history of episodes of aggression resulting in assaults on another individual or significant damage to property. The behavior is completely out of proportion to any precipitating stress. There is no diagnosis of another mental or physical disorder that would better explain the outbursts. Individuals typically report aggressive impulses that are experienced as a need to attack, strike out, or defend oneself before the explosive acts. Many individuals report a feeling of tension with aggressive impulses and obtain relief or even pleasurable feelings with the explosive acts. About one-third of individuals report physical symptoms such as rapid or irregular heartbeat, tingling, shaking, chest tightness, or head pressure before or during the aggressive episodes. About one-half report change in or loss of awareness with the explosive episodes although they still remember the episodes. Changes in mood and energy frequently accompany the outbursts.

Physical exam: The exam does not confirm this diagnosis, but can reveal nonspecific, mild neurological findings. Observation of the individual's orientation, dress, mannerisms, behavior, and content of speech provide essential signs in diagnosing the illness.

Tests: Tests do not establish the diagnosis, but nonspecific electroencephalogram (EEG) changes may be observed.

Treatment

Drug therapy may include antidepressants such as tricyclic antidepressants or serotonin reuptake inhibitors, and mood-stabilizers such as lithium, anticonvulsants, or beta-blockers. Antianxiety medication may be helpful to reduce any precipitating anxiety. Psychotherapy is also useful to establish a trusting alliance that can be useful in times of stress.

Prognosis

The course of this illness is episodic and unpredictable.

Differential Diagnosis

Medical possibilities are temporal lobe epilepsy or brain tumor. Other psychiatric diagnoses are antisocial personality disorder, manic episode, dissociative disorder, paranoid schizophrenia, delirium, dementia, and substance intoxication or withdrawal. Malingering is also a possibility.

Specialists

- Neurologist
- Psychiatrist

Work Restrictions / Accommodations

Tolerance for explosive rage is minimal in the workplace, particularly in light of concern for the safety of coworkers. Frequency of episodes has a direct bearing on employability. Job accommodations, when possible, should include a quiet, predictable low stress environment; work that is completed independent of coworkers; provisions for flexible breaks to control stress and anger levels; and flexibility in schedule to contact support system and attend treatment programs, meetings among the employer, supervisor, and job coach to explore sources of tension on the job, and any solutions or other accommodations.

Comorbid Conditions

Comorbid conditions that may lengthen disability are alcohol abuse or drug use or the presence of another psychiatric illness.

Complications

The disorder often results in repeated loss of employment, damage to personal relationships, divorce, and social isolation. Accidental injury and confinement in prison can also occur.

Factors Influencing Duration

The discovery of an underlying, treatable condition such as alcohol or drug abuse may influence disability. Response to treatment, frequency and severity of outbursts, legal consequences of explosive outbursts, and specific job responsibilities all influence length of disability.

Length of Disability

This condition represents a life-long pattern of behavior. In most cases, no disability is expected, though the individual may be removed from the workplace for safety reasons. Duration depends on severity of manifestations and exacerbating factors.

Failure to Recover

If an individual fails to recover within the maximum duration expectancy period, the reader may wish to reference the following questions to assist in better understanding the specifics of an individual's medical case.

Regarding diagnosis:

- Does individual's behavior fit the criteria for explosive personality disorder? If not, how does it differ?
- Has diagnosis been confirmed?
- Have other psychiatric disorders, substance abuse, and medical conditions been ruled out?

Regarding treatment:

- Does individual's treatment plan include drug therapy? If not effective in controlling episodes or aggression, what other options are available?
- If individual is involved in psychotherapy, does it appear to be effective in lowering stress and establishing a trusting alliance during times of stress?

Regarding prognosis:

- Although the course of this illness is episodic, unpredictable, and difficult to predict, what does physician/therapist see as a realistic prognosis or goal?
- Is there evidence that individual could be hiding behind this behavior to avoid responsibility for his/her behavior?

References

Lion, J.R. "The Intermittent Explosive Disorder." Psychiatric Annals 22 (1992): 64-66.

McElroy, Susan. "Recognition and Treatment of DSM-IV Intermittent Explosive Disorder." Journal of Clinical Psychiatry 60 Suppl. 15 (1999): 12-16.

Face Lift

Other names / synonyms: Cosmetic Surgery, Plastic Surgery, Rhytidectomy

86.25, 86.82, 86.92, 86.93

Definition

A face lift (rhytidectomy) describes various surgical procedures aimed at minimizing skin wrinkles (rhytids) on the face and neck.

The individual undergoing this usually elective procedure typically wants to achieve a more youthful or aesthetically pleasing appearance. A face lift often takes place in conjunction with other surgical procedures that reshape the nose (rhinoplasty), chin (mentoplasty), eyebrows, eye area (blepharoplasty), lips (augmentation), ears (otoplasty), or other facial features. Fat transfers using tissue from other parts of the body (collagen injection) also might be used for sculpting facial features or smoothing wrinkles.

The Plastic Surgery Information Service estimates that about 72,800 face lifts were performed in the US in 1999.

Reason for Procedure

A face lift tightens muscles and removes excess skin, which, in older adults, begins to sag and wrinkle partly because of gravity's long-term effects as aging skin loses its elasticity. Loose skin or jowls may form on both sides of the bottom of the face, creating a "square" appearance. Deeper lines begin to form in the face, while clusters of wrinkles develop particularly around the lips and eyes. Sagging skin may also droop from the neck. Individuals often seek face lifts for professional reasons, particularly when jobs might require a high public profile and youthful, energetic demeanor. Other often complex social or psychological factors might motivate the individual to seek cosmetic surgery. Surgeons often will query individuals in-depth to assess expectations before proceeding with a face lift.

Description

Prior to surgery, individuals are instructed to avoid substances such as nicotine and alcohol along with certain vitamins and medications that might hamper the healing process. While most procedures are done under local anesthesia on an outpatient basis, the individual will need a ride home after the surgery. Some surgeons require hospitalization of individuals the night before the procedure. In some cases where specific health issues are involved or complicated procedures are planned, the individual will undergo general anesthesia. In this case, a tube is usually inserted in the throat to keep the airway open while the individual is unconscious. A sedative often is administered prior to surgery involving local anesthesia.

The most commonly practiced method of face lift is a technique called SMAS (Superficial Muscular Aponeurotic System). With this system, the surgeon uses the hairline to hide a row of incisions that outline the face in a line that dips behind the ears. Some surgeons use a small, tube-like instrument with a lighted camera to achieve tiny incisions (endoscopy). Face and neck skin is then smoothed and tucked, while excess fat is removed (liposuction). Collagen injections might be added to contour the face. Sutures and staples are used to close incisions and tighten the skin. The procedure usually lasts about 5 hours. Depending on the extent of procedures, 2 sessions might be required.

After surgery, the individual will be required to wear dressings for a few days. During this time, the individual also may be instructed to rest and keep the head elevated. Sutures or staples may be removed in about a week. Persistent pain is unlikely, although some numbness might be noted for the next few weeks or months. Pain relievers (analgesics) may be prescribed if pain lingers. After wrappings are removed, considerable bruising and swelling (edema) on the face likely will be apparent. Most individuals are advised to rest for at least a week. Scars usually hidden in the hairline may take as long as a year to completely heal. The face may not appear completely normal for several weeks or months. Direct sun exposure also should be avoided for several months. Camouflage makeup might be needed during the healing process. The procedure is not permanent, and may need to be repeated or enhanced every 5-10 years.

Prognosis

The individual almost always achieves a more youthful appearance, which will diminish over time as the aging process continues. Typically, enhancements or repeats of the procedure must be performed every 5-10 years. Scarring may not resolve until after about a year. Men may have to shave in new places such as behind the ears because of the re-positioning of skin. The face lift procedure will address only certain features and, alone, will not smooth wrinkles in the area around the forehead and eyes.

Specialists

- Dermatologist
- Ophthalmologist
- Oral Surgeon
- Otolaryngologist
- Plastic Surgeon

Work Restrictions / Accommodations

Individuals who receive a face lift typically must receive time off work for about 2 weeks after the procedure. At work, individuals must avoid strenuous activity and avoid exposure to the sun for about 6 weeks. Complications such as infection may extend the individual's need for time off or accommodation.

Comorbid Conditions

Individuals with thicker skin and wider and shorter necks likely will not receive optimal results from a face lift.

Procedure Complications

Some complications of face lift include collection of blood under the skin (hematoma) that may require surgical removal. Post-operative infection, allergic reaction to anesthesia, slow wound healing, bleeding, scarring, and nerve injuries are possible. In rare cases, collagen injections have caused vision loss and stroke (cerebral infarction). Hair loss (alopecia) may occur if hair follicles are damaged during the procedure.

Factors Influencing Duration

Those who are slow to heal will have more difficulty recovering from the procedure. Complications such as infection may lengthen disability. If the individual has several cosmetic procedures done in addition to a face lift, recovery time may need to be extended.

Length of Disability

The length of disability may depend on the individual's work tasks, particularly if strenuous activity and heavy lifting are required.

Duration in Days

Job Classification	Minimum	Optimum	Maximum
Any work	3	7	14

References

Rhytidectomy: Face Lift and Neck Lift. Mayo Clinic. 12 Jan 2000. 28 Sept 2000 <http://www.mayo.edu/staff/plastic/Cosmetic/CSOLFacelift.html>.

Deckerd, Michael E., et al. Rhytidectomy: The Basics. University of Texas Medical Branch at Galveston Department of Otolaryngology. 13 Oct 1999. 27 Sept 2000 <http://www2.utmb.edu/otoref/Grnds/Rhytidectomy-991013/Rhytidectomy-991013.htm>.

Factitious Illness with Physical Symptoms

Other names / synonyms: Hospital Addiction, Munchausen's Syndrome, Polysurgical Addiction, Professional Individual Syndrome

300.12, 300.19, 301.51, 306, 306.0, 306.3, 306.5, 306.6, 306.7, 306.8

Definition

In factitious illness, an individual intentionally produces physical or psychological symptoms of medical or mental disorders. The individual's motivation and purpose is to assume the sick role, not to avoid responsibilities or to realize financial gain. Goals may include hospitalization, undergoing complex and risky medical procedures, and obtaining drugs especially narcotics. In some cases, moving from one hospital to another or from one physician to another becomes a way of life.

Although the behaviors are compulsive in origin and cannot be controlled, they are considered voluntary in that they are deliberate and purposeful. Individuals present their history and physical symptoms expertly. As they become very knowledgeable about medical diagnosis, they can even fool a seasoned clinician. Individuals may feign pain, fever, low blood sugar, bruises, contaminated urine, seizures, vomiting, rashes, dizziness, and fainting spells. They commonly have multiple scars from previous surgical procedures. After the test results begin to expose their deception, they move on to another hospital and start the process over again.

The psychological basis for factitious disorders is poorly understood. In some cases, it has been traced to childhood trauma either physical or mental. Families of origin often reveal a rejecting mother or absent father. Factitious illness is used to re-create the desired parent-child bond. It is an attempt to resolve the conflict of seeking acceptance and love from an absent or rejecting parent.

Factitious illness syndrome is rare. It peaks in young to middle-aged adults but has been reported from childhood through old age.

Diagnosis

History: A typical history includes multiple prior hospitalizations, workups, surgeries, and frequent office visits to healthcare providers including psychiatric institutions. The diagnosis is often made only on the basis of this history. Factitious illness is characterized by dramatic presentations of apparently severe illnesses with reported symptom patterns that are too perfect and too much like a textbook presentation. However, individuals may also be vague or inconsistent when reporting the details of their medical problems.

Because individuals with factitious illness misrepresent their histories and symptoms, obtaining and verifying prior hospitalizations and medical care is important. There may be evidence of pathological lying in areas other than medical history. Information from any available friend, relative, coworker, or other reliable sources often confirm the deception. Individuals who present with symptoms of pain warranting a prescription for narcotics may enlist a cohort to bolster their story.

Physical exam: As the individual is skilled at appearing ill and knowledgeable about symptoms and physical signs, it is possible that the examiner may find physical signs in single or multiple systems. For example, individuals may scratch their skin to feign an itching rash, use medications that will increase or decrease their heart rate or blood pressure, or use eye drops to dilate one eye to feign a neurological disorder. Although the examiner may be correct in diagnosing factitious illness, for medicolegal reasons, the history and physical findings should be the guide in ordering appropriate tests. Observation of the individual's orientation, dress, mannerisms, behavior, and content of speech provide essential signs to diagnose the illness.

Tests: Testing is limited to the least expensive approach (usually routine laboratory tests and x-rays) that can discount the related symptoms. An atypical pattern of lab results may help to diagnose the condition. However, a complete workup of complex, invasive medical procedures may sometimes be necessary to rule out physical causes of symptoms. Psychological testing may reveal a poor sense of identity, related personality disorders, poor sexual adjustment, a low tolerance for frustration, strong dependency issues and, in some individuals, an inflated sense of self-worth.

Treatment

An effective treatment for factitious disorder has yet to be identified. The foundation of the illness precludes the individual from seeking effective therapy. Instead of wanting to get better, they want to maintain the sick role. Early recognition by a physician may prevent the individual from undergoing further potentially dangerous diagnostic and therapeutic interventions.

If the diagnosis is in doubt, appropriate specialists should be consulted. Hospitalization for physical workup may be needed. When the diagnosis is clearly established, psychiatric referral should always be offered. As psychiatric treatment is usually declined, this refusal should be documented in the individual's record. Antipsychotic drugs are sometimes given but there is no evidence they have any effect on the course or prognosis.

Prognosis

Prognosis in most cases is poor, though not for all individuals. Successful psychiatric intervention favors a good prognosis. Morbidity and mortality as a result of needless medication and invasive procedures is possible.

Differential Diagnosis

A factitious disorder should be differentiated from severe personality disorders, somatoform disorders, malingering, and substance abuse. In conversion disorders, but not in factitious illness, motivation is subconscious and symptoms are not subject to voluntary control. In both malingering and factitious disorder, individuals feign illness. However, malingering individuals do so for financial gain whereas individuals with factitious disorder feign illness solely to maintain the sick role. The sick role is a reward in itself. Individuals with factitious disorder may have many unpleasant personality traits, making it sometimes difficult to distinguish them from individuals with other personality disorders. In fact, individuals with factitious illness may frequently also suffer from a personality disorder.

Specialists

- Psychiatrist
- Psychologist

Work Restrictions / Accommodations

Working around drugs, chemicals, and hazardous materials should be restricted. The individual may use these materials in an attempt to feign physical illness with serious or life-threatening consequences.

Comorbid Conditions

Coexisting conditions that may affect recovery and lengthen disability include substance abuse particularly of prescribed analgesics and sedatives and personality disorders.

Complications

In factitious disorder, the invention of physical and/or psychological symptoms is a complication in itself. If real physical or mental symptoms appear, hospital staff, clinicians, and therapists are likely to dismiss them as factitious given the individual's past medical history. Coexisting psychiatric illnesses including substance abuse makes diagnosis almost impossible.

Individuals with factitious disorder go to great lengths to feign symptoms even to the point of taking drugs or exposing themselves to chemicals that may cause injury or real medical problems. Treatment of the feigned illness with drugs or surgery can also produce real physical symptoms or mental signs that cloud the true clinical picture. Many treatments and procedures carry the possibility of medical complications.

Factors Influencing Duration

Delays in properly diagnosing this disorder are inherent in the disorder. Multiple operations and medical treatments may produce their own disabilities. Positive influences include early detection, psychiatric treatment, and a strong family support system.

Length of Disability

Maximum duration may include hospitalization.

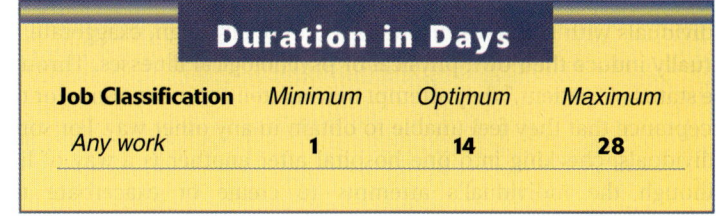

Job Classification	Minimum	Optimum	Maximum
Any work	1	14	28

Failure to Recover

If an individual fails to recover within the maximum duration expectancy period, the reader may wish to reference the following questions to assist in better understanding the specifics of an individual's medical case.

Regarding diagnosis:

- If individual states a history of multiple hospitalizations (including psychiatric institutions) and frequent office visits to health care providers, have prior hospitalizations and medical care been verified?
- For medicolegal reasons, have appropriate diagnostic tests been performed?
- Have legitimate medical conditions been identified or ruled out?
- If initial chief complaint proved negative, has the individual complained of another physical problem and produced more symptoms?
- Is the individual eager to undergo multiple invasive procedures or operations?

Regarding treatment:

- How long has this condition been going on before the individual sought treatment with the current health care provider?
- If the diagnosis is in doubt, have appropriate specialists been consulted?
- Is hospitalization for physical workup warranted?
- Once diagnosis was clearly established, was psychiatric referral offered?
- If psychiatric treatment was declined, was refusal documented in the individual's record?

Factitious Illness with Physical Symptoms 867

Regarding prognosis:

- Although an effective treatment for factitious disorder has yet to be identified, was an attempt made to provide a way for the individual to give up the symptoms while still saving face?

- Does the individual's history of needless medications and invasive procedures pose a threat to his or her current health status?

References

Ernoehazy, William Jr. Munchausen Syndrome. eMedicine.com. 15 Sep 2000. 13 Oct 2000 <http://www.emedicine.com/emerg/topic322.htm>.

Tierney, L.M. Jr., S.J. McPhee, and M.A. Papadakis. Current Medical Diagnosis and Treatment, 36th ed. Stamford: Appleton & Lange, 1997.

Factitious Illness with Psychological Symptoms

Other names / synonyms: Compensation Neurosis, Munchausen Syndrome
300.16

Definition

Individuals with factitious disorders intentionally feign, exaggerate, or actually induce their own physical or psychological illnesses. Through the status of "patient," they attempt to win attention, nurturance, or the acceptance that they feel unable to obtain in any other way. For some individuals, checking into one hospital after another is a way of life. Although the individual's attempts to create or exacerbate the symptoms of an illness are voluntary, such behavior is neurotic because the individual is unable to refrain from it.

The psychological basis for factitious disorders is uncertain. Some cases have been traced to physical or mental childhood trauma. Traumatic events, illnesses, and hospitalizations may be used to recreate the desired parent-child bond they lacked in reality.

The course and prognosis of factitious disorder with psychological symptoms is not fully known because individuals are usually lost in the follow-up stages of research. The disease is usually chronic. In some cases there is an array of hospitalizations beginning in adolescence or early adulthood and extending to the late forties. Factitious disorders appear to be rare in individuals older than age forty-five. This is thought to be the case because (1) individuals in contact with the "genuine" pathology become more skilled in faking those conditions, thus making it more difficult to diagnose as a factitious disorder; and (2) aging individuals may develop, whether or not in connection with their factitious disorder and/or treatments, a genuine illness that allows them to assume the "patient" role without faking.

Because of the difficulty in establishing the diagnosis, epidemiological data is not available on the prevalence of factitious disorder with psychological symptoms in the general population. Two studies have attempted to evaluate the frequency of factitious disorder in psychiatric settings. One study found a prevalence of 4.1% of definitely factitious individuals (an additional 2.3% possible) in a sample of 219 individuals diagnosed as psychotic. The second study found only 0.5% factitious disorder among individuals admitted to a psychiatric hospital. Researchers strongly suspect that this could be an underestimate.

Diagnosis

Based on 2 widely used diagnostic systems (the Diagnostic and Statistical Manual of Mental Disorders, or DSM-IV; and the International Classification of Diseases, or ICD-10) the diagnostic criteria for psychiatric factitious disorder is identical to the criteria for physical factitious disorder. For this reason, researchers and medical professionals believe that the condition is underdiagnosed. It may also be misreported as factitious cases of post-traumatic stress disorder (PTSD) or factitious bereavement.

Both the DSM-IV and the ICD-10 criteria require that the individual feign or produce symptoms in an apparent effort to assume the sick role. The DSM-IV emphasizes the lack of external incentives, and the ICD-10 notes the frequent association with marked personality disorders.

Researchers in this disorder have proposed more practical diagnostic criteria. This disorder should be severe enough to prevent steady employment and hinder family and social relationships. Onset is in early adulthood, with a chronic course. Symptoms change dramatically from one day to the next, or from one hospitalization to the next. While not related to treatment, the symptoms are often influenced by environment. The individual may change the symptoms or get worse when he/she feels observed, in response to the suggestions of others, or by mimicking other individuals around him. Symptoms are unconventional and fantastic. A large number of symptoms usually associated with several different psychiatric disorders may occur simultaneously or in rapid succession. The condition may be associated with other factitious disorders, such as factitious disorder with physical signs, or factitious bereavement. The individual's real medical history and biographical data are difficult to confirm because of vague, exaggerated, or dramatically reported history (pseudologia phantastica). Usually there are few or no visitors because the individual prevents medical staff from contacting family members or friends. External, material incentives for playing the sick role are either absent or minimal.

History: Care should be taken when making a diagnosis from an individual's report of hospitalizations, stays at psychiatric institutions, and office visits. Obtaining verification for these reports is important because much of the report is likely to be factitiously presented by the afflicted individual. Many physicians try to obtain information from the individual's friends, relatives, co-workers, and other reliable sources before confirming the diagnosis. Because factitious psychological illness often has its roots in family dynamics, some physicians also try to interview a close relative.

Physical exam: General physical and neurological exams are usually normal. Although the examiner may be correct in diagnosing factitious illness, for medicolegal reasons, the history and physical findings should be the guide in ordering appropriate tests. Observation of the individual's orientation, dress, mannerisms, behavior, and content of speech provide essential signs to diagnose the illness.

Tests: Testing is limited to the least expensive approach (usually routine laboratory tests and x-rays) that can discount the related symptoms. An atypical pattern of lab results may help to diagnose the condition. However, a complete work-up of complex, invasive medical procedures may sometimes be necessary to rule out physical causes of symptoms. Psychological testing may reveal a poor sense of identity, related personality disorders, poor sexual adjustment, a low tolerance for frustration, strong dependency issues and, in some individuals, an inflated sense of self-worth.

Treatment

An effective treatment of factitious disorders has yet to be identified. The desire to maintain the sick role prevents the individual from seeking effective therapy.

Treatment may be most effective when the focus is on management rather than on cure. The first and most important step in successful management is early recognition of the disorder. A second, essential, and probably more difficult step is securing an enduring, stable patient-physician relationship. Once such a relationship is established, management of the disorder must be oriented to avoid unnecessary hospitalizations and medical procedures.

Some mental health professionals use analytical and cognitive-behavioral approaches to treat factitious disorders. Treatment may also include pharmacological agents such as antipsychotic drugs and selective serotonin re-uptake inhibitors (SSRIs).

Prognosis

Overall, treatment reports for this disorder are disappointing. Outcome can be even worse than in cases of genuine psychoses. Self-injury, attempted suicide, and suicide are not uncommon. The individual's willingness to undergo treatment with unnecessary high doses of antipsychotic and antidepressant medication or with ECT can lead to severe adverse reactions. Outcome may be somewhat better with analytical and cognitive-behavioral approaches. Good responses to antipsychotic drugs and selective serotonin re-uptake inhibitors (SSRIs) have also been reported.

Differential Diagnosis

Differential diagnosis might include severe personality disorders, schizophrenia, somatoform disorder, substance abuse disorders (drug and alcohol abuse), hysteria, malingering, and conversion disorders. Factitious disorders can be distinguished from hysteria because in hysteria the symptoms are produced unconsciously. In factitious disorders, symptoms are voluntarily self-induced. Factitious disorders can be distinguished from malingering because in malingering, symptoms are intended to obtain some kind of discernible gain or to avoid an unpleasant situation; in factitious disorders, individuals do not seek external gains. In conversion disorders, both the motivation to produce psychological symptoms and their production are unconscious. Also included in the differential diagnosis could be the illness the individual is feigning.

Specialists

- Psychiatrist
- Psychologist

Work Restrictions / Accommodations

Individual should be restricted from working with or around chemicals, medications, and hazardous materials or situations. In an attempt to feign physical signs, individuals may attempt to injure themselves or to use drugs to induce abnormal findings, causing serious or life-threatening consequences for themselves and their co-workers.

Comorbid Conditions

Coexisting conditions that may affect recovery and lengthen disability include substance abuse (particularly of prescribed analgesics and sedatives) and personality disorders.

Complications

Fabrication of psychiatric symptoms, such as depression, hallucinations, and suicidal ideation, makes it difficult to diagnose the illness. Delayed diagnosis may preclude treatment. Treatment of the feigned illness can produce real symptoms and physical or mental signs, thus clouding the true clinical picture. The individual may be willing to take large doses of powerful sedatives and even undergo electroconvulsive therapy. If real physical or mental symptoms appear, hospital staffs, clinicians, and therapists are likely to dismiss them as factitious given the individual's track record.

Factors Influencing Duration

Delays in the management and diagnosis of the disorder increase the length of disability. Early detection, good response to treatment, establishment of a therapeutic patient-doctor relationship, and strong family supports would tend to decrease length of disability.

Length of Disability

Maximum duration may include hospitalization.

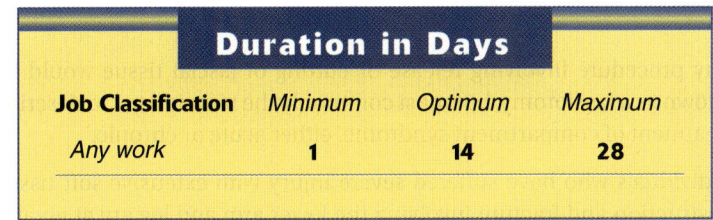

Duration in Days

Job Classification	Minimum	Optimum	Maximum
Any work	1	14	28

Failure to Recover

If an individual fails to recover within the maximum duration expectancy period, the reader may wish to reference the following questions to assist in better understanding the specifics of an individual's medical case.

Regarding diagnosis:

- Has diagnosis been confirmed?
- Was diagnosis based on the individual's past health history of multiple hospitalizations (including psychiatric institutions) and frequent office visits to healthcare providers?
- Have prior hospitalizations and medical care been verified?
- With medicolegal issues in mind, have appropriate diagnostic tests been done?
- Have legitimate medical conditions been identified or ruled out?

- When extensive work-up of the initial complaint proves negative, has the chief complaint or symptoms changed?
- Is the individual eager to undergo multiple invasive procedures or operations?

Regarding treatment:

- Has treatment focused on management, to avoid unnecessary hospitalizations and medical procedures, rather than on cure?
- Because a trusting relationship with the physician is essential to treatment, has the individual been able to establish a good doctor-patient relationship? If not, what can be done to build or restore this relationship?

- Have analytical and cognitive-behavioral approaches been used effectively?
- Would the individual benefit from the addition of pharmacological agents such as antipsychotic drugs and selective serotonin reuptake inhibitors (SSRIs)?

Regarding prognosis:

- How long has this condition been going on before the individual sought treatment with the current healthcare provider?
- Does the history of needless medications and invasive procedures pose a threat to individual's current health status?

References

Factitious Disorders (Munchausen Syndrome). Szoke, Andrei, MD. 30 Nov 1999. 1 Jan 2001 <http://perso.club-internet.fr/andreisz/index.html>.

Feldman, Marc. Dr. Marc Feldman's Munchausen Syndrome, Factitious Disorder, and Munchausen by Proxy Page. 09 Feb 2001. 15 Feb 2001 <http://ourworld.compuserve.com/homepages/Marc_Feldman_2/>.

Fasciotomy
83.14

Definition

Fasciotomy is a surgical procedure to reduce pressure around muscles, nerves, tendons and vessels. These structures are encased in a fibrous, fairly rigid capsule (compartment) that may not be able to expand enough to accommodate swelling inside the compartment (compartment syndrome). The swelling and increased pressure result from either injury or more chronic overuse stress.

The most common areas of involvement are the lower leg and the arm below the elbow. Fingers may be involved in crushing injuries or snake bites.

Any procedure involving release or cutting of fascial tissue would be known as a fasciotomy, but most commonly the term is used to describe treatment of compartment syndrome, either acute or chronic.

Individuals who have suffered severe injury with extensive soft tissue destruction and fracture involving the lower arm and leg are at greater risk for acute compartment syndrome requiring a fasciotomy. The muscle compartments in these locations are smaller and more confining. Individuals who suddenly change work loads to their forearm or lower leg, have poor training technique for sports or work, wear ill-fitting shoes with worn soles, walk/run on tilted surfaces such as roads are at greater risk for chronic compartment syndrome. Any activity that requires jumping or standing on your toes also increases the risk for more chronic compartment syndrome symptoms.

Reason for Procedure

This procedure is used to relieve pressure in an area that might result in vascular compromise (compartment syndrome). In acute injuries or post-fracture care, failure to relieve this pressure could result in neurovascular compromise and, ultimately, in loss of function of the affected limb or extremity. Severe compartment syndrome left untreated could lead to amputation.

When the pressure rises acutely as in trauma or post-fracture care, the situation may be limb-threatening and is treated as an acute emergency.

In more chronic situations, the pressure in the compartment may rise and fall based on activity. If change in activity or conditioning do not relieve the pain, elective surgery (fasciotomy) may be performed. In either situation, the sheath surrounding the muscle (fascia) is opened to allow the muscle to expand, increasing circulation and decreasing pressure.

In more chronic overuse-type conditions, especially in the lower leg, fasciotomy is performed when conservative measures have failed, to relieve pain and improve function.

Description

Fasciotomy involves incisions through the skin over the affected compartment, most commonly in the lower leg or forearm. The incision and dissection is carried down to the fascia surrounding the muscles. Careful attention must be paid to the nerves and vessels in the area. Sometimes multiple small incisions are made in the skin and fascia; in other situations long continuous incisions are made over the entire compartment.

In acute situations, the incisions may be left open and covered with wet sterile dressings, which allow the muscle to swell up and out of the skin. Once the pressure is relieved, circulation is restored and swelling is relieved, along with decrease in pain and restoration of muscle function. The individual then returns to the operating room for secondary wound closure, perhaps with skin grafting.

When treating more chronic compartment syndrome, the fascia is left open and the overlying layers of tissue and skin are closed with sutures.

The procedure requires anesthesia and except in extreme emergencies is performed in the operating room. Compartment pressure readings are monitored during and after the procedure.

Prognosis

Return to normal function after a fasciotomy usually takes 2-3 months.

Specialists

- Hand Surgeon
- Occupational Medicine Physician
- Orthopedic Surgeon
- Physiatrist
- Physical Therapist
- Plastic Surgeon

Rehabilitation

Physical therapy after a fasciotomy in chronic situations follows the same general procedure no matter the location of the surgery.

The first part of therapy is to control pain. The individual may be required to elevate the limb If the fasciotomy was performed to the hands, the hand should be held overhead and light fist motions made with the injured hand. If the surgery was performed to the leg area, the leg should be elevated higher than the heart while in a reclined position. T.E.N.S. (Transcutaneous Electrical Nerve Stimulation), where electrodes are placed on the skin over or near the area of pain to stimulate nerve fibers, can be used to help reduce pain associated with the inflammatory response. After the second or third day post surgery, walking or hand movement may be initiated.

During the range-of-motion phase of therapy, the individual may engage in exercises that help increase limb movement. For example, if the individual is being treated for shin splints, the therapist may start active range-of-motion exercises in which the foot points down or moves side to side. The duration and intensity of each exercise session depends on the underlying cause of the injury. An individual receiving therapy for a hand injury may engage in hand exercises such as opening and closing the hand on an hourly basis.

Once pain and swelling have subsided, more resistive exercises like pointing and flexing the toe while using a towel for resistance can be performed. The goal in this stage is to build muscle strength and flexibility of the affected area. Individuals may begin doing more functional activities such as riding a stationary bike at low resistance or starting to grip objects. Alternative methods of therapy during this stage may include a whirlpool or full aqua therapy.

One major aspect of therapy is to regain muscle balance in the effected limb. For example, building muscles of the wrist and fingers (including the thumb) is crucial for proper hand function. Muscle imbalances cause uneven loading to the limb while tasks are performed causing further injury. Possible exercises include wrist curls, where the individual lays the forearm on a bench or therapy table with the hand free and a weight gripped in the affected hand with palm facing down. The individual then raises the weight so that the hand curls upward toward the ceiling. This exercise can be performed with the palm facing up; the movement is still with the hand curling up toward the ceiling. The functional phase can combine several different techniques such as using a balancing platform to build lower body reaction.

Work Restrictions / Accommodations

Individuals with lower extremity involvement and who have jobs that require long periods of standing or walking may need to be reassigned to more sedentary duties. Individuals with upper extremity involvement may need to avoid repetitive gripping, twisting, and lifting duties requiring extensive use of the arm or wrist. These individuals may need to be temporarily or permanently assigned to other duties. Reconditioning of the affected muscle groups is important postoperatively.

Comorbid Conditions

Any condition that would impair healing, such as diabetes or AIDS, may influence length of disability.

Procedure Complications

Possible complications of the procedure include skin sluff; infection; nerve, blood vessel, and muscle damage; and scarring. Contractures of the skin and soft tissue may result from either the initial procedure or secondary wound closure. If skin grafting is required, there could be infection, scarring, and contracture at the donor site. Muscle weakness may also occur.

Factors Influencing Duration

Factors include site of treatment, duration and extent of condition, development of necrosis or other complications, individual compliance, the individual's job requirements and ability to modify such activities, and particular type of physical activity the individual pursues.

Length of Disability

If the fasciotomy was done in an acute injury, length of disability would be dependent recovery of the underlying injury as well as the fasciotomy. Job requirements and inability to adapt to activity changes may prolong disability.

For the forearm, duration for sedentary and light work may be shorter if one-handed work is available (modified duty). For the leg, duration for sedentary and light work may be shorter if work can be performed in a sitting position.

Forearm.

Duration in Days

Job Classification	Minimum	Optimum	Maximum
Sedentary work	14	28	56
Light work	21	42	70
Medium work	42	42	91
Heavy work	70	91	119
Very Heavy work	91	119	Indefinite

Leg.

Duration in Days

Job Classification	Minimum	Optimum	Maximum
Sedentary work	14	42	63
Light work	21	63	91
Medium work	42	91	119
Heavy work	63	119	182
Very Heavy work	63	182	Indefinite

References

Bednar, Michael MD, and Terry Light, MD. "Hand Surgery." Current Diagnosis and Treatment in Orthopedics. Skinner, Harry B., and J.B. Skinner, eds. Norwalk: Appleton & Lange, 1995. 485-486.

Hunter, James, et al. Rehabilitation of the Hand: Surgery and Therapy, 3rd ed. St. Louis: The C.V. Mosby Company, 1990.

Fever
Other names / synonyms: Pyrexia
780.6

Definition

A fever (pyrexia) is defined as an increase in an individual's temperature above the temperature normally maintained by that individual. Fever is one of the most recognized features of infectious diseases. Temperature may be taken in the mouth, rectum, the armpit (axilla), or ear, although these temperatures will vary (the rectum is about 0.5 F degrees warmer than the mouth and 1.5 degrees warmer than the axilla).

Historically, the normal body temperature is identified as 98.6 degrees F. It is now known however that temperature normally varies between people and fluctuates about one degree throughout the 24-hour cycle. Body temperature is very tightly controlled. A temperature is considered low if under 96.0 degrees F (35.0 degrees C). Fever or high temperature is above 99.5 degrees F (37.5 degrees C) orally or above 100.5 degrees F (38.0 degrees C) rectally. This means that the "normal" temperature can range from 96.0 to 99.5 degrees F (35.0 to 38.0 degrees C) if measured orally.

The hypothalamus in the brain controls temperature. Fever is brought about by production of immune mediators, interleukin 1, tumor necrosis factor, and interferon. These compounds affect the hypothalamus and cause shivering, which leads to a rise in temperature.

Fever is a symptom. Almost any infection may be accompanied by fever although the absence of fever does not exclude infection. Fever may occur with myocardial infarction, pulmonary embolism, drug reactions, autoimmune disease, trauma, and tumors.

Diagnosis

History: The individual may report fever, chills, shaking, sweating, muscle pain (myalgia), and malaise. Prolonged temperature elevation can cause fatigue, weakness, and lack of strength and energy (asthenia). Individuals may also have localized symptoms resulting from the specific illness such as a sore throat, cough, or painful burning urination.

Physical exam: The exam may reveal an elevated temperature, chills, sweats, and malaise. The individual may have signs of an overwhelming infection (sepsis) that includes rapid breathing (tachypnea), rapid heart rate (tachycardia), and low blood pressure (hypotension). The individual may appear acutely ill. Physical examination may reveal a wide range of abnormal signs depending on the severity of the fever and causative agent or condition. These may include an altered mental status, inflamed tympanic membranes, drainage from the throat or nasal passages, swollen lymph nodes, evidence of pulmonary congestion, abdominal tenderness, flank or kidney tenderness, vaginal drainage, rectal tenderness or drainage, skin rashes, and signs of joint inflammation such as redness, tenderness, swelling, and joint effusion.

Tests: Tests depend on the suspected causative agent. They can include a culture for streptococcal bacteria in the throat if individual complains of a sore throat, urinalysis for urinary symptoms, or a chest x-ray if there is a productive cough. A complete blood count may be ordered. Cultures of the blood, urine, or vaginal drainage may be obtained. Sometimes a stool culture may be requested.

Treatment

Treatment depends on the underlying cause. Antipyretic drugs (e.g., acetaminophen and nonsteroidal anti-inflammatory agents) can lower a temperature. The individual should also be replenished with fluids.

Certain groups of individuals may be treated more aggressively because of an increased risk of complication for high fevers. These individuals include those with heart disease (since fever increases the oxygen demand placed on the heart), those at risk for seizures, and pregnant women (because high fever may cause abnormalities to the fetus).

Prognosis

The outcome depends on the underlying condition. Fever generally resolves without complications. Temperatures above 106 degrees F are life-threatening.

Differential Diagnosis

Fever is the most prevalent symptom of infection but is also a manifestation of many other medical disorders. Common infections causing fever include upper respiratory infection, lower respiratory infection, and urinary tract infections. Less common infections include extrapulmonary and miliary tuberculosis, atypical Mycobacteria and fungal infections, catheter-related endocarditis, meningococcemia, gonococcemia, Listeria, Brucella, rat-bite fever, relapsing fever, mononucleosis, cytomegalovirus, human immunodeficiency virus, hepatitis, Q fever, psittacosis, amebiasis, malaria, and toxoplasmosis.

Fever may occur with medical disorders such as rheumatic fever, systemic lupus erythematosus, rheumatoid arthritis, vasculitis (inflammation of the blood vessels), sarcoidosis (a chronic condition characterized by formation of nodules in the lungs, spleen, liver, skin, mucous membranes, lacrima, and salivary glands), granulomatous hepatitis, Crohn's disease, pulmonary emboli, sickle cell disease, hemolytic anemia, lymphoma, leukemia, cancers, familial Mediterranean fever, Fabry disease (an uncommon familial disease), and cyclic neutropenia (a decrease in the number of neutrophils, a type of white blood cell).

Fever may also occur with use of certain medications such as sulfonamides, penicillins, thiouracils, barbiturates, quinidine, and some laxatives.

An individual's temperature may increase with strenuous exercise or in high, ambient heat, causing malignant hyperthermia.

Specialists

- Infectious Disease Physician
- Internist

Work Restrictions / Accommodations

Restrictions and accommodations will be determined based on the specific diagnosis. Generally, individuals with contagious disease should not be in the workplace.

Complementary and Alternative Therapies

Content is intended for awareness only. Treatments may or may not be effective. Scientific evidence may be lacking and some substances have potentially toxic effects. Dr. Presley Reed and the editors do not endorse the use of these therapies in the absence of consultation with a licensed medical professional.

Acupressure and Acupuncture - May help reduce fever.

Aromatherapy - Essential oils of bergamot, chamomile, or eucalyptus when applied as a compress or inhaled may help reduce fever.

Detoxification, fasting, and colon therapy - During the fever, water or herbal tea fasts or juice diets may be beneficial.

Boneset, Lemongrass - May encourage the action and completion of a fever.

Comorbid Conditions

Comorbid conditions include heart disease, pregnancy, and whether individuals are prone to seizures.

Complications

High fever may be complicated by seizures, tachycardia, low fluid volume (dehydration), hypotension, and the inability to supply blood to the body (circulatory collapse). High fever in pregnant women may cause congenital abnormalities (teratogenic).

Factors Influencing Duration

The severity of underlying disease, complications, and the effectiveness of treatment influence the length of disability.

Length of Disability

Duration depends on underlying cause and/or procedure. Additional diagnostic information is necessary to determine disability duration.

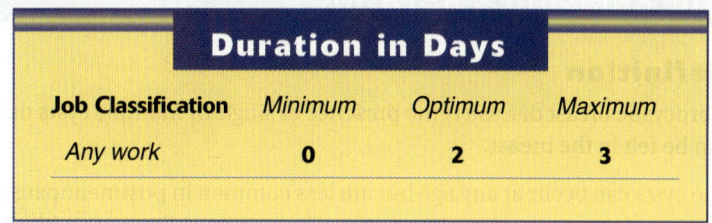

Duration in Days

Job Classification	Minimum	Optimum	Maximum
Any work	0	2	3

Failure to Recover

If an individual fails to recover within the maximum duration expectancy period, the reader may wish to reference the following questions to assist in better understanding the specifics of an individual's medical case.

Regarding diagnosis:

- Has the cause of fever been identified?
- Was there a prolonged temperature elevation?
- Were localized symptoms present?
- Were signs of sepsis (tachycardia, hypotension, tachypnea) present?
- Did the individual appear acutely ill?
- Was mental status altered?
- Were appropriate diagnostic tests performed such as cultures, chest x-ray, blood studies, and/or urinalysis?
- Were additional specific tests performed depending on the underlying condition?

Regarding treatment:

- Has fever persisted despite treatment of the underlying cause?
- While low-grade fevers do not necessarily require treatment, was fever addressed because individual was at increased risk of complications (i.e., those with heart disease, those who are at risk of seizures or those who are pregnant)?
- Was treatment effective in resolving fever?

Regarding prognosis:

- How severe was fever? What was its duration?
- Has underlying condition been controlled or resolved? Has fever persisted despite treatment of underlying cause?
- Should diagnosis be revisited?
- Has individual experienced any complications such as seizures, tachycardia, dehydration, hypotension, or circulatory collapse?
- Does individual have an underlying condition that may impact recovery such as heart disease, pregnancy, or being prone to seizures?

References

Beutler, Bruce, and Steven M. Beutler. "The Pathogenesis of Fever." Cecil Textbook of Medicine, 20th ed. Bennett, J. Claude, and Fred Plum, eds. Philadelphia: W.B. Saunders Company, 1996. 1533-1535.

McPhee, Stephen J., and Stephen A. Schroeder. "General Approach to the Patient: Health Maintenance and Disease Prevention; and Common Symptoms." Current Medical Diagnosis and Treatment. Tierney, Lawrence M., Stephen J. McPhee, and Maxine A. Papadakis, eds. New York: Lange Medical Books/McGraw-Hill, 2000. 1-34.

Fibrocystic Breast Disease

Other names / synonyms: Cystic Breast, Diffuse Cystic Mastopathy, Mammary Dysplasia

610, 610.1, 610.2, 610.8, 610.9

Definition

Fibrocystic breast disease is the presence of single or multiple cysts that can be felt in the breast.

The cysts can occur at any age but are less common in postmenopausal women who are not taking hormones. The cysts may fluctuate with the menstrual cycle and are common during periods of hormonal irregularity. The cysts are characteristically firm, mobile, contain fibrous connective tissue, and can be fluid filled and tender.

The cysts are noncancerous (benign) and a common cause of breast masses in premenopausal women more than 40 years of age, but can occur in younger women. Even though they are benign, they must be treated as potentially cancerous and observed carefully for growth or change. In one study, cysts accounted for 10% of breast masses in women less than 40 years of age.

Diagnosis

History: Women may report a breast lump or lump(s) that may be painful and tender, frequently beginning 7 to 10 days before menstruation and resolving as menstruation progresses. The lump(s) may fluctuate in size with the menstrual cycle.

Physical exam: The exam may reveal a well-demarcated cyst or cysts from the surrounding breast tissue, that are typically firm and mobile. It is difficult to distinguish a cyst from a solid mass on physical examination.

Tests: Ultrasonography or aspiration of the cyst must be used for diagnostic purposes. Ultrasound imaging reveals a round or oval shaped cyst with defined margins. A simple cyst can be aspirated and a biopsy performed if it is without symptoms (asymptomatic). Aspiration can be performed using ultrasound to locate the cyst if the mass cannot be felt. Cysts require a surgical biopsy only if the aspirate fluid is bloody, the abnormality does not resolve after the aspiration of fluid, or the same cyst recurs multiple times in a short period of time. A mammogram can detect masses, including small masses that cannot be felt (nonpalpable), but it cannot distinguish between a benign and cancerous lump. Cysts that cannot be felt upon examination can be identified by mammography and confirmed to be simple cysts by ultrasound examination.

Treatment

In most cases, no treatment is required. Eliminating caffeine and chocolate in the diet and taking supplemental vitamin E may be effective in helping alleviate breast tenderness. Breast pain may be treated with pain medication and wearing a firm support brassiere. Aspiration is an appropriate first step in the management of breast cysts, but clinical follow-up after aspiration is essential. For recurrent cysts, reexamination and biopsy is indicated. An individual must be shown any cysts present and taught to examine her breasts and report any changes to the physician. Reassurance should be given that the condition is very common and generally not associated with cancer.

Prognosis

Most often, the cysts are benign breast disease. Breast pain alone is rarely a presenting symptom of cancer. Breast cysts can be diagnosed and effectively treated with aspiration. Individuals with a single breast cyst should be reexamined four to six weeks after cyst aspiration to determine if the cyst has recurred. In one follow-up study, of 389 women who had cyst aspiration, 44 women had a recurrent cyst and 20 had a solid mass at the aspiration site. In biopsies of the 20 solid masses, two were cancerous.

Differential Diagnosis

Breast cancer and benign solid breast masses are other diagnostic possibilities. Definitive diagnosis is made with a breast biopsy.

Specialists

- General Surgeon
- Gynecologist

Work Restrictions / Accommodations

Work restrictions or accommodations are not usually associated with this condition. If surgery is performed, lifting and reaching above shoulder level should be restricted for a brief period after surgery.

Comorbid Conditions

Abscess of the breast may influence disability.

Complications

Presence of fibrocystic breast disease can complicate the diagnosis of breast cancer.

Factors Influencing Duration

With medical treatment, no disability is expected. Factors that might influence disability include age of individual and if the cyst recurs or is cancerous.

Length of Disability

With medical treatment, no disability is expected.

Needle aspiration.

Duration in Days

Job Classification	Minimum	Optimum	Maximum
Sedentary work	1	1	1
Light work	1	1	1
Medium work	1	1	2
Heavy work	1	2	3
Very Heavy work	1	2	3

Open biopsy.

Job Classification	Duration in Days		
	Minimum	Optimum	Maximum
Sedentary work	1	3	14
Light work	1	3	14
Medium work	1	3	14
Heavy work	3	7	21
Very Heavy work	3	7	21

Failure to Recover

If an individual fails to recover within the maximum duration expectancy period, the reader may wish to reference the following questions to assist in better understanding the specifics of an individual's medical case.

Regarding diagnosis:

- Does the individual report a breast lump or lump(s) that are painful and tender?
- Does it appear 7 to 10 days before menstruation?
- Does it resolve as menstruation progresses?
- Does the lump fluctuate in size with the menstrual cycle?
- Did physical exam reveal a well-demarcated cyst or cysts?
- Is the lump firm and mobile?
- Has the individual had ultrasound or cyst aspiration?
- Was it necessary to do a surgical biopsy?
- Has the individual had a mammogram?
- Have conditions with similar symptoms been ruled out?

Regarding treatment:

- Has the individual eliminated caffeine and chocolate?
- Are they taking supplemental vitamin E?
- Does the individual wear a brassiere with good support?
- Does she know where the cyst(s) is? Has she been shown how to do breast self-exams?
- Is she scheduled for follow-up appointments as needed?

Regarding prognosis:

- If necessary is the individual's employer able to accommodate restrictions?

References

Apantaku, Lecia M. "Breast Cancer Diagnosis and Screening." American Family Physician 10 (2000): 10. 07 Dec 2000 <http://www.aafp.org/afp/20000801/596.html>.

Morrow, Monica. "The Evaluation of Common Breast Problems." American Family Physician 5 (2000): 11. 12 Dec 2000 <http://www.aafp.org/afp/20000415/2371.html>.

Fibroid Tumor of Uterus

Other names / synonyms: Fibroids, Fibroleiomyoma, Fibromyoma, Leiomyoma, Myoma, Uterine Leiomyoma, Uterine Myoma

218, 218.0, 218.1, 218.2, 218.9, 219, M8890/0

Definition

Fibroid tumors of the uterus (fibroids) are growths of tissue in the uterus. While the growths are abnormal, they are not cancerous. They are benign. The tissue growths are made up of fibrous connective tissue. They develop as distinct, firm, and round masses, often occurring in groups.

Fibroids are classified as one of three types depending on where they are located. Intramural fibroids are located within the muscular wall of the uterus. Subserous fibroids are located on the outside surface of the uterus. Submucous fibroids are located inside the uterine lining. Most fibroids (95%) are intramural or subserosal, but many fibroids are a combination of types. For example a fibroid may be on the outside surface of the uterus, yet extend into the muscular wall. A subserosal and submucous fibroid sometimes attaches by a stalk. This is called a pedunculated fibroid. This type of fibroid can easily become twisted, cutting off its blood supply. The tissue then begins to die (necrosis) and can become infected

Fibroids can develop in relation to the main part, or body of the uterus. They also can develop in relation to the narrowed opening to the uterus called the cervix. Some fibroids are considered "parasitic." This means they are made up of uterine tissue, but get their blood supply from another adjacent organ. Intraligamentous fibroids are found within the broad ligaments attached to the uterus.

The growth of fibroids is associated with the female hormone estrogen. Fibroids tend to enlarge with pregnancy and decrease with menopause. If estrogen replacement therapy is used after menopause, fibroids may continue to grow.

Fibroids typically occur during the reproductive years. At least 20% women of reproductive age have known uterine fibroids. Studies suggest, however, that up to 80% of women have undetected fibroids. Estimates are that only 20-50% of women with fibroids have related symptoms.

In addition to age, increased body mass is a risk factors for fibroids. Black women have up to 9 times higher incidence of fibroids than white women. The risk of fibroids appears to be less in women who smoke (because of an antiestrogenic effect) and who have given birth. Evidence regarding the risk posed by oral contraceptives is contradictory. Some experts believe them to be a risk factor for fibroids. Evidence exists, however, that demonstrates women who take oral contraceptives actually have a lower incidence of fibroids.

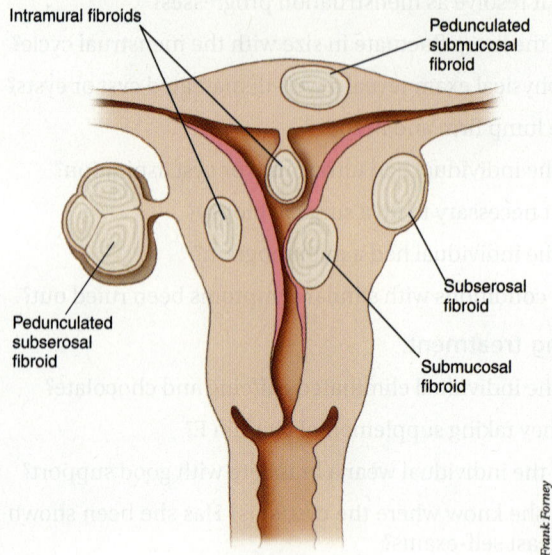

Diagnosis

History: Fibroids frequently cause no symptoms. If symptoms are present, they typically involve abnormal uterine bleeding and pelvic pressure. Abnormal uterine bleeding takes the form of excessive menstrual bleeding (menorrhagia), bleeding between periods (metrorrhagia), or painful menstrual periods (dysmenorrhea). Pelvic pressure from the growing fibroid causes frequent or painful urination and constipation. Severe pain may result from a twisted pedunculated fibroid.

The individual may have a history of infertility. Infertility has been associated with uterine fibroids. In pregnancy, fibroids may cause miscarriage (spontaneous abortion) by the second month.

Physical exam: Fibroids of sufficient size may be discovered during a bimanual pelvic exam (one hand on top of the abdomen during exam). They also may be discovered by pressing down on the abdomen with one or both hands (palpation). Sometimes a fibroid may be seen extending out of the cervix into the vagina. This is called a prolapsed fibroid.

Tests: A pelvic ultrasound can assist in the diagnosis and exclude pregnancy as the cause of uterine enlargement. Transvaginal ultrasound can provide information about fibroids inside the uterus. An ultrasound probe is inserted into the uterus through the vagina. More detail may be seen if the uterus is filled with saline before the ultrasound procedure. This is called sonohysterography.

Hysteroscopy is another procedure in which the inside of the uterus can be examined. A thin flexible tube is inserted into the uterus through the vagina. On one end of the tube is a camera through which the physician can see inside the uterus. If anything looks abnormal during this procedure, the physician may remove a tiny piece of tissue (biopsy). This tissue is examined under a microscope. Magnetic resonance imaging (MRI) is another imaging procedure to help study the uterus in detail.

The amount of bleeding may be estimated by a hematocrit or hemoglobin blood test. A pregnancy test may be given to rule out pregnancy. A pap smear may be done to rule out malignancy.

Treatment

Small, asymptomatic fibroids are usually not treated. They should, however, be monitored for growth by pelvic examinations every 6 months. If treatment for fibroids becomes necessary, surgery and hormone therapy are the two options.

Surgery is considered only under certain circumstances: when bleeding is so significant as to cause anemia, if pain is severe or chronic, if there is evidence of a twisted deteriorating pedunculated fibroid, or if the fibroid is extending (prolapsed) through the cervix, causing urinary symptoms, or growing significantly.

Surgery options include hysterectomy or myomectomy. A hysterectomy is the removal of the complete uterus. This is the only procedure that will remove current fibroids and also removes the chance of future fibroids. Myomectomy removes only the fibroids, leaving the uterus intact. Hysterectomy and myomectomy can be performed either through open abdominal surgery or vaginally using a laparoscopic procedure. Hysterectomy removes all chance of a future pregnancy. In contrast, myomectomy preserves fertility.

Gonadotropin-releasing hormone (GnRH) agonists simulate menopause. The decreased estrogen level then stops the growth of fibroids. It also stops menstrual bleeding. The result, however, is short-term. About half the fibroids regrow when the medication is discontinued.

GnRH agonists are used only for limited time periods, usually not longer than 6 months. They are taken to control fibroid growth in women who want to preserve their fertility, to control blood loss and correct anemia before surgery, and to shrink a large fibroid before surgery. They are also used as an option for women who are near menopause and for whom surgery is not indicated.

Androgenic drugs and progestins have been used to control menstrual bleeding. They do not, however, consistently decrease uterine or fibroid size.

Prognosis

Half of fibroids don't cause symptoms and don't require treatment. For fibroids that do cause symptoms, surgical removal of the uterus (hysterectomy) is the only sure cure. Surgical removal of the fibroids only (myomectomy) successfully removes present fibroids in 80% of individuals, but approximately 10% of fibroids will regrow. Gonadotropin-releasing hormone (GnRH) agonists bring about a 40-60% decrease in fibroid size after 3 months of treatment. Half the fibroids regrow, however, after treatment is discontinued. Fibroids typically stop appearing and growing once a woman reaches menopause.

Differential Diagnosis

Conditions with similar symptoms include uterine cancer, leiomyosarcoma, ovarian mass (benign or cancerous), an inflammatory mass, endometriosis, or pregnancy.

Specialists

- Fertility Specialist
- Gynecologist
- Surgeon

Work Restrictions / Accommodations

Pain and excessive blood loss may interfere with work and require a less strenuous workload or time off from work. If surgery is performed, a recovery period must be allowed. Hysterectomy requires a longer recovery period than myomectomy, up to a total of 6 weeks. Laparoscopic procedures have a shorter recovery period than open abdominal surgeries.

Comorbid Conditions

Fibroids usually get worse during pregnancy.

Complications

Fibroids can result in excessive bleeding and pain. Submucous fibroids develop infection at a greater rate than other types of fibroids. Pedunculated fibroids have a tendency to become twisted. This cuts off their blood supply, and leads to tissue death (necrosis), severe pain, and infection.

In pregnancy, a fibroid may cause miscarriage (spontaneous abortion), premature labor, pain, prolonged labor, obstructed labor, failure of the head to engage the birth canal, and postpartum hemorrhage. Depending upon where it is located within the uterus, a fibroid may necessitate a cesarean section rather than a vaginal birth.

Fibroids are associated with infertility in approximately 2-3% of infertile individuals. This may be because they interfere with implantation of the embryo or movement of sperm, obstruct the fallopian tubes, or change the shape of the uterine cavity.

Although fibroids are benign, cancerous changes do develop in rare cases (0.1-1.0% of fibroids).

Factors Influencing Duration

Fibroid size and location, extent of pain and bleeding, nearness to menopause, need for surgery, and response to treatment will influence length of disability due to fibroids.

Length of Disability

Myomectomy.

Duration in Days

Job Classification	Minimum	Optimum	Maximum
Sedentary work	3	7	21
Light work	3	7	21
Medium work	7	14	28
Heavy work	7	21	35
Very Heavy work	14	21	35

Hysterectomy, laparoscopic or vaginal.

Duration in Days

Job Classification	Minimum	Optimum	Maximum
Sedentary work	21	28	42
Light work	21	28	42
Medium work	28	42	56
Heavy work	28	56	70
Very Heavy work	28	70	84

Hysterectomy, abdominal.

Duration in Days

Job Classification	Minimum	Optimum	Maximum
Sedentary work	28	42	56
Light work	28	42	56
Medium work	42	56	56
Heavy work	42	70	84
Very Heavy work	42	84	98

Duration Trend from Normative Data*

Cases	Mean	Min	Max	No Lost Time	Over 6 Months
23322	50	0	411	0.08%	0.17%

Percentile:	5th	25th	Median	75th	95th
Days:	14	33	45	59	110

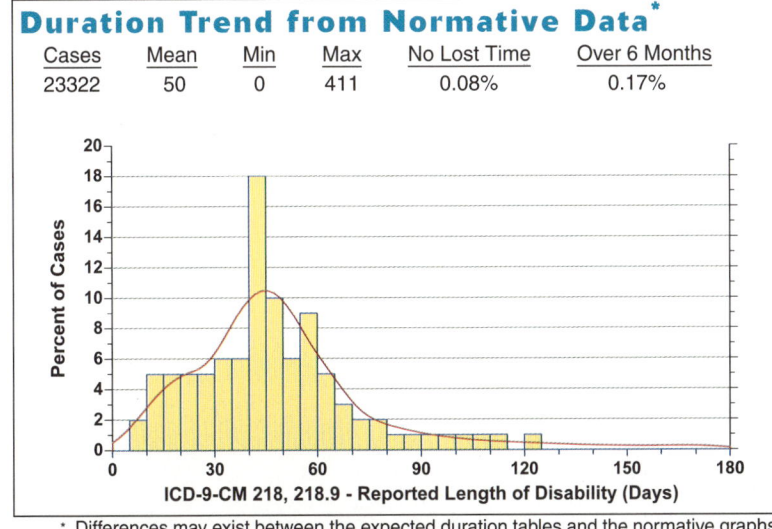

ICD-9-CM 218, 218.9 - Reported Length of Disability (Days)

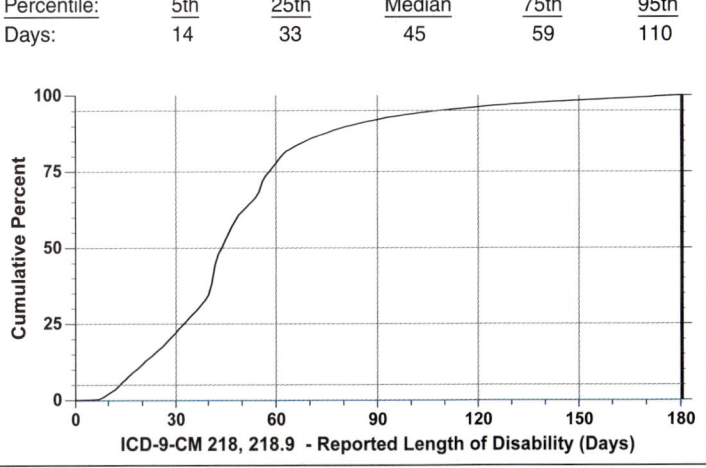

ICD-9-CM 218, 218.9 - Reported Length of Disability (Days)

* Differences may exist between the expected duration tables and the normative graphs. Duration tables provide expected recovery periods based on the type of work performed by the individual. The normative graphs reflect the actual observed experience of many individuals across the spectrum of physical conditions, in a variety of industries, and with varying levels of case management.

Fibroid Tumor of Uterus

Failure to Recover

If an individual fails to recover within the maximum duration expectancy period, the reader may wish to reference the following questions to assist in better understanding the specifics of an individual's medical case.

Regarding diagnosis:

- Is individual of reproductive age?
- Is there a history of infertility?
- Does individual have increased body mass?
- Does individual report excessive menstrual bleeding (menorrhagia), bleeding between periods (metrorrhagia), or painful menstrual periods (dysmenorrhea)?
- Is there frequent or painful urination or constipation?
- Does individual report severe pain, possibly suggesting twisted pedunculated fibroid?
- Was a pelvic ultrasound done to exclude pregnancy as the cause of uterine enlargement? Was transvaginal ultrasound done?
- Was hysteroscopy performed? If so, were tissue samples taken (biopsy)? Was MRI required? Were complete blood count (CBC), pregnancy test, or Pap smear taken to rule out bleeding, pregnancy, and malignancy, respectively?
- Was a diagnosis of uterine fibroid(s) confirmed?

Regarding treatment:

- If fibroids are small and without symptoms (asymptomatic), does individual undergo pelvic examinations every 6 months?
- Does individual require surgery for bleeding that has caused anemia, chronic or severe pain, a twisted deteriorating pedunculated fibroid, or a fibroid extending (prolapsed) through the cervix?
- If surgery is required, will only the fibroid be removed (myomectomy) or the entire uterus (hysterectomy)? If hysterectomy is required, does individual understand this will eliminate all possibility of becoming pregnant?
- Are gonadotropin-releasing hormone (GnRH) agonists a treatment option, considering that approximately half the fibroids regrow when medication is discontinued?

Regarding prognosis:

- Is this an initial diagnosis or has the fibroid recurred?
- Did individual require treatment?
- If surgical intervention was required, was a myomectomy or hysterectomy performed?
- Did any postsurgical complications occur? If so, what were they and what is the expected recovery time?
- Is individual nearing the age of menopause when fibroids generally stop appearing and growing?
- Has individual experienced excessive bleeding, pain, or infection?
- If individual was pregnant, did the fibroid cause miscarriage (spontaneous abortion), premature labor, pain, prolonged labor, obstructed labor, failure of the head to engage the birth canal, or postpartum hemorrhage? Did individual require cesarean section rather than a vaginal birth?
- Has the fibroid caused infertility? If so, would individual benefit from counseling to cope with the impact of this condition?

References

Dambro, Mark, and Jo Griffith. Griffith's 5-minute Clinical Consult. Philadelphia: Lippincott Williams & Wilkins, 1999.

Ryan, Kenneth, et al. Kistner's Gynecology and Women's Health, 7th ed. St. Louis: Mosby, 1999.

Fibromyalgia and Myofascial Pain Syndrome

Other names / synonyms: Fibromyositis, Fibrositis, Muscular Rheumatism, Myofasciitis

729.1, 729.89

Definition

Considerable controversy continues to surround the cause (etiology), definition, diagnosis and treatment of persons with these disorders.

Fibromyalgia (FM) is a syndrome of widespread pain, decreased pain threshold (tenderness) and other characteristic symptoms including nonrestorative sleep, fatigue, mood disturbance, stiffness, irritable bowel symptoms and headache. Widespread pain is defined by the number of body regions involved (greater than 3) and by a pattern of pain symptoms that involves upper and lower body, both sides of the body and axial skeleton. Decreased pain threshold (tenderness) is indicated by the proportion of specific sites that elicit symptoms of pain on palpation.

Myofascial Pain Syndrome (MPS) is a syndrome in which pain and tenderness are localized to one or a few discrete areas. Persons with FM are distinguished from those with MPS because FM is a generalized pain syndrome characterized by symptoms of widespread pain. Persons with MPS report pain in one quadrant of the body or at one anatomical site. Palpation in the symptomatic region reveals a discrete area of localized tenderness within a so-called 'taut band' which is an area of increased consistency or hardness. The localized tenderness within the taut band is known as a "trigger point." Palpation of the trigger point is said to reproduce the person's pain symptoms or refer the pain to another location.

Diagnosis

History: Individuals with FM report pain in the left and right sides of the body, pain above and below the waist, pain in the axial skeleton (cervical spine, anterior chest, thoracic spine or low back) and other symptoms (poor sleep, fatigue, stiffness, anxiety, headache, mental stress and irritable bowel symptoms). Persons with MPS report pain which is localized to one or a few discrete anatomical sites.

Physical exam: Individuals with FM have a normal objective physical examination. However, persons with FM report pain on digital palpation in at least 11 of 18 specific tender point spots located in many different body regions. Persons with MPS have a normal objective physical examination. However, it is said that palpation of the affected areas reveals an area of localized tenderness known as a trigger point.

Tests: There are no routine hematologic, urine, biochemical or imaging tests that are diagnostically or prognostically useful in FM or MPS. Since the symptoms of FM or MPS are common, testing may be performed to exclude or evaluate other conditions which could account for the symptoms. Extensive diagnostic testing is not useful, is not cost-effective and is discouraged.

The 1990 American College of Rheumatology Criteria for the Classification of Fibromyalgia are often used for diagnosis of FM. These criteria require a history of widespread pain and the presence of pain on palpation at 11 or more of 18 specified tender point sites. Since persons with FM have no objective abnormalities on physical examination and no abnormalities on diagnostic testing, the diagnosis is based upon the person's subjective report and subjective response to physical examination.

Unlike FM, the diagnostic criteria for MPS have not been established. The diagnosis is usually based upon a regional (localized) pain symptom, spot tenderness and reproduction of pain symptoms by pressure on the tender spot.

The diagnostic criteria for FM and MPS are subjective since there are no reproducible, biochemical, immunologic, electrodiagnostic or histopathologic correlates with these diagnoses.

Treatment

Because of their putative specific effect on sleep disturbance, tricyclic antidepressants have been the therapy most frequently used in the treatment of FM. Amitriptyline appears to have modest short-term benefit for some of the symptoms of FM, but no long term benefit has been established. Non-steroidal anti-inflammatory drugs and corticosteroids are not effective. Cognitive behavioral therapy has shown some benefit in uncontrolled studies. No defined, prospective, controlled, double-blind randomized trials, with long-term quantitative assessment of outcome are reported for treatments of MPS. Non-proven treatments for MPS include: stretch and spray therapy, trigger point injections, physical therapy, non-steroidal anti-inflammatory drugs and corticosteroids.

Prognosis

Most studies have indicated that FM tends to be a chronic syndrome; however, good outcomes in which the majority of persons improve or no longer satisfy the criteria for FM have also been reported. An important limitation to these studies is that they come from specialty centers where the admission process selects for severity and chronicity. No data are available concerning prognosis of FM in the community, in the primary care setting or in the workplace.

No long-term studies have been done to determine the natural history of MPS. No data are available concerning prognosis of MPS in the community, in the primary care setting or in the workplace.

Differential Diagnosis

Because the symptoms of FM and MPS are common, the list of other conditions which could account for the symptoms is large and includes: multiple sclerosis, rheumatoid arthritis, osteoarthritis, systemic lupus erythematosus, bursitis, tendinitis-tenosynovitis, ligament strain, polymyalgia rheumatica, trauma, tumor, polymyositis, ankylosing spondylitis, Reiter's syndrome, hypothyroidism, Parkinson's disease, mental and behavioral disorders (depression, somatoform disorders, factitious illness) and malingering.

Specialists

- Internist
- Neurologist
- Pain Specialist
- Physiatrist
- Primary Care Provider
- Rheumatologist

Work Restrictions / Accommodations

Persons with FM and MPS have no identifiable objective medical basis for their symptoms. That is, persons with these disorders report symptoms but have normal physical examinations and normal findings on diagnostic testing. Consequently, there is no objective medical basis upon which to predicate work restrictions or accommodations.

Comorbid Conditions

Concurrent mental or behavioral disorders including depression, somatoform disorders, factitious disorders, can contribute to symptom production in FM and MPS.

Complications

Complications can arise from treatment (i.e., unwanted side effects or reinforcement of counterproductive behaviors) or from the person's behavior (i.e., self-limitation of personal or occupational activities of daily living).

Factors Influencing Duration

In both FM and MPS, the factors influencing perceived disability are unknown due to an absence of scientifically valid studies addressing this issue.

Complementary and Alternative Therapies

Content is intended for awareness only. Treatments may or may not be effective. Scientific evidence may be lacking and some substances have potentially toxic effects. Dr. Presley Reed and the editors do not endorse the use of these therapies in the absence of consultation with a licensed medical professional.

Exercise -	Aquatic exercise, swimming, walking, and stretching exercises can relieve symptoms through improved physical fitness.
Heat therapy -	Local heat, using heating pad or warm compress, can provide pain relief to affected muscles.
Massage -	Therapeutic massage can relax muscles, providing pain relief.
Relaxation techniques -	Various stress reduction methods such as biofeedback and breathing exercises may help ease symptoms.
Visualization techniques -	Helps individual to learn pain control techniques.

Length of Disability

Although persons with FM or MPS may self-limit their work or social activities, there may be no objective medical basis for disability. This is a controversial diagnosis. Contact physician for more information.

Duration Trend from Normative Data*

Cases	Mean	Min	Max	No Lost Time	Over 6 Months
5717	62	0	709	0.39%	1.70%

Percentile:	5th	25th	Median	75th	95th
Days:	10	22	43	84	162

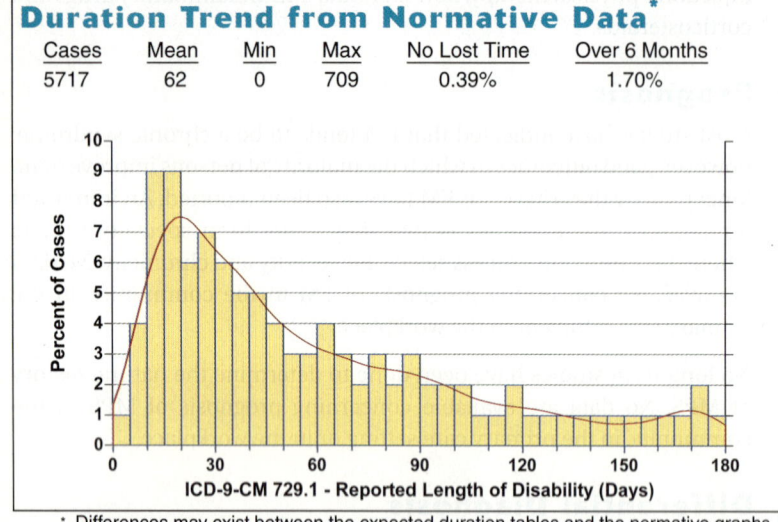
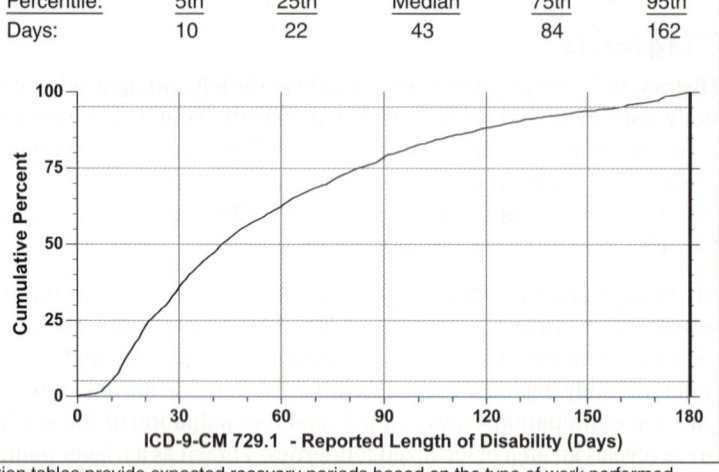

ICD-9-CM 729.1 - Reported Length of Disability (Days)

* Differences may exist between the expected duration tables and the normative graphs. Duration tables provide expected recovery periods based on the type of work performed by the individual. The normative graphs reflect the actual observed experience of many individuals across the spectrum of physical conditions, in a variety of industries, and with varying levels of case management.

Failure to Recover

If an individual fails to recover within the maximum duration expectancy period, the reader may wish to reference the following questions to assist in better understanding the specifics of an individual's medical case.

Regarding diagnosis:

- Have similar conditions been ruled out?
- Has diagnosis of FM or MPS been established?

- Does individual have a comorbid condition that may impact recovery?

Regarding treatment:

- Has there been an adequate trial of amitriptyline?
- Has there been a trial of cognitive behavioral therapy?
- Have treatments resulted in unwanted side-effects?
- Have treatment methods reinforced inappropriate illness behaviors?

Regarding prognosis:

- Have psychosocial factors, i.e., family and workplace dynamics, been considered?
- Have mental and behavioral disorders (depression, somatoform disorders, factitious disorders) been considered?
- Have inappropriate illness behaviors (symptom exaggeration, malingering) been considered?

References

Gordon, Stacey, and Candis Morrison. "Fibromyalgia and its Primary Care Implications." MEDSURG Nursing 7 01 Aug 1998 207-214. Electric Library. 20 Nov 2000 <http://wwws.elibrary.com/=>.

Millea, Paul J., MD, MS, and Richard Holloway, PhD. "Diagnosis and Treatment of Fibromyalgia." Medical College of Wisconsin Physicians and Clinics. 26 Dec 2000. 26 Jan 2001 <http://healthlink.mcw.edu>.

Filariasis

Other names / synonyms: Bancroftian Filariasis, Brugian Filariasis, Lymphatic Filariasis, Malayan Filariasis, Timorean Filariasis

125, 125.6, 125.9

Definition

Filariasis is a general term applied to infection caused by parasitic filarial roundworms (nematodes). Usually, however, the term is used to describe one type of filarial infection "lymphatic filariasis," which is caused by one of three species of filarial worms: Wuchereria bancrofti, Brugia malayi, and Brugia timori. The infection is spread by blood-sucking insects (arthropods), primarily mosquitoes.

The adult forms of these three species of worms live in the lymphatic vessels of people. These threadlike worms, measuring 2 to 4 inches long, produce microscopic larvae (microfilariae), which move into the blood stream. A mosquito ingests the microfilariae while feeding on blood from an infected individual. In the mosquito, the microfilariae mature into an infective larvae stage over a period of weeks. During a future bite, the infected mosquito will deposit the infective larvae into the bloodstream of a new host. These larvae will eventually travel to and reside in the lymphatic vessels or lymph nodes of their new host. The cycle begins again as the larvae mature into adult worms, producing microfilariae that migrate to the bloodstream.

Inflammation, a process triggered by the body's own immune reaction to the worms, results in swelling of tissue, primarily lymphatic tissue, the accumulation of fluid, and pain. Outward symptoms may take years to develop. In fact, some people never have outward symptoms, despite hidden (occult) internal damage. Although the infection is not fatal, its manifestations cause it to be considered the second leading cause of permanent disability worldwide.

Lymphatic filariasis affects 120 million people. The worms that cause it are found in at least 80 countries; they are not, however, found in the US. The vast majority (90%) of these infections are caused by Wuchereria bancrofti. This species is found in most tropical countries, including Latin America, Africa, Asia, and the Pacific Islands. Brugia malayi is the next most common cause of infection. It is found in rural southwest India, southeast Asia, and coastal regions of China and South Korea. Brugia timori is found in rural islands of southeast Indonesia.

Any cases of lymphatic filariasis in the US are due to travel to other countries where the worms are found.

Diagnosis

History: The individual has a history of travel in tropical or subtropical areas, and significant history of insect bites. For a traveler, symptoms will develop at least 8 months after this exposure. For an individual native to a country where filariasis is prevalent, the time from exposure to the onset of symptoms may be 2 to 3 years.

Symptoms of acute disease include episodes of fever with pain and/or swelling of lymph nodes (lymphadenitis) and lymphatic vessels (lymphangitis). Individuals may report that these episodes occur at irregular intervals and last several days. Enlarged lymph nodes may remain after the episodes. As the disease progresses, other body sites, such as the genitalia, may become intermittently inflamed. Infected travelers may have symptoms of allergy, such as hives and rashes. Individuals with chronic disease may show symptoms of obstruction and interference with normal lymphatic flow, such as a rapid increase in the size (mass) of the extremities, genitals, or breasts. Episodic nighttime coughing or wheezing may be reported.

Physical exam: Characteristic painful/swollen lymph nodes (lymphadenitis) may be evident. The primary affected node is the most severe, with pain and swelling decreasing in intensity with distance from the node (retrograde). In later stages, involvement of the lymphatics in the tissue that lines the abdomen and covers the internal organs (the peritoneum) will also occur. Examination of the abdomen by pressing with the hands (abdominal palpation) may reveal a swollen spleen or liver.

In chronic cases, swelling of the scrotum and enlarged lymphatic vessels are characteristic physical symptoms. The infected area, commonly a limb or the scrotum, becomes enormously enlarged (elephantiasis), and the skin becomes thick, coarse, and cracked. Hard masses may accumulate in the breasts, legs, hands or testicles. A milky, white substance (chyle) may appear in the urine as a result of lymphatic vessel rupture into the urinary tract.

Tests: The diagnosis of filariasis may be made by microscopic examination of blood for the presence of microfilariae. Worms may also be present in fluids drawn from swollen areas. Each species of filarial nematode will show characteristic structure and form (morphology) under microscopic examination. This test, however, may be negative, despite the fact that the individual does have filariasis. For example, one form of W. bancrofti microfilariae is present in the blood all the time, but in highest concentration during the daytime. Another form is present only at night, particularly from 10 p.m. to 2 am. Unless the timing of the blood collection takes this into consideration, the test result may be a false negative. Some infected individuals never, or seldom, have microfilariae in their blood. In addition it takes time for the microfilariae to be found in the blood: 3 to 12 months for a traveler, 2 to 3 years for an indigenous individual.

A more reliable alternative is a blood test that tests for the presence of filarial protein (antigen). This test is positive in almost all individuals with filariasis, whether or not they have microfilariae in their blood. This antigen test is available only for infection caused by W. bancrofti. It is not available for B. malayi or B timori filariasis.

Other blood tests that may be used to diagnose infection in cases where microfilariae are not actively present in the blood include DNA tests that can detect infection with either W. bancrofti or B. malayi, filarial antibody tests, and tests for IgE (individuals with filariasis typically have extremely high IgE levels).

Ultrasonography may reveal adult worms in lymphatic tissue, particularly of the scrotum in men, and of the breast and retroperitoneal lymphatics in women. If the lungs are involved, x-rays may show scattered, small nodular lesions on the lungs. There may be increased evidence of vascular damage on the chest films.

Specialists

- Immunologist
- Infectious Disease Physician
- Plastic Surgeon
- Pulmonologist
- Surgeon

Treatment

Filariasis may be treated in early, mild cases with a 6 to 12 day course of antifilarial drugs. This treatment usually eliminates the microfilariae from the blood, but it may not kill all the adult worms in the lymph, and small numbers of microfilariae may reappear in the blood after treatment. To boost the effectiveness of the drug therapy, antifilarial drugs should be repeated at various intervals such as yearly, every 1 to 6 months, or for 2 days every month for 1 year.

If the infected individual lives in an area endemic for the species of filarial roundworm that cause onchocerciasis (Onchocerca volvulus) or loiasis (Loa loa), he or she should be checked for a coinfection with these worms before beginning treatment. Different drugs may be required.

The first 24 hours of drug treatment may cause a reaction marked by fever, illness, and muscle or joint pain. This is due to the rapid kill-off of microfilariae. These symptoms may be treated with antipyogenic or antihistamine drugs, or corticosteroids.

Treatment for symptomatic relief includes bed rest, antibiotic use for secondary infections, elastic stockings and pressure bandages to reduce swelling and fluid accumulation, and suspensory bandaging for swollen testicles or breasts. Local injection of hardening (sclerosing) agents or surgical drainage may help dry up accumulations of fluid (hydroceles). A procedure in which a shunt is placed between a lymph vessel and a blood vessel (lymphovenous shunt procedure) may help drain and eliminate the accumulated lymph associated with elephantiasis. Elephantiasis may also improve following other types of drainage and the surgical removal of excess fatty and fibrous tissue (debulking surgery).

Good hygiene is vital in the management of elephantiasis. The affected area should be washed twice daily with soap and water and raised at night. Shoes should be worn and nails kept clean and trimmed at all times. Small wounds, cuts, or scratches should be treated with antiseptic or antibiotic creams. Counseling may be needed to handle the psychological and social stresses associated with this condition.

Prognosis

Early or mild filariasis typically responds well to treatment. The response of advanced infection is poor. Although not fatal, the disease can leave an individual severely disabled with genital damage or elephantiasis.

Lymphatic swelling, caught early, will resolve with treatment of the infection. Swelling that has advanced to elephantiasis may be irreversible. If the affected area is kept free of bacterial or fungal infection, other nearby lymph vessels can sometimes successfully reestablish lymph flow, decreasing the amount of tissue damage and disfigurement. Debulking surgery, in which excess tissue is removed, may also be successful in reducing disfigurement.

Differential Diagnosis

Many other infectious diseases give symptoms of lymphadenitis, lymphangitis, and mild fever. Epididymitis or swelling of the testicles and breast may resemble symptoms of mumps. Malignancies and a number of nonmalignant diseases may result in vessel blockage or lung obstruction.

Rehabilitation

Individuals with the diagnosis of filariasis may require rehabilitation. The time frame and type of therapy necessary is based on the severity and type of complications.

If the lymphatic system is involved, the primary goal of therapy is to reduce swelling. Elevating the swollen leg or arm above the level of the heart helps to decrease swelling. Performing ankle pumps, in which the toes are pointed and extended, or squeezing therapy putty to engage the muscles helps to mobilize excess fluid out of the involved leg or arm. Therapists may manually massage the affected leg or arm from the farthest point of the extremity toward the torso.

In the case of lymphatic involvement, therapists may provide individuals with elastic stockings that reduce the incidence of swelling in the affected limb. Therapists also instruct individuals to avoid overloading the lymphatic system in the following ways: by allowing the affected limb to rest below the level of the heart, using heating pads, and using the muscles in the affected limb for a prolonged period of time. This will help prevent swelling.

Individuals who have lung disease as a result of filariasis may require respiratory, occupational, and physical therapy to improve lung functioning. Respiratory therapists help to facilitate the expulsion of lung secretions through chest therapy. While undergoing chest therapy, individuals are positioned to maximize the expulsion of secretions (for example, lying on the stomach with the head lower than the legs). Respiratory therapists then cup their hands and strike the individual's chest wall in a rhythmic manner (percussion), or compress and vibrate the chest wall with their hands (vibration, shaking).

Respiratory therapy addresses increasing lung capacity and decreasing the risk for the buildup of lung secretions. Respiratory therapists teach individuals pursed lip breathing to increase the airflow to the lungs. Individuals may also use an incentive spirometer, which is a device that measures and displays the amount of air inspired to help motivate individuals to take deeper breaths. Individuals also learn to produce an effective cough through techniques such as huffing, in which air is breathed out forcefully while the mouth is open. Individuals also learn positions to relieve shortness of breath such as leaning forward while sitting, with the arms resting on the thighs.

Occupational therapy addresses any fatigue or shortness of breath that may occur during activities of daily living. Individuals learn to utilize equipment such as a shower chair to decrease the energy expended during bathing, or a long-handled sponge to decrease the amount of forward bending an individual has to perform.

Physical therapy addresses decreases in endurance and strength. Individuals perform strengthening exercises of the arms and legs to improve overall endurance. In addition to strengthening the arms and legs, the muscles of the upper back are strengthened. Individuals may perform aerobic activity such as walking on a treadmill or riding a stationary bicycle to further increase endurance.

Work Restrictions / Accommodations

Individuals with an enlarged spleen should be restricted from heavy lifting or strenuous work. Accommodations may be required if chronic lung disease, excessive fluid accumulation, or hospitalization interfere with normal work activities.

This infection is not spread from individual to individual so interpersonal on-the-job infection control measures are not required.

Comorbid Conditions

Individuals coinfected with other filarial species that cause onchocerciasis or loiasis may not be able to safely use the drugs typically used to treat lymphatic filariasis. Any condition that prolongs wound healing or interferes with circulation in the lower extremities, such as diabetes, may delay healing and prolong disability.

Complications

The infection may be complicated if it develops into chronic disease with fluid accumulation and lymphatic vessel blockage or rupture. Chronic lung damage may result from worm invasion of the lungs. Relapses may occur. Antifilarial drug treatment may lead to systemic allergic reactions to the dying worms. Dead adult worms may calcify and create abscesses in the tissues. The disfigurement associated with elephantiasis has profound psychological and social consequences, including sexual dysfunction.

Factors Influencing Duration

Length of disability may be influenced by the severity of symptoms, onset of complications, and the possibility of recurrent episodes with gradually increasing severity. Chronic disease may require longer periods of disability because it often requires hospitalization and may result in permanent disability, especially when the lungs become involved.

Length of Disability

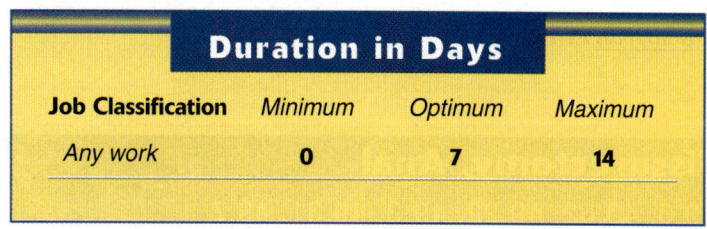

Job Classification	Minimum	Optimum	Maximum
Any work	0	7	14

Duration in Days

Failure to Recover

If an individual fails to recover within the maximum duration expectancy period, the reader may wish to reference the following questions to assist in better understanding the specifics of an individual's medical case.

Regarding diagnosis:

- Has the individual traveled outside the US?
- Has the individual had episodic fever with pain? Lymphadenitis? Lymphangitis?
- Have the genitalia become inflamed?
- Has the individual had hives or rashes?
- Has there been a rapid increase of the size of legs, breasts, or genitals?
- Does the individual have episodic nighttime cough or wheezing?
- On physical exam, was lymphadenitis evident? Was the primary node very tender?
- Is there evidence of involvement of the peritoneal lymphatics?
- Were the spleen or liver palpable?
- Has the individual had a microscopic examination of the blood? Filarial antigen? DNA? IgE? Ultrasound? Chest x-ray?
- Have conditions with similar symptoms been ruled out?

Regarding treatment:

- Has the individual been treated with antifilarial drugs?
- Are treatments scheduled at various intervals for a year?
- Were there any side effects of treatment?

Regarding prognosis:
- Is the individual active in rehabilitation?
- Can individual's employer accommodate any necessary restrictions?
- Does the individual have any conditions that may affect ability to recover?
- Has the individual developed a systemic allergic to the antifilarial drugs?
- Have relapses occurred?
- Does the individual have elephantiasis?
- Has the individual sought counseling?

References

"Campaign to Eliminate Lymphatic Filariasis Leads to Expanded Role for DPD." CDC/NCID Focus 7 2 (1995): 1.

Comley, J.C. "New Macrofilaricidal Leads from Plants." Tropical Medical Parasitology 41 1 (1990): 1-9.

Fissurectomy, Anal
49.0, 49.02, 49.22, 49.3, 49.31, 49.7

Definition

An anal fissurectomy is the removal (excision) of painful cracks or tears that develop in the anal canal (anal fissure).

Anal fissurectomy involves dilation of the circular muscles at the opening of the anus controlling defecation (anal sphincter) and often, placement of an incision in the anal sphincter (sphincterotomy).

The muscles of the anal sphincter may contract excessively (spasm) and result in trauma as stool passes. Anal fissures may occur as a result of trauma to the anal canal. Trauma can occur due to straining with defecation such as with constipation. Individuals at risk for development of anal fissures have frequent constipation.

Reason for Procedure

An anal fissurectomy treats anal fissures that do not heal with conservative treatment (avoidance of diarrhea or constipation, bulk laxatives, stool softeners, local anesthetics or mild non-narcotic analgesics, and sitz baths).

The fissures most commonly occur along the midline of the anal canal toward the back (posterior). Sometimes the fissure occurs along the front (anterior) midline. Fissures that occur on either side are often associated with other conditions such as Crohn's disease, inflammation of the rectum and anus (proctitis), leukemia, cancer, syphilis, or tuberculosis.

Sphincterotomy releases sphincter contraction (spasm), relieves pain, and allows healing of the fissure (lateral internal anal sphincterotomy). Sphincterotomy can be performed at the same time as a fissurectomy or may be performed in place of a fissurectomy for treatment of anal fissures.

Description

The procedure is usually performed on an outpatient basis using local anesthesia.

To perform a fissurectomy, the anal canal is first opened more widely (dilated). The fissure is removed (excised) and any blood vessels that bleed are closed with a small suture (ligated) or sealed with electrocoagulation.

The most commonly used method of treating an anal fissure involves cutting a small portion of the internal sphincter (lateral internal anal sphincterotomy) to release abnormal contraction of the sphincter (sphincter spasm), relieve pain, and allow healing of the fissure. If sphincterotomy is also to be performed, an incision is made in the sphincter.

When the procedure is completed, a drain or packing material is placed in the anal canal and a dressing applied.

Prognosis

The outcome is generally good. Women are more likely than men to experience incontinence of stool following the procedure, although this is rare. Unfortunately, anal fissures can recur.

Specialists

- Colorectal Surgeon
- General Surgeon

Work Restrictions / Accommodations

After recovery, no work restrictions or special accommodations are required.

Comorbid Conditions

Disability may be lengthened by hemorrhoids.

Procedure Complications

A complication of anal fissurectomy is minor incontinence of stool.

Factors Influencing Duration

The depth of the incision and any complications affect length of disability.

Length of Disability

Job Classification	Duration in Days		
	Minimum	Optimum	Maximum
Any work	7	14	21

References

Dayton, Merril T., and Judith L. Trudel. "Colon, Rectum, and Anus." Essentials of General Surgery, 3rd ed. Lawrence, Peter F., ed. Philadelphia: Lippincott Williams & Wilkins, 2000. 265-298.

Petty, Lynda R. "Gastrointestinal Surgery." Alexander's Care of the Patient in Surgery, 11th ed. Meeker, Margaret H., and Jane C. Rothrock, eds. St. Louis: Mosby, 1999. 313-370.

Folic Acid Deficiency Anemia

Other names / synonyms: Congenital Folate Malabsorption, Folate Acid Deficiency

281.2

Definition

Folic acid deficiency anemia is a form of anemia caused by a deficiency of the vitamin called folic acid that is needed for normal red blood cell formation. Folic acid is not made or stored in the body in adequate amounts, so it must be absorbed from food and is found in most fruits and vegetables, particularly greens and legumes. Sufficient amounts are usually available in a balanced diet.

Reasons for folic acid deficiency include pregnancy, lactating women, inadequate dietary intake from restricted diets or overcooking foods, excess alcohol use, chronic hemolytic anemia, malabsorption syndromes, and drugs, especially methotrexate, trimethoprim, pentamidine, phenytoin, and phenobarbital.

Diagnosis

History: An individual with mild anemia may have no symptoms and the anemia may only be recognized because of abnormal laboratory tests. More severe anemia may have many of the nonspecific symptoms of anemia including fatigue, weakness, dizziness, shortness of breath, and decreased exercise capacity.

Physical exam: Findings may include pallor of the skin and gums and elevated respiratory and heart rates, even at rest.

Tests: A complete blood count (CBC) usually shows oversized red blood cells (macrocytosis), a low level of hemoglobin (the oxygen-carrying molecule of blood), and a low folic acid level. A more specific blood test for a red blood cell folate level will confirm the diagnosis, as will a bone marrow biopsy that shows large numbers of abnormal, large red blood cells (megaloblasts). Additional diagnostic tests may also be needed to determine the underlying cause of the deficiency.

Treatment

When due to a poor diet, treatment includes proper nutrition and a short course of a daily folic acid supplement. If the anemia is due to another underlying problem such as alcoholism, hemolytic anemia, or malabsorption, the underlying problem must be corrected in addition to taking daily folic acid supplements.

Prognosis

With adequate treatment, most individuals feel better within 5 to 7 days, and the anemia is fully corrected within 1 to 2 months. When due to pregnancy, the anemia usually resolves after delivery but may recur with another pregnancy.

Differential Diagnosis

Other conditions causing large red blood cells (megaloblastosis) include vitamin B_{12} (cobalamin) deficiency, hemolytic anemia, phenytoin, and many antineoplastic and immunosuppressant drugs including hydroxyurea, fluorouracil, azathioprine, and mercaptopurine. Conditions with similar symptoms also include aplastic anemia or leukemia.

Specialists

- Hematologist
- Internist

Work Restrictions / Accommodations

If an individual has chest pain, shortness of breath, or decreased exercise capacity, activity at work may have to be restricted until the anemia is corrected, otherwise, work restrictions or accommodations are not usually needed.

> ### Complementary and Alternative Therapies
>
> Content is intended for awareness only. Treatments may or may not be effective. Scientific evidence may be lacking and some substances have potentially toxic effects. Dr. Presley Reed and the editors do not endorse the use of these therapies in the absence of consultation with a licensed medical professional.
>
> Diet modification - Adding foods that are high in folic acid to the diet may help treat the anemia. The liver can store folic acid for a limited period of time. Good sources include asparagus, beef liver, broccoli, collards, mushrooms, oatmeal, peanut butter, red beans, and wheat germ.
>
> Supplement therapy - Certain food items are now supplemented with folic acid because of the prevalence of folic acid deficiency in pregnant women.

Comorbid Conditions

Vitamin B_{12} deficiency, iron deficiency, alcoholism, and malabsorption may lengthen the time of disability.

Complications

If severe, the anemia can lead to shortness of breath or in individuals with heart disease, chest pain (angina pectoris) or congestive heart failure. During pregnancy, folic acid deficiency may negatively affect the fetus by causing defects in the folds from which the brain and spinal cord arise in the developing fetus (neural tube).

Factors Influencing Duration

The severity of the anemia, response to treatment, and nature of any underlying condition will influence the length of disability.

Length of Disability

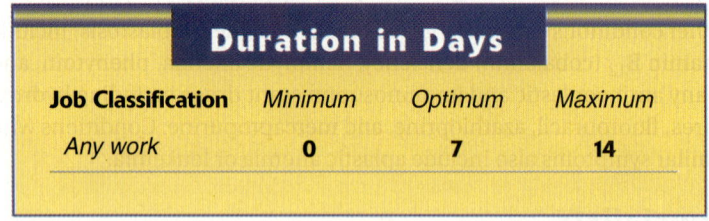

Duration in Days

Job Classification	Minimum	Optimum	Maximum
Any work	0	7	14

Failure to Recover

If an individual fails to recover within the maximum duration expectancy period, the reader may wish to reference the following questions to assist in better understanding the specifics of an individual's medical case.

Regarding diagnosis:

- Is individual pregnant or breastfeeding (lactating)?
- Is individual on a restricted diet causing inadequate intake of folic acid?
- Does individual have a history of chronic hemolytic anemia or malabsorption syndrome?
- Does individual take medications such as methotrexate, trimethoprim, pentamidine, phenytoin, or phenobarbital?
- Does individual complain of fatigue, weakness, dizziness, shortness of breath, and decreased exercise capacity suggesting severe anemia? Are the skin and gums pale (pallor)?
- Was a complete blood count (CBC) done revealing a low level of the oxygen-carrying molecule of blood (hemoglobin)? Was a red blood cell folate level done to confirm the diagnosis?
- Was a bone marrow biopsy required? If so, did it reveal large numbers of abnormal, large red blood cells (megaloblasts)?
- Was the diagnosis of folic acid deficiency confirmed?

Regarding treatment:

- If the deficiency was caused by poor diet, is individual willing and/or capable of correcting dietary deficiencies?
- Would individual or caregiver benefit from consultation with a nutritionist or dietitian?
- Are folic acid supplements being given?
- Is individual compliant with the supplementation regimen?
- Were other underlying causes identified? Is the underlying condition responding to treatment?
- If the deficiency was caused by medication use, are alternate medications available?

Regarding prognosis:

- Are symptoms persisting even with treatment?
- Is individual compliant with all diet recommendations and with taking the folic acid supplement, as directed?
- Is an underlying condition impacting recovery? How can the underlying condition be corrected?
- If pregnant, does individual understand that not taking folic acid supplements could negatively affect the fetus?
- How severe is the anemia and how will it affect daily activities of individual?

References

Babior, Bernard M., and H. Franklin Bunn. "Megaloblastic Anemias." Harrison's Principles of Internal Medicine. Fauci, Anthony S., et al., eds. New York: The McGraw-Hill Companies, Inc, 1998. 653-659.

Schrier, S.L., MD. "Chapter III: Anemia: Production Defects." Scientific American® Medicine Online Dale, D.C., and D.D. Federman, eds. New York: WebMD Corporation, 2000 Scientific American Medicine. 24 Jan 2000 <http://www.samed.com/sam/forms/index/htm>.

Folliculitis

Other names / synonyms: Acne Miliaris

704.8, 706.1

Definition

Folliculitis is a superficial or deep infection and inflammation of hair follicles usually arising from blockage of the associated oil (sebaceous) gland. The infection and inflammation may spread to areas around the affected follicles. Folliculitis can be bacterial (most often staphylococcus), fungal (Candida), or viral (herpes simplex or molluscum contagiosum).

Factors that promote folliculitis include shaving, friction from clothing, athletic padding, mineral oil on the skin, and the use of wax to remove hair (wax epilation). Folliculitis may occur anywhere on the skin surface but is commonly found on the extremities, scalp, and face. It usually occurs in areas with short, coarse hairs. Chronic folliculitis of the bearded area is called barber's itch (sycosis barbae) and is most common in black males.

Less common causes of folliculitis are the klebsiella, proteus, and pseudomonas bacteria. Klebsiella or proteus can cause folliculitis in individuals on long-term antibiotic treatment for acne. Pseudomonas causes "hot tub" or "spa pool" folliculitis and is contracted by individuals using a contaminated, inadequately chlorinated hot tub. Hot tub folliculitis may also be contracted from swimming pools or a contaminated sponge or loofah.

Folliculitis is a common skin infection, however, incidence of chronic folliculitis is uncommon.

Diagnosis

History: The individual complains of pus-filled pimples (pustules) associated with hair follicles. The individual may complain of pain and itching (pruritus) in the affected area. Individuals with widespread folliculitis may report recent use of a hot tub. Individuals with hot tub folliculitis may also complain of headache, low-grade fever, sore throat, sore eyes, dizziness, and a feeling of discomfort and fatigue (malaise).

Physical exam: Diagnosis is made based on the clinical appearance of small, dome-shaped, yellowish pustules occurring at the opening of a hair follicle, often on the scalp or bearded area of the face. Folliculitis restricted to the trunk, legs, and arms suggests hot tub folliculitis.

Tests: Culture of the pus may be performed to identify the causative agent, especially in deep and chronic cases. Skin samples (biopsy) may be taken to diagnose a possible viral infection in individuals with folliculitis that fails to respond to standard antibiotic or antifungal treatment.

Treatment

Treatment with warm saline compresses and local (topical) antibiotics or antifungals is usually sufficient to control bacterial or fungal infection, respectively. Folliculitis of the scalp is treated with selenium sulfide shampoo and antibiotic and corticosteroid creams. Viral folliculitis may be treated with antiviral agents or by scraping (curettage). Individuals with extensive folliculitis require oral antibiotic therapy. Individuals should stop shaving the affected area until the folliculitis clears. Switching from a blade to an electric razor may be beneficial. Razor blades should be changed and the heads of electric razors decontaminated daily to prevent reinfection.

Prognosis

The outcome is good with complete resolution usually occurring within 10 days. Folliculitis generally resolves without scarring except in deep follicles or complicated cases. Folliculitis may be chronic in areas with multiple, deep follicles (bearded area). Recurrence is possible.

Differential Diagnosis

Acne vulgaris, chloracne, drug-induced acne, pustular psoriasis, bullous impetigo, rosacea, ingrown hair (pseudofolliculitis barbae), tinea barbae, contact dermatitis, and chronic discoid lupus erythematosus can present with similar signs and symptoms.

Specialists

- Dermatologist
- Infectious Disease Physician

Work Restrictions / Accommodations

Contact with oils and greases should be avoided. Individuals should practice ordinary hygienic measures that include daily showers and changes of clothing. Clothing should be loose to minimize sweating and irritation. The use of personal protective equipment (respirator) may be affected depending on the location of the folliculitis.

Comorbid Conditions

Comorbid conditions that may influence the length of disability are diabetes, acne vulgaris, AIDS, organ transplantation, cancer, obesity, and diseases causing impaired circulation (e.g., arteriosclerosis).

Complications

Complications include boils (furunculosis), clusters of boils (carbuncles), aggregations of immune cells (granulomas), ulcerations, subcutaneous abscesses, chronicity, neurodermatitis, and scarring. Chronic, deep folliculitis of the scalp (folliculitis decalvans) can cause hair loss (alopecia).

Factors Influencing Duration

Location and extent of the lesions, complications, and response to treatment may influence the length of disability.

Length of Disability

In most cases, no disability is expected.

Failure to Recover

If an individual fails to recover within the maximum duration expectancy period, the reader may wish to reference the following questions to assist in better understanding the specifics of an individual's medical case.

Regarding diagnosis:

- Does the individual have a recent history of hot tub use?
- Are the skin symptoms isolated to the trunk and extremities?
- Has the individual been on long-term antibiotic use for acne?
- Have cultures of the pus been performed?
- Has the individual been tested to determine if they are a carrier of staphylococcus aureus?
- Has a skin biopsy been performed?
- Has blood work been done or other tests performed to diagnose a potential underlying condition (i.e., immune suppression)?

Regarding treatment:

- Is the appropriate antibiotic being used for the specific type of bacteria?
- Is the individual complying with treatment recommendations?
- Does the folliculitis recur in the shaved areas of skin? Has the individual been instructed to use an electric razor?
- Is the individual being treated with oral antibiotics?

Regarding prognosis:

- Have the symptoms persisted despite treatment?
- Was a repeat culture and sensitivity done to rule out secondary infection or a antibiotic resistant bacteria?
- Have appropriate adjustments in antibiotic therapy been made?
- Does the individual have any underlying conditions such as diabetes, acne vulgaris, AIDS, organ transplantation, cancer, obesity, and diseases causing impaired circulation (e.g., arteriosclerosis, that may impact recovery and prognosis?
- Has the individual experienced any complications (boils, granulomas, ulcerations, subcutaneous abscesses, chronicity, neurodermatitis, or scarring) that may impact recovery and prognosis?

References

Aly, Raza. "Gram-negative Infections: Folliculitis, Toe Web, Others." Atlas of Infections of the Skin. Aly, Raza, and Howard Maibach, eds. New York: Churchill Livingstone, Inc, 1999. 133-135.

Aly, Raza. "Staphylococcal Infections." Atlas of Infections of the Skin. Aly, Raza, and Howard Maibach, eds. New York: Churchill Livingstone, Inc, 1999. 118.

Andersen, Philip, and Kristin Malaker. "Other Common Disorders." Managing Skin Disease. Hiscock, Tim, ed. Baltimore: Williams & Wilkins, 1999. 139-140.

Hall, John. "Dermatologic Bacteriology." Sauer's Manual of Skin Diseases. Hall, John, ed. Philadelphia: Lippincott, Williams & Wilkins, 2000. 148-150.

Jang, K., et al. "Viral Folliculitis on the Face." British Journal of Dermatology 142 (2000): 555-559.

Pray, Steven. "Bacterial Infections of the Hair Follicles." U.S. Pharmacist 25 4 (2000). 14 Aug 2000 <http://www.uspharmacist.com/NewLook/DisplayArticle.cfm?item_num=506>.

Food Poisoning

Other names / synonyms: Food-Borne Disease, Foodborne Illness

003, 004, 005, 005.0, 005.1, 005.2, 005.3, 005.4, 005.8, 005.9, 988, 988.8, 988.9

Definition

Food poisoning (food-borne illness) is the general term used for any condition associated with ingestion of food or water that has been contaminated with microorganisms (bacteria, parasites, or viruses), microbial toxins, poisonous plants, or chemicals. Despite the popularity of this term, food poisoning is misleading because the illness is caused by a contaminant, not the food itself.

Bacteria are common causes of food-borne illness. Common culprits include Staphylococcus aureus, Bacillus cereus, Clostridium perfringens, Campylobacter jejuni, Yersinia enterocolitica, Escherichia coli, Vibrio parahaemolyticus, Shigella species, salmonella species, Clostridium botulinum, and Listeria monocytogenes. Some bacteria cause illness directly. Others produce a poison (toxin) that causes illness. Many types of bacteria normally inhabit the intestines of farm animals and poultry. Improper slaughtering and/or butchering techniques can bring these bacteria into contact with the meat products. Improper cooking can then lead to illness.

Another common method of transmission occurs when meat or poultry are not properly handled in the kitchen. For instance, a cutting board and knife used to prepare uncooked meat can contaminate raw vegetables if the knife and cutting board are not thoroughly washed with hot soapy water prior to contact with the vegetables. In this instance, cooking the meat will eliminate the risk of transmission from the meat itself, but the raw vegetables that have become contaminated, may still cause illness.

Many bacteria are normal inhabitants of the human body but when ingested can cause illness, e.g., E. coli (normally found in the human intestine), and S. aureus (commonly found in the nose and sometimes on the skin). Handling food without thoroughly washing hands after using the restroom, changing a baby's diaper, or blowing the nose can cause illness. Some bacteria (S. aureus, C. botulinum) form toxins that are difficult to destroy even with thorough cooking.

Raw sewage spilled into a body of water where fish or shellfish are harvested can cause food-borne illness particularly if the fish/shellfish is eaten raw or rare. Bacteria can also contaminate drinking water.

Viruses commonly responsible for causing food poisoning are the Norwalk virus (a common contaminant of shellfish), the hepatitis virus, and the rotavirus. Food-borne viruses are usually associated with undercooked or raw contaminated fish and shellfish although other types of food can also transmit viral illness.

Noninfective causes of food-borne illness include poisonous mushrooms and toadstools. Fresh fruit and vegetables can cause illness if they have accidentally been contaminated with high doses of insecticide, or if fertilized with manure and not thoroughly washed before eating. Food stored in an unsuitable container can cause chemical poisoning, e.g., food stored in a metal container (made partly of zinc) that has previously held poison or acidic fruit juice. If animals have eaten a poisonous product, this poison can be passed to individuals ingesting the animal product, e.g., shellfish that feed on poisonous plankton can cause illness when eaten.

Certain exotic foods are poisonous if improperly prepared or cooked and can lead to serious illness or death. These include the Japanese puffer fish or the tropical cassava.

Food-borne illness is a problem affecting millions of individuals worldwide. Food-borne illness due to bacterial infection alone accounts for approximately 76 million illnesses and 5,000 deaths in the US each year. In the US, most cases of food-borne illness are attributed to C. jejuni. The very young and the elderly are at an increased risk of serious disease or death from food-borne illnesses. Prompt notification of concern to the local health authority when common exposures are recognized (among multiple individuals eating at the same picnic, restaurant).

Diagnosis

History: Symptoms vary according to the type of poisoning, how heavily the food was contaminated, and how much of the food was ingested. In general, symptoms usually include stomach pain, nausea, vomiting, and diarrhea. In severe cases, shock, collapse, or paralysis may occur. Fever may be present. Individuals may report that others sharing the same food or foods also became ill.

Physical exam: The exam may be normal or reveal abdominal tenderness. General findings can apply to numerous illnesses (nonspecific). The individual may have signs of dehydration including blood pressure that changes with body position changes (orthostatic hypotension), dry mucous membranes, a sunken appearance of the eyes, and decreased skin tension (turgor). The rectal exam may be painful due to inflammation caused by constant diarrhea. The individual should be questioned regarding the onset of symptoms and the timing of the suspected meal. In chemical poisoning, symptoms occur quickly, usually within 1 hour. Bacterial infection tends to occur within 1 to 12 hours, but can be delayed as long as 3 days for certain bacteria (e.g., salmonella). Toxins produce symptoms anywhere from 1 hour to 6 days after ingestion. Most viruses produce symptoms within 2 to 5 days after ingestion.

Tests: The tests used may vary with the suspected causative agent and usually include microscopic examination or cultures of stools, vomit, or blood. Cultures may be done on remaining suspected food, food preparation area, or the food handlers. Other tests to identify the causative organism include gel diffusion, radioimmunoassay (RIA), enzyme-linked immunoassay (ELISA), latex agglutination, serotyping of suspected organism, gene probe for toxin, tissue culture assays, and immunoelectron microscopy.

Treatment

Treatment depends on the causative agent. Most cases of food poisoning are self-limited and require only supportive care. Recovery is often complete within 24 hours from the onset of symptoms.

Poisoning due to a chemical or bacterial toxin may need to be washed out of the stomach (gastric lavage). If vomiting does not occur naturally, drugs may be given to encourage vomiting (emetics) as a way to clear the stomach of contaminated food. If the individual has been vomiting for an extended period of time, however, drugs may be given to help stop vomiting (antiemetics). Other medications include antibiotics, antiviral agents, pain relievers (analgesics), or fever-reducing medication (antipyretics). Severe dehydration may require hospitalization with intravenous replacement of fluid and electrolytes.

Infections inherently more serious than others may require hospitalization and include infections in the bloodstream (septicemia), the brain or spinal cord (meningitis), and toxins affecting the nervous system (toxin produced by C. botulinum).

Prognosis

Food-borne illness is not life-threatening in the vast majority of cases. Most individuals will experience complete recovery even in the absence of medical treatment. Severe or complicated cases may, however, require treatment for recovery particularly where diarrhea and vomiting caused dehydration.

In rare cases, a food-borne illness can result in a life-threatening illness. For example, toxin produced by C. botulinum affects the nervous system causing muscle paralysis. If the toxin reaches the heart or the diaphragm, death can occur quickly. Overall, mortality due to food-borne illness is approximately 5,000 cases per year in the US.

Differential Diagnosis

Conditions with similar symptoms include other bacterial or viral infections, inflammatory bowel disease, appendicitis or other acute abdominal disorders, heavy metal poisoning, endocrine disorders, and acquired enzyme deficiency.

Specialists

- Gastroenterologist
- Infectious Disease Physician
- Primary Care Provider

Work Restrictions / Accommodations

Accommodations and work restrictions are not generally required. Heavy lifting, extensive walking, or strenuous physical activity may need to be modified until physical stamina returns. Work in especially hot, humid environments (high heat stress) require special attention to accommodation.

Complementary and Alternative Therapies

Content is intended for awareness only. Treatments may or may not be effective. Scientific evidence may be lacking and some substances have potentially toxic effects. Dr. Presley Reed and the editors do not endorse the use of these therapies in the absence of consultation with a licensed medical professional.

Kaolin - Said to increase the bulk of feces and may be found in many antidiarrheal preparations. Kaolin does not have any antibacterial activity so it should not be used as the sole treatment in infectious diarrheas.

Yogurt - Said to reestablish normal flora in the intestines.

Comorbid Conditions

Any concurrent illness associated with dehydration, weakness, or anorexia may lengthen disability. Immune deficiency may also lengthen disability.

Complications

Complications include cardiovascular collapse, irregular heartbeat (arrhythmias) due to electrolyte imbalance, hemolytic uremic syndrome, Guillain Barré syndrome, Reiter syndrome, severe dehydration, respiratory failure, neurological problems, abscess formation, infection in the blood (sepsis), and infection of other body organs (metastatic infection). Coma, paralysis, and shock can also complicate food-borne illness.

Factors Influencing Duration

Factors that might influence length of disability include age, causative agent, severity of symptoms, response to treatment, and the presence of complications or underlying medical conditions such as immunosuppressive disorders.

Length of Disability

Most cases will resolve completely within one day from the onset of symptoms. Complications and/or severe disease may require a longer recovery period.

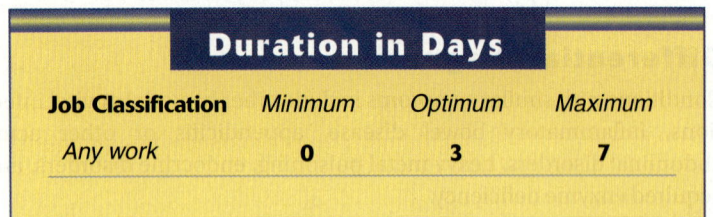

Duration in Days

Job Classification	Minimum	Optimum	Maximum
Any work	0	3	7

Failure to Recover

If an individual fails to recover within the maximum duration expectancy period, the reader may wish to reference the following questions to assist in better understanding the specifics of an individual's medical case.

Regarding diagnosis:

- Has the diagnosis of food-borne illness been confirmed? Has causative agent been identified? Have other possible causes of infection or poisoning been ruled out?
- How timely was medical attention sought? Had complications (such a dehydration) already occurred?
- Have underlying medical conditions that may impact recovery been identified or ruled out (i.e., immunosuppressed disorders)?

Regarding treatment:

- Was the treatment appropriate for the underlying cause and symptoms present? Was antimicrobial (antibiotic, antiparasitic, etc) medication warranted? Were symptoms of fever and/or dehydration addressed in the treatment plan?
- Were the symptoms serious enough to warrant hospitalization?

Regarding prognosis:

- Based on the underlying cause, severity of symptoms and general health of the individual what was the expected outcome? Did adequate time elapse for complete recovery?
- Did symptoms persist despite treatment? If so, did the individual receive repeat or additional diagnostic testing to rule out the possibility of bacterial resistance, secondary infection or associated complications? Were appropriate adjustments made in the current treatment to address any bacterial resistance or complications?
- If slow recovery is due to poor general health or underlying medical conditions (such as immunosuppressed disorders), what is being done to address these issues? Is individual receiving appropriate treatment?

References

Foodborne diseases. National Institute of Allergy and Infectious Disease. 01 Sep 2000. 14 Oct 2000 <http://www.niaid.nih.gov/factsheets/foodbornedis.htm>.

Dambro, Mark. "Food Poisoning, Bacterial." Griffith's 5-minute Clinical Consult. New York: Lippincott, Williams & Wilkins, 2000. 408-409.

Foreign Body, Cornea
930, 930.0

Definition

A corneal foreign body is a piece of material on or embedded in the transparent structure at the front of the eye (cornea).

Corneal foreign bodies usually fall under the category of minor ocular trauma. They usually occur when some force (e.g., wind or backdraft from a power tool) blows a small particle into the eye and the particle becomes lodged in the surface layer of the cornea (corneal epithelium). The particle material is usually metal, glass, or organic material.

Risk factors include occupational hazards such as working around substances that could end up in the eye (metal filings and sawdust).

Corneal foreign bodies are one of the most common causes for ophthalmic emergency visits. Superficial corneal foreign bodies are much more common than deeply embedded corneal foreign bodies. As for most other traumatic injuries, the incidence in males is much higher than in females; the peak incidence occurs in the second decade and generally occurs in individuals under 40 years old and in workers who fail to wear proper personal protective equipment such as safety glasses, goggles, and full face shields.

Diagnosis

History: Individuals may complain of pain in the eye, foreign body sensation, sensitivity to light (photophobia), excessive tearing, and redness of the affected eye.

Physical exam: A visual acuity exam will be normal or decreased. Ocular examination may reveal redness of the eyes (conjunctival injection), swelling of the cornea (corneal edema), a rust ring (if the foreign body is metallic), and a visible foreign body.

Tests: A slit-lamp examination with fluorescein dye will confirm the presence of aqueous humor leakage (Seidel's sign). A Woods lamp examination with ultraviolet stain will confirm an epithelial defect caused by the foreign body.

Treatment

Once it has been established that the object has not perforated the cornea, the foreign body will be removed by a qualified health professional using a sterile fine-gauge needle or cotton swab or pledget and a slit-lamp or binocular lens. If the material is superficial enough, a direct stream of irrigating fluid or a cotton swab may be used to remove it. Antibiotic ointment will be applied and the eye will be patched at least overnight. Frequently, follow-up exams are scheduled.

Prognosis

The corneal surface will usually heal when the foreign body is removed. The eye may be patched for 1 to 3 days. There is usually no permanent visual deficit. Prognosis is excellent unless a rust ring or scarring involves the visual axis. If infection develops, the prognosis is more guarded. Foreign bodies that penetrate the globe and intraocular foreign bodies are separate categories and have worse prognoses.

Differential Diagnosis

Conditions that may present with similar symptoms include a conjunctival foreign body, conjunctivitis, blepharitis, eyelids that turn inwards (entropion), dry eye syndrome, corneal abrasions and ulcers, intraocular foreign bodies, keratitis (bacterial or fungal), corneal melt, and iritis.

Specialists

- Ophthalmologist

Work Restrictions / Accommodations

Following treatment for a corneal foreign body, an eyepatch may be worn for 1 to 3 days. Accommodations may be necessary for work duties that require excellent visual acuity and depth perception (e.g., drivers and pilots may need to have restricted duties). To prevent further or future injury, protective eyewear should be used when the individual is engaged in any high risk activities (e.g., using power tools, chemicals, or engaging in sports activities).

Comorbid Conditions

Existing conditions that could impact ability to recover and further lengthen disability include dry eye syndrome (keratoconjunctivitis sicca), blepharitis, lagophthalmos, meibomian gland dysfunction, herpes simplex keratitis, and neurotrophic keratitis.

Complications

Possible complications that may arise include a rust ring (usually from an iron foreign body), infection of the cornea (infectious keratitis, usually caused by organic foreign bodies), globe perforation, and scarring in the visual axis.

Factors Influencing Duration

The type of material comprising the foreign body, the promptness of treatment, the presence of any complications, and the individual's response to treatment will determine the length of disability.

Length of Disability

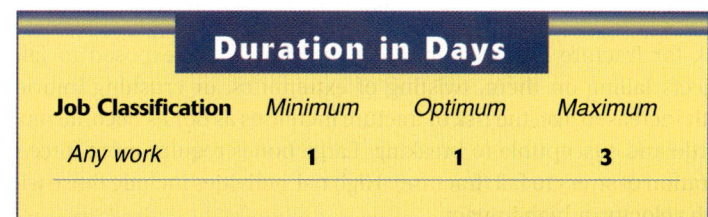

Job Classification	Minimum	Optimum	Maximum
Any work	1	1	3

Duration in Days

Failure to Recover

If an individual fails to recover within the maximum duration expectancy period, the reader may wish to reference the following questions to assist in better understanding the specifics of an individual's medical case.

Regarding diagnosis:

- Has diagnosis been confirmed? Through what process? Visual examination? A slit-lamp examination with fluorescein dye? A Woods lamp examination with ultraviolet stain?
- Was a foreign body present?
- Has individual experienced any complications?
- Does individual have an underlying condition that may impact recovery?

Regarding treatment:

- Did individual use ocular antibiotics and follow the treatment plan as prescribed?
- Have subsequent exams indicated that the injury is healing/has healed without infection or other complications?

Regarding prognosis:

- If individual experienced complications, are they resolving with treatment? If not, what does the current treatment plan now entail?

References

Corneal Foreign Body. Review of Optometry. 2001. 01 Jan 2001 <http://www.revoptom.com/handbook/SECT3G.HTM>.

Corneal Injury. drkoop.com. 01 Jan 1998. 01 Jan 2001 <http://www.drkoop.com/conditions/ency/article/001017.htm>.

Fracture

Other names / synonyms: Bone Break, Compound, Crack Fracture, Failed-Union Fracture, Greenstick Fracture, March Fracture, Non-Union Fracture, Open Fracture, Split Fracture, Stress Fracture

800, 802, 802.0, 802.2, 802.4, 803, 807.0, 811, 821, 822, 827.0, 827.1

Definition

Fractures are any break in a bone, no matter how small. Bones are composed of many layers, and a disruption of the layers results in a fracture. There are many types of fractures, defined by the number of bone fragments and their position. The fracture occurs when force is applied to the bone in an amount greater than it can support. This may be direct force as in a blow, a twisting force, or repeated pounding on the same bone. The amount of force required to cause a fracture depends on the composition and strength of the bone.

All fractures are described with terms from each of 5 different categories: location of the bone in the body (anatomic location), direction of the fracture lines (transverse, oblique, spiral, comminuted, or impacted) the relation of the bone pieces to each other (alignment and apposition), the stability of the fracture and the amount of soft tissue damage around the fracture (simple or closed, compound or open, complicated, uncomplicated).

The muscles attached to the bones often pull the fracture fragments out of position, especially if the muscles go into spasm. This can change the status of a fracture from one where the fragments are in position (nondisplaced) to one with fragments that have shifted (displaced).

Risk for fracture is increased when individuals are exposed to falls, objects falling on them, twisting of extremities, or crushing injuries. With increased age, the risk of fracture increases as bones become more brittle and susceptible to breaking. Large bones require more force or duration of stress to fail (fracture). High risk activities include those with high velocity or high impact.

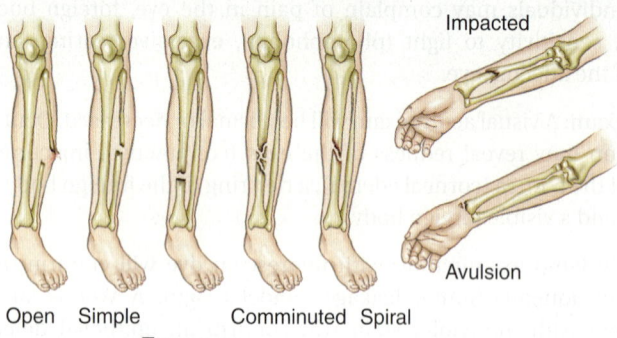

Open, Simple, Transverse, Comminuted, Spiral, Impacted, Avulsion

Laurie O'Keefe

Diagnosis

History: Fractures are either the result of a traumatic event or repeated stress to an area. Individuals will describe an injury such as a fall or an object falling on them. Pounding on an area over and over can cause a break (stress fracture); for example, marching or running. These individuals may not remember a specific injury. Individuals may have obviously misshapen (deformed) bones, swelling, pain and/or lack of feeling (decreased sensation) near the area. The ability to use an injured body part does not exclude a fracture. Individuals should be questioned about previous injuries.

Physical exam: Visual examination may be diagnostic because of the amount of deformity. Touching the area (palpation) reveals pain or tenderness over the area. There may be decreased sensation beyond the fracture. Swelling and bruising (ecchymosis) is usually present. Joint looseness (laxity) and changes in range of motion may be evident.

Tests: Plain x-rays are used to determine the severity of the fracture and position of the fragments. X-rays include the joint above and below the injury site. Subtle (occult) fractures may not be apparent on x-ray exam for up to 2 weeks after time of fracture. CT scans and/or MRI may be needed to further define the fracture and its effect on surrounding joints. EMG and angiography can be required to evaluate damage to nerves and vessels. A bone scan may show a subtle fracture not easily recognized on plain x-rays.

Treatment

If the bone fragment ends are in adequate position to allow for healing to occur, protective rest (immobilization) may be all that is needed. The device used for immobilization may range from a sling, to a brace, to a cast. Measures to decrease swelling and pain include ice, elevation, and medication.

Fractures that are not in correct position (alignment) will require repositioning (reduction). This may be accomplished with gentle pressure to the bones after pain relief has been gained (closed reduction). If this maneuver is not successful or not desirable, surgery may be indicated to realign the bone fragments (open reduction). Fractures that change position (unstable) will often require that metal implants (fixation devices) be inserted into the fragments to hold them in correct position. The material used is known as "hardware" and could be wire, screws, pins, rods, or plates (open reduction, internal fixation, or ORIF), or external fixation devices (external fixator.)

Bone fragments that protrude through the skin, even if they slip back into place (compound fracture), need to be treated in the operating room. The wound will require cleaning and treatment. Reduction of this type of fracture is a surgical procedure (open treatment of open fracture). These individuals require antibiotic therapy, perhaps for several weeks.

Joints that have been dislocated and fractured may require surgical repair of the supporting structures as well as treatment of the fracture. Injuries that result in the pulling away of tendons from the bone (avulsion fracture) are sometimes treated surgically to reattach the bone fragment and, therefore, the tendon. This is common in injuries to the fingers and ankle. The process of bone healing may be stimulated or accelerated with electromagnetic coils applied over the skin or placed over the fracture during surgery. Some fractures can also be treated with ultrasound to accelerate healing.

Pain over an area with a high incidence of occult fractures may be treated with a protective splint or cast and reexamined in 2 weeks. This is common in the wrist (scaphoid or navicular bone) and foot. Fractures can occur because of diseases that affect the strength of the bone or the protective structures around it (pathological fractures, fractures of bone tumors).

Prognosis

Simple, uncomplicated fractures usually heal in 6-12 or more weeks without loss of function. Any increase in severity of the fracture or added complications will delay recovery for weeks to months and may compromise function. While the fracture may heal, damage to the surrounding structures could result in poor function of an extremity and less than optimum outcome.

Differential Diagnosis

Dislocated joints may appear to be fractures. Swelling in a localized area could appear to be a fracture. This is not uncommon in individuals with rheumatoid arthritis or other inflammatory diseases. Pathological fractures are still fractures, but the underlying disease must be evaluated as well.

Specialists

• Orthopedic Surgeon	• Physiatrist

Rehabilitation

See specific fracture for rehabilitation.

Work Restrictions / Accommodations

Individuals will require some kind of immobilizing device, which could present safety hazards to themselves or coworkers. Assistive devices for walking such as crutches and canes need to be used only on dry, hard surfaces, and these will decrease manual dexterity. Individuals will need frequent rest periods and an area to elevate the injured extremity, perhaps even a cot or bed, during the early weeks of treatment. Access to ice is advisable.

There may be extensive physical and/or occupational therapy appointments to facilitate optimum results. Work release time is usually needed for these visits. Occupational therapy work site evaluation of safety issues and work feasibility will be beneficial in situations that seem challenging to the individual and/or employer. Medication use for control of pain and swelling is probable during the first weeks of treatment. If use is allowed during work time, safety issues need to be addressed and well as drug testing policies.

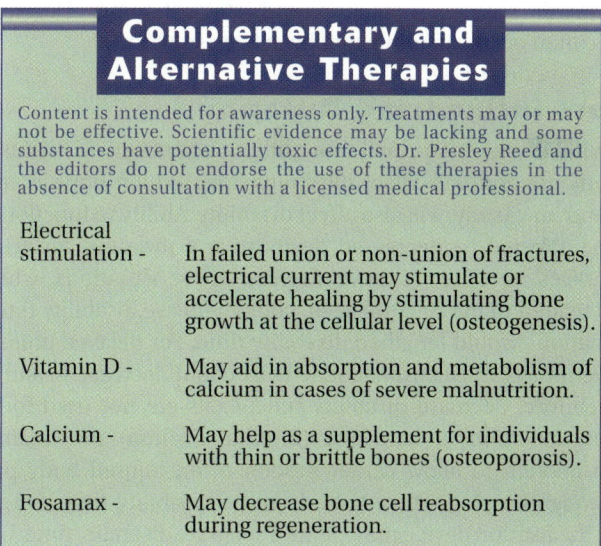

Complementary and Alternative Therapies

Content is intended for awareness only. Treatments may or may not be effective. Scientific evidence may be lacking and some substances have potentially toxic effects. Dr. Presley Reed and the editors do not endorse the use of these therapies in the absence of consultation with a licensed medical professional.

Electrical stimulation -	In failed union or non-union of fractures, electrical current may stimulate or accelerate healing by stimulating bone growth at the cellular level (osteogenesis).
Vitamin D -	May aid in absorption and metabolism of calcium in cases of severe malnutrition.
Calcium -	May help as a supplement for individuals with thin or brittle bones (osteoporosis).
Fosamax -	May decrease bone cell reabsorption during regeneration.

Comorbid Conditions

Any chronic medical condition that compromises skin and bone healing would lengthen disability from fractures. This would include such conditions as diabetes, peripheral vascular disease, inflammatory diseases, osteoporosis, or malnutrition. Smoking and obesity have a negative impact on bone healing, as does inactivity. Infection would delay healing and prolong recovery. Associated injuries such as tendon lacerations and compartment syndrome would also delay recovery.

Complications

Serious and life-threatening complications can occur to other parts of the body from material released into the bloodstream at the time of fracture. These include injury to the lungs (emboli of fat or blood), blood vessels (vein thrombosis, compartment syndrome) and infection. Fat embolism, an occasional complication of long bone fractures, can occur as a result of bone marrow releasing fat into the veins following a fracture. This fat can lodge in the lungs where it obstructs blood flow or pass into the arteries where it can cause central nervous system changes. Fat embolism occurs 12-48 hours following fracture and is capable of producing a wide range of symptoms. These include fever, increased heart rate and breathing, blood-tinged sputum, cyanosis, anxiety, restlessness, altered level of consciousness, convulsions, coma, and rash. Fat embolism is rare but may occur with tibial or femoral shaft fractures. Damage to any of the structures near the fracture such as blood vessels, nerves or ligaments will complicate treatment and adversely effect the outcome. Complex regional pain syndrome (RSD) is an example of these problems.

Infection in either the bone (osteomyelitis), joint, or in the soft tissues requires treatment, and can delay healing. Fractures that have been successfully reduced may later shift out of position. This is especially true of fractures around the wrist. Stiffening of joints (contracture) or damage resulting in looseness of the joint (laxity) prolongs treatment. Coexisting trauma that would delay treatment of the fracture can complicate healing.

Cigarette smoking delays bone healing, as does any other problem with blood or oxygen circulation. Noncompliance with treatment (such as removing protective devices) results in motion across the fracture, which prevents or delays healing (nonunion or delayed union). Weakening of the bone from disuse (osteopenia) and weak (atrophied) muscles will require protection and strengthening. Degenerative arthritis often occurs in joints that have been injured.

Factors Influencing Duration

Dominant versus non-dominant side, weightbearing status, and treatment method will affect disability time. Which bone is broken, where and how badly, will also affect disability. Ability to function safely could be affected by decreased dexterity and the need for crutches, casts, braces, or other assistive devices. These situations, while not directly related to the fracture itself, could increase disability time. Any complications would lengthen disability time. For delayed unions, the implementation of electromagnetic coils could decrease healing time and, therefore, decrease disability time. Coils are not used for acute fractures. Insertion of hardware (internal fixation) may stabilize a fracture enough to allow earlier motion of an injured body part, or earlier weightbearing. This could decrease disability time. Surgery to remove the fixation device may create a separate disability time, but this is usually brief.

Length of Disability

Failure of the bone to heal (malunion or nonunion) would prolong recovery and may create a permanent disability. Duration depends on specific bone, where the fracture occurred within the bone, and the severity of the fracture.

Femur (thigh).

Duration in Days

Job Classification	Minimum	Optimum	Maximum
Sedentary work	14	28	84
Light work	18	42	182
Medium work	119	182	224
Heavy work	161	224	273
Very Heavy work	182	273	Indefinite

Mandible (lower jaw).

Duration in Days

Job Classification	Minimum	Optimum	Maximum
Sedentary work	7	21	42
Light work	7	21	42
Medium work	7	21	42
Heavy work	7	21	42
Very Heavy work	7	21	42

Maxilla (upper jaw).

Duration in Days

Job Classification	Minimum	Optimum	Maximum
Sedentary work	7	14	42
Light work	7	14	42
Medium work	7	14	42
Heavy work	7	14	42
Very Heavy work	7	14	42

Nose.

Duration in Days

Job Classification	Minimum	Optimum	Maximum
Sedentary work	1	3	7
Light work	1	3	7
Medium work	1	4	7
Heavy work	1	7	14
Very Heavy work	1	7	14

Patella (kneecap).

Duration in Days

Job Classification	Minimum	Optimum	Maximum
Sedentary work	7	14	28
Light work	14	21	42
Medium work	14	28	56
Heavy work	21	56	91
Very Heavy work	28	84	112

Scapula (shoulder blade).

Job Classification	Duration in Days		
	Minimum	Optimum	Maximum
Sedentary work	3	14	21
Light work	7	14	28
Medium work	14	28	42
Heavy work	28	42	56
Very Heavy work	42	56	70

Failure to Recover

If an individual fails to recover within the maximum duration expectancy period, the reader may wish to reference the following questions to assist in better understanding the specifics of an individual's medical case.

Regarding diagnosis:

- Were symptoms of a fracture (pain, obvious deformity, swelling, loss of strength and motion) noted on the initial exam?
- Was the diagnosis of fracture confirmed with x-ray? If not, were a follow-up x-ray or bone scan done to rule out a subtle fracture?
- Was the possibility of joint dislocation ruled out?

Regarding treatment:

- Was treatment appropriate to type and location of fracture?
- Would individual benefit from a consultation with a specialist (orthopedic surgeon, hand surgeon, foot surgeon)?
- Was open reduction and internal fixation required? What is the expected outcome?

Regarding prognosis:

- Based on the type of treatment required has adequate time elapsed for recovery (6-12 weeks)?
- Did the individual experience any complications that may impact recovery (i.e., fat emboli, DVT, compartment syndrome or infection)?
- Has individual followed prescribed rehabilitative therapy?
- If the recovery has been longer than expected, has the individual be re-examined to rule out the possibility of a malunion or nonunion?
- Does individual have an underlying condition (diabetes, vascular disease, inflammatory disease, osteoporosis, or malnutrition) or associated injury (tendon laceration, compartment syndrome) that may impact recovery?

References

Rockwood and Green's Fractures in Adults. Rockwood, Charles A., David P. Green, and Robert Bucholz, eds. Philadelphia: Lippincott, Williams & Wilkins, 1998.

Simon, Robert R., MD, and Steven Koenigsknecht, MD. Emergency Orthopedics: The Extremities, 3rd ed. Stamford: Appleton & Lange, 1996.

Fracture, Ankle

Other names / synonyms: Ankle Fracture, Bimalleolar Fracture, Broken Ankle, Fracture of the Lateral Malleolus, Fracture of the Medial Malleolus, Fracture of the Posterior Malleolus, Lateral Malleolus Fracture, Malleolar Fracture, Medial Malleolus Fracture, Posterior Malleolar Fracture, Trimalleolar Fracture

824, 824.0, 824.1, 824.2, 824.3, 824.4, 824.5, 824.6, 824.7, 824.8, 824.9

Definition

Fractures of the ankle describe injury to the medial and posterior tibia or the lateral fibula. Ankle fractures occur most commonly when the ankle rolls in or out, and are the result of force on the foot rotating or impacting against the talus and transmitting to the tibia and fibula. The direction of this force is known as the mechanism of injury. Any type of ankle fracture can be displaced or nondisplaced. A displaced fracture has separation of the fractured bone segments, while a nondisplaced ankle fracture is a crack in the bone without separation. Any type of ankle fracture can affect the joint surface and joint motion (articulation) and almost always involves ligament injuries.

Ankle fractures are often associated with dislocations of the joint. Although the ankle joint is composed of three bones (tibia, fibula, and talus), fractures of the talus are not included in the diagnosis "ankle fracture." The protruding areas on the sides of the ankle are the most commonly injured areas. The prominence on the inside of the ankle is called the medial malleolus and is part of the tibia, while the prominence on the outside of the ankle is called the lateral malleolus and is part of the fibula. The posterior lip of the tibia lies under the Achilles tendon and is not easily felt. It is called the posterior malleolus. When this is fractured, the injury is known as the trimalleolar fracture.

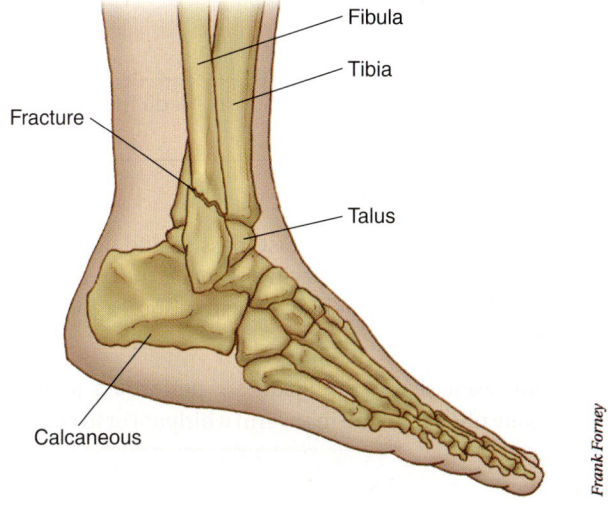

Fracture, Ankle

Diagnosis

History: Ankle fractures usually occur as a result of a traumatic event such as a fall with a twisting motion about the ankle. The ankle will be swollen, painful, and often discolored. The ability to bear weight will be limited.

Physical exam: Swelling, bruising (ecchymosis), deformity, and loss of motion will be noted. Using the fingers to feel the ankle (palpation) usually pinpoints the area of fracture. Ligamentous stability must be tested as pain allows. Neurovascular examination of the foot and ankle must be included.

Tests: Routine plain ankle x-rays followed by stress views, if indicated, will assess stability. Occasionally, a CT or MRI may be ordered to evaluate joint surface changes and fracture position. Postreduction and follow-up x-rays will be necessary.

Treatment

If the fracture is not displaced, treatment with cast or brace (immobilization) is usually sufficient. If the fracture is displaced, restoring the fracture to its normal position is necessary by either closed reduction or open reduction with internal fixation (ORIF). Stability of the fracture after reduction is critical in order to maintain ankle motion and prevent complications such as degenerative arthritis. Because joint stability is dependent on both bone position and ligament support, any injured ligament must be treated along with the reduction of the fracture so that ankle stability can be restored. Postreduction immobilization is necessary to maintain this stability while healing occurs. Weight-bearing is restricted for a period of time based on the type of fracture, stability, and bone healing. Early mobilization of the joint while maintaining reduction of the fracture should begin as soon as possible.

Prognosis

An ankle fracture that heals in perfect alignment usually leaves little or no impairment. Some individuals, however, may be left with traumatic arthritis of the ankle joint, continued pain, or a tendency for recurrent ankle sprains. If the weight-bearing surface of the tibia was fractured, post traumatic arthritis is much more likely.

Differential Diagnosis

Conditions that present with similar findings include ankle sprain, Achilles tendon rupture, and dislocation of the talus.

Specialists

- Orthopedic Surgeon
- Podiatrist
- Sports Medicine Physician

Rehabilitation

If immobilization is required with a cast, passive and active range-of-motion exercises of the ankle joint begin as soon as the cast is removed. If no cast is used, these exercises should begin as soon as possible after fracture reduction.

Range-of-motion exercises to the ankle are performed as tolerated. These exercises are often initiated in a warm whirlpool or in conjunction with another form of heat treatment, and continued until all movement is restored.

In this early phase of strengthening, isometric exercises begin with contraction of the muscles around the ankle joint without any movement at the joint.

The next phase of rehabilitation involves movement at the joint called isotonic exercise. An example of this rehabilitation exercise is the use of weights and elastic bands for ankle strengthening. As the resistance is lifted or pulled throughout the range of motion, the muscle shortens and lengthens. Strength training of this type will also include weight equipment and machines.

Work Restrictions / Accommodations

Restrictions and accommodations include limited or no weight-bearing for several weeks; use of crutches, canes, walker, or wheelchair; and limited standing, stair climbing, or walking. Use of medications for pain control and inflammation will require review of drug policies. Rest periods may be necessary to allow for elevation of the foot and lower leg.

Comorbid Conditions

Coexisting conditions that might impact recovery and further lengthen disability include obesity, diabetes mellitus, peripheral vascular disease, generalized arthritis, any neurologic disease causing loss of sensation to the foot and ankle, malnutrition, osteoporosis, deconditioning due to advanced age, and other injuries sustained with the ankle fracture such as spinal compression fractures.

Complications

Complications may include tendon subluxation or disruption, wound infection, injury to the nerves and vessels in the area, nonunion of the fracture, ankle joint instability, degenerative arthritis, complex regional pain syndrome (RSD), and calcification of the ligaments. Delay in surgical treatment of a complex fracture or ligament injury can lead to a higher complication rate.

Factors Influencing Duration

Factors that might influence the length of disability include the individual's age, general health, severity of the fracture, concomitant ligament injury, amount of weight-bearing allowed, response to treatment, and job requirements. Early mobilization of the ankle joint hastens recovery.

Length of Disability

Bimalleolar. Closed.

Duration in Days

Job Classification	Minimum	Optimum	Maximum
Sedentary work	7	14	42
Light work	14	21	56
Medium work	42	70	112
Heavy work	56	112	168
Very Heavy work	70	112	168

Lateral malleolus.

Duration in Days

Job Classification	Minimum	Optimum	Maximum
Sedentary work	7	14	42
Light work	14	28	56
Medium work	28	56	84
Heavy work	42	84	112
Very Heavy work	42	112	168

Reduction of Fracture, ankle (open) with or without internal fixation.

Duration in Days

Job Classification	Minimum	Optimum	Maximum
Sedentary work	14	28	42
Light work	56	70	84
Medium work	70	84	98
Heavy work	84	98	112
Very Heavy work	84	98	112

Reduction of Fracture, ankle (closed).

Duration in Days

Job Classification	Minimum	Optimum	Maximum
Sedentary work	1	7	14
Light work	7	14	28
Medium work	21	42	70
Heavy work	70	77	84
Very Heavy work	84	98	112

Trimalleolar.

Duration in Days

Job Classification	Minimum	Optimum	Maximum
Sedentary work	14	28	42
Light work	84	91	112
Medium work	112	119	140
Heavy work	140	154	168
Very Heavy work	140	154	252

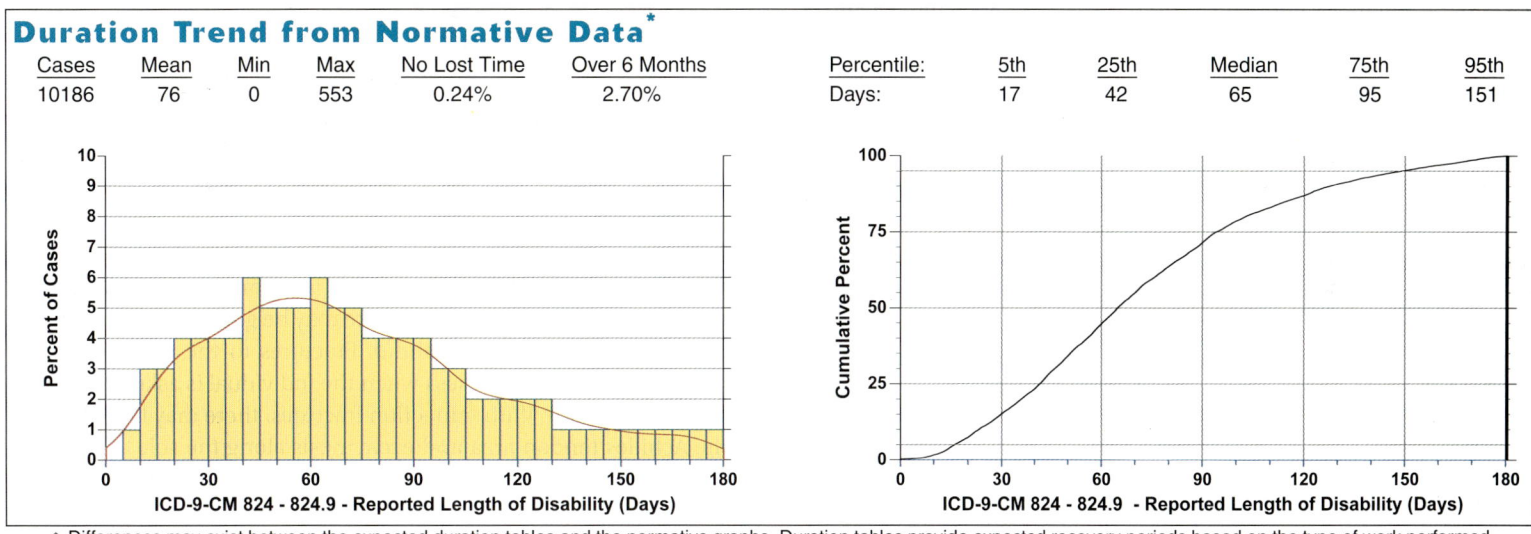

Duration Trend from Normative Data*

Cases	Mean	Min	Max	No Lost Time	Over 6 Months
10186	76	0	553	0.24%	2.70%

Percentile:	5th	25th	Median	75th	95th
Days:	17	42	65	95	151

* Differences may exist between the expected duration tables and the normative graphs. Duration tables provide expected recovery periods based on the type of work performed by the individual. The normative graphs reflect the actual observed experience of many individuals across the spectrum of physical conditions, in a variety of industries, and with varying levels of case management.

Failure to Recover

If an individual fails to recover within the maximum duration expectancy period, the reader may wish to reference the following questions to assist in better understanding the specifics of an individual's medical case.

Regarding diagnosis:

- Was the individual's joint also dislocated?
- Was the weight bearing surface of the tibia (plafond) also fractured?
- Was the fracture displaced? Was closed or open reduction done?
- Does the post operative x-ray show "anatomic" or perfect position of the fracture pieces or part of the fracture still out of position?
- Has the individual had routine ankle x-rays followed by stress views?
- Has the individual had a CT scan or MRI?
- Were post-reduction x-rays done? Follow-up x-rays?
- Are there loose bodies within the joint?

Regarding treatment:

- Was the fracture non-displaced? Was the joint immobilized? Was ORIF done?

Fracture, Ankle

- Were other injuries also repaired? Is the joint immobilized?
- Is the individual non-weight bearing?

Regarding prognosis:

- Has the individual started an exercise program at the appropriate time?
- Is the individual actively involved in physical therapy to strengthen the ankle?
- Does the individual have any conditions that may affect ability to recover?
- Does the individual have any complications?

References

Chapman, Michael W. "Fractures and Fracture-dislocations of the Ankle." Surgery of the Foot and Ankle, 6th ed, vol 2. Mann, Roger A., and Michael J. Coughlin, eds. St. Louis: Mosby, 1993. 1439-1464.

Malone, Terry R., Thomas McPoil, and Arthur J. Nitz. Orthopedic and Sports Physical Therapy. St. Louis: Mosby, 1997.

Fracture, Calcaneus

Other names / synonyms: Calcaneal Fracture, Calcaneus Fracture, Heel Fracture

825.0, 825.1

Definition

A fracture of the calcaneus is a breakage (fracture) of the heel (calcaneus), which is the largest bone in the foot.

Calcaneus fractures can occur from a direct blow to the sole of the foot (plantar surface) resulting from traumas such as a fall from a height or a motor vehicle accident. As a result, calcaneus fractures are often associated with other injuries. A significant number of fractures of the calcaneus result in disruption of the joint surface between the calcaneus and ankle bone (talus).

Calcaneal fractures are classified by their location, either through the body of the bone or of the prominence on the sides. They are further defined by the amount of disruption of the joint surface and amount of bone fragment movement away from the normal positioning (displacement).

Individuals who are at risk for calcaneus fracture are those who participate in sports who have the potential for falling from a height, such as pole-vaulting, high-jumping, gymnastics, or skating. Also at risk are individuals whose work involves jumping down from a height such as construction workers, warehouse workers, truck loaders, and agricultural workers.

Calcaneus fractures account for 10% of all fractures in the foot. Men are 5 times more than women likely to sustain a calcaneus fracture. Calcaneus fractures occur most frequently in individuals between the ages of 30-50 years.

Diagnosis

History: Individuals may describe a traumatic event such as a fall or jump onto the heel. There may be pain, swelling, and discoloration around the foot and ankle. Individuals are often unable to bear weight on the injured foot. Individuals may complain of lower back pain, as up to 10% of individuals with calcaneus fracture also sustain compression fractures of the lower (lumbar) spine.

Physical exam: Swelling and bruising (ecchymosis) are noted around the ankle. An open wound may be present, especially if the injury was sustained during a motor vehicle accident. Feeling with the hands (palpation) would reveal pain over the calcaneal protuberances (tuber-

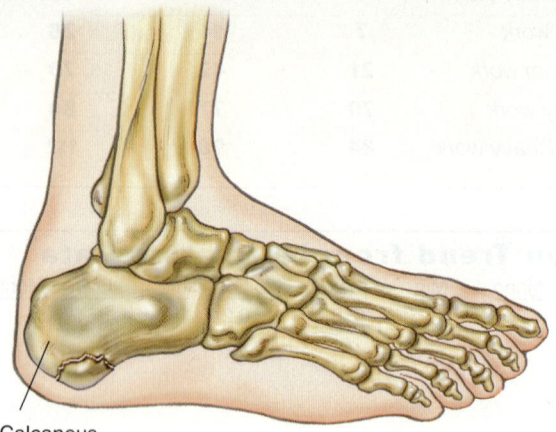
Calcaneus

osities) or the hindfoot. Deformity of the hindfoot, such as shortening, widening, or crookedness (angulation) is common. Blisters may be present along the foot and ankle. There may be good ankle motion, but extremes of motion will be painful. Fractures to the rear (posterior) tuberosity may cause weakness when the individual is asked to point a toe (plantar flexion). With impaction fractures, there may be deformity in the Achilles tendon area and ecchymosis along the sole of the foot. Examination of the spine and lower legs is necessary to rule out injury to these areas.

Tests: Multiple angle plain x-rays are ordered first, followed by CT and MRI scan to evaluate joint surface integrity and position of fracture fragments.

Treatment

Calcaneus fractures with a skin wound are cleaned (irrigation and debridement) and the individual is treated with intravenous antibiotics. Fractures that are not displaced or located away from the joint (extra-articular) are managed conservatively by application of a cast or compression dressing. Unstable and/or displaced fractures are treated surgically (open reduction and internal fixation) using screws and/or plates to stabilize the bone fragments. A bone graft may be necessary to fill in bone defects resulting from fragments having been crushed. A soft compressive dressing may be applied for 5-7 days to control swelling before open reduction is attempted.

Fractures associated with significant soft tissue damage may be treated by closed reduction in which the stabilizing screws or pins are inserted through the skin (percutaneous osteosynthesis). As an alternative, external fixators are sometimes used. These procedures are usually performed within 48 hours of injury. Antibiotics and analgesics are prescribed as needed. Weight bearing on the heel should be avoided for 6-8 weeks. Full weight bearing is usually permitted after 3 months.

Prognosis

Conservative treatment of fractures that do not involve the joint surface and are not displaced (which accounts for only about 25% of calcaneal fractures) usually results in a positive outcome.

The prognosis for chronic pain and stiffness is worse if the calcaneus heals with significant deformity (widening) and if the fracture involves the subtalar joint.

Operative treatment (open or closed reduction) of displaced fractures has a good to excellent outcome in 61-85% of the cases. The success rate decreases as the number of bone fragments increases. For example, only 9% of individuals with 4 or more calcaneus bone fragments have a good to excellent outcome. The success rate is poor for fractures in which the calcaneus is broken into many small pieces (comminuted fracture). Early heel joint motion is critical for eventual function.

Differential Diagnosis

A dislocation or severe sprain of the ankle joint could have similar symptoms.

Specialists

- Orthopedic Surgeon
- Physical Therapist
- Sports Medicine Physician

Rehabilitation

Physical therapy may be helpful for recovery from calcaneal fracture. Hot packs and ultrasound decrease pain and stiffness prior to therapy sessions. Cold packs may decrease pain and swelling.

Regaining flexibility is crucial to rehabilitation. Physical therapists may stretch the injured foot and ankle and perform joint mobilizations to further increase range of motion. Individuals learn to perform stretches at home such as placing a towel under the ball of the foot and pulling to stretch the Achilles tendon. Active flexibility exercises such as making circular motions with the foot or writing the alphabet with the toes also stretch the injured ankle.

Strengthening exercises improve function. Therapists may manually resist the foot as an individual plantarflexes, dorsiflexes, inverts, and everts the foot. Elastic tubing with progressively increasing resistances can be used to strengthen the ankle in these motions as well. Standing heel and toe raises can be performed while standing on both feet or while standing on the injured foot.

Balance exercises may be helpful. Individuals can start with single leg standing on the injured foot. This can be progressed to walking on a gymnastic mat without wearing shoes and standing on the injured leg while throwing and catching a ball. Individuals can also perform dynamic balance exercises such as running laterally or skipping.

Work Restrictions / Accommodations

Work restrictions and accommodations may include no weight bearing for 6-8 weeks, along with use of crutches, walker, or wheelchair. These restrictions will interfere with manual dexterity and the ability to climb stairs, stand for long periods of time, walk long distances, and drive a car or other motor vehicle. The ability to maneuver in small or congested areas may also be affected. Frequent rest periods, including the ability to elevate the affected leg, will be necessary.

Comorbid Conditions

Osteoporosis, obesity, diabetes, peripheral vascular disease, and other injuries (lacerations, damage to ligaments or cartilage) sustained during the traumatic event may influence the length of disability.

Complications

Nerve entrapment and peroneal tendon dislocation or entrapment can occur with the fracture. Severe degenerative arthritis, stiffness of the calcaneus and talus (subtalar) joint, chronic pain, fracture blisters, pressure sores, and infection leading to skin loss are possible complications of the injury and treatment. With displaced fractures, the bone fragments may align incorrectly (malunion) or fail to join (nonunion). Pressure from swelling or bleeding can result in compartment syndrome, which can cause permanent muscle and nerve damage. Injuries to the foot can cause the toes to stiffen into nonfunctional positions (contractures). A decreased blood supply can lead to tissue breakdown (avascular necrosis), which can result in the collapse of the foot bone (talus) that connects to the lower leg bones. With heel fractures, there is a very high incidence of an associated injury to the spine and forearm (the "lovers triad") as well as injuries to the ligaments and cartilage of the foot. Fracture of the ankle, thighbone (femur), and elbow are also common concomitant injuries.

Factors Influencing Duration

The type of fracture, amount of joint surface disrupted, treatment required, complication rate, and amount of weight bearing required for job activities may affect disability.

Length of Disability

Duration of disability depends on job requirements and whether job duties can be performed in a seated position. Heavy work is not usually compatible with intra-articular fracture of the calcaneal body and disability may be permanent.

Anterior process.

Duration in Days

Job Classification	Minimum	Optimum	Maximum
Sedentary work	1	3	7
Light work	1	3	7
Medium work	14	42	70
Heavy work	56	84	112
Very Heavy work	56	84	112

Calcaneal body, intra-articular.

Job Classification	Duration in Days			
	Minimum	Optimum	Maximum
Sedentary work	14	21	28
Light work	56	63	70
Medium work	84	98	112
Heavy work	112	168	Indefinite
Very Heavy work	168	252	Indefinite

Reduction of Fracture, calcaneus (closed).

Job Classification	Duration in Days			
	Minimum	Optimum	Maximum
Sedentary work	14	21	28
Light work	42	56	70
Medium work	84	98	112
Heavy work	112	140	168
Very Heavy work	168	168	252

Sustenaculum tali.

Job Classification	Duration in Days			
	Minimum	Optimum	Maximum
Sedentary work	1	2	3
Light work	2	3	4
Medium work	7	14	21
Heavy work	42	56	84
Very Heavy work	42	56	112

Tuberosity (horizontal fracture).

Job Classification	Duration in Days			
	Minimum	Optimum	Maximum
Sedentary work	7	9	14
Light work	42	56	63
Medium work	56	70	84
Heavy work	84	98	168
Very Heavy work	168	252	Indefinite

Tuberosity (vertical fracture).

Job Classification	Duration in Days			
	Minimum	Optimum	Maximum
Sedentary work	3	14	7
Light work	14	21	28
Medium work	28	35	84
Heavy work	56	70	168
Very Heavy work	56	70	224

Failure to Recover

If an individual fails to recover within the maximum duration expectancy period, the reader may wish to reference the following questions to assist in better understanding the specifics of an individual's medical case.

Regarding diagnosis:

- Has diagnosis of fractured calcaneus been confirmed?
- Has individual experienced any complications?
- Have plain x-rays been taken during the recovery phase?
- Does the individual have intense pain associated with the foot and lower leg indicating compartment syndrome?
- Does the individual experience heel pain during or after physical activity?
- Does individual smoke? Does individual have poor blood circulation to the legs?

Regarding treatment:

- Was a displaced fracture treated without surgery?
- Have complications occurred?
- What treatment options are now being considered?
- Was the displaced fracture managed soon after the injury occurred?
- Was surgery performed? What type? Was surgery performed within 48 hours?
- Was individual too active or weight bearing too soon? What are the consequences?

Regarding prognosis:

- Has nonunion occurred in an individual who also suffers from malalignment, bone loss, and/or infection?
- How severe are the symptoms? Are they incapacitating?
- Can the individual walk with use of a cane or crutches?
- Can the individual perform the normal activities of daily life?

References

Apley, A. Graham, and Louis Solomon. "Injuries of the Lower Limb." Concise System of Orthopaedics and Fractures. Oxford: Butterworth-Heinemann Ltd, 1994. 317-344.

Borrelli, Joseph, and Robert Dunbar. "Fractures of the Calcaneus and Talus." Clinical Orthopaedics. Craig, Edward, ed. Philadelphia: Lippincott, Williams & Wilkins, 1999. 920-936.

Kisner, Carolyn, and Lynn Allen Colby. Therapeutic Exercise: Foundations and Techniques, 2nd ed. Philadelphia: F.A. Davis, 1990.

Trafton, Peter. "Lower-extremity Fractures and Dislocations." Trauma. Mattox, Kenneth, David Feliciano, and Ernest Moore, eds. New York: McGraw-Hill, 2000. 981-1009.

Fracture, Carpal Bones

Other names / synonyms: Broken Wrist, Fractured Wrist, Wrist Fracture

814, 814.0, 814.00, 814.01, 814.02, 814.03, 814.04, 814.05, 814.06, 814.07, 814.08, 814.09, 814.1, 814.10, 814.11, 814.12, 814.13, 814.14, 814.15, 814.16, 814.17, 814.18, 814.19

Definition

A carpal fracture is a break of one of the eight small bones of the wrist (carpus), which are the scaphoid, lunate, capitate, triquetrum, hamate, pisiform, trapezium, and trapezoid.

Fractures of a carpal bone usually do not involve a break in the skin (closed fracture). Carpal fractures may be either stable or unstable. The fragments can be out of the normal positioning (displaced) or in normal alignment (nondisplaced). Carpal fractures can occur with or without joint dislocation. Nondisplaced fractures are the most common.

The usual cause is a fall onto the outstretched hand. Other causes include a motor vehicle accident (when the individual straightens the arm for protection before an impact), collisions between sports participants, or a sudden blow to the palm by a baseball bat or golf club. Stress fractures of the carpal bones can occur in individuals suffering from repetitive trauma such as those who use a jackhammer.

The specific carpal bone that is fractured depends on the position of the hand at impact and the exact forces exerted on the hand. Use of golf clubs, bats, or racquets in sports can fracture the hooked portion of the hamate bone. The scaphoid is the most frequently fractured carpal bone, accounting for two-thirds of all carpal fractures. Scaphoid fractures are the most disabling, require more prolonged treatment (with the possibility of surgery), and are more prone to complications than fractures of the other carpal bones.

The triquetrum is the second most common carpal fracture. Individuals at risk for sustaining a carpal fracture include athletes, laborers, and those whose activity places them at risk for repetitive hand or wrist trauma (e.g., use of a jackhammer and gymnasts). Carpal fractures are fairly common injuries in athletes.

Half of scaphoid fractures occur in males under age 30 but they occur in all age groups, usually in the dominant hand.

Diagnosis

History: The individual reports a trauma, most commonly a fall onto the hand that is immediately followed by wrist pain. The individual may experience decreased grip strength or pain while moving the wrist.

Physical exam: Swelling and localized tenderness over the fracture may be evident. Pain caused by pinching the thumb or pressing the triangular depression at the outer side of the wrist (anatomical snuff box) are characteristic of a fractured scaphoid bone. Deformity of the wrist may be seen. Range of motion in the wrist is limited with pain at the extremes of motion. Instability of the wrist can be demonstrated by several stress tests. Numbness and weakness may occur in the distribution of the median nerve on the palm side of the thumb and the index and long fingers.

Tests: Plain x-rays can diagnose most carpal fractures but must be taken carefully. Special views may be required for some of the carpals, but despite careful attention, a carpal fracture can easily be missed or diagnosed late. A repeat plain x-ray taken 1 to 2 weeks after injury may

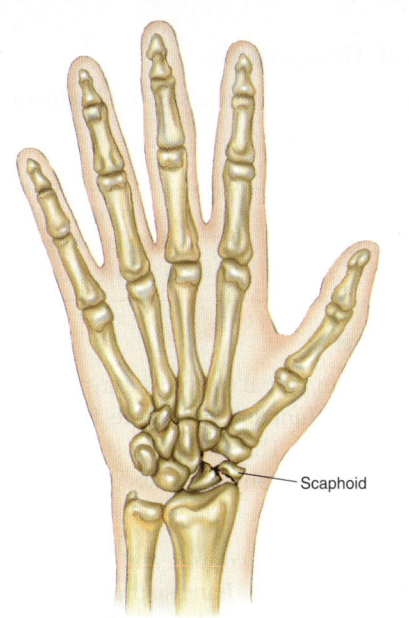

detect a subtle scaphoid fracture not visible on x-rays taken on the day of injury. Stress x-rays can demonstrate an unstable fracture.

Occasionally other tests such as tomograms, MRI, CT, or a bone scan are needed if pain persists and plain x-rays remain normal.

Treatment

Treatment of nondisplaced fractures usually consists of immobilization of the wrist in a cast extending from proximal forearm to just above the knuckles, leaving the thumb and fingers free to move. However, if the scaphoid bone is involved, the cast often extends above the elbow for the first 6 weeks, and also incorporates the thumb. Follow-up x-rays will be needed to monitor healing and detect any displacement of the fracture (loss of the reduction). The wrist may be immobilized for up to 3 or 4 months.

Displaced and unstable fractures often require surgery (open reduction) to ensure proper healing and restoration of function. It is usually an open procedure (arthrotomy) but some surgeons prefer to reduce wrist fractures arthroscopically. Surgery may involve external or internal fixation with pins, wires, screws, or plates, especially if there is also a fracture of the outer lower forearm bone (distal radius) extending into the wrist joint. The hardware may need to be removed at a later date.

A bone graft may be done when the bone is broken into many pieces (comminuted fracture) with bone loss especially if the joint with the thumb is involved. When fracture healing is delayed (delayed union) or has failed (nonunion) electromagnetic bone stimulation may be used. Bone grafting may also be done for nonunion. Other late surgery, for post-traumatic arthritis or avascular necrosis, may involve fusion (arthrodesis) or removal of several wrist bones (proximal row carpectomy).

Prognosis

Most (95%) of scaphoid fractures heal satisfactorily even with delayed diagnosis and treatment. Lunate fractures are rare but usually heal. Fractures of the other carpals have a generally satisfactory outcome. Surgical treatment of carpal fractures has a favorable outcome. Nonunion, avascular necrosis, or posttraumatic arthritis of a carpal fracture may lead to permanent disability.

Differential Diagnosis

Acute pain in the wrist may be the result of a ligament tear (sprain).

Specialists

- Hand Surgeon
- Orthopedic Surgeon
- Physiatrist
- Physical Therapist
- Plastic Surgeon
- Sports Medicine Physician

Rehabilitation

Individuals who sustain carpal fractures may require rehabilitation to regain hand and wrist function. Once the fractured wrist is healed, outpatient therapy begins. The individual should be seen by either an occupational therapist or a physical therapist who is a certified hand therapist.

Therapy first addresses pain control and the reduction of swelling. Individuals learn to position the hand so that it rests above the elbow on a pillow. This position helps decrease swelling in the hand. Hot packs and hot paraffin wax decrease joint stiffness prior to therapy. Therapists may perform scar massage to promote healing and scar mobility over any surgical site. Ice packs decrease pain and swelling after exercise.

Stretching techniques are necessary to increase range of motion at the wrist and forearm. Therapists may passively stretch the wrist to increase flexion and extension and the forearm to increase rotation. Individuals learn to stretch the wrist by holding the elbow straight and using their other hand to help bend the wrist into flexion and extension. Individuals stretch the forearm by placing their other hand on the forearm and using it to help turn the forearm in the two rotational directions.

Strengthening exercises are necessary to restore function and prevent reinjury. Individuals may use light hand weights to strengthen wrist flexion and extension and forearm rotation while placing the forearm on a table for support. Individuals also squeeze therapy putty to restore hand strength. Exercises such as turning a doorknob or pages in a book increase the function of the wrist and forearm.

Work Restrictions / Accommodations

Any use of the injured arm is very limited while the wrist is immobilized. The individual is temporarily unable to lift and carry heavy or bulky objects, operate equipment, drive a motor vehicle, or perform other tasks that require use of both hands. If the dominant arm or hand is affected, the individual may be unable to write legibly or type well. Likewise, carpal fracture in the dominant hand affects fine motor skills such as those needed to work in a laboratory or on an assembly line. Therefore, individuals whose dominant arm or hand is affected may require a temporary or permanent reassignment of duties. After the cast or splint is removed, work may have to be temporarily modified to allow for stiffness, weakness, and lack of endurance in the hand and shoulder.

Complementary and Alternative Therapies

Content is intended for awareness only. Treatments may or may not be effective. Scientific evidence may be lacking and some substances have potentially toxic effects. Dr. Presley Reed and the editors do not endorse the use of these therapies in the absence of consultation with a licensed medical professional.

Cryotherapy - After cast is removed, frequent ice massages or ice packs may decrease pain and swelling.

Heat therapy - After cast is removed, hot packs and hot paraffin wax may decrease joint stiffness.

Massage - Scar massage may promote healing and scar mobility over any surgical site.

Comorbid Conditions

Osteoarthritis, rheumatoid arthritis, and other injuries to the wrist, hand, or arm can increase the length of disability.

Complications

Incorrect alignment (malunion), nonunion (especially the scaphoid), delayed union, and collapse of the bone (avascular necrosis) can occur. For example, the scaphoid has a 10% rate of nonunion as well as frequent malunion. The hamate fracture is hard to see on x-ray and can show no x-ray changes until much later when it is more difficult to treat. Fracture of the lunate can lead to Kienböck's disease where the bone becomes soft and granular and breaks into pieces (fragments).

Joint pain, stiffness, limitation in wrist movement, and weakness of grip can persist. There can be wrist instability and posttraumatic arthritis especially if there is also an associated fracture of the radius. As a late complication, posttraumatic arthritis can damage the tendons to the fingers with the possibility of tendon rupture.

A median nerve injury can result from excessive flexion of the wrist in a cast, by direct injury, stretching, or compression from bleeding. Carpal tunnel syndrome can occur. Pressure on the local blood vessels from swelling while wearing a cast can result in compartment syndrome that can cause permanent muscle and nerve damage and persistent clawing of the fingers. Shoulder stiffness and pain can develop if the arm stays immobile in a sling after the injury (shoulder-hand syndrome). Complex regional pain syndrome (RSD) is a serious complication with potential long-term disability.

Factors Influencing Duration

The severity of the fracture, any complications, and whether the dominant hand or nondominant hand was injured influence the length of disability.

Length of Disability

Duration depends on job requirements and the bone involved. Disability is longer when job duties require use of both hands for heavy work. The forearm and hand may be in a cast for six to twelve weeks. If one-handed work is available for sedentary and light work, individuals may be able to return to work sooner. Medium to very heavy work requires that the bone is healed on x-ray and the extremity is rehabilitated.

Duration in Days

Job Classification	Minimum	Optimum	Maximum
Sedentary work	3	7	14
Light work	3	14	28
Medium work	28	84	119
Heavy work	42	147	182
Very Heavy work	42	182	182

Failure to Recover

If an individual fails to recover within the maximum duration expectancy period, the reader may wish to reference the following questions to assist in better understanding the specifics of an individual's medical case.

Regarding diagnosis:

- Did the individual present with a sudden onset of pain in the wrist?
- Has diagnosis of carpal fracture been confirmed through plain x-rays?
- If a fracture was not visible on plain x-ray films, were repeat films taken 1 to 2 weeks later? Were at least four different views taken?
- If plain x-rays were negative for carpal fracture even though the symptoms strongly suggested a fracture, were MRI, CT, or bone scans conducted?
- Does individual have an underlying condition (i.e., osteoarthritis, RA or other associated injuries) that may impact recovery?

Regarding treatment:

- Was the fracture nondisplaced? If so, was closed reduction and immobilization indicated?
- Has the fracture not healed even after 3 to 4 months of immobilization in a cast?
- Were follow-up x-rays done to monitor healing?
- Does the individual have a delayed union or nonunion?
- Has the individual experienced any complications related to fracture or treatment of fracture (malunion, nonunion, avascular necrosis, nerve injury, etc)? If so, have the complications been addressed in the treatment plan?
- Did surgery involve external or internal fixation with pins, wire, screws, or plates?
- Will the hardware need to be removed at a later date?
- Was bone graft required?

Regarding prognosis:

- Does the individual have an established nonunion from a previous, undiagnosed injury that was aggravated by a recent injury?
- Does the individual have a nonunion of the carpal fracture despite appropriate treatment and adequate time for healing?
- Has avascular necrosis occurred?
- Is individual now a candidate for surgical intervention?
- Has the individual experienced any long-term sequelae (nerve injury, regional pain syndrome) from the fracture that be potentially disabling?

References

Adams, John, and David Hamblen. "Wrist and Hand." Outline of Fractures: Including Joint Injuries. Adams, John, and David Hamblen, eds. Edinburgh: Churchill Livingstone, 1999. 177-194.

Apley, A. Graham, and Louis Solomon. "Injuries of the Upper Limb." Concise System of Orthopaedics and Fractures. Oxford: Butterworth-Heinemann Ltd, 1994. 270-298.

Griffith, H. Winter, MD. Complete Guide to Sports Injuries. New York: The Berkley Publishing Group, 1997.

Kisner, Carolyn, and Lynn Allen Colby. Therapeutic Exercise: Foundations and Techniques, 2nd ed. Philadelphia: F.A. Davis, 1990.

Pruitt, Donald. "Fractures and Dislocations of the Wrist." Handbook of Fractures. Perry, Clayton, and John Elstrom, eds. New York: McGraw-Hill, 2000. 160-173.

Salter, Robert. "Specific Fractures and Joint Injuries in Adults." Textbook of Disorders and Injuries of the Musculoskeletal System. Baltimore: Williams & Wilkins, 1999. 561-655.

Fracture, Cervical Spine (With or Without Spinal Cord Injury)

Other names / synonyms: Broken Neck, Upper Spine Fracture

805.0, 805.00, 805.01, 805.02, 805.03, 805.04, 805.05, 805.06, 805.07, 805.08, 805.1, 805.10, 805.11, 805.12, 805.13, 805.14, 805.15, 805.16, 805.17, 805.18, 806.0, 806.00, 806.01, 806.02, 806.03, 806.04, 806.05, 806.06, 806.07, 806.08, 806.09, 806.1, 806.10, 806.11, 806.12, 806.13, 806.14, 806.15, 806.16, 806.17, 806.18, 806.19

Definition

Fracture of the cervical spine is a fracture of one or more of the seven connected bones (vertebrae) in the neck (cervical) region. Cervical spine and spinal cord injuries are primarily the result of traumatic injuries to the head and neck. The most frequent injuries result from vehicle collisions, diving into shallow water, and gunshot wounds to the neck. Neurological injury occurs in 40% of individuals with fracture at the cervical level. The further the fracture is up the spine, the more function the individual is likely to lose. When the spinal cord has been injured, the difference between an individual losing function in legs (becoming a paraplegic) and losing function in arms and legs (becoming quadriplegic) depends on which vertebrae was fractured. An individual with an unstable fracture is at risk for spinal cord injury unless the fracture is stabilized.

Spinal cord injuries occur in approximately 12,000 to 15,000 individuals a year in the US. According to a Pennsylvania study of 111,219 individuals entering US trauma centers, overall incidence of all types of cervical spinal injury was 4.3%, cervical spinal injury without spinal cord injury was 3.0%, spinal cord injury without fracture was 0.70%, and delayed diagnosis of all types of cervical spinal injury was 0.01%. Another study of 5,021 individuals consecutively admitted to a US trauma center determined that 2% had cervical spine injury with spinal cord injuries. A Swedish study found that cervical spine fracture leads to earlier death in individuals over 65.

Neurologic injury from cervical spine fracture does decrease predicted life expectancy, with more severe paralysis and higher level fracture predicting the greatest decreases in life expectancy.

Diagnosis

History: Fracture or dislocation of the cervical spine is suspected in any individual who complains of pain in the neck area following an injury. Careful history is recorded regarding the nature of the accident. Individuals may report being thrown from a vehicle and striking the head. At the time of the accident, the individual may already show signs of paralysis. Individuals who lose function in all four limbs (quadriplegia) may initially move hands or feet briefly following the injury. This is important for the diagnosis and prognosis of neurological injury. There may also be a history or previous episodes of cervical spine disease such as injuries, paralysis, weakness, spondylosis, or seizures.

Physical exam: A neurosurgeon or orthopedic spine surgeon must examine the individual frequently in the days after the injury. The neurologist will determine which limbs and other parts of the body are unresponsive to stimuli and whether function is likely to return.

Tests: X-rays, CT, and complex-motion tomographic studies (TOMOS) will determine the site and extent of the fracture. MRI is also usually obtained.

Treatment

Because neurological damage often occurs after the injury and the extent of damage to the spinal cord is not fully determined, individuals with broken necks and neurologic deficit are generally administered massive doses of steroids to facilitate neurological recovery as soon as possible after injury (within 4 hours). Management of acute cervical spine injuries with neurologic deficit consists of bed-based skeletal traction until all non-neurological injuries are evaluated. Early application of a whole body apparatus to restrict movement (halo body vest) provides immediate cervical stabilization and facilitates the diagnostic work up and treatment of individuals with multiple injuries.

It is imperative to realign the bony fragments in the cervical spine and reduce the joint dislocation as quickly as possible. This can be done using skeletal traction, a halo body vest, and/or operative internal stabilization for unstable fractures. Pain relievers (analgesics) may be given.

Prognosis

The prognosis for individuals with cervical spine fracture ranges from never using any limbs again (quadriplegia) to recovering completely after the fracture heals, depending on whether there is a spinal cord injury. The outcome for an individual with lost limb function depends greatly on the cause of the cervical spine fracture and spinal cord injury.

Partial spinal cord injuries usually demonstrate some degree of neurologic improvement over time, unlike injuries with immediate, complete and persisting loss of function below the level of injury.

Differential Diagnosis

Fracture of the upper thoracic spine may present with similar symptoms.

Specialists

- Neurologist
- Neurosurgeon
- Occupational Therapist
- Orthopedic Surgeon
- Physiatrist
- Physical Therapist
- Spine Surgeon

Rehabilitation

Rehabilitation of a fracture to the cervical spine depends on fracture type, whether there is an associated spinal cord injury, and the individual's age and general health. In a cervical spine fracture without a spinal cord injury, fractures are classed as stable or unstable, and those are treated differently.

It is not uncommon for the individual to also have the cervical spine immobilized with a cervical collar or a halo brace for 6 to 12 weeks to reduce unwanted movement of the healing vertebrae. Immobilization of the fracture site can be either external (outside of the body) or internal (within the body by the use of surgical hardware attached directly to the vertebra). The primary goal of immobilization whether external or internal fixation is to reduce movement of the fracture site long enough for healing to initiate and progress. Once the fracture is stable, individuals with fractures of the cervical spine without spinal cord injury require outpatient physical therapy.

Treatments involving cold or heat help control pain. Heat treatment may include ultrasound where high frequency sound waves produce heat that penetrates deep into the involved muscles.

Electrical stimulation, such as T.E.N.S., combined with heat or cold treatment is a technique used in physical therapy to relax muscles around the dislocated joint.

Once the fracture has healed by x-ray studies, it is necessary to restore range of motion at the neck. Physical therapists may passively stretch the neck into rotation, side bending, flexion, and rotation. Individuals learn to actively move the neck in each of these directions to further increase motion. Individuals can increase the stretch in the neck by applying manual overpressure as the neck is moved in each of these directions.

Exercises helpful in improving stability around the fracture site begin with isometric exercises. This form of straightening helps strengthen the muscles of the neck without moving the neck through the range of motion. In these exercises, the individual uses one hand for light resistance while the neck is moved into each available direction.

Strengthening of the upper extremities begins slowly by addressing endurance with low resistance and high repetitions then progresses to focus more on strengthening by fewer repetitions and heavier resistance. Because of the various degrees of myelopathy affecting the involved cervical and/or upper extremity muscles, some restrictions may be placed on the progression of the range of motion and strengthening.

If an individual sustains a spinal cord injury with a cervical spine fracture, there is a lengthy rehabilitation process. Physical therapists stretch all of an individual's joints to maintain flexibility and prevent the joints from contracture. If the individual's respiratory system is affected by the injury, respiratory therapists teach deep breathing exercises and perform chest percussions to keep the lungs clear of mucus. Respiratory therapists also routinely assess individuals on ventilators to determine continued need for assisted breathing.

Achieving independence in self-care is the primary goal of occupational therapists. As rehabilitation progresses, occupational therapists assess an individual's potential for self-care and work with the physical therapist to increase general strength and improve sitting tolerance and balance. Occupational therapists teach dressing, grooming, and feeding techniques to individuals with cervical fractures of C5 and below. Individuals with fractures above C5 cannot perform self-care because of the effect the injury has on the nerves important for upper limb movement.

Both occupational and physical therapists develop strengthening exercises for any arm muscles that have movement and a flexibility program initiated for all joints. Family members are instructed in these specific exercises.

Once individuals are medically stable, they are transferred to a rehabilitation hospital for several months. Therapy lasts for several hours each day. Special equipment can increase the independence of individuals with spinal cord injuries. Physical and occupational therapists order and fit wheelchairs with a specific seat cushion system that maintains correct posture and sitting balance. Occupational therapists utilize adaptive equipment to progress with self-care such as special utensils with thick handles to allow for a better grasp.

Physical therapists teach individuals and their families strategies for rolling and transferring to and from the bed, the wheelchair, shower, and the car. Slight changes in position made while sitting in a wheelchair are taught to prevent skin breakdown. Rehabilitation also includes speech therapy that helps increase the volume of speech for all individuals and sets up communicating strategies for ventilator-dependent individuals.

Work Restrictions / Accommodations

For a quadriplegic individual to return to work, the job must not require the use of any of the four limbs and must be voice-activated wheelchair-accessible. Individuals will need time off for follow-up visits to physicians and therapists. For the individual with a fracture without a spinal cord injury, he or she will not be able to lift or stretch until the fracture heals (sedentary or light work), and will need time off for visits to physicians and therapists. The individual may take medications for pain so should not operate heavy machinery or fly airplanes until the fracture heals.

Comorbid Conditions

Comorbid conditions that slow full recovery include osteoporosis, diabetes, previous neurological damage, heart disease, bone cancer, and other advanced cancers.

Complications

Complications include infection after open fractures or open reduction, nerve damage in displaced fractures or fracture dislocations, and bone healing with faulty alignment (malunion). If the spinal cord is damaged, additional complications from paraplegia or quadriplegia include pneumonia, recurring urinary infections, decubitus ulcers, nephrolithiasis, and osteoporosis.

Factors Influencing Duration

The most important factors that determine the long-term functional results after injuries in the cervical spine include the level of trauma to the vertebrae, whether the individual sustained additional trauma to the rest of the body, position of the affected vertebrae, if the fracture is stable or unstable, individual's health (excellent or poor) at the time of trauma, and, most importantly, the severity of the initial neurological deficit. The nature of an individual's work, age, complications from the injury, and stability of the fracture will also influence the length of disability.

Length of Disability

Fractures that heal with significant deformity may be incompatible with heavy or very heavy work. Spinal cord injury, even with partial neurologic recovery, usually precludes moderate and heavy work, so disability may be permanent for heavy work. The US Social Security Administration's criteria for permanent and total disability due to spinal cord injury are "significant and persistent disorganization of motor function in two extremities, resulting in sustained disturbance of gross and dexterous movements or station and gait."

Closed, without spinal cord injury. Stable fracture.

Duration in Days

Job Classification	Minimum	Optimum	Maximum
Sedentary work	3	14	21
Light work	5	21	28
Medium work	28	56	91
Heavy work	42	91	119
Very Heavy work	42	119	182

Open or closed, with spinal cord injury.

Duration in Days

Job Classification	Minimum	Optimum	Maximum
Sedentary work	119	182	Indefinite
Light work	119	182	Indefinite
Medium work	Indefinite	Indefinite	Indefinite
Heavy work	Indefinite	Indefinite	Indefinite
Very Heavy work	Indefinite	Indefinite	Indefinite

Failure to Recover

If an individual fails to recover within the maximum duration expectancy period, the reader may wish to reference the following questions to assist in better understanding the specifics of an individual's medical case.

Regarding diagnosis:

- What level in the neck did the injury occur?
- Does the individual have a stable fracture? An unstable fracture?
- What was the mechanism of injury?
- Did the individual show any signs of paralysis right away?
- Was the onset of paralysis delayed?
- Does the individual have any history of previous injuries, paralysis, weakness or spondylosis?
- Does the individual have a history of seizures?
- Has the individual been examined frequently by a neurologist?
- Has the individual had x-rays, CT scan and TOMOS?
- Has other neurological testing been done? Controlled diagnostic blocks?
- Have conditions with similar symptoms been ruled out?

Regarding treatment:

- Was the individual given massive doses of steroids within 4 hours of the injury?
- Was the individual's cervical spine stabilized with a halo body vest? With a whole body apparatus?
- Were any bony fragments realigned as quickly as possible?
- Was any joint dislocation realigned as quickly as possible?
- Did the individual have a spinal cord injury?

Regarding prognosis:

- Has the physical therapist shown the individual how to do range of motion exercises? Has the individual incorporated them into their home exercise program?
- Is the individual on a ventilator?
- Is the respiratory therapist involved in the care?
- Is the occupational therapist working with physical therapy to maximize the individual's recovery?
- Is a speech therapist on the treatment team?
- Is there a psychologist or psychiatrist on the treatment team?
- Does the individual have any conditions that may affect their ability to recover?
- Has the individual had any complications such as infection, nerve damage, malunion, paraplegia, quadriplegia or pneumonia?

References

Apley, A. Graham, and Louis Solomon. "Injuries of the Spine, Thorax, and Pelvis." Concise System of Orthopaedics and Fractures. Apley, A. Graham, and Louis Solomon, eds. Oxford: Butterworth-Heinemann Ltd, 1994. 299-316.

Kisner, Carolyn, and Lynn Allen Colby. Therapeutic Exercise: Foundations and Techniques, 2nd ed. Philadelphia: F.A. Davis, 1990.

Scully, Rosemary M., and Marylou R. Barnes. Physical Therapy. Philadelphia: J.B. Lippincott Company, 1989.

Somers, Martha Freeman. Spinal Cord Injury: Functional Rehabilitation. East Norwalk: Appleton & Lange, 1992.

Fracture, Clavicle

Other names / synonyms: Broken Collarbone, Clavicle Fracture, Collarbone Fracture

810

Definition

Fracture of the collarbone (clavicle) can occur when force or stress is applied to the upper chest.

The clavicle is a round, slightly "s"-shaped bone that rests across the top of the chest. One end attaches to the breastbone (sternum), the other attaches to the acromion, which is part of the shoulder blade (scapula). The clavicle supports the arm, transmitting forces from the arm to the central skeleton. The ligaments connecting the clavicle to the sternum and scapula are very strong. Therefore, the clavicle is rarely dislocated but frequently broken.

Most fractures of the clavicle result from a direct blow, a fall onto the shoulder, or a fall on the outstretched arm. Because of its "s" shape, the clavicle is vulnerable to fracture, especially near the curves. Fractures are classified by the position along the bone and also by the amount of separation (displacement) between the bone fragments. Fracture of the middle third segment (Grade 1 fracture) accounts for 80% of all clavicle fractures, and those of the lateral third (Grade 2 fracture) or medial third (Grade 3 fracture) account for 15% and 5%, respectively. Most fractures of the clavicle are uncomplicated. Damage to nerves (brachial plexus) or blood vessels can occur, but is uncommon. Because the clavicle provides suspension of the shoulder to the trunk, an injury to the clavicle can be thought of as an injury to the entire shoulder area. The clavicle is one of the most frequently broken bones, and accounts for 5-10% of all skeletal injuries. Individuals at risk for a clavicle fracture are those who participate in contact sports such as football, wrestling, softball, baseball, and boxing.

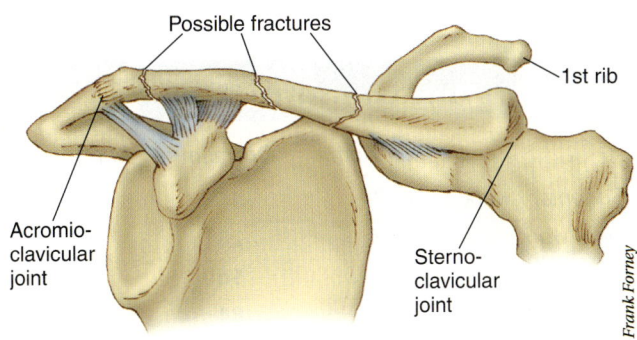

Diagnosis

History: The individual may report a recent injury, usually a fall or blow. Symptoms may include pain and local swelling. The affected arm may feel numb and be immobile. The affected shoulder may droop or fall forward. Holding the injured shoulder rigid may cause muscle spasm and additional pain across the upper shoulder and neck.

Physical exam: Swelling and pain around the site are usually present. The affected shoulder may slope downward and forward from loss of support. Bruising (ecchymosis) may be noted around the fracture site. Movement and strength of the shoulders may be impaired. The location of the fracture may be detected by feeling with the hands (palpation). Because major blood vessels (subclavian) and nerves (brachial plexus) lie under the clavicle, a neurovascular evaluation is routine.

Tests: Plain x-rays of the clavicle or upper chest usually are adequate to determine the location and severity of the fracture. In the case of severe trauma, a chest film may also be required. Electromyography (EMG), which measures the electrical activity of muscles, may be warranted to rule out nerve damage. If injury to a major blood vessel is suspected, angiography or venography may be done to assess the damage.

Treatment

Most fractures can be treated conservatively through the use of a figure-8 harness for 4-6 weeks. The straps wrap around the arms and can cause skin irritation and breakdown, so the individual and family need to be instructed in proper use of the harness and in skin care. Many fractures are treated just as well with a sling.

If the broken bone ends have become separated or are in an abnormal position (displaced fracture), the bones need to be restored to their normal position (reduction). The reduction does not have to be exact. Reduction can usually be accomplished without surgery (closed reduction) by manipulation and use of a figure-8 harness.

Severely displaced fractures, which are difficult to reposition by closed methods, may require surgical intervention (open reduction) and internal fixation with pins, screws, and/or plates.

Fractures of the tip of the clavicle nearest the shoulder (distal end) are treated like a shoulder (acromioclavicular) joint separation or sprain. This is usually accomplished by immobilization through the use of braces or a sling. Often, however, surgery (arthroplasty) is recommended to reduce the fracture and repair the joint.

Fractures near the breastbone (sternum) are treated with comfort measures, such as a sling for support, after a thorough examination for more extensive trauma to the chest area. This type of fracture is fairly uncommon. Treatment for all types of fracture usually includes cold therapy (ice), analgesics, and education in proper posture. Electromagnetic current or ultrasonic pulse may be utilized for fractures that are not healing (nonunion) but are not as effective as bone grafting and internal fixation.

Prognosis

Whether treated conservatively or by open or closed reduction, clavicle fractures have an excellent outcome. Most fractures heal within 6-8 weeks without complications or residual disability. Fractures in the middle one-third of the clavicle have a higher risk of not healing (nonunion). Fractures that involve the shoulder (acromioclavicular) joint have a risk of developing degenerative arthritis.

Differential Diagnosis

Before x-ray verification, shoulder (acromioclavicular) joint dislocation or sprain may be very difficult to differentiate from a distal clavicle fracture. The two injuries may occur at the same time. Dislocation at the sternum (sternoclavicular) without a fracture is rare, but could mimic a clavicle fracture near the sternum. Other possibilities include rotator cuff injury, rib fracture, and an accumulation of air in the space surrounding the lung (pneumothorax).

Specialists

- Orthopedic Surgeon
- Physical Therapist

Rehabilitation

Individuals who sustain a clavicle fracture may benefit from outpatient physical therapy. Individuals first learn pain control. Hot packs are applied to the shoulder prior to therapy to relax the shoulder musculature. Individuals also learn pendulum exercises for pain control in which an individual bends over to let the injured arm dangle and circles it slowly in a clockwise and then counter-clockwise motion. Ice packs should be applied to the shoulder for 15 minutes after exercise to reduce pain and swelling.

Range of motion is restored through a series of stretching exercises. Individuals perform wand exercises in which a stick is grasped by both hands and the non-injured arm assists the injured shoulder into flexion, abduction, extension, and external rotation. Individuals stretch the shoulder into internal rotation by clasping the hand of the injured shoulder behind the back with the other hand. The non-injured hand assists in moving the other hand up the lower back.

Strengthening exercises are necessary to restore shoulder function. The injured shoulder is moved into flexion, abduction, extension, internal rotation, and external rotation while the hand grasps resistive tubing. Individuals perform push-ups in a standing position against a wall.

Work Restrictions / Accommodations

Restrictions include no lifting, carrying, or overhead work for a few weeks after the fracture has healed. Activities of both arms may be restricted if a harness or sling is used to maintain proper posture and fracture alignment. The individual with a clavicle fracture may be temporarily unable to write legibly, type well, perform activities that require fine motor skills such as those needed to work in a laboratory or on an assembly line, operate equipment, and operate a car or other motor vehicle. The union may not be strong enough for 16-24 weeks to allow lifting heavy weights above the shoulder. When comfortable, the arm can be used at waist height without any weight. Ice packs and rest periods may be necessary to control swelling and numbness of the arm during the first 1-2 weeks. Elevated worktables to use while standing may allow earlier return to work. Work site visits by an occupational therapist may identify other accommodations or restrictions.

Comorbid Conditions

Osteoporosis and other injuries (e.g., other fractures, damage to ligaments or cartilage) sustained during the traumatic event may influence the length of disability.

Complementary and Alternative Therapies

Content is intended for awareness only. Treatments may or may not be effective. Scientific evidence may be lacking and some substances have potentially toxic effects. Dr. Presley Reed and the editors do not endorse the use of these therapies in the absence of consultation with a licensed medical professional.

Electromagnetic current - Said to promote healing in fractures that are not healing (nonunion).

Ultrasonic pulse - Said to promote healing in fractures that are not healing (nonunion). These therapies, however, are not considered as effective as bone grafting and internal fixation.

Complications

In a fracture, damage can also occur to the underlying nerves (brachial plexus) and subclavian blood vessels or to the ligaments around the acromioclavicular joint. Incorrect fusion (malunion) or failure of the bone ends to fuse together (nonunion) can result from inadequate reduction or the failure to maintain reduction of a displaced fracture. Malunion can cause a large bony deformity that may compress adjacent blood vessels or nerves (brachial plexus) resulting in thoracic outlet syndrome.

Factors Influencing Duration

Factors include the degree of displacement, the presence or absence of damage to adjacent blood vessels or nerves (brachial plexus), whether reduction was closed or open, whether the dominant or non-dominant side is involved, and the individual's job requirements.

Length of Disability

Duration depends on job requirements.

Duration in Days

Job Classification	Minimum	Optimum	Maximum
Sedentary work	7	14	28
Light work	14	28	42
Medium work	21	56	84
Heavy work	28	84	112
Very Heavy work	28	84	182

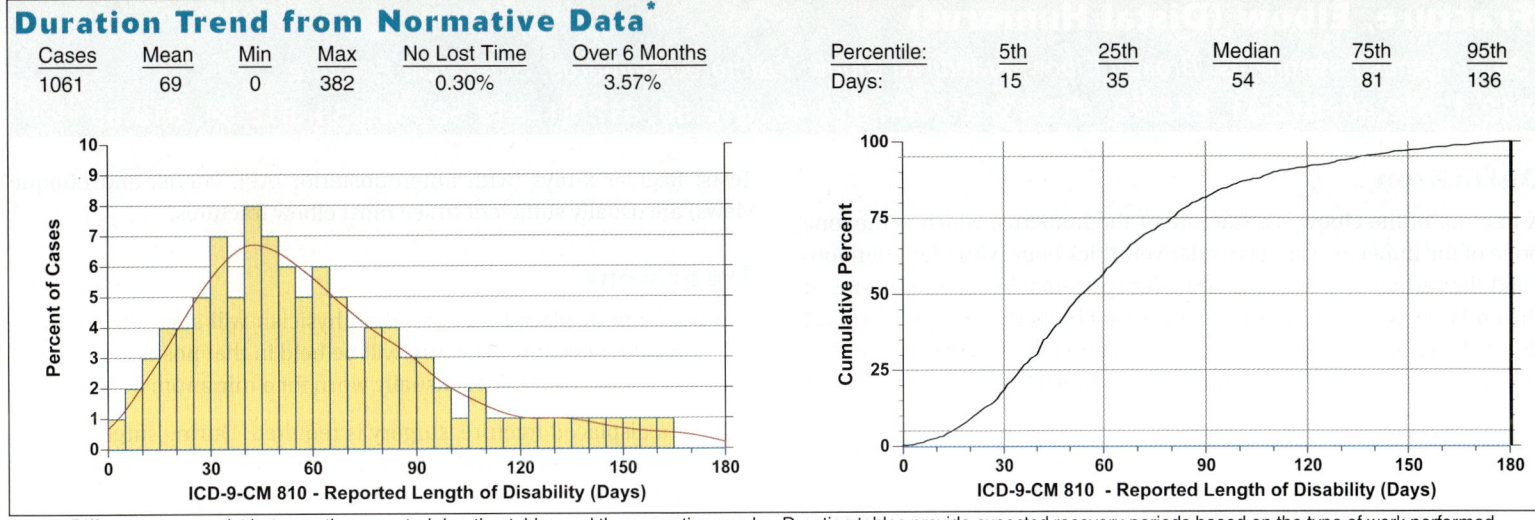

Failure to Recover

If an individual fails to recover within the maximum duration expectancy period, the reader may wish to reference the following questions to assist in better understanding the specifics of an individual's medical case.

Regarding diagnosis:

- Has the individual experienced a direct blow to the shoulder, a fall onto the shoulder, or a fall on the outstretched arm?
- Does the individual report pain and local swelling?
- Does the affected arm feel numb or have a sensation of burning or prickling (paresthesia)?
- Is the arm immobile?
- Does the affected shoulder droop or fall forward?
- Does the individual report that holding the injured shoulder rigid causes muscle spasm and additional pain across the upper shoulder and neck?
- Were plain x-rays of the clavicle or chest done?
- Was electromyography (EMG) done to rule out nerve damage?

Regarding treatment:

- Was conservative treatment, through the use of a figure-8 harness for 4-6 weeks, sufficient to resolve the fracture?
- Were the broken bone ends separated or in an abnormal position (displaced fracture), requiring restoration to their normal position without surgery (closed reduction)?
- If the fracture was severely displaced, was surgical intervention (open reduction) and internal fixation with pins, screws, and/or plates required?
- Was surgery successful? Did the individual experience any post-surgical complications?
- Was joint repair (arthroplasty) also required?
- Were cold therapy (ice), analgesics, and education in proper posture given?
- Did the individual participate in a physical therapy regimen?

Regarding prognosis:

- What was the location and extent of the fracture and associated injuries?
- Did the individual require conservative treatment, open reduction, or closed reduction of the fracture?
- Was the fracture in the middle one-third of the clavicle, causing a higher risk for not healing (nonunion)?
- Did individual receive comprehensive rehabilitation? Would individual benefit from additional therapy?
- Are any underlying injuries or illnesses affecting recovery?
- How severe are the symptoms? Are they incapacitating?
- Can the individual perform tasks using the unaffected arm?
- Can the individual perform activities of daily life?

References

Apley, A. Graham, and Louis Solomon. "Injuries of the Upper Limb." Concise System of Orthopaedics and Fractures. Apley, A. Graham, and Louis Solomon, eds. Oxford: Butterworth-Heinemann Ltd., 1994. 270-298.

Kisner, Carolyn, and Lynn Allen Colby. Therapeutic Exercise: Foundations and Techniques, 2nd ed. Philadelphia: F.A. Davis, 1990.

Fracture, Elbow (Distal Humerus)

Other names / synonyms: Broken Elbow, Fractured Elbow, Fractured Humerus, Sideswipe Fracture

812.4, 812.40, 812.41, 812.42, 812.43, 812.44, 812.49, 812.50, 812.51, 812.52, 812.53, 812.54, 812.59

Definition

A fracture of the elbow is a fracture of the humerus, which is the long bone of the upper arm, and is a relatively thick bone with a large smooth head that articulates with the shoulder (proximal head) and bumps at the end that articulates at the elbow (distal humerus). These bumps at the distal end of the humerus are called condyles (medial epicondyle and lateral epicondyle). The condyles are attachment sites for muscles that move the forearm.

Fractures to the distal humerus usually involve both condyles. There may be damage to the humerus, the elbow joint, and to soft tissue around the fracture site (e.g., nerves, tendons, ligaments, and blood vessels). Fractures can be categorized in several ways. Perhaps the most useful distinction for fractures is between nondisplaced and displaced fractures. Nondisplaced fractures are less severe, and the fracture does not separate. Displaced fractures may involve both condyles and the surface of the elbow joint. The bone fragments separate completely and need to be rejoined.

Fractures of the distal humerus are relatively uncommon, accounting for only 2% of fractures in adults.

Fractures of the distal humerus are most often the result of a fall or direct blow onto the back of the upper arm when the elbow is flexed.

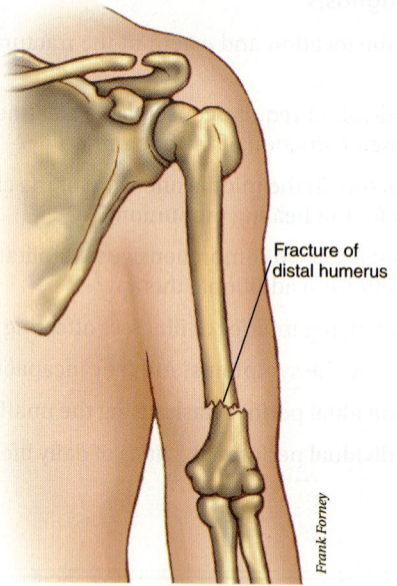
Fracture of distal humerus

Diagnosis

History: Most individuals will relate a history of either direct elbow trauma or a fall onto an outstretched hand. Individuals may complain of pain, swelling, and decreased range of motion.

Physical exam: Upon examination, the individual is unable to fully extend the elbow, and pain increases with pronation/supination of the hand. Swelling and bruising (edema and ecchymosis) may be evident around the elbow.

Tests: Regular x-rays (with anteroposterior [AP], lateral, and oblique views) are usually sufficient to see most elbow fractures.

Treatment

To treat a nondisplaced fracture, the physician will align the arm in a proper healing position. The arm will be held in that position by a hard posterior splint. The splint is usually worn for a minimum of 10 days.

To treat a displaced fracture, surgery is required. During surgery (open reduction and internal fixation), the bone fragments will be internally stabilized with plates or a combination of wires, pins, and screws. General anesthesia will be used.

For both nondisplaced and displaced fractures, analgesia will be prescribed for pain control. The individual will be instructed to keep the injured arm elevated in order to reduce or control swelling.

When the sling and cast are removed, prior to starting rehabilitation exercises, the arm may initially be treated with rest, ice, compression, and elevation.

Prognosis

The distal humerus usually fractures only during severe trauma. Even the best surgical repairs can lead to stiffness and traumatic arthritis. Regardless of treatment, there is usually some decrease in range of motion but without any accompanying functional deficit.

Differential Diagnosis

Other conditions that may present with similar findings include elbow dislocations, forearm fractures, proximal humerus fractures, severe bone bruises of the bones of the elbow, and bursitis.

Rehabilitation

Individuals who sustain fractures of the distal humerus may require outpatient physical therapy. Therapy initially addresses the reduction of pain and swelling. Individuals are taught to position the hand above the elbow on pillows to reduce swelling in the hand. Hot packs applied to the shoulder and elbow relax the musculature of the arm. Ice packs reduce pain and swelling at the shoulder and elbow and are applied for 15 minutes after exercising.

Restoration of range of motion is the second goal of physical therapy. Therapists may passively stretch the shoulder and elbow to restore any limited range of motion. Individuals can stretch the shoulder into internal rotation by clasping the hand of the injured shoulder behind the back with the other hand. The noninjured hand assists in moving the other hand up the lower back. Elbow flexion and extension are increased with the use of overpressure of the noninjured hand to help bend and extend the elbow.

Strengthening exercises restore elbow and shoulder function. The injured shoulder is moved into flexion, abduction, extension, internal rotation, and external rotation while the hand grasps resistive tubing. Biceps curls and triceps kickbacks with light hand weights increase elbow flexion and extension strength.

Work Restrictions / Accommodations

Soon after a fracture, ice packs and a place to rest and elevate the arm may be required. Breaks and rest may be necessary every 2 hours or as pain and swelling dictate. There may be a decreased range of motion in the elbow and lifting or carrying assignments may need to be reduced or temporarily eliminated.

In a best-case scenario, individuals with fractures of their nondominant arm that did not require surgery could return to work (modified duty) in 1-2 weeks. Individuals with more severe fractures requiring surgery and/or fractures involving the dominant arm will require longer periods of work restrictions, depending on the individual's situation. If use of pain medication is allowed while working, modification of any drug testing policies may be necessary.

Specialists

- Neurologist
- Orthopedic Surgeon
- Physiatrist
- Sports Medicine Physician
- Vascular Surgeon

Comorbid Conditions

Conditions that could impact ability to recover and further lengthen disability include arthritis, bursitis, osteoporosis, and tumors affecting the elbow joint.

Complications

Fractures that are immobilized for prolonged periods of time may result in permanent decreased range of motion. Distal humerus fracture may lead to muscle ischemia and permanent muscle contracture, a form of compartment syndrome called Volkmann ischemia. Nerve dysfunction (e.g., ulnar nerve palsy, iatrogenic posterior interosseous nerve palsy), infection, and mal-union are other possible complications.

Factors Influencing Duration

Individuals with fractures of their nondominant arm not requiring surgery may return to work sooner than those with the same injuries to the dominant side, depending on the amount of swelling and tolerance of pain. Use of pain medication may be necessary for comfort and to increase rehabilitation effort, but may put most individuals at risk if they are working; therefore, return to work may be delayed.

Changes in the structure of the elbow may also affect the function of the wrist and hand, which might require treatment. Duration depends on severity of injury, whether the dominant or nondominant arm is involved, type of treatment, and complications.

Length of Disability

Duration in Days

Job Classification	Minimum	Optimum	Maximum
Sedentary work	7	14	28
Light work	14	21	91
Medium work	63	91	147
Heavy work	119	182	238
Very Heavy work	119	182	273

Failure to Recover

If an individual fails to recover within the maximum duration expectancy period, the reader may wish to reference the following questions to assist in better understanding the specifics of an individual's medical case.

Regarding diagnosis:

- Does the individual report a fall or direct blow to the back of the upper arm when the elbow is flexed?
- Are there complaints of pain and swelling?
- Does the individual report decreased ability to move the elbow?
- Does pain increase with movement of the hand?
- Were x-rays (with anteroposterior [AP], lateral, and oblique views) of the elbow taken?
- Was the diagnosis of fractured elbow confirmed?

Regarding treatment:

- Were bone fragments completely separated (displaced fracture) or not (nondisplaced fracture)?
- For nondisplaced fracture, was the bone realigned and splinted for a minimum of 10 days?
- If the individual experienced a displaced fracture, was surgical re-alignment (open reduction and internal fixation) done?
- If open reduction was required, did any complications occur postsurgically?
- For both types of fracture, were rest, ice compresses, and elevation recommended?
- Were analgesics required to relieve pain?
- Was the individual compliant with the all treatment recommendations (rest, ice, and elevation)?
- Was physical therapy recommended for this individual?

Regarding prognosis:

- Was this an uncomplicated, nondisplaced fracture or a displaced fracture? If displaced, was there joint, nerve, or tissue damage, requiring significant time from which to recover?
- Has physical therapy been completed as recommended? Would additional therapy benefit the individual?
- Did adequate time elapse for full recovery?
- How does the injury affect the daily activities of the individual?

References

Distal Humerus Fractures - Supracondylar Fractures. EMBBS. 2000. 20 Nov 2000 <http://www.embbs.com/ortho/suprc.html>.

Kisner, Carolyn, and Lynn Allen Colby. Therapeutic Exercise: Foundations and Techniques, 2nd ed. Philadelphia: F.A. Davis, 1990.

Fracture, Femoral Neck

Other names / synonyms: Broken Hip, Fracture, Hip Fracture, Intracapsular Fracture of the Femoral Neck, Unsolved Fracture

820, 820.0, 820.00, 820.01, 820.02, 820.03, 820.09, 820.1, 820.10, 820.11, 820.12, 820.13, 820.19, 820.2, 820.20, 820.21, 820.22, 820.3, 820.30, 820.31, 820.32, 820.8, 820.9

Definition

A femoral neck fracture is a hip fracture in which the neck of the thigh bone (femur) is broken. Femoral neck fractures may occur as a result of a fall, motor vehicle accident, or spontaneously because of a disease process, such as osteoporosis. Stress fractures can result from repetitive mechanical stress or structural defects in the bone making it weak or brittle. Risk factors for femoral neck fracture include diabetes, osteoporosis (particularly in postmenopausal women), osteomalacia, irradiation, metastatic cancer, rheumatoid arthritis, neurological disease, or hyperparathyroidism associated with severe renal disease. Military recruits, long-distance runners, and ballet dancers are at risk for suffering a stress fracture of the femoral neck.

Fractures of the femoral neck are divided into 4 types according to the Garden system, which describes fractures according to their degree of completeness and displacement. In a complete fracture, the 2 bone fragments are no longer connected. In a displaced fracture of the femoral neck, usually caused by trauma, the bone has been moved out of its original position, 2 bone fragments fail to line up, or 1 bone fragment becomes rotated about its axis. Garden Type I fracture is incomplete or twisted (valgus impacted); Type II is complete but not displaced; Type III is complete and partially displaced; and Type IV is complete and totally displaced. Type I fractures are considered stable, while the other classes of fractures are considered unstable. An impacted fracture, in which the surfaces are crushed together, must be distinguished from a nondisplaced fracture. A nondisplaced fracture has no impaction and no inherent instability.

Femoral neck fractures occur most often in the elderly. In fact, 80% occur in those over the age of 60, particularly in postmenopausal women. Femoral neck fractures in the elderly occur spontaneously or following low-energy trauma. In young adults, femoral neck fracture is usually caused by high-energy trauma.

Diagnosis

History: The most prominent symptom associated with a femoral neck fracture is pain in the hip, groin, or thigh, usually following a fall or accident; or in an elderly person with any of the risk factors described above. Hip pain associated with a displaced fracture is typically more severe than in a nondisplaced fracture. Pain is sometimes felt in other areas of the body, such as the knee (referred pain). Additional symptoms may include swelling, point tenderness, paleness (pallor), tingling sensation (paresthesia), paralysis, deformity, discoloration, grating sound upon movement (crepitus), and loss of mobility.

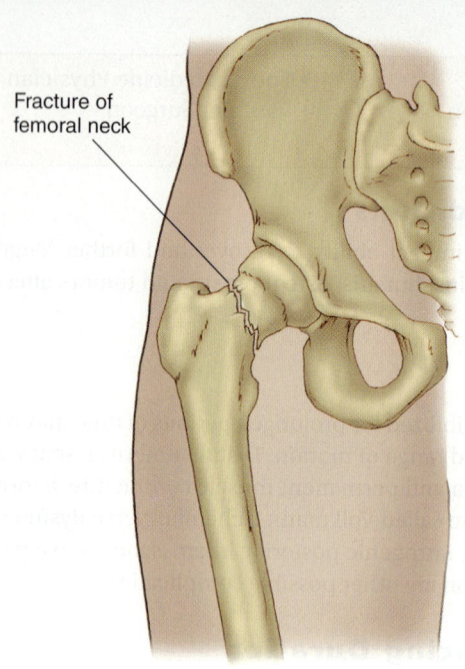

Frank Forney

Physical exam: The exam usually reveals tenderness and swelling of the affected area, decreased ability or inability to move, and groin pain with hip motion. The broken leg may look shorter than the other or appear to be bent (flexed) and turned outward (externally rotated). There may be associated bruising and discoloration and a loss of pulse in the affected leg. If the fracture is open, an obvious skin wound will be present.

Tests: X-rays of the hip, pelvis, femur, knee, and other tender or painful areas determine the extent of the hip fracture and whether or not secondary fractures are also present. CT scan or MRI may also be used if a suspected fracture is not readily visible by plain x-rays. Technetium bone scan may be done to confirm a suspected fracture or to assess whether or not the femoral head has lost its blood supply because of the fracture. Tomogram may help identify stress fracture. Routine laboratory blood and urine tests will be needed before surgery, including complete blood count (CBC), chemical profile, blood clotting profile, and electrolytes. Chest x-ray and electrocardiogram (EKG) are usually done to assess the risk of anesthesia.

Treatment

Femoral neck fractures are treated as semi-emergencies because the consequences of delaying treatment can be severe, even life threatening. Gentle traction may be used during transport to the hospital and prior to surgery. The leg should be immobilized or splinted, a cold pack applied, and the leg elevated to reduce pain and swelling. Open wounds are carefully cleaned, a tetanus vaccination is given, antibiotics are administered, and surgery may be necessary to repair injury to soft tissue.

Surgical repair of the fracture is nearly always indicated and is performed as soon as possible after the injury. Nonoperative management (bedrest followed by early mobilization) may be appropriate for certain elderly individuals who were sedentary prior to fracture and are not experiencing significant pain. Nondisplaced fractures are usually treated by fixation with 3-4 screws, which may be inserted through the skin. Treatment of displaced fractures is directed at preservation of life and restoration of hip function. Type III displaced fractures are treated with reduction (open or closed) and rigid internal fixation (screws and a plate) to restore normal positions to the bone fragments. In elderly persons, the affected hip joint may be replaced by a prosthetic (hemiarthroplasty). Hip hemiarthroplasty is normally reserved for Type IV displaced fractures and in cases in which there was a pre-existing abnormal condition (such as arthritis). Total hip replacement (arthroplasty) may be required in some cases, especially when individuals sustain a fracture of a hip with pre-existing significant arthritis. Individuals with femoral neck fractures secondary to radiation are treated conservatively, using internal fixation devices, although hemiarthroplasty may also be performed.

Individuals are encouraged to get up and walk as soon as possible following surgery to prevent complications such as deep vein thrombosis, pulmonary embolism, bedsores, and pneumonia due to prolonged immobilization. Plain x-rays are taken of the hip every 8-12 weeks until the fracture has healed completely. Osteoporosis, which is often present, is treated with calcium supplementation and hormone replacement in postmenopausal women.

Prognosis

The outcome is extremely variable depending on the type of injury, presence of pre-existing conditions, and treatment required. Most individuals (65%) fully recover following a hip fracture. In older individuals, however, there is a 10-20% mortality rate within 3 months, and for debilitated individuals, the mortality rate at 1 year approaches 30 percent. Elderly individuals may experience some degree of temporary mental deterioration following femoral neck fracture surgery caused by undetermined factors that may include general anesthesia, depression, or awareness of age-related changes.

Failure to heal (nonunion) occurs in 10-30% of displaced femoral neck fractures. Approximately 25-30% of femoral neck fractures ultimately require a prosthetic replacement due to osteonecrosis resulting from inadequate circulation. In a 2000 Swiss study, total hip replacements using different materials for the artificial joint had a similar outcome, with mechanical failure in 2% of 56 individuals followed over a 4-7 year period. More than 90% of individuals rated their own outcome as excellent or very good.

Differential Diagnosis

Primary or metastatic malignancy can cause symptoms that mimic femoral neck fracture.

Specialists

- Orthopedic Surgeon
- Physiatrist

Rehabilitation

Rehabilitation of femoral neck fracture can take up to 6 months and involves physical therapy designed to increase range of motion and muscle strength. Therapy is different depending on whether the fracture has been percutaneously pinned, has undergone open reduction and internal fixation (nailing), or has been prosthetically replaced.

During the first phase, the therapist will allow weight bearing to tolerance. The therapist may instruct the individual in quadriceps exercises, gluteal exercises and ankle exercises.

The therapist may instruct the individual in range of motion exercises for hip, leg and knee. In addition, individuals may use a stationary bicycle for range of motion and strengthening

The following phase, the individual will continue to progress to full weight bearing. The individual should also begin more strength work by performing partial weight bearing or full weight bearing closed-chain exercises. Partial weight bearing (PWB) exercises may include PWB minisquats, wall sits, lunges and proprioception using BAPS board (balance exercises). Full weight bearing closed-chain exercises may include wall sits, minisquats with or without resistance, lunges, proprioception, and step-ups.

During last phase of rehabilitation, the therapist works with the individual continuing in closed-chain exercises until the individual obtains full knee and hip range of motion, can perform a full squat, and can climb and descend stairs full weight bearing. The goal is to get the thigh circumference almost equal to the uninjured side.

Work Restrictions / Accommodations

Individuals requiring total hip arthroplasty may require extended work leave or leave of absence. Because of the extensive physical therapy that may be needed, additional time off may be required. Most surgeons would prohibit moderate (50 pounds) lifting for at least one year to observe for avascular necrosis of the femoral head. Persons whose jobs require prolonged standing may need temporary reassignment to sedentary duties. If crutches are required, relocation to an area of the workplace near an exit may be required, and additional safety precautions may need to be taken. Walking canes or walkers may be necessary to aid those with an unsteady gait, and rails should be installed in the bathroom and on stairs as precautionary measures to help prevent recurrence.

Comorbid Conditions

Arthritis, cancer, diabetes, cardiopulmonary and cerebrovascular disease, general debility, hypertension, malnutrition, and obesity may increase the length of disability.

Complications

Complications associated with a femoral neck fracture include the possibility of permanent deformity and dysfunction if the bones fail to heal (nonunion) or heal incorrectly (malunion), or muscle contractures. There may be a delay in diagnosing femoral neck stress fracture. Nondisplaced fractures may become displaced prior to treatment. High-energy femoral neck fractures are often associated with other injuries including pelvis fracture, knee injuries, and chest contusions following a motor vehicle accident, and wrist, shoulder, and rib fractures following a major fall. Femoral neck fracture can disrupt the blood supply to the femoral head (avascular necrosis or osteonecrosis of the femoral head) in about 40% of individuals, with subsequent collapse and arthritis of the hip. This manifests as late pain and stiffness beginning months after the fracture. Prolonged immobility can lead to kidney stones (renal calculi), blood clots (thromboembolism), pneumonia, or bed sores. Especially in the elderly, these complications can be life-threatening. Even in younger individuals, fat released from the broken bone (fat embolism) can enter the blood stream, causing stroke or even death. Long term complications of femoral neck fracture include the possibility of developing degenerative or posttraumatic arthritis, hardware failure, and infection.

Factors Influencing Duration

Factors influencing length of disability include the location and type of fracture, the cause of the fracture, the presence of underlying diseases or pathologic conditions that precipitate fractures, the specific treatment or surgical intervention provided, the development of complications, the individual's age, general health, and ability to ambulate shortly after surgery, and the individual's job requirements.

Length of Disability

If work can be performed sitting instead of standing, return to work should occur much earlier. Heavy and very heavy work is rarely possible after a femoral neck fracture. Disability may be permanent.

Duration in Days

Job Classification	Minimum	Optimum	Maximum
Sedentary work	42	56	84
Light work	42	56	84
Medium work	56	84	112
Heavy work	Indefinite	Indefinite	Indefinite
Very Heavy work	Indefinite	Indefinite	Indefinite

Failure to Recover

If an individual fails to recover within the maximum duration expectancy period, the reader may wish to reference the following questions to assist in better understanding the specifics of an individual's medical case.

Regarding diagnosis:

- Were the individual's presenting symptoms consistent with those of a femoral neck fracture?
- Was the diagnosis confirmed with x-rays, CT scan, or MRI?
- If the diagnosis was uncertain, was the possibility of malignant femur tumor ruled out?
- Did the individual suffer any complications that would prolong recovery?
- Does the individual have any condition that may contribute to prolonged disability?

Regarding treatment:

- Was the fracture treated promptly and appropriately?
- Was surgery required?

Regarding prognosis:

- Considering the type of fracture, the presence of pre-existing conditions, age and general health of the individual, what was the expected outcome?
- Did the individual participate in physical therapy and rehabilitation exercises as directed?
- Has adequate time elapsed to allow for recovery?
- Are there other conditions (such as advanced age, decreased mental alertness, debilitating health problems) that impair the individual's ability to participate in physical therapy?
- Is pain interfering with rehabilitation? If so, have alternative pain relief interventions been tried?
- Is the individual motivated to adhere to the prescribed physical therapy?
- If there is lack of motivation, have interventions such as making adjustments in the rehabilitation prescription, changing the physical therapist, or seeking a rehabilitation group that is a similar age?
- Have accommodations and work restrictions been addressed?

References

Dijkstra, J.B., P.J. Houx, and J. Jolles. "Cognition After Major Surgery in the Elderly: Test Performance and Complaints." British Journal of Anaesthesia 82 6 (1999): 867-874.

Egol, Kenneth, et al. "Stress Fractures of the Femoral Neck." Clinical Orthopaedics and Related Research 348 (1998): 72-78.

Jagmin, M.G. "Postoperative Mental Status in Elderly Hip Surgery Patients." Orthopaedic Nursing 17 6 (1998): 32-42.

Koval, Kenneth, Kenneth Egol, and Joseph Zuckerman. "Hip Fractures and Dislocations." Principles of Orthopaedic Practice. Dee, Roger, et al., eds. New York: McGraw-Hill, 1997. 465-472.

Perry, Clayton. "Intracapsular Fractures of the Proximal Femur." Handbook of Fractures, 2nd ed. Perry, Clayton, and James Elstrom, eds. New York: McGraw-Hill, 2000. 250-266.

Taylor, Kenneth, and Vasantha Murthy. "Femoral Neck Fractures." Treatment and Rehabilitation of Fractures. Hoppenfeld, Stanley, and Vasantha Murthy, eds. Philadelphia: Lippincott Williams and Wilkins, 2000. 257-272.

Fracture, Fingers and Thumb

Other names / synonyms: Broken Finger, Broken Thumb, Fractures of the Phalanges of Hand

816, 816.0, 816.00, 816.01, 816.02, 816.03, 816.1, 816.10, 816.11, 816.12, 816.13

Definition

This refers to a disruption, or break, in any of the bones of the fingers or thumbs. The bones of the fingers are called phalanges (plural) or a phalanx (singular): distal, middle, and proximal. Each finger (digit) has 3 small bones connected at the knuckles (joints). The thumb, being shorter, has only 2 bones and 2 joints. The bones can be fractured by a direct blow, rotation, twisting, and by crushing injuries. The fractures may be accompanied by dislocations and/or open wounds. Fractures of the end of the finger (distal phalanx) may include an injury to the nail bed, which means the fracture must be treated as an open fracture. When the fingers are injured, soft tissue structures can get between the fragments, making reduction difficult and tendon or ligament damage likely.

Finger fractures are known by the descriptive fracture name and the location (for example, nondisplaced spiral fracture of the proximal phalanx). The fragments may protrude through the skin (open or compound fracture) or may cause deformity of the finger without tearing the skin (closed fracture). Function of the hand is maintained when the fingers and thumb are able to move in correct relation to each other and to the wrist bones. A fracture to any of the small bones has the potential to change this relationship, which can be painful and debilitating. Tendon rupture is a significant injury and often accompanies finger fractures.

Metacarpal and phalangeal fractures make up 10% of all fractures. More than 50% of finger fractures due to injury are work-related. The distal phalanx (with associated nail bed injury) accounts for 45-50% of finger fractures, while the metacarpals account for 30-35%, the proximal phalanx 15-20%, and the middle phalanx 8-12 percent.

The risk of finger/thumb fractures increases with contact sports (e.g., hockey, football), skiing, bone or joint disease (e.g., osteoporosis), and poor nutrition (e.g., calcium deficiency).

Diagnosis

History: Individuals present with pain, swelling, sensations of numbness or coldness, and decreased range of motion in the affected digit. There may be a history of trauma, perhaps thought of as insignificant at the time.

Physical exam: Pressure applied to the finger (palpation) reveals pain and swelling. Range-of-motion (ROM) evaluation may indicate loss of tendon function. Sensory testing is included to evaluate nerve damage. There may be observable deformity, but the cause may be tendon damage or joint dislocation without fracture.

Examination of the skin and nail bed for bloody effusion or open wounds must be done to evaluate the need for antibiotics. It is important to separate new and old injuries during the examination. It is not uncommon for previous tendon and bone injuries to complicate the findings.

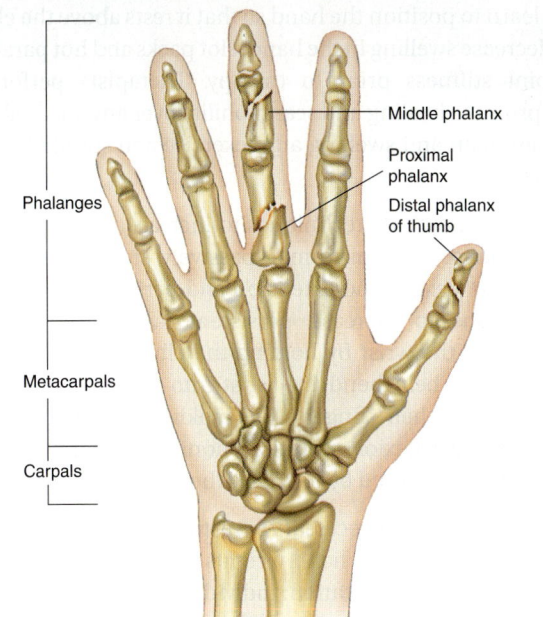

Tests: Plain x-rays with anteroposterior (AP), lateral, and oblique views will show the fracture position. Strength testing of each digit and joint establishes tendon and ligament integrity.

Treatment

Treatment for finger and thumb fractures depends on the type of break. It may consist of buddy taping to an adjacent finger, splinting, or casting, with attempts to move the involved digit as soon as possible, and uninvolved digits immediately. More severe or open fractures require surgery, using pins, screws, or wires to hold the bone fragments in place (open reduction and internal fixation; ORIF).

Prognosis

Restoration of function and healing of the fracture can be expected in uncomplicated fractures. Permanent disability may occur if the rotation and alignment are not obtained and maintained during healing or if complications are encountered. Prognosis is excellent with good care and proper rehabilitation. The biggest problem after healing is stiffness. The best way to prevent stiffness is to move the fingers as soon as possible.

Differential Diagnosis

Conditions that present with similar symptoms include hand dislocations, wrist dislocations, hand infections, and numerous soft-tissue injuries of the hand. Additionally, individuals with rheumatoid arthritis can have fingers deformed by the disease that appear to be fractured.

Specialists

- Hand Surgeon
- Occupational Therapist
- Orthopedic Surgeon
- Physiatrist

Rehabilitation

Individuals who sustain fractures of the fingers or thumb may require outpatient therapy. The individual should be seen by either an occupational therapist or a physical therapist who is a certified hand therapist.

Therapy first addresses pain control and the reduction of swelling. Individuals learn to position the hand so that it rests above the elbow on a pillow to decrease swelling in the hand. Hot packs and hot paraffin wax decrease joint stiffness prior to therapy. Therapists perform scar massage to promote healing and scar mobility over any surgical site. Ice packs decrease pain and swelling after exercise and should be applied for 15 minutes.

Individuals learn stretching techniques to increase range of motion at the wrist and hand. Therapists may passively stretch the wrist and fingers to increase flexion and extension and perform interphalangeal joint mobilizations to increase persistent lack of finger flexion. Individuals stretch the wrist by holding the elbow straight and using their other hand to help bend the wrist into flexion and extension. Individuals stretch their fingers by making a fist and adding overpressure to finger flexion with their noninjured hand. Finger and thumb opposition is restored by touching the thumb to each finger.

Strengthening exercises are necessary to restore function and to prevent reinjury. Individuals use light hand weights to strengthen wrist flexion and extension and forearm rotation; individuals place the forearm on a table for support for these exercises. Individuals squeeze therapy putty to restore hand strength. The muscles of the fingers should be strengthened by pinching therapy putty between the fingers, or by placing a rubber band around 2 fingers at a time and spreading them apart. Individuals learn functional exercises such as turning a doorknob and grasping/turning a key and perform exercises that emphasize dexterity such as picking up pegs and placing them in a pegboard.

Work Restrictions / Accommodations

Work restrictions and accommodations will vary with severity of the fracture and the amount of physicality or dexterity required for the individual's job. For example, typists or surgeons would require the use of all digits to perform their duties and may need to reduce or modify their duties until fully healed. Individuals with finger and thumb injuries may need to take breaks to elevate and ice the injured hand to reduce swelling and pain. Individuals who require great grip strength to perform their duties may need to modify their duties until healed.

Complementary and Alternative Therapies

Content is intended for awareness only. Treatments may or may not be effective. Scientific evidence may be lacking and some substances have potentially toxic effects. Dr. Presley Reed and the editors do not endorse the use of these therapies in the absence of consultation with a licensed medical professional.

Hydrotherapy - After splint is removed, ice soaks/massage and whirlpool treatments may relieve pain and help decrease stiffness.

Comorbid Conditions

Conditions that could impact ability to recover and further lengthen disability include degenerative arthritis, osteoporosis, calcium deficiency, Paget's disease, and tumors or cysts of the affected bones.

Complications

Possible complications of finger/thumb fractures include mal-rotation, degenerative arthritis, adhesion of tendon to bone (more likely to occur with open or widely angulated fractures), and non-union. Improperly treated middle phalanx fractures may be complicated by a deformity characterized by flexion of the proximal joint and hyperextension of the distal joint (Boutonniere deformity). The most common complication of phalangeal fractures is stiffness.

Factors Influencing Duration

Disability is dependent on whether the dominant versus nondominant hand is involved, work requirements, the digit/digits involved, and the presence of complications.

Length of Disability

Duration depends on whether dominant or non-dominant hand is involved. Loss of function may be permanent with complications.

Closed, with internal fixation or open.

Duration in Days

Job Classification	Minimum	Optimum	Maximum
Sedentary work	1	3	42
Light work	1	3	42
Medium work	14	21	56
Heavy work	28	42	70
Very Heavy work	28	42	112

Open, with internal fixation.

Duration in Days

Job Classification	Minimum	Optimum	Maximum
Sedentary work	3	7	42
Light work	3	7	42
Medium work	21	28	56
Heavy work	28	42	70
Very Heavy work	28	42	112

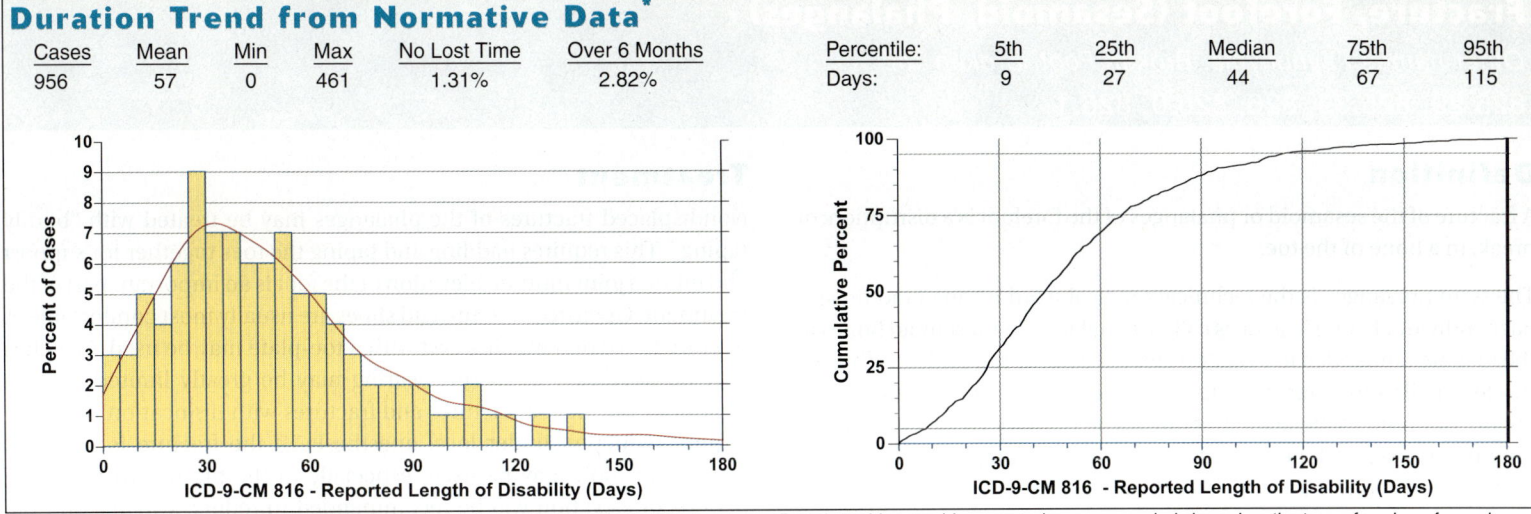

Failure to Recover

If an individual fails to recover within the maximum duration expectancy period, the reader may wish to reference the following questions to assist in better understanding the specifics of an individual's medical case.

Regarding diagnosis:

- Was diagnosis of fracture confirmed by x-ray?
- Did individual experience any complications?
- Does individual have an underlying condition that may impact recovery?

Regarding treatment:

- Was treatment appropriate to type and location of fracture?
- Would individual benefit from a consultation with a specialist (orthopedic surgeon, hand surgeon, occupational therapist, physiatrist)?
- Was open reduction and internal fixation required?
- What is the expected outcome?

Regarding prognosis:

- Has individual followed prescribed rehabilitative therapy?
- Have there been any complications?
- Would the individual benefit from a consultation with a specialist (orthopedic surgeon, hand surgeon, occupational therapist, physiatrist)?

References

Finger Fractures. e-hand.com. 2000. 4 Dec 2000 <http://www.eatonhand.com/hw/hw010.htm>.

Fracture of Finger/Thumb. IntraCorp. 2000. 4 Dec 2000 <http://iconline.intracorp.com/ecomm/icportal/profiles/ClaimsProfessional/ic-art/html/FxFingThDescART.html>.

Apley, A. Graham, and Louis Solomon. "Injuries to the Upper Limb." Concise System of Orthopaedics and Fractures. Oxford: Butterworth-Heinemann Ltd, 1994. 270-298.

Fraser, William R., DO. Fractures, Hand. eMedicine.com. 17 Feb 2001. 24 Mar 2001 <http://www.emedicine.com/emerg/topic197.htm>.

Griffith, H. Winter. Complete Guide to Sports Injuries. New York: The Berkley Publishing Group, 1997.

Kisner, Carolyn, and Lynn Allen Colby. Therapeutic Exercise, Foundations and Techniques, 2nd ed. Philadelphia: F.A. Davis, 1990.

Fracture, Forefoot (Sesamoid, Phalanges)

Other names / synonyms: Broken Foot, Broken Toe
825.29, 825.39, 826, 826.0, 826.1

Definition

A fracture of the sesamoid or phalanges of the forefoot is a disruption, or break, in a bone of the toe.

The term phalanges is the technical medical word for toe (and finger). Each individual bone in a toe is called a phalanx. The sesamoid bones in the toes are embedded in a tendon located behind and under the big toe (under the first metatarsal bone in the foot). Sesamoid stress fractures are uncommon, as are acute fractures. The primary cause of sesamoid fractures is overwork and excessive pressure on that area of the foot. Dancers and runners are at risk for these fractures.

Broken toes are usually the result of an accident or stubbing the toe. The great toe is the most frequently broken toe. Causes include a direct blow to the area, a fall, or an automobile accident. Stubbing a toe while barefoot is a common cause of fracture for the fifth toe. Individuals with osteoporosis are at greater risk for toe fractures.

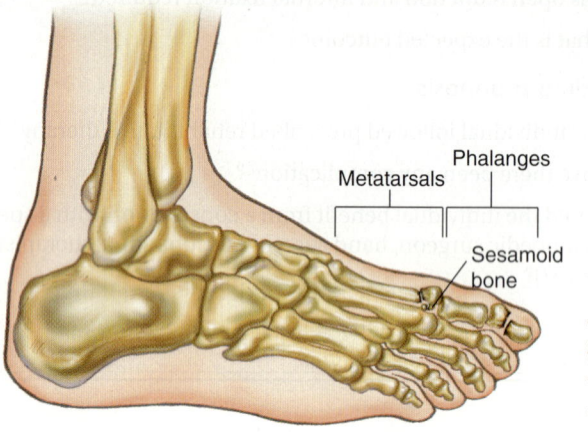

Diagnosis

History: For a toe fracture, the individual will complain of pain and tenderness over the fracture site. The individual may relate an injury to the area. The individual will also complain of increased pain upon walking or weight bearing. For a sesamoid fracture, the individual will complain of either dull, intermittent pain in the general area of the sesamoids or severe throbbing pain in that area. The individual may relate the feeling to a bruising sustained from walking with a stone in their shoe.

Physical exam: Upon examination of a toe fracture, there may be swelling, bruising, numbness, or tingling of the toe. If the fracture is displaced, the toe will have a misshapen or deformed appearance. Upon examination of a sesamoid fracture, there will be pain upon pressing (palpation) in the area of the sesamoids. Pulling on the great toe will also cause discomfort.

Tests: Routine x-rays will reveal fractures of the toes with special views required for confirming sesamoid fractures. Dislocations may be subtle, and comparison views of the other foot may be necessary. Postreduction films will be taken, as will follow-up films.

Treatment

Nondisplaced fractures of the phalanges may be treated with "buddy taping." This requires padding and taping the toes together for support and limited joint motion. Elevation of the foot is an important part of the treatment. Open-toed, semi-rigid shoes are usually most comfortable. A fracture brace or a walking cast with a toe-plate may be used. Crutches may be necessary as weight bearing may be greatly limited early in treatment. Displaced fractures and fractures with dislocation will often require reduction under local anesthesia. If the fracture is unstable, internal fixation may be used, especially in the big (great) toe. Long periods of elevation will be recommended to reduce swelling and the risk of complications. Treatment of these fractures usually includes a walking boot or cast, and crutches with protected weight bearing for 6-8 weeks.

Fractures of the sesamoid are treated with rest, anti-inflammatory medications, protective padding, a semi-rigid soled shoe, and arch supports to relieve tension on the tendon. Partial weight bearing may be required for a few days to weeks. If symptoms persist for 6 months after a sesamoid fracture, are unrelieved by a cortisone injection, and cause functional disability, the sesamoid may be surgically removed (excised).

Prognosis

Generally, nondisplaced, uncomplicated fractures can be expected to heal in 6-8 weeks without residual damage. During that time, the ability to walk may be severely impaired. Recovery from fractures that require reduction and fixation may take several weeks. This is true for soft tissue damage as well. Complications of the injury will extend the recovery period and may have a less successful outcome.

Following conservative treatment of a sesamoid fracture, individuals may begin to resume bearing weight. Stiff-soled shoes should be worn until pain is gone. Following a sesamoid fracture, dancers and athletes may require a full year for complete recovery.

Differential Diagnosis

Conditions that present with similar symptoms include soft-tissue injuries of the ankle, lower extremity compartment syndrome, and foot dislocations.

Specialists

- Orthopedic Surgeon
- Physiatrist
- Podiatrist
- Sports Medicine Physician

Work Restrictions / Accommodations

Restrictions and accommodations may include limited or no weight bearing and limited walking, climbing, and squatting. Use of assistive devices such as a cane, crutches, or walker may be necessary. With severe injuries involving soft tissue damage to both feet, a wheelchair may be necessary to provide elevation and restricted weight bearing. Frequent rest periods to elevate the foot, including a facility to allow the individual to lie down with the foot elevated, will be needed. It should be noted that while the injury may appear trivial, the pain and restriction of activity can be quite dramatic. Temporary work restrictions may be necessary due to special footwear requirements.

Comorbid Conditions

Conditions that could impact ability to recover and further lengthen disability include diabetes, peripheral vascular disease, obesity, degenerative arthritis of the feet, osteoporosis, calcium deficiency, tendinitis, bursitis, and sesamoiditis.

Complications

Because many of these fractures are associated with crushing trauma to the forefoot, extensive soft tissue damage may be the greater problem. Infection, nerve and tendon destruction, and vascular compromise may complicate the injury and treatment. Fracture dislocation, especially of the great toe, will be more challenging to treat. Any underlying medical condition that affects circulation of the foot will complicate treatment. As with all fractures, osteoarthritis and osteomyelitis are possible complications.

Surgical removal of either or both sesamoids may lead to a variety of foot deformities.

Factors Influencing Duration

Type and severity of fracture, age, complications of the injury, ability to modify work activities, and rate of healing may affect disability periods.

Length of Disability

For toe fractures, duration depends on which digit is involved.

Phalanges (toes).

Duration in Days

Job Classification	Minimum	Optimum	Maximum
Sedentary work	1	3	14
Light work	3	7	21
Medium work	14	21	28
Heavy work	28	35	42
Very Heavy work	28	35	42

Sesamoid bones.

Duration in Days

Job Classification	Minimum	Optimum	Maximum
Sedentary work	1	2	3
Light work	1	3	7
Medium work	3	7	14
Heavy work	35	49	84
Very Heavy work	42	49	112

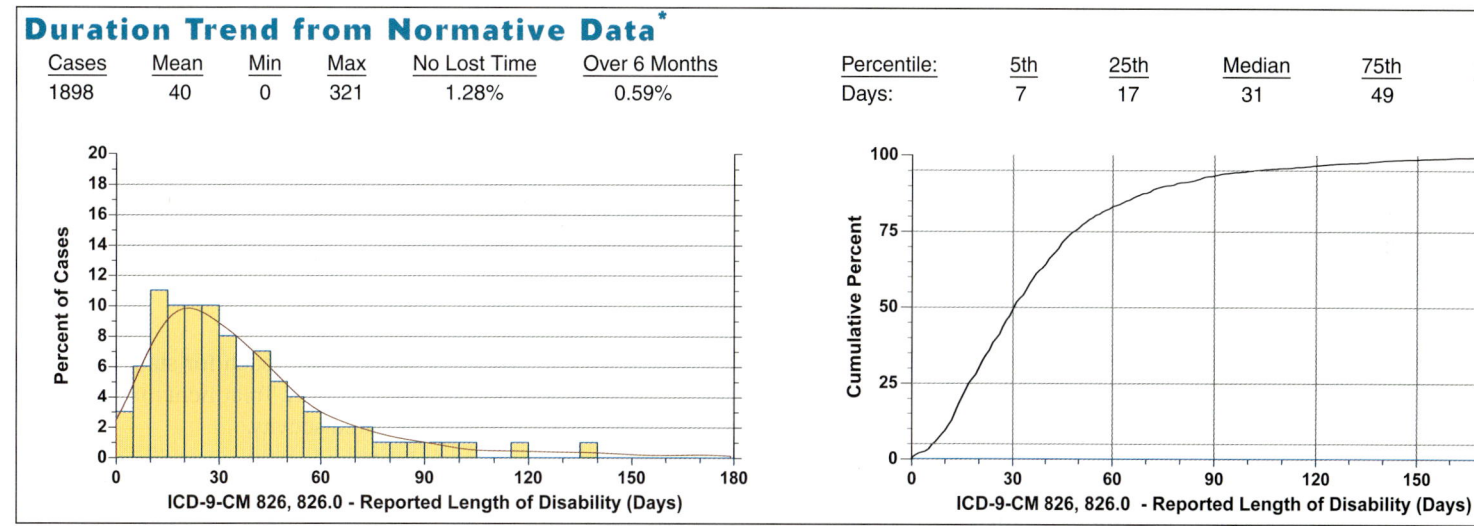

Duration Trend from Normative Data*

Cases	Mean	Min	Max	No Lost Time	Over 6 Months
1898	40	0	321	1.28%	0.59%

Percentile:	5th	25th	Median	75th	95th
Days:	7	17	31	49	102

ICD-9-CM 826, 826.0 - Reported Length of Disability (Days)

* Differences may exist between the expected duration tables and the normative graphs. Duration tables provide expected recovery periods based on the type of work performed by the individual. The normative graphs reflect the actual observed experience of many individuals across the spectrum of physical conditions, in a variety of industries, and with varying levels of case management.

Failure to Recover

If an individual fails to recover within the maximum duration expectancy period, the reader may wish to reference the following questions to assist in better understanding the specifics of an individual's medical case.

Regarding diagnosis:

- Was the individual's presenting symptoms consistent with a diagnosis of forefoot fracture?
- Was the diagnosis confirmed with x-rays?
- If the diagnosis was uncertain, were other conditions ruled out?
- Is the individual obese?
- Does the individual have degenerative arthritis of the feet, osteoporosis, calcium deficiency, tendinitis, bursitis, sesamoiditis, diabetes, or peripheral vascular disease?

Fracture, Forefoot (Sesamoid, Phalanges)

Regarding treatment:
- Was the treatment appropriate for the type of fracture?
- Was surgery required?
- Was the pain managed effectively with anti-inflammatory medications?
- If not, were other pain management interventions tried?

Regarding prognosis:
- Has adequate time elapsed for recovery?
- Have appropriate accommodations and job reassignments been made?
- Did the individual suffer any complications that could impact recovery?

References

Toe Fracture. HealthGate. 23 Jun 1999. 1 Dec 2000 <http://www.healthgate.com/sport/sport124.shtml>.

Apley, A. Graham, and Louis Solomon. "Injuries to the Lower Limb." Concise System of Orthopaedics and Fractures. Oxford: Butterworth-Heinemann Ltd, 1994. 316-344.

Churchill, R.S., and B.G. Donley. "Managing Injuries of the Great Toe." The Physician and Sportsmedicine 26 (1998): 11. 1 Dec 2000 <http://www.physsportsmed.com/issues/1998/09sep/donley.htm>.

Kisner, Carolyn, and Lynn Allen Colby. Therapeutic Exercise: Foundations and Techniques, 2nd ed. Philadelphia: F.A. Davis, 1990.

Fracture, Lumbosacral Spine (With or Without Spinal Cord Injury)
Other names / synonyms: Broken Back, Spinal Fracture
805.4, 805.5, 806.4, 806.5

Definition

A fracture of the lumbosacral spine is a fracture of 1 or more bones of the spine (vertebrae) in the lower back (lumbosacral) region. There are 5 lumbar vertebrae.

Fractures in the lumbar spine are classified as stable or unstable. They are also categorized as compression fractures, fractures of the transverse process, flexion-rotation injuries, and pathological fractures. Most fractures of the lumbar spine are not severe or complicated.

Compression fractures occur most commonly after falls from a height, with the individual landing on his/her heels. Compression fractures can also occur as the result of a motor vehicle accident and are sometimes overlooked because of other, more serious injuries.

Fractures of the transverse process are most often the result of direct violence.

Fractures resulting from forceful flexion and rotation are also common in traffic accidents and mining accidents. Fractures caused by acute flexion of the spine are most often sustained in a motor vehicle accident by individuals wearing a lap seat belt without a shoulder harness (seat belt injuries).

Pathological fractures are seen in individuals with osteoporosis or other disease conditions, which compromise bone strength.

The spinal cord ends at lumbar vertebra number 1 (L1), so fractures at the thoracolumbar junction (T12-L1) can cause injury to the end of the spinal cord. Fractures lower in the lumbar spine can cause damage to the nerve roots (including cauda equina syndrome) but cannot damage the spinal cord.

Diagnosis

History: Individuals will often complain of localized pain in the lumbar region, perhaps specifically over the injured vertebrae. There may be pain with motion, bruising (ecchymosis), and swelling. There may also be changes in sensation or inability to move the lower extremities, along with loss of bowel and bladder function.

Physical exam: Individuals may present with obvious swelling, bruising (ecchymosis), and deformity. Tenderness of the spine may be evident upon touch (palpation). To evaluate nerve damage resulting from injury sustained during the fracture, a neurological screening exam is done. This includes testing of the reflexes by percussion, muscle function with resisted range of motion, and sensitivity to touch (complete neurological examination). Nerve damage will be evident with either decreased or hyperactive reflexes, decreased muscle function, and diminished perception of touch.

Tests: AP, Lateral, and Oblique x-rays of the spine will be ordered to establish the diagnosis of bone fracture. CT and/or MRI scans may be necessary to determine fragment position and soft tissue involvement. Neurological studies may include EMG and nerve conduction studies. Lab studies will include urinalysis to screen for genital-urinary tract injury.

Treatment

Nonoperative treatment is the standard approach for stable fractures that do not have a tendency to late deformity. Treatment may include a custom brace or cast, bed rest, or limited activity.

For unstable fractures, surgery offers the advantage of better neurologic improvement and shortened rehabilitation time compared to bedrest. However, neurologic deficit sometimes worsens with surgical treatment. Surgical procedures include fusion, internal fixation with hardware insertion (instrumentation) and removal of fragments. Treatment of spinal cord injuries may also be necessary during the procedure. Postoperative care may involve prolonged bed rest until evidence of healing is demonstrated on x-rays. Individuals with associated spinal cord injuries or internal organ damage may require additional surgery during recovery.

Prognosis

Stable, uncomplicated fractures of the vertebrae in the lumbar area usually heal without difficulty using only conservative, nonoperative treatment in 6-10 weeks. Those cases requiring surgery to stabilize fracture fragments usually go on to recovery if there is no neurological damage or progressive underlying disease such as osteoporosis or cancer. The need for surgical stabilization does not necessarily mean a longer recovery. There is a possibility of partial body paralysis (paraplegia) with spinal cord or nerve root damage from the original injury.

Differential Diagnosis

Lumbar strain, kidney disease, prostrate disease, and degenerative lumbar disc disease will most likely be excluded by the history of trauma, but could present with somewhat similar pain symptoms.

Specialists

- Neurosurgeon
- Orthopedic Surgeon
- Physiatrist

Rehabilitation

Outpatient physical therapy begins when the fracture is healed and the individual is allowed to remove the brace. Therapists initially focus on pain control and the reduction of swelling. Increasing range of motion is the second objective of rehabilitation. Stretching exercises are also taught. Individuals perform lower trunk rotation stretches by lying on the back (supine) and moving bent knees from one side to the other. The therapist may also instruct the individual in a hamstring stretch in which the individual lies on the back and, using a strap or belt, pulls the foot up toward the ceiling while the opposite leg is stretched out straight on the floor.

Strengthening the back and abdominal muscles prevents future injury. The abdominal muscles are strengthened by performing curl-ups, pelvic tilts, and single knee lifts. The muscles of the back are strengthened by performing back extension exercises.

Muscle stabilization exercises should also be done to keep the body's core strong and to prevent injury. The therapist will include such exercise as bridging, the plank, push-ups from the plank position, and squats. In addition to strengthening exercises, a cardiovascular routine such as brisk walking, cycling, aquatics, swimming, cross-country skiing, skiing, or low-impact aerobics should be established to maintain overall body strength and to prevent any reoccurrence of injury.

Therapy should also address correct posture, proper body mechanics, and proper lifting techniques.

Lumbar spine fractures with significant neurologic deficit (cauda equina syndrome) have paraparesis or paraplegia and require extensive rehabilitation.

Work Restrictions / Accommodations

Depending on the level of injury, the individual may need job retraining. For an individual who has a fracture without spinal cord or nerve root injury, there will be restrictions of physical activities such as lifting, standing, stair climbing, overhead work, bending, or squatting until the fracture has healed. Permanent restrictions may or may not be needed depending on whether or not the fracture healed with significant deformity, pain, or neurologic deficit.

In cases of paraplegia, the facility will need to be wheelchair accessible.

Rehabilitation may be extensive and ongoing, requiring absence from work.

Comorbid Conditions

Spinal cord injury of any degree would lengthen recovery as would damage to internal organs. Osteoporosis, neurologic disease, and metastatic disease may preclude full recovery. Obesity and smoking would impact healing of the fracture.

Complications

Complications of fractures include infection after surgery, nerve damage in displaced fractures, and faulty alignment of the healed vertebrae (malunion).

In cases of severe trauma with multiple injuries, spinal cord damage and damage to the abdominal organs can occur. The complication could be as severe as paraplegia.

Factors Influencing Duration

Factors that may influence length of disability are spinal cord or nerve root injury, the individual's age, any complications, and the stability of the fracture. Duration depends on which vertebra or joint is involved, and whether the fracture is stable or unstable, treated conservatively or surgically.

Length of Disability

Stable fractures without complications may not complicate recovery beyond bone healing. Unstable fractures, those with spinal cord or nerve root injury, or internal organ injury may have a protracted recovery, beyond the healing of the fracture. For these individuals, disability may be permanent. Unstable fractures and spinal cord injury that require internal fixation (surgical treatment) are incompatible with return to moderate or heavy work. The US Social Security Administration's criteria for permanent and total disability due to spinal cord or cauda equina injury are "significant and persistent disorganization of motor function in two extremities resulting in sustained disturbance of gross and dexterous movements, or gait and station."

Stable, treated with brace.

Duration in Days

Job Classification	Minimum	Optimum	Maximum
Sedentary work	7	14	28
Light work	14	21	42
Medium work	42	56	91
Heavy work	91	119	147
Very Heavy work	119	147	182

Surgical treatment of unstable fracture without neurologic deficit.

Duration in Days

Job Classification	Minimum	Optimum	Maximum
Sedentary work	21	28	91
Light work	42	91	119
Medium work	91	168	182
Heavy work	Indefinite	Indefinite	Indefinite
Very Heavy work	Indefinite	Indefinite	Indefinite

With spinal cord injury.

Duration in Days

Job Classification	Minimum	Optimum	Maximum
Sedentary work	119	182	Indefinite
Light work	119	182	Indefinite
Medium work	Indefinite	Indefinite	Indefinite
Heavy work	Indefinite	Indefinite	Indefinite
Very Heavy work	Indefinite	Indefinite	Indefinite

Failure to Recover

If an individual fails to recover within the maximum duration expectancy period, the reader may wish to reference the following questions to assist in better understanding the specifics of an individual's medical case.

Regarding diagnosis:

- How did the accident occur?
- What position was the individual in when the accident occurred?
- What type of fracture does the individual have?
- What symptoms does the individual have? Is there decreased sensation in the perianal region? Is there bladder or bowel dysfunction?
- Were plain x-rays taken? Has an MRI been performed?
- Has the individual received adequate testing to establish the diagnosis?
- Have these conditions with similar symptoms been ruled out?

Regarding treatment:

- Was the fracture stable or unstable?
- Was surgery necessary?
- Did the individual who had nonoperative treatment show signs of neurological deficit?

Regarding prognosis:

- Is the individual active in physical therapy?
- Does the individual have a home exercise program?
- Is the individual's employer able to accommodate the necessary restrictions?
- Does the individual have any complications?

References

"Disorders, Diseases and Injuries of the Spine." Current Diagnosis and Treatment in Orthopedics. Skinner, J.B., and Harry B. Skinner, eds. Norwalk: Appleton & Lange, 1995. 231-236.

Kisner, Carolyn, and Lynn Allen Colby. Therapeutic Exercise: Foundations and Techniques, 2nd ed. Philadelphia: F.A. Davis, 1990.

Fracture, Metacarpal Bones

Other names / synonyms: Bennett's Fracture, Boxer's Fracture, Broken Hand, Rolando's Fracture

815, 815.0, 815.00, 815.01, 815.02, 815.03, 815.04, 815.09, 815.1, 815.10, 815.11, 815.12, 815.13, 815.14, 815.19

Definition

A metacarpal bone fracture is a break in 1 of the 5 metacarpal bones in each hand.

These long, thin bones are located between the carpal bones in the wrist and the phalanges in the fingers. Metacarpal fractures are categorized as head, shaft, neck, and base fractures. The most common metacarpal fracture is a fracture of the neck of the fifth metacarpal (boxer's fracture).

Fractures of the first metacarpal (thumb) are fairly rare, as the bone is quite mobile. Two such fractures are Bennett's fracture and Rolando's fracture. The Rolando fracture is an intra-articular fracture of the base of the first metacarpal (thumb) where the bone is crushed into several pieces at the fracture site (comminuted), and the Bennett fracture is a noncomminuted fracture in a similar location.

Most metacarpal fractures are caused by a direct blow (e.g., a striking blow with a fist) or indirect stress to the affected bone (e.g., twisting or violent muscle contraction). Individuals who compete in contact sports (e.g., football and boxing), have a history of bone or joint disease (e.g., osteoporosis), or suffer from poor nutrition (e.g., calcium deficiency) are at increased risk for metacarpal fractures.

Males experience more metacarpal fractures than females by a 3 to 1 ratio. Metacarpal and phalangeal fractures make up approximately 10% of all fractures. Approximately 30-35% of all hand fractures are metacarpal fractures. However, the overall national incidence of metacarpal fractures cannot be readily estimated because many types of fractures are treated in outpatient settings.

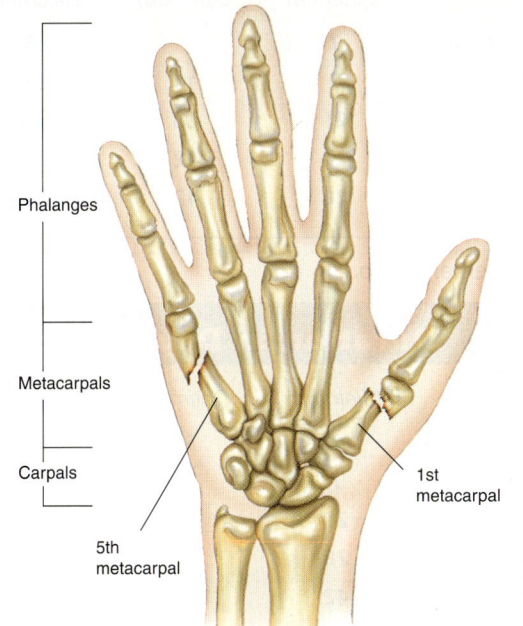

Diagnosis

History: Most fractures are the direct result of trauma. Individuals will complain of severe hand pain, swelling of soft tissue (edema) around the fracture, and numbness and/or coldness beyond the fracture site (if the blood supply is impaired).

Physical exam: Upon examination, a visible deformity may be present if the fracture is complete. Localized swelling and tenderness to the touch may be noted around the fracture site. Decreased grip strength may be noted. If there was any delay in seeking treatment, the pain and swelling may be more generalized. A complete neurovascular exam of the arm, hand, and fingers should be performed.

Tests: Routine x-rays include 3 views (anteroposterior [AP], lateral, and oblique) to properly assess angulation of the fracture fragments as well as involved joint surfaces. CT scans may be ordered to evaluate the metacarpal-carpal joints in complicated fractures.

Treatment

These fractures must heal properly to maintain good hand mechanics. This is especially true of the second and third metacarpals (index and middle finger), which act as anchors for the others. Progressively more angulation can be tolerated with fractures of the third, fourth, and fifth metacarpals. However, rotation and excessive shortening should be avoided in any of them; and normal (anatomic) position is the goal of treatment.

Either closed or open reduction is used to reduce displaced fractures, and metal wires, pins, or screws may be necessary to maintain the position once obtained (open reduction with internal fixation, ORIF). Open reduction has the advantage of being able to obtain perfect, or nearly normal position of the fracture fragments; and internal fixation allows early motion of the fingers in physical therapy. Casts, splints, and braces are often used to maintain position, whether the fracture is treated surgically or not.

Severe fractures with multiple pieces (comminuted) may require the use of an external metal device that maintains position of the fragments while allowing motion of the joints (external fixator). Any open wounds also require antibiotics in the emergency room and follow-up wound care. Individuals with massive crushing injuries to the hand are often hospitalized to control swelling and treat or prevent infection.

Prognosis

For both closed and open reduction, the prognosis is excellent with proper treatment and good rehabilitation. Uncomplicated fractures heal in 4 to 8 weeks. Any complication will delay recovery.

Differential Diagnosis

Conditions that present with similar symptoms include hand dislocations, wrist dislocations, hand infections, numerous soft-tissue injuries of the hand, and cysts and tumors. Additionally, individuals with rheumatoid arthritis can have disease-related deformities at the metacarpo-phalangeal joint that appear to be fracture/dislocations.

Specialists

- Hand Surgeon
- Hand Therapist
- Orthopedic Surgeon
- Physiatrist
- Sports Medicine Physician

Rehabilitation

Individuals who sustain metacarpal fractures may require outpatient therapy. The individual should be seen by either an occupational therapist or a physical therapist who is a certified hand therapist.

Therapy first addresses pain control and the reduction of swelling. Individuals learn to position the hand so that it rests above the elbow on a pillow to decrease swelling in the hand. Hot packs and hot paraffin wax decrease muscle stiffness prior to therapy. If there is surgical repair, therapists perform cross-friction massage to surgical scars to promote healing and instruct individuals in self-massage. Ice packs decrease pain and swelling after exercise.

Individuals learn stretching techniques to increase range of motion at the wrist and forearm. Therapists may passively stretch the wrist to increase flexion and extension, the forearm to increase rotation, and the hand to increase finger flexion and extension. Individuals stretch the wrist by holding the elbow straight and using their other hand to help bend the wrist into flexion and extension. Forearm stretches are performed by placing the other hand on the forearm and using it to help turn the forearm in the 2 rotational directions. Finger stretches are performed by making a fist and by extending the fingers and adding overpressure with the noninjured hand to increase these motions. Finger and thumb opposition is restored by touching the thumb to each finger.

Strengthening exercises are necessary to restore function and to prevent reinjury. Individuals use light hand weights to strengthen wrist flexion and extension and forearm rotation; individuals place the forearm on a table for support for these exercises. Individuals can squeeze therapy putty to restore hand strength. The muscles of the fingers should be strengthened by pinching therapy putty between the fingers, or by placing a rubber band around 2 fingers at a time and spreading them apart. Individuals learn functional exercises such as turning a doorknob and grasping/turning a key and perform exercises that emphasize dexterity such as picking up pegs and placing them in a pegboard.

Work Restrictions / Accommodations

Work restrictions and accommodations will vary with severity of the fracture and the amount of physicality or dexterity required for the individual's job. Total use of the injured hand (and fingers) may be restricted until the fracture is healed. Rest periods to allow elevation of the hand are important to avoid complications. Any work task that requires 2 hands may need to be eliminated for 4 to 8 weeks (during healing) and then added back gradually during rehabilitation.

Comorbid Conditions

Existing conditions that could impact ability to recover and further lengthen disability include degenerative arthritis, osteoporosis, calcium deficiency, Paget's disease, and tumors or cysts of the affected bones.

Complications

Possible complications of metacarpal fractures include malunion (causing pain on gripping), nonunion (necessitating reconstructive surgery), metacarpal phalangeal joint extension contractures, intrinsic muscle contractures, infection (especially pin tract), tendon adherence, and refracture.

Factors Influencing Duration

Disability is dependent on whether the dominant versus nondominant hand is involved, work requirements, the digit/digits involved, and the presence of complications.

Length of Disability

Duration depends on dominant or non-dominant hand is involved.

Open, with internal fixation.

Duration in Days

Job Classification	Minimum	Optimum	Maximum
Sedentary work	7	7	28
Light work	7	14	28
Medium work	21	28	56
Heavy work	28	42	70
Very Heavy work	28	42	112

Closed, with internal fixation.

Duration in Days

Job Classification	Minimum	Optimum	Maximum
Sedentary work	1	7	42
Light work	7	14	42
Medium work	21	28	56
Heavy work	28	42	70
Very Heavy work	42	42	112

Duration Trend from Normative Data*

Cases	Mean	Min	Max	No Lost Time	Over 6 Months
3834	55	0	458	0.29%	1.89%

Percentile:	5th	25th	Median	75th	95th
Days:	15	31	45	63	111

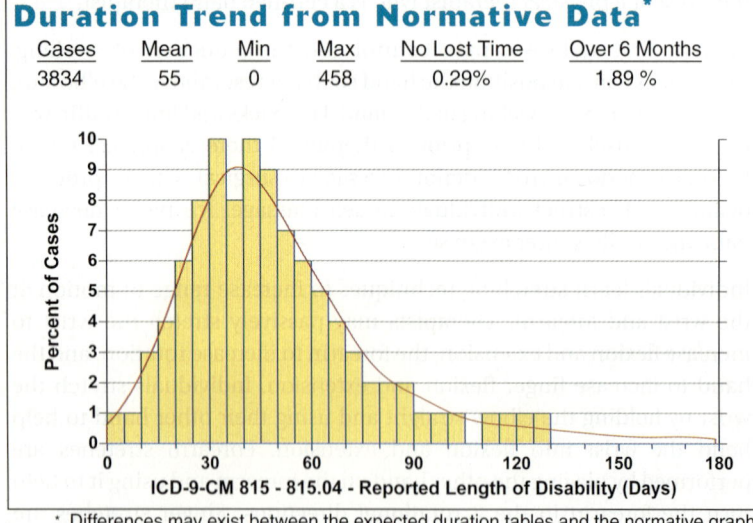
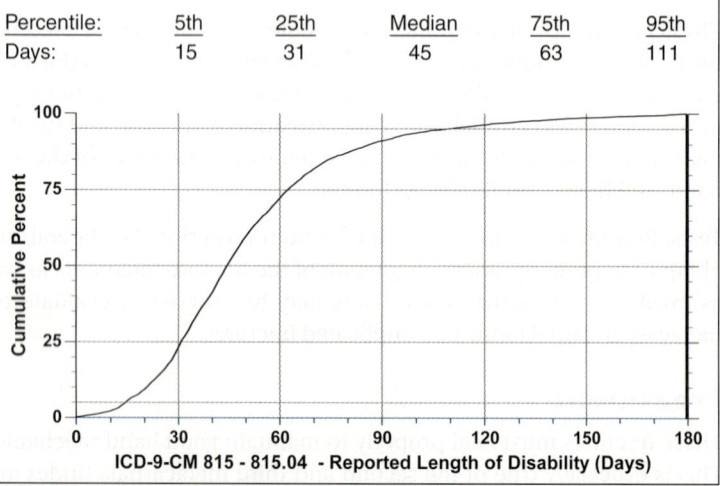

ICD-9-CM 815 - 815.04 - Reported Length of Disability (Days)

* Differences may exist between the expected duration tables and the normative graphs. Duration tables provide expected recovery periods based on the type of work performed by the individual. The normative graphs reflect the actual observed experience of many individuals across the spectrum of physical conditions, in a variety of industries, and with varying levels of case management.

Failure to Recover

If an individual fails to recover within the maximum duration expectancy period, the reader may wish to reference the following questions to assist in better understanding the specifics of an individual's medical case.

Regarding diagnosis:

- Did the individual present with symptoms consistent with a metacarpal bone fracture?
- Was an x-ray done to confirm the diagnosis?
- If the diagnosis was uncertain, were other conditions with similar symptoms ruled out?

- Does individual have an underlying condition (such as degenerative arthritis, osteoporosis, calcium deficiency, Paget's disease, and tumors or cysts of the affected bones) that may impact recovery?

Regarding treatment:

- Was treatment appropriate to type and location of fracture?
- Was the individual's pain adequately managed?
- Would individual benefit from consult with a specialist (orthopedic surgeon, hand surgeon, occupational therapist, physiatrist)?

Regarding prognosis:

- Has adequate time elapsed for healing?
- Did the individual participate in the recommended occupational or physical therapy?
- Would the individual benefit from therapy with a certified hand therapist?
- Did the individual suffer any associated complications that may contribute to a delayed or incomplete recovery?
- Has change of duties or temporary job reassignment been considered as appropriate?

References

Boxer's Fracture. Eaton Hand. 2000. 1 Jan 2000 <http://www.eatonhand.com/hw/hw005.htm>.

Apley, A. Graham, and Louis Solomon. "Injuries to the Upper Limb." Concise System of Orthopaedics and Fractures. Oxford: Butterworth-Heinemann Ltd, 1994. 270-298.

Fracture, Metatarsal Bones
Other names / synonyms: Broken Foot, Chopart's Fracture, Jones Fracture, Lisfranc's Fracture
825, 825.2, 825.25

Definition

A metatarsal bone fracture is a break in 1 of the 5 metatarsal bones in each foot. These long thin bones are located between the tarsal bones in the hindfoot and the phalanges in the forefoot.

Fractures of the metatarsal bones are often associated with dislocations and are often unstable. They are classified by their location: head, shaft/neck, or base. The most common fracture is of the base of the fifth metatarsal (Jones fracture), and is the result of twisting the forefoot. The location must be carefully evaluated as the treatment is radically different from fractures of the shaft of the fifth metatarsal. Fractures may develop in the metatarsals from repetitive use as well as from acute injury. Stress fractures and bone remodeling from stress are common in the second or third metatarsal (sometimes called a March fracture).

Most metatarsal fractures are caused by twisting injuries or direct impact (e.g., a heavy object falling on the foot). Athletes, individuals who are obese, and individuals with osteoporosis have an increased risk of metatarsal fractures.

The overall national incidence of metatarsal fractures cannot be readily estimated because many types of fractures are treated in outpatient settings, which are not linked to integrated databases.

Diagnosis

History: Individuals will report sharp pain in the forefoot that is aggravated by walking. Individuals may also report swelling (edema) and discoloration of the skin (ecchymosis). Most individuals will report a trauma prior to the beginning of the symptoms. Stress fractures will not be associated with a single trauma but rather with repetitive activity like jogging, ballet dancing, etc.

Physical exam: The foot may appear swollen over the suspected fracture site, deformity may be apparent, and pain will usually be localized. With

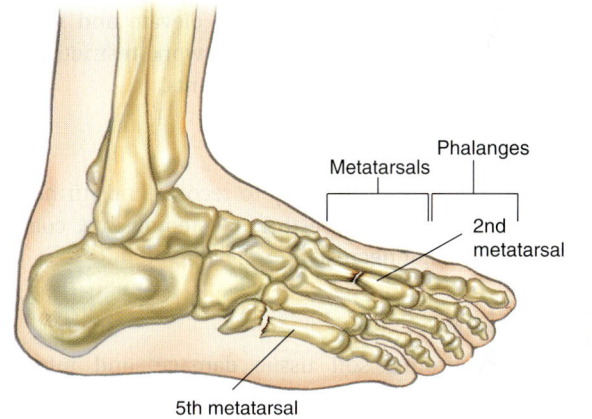

severe injuries, soft tissue damage may be apparent. Forefoot motion will be limited by pain. In more chronic cases, pain may be more diffuse and swelling minimal.

Tests: Routine x-rays (AP, lateral, and oblique views) are usually sufficient to diagnose the fracture. Comparison views of the other foot may be necessary. CT scans or MRI may be needed to rule out other injuries.

Treatment

Nondisplaced fractures of the shaft are the least difficult to manage. Treatment for minor metatarsal fracture will include R.I.C.E. therapy (rest, ice, compression, and elevation). Conservative treatment for minor metatarsal fractures will continue with a stiff-soled shoe, fracture brace, or walking cast. More severe fractures may require a non-weight-bearing cast for several weeks.

Displaced fractures may require open reduction and fixation. In areas of the foot where there is poor blood supply or in cases of significant dislocation, surgery (open reduction and internal fixation; ORIF) may be necessary.

Prognosis

A good outcome can be expected for simple, nondisplaced fractures without complications. Healing usually is noted within 6 to 8 weeks. Complicated fractures with associated injuries (e.g., dislocations) that require surgery will take longer to heal and the outcome may be less successful, especially if treatment has been delayed and circulation compromised.

Differential Diagnosis

Conditions that present with similar clinical findings include various ankle sprains, lower extremity compartment syndrome, and foot dislocations.

Specialists

- Orthopedic Surgeon
- Physiatrist
- Podiatrist
- Sports Medicine Physician

Work Restrictions / Accommodations

Weight bearing may be restricted for several weeks. This will affect the individual's ability to climb stairs, stand for even short periods of time, stoop, squat, or walk short distances. Crutches, canes, walkers, or wheelchairs may be required. Safety issues concerning work in confined space, limited dexterity, and ability to ambulate should be reviewed. Frequent rest periods with the ability to elevate and ice the lower extremity may be necessary. Temporary work restrictions may be necessary due to special footwear requirements.

Comorbid Conditions

Conditions that could impact ability to recover and further lengthen disability include obesity, osteoarthritis, osteomyelitis, compartment syndrome, and avascular necrosis.

Complications

Compartment syndrome, soft tissue damage, and infection may complicate the injury. Nonunion, infection, loss of reduction, or compartment syndrome could be complications of treatment. Chronic pain, callus growth on the sole of the foot, and traumatic degenerative arthritis could be long-term complications of the injury.

Factors Influencing Duration

The type and severity of the fracture, associated injuries, treatment required, and response to treatment may affect disability. The ability to modify work requirements and the rate of healing may also affect the disability period.

Length of Disability

Duration depends on fracture type.

1st metatarsal fracture.

Duration in Days

Job Classification	Minimum	Optimum	Maximum
Sedentary work	1	2	3
Light work	42	56	84
Medium work	70	84	112
Heavy work	112	140	168
Very Heavy work	112	140	168

Closed.

Duration in Days

Job Classification	Minimum	Optimum	Maximum
Sedentary work	1	7	14
Light work	7	14	28
Medium work	28	42	70
Heavy work	56	70	84
Very Heavy work	56	70	112

Distal metatarsal 2, 3, 4, or 5 (neck) fracture.

Duration in Days

Job Classification	Minimum	Optimum	Maximum
Sedentary work	7	9	14
Light work	21	28	35
Medium work	42	49	70
Heavy work	70	77	84
Very Heavy work	70	77	112

Proximal 5th metatarsal (Jones fracture).

Duration in Days

Job Classification	Minimum	Optimum	Maximum
Sedentary work	1	2	3
Light work	1	2	3
Medium work	14	21	28
Heavy work	35	42	56
Very Heavy work	35	42	56

Stress fracture of 2nd metatarsal.

Duration in Days

Job Classification	Minimum	Optimum	Maximum
Sedentary work	1	1	1
Light work	1	2	3
Medium work	7	14	21
Heavy work	21	28	84
Very Heavy work	21	28	84

Duration Trend from Normative Data*

Cases	Mean	Min	Max	No Lost Time	Over 6 Months
3606	59	0	384	0.18%	0.79%

Percentile:	5th	25th	Median	75th	95th
Days:	14	32	48	75	131

ICD-9-CM 825, 825.25 - Reported Length of Disability (Days)

* Differences may exist between the expected duration tables and the normative graphs. Duration tables provide expected recovery periods based on the type of work performed by the individual. The normative graphs reflect the actual observed experience of many individuals across the spectrum of physical conditions, in a variety of industries, and with varying levels of case management.

Failure to Recover

If an individual fails to recover within the maximum duration expectancy period, the reader may wish to reference the following questions to assist in better understanding the specifics of an individual's medical case.

Regarding diagnosis:

- Did the individual present with symptoms consistent with a metatarsal bone fracture? Was the diagnosis confirmed with an x-ray?
- If the diagnosis was uncertain, were other conditions with similar symptoms ruled out?
- Does the individual have any condition that might impact ability to recover?

Regarding treatment:

- Was the treatment appropriate for the type of fracture?
- Was surgery required? Are the weight bearing ends of all 5 metatarsals on the same level, or is one or more of the metatarsals healed in poor position causing pain and calluses on the bottom of the foot?
- Would the individual benefit by consultation with a specialist (orthopedic surgeon, podiatrist, sports medicine specialist, or physiatrist)?

Regarding prognosis:

- Has individual followed prescribed rehabilitative therapy?
- Did the individual suffer any complications that may impact ability to recover?
- Have appropriate work reassignments and accommodations been made?

References

Metatarsal Fractures. EMEDx. 2000. 1 Jan 2000 <http://www.emedx.com/pt/dx_info/foot-ankle/metatarsal-fractures.htm>.

Kisner, Carolyn, and Lynn Allen Colby. Therapeutic Exercise: Foundations and Techniques, 2nd ed. Philadelphia: F.A. Davis, 1990.

Fracture, Midfoot (Cuboid, Cuneiform, Navicular)

Other names / synonyms: Foot Fracture, Lisfranc's Fracture

825.22, 825.23, 825.24

Definition

A midfoot fracture is a fracture of one or all of the bones in the midfoot (cuboid, cuneiform, and navicular). Fractures of the bones in the midfoot are usually not isolated injuries; there are often multiple fractures or fracture dislocations. The midfoot is fairly rigid and stable, and when injuries occur, the force is often transmitted across the rows of bones.

Navicular fractures are the most common midfoot fractures (62% of all midfoot fractures). Navicular fractures are classified as dorsal avulsion fractures, tuberosity fractures, nondisplaced body fractures, displaced body fractures, or osteochondral fractures. Dorsal avulsion fractures are the most common navicular fracture accounting for 47% of all navicular fractures.

Cuboid fractures can occur in isolation, but are more often seen in conjunction with other fractures. Cuboid fractures are classified as avulsion (most occur on the lateral side) or body fractures (may be simple, stress, comminuted, crush, or fracture/dislocation).

Cuneiform fractures are classified as avulsion fractures, body fractures, or fracture/dislocations.

Midfoot fractures are rare, with only about 0.5% of all fractures involving the midfoot. One retrospective study showed that midfoot fractures affected men more than women by a ration of 3:1, but there are few epidemiological statistics available for this condition. Athletes, especially runners, are at risk for midfoot stress fractures.

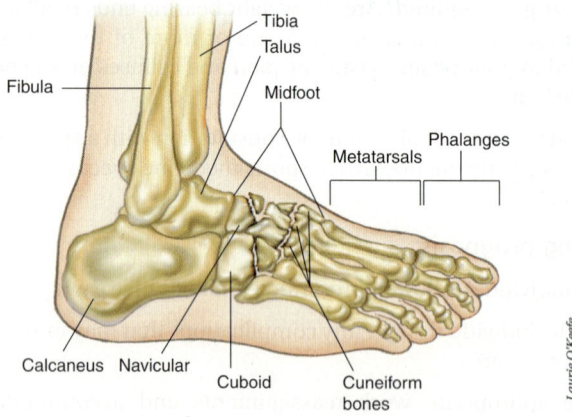

Diagnosis

History: The individual will report marked pain and swelling, and limited ability to move the foot and bear weight. There may be open wounds or severe soft tissue damage if the fractures are the result of a crushing injury.

Physical exam: Localized pain, swelling, and possible deformity may be noted. Attention must be paid to skin integrity and neurovascular status. The exam must rule out dislocations of the metatarsal bones, as they are commonly associated injuries.

Tests: Anterior-posterior (AP), lateral, and oblique x-rays with comparison views from the other foot are necessary, as these fractures are often difficult to detect due to overlapping bone outlines. A CT scan may be necessary to confirm the diagnosis.

Treatment

Depending on the type of fracture, treatment may range from a weight-bearing fracture brace or cast until asymptomatic (approximately 3 weeks) to open reduction and internal fixation (ORIF) followed by a nonweight-bearing cast until healed. Unstable, comminuted, or displaced fractures that cannot be simply reduced are treated surgically, as are fracture/dislocations.

Prognosis

The outcome depends on the severity of the fracture, the treatment required, and the development of complications. Nondisplaced fractures generally have an excellent prognosis with appropriate treatment. In fractures are severe enough to require surgery, healing times may be extended by 1-3 weeks, but the overall outcome is still good.

Differential Diagnosis

Conditions that present with similar symptoms include soft-tissue injuries of the ankle, lower extremity compartment syndrome, and foot dislocations.

Specialists

- Orthopedic Surgeon
- Physiatrist
- Podiatrist
- Sports Medicine Physician

Work Restrictions / Accommodations

Weight bearing may be restricted for several weeks. This will affect the individual's ability to climb stairs, stand for even short periods, or walk short distances. Crutches, canes, walkers, or wheelchairs may be required. Stooping and squatting should be restricted until the individual has regained full range of motion through stretching and physical therapy. Safety issues concerning work in confined space, limited dexterity, and ability to ambulate should be reviewed. Frequent rest periods with the ability to elevate the lower extremity may be necessary.

> **Complementary and Alternative Therapies**
>
> Content is intended for awareness only. Treatments may or may not be effective. Scientific evidence may be lacking and some substances have potentially toxic effects. Dr. Presley Reed and the editors do not endorse the use of these therapies in the absence of consultation with a licensed medical professional.
>
> Cryotherapy - After cast is removed, frequent ice massages or ice packs may decrease pain and swelling.
>
> Heat therapy - After cast is removed, hot packs and hot paraffin wax may decrease joint stiffness.
>
> Massage - Scar massage may promote healing and scar mobility over any surgical site.

Comorbid Conditions

Conditions that could impact ability to recover and further lengthen disability include diabetes, peripheral vascular disease, obesity, osteoarthritis, osteomyelitis, compartment syndrome, and avascular necrosis.

Complications

Compartment syndrome is the most dangerous acute complication of midfoot fractures. Compartment syndrome is most commonly associated with fractures sustained from a crushing injury. Long-term complications of midfoot fractures include infection, degenerative arthritis, nonunion or instability, and gait disturbances.

Factors Influencing Duration

Type and severity of fracture, age, complications of the injury, ability to modify work activities, and rate of healing may affect disability periods.

Length of Disability

Cuboid bone of foot.

Job Classification	Duration in Days		
	Minimum	Optimum	Maximum
Sedentary work	1	2	3
Light work	1	2	3
Medium work	14	28	42
Heavy work	42	56	84
Very Heavy work	56	70	112

Cuneiform bones of foot.

Job Classification	Duration in Days		
	Minimum	Optimum	Maximum
Sedentary work	1	2	3
Light work	1	2	3
Medium work	14	28	42
Heavy work	42	56	84
Very Heavy work	56	70	112

Navicular bone of foot. Body fracture, displaced.

Job Classification	Duration in Days		
	Minimum	Optimum	Maximum
Sedentary work	7	9	14
Light work	42	49	56
Medium work	56	63	112
Heavy work	112	126	168
Very Heavy work	112	126	224

Navicular bone of foot. Body fracture, undisplaced.

Job Classification	Duration in Days		
	Minimum	Optimum	Maximum
Sedentary work	1	2	3
Light work	1	2	3
Medium work	21	28	112
Heavy work	70	77	168
Very Heavy work	70	77	224

Navicular bone of foot. Dorsal avulsion fracture.

Job Classification	Duration in Days		
	Minimum	Optimum	Maximum
Sedentary work	1	2	3
Light work	1	2	3
Medium work	14	21	28
Heavy work	28	35	56
Very Heavy work	28	35	56

Navicular bone of foot. Stress fracture.

Job Classification	Duration in Days		
	Minimum	Optimum	Maximum
Sedentary work	1	3	7
Light work	14	21	28
Medium work	56	63	112
Heavy work	84	112	168
Very Heavy work	84	112	168

Navicular Bone of Foot. Tuberosity fracture.

	Duration in Days		
Job Classification	Minimum	Optimum	Maximum
Sedentary work	7	10	14
Light work	7	14	21
Medium work	14	21	42
Heavy work	14	28	56
Very Heavy work	21	42	56

Failure to Recover

If an individual fails to recover within the maximum duration expectancy period, the reader may wish to reference the following questions to assist in better understanding the specifics of an individual's medical case.

Regarding diagnosis:

- Has diagnosis been confirmed by x-ray and CT scan?
- Is a "Lisfranc" tarsal-metatarsal fracture dislocation present but unrecognized?
- Has individual experienced any complications related to fracture or treatment?
- Does individual have an underlying condition such as diabetes, peripheral vascular disease, obesity or other conditions that may impact recovery?

Regarding treatment:

- Was the individual placed in a cast?
- Was surgical intervention necessary?

Regarding prognosis:

- If symptoms persist past expected recovery, have x-rays been repeated to rule out nonunion or malunion?
- Are other complications present?
- Is individual following prescribed rehabilitative therapy?
- Has individual resumed weight-bearing too soon?

References

Apley, A. Graham, and Louis Solomon. "Injuries to the Lower Limb." Concise System of Orthopaedics and Fractures. Oxford: Butterworth-Heinemann Ltd, 1994. 317-344.

Silbergleit, Robert, MD. "Fractures, Foot." eMedicine.com. 07 Feb 2001. 22 Feb 2001 <http://www.emedicine.com/emerg/topic195.htm>.

Fracture, Pelvis

Other names / synonyms: Fracture of Bones within the Pelvis, Pelvic Fracture
808, 808.2, 808.3, 808.4, 808.41, 808.42, 808.43, 808.49, 808.5, 808.51, 808.52, 808.53, 808.59, 808.8, 808.9

Definition

The pelvis is formed by a group of bones arranged in a large ring. The ileum, ischium, pubis, sacrum, and coccyx form the pelvis (pelvic ring or pelvic girdle) supporting the spine and joining to the lower extremities. Any or all of these bones can be broken (fractured).

These fractures can be categorized as low- or high-energy fractures depending on the amount of force delivered to the pelvic bones. A low-energy fracture results in a fracture of an individual bone in the group (pelvic ring) without disrupting pelvic alignment, while a high-energy fracture disrupts the overall alignment of the pelvic ring and is likely to have associated damage to the organs contained within the pelvis. Half of all pelvic fractures are less serious in that they do not involve injury to organs of the urinary, reproductive, and digestive systems within the pelvic girdle.

Individuals using moving equipment or being hit by falling objects are at greater risk for pelvic fractures. Pelvic fractures seen in young adults are most often from direct trauma. Pelvic fractures in the elderly (especially women) are usually the result from thinning of the bone (osteoporosis).

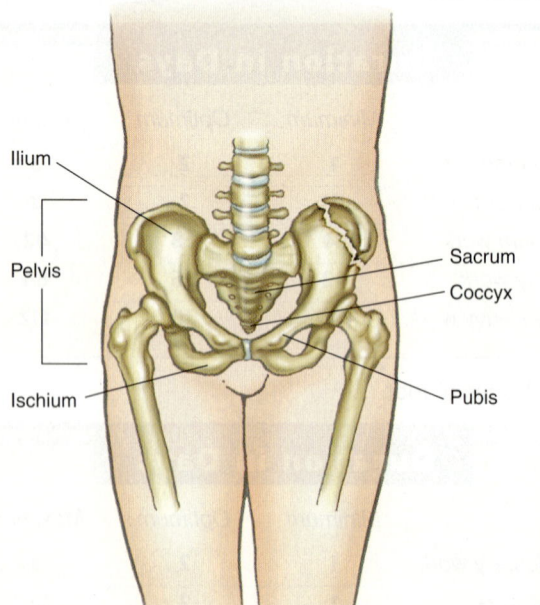

Diagnosis

History: Individuals may report a fall, being thrown from a moving object, or crushed under a heavy object. The fall could be onto the side or straddling a fixed object. Pain in the pelvis follows immediately and is constantly present. It is painful to walk and/or sit.

Physical exam: Compressing the sides of the hips together or pressing on the pubic symphysis produces pain. Blood may be noted in the urethra. A rectal and vaginal exam may reveal associated injuries. Blood pressure and heart rate changes may indicate blood loss.

Tests: Plain x-rays demonstrate many pelvic fractures, but a CT may be required in some cases. MRI may be ordered especially if internal organ damage needs to be ruled out. A urinalysis is done to detect blood in the urine, which is a sign of injury to the urinary tract. If a stress fracture is suspected, a bone scan may be ordered.

Treatment

If the pelvic fracture is only minimally displaced, bed rest and subsequent walking with crutches may be sufficient treatment along with pain medication. Surgery (external fixation or open reduction with internal fixation, or ORIF) may be needed for an unstable, displaced fracture. Emergency surgery is needed to control bleeding or repair damage to the intestinal or urinary systems. A less common fracture is from cancer in the bone that may be treated with radiation therapy and surgical stabilization (ORIF).

Prognosis

Outcome depends on the severity of the fracture and any associated injuries. The majority of those with nondisplaced fractures will be pain-free and without organ dysfunction after treatment. If pelvic distortion remains, the majority of individuals will have continued pain and dysfunction.

Open pelvic fractures are the most serious due to hemorrhage and sepsis, with up to a 50% mortality rate. Overall, those suffering an open fracture, one-third will have some sexual dysfunction, and one-third will change jobs as a result of the injury.

Differential Diagnosis

Avascular necrosis of the hip region, osteomyelitis, cancer, and osteoporosis may present with similar symptoms. These conditions are not the result of trauma but may be discovered when evaluating pelvic pain.

Specialists

- General Surgeon
- Gynecologist
- Orthopedic Surgeon
- Physiatrist
- Physical Therapist
- Radiologist
- Urologist
- Vascular Surgeon

Rehabilitation

Pelvic fractures vary from stable and uncomplicated fractures, like a non displaced fracture of the pubic ramus, to severe displaced fractures of the weight bearing portion of the pelvis with associated major injuries to the gastrointestinal tract and/or genitourinary tract.

At the time when weight bearing is to begin, the therapist may be involved in teaching ambulation skills. Later, when the fracture has healed sufficiently, exercises to restore strength, flexibility and endurance are appropriate. Specific therapy instructions will be determined by the treating surgeon, based on many factors related to the fracture and associated injuries.

A flexibility program helps maintain range of motion at the hip. Strengthening exercises may help prevent reinjury of the pelvis.

Work Restrictions / Accommodations

Standing, walking, and sitting may all need to be temporarily limited. The pelvis supports the weight of the upper body during standing and sitting, so a fracture will make these functions painful until healing occurs. Allowances should be made for individuals to change positions frequently.

During early recovery, wheelchair ambulation or a walker, crutches, and, later, a cane may be required for standing and walking. Safety issues need to be addressed with the use of assistive devices. Stair climbing is difficult during this period of recovery.

Comorbid Conditions

Healing of the pelvic fracture can be delayed by smoking, malnutrition, blood disorders, radiation therapy, osteoporosis, and obesity.

Complications

Immediate complications include hemorrhage and shock seen in a serious pelvic injury especially an open pelvic fracture. The bladder or urethra may be torn. There can be laceration or perforation of the rectum, anus, and small or large bowel. These may require a temporary colostomy. Lacerations may occur to the genitalia that may be overlooked in women. Individuals with pelvic fractures may also have injuries to the head, chest, or abdomen.

Other complications include infection either from outside contamination of the wound or from intestinal leakage. Peritonitis or retroperitoneal abscess can result from laceration of the rectum with possible sepsis. Bowel obstruction can occur either from a reflex ileus or entrapment of bowel in the fracture. Blood can clot in pelvic veins and then spread through the circulation (thromboembolism).

Later complications include bowel dysfunction or sexual dysfunction including impotence. Mal-union of the fracture can result in an abnormal gait, difficulty sitting, and back pain. Low back pain can also result from a fracture involving the sacroiliac joint. If the fracture involves the hip joint, degenerative arthritis of the hip can follow. Damage to lumbar and sacral nerves can leave weakness or disturbed sensation resulting in a gait disturbance. If the fracture heals with a deformed pelvis, this can interfere with future vaginal deliveries and require a cesarean delivery.

Factors Influencing Duration

The severity of the fracture and resultant treatment along with any associated internal organ damage/treatment influence disability.

Length of Disability

The extent of the fracture and treatment required will determine length of disability. Individuals with multiple injuries with or without complications may be permanently disabled. Follow-up surgeries to alleviate pain commonly in the back may be necessary if conservative treatment is not successful.

Not including acetabulum.

Duration in Days

Job Classification	Minimum	Optimum	Maximum
Sedentary work	14	42	56
Light work	28	56	84
Medium work	42	70	112
Heavy work	56	84	140
Very Heavy work	84	98	140

Acetabulum.

Duration in Days

Job Classification	Minimum	Optimum	Maximum
Sedentary work	70	84	112
Light work	70	84	112
Medium work	84	112	140
Heavy work	112	140	168
Very Heavy work	112	140	168

Failure to Recover

If an individual fails to recover within the maximum duration expectancy period, the reader may wish to reference the following questions to assist in better understanding the specifics of an individual's medical case.

Regarding diagnosis:

- Did the individual report a fall, thrown from a moving object, or crushed?
- How old is the individual?
- Does he/she have osteoporosis?
- What type of fracture was sustained? Low- or high-energy?
- Was there damage to organs in the pelvis?
- Did x-ray reveal pelvic fracture? Did MRI reveal internal organ damage?
- Were other conditions such as avascular necrosis of the hip region, osteomyelitis, cancer, and osteoporosis ruled out?

Regarding treatment:

- Was pelvic fracture minimally displaced?
- Did individual use crutches and later a cane when standing or walking?
- Was surgery necessary to repair any damage?
- Was there bleeding or damaged to the intestinal or urinary systems that required emergency surgery?

Regarding prognosis:

- Was individual pain-free and without organ dysfunction after treatment?
- Is the individual using a wheelchair, walker, cane or crutches?
- Is the individual still taking pain medication?
- Is the individual a smoker or obese?
- Does the individual have malnutrition, blood disorders, radiation therapy, or osteoporosis?
- Does the individual have a gait disturbance, difficulty sitting, back pain, or degenerative arthritis?

References

Anderson, Bruce. Office Orthopedics for Primary Care, 2nd ed. Philadelphia: W.B. Saunders Company, 1999.

Apley, A. Graham, and Louis Solomon. "Injuries of the Spine, Thorax, and Pelvis." Concise System of Orthopaedics and Fractures. Oxford: Butterworth-Heinemann Ltd, 1994. 299-316.

Browne, Patrick. Basic Facts of Fractures. Boston: Blackwell Scientific Publications, 1983.

Kisner, Carolyn, and Lynn Allen Colby. Therapeutic Exercise: Foundations and Techniques, 2nd ed. Philadelphia: F.A. Davis, 1990.

Fracture, Radius and Ulna, Distal

Other names / synonyms: Barton's Fracture, Buckle Fracture, Colles' Fracture, Pouteau Fracture, Smith's Fracture, Transverse Wrist Fracture, Wrist Fracture

813, 813.00, 813.01, 813.02, 813.03, 813.1, 813.2, 813.3, 813.4, 813.40, 813.41, 813.42, 813.43, 813.44, 813.5, 813.50, 813.51, 813.52, 813.53, 813.54, 813.80, 813.81, 813.82, 813.83, 813.90, 813.91, 813.92, 813.93

Definition

A fracture of the distal radius or ulna (or wrist fracture) is a break in 1 of 2 bones of the forearm near where they form part of the wrist joint. The radius is the bone located on the thumb side of the forearm, and the ulna is the bone located on the side of the small finger.

Such fractures usually involves not only the ends of the bone but also injury to the many small ligaments in the wrist. This may further decrease stability of the wrist joint creating problems with function of the wrist and hand.

This type of injury most often results from a fall with the hand extended during landing. Fractures of the distal radius and ulna are described by their location and position; for example, fragmented (comminuted) or displaced. A displaced fracture is one in which the bone has shifted its position. In addition, common descriptive names include Colles, Smith, and Barton fractures. A Colles fracture describes a break across the ends of both the radius and ulna, which results in a backward and outward position of the hand relative to the wrist. Colles fracture is the most common wrist fracture. A Smith's fracture describes the end of the radius heading downward, toward the palm. This fracture is sometimes called a reverse Colles. A Barton's fracture involves the upper (dorsal) edge of the radius and the joint surface. In cases where the force of the impact drives the bone fragments through the skin, or the skin is torn away from the area, exposing the bone and surrounding tissues, the fracture is referred to as an open fracture. If the skin remains intact, the fracture is considered closed.

Colles fractures are very common among adults, particularly middle-aged to elderly women who have osteoporosis. In the US, approximately 150,000 to 200,000 Colles fractures are reported annually. The incidence of forearm fracture in 35 to 44-year-old women is double that of men in the same age group, and the lifetime risk of Colles fracture is about 15% for women. Over the age of 35, the incidence ratio of wrist fractures in women compared to men is over four to one. The incidence plateaus at about the age of 60 for women and 59 for men. At age 80 and over, the annual incidence is 593 per 100,000 women and 78 per 100,000 men. There is an increased risk of wrist fractures in individuals who smoke.

Diagnosis

History: Individuals may relate a history of a fall or other traumatic event. Individuals may complain of pain, swelling, numbness, and perhaps deformity of the wrist.

Physical exam: It is very important to remove all rings and bracelets as soon as possible. Upon examination, skin breakdown, swelling, hematoma formation, deformity, and discoloration may be noted over the fracture site. Application of gentle pressure (palpation) to the wrist and forearm may reveal tenderness. Vascular examination and neurological assessment with 2-point discrimination to rule out concomitant injuries of the neurovascular structures in the area are part of the examination. Tendon and muscle function are evaluated via range of motion of the wrist and fingers (ability to move the wrist and fingers does not exclude a fracture).

Tests: Plain x-rays with multiple angles are necessary to verify alignment, fragment position, and articular surface involvement. X-rays are repeated after reduction and again at weekly intervals until stability of the fracture is assured. Complicated fractures may require CT or MRI scans before and after reduction. If there is suspicion of nerve or vessel injury, nerve conduction studies and vascular studies may be ordered.

Treatment

Closed fractures that are not displaced may be treated with a short arm cast or splint if the fracture appears stable. Because of the many pulling forces of ligaments and muscles near the wrist, the fragments may slip out of position, so close monitoring is required.

Closed fractures with fragments out of position will require manipulation (reduction), either closed with local or regional anesthesia or during surgery (open reduction). Again, because of the many forces pulling on the wrist, the fragments may slip after reduction. Turning the palm of the hand over rotates the radius and ulna, which can also cause displacement of the fracture, therefore the elbow is included in any splint or cast that is applied (sugar tong or long arm cast). This locks the elbow and hand, preventing rotation of the radius and possible displacement of the fracture.

If the fracture is unstable, metal hardware may be used to hold the fragments in position during healing. This hardware may be inserted directly into the fragments during surgery (open reduction with internal fixation, or ORIF). Traction and fixation may be accomplished with attached long pins passing through the skin and bone from one side to the other. These devices, called external fixators, may have hinges that allow wrist flexion while maintaining reduction of the fracture with traction. Some individuals require use of a sling, but elevation of the wrist and forearm during the early stages of healing is important to prevent complications.

Motion of the fingers and shoulder is encouraged. Medications for pain and swelling will be needed. Ice packs over the cast or splint can be helpful in reducing swelling and pain. Early motion of the wrist helps prevent stiffness and arthritis. Sometimes a removable splint can be used during the late stages of healing to encourage motion exercises. Referral to a hand therapist can be invaluable, even early in treatment. In very severe cases in which a wrist fracture is not healed after 4 months, or when the bones have been so displaced and fragmented that they can't be repaired, wrist replacement surgery (wrist arthroplasty) is indicated.

Prognosis

Uncomplicated distal radius and ulna fractures treated conservatively usually have an excellent outcome and should heal in about 6 weeks. There may be stiffness and swelling with activity for a few weeks. Fractures with open wounds, fractures requiring fixation (ORIF), or fractures requiring repeat reduction will have a longer recovery and may have poorer outcomes. In very severe cases in which wrist arthroplasty is performed, recovery is slower; however, the outcome is much better in these cases than if no replacement had been performed.

Differential Diagnosis

Fracture of any of the carpal bones (especially the scaphoid), ligament injuries in the hand or radioulnar joint, and aseptic necrosis could present with similar findings.

Specialists

- Hand Surgeon
- Neurosurgeon
- Occupational Therapist
- Orthopedic Surgeon
- Physiatrist
- Sports Medicine Physician
- Vascular Surgeon

Rehabilitation

Physical and/or occupational therapy may start immediately after treatment. Frequency and methods of therapy depend on the amount of nerve or tissue damage, as well as treatment and fracture type (e.g., an external fixation or open fracture may take longer). During rehabilitation, therapists should look for signs of nonunion, carpal tunnel, or other nerve damage.

Initially, range-of-motion and isometric exercises for unaffected areas of the limb such as digits, elbow, and shoulder are implemented. Digit exercises may include adduction and abduction finger exercises, such as spreading the fingers apart and then back together to help decrease swelling without turning the wrist. To reduce stiffening of the finger joints, the individual can perform exercises that provide extension of the metacarpophalangeal (MCP) and flexion of interphalangeal (IP) joints by extending the MCP joint and flexing each IP joint, and then pushing the fingertips outward so that the MCP joints are now extended and the IP joints are flexed. Shoulder and elbow exercises can be done either lying down or standing. Arm raises in multiple planes (e.g., across the body as well as straight up and down) and arm bends are typical shoulder and elbow exercises.

As the fracture becomes more stable, the individual may be fitted with a removable cast or brace. This fixation device is removed during therapy so that full active range of motion of the wrist and gentle resistive training (ball squeezes) can be introduced. To increase grip strength, gripping exercises are performed using putty or a soft rubber ball. A technique called joint blocking can be effective in increasing individual finger strength. For example, the therapist can block the MCP joint of the thumb by applying gentle pressure at the joint so that it cannot bend, and have the individual try to push the thumb back (extend) against the resistive force of a rubber band. Flexion and extension exercises for the wrist are performed with the forearm stabilized along a flat surface (arm of a chair or therapy table) with the wrist able to move freely in an up-and-down motion either with the palm facing up or down. If the individual is working to improve wrist flexors, the individual's palm should be face up; then, with a loosely closed fist, the hand is raised and lowered in a controlled motion with movement only from the wrist. By turning the palm down, and repeating the motion outlined above, the individual can engage the extensors of the wrist. Passive stretching for the wrist and forearm is also implemented.

Once pins and/or cast are removed, more functional activities (writing, opening doors) as well as weight training can begin. The wrist can be placed in more functional positions such as pronation where the individual holds the butt of a 1-2 pound weight with the palm facing down. The movement is a rotation from the wrist in a clockwise fashion from 9 to 1 o'clock from the right side, and 3 to 11 o'clock on the left. To perform resistive supination exercises, the exercises above are performed with the palm up. Other exercises such as sitting push-ups and wall push-ups can facilitate joint stability and start to engage the hand, wrist, elbow, and shoulder in functional retraining.

Work Restrictions / Accommodations

If the fracture is unstable, the arm should not be used for several weeks. The wrist should not be rotated until the fracture is healed. Lifting, carrying, and pushing should be limited. Use of a cast, splint, external fixation, and/or sling will affect dexterity; therefore, if the dominant side is injured, work restrictions may be more extensive (e.g., if an individual is right-handed and must write or perform fine motor skills with their dominant hand, they will experience more work limitations than if the nondominant hand were injured). Rest periods for elevation of the hand and forearm may be necessary during the initial stage of recovery. Use of medication for pain and swelling would require review of individual and co-worker safety and drug testing policies.

Comorbid Conditions

Comorbid conditions that would impact recovery include degenerative arthritis, osteoporosis, and any condition that inhibits the individual's ability to adhere to a rehabilitative exercise program.

Complications

Stiffness of the wrist joint is a frequent complication. Other complications include failure to regain full mobility of the wrist, chronic pain due to ligament injury, post-traumatic arthritis, and median nerve damage or compression leading to carpal tunnel syndrome. Swelling may cause the serious complication of compartment syndrome. Complex regional pain syndrome is not uncommon after wrist fractures. Tendon rupture, particularly an extensor tendon, may be a late complication.

Factors Influencing Duration

Loss of reduction, infection, aseptic necrosis, ligament injury, and concomitant carpal injury would lengthen treatment and recovery. Other factors that could influence disability include age, type of fracture, whether the dominant or nondominant hand is involved, stability of the fracture, and job requirements.

Length of Disability

Disability will be longer when distal (intra-articular). Disability may be permanent for individuals who perform heavy and very heavy work.

Distal.

Duration in Days

Job Classification	Minimum	Optimum	Maximum
Sedentary work	3	7	21
Light work	7	14	91
Medium work	63	91	147
Heavy work	119	182	238
Very Heavy work	119	182	273

Radius or radius with ulna.

Duration in Days

Job Classification	Minimum	Optimum	Maximum
Sedentary work	3	7	21
Light work	7	21	91
Medium work	28	91	119
Heavy work	56	119	147
Very Heavy work	70	147	168

Ulna.

Duration in Days

Job Classification	Minimum	Optimum	Maximum
Sedentary work	3	7	21
Light work	7	14	91
Medium work	28	70	119
Heavy work	56	91	147
Very Heavy work	70	147	168

Duration Trend from Normative Data*

Cases	Mean	Min	Max	No Lost Time	Over 6 Months
988	85	1	444	0.32%	7.37%

Percentile:	5th	25th	Median	75th	95th
Days:	19	45	65	93	140

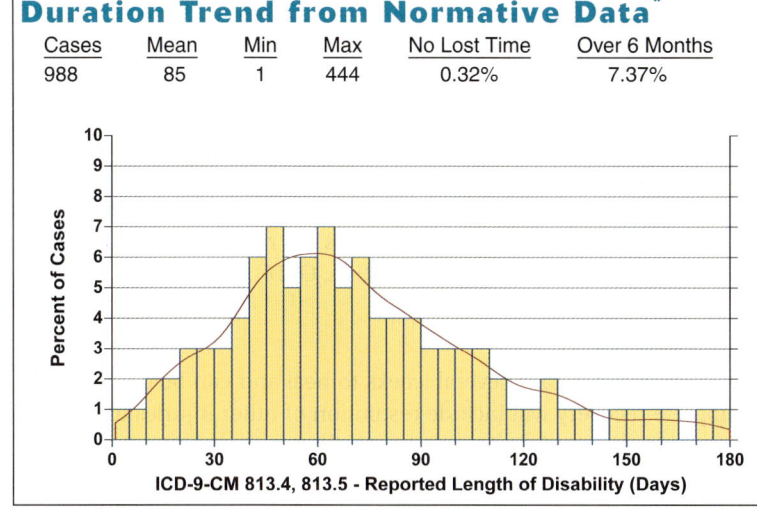

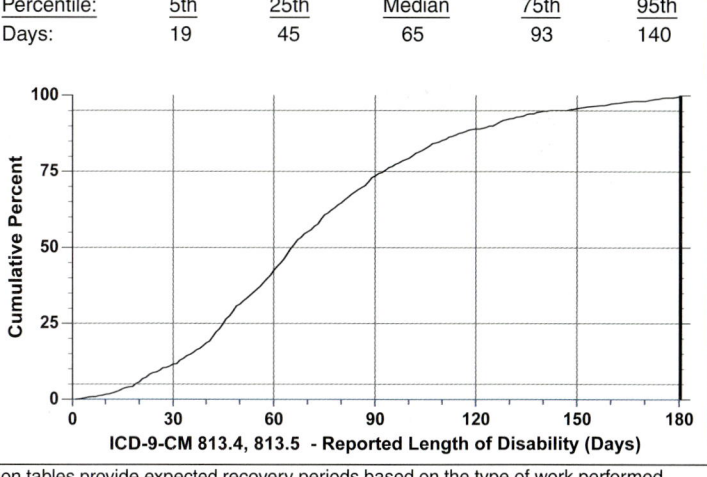

ICD-9-CM 813.4, 813.5 - Reported Length of Disability (Days)

* Differences may exist between the expected duration tables and the normative graphs. Duration tables provide expected recovery periods based on the type of work performed by the individual. The normative graphs reflect the actual observed experience of many individuals across the spectrum of physical conditions, in a variety of industries, and with varying levels of case management.

Failure to Recover

If an individual fails to recover within the maximum duration expectancy period, the reader may wish to reference the following questions to assist in better understanding the specifics of an individual's medical case.

Regarding diagnosis:

- Does individual complain of pain, swelling, numbness, and perhaps deformity of the wrist?
- Did individual present with symptoms consistent with a fracture of the radius or ulna?
- Was the fracture confirmed with an x-ray?
- If the diagnosis was uncertain, were other conditions with similar symptoms ruled out?

Regarding treatment:

- Was the treatment appropriate for this type of fracture?

- Was surgery required? Were any complications associated with the procedure?
- Would individual benefit by consultation with a specialist (orthopedic surgeon, hand surgeon, occupational therapist, vascular surgeon, neurosurgeon, sports medicine specialist, and physiatrist)?
- Did individual receive rehabilitation therapy, in particularly with a therapist specializing in the treatment of hands?

Regarding prognosis:

- Does individual have any condition that may inhibit his/her ability to adhere to a rehabilitative exercise program?
- Has adequate time elapsed for recovery? What is the expected prognosis?
- Has individual followed prescribed rehabilitative therapy?
- Did individual have any injury-related complications such as persistent immobility of the wrist, nonunion of the fracture, infection, chronic pain, post-traumatic arthritis, tendon rupture, compartment syndrome, or median nerve damage? If so, were complications addressed in the overall treatment plan?
- Does individual have any underlying condition such as degenerative arthritis or osteoporosis that may impact recovery?

References

Colles Fracture. American Academy of Orthopedic Surgeons. 2000. 01 Jan 2000 <http://orthoinfo.aaos.org/fact/thr_report.cfm?Thread_ID=150&topcategory=Arm>.

Wrist Fractures - Incidence/Prevalence. Merck & Co., Inc. 1995. 01 Jan 2000 <http://www.merck.com/pro/osteoporosis/inde91.htm>.

Fracture, Rib
Other names / synonyms: Broken Rib, Cracked Rib
807.0, 807.09, 807.1

Definition

Rib fractures are a disruption in the rib bone anywhere in the rib cage. There may be single fractures to one rib, multiple fractures to many ribs, or multiple fractures (comminuted) to the same rib. The fractures are classified by location (rib number and then right or left), then by position (displaced, nondisplaced).

Rib fractures are caused by blunt trauma to the chest, strong episodes of coughing that increase pressure and motion of the chest wall, or from disease of the rib bone which renders it weak. There does not seem to be a gender-specific tendency for rib fracture, although job requirements for heavy labor create a greater risk from blunt trauma, so males may appear at greater risk for rib fracture. In the older population, a higher incidence of osteoporosis among women may lead to a higher risk.

Diagnosis

History: Individuals may complain of pain with breathing, coughing, or using muscles along the chest wall. Individuals may feel a lump over the fracture or feel the rib move abnormally, either out of position or not in rhythm. In situations of severe trauma, the individual may also complain of the inability to breath normally.

Physical exam: Tenderness over the fracture, with possible displacement may be felt. Changes in breath sounds may be heard (auscultated), crunching (crepitus) felt in the soft tissue around the fracture site (air which has leaked out of the chest cavity and is trapped in the tissue), and abnormal expansion of the chest wall (flail chest) may be noted.

Tests: Chest and rib x-rays are ordered to locate the fracture(s). In severe trauma cases, CT scan, MRI scan, pulmonary function screening, ventilation quotient (VQ) scan, and pulse oximetry may be ordered to establish respiratory function.

Treatment

Uncomplicated rib fractures are treated symptomatically. This includes medications to decrease pain, suppress coughing, and decrease inflammation. Ice placed over the tender area, support from a rib belt or corset (with risk of pneumonia or lung collapse if over-used or improperly applied), and an intercostal nerve block if pain is severe and localized are examples of progressive, symptomatic treatment.

In cases of nonunion or malunion, electrical stimulation may be used to stimulate bone growth.

Rarely do rib fractures require surgical management, unless the fractures are a part of major trauma to the chest with multiple complications. Surgical procedures would include removal of bone fragments (rib resection) or use of fixation devices for rigid stabilization during healing (open reduction internal fixation, ORIF).

Prognosis

Rib fractures may take several weeks to heal and can be quite painful. Complete recovery will include resolution of other injuries in multiple trauma cases.

Rib fractures treated with non surgical methods (conservative treatment) will heal in 6-10 weeks, but may be quite painful during that period.

When surgical intervention (ORIF) is required, the rib should heal in approximately 6 weeks if there is no underlying condition affecting bone healing. Associated conditions such as injury to the major organs and vessels in the chest (thorax) may take longer to heal than an isolated rib fracture.

Differential Diagnosis

Pleurisy, costochondritis, and shingles may present with similar pain symptoms.

Specialists

- Internist
- Orthopedic Surgeon
- Pulmonologist
- Thoracic Surgeon

Rehabilitation

A rib fracture may require rehabilitation in the event additional structures including muscles and ligaments associated with the rib are also affected. At the onset of the rehabilitation, the physical therapist may apply treatments utilizing ice or heat to minimize swelling and pain.

Electrical stimulation combined with heat or cold treatment is another technique used in physical therapy to relax muscles around the fracture site. Transcutaneous electrical nerve stimulation (T.E.N.S.) consists of a battery powered device with electrodes placed on the skin in the region of the pain. An electrical impulse predetermined by the physical therapist produces a high frequency tingling sensation that blocks pain at that level of the spine. In cases of nonunion or malunion, electrical stimulation may be used to stimulate bone growth.

Once pain and swelling are reduced, the physical therapist performs stretching exercises to help restore full motion to an affected joint and/or upper limb. If the individual experiences a decrease in shoulder motion because of tight muscles attaching to the rib, stretching exercises consist of the physical therapist moving the arm with no effort by the individual.

The physical therapist may need to make modifications for those individuals with severely affected range of motion to any joints near the rib fracture. Modifications may also be needed in the event that the rib fracture results in pneumonia. Physical therapy addresses this possible complication by increasing ventilation with breathing exercises localized to the area of involvement followed by a gradual strengthening program. An exercise promoting both relaxation and a postural alteration for the muscles that aid in breathing begins with the individual assuming a relaxed sitting position while leaning forward, resting the forearms on the thighs or a pillow in the lap.

Until the rib is fully healed and shoulder/trunk motion returns, the individual should refrain from heavy lifting or contact sports.

Work Restrictions / Accommodations

Modifications of job requirements for upper body activities involving reaching, carrying, lifting, or overhead work would be necessary. Individuals with rib fracture(s) may not be able to tolerate heavy exertion in any position due to difficulty breathing.

Complementary and Alternative Therapies

Content is intended for awareness only. Treatments may or may not be effective. Scientific evidence may be lacking and some substances have potentially toxic effects. Dr. Presley Reed and the editors do not endorse the use of these therapies in the absence of consultation with a licensed medical professional.

Magnet Therapy - Magnets may be effective over persistently painful fracture sites.

Comorbid Conditions

Any acute or chronic respiratory illness would impact recovery from a rib fracture. Individuals with chronic obstructive lung disease (COPD), emphysema, or asthma may need to be hospitalized for respiratory support and management during the acute healing stage.

Chronic diseases affecting bone strength such as osteoporosis, cancer, or treatment for cancer would complicate recovery.

Complications

Individuals with chronic obstructive lung disease (COPD), emphysema, or asthma may need to be hospitalized for respiratory support and management.

Nonunion or failed union of the fracture can occur.

Collapsed lung (hemothorax or pneumothorax), flail chest, respiratory distress, pneumonia, damage to organs and bones in the chest cavity (thorax) could result from severe rib fractures.

Factors Influencing Duration

Inadequate healing of the fracture would impact disability. Recovery may be delayed by the concomitant injury.

Length of Disability

Duration depends on single or multiple ribs. Recovery from the pain of simple rib fractures may take weeks, longer than expected for bone healing.

Duration in Days

Job Classification	Minimum	Optimum	Maximum
Sedentary work	3	14	21
Light work	7	21	28
Medium work	14	28	42
Heavy work	21	42	56
Very Heavy work	21	42	70

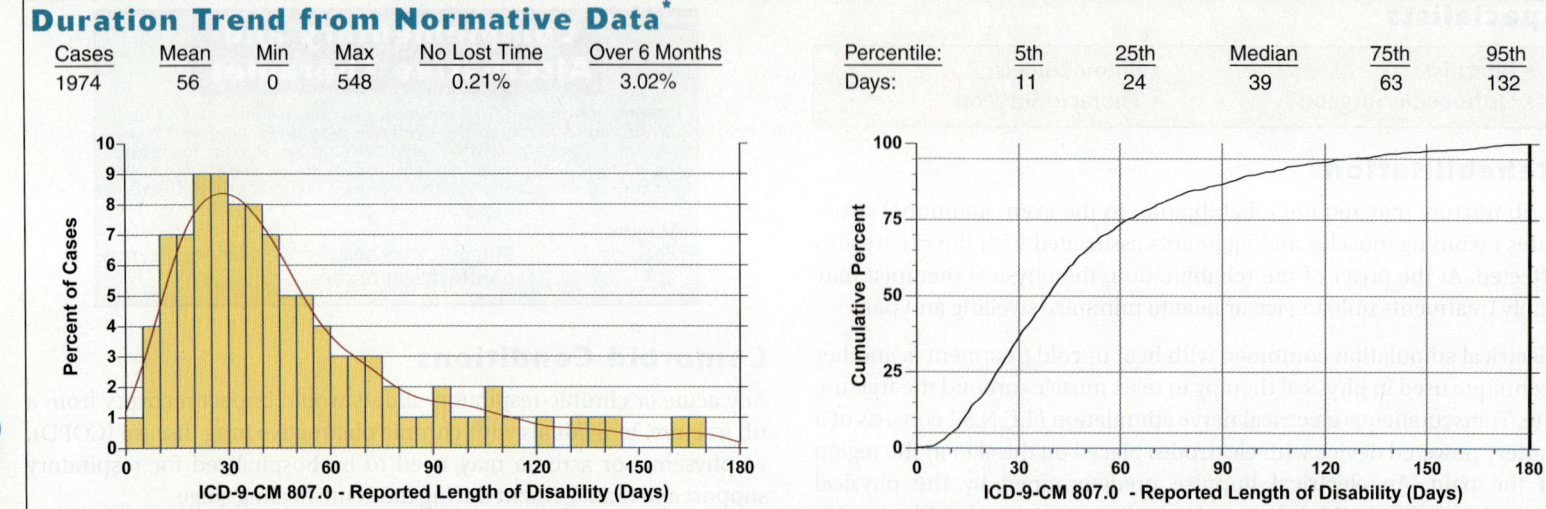

Duration Trend from Normative Data

Cases	Mean	Min	Max	No Lost Time	Over 6 Months
1974	56	0	548	0.21%	3.02%

Percentile:	5th	25th	Median	75th	95th
Days:	11	24	39	63	132

ICD-9-CM 807.0 - Reported Length of Disability (Days)

* Differences may exist between the expected duration tables and the normative graphs. Duration tables provide expected recovery periods based on the type of work performed by the individual. The normative graphs reflect the actual observed experience of many individuals across the spectrum of physical conditions, in a variety of industries, and with varying levels of case management.

Failure to Recover

If an individual fails to recover within the maximum duration expectancy period, the reader may wish to reference the following questions to assist in better understanding the specifics of an individual's medical case.

Regarding diagnosis:

- Did the individual have any trauma to the chest?
- Does the individual have pain with breathing?
- Does the individual feel a lump on the chest wall?
- On physical exam, were any abnormalities found such as abnormal breath sounds, crepitus, or flail chest?
- Did the individual receive adequate testing to establish the diagnosis (i.e., chest x-ray, bone scan, MRI)?
- Have conditions with similar symptoms such as pleurisy, costochondritis, and shingles been ruled out?

Regarding treatment:

- Has the individual responded to rest and analgesics? If not, were other interventions such as electrical stimulation considered?
- Was surgery indicated? What procedure was done?
- Is the individual participating in physical therapy?

Regarding prognosis:

- Has adequate time elapsed for recovery?
- Does the individual have any underlying conditions that would impair recovery, such as acute or chronic respiratory illness, chronic obstructive lung disease (COPD), emphysema, or asthma?
- Has the individual experienced any associated injury or complications such as pneumonia, respiratory distress, hemothorax or pneumothorax, or organ injury that could impact recovery and prognosis?
- Have appropriate work accommodations been made to allow the individual to return to work safely?

References

Anderson, Bruce. Office Orthopedics for Primary Care, 2nd ed. Philadelphia: W.B. Saunders Company, 1999.

Sloan, J.P., C.L. Muwanga, and E.A. Waters. "Multiple Rib Fractures: Transcutaneous Nerve Stimulation Versus Conventional Analgesia." Journal of Trauma 26 12 (1986): 1120-1122.

Fracture, Sacrum

Other names / synonyms: Os Sacrum Fracture, Spine Fracture

805.6, 805.7, 806.6, 806.60, 806.61, 806.62, 806.69, 806.7, 806.70, 806.71, 806.72, 806.79, 806.8, 806.9

Definition

A sacral fracture is a complete or incomplete break in the sacrum, which is a part of the spinal column made up of 5 fused vertebrae (the sacral vertebrae) between the lumbar vertebrae and the coccyx (tailbone). The sacrum anchors the spine to the pelvic girdle (between the 2 hip bones).

Traumatic fracture of the sacrum can occur as a result of a direct blow to the back, which is often associated with other pelvic injury. It can also occur due to indirect stress caused by twisting or other injury. In the elderly, a sacral fracture can occur secondary to osteoporosis with minimal or no trauma.

Sacral fractures are classified according to location: Vertical fractures are classified by the location of the fracture in relation to the neural foramen. Zone I fractures occur across the wing-like structures of the sacrum (sacral ala), and can cause lumbar L5 nerve root impingement; Zone II fractures occur through the tunnel-like openings in the sacral canal (neuroforamina), and can cause one-sided numbness in the sacral region; Zone III fractures occur through the body of the sacrum, and can result in a syndrome characterized by urinary and rectal dysfunction (cauda equina syndrome) or bladder dysfunction (neurogenic bladder), and about half of individuals will show neurological injuries. Transverse fractures commonly occur between S1 and S3, and frequently have associated bladder dysfunction. Osteoporotic fractures usually involve just the sacrum. Most other sacral fractures are the result of high-energy injuries, with a high incidence of associated injuries. Sacral fractures usually involve injury not only to the sacrum, but also to the hip joint (sacroiliac joint) and the soft tissue surrounding the fracture, e.g., muscles, nerves, tendons, ligaments, blood vessels, and bone covering (periosteum).

Individuals who are at particular risk of developing a sacral fracture include those who play contact sports, skaters, and individuals with a history of bone or joint disease, such as osteoporosis. Postmenopausal women, individuals taking long-term corticosteroid treatments, those with rheumatoid arthritis, and those who have undergone radiation therapy are at increased risk of stress fractures of the sacrum.

Diagnosis

History: The individual may report severe pain in the lower back, tenderness to the touch, and occasionally numbness. In some cases, the individual may report a direct blow to the back.

Physical exam: The exam may reveal swelling and bruising of the soft tissue surrounding the fracture and a deformity that the physician can feel (palpate) in rare cases of complete fracture where the bone fragments have separated enough to cause noticeable distortion. Often, there may be damage to the nerves that supply the rectum, bladder, and genitals. Indications of nerve damage may not be evident for several days after the injury.

Tests: Plain x-ray will usually identify the fracture. A bone scan or CT scan might be necessary to detect stress fractures (also called insufficiency fractures).

Treatment

Most sacral fractures are stable, and bed rest is the prescribed treatment, along with a sacral corset or brace for comfort while the fracture heals. Medications (analgesics) may be recommended for pain. For osteoporotic and/or stress fractures, walker ambulation and analgesics are appropriate. For fractures that are displaced, unstable, or complicated by neurologic deficit, surgery may be necessary.

Surgery is performed under general anesthesia. Surgical treatment may entail open reduction and internal fixation (ORIF) of the sacrum or removal of part of a vertebra (sacral laminectomy). In an ORIF procedure, the bones are replaced to the proper position (reduced) and secured with internal fixation (hardware). In a sacral laminectomy, part of a sacral vertebra is removed (excision of the posterior arch of the vertebra).

Prognosis

Prognosis will depend on the severity and location of the fracture. The average healing time for a nondisplaced sacral fracture is 6 to 8 weeks. The average healing time for a displaced sacral fracture (requiring surgical intervention) is 8 to 12 weeks. In both medically and surgically treated fractures, complete healing is likely, and is indicated by no pain at the fracture site and an x-ray showing complete bone union. Stress fractures of the sacrum may take up to 9 months to heal completely.

Differential Diagnosis

An acutely herniated L5-S1 intervertebral disc could produce similar pain. Other possible diagnoses include sacroiliac dislocation and cancer (metastatic lesions that may appear as stress fractures). A sacral fracture could be due to erosion of bone by cancer (a pathological fracture).

Specialists

- Orthopedic Surgeon
- Physiatrist
- Sports Medicine Physician

Rehabilitation

In most cases of sacral fracture there is minimal displacement of the sacrum bone fragments. If there is no neural damage or need for operative procedures, therapy for a sacrum fracture is minimal. A physical therapist may apply modality treatments such as ice or heat to minimize swelling and pain and/or supervise a progressive body maintenance program. The individual is encouraged to sit on a soft cushion and to limit sitting activity up to 30-minute intervals.

More serious sacral fractures may be accompanied with sacroiliac joint strain that will lead to low back pain. In either the mild or serious case, the goal of therapy is to reduce lower back and pelvic pain as well as restoring proper gait and functional mechanics by strengthening low back, abdominal, and hip muscles.

Forces that create strain on the lower back or pelvis during the early phases of treatment are contraindicated. The individual is taught good form when performing any movement to avoid arching the back or placing unnecessary loads on the sacroiliac joint. Exercises and stretching for the lower and upper body may be performed in prone (face down) or supine (face up) positions to eliminate undo stress to the sacral area. Once pain has diminished, therapy may focus on strengthening the hip, lower back, and abdominal muscles. To continue to protect the healing fracture, the individual may engage in aqua therapy.

Once the individual is pain-free and the sacral fracture is stable, the individual may engage in shallow water training that helps them return to normal weight bearing. Walking forward, backward, and laterally, and minisquat exercises all help restore normal gait pattern.

Aqua therapy progresses with varying intensity and duration of exercises until the individual is pain-free and able to return to gravity-based therapy. The length of any therapy program depends on the seriousness of the sacral fracture. As well, occupational therapy may also be implemented if the individual experiences more permanent damage and needs to adjust the environment, such as by placing special cushions in the car while driving or adjusting the work environment if tasks like reaching, bending, or sitting for prolonged periods of time are performed.

Work Restrictions / Accommodations

Individuals may need to wear a corset or brace for support while healing, and will need to avoid physical labor (lifting, carrying, etc). Prolonged sitting or standing may temporarily need to be limited. Accommodation for frequent bathroom visits could be necessary. Individuals with stress fractures of the sacrum require avoidance of weight bearing due to the risk of late displacement and possible malunion of the fracture.

Comorbid Conditions

Comorbid conditions that may lengthen the recovery time include obesity, poor nutrition (especially calcium deficiency), diabetes mellitus, rheumatoid arthritis, and any condition that inhibits the individual's ability to engage in rehabilitative exercise therapy.

Complications

Pain with sitting or standing could be prolonged. About 60% of individuals who experience a sacral fracture will have some sort of neurological complication. These include cauda equina syndrome, in which the individual experiences urinary retention, numbness, and loss of rectal tone, and bladder dysfunction caused by nerve injury (neurogenic bladder). Sexual, bladder, or bowel dysfunction could persist due to postoperative swelling and pressure on nerves and blood vessels. Other possible complications include death of the bone cells (avascular necrosis) due to inadequate blood supply, excessive bleeding, infection, and an unstable or arthritic spinal joint following repeated injury.

Factors Influencing Duration

Length of disability may be influenced by age, type of fracture, presence or absence of neurologic deficit, presence or absence of other pelvic fractures, and whether the individual has a smoking habit or regularly uses mind-altering drugs.

Length of Disability

Stable fracture. No neurologic deficit.

Duration in Days

Job Classification	Minimum	Optimum	Maximum
Sedentary work	7	14	28
Light work	7	14	28
Medium work	7	21	42
Heavy work	28	42	70
Very Heavy work	28	42	91

Failure to Recover

If an individual fails to recover within the maximum duration expectancy period, the reader may wish to reference the following questions to assist in better understanding the specifics of an individual's medical case.

Regarding diagnosis:

- Did the individual present with symptoms consistent with a sacral fracture?
- Diagnosis is usually confirmed by an x-ray of the sacrum. Was the diagnosis confirmed with x-ray?
- If the diagnosis was uncertain, were other conditions with similar symptoms ruled out?

Regarding treatment:

- Was the treatment appropriate for the type of fracture?
- Was surgery required?
- Was the individual's pain controlled with ice and analgesics? If not, were other interventions tried (relaxation, visualization, alternative analgesics, or dose adjustments)?
- Did the individual comply with the treatment recommendations?
- Would the individual benefit from consultation with a specialist (orthopedic surgeon, physiatrist, and sports medicine specialist)?

Regarding prognosis:

- Has adequate time elapsed for healing?
- Has the individual participated in physical therapy and aqua therapy as recommended?
- Does the individual have any conditions that may impact ability to recover?
- Has the individual experienced any complications? If so, have the complications been addressed in the treatment and rehabilitation plan (i.e., bladder training for those with bladder dysfunction)?

References

Sacrum and Sacral Fractures. Wheeless' Textbook of Orthopaedics. 01 Aug 1999. 01 Jan 2000 <http://www.medmedia.com/o11/27.htm>.

Spine Fracture, Sacrum. HealthGate.com. 23 Jun 1999. 01 Jan 2000 <http://www.healthgate.com/sport/sport121.shtml>.

Eismont, Frank, and Scott Kitchel. "Thoracolumnar Spine." Orthopaedic Sports Medicine: Principles and Practice Volume 2. DeLee, Jesse, and David Drez, eds. Philadelphia: W.B. Saunders Company, 1994. 1028.

Reid, David. "Soft Tissue Injuries of the Thigh." Sports Injury Assessment and Rehabilitation. Reid, David, ed. New York: Churchill Livingstone, 1992. 641.

Fracture, Skull (Closed)

Other names / synonyms: Closed Head Injury, Cranial Fracture, Fractured Cranium, Fractured Skull

801.0, 801.09, 801.1, 801.2, 801.3, 801.5, 801.8, 803.0

Definition

A closed skull fracture is a break in one or more of the bones of the head (cranium) without an accompanying wound to the skin.

Closed skull fractures can be classified as linear (simple), basilar, or depressed fractures. A simple skull fracture is a break in the form of a thin line and is not associated with any distortion of the bone. Simple skull fractures account for 80% of all skull fractures. Basilar skull fractures, which are fractures of the base of the skull, are common. A depressed brain fracture is one in which the skull bones are pushed inward or crushed. This can compress the brain and/or damage it with bone fragments.

Individuals who are at risk of sustaining a skull fracture include construction workers, warehouse workers, and those who have a risk of falls or heavy objects falling onto them. In addition, individuals who participate in contact sports (e.g., football, hockey, soccer), especially when protective equipment is not worn, and sports that involve heavy equipment (e.g., baseball, golf, tennis) are at risk of sustaining a skull fracture.

Roughly two-thirds of skull fractures are accompanied by serious injury to the brain. Skull fractures are usually caused by a severe blow to the head, by falls, physical assault, motor vehicle accidents, and contact sports. Head injury is the leading cause of death in men under the age of 35 years. There are approximately 2 million skull fractures in the US each year.

Diagnosis

History: The individual would have a history of a severe blow to the head. He or she may complain of headache and/or pain at the site of injury. The individual may have lost consciousness following the blow. If the injury is severe, the individual may experience weakness, confusion, fatigue, seizures, dizziness, vomiting, drowsiness, speech difficulties, and vision problems, or may display early symptoms of inflammation of the membranes that surround the brain and spinal cord (meningitis), which include a stiff neck, confusion, and fever.

Physical exam: Tenderness and swelling over the fracture is usually present. The deformity of a depressed skull fracture is sometimes felt by touch (palpation). The individual would be examined for bleeding from the ear(s), bruising at the site of injury, behind the ears, and around the nose and eyes (known as "raccoon eyes"), and a watery discharge from the ears and nose. The individual's eyes, vision, speech, and memory may be checked.

Tests: Tests may include a skull x-ray, CT scan, and MRI. An EEG to measure and monitor brain activity may be performed. Because of the absence of an obvious wound to the skin, closed skull fractures can be difficult to detect without advanced diagnostic testing.

Treatment

Simple skull fractures often require no specific treatment other than monitoring the individual for 12 to 24 hours for signs of neurological complications. The primary concern is whether there is underlying brain damage. The individual may be observed in the emergency room and discharged with the instruction that someone must wake the individual every hour to ensure that the individual has not sustained a brain injury. The standard treatment plan of rest, ice, compression, and elevation (R.I.C.E.) may be followed. Analgesics may be taken. Surgery (open reduction) is necessary if the bone fragments are out of alignment (depressed brain fracture).

Prognosis

Uncomplicated skull fractures heal within 4-6 weeks, after which the individual can return to normal levels of functioning. Open reduction of depressed skull fracture has a good outcome, provided there was no brain injury. Individuals with brain injury can have residual problems that may lead to permanent disability.

Differential Diagnosis

The diagnosis is evident based upon the history of a trauma and x-ray exam.

Specialists

- Neurologist
- Neurosurgeon
- Orthopedic Surgeon
- Physiatrist
- Physical Therapist

Rehabilitation

There is no true rehabilitative procedure for a closed skull fracture. Rehabilitative therapy beyond initial trauma usually occurs in those individuals who suffer brain injury as a result of the skull fracture (e.g., cerebral concussion, coup, and contrecoup contusions). If brain injury results, the individual participates in an integrated rehabilitation plan that consists of physical, occupational, neuropsychological, and vocational therapies. These therapies can last for 6 months to 2 years. Prolonged treatment is dependent on the severity and permanency of the brain injury.

Assuming that the individual has no brain injury or blood clot outside the brain covering (hematoma), an individual may start a therapeutic exercise routine if they are free of headaches and nausea. Exercise selection depends on the location of the skull fracture as well as accompanying symptoms such as neck and upper back tightness.

Initially, range-of-motion exercises for the arms and lower body may be implemented. Arm movements may include straight-arm raises, where the individual lies face up with their hands to their side and palms facing their thighs, raising their arms overhead one at a time. Ultrasound and stretches for the upper back (especially the trapezius) may also accompany range-of-motion exercises.

When the skull fracture becomes more stable, a walking and/or stationary bike program is implemented to the tolerance of the individual. Progressively, arm exercises may be added while the individual rides the bike or separately as part of a different routine. As well, leg extension exercises where the individual sits at the end of a therapy table or bench with the legs perpendicular to the floor, and then extends them until they are parallel to the floor can be utilized. Weight is eventually added as the routines become progressively more functional in nature. Full weight bearing may be allowed after the individual exhibits good balance and muscular coordination.

Work Restrictions / Accommodations

Individuals with uncomplicated skull fractures are typically able to resume normal activities within a few weeks. Skull fracture without brain damage generally does not require restrictions. However, pain medication can affect mental alertness and the ability to operate machinery, and may require alteration of drug-use and testing policies by the employer.

Comorbid Conditions

Osteoporosis, poor nutrition, and other injuries sustained during the traumatic event may influence the length of disability.

Complications

Complications of a closed skull fracture include concussion, brief coma, hemorrhage, nerve damage, leakage of the fluid that bathes the brain and spinal cord (cerebrospinal fluid), meningitis, collection of blood (hematoma) in the brain, brain abscess, temporary or permanent loss of vision, significant impairments to mental function, and post-traumatic epilepsy. Postconcussion syndrome effects (e.g., headache, dizziness, fatigue, memory loss, personality change) can last from weeks to months, even years. Neuropsychological testing can be performed to better assess these residuals.

Factors Influencing Duration

The severity of the fracture, whether or not surgery was required, underlying brain damage, job demands, and the presence of complications will influence the length of disability.

Length of Disability

Disability may be permanent for individuals who have certain residual sequelae due to a severe head injury.

Without brain injury.

Duration in Days

Job Classification	Minimum	Optimum	Maximum
Sedentary work	3	7	21
Light work	7	14	28
Medium work	10	21	35
Heavy work	14	28	42
Very Heavy work	14	35	42

Failure to Recover

If an individual fails to recover within the maximum duration expectancy period, the reader may wish to reference the following questions to assist in better understanding the specifics of an individual's medical case.

Regarding diagnosis:

- Was a skull fracture confirmed by a skull x-ray?
- Was a CT scan or MRI conducted to rule out associated brain injury?
- Have conditions with similar symptoms been ruled out?

Regarding treatment:

- Did the individual receive the appropriate treatment and monitoring for the injury sustained?
- Was surgery required? What was the expected outcome?
- Did the individual participate in appropriate neurological rehabilitation?
- Are there barriers that prevent the individual from participating in neurological rehabilitation, such as lack of insurance coverage, lack of transportation, lack of motivation?
- Would the individual benefit from consultation with a specialist (neurosurgeon, neurologist, orthopedic surgeon, physiatrist)?
- Does the individual have adequate psychosocial support (family, friends, head injury support group)?

Regarding prognosis:

- Has adequate time elapsed for complete recovery?
- What was the expected outcome (full recovery, partial disability, etc.)?
- Does the individual have any coexisting conditions that may impact recovery?
- Did the individual experience any complications associated with the injury?
- If so, have the complications been addressed in the treatment plan?
- Are work accommodations appropriate for the severity of the disability?

References

"Skull Fracture." The PDR® Family Guide Encyclopedia of Medical Care. 1999. 27 Dec 2000 <http://www.healthsquare.com/mc/fgmc9048.htm>.

Head and Spinal Chord Trauma. Columbia University. 01 Jan 2000. 7 July 2000 <http://cpmcnet.columbia.edu/texts/guide/hmg26_0007.html>.

Head Injury: Skull Fracture. HealthGate.com. 23 June 1999. 27 Dec 2000 <http://www.healthgate.com/sport/sport101.shtml>.

Torg, Joseph, and Thomas Gennarelli. "Head and Cervical Spine Injuries." Orthopaedic Sports Medicine: Principles and Practice Volume 1. DeLee, Jesse, and David Drez, eds. Philadelphia: W.B. Saunders Company, 1994. 417-462.

Fracture, Sternum (Closed)

Other names / synonyms: Fractured Sternum, Sternal Fracture

807.2, 807.3

Definition

Fracture of the sternum is a break (fracture) of the breastbone (sternum) that occurs without an associated skin injury (closed).

The majority of sternum fractures are caused by blunt trauma to the chest. Uncommonly, sternum fracture occurs from vertical compression of the rib cage. Most sternum fractures are merely a crack but, less commonly, violent trauma pushes (displaces) the sternum into the chest. Sternum fractures can also be caused by repeated stress (stress fracture) or spontaneously because of bone weakness (insufficiency fracture). Most (60-90%) sternum fractures are caused by a motor vehicle accident. Most of the remaining sternum fractures are caused by falls, assaults, motor vehicle accidents (a car hitting a pedestrian), and direct impact sports. Stress fractures and insufficiency fractures of the sternum are rare.

Individuals who are at risk of falling from a height (e.g., construction workers, warehouse workers) and those who participate in direct contact sports (e.g., hockey, football) are at an increased risk of sustaining a sternum fracture. Golfers, weight lifters, and other athletes in non-contact sports are at an increased risk of developing stress fractures. Individuals with osteoporosis, osteopenia, or severe hunchback (kyphosis), and those who are on long-term steroid therapy are at an increased risk of insufficiency fractures. The use of seat belts has led to an increase in the number of sternum fractures; however, the severity of injuries has decreased.

Each day, 12 out of every 1 million individuals in the US suffer a chest (thoracic) injury. Sternum fractures occur more frequently in women than in men and are more common in individuals over the age of 50 years.

Diagnosis

History: Most individuals have a history of trauma such as a motor vehicle accident, fall, or contact sport injury. The individual may complain of intense chest pain that is localized to the sternum. Individuals with an insufficiency fracture may complain of pain throughout the chest. Some individuals may complain of breathing difficulty (dyspnea).

Physical exam: The significant majority of those with a sternal fracture present with pain and tenderness when the sternum is felt with the hands (palpated). Palpation may detect sternal displacement and/or a grating sensation (crepitation). Approximately 50% of those with a sternal fracture present with breathing difficulty (dyspnea). The individual may have bruising or swelling (edema) over the sternum. Individuals with an insufficiency fracture usually display an exaggerated hunch back (kyphosis). A thorough exam includes listening to the heart and lungs with a stethoscope and observation and palpation for other chest injuries.

Tests: Tests include chest x-rays (posteroanterior, lateral, and sternal views). CT scanning or ultrasonography may be performed. ECG, cardiac monitoring, pulse oximetry, and blood tests for cardiac enzymes may be performed on individuals who sustained a significant blunt injury.

Treatment

A minor sternal fracture is treated with analgesics (NSAIDs and opiates) and restricted activities for several weeks. Intercostal nerve blocks may be used for pain control. Treatment of a displaced sternum may require making a small cut (incision) into the chest so that a hook can be used to pull the sternum into the proper position. Compression fractures of the sternum are treated the same as a minor sternal fracture.

Prognosis

Most sternum fractures will heal on their own; however, adherence to the treatment guidelines can prevent delays in the recovery process. Although sternum fractures take several weeks to heal, a complete recovery can be expected. The prognosis is excellent for sternum fractures in the absence of other significant injuries.

Differential Diagnosis

A fractured sternum is a specific physical finding. Prior to x-ray confirmation, spontaneous fractures may simulate a heart attack (myocardial infarction) or pulmonary emergency.

Specialists

- Orthopedic Surgeon
- Physiatrist
- Physical Therapist
- Sports Medicine Physician

Rehabilitation

A fracture of the sternum may require rehabilitation in the event additional structures including muscles and ligaments associated with the sternum are also affected.

At the onset of the rehabilitation, the physical therapist may apply treatments utilizing ice or heat to minimize swelling and pain. Once pain and swelling have been reduced, the physical therapist performs stretching exercises to help restore full motion to an affected joint and/or limb. If the individual experiences a decrease in shoulder motion because of tight muscles attaching to the sternum and arm bone (humerus), stretching exercises consist of the physical therapist moving the arm while no effort is provided by the individual.

The affected muscles and/or ligaments are placed upon a mild stretch. Modifications may need to be made by the physical therapist for those individuals with severely affected range of motion to any joints near the sternum.

Until the sternum is fully healed and shoulder motion has returned, the individual should refrain from heavy lifting or contact sports.

Work Restrictions / Accommodations

Overhead lifting, pushing, pulling, and lifting objects that weigh more than 5 pounds should be eliminated from duties until the fracture has healed. After the fracture has healed, there should be a gradual return to normal activities. A temporary reassignment of duties may be necessary. Pain medication can affect mental alertness and the ability to operate machinery and may require alteration of drug-use and testing policies by the employer.

Comorbid Conditions

Associated injuries (e.g., spine fracture, major chest injury), osteoporosis, osteopenia, and diabetes may influence the length of disability.

Complications

Complications are rare and include cardiac concussion, cardiac contusion, osteomyelitis, abscess, pneumothorax, aortic rupture, mediastinitis, nonunion, and pseudarthrosis. Fractures resulting from compression of the rib cage are usually associated with fracture of the upper (thoracic) back.

Factors Influencing Duration

The severity of the fracture, presence of complications, and effectiveness of pain management can influence the length of disability.

Length of Disability

Duration depends on the severity of the fracture and related symptoms, if any. Duration may be longer for individuals whose duties involve heavy and very heavy work.

Duration in Days

Job Classification	Minimum	Optimum	Maximum
Sedentary work	7	14	28
Light work	7	21	42
Medium work	14	42	91
Heavy work	42	91	119
Very Heavy work	56	119	182

Failure to Recover

If an individual fails to recover within the maximum duration expectancy period, the reader may wish to reference the following questions to assist in better understanding the specifics of an individual's medical case.

Regarding diagnosis:

- Did the individual present with findings consistent with a sternal fracture (pain, bruising, and swelling of the sternum)?
- Was a fracture confirmed on x-ray?
- Was a CT scan of the chest, 12-lead ECG, spinal x-rays, cardiac isoenzymes and pulse oximetry done to rule out other associated injuries or other conditions?
- Would the individual benefit from consultation with a specialist (orthopedic surgeon, cardiologist, pulmonologist, traumatologist, cardiovascular surgeon)?

Regarding treatment:

- Was the treatment appropriate for the type of fracture and associated injuries?
- Is pain being adequately controlled with analgesics? If not, has an intercostals nerve block been considered?
- Did the individual suffer any associated injuries that may influence length of disability? If so, are the injuries being addressed in the treatment and rehabilitation plan?

Regarding prognosis:

- Has adequate time elapsed for recovery?
- Does the individual have any comorbid conditions such as cardiac disease, osteoporosis, chronic pulmonary disease, or bleeding disorders that may impact ability to recover?
- What was the expected outcome?

References

Adams, John, and David Hamblen. "Spine and Thorax." Outline of Fractures including Joint Injuries. Adams, John, and David Hamblen, eds. Edinburgh: Churchill & Livingstone, 1000. 99-110.

Scully, Rosemary M., and Marylou R. Barnes. Physical Therapy. Philadelphia: J.B. Lippincott Company, 1989.

Fracture, Talus

Other names / synonyms: Shepherd Fracture, Talar Fracture

825.21

Definition

Fracture of the talus is a fracture of one of the three bones in the ankle. The talus is the second most commonly fractured of the seven tarsal bones. No muscles are attached to the talus and the blood supply is limited to the ligament and the joint capsule.

The human ankle is a complex joint that consist of three bones, the tibia, the fibula, and the talus. The three bones work in unison to provide the range of motion necessary for daily and recreational activities (e.g., running, jumping, walking). The range of motion of the ankle joint is so unique that medical scientists have not been able to successfully duplicate the joint with an implant.

There are four main types of talar fractures. Neck and body fractures are the most common talar fracture and may be associated with subtalar dislocation. Lateral process fractures used to be rare but are becoming more common with the rise in popularity of snowboarding. Posterior process fractures or Shepherd fractures are caused by damage to the posterior process of the talus by either sudden extension of the foot so that the forefoot is depressed relative to the heel (plantarflexion) or by repetitive motion (especially in athletes or dancers). Talar dome fractures (transchondral or osteochondral) are caused by small cartilaginous avulsions or body chips at the tibial articulation site.

Fractures of the talus are rare, but are often associated with long term disability.

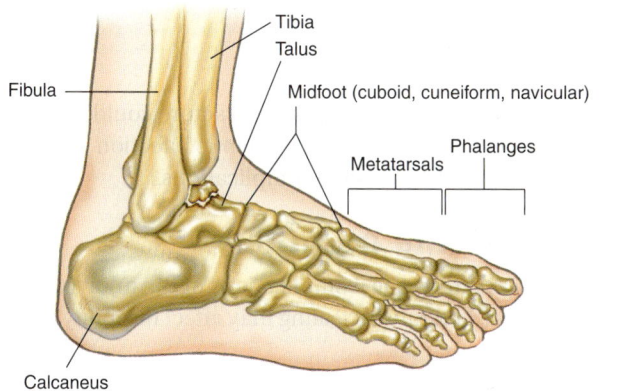

Diagnosis

History: Individuals usually complain of swelling, stiffness, and pain with ankle motion and weight bearing. The individual will usually relate a history of a twisting ankle or foot injury, jumping and landing on the foot, or jamming the foot and ankle. The individual may have heard a "pop" during the injury.

Physical exam: The exam may reveal a crackling noise or sensation upon movement of the ankle joint (crepitus), joint locking, laxity of lateral and anterior ankle ligaments, and pain or tenderness with movement of the foot backward at the ankle (dorsiflexion).

Tests: Routine ankle x-rays show the fracture. A CT scan may be necessary to evaluate the fragment position and status of the joint surface.

Treatment

Treatment varies with the different types of talar fractures. Talar head fractures that are nondisplaced are treated with below-the-knee casting or a fracture brace for 6 to 10 weeks.

Displaced fractures require open reduction and internal fixation (ORIF).

Nondisplaced neck and body fractures are treated with a short leg cast or fracture brace and no weight bearing for 6 to 10 weeks. Displaced neck and body fractures usually require ORIF.

Treatment of lateral process fractures depends on the size of the fragment and the degree of displacement. Nondisplaced fractures should be immobilized with a cast or fracture brace and weight bearing should be avoided. Displaced lateral process fractures usually require ORIF.

Initial therapy for talar dome fractures includes immobilization without weight bearing, followed by arthroscopic debridement, subchondral drilling, synovectomy, and bone graft, depending on the severity of the injury.

Posterior process (Shepherd) fractures are treated by immobilization with either partial or full weight bearing.

Prognosis

Most talar fractures go on to heal, but the recovery may be slowed dramatically by complications.

Talar head fractures that are nondisplaced are treated with below-the-knee casting or bracing. Displaced fracture require ORIF. There is a low incidence of osteoarthritis of the talonavicular joint.

Talar neck and body fractures are usually treated with ORIF and have a high incidence of avascular necrosis and osteoarthritis of the ankle and subtalar joint.

Both nondisplaced lateral talar process fractures treated with below-the-knee casting or bracing and displaced lateral talar process fractures treated with ORIF yield a high proportion of individuals with residual subtalar joint pain.

Talar dome fractures may be treated with immobilization without weight bearing, followed by arthroscopic debridement, subchondral drilling, synovectomy, and bone graft. Long-term follow-up of talar dome fractures shows that despite the type of treatment, most individuals will have chronic ankle pain and swelling.

Posterior process (Shepherd) fractures treated with immobilization with partial or full weight bearing have a generally good outcome with a possibility for some residual pain and stiffness.

Differential Diagnosis

Other conditions that may present with similar findings include second or third degree ankle sprains, dislocation of the talus, osteochondritis dissecans, injury to the deltoid ligament or ankle syndesmosis, compartment syndrome and fractures of the other tarsal bones.

Specialists

- Orthopedic Surgeon
- Physiatrist
- Podiatrist
- Sports Medicine Physician

Rehabilitation

Rigid fixation usually provides quicker return to function than fracture-stabilizing methods such as casting. Although stabilizing methods dictate when progressive stages of therapy are reached, each type of fixation eventually follows the same rehabilitative procedure.

For the first few weeks, only range of motion exercises are usually permitted for the toes and knee. To prevent muscle atrophy, muscle-sets or isometric tightening of a set of muscles (for example, the quadriceps or the gastrocnemius--holding the contraction for 5 seconds) can be initiated while the foot is still immobilized. In addition, electromuscular stimulation may be used for accessible leg muscles such as quadriceps, gastrocnemius, and tibialis anterior. All treatments are performed to pain tolerance.

As the fracture becomes more stable and fixators or casts are removed, dorsi and plantar flexion exercises for the foot--partial to full weight bearing--are allowed. Heat in the form of hot packs or ultrasound may be used prior to each session to increase range of motion. The therapist usually performs range of motion techniques on the foot and ankle manually until the individual can actively move the foot. Cryotherapy (ice massage) may be used after each session to decrease swelling and pain. Depending on the fracture, resistive exercises may not be implemented until later in therapy.

Hydrotherapy (aquatic rehabilitation) may be necessary to increase range of motion and weight bearing without maximal forces of gravity. Exercising in neck-level water allows for approximately 10% weight bearing. The individual can engage in gait re-training through walking laps (forward and backward) or strength training through toe raises. Once the individual can tolerate his/her full weight, the routine can be split between aquatic and standard exercises. High-impact activities are contraindicated for approximately 6 months after therapy has completed.

Work Restrictions / Accommodations

Use of a cast, walking cast shoe, ankle brace with crutches, cane, walker, or wheelchair will be necessary for a period of days to months. Therefore, work restrictions or accommodations should include no prolonged standing (weight bearing), walking, and stair climbing. Frequent rest periods to elevate or ice the ankle may be necessary. After the cast is removed, stooping and squatting should be avoided pending release from physical therapy.

Use of medication for control of pain and inflammation will require review of drug policies. Driving and operation of heavy machinery may need to be reduced or eliminated. Safety issues concerning work in a confined space on uneven or slick surfaces should be considered.

Complementary and Alternative Therapies

Content is intended for awareness only. Treatments may or may not be effective. Scientific evidence may be lacking and some substances have potentially toxic effects. Dr. Presley Reed and the editors do not endorse the use of these therapies in the absence of consultation with a licensed medical professional.

Capacitive coupled electric fields -	A bone healing stimulation method promoting bone formation by application of alternating current in the form of a sinusoidal wave. This method has been purported to be successful in the treatment of stress fractures.
Cryotherapy -	After cast is removed, frequent ice massages or ice packs may decrease pain and swelling.
Heat therapy -	After cast is removed, hot packs and hot paraffin wax may decrease joint stiffness.
Hydrotherapy (aquatic rehabilitation) -	May help to increase range of motion and weight bearing without maximal forces of gravity.
Massage -	Scar massage may promote healing and scar mobility over any surgical site.

Comorbid Conditions

Conditions that could impact ability to recover and further lengthen disability include obesity, arthritis, compartment syndrome, and avascular necrosis.

Complications

Due to the poor blood supply, any displaced fracture could be complicated by avascular necrosis. Localized or systemic infection and degenerative joint disease are other possible complications.

Factors Influencing Duration

Type and severity of fracture, age, complications of the injury, ability to modify work activities, and rate of healing may affect disability periods.

Length of Disability

Avulsion fracture.

Duration in Days

Job Classification	Minimum	Optimum	Maximum
Sedentary work	1	3	7
Light work	1	3	7
Medium work	14	21	28
Heavy work	28	35	84
Very Heavy work	42	49	112

Osteochondral fracture (excision with osteotomy).

Job Classification	Duration in Days		
	Minimum	Optimum	Maximum
Sedentary work	7	9	14
Light work	42	49	56
Medium work	56	70	70
Heavy work	84	98	168
Very Heavy work	112	126	224

Osteochondral fracture (open reduction and internal fixation).

Job Classification	Duration in Days		
	Minimum	Optimum	Maximum
Sedentary work	7	9	14
Light work	56	70	84
Medium work	84	98	112
Heavy work	112	126	168
Very Heavy work	112	126	224

Osteochondral fracture of talar dome (excision of fragment without osteotomy).

Job Classification	Duration in Days		
	Minimum	Optimum	Maximum
Sedentary work	1	3	7
Light work	14	21	28
Medium work	42	49	56
Heavy work	70	84	98
Very Heavy work	84	98	112

Talar body fracture, displaced, comminuted.

Job Classification	Duration in Days		
	Minimum	Optimum	Maximum
Sedentary work	14	21	28
Light work	84	98	112
Medium work	112	126	168
Heavy work	140	154	224
Very Heavy work	140	154	224

Talar body fracture, undisplaced.

Job Classification	Duration in Days		
	Minimum	Optimum	Maximum
Sedentary work	7	9	14
Light work	42	49	56
Medium work	56	63	70
Heavy work	70	77	84
Very Heavy work	70	77	112

Talar neck fracture (vertical) with dislocation of talus.

Job Classification	Duration in Days		
	Minimum	Optimum	Maximum
Sedentary work	7	14	21
Light work	56	70	84
Medium work	84	98	168
Heavy work	112	126	Indefinite
Very Heavy work	126	140	Indefinite

Talar neck fracture (vertical) without dislocation of talus.

Job Classification	Duration in Days		
	Minimum	Optimum	Maximum
Sedentary work	3	4	7
Light work	14	21	28
Medium work	42	49	168
Heavy work	70	91	224
Very Heavy work	84	105	224

Failure to Recover

If an individual fails to recover within the maximum duration expectancy period, the reader may wish to reference the following questions to assist in better understanding the specifics of an individual's medical case.

Regarding diagnosis:

- Has diagnosis of fractured talus been confirmed by x-ray and/or CT scan?
- Has individual experienced any complications related to the fracture or treatment?
- Does individual have any underlying conditions that may impact recovery?

Regarding treatment:

- What type of fracture occurred (displaced, nondisplaced, lateral process, posterior process or Shepherd fracture)?

- Where was the fracture located (talar head, neck or body, talar dome)?
- Did individual require ORIF?
- Did the individual require casting or a fracture brace?
- Has arthroscopic procedure been performed? What interventions were required?

Regarding prognosis:
- Has recovery been impacted by complications or residual pain? To what extent is function impaired? What else can be done?
- Is individual following prescribed rehabilitative therapy?

References

Foot and Ankle Care: Talar Dome Fractures. Oman Enterprises. 2000. 15 Nov 2000 <http://www.omanenterprises.com/conditions/talardomefractures.htm>.

Kippen, Cameron. Fractures of the Foot. Curtin Educational. 2000. 15 Nov 2000 <http://www.curtin.edu.au/curtin/dept/physio/podiatry/podology/257/fractures.html>.

Fracture, Thoracic Spine (With or Without Spinal Cord Injury)

Other names / synonyms: Broken Back

805.2, 805.3, 806.2, 806.20, 806.21, 806.22, 806.23, 806.24, 806.25, 806.26, 806.27, 806.28, 806.29, 806.3, 806.30, 806.31, 806.32, 806.33, 806.34, 806.35, 806.36, 806.37, 806.38, 806.39

Definition

Fracture of the thoracic spine is a break (fracture) of one or more bones of the spine (vertebrae) in the upper back (thoracic) region.

There are 12 thoracic vertebrae. There are 4 major types of thoracic spine injuries including compression, burst, flexion-distraction, and fracture-dislocation. Compression fractures are the most common type of thoracic spine fracture. They occur when the spine is bent forward (forward flexion) or sideways (lateral flexion) at the moment of trauma, causing the front (anterior) or side (lateral) region of the vertebra, respectively, to be crushed. Compression fractures are common because of the natural curve in the thoracic spine. Burst fractures are similar to compression fractures except that the entire vertebra is evenly crushed. This "pancaking" of the vertebra often pushes bone fragments into the spinal column. Burst fractures are uncommon because of the curve to the thoracic spine. Loss of motor, sensory, and reflex functions (neurologic deficits) commonly occurs with a burst fracture.

Compression and burst fractures are usually caused by a fall from a height onto the buttocks or feet, respectively. Flexion-distraction fractures (seat belt injury, lap belt injury, chance fracture) involve the separation (distraction) of the fractured vertebra and are caused by hyperflexion during the traumatic event. Flexion-distraction fractures rarely occur in the thoracic spine but can occur during a motor vehicle accident if the seat belt is worn high and without a shoulder harness. Fracture-dislocations, in which vertebral fractures are found in combination with displacement (dislocation) of adjacent vertebrae, are caused by high energy traumas. Fracture-dislocations are very unstable and cause a complete neurological deficit (paraplegia) for 75% of the individuals. Spinal cord injury can be classified as complete, which is associated with permanent paralysis, or incomplete, with the potential for neurologic improvement.

The most common causes of fractures to the thoracic spine are motor vehicle accidents, falls, sports injuries, and acts of violence, including gun shot wounds. Also, minor trauma can cause a thoracic spine fracture in individuals with a loss of bone mass (osteoporosis). Males are injured 4 times more frequently than females. Most thoracic spine fractures are caused by accidents, but individuals who are at an increased risk of this fracture include athletes, those with osteoporosis, and those whose work or recreation places them at risk of falling from a height. Thoracic fracture is a relatively common injury.

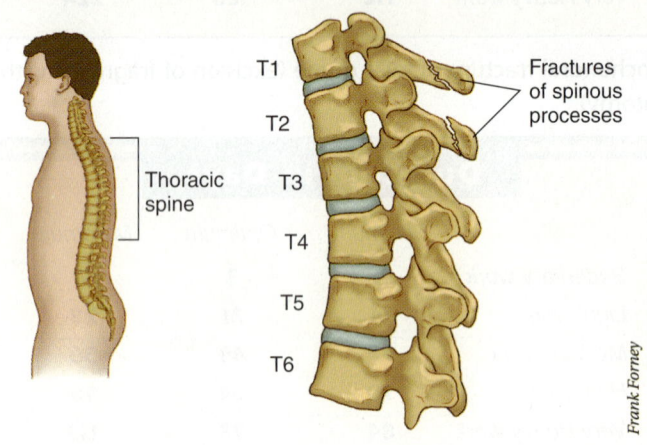

Diagnosis

History: The individual may report tenderness over the area of the fracture and temporary or persisting paralysis (or even numbness or tingling) of the arms or legs. Movement of the back causes pain. The individual may seem to be completely paralyzed below the waist, but reports a period of sensation around the anus (perianal) or in the legs or movement of the legs. Subtle signs of neurological injury include bladder or bowel dysfunction and changes in sensations of the perianal region. The individual should be specifically questioned as to previous spine injury, prior neurologic deficits, and the details of the mechanism of the current injury. If the individual is unable to respond, an attempt to interview family members or observers would be made.

Physical exam: The back may have cuts (abrasions), bruising, and deformity. Shifting of the vertebral bodies may be detected by touching with the hands (palpation). The individual may have chest or abdominal trauma (e.g., shoulder harness or lap seat belt markings). The individual may have difficulty moving his or her arms and legs. A finger (digital) rectal exam may reveal changes in voluntary or reflexive anal sphincter contraction. The unconscious or intoxicated individual is difficult to assess in terms of pain and motor sensory function. Careful observation of spontaneous extremity motion may be the only information indicating spinal cord function until a detailed exam is performed.

Tests: X-rays (anteroposterior and lateral views), CT scans, and MRI are the usual methods used to diagnose thoracic fractures. MRI permits visualization of the spinal cord and other soft tissues.

Treatment

Nonsurgical treatment is used to treat any stable fracture in the absence of neurologic deficits including most compression fractures, some burst fractures, and flexion-distraction fractures without ligament injuries. Nonsurgical treatment involves wearing a hyperextension orthosis, cast, or brace for 4-6 weeks. Longer periods of immobilization may be needed for individuals with more severe injuries and for those with osteoporosis. Bed rest for 1-3 weeks is common.

Veterbroplasty, or kyphoplasty, is a method of decreasing the deformity of compression fractures. The deformity is reduced, and bone cement (polymethyl methacrylate) is injected through a needle to stabilize the fracture with minimal deformity.

Individuals with unstable fractures including severe compression fractures, fracture-dislocations, flexion-distraction fractures with ligamentous injuries, and most burst fractures may be treated surgically. The goals of surgical treatment are to realign the spine, stabilize the spine, and prevent (or improve) neurologic deficits. The treatment method depends on the severity of the fracture, presence of a spinal cord injury, overall health of the individual, age of the individual, and surgeon's preference.

Spinal surgery is performed as an open procedure using general anesthesia. All surgical methods involve fusion (arthrodesis) of adjacent vertebrae by using metal plates, rods, wires, and/or screws to stabilize the spine. Following surgery, bracing is used as for nonsurgical treatment. Corticosteroids may provide potential benefit to the individual with a spinal cord injury. Analgesics may be prescribed as needed.

Prognosis

With either surgical or nonsurgical treatment, the outcome is excellent provided there is no neurological damage. Bone healing is complete between 8-16 weeks. The more severe the final deformity, the more likely persisting pain, or late onset pain, will be a problem. There is potential for below-the-waist paralysis (paraplegia) if complete spinal cord injury occurred. Surgical treatment can lead to significant improvement of neurological deficits caused by incomplete spinal cord injuries.

Differential Diagnosis

Fracture of the thoracic spine is a specific diagnosis.

Specialists

- Neurologist
- Neurosurgeon
- Orthopedic Surgeon
- Physiatrist
- Physical Therapist

Rehabilitation

For a fracture of the thoracic spine, rehabilitation can take up to 6 months even without neurological damage. Therapy for thoracic spine fracture without spinal cord injury, regardless of the method of fracture stabilization (brace or cast), is usually the same, and full return of function is expected. The team caring for an individual with a spinal cord injury may include a social worker, vocational specialist, and/or occupational therapist. Therapeutic outcomes for individuals with spinal cord injury concomitant with a thoracic spine fracture are variable, and may include full or partial paralysis.

Therapy may consist of range-of-motion exercises for the noninjured areas of the body only, with some isometric strength training for the abdomen, gluteus, and hamstring muscles. Progressive resistive exercises to strengthen erector spinae and other lower back muscles may be introduced as therapy continues. Strength and flexibility must be accompanied by functional training so the individual is able to maintain trunk control through all movements. A Swiss ball can be introduced during the functional phase of rehabilitation to help improve back stabilization.

Individuals without spinal cord injury may benefit from hydrotherapy to increase flexibility and strength.

Work Restrictions / Accommodations

To reduce the risk of complications, the individual may not be allowed to work during the early recovery period. Prolonged sitting, standing, heavy lifting, bending, overhead (spine extension) work, and climbing long flights of stairs may be temporarily restricted. Adjusting worktable height, chair height, and use of foot rests are all beneficial for individuals with back problems. The individual may require frequent breaks. Temporarily working reduced hours may be necessary. Permanent restrictions may include heavy lifting, carrying moderate to heavy loads, and overhead work. If spinal cord injury is present, the facility will need to be wheelchair accessible. Additional time off for doctor visits may be necessary. Depending on the job duties, the individual may require a permanent reassignment of duties, which may necessitate retraining.

Complementary and Alternative Therapies

Content is intended for awareness only. Treatments may or may not be effective. Scientific evidence may be lacking and some substances have potentially toxic effects. Dr. Presley Reed and the editors do not endorse the use of these therapies in the absence of consultation with a licensed medical professional.

T.E.N.S. - May produce significant pain relief.

Acupuncture - May help in the treatment of chronic pain. The mechanism of action is unknown.

Comorbid Conditions

Osteoporosis, rheumatoid arthritis, osteoarthritis, damage to the thoracic spine ligaments, injury to other regions of the spine, and other injuries sustained during the traumatic event may influence the length of disability.

Complications

Complications of thoracic fractures include neurologic deficits (including paraplegia), hunchback (kyphosis), disc herniations, and bone healing with faulty alignment (malunion).

Factors Influencing Duration

Factors that may influence length of disability are the presence of neurological damage, age of the individual, presence of complications, and stability of the fracture. Duration also depends on which type of fracture occurred.

Length of Disability

Duration depends on job requirements. Disability may be shorter for individuals whose job duties are sedentary in nature (e.g., desk work). Stable fractures with significant deformity may not be compatible with heavy or very heavy work. Unstable fractures requiring internal fixation (surgical treatment) are incompatible with heavy and, perhaps, medium work. Spinal cord injury, even with partial neurologic recovery, usually precludes moderate and heavy work. Disability may be permanent.

Stable fractures. Brace.

Duration in Days

Job Classification	Minimum	Optimum	Maximum
Sedentary work	7	14	28
Light work	14	21	42
Medium work	42	56	91
Heavy work	91	119	154
Very Heavy work	119	154	182

Surgical treatment of unstable fracture without neurologic deficit.

Duration in Days

Job Classification	Minimum	Optimum	Maximum
Sedentary work	21	28	91
Light work	42	91	119
Medium work	91	168	182
Heavy work	Indefinite	Indefinite	Indefinite
Very Heavy work	Indefinite	Indefinite	Indefinite

Open or closed, with spinal cord injury.

Duration in Days

Job Classification	Minimum	Optimum	Maximum
Sedentary work	119	182	Indefinite
Light work	119	182	Indefinite
Medium work	Indefinite	Indefinite	Indefinite
Heavy work	Indefinite	Indefinite	Indefinite
Very Heavy work	Indefinite	Indefinite	Indefinite

Failure to Recover

If an individual fails to recover within the maximum duration expectancy period, the reader may wish to reference the following questions to assist in better understanding the specifics of an individual's medical case.

Regarding diagnosis:

- Did the individual present with findings consistent with a thoracic spine fracture? Were their symptoms consistent with injury to the spinal cord?
- Was the diagnosis confirmed on x-ray?
- Was an MRI done to determine if there was associated injury to the spinal cord or soft tissues?

Regarding treatment:

- Was the treatment appropriate for the type of fracture?
- Was surgical stabilization required?
- Were analgesics effective in controlling pain?
- Would the individual benefit from consultation by a specialist (neurosurgeon, orthopedic surgeon, physiatrist)?
- Was the individual compliant with treatment recommendations?
- Did the individual participate in rehabilitation as recommended?
- Are there barriers preventing the individual from participating with rehabilitation (insurance limitations, lack of transportation, lack of motivation, pain)?

Regarding prognosis:

- Has adequate time elapsed to allow for recovery?
- Was there associated spinal cord injury?
- What was the expected outcome?
- Does the individual have any pre-existing conditions that may influence the length of disability?
- Did the individual suffer any complications associated with the injury?
- Have appropriate work accommodations been considered?

References

Adams, John, and David Hamblen. "Spine and Thorax." Outline of Fractures: Including Joint Injuries. Adams, John, and David Hamblen, eds. Edinburgh: Churchill Livingstone, 1999. 99-110.

Hoppenfield, Stanley, and Vasantha Murthy. Treatment and Rehabilitation of Fractures. Philadelphia: Lippincott Williams & Wilkins, 2000.

Fracture, Tibia or Fibula

Other names / synonyms: Broken Leg, Leg Fracture

823, 823.0, 823.00, 823.01, 823.1, 823.10, 823.11, 823.2, 823.20, 823.21, 823.22, 823.3, 823.30, 823.31, 823.8, 823.80, 823.81, 823.9, 823.91, 823.92

Definition

A fracture of the tibia or fibula is a fracture of the 2 bones of the lower leg. This fracture can occur anywhere between the knee and ankle.

The fracture may result from a direct injury (such as a motor vehicle accident) or a twisting force (such as a sports injury). With a serious direct impact, the bone may fracture in several places (a comminuted or segmental fracture) and is likely to break the skin (open fracture). A twisting force can cause a spiral fracture. Fractures can also result from minimal injury. They may be due to fatigue (stress fracture), from repetitive impact as in jogging, or from thinning of the bone (osteoporosis). Fractures from low-energy trauma are often stable and minimally displaced. A high-energy injury can result in damage to the soft tissues including muscle, ligaments, blood vessels, and nerves.

The tibia is the most frequently fractured of the long bones. Tibia and fibula fractures due to trauma are most common in young males.

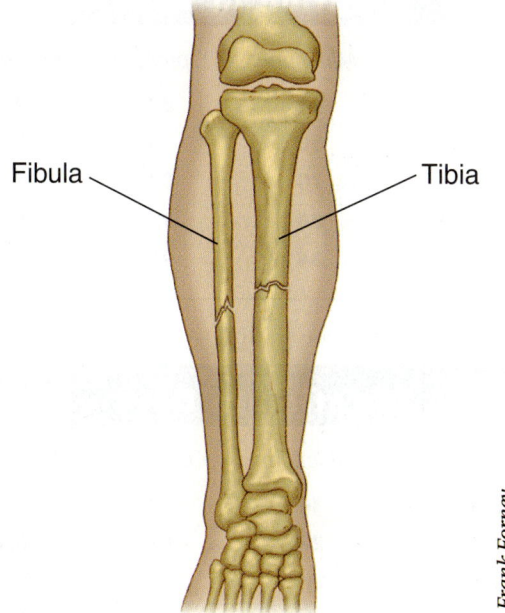

Fibula — Tibia

Frank Forney

Diagnosis

History: The individual may report a recent trauma, such as a motor vehicle accident, a sports injury, or a severe fall. The individual may also report severe pain and inability to bear full weight on the leg (but walking is possible if only the fibula is fractured).

Physical exam: The exam may reveal swelling and bruising at the fracture site. If the fracture is displaced, a deformity may be noted. Tenderness is present over the fracture. Examination might demonstrate an injury affecting sensation in the foot, muscle strength, or blood supply. An open wound may be noted with some fractures.

Tests: Plain x-rays will establish the diagnosis. CT scan and MRI are rarely needed, unless the fracture extends into the knee joint. A bone scan can show the earliest sign of a stress fracture.

Treatment

Many treatments are possible, depending on the location and severity of the fracture(s). A stress fracture in an athletic adult can be treated by rest and perhaps a leg brace and avoidance of the repetitive activity for 6 to 10 weeks. For uncomplicated fractures, closed reduction and a cast may be the only treatment required. Most closed fractures are treated nonsurgically.

More complicated fractures may require pins placed externally (external fixation devices), or surgery for open reduction and internal fixation (ORIF) with pins, plates, screws, or intramedullary rods. Open fractures are treated with surgery to remove contaminated tissue (open debridement) and left open with drains to the wound. Wound closure then requires a second operation in about 5 days. Bone grafting may be done early or late in the course of treatment. Medications include analgesics for pain and antibiotics and a tetanus shot for open fractures.

Prognosis

In general, the chances of complete healing of a tibial or fibular fracture is good. However, outcome depends on the location, severity of the fracture, and the extent of soft tissue injury, along with the presence of any complications. The tibia is the most common fracture to remain unhealed (non-union).

Differential Diagnosis

ItPrinciples could be a pathologic fracture from a disease of bone itself, such as Paget's disease or osteomalacia, or from cancer in the bone. Infection could also result in pathologic fracture if the individual has an immune system deficiency. Other possible diagnoses include soft tissue injury to the ankle or knee, ankle or knee fractures, and peripheral vascular injury or trauma.

Specialists

- Orthopedic Surgeon
- Plastic Surgeon
- Vascular Surgeon

Rehabilitation

Depending on the type and location of the fracture, physical therapy may not be prescribed (e.g., fibula shaft fracture with nondisplacement). Fractures of the tibia, primary weight-bearer of the lower extremity, as well as lower fibula may require physical therapy.

Rehabilitation techniques are also determined by orthopedic methods of stabilizing the fracture (cast or fixation). Certain types of fixation (rod insertion along the tibial shaft) may allow for increased weight bearing and quicker return to function of the ankle and knee through isometric, isotonic, and range-of-motion exercises. Other instances of fixation may impede weight bearing (e.g., fibular fixation near the ankle) and slow the rehabilitation process.

Typically, all joints that do not require immobilization should be mobilized to avoid post-fracture joint stiffness. Initial rehabilitation programs may include range-of-motion and isometric exercises for the toe, knee, and hip joints.

Once cast and/or pins are removed (usually around 8 weeks), progressive strength training and range-of-motion exercises can be implemented. Heat, ice, nonsteroidal anti-inflammatory drugs (NSAID) are some of the modalities that therapists use to decrease pain and other symptoms during this treatment phase. One major concern after prolonged immobilization is mobilizing the ankle and foot joints to ensure proper flexibility and biomechanics. The therapist may assist by manually mobilizing joints through techniques such as talocrural joint traction where the therapist holds the mid-foot and heel of the individual's upright foot and pulls forward. The individual is taught active flexibility activities (active stretches) and isometric exercises. Closed chain compressive movements such as seated calf raises and stationary cycling may also introduced to increase ankle stability.

Prior to full weight bearing, the individual may engage in functional balance or proprioceptive training and may use either a simple balance board that moves laterally or a Biomechanical Ankle Platform System (BAPS) that moves in multiple directions.

Work Restrictions / Accommodations

Prolonged standing and walking will be temporarily limited. Any physical activity requiring leg strength (lifting, construction, etc.) will also be limited. The individual may be unable to drive for some time. Provisions should be made to allow periodic elevation of the individual's leg.

Comorbid Conditions

Diabetes mellitus, peripheral vascular disease, osteoporosis, Paget's disease, obesity, compartment syndrome, and immune conditions (such as AIDS) may lengthen disability.

Complications

Possible complications are delayed union or non-union, misalignment of the knee and ankle, or rotation of the foot (mal-union), refracture, or leg shortening, in the case of a seriously comminuted fracture. Skin loss due to the thinness of skin over the tibia, infection in the bone (osteomyelitis), joint stiffness or loss of knee flexion are other complications. If the fracture involves the knee or ankle joint, traumatic arthritis may cause complications. Other complications include anterior compartment syndrome, nerve damage such as a peroneal nerve injury with foot drop, and arterial injury, especially with upper tibial fractures. Complex regional pain syndrome, fat embolism, or the need for amputation if there is massive damage to soft tissues in the leg may also occur.

Factors Influencing Duration

The severity of the fracture (open or closed, simple or comminuted) will affect disability. The age of the individual and any complications may also affect disability.

Length of Disability

Open fractures will take longer to heal. Sedentary and light work duration reflects work in a brace or cast.

Fracture, fibula. Open or closed.

Duration in Days

Job Classification	Minimum	Optimum	Maximum
Sedentary work	1	7	14
Light work	7	14	28
Medium work	21	42	70
Heavy work	70	77	84
Very Heavy work	84	98	112

Fibula. Open with internal fixation.

Duration in Days

Job Classification	Minimum	Optimum	Maximum
Sedentary work	14	28	42
Light work	56	70	84
Medium work	70	84	98
Heavy work	84	98	112
Very Heavy work	84	98	112

Tibia.

Duration in Days

Job Classification	Minimum	Optimum	Maximum
Sedentary work	14	28	84
Light work	28	42	182
Medium work	119	182	224
Heavy work	161	224	273
Very Heavy work	182	273	Indefinite

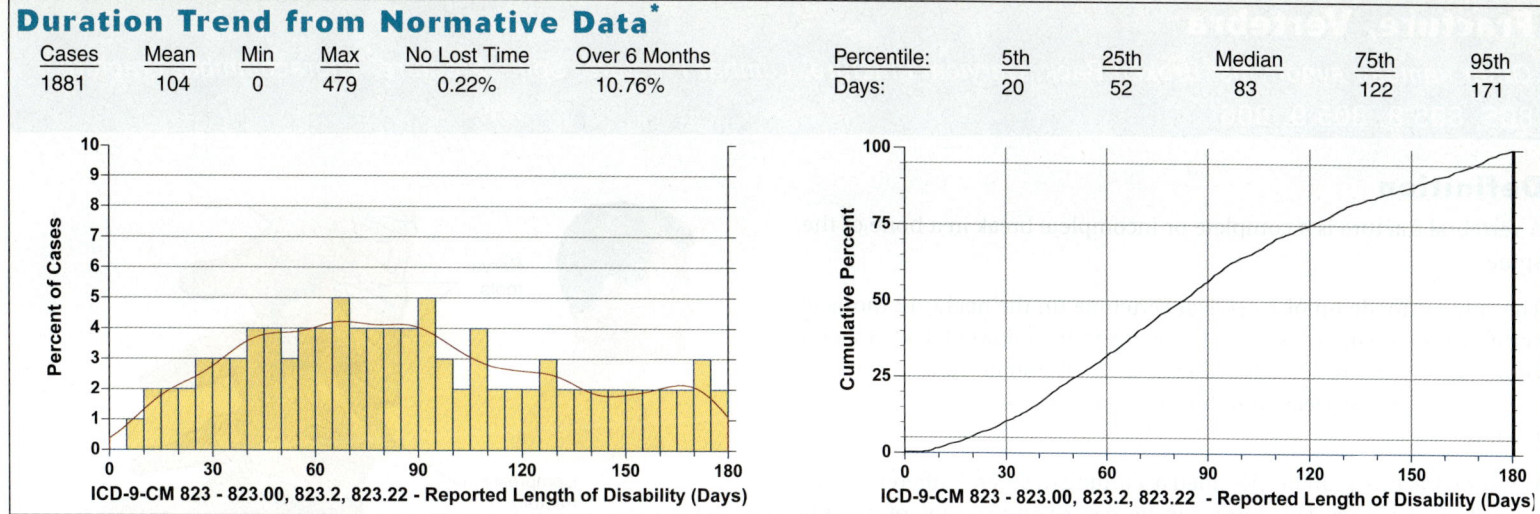

Failure to Recover

If an individual fails to recover within the maximum duration expectancy period, the reader may wish to reference the following questions to assist in better understanding the specifics of an individual's medical case.

Regarding diagnosis:

- Did the individual present with symptoms consistent with a fracture of the tibia or fibula?
- Was the fracture confirmed on x-ray?
- Was a bone scan done to rule out a stress fracture?
- If the diagnosis was uncertain, were other conditions with similar symptoms ruled out?

Regarding treatment:

- Was the treatment appropriate for the type of fracture?
- Was the individual's pain controlled with ice and analgesics? If not, were other interventions tried (TENS, relaxation, visualization, alternative analgesics, or dose adjustments)?
- Was surgery required? In cases of open fractures, was surgery initiated within 12 hours of injury?
- Did the individual participate in physical therapy as recommended?
- Does the individual have any conditions that may impact ability to recover?
- Did the individual return to activity too early?
- Would the individual benefit from consultation with a specialist (orthopedic surgeon, vascular surgeon, plastic reconstructive surgeon, sports medicine specialist, or physiatrist)?

Regarding prognosis:

- Did the individual experience any complications that may influence length of disability?

References

Colton, C. "Injuries of the Ankle." Watson-Jones Fractures and Joint Injuries. Wilson, J., ed. London: Churchill Livingstone, 1982. 1104-1151.

Steele, Mark. Fractures, Tibia and Fibula. eMedicine.com. 18 Feb 2001. 18 Feb 2001 <http://www.emedicine.com/emerg/topic207.htm>.

Fracture, Vertebra

Other names / synonyms: Broken Back, Cervical Fracture, Lumbar Fracture, Spine Fracture, Thoracolumbar Fracture

805, 805.8, 805.9, 806

Definition

A vertebral fracture is a complete or incomplete break in a bone of the spine.

The spine is made up of 7 cervical vertebrae (in the neck), 12 thoracic vertebrae (in the upper back), 5 lumbar vertebrae (lower back), 5 sacral vertebrae (which are fused together at end of the spine), and the coccyx (tailbone). The cervical and lumbar vertebrae are most prone to fracture.

Vertebral fractures can be classified according to several different types as well as locations. The spine can be described in terms of 3 load-bearing columns (as viewed from the side): the anterior column (which is toward the front), the middle column, and the posterior column (toward the back).

There are 4 types of vertebral fractures: compression fractures, flexion-distraction fractures, burst fractures, fracture-dislocations. Compression fractures, which are the most common type of thoracolumbar fracture, occur when the anterior part of the vertebrae are forced together.

Flexion-distraction fractures are the type that can occur as the result of an automobile accident while wearing a seat belt, when extreme force is placed on a few vertebrae by the rapid deceleration of the car.

Burst fractures result from extreme force applied straight down on the vertebrae (e.g., when an individual falls from a height and lands on the feet), and involve both the anterior and middle columns.

Fracture-dislocations are the result of a twisting or shear force and involve displacement of the vertebrae, and involve all 3 columns.

Vertebral fractures may be the result of a traumatic injury or indirect stress due to excessive spinal flexing, extension, rotation, or bending. The most common causes of injuries to the lumbosacral spine are motor vehicle accidents, falls, sports injuries, and acts of violence. Sports activities that are associated with the highest risk of cervical fracture include diving, equestrian activities, football, gymnastics, skiing, and hang gliding. In older individuals (75 and older), falls account for 60% of spinal fractures. Neurologic injury occurs in 40% of individuals with fractures at the cervical level. Cervical spine injuries result in approximately 6000 deaths and 5000 new cases of quadriplegia each year, and about 80% of individuals with cervical spine fractures are between the ages of 18 and 25 years.

The lifetime risk of vertebral fracture is about 15% in white women and 5% in white men. However, cervical fractures occur in males more frequently than in females by a ratio of four to one. The incidence of vertebral fracture in women is estimated to be approximately 200 per 10,000 person years.

Diagnosis

History: Individuals may be free of symptoms or they may report transient paralysis or numbness or tingling of the extremities. This suggests that the spinal cord and/or its roots have been injured. Individuals with cervical spine fractures may report posterior neck pain,

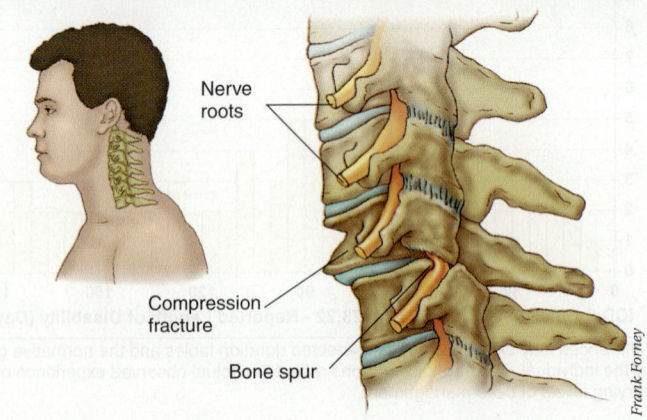

limited range of motion associated with pain, and weakness, numbness, or tingling along the affected nerve roots. Individuals with thoracolumbar fractures may report pain, limited motion, and lack of feeling or strength in the legs. Pain may not begin until hours after the injury.

Physical exam: Swelling of the soft tissue may be present around the site of the vertebral fracture. Touching of the area (palpation) may reveal tenderness. Individuals with cervical fractures present with limited range of motion that is associated with pain. However, clinical evaluation of individuals with cervical spine fracture is rarely enough for a diagnosis; radiologic evaluation is essential. Individuals with thoracolumbar fractures may show visible deformity if the fracture is complete and is severe enough to distort normal back contours. Paralysis of the legs and muscles may be present if concomitant spinal cord injury has occurred.

Deformities, abrasions, and bruising may be present over affected areas along the length of the spine. Palpation of the parts of the spine that are easily felt as the bumps down the center of the back (spinous processes) may reveal shifting of the vertebral bodies. Lateral turning may be accomplished with a backboard. Inspection of the abdomen may reveal trauma such as lap seat belt markings, which are often associated lumbosacral spine injury. A neurological examination may reveal sensory deficits (e.g., digital rectal examination for voluntary or reflex anal sphincter contraction).

Tests: X-rays (anteroposterior [AP] and lateral views), CT scans, and MRI are the usual methods used to diagnose spinal fractures. MRI permits visualization of the spinal cord. The large majority of cervical spine fractures (85-90%) are evident on lateral views; other useful views are oblique, odontoid, and swimmer's, as well as AP.

Treatment

Generally speaking, treatment consists of nonsurgical or surgical alignment (or realignment) and holding of the spine in its correct position; this can be accomplished in a number of ways. The first step in treatment of any suspected vertebral fracture is immobilization to protect the spinal cord. Once the location of the fracture and the extent of spinal cord injury are determined (via x-rays, CT scan, and/or MRI), treatment will depend on the type of fracture, its location, and any nerve damage, and may vary from a conservative approach to surgical intervention.

One of the factors in determining whether to treat conservatively (nonsurgically) or surgically is the stability of the fracture. In general, if a fracture is stable, the affected area (neck or back) is immobilized with the use of orthotics (braces or corsets) or casts. Mild thoracolumbar fractures with a low risk of progression usually require only minimally immobilizing orthoses (e.g., a lumbosacral corset) to restrict gross trunk motion. More moderate injuries, such as severe compression fractures and moderate burst fractures, may require a more rigid brace. Milder cervical fractures may be treated with traction, applied to slowly manipulate broken bones back to their proper position.

Severe injuries, such as fracture-dislocations and multilevel burst fractures, are usually unstable, such that orthotics would not provide enough support to ensure protection from further injury. Unstable fractures that produce deformity generally require surgical decompression, stabilization, and fusion (with pedicle screws, rods, hooks). There is some evidence that conservative treatment of well-selected unstable fractures may provide equally beneficial outcomes to surgery; however, this choice is highly individualized and varies depending upon a number of factors, including potential for neurological injury.

Following immobilization procedures, treatment consists of bed rest, ice (or heat), whirlpool treatments if available, and gentle massage to minimize swelling. Medications may include narcotic pain relievers for severe pain, over-the-counter analgesics (e.g., acetaminophen) for milder pain, antibiotics to fight infection if the skin was broken or if surgery was performed, and stool softeners if necessary to prevent constipation due to inactivity. Prophylactic corticosteroids are used when there is the possibility of spinal cord injury (to reduce swelling and minimize damage).

Prognosis

Predicted outcome depends upon the severity of the fracture and the extent of accompanying neurological damage. The probability for complete healing and no pain following cervical fractures with no neurological damage is very good with conservative treatment; average healing time is 6 to 12 weeks in traction, followed by 2 months in a neck brace. Thoracolumbar fractures that are not associated with instability have a very good prognosis, and usually heal satisfactorily within 6 to 12 weeks with conservative treatment.

Surgical treatment is often the only choice in cases of unstable fractures. Surgery (decompression, stabilization, and fusion) is usually successful at immobilizing the vertebral column, but may be associated with residual pain and/or reduced mobility in the affected area of the back. Because there is the potential for varying degrees of paralysis if the spinal cord is injured, prognosis in these cases varies widely (from full recovery to total paralysis).

Differential Diagnosis

Signs and symptoms of spine fractures may be similar to those seen with cauda equina syndrome, cervical strain, hanging injuries and strangulation, neoplasms of the spinal cord, septic shock, spinal cord infections, thoracic outlet syndrome, and torticollis.

Specialists

- Neurosurgeon
- Orthopedic Surgeon
- Physiatrist

Rehabilitation

Rehabilitative therapy for vertebral fractures differs based on location, severity, and cause of fracture. Deviations in therapeutic procedures are also dictated by mode of fracture stabilization. In general, for fractures with neurologic deficit, most rehabilitation programs include progressive physical and occupational therapy over a period of 3-6 months. Vocational rehabilitation may be necessary for more impaired individuals. Complete healing time for the vertebral fractures is between 6-8 weeks or when the union of vertebral bones is complete.

Individuals who experience operative spinal stabilization through vertebral fusion or other fixation methods will engage in similar routines as those who received nonoperative stabilization. However, their rate of progression and chosen exercises will take into account the limitations imposed by the operative procedure. In either case, therapeutic exercises for muscle groups not immobilized are initiated immediately to increase spine alignment and healing.

In order to alleviate stress on the spine, the individual may engage in short arc exercises. Ice massage or heat may be applied to the fracture site if the area is not casted. Hydrotherapy may be initiated to assist in regaining normal gait pattern. Functional exercises may be introduce to help restore normal gait pattern. Progressive resistive exercises to strengthen erector spinae and other lower back muscles may also be taught.

Strength and flexibility must be accompanied by functional training so the individual is able to maintain trunk control through all movements.

Work Restrictions / Accommodations

An individual with a fracture and no spinal cord injury will be restricted in most physical activities for several weeks after the injury; these individuals must especially refrain from physical labor, such as lifting, running, walking, or standing for extended periods of time, carrying, bending, climbing ladders, and twisting. Individuals who require surgical intervention that includes fusion of the vertebral column for stability may be permanently disabled from certain of these activities. The individual may need to be able to take rest breaks (recline) periodically throughout the day, and may need time off for therapy. Numerous additional work restrictions and accommodations may be necessary if the spinal cord was injured, and the extent required will be dependent upon the severity of the injury. The individual may be permanently disabled from performing duties requiring physical strength or dexterity. In extreme cases (for example, in cases of paralysis) the work place will need to be wheelchair-accessible and will require standard facilities for disabled persons.

Comorbid Conditions

Comorbid conditions that may affect recovery include obesity, history of bone or joint disease, such as osteoporosis, arthritis, and drug addiction.

Complications

The most serious complication of vertebral fractures is spinal cord injury, which can result in paralysis. Approximately 39% of cervical fractures have some degree of associated neurologic deficit. Other complications of vertebral fractures include infection, nerve damage in displaced fractures, faulty alignment of the healed vertebrae (malunion), chronic obstructive airways disease, gastrointestinal disease, further instability or arthritis in the area, impaired blood supply to the fracture site, and avascular necrosis. Chronic pain as a result of vertebral fracture can lead to depression. Vertebral fractures can cause postural changes, leading to the development of hunchback (kyphosis). More severe kyphosis causes the individual to hyperextend the neck, leading to neck pain and muscle fatigue. Kyphosis can also limit total lung capacity and exercise tolerance. Cervical spine fractures may be complicated by spinal shock, neurogenic shock, complete and incomplete cord syndromes, Brown-Sequard syndrome, and Horner syndrome.

Factors Influencing Duration

Factors influencing the length of disability include the presence of spinal cord injury, the individual's age, any complications, and stability of the fracture.

Length of Disability

Disability depends upon severity, location, and extent of underlying pathology, if any. In some cases, disabillity may be permanent. Contact physician for additional information on location of fracture.

Failure to Recover

If an individual fails to recover within the maximum duration expectancy period, the reader may wish to reference the following questions to assist in better understanding the specifics of an individual's medical case.

Regarding diagnosis:

- Did the individual present with symptoms consistent with a vertebral fracture?
- Did the individual present with neurological deficits?
- Was the fracture confirmed with an x-ray?
- Was a CT scan done to rule out spinal cord injury?
- If the diagnosis was uncertain, were other conditions with similar symptoms ruled out?

Regarding treatment:

- Were analgesics effective in controlling pain? If not, were alternative pain management techniques (TENS, relaxation exercises, hydrotherapy, visualization) tried?
- Was the individual compliant with treatment recommendations?
- Would the individual benefit from consultation by a specialist (neurosurgeon, orthopedic surgeon, physiatrist)?
- Did the individual participate in rehabilitation as recommended?
- Are there barriers preventing the individual from participating with rehabilitation (insurance limitations, lack of transportation, lack of motivation, pain)?

Regarding prognosis:

- Was the fracture associated with injury to the spinal cord?
- What was the expected outcome?
- Does the individual have any comorbid conditions that may impact ability to recover?
- Did the individual suffer any complications or have any concurrent injuries that may influence length of disability?
- Have appropriate work accommodations been considered?

References

Neck (Cervical Spine) Fracture. HealthGate.com 23 Jun 1999. 1 Jan 2001 <http://www.healthgate.com/sport/sport110.shtml>.

DeLee, Jesse, and David Drez. Orthopaedic Sports Medicine: Principles and Practice. Philadelphia: W.B. Saunders Company, 1994.

Fracture, Vertebra (Pathological)

Other names / synonyms: Pathologic Fracture, Pathological Cervical Fracture, Pathological Compression Fracture, Pathological Lumbar Fracture, Pathological Spine Fracture, Pathological Thoracolumbar Fracture

733.13

Definition

Pathological fractures of the vertebrae are breaks in the spine that occur due to weakening of the bone by an underlying, pre-existing disease or condition. When the structure of the normal bone is altered by the underlying disease, the vertebra gives way with a spontaneous fracture, or with a fracture caused by minimal trauma.

The fracture may be a result of trauma or what would seem to be normal activities. The fracture occurs through the weakened vertebral body, causing it to collapse. This type of fracture is often referred to as a compression fracture. The most common area of involvement is the thoracolumbar region.

Individuals at increased risk of pathological fractures of the vertebra include those with certain underlying infections, metabolic bone diseases, or cancers that cause a weakening of the vertebral bone. Such disorders include bone infections such as hematogenous osteomyelitis and bone tuberculosis; metabolic bone diseases such as osteoporosis, osteomalacia, hyperparathyroidism, renal osteodystrophy; and tumors, such as multiple myeloma, chordoma, and metastatic carcinoma.

Individuals on chronic corticosteroid treatment can also have weakening of the vertebra that can predispose them to fractures.

Approximately 9 out of 10,000 individuals sustain vertebral fractures in the general population. One of the most common causes of pathological vertebral fractures is osteoporosis, which occurs most often in postmenopausal women. Pathological vertebral fractures are more common in the elderly than in younger individuals. However, because of the lack of a standardized definition of a vertebral fracture and the fact that mild pathological compression fractures are often missed, prevalence estimates vary.

Diagnosis

History: The individual may complain of the sudden onset of back pain, often with lifting, although there may not be any history of trauma or change in activity level. If the collapse of the vertebra occurs more slowly, the individual may report milder back pain with more gradual onset. An increase in the curve of the upper back may be noted by the individual. Depending on the location of the fracture, the individual may report problems with urination or bowel movements. If there is pressure on the spinal cord, the individual may report numbness, tingling, or weakness. In some cases, there may be only very mild or no symptoms of compression fracture.

Unlike traumatic, nonpathologic fractures in which pain decreases with time as the fracture heals, pathologic fractures secondary to bone infection or tumor usually have pain that worsens over time, until the infection of tumor is recognized and treated.

Physical exam: Inspection and touching (palpation) of the affected part helps localize the affected area to be x-rayed. In some cases, the individual may show signs of hunchback (kyphosis). Attention must also be given to the causative disease process involved, although it may not be discovered until after initial x-rays are taken.

Tests: X-rays (anteroposterior [AP] and lateral views), CT, and MRI are the usual methods used to diagnose spinal fractures. MRI permits visualization of the spinal cord. Although the fracture may be evident with plain x-rays, a bone scan is often required to detect a compression fracture. Bone scans are often ordered to determine if the bone infection or bone tumor is present in other bones, in addition to the vertebra with the pathologic fracture. Measuring bone density by photon scan or CT may be part of testing for osteoporosis. Various additional tests may be performed depending on the suspected underlying disease process.

Treatment

Treatment is primarily determined by the underlying bone pathology. Osteoporotic fractures generally heal normally. If deformity is significant, vertebroplasty, or reduction of the deformity, and stabilization by injection of bone cement (polymethyl methacrylate) may be utilized. In general, pathologic fractures secondary to infection or tumor will not begin to heal until definite treatment of the infection or tumor has occurred. Most fracture pain responds to medication. Some type of orthotic (brace or corset) may be recommended for comfort. Ice (or heat), whirlpool treatments if available, and gentle massage may also be recommended. Supplemental medical treatment may be recommended in cases of osteoporosis.

Prognosis

The outcome varies tremendously with the underlying diagnosis. Most osteoporotic compression fractures heal within 6 to 8 weeks with conservative treatment, whereas fractures caused by metastatic disease may not have successful outcomes. Fractures of the spine resulting from osteoporosis may heal but with residual deformity, which may cause pain. Vertebroplasty significantly decreases the deformity and chance of chronic pain.

Surgical treatment (stabilization or fusion) of pathological vertebral fractures is a highly specialized decision, due to large variations in actual outcome. Recurrence of pathological vertebral fractures is common, since the underlying disease condition is often chronic.

Differential Diagnosis

Signs and symptoms of spine fractures may be similar to those seen with cauda equina syndrome, neoplasms of the spinal cord, septic shock, spinal cord infections, thoracic outlet syndrome, torticollis, and other degenerative conditions of the spine. A stress fracture may present with a similar pain pattern but with a much better prognosis.

Specialists

- Endocrinologist
- Infectious Disease Physician
- Oncologist
- Orthopedic Surgeon

Rehabilitation

There is no single therapeutic strategy employed for vertebral fractures caused by underlying pathology. The individual may participate in physical and occupational therapy to improve level of function after such an injury, but not the underlying condition.

Rehabilitation of a fracture to the vertebrae depends on the disease predisposing to the pathologic fracture, fracture type, severity, the individual's age, and general health.

In all cases, pain management is a must. An occupational therapist may evaluate work and home conditions to make adjustments that will help decrease mechanical stress as the pathological conditions progress.

Work Restrictions / Accommodations

Restrictions and accommodations are dependent on the underlying disease process, and thus the predicted life expectancy of the individual, the number of vertebrae involved, work expectations, and the type of treatment the individual receives for the underlying condition. Restrictions would include avoidance of any lifting, overhead work, carrying, pushing, and prolonged standing or sitting. Use of a corset should not affect dexterity. Safety issues and drug testing policies must be reviewed if pain medication is required.

Comorbid Conditions

Comorbid conditions that could influence disability are the underlying diseases that predispose the individual to the pathological factor, including hematogenous osteomyelitis, bone tuberculosis, osteoporosis, osteomalacia, hyperparathyroidism, renal osteodystrophy, Paget's disease, multiple myeloma, chordoma, and metastatic carcinoma, as well as obesity, arthritis, calcium deficiency, insufficient protein intake, and drug addiction.

Complications

The most common complications of pathological vertebral fractures are hunchback (kyphosis) and shortened height. Compression fractures of the vertebrae can also cause compression and irritation of spinal nerve roots and/or the spinal cord. Multiple vertebral compression fractures of the thoracic spine with accompanying kyphosis can cause the individual to hyperextend the neck, leading to neck pain and muscle fatigue. Kyphosis can also limit total lung capacity and exercise tolerance. Chronic pain as a result of vertebral fracture can lead to depression.

Factors Influencing Duration

The underlying disease that resulted in the fracture is the greatest influence on the disability. Other factors include the individual's age, severity of the injury, the amount of impingement on the spinal cord and nerve roots, the presence of complications (e.g., infection), the individual's occupation, and risk factors involved with work. Pain tolerance and ability to change job responsibilities may affect the length of disability.

Length of Disability

In some cases, disability may be permanent. Duration depends on which vertebra, whether fracture is stable or unstable, degree of bone deformity, and neurological deficit. Diagnosis is usually incompatible with heavy and very heavy work.

Single vertebra, mild to moderate deformity. Fracture secondary to osteoporosis.

Duration in Days

Job Classification	Minimum	Optimum	Maximum
Sedentary work	21	28	42
Light work	42	49	56
Medium work	70	77	84
Heavy work	Indefinite	Indefinite	Indefinite
Very Heavy work	Indefinite	Indefinite	Indefinite

Failure to Recover

If an individual fails to recover within the maximum duration expectancy period, the reader may wish to reference the following questions to assist in better understanding the specifics of an individual's medical case.

Regarding diagnosis:

- Does individual have any underlying infections? Are they on chronic corticosteroid treatment?
- Does individual have any metabolic bone diseases or cancers?
- Have conditions with similar symptoms been ruled out?
- Did the individual have sudden onset of back pain while lifting? Did the individual report milder back pain with more gradual onset?
- Is there an increase in the curve of the upper back?
- Does the individual report problems with urination or bowel movements? Does the individual report numbness, tingling, or weakness?
- On palpation of the affected part, was the physician able to localize the affected area? Was kyphosis present?
- Is the causative disease process apparent?
- Has the individual had x-rays, CT, and MRI?
- Was a bone scan done?
- Has a bone biopsy proven the diagnosis of the underlying disorder?

Regarding treatment:

- Has consultation with the appropriate specialist been obtained?
- Did the individual respond to medication?
- Was an orthotic recommended for comfort?
- Were ice, heat, whirlpool treatments, and gentle massage utilized?
- Is the underlying condition being treated?

Regarding prognosis:

- Is individual active in rehabilitation?
- Is the individual's employer able to accommodate any necessary restrictions?
- Does the individual have kyphosis and shortened height?
- Is there irritation of spinal nerve roots?
- Does individual have multiple vertebral compression fractures?
- Does individual hyperextend the neck, leading to neck pain and muscle fatigue?
- Is there limited total lung capacity and exercise tolerance?
- Is depression present secondary to chronic pain?

References

Compression Fractures of the Back. drkoop.com. 1998. 01 Jan 2001 <http://www.drkoop.com/conditions/ency/article/000443.htm>.

Mellors, Robert. Bone. Cornell University Medical College. 01 Apr 1998. 01 Jan 2001 <http://edcenter.med.cornell.edu/CUMC_PathNotes/Skeletal/Bone.html>.

Frostbite

Other names / synonyms: Cold Injury

991.0, 991.1, 991.2, 991.3, 991.9

Definition

Frostbite is an injury to the skin and underlying tissues as a result of severe environmental cold exposure or direct contact with a very cold object. The tissue injury in frostbite results from both freezing temperatures and compromised circulation (vasoconstriction). The circulation ceases and tiny clots (thrombi) form in the blood vessels. The parts of the body most often affected by frostbite are the hands, feet, nose, and ears.

Frostbite starts with a mild form of cold injury called frostnip. Frostnip represents reversible damage. There is discomfort, blanching, and numbness of the skin that is relieved by rewarming. Superficial frostbite is limited to the skin and subcutaneous tissues. Severe frostbite involves the muscles, nerves, and deeper blood vessels and may result in tissue death (necrosis) and decay (gangrene), and loss of digits.

Mountain frostbite is a variation seen among mountain climbers and others exposed to extremely cold temperatures at high altitude. It combines tissue freezing with lack of oxygen (hypoxia) and general body dehydration.

Most cases of frostbite are seen in workers and soldiers, those who work outdoors in the cold, and among winter outdoor enthusiasts. Predisposing factors for frostbite include inadequate clothing, high humidity, vascular disease, nicotine, and alcohol. Individuals at the greatest risk for frostbite may include those stranded in cold weather, work in cold environments, winter athletes, homeless or improperly clothed, or have had a previous cold injury. In addition, elderly, immobile, mentally impaired, or malnourished individuals may have greater risk of developing frostbite.

As a result of inconsistent reporting systems and data, the exact prevalence of frostbite is unknown. In wartime situations, however, frostbite occurred more frequently in blacks and those from warm climates. In North America, frostbite is uncommon and occurs primarily in the northern states, Alaska, and Canada. The majority of frostbite victims are male.

Diagnosis

History: The individual may complain of pain, prickling and itching, pins and needles (paresthesias), or numbness particularly in the hands and feet. Individuals may report recent exposure to extreme cold or a prolonged exposure to cold. Although the hands and feet are most often affected, individuals may also have symptoms affecting the shins, cheeks, nose, ears, and eyes. Following warming, the individual often describes tenderness or burning pain.

Physical exam: An early sign of frostbite is white, waxy skin with decreased sensitivity. After thawing, the skin is reddened with superficial blisters and swelling. If frostbite has affected deeper tissue, gangrene and necrosis may occur.

Tests: Lab studies are not important in the initial diagnosis and management of frostbite. They may be helpful, however, in identifying delayed systemic complications such as wound infection or underlying hypothermia. A complete blood count (CBC) and chemistry panel is commonly ordered. A radioisotope scan called Tc-99m (Technetium 99) pertechnetate scintigraphy is useful in detecting tissue injury.

Treatment

Treatment is first directed at managing life-threatening conditions. Administration of warm, intravenous fluids may be used as a warming measure to enhance blood flow especially in individuals with mountain frostbite or hypothermia. Frostbitten areas are treated with slow rewarming in cool water that is raised gradually over an hour to a maximum temperature of 104 degrees F.

Tissue damage increases with trauma to the involved areas or with warming and refreezing therefore affected areas should not be massaged or rewarmed if the areas are still exposed to the cold environment. It is important not to walk, bear weight, or put pressure on affected areas. Bed rest, elevation of the affected area, tetanus toxic administration, and administration of antibiotics is necessary if infection is present. Analgesics or narcotics are used for pain. In the case of necrosis or gangrene, resection of the dead tissue or amputation is performed.

Prognosis

If treated early, frostbite is reversible by simple warming. Recovery is most often complete if not complicated by infection or gangrene. Early return of sensation and healthy skin color are signs of a favorable outcome. On the other hand, persistent blue discoloration (cyanosis) and blood blisters (hemorrhagic blebs) are signs of necrosis and a less favorable outcome.

Long-term effects include altered sensation of affected area, damage to sweat glands, cracking skin and loss of nails, abnormal color changes of area, cold sensitivity, joint stiffness, tremor, and osteoporosis. Muscle weakness and phantom pain may occur in amputated extremities.

Differential Diagnosis

Other conditions with similar symptoms include frostnip, Pernio (chilblains), and trench foot.

Specialists

- Dermatologist
- Emergency Medicine
- General Surgeon
- Internist
- Physiatrist
- Plastic Surgeon

Rehabilitation

Superficial frostbite (involving the skin only) does not need advanced therapeutic intervention. However, for deep frostbite (involving the skin and underlying tissue) therapy is initiated immediately after rewarming

With diminished pain and swelling, the individual begins a routine of active range of motion exercises. Passive range of motion where the therapist assists the individual beyond the active range is prohibited as the tissue is too weak and may cause further tissue damage.

During the early stages of healing, pain is quite pronounced and may require Transcutaneous Nerve Stimulation (TENS). The intensity of stimulation can be controlled to apply a low activation to the affected area that allows for reduction of fluid in the joint and tissues ultimately relieving pressure and decreasing pain. This modality may also be used in conjunction with exercise of the extremity to increase range of motion and avoid the formation of joint contracture. As well, the area of exposure may be highly sensitive and require desensitization therapy for proper healing to continue. In addition to massage desensitization exercises such as handling objects of differing textures are implemented until the affected area responds without irritation.

The individual may be assessed for vascular status of the affected area with an angiogram (technique to find the size and shape of blood vessels) and bone scintigram (technique to determine the function of tissues). These tests may determine if amputation is necessary.

For hand treatment, splinting may be necessary for up to six months post exposure. An intense program to regain proper hand function is initiated once the skin and underlying tissue are able to tolerate force without risk of further damage. Gripping exercises such as squeezing a tennis ball or putty and more functional exercises such a picking up objects are gradually added to the routine. As therapy progresses, exercises should be reflective of the work environment. The individual should be reintroduced to tools associated with their occupation such as a hammer. In the final phase of therapy, the individual must work to improve hand endurance. The work environment of the individual must be re-assessed in preparation for the individual's return to work. Changes in job environment may include wearing a splint while performing tasks that require continuous wrist motion or rotating tasks that may induce repetitive strain to the thumb. Protective clothing must continually be worn if the individual works in an outdoor environment.

Lower extremity therapy may initially include bracing the foot or feet. The individual may be required to use crutches or a wheel chair to ambulate. One major concern after prolong immobilization is mobilizing the ankle and foot joints to ensure proper flexibility and biomechanics. Once the tissue can tolerate applied force, the therapist may assist by manually mobilizing joints through techniques such as talocrural joint traction where the therapist holds the mid-foot and heel of the individual's upright foot and pulls forward. Progressive active flexibility activities include towel stretches. These active stretch exercises are eventually replaced by isometric exercises that use the same movements. These exercises are geared to restore full toe and foot biomechanics that are necessary for proper walking.

Prior to full weight bearing, the individual may engage in functional balance or proprioceptive training.

Work Restrictions / Accommodations

With complete recovery, restrictions or accommodations are not necessary. Personal protective equipment should be considered for individuals who work outdoors. Any amputation of the digits may require a change in individual's work duties.

Comorbid Conditions

Comorbid conditions that may impact ability to recover and further lengthen disability include atherosclerosis, peripheral vascular disease, diabetes, thyroid dysfunction, arthritis, and nicotine use.

Complications

Thawing and refreezing of the affected areas and trauma to the frozen area increase tissue damage. Other complications include hypothermia, infection, and gangrene.

Factors Influencing Duration

Location of the frostbite, extent of tissue damage, and infection lengthen the period of disability. Surgery for possible complications will also influence the length of disability.

Length of Disability

Duration depends on site and extent.

Without gangrene.

Duration in Days

Job Classification	Minimum	Optimum	Maximum
Sedentary work	1	7	14
Light work	1	7	14
Medium work	7	14	21
Heavy work	28	35	42
Very Heavy work	28	35	42

With gangrene.

Duration in Days

Job Classification	Minimum	Optimum	Maximum
Sedentary work	7	14	21
Light work	14	21	28
Medium work	28	42	56
Heavy work	42	56	70
Very Heavy work	42	56	70

Failure to Recover

If an individual fails to recover within the maximum duration expectancy period, the reader may wish to reference the following questions to assist in better understanding the specifics of an individual's medical case.

Regarding diagnosis:

- Does individual have a history of exposure to extreme cold or a prolonged exposure to cold?
- Are the symptoms and physical exam findings consistent with the diagnosis of frostbite such as pain, prickling and itching, pins and needles (paresthesias), or numbness particularly in the hands and feet? After warming was there tenderness or burning pain?
- On exam, is skin white and waxy with decreases sensitivity?
- Were other conditions with similar symptoms ruled out?

Regarding treatment:

- Was treatment of any life-threatening conditions such as hypothermia necessary?
- Were frostbitten areas rewarmed slowly?
- Were the affected areas protected from pressure or rubbing to prevent further damage?
- Did individual receive other appropriate interventions such as tetanus toxoid administration?

Regarding prognosis:

- Was treatment prompt and appropriate?
- Did individual experience any complications such as gangrene that may impact recovery?
- Did individual experience any long-term effects such as altered sensation of affected area, damage to sweat glands, cold sensitivity, joint stiffness, tremor, osteoporosis that may impact prognosis?
- Does individual have any comorbid conditions such as atherosclerosis, peripheral vascular disease, diabetes, thyroid dysfunction, arthritis, or nicotine use that would impact recovery?

References

Frostbite. Indiana Hand Center.com. 09 Oct 2000. 14 Jan 2001 <http://www.indianahandcenter.com/hot_frost.html>.

Reamy, Brian, MD. "Frostbite: Review and Current Concepts." Journal of the American Board of Family Practice 11 1 (1998): 9. 14 Jan 2001 <http://www.familypractice.com/journal/1998/v11.n01/1101.05/art-1101.05.htm>.

Furuncle
Other names / synonyms: Boil, Furunculosis
680, 680.9

Definition

A furuncle is a pus-filled hair follicle resulting from infection by bacteria, usually Staphylococcus aureus. Often it is preceded by a superficial or deep infection and inflammation of hair follicles (folliculitis). Furuncles can be multiple and recurrent. They affect only areas where hair follicles are present particularly regions subject to friction and perspiration such as the neck, face, armpits, and buttocks.

Predisposing factors include obesity, diabetes mellitus, treatment with corticosteroids or cytotoxic agents (e.g., anticancer medications), immunodeficiency conditions, mite infestation (scabies), carriage of Staphylococcus aureus, dermatitis with scratches and cracks (excoriations), skin trauma caused by friction from clothing, poor hygiene, and malnutrition. Individuals with oily skin, dark complexion, acne, and dandruff (acne-seborrhea complex) are at an increased risk of developing furuncles.

Furuncles are very common and nearly everyone has one at some point in their life. Furuncles usually occur in young adults and are associated with hormonal changes. Men and women are equally affected.

Diagnosis

History: The individual may complain of a hard, tender, red, enlarged, and painful nodule on the skin. The nodule may be swollen because of pus accumulation. If the nodule had ruptured, the discharge of pus may lead to a decrease in the swelling, redness, and pain. The individual may have a history of folliculitis or previous furuncles.

Physical exam: The exam may reveal a reddened nodule that may be hard, tender, warm, and painful to the touch. The boils may be swollen and discharge may occur.

Tests: Culture of the pus is occasionally needed to determine the specific causative bacteria. In addition, the antibiotic sensitivities of the causative organism may be determined.

Treatment

Furuncles are treated with oral antibiotics and by application of moist heat to hasten drainage. Furuncles may need to be lanced and drained (incision and drainage). General skin care should include use of antimicrobial soap solution, wearing a protective bandage, and avoidance of skin irritants (e.g., strong soaps, deodorants). Clothing should be loose, lightweight, and porous.

Furuncles with surrounding skin inflammation (cellulitis) or associated with fever should be treated with intravenous antibiotics.

Prognosis

The outcome is very good in most cases but depends on the severity of the infection, response to treatment, and the individual's overall condition and ability to resist infection. Furunculosis is often recurrent. Deep furuncles may lead to scarring.

Differential Diagnosis

Infected sebaceous or epithelial inclusion cyst, folliculitis, fungal infection (tinea), herpes simplex infection, allergic contact dermatitis, hidradenitis, and botfly infestation are other possible diagnoses.

Specialists

- Dermatologist
- General Surgeon
- Infectious Disease Physician

Work Restrictions / Accommodations

Hands should be thoroughly washed after contact with the lesions. Exposure to chemicals and oils should be avoided. Situations that might cause individuals to sweat should be avoided. If individuals are required to wear uniforms, pressure from tight clothing or belts should be avoided. Depending on the location of the furuncle, excessive sitting or walking may need to be restricted and the use of personal protective equipment (e.g., respirator) may be affected.

Comorbid Conditions
Diabetes, AIDS, organ transplantation, cancer, and obesity may influence the length of disability.

Complications
Complications may be either local such as skin inflammation (cellulitis) or a walled-off focus of infection (abscess) or systemic when the infection is spread via the bloodstream. The latter complication is life-threatening because it may cause infection of the heart (endocarditis), inflammation of bone (osteomyelitis), or brain abscess. Squeezing furuncles located about the lips, nose, or spine can spread the infection even more rapidly and form a brain or spinal abscess. Multiple furuncles can merge and form a carbuncle.

Factors Influencing Duration
Location and extent of the lesions, complications, and response to treatment may influence the length of disability.

Length of Disability
Duration depends on site and job requirements. Recurrence is common.

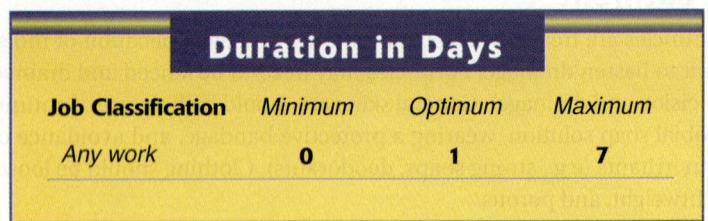

Duration in Days

Job Classification	Minimum	Optimum	Maximum
Any work	0	1	7

Failure to Recover
If an individual fails to recover within the maximum duration expectancy period, the reader may wish to reference the following questions to assist in better understanding the specifics of an individual's medical case.

Regarding diagnosis:
- Does individual complain of a hard, tender, red, enlarged, and painful nodule on the skin? Has the nodule ruptured?
- Does individual have a history of folliculitis?
- Has diagnosis of folliculitis been confirmed?
- Does individual have any predisposing factors for folliculitis such as obesity, diabetes mellitus, treatment with corticosteroids or cytotoxic agents (e.g., anticancer medications), immunodeficiency conditions, mite infestation (scabies), carriage of Staphylococcus aureus, dermatitis with scratches and cracks (excoriations), skin trauma caused by friction from clothing, poor hygiene, and malnutrition?
- Does individual have oily skin, dark complexion, acne, and dandruff (acne-seborrhea complex)?
- Were conditions with similar symptoms ruled out?

Regarding treatment:
- Was culture and sensitivity done to identify the infectious organism and determine the most effective antibiotic to use?
- Do symptoms persist despite treatment?
- Were antibiotic-resistant organisms ruled out?
- Were incision and drainage successful in relieving pain and helping to resolve the infection?
- Was individual compliant with the skin care program?
- If cellulitis or fever developed, was individual treated with IV antibiotics? Has cellulitis resolved?

Regarding prognosis:
- Does individual have any conditions that may impact recovery such as diabetes, AIDS, organ transplantation, cancer, or obesity?
- Has individual experienced any complications, either local or systemic, associated with the furuncle? Have complications responded to treatment?
- Does individual suffer from recurrent furuncles?
- Is there anything that can be done to prevent further occurrences?

References
Anderson, Philip, and Kristin Malaker. "Most Common Skin Disorders." Managing Skin Diseases. Hiscock, Tim, ed. Baltimore: Williams & Wilkins, 1998. 91-95.

Pray, Steven. "Bacterial Infections of the Hair Follicles." U.S. Pharmacist 25 4 (2000): 1-3. 14 Aug 2000 <http://www.medscape.com/jobson/USPharmacist/2000/v25.n04/usp2504.01/pnt-usp2504.01.html>.

Ganglionectomy (Wrist)
Other names / synonyms: Excision of Synovial Cyst
82.21

Definition
Ganglionectomy is a surgical procedure to remove a ganglion or synovial cyst. The procedure can be simple or complex, depending on the location and size of the cyst.

Ganglions are synovial fluid-filled cysts that most commonly form in the wrist, ankle, and fingers. A tunnel (sinus tract) forms from the lining of a joint or tendon (synovium) allowing for leakage of synovial fluid and accumulation in the soft tissue, resulting in the formation of a cyst (ganglion). The ganglion may feel like a lump just under the skin and cause pain, tingling, and restricted motion. If the ganglion is deep along a buried tendon, only the symptoms may be apparent. Some ganglions are only unsightly, but don't cause any other symptoms.

A ganglion can be found in any joint or along any tendon in the body. Most commonly, those requiring surgical removal are in the wrist and hand, knee, and ankle areas.

Ganglions are most likely to form in areas exposed to repetitive stress such as twisting the wrist while gripping or in individuals with inflammatory diseases such as rheumatoid arthritis.

Reason for Procedure
Depending on its size and location, a ganglion can cause pressure on surrounding tendons, nerves, or blood vessels. A ganglionectomy is necessary to remove (excise) a ganglion that is causing pain, numbness, tingling, or restricted motion.

Ganglionectomy is used when conservative measures such as needle aspiration, installation of steroids and restricted activity are not successful.

Description
Depending on the ganglion's size and location, either local or regional anesthesia may be used. The procedure can done on an outpatient basis.

Ganglions are most often superficial, and can be cut (dissected) free from surrounding tissues through a small skin incision. Ganglion cysts originating from deep tendon sheaths or joint capsules, will require more extensive surgery to completely locate and remove them. Once located, the ganglion is cut free from the joint or tendon, and removed. Care is taken to also remove the attachment (sinus tract) to the synovium beneath the cyst, decreasing the likelihood of recurrence. Particular care must be taken to avoid injury to the radial artery when excising ganglions about the volar radial wrist. After the wound is closed, bulky compressive dressings are placed over the incision. Sometimes a protective splint to restrict motion is also applied.

Prognosis
Most individuals recover completely without complication, relieving the symptoms of pain and changes in sensation (paraesthesia). Recurrence is possible, but less likely than when the ganglion is treated by aspiration and injection.

Specialists
- General Surgeon
- Orthopedic Surgeon
- Neurosurgeon
- Plastic Surgeon

Rehabilitation
After surgical treatment for a ganglion cyst on the wrist, bandages may not be removed for approximately 72 hours. The main concern for the first few days is the swelling and bruising due to surgery. Applying ice to the wrist may help contain the swelling (edema). Finger, wrist, and forearm exercises are implemented once the bandage is removed.

The individual can perform functional activities such as brushing teeth and picking up objects. Light stretches to improve wrist extension and flexion are performed daily, such as holding one arm out straight and gently applying pressure so that the hand bends downward from the wrist and holding for a count of twenty. In addition, squeezing exercises may be performed with a ball or putty. Care must be taken not to pull out stitches when performing any wrist movement.

After a week, postsurgery activities such as driving can be resumed. Stitches are usually removed 1-2 weeks after the operation. At this point, wrist exercises may progress to using light weights. Ice massage after exercise may help to reduce inflammation. Once the tissue around the incision is healed, the individual may benefit from hand and wrist exercises performed in a heated whirlpool.

It is important to include exercises such as resistive pronation and supination to work the wrist in different functional directions. Pronation and supination exercises are performed with the forearm stabilized along a bench or table with the wrist and hand free and the palm toward the wall. The individual holds a weight perpendicular to the floor (at 12 o'clock) and rotated either to 9 o'clock (palm facing down) or 3 o'clock (palm facing up).

Work Restrictions / Accommodations
Individuals returning to work while still wearing a bandage will require accommodations to keep the dressing clean and dry.

Because of pain during early healing, the individual may need to be reassigned duties that do not involve use of the wrist or involved joint. Restriction of aggravating activities is necessary, such as repetitive wrist motion. Protective splints or braces may be required both during recovery and as a preventative measure.

Comorbid Conditions
Inflammatory diseases such as rheumatoid arthritis may complicate recovery.

Procedure Complications
Possible complications could include skin sloughing, infection, nerve or vessel damage, and failure to alleviate the symptoms. Recurrence is possible.

Factors Influencing Duration

Factors influencing length of disability include presence of complications, the individual's job requirements, and any aggravating activities associated with job requirements. Overuse in the early postoperative period could delay healing.

Length of Disability

Duration depends on site and whether dominant or non-dominant limb is involved. Individuals may be able to return quickly to modified work or work not involving the operative site.

Duration in Days

Job Classification	Minimum	Optimum	Maximum
Sedentary work	1	3	14
Light work	1	3	14
Medium work	7	14	21
Heavy work	14	21	28
Very Heavy work	14	28	42

References

Anderson, Bruce. *Office Orthopedics for Primary Care*. Philadelphia: W.B. Saunders Company, 1999.

Prentice, William. *Rehabilitation Techniques in Sports Medicine*. St. Louis: Mosby, 1994.

Gangrene

Other names / synonyms: Dry Gangrene, Fournier's Gangrene, Gas Gangrene, Meleney's Synergistic Gangrene, Moist Gangrene, Myonecrosis, Necrotizing Fascitis, Tissue Necrosis

785.4

Definition

Gangrene is tissue destruction (necrosis) from partial or total loss of the blood supply. Deprived of oxygen and nutrients, the cells slowly die and, in most cases, bacterial infections develop. It can involve small areas or total organs and limbs.

Causes of gangrene can be external injuries or internal interruption of blood supply. External causes include skin ulcers or wounds, crushing injuries, deep burns, frostbite, boils, and chemical damage of the skin. Internal causes include blood clotting (thrombosis) in a diseased artery, an embolus, severe arteriosclerosis, diabetes, a strangulated hernia, torsion of the testes, or some vascular disorders.

The three major types of gangrene include moist, dry, and gas gangrene. Moist and dry gangrene develop from impaired circulation. Moist gangrene usually occurs in the toes, feet, or legs after a crushing injury or some other factor that causes a sudden interruption of the blood supply (both venous and arterial). An infection occurs and overwhelms the body's normal defenses, resulting in rapid tissue destruction.

Dry gangrene occurs in the absence of bacterial infection. It is characterized by a discoloration and drying out of tissue. Dry gangrene occurs most often as a complication of advanced diabetes or arteriosclerosis.

Gas gangrene is a progressive gangrene characterized by gas bubbles in the dead and dying tissue. The gangrene and formation of gas are a result of one or more toxin-producing bacteria called clostridium entering the body through wounds. The clostridium species thrive in the environment of deep, enclosed areas where oxygen levels are low such as the uterus, gastrointestinal tract, gallbladder, and deep penetrating wounds of the muscles. This form of gangrene spreads very quickly and causes rapid death.

The most frequent traumatic injuries are vehicular or agricultural accidents with open fractures. Crush injuries, industrial accidents, and gunshot wounds are other types of injuries that may lead to gangrene. In the surgical setting, intestinal surgery, especially resection of the bowel and biliary tract, is the most common cause of gas gangrene. Less frequently, gas gangrene is associated with vascular insufficiency in the lower extremities. Sometimes gas gangrene occurs as a complication of burns or amputation. Other cases have infrequently occurred after injections or gynecological procedures.

There are approximately 1,000 to 3,000 cases of gas gangrene due to trauma or surgery in the US each year. Approximately half of the gas gangrene cases are related to trauma.

Diagnosis

History: The individual may report a history of appendicitis, cholecystitis, intestinal obstruction, hernia, frostbite, crush injury, abortion, surgical or traumatic wounds, intramuscular injection sites (commonly seen in drug addicts), diabetes mellitus, or circulatory problems. Individuals may have moderate to severe pain and swelling around an injury site. They may also complain of nausea, vomiting, fever, and chills.

Physical exam: The exam may reveal fever, pain, darkening of tissue, and unpleasant odor. The area may be swollen with blisters or have drainage from the tissues. The individual may have an elevated temperature, rapid heart rate, and cool, clammy skin. In some cases, excessive breakdown of blood cells from the infection will cause the skin to become yellow-colored (jaundiced).

Tests: Lab tests include a complete blood count (CBC), blood cultures, and cultures of the infected tissue and drainage. Sometimes exploratory surgery is required to obtain cultures and determine the source or extent of the infection. Imaging studies, such as plain x-rays, CT, and MRI may be helpful.

Treatment

Prompt surgical removal of dead, damaged, and infected tissue (debridement) is always necessary. If a crush injury occurs, the associated swelling of the muscle compartments may impair circulation. Under these circumstances, surgical incisions to release excess pressure in muscle compartments (fasciotomy) or excision of involved muscles (myectomy) may be needed to restore circulation. If the process is extensive and there are irreversible changes in an extremity, amputation becomes necessary. Plastic reconstruction may be needed if the surgical excisions involve a large area of tissue and/or muscle.

Administering pressurized, 100% oxygen (hyperbaric oxygen therapy) may limit the area of tissue destruction and reduce the amount of the tissue excision necessary. This intervention has varying degrees of success.

Blood transfusions, plasma infusions, and electrolyte replacement may be needed to treat associated blood loss, fluid loss, and shock. Antibiotics are given through a vein (intravenously). Pain medications may be used to control pain.

Prognosis

Without treatment, gas gangrene has a mortality rate approaching 100% within 48 hours of the onset of symptoms. Prompt surgical excision of diseased tissue in conjunction with fluid replacement and antibiotic therapy is associated with an overall mortality rate of 15-30%.

Other forms of gangrene have more favorable outcomes following prompt surgical treatment. However, many individuals are left severely crippled or disfigured by the surgery.

Differential Diagnosis

Cellulitis, peritonitis, and staphylococcal infection are possible differential diagnoses.

Specialists

- General Surgeon
- Internist
- Plastic Surgeon

Rehabilitation

Individuals with gangrene may require surgical excision of the gangrene or amputation. Individuals who undergo excision of the gangrene may require physical and occupational therapy prior to discharge from the hospital in order to increase endurance.

In general, occupational therapy addresses any fatigue that may occur during activities of daily living. Individuals learn to utilize equipment such as a shower chair to decrease the energy expended during bathing or a long-handled sponge to decrease the amount of arm work. Occupational therapists may teach energy conservation techniques where activities of daily living such as meal preparation are broken into smaller components that make tasks more manageable.

Physical therapy addresses decreased endurance, strength, and range of motion. Individuals perform stretching and strengthening exercises of the arms and legs in order to improve overall endurance. Individuals may perform aerobic activity such as walking on a treadmill or riding a stationary bicycle to further increase endurance. Both disciplines ensure that the individual is capable of performing the skills essential to daily living upon returning home.

Individuals requiring amputation may need physical and occupational therapy as well as psychological counseling and a consultation with a prosthetist depending on the nature of the amputation. Individuals with one or more toes amputated may require a few physical therapy sessions to relearn the mechanics of walking as a result of decreased stability. Individuals learn to walk with a cane or may require a prosthesis that fits over the foot to increase stability. Individuals with foot or lower extremity amputation require extensive physical therapy both in the hospital and on an outpatient basis. Individuals learn to wrap the end of the amputation (the residual limb) to prevent swelling so that a prosthetic limb may be fitted. Individuals also inspect the skin for any sign of infection or irritation so as to prevent further amputation.

Individuals learn to bear weight on the residual limb through exercises such as bridging where the individual lies on the back, bends the knees up, and lifts the buttocks. Pillows are placed under the residual limb to provide weight-bearing ability. Individuals with one or more fingers amputated may require occupational therapy to relearn tasks such as writing, grasping different objects, and dressing.

Individuals who sustain amputation may require counseling to deal with their altered body image. They typically undergo a period of grieving for their missing body part and should work through these feelings of loss with a psychologist trained in this area. Counseling is necessary to enable the individual to maintain motivation for learning new skills so that recovery is possible.

Work Restrictions / Accommodations

Many individuals are left severely crippled or disfigured by surgery. Job responsibilities may need to be adjusted according to the functional capacity of the individual. Occupational assistive devices are helpful for those with amputated fingers.

Complementary and Alternative Therapies

Content is intended for awareness only. Treatments may or may not be effective. Scientific evidence may be lacking and some substances have potentially toxic effects. Dr. Presley Reed and the editors do not endorse the use of these therapies in the absence of consultation with a licensed medical professional.

T.E.N.S. - Has shown some benefit as an alternative to drug therapy in treating arterial circulatory disturbances of the lower extremities.

Comorbid Conditions

Vascular disease, diabetes mellitus, malnutrition, alcoholism, immunodeficiency diseases, and bleeding disorders are conditions that may decrease recovery and lengthen disability.

Complications

Spread of infection systemically throughout the body (sepsis), shock, and multiple organ failure are the most serious complications associated with gangrene.

Factors Influencing Duration

The factors that determine the period of disability include the timeliness of the diagnosis, location and extent of the disease when diagnosed, type of gangrene, microorganism responsible for the infection, and response to antibiotic therapy and débridement or surgery. The extent and nature of surgery will dictate the length of disability.

Length of Disability

Duration depends on extent, location, and cause of gangrene, its response to treatment and whether amputation is necessary. Contact physician for more specific information.

Failure to Recover

If an individual fails to recover within the maximum duration expectancy period, the reader may wish to reference the following questions to assist in better understanding the specifics of an individual's medical case.

Regarding diagnosis:

- Does individual have history of appendicitis, cholecystitis, intestinal obstruction, hernia, frostbite, crush injury, abortion, surgical or traumatic wounds, intramuscular injection sites (commonly seen in drug addicts), diabetes mellitus, or circulatory problems?
- Is there moderate to severe pain and swelling around an injury site?
- Is there evidence of persistent infection at the wound site?
- Does individual complain of nausea, vomiting, fever, and chills?
- On exam, is there fever, pain, darkening of tissue, and unpleasant odor? Swollen with blisters or drainage from the tissues? Does individual have an elevated temperature, rapid heart rate, and cool, clammy skin? Jaundiced?
- Were wound and tissue cultures done?
- Has diagnosis of gangrene been confirmed? What type? Moist, dry, or gas gangrene?

Regarding treatment:

- Was culture and sensitivity done to positively identify the causative organism and determine the most effective antibiotic to use?
- Were antibiotic-resistant organisms ruled out?
- If process was extensive and irreversible changes in the extremity occurred, was amputation necessary?
- Did individual undergo hyperbaric oxygen therapy? With what degree of success?
- Since administering pressurized, 100% oxygen may limit the area of tissue destruction and reduce the amount of the tissue excision necessary, would this therapy still be an option?
- Has individual received or is individual scheduled for plastic reconstruction?

Regarding prognosis:

- Was diseased tissue successfully removed?
- Did culture and sensitivity confirm the most effective choice of antibiotic therapy?
- Was individual left severely crippled or disfigured by the surgery?
- Is individual scheduled for plastic reconstruction?
- Has individual received appropriate and well-fitting prosthetic device?
- Did individual receive comprehensive physical rehabilitation?
- Does individual have an underlying condition such as vascular disease, diabetes mellitus, malnutrition, alcoholism, immunodeficiency diseases, or a bleeding disorder that may impact recovery?
- Has individual been allowed to go through an appropriate period of grieving for the lost body part? Would individual benefit from working through these feelings of loss with a psychologist trained in this area?
- Does individual demonstrate signs of depression such as apathy, helplessness, fatigue, or loss of appetite? Would additional psychological counseling help individual deal with his/her altered body image?

References

Brannon, Linda, and Jess Feiss. Health Psychology. Belmont: Wadsworth Publishing Company, 1992.

May, Bella. "Assessment and Treatment of Individuals Following Lower Extremity Amputation." Physical Rehabilitation: Assessment and Treatment. O'Sullivan, Susan B., and Thomas J. Schmitz, eds. Philadelphia: F.A. Davis Company, 1994. 375-396.

Gas Gangrene

Other names / synonyms: Bacillus Gangrene, Clostridial Myonecrosis

040.0

Definition

Gas gangrene is a rapidly progressive, life-threatening, toxemic infection of skeletal muscle caused by a dangerous strain of bacteria (Clostridium) that destroys muscle. The infection rapidly spreads to involve additional muscle. It is a true medical emergency, and death can result in as little as one day.

Gas gangrene infections are usually the result of obstructed blood supply to an organ or tissue due to injury (trauma), surgery, or as a complication of gangrene caused by blocked blood supply but without infection (dry gangrene). Post-traumatic gas gangrene may occur following a compound fracture, burns, or subcutaneous or intramuscular injection (insulin or epinephrine). The presence of dead (devitalized) tissue and the presence of foreign bodies in the wound increase the risk of gas gangrene. Postsurgical gas gangrene occurs most often following surgery of individuals with diabetes or other chronic debilitating disease. Spontaneous gas gangrene may occur in association with an underlying cancer. The time between injury and onset of disease (incubation period) can range from 6 hours to 2 days. The prevalence of gas gangrene in the US annually is 0.1 case per 100,000 people.

Diagnosis

History: There may be a history of trauma, surgery, or cancer. Individuals will relate a history of fever with sudden, increasing pain in affected area. The individual may notice a foul odor from the wound. Once the tissue dies, it becomes numb. In the final stages of the disease, confusion (delirium), decreasing responsiveness (stupor), and coma occur.

Physical exam: The exam may reveal black, discolored skin surrounded by redness and swelling with oozing pus. Fluid accumulation beneath the skin in blisters (bullae) produces a foul-smelling, blood-tinged discharge. Gas may be felt (palpable) in the tissues in 80% of cases. The wound site may be pale originally, but then turns red or bronze, then finally blackish-green. Surgical exploration demonstrates muscle that does not bleed or contract when stimulated. This muscle will initially appear lusterless pink, then deep red, then gray-green or mottled purple. Symptoms also include increased heart rate, fall in blood pressure, and increased respiration.

Tests: Gram stain of the wound discharge shows remarkable absence of white blood cells (leukocytes) and the presence of gram-positive rods. An anaerobic (absence of oxygen) culture confirms the diagnosis. X-rays of the soft tissue, CT scan, or MRI may show gas within the soft tissues, but since other organisms also produce gas, this is not enough to make the diagnosis.

Treatment

Immediate surgery is done to remove the dead tissue (debridement). Treatment may also include increasing the amount of oxygen in the tissues by exposing the individual to oxygen at a much higher concentration than normal atmospheric pressure (hyperbaric oxygen therapy, or HBO). Amputation of the infected part and adjacent tissue is often necessary. Appropriate antibiotics are administered intravenously. Hospitalization with intensive therapy combining surgery, HBO, intravenous antibiotics, and supportive medical therapy is required to prevent death from sepsis.

Prognosis

If the individual receives rapid, aggressive treatment with hospitalization, debridement, and intravenous antibiotics, prognosis is generally good, and 80% of such individuals survive. However, 15-20% of individuals will require some level of amputation. Most of these amputations are of the lower extremity, and successful rehabilitation and fitting with a prosthetic device allow the majority of individuals to obtain a good functional recovery.

Differential Diagnosis

Other possibilities include simple contamination, anaerobic cellulitis, streptococcal myositis, necrotizing fasciitis, and infection with Aeromonas hydrophilia.

Specialists

- General Surgeon
- Infectious Disease Physician
- Vascular Surgeon

Rehabilitation

When gangrenous tissue cannot be restored to life and surgical resection/amputation is required, rehabilitation for gas gangrene is an important aspect of treatment. Once pain and swelling subside following an amputation for gas gangrene, rehabilitation emphasizes regaining range of motion and strength to the remaining region of the body and/or joints of an affected extremity (or residual limb). Flexibility of specific muscles is important to help the individual return to as normal function as possible. For example, if the amputation is below the knee, keeping the back thigh muscles (hamstrings) flexible is critical. If the amputation is above the knee, the focus is on the hip muscles, both in front and back of the thigh.

Strengthening a residual limb begins early in rehabilitation along with training in the use of a temporary prosthesis, if indicated. Functional training exercises are important in rehabilitation and focus on the individual's physical demands at home and in preparation for return to work. Such activities more closely match normal requirements of activities of daily living (ADLs). A home exercise program is started at the time of the physical therapy evaluation (at the hospital), with gradual progression in difficulty up to the date of discharge. The final step is to incorporate activities that help individuals return to their home and previous work environment. This includes exercises resembling work requirements, and instruction on placement and removal of the prosthesis, if indicated.

The physical therapist may need to make modifications for those individuals whose amputation resulted from gas gangrene. Variations in rehabilitation depend on the part of the body amputated and whether prosthesis is required.

Work Restrictions / Accommodations

Extended work leave or temporary transfer to sedentary duties may be required. If amputation of a limb is necessary, appropriate accommodations will be necessary based on the individual's functional status with or without a prosthetic device (artificial limb). Because the lower extremity is most commonly amputated, accommodations may be necessary to allow the individual to have sedentary duties, or to be allowed to use a wheelchair or crutches.

Comorbid Conditions

Diabetes mellitus and peripheral vascular disease may lengthen disability.

Complications

Complications include sepsis (presence of the bacteria or their poisons throughout the bloodstream) and death.

Factors Influencing Duration

Length of disability may be influenced by the location and extent of the gangrene, type of effectiveness of treatment given, and the individual's work requirements.

Length of Disability

Length of disability will be determined by the need for amputation, the affected limb, and dominant verus non-dominant limb. Contact physician for more specific information.

Failure to Recover

If an individual fails to recover within the maximum duration expectancy period, the reader may wish to reference the following questions to assist in better understanding the specifics of an individual's medical case.

Regarding diagnosis:
- Has diagnosis of gas gangrene been confirmed by an anaerobic culture?
- Has the individual exhibited any indication of sepsis?
- Does the individual have an underlying condition that may impact recovery?

Regarding treatment:
- Did individual receive prompt, aggressive treatment?
- Would individual benefit from additional HBO treatment?

Regarding prognosis:
- Was amputation necessary?
- Did individual receive successful fitting with a prosthetic device?
- Was individual enrolled in a comprehensive rehabilitation program?

References

Scully, Rosemary M., and Marylou R. Barnes. Physical Therapy. Philadelphia: J.B. Lippincott Company, 1989.

Swartz, Morton N. "Myositis." Principles and Practice of Infectious Diseases, 4th ed, vol 1. Mandell, Gerald L., John E. Bennett, and Raphael Dolin, eds. New York: W.B. Saunders Company, 1995. 931-936.

Gastrectomy

Other names / synonyms: Billroth I Procedure, Billroth II Procedure, Complete Gastrectomy, Gastrectomy with Anastomosis, Gastroduodenostomy, Gastrojejunostomy, Gastrojejunostomy, Hofmeister Gastrectomy, Partial Gastrectomy, Polya Gastrectomy, Proximal Gastrectomy, Radical Gastrectomy, Subtotal Gastrectomy, Total Gastrectomy

43.5, 43.6, 43.7, 43.89, 43.99, 44.3, 44.39

Definition

A gastrectomy is a surgical procedure to remove part or all of the stomach. The procedure may be indicated for stomach cancer, or in cases of peptic ulcer disease that are unresponsive to medical interventions.

In most cases, half to two-thirds of the stomach is removed (partial or subtotal gastrectomy). In a total gastrectomy, the whole stomach is removed.

Once the gastrectomy is performed, the surgeon must connect the remaining portion of the stomach directly to the small intestines (gastroenterostomy). When the remaining part of the stomach is joined to the duodenum (the first part of the small intestine); the procedure is called a gastroduodenostomy. When joined to the middle section of the small intestine (jejunum), the procedure is called a gastrojejunostomy.

When the esophagus is joined directly to the jejunum, the procedure is a total gastrectomy.

Gastric cancer occurs most frequently in men over 40 years old. The incidence of gastric cancer is 2 out of 10,000 people and is more common in Japan, Chile, and Iceland. Risk factors for gastric cancer are a family history of gastric cancer, blood type group A, history of pernicious anemia, history of chronic stomach inflammation (gastritis), or history of gastric polyp.

Peptic ulcers are lesions of the gastrointestinal tract that destroy the inner lining of the gastrointestinal tract (mucosa). The most common peptic ulcer sites are the first few centimeters of the duodenum (duodenal ulcer) or the lesser curvature of the stomach (gastric ulcer).

There are about 500,000 new cases of peptic ulcers each year in the US. They occur in about 10% of the adult population. They are 5 times more common in the duodenum than in the stomach (gastric ulcers). Peptic ulcers are slightly more common in men than women. Ulcers in the duodenum are most common in ages 30 to 55, while gastric ulcers are more common between 55 and 70 years of age. Ulcers are more common in smokers and in individuals who used nonsteroidal anti-inflammatory drugs (NSAIDs) on a chronic basis. The role of emotional stress in the development of ulcers is uncertain. Other conditions that play a role in the development of peptic ulcers are chronic stomach infection with bacteria called Helicobacter pylori and gastric acid hypersecretion states, such as Zollinger-Ellison syndrome. It is believed that 70-75% of duodenal ulcers are associated with H. pylori infections.

For the most part, peptic ulcers are treated successfully with medical interventions or endoscopic procedures. Occasionally, some cases of peptic ulcer disease are unresponsive to these interventions and ultimately require a gastrectomy. A partial gastrectomy is done to remove the segment of the stomach affected by the disease. In addition, other surgical interventions (such as vagotomy or vagotomy and pyloroplasty) are usually done to reduce acid production and prevent recurrence of ulcers in the remaining parts of the stomach.

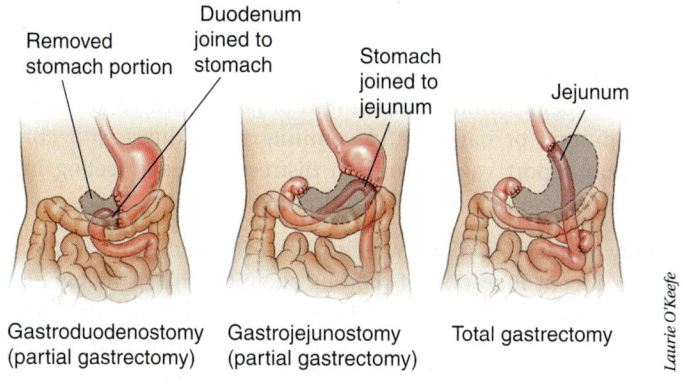

Reason for Procedure

A partial gastrectomy is used to manage large bleeding stomach ulcers or ulcers that break through (perforate) the stomach or duodenal wall. It is also used to treat cancers that are located closer to the end of the stomach.

A total gastrectomy is a rare procedure used for treating certain stomach cancers. In some cases, it is used for individuals with terminal stomach cancer to provide relieve discomfort in the remaining months of their lives.

Description

General anesthesia is administered. The abdomen is scrubbed and shaved. A tube may be inserted to drain bladder (urinary catheter) and one to drain the stomach contents (nasogastric tube).

The surgeon creates an incision that runs midline from the ribcage to the lower abdomen. After locating the injured or diseased area of the stomach, the surgeon will use a stapling device to section off the healthy stomach from the diseased stomach. If necessary, the free end of the stomach will be joined to a healthy segment of the small intestine.

One or more small drains may be placed at the surgical site to allow for drainage of blood and fluid. The abdominal wound is closed in layers. The final skin layer will be closed with a small stapling device.

Prognosis

The outcome is dependent on the underlying disease, the extent of the disease, and the extent of surgery required. In the treatment of stomach cancer, a gastrectomy has a favorable outcome (5-year survival of over 45%) if the surgery is done before the cancer spreads to the lymph nodes or elsewhere. In metastatic stomach cancer, a gastrectomy is generally effective at reducing pain and discomfort. However the 5-year survival is less than 20%, due to the underlying cancer.

In large stomach ulcers with significant bleeding, an emergency gastrectomy is generally successful in controlling bleeding.

Gastrectomy is not 100% effective in treating gastric ulcers. Approximately 5-10% of the individuals will have recurrence of ulcers.

Specialists

- Gastroenterologist
- General Surgeon

Work Restrictions / Accommodations

Early in the recovery (2 to 4 weeks postoperatively) individuals may need to avoid strenuous activities or heavy lifting. The individual's schedule should be modified to allow for 2-3 small meal breaks during the work day rather than the single, traditional lunch hour.

Comorbid Conditions

Comorbid conditions of immune suppression and bleeding disorders may impact ability to recover and further lengthen disability.

Procedure Complications

The most common complications from the procedure include wound infection, leaking at the site where the stomach is joined to the intestine (anastomosis), lung congestion (atelectasis), and bleeding. Less common complications include shock (from bleeding) or cardiac arrest. Late complications include recurrent ulcers, diarrhea (from sugar and carbohydrate intolerance), and iron deficiency anemia.

Factors Influencing Duration

Length of disability may be influenced by the underlying condition, the extent of the surgery (partial or total gastrectomy), the presence of post-gastrectomy syndromes (side effects after gastric surgery), or the presence of surgical complications.

Length of Disability

Partial gastrectomy, with or without vagotomy.

Duration in Days

Job Classification	Minimum	Optimum	Maximum
Sedentary work	28	35	42
Light work	28	35	42
Medium work	42	49	56
Heavy work	42	49	56
Very Heavy work	42	49	56

Total.

Duration in Days

Job Classification	Minimum	Optimum	Maximum
Sedentary work	28	42	56
Light work	28	42	56
Medium work	42	56	70
Heavy work	42	56	70
Very Heavy work	42	56	70

References

Sabiston, David C., and H. Kim Lyerly. Textbook of Surgery, 15th ed. Philadelphia: W.B. Saunders Company, 1997.

Gastritis

Other names / synonyms: Acute Gastritis, Atrophic Gastritis, Erosive Gastritis, Gastric Inflammation, Stomach Inflammation

535.0, 535.1, 535.2, 535.3, 535.4, 535.5, 535.6

Definition

Gastritis is a common ailment involving inflammation of the stomach lining that causes general discomfort and, rarely, gastrointestinal bleeding.

There are two forms of gastritis. Acute gastritis is mild and temporary, lasting 1 to 2 days and can result from any number of causes. Acute gastritis may be caused by stomach acid-induced damage, excessive smoking or alcohol consumption, or as a side effect of aspirin, certain prescription medications such as nonsteroidal anti-inflammatory drugs (NSAIDs), or foods contaminated with certain bacteria. Accidental or purposeful ingestion of ammonia, lye, Lysol, or other cleaning agents (corrosive alkali) or acids can lead to corrosive acute gastritis. Conditions that produce severe stress such as shock, trauma, or major surgery may also cause gastritis. Finally, acute gastritis may be caused by certain medical procedures (iatrogenic) including radiation therapy and administration of anticancer drugs (chemotherapeutic agents).

Chronic gastritis is a progressive, irreversible decay (atrophy) of the lining (gastric mucosa) and glandular tissue within the stomach. This leaves a less effective barrier to the corrosive and digestive properties of hydrochloric acid and pepsin contained within the stomach. There are two forms of chronic gastritis. Type A gastritis (also known as autoimmune atrophic gastritis) may be triggered by a physical or psycho-emotional stressor that causes the individual's immune system to produce antibodies against certain cells in the stomach (parietal cells). Destruction of these cells results in atrophy of the stomach tissue. Type B gastritis (or simple atrophic gastritis) is more common and is strongly associated with the presence of a certain bacterium (Helicobacter pylori or H. pylori) in the stomach mucosa. Other causes of simple atrophic gastritis may include chronic alcohol or cigarette use, exposure to toxins such as lead, and certain metabolic conditions that may occur during renal failure (uremia).

The frequency of gastritis increases as individual's age. Men and women are affected equally. In the US and other countries, the overall prevalence of atrophic gastritis ranges from 20-42% except in Colombia and Japan where the overall incidence ranges from 40-90%. Atrophic gastritis is found in 32% of Americans age 60 or older and affects nearly 100% of individuals who are at least 70.

Diagnosis

History: Individuals with acute gastritis may report lack of appetite (anorexia), upper abdominal discomfort or pain, diarrhea, blood in the stool or sputum, or nausea and vomiting. Individuals with chronic gastritis may report vague stomach distress, a heavy feeling in the stomach after meals, or ulcer-like symptoms.

There may be a history of ulcer, recent use of steroidal or NSAIDs such as aspirin, recent ingestion of food or chemical that is highly acidic, recent radiation or surgical procedure, or past gastrointestinal illness. The individual history should include information regarding eating, drinking, and smoking habits as well as prescription and nonprescription drug use.

Physical exam: The exam results are most often normal. Rarely is there abdominal tenderness, pale skin, rapid heartbeat (tachycardia), and low blood pressure (hypotension).

Tests: Gastritis is typically diagnosed by the history and physical examination. The inner lining of the stomach may be visualized using a flexible fiber-optic microscope (endoscope). A tissue sample of the stomach mucosa may also be taken for analysis during this procedure (endoscopic biopsy). The stomach can also be visualized after swallowing a radiopaque contrast medium (barium) and taking x-rays. Other tests that may be done include various blood tests (hematocrit and hemoglobin indices) for low hemoglobin in the bloodstream (anemia), blood tests for markers of H. pylori infection, or insertion of a tube through the nose and into the stomach (nasogastric tube) to obtain samples of stomach secretions (gastric analysis).

Treatment

Treatment is primarily supportive and antacids in either liquid or tablet form may be sufficient to treat cases of mild gastritis. Antacids may also be used if the gastritis is associated with an ulcer. Gastritis caused by NSAID usage may be treated by discontinuing the drug, decreasing the dose, or taking the drug with food. Excess stomach acid production may be treated with drugs such as a histamine receptor antagonist or a proton pump inhibitor. Gastritis due to alcohol consumption is usually mild and treated by counseling the individual to either stop or decrease the amount of alcohol consumed. Should the individual be deficient in vitamin B_{12}, shots must be received on a monthly basis. A blood transfusion may be required if severe bleeding has occurred. Surgery to remove part of the stomach (subtotal gastrectomy) is indicated in rare instances. Chronic gastritis caused by Helicobacter pylori may be treated with antibiotics.

Prognosis

The predicted outcome associated with acute gastritis is related to the cause of the gastritis. Most individuals with acute gastritis recover completely within 48 hours of starting treatment. Acute gastritis due to stress or associated with bleeding has a poorer prognosis and longer recovery times may be expected. Type A gastritis (autoimmune atrophic gastritis) can result in destruction of a compound secreted by the stomach (intrinsic factor) that allows vitamin B_{12} to be absorbed. A form of anemia (pernicious anemia) may result if the individual becomes deficient in vitamin B_{12}. Injections of vitamin B_{12} can alleviate this condition.

Chronic gastritis associated with H. pylori infection (type B gastritis) may progress to ulceration, necessitating a longer course of treatment. If a stomach ulcer is present, subtotal gastrectomy may be used as a treatment. There is usually some degree of postoperative morbidity following gastrectomy (including weight loss, cramping, or diarrhea) and mortality resulting from this procedure ranges from 2.4-5.6%. Gastrectomy may be used in combination with selective cutting of the vagus nerve (highly selective vagotomy) and ulcer recurrence is rare (1%) following this treatment.

Differential Diagnosis

Conditions that present with similar symptoms include lesions in the mucosal lining of the stomach (gastric ulcer), perforation of the stomach, gastric cancer, regurgitation of acid from the stomach into the esophagus (gastroesophageal reflux, heartburn), food poisoning, inflammation of the gut that is caused by a virus (viral gastroenteritis), and stomach indigestion (dyspepsia).

Specialists

- Gastroenterologist
- Internist

Rehabilitation

Regular physical activity on a daily basis is recommended to relieve stress that may exacerbate gastritis. Aerobic exercise such as walking, jogging, or swimming (30 to 45 minutes per session) is usually beneficial. In the rare instance where a portion of the stomach is removed surgically (subtotal gastrectomy), intermittent positive pressure breathing exercises may be necessary to prevent pulmonary complications.

Work Restrictions / Accommodations

No work restrictions and accommodations are usually required following the recovery period. If the individual is treated with a subtotal gastrectomy, recovery may be 4 to 6 weeks. During this time, heavy lifting should be restricted and a more sedentary job may be necessary.

Complementary and Alternative Therapies

Content is intended for awareness only. Treatments may or may not be effective. Scientific evidence may be lacking and some substances have potentially toxic effects. Dr. Presley Reed and the editors do not endorse the use of these therapies in the absence of consultation with a licensed medical professional.

Acupuncture - Insertion of needles at specific points on the body may alleviate symptoms of gastritis.

Electro-acupuncture - Insertion of needles at specific body points in combination with mild electric current may decrease secretion of gastric acid.

Chinese medicines - Traditional Chinese herbal medicines may be therapeutic for gastritis.

Comorbid Conditions

Existing conditions that may affect an individual's ability to recover from gastritis include pyloric ulcer disease, stomach cancer, and inflammation of the duodenum (duodenitis) any of which can exacerbate inflammation of the stomach.

Complications

Complications associated with acute gastritis can include formation of lesions in the mucosal lining of the stomach (ulceration) and bleeding (hemorrhage) from the wall of the stomach. Chronic gastritis is often without symptoms for a period of time until atrophy of the stomach becomes severe enough that it interferes with digestion and emptying of food into the small intestine. Resulting complications may include fatigue and vague discomfort after eating.

Factors Influencing Duration

Factors that may influence the length of disability include the underlying cause of the gastritis, degree of inflammation, treatment prescribed, and development of complications.

Length of Disability

Acute. Medical treatment.

Duration in Days

Job Classification	Minimum	Optimum	Maximum
Sedentary work	0	3	7
Light work	0	3	7
Medium work	0	3	7
Heavy work	0	3	7
Very Heavy work	0	3	7

Partial gastrectomy, with or without vagotomy.

Duration in Days

Job Classification	Minimum	Optimum	Maximum
Sedentary work	28	35	42
Light work	28	35	42
Medium work	42	49	56
Heavy work	42	49	56
Very Heavy work	42	49	56

Duration Trend from Normative Data*

Cases	Mean	Min	Max	No Lost Time	Over 6 Months
331	31	0	394	2.42%	1.52%

Percentile:	5th	25th	Median	75th	95th
Days:	4	10	16	31	102

ICD-9-CM 535.0 - Reported Length of Disability (Days)

* Differences may exist between the expected duration tables and the normative graphs. Duration tables provide expected recovery periods based on the type of work performed by the individual. The normative graphs reflect the actual observed experience of many individuals across the spectrum of physical conditions, in a variety of industries, and with varying levels of case management.

Failure to Recover

If an individual fails to recover within the maximum duration expectancy period, the reader may wish to reference the following questions to assist in better understanding the specifics of an individual's medical case.

Regarding diagnosis:

- Did the individual present with symptoms of (anorexia), upper abdominal discomfort or pain, vomiting or diarrhea?
- Was the possibility of food poisoning ruled out?
- Does the individual have a history of chronic alcohol or NSAID use?
- Has the diagnosis of gastritis been determined by history and physical exam?
- If the diagnosis was uncertain, were other diagnostic studies done (i.e., gastrointestinal x-rays or endoscopy) to rule out other conditions such as gastric ulcer, perforation of the stomach, gastric cancer, gastroesophageal reflux?

Regarding treatment:

- If elimination of gastric irritants and administration of antacids was not effective, what treatment options are now being considered?
- Is drug treatment or proton pump inhibitor necessary? Has individual been following drug therapy regimen as prescribed?
- Has the individual been tested for the presence of H. pylori? If so, is this infection being addressed in the treatment plan?
- Have blood tests been done to rule out the possibility of associated pernicious anemia? Has the individual received vitamin B_{12} injections as needed to treat pernicious anemia?
- Was condition severe enough that emergency treatment and/or hospitalization was necessary? Was surgery necessary? If so, what procedure?

Regarding prognosis:

- Based on the underlying cause of the gastritis, has adequate time elapsed for recovery (48 to 72 hours)?
- Has individual been successful in limiting alcohol intake? Would individual benefit from counseling or enrollment in a community program?
- Has individual been compliant with monthly injections of vitamin B_{12}? If not, what can be done to increase compliance?
- Is individual receiving appropriate antibiotic therapy in regards to H. pylori infection?
- If the symptoms have persisted, is surgery indicated?
- Has individual experienced any complications (such as ulceration, chronic gastritis, or hemorrhage) that could impact recovery and prognosis?
- Is there an underlying condition (bleeding disorders, cancer, peptic ulcer disease) that could impact recovery?

References

Chen, R., and M. Kang. "Observation on Frequency Spectrum of Electrogastrogram (EGG) in Acupuncture Treatment of Functional Dyspepsia." Journal of Traditional Chinese Medicine 18 3 (1998): 184-187.

Wu, Y.L., S.F. Chen, and L.L. Pan. "Effect of Electroacupuncture on Gastric Acid Secretion and Gut Hormones." Chung-Kuo Chung Hsi i Chieh Ho Tsa Chih 14 12 (1994): 709-711.

Gastroenteritis, Infectious
Other names / synonyms: Diarrhea, Food Poisoning, Infectious Colitis, Stomach Flu, Traveler's Diarrhea
009.0, 009.1, 009.2, 009.3

Definition

Gastroenteritis is a general or nonspecific term given to a variety of conditions causing inflammation of the stomach and intestinal tract. Infectious gastroenteritis occurs when microorganisms such as bacteria, protozoa, or viruses infect the stomach or intestines. Bacteria that can cause gastroenteritis include staphylococci, clostridia, Bacillus cereus, salmonella, E. coli, shigella, and vibrios. Protozoa that can cause gastroenteritis include Entamoeba histolytica and Giardia. A common virus that causes gastroenteritis is the rotavirus.

The most notable sign of gastroenteritis is diarrhea. Gastroenteritis can be transmitted by contaminated food, water, or by individual-to-individual contact. Most cases occur in the summer months. Travelers to developing countries should avoid fresh foods and water that may be contaminated. Eating improperly cooked food especially contaminated shellfish can cause gastroenteritis. Daycare centers are common places for outbreaks of gastroenteritis because the disease can be spread through diaper changing. A similar situation occurs in nursing homes. Occasionally, gastroenteritis can be a symptom of a more serious disease such as typhoid or cholera.

Gastroenteritis occurs all over the world although specific microorganisms may be more prevalent in one part of the world versus another. Gastroenteritis caused by rotavirus is most common in Asia, Africa, and South America. Vibrio bacteria cause gastroenteritis in Asia. Shigella causes epidemics of gastroenteritis in Central and South America, South Asia, and sub-Saharan Africa.

In the US, an estimated 100 million cases of gastroenteritis occur annually. An estimated 90,000 of these are due to food poisoning. Most of these cases, however, do not require medical attention. An estimated 3 to 5 billion cases occur on a worldwide basis each year. In some developing countries, diarrhea is a leading cause of death.

Diagnosis

History: Symptoms of gastroenteritis can vary depending on the microorganism causing the disease. In general, onset is sudden. Individuals may report loss of appetite, nausea or vomiting, abdominal pain or cramping, and diarrhea. Aching muscles and exhaustion may also be present. The individual may or may not report ingestion of suspect food or water or contact with an infected individual.

The individual's medical history is pertinent as certain medications and underlying illnesses may make and individual more susceptible (predispose) to infectious gastroenteritis. When isolation of the particular agent is not feasible or cost-effective, diagnosis may rest on the individual's recent history, ruling out other causes, and symptoms of infectious disease that appear in many individuals at the same time in the same geographical area (the epidemiologic setting).

Physical exam: Bowel sounds may be hyperactive and individual may have abdominal tenderness. Intestine may be swollen or inflated (distended). Irritation of the perianal area or throat may be present due to repeated bouts of diarrhea and vomiting. There may also be signs of dehydration such as dry mucous membranes, sunken eyes, decreased skin tension (turgor), lethargy, increased heart rate, or changes in blood pressure when individual changes position (orthostatic).

Tests: When isolation of the particular agent is not feasible or cost-effective, diagnosis may be made on symptoms alone. In infectious diarrhea, visual (gross) examination of the stool is the single most important test. If it contains blood or mucus, microscopic examination should be done to look for ova (eggs) and parasites. Since a single stool may not reveal parasites even when present, three fresh, separate stools should be tested if blood or mucus is found in the first sample. If symptoms persist beyond 3 to 4 days, when fever or bloody diarrhea occurs, or if the individual's immune system is deficient (immunocompromised), a culture should be done on the stool to isolate the infective organism.

Treatment

Treatment of gastroenteritis depends on the cause of the illness. Most cases resolve in 3 to 4 days. Lost fluid should be replaced by drinking fluids. Gatorade, water, diluted tea, or juices can replace lost sugars and electrolytes. In severe cases, dehydration may need to be treated by administration of intravenous fluids.

Viral gastroenteritis is self-limited. Treatment involves resting the stomach and intestines and allowing the diarrhea to run its course. Fluid intake should be enough to prevent dehydration, but solid food should not be eaten until symptoms subside.

When symptoms are severe, persist for longer than 72 hours, or if bloody diarrhea occurs, medical assistance is required. A specific diagnosis must be made so that appropriate antibiotics can be started.

Parasitic infections are more difficult to treat, although a number of effective antiparasitic drugs are available.

Although drugs that decrease the movement of the intestines (antimotility or antidiarrheal drugs) may be used safely in mild to moderate diarrhea, they should not be used when blood, high fever, or systemic toxicity is present for fear of worsening the condition. They should also be discontinued when diarrhea worsens despite treatment.

In rare cases, preventative medication including antibiotics and drugs that coat the stomach (bismuth sulfate) can prevent gastroenteritis for individuals traveling to areas where diarrheal illnesses are endemic.

Prognosis

In most cases, the prognosis is very good. Symptoms of gastroenteritis usually subside within 48 to 72 hours.

While infectious gastroenteritis is usually acute (rapid onset with a short duration), certain parasites such as Giardia can cause chronic diarrhea. For more severe or prolonged cases, prognosis depends on the organism causing the gastroenteritis and the effectiveness of treatment. Recovery can be delayed by an extensive infection, unusual reactions to medicines, or infection from bacteria that produce a more powerful toxin. Without replacement, extreme loss of body fluid and electrolytes can lead to hypovolemic shock, coma, or death.

Differential Diagnosis

Although a diagnosis of gastroenteritis may be based on the symptoms, pinpointing the cause may be more difficult. In addition to infection, certain drugs, stress, or foods can cause gastroenteritis.

Specialists

- Gastroenterologist
- Internist
- Infectious Disease Physician

Work Restrictions / Accommodations

Because the infectious organisms may inadvertently be spread through poor hygiene practices, workers should not be allowed to handle food or beverages until symptoms resolve. In cases of severe fluid loss, restrictions on heavy lifting or operation of machinery may be considered until the individual recovers his or her strength.

Complementary and Alternative Therapies

Content is intended for awareness only. Treatments may or may not be effective. Scientific evidence may be lacking and some substances have potentially toxic effects. Dr. Presley Reed and the editors do not endorse the use of these therapies in the absence of consultation with a licensed medical professional.

Ipecac -	With its amebicidal components, ipecac is said to have been effectively used to treat mild cases of dysentery. It should not be confused with syrup of ipecac, however. Ipecac extracts can be highly toxic and misuse can lead to serious acute and chronic toxicities.
Kaolin -	Said to increase the bulk of feces and may be found in many antidiarrheal preparations. Kaolin does not have any antibacterial activity so it should not be used as the sole treatment in infectious diarrheas.
Yogurt -	Said to reestablish normal flora in the intestines.
Berberine -	May have antiprotozoan activity for mild cases of amebiasis.
Grapefruit seed extract -	May be helpful in eliminating Giardia.

Comorbid Conditions

Prolonged infections lower the body's immunity (defense system) and may result in the establishment of secondary or opportunistic infections. Factors that can lower immunity include infection with other organisms such as human immunodeficiency virus (HIV), treatment with steroidal drugs, underlying conditions such as lymphoma, leukemia, generalized cancer (malignancy), and even fatigue. Individuals with underlying diseases such as inflammatory bowel disease, diabetes, and heart disease may suffer more severe cases of gastroenteritis. Elderly individuals are more prone to complications of diarrhea.

Multiple infections in the body often make a definitive diagnosis of infectious gastroenteritis difficult. Simultaneous treatment for multiple infections can reduce the effectiveness of therapy on either or both infections.

Complications

Severe or prolonged diarrhea and vomiting may result in the loss of essential body fluids and nutrients causing dehydration, shock, and collapse. Certain types of microorganisms, such as E. coli 0157 can cause more serious conditions such as hemorrhagic colitis. When bacterial or parasitic infections are inadequately treated, the infection may spread to other areas of the body, especially the liver.

Factors Influencing Duration

The source of illness, severity of symptoms, response or adverse reaction to medication, or the development of complications may influence length of disability. For some parasitic infections, treatment with antiparasitic drugs can cause side effects that extend the required period of disability.

Length of Disability

Duration depends on cause.

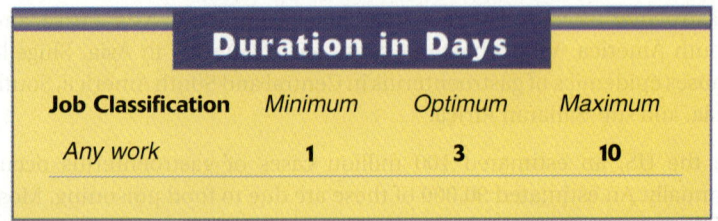

Duration in Days			
Job Classification	Minimum	Optimum	Maximum
Any work	1	3	10

Failure to Recover

If an individual fails to recover within the maximum duration expectancy period, the reader may wish to reference the following questions to assist in better understanding the specifics of an individual's medical case.

Regarding diagnosis:

- Has individual had any recent infectious exposure or immune suppressive condition?
- Has diagnosis of infectious gastroenteritis been confirmed or just assumed due to symptoms?
- Did stool samples reveal the presence of intestinal parasite or bacteria infection?

- If the diagnosis was uncertain, were other conditions with similar symptoms (i.e., inflammatory bowel disease, biliary infection, pancreatitis) ruled out?

Regarding treatment:

- Has the organism causing the gastroenteritis been identified so that appropriate antimicrobial therapy can be used?
- If individual does not respond to current treatment, would a change in antibiotic be warranted? Should diagnosis be revisited?
- Has individual received appropriate supportive care and interventions to help relieve symptoms (i.e., antipyretics, fluids)?
- Is individual experiencing a reaction to the current medication?

Regarding prognosis:

- Based on the underlying cause, severity of symptoms and general health of individual, what was the expected outcome? Has adequate time elapsed for complete recovery?
- If the symptoms have persisted despite treatment, has individual been reevaluated to rule out the possibility of bacterial resistance or secondary infection?
- Did individual suffer any associated complications such as severe dehydration, shock, or systemic infection that could impact recovery and prognosis?

References

Brooks, G.F., J.S. Butel, and S.A. Morse. Medical Microbiology. Stamford: Appleton & Lange, 1998.

Tierney, L.M., S.J. McPhee, and M.A. Papadakis. Current Medical Diagnosis and Treatment. Stamford: Appleton & Lange, 1998.

Gastroenteritis, Non-Infectious
Other names / synonyms: Non-Infectious Colitis, Non-Infectious Diarrhea
558.9, 787.91

Definition

Noninfectious gastroenteritis is an inflammation of the stomach and intestines that often occurs unexpectedly in a very short period of time with extreme force and intense activity. Its severity may vary from mild and inconvenient to severe and life-threatening. Gastroenteritis is the sudden onset of frequent bowel movements of watery consistency (diarrhea), nausea, vomiting, abdominal cramping, abdominal pain, weakness, and sometimes either fever or chills.

The causes of noninfectious gastroenteritis may include extreme emotional stress, adverse reactions to a food or a food ingredient (food intolerance, food allergies, food poisoning), very spicy foods, toxic substances, or excessive intake of alcohol. Certain drugs (including antibiotics) upset the balance of bacteria that is naturally present in the intestines causing symptoms of gastroenteritis.

The frequency with which noninfectious gastroenteritis occurs is difficult to determine due to under-reporting, especially with mild illnesses. This results in wide variations in estimated numbers of cases, hospitalizations, and deaths. There are up to 90 million cases per year, several million physician visits, and thousands of hospitalizations.

Diagnosis

History: Noninfectious gastroenteritis is characterized by any or all of the following symptoms: nausea, vomiting, diarrhea, abdominal cramps, abdominal pain, loss of appetite (anorexia), unintentional weight loss, and vague abdominal discomfort. Symptoms may be mild, or sudden and violent. Usually lasting only 2-3 days, the individual tends to recover without any specific treatment other than replacement of lost fluids and salts (electrolytes).

Physical exam: The exam may reveal an elevated heart rate, fever, paleness of the skin, and a soft but distended abdomen. The mucous membranes of the mouth are usually pink but may appear dry and the tongue may appear whitish or "coated." Blood pressure may fluctuate with changes in position, indicating dehydration.

Tests: In mild cases, the symptoms alone are usually sufficient to diagnose gastroenteritis. In more serious cases, diagnostic tests may be needed to rule out infection, including a complete blood count (CBC) and electrolyte panel. Other tests, such as stool cultures for pus cells and infectious organisms, such as pathogenic bacteria and parasites, may be done (especially if the person's history includes foreign travel or drinking mountain water).

Urinalysis may be performed to rule out urinary tract infection or kidney stones. Liver profile and amylase may be used to rule out disease of the gallbladder or pancreas. X-rays of the abdomen may be taken to rule out bowel obstruction.

Treatment

General measures include rest, and taking fluids to replace the body's fluids and electrolytes (salts and sugars) that were lost through vomiting or diarrhea. Solid food is avoided until symptoms subside. If the individual cannot take fluids by mouth, intravenous (IV) replacement will be necessary to prevent or correct dehydration. Spicy foods or those to which there is an intolerance should be avoided. Alcohol intake needs to be decreased. Treatment of gastroenteritis caused by stress or excess stomach acid may include medications that neutralize the acid (antacids) or block acid secretion.

Gastroenteritis due to adverse drug effects can sometimes be relieved by taking the drug with food or antacids. In some cases, however, the dosage may need to be altered, medication changed, or drug discontinued.

Gastroenteritis may be prevented by never eating protein-rich foods (such as meat, eggs, and cream) that have been undercooked or stored without refrigeration.

Prognosis

Usually lasting only 2 to 3 days, the individual tends to recover without any specific treatment other than replacement of lost fluids and salts (electrolytes). Recovery is usually complete and without complications. Failure to improve within 2 weeks should bring the diagnosis into question.

Differential Diagnosis

Conditions with similar symptoms include infectious gastroenteritis, inflammatory bowel disease, and ischemic colitis.

Specialists

- Gastroenterologist
- Internist

Work Restrictions / Accommodations

Part-time work or less rigorous physical demands may be required for a few days until complete recovery is assured. Adequate access to toilet facilities should be available.

Complementary and Alternative Therapies

Content is intended for awareness only. Treatments may or may not be effective. Scientific evidence may be lacking and some substances have potentially toxic effects. Dr. Presley Reed and the editors do not endorse the use of these therapies in the absence of consultation with a licensed medical professional.

Lactobacillus - May build up the intestines' store of "good bacteria" and lessens the body's susceptibility to invading bacteria.

Comorbid Conditions

Ulcers, inflammatory bowel disease, food intolerance, diabetes, heart disease, liver disease, and kidney disease may worsen the effects of noninfectious gastroenteritis.

Complications

Dehydration is the most frequent complication of both vomiting and diarrhea. Frequent vomiting may lead to irritation of the esophagus and unrelenting burning in the chest (esophagitis) because of the refluxing of stomach acids. Accidentally inhaling (aspiration) vomit can cause severe pneumonia.

Irritation of the stomach (gastritis) or ulceration of the stomach can also be associated with prolonged or severe vomiting. Frequent loose stools may irritate the anus or result in the development of hemorrhoids or anal tears that can cause rectal bleeding. Inability to take routine medications due to nausea may worsen other ongoing medical conditions.

Factors Influencing Duration

Length of disability may be influenced by the inability either to control fluid losses (through persistent or severe vomiting and diarrhea) or replace lost fluids.

Length of Disability

Duration depends on cause.

Duration in Days

Job Classification	Minimum	Optimum	Maximum
Any work	1	3	7

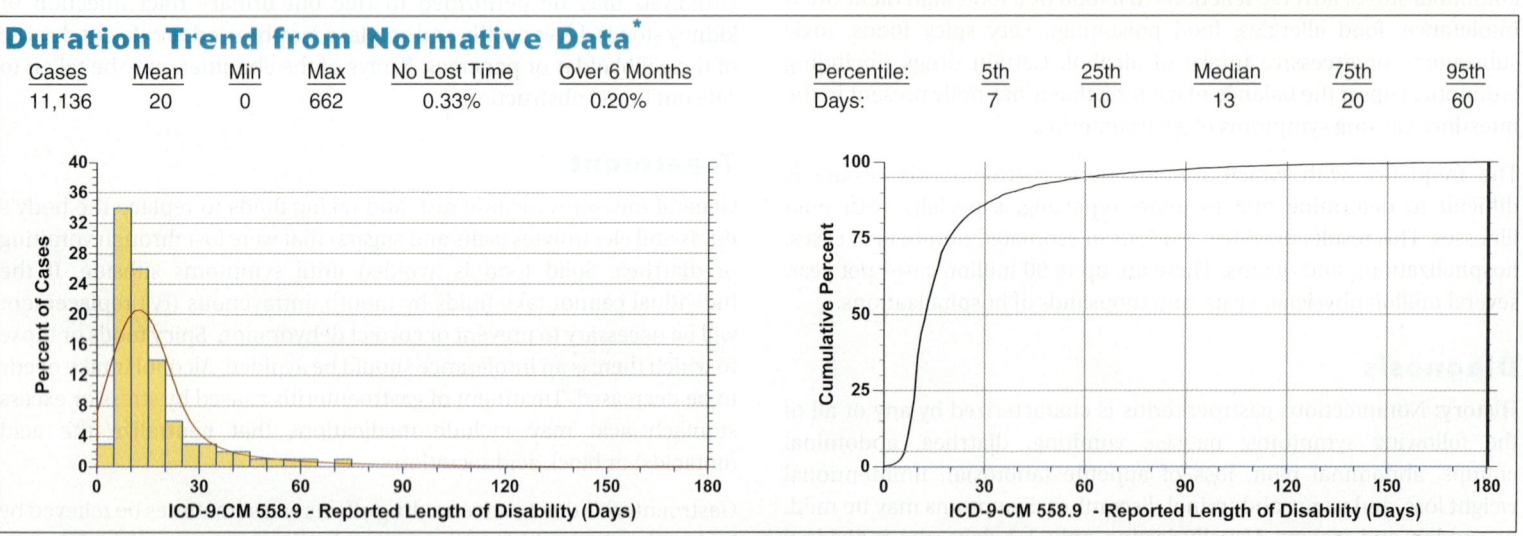

Duration Trend from Normative Data*

Cases	Mean	Min	Max	No Lost Time	Over 6 Months
11,136	20	0	662	0.33%	0.20%

Percentile:	5th	25th	Median	75th	95th
Days:	7	10	13	20	60

ICD-9-CM 558.9 - Reported Length of Disability (Days)

* Differences may exist between the expected duration tables and the normative graphs. Duration tables provide expected recovery periods based on the type of work performed by the individual. The normative graphs reflect the actual observed experience of many individuals across the spectrum of physical conditions, in a variety of industries, and with varying levels of case management.

Failure to Recover

If an individual fails to recover within the maximum duration expectancy period, the reader may wish to reference the following questions to assist in better understanding the specifics of an individual's medical case.

Regarding diagnosis:

- Are symptoms of noninfectious gastroenteritis present such as nausea, vomiting, diarrhea, abdominal cramps, abdominal pain, loss of appetite (anorexia), unintentional weight loss, and vague abdominal discomfort?
- Does exam reveal an elevated heart rate, fever, paleness of the skin, and a soft but distended abdomen? Are the mucous membranes of the mouth pink? Dry? Is the tongue whitish or coated?
- Was the cause of the noninfectious gastroenteritis (which may include extreme emotional stress, adverse reactions to a food or food ingredient, very spicy foods, toxic substances, or excessive intake of alcohol) identified?
- While in mild cases the symptoms alone are usually sufficient to diagnose gastroenteritis, if this was a more serious case, were diagnostic tests (including CBC and electrolyte panel) done to rule out infection?
- Has individual been taking antibiotics?
- Has diagnosis of noninfectious gastroenteritis been confirmed?
- Were other conditions with similar symptoms such as infectious gastroenteritis, inflammatory bowel disease, or ischemic colitis ruled out?

Regarding treatment:

- Has individual maintained hydration and electrolyte balance? Were IV fluids necessary to prevent or correct dehydration?
- If condition is associated with the taking of prescribed antibiotics, was the full course of antibiotics completed yet? Are there alternative medications that individual could be taking instead?
- Was food intolerance identified?
- Was excessive stomach acid successfully resolved?
- Is stress aggravating the condition? Has individual participated in a stress management program?

Regarding prognosis:

- Has individual adhered to dietary modifications such as avoidance of spicy foods? Has individual reduced alcohol intake?
- Does individual have a coexisting condition such as ulcers, inflammatory bowel disease, food intolerance, diabetes, heart disease, liver disease, or kidney disease that may worsen the effects of noninfectious gastroenteritis or impact recovery?
- Has individual experienced any complications associated with noninfectious gastroenteritis such as dehydration or aspiration pneumonia? Are complications being addressed in the treatment plan?
- Would individual benefit from additional stress management or coping techniques?
- Are workplace accommodations or a temporary transfer to less demanding occupational duties warranted?

References

A Guide to Alternative Medicine: Gastroenteritis. Knowledge Center. 2000. 01 Jan 2001 <http://www.knowledgecenters.versaware.com/notoc/getPage.asp?book=alternativemedicine&page=060000251.asp>.

Diskin, Arthur, MD. "Gastroenteritis." eMedicine.com 08 Feb 2001. 131 Feb 2001 <http://www.emedicine.com/emerg/topic213.htm>.

Gastroenterostomy

Other names / synonyms: Gastrectojejunostomy, Gastroduodenostomy, Gastroenterostomy Bypass, Gastrojejunostomy

44.3, 44.39, V45.3

Definition

A gastroenterostomy is a general term to describe 2 types of surgical procedures in which the stomach is surgically joined to the small intestines. It usually accompanies removal of part or all of the stomach due to disease (gastrectomy). Once the gastrectomy is performed, the surgeon must join (anastomosis) the remaining part of the stomach to the small intestine to allow for movement of digested food and fluids from the stomach to the intestines. If the remaining part of the stomach is joined to the first part of the small intestine (duodenum), the procedure is called a gastroduodenostomy. When joined to the middle section of the small intestine (jejunum), the procedure is called a gastrojejunostomy.

A gastroenterostomy may be indicated for those with benign or cancerous tumors of the stomach, peptic ulcer disease that is unresponsive to medical therapy, and slowed gastric motility (gastroparesis).

Gastric cancer occurs most frequently in men over 40 years old. The incidence of gastric cancer is 2 out of 10,000 people and is more common in Japan, Chile, and Iceland. Risk factors for gastric cancer are a family history of gastric cancer, blood type group A, history of pernicious anemia, history of chronic stomach inflammation (gastritis), or history of gastric polyp.

Peptic ulcer disease is a collective term to describe ulcers that arise in the stomach or first part of the small intestine (duodenum) as a result of an overproduction of acid and pepsin (an enzyme). The incidence of duodenal ulcers is 7 out of 1000 people. They are more common in young adults (age 30 to 40), who have a family history of peptic ulcers, have presence of Helicobacter pylori bacteria in the stomach, have group O blood type, or have chronic use of nonsteroidal anti-inflammatory drugs (NSAIDs). The incidence of gastric ulcers is 8 out of 10,000 people. They are more common in those over 50, and are associated with blood type group A, NSAID use, and chronic gastric inflammation (gastritis).

The exact cause of gastroparesis is not known. However, a disruption of the nerve stimulation in the intestine seems to be a factor. It is a common complication of diabetes or visceral nerve disease such as seen with systemic sclerosis. It may also be a complication following surgical cutting of the vagus nerve (vagotomy). About 3 out of 1,000 individuals suffer from gastroparesis.

Reason for Procedure

A gastroenterostomy may be done as a surgical intervention for peptic ulcer disease, to remove tumors of the stomach, or to facilitate emptying of the stomach in conditions of slowed gastric motility. A gastroenterostomy usually accompanies a surgical resection of the stomach (gastrectomy). Once the gastrectomy is performed, the surgeon must create a new opening from the stomach to the intestines (enterostomy). Depending on the extent of the stomach resection, the stomach may be joined either to the first part of the small intestine (gastroduodenostomy) or to the second part of the small intestine (gastrojejunostomy).

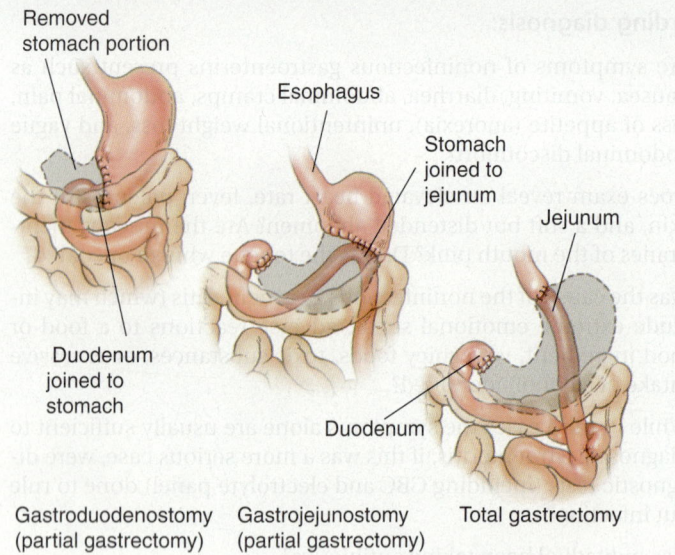

Gastroduodenostomy (partial gastrectomy)   Gastrojejunostomy (partial gastrectomy)   Total gastrectomy

Description

General anesthesia is administered. A tube may be inserted to drain the bladder (urinary catheter) and one to drain the stomach (nasogastric tube) contents. The surgeon creates an incision that runs midline from the ribcage to the lower abdomen. The surgeon uses either surgical stitches or a stapling device to join the stomach to a healthy segment of the small intestine so there is an passageway (enterostomy) between the stomach and the intestine. One or more small drains may be placed at the surgical site to temporarily allow for drainage of blood and fluid. The abdominal wound is closed in layers. The final skin layer will be closed with a small stapling device.

Prognosis

The outcome is dependent on the underlying disease, the extent of the disease and the extent of surgery required. Generally, the procedure is successful in providing an alternative conduit (enterostomy) between the stomach and the small intestine.

Specialists

- Surgeon

Work Restrictions / Accommodations

Early in the recovery period (2 to 4 weeks postoperatively) the individual may need to avoid strenuous activity of heavy lifting. The individual may require modifications in the work schedule allowing for 3 small meals during the work day, rather than 1 traditional lunch hour.

Comorbid Conditions

Comorbid conditions of immune suppression and bleeding disorders may impact ability to recover and further lengthen disability.

Procedure Complications

The most common complications from the procedure include wound infection, leaking at the site where the stomach is joined to the intestine (anastomosis), lung congestion (atelectasis), and bleeding. Less common complications include shock (from bleeding) or cardiac arrest. Late complications include recurrent ulcers, diarrhea (from sugar and carbohydrate intolerance), and iron deficiency anemia.

Factors Influencing Duration

Length of disability may be influenced by the underlying reason for the gastrectomy, the extent of gastrectomy (partial or total), the site of the gastroenterostomy, the presence of side effects after gastric surgery (post-gastrectomy syndromes), or the presence of surgical complications.

Length of Disability

Duration includes hospitalization.

Duration in Days

Job Classification	Minimum	Optimum	Maximum
Sedentary work	28	35	42
Light work	28	35	42
Medium work	42	49	56
Heavy work	42	49	56
Very Heavy work	42	49	56

References

Tierney, Lawrence M., Stephen J. McPhee, and Maxine A. Papadakis, eds. Current Medical Diagnosis and Treatment, 39th ed. New York: Lange Medical Books/McGraw-Hill, 2000.

Gastroesophageal Reflux

Other names / synonyms: Esophageal Reflux, Gastroesophageal Reflux Disease, GERD, Heartburn

530.81

Definition

Gastroesophageal reflux refers to a backflow of stomach contents into the esophagus.

The esophagus is the muscular tube that carries food from the throat to the stomach. Food is carried along the esophagus by waves of contraction and relaxation of its muscular walls (peristalsis). The part of the esophagus closest to the stomach is surrounded by a sphincter (circular muscle capable of opening and closing). During peristalsis, the lower esophageal sphincter relaxes, allowing food to enter the stomach. In the resting state, this sphincter is closed, preventing backflow (reflux) of stomach contents into the esophagus. However, a drop in pressure in the lower esophagus or a weakening of the sphincter muscle can permit a backflow of powerful stomach acids into the esophagus. While the lining of the stomach protects it from the effects of its own acids, the esophagus lacks this protective lining. A backflow of stomach acid into the esophagus can cause pain, inflammation (esophagitis), and damage. The degree of inflammation depends on the acidity of the stomach contents and the amount of stomach acid refluxed into the esophagus.

Certain foods or circumstances also increase the risk of reflux. Exercising or bending over after a large meal can pressure the sphincter and allow stomach acid to flow back into the esophagus. When an individual is lying down, gravity contributes to reflux. Overeating, fatty or spicy foods, alcohol, caffeine, cigarette smoking, and certain medications can lead to acid indigestion. Reflux can also be caused by anything that increases abdominal pressure such as clothing or belts too tight around the waist. Reflux may occur in association with pregnancy or obesity.

Reflux is also associated with hiatal hernia. The esophagus enters the stomach just after passing through a band of muscle called the diaphragm. In a hiatal hernia, the opening (hiatus) in the diaphragm through which the esophagus passes is enlarged. This allows the lower esophagus and upper part of the stomach that normally stay beneath the diaphragm to slide through the hiatus, move above the diaphragm, and into the chest cavity. This makes it difficult for the sphincter to work correctly, partially because the angle between the esophagus and stomach (gastroesophageal angle) is changed.

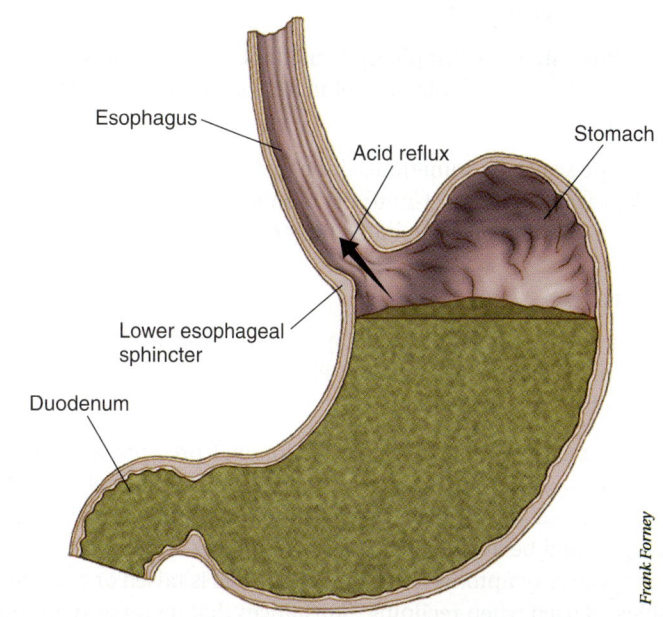

Diagnosis

History: The most common symptom of gastroesophageal reflux is heartburn, a burning pain in the lower chest usually below the sternum. The pain may range from mild to so severe that it mimics a heart attack (myocardial infarction). Gastroesophageal reflux, however, is not related to the heart.

The pain typically occurs 30 to 60 minutes after eating and is often precipitated by other common symptoms of reflux. These include a reflex increase in salivation (water brash) and backward flow of stomach contents into the mouth (regurgitation). Inhalation (aspiration) of regurgitated material can occur especially during sleep. This may result in respiratory symptoms such as hoarseness, wheezing, cough, and difficulty breathing. Difficulty swallowing (dysphagia) is often a symptom of complicated reflux disease. Painful swallowing (odynophagia) may indicate esophageal inflammation or an ulcer.

Physical exam: The diagnosis is usually suspected from the history, however, in some individuals it may be necessary to rule out a cardiac source of pain (myocardial infarction, angina pectoris) and other gastrointestinal disease.

Tests: The healthcare provider may order an upper gastrointestinal x-ray and/or a direct examination of the esophagus through a flexible viewing tube (endoscopy). An upper GI series (barium x-ray of the upper gastrointestinal tract) can detect ulcers or narrowing of the esophagus.

Regardless of x-ray or endoscopic findings, proof that the symptoms are caused from acid reflux is best obtained through a tissue sample (biopsy) and microscopic examination.

When symptoms are not typical, special studies may be required to make the diagnosis. The simplest of these tests is the Bernstein acid perfusion test. In this test, a specific concentration of hydrochloric acid is instilled into the esophagus. If the individual's pain is reproduced by this procedure and relieved by instillation of saline solution, it is an indication that acid reflux is the cause of the pain. In some cases, ambulatory pH monitoring may be helpful. By continuously monitoring the degree of acidity (pH) of the esophagus for up to 24 hours, the individual's daily pattern of reflux and its relationship to symptom occurrence can be documented.

Pressure measurement (esophageal manometry) at the lower esophageal sphincter can indicate sphincter strength and abnormal functioning.

Radioisotope scans are sometimes done to demonstrate reflux. A reflux scan is less sensitive than 24-hour pH monitoring, however, it can help document aspiration of regurgitated material.

Treatment

Treatment of symptomatic reflux may be considered in several phases. Phase I consists of general measures, Phase II is medical treatment, and Phase III is surgical intervention.

In Phase I, measures that decrease abdominal pressure are helpful. Weight loss may make a difference for overweight people. Tight clothing and belts should be avoided. Meals should be small and frequent. Reclining should be avoided for at least two hours after meals. Gravity may help relieve symptoms if the head of the bed is raised or more then one pillow is used when reclining. Substances that increase symptoms should be avoided such as alcohol, tobacco, caffeine, acidic foods and drink (e.g., citrus and tomatoes), fats, chocolates, and peppermint.

Medications should be reviewed since certain medications (anticholinergic drugs, calcium-channel blockers) can decrease lower esophageal sphincter tone. Others such as potassium supplements and certain antibiotics may be irritating to the esophagus. Medication such as cimetidine or ranitidine can reduce stomach acidity. The acid neutralizing effect of antacids may also be helpful when taken after meals and at bedtime. However, this relief is only short-term.

When the above measures are unsuccessful in controlling symptoms, histamine (H2) antagonists are introduced in Phase II treatment. By blocking histamine receptors, these medications decrease the secretion of gastric acid. If the response is incomplete, cholinergic drugs or other motility promoting agents may be added. These medications increase esophageal and gastric movement (motility), increase lower esophageal sphincter tone, and promote gastric emptying. Medication to protect the mucous lining may also be tried. While uncomplicated disease usually responds well to Phase I or II therapy, complications generally require Phase II treatment.

If severe reflux esophagitis is present, a proton pump inhibitor medication may be tried. This medication directly blocks the secretion of acid (hydrogen ions or protons) by the stomach. Although the medication often produces complete healing in 4 to 8 weeks, most have reoccurrence after the drug is discontinued. Currently, proton pump inhibitors are approved for short-term use only.

Antireflux surgery or Phase III is indicated when symptoms persist or recur despite conservative treatment. A weakened esophageal sphincter can be surgically strengthened. A hiatal hernia can be reduced by surgically returning the stomach and esophagus to their normal position in the abdominal cavity. The hiatal opening is then secured with sutures. Another procedure called fundoplication creates a high-pressure area in the lower esophagus, preventing reflux.

Prognosis

The clinical course of gastroesophageal reflux varies. While some symptoms resolve, others may be resistant to therapy. Most individuals with mild disease will continue to experience symptoms of varying degrees and frequency. When symptoms are severe or resistant to treatment, surgery may be required.

Differential Diagnosis

Other conditions that may present with similar symptoms include infectious esophagitis, hiatal hernia, ischemic heart disease, and other esophageal disorders such as narrowed areas (strictures), cancer, spasm, inability to relax (achalasia), and motility disorders.

The relationship between Helicobacter pylori (H. pylori) infection and gastroesophageal reflux disease (GERD) is not well known. Gastritis secondary to H. pylori infection may protect against GERD based on geographic and ethic distributions of GERD.

Specialists

- Gastroenterologist
- Internist

Work Restrictions / Accommodations

Restrictions or accommodations may not be necessary.

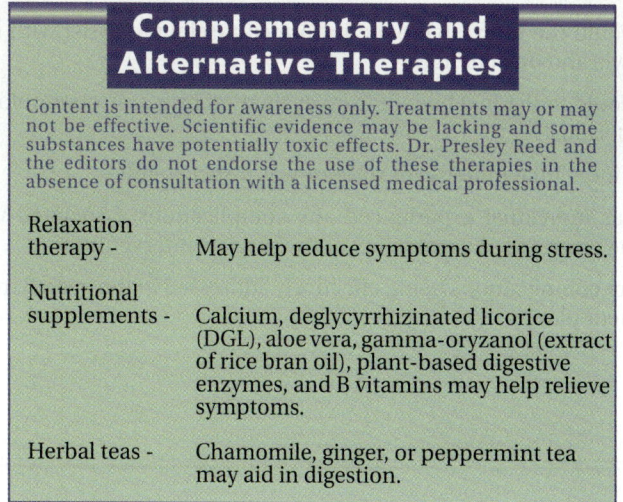

Complementary and Alternative Therapies

Content is intended for awareness only. Treatments may or may not be effective. Scientific evidence may be lacking and some substances have potentially toxic effects. Dr. Presley Reed and the editors do not endorse the use of these therapies in the absence of consultation with a licensed medical professional.

Relaxation therapy - May help reduce symptoms during stress.

Nutritional supplements - Calcium, deglycyrrhizinated licorice (DGL), aloe vera, gamma-oryzanol (extract of rice bran oil), plant-based digestive enzymes, and B vitamins may help relieve symptoms.

Herbal teas - Chamomile, ginger, or peppermint tea may aid in digestion.

Comorbid Conditions

Anticholinergic drugs commonly used for asthma increase the tendency of the lower esophageal sphincter to leak and may lengthen disability. Cigarette smoking contributes to esophageal reflux.

Complications

Complications include vomiting, aspiration, hoarseness, chronic cough, recurrent disease, and choking sensations. Approximately 10% of the individuals with severe reflux esophagitis develop narrowing or constriction of the esophagus (peptic stricture). Barrett's esophagus is a precancerous condition and involves changes in the esophageal lining due to damage from persistent reflux acid. This condition may occur in those with peptic strictures. Complications may also include painful swallowing (odynophagia) and noncardiac chest pain that may indicate the development of ulcers.

Factors Influencing Duration

Length of disability may be influenced by the severity of symptoms, type of treatment (Phases I, II, or III), compliance with and response to treatment, and the presence and severity of reflux complications. If the treatment is surgical, length of disability also depends on the type of surgery and any surgical complications.

Length of Disability

Medical treatment.

Duration in Days

Job Classification	Minimum	Optimum	Maximum
Any work	0	1	3

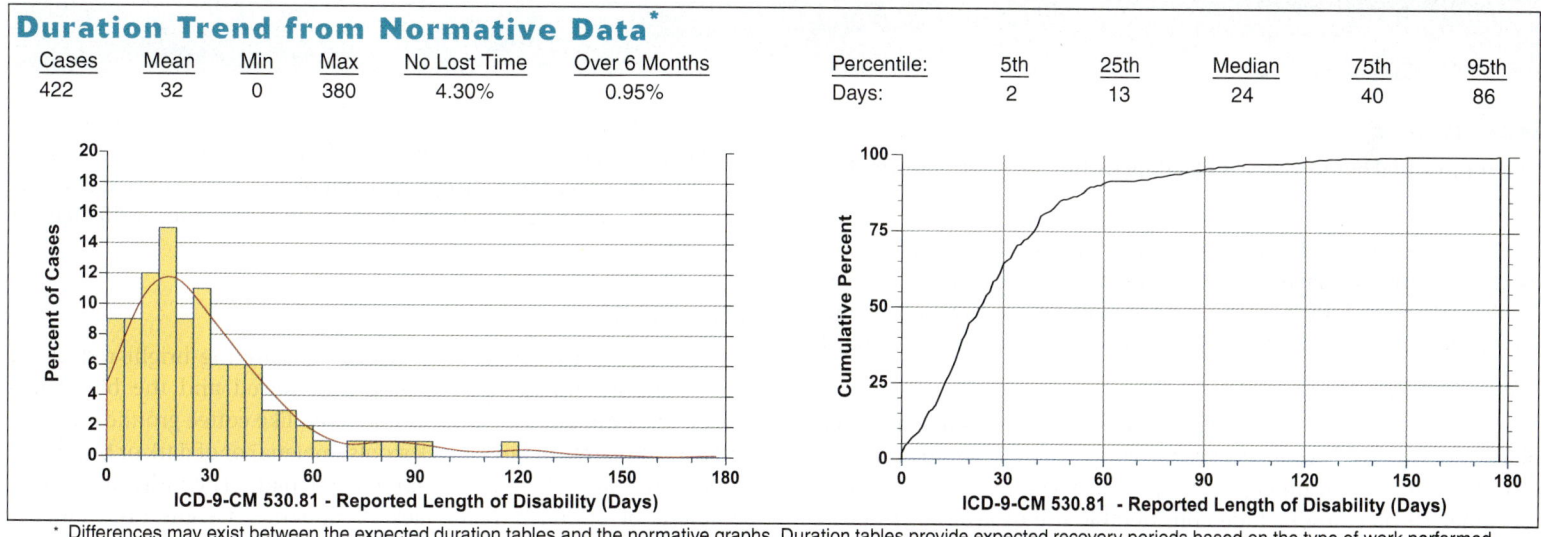

Duration Trend from Normative Data*

Cases	Mean	Min	Max	No Lost Time	Over 6 Months
422	32	0	380	4.30%	0.95%

Percentile:	5th	25th	Median	75th	95th
Days:	2	13	24	40	86

ICD-9-CM 530.81 - Reported Length of Disability (Days)

* Differences may exist between the expected duration tables and the normative graphs. Duration tables provide expected recovery periods based on the type of work performed by the individual. The normative graphs reflect the actual observed experience of many individuals across the spectrum of physical conditions, in a variety of industries, and with varying levels of case management.

Failure to Recover

If an individual fails to recover within the maximum duration expectancy period, the reader may wish to reference the following questions to assist in better understanding the specifics of an individual's medical case.

Regarding diagnosis:

- Has diagnosis of gastroesophageal reflux been confirmed?
- Was it confirmed by esophagoscopy, biopsy, upper gastrointestinal (GI) series, and/or Bernstein test?
- Have conditions with similar symptoms been ruled out?
- Have associated causes or conditions that may aggravate the condition been identified?

Regarding treatment:

- Has individual been instructed in lifestyle and diet modifications, including losing weight, abstaining from alcohol, tobacco, caffeine, acidic and fatty foods, and wearing nonrestrictive clothing? Is the individual complying with recommended changes? What can be done to enhance compliance?
- Have medications taken for other conditions been reviewed? Can any that may contribute to reflux be replaced or eliminated?
- Is the use of histamine (H2) antagonists, cholinergics, or a proton pump inhibitor medication effectively controlling symptoms?
- If symptoms are severe or resistant to treatment, is/was surgery required?
- Which of the following procedures was performed or is scheduled to be performed: surgical strengthening of the esophageal sphincter; correction of a hiatal hernia; or a fundoplication to create a high-pressure area in the lower esophagus?

Regarding prognosis:

- Do symptoms persist despite medical treatment? How severe are the symptoms?
- Would the individual benefit from counseling to assist with lifestyle and diet changes?
- Would individual benefit from evaluation by a gastroenterologist specialist?
- If individual underwent surgery, was it successful?
- Has individual experienced any complications associated with the gastroesophageal reflux or the surgical intervention?
- Are complications being effectively addressed in the overall treatment plan?

References

Gastroesophageal Reflux Disease (Hiatal Hernia and Heartburn). National Digestive Diseases Information Clearinghouse. 12 Feb 1998. 13 Mar 2000 <http://www.niddk.nih.gov/health/digest/pubs/heartbrn/heartbrn.htm>.

Ferri, Fred. Ferri's Clinical Advisor. St. Louis: Mosby, 2000.

Lamb, Joe, MD. "Supplement Recommendations for Heartburn." WholeHealthMD.com 2000. 26 June 2000 <http://www.wholehealthmd.com/hc/resourceareas_supp/0,1442,472,00.html>.

McDonald-Haile, J., et al. "Relaxation Training Reduces Symptom Reports and Acid Exposure in Patients with Gastroesophageal Reflux Disease." Gastroenterology 107 1 (1994): 61-69.

McQuaid, Kenneth. "Alimentary Tract." Current Medical Diagnosis and Treatment. Tierney, Lawrence, Stephen McPhee, and Maxine Papadakis, eds. New York: Lange Medical Books/McGraw-Hill, 2000. 553-655.

Sonnenberg, A., and H.B. El-Serag. "Clinical Epidemiology and Natural History of Gastroesophageal Reflux Disease." Yale Journal of Biology and Medicine 72 2-3 (1999): 81-92.

Gastrointestinal Hemorrhage

Other names / synonyms: Gastrointestinal Bleeding, Lower Intestinal Bleeding, Upper Gastrointestinal Bleeding

578, 578.0, 578.1, 578.9

Definition

Gastrointestinal hemorrhage is bleeding within the gastrointestinal (GI) tract.

The GI system is divided into the upper GI tract, which includes the esophagus and stomach, and the lower GI tract, which includes the small intestine and the large intestine (colon). Severe bleeding warrants emergency treatment and usually occurs more often in the upper GI tract than in the lower GI tract.

The most frequent cause of upper GI bleeding is stomach (peptic) ulcers, but ruptured esophageal veins (varices) and inflammation of the esophagus (erosive esophagitis) may cause bleeding also. Risk factors for upper GI bleeding include considerable use of aspirin or nonsteroidal anti-inflammatory drugs (NSAIDs), which can cause erosion of the protective lining (mucosa) in the GI tract, and alcohol consumption.

Lower GI hemorrhage occurs most often in the large intestine (colon) and may rarely be caused by lesions in the small intestine. Frequently, the cause for lower GI bleeding is diverticulosis. Diverticula are pouches on the colon, much like the appendix, that push through the lining of the colon and into the muscle tissue. When diverticula become inflamed (diverticulitis), they can cause hemorrhage. Other causes for lower GI bleeding include inflammation of the colon because of infection (infectious colitis), ulcerations on the colon (ulcerative colitis), cancer, hemorrhoids, and inflammatory bowel disease (IBD).

Hospital admissions in the US for GI bleeding number greater than 300,000 per year, and the rate at which GI bleeding occurs (incidence) increases with age. Ten to twenty percent of all GI bleeding cases occur in the large intestine (colon) and the majority of individuals affected are the elderly.

Diagnosis

History: The individual may complain of vomiting bright red blood (hematemesis), but if the bleeding has slowed and the blood has darkened, complaints of vomitus that looks like coffee grounds may be noted. Complaints of tarry, black stools (melena) or of dark or bright red blood in the stool (hematochezia) may be made. The individual might complain of stomach pain, lack of appetite, weight loss, fatigue, weakness, dizziness, or chest pain.

Physical exam: The individual may appear to be pale (pallor) and/or weak, and the extremities may be moist and cool. Blood pressure and pulse measurements may reflect changes when the individual moves from a lying or sitting position to a standing position (orthostatic measurements). Orthostatic changes are evident when a change in the pulse rate of greater than 10 beats/minute or a drop in blood pressure of 10 points (mmHg) occur. Listening to the abdomen with a stethoscope (auscultation) may reveal overactive sounds in the bowel (hyperactive bowel sounds) if blood is present. Insertion of the finger into the anus and up into the rectum (digital rectal exam) is done to check for masses, hemorrhoids, or ulcerations.

Tests: Blood tests may include a complete blood count (CBC) to monitor hemoglobin and hematocrit for anemia, and to monitor clotting (coagulation) parameters, such as platelet count and prothrombin time. The blood may be typed and cross-matched in the event that the individual requires a blood transfusion. Blood tests to determine liver function abnormalities should also be done. Chemical testing of the stool for blood should be done.

Imaging tests for the upper GI tract involve insertion of a viewing tube (endoscope) through the nose, into the esophagus, and down into the stomach (panendoscopy) to determine the source of bleeding. During the procedure, it is possible for the physician to insert various instruments through the endoscope to stop bleeding or to take a tissue sample for exam under a microscope (biopsy). If the panendoscopy is not diagnostic or not available, an x-ray can be taken. The x-ray is taken after the individual ingests contrast medium (barium) so the upper GI tract can be viewed.

Lower GI tract diagnostic tests also require that various endoscopic procedures be performed. The anus (anoscopy), the lower portion of the large intestine (sigmoid colon) above the rectum (sigmoidoscopy), and the entire large intestine, or colon (colonoscopy) can be viewed. As with endoscopic procedures for upper GI bleeding, bleeding may be stopped and biopsies may be taken through these viewing scopes also.

Treatment

Any bright, red blood in vomitus or stool, and any black, tarry stools are considered medical emergencies until otherwise proven. The individual is placed on intravenous (IV) fluids. Blood replacement is given, if needed. A tube, attached to a pump, is inserted through the nose into the stomach (nasogastric or NG tube) so that blood can be removed and the GI tract can rest; nothing is given to the individual by mouth. If endoscopic exams of the upper or lower GI tract reveal bleeding, the bleeding may be stopped by applying electrical charges (bipolar electrocoagulation) or lasers to the bleeding areas (cauterization). If the bleeding is severe, surgical correction, such as removing part of the stomach (gastric resection) or cutting part of the vagus nerve (vagotomy) may be necessary.

The individual will be instructed to refrain from alcohol, caffeine, and from smoking cigarettes.

Prognosis

Eighty to ninety percent of GI bleeding stops on its own with excellent outcome provided the individual follows instructions such as no alcohol or caffeine, and no smoking. The overall death (mortality) rate, however, is 5-14 percent. This rate is due, in part, to the increasing age of the population. Individuals who are less than 60 years old, however, and have no underlying medical problems have a mortality rate of less than 1 percent.

Those who must undergo surgical correction (vagotomy or gastric resection) may have very good outcomes, but this depends on the underlying cause for the bleeding and the severity of the blood loss.

Differential Diagnosis

Differential diagnoses include cirrhosis of the liver; ingestion of iron, bismuth, or other foods that darken the stool; valvular heart disease; arteriovenous malformation; scleroderma; and mixed connective tissue disease.

Specialists

- Gastroenterologist
- Internist

Work Restrictions / Accommodations

There may be activity or lifting restrictions if surgery is performed. The individual may benefit from avoiding stressful situations. Individuals will need a gradual increase in normal activities to rebuild stamina and strength.

Comorbid Conditions

Conditions that might influence length of disability include cardiovascular disease, liver disease, alcoholism, diabetes mellitus, increased blood pressure (hypertension), kidney (renal) disease, and lung (pulmonary) disease.

Complications

Complications of GI hemorrhage include anemia, chemical and fluid imbalances in the body, recurrent bleeding, or significant loss of blood leading to shock (hemorrhagic shock).

Factors Influencing Duration

The age of the individual, the recurrence of bleeding, persistent anemia, and the individual's response to treatment may influence the length of disability.

Length of Disability

Duration of disability will depend upon the underlying cause and severity of the condition. In some cases, disability may be permanent.

Failure to Recover

If an individual fails to recover within the maximum duration expectancy period, the reader may wish to reference the following questions to assist in better understanding the specifics of an individual's medical case.

Regarding diagnosis:

- Does the individual have a history of stomach (peptic) ulcers or inflammation of the esophagus (erosive esophagitis)?
- Does the individual take considerable amounts of aspirin or non-steroidal anti-inflammatory drugs (NSAIDs)?
- How much alcohol does the individual consume and how often?
- Does the individual have a history of diverticulosis, colitis, cancer, hemorrhoids, or inflammatory bowel disease (IBD)?
- Does the individual complain of vomiting bright red blood (hematemesis) or of vomitus that looks like coffee grounds?
- Has the individual noticed tarry, black stools (melena) or dark or bright red blood in the stool (hematochezia)?
- Does the individual report stomach pain, lack of appetite, weight loss, fatigue, weakness, dizziness, or chest pain?
- Was a complete blood count (CBC) done to monitor hemoglobin and hematocrit for anemia?

- Were clotting (coagulation) parameters measured?
- Were blood tests done to determine liver function abnormalities?
- Was the stool tested for the presence of blood?
- Were imaging tests for the upper GI tract done, including upper GI x-rays or insertion of a viewing tube through the nose, into the esophagus, and down into the stomach (panendoscopy)?
- Was the lower GI tract viewed either by anoscopy, sigmoidoscopy, or colonoscopy?
- Was the diagnosis of upper or lower GI tract hemorrhage confirmed?

Regarding treatment:

- Did the individual require emergent medical care for bright, red blood in vomitus or stool, or for black, tarry stools?
- Did the individual require intravenous (IV) fluid and blood replacement?
- Was a nasogastric (NG) tube placed for blood removal and for the GI tract to rest?
- If endoscopic exams of the upper or lower GI tract revealed bleeding, was the bleeding stopped with electrical charges (bipolar electrocoagulation) or lasers (cauterization)?
- Did severe bleeding require surgical correction, such as removing part of the stomach (gastric resection) or cutting part of the vagus nerve (vagotomy)?
- If surgery was done, did it stop the bleeding completely?
- Has the individual been instructed to refrain from alcohol, caffeine, and from smoking cigarettes?

Regarding prognosis:

- Did the individual experience upper or lower GI bleeding?
- Did the bleeding stop on its own or was intervention required?
- How severe was blood loss?
- If severe, how will this affect the daily activities of the individual and for how long?
- Was this an initial bleeding episode, or a recurrence?
- Is the individual compliant with refraining from alcohol, caffeine, and smoking?
- Does the individual have an underlying condition that might prolong recovery?
- What is the condition and how can it be treated?
- If surgery was required, did any postsurgical complications occur? If so, what were they and what is their expected outcome with treatment?
- Has the individual developed anemia or chemical and fluid imbalances?
- If so, how will these be treated and what is their expected outcome with treatment?

References

"Gastrointestinal Bleeding." Merck Manual of Diagnosis and Therapy, 17th ed. Beers, Mark H., and Robert Berkow, MD, eds. Whitehouse Station, NJ: Merck & Co. Inc., 1999. 05 Dec 2000 <http://www.merck.com/mmanual/section3/chapter22/22a.htm>.

Cohen, Lisa, et al. Nurse's Clinical Library Gastrointestinal Disorders. Springhouse, PA: Springhouse Corporation, 1985.

Gastrostomy

Other names / synonyms: Beck-Jianu Gastrostomy, Brunschwig's Gastrostomy, Decompression Gastrostomy, Janeway Gastrostomy, PEG, Percutaneous Endoscopic Gastrostomy, Permanent Gastrostomy, Spivack's Gastrostomy, Ssabanejew-Frank Gastrostomy, Stamm-Kader Gastrostomy, Temporary Gastrostomy

43.11, 43.19, V55.1

Definition

Gastrostomy is a procedure that creates an artificial opening (ostomy) between the stomach and the surface of the abdomen. Usually, a tube is placed through the abdominal wall directly into the stomach. These tubes are used as an access to provide nutrition, either temporarily or permanently, for individuals that are unable to take adequate amounts of food orally. The procedure may be done in the operating room under general anesthesia or may be done with local anesthesia using an endoscope (percutaneous gastrostomy).

It is difficult to identify a particular population who is more likely to undergo a gastrostomy, as the procedure is indicated in a variety of conditions. A gastrostomy may be done to temporarily avoid disturbing a fresh surgical incision when there has been surgery to the mouth, pharynx, or esophagus. In addition, severe facial, head, or spinal trauma and neuromuscular weakness associated with stroke and some neurological disorders can impair swallowing, which may be an indication for a gastrostomy.

Reason for Procedure

A gastrostomy is done to provide a route for liquid nutritional support when an individual is unable to take sufficient food orally to maintain adequate nutrition. This may be due to anatomical, surgical, or traumatic derangement of the mouth, pharynx, esophagus, or the upper stomach. Sometimes, gastrostomies are used temporarily to avoid disturbing fresh surgical sites following surgery to the mouth, pharynx, esophagus, or upper stomach. Other indications for a gastrostomy are swallowing problems secondary to decreased level of consciousness or neurological disorders.

Description

With percutaneous gastrostomy, the stomach is entered with a scope (endoscopically) and the gastric and abdominal walls punctured with endoscopic guidance. The gastrostomy tube is introduced through the mouth, passed into the stomach, out through the stomach and abdominal wall, and secured in place. This is a routine technique that can be performed under local anesthesia.

Other gastrostomies are usually performed with conventional surgery. The individual is given general anesthesia. The surgeon creates a small opening through the abdominal wall and wall of the stomach. The stomach is stitched (tacked) up to the abdominal wall. Sometimes a rubber cuff (bolster) is attached to the opening to protect the skin surface. A flexible feeding tube is inserted into the stomach through the opening.

Generally, both the endoscopic or conventional surgical approach can be performed as an outpatient surgery. After the wound has healed, the feeding tube can be removed and then inserted as needed for feeding. A small, plastic plug can be placed over the opening (stoma) when not in use for feeding. This allows the individual to carry out normal daily activities (bathing, working, etc.) without restrictions.

Prognosis

The procedure is generally safe and successful at providing either temporary or permanent access for administering liquid feedings.

Specialists

- Gastroenterologist
- General Surgeon

Work Restrictions / Accommodations

A gastrostomy may be either temporary or permanent. After removal of a temporary gastrostomy and the wound has healed, there are no work restrictions or accommodations necessary.

In individuals with a permanent gastrostomy, once the surgical wound is healed, the feeding tube can be removed after each feeding. The opening is covered with a small, plastic plug that allows individuals to perform normal activities without restrictions. However, individuals who require feeding via a gastrostomy tube may need more frequent breaks to allow for administration of small, frequent, liquid meals.

Comorbid Conditions

Comorbid conditions of malnutrition, immune suppression, bleeding disorders, or cancer may impact ability to recover and further lengthen disability.

Procedure Complications

The procedure has few risks. If the procedure is done under general anesthesia, then complications associated with anesthetic use are possible (i.e., breathing problems, heart abnormalities, drop in blood pressure or pulse). Other complications, though rare, include bleeding, perforation of adjacent structures, infection, and movement (migration) of the feeding tube.

Some individuals develop nausea, vomiting or diarrhea with the initiation of liquid nutrition. These problems usual subside over a period of a couple of weeks.

Factors Influencing Duration

The age and general health of the individual, and type of gastrostomy performed will influence the length of disability.

Length of Disability

Open gastrostomy.

Duration in Days

Job Classification	Minimum	Optimum	Maximum
Sedentary work	28	35	42
Light work	28	35	42
Medium work	42	49	56
Heavy work	42	49	56
Very Heavy work	42	49	56

References

Clochesy, John M., et al. Critical Care Nursing, 2nd ed. Philadelphia: W.B. Saunders Company, 1996.

General Paresis

Other names / synonyms: Brain Syphilis, Dementia Paralytica, General Paralysis of the Insane, Paralytic Dementia, Paresis, Syphilitic Meningoencephalitis

094, 094.0, 094.1, 095, 095.8, 095.9, 096

Definition

General paresis is a chronic inflammation of the brain and its lining (meningoencephalitis) that occurs in the late stages of syphilis. The infection causes gradual, widespread damage to the nerves of the brain, resulting in a variety of physical and psychological changes.

General paresis is a progressive, disabling, and life-threatening condition. Since it is a complication of syphilis, the primary risk factor is previous syphilis infection. Previous infection with another sexually transmitted disease such as gonorrhea is also a risk factor as such diseases can hide the symptoms of a syphilis infection.

Approximately 1 in 1 million individuals (i.e., 5% of individuals with untreated syphilis) develop general paresis within 10 to 15 years after the primary infection. General paresis develops more often in men than in women and occurs more often in whites than blacks.

Diagnosis

History: The individual may report irritability, memory loss, personality changes, impaired concentration, carelessness, headache, and insomnia. In the later stages of this condition, symptoms include muscle weakness, defective judgment, depression, psychosis, confusion, disorientation, paranoia, and seizures. The final stage of the disease may include frequent seizures, incontinence, and recurrent strokes. The individual may voluntarily report prior syphilis infection, but since the initial infection may have occurred several years previously, the individual may not make the association between the current symptoms and the previous infection.

Physical exam: Individuals may present with tremors of the lips, tongue, and fingers, slurred speech, difficulty writing, unsteadiness, decreased muscle tone, muscle weakness, lack of facial expressions, and small, nonreactive pupils. Other conditions associated with late-stage syphilis infection may also be present such as tabes dorsalis, another disease that affects the nervous system.

Tests: Blood (serologic) tests are first conducted to identify the cause of infection. If syphilis is detected, then a lumbar puncture procedure is performed to obtain a small amount of cerebrospinal fluid (CSF). Study of the CSF fluid can confirm diagnosis and provide a baseline to gauge the effectiveness of future treatment.

Treatment

The goals of treatment are to cure the underlying infection and reduce progression of the disorder. Treatment of the infection reduces new nerve damage but will not reverse damage that has already occurred. Antibiotic medication may be prescribed. It is important that individuals treated for general paresis have periodic tests of the CSF to ensure that the infection is responding. If the CSF fails to return to normal after 6 months, the individual is treated again. Individuals with neurosyphilis may need to be retested up to 2 years after treatment.

Damage already done to body organs cannot be reversed but can be treated symptomatically. Emergency treatment of seizures may be required. Anti-seizure medicine may be prescribed for controlling seizures. Assistance or supervision with activities such as eating and dressing may be required if the individual can no longer care for him/herself. Physical or occupational therapy may be required for those with muscle weakness.

Prognosis

General paresis can lead to the inability to care for oneself and communicate or interact with others. Progressive disability is likely, although treatment can reduce (but not necessarily stop) the progression of nerve damage. Damage already done to body organs cannot be reversed. If untreated, this condition is fatal with death typically occurring within 5 to 6 years following the development of symptoms.

Differential Diagnosis

Conditions with similar symptoms include cerebral tumor, subdural hematoma, cerebral arteriosclerosis, Alzheimer's disease, multiple sclerosis, and chronic alcoholism.

Specialists

- Infectious Disease Physician
- Internist
- Neurologist
- Physical Therapist

Rehabilitation

Physical and/or occupational therapy may help individuals with muscle weakness. The duration and frequency of such therapy vary considerably depending on the extent and severity of symptoms and the individual's response to treatment. In general, therapy focuses on maintaining range of motion, increasing strength, and improving coordination, balance, and functional abilities such as gait.

Individuals with weakness and decreased function in their arms and/or legs require a comprehensive stretching program to maintain range of motion in the joints. Occupational and physical therapists instruct individuals and their family members on how to safely stretch the arms and legs.

A strengthening program helps maintain or improve functional abilities of the arms and legs. Individuals perform arm exercises such as elbow extension with light hand weights to enable them to use crutches or a walker. Bridging exercises may be performed where the individual lies on the back with the knees bent and lifts the buttocks up from the bed. This promotes the ability to get out of a chair.

Individuals may have impaired coordination. An occupational therapist instructs individuals in performing fine motor coordination exercises such as picking up pegs and placing them in a pegboard. Practical coordination exercises include fastening buttons or practicing signatures. Individuals work on gross motor coordination in physical therapy such as kicking a soccer ball rolled toward them or throwing beanbags at a target.

Physical and occupational therapists also help individuals with their sitting and standing balance. Dynamic sitting balance exercises that promote dressing and grooming abilities include having an individual sit on a therapy ball while attempting to reach for objects placed at various distances. Physical therapists may focus on standing balance to preserve the ability to walk with exercises such as walking heel to toe in a set of parallel bars.

The main focus of physical and occupational therapy is to maximize functional capabilities. Occupational therapists teach individuals skills such as getting in and out of the shower, dressing, and meal preparation. They may order equipment such as a tub seat, a long-handled shoehorn, or kitchen utensils with thick handles to make these tasks easier. Physical therapists teach skills such as getting in and out of bed, walking, or using a wheelchair. They may order equipment such as crutches, a cane, or wheelchair, as appropriate. Physical therapists may also refer an individual to an orthotist if leg braces are necessary.

Work Restrictions / Accommodations

Extended sick leave for hospitalization and treatment may be needed. Other accommodations vary depending on the extent and severity of symptoms. Work responsibilities may need to be modified to duties requiring minimal intellectual and/or physical activity. Disability may be permanent.

Comorbid Conditions

Infection with HIV or hepatitis B may lengthen the disability period.

Complications

Complications include injury caused from falls or during seizures.

Factors Influencing Duration

Length of disability may be influenced by the timeliness and accuracy of the diagnosis, nature and severity of symptoms, response to treatment, any other forms of neurosyphilis such as tabes dorsalis, or any complications. Treatment may stop the progression in some cases but will not reverse the disability.

Length of Disability

Disability may be permanent.

Failure to Recover

If an individual fails to recover within the maximum duration expectancy period, the reader may wish to reference the following questions to assist in better understanding the specifics of an individual's medical case.

Regarding diagnosis:

- Has diagnosis of general paresis been confirmed?
- Have conditions with similar symptoms been ruled out?

Regarding treatment:

- Has individual taken antibiotics as prescribed? Was culture and sensitivity done to determine the most effective antibiotic therapy and to rule out antibiotic-resistant organisms?
- Since individuals with neurosyphilis may need to be retested for up to 2 years following treatment, was the individual compliant with CSF testing regimen?
- If the CSF failed to return to normal after 6 months, was the individual retreated?
- Has the individual followed the physician's instructions regarding the use of anti-seizure medications?
- Does the individual have muscle weakness?
- Does the individual have an underlying condition that may complicate treatment or impact recovery?

Regarding prognosis:

- Is individual able to care for him/herself? Does individual need assistance with daily activities such as eating and dressing?
- Has the individual received appropriate physical and/or occupational therapy?
- Has treatment been effective in reducing nerve damage progression? If not, is it due to the infection not responding to antibiotic therapy?
- Has individual received a second course of treatment?
- Has the individual experienced any complications associated with the general paresis?
- Is individual compliant with CSF testing regimen? If not, what can be done to increase compliance?

References

Encyclopedia Britannica. "Paresis." Britannica Online. 2000. 15 Oct 2000 <http://www.britannica.com/bcom/eb/article/9/0,5716,59909+1+58448,00.html?query=paresis>.

Guccione, Andrew A. "Functional Assessment." Physical Rehabilitation: Assessment and Treatment. O'Sullivan, Susan B., and Thomas J. Schmitz, eds. Philadelphia: F.A. Davis Company, 1994. 193-208.

Lister, Marilyn J., ed. Contemporary Management of Motor Control Problems. Alexandria: Foundation for Physical Therapy, 1991.

O'Sullivan, Susan B. "Strategies to Improve Motor Control and Motor Learning." Physical Rehabilitation: Assessment and Treatment. O'Sullivan, Susan B., and Thomas J. Schmitz, eds. Philadelphia: F.A. Davis Company, 1994. 225-250.

Gestational Diabetes
648.8

Definition

Gestational diabetes is the onset of diabetes during pregnancy. During pregnancy, the production of certain hormones can change the way sugar is utilized in the body. These hormones can partly block the effect of insulin, another hormone that controls the amount of sugar in the blood. After delivery, this diabetic condition usually resolves, but not always.

Pregnant women should be screened for gestational diabetes between the 24th and 28th week of pregnancy. Women with known risk factors should be screened for diabetes at the first prenatal visit. This condition usually begins in the fifth or sixth month of pregnancy.

Risk factors include excessive sugar in the urine (glycosuria), a history of gestational diabetes, stillbirth or miscarriage, congenital malformation, obese women with a body mass index (BMI) greater than 27, and a history of delivering large babies larger than or equal to nine pounds.

Gestational diabetes affects about 2% of all pregnant women in the US. In Denmark, the incidence of gestational diabetes is also about 2%. Universal screening detected a prevalence of 2.7%. The incidence of gestational diabetes in adolescent Hispanic Americans is low at 1.5%. In countries such as Ethiopia where chronic malnutrition is a problem, prevalence of gestational diabetes is high compared to other parts of Africa.

Diagnosis

History: Individuals may report similar symptoms of diabetes mellitus such as excessive thirst and increased urine production, however, typically, there are no symptoms.

Physical exam: The exam includes assessment of the mother's vital signs (blood pressure, pulse), body weight, and nutritional status.

Tests: Diagnosis is confirmed by screening glucose test and follow up test if positive.

Treatment

Treatment of gestational diabetes consists of modifying the diet, monitoring blood sugar levels, and exercising regularly. Diet modification includes eating well-balanced meals and reducing intake of foods high in sugar. Depending on weight gain during pregnancy, the doctor may recommend eating less at each meal. In some cases, insulin replacement may be required. The glucose level should be monitored weekly at varying times during the day.

Prognosis

The condition usually resolves after delivery although it may take several weeks to completely resolve. In some cases, if the woman becomes pregnant again, gestational diabetes may return. Gestational diabetes also increases the risk of developing diabetes mellitus later in life.

If gestational diabetes is not recognized and treated, the risk for fetal and newborn death increases. Nausea and vomiting during pregnancy can complicate the management of gestational diabetes. Alterations in lifestyle and reduction of risk factors can delay or prevent this development.

Differential Diagnosis

Impaired glucose tolerance may be the result of disease of the pancreas or kidney insufficiency.

Specialists

- Endocrinologist
- Obstetrician
- Perinatologist

Work Restrictions / Accommodations

Individuals may need frequent meals and restroom breaks. In more severe cases, insulin therapy is needed.

Comorbid Conditions

Preeclampsia is a comorbid condition that may further lengthen disability.

Complications

Complications include increased risk of preeclampsia, miscarriage, fetal growth problems, and intrauterine fetal demise (IUFD) as well as the complications associated with diabetes mellitus. Babies of mothers who developed gestational diabetes may grow somewhat larger than average due to the extra sugar in the blood that feeds the baby more. If the baby is very large (macrosomic), the mother may have a difficult labor or need a cesarean section.

Nausea and vomiting during pregnancy can complicate the management of gestational diabetes. Gestational diabetes may cause problems for the baby at birth such as low blood sugar level or jaundice (yellowish skin color). These complications however, are usually not serious and are easily treated with extra glucose (sugar) to bring the blood sugar to normal and special lights to correct the jaundice condition.

Factors Influencing Duration

Duration depends on the month of pregnancy when diagnosis was made. The extent to which this disorder is controlled by dietary modification and/or medication may influence the length of disability.

Length of Disability

Duration depends on severity of the diabetes and may continue until delivery. The majority of gestational diabetes can be managed with dietary changes and increased pregnancy monitoring and is therefore not source of disability unless complications are documented.

Single episode, without additional complications.

Duration in Days

Job Classification	Minimum	Optimum	Maximum
Any work	1	7	14

Failure to Recover

If an individual fails to recover within the maximum duration expectancy period, the reader may wish to reference the following questions to assist in better understanding the specifics of an individual's medical case.

Regarding diagnosis:

- Considering the individual's history, was the woman screened for diabetes at the appropriate stage of her pregnancy?
- Was diagnosis of gestational diabetes confirmed?
- Were other conditions associated with impaired glucose tolerance ruled out?

Regarding treatment:

- Does individual keep regular follow-up appointments?
- Was individual adequately instructed in diet modification and exercise recommendations?
- Does individual continue to have elevated blood sugars despite diet and activity changes?
- Is individual compliant in following the recommendations? Are barriers preventing her from complying (language barrier, lack of motivation, lack of understanding)?
- Was more aggressive treatment initiated (such as insulin replacement)?

Regarding prognosis:

- Did gestational diabetes respond to treatment?
- Has pregnancy been completed? Was a cesarean section necessary?
- Did mother or infant experience any complications related to the gestational diabetes? Are complications being addressed in the overall treatment plan?
- Has elevated blood sugar continued after delivery of the baby?
- Does individual continue with diet modifications and exercise recommendations? If not, what can be done to enhance compliance?
- Would individual benefit from consultation with an endocrinologist?

References

Lee, L. "Introducing Herbal Medicine into Conventional Health Care Settings." Journal of Nurse-Midwifery 44 3 (1999): 253-266.

McFarland, M.B., et al. "Dietary Therapy for Gestational Diabetes: How Long is Enough?" Obstetrics and Gynecology 93 (1999): 978-982.

Giardiasis

Other names / synonyms: Beaver Fever, Lambliasis
007, 007.1, 007.3, 007.8, 007.9

Definition

Giardiasis is an intestinal infection caused by a protozoan parasite called Giardia lamblia. The infection occurs when the parasite is ingested usually from water contaminated by feces. It is highly transmittable and multiple infections are usually seen within a household or daycare setting.

The disease results in very foul-smelling diarrhea, gas, and bloating. It develops 1 to 3 weeks after exposure and lasts 7 to 10 days. While most cases are mild or without symptoms, in rare cases giardiasis can become chronic and result in the individual being unable to absorb important nutrients from food (malabsorption syndrome).

Worldwide, giardiasis is usually associated with developing countries with poor sanitary conditions. In the US and Europe, giardiasis is considered the most common parasitic infection of the intestine. Individuals at risk include travelers to developing countries, campers drinking unpurified water from contaminated streams, individuals with impaired immune systems, and male homosexuals. It is not, however, an opportunistic infection of AIDS.

Diagnosis

History: Symptoms may be absent (asymptomatic) or include diarrhea. Ranging from mild to severe, the watery diarrhea is typically very odorous, frothy, and greasy but free of blood or pus. Individuals may also report weakness, loss of appetite (anorexia), nausea, vomiting, abdominal bloating and discomfort, and flatulence. In severe or chronic infections, significant weight loss can occur if the individual has malabsorption syndrome). History may include travel abroad or into the wilderness, or contact with an infected individual especially if oral-anal contact was involved. The individual may have contracted the disease through contact with an asymptomatic carrier.

Physical exam: The exam may reveal abdominal tenderness and distention with overactive bowel sounds. Evidence of weight loss or generalized weakness may also be present.

Tests: Diagnosis is made when the Giardia parasite is detected in the individual's stool. Stool samples are typically collected and examined over a period of 3 days. Because parasites may be excreted at unpredictable intervals, stool samples may need to be collected over a longer period of time. Stained smears of the stool may reveal the Giardia parasite. Tests performed on Entero-Test capsules or fluid suctioned from the small intestine (duodenum) can help confirm diagnosis. Although blood tests (ELISA, IgM) may show Giardia antigen, they cannot always distinguish present from past infections. In rare cases, biopsy of the small intestine may be needed to identify the organism.

Treatment

Giardiasis can be treated with a number of antiprotozoan drugs. The mainstay of treatment is metronidazole taken 3 times a day by mouth for 5 days. For severe cases of diarrhea, fluids and nutrients may need to be replaced intravenously. Although treatment of asymptomatic cases of giardiasis is controversial, treatment prevents transmission of the disease.

Prognosis

The prognosis for giardiasis is good. Prompt, appropriate treatment usually affects a cure. Relapses may occur. Although the infection may become chronic in some individuals, it does not appear to last indefinitely.

Differential Diagnosis

Conditions with similar symptoms include other protozoa, viral or bacterial enteritis, and peptic stomach disease.

Specialists

- Gastroenterologist
- Parasitologist
- Infectious Disease Physician

Work Restrictions / Accommodations

Individuals weakened by excessive diarrhea should avoid strenuous work until strength returns. The individual may need to incrementally increase workload as tolerated.

Complementary and Alternative Therapies

Content is intended for awareness only. Treatments may or may not be effective. Scientific evidence may be lacking and some substances have potentially toxic effects. Dr. Presley Reed and the editors do not endorse the use of these therapies in the absence of consultation with a licensed medical professional.

Kaolin -	Said to increase the bulk of feces and may be found in many antidiarrheal preparations. Kaolin does not have any antibacterial activity so it should not be used as the sole treatment in infectious diarrheas.
Yogurt -	Said to reestablish normal flora in the intestines.
Berberine -	May have an antiprotozoan activity for mild cases of giardiasis.
Grapefruit seed extract -	May be helpful in eliminating Giardia.

Comorbid Conditions

Coexisting conditions that may impact recovery include decreased stomach acidity (hypochlorhydria or achlorhydria), malnutrition, and impaired or depressed immune system function.

Complications

When prompt, accurate diagnosis is delayed, diarrhea and poor intestinal absorption may result in significant loss of fluids and nutrients. In severe or chronic infections, significant weight loss and debility can occur if the individual cannot absorb important nutrients from food.

Factors Influencing Duration

The length of disability is affected by the severity of symptoms, delay in diagnosis or treatment, and individual's response to treatment.

Length of Disability

Duration in Days

Job Classification	Minimum	Optimum	Maximum
Any work	3	7	14

Failure to Recover

If an individual fails to recover within the maximum duration expectancy period, the reader may wish to reference the following questions to assist in better understanding the specifics of an individual's medical case.

Regarding diagnosis:

- Has diagnosis of giardiasis been confirmed? Are further diagnostic tests pending or being considered?
- Have underlying conditions that may impact recovery (immune suppression) been identified or ruled out?
- Has individual experienced a significant weight loss indicating malabsorption syndrome?

Regarding treatment:

- Has the individual received the appropriate antimicrobial therapy?
- Have the symptoms persisted despite treatment? If so, have antiprotozoal drugs been considered as an alternative treatment?
- Is the individual experiencing a reaction to the current medication? Has this interfered with compliance in taking the medication?
- If malabsorption syndrome occurs, has individual been treated with intravenous nutrition support?

Regarding prognosis:

- Has condition persisted beyond expected recovery? Did individual delay seeking treatment?
- Did individual appear to recover only to become ill again? If so, was the individual re-examined to rule out the possibility of chronic infection or secondary infection?
- Has the individual suffered any associated complications such as nutritional deficiencies? If so, are appropriate nutritional supplementations being administered?

References

Agarwal, A.K., and D.M.Tripathi. "Management of Giardiasis by a Herbal Drug Pippali Rasayana: A Clinical Study." Journal of Ethnopharmacology 56 3 (1997): 233-6.

Vesy, C.J., and W.L.Peterson. "Review Article: The Management of Giardiasis." Ailment Pharmacol Ther 13 7 (1999): 843-850.

Gingival Abscess
Other names / synonyms: Alveolar Process Fistula, Dental Fistula, Parulis, Periapical Abscess with Sinus
522.7, 523.3

Definition

A gingival abscess is a pus-filled sac that forms in the gumline (gingiva) of the teeth.

Gingival abscess is one of three kinds of dental abscesses that resemble each other. The other two kinds are periodontal and periapical abscesses. A periodontal abscess occurs when the infection of a gingival abscess moves deep into gum pockets and drainage of pus is blocked. A periapical abscess occurs when the inner layer of a tooth (pulp) becomes infected, usually secondary to tooth decay.

Gingival abscess is caused by infection from bacteria that enter the gums following injury from aggressive tooth brushing, toothpick punctures, or from food that is forced into the gumline. The infection may spread into surrounding tissue, and if left untreated, it can progress, damaging the support structure of the teeth.

According to reports issued by the Centers for Disease Control and Prevention (CDC) in 1998, 11,000 cases of gingival abscess were diagnosed in the US.

Diagnosis

History: Although most gingival abscesses develop quickly, a slow-developing gingival abscess may go unnoticed and present no symptoms until it has become severe. Symptoms may include tenderness and swelling in the gumline, a feeling of loose teeth, or teeth that have become unusually sensitive to heat and cold. If the abscess has progressed, it may be releasing a foul-tasting pus. Severe abscesses can cause fever, headache, and a dull, throbbing pain.

Physical exam: In its initial stages, a gingival abscess causes the gumline to swell and appear red and shiny. A point may appear from which pus can be released under gentle pressure. Lymph nodes in the neck may also be swollen.

Tests: Tests are usually not required to diagnose a gingival abscess. An x-ray will help to determine the exact location of the abscess and to see if the abscess has penetrated the structure supporting the teeth (periodontal structure).

Treatment

The first step of treatment is to drain all pus that has accumulated in the abscess. One way to accomplish the drainage is to pass a probe into the abscess and to gently scrape away the infected material. It may be necessary to make a small incision in the gums in order to reach the abscess. If the abscess has not progressed into the periodontal structure, antibiotic therapy is usually effective in eliminating the infection.

If the abscess has progressed into the periodontal structure, deep cleaning will be recommending for the gum pocket. If too much bony support and periodontal ligament attachment have been lost or if the tooth is too loose, the tooth may need to be removed (dental extraction).

Prognosis

Following drainage, if the abscess has not progressed into periodontal structure, antibiotic therapy is effective in eliminating the infection.

The prognosis is poor if the abscess has progressed into the periodontal structure. If too much of the bony support and periodontal ligament attachment have been lost, the tooth will have to be removed (tooth extraction).

Differential Diagnosis

Conditions with symptoms similar to gingival abscess include acute gingivitis and periodontal and dentoalveolar abscesses.

Specialists

- Dentist

Work Restrictions / Accommodations

Restrictions are necessary for the individual whose duties involve telephone communication, giving in-house or sales presentations, conducting interviews, or any other work responsibilities where the individual is required to talk. Work responsibilities may need to be shifted, temporarily, to less verbally demanding duties.

Comorbid Conditions

Comorbid conditions that might influence the length of disability after treatment for gingivitis include medically compromising conditions, such as diabetes mellitus and human immunodeficiency virus (HIV) infection. Also, individuals on medications that cause dry mouth are at higher risk for bacterial infections.

Complications

A gingival abscess near a molar rarely progresses into an abscess involving a tooth root (dentoalveolar abscess). Pus from an abscess may be discharged into the jaw and throughout the floor of the mouth, causing difficulty in swallowing and breathing. The discharge of pus may also cause swelling so severe that breathing is obstructed, making it necessary to create a surgical opening in the trachea (emergency tracheostomy).

Factors Influencing Duration
Length of disability may be influenced by the severity and extent of the abscess, and by the individual's response to the antibiotic treatment.

Length of Disability
Gingivectomy.

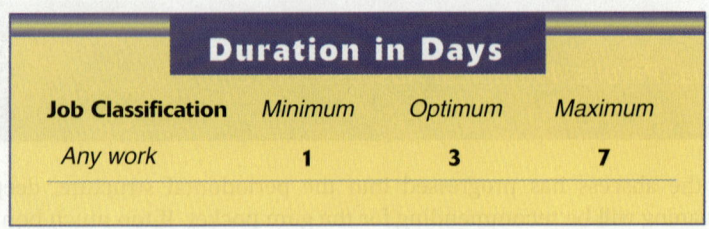

Job Classification	Minimum	Optimum	Maximum
Any work	1	3	7

Failure to Recover
If an individual fails to recover within the maximum duration expectancy period, the reader may wish to reference the following questions to assist in better understanding the specifics of an individual's medical case.

Regarding diagnosis:
- Have the gums had injuries from aggressive tooth brushing, toothpick punctures or food that has been forced into the gumline?
- Was the diagnosis confirmed with a dental exam?
- Did the abscess develop quickly or gradually?
- Was an x-ray done? Did the abscess penetrate the periodontal structure?
- Were other similar conditions, such as acute gingivitis, periodontal or dentoalveolar abscesses ruled out?

Regarding treatment:
- Was the pus drained from the abscess?
- Was the individual given antibiotics?
- Did it become necessary to remove the tooth because of severe damage?

Regarding prognosis:
- Have the symptoms persisted despite treatment? Was the individual re-examined by the dentist to rule out the possibility of complications?
- Does the individual's employer have work they can do on a temporary basis that involves minimal talking?
- Has the individual experienced any associated complications such as dentoalveolar abscess that may impact recovery and prognosis?
- Does the individual have any existing conditions such as diabetes mellitus or HIV of that may impact recovery and prognosis?

References
"Chapter 106: Teeth and Periodontium." Merck Manual of Diagnosis and Therapy, 17th ed. Beers, Mark H., and Robert Berkow, MD, eds. Whitehouse Station, NJ: Merck & Co. Inc., 1999. 20 Jan 2001 <http://www.merck.com/pubs/mmanual/section9/chapter106/106e.htm>.

Oral Abscess. Healthseva.com. 01 Jan 2000. 20 Jan 2001 <http://www.healthseva.com/content/dentistry/oralabcess_2.php3>.

Gingivectomy
Other names / synonyms: Excision of Gingival Tissue, Gingivoplasty, Gum Resection
24.31

Definition
Gingivectomy is a dental surgical procedure that is used to treat gum disease (gingivitis) after nonsurgical methods, such as root planing and scaling, have been unsuccessful in the removal of below-the-gum (subgingival) deposits (plaque and calculus).

Accumulation of bacterial plaque deposits causes the gums to swell and pull away from the teeth, forming pockets that trap food, providing a breeding environment for bacteria and making it more difficult to properly clean the teeth.

During the procedure, loose, diseased gum tissue is trimmed to reduce the size of deepened pockets that have formed between the gum and the tooth.

Another indication for gingivectomy is severe gingival overgrowth (gingival hyperplasia), which may be genetic or drug-induced. Removal of excess gingival tissue via the gingivectomy procedure dramatically improves the individual's appearance.

Reason for Procedure
Gingivectomy treats gingivitis by removing damaged, excess gum tissue and restoring a normal pocket depth between the gum and tooth. Experts estimate that at least 75% of the US population has some form of gingivitis, which is usually caused by poor oral hygiene.

Gingivectomy also removes excess gingival tissue (gingival hyperplasia), which is usually due to hereditary or drug-induced causes.

Description
A gingivectomy is usually performed by a dentist who specializes in the treatment of gum disease (periodontist). The periodontist starts by numbing the gums with a substance on an applicator so that the injection of the local anesthetic into the gums will be less painful. Once the gums are numbed, the periodontist cuts away the excess gum tissue using a scalpel or a laser.

After the gum tissue has been trimmed, the periodontist applies a puttylike substance (packing) over the gum line to prevent discomfort while eating and to allow new tissue to grow. The packing usually stays in place for about a week.

Prognosis

The prognosis for gingivectomy in treating gum disease (gingivitis) and gingival overgrowth (gingival hyperplasia) is good. It is important that the individual be committed to good dental care habits after the procedure in order to maintain the positive results.

Specialists

- Dentist

Work Restrictions / Accommodations

The individual who has been treated for gingivitis may need to use a lavatory for brushing and flossing his or her teeth after lunch and after snacks.

Comorbid Conditions

Comorbid conditions that might influence the length of disability after gingivectomy include medically compromising conditions, such as diabetes mellitus and human immunodeficiency virus (HIV) infection.

Also, individuals on medications that cause dry mouth are at higher risk for bacterial infections.

Procedure Complications

As with most surgical problems, infection and hemorrhage are possible complications.

Factors Influencing Duration

Most individuals should be able to return to work soon after a gingivectomy is performed, though they may need a follow-up visit with the dentist or periodontist about a week later to remove the packing.

Length of Disability

Length of disability varies depending on complications from the procedure and the level of physical demand of the individual's job.

Duration in Days

Job Classification	Minimum	Optimum	Maximum
Any work	1	3	7

References

Gingivectomy for Gum Disease. Healthwise, Incorporated. 01 Jan 2000. 19 Jan 2001 <http://www.healthynetwork.com/kbase/topic/detail/surgical/hw146210/detail.htm>.

Hasan, Asad. Oracare Dental. Oracare Dental, Inc. 10 Jun 2000. 6 Feb 2001 <http://www.oracare-dental.com/gum_disease.htm>.

Gingivitis

Other names / synonyms: Gingivostomatitis, Hyperplastic Gingivitis, Ulcerative Gingivitis
523.0, 523.1, 523.2, 523.9

Definition

Gingivitis is an inflammation of the soft gum tissue (gingiva). It is the mildest stage of gum disease. It is a common condition, and it is estimated that at least half of Americans of all ages develop the problem at some time.

Typically, gingivitis is painless and reversible with a regimen that includes daily tooth brushing, flossing, and regular dental checkups that include cleanings. Left untreated, however, gingivitis can lead to serious infection of the tissue that surrounds and supports the teeth, ultimately damaging the periodontal ligaments, the bone that surrounds the teeth, and the gums.

Gingivitis is most often caused by the bacteria found in plaque. Plaque, the sticky material that develops on the exposed surfaces of the teeth, is composed of mucus, food debris, saliva, and bacteria. When not removed, plaque mineralizes into a hard deposit called calculus (tartar) that becomes trapped at the base of the tooth. Plaque and calculus cause mechanical irritation and inflammation of the gingiva. Bacteria, and the toxins produced by the bacteria, cause the gums to become infected, swollen, and tender.

Other causes of gingivitis include injury to the tissue from improper brushing and flossing techniques, ill-fitting dentures, vitamin C deficiency (scurvy), dry mouth (as a side effect of some medications),

generalized inflammation of the mouth (stomatitis), overgrowth (hyperplasia) of gum tissue due to long-term use of some medications (such as Dilantin), glandular disorders (including thyroid disorders), exposure to heavy metals (e.g., lead), complications during pregnancy, diabetes, misaligned teeth, rough filling edges, and mouth appliances that irritate the gums, and blood diseases (such as leukemia).

Changes in hormones during pregnancy, menstruation, puberty, and menopause and taking oral contraceptives can make the gum tissues more susceptible to inflammation.

Diagnosis

History: The first sign of gingivitis is gums that bleed when the teeth are brushed; it will appears on the individual's toothbrush even with gentle brushing. In contrast to healthy gums that are coral pink and firm, unhealthy gingival tissue looks infected and is inflamed, swollen, dark red, and recedes from the teeth. Symptomatic individuals may also present with a bad taste in their mouth or have bad breath (halitosis).

Physical exam: When the dentist examines the individual's mouth and teeth, soft, swollen, shiny, red-purple gingiva are seen. Deposits of plaque may be visible at the base of the teeth and gums. There may be also sores in the mouth. Gums will usually be pain free or mildly tender when touched.

Tests: Although no further testing is usually necessary for diagnosis of gingivitis, dental x-rays (radiographs) may be ordered to determine whether there has been spread of inflammation to supporting structures of the teeth (periodontitis).

Treatment

The goal of treatment is to reduce gingival inflammation.

First, the teeth are cleaned thoroughly by the dentist or dental hygienist. This may involve using various instruments or devices to loosen and remove deposits from the teeth (scaling).

A meticulous regime of oral hygiene must be initiated thereafter. Professional tooth cleaning, in addition to frequent, careful brushing and flossing, will be recommended twice per year, or more frequently for severe cases. Antibacterial mouth rinses or other aids may also be recommended.

Repair or replacement of dental and/or orthodontic appliances or misaligned teeth may be recommended.

Systemic illnesses or other conditions should be treated and monitored.

Prognosis

Most individuals see a dramatic improvement (decrease in bleeding and tenderness) in their gums within a few weeks after the professional dental cleaning and the institution of careful, at-home, oral hygiene. Strict, lifelong oral hygiene must be maintained or gingivitis will recur.

Differential Diagnosis

Gingivitis may be a warning sign of a systemic disorder, such as primary herpes simplex, hypovitaminosis, vitamin C deficiency, an allergic reaction, diabetes mellitus, leukemia, eating disorders, or a debilitating disease (e.g., AIDS).

Specialists

- Dentist

Work Restrictions / Accommodations

Most individuals benefit by having access to a lavatory where they can brush and floss their teeth after lunch and after snacks.

Comorbid Conditions

Comorbid conditions that might influence the length of disability after treatment for gingivitis include medically compromising conditions, such as diabetes mellitus and human immunodeficiency virus (HIV) infection. Also, individuals taking medications that cause dry mouth are at higher risk for bacterial infections.

Complications

Gingivitis affects only gum tissue. If left untreated, the bacteria causing the inflammation will eventually attack other tissues. This may lead to more serious dental disease, such as periodontitis, that will permanently damage the supporting structures of the teeth.

Individuals with some heart conditions such as valvular disease, atrial fibrillation, or foreign bodies are at risk for bacterial endocarditis if treatment for gingivitis is begun without prophylactic antibiotic therapy.

Factors Influencing Duration

Length of disability may be influenced by the extent of the disease, the individual's response to treatment, and the development of complications. Most individuals require little or no recuperation time.

Length of Disability

No disability is expected.

Failure to Recover

If an individual fails to recover within the maximum duration expectancy period, the reader may wish to reference the following questions to assist in better understanding the specifics of an individual's medical case.

Regarding diagnosis:

- Has the individual started a good dental hygiene program including proper brushing, flossing and regular dental checkups?
- Does the individual get their teeth cleaned on a regular basis?
- Has the individual noticed bleeding when brushing their teeth?
- Do the gums appear pink and firm or are they swollen, dark red and receding from the teeth?
- Does the individual have bad breath?
- Were the individual's gums injured?
- Does the individual have a Vitamin C deficiency, dry mouth or stomatitis?
- Do they have overgrowth of the gum tissue as a side effect of certain medications?
- Has the individual been exposed to heavy metals? Is the individual pregnant?
- Does the individual have leukemia?
- Was the diagnosis confirmed with a dental exam?

Regarding treatment:
- Has the individual seen their dentist for an exam and cleaning?
- Was the individual trained in a meticulous oral hygiene program? Do they follow it?
- If the cause is faulty dental appliances, have they been repaired or replaced?

Regarding prognosis:
- Does the individual have any comorbid conditions such as diabetes, or HIV infection that could impact recovery or prognosis?
- Does the individual have a good understanding of the importance of preventing periodontal disease?

References

Gingivitis. HealthCentral.com Inc. 01 Jan 1999. 19 Jan 2001 <http://www.healthcentralsympatico.com/mhc/top/001056.cfm>.

MD Consult L.L.C. - Gingivitis. Clinical Reference Systems 2000. 01 Jan 2000. 19 Jan 2001 <http://home.mdconsult.com/ >.

Glaucoma, Acute (Angle-Closure)
365, 365.20, 365.21, 365.22, 365.23, 365.24

Definition

Glaucoma is a disease that damages optic nerves because of elevated pressure within the eye (intraocular pressure). Acute (angle-closure) glaucoma occurs in individuals with abnormal eye structures that trap fluid behind the colored portion of the eye (iris) and prevents proper drainage. When the fluid is unable to circulate properly, it cannot exit the eye through natural channels and begins to build pressure much as water does when trapped behind a dam. With angle-closure glaucoma, this blockage may cause rapid rise in intraocular pressure.

While other types of glaucoma may exist for years without detection, the acute form of the disease may manifest as an emergency due to sudden onset. If not treated promptly, acute glaucoma may cause permanent vision loss. The acute closed angle variety of glaucoma occurs in about 10% of all US glaucoma cases. It is more common in older age groups, since the aging process may cause the lens of the eye to thicken and block normal flow of fluids.

Diagnosis

History: Individual may complain of headache, blurred vision with halos around lights, and a red painful eye. Pain may be severe and accompanied by nausea and vomiting.

Physical exam: A red eye with a dilated pupil may be detected during physical examination.

Tests: Intraocular pressure may be quite high after measurement (tonometry). Examination of the interior eye structure using a specialized contact lens (gonioscopy) helps identify possible structural defects creating blockages of the eye's fluids.

Treatment

In an acute attack, oral and/or intravenous medication such as beta blockers may be used to lower eye pressure. When the eye has stabilized, laser incision of the iris (iridotomy) or removal of part of the iris (iridectomy) is performed. This usually opens drainage systems and prevents any further attacks. Acute glaucoma often develops later in the unaffected eye, which may also be treated as a precautionary measure.

Prognosis

Untreated acute glaucoma may result in severe and permanent visual loss within 2 to 5 days of onset of symptoms. If treatment is timely, a laser iridectomy or other appropriate procedures may cure or alleviate the condition.

Differential Diagnosis

Inflammation of the iris (uveitis), conjunctivitis, and corneal disorders exhibit similar symptoms.

Specialists

- Ophthalmologist

Work Restrictions / Accommodations

If visual acuity is a job requirement, permanent vision damage may prevent or hinder performance of previous duties. In cases where vision loss has occurred, larger computer screens or the availability of magnifying lenses may be helpful.

Comorbid Conditions

Clouding in the transparent front portion of the eye (cornea) sometimes accompanies onset of acute glaucoma, and may hamper tests needed to examine the eye's interior structure.

Complications

Structural defects within the eye may cause blockages of channels that drain fluids and result in acute angle-closure glaucoma. Inflammation in the eye (anterior uveitis) may cause an onset of the disease. Other conditions associated with the disease include dislocation of the eye's lens, emotional stress, diabetes, and use of certain antihistamines, antidepressants, or other drugs. Trapped fluid (ciliary block) may also result as a complication of eye surgery. Cataracts are also known to be associated with glaucoma.

Factors Influencing Duration

Length of disability depends on the extent of damage caused by the condition, the severity of the attack, promptness of treatment, and the individual's response to treatment.

Length of Disability

Physical disability may be limited, but visual loss may be persistent or permanent. Permanent damage may impair the individual's ability to perform tasks requiring visual acuity.

Medical treatment.

Duration in Days

Job Classification	Minimum	Optimum	Maximum
Sedentary work	1	2	3
Light work	1	2	3
Medium work	1	2	3
Heavy work	1	2	3
Very Heavy work	1	2	3

Laser treatment (laser iridectomy)

Duration in Days

Job Classification	Minimum	Optimum	Maximum
Sedentary work	1	2	3
Light work	2	3	7
Medium work	3	7	14
Heavy work	3	7	14
Very Heavy work	3	7	14

Surgical treatment (open iridectomy)

Duration in Days

Job Classification	Minimum	Optimum	Maximum
Sedentary work	7	9	14
Light work	7	9	14
Medium work	14	21	28
Heavy work	14	21	28
Very Heavy work	14	21	28

Failure to Recover

If an individual fails to recover within the maximum duration expectancy period, the reader may wish to reference the following questions to assist in better understanding the specifics of an individual's medical case.

Regarding diagnosis:

- Have conditions with similar symptoms such as, uveitis, conjunctivitis, or corneal disorders, been ruled out?
- Has diagnosis of acute (angle-closure) glaucoma been confirmed?
- Has individual's eye been tested thoroughly for presence of structural defects that could be causing the condition?
- Does individual have an underlying condition such as, anterior uveitis, dislocation of the eye's lens, emotional stress, diabetes, cataracts, and use of certain antihistamines, antidepressants or other drugs, or trapped fluid (ciliary block) that may contribute to the condition or impact recovery?
- Are underlying conditions receiving appropriate treatment?

Regarding treatment:

- Has individual received laser surgery or other appropriate treatment to encourage proper drainage of fluids that might be trapped within the eye?
- Has individual received oral and/or intravenous medication such as beta-blockers to lower eye pressure?
- Has the other eye been treated as a precautionary measure?
- Has individual been taking medication (antihistamines, antidepressants, and certain other drugs) that may contribute to onset of the disease?
- Are alternative medications available that would be just as effective?
- Has individual been under increased emotional stress recently?
- Has individual been instructed in stress reduction techniques?
- Is age a factor in the severity of the condition?

Regarding prognosis:

- Was treatment given promptly (within 2 to 5 days) after onset of the disease?
- Have underlying conditions that may contribute to this disease been identified and properly addressed? Are underlying conditions responding to treatment?

References

"Chapter 100. Glaucoma." Merck Manual of Diagnosis and Therapy, 17th ed. Beers, Mark H., and Robert Berkow, MD, eds. Whitehouse Station, NJ: Merck & Co. Inc., 1999. 25 June 2000 <http://www.merck.com/pubs/mmanual/section8/chapter100/100c.htm>.

Glaucoma, Chronic (Open-Angle)

Other names / synonyms: Simple Glaucoma

365, 365.01, 365.1, 365.11, 365.15

Definition

Chronic glaucoma occurs when fluids (aqueous humor) trapped within the eye fail to drain properly, typically causing a gradual build-up of pressure (intraocular pressure). Small blood vessels eventually collapse and cut off supplies of nutrients and oxygen to the retina and optic nerve. As retinal cells and nerve fibers die, the field of vision progressively narrows until the individual can see only straight ahead (tunnel vision). If untreated, the disease can cause total blindness.

The aging process often contributes to development of chronic glaucoma when cells necessary to maintain proper drainage channels in the eye begin to deteriorate and fluids become trapped. Other risk factors are associated with genetic defects, such as a propensity to form proteins that clog drainage channels or abnormal tissue development that creates blockages. Abnormal brain chemicals also may be released, which cause optic nerve fibers to die. Glaucoma is thought to affect about 3 million US citizens at any given time.

Diagnosis

History: Glaucoma progresses gradually. The disease usually has no symptoms until optic nerve fibers are damaged and the individual's field of vision begins to decrease. Elevated intraocular pressure sometimes, but not always, indicates presence of the disease.

Physical exam: The exam of the retina may show characteristic changes in the optic nerve, but the disease by that time probably has created permanent damage.

Tests: Measuring the pressure inside the eye (tonometry) at one time was thought to establish the diagnosis, but now is considered to be only one tool in the attempt to identify the disease. Individuals with low intraocular pressure may have glaucoma, just as individuals with high intraocular pressure may have no sign of the disease. A test of visual fields also helps determine whether glaucoma is present. The type of glaucoma is established through use of a specialized contact lens for examining the eye's interior to rule out structural defects (gonioscopy). Inadequate drainage of the eye's fluids in the absence of obvious blockages is considered to be open-angle glaucoma.

Treatment

In chronic open-angle glaucoma, medication may be used to decrease pressure within the eye, by either enhancing outflow of fluid or inhibiting the formation of fluid.

Surgery is increasingly becoming an option for improving drainage of fluid out of the eye. A trabeculectomy involves surgical removal of part of the fluid drainage system, while a laser is used in a trabeculoplasty to burn off part of the system to encourage increased fluid outflow. Incisions are made into the drainage system to relieve pressure in a trabeculotomy.

Loss of vision can be prevented only if glaucoma is detected in its early stages. To prevent permanent damage, early diagnosis is crucial. Regular eye examinations are recommended, particularly for individuals of ages 40 or older. Regular testing also is important for individuals considered at higher risk for glaucoma, including those with a family history of the disease.

Prognosis

With early diagnosis and treatment, useful vision is preserved for life in most cases. Surgical procedures that open or relieve pressure on the eye's fluid drainage systems (trabeculectomy, trabeculoplasty, trabeculotomy) are successful in the short term more than 80% of the time in lowering eye pressure and improving vision. However, surgical procedures are not a permanent solution and many individuals eventually will need re-treatment.

Without treatment, the optic nerve will continually be damaged and the individual's field of vision will decrease. Untreated chronic glaucoma that begins at middle age may cause complete blindness by age sixty-five.

Differential Diagnosis

Other possibilities are narrow-angle glaucoma and secondary glaucoma (from trauma, inflammation, or complications of eye surgery).

Specialists

- Ophthalmologist

Work Restrictions / Accommodations

If visual acuity is a job requirement, glaucoma that has created permanent damage may prevent the individual from performing certain tasks. Some individuals with permanent eye damage and limited field of vision may need to be assigned duties that do not require fully functioning side vision (peripheral vision). Work stations may also need adjustment to accommodate limited field of vision. Larger and glare-free computer screens along with lenses providing magnification may be needed.

Complementary and Alternative Therapies

Content is intended for awareness only. Treatments may or may not be effective. Scientific evidence may be lacking and some substances have potentially toxic effects. Dr. Presley Reed and the editors do not endorse the use of these therapies in the absence of consultation with a licensed medical professional.

THC - Systemic delta 9-tetrahydrocannabinol (or THC) lowers intraocular pressure in various glaucomas, but at the expense of significant decreases in blood pressure.

Comorbid Conditions

Eye inflammation and a tendency to form scar tissue decrease chances of successful surgery.

Complications

Glaucoma may be associated with certain medical conditions such as diabetes mellitus and extreme nearsightedness (myopia). The disease also might manifest as a complication of eye surgery.

Factors Influencing Duration

Length of disability depends on the extent of visual loss at the time treatment begins, the method of treatment, and the response to treatment.

Length of Disability

Physical disability may be limited, but visual loss may be persistent or permanent. Permanent damage may impair the individual's ability to perform tasks requiring visual acuity.

Medical treatment.

Duration in Days

Job Classification	Minimum	Optimum	Maximum
Sedentary work	1	1	3
Light work	1	1	3
Medium work	1	2	3
Heavy work	1	2	3
Very Heavy work	1	2	3

Trabeculoplasty.

Duration in Days

Job Classification	Minimum	Optimum	Maximum
Sedentary work	1	2	3
Light work	3	4	7
Medium work	3	4	7
Heavy work	7	9	14
Very Heavy work	7	9	14

Surgical treatment (trabeculectomy).

Duration in Days

Job Classification	Minimum	Optimum	Maximum
Sedentary work	3	9	14
Light work	3	9	14
Medium work	14	21	28
Heavy work	14	21	28
Very Heavy work	14	21	28

Failure to Recover

If an individual fails to recover within the maximum duration expectancy period, the reader may wish to reference the following questions to assist in better understanding the specifics of an individual's medical case.

Regarding diagnosis:

- Does individual notice a decrease in the field of vision (tunnel vision)?
- Did the physician note changes in the optic nerve when examining the eye with an ophthalmoscope?
- What is individual's age?
- Is there a family history of glaucoma?
- Has individual been thoroughly tested for signs of high and low intraocular pressure (individuals with low intraocular pressure may have glaucoma, just as individuals with high intraocular pressure may have no sign of the disease)?
- Is there a reduced field of vision?

Regarding treatment:

- Was glaucoma diagnosed in its early stages, or has it progressed? How far has it progressed?
- Does individual obtain regular eye examinations?
- Is individual over 40, or is there a family history of glaucoma, putting individual at higher risk for the disease?
- Is individual compliant with medications regimens used to decrease pressure within the eye, to enhance outflow of fluid, or to inhibit the formation of fluid?
- Would individual benefit from surgical intervention?

Regarding prognosis:

- Did diagnosis and treatment occur early in the disease process?
- What surgical procedure (trabeculectomy, trabeculoplasty, trabeculotomy) was required?
- Did surgical intervention treat the disease successfully?
- Have postsurgical complications developed, such as bleeding or infection?
- What is the treatment for the complication and what is the expected outcome of this treatment?
- Does individual require additional treatment?
- How significant is vision loss?
- How will this affect individual's activities of daily living?

References

Cassin, Barbara, et al. Dictionary of Eye Terminology, 3rd ed. Gainesville, FL: Triad Publishing Co, 1997.

Merritt, J.C., D.D. Perry, and D.N. Russell. "Topical Delta 9-tetrahydrocannabunol and Aqueous Dynamics in Glaucoma." Journal of Clinical Pharmacology 21 8-9 Suppl (1981): 467S-471S.

Glioma

Other names / synonyms: Brain Tumor, Oligodendroglioma
191.9, 192.8, M9450/3

Definition

Gliomas are brain tumors, of unknown origin, and are associated with specific types of brain cells, eg, astrocytes, oligodendrocytes, ependymal cells, and microglial cells.

The most common gliomas are tumors affecting astrocytes (astrocytomas). Tumors affecting oligodendrocytes (oligodendrogliomas) make up only 5-15% of all gliomas. Other types of gliomas are rare in adults. Gliomas can also be "mixed," arising from more than one type of cell.

Gliomas can arise in any area within the brain (temporal, frontal, occipital, parietal, brainstem), and their location will dictate the symptoms that present.

Gliomas can occur at any stage in life. Depending upon the characteristics of the tumor (tumor grade), it may be benign or rapidly fatal. Typically, brain tumors are graded on a scale of 1 to 4 as to their malignancy potential. Low-grade tumors (Grades 1 and 2) grow more slowly and are associated with longer survival times, while individuals with high-grade tumors (Grades 3 and 4) are typically given a poorer prognosis.

Gliomas are the most common type of brain tumor and account for approximately 45-60% of all intracranial tumors. About 10,000 new cases of gliomas are reported per year in the US. Astrocytomas are slightly more common in whites than in blacks, and in males than females. Oligodendrogliomas are slightly more common in males than in females.

Diagnosis

History: The individual may report a history of a seizure. The individual may also complain of headache, gastrointestinal upset, personality changes, slowing of psychomotor function, and focal symptoms. Headache is usually worse upon awakening early in the morning. Gastrointestinal symptoms include loss of appetite, queasiness, nausea, and occasional vomiting. Changes in intellectual capacity (cognitive), behavior, or personality may also be reported by the individual or his or her family.

Focal symptoms depend upon the general area of the brain where the tumor is located: frontal, parietal, temporal, or occipital. Symptoms associated with a frontal tumor include mild mental slowing, mood changes or dementia, arm or leg weakness, difficulty with speech, or the individual may essentially be without symptoms. Symptoms of a parietal tumor include sensory and perceptual changes, loss of spatial orientation, and the inability to recognize once familiar objects or persons. Temporal tumors can cause epilepsy, affect memory, may cause auditory hallucinations, changes in verbal ability, or aggressive behavior. Finally, occipital tumors may cause visual disturbances, even blindness.

Physical exam: Depending upon the type, size, and location of the tumor, the physical or neurologic examination may be normal or reveal subtle changes in the above areas.

Tests: X-rays are performed to confirm a tumor mass. CT scan and/or MRI are used to better visualize the type and extent of tumor growth. A tumor biopsy may be performed to establish a diagnosis. Cerebrospinal fluid may be drawn and used to diagnose and follow the individual's response to therapy.

Treatment

Tumors are often more extensive than can be seen on scans and by the naked eye. Because of this, it is not possible to cure a malignant primary brain tumor by surgery alone. Extensive surgery may help relieve symptoms in some cases, but runs a high risk of causing damage to normal brain tissue. Therefore, the course of treatment depends upon the type, location, and grade of the tumor. Generally, however, while treatment can consist of a combination of surgery (craniotomy with internal decompression or with stereotactic volumetric reduction), and/or chemotherapy (eg, nitrosoureas alkylating agents, miscellaneous alkylating agents, and miscellaneous antineoplastics), stereotactic radiosurgery or radiotherapy is now felt to be the treatment of choice. This allows a narrow beam of radiation to specifically target only the glioma, sparing the normal brain from significant exposure. Astrocytomas are usually treated with a combination of chemotherapy and radiotherapy while oligodendrogliomas can be treated with surgery, radiotherapy, and chemotherapy. High-grade gliomas, regardless of type, may require surgery to reduce the size and symptoms associated with the tumor (palliative treatment).

Prognosis

Outcome is dependent on the type of tumor, tumor location, and the stage of disease. Certain gliomas can be removed surgically and have a good prognosis. Certain slow-growing tumors such as gangliogliomas, dysembryoplastic neuroepithelial tumors (DNETs), and pilocytic astrocytomas can be cured with surgical removal. Oligodendrogliomas can be removed surgically only if they are in nonessential brain areas; the survival rate for these individuals is 10 to 15 years. These tumors, however, tend to recur.

With treatment (surgical removal or reduction, radiotherapy, chemotherapy, or a combination), individuals with low-grade oligodendrogliomas survive an average of 9 years, while those with high-grade tumors survive an average of 2 years. Individuals with low-grade astrocytomas (grades 1 and 2) have a median survival time of 7.5 years. Individuals with grade 2 astrocytoma have a 5-year survival rate of about 34% without treatment, and about 70% with radiation therapy, and a median survival time of 4 years. Individuals with grade 3 astrocytoma have a median survival time of 18 months with treatment (radiation plus chemotherapy). Individuals with grade 4 astrocytoma have a median survival time of 17 weeks without treatment, 30 weeks with radiation, and 37 weeks with surgical removal of most of the tumor plus radiation.

Differential Diagnosis

Differential diagnoses include benign tumor of the brain, brain abscess, stroke, aneurysm, inflammation of the brain and its lining (meningoencephalitis), metabolic dysfunction, hydrocephalus, hematoma, brain abscess, cavernous sinus syndrome, cluster headache, head injury, intracranial hemorrhage, multiple sclerosis, and Tolosa-Hunt syndrome.

Specialists

- Neurologist
- Neurosurgeon
- Oncologist

Work Restrictions / Accommodations

Impairment in intellectual function, physical capacity, and vision may necessitate a change of job duties. Additionally, neuromuscular impairment may necessitate a change to sedentary duties. Extended work leave for treatment and recuperation will be required; this will need to be evaluated on a case-by-case basis.

Complementary and Alternative Therapies

Content is intended for awareness only. Treatments may or may not be effective. Scientific evidence may be lacking and some substances have potentially toxic effects. Dr. Presley Reed and the editors do not endorse the use of these therapies in the absence of consultation with a licensed medical professional.

Hydrazine sulfate - Has been used as an antitumor agent and said to act as a treatment for body wasting (cachexia) associated with advanced cancer.

Coenzyme Q10 - Analogs of this substance may suppress cancer growth directly.

Cancell/Entelev - Said to slow or inhibit cancer cell formation.

Comorbid Conditions

Any immunosuppressive condition may influence length of disability.

Complications

Complications associated with gliomas include neurological impairment, seizure, bleeding, and stroke. Up to 30% of individuals with malignant brain tumors develop blood clots (deep venous thrombosis).

Factors Influencing Duration

Factors influencing the length of disability include the type and grade of the tumor, location of the tumor, the age of the individual at diagnosis, the type and efficacy of treatment (for example, the completeness of removal or resection), and the development of complications.

Length of Disability

Duration depends on size, site, and stage. Disability may be permanent.

Medical or surgical treatment.

Duration in Days

Job Classification	Minimum	Optimum	Maximum
Any work	42	182	Indefinite

Failure to Recover

If an individual fails to recover within the maximum duration expectancy period, the reader may wish to reference the following questions to assist in better understanding the specifics of an individual's medical case.

Regarding diagnosis:

- Has diagnosis of glioma been confirmed?
- Has individual experienced any complications related to the glioma, such as neurological impairment, seizure, bleeding, stroke or deep venous thrombosis?

Regarding treatment:

- What is the type, location and grade of the tumor?
- Was surgical removal of all or part of the tumor possible?
- Were radiation and/or chemotherapy prescribed?
- Regardless of the type, could surgery be done to reduce the size and symptoms associated with the tumor (palliative treatment)?

Regarding prognosis:

- What was response to treatment?
- Based on known factors, what is the prognosis?
- Would individual benefit from a second opinion?
- Is the individual experiencing neurological deficits?
- Does impairment in intellectual function or neuromuscular impairment necessitate a change in occupational duties?
- Is individual realistic about prognosis?
- Would individual/family benefit from counseling or enrollment in a support group?

References

"CNS Neoplasms: Intracranial Neoplasms (Brain Tumors)." Merck Manual of Diagnosis and Therapy, 17th ed. Beers, Mark H., and Robert Berkow, MD, eds. Whitehouse Station, NJ: Merck & Co. Inc., 1999. 02 Jan 2001 <http://www.merck.com/pubs/mmanual/section14/chapter177/177b.htm>.

Glioma. Boston Neurosurgery. 2000. 4 Jan 2001 <http://www.prattneurosurgery.com/glioma.htm>.

Glomerulonephritis, Acute

Other names / synonyms: Acute Poststreptococcal Glomerulonephritis, Glomerular Disease, Infectious Glomerulonephritis, Postinfectious Glomerulonephritis

Definition

Acute glomerulonephritis is a condition where the structures in the kidney that filter waste and protein from the blood (glomeruli) become inflamed and unable to function properly. There are two forms of acute glomerulonephritis and these are postinfectious glomerulonephritis and infectious glomerulonephritis. Postinfectious glomerulonephritis typically occurs about 21 days following a respiratory or skin infection with a certain type of bacteria (streptococcus). Infectious glomerulonephritis occurs during or within a few days of streptococcal infection.

Of the two types, postinfectious glomerulonephritis (also called acute poststreptococcal glomerulonephritis) is the most common. A common risk factor for development of postinfectious glomerulonephritis is a skin infection that is caused by streptococcal bacteria (impetigo). Other infectious diseases that are risk factors for either infectious or postinfectious glomerulonephritis include syphilis, malaria, typhoid fever, mononucleosis, mumps, measles, hepatitis, Berger's nephropathy, systemic lupus erythematosus, and Henoch-Schönlein purpura.

Acute glomerulonephritis may occur at any age although it is more rare in adults.

There has been a significant decline in the incidence of acute glomerulonephritis in developed countries such as the United States and in Europe, and cases are reported only sporadically. The reasons for declining incidence rates are probably related to improved nutritional status in these countries and more liberal use of antibiotics. Developing countries, such as in Africa and the Caribbean, appear to have higher potential for development of streptococcal infections and the incidence of acute glomerulonephritis is proportionally higher in these areas.

Diagnosis

History: Individuals may report a recent streptococcal or viral illness. In some cases, symptoms are mild and the individual may report only vague weakness, loss of appetite (anorexia), and lethargy. In more severe cases, they may complain of cola- or tea-colored urine, fever, chills, weakness, headache, blurred vision (reduced visual acuity), abdominal or flank pain, reduced or no urine output (oliguria or anuria, respectively) for several days, nausea, and vomiting.

Physical exam: Examination usually reveals generalized swelling (edema) particularly around the face and eyes (periorbital), fluid in the abdomen (ascites), fluid in the lungs (pulmonary edema) and chest cavity (pleural effusion), and elevated blood pressure (hypertension).

Tests: Visual examination of the urine usually provides enough information necessary for a definitive diagnosis of acute glomerulonephritis. The urine, which may be scanty in amount, will typically be dark, smoky or cola-colored, or red or brown in hue. There is usually a persistent and excessive foam in the specimen. Throat or skin cultures may reveal group A streptococci. A laboratory test of the urine (urinalysis) may show that the urine is acidic (low pH) and has mid- to high-normal range values for specific gravity. Other laboratory tests may include an analysis of how well the kidneys are working (renal function test) and specific blood tests for serum urea nitrogen, creatinine, hyaluronidase, deoxyribonuclease B, and serum complement. The number of red blood cells (hematocrit) and the amount of hemoglobin in the blood can be measured using a complete blood count (CBC) test.

Treatment

Treatment for acute glomerulonephritis is dependent upon the underlying cause of the disease and, in most cases, it is designed to relieve symptoms and reduce the potential for complications. Antibiotic therapy is used to treat the infection that resulted in acute glomerulonephritis (e.g., penicillin is given for streptococcal bacteria). Fluid retention (edema) and high blood pressure (hypertension) are treated with drugs that promote fluid loss (diuretics) and lower blood pressure (angiotensin converting enzyme (ACE) inhibitors). Other drug treatments may include anti-inflammatory drugs (corticosteroids), drugs that decrease the response of the immune system (immunosuppressive agents or antiplatelet agents), and drugs that prevent clotting (anticoagulants). Usually, dietary salt (sodium) and water will be restricted.

Prognosis

The predicted outcome is extremely variable and there is very little information from any clinical study regarding treatment effects that is not contradicted by the results from other published studies. Generally, adults have a worse prognosis for acute glomerulonephritis than do young individuals. However, drug treatments are usually effective and very few individuals die as a result of fluid in the lungs (pulmonary edema), brain inflammation (hypertensive encephalopathy), or uncontrolled infection. Approximately 1% of individuals with acute glomerulonephritis develop kidney damage that is severe enough to cause progressive and irreversible renal failure. Individuals who lose kidney function will have to be treated on an ongoing basis with dialysis or have surgical transplantation of a donor kidney.

Differential Diagnosis

Conditions that present with symptoms similar to acute glomerulonephritis include chronic renal failure, allergic interstitial nephritis, atheroembolism, hemolytic uremic syndrome, thrombotic thrombocytopenia purpura (TTP), endocarditis, cryoglobulinemia, vasculitis, Goodpasture's syndrome, acute pancreatitis, and system infection (sepsis).

Specialists

- Internist
- Nephrologist

Work Restrictions / Accommodations

Rest is an important part of recovery from acute glomerulonephritis. Bed rest followed by a period of very limited activity may continue for several weeks to months. Individuals who are able to return to work will be very limited in their capacity to perform physical labor and they may have to be reassigned to a desk job for a period of time. If kidney dialysis is required, the individual may require an extended leave of absence or a switch to part-time or flex-time to accommodate their treatment schedule. Individuals who are receiving dialysis treatments should be assigned more sedentary duties.

Comorbid Conditions

Existing conditions that may impact an individual's ability to recover and further lengthen disability include other kidney diseases that affect function of the glomeruli (e.g., rapidly progressive nephritic syndrome; asymptomatic glomerulopathy; hematuria; chronic glomerular syndrome), or diseases that affect the cardiovascular system (e.g., congestive heart failure; hypertension), immune system (e.g., systemic lupus erythematosus or SLE), or metabolic state (e.g., diabetes mellitus; thyrotoxicosis).

Complications

Complications of acute glomerulonephritis include elevated blood pressure (hypertension), urinary tract or kidney infection (pyelonephritis), inflammation of the brain tissue (hypertensive encephalopathy), and decreased pumping ability of the heart (congestive heart failure). Approximately 30% of adult individuals who develop acute glomerulonephritis will progress to a condition where their kidneys are nonfunctional (chronic renal failure).

Factors Influencing Duration

Factors that might influence disability include the severity of the disease symptoms, the progression of the disease, and the individual's response to treatment for the underlying cause. Advanced age may also further lengthen disability, as older individuals are slower to recover and are more susceptible to recurrent infection. Because acute glomerulonephritis requires extensive bed rest and inactivity for proper recovery, the individual's mental health is of primary importance.

Length of Disability

Professional guidance may be necessary to minimize depression and anxiety about the condition.

Duration in Days

Job Classification	Minimum	Optimum	Maximum
Sedentary work	14	28	42
Light work	14	28	42
Medium work	14	28	42
Heavy work	28	42	42
Very Heavy work	28	42	42

Failure to Recover

If an individual fails to recover within the maximum duration expectancy period, the reader may wish to reference the following questions to assist in better understanding the specifics of an individual's medical case.

Regarding diagnosis:
- Has diagnosis of acute glomerulonephritis been confirmed?
- Has individual experienced any complications related to the glomerulonephritis?
- Does individual have an underlying condition that may impact recovery? Is this condition receiving appropriate treatment?

Regarding treatment:
- Is individual taking medication as prescribed?
- Is individual compliant with dietary modifications?
- Is individual receiving adequate rest for optimal recovery?

Regarding prognosis:
- Do symptoms persist despite treatment?
- Did individual experience residual kidney impairment?
- Was hypertension effectively resolved?
- Is additional drug therapy warranted?
- Did individual experience permanent kidney damage?
- Is dialysis required?
- Is individual a candidate for a kidney transplant?
- Is individual on local/national transplant lists?

References

Chen, M.F. "Recent Advances in the Prophylaxis and Treatment of Chronic Glomerulonephritis with Combined TCM and WM." Journal of Traditional Chinese Medicine 3 2 (1983): 151-162.

Holub, T.I. "The Effect of Reflexotherapy on the Hemostatic System of Patients with Glomerulonephritis." Likarska Sprava 3 (1999): 157-161.

LeMone, P., and K.M. Burke. Medical-Surgical Nursing. Upper Saddle River, NJ: Prentice Hall Health, 2000.

Llach, F. Clinical Nephrology. Boston: Little, Brown and Company, 1993.

Glomerulonephritis, Chronic

Other names / synonyms: Chronic Diffuse Glomerulonephritis, Chronic Glomerular Syndrome, Chronic Progressive Glomerular Syndrome

582

Definition

Chronic glomerulonephritis is a condition where the structures in the kidney that filter waste and protein from the blood (glomeruli) slowly and progressively become unable to function properly. As the glomeruli are destroyed, the kidneys shrink and become severely contracted. Fibrous and scar tissue eventually replaces functional kidney tissue although the rate of destruction varies between individuals. Many years may pass before the affected individual starts to experience the symptoms of kidney (renal) failure.

Chronic glomerulonephritis actually refers to a diverse category of diseases all of which have varying causes. There are a number of different forms of glomerulonephritis (including acute glomerulonephritis, membranoproliferative glomerulonephritis, rapidly progressive glomerulonephritis, idiopathic membranous glomerulonephritis, and IgA nephropathy) any of which can progress to chronic glomerulonephritis.

Diseases that are risk factors for acute glomerulonephritis (which, as indicated, may progress to chronic glomerulonephritis) include syphilis, malaria, typhoid fever, mononucleosis, mumps, measles, and Henoch-Schönlein purpura. Chronic glomerulonephritis may also develop secondarily to other diseases including diabetes mellitus, systemic lupus erythematosus, hepatitis C, and acquired immunodeficiency syndrome (AIDS).

Chronic glomerulonephritis is rare and it affects only 4 out of every 100,000 individuals. Twenty to fifty percent of individuals with acute glomerulonephritis will eventually develop chronic glomerulonephritis. Approximately 25% of individuals with chronic glomerulonephritis have no prior history of kidney disease, and in these cases, the disorder first appears as chronic renal failure.

Diagnosis

History: Individuals with chronic glomerulonephritis may report a vague feeling of weakness or discomfort (malaise), increasing irritability and mental cloudiness, a metallic taste in the mouth, excretion of large amounts of urine (polyuria), excessive urination at night (nocturia), headache, dizziness, and digestive disturbances. If the disease has progressed, the individual may complain of breathing difficulties (dyspnea) and pain in the chest (angina).

Physical exam: Examination may reveal weight loss, fluid retention (edema), and most often, high blood pressure (hypertension). It is not uncommon for the individual with chronic glomerulonephritis to have nosebleeds, signs of blocked arteries (arteriosclerosis), an enlarged heart (cardiomegaly), and bleeding (hemorrhage) into the kidneys, lungs, eye tissue (retina), and brain (cerebrum). Physical examination of the back (fundus) of the eye may reveal blood vessel changes and edema of the optic discs.

Tests: A laboratory test of the urine (urinalysis) should be done to determine its specific gravity and protein content, and to determine if it contains white blood cells, kidney tubular cells, and hemoglobin. Blood tests should include a complete blood count (CBC) to test for low hemoglobin in the blood stream (anemia). High frequency sound waves (ultrasound) and computer-aided x-ray analysis (computerized tomography) may be used to visualize the kidneys. A small sample of tissue may be taken from the kidney (renal biopsy) for microscopic examination to verify diagnosis in those individuals who have no prior history of kidney disease.

Treatment

The initial step in treatment of chronic glomerulonephritis should include therapy for the underlying disease that precipitated the condition. Symptoms that occur as a result of chronic glomerulonephritis itself may be treated using various drug therapies. Fluid retention (edema) and high blood pressure (hypertension) are treated with drugs that promote fluid loss (diuretics) and lower blood pressure (angiotensin converting enzyme (ACE) inhibitors). Other drug treatments may include anti-inflammatory drugs (corticosteroids), drugs that decrease the response of the immune system (immunosuppressive agents), and drugs that prevent clotting (anticoagulants or antiplatelet agents). Usually, dietary salt (sodium) and water will be restricted. Kidney dialysis or transplantation may become necessary if the individual begins to develop progressive renal failure leading to end-stage renal disease.

Prognosis

Chronic glomerulonephritis is a gradual (insidious) disease that develops over an extended period of time (often as long as 30 years). The treatment outcome is dependent upon the cause and the severity of the high blood pressure (hypertension) and protein loss in the urine (proteinuria). Drug treatments may slow or stabilize this progression in some individuals. If left untreated, chronic glomerulonephritis will progress to irreversible end-stage renal failure. The individual will then develop massive infiltration of fluid into connective tissues of the body (anasarca) unless dialysis treatments are initiated. Very few individuals spontaneously survive this stage of the disease and enter remission. Without dialysis treatment or kidney transplantation, most individuals die within two years.

Differential Diagnosis

Conditions that present with symptoms similar to chronic glomerulonephritis include chronic renal failure, allergic interstitial nephritis, hemolytic uremic syndrome, thrombotic thrombocytopenia purpura (TTP), endocarditis, cryoglobulinemia, vasculitis, Goodpasture's syndrome, acute pancreatitis, and system infection (sepsis).

Specialists

- Internist
- Nephrologist

Work Restrictions / Accommodations

If kidney dialysis is required, individuals may require an extended leave of absence or a switch to part-time or flex-time to accommodate their treatment schedule. Individuals who are receiving dialysis treatments should be assigned more sedentary duties.

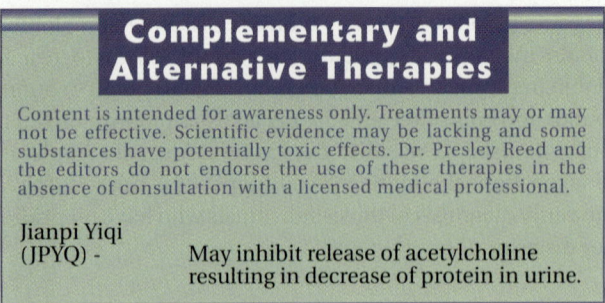

Complementary and Alternative Therapies

Content is intended for awareness only. Treatments may or may not be effective. Scientific evidence may be lacking and some substances have potentially toxic effects. Dr. Presley Reed and the editors do not endorse the use of these therapies in the absence of consultation with a licensed medical professional.

Jianpi Yiqi (JPYQ) - May inhibit release of acetylcholine resulting in decrease of protein in urine.

Comorbid Conditions

Existing conditions that may impact an individual's ability to recover and further lengthen disability include other kidney diseases that affect function of the glomeruli (e.g., rapidly progressive nephritic syndrome; asymptomatic glomerulopathy; hematuria; chronic glomerular syndrome), or diseases that affect the cardiovascular system (e.g., congestive heart failure; hypertension), immune system (e.g., systemic lupus erythematosus or SLE), or metabolic state (e.g., diabetes mellitus; thyrotoxicosis).

Complications

A primary complication of chronic glomerulonephritis is elevated blood pressure (hypertension). Other complications may include urinary tract or kidney infection (pyelonephritis), inflammation of the brain tissue (hypertensive encephalopathy), decreased pumping ability of the heart (congestive heart failure), and chronic kidney (renal) failure with progression to end-stage renal disease.

Factors Influencing Duration

Factors that might influence the length of disability include the individual's age and general health, the severity and extent of the disease at initial presentation, the development and persistence of complications, and the length of time the disease has been present.

Length of Disability

Duration depends on cause and on the job requirements. Individuals who are receiving dialysis may need to be reassigned to sedentary duties on the days of treatment. Disability may be permanent if the individual does not respond to drug treatments or if their condition progresses to end-stage renal failure.

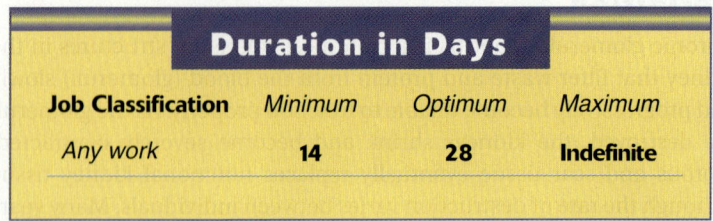

Duration in Days

Job Classification	Minimum	Optimum	Maximum
Any work	14	28	Indefinite

Failure to Recover

If an individual fails to recover within the maximum duration expectancy period, the reader may wish to reference the following questions to assist in better understanding the specifics of an individual's medical case.

Regarding diagnosis:

- Does the individual have any risk factors?
- What symptoms does the individual have?
- What were the findings on physical exam?
- Has the individual received appropriate testing to establish the diagnosis?
- Have conditions with similar symptoms been ruled out?

Regarding treatment:

- Has the underlying conditions responded to treatment?
- Has dialysis become necessary? Kidney transplant?
- Does the individual follow their dietary restrictions?

Regarding prognosis:

- Is the individual's employer able to accommodate any necessary restrictions?
- Does the individual have any of these conditions?
- Does the individual have any complications?

References

Deligiannis, A., et al. "Cardiac Effects of Exercise Rehabilitation in Hemodialysis Patients." International Journal of Cardiology 70 3 (1999): 253-266.

Llach, F. Clinical Nephrology. Boston: Little, Brown and Company, 1993.

Glomerulosclerosis

Other names / synonyms: Focal and Segmental Hyalinosis, Focal Glomerulosclerosis, Focal Sclerosis with Hyalinosis, Glomerular Sclerosis, Segmental Glomerulosclerosis, Segmental Hyalinosis

582, 582.1, 587

Definition

Glomerulosclerosis refers to deposits or scarring in the kidneys' tiny blood vessels (glomeruli). Glomeruli filter impurities from the blood, and then excrete them as urine.

Glomerulosclerosis may be the result of an underlying disease process including chronic liver disease (cirrhotic glomerulosclerosis), hardening of the arteries in the kidneys (renal arteriosclerosis), severe inflammation of the glomeruli (glomerulonephritis) with progressive kidney damage, and idiopathic nephrotic syndrome (focal glomerulosclerosis). Glomerulosclerosis can be associated with diabetes mellitus or a condition in which urine flows from the bladder backwards into the kidney (reflux nephropathy). High blood pressure (hypertension) or intravenous drug abuse may also cause glomerulosclerosis.

Mild glomerulosclerosis occurs normally with age. Renal function decreases 10% each decade after age 30; up to a 75% reduction in renal function may still be compatible with normal life. Focal glomerulosclerosis without a known cause primarily affects males. Blacks have a much higher risk of developing the disease than whites due to an increased incidence of uncontrolled and untreated hypertension.

Diagnosis

History: The main result of focal segmental glomerulosclerosis is "nephrotic syndrome," which causes about 10-15% of cases. This syndrome is a group of signs and symptoms that includes protein in the urine, low blood protein, and swelling due to fluid accumulation (edema). The urine may also contain fat visible under the microscope, and a rise in blood cholesterol. Individuals may experience symptoms including increased or decreased urine output, edema in the ankles or abdomen, blood in the urine (hematuria), foamy urine, unintentional weight gain, and poor appetite (anorexia).

Physical exam: The exam may reveal high blood pressure (hypertension). Signs of chronic renal failure and associated fluid overload may develop as the disorder progresses. Symptoms of this include nausea and vomiting, unintentional weight loss, general ill feeling (malaise), fatigue, headache, generalized itching (pruritus), increased or decreased urine output, nocturnal urination, early bruising or bleeding, decreased alertness, confusion, muscle twitching or cramps, decreased sensation in the hands or feet, excessive thirst, and seizures.

Tests: Excess protein in the urine (proteinuria) is a sign of glomerulosclerosis. However, since only 15% of individuals with proteinuria have glomerulosclerosis, microscopic examination of a kidney tissue sample extracted using a needle (renal biopsy) may be necessary; it may show scarring of parts of a glomerulus (focal) or of only some of the glomeruli (segmental). An immunofluorescence microscopy may show deposits of one of the glycoproteins that function as antibodies, immunoglobulin IgM.

Treatment

Scarred glomeruli cannot be repaired; treatment of this condition may be chronic and lifelong. The goal of treatment is to slow progression of the condition. Although the disorder seems to be immune-system related, and response to corticosteroid or immunosuppressive medications is inconsistent, these medications are often prescribed. Underlying diabetes and hypertension must be controlled, usually by medication such as ACE inhibitors. Liver transplant may be required for individuals with cirrhosis. Treatment of high blood cholesterol and triglyceride levels, also common with this disorder, may be recommended to reduce potential for developing atherosclerosis, and can be achieved with medication. To lighten the waste load on the kidneys, a low protein, low cholesterol, and low saturated fat diet is generally recommended; low-sodium diets may help control edema. Kidney dialysis or a kidney transplant may be necessary if renal failure develops.

Prognosis

The 10-year survival rate for mild glomerulosclerosis is 85-90%; it drops to 25-55% for individuals with nephrotic syndrome. Most individuals with glomerulosclerosis progress to kidney failure (end-stage renal disease), eventually requiring external cleansing of the blood (dialysis) or a kidney transplant within 15 years. Spontaneous remission occurs in fewer than 6% of individuals with glomerulosclerosis.

Differential Diagnosis

A condition with similar symptoms is acute nephritic syndrome.

Specialists

• Gastroenterologist	• Transplant Surgeon
• Nephrologist	• Urologist

Work Restrictions / Accommodations

Work restrictions or accommodations depend on the severity of the condition, underlying disease, treatment required, and the nature of the work responsibilities. An individual who has received the diagnosis of glomerulosclerosis and is under treatment to slow its progression may be able to work for years until kidney failure sets in.

Comorbid Conditions

Comorbid conditions include diabetes, hypertension, and AIDS.

Complications

Complications include nephrotic syndrome, chronic renal failure, end-stage renal disease, malnutrition, and enhanced susceptibility to infections.

Factors Influencing Duration

Progression of the condition and development of nephrotic syndrome will increase the length of disability.

Length of Disability

Disability may be permanent if the individual progresses to kidney failure and is either not a candidate for a transplant, or a donor kidney is not available. In that case, the need for frequent dialysis may make a regular work schedule impractical.

Medical treatment.

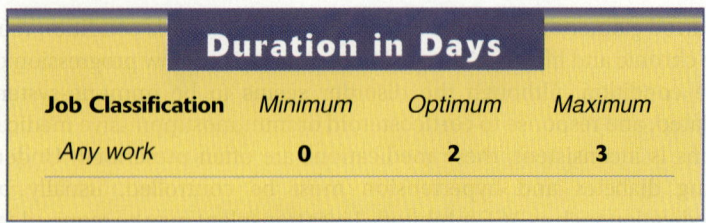

Job Classification	Minimum	Optimum	Maximum
Any work	0	2	3

Failure to Recover

If an individual fails to recover within the maximum duration expectancy period, the reader may wish to reference the following questions to assist in better understanding the specifics of an individual's medical case.

Regarding diagnosis:

- Does individual have diabetes mellitus or reflux nephropathy? High blood pressure (hypertension)?
- Does individual abuse intravenous drugs?
- Were signs of chronic renal failure present such as nausea and vomiting, unintentional weight loss, general ill feeling (malaise), fatigue, headache, generalized itching (pruritus), increased or decreased urine output, nocturnal urination, early bruising or bleeding, decreased alertness, confusion, muscle twitching or cramps, decreased sensation in the hands or feet, excessive thirst, and seizures?
- Was nephrotic syndrome with associated symptoms such as protein in the urine, low blood protein, and swelling due to fluid accumulation (edema) ruled out?
- Does individual experience increased or decreased urine output, edema in the ankles or abdomen, blood in the urine (hematuria), foamy urine, unintentional weight gain, and poor appetite (anorexia)?
- Was the diagnosis confirmed with a renal biopsy and immunofluorescence microscopy?

Regarding treatment:

- Was individual given a trial of corticosteroids or immunosuppressive medications? Were they helpful?
- If individual is diabetic or hypertensive, are these conditions under good control?
- Is individual on medications to control blood lipids, if needed?
- Is individual compliant with the dietary restrictions, i.e., low protein, low cholesterol, and low saturated fat diet?
- Was kidney dialysis necessary?
- Is a kidney transplant being considered?

Regarding prognosis:

- Does individual any underlying conditions such as diabetes, hypertension, or AIDS that may impact recovery?
- Have any complications developed such as nephrotic syndrome, chronic renal failure, end-stage renal disease, malnutrition, and enhanced susceptibility to infections?

References

"Focal Segmental Glomerulosclerosis." National Library of Medicine. 01 Jan 2000. 1 Jan 2001 <http://medlineplus.adam.com/ency/article/000478.htm>.

Korbet, S. "Clinical Picture and Outcome of Primary Focal Segmental Glomerulosclerosis." Nephrology Dialysis Transplantation 14 90003 (1999): 68-73.

Glycosuria

Other names / synonyms: Glucosuria

271.4, 791.5

Definition

Glycosuria is defined as abnormal levels of sugar (glucose) in the urine. It occurs when the amount of glucose in the blood exceeds the maximum amount that the kidneys can resorb.

Glycosuria may result when the pancreas does not produce enough insulin (diabetic glycosuria), too much starch or sugar is ingested (alimentary glycosuria), the endocrine glands (particularly the thyroid, ovaries, adrenal, or pituitary) are not functioning properly, or the kidneys have a reduced ability to resorb glucose (renal glycosuria). In addition, emotional stress can cause glycosuria (emotional glycosuria). Excessive amounts of glucose in the blood (hyperglycemia), physical damage to the kidney, and changes in hormone levels during pregnancy can also cause glycosuria. Renal glycosuria tends to run in families.

Diagnosis

History: Glycosuria does not exhibit any symptoms that would prompt an individual to seek the attention of a physician.

Physical exam: Glycosuria is usually discovered during a routine examination. It is often identified when a physician attempts to rule out diabetes mellitus.

Tests: Urinalysis will reveal excessive amounts of glucose in the urine.

Treatment

Glycosuria alone is not necessarily a serious condition. Treatment is not usually necessary, however the underlying cause may require therapy.

Prognosis

Depending on the underlying cause, glycosuria may be chronic or acute, but the lifespan of the affected individual is not likely to be affected.

Differential Diagnosis

Glycosuria is often a symptom of another disease. Diabetes mellitus, acute renal insufficiency, and chronic renal insufficiency are all associated with glycosuria. One of the normal maternal physiologic adaptations during pregnancy is an increase in the renal excretion of glucose. Examination of up to 50% of healthy pregnant women shows detectable glycosuria at some stage.

Specialists

- Endocrinologist
- Internist
- Nephrologist

Comorbid Conditions

The presence of kidney disease would affect the length of disability.

Complications

Complications from glycosuria are rare. Renal glycosuria is a complex HLA-linked disease with increased susceptibility to multiple autoantibody production, which urges caution with respect to its classical definition as a benign condition.

Factors Influencing Duration

Some individuals may develop diabetes mellitus that could lengthen the recovery period.

Length of Disability

No disability is associated with this condition.

Failure to Recover

If an individual fails to recover within the maximum duration expectancy period, the reader may wish to reference the following questions to assist in better understanding the specifics of an individual's medical case.

Regarding diagnosis:

- Does individual have a history of diabetes, an endocrine disorder, or kidney disorder?
- Has individual undergone recent emotional stress?
- Is individual pregnant?
- Has the diagnosis of glycosuria been confirmed by urinalysis?

Regarding treatment:

- Has the underlying cause of this condition been identified and treated adequately?
- What type of treatment is required?
- How long will individual require treatment?
- Is individual compliant with the treatment regimen?

Regarding prognosis:

- Is the underlying cause of the glycosuria a chronic or acute condition?
- Though the probability is rare, has individual developed complications?
- Does individual have renal glycosuria? If so, has individual developed antibodies against their own immune system?

References

Brazy, Peter. "Metabolic and Congenital Kidney Disorders." Merck Manual of Medical Information. Berkow, Robert New York: Pocket Books, 1997. 672-679.

Lind, T. "Antenatal Screening Using Random Blood Glucose Values." Diabetes 34 Suppl 2 (1985): 17-20.

Goiter

Other names / synonyms: Enlarged Thyroid Gland, Struma

240, 240.0, 240.9, 246.1

Definition

Goiter refers to an enlarged thyroid gland. Multiple growths (nodules and cysts) may also be present. Located in the front of the neck, the thyroid gland secretes hormones (thyroxine and triiodothyronine) that play an important role in controlling the body's metabolism. There are several different types of goiter depending on the underlying cause.

A toxic goiter is associated with overactivity of the thyroid gland and can lead to a harmful condition caused by excessive thyroid hormones (thyrotoxicosis). An enlarged thyroid gland may occur without any disruption of its function at the onset of puberty, during pregnancy, as a result of taking birth control pills, or at menopause due to hormonal disturbance.

The thyroid gland requires iodine in order to produce thyroxine. Insufficient iodine in the diet causes the gland to swell. Goiters have historically been a constant (endemic) problem in developing countries, parts of Europe, and in the Great Lakes region (before iodine was added to the US salt supply). Approximately 75% of the individuals with goiters live in parts of the world where iodine is deficient in the diet. Although iodine deficiency is the most common cause of endemic goiter, certain foods and water pollutants can themselves cause goiter or aggravate a tendency toward goiter.

A goiter may be associated with certain conditions where the immune system reacts against the body's own tissues (autoimmune disorders) and include Hashimoto's thyroiditis and Graves' disease. Blocked thyroid hormone production (hypothyroidism) or overproduction of thyroid hormone (hyperthyroidism) can result in goiters. Goiters can also be caused by noncancerous (benign) or cancerous (malignant) tumors, thyroid enzyme deficiency present at birth, or by taking certain drugs for the treatment of an overactive thyroid gland.

Because several different conditions can cause goiter, it is difficult to determine the incidence or prevalence of this condition. Thyroid disease in general affects an estimated 13 million individuals in the US although half of them remain undiagnosed. Women are 5 to 8 times more likely than men to have a thyroid disorder, with 1 in 8 women developing some form of thyroid disorder in her lifetime. The risk of thyroid disorder increases with age. A small percentage of women (5-8%) develop thyroid abnormalities after delivering a baby (postpartum).

Diagnosis

History: Goiters can range in size from a barely noticeable lump to visible swelling on the neck. An individual may notice swelling in the Adam's apple area of the neck where the thyroid gland is located. A large goiter may press on the food pipe (esophagus) or windpipe (trachea), making swallowing or breathing difficult. Pregnant women may notice discomfort in swallowing. In thyrotoxicosis, a condition caused by a toxic goiter (one that produces excessive hormones), symptoms may include increased appetite, warm dry skin, weight loss, trembling (tremor), difficulty sleeping (insomnia), heart racing, and occasional muscle weakness and restlessness (agitation). Goiters due to Graves' disease can present with bulging eyes (exophthalmos).

Physical exam: A goiter can be easily felt when the doctor gently presses on the area of the thyroid and asks the individual to swallow water.

Tests: A goiter refers only to an enlarged thyroid, so diagnosis is usually made by physical exam, or as an incidental finding of another test such as ultrasound of the carotids, or CT scan of the chest. Thyroid function tests are then done to learn if there is a functional as well as structural problem. A small sample of tissue is removed from the thyroid gland for microscopic examination (fine needle aspiration biopsy) to determine whether or not nodules (if present) are cancerous (malignant). Ultrasound can distinguish between fluid-filled sacs (cysts) and tumors.

Treatment

Treatment depends on the underlying cause. Goiters not caused by disease may eventually disappear without treatment. Very small goiters may not require any treatment. Large or unsightly goiters or those that cause difficulties with swallowing or breathing may require partial or total removal of the thyroid gland (thyroidectomy). In cases where nodules are present, medications may be prescribed to shrink the nodules. The nodules can also be removed surgically. Iodine deficiency is corrected by dietary changes and the intake of salt supplemented with iodine (iodized salt). When a goiter is the result of a disease process, treatment is aimed at the underlying disorder and may include taking hormone pills.

Prognosis

Results vary widely with little predictability. Early stage cases of goiter often respond well to medication (hormone therapy) and diminish or disappear within 3 to 6 months. Where nodules are present, only about one-third of individuals see reduction in gland size after hormone therapy. Surgery (thyroidectomy) is generally effective. Even in cases where the goiter regresses with treatment, it may recur in later months or years. Undiagnosed progressive thyroid cancer can be fatal.

Thyrotoxicosis, caused by a toxic goiter, can lead to serious heart (cardiac) complications.

Differential Diagnosis

Conditions with symptoms similar to goiter include thyroid cancer and tumors of other structures in the neck.

Specialists

- Endocrinologist
- Surgeon

Work Restrictions / Accommodations

A goiter does not generally require work restrictions or accommodations. If surgery is indicated for treatment, extended sick leave may be necessary while the individual recovers.

Complementary and Alternative Therapies

Content is intended for awareness only. Treatments may or may not be effective. Scientific evidence may be lacking and some substances have potentially toxic effects. Dr. Presley Reed and the editors do not endorse the use of these therapies in the absence of consultation with a licensed medical professional.

Diet - Iodine may help treat goiter. Seafood is a rich source of iodine. Iodized salt is commercial table salt where iodine has been added. Drinking water contains varying amounts of iodide (a form of iodine) depending on the iodide content of the local soil. However, in cases of goiter in iodine sufficient societies, increasing iodine intake has not been shown to be helpful. In toxic goiter, excessive iodine can precipitate thyroid storm.

Comorbid Conditions

Malnutrition or anorexia nervosa may prolong the period of disability if the underlying cause is due to a deficiency of iodine.

Complications

An unusually large goiter can displace the food pipe (esophagus) or the windpipe (trachea) causing difficulties in breathing and swallowing. Thyrotoxicosis, caused by a toxic goiter, can lead to serious cardiac complications and contribute to osteoporosis. Muscle weakness due to thyroid myopathy can cause prolonged disability.

Factors Influencing Duration

Length of disability is determined by the severity of symptoms, any underlying medical conditions that may be causing the goiter, and method of treatment.

Length of Disability

Duration depends on cause. In most cases, goiter does not result in disability. Duration depends on partial versus complete.

Medical treatment.

Duration in Days

Job Classification	Minimum	Optimum	Maximum
Sedentary work	0	3	7
Light work	0	3	7
Medium work	0	3	7
Heavy work	0	3	7
Very Heavy work	0	3	7

Surgical treatment (thyroidectomy).

Duration in Days

Job Classification	Minimum	Optimum	Maximum
Sedentary work	7	14	21
Light work	7	14	21
Medium work	14	21	28
Heavy work	14	28	42
Very Heavy work	14	28	42

Failure to Recover

If an individual fails to recover within the maximum duration expectancy period, the reader may wish to reference the following questions to assist in better understanding the specifics of an individual's medical case.

Regarding diagnosis:

- Has the diagnosis of goiter been confirmed by blood tests, x-rays, ultrasound, and/or iodine uptake test? Has malignancy been eliminated as a possibility?
- Has the neck been thoroughly examined to rule out masses (tumors, cysts, nodules) on any other structures?
- Is the goiter unusually large?
- Does individual have increased appetite, warm dry skin, weight loss, trembling (tremor), difficulty sleeping (insomnia), occasional muscle weakness, and restlessness (agitation)?
- Does the individual have thyrotoxicosis? Is there swelling in the Adam's apple area of the neck?
- Is individual having trouble breathing?

Regarding treatment:

- If dietary changes have not been effective in resolving the goiter, are medications being considered?
- Is surgery being considered? Partial or total thyroidectomy?
- Is underlying condition being effectively controlled?
- Are there other treatment options that may be more effective?
- Would individual benefit from consultation with a specialist (endocrinologist, surgeon)?

Regarding prognosis:

- Has medication been effective in diminishing or resolving goiter?
- Has individual been compliant with dietary changes and addition of iodized salt? Does individual have an underlying condition such as malnutrition or anorexia nervosa that may impact recovery? If so, is this condition being effectively treated? Has underlying condition responded favorably to treatment? If medication was not effective or if goiter recurs, is individual now a candidate for surgery?

References

Facts About Thyroid Disease. American Association of Clinical Endocrinologists. 10 Nov 2000 <http://www.aace.com/pub/spec/tam/facts.htm>.

Levy, Richard. "Hyperthyroidism." Griffith's 5-minute Clinical Consult. Dambro, Mark, ed. Philadelphia: Lippincott, Williams & Wilkins, 2000. 532-533.

Gonorrhea

Other names / synonyms: Arthritis-Dermatitis Syndrome, Clap, Disseminated Gonococcal Disease, Gonococcal Arthritis, Gonococcal Cervicitis, Gonococcal Proctitis, Gonococcal Urethritis, Gonorrhea

098, 098.0, 098.1, 098.2, 098.3, 098.4, 098.5, 098.6, 098.7, 098.8

Definition

Gonorrhea is a highly contagious venereal disease caused by the bacterium Neisseria gonorrhea. The disease is spread through sexual contact and initially causes an infection in the lower reproductive tract (the cervix, vagina, and urethra in women or the urethra in men). With anal sex, the infection occurs in the rectum. With oral sex, the infection can begin in the throat (pharynx). If the disease is not treated, the infection can move up the reproductive tract to the prostate, epididymis, and testis in men, and the pelvic organs in women. It can then enter the blood, affecting the joints and major organs of the body (disseminated gonorrhea). Because symptoms can be delayed, however, it is often spread before individuals realize they are infected. It can also be transmitted from an infected mother to her newborn infant during childbirth that may cause an eye infection in the newborn. Gonorrhea is not spread, as some believe, by touching doorknobs and toilet seats.

Gonorrhea is one of the oldest sexually transmitted diseases known and is the most common one in the US today. The number of estimated yearly cases of gonorrhea in the US is between 1.5 and 3 million. Worldwide there are about 62 million cases annually. The disease is prevalent in both industrialized and nonindustrialized nations. While all social strata in the US can be affected, gonorrhea is especially common in low socioeconomic settings. Cases of gonorrhea decreased from the mid-1970s to the early 1990s, probably due to safer sexual practices. The decline has since ceased, however, with 600,000 new cases reported each year in the US. Gonorrhea affects women more than men, and blacks more than whites and Hispanics. It is most common in sexually active individuals between the ages of 15 and 29.

Diagnosis

History: Individuals may report history of sexual contact with a new or multiple partners. Symptoms usually appear 3 days to 2 weeks after infection. However, some individuals, especially women, may not experience any symptoms (asymptomatic). Common symptoms include frequent urination with pain, burning, and occasional bleeding. A discharge from the vagina or penis may be present, and the penal opening may become red and swollen. As the disease progresses, there may be fever, deep abdominal pain, discomfort during intercourse, or bleeding between menstrual periods in women. Depending on specific sexual practices, the infection may occur in the throat, causing pain and inflammation (gonococcal pharyngitis), or in the rectum causing itching, discharge, and painful bowel movements. If infected fluid enters the eye, redness and inflammation may occur (gonorrheal conjunctivitis).

Physical exam: Men will usually exhibit a thick discharge from the penis. A similar discharge from the cervix may be found in women with possible tenderness of the fallopian tubes. Abscesses of the tubes can sometimes be detected by a pelvic examination. A sore throat, difficulty swallowing, and swelling of lymph nodes in the neck may suggest throat infection.

Because an infected woman may have no symptoms for weeks or even months, the disease may only be discovered after her partner is diagnosed and she is identified as his contact.

Tests: Microscopic examination of pus may reveal characteristic-appearing bacteria. Culture of pus positive for growth of Neisseria gonorrhea confirms the diagnosis. Once bacteria are grown in culture, specific antibiotics that kill these bacteria can also be identified, ensuring effective treatment. Tests that look for specific proteins or DNA of the gonorrheal bacteria are faster and simpler. Unfortunately these tests, including enzyme-linked immunosorbent assay (ELISA or EIA) and direct immunofluorescence test (DFA), are less sensitive in detecting the infection and do not provide any information on antibiotic sensitivity. A newer DNA probe test can be used to detect specific bacterial genes. Combining a pus sample from an affected area with a chemical that agitates the bacteria causes it to release DNA. Analyses of these DNA samples allow for a specific diagnosis.

Treatment

Gonorrhea is treated with antibiotics either orally or by injection. Although penicillin was once the drug of choice over the past two decades, many cases of gonorrhea have been found that are resistant to penicillin, ampicillin, and tetracycline. In these cases, alternative antibiotics must be used. More than 97% of uncomplicated gonorrheal urethral and cervical infections are eradicated by a large single dose of the appropriate antibiotic. Anal and throat infections are more likely to need multiple doses. Because nongonococcal urethritis and chlamydia infections often coexist with gonorrhea, these diseases may also need to be treated with a broad-spectrum antibiotic.

Latex condoms may prevent infection if used properly. The use of diaphragms may also help prevent cervical infection.

All sexual partners of the infected individual should be treated. Because asymptomatic infection is common, routine screening is recommended for women who are sexually active with new or multiple partners, or with a partner diagnosed with a sexually transmitted disease. Women younger than age 20, and those whose partners do not use condoms, are particularly at risk. All women with positive screening cultures should be treated with appropriate antibiotics.

Prognosis

With early antibiotic treatment, the prognosis for gonorrhea is good. The infection usually clears in 2 to 4 weeks provided the bacteria are susceptible to the chosen antibiotic. With an impaired immune system, infections may last for months and become more severe.

Untreated or improperly treated infection can cause complications. In men, urethral gonorrhea infections can result in acute or chronic prostate gland inflammation or testicular infection. In women, infection can spread to the uterus and fallopian tubes causing sterility, ectopic (tubal) pregnancy, or pelvic inflammatory disease. In pregnant women, infection can lead to spontaneous abortion, premature rupture of the membranes, premature delivery, and stillbirth.

Differential Diagnosis

Gonorrhea must be differentiated from other nongonococcal infections of the urethra, cervix, rectum, or vagina. Other conditions with similar symptoms include pelvic inflammatory disease, arthritis, and Reiter's disease.

Specialists

- Cardiologist
- Dermatologist
- Gynecologist
- Infectious Disease Physician
- Neurologist
- Rheumatologist
- Urologist

Work Restrictions / Accommodations

There are no anticipated work restrictions or accommodations for uncomplicated gonorrhea. Although some accommodations may be required if complications are present, the nature and extent of the accommodations will depend on the severity of the symptoms. Long-term disability is not expected.

Comorbid Conditions

With an impaired immune system, gonorrhea infections may last for months and become more severe. In pregnant women, the infection can lead to spontaneous abortion, premature rupture of the membranes, premature delivery, and stillbirth.

Complications

Gonorrhea bacteria spreading through the bloodstream (disseminated gonococcal disease) can cause fever, rash, and joint pain. Although fever and rash resolve, one or more joints may become swollen with infected fluid, and red pus-filled lesions may appear on the skin (arthritis-dermatitis syndrome). This complication is more common in women, especially during menstruation or in the second and third trimesters of pregnancy. Arthritis-dermatitis syndrome is the most common cause of infectious arthritis in young adults.

Involvement of the heart or brain can cause endocarditis or meningitis. Liver involvement in women can cause perihepatitis or Fitz-Hugh-Curtis syndrome. Infection of the eyes causes conjunctivitis.

In pregnant women, infection can lead to spontaneous abortion, premature delivery, and low birth weight babies. Gonorrhea leads to pelvic inflammatory disease in 10-20% of infected women. Scarring of the fallopian tubes and other pelvic organs can cause chronic pain and infertility. Infection of the Bartholin's gland near the vagina may lead to painful abscess formation.

Factors Influencing Duration

The length of disability will be influenced by the response to treatment or if there are any complications. Antibiotic-resistant infections may be more severe and require prolonged treatment. Pregnancy complications, including infection of the developing fetus, may extend disability. Untreated heart or brain involvement can lead to long-term disabilities.

Length of Disability

For complicated gonorrhea, the length of disability will depend upon the severity and therapeutic treatment of the disease.

Acute, Uncomplicated infection.

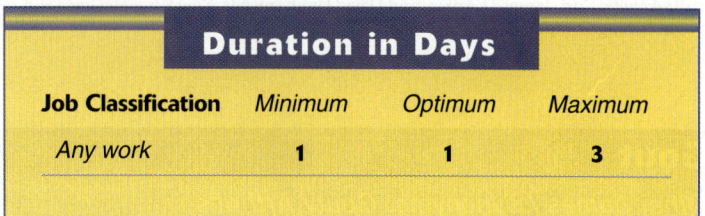

Job Classification	Minimum	Optimum	Maximum
Any work	1	1	3

Failure to Recover

If an individual fails to recover within the maximum duration expectancy period, the reader may wish to reference the following questions to assist in better understanding the specifics of an individual's medical case.

Regarding diagnosis:

- Has diagnosis of gonorrhea been confirmed?
- Did the infection include more than one sexually transmitted disease?
- Did the individual experience any secondary infections or complications?
- Does the individual also have nongonococcal urethritis or a chlamydia infection?
- Does the individual have an impaired immune system?

Regarding treatment:

- Was infection treated orally or by injection of antibiotics? Are multiple doses required?
- Was effectiveness verified by follow-up culture?
- Was a culture and sensitivity test done to indicate the most effective antibiotic?
- Where was infection located?
- Does the bacterium appear resistant to the antibiotic used?
- If complications occurred, should individual be hospitalized for intravenous antibiotics?
- Would the individual benefit from consultation with an appropriate specialist for further treatment recommendations?
- Were contacts located and treated?

Regarding prognosis:

- Was follow-up culture done to confirm that the infection was completely eradicated?
- Was the individual educated about future prevention and the risks of reinfection?

References

"Sexually Transmitted Diseases." Scientific American Medicine. 01 Jan 2000. 13 Oct 2000 <http://www.samed.com/sam/forms/index.htm>.

Mansen, Thom J. "Sexually Transmitted Diseases." Pathophysiology. McCance, Kathryn L., and Sue E Heuther, eds. St. Louis: Mosby, 1994. 800-859.

References (Continued)

Brooks, G.F., J.S. Butel, and S.A. Morse. Medical Microbiology. Stamford: Appleton & Lange, 1998.

Hyde, Janet Shibley. "Sexually Transmitted Diseases." Understanding Human Sexuality. Berkowitz, Curt, James D. Anker, and David Dunham, eds. New York: McGraw-Hill Publishing Company, 1990. 550-579.

National Institute of Allergy and Infectious Diseases. Fact Sheet: Gonorrhea. National Institutes of Health. 01 Jun 1998. 01 Sept 2000 <http://www.niaid.nih.gov/factsheets/stdgon.htm>.

Tierney, L.M., S.J. McPhee, and M.A. Papadakis. Current Medical Diagnosis and Treatment. Stamford: Appleton & Lange, 1998.

Gout

Other names / synonyms: Gouty Arthritis
274, 274.0, 274.1, 274.8, 274.9

Definition

Gout is a type of arthritis caused by the accumulation of uric-acid crystals in one or more joints, most often the big toe.

Gout can occur alone or in combination with any of the following: abnormal amounts of uric acid in the blood (hyperuricemia), acute inflammatory arthritis, deposits of sodium biurate (tophi) in tissues near a joint or in the kidney (renal tophi), and urinary stones (urolithiasis). Either an overproduction or an under-excretion of uric acid may cause gout. However, an elevated uric acid level does not always result in gout.

In gout, deposits of uric acid in the joints and in cartilage cause inflammation, swelling and severe pain.

Most attacks occur without apparent cause. Occasionally, an attack may follow an operation, infection, trauma, alcohol ingestion, starvation, over indulgence in foods with high purine content (meat, fish, fowl, and certain vegetables), ingestion of drugs that cause changes in urate concentration, or minor irritations. Gout may be associated with obesity, high blood pressure (hypertension), narrowing of blood vessels due to atherosclerosis, and elevated lipids (hyperlipidemia).

The first attacks of gout most often occur between the ages of 40 to 60 years. Males are affected by gout more than females. Gout tends to primarily involve the lower extremities. Joints most often involved include the great toe, instep, ankle, heel, wrist, elbows and fingers. Over time, deposits of uratic acid crystals in these joints may cause deformity of the joints.

Diagnosis

History: The individual may complain of a sudden, unexplained onset of severe joint pain. They often report that the pain is limited to one joint. However, occasionally they may have pain in multiple joints. Often the pain occurs at night and is severe enough to wake the individual from sleep. Some may report that the pain disappears after a few hours while others may have pain that lasts for several weeks. The individual may report that the pain disappears spontaneously and then returns after a period of months.

Physical exam: Findings on physical exam may include a warm, swollen, tender joint. Pain is elicited with slight pressure. If the individual has had several attacks of gout, he or she may also have excess fibrous buildup in the ears, hands, feet and elbows. The physical exam may be normal if the individual does not seek treatment during an acute attack, however.

Tests: Diagnosis involves aspiration of the joint (arthrocentesis) with examination for urate crystals, or tissue biopsy for evaluation of sodium biurate deposits (tophi) are performed. Sedimentation rate, complete blood count (CBC) with differential and a 24-hour urine collection are done to assess uric acid levels. X-rays of the involved joint may be done to rule out other conditions. A bone scan or magnetic resonance imaging (MRI) may be used to detect all areas involved.

Treatment

Medications are the mainstay of treatment. During an acute attack, these may include non-steroidal anti-inflammatory agents (e.g., aspirin or ibuprofen) or corticosteroids, pain relievers (analgesics), and a specific anti-gout agent called colchicine. The individual's response to colchicine may be used for diagnosis as well as treatment. In chronic gout, medications that increase the excretion of uric acid in the urine (uricosuric agents) and those that block the production of uric acid (allopurinol) are used. Most individuals are urged to limit their consumption of organ meats and alcohol (both of which are known to interfere with the elimination of uric acid) and to lose weight if they are obese, to ease the strain on the affected joints.

Prognosis

When the treatment is initiated when symptoms first arise, total control usually is attained. If attacks recur, successful uric acid adjustment (requiring lifelong use of medication) usually is effective. Kidney damage occurs in up to 10% of individuals with gout.

Differential Diagnosis

Other possibilities include rheumatoid arthritis, cellulitis, calcium pyrophosphate dihydrate crystal deposition disease (CPPD), osteoarthritis, septic arthritis, traumatic arthritis, bursitis, and tendinitis.

Specialists

- Internist
- Nephrologist
- Rheumatologist

Rehabilitation

In general, rehabilitation recommendations for those with gout are similar to individuals with other forms of arthritis. Individuals who suffer from complications of joint deformity and immobility may benefit from outpatient physical therapy for range of motion exercises, to control of pain and inflammation, and to increase flexibility.

Therapists instruct individuals in the use of heating pads to decrease joint stiffness and pain. Individuals learn to apply heat as needed for pain control. Therapists instruct in gentle stretching and strengthening exercises for the affected joints. Individuals also perform low-impact aerobic exercise such as walking or swimming to increase strength and endurance, and decrease fatigue. Individuals who are unable to perform exercises due to pain may benefit from an aquatic therapy program in a heated pool, which reduces the stress through an individual's joints due to the buoyant properties of water.

Work Restrictions / Accommodations

Most individuals will require sick leave during an acute attack. If the person continues to work, temporary assignment to sedentary duties may be required. Reassignment may be necessary for individuals whose jobs require prolonged standing or walking.

Complementary and Alternative Therapies

Content is intended for awareness only. Treatments may or may not be effective. Scientific evidence may be lacking and some substances have potentially toxic effects. Dr. Presley Reed and the editors do not endorse the use of these therapies in the absence of consultation with a licensed medical professional.

Folate-	Said to be a preventive treatment for gout.
Devil's claw-	This herb is said to be an effective pain reliever in various types of arthritis and thus is sometimes recommended for pain relief in those with gout.
Supplement therapy -	Fish oil, vitamin E, vitamin A, selenium, bromelain, and aspartic acid may aid in the treatment of symptoms and prevention of gout.

Comorbid Conditions

Comorbid conditions that also affect joint mobility such as osteoarthritis, rheumatoid arthritis, and bony deformities of the feet (such as bunions, hammertoes or fractures) may impact ability to recover and further lengthen disability.

Complications

Complications include death of bone tissue due to insufficient blood supply (avascular necrosis), bone deformity, kidney damage, chronic arthritis, and high blood pressure (hypertension).

Factors Influencing Duration

Length of disability may be influenced by the duration of the disease, the method and effectiveness of treatment, the joint affected, and the individual's job requirements.

Length of Disability

Duration in Days

Job Classification	Minimum	Optimum	Maximum
Sedentary work	0	3	7
Light work	3	7	14
Medium work	3	7	14
Heavy work	3	7	14
Very Heavy work	3	7	14

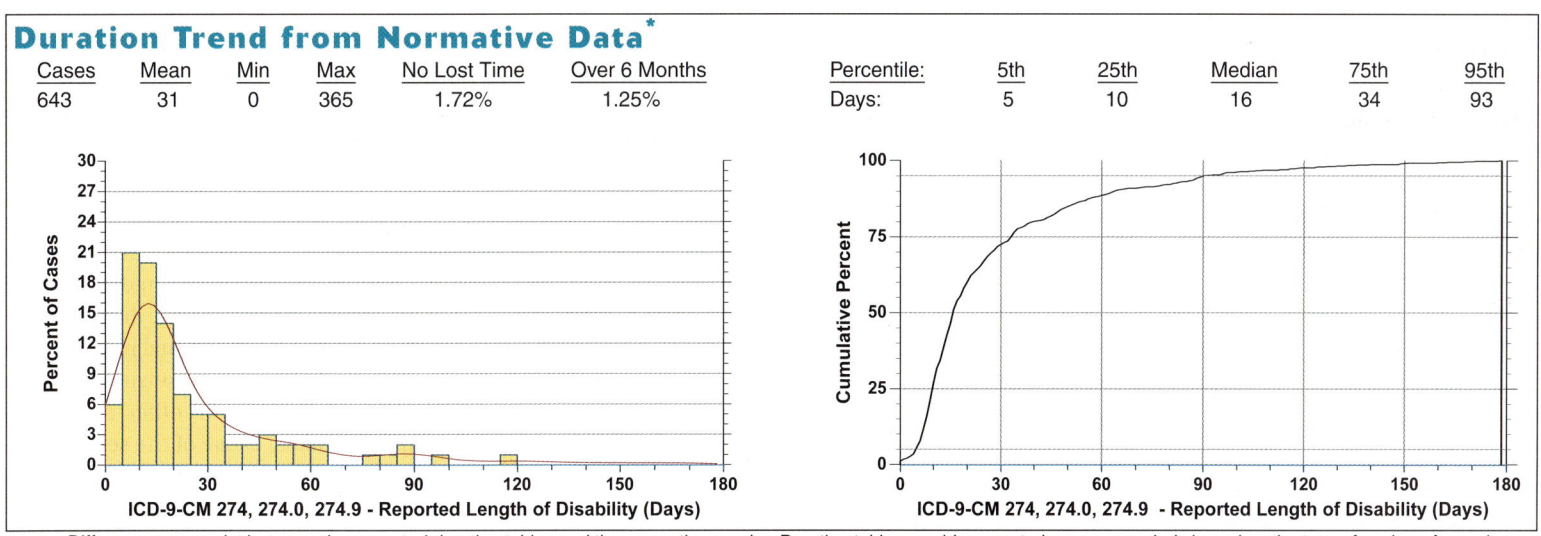

Duration Trend from Normative Data*

Cases	Mean	Min	Max	No Lost Time	Over 6 Months
643	31	0	365	1.72%	1.25%

Percentile:	5th	25th	Median	75th	95th
Days:	5	10	16	34	93

ICD-9-CM 274, 274.0, 274.9 - Reported Length of Disability (Days)

* Differences may exist between the expected duration tables and the normative graphs. Duration tables provide expected recovery periods based on the type of work performed by the individual. The normative graphs reflect the actual observed experience of many individuals across the spectrum of physical conditions, in a variety of industries, and with varying levels of case management.

Failure to Recover

If an individual fails to recover within the maximum duration expectancy period, the reader may wish to reference the following questions to assist in better understanding the specifics of an individual's medical case.

Regarding diagnosis:

- Was diagnosis of gout confirmed through aspiration of the joint (arthrocentesis) with examination for urate crystals or by tissue biopsy for evaluation of sodium biurate deposits (tophi)?

Gout 1013

- Was a sedimentation rate, complete blood count (CBC) with differential and a 24-hour urine collection done to assess uric acid levels?
- Were X-rays of the involved joint done to rule out other conditions with similar symptoms?
- Does individual have any coexisting conditions that may complicate treatment or impact recovery?

Regarding treatment:

- Has individual been placed on appropriate medications such as anti-inflammatory agents, analgesics, corticosteroids or anti-gout medications?
- Has drug therapy included the use of medications to lower the uric acid levels?
- Has the individual been instructed to follow a diet low in purines? Would individual benefit from consultation with a nutritionist?
- If appropriate, has individual been instructed to lose weight? Would individual benefit from enrollment in a community weight loss program?

Regarding prognosis:

- Did the individual seek treatment when symptoms first occurred?
- Is the individual compliant with the treatment plan? If not, what can be done to enhance compliance?
- If attacks recur, is individual on a successful program of uric acid adjustment (requiring lifelong use of medication)? Is individual capable of following a long-term medication regimen?
- Has individual developed complications such as avascular necrosis, bone deformity, kidney damage, or chronic arthritis? if so, are complications being adequately addressed in the overall treatment plan?

References

Conditions: Gout. The Natural Pharmacist. 2001. 22 Feb 2001 <http://www.tnp.com/topic.asp?ID=117>.

Guccione, Andrew A. "Arthritis." Physical Rehabilitation: Assessment and Treatment. O'Sullivan, Susan B., and Thomas J. Schmitz, eds. Philadelphia: F.A. Davis Company, 1994. 423-449.

Kaplan, Joseph. "Gout and Pseudogout." eMedicine.com. 09 Feb 2001. 22 Feb 2001 <http://www.emedicine.com/emerg/topic221.htm>.

Kisner, Carolyn, and Lynn Allen Colby. Therapeutic Exercise: Foundations and Techniques. Philadelphia: F.A. Davis Company, 1990.

Shen, Harry, MD, and Cheryl Solimini. Living with Arthritis. New York: Plume, 1993.

Tierney, Lawrence M., Stephen J. McPhee, and Maxine Papadakis, eds. Current Medical Diagnosis and Treatment, 39th ed. New York: Lange Medical Books/McGraw-Hill, 2000.

Grand Mal Seizure

Other names / synonyms: Convulsion, Epilepsy, Generalized Convulsive Epilepsy, Major Epilepsy, Tonic-Clonic Convulsion, Tonic-Clonic Seizure

345.1, 345.3, 345.8

Definition

Grand mal seizures are caused by abnormal electrical activity of the brain. Normal human activities, thoughts, perceptions, and emotions are produced by electrical impulses that stimulate nerve cells in the brain. During a seizure, the usual electrical communication in the brain is disrupted by a chaotic and unregulated discharge. Seizures are a symptom of brain dysfunction and can be the result of a wide variety of diseases or injuries. Seizures may be associated with birth trauma, head injury, central nervous system infections, brain tumor, stroke, ingestion of toxic substances, or metabolic imbalance.

A grand mal seizure starts with opening of the mouth and eyes. The arms are thrown out and up and the legs straighten. The respiratory muscles contract, forcing air out of the lungs and creating a sound like a cry or a grunt. The jaws clamp shut and the individual may bite the tongue. Breathing ceases and the bladder can contract releasing urine (incontinence). The body collapses and is rigid. The individual loses consciousness. This is called the tonic phase of the seizure and lasts for about 15 to 30 seconds.

The clonic phase immediately follows and is characterized by violent rhythmic muscular contractions of the entire body including the muscles of the face and eyes. The individual does not breathe normally as the respiratory muscles are also involved (apnea). The movements gradually subside and the seizure is over in 1 to 2 minutes. Breathing becomes regular and the individual falls asleep. Individuals may waken within a few minutes but will be confused, lethargic, and fatigued. This mental state may persist for hours. They often have a headache and fail to remember the seizure or events preceding it. This is called the postictal phase.

Seizures with no apparent cause are called idiopathic seizures. They account for 75% of the cases of grand mal seizures in adults. They may actually be due to microscopic brain lesions that occurred at birth or from trauma, or may be caused by unexplained metabolic disturbances. The term epilepsy is a diagnosis given when an individual has repeated seizure episodes over a period of time. If a grand mal seizure follows a localized seizure (partial seizure) with jerking or other symptoms involving only one part of the body, the likely cause of the seizures is a lesion in a small area of the brain. About 25% of individuals develop grand mal seizures after partial seizures.

Grand mal seizures may accompany meningitis, herpes simplex virus infections, cerebral tuberculomas, brain tumors, degenerative diseases of the brain, diabetes, inflammatory disorders of blood vessels (vasculitis), drug abuse, alcohol abuse, withdrawal from antianxiety or antidepressant drugs, traumatic injury to the brain, and occupational exposure to chemicals. Grand mal seizures can occur for no reason (idiopathic grand mal seizures). Even when there is no clear cause, idiopathic grand mal seizures recur in 30-70% of individuals.

In the US, 2.5 million Americans have been diagnosed with epilepsy. Between 1,375 and 23,250 individuals every year die suddenly during a grand mal seizure.

Grand mal seizures affect approximately 2 out of 10,000 individuals with about 5% of the population having at least one seizure. Most seizures that occur as a single episode are grand mal seizures.

Diagnosis

History: History of seizure from the family or other witnesses is important in diagnosis unless the healthcare provider witnesses an episode. Before a grand mal seizure, individuals may report warning symptoms (aura) such as smelling unpleasant odors or experiencing distortions of space and time. There may be a history of incontinence during the seizure in addition to tongue biting or other self-injury. After a grand mal seizure, an individual often reports a severe, throbbing headache, and/or severe fatigue. Between seizures, there may be a history of headaches, visual symptoms, weakness or numbness of an arm or leg, or speech disturbance. These provide important clues about the underlying cause and location of any structural defect in the brain.

Most individuals report a history of epilepsy since childhood. If the grand mal seizure was the first one experienced, the individual may have had trauma to the head. Individuals may have diseases affecting the brain (i.e., meningitis), psychological stress, a history of taking mood altering drugs (prescribed or illegal), or alcohol abuse. An important part of the history with a grand mal seizure is to discover if the generalized convulsion was preceded by a focal or partial seizure. This type of seizure can be limited to a single part of the body and then spreads or evolves into a grand mal seizure. This may imply dysfunction in a limited area of the brain related to birth injury, trauma, tumor, abscess, stroke, abnormal blood vessels (vascular malformation), or some other structural abnormality.

Physical exam: The immediate concern of the physician or emergency personnel first examining the individual is to make sure the individual's airway is open and unobstructed. If fever is noted, it could be the cause of the seizure or a sign of infection. Any contusions, lacerations, or fractured bones the individual may have sustained during the seizure are noted. A brief neurological examination is performed. A more thorough examination is postponed until the individual is alert and able to follow directions. After the seizure (post-ictal phase) some neurological findings may be absent or equivocal. When the individual regains consciousness, he or she may not react appropriately to stimuli and may be temporarily paralyzed on one side (Todd's post-ictal paralysis). The neurological exam usually focuses on finding specific, localized neurological deficits that may indicate areas of brain lesions.

Tests: Blood tests detect any metabolic abnormalities. A drug screen including a blood alcohol level may be warranted. If the seizure was preceded by fever or a change in mental status, an immediate spinal tap (lumbar puncture) is performed to check the spinal fluid for signs of an infection (meningitis, encephalitis) that may have led to a generalized seizure. However, if signs of increased pressure within the brain (increased intracranial pressure) are evident, brain CT or MRI should be done first. Further testing depends on whether or not this was the first seizure the individual has had. If it is the first episode without an apparent cause, extensive testing is necessary.

An electroencephalogram (EEG) may show characteristic changes or electrical abnormalities in the region(s) of the brain where the seizure began. If EEG is normal, longer periods of EEG monitoring in an overnight sleep laboratory or the use of a tape recorder to monitor brain wave activity during daily activities may be helpful. Other tests include cerebral angiogram to rule out aneurysm or arteriovenous malformation. In some cases, positron emission tomography (PET) can help determine whether the individual suffering recurring grand mal seizures is a candidate for surgery since this test helps localize the area of the brain where seizures originate.

Treatment

When an individual is brought to the emergency room during or following a grand mal seizure, airway and circulation must first be protected then any associated injuries or medical problems (i.e., stroke, drug overdose or withdrawal, infection, or complications of diabetes) treated. The individual should be protected from self-injury. Cardiopulmonary respiration (CPR) may be needed in some cases. If the seizure is ongoing, thiamine and sugar solution (glucose) should be given intravenously. Both thiamine deficiency and low blood sugar (hypoglycemia) can cause grand mal seizure and are easily treated with no side effects.

A single idiopathic seizure after extensive testing is generally not treated, although the individual should be followed closely. If the individual had only one grand mal seizure as a result of an illness in the brain, the illness or structural defect is treated. Generally no further treatment is necessary once the illness resolves.

When the seizure is caused by a structural problem in the brain that cannot be treated, the individual is at risk for continued seizures and may need ongoing medical treatment. An individual with ongoing grand mal seizures is treated with anticonvulsant drugs either individually or in combination. Side effects and continued seizures despite drug therapy may necessitate frequent changes in drug regimen. Depending on the cause of the seizure and if no seizures occur for 2 to 3 years, the medication dose may be reduced or stopped. Prolonged or repeated seizures (when the individual does not regain consciousness) denote a condition called status epilepticus that can be fatal without emergency treatment using intravenous anticonvulsant drugs.

Surgery is only considered if the individual has daily grand mal seizures, if the part of the brain where the seizure originates is known, and if life is unbearable both because of the constant seizures or the side effects from the anticonvulsant drugs. If the cause can be localized with certainty to a specific area of the brain such as the temporal lobe, the area can be removed surgically. Seizures may respond to surgery that cuts connections between the two halves (hemispheres) of the brain (corpus callosotomy). Brain damage may complicate epilepsy surgery so should only be used in intractable cases.

Prognosis

An individual who experienced a single grand mal seizure and where treatment was considered unnecessary will likely never have another one. An individual with grand mal seizures that are well controlled with anticonvulsant drugs can lead a reasonably normal life. The individual experiencing surgery (had part of the brain removed) may no longer need anticonvulsant drugs, but may suffer from subtle impairments related to loss of these brain structures such as memory loss, language difficulties, or detrimental changes in personality, emotions, or behavior. Brain surgery stops recurrent seizures in most individuals and reduces seizures in most others.

Differential Diagnosis

A grand mal seizure can be misdiagnosed as a bad reaction to illegal drug use or a behavior disorder. Episodes resembling seizures but without abnormal electrical activity on EEG (pseudoseizures) may occur in conversion disorder, hysteria, or somatoform disorder. If the episodes are not witnessed and the history is unclear, they may be confused with transient ischemic attack (TIA) or fainting (syncope).

Specialists

- Internist
- Neurologist
- Neurosurgeon
- Radiologist

Work Restrictions / Accommodations

Individuals with recurring seizures and who are on drug therapy should not operate machinery, motor vehicles, or work from heights. If work involves driving, flying, or piloting a boat, the individual may be advised to find another line of work. Individuals who have been seizure-free for a year or more and have permission from a neurologist should not be restricted in their work-related activities. No restrictions should be placed on individuals who have only had one seizure if the cause of that seizure has been removed (e.g., if seizure was the result of discontinuing an antianxiety drug). Disruptions in sleep related to working night shifts or undue stress may exacerbate a tendency to have seizures and should be avoided if possible.

Comorbid Conditions

Comorbid conditions that slow full recovery include diseases affecting the brain such as cancers and meningitis, excessive consumption of alcohol, and use of illegal recreational drugs. Pregnancy may complicate recovery by exacerbating seizures and limiting drugs used since some may induce birth defects.

Complications

A single grand mal seizure while driving a car, flying an airplane, or swimming alone can be fatal. Operating a car, other vehicle, or heavy machinery when having a seizure can injure self and others. Constant seizures (some individuals have more than 50 per day) decrease quality of life. Tongue biting, limb fracture, head trauma, and other injuries may accompany grand mal seizures. The lack of oxygen and blood flow to the brain during repeated seizures or status epilepticus can cause brain damage. During a seizure, the individual may choke on saliva or stomach contents (aspiration) that can lead to loss of oxygen or pneumonia.

Factors Influencing Duration

The main factor influencing the length of disability is how fast the individual can be stabilized, whether on anticonvulsant drugs or following brain surgery. Side effects from anticonvulsant medications that may hinder return to work include dizziness, fatigue, and memory problems.

Length of Disability

With effective treatment and control of the seizures, there may be no disability. The length of disability would be the time necessary to stabilize medications. An isolated seizure episode may not carry any period of disability. Length of disability can vary from a few weeks to permanent disability depending on whether seizures can be controlled with drugs or surgery. If the seizures have caused permanent brain damage, the disability may be permanent.

Medical treatment.

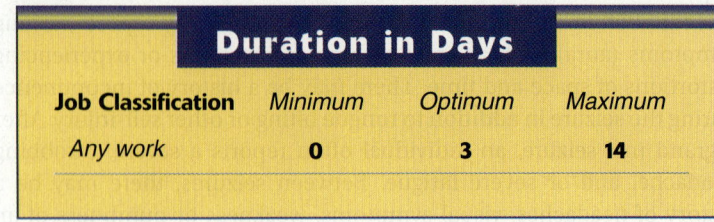

Duration in Days

Job Classification	Minimum	Optimum	Maximum
Any work	0	3	14

Failure to Recover

If an individual fails to recover within the maximum duration expectancy period, the reader may wish to reference the following questions to assist in better understanding the specifics of an individual's medical case.

Regarding diagnosis:

- Did individual have any birth trauma or head injury? A central nervous system infection? Brain tumor or stroke?
- Did individual ingest a toxic substance? Have a metabolic imbalance?
- Has individual had a witnessed seizure? Has individual been injured during a seizure?
- Does individual have an aura?
- Do headaches, visual symptoms, extremity weakness, or speech disturbance occur between seizures?
- How old was individual at onset of seizures?
- Does individual currently have any psychological stress?
- Has individual taken mood altering drugs (prescribed or illegal)? Abuse alcohol?
- Was a blood test done? Drug screen including blood alcohol? If fever is present, was a lumbar puncture done? Brain CT or MRI? EEG? Has individual had a cerebral angiogram or PET scan?
- Is individual a candidate for surgery?
- Have conditions with similar symptoms been ruled out?

Regarding treatment:

- If the seizure was a single idiopathic seizure, was the underlying cause treated?
- Have the appropriate anticonvulsant drugs been prescribed? Does individual take them as prescribed? Has individual had blood levels done to insure the drugs are in the therapeutic range?
- Has surgery become necessary?

Regarding prognosis:

- Does individual see a neurologist on a regular basis?
- Does individual have any conditions that may affect ability to recover?
- Has individual had a seizure while driving a car or flying an airplane? Was license to do these things revoked?
- If seizures cannot be controlled on anticonvulsant drugs, should surgery be considered?

References

Kumar, S.K., and B.J. Freeman. "Quadriplegia Following Grand Mal Seizures." Injury 30 9 (1999): 626-629.

Theune, M., et al. "Grand Mal Series After Ecstasy Abuse." Nervenarzt 70 12 (1999): 1094-1097.

Graves' Disease

Other names / synonyms: Basedow's Disease, Diffuse Thyrotoxic Goiter, Exophthalmic Goiter, Parry's Disease, Thyrotoxicosis, Toxic Goiter

242, 242.0, 242.00, 242.01

Definition

Graves' disease is a complex disease in which the immune system reacts against the body's own tissues (an autoimmune disease). The thyroid gland is an endocrine gland located in the front of the neck, near the "Adam's apple." This gland produces certain hormones that are important for controlling the body's metabolism and regulating calcium balance. In Graves' disease, the thyroid gland becomes overactive and enlarged (goiter), and begins producing excessive amounts of hormones (hyperthyroidism). Thyroid disorders may result from defects in the gland itself, or from disruption of the calcium control system involving the parathyroid gland.

If left undiagnosed or inadequately treated, Graves' disease can put individuals at risk for a potentially fatal condition in which there is severe worsening or exaggeration of the symptoms of thyroid overactivity called thyroid storm or thyroid crisis. On the other hand, a unique characteristic of this disorder is the complete or partial disappearance of symptoms for unknown reasons (spontaneous remissions) in up to 50% of the cases.

Graves' disease affects 5 out of every 10,000 individuals. It is more common in women than in men, and usually develops after 20 years of age, with the majority of cases occurring in women between 20-40 years of age. Although the cause remains unknown, Graves' disease typically follows an illness or stress, and tends to run in families. It is sometimes found in conjunction with other autoimmune diseases such as pernicious anemia, myasthenia gravis, and diabetes. Because the exact cause of Graves' disease is unknown, specific risk factors and preventative measures are also unknown.

Diagnosis

History: General symptoms due to increased levels of thyroid hormones (hyperthyroidism) include weight loss, increased appetite, hand tremors, nervousness, restlessness, fatigue, heat intolerance, sweating, muscle cramps, breathlessness, blurred or double vision, diarrhea or frequent bowel movements, menstrual irregularities, difficulty climbing stairs, and a fluttering in the chest (heart palpitations). In rare cases, individuals may experience temporary paralysis lasting 7-72 hours, typically after strenuous exercise. Additional symptoms may include eye irritation, eye sensitivity, or pressure behind the eyes; individuals may notice their eyes appear to bulge (exophthalmos), causing eye irritation and tearing.

Individuals in advanced stages of Graves' disease may have symptoms of a condition called thyroid storm, which include a rapid pulse, delirium, nausea, diarrhea, dehydration, fever, and generalized weakness (malaise).

Physical exam: The exam will usually reveal an enlarged thyroid gland (goiter) and unusual bulging of the eyeballs (exophthalmos). Other symptoms may include swollen glands, an irregular heartbeat, increased heart rate, and an "orange-peel" skin texture (myxedema) on the front of the shins.

Tests: Diagnosis is confirmed by thyroid function and radioactive iodine uptake tests. Blood tests measure hormone (TSH, T3, T4, TSI) levels in the blood. In radioactive iodine uptake tests, the individual is given a small quantity of a radioactive chemical (either orally or by injection). The chemical is absorbed by either healthy or diseased tissue, depending on the disease process and the type of scan. The emitted radioactivity produces an image of the thyroid on film for evaluation of abnormalities. A high uptake, distributed evenly throughout the gland, with low TSH levels in the blood confirms the diagnosis and differentiates it from thyroiditis, which is treated very differently.

Diagnostic imaging tests (MRI, CAT scan, and ultrasound) may be recommended to rule out thyroid tumor as the underlying cause of the hyperthyroid symptoms, or an eye tumor as the underlying cause for exophthalmos.

Treatment

Treatment is aimed at controlling the overactivity of the thyroid gland. This can be most quickly achieved with antithyroid medications. Medications to relieve heart symptoms, sweating, and anxiety may also be prescribed. When medication is unsuccessful or if the individual prefers, outpatient administration of radioactive iodine may be given in liquid form. The radioactive iodine concentrates in the thyroid gland, destroying overactive thyroid tissue (ablation). Individuals who do not respond well to these approaches may need to have part or all of the thyroid gland removed (thyroidectomy), which can result in hypothyroidism due to the underproduction or absence of the thyroid hormones. Eye problems usually resolve with treatment of the underlying disorder. Sometimes prednisone is required for severe inflammation, and eyes may need to be taped closed at night so they do not dry out; wearing sunglasses and using eyedrops may lessen irritation.

Rarely, surgical decompression of the orbit may be required. Even with good response to treatment, lifelong monitoring by a physician is important because of the serious complications associated with the disease.

Prognosis

Graves' disease may subside for no apparent reason, or may result in a deficiency of thyroid hormone (hypothyroidism), also for no apparent reason. Though treatment for the thyroid problem itself can be successful, in most cases the disorder progresses. Eye, heart, and psychological complications such as depression may remain after treatment. Graves' disease often recurs requiring life-long antithyroid treatment. Weight gain is a frequent consequence of treatment.

Untreated or poorly treated Graves' disease can lead to a serious condition called thyroid storm or thyroid crisis, which can lead to death.

Differential Diagnosis

Bulging eyes (exophthalmos) can be caused by a tumor in the eye socket that causes the eyeball to be pushed forward. The other symptoms of Graves' disease are similar to those found in a non-thyroid disorder called pheochromocytoma. Only laboratory tests can confirm the diagnosis. The most important differential diagnoses are other causes of hyperthyroidism including thyroiditis, toxic goiter, hot nodule, and facetious thyroid hormone ingestion.

Specialists

- Endocrinologist
- General Surgeon
- Ophthalmologist
- Otolaryngologist
- Psychiatrist
- Psychologist

Work Restrictions / Accommodations

Work restrictions or accommodations are not usually necessary. Individuals with protruding eyes (exophthalmos) may be more sensitive to bright light, fumes, wind, or dust, and may require protective eyewear or reassignment to a position where these conditions can be avoided. Exophthalmos also causes eye irritation and dryness, which may be alleviated by frequently using eye drops. If surgery is required, extended sick leave may be required during the recovery period.

Comorbid Conditions

Individuals with other autoimmune diseases (AIDS) may experience more severe symptoms.

Complications

Anti thyroid drugs can cause jaundice or, rarely, neutropenia. Graves' disease can cause heart disease (atrial fibrillation or congestive heart failure). Surgical removal of all or part of the thyroid gland (thyroidectomy) can result in a decrease in thyroid hormones (hypothyroidism). It can also result in vocal cord damage and permanently reduced function of the parathyroid glands (hypoparathyroidism). During treatment, individuals may experience a number of temporary side effects associated with the drugs they are taking. RAI usually results in permanent hypothyroidism, requiring treatment with thyroid hormones for life.

Factors Influencing Duration

The length of disability may be influenced by the severity of the symptoms, complications resulting from the disease, and the method of treatment.

Length of Disability

Remission occurs in approximately 30% of cases treated with antithyroid drugs, most of which recur within 5 years. For Thyroidectomy, durations include hospitalization.

Medical treatment.

Duration in Days

Job Classification	Minimum	Optimum	Maximum
Sedentary work	1	3	7
Light work	1	3	7
Medium work	1	3	7
Heavy work	1	3	7
Very Heavy work	1	3	7

Surgical treatment (thyroidectomy).

Duration in Days

Job Classification	Minimum	Optimum	Maximum
Sedentary work	7	14	21
Light work	7	14	21
Medium work	14	21	28
Heavy work	14	28	42
Very Heavy work	14	28	42

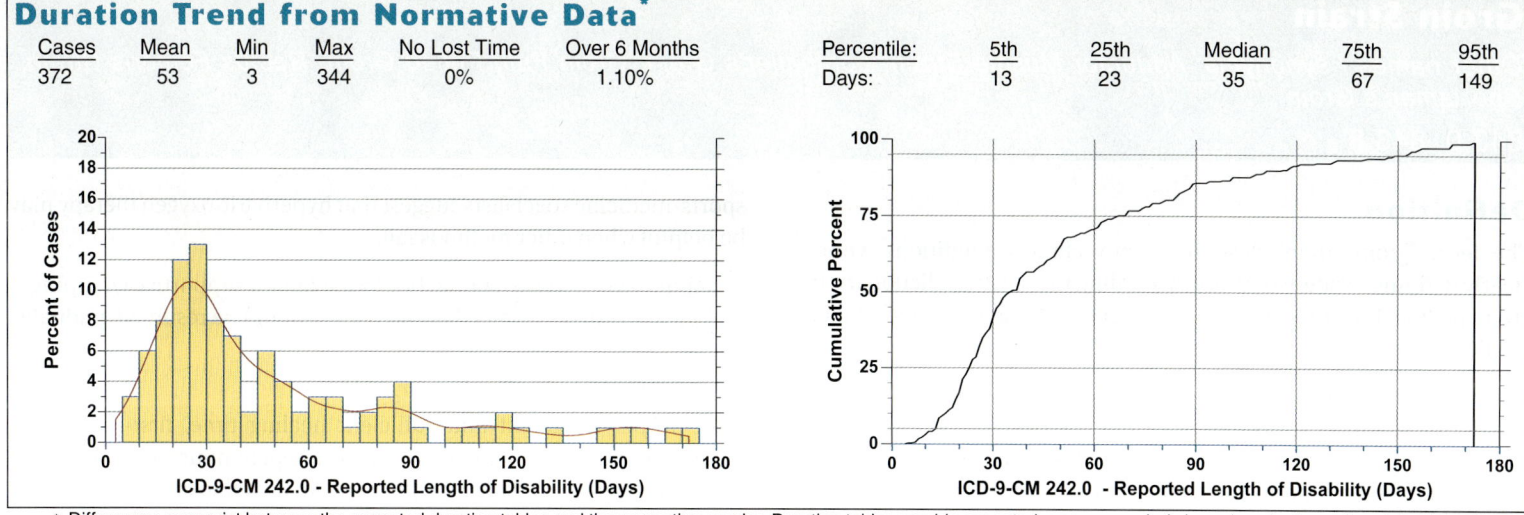

* Differences may exist between the expected duration tables and the normative graphs. Duration tables provide expected recovery periods based on the type of work performed by the individual. The normative graphs reflect the actual observed experience of many individuals across the spectrum of physical conditions, in a variety of industries, and with varying levels of case management.

Failure to Recover

If an individual fails to recover within the maximum duration expectancy period, the reader may wish to reference the following questions to assist in better understanding the specifics of an individual's medical case.

Regarding diagnosis:

- Does the individual have a history of hyperthyroidism?
- Are symptoms indicative of increased thyroid hormone levels, such as weight loss, increased appetite, hand tremors, nervousness, restlessness, fatigue, heat intolerance, sweating, muscle cramps, breathlessness, blurred or double vision, diarrhea or frequent bowel movements, menstrual irregularities, difficulty climbing stairs, and a fluttering in the chest (heart palpitations)?
- Does the individual have a goiter? Are the eyes bulging (exophthalmos)?
- Does the individual have an "orange-peel" skin texture (myxedema) on the front of the shins?
- Does the individual have symptoms of thyroid storm, including rapid pulse, delirium, nausea, diarrhea, dehydration, fever, and generalized weakness (malaise)?
- Has diagnosis been confirmed by thyroid function and radioactive iodine uptake tests?
- Are imaging tests (MRI, CAT scan, and ultrasound) required to rule out thyroid tumor or eye tumor?

Regarding treatment:

- Have antithyroid medications been prescribed? Is the individual compliant with the treatment regimen?
- Are medications controlling symptoms?
- Has the individual had careful follow-up to monitor the serum thyroid levels and make dosage adjustments in the medication?
- Would the individual benefit from radioactive iodide treatment?
- Has surgical treatment been considered?

Regarding prognosis:

- Based on the severity of symptoms and general health of the individual, what was the expected outcome?
- Were the symptoms severe enough to warrant hospitalization (i.e., thyroid storm)?
- Has the individual experienced any associated complications such as atrial fibrillation or congestive heart failure? Have these conditions been addressed in the treatment plan?
- Did the individual experience any complications associated with surgical intervention such as vocal cord damage or hypoparathyroidism?

References

"Graves' Disease." MSN Health. 1999. 10 Nov 2000 <http://content.health.msn.com/content/asset/adam_disease_graves_disease>.

"Thyroid Gland Disorders." The Merck Manual of Medical Information. Berkow, Robert, Mark Beers, and Andrew Fletcher, eds. New York: Pocket Books, 1997. 773-781.

Groin Strain

Other names / synonyms: Adductor Muscle Strain, Footballer's Groin, Groin Pull, Pulled Groin, Rectus Femoris Strain, Sportsman's Groin

843.0, 843.8

Definition

The term "groin strain" describes many clinical conditions without clearly defining location or cause. According to Webster's dictionary, the groin is "the fold or depression between belly and thighs." Taber's medical dictionary describes the groin as "the inguinal region."

Groin strains can occur at two different locations on the upper thigh. A "hip flexor strain" involves muscles along the front of the upper thigh, while an "adductor strain" involves muscles along the inside of the upper thigh. These injuries can result from a variety of causes, including poor flexibility, inadequate warm-up, muscle strength imbalance, muscle weakness, fatigue, or a single violent force applied to the muscle. Chronic strains are caused by overuse. Acute strains are caused by direct injury or overstress.

Groin strains are categorized as mild, moderate, or severe. A mild strain involves a slightly pulled muscle without tearing of muscle or tendon fibers; there is no associated loss of strength. A moderate strain involves tearing of fibers in a muscle, tendon, or at the attachment to the bone; strength is diminished. A severe strain involves rupture of the muscle-tendon-bone attachment with separation of fibers.

Groin strains occur frequently to individuals involved in professional and recreational sports. However, they can also occur during daily activities such as lifting and reaching.

Diagnosis

History: The individual usually complains of pain and tenderness in the groin area. Bruising or skin discoloration may also be present. There may be swelling in the groin. Individuals may report muscle spasms in the abdomen and thigh.

Physical exam: Tenderness, swelling and/or bruising may be evident upon examination with palpation. A crackling sound (crepitation) may be evident in the injured area.

Tests: Plain x-rays may reveal calcification of muscle or tendon. The doctor may order further tests if a hernia is suspected.

Treatment

Particularly for the "weekend athlete" who suffers a one-time groin strain, pain and tenderness usually disappear without professional treatment within a few days to a week. Recovery can be aided by the R.I.C.E. approach (rest, ice, compression and elevation). Walking and any painful motion should be limited as much as possible. Treatment may also include massaging the area with ice. NSAIDs and topical liniments may be used for minor discomfort. For moderate or severe strains, crutches may be used for 3 to 5 days.

If the pain does not resolve, the individual may be advised to consider steroid or painkiller injections, which usually provide relief. Some sports-medicine specialists suggest that hyperbaric oxygen therapy may be helpful when other methods fail.

Rehabilitative exercises should be started once a supportive wrapping is no longer needed. Normal daily activities should be resumed gradually.

Prognosis

With proper treatment and sufficient healing time, first-time groin strains should heal completely. If this is a repeat injury, complications such as proneness to repeated injury and an unstable or arthritic hip are more likely to occur.

Differential Diagnosis

Conditions with a similar presentation include prostatitis, epididymitis, hydrocele/varicocele, testicular torsion, testicular neoplasm, inguinal hernia, femoral hernia, iliopectineal bursitis, osteoarthritis, pubic ramus fracture, and Legg-Calve-Perthes disease.

Specialists

- Internist
- Physiatrist
- Sports Medicine Physician

Rehabilitation

Rehabilitation from a groin strain usually requires progressive stretching and bilateral muscle strength balancing. Modalities are an important part of groin strain therapy. Pulsed ultrasound and electrical muscle stimulation (EMS) can greatly reduce pain and inflammation while increasing range of motion. The therapist can cool the muscles either through ice massage or mist spray prior to stretching (cryo-stretching) for active hip abduction and flexion, which helps facilitate movement without strain. Both gentle stretching for the groin and hamstring as well as adduction and flexion exercises without resistance can be started after initial pain and swelling subsides. Hip flexion exercises, such as standing with both legs together and flexing the hip so that one leg rises in front with the quadriceps parallel to the floor and the bent knee before returning the foot to the floor, may be performed.

Stair climbing and cycling exercises are "closed chain exercises" that begin when the individual can tolerate the activity. Once range of motion for the injured leg comes within 10 degrees of the non-injured leg, more advanced stretches and strength training are integrated into therapy. This phase of therapy may include aqua exercises such as jogging in place, squat lunges in shallow water, and leg lifts stressing adductor and hip flexor muscles. Strength training-- stressing adductor and hip flexor muscles--continues until muscle strength proportions between and within both legs are balanced. To remain injury free, the individual should continue to follow an overall body flexibility and strength-training routine.

Work Restrictions / Accommodations

If the strain is moderate to severe, crutches may be necessary. No work restrictions or accommodations should be necessary unless the individual's work responsibilities are physically demanding; in this case, the individual would need to avoid prolonged walking, standing, bending, lifting, and excessive reaching and twisting. A gradual return to daily activities is best.

Comorbid Conditions

Conditions that could impact ability to recover and further lengthen disability include obesity, history of previous groin injury, underlying cardiovascular condition that results in decreased circulation, or bleeding disorders.

Complications

Possible complications that may arise in the course of this disease include inflammation at the site of the muscle/tendon attachment to the bone (periostitis), unstable or arthritic hip following repeated injury, proneness to repeated injury, and prolonged healing time if activity is resumed too early.

Factors Influencing Duration

Factors include severity of strain, response to treatment, activities and/or responsibilities of the individual. Returning to activities too soon invites further injury.

Length of Disability

Duration in Days

Job Classification	Minimum	Optimum	Maximum
Sedentary work	0	3	7
Light work	0	3	7
Medium work	3	7	14
Heavy work	7	10	21
Very Heavy work	7	10	21

Failure to Recover

If an individual fails to recover within the maximum duration expectancy period, the reader may wish to reference the following questions to assist in better understanding the specifics of an individual's medical case.

Regarding diagnosis:

- Did the individual have a history of a physical event that may have precipitated a groin strain?
- Did the individual experience pain and symptoms in the areas commonly associated with the diagnosis of a groin strain?
- Were conditions with similar symptoms considered in the differential diagnosis?

Regarding treatment:

- Has the individual adhered to a regimen of rest, ice, compression, elevation, and NSAIDs?
- Is the individual following prescribed physical therapy? If not, are there barriers preventing the individual from receiving appropriate physical therapy (insurance limits, lack of motivation, lack of time)?
- If pain did not resolve following conservative treatment, were other more aggressive interventions considered?

Regarding prognosis:

- Has adequate time elapsed for complete healing?
- Did the individual resume activity too soon?
- Was this a repeat injury?
- Did the individual suffer any associated complications that may impact recovery and prognosis?
- Does the individual have any underlying conditions that may impact ability to recover?

References

Groin Strain. HealthGate.com. 23 Jun 1999. 13 Nov 2000 <http://www.healthgate.com/sport/sport36.shtml>.

Hunter-Griffin, Letha. "Rehabilitative Techniques." Athletic Training and Sports Medicine. Rosemont: American Academy of Orthopaedic Surgeons, 1991. 822-825.

Kelly, Christine Kuehn. Groin Strain. City: Seattle - Health and Fitness. 2000. 14 Nov 2000 <http://home.digitalcity.com/seattle/health/conditions.dci?condition=groinstrain>.

Lacroix, Vincent J. "A Complete Approach to Groin Pain." The Physician and Sportsmedicine 28 (2000): 15. 14 Nov 2000 <http://www.physsportsmed.com/issues/2000/01_00/lacroix.htm>.

Reid, David. "Soft Tissue Injuries of the Thigh." Sports Injury Assessment and Rehabilitation. New York: Churchill Livingstone, 1992. 589-592.

Ruane, Joseph, and Thomas Rossi. "When Groin Pain is More than Just a Strain: Navigating a Broad Differential." The Physician and Sportsmedicine 26 (1998): 15. 14 Nov 2000 <http://www.physsportsmed.com/issues/1998/04apr/ruane.htm>.

Guillain-Barré Syndrome

Other names / synonyms: Acute Idiopathic Polyneuritis, Acute Idiopathic Polyradiculitis, Acute Infective Polyradiculitis, Acute Inflammatory Demyelinating Polyneuropathy, Landry's Ascending Paralysis, Landry's Paralysis, Miller-Fisher's Syndrome

357.0

Definition

Guillain-Barré syndrome is an inflammatory disease of the peripheral nervous system, those nerves outside the brain and spinal cord. As these nerves become inflamed, both movement (motor), and sensation (sensory) functions are impaired. This syndrome is characterized by the rapid onset of weakness, sensory loss, and impairment of reflexes; often paralysis of the legs, arms, breathing muscles, and face develops. Because it involves more than one nerve, it is considered a polyneuropathy.

In 60% of individuals, a mild respiratory or gastrointestinal infection precedes the symptoms by 1-3 weeks or longer. Recent studies show that a certain type of bacteria called Campylobacter jejuni is the most frequent preceding infection. Other less frequent preceding events or illnesses include surgical procedures, other bacterial infections, exposure to thrombolytic agents, or lymphoma (Hodgkin's disease). Some theories suggest an autoimmune mechanism in which the person's defense system of antibodies and white blood cells are triggered into damaging the nerve covering, leading to weakness and abnormal sensation. The administration of antirabies and the swine influenza vaccines given in 1976 was associated with an increase in the incidence of Guillain-Barré Syndrome.

Guillain-Barré syndrome occurs in all parts of the world and in all seasons. It affects adults of all ages and both sexes, although females seem to be more susceptible to the disease, and attack rates are highest in individuals 50-74 years of age. The reported incidence rate worldwide varies from 0.4-1.7 cases per 100,000 persons per year.

Diagnosis

History: Guillain-Barré syndrome is easily recognized. Tingling and burning sensations (paresthesias) and numbness are frequently reported by individuals, although these symptoms may be absent in a few cases. Most individuals report weakness starting in the limb muscles farthest from the point of origin (distal); it generally develops in the legs before the arms or the trunk, and spreads to the neck and cranial muscles later. The weakness can progress to total motor paralysis. More than 50% of individuals report pain and an aching discomfort in the muscles, especially in the hips, thighs, and back. Occasionally facial, eye (ocular), or throat (oropharyngeal) muscles are affected. Individuals may report difficulty swallowing (dysphagia), visual disturbances, or speech impairment (dysarthria).

Physical exam: Deep tendon reflexes begin by being reduced and eventually become absent. In rare cases, only the ankle reflexes are lost during the first week of the illness. In the early stage, arm muscles will be less weak than the leg muscles, or they may be spared entirely. Disturbances of the autonomic (functionally independent) system including facial flushing, rapid heart beat (sinus tachycardia), alternating high blood pressure (hypertension) and low blood pressure (hypotension), and either loss of sweating or profuse sweating (diaphoresis) are commonly found but usually do not persist longer than a week or two. Urinary retention occurs in about 15% of individuals.

Tests: Electrodiagnostic tests, including electromyography (EMG) and nerve conduction velocity (NCV), which demonstrate significantly slowed or blocked impulses support the diagnosis. A lumbar puncture is performed and a sample of cerebral spinal fluid (CSF) is analyzed. Elevated protein in the CSF is seen in most individuals, but may be normal the first few days after onset. The CSF cell count is usually normal, but in about 10% of cases there may be an elevated white blood cell count. Precursor viral infections may also be documented by blood tests.

Treatment

Because progression of this disease in its early stages is unpredictable, most individuals are initially hospitalized in an intensive care unit (ICU) so breathing and other body functions can be monitored. The treatment for acute, severe cases of Guillain Barré is respiratory assistance and careful nursing. Some individuals may require a respirator (mechanical ventilation) for breathing. Individuals with swallowing weakness (dysphagia) may require intubation to prevent aspiration of food particles. Other major components of therapy include support of blood pressure by volume infusion, administration of medication to manage low blood pressure, and prevention of sodium, potassium, and chloride (electrolyte) imbalance. Only extreme cases of high blood pressure (hypertension) require treatment with anti-hypertensive agents.

Plasmapheresis has been found to be effective in severe cases. In this procedure, blood is withdrawn and the plasma is removed and replaced with fresh frozen plasma or albumin. Individuals who are treated within 2 weeks of onset experience a distinct reduction in hospitalization time and better recovery of walking ability. Intravenous (IV) administration of immune globulin is as effective as plasma exchange; it is also safer and more immediately available. Physical therapy should be started once the individual is able to tolerate it.

Prognosis

About 85% of individuals completely recover from the condition, and about 10-12% recover with severe residual effects; 3-5% do not survive the illness. In the early stages, death is often due to cardiac arrest, but later in the illness, pulmonary embolism and other complications, such as infection, are the main causes. Of those individuals who recover with severe residual effects, most had either a severe form of the disease, widespread nerve damage, or required prolonged mechanical ventilation. Individuals who recover completely either have no residual effects or mild motor deficits in the legs or feet.

Recovery usually occurs within a few weeks or months, unless there is severe nerve damage; then it takes 6-18 months to regenerate the nerves. Older individuals recover more slowly than younger ones and are more likely to have residual weakness. Individuals who have pronounced sensory loss and imbalance are likely to have these difficulties indefinitely. About 5-9% of individuals will experience one or more recurrences of polyneuropathy. In these cases, the nerves may become enlarged and the neuropathy may become chronic; this should be distinguished from acute Guillain-Barré syndrome. The routine use of gamma globulin and plasma exchange has led to a higher rate of relapse during the first month of the illness. Most individuals with relapse respond to re-treatment and only a few become chronically disabled.

Differential Diagnosis

Differential diagnoses include other types of acute polyneuropathy that can cause respiratory failure, acute spinal cord disease, acute myasthenia gravis, and tick paralysis. Other conditions with similar symptoms include hexacarbon abuse, acute alcoholic neuropathy, basilar artery thrombosis or embolism, neuromuscular junction disease, "locked-in" syndrome, chronic demyelinating polyradiculopathy with acute presentation, acute pandysautonomia, acute transverse myelopathy, botulism poisoning, poliomyelitis, saxitoxin poisoning, diphtheria, and heavy metal intoxication.

Specialists

- Neurologist
- Physical Therapist
- Psychiatrist
- Psychologist
- Pulmonologist
- Respiratory Therapist

Rehabilitation

Individuals with Guillain-Barré Syndrome may require respiratory, speech, physical, and occupational therapy depending upon the extent of disability.

Inpatient respiratory therapy may be required if the individual presents with weakness of the diaphragm and the muscles of the ribcage (intercostal muscles). Individuals learn to use an incentive spirometer, a device that measures the volume of inspired air, to help support respiration and decrease the risk of pulmonary complications. Individuals also learn how to produce an effective cough through techniques such as huff coughing, in which the individual produces a sound like the letter "H" to prevent the build up of secretions in the lungs. For individuals who have severely weakened respiratory muscles, a ventilator may be required temporarily.

Individuals require inpatient speech therapy if they are on a ventilator. Individuals require physical and occupational therapy on an inpatient as well as an outpatient basis. Rehabilitation needs vary among individuals, as do rehabilitation treatments. Initially, therapy goals are more supportive, than rehabilitative. Occupational and physical therapists focus on preventing joint contractures through passive and active range of motion exercises to all joints. All active range of motion exercises should be performed in low repetitions to prevent further damage to the nervous system.

Once individuals are stabilized and function has begun to return, inpatient rehabilitation can begin. Individuals begin a sub-maximal strengthening program in occupational and physical therapy for the arms and legs to maintain functional abilities. Individuals perform arm exercises such as elbow extension so that crutches or a walker could be used. Lower extremity exercises such as bridging may be performed, in which the individual lies on the back with the knees bent and lifts the buttocks up from the bed. This promotes the ability to get up out of a chair.

Individuals may have impaired coordination. Individuals perform fine motor coordination exercises in occupational therapy such as picking up pegs and placing them in a pegboard or may work on practical coordination exercises such as fastening buttons or practicing their signatures. Individuals work on gross motor coordination in physical therapy such as kicking a soccer ball that is rolled towards them or throwing beanbags at a target.

Individuals work on sitting and standing balance in physical and occupational therapy. The main focus of physical and occupational therapy is to maximize functional capabilities (getting in and out of the shower, dressing, and meal preparation). Physical therapists teach skills such as getting in and out of bed, walking, or using a wheelchair.

Work Restrictions / Accommodations

Extended leave from work may be required for individuals with respiratory complications, severe residual effects from the condition, and for those who need physical therapy during recovery. Even for those who recover with few residual side effects, work duties requiring minimal physical activity and mobility may be necessary for a while.

Comorbid Conditions

Other diseases of the peripheral nerves, such as peripheral neuropathies, would impact the ability to recover and further lengthen the disability.

Complications

Complications include blood clots to the lung (pulmonary embolism), partial or complete collapse of a lung (atelectasis), tracheal erosion, respiratory infection such as aspiration pneumonia, increased intracranial pressure, other additional infections such as infections of the urinary tract (UTI) or skin (cellulitis), and psychological stress.

Factors Influencing Duration

The severity of respiratory symptoms, degree of muscle paralysis, and the presence of other peripheral nerve diseases (neuropathies) will influence the length of the disability.

Length of Disability

Most individuals recover fully within six months. The length of disability depends on the particular job requirements, particularly whether or not heavy work needs to be performed. If the individual recovers completely or nearly completely, light to moderate work may be done depending on the presence or degree of motor deficits in the arms, hands, feet, or legs. Disability may be permanent.

Duration in Days

Job Classification	Minimum	Optimum	Maximum
Sedentary work	28	84	Indefinite
Light work	28	84	Indefinite
Medium work	42	112	Indefinite
Heavy work	42	112	Indefinite
Very Heavy work	56	168	Indefinite

Failure to Recover

If an individual fails to recover within the maximum duration expectancy period, the reader may wish to reference the following questions to assist in better understanding the specifics of an individual's medical case.

Regarding diagnosis:

- Were other neuropathies and spinal cord diseases (other types of acute polyneuropathy, acute spinal cord disease, acute myasthenia gravis, tick paralysis, hexacarbon abuse, acute alcoholic neuropathy, basilar artery thrombosis or embolism, neuromuscular junction disease, "locked-in" syndrome, chronic demyelinating polyradiculopathy with acute presentation, acute pandysautonomia, acute transverse myelopathy, botulism poisoning, poliomyelitis, saxitoxin poisoning, diphtheria, and heavy metal intoxication) ruled out?
- Has diagnosis of Guillain-Barré syndrome been confirmed? Based on what criteria?
- Has individual experienced any complications, such as pulmonary embolism, atelectasis, tracheal erosion, respiratory infection such as aspiration pneumonia, increased intracranial pressure, other additional infections such as infections of the urinary tract or cellulitis, and psychological stress. ?
- Does individual have an underlying condition, such as peripheral neuropathies, that may impact recovery?

Regarding treatment:

- Did individual require mechanical ventilation or intubation?
- Has independent function been restored?
- Were therapies such as plasma exchange and immune globulin utilized? With what result?
- Was physical therapy initiated at the appropriate time?
- Would individual benefit from additional physical therapy?

Regarding prognosis:

- Does individual have residual impairment? To what degree is function impacted?
- How old is individual?
- How long since initial onset of Guillain-Barré syndrome?
- Have more than 18 months passed?
- Has sensory loss and imbalance resolved to any degree during that time?
- Has individual experienced recurrence of polyneuropathy?
- Has individual experienced a relapse?
- Has condition responded to treatment?

References

Adams, Raymond D., Maurice Victor, and Allan H. Ropper. Principles of Neurology, 6th ed. New York: McGraw Hill, 1997.

Boss, Barbara J. "Alterations of Neurologic Function." Pathophysiology. McCance, Kathryn L., and Sue E. Heuther, eds. St. Louis: Mosby-Year Book, Inc, 1994. 527-586.

Burrows, D.S., and A.C. Cuetter. "Residual Subclinical Impairment in Patients Who Totally Recovered from Guillain-Barre Syndrome: Impact on Military Performance." Military Medicine 155 (1990): 438-440.

Watchie, Joanne. Cardiopulmonary Physical Therapy. Philadelphia: W.B. Saunders Company, 1995.

Gynecomastia

Other names / synonyms: Breast Hypertrophy

611.1

Definition

Gynecomastia is a descriptive term for female breast development in the male. It can involve one or both breasts. Both sexes normally have a balance of male hormones (androgens or testosterone) and female hormone (estrogen). Gynecomastia occurs when this balance is disturbed. This condition is quite common during puberty (physiologic gynecomastia). The appearance of gynecomastia in elderly men is not unusual, as about 40% of men over 65 exhibit some breast tissue. The reasons for this are unclear.

In pathologic gynecomastia, the increased estrogen effects can be caused by estrogen-secreting tumors of the testicles and adrenal glands, an overactive thyroid gland (hyperthyroidism and thyrotoxicosis), and liver disease, notably cirrhosis of the liver. Tumors that secrete human chorionic gonadotropin, such as carcinoma of the lung, can stimulate estrogen production. Decreased androgen production or its effects is largely due to congenital disorders (genetic defects) or testicular atrophy.

Drugs can cause gynecomastia when they have an estrogen-like effect or somehow block the action of testosterone. Alcoholics may have gynecomastia because of liver damage and shrinkage (atrophy) of the testicles. Hormonal treatment for prostate cancer may also lead to this condition.

Diagnosis

History: An understandable concern with appearance and anxiety about possible breast cancer may prompt a man to seek medical advice. There could be some tenderness in the gynecomastia associated with puberty. A careful drug history should note all current and past drug use. A history of alcoholism would be significant.

Physical exam: The appearance can range from apparently normal male breasts to fully developed female breasts. Palpation of the breasts around and under the nipple (the areola) will reveal a granular consistency that is characteristic of gland development. This is important, as obese men can have fat deposits that mimic the appearance of gynecomastia.

Findings such as discoloration, skin fixation, nipple discharge, or other masses could suggest cancer of the breast. The liver is examined for changes of cirrhosis. The testicles are examined for size and uniformity.

Tests: Adolescents with minimal gynecomastia of less than 3 years duration are excluded from further testing. Without a clear history of drug-induced gynecomastia, liver function, thyroid tests, and blood levels for certain hormones are checked.

Treatment

If the individual is an adolescent undergoing normal changes of puberty, no treatment is necessary as the condition is self-limiting. Otherwise, treatment depends on the cause of the gynecomastia. A satisfactory diagnosis is made in less than half of the cases.

Drug-induced gynecomastia may be resolved by stopping that drug or changing to an alternative drug. If the hormone imbalance is caused by a tumor, treatment is directed toward the particular cancer. Low-dose tamoxifen may be useful in treating painful gynecomastia for those individuals on flutamide/finasteride combination therapy for advanced prostate cancer. Thyroid conditions would be treated accordingly. Gynecomastia associated with cirrhosis of the liver is not treated. Replacement hormone therapy is given to men with testicular insufficiency.

If gynecomastia has progressed to the stage where there are permanent changes in the breast tissue, such as fat deposition and fibrosis, the enlarged breasts will not resolve and cosmetic surgery (reduction mammoplasty) is an option. Tissue can also be removed by a surgical technique in which a suction tube is inserted through a small incision into the breast.

Prognosis

Mild cases of gynecomastia, if not due to an underlying disease, usually resolve without treatment. The prognosis for gynecomastia resulting from a disease (cirrhosis of the liver, testicular cancer) depends on the outcome of that underlying disease. Drug-induced gynecomastia usually resolves when the drug is stopped.

Differential Diagnosis

Although rare, breast cancer in men but is an alternative diagnosis in the case of a breast mass.

Specialists

- Endocrinologist
- Plastic Surgeon

Work Restrictions / Accommodations

If surgery is required, lifting and reaching above shoulder height may be limited for a brief period.

Comorbid Conditions

Length of disability may be influenced by the underlying medical condition including: adrenal tumor, prostate cancer, carcinoma of the lung, cirrhosis of the liver, hyperthyroidism, and thyrotoxicosis. Anxiety, extreme preoccupation with appearance, or gender disassociation may also impact the length of disability.

Complications

As gynecomastia is not a disease, it has no complications other than psychological effects. Anxiety and concern about appearance are common.

Factors Influencing Duration

Disability is not usually associated with this condition. Any disability would be governed by the disease or factors that caused the gynecomastia.

Length of Disability

Surgical treatment. Reduction mammoplasty.

Duration in Days

Job Classification	Minimum	Optimum	Maximum
Sedentary work	5	7	10
Light work	5	7	10
Medium work	5	14	21
Heavy work	10	21	28
Very Heavy work	10	28	35

Duration Trend from Normative Data*

Cases	Mean	Min	Max	No Lost Time	Over 6 Months
1422	33	2	482	0%	0.28%

Percentile:	5th	25th	Median	75th	95th
Days:	12	19	27	40	68

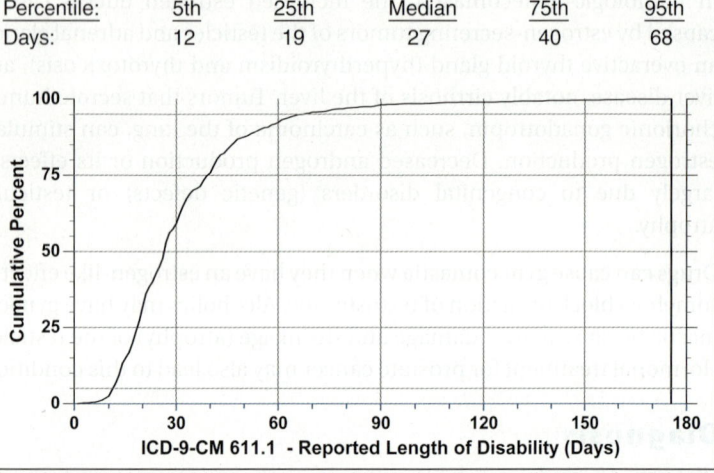

ICD-9-CM 611.1 - Reported Length of Disability (Days)

* Differences may exist between the expected duration tables and the normative graphs. Duration tables provide expected recovery periods based on the type of work performed by the individual. The normative graphs reflect the actual observed experience of many individuals across the spectrum of physical conditions, in a variety of industries, and with varying levels of case management.

Failure to Recover

If an individual fails to recover within the maximum duration expectancy period, the reader may wish to reference the following questions to assist in better understanding the specifics of an individual's medical case.

Regarding diagnosis:

- Has diagnosis of gynecomastia been confirmed?
- Have other conditions with similar symptoms been ruled out?
- Has individual undergone a comprehensive physical exam in order to try to determine the cause of the gynecomastia?
- Because gynecomastia may be due to alcoholic-related liver damage, has physician taken a complete drug and alcohol history?
- Does individual have a coexisting condition (such as being on hormonal treatment for prostate cancer) that may complicate treatment or impact recovery?

Regarding treatment:

- If gynecomastia is drug-induced, can it be resolved by stopping that particular drug or changing to an alternate drug?
- If hormone imbalance is caused by a medical condition, is underlying cause responding to treatment?
- If symptoms persist despite treatment, what other options are available?
- If gynecomastia has progressed to the stage where there are permanent changes in the breast tissue, is individual a candidate for surgical intervention?

Regarding prognosis:

- If symptoms persist despite treatment of underlying cause, would individual benefit from consultation with a specialist (endocrinologist, plastic surgeon)?
- Is surgical removal of excess breast tissue warranted?
- If individual is experiencing emotional trauma due to body image, would psychological counseling be beneficial?

References

Staiman, V.R., and F.C. Lowe. "Tamoxifen for Flutamide/Finasteride-induced Gynecomastia." Urology 50 6 (1997): 929-933.

Thornton, Yvonne S. Woman to Woman. New York: Penguin, 1997.

Hallux Rigidus

Other names / synonyms: Arthrosis, First Metatarsophalangeal Joint Arthritis, Hallux Limitus

735.2, 735.9, 755.66

Definition

Hallux rigidus is a degenerative arthritic condition that affects the large joint at the base of the great toe (metatarsophalangeal joint or MTP joint). When the joint becomes so arthritic that it is stiff (almost no motion or no motion), it is called hallux rigidus. The ends of the bones at the MTP joint are covered with a slick coating (articular cartilage). Hallux rigidus develops when this cartilage begins to wear away (degenerate) and raw bone rubs against raw bone.

For some individuals, the condition begins when there is an injury to the joint cartilage. The injury sets a degenerative process in motion that may last for years before symptoms appear. In most individuals, however, there is no definitive cause. The condition just develops, although it is believed that minor anatomical differences in the foot may make it more likely that certain individuals develop hallux rigidus. The most probable cause of the condition is the tremendous stress placed on this joint during walking. With each step, a force equal to twice the body weight passes through this joint. In some individuals, hallux rigidus may be secondary to some other medical condition (e.g., gout or infection of the joint).

Hallux rigidus is fairly common and not influenced by age or gender. Sports that involve running or jumping may predispose an individual to hallux rigidus.

Diagnosis

History: This condition develops gradually so individuals may mistakenly associate it with the activity they were doing when pain was first noticed. Symptoms include pain, intermittent swelling, and a stiffness or loss of motion in the joint at the base of the big toe (MTP joint). Pain is worse during walking or running because the MTP joint does not have the ability to move enough to allow the foot to roll through with each step.

Physical exam: Physical exam reveals swelling, tenderness, and very restricted motion of the great toe (MTP joint). The joint is painful when moved. In severe cases, the ability to bend the toe upward (dorsiflexion) may be lost completely.

Tests: X-rays are taken in order to evaluate the full extent of joint degeneration, bone spur (osteophyte) formation on the metatarsal head, and loss of joint space.

Treatment

Treatment usually begins with anti-inflammatory medications to control the inflammation associated with the degenerative arthritis. Cortisone injected directly into the affected joint may give temporary relief.

Special shoes that reduce the amount of bending the toe incurs during walking also help lessen the symptoms. A rocker-type sole (addition of a metatarsal bar) allows the shoe to take some of the bending force. In some cases, this can be combined with a metal brace (steel shank) in the sole to limit its flexibility, thereby reducing motion in the MTP joint.

If other treatments fail, surgery may be suggested. One procedure called a cheilectomy involves removing bone spurs at the top of the MTP joint so they don't bump together when the toe extends. This procedure permits the toe to bend better and reduces pain with walking.

Another surgical alternative is to remove the MTP joint between the two bones and fixing the bones with a metal pin or screw, thus allowing them to grow or fuse together (arthrodesis). This procedure results in a joint that no longer moves so a rocker-sole shoe is usually needed after arthrodesis to improve gait.

Replacing the joint with an artificial joint (arthroplasty) similar to that of a knee or hip replacement can both relieve pain and preserve joint motion. In this outpatient procedure, one of the joint surfaces is removed and replaced with a plastic surface.

Prognosis

Conservative treatment with anti-inflammatory medications and special footwear can effectively treat symptoms and yield a good long-term outcome for many individuals. When symptoms become refractory to this type of treatment, surgery may be performed. A cheilectomy will lessen or even eliminate pain during walking and allow bending of the joint. Because of the progressive degenerative nature of arthritis, however, additional treatment will be necessary. Fusion of the MTP joint alleviates pain but leaves the individual with a joint that no longer moves causing a persisting limp. Wearing a shoe with a rocker-type sole may improve the gait following a fusion procedure. Arthroplasty may relieve pain and preserve joint motion, however, the artificial joint will probably not last a lifetime and will require repeat surgery when it fails.

Differential Diagnosis

Other conditions that present with similar symptomatology include gout, fracture, neoplasm of bone and soft tissue, sesamoiditis, bursitis, tendinitis, and presence of a foreign body.

Specialists

- Orthopedic Surgeon
- Podiatrist
- Rheumatologist

Work Restrictions / Accommodations

Since the pain is worsened by weight-bearing, activities such as squatting, walking, lifting, or prolonged periods of standing may be restricted. According to the individual's job requirements, other accommodations (e.g., use of crutches or a cane) may be needed.

> **Complementary and Alternative Therapies**
>
> Content is intended for awareness only. Treatments may or may not be effective. Scientific evidence may be lacking and some substances have potentially toxic effects. Dr. Presley Reed and the editors do not endorse the use of these therapies in the absence of consultation with a licensed medical professional.
>
> Glucosamine and chondroitin sulfate - May help relieve pain and actually grow new articular cartilage.

Comorbid Conditions

Conditions that could impact ability to recover and further lengthen disability include peripheral vascular disease, obesity and gout or bursitis of the affected toe joints.

Complications

In the majority of individuals, the joint remains arthritic and stiff and tends not to get much worse. However, in approximately 20-25% of individuals, the joint becomes progressively more stiff and painful. As with any foot problem, pain may lead to an altered gait. This can place abnormal stress on other parts of the foot, ankle, and knee, creating pain in these joints and eventually causing back pain.

Factors Influencing Duration

Factors that may influence length of disability include the individual's age, whether one or both feet are involved, whether the individual had surgery, and individual's basic job requirements.

Length of Disability

Medical treatment.

Duration in Days

Job Classification	Minimum	Optimum	Maximum
Sedentary work	5	7	14
Light work	5	7	14
Medium work	5	7	14
Heavy work	5	7	14
Very Heavy work	5	7	14

Surgical treatment.

Duration in Days

Job Classification	Minimum	Optimum	Maximum
Sedentary work	7	14	21
Light work	7	21	21
Medium work	14	21	28
Heavy work	28	35	42
Very Heavy work	28	35	42

Failure to Recover

If an individual fails to recover within the maximum duration expectancy period, the reader may wish to reference the following questions to assist in better understanding the specifics of an individual's medical case.

Regarding diagnosis:

- Was the cause of hallux rigidus determined?
- Was there a previous injury to the joint cartilage?
- Were there secondary medical conditions that may have contributed to the development of hallux rigidus?
- Does individual participate in a sport that involves running or jumping?
- Does individual experience pain, intermittent swelling, or stiffness or loss of motion in the MTP joint? Is the pain aggravated during walking or running?
- Were conditions with similar symptoms of hallux rigidus ruled out?
- Did x-rays confirm arthritic changes? Were bone spurs present?

Regarding treatment:

- Was individual given anti-inflammatory medications and Cortisone injections?
- Was individual supplied with special shoes with a rocker-type sole? Was a metal brace in the sole also used?
- Did conservative treatments fail to alleviate the condition?
- Was surgery performed? If so, what type of surgery was necessary? Cheilectomy, fusion of the MTP joint, or arthroplasty?

Regarding prognosis:

- Is the individual's employer able to accommodate any necessary restrictions?
- Does individual have any conditions that may affect ability to recover?
- Did the joint become progressively more stiff and painful?
- Did pain cause individual to alter gait?
- Did back pain occur?

References

Apley, A. Graham, and Louis Solomon. "The Ankle and Foot." Concise System of Orthopaedics and Fractures. Oxford: Butterworth-Heinemann Ltd, 1994. 209-223.

Magee, David J. "The Lower Leg, Ankle, and Foot." Orthopedic Physical Assessment. Bilbis, Margaret M., ed. Philadelphia: W.B. Saunders Company, 1992. 448-515.

Hammertoe

Other names / synonyms: Claw Toe, Hammer Digit Syndrome

735.4

Definition

A hammertoe is a crooked (contracted) toe deformity in which the toe bends upward like a claw. It usually involves the second through fifth toes (lesser toes).

Hammertoes result from a buckling (contracture) of the toe joints (metatarsophalangeal and proximal interphalangeal joints). Pressure points form on the bottom of the metatarsal bone and on the top of the middle joint of the toe.

If the second joint (distal interphalangeal joint) of the toe also bends down, the deformity is known as a "clawtoe." If the distal interphalangeal joint alone is contracted, the condition is known as a "mallet toe." Hammertoes can overlap or underlap each other. Friction between hammertoes can result in the enlargement of the toe bones in such a manner that a spur (exostosis) forms. A corn may form over such a spur between 2 toes, and may be painful. Hammertoes may be painful due to pressure from shoes, from corns, or from arthritis, which often develops in the contracted joint. Hammertoes may be hereditary, or may develop due to musculoskeletal imbalances of the foot.

Hammertoes are more common in females than males, and more common in blacks than in whites. The incidence of hammertoes increases with age. In the 15-30 year-old group, the incidence is 1 in 100 among whites, and 1 in 33 among blacks, with a 9:1 female to male preponderance. In 31-60 year olds, the incidence is 1 in 15 whites, one in 5 blacks, and has a 2.5:1 female preponderance. In the over 60-year-old group, the incidence is 1 in 10 whites, 1 in 9 blacks, with a 3:1 female preponderance.

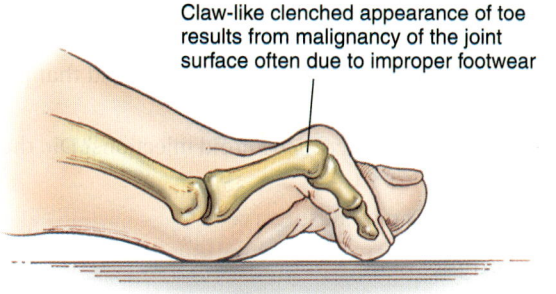

Claw-like clenched appearance of toe results from malignancy of the joint surface often due to improper footwear

Laurie O'Keefe

Diagnosis

History: Individuals may report painful calluses on the top of the toe and under the metatarsal head (ball of the foot) of the corresponding toe. Individuals may also report that the joints of the toe are painful, that the toe is becoming crooked, and that the pressure from the shoe is causing pain.

Physical exam: The exam may reveal a toe in which the near bone of the toe (proximal phalanx) is angled upward, and the middle bone of the toe points the opposite direction (plantar flexed). Toes may appear crooked or rotated as well. The involved joint may be painful when moved, or may be stiff. There may be areas of thickened skin (corns) on top of or between the toes.

Tests: X-rays will demonstrate the contractures of the involved joints, as well as possible arthritic changes and bone enlargements (spurs; exostoses).

Treatment

Hammertoes that are not painful (asymptomatic) may not require treatment. In mild cases, wearing open-toed shoes or wider shoes may provide relief. Foam or moleskin pads can provide symptomatic relief by reducing pressure. Periodic trimming (debridement) of corns (clavi, helomata) by a podiatrist can provide temporary relief. Corticosteroid injections are often very effective in reducing pain. Surgical correction is necessary in more severe cases, and may consist of removing a bone spur (exostectomy); removing the enlarged bone and straightening the toe (arthroplasty), sometimes with internal fixation with a pin; fusing the toe joint and then straightening the toe (arthrodesis); or simple tendon lengthening and capsule release in milder, flexible hammertoes (tenotomy and capsulotomy).

Prognosis

In mild cases, conservative treatment provides relief of symptoms. Individuals treated surgically usually heal well with complete symptomatic relief. Joint fusion procedures are successful in relieving pain, but they leave the toes stiff.

Differential Diagnosis

Involvement of all toes can be due to rheumatoid arthritis, pes cavus deformity, or Charcot-Marie-Tooth disease, or other peripheral neuropathies.

Specialists

- Orthopedic Surgeon
- Podiatrist
- Sports Medicine Physician

Work Restrictions / Accommodations

Work requiring walking or prolonged standing may have to be restricted or modified if surgery is performed. This restriction will continue until the surgical areas are healed. The individual may wear a surgical shoe and may be restricted from driving. If the individual requires postoperative pain medications, drug policies need to be reviewed.

Comorbid Conditions

Comorbid conditions include diabetes mellitus, peripheral vascular disease, and various types of arthritis.

Complications

Long-standing hammertoe deformity can result in arthritic changes in the joint, causing the joint to become stiff or fixed (ankylosis), or causing the formation of arthritic bone enlargements (spurs or exostoses).

Factors Influencing Duration

The method of treatment may influence the length of disability, with surgical treatment requiring the longest disability.

Length of Disability

Surgical treatment.

Duration in Days

Job Classification	Minimum	Optimum	Maximum
Sedentary work	3	7	14
Light work	7	21	21
Medium work	14	21	28
Heavy work	28	35	42
Very Heavy work	28	35	42

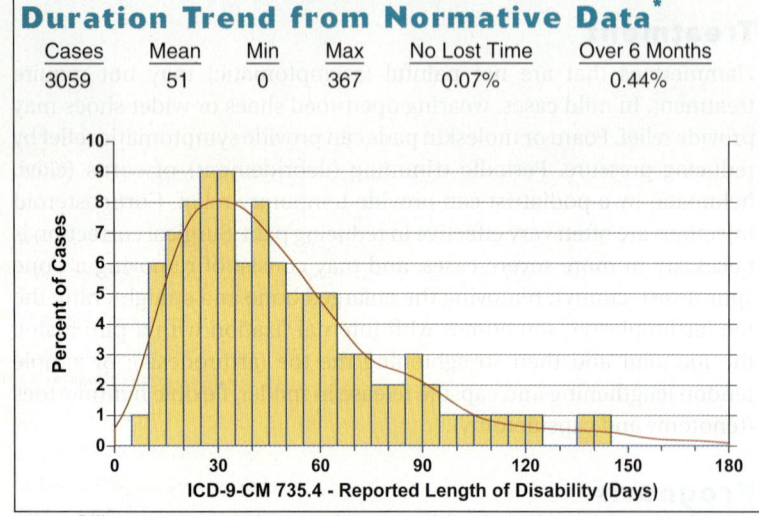

Duration Trend from Normative Data*

Cases	Mean	Min	Max	No Lost Time	Over 6 Months
3059	51	0	367	0.07%	0.44%

ICD-9-CM 735.4 - Reported Length of Disability (Days)

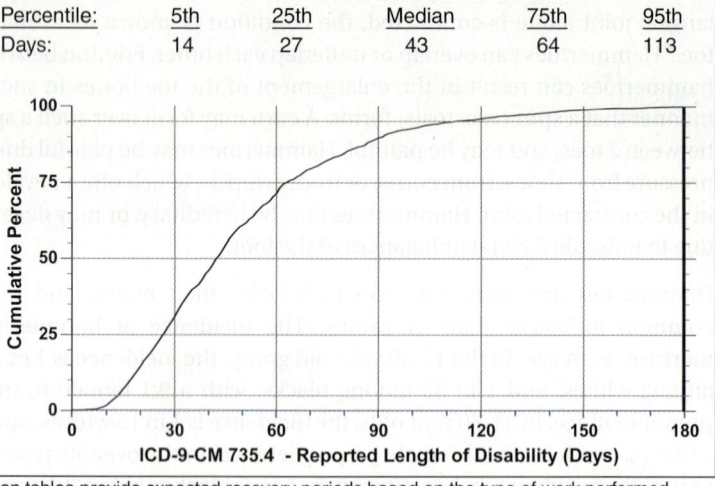

Percentile:	5th	25th	Median	75th	95th
Days:	14	27	43	64	113

ICD-9-CM 735.4 - Reported Length of Disability (Days)

* Differences may exist between the expected duration tables and the normative graphs. Duration tables provide expected recovery periods based on the type of work performed by the individual. The normative graphs reflect the actual observed experience of many individuals across the spectrum of physical conditions, in a variety of industries, and with varying levels of case management.

Failure to Recover

If an individual fails to recover within the maximum duration expectancy period, the reader may wish to reference the following questions to assist in better understanding the specifics of an individual's medical case.

Regarding diagnosis:

- What type of deformity of the toes does the individual have? Is it painful?
- Did x-rays confirm the diagnosis?
- Has the individual tried open-toed or wider shoes? Did that provide relief?
- Were conditions with similar symptoms ruled out?

Regarding treatment:

- Did the individual try foam or moleskin pads? Did that provide relief?
- Did the individual have the corns trimmed? Did that provide relief?
- Did the individual have corticosteroid injections? Did that reduce the pain?
- Did the individual require surgery?

Regarding prognosis:

- Does the individual have any pre-existing conditions, such as diabetes or peripheral vascular disease that might influence disability?
- Has the individual developed arthritic changes?

References

Apley, A. Graham, and Louis Solomon. "The Ankle and Foot." Concise System of Orthopaedics and Fractures. Oxford: Butterworth-Heinemann Ltd, 1994. 209-223.

Kisner, Carolyn, and Lynn Allen Colby. "The Ankle and Foot." Therapeutic Exercise: Foundations and Techniques, 2nd ed. Philadelphia: F.A. Davis Company, 1990. 385-408.

Magee, David J. "Lower Leg, Ankle, and Foot." Orthopedic Physical Assessment. Biblis, Margaret M., ed. Philadelphia: W.B. Saunders Company, 1992. 448-515.

Trepal, Michael J. Preferred Practice Guidelines: Hammer Toe Syndrome. Park Ridge, IL: American College Of Foot and Ankle Surgeons, 1992.

Head Injury, Superficial

Other names / synonyms: Minor Head Injury
910, 910.9, 920

Definition

A superficial head injury is an injury to the head that does not involve damage to the skull or brain. Injuries can include scrapes (abrasions), cuts (lacerations), bruises (contusions), burns, or animal bites. The formal definition of minor head injury is loss of consciousness for less than 10 minutes, no amnesia, no coma (Glasgow Coma Scale 15), no skull fracture, no new neurological damage, and no detected brain injury.

Most, if not all, individuals in the US experience a minor injury to their heads at least once in their lives from minor traffic accidents, sports injuries, falls, criminal violence, and accidents at work or home. Airbags prevent serious head injury in vehicle crashes but can themselves cause minor injuries to the head, neck, and upper body. A US study found that more than 5% of airbag injuries are superficial burns to the upper extremity or head and neck. A 1993 German evaluation of 119 individuals involved in vehicle accidents (who were airbag-protected) showed them having predominant minor injuries on the head, cervix, and thorax.

Diagnosis

History: The individual may report a recent bite, bump, cut, or scrape to the head causing minor bleeding that stops within a few minutes. Superficial head injuries should not include the symptoms of persistent or severe headache, blurred or double vision, difficulty walking or maintaining balance, lethargy or inability to arouse from sleep, blurred speech, numbness or loss of sensation, bleeding, or drainage of fluid from the nose, mouth, or ear.

Physical exam: The pulse should be above 50 beats per minute in adults. The neurological exam can rule out a more severe head injury. Pupils are equal in size and react equally to light. The individual must be totally oriented (person, place, and time).

Tests: Skull x-ray rules out skull fractures. CT scanning rules out delayed bleeding into the brain (hematoma) and MRI determines brain injury. These tests are generally only required if physical signs give any suggestion that the head injury is more serious.

Treatment

Minor head injuries are treated as minor scrapes and injuries through use of ice packs, bandages, and mild pain relievers (analgesics). Cuts deeper than 1 mm may be closed with stitches after the individual is given a topical anesthetic. A superficial animal bite is additionally treated with a course of antibiotics. The individual is observed for development of symptoms associated with more serious head injury. Individual may be admitted into the hospital for overnight observation if they start showing signs of concussion or brain injury after an initial diagnosis of minor head injury.

Prognosis

Wounds treated with stitches should heal within 10 days, depending on the depth of injury. Full recovery is expected within a few days for an individual with a superficial head injury that needs no special treatment.

Differential Diagnosis

An individual with a head injury may have a minor head injury or may have a more serious skull fracture, concussion, penetrating injury, and bleeding into the brain (hematoma).

Specialists

- Emergency Medicine
- Neurologist

Work Restrictions / Accommodations

A superficial head injury should not require any work restrictions or accommodations.

Comorbid Conditions

Comorbid conditions that slow full recovery include a previous head injury and hemophilia.

Complications

An injury to the head such as a blow may cause injury to the brain even if there are no signs of external damage. Because the signs of brain injury may not show up immediately, it may be difficult to differentiate a damaging blow from an insignificant one. Up to 50% of individuals diagnosed with a minor head injury develop symptoms of minor brain injury (postconcussive syndrome) within one month of injury. Because of this complication, the individual should have a follow-up visit to a neurologist within 1 to 2 weeks of the injury.

Factors Influencing Duration

The location, severity, and extent of the injury influence the length of disability.

Length of Disability

The individual requiring stitches to close a wound will not have a prolonged disability but will need to schedule a visit to a general practitioner to have the stitches removed after 7 to 10 days. During the follow-up visit, the diagnosis will either be confirmed and the individual can return to all his/her duties, or the diagnosis will be changed to something more serious. A changed diagnosis can lengthen the disability.

Duration in Days

Job Classification	Minimum	Optimum	Maximum
Sedentary work	0	1	3
Light work	0	1	3
Medium work	0	3	7
Heavy work	0	3	7
Very Heavy work	0	3	7

Notes

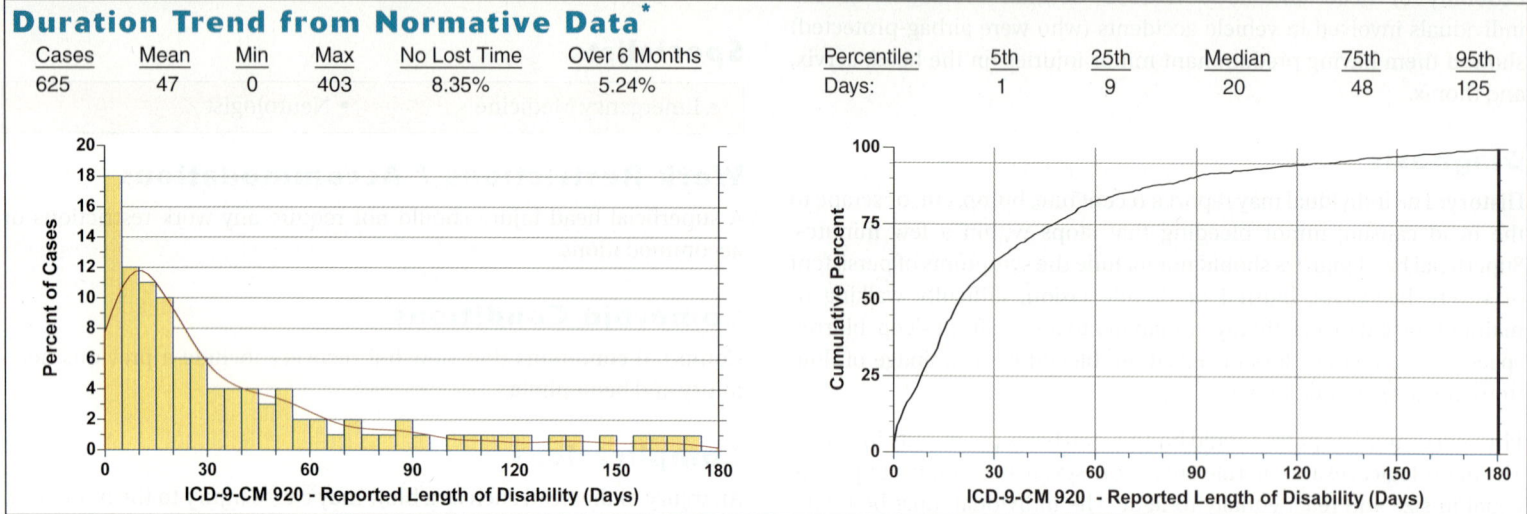

Duration Trend from Normative Data*

Cases	Mean	Min	Max	No Lost Time	Over 6 Months
625	47	0	403	8.35%	5.24%

Percentile:	5th	25th	Median	75th	95th
Days:	1	9	20	48	125

ICD-9-CM 920 - Reported Length of Disability (Days)

* Differences may exist between the expected duration tables and the normative graphs. Duration tables provide expected recovery periods based on the type of work performed by the individual. The normative graphs reflect the actual observed experience of many individuals across the spectrum of physical conditions, in a variety of industries, and with varying levels of case management.

Failure to Recover

If an individual fails to recover within the maximum duration expectancy period, the reader may wish to reference the following questions to assist in better understanding the specifics of an individual's medical case.

Regarding diagnosis:

- Has the diagnosis of superficial head injury been confirmed?
- Did individual suffer a more serious injury such as a skull fracture, concussion, penetrating injury, or hematoma?
- Did MRI and CT rule out brain injury?
- Did a neurologist examine individual?
- Has follow-up in 1 to 2 weeks of injury been scheduled with neurologist?

- Does individual have an underlying condition that may impact recovery such as a previous head injury or hemophilia?

Regarding treatment:

- Did individual follow the prescribed therapy?
- Have there been any complications (such as a wound infection) despite treatment? What additional treatment has been required?
- Was individual admitted for observation? Was diagnosis updated to a more serious or more specific diagnosis?

Regarding prognosis:

- Has diagnosis been revised?
- Has individual had an additional head injury since the one causing the disability?
- Since the disability, has individual reported blackouts or other symptoms indicating postconcussive syndrome?

References

Bazarian J., M. Hartman, and E. Delahunta. "Minor Head Injury: Predicting Follow-up After Discharge From the Emergency Department." Brain Injury 14 3 (2000): 285-294.

Thornhill, S., et al. "Disability in Young People and Adults One Year After Head Injury: Prospective Cohort Study." British Medical Journal / British Medical Association 320 7250 (2000): 1631-1635.

Headache

Other names / synonyms: Benign Headache, Cephalgia, Cluster Headache, Histamine Headache, Muscle Contraction Headache, Pain in the Head, Tension Headache

307.81, 784.0

Definition

Headache is a general description for a pain in the head. It is the most common pain complaint, and although painful and annoying, the vast majority do not indicate a serious disorder.

There are several distinct types of headaches: tension, caused by muscle contraction, and vascular, which includes migraine, or cluster, or a combination of the two.

Headache may occur without any known cause or can be a symptom of a variety of other disorders (e.g., infections in the sinuses, meninges, or brain), severe long-standing high blood pressure, bleeding or tumor in the brain, and alcohol overuse. It may also occur without any known cause. A headache can also occur as a result of hunger, and rebound headaches can develop when the frequent use of certain analgesics is stopped. Most people have experienced a headache caused by muscular tension at one time or another. These tension headaches may result from acute stress or may be associated with chronic anxiety or depression.

Vascular headaches may be caused by dilation of blood vessels in the brain and/or scalp. Migraine is the most common type of vascular headache. Cluster headaches are a less common variation of migraine headaches and are possibly associated with the release of histamine from body tissues and the enlargement of the carotid arteries of the neck.

Many disorders involving structures of the head and face can cause headaches or facial pain. Among these are acute or chronic sinusitis, middle ear infection (otitis media), mastoiditis, dental disorders, and temporomandibular joint (TMJ) syndrome. Headaches may also result from eyestrain or can be a symptom of an eye disease such as iritis or glaucoma. Facial pain can be caused by nerve disorders such as tic douloureux or herpes zoster.

Headaches may be a symptom of a central nervous system (CNS) disease. CNS infections (meningitis and encephalitis) and space-occupying lesions (cerebral hemorrhage, subdural hematoma, brain cancer, or brain abscess) may be accompanied by headache. Headache may also occur in system-wise (systemic) diseases affecting the CNS (severe hypertension and systemic lupus erythematosus). An extremely severe headache is the primary symptom of a ruptured cerebral aneurysm. A head injury (concussion or cerebral contusion) may be followed by post-traumatic headaches. Headache may also occur after a spinal tap (lumbar puncture).

Pain may be referred to the head from other areas of the body particularly the neck, shoulders, or back. Disorders of the spine (intervertebral disc disorders) or the brachial plexus (thoracic outlet syndrome) may produce headaches. Headaches may also arise from disorders of muscle and fascia (neck or back strains, myofascial pain syndrome, and fibromyalgia).

Headaches may be toxic in origin (e.g., alcoholism, lead poisoning, and renal failure). Caffeine withdrawal is often overlooked as a cause of headaches. Headache may also be an adverse effect of certain medications such as those used to treat angina (nitrates). In some people, glare or certain foods may trigger headaches; heavy smokers may be more prone to headaches. In addition, fever from any cause may be accompanied by headache.

In the US, there are about 20 million outpatient visits every year for headaches. In general, headache affects more women than men, however cluster headaches affects more men than women.

Diagnosis

History: Individuals may report associated symptoms including anorexia, nausea, vomiting, a runny nose, or depression. The history provides the most important diagnostic information and should include onset (sudden, chronic, age at onset), location (unilateral or bilateral; back of the neck, head, behind the eye), character of the pain (violent, throbbing, pressure or ache, boring, shock-like, worsening over time), and trigger factors (hormonal changes, menses, changes in sleep, post-stress, foods, missing a meal, or weather changes).

Physical exam: The exam of an individual with a benign headache disorder is normal. Physical examination of an individual with a headache secondary to an organic disorder may reveal tender temporal arteries, swelling of the optic disc (papilledema), fever and neck rigidity, loss of neurologic function (e.g., loss of sight, speech changes), or personality changes.

Tests: If history and physical exam suggest a typical headache history, testing is not necessary. If sinusitis is suspected as the cause of headache, sinus x-rays may confirm it. Tests recommended for acute, severe headaches may include CT scan, MRI, and lumbar puncture in order to exclude organic abnormalities. Other tests may be recommended for individuals over 60 who have a new onset of headache or a change in the headache pattern. Tests recommended may include sedimentation rate or C-reactive protein or a temporal artery biopsy to rule out giant cell arteritis.

Treatment

Treatment and prognosis depend on the specific diagnosis. Appropriate treatment for any specific underlying conditions is necessary.

Preventative (prophylactic) medications used for the treatment of tension headaches may include over-the-counter analgesics, NSAIDs, antidepressants, and muscle relaxants. Medications to stop a headache that has begun (abortive medications) include NSAIDs and muscle relaxants.

Prophylactic medications used for the treatment of migraine headaches may include beta-blockers, calcium-channel blockers, for nonsteroidal anti-inflammatory drugs (NSAIDs), antidepressants, serotonin agonists, antihistamines, or anticonvulsants. Medications recommended to abort a migraine headache may include serotonin agonists, NSAIDs, antiemetics, and analgesics.

Prophylactic medications used for the treatment of cluster headaches may include calcium channel blockers, corticosteroids, serotonin agonists, and lithium. Abortive medications may include inhalation of 100% oxygen, serotonin agonists, a local anesthetic, analgesics, or glucocorticoids. Triggers factors such as cigarette smoke, alcohol, and specific foods should be avoided.

Treatment for all types of headache also includes nonpharmacologic treatment. Treatment may also include biofeedback, physical therapy, and guided imagery. Stress management strategies, relaxation techniques, good posture, adequate sleep, and massage may help the headache sufferer.

Prognosis

Prognosis depends on the identified cause.

Differential Diagnosis

Headache can occur with sinusitis, otitis media, mastoiditis, dental disorders, and TMJ syndrome. It may be the result of eyestrain or a symptom of an eye disease such as iritis or glaucoma. Facial pain can be caused by nerve disorders such as tic douloureux or herpes zoster.

Headache may be a symptom of CNS disease. CNS infections (meningitis and encephalitis) and space-occupying lesions (cerebral hemorrhage, subdural hematoma, brain cancer, or brain abscess) may be accompanied by headache. Headache may also occur in systemic diseases affecting the CNS (severe hypertension and systemic lupus erythematosus). A head injury (concussion or cerebral contusion) may be followed by post-traumatic headaches. Headache also may occur after a spinal tap (lumbar puncture). A severe headache will be the first symptom of a ruptured cerebral aneurysm.

Pain may be referred to the head from other areas of the body particularly the neck, shoulders, or back. Disorders of the spine (intervertebral disc disorders) or the brachial plexus (thoracic outlet syndrome) may produce headaches. Headaches may also arise from disorders of muscle and fascia (neck or back strains, myofascial pain syndrome, or fibromyalgia).

Headaches may be toxic in origin (e.g., alcoholism, lead poisoning, and renal failure). Caffeine withdrawal is a cause of headaches. Headache may also be an adverse effect of certain medications such as those used to treat angina (nitrates). In addition, fever from any cause may be accompanied by headache.

Headache may be due to physical causes such as inflammation of the blood vessels (vasculitis), giant cell arteritis, hyperthyroidism, hypothyroidism, inadequate output of hormones from the adrenal gland (adrenal insufficiency), hyperparathyroidism/hypercalcemia, hyponatremia, a tumor on the adrenal gland (pheochromocytoma), fever, infection, sleep apnea, chronic renal failure, depression, excess red blood cells (polycythemia), anemia, and hypoxemia.

Specialists

- Neurologist

Rehabilitation

Individuals with headaches resulting from tight neck and shoulder musculature may receive massages to decrease muscle stiffness.

A heating pad may be applied as needed to decrease muscle spasm. Simple stretches are also performed throughout the day that decrease muscle tension (shoulder rolls backward and bending the neck forward, backward, sideways, and rotationally).

Biofeedback also helps decrease muscle tension. For individuals who cannot adequately manage their muscle tension, referral to a certified massage therapist may be appropriate for ongoing massage treatments.

Individuals suffering from tension and migraine headaches may require psychological counseling to help reduce stress and manage pain. Psychologists discuss possible coping mechanisms that help reduce tension headaches.

Individuals learn progressive muscle relaxation that combines deep breathing with progressively tensing and relaxing muscle groups in sequence. Finally, individuals may use meditation in order to promote relaxation.

Work Restrictions / Accommodations

Work restrictions and accommodations depend on the type of headache and the underlying cause.

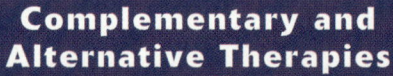

Complementary and Alternative Therapies

Content is intended for awareness only. Treatments may or may not be effective. Scientific evidence may be lacking and some substances have potentially toxic effects. Dr. Presley Reed and the editors do not endorse the use of these therapies in the absence of consultation with a licensed medical professional.

Acupuncture - May aid in pain relief.

Comorbid Conditions

Comorbid conditions depend on the underlying cause, if present.

Complications

Regular use of pain medications can become a distinct problem, both in the treatment of the headache (creating rebound headaches) and the problem of dependency.

Factors Influencing Duration

Length of disability depends on the severity of the symptoms, specific diagnosis, and response to prophylactic and abortive medications.

Length of Disability

Vague diagnosis. Duration depends on type and underlying condition. Contact physician for more specific headache diagnosis (tension, cluster, migraine).

Duration in Days

Job Classification	Minimum	Optimum	Maximum
Any work	0	1	3

Failure to Recover

If an individual fails to recover within the maximum duration expectancy period, the reader may wish to reference the following questions to assist in better understanding the specifics of an individual's medical case.

Regarding diagnosis:

- Has the cause or the source of the headache been identified and confirmed?
- Are clinical findings present that may be associated with underlying conditions (tender temporal arteries, papilledema, fever and neck rigidity, loss of neurologic function)?
- Is underlying condition receiving appropriate treatment?
- Has individual experienced complications, such as rebound headaches or drug dependency, relating to the headache?

Regarding treatment:

- Has underlying condition responded to treatment? If not, what treatment options are now available?
- Did headache symptoms respond to prophylactic or abortive therapy? Have prophylactic measures been effective in preventing headaches? Have prophylactic measures been effective in reducing intensity or frequency of headaches?
- Have trigger factors been identified? Is the headache associated with hormonal changes, menses, changes in sleep, poststress, type of food, missing a meal, or weather changes?
- Has treatment plan included biofeedback, physical therapy, and guided imagery? Would individual benefit from including these measures in current treatment regimen?

Regarding prognosis:

- Has underlying condition responded favorably to treatment? What is current prognosis for underlying condition? How will this affect headaches?
- How disabling are headache symptoms?
- Has severity or frequency of headaches diminished with prophylactic or abortive therapy?

References

Astin, John A. "Why Patients Use Alternative Medicine." JAMA 279 19 (1998): 1548-1553.

Benjamin, Samuel D., et al. "CAM Strategies to Promote Wellness." Patient Care (1999): 143-145, 149-1.

Brannon, Linda, and Jess Feist. "Understanding Pain." Health Psychology. King, Kenneth, ed. Belmont: Wadsworth, Inc, 1992. 110-138.

Brannon, Linda, and Jess Feist. "Coping with Stress and Pain." Health Psychology. King, Kenneth, ed. Belmont: Wadsworth, Inc, 1992. 138-164.

Gordon, James S. "Alternative Medicine and the Family Physician." American Family Physician 54 7 (1996): 22052215.

Poe, Wendy. "Electromyographic Biofeedback." Manual for Physical Agents. Hayes, Karen W., ed. Norwalk: Appleton & Lange, 1993. 151-155.

Solomon, Glen D. "Headache." Saunders Manual of Medical Practice, 2nd ed. Rakel, Robert E., ed. Philadelphia: W.B. Saunders Company, 2000. 1341-1344.

Welch, K., MA. "Headache." Scientific American Medicine. Dale, D.C., and D.D. Federman New York: Scientific American, Inc, 1997. Neuro VIII.

Hearing Loss

Other names / synonyms: Conductive Hearing Loss, Deafness, Neural Hearing Loss, Sensory Hearing Loss

389, 389.0, 389.1, 389.12, 389.14, 389.7, 389.8, 389.9

Definition

Hearing loss (deafness, hearing impairment) refers to the partial or complete inability to hear sounds in one or both ears. Hearing loss can be categorized into 3 basic types: conductive, sensori-neural, and mixed. It can be genetic, congenital, an aftermath of an infectious process, the result of trauma or toxins, related to age, due to some disease, or the result of damage from excessive noise and vibration such as occurring in certain occupations or forms of entertainment.

Conductive hearing loss is the poor transmission of sound waves through the external ear canal to the bones (ossicles) of the middle ear. Specific causes of conductive hearing loss are obstruction (impacted earwax or cerumen), accumulation of fluid in the middle ear (middle ear effusion), or disturbances affecting the continuity of the ossicles of the middle ear (otosclerosis). The most common causes of temporary conductive hearing loss are impacted earwax and acute middle ear infection (acute otitis media) with effusion. Persistent conductive losses usually result from chronic otitis media, trauma, or otosclerosis.

Sensori-neural hearing loss (sensory or nerve hearing loss) is the poor transmission of sound waves into the inner ear or hearing nerves as a result of damage to the essential organ of hearing that forms the inner ear (cochlea) and/or damage to the eighth cranial nerve (vestibulocochlear nerve). Sensori-neural hearing loss can be caused by prolonged noise trauma, the aging process (presbycusis), drugs that are harmful to some part of the hearing mechanism (ototoxic drugs), endolymphatic hydrops (Ménière's syndrome), brain tumors, and head trauma. Sensori-neural hearing loss can also be the result of other problems affecting the eighth cranial nerve (vestibulocochlear nerve) such as acoustic neuroma, other systemic diseases like multiple sclerosis, diabetes, Paget's disease, cerebrovascular disease, and immunosuppressive diseases.

Mixed hearing loss refers to a combination of conductive and sensori-neural hearing loss. In individuals with mixed hearing loss, it is important to note that although the conductive portion of the hearing loss may be helped by medical or surgical treatment, the sensori-neural hearing loss is permanent. Functional hearing loss is caused by emotional or psychological factors. The individual does not seem to hear, but there is no organic cause or history of deafness in the family.

Hearing loss is one of the primary handicapping disabilities in the US, and affects approximately 13 million people of working age.

Diagnosis

History: Individuals with hearing loss are often unaware of their problem. They frequently agree to see a physician at the urging of family members, friends, or co-workers who have had trouble communicating with them. Presbycusis involves a progressive loss of hearing, beginning with high-frequency sounds such as speech and is related to the aging process.

Individuals with conductive hearing loss may simply report that sounds are more quiet and distant than before. Their own voices sound loud to themselves, and consequently, they tend to speak softly. Because of this, they may be frequently asked to repeat things they say.

The individual with sensori-neural hearing loss may report that sounds are not only quieter than before but also distorted and less clear. High-pitched tones are harder to hear (less audible) than low ones, words are difficult to distinguish, and sounds are muffled. The sounds "s," "f," and "z" are not heard, but consonants such as "c" come through more clearly. These individuals may tend to speak loudly because they have difficulty hearing their own voices and consequently cannot modulate them. Individuals with conductive or sensori-neural hearing loss may report ringing in the ear (tinnitus) and balance disturbances (vertigo), sometimes accompanied by nausea, vomiting, and a rhythmic jerking of the eyes (nystagmus).

Physical exam: In the office, an otoscopic examination is performed. Hearing loss may be estimated by having the individual repeat out loud words that are presented by the physician in a soft whisper, a normal spoken voice, or a shout. Tuning forks are useful in differentiating between conductive and sensori-neural hearing losses. During the Weber test, the tuning fork is placed on the forehead or front teeth. If the loss is conductive, the sound will appear louder in the poorer hearing ear because bone conduction is better than air conduction in this type of hearing loss. In sensori-neural losses, the sound will radiate to the better side. In the Rinne test, the tuning fork is placed alternately behind the ear on the mastoid bone and in front of the ear canal. In conductive losses, bone conduction of sound (from behind the ear) will exceed air conduction (from in front of the ear). In sensori-neural losses, the opposite will be true.

In conductive hearing loss, external ear or middle ear abnormalities may be found including earwax (cerumen) obstruction, an inflamed eardrum (tympanic membrane) with evidence of fluid buildup behind it, or a ruptured eardrum (tympanum perforation). Great care and patience must be taken to communicate effectively with the hearing-impaired individual in order to obtain an adequate history. Visual aids may be needed. A balance disorder accompanied by nystagmus may be observed in the individual with hearing loss, depending on the nature of the hearing problem.

Tests: Audiometric studies are performed in a soundproof room. Based on the results of the audiogram, conductive hearing loss can be classified by the decibel level, with a range of 0 to 15 decibels (dB) being normal hearing. This is equivalent to hearing a soft whisper. A mild hearing loss is 16 to 25 dB, the equivalent of hearing a soft-spoken voice. Moderate hearing loss ranges from 41 to 55 dB, the equivalent of hearing a normally spoken voice. A moderately severe hearing loss ranges from 56 to 70 dB. A severe loss is in the range of 71 to 90 dB, the equivalent of hearing only a loud-spoken voice. Profound hearing loss is a reading above 91 dB, the equivalent of hearing only a loud shout.

Sensori-neural hearing loss is evaluated by speech discrimination testing of the individual's ability to distinguish certain sounds and words. Results are reported as the percentage of correct answers (90-100% correct is normal). An electrophysiologic test (auditory brain stem evoked potential) can determine whether the problem affects the cochlea or the central nervous system.

Electronystagmography (ENG), a test where warm or cold water is used to stimulate the inner ear (caloric test), may be ordered if balance disorders are suspected. Skull x-rays, a CAT scan, or MRI of the ear or head help rule out head trauma and diseases of the central nervous system. Electromyography (EMG) may be ordered to rule out diseases of the neurological system. Using sound energy flow (tympanometry), an indirect measurement of the mobility of the tympanic membrane and ossicles can be taken.

Treatment

Some hearing loss may not be correctable, so treatment is aimed at improving residual hearing and developing coping skills. Treatment of conductive hearing loss is aimed at the specific underlying cause within the ear. Temporary conductive hearing loss is correctable. Cerumen impaction can be mechanically removed in the physician's office or flushed from the ear with warm water. To treat middle ear infections, fluid in the middle ear can be drained (myringotomy) and the individual treated with antibiotics. If the infection is chronic and has spread to the mastoid bone, a mastoidectomy can be performed with or without the removal of a cyst-like mass in the middle ear or mastoid (cholesteatoma), in conjunction with antibiotic therapy.

A perforated eardrum usually heals by itself or can be surgically repaired (tympanoplasty, myringoplasty). Medical and surgical treatment can generally improve hearing loss due to conductive problems. Hearing loss from otosclerosis is usually treated by a surgical procedure in which the stapes (a middle ear bone) is replaced with prosthesis (stapedectomy). A hearing aid (amplification) may be useful for some conductive hearing loss, depending on the cause.

Most sensori-neural hearing losses are not correctable with medical or surgical therapy, but often may be stabilized. Sensori-neural hearing losses are generally treated by providing hearing aids (amplification) specifically fitted to the individual's hearing loss by an audiologist or speech and hearing specialist. The volume of sound will be increased through amplification, but sounds will remain muffled. Digitally programmable aids are now available that can be tuned to deal with difficult listening circumstances. Other assistive devices that attach to the television set, radio, or telephone may be recommended.

Sensori-neural hearing losses caused by certain metabolic diseases (diabetes, hypothyroidism, hyperlipidemia, and renal failure) or autoimmune disorders (polyarteritis and lupus erythematosus) may respond to medical treatment of the underlying diseases. Some individuals with profound sensori-neural hearing loss may be appropriate candidates for surgical implantation of an electronic device behind the ear to stimulate the auditory nerve (cochlear implant/cochlear implantation).

Depression may accompany loss of hearing, and should be treated with counseling and antidepressant medications. Consultation with a social worker may help the individual and the individual's family sort out the social issues associated with living with hearing loss, and help them find supportive resources within their community. Instruction in speech reading (commonly known as lip reading) may help those committed to learning this form of communication.

Prognosis

The predicted outcome for conductive hearing loss is restored or improved hearing, elimination of infection, and removal of invasive masses. Individuals with earwax impactions will immediately be able to hear as well as they did before the impaction. Most individuals with acute otitis media improve after 48 hours on antibiotic therapy, and may be symptom-free after several days.

Outcomes for chronic otitis media are less predictable, and outpatient treatment tends to be ongoing. Following a tympanoplasty, and if the eardrum was successfully reconstructed, the individual's hearing should be markedly improved. Following a mastoidectomy, the mastoid air cells should be clear of infection, but permanent hearing loss may result from the effects of long-term infection on the bones of the middle ear. Similarly, removal of cysts within the middle ear or mastoid (cholesteatoma) will result in marked improvement of hearing unless the middle ear bones were destroyed by its growth and development.

Without a stapedectomy, the hearing loss of an individual with otosclerosis will progress until middle age (age 45 to 50) and then stabilize. Ninety percent of individuals having a stapedectomy procedure to treat otosclerosis will experience significant improvement in hearing postoperatively, and frequently will enjoy near-normal hearing. Improvement in hearing will often be apparent within 3 weeks following surgery, and maximum hearing realized in approximately 4 months.

Following successful surgery, tinnitus is reduced or eliminated in about 50% of all individuals.

Ten percent of individuals with otosclerosis experience no improvement in hearing following a stapedectomy, and 3% will suffer persistent, profound sensori-neural hearing loss. Most sensori-neural hearing losses are not correctable with medical or surgical therapy, but the speed of deterioration can sometimes be stabilized if the cause of the loss is removed or lessened (noise associated with work or recreation). Sensori-neural hearing losses caused by certain metabolic diseases (diabetes, hypothyroidism, hyperlipidemia, and renal failure) or autoimmune disorders (polyarteritis and lupus erythematosus) may respond to medical treatment of the underlying diseases. Individuals with profound sensori-neural hearing loss will be able to hear environmental sounds after cochlear implantation.

Differential Diagnosis

Differential diagnoses for hearing loss include cerumen impaction, foreign body in the ear, barotrauma, tympanum perforation, otitis externa (infective), neoplasm of the ear canal, otitis externa (malignant), serous otitis media, acute otitis media, middle ear effusion, chronic otitis media with formation of cholesteatoma, mastoiditis, otosclerosis, middle ear trauma, middle ear tumor, viral inner ear infection (labyrinthitis), endolymphatic hydrops (Ménière's syndrome), presbycusis, noise trauma, head trauma, ototoxicity, acoustic neuroma, multiple sclerosis, cerebrovascular disease, vascular occlusion of the internal auditory artery, diabetes mellitus, hypothyroidism, hyperlipidemia, renal failure, measles, mumps, syphilis, polyarteritis, lupus erythematosus, and damage resulting from radiation therapy.

Specialists

- Otolaryngologist

Rehabilitation

Individuals with hearing loss may require consultation with a speech therapist. The frequency and duration of speech therapy is contingent upon the degree of hearing loss. Individuals with conductive hearing loss may be able to function with the use of hearing aids. Individuals with sensori-neural hearing loss may require pocket amplification devices.

Individuals with cochlear implants require extensive training in use of the implant, and may also need speech therapy if experiencing profound deafness for a long period of time.

Speech therapists also teach lip reading or sign language for communication. They provide suggestions for coping with hearing loss such as eliminating environmental background noise through the use of carpeting, drapes, and upholstered furniture to absorb the noise. Speech therapists also assist individuals in obtaining equipment to compensate for hearing loss, such as TDD telephones and doorbells, as well as smoke detectors that utilize flashing lights instead of sound as a signal. Occupational and vocational therapy may be needed to help individuals adapt to their environments.

Individuals with persistent balance disorders may benefit from an exercise program designed to take advantage of the brain's tendency to eventually adapt (habituate) to the repetition of a specific stimulus, causing an individual's sensation of rotation or movement of themselves or their surroundings (vertigo and vestibular rehabilitation). Although sitting or lying with the head perfectly still may feel more comfortable, this immobility can prolong or even prevent the adaptation process and should be avoided as much as possible.

Traditional physical therapy addresses secondary symptoms associated with the inactivity accompanying persistent balance disorders. These secondary symptoms include decreased strength, loss of the range of motion, and increased tension, particularly in the cervical and shoulder region that can lead to muscle fatigue and headaches.

Work Restrictions / Accommodations

Work restrictions and accommodations may be required for individuals who continue to experience balance disturbances. This is for their own protection, as well as the safety of others. Individuals with persistent temporary or permanent hearing loss following medical or surgical treatment may require vocational or occupational therapy to help them prepare for a different job. The use of hearing aids may be necessary depending on the severity of the hearing loss. Persistent facial paralysis or palsy may also require accommodations if the individual's job requires distinct speech and/or contact with the public. While exposure to noise in the work place should be reduced for all workers through use of protective ear-wear; this protection is critical to the individual with a hearing loss. Various aids such as an amplifier for the earpiece of a telephone are available for the hearing-impaired.

Comorbid Conditions

Comorbid conditions include chronic pulmonary or cardiovascular diseases that increase an individual's risk during surgical procedures, requiring sedation or a general anesthetic, and diseases, conditions, and medications that weaken immune systems (immunosuppression).

Complications

Interference in the ability to communicate adversely affects an individual's interaction with co-workers, family, friends, and the general public, and can be the source of social isolation. The loss of speech clarity that confronts the individual with sensori-neural hearing loss is especially frustrating because they hear what is spoken but cannot decipher the words.

Some medical complications of hearing loss are related to persistent middle ear infections such as meningitis, subdural infection, brain abscess, infection of the petrous bone (petrous apicitis), infection of the temporal bone (osteomyelitis), facial paralysis from inflammation of the facial nerve, facial palsy from chronic pressure on the facial nerve, and thrombosis of the sigmoid sinus (leading to sepsis and increased intracranial pressure).

Other complications are related to surgical complications following a corrective procedure. These may include tympanic membrane perforation (requiring additional surgery), persistent conductive hearing loss (resulting from middle ear effusion, a loose or displaced prostheses), sensori-neural hearing loss, cochlear deafness, alterations in taste, dryness of the mouth from potential injury to the chorda tympani nerve, temporary or persistent balance disorders, persistent tinnitus, facial nerve palsy, facial nerve paralysis (uncommon), perilymph fistula (due to incomplete closure of the oval window), and nystagmus.

Individuals receiving fluoride therapy for treatment of cochlear otosclerosis may experience gastrointestinal irritation (nausea and vomiting) that usually responds to dosage adjustments. Unresolved nausea and vomiting associated with balance disturbances can result in blood electrolyte disturbances. Although lying perfectly still provides some relief for individuals suffering from balance disorders, physical weakness can result from immobility.

Acute otitis media in the postoperative period is a rare but very serious comorbid condition that threatens the hearing in the operated ear. Middle ear infection can quickly involve the inner ear and, in rare cases, lead to meningitis.

Factors Influencing Duration

Factors influencing the length of disability and pertaining to surgical procedures (e.g., otosclerosis or mastoidectomy) include the general health and fitness of the individual before surgery, evidence of preexisting diseases affecting any of the major body systems that might interfere with the healing process, the general ability to heal, and compliance with postoperative orders.

Length of Disability

Length of disability for individuals with hearing loss depends on the extent of loss, the underlying cause, and the requirements of the job. Individuals with conductive hearing loss may have persistent hearing loss and balance disturbances even after the immediate cause is either medically or surgically corrected.

Failure to Recover

If an individual fails to recover within the maximum duration expectancy period, the reader may wish to reference the following questions to assist in better understanding the specifics of an individual's medical case.

Regarding diagnosis:

- Has diagnosis for cause of hearing loss been confirmed?
- Has an MRI or CT been done to determine the presence of a middle ear tumor or skull fracture, as well as the extent of the infection in the middle ear, mastoid area, and brain?
- Have pain and fever persisted despite appropriate treatment?
- Is the ear still draining?

- Has nausea, vomiting, and vertigo persisted?
- Should diagnosis be revisited?
- Has individual experienced any complications from infection or corrective procedures?
- If healing of the perforation or recovery from surgery is slow, have tests for diabetes, HIV/AIDS, leukemia, and other immunosuppressive diseases been performed?

Regarding treatment:
- Was the ear examined by using a microscope (rather than an otoscope) for better visualization?
- Did the individual tell the physician about recent head trauma, all current medications, and the history of treatment for diseases of the neurological or cardiovascular system?
- Was the individual questioned about recent middle ear infections or ear injuries, treated or untreated?
- Was culture and sensitivity testing performed on the ear discharge?
- Was the individual treated with antibiotics based on the results of culture and sensitivity testing of the ear drainage?
- Was the individual asked about past responses to infection with regard to resistance to treatment?
- Is the individual still being treated with antibiotics?
- Has the individual been compliant with taking the prescribed dose of antibiotic at the prescribed time in the prescribed manner?
- Has the individual complied with prescribed therapy (physical therapy or vestibular rehabilitation therapy)?
- Has the individual followed recommended restrictions on activity (flying, underwater diving, insertion of objects into the ear)?
- Has the individual kept the ear dry by using earplugs during bathing?

Regarding prognosis:
- If underlying condition is not resolving, have specialists been consulted to rule out systemic diseases that can cause hearing loss?
- Has the individual been seen by specialists in infectious disease and/or hematology?
- What has been done to enhance existing hearing?
- What accommodations are necessary to enable individual to return to occupational duties?

References

Craik, Rebecca L. "Sensorimotor Changes and Adaptation in the Older Adult." Geriatric Physical Therapy. Guccione, Andrew A., ed. St. Louis: Mosby-Year Book, 1993. 71-97.

Lewis, Sharon, Margaret Heitkemper, and Shannon Dirksen. Medical-Surgical Nursing. St. Louis: Mosby, 2000.

Tierney, Lawrence, Stephen McPhee, and Maxine Papadakis. Current Medical Diagnosis and Treatment. New York: McGraw-Hill, 2000.

Wyatt, Carol A. "Hearing Disorders and the Aging Process." Otoscope 8 2 (1991): 1-2.

Heart Block

Other names / synonyms: Atrioventricular (AV) Block, Atrioventricular Block, AV Block, Stokes-Adams Syndrome, Unspecified Conduction Defect

426.1, 426.8, 426.9

Definition

Heart block is a general term for disorders of the electrical conduction system in the heart. Specifically, electrical impulses originating in the atrium or sinus node are blocked at the atrioventricular node preventing them from traveling down to the ventricles. There are three degrees of heart block ranging in severity from incomplete blockage of electrical impulses (first- and second-degree) to complete (third-degree) blockage.

The reasons for heart block are varied although a common cause is a decreased blood supply to the heart muscle as a result of myocardial infarction (MI) or chronic ischemic heart disease. Heart block is often a result of taking certain prescription drugs. Many of these drugs (including digitalis, beta- and calcium-channel blockers, and antiarrhythmics) are prescribed for diseases of the cardiovascular system. Heart block can be a response to elevated blood potassium levels (hyperkalemia).

Other common causes of heart block are congenital heart disease, aging (Lenegre's syndrome), diseases of the aortic and mitral valves, and postoperative complications. Infectious diseases that may cause heart block include acute rheumatic fever, endocarditis, myocarditis, Lyme disease, and almost any other systemic infectious disease such as mononucleosis. Less common causes include infiltrative and connective tissue diseases such as tumors, sarcoidosis, and amyloidosis.

The incidence of heart block increases with age and in individuals with heart disease. Heart block is rarely found in young, healthy adults. Studies indicate that first-degree block occurs in 5% of men older than 60 years, and this increases to 10% if cardiac disease is present. Third-degree heart block occurs most often in individuals older than 70 years. Forty percent of elderly individuals with third-degree block are women.

Diagnosis

History: History depends on the particular type of heart block. Individuals with first-degree block often have no symptoms while those with second- or third-degree block usually complain of reduced exercise tolerance. Second- or third-degree heart block can also produce fatigue or shortness of breath and dizziness, and these individuals may periodically experience near loss or loss of consciousness (Adams-Stokes syndrome). Varying degrees of seizure activity may be associated with fainting spells (syncope).

Physical exam: Individuals with first-degree heart block usually have no symptoms upon physical examination. Individuals with third-degree heart block may have a low ventricular heart rate (bradycardia), low blood pressure (hypotension), and chest pain (angina pectoris).

Tests: An electrocardiogram (ECG) will differentiate the types of heart block. Exercise testing may further disclose significant ECG abnormalities. First-degree heart block can be identified on an ECG by a prolonged PR interval (greater than 0.2 seconds), while second-degree heart block results in intermittently dropped QRS complexes. The two recognized subdivisions of second-degree AV block are Mobitz type I (Wenckebach phenomenon) and Mobitz type II. Mobitz type I does not usually produce symptoms because the individual has an adequate ventricular heart rate, however, their pulse may be irregular. For Mobitz type II, an ECG shows sudden missing of a ventricular beat. Individuals with third-degree heart block have complete disassociation between atrial and ventricular beats. A portable Holter monitor may be worn so ECG tracing can be recorded continuously over the period of a day or more. Ultrasound may also be used to identify other structural abnormalities often associated with third-degree heart block.

Treatment

Treatment depends on the type of block. First-degree heart block requires no treatment. Exercise or drug treatment that decreases vagal tone (anticholinergics) may reverse Mobitz type I, but generally, this type requires no treatment as long as the ventricular heart rate remains normal. Should the ventricular rate become low or the condition progresses to Mobitz type II, a drug that speeds the rate of electrical impulse conduction (anticholinergics or sympathomimetics) may be prescribed and cardiac depressants withheld. If Mobitz type II develops following MI, a temporary pacemaker may be inserted prophylactically. For third-degree heart block, anticholinergics or sympathomimetics may be prescribed and a temporary or permanent pacemaker inserted.

Prognosis

Individuals with first-degree or Mobitz type I heart block can expect no adverse effects unless there is progression to more severe forms of the condition. Mobitz type II often progresses to third-degree AV block especially in individuals with MI. This condition can result in unpredictable incidence of fainting (syncope) and sudden cardiac death if left untreated. After pacemaker implantation, however, most individuals show improvement within 1 month and can usually resume most tasks associated with daily living.

Differential Diagnosis

Certain symptoms of severe heart block are characteristic of several other conditions and disease states. Vestibular abnormalities or psychiatric disorders may cause dizziness. Syncope may be cardiac or noncardiac related or multi-causal in origin. Certain drugs (digitalis, beta-blockers, and calcium-channel blockers) may aggravate syncope.

Specialists

- Cardiologist
- Cardiovascular Surgeon

Rehabilitation

The individual with any of the various types of heart blocks may benefit from therapy.

In the hospital, low levels of exercise help prevent the hazards of bed rest, reduce episodes of low blood pressure when changing positions (orthostatic hypotension), and maintain overall mobility of the body. Low-level exercise may begin in the coronary care unit of a hospital with the individual on his or her back (supine position). The individual progresses to sitting and eventually to standing. Progressive walking (ambulating) and eventual stair climbing are an important part of the individual's inpatient exercise program. Intensity gradually increases until discharge from the hospital.

After discharge from the hospital or for individuals not hospitalized, goals are to improve functional capacity by increasing physical endurance and promoting return to activity. This is done in an outpatient setting. Individuals are usually attached to an electrocardiograph (EKG) monitor, a device used to record the continuous electrical activity of the heart muscle. A physical therapist keeps a daily log of the individual's blood pressure, heart rate, and cardiac rhythm.

Phase three continues in an outpatient setting. Individuals may stay involved with an outpatient program for up to a year in order to accomplish all their goals while still at modified work duty. Higher levels of exercise are eventually added including recreational activities such as swimming and outdoor hiking. Light jogging at approximately 5 miles per hour (mph) and cycling at approximately 12 mph are appropriate as long as the individual tolerates the rehabilitation program well. Individuals with a history of coronary artery disease, heart valve disorders, or other cardiac disorders are at higher risk for various forms of heart blocks. Because of the varying degrees and types of heart blocks and the amount of damage the heart may have sustained from this condition, the program may need to be modified for those individuals experiencing a heart block.

Work Restrictions / Accommodations

Individuals who experience dizziness or syncope may need restrictions from hazardous work, dangerous machinery, or exposed heights.

Comorbid Conditions

Conditions such as MI or chronic ischemia that decrease blood flow to the AV junction may impact the ability to alleviate heart block. Trauma to the AV node resulting from cardiac surgery may have a similar effect. Hyperkalemia, congenital heart disease, aortic and mitral valvular disease, diabetes mellitus, pulmonary insufficiency, and renal disease requiring dialysis can further lengthen disability. Less commonly, infiltrative and connective tissue diseases can have detrimental effects.

Complications

Third-degree heart block can lead to decreased cardiac output, circulatory impairment, and heart failure. Other complications may include excessive urea in the blood (uremia) and low blood hemoglobin (anemia).

Factors Influencing Duration

The type of heart block, its cause, treatment, and the response to the particular treatment can all affect length of disability. Age may also be a factor since severe heart block is more common in the elderly.

Length of Disability

Disability does not usually occur in individuals with first-degree or Mobitz type I heart block. For more severe forms of heart block, disability may be permanent if job requirements are physically demanding.

Failure to Recover

If an individual fails to recover within the maximum duration expectancy period, the reader may wish to reference the following questions to assist in better understanding the specifics of an individual's medical case.

Regarding diagnosis:

- Was the correct diagnosis made as to first-, second-, or third-degree heart block?
- Was an electrocardiogram (ECG) used to differentiate the types of heart block? Did Holter monitor and/or exercise testing further disclose significant ECG abnormalities?
- Was an ultrasound used to identify other structural abnormalities often associated with third-degree heart block?
- Has cause of heart block been identified?

Regarding treatment:

- If individual has a low heart rate, would he/she benefit from taking drugs that speed the rate of electrical impulse?
- Would the individual benefit from placement of a temporary or permanent pacemaker?
- If heart block is the result of certain drugs prescribed for diseases of the cardiovascular system, should medication be stopped?

Regarding prognosis:

- Do symptoms persist despite treatment?
- Has the individual's condition progressed to Mobitz type II or to third-degree heart block?
- Is the pacemaker functioning properly?
- Does individual have a coexisting condition (such as MI, chronic ischemia, trauma to the AV node from cardiac surgery, hyperkalemia, congenital heart disease, aortic and mitral valvular disease, diabetes mellitus, pulmonary insufficiency, renal disease, infiltrative and connective tissue diseases) that may complicate treatment or impact recovery?

References

Bexton, R.S., and A.J. Camm. "Second Degree Atrioventricular Block." European Heart Journal 5 Suppl A (1984): 111-114.

Luckman, Joan, and Karen C. Sorensen. "Nursing People Experiencing Cardiac Arrhythmias." Medical-Surgical Nursing. Kay, Dudley, ed. Philadelphia: W.B. Saunders Company, 1987. 901-926.

Heart Failure, Congestive

Other names / synonyms: Cardiac Decompensation, Cardiac Insufficiency, CHF, Compensated Heart Failure, Congestive Heart Failure, Decompensated Heart Failure, Heart Failure, Left Ventricular Failure, Ventricular Failure

428, 428.0, 428.1, 428.9, 429.9

Definition

Congestive heart failure (CHF) occurs when the heart is unable to pump an adequate amount of blood to meet the metabolic demands of the body at rest or during exercise. That is, the amount of blood coming out of the heart is decreased and this leads to inadequate blood flow to the various body organs (decreased tissue perfusion). In response to decreased tissue perfusion, the body activates certain normal, compensatory mechanisms. However, these mechanisms may result in increased pressure and congestion in the blood vessels (hence the term congestive heart failure). Eventually, as the body uses up all its compensatory mechanisms, the heart begins to fail, and this is usually followed by increased morbidity and death.

Heart failure is not a disease itself; rather, the term denotes all of the body's responses to inadequate pumping ability of the heart. CHF may be categorized in a number of different ways. Most commonly, the classification of left or right ventricular failure is utilized. Left or right ventricular failure refers to failure of the left or right lower pumping chambers (ventricles) of the heart. Left ventricular failure typically results from high blood pressure (hypertension), decreased blood flow to the heart muscle (ischemic heart disease), or diseases of the valves within the left heart (aortic or mitral valvular disease).

Right ventricular failure may develop independently, or more commonly, it may follow (and be a result of) development of left ventricular failure. Causes of right ventricular failure that develop independently of left ventricular failure include low blood flow (infarction) of the right ventricle, lung diseases (chronic obstructive lung disease or COPD), inflammation of the tissue that surrounds the right ventricle (constrictive pericarditis), or diseases of the valves within the right heart (tricuspid or pulmonic valvular disease).

Other risk factors for development of CHF include defects in the tissue that separates the left and right ventricles (ventricular septal defect), any disease that affects the heart muscle (cardiomyopathy), decreased oxygen-carrying capacity of the blood (anemia), over-active thyroid gland disease (thyrotoxicosis), diabetes, smoking tobacco, obesity, sedentary lifestyle, pregnancy, prolonged fever, blood clots in the lungs (pulmonary embolism), rheumatic fever, and abnormal heart beat (dysrhythmia).

Estimates of the number of individuals suffering from CHF in the US range from 2.5 million to over 4 million (approximately 2% of the US population). Approximately 400,000 individuals die of CHF in the US each year. The incidence of this condition increases significantly with age and the prevalence of CHF approximately doubles with each decade of life. It affects approximately 3% of middle-aged adults and 10% or more of people aged 75 years or older. The annual incidence of CHF in men is almost twice that in women and the average survival time following diagnosis is 2.2 years greater in women than in men (5.4 years vs. 3.2 years for women and men, respectively).

Diagnosis

History: Individuals with CHF may report a history of diabetes or chronic alcohol abuse. Those with left ventricular heart failure may complain of fatigue and activity intolerance, weakness, dizziness, brief fainting spells (syncope), shortness of breath, dry hacking cough, breathing difficulty (dyspnea), and difficulty in breathing when lying down (orthopnea). Individuals with right ventricular failure will often experience these same symptoms, and in addition, they may report swelling (edema) in the feet and legs, pain in the upper right part of the abdomen (upper right quadrant), nausea, loss of appetite (anorexia), and excessive urination at night (nocturia). Individuals with both right and left ventricular failure (biventricular failure) may report all the symptoms listed above as well as the experience of awakening at night acutely short of breath (paroxysmal nocturnal dyspnea).

Physical exam: The veins in the neck may be enlarged (jugular venous distention), and the arms, hands, ankles and lower back may show signs of water retention and swelling (edema). The heart rate may be high even when the individual is sitting or laying down (resting tachycardia). Abnormal heart sounds may occur (displaced apex beat; third heart sound). Using a stethoscope, popping sounds might be heard in the individual's chest when they breath (pulmonary crackles). The abdomen may fill with fluid (ascites) and nausea, vomiting, and intestinal upset can be present.

Tests: Laboratory tests that may be performed include measurement of sodium, potassium, chloride, and total electrolytes in the blood (serum electrolyte test). Other blood tests may include serum bilirubin, assessment of coagulation capabilities, albumin levels, and liver enzymes (liver function test). The amount of oxygen and carbon dioxide in the blood stream can be measured using an arterial blood gas (ABG) analysis. A chest x-ray may show if the heart has increased in size (hypertrophied or dilated) in response to increased pressure in the heart blood vessels (vascular congestion). High frequency sound waves (ultrasound) may be used to evaluate function of the left ventricle and to obtain evidence of ventricular dilation and enlargement (hypertrophy). Electrocardiography (ECG) is used to identify changes associated with ventricular enlargement, and to detect abnormal heart rhythm (dysrhythmias), decreased blood flow to the heart (myocardial ischemia), or tissue death due to absence of blood flow to a certain region of the heart (myocardial infarction). Monitoring the heart with ECG while the individual exercises on a treadmill (cardiac stress test) may also be useful to identify cardiac abnormalities associated with congestive heart failure.

Treatment

Individuals with CHF typically receive several different medications to treat their condition. Most commonly, drugs to prevent formation of angiotensin II (angiotensin converting enzyme or ACE inhibitors), to increase urine output (diuretics), to increase the strength of the heart (inotropic medications), to relax the blood vessels (vasodilators), and to prevent abnormal heart rhythm (antidysrhythmics) are used. Also, individuals are commonly put on a diet that contains very little salt (sodium). Devices that assist the heart in pumping blood (mechanical circulatory support devices) may be implanted into arteries or into the heart itself. Any other surgical treatment for CHF is usually reserved for individuals in end-stage disease who cannot be treated using drug therapy only. The main surgical option is replacement of the diseased heart with the heart of a donor (cardiac transplantation).

Prognosis

Congestive heart failure is most often a progressive and deteriorating condition. The outlook may depend upon the age of the individual, severity of the failure, and the underlying cause for the condition. There is an increased risk of sudden death, and overall, approximately 50% of individuals die within 1-2 years of diagnosis. Drug treatment may decrease the mortality rate approximately twenty percent. Implantation of mechanical circulatory support devices provide only temporary support for individuals who are waiting for a donor heart to become available so they may undergo cardiac transplantation. Following cardiac transplantation, the percentage of individuals that survive 1, 5, and 10 years after surgery are 85%, 67%, and 40%, respectively.

Differential Diagnosis

Conditions that present with similar symptoms as congestive heart failure include primary lung (pulmonary) disorders such as acute respiratory distress syndrome (ARDS), trauma, sepsis, drug overdose, or nerve disorders related to these conditions.

Specialists

- Cardiologist
- Critical Care Specialist

Rehabilitation

Early incorporation of a physical rehabilitation program for CHF may increase survival time. Individuals with the diagnosis of CHF may attend outpatient physical and occupational therapy at a clinic specializing in cardiac rehabilitation. Cardiac rehabilitation centers offer ECG monitoring of all participants during exercise sessions.

Individuals learn to self-monitor their pulse and rate the amount of energy they expend by utilizing a rating of perceived exertion scale. This is a numbered scale that rates exercises from very, very light to very, very hard. Individuals use this scale and their pulse to stay within safe exercise parameters predetermined by their physicians. Individuals also learn to monitor their weight daily to determine if they are gaining fluid and are instructed to inform their physicians if more than 2 pounds are gained over a period of 24r to 48hours.

Individuals attend physical therapy to learn basic conditioning and stretching exercises. Aerobic exercises are performed such as treadmill walking or stationary bicycling. Initial activities may include limited walking, range-of-motion, and treadmill exercises. Eventually, more frequent walks, walk-jog, biking, and arm ergometer exercises may be encouraged. The walking program aims toward a goal of 2 miles in less than 60 minutes. Eventually, exercise may become more strenuous with a goal of attaining 75-85% maximum intensity while walking, jogging, biking, swimming, performing calisthenics, and/or weight training.

Occupational therapy addresses any fatigue or shortness of breath that may occur during activities of daily living. Individuals learn to utilize equipment such as a shower chair to decrease the energy expended during bathing or a long-handled sponge to decrease the amount of arm activity necessary for bathing. (Excessive arm activity is more taxing on the heart and can lead to fatigue). Occupational therapists also teach energy conservation techniques where activities of daily living such as meal preparation are broken into smaller components that make tasks more manageable.

Work Restrictions / Accommodations

Work activities may be continued and encouraged to the extent that the individual's symptoms allow them to perform their duties. Modifications and/or restrictions may be required with work duties that require medium to heavy physical activity. In this situation, it may be necessary for the individual to return to work at a completely different level, job function, or activity. In work settings that are primarily sedentary, materials and supplies should be organized nearby and restroom facilities should be easily accessible. Ergonomic seating with the ability to raise the legs may be needed. It may be necessary to limit walking distances that are required to function at work. There should be easy access to the work area and facilities such as parking, elevators, and lunch or break areas. Alternating physical activities with rest periods may be necessary. Shortened work hours or work weeks may be necessary, however, this will vary according to the severity of the individual's symptoms.

Complementary and Alternative Therapies

Content is intended for awareness only. Treatments may or may not be effective. Scientific evidence may be lacking and some substances have potentially toxic effects. Dr. Presley Reed and the editors do not endorse the use of these therapies in the absence of consultation with a licensed medical professional.

Natural supplements -	Natural foods such as hawthorn, garlic, soy protein, and Cholestin may help reduce cholesterol and fats to lower risk factors for CHF.
Neuromuscular electrical stimulation -	Stimulation of muscles in legs and arms with low-voltage electrical current may help maintain strength in individuals with CHF.
Biofeedback -	Changes in skin temperature may be used as a biofeedback-relaxation monitoring mechanism to decrease stress on the failing heart.

Comorbid Conditions

Pre-existing conditions that might impact an individual's ability to recover and further lengthen disability from congestive heart failure include older age, existence of a prior heart attack (myocardial infarction), obesity, high blood pressure (hypertension), diabetes mellitus, pregnancy, blood lipid disorders (hyperlipidemia), low hemoglobin in the blood (anemia), an overactive thyroid gland (hyperthyroidism) leading to toxic levels of thyroid gland hormone (thyrotoxicosis), kidney (renal) failure, and infection.

Complications

Possible complications of congestive heart failure include difficulty in breathing when laying down (orthopnea), abnormal (cyclic) breathing (Cheyne-Stokes respiration), fluid in the lungs (pulmonary edema), decreased oxygen to the brain (cerebral hypoxia), fatigue and muscular weakness, and water accumulation (congestion) in various body organs.

Factors Influencing Duration

Factors that might influence the length of disability include the type of treatment that is utilized, the presence or absence of complications, and the availability of lighter or part-time work on either a temporary or permanent basis. The individual's willingness to address correctable risk factors (i.e., smoking, sedentary lifestyle, obesity) may be a fundamental determinant of the length of disability. A cardiac rehabilitation program may facilitate recovery and shorten the period of disability. Severe mental stress or exertion may trigger increased symptoms and complications.

Length of Disability

The duration of disability will depend upon cardiac function, the severity of the heart failure, the underlying cause for development of the condition, and the treatment that is utilized. Also, physical demands of the job will be a major determining factor in the expected length of disability. Individuals with severe CHF may be permanently disabled depending upon the requirements of the job.

Medical treatment.

Job Classification	Minimum	Optimum	Maximum
Sedentary work	21	42	Indefinite
Light work	21	42	Indefinite
Medium work	28	56	Indefinite
Heavy work	28	84	Indefinite
Very Heavy work	28	112	Indefinite

Duration in Days

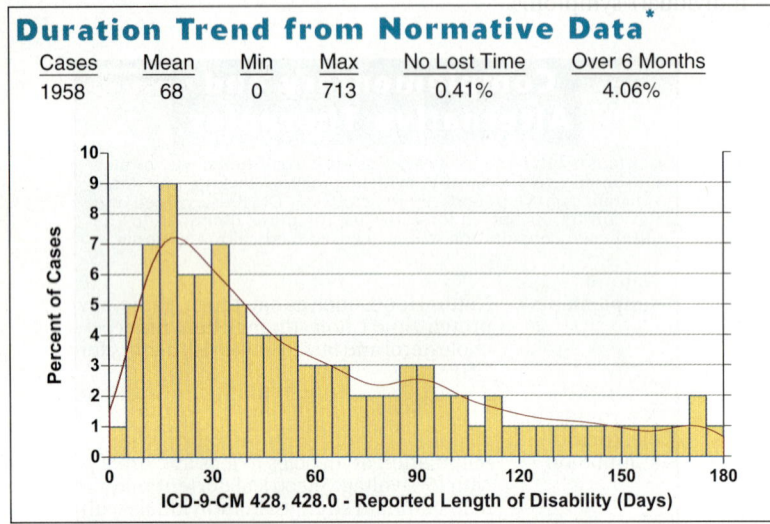
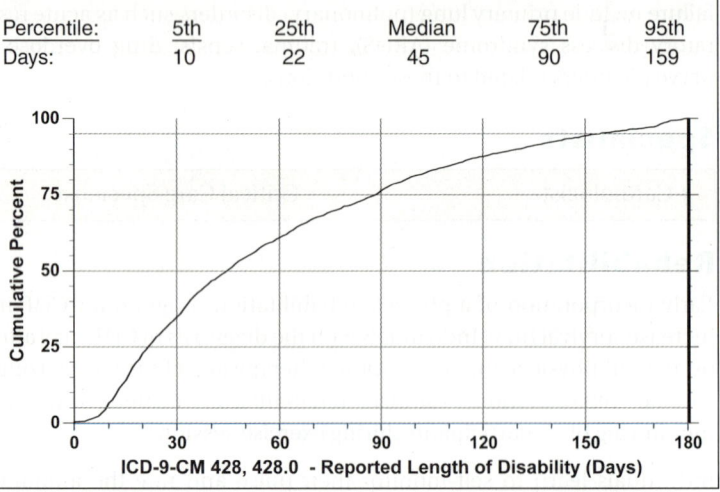

* Differences may exist between the expected duration tables and the normative graphs. Duration tables provide expected recovery periods based on the type of work performed by the individual. The normative graphs reflect the actual observed experience of many individuals across the spectrum of physical conditions, in a variety of industries, and with varying levels of case management.

Failure to Recover

If an individual fails to recover within the maximum duration expectancy period, the reader may wish to reference the following questions to assist in better understanding the specifics of an individual's medical case.

Regarding diagnosis:

- Has individual had a history of underlying heart conditions or precipitating events that are known to contribute to congestive heart failure?
- Did individual present with symptoms and clinical findings consistent with the diagnosis of congestive heart failure?
- Is the condition new or is individual presenting with worsening symptoms, associated with the progression of the heart failure?
- If the diagnosis or cause was uncertain, were additional diagnostic tests done to rule out other possible conditions?
- Would individual benefit from consultation with a specialist (cardiologist, cardiac surgeon)?

Regarding treatment:

- Was any underlying cause addressed in the treatment plan?
- Did the treatment provide appropriate medications to maximize heart function and minimize symptoms?
- Did the severity of the heart failure warrant intervention with cardiac assist devices?
- Was individual considered for cardiac transplantation?

Regarding prognosis:

- Based on individual's age, severity of heart failure and treatment, what is the expected outcome?
- Did individual participate in a cardiac rehabilitation program as recommended? If not, are there obvious barriers to participation (insurance limits, transportation, motivation)?
- Does individual have any pre-existing conditions that could impact ability to recover? Are these pre-existing conditions being addressed in the treatment plan?
- Did individual suffer any associated complications that would influence length of disability and prognosis? If so, has adequate time elapsed for recovery?

References

Clochesy, John M., et al. Critical Care Nursing, 2nd ed. Philadelphia: W.B. Saunders Company, 1996.

Hochman, J.S., and B.J. Gersh. "Acute Myocardial Infarction: Complications." Textbook of Cardiovascular Medicine. Topol, E.J., ed. Philadelphia: Lippincott-Raven Publishers, 1998. 437-480.

LeMone, P., and K.M. Burke. Medical-Surgical Nursing. Upper Saddle River, NJ: Prentice Hall Health, 2000.

Morelli, V., and R.J. Zoorob. "Alternative Therapies: Part II. Congestive Heart Failure and Hypercholesterolemia." American Family Physician 62 6 (2000): 1325-1330.

Moser, D.K., et al. "Voluntary Control of Vascular Tone by Using Skin Temperature Biofeedback-relaxation in Patients with Advanced Heart Failure." Alternative Therapies in Health and Medicine 3 1 (1997): 51-59.

O'Connor, C.M., and C.F. Gottlieb. "Aging and the Heart." Textbook of Cardiovascular Medicine. Topol, E.J., ed. Philadelphia: Lippincott-Raven Publishers, 1998. 817-840.

Quittan, M., et al. "Strength Improvement of Knee Extensor Muscles in Patients with Chronic Heart Failure by Neuromuscular Electrical Stimulation." Artificial Organs 23 5 (1999): 432-435.

Watchie, Joanne. Cardiopulmonary Physical Therapy. Philadelphia: W.B. Saunders Company, 1995.

Heart Murmur
Other names / synonyms: Murmur
785.2

Definition

A heart murmur is a sound produced by blood crossing a valve within the heart. A valve is a thin door-like structure between two chambers of the heart. When open, a valve allows blood to cross it in a forward fashion and when closed, prevents blood from crossing it in a backward fashion. Heart murmurs are audible with a stethoscope.

There are four chambers and four valves within the heart. The valves are called the tricuspid, pulmonic, mitral, and aortic. Normal valves do not produce murmurs except in children. Murmurs produced by normal valves in children are termed functional or innocent murmurs.

Murmurs produced when blood is moving across a valve in a forward fashion are called systolic murmurs. Murmurs produced by blood going in the opposite direction are called diastolic.

Valves that are too narrow (stenotic) cause systolic murmurs and those that are too leaky (insufficient) cause diastolic murmurs. Murmurs are designated according to the responsible valve and whether it is stenotic or insufficient. The most common murmur is mitral insufficiency.

In adults, the most common cause of heart murmurs is rheumatic fever during childhood, and often individuals are not aware they had the disease. Other causes include high blood pressure (hypertension), degeneration and calcification of the valve due to hardening of the arteries (atherosclerosis), infection due to endocarditis, and trauma.

Sometimes systolic murmurs are generated by blood crossing a normal valve too rapidly. Increased velocity of blood flow is caused by fever, a low blood count (anemia), an over active thyroid (hyperthyroidism), and exercise. Since each of these causes of increased flow is transient, the murmur disappears when the cause goes away.

Diagnosis

History: A history of a murmur since birth establishes it as congenital. A history of frequent strep throats during childhood raises the specter of rheumatic fever that may have been overlooked. If individual reports a murmur never heard before, this indicates that the murmur was recently acquired suggesting atherosclerosis, hypertension, or endocarditis. Heart murmurs can also develop after heart attacks.

Physical exam: Murmurs are best identified with a stethoscope and are rated according to their intensity with Grade 1 being barely audible and Grade 6 audible even with the stethoscope off of the chest. The location on the chest wall where the murmur is best heard and the areas to which it radiates can be helpful in identifying the cardiac structure from which the murmur originates. For example, a murmur produced by mitral regurgitation is usually loudest at the apex of the heart (5th intercostals space, mid clavicle) and may radiate toward the sternum. Likewise, where the murmur occurs in the cardiac cycle may be noted. For example, whether the murmur occurs in the resting stage (diastole) or contracting stage (systole), whether it is early or late in the stage, or whether it occurs throughout the heartbeat, are important clues to the cause of the murmur.

Soft or hard to hear systolic murmurs can often be made louder by having the individual strain down as if attempting to lift a heavy object (Valsalva maneuver) or briefly inhale a substance called amyl nitrite that increases the flow of blood across a valve.

Tests: As heart murmurs may develop due to a variety of underlying causes, the diagnostic testing required will vary. Chest x-ray, electrocardiogram, cardiac catheterization, echocardiography, treadmill, and angiography are typical diagnostic tests.

Treatment

Appropriate therapeutic intervention is based on the underlying medical condition responsible for the heart murmur. Functional heart murmurs require no treatment. Functional murmurs are not caused by valvular or septal defects and pose no danger to the individual. Murmurs of a significant nature require medical treatment. Antibiotics are prescribed to treat and/or prevent infection. Antihypertensives decrease pressure and stress on the heart. Open or closed surgical repair of valves is performed in serious instances. This may include valve replacement with synthetic or natural grafts.

Prognosis

An individual may have a benign functional murmur without any problems or effect on longevity. A murmur associated with valvular stenosis or insufficiency can result in significant complications that must be managed. Generally, medical management of heart murmurs is very good. Surgical valve replacement has good success rates, although the procedure itself is not without morbidity/mortality. Prognosis depends upon the degree of impairment.

Differential Diagnosis

Adults may sometimes have unexpected sounds called bruits in the neck indicating disease of the carotid arteries due to atherosclerosis. Inflammation of the surface of the heart (pericarditis) can produce a sound called a pericardial friction rub.

Specialists

- Cardiologist

Rehabilitation

Individuals with heart murmurs due to serious underlying medical conditions may attend outpatient physical and occupational therapy at a clinic specializing in cardiac rehabilitation. Cardiac rehabilitation centers offer ECG monitoring of all participants during the exercise sessions. Individuals learn to self-monitor their pulse and rate the amount of energy they expend by utilizing a rating of perceived exertion scale. This is a numbered scale that rates exercises from "very, very light" to "very, very hard". Individuals use this scale and their pulse to stay within safe exercise parameters predetermined by their physicians.

Individuals also perform aerobic exercise such as treadmill walking or stationary bicycling. Occupational therapy addresses any fatigue or shortness of breath that may occur during activities of daily living. Individuals learn to utilize equipment such as a shower chair to decrease the energy expended during bathing or a long-handled sponge to decrease the amount of arm activity necessary for bathing. (Excessive arm activity is more taxing on the heart and can lead to fatigue). Occupational therapists may teach energy conservation techniques where activities of daily living such as meal preparation are broken up into smaller components to make tasks more manageable.

Work Restrictions / Accommodations

No work restrictions or special accommodations are required for an individual with a heart murmur. However, if the associated valvular stenosis or insufficiency results in a significant complication, the complication may dictate work restrictions or accommodations. Job stress and physical activity should correspond to worker fitness. Individuals may be advised to resume work on a part-time basis following surgery.

Comorbid Conditions

Any condition that compromises cardiac function would exacerbate disability. Examples include atherosclerosis, obesity, diabetes, or smoking.

Complications

Abnormal murmurs predispose the individual to an infection on the valve called endocarditis. Endocarditis is most often acquired from dental work resulting in bleeding of the gums that allows bacteria in the mouth to enter the bloodstream. Bacteria then settle on the abnormal valve and cause a potentially serious infection. This infection can be easily prevented with penicillin or a related antibiotic before the dental work is performed. Individuals with a murmur should inform their dentist of this condition before any work (including cleaning) is done.

Incompetent or stenotic valves can, over time, lead to heart failure, irregular heart beats, or heart attack.

Factors Influencing Duration

The length of disability may be influenced by the nature of the murmur and the required treatment. Age and the severity of the symptoms will also influence length of disability.

Length of Disability

This is a vague diagnosis. Contact physician for more specific information regarding type and cause of murmur.

Failure to Recover

If an individual fails to recover within the maximum duration expectancy period, the reader may wish to reference the following questions to assist in better understanding the specifics of an individual's medical case.

Regarding diagnosis:

- Does the individual complain of dizziness, chest pain, or fluttering heart?
- Has the individual had an ECG to rule out heart rhythm disturbances? Has the individual had an echocardiogram? Has the individual had a chest x-ray to rule out congestive heart failure?

Regarding treatment:

- What treatments have been tried? Medications?
- Has the individual had surgery or being considered for surgery?

Regarding prognosis:

- Does the individual demonstrate symptoms of congestive heart failure such as shortness of breath, low blood pressure, weight gain, or swelling of legs and feet?
- Does individual have a murmur associated with valvular stenosis or insufficiency? Did complications occur? Are they being managed?

References

Clochesy, John M., et al. Critical Care Nursing, 2nd ed. Philadelphia: W.B. Saunders Company, 1996.

Watchie, Joanne. Cardiopulmonary Physical Therapy. Philadelphia: W.B. Saunders Company, 1995.

Heart Valve Replacement

Other names / synonyms: Aortic Valve Replacement, Heart Valve Prosthesis, Heart Valve Replacement, Mitral Valve Replacement, Tricuspid Valve Replacement

35.2, 35.20, 35.21, 35.22, 35.23, 35.24, 35.25, 35.26, 35.27, 35.28

Definition

Heart valve replacement refers to the substitution of a natural (native) heart valve with an artificial one (prosthetic valve). There are two types of prosthetic valves. The oldest type is composed of synthetic materials (mechanical valves) and the other from natural sources either animals or humans.

These natural valves are called tissue valves or bioprosthesis. Tissue valves are subclassified according to their source. Heterograft valves or xenografts are taken from pigs (porcine) or cows (bovine). Homografts or allografts are valves removed from human cadavers. Autografts are live valves transferred from one position to another in the same individual. For example, an individual's aortic valve can be replaced with his or her pulmonic valve. The pulmonic valve is then replaced with a homograft valve.

Both types of prosthetic valves have their advantages. Mechanical valves have the advantage of lasting longer (more durable). The disadvantage is that the individual will need to take a blood thinner (anticoagulant) called warfarin (Coumadin) indefinitely. Conversely, tissue valves offer the advantage of not requiring anticoagulants and the disadvantage of being less durable. The type of prosthetic valve chosen for implantation depends primarily on individual's age and preference to take an anticoagulant indefinitely.

In general, individuals under age 35 receive mechanical valves because of durability and the reduced likelihood of needing a second operation later in life. They do however require lifelong anticoagulation therapy. Individuals over age 35 often receive tissue valves since durability is less of an issue.

Individuals with coronary artery disease or rheumatic heart disease or who have had rheumatic fever or bacterial endocarditis are at higher risk for requiring heart valve replacement.

Approximately 70,000 to 80,000 diseased or damaged heart valves are replaced annually in the US.

Reason for Procedure

The major reason for valve replacement surgery is to replace valves that are narrow (stenotic) or leaky (insufficient). These structural problems are due to either a congenital abnormality or acquired diseases such as rheumatic fever or atherosclerosis.

Description

The individual's skin and underlying tissue and muscle are cut (incised) from the notch at the top of the breastbone (sternum) to the bottom of the breastbone (xiphoid process). The breastbone is divided with an electric saw. A sternal retractor is inserted, separating the two sides of the split sternum and ribs and exposing the heart.

The membrane covering the heart (pericardium) is incised and held back with lengths of surgical thread (suture). The individual is then placed on cardiopulmonary bypass (CPB). During CPB, the individual's blood flow is diverted from the heart and lungs through tubing connected to a heart-lung machine. Anticoagulants are added to the blood to prevent clots from forming on the tubing's artificial surface and traveling to the brain or other vital organs. As blood passes through the heart-lung machine, the pump oxygenator removes carbon dioxide and adds oxygen. The heart-lung machine then pumps the oxygenated blood back to the body through another set of tubing. This artificial circulation allows the cardiovascular surgeon to work in a nearly motionless and bloodless surgical field without endangering the flow of blood and oxygen to the individual's vital organs and other tissue. Under these optimal conditions, the surgeon cuts away (excises) the diseased heart valve and sutures a replacement valve into position.

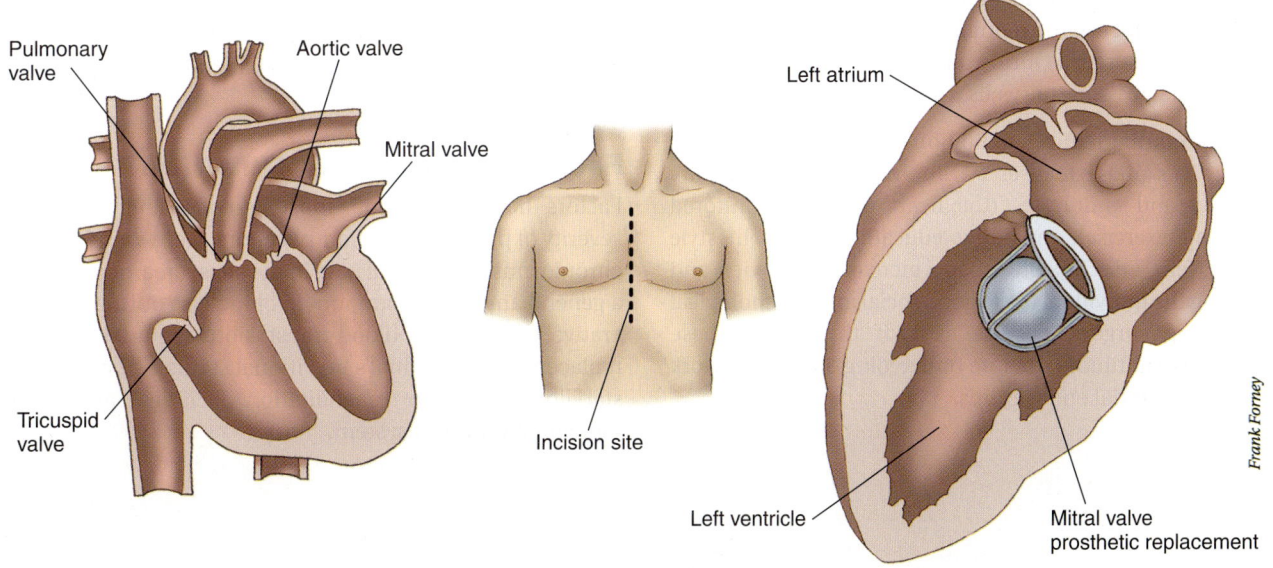

Because the heart and lungs receive no blood or oxygen (and other vital organs receive a reduced amount of oxygen) while the individual is on CPB, measures need to be taken to reduce the body's need for oxygen by reducing body temperature. This is accomplished with the heat exchanger portion of the heart-lung machine. Cooling the body's temperature to approximately 82 degrees F reduces its need for oxygen by 50%. Cooling the temperature to 68 degrees F reduces the body's need for oxygen another 25%.

When the surgeon has completed the surgical repair, the individual's body is warmed the same way it was cooled. The sternum is closed with metal wires and the skin sutured closed.

Prognosis

The operative mortality for heart valve replacement is about 5%. The overall survival is about 60% at 10 years. A given individual's risk of death within 10 years after surgery is related to the individual's age, overall function of the heart, durability of the valve, and need for anticoagulant therapy.

Rate of success for heart valve replacement surgery is high and increasing. Individuals who recover from this procedure usually lead normal lives with relatively few symptoms of chronic heart disease.

Specialists

- Cardiologist
- Cardiothoracic Surgeon

Rehabilitation

Respiratory therapy may begin in the intensive care unit as soon as the breathing tube (endotracheal tube) is removed. Respiratory therapy focuses on preventing the buildup of lung secretions that can lead to pneumonia and reinflating the lungs to their presurgical condition. Respiratory therapists teach individuals pursed lip breathing to increase the airflow to the lungs. Individuals may also use an incentive spirometer. This is a device that measures and displays the amount of air inspired and helps motivate individuals to take deeper breaths. Individuals also learn to produce an effective cough through techniques such as huffing where air is breathed out forcefully with the mouth open.

Cardiac rehabilitation begins in the hospital shortly after the immediate postoperative period and focuses on helping individuals resume a more normal lifestyle following surgery. During phase I, the individual begins walking in the hospital halls and stairwells with assistance.

Phase II begins in an outpatient rehabilitation facility after discharge from the hospital. This phase focuses on improving the individual's capacity for activity and endurance (the heart may be monitored electronically during exercise), providing education about lifestyle changes, reducing fear and anxiety about increasing activity and exercise, and helping the individual make good social and psychological adjustments following surgery. For the rest of their lives, these individuals need to take antibiotics before undergoing any dental work or surgery to prevent bacterial endocarditis.

Phase III is a continuation of phase II and focuses on providing an ongoing exercise and diet program while continuing to help the individual resolve psychosocial issues. Electronic heart monitoring is available during exercise, but is not required. Phase IV provides continuing exercise, diet, and psychosocial support, if needed.

Work Restrictions / Accommodations

After 6 postoperative weeks, individuals who have had successful heart valve replacement surgery without experiencing serious postoperative complications or disabilities can usually return to work part-time with few if any restrictions on activity with the exception of heavy lifting. Hours of work may be gradually increased over the next 6 to 8 weeks until the individual is working a full day. Individuals with residual chronic heart disease or chronic chest pain may require work restrictions and accommodations that conserve their energy and reduce strain on their hearts. Other medical problems or permanent disabilities because of underlying medical conditions (i.e., diabetes, chronic obstructive lung disease, or chronic renal failure requiring dialysis) or postoperative complications (i.e., partial paralysis or speech impairment because of stroke) may also require work restrictions and accommodations.

Comorbid Conditions

For the individual undergoing heart valve replacement surgery, comorbid conditions that may influence length of disability include previous cardiac surgery, pre-existing diseases affecting any of the major body systems (i.e., high blood pressure, chronic kidney disease, bleeding disorders, diabetes mellitus, chronic obstructive lung disease, chronic heart disease, and immunosuppressive diseases), obesity, and history of smoking, alcoholism or other substance abuse.

Procedure Complications

Operative complications common to both types of valves include bleeding, arrhythmias, infection, dehiscence of the sternum, thrombophlebitis, pulmonary emboli, stroke, acute myocardial infarction, and respiratory and kidney failure. The major complication of tissue valves over time is degeneration that requires a second operation. The major complications of mechanical valves are related to the need for anticoagulant therapy to prevent clot (thrombus) formation in the valve. Pieces of thrombus (emboli) may break off and lodge in any organ resulting in serious consequences such as a stroke. Long-term complications common to both types of valves include bacterial endocarditis and paravalvular leaks.

Factors Influencing Duration

Factors that may influence the length of disability include number and severity of postoperative complications (i.e., wound infection, bleeding, chronic musculoskeletal pain in the chest area, or an adverse reaction to a general anesthetic), amount of blood loss during surgery and postoperatively, number of blood transfusions required, success of the valve replacement, individual's nutritional status and mental and emotional stability, access to rehabilitation facilities, and strength of the individual's support system.

Length of Disability

Individual is anticoagulated. Disability may be permanent.

Duration in Days

Job Classification	Minimum	Optimum	Maximum
Sedentary work	28	42	56
Light work	28	42	56
Medium work	56	70	84
Heavy work	Indefinite	Indefinite	Indefinite
Very Heavy work	Indefinite	Indefinite	Indefinite

References

Meeker, Margaret, and Jane Rothrock. Alexander's Care of the Patient in Surgery. St. Louis: Mosby, 1999.

Sundt, Thoralf M., MD. Aortic Valve Replacement. The Society of Thoracic Surgeons. 12 Oct 2000. 13 Oct 2000 <http://www.sts.org/doc/3621>.

Heat Exhaustion

Other names / synonyms: Heat Prostration

992.3, 992.4, 992.5

Definition

Heat exhaustion is an acute heat-related illness characterized by dehydration and elevated body temperature. It occurs when the body can no longer adequately cool itself due to extreme environmental conditions or excess heat production as during exercise.

This heat illness and other heat syndromes such as heat stroke occur most frequently when the air temperature rises above 90 degrees F and humidity is greater than 60%. Heat exhaustion is seen most frequently during the first few days of a heat wave. This is because the body's cooling mechanism takes about 7 to 14 days to adapt to high environmental temperatures. Until adaptation takes place, the body is inefficient at cooling and can easily become overheated and dehydrated when exposed to a high temperature for an extended period of time.

Heat exhaustion can progress quickly to a more serious form of heat illness called heat stroke. Heat stroke occurs in two forms. One is exertional heat stroke that typically occurs in healthy, younger individuals exercising at ambient temperatures above 90 degrees F. The other is nonexertional heat stroke that usually occurs either at rest or during ordinary activities in older individuals with pre-existing chronic illnesses, especially heart disease.

Heat exhaustion with water depletion can occur in any individual who fails to take in enough fluids or is taking a medication to rid the body of water (diuretic). Other circumstances that can increase the risk of heat exhaustion include exercising in a hot environment, lack of air conditioning or proper ventilation, inappropriate clothing (e.g., occlusive, heavy, or vapor-impermeable), decreased fluid intake, certain pre-existing illnesses, use of diuretics, and spending extended time in hot, enclosed environments (e.g., inside of tents or autos in the sun, hot tubs, or saunas).

In an average year in the US, about 175 to 200 individuals die from heat-related disorders including heat stroke. This number increases to over 1,500 during heat waves. Geographically, heat exhaustion and other heat-related illnesses occur most frequently in areas with high air temperatures. Heat-related illnesses occur with equal frequency in males and females. Infants and the elderly are more prone to heat exhaustion as a result of inadequate body temperature regulation (thermoregulatory) mechanisms.

Diagnosis

History: The individual usually reports recent exposure to a temperature above 90 degrees F or participated in prolonged or heavy physical activity at a somewhat lower temperature. Individual may complain of headache, dizziness, weakness, thirst, fatigue, loss of appetite, or nausea and vomiting.

Physical exam: Individual appears flushed, warm, and perspires heavily. They may be anxious or confused. An elevated temperature and a rapid respiratory rate are present.

Tests: A complete blood count (CBC) and measurement of the serum sodium, potassium, chloride, and bicarbonate (electrolytes) should be obtained.

Treatment

Therapy consists of moving the individual to cooler surroundings, providing rest, and rehydration with fluids containing sodium and potassium. Ideally, the individual should be treated at an emergency department or urgent care clinic. If such a facility is not available, administration of sports drinks and even soda drinks can help replace fluids. Fluid replacement should be given slowly and continued for at least 6 to 9 hours or until adequate hydration is achieved. Blood pressure, pulse, temperature, and urine output are monitored to assess severity of illness and guide fluid replacement. In severe cases, hospitalization is required for administration of intravenous fluids. Cool washcloths or ice packs may be placed on the neck, groin, or armpits to hasten cooling. Rest and fluid replacement should continue for at least 24 hours.

Prognosis

With prompt treatment, individuals with heat cramps and heat exhaustion should have full recovery with no residual effects.

Differential Diagnosis

Heat stroke, fever from infection, malignant hyperthermia, hypothalamic infarct, and drug-induced fluid loss have similar symptoms to heat exhaustion.

Specialists

- Emergency Medicine
- Internist

Work Restrictions / Accommodations

Individuals should avoid activity in the heat for approximately 24 to 48 hours following heat exhaustion.

The Occupational Safety and Health Administration (OSHA) and National Institute of Occupational Safety and Health (NIOSH) have published guidelines regarding work accommodations to prevent heat-related illness. In general, recommendations include heavy work scheduled for the coolest part of the day, frequent rest breaks in cool areas, adequate amounts of cool water provided for workers, and light-duty assignments for those at greatest risk of heat-related illnesses (obese, elderly, those not acclimated to the heat and on medications).

Comorbid Conditions

Advanced age, obesity, and concomitant medication use especially diuretics are conditions that may impact the ability to recover and lengthen the time of disability.

Complications

Heat exhaustion can quickly progress to heat stroke associated with low blood pressure, shock, organ dysfunction, and even death.

Factors Influencing Duration

The severity of the heat exhaustion, certain pre-existing medical conditions, working conditions (ambient temperature), and the individual's job requirements influence the length of disability.

Length of Disability

Duration depends on severity of heat exhaustion, work conditions (ambient heat), and individual's job requirements.

Duration in Days

Job Classification	Minimum	Optimum	Maximum
Any work	0	1	3

Failure to Recover

If an individual fails to recover within the maximum duration expectancy period, the reader may wish to reference the following questions to assist in better understanding the specifics of an individual's medical case.

Regarding diagnosis:

- Has individual been exposed to air temperature over 90 degrees F with humidity greater than 60%?
- Did individual fail to drink adequate amounts of fluid? Are they taking diuretics?
- Was individual wearing inappropriate clothing?
- Does individual have inadequate thermoregulatory mechanisms?
- Does individual complain of a headache, dizziness, fatigue, or weakness? Is there increased thirst, loss of appetite, or nausea and vomiting? Does individual appear warm and flushed? Perspiring heavily? Is individual anxious or confused?
- Was body temperature elevated? Were rapid respirations evident?
- Was a CBC and electrolyte test performed?

Regarding treatment:

- "In the field" was individual moved to cooler surroundings? Were sports drinks given? Were ice packs to the neck, groin, or neck used to facilitate cooling?
- Was individual then taken to the emergency room? Was IV fluid replacement needed?
- Was it necessary to hospitalize the individual?

Regarding prognosis:

- Can individual's employer accommodate any necessary restrictions?
- Does individual have any conditions that may affect ability to recover?
- Did individual have any complications such as heat stroke associated with low blood pressure, shock, organ dysfunction, or death?

References

Center for Disease Control and Prevention. "Publications." Resources. National Institute of Occupational Safety 01 Oct 2000. 04 Oct 2000 <http://www.cdc.gov/niosh/pubs.html>.

Tierney, Lawrence M., Stephen J. McPhee, and Maxine A. Papadakis, eds. Current Medical Diagnosis and Treatment, 39th ed. New York: Lange Medical Books/McGraw-Hill, 2000.

Heat Stroke

Other names / synonyms: Siriasis, Sunstroke, Thermic Fever

992.0

Definition

Heat stroke is the most serious of several similar heat-related illnesses. It is a life-threatening medical emergency resulting from failure of the body's temperature regulation (thermoregulation) mechanism. Unlike other heat illnesses, heat stroke is characterized by extreme elevation of body temperature (hyperthermia) and associated central nervous system dysfunction and organ dysfunction.

Normally, the process of sweating and evaporation of sweat facilitates body cooling. In extreme temperatures, the amount of heat produced exceeds the cooling effect of sweat evaporation. Likewise, if humidity reaches 100%, evaporation of sweat is no longer possible and the body loses its ability to dissipate heat. Eventually the body's temperature rises leading to severe dehydration, swelling of brain tissue, low blood pressure, organ damage, and, possibly, death.

Heat stroke traditionally is divided into exertional and classic varieties, distinguished by the underlying etiology. Exertional heat stroke typically occurs in younger athletic individuals who exercise vigorously in the heat until the body's normal thermoregulatory mechanisms are overwhelmed. Classic heat stroke more commonly occurs in older individuals, or in those with underlying illnesses who are exposed to extreme environmental temperatures and/or humidity. Another less common type of heat stroke is sunstroke which is heatstroke caused by direct exposure to the sun.

Generally, prolonged exposure to temperatures in excess of 90 degrees Fahrenheit or humidity in excess of 65% presents the greatest risk of developing heat-related illnesses. However, heat illnesses can occur under more moderate environments in the obese because of inadequate thermoregulatory mechanisms. Geographically, heat stroke and other heat-related illnesses occur most frequently in areas with high air temperatures.

Other circumstances that may increase the risk of developing heat stroke include exercising in a hot environment, lack of air conditioning or proper ventilation, inappropriate clothing (e.g., occlusive, heavy or vapor-impermeable), decreased fluid intake, pre-existing illness or medication use, or spending extended time in hot environments (e.g., inside of tents or autos in the sun, hot tubs, or saunas).

About 175-200 persons die from heat-related disorders (which includes heat stroke) during an average year in the US. This statistic rises to over 1,500 persons during heat waves. Heat related illnesses occur with equal frequency in males and females. Older individuals are more prone to developing heat exhaustion as a result of inadequate body temperature regulation (thermoregulatory) mechanisms. The exact number of persons seeking treatment for heat-related disorders is not recorded but reaches into the thousands.

Diagnosis

History: The individual may complain of headache, dizziness, thirst, fatigue, weakness, loss of appetite, nausea, and vomiting. Individuals may report a recent history of heavy or prolonged physical exertion or exposure to intense sun or a warm, possibly humid, environment.

Physical exam: The critical feature of heat stroke is neurological dysfunction, which has a sudden onset in 80% of cases. This may be manifested by confusion, disorientation, hallucinations, bizarre behavior, problems with walking or coordination, seizures, pupil dilation, or even coma. Vital signs will reveal a core temperature range of 104 degrees F to 106 degrees F, increased heart rate, and rapid, shallow respirations. Sweating may or may not be present. Urine output may be scant or absent. There may be symptoms that suggest bleeding tendencies such as small hemorrhages in the whites of the eyes (conjunctival hemorrhage), bruising, bloody stools, bloody sputum (hemoptysis), or blood in the urine (hematuria).

Tests: Appropriate laboratory tests are done to determine the degree of fluid and electrolyte loss and to detect any signs of organ dysfunction. This may include complete blood count (CBC), chemistry panel, liver enzymes, blood urea nitrogen (BUN) and creatinine, a urinalysis and urine specific gravity, cardiac isoenzymes, and arterial blood gases (ABGs).

X-rays may include a chest x-ray to determine if lung damage has occurred. A computed tomography (CT) of the head to look for brain swelling or bleeding. An electrocardiogram may be done to detect heart rhythm disturbances or evidence of heart damage.

Treatment

Primary treatment includes initial stabilization of airway, breathing, and circulation. Supplemental oxygen and IV fluids may be given. Heat stroke requires lowering the body temperature quickly to prevent seizures, organ damage or death, and to maintain adequate breathing. Lowering the body temperature is usually accomplished by moving the person to a cool environment, removing the clothing, fanning, and bathing the skin with cool water. Ice packs can be applied to the neck, armpits, and groin. Medications to suppress shivering (Thorazine) or control seizures (benzodiazepines) may be given as needed. Heat stroke victims may be admitted to the hospital for continued monitoring, cooling interventions, and fluid administration.

Prognosis

With rapid cooling, adequate rehydration, and aggressive treatment of complications, the survival rate approaches 90% for those with heat stroke. Mortality may reach 70% if initial treatment is delayed beyond 2 hours. Prolonged temperature elevation (greater than 104 degrees F), coma lasting longer than 4 hours, or complications of bleeding disorders or organ failure are associated with a poor outcome.

Differential Diagnosis

Other possibilities include fever from infection, central nervous system dysfunction, or drug-induced fluid loss.

Specialists

- Critical Care Specialist
- Emergency Medicine
- Internist

Work Restrictions / Accommodations

Both OSHA and NIOSH have specific recommendations to prevent heat-related illnesses for workers in hot environments. The following summarizes the general recommendations: Heavy work should be scheduled at the coolest part of the day. Proper clothing should be worn. Frequent rest breaks in cool areas should be provided. Cool water, as much as a quart per hour, should be provided. Employees should be trained to recognize symptoms of heat stress. Heat measurements should be done if there is a potential for heat stress, exhaustion, and heat stroke. Modified duty should be considered for those at greatest risk for heat illnesses (elderly, obese, or individuals on medications). Those returning from illness should be allowed approximately 5-7 days to acclimate to the hot environment before performing heavy labor.

Those with secondary brain or organ system dysfunction may have more specific work restrictions or accommodations recommended by their physician.

Comorbid Conditions

Comorbid conditions of obesity, heart disease, hyperthyroidism, diabetes, and some neurologic diseases such as Parkinsonism may impact ability to recover and further lengthen disability.

Complications

Temperatures above 105 degrees F increase the seriousness of the illness. Complications may include brain damage, kidney failure, liver failure, pneumonia, seizures, heart damage, skeletal muscle breakdown (rhabdomyolysis), and bleeding disorders (DIC).

Factors Influencing Duration

Disability factors include the degree of the temperature, the time period the individual remains with a high temperature, age, overall state of health, and amount of hydration prior to the occurrence of the heat stroke.

Length of Disability

The expected length of disability is variable. Duration depends on severity, presence of convulsions, work conditions (ambient heat), or permanent tissue damage.

Duration in Days

Job Classification	Minimum	Optimum	Maximum
Sedentary work	2	3	14
Light work	2	3	14
Medium work	3	4	14
Heavy work	7	8	14
Very Heavy work	7	8	14

Failure to Recover

If an individual fails to recover within the maximum duration expectancy period, the reader may wish to reference the following questions to assist in better understanding the specifics of an individual's medical case.

Regarding diagnosis:

- Was diagnosis of heat stroke confirmed?
- Have other conditions such as fever from infection, central nervous system dysfunction, or drug-induced fluid loss, been ruled out?
- Does individual have signs of neurological dysfunction such as disorientation, decreased level of consciousness, impaired memory, and persistent seizure activity?
- Does individual have symptoms of other organ system dysfunction such as elevated liver enzymes or kidney function tests (BUN and creatinine)?
- Did individual experience complications such as, brain damage, kidney failure, liver failure, pneumonia, seizures, heart damage, skeletal muscle breakdown (rhabdomyolysis), and bleeding disorders (DIC), resulting from heat stroke?
- Does individual have an underlying condition such as, obesity, heart disease, hyperthyroidism, diabetes, and some neurologic diseases such as Parkinsonism, that may impact ability to recover?

Regarding treatment:

- Did individual receive prompt emergency room treatment (within 2 hours) with appropriate cooling measures?
- Was hospitalization required?

Regarding prognosis:

- If individual received prompt, aggressive treatment, what is the reason for delayed recovery?
- Did individual experience complications such as, prolonged temperature elevation (greater than 104 degrees F), coma lasting longer than 4 hours, or complications of bleeding disorders or organ failure, despite treatment?
- Is residual impairment present?
- How does impairment impact daily activity or occupational function?

References

Curtis, Rick. "Outdoor Action Guide to Heat-related Illnesses and Fluid Balance." National Institute of Occupational Safety. 1 Oct 2000. 4 Oct 2000 <http://www.cdc.gov/niosh/nasd/docs5/nj98004.html>.

Tierney, Lawrence M., Stephen J. McPhee, and Maxine A. Papadakis, eds. Current Medical Diagnosis and Treatment, 39th ed. New York: Lange Medical Books/McGraw-Hill, 2000.

Heel Spur (Calcaneal)

Other names / synonyms: Calcaneal Spur, Exostosis of the Heel, Jogger's Heel

726.73, 736.76

Definition

The calcaneus bone is more commonly known as the heel of the foot. A bony growth on the undersurface of this bone is a heel spur (calcaneal, exostosis).

The spur can be seen on x-ray and is often discovered when x-rays are done for another reason. Pain in this region is not the result of the spur, but from inflammation of the tissue in the area. Many people have heel spur(s) and do not have pain in the area.

Common causes of pain in the heel include a bruise (contusion) of the fat pad in the heel, plantar fasciitis and inflammatory diseases including Reiter's syndrome. For additional specific information, see Plantar Fasciitis.

Hematosalpinx

Other names / synonyms: Fallopian Tube Infarction

620.8

Definition

Hematosalpinx is an accumulation of blood in the uterine (fallopian) tube, also called the salpinx, that extends from the upper uterus to the region of the ovary of the same side. Hematosalpinx can result from menstrual blood that has flowed into the fallopian tube (retrograde menstruation) instead of out through the vagina. Blood in the fallopian tube can be associated with endometriosis, a condition in which cells that normally line the uterus are also found in the pelvic cavity or some other area within the abdominal cavity.

Hematosalpinx is often a complication of a pregnancy that has developed outside of the uterine cavity, usually within the fallopian tubes (ectopic pregnancy). Hematosalpinx may also result from tubal disease such as inflammation of the fallopian tube (salpingitis). Another risk factor for hematosalpinx is advanced maternal age (the risk increases with age). Black women have a higher risk of death due to hemorrhage than white women; this may be related to decreased access to proper health care.

Incidence is difficult to estimate because hematosalpinx is often associated with a tubal pregnancy, and may not be included in the final diagnosis.

Diagnosis

History: Hematosalpinx may have no symptoms (asymptomatic), or the symptoms may be that of the condition with which it is associated. Symptoms associated with endometriosis may include severe abdominal or lower back pain during menstruation (dysmenorrhea), and painful intercourse (dyspareunia). In rare cases, irritation caused by endometrial fragments may cause infection or abscesses. Ectopic pregnancy symptoms include a positive pregnancy test accompanied by severe abdominal pain and vaginal spotting. Salpingitis symptoms may include severe abdominal pain, fever, and frequent urination.

Physical exam: Physical and pelvic exams will reveal symptoms of pain and irritation, and can help rule out conditions with similar symptoms, such as appendicitis, pelvic inflammatory disease (PID), or endometriosis.

Tests: Laboratory evaluation includes pregnancy testing for women of childbearing age. A complete blood count will provide evidence of blood loss and an adequate platelet level. Cervical cultures and a Papanicolaou (PAP) smear will identify the presence of cervical dysplasia or a sexually transmitted disease (STD). A test in which radiopaque is injected into the uterus and tubes and observed radiographically (hysterosalpingogram) can identify fallopian tube blockage.

Treatment

Treatment is directed at the underlying cause. A surgical procedure (salpingostomy) may be done to drain the fallopian tube of fluid and reopen the tube if it has been blocked. A removal of the entire tube (salpingectomy) may be necessary, as is the case with an ectopic pregnancy. Inflammation of the fallopian tube (salpingitis) is treated with antibiotics or surgery if the disease persists. Areas of endometrial tissue (endometriosis) that are detected on or around the outside of the fallopian tubes or ovaries, or elsewhere within the pelvis or abdomen, may be surgically removed.

Prognosis

Treatment is directed at resolving the underlying condition. If endometriosis is present, progression of ectopic growth is usually halted with treatment. With an ectopic pregnancy, outcome is related to where implantation has occurred within the fallopian tube, how advanced the pregnancy is, and condition of the mother. Salpingitis usually resolves with specific treatment for the infection. If the fallopian tube must be removed, fertility may be affected.

Differential Diagnosis

A collection of pus within the fallopian tube (pyosalpinx), and clear fluid collection within the fallopian tube (hydrosalpinx) as the end-stage of pyosalpinx, may present with similar symptoms.

Specialists

- General Surgeon
- Gynecologist

Work Restrictions / Accommodations

Work restrictions or accommodations are directly dependent upon the diagnosis and treatment of the underlying cause. Endometriosis may require time off from work depending on severity of painful symptoms. Ectopic pregnancy may result in time off from work for surgery and recuperation time. Salpingitis usually resolves after treatment, enabling the woman to return to work. If fertility has been affected, depression may result and time off may be needed for psychological counseling.

Comorbid Conditions
A comorbid condition is painful menstruation (dysmenorrhea).

Complications
An ectopic pregnancy carries with it the life-threatening risk of fallopian tube rupture and resulting hemorrhage. Another possible complication of a hematosalpinx may occur when part of the tube becomes twisted (torsion); this can result in death if not corrected. Torsion would require additional diagnostic measures to detect the underlying disease associated with the hematosalpinx (such as genital tuberculosis). Fertility may be affected if treatment involves removal of fallopian tube, or if endometriosis remains untreated.

Factors Influencing Duration
The underlying cause and type of treatment directly affects the length of disability.

Length of Disability
Length of disability is related to underlying cause and need for additional evaluation, procedures, and/or surgery.

Medical treatment.

Duration in Days

Job Classification	Minimum	Optimum	Maximum
Sedentary work	7	14	28
Light work	7	14	28
Medium work	7	14	28
Heavy work	7	14	28
Very Heavy work	7	14	28

Laparoscopic salpingectomy.

Duration in Days

Job Classification	Minimum	Optimum	Maximum
Sedentary work	3	7	21
Light work	3	7	21
Medium work	7	14	28
Heavy work	7	21	35
Very Heavy work	14	21	35

Failure to Recover
If an individual fails to recover within the maximum duration expectancy period, the reader may wish to reference the following questions to assist in better understanding the specifics of an individual's medical case.

Regarding diagnosis:
- Was individual pregnant at the time of presentation?
- Does individual have a history of endometriosis, salpingitis, or retrograde menstruation?
- Does individual have symptoms or clinical findings consistent with the diagnosis of hematosalpinx?
- Are symptoms such as, severe abdominal or lower back pain during menstruation, vaginal spotting, fever, or frequent urination, present?
- Was the diagnosis confirmed with a pelvic exam ad hysterosalpingogram?
- Did individual receive a prompt consultation with a specialist (gynecologist)?
- Were other similar conditions (pyosalpinx and hydrosalpinx) ruled out in the differential diagnosis?

Regarding treatment:
- Was the treatment appropriate for the underlying condition?
- Was surgical intervention (salpingectomy or salpingostomy) indicated?
- Was a course of antibiotics prescribed?

Regarding prognosis:
- Based on the underlying cause and type of treatment required, what was the expected outcome?
- Was individual pregnant?
- Did individual have a fallopian tube rupture and hemorrhagic shock?
- Was torsion present? If so, was treatment prompt?

References

Facts About Endometriosis. National Institute of Child Health and Human Development. 27 Sep 2000. 15 Feb 2001 <http://156.40.88.3/publications/pubs/endomet.htm>.

Braunwald, Eugene, et al. Harrison's Principles of Internal Medicine, 11th ed. New York: McGraw-Hill Book Company, 1987.

Fujimoto, V.Y., N.A. Klein, and P.B. Miller. "Late Onset Hematometra and Hematosalpinx in a Woman with a Noncommunicating Uterine Horn. A Case Report." Journal of Reproductive Medicine 43 5 (1998): 465-467.

Oriel, K.A., and S. Schrager. "Abnormal Uterine Bleeding." American Family Physician 6 9 (1999): 1371-1378.

Hematuria

Other names / synonyms: Blood in the Urine

599.7

Definition

Hematuria is the presence of red blood cells in the urine. It is a symptom of an underlying condition rather than a disease; most causes are not serious.

Hematuria occurs when blood enters the urine from any point along the urinary tract, from the kidney to the urethral opening. One of the most common causes of hematuria is an infection that causes inflammation in the urethra (urethritis), the bladder (cystitis), or ureters and kidneys (pyelonephritis). An inflammation of the prostate gland (prostatitis) or benign prostate enlargement (benign prostatic hypertrophy, or BPH) can cause hematuria in men. Glomerulonephritis, an inflammation of the glomeruli (filtering units in the kidney), can also cause blood in the urine. Other causes of hematuria include cysts, tumors, kidney or bladder stones, trauma (injury), or bleeding disorders. Occasionally, excessive high-impact exercise such as jogging can cause hematuria. A small percentage of the population has hematuria that is not detectable by the naked eye but which under a microscope shows a high number of red blood cells (microscopic hematuria). Gross hematuria can be easily seen; the urine is red or the color of cola.

The overall prevalence of hematuria is about 9% in women and 6% in men.

Diagnosis

History: The individual may report seeing blood in the urine or experiencing pain with urination. A fever, rash, or lower abdominal pain may also be present. Frequent urination may later change to urinary retention. Recent trauma to the abdomen or lower back may be reported.

Physical exam: The blood may be clearly visible as the urine comes out red; small amounts of blood may give the urine a clouded or smoky appearance; or blood may not be visible at all except under a microscope. Fever, rash, or elevated blood pressure (hypertension) may be present. A mass in the abdomen or pelvic region may be apparent upon applying pressure to the abdominal area (palpation).

Tests: Diagnostic tests should include a urinalysis and urine culture. Urine samples should be carefully collected in sequential portions (known as aliquots) to help isolate the potential source of bleeding. For example, hematuria in the first voided aliquot indicates that the bleeding may originate from the urethra and/or the prostate. In additional to red blood cells, a urinalysis may reveal white blood cells indicative of a urinary tract infection. An analysis of chemical components may reveal excess protein, which may be a sign of poor kidney function. Casts (groups of cells molded together in the shape of the kidneys' tiny filtering tubes) can signal kidney disease. High levels of wastes usually excreted by the kidneys (filtered out from the blood) into the urine may be detected in blood and is additional evidence of kidney disease. The presence of cysts, stones, or tumors can be detected through images of the urinary tract using ultrasound or CT scan. Intravenous pyelography (IVP) follows the route of a dye through the urinary tract using x-ray imaging and gives important information about the kidneys, ureters, and bladder. Angiography is a procedure that enables the blood vessels in the kidneys to be seen on film after they have been filled with a substance that shows up on x-ray (contrast medium). Direct examination of the bladder and ureters may be achieved using a fiber-optic instrument inserted through the urethra (cystoscopy and ureteroscopy).

Treatment

Hematuria or blood in the urine is a symptom rather than a diagnosis. Treatment is determined by the underlying condition. In many cases, the underlying cause is not serious, and no treatment is necessary. If the hematuria is the result of an infection, the infection is generally treated with antibiotics.

Prognosis

Since hematuria is a symptom, not a diagnosis, outcome depends on the underlying condition and treatment of that problem. Most causes of hematuria either require no treatment or are easily treatable. However, hematuria is sometimes evidence of a more serious condition such as kidney disease or bladder cancer.

Differential Diagnosis

Hematuria is a symptom common to a variety of conditions including cystitis, urethritis, pyelonephritis, prostatitis, cysts, tumors, kidney or bladder stones, glomerulonephritis, trauma, and bleeding disorders.

Specialists

- Gynecologist
- Nephrologist
- Urologist

Work Restrictions / Accommodations

Work restrictions or accommodations will be specific to diagnosis of the underlying condition and treatment of that problem.

Comorbid Conditions

Comorbid conditions include immune system suppression and bleeding disorders.

Complications

Potential complications are determined by the underlying condition.

Factors Influencing Duration

For hematuria due to trauma or exercise, duration depends on whether the job requirements are physically strenuous. For hematuria due to a urinary tract infection, length of disability may depend on availability of convenient restroom facilities and frequent breaks.

Length of Disability

This is a vague diagnosis. Duration depends on cause. Contact physician for more specific information.

Failure to Recover

If an individual fails to recover within the maximum duration expectancy period, the reader may wish to reference the following questions to assist in better understanding the specifics of an individual's medical case.

Regarding diagnosis:

- Is individual a runner or jogger?
- Is there a history of a bleeding disorder? Trauma to the urinary system? Prostate enlargement? Infection in the bladder, ureters, or kidneys? Glomerulonephritis?
- Was a microscopic examination done of the urine?
- Has individual had any pain with urination?
- Has individual had any recent trauma to the abdomen or lower back?
- Is fever, rash, or lower abdominal pain present?
- Was a urinalysis and urine culture done?
- Were tests done to rule out kidney disease?
- Did individual have imaging tests to rule out cysts, stones, tumors, or abnormalities in the blood vessels in the kidneys?
- Did individual have a cystoscopy and ureteroscopy?
- Were conditions such as cystitis, urethritis, pyelonephritis, prostatitis, cysts, tumors, kidney or bladder stones, glomerulonephritis, trauma, or bleeding disorders ruled out?

Regarding treatment:

- Has the underlying cause of the hematuria been accurately diagnosed?

Regarding prognosis:

- What is the underlying condition?
- Has there been sufficient time to heal from trauma?
- Have job requirements been modified?

References

Hematuria (Blood in the Urine). National Institute of Diabetes and Digestive and Kidney Diseases. 01 May 1999. 1 Jan 2001 <http://www.niddk.nih.gov/health/urolog/summary/hematuri/>.

Beers, Mark H., and Robert Berkow. The Merck Manual of Diagnosis and Therapy. Whitehouse Station, NJ: Merck & Co, 1999.

Hemiplegia

Other names / synonyms: Hemiparalysis, Hemiparesis
342, 342.0, 342.1, 342.8, 342.9

Definition

Hemiplegia is paralysis of one side of the body and is the most common form of paralysis. It involves the arm, leg, and sometimes the face on one side of the body.

The main causes of hemiplegia are brain hemorrhage (hemorrhagic stroke) and diseases of the blood vessels of the cerebrum and brain stem that cause interruption of blood supply to the brain (ischemic stroke). Trauma (brain injury) is another cause of hemiplegia. Other important but less acute in onset causes include brain tumor or lesion, brain abscess, diseases that destroy the sheath surrounding nerve cells (such as multiple sclerosis), blood vessel (vascular) complications of viral or bacterial infection (meningitis), and inflammation of the brain (encephalitis). With rare exceptions, hemiplegia is caused by a brain or spinal cord lesion on the side opposite to the paralysis. It is rarely caused by a few unusual cases of infectious disease caused by the poliovirus (poliomyelitis) or a disorder of motor nerve cells (neurons) in the spinal cord, brainstem, and motor cortex (motor system disease).

Brainstem lesions in other areas of the brain, such as the medulla, can cause paralysis of other parts of the body, including the tongue and sometimes the pharynx and larynx on one side, and the arm and leg on the other. These are called "crossed paralyses," and are typical of brainstem lesions. Rarely, a lesion in the spinal cord can cause hemiplegia, but more often these lesions induce paralysis on both sides of the body. A paralysis that spares the face, combined with a loss of vibratory and position sense on the same side, and a loss of pain and temperature sensation on the opposite side, signifies disease of one side of the spinal cord (Brown-Sequard syndrome).

The incidence of hemiplegia due to stroke events is approximately 11% in the US, and has been shown to be slightly higher in other countries such as Poland, where it is approximately nineteen percent. Overall incidence, which includes causes other than stroke, is difficult to predict. Hemiplegia affects the population worldwide.

Diagnosis

History: Individuals report weakness or paralysis on one side of the body. This may include the arms, legs, facial muscles, tongue, and swallowing muscles. There may be defects in speech (aphasia) or difficulty in swallowing (dysphagia).

Physical exam: Muscle weakness is evaluated during the physical and neurological examination. Identifying the pattern of muscle weakness or paralysis can help the physician identify where the damage has occurred in the nervous system. Muscle atrophy may be seen in the limbs or trunk of one side of the body. The face, an arm, a leg, or the entire side of the body may be affected. Individuals with hemiplegia may have difficulty with walking or grasping objects. A loss of ability to coordinate movement (ataxia) may be evident, and manifest as problems with body posture, walking, and balance.

Tests: MRI, CT scan, and cerebral angiogram are the most useful diagnostic tests to confirm the cause of hemiplegia and the area of brain injury.

Treatment

Medication to lower blood pressure and blood cholesterol levels may be used in individuals with hemiplegia caused by stroke and who have risk factors for stroke recurrence such as high blood pressure (hypertension) and heart disease. Drug therapy to reduce the swelling of the brain and emergency brain surgery to relieve pressure (decompression) may be necessary in cases of head injury, brain hemorrhage, brain tumors, or brain abscess. Surgery may also be used to repair blockage of the blood vessels (carotid endarterectomy) or malformations in and around the brain (total surgical excision or tumor resection). Treatment to prevent formation of blood clots in the bedridden individual should be immediate or complications can occur.

As soon as the individual has stabilized, physical therapy may begin. This is to prevent stiffening (contractures) of the arms and legs. In many cases, there can be a return of some function of affected areas for 1-2 years. The individual must be taught self-exercises to maintain body alignment. Assessment of mental status should be made to determine the presence and degree of mental impairment and depression. Treatment with antidepressant drugs may be required.

Prognosis

Hemiplegia can be severe and permanent as a consequence of lesions of the brain and spinal cord. The distribution of the paralysis due to these lesions varies with the location of the lesion and affects a group of muscles, never individual muscles. The paralysis never involves all of the muscles on one side of the body, even in the most severe forms of hemiplegia.

Hemiplegia resulting from stroke is usually permanent. In cases of head injury, there may be partial or near complete recovery. In other causes less acute in onset, recovery may be possible if the condition is treated promptly (removal of a brain tumor or treatment of a viral infection). The degree of recovery depends on the extent of the damage to the brain or spinal cord. In all cases, there is the possibility of some degree of recovery with appropriate rehabilitation (physical therapy).

In addition to physical limitations, the mental status of the individual is an essential element for recovery. Brain damage can cause loss of normal thought processes (cognitive disorders) and balance may be impaired. Even if the individual can think and speak clearly, the devastating loss of normal control of the body affects each individual differently and a reactive depression is not uncommon. Sometimes control of emotions and behavior are impaired. Speech and behavioral therapies can result in some degree of recovery.

Differential Diagnosis

A mental disorder called conversion disorder characterized by symptoms of loss or alteration of physical function suggesting physical illness of the sensorimotor system, such as paralysis, may be a possible explanation of hemiplegia when no other physical cause has been identified. Psychiatric evaluation should reveal the diagnosis.

Specialists

- Internist
- Neurologist
- Neurosurgeon
- Occupational Therapist
- Physical Therapist
- Psychiatrist

Rehabilitation

Individuals who suffer from hemiplegia may require various rehabilitation services that include physical therapy, occupational therapy, speech therapy, and orthotic management.

Occupational therapy focuses on regaining the ability to perform activities of daily living. Occupational therapists teach individuals to perform activities such as washing dishes and doing the laundry while maintaining their balance. Individuals also learn dressing and bathing techniques. Occupational therapists may order equipment such as a tub transfer bench to assist individuals in utilizing the bathtub or elastic shoelaces to promote ease of dressing.

Occupational therapists also promote the return of upper extremity and hand function through a variety of activities. Often the upper arm separates (subluxes) from the shoulder girdle due to the loss of muscle tone. Occupational therapy may use neuromuscular electrical stimulation (NMES), which uses electrodes to provide external stimulation to the muscles to counteract this symptom. More frequently, individuals are provided with a hemi-sling that helps support the arm to prevent subluxation. Occupational therapists may stretch the upper extremity and teach self-stretching techniques so that the arm can regain maximum potential. Individuals perform strengthening exercises such as shoulder shrugs, biceps curls, and hand grasps. Individuals perform tasks that require weight bearing through the affected hand to provide nervous impulses to the brain so that damaged neural paths can begin to heal. An example of a weight bearing activity is placing the hands on the bed while seated to help maintain an upright posture. Individuals engage in tasks that utilize both hands such as holding a cup with the hemiplegic hand while pouring a drink using the good hand. As function returns, individuals may engage in fine motor tasks such as handwriting.

Physical therapy focuses on stretching and strengthening the hemiplegic side. Physical therapy also focuses on transfer training. Physical therapists teach individuals to roll in bed, to transfer from lying to sitting, and to transfer from sitting to standing. Therapy teaches the individual to roll to both sides and to bear weight evenly when sitting and standing so that the individual is aware of the hemiplegic side. Individuals also learn mobility techniques such as walking and climbing stairs utilizing a pyramid cane or 4-pronged cane.

Orthotic management may also be required for individuals to regain function. Speech therapy may be required to strengthen the muscles of the face for improved speech and swallowing.

Work Restrictions / Accommodations

Work restrictions and accommodations will depend on the job requirements and level of activity involved. Wheelchair accessibility in and out of buildings and handicapped facilities may be needed. Although only one side of the body is affected in hemiplegia, activities that require coordination and balance are affected and impact the ability to perform physical work. However, vocational therapists may help an individual with hemiplegia identify vocational strengths and develop resumes that highlight those strengths. Stroke vocational rehabilitation agencies may help an individual find a job that is tailored to his/her specific needs and appropriate for the degree of disability. Occupational therapists also are instrumental in helping an individual perform self-directed activities or occupations such as housecleaning, gardening, and practicing arts and crafts. They also help individuals learn how to adapt to driving and provide on-road training, which may be an important consideration in returning to work.

Comorbid Conditions

Diseases that can cause muscle atrophy or weakness such as cerebral palsy and multiple sclerosis would impact the ability to recover and further lengthen disability.

Complications

Muscles can become permanently contracted if a physical therapy program with specific exercises to increase range of motion is not instituted. Skin can break down due to increased pressure and form pressure (decubitus) ulcers if position changes and skin care are not done regularly to relieve pressure. Pneumonia and blood clots (deep vein thrombosis) are other complications.

Factors Influencing Duration

The length of disability will be determined by the cause of the hemiplegia, the severity and area of the paralysis, the duties or activity level required of the individual, and which side of the body was affected. An individual who has a job that involves moderate to heavy physical activity would be considered permanently disabled. Duties that are more sedentary might not present as many problems if intellectual capacity appropriate for the work is present.

Length of Disability

The length of disability will be influenced by the individual's job requirements and severity of the paralysis, especially if the job requires heavy work. Disability may be permanent. If the dominant cerebral hemisphere is involved, speech may be lost (aphasia), as well as other motor functions.

Duration in Days

Job Classification	Minimum	Optimum	Maximum
Sedentary work	70	112	Indefinite
Light work	91	182	Indefinite
Medium work	91	182	Indefinite
Heavy work	91	182	Indefinite
Very Heavy work	91	182	Indefinite

Failure to Recover

If an individual fails to recover within the maximum duration expectancy period, the reader may wish to reference the following questions to assist in better understanding the specifics of an individual's medical case.

Regarding diagnosis:

- Has diagnosis of hemiplegia been confirmed?
- Has there been psychiatric evaluation?
- Was a complete neurological evaluation performed with appropriate imaging studies to ascertain the area of brain involvement?

Regarding treatment:

- If individual has hypertension, high blood cholesterol, or heart disease, as a cause of stroke, was medication prescribed to control these conditions?
- Did individual receive appropriate treatment for a causative condition such as encephalitis, meningitis, or brain abscess?
- Was surgery required to repair blockage to the blood vessels (carotid endarterectomy) or malformations in and around the brain (total surgical excision or tumor resection)? With what success?
- Has individual complied with a physical therapy program for rehabilitation?
- Has mental status been assessed?
- Would individual benefit from treatment with antidepressant drug therapy?

Regarding prognosis:

- Did individual receive prompt, appropriate treatment for a causative condition such as encephalitis, meningitis, or brain abscess?
- How extensive is impairment?
- Can additional function be restored to this individual through physical therapy?
- Is individual receiving appropriate rehabilitative (speech, behavioral, or psychological) therapy?
- Would individual benefit from extended length or additional forms of therapy?
- Does individual have an underlying condition that may impact recovery such as cerebral palsy, multiple sclerosis, or other diseases that can cause muscle atrophy/weakness?

References

Adams, Raymond H., Maurice Victor, and Allan H. Ropper. Principles of Neurology, 6th ed. New York: McGraw Hill, 1997.

O'Sullivan, Susan B. "Stroke." Physical Rehabilitation: Assessment and Treatment. O'Sullivan, Susan B., and Thomas J. Schmitz, eds. Philadelphia: F.A. Davis Company, 1994. 327-360.

Hemolytic Anemia

Other names / synonyms: Acquired Hemolytic Anemia, Autoimmune Hemolytic Anemia, Drug-Induced Hemolytic Anemia, Idiopathic Anemia, Inherited Hemolytic Anemia, Nonimmune Hemolytic Anemia

282, 282.1, 282.2, 282.3, 282.8, 282.9, 283, 283.0, 283.1, 283.2, 283.9, 773, 773.0, 773.1, 773.2

Definition

Hemolytic anemia is a general term applied to conditions in which red blood cells have a shortened life span. For a variety of reasons, the red blood cells are broken down or removed from circulation faster than they can be produced. Anemia is due to abnormally low number of red blood cells in circulation.

Hemolytic anemia may result from disorders that are either inherited or acquired. The anemia-producing inherited disorders are generally responsible for abnormalities within the red blood cell. These genetically determined defects include defects of the cell membrane (as in hereditary spherocytosis), defects in the structure or production of hemoglobin (as in sickle cell anemia or thalassemia), or deficiencies of needed enzymes (as in pyruvate kinase deficiency).

Many of the acquired disorders that cause hemolytic anemia involve the immune system. In autoimmune hemolytic anemia, red blood cells are destroyed by antibodies produced by the individual's own immune system. In a transfusion reaction, antibodies destroy red blood cells as a result of mismatched blood. Acquired disorders that don't involve the immune system include conditions that cause the red blood cells to break into fragments (as in some coagulation disorders or complications of mechanical heart valves); intracellular infections, such as malaria; exposure to toxic chemicals; adverse drug reactions; excessive trapping of blood cells in the spleen (hypersplenism); or other acquired diseases, such as a bone marrow disorder that predisposes blood cells to early destruction (paroxysmal nocturnal hemoglobinuria).

Approximately 4 of 100,000 individuals have hemolytic anemia. A little less than half of these (1-2 of 100,000) have autoimmune hemolytic anemia. Risk factors for developing hemolytic anemia vary according to the cause of the anemia. For example, the risk of developing hemolytic anemia due to sickle cell anemia is higher in blacks than in whites. The risk of developing many of the inherited disorders depends on whether or not the disorder, or the gene for the disorder, is already present in the family. In contrast, the risk of autoimmune hemolytic anemia does not vary with racial groups, nor does it seem to be influenced by genetic factors.

Diagnosis

History: Symptoms will vary depending on how quickly the hemolytic anemia develops and progresses. An individual with slow development may report only some yellowing of the skin and eyes (jaundice). Individuals with a more rapid onset of anemia may have fatigue and shortness of breath. With an acute onset, there may be fever, chills, headache, and pain in the back, abdomen, or extremities. Individuals may report urine that is red or dark. Individuals with hemolytic anemia typically do not have abnormal bleeding.

Physical exam: Findings may include paleness of the skin (pallor), rapid heart rate, and rapid breathing. Mild yellowing of the skin and eyes due to the presence of bile in the blood (jaundice) is usually present. The spleen and liver may be enlarged. Signs of heart failure can be seen with severe anemia.

Tests: A complete blood count (CBC) shows an abnormally low number of red blood cells and a low hemoglobin level. These findings correlate with the degree of anemia. A count of immature red blood cells (reticulocyte count) shows an increased number. A peripheral blood smear may show abnormally shaped red blood cells and cell fragments.

Serum bilirubin will be elevated. The direct Coombs test will be positive in immune hemolytic anemias. Other tests, specific to the suspected cause of the hemolytic anemia, will vary.

Treatment

Medical treatment is given that is specific for the disorder that is causing the anemia. In general, surgical removal of the spleen (splenectomy) and oral folic acid supplements may be recommended.

Some cases of immune hemolytic anemias are mild enough that no treatment is required. Significant anemia may be treated with steroids or other immunosuppressive drugs. A minority of individuals may need a blood transfusion to replace destroyed red blood cells. Life-threatening immune hemolytic anemia may be treated with plasmapheresis, a procedure in which an individual's plasma is removed and replaced.

Prognosis

Outcome varies widely among the various hemolytic anemias and is dependent on the causative disorder.

Removal of the spleen (splenectomy) effectively stops the entrapment and removal of normal red blood cells by an enlarged spleen (hypersplenism), thereby boosting the number of red blood cells in the circulation. Splenectomy, however, does not correct the original red blood cell defect or condition affecting the red blood cells. Transfusion of red blood cells temporarily increases the number in circulation. Folic acid supplements will help increase hemoglobin levels, helping to counteract the effects of the hemolytic process.

Up to 80% of individuals with immune hemolytic anemia respond to steroid treatment, and up to 50% respond to other immunosuppressive medications. The effects of the removal of plasma (plasmapheresis), which contains the destructive antibodies, are short-term, but life-saving in an hemolytic emergency.

Differential Diagnosis

Individuals with malignancy may present with symptoms of fatigue, pallor, and jaundice. Individuals with liver disease or pancreatic disease will appear jaundiced. Some malignancies (particularly lymphoma) are often accompanied by an enlarged spleen (splenomegaly). Heart failure produces many of the signs and symptoms associated with anemia.

Specialists

- Hematologist

Work Restrictions / Accommodations

A persistent anemia may require reduction in the physical requirements of work. This reduction may be temporary or permanent depending on the availability of and response to treatment. If splenectomy is performed, time off for recovery will be needed.

Comorbid Conditions

Comorbid conditions include underlying cardiovascular disease and liver disease, and other underlying disease, such as malignancy.

Complications

The increased breakdown of red blood cells can result in bile blockage in the liver and gallstone formation. Non-healing leg ulcers can be seen. Kidney failure and even shock can result from acute, severe destruction (hemolysis) of red blood cells. Severe anemia can result in heart failure.

Factors Influencing Duration

Severity of the anemia, availability of treatment, and response to treatment will influence the length of disability.

Length of Disability

Duration depends on cause. Disability may be permanent.

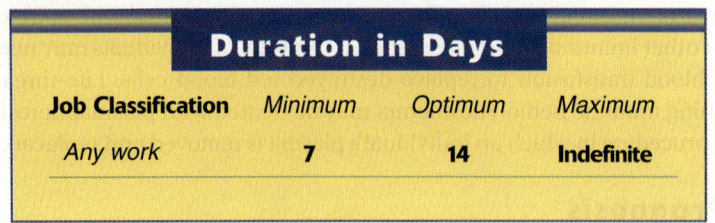

Duration in Days

Job Classification	Minimum	Optimum	Maximum
Any work	7	14	Indefinite

Failure to Recover

If an individual fails to recover within the maximum duration expectancy period, the reader may wish to reference the following questions to assist in better understanding the specifics of an individual's medical case.

Regarding diagnosis:

- Was diagnosis of hemolytic anemia been confirmed?
- Was specific disorder causing the hemolytic anemia been identified?
- Has individual experienced any complications from the hemolytic anemia?
- Does individual have an underlying condition that may impact recovery such as cardiovascular disease, liver disease, or malignancy?

Regarding treatment:

- Is underlying condition responding to treatment?
- If not, what other treatment options are available?
- If condition is caused by reaction to a drug, has individual stopped taking that drug?
- Was another medication been successfully substituted?
- Would individual benefit from supplemental oral folate?
- Has individual taken steroids or immunosuppressive drugs as prescribed? If not, what can be done to increase compliance?
- Was splenectomy, blood transfusion or plasmapheresis required? With what results?

Regarding prognosis:

- What is the current prognosis for the underlying condition?
- Would individual benefit from steroid or immunosuppressive therapy?
- Since many therapies help only on a short-term basis, what is the long-term treatment plan?
- Is individual's red blood cell count monitored on a regular basis?

References

Hemolytic Anemia. National Library of Medicine. 1999. 14 Aug 2000 <http://medlineplus.adam.com/ency/article/000571.htm>.

Szchzepiorkowski, Zbigniew, and Ronald Sacher. "Autoimmune Hemolytic Anemia." Conn's Current Therapy 2000, 52nd ed. Rakel, Robert, ed. Philadelphia: W.B. Saunders Company, 2000. 359-363.

Hemophilia A

Other names / synonyms: Classic Hemophilia, Congenital Factor VIII Disorder, Factor VIII Deficiency, Factor VIII Deficiency Hemophilia

286.0

Definition

Hemophilia A is the most common severe bleeding disorder. Blood clotting depends on the presence of specific substances in the blood called clotting factors. Individuals with hemophilia A do not have factor VIII, one of these important clotting factors. Without an adequate amount of factor VIII, spontaneous bleeding can occur and blood cannot clot normally following an injury. The most common sites for bleeding are into the joints (knees, ankles, and elbows), muscles, and from the mucous membranes.

The severity of the condition varies according to how much factor VIII activity the individual retains. Up to 70% of individuals with hemophilia A retain less than 1% of normal factor VIII activity, and consequently have severe hemophilia. The remaining individuals either have factor VIII levels between 1% and 5% of normal and a moderate condition, or greater than 5% and a mild condition.

Hemophilia A is an inherited disorder. Because the gene for this disease is on the X chromosome, it is a sex-linked disease that only affects males. The gene is carried by women without symptoms and is passed to their daughters and sons. When a daughter inherits the gene, she also becomes a carrier and is asymptomatic but when a son inherits the gene, he is affected by hemophilia A. Up to 30% of cases, however, occur from a new gene mutation not present in the mother.

All races and ethnic groups are equally affected by hemophilia A with about 100 cases for every 1 million individuals. The peak prevalence is in young adult males between the ages of 20 and 30. Before 1985 when screening blood products for HIV began, many hemophiliacs were exposed to HIV in factor replacement products. An estimated 75% of individuals with hemophilia are now reported to be HIV-positive.

Diagnosis

History: The amount of factor VIII determines the severity of hemophilia A and therefore the symptoms that present. Individuals with severe anemia have frequent spontaneous bleeding into joints and other tissues, leaving those joints and tissues stiff and painful. After trauma, injury, or surgery, these anemic individuals typically experience severe bleeding. Among individuals with mild or moderate hemophilia, spontaneous bleeding is uncommon, although bleeding can occur after trauma, injury, or surgery.

Individuals with severe hemophilia are typically diagnosed following an episode of active bleeding during childhood. Individuals with mild or moderate hemophilia, however, may not be diagnosed until adulthood when bleeding occurs in association with an injury, dental work, or surgery.

Physical exam: Evidence of active bleeding may be present such as blood in the urine or large areas of bruising (hematomas). Joints may be swollen and stiff, hot and tender, and there may be a rash on the skin covering the joint. Mobility of the joint may be reduced.

Tests: A panel of coagulation studies is done to identify the clotting factor deficiency. In hemophilia A, a factor VIII assay is reduced.

Treatment

Treatment is directed at stopping and preventing the bleeding. Both are accomplished by the infusion of factor VIII replacement. The two types of available replacement products are factor VIII concentrate made from purified pooled human plasma, and a newer product called recombinant DNA-derived factor VIII. The recombinant DNA product has an advantage. Since it is not made from human plasma, it cannot transmit blood-borne viruses such as HIV or hepatitis B and C. Individuals who are HIV-positive may benefit from products that have been additionally purified.

To stop or prevent imminent bleeding, factor VIII replacement is given in sufficient quantity to bring up levels to 25-30% of normal for minor bleeding, to 50% for severe bleeding, surgery, or trauma, or up to 80-100% for life-threatening bleeding, major surgery, or trauma. Primary preventive (prophylaxis) treatment prevents spontaneous bleeding. This treatment involves the administration of factor VIII replacement twice a week to maintain levels at greater than 1-2% of normal. A permanent indwelling catheter is implanted that enables the individual to self-administer the treatment without repeated needlesticks. Prophylaxis treatment may not be necessary for an individual with mild hemophilia.

Another major goal of primary prophylaxis treatment is to prevent joint deformity caused by repeated bleeding into joints (hemarthrosis). Pain associated with hemarthrosis is treated with narcotic analgesics, temporary immobilization, restrain from weight bearing, acupuncture, transdermal nerve stimulation, and hypnosis.

The progression of joint damage may be delayed by removing all or part of a joint's synovial membrane (synovectomy). This may be done during open surgery or by arthroscopy. The inflamed tissue is removed, thereby reducing bleeding and pain. An alternative procedure called synoviorthosis is a nonsurgical synovectomy that uses an injection of a radio-isotope.

If the joint pain is unrelenting or if the joint destruction is severe, a prosthetic replacement may be necessary. Chronic ankle pain may require surgical joint fusion (arthrodesis).

Additional agents are available to help stop bleeding. Antifibrinolytic agents may be used to stop bleeding from mucous membranes and fibrin glue can stop bleeding at the site of the injury. A specific antidiuretic hormone may be used intravenously or in a nasal spray to temporarily raise factor VIII levels in the blood.

Individuals must be advised to never take aspirin or nonsteroidal anti-inflammatory drugs as either would interfere with platelet function and thereby increase the risk of bleeding. All individuals with hemophilia should be vaccinated against hepatitis A and B.

Prognosis

Life expectancy is related to the severity of the hemophilia. The mortality rate is 4 to 6 times greater in individuals with a severe condition than those with a mild condition. HIV-negative individuals with mild hemophilia have a normal life expectancy.

Replacement of factor VIII stops bleeding quickly during an active bleeding episode and promptly reverses joint pain, stiffness, and swelling. If factor VIII levels are maintained at greater than 1-2% of normal, spontaneous bleeding is prevented and overall health is improved.

HIV is the major cause of death among hemophiliacs and is responsible for 55% of these deaths. An individual with HIV has a 2-8% lifetime risk of intracranial hemorrhage, the second leading cause of death.

Damage to a particular joint is delayed but not completely stopped by the surgical removal of a portion of the synovial membrane (synovectomy). Prosthetic joint replacement stops unremitting joint pain and halts destruction. Joint fusion (arthrodesis) brings relief to chronic ankle pain.

Differential Diagnosis

Hemophilia B has the identical clinical course as hemophilia A. Conditions with similar symptoms include other clotting factor deficiencies such as von Willebrand's disease or vitamin K deficiency, platelet function disorders, liver disease, and anticoagulant overdose. Blood in the genitourinary tract must be distinguished from bleeding due to kidney stones or infection.

Specialists

- Hematologist
- Orthopedic Surgeon

Rehabilitation

Individuals with arthritis associated with hemophilia A require physical and occupational therapy since both disciplines address arthritis symptoms. Therapists instruct individuals in the use of heating pads to decrease joint stiffness and pain. Therapists instruct in stretching and strengthening exercises for the affected joints. Individuals learn to perform these exercises independently to help reduce impairment due to arthritis. Individuals also perform low-impact aerobic exercise such as walking or swimming to increase strength and endurance, and decrease fatigue.

For those individuals with arthritis in the fingers, wrist, and hand, occupational therapists can order adaptive equipment such as jar-openers and elastic shoelaces that help decrease the stress these joints experience in daily activities. Occupational therapists may also teach energy conservation techniques where activities of daily living such as meal preparation are broken into smaller components to make tasks more manageable.

Work Restrictions / Accommodations

Individuals with hemophilia need a safe work environment where they can avoid the risk of personal injury that could trigger an acute bleed. Where indicated, protective gear, especially to the head, should be worn. Office work or sedentary work would probably be more appropriate than strenuous work involving heavy lifting or other physical exertion. The employer should be aware of the condition so that the appropriate level of care can be obtained quickly in the event of an on-the-job injury. Joint pain and lack of mobility may require specific accommodations. Time off will be needed if joint surgery (arthrodesis, synovectomy, or prosthetic joint replacement) or treatment of a severe bleeding episode is required.

Comorbid Conditions

Hepatitis A, B, or C infection, chronic posthepatitic cirrhosis, parvovirus infection, HIV infection, or AIDS will cause additional disability. Gastrointestinal lesions such as ulcers or hemorrhoids increase the risk of bleeding.

Complications

Individuals may develop severe, life-threatening bleeding episodes. Bleeding may occur anywhere, particularly inside the skull, central nervous system, genitourinary tract, and abdominal cavity. Intracranial hemorrhage is the second most common cause of death among individuals with hemophilia. Bleeding of the tongue or back of the throat can cause life-threatening blockage of the airway.

Bleeding into joints causes joint disease (arthropathy). Repeated bleeding into a joint leads to permanent damage and deformity. Bleeding can also occur into muscles. Continued bleeding into muscles can cause cysts to develop within the muscle tissue or on the covering of bone. These cysts are also called pseudotumors and are painful and must be surgically excised.

Individuals may develop antibodies against the replaced clotting factor VIII. It was formerly estimated that up to 15% of individuals with hemophilia A had these antibodies. Newer replacement products, however, illicit this immune response in fewer individuals, bringing present estimates of individuals with antibody formation closer to 5%.

Infections (e.g., HIV, hepatitis A, B, and C) spread through blood products and have historically been a source of tremendous complications for individuals with hemophilia. The products currently used, however, are relatively safe. Since 1986 there have been no transmissions of HIV through a factor concentrate. All blood products are now screened before usage for potential viruses including HIV, hepatitis A, B, and C, and parvovirus.

In addition, factor VIII concentrates from pooled human plasma have been through a purification viral inactivation process that kills HIV, hepatitis B and C. Hepatitis A and parvovirus are unfortunately not killed by the inactivation process.

Factors Influencing Duration

Factors include the severity of the disorder, degree of joint involvement, location of external bleeding, complications of the disease, ability to maintain adequate levels of factor VIII, and development of antibodies to replacement factor VIII.

Length of Disability

Disability may result from trauma or other complications of disease or treatment. Duration depends on job requirements and if the individual has frequent, severe bleeding episodes. Disability may be permanent.

Single episode.

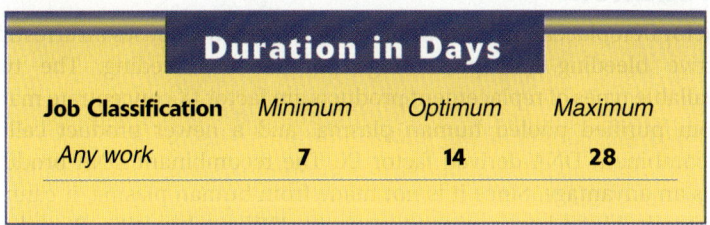

Job Classification	Minimum	Optimum	Maximum
Any work	7	14	28

Failure to Recover

If an individual fails to recover within the maximum duration expectancy period, the reader may wish to reference the following questions to assist in better understanding the specifics of an individual's medical case.

Regarding diagnosis:

- Was diagnosis of hemophilia A made by testing the coagulation ability of factor VIII? Is the deficiency of factor VIII mild, moderate, or severe?
- Does individual complain of stiff and painful joints?
- Has individual recently experienced trauma or injury, undergone surgery, or had dental work done?
- Does individual participate in contact sports or other activities with an increased risk of injury? Does individual understand the risk?
- Has individual noted blood in the urine, bruising of the skin, or a rash?

Regarding treatment:

- Did individual experience a bleeding episode? Have episodes of bleeding been successfully managed?
- Is prophylactic treatment successful in maintaining factor VIII levels?
- If individual has a permanent, indwelling catheter, is it functioning properly?
- Are joints frequently stiff and painful due to bleeding inside the joint?
- Is pain successfully managed? If not, have all treatments for pain such as, narcotic analgesics, temporary immobilization, restrained from weight bearing, acupuncture, transdermal nerve stimulation, or hypnosis, been tried?
- Has an orthopedic surgeon been consulted regarding surgical procedures to help slow the progression of joint disease or repair damaged areas?
- Are additional agents required to help stop bleeding?
- Did individual take aspirin or nonsteroidal anti-inflammatory drugs?

Regarding prognosis:

- Has individual undergone surgical procedures such as, synovectomy, synoviorthosis, or arthrodesis?
- What is the severity of the disease? Does individual have HIV infection?
- Has individual experienced one or more life-threatening bleeding episodes?
- Has individual formed antibodies against factor VIII?
- Does individual have any infections, including hepatitis A, B, C, HIV, or parvovirus?
- Has individual been vaccinated against hepatitis A and B?
- Does individual have adequate family, social, and economic support to meet the challenges of the disease?

References

Hemophilia. National Heart, Lung, and Blood Institute. 12 Oct 1999. 31 Aug 2000 <http://www.nhlbi.nih.gov/health/public/blood/other/hemophel.htm>.

Recommendations Concerning the Treatment of Hemophilia and Related Bleeding Disorders. Medical and Scientific Advisory Council of the National Hemophilia Foundation. 10 Jun 2000. 31 Aug 2000 <http://www.hemophilia.org/research/news/masac100.html>.

Andrews, Margaret M., and Kathleen Hardin Mooney. "Alterations of Hematologic Function in Children." Pathophysiology. McCance, Kathryn L., and Sue E. Heuther, eds. St. Louis: Mosby, 1994. 908-942.

Ferri, Fred. Ferri's Clinical Advisor. St. Louis: Mosby, 2000.

Goroll, Allan, Lawrence May, and Albert Mulley. Primary Care Medicine, 3rd ed. Philadelphia: Lippincott-Raven, 1995.

Guccione, Andrew A. "Arthritis." Physical Rehabilitation: Assessment and Treatment. O'Sullivan, Susan B., and Thomas J. Schmitz, eds. Philadelphia: F.A. Davis Company, 1994. 423-450.

Kessler, Craig. "Coagulation Factor Deficiencies." Cecil Textbook of Medicine, 21st ed. Goldman, Lee, and J. Claude Bennett, eds. Philadelphia: W.B. Saunders Company, 2000. 1004-1012.

Shapiro, Am, and Keith Hoots. "Hemophilia and Related Conditions." Conn's Current Therapy 2000, 52nd ed. Rakel, Robert, ed. Philadelphia: W.B. Saunders Company, 2000. 390-397.

Shenm Harry, MD, and Cheryl Solimini. Living with Arthritis. New York: Plume, 1993.

Tierney, Lawrence, Stephen McPhee, and Maxine Papadakis. Current Medical Diagnosis and Treatment, 39th ed. New York: Lange Medical Books/McGraw-Hill, 2000.

Hemophilia B

Other names / synonyms: Christmas Disease, Factor IX Deficiency, Factor IX Hemophilia

286.1

Definition

Hemophilia B is a severe bleeding disorder caused by a deficiency of a substance in the blood (a clotting factor) called factor IX that is necessary for blood clotting. A deficiency of factor IX can result in spontaneous bleeding and an inability of the blood to clot normally following an injury. The most common sites for bleeding are into the joints (knees, ankles, and elbows) and muscles and from mucous membranes.

The severity of the condition depends on the degree of factor IX deficiency. Up to 45% of individuals with hemophilia B have less than 1% of normal factor IX and consequently have severe hemophilia. The remaining individuals either have factor IX levels between 1% and 5% of normal and a moderate condition, or greater than 5% and a mild condition.

Hemophilia B is an inherited disorder that affects only males. The gene for this sex-linked disease is on the X chromosome and is carried by women without symptoms and passed to their daughters and sons. When a daughter inherits the gene, she also becomes an asymptomatic carrier but when a son inherits the gene, he is affected by the disease hemophilia B. Up to 30% of cases, however, occur from a new gene mutation not present in the mother.

There are approximately 20 cases of hemophilia B for every 1 million individuals. The disease affects all races and ethnic groups equally. The peak prevalence is in young adult males between the ages of 20 and 30. Before 1985 when screening blood products for HIV began, many hemophiliacs were exposed to HIV in factor replacement products. An estimated 75% of individuals with hemophilia are now reported to be HIV-positive.

Diagnosis

History: Symptoms reflect the severity of the disease and the level of factor IX. Individuals with severe anemia have frequent spontaneous bleeding into joints and other tissues, leaving those joints and tissues stiff and painful. Severe bleeding typically follows trauma, injury, or surgery. Individuals with mild or moderate hemophilia can experience bleeding after trauma, injury, or surgery, but spontaneous bleeding is uncommon.

Individuals with severe hemophilia are typically diagnosed following an episode of active bleeding during childhood. Individuals with mild or moderate hemophilia, however, may not be diagnosed until adulthood when bleeding occurs in association with an injury, dental work, or surgery.

Physical exam: Evidence of active bleeding can be present such as blood in the urine or large areas of bruising (hematomas). Joints may be swollen and stiff, hot and tender, and there may be a rash on the skin covering the joint. Mobility of the joint may be reduced.

Tests: A panel of coagulation studies is done to identify the clotting factor deficiency. In hemophilia B, the partial thromboplastin time (PTT) is prolonged and a factor IX assay reduced. The prothrombin time (PT) is normal.

Treatment

Factor IX replacement is the primary treatment and focuses on arresting active bleeding and preventing spontaneous bleeding. The two available types of replacement products are factor IX concentrate made from purified pooled human plasma, and a newer product called recombinant DNA-derived factor IX. The recombinant DNA product has an advantage. Since it is not made from human plasma, it cannot transmit blood-borne viruses such as HIV or hepatitis B and C. Individuals who are HIV-positive may benefit from products that have been additionally purified.

To stop or prevent imminent bleeding, factor IX replacement is given in sufficient quantity to bring up levels to 25-30% of normal for minor bleeding, to 50% for severe bleeding, surgery, or trauma, or up to 80-100% for life-threatening bleeding, major surgery, or trauma. Primary preventive (prophylaxis) treatment prevents spontaneous bleeding. This treatment involves the administration of factor IX replacement 3 times a week to maintain levels at greater than 1-2% of normal. A permanent indwelling catheter is implanted that enables the individual to self-administer the treatment without repeated needlesticks. Prophylaxis treatment may not be necessary for an individual with mild hemophilia.

Another major goal of primary prophylaxis treatment is to prevent joint deformity caused by repeated bleeding into joints (hemarthrosis). Pain associated with hemarthrosis is treated with narcotic analgesics, temporary immobilization, restrain from weight bearing, acupuncture, transdermal nerve stimulation, and hypnosis.

The progression of joint damage may be delayed by removing all or part of a joint's synovial membrane (synovectomy). This may be done during open surgery or by arthroscopy. The inflamed tissue is removed, thereby reducing bleeding and pain. An alternative procedure called synoviorthosis is a nonsurgical synovectomy that uses an injection of a radioisotope.

If the joint pain is unrelenting or if the joint destruction is severe, a prosthetic replacement may be necessary. Chronic ankle pain may require surgical joint fusion (arthrodesis).

Additional agents are available to help stop bleeding. Antifibrinolytic agents may be used to stop bleeding from mucous membranes. Fibrin glue can stop bleeding at the site of the injury. Individuals must be advised to never take aspirin or nonsteroidal anti-inflammatory drugs as either would interfere with platelet function and thereby increase the risk of bleeding. All individuals with hemophilia should be vaccinated against hepatitis A and B.

Prognosis

Life expectancy is related to the severity of the hemophilia. The mortality rate is 4 to 6 times greater in individuals with a severe condition than those with a mild condition. HIV-negative individuals with mild hemophilia have a normal life expectancy.

Replacement of factor IX stops bleeding quickly during an active bleeding episode and promptly reverses joint pain, stiffness, and swelling. If factor IX levels are maintained at greater than 1-2% of normal, spontaneous bleeding is prevented and overall health is improved.

HIV is the major cause of death among hemophiliacs and is responsible for 55% of these deaths. An individual with HIV has a 2-8% lifetime risk of intracranial hemorrhage, the second leading cause of death.

Damage to a particular joint is delayed but not completely stopped by the surgical removal of a portion of the synovial membrane (synovectomy). Prosthetic joint replacement stops unremitting joint pain and halts destruction. Joint fusion (arthrodesis) brings relief to chronic ankle pain.

Differential Diagnosis

Hemophilia A has the identical clinical course as hemophilia B. Conditions with similar symptoms include other clotting factor deficiencies such as von Willebrand's disease or vitamin K deficiency, platelet function disorders, liver disease, and anticoagulant overdose. Blood in the genitourinary tract must be distinguished from bleeding due to kidney stones or infection.

Specialists

- Hematologist
- Orthopedic Surgeon

Rehabilitation

Rehabilitation for hemophilia B may be necessary if repeated episodes of bleeding into the individual joints (hemarthrosis) has resulted in the destruction of joint structures. In severe cases, the individual may need an affected joint replaced with an artificial joint. If this is the case, the rehabilitation program begins with range-of-motion exercises that return joint mobility and then followed by progressive strengthening exercises.

Stretching exercises consist of the therapist moving the affected limb with no effort initiated by the individual. The muscles of the involved joint are placed in a mild stretch. Once range of motion returns to the joint, mild strengthening begins, as tolerated. Nonweight-bearing exercises like swimming or isometrics strengthen muscles around the joints and help keep the joints stable and mobile.

The physical therapist may need to modify the program for individuals with hemophilia B with associated joint pain (arthralgia) depending on the location of the affected joint, the origin and stage of the condition, and whether surgery on the joint was required.

Work Restrictions / Accommodations

Individuals with hemophilia need a safe work environment where they can avoid the risk of personal injury that could trigger an acute bleed. Where indicated, protective gear, especially to the head, should be worn. Office work or sedentary work would probably be more appropriate than strenuous work involving heavy lifting or other physical exertion. The employer should be aware of the condition so that the appropriate level of care can be obtained quickly in the event of an on-the-job injury. Joint pain and lack of mobility may require specific accommodations. Time off will be needed if joint surgery (arthrodesis, synovectomy, or prosthetic joint replacement) or treatment of a severe bleeding episode is required.

Comorbid Conditions

Hepatitis A, B, or C infection, chronic posthepatitic cirrhosis, parvovirus infection, HIV infection, or AIDS will cause additional disability. Gastrointestinal lesions such as ulcers or hemorrhoids increase the risk of bleeding.

Complications

Individuals may develop severe, life-threatening bleeding episodes. Bleeding may occur anywhere, particularly inside the skull, central nervous system, genitourinary tract, and abdominal cavity. Intracranial hemorrhage is the second most common cause of death among individuals with hemophilia. Bleeding of the tongue or back of the throat can cause life-threatening blockage of the airway.

Bleeding into joints causes joint disease (arthropathy). Repeated bleeding into a joint leads to permanent damage and deformity. Bleeding can also occur into muscles. Continued bleeding into muscles can cause cysts to develop within the muscle tissue or on the covering of bone. These cysts are also called pseudotumors and are painful and must be surgically excised.

Pooled plasma factor IX replacement may trigger thrombotic (harmful blood clots) episodes. Individuals may also develop antibodies against the replaced clotting factor IX. Approximately 2.5% of individuals with hemophilia B have these antibodies.

Infections (e.g., HIV, hepatitis A, B, and C) spread through blood products and have historically been a source of tremendous complications for individuals with hemophilia. The products currently used, however, are relatively safe. Since 1986 there have been no transmissions of HIV through a factor concentrate. All blood products are now screened for potential viruses including HIV, hepatitis A, B, and C, and parvovirus before being used. In addition, factor IX concentrates from pooled human plasma have been through a purification viral inactivation process that kills HIV, hepatitis B and C. Hepatitis A and parvovirus are unfortunately not killed by the inactivation process.

Factors Influencing Duration

Factors include the severity of the disorder, degree of joint involvement, location of external bleeding, complications of the disease, ability to maintain adequate levels of factor IX, and development of antibodies to replacement factor IX.

Length of Disability

Disability may result from trauma or other complications of disease or treatment. Disability may be permanent.

Single episode.

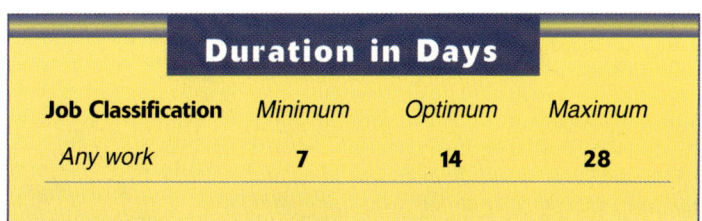

Job Classification	Minimum	Optimum	Maximum
Any work	7	14	28

Hemophilia B 1065

Failure to Recover

If an individual fails to recover within the maximum duration expectancy period, the reader may wish to reference the following questions to assist in better understanding the specifics of an individual's medical case.

Regarding diagnosis:

- Does the individual complain of stiff and painful joints?
- What level of factor IX does the individual have?
- Has the individual recently experienced trauma or injury, undergone surgery, or had dental work done?
- Does the individual participate in contact sports or other activities with an increased risk of injury?
- Has the individual noted blood in the urine, bruising of the skin, or a rash?
- Is the partial thromboplastin time (PTT) prolonged, but the prothrombin time (PT) normal?
- Is a factor IX assay decreased?

Regarding treatment:

- Is primary prophylaxis therapy successful in maintaining factor IX levels?
- Have episodes of active bleeding been effectively managed?
- Is joint pain successfully managed? If not, have all treatments for pain been tried?
- Has an orthopedic surgeon been consulted regarding surgical procedures to help slow the progression of joint disease or repair damaged areas?
- What procedure is required?

Regarding prognosis:

- What is the severity of the disease?
- Does the individual have HIV infection?
- Has the individual experienced one or more life-threatening bleeding episodes?
- Does the individual have permanent joint damage?
- Have blood clots formed?
- Has the individual developed antibodies to factor IX replacement? If so, has alternative therapy been started?
- Does the individual have any infection, including hepatitis A, B, C, or parvovirus?

References

Hemophilia. National Heart, Lung, and Blood Institute. 12 Oct 1999. 31 Aug 2000 <http://www.nhlbi.nih.gov/health/public/blood/other/hemophel.htm>.

Recommendations Concerning the Treatment of Hemophilia and Related Bleeding Disorders. Medical and Scientific Advisory Council of the National Hemophilia Foundation. 10 Jun 2000. 31 Aug 2000 <http://www.hemophilia.org/research/news/masac100.html>.

Ferri, Fred. Ferri's Clinical Advisor. St. Louis: Mosby, 2000.

Goroll, Allan, Lawrence May, and Albert Mulley. Primary Care Medicine, 3rd ed. Philadelphia: Lippincott-Raven, 1995.

Kessler, Craig. "Coagulation Factor Deficiencies." Cecil Textbook of Medicine, 21st ed. Goldman, Lee, and J. Claude Bennett, eds. Philadelphia: W.B. Saunders Company, 2000. 1004-1012.

Kisner, C., and L. Colby. Therapeutic Exercise Foundations and Techniques. Philadelphia: F.A. Davis Company, 1990.

Shapiro, Amy, and Keith Hoots. "Hemophilia and Related Conditions." Conn's Current Therapy 2000, 52nd ed. Rakel, Robert, ed. Philadelphia: W.B. Saunders Company, 2000. 390-397.

Tierney, Lawrence, Stephen McPhee, and Maxine Papadakis. Current Medical Diagnosis and Treatment, 39th ed. New York: Lange Medical Books/McGraw-Hill, 2000.

Hemoptysis

Other names / synonyms: Bloody Sputum, Pulmonary Hemorrhage

786.3

Definition

Hemoptysis is the symptom of coughing up blood or blood-streaked phlegm (sputum) as a result of bleeding from the respiratory tract. The blood or blood-streaked sputum may appear bright red or may look frothy because it is mixed with air from the lungs.

The source of hemoptysis may be bleeding in the lung circulation (pulmonary vessels or bronchial vessels) or the tissue (granular). Inflammatory conditions of the airways (bronchitis, bronchiectasis, laryngitis) account for about 70% of hemoptysis cases. Primary tumors (especially carcinoma) of the lung account for about 20% of cases. These tumors are most common in persons over 40 years old who are smokers. However, lung cancers that have spread from other primary sites (metastatic lung cancers) rarely causes hemoptysis.

Other causes of hemoptysis are inflammatory lesions of the lung such as tuberculosis or pulmonary emboli. The autoimmune disorders of systemic lupus erythematosus, Goodpasture's syndrome and Wegener's granulomatosis, may also have the symptom of hemoptysis. Occasionally, hemoptysis can result from lung trauma following medical procedures, (bronchoscopy, lung biopsy, pulmonary artery catheterization). However, in many cases, the exact cause of hemoptysis is not found.

Diagnosis

History: In addition to reporting the symptom of coughing up blood, the individual may complain of fever, night sweats, weight loss, loss of appetite, difficulty breathing or chest pain. Individuals may provide additional information such as a history of lung infections, cancer, or cigarette smoking.

Physical exam: Depending on the cause, the physical exam may reveal pain over the sinuses or inflammation of the nose or throat. Abnormal lung sounds such as wheezes, crackles, or diminished breath sounds may be present. Distended neck veins, generalized swelling of extremities, extra heart sounds and poor color are other possible associated findings. Localized pain or masses may be present and are suggestive of tumors.

Tests: Tests should be aimed at determining the underlying cause of the hemoptysis. Sputum may be collected and analyzed to check for bacteria, tuberculosis, or malignancy. Coagulation studies, arterial blood gases, CT scan, BUN/creatinine, and serologic studies may be performed. Bronchial arteriography to help localize the site of bleeding may be used. Computerized tomography (CT) or magnetic resonance imaging (MRI) may detect lung or other body system masses or lesions.

Treatment

Effective treatment is dependent on the underlying cause of hemoptysis. Therapy should focus on stopping the bleeding, controlling cough, preventing any spread of infection and alleviating the individual's fear and apprehension.

Often mild bleeding stops spontaneously. However, massive or continuous bleeding (greater than 600cc in 24 hours) can be life-threatening and require immediate intervention. Bronchial artery embolization is one intervention used to control massive lung bleeding. Laser therapy is another treatment modality to arrest bleeding in those with massive hemoptysis. Surgical intervention (thoracotomy) may be considered for individuals with massive bleeding from an identifiable lung lesion.

The cough may be treated with respiratory therapy and medications to reduce inflammation or treat and control an infection. Sedatives and narcotics are avoided, since they can depress respirations.

Prognosis

Depending on the underlying cause, the outcome of hemoptysis is generally good, with most individuals surviving. However, those with bleeding disorders, usually have a greater amount of bleeding and a high mortality rate, probably due to the difficulty in controlling the bleeding. Extensive or prolonged bleeding has a mortality rate of 50-100% regardless of the underlying cause. Likewise those with lung cancer have a high mortality rate. Their mortality is most often due to the complication of infection rather than the initial bleeding, however.

In general, bronchial artery embolization results in long-term control of bleeding in only about 50% of the cases. Data on outcomes for surgical treatments (thoracotomy or laser therapy) for inflammatory or cancerous causes of hemoptysis is scarce. On the average, there is about a 50%, five-year survival rate following thoracotomy or laser therapy. Both procedures carry the risk of mortality due to complications of infection, bleeding and respiratory failure.

Differential Diagnosis

Bleeding from the esophagus or stomach (hematemesis) or higher up in the respiratory system such as from the larynx or sinuses will present similarly.

Specialists

- Emergency Medicine
- Infectious Disease Physician
- Internist
- Otolaryngologist
- Pulmonologist

Work Restrictions / Accommodations

Any work restrictions and accommodations will be dependent upon the cause of hemoptysis. Those who have residual shortness of breath may require modified duty with frequent rest breaks.

Comorbid Conditions

Comorbid conditions of obesity, chronic pulmonary disease, immune suppression (ie. HIV or AIDS), bleeding disorders, liver disease, or congestive heart failure may impact ability to recover and further lengthen disability.

Complications

Massive blood loss may lead to asphyxia, shock, and anemia.

Factors Influencing Duration

The length of disability is dependent on the age of the individual, the underlying cause, the individual's response to treatment and the individual's compliance with the treatment regimen.

Length of Disability

Duration depends on cause. Contact physician for more specific information.

Failure to Recover

If an individual fails to recover within the maximum duration expectancy period, the reader may wish to reference the following questions to assist in better understanding the specifics of an individual's medical case.

Regarding diagnosis:

- Has the cause of the hemoptysis been identified?
- Is bleeding recurrent or significant?
- Has bronchoscopy or perfusion scan been done to identify the bleeding point?
- Does individual have an underlying condition that may impact recovery?

Regarding treatment:

- If bleeding stopped spontaneously, has it recurred?
- Does source need to be identified or re-evaluated?
- Has the individual been considered for a pulmonary rehabilitation program?
- Was procedure successful in resolving the bleeding? Is additional therapy required?

Regarding prognosis:

- Has hemoptysis recurred despite treatment of underlying condition?
- Does bleeding source need more aggressive resolution?
- Would individual benefit from evaluation by a specialist or enrollment in a pulmonary rehabilitation program?
- Does individual have an underlying disorder that may impact recovery?

References

"Hemoptysis." Merck Manual of Diagnosis and Therapy, 17th ed. Beers, Mark H., and Robert Berkow, MD, eds. Whitehouse Station, NJ: Merck & Co. Inc., 1999. 18 Oct 2000 <http://www.merck.com/pubs/mmanual/section6/chapter63/63g.htm>.

Tierney, Lawrence M., Stephen J. McPhee, and Maxine A. Papadakis, eds. Current Medical Diagnosis and Treatment, 39th ed. New York: Lange Medical Books/McGraw-Hill, 2000.

Hemorrhage of Rectum and Anus
Other names / synonyms: Anorectal Hemorrhage
569.3

Definition

Bleeding or hemorrhage of the rectum or anus is a symptom associated with a variety of disorders in the lower gastrointestinal (GI) tract.

Hemorrhoids are the most common cause of visible blood from the anus or rectum. Hemorrhoids are enlarged veins in the anal area that can rupture and produce bright red blood that can show up in the toilet or on toilet paper. Internal hemorrhoids (those that do not protrude from the rectum) commonly produce painless bleeding from the rectum. Factors associated with hemorrhoids are low fiber diet, constipation, pregnancy, heavy lifting, or repeated, vigorous coughing and sneezing.

If the bleeding is associated with pain during bowel movements, it is more likely due to cuts (fissures) of the anus or rectum. Anal fissures are most commonly caused by passage of a large, hard stool.

Inflammation or tumors of the colon or rectum can cause bleeding. Extensive bleeding from the colon passed out the anus with stool may occur. Ulcerative colitis can produce inflammation and extensive surface bleeding from tiny ulcerations. Crohn's disease of the large intestine can produce spotty bleeding. Diverticular disease caused by inflammation of outpouchings (diverticula) of the colon wall may result in heavy bleeding.

Benign growths or polyps of the colon are very common and may be forerunners of cancer. These growths and cancerous tumors can cause bright red blood to be passed from the rectum. Cancer of the colon and rectum is the second most frequent of all cancers in the US and is usually associated with either hidden or obvious bleeding from the lower intestine and rectum.

Hemorrhoids are present in about 5% of the general adult population with the incidence increasing to about 50% in adults over age 50. Anal fissures are primarily seen in young adults and affect both genders equally. Ulcerative colitis and Crohn's disease (inflammatory bowel diseases) affect women and men equally. About half of all Americans age 60 to 80 and almost everyone over 80 have diverticular disease.

Diagnosis

History: The individual reports a history of passing blood from the rectum or anus. They may describe the blood as being bright or dark red and passed alone or along with stool (hematochezia) or mucus. The bleeding may be intermittent or constant. Individuals may report bright red blood on toilet tissue. Pain in the anus and rectum or crampy abdominal pain may occur. Those with significant or prolonged bleeding may complain of fatigue, dizziness, shortness of breath, or other signs of anemia or shock.

Physical exam: Blood may be present in the rectum upon digital anorectal exam (gloved finger inserted into anus). The digital anorectal exam may reveal cuts (fissures) or protrusions in the anus and rectum such as hemorrhoids or polyps. Bowel sounds may be hyperactive in inflammatory bowel conditions. The abdomen may be distended in bowel disorders.

Tests: Barium x-rays, x-rays that highlight blood vessels (angiography), and radionuclide scans can be used to locate sources of bleeding. A lighted scope can directly visualize the anus (anoscopy), rectum (sigmoidoscopy), or colon (colonoscopy). Bleeding and clotting time are determined. A complete blood count (CBC) is done to check for anemia. Stool is checked for hidden blood (occult).

Treatment

Treatment is directed at the underlying problem. If bleeding is significant, intravenous fluids and blood may be given. The site of the bleeding is promptly controlled with an electrical device that coagulates blood (electrocautery) during endoscopy.

A variety of endoscopic therapies are useful for treating GI tract bleeding. Active bleeding from the intestines is often controlled through injection of chemicals directly into a bleeding site with a needle introduced through the endoscope. A bleeding site and surrounding tissue can also be cauterized or heat-treated with a heater probe or electrocoagulation device passed through the endoscope. Removal of polyps with an endoscope can control bleeding from colon polyps.

Removal of hemorrhoids by banding or various heat or electrical devices is effective in individuals who suffer hemorrhoidal bleeding on a recurrent basis. Serious, ongoing bleeding may require surgery (laparoscopy) to control the site of bleeding. In general, medications known to cause intestinal bleeding such as aspirin or other anti-inflammatory agents are discontinued. Warm water, showers, or baths after bowel movement, analgesics, stool softeners, and a high fiber diet are recommended for ongoing management of anal fistulas or hemorrhoids.

Prognosis

Outcome depends on the underlying cause, amount of bleeding, and type of treatment required. The prognosis is generally good with early detection. Bleeding stops spontaneously in 90% of all lower GI hemorrhages. However, recurrences are common until the underlying cause is treated. In most cases, endoscopic treatment is effective at controlling recurrent or persistent bleeding from the rectum or anus. Persistent or recurrent bleeding from hemorrhoids is effectively managed with removal of the hemorrhoids.

Differential Diagnosis

A variety of conditions with similar symptoms include colon cancer, diverticular disease, colon polyps, or inflammatory bowel disease. In addition, ingestion of medications such as iron, bismuth or other foods such as beets can discolor the stool and be confused with rectal or anal bleeding.

Specialists

- Emergency Medicine
- Gastroenterologist
- General Surgeon
- Primary Care Provider
- Proctologist

Work Restrictions / Accommodations

Work restriction and accommodations may vary according to the underlying condition. The individual's physician can provide specific details regarding appropriate work accommodations. For example, lifting or activity restrictions may be applied following surgical intervention. Some individuals may need to avoid prolonged periods of sitting.

Comorbid Conditions

Comorbid conditions such as diabetes, immune system disorders, or bleeding disorders may impact ability to recover and further lengthen disability.

Complications

Depending on the underlying cause of the bleeding, complications may include anemia, hemorrhagic shock (rare), perforation of bowel, infection or abscess, and the development of an abnormal passage between the lower intestine and the abdomen (fistula).

Factors Influencing Duration

The underlying cause and treatment, recurrence of bleeding, any complications, and response to treatment influence the length of disability.

Length of Disability

Duration in Days

Job Classification	Minimum	Optimum	Maximum
Any work	1	7	14

Failure to Recover

If an individual fails to recover within the maximum duration expectancy period, the reader may wish to reference the following questions to assist in better understanding the specifics of an individual's medical case.

Regarding diagnosis:

- Does individual have a history of hemorrhoids, fissures, or inflammatory bowel diseases?
- Does individual have a bleeding disorder that may contribute to persistent bleeding?
- Does individual report passing blood from the anus? Is the blood bright or dark red? Was it seen on the toilet paper or did it pass with stool (hematochezia) or mucus?
- Are there complaints of pain in the anus and rectum or crampy abdominal pain? Has the bleeding been prolonged? If so, does individual complain of fatigue, dizziness or shortness of breath?
- Does the physician note the presence of blood in the rectum upon digital anorectal exam (gloved finger inserted into anus)?
- Does the digital anorectal exam reveal cuts (fissures) or protrusions in the anus and rectum such as hemorrhoids or polyps?
- Does the physician hear hyperactive bowel sounds when listening with a stethoscope (auscultation)?

- Has individual received intestinal x-rays and endoscopy to determine the source of the bleeding?
- Are bleeding and clotting times normal?
- Is the CBC normal or is individual anemic?
- Was there evidence of occult blood in the stool?

Regarding treatment:

- What was the cause of bleeding and is that under control?
- What treatment was required to stop the bleeding?
- Electrocautery, sclerotherapy, or electrocoagulation during endoscopy?
- Were bleeding polyps and hemorrhoids removed endoscopically?
- Did individual lose a significant amount of blood?
- Was laparoscopy necessary?

- Have all medications such as aspirin and other anti-inflammatory agents known to cause GI bleeding been discontinued?
- Does individual take analgesics and stool softeners as prescribed?
- If individual has anal fissures or hemorrhoids, are high fiber foods included in their diet?

Regarding prognosis:

- Has the underlying cause been addressed? If so, why is the bleeding recurring?
- Did individual experience significant blood loss?
- Has individual developed any complications such as anemia, hemorrhagic shock (rare), perforation of bowel, infection or abscess, and the development of an abnormal passage between the lower intestine and the abdomen (fistula)?

References

Tierney, Lawrence M., Stephen J. McPhee, and Maxine Papadakis. Current Medical Diagnosis and Treatment, 39th ed. New York: Lange Medical Books/McGraw-Hill, 2000.

Hemorrhoid Treatment

Other names / synonyms: Hemorrhoid Cryosurgery, Hemorrhoid Ligation, Hemorrhoid Sclerotherapy, Hemorrhoidectomy, Piles, Prolapsed Rectal Blood Veins

49.42, 49.44, 49.45, 49.46

Definition

Hemorrhoids can be treated by a variety of procedures including conservative medical treatment, injection (sclerotherapy), rubber band ligation, freezing (cryosurgery), heat (thermal coagulation), infrared coagulopathy, laser removal, or the evacuation of a blood clot (thrombosed hemorrhoid), hemorrhoidectomy (surgical removal of hemorrhoids). The choice of treatment depends on the type of hemorrhoids (internal or external) and the severity of symptoms. External hemorrhoids need treatment only when an acute blood clot (thrombosis) is present. Preventive measures include dietary modifications including bulk-forming foods and fluids or stool modifiers or laxatives.

Hemorrhoids are a normal feature of the anal area and consist of swollen or dilated blood veins located either externally or internally around the anus. As internal hemorrhoids become larger, they extrude from the anus and become external hemorrhoids.

Hemorrhoids may worsen because of increased pressure in the anal veins due to straining attempts to pass hard feces, pressure during pregnancy, or pressure from childbirth. Weakness of the anal veins can be a congenital condition (present at birth), making hemorrhoids more likely. Hemorrhoids are common in both men and women and occur in about half of the population by age fifty. First-degree hemorrhoids bleed but do not prolapse through the anus/rectum. Second-degree hemorrhoids prolapse during bowel movements but then withdraw back up into the rectum. Third-degree hemorrhoids remain prolapsed unless pushed gently back into the rectum, while fourth-degree hemorrhoids cannot be pushed back into the rectum.

Reason for Procedure

Procedures to treat hemorrhoids are performed only when hemorrhoids become symptomatic. Typical symptoms are bleeding, protrusion outside the anus, itching, and pain. Less common symptoms of internal hemorrhoids are mucus discharge and a sensation of incomplete evacuation. Hemorrhoids that have become ulcerated or those in which a blood clot has formed (thrombosed) may be very painful. External hemorrhoids make the anal region difficult to clean. If not corrected, hemorrhoids can cause rectal bleeding and increasing discomfort with defecation. A prolapsed hemorrhoid can strangle, reducing its blood supply, or painful blood clots can form within the vein.

Description

Diagnosis of internal hemorrhoids may require the use of an instrument to look into the rectum (proctoscopy) or the lower part of the colon (sigmoidoscopy).

Conservative medical treatment includes having the individual sit in a warm bath for up to ten minutes several times a day, correction of diet to add more fiber and fluids, stool modifiers (softeners or bulk formers), or the application of external creams to relieve pain or itching and other symptoms.

Rubber band ligation can also be used to treat bleeding or prolapsed internal hemorrhoids. The hemorrhoid is grasped by forceps and drawn into a banding instrument. Tight rubber bands are squeezed onto the neck of the hemorrhoid, tightly constricting its base. The bands cut off the blood supply to the hemorrhoid, causing it to wither and slough off in seven to ten days. Because loss of blood to the vein may produce pain, painkillers (analgesics) may be required for several days after the procedure.

Sclerotherapy is used to treat internal hemorrhoids that bleed or protrude outside the anus (prolapsing hemorrhoids). An irritating solution is injected into the tissue around the hemorrhoids resulting in the collapse of dilated veins.

Cryosurgery is an alternative to ligation. Using a coolant, such as liquid nitrogen, internal hemorrhoids may be frozen with a cryoprobe (device used to apply extreme cold to tissue). The freezing shrinks and destroys the veins, which then slough off. Sloughing results in an anal discharge lasting two to three weeks. Painkillers (analgesics) may be required.

Thermal coagulation and direct current electrocoagulation can also be used to treat hemorrhoids. The hemorrhoid tissue is destroyed (coagulated) using high frequency currents. There is usually no discomfort associated with this procedure, which is most effective for treating hemorrhoids too small to be ligated with rubber bands.

Infrared light coagulation is another technique used to destroy swollen hemorrhoidal tissue. It uses infrared radiation to produce death (necrosis) of the tissue at the apex (area next to the skin) of the hemorrhoid.

When a hemorrhoid is prolapsed (protruding outside the anus), a blood clot can form in the vein. Because the vein can no longer spring back into position in the anus, its blood supply is reduced, causing extreme pain. Evacuation of a clotted (thrombosed) hemorrhoid is possible only if the individual is seen soon after the formation of the clot. Under local anesthetic, a small incision is made in the vein through which the clot is squeezed out. Pain relief is rapid.

Hemorrhoidectomy is the surgical removal of hemorrhoids. A hemorrhoidectomy tends to be reserved for the treatment of large, protruding (prolapsing), bleeding hemorrhoids when other, simpler methods of treatment have failed to correct the problem. External hemorrhoids can be surgically removed under local anesthetic as an outpatient procedure. The removal of internal hemorrhoids is usually performed in the hospital under a general or spinal anesthetic because it is a more invasive procedure. An examination of inside of the rectum through a viewing instrument (proctoscopy) is first performed to exclude tumors. The hemorrhoid is then grasped with forceps and removed. Excision can be performed with a knife (scalpel), cautery device, or a laser. The wound is closed by either sewing it closed (suture) or searing the edges with a hot instrument (cautery).

Prognosis

Conservative measures (warm baths, stool modifiers, external creams) offer symptom relief but, if the veins continue to swell, symptoms may return. Pregnancy-related hemorrhoids frequently resolve spontaneously over several weeks to months after childbirth.

Rubber-band ligation results in 80-90% of symptom relief, although up to 40% of individuals may develop recurrent symptoms within 5 years.

Sclerotherapy is used less often than ligation, because it is more difficult to perform and yields less successful results than ligation.

Thermal coagulation and direct current electrocoagulation have generally good results, but may require several treatments, and may cause enough discomfort to cause 12-15% of individuals to refuse further treatments.

Infrared light coagulation yields success rates similar to that of rubber-band ligation.

Blood clot evacuation brings almost instant pain relief. Other measures may be needed to treat the hemorrhoidal tissue.

Fewer than 10% of hemorrhoids require surgical intervention. Hemorrhoidectomy, the surgical treatment of choice, is used when third- or fourth-degree hemorrhoids do not respond to other treatment methods. Hemorrhoidectomy usually results in complete removal of the affected tissue and usually total symptom relief, after a period of surgical recovery of up to 2-4 weeks, with only a 5-8% recurrent rate.

Specialists

| • Proctologist | • Surgeon |

Work Restrictions / Accommodations

Straining or heavy lifting may be temporarily restricted. The individual may be more comfortable with cushioned seating. After the initial recovery period of several days to several weeks, depending upon the treatment, individuals should have no restrictions except those of comfort. Since non-surgical treatments may not excise all hemorrhoids, or there may be a recurrence, symptoms may be more noticeable for some occupations, such as professional drivers.

Comorbid Conditions

Other benign anorectal conditions such as an abnormal pathway from the mucosal lining of the anus to the skin (anal fistula), abnormal tissue growth on the wall of the rectum (rectal polyps), a tear in the anal canal (fissure), or colon cancer are possible comorbid conditions.

Procedure Complications

Complications of surgery, ligation, or other removal techniques include pain, excessive bleeding, infection at the surgical site, fever, or urinary retention.

Factors Influencing Duration

Length of disability may be influenced by the type, number, and severity of the hemorrhoids, the method and response to treatment, or the presence of complications. There is usually no period of disability for thermal coagulation and evacuation.

Length of Disability

After uncomplicated treatment of hemorrhoids, there is usually no disability. Untreated, painful hemorrhoids may interfere with an individual's ability to sit comfortably or to lift or strain.

Sclerotherapy.

Duration in Days

Job Classification	Minimum	Optimum	Maximum
Sedentary work	1	2	3
Light work	1	2	3
Medium work	1	3	7
Heavy work	1	4	7
Very Heavy work	1	4	7

Rubber band ligation and cryosurgery.

Duration in Days

Job Classification	Minimum	Optimum	Maximum
Sedentary work	1	7	14
Light work	1	7	14
Medium work	1	7	14
Heavy work	1	7	14
Very Heavy work	1	7	14

Hemorrhoidectomy.

Duration in Days

Job Classification	Minimum	Optimum	Maximum
Sedentary work	14	21	28
Light work	14	21	28
Medium work	21	28	42
Heavy work	21	35	42
Very Heavy work	21	35	42

References

Hemorrhoids. MedicineNet.com. 22 Jul 2000. 18 Jan 2001 <http://www.aboutdigestion.com/script/main/art.asp?li=DIG&ArticleKey=383&page=1#1whatexactly>.

Beers, Mark H., and Robert Berkow, eds. "Anorectal Disorders." Merck Manual of Diagnosis and Therapy, 17th ed. Beers, Mark H., and Robert Berkow, eds. Whitehouse Station, NJ: Merck Research Laboratories, 1999. 336-342.

Kranzfelder, Kathy, and Toni Dove. Hemorrhoids. National Institute of Diabetes and Digestive and Kidney Diseases (NIDDK). 01 Oct 1999. 18 Jan 2001 <http://www.niddk.nih.gov/health/digest/pubs/hems/hemords.htm>.

Murray, John J. "Hemorrhoids, Anal Fissure, and Anorectal Abscess and Fistula." Conn's Current Therapy. Rakel, Robert E., ed. Philadelphia: W.B. Saunders Company, 2000. 492-495.

Hemorrhoids

Other names / synonyms: External Hemorrhoids, Internal Hemorrhoids, Lump in the Rectum, Piles, Rectal Lump

455, 455.0, 455.1, 455.2, 455.3, 455.4, 455.5, 455.6, 455.7, 455.8, 455.9

Definition

Hemorrhoids are swollen, enlarged veins in and around the anus and lower portion of the rectum. Internal hemorrhoids are located near the beginning of the anal canal, about one inch inside the rectum, and are covered with mucous membrane. External hemorrhoids are located under the skin surrounding the anal opening. Internal and external hemorrhoids can occur at the same time or separately.

Hemorrhoids are caused by increased pressure in the veins of the rectum and anus. The most common cause of this increased pressure is excessive straining at bowel movements, usually due to constipation. Other causes of increased pressure in the veins of the rectum and anus include prolonged sitting on the toilet, pregnancy and the strain of childbirth, and obesity. Other factors that contribute to hemorrhoid formation include anal infection, diarrhea, delaying the urge to empty the bowels, prolonged sitting, a family history of hemorrhoids, and liver disease.

Hemorrhoids are one of the most common problems of the lower digestive tract. It has been estimated that hemorrhoids affect over 10 million individuals in the US. It has been suggested that 2 out of 1000 people develop hemorrhoids, and that one-half of Americans over the age of 50 have suffered from hemorrhoids.

Diagnosis

History: Individuals who suffer from both internal and external hemorrhoids may complain of rectal bleeding after bowel movements and/or bright red blood in the stool; however, the individuals with external hemorrhoids will also report pain during bowel movements and anal itching. Individuals with internal hemorrhoids usually do not experience pain unless the hemorrhoids protrude out through the anus (prolapse).

Physical exam: A rectal examination with a gloved hand is usually sufficient to diagnose both internal and external hemorrhoids.

Tests: A stool guaiac test may be performed to confirm the presence of blood in the stool. Because rectal bleeding may be indicative of diseases more serious than hemorrhoids, anoscopy, proctoscopy, or sigmoidoscopy may be performed to rule out any other source of bleeding.

Treatment

Conservative treatment often is sufficient for mild hemorrhoids, especially those that occur during pregnancy, since they tend to disappear after delivery. General treatment measures include a high-fiber diet and adequate fluid intake to avoid constipation. Stool softeners may also be given, and cultivating regular toilet habits may help. Irritation of the skin around the anus may be relieved by ointments or suppositories. Moisturized cleansing pads may be used after bowel movements to keep the anal area clean. Topical application of corticosteroid creams may help reduce pain and swelling.

If bleeding is a problem, injecting a substance into the vein that causes internal scarring (sclerosis), thus blocking the vein (sclerotherapy) of internal hemorrhoids may be effective. The bleeding usually stops within days after the injection; however, it may recur. Since injection has little effect on prolapse, rubber band ligation may be indicated for significant vein prolapse. Alternatives include freezing the hemorrhoid (cryotherapy) and/or heating it (thermal coagulation).

Acute clotting (thrombosis) or ulceration of internal hemorrhoids may also be treated conservatively. Bedrest is prescribed to minimize swelling and prevent further thrombosis. Analgesics and sedatives may be helpful. Warm sitz baths relieve pain and swelling, and help prevent infection. Suppositories or astringent compresses also may be used to relieve symptoms. Antibiotics are sometimes indicated. The acute pain subsides over a period of 1 to 2 weeks, with the thromboses gradually being reabsorbed over a 1 to 2 month period. After the acute attack, the hemorrhoids may be ligated or removed surgically (hemorrhoidectomy). Surgery is usually reserved for either reducible or non-reducible hemorrhoids that have severe symptoms or complications.

If the individual is seen within the first 48 hours, an acutely thrombosed external hemorrhoid may be relieved by removing the obstructing clot through a small incision. After that period, the clot cannot usually be removed, and is then treated conservatively; the pain usually subsides over several days.

Prognosis

The prognosis for both internal and external hemorrhoids is good. For mild hemorrhoids, conservative treatment is usually effective, but recurrences can occur if a high-fiber diet with adequate fluid intake is not adopted. If surgery (hemorrhoidectomy, rubber band ligation, or sclerotherapy) becomes necessary, it is usually highly successful. There is a 10 - 50% rate of recurrence.

Differential Diagnosis

Conditions that may present with similar symptoms include neoplasm, diverticulosis, rectal polyps, anorectal abscess, anorectal fistula, impaction, levator syndrome, anal fissure, rectal trauma, gay bowel syndrome, infections (sexually transmitted diseases - STDs), fistula, rectal prolapse, eczema, fungal infection, and anogenital warts (condyloma acuminata).

Specialists

- Colorectal Surgeon
- Gastroenterologist
- General Surgeon
- Internist
- Primary Care Provider
- Proctologist

Work Restrictions / Accommodations

The extent of disability may depend on whether the individual's job involves heavy lifting, or prolonged sitting or standing. This condition is particularly prevalent among, and difficult for long-haul truck drivers as it combines prolonged sitting and jouncing-type pressure on the rectum and anus. Temporary accommodations may be necessary.

Comorbid Conditions

Existing conditions that could impact ability to recover and further lengthen disability anorectal infections, fecal impaction, and rectal neoplasms.

Complications

Hemorrhoids can be the source of many uncomfortable, yet generally non-serious problems. Formation of a blood clot (thrombosis) may cause severe pain. External hemorrhoids can be extremely itchy and irritated especially if the area is allowed to remain moist. Both internal and external hemorrhoids can result in fresh red blood oozing. This blood dripping from the anus into the toilet can be quite disconcerting; it may also stain undergarments. Iron deficiency anemia may result from prolonged blood loss.

Factors Influencing Duration

Length of disability depends on the type of hemorrhoids (internal or external), presence and degree of prolapse, presence of thrombosis or ulceration, severity of symptoms, method of treatment, and presence or absence of complications such as infection.

Length of Disability

Medical treatment.

Duration in Days

Job Classification	Minimum	Optimum	Maximum
Sedentary work	0	7	14
Light work	0	7	14
Medium work	0	10	14
Heavy work	0	14	21
Very Heavy work	0	14	21

Rubber band ligation or cryosurgery.

Duration in Days

Job Classification	Minimum	Optimum	Maximum
Sedentary work	1	7	14
Light work	1	7	14
Medium work	1	7	14
Heavy work	1	7	14
Very Heavy work	1	7	14

Sclerotherapy.

Duration in Days

Job Classification	Minimum	Optimum	Maximum
Sedentary work	1	2	3
Light work	1	2	3
Medium work	1	3	7
Heavy work	1	4	7
Very Heavy work	1	4	7

Surgical treatment. Hemorrhoidectomy.

Duration in Days

Job Classification	Minimum	Optimum	Maximum
Sedentary work	14	21	28
Light work	14	21	28
Medium work	21	28	42
Heavy work	21	35	42
Very Heavy work	21	35	42

Duration Trend from Normative Data*

Cases	Mean	Min	Max	No Lost Time	Over 6 Months
461	29	0	222	0.87%	0.22%

Percentile:	5th	25th	Median	75th	95th
Days:	8	15	23	34	66

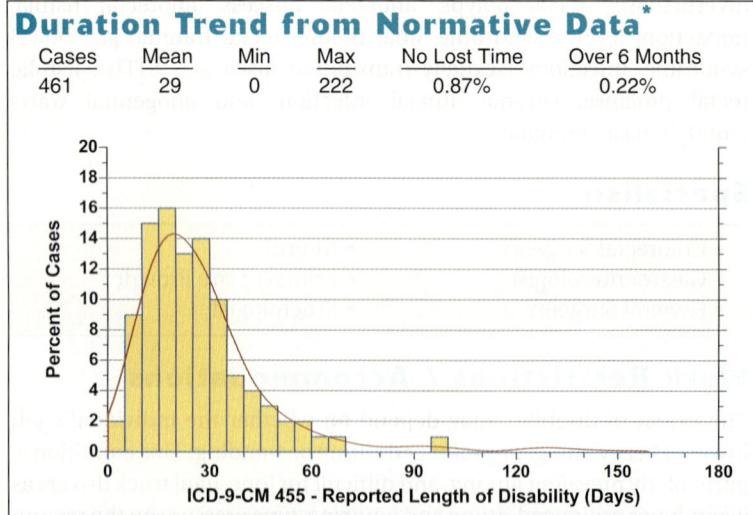
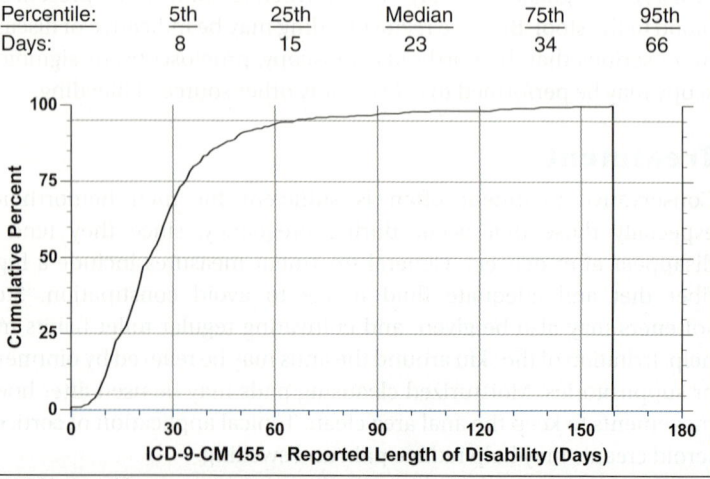

ICD-9-CM 455 - Reported Length of Disability (Days)

* Differences may exist between the expected duration tables and the normative graphs. Duration tables provide expected recovery periods based on the type of work performed by the individual. The normative graphs reflect the actual observed experience of many individuals across the spectrum of physical conditions, in a variety of industries, and with varying levels of case management.

Failure to Recover

If an individual fails to recover within the maximum duration expectancy period, the reader may wish to reference the following questions to assist in better understanding the specifics of an individual's medical case.

Regarding diagnosis:

- Did the individual present with symptoms and a clinical presentation consistent with the diagnosis of hemorrhoids?
- Was the diagnosis confirmed with a rectal exam?
- If the diagnosis was uncertain, were other diagnostic tests (anoscopy, sigmoidoscopy, colonoscopy) done to rule out conditions with similar symptoms?

Regarding treatment:

- Were conservative measures successful?
- Was individual compliant with treatment recommendations?
- Did individual experience complications such as persistent bleeding or prolapsed hemorrhoids?
- Were hemorrhoids treated with more aggressive measures, such as injection sclerotherapy, band ligation, cryotherapy, or thermal coagulation?
- Is surgical intervention (hemorrhoidectomy) indicated?

Regarding prognosis:

- Did symptoms persist or worsen despite treatment?
- Was individual compliant with treatment recommendations?
- Would the individual benefit from dietary counseling?
- Have hemorrhoids recurred, even after surgical treatment?
- Does individual have a coexisting condition that could impact ability to recover such as anorectal infections, fecal impaction, and rectal neoplasms?
- Would the individual benefit from consultation with a specialist (gastroenterologist, general surgeon)?

References

Hemorrhoids. drkoop.com. 2000. 11 Dec 2000 <http://www.drkoop.com/conditions/ency/article/000292.htm>.

Hemorrhoids. Jackson Gastroenterology. 1998. 11 Dec 2000 <http://www.gicare.com/pated/ecdgs10.htm>.

Hemothorax, Traumatic
860.2, 860.3

Definition

Hemothorax is a bleeding into the chest cavity between the lung and internal chest wall (pleural cavity). Hemothorax is classified according to the amount of blood present: minimal, moderate, or massive. Traumatic hemothorax is caused by blunt or penetrating trauma to the chest. In a chest injury, a rib may lacerate lung tissue or an artery, causing blood to collect in the pleural space. A large hemothorax is often the cause of shock in a trauma victim. Hemothorax may also be associated with pneumothorax (collapsed lung).

Men are as likely to suffer hemothorax as women. In the US, hemothorax incidence is 6 out of 100,000 individuals per year. Free blood in the chest is seen in 23-51% of blunt trauma victims and 64-82% of penetrating trauma victims. Usually this blood comes from cut or torn low-pressure pulmonary vessels and thoracic veins. In a study from South Africa, less than 10% of hemothorax cases required surgical intervention. A Japanese study found that the cause of blunt thoracic injury in 80.7% of individuals was traffic accidents, and 56% of all individuals were diagnosed with hemothorax.

Diagnosis

History: The individual or family member will give a history of blunt injury to the chest (such as from an automobile accident) or penetrating wound (such as from a gunshot). In the absence of an obvious wound, the individual may also complain of shortness of breath and moderate to severe chest pain.

Physical exam: Most individuals have decreased breath sounds over the hemothorax. They may also have dulled sounds after tapping over the involved area. They may be anxious and restless and have a rapid heartbeat.

Tests: Signs of hemothorax may be evident with chest x-ray, removal of fluid through a needle from the pleural cavity (thoracentesis), and visual or microscopic analysis of this fluid (pleural fluid analysis).

Treatment

The objective of treatment is to stabilize the condition of the affected individual, stop the bleeding, and remove the blood in the pleural space, and re-inflate the collapsed lung. A chest tube is pushed through a small hole (between two ribs) in the chest wall to drain the blood (thoracentesis). The chest tube is left in place for several days to re-expand the lung.

The cause of the hemothorax will also be treated. Frequently, surgery is performed because of the nature of injury sustained by trauma. Less than 10% of hemothorax cases require surgical intervention (thoracoscopy) for opening the thorax and cleaning out any clotted blood. Surgery can also involve repairing and sewing muscle, blood vessels, and internal organs (thoracotomy).

Prognosis

As long as the individual has no additional serious wounds or illnesses and he or she receives the described therapy, he or she is likely to recover completely. The outcome after surgery for the otherwise healthy individual is excellent. Respiratory failure and death is the likely result from traumatic hemothorax if blood leakage is not stopped either because the individual cannot get treatment or because he or she does not get treatment soon enough. The outcome is not predictable if the individual sustained other serious wounds apart from the one that caused the hemothorax.

Differential Diagnosis

Individuals who have the symptoms of hemothorax can also be diagnosed with gas in the cavity between the lungs and the lung sacs (pneumothorax), lung bruising (pulmonary contusion), and air in the space between the lungs (pneumomediastinum).

Specialists

- Cardiothoracic Surgeon
- Emergency Medicine
- General Surgeon
- Pulmonologist

Rehabilitation

Individuals who suffer from traumatic hemothorax will either require the placement of a chest tube or a thoracotomy. Either of these procedures may necessitate occupational, physical, and respiratory therapy.

Respiratory therapy addresses increasing lung capacity and decreasing the risk for the buildup of lung secretions. Respiratory therapists teach individuals pursed lip breathing to increase the airflow to the lungs. Individuals may also use an incentive spirometer, which is a device that measures and displays the amount of air inspired to help motivate individuals to take deeper breaths. Individuals also learn to produce an effective cough through techniques such as huffing, in which air is breathed out forcefully while the mouth is open. Individuals learn to hold a pillow to the incision area when coughing, laughing, or performing activity such as walking. This technique (splinting) can help alleviate pain at the incision site. Individuals also learn positions to relieve shortness of breath, such as leaning forward while sitting with the arms resting on the thighs.

Occupational therapy addresses any fatigue or shortness of breath that may occur during activities of daily living. Individuals learn to utilize equipment such as a shower chair to decrease the energy expended during bathing, or a long-handled sponge to decrease the amount of forward bending an individual has to perform. Occupational therapists may also teach energy conservation techniques.

Work Restrictions / Accommodations

When the individual returns to work, recovery from surgery will restrict work to sedentary duties for the otherwise healthy individual for 6 weeks.

Comorbid Conditions

Comorbid conditions that slow full recovery include other injuries that are sustained after a serious vehicle accident or work-related accident, lung cancer, emphysema, diabetes, heart disease, obesity, hemophilia, HIV/AIDS.

Complications

Complications include shock due to massive bleeding from cut blood vessels and organs before surgery, lung abscess (empyema), or fibrous clot within the pleural cavity (fibrothorax).

Factors Influencing Duration

Factors that influence length of disability include the underlying cause for treatment and the presence of other injuries.

Length of Disability

Length of disability depends on extent of hemothorax, complications and work requirements. An individual with additional serious wounds may take longer. An individual with underlying serious illness (such as diabetes) or whose hemothorax was caused by cancer may have permanent disability. Duration figures reflect recovery times for the procedure only.

Thoracostomy (chest tube).

Duration in Days

Job Classification	Minimum	Optimum	Maximum
Sedentary work	3	14	28
Light work	3	14	28
Medium work	3	21	42
Heavy work	7	21	42
Very Heavy work	7	21	42

Failure to Recover

If an individual fails to recover within the maximum duration expectancy period, the reader may wish to reference the following questions to assist in better understanding the specifics of an individual's medical case.

Regarding diagnosis:

- Was diagnosis of hemothorax confirmed?
- Was hemothorax diagnosed by x-ray?
- Was fluid removed from the pleural cavity and analyzed for signs of blood?
- Did individual sustain any injuries elsewhere in the body?
- Has individual experienced complications such as shock due to massive bleeding from lacerated blood vessels or organs, empyema, or fibrothorax?
- Does individual have an underlying condition that may impact recovery?
- Has individual been examined for other lung diseases such as lung cancer, or emphysema?

Regarding treatment:

- Was treatment prompt and appropriate?
- Did individual require surgery to remove clotted blood?
- Was surgery required to repair muscle, blood vessels, and/or internal organs?
- Was treatment effective?

Regarding prognosis:
- Did unexpected complications occur?
- Can delayed recovery be explained through other factors?
- Are wounds healing as expected?
- In what way is recovery impacted?

References

Briusov, P.G., A.N. Kuritsyn, and N.I. Urazovskii. "The Operative Videothoracosopy in Rendering Emergency Surgical Care in Penetrating Gunshot Chest Wounds." Voen Med Zh 319 2 (1998): 21-68.

Guccione, Andrew A. "Functional Assessment." Physical Rehabilitation: Assessment and Treatment. O'Sullivan, Susan B., and Thomas J. Schmitz, eds. Philadelphia: F.A. Davis Company, 1994. 193-208.

Rodseth, C.P., et al. "Immediate Physiotherapy in Perforating Wounds of the Pleural Cavity and Underlying Lung." South African Medical Journal 54 20 (1978): 814-816.

Watchie, Joanne. Cardiopulmonary Physical Therapy. Philadelphia: W.B. Saunders Company, 1995.

Hepatic Angiosarcoma

Other names / synonyms: Angioblastic Sarcoma, Angioplastic Sarcoma, Angiosarcoma Endothelioblastoma, Hemangioendothelial Sarcoma, Kupffer Cell Sarcoma, Malignant Hemangioendothelioma

155.2

Definition

Hepatic angiosarcoma is a rare type of liver cancer that develops in the cells (Kupffer and endothelial cells) lining the blood vessels of the liver. The normal function of Kupffer cells is to filter bacteria and foreign molecules from the blood as it passes through the liver. Endothelial cells normally act as a leaky, semipermeable barrier between the blood circulating through the vessel and the liver tissue surrounding it.

Risk factors for hepatic angiosarcoma include prior exposure to certain compounds (monomeric vinyl chloride or inorganic arsenic) used in the chemical, plastic, and tire industries. The link between angiosarcoma and monomeric vinyl chloride is particularly strong. This compound may also be found in insecticides, commercial hair spray propellants, and cigarette smoke. The condition has also been linked with exposure to certain radioactive compounds (radium, thorium oxide, or thorotrast) previously used in radiology studies and male sex hormones (androgenic anabolic steroids). Hepatic angiosarcoma may also result from exposure to the herbicide dioxin (2,4,5-trichlorophenoxyacetic acid or 2,4,5-T), a component of the defoliant Agent Orange used by the US military in areas of Southeast Asia from 1965 to 1970. Exposure to copper and oral contraceptives have also been implicated as causative agents although their role remains unproved.

The latency period between exposure to vinyl chloride and the development of hepatic angiosarcoma has a reported range of 9 to 37 years. Hepatic angiosarcoma constitutes only 2% of all primary tumors of the liver with approximately 25 cases occurring each year in the US. Only about 4 cases a year were reported in Great Britain. The male to female ratio is 3:1 and the average age of occurrence is 53 years.

Diagnosis

History: Individuals may report no symptoms until late in the disease when they usually experience abdominal and shoulder pain, fatigue, weight loss, and fever. Individuals may also report a yellow discoloration (jaundice) of the skin, whites (sclera) of the eyes, and mucous membranes. These symptoms may be present for a considerable time prior to diagnosis of the disease.

Physical exam: An enlarged liver (hepatomegaly) and fluid in the abdominal cavity (ascites) are commonly seen on physical examination. The ascites fluid may be bloodstained (hemoperitoneum). Listening to the blood flow over the area of the tumor may reveal a low-frequency noise (vascular hum). Destruction of red blood cells (microangiopathic hemolytic anemia), reduction of the number of platelets (thrombocytopenia), and an inability of the blood to coagulate (consumption coagulopathy) also may be observed.

Tests: Visualization of the tumor(s) within the vessels may be done using x-rays after injection of a radiopaque dye (angiography), the single best noninvasive diagnostic tool available. CT, high-frequency sound waves (ultrasonography), or low-frequency radio waves (MRI) may also prove useful. Hepatic angiosarcoma will appear as either a single, solitary mass or as many small nodules ranging from pinpoint size to several centimeters in diameter. A definitive diagnosis of the disease can only be made by microscopically examining a biopsy specimen. A liver biopsy may be done using either an incision through the abdominal wall (laparotomy) or insertion of a needle through the abdominal wall and directly into the liver (percutaneous needle biopsy).

Treatment

Hepatic angiosarcoma can be treated by surgical removal of the diseased portion of the liver (resection). Unfortunately, liver resection is possible in very few cases. It may be considered, however, a viable treatment if the disease is limited to a single lobe of the liver and the rest of the organ is essentially normal. Chemotherapy may be useful to improve liver function and slow the progression of the disease in some cases. Angiosarcoma seems resistant to radiation treatment.

Prognosis

Angiosarcoma tumors spread quickly and 60% of individuals will have metastasis into other organs at the time of diagnosis. Very few individuals present with a tumor that is limited in size and amenable to surgical resection. The tumor is usually found in both lobes of the liver making surgical cure impossible. The predicted outcome for an individual with hepatic angiosarcoma is extremely poor with an average life expectancy of 6 months following diagnosis. However, individuals with well-defined tumors that are treated surgically may survive anywhere from 1 to 3 years. The longest reported survivor lived for 7 years.

Differential Diagnosis

Conditions presenting with similar symptoms as hepatic angiosarcoma include other harmless (benign) or cancerous (malignant) liver tumors. A fluid- or tissue-containing sac (cyst) may resemble angiosarcoma, and cirrhosis or cancer spread from other organs (metastatic cancer) is another possibility.

Specialists

- Gastroenterologist
- General Surgeon
- Oncologist
- Radiation Oncologist

Work Restrictions / Accommodations

With few exceptions, individuals with hepatic angiosarcoma will not return to work in any capacity because of the poor survival rate. The rare individual whose life is prolonged by treatment may require more sedentary work for a period of time due to weakness and fatigue following surgery, radiation therapy, or chemotherapy. Factors influencing the length of disability include the type and stage of disease at initial presentation, the presence of concurrent infection and overall general health, the type of treatment pursued, and the presence of complications.

Comorbid Conditions

Existing conditions that may impact an individual's ability to recover from hepatic angiosarcoma include prior liver disease, prolonged malnutrition, heart disease, or any systemic disease such as diabetes.

Complications

Complications of hepatic angiosarcoma include congestive heart failure and circulation problems in the liver itself (hepatic bruits). Other complications may include abnormal tissue growth (fibrosis) leading to decreased liver function (cirrhosis) and an increased risk of bleeding (hemorrhage). The liver is located close to several vital organs including the lung and spleen. Angiosarcoma may spread (metastasize) into these organs directly or indirectly via the lymphatic or vascular systems, which can lead to widespread cancer throughout the body.

Factors Influencing Duration

Factors that may influence the length of disability include the age of the individual, the stage of the tumor at initial diagnosis, degree of metastasis, presence of concurrent infections and overall general health, type of treatment, and other complicating diseases.

Length of Disability

Disability is permanent for most individuals and usually there is no recovery. The few individuals able to return to the job may require more sedentary work until recovery from surgery, chemotherapy, and radiation treatment is complete. Surgery, radiation therapy, or chemotherapy may prolong the length of disability. For surgical treatment, durations reflect recovery from procedure only.

Chemotherapy.

Duration in Days

Job Classification	Minimum	Optimum	Maximum
Sedentary work	14	21	28
Light work	14	21	28
Medium work	21	28	42
Heavy work	21	35	42
Very Heavy work	21	35	42

Surgical treatment.

Duration in Days

Job Classification	Minimum	Optimum	Maximum
Sedentary work	28	35	42
Light work	28	35	42
Medium work	42	49	56
Heavy work	56	70	84
Very Heavy work	56	70	84

Failure to Recover

If an individual fails to recover within the maximum duration expectancy period, the reader may wish to reference the following questions to assist in better understanding the specifics of an individual's medical case.

Regarding diagnosis:

- Was diagnosis of hepatic angiosarcoma confirmed? Was biopsy performed?
- Were other conditions such as, benign or malignant liver tumors, cysts, cirrhosis, or cancer spread from other organs (metastatic cancer), ruled out?
- Has individual experienced any complications such as, congestive heart failure, hepatic bruits, fibrosis leading to cirrhosis, or increased risk of hemorrhage, that may impact recovery?
- Does individual have an underlying condition such as, prior liver disease, prolonged malnutrition, heart disease, or any systemic disease such as diabetes, that may impact recovery?

Regarding treatment:

- If disease was limited to a single lobe of the liver and the rest of the organ is essentially normal, was resection successful in removing all the cancerous tissue?
- Would chemotherapy be beneficial in this case?

- Did individual sustain residual neurologic abnormalities such as tremor of the head or arms, speech disturbances, alterations in gait, or impairment of intellectual functioning?
- Can therapy help individual compensate for impairment?
- Would work accommodations allow individual to continue in present occupation?
- Have complications developed such as hemorrhage, infection, dehydration, or kidney failure that may impact recovery and length of disability?

References

Clochesy, John M., et al. Critical Care Nursing, 2nd ed. Philadelphia: W.B. Saunders Company, 1996.

Hepatitis A

Other names / synonyms: Infectious Hepatitis, Viral Hepatitis Type A
070.0, 070.1, 573.1

Definition

Viral hepatitis type A, formerly called infectious hepatitis, is a highly contagious disease spread by a viral infection that causes liver inflammation. Rarely fatal, the disease typically runs its course in 2-6 months.

As the virus is spread primarily by food or water contaminated with feces, the disease is very common in developing countries with inadequate sanitation systems. Many cases occur among travelers who have recently returned from an area where the virus is prevalent and hygiene standards are low. Consumption of raw shellfish from contaminated waters may also cause infection.

Hepatitis A infections may be spread through daycare centers where good hygiene such as hand-washing is absent or by food handlers who sometimes are the source of epidemics. Individuals spreading the infection may have no symptoms (carriers) or their symptoms are not yet apparent. The disease also may be transmitted sexually through oral or anal contact, or intravenously in drug users through shared needles.

Since symptoms aren't always present, prevalence is difficult to determine. Each year, approximately 1.4 million people worldwide, and 125,000-200,000 in the US, become infected with hepatitis A. It is the seventh most commonly reported infectious disease in the US, and accounts for up to 65% of all viral hepatitis cases in the US each year. Reported cases are about 1 in 10,000 people. Almost all adults in certain underdeveloped countries and as many as 35-40% of adults in the US are thought to have been exposed to the disease.

Diagnosis

History: Individuals may have an abrupt onset of the disease, accompanied by loss of appetite, nausea, body aches, and fatigue. Fever is common, but rarely higher than 102 degrees F. Dark urine and light-colored stools may also be reported, along with a yellowing of the eyes and skin (jaundice). Symptoms develop within 3-6 weeks after exposure. Individuals may report recent travel to underdeveloped countries or close contact with an individual infected with hepatitis A.

Physical exam: Even when an individual is infected, the physical examination may be unrevealing. The liver may be enlarged (hepatomegaly) and tender. Occasionally, the spleen is also enlarged (splenomegaly). A yellow discoloration of the eyes and skin (jaundice) may be present.

Tests: Blood tests of liver function show significantly elevated levels of AST, ALT, and bilirubin. A positive test specific for hepatitis A (Hepatitis A IgM antibody) is necessary for a definitive diagnosis.

Treatment

Rest is usually the only treatment for hepatitis A. The duration of recommended rest depends on the severity of symptoms. Appropriate fluid and food intake also are recommended. Alcohol and other substances toxic to the liver should be avoided. In the unlikely event that abnormalities persist for more than six months, a liver biopsy may be indicated. Those in close contact with someone with hepatitis A should consider receiving a protective injection of immune globulin, which is effective for about 3-6 months. A vaccine that must be given before exposure to the virus is also available for those in high-risk occupations or traveling to high-risk countries. This offers longer-term protection, and consists of an initial shot followed by a booster shot in about 6-18 months. Serious reactions to the vaccine are rare, but local reactions including pain, redness, tenderness, and warmth are common at the vaccination site. Fever, abdominal pain, headache, fatigue, and allergic reactions may also occur. Preventative measures also include frequent hand-washing before handling food and after using the toilet or changing diapers, avoiding untreated tap water and unpeeled fruit or raw vegetables when traveling to high risk areas, and not eating raw shellfish.

Prognosis

Most people with hepatitis A infection recover completely, although about 100 Americans annually die from the disease. In 1-2 months the liver is completely healed. The first signs of recovery are the disappearance of nausea and the return of appetite.

Differential Diagnosis

The symptoms of hepatitis A virus infection are often the same as other types of viral hepatitis, which include hepatitis B, C, and E, infectious mononucleosis, and cytomegalovirus. Jaundice can also result from many noninfectious causes of hepatitis, including prescription drugs, poisons, alcohol, or gallstones.

Specialists

- Gastroenterologist
- Hepatologist
- Infectious Disease Physician

Work Restrictions / Accommodations

Absence of jaundice is not required before returning to work, but employees who have significant social interaction may need to limit their contact with the public. Good hygiene is crucial. Customers at a restaurant or other place of business may be wary of employees who are jaundiced for fear of exposure to a contagious disease. Employees required to perform strenuous tasks may need to limit their job-related activities in the first few days after returning to work.

Comorbid Conditions

Individuals with chronic liver disease or who have received liver transplants might have a difficult recovery or complications. The disease also would likely be more severe in individuals who have a blood clotting disorder such as hemophilia. Any chronic illness may prolong recovery.

Complications

Hepatitis A rarely has complications. Recovery usually begins within 3 weeks, but rarely, jaundice and other symptoms can last for 2-6 months or more (prolonged cholestatic jaundice). Chronic liver disease does not occur, but 15% may have prolonged or recurrent (relapsing) hepatitis.

Factors Influencing Duration

In some individuals, prolonged fatigue may persist for months, even after liver function tests have returned to normal. Commercial food handlers, daycare workers, and healthcare workers should be off work as long as symptoms persist, and for at least 1 week after symptoms have resolved.

Length of Disability

Since hepatitis A is highly contagious, length of disability may depend on the individual's occupation and the need to avoid exposing the public to contamination.

Duration in Days

Job Classification	Minimum	Optimum	Maximum
Any work	7	21	42

Failure to Recover

If an individual fails to recover within the maximum duration expectancy period, the reader may wish to reference the following questions to assist in better understanding the specifics of an individual's medical case.

Regarding diagnosis:

- Was diagnosis of viral hepatitis type A confirmed by testing for Hepatitis A IgM antibody?
- Were other conditions such as, other types of viral hepatitis, (hepatitis B, C, and E), infectious mononucleosis, cytomegalovirus, or jaundice caused by prescription drugs, poisons, alcohol, or gallstones, ruled out?
- Does individual have an underlying condition such as, liver transplant or blood clotting disorder such as hemophilia that might impact recovery?

Regarding treatment:

- Has individual been compliant with prescribed treatment plan?
- Has individual been receiving sufficient rest to recover from the disease?
- Has individual avoided substances toxic to the liver such as alcohol?

Regarding prognosis:

- If symptoms have persisted past the expected duration, should diagnosis be revisited?
- Does individual's condition demonstrate a relapsing pattern?
- If abnormalities persist, is a liver biopsy indicated?

References

Hepatitis A. Merck Vaccine Division. 1995. 8 Nov 2000 <http://www.merck.com/disease/preventable/hepa/>.

Viral Hepatitis A. Centers for Disease Control and Prevention. 19 Apr 2000. 23 Aug 2000 <http://www.cdc.gov/ncidod/diseases/hepatitis/a/index.htm>.

Hepatitis B
070.2, 070.3, 070.30

Definition

Sometimes described as a "silent killer," viral hepatitis type B is an inflammation of the liver caused by a viral infection. The acute and most common form of the disease typically clears up within several months. If the disease persists beyond 6 months, the individual is thought to have a chronic form. Up to 17% of those infected develop chronic hepatitis B that may be present throughout the individual's lifetime. Often undetected in its early stages, the disease (over a period sometimes lasting decades) may slowly destroy the liver or lead to liver cancer.

The two ways to spread hepatitis B are by sharing needles between intravenous drug users and sexual activity (both heterosexual and homosexual). Bodily fluids are often the source of infection among family members or others living in the same household. Healthcare personnel are also at risk usually through accidental punctures from needles contaminated with an infected individual's blood. In the past, the virus was spread primarily by transfusions of contaminated blood and blood products. This form is called serum hepatitis and has virtually been eliminated because of screening for the virus by blood banks. Since 1993, an increase in hepatitis B infection has occurred in three major risk groups: sexually active heterosexuals, homosexual men, and injection drug users.

Most hepatitis B virus infections occur in young adults. Only 20% of infections reveal any overt illness commonly associated with hepatitis. The hepatitis B virus is thought to infect about 350 million people worldwide. It is found in up to 20% of the population in some parts of the world including Africa and Asia, and in about 5% of all individuals in the US. Of the 140,000 to 320,000 infections each year in the US, only 70,000 to 160,000 are symptomatic. Despite recent widespread US vaccination programs aimed primarily at children and those in high-risk occupations such as healthcare workers, hepatitis B kills up to 5,000 individuals each year in the US and about 1 million individuals worldwide.

Diagnosis

History: Fifty percent of individuals infected have no symptoms. Individuals may report early symptoms of the disease including muscle and joint aches, headache, and weakness. There may also be complaints of bad breath and a bitter taste in the mouth. Loss of appetite and nausea are common and accompanied by weight loss. A low-grade fever, diarrhea, and constipation may variably occur. The urine may be dark and the stools light-colored. Yellow skin and eyes (jaundice) develop soon thereafter. At this point in the illness, the fever and aches may subside. Individuals with a chronic form of the disease may also report chest pain or itchy skin eruptions.

Physical exam: The exam commonly reveals tenderness over the liver when pressure is applied just below the ribs on the right side of the body. Enlargement of the liver (hepatomegaly) and occasionally the spleen (splenomegaly) may be detected. The appearance of jaundice may occur but is variable.

Tests: Blood tests (serology) will show general signs of impaired liver function (high ALT, AST, and bilirubin). To specifically diagnose hepatitis B, other blood tests are needed for detection of HBsAg and anti-HBc IgM antibody.

Treatment

Drugs with antiviral properties (interferons) are sometimes injected to help stimulate immune responses. In experimental programs, drugs that suppress the immune system (corticosteroids) may also be included as part of the therapy to improve the effectiveness of interferons. Other treatment includes rest as needed to alleviate symptoms. Liver transplants are an option for those with an advanced form of the disease, but availability of organs is limited.

Adequate fluid and food intake are also important. Preventive treatment is recommended for the sexual partners of an individual with acute hepatitis B. An immune globulin injection and hepatitis B vaccination may be recommended for individuals who have been exposed. The vaccine alone is recommended for individuals with household contacts who are chronic carriers of the hepatitis B virus. Hepatitis B vaccinations are required in some states, but to be effective, they must be given prior to exposure to the virus. Routine vaccination is recommended in infants and 11- and 12-year-olds, and in high-risk groups of all ages.

Prognosis

The duration of acute hepatitis B illness is quite variable. Most healthy adults with hepatitis B usually recover completely within 6 months, but about 17% develop a chronic form. In less than 3% of cases, the disease worsens over a period of 1 to 3 months (subacute hepatic necrosis). In less than 1% of cases, there is massive death of liver tissue (fulminant hepatitis). Between 1-5% of adults become chronic carriers of the virus. Up to 15-25% of Western whites with chronic hepatitis B infection die prematurely of either cirrhosis or liver cancer.

Severity of the disease is directly related to how young the individual is when first infected. Individuals with chronic hepatitis B infection since childhood or adolescence have a 15% chance of dying from liver disease. Those who develop liver cancer have an average survival rate of 1 year following diagnosis. Individuals infected with chronic hepatitis B who are considered good candidates for interferon drug therapy have a 40% chance of recovery following treatment. Coinfection with hepatitis D (delta antigen) can lead to a more prolonged and severe disease course.

Differential Diagnosis

The symptoms of hepatitis B viral infection are often the same as for other types of viral hepatitis that include hepatitis A, C, and E, infectious mononucleosis, and cytomegalovirus. Jaundice can result from many noninfectious causes of hepatitis including prescription drugs, poisons, alcohol, or gallstones.

Specialists

- Gastroenterologist
- Hepatologist
- Infectious Disease Physician
- Preventative Medicine Specialist

Rehabilitation

Individuals with hepatitis B require no specific physical rehabilitation. They may wish to consult with a physical therapist and develop an exercise program to maintain endurance and strength. Adherence to a regular exercise program is critical in maintaining overall health and is particularly important in individuals with compromised immune systems. Aerobic exercise increases cardiopulmonary fitness, improves muscle function, enhances weight gain, and improves mood and coping behavior. Exercise should be undertaken with a goal of attaining 75-85% maximum intensity while walking, jogging, biking, swimming, performing calisthenics, and/or weight training.

Work Restrictions / Accommodations

Individuals usually do not work during the jaundice period of hepatitis B, but this recommendation varies depending on the type of job. Absence of jaundice is not required before a return to work, but employees with significant social interaction may need to limit their contact with the public. Customers at a restaurant or other places of business may fear contact with a contagious disease when it is obvious that an employee is jaundiced. Employees required to perform strenuous tasks may need to limit their job-related activities in the first few days after returning to work. Individuals who develop complications from hepatitis B such as paralysis or joint pain may need easy accessibility to work stations and accommodation such as appropriate seating and support.

Complementary and Alternative Therapies

Content is intended for awareness only. Treatments may or may not be effective. Scientific evidence may be lacking and some substances have potentially toxic effects. Dr. Presley Reed and the editors do not endorse the use of these therapies in the absence of consultation with a licensed medical professional.

Milk thistle -	Contains Silymarin, which may reduce liver damage in cirrhosis and acute and chronic hepatitis.
St. John's wort -	Said to promote antiviral activity.
Acupuncture -	May help relieve symptoms.
Turmeric -	May protect liver from tumor development.
Shiatsu massage -	May help to relieve some symptoms.
Vitamin E -	May protect the liver and prevent tumor development by decreasing free radical formation.

Comorbid Conditions

Individuals with blood clotting disorder, chronic liver disease, or liver transplants have greater difficulty recovering from hepatitis B. Alcoholism also impairs liver function and may hamper recovery. Any chronic illness may affect recovery.

Complications

Progressive liver disease (cirrhosis) may develop annually in 1-12% of individuals with hepatitis B. Every year, about 1.5% of individuals in the US with cirrhosis and 2-4% of individuals in other countries may develop liver cancer (hepatocellular carcinoma). Other possible complications include arthritis and inflammation of the arteries (polyarteritis nodosa); inflammation of small structures in the kidney (membranous glomerulonephritis); and reversible nerve damage causing paralysis of the arms, legs, eyes, lungs, neck, and diaphragm (Guillain-Barré syndrome). Inflammation may also affect the heart muscle or tissue (myocarditis). Individuals over 40 and drug addicts are more likely to develop a worsening of the disease (subacute hepatic necrosis). Older individuals may also develop muscle pain similar to rheumatism (polymyalgia rheumatica).

Factors Influencing Duration

The illness usually lasts 1 to 2 months and it may take as long as 6 months for the liver to regain proper function. If recovery does not take place within that time frame, the individual may have a chronic and possibly incurable form of hepatitis B. Liver damage and accompanying complications may cause the individual's condition to gradually worsen.

Length of Disability

The severity of symptoms and response to treatment determine if individuals can manage tasks demanding physical strength. Specific job duties may influence expected length of disability.

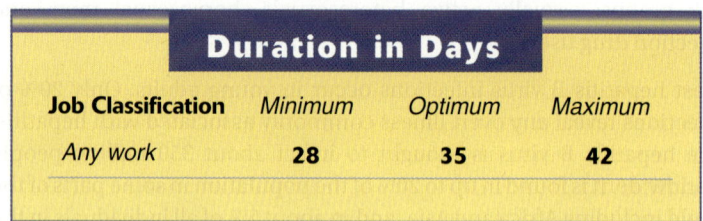

Job Classification	Minimum	Optimum	Maximum
Any work	28	35	42

Failure to Recover

If an individual fails to recover within the maximum duration expectancy period, the reader may wish to reference the following questions to assist in better understanding the specifics of an individual's medical case.

Regarding diagnosis:

- Has diagnosis of viral hepatitis type B been confirmed?
- Has individual had appropriate blood tests to confirm impaired liver function and the specific presence of the hepatitis B virus?
- Were other conditions such as other types of viral hepatitis including hepatitis A, C, and E, infectious mononucleosis, cytomegalovirus, or jaundice resulting from prescription drugs, poisons, alcohol, or gallstones ruled out?
- Has individual developed complications such as, cirrhosis, arthritis, polyarteritis nodosa, membranous glomerulonephritis, Guillain-Barré syndrome, myocarditis, subacute hepatic necrosis, or polymyalgia rheumatica?
- Does individual have an underlying condition such as alcoholism, blood clotting disorder, chronic liver disease, or liver transplant that may impact recovery?
- Has coinfection with hepatitis D (delta antigen) been identified?

Regarding treatment:

- Is individual considered a candidate for newer therapies such as interferon injections?
- Has individual received adequate rest, nutritional, and fluid intake?
- Is individual registered in an organ transplant program?

Regarding prognosis:

- Since the virus must run its course, has individual had an appropriate length of time to recover?
- Does disease appear to be progressing? Is there evidence of liver tissue death?
- Is a more aggressive treatment now indicated?
- Is individual a carrier?
- What precautions must individual now take for self and for others with whom he/she comes in contact?
- Does individual's age at onset impact this prognosis?
- Is there evidence of liver cancer?
- Is individual a candidate for interferon drug therapy? If not, why not?
- Have all associated individuals received appropriate vaccination for Hepatitis B, or treatment with immune globulin injection?

References

Viral Hepatitis B. Center for Disease Control. 01 Jan 2000. 8 Nov 2000 <http://www.cdc.gov/ncidod/diseases/hepatitis/b>.

Kisner, Carolyn, and Lynn Allen Colby. Therapeutic Exercise: Foundations and Techniques, 2nd ed. Philadelphia: F.A. Davis Company, 1990.

Hepatitis C
Other names / synonyms: Non-A Hepatitis
070.41, 070.5, 070.51

Definition

Hepatitis C is a viral infection that causes liver inflammation. The virus is most frequently transmitted through sharing of needles, sexual contact, hemodialysis, and accidental exposure of healthcare workers to infected blood. While in modern times screening by blood banks has virtually eliminated exposure through transfusions, many people were infected in this way prior to 1992. In many individuals, the source of infection is unknown.

Identified for the first time in the late 1980s, the virus is considered to be the most insidious of the various types of hepatitis because symptoms tend to occur only in late stages of the disease. The virus undergoes mutations, which help it evade immune responses. An infection may be undetected for decades, until some afflicted individuals finally experience symptoms that may indicate extreme liver damage or outright failure.

The disease is chronic in about 85% of all cases. Almost 2% of US citizens are thought to have hepatitis C, but may be unaware of the infection because of lack of symptoms. Between 8,000-10,000 US residents die from the disease each year. About 3% of the world's population is thought to have the disease. About 20% of chronic cases develop liver damage (cirrhosis), and about 10% develop liver cancer (hepatocellular carcinoma).

Diagnosis

History: While early symptoms of the disease often are absent, individuals may report muscle and joint aches, headache, weight loss, and weakness. Other prominent symptoms may include loss of appetite and nausea. Diarrhea, constipation, and low-grade fever occur occasionally, along with the development of yellow skin and eyes (jaundice). Individuals may also report abdominal pain. Because laboratory tests are not always definitive, the individual's clinical and social history are important for diagnosis in the early stages of the disease.

Physical exam: The exam may show enlargement of the liver (hepatomegaly) and spleen (splenomegaly). Progressive liver disease may be indicated by visible branching capillaries on the skin (spider nevi), redness of the palms of the hand (palmar erythema), and a liver that is firm on examination.

Tests: Blood tests (serology) of liver function will show high or fluctuating levels of the enzyme ALT. A specific indicator of this infection, HCV antibody, does not occur in detectable amounts until about 15 weeks after onset of the disease. Additional blood tests (EIA, RIBA-2) are frequently necessary to aid in diagnosis.

Progressive liver disease may be indicated if abnormal values in other blood tests are found, such as serum albumin or the platelet count. In this case, a small piece of the liver may be removed for microscopic examination (liver biopsy). Some specialists recommend liver biopsies be performed in all cases where hepatitis C has been identified to rule out liver damage.

Treatment

Usually the hepatitis clears up without treatment. Recommendations include rest when needed. Adequate fluid and food intake is also recommended. Drugs with anti-viral properties (interferons) may help to clear the virus, but these are administered only to individuals who meet certain guidelines. Up to 30% of those treated with interferon experience improvement. Use of an anti-viral drug, ribavirin, also has produced positive results when used in combination with interferon. In extreme cases, a liver transplant may be performed depending on availability and prognosis for the individual. Unlike for hepatitis A and B, a preventive vaccine has not yet been developed for hepatitis C.

Prognosis

Most individuals diagnosed with the disease do not develop life-threatening conditions. Many individuals with this form of hepatitis have few, if any, symptoms, particularly in the early stages of the disease. Many times the disease will clear up on its own. Even without symptoms, the disease, in a small percentage of cases, may progress and create liver damage over the course of decades. About 20% of chronic cases may develop into permanent liver damage or liver failure, while 10% of such cases lead to liver cancer. Individuals who develop liver cancer survive an average of about 1 year.

Genetic testing can reveal individuals infected with a viral genotype that predicts a less successful response to treatment. Older age and viral load are also variables associated with reduced response to treatment.

Differential Diagnosis

The symptoms of hepatitis C virus infection are often the same as other types of viral hepatitis, which include hepatitis A, B, and E; infectious mononucleosis; and cytomegalovirus. Jaundice can result from many non-infectious causes of hepatitis, including prescription drugs, poisons, alcohol, or gallstones.

Specialists

- Gastroenterologist
- Hepatologist
- Infectious Disease Physician
- Preventative Medicine Specialist

Work Restrictions / Accommodations

While in a state of jaundice, individuals usually do not work. However, absence of jaundice is not required before returning to work depending on the amount of contact the individual has with the public. Employees required to perform strenuous tasks may need to limit their job-related activities in the first few days after returning to work.

Complementary and Alternative Therapies

Content is intended for awareness only. Treatments may or may not be effective. Scientific evidence may be lacking and some substances have potentially toxic effects. Dr. Presley Reed and the editors do not endorse the use of these therapies in the absence of consultation with a licensed medical professional.

Glycyrrhizin -	Said to exhibit a protective effect on induced liver damage in rats. The mechanism is not known.
Green tea -	May reduce membrane fluidity and provide a protective effect to the liver.
Silymarin -	Said to stimulate the process of liver regeneration.
Bougainvillea spectabilis Wild -	Contains spinasterol and caffeic acid, which are said to exhibit strong inhibition of xanthine oxidase, levels of which are elevated in liver tumors.
Vitamin E -	Said to be effective in the treatment of liver damage associated with hepatitis C.
N-acetyl-cysteine -	Said to be effective in the treatment of liver damage associated with hepatitis C.

Comorbid Conditions

Individuals with blood clotting disorders, chronic liver disease, or liver transplants would have greater difficulty recovering from hepatitis C. Alcoholism and drug addiction impair liver function and might hamper recovery.

Complications

Chronic cases may develop into liver damage (cirrhosis) or liver cancer (hepatocellular carcinoma). As more has become known about the newly discovered disease, many other complications have been found to be associated with development of hepatitis C, including thyroiditis, vasculitis, and various immune disorders.

Factors Influencing Duration

Although recent progress has been made in the diagnosis and description of hepatitis C infection, many factors influencing the severity of the disease have not yet been determined. Infection by transfusion may lead to a higher incidence of chronic liver disease and cirrhosis. Alcohol use has been shown to accelerate progression of the disease.

Length of Disability

The severity of symptoms, response to treatment, and existence of complications will influence the individual's degree of recovery and ability to perform tasks such as heavy lifting.

Duration in Days

Job Classification	Minimum	Optimum	Maximum
Any work	28	35	84

Failure to Recover

If an individual fails to recover within the maximum duration expectancy period, the reader may wish to reference the following questions to assist in better understanding the specifics of an individual's medical case.

Regarding diagnosis:

- Has diagnosis of viral hepatitis C been confirmed?
- Does individual have a coexisting condition (such as an alcohol or drug addiction) that may impact recovery?
- Have conditions with similar symptoms such as viral hepatitis (hepatitis A, B, and E), infectious mononucleosis, and cytomegalovirus been ruled out?
- Have blood tests (EIA, RIBA-2) been done to ensure proper diagnosis?

Regarding treatment:

- Has individual been compliant with treatment recommendations?
- What can be done to increase compliance?
- Is individual a good candidate for drug therapies addressing hepatitis C?

- Is individual being considered for a liver transplant? Is individual on local/national transplant lists?

Regarding prognosis:

- If symptoms persist longer than expected, should diagnosis be revisited?

- Has genetic testing been performed?
- Would individual benefit from consultation with a specialist (gastroenterologist, hepatologist, infectious disease specialist)?
- Does the individual have permanent liver damage or liver cancer?
- Is individual being considered for a liver transplant?

References

Patrick, L. "Hepatitis C: Epidemiology and Review of Complementary/Alternative Medicine Treatments." Altern Med Rev 4 4 (1999): 220-238.

Talan, Jamie. "The ABC's of Hepatitis." Newsday 28 Jul 1998 6. Electric Library. 23 Aug 2000 <http://www.elibrary.com/>.

Hepatitis, Alcoholic
Other names / synonyms: Acute Alcoholic Liver Disease
571, 571.0, 571.1, 571.2, 571.3

Definition

Alcoholic hepatitis is a form of liver damage where the liver, which has been working to neutralize alcohol's toxic effects, becomes inflamed.

Over a period of years, about half of individuals considered heavy drinkers of alcohol develop some form of liver damage including alcoholic hepatitis.

Since not all heavy drinkers or alcoholics develop liver disease, some researchers believe other factors such as heredity and diet contribute to development of alcoholic hepatitis. Overuse of alcohol tends to be associated with poor eating habits and a lack of nutrients that otherwise help maintain health. The affected individual may fail to eat properly when calories from alcohol decrease the urge to consume regular (not snacks) foods.

Women who consume the same amount of alcohol as men considered excessive drinkers are at higher risk of developing liver disease, as they are less able to metabolize the substance. Even after choosing to abstain, women are more likely to experience progressive liver damage. About 10% of men and 3% of women worldwide may have alcohol addiction problems. It is estimated that about 3 of every 10,000 individuals have alcoholic hepatitis.

Diagnosis

History: Individuals may complain of flu-like symptoms such as fatigue, abdominal pain, low-grade fever, appetite loss, nausea and vomiting, and/or yellowing of the skin and whites of the eyes (jaundice). The individual may experience swollen ankles or abdomen. Individuals with severe alcoholic hepatitis may have high fever. As the disease progresses, individual may have difficulty concentrating, which indicates possible impending liver failure. When asked, most individuals report a history of excessive alcohol consumption.

Physical exam: Pressure applied to the area of the liver (palpation) may detect an enlarged liver (hepatomegaly) and spleen (splenomegaly) and/or abdominal tenderness. An enlarged abdomen may indicate fluid retention (ascites). The physical exam may also reveal an enlarged salivary gland below the ear (parotid gland), breast development in a male (gynecomastia), and decreased testicle size. Spider veins and yellowing (jaundice) of the skin or the white of the eye (sclera) may be observed.

Tests: Blood tests (serology) to detect abnormal liver function include measurements of key liver enzymes (GGT, AST, ALT) and blood components including bilirubin, red blood cells (hematocrit), and mean corpuscle volume. Imaging of the liver may be needed through tests including use of high power magnets and computers (MRI) or high frequency sound waves (ultrasonography). However, for a definitive diagnosis, a small piece of liver tissue removed through a needle (liver biopsy) and followed by microscopic examination needs to be performed.

Treatment

To stop further inflammation and allow the liver sufficient time to heal, individuals are instructed to stop drinking alcohol permanently. Individuals may also be asked to cease taking certain medications that may worsen the condition due to the liver's inability to metabolize and excrete certain compounds during the illness. Researchers are exploring new medications that show promise in helping inhibit damage created by alcohol.

In addition, nutritional advice and supplementation is provided. After initial onset of the illness, protein may be withdrawn from the diet because of the liver's inability to break down the substance. To prevent dehydration, the individual may need to be fed nutrients and fluids by vein (intravenous). In severe cases, anti-inflammatory drugs (corticosteroids) may be administered. Hospitalization may be required for treatment of side effects from alcohol withdrawal including tremors, hallucinations, or seizures (delirium tremens). Accompanying metabolic disorders or infections that may have developed with long-term alcohol addiction may also require treatment. The individual is referred to alcohol rehabilitation counseling and support groups. In extreme cases where damage has caused liver failure, an organ transplant may be considered for individuals abstaining from alcohol use.

Prognosis

Individuals who permanently abstain from alcohol use and who have mild or moderate disease usually recover completely. Recovery time, however, can take months. Alcohol is a factor in about half of all cases of liver disease requiring hospitalization. Approximately 40% of individuals with severe disease die within one month of hospitalization.

Individuals with less serious alcoholic hepatitis typically have a lower mortality rate in the range of 7-8%.

Qualified individuals who undergo liver transplants have about an 85% chance of surviving past one year and a 76% chance of surviving three years.

Differential Diagnosis

Conditions with similar symptoms may include biliary tract obstruction such as gallstones, idiopathic hemochromatosis, nonalcoholic steatohepatitis, viral hepatitis, primary biliary cirrhosis, hepatocellular carcinoma, infectious mononucleosis, and cytomegalovirus. Jaundice can result from non-alcohol-related causes of hepatitis such as prescription drugs or poisons.

Specialists

- Gastroenterologist

Work Restrictions / Accommodations

Individuals with mild or moderate forms of alcoholic hepatitis may require extended time off or temporary leave of absence during initial stages of recovery. Even after returning to work, the individual may be unable at first to perform tasks requiring physical endurance or stamina. Temporary assignment to less strenuous duties may be required until recovery is complete.

Complementary and Alternative Therapies

Content is intended for awareness only. Treatments may or may not be effective. Scientific evidence may be lacking and some substances have potentially toxic effects. Dr. Presley Reed and the editors do not endorse the use of these therapies in the absence of consultation with a licensed medical professional.

Antibiotic therapy - Eliminating certain bacteria in the intestinal tract may help reduce alcohol-caused liver damage.

Supplement Therapy- Vitamins A and E may help alleviate symptoms but should be taken only under consultation with a physician.

Comorbid Conditions

Heavy smoking combined with alcohol use significantly increases the chance of severe liver disease. Individuals with other forms of hepatitis will likely experience even greater liver damage.

Complications

Alcohol addiction combined with heavy smoking triples the possibility that liver scarring (cirrhosis) will develop. Autopsy studies reveal that from 10-15% of alcoholics have developed cirrhosis at the time of their deaths. Other complications associated with alcoholic hepatitis include bleeding, liver failure, brain injury (hepatic encephalopathy), inflammation of the pancreas (pancreatitis), liver scarring (cirrhosis), delirium tremens, fluid retention in the abdomen (ascites), blood coagulation disorders, high blood pressure within the liver (portal hypertension), coma, liver failure, and death. Long-term alcohol addiction can also cause numerous associated diseases such as infections and malnutrition.

If a new organ is needed, individuals with extreme liver damage who continue to consume alcohol are rejected as candidates for liver transplants.

Factors Influencing Duration

The main factor influencing length of disability is the individual's ability to cease alcohol consumption permanently in order to prevent or reverse liver damage. Severity of the disease upon initial diagnosis and presence of complications such as liver scarring (cirrhosis) also affect the individual's disability status.

Length of Disability

If liver damage is extensive, disability may be permanent.

Duration in Days

Job Classification	Minimum	Optimum	Maximum
Sedentary work	14	56	84
Light work	14	56	84
Medium work	28	84	112
Heavy work	56	112	168
Very Heavy work	56	112	168

Failure to Recover

If an individual fails to recover within the maximum duration expectancy period, the reader may wish to reference the following questions to assist in better understanding the specifics of an individual's medical case.

Regarding diagnosis:

- Does individual have history of excessive alcohol consumption?
- Does individual complain of flu-like symptoms such as fatigue, abdominal pain, low-grade fever, appetite loss, nausea and vomiting, and/or yellowing of the skin and whites of the eyes (jaundice)? Swollen ankles or abdomen? Is high fever present?
- When pressure is applied to the area of the liver (palpation), are an enlarged liver (hepatomegaly) and spleen (splenomegaly) and/or abdominal tenderness detected? Is the salivary gland below the ear (parotid gland) enlarged?
- Has breast development in a male (gynecomastia) occurred? Decrease in testicle size?
- Were spider veins and yellowing (jaundice) of the skin or the white of the eye (sclera) may be observed?
- Does individual have difficulty concentrating?
- Were blood tests (serology) performed such as measurements of key liver enzymes (GGT, AST, ALT) and blood components including bilirubin, red blood cells (hematocrit), and mean corpuscle volume for detection of abnormal liver function?
- Was imaging of the liver done using high power magnets and computers (MRI) or high frequency sound waves (ultrasonography)?
- Was a liver biopsy performed and followed by microscopic examination?

- Was diagnosis of alcoholic hepatitis confirmed? If diagnosis is uncertain, were conditions with similar symptoms ruled out?

Regarding treatment:

- Has individual abstained from alcohol use? Were referrals made for support group and counseling?
- Is individual enrolled in a comprehensive alcohol detoxification and rehabilitation program?
- Was nutritional supplementation effective in correcting malnutrition?
- Are underlying metabolic disorders and/or infections being effectively addressed?
- Since heavy smoking combined with alcohol use significantly increases the chance of severe liver disease, was individual instructed to stop smoking? Would individual benefit from enrollment in a community stop smoking program?

Regarding prognosis:

- Has individual continued to use alcohol even when liver damage was confirmed and referrals made for support groups and counseling? What can be done to enhance compliance?
- Does individual have a coexisting condition such as another form of hepatitis that may complicate treatment or impact recovery?
- Have any complications developed that may lengthen disability?

References

Maher, Jacquelyn J. "Exploring Alcohol's Effects on Liver Function." Alcohol Health and Research World 21 01 Jan 1997 5(7). Electric Library. 26 Dec 2000 <http://wwws.elibrary.com/ >.

Hepatitis, Chronic

Other names / synonyms: Chronic Active Hepatitis, Chronic Persistent Hepatitis

571.4

Definition

Chronic hepatitis is a broad term for various types of liver inflammation lasting a minimum of 6 months.

The condition may be caused by infection (hepatitis B, C, and D or other viruses), chronic exposure to toxins (alcohol, prescription drugs), or some birth defects related to inadequate metabolism (alpha-1-antitrypsin deficiency, Wilson's disease). Diseases linked to immune disorders such as systemic lupus erythematosus or rheumatoid arthritis may also cause chronic hepatitis.

There are two forms of chronic hepatitis. The milder of the two forms is called chronic persistent hepatitis and generally does not progress to liver scarring (cirrhosis) and/or possible failure. The cause of this form of the disease is often difficult to determine.

The most common form of the disease is called chronic active hepatitis and develops over a long period of time with great potential for progression to cirrhosis and liver failure.

At least 50% of chronic hepatitis cases are associated with hepatitis C viral infection. Twenty percent are due to hepatitis B infection with or without concurrent infection with the hepatitis D virus. In some cases, a reaction to a specific medication can also cause chronic hepatitis. Alcohol use is a factor in almost half of hospitalizations related to chronic hepatitis and in almost half of all fatal cases of chronic hepatitis.

Chronic active hepatitis occurs in all ages but women are more likely to experience liver damage than men. Hepatitis C, which is chronic in about 85% of cases, is found in 2% of the US population and 3% of the world population. About 5% of individuals worldwide are considered chronic carriers of the hepatitis B virus.

Diagnosis

History: Individuals with chronic persistent hepatitis often report milder symptoms such as fatigue, loss of appetite, and nausea or vomiting. Individuals in the early stages of active or chronic persistent hepatitis may complain of these and other symptoms such as a general sensation of poor health (malaise), joint pain, headache, absence of menstrual periods (amenorrhea), chest pain, and abdominal tenderness. More severe symptoms of chronic active hepatitis may include fever and yellowing of the skin and whites of the eyes (jaundice).

Physical exam: Examination may reveal abdominal tenderness, dry eyes and mouth, skin rash, persistent or recurring yellowing (jaundice) of the skin and whites of the eye (sclera), enlarged liver (hepatomegaly), enlarged spleen (splenomegaly), painful joints, and an enlarged thyroid gland (goiter). Young women with chronic active hepatitis may have acne and increased hair growth in a pattern similar to men (hirsutism). Progressive liver disease may be indicated by visible branching capillaries on the skin (spider nevi) and redness of the palms of the hand (palmar erythema).

Tests: Blood tests (serology) may be performed including the measurement of key liver enzymes (GGT, AST, ALT) and blood components including bilirubin, red blood cells (hematocrit), mean corpuscle volume, and viral antibodies. Imaging tests using high power magnets and computers (MRI) and high frequency sound waves (ultrasonography) may aid in the diagnosis. Removal of liver tissue with a needle (liver biopsy) for microscopic examination may also be needed.

Treatment

Chronic persistent hepatitis may initially be diagnosed as acute viral hepatitis with no treatment except bed rest generally required. Should liver enzymes remain elevated and symptoms unresponsive to rest, a diagnosis of chronic persistent hepatitis may be made. Since this condition tends to resolve on its own and symptoms are mild, no treatment other than rest is usually recommended.

Treatment for chronic active hepatitis consists of general supportive care, hospitalization, and, in some cases, administration of anti-inflammatory drugs such as corticosteroids or interferons. Nutritional supplementation is provided during first onset (acute) phase of the illness to prevent dehydration and because the liver is unable to break down proteins.

For those cases of chronic active hepatitis not caused by infection, corticosteroid therapy is generally the treatment of choice. Drugs may be required for up to a year following the disappearance of symptoms. In some severe cases when the individual fails to respond to treatment, a liver transplant may be considered.

Complementary and Alternative Therapies

Content is intended for awareness only. Treatments may or may not be effective. Scientific evidence may be lacking and some substances have potentially toxic effects. Dr. Presley Reed and the editors do not endorse the use of these therapies in the absence of consultation with a licensed medical professional.

Supplement Therapy - Vitamins A and E may help alleviate symptoms but should be undertaken only under consultation with a physician. Vitamin E is thought to help improve the liver's function as a detoxifier.

Antibiotic therapy - Eliminating certain bacteria in the intestinal tract may help reduce alcohol-caused liver damage.

Prognosis

The outcome is highly variable. Chronic persistent hepatitis generally has a favorable outcome since cirrhosis and liver failure are unlikely to occur.

However, in chronic active hepatitis, the disease may disappear completely or may progress to cirrhosis. The outcome is highly dependent on the cause. Overall, if the condition remains untreated, 50-75% of individuals with chronic active hepatitis die within the first few years. Approximately 60-80% of individuals recover completely with corticosteroid and other treatment. However, other individuals appear to recover with treatment and then suffer relapses.

As many as 50% of individuals with chronic hepatitis B and cirrhosis die within the first five years following symptom onset. Chronic hepatitis C is most often a long, slow disease that, after years of few or no symptoms or laboratory abnormalities, may develop into cirrhosis or liver cancer. Hepatitis D may be associated with an increased incidence of liver failure. About half of individuals with chronic hepatitis related to immune disorders are likely to experience relapse following treatment. Individuals who undergo liver transplants have about an 85% chance of surviving past one year and a 76% chance of surviving three years.

Differential Diagnosis

Other differential diagnoses include acute infectious hepatitis, rheumatoid arthritis, systemic lupus erythematosus, and cryptogenic cirrhosis. Other conditions with similar symptoms are biliary tract obstruction such as gallstones, primary biliary cirrhosis, hepatocellular carcinoma, infectious mononucleosis, and cytomegalovirus. Jaundice can result from non-alcohol related causes of hepatitis such as prescription drugs or poisons.

Specialists

- Critical Care Specialist
- Gastroenterologist
- Neurologist

Work Restrictions / Accommodations

Work restrictions are highly dependent on the cause and severity of chronic hepatitis as well as effectiveness of treatment. Hospitalization may be needed. Individuals may need extended time off or a leave of absence from work for complete recovery that could take months. If liver damage is severe, permanent disability may result.

Comorbid Conditions

Excessive alcohol consumption can cause chronic hepatitis and worsen the prognosis for viral forms of the disease. Heavy smoking can also greatly increase the risk of liver damage in association with alcohol use. Individuals with blood clotting disorders (hemophilia) or liver transplants have greater difficulty recovering from chronic hepatitis.

Complications

Complications associated with chronic hepatitis include bleeding, liver failure, brain injury (hepatic encephalopathy), inflammation of the pancreas (pancreatitis), liver scarring (cirrhosis), liver cancer (hepatocellular carcinoma), delirium tremens associated with alcohol use, blocked bile ducts from scarring (primary sclerosing cholangitis), damage to bile ducts from inflammation (primary biliary cirrhosis), and fluid retention in the abdomen (ascites). Inflammation and pain in the joints (arthritis) may occur along with itchy skin eruptions. Inflammation of the arteries in widespread areas (polyarteritis nodosa) has been observed. Inflammation of small structures in the kidney (membranous glomerulonephritis) can develop. Inflammation may also affect heart muscles or tissue (myocarditis). Individuals older than 40 and drug addicts are more likely to develop a worsening of the disease (subacute hepatic necrosis). Older individuals may also develop muscle pain similar to rheumatism (polymyalgia rheumatica). Other complications associated with development of chronic hepatitis C in particular may include thyroiditis, vasculitis, and various immune disorders. Other complications are anorexia, arthralgia, glomerulonephritis, skin rashes, and amenorrhea.

Factors Influencing Duration

Factors that may influence the length of disability include underlying cause of the liver inflammation and presence of liver scarring (cirrhosis). Type of treatment provided and individual's response influence recovery time. Individual's age and general health at the time of initial diagnosis can also influence possible development of complications such as bleeding or infection.

Length of Disability

Disability may be permanent depending upon extent of liver damage and job demands.

Failure to Recover

If an individual fails to recover within the maximum duration expectancy period, the reader may wish to reference the following questions to assist in better understanding the specifics of an individual's medical case.

Regarding diagnosis:

- Does individual have any past history of congenital biliary abnormalities or exposure to viral hepatitis or hepatic toxins?
- Does individual report fatigue, loss of appetite, and nausea or vomiting? Does individual have a general sensation of poor health (malaise), joint pain, headache, absence of menstrual periods (amenorrhea), chest pain, and abdominal tenderness? Fever and yellowing of the skin and whites of the eyes (jaundice)?
- Does exam reveal abdominal tenderness, dry eyes and mouth, skin rash, persistent or recurring yellowing (jaundice) of the skin and whites of the eye (sclera), enlarged liver (hepatomegaly), enlarged spleen (splenomegaly), painful joints, and an enlarged thyroid gland (goiter)?
- If a young woman, does individual have acne and increased hair growth in a pattern similar to a man (hirsutism)?
- Are visible branching capillaries on the skin (spider nevi) and redness of the palms of the hand (palmar erythema) present?
- Was the diagnosis confirmed with liver enzyme and viral antibody tests?
- If the diagnosis was uncertain, were additional tests done to rule out the possibility of other conditions with similar symptoms?

Regarding treatment:

- Was treatment appropriate for the type and severity of the hepatitis?
- Did treatment include physical rest, good nutrition or nutritional support, and avoidance of any medications or toxins metabolized by the liver (e.g., alcohol, Tylenol)?
- Was individual compliant with treatment recommendations? If not, would counsel or support groups be beneficial?
- For advanced stages of chronic active hepatitis, did aggressive treatment include administration of corticosteroids or interferon?
- If facing liver failure, is individual a candidate for liver transplant?

Regarding prognosis:

- If diagnosis is chronic persistent hepatitis, what is expected outcome?
- In chronic active hepatitis, has the disease progressed to cirrhosis?
- Does individual have a coexisting condition such as substance abuse, alcohol use, immune suppression, cancer, or clotting abnormalities that may complicate treatment or impact recovery?
- Have any complications developed that may impact recovery?
- Did individual require liver transplantation? If so, has adequate time elapsed for complete recovery?

References

Goldman, Lee, and J. Claude Bennett. Cecil Textbook of Medicine, 21st ed. Philadelphia: W.B. Saunders Company, 2000.

Keeffe, Emmet B. "Chronic Hepatitis." Dale, D.C., and Daniel D. Federman, MD, eds. New York: WebMD Corporation, 2000 Scientific American Medicine. 26 Dec 2000 <http://www.samed.com/sam/forms/index.htm>.

Hepatitis, Viral

Other names / synonyms: Fulminant Hepatitis, Viral Hepatitis
070, 070.9

Definition

Viral hepatitis is a disease that causes liver inflammation and is found in various forms. The main varieties of viral hepatitis track the alphabet under the names of A, B, C, D, and E. The first 3 types are the most common, while the last 2 have been identified only in recent years. Newer forms of the disease often are designated as non-A-E hepatitis, including a recently discovered group of G and GB viruses, and a very isolated form of F identified in France.

Individuals with weakened immune systems particularly are susceptible to other sources of viral hepatitis such as infectious mononucleosis (linked to the Epstein-Barr virus), yellow fever, and a form of herpes virus known as cytomegalovirus. Symptoms of infection such as yellow skin and eyes (jaundice) are similar for the different viruses. But each form has distinct routes of infection along with varying complications and prognosis. The main diagnostic categories are hepatitis A, B, or C.

Viral hepatitis may spread through sexual contact or ingestion of contaminated food or water. Contaminated blood supplies used in transfusions sometimes spread infections, although recent blood bank screening processes have decreased the risk considerably. Healthcare workers are considered a high risk group because of the possibility of infection from accidental needle pricks. More than 1 type of hepatitis virus sometimes is involved in an infection.

In the US, viral hepatitis commonly is found on Native American reservations or in Alaskan villages. Travelers to international destinations, particularly in developing countries, are at higher risk of exposure. As many as 40% of US adults are thought to have had some form of hepatitis A, which many times has no symptoms. In cases with symptoms obvious enough to be reported, the prevalence of hepatitis A is about 1 in 10,000 people. In undeveloped countries, almost all adults are thought to have been exposed to the disease. About 10 million cases of hepatitis A occur annually worldwide. The hepatitis B virus, which typically is ongoing (chronic), infects about 350 million people worldwide. About 5% of all US citizens have hepatitis B, while about 2%

have hepatitis C. About 3% of the world's population is thought to have hepatitis C, which also often is chronic. Reporting is sporadic for D, E, F and G types of viral hepatitis, which tend to be rare, especially within the US.

Diagnosis

History: Nausea, diarrhea, appetite loss, fatigue, and yellow skin and eyes (jaundice) often are reported as early symptoms of various forms of viral hepatitis. General itching and lightening of stools may also be reported. The individual could have just returned from travel to an undeveloped area, where substandard sanitation practices may increase the risk of developing hepatitis A. In the case of hepatitis B, individuals may also complain of bad breath and a bitter taste in the mouth.

Later symptoms related to various forms of hepatitis may include headache, fever, influenza-like symptoms, muscle pain (arthralgia), or rash. Symptoms may last only a few weeks or linger for months. Symptoms accompanying hepatitis B or C may be ongoing (chronic). Occasionally, individuals with viral hepatitis such as B or D report that the disease appears to have ended, only to be followed by repeated relapses of symptoms.

Physical exam: The exam may reveal jaundice and dark urine. Enlargement of the liver (hepatomegaly) and spleen (splenomegaly) may be detected. Progressive liver disease may be indicated by visible branching capillaries on the skin (spider nevi), redness of the palms of the hand (palmar erythema), and a liver that is firm on examination (palpable). A severe form of hepatitis (fulminant) is indicated when the individual displays abnormal behavior, drowsiness, confusion, sleepiness, and possibly coma.

Tests: Various blood tests (serology) will help determine liver function and possibly lead to identification of the form of hepatitis causing the infection. Analysis of serum albumin or blood platelet count may help identify progressive liver disease. A small piece of the liver may be removed for microscopic examination (liver biopsy). Liver biopsies sometimes are recommended for all cases involving hepatitis C to rule out liver damage.

Treatment

Prevention is the best treatment for viral hepatitis. Vaccines are available for hepatitis types A and B, including a combined vaccine. Usually, three injections over a period of 6 months are required to give optimal protection. However, even one vaccination, even on the way to the airport, is better than none. Vaccination is recommended for people at high-risk such as healthcare workers, individuals undergoing kidney dialysis, individuals who practice promiscuous sexual activity, and individuals traveling to areas where hepatitis infection rates are high. More widespread vaccination programs also are underway in efforts to eradicate the B form of hepatitis. Sterile or disposable needles should be used for acupuncture, ear piercing, or tattooing. Preventive treatment such as an immune globulin injection may be recommended for household members or sexual partners of an infected individual.

After hepatitis has been diagnosed, consumption of alcoholic beverages should be avoided. Ample rest and fluids are recommended. Meals should be limited in caloric intake to minimize nausea and help overcome loss of appetite. In severe cases, intravenous feeding may be required. Liver transplantation may be performed in some cases of fulminant hepatitis.

Drugs with antiviral properties (interferons) sometimes are injected to help stimulate immune responses in individuals with hepatitis B or C. Drugs now used experimentally help suppress the immune system (corticosteroids), and may also be included as part of the therapy to improve the effectiveness of interferons.

Prognosis

Symptoms of short-term (acute) viral hepatitis often resolve in 2-8 weeks. Damage to the liver may heal within 3-6 months after the cessation of active viral infection. No long-term effects are expected from uncomplicated acute viral hepatitis.

The disease tends to be more severe and is more likely to become chronic in individuals who are older, pregnant, or immunodeficient. Liver cancer may occur as a result of hepatitis B and C infections. The average survival rate for those diagnosed with liver cancer is 1 year.

Fulminant hepatitis also may result in death, unless liver transplantation is performed quickly. The long-term impact of the transplantation will depend upon the individual's health. Older individuals and those suffering from immunodeficiencies may have greater difficulty recovering from transplant surgery. About 70% of transplanted livers continue to function at least 3 years after surgery, while about 76% of individuals survive at least 3 years after transplant surgery even if the organ fails.

Type E hepatitis causes death in almost 20% of cases involving pregnant women.

Differential Diagnosis

Other viral sources of hepatitis are infectious mononucleosis, yellow fever, Q Fever, and cytomegalovirus. Jaundice often is associated with noninfectious causes of hepatitis, including prescription drugs, poisons, alcohol, or gallstones.

Specialists

- Gastroenterologist
- Hepatologist
- Infectious Disease Physician

Work Restrictions / Accommodations

Persons with more severe disease or who are expected to perform strenuous activities will require extended periods of partial disability. If fulminant hepatitis develops, a longer recovery time will be needed, especially if surgery is required. Some individuals who appear to have recovered may have relapses, requiring additional time off from work.

If the Hepatitis A affected individual works in a food-handling job, some states/countries may require their exclusion from food contact until fully recovered. Theoretically, adequate hygiene including meticulous hand washing and wearing of gloves and facial masks should allow even infected workers to work safely.

Comorbid Conditions

Alcoholism may complicate and lengthen symptoms. Individuals with weakened immune systems are particularly susceptible to other sources of viral hepatitis, such as infectious mononucleosis (linked to the Epstein-Barr virus), yellow fever, and cytomegalovirus.

Complications

The type of virus influences the severity of acute viral hepatitis, which may persist and turn into an ongoing (chronic) form. Other complications have been found to be associated with hepatitis C including thyroiditis, vasculitis, and various immune disorders. When viral hepatitis progresses rapidly with increasingly severe symptoms, it is considered to be in a fulminant form. Simultaneous infection with multiple types of hepatitis viruses may complicate the condition and contribute to the development of more serious symptoms.

Infection with hepatitis B may lead to inflammation and joint pain (arthritis) and skin eruptions, widespread inflammation of arteries (polyarteritis nodosa), inflammation of small structures in the kidney (membranous glomerulonephritis), and nerve paralysis (Guillain-Barré syndrome). Inflammation associated with hepatitis B complications may also affect heart muscles or tissue (myocarditis). Persons older than 40 years of age and drug addicts are more likely to develop a worsening of the disease (subacute hepatic necrosis). Older individuals also may develop muscle pain similar to rheumatism (polymyalgia rheumatica).

Factors Influencing Duration

The length of disability will be influenced by the type of hepatitis virus causing the infection, the individual's age, other medical conditions affecting immunity, complications, and the need for surgical intervention. Any of these factors may extend the expected period of disability for acute viral hepatitis. If surgery is required, overall disability may last several months. Chronic forms of hepatitis could result in permanent disability.

Length of Disability

Duration depends on type, see specific diagnosis for duration information. Disability may be permanent for individuals with chronic forms of hepatitis.

Failure to Recover

If an individual fails to recover within the maximum duration expectancy period, the reader may wish to reference the following questions to assist in better understanding the specifics of an individual's medical case.

Regarding diagnosis:

- Has diagnosis of viral hepatitis been confirmed?
- Has the individual experienced any complications?
- Does individual have an underlying condition that may impact recovery?
- Does the individual live on an Indian reservation or work on a reservation?
- Has the individual traveled recently? Internationally? To a developing country?

Regarding treatment:

- Has individual complied with prescribed treatment regarding rest, fluids, limited calorie intake, and abstaining from alcohol?
- Has the individual received appropriate tests to identify the form of viral hepatitis to ascertain proper treatment?
- If the individual has severe symptoms, has a liver transplant been considered as an option?

Regarding prognosis:

- Does the individual have a weakened immune system?
- Is the individual an alcoholic?
- Is extended disability related to factors such as age, pregnancy, or immunodeficiency?
- Has the individual been diagnosed with liver cancer?

References

Viral Hepatitis: An Epidemic in the Making?. American Digestive Health Foundation (ADHF). 17 Aug 2000. 1 Jan 2001 <http://www.gastro.org/adhf/viral-hep.html>.

DerMarderosian, Ara, PhD, ed. The Review of Natural Products. St. Louis: Facts and Comparisons, 2000.

Hernia Repair

Other names / synonyms: Herniorrhaphy

53.0, 53.1, 53.2, 53.3, 53.4, 53.5, 53.7

Definition

A hernia is a defect in a muscular wall that allows a portion of the intestine or other organ or piece of tissue to protrude through the weakened area. A hernia repair is a surgical procedure in which the protruding organ or tissue is positioned back into its appropriate body cavity and the weakened muscular wall is repaired so that the hernia will not recur.

The most common hernia sites are the groin (inguinal) area or around the umbilical area. Hernias can also form around the esophagus (hiatal hernia) or at the site of a previous incision (incisional hernia). There are numerous causes of hernias, including upright stance (which creates stretching of the muscular wall), muscular deficiency, connective tissue destruction, smoking, aging, increased abdominal pressure, peritoneal dialysis (individuals with end-stage renal disease who receive dialysis through an opening in the peritoneum), and obesity.

Some hernias can become strangulated; that is, the blood supply becomes compromised. When this happens, the individual usually experiences pain and tenderness. Symptoms of a hernia include a lump or swelling in the location of the hernia, pain upon standing, and/or colicky abdominal pain. To diagnose a hernia, the mass should be able to be pushed back into the body cavity with gentle pressure (reducible). If the mass is not reducible, then a hernia can be diagnosed by using an ultrasound test (using sound waves to detect abnormalities within the body), or herniography (injecting dye into the peritoneal cavity, which will outline the site in question).

Hernias tend to be more frequent in males than in females; inguinal hernias occur in about 2% of males.

Reason for Procedure

Hernia repairs are done in order to relieve symptoms of pain or tenderness and to prevent or resolve complications, such as incarcerated or strangulated hernias. An incarcerated hernia is one in which the intestine becomes trapped in the opening in the muscle wall. A strangulated hernia is one in which the intestinal blood supply is impaired, due to the hernia. Both incarcerated and strangulated hernia repairs are considered urgent because of the possible complications of intestinal blockage or infection.

Description

Inguinal hernias may be repaired using a traditional surgical approach or a laparoscopic approach. If there are bilateral inguinal hernias, either one or both can be done at the same time. If both are done, general anesthesia is usually required. If only one at a time is done (staged procedure), local anesthesia may be used. An incision is made over the area of the hernia and the bulging tissue or organ is replaced inside the muscle wall or body cavity. The muscle tissue is then repaired with sutures or sometimes with an artificial material, such as a specialized type of mesh, which reinforces the muscle wall. Lastly, the skin is closed with sutures or staples.

There are several common approaches for laparoscopic inguinal hernia repair, including those in which the incision is placed through the abdominal muscle wall (transabdominal), through the inguinal area (anterior inguinal), outside of the peritoneum (extraperitoneal, the peritoneum being the membrane that lines the abdominal and pelvic areas), or anterior to the peritoneum (preperitoneal). The approach used depends upon a variety of factors, including surgeon's preference, instrumentation, obesity, and comorbidity.

Prognosis

Surgical treatment of uncomplicated hernias usually results in complete recovery, after a period of up to 6 weeks recovery. Inguinal hernias repaired without mesh may have up to a 20% recurrence, while those made with mesh have only a 5% recurrence rate.

Specialists

- General Surgeon
- Urologist

Work Restrictions / Accommodations

Upon return to work, individuals should not lift anything heavy for 6-8 weeks after surgery. Standing and walking can be done to comfort level. Sanctions against heavy lifting usually include other types of strain, such has pushing heavy items, since this also puts a strain on the healing muscle layers of the abdomen or inguinal area.

Comorbid Conditions

The presence of a testicular problem, such as a twisted testicle (testicular torsion), scrotal disorders, such as a collection of fluid within the scrotum (hydrocele), or obesity may lengthen disability.

Procedure Complications

Surgical complications may include allergic or abnormal reactions to anesthesia, excessive bleeding, urinary retention, surgical-wound infection, damage to the testicle's blood supply or nerve supply, or recurrent hernia.

Factors Influencing Duration

The location of the hernia, the surgical approach and the presence of any complications, such as a strangulated hernia, may influence the length of disability.

Length of Disability

For incisional, duration depends on size.

Hiatal or diaphragmatic.

Duration in Days

Job Classification	Minimum	Optimum	Maximum
Sedentary work	14	21	28
Light work	14	21	28
Medium work	21	28	42
Heavy work	28	42	56
Very Heavy work	28	56	70

Inguinal or femoral hernia. Conventional method.

Duration in Days

Job Classification	Minimum	Optimum	Maximum
Sedentary work	7	10	21
Light work	7	10	21
Medium work	14	28	42
Heavy work	35	42	56
Very Heavy work	42	56	70

Incisional or ventral.

Duration in Days

Job Classification	Minimum	Optimum	Maximum
Sedentary work	7	14	21
Light work	14	21	28
Medium work	21	28	42
Heavy work	42	49	56
Very Heavy work	49	56	63

Umbilical.

Duration in Days

Job Classification	Minimum	Optimum	Maximum
Sedentary work	7	14	28
Light work	7	14	28
Medium work	14	21	42
Heavy work	21	28	42
Very Heavy work	21	42	56

Inguinal or femoral hernia. Canadian/Shouldice method.

Duration in Days

Job Classification	Minimum	Optimum	Maximum
Sedentary work	2	4	7
Light work	7	9	14
Medium work	14	21	28
Heavy work	35	42	49
Very Heavy work	42	49	56

Duration Trend from Normative Data*

Cases	Mean	Min	Max	No Lost Time	Over 6 Months
992	28	2	340	0%	0.10%

Percentile:	5th	25th	Median	75th	95th
Days:	9	13	20	32	81

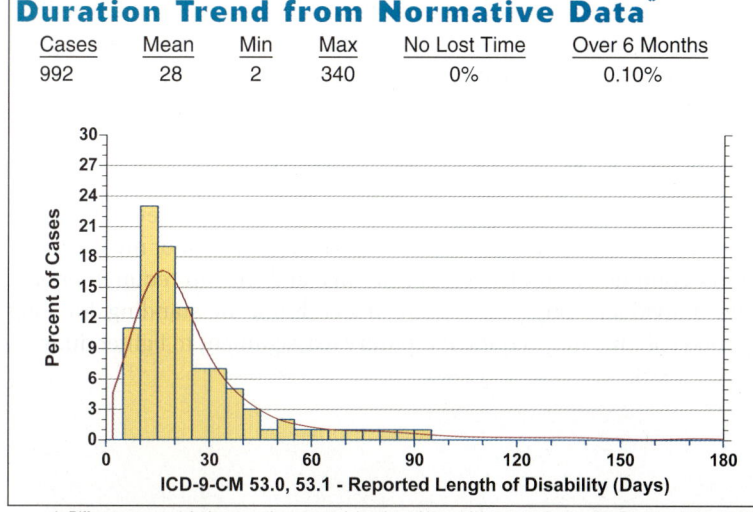

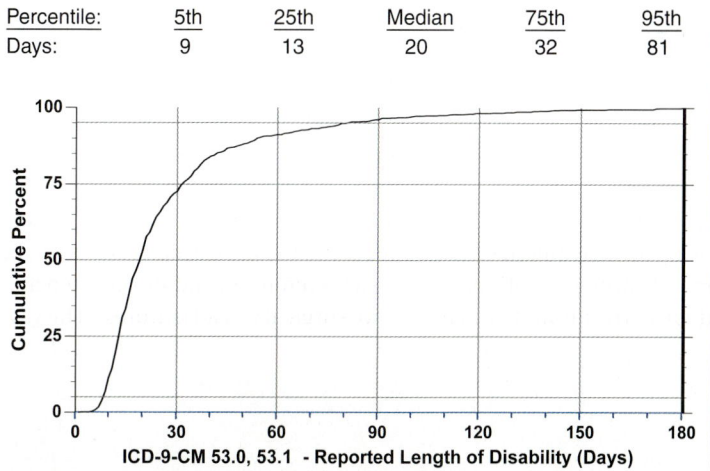

ICD-9-CM 53.0, 53.1 - Reported Length of Disability (Days)

* Differences may exist between the expected duration tables and the normative graphs. Duration tables provide expected recovery periods based on the type of work performed by the individual. The normative graphs reflect the actual observed experience of many individuals across the spectrum of physical conditions, in a variety of industries, and with varying levels of case management.

Hernia Repair 1095

References

Hernia Repair. WebMD.com. 1999. 18 Jan 2001 <http://my.webmd.com/content/asset/adam_surgery_herniorrhaphy >.

Soares, Robert L., and Joseph F. Amaral. "Laparoscopic Inguinal Hernia Repair." Current Review of Minimally Invasive Surgery. Brooks, David C., ed. New York: Springer-Verlag, 1998. 77-86.

Hernia Repair, Vaginal
Other names / synonyms: Cystocele Repair, Rectocele Repair, Transvaginal Enterocele Repair
70.5, 70.51, 70.52, 70.71, 70.8

Definition

A vaginal hernia repair is a surgical procedure used to correct the presence of a protrusion (herniation) of the bladder into the vaginal area (cystocele) or a part of the intestine or intestinal wall into the vaginal area (enterocele).

Cystoceles and enteroceles are types of hernias since they are the result of body tissue that has herniated into other areas.

Cystocele and enterocele occur when the muscles surrounding the vaginal area (pelvic floor muscles) become weak. This muscle weakness may occur at birth (congenital defect), or after pregnancy or removal of the uterus (hysterectomy), or in conditions, such as obesity, that cause chronic increased intra-abdominal pressure. The protrusion of the bladder may include just a small part of the bladder wall or all of the bladder and the tube leading from the bladder to the outside of the body (urethra). An enterocele may occur after previous vaginal surgery in 3-17% of cases. Cystocele and enterocele repairs may be done separately or at the same time, depending upon whether they occur separately or together.

Reason for Procedure

Cystocele repair is indicated if there is the inability to stop the flow of urine (urinary incontinence), obstruction of the urinary tract or urethra because of the severity of the cystocele, difficulty emptying the bladder, or if the cystocele exists at the entrance of the vagina. Enterocele repair is indicated if there is discomfort related to the enterocele at the entrance of the vagina, urinary incontinence, difficulty emptying the bladder, or constipation. If repair of either type of herniation is delayed, painful vaginal wall ulceration may occur.

Description

Vaginal hernia repair can be done on an inpatient or outpatient basis.

The woman receives either a general or epidural anesthesia and is placed on her back with her buttocks on the edge of the surgical table and her legs elevated and positioned in a support device that includes stirrups for the feet (dorsal lithotomy position). The vagina is opened, using an instrument called a speculum, the prolapsed tissue is put back into its proper position, extra tissue is removed, and the affected area is then sewn (sutured) into place with surgical thread (sutures). The vagina may be packed with antibiotic soaked material for about a day. Oral or intravenous antibiotics may be administered. The individual may have a rubber tube placed into the bladder for a few days if she is unable to empty her bladder after the procedure.

Prognosis

Success rates and relief of symptoms for cystocele repair vary from 70-96%, depending on the severity of the prolapsed/herniated bladder. Enterocele repair yields a good outcome with relief of symptoms in 86-96% of cases.

Specialists

- Gynecologist

Work Restrictions / Accommodations

Lifting and strenuous activity or excessive standing may need to be restricted for a period of several weeks. Driving a motor vehicle may be restricted for up to 2 weeks after surgery. Avoidance of sexual activity is required for several weeks.

Comorbid Conditions

The presence of severe obesity or other vaginal conditions such as uterine prolapse may lengthen recovery time.

Procedure Complications

Possible complications may include allergic or abnormal reactions to anesthesia, continuing difficulty emptying the bladder, or recurrence of symptoms of urinary incontinence. Persistent pain, infection, bleeding, scarring of the vaginal wall, an abnormal opening between the vaginal wall and other areas (fistula), or painful urination are other risks of surgery.

Factors Influencing Duration

Factors influencing length of disability include the severity of the cystocele or enterocele, presence of coexisting pelvic floor muscle relaxation conditions, surgical complications, and the job requirements of the individual. Jobs that require heavy lifting or standing for long periods of time may require temporary reassignment to lighter duties.

Length of Disability

Uncomplicated vaginal hernia repair is not associated with any permanent disability after the recovery period of 4 to 6 weeks.

Duration in Days

Job Classification	Minimum	Optimum	Maximum
Sedentary work	28	42	56
Light work	28	42	56
Medium work	42	42	56
Heavy work	42	56	70
Very Heavy work	42	56	70

References

Nitti, Victor W. "Transvaginal Enterocele Repair." Glenn's Urologic Surgery, 5th ed. Graham, Sam D. Jr, ed. Philadelphia: Lippincott-Raven Publishers, 1998. 373-381.

Rovner, Eric S., David A. Ginsberg, and Shlomo Raz. "Cystocele." Glenn's Urologic Surgery, 5th ed. Graham, Sam D. Jr., eds. Philadelphia: Lippincott-Raven Publishers, 1998. 361-369.

Hernia, Hiatal

Other names / synonyms: Diaphragmatic Hernia, Hiatus Hernia, Mixed Hernia, Paraesophageal Hernia, Sliding Hernia, Type I Hernia, Type II Hernia, Type III Hernia, Type IV Hernia

551.3, 552.3, 553.3, 553.8, 553.9

Definition

A hiatal hernia occurs when the stomach protrudes (herniates) into the chest cavity through the opening in the diaphragm (hiatus) through which the esophagus passes.

Generally, there are 2 types of hiatal hernias: type I (sliding or diaphragmatic) and type II (rolling or paraesophageal) hernias. Sliding hiatal hernia occurs when the junction of the esophagus and stomach (gastroesophageal junction) that is normally situated below the diaphragm slides into the chest cavity. Rolling hiatal hernia occurs when the esophageal junction remains below the diaphragm and a portion of the stomach herniates through the esophageal hiatus into the chest cavity. Occasionally, an individual may present with a type III (mixed) hiatal hernia, which occurs when almost all of the stomach herniates into the chest cavity. In this case, the gastroesophageal junction may lie either above or below the diaphragm. A small portion of the gut (small bowel or colon) may protrude through the diaphragm along with the stomach and, in this case, the hernia is referred to as a type IV hernia.

Risk factors for developing hiatal hernia include any action that increases pressure in the abdominal cavity such as coughing, vomiting, straining during bowel movements, sudden exertion, pregnancy, or obesity.

Hiatal hernia may occur in as much as 4-7% of the general population who have no other pathological symptoms. Over half of the individuals who develop hiatal hernia will remain symptom-free. Eighty percent of hiatal hernias are sliding, 15% are rolling, and 5% are mixed. Type IV hernias are very rare. Sixty percent of individuals with hiatal hernia are between 40 and 70 years of age, and the incidence increases in the elderly. Women develop rolling hiatal hernias more often than do men at a ratio of three to one. Men and women develop sliding hernias at an equal rate.

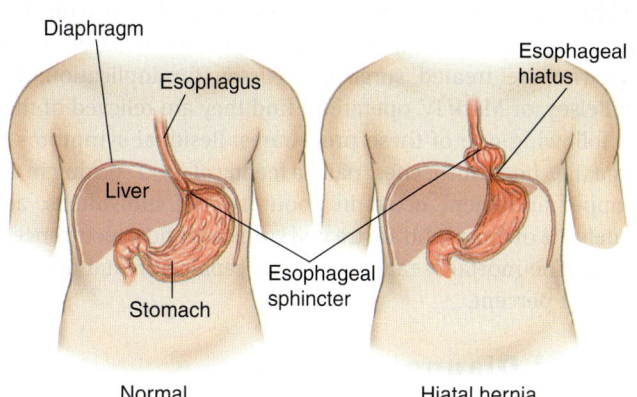

Diagnosis

History: Individuals may report heartburn or chest pain that is more pronounced when they are lying flat. Heartburn may sometimes wake the individual at night or it may be more noticeable in the morning. Heartburn is often reported 30-60 minutes after eating or drinking. The individual may report the sensation that food is sticking in the chest or upper abdomen, and they may complain of food or stomach acid regurgitation into the mouth.

Physical exam: The exam is not helpful for this diagnosis.

Tests: The esophagus and stomach can be visualized using x-rays after swallowing a radiopaque dye (barium swallow). A flexible fiber-optic microscope can be inserted into the esophagus (esophagoscopy) for further visualization and diagnosis. A tissue sample (biopsy) of the esophagus may be taken during esophagoscopy for microscopic analysis. Another test may include a study to determine if the esophagus and stomach are contracting properly during swallowing and digestion (motility study). A complete blood count (CBC) should be done to determine if the individual has low hemoglobin in the blood stream (anemia). Other tests may include measurement of pressure in the esophagus (esophageal manometry), measurement of stomach acid production (pH telemetry), determination of how well the esophagus is functioning (esophageal clearance studies), and an assessment of the heart (electrocardiogram, or ECG).

Treatment

Initial treatment includes administration of antacids and drugs (histamine receptor blocker, proton pump inhibitor) that decrease stomach acid secretion. Elevation of the head of the bed; avoidance of large late evening meals; avoidance of highly seasoned foods, citrus juices, and alcohol; wearing loose-fitting clothing; and eating small, frequent, bland meals may also be of benefit. Surgery (Nissen fundoplication; Hill operation; Belsey, or Mark IV, operation) to narrow the esophageal hiatus and restore the hernia below the diaphragm may be necessary in those individuals with sliding hernia who do not respond to drug treatments and other modifications. It is recommended that all individuals with rolling hernia undergo surgical repair using the same surgical techniques that are used to treat sliding hernia. Again, surgery will serve to narrow the esophageal hiatus and return the stomach to its normal location in the abdominal cavity.

Prognosis

Most individuals with sliding hernia can expect relief of their symptoms by antacid, drug, and/or other treatment modifications. Over 90% of individuals who are treated surgically (Nissen fundoplication; Hill operation; Belsey, or Mark IV, operation) find they are relieved of their symptoms following one of these procedures. Residual symptoms of hiatal hernia (i.e., heartburn, chest pain, a feeling of food sticking in the chest or upper abdomen) occur in about 10% of individuals, and approximately 7% of those who are treated surgically show recurrence of the condition. The mortality rate for surgical repair of hiatal hernia is approximately 1 percent.

Differential Diagnosis

Conditions that present with symptoms similar to hiatal hernia include ischemic heart disease, dyspepsia, biliary colic, stomach cancer, and peptic ulcer disease.

Specialists

- Gastroenterologist
- General Surgeon

Work Restrictions / Accommodations

Restrictions on lifting, climbing, and strenuous physical activity should be expected following surgical repair of hiatal hernia. Recurrence of hiatal hernia is not uncommon (approximately 7% of the time following surgical treatment), and permanent work restrictions and accommodations may include avoidance of bending, lifting, and abdominal straining. Also, the individual should not be subjected to any sort of abdominal constriction and loose, non-constrictive clothing should be worn. The individual will benefit if they are able to eat small, frequent meals (rather than a single, large meal) while at work. The individual should be able to eat meals in the sitting position.

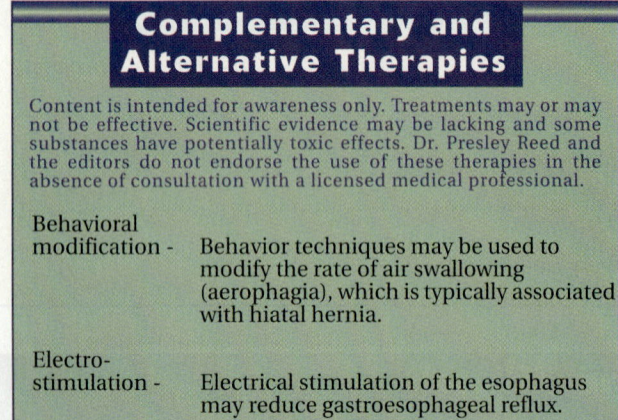

Complementary and Alternative Therapies

Content is intended for awareness only. Treatments may or may not be effective. Scientific evidence may be lacking and some substances have potentially toxic effects. Dr. Presley Reed and the editors do not endorse the use of these therapies in the absence of consultation with a licensed medical professional.

Behavioral modification - Behavior techniques may be used to modify the rate of air swallowing (aerophagia), which is typically associated with hiatal hernia.

Electro-stimulation - Electrical stimulation of the esophagus may reduce gastroesophageal reflux.

Comorbid Conditions

Inflammation of the esophagus (esophagitis) may impact an individual's ability to recover, and further lengthen the disability. Obesity may also have an effect as overweight individuals tend to heal more slowly and progress toward recovery at a slower rate. Any condition that increases pressure in the abdominal cavity such as coughing, vomiting, straining during bowel movements, or pregnancy may impact an individual's ability to recover.

Complications

Possible complications of hiatal hernia may include reflux of stomach acid into the esophagus (esophageal reflux), which can cause the esophagus to bleed and erode (ulcerate). Respiratory infection may occur as a result of inhaling stomach acid while asleep. Excessive gas (flatulence) and swelling of the upper abdomen (epigastric distention), presumably from stomach swelling, may also occur. An abnormal narrowing (stricture) of the esophagus or stomach is another potential complication. Also, low blood hemoglobin (anemia) can result from bleeding that may occur in the lower esophagus or from the inner lining of the stomach. Occasionally, the stomach may twist on itself (organo-axial gastric volvulus) producing pain, nausea, vomiting, and tissue death (necrosis). This condition is potentially a life-threatening situation.

Factors Influencing Duration

Factors that might influence the length of disability include the type and severity of the hernia, the surgical procedure used to fix the hernia, the presence and nature of complications, and the individual's age and job requirements. The length of disability will be significantly prolonged if the hernia recurs.

Length of Disability

The duration of disability following treatment for hiatal hernia depends upon the requirements of the job. Recurrence of a hernia may occur, and this should be a consideration upon return to work.

Medical treatment.

Duration in Days

Job Classification	Minimum	Optimum	Maximum
Sedentary work	0	2	3
Light work	0	2	3
Medium work	0	2	4
Heavy work	0	3	4
Very Heavy work	0	3	4

Surgical treatment.

Duration in Days

Job Classification	Minimum	Optimum	Maximum
Sedentary work	14	21	28
Light work	14	21	28
Medium work	21	28	42
Heavy work	28	42	56
Very Heavy work	28	56	70

Failure to Recover

If an individual fails to recover within the maximum duration expectancy period, the reader may wish to reference the following questions to assist in better understanding the specifics of an individual's medical case.

Regarding diagnosis:

- Does the individual have coughing, vomiting, or straining during bowel movements?
- Is the individual pregnant or obese?
- Does the individual report heartburn or chest pain that is worse when lying flat?
- Does heartburn sometimes wake them at night? Is it more noticeable in the morning?
- Does the individual have the sensation that food is sticking in the chest or upper abdomen?
- Does the individual complain of food or stomach acid regurgitation into the mouth?
- Has the individual had a barium swallow and esophagoscopy?
- Was a biopsy of the esophagus done?
- Was a motility study done?
- Did the individual have a CBC?
- Did the individual also have esophageal manometry, pH telemetry, esophageal clearance studies, and an ECG?
- Have conditions with similar symptoms been ruled out?

Regarding treatment:

- Have antacids and drugs that decrease stomach acid secretion been prescribed?
- Does the individual elevate of the head of their bed?
- Does the individual avoid large late evening meals, highly seasoned foods, citrus juices, and alcohol?
- Does the individual wear loose-fitting clothing?
- Does the individual eat small, frequent, bland meals?
- Was surgery necessary?

Regarding prognosis:

- Is the individual's employer able to accommodate any necessary restrictions?
- Does the individual have any conditions that could affect their ability to recover?
- Does the individual have esophageal reflux?
- Does the individual have a respiratory infection because of inhaling stomach acid while asleep?
- Does the individual have flatulence and epigastric distention?
- Does the individual have a stricture of the esophagus or stomach?
- Does the individual have anemia?
- Has the stomach twisted back on itself?

References

Calloway, S.P., et al. "Behavioural Techniques in the Management of Aerophagia in Patients with Hiatus Hernia." Journal of Psychosomatic Research 27 6 (1983): 499-502.

LeMone, P., and K.M. Burke. Medical-Surgical Nursing. Upper Saddle River, NJ: Prentice Hall Health, 2000.

Hernia, Incisional

Other names / synonyms: Ventral Hernia

551.2, 551.21, 552.2, 553.2, 553.21

Definition

An incisional hernia occurs when abdominal organs (e.g., intestine or connective tissue) bulge out of the incision site from a previous surgery.

Incisional hernia is usually a result of inadequate healing of the incision site wound and occurs most commonly following lower midline incisions. The major risk factor for this condition is infection of the incision site that can lead to accumulation of fluid (edema) and softening of the tissues held together by the stitches (sutures). As a result, the tissue weakens and the sutures cut through the tissue. The wound will eventually reopen, allowing the abdominal organs to bulge through the incision site.

Vertical incisions are more prone to hernia than horizontal (transverse) incisions. The material used to close the incision may lead to incisional hernia. Other risk factors include poor wound closure technique, advanced age or debility, inadequate nutrition, and any action that increases pressure in the abdominal cavity such as coughing, vomiting, heavy lifting, or straining during bowel movements. Diseases such as syphilis, diabetes, tuberculosis, and cancer may predispose an individual to incisional hernia following surgery.

Incisional hernia occurs approximately 1-3% of the time following abdominal surgery and usually develops in individuals older than thirty-five. Incisional hernia develops in over 60% of individuals within 2 months of their operation; however, it may occur as late as 5 to 10 years following surgery. Thirty-four percent of all incisional hernias occur through low midline incisions. Incisional hernias are more common in women than men with a 2.3 to 1 ratio. The higher incidence in women is most likely the result of more lower midline incisions performed on females than males.

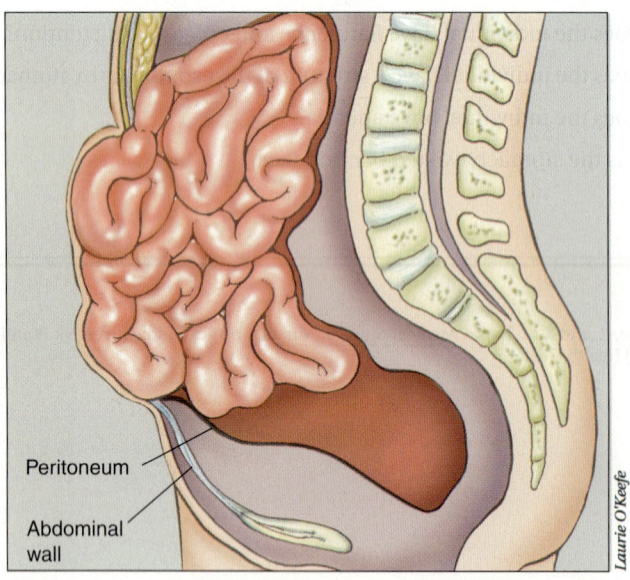

Diagnosis

History: Individual may complain of pain in the area of incision from a previous operation. In addition, a bulge may appear in the abdomen near the incisional site that is accompanied by a dull, aching sensation. The onset of an incisional hernia may be sudden or happen in a delayed, insidious manner (more common). The appearance of an incisional hernia may or may not coincide with heavy lifting or abdominal straining.

Physical exam: An incisional hernia is identified from a bulging or weakness in the area of a surgical incision site. The extent of the herniation can usually be felt by hand (palpation). In general, the mass that protrudes through the incision site can be pushed back into the abdominal cavity with a finger (reducible).

Tests: Diagnosis ordinarily presents no difficulties and tests may not be needed. In some cases, CT, high-frequency sound waves (ultrasound), or introduction of a contrast material into the area of herniation and subsequent x-ray analysis (herniography) can visualize an incisional hernia.

Treatment

Incisional hernias require surgical repair. Small hernias may be repaired through sewing closed the defect in the abdominal wall. Large incisional hernias may require more extensive treatment using a specific open-surgery technique (e.g., Babcock operation or Koontz technique). A multitude of different open-surgical repairs for incisional hernia are available depending on the location and severity of the defect. The incision may sometimes be closed using a patch of polypropylene mesh material as added support. As an alternative to open-surgery, incisional repair and mesh implantation may be done using a device that allows visualization of the wound and inner abdomen through a fiber-optic tube (laparoscope). If the individual does not want surgery or is a poor risk for the procedure, an elastic corset may be used to control the symptoms.

Prognosis

The outcome for open-surgical treatment of incisional hernia depends primarily on the size of the hernia and its location. Small incisional hernias respond well to surgical treatment although they are more difficult to repair if located on the abdomen immediately below the ribs (costal margin) or immediately above the pubic bone. Large incisional hernias tend to recur often (25-52% of the time) following open-surgery. Recurrence tends to be lower if a polypropylene mesh support is implanted during surgery. Use of a laparoscope to perform the surgery and mesh implantation (laparoscopy) may reduce the recurrence to 3-15 percent.

Differential Diagnosis

A condition that presents with similar symptoms as incisional hernia is abnormal separation of the abdominal muscles (diathesis recti) and may occur in severely obese individuals. An abdominal tumor or cyst may also present with similar symptoms.

Specialists

- General Surgeon

Rehabilitation

Following abdominal surgery, intermittent positive pressure breathing exercises may be necessary to prevent pulmonary complications. Also, certain exercises may be performed to reduce postoperative pain and speed recovery including progressive relaxation and deep breathing techniques. These exercises may be performed several times a day until pain from inhalation/exhalation is less noticeable. Moving and walking is recommended the day after surgery. The individual is restricted in lifting heavy weights and engaging in any exercise that may place strain on the incision area for at least 6 weeks postsurgery. Ongoing exercise therapy may be required, however, to educate the individual as to proper body mechanics. Since recurrent herniation is usually due to excess weight, an individual should be encouraged to maintain optimal body weight through proper eating habits.

To reduce body weight, an individual may be placed on a food intake regimen and prescribed daily exercise such as walking. During this time, the individual may also engage in a specialized exercise program with a physical therapist geared to improve functional biomechanics. This program may initially begin in an aqua environment where strain on the incision site will be minimal. Once the incisional site heals, the program may progress to the use of a fitness ball (i.e., Swiss ball).

Exercises performed on the Swiss ball provide sensory, balance, and postural retraining. As soon as the hernia site is stable, an individual may start restoring posture and muscle balance in the torso (abdominals, chest, shoulders, and upper back). As a warm-up, the individual may engage in light bouncing centered on the ball with hip and knees bent at 90 degrees and feet planted on the floor. While avoiding pressing the rib cage forward or arching the lower back, the individual tightens the thigh and hip muscles while bouncing up and down on the ball in a controlled manner. Bouncing may be integrated into a progressive routine by adding arms or legs to the movement and later adding resistance.

The therapist may apply ice or mild heat to the incision site before or after treatment to continue to reduce pain.

Work Restrictions / Accommodations

Restrictions on lifting, climbing, and strenuous physical activity should be expected for several weeks following surgical repair of incisional hernia. After recovery, the individual should return to work in full capacity with no disability.

Complementary and Alternative Therapies

Content is intended for awareness only. Treatments may or may not be effective. Scientific evidence may be lacking and some substances have potentially toxic effects. Dr. Presley Reed and the editors do not endorse the use of these therapies in the absence of consultation with a licensed medical professional.

Electrical stimulation - Implantation of an electrical stimulator after the initial surgical procedure may prevent the occurrence of incisional hernia.

Comorbid Conditions

Existing conditions that may impact an individual's ability to recover and further lengthen disability include severe obesity, and systemic diseases such as syphilis, diabetes, tuberculosis, and cancer.

Complications

The intestine and connective tissue (omentum) bulging through the incision site may become pinched (strangulated) and lead to obstruction of the intestine. Tissue death (necrosis) and decay (gangrene) can occur and may lead to production of toxic substances by bacteria in the tissue (toxemia).

Factors Influencing Duration

Factors that may influence the length of disability include the location and severity of the hernia, surgical procedure, the presence and nature of complications, and the individual's job requirements. Older individuals (over 35) tend to have a longer period of disability.

Length of Disability

Duration depends on size of hernia and job requirements. Recurrence of incisional hernia is not uncommon and this should be a consideration when individual returns to work.

Surgical repair.

Duration in Days

Job Classification	Minimum	Optimum	Maximum
Sedentary work	7	14	21
Light work	14	21	28
Medium work	21	28	42
Heavy work	42	49	56
Very Heavy work	49	56	63

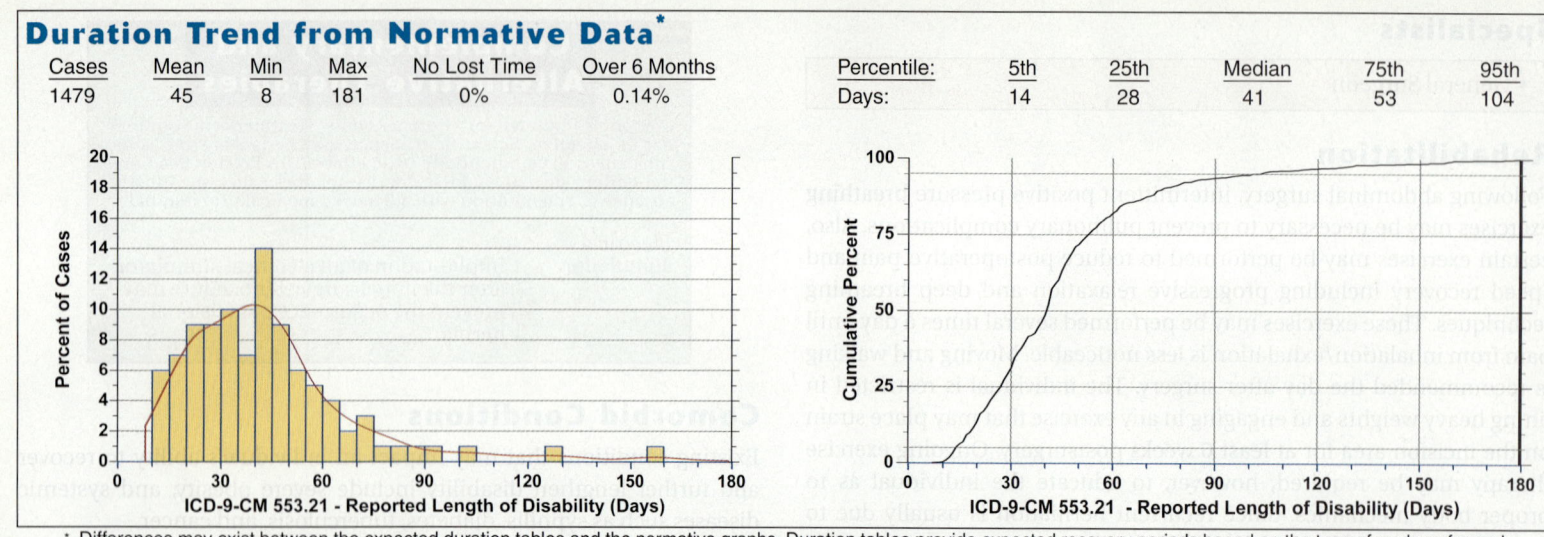

Duration Trend from Normative Data*

Cases	Mean	Min	Max	No Lost Time	Over 6 Months
1479	45	8	181	0%	0.14%

Percentile:	5th	25th	Median	75th	95th
Days:	14	28	41	53	104

* Differences may exist between the expected duration tables and the normative graphs. Duration tables provide expected recovery periods based on the type of work performed by the individual. The normative graphs reflect the actual observed experience of many individuals across the spectrum of physical conditions, in a variety of industries, and with varying levels of case management.

Failure to Recover

If an individual fails to recover within the maximum duration expectancy period, the reader may wish to reference the following questions to assist in better understanding the specifics of an individual's medical case.

Regarding diagnosis:

- Did individual have surgery that involved a lower midline incision?
- Did the wound heal inadequately?
- Did individual have a wound infection?
- What material was used to close the wound?
- Is individual older? Debilitated? Malnourished?
- Does individual do heavy lifting? Strain with bowel movements?
- Does individual have syphilis, diabetes, tuberculosis, or cancer?
- Does individual have pain in an incision? Is there a bulge present?
- Was the onset gradual or sudden?
- On exam was a bulge visible or palpable? Is it reducible?
- Were CT scan, ultrasound, or herniography done?
- Have conditions with similar symptoms been ruled out?

Regarding treatment:

- Has surgery been done? Was it refused?
- Does individual use a corset?

Regarding prognosis:

- Is individual's employer able to accommodate any necessary restrictions?
- Does individual have any conditions that may affect their ability to recover?
- Did individual develop a strangulation?
- Was necrosis or gangrene present?

References

Hamlin, J.A., and A.M. Kahn. "Hernioigraphy: A Review of 333 Herniograms." American Surgeon 64 10 (1998): 965-969.

Larson, G.M. "Ventral Hernia Repair by the Laparoscopic Approach." Surgical Clinics of North America 80 4 (2000): 1329-1340.

Hernia, Inguinal and Femoral

Other names / synonyms: Crural Hernia, Femoral Herniation, Inguinal Herniation

550, 550.0, 550.00, 550.01, 550.02, 550.03, 550.1, 550.10, 550.11, 550.12, 550.13, 550.9, 550.90, 550.91, 550.92, 550.93, 551, 551.0, 551.8, 552.0, 553.0, 553.00, 553.01, 553.02, 553.03

Definition

A hernia is the abnormal protrusion of an organ or tissue through the structure that usually contains it. Hernias may occur in the abdominal area when a loop of intestine bulges through a weakness or abnormal opening in the muscular wall of the abdomen (abdominal hernia). The abdominal wall is relatively weak at the groin (where the lower abdomen meets the thigh) and there are 3 types of abdominal hernias that are seen typically in this region: indirect inguinal, direct inguinal, and femoral.

The incidence of indirect inguinal hernias rises among individuals in their fifties and then tapers off in later years. The condition is far more common in males than females. Normally, an opening through the lower abdominal wall (inguinal canal) closes off with the spermatic cord (males) or a small fibrous ligament (females) running through it. However, in some individuals the canal does not close off tightly and increased pressure inside the abdomen, as during strenuous activity, may force it open. A hernial sac (containing clear, membrane-like abdominal tissue (omentum), portions of bowel, or parts of the urinary bladder then may form, which protrudes into and through the inguinal canal. As the hernial sac enlarges, it may extend into the scrotum (males) or into the groin (females).

Direct inguinal hernias are seen most commonly in men over age forty. This type of hernia passes straight through the abdominal wall (rather than through a canal) in an area of muscular weakness. The abdominal weakening occurs usually from a combination of aging and increased abdominal pressure that can result from chronic coughing or straining.

Femoral hernias rarely occur before the age of puberty and are much more likely to affect women than men. In a femoral hernia, the hernial sac protrudes downward through the opening (femoral canal) where large blood vessels (the femoral artery and vein) pass into the thigh. Femoral hernia is a type of indirect hernia.

Each of these three types of hernias can be described as reducible or incarcerated. A reducible hernia is one in which the hernial sac can be pushed back into the abdomen by manipulation using a finger. With an incarcerated hernia, the hernial sac has become trapped so that it cannot be pushed back into the abdominal cavity using finger manipulation. In this case, the blood supply may be cut-off (strangulation) and tissue death (necrosis) may be the result.

Any condition that increases pressure in the abdomen (such as obesity, chronic cough, or chronic straining) may encourage the development of a hernia. Hernias often occur as a complication of straining during urination due to an enlarged prostate gland (prostatic hypertrophy). Hernias are also seen in individuals who are chronically constipated and who must strain to move their bowels. Pregnancy may also be a contributing factor.

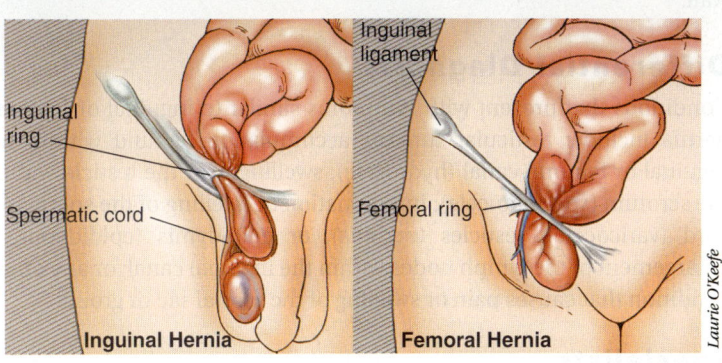
Inguinal Hernia / Femoral Hernia

Diagnosis

History: The individual reports a swelling in the groin area. It may be painless, or discomfort may be reported with straining or coughing. The individual might associate onset of the swelling with an episode of heavy lifting.

Physical exam: A bulge or swelling appears in the groin area or within the scrotal sac with an inguinal hernia. The bulge will appear lower on the abdomen (near the area of the upper thigh) with a femoral hernia. It may be possible to determine if the hernia is reducible or incarcerated by finger manipulation. The exact diagnosis cannot be confirmed until the time of surgery.

Tests: Tests are not needed in the diagnosis of inguinal or femoral hernias. However, in rare cases, it may be useful to examine the abdominal cavity through a small incision in the abdominal wall using an illuminated optical tube (laparoscopy).

Treatment

Surgical repair is the treatment for inguinal or femoral hernia. Most hernias in the inguinal or femoral region are uncomplicated and can be repaired under local anesthesia in an outpatient setting. Conventional hernia surgery (Lichtenstein open mesh technique or Shouldice repair) or endoscopic (transabdominal preperitoneal; TAPP repair) have been compared. Long-term evaluation demonstrated greater satisfaction with the result of the repair in those who had the endoscopic repair. If the hernia is in the upper abdominal region it is considered more complicated and general anesthesia is usually used during surgical repair. Consequently, a short hospital stay may be required.

Prognosis

Complete recovery is expected after surgical repair of a hernia in most cases. However, mortality becomes a consideration if strangulation is a complicating factor. Mortality rate is approximately 5% when strangulation is treated within 12 hours. This rate rises to 10% when treatment for strangulation occurs within the second 12 hours, and rises thereafter, to between 40-70% at the end of 4 days.

Recurrence of a hernia may occur, and this happens approximately 11-17% of the time with indirect and direct hernias, respectively. The likelihood of recurrence depends upon the size and severity of the hernia, history of any previous recurrence, presence of predisposing factors, and the surgical technique used for repair. The risk of recurrence may be lessened by using a synthetic patch to strengthen the abdominal wall.

Differential Diagnosis

Conditions that present with symptoms similar to inguinal or femoral hernia include: testicular tumors; accumulation of fluid within the inguinal or femoral canal (hydrocele); swelling near the testicle within the scrotum (spermatocele); inflammation or swelling of the spermatic cord (varicocele), testicles (orchitis), or epididymis (epididymitis); enlargement of the lymph nodes within the inguinal canal; or any other condition that causes pain or swelling of the scrotal sac or groin.

Specialists

- General Surgeon

Rehabilitation

Following abdominal surgery to repair a hernia, intermittent positive pressure breathing exercises may be necessary to prevent pulmonary complications. Certain exercises such as progressive relaxation and deep breathing techniques may be performed to reduce postoperative pain and speed recovery. These may be performed several times a day until pain from inhalation/exhalation is less noticeable. Physical therapists instruct individuals to hold a pillow to the abdomen when walking, coughing, or laughing. The pillow acts as a splint in place of the weakened abdominal muscles and decreases the amount of perceived pain during these activities. While lying on the back, the individual performs exercises such as pelvic tilts where the lower back is flattened against the bed, and neck bends where the neck is bent forward. These exercises strengthen the abdominal muscles.

Work Restrictions / Accommodations

Lifting or climbing should be avoided or greatly limited during the recovery period following surgical repair of an inguinal or femoral hernia.

Comorbid Conditions

Obesity or advanced age can lengthen disability as these individuals tend to heal more slowly and progress at a slower rate.

Complications

The hernial sac may become trapped (incarcerated), which can lead to obstruction of intestinal food contents or elimination of blood flow to the protruding organ (strangulation). This condition is more common in indirect and femoral hernias because these pass through a ring of muscular tissue (hernia ring) that comprises the inguinal or femoral canal. Strangulation is a medical emergency and immediate surgery is required to prevent tissue death (necrosis) within the trapped tissue. Recurrence of the hernia is another possible complication.

Factors Influencing Duration

Factors that might influence the length of disability include the type and severity of the hernia, the surgical procedure used to fix the hernia, the presence and nature of complications, and the individual's job requirements. The length of disability will be significantly prolonged if the hernia recurs.

Length of Disability

Duration of disability depends upon job requirements. If heavy lifting or strenuous activity is required, disability may last weeks to months. Recurrence of a hernia may occur, and this should be a consideration upon return to work.

Surgical treatment (Canadian/Shouldice method).

Duration in Days

Job Classification	Minimum	Optimum	Maximum
Sedentary work	2	4	7
Light work	7	9	14
Medium work	14	21	28
Heavy work	35	42	49
Very Heavy work	42	49	56

Conventional surgical treatment.

Duration in Days

Job Classification	Minimum	Optimum	Maximum
Sedentary work	7	10	21
Light work	7	10	21
Medium work	14	28	42
Heavy work	35	42	56
Very Heavy work	42	56	70

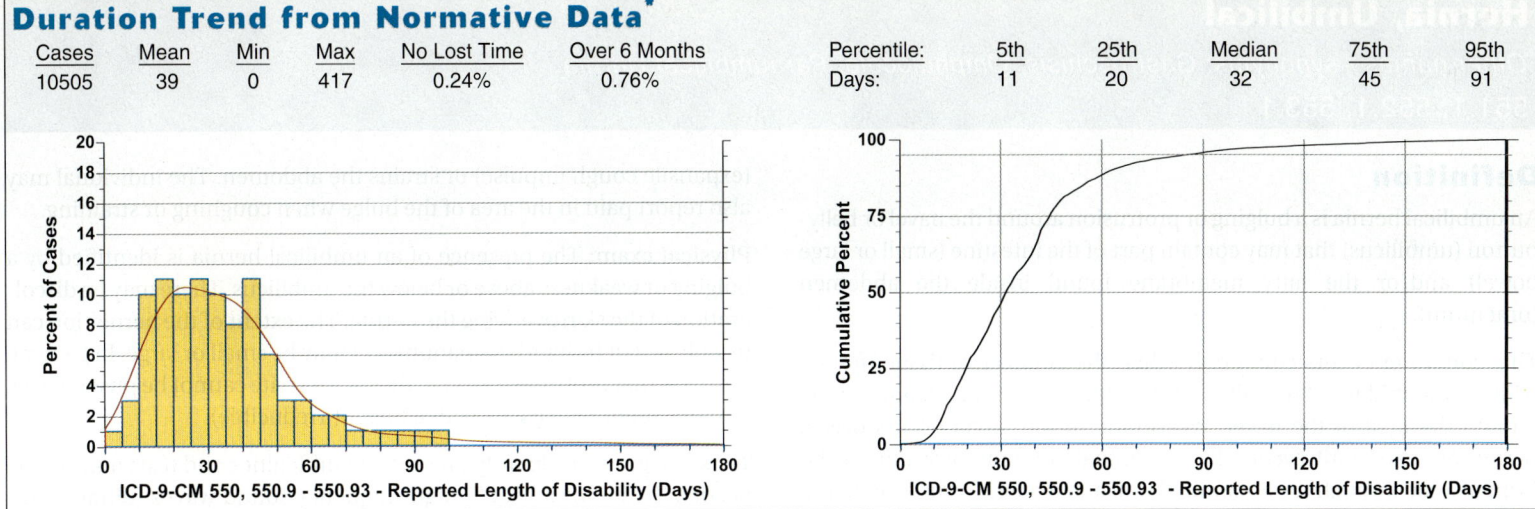

* Differences may exist between the expected duration tables and the normative graphs. Duration tables provide expected recovery periods based on the type of work performed by the individual. The normative graphs reflect the actual observed experience of many individuals across the spectrum of physical conditions, in a variety of industries, and with varying levels of case management.

Failure to Recover

If an individual fails to recover within the maximum duration expectancy period, the reader may wish to reference the following questions to assist in better understanding the specifics of an individual's medical case.

Regarding diagnosis:

- Does individual have swelling or a bulge in the groin area or within the scrotal sac? If so, is the bulge lower on the abdomen (near the area of the upper thigh)? Is it painless or is discomfort reported with straining or coughing?
- If diagnosis is uncertain, were other conditions with similar symptoms ruled out?
- Was diagnosis of inguinal or femoral hernia confirmed?

Regarding treatment:

- Since surgical repair is the treatment for inguinal or femoral hernia, was hernia repair successful?
- Was hernia repaired under local anesthesia in an outpatient setting?
- If the hernia was located in the upper abdominal region, were general anesthesia and a short hospital stay required?
- Did individual experience any complications from the surgical procedure or anesthesia?

Regarding prognosis:

- Was strangulation or tissue necrosis present? Will further procedures be required?
- Does individual have a coexisting condition such as obesity or advanced age that may complicate treatment or impact recovery?
- Based on known factors (size and severity of the hernia, history of any previous recurrence, presence of predisposing factors, and the surgical technique used for repair), is individual at risk for hernia recurrence?
- Was a synthetic patch used to strengthen abdominal wall and lessen risk of recurrence?
- Have any complications developed that may impact recovery?

References

Allison, John G. "Groin Hernias." Hernias of the Diaphragm and Abdominal Wall. Shirazi, Siroos S., ed. Garden City: Medical Examination Publishing Co., Inc, 1981. 117-150.

Danielsson, P., S. Isacson, and M.V. Hansen. "Randomised Study of Lichtenstein Compared with Shouldice Inguinal Hernia Repair by Surgeons in Training." European Journal of Surgery 165 1 (1999): 49-53.

Davenport, Horace W. Physiology of the Digestive Tract. Chicago: Year Book Medical Publishers, Inc, 1982.

Evans, M.M., and P.A. Rubio. "Music: A Diversionary Therapy." Today's OR-Nurse 16 4 (1994): 17-22.

Kisner, Carolyn, and Lynn Allen Colby. "The Spine: Posture." Therapeutic Exercise: Foundations and Techniques. Philadelphia: F.A. Davis Company, 1990. 429-471.

Koontz, Amos R. Hernia. New York: Meredith Publishing Company, 1963.

Leibl, B.J., P. Daubler, and C.G. Schmedt. "Long-Term Results of a Randomized Clinical Trial Between Laparoscopic Hernioplasty and Shouldice Repair." British Journal of Surgery 87 6 (2000): 780-783.

Luckmann, Joan, and Karen C. Sorensen. Medical-Surgical Nursing. Philadelphia: W.B. Saunders Company, 1987.

Schwager, K.L., D.B. Baines, and R.J. Meyer. "Acupuncture and Postoperative Vomiting in Day-stay Pediatric Patients." Anesthesia and Intensive Care 24 6 (1996): 674-677.

Smedley, F., M. Taube, and C. Wastell. "Transcutaneous Electrical Nerve Stimulation for Pain Relief Following Inguinal Hernia Repair: A Controlled Trial." European Surgical Research 20 4 (1988): 233-237.

Hernia, Umbilical

Other names / synonyms: Gastroschisis, Omphalocele, Paraumbilical Hernia

551.1, 552.1, 553.1

Definition

An umbilical hernia is a bulging or protrusion around the navel or belly-button (umbilicus) that may contain part of the intestine (small or large bowel) and/or the fatty membrane found inside the abdomen (omentum).

This condition occurs commonly when the connective tissue (fascia) lying in the midline (linea alba) of the abdominal wall becomes weak around the area of the navel. Weakening of the fascia occurs over a period of years until eventually abdominal contents protrude in the form of a sac through the abdominal wall and a bulge forms around the umbilicus. A newly formed umbilical hernia is usually small and contains only omentum. This type of hernia can attain massive proportions however, as more of the abdominal contents (transverse colon, small intestine, great omentum) are pushed into the sac. An exceedingly small number of umbilical hernias in adults may be the reappearance of a weakness in the area of the navel they experienced as an infant.

Obese individuals are at major risk in developing umbilical hernia because of their increased intra-abdominal pressure. Other risk factors may include multiple pregnancies with prolonged labor, fluid in the abdomen (ascites), bronchitis, asthma, and large abdominal tumors. Any action that increases pressure in the abdominal cavity such as coughing, vomiting, heavy lifting, or straining during bowel movements also increases the risk for developing umbilical hernia.

Umbilical hernias are more common in women than men with a ratio of 1.15 to 1. They may occur at any age (average age of occurrence is 53) but are more common in elderly individuals. Eighty-six percent of umbilical hernias occur in whites.

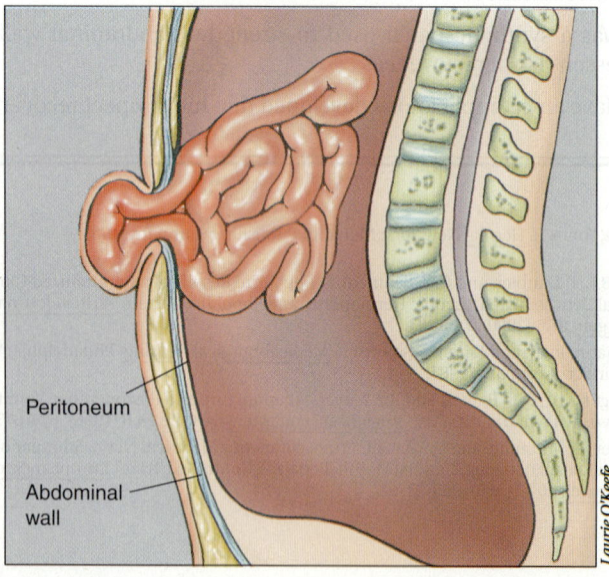

Diagnosis

History: Individuals with umbilical hernia report a protrusion above or below the umbilicus that expands when the individual coughs (expansile cough impulse) or strains the abdomen. The individual may also report pain in the area of the bulge when coughing or straining.

Physical exam: The presence of an umbilical hernia is identified by a bulging or weakness above or below the umbilicus. There may be discoloration of the skin overlying the hernia. The extent of the herniation can usually be felt by hand (palpation) and may be small or large. In general, the mass that protrudes through the incision site cannot be pushed back into the abdominal cavity with a finger (irreducible).

Tests: Diagnosis ordinarily presents no difficulties and tests may not be needed. In some cases, CT, high-frequency sound waves (ultrasound), or introduction of a contrast material into the area of herniation and subsequent x-ray analysis (herniography) may be used to visualize an umbilical hernia.

Treatment

A small umbilical hernia easily pushed back into the abdomen (reducible) in an adult of normal weight may be ignored or held in place and controlled by a special belt (truss). This type of treatment may also be used for those individuals who are not good surgical risks or the elderly who may not tolerate surgery. Large umbilical hernias are usually best treated with surgery (Mayo procedure) that incorporates implantation of a polyurethane mesh to provide support and hold the herniated sac inside the abdomen. Very large umbilical hernias are common in extremely obese individuals and it may be necessary to remove large portions of fat (lipectomy) in order to perform the hernial repair.

Prognosis

The predicted outcome for an individual with a small umbilical hernia treated only with a truss is generally good. If left untreated, however, small umbilical hernias can expand and become problematic. Greater than 90% of healthy individuals treated surgically with mesh repair can be discharged from the hospital on the same day as the surgery. Rarely is there recurrence of the condition following surgical treatment (<3% of the time). About 5% of individuals experience complications from surgery such as infection or bleeding.

Differential Diagnosis

Conditions that may present with similar symptoms as umbilical hernia include abnormal separation of the abdominal muscles (diathesis recti) and incisional hernia. An abdominal tumor or cyst may also present with similar symptoms.

Specialists

- General Surgeon

Rehabilitation

Following abdominal surgery to repair a hernia, intermittent positive pressure breathing exercises may be necessary to prevent pulmonary complications. Certain exercises such as progressive relaxation and deep breathing techniques may be performed to reduce postoperative pain and speed recovery. These may be performed several times a day until pain from inhalation/exhalation is less noticeable. Physical therapists instruct individuals to hold a pillow to the abdomen when walking, coughing, or laughing. The pillow acts as a splint in place of the weakened abdominal muscles and decreases the amount of perceived pain during these activities. While lying on the back, the individual performs exercises such as pelvic tilts where the lower back is flattened against the bed, and neck bends where the neck is bent forward. These exercises strengthen the abdominal muscles.

Work Restrictions / Accommodations

Restrictions on lifting, climbing, and strenuous physical activity should be expected for several weeks following surgical repair of umbilical hernia. After recovery, the individual can usually return to work in full capacity with no disability. It is rare when an umbilical hernia repaired surgically reoccurs. If this is the case, however, reassignment to an alternative position requiring less physical strain may be considered.

Comorbid Conditions

Existing conditions that may impact an individual's ability to recover and further lengthen disability include severe obesity and systemic diseases such as syphilis, diabetes, tuberculosis, and cancer.

Complications

Complications of umbilical hernia may include trapping (incarceration) of the intestine or omentum contained within the herniated sac so that it cannot be pushed back into the abdomen. Consequently, the flow of blood to the tissue within the incarcerated sac may be cut off (strangulation) and the tissue may then start to die (necrose). The individual experiences pain, vomiting, complete constipation, and shock. This condition is a surgical emergency. Other possible complications of umbilical hernia include rupture of the hernial sac, ascites, infection, abdominal distention, pneumonia, fluid in the lungs (pulmonary edema), heart problems (cardiac insufficiency), skin discoloration due to liver dysfunction (jaundice), intestinal bleeding (hemorrhage), and kidney (renal) problems.

Factors Influencing Duration

Factors that may influence the length of disability include the severity of the hernia, surgical procedure used as treatment, presence and nature of complications, and the individual's job requirements. Older individuals (>35 years of age) tend to have a longer period of disability.

Length of Disability

Duration of disability from umbilical hernia depends on the requirements of the job. Recurrence of umbilical hernia should also be a consideration when individual returns to work.

Surgical repair.

Duration in Days

Job Classification	Minimum	Optimum	Maximum
Sedentary work	7	14	28
Light work	7	14	28
Medium work	14	21	42
Heavy work	21	28	42
Very Heavy work	21	42	56

Duration Trend from Normative Data*

Cases	Mean	Min	Max	No Lost Time	Over 6 Months
2064	35	0	216	0.05%	0.10%

Percentile:	5th	25th	Median	75th	95th
Days:	12	20	31	42	70

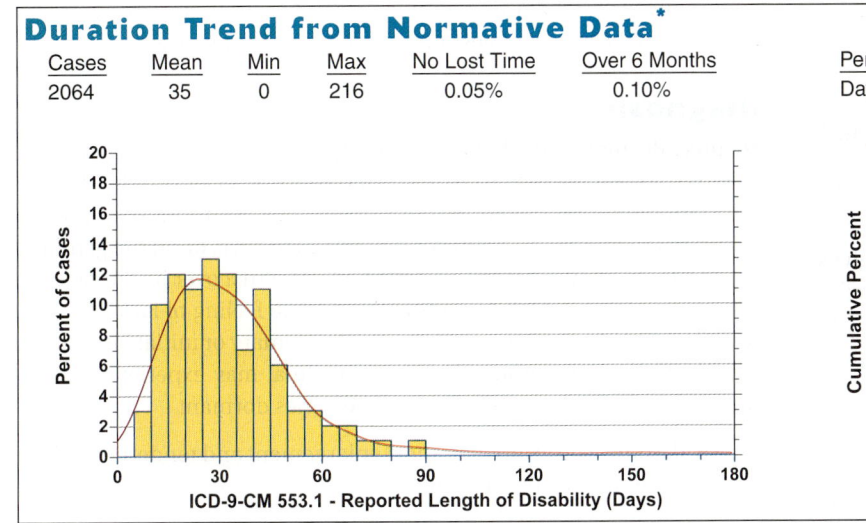
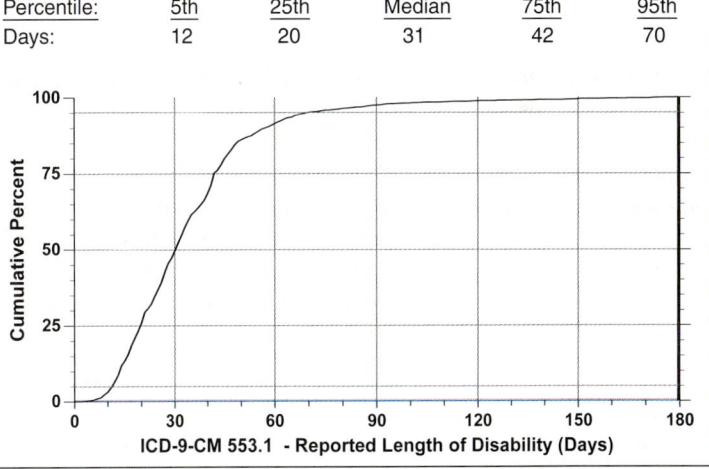

* Differences may exist between the expected duration tables and the normative graphs. Duration tables provide expected recovery periods based on the type of work performed by the individual. The normative graphs reflect the actual observed experience of many individuals across the spectrum of physical conditions, in a variety of industries, and with varying levels of case management.

Failure to Recover

If an individual fails to recover within the maximum duration expectancy period, the reader may wish to reference the following questions to assist in better understanding the specifics of an individual's medical case.

Regarding diagnosis:

- Does individual have a protrusion above or below the umbilicus that expands when individual coughs (expansile cough impulse) or strains the abdomen? Does pain occur in the area of the bulge when coughing or straining?
- Is skin overlying the hernia discolored?
- Can the mass that protrudes through the incision site be pushed back into the abdominal cavity with a finger (irreducible)?

- While diagnosis ordinarily presents no difficulties, was ultrasound or herniography needed to visualize hernia and confirm diagnosis?
- If diagnosis is uncertain, were other conditions with similar symptoms ruled out?
- Was diagnosis of umbilical hernia confirmed?

Regarding treatment:

- If surgical repair was not an option, what were extenuating circumstances?
- Was surgical repair successful?
- Did individual experience any complications associated with the hernia such as tissue necrosis? Will further procedures be necessary?
- Were any complications associated with the procedure or anesthesia?

Regarding prognosis:

- Since even small hernias can expand, has umbilical hernia now become problematic? Is surgical repair now warranted?
- Did the hernia recur despite surgical repair?
- Does individual have a coexisting condition such as severe obesity, syphilis, diabetes, tuberculosis, or cancer that may complicate treatment or impact recovery?

References

Abramov, D., et al. "Antibiotic Prophylaxis in Umbilical and Incisional Hernia Repair: A Prospective Randomized Study." European Journal of Surgery 162 12 (1996): 945-948.

Baccari, E.M., B. Breiling, and C.H. Organ, Jr. "A Study of the Maturity Onset of Adult Umbilical Hernia." The American Surgeon 37 (1971): 385-388.

Davis, A.B. "Laparoscopic Hernia Repair in the Community Hospital Setting." Surgical Laparoscopy, Endoscopy and Percutaneous Techniques 6 6 (1996): 448-452.

Feleshtinskii, I.P. "Ways of Improvement of Surgical Results for Umbilical Hernia in Elderly and Old Patients." Klinichna Khirurhiia 7-8 (1997): 36-38.

Gianetta, E., et al. "Hernia Repair in Elderly Patients." British Journal of Surgery 84 7 (1997): 983-985.

Kisner, Carolyn, and Lynn Allen Colby. Therapeutic Exercise: Foundations and Techniques, 2nd ed. Philadelphia: F.A. Davis Company, 1990.

LeMone, P., and K.M. Burke. Medical-Surgical Nursing. Upper Saddle River, NJ: Prentice Hall Health, 2000.

Park, S., et al. "Repair of Mild Umbilical Hernia." Annals of Plastic Surgery 42 6 (1999): 634-637.

Herpes Simplex

Other names / synonyms: Cold Sore, Fever Blister, Genital Herpes, Oral Herpes

054, 054.0, 054.1, 054.2, 054.3, 054.4, 054.43, 054.5, 054.6, 054.7, 054.8, 054.9

Definition

Herpes simplex is a virus that causes infections characterized by an eruption of small fluid filled blisters (vesicles) or lesions on the skin accompanied by burning and itching.

There are two general types of herpes infections; oral herpes, usually caused by herpes simplex virus type-1 (HSV-1), and genital herpes, which is usually caused by herpes simplex virus type-2 (HSV-2). Genital herpes can cause lesions on the penis, the labia, the perianal skin, or the buttocks. Herpes can also cause infections inside the mouth (gingivostomatitis), in the eye (keratoconjunctivitis), or on the skin, as well as more serious infections of the nervous system and brain (encephalitis). The most common form of herpes, however, is a cold sore that appears at the edge of the lip.

Between 70-90% of adults have been infected with HSV-1. Most individuals initially acquire HSV-1 between the ages of 1-5 years of age by direct contact with an infected person or through infected saliva. Transmission of the virus can occur during periods of viral shedding which may or may not be accompanied by a lesion. It is estimated that over 80% of the population has been infected with HSV-1, and 1-5% of adults are excreting the virus at any one time.

HSV-2 is acquired through sexual contact and is not as common as HSV-1. In the US, approximately 65% of black adults and 20% of white adults have had HSV-2. Once either virus has been acquired, it can reside in a latent form within nerve tissue indefinitely, causing recurrences in the form of a cold sore or fever blister for HSV-1 or a genital lesion for HSV-2.

The frequency of recurrences is quite variable between individuals but commonly occur following minor infections, trauma, stress, excess exposure to the sun, or ingestion of certain foods and drugs.

Diagnosis

History: Burning and stinging at the site of infection accompanied by lesions that appear as a group of small blisters (vesicles) on the skin are the main symptoms of herpes infections. These lesions most frequently occur on the mouth, lips, and conjunctiva of the eye, or on the genitalia in the case of genital herpes. Lesions typically crust over in 7-10 days. A sore throat, fever, irritability, and an indefinite feeling of lack of health (malaise) can also accompany herpes. The primary or initial infection is usually without symptoms, but the individual may experience a sore throat or mouth sore before the virus becomes dormant.

Physical exam: The exam may show enlargement and tenderness of the lymph nodes in the neck or groin.

Tests: Tests are seldom done to diagnose herpes, but can include samples from the lesion for viral culture. Microscopic examination of the infected skin cells, or a Tzanck smear, can indicate abnormalities. For rapid diagnosis when encephalitis is suspected, an antibody test on a brain biopsy can be performed.

Treatment

Herpes lesions are typically self-limiting and extensive treatment is not warranted. The lesion should be kept clean and dry to prevent spreading and the development of bacterial infections. For more severe cases of herpes, antiviral medications are given. Since the use of these antiviral medications, resistant strains of the virus have been reported. Many individuals find over-the-counter remedies such as camphor to be effective. Mouth rinses that contain lidocaine may provide pain relief. No treatment can prevent the virus from becoming dormant in the body.

Using condoms during sexual contact can reduce the risk of contracting genital herpes. The risk of oral herpes may be reduced by using a lip balm containing sunscreen or by otherwise decreasing sun exposure.

Prognosis

Herpes lesions of the mouth or genitals typically clear up in 7-10 days. Serious infections that have spread to the brain take longer to treat and can be fatal, but that is rare. Genital herpes infections during pregnancy can cause infection in the fetus, and can result in spontaneous abortion, premature birth, or congenital abnormalities.

Differential Diagnosis

Conditions that resemble herpes simplex include a nonviral canker sore, allergic reaction, other viral or bacterial infection, and dermatitis.

Specialists

- Infectious Disease Physician
- Primary Care Provider

Work Restrictions / Accommodations

Individuals may not be able to use their mouths or lips for a period of time, which may interfere with some types of work. More serious forms of the disease may require more work restrictions. Individuals with open sores should be isolated from other employees so as not to spread the virus to co-workers.

Comorbid Conditions

Immunosuppressive conditions such as AIDS can result in a more serious case of the disease. Herpes that occurs on the skin of individuals with eczema or burns can be more serious.

Complications

Complications include systemic infections, meaning that the virus spreads throughout the body. Rarely, encephalitis, inflammation of the bone marrow (myelitis), meningitis, and pain in the nerves can occur. In pregnant women, it can result in a serious form of the disease that may be fatal, cause spontaneous abortion, or infect the fetus, causing abnormalities.

Factors Influencing Duration

If the disease has spread to become systemic or caused infection of any organs, the disability will be extended.

Length of Disability

In most cases, no disability is expected.

Without complication.

Duration in Days

Job Classification	Minimum	Optimum	Maximum
Any work	0	7	14

Failure to Recover

If an individual fails to recover within the maximum duration expectancy period, the reader may wish to reference the following questions to assist in better understanding the specifics of an individual's medical case.

Regarding diagnosis:

- Has diagnosis of herpes simplex virus been confirmed?
- Have other conditions with similar symptoms been ruled out?
- Does individual have a coexisting condition that may complicate treatment or impact recovery?

Regarding treatment:

- Although usually self-limiting, have symptoms persisted past expected resolution?
- If complications occurred (such as systemic infections, encephalitis, myelitis, meningitis, neuralgia, or spontaneous abortion), have they responded to treatment?
- Does individual's condition warrant a more aggressive treatment with antiviral medication?

Regarding prognosis:

- Does individual have a lowered or suppressed immune system resulting in disease episodes that are more severe, last longer and often show long-term effects of the infection?
- Would individual benefit from consultation with an infectious disease specialist?
- If individual is pregnant, has she informed her obstetrician or health care provider about her HSV history?

References

Brooks, George F., Janet S. Butel, and Stephen A. Morse. <u>Medical Microbiology.</u> Stamford: Appleton & Lange, 1998.

Herpes Zoster

Other names / synonyms: Shingles

053, 053.9

Definition

Herpes zoster, or shingles, is a reactivation of the chickenpox or varicella-zoster virus.

After an attack of chickenpox, the varicella-zoster virus can become dormant in a group of nerve cells or ganglia. Many years later, the virus becomes active again and moves through the nerve tract to the skin. It is characterized by red patches of skin covered with small blisters (lesions). These blisters contain the virus, which can cause chickenpox in susceptible individuals.

Herpes zoster occurs in about 10-20% of adults at some point during their lives. It is not known why this reactivation occurs in some people and not others. It most commonly occurs in individuals over the age of 50 years. Although most individuals are immune to additional attacks of herpes zoster, recurrent attacks can occur in immunocompromised individuals, those with Hodgkin's' disease, other cancers, atopic dermatitis, or those with AIDS.

Diagnosis

History: Individuals may report initial symptoms of chills, fever, nausea, diarrhea, and sometimes difficulty in urinating. This may be followed a few days later by nerve and skin pain and tingling in the affected area and reddened, fluid-filled blisters on the skin. Blisters may appear on the trunk, from the spine to the breastbone, and on the legs and face. Individuals may complain of sensitive skin that is painful. Often, this extremely painful skin, especially over the anterior chest wall, may precede the onset of any visible signs of the condition.

Physical exam: The exam may reveal very sensitive skin in the affected area. Although diagnosis is difficult before the blisters arise, a description of vague pain on one side of the body can be useful in diagnosing herpes zoster. The distribution of skin lesions is typically in an area controlled by a single spinal nerve (dermatome), although some may lie outside this area. Lymph node swelling sometimes occurs. Depending upon the area affected, there may be vision abnormalities, taste abnormalities, drooping eyelid, hearing loss, or joint pain. The individual usually has a history of having chickenpox.

Tests: Tests are rarely done to diagnose herpes zoster, but may include a viral culture of the skin lesion or a microscopic examination of skin cells (Tzanck test). Blood tests may indicate an elevated white blood cell count.

Treatment

Herpes zoster is usually self-limiting and no treatment is given unless needed to treat the symptoms. No drug can eliminate the virus, but antiviral drugs may shorten the duration of the disease, especially in immunocompromised individuals.

Corticosteroids have been used to reduce the inflammation associated with shingles, but may worsen the disease by interfering with the immune system.

Analgesics such as aspirin or narcotics in severe cases can be used to reduce the pain associated with the disease. Antihistamines may also reduce pain and itching.

Calamine or starch lotions applied topically can relieve itching. The skin should be kept clean to prevent secondary bacterial infections.

Post-herpetic neuralgia may be treated with regional nerve blocks such as an epidural.

There is currently a vaccine to prevent chickenpox. It is not known what effect this vaccine has on herpes zoster.

Prognosis

Most individuals recover without complications in 2-6 weeks. Blisters crust over and begin to heal in about 5 days. Sometimes scarring of the skin can occur. Rarely, temporary or permanent paralysis or nerve pain can occur in the affected area.

Differential Diagnosis

The vague pain that occurs with herpes zoster can be similar to that felt with appendicitis, kidney stones, gallstones, or inflammation of the large intestine. Dermatitis such as poison oak or poison ivy as well as herpes simplex may look similar to herpes zoster.

Specialists

- Neurologist
- Primary Care Provider

Work Restrictions / Accommodations

Severe pain may restrict work for some individuals. If individuals take narcotics as a pain reliever, they should not operate machinery or do other types of work requiring quick reaction times. In the case of paralysis or other complications, additional work restrictions may be necessary.

Complementary and Alternative Therapies

Content is intended for awareness only. Treatments may or may not be effective. Scientific evidence may be lacking and some substances have potentially toxic effects. Dr. Presley Reed and the editors do not endorse the use of these therapies in the absence of consultation with a licensed medical professional.

Acupuncture -	May help relieve pain, especially if neuralgia develops.
Capsaicin -	An ointment containing capsaicin, an extract of pepper, applied to painful areas may gradually ease the pain of shingles.
Hypnotherapy -	May help relieve the burning pain of shingles. Also may promote relaxation, which also aids in managing shingles.
Vitamin B complex -	May help nerve cells regenerate.

Comorbid Conditions

The presence of an immunosuppressive disorder such as AIDS or cancer can lengthen the duration of herpes zoster.

Complications

Secondary bacterial infection can occur. If the facial nerves are affected, more serious complications can occur, such as blindness if the eye is involved, facial paralysis or hearing loss. Post-herpetic neuralgia can occur, which involves the persistence of pain in the area where shingles occurred. This may last for months or years, and is more common in individuals over the age of 60 years.

Factors Influencing Duration

The length of disability depends upon which nerve group is affected and how much pain is experienced. If paralysis, deafness, or blindness occur, disability will increase. If neuralgia occurs, disability will also be extended.

Length of Disability

Acute infection without complication.

Duration in Days

Job Classification	Minimum	Optimum	Maximum
Sedentary work	0	7	14
Light work	0	7	14
Medium work	0	7	14
Heavy work	0	7	21
Very Heavy work	0	7	21

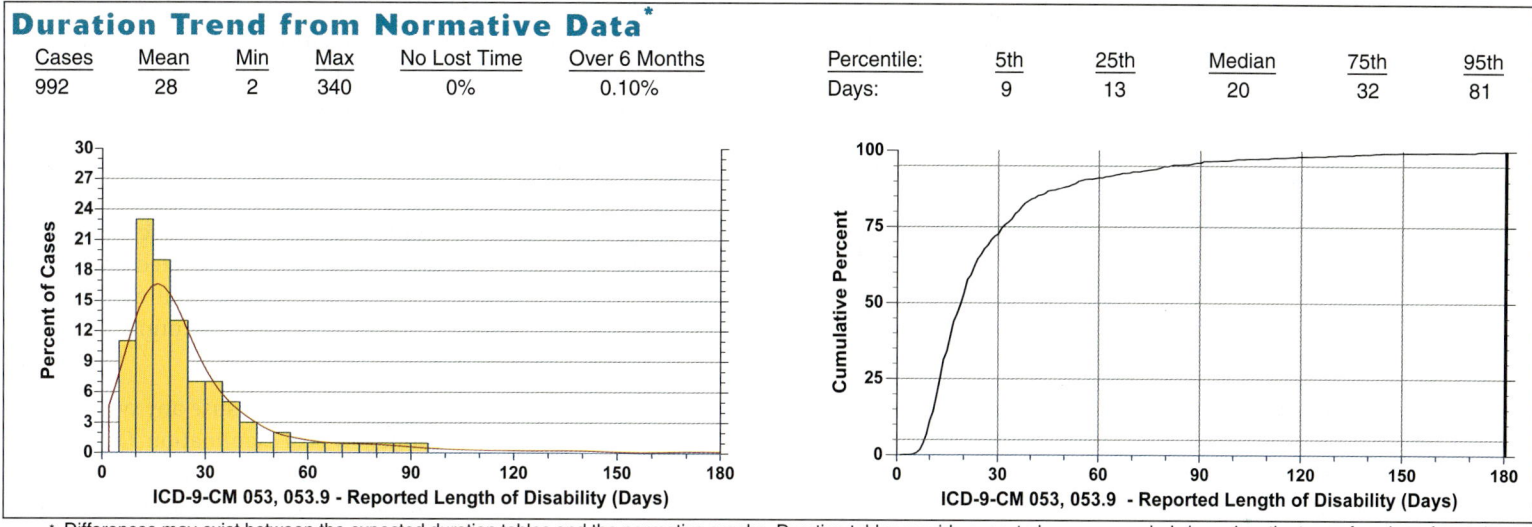

* Differences may exist between the expected duration tables and the normative graphs. Duration tables provide expected recovery periods based on the type of work performed by the individual. The normative graphs reflect the actual observed experience of many individuals across the spectrum of physical conditions, in a variety of industries, and with varying levels of case management.

Failure to Recover

If an individual fails to recover within the maximum duration expectancy period, the reader may wish to reference the following questions to assist in better understanding the specifics of an individual's medical case.

Regarding diagnosis:

- Has diagnosis of herpes zoster been confirmed?
- Has the individual experienced extremely painful skin, especially over the chest wall?
- If diagnosis was uncertain, have conditions with similar symptoms been ruled out?
- Has individual experienced any complication related to the herpes zoster?

Regarding treatment:

- Do symptoms persist despite treatment?
- Would individual benefit from antiviral drug therapy?
- Would a regional nerve block be appropriate for this individual?
- Do symptoms impair function?
- If affected by paralysis, is physical or occupational therapy indicated?

Regarding prognosis:

- If symptoms persist beyond expected duration, has temporary or permanent paralysis or post-herpetic neuralgia occurred in the affected area?
- Does individual have a coexisting condition, such as an immunosuppressive disorder (AIDS or cancer), that may complicate treatment or impact recovery?
- Would individual benefit from pain management techniques or enrollment in a chronic pain clinic?
- Is transition to less demanding duties, isolation from vulnerable co-workers, or limited disability warranted?

References

Herpes Zoster. American Academy of Dermatology. 1999. 22 Feb 2001 <http://www.aad.org/pamphlets/herpesZoster.html>.

Brooks, George F., Janet S. Butel, and Stephen A. Morse. Medical Microbiology. Stamford: Appleton & Lange, 1998.

High Blood Pressure, Benign

Other names / synonyms: Benign Hypertension, Essential Hypertension, High Blood Pressure, Hypertension, Primary Hypertension

401, 401.1, 401.9

Definition

High blood pressure or hypertension occurs when smaller blood vessels (arterioles) narrow causing the blood to exert excessive pressure against the blood vessel walls, making the heart work harder to maintain this higher pressure. Although blood pressure usually varies during the day and often increases as a normal response to stress and physical activity, an individual with hypertension has high blood pressure even at rest.

Blood pressure is recorded as two numbers. The top number (systolic pressure) represents pressure in the arteries when the heart muscle contracts to pump blood. The bottom number (diastolic pressure) represents pressure in the arteries between heartbeats when the heart is at rest. Hypertension is usually defined as a resting systolic pressure greater than or equal to 140 mm Hg (millimeters of mercury) or resting diastolic pressure greater than or equal to 90 mm Hg. Normal blood pressure is considered below 130/85. Mild hypertension ranges from 140-159/90-99, moderate from 160-179/100-109, and severe from 180-209/110-119. Very severe hypertension is over 210/120. According to 1999 World Health Organization guidelines, individuals with kidney disease are considered to have high blood pressure if systolic blood pressure is greater than 125 mm Hg or diastolic blood pressure is greater than 75 mm Hg. In diabetes, diastolic blood pressure over 80 is considered elevated.

Although no single cause for primary hypertension has been identified, several genetic and environmental or lifestyle factors increase the risk of developing the disease. Environmental factors that increase the risk for hypertension include obesity, high dietary salt (sodium) intake, tobacco use, high-fat diet, excessive use of alcohol, stressful lifestyle, lack of exercise, anxiety or depression, and living in the southeast region of the US.

Essential hypertension may be inherited in 30-60% of cases. Specific genetic risk factors include abnormalities in angiotensin-renin genes and inherited abnormalities of the sympathetic nervous system controlling heart rate, blood pressure, and blood vessel diameter. Hypertension occurs four times more frequently among blacks than whites. Blood pressure increases with increasing age, as up to 50% of the population over age 50 suffer from primary hypertension. Men and postmenopausal women have a higher risk of developing hypertension. Diabetes also increases risk of hypertension.

Hypertension is an extremely common disorder affecting approximately 15% of the US population, 25% of all adults or 50 to 60 million individuals. Ninety percent of all cases of hypertension have no obvious cause (essential, primary, or benign hypertension). Secondary hypertension, a result of another (primary) disorder such as kidney disease, accounts for the remaining 10% of cases.

Diagnosis

History: For most individuals, primary hypertension causes no symptoms for years. As the disease progresses, damage to the brain, eyes, heart, and kidneys may occur. Symptoms of severe hypertension or its complications may include headache, dizziness, racing or irregular heartbeat, tiring easily, impotence, nosebleeds, chest pain, or shortness of breath. Family or past history may reveal high blood pressure, stroke, heart problems, kidney disease, or diabetes. Individual may present with risk factors for high blood pressure such as tobacco use, salt intake, obesity, sedentary lifestyle, and elevated cholesterol. Medication history may reveal use of medications that elevate blood pressure. Social history may suggest emotional or environmental factors that could affect blood pressure.

Physical exam: Because hypertension does not cause any symptoms, it is usually detected during a routine physical examination. Once hypertension is suspected, evaluation may include blood pressure readings recorded in both arms and repeated after the individual sits or lies down for 5 minutes (and at least 30 minutes after smoking or coffee ingestion). If a person has a high reading, blood pressure is immediately measured again, and then twice on at least 2 other days to make sure the high blood pressure persists. Readings may need to be repeated at home, as some individuals have elevated blood pressure in the doctor's office because of anxiety (white-coat syndrome). If blood pressure is elevated, physical exam should determine if the neck veins are swollen (distended), the thyroid or heart is enlarged, the presence of any heart murmurs, and if characteristic changes in the eyes are evident using an ophthalmoscope.

Tests: No laboratory tests are used to diagnose primary hypertension. After hypertension is diagnosed, however, laboratory tests are usually performed to rule out secondary causes of hypertension. These tests may include urine and blood tests, a chest x-ray, and an electrocardiogram. A blood test for renin may identify increased production of angiotensin, a chemical that narrows blood vessels. High renin levels may predict heart attacks in white males with high blood pressure. An exercise stress test performed on individuals with borderline elevated pressure may predict risk of enlargement of the left side of the heart (left ventricular hypertrophy).

Treatment

Primary hypertension cannot be cured but can be treated to prevent complications. Treatment of hypertension usually follows a progressive (stepped-care) approach. With this approach, each step is slightly more aggressive than the previous one until blood pressure is controlled.

Step 1 includes lifestyle modifications such as losing weight (especially in the abdominal area), increasing exercise, moderating alcohol and caffeine intake, stopping smoking, and making dietary changes that include a reduction in salt intake, saturated fat, and cholesterol and an increase in fruits, vegetables, and low-fat dairy foods. The DASH (Dietary Approaches to Stop Hypertension) diet is low in saturated fat, rich in whole grains, fruits and vegetables, and contains modest amounts of protein, preferably from fish, poultry, low-fat dairy, or soy products. This diet contains more than twice the amounts of potassium, calcium, and magnesium than the average American diet. If blood pressure is not controlled with lifestyle modifications, the individual will proceed to step 2, involving drug therapy. It is important to note that lifestyle modifications should continue throughout all steps of therapy.

Drug therapy at step 2 usually begins with a diuretic or beta-blocker. If these agents do not work or lead to unwanted side effects, an angiotensin-converting enzyme inhibitor, calcium-channel blocker, alpha-1-receptor blocker, or alpha-beta blocker may be used instead. If blood pressure is still not adequately controlled at step 2, the individual proceeds to step 3.

This third step involves increasing the drug dosage, substituting a drug in the same class, or switching to a drug in a different class. If blood pressure is still not controlled, the individual proceeds to step 4.

This fourth step involves combination drug therapy where a second or third agent is added to the drug regimen. This second or third agent should include a diuretic, if not already used, or drugs such as vasodilators, alpha1-antagonists, peripherally acting adrenergic neuron antagonists, angiotensin-converting enzyme (ACE) inhibitors, angiotensin II receptor antagonists, or calcium-channel blockers.

Prognosis

With appropriate lifestyle changes and the wide variety of drugs available, most individuals with high blood pressure can control the condition. However, hypertension rarely has symptoms and individuals do not feel sick so they may not feel compelled to make lifestyle changes or follow medication regimens (noncompliance). This could lead to further complications from hypertension. High blood pressure was responsible for more than 40,000 deaths in the US in 1996, and may have contributed to more than 200,000 deaths. Mortality rate from high blood pressure rose 6.8% over the previous 10 years and the actual number of deaths increased by one-third. Blacks are especially affected as death occurs in 30% of the men and 20% of the women with hypertension.

Differential Diagnosis

Conditions with similar symptoms and presentation include secondary hypertension where elevated blood pressure is caused by an underlying disease. Pregnancy, cirrhosis, kidney disease, or Cushing's disease may all cause temporary high blood pressure. Many medications can also elevate blood pressure transiently, as can caffeine, stress, exercise, excessive consumption of licorice, and even mobile phone use. Exposure to lead may cause high blood pressure in adults. Some individuals with elevated blood pressure when in the doctor's office may have white-coat syndrome where blood pressure is elevated because of anxiety in the medical setting. Readings should be done at home to avoid unnecessary drug treatments.

Specialists

- Internist
- Radiologist

Rehabilitation

Although benign high blood pressure may appear to have no cause, an elevated blood pressure is always considered a risk because of the potential for related cardiovascular disease. The principles of aerobic conditioning in physical therapy were used to develop a program for high blood pressure, benign or malignant. Such a rehabilitation program occurs in several phases and follows a similar progression to that of other related cardiac diseases.

At the initial rehabilitation stage during low demand aerobic activities that use large muscle groups such as the lower extremities, individuals may be monitored for heart rate and rhythm and blood pressure. Initial exercises include calisthenics of varying intensity like marching in place or raising both arms overhead. The individual is continuously monitored while walking (ambulating) for an initial 2 to 5 minutes and progresses to 15 to 20 minutes. Under supervision, the individual may use a stationary bicycle set at 50 RPM (revolutions per minute) for 3 minutes.

Rehabilitation professionals experienced in cardiac rehabilitation often keep a daily log of the individual's blood pressure, heart rate, and cardiac rhythm. Individuals with significantly high blood pressure are typically tested using an electrocardiograph (ECG), a device that records the continuous electrical activity of the heart muscle. Higher levels of exercises are given in addition to recreational activities such as swimming and outdoor hiking. Light jogging (at approximately 5 mph) and cycling (at approximately 12 mph) are appropriate as long as the individual tolerates the rehabilitation program well.

The later part of the program for benign high blood pressure involves aerobic exercises to increase cardiovascular fitness. These exercises include walking briskly, running, jogging, swimming, climbing stairs, or bicycling. The American Heart Association recommends 30 to 60 minutes of aerobic activity 3 or 4 times a week to help keep high blood pressure under control. Throughout all stages of the rehabilitation program for high blood pressure, the healthcare team closely monitors the individual to assure that the heart rate slowly returns to normal after the exercises.

Work Restrictions / Accommodations

Work restrictions or special accommodations are not usually required for mild cases of benign primary hypertension. Some individuals, however, may need a less stressful environment.

Complementary and Alternative Therapies

Content is intended for awareness only. Treatments may or may not be effective. Scientific evidence may be lacking and some substances have potentially toxic effects. Dr. Presley Reed and the editors do not endorse the use of these therapies in the absence of consultation with a licensed medical professional.

Biofeedback -	Uses sensitive electronic equipment to teach individuals to identify and self-regulate the body's response to stress, injury, and illness. The latest advances include specialized equipment that help train an individual to control heart rate and blood pressure.
Vitamin C -	Widens blood vessels; scientists speculate that constricted arteries may be partly caused by the type of cell damage that vitamin C intake corrects.
Vitamin D -	May affect hormones involved in blood pressure.
Calcium -	Lowers blood pressure and involved in muscle contraction, making it good for the heart and blood vessels.
Magnesium -	Relaxes the muscles that control blood vessels permitting blood to flow more freely; also helps maintain a balance between potassium and sodium in the blood, which has a positive effect on blood pressure.
Hawthorn -	May help widen blood vessels and moderate heart rate.
Coenzyme Q10 -	Unknown mechanism of action in high blood pressure, but more than one-third of individuals are thought to have an inadequate supply of this substance.
Essential fatty acids -	May help foster good circulation.
Taurine -	May help normalize increased nervous system activity and, used with arginine, may widen blood vessels.

Comorbid Conditions

Obesity, diabetes, lack of physical exercise (sedentary lifestyle), heart disease, and kidney disease may make hypertension more difficult to treat.

Complications

Obesity significantly increases the risk of hypertension and smoking tobacco appears to intensify its effects. Increased blood pressure can damage the inner linings of the arteries leading to atherosclerosis or thickening of the walls of the arteries. This in turn leads to increased hypertension and heart disease as the heart becomes enlarged (hypertrophy).

Complications of untreated hypertension also include injury to blood vessels in the kidneys, brain, heart, and eyes that may cause kidney failure, stroke, heart failure, and retinopathy (impaired vision due to retinal damage at the back of the eye). High blood pressure increases the elimination of calcium in the urine that may lead to loss of bone mineral density, osteoporosis, and fractures, especially in elderly women. Sexual dysfunction occurs in 17% of hypertensive men. Long-term (chronic) high blood pressure may lead to decreased memory and mental function in the elderly. Women with high blood pressure before they become pregnant are at greater risk for preeclampsia, a severe, sudden increase in blood pressure during pregnancy that can be very serious for both mother and child. If primary hypertension is untreated, it can lead to malignant hypertension with severe blood pressure elevations that can be life threatening.

Factors Influencing Duration

Length of disability may be influenced by the cause and severity of the hypertension, response to treatment, and whether or not the individual is compliant with treatment recommendations for lifestyle changes and drug therapy. Complications may produce a period of disability.

Length of Disability

No disability is expected for individuals with mild primary hypertension that responds to treatment, but complications may be associated with disability depending on their severity.

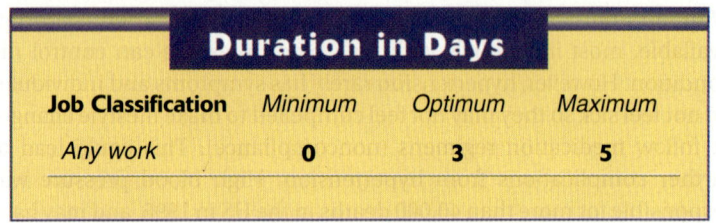

Duration in Days

Job Classification	Minimum	Optimum	Maximum
Any work	0	3	5

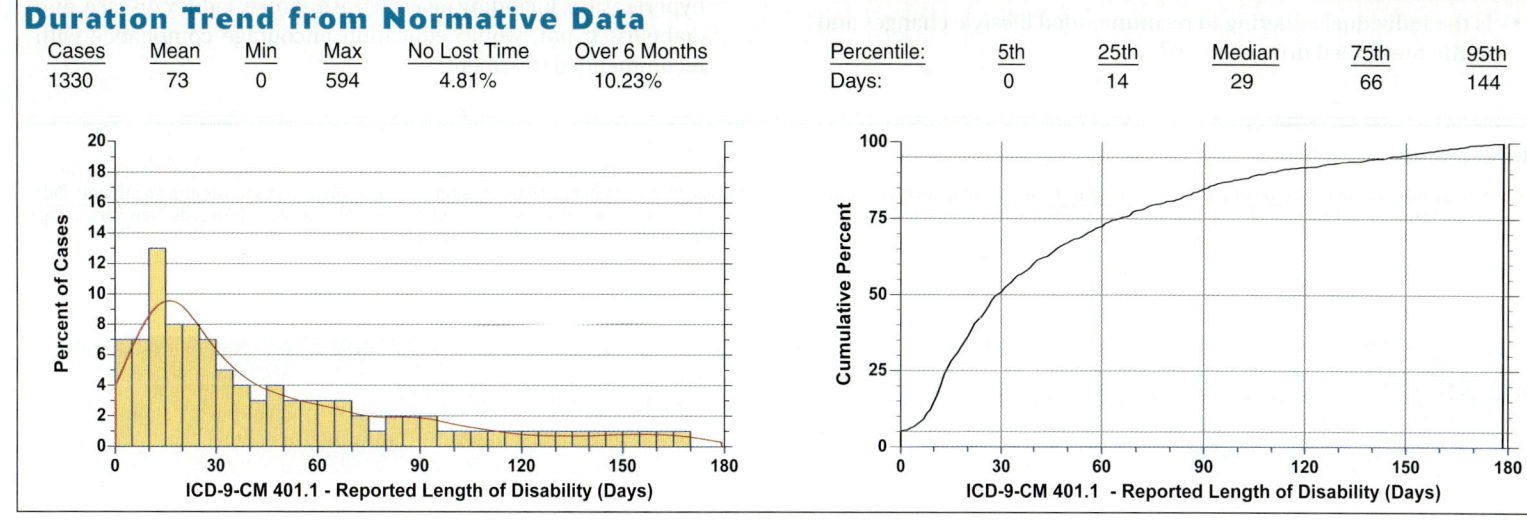

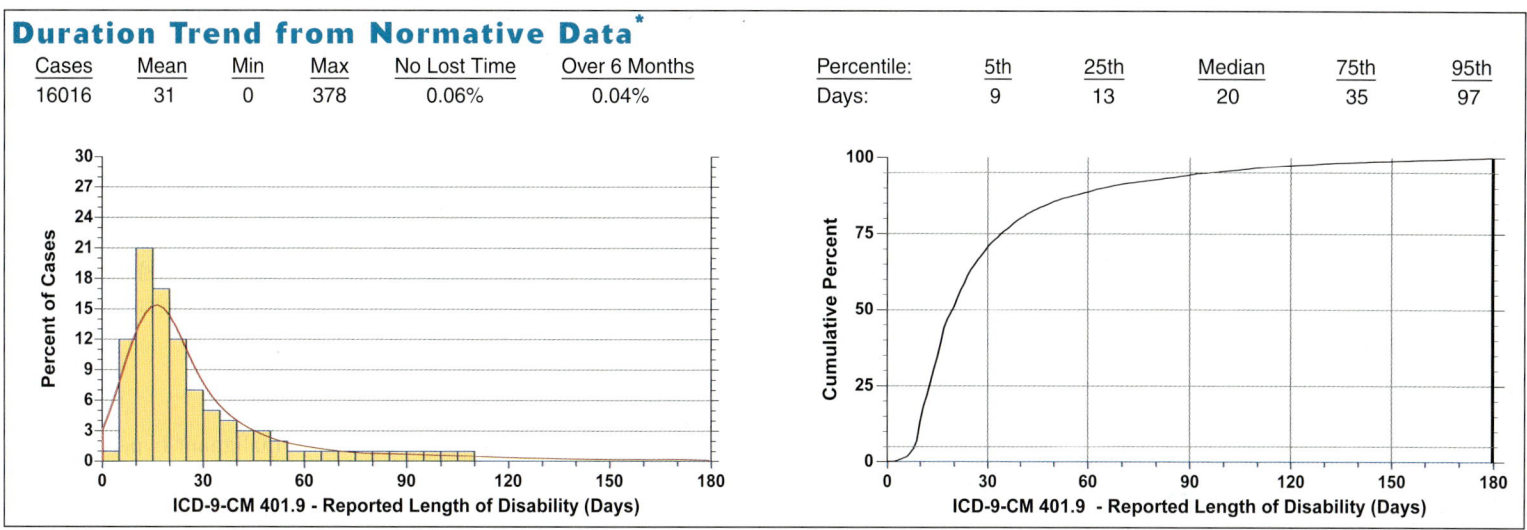

* Differences may exist between the expected duration tables and the normative graphs. Duration tables provide expected recovery periods based on the type of work performed by the individual. The normative graphs reflect the actual observed experience of many individuals across the spectrum of physical conditions, in a variety of industries, and with varying levels of case management.

Failure to Recover

If an individual fails to recover within the maximum duration expectancy period, the reader may wish to reference the following questions to assist in better understanding the specifics of an individual's medical case.

Regarding diagnosis:

- Does the individual have a family history of hypertension?
- Does the individual smoke, use salt, or have a sedentary lifestyle?
- Is the individual overweight?
- Is the individual's cholesterol elevated?
- Does the individual complain of headache, dizziness, irregular heartbeat, tiring easily, impotence, nosebleeds, chest pain, or shortness of breath?
- Are medications or emotional or environmental factors contributing to hypertension?
- Are blood pressure readings elevated consistently?
- Does the individual have distension of neck veins, enlarged thyroid, heart murmur(s), or changes in the eyes?

- Has a urine analysis been done?
- Have blood tests, including a test for renin, which often identifies an increase in the chemical that narrows blood vessels (angiotensin) been done?

Regarding treatment:

- Has the individual attempted to make lifestyle changes?
- Does the individual require assistance such as a weight loss program, counseling with a dietitian, an exercise regimen designed for the individual, or a cease smoking program?
- What drug has the individual taken? Has the dosage been increased?
- Is another drug of the same class required?
- Is a drug in a different class required?
- Is noncompliance with the treatment regimen an issue?
- What second or third drug has been added to the individual's drug regimen?
- Is noncompliance with the treatment regimen an issue?

High Blood Pressure, Benign

Regarding prognosis:

- Is the individual adhering to recommended lifestyle changes and to the prescribed drug regimen?
- Does the individual understand the potential risks of untreated hypertension, including heart disease, stroke, kidney disease, and diabetes? If not, would education encourage compliance with recommended treatment?

References

"Cardiovascular Disorders." Professional Guide to Diseases. 6th ed. Weinstock, Doris, and Marcia Andrews Springhouse, NJ: Springhouse Corporation, 1998. 1061-1151.

Massie, Barry. "Systemic Hypertension." Current Medical Diagnosis and Treatment, 39th ed. Tierney, Lawrence, Stephen McPhee, and Maxine Papadakis, eds. New York: Lange Medical Books/McGraw Hill, 2000. 444-466.

High Blood Pressure, Malignant

Other names / synonyms: Hypertensive Emergency
401, 401.0, 401.9

Definition

Malignant hypertension is a condition of severe high blood pressure that is characterized by swelling of the optic disc (papilledema) and destruction of arteries and arterioles. Systolic pressure is usually >180mm Hg. Diastolic blood pressure is in the range of 120-140 mm Hg. Serious organ damage or death may occur if blood pressure is not promptly reduced.

Malignant hypertension can occur in the course of hypertension with no obvious cause (essential hypertension), but is most often associated with renovascular hypertension, acute kidney disease (glomerulonephritis), chronic kidney failure (renal failure), inflammation of blood vessels in the kidney (renal vasculitis), and toxic pregnancy (preeclampsia). Often, the underlying cause for the condition is unknown.

Malignant hypertension occurs in 1-5% percent of individuals with high blood pressure. It is more common in individuals who are young, black, or male.

Diagnosis

History: Symptoms may include headache, irritability, restlessness, confusion, prolonged drowsiness, blurred vision, nausea, vomiting, malaise, dizziness, chest pain, palpitations, or shortness of breath. Blood pressure elevates to an extreme, often suddenly. Surprisingly, in some individuals the condition is discovered without any symptoms.

Physical exam: An exam shows systolic blood pressure elevation and diastolic blood pressure readings rapidly accelerating (usually to 130 mmHg or higher). Symptoms may also include evidence of damage to retina at back of the eye (retinopathy), and swelling of the head of the optic nerve (papilledema). Blood and protein in the urine indicate progressive kidney involvement (hypertensive nephropathy).

Tests: The diagnosis of malignant hypertension is based on accelerated hypertension, along with the results of a chest x-ray, record of the electrical activity of the heart (electrocardiogram), complete blood count (CBC), blood urea nitrogen, creatinine, electrolytes, and urinalysis. Analysis of urine sediment reveals red cell casts, protein, and/or blood indicating kidney involvement. Blood tests may reveal signs of anemia, coagulation disorders, or elevated levels of renin (enzyme produced by the kidney which is elevated in some forms of hypertension), and aldosterone (hormone elevated in hypertension).

Treatment

Malignant hypertension requires immediate hospitalization, often in an intensive care unit. The goal of treatment is to lower the blood pressure and to stabilize and reverse the damage to target organs. Antihypertensive drugs are given to promptly, yet gradually, reduce systolic and diastolic pressure to levels just above normal. Although intravenous antihypertensive drug therapy is usually indicated, for some individuals oral drugs can also be used successfully. Therapy also usually includes a diuretic to remove excess fluid from the body. If renal failure is involved, dialysis may be needed to remove fluid and wastes from the body until kidney function can be restored. If the underlying cause for the condition is known, it should be specifically treated.

Prognosis

Without prompt and aggressive treatment, malignant hypertension is always fatal. Death is typically due to brain or renal damage. With antihypertensive treatment, however, 90% of individuals live 1 year, and 75-80% live 5 years. The prognosis varies between individuals and depends primarily on the degree of renal damage.

Differential Diagnosis

Similar symptoms may be seen in acute ventricular failure, uremia, cerebrovascular accident, subarachnoid hemorrhage, brain tumor, head injury, epilepsy, collagen disease (such as lupus), encephalitis, drug overdose or withdrawal, and acute anxiety disorder.

Specialists

- Cardiologist

Rehabilitation

Because malignant high blood pressure can be an emergency requiring immediate treatment in the hospital, rehabilitation for this form of high blood pressure begins after the underlying cause has been identified and treated. As with rehabilitation for other forms of high blood pressure, an exercise program developed by a healthcare professional is important and focuses on aerobic exercise, as this type of exercise is better for reducing blood pressure. The conventional recommendation for exercise is 30 minutes a day for 5 days a week to get the maximum cardiovascular benefit. The traditional recommendation for exercise programs for individuals recovering from the effects of malignant hypertension is aerobic exercise for 30-45 minutes at least 3 days a week.

Rhythmic forms of moderate exercise are used in the rehabilitation of most forms of high blood pressure such as jogging, bicycling, swimming. The benefits come from the expansion of the blood vessels in the working muscles. This decreases the total resistance in blood vessels throughout the body and enhances blood flow. Thirty to forty-five minutes of mild-to-moderate exercise such as brisk walking or bike riding 4-5 days per week is recommended. This can lower blood pressure. If rehabilitation is done at a cardiac center, workouts may last up to an hour. In this setting, an electrocardiograph is used to record the continuous electrical activity of the heart muscle. A physical therapist experienced in cardiac rehabilitation keeps a daily log of the individual's blood pressure, heart rate, and cardiac rhythm.

Throughout the course of rehabilitation for high blood pressure, patient and family education is necessary to establish a program the individual can continue once discharged from the care of the rehabilitation professional. A 6-month exercise program contributes to a decrease in the resistance of blood flow within the body. This results in a subsequent decrease in blood pressure. Because most individuals with malignant high blood pressure are managed with medication, it is important that the therapist has a medication history for each individual as many of these drugs alter the acute and chronic response to exercise.

Work Restrictions / Accommodations

Work restrictions or special accommodations need to be determined on an individual basis. They depend on the degree of organ damage or impairment resulting from the hypertension.

Comorbid Conditions

Persistence of any condition that leads to or worsens high blood pressure, such as coronary artery disease or renovascular disease, prolongs disability.

Complications

Possible complications include acute brain dysfunction, fluid accumulation in the lungs (pulmonary edema), kidney damage (nephropathy), renal failure, damage to the retina at the back of the eye (retinopathy), insufficient blood supply to the heart muscle, and heart failure or heart attack (myocardial infarction).

Factors Influencing Duration

Length of disability may be influenced by the cause of hypertension, degree of damage to the kidneys and other target organs, the response to treatment, or the presence of complications.

Length of Disability

Disability may be permanent.

Duration in Days

Job Classification	Minimum	Optimum	Maximum
Sedentary work	14	14	28
Light work	14	14	28
Medium work	14	21	42
Heavy work	14	28	56
Very Heavy work	14	28	56

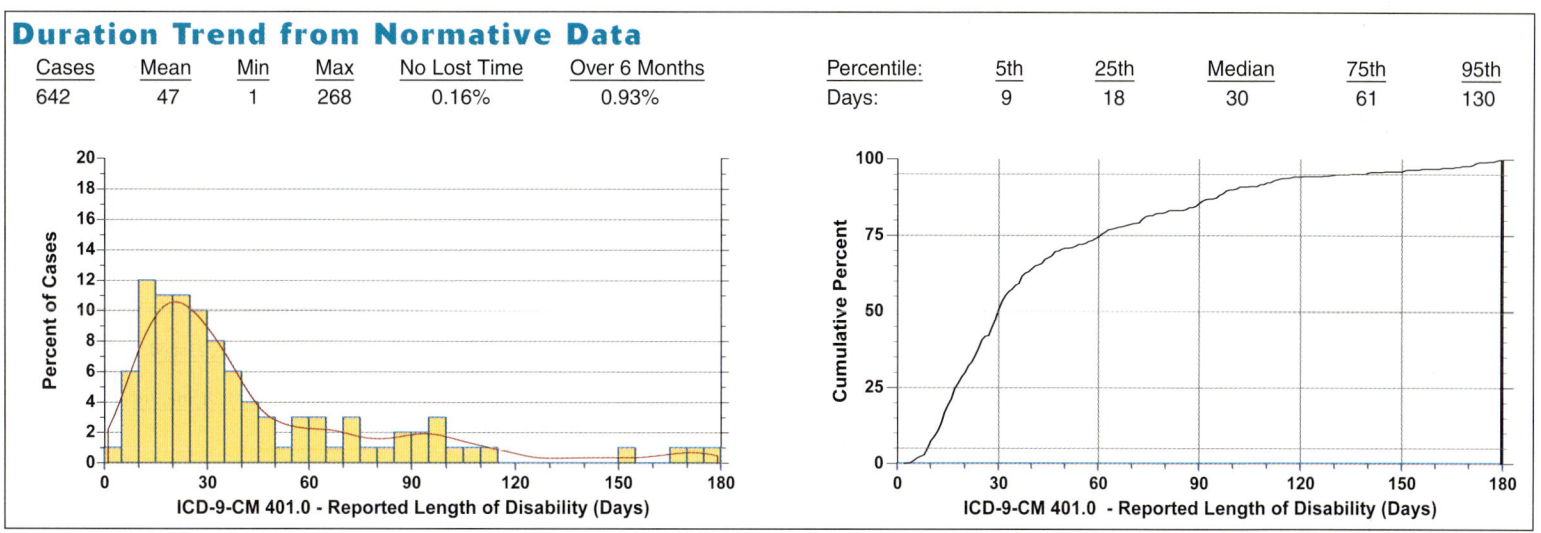

Duration Trend from Normative Data

Cases	Mean	Min	Max	No Lost Time	Over 6 Months
642	47	1	268	0.16%	0.93%

Percentile:	5th	25th	Median	75th	95th
Days:	9	18	30	61	130

High Blood Pressure, Malignant

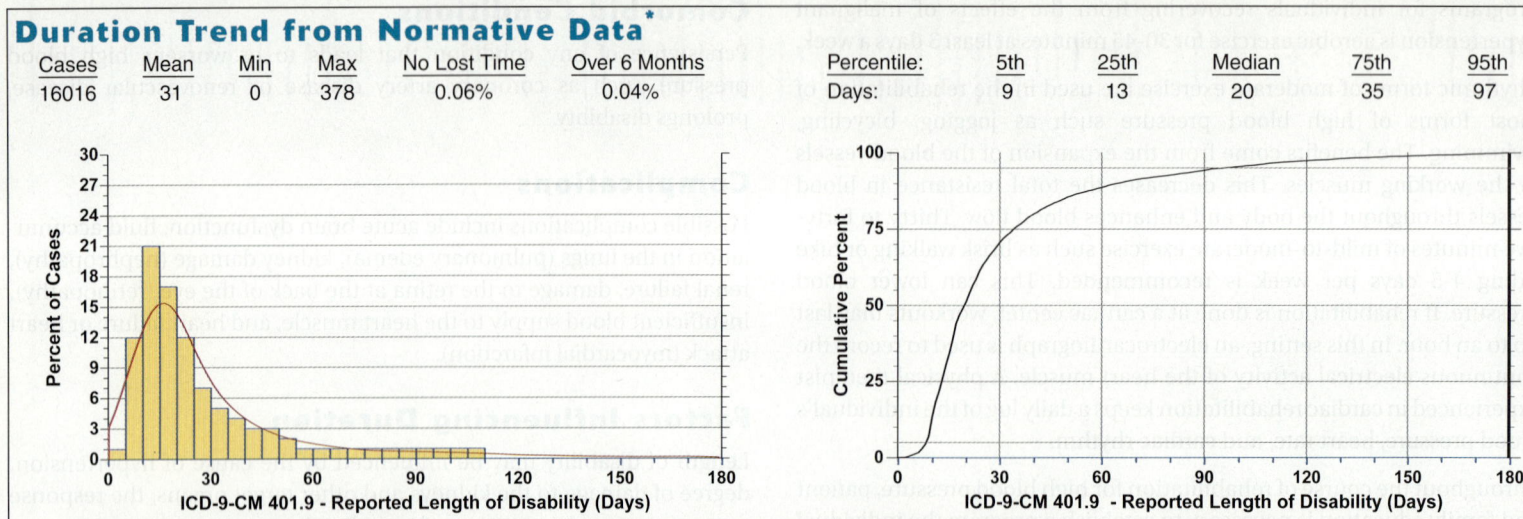

* Differences may exist between the expected duration tables and the normative graphs. Duration tables provide expected recovery periods based on the type of work performed by the individual. The normative graphs reflect the actual observed experience of many individuals across the spectrum of physical conditions, in a variety of industries, and with varying levels of case management.

Failure to Recover

If an individual fails to recover within the maximum duration expectancy period, the reader may wish to reference the following questions to assist in better understanding the specifics of an individual's medical case.

Regarding diagnosis:

- Has diagnosis of malignant hypertension been confirmed?
- Have other conditions with similar symptoms been ruled out?
- Has the underlying cause of malignant hypertension been identified?
- Has individual experienced any complications related to the malignant hypertension?

Regarding treatment:

- Has blood pressure been stabilized? Was blood pressure successfully sustained at acceptable levels?
- Has individual sustained organ damage? Is damage reversible?
- If renal failure was involved, was dialysis necessary? Are kidneys again functional?
- If the underlying cause for the condition is known, has it responded favorably to treatment?

Regarding prognosis:

- Does individual's condition continue to be monitored by a physician?
- Has individual responded favorably to antihypertensive treatment?
- Has blood pressure remained within acceptable limits?
- Did individual sustain permanent organ damage?
- Does individual have a coexisting condition, such as coronary artery disease or renovascular disease that may complicate treatment or impact recovery?
- Is the individual participating in a comprehensive rehabilitation program?

References

Braunwald, Eugene. Heart Disease: A Textbook of Cardiovascular Medicine, 5th ed. Philadelphia: W.B. Saunders Company, 1997.

Brenner, Barry. Brenner and Rector's The Kidney, 6th ed. Philadelphia: W.B. Saunders Company, 2000.

Cotran, Ramzi, Vinay Kumar, and Tucker Collins. Robbins Pathologic Basis of Disease, 6th ed. Philadelphia: W.B. Saunders Company, 1999.

Ferri, Fred. Ferri's Clinical Advisor. St. Louis: Mosby, 2000.

Goldman, Lee, and J. Claude Bennett. Cecil Textbook of Medicine, 21st ed. Philadelphia: W.B. Saunders Company, 2000.

Goroll, Allan, Lawrence May, and Albert Mulley. Primary Care Medicine, 3rd ed. Philadelphia: Lippincott-Raven, 1995.

Hip Replacement, Total

Other names / synonyms: Hip Arthroplasty, THR, TJR, Total Joint Arthroplasty

81.51, 81.52

Definition

A total hip replacement (THR) is a surgical procedure whereby the diseased cartilage and bone of the hip joint are surgically replaced with artificial materials. The hip joint is a ball and socket joint. The ball is the head of the thighbone (femur). The socket is a "cup-shaped" bone of the pelvis called the acetabulum.

During hip replacement surgery, the ball (head of the femur) is removed and replaced with a metal ball set on a stem. The stem is inserted into the canal of the thighbone and may be fixed in place with cement or the stem may be designed for placement without bone cement. The socket is sanded down to healthy bone and a plastic cup or socket is held in place with screws and/or bone cement.

THR is performed more than 120,000 times per year in the US. Sixty-two percent of all THR procedures in the US are performed in women. Two-thirds of all THR procedures are performed in individuals who are older than 65 years of age. Most THR procedures are performed on whites. The prevalence rate of hip implants (fixation devices and artificial joints) is 4.2 per 1,000 in whites compared with 1.7 per 1,000 in blacks. The disparity by race increases markedly with age.

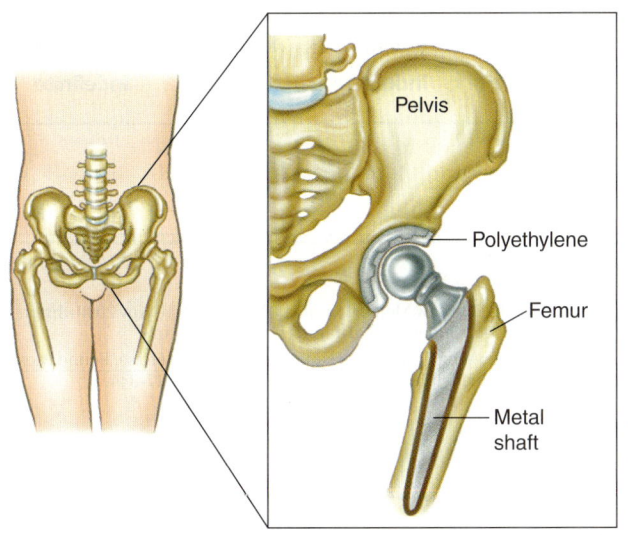

Reason for Procedure

The most common reason for performing the total hip replacement procedure is progressively severe arthritis in the hip joint. The most common type of arthritis leading to THR is degenerative arthritis (osteoarthritis) of the hip. Other conditions leading to THR include bony fractures of the hip joint and death (necrosis) of the hip bone.

Hip joints are replaced when individuals have severe pain, significant loss of motion, and an inability to perform routine and recreational activities. THR is elective surgery. The decision to proceed is largely the individual's and is based primarily on pain.

Hip replacement cannot be done if there is active infection in the joint or if the quality of the bone will not support the implants and increased weight-bearing.

Description

Hip replacement surgery is normally performed with the individual under general anesthesia. During hip replacement surgery, the surgeon removes the diseased bone tissue and cartilage from the hip joint. The healthy parts of the hip are left intact. Then, the surgeon replaces the head of the femur (the ball) and the acetabulum (the socket) with new, artificial parts.

The surgeon may sometimes use a special glue or cement to bond the new parts of the hip joint to the existing, healthy bone. This is referred to as a "cemented" procedure. In an "uncemented" procedure, the artificial parts are made of a porous material that allows the individual's own bone to grow in to the pores and hold the new parts in place. Sometimes a "hybrid" procedure replacement is performed, which consists of a cemented "ball" and an uncemented "socket." Hip replacement surgery usually lasts between 2-3 hours.

When the individual awakens, there will be an IV tube in place for fluids, pain medication, and antibiotics. There will be a small drainage tube called a "Hemovac" collecting blood from the surgical site. A Foley catheter will be in place to drain the bladder until the individual is able to urinate on his/her own. A firm pillow will be between the individual's legs to prevent turning the hip or crossing the legs. The individual will be hospitalized for a short time.

Prognosis

Results are generally very good, and most individuals are relieved of all of their hip and groin pain. Approximately 90% of total hip replacements will last 10 years, and 80% will last 20 years.

Specialists

• Orthopedic Surgeon	• Physiatrist

Rehabilitation

Individuals who have a total hip replacement require both physical and occupational therapy. Occupational therapy is needed during an individual's hospitalization after surgery. Individuals learn how to dress, bathe, and cook for themselves safely without injuring the new hip joint. Occupational therapists may order equipment such as tub seats and long handled sponges and shoehorns to help the individual accomplish these tasks.

Physical therapy begins in the hospital and continues on an outpatient basis. The first goal of therapy is to teach precautionary measures to the individual. These include not bending the hip past a 90 degree angle, not crossing the legs, and not rotating the leg so that the toes point inward, as these activities risk dislocation of the prosthesis.

The second goal of physical therapy is the control pain. Individuals accomplish this through the use of ice packs applied as needed to the hip for 15 minutes.

The third goal of physical therapy is increasing the strength and range of motion of the hip. Examples of these types of exercises include heel slides, isometric gluteus maximus sets, and supine hip abduction.

Individuals may perform knee and ankle strengthening exercises to decrease the amount of stress through the hip joint.

The final goal of physical therapy is increasing functional abilities. Physical therapists teach individuals how to walk using a walker or crutches. Individuals progress to walking with a cane and then walking without any assistance as they are able. Individuals may walk on a treadmill to help normalize their gait pattern. Individuals learn to ascend and descend stairs while using crutches, and are eventually progressed to negotiating stairs without assistance. Individuals also learn to perform transfers to the bathtub, bed, and chair within the learned precautionary measures.

Work Restrictions / Accommodations

Riding in a car is permitted, but frequent stops (hourly) must be made to get out and walk and stretch. Work restrictions or accommodations should include no prolonged standing, limited stair climbing, frequent rest periods, and use of a walker or cane during early recovery stages. Stooping, squatting, and excessive forward bending should be avoided for 6 weeks.

A higher chair or firm cushions added to a low chair will be necessary to assist in standing. A chair with arm rests to assist in standing may be needed.

With proper physical therapy, the individual should be able to return to an active lifestyle.

Comorbid Conditions

Conditions that could impact the ability to recover and further lengthen disability include obesity, rheumatoid arthritis, osteoarthritis, bursitis, and other musculoskeletal disorders of the back, pelvis, and lower limbs, but especially the presence of disease in the other (contralateral) hip joint.

Procedure Complications

As with all major surgical procedures, complications can occur. The most common complications following hip replacement surgery are thrombophlebitis, infection, dislocation, and loosening.

Thrombophlebitis (deep vein thrombosis) can occur after any operation but is more likely after surgery on the hip, pelvis, or knee. Deep vein thrombosis occurs when blood clots form within the large veins of the leg. Pressure stockings to keep blood circulating and medications to thin the blood can be used for prevention.

Factors Influencing Duration

Length of disability may be influenced by complications from the procedure, the underlying disease process, age, and the individual's job requirements. Sedentary and light work can be performed sooner if done sitting. Hip replacement is not compatible with heavy work. Disability may be permanent.

Length of Disability

Job Classification	Minimum	Optimum	Maximum
Sedentary work	28	63	84
Light work	42	112	140
Medium work	84	112	182
Heavy work	Indefinite	Indefinite	Indefinite
Very Heavy work	Indefinite	Indefinite	Indefinite

Duration in Days

References

A Patient's Guide to Artificial Hip Replacement. Medical Multimedia Group. 26 Mar 1998. 10 Nov 2000 <http://www.sechrest.com/mmg/thr/>.

Questions and Answers About Hip Replacement. NIH. 2000. 09 Nov 2000 <http://www.nih.gov/niams/healthinfo/hiprepqa.htm>.

Total Hip. Johns Hopkins Bayview Medical Center. 01 Apr 1999. 10 Nov 2000 <http://www.bayviewortho.com/patients/education/Hip/totalhip.htm>.

Kisner, Carolyn, and Lynn Allen Colby. "The Hip." Therapeutic Exercise: Foundations and Techniques, 2nd ed Philadelphia: F.A. Davis Company, 1990. 317-344.

Histoplasmosis

Other names / synonyms: Darling's Disease

115, 115.0, 115.10, 115.12, 115.13, 115.14, 115.15, 115.5, 115.90

Definition

Histoplasmosis is a fungal infection that usually invades the lungs. Spread by inhalation of spores from the histoplasma capsulatum fungus, the spore cells reproduce in the lungs but may spread into other parts of the body (disseminated histoplasmosis). Individuals with weakened immune systems are the most susceptible to this disease. The disease also tends to be more aggressive in individuals exposed to large quantities of spores.

The acute form of the disease usually manifests as a short-term upper respiratory tract infection typical of epidemics. Histoplasmosis can be dormant for years after initial exposure to the fungus, with delayed or recurring symptoms (reactivation histoplasmosis) often appearing in individuals with significantly impaired immune systems.

The fungus carrying the disease exists worldwide, but is found in abundance in soils of the Ohio and Mississippi River Valleys in the US, Central and South America, the Caribbean, France, Africa, and the Far East. The fungus is associated with areas where bird or bat droppings have accumulated over several years. Fungal spores may be disturbed and become airborne at work sites such as building ventilation systems near pigeon droppings, dirt floors of chicken coops, and caves with roosting bats. These sites create a potential work hazard that has prompted the National Institute for Occupational Safety and Health to release safety guidelines, e.g., notifying workers of potential risks where exposure is likely to occur. Those in occupations considered at risk for exposure to histoplasmosis include construction workers, farmers, gardeners, roofers, and bridge inspectors.

While not usually affecting healthy individuals, about 2% of individuals with AIDS have the progressive disseminated form of histoplasmosis. In these cases, toxins in the bloodstream (sepsis) may cause widespread tissue damage that can lead to failure of organs such as the kidney and liver. In areas of the US where histoplasma capsulatum fungus is prevalent, about 250,000 individuals are infected annually. Although symptoms are absent in most cases, studies reveal that up to 80% of residents living in areas where the fungus is abundant test positive for the presence of histoplasmosis infection.

Diagnosis

History: In the acute form, symptoms may develop within days or weeks after exposure to a site where bird or bat droppings have accumulated. Even when infected, healthy individuals may have no symptoms (asymptomatic) or exhibit a relatively mild illness. If symptoms are present, they may be flu-like and include chills, cough, fever, headache, abdominal pain, chest pain, or difficulty breathing. Skin lesions and joint pain may also be reported. The individual may also have a pre-existing condition such as emphysema or an immune disorder that has worsened. In the progressive disseminated form of histoplasmosis, symptoms may worsen slowly or very rapidly.

Severe or chronic (chronic cavitary histoplasmosis) forms of the disease develop gradually over several weeks. Symptoms may include a feeling of illness (malaise), gastrointestinal disturbances, diarrhea, weight loss, chronic mild fever, cough that produces yellow or green sputum (phlegm), confusion, disorientation, and neck pain. Complaints in rare cases may include impaired vision or blindness (presumed ocular histoplasmosis).

Physical exam: Milder cases resemble upper respiratory infections. In progressive forms of the disease, ulcers of the mucous membranes in the mouth and throat may be present. When pressure is applied by hand (palpation), enlarged lymph nodes (lymphadenopathy), spleen (splenomegaly), and/or liver (hepatomegaly) may be detected. Individuals with immune disorders or pre-existing related conditions may have difficulty in breathing. Continual weight loss (wasting syndrome) may be evident.

Tests: The diagnosis can be confirmed by microscopic examination of specimens taken from phlegm, blood, or tissue biopsies to confirm the presence of targeted microorganisms. Blood and urine tests (serology) may also help identify specific antibodies produced by the immune system as a defense against antigens associated with the disease. Investigations are being done on new laboratory methods that use polymerase chain reaction (PCR) technology to directly identify specific genes or DNA sequences of the organism.

Chest x-rays may help reveal abnormalities in the lungs, but these could be variable and nonspecific. Moderately severe infections may be recognized in the x-rays as an atypical pneumonia. Other diagnostic tests may be performed to rule out complications or coexisting conditions. A complete blood count (CBC), detection of total percentage of red blood cells (hematocrit), and hemoglobin analysis can rule out anemia. Liver and kidney function tests indicate possible impending failure of these organs. CT scans obtain images of the head and abdominal areas to help detect presence of the disease. Tests may also be conducted to determine whether lungs are functioning adequately (pulmonary function tests). In individuals with AIDS, bacteria in the blood (bacteremia) should be investigated. A urine antigen test is very helpful in the diagnosis and follow up of histoplasmosis in individuals with AIDS.

Skin testing is generally not useful in diagnosing histoplasmosis. Many residents living in an affected area will test positive without having symptoms. In disseminated histoplasmosis, half of those with the condition will have negative results after skin testing.

Treatment

In milder, acute cases, symptoms usually clear up without treatment. More severe forms of histoplasmosis are treated with oral or intravenous antifungal drugs. Treatment usually lasts about 2 weeks but this may need to be extended up to 6 months for more severe cases. Individuals with AIDS-related histoplasmosis may require lifelong suppressive treatment. Fluid can be drawn from the lung through a needle (thoracentesis) to relieve congestion.

In extreme cases of chronic pulmonary histoplasmosis, surgical intervention may be warranted to correct cavities that have formed in the lungs (surgical resection). In individuals with visual problems such as abnormal membrane formation in the back of the eye (choroiditis), laser treatment may be needed (photocoagulation).

Prognosis

For most healthy individuals, symptoms are relatively mild to nonexistent. Mild cases are seldom fatal and usually clear up in a few weeks. Massive exposure to a source of histoplasmosis or the development of complications, however, may result in a chronic condition requiring continual monitoring and medical treatment for up to 6 months. Chronic lung disease (chronic pulmonary histoplasmosis) may develop in some cases, particularly among individuals with emphysema. Bacterial invasion or lung damage may eventually result in death.

For those who undergo surgical resection of lung cavities, outcomes are usually good unless the individual is severely malnourished or has other complications affecting the ability to recover.

Without treatment, infection can spread and begin to destroy different organs of the body such as the liver and kidneys. Untreated progressive disseminated histoplasmosis is up to 90% fatal. Histoplasmosis-infected individuals with AIDS require lifelong therapy.

Differential Diagnosis

Histoplasmosis symptoms are similar to a variety of respiratory illnesses including influenza, asthma, respiratory tuberculosis, emphysema, lung tumor, pneumonia, and silicosis. Similar symptoms are also found in other fungal infections such as aspergillosis, blastomycosis, and San Joaquin Valley Fever (coccidioidomycosis). Sarcoidosis creates inflammation of tissue in the eyes, lungs, liver, lymph nodes, and other areas.

Specialists

- Cardiologist
- Internist
- Neurologist
- Ophthalmologist
- Radiologist

Work Restrictions / Accommodations

Individuals who develop complications such as chronic lung infection may be unable to perform tasks that require endurance or physical exertion. Workers should be notified of possible exposure risks. Protective equipment such as respirators may be required.

Comorbid Conditions

Pre-existing immune disorders hamper the body's ability to fight off infection and may lengthen recovery time. Individuals with HIV or AIDS are more likely to develop the progressive disseminated form of histoplasmosis. Heavy smoking delays recovery.

Complications

Immune disorders that impair the individual's ability to fight off infection may cause the development of additional conditions such sepsis or chronic lung disease with symptoms similar to tuberculosis. Anemia may also occur if the bone marrow is affected.

Impaired vision and/or blindness may develop. Inflammation and fluid may form around the heart (pericarditis). Scarring in the chest cavity (fibrosing mediastinitis) may also occur. Individuals taking drugs that impair immune responses such as those associated with organ transplants are also susceptible to spread of the infection. Heavy smoking greatly increases the risk of chronic lung disease with accompanying complications.

Factors Influencing Duration

Length of disability may be influenced by the stage and severity of the disease at the time of diagnosis, the treatment, response to treatment, and the presence of other chronic medical conditions such as lung disease. If drug-resistant forms of the fungus are present, the disease may progress until an effective compound is found.

Length of Disability

For chronic cases, disability may be permanent.

Acute.

Duration in Days

Job Classification	Minimum	Optimum	Maximum
Sedentary work	0	7	14
Light work	0	7	14
Medium work	0	7	14
Heavy work	0	7	14
Very Heavy work	0	7	14

Chronic.

Duration in Days

Job Classification	Minimum	Optimum	Maximum
Sedentary work	14	28	56
Light work	14	28	56
Medium work	28	56	84
Heavy work	84	112	168
Very Heavy work	84	112	168

Failure to Recover

If an individual fails to recover within the maximum duration expectancy period, the reader may wish to reference the following questions to assist in better understanding the specifics of an individual's medical case.

Regarding diagnosis:

- Does the individual work or play in areas where bird or bat droppings accumulate?
- Is the individual a heavy smoker?
- Does the individual have flu-like symptoms including chills, cough, fever, headache, abdominal pain, chest pain, or difficulty breathing?
- Does the individual report skin lesions, joint pain or weight loss?
- Does the individual have a pre-existing condition such as emphysema or an immune disorder that has worsened?
- Has the individual developed malaise, gastrointestinal disturbances, diarrhea, weight loss, chronic mild fever, productive cough with yellow or green sputum, confusion, disorientation, or neck pain?
- Does the individual have ulcers of the mucous membranes in the mouth and throat?

- On palpation, are lymphadenopathy, splenomegaly, and/or hepatomegaly detected?
- Does the individual have difficulty breathing?
- Has the individual had microscopic examination of specimens taken from phlegm, blood, or tissue biopsies?
- Has the individual had a chest x-ray, CBC, serology testing, urinalysis, CT scan and pulmonary function tests?
- Have conditions with similar symptoms been ruled out?

Regarding treatment:

- Does the individual have a milder acute case? Did symptoms resolve without treatment?
- Does the individual have a more severe acute case? Was the individual treated with IV antifungal drugs for 2 weeks up to 6 months?
- Does the individual have AIDS-related histoplasmosis? Will the individual receive lifelong suppressive treatment?
- Was it necessary to do a thoracentesis?
- Was it necessary to perform a surgical resection of the lungs?
- Were laser treatments necessary for choroiditis?

Regarding prognosis:

- Is the individual's employer able to accommodate any necessary restrictions?
- Does the individual have any conditions that may affect ability to recover?
- Does the individual have any complications such as chronic lung disease, anemia, impaired vision, blindness, pericarditis, fibrosing mediastinitis or sepsis?

References

Chang, Ryan C., and Susanto, Irawan. Histoplasmosis. eMedicine.com. 06 Jul 2000. 26 Aug 2000 <http://www.emedicine.com/med/topic1021.htm>.

Wheat, Joe. Histoplasmosis Information Guide. Indiana University Histoplasmosis Reference Laboratory. 2000. 28 Aug 2000 <http://www.iupui.edu/~histodgn/his-edu.html>.

Hodgkin's Disease

Other names / synonyms: Hodgkin's Lymphoma, Lymphadenoma, Lymphatic Cancer

200.1, 201, 201.0, 201.00, 201.08, 201.1, 201.10, 201.18, 201.2, 201.20, 201.28, 201.4, 201.40, 201.48, 201.5, 201.50, 201.58, 201.6, 201.60, 201.68, 201.7, 201.70, 201.78, 201.9, 201.90, 201.98

Definition

Hodgkin's disease is an abnormal, cancerous growth of lymph tissue (lymphoma).

Lymph tissue is found within the lymphatic system, which is a vast network of tubes that transports a clear, plasma-like fluid called lymph. Hodgkin's disease occurs when a certain cell type (Reed-Sternberg cells) of the lymphatic tissues multiply uncontrollably and destroy the normal structure of the tubes within the lymph system.

Hodgkin's disease usually begins as a painless swelling of the lymph nodes. It may also spread to the bone marrow and to nonlymphatic structures. There is no known cause for Hodgkin's disease but it may be related to a viral infection (Epstein-Barr virus, or EBV). The Epstein-Barr virus is frequently found in tumors taken from individuals with Hodgkin's disease. Furthermore, individuals who have ever contracted mononucleosis (a disease caused by the EBV) have about a three-fold increased risk of contracting Hodgkin's disease. Thus, it is now generally accepted that the Epstein-Barr virus likely plays a primary role in the development of this form of cancer. Another risk factor for Hodgkin's disease may include the human immunodeficiency virus (HIV). Individuals with HIV have a 5 to 8-fold greater risk of Hodgkin's disease. Some occupations may also be associated with a greater risk (woodworkers have a moderate association with this condition). Individuals who have been farmers for more than 10 years have a 2-fold risk, and this increases to 3.2-fold or 3.4-fold in farmers with pesticide or livestock and meat processing exposures, respectively. There may be a genetic predisposition toward Hodgkin's and about 1% of individuals with this condition will have a family history of the disease.

The incidence of Hodgkin's disease varies widely worldwide from 0.8 per 100,000 people in Asia to 3.7 per 100,000 people in all of North America. Europe shows rates that are intermediate between these 2 extremes; while in the US, the incidence rate is 2.9 per 100,000 people. The incidence rates are lower in women than men in all geographic areas (male:female incidence ratio in the US is 1.4:1). In the US, the rates in blacks and Asians are lower than those in whites. Generally, Hodgkin's disease appears to affect predominantly young adults (15-34 years of age) or older individuals (50 years or older). All incidence rates seem to be decreasing over time in most areas.

Diagnosis

History: Individuals will report a painless mass in the neck. Individuals may find a mass on the inner thigh area (ilioinguinal-femoral region). Other symptoms such as persistent fever, weight loss, night sweats, itching (pruritus), and fatigue may occur in one-third of individuals. Fever that is associated with Hodgkin's disease usually appears or is more noticeable in the evening. Characteristically, the fever is cyclic (Pel-Ebstein fever) and it may recur at variable intervals of several days to many weeks. Individuals may also report pain that is induced by alcohol ingestion. This pain is sudden and severe, and occurs within a few minutes of ingesting even a very small amount of alcohol. Often, the pain will occur at a site of bone (osseous) involvement with the disease.

Physical exam: Enlarged lymph nodes, nearly always in the neck or armpit but occasionally in the groin, are usually noted during physical examination. Enlargement of both the spleen (splenomegaly) and liver (hepatomegaly) may be noticed during finger or hand manipulation (palpation) of the abdomen. If the cancer is advanced, large tumor masses may appear on the neck producing the so-called bull-neck appearance of Hodgkin's disease.

Tests: Definite diagnosis of Hodgkin's disease requires taking a sample of tissue (biopsy) from an enlarged lymph node. Other tests may include a routine x-ray (chest radiographic examination), which could reveal a mass in the middle of the chest (mediastinal mass). Computer-aided x-ray analysis (computerized tomography), low-frequency radio waves (magnetic resonance imaging, or MRI), or exploratory surgery into the abdomen (laparotomy) may aid in determining the spread of the disease. A sample of bone marrow (bone marrow biopsy) may reveal the extent of bone involvement. Blood analysis can be run (serum alkaline phosphatase test) to determine the extent of liver involvement and high frequency sound waves (ultrasound) may be used to determine liver enlargement. A complete blood count (CBC) will provide information regarding the number of white blood cells (leukocytes) and platelets in the blood stream, both of which are usually elevated. Other blood tests may include serum albumin level, serum lactate dehydrogenase, and serum Beta-2 microglobulin level. A hemoglobin level test may reveal a low concentration of hemoglobin in the red blood cells (anemia). A test to identify a generalized inflammatory condition (erythrocyte sedimentation rate, or ESR) may be done, and it is usually elevated in individuals with Hodgkin's disease.

Treatment

Treatment depends upon the stage of the disease at diagnosis. Individuals who have limited disease without systemic symptoms (stages IA and IIA) are usually treated with radiation therapy only (full-dose, extended-field irradiation). Usually, the neck region and the upper abdominal area receive radiation treatment if the disease is found only above the diaphragm (supradiaphragmatic). Also, individuals who present with disease that is limited to the pelvis or abdomen are usually treated with irradiation only. Those who have otherwise limited disease symptoms but have one or more large tumor masses (bulky disease) in the chest area (mediastinum) are best treated with one or more chemotherapeutic agents (combination chemotherapy) along with irradiation (combined modality therapy). Additionally, individuals who have extensive involvement with their spleen may receive combined modality therapy. Those who have limited disease with systemic symptoms such as fever, weight loss, night sweats, itching (pruritus), and fatigue (stages I and IIB) may be treated with irradiation and surgical removal of the spleen (splenectomy). Certain subgroups of individuals with stages I or IIB Hodgkin's disease may require chemotherapy treatment only, or chemotherapy in combination with radiation treatment. Bulky disease (limited to the mediastinum) in combination with systemic symptoms (stage IB) is rare and usually the disease is found to be more widespread. Individuals with non-bulky disease and limited upper abdominal disease (stage IIIA) may be cured by irradiation and/or combination chemotherapy. Stage IIIA disease that has extensive involvement of the spleen is best treated with chemotherapy alone or combined modality therapy. Chemotherapy is the primary treatment for individuals with stage IIIB disease in which there are sites of initial bulky disease and upper abdominal involvement. Stage IV disease in which there is spread to other organs such as bone and/or liver requires combination chemotherapy as the primary treatment. However, there may be selected situations in which irradiation should be used as well.

Prognosis

Hodgkin's disease is very treatable and, overall, 75% of individuals with this condition are cured. Ten-year survival rates range between 80-95%, although more advanced-stage cancers have a poorer prognosis. Also, the general population of individuals with Hodgkin's have a higher mortality rate than all nonaffected individuals primarily due to treatment-related mortality. That is, individuals with Hodgkin's disease ultimately have higher death rates because of nondisease-related effects of chemotherapy or radiation treatments. Most recurrences of Hodgkin's (approximately 30% of early-stage cases) occur in the first 2-3 years after diagnosis, and these usually are effectively treated with chemotherapy. Approximately 13% of all individuals with Hodgkin's disease relapse at a later time (3-20 years following treatment).

Differential Diagnosis

Conditions that present with symptoms similar to Hodgkin's disease include non-Hodgkin's lymphoma or other lymphomas, mononucleosis, HIV infection, lupus, and tuberculosis.

Specialists

- General Surgeon
- Hematologist
- Oncologist
- Radiation Oncologist

Work Restrictions / Accommodations

Individuals with Hodgkin's disease will experience high levels of fatigue with normal levels of physical exertion. Chemotherapy and radiation therapy can cause additional weakness and fatigue. Work responsibilities may need to be modified until recovery is complete. Also, individuals who have exploratory abdominal surgery (laparotomy) may require more sedentary, nonphysical work for a period of time.

Complementary and Alternative Therapies

Content is intended for awareness only. Treatments may or may not be effective. Scientific evidence may be lacking and some substances have potentially toxic effects. Dr. Presley Reed and the editors do not endorse the use of these therapies in the absence of consultation with a licensed medical professional.

Massage therapy - May help with relaxation and well being.

Acupuncture - Needles inserted into certain points on the body may help to alleviate pain from Hodgkin's disease.

Comorbid Conditions

Conditions that may impact an individual's ability to recover from Hodgkin's disease include prior liver disease, heart disease, or any systemic disease such as diabetes.

Complications

Complications of Hodgkin's disease can include several emergency situations that may result from the condition. These include lymph node enlargement or fluid accumulation in various organs to the point where there is airway obstruction, obstruction of the major vein that returns blood to the heart (superior vena caval obstruction), compression of the heart (pericardial tamponade), spinal cord compression, obstruction of the bile duct (extrahepatic biliary obstruction), or pressure on nerves in the head or periphery (cranial and peripheral neuropathies). Complications of radiation treatment for Hodgkin's disease include development of secondary cancers such as acute nonlymphocytic leukemia, radiation-induced carcinomas and sarcomas, and non-Hodgkin's lymphoma. Also, radiation therapy to the neck region may result in an underactive thyroid (hypothyroidism) several years after treatment is complete. Chemotherapy treatments often result in acute (but reversible) toxicity leading to nausea, vomiting, and neurologic disorders. Infections may occur as a result of depression of the immune system by chemotherapy treatment or as a result of the Hodgkin's disease itself. Other complications of chemotherapy may include heart or lung disorders and female infertility. Finally, psychological problems may occur in individuals with grossly enlarged lymph nodes. These may increase in size significantly to the point where the individual's appearance is referred to clinically as the bull-neck that is associated with Hodgkin's disease. Such changes may produce problems with the affected individual's body image, self-esteem, and interpersonal relationships.

Factors Influencing Duration

Factors that influence length of disability include the stage of the disease when it is first detected, methods and complexity of treatment, and the individual's response to treatment. Individuals older than 50 years tend to have more advanced disease and do less well in response to combination chemotherapy and irradiation than do younger individuals. Disability may result from the adverse effects of radiation or chemotherapy and not only from the disease itself.

Length of Disability

Duration depends on stage, severity of symptoms, type of treatment and dosage. Heavy physical labor is usually restricted following surgery (laparotomy), chemotherapy, and/or radiation therapy treatments. For treatment with radiation or chemotherapy, durations reflect recovery period for treatment only, not for the disease itself. Disability may be permanent.

Radiation or chemotherapy.

Duration in Days

Job Classification	Minimum	Optimum	Maximum
Sedentary work	2	7	14
Light work	2	7	14
Medium work	3	7	14
Heavy work	7	14	21
Very Heavy work	7	14	21

Failure to Recover

If an individual fails to recover within the maximum duration expectancy period, the reader may wish to reference the following questions to assist in better understanding the specifics of an individual's medical case.

Regarding diagnosis:
- Does individual have a history of infection with the Epstein-Barr virus (EBV), particularly mononucleosis?
- Is individual infected with the human immunodeficiency virus (HIV)?
- Has individual been a farmer for more than 10 years or worked with wood?
- Is there a family history of Hodgkin's disease?
- Does individual report a painless mass in the neck or in the inner thigh area (ilioinguinal-femoral region)?
- Has individual noted persistent fever, weight loss, night sweats, itching (pruritus), or fatigue?
- Does individual report pain that is induced by alcohol ingestion?
- Has a tissue sample (biopsy) been taken from an enlarged lymph node to make a definitive diagnosis of Hodgkin's disease?
- Were a chest x-ray, computed tomography (CT scan), magnetic resonance imaging (MRI), or exploratory surgery into the abdomen (laparotomy) required to determine the extent of the disease?
- Was a bone marrow biopsy done to reveal the extent of bone involvement?
- Were complete blood count (CBC), liver function tests, serum albumin, serum lactate dehydrogenase, and/or serum Beta-2 microglobulin levels taken?
- Was the diagnosis of Hodgkin's disease confirmed?

Regarding treatment:
- At what stage of the disease was individual at time of diagnosis?
- If at stage IA and IIA, did individual receive radiation therapy only (full-dose, extended-field irradiation)?
- If individual also had one or more large tumors in the chest area (mediastinum), was chemotherapy given?
- If the spleen was involved, did individual require both radiation therapy and chemotherapy?
- If at stage I and IIB, did individual receive radiation therapy and surgical removal of the spleen (splenectomy)?
- If at stage IIIA, was individual treated with radiation therapy, chemotherapy, or both? Did individual at stage IIIA disease receive only chemotherapy?
- If at stage IV, in which there is spread to other organs such as bone or liver, did individual receive combination chemotherapy as the primary treatment?
- How did individual respond to the treatment? Was the treatment successful?

Regarding prognosis:
- Was treatment begun at an early stage of the disease?
- Has the disease spread (metastasized) to other parts of the body?
- Is this a recurrence (approximately 3 years after diagnosis) or a relapse (3-20 years after treatment)? Have complications resulted from chemotherapy and/or radiation therapy?
- Has individual developed lymph node enlargement causing compression or obstruction of other organs or nerves?
- How will complications be treated and what is the expected outcome with treatment?
- Has individual experienced grossly enlarged lymph nodes (bull-neck), altering individual's appearance?

- Have complications of the disease produced problems with individual's body image, self-esteem, and interpersonal relationships?
- Would individual benefit from psychological counseling?

References

LeMone, P., and K.M. Burke. Medical-Surgical Nursing. Upper Saddle River, NJ: Prentice Hall Health, 2000.

Mueller, N.E., and S. Grufferman. "The Epidemiology of Hodgkin's Disease." Hodgkin's Disease. Mauch, P.M., et al., eds. Philadelphia: Lippincott Williams & Wilkins, 1999. 61-78.

Rosenberg, S.A., and G.P. Canellos. "Hodgkin's Disease." The Lymphomas. Canellos, G.P., T.A. Lister, and J.L. Sklar, eds. Philadelphia: W.B. Saunders Company, 1998. 305-331.

Thwaite, J. "Complementary Therapies: A Patient's Choice." Complementary Therapies in Nursing & Midwifery 2 3 (1996): 68-70.

Human Immunodeficiency Virus

Other names / synonyms: HIV

042.0, 042.1, 042.2, 043, 043.0, 043.1, 043.2, 043.3, 044, 044.0, 044.9

Definition

Human immunodeficiency virus (HIV) is a subgroup of retroviruses known for a period of seeming inactivity (latency), persistent presence of viruses (viremia), infection of the nervous system, and weak host immune responses. It infects white blood cells (WBCs), the cells that help the body fight infections and other diseases; in particular, those WBCs which have the CD4+ molecule (CD4+ T lymphocyte or T-cells) on their surface. HIV-infected CD4+ T lymphocytes are eventually destroyed because HIV binds to them and they become internalized, permitting the HIV to replicate within the cell. Consequently, after a period of time (latency period) in which the HIV continues to replicate, the number of CD4+ T lymphocyte cells decrease, the immune system weakens, and the individual becomes highly susceptible to parasitic, fungal, bacterial, or other viral infections. Eventually, the HIV-infected individual will develop acquired immune deficiency syndrome (AIDS). AIDS is characterized by normally harmless infections turning deadly as a result of the individual's compromised immune system (opportunistic infections). The time between initial HIV infection and the onset of AIDS is quite variable, and may last from a few months to 10 years or more.

HIV is transmitted primarily through sexual contact (over 70%). Fluids containing the virus must enter the bloodstream in order for infection to occur. HIV may enter the body through cuts or breaks in the skin, mouth, vagina, anal canal, or rectum. HIV has been found in a variety of body fluids and the importance of these in HIV transmission varies depending upon the concentration (viral load) they contain.

In the US, the Centers for Disease Control (CDC) recommends that precautions be used when coming in contact with blood, semen, or vaginal secretions; fluid from the brain or spinal cord (cerebrospinal fluid); joint (synovial), chest (pleural), or heart (pericardial) fluid; or uterine (amniotic) fluid from a pregnant female. Precautions should also be employed for exposure to feces, nasal secretions, sputum, sweat, tears, urine, vomit, and breast milk that contains visible blood.

The primary way HIV is transmitted is by intimate sexual contact (either homo- or heterosexual) with an HIV-infected person. Other methods of transmission include exposure to HIV-contaminated blood or blood products by direct injection, sharing of syringes or needles, transfusion, or any other method of cross-contamination. Another method of transmission occurs when the virus is passed from an HIV-infected mother to her unborn baby during development in utero, or to her newborn baby during labor and delivery, or when breast feeding. Twenty-thirty percent of babies born to HIV-positive mothers will be infected with the virus, although this may drop as low as 13% in some developed countries. Transmission rates from mother to child can be reduced to 8% by giving the drug AZT (zidovudine) to HIV-infected women during pregnancy, and to their infants after birth. There is no evidence that HIV can be transmitted through casual contact or even close nonsexual contact (such as that which occurs in families, at school, or in the workplace), or from insects or respiratory droplets.

High risk behaviors for transmission of HIV include homo- or heterosexual practices in which condoms are not worn (unprotected sex), using condoms made of natural or non-latex membranes, sharing needles or syringes for drug self-injection, and tattooing or body piercing. Safe sex requires men to consistently and correctly use latex condoms, and women to use lubricated polyurethane condoms. It is not recommended that a male and female wear condoms at the same time because friction between the two materials may cause tears or slippage of either condom. The safest form of sex is abstaining from risky behaviors for 6 months, followed by testing for HIV. A negative result would indicate safety in engaging in sexual acts with only a single HIV-free partner who has undergone the same testing measures. HIV transmission through infected blood components, such as clotting factor concentrates and blood transfusions, has been reduced markedly in the US but not completely eliminated. It has been estimated that 1 in 450,000-660,000 transfusions per year transmits HIV. This figure may be higher in certain urban areas such as New York and San Francisco, and reduced in certain rural areas that have a low prevalence of HIV.

More than 30 million people worldwide are infected with HIV and most of these infections have occurred as a result of heterosexual contact. In the US, men comprise 80-90% of HIV-infected individuals, and homosexual contact is the most frequently reported high-risk behavior within this group. In recent years, however, male-to-male sexual contact has accounted for a decreasing number of HIV infections. Women account for a minority of HIV infections in the US, but the proportion of cases among females has risen steadily from 7% in 1985 to 23% in 1998. In the US, a disproportionately high HIV infection rate for adults occurs among blacks (36%) and Hispanics (18%).

Diagnosis

History: An HIV-infected individual may report high-risk sexual behavior, intravenous drug use, or rarely, multiple transfusions of blood or blood products. Two-to-four weeks after the initial infection, individuals will experience a brief flu-like illness with a sore throat, weakness, fever, or rash. These symptoms will disappear within a few days or weeks and are followed by a long incubation (latency) period during which there are no overt signs of infection. After this latency period, HIV-infected individuals most often progress to acquired immune deficiency syndrome (AIDS), reporting altered mental status including short-term memory loss, concentration difficulties, mood changes (usually toward depression, apathy, or suicidal ideation) or dementia, cough, shortness of breath, night sweats, skin growths, easy bruising, unexpected nosebleeds, difficulty swallowing (dysphagia), chest pain, persistent fever, diarrhea, abdominal pain, vomiting, headaches, and/or weight loss.

Physical exam: The HIV-infected individual may have a fever, skin rash, and/or enlarged lymph nodes that show up 2-4 weeks after initial infection. This is followed by a latent phase that can last up to 10 years or more. During this phase there are no clear physical signs except for occasional non-threatening infections like chronic herpes (shingles), or thrush (oral fungal infection with Candida). HIV-infected individuals who have developed AIDS may have lesions in the mouth that are characteristic of yeast infections, plaque-like lesions in the mouth (oral hairy leukoplakia), or raised blue or purple spots anywhere on the body (Kaposi's sarcoma). An eye examination may reveal blurry vision, spots before the eyes (floaters), or loss of vision. It may be difficult to visualize the retina during an eye examination, and the retina may have a "cottage cheese and ketchup" appearance. Wheezes or crackle (dry rales) sounds in the lungs, enlarged lymph nodes, abdominal masses, fluid in the abdominal cavity (ascites), enlarged liver (hepatomegaly), enlarged spleen (splenomegaly), reflex abnormalities, gait problems, and cranial nerve impairment may also be noted during physical examination.

Tests: HIV infection can be determined by blood or urine tests, or by home testing.

Blood Tests: HIV infection can be determined by either direct detection of the virus or detection of the antibodies that the individual produces in response to the HIV. Direct detection of the virus may be done at any time following infection, and the HIV polymerase chain reaction (PCR) or HIV culture tests are commonly used. However, with antibody detection tests, there is a time delay before the immune system will mount a response against HIV, and a waiting period of 6 months following infection is usually recommended to increase reliability. The most common types of antibody tests for HIV diagnosis include the enzyme-linked immunoabsorbent assay (ELISA), Western blot, immunofluorescence, radioimmune-precipitation, and hemagglutination.

Oral/Urine Tests: Currently, there is one oral test that has been approved by the Food and Drug Administration (FDA). The Oral Fluid Vironostika HIV-1 MicroElisa System and the OraSure HIV-1 WB kit in combination with the OraSure Collection system have been found to be highly reliable in identifying HIV-infected individuals. The FDA has approved a urine HIV-1 antibody ELISA; however, it has not been approved as a stand-alone diagnostic test, so individuals with reactive urine specimens should be retested using a blood test.

Home Tests: The FDA has approved the Home Access and Home Access Express tests. With these, the individual is provided with a specimen collection device with which to obtain a drop of blood, which is then blotted onto a card. The specimen card is mailed to a central testing service and the individual is informed anonymously of the results by telephone. Post-test counseling is also provided.

The rate of HIV disease progression is measured by the rate of increased viral particles (viral load) in the bloodstream or tissue of an infected individual. Thus, viral load measurement can serve as both an accurate predictor of disease progression, and an indicator of the effectiveness of anti-viral drug treatment. Viral load can be determined by measuring HIV ribonucleic acid (RNA) in plasma. Commonly, three types of assays are used to measure HIV RNA: reverse transcription polymerase chain reaction (RT-PCR), the branched deoxyribonucleic acid (bDNA) test, or the nucleic acid sequence-based amplification (NASBA). Other tests may be performed to monitor the extent of damage the virus has done to the immune system. The most important of these counts the number of CD4+ T-lymphocytes (T-cells) in the blood stream using flow cytometry. This test is also used to monitor the effectiveness of antiretroviral drug therapy, to determine the risk for opportunistic diseases and the need for preventative (prophylactic) drug administration, and to assess the prognosis for the HIV-infected individual. Other tests may include a complete blood count (CBC) with a white blood cell differential count, blood urea nitrogen (BUN) and creatinine, liver function tests, glucose and lipid profiles, arterial blood gases (ABGs), blood serum chemistries, electrolytes, blood culture, stool culture, a rapid plasma reagin (RPR) test or a Venereal Disease Research Laboratory (VDRL) test for syphilis, a hepatitis B core antibody test, hepatitis C and toxoplasmosis serology, a purified protein derivative (PPD) test for tuberculosis, and a Pap smear in women. In some clinical settings, urinalysis, cytomegalovirus (CMV) serology, and a qualitative test for glucose-6-phosphate dehydrogenase (G6PD) may be advisable. Additional diagnostic tests include chest x-ray, head CAT scan, cerebrospinal fluid analysis, and lumbar puncture.

Treatment

Important advances have been made in drug treatments that can slow the progression of disease following HIV infection. Drug treatment must be individualized and take into account the disease progression (viral load) and the degree of immunodeficiency as determined by the CD4+ T lymphocyte cell (T-cell) count. No study has determined specifically the best time to start drug treatment; however, it is believed that initiating highly active anti-retroviral therapy (HAART) as early as possible offers the best chance for minimizing both viral load and disease progression. Combination therapy using two nucleoside reverse transcriptase inhibitors (NRTIs) in conjunction with a protease inhibitor (PI) or a nonnucleoside reverse-transcriptase inhibitor (NNRTI) is recommended as initial therapy for most individuals. The drug regimen may be modified if the individual cannot tolerate one or more of the drugs, or if there is a rising viral load, a declining CD4+ T lymphocyte count, or progression of clinical diseases characteristic of AIDS.

Resistance to drug therapy is also a consideration, because the high rate of HIV turnover in the body often produces drug-resistant forms of the virus. Additionally, preventative (prophylactic) drug treatment for a common opportunistic disease, Pneumocystis carinii Pneumonia (PCP), is usually prescribed. The current drug of choice for PCP prophylaxis is trimethoprim-sulfamethoxazole (TMP-SMX). Oxygen is administered for those with difficulty breathing (dyspnea), and intravenous (IV) fluids are given for dehydration or low blood pressure (hypotension). Finally, psychosocial issues are important at all stages following viral infection because adjustment or anxiety disorders, depression, and substance abuse are common among HIV-infected individuals. Psychological testing, antidepressant therapy, and/or community support groups are important adjunctive treatment for HIV.

Tremendous effort has been put forth attempting to develop a vaccine that will either prevent infection by HIV or boost the immune systems of infected individuals. Several vaccines have been partially successful in preventing HIV infection in non-human primates; however, these results have not been replicated in people. Clinical trials with experimental vaccines began in 1987 and these experiments are on-going. A few vaccines have moved into advanced (phase 3) clinical trials, although most have not gone beyond initial (phase 1) testing. Vaccine development has proven extraordinarily difficult because HIV mutates frequently. Consequently, scientists have had a difficult time producing one or a combination of vaccines that will overcome the mutated viruses that escape immune recognition.

Prognosis

There is no evidence that any HIV-infected individual has ever been cured or become non-infectious. At this time, there is no recovery and the disease is inevitably fatal. However, individuals with recent HIV infection can remain symptom-free for 10 years or more, even without drug therapy. The period of time without apparent disease expression may be increased by years or perhaps decades by using combination anti-retroviral drug therapy. Approximately two-thirds of HIV-positive individuals who start combination anti-retroviral therapy have an undetectable viral load after 3 years of treatment. Other studies have suggested that after 6 months of drug treatment, HIV replication is totally suppressed and 99.9% of the virus is eliminated. Nevertheless, some virus still remains, and the individual is still infectious, and long-term drug therapy will be necessary.

Differential Diagnosis

Conditions that present with symptoms similar to HIV include infectious mononucleosis, Epstein-Barr virus, toxoplasmosis, rubella, syphilis, viral hepatitis, disseminated gonococcal infection, herpes simplex virus, typhus, Crohn's disease, or a number of other viral or parasitic infections.

Specialists

- Dentist
- Dermatologist
- Hematologist
- Infectious Disease Physician
- Internist
- Neurologist
- Oncologist
- Pathologist
- Pulmonologist

Rehabilitation

Individuals who test positive for the HIV virus require no specific physical rehabilitation. Individuals may wish to consult with a physical therapist or exercise pathologist to develop an exercise program. Individuals should be encouraged to begin an exercise program as early as possible following HIV infection. Aerobic exercise has been found to increase cardiopulmonary fitness, improve muscle function, enhance weight gain, and improve mood state and coping behavior. Most importantly, recent studies indicate that exercise may increase CD4+ T lymphocyte cell counts in HIV-infected individuals. Individuals should exercise with a goal of attaining 75-85% maximum intensity while walking, jogging, biking, swimming, performing calisthenics, and/or weight training.

Also important in the rehabilitation of individuals infected with the HIV virus are the disciplines of psychology and social work. Individuals infected with HIV eventually develop AIDS, a disease with no known cure. Psychological counseling may help individuals deal with fears of dying and depression that accompany the diagnosis of HIV infection. Because distress and depression have been shown to lower the immune system, counseling has a beneficial effect on an individual's physical health. Psychologists and psychiatrists also work with individuals who have become infected through intravenous drug use through behavior modification programs at drug treatment centers. These programs can be successful in helping individuals recover from drug addiction.

Social workers can also assist individuals diagnosed with HIV. The newer treatments for HIV infection are expensive and often not covered by health insurance. Social workers can direct individuals to programs that subsidize treatment. For those individuals who have become infected through intravenous drug use, social workers can aid in placement at drug rehabilitation centers.

Work Restrictions / Accommodations

HIV-infected individuals may need to be transferred to a job requiring less physical activity, extended sick leave, or a leave of absence. In the workplace, HIV is an important component of a comprehensive infectious disease policy, and universal precautions should be incorporated into all procedures regardless of the HIV status of employees. Risk of exposure to blood-borne HIV can be modified by on-going education, engineering controls, and the use of safety devices. Universal precautions include hand washing, protecting intact skin, caring for and appropriately covering damaged skin, properly handling and disposing of sharp objects, and carefully handling all blood and body fluids. Disposable latex gloves should be worn during all medical procedures and emergencies, and during industrial accidents. A plan for rapid evaluation and management should be in place in case HIV exposure occurs. Neurocognitive impairment may adversely affect work with essential job functions requiring complex cognitive function.

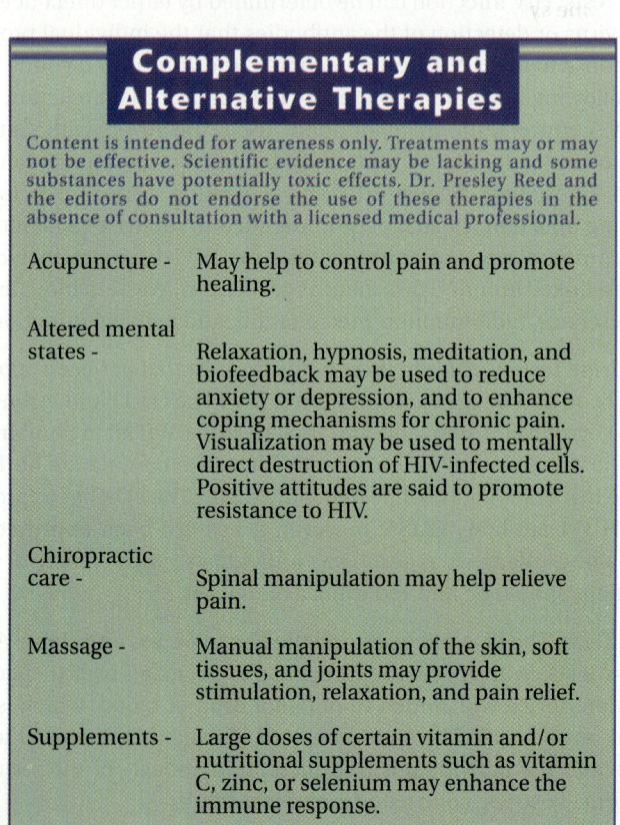

Complementary and Alternative Therapies

Content is intended for awareness only. Treatments may or may not be effective. Scientific evidence may be lacking and some substances have potentially toxic effects. Dr. Presley Reed and the editors do not endorse the use of these therapies in the absence of consultation with a licensed medical professional.

Acupuncture -	May help to control pain and promote healing.
Altered mental states -	Relaxation, hypnosis, meditation, and biofeedback may be used to reduce anxiety or depression, and to enhance coping mechanisms for chronic pain. Visualization may be used to mentally direct destruction of HIV-infected cells. Positive attitudes are said to promote resistance to HIV.
Chiropractic care -	Spinal manipulation may help relieve pain.
Massage -	Manual manipulation of the skin, soft tissues, and joints may provide stimulation, relaxation, and pain relief.
Supplements -	Large doses of certain vitamin and/or nutritional supplements such as vitamin C, zinc, or selenium may enhance the immune response.

Comorbid Conditions

Factors that may influence the length of disability from HIV infection include the stage of the disease, the viral load, the number of CD4+ T lymphocytes present in the bloodstream, the presence of opportunistic infections during the course of the disease, and the response to drug treatment.

Complications

Individuals with HIV may experience a number of complications during the course of their illness, as it progresses into AIDS. Drug therapy may cause adverse side effects including nausea, severe headache, insomnia, or anemia.

The type, number, and severity of complications as a result of the disease varies with the status of immune system functioning and progression of the disease. Typical complications include fatigue, dizziness, anorexia and weight loss, nausea and vomiting, diarrhea, cough, difficulty in swallowing (dysphagia), difficulty breathing (dyspnea), pain, fever, itching (pruritus), sleep disturbances, night sweats, and psychological distress. Other complications may include skin diseases (dermatophytosis, psoriasis), inflammation of hair follicles (folliculitis), arthritis (Reiter's syndrome), decreased hemoglobin in the blood (anemia), bleeding into the skin or other organs (idiopathic thrombocytopenic purpura or ITP), decreased white blood cell count (leukopenia), kidney disorders (nephropathy), chronic herpes (shingles), mental disorders (dementia), a variety of cancerous tumors (Kaposi's sarcoma, Hodgkin's lymphoma, non-Hodgkin's lymphoma, and squamous cell carcinoma), mouth sores and lesions (oral hairy leukoplakia), an oral fungal infection (thrush), and a variety of tooth and gum (periodontal) diseases (linear gingival erythema, necrotizing ulcerative gingivitis).

Most complications arise as a product of opportunistic infections when the immune system is in a weakened (compromised) state. Many of the diseases associated with opportunistic infections in HIV-infected individuals arise from fungal infections (Pneumocystis carinii pneumonia or PCP, aspergillosis, candidiasis, cryptococcosis, histoplasmosis, coccidioidomycosis, penicilliosis), parasitic infections (cryptosporidiosis, isosporiasis, toxoplasmosis, microsporidiosis, Strongyloides stercoralis, Cyclospora cayetanensis), viral diseases (cytomegalovirus or CMV, herpes simplex virus types 1 and 2 (HSV-1 and HSV-2), varicella-zoster virus or VZV, Epstein-Barr virus or EBV, polyomavirus, poxvirus, parvovirus, human papillomavirus or HPV, hepatitis virus), and bacterial infections (mycobacteria, nocardiosis, Bartonella, Rhodococcus, Haemophilus influenzae, Pseudomonas aeruginosa, Staphylococcus aureus, Salmonella).

Factors Influencing Duration

Factors that might influence the length of disability include other diseases that may increase the severity of symptoms associated with various opportunistic infections. These include infectious diseases such as hepatitis B and tuberculosis, as well as chronic infections or parasitic diseases such as malaria. Immunosuppressant drugs, pregnancy, malnutrition, genetic susceptibility, infection with other sexually transmitted diseases, and stress may also have effects. Advancing age appears to be a major determinant in how rapidly the disease progresses.

Length of Disability

The duration of disability depends upon the requirements of the job and the degree of disability experienced by the HIV-infected individual. Progression of HIV will be more rapid with higher viral loads and lower CD4+ T lymphocyte cell counts. Disability may be permanent if the disease has progressed to full-blown AIDS.

Failure to Recover

If an individual fails to recover within the maximum duration expectancy period, the reader may wish to reference the following questions to assist in better understanding the specifics of an individual's medical case.

Regarding diagnosis:

- Has diagnosis of HIV infection been confirmed?
- Have conditions with similar symptoms been ruled out?
- Which factors (stage of disease, viral load, number of CD4+ T lymphocytes present, complications, associated opportunistic infections) may complicate treatment and impact recovery?

Regarding treatment:

- Has drug treatment plan been individualized, taking into account the disease progression and degree of immunodeficiency?
- Although there is not a general consensus of the best time to start drug treatment for HIV, is drug therapy appropriate for this individual at this time?
- Is a combination anti-retroviral drug treatment available to individual?
- Is the present combination of drugs being administered appropriate for this individual?
- Can drug regimen be modified if the individual cannot tolerate one or more of the drugs, or if there is a rising viral load, a declining CD4+ T lymphocyte count, or progression of clinical diseases characteristic of AIDS?
- What can be done to lessen adverse effects? Have alternate drug combinations been as effective?
- Because the high rate of HIV turnover in the body often produces drug-resistant forms of the virus, what is being done to monitor the efficacy of the current drug therapy?
- Is individual receiving prophylactic drug therapy against common opportunistic diseases?

Regarding prognosis:

- Have the benefits of drug therapy been explained to the individual?
- Does individual understand that the period of time without apparent disease expression may be increased by years or perhaps decades by using combination anti-retroviral drug therapy?
- Is individual involved in appropriate drug therapy at this time? If not, is it available to him/her?
- If not available, how can the individual access combination anti-retroviral drug therapy?
- Can individual be compliant with long-term drug therapy?
- Has individual experienced complications, such as opportunistic infections? Are complications being effectively treated under current treatment plan?

- Does individual have realistic expectations?
- Because psychosocial issues are important at all stages following viral infection, has individual received psychological testing?
- Would individual benefit from antidepressant therapy?
- Would individual and/or family benefit from psychological counseling?
- Is individual involved in a community support group?

References

Berger, Barbara, and Vida M. Vizgirda. "Preventing HIV Infection." The Person with HIV/AIDS. Nursing Perspectives. Durham, Jerry D. and Felissa R. Lashley, eds. New York: Springer Publishing Company, Inc, 2000. 97-138.

Brannon, Linda, and Jess Feist. "Living with Chronic Illness." Health Psychology. King, Kenneth, ed. Belmont: Wadsworth Publishing Company, 1992. 275-315.

LaPerriere, A., et al. "Change in CD4+ Cell Enumeration Following Aerobic Exercise Training in HIV-1 Disease: Possible Mechanisms and Practical Applications." International Journal of Sports Medicine 18 Suppl 1 (1997): S56-61.

Lashley, Felissa R. "The Etiology, Epidemiology, Transmission, and Natural History of HIV Infection and AIDS." The Person with HIV/AIDS. Nursing Perspectives. Durham, Jerry D., and Felissa R. Lashley, eds. New York: Springer Publishing Company, Inc, 2000. 1-73.

Libman, Howard, Raymond Powrie, and Michael Stein. "Primary Care of HIV Disease." HIV. Libman, Howard, and Harvey J. Makadon, eds. Philadelphia: American College of Physicians, 2000. 63-94.

Mansen, Thom J. "Sexually Transmitted Diseases." Pathophysiology. McCance, Kathryn L., and Sue E. Heuther, eds. St. Louis: Mosby, 1994. 800-829.

McCutchan, J. Allen. "Alternative, Unconventional, and Unproven Therapies." Textbook of AIDS Medicine. Merigan, Thomas C., et al., eds. Baltimore: Williams & Wilkins, 2000. 903-909.

Perna, F.M., et al. "Cardiopulmonary and CD4 Cell Changes in Response to Exercise Training in Early Symptomatic HIV Infection." Medicine and Science in Sports and Exercise 31 7 (1999): 973-979.

Wightman, Susan L., and Michael K. Klebert. "The Medical Treatment of HIV Disease." The Person with HIV/AIDS. Nursing Perspectives. Durham, Jerry D., and Felissa R. Lashley, eds. New York: Springer Publishing Company, Inc, 2000. 311-350.

Zeller, Janice M., and Barbara Swanson. "The Pathogenesis of HIV Infection." The Person with HIV/AIDS. Nursing Perspectives. Durham, Jerry D., and Felissa R. Lashley, eds. New York: Springer Publishing Company, Inc, 2000. 75-96.

Humidifier Fever
Other names / synonyms: Ventilation Pneumonitis
495.9

Definition

Humidifier fever is a form of sick building syndrome that usually develops on Monday or the first workday of the week. Humidifier fever can be caused by a number of different agents including amoebas, bacteria, and fungi. Mold and mildew refer to growths of fungi that may live in the moist environment of a humidifier or any moisture-laden atmosphere.

Humidifier fever is a benign variant of inflammation of the alveoli in the lungs (allergic alveolitis) and occurs sporadically in a wide range of settings. The office environment continues to be an occasional source of this condition. The areas where microbes reside can be difficult to locate and may be well hidden, often in heating and air-conditioning systems remote from the individual's work area.

Humidifier fever refers to the disease and not to the mechanism by which it is transmitted. The agents causing it can be found in any location and atmosphere where moisture is present in any form. The moisture does not need to be standing water. It can be in the form of mist or condensation on any surface and in any cavity in a building.

The problems of mold and mildew can be just as extensive in cooling climates as in heating climates. Either surfaces are too cold, moisture levels are too high, or both. A common example of mold growth in cooling climates is found in rooms where conditioned cold air blows against the interior surface of an exterior wall.

Various levels of the disease have been reported in most industrialized countries.

Diagnosis

History: The affected individual may report symptoms such as chest tightening, runny nose, and slight breathing discomfort. The symptoms usually occur on Monday morning or early in the workweek. The hallmark of the disease is the sudden onset of fever. Other features may include muscle aches and pains and mild shortness of breath.

Physical exam: The exam may reveal a slightly elevated temperature, mild to moderate respiratory distress, cough, and a crackling sound when breathing (rales).

Tests: Complete blood count, white blood cell count, and chest x-ray should be done. Lung function tests including spirometry testing should be conducted. Spirometry monitoring should continue in the workplace. Cultures to identify any offending organisms or suspected organisms may be needed. Lung biopsy helps rule out infections from other sources.

Treatment

Humidifier fever typically resolves once the individual is no longer exposed to the causative agent. Mild fevers may be treated with the proper agent to reduce fever (antipyretic). Rest and supportive care away from the source of the irritant may be needed.

Cleaning and disinfecting the air conditioning/heating/ventilation system with nonpolluting cleaners and antimicrobial agents provides protection against mold growth. However, it is virtually impossible to eliminate all nutrients that support the growth of infectious materials such as bacteria, fungi, and amoebas. Moisture control is thus an important strategy for reducing mold growth.

Prognosis

Recovery usually occurs when the individual is no longer exposed to the causative agent. The outcome is good when proper treatment and precautions are taken. Precautions need to be taken while in the home environment to avoid recurring bouts of humidifier fever due to exposure to pathogens and organisms in any moisture-laden air. Re-exposure has a negative effect on recovery.

Differential Diagnosis

Hypersensitivity pneumonitis, asthma, bronchitis, influenza, and emphysema may all present with similar signs and symptoms.

Specialists

- Occupational Medicine Physician
- Pulmonologist

Work Restrictions / Accommodations

Individuals may need to be transferred to exposure-free departments. This would allow most individuals to be kept at work.

Mold and mildew growth can be reduced where relative humidities near surfaces can be maintained below the dew point. This is done by reducing the moisture content (vapor pressure) of the air, increasing air movement at the surface, or increasing the air temperature (either the general space temperature or the temperature at building surfaces).

Mold and mildew that depend on vapor pressure can be reduced by source control (e.g., direct venting of moisture-generating activities such as showers) to the exterior, dilution of moisture-laden indoor air with outdoor air that is at a lower absolute humidity, or dehumidification.

Comorbid Conditions

Coexisting lung diseases such as emphysema, asthma, and chronic bronchiolitis seen in smokers may lengthen disability. A weakened immune system prolongs recovery time and may prolong disability.

Complications

Continuing exposure to the organisms can result in chronic bronchitis or inflammation of the lung. Allergic reactions may also develop.

Factors Influencing Duration

Workers with breathing difficulties and weakened physical condition are more at risk for disability.

Length of Disability

Duration in Days

Job Classification	Minimum	Optimum	Maximum
Any work	1	3	7

Failure to Recover

If an individual fails to recover within the maximum duration expectancy period, the reader may wish to reference the following questions to assist in better understanding the specifics of an individual's medical case.

Regarding diagnosis:

- Does individual have symptoms such as chest tightening, runny nose, slight breathing discomfort, or muscle aches and pains? Do these symptoms occur on Monday morning or early in the work-week?
- Does individual have the hallmark of the disease, i.e., sudden onset of fever?
- On exam, did individual have a slight fever, mild to moderate respiratory distress, cough, and rales?
- Was a CBC with WBC done? Chest x-ray? If necessary, were cultures done? Was it necessary to do a lung biopsy?
- Were conditions with similar symptoms ruled out?

Regarding treatment:

- Was individual removed from exposure to the causative agent?
- Was any fever treated with an antipyretic?
- Was an attempt made to clean the offending ventilation system? Control moisture?

Regarding prognosis:

- Can individual's employer accommodate any necessary restrictions?
- Does individual have any conditions that may affect ability to recover?
- Have any complications developed such as chronic bronchitis, inflammation of the lung, or allergic reactions?

References

Humidfier Fever. MedicineNet, Inc. 2000. 16 Nov 2000 <http://www.medterms.com/script/main/art.asp?articlekey=13144>.

Cullen, Mark, and Linda Rosenstock, MD. "Occupational Safety and Health." Scientific Amercian Medicine Online. HealtheonWebMD/Corp. 2000. 16 Nov 2000 <http://www.samed.com>.

Huntington's Chorea

Other names / synonyms: *Huntington's Disease*

333.4

Definition

Huntington's chorea is an inherited neurological disease resulting from degeneration of nerve cells (neurons) in certain areas of the brain involved in controlling movement, coordination, speech, thoughts, memory, and perception.

Uncontrollable jerking movements (chorea) are the hallmark of this disorder. Huntington's chorea is also associated with depression and intellectual loss. A child of a parent with Huntington's chorea has a 50% chance of developing the disease (autosomal dominant inheritance with complete penetrance). A specific gene for Huntington's disease has been identified, producing an abnormal protein product called huntingtin. It is not yet known how this protein is linked to the selective death of groups of nerve cells.

In the US, only about 30,000 people have Huntington's chorea (prevalence 5.15 per 100,000). The disease is found in all ethnic groups with an equal number of males and females affected. The age of onset varies, but adult-onset chorea usually begins at middle age and continues to deteriorate with death occurring 15 to 25 years later.

Diagnosis

History: As Huntington's chorea is a familial disease passed from parent to child, family history is extremely important for diagnosis. Individuals may report mood swings, irritability, depression, apathy, or anger. Impairment of memory, judgment, and other cognitive functions may also occur before the involuntary movements are noticed. Mental deterioration is usually accompanied by moodiness, irritability, or antisocial behavior. Individuals may report feeling depressed and may discuss thoughts of suicide.

Some individuals with Huntington's chorea have initial complaints of involuntary movements or rigidity. The movement disorder consists of uncontrolled dance-like jerking movements (chorea) in the fingers, feet, face, and trunk. These may resemble piano-playing movements of the fingers, facial grimaces, or dancing gait. Clumsiness and problems with balance and coordination may be reported as the disease progresses. Intellectual deterioration and jerky movements of the extremities and face worsen until individuals eventually lose the ability to care for themselves as they become unable to walk and function intellectually.

Physical exam: Abnormalities of rapid eye movements may be evident. Initially, periodic twitching in the face or extremities is seen and these movements become more pronounced and frequent as the disease progresses. Walking becomes unsteady. More generalized and sustained writhing motions are later observed with the muscles becoming more rigid (dystonia). Speech becomes hard to understand and swallowing becomes difficult.

Tests: Genetic testing (DNA analysis) reveals the specific gene associated with Huntington's disease. Brain imaging testing such as CT and MRI show shrinking (atrophy) of the deep structures involved in movement control (basal ganglia) in later stages. Levels of certain neurochemicals may be decreased including gamma-aminobutyric acid and glutamic acid decarboxylase.

Treatment

There is no treatment to stop or reverse the course of the disease. Only the symptoms of Huntington's chorea are treated and not the disease itself. Abnormal movements and mental disturbances may be alleviated with antipsychotic drugs that may have severe side effects including sedation.

For depression, serotonin reuptake inhibitors may be used. Tranquilizers may help anxiety and other medications may be used to control obsessive-compulsive behavior. Genetic counseling should be offered to the children of individuals with Huntington's chorea. DNA testing determines whether or not the offspring also carry the affected gene and are at risk of developing the disease and/or passing the risk to their children. Psychological counseling should be offered both before and after genetic testing to help the individual cope with emotional issues uncovered by the results.

Prognosis

The prognosis is poor and most individuals require constant care in an institutional setting at the end stage of the disease. In some individuals, the disease may progress to the point where speech is slurred and vital functions such as swallowing, eating, speaking, and walking decline. Some individuals may not be able to recognize their family members. Problems with balance and coordination manifest initially and develop into dance-like (choreic), irregular, spasmodic, involuntary movements as the disease progresses. Problems with walking may result in an increase of falls. Individuals who develop symptoms of Huntington's disease by age 35 often become bedridden within 15 to 20 years. Death usually occurs 15 to 25 years after neurological or psychological impairment begins and may be caused by pneumonia or heart failure. Some individuals commit suicide soon after diagnosis.

Differential Diagnosis

Relatively benign, nonprogressive conditions associated with chorea include benign familial chorea, chorea gravidarum seen with pregnancy, senile chorea, and essential chorea. Neurodegenerative conditions that may be associated with intellectual deterioration and/ or involuntary movement and rigidity are Parkinson's disease, Alzheimer's disease, and Pick's disease. Stroke, tumor, or other lesions affecting the basal ganglia or subthalamic nucleus may give rise to a similar movement disorder. Alcoholism and drug-induced movement disorder may be associated with intellectual changes and involuntary shaking. Bipolar disorder can resemble the emotional and psychiatric changes seen in Huntington's disease. Other possibilities include Giles de La Tourette's Syndrome, neuroacanthocytosis, Wilson's disease, hyperglycemic nonketotic encephalopathy, periarteritis nodosa, and Creutzfeldt-Jacob disease.

Specialists

- Neurologist
- Physiatrist

Rehabilitation

Because of the progressive nature of Huntington's chorea, rehabilitation is focused on maintaining the individual's optimal quality of life. The physical, occupational, and speech therapist can help in the individual's maintenance of functional skills and advise the family on adaptive equipment. Adaptive equipment becomes important with activities needed throughout daily living such as self-care, walking and eating. Physical therapists instruct the individual on the proper use of a cane or walker to assist with walking whereas the occupational therapist is helpful in teaching techniques for easier dressing and other self cares. The occupational therapist also offers instruction of adaptive equipment such as splints for the hand and/or wrist to aid in eating or other devices to aid in reaching and/or grasping objects.

Traditional relaxation exercises are helpful early in the disease and include gentle rocking and/or rotation of the extremities in a sitting position. However, with progression of Huntington's chorea, techniques of stretching help reduce uncontrolled muscle spasm and inflexibility (muscle tone). These techniques offered by both physical and occupational therapy reduce movements associated with this disease. Passive stretching exercises to the affected limbs/joints are performed and described as the therapist placing the muscle and/or joint on a mild stretch without any assistance or resistance coming from the individual.

Increasing stability about the shoulders, trunk, neck and hips will help maintain function. Sitting control is improved by sitting in a chair that does not have arms or back while the therapist applies mild pressure at various regions of the trunk while instructing the individual to resist movement by the therapist. Individuals learn exercises such as shifting their weight in all directions while sitting progressing to the same activities in a standing position. Standing exercises are advanced to activities such as placing one foot forward and backward on a straight line and walking between two parallel lines. If the individual is able to continue working early on in the disease process and job duties require fine motor movements, job reassignment and vocational rehabilitation may be needed.

Speech therapy can be helpful with maintaining oral (mouth) motor control as the condition progresses and swallowing and speech become difficult. Speech therapy is also helpful in addressing loss of memory and perception. Eventually goals are aimed at preventing total loss of mobility for the individual afflicted with Huntington's chorea.

Work Restrictions / Accommodations

Because of involuntary movements, individuals cannot work around moving machinery or in any position that would put them in danger of injury to others or themselves. Behavioral manifestations usually prevent individuals from interacting with the public. Intellectual decline may lead to permanent disability.

Comorbid Conditions

Other neurological or psychiatric disorders may lengthen disability.

Complications

Complications of the illness include gradual loss of mental faculties that evolve into dementia. Severe depression may result in suicide. The involuntary movements may progress to more uncontrolled movements resulting in the inability to walk. Weight loss may be dramatic due to excessive calories burned by constant involuntary movements.

Factors Influencing Duration

This condition progresses to permanent disability.

Length of Disability

Duration depends on severity of manifestations. Disability may be permanent. Contact physician for additional case information.

Failure to Recover

If an individual fails to recover within the maximum duration expectancy period, the reader may wish to reference the following questions to assist in better understanding the specifics of an individual's medical case.

Regarding diagnosis:

- Does the individual have a family history of the disease?
- Does the individual report mood swings, irritability, depression, apathy, or anger?
- Does the individual report impairment of memory, judgment, and other cognitive functions?
- Does the individual have suicidal ideation?
- Does the individual have uncontrolled dance-like jerking movements (chorea) in the fingers, feet, face, and trunk? Do they resemble piano-playing movements of the fingers, facial grimaces, or dancing gait?
- Does the individual have clumsiness and problems with balance and coordination?
- Is the individual's condition deteriorating? Are they unable to care for themselves?
- On physical exam were rapid eye movements, periodic twitching in the face and extremities present? Have these become more pronounced?
- Does the individual have an unsteady gait?
- Is it hard to understand the individual's speech?
- Does the individual have difficulty swallowing?
- Has the individual had DNA analysis? Neurochemical testing?
- Has the individual had a CT scan and MRI?
- Have conditions with similar symptoms been ruled out?

Regarding treatment:

- Is the individual receiving symptomatic treatment?
- Is the individual being treated with antipsychotic drugs for the abnormal movements and mental disturbances? Serotonin reuptake inhibitors? Tranquilizers?
- Have the individual's children been offered genetic counseling?
- Has the individual received psychological counseling?

Regarding prognosis:
- Does the individual exercise regularly?
- If the individual is able to work, is their employer able to accommodate any necessary restrictions?
- Does the individual have any conditions that may affect the course of the disease? Does the individual have any complications such as dementia, severe depression, suicide, inability to walk, or weight loss?

References

Huntington's Disease - Hope Through Research. National Institute of Neurological Disorders and Stroke. 27 Jun 2000. 04 July 2000 <http://www.ninds.nih.gov/health_and_medical/pubs/huntington_disease-htr.htm>.

Gottlieb, Bill, ed. New Choices in Natural Healing. Englewood: Rodale Press, Inc, 1995.

Hydatidiform Mole
Other names / synonyms: Gestational Trophoblastic Disease, Gestational Trophoblastic Neoplasia, GTN, Hydatid Mole, Molar Pregnancy
630

Definition

Hydatidiform mole is a noncancerous (benign) tumor that develops from a fertilized egg (ova) at the beginning of a pregnancy. It is often referred to as a molar pregnancy.

Instead of the normal embryonic cell division that results in development of an infant, the placental material grows uncontrolled and develops into a shapeless mass of watery small blister-like sacs (vesicles). Frequently there is no fetus at all. There are three types of molar pregnancy: complete mole, partial mole, and transitional mole.

A complete mole is the fertilization of an "empty" egg. It can contain products of conception (conceptus, which would normally develop into an embryo) but no fetal parts or outermost cellular membrane (chorion) that develops small finger-like projections (chorionic or placental villi) and later a placenta. The conceptus can never develop into an embryo. Twenty percent of complete moles become malignant. In a partial mole (an incomplete mole), an embryo or fetus (the term used after the eighth week of pregnancy) develops, but usually dies by the ninth week. On occasion, the fetus can survive into the final 3 months of pregnancy (third trimester). The placental villi are less abnormal and only occur in limited areas (focal). Eighty to ninety percent of women with a partial mole have uterine bleeding, an early onset of pregnancy complications that includes hypertension, edema, and protein in the urine (preeclampsia), and a uterus too small for gestational dates. Although fetal heart tones will be absent, the fetus may be identifiable on ultrasound. Very rarely the infant may be born alive, but will have such severe genetic abnormalities that death usually occurs in a few days. There is no potential for malignancy with this type of mole. Two percent of partial moles are "complete mole with coexistent fetus" in which the pregnancy results in identical twins; one twin will develop normally and the other develop abnormally as a molar pregnancy.

The third type of hydatidiform mole, the transitional mole, is also known as a blighted ovum with hydropic (swollen) chorionic villi. The villi then degenerate into a shapeless mass of watery vesicles, resembling a bunch of small grapes. The cells that form the outer layer of cells around the developing embryo (trophoblast) may be normal in size or underdeveloped. The embryo will be stunted and levels of the hormone hCG low.

The exact number of pregnancies that result in hydatidiform moles is not clear. It may range from 1 out of every 85 to 1,724 pregnancies (obtained from hospital studies), to 1 out of every 522 to 1,560 pregnancies (obtained from studies of the general population).

The cause of hydatidiform mole is unknown. Women at greatest risk include women who are either under 20 or over 40 years old, of low socioeconomic status, and of Asian ethnicity. Women who have had one hydatidiform mole are at increased risk (30%) of developing another with a future pregnancy.

Some women are at decreased risk for development of a molar pregnancy. In the US, black women have half the risk for developing hydatidiform mole as other women. Women that have had 1 or more previous normal term pregnancies also have a reduced risk for molar pregnancy. The incidence is higher in Mexico and some Asian countries.

Diagnosis

History: The most common sign the woman may report is abnormal bleeding from the uterus and passage of tissue, which is actually grapelike vesicles, through the vagina during the first 3 months of pregnancy. Women also report abdominal pain and excessive nausea and vomiting (hyperemesis gravidarum).

Physical exam: The exam reveals an abnormal uterine size. This is the most common sign of a hydatidiform mole. In about half of the cases, the uterus is larger than it should be. In another third, the uterus is smaller than expected. Physical examination generally reveals an absence of fetal heart tones. Toxemia may develop in the first 24 weeks of pregnancy (the first or early second trimester); this is a highly unusual finding in a normal pregnancy.

Tests: The mole produces excessive amounts of the hormone human chorionic gonadotropin (hCG) that can be detected in the blood and urine. Careful monitoring of these levels is necessary for diagnosis, treatment, and follow-up care.

An ultrasound scan is the diagnostic method of choice because it is safe and noninvasive (does not actually enter the body).

Treatment

Termination of the pregnancy is the method of treatment of hydatidiform mole. Treatment should not be delayed any longer than is necessary to confirm diagnosis, and to emotionally and medically prepare the woman for treatment. The woman's cardiovascular, respiratory, and kidney status are evaluated prior to the procedure. The mole is usually removed from the uterus by suction curettage (suctioning the contents of the uterus) or removal of the uterus (hysterectomy) if no further pregnancies are planned. If further pregnancies are planned, and the mole is advanced, a procedure in which an incision is made through the abdomen into the uterus (abdominal hysterotomy) may be necessary to remove it.

Contraception is needed following evacuation of molar pregnancy to prevent pregnancy during the follow-up period to ensure HGC levels return to normal and there is no residual molar tissue.

Anticancer medications may be recommended in cases in which the hCG level does not return to normal, or increases following evacuation of the molar pregnancy. It is also indicated for women with a tumor of the chorion (choriocarcinoma).

Prognosis

Prognosis for treated individuals is excellent. Mortality from hydatidiform mole is almost zero due to early diagnosis and appropriate treatment. Unfortunately, even after evacuation, complete moles may progress to malignancy. Levels of hCG need to be monitored regularly after evacuation to detect possible progression to malignancy.

Differential Diagnosis

Conditions with symptoms similar to a hydatidiform mole include normal pregnancy in which the dates are incorrect. It may be mistaken for normal pregnancies in which a uterine fibroid or an ovarian tumor is also present. It may also be pregnancy with twins. Hydatidiform mole may appear similarly to a condition in which there is an excess of fluid within the placenta (hydramnios), causing the uterus to be larger than normal. Death of a normal infant (intrauterine fetal death) must also be considered in the diagnosis. Hydatidiform mole may also be a different type of trophoblastic tumor (choriocarcinoma, chorioadenoma).

Specialists

- Gynecologist
- Obstetrician
- Oncologist
- Perinatologist

Work Restrictions / Accommodations

If a surgical procedure is performed (suction curettage, hysterectomy, abdominal hysterotomy), heavy lifting or work requiring long periods of standing may need to be modified during the recovery period. Time off from work may be needed for appointments with the doctor and for therapeutic procedures. In cases in which premature delivery occurred, time off from work for recovery may be needed. In addition, if an infant was born alive, and died in a few days, time off from work may be needed for grieving. Additional time off from work may be needed if anticancer medication (chemotherapy) is to be given. Specific restrictions must be individualized based on circumstances of presentation.

Comorbid Conditions

A comorbid condition is pregnancy with twins.

Complications

Complications can include anemia (from chronic blood loss), toxemia, hyperthyroidism, heart failure, release of the trophoblast into the blood stream (trophoblastic embolization), hemorrhage, and sepsis. Trophoblastic embolization may result in severe respiratory problems (acute pulmonary insufficiency). Ovarian cysts develop in 25-50% of women who had hydatidiform mole, and may be the result of the high hCG levels.

Some moles are considered to be invasive. This occurs when the mole extends into the wall of the uterus. Even though this type of mole is aggressive and can spread, it is not a cancer. Invasive moles occur in about 5-10% of cases. Invasive moles may even rupture the wall of the uterus. Rupture of the uterine wall may result in hemorrhage and spread of molar tissue to distant organs.

Further complications may include the development of a malignancy (choriocarcinoma); this occurs in 3-7% of cases. This is a highly aggressive form of cancer that spreads rapidly to the lungs, lower genital tract, brain, liver, kidney, and gastrointestinal tract. Treatment of choriocarcinoma is immediate tumor removal, and monitoring hCG levels in the blood for 6 months to 1 year.

Because of the risk of invasive moles and choriocarcinoma, the hCG level is monitored after molar pregnancy. Initially, monitoring is weekly. The hCG generally drops to normal within 14 weeks following evacuation of the mole. Following that, monitoring is conducted every other week for another 6 to 12 months. Because there is a risk of the growth recurring in a future pregnancy, a woman should not become pregnant again during the follow-up period.

Factors Influencing Duration

If a hysterectomy or abdominal hysterotomy is done, the normal postoperative recovery period is necessary. Chemotherapy, sometimes given to prevent progression to malignancy, may also prolong the recovery period.

Length of Disability

Suction and curettage.

Duration in Days

Job Classification	Minimum	Optimum	Maximum
Sedentary work	2	3	7
Light work	2	3	7
Medium work	3	4	7
Heavy work	3	4	7
Very Heavy work	3	4	7

Failure to Recover

If an individual fails to recover within the maximum duration expectancy period, the reader may wish to reference the following questions to assist in better understanding the specifics of an individual's medical case.

Regarding diagnosis:

- Is individual under age 20 or over 40? Is the father over 45?
- Does individual have a history of molar pregnancy(ies) or of spontaneous miscarriages?

- Does individual report abnormal bleeding from the uterus and passage of tissue, which is actually grapelike vesicles, during the first 3 months of pregnancy?
- Does individual report abdominal pain and excessive vomiting (hyperemesis gravidarum)?
- Does individual exhibit signs of toxemia (preeclampsia), including high blood pressure (hypertension) and fluid retention (edema), in the first 24 weeks of pregnancy (the first or early second trimester)?
- Were blood and urine obtained to test for excessive amounts of the hormone human chorionic gonadotropin (hCG)?
- Was an ultrasound done to confirm the diagnosis?
- Was the diagnosis of hydatiform mole confirmed?

Regarding treatment:

- Was the pregnancy terminated?
- Were the contents of the uterus removed with suction (suction curettage) or, if no further pregnancies were planned, was the uterus removed (hysterectomy)?
- Did any complications occur as a result of either of these procedures?
- If individual plans further pregnancies, was abdominal hysterotomy required to remove the hydatiform mole?
- Did HCG levels return to normal following evacuation? If not, were anticancer medications given?
- Was contraception used to prevent pregnancy during the follow-up period?

Regarding prognosis:

- Was the hydatiform mole treated, or did it result in spontaneous expulsion?
- After evacuation, were HCG levels monitored regularly to detect possible progression to malignancy?
- If the mole was invasive, did rupture of the uterine wall and hemorrhage occur? If so, how severe was blood loss?
- Did the invasive mole spread to other organs?
- Has individual developed cancer from the hydatiform mole (choriocarcinoma)?
- If so, was the tumor removed completely?
- Has individual experienced other complications, such as anemia, hyperthyroidism, heart failure, release of the trophoblast into the blood stream (trophoblastic embolization), or sepsis?
- What is the treatment for any complications that have developed, and what is the expected outcome with treatment?

References

Copeland, Larry J. "Gestational Trophoblastic Neoplasia." Textbook of Gynecology, 2nd ed. Copeland, Larry J., ed. Philadelphia: W.B. Saunders, 2000. 1409-1430.

Cunningham, F., et al. "Diseases and Abnormalities of the Placenta." Williams Obstetrics, 20th ed. Appleton & Lange, 1997. 669-691.

Hahn, Yong H., MD. "Hydatiform Mole." Medical College of Wisconsin. 28 Feb 2001. 28 Feb 2001 <http://chorus.rad.mcw.edu/doc/00948.html>.

Morrow, C. Paul, and John P. Curtin. "Tumors of the Placental Trophoblast." Synopsis of Gynecologic Oncology, 5th ed. New York: Churchill Livingstone, 1998. 315-351.

Hydrocele

Other names / synonyms: Processus Vaginalis
603, 603.1, 603.8, 603.9

Definition

Hydrocele refers to a soft, painless swelling in the scrotum that is caused by excessive fluid along the spermatic cord in the space around the testes (scrotum).

As fluid collects around the testes, the resulting mass gradually grows. The mass may be soft and resemble a fluid-containing sac (cystic), or it may be quite hard and tense. The fluid is clear and yellow. In adults, a hydrocele may develop rapidly in response to local injury to the testis, radiation exposure (radiotherapy), inflammation of the sperm ducts (epididymis) leading away from the testis (acute epididymitis), by fluid or blood obstruction within the spermatic cord, or inflammation of the testis (orchitis). More commonly, hydrocele is an ongoing (chronic) condition of unknown cause. Hydroceles are common in the newborn infant when the tract through which the testes descend from the abdomen into the scrotum fails to close, and peritoneal fluid drains through the open tract becoming trapped in the scrotum.

Risk factors for development of hydrocele include inflammation, infection, or injury to the testis. Hydroceles occur in an estimated 1% of all males; the incidence is higher in tropical countries. In adults, the condition occurs most frequently after 30 years of age. The right testicle is affected slightly more often than the left, and in 10-15% of cases, the hydrocele is found around both testes (bilateral).

Diagnosis

History: The individual usually describes a mass that may be small and soft in the morning but larger and more tense at night. Most often, individuals will not report pain, however, they may complain of its bulk or weight, which can be uncomfortable.

Physical exam: Manipulation of the mass with the fingers (palpation) will reveal a rounded, unstable, fluid-filled (cystic) mass in the scrotum that is non-tender to touch unless some other underlying disease causing the inflammation is present. An enlargement may be noted in the upper part of the scrotum or groin (cystic fusiform swelling) if the hydrocele is enclosed within the cord (spermatic cord or funiculus spermaticus), which suspends the testis within the scrotum.

Tests: A light can be held behind the scrotum (transilluminate) to differentiate between a tense hydrocele and a tumor of the testis, which will not allow light to pass through. Also, high-frequency sound waves (ultrasound) may be used to rule out a cancerous tumor or infection. Reflection of sound waves (Doppler flow study) may also be used to assess blood flow to the testes. Radioactive material may be injected (testicular scintigraphy) to identify other abnormal conditions such as twisting of the testis (testicular torsion). A blood test, including a complete blood count (CBC), will identify an inflammatory process; a urinalysis can detect protein in the urine.

Treatment

Active treatment of a hydrocele is not usually necessary unless it is firm (tense), potentially compromising circulation to the testis. Treatment is also warranted if the hydrocele is a large, bulky mass that causes discomfort or is unsightly.

One treatment option includes removing fluid from the hydrocele with a needle (aspiration) followed by an injection of a thickening or hardening (sclerosing) medication to close off (obliterate) the opening through which fluid accumulates (sclerotherapy). A more common approach is a minor surgical procedure to tighten or remove the sheath of tissue that surrounds the hydrocele (hydrocelectomy). This procedure is performed under either general or spinal anesthesia. A drainage tube is usually inserted into the scrotum during the surgery and kept in place for 1-2 days, or until there has been sufficient recovery.

Prognosis

Most often, a hydrocele will go away without any medical intervention. The outcome following aspiration or sclerotherapy treatment is generally not good. There is a high risk of infection, unwanted tissue growth (fibrosis) and mild to moderate pain; frequently the hydrocele will return following either of these procedures. An excellent outcome can be expected following hydrocelectomy as this procedure eliminates the condition in virtually all cases. Possible complications of this procedure include the formation of a blood clot (hematoma), abscess, or injury to scrotal tissue or structures.

Differential Diagnosis

Conditions that present with similar symptoms as hydrocele include acute epididymitis, acute orchitis, torsion of the spermatic cord, and strangulated hernia.

Specialists

- Urologist

Work Restrictions / Accommodations

Heavy lifting and physical labor may need to be modified or restricted for a period of time if the individual had surgery.

Comorbid Conditions

Existing conditions that may impact an individual's ability to recover and further lengthen disability include circulatory problems to the testis (such as varicocele) or inflammatory conditions within the scrotum (e.g., epididymitis; orchitis). The presence of an inguinal hernia will necessitate a hydrocelectomy.

Complementary and Alternative Therapies

Content is intended for awareness only. Treatments may or may not be effective. Scientific evidence may be lacking and some substances have potentially toxic effects. Dr. Presley Reed and the editors do not endorse the use of these therapies in the absence of consultation with a licensed medical professional.

Massage - Chinese massage techniques have been used to treat hydrocele. Effectiveness is uncertain.

Complications

Possible complications of hydrocele include compression of the blood supply to the testicle. This may lead to wasting (atrophy) of the testicular tissue and bleeding (hemorrhage) into the hydrocele sac. Other complications include infection, fluid reaccumulation, hematoma, hemorrhage, and fibrosis.

Factors Influencing Duration

Length of disability may be influenced by the size of the hydrocele and the severity of symptoms, the type of treatment required, and the individual's job responsibilities. Age may be a factor for those who have surgical repair.

Length of Disability

Disability may be longer for individuals who had surgery and who do heavy physical work. For surgical treatment, duration depends on size of hydrocele and severity of symptoms.

Medical treatment.

Job Classification	Minimum	Optimum	Maximum
Sedentary work	0	1	3
Light work	0	1	3
Medium work	0	1	3
Heavy work	0	1	7
Very Heavy work	0	1	7

Surgical treatment.

Job Classification	Minimum	Optimum	Maximum
Sedentary work	3	7	14
Light work	3	7	14
Medium work	3	7	21
Heavy work	3	14	21
Very Heavy work	3	14	21

Failure to Recover

If an individual fails to recover within the maximum duration expectancy period, the reader may wish to reference the following questions to assist in better understanding the specifics of an individual's medical case.

Regarding diagnosis:

- Has diagnosis of hydrocele been confirmed?
- If diagnosis uncertain, were transilluminate, ultrasound, Doppler flow study, and/or testicular scintigraphy done to rule out other conditions with similar symptoms?
- Has individual experienced any complications related to the hydrocele, such as hemorrhage or atrophy of testicular tissue?

Regarding treatment:

- Did hydrocele disappear after a period of watchful waiting?
- For what reason does hydrocele require treatment?
- If aspiration and sclerotherapy was performed, did infection or fibrosis occur?
- Was surgical intervention (hydrocelectomy) necessary?

Regarding prognosis:

- By what method was hydrocele corrected?
- Has hydrocele recurred?
- What further treatment is being considered?
- Does individual have an coexisting condition, such as varicocele, epididymitis or orchitis, that might complicate treatment or impact recovery?

References

LeMone, P., and K.M. Burke. Medical-Surgical Nursing. Upper Saddle River, NJ: Prentice Hall Health, 2000.

McAninch, J.W. "Disorders of the Testis, Scrotum, and Spermatic Cord." Smith's General Urology. Tanagho, Emil A., and Jack W. McAninch, eds. Norwalk: Appleton & Lange, 1995. 681-690.

Nistal, M., and R. Paniagua. Testicular and Epididymal Pathology. New York: Thieme-Stratton Inc, 1984.

Wang, R. "Treatment of 40 Cases of Hydroceles with Massage at Qichong (St 30)." Journal of Traditional Chinese Medicine 18 3 (1998): 218-219.

Hydronephrosis

Other names / synonyms: Hydrocalycosis, Nephrydrosis
591

Definition

Hydronephrosis is a condition in which the kidney swells with urine, due to blockage of the urinary drainage system.

The build-up of urine in the kidney creates excessive pressure within the kidney. With build-up and swelling of the kidney with urine, kidney damage and infection occur, which can result in permanent injury and kidney failure if left unchecked. Either one or both kidneys may be affected. The blockage causing hydronephrosis may occur over the course of a few days, causing symptoms and problems very quickly (acute), or it may be a slowly progressive condition that develops over the course of several weeks or months, causing symptoms and problems only as it becomes more severe (chronic).

Several conditions may place individuals at increased risk for development of hydronephrosis. Individuals may have blockage from a stone (calculi) lodged in a kidney (kidney stone) or in a tube that drains urine from the kidney, the ureter (ureteral stone). Narrowing (stenosis) of a ureter can also cause urine to back-up into the kidney. Back-up of urine from the bladder can also cause hydronephrosis. This is often due to retention of urine in the bladder, usually due to blockage of the urethra (from benign prostatic hypertrophy, for example). Cancer of the urinary tract or anatomic abnormalities in the development of the urinary system can also lead to hydronephrosis.

Hydronephrosis has been found in about 4% of all individuals at autopsy.

Diagnosis

History: The individual may report a history of benign prostatic hypertrophy and increasing difficulty on urination. The individual may report a history of kidney stones. Some individuals may report a history of cancer. The individual may note flank pain, especially if it is from acute obstruction. The pain may be colicky in nature, and it may extend (radiate) to the groin, vulva, or testes. Fever, nausea, vomiting, and painful or difficult urination might also be reported. There may be blood or pus in the urine. Sometimes, the individual may note alternating periods first when there is no urine (oliguria) and then periods of excessive urine (polyuria). The individual may feel a lump or mass over one or both kidneys. If obstruction occurs gradually, symptoms may be absent.

Physical exam: Feeling the area with the fingers (palpation) might reveal tenderness over the affected kidney with acute obstruction. It may also reveal the presence of a lump or mass in one or both flank areas. An elevated blood pressure may be noted.

Tests: A catheter may be inserted into the bladder to empty the bladder and to measure the amount of urine in the bladder after urination (residual urine). A large amount of residual urine may indicate obstruction to urine flow out of the bladder. Inability to insert a catheter into the bladder through the urethra is indicative of urethral obstruction (usually due to prostate disease or a urethral stricture). Diagnostic tests may include laboratory testing of the blood and urine, diagnostic imaging procedures, and surgical procedures to visualize the urethra and bladder. Laboratory tests of the blood may include a complete blood count (CBC), which may reveal a reduction in the number of red blood cells (anemia). Blood tests may also include measurement of the blood urea nitrogen (BUN) and creatinine, which are tests of kidney function. If kidney function has been compromised, the BUN and creatinine will be elevated. Laboratory tests of the urine may include analysis of the urine (urinalysis) and a culture to determine the presence of bacteria. Urinalysis may reveal blood, pus, or other abnormal elements. Diagnostic imaging tests may include x-ray and other imaging studies. An x-ray of the abdomen that shows the kidneys, ureter, and bladder may be performed (often referred to as a KUB). An x-ray may reveal enlargement of the renal shadows or calcifications (which may be stones or tumor metastases to the bones). X-rays of the kidneys and urinary tract may be taken using radiopaque dyes, including an intravenous pyelography (IVP), and retrograde pyelography. These x-rays reveal changes in the bladder and/or an obstructive lesion. Ultrasonography and CT scanning may reveal the extent of enlargement (dilation) and wasting of the functional cells of the kidneys (atrophy) that has occurred as a result of the dilation and pressure within the kidney. Surgical procedures that may be performed for diagnosis include visual examination of the urethra, bladder, and ureters with a lighted fiberoptic tube that is inserted through the urethra (cystoscopy). Cystoscopy may reveal obstruction, and urine samples may be obtained from the kidneys for analysis and culture.

Treatment

Treatment is twofold. The aims of treatment are to quickly reduce the amount of extra urine in the kidney caused by the backup and to correct/treat the underlying cause. Either medical or surgical treatment or both may be necessary. Medical treatment may be used to treat infection. Antibiotics are given to treat the infection and bedrest aids in recovering from any infection.

The cause of the urinary blockage must be surgically corrected. Cystoscopy may be performed to remove kidney stones from the ureters. Stones that are too large for removal by cystoscopy may be treated first with extracorporeal shock wave lithotripsy (ESWL). In ESWL, kidney stones are broken apart using shock waves that are transmitted through the skin. The fragments may then pass during urination, or they may then be removed using cystoscopy procedures. A small tube (stent) may be placed during cystoscopy in the ureter to enable passage of kidney stones. Surgical treatment of the prostate may be necessary to reduce obstruction of the urethra.

If the hydronephrosis is due to benign prostatic hypertrophy (BPH), treatment options include transurethral resection of prostate (TURP), transurethral incision of prostate (TUIP), and transurethral laser-induced prostatectomy (TULIP). Tumors affecting outflow of urine from the kidneys or that block the ureters, bladder, or urethra are removed surgically. In some cases, a tube may be inserted directly into the kidney to drain the kidney (percutaneous nephrostomy).

Prognosis

Outcome of hydronephrosis should be favorable if the underlying cause is not cancer, and if the obstruction can be relieved and kidney function preserved. Damage to the kidneys may be permanent, requiring lifelong treatment and follow-up. The outcome of the underlying condition varies with cause. Most infections respond well to antibiotic treatment, although some may require prolonged therapy for adequate treatment. The outcome of kidney stones is usually good, but they may reoccur. Long-term treatment of conditions increasing development of kidney stones may be needed. The outcome of prostatectomy procedures is generally favorable, resulting in decreased symptoms associated with the enlarged prostate. The outcome of surgical treatment to treat tumors varies with the type of cancer, the extent of the disease, and the spread to distant organs.

Differential Diagnosis

A kidney cyst or a solid kidney mass may appear similarly to hydronephrosis.

Specialists

- Nephrologist
- Urologist

Work Restrictions / Accommodations

Time off from work will be needed in many cases for diagnostic procedures and for treatment. Work restrictions are generally not needed for cystoscopy procedures. Surgical procedures performed through abdominal incisions may require several days of hospitalization, and prolonged (6-8 week) recovery periods. Individuals can return to duties gradually after surgery. Lifting should be restricted for a short period.

Comorbid Conditions

Comorbid conditions may include infection of the urinary tract.

Complications

Complications of hydronephrosis include infection (pyelonephritis) and acute or chronic kidney failure.

Factors Influencing Duration

The underlying cause and the severity of symptoms related to the hydronephrosis will influence the length of disability. Response to treatment and development of any complications will also influence length of disability.

Length of Disability

Duration depends on cause.

Acute.

Duration in Days

Job Classification	Minimum	Optimum	Maximum
Sedentary work	7	14	21
Light work	7	14	21
Medium work	7	14	21
Heavy work	7	14	21
Very Heavy work	7	14	21

Cystoscopy.

Job Classification	Duration in Days		
	Minimum	Optimum	Maximum
Sedentary work	1	3	4
Light work	1	3	4
Medium work	1	3	4
Heavy work	1	3	4
Very Heavy work	1	3	4

Lithotripsy, extracorporeal shock wave.

Job Classification	Duration in Days		
	Minimum	Optimum	Maximum
Sedentary work	1	2	7
Light work	1	2	7
Medium work	1	2	7
Heavy work	1	2	7
Very Heavy work	1	2	7

Transurethral resection of prostate.

Job Classification	Duration in Days		
	Minimum	Optimum	Maximum
Sedentary work	7	9	14
Light work	7	9	14
Medium work	14	16	21
Heavy work	21	24	28
Very Heavy work	21	24	28

Failure to Recover

If an individual fails to recover within the maximum duration expectancy period, the reader may wish to reference the following questions to assist in better understanding the specifics of an individual's medical case.

Regarding diagnosis:

- Does the individual have any risk factors?
- What symptoms does the individual have?
- What were the findings on physical exam?
- Has the individual received appropriate diagnostic testing to establish the diagnosis?
- Have conditions with similar symptoms been ruled out?

Regarding treatment:

- Has the individual received appropriate treatment?

Regarding prognosis:

- Is the individual's employer able to accommodate any necessary restrictions?
- Does the individual have any comorbid conditions?
- Does the individual have any complications?

References

Amend, William J.C., and Flavio G. Vincenti. "Oliguria; Acute Renal Failure." Smith's General Urology, 15th ed. Tanagho, Emil A., and Jack W. McAninch, eds. New York: Lange Medical Books/McGraw-Hill, 2000. 605-609.

Cutler, Ralph E. "Obstructive Uropathy." The Merck Manual of Diagnosis and Therapy, 17th ed. Beers, Mark H., and Robert Berkow, eds. Whitehouse Station, NJ: Merck Research Laboratories, 1999. 1827-1829.

Kogan, Barry A., Robert S. Hattner, and Jeffrey A. Cooper. "Radionuclide Imaging." Smith's General Urology, 15th ed. Tanagho, Emil A., and Jack W. McAninch, eds. New York: Lange Medical Books/McGraw-Hill, 2000. 183-195.

Nagle, Gratia M. "Genitourinary Surgery." Alexander's Care of the Patient in Surgery, 11th ed. Meeker, Margaret H., and Jane C. Rothrock, eds. St. Louis: Mosby, 1999. 501-598.

Stoller, Marshall L., and Damian M. Bolton. "Urinary Stone Disease." Smith's General Urology, 15th ed. Tanagho, Emil A., and Jack W. McAninch, eds. New York: Lange Medical Books/McGraw-Hill, 2000. 291-320.

Tanagho, Emil A. "Urinary Obstruction and Stasis." Smith's General Urology, 15th ed. Tanagho, Emil A., and Jack W. McAninch, eds. New York: Lange Medical Books/McGraw-Hill, 2000. 208-220.

Hyperbaric Oxygenation

Other names / synonyms: Hyperbaric Oxygen (HBO or HBO2), Hyperbaric Oxygen Therapy (HBOT), Recompression Therapy

93.95

Definition

Hyperbaric oxygen, or HBO, is a treatment in which 100% oxygen is administered at increased pressure (typically 2-3 times atmospheric pressure) inside an enclosed pressure vessel referred to as a hyperbaric chamber.

The effects of HBO are mainly due to the increased oxygen tension and content in the blood, and hence the tissues. At one atmosphere pressure breathing high oxygen concentrations imparts only a small increment of oxygen into physical solution in the blood. However, at 2-3 atmospheres pressure, the additional dissolved oxygen in the blood is significant, and can facilitate normal oxygenation of ischemic tissues. In cases of iatrogenic or diving-related gas embolism or decompression sickness an additional mechanism of action is the physical reduction in bubble size. Placement of a single limb inside a chamber that is compressed with oxygen does not significantly raise tissue oxygen tension and is not considered HBO treatment.

Most hyperbaric chambers are large enough to hold a single individual (monoplace chamber), but some are large enough to accommodate more than one individual and a health provider (multiplace chamber).

Reason for Procedure

Hyperbaric oxygen is a useful primary treatment or adjunct for a variety of medical conditions and injuries. The Undersea and Hyperbaric Medical Society has approved 13 indications for the use of HBO. These indications are air or gas embolism; carbon monoxide (CO) poisoning; CO poisoning complicated by cyanide poisoning; clostridial myositis and myonecrosis (gas gangrene); crush injuries, compartment syndromes, and other acute traumatic peripheral ischemias; decompression sickness; enhancement of healing in selected problem wounds; exceptional blood loss anemia; intracranial abscess; necrotizing soft tissue infections; osteomyelitis (refractory); delayed radiation injury (soft tissue and bony necrosis); skin grafts and flaps (compromised); and thermal burns.

Description

Suitability for HBO treatment includes the presence of a disease for which HBO has been demonstrated to have efficacy and absence of conditions that preclude safe treatment. Because hyperbaric oxygen therapy involves the contraction and expansion of air spaces within the body, illnesses that may interfere with this process and cause tissue damage require individual consideration. For example, eustachian tube dysfunction, which precludes equalization of middle ear and ambient pressures, may require myringotomy or tympanostomy tube placement before treatment. Bullous lung disease, which could predispose to pneumothorax or arterial gas embolism, is a relative contraindication.

During hyperbaric treatment, individuals are usually placed in a sitting or supine position inside the chamber. In the smaller monoplace chambers, the individual lies flat while the chamber is filled with 100% oxygen. In the larger multiplace chambers, oxygen is delivered by way of a tightly fitting demand valve mask, similar to ones used by aviators, or via an oxygen hood, which is a clear plastic device that completely covers the head and neck.

Treatments may consist of only one recompression for acute conditions, or may include 20-40 or more treatments for more chronic medical conditions. Each treatment usually lasts 1-2 hours; the number of treatments is dependent upon the progress of the individual and the alleviation of symptoms. For each treatment, the chamber pressure and duration are set according to the diagnosis and the treatment policy and procedures of a given facility.

Individuals are required to wear special hospital clothing to enter the hyperbaric chamber and petroleum based flammable material, including patient dressings, and spark-generating products are not allowed to accompany the individual into the chamber.

Prognosis

Outcome depends on the disease process.

Specialists

- Emergency Medicine

Work Restrictions / Accommodations

Besides wearing special hospital clothing while in the hyperbaric chamber and the avoidance of any flammable materials, the individuals will be located inside a hyperbaric chamber and isolated from total bedside care. Claustrophobic individuals may not tolerate the chamber environment. Individuals are advised against smoking between treatments, as the ensuing vasoconstriction may limit the effectiveness of hyperbaric oxygen therapy.

Comorbid Conditions

Any condition that might impair the oxygenation of blood or the flow of blood into the body tissues reduces the effectiveness of hyperbaric oxygen therapy. Cystic or bullous lung disease and diffuse airways obstruction may pose a risk of pulmonary barotrauma during chamber decompression. Hyperbaric oxygen therapy is not recommended for pregnant women except for the treatment of acute illness in which the risk of withholding treatment exceeds the potential risk of exposure of the fetus to hyperbaric treatment. Adequate monitoring of critically ill individuals, including those requiring mechanical ventilation, can be achieved in a hyperbaric chamber, which may serve as an extension of the intensive care unit.

Procedure Complications

Oxygen can be toxic when breathed at high ambient pressure. During most commonly used hyperbaric treatment schedules, pulmonary toxicity is uncommon, although tracheobronchitis due to O2 toxicity can occur during prolonged treatments (e.g., for serious decompression sickness). The earliest symptoms of pulmonary O2 toxicity are substernal chest pain and cough, which generally resolve within 12-72 hours after cessation of treatment. Central nervous system toxicity can also occur, manifesting as nausea, muscle twitching or grand mal seizures. Individuals must be closely observed for signs and symptoms of oxygen toxicity during HBO treatment.

Hyperbaric oxygen may also cause a change in the refractive index of the lens of the eye, producing near-sightedness (myopia). This usually occurs after 40 or more repeated exposures and is generally, but not always, reversible after treatments have stopped.

Factors Influencing Duration
Factors that influence disability include the severity of the underlying condition, the number of treatments, and the presence of complications.

Length of Disability
No disability is expected to result from this therapy. Disability may occur as a result of an underlying condition.

References
Hampson, Neil B., ed. Hyperbaric Oxygen Therapy: 1999 Committee Report. Kensington, MD: Undersea and Hyperbaric Medical Society, 1999.

Piantadosi, Claude. "Physiology of Hyperbaric Hyperoxia." Respiratory Care Clinics of North America. Moon, Richard E., and Enrico M. Camporesi, eds. Philadelphia: W.B. Saunders Company, 1999. 7-19.

Hyperemesis Gravidarum
Other names / synonyms: Morning Sickness
643, 643.0, 643.1, 643.2, 643.8, 643.9

Definition
Hyperemesis gravidarum is a rare disorder characterized by nausea and vomiting during pregnancy that is so severe and persistent it causes weight loss, dehydration, nutritional deficiencies, electrolyte imbalance, pH imbalance (metabolic acidosis), and possible liver damage. Symptoms are often severe enough that the individual requires hospitalization.

Hyperemesis gravidarum may be related to the high hormonal levels in the blood from pregnancy, although the exact cause is not known. Most women experience some nausea and vomiting during the first trimester of pregnancy, but a few will have nausea and vomiting that persists.

While nausea and vomiting during pregnancy (morning sickness) occur in up to 70% of all pregnancies, only about 2 out of every 1,000 pregnant women have their pregnancies complicated by hyperemesis gravidarum. A woman vomiting during pregnancy but who continues to gain weight and is not dehydrated does not have hyperemesis gravidarum.

Diagnosis
History: Beginning early in pregnancy, a woman may complain of vomiting that becomes so persistent and severe it leads to progressive weight loss (larger than 5% of original body weight) and dehydration. Eventually she may be unable to keep down any solids or liquids. The individual may also complain of excessive salivation (ptyalism) and a rapid heartbeat (tachycardia).

Physical exam: The woman may present with weight loss of 5 to 35 pounds or a failure to gain weight. There may be signs of dehydration (dry mucous membranes, poor skin turgor), yellow coloring to skin or whites of eyes (jaundice), tachycardia, and/or a low-grade fever. Ophthalmic examination may reveal bleeding into the retina of the eye (hemorrhagic retinitis). Individuals may also have a distinct odor to their breath (ketonic odor).

Tests: Blood studies assess the electrolyte levels and rule out electrolyte imbalance. Serum bicarbonate and urine ketones are checked to help detect acidosis. Liver function tests, white blood cell count, and urinalysis are performed to rule out other causes. Thyroid dysfunction can be associated with hyperemesis gravidarum therefore a TSH and a free T4 may be done to evaluate thyroid function. A fetal ultrasound evaluation may help rule out the possibility of a hydatidiform mole instead of a pregnancy.

Treatment
Affected individuals should be hospitalized immediately to restore fluids and replace electrolytes (intravenously). No food should be given by mouth (orally) until vomiting ceases and dehydration is corrected. Nourishment may be supplied via the intestines (enteral feeding) or by injection (parenteral feeding). Vitamin supplementation is often recommended (especially vitamins B_6 [pyridoxine], C [ascorbic acid], and B_1 [thiamine]). Thiamine is recommended to prevent the development of a rare neurological disorder (Wernicke's encephalopathy).

Antiemetics may be required; however, the risk of using antiemetics must be carefully weighed against the possibility of prolonged starvation and dehydration.

Total parenteral nutrition (TPN) is sometimes required.

Prognosis
The predicted outcome is excellent. The condition is generally self-limiting and usually resolves during the second half of the pregnancy; however, death and serious complications are possible. If left untreated, hyperemesis gravidarum can be fatal. With increasing sophistication of home care, there is little reason for long-term hospitalization.

Differential Diagnosis
Conditions with similar symptoms include peptic ulcer, gastritis, gastroenteritis, pyelonephritis, pancreatitis, cholelithiasis, cholecystitis, hepatitis, acute appendicitis, diabetic ketoacidosis, pseudotumor cerebri, and hydatidiform mole.

Specialists

- Dietary Advisor
- Gynecologist
- Obstetrician
- Perinatologist

Work Restrictions / Accommodations

Hospitalization may be required until dehydration and electrolyte imbalance are successfully treated. Individuals may require many breaks during the working day to consume frequent but small, bland meals. Nausea and vomiting can be triggered by bad odors. Individuals who work around these types of odors may need to be assigned different duties on a temporary basis. Once individuals are in positive caloric status, they can usually resume normal duties for the duration of the pregnancy.

Comorbid Conditions

Hyperthyroidism, pyridoxine deficiency, Helicobacter pylori infection, multiple gestation, and psychological factors can all impact the ability to recover from hyperemesis gravidarum and lengthen the disability time.

Complications

Complications from vomiting are rare but may include a tear in the mucosa at the junction of the esophagus and stomach (Mallory-Weiss tear) or an esophageal perforation.

Without thiamine supplementation, a neurological disorder characterized by confusion, disorientation, nystagmus, diplopia, and coma (Wernicke's encephalopathy) may occur.

When acid levels within the blood increase due to the loss of fluids, a serious condition called acidosis may occur. Acidosis depresses the central nervous system by interfering with the ability of the nerves to communicate with each other (synaptic transmission). As the acid level rises, the malfunction of the nervous system worsens, and the individual may become disoriented, comatose, or even dies.

Severe dehydration can lead to an abnormally low volume of blood circulating in the body (hypovolemia). Untreated, hypovolemia can lead to shock and be potentially fatal. Another serious complication of hyperemesis gravidarum is bleeding within the retinas of the eye (hemorrhagic retinitis). Hyperemesis gravidarum sometimes affects the liver where the tissue deteriorates similar to that found in starvation. Maternal failure to gain weight can cause extrauterine growth retardation.

Factors Influencing Duration

The severity of symptoms and response to treatment influence the length of disability.

Length of Disability

Duration depends on the severity of the condition and may continue until delivery. Contact physician for more specific information.

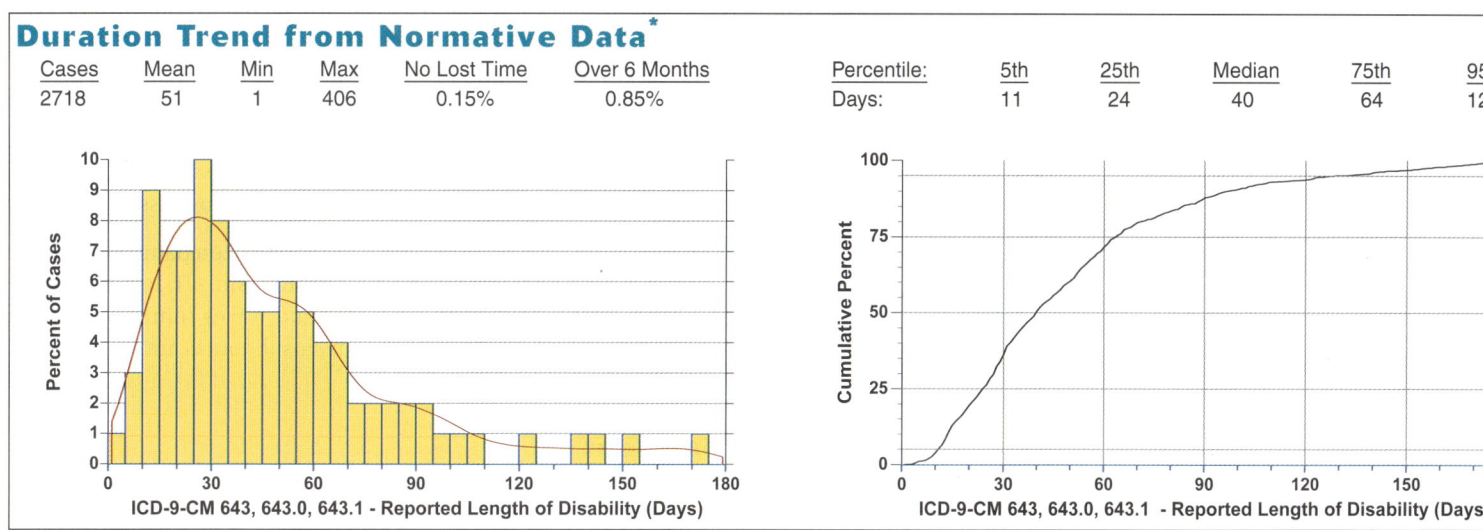

* Differences may exist between the expected duration tables and the normative graphs. Duration tables provide expected recovery periods based on the type of work performed by the individual. The normative graphs reflect the actual observed experience of many individuals across the spectrum of physical conditions, in a variety of industries, and with varying levels of case management.

Failure to Recover

If an individual fails to recover within the maximum duration expectancy period, the reader may wish to reference the following questions to assist in better understanding the specifics of an individual's medical case.

Regarding diagnosis:

- Was diagnosis of hyperemesis gravidarum confirmed?
- Have other conditions with similar symptoms been ruled out?
- Does individual have a coexisting condition such as hyperthyroidism, pyridoxine deficiency, Helicobacter pylori infection, or psychological factors that may complicate treatment or impact recovery?

Regarding treatment:

- Was individual promptly hospitalized for replacement of fluids and nutritional support?
- If symptoms persisted despite treatment, was nourishment supplied via enteral or parenteral feeding?
- Did treatment include vitamin supplementation?

- Were injectable steroids considered in the treatment plan?
- If psychological factors are present, would individual benefit from psychological counseling?

Regarding prognosis:

- Was condition so severe and persistent that it caused weight loss, dehydration, nutritional deficiencies, electrolyte imbalance, pH imbalance (metabolic acidosis), or liver damage? Have these complications responded to treatment?
- With increasing sophistication of home care, can individual continue to receive treatment at home rather than through long-term hospitalization?

References

Hyperemesis Gravidarum. drkoop.com. 1998. 1 Jan 2001 <http://www.drkoop.com/conditions/ency/article/001499.htm>.

Golaszewski, T.P. Frigo, and H.E. Mark. "Treatment of Hyperemesis Gravidarum by Electrostimulation of the Vestibular Apparatus." Z Geburtshilfe Neonatol 199 3 (1995): 107-110.

Mahan, Kathleen L., and Sylvia Escott-Stump, eds. Krause's Food, Nutrition, and Diet Therapy, 10th ed. Philadelphia: W.B. Saunders Company, 2000.

Tierney, Lawrence M., Stephen J. McPhee, and Maxine A. Papadakis, eds. Current Medical Diagnosis and Treatment, 39th ed. New York: Lange Medical Books/McGraw-Hill, 2000.

Hyperinsulinism

Other names / synonyms: Endogenous Hyperinsulinism
251.1

Definition

Hyperinsulinism (also called endogenous hyperinsulinism) refers to abnormally high levels of insulin in the bloodstream in association with documented low blood sugar (hypoglycemia).

Insulin is a hormone produced by cells (beta or islet cells) located within the pancreas. Insulin helps regulate sugar (glucose) levels in the blood by promoting its uptake from the blood into tissue. Therefore, insulin's effect is to lower blood sugar concentrations. During hyperinsulinism, when insulin levels in the blood are very high, blood sugar is abnormally low.

The primary risk factor for hyperinsulinism is the presence of a cell growth (insulinoma or islet cell tumor) in the pancreas that secretes unusually high amounts of insulin. Other risk factors may include an increase in the number of islet cells in the pancreas (islet cell hyperplasia or nesidioblastosis), obesity, and consumption of a diet rich in carbohydrates.

Up to 85% of individuals with hyperinsulinism have a pancreatic insulinoma. Insulinomas are usually noncancerous (benign); however, 10% of them will be deadly (malignant). Insulinomas occur in all age groups, although they are most common between the ages of forty and sixty. The average age for occurrence of insulinoma is 47 years. Hyperinsulinism occurs more frequently in women than men, with a 1.5 to 1 female to male ratio.

Diagnosis

History: Individuals may complain of double vision (diplopia), blurred vision, sweating, weakness, increased heart rate (palpitation), and more rarely, epileptic-like (grand mal) seizures. They may also report headaches, menstrual problems, muscle cramps, and hair loss.

Physical exam: The exam may reveal obesity, elevated blood pressure, confusion or abnormal behavior, lethargy, occasional amnesia, and drowsiness. If the hyperinsulinism is caused by a pancreatic islet cell tumor that has spread (metastasized) into other organ systems, the individual may show signs of bile duct obstruction such as yellowing of the skin (jaundice), dehydration, and diarrhea. Hand manipulation (palpation) of the abdomen may reveal an enlarged liver (hepatomegaly).

Tests: Hyperinsulinism is characterized by high blood concentrations of insulin and low concentrations of blood sugar even after a period of time without food (fast). Fasting insulin concentration in the blood can be measured using a radioactive binding technique (insulin radioimmunoassay). A blood glucose test can determine the sugar concentration in the bloodstream. Another type of radioimmunoassay measures the molecule precursor of insulin (proinsulin radioimmunoassay).

Intraoperative ultrasound is the best way to visualize a pancreatic tumor (insulinoma) that may be causing hyperinsulinism. CT, low-frequency radio waves (MRI), or high-frequency sound waves (ultrasound) may also help visualize tumors; however, most insulinomas are too small for these tests to be beneficial.

Treatment

The majority of individuals with hyperinsulinism have benign insulin-secreting insulinomas. These are usually treated by surgical removal (enucleation). A portion of the pancreas may have to be removed (partial pancreatectomy) if there are multiple insulinomas. Individuals who cannot tolerate surgery may be treated using drugs that inhibit insulin secretion (diazoxide) and raise blood glucose levels (phenytoin, glucocorticoids, propranolol, or chlorpromazine).

Prognosis

Individuals with hyperinsulinism due to a localized pancreatic tumor and are treated surgically should have a successful outcome 75% of the time. Individuals treated with drug therapy may expect less severe hypoglycemia 62% of the time. Twenty-six percent of individuals treated with drug therapy should expect blood concentrations of insulin and glucose to return to normal.

Differential Diagnosis

Conditions that present with similar symptoms as hyperinsulinism include injection of insulin by the individual (factitious hypoglycemia), nonislet cell tumor hypoglycemia, adrenal insufficiency, liver failure with accompanying infection (sepsis), uremia, and various autoimmune syndromes.

Specialists

- Endocrinologist
- Gastroenterologist
- General Surgeon
- Oncologist

Rehabilitation

Initially, education is necessary for the individual to understand the role of insulin in the body and the effects of food and exercise on insulin levels. Even if the cause of hyperinsulinism is assessed as insulinoma (tumor of the islets of Langerhans in the pancreas), proper diet and exercise are crucial for maintaining insulin levels within the body. Also, central obesity (excess fat is stored in the abdominal area), which currently affects more men than women, is an independent risk factor for insulin resistance, diabetes, and coronary heart disease. Individuals should be made aware that their current lifestyle of overeating, inactivity, smoking, etc. might be contributing to their problems with insulin.

The individual will typically undergo a nutritional assessment by a licensed nutritionist. A strict diet regimen is usually established. A typical diet plan may include caloric levels of 1,200, 1,500, and 1,800. Saturated fats should be limited to 5-10% of their daily intake, while percentages of complex carbohydrate intake should range form 30-45%, depending on the nutritionist's evaluation. Excess calories that are not utilized through everyday activity should be expired through regular exercise.

Before engaging in an exercise program, the individual is usually screened for any condition such as hypertension or arthritis that may require a specialized protocol. Exercise should be a regular part of daily life. Moderate-to-intense aerobic exercises such as brisk walking or stationary cycling should be performed. Insulin lowering effects are seen up to 48 hours after aerobic exercise; however, if not performed continuously, exercise benefits cease. Targeted heart rate for exertion control is set based on age, and should be followed to prevent over- or under-exertion. An aqua therapy routine may be prescribed for those individuals whose weight makes it difficult to perform aerobic exercises such as walking for prolonged periods of time. As well, the aqua environment helps to alleviate stress on joints and creates a protective environment for individuals who fear injury. In some instances, a reduction in body weight by as little as 10% shows marked improvement in insulin stabilization.

Behavior modification such as smoking cessation and weight management may be helpful. In any case, if hyperinsulinism is not controlled, exercise and diet management is ongoing.

Work Restrictions / Accommodations

If treatment includes surgery, individuals may need light-to-sedentary work for 2 to 4 weeks until recovery is complete. Otherwise, no work restrictions or accommodations are usually required.

Complementary and Alternative Therapies

Content is intended for awareness only. Treatments may or may not be effective. Scientific evidence may be lacking and some substances have potentially toxic effects. Dr. Presley Reed and the editors do not endorse the use of these therapies in the absence of consultation with a licensed medical professional.

Aerobic exercise -	Regular aerobic exercise is said to be an effective method of controlling high insulin levels. Excess calories that are not utilized through everyday activity should be expired through regular exercise.
Diet modification -	A strict diet regimen may help to regulate the intake of saturated fats and carbohydrates.

Comorbid Conditions

Existing conditions that may impact an individual's ability to recover and further lengthen the duration include obesity and adult onset (type II) diabetes.

Complications

Possible complications of hyperinsulinism include development of noninsulin-dependent diabetes mellitus (also called type II or adult onset diabetes mellitus). Noninsulin-dependent diabetes often leads to high blood pressure (hypertension), increased fat in the bloodstream (hypertriglyceridemia), and blockage of the blood vessels in the heart (coronary artery disease) that can result in a heart attack (myocardial infarction). Other complications may include stoppage of blood flow to the brain (stroke) and kidney failure (nephropathy).

Factors Influencing Duration

Factors that may influence the length of disability include hypertension, atherosclerosis, and/or disorders of lipid metabolism. The individual's age may be a factor in the response to treatment. Older individuals are not expected to recover from surgery as quickly as younger ones.

Length of Disability

The duration of disability depends on the severity of the condition, treatment received, and requirements of the job. In most cases, no disability is expected.

Failure to Recover

If an individual fails to recover within the maximum duration expectancy period, the reader may wish to reference the following questions to assist in better understanding the specifics of an individual's medical case.

Regarding diagnosis:

- Has diagnosis of hyperinsulinism been confirmed?
- Has individual experienced any complications related to the hyperinsulinism?

Regarding treatment:	Regarding prognosis:
• Do symptoms persist despite surgical removal of insulinomas? • What additional treatment options are available to this individual? • If drug treatment is not adequate, is surgical intervention now an option? • Would individual benefit from diet modification and enrollment in a weight loss program?	• If symptoms persist despite treatment, would individual benefit from further evaluation by a specialist? • Would individual benefit from consultation with a nutritionist/dietitian? • Is individual currently enrolled in a weight loss program?

References

Syndrome X Web. Shaman Pharmaceuticals, Inc. 12 Oct 2000. 14 Jan 2001 <http://syndromexweb.com>.

Cryer, P.E. "Glucose Homeostasis and Hypoglycemia." Textbook of Endocrinology. Wilson, J.D., and D.W. Foster, eds. Philadelphia: W.B. Saunders Company, 1985. 989-1017.

Eastman, R.C., R.S. Rittmaster, and C.R. Kahn. "Hypoglycemia." Clinical Endocrinology. Kohler, P.O., ed. New York: John Wiley & Sons, 1986. 465-490.

Grieger, Lynn. "Syndrome X and Diet Recommendations." Heart Information Network. 23 Dec 2000. 14 Jan 2001 <http://www.heartinfo.org/news2000/syndx082500.htm>.

Karam, J.H., and C.W. Young. "Hypoglycemic Disorders." Basic and Clinical Endocrinology. Greenspan, F.S., and J.D. Baxter, eds. Norwalk: Appleton & Lange, 1994. 635-648.

Service, F.J., et al. "Functioning Insulinoma - Incidence, Recurrence, and Long-term Survival of Patients: A 60-year Study." Mayo Clinic Proceedings 66 7 (1991): 711-719.

Hyperkalemia
276.7

Definition

Hyperkalemia is a serious condition in which excess amounts of potassium are in the bloodstream. Potassium is necessary for normal cellular metabolism and electrical impulse transmission in nerves and muscles, which in turn is necessary for normal nervous system function and muscle contraction. Potassium is found in foods such as bananas, oranges, baked potatoes, fish, beans, dairy products, and salt-substitutes. Any excess potassium is usually eliminated by the kidneys. When this does not occur and potassium levels build up, the result can be muscle weakness or paralysis, heart problems, and death in severe cases.

Hyperkalemia is found most often in individuals with kidney problems, especially those with diabetes and aldosterone abnormalities (type 4 renal tubular acidosis, adrenal insufficiency). It can also develop in individuals taking oral potassium supplements or certain medications (potassium-sparing diuretics such as amiloride, triamterene, and spironolactone, and the antibiotic trimethoprim), and as a complication of dehydration, severe burns, internal bleeding, and muscle trauma.

Diagnosis

History: Mild hyperkalemia usually has no symptoms and may be recognized only because of an abnormally high potassium blood test result, while individuals with moderate or severe hyperkalemia may report weakness, numbness, muscle paralysis, an irregular heart beat, or confusion.

Physical exam: Findings may include weakness, poor reflexes, a slow or irregular heart beat, trouble breathing due to a weak respiratory effort, and respiratory and cardiac arrest in the most severe cases.

Tests: A blood test to measure potassium will demonstrate an elevated potassium measurement, defined as a potassium value of greater than 5 mmol/liter. An electrocardiogram is usually done to determine any impact on the heart, and additional tests may be done to determine the cause of the hyperkalemia if it is not obvious.

Treatment

When hyperkalemia is the result of a drug complication, removing the offending drug will usually correct the problem. When hyperkalemia is chronic and not life-threatening, treatment measures include a diet low in potassium, avoiding medications that can raise potassium (beta-blockers, ACE-inhibitors, potassium-sparing diuretics, nonsteroidal anti-inflammatory drugs, and trimethoprim), and use of loop diuretics such as furosemide, which promote potassium elimination by the kidneys, oral potassium-binding resins such as Kayexalate (sodium polystyrene sulfonate), and aldosterone replacement therapy, which also helps promote potassium elimination by the kidneys. When hyperkalemia is severe, hospitalization for more urgent therapy given by vein (intravenous) is needed, including some combination of calcium salts, fluids containing glucose, insulin, loop diuretics, and sodium bicarbonate. In addition, potassium-binding resins, given orally or by enema, and nebulizer treatments containing albuterol may be used. These treatments all work in various ways to help lower the blood level of potassium. If the hyperkalemia does not improve, dialysis may be needed.

Prognosis

Most individuals with hyperkalemia respond favorably to treatment, and it is the underlying cause of the hyperkalemia, such as diabetes or chronic renal failure, that affects the long-term outcome.

Differential Diagnosis

Hyperkalemia can be a sign of adrenal insufficiency and hypoaldosteronism. Heparin has the potential to induce hyperkalemia. Breakdown of red blood cells in the test tube (hemolysis) due to delay in testing the sample, or high numbers of white blood cells or platelets in the individual's blood can all result in an elevated potassium test result that does not reflect true hyperkalemia in the body and does not need treatment (a situation called pseudohyperkalemia). True hyperkalemia always has an underlying cause that must be identified.

Specialists

- Endocrinologist
- Internist
- Nephrologist

Work Restrictions / Accommodations

Weakness, fatigue, or an irregular heart beat may require decreased activity; but generally, any restrictions or accommodations would be more likely related to the underlying cause of the hyperkalemia, and not the hyperkalemia itself. No restrictions or accommodations should be necessary once the individual returns to work.

Comorbid Conditions

Kidney disease, diabetes mellitus, and gastrointestinal and cardiac conditions may lengthen disability.

Complications

Hyperkalemia can be complicated when individuals take blood pressure medications and for those who have kidney disease, diabetes, or heart problems. Hyperkalemia resulting from digoxin therapy is a well-recognized phenomenon. Undiagnosed and untreated, severe hyperkalemia may be complicated by weakness, muscle paralysis, a slow or irregular heart beat, and, in the most severe cases, respiratory or cardiac arrest.

Factors Influencing Duration

Disability time varies according to the underlying problem and type of treatment required. In mild cases with a reversible problem, such as a drug side effect, disability time should be minimal. More serious hyperkalemia that involves hospitalization or regular dialysis may require more lengthy disability time.

Length of Disability

The length of disability is usually dependent most on the underlying cause.

Duration in Days

Job Classification	Minimum	Optimum	Maximum
Sedentary work	0	2	3
Light work	0	2	3
Medium work	0	2	3
Heavy work	3	3	5
Very Heavy work	3	3	5

Failure to Recover

If an individual fails to recover within the maximum duration expectancy period, the reader may wish to reference the following questions to assist in better understanding the specifics of an individual's medical case.

Regarding diagnosis:

- Has diagnosis of hyperkalemia been confirmed?
- Because hemolysis due to delay in testing a blood sample, or high numbers of white blood cells or platelets in the blood can all result in an elevated potassium test result (pseudohyperkalemia), is this a case of true hyperkalemia?
- Has underlying cause of the hyperkalemia been identified?
- Does individual have a coexisting condition, such as kidney disease, diabetes mellitus, gastrointestinal or cardiac condition that may complicate treatment or impact recovery?

Regarding treatment:

- If hyperkalemia was the result of a drug complication, did removing the offending drug correct the problem?
- Has individual been able to comply with a diet low in potassium? Would individual benefit from consultation with a nutritionist?
- Has drug therapy effectively lowered the blood potassium level?
- If hyperkalemia did not improve with drug therapy, did hyperkalemia respond to dialysis? Is continued or future dialysis anticipated?

Regarding prognosis:

- Has the underlying cause of the hyperkalemia, such as diabetes or chronic renal failure, responded to treatment? What does follow-up entail?
- Would individual benefit from consultation with a specialist (internist, nephrologist, endocrinologist)?

References

Black, Robert M., MD. "Hyperkalemia." Disorders of Acid-Base and Potassium Balance. Dale, D.C., and Daniel D. Federman, MD, eds. New York: WebMD Corporation, 2000 Scientific American Medicine. 28 June 2000 <http://www.samed.com/sam/forms/index.htm>.

Fenton, F., A.J. Smally, and J. Laut. "Hyperkalemia and Digoxin Toxicity in a Patient with Kidney Failure." Annals of Emergency Medicine 28 4 (1996): 440-441.

Sherman, D.S., C.L. Kass, and D.N. Fish. "Fludrocortisone for the Treatment of Heparin-induced Hyperkalemia." Annals of Pharmacotheraphy 34 5 (2000): 606-610.

Singer, Gary G., and Barry M. Brenner. "Fluid and Electrolyte Disturbances." Harrison's Principles of Internal Medicine. Fauci, Anthony S., et al., eds. New York: The McGraw-Hill Companies, Inc, 1998. 265-277.

Hyperparathyroidism

Other names / synonyms: Overactive Parathyroid Glands, Parathyroid Adenoma

252.0

Definition

Hyperparathyroidism is a disorder in which any of the 4 glands located next to the thyroid gland near the front of the neck (parathyroid) release an excessive amount of parathyroid hormone. Increased parathyroid hormone (the substance that keeps calcium levels in check) results in an increased calcium level in the blood (hypercalcemia) and urine (hypercalciuria).

Primary hyperparathyroidism is usually the result of small benign tumors, or adenomas, on the parathyroid glands. Hyperparathyroidism can also be due to an enlargement of the glands, the cause of which is unknown. Secondary hyperparathyroidism may be caused by a chronic hypocalcemia (decreased level of calcium) that originates elsewhere in the body, such as hypercalciuria, or it can be caused by a vitamin D deficiency.

Occurring in about 40 out of 1,000 individuals, the disease is found approximately twice as common in women as in men. It occurs predominantly in women over age forty.

Diagnosis

History: Hyperparathyroidism may not cause any symptoms (asymptomatic). It may cause generalized aches and pains, depression, or abdominal pain. Often, the only symptoms are those of kidney stones (urinary tract calculi). In severe cases, the symptoms are those of hypercalcemia (nausea, vomiting, tiredness, excessive urination, excessive thirst, muscle weakness, depression, personality disturbance, abnormal behavior and/or confusion).

Physical exam: The exam may reveal muscle weakness or calcium precipitate in the tissues due to the hypercalcemia. Abnormal deposits of calcium (calcinosis) may occur in joints causing a type of arthritic inflammation known as pseudogout. Eye (ophthalmic) exam may reveal calcium precipitate in the corneas (band keratopathy). Enlargement or tumor of the parathyroid gland may be evident.

Tests: Diagnosis of hyperparathyroidism is confirmed by tests to measure the level of calcium, phosphorus, and parathyroid hormone in the blood. In about 50% of cases, individuals are unaware of the disorder and discover it only through routine multi-panel blood work that reveals high levels of calcium and parathyroid hormone, or through urinalysis that shows high calcium levels. Twenty-four hour urine for calcium level is critical to differentiate from FHH (familial hypocalciuria and hypocalcemia), which needs no treatment.

X-ray tests may also be used to diagnose hyperparathyroidism. X-ray films can show evidence of excess parathyroid hormone action on certain bones. Occasionally, a routine chest x-ray may reveal a parathyroid mass.

Treatment

Primary hyperparathyroidism is typically treated by surgically removing all abnormal parathyroid tissue (parathyroidectomy). Rehydration (including intravenous fluids) and using diuretics to force the kidneys to pass large amounts of urine (diuresis) may be used to help dilute blood calcium levels, if they are particularly high. Diuretics should only be used in conjunction with aggressive rehydration. In addition, the individual may be advised to reduce or avoid calcium in the diet, increase fluids, and continue to take diuretics to effectively flush excess calcium levels out of the body.

When hyperparathyroidism causes severe hypercalcemia that cannot be controlled by diet and/or diuretics, drugs such as plicamycin, gallium nitrate, calcitonin, bisphosphonates, or corticosteroids may be required. Mild cases not associated with osteoporosis, nephrolithiasis, or symptoms of hypercalcemia, may be managed with watchful waiting and do not always require surgery.

Hyperparathyroidism will compound the already significant risk of osteoporosis in postmenopausal women. Therefore, postmenopausal women with this disease are usually counseled to have the problem fixed rather than watched conservatively.

Treatment for secondary hyperparathyroidism focuses on addressing the underlying cause of the problem. The individual may require vitamin D therapy and, in some cases, dialysis to remove excess calcium from the blood. General weakness that is commonly observed in individuals with secondary hyperparathyroidism is found more frequently in women, and in individuals with diabetic nephropathy or hypertensive nephropathy. Parathyroidectomy and autotransplantation can achieve improvement in muscle power and general weakness in cases of tertiary hyperparathyroidism.

Prognosis

Hyperparathyroidism is usually a chronically progressive disease unless surgically cured. Therefore, individuals who receive medical treatment only (without surgery) must be carefully monitored. With surgery (parathyroidectomy), most individuals are successfully cured. Bones may heal once a parathyroid tumor is removed. However, kidney or pancreas damage resulting from the hypercalcemia may persist.

Differential Diagnosis

Other conditions with symptoms similar to hyperparathyroidism include adrenal insufficiency, hyperthyroidism, excessive calcium or vitamin D ingestion, familial hypocalciuric hypercalcemia, and certain malignant tumors or myelomas.

Specialists

- Endocrinologist
- Gastroenterologist
- Internist
- Nephrologist
- Neurologist
- Surgeon

Work Restrictions / Accommodations

Individuals with hyperparathyroidism may require an extended medical leave if surgery or hospitalization is required for treatment of the disease. Due to the increased risk for bone fractures, it may be necessary to limit strenuous activity in individuals with coexisting osteoporosis.

Complementary and Alternative Therapies

Content is intended for awareness only. Treatments may or may not be effective. Scientific evidence may be lacking and some substances have potentially toxic effects. Dr. Presley Reed and the editors do not endorse the use of these therapies in the absence of consultation with a licensed medical professional.

Diet modification - Reducing or avoiding calcium in the diet, plus increased fluids, may help decrease excess calcium levels in the blood and urine.

Ethanol injection - Ultrasonically guided ethanol injection through the skin (percutaneous) into parathyroid adenomas may destroy the adenoma tissue. It may be a useful alternative therapy in individuals not suitable for surgery.

Comorbid Conditions

Coexisting conditions that may impact recovery include chronic renal insufficiency, malabsorption of vitamin D and calcium due to small bowel disease or following gastrectomy, vitamin D deficiency due to malnutrition, hypomagnesemia (due to chronic alcohol abuse, vomiting, diarrhea, nasogastric suction, diuretic therapy, or renal disease), and drug-induced osteomalacia. Hyperparathyroidism may also occur as part of a rare hereditary condition known as multiple endocrine neoplasia syndrome.

Complications

Individuals with hyperparathyroidism are at increased risk for a variety of diseases/conditions due to the excessive amounts of calcium in the blood and urine. These complications include: excessive urination, kidney stones, kidney failure, thinning and weakening bones (leading to increased risk of fracture), depression, abnormal behavior, personality disturbance, drowsiness, tiredness, excessive thirst, seizures, coma, nausea, vomiting, constipation, abdominal pain, flatulence, intestinal obstruction, inflammation of the pancreas (pancreatitis), ulceration of the stomach (peptic ulcer), inflammation of the joints (pseudogout), and muscle weakness. Dehydration, irregular heartbeat (arrhythmia), and death can also occur.

Factors Influencing Duration

Length of disability depends on the severity of the symptoms, the underlying cause of the condition, method of treatment, and the presence of any complications.

Length of Disability

Most individuals will recover completely. Those with severe disease or those who experience complications may experience a prolonged recovery time or even permanent disability.

Surgical removal of tumor (parathyroidectomy).

Duration in Days

Job Classification	Minimum	Optimum	Maximum
Sedentary work	7	14	28
Light work	7	14	28
Medium work	7	21	35
Heavy work	7	21	42
Very Heavy work	7	21	42

Failure to Recover

If an individual fails to recover within the maximum duration expectancy period, the reader may wish to reference the following questions to assist in better understanding the specifics of an individual's medical case.

Regarding diagnosis:

- Has the diagnosis of hyperparathyroidism been confirmed through blood test and/or x-ray?
- Has the correct gland been removed?
- Are other or are all 4 glands hyperplastic?
- Has individual experienced any complications?
- Does individual have an underlying condition that may impact recovery?

Regarding treatment:

- If parathyroidectomy is not an option, what are the extenuating circumstances?
- Has individual been compliant with prescribed treatment?
- Has drug therapy effectively controlled blood calcium levels?
- If postmenopausal, has individual had bone density test and been treated with estrogen or bisphosphonates if needed?
- Has any underlying condition been effectively treated or controlled? Is this enough to resolve hyperparathyroidism?
- If tertiary hyperparathyroidism, is individual a candidate for a parathyroidectomy?

Regarding prognosis:

- Has medical treatment alone been effective?
- At what point will parathyroidectomy be an option?
- To what extent does damage impair function?

References

Lewis, James III. "Salt Balance." Merck Manual of Medical Information. Berkow, Robert, ed. New York: Pocket Books, 1997. 731-742.

Hypersensitivity Pneumonitis

Other names / synonyms: Bird Fancier's Disease, Byssinosis, Cork Worker's Lung, Cotton Worker's Disease, Extrinsic Allergic Alveolitis, Farmer's Lung, Hot Tub Lung, Industrial Bronchitis, Machine Operator's Lung, Mushroom Worker's Lung, Pigeon Breeder's Disease, Sugar Cane Disease (Bagassosis)

495, 495.0, 495.1, 495.2, 495.5, 495.8, 495.9

Definition

Hypersensitivity pneumonitis is an inflammation of the lungs and bronchi from an allergic or hypersensitive reaction. It is an immune reaction to antigens found on a variety of inhaled agents small enough to enter the terminal airways in the lungs (bronchioles and alveoli).

The number of specific substances known to be capable of causing hypersensitivity pneumonitis is increasing. Most commonly, the agent is a microorganism or an animal or vegetable protein. However, simple chemicals, when inhaled in considerable amounts, may also cause the disease. The most common form of hypersensitivity pneumonitis, called farmer's lung, is caused by inhalation of an organism that thrives at warm temperatures (thermophilic) present in moldy hay and grain. Other relatively common causes of hypersensitivity pneumonitis include pigeon breeder's disease and bird fancier's disease, in which inhaled serum proteins from pigeons or pet birds induce the syndrome. The list of agents may also include wood and plant dusts, molds and fungi, enzymes and other proteins, cereal and grain dust, chemicals, pesticides, and cigarette smoke. The disease is often occupational.

A number of illnesses such as sugar cane disease (bagassosis), cotton worker's disease (byssinosis), cork worker's lung, hot tub lung, farmer's lung, mushroom worker's lung, bird fancier's disease, industrial bronchitis, and machine operator's lung are classified as hypersensitivity pneumonitis. In acute cases, symptoms typically appear between 2-9 hours after exposure, and usually disappear within a few days after the individual avoids the agent that caused the reaction. Chronic hypersensitivity pneumonitis can develop after months or years of exposure and is more difficult to diagnose and treat and can lead to pulmonary fibrosis. A very severe reaction can cause low blood oxygen (hypoxia) and respiratory failure.

There is a great variability of susceptibility in exposed populations and apparent resistance to illness in most exposed persons. The incidence varies considerably. Studies have documented between 8-540 cases per 100,000 per year for farmers, and rates of 6000-21,000 per 100,000 per year for pigeon breeders. High attack rates have been documented in sporadic outbreaks. Prevalence varies by region, climate, and farming practices. The disease affects 0.4-7% of farming population. Reported prevalence among bird fanciers is estimated from 20-20,000 per 100,000 persons at risk.

Diagnosis

History: Hypersensitivity pneumonitis exists in 2 basic clinical forms: acute and chronic. Acute hypersensitivity pneumonitis is characterized by fever, chills, cough, difficulty in breathing (dyspnea), nausea, muscle aches, fatigue, and malaise that typically occurs 4 to 8 hours after antigenic exposure. In chronic hypersensitivity pneumonitis, there are usually no systemic symptoms; rather, chronic shortness of breath and cough on exertion mark the symptom complex.

Physical exam: Typical findings include fever, mild-to-moderate respiratory distress, cough, and rales. There is no single diagnostic test that can be used to establish an unequivocal diagnosis of hypersensitivity pneumonitis. Therefore, one must rely on a combination of history, radiography, serologic study, and exclusion of other possible causes. A history of previous episodes of acute hypersensitivity pneumonitis is of diagnostic value.

Tests: Blood tests that include a complete blood count and culture examination for specific antigens may be done. Chest x-rays, lung function studies, and/or aspiration of lung fluid for microscopic examination and culture should be done. Samples of lung tissue may be taken (biopsy) for examination for infectious organisms.

Treatment

The first step of treatment is to remove the agent that is causing the problem, or if that is not possible, the individual must leave the offending environment. Some individuals may require emergency treatment and hospitalization. Most individuals require corticosteroids to reduce inflammation. Antibiotics are not indicated unless there are accompanying infections.

Prognosis

Recovery is usually complete once the offending agent is removed. In the case of individuals who have contracted the disease from their work place, resolution of the pneumonitis may require a change of occupation.

Differential Diagnosis

Hypersensitivity pneumonitis can be difficult to diagnose, particularly if the individual has had long-term exposure to the offending agent. Certain tests may be necessary to rule out more serious lung diseases such as infectious pneumonia and pulmonary fibrosis.

Specialists

- Allergist
- Occupational Medicine Physician
- Pulmonologist

Work Restrictions / Accommodations

The individual who contracts hypersensitivity pneumonitis in the work place often must change his work location to avoid the offending agent. However, socioeconomic factors may preclude a complete change of environment. Restrictions may be necessary for individuals in hazardous waste operations. Some individuals obtain good results by wearing special masks or helmets. Dust control or the use of protective masks to filter the causative dust particles in contaminated areas may be effective. Sometimes, chemical means may be used to prevent the growth of antigenic microorganisms (e.g., in hay).

Comorbid Conditions

Coexisting lung diseases, such as emphysema, asthma, and chronic bronchiolitis, seen in smokers, may lengthen disability.

Complications

Severe hypersensitivity pneumonitis may result in chronic bronchitis and permanent lung damage.

Factors Influencing Duration

Factors include type of and response to treatment and the individual's occupation and availability of another job without the presence of the inhaled agent. Age, general state of health, physical condition, and nutritional status may influence the individual's ability to undergo treatment and recover.

Length of Disability

Duration in Days

Job Classification	Minimum	Optimum	Maximum
Sedentary work	3	7	21
Light work	3	7	28
Medium work	5	14	42
Heavy work	7	21	42
Very Heavy work	7	21	56

Failure to Recover

If an individual fails to recover within the maximum duration expectancy period, the reader may wish to reference the following questions to assist in better understanding the specifics of an individual's medical case.

Regarding diagnosis:

- Does the individual have an occupation in which inhalation of microorganisms or animal or vegetable protein may be present, particularly those who work on farms and those who work with birds?
- Has the individual recently worked in another organization where chronic exposure is higher?
- Could exposure be occurring outside the workplace; i.e., in the home, in the community, or in recreational activities?
- Has the individual experienced previous episodes of hypersensitivity pneumonitis?
- Does the individual complain of fever, chills, cough, difficulty in breathing (dyspnea), nausea, muscle aches, fatigue, and malaise?
- Did these symptoms occur 4 to 8 hours after antigenic exposure, suggesting an acute episode?
- Does the individual complain of chronic shortness of breath and cough on exertion, suggesting a chronic condition?
- Were blood tests done to include a complete blood count (CBC) and culture examination for specific antigens?
- Were chest x-ray, lung function studies, and/or aspiration of lung fluid for microscopic examination done?
- Were samples of lung tissue (biopsy) taken for examination for infectious organisms?
- Was the diagnosis of hypersensitivity pneumonitis confirmed?

Regarding treatment:

- Has the individual completely been removed from the agent that caused the problem?
- Did the individual require emergency medical treatment and hospitalization?
- Were corticosteroids given to reduce inflammation?
- If there was accompanying infection, were appropriate antibiotics prescribed?
- Was the individual compliant with all medications?

Regarding prognosis:

- Does the individual require a change of occupation or work location to prevent exposure to the offending agent?
- Does the individual smoke? If so, would a smoking cessation program be appropriate for this individual?
- Has the individual developed chronic bronchitis and permanent lung damage?
- If so, how will they be treated and what is the expected outcome?
- How severe is the lung damage?
- How will this damage affect the individual's activities of daily living?

References

"Chapter 76. Hypersensitivity Diseases of the Lungs." Merck Manual of Diagnosis and Therapy, 17th ed. Beers, Mark H., and Robert Berkow, MD, eds. Whitehouse Station, NJ: Merck & Co. Inc, 1999 18 Nov 2000 <http://www.merck.com/pubs/mmanual/section6/chapter76/76b.htm>.

Hypersensitivity Pneumonitis. National Library of Medicine. 01 Jan 2001. 1 Jan 2001 <http://medlineplus.adam.com/ency/article/000109.htm>.

Hypersomnia

Other names / synonyms: Excessive Daytime Sleepiness, Idiopathic Hypersomnia, Narcolepsy, Sleep Apnea

708.5, 780.54

Definition

Hypersomnia is excessive, involuntary, and constant sleepiness during waking hours. An individual with hypersomnia has difficulty staying awake and has problems with motor control and concentration. The three types of hypersomnia are sleep apnea, narcolepsy, and hypersomnia of no clear cause (idiopathic).

Sleep apnea occurs when the back of the throat blocks the air to the lungs during sleep causing the individual to gasp for air. The three different kinds of sleep apnea are obstructive, central, and mixed.

Obstructive sleep apnea (OSA) is the most common form of apnea. When the collapse of the back of throat blocks the airway, the individual gasps for air but does not fully awaken. Breathing may stop hundreds of times at night usually for periods of 10 seconds or longer. Central sleep apnea is less common and caused by failure of the brain to signal the muscles to breathe. This awakens the individual as oxygen levels in the blood drop abruptly. Mixed sleep apnea refers to both obstructive and central sleep apneas occurring together. Risk factors for sleep apnea include family history of apnea, snoring, smoking, obesity, sleeping on the back rather than on the side, and medical conditions such as heart failure and gastroesophageal reflux disease (GERD).

Individuals with narcolepsy experience sleepiness during the day usually at inappropriate times. More than half may experience an abrupt loss of muscle tone and weakness (cataplexy) triggered by sudden emotion, as well as sleep paralysis where they are momentarily unable to move or speak when they awaken. About half of individuals with narcolepsy go through dream-like states between sleep and wakefulness (hypnagogic hallucinations). Narcolepsy is caused from low levels of chemical messengers in the brain (dopamine and norepinephrine) and genetic factors. It typically starts in the second or third decade of life.

Hypersomnia has been associated with high levels of certain immune factors (tumor necrosis factor-alpha) and interleukin 6. More than half of obese individuals in one study reported daytime sleepiness compared with only 2% of those who were not obese. Other factors predisposing to hypersomnia include female sex (in forms of hypersomnia other than sleep apnea), night-shift work, major depression, and long-haul truck driving.

It is estimated that about 18 to 25 million individuals have sleep apnea but only less than a million know they have it. The full syndrome affects about 4% men and 2% women. Blacks are at higher risk compared to other ethnic groups in the US. Sleep apnea is more likely to occur in individuals over age 40.

It is estimated that about 0.2 to 2.6 per 1,000 individuals suffer from narcolepsy but about 85% are not correctly diagnosed.

Diagnosis

History: The individual may report headaches in the morning, unrefreshing sleep, trouble with mental or emotional functioning, excessive sleepiness during the daytime, and fatigue. In sleep apnea, the sleep partner may report gasping for air, or snoring during sleep. In narcolepsy, individuals and their families may report falling asleep at inappropriate times, loss of postural and motor control when excited (cataplexy), dreamlike visions while falling asleep (hypnagogic hallucinations), and momentarily being unable to move or speak upon awakening (sleep paralysis). Drug and medication history are important to rule out daytime sleepiness associated with substance use.

Physical exam: The exam may reveal upper airway problems including soft palate abnormalities or enlarged tonsils. Obesity, wide neck, and distinctive heartbeat are indicators of sleep apnea. Measurements of body mass, neck circumference, and four areas inside the mouth assist in diagnosis of sleep apnea.

Tests: Polysomnography is an overnight test where monitoring devices hooked up to the individual assess various sleep stages for the electrical activity of the brain (electroencephalogram or EEG), the heart (electrocardiogram), and movements of the muscles (electromyogram) and eyes (electrooculogram). Oxygen levels in the blood and changes in breathing are also monitored. Multiple Sleep Latency Test (MSLT) measures the time it takes to fall sleep during the day in a quiet room. Other tests may include the Maintenance of Wakefulness Test and the Epworth Sleepiness Scale.

Treatment

Treatment for hypersomnia depends on the underlying cause. Treatment of sleep apnea includes changes in sleeping habits such as trying to roll over on the side and using a special pillow that helps to stretch the neck. Weight loss and other lifestyle changes such as quitting smoking and avoiding alcohol within four hours of sleep are recommended. The continuous positive airway pressure (CPAP) is another treatment for obstructive sleep apnea.

Other treatments include the use of dental devices similar to sports mouth guards, an orthodontic treatment called rapid maxillary expansion, and oxygen therapy. Medications such as thyroid hormone, asthma medications, and gastroesophageal reflux disorder medications may also be used. Removal of soft tissue on the back of the throat and palate (uvulopalatopharyngoplasty) or a procedure where an opening is created in the neck into the windpipe and a tube inserted (tracheostomy) may be performed.

Treatment for narcolepsy includes regularly scheduled naps several times a day and use of medications such as stimulants, modafinil, antiseizure drugs, opiates, and some monoamine oxidase inhibitors.

Prognosis

Outcome depends on method of treatment and compliance. Because many of the treatment methods are cumbersome, the compliance rate is often low. Rolling over to one side and use of nasal strips may reduce snoring and improve sleep. Use of CPAP can result in improvements in memory, mood, concentration, and health. Dental devices work very well for mild to moderate apnea. In general, medications are not very successful in treating sleep apnea. Tracheostomy is used in life-threatening circumstances and has a high success rate. Uvulopalatopharyngoplasty is successful in 50-60% of the cases.

Taking regularly scheduled naps during the day helps reduce abrupt sleepiness and improves narcolepsy.

Differential Diagnosis

Conditions that may present with similar symptoms include chronic fatigue syndrome, depression, epilepsy, low blood sugar (hypoglycemia), influenza, or any chronic illness.

Specialists

- Neurologist

Work Restrictions / Accommodations

Individuals who work with heavy machinery or work at heights may need to be reassigned. Individuals who stand up during work may need to use a chair and do their work sitting down to prevent falls. More breaks may be needed for these individuals to take naps or change work routine to stay awake. Driving especially for long distances should be avoided. Narcoleptic individuals with cataplexy should not have to deal with emotionally charged situations or those that could provoke excitement.

Comorbid Conditions

Comorbid conditions include obesity, cold and influenza, asthma, respiratory infections, alcoholism, anxiety, and fatigue. Chronic or acute illness may aggravate daytime sleepiness.

Complications

Accidents may occur as a result of individuals falling asleep while driving. Individuals deprived of sleep may eat more and exercise less that can lead to obesity. A rise in the pressure inside the blood vessels of the lungs (pulmonary hypertension) can develop in individuals with sleep apnea. Higher carbon dioxide and lower oxygen levels in the blood at night may increase the risk of high blood pressure, stroke, heart attack, heart failure, diabetes, and kidney failure. Sleep apnea may affect higher brain functions such as memory and concentration. It may also cause headaches and irregular menstrual periods in females.

Psychological and social dysfunction in all aspects of life is common in individuals with narcolepsy. Other complications include depression, headaches, injury caused by sudden falls, and stimulant dependence or abuse.

Factors Influencing Duration

Factors that may influence disability include age, gender, response to treatment, severity of the condition, presence of any underlying conditions, and specific job duties.

Length of Disability

Duration of disability depends on job requirements and accommodations available at work. Disability may be permanent for individuals who work with heavy machines, at heights, or standing.

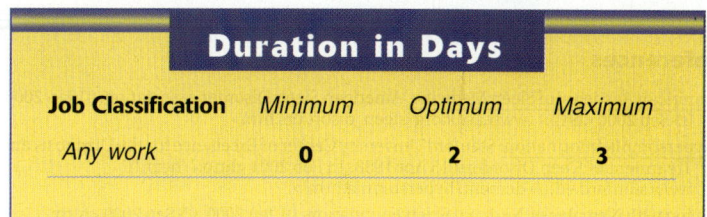

Duration in Days

Job Classification	Minimum	Optimum	Maximum
Any work	0	2	3

Failure to Recover

If an individual fails to recover within the maximum duration expectancy period, the reader may wish to reference the following questions to assist in better understanding the specifics of an individual's medical case.

Regarding diagnosis:

- Does individual have a history of sleep apnea or narcolepsy? History of neurological or psychiatric disorders?
- Is individual using medications that could aggravate symptoms?
- Does individual have headaches in the morning, nonrestorative sleep, heartburn, trouble with mental or emotional functioning, loss of urine control (incontinence), sleepiness during the daytime, and fatigue?
- Does individual's sleep partner report individual gasps for air, chokes, or snores during sleep?
- Does individual or family report that the individual falls asleep at inappropriate times, loses postural and motor control when excited (cataplexy), has dreamlike visions while falling asleep (hypnagogic hallucinations), or is momentarily unable to move or speak upon awakening (sleep paralysis)?
- Does individual ingest caffeine and alcohol or work different shifts?
- Was polysomnography done? CT or MRI?
- Was diagnosis of hypersomnia confirmed?

Regarding treatment:

- Is any underlying condition being treated appropriately?
- Were nasal strips used for sleep apnea?
- Is individual a candidate for surgery for sleep apnea?
- Was narcolepsy treated with stimulants or antidepressants? Were these medications effective or are other medications being considered?
- Has individual implemented appropriate behavioral changes and good sleep hygiene?
- Is individual avoiding shift work, alcohol, and caffeine?

Regarding prognosis:

- Is individual complying with the prescribed treatment plan?
- Does hypersomnia persist despite treatment? Could other factors be causing the symptoms?
- Does the diagnosis need to be revisited?
- If hypersomnia is caused by alcohol or drug abuse, would individual benefit from participation in a chemical dependency program?

References

American Academy of Sleep Medicine. American Sleep Disorder Association. 01 Jan 2000. 05 Sep 2000 <http://www.asda.org/sleep_disorders.htm>.

Hypersomnia Information. Stanford University Center of Excellence for the Diagnosis and Treatment of Sleep Disorders. 15 Apr 1998. 15 Feb 2001 <http://http://www.stanford.edu/~dement/hypersomnia.html>.

Living with Narcolepsy. National Sleep Foundation. 01 Jan 2000. 05 Sep 2000 <http://www.sleepfoundation.org/publications/livingnarcolepsy.html>.

Sleep Apnea and Narcolepsy (Hypersomnia). WebMD. 1999. 13 Mar 2001 <http://my.webmd.com/content/dmk/dmk_article_40080>.

Sleep Hygiene. University of Iowa Health Care. 31 Jan 2000. 15 Feb 2001 <http://http://www.vh.org/Patients/IHB/Psych/PatientEdMaterials/sleephygiene.html>.

Bassetti, C. "Narcolepsy." Current Treatment Options in Neurology 1 4 (1999): 291-298.

Beers, Mark, and Robert Berkow. The Merck Manual of Diagnosis and Therapy. Whitehouse Station, NJ: Merck Research Laboratories, 1999.

Harsh, J., et al. "Night-time Sleep and Daytime Sleepiness in Narcolepsy." Journal of Sleep Research 9 3 (2000): 309-316.

Hoover-Stevens, S., and R. Kovacevic-Ristanovic. "Management of Narcolepsy in Pregnancy." Clinical Neuropharmacology 23 4 (2000): 175-181.

Inoue, Y., et al. "Sleep Problems in Japanese Industrial Workers." Psychiatry Clinics of Neuroscience 54 3 (2000): 294-295.

Thomas, Clayton L., MD. Taber's Cyclopedic Medical Dictionary. Philadelphia: F.A. Davis Company, 1997.

Zeman, A., N. Douglas, and R. Aylward. "Lesson of the Week: Narcolepsy Mistaken for Epilepsy." British Medical Journal 322 7280 (2001): 216-218.

Hypersplenism

Other names / synonyms: Big Spleen Syndrome, Dyssplenism, Hypersplenia, Splenic Anemia

289.4

Definition

Hypersplenism is a disorder in which the spleen becomes increasingly active and rapidly and prematurely destroys and removes blood cells. One of the major functions of the spleen (which is located in the upper left abdomen) is to remove those blood cells from the body's bloodstream that are abnormal, aging, or covered with antibodies. In hypersplenism, the spleen's normal function accelerates such that the spleen begins to automatically remove blood cells that may still be normal in function.

Hypersplenism is thought to be caused by a variety of other disorders. When hypersplenism is brought on by a problem with or a disorder within the spleen itself, it is referred to as idiopathic or primary hypersplenism. When brought on by another disease, such as chronic malaria, rheumatoid arthritis, tuberculosis, or by a tumor, the disorder is referred to as secondary hypersplenism. Research has shown that, in general, spleen disorders are almost always secondary in nature.

According to reports issued by the Centers for Disease Control and Prevention (CDC) in 1998, the number of diagnoses listed for hypersplenism in the US was small (about 10,000 total) for both males and females.

Diagnosis

History: A diagnosis of hypersplenism requires that the individual experience such symptoms as easy bruising, easy contracting of bacterial diseases, fever, weakness, heart palpitations, and ulcerations of the mouth, legs, and feet. Individuals with hypersplenism may also bleed unexpectedly and heavily from the nose or other mucous membranes, and from the gastrointestinal or urinary tracts. Many individuals will develop an enlarged spleen (splenomegaly), which (because of its encroachment on the stomach) may cause stomach pain on the left side as well as a premature feeling of fullness after eating (early satiety). Other symptoms may stem from the underlying disease (such as malaria and tuberculosis) that has caused the disorder.

Because there is such a wide range of possible symptoms for this disorder, a thorough patient history is very helpful.

Physical exam: The physician's manipulation and pressing on the abdominal area (palpation) may reveal an abnormally enlarged spleen (splenomegaly) or a shrunken, hard liver (cirrhosis). Examination with a stethoscope may reveal abnormal vascular sounds (bruits). Fever, bruising, and ulceration may also be confirmed during this exam.

Tests: Blood tests, including a complete blood count (CBC), are taken to check counts of the various types of blood cells. These tests usually reveal decreases in white blood cells (leukopenia), red blood cells (anemia), and platelets (thrombocytopenia). Other diagnostic tests (such as liver function tests, CT scans, and ultrasound exams) are used to confirm an enlarged spleen (splenomegaly), which because of its accelerated function of removal of blood cells is responsible for the decreases in blood cells. Finally, bone marrow aspiration can help to identify many of the causes of hypersplenism, such as leukemia, lymphoma, and metastatic cancer.

Treatment

Most individuals with hypersplenism require therapy for the underlying disease (secondary hypersplenism) rather than spleen removal (splenectomy), which is often used to treat primary hypersplenism. In secondary hypersplenism, the underlying disease (e.g., chronic malaria or tuberculosis) must be treated to prevent further destruction of blood cells and possible spleen enlargement. In general, treatments for possible underlying diseases should be attempted prior to consideration for removal of the spleen (splenectomy).

Instances where splenectomy is considered include an indication of severe reduction of platelets or immune cells, direct involvement of the spleen (idiopathic or primary hypersplenism) in a disorder (as in leukemia and lymphoma), and spread of cancer from other organs to the spleen.

Prognosis

For those individuals who require therapy for the underlying condition causing hypersplenism, outcome is usually favorable. However, if massively enlarged spleens (splenomegaly) are not treated promptly, they can destroy blood products, causing low red blood cell count (anemia), low white blood cell count (leukopenia), and low platelet count (thrombocytopenia). Such low blood cell counts can lead to complications that include mucosal bleeding, bleeding from abnormally dilated or swollen veins, arteries, or lymph vessels (varices) in the esophagus, and recurrent infections.

When treatment for hypersplenism includes removal of the spleen (splenectomy), outcome is often unfavorable because the individual becomes more vulnerable to severe bacterial infections, such as Streptococcus pneumoniae. This is the case because the systems of individuals without spleens become less effective in filtering bacterial pathogens from the blood stream, predisposing the individual to a more severe infection of the blood (septicemia). Individuals without spleens are also more susceptible to attacks of malaria.

Differential Diagnosis

Differential diagnoses include myeloproliferative disorders, lymphomas, and Hodgkin's Disease.

Specialists

- Gastroenterologist
- General Surgeon
- Hematologist

Work Restrictions / Accommodations

Appropriate limitation of activity at work is an important restriction because it can help to minimize trauma that might cause the spleen to rupture.

Individuals with hypersplenism may need frequent sick leave for treatment of the disorder and its complications. If surgery is required, an extended leave of absence may be required for rest and recuperation.

Comorbid Conditions

Research has shown spleen disorders to be almost always secondary in nature. Diseases with which they are associated include chronic malaria, rheumatoid arthritis, tuberculosis, or tumor.

Complications

A number of complications may occur when the spleen enlarges or when hypersplenism is left untreated. First, the low blood cell count in both of these instances may lead to mucosal bleeding, bleeding from abnormally dilated or swollen veins, arteries, or lymph vessels (varices) in the esophagus, and recurrent infections. Second, the spleen may become uncomfortably large. Third, rupture of the enlarged spleen is a complication that is particularly possible when the underlying cause is infectious mononucleosis.

Factors Influencing Duration

In most cases, no disability is expected. Factors that might influence length of disability as well as the intensity and complications of the disorder include the cause of the hypersplenism, the complications, and the treatment. For instance, if the treatment includes surgical removal of the spleen (splenectomy), length of disability will be increased.

Length of Disability

Medical treatment.

Duration in Days

Job Classification	Minimum	Optimum	Maximum
Sedentary work	3	5	10
Light work	3	5	10
Medium work	3	5	14
Heavy work	5	7	28
Very Heavy work	5	7	28

Surgical treatment (splenectomy).

Duration in Days

Job Classification	Minimum	Optimum	Maximum
Sedentary work	14	21	28
Light work	14	21	28
Medium work	28	35	42
Heavy work	35	42	56
Very Heavy work	35	42	70

Failure to Recover

If an individual fails to recover within the maximum duration expectancy period, the reader may wish to reference the following questions to assist in better understanding the specifics of an individual's medical case.

Regarding diagnosis:

- Does individual have primary or secondary hypersplenism?
- Has individual noticed that they bruise easily?
- Do they seem to become ill more easily?
- Have they had weakness, heart palpitations, or ulcerations of the mouth, legs, and feet?
- Have they had unexpected bleeding from the nose? GI tract? Urinary tract?
- Do they have left-sided abdominal pain?
- Do they feel full after eating a small amount?
- On physical exam, did palpation reveal splenomegaly or cirrhosis?
- Were any bruits heard?
- Were fever, bruising, or ulcerations noted?
- Has individual had a CBC and liver function tests? CT scan? MRI?

- Was a bone marrow aspiration done?
- Have conditions with similar symptoms been ruled out?

Regarding treatment:
- Has individual received treatment for the underlying disease and hypersplenism?
- Did individual have a splenectomy?

Regarding prognosis:
- Is individual's employer able to accommodate any necessary restrictions?
- Does individual have any conditions that may affect their ability to recover?
- Has individual had any complications such as bleeding or recurrent infections?
- Has the spleen become uncomfortably large?

References

Mayon-White, Dick. Factsheet on Splenectomy and Infection. Leukemia Research Fund. 01 Jan 2000. 01 Jan 2001 <http://www.leukaemia.demon.co.uk/spleen.htm>.

Hypertensive Heart Disease

Other names / synonyms: Arterial Hypertension, Essential Hypertension, Hypertension, Hypertensive Cardiomegaly, Hypertensive Cardiomyopathy, Hypertensive Cardiopathy, Hypertensive Cardiovascular Disease, Left Ventricular Hypertrophy

402, 402.9

Definition

Hypertensive heart disease refers to heart conditions that develop as a result of high blood pressure (hypertension). Ten percent of individuals with chronic hypertension have enlarged left ventricles (left ventricular hypertrophy). This puts the individual at a seven-fold risk of illness and death (morbidity and mortality) due to congestive heart failure, disturbances of heart rhythms (ventricular arrhythmias), and heart attack (myocardial infarction). For these reasons, an enlarged left ventricle in association with hypertension and is considered the definitive sign of hypertensive heart disease.

Although an enlarged ventricle indicates that heart disease is present, early treatment can prevent future serious heart complications. Fortunately, most individuals respond well to drug therapy, which usually results in a reduction of the size of the left ventricle. Most cases of hypertension have no discernible cause (essential hypertension). A chronic but treatable disease, essential hypertension as yet has no cure.

Diagnosis

History: Individuals with hypertensive heart disease may have symptoms of coronary artery disease (angina), fatigue, and shortness of breath with exertion and/or at rest. Congestive heart failure can include episodes of interrupted sleep due to breathing problems (paroxysmal nocturnal dyspnea).

Physical exam: High blood pressure (hypertension) is present in varying degrees of severity. Changes in the small blood vessels (arterioles) of the eyes may be noted during examination. Pulse may be irregular. Listening to the heart through a stethoscope (auscultation) may reveal an irregular pulse, heart murmurs, or extra heart sounds (gallops). In advanced cases of hypertensive heart disease, the individual may have an enlarged liver, swelling of the feet and ankles, and other signs of congestive heart failure.

Tests: An electrocardiogram, echocardiogram, and chest x-ray are used to confirm an enlarged left ventricle.

Treatment

Intervention for hypertensive heart disease includes drug therapy and modification of lifestyle. Several classes of drugs may be prescribed in the treatment of hypertension. These include diuretics, beta-blockers, ACE inhibitors, calcium channel blockers, angiotensin II receptor antagonists, and alpha-blockers. The type of drug therapy selected is based on coexisting medical conditions, lifestyle issues, safety, and tolerance of the drug.

A combination of drugs may be more effective when controlling blood pressure and symptoms in individuals whose hypertension is resistant to ordinary treatment (refractory) or whose hypertension is complicated by other underlying medical conditions. For example, if a beta-blocker, ACE inhibitor, or angiotensin II blocker were used as the primary drug, a diuretic could be added as a secondary drug. Another approach may be to use low-dose combinations of complementary anti-hypertensive drugs, such as a beta-blocker with a calcium channel blocker.

Lifestyle modification, a cornerstone of therapy, can substantially reduce illness and death (morbidity and mortality). In general, individuals are advised to reduce salt and alcohol in the diet, abstain from smoking, lose weight, and exercise regularly.

Prognosis

Drug therapy and lifestyle modifications can reduce the blood pressure, lessen the risk of congestive heart failure, and are usually successful in reducing left ventricular enlargement.

Differential Diagnosis

Left ventricular hypertrophy may be secondary to stenosis of the aortic valve or idiopathic hypertrophic subaortic stenosis.

Specialists

- Cardiologist

Rehabilitation

Physical therapy may benefit individuals with hypertensive heart disease by applying principles of aerobic conditioning.

Individuals are monitored for heart rate, rhythm, and blood pressure. At this stage, exercise is aimed primarily at preventing the hazards of bedrest, reducing episodes of low blood pressure when changing positions (orthostatic hypotension), and maintaining overall mobility of the body. Exercise at low levels often begins with the individual on his or her back (supine position). The individual progresses from exercises to sitting and eventually to standing. Progressive walking (ambulating) with continuous monitoring for 2-5 minutes and progressing to 15-20 minutes is also part of this phase. Eventually stair climbing becomes an important part of individual's exercise program while hospitalized. Intensity is gradually increased until discharge from the hospital.

After the individual is discharged from the hospital, similar exercises as in phase one are performed with progression of time and intensity that varies from individual to individual. Goals are to improve functional capacity by increasing physical endurance and promoting return to activity. This is done in an outpatient setting such as a rehabilitation center. An electrocardiograph is used to record the continuous electrical activity of the heart muscle and is attached to the individual. A physical therapist keeps a daily log of the individual's blood pressure, heart rate, and cardiac rhythm.

Phase three continues and, depending on the individual's condition, this phase may last for several months. Individuals may stay involved with an outpatient program for up to a year to accomplish all of the their goals while still at modified work duty. Eventually higher levels of exercise comprise this phase with the addition of recreational activities such as swimming and outdoor hiking. Light jogging at approximately 5 miles per hour and cycling at approximately 12 miles per hour is appropriate as long as the individual is tolerating the rehabilitation program well. Modifications may need to be made to the rehabilitation program as surgery may or may have not been performed after the onset of the heart attack, and the individual may have additional medical conditions.

Phase four of cardiac rehabilitation for hypertensive heart disease occurs after discharge from the hospital. Long-term maintenance of performance levels reached during phase two and three are concerns at this time. Aerobic exercises that increase cardiovascular fitness are emphasized and include exercises such as walking briskly, running, jogging, swimming, climbing stairs, or bicycling. The American Heart Association, the Centers for Disease Control and Prevention (CDC), and the American College of Sports Medicine recommend 30-60 minutes of aerobic activity 3-4 times a week to help keep high blood pressure under control. Throughout all phases, it is important to allow the heart rate to slowly return to normal after the exercises.

Work Restrictions / Accommodations

A change may need to be made to lower-stress duties. For instance, individuals with jobs that require exertion, operation of commercial vehicles, or operation of heavy equipment may need to be reassigned to less strenuous duties.

Complementary and Alternative Therapies

Content is intended for awareness only. Treatments may or may not be effective. Scientific evidence may be lacking and some substances have potentially toxic effects. Dr. Presley Reed and the editors do not endorse the use of these therapies in the absence of consultation with a licensed medical professional.

Biofeedback -	May be used as a relaxation method to reduce stress.
Massage -	May reduce tension, promote relaxation, reduce stress.
Tai Chi -	May help reduce stress, and, in turn, hypertension.
Yoga -	Relaxation, breathing techniques, and meditation may help lower blood pressure.
Garlic -	Said to help lower diastolic (but not systolic) blood pressure.

Comorbid Conditions

Coronary artery disease, obesity, tobacco use, sedentary lifestyle, and alcohol abuse increase the individual's risk for developing serious cardiovascular disease. Underlying renal disease, liver disease, and diabetes mellitus may also lengthen disability.

Complications

Cardiac complications of hypertension include left ventricle hypertrophy, left ventricular diastolic dysfunction, asymptomatic coronary artery disease, congestive heart failure, ventricular arrhythmias, myocardial ischemia, and sudden death.

Factors Influencing Duration

Factors that may influence disability include severity of symptoms, response to treatment, persistence of hypertension, poor cardiac performance (measured with treadmill exercise test), depression or emotional problems, and cognitive dysfunction.

Length of Disability

Duration depends on severity and specific diagnosis. Contact attending physician to obtain specific diagnostic information. Disability may be permanent.

Duration in Days

Job Classification	Minimum	Optimum	Maximum
Sedentary work	14	14	28
Light work	14	14	28
Medium work	14	21	42
Heavy work	14	28	56
Very Heavy work	14	28	56

Failure to Recover

If an individual fails to recover within the maximum duration expectancy period, the reader may wish to reference the following questions to assist in better understanding the specifics of an individual's medical case.

Regarding diagnosis:

- Has diagnosis of hypertensive heart disease been confirmed?
- Does individual have an enlarged left heart ventricle (left ventricular hypertrophy)?
- Does individual continue to complain of symptoms associated with congestive heart failure such as shortness of breath, weight gain, swollen ankles, cough, and nocturnal dyspnea?

Regarding treatment:

- Has drug therapy been effective?
- Is individual's current drug therapy based on coexisting medical conditions, lifestyle issues, safety, and tolerance of the drug?
- Would a combination of drugs be more effective?
- Has individual complied with lifestyle modifications such as reducing salt in the diet, limiting alcohol consumption, and losing weight?
- Has individual been able to stop smoking?
- Has individual replaced sedentary lifestyle with regular exercise?

Regarding prognosis:

- Do symptoms persist despite treatment?
- What alterations in drug therapy can now be made that might better accomplish treatment goals?
- Has individual been able to accomplish lifestyle modifications?
- Would individual benefit from enrollment in community support programs such as an alcohol treatment program (AA), smoking cessation program, exercise program (through local gym or recreation service), or weight loss program (such as Weight Watchers)?
- Would individual benefit from nutrition counseling?
- Does individual have a coexisting condition (such as coronary artery disease, renal disease, liver disease, diabetes mellitus) that may complicate treatment or impact recovery?

References

The Natural Pharmacist. Natural Treatments for Heart Disease. Prima Communications, Inc. 20 Jun 2000. 20 June 2000 <http://www.tnp.com/indepth-page.asp?ID=33&Area=15&Page=5>.

Scully, Rosemary M., and Marylou R. Barnes. Physical Therapy. Philadelphia: J.B. Lippincott Company, 1989.

Hyperthyroidism

Other names / synonyms: Overactive Thyroid

242.1, 242.10, 242.11, 242.2, 242.20, 242.21, 242.3, 242.30, 242.31, 242.8, 242.80, 242.81, 242.9, 242.90, 242.91

Definition

Hyperthyroidism is a condition in which the thyroid gland is overactive. The thyroid gland is located in the front of the neck near the Adam's apple. This gland produces hormones (thyroid hormones) that play an important role in controlling the body's metabolism.

There are several different causes of hyperthyroidism. The most common is called Graves' disease. Other causes include inflammation of the thyroid gland (thyroiditis), enlargement of the thyroid with many small growths (toxic multinodular goiter), a single overactive thyroid growth, and overdose of the medication used to treat an underactive thyroid (thyroid hormone pills). In rare cases, hyperthyroidism can result from tumors of the pituitary gland or other tumors, or as a side effect of certain medications that interfere with the body's levels of iodine.

Hyperthyroidism affects 1 in 10,000 women and 1 in 30,000 men. It can occur at any age but is most common in individuals between the ages of 30 and 40. Hyperthyroidism tends to run in families. The elderly have fewer symptoms, making the condition harder to diagnose.

Diagnosis

History: Individuals may have a family history of hyperthyroidism. The individual may complain of multiple symptoms including a sensation that the heart is pounding and/or beating rapidly or a fluttering in the chest (heart palpitations). The individual may complain of being hot even when the room feels cool or comfortable to others. Profuse sweating may be reported. Individuals often complain of increased appetite with unintentional weight loss. The hands may tremble. Many complain of feeling nervous, restless or anxious, tired and/or weak with difficulty sleeping yet report increased activity levels. Frequent bowel movements and occasional diarrhea are also common symptoms. Difficulty swallowing can occur in the setting of an enlarged thyroid (goiter).

Physical exam: The exam may reveal elevated blood pressure. The heart rate may be rapid and an irregular heart rhythm (atrial fibrillation) may be present especially in the elderly. Reflexes are very brisk. The eyes may appear to be bulging with eyelids wide open. The skin may be warm and moist. A tremor can be seen in the hands and tongue. Enlargement of the thyroid gland (goiter) is often noted.

Tests: Blood tests reveal abnormal levels of thyroid hormones. The blood cholesterol is often low. An electrocardiogram (ECG) can identify heart rhythm abnormalities. The thyroid can be inspected for uptake the radioactive iodine uptake test. In this test, the individual is given a small quantity of a radioactive chemical (either orally or by injection). The chemical is absorbed by either healthy or diseased tissue (depending on the disease process and type of scan). The emitted radio-activity produces an image of the thyroid on film for evaluation of abnormalities and differentiation of the cause for the hyperthyroidism.

Treatment

Most cases are treated with medications that interfere with the thyroid hormones (antithyroid medications). Once the excess thyroid hormones are controlled, the majority of symptoms will decrease or disappear. Other medications (beta-blockers) may also be prescribed to alleviate rapid heartbeat and trembling. Antithyroid medications usually continue for 3 to 12 months. The thyroid levels are then reevaluated after this period. Depending on the results, medication may be resumed, modified, or discontinued. In some cases, radioactive iodine therapy may be indicated. Surgical removal of a portion of the thyroid gland (partial or subtotal thyroidectomy) is rare but can be especially helpful in cases of a single toxic nodule when the rest of the gland is completely suppressed, increasing the chances of a full recovery without needing lifelong thyroid hormones.

Prognosis

Hyperthyroidism is usually treatable with no long-term adverse effects. Side effects of medications used to treat hypothyroidism may be more problematic in older individuals. Surgical removal of a portion of the thyroid (subtotal thyroidectomy) is generally effective but can result in inadequate production of thyroid hormone in the body. Older individuals are also at increased risk for complications such as cardiac failure.

Hyperthyroidism due to Graves' disease can result in the complication of thyroid storm, which if not promptly treated is almost always fatal.

Differential Diagnosis

Psychological disorders (i.e., anxiety, panic attacks, or manic-depressive disorder) and cocaine or amphetamine abuse may present with some of the symptoms and signs of hyperthyroidism. Hyperthyroidism may occasionally be confused with widespread cancer, hyperparathyroidism, or myasthenia gravis. Pregnancy should also be ruled out.

Specialists

- Endocrinologist
- General Surgeon
- Nuclear Medicine Physician
- Ophthalmologist

Work Restrictions / Accommodations

In general, work restrictions and accommodations are not necessary. Individuals with bulging eyes (exophthalmos) have eye irritation, increased tearing, possible eye pain, and increased sensitivity to bright light, dust, fumes, or wind. Depending on the individual's job requirements, special eyewear may be helpful. Frequent breaks to instill eye drops may also be necessary. If surgery is required for treatment of hyperthyroidism, extended sick leave may be required for recovery from the procedure. If radioactive treatment is used, extended sick leave may be required if the individual experiences significant post-iodine thyroiditis and exacerbation of hyperthyroidism. Disability due to hyperthyroidism after this phase can also occur, with symptoms of ever fatigue, cold intolerance, and unexplained weight gain.

Comorbid Conditions

Pregnant women may have a longer recovery period from hyperthyroidism since treatment options are limited.

Complications

An eye condition called exophthalmos can develop despite adequate treatment of hyperthyroidism. Underactive thyroid function (hypothyroidism) can result after treatment of hyperthyroidism. Heart rhythm disturbances and high-output heart failure are other possible complications. Older individuals are more likely to experience cardiac failure. Muscle weakness and bone demineralization can occur.

When hyperthyroidism is due to underlying Graves' disease, a serious complication of thyroid storm can develop. Thyroid storm is an unusual and life-threatening condition characterized by a severe increase in thyroid hormone levels with overstimulation of the heart and brain, and a high fever. Prompt medical treatment is necessary to prevent death.

Factors Influencing Duration

The age of the individual and the underlying cause of the disease may influence the length of disability. The length of disability depends on the type of treatment administered and the individual's response to therapy. The development of hypothyroidism after treatment will prolong recovery.

If radioactive treatment is used, extended sick leave may be required if the individual experiences significant post-iodine thyroiditis and exacerbation of hyperthyroidism. Disability due to hyperthyroidism after this phase can also occur, with symptoms of severe fatigue, cold intolerance, and unexplained weight gain.

Length of Disability

Hyperthyroidism is generally responsive to treatment, and prolonged disability is not anticipated. Duration depends on partial versus complete.

Medical treatment.

Duration in Days

Job Classification	Minimum	Optimum	Maximum
Sedentary work	0	3	7
Light work	0	3	7
Medium work	0	3	7
Heavy work	0	3	7
Very Heavy work	0	3	7

Surgical treatment (thyroidectomy).

Duration in Days

Job Classification	Minimum	Optimum	Maximum
Sedentary work	3	7	14
Light work	3	7	14
Medium work	7	14	21
Heavy work	7	28	42
Very Heavy work	7	28	42

Duration Trend from Normative Data*

Cases	Mean	Min	Max	No Lost Time	Over 6 Months
443	59	6	360	0%	0.68%

Percentile:	5th	25th	Median	75th	95th
Days:	14	26	41	79	160

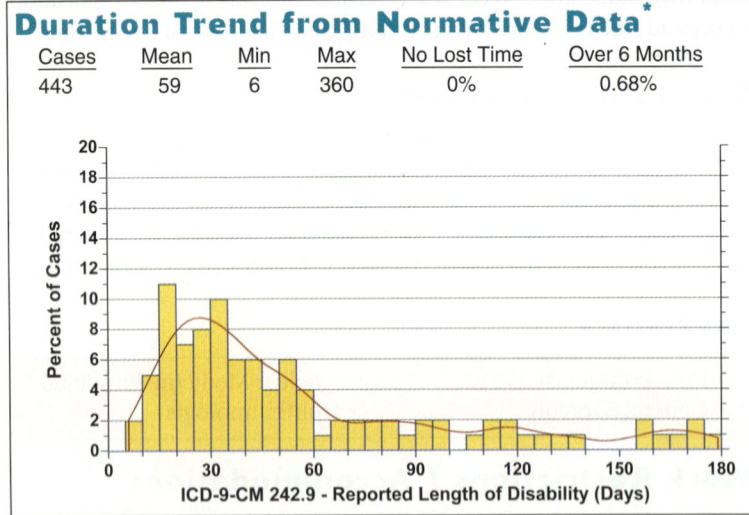
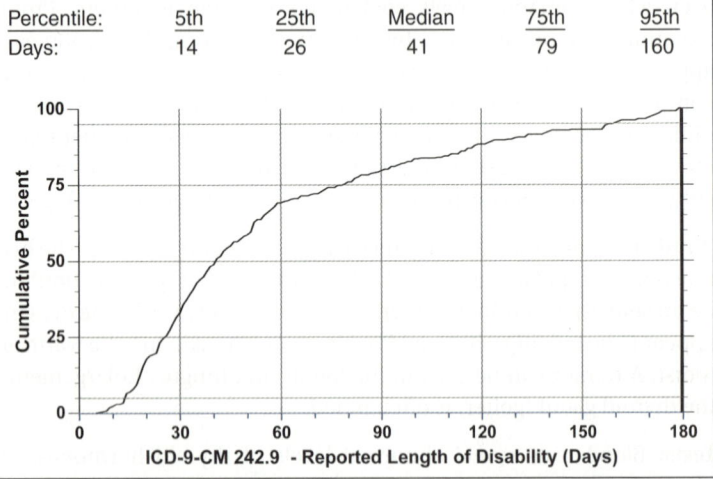

ICD-9-CM 242.9 - Reported Length of Disability (Days)

* Differences may exist between the expected duration tables and the normative graphs. Duration tables provide expected recovery periods based on the type of work performed by the individual. The normative graphs reflect the actual observed experience of many individuals across the spectrum of physical conditions, in a variety of industries, and with varying levels of case management.

Failure to Recover

If an individual fails to recover within the maximum duration expectancy period, the reader may wish to reference the following questions to assist in better understanding the specifics of an individual's medical case.

Regarding diagnosis:

- Does the individual have a family history of hyperthyroidism?
- Does the individual have Graves' disease, thyroiditis, toxic multinodular goiter, a single overactive thyroid growth, or overdose of thyroid hormone pills?
- Does the individual have tumors of the pituitary gland or other tumors, or side effects of certain medications that interfere with the body's levels of iodine?

- Does the individual complain of heart palpitations, feeling hot even when the room feels cool or comfortable to others, profuse sweating, increased appetite, difficulty swallowing, or unintentional weight loss?
- Does the individual complain of feeling nervous, restless or anxious, trembling hands, tired and/or weak with difficulty sleeping yet report increased activity levels?
- Does the individual complain of frequent bowel movements or occasional diarrhea?
- On exam did the individual have hypertension, tachycardia or atrial fibrillation?
- Did the individual have brisk reflexes, warm moist skin, tremor in the hands and tongue, goiter or eyes appear to be bulging with eyelids wide open?
- Has the individual had complete thyroid hormone testing, cholesterol testing, ECG, and radioactive iodine uptake test?
- Have conditions with similar symptoms been ruled out?

Regarding treatment:

- Is the individual being treated with antithyroid medications? Beta-blockers?
- Was the individual treated with radioactive iodine therapy?
- Did it become necessary to perform a subtotal thyroidectomy?
- Is the individual compliant with their treatment regime?

Regarding prognosis:

- Is the individual's employer able to accommodate any necessary restrictions?
- Does the individual have any conditions that may affect their ability to recover?
- Does the individual have any complication such as exophthalmos, hypothyroidism, heart rhythm disturbances, high-output heart failure, muscle weakness or bone demineralization? Has the individual had a thyroid storm?

References

"Thyroid Gland Disorders." The Merck Manual of Medical Information. Berkow, Robert, Mark Beers, and Andrew Fletcher, eds. New York: Pocket Books, 1997. 773-781.

Levy, Richard. "Hyperthyroidism." Griffith's 5-minute Clinical Consult. Dambro, Mark, ed. Philadelphia: Lippincott, Williams & Wilkins, 2000. 532-533.

Hyperventilation Syndrome
Other names / synonyms: Over-Breathing Syndrome, Psychogenic Hyperventilation
306.1

Definition

Hyperventilation syndrome is a condition where an individual breathes excessively and at a more rapid rate than necessary for the body's needs resulting in changes in blood flow and body chemistry that produce characteristic symptoms. Overbreathing changes blood chemistry, affects the function of nerves and muscles, and also decreases blood flow to the brain. Individuals with this disorder usually seek medical attention and fear that something is happening to their body. The symptoms often reinforce the individual's belief there is imminent danger of bodily harm, further increasing the level of anxiety.

Hyperventilation syndrome is usually generated by intense fear or anxiety.

Individuals are not often aware they have altered their breathing. Symptoms can be seen during prolonged crying either from normal grieving or a depressive disorder. Acute hyperventilation syndrome accounts for only 1% of cases but is easier to diagnose than chronic hyperventilation syndrome that can present with respiratory, heart, neurologic, or gastrointestinal symptoms without apparent overbreathing.

The underlying mechanism is unknown but certain triggers may provoke an exaggerated respiratory response in susceptible individuals. Triggers may include emotional distress, lactic acid levels that build up in response to exercise, caffeine, carbon dioxide, certain medications such as isoproterenol, and some hormones such as cholecystokinin. Individuals with hyperventilation syndrome tend to breathe using the upper chest muscles rather than the diaphragm so that their lungs are chronically overinflated. When stress induces the need to take a deep breath, the individual feels short of breath, which creates more anxiety and begins a vicious circle.

Although there is considerable overlap in symptoms between hyperventilation syndrome and panic disorder, these conditions are separate. Approximately 50% of individuals with panic disorder have hyperventilation symptoms and 25% of individuals with hyperventilation syndrome also have panic disorder.

No clear genetic factors have been found but close relatives of individuals with hyperventilation syndrome are more likely to have the disorder. Up to 10% of individuals in a general internal medicine practice in the US had a primary diagnosis of hyperventilation syndrome. Women are from 2 to 7 times more likely to have the disorder than men. Peak age of incidence is 15 to 55 but cases are reported in all age groups except infants.

Diagnosis

History: Individual may have a history off recurrent episodes of breathlessness, feeling short of breath, and being unable to fill the lungs. Other symptoms are pins-and-needles feelings (paresthesias) in fingers, toes, and around the mouth. Individual may report spasm in muscles of the hands and/or feet (carpopedal spasm). The individual may feel lightheaded or faint or have feelings of a distorted reality. There are often concerns of a heart attack, stroke, suffocation, or other bodily harm. Feeling that the heartbeat is heavy and rapid (palpitations) is common. Attention and concentration are limited because of fear or panic. Each episode is experienced as intensely as the first one.

Acute hyperventilation syndrome may present with great agitation and anxiety. History more often includes sudden onset of chest pain, shortness of breath, or neurologic symptoms such as dizziness, weakness, fainting, or paresthesias after a stressful event. Swallowing air when overbreathing may lead to gastrointestinal symptoms including bloating, belching, excess gas, and a pressure sensation over the upper abdomen.

Physical exam: The individual may be asked to hyperventilate. If this reproduces their symptoms, the diagnosis is confirmed. In acute hyperventilation syndrome, it may be obvious that the individual is breathing rapidly and deeply. The upper chest wall may be tender from muscle fatigue. Chemical changes associated with decreased carbon dioxide levels may cause carpopedal spasm, wheezing, or decreased blood calcium levels associated with characteristic abnormalities in muscular contraction (Chvostek's or Trousseau's signs). Physical signs of anxiety may include shaking (tremor), dilated pupils (mydriasis), pale skin (pallor) and rapid heart beat (tachycardia). In chronic hyperventilation syndrome, rapid or deep breathing is usually not apparent but the individual may sigh deeply 2 to 3 times a minute.

Tests: Tests may establish a medical diagnosis to account for the hyperventilation. Electrocardiogram (ECG) may reveal characteristic changes. Blood gases can show characteristic abnormalities associated with overbreathing. Chest x-ray is indicated when disease of the heart or lungs is suspected.

Treatment

If presumed acute hyperventilation syndrome is not yet diagnosed, transport to the hospital for further evaluation may be indicated. Individuals should be made more aware of their breathing and trained to use the diaphragm and abdomen rather than the upper chest. The individual may be instructed to breathe through the nose and not the mouth during an attack as a way to limit the overbreathing. Individuals can breathe into a paper bag to avoid the blood chemistry changes and other symptoms of hyperventilation. However, rebreathing from a paper bag can be dangerous in individuals with undiagnosed lung or heart disease and is not recommended.

Supportive psychotherapy can reassure the individual that he or she is getting enough oxygen during an attack. Any underlying psychological disorder should be treated if the individual is able to change his or her focus from physical to psychological matters. Antianxiety medications, sedatives, beta-blockers, and tricyclic antidepressants may be useful in selected individuals but should not be given for prolonged periods.

Prognosis

Most individuals can be taught to manage this syndrome themselves. Some will remain fixated on their physical symptoms however, even with the most skillful psychotherapist, and continue to experience episodes of hyperventilation.

Death is extremely rare but may result from heart attack (myocardial ischemia) in individuals with pre-existing coronary artery disease. Complications may occur from unneeded tests such as angiography or with treatment such as blood thinners. In a study of 45 individuals with normal coronary arteries and chest pain caused by hyperventilation syndrome, two-thirds returned to the emergency room for chest pain and 40% were readmitted to rule out heart attack within 3.5 years.

Differential Diagnosis

Medical diseases in the differential diagnosis include acute respiratory distress syndrome, epilepsy, acute asthmatic attack, atrial fibrillation or flutter, dilated or restrictive cardiomyopathy, chronic obstructive pulmonary disease and emphysema, costochondritis, hyperthyroidism, very low blood sugar levels (hypoglycemia) or very high levels (diabetic ketoacidosis), other metabolic acidosis, methemoglobinemia, heart attack (myocardial infarction), pleural effusion, pneumonia, pneumothorax, pulmonary embolism, smoke inhalation, venous air embolism, withdrawal syndromes, and Ménière's disease. Psychological diseases resembling hyperventilation syndrome include conversion disorder, panic disorder, schizophrenia, borderline or histrionic personality disorder, or a specific phobia.

Specialists

- Cardiologist
- Gastroenterologist
- Neurologist
- Psychiatrist
- Psychologist
- Pulmonologist
- Respiratory Therapist

Work Restrictions / Accommodations

Accommodations may include modifying identifiable work situations that provoke the hyperventilation such as having to wear protective gear on the face or being in a crowded, noisy workplace. The individual should be introduced to stressful situations gradually under appropriate supervision and support. Other accommodations may include providing flexible work schedule for medical or psychiatric appointments; and allowing break time according to individual's needs rather than a fixed schedule. Highly stressful activities such as operating machinery should be temporarily adjusted. The workspace can also be modified to reduce noise or visual distractions.

Comorbid Conditions

Asthma or other pulmonary disease, coronary heart disease or other cardiac disease, or the presence of a psychiatric illness may lengthen disability.

Complications

Individual may faint since the amount of carbon dioxide decreases with overbreathing, causing decreased blood flow to the brain. If the individual falls while fainting, there may be injury from the fall. If forced to remain standing, individual may have a seizure or further decrease in blood flow to the brain. Changes in blood chemistry associated with overbreathing may include decreased calcium that causes muscle twitching or spasm, decreased potassium that causes generalized weakness, or decreased phosphate that may cause pins-and-needles sensations (paresthesias) and weakness.

Heart rhythm disturbances can be a result, not a cause, of hyperventilation. Hyperventilation syndrome can develop into such a concern about heart disease (cardiac neurosis) that individuals impose limits on their activities. In older individuals with coronary artery disease, decreased carbon dioxide levels associated with overbreathing may further narrow blood vessels supplying the heart and cause damage to the heart muscle.

Factors Influencing Duration

Successful treatment of an underlying psychological or physical cause may shorten disability duration.

Length of Disability

Duration of disability depends on response to medications and psychotherapy and other psychiatric or medical disorders. Disability is limited to the duration of the hyperventilation attacks, which is usually quite brief. In most cases, no disability is expected. However, an association with panic episodes could significantly increase duration of disability.

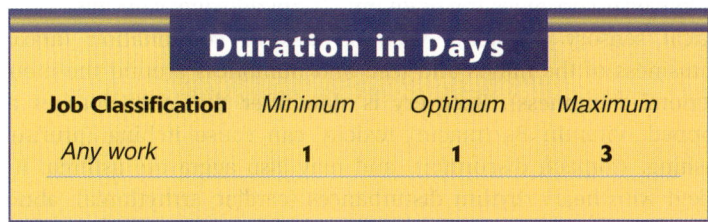

Job Classification	Minimum	Optimum	Maximum
Any work	1	1	3

Failure to Recover

If an individual fails to recover within the maximum duration expectancy period, the reader may wish to reference the following questions to assist in better understanding the specifics of an individual's medical case.

Regarding diagnosis:

- Does the individual have intense fear or anxiety? Emotional distress?
- Is the individual taking isoproterenol or cholecystokinin?
- Does the individual have recurrent episodes of breathlessness, feeling short of breath, and being unable to fill the lungs?
- Does the individual have paresthesias in the fingers, toes, and around the mouth? Does the individual have carpopedal spasm?
- Does the individual express concerns of a heart attack, stroke, or suffocation?
- Does the individual complain of palpitations?
- Did the individual present with great agitation and anxiety?
- Did the individual have a sudden onset of chest pain, shortness of breath, or neurologic symptoms such as dizziness, weakness, fainting, or paresthesias after a stressful event? Has the individual swallowed air?
- Does the individual complain of symptoms including bloating, belching, excess gas, and a pressure sensation over the upper abdomen?
- Has the individual had tests to establish a medical diagnosis to account for the hyperventilation, such as ECG, blood gases or a chest x-ray?
- Have conditions with similar symptoms been ruled out?

Regarding treatment:

- What is the underlying cause of the hyperventilation? Is it being treated?
- Has the individual been made more aware of the pattern of breathing?
- Has the individual been trained to use the diaphragm and abdomen rather than the upper chest?
- Is the individual participating in psychotherapy?
- Have antianxiety medications, sedatives, beta-blockers or tricyclic antidepressants been tried?

Regarding prognosis:

- Is the individual's employer able to accommodate any necessary restrictions?
- Does the individual have any conditions that may affect the ability to recover?
- Does the individual have any complications such as fainting, injuries from falling, changes in blood chemistry, paresthesias, weakness, or heart rhythm disturbances?
- Has the individual developed a cardiac neurosis?

References

New England Journal of Medicine. Gottlieb, Bill, ed. Emmaus, PA: Rodale Press, Inc, 1995.

Hall, Laura Lee. "Making the ADA Work for People with Psychiatric Disabilities." Mental Disorder, Work Disability, and the Law. Bonnie, Richard J., and John Monahan, eds. Chicago: The University of Chicago Press, 1997. 241-280.

Hypervitaminosis

Other names / synonyms: Vitamin Overdose, Vitamin Toxicity

278.8, 963.5

Definition

Hypervitaminosis refers to adverse health effects arising from the ingestion of excessive amounts of a vitamin or vitamins. Effects can range from mild to serious. The fat-soluble vitamins A, D, E, and K are absorbed and eliminated more slowly than the water-soluble vitamins. They are stored in fatty tissues and organs, such as the liver and are more toxic than the water-soluble vitamins.

Most vitamin toxicities do not occur from dietary intakes of foods; they usually come from taking high potency vitamin supplements. Much of the data on the adverse health effects of taking large amounts of vitamins pertain to acute rather than chronic use. Because nutrients work together, consuming excessive amounts of one nutrient can cause a deficiency of another. Because supplements are legally considered to be foods not drugs, the Food and Drug Administration has few regulations concerning them.

The common misconception about vitamins is that if taking some is good then more must be better. The majority of over-the-counter vitamin supplements are safe when taken in the recommended dosages. The benefits and safety of large or megadose vitamin therapy are unproved and may be dangerous. Toxicity usually occurs only when very large doses of the fat-soluble vitamins are taken over a prolonged period of time.

The water-soluble vitamins are eliminated in the urine and perspiration. Vitamin C (ascorbic acid) is often taken in megadoses for its purported efficacy in building resistance to the common cold. Doses of Vitamin B_6 that are low can antagonize the effects of a drug used to treat Parkinson's disease, and interfere with drugs used to treat epilepsy. Vitamin B_3 (niacin) is taken in large doses to treat high cholesterol.

Morbidity and mortality are rare from pure vitamins. One study of acute or chronic overdoses with more than 40,000 exposures reported 1 death and 8 major adverse outcomes.

Diagnosis

History: The individual may present with nonspecific symptoms, such as nausea, vomiting, diarrhea, and rash. Vitamin-caused symptoms may be secondary to those caused by additives (e.g., mannitol), colorings, or binders, but those symptoms are usually not severe. Individuals who have taken too much Vitamin A may also report headache, decreased appetite, irritability, itching (pruritus), hair loss (alopecia), cracks at the corner of the mouth, seborrhea-type dermatitis, drowsiness, and/or peeling skin in the form of scales (desquamation) after 24 hours. Chronic toxicity results in bone pain.

Too much Vitamin D may result in additional initial reports of anorexia, followed by increased urination (polyuria), excessive thirst (polydipsia), weakness, nervousness, itching (pruritus), muscle weakness, apathy, headache, and bone pain. Renal function may be impaired, and kidney calcifications (kidney stones) may develop. As the result of too much Vitamin E, individuals may report additional symptoms of fatigue, headache, easy bruising and bleeding, double vision (diplopia), muscle weakness, and presence of creatine in the urine (creatinuria).

Excessive amounts of Vitamin C can also cause increased estrogen hormone levels in women, interference with the absorption of Vitamin B_{12}, and the possible development of kidney stones. Large doses during pregnancy may affect the developing fetus and cause a rebound effect in the newborn infant that resembles a vitamin C deficiency.

Prolonged excess ingestion of Vitamin B_6 (pyridoxine) can cause neurological sensory problems such as lack of coordination (ataxia), clumsiness of the hands and feet, and numbness around the mouth (perioral numbness). Recovery is slow after the large dosages are stopped. Vitamin B_3 (niacin) toxicity can cause itching (pruritus), flushing, stomach discomfort, and may also aggravate asthma. It is linked with heart rhythm disturbances (cardiac arrhythmia), abnormally increased skin pigment (hyperpigmentation), and liver problems.

Physical exam: Some chronic vitamin toxicity affects the skin and mucous membranes, and the musculoskeletal and neurological systems. Individuals may present with redness (erythema), eczema-type dermatitis, itching (pruritus), dry and cracked skin, inflammation of the membrane covering the eyes (conjunctivitis), peeling on the palms of the hands and the soles of the feet, and hair loss (alopecia). Musculoskeletal effects include pain and tenderness, particularly over the long bones of the upper and lower extremities. Neurological effects include frontal headache and blurred vision. Findings may also include swelling of the optic disk (papilledema), enlarged liver (hepatomegaly), fluid in the abdominal cavity (ascites), and increased intracranial pressure.

Other findings may include constipation, backache, excess fats in the blood (hyperlipidemia), and excess calcium in the blood (hypercalcemia). Findings may also include high blood pressure (hypertension) and irregular heartbeats (cardiac arrhythmias) and hidden (occult) rectal bleeding.

Tests: Urinalysis, complete blood count (CBC), electrolytes (if there has been severe vomiting or diarrhea); the bleeding time tests, prothrombin time (PT), and partial thromboplastin time (PTT), may be needed if there is evidence of bruising or bleeding, or if the individual is taking an anticoagulant. Specific tests for individual vitamins should be done. A liver function test may be needed. Calcium levels in the blood should be determined; phosphate levels may increase with calcium levels. Urinalysis should be checked for uric acid (uricosuria). There may be a false-negative test for glucose in the urine (glucosuria). Kidney (renal) function tests should be done.

With chronic vitamin A and D toxicity, skeletal x-rays may be taken to check for evidence of calcifications. A lumbar puncture (LP) may be needed to rule out increased intracranial pressure (ICP) in individuals with vitamin A toxicity. An x-ray of the kidney after dye has been injected (intravenous pyelogram), or a computerized axial tomography (CAT scan) should be done for suspected kidney stones (nephrolithiasis) in individuals with vitamin C toxicity. An electrocardiogram (EKG) should be done to evaluate for the effects of hypercalcemia in individuals with vitamin D toxicity.

Treatment

In most cases, hypervitaminosis is successfully treated by reducing the offending vitamin to normal amounts or eliminating it completely. Symptoms are treated as they occur.

If there have been potentially lethal ingestions, the stomach may be washed out (gastric lavage), activated charcoal may be used, and oxygen, IV, cardiac monitoring and airway maintenance may be indicated. Counseling may be needed.

Prognosis

The prognosis for a complete recovery is generally excellent. There are likely to be no residual effects when treatment is given promptly and appropriately.

Differential Diagnosis

The different possible diagnoses that might be considered depend on the particular vitamin toxicities. Vitamin A, C, D, or E overdosages, either singly or in combination, may present with signs and symptoms similar to gastroenteritis, gastrointestinal bleeding, iron toxicity, dermatitis, fish poisoning, fluoride poisoning, or migraine headache.

Specialists

- Emergency Medicine

Work Restrictions / Accommodations

The individual should need no special accommodations or restrictions.

Comorbid Conditions

Pre-existing liver disease, kidney disease, stomach disorders, or blood disorders may also affect the outcome of vitamin overdosage. Emotional or psychological factors may interfere with clinical presentation.

Complications

Various complications (depending on the vitamin) may occur when the individual does not follow medical and dietary advice. If individuals continue to take the vitamins in large doses, an easily treated problem will be unnecessarily complicated.

Factors Influencing Duration

Age, physical condition, the particular complications of the disease, and nutritional status will influence recovery and have an effect on any disability.

Length of Disability

Duration of disability depends on the specific vitamin and the severity of the reaction. In most cases, no disability is expected.

Failure to Recover

If an individual fails to recover within the maximum duration expectancy period, the reader may wish to reference the following questions to assist in better understanding the specifics of an individual's medical case.

Regarding diagnosis:

- Has diagnosis of hypervitaminosis been confirmed?
- Is there a history of intentional vitamin overdosage or exposure?
- Is the exposure dose within the range of doses believed to cause such effects?

Regarding treatment:

- Was ingestion acute? Was it a mistake or intentional?
- If hypervitaminosis was the result of chronic overuse, did symptoms resolve with reducing or eliminating vitamin use?
- What can be done to expedite elimination of vitamin from body?

Regarding prognosis:

- If symptoms persist, should diagnosis be revisited?
- Has individual been instructed in the proper use/amount of vitamins?
- Would individual benefit from consultation with a nutritionist?
- If individual is incapable of following instructions, can someone else in the home supervise vitamin use?
- Does individual have an underlying condition that may impact recovery such as a pre-existing liver disease, kidney disease, stomach disorders or blood disorders?

References

Rosenbloom, Mark, MD. Vitamin Toxicity. eMedicine.com. 31 Jan 2001. 01 Mar 2001 <http://emedicine.com/emerg/topic638.htm>.

Hypervitaminosis A

Other names / synonyms: Acute Chronic Vitamin A (Retinol) Toxicity, Vitamin A Overdose

278.2, 963.5

Definition

Hypervitaminosis A or vitamin A toxicity refers to adverse health effects from chronic and acute overdoses of vitamin A. Retinol is the chemical name of vitamin A. Retinol is manufactured in the liver from beta carotene obtained in the diet.

Foods containing beta-carotene include dark-green leafy vegetables, yellow fruits and carrots, egg yolks, butter, cream, liver, fish liver oils, and fortified margarine. The only adverse effect from consuming too much beta-carotene is a change in skin pigmentation to a yellowish hue that dissipates when these foodstuffs are eliminated or reduced in the diet.

Vitamin A is essential for good vision, healthy skin, and normal metabolism. Most individuals derive adequate amounts of the vitamin from the foods they eat. Problems occur when there is accidental or intentional ingestion of large quantities of vitamin A from either the diet or from vitamin A preparations.

Most nutrient toxicities don't occur from dietary intakes of foods. Vitamin toxicities usually come from taking high potency vitamin supplements. Much of the data on adverse health effects from taking large amounts of a vitamin pertain to acute rather than chronic use. Because nutrients work together, consuming excessive amounts of one nutrient can cause a deficiency of another. Some supplements have been contaminated and some have failed to meet advertised claims. Because supplements are legally considered to be foods not drugs, the Food and Drug Administration has few regulations concerning them.

Data from the 1998 American Association of Poison Control Centers' Toxic Exposure Surveillance System notes the following total number of exposures for Vitamin A (2146); the number of those individuals with major adverse outcomes (zero); the number of deaths from that ingestion (zero). Overall, a total of 49,709 exposures to different types of vitamins were reported to the poison control centers across the US in 1998, accounting for a total of 14 major adverse outcomes, and no deaths. Of that total, 39,396 exposures were in children younger than 6 years.

Diagnosis

History: Acute vitamin A toxicity from a single massive dose causes nausea, vomiting and abdominal pain, and neurological symptoms of headache, drowsiness, irritability, and dizziness. Chronic ingestion of over 50,000 units of vitamin A per day for more than three months produces symptoms of fever, bone and joint pain, hair loss (alopecia), dry, cracked lips and itchy skin (pruritus), anorexia and weight loss.

Physical exam: Acute toxicity causes increased pressure on the brain (intracranial pressure) revealed by changes in the retina of the eye (papilledema). It is followed by peeling skin (desquamation). Physical findings in chronic toxicity include low-grade fever, swelling of the optic disc (papilledema), dry and fissured lips, dry skin, and enlarged liver and spleen (hepatosplenomegaly). A yellow skin pigmentation (hypercarotenosis) is differentiated from jaundice in that it does not involve the whites of the eyes (sclera).

Tests: Blood tests will confirm the diagnosis by demonstrating elevated levels of vitamin A (retinol). A complete blood count (CBC) should be done to rule out low white blood cells (leukopenia). The blood should also be checked for calcium, glucose, and liver function tests (LFTs). Skeletal x-rays should be obtained to demonstrate calcifications in chronic vitamin A toxicity.

Treatment

In most cases, hypervitaminosis is successfully treated by reducing the vitamin A to normal amounts and, in some cases, eliminating it completely. Symptoms are treated as they occur. All ingestions require only supportive measures and an IV. All serious ingestions need hydration if vomiting or diarrhea is present. Oxygen supplementation, cardiac monitoring and airway maintenance are essential if the condition becomes life-threatening. The stomach may be washed out (lavage) where there are potentially lethal ingestions generally less than one hour after the ingestion. Activated charcoal may be used for acute overdoses. Antiemetics or antidiarrheals may be used if needed.

Acute and chronic toxicity is resolved by eliminating vitamin A supplements from the diet.

Skin pigmentation due to over-ingestion of yellow fruits and vegetables is not considered a toxic condition.

Prognosis

The prognosis is generally excellent. All symptoms usually resolve after stopping excessive vitamin A supplement, instituting supportive therapy and returning to normal dietary intake of vitamin A. Treatment usually reverses all symptoms. A yellow skin pigmentation resolves quickly with modifications to the diet. A study of 40,000 acute and chronic overdoses reported only 1 death and 8 major adverse outcomes.

Differential Diagnosis

A related problem often mistaken as hypervitaminosis A, though not a serious one, is carotenemia (or hypercarotenosis), the yellow/orange coloring of skin that can arise from over-ingestion of yellow fruits and vegetables, especially carrots. Over-active parathyroid (hyperparathyroidism), excessive calcium in the blood (hypercalcemia), gastroenteritis, and iron toxicity may present with similar signs and symptoms.

Specialists

- Dietary Advisor
- Endocrinologist
- Hepatologist
- Internist
- Medical Toxicologist
- Nephrologist
- Obstetrician
- Physical Therapist

Work Restrictions / Accommodations

No work restrictions or accommodations should be necessary.

Comorbid Conditions

Liver disease, kidney disease, and gastrointestinal disorders may worsen the effects of vitamin A overdose.

Complications

In pregnant women, over-consumption of vitamin A or absorption through the skin from topical treatments for skin problems may cause birth defects in infants.

If the vitamin toxicity has led to an enlarged liver, this may progress to cirrhosis. In rare cases, vitamin A toxicity can lead to excessive calcium (hypercalcemia), a serious condition that causes the blood to reabsorb calcium from the bones.

Factors Influencing Duration

Factors include related complications, if any. Age, physical condition, health status, and mental status may influence the ability of the individual to undergo treatment and therapy for excessive vitamin usage.

Length of Disability

Duration in Days

Job Classification	Minimum	Optimum	Maximum
Sedentary work	0	3	5
Light work	0	3	5
Medium work	0	3	5
Heavy work	0	5	10
Very Heavy work	0	5	14

Failure to Recover

If an individual fails to recover within the maximum duration expectancy period, the reader may wish to reference the following questions to assist in better understanding the specifics of an individual's medical case.

Regarding diagnosis:

- Did individual have clinical characteristics consistent with the diagnosis of hypervitaminosis A (i.e., dry lips, dryness of nose and eyes, peeling skin, hair loss, bone or joint pain headache, and nausea and vomiting)?
- Was the underlying cause of the hypervitaminosis determined? Did it appear chronic or acute?
- Was the diagnosis confirmed with serum retinol levels? Was any liver dysfunction detected with liver function tests?
- If the diagnosis was uncertain, were other conditions with similar symptoms ruled out (i.e., hyperparathyroidism, excessive calcium in the blood (hypercalcemia), gastroenteritis, and iron toxicity)?

Regarding treatment:

- Were sources of vitamin A limited or eliminated?
- Did individual require fluid replacement or administration of antidiarrheals or antiemetics?
- Was gastric lavage or administration of activated charcoal warranted?

Regarding prognosis:

- Was the treatment successful in lowering the serum retinol levels to normal?
- Does individual have any pre-existing conditions such as liver, kidney, or gastrointestinal disorders that may impact recovery?
- Did individual suffer from complications of liver dysfunction or hypercalcemia?

References

"Chapter 3: Vitamin Deficiency, Dependency, and Toxicity." Merck Manual of Diagnosis and Therapy, 17th ed. Beers, Mark H., and Robert Berkow, MD, eds. Whitehouse Station, NJ: Merck & Co. Inc., 1999. 14 Oct 2000 <http://www.merck.com/pubs/mmanual/section1/chapter3/3c.htm>.

Rosenbloom, M. "Toxicity, Vitamin from Emergency Medicine/Toxicology." eMedicine.com. 31 Jan 2001. 22 Feb 2001 <http://www.emedicine.com/emerg/topic638.htm>.

Hypervitaminosis D

Other names / synonyms: Vitamin A Overdose, Vitamin D Overdose

278.4

Definition

Hypervitaminosis D is an uncommon condition that refers to the adverse health effects of excessive amounts of vitamin D in the bloodstream. Usually precipitated by over-ingestion of vitamin D supplements, it is also a complication of treating a deficiency of parathyroid hormone (hypoparathyroidism). The formation of nodules in the lymph nodes, lungs, bones, and skin (sarcoidosis) interrupts the metabolism of vitamin D and leads to elevated levels of the vitamin. Vitamin D is synthesized by the body after exposure to sunlight and is found in foods such as fortified milk, margarine, egg yolks, and fish oils. Vitamin D helps the body absorb calcium and phosphorus. It is essential to the formation of bones and teeth. An excess of the vitamin can lead to kidney damage and elevated blood calcium levels (hypercalcemia).

Most nutrient toxicities don't occur from dietary intakes of foods. Vitamin toxicities usually come from taking high potency vitamin supplements. Much of the data on adverse health effects from taking large amounts of a vitamin or mineral pertain to acute rather than chronic use. Because nutrients work together, consuming excessive amounts of one nutrient can cause a deficiency of another.

There are no available or reliable data on the extent and range of vitamin D overdosage in the US or worldwide. Overall, a total of 49,709 exposures to different types of vitamins were reported to the poison control centers across the US in 1998, accounting for a total of 14 major adverse outcomes, and no deaths. Of that total, 39,396 exposures were in children younger than 6 years. Morbidity and mortality are rare from pure vitamins. One study of acute or chronic overdoses, with more than 40,000 exposures, reported 1 death and 8 major adverse outcomes.

Because supplements are legally considered to be foods not drugs, the Food and Drug Administration has few regulations concerning them.

Diagnosis

History: Individuals may complain of headache, irritability, nausea, and weight loss. If the toxicity is severe, they may also complain of excessive thirst, weakness, anxiety, and itching. Chronic toxicity effects may also include constipation, loss of appetite (anorexia), excessive thirst (polydipsia), excessive secretion of urine (polyuria), backache, excessive fat in the blood (hyperlipidemia), and abnormally high concentration of calcium in the blood (hypercalcemia).

Physical exam: Long-term overdoses of vitamin D can cause retarded growth in children. Findings may also include hypertension and irregular heart beats (cardiac arrhythmias). There are no other notable physical findings.

Tests: The definitive test is demonstration of elevated levels of 25-hydroxyvitamin D in the blood. Electrolytes in the blood should be determined if there is severe vomiting or diarrhea. Calcium levels should also be determined. Abnormally high levels of calcium indicate vitamin D toxicity. Phosphate levels may also increase with increasing calcium levels. Kidney (renal) function tests are necessary to evaluate possible kidney damage from excessive calcium in the urine (hypercalciuria). Skeletal x-rays should be obtained to demonstrate abnormal deposits of calcium (calcifications) in chronic vitamin D toxicity.

Treatment

Treatment begins by immediately stopping any vitamin D supplements and restriction of dietary calcium if hypercalcemia has developed. The individual with vitamin D toxicity should be placed on a low-calcium diet. An oral drug (calcium disodium edetate) should be considered to increase the fecal excretion of calcium. In severe hypercalcemia, the individual may need hydration, diuretics, steroids, or other drugs. Ample fluids are encouraged. Removal of substances and water via the abdominal lining (peritoneal dialysis) or via the blood (hemodialysis) may be necessary if the individual is unable to take large amounts of fluids by mouth.

Prognosis

Treatment is usually successful, but because vitamin D is stored in fat (fat-soluble), reserves can be substantial. Symptoms may persist for several weeks after treatment. In addition, if the hypercalcemia has progressed to the point of causing kidney damage, it may be irreversible, even with treatment. Removal of substances and water via the abdominal lining (peritoneal dialysis) or via the blood (hemodialysis) are successful in removing excess calcium in individuals when they have been unable to take fluids by mouth.

Differential Diagnosis

Some of the symptoms of hypervitaminosis D are similar to those of hypercalcemia itself. Migraine headache, excess parathyroid hormone (hyperparathyroidism), fluoride poisoning, iron toxicity, gastroenteritis, and food poisoning may all present with similar signs and symptoms. Therefore, the first step of diagnosis must be to establish whether the individual has been taking high doses of vitamin D.

Specialists

- Dietary Advisor
- Endocrinologist
- Hepatologist
- Internist
- Medical Toxicologist
- Nephrologist
- Obstetrician
- Physical Therapist

Work Restrictions / Accommodations

No work restrictions or accommodations should be necessary.

Comorbid Conditions

Liver disease, kidney disease, and gastrointestinal disorders may worsen the effects of vitamin D overdose.

Complications

Excess vitamin D can lead to kidney disorders and skeletal problems from hypercalcemia.

Factors Influencing Duration

Length of disability depends on whether there are any complications from the megadoses of vitamin D. If hypercalcemia is present, and it almost always is, duration will be extended.

Length of Disability

Duration may be longer if hypercalcemia is present.

Job Classification	Duration in Days		
	Minimum	Optimum	Maximum
Sedentary work	0	3	5
Light work	0	3	5
Medium work	0	3	5
Heavy work	0	5	10
Very Heavy work	0	5	14

Failure to Recover

If an individual fails to recover within the maximum duration expectancy period, the reader may wish to reference the following questions to assist in better understanding the specifics of an individual's medical case.

Regarding diagnosis:

- Did the individual have a history of vitamin D supplementation?
- Were the clinical findings characteristic of hypervitaminosis D (nausea, vomiting, weight loss, constipation, thirst, high urine output, backache, hyperlipemia, hypercalcemia)?
- Was the diagnosis confirmed by measuring the serum 25-hydroxyvitamin D?
- If the diagnosis was uncertain, were other causes of hypercalcemia ruled out?
- Were other conditions with similar symptoms ruled out, such as fluoride poisoning, iron toxicity, gastroenteritis or food poisoning?

Regarding treatment:

- Were sources of vitamin D and calcium eliminated as appropriate?
- Was treatment with calcium disodium edetate needed to help lower serum calcium levels?
- Did the individual receive oral or intravenous fluids for hydration?

Regarding prognosis:

- Did adequate time elapse for recovery (several weeks)?
- Did the individual have any pre-existing conditions such as, liver, kidney or gastrointestinal disorders that would impact recovery?
- Did the individual have associated hypercalcemia?
- Did the individual suffer any kidney damage secondary to the hypercalcemia? If so, was this addressed in the treatment plan?

References

"Chapter 3: Vitamin Deficiency, Dependency, and Toxicity." Merck Manual of Diagnosis and Therapy, 17th ed. Beers, Mark H., and Robert Berkow, M.D, eds. Whitehouse Station, NJ: Merck & Co. Inc., 1999. 14 Oct 2000 <http://www.merck.com/pubs/mmanual/section1/chapter3/3d.htm>.

Vitamin D Homepage. Vitamins Plus. 1998. 15 Oct 2000 <http://www.vitaminsplus.com/library/vitamins/vitamind.asp>.

Mahan, Kathleen L., and Sylvia Escott-Stump, eds. Krause's Food, Nutrition, and Diet Therapy, 10th ed. Philadelphia: W.B. Saunders Company, 2000.

Rosenbloom, Mark, MD. "Toxicity, Vitamin." eMedicine.com 01 Oct 2000. 21 Oct 2000 <http://www.emedicine.com/emerg/topic638.htm>.

Hypochondriasis

Other names / synonyms: Atypical Somatoform Disorder, Hypochondria, Hypochondriacal Neurosis

300.7

Definition

Hypochondriasis is a mental disorder in which the individual believes that real or imagined physical symptoms are signs of a serious illness despite medical reassurance that they are not. More specifically, the disorder is characterized by a preoccupation with bodily functions and the interpretation of normal sensations (such as heart beats, sweating, peristaltic action, and bowel movements) or minor abnormalities (such as a runny nose, minor aches and pains, or slightly swollen lymph nodes) as indications of highly disturbing problems needing medical attention. An individual with hypochondriasis might think to himself or herself this thought: "I have a headache; therefore, I must have a brain tumor."

Negative results of diagnostic evaluations and reassurance by physicians only increase the individual's anxious concern about his or her health; the individual feels distressed because of the negative findings and seeks further medical attention. The ability of many hypochondriacs to function in social, occupational, and interpersonal roles may be impaired.

No specific cause has been found for this disorder, but it frequently develops in individuals or relatives of individuals who have had a particular disease. Frequent appointments with healthcare providers are typical and time from work is often taken for doctors' appointments, treatments, lab tests, and so on.

Hypochondriasis occurs at any age, but most commonly between 20-30 years of age. The disorder's prevalence in the US is estimated to be between 4-9%. Men and women appear to be affected equally, and social, educational, and marital factors do not appear to affect the diagnosis.

Diagnosis

History: A diagnosis of hypochondriasis requires that the individual experiences a preoccupation with fear of illness, and that the fear be persistent (for a duration of least 6 months) despite the absence of an apparent physical disorder to account for the symptoms and abnormal medical findings confirming the disorder. The individual's belief that he or she has a serious illness is usually based on a misinterpretation of symptoms that may shift, change, and/or be vague or specific.

Physical exam: The exam is usually normal.

Tests: Invasive diagnostic tests should be minimized but appropriate psychological and psychiatric evaluation should be performed to rule out other related disorders.

Treatment

Improvement may result from reassurance through regular physician visits. Group rather than individual therapy is most helpful. Coexisting psychiatric conditions should be treated. Hypochondriasis is sometimes episodic, suggesting that it may be related to stressful life events.

From a psychological point of view, current research indicates that techniques used to treat obsessive compulsive disorder (OCD) are also effective for hypochondriasis. Two such techniques--cognitive therapy and exposure and response prevention (ERP)--are showing favorable research results. Pharmacotherapy tends to be effective in instances when hypochondriasis coexists with a depressive or anxiety disorder. In those instances, antidepressants and antianxiety medications are usually prescribed.

Prognosis

Some sources report that one-third to one-half of all hypochondriacs eventually experience a significant improvement. Hypochondriasis has been shown to have fluctuations in intensity with periods of relative remission and exacerbation of acuity that may create destruction in the individual's life. Prognosis varies depending on the individual's personality structure, education, social support system, intelligence, and motivation for change. Many psychiatrists consider the prognosis for this condition to be poor when treated with a psychoanalytic approach. When hypochondriasis is present along with depression, the prognosis is particularly poor.

As noted elsewhere in this report, the course of this condition is generally chronic and only a very small number of individuals, perhaps 5% at most, recover permanently.

Differential Diagnosis

The possibility exists that the symptoms reported by an individual with hypochondriasis are bona fide symptoms of a medical disorder. Such medical disorders include multiple sclerosis, myasthenia gravis, systemic lupus erythematosus, and acquired immune deficiency syndrome (AIDS).

The possibility exists also that hypochondriasis could be misdiagnosed as another mental disorder, such as somatization disorder. The two disorders differ, however, in that in somatization disorder, the individual's concern is about many symptoms. With hypochondriasis, the individual's concern is about having a disease. Other somatoform disorders that have been known to resemble hypochondriasis are conversion disorder pain disorder and body dysmorphic disorder. Depressive disorder, anxiety disorder, and panic disorder sometimes coexist as separate mental disorders with hypochondriasis. Factitious illness with physical symptoms and malingering have presented with manifestations of this disorder. The delusional hypochondriacal beliefs in schizophrenia and other psychotic disorders are differentiated from hypochondriasis by their delusional intensity and the presence of other psychotic symptoms.

Specialists

- Internist
- Neurologist
- Psychiatrist
- Psychologist

Work Restrictions / Accommodations

Work restrictions or accommodations are necessary only infrequently, for the most serious cases. In these instances, time-limited restrictions and work accommodations should be individually determined based on the characteristics of the individual's response to the disorder, the functional requirements of the job and work environment, and the flexibility of the job and work site. The purpose of the restrictions/accommodations is to help maintain the worker's capacity to remain at the workplace without a work disruption or to promote timely and safe transition back to full work productivity.

Comorbid Conditions

In most cases, no disability is expected. Comorbid conditions could, however, influence the intensity of the disorder and tendency to relapse. Such conditions include alcohol abuse, drug abuse, depression, and the presence of a personality disorder.

Complications

A coexisting anxiety or mood disorder, especially major depression, complicates the course and prognosis of hypochondriasis. The individual's refusal of psychological treatment and his or her experience with life-circumstance problems (e.g., financial, marital, legal, occupational) have also been associated with complication and exacerbation of the disorder. Another complication is the possibility that a bona fide disease may be overlooked and go untreated because of the individual's previously unfounded complaints.

Factors Influencing Duration

In most cases, no disability is expected. Factors that might influence the intensity of the disorder and the tendency to relapse are severity of associated disorders, intensity of belief system, and willingness to undergo psychotherapy. Psychosocial stressors may influence the time between exacerbations of the disorder. The social support and social interaction that would come from group therapy would ease the exacerbations.

Length of Disability

In most cases, no disability is expected.

Duration in Days

Job Classification	Minimum	Optimum	Maximum
Any work	1	1	7

Failure to Recover

If an individual fails to recover within the maximum duration expectancy period, the reader may wish to reference the following questions to assist in better understanding the specifics of an individual's medical case.

Regarding diagnosis:

- Have actual existing medical conditions been ruled out through medical history and physical exam by a physician?
- Has a psychological evaluation been performed?
- What is the individual's health care history?
- Has the individual previously been under medical supervision by other health care professionals for this same problem?
- Was medical condition previously established or ruled out?

Regarding treatment:

- Were physical exam and diagnostic testing performed to identify or rule out an organic basis for complaints?
- Were existing complaints treated symptomatically as appropriate?
- Is the individual scheduled for or receiving regular follow-up visits?
- Because it is very difficult for the individual to accept the conclusion that the health problem is not a serious organic illness, is the individual and/or family receiving psychotherapy or counseling to help deal with this situation?
- Is the individual involved in a group therapy that provides needed support and social interaction? Is therapy sufficient to reduce fear and anxiety?

Regarding prognosis:

- Is the individual making an effort to avoid going to different doctors and getting repeat medical tests?
- Is the individual involved in an effective group therapy?
- Is the individual able to focus on other aspects of life and move on?
- Would additional psychotherapy help?

References

DSM-IV: Hypochondriasis. American Psychiatric Association. 01 Jan 1994. 23 Aug 2000 <http://www.behavenet.com>.

Hypochondriasis. Adam.com, Inc. 01 Jan 1999. 19 Aug 2000 <http://adam.com/ency/article/001236.htm>.

What is Hypochondriasis? Bio-Behavioral Institute. 01 Jan 2000. 23 Aug 2000 <http://www.bio-behavioral.com/hypochondriasis.html>.

Torem, Moshe. "Hypochondriasis." Griffith's 5-minute Clinical Consult. Dambro, M., and Jo A. Griffith, eds. New York: Lippincott, Williams and Wilkins, 1999. 534-540.

Hypoglycemia
Other names / synonyms: Low Blood Glucose, Low Blood Sugar
251.2

Definition

Hypoglycemia is a condition in which blood sugar (glucose) levels are abnormally low. This is a serious condition, because the body uses glucose for fuel, and when levels are too low, many organ systems (particularly the brain and nervous system) malfunction.

Hypoglycemia can result when an individual with diabetes mellitus (a diabetic) accidentally takes too much of the medicine (insulin, sulfonylureas) he or she uses to reduce glucose levels. Many other drugs that are not related to treatment of diabetes can also cause hypoglycemia.

Meals high in refined carbohydrates, excessive alcohol consumption, and certain types of gastrointestinal surgery can produce an episode of hypoglycemia. Starvation and strenuous exercise can lead to hypoglycemia in rare instances, but this usually happens in individuals with some other underlying disease (e.g., pituitary or adrenal gland disease, liver disease).

Excessive production of insulin (usually caused by a tumor of certain cells in the pancreas), kidney failure, heart failure, malnutrition, cancer, shock, severe infection, and extensive liver disease can all produce hypoglycemia.

Aside from the diseases and conditions listed above, females and older individuals are at risk. Because hypoglycemia is not a disease itself but rather a sign of some other illness, incidence and prevalence are unknown.

Diagnosis

History: The individual may have a history of passing out or complain of hunger, headache, weakness, a pounding in the chest (cardiac palpitations), sweating, feelings of anxiousness, and difficulty concentrating. Family members may notice confusion or personality changes in the individual.

Physical exam: On examination, the heart rate may be above 100 beats per minute (tachycardia) and the blood pressure may be high (hypertension). The skin will be pale and feel cool and clammy. The individual may be unconscious or have involuntary muscle jerking (convulsions).

Tests: A blood test reveals abnormally low levels of glucose. This is definitive for this condition. The physician may order a test to measure blood glucose level after eating (nonfasting or postprandial) or after 12 hours of fasting. Insulin levels should also be measured in all cases during an episode, if possible. Insulin levels are not helpful if the simultaneous glucose level is not low.

Treatment

Hypoglycemia is treated by having the individual (if conscious) consume sugar in any form (candy, fruit juice, glucose tablets, milk). This is often followed by more sustaining carbohydrates such as crackers with peanut butter. If the individual is unconscious, intravenous glucose is given. These methods successfully restore glucose levels within minutes.

Long-term treatment includes education on the symptoms for early detection and intervention. If the individual is diagnosed as a diabetic, education and a thorough understanding of the disease and its treatment is perhaps the best therapy. Dietary changes may include small, frequent meals instead of three large meals per day. Those at risk for severe episodes of hypoglycemia may benefit from having a hormone called glucagon handy at all times. This medication is given by injection and returns glucose levels to normal within minutes.

In the extremely rare cases where a tumor is causing too much insulin to be secreted, surgical removal is indicated. The success of this procedure varies depending on the experience of the surgeon, the ability to locate all tumors (there are often multiple and they are usually very small), and the individual's response to surgery.

Prognosis

With early intervention, the outcome is good. Patient education and dietary changes are very effective in preventing or limiting episodes of hypoglycemia. In cases when glucagon is administered, hypoglycemia will generally resolve within minutes.

In the rare cases where surgical removal of pancreatic tumors is necessary, the outcome will depend on the skill of the surgeon, the ability of the surgeon to locate and remove all tumors, the presence of surgical complications, and the individual's response to the surgery.

The long-term outcome is based on the underlying cause and the individual's response to treatment.

Differential Diagnosis

Other diagnoses may include electrolyte imbalance, cardiac rhythm abnormalities, central nervous system disease, psychological disorders, myocardial infarction, stroke, hyperpituitarism, or hyperthyroidism.

Specialists

- Endocrinologist

Work Restrictions / Accommodations

Accommodations include flexibility in work schedule to allow for prevention or response to symptoms of hypoglycemia. Other restrictions may include working at consistent levels of physical exertion, limiting work in high places, and limiting operation of vehicles or high-speed equipment. Individuals should not work in isolated areas or without a coworker. Due to the risk of losing consciousness, sedentary positions might be preferable.

Complementary and Alternative Therapies

Content is intended for awareness only. Treatments may or may not be effective. Scientific evidence may be lacking and some substances have potentially toxic effects. Dr. Presley Reed and the editors do not endorse the use of these therapies in the absence of consultation with a licensed medical professional.

Dietary modifications - Individuals prone to hypoglycemia may be able to avoid episodes through dietary changes that include small, frequent meals instead of three large meals a day. A diet including longer-lasting carbohydrates such as bread or crackers may also be helpful.

Comorbid Conditions

Alcoholism or anorexia nervosa may lengthen disability.

Complications

Complications may include seizures, coma, or death. Complications are based on degree and timing of medical intervention and the severity of the underlying cause.

Factors Influencing Duration

Factors influencing the length of disability may include the control of underlying disease, the individual's awareness of hypoglycemic symptoms, and ability to self-intervene. Progression of other underlying causes/diseases (i.e., tumor of pancreas) also influences the length of disability.

Length of Disability

Episodes of hypoglycemia generally respond completely to treatment within minutes. Duration depends on underlying cause and severity of symptoms.

Duration in Days

Job Classification	Minimum	Optimum	Maximum
Any work	0	2	3

Failure to Recover

If an individual fails to recover within the maximum duration expectancy period, the reader may wish to reference the following questions to assist in better understanding the specifics of an individual's medical case.

Regarding diagnosis:

- Has hypoglycemia been confirmed?
- Have conditions with similar symptoms been ruled out?
- Has underlying cause of hypoglycemia been identified? If cause is undetermined, is inpatient observation and testing beneficial?

Regarding treatment:

- If at risk for hypoglycemic episodes, does individual recognize early symptoms?
- Does individual carry a form of glucose or glucagon with him/her at all times?
- Is individual eating small, frequent meals instead of three large meals a day? Does regular diet include longer-lasting carbohydrates such as bread or crackers? Would individual benefit from consultation with a nutritionist?
- Is surgical removal of insulin-secreting tumors an option? Is surgeon a specialist experienced in this type of tumor?
- If symptoms persist despite treatment, is it possible that not all the tumors were removed?

Regarding prognosis:

- Is individual diligent in preventing hypoglycemic episodes? If episodes do occur, does individual recognize early symptoms and seek appropriate intervention?
- Does individual wear a medical ID tag to alert emergency medical personnel about hypoglycemic condition?
- Has primary cause of hypoglycemia been identified?
- Has treatment of underlying condition been effective in reducing hypoglycemic episodes?
- If symptoms persist despite treatment, does diagnosis need to be revisited?
- Would individual benefit from evaluation by an endocrinologist?

References

Florence, Joseph. "Diabetic Hypoglycemia." Griffith's 5-minute Clinical Consult. Dambro, Mark, ed. Philadelphia: Lippincott, Williams & Wilkins, 2000. 538-539.

Schneider, F. David. "Nondiabetic Hypoglycemia." Griffith's 5-minute Clinical Consult. Dambro, Mark, ed. Philadelphia: Lippincott, Williams & Wilkins, 2000. 540-541.

Hypoparathyroidism
Other names / synonyms: Hypoparathyreosis, Underactive Parathyroid
252.1

Definition

Hypoparathyroidism is a rare hormone (endocrine) disorder in which the glands located near the thyroid gland at the front of the neck (parathyroid glands) fail to produce enough parathyroid hormone. This hormone, along with vitamin D and a hormone produced by the thyroid gland (calcitonin), regulates the level of calcium in the body. Deficiency of parathyroid hormone reduces calcium levels in the blood (hypocalcemia). A low level of calcium in the body can lead to a condition (tetany) that causes muscle spasms, twitches, convulsions or seizures.

Hypoparathyroidism can be classified as either hereditary or acquired. In hereditary hypoparathyroidism, the parathyroid glands may be absent from birth (congenital hypoparathyroidism), or they may cease to function for no apparent reason (idiopathic hypoparathyroidism). Acquired hypoparathyroidism most often occurs following surgery on the thyroid gland or when a portion of the parathyroid glands are removed in the treatment of overproduction of the parathyroid hormone (hyperparathyroidism). Acquired hypoparathyroidism is less common than it once was, as doctors have learned the importance of preserving the parathyroid glands during surgery.

Hypoparathyroidism can occur after exposure to toxic heavy metals or radiation therapy, or can be the result of tumors or infection. Functional hypoparathyroidism, caused by magnesium deficiency, prevents the secretion of the parathyroid hormone.

Hypoparathyroidism is a very rare disease, affecting only about 4 in every 100,000 people. It affects men and women equally, and tends to occur in those younger than 16 years or older than 40 years of age. Risk factors include a family history of hypoparathyroidism, recent surgery of the thyroid or parathyroid, and the presence of certain diseases (e.g., Addison's disease) in which the body's immune system attacks its own tissues (autoimmune disease).

Diagnosis

History: Symptoms may include tingling in the lips or painful cramplike spasms of the face, hands, arms and sometimes feet. In severe cases, a life-threatening syndrome known as tetany may occur. Symptoms of tetany include scattered muscle twitching, cramps, difficulty in swallowing, difficulty breathing, or generalized seizures. When the disease is ongoing (chronic), the individual may experience fatigue, anxiety, or personality changes. Blurred vision may be reported.

Physical exam: Findings on physical exam may include thin, brittle nails, dry, scaly skin and hair loss (particularly eyebrows). Yeast infections (Candidiasis) of the fingers, toenails, skin, mouth (thrush) or vagina may be noted. Eye examination may reveal a condition in which the lens of the eye becomes cloudy (cataract). Irregular heartbeat may also be noted.

Tapping on a facial nerve located in front of the ear will cause contraction of a facial muscle (Chvostek's sign) in hypoparathyroidism. In addition, pressing on the nerves and vessels of the upper arm will cause muscle spasm (Trousseau's phenomenon) in hypoparathyroidism.

Tests: Blood tests measure levels of the calcium, phosphate, magnesium, and parathyroid hormone in the blood. An electrocardiogram (ECG) often detects an abnormality in the electrical activity of the heart.

Treatment

Hypoparathyroidism resulting from surgery may resolve itself without treatment. In most cases, however, individuals begin a lifelong regimen of oral calcium and vitamin D supplements in order to maintain the blood calcium at a normal level. Vitamin D is necessary to increase the absorption of calcium from the diet. Functional hypoparathyroidism, caused by magnesium deficiency, is easily corrected by taking magnesium supplements.

In severe cases, a serious condition called tetany may be present. Tetany is characterized by twitching and painful muscle spasms and possibly generalized seizures. Immediate treatment with intravenous calcium in a hospital setting is necessary. Spasm of the throat muscles can make breathing difficult, necessitating a procedure called intubation, or surgery (tracheostomy), in order to keep the airway open.

Prognosis

Short-term (acute) hypoparathyroidism usually responds well to treatment, particularly if it occurs as a complication of surgery and is detected quickly. When the disease has been chronic, permanent damage such as calcium deposits in the brain, or clouding of the lens of the eye (cataracts) can occur.

Differential Diagnosis

Hypoparathyroidism can be mistaken for asthma, a brain tumor, epilepsy, or a condition characterized by involuntary muscle spasms and movements (choreoathetosis).

Specialists

- Endocrinologist

Work Restrictions / Accommodations

No work restrictions or accommodations should be necessary once the individual has received treatment.

Comorbid Conditions

Presence of other conditions such as nutritional disorders other hormone disorders may result in more severe symptoms and a delayed recovery.

Complications

Hypoparathyroidism may be associated with disorders in which the immune system reacts against the body's own tissues (autoimmune) such as sprue syndrome, pernicious anemia, or Addison's disease. Long standing cases may involve cataract formation or formation of calcium deposits in brain tissue. Over-treatment with calcium or vitamin D may cause kidney damage and impair renal function. Hypoparathyroidism increases the risk of developing Parkinson's disease.

Factors Influencing Duration

Length of disability may be influenced by severity of symptoms, presence of complications or associated disorders, and the individual's response to treatment.

Length of Disability

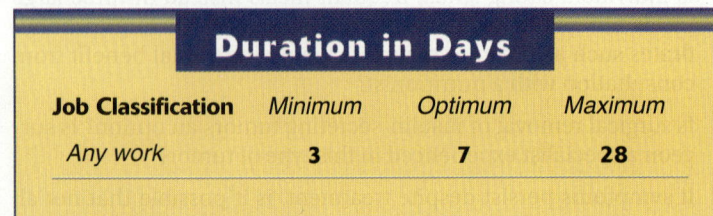

Duration in Days

Job Classification	Minimum	Optimum	Maximum
Any work	3	7	28

Failure to Recover

If an individual fails to recover within the maximum duration expectancy period, the reader may wish to reference the following questions to assist in better understanding the specifics of an individual's medical case.

Regarding diagnosis:

- Has the diagnosis of hypoparathyroidism been confirmed?
- Has the underlying cause been identified? Is the underlying cause receiving appropriate treatment?
- Has individual experienced any complications related to the hypoparathyroidism?
- Does individual have an underlying condition that may impact recovery?

Regarding treatment:

- Is the individual compliant with the physician's instructions for treatment of this condition as well as the treatment of any underlying condition? Has hypoparathyroidism responded to treatment?
- Does individual experience episodes of tetany? Is emergency intervention available? Has individual (or caretaker) been educated in early symptoms and how to access emergency intervention?

Regarding prognosis:

- Was hypoparathyroidism detected early and treated effectively? If symptoms persist, has underlying condition been resolved?
- Is individual receiving appropriate follow-up? Does individual comply with follow-up regimen?
- With long-standing or chronic hypoparathyroidism, permanent damage such as calcium deposits in the brain or cataracts can occur. Has permanent damage occurred? To what extent does it impact functioning?

References

Levy, Richard. "Hypoparathyroidism." Griffith's 5-minute Clinical Consult. Dambro, Mark, ed. Philadelphia: Lippincott, Williams & Wilkins, 2000. 548-549.

Hypoproteinemia

Other names / synonyms: Decreased Serum Protein, Hypoalbuminemia

273.8

Definition

Hypoproteinemia is a decreased level of protein in the blood. Hypoproteinemia results when protein is not being properly absorbed (malabsorption) during digestion. Malabsorption can be caused by numerous diseases/conditions including inflammation of the pancreas (pancreatitis), cystic fibrosis, obstruction of the bile duct, deficiency of the enzyme lactase, excess stomach acid, an imbalance of the bacteria in the small intestine, bowel infection (gastroenteritis), Crohn's disease, lymphoma, or poor blood supply to the intestine. In addition, individuals who have had part of the intestine removed surgically may experience hypoproteinemia. Certain drugs (neomycin, alcohol) may affect absorption, thereby resulting in hypoproteinemia. Finally, a severe lack of protein in the diet (malnutrition) could also cause hypoproteinemia.

Diagnosis

History: Hypoproteinemia does not have any symptoms that would prompt an individual to visit a physician. Symptoms will be specific to the underlying disease.

Physical exam: Hypoproteinemia is often not evident upon physical examination. In some cases, where there is a deficiency in serum albumin specifically, peripheral edema may be evident.

Tests: Hypoproteinemia can be confirmed by a routine blood test, specifically serum albumin and total protein levels.

Treatment

Since hypoproteinemia is a sign of an underlying disease, treatment is directed at the disease process itself.

Prognosis

The outcome of the individual's condition with hypoproteinemia is based on the individual's primary disease prognosis.

Differential Diagnosis

Because hypoproteinemia is a symptom of many primary diseases, there are no differential diagnoses.

Specialists

- Gastroenterologist
- Internist

Work Restrictions / Accommodations

In order to control peripheral edema, individuals with a low serum protein need to be assigned sedentary duties or duties that would not require individuals to be on their feet all day. Other restrictions and accommodations may be necessary depending on the primary disease.

Comorbid Conditions

Comorbid conditions depend on the individual's primary disease.

Complications

Hypoproteinemia does not have any complications. Instead, it is a complication of the individual's primary disease.

Factors Influencing Duration

Length of disability is based solely on the individual's primary disease and not on hypoproteinemia.

Length of Disability

No disability is associated with hypoproteinemia. Duration depends on underlying condition.

Failure to Recover

If an individual fails to recover within the maximum duration expectancy period, the reader may wish to reference the following questions to assist in better understanding the specifics of an individual's medical case.

Regarding diagnosis:

- Does the individual have any underlying conditions that can cause malabsorption such as pancreatitis, cystic fibrosis, obstruction of the bile duct, deficiency of the enzyme lactase, excess stomach acid, an imbalance of the bacteria in the small intestine, gastroenteritis, Crohn's disease, lymphoma, or poor blood supply to the intestine?
- Has part of individual's intestine been removed surgically?
- Has individual been on Neomycin? Use alcohol? Is individual malnourished?
- Does individual have peripheral edema?
- Have blood serum albumin and total protein testing been done?

Regarding treatment:

- What is the underlying condition? Is it responding to treatment?

Regarding prognosis:

- Can individual's employer accommodate any necessary restrictions?
- Is individual compliant with the treatment regime?

References

Watson, William. "Malabsorption Syndromes." The Merck Manual of Medical Information. Berkow, Robert, ed. New York: Pocket Books, 1997. 585-590.

Hypoprothrombinemia

Other names / synonyms: Factor II Deficiency, Prothrombin Deficiency

286.3

Definition

Hypoprothrombinemia is a blood clotting (coagulation) disorder in which there is an absence of or abnormally low levels of prothrombin, a protein essential for normal clotting. Hypoprothrombinemia may be congenital or acquired.

Congenital hypoprothrombinemia is an inherited condition. An individual must inherit 2 copies of the gene for this disorder, 1 from each parent, in order to show symptoms. Low prothrombin levels are the result of decreased production of prothrombin.

Acquired hypoprothrombinemia is caused by several conditions that either interfere with the production of prothrombin or reduce its level after production. Liver disease, such as cirrhosis, hepatitis, or malignancy, reduces prothrombin levels because prothrombin is made in the liver. Obstruction of the bile tract (obstructive biliary disease), caused by tumor, gallstones, infection, or drugs, interferes with fat absorption (bile is needed to absorb fat). This, in turn, interferes with the absorption of vitamin K. Without adequate amounts of vitamin K, prothrombin can't be produced. A deficiency of vitamin K in the diet or a malabsorption syndrome has the same effect. Low levels of functional prothrombin may be caused by some medications, such as anticoagulants, and toxic amounts of salicylate. Kidney disease that results in the loss of large amounts of protein, including prothrombin, in the urine, will decrease prothrombin levels. Individuals with lupus have a substance in their blood called the lupus anticoagulant. Up to 75% of these individuals also have antibodies against prothrombin, and 25% have antibody action significant enough to produce low prothrombin levels. These antibodies bind to prothrombin and cause it to be removed from the bloodstream. The risk of acquiring hypoprothrombinemia follows the risk of developing these conditions that affect prothrombin levels.

Up to 68% of individuals taking certain antibiotics will develop hypoprothrombinemia. Congenital hypoprothrombinemia is very rare, with fewer than 100 cases on record.

Diagnosis

History: Individuals may have a history of easy bruising, nosebleeds, gum bleeding, blood in the urine or stool, postpartum hemorrhage, excessive or prolonged menstrual bleeding, and excessive bleeding following surgery or trauma. Spontaneous severe bleeding (hemorrhage) is uncommon. In cases of congenital hypoprothrombinemia, an accurate family history may show evidence of the disorder in another family member.

Physical exam: Bruising and bleeding gums may be evident. Some individuals will have bleeding into the joints (hemarthrosis) or muscles (intramuscular hematoma). The individual also may present during an episode of active bleeding.

Tests: Blood tests that check clotting (coagulation tests) are performed, particularly prothrombin time (PT), and partial thromboplastin time (PTT). A prothrombin assay is performed to measure the actual amount of prothrombin in the blood.

Treatment

Treatment depends upon the severity of the bleeding and the cause of the hypoprothrombinemia. Mild hypoprothrombinemia may not require treatment, as prothrombin levels must fall to a very low level before abnormal bleeding occurs.

Vitamin K is given when the cause is based on vitamin K deficiency, as in obstructive biliary disease, dietary vitamin K deficiency, or salicylate poisoning. Congenital hypoprothrombinemia and liver disease do not respond to vitamin K, but require replacement of prothrombin (prothrombin replacement therapy). This is given in the form of plasma or a concentrate of prothrombin (prothrombin complex concentrate). Because the effects of either of these blood products are short-lived, they are given only during active bleeding or before any type of surgical procedure (due to the inherent risk of bleeding during surgery). Prothrombin replacement therapy is also given during any period of severe bleeding, despite the type of hypoprothrombinemia. Androgen hormones may help raise prothrombin levels in some individuals. Individuals with hypoprothrombinemia associated with lupus may be treated with steroids.

Prognosis

Prothrombin levels begin to rise within 24-36 hours after the administration of vitamin K. Given during a period of active bleeding or before surgery, plasma or prothrombin complex concentrate result in an immediate rise in prothrombin levels.

Congenital hypoprothrombinemia is an incurable, lifelong condition. Individuals may experience episodes of bleeding that require medical treatment. Life expectancy is normal, however, with care and replacement therapy.

In many cases, acquired hypoprothrombinemia will disappear once the causative disorder is corrected. For example, once the biliary obstruction is removed or the vitamin K deficiency corrected, normal prothrombin synthesis is restored. Resolution of hypoprothrombinemia due to liver disease depends on the severity and permanence of the cellular damage. If liver cells remain permanently damaged, prothrombin synthesis may not be restored.

Differential Diagnosis

Differential diagnoses include deficiencies of other clotting factors. Once the deficiency of prothrombin has been confirmed, one of several causative conditions must be confirmed: congenital hypoprothrombinemia, liver disease, obstructive biliary disease, dietary vitamin K deficiency, malabsorption, kidney disease, use of certain medications, or lupus.

Specialists

- Hematologist
- Internist
- Rheumatologist

Work Restrictions / Accommodations

No work restrictions or accommodations are usually required with this condition. Care should be taken to ensure that the individual is working in a relatively safe environment. Where indicated, protective gear, especially to the head, should be worn. The employer should be aware of the condition so that the appropriate level of care can be obtained quickly in the event of an on-the-job injury.

Comorbid Conditions

Diarrhea or any condition interfering with absorption of nutrients will exacerbate hypoprothrombinemia. Deficiency of other clotting factors may also result from vitamin K deficiency or liver disease, complicating the control of bleeding.

Complications

Complications associated with this disorder include severe, life-threatening bleeding (hemorrhage), particularly inside the skull (intracranial bleeding). Hemorrhage may follow surgery or trauma.

Factors Influencing Duration

Factors include surgery, trauma, use of certain medications that affect prothrombin, alcohol use, dietary intake of vitamin K, the presence of lupus, or the development of severe hemorrhage.

Length of Disability

No disability is associated with this condition unless bleeding occurs as a response to surgery or trauma.

Failure to Recover

If an individual fails to recover within the maximum duration expectancy period, the reader may wish to reference the following questions to assist in better understanding the specifics of an individual's medical case.

Regarding diagnosis:

- Is the individual's hypoprothrombinemia congenital or acquired?
- Does the individual have any liver diseases such as cirrhosis, hepatitis, or malignancy?
- Does the individual have obstructive biliary disease?
- Does the individual have a dietary deficiency of vitamin K or a malabsorption syndrome?
- Does the individual have lupus?
- Does the individual have a history of easy bruising, nosebleeds, gum bleeding, blood in the urine or stool, postpartum hemorrhage, excessive or prolonged menstrual bleeding, and excessive bleeding following surgery or trauma?
- On exam was bruising and bleeding gums evident?
- Did the individual have hemarthrosis? Intramuscular hematoma?
- Has the individual had complete coagulation testing done?
- Have conditions with similar symptoms been ruled out?

Regarding treatment:

- What is the severity of the individual's disease?
- Is the individual receiving Vitamin K if necessary?
- Is the individual receiving prothrombin replacement therapy if necessary?
- Were androgen hormones tried?
- If the individual has lupus, were they treated with steroids?

Regarding prognosis:

- Is the individual's employer able to accommodate any necessary restrictions?
- Does the individual have any conditions that may affect their ability to recover?
- Does the individual have any complications such as severe, life-threatening hemorrhage, particularly intracranial bleeding or hemorrhage following surgery or trauma?

References

Dambro, Mark, and Jo Griffith. Griffith's 5-minute Clinical Consult. Philadelphia: Lippincott Williams & Wilkins, 1999.

Pagana, Kathleen, and Timothy Pagana. Mosby's Manual of Diagnostic and Laboratory Tests. St. Louis: Mosby, 1998.

Hypotension

Other names / synonyms: Low Blood Pressure

458, 458.8

Definition

Hypotension is an abnormal condition in which an individual's blood pressure is too low for normal functioning.

Blood pressure is measured in millimeters of mercury (mmHg); the first number represents the maximum pressure exerted in the blood vessels when the heart contracts (systolic blood pressure), and the second number represents the pressure between contractions when the heart is at rest (diastolic blood pressure). Hypotension is diagnosed if an individual's blood pressure falls below 90/60 mmHg (or 90/60). Hypotension may also be diagnosed if an individual has a sudden large drop in blood pressure of more than 30 mmHg or more from their baseline, or more than 20 mmHg systolic or 10 mmHg diastolic blood pressure. In such cases, the blood pressure may remain higher than 90/60 mmHg, but the sudden drop may cause symptoms. Orthostatic hypotension (also called postural hypotension) is when a sudden decrease in blood pressure occurs as an individual makes a sudden change in body position, usually from a lying to an upright position.

Hypotension can be caused by a number of conditions, including dehydration or electrolyte loss due to physical exertion, diarrhea, or vomiting; vasovagal syncope (blood vessels' response to stimulation of the vagus nerve); anaphylaxis (life-threatening allergic response); excessive dieting; pregnancy; trauma; shock; stress; allergic reactions; anxiety; depression; alcohol toxicity; or from certain drugs, such as those used to treat high blood pressure (hypertension), drugs that cause a decrease in fluid volume in the body (hypovolemia), anesthesia, calcium channel blockers, diuretics, antiarrhythmics, vasodilators, and drugs used to treat Parkinson's disease. Hypovolemic shock should be considered in situations where significant blood or fluid loss has occurred and/or may be continuing, including hemorrhage following trauma, diuresis secondary to hyperglycemia, or polyuria due to diabetes insipidus. Failure of cardiac contractility (cardiogenic shock) may occur as a manifestation of longstanding congestive heart failure or secondary to acute coronary ischemia. Chronic orthostatic hypotension may be caused by an underlying disease condition such as diabetes, Addison's disease, build-up of fatty deposits on the arteries (atherosclerosis), Shy-Drager syndrome, cardiovascular disease, alcoholism, and nutritional diseases.

While hypotension affects men and women equally, and can occur in individuals of any age, the incidence of hypotension and orthostatic hypotension increases with age. Approximately 10-20% of elderly people have postural hypotension. Hypotension that occurs after meals (postprandial hypotension) occurs in up to 33% of elderly people.

Diagnosis

History: Individuals may report lightheadedness; dizziness; fainting (syncope); unsteadiness; blurred vision; fatigue; recent illness, accident, or trauma; nausea; or loss of consciousness. Individuals should be asked what their normal blood pressure reading is.

Physical exam: Frequent monitoring of vital signs (blood pressure, pulse, rate of breathing, temperature) will be necessary. Blood pressure is measured with an instrument called a sphygmomanometer. Orthostatic hypotension is evaluated by measuring the individual's blood pressure and pulse rate while he or she is reclining and again after the individual swiftly moves to a standing position. Because the hypotensive response may be delayed, prolonged standing or a tilt test may be required to detect a delayed hypotensive response. In general, blood pressure that drops below 90/60 mmHg results in a diagnosis of hypotension. Other physical exam findings may include an abnormally low pulse rate and signs of dehydration in the mucous membranes.

Tests: Diagnostic tests that may be performed include blood tests (CBC to detect electrolyte imbalances, blood cultures), an electrocardiogram (EKG), urinalysis, and x-rays of the abdomen and chest.

Treatment

Chronic hypotension that is not caused by an underlying disease can often be treated with diet and lifestyle changes. This may include a diet higher in salt, and drinking plenty of fluids (particularly while exercising, during hot weather, or when sick with a viral illness), getting regular exercise to promote blood flow, stretching prior to moving from a reclining to a standing position, drinking caffeinated beverages, eating smaller, more frequent meals (in cases of postprandial hypotension), and avoiding prolonged exposure to hot water. If these measures do not alleviate the condition, medications such as steroids that promote fluid retention, or drugs that cause constricting of the blood vessels may be prescribed.

Prognosis

The prognosis for individuals with hypotension depends on the underlying cause of the condition. Chronic low blood pressure is usually not serious. However, hypotension may be due to more serious underlying conditions such as Shy-Drager syndrome or certain cancers, for which the prognosis is often less optimistic. Hypotension that occurs when an individual experiences shock (a condition in which the cardiovascular system is unable to provide adequate blood circulation to the body) is life-threatening.

Differential Diagnosis

The most common symptoms of hypotension (dizziness and lightheadedness) can be caused by any one of a very large number of other conditions. Orthostatic hypotension can be associated with a number of serious underlying disorders, including Addison's disease, atherosclerosis, diabetes, and certain neurological disorders such as Shy-Drager syndrome.

Specialists

- Cardiologist
- Internist

Work Restrictions / Accommodations

Individuals susceptible to hypotension should avoid lengthy exposure to heat, long periods of physical exertion, and heavy lifting. Individuals with orthostatic hypotension should have the opportunity to take short walking breaks throughout the day.

Comorbid Conditions

Increased age, obesity, pregnancy, diabetes, and Shy-Drager syndrome may prolong the duration of symptoms.

Complications

The most common complications of hypotension are lightheadedness and dizziness; both can result in falls and/or injury. Extremely low blood pressure can result in shock.

Factors Influencing Duration

The length of the disability depends on the cause of the hypotension. Hypotension can often be controlled with diet and exercise. If the hypotension is due to a medication the individual is taking, switching to an alternative medication may alleviate the problem. The disability may be more lengthy and/or severe if the individual suffers from a chronic underlying disease that causes the hypotension (Shy-Drager syndrome).

Length of Disability

Duration in Days

Job Classification	Minimum	Optimum	Maximum
Any work	1	3	7

Failure to Recover

If an individual fails to recover within the maximum duration expectancy period, the reader may wish to reference the following questions to assist in better understanding the specifics of an individual's medical case.

Regarding diagnosis:

- Is individual's blood pressure under 90/60?
- What is individual's normal blood pressure?
- Does individual have orthostatic hypotension?
- Is individual dehydrated?
- Does individual have vasovagal syncope? Anaphylaxis? Excessive dieting? Pregnancy? Trauma or shock? Stress, anxiety, or depression;? Alcohol or drug toxicity?
- Has individual had significant blood or fluid loss? Diuresis secondary to hyperglycemia, or polyuria due to diabetes?
- Does individual have longstanding congestive heart failure or acute coronary ischemia?
- Does individual have Addison's disease, atherosclerosis, Shy-Drager syndrome, alcoholism, or nutritional diseases?
- Does individual report lightheadedness, dizziness, syncope, unsteadiness, blurred vision, fatigue, recent illness, accident, or trauma, nausea, or loss of consciousness?
- Has individual had blood tests, urinalysis, ECG, and x-rays of the abdomen and chest?
- Have conditions with similar symptoms been ruled out?

Regarding treatment:

- Has individual made diet and lifestyle changes including a diet higher in salt, drinking plenty of fluids, getting regular exercise to promote blood flow, stretching prior to moving from a reclining to a standing position, drinking caffeinated beverages, eating smaller, more frequent meals and avoiding prolonged exposure to hot water?
- Was it necessary to use medications such as steroids to promote fluid retention, or drugs that cause constriction of the blood vessels?

Regarding prognosis:

- What is the underlying cause for individual's hypotension?
- Does individual have any conditions that may affect ability to recover?
- Does individual have any complications such as falls, injury, or shock?

References

"Blood Pressure, Low." General Health Encyclopedia. HealthCentral.com 01 Jan 2000 01 Jan 2001 <http://www.healthcentral.com/mhc/top/003083.cfm>.

Orthostatic Hypotension. National Institute of Neurological Diseases and Stroke. 27 Jun 2000. 01 Jan 2001 <http://www.ninds.nih.gov/health_and_medical/disorders/orthosta_doc.htm>.

Hypothyroidism

Other names / synonyms: Myxedema, Thyroid Insufficiency, Underactive Thyroid Gland

243, 244, 244.0, 244.1, 244.2, 244.3, 244.8, 244.9

Definition

Hypothyroidism is the underproduction of hormones by a gland in the neck called the thyroid gland. The thyroid gland is located in the front of the neck, near the "Adam's apple." Its function is to produce hormones (thyroid hormones) that are responsible for regulating the body's metabolism. When the thyroid doesn't produce sufficient levels of thyroid hormones, many body systems are affected. The body essentially slows down.

There are several causes of hypothyroidism. This condition can result when the thyroid gland itself becomes damaged or diseased (e.g., Hashimoto's thyroiditis), after surgical removal of the thyroid, or after treatment of an overactive thyroid (hyperthyroidism). Hypothyroidism can also result when another hormone-producing gland (the pituitary gland) or a part of the brain (hypothalamus) fails to stimulate the activity of the thyroid. Sometimes, hypothyroidism is due to a lack of iodine in the diet, although this has become increasingly rare with the availability of iodine-supplemented salt (iodized salt).

Hypothyroidism is the most common type of thyroid disorder, far more common than overactive thyroid (hyperthyroidism). In general, it affects 5-10 per 1000 people. It affects women 5-10 times more often than men. It can occur at any age, but typically strikes those over the age of 40. Older individuals (over 65 years of age) are at an even greater risk, with the incidence in this age group increasing to 6-10% of women and 2-3% of men. There is no known genetic predisposition to hypothyroidism.

Diagnosis

History: Individuals may complain of fatigue and sluggishness despite increased sleep time, intolerance to cold, impaired memory and concentration, weight gain, hoarseness, facial swelling (edema), depression, and constipation. Women may report heavier than normal menstrual flow. In mild cases, symptoms may not be noticed.

Physical exam: The exam may reveal swelling of the legs and face (particularly the area around the eyes) due to fluid accumulation (edema). The skin may be coarse and dry, and may feel cool to the touch. The body temperature may be low. Hair may be unusually dry or thin. Reflexes may be sluggish. The thyroid gland may or may not feel enlarged. The heart rate may be low (bradycardia).

Tests: A high blood level of thyroid stimulating hormone (TSH) and a low level of thyroid hormone indicates hypothyroidism. Blood tests may also show associated abnormalities of liver or kidney function, as well as elevated cholesterol levels.

Treatment

Hypothyroidism is treated with thyroid hormone replacement medication. Routine monitoring of thyroid hormone levels is necessary, and adjustments to the medication dose may be required periodically. Because the cause of thyroid failure is likely to be progressive and permanent, hormone replacement medications are usually taken for life.

In cases where hypothyroidism is caused by another disease, treatment of that disease may lessen or eliminate the symptoms of hypothyroidism.

Prognosis

With treatment, the prognosis is excellent. Hypothyroidism is readily cured with hormone replacement therapy, and there are usually no long-term adverse effects. But hypothyroidism can recur if individuals stop hormone replacement therapy without medical supervision. If hypothyroidism is not treated, it can progress to coma and possible death.

Differential Diagnosis

Several other conditions share symptoms and/or signs with hypothyroidism including chronic kidney failure (nephrotic syndrome), chronic nephritis, neurasthenia, depression, euthyroid sick syndrome, congestive heart failure, primary amyloidosis, and dementia from other causes.

Specialists

- Endocrinologist
- General Surgeon
- Primary Care Provider

Work Restrictions / Accommodations

Individuals with mild hypothyroidism would not need work restrictions or accommodations. Accommodations depend on the type and severity of symptoms as well as the individual's job requirements. Working outdoors in cold weather may be unbearable, requiring reassignment to an indoor position. Fatigue may make strenuous work difficult or impossible, making transfer to a more sedentary position necessary. But, these symptoms, if due to hypothyroidism, should disappear within 3 months of normalization of thyroid blood tests.

Comorbid Conditions

Individuals with a compromised immune system, a current infection, or pre-existing heart condition are more likely to have severe symptoms and complications.

Complications

Individuals with hypothyroidism are at a greater risk for high cholesterol (hypercholesterolemia), hardening of the arteries (arteriosclerosis), and subsequent heart disease. Medications characterized as depressants (such as certain painkillers, general anesthesia, opiates, etc.) and alcoholic beverages may have an unusually pronounced effect. Emotional depression is commonly seen. Fifteen percent of individuals who seek therapy for depression have undiagnosed hypothyroidism. Some individuals develop paranoia. Increased susceptibility to infections, extreme dilation of the colon (megacolon), and infertility can also result.

Factors Influencing Duration

Factors include the severity of symptoms, presence of complications, and the individual's response to treatment.

Length of Disability

Most individuals will respond well to treatment. Symptoms can recur as the underlying disease progresses. Untreated cases can be fatal.

Duration in Days

Job Classification	Minimum	Optimum	Maximum
Sedentary work	0	14	28
Light work	0	14	28
Medium work	0	21	42
Heavy work	0	28	56
Very Heavy work	0	28	56

Duration Trend from Normative Data*

Cases	Mean	Min	Max	No Lost Time	Over 6 Months
469	56	0	643	0.65%	1.94%

Percentile:	5th	25th	Median	75th	95th
Days:	11	20	36	70	147

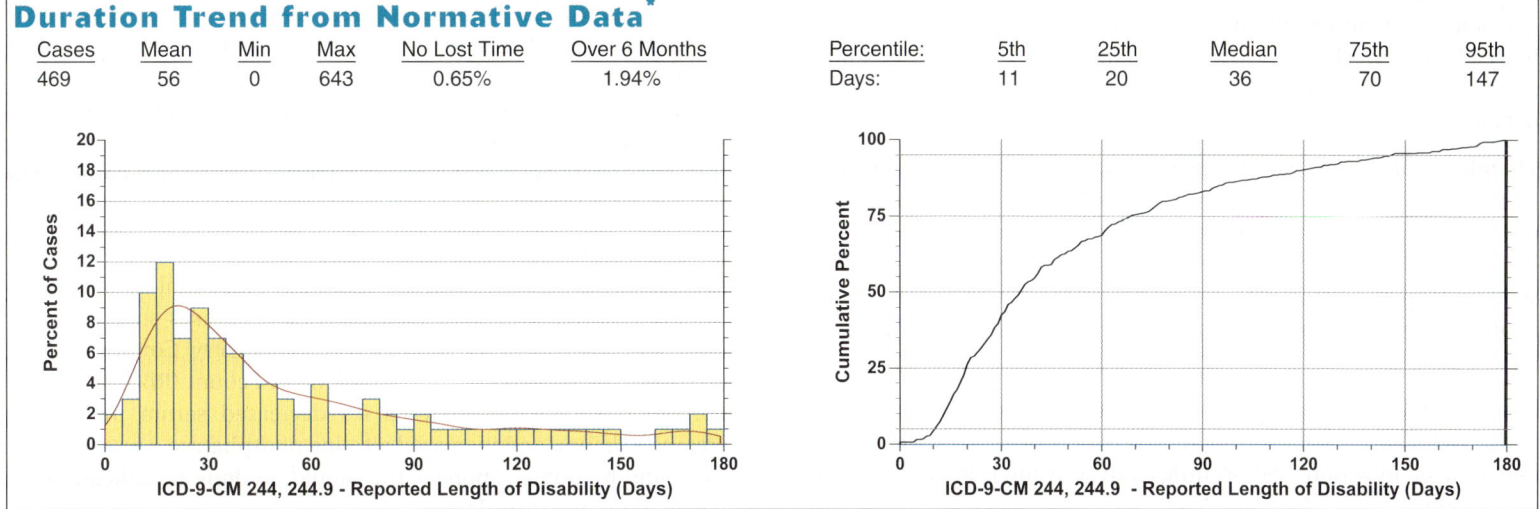

ICD-9-CM 244, 244.9 - Reported Length of Disability (Days)

* Differences may exist between the expected duration tables and the normative graphs. Duration tables provide expected recovery periods based on the type of work performed by the individual. The normative graphs reflect the actual observed experience of many individuals across the spectrum of physical conditions, in a variety of industries, and with varying levels of case management.

Failure to Recover

If an individual fails to recover within the maximum duration expectancy period, the reader may wish to reference the following questions to assist in better understanding the specifics of an individual's medical case.

Regarding diagnosis:

- Does the individual complain of fatigue and sluggishness despite increased sleep time? Does the individual have an intolerance to cold, impaired memory or concentration?
- Does the individual report weight gain, hoarseness, facial edema, depression, and constipation?
- If female, does the individual report heavier than normal menstrual flow?
- On physical exam does the individual have edema of the legs and face (particularly the area around the eyes)?
- Is skin coarse and dry, and cool to the touch? Is the body temperature low?
- Is the individual's hair unusually dry or thin? Are the reflexes sluggish?
- Is the thyroid gland palpable? Does the individual have bradycardia?
- Has the individual had complete blood thyroid testing done?
- Were liver and kidney functions tests done? Blood cholesterol?
- Have conditions with similar symptoms been ruled out?

Regarding treatment:

- Is the individual being treated with thyroid hormone replacement medication?
- Does the individual see their physician regularly to monitor the condition?
- If there is an underlying condition, is it being treated?

Hypothyroidism 1181

Regarding prognosis:

- Does the individual have any conditions that may affect their ability to recover?

- Does the individual have any complications such as hypercholesterolemia, arteriosclerosis, and subsequent heart disease? Does the individual have an unusually pronounced effect form depressant medications and alcoholic beverages? Does the individual have emotional depression or paranoia? Does the individual have increased susceptibility to infections, megacolon or infertility?

References

Hypothyroidism. American Thyroid Association. 1996. 10 Nov 2000 <http://www.thyroid.org/patient/brochur5.htm>.

Majeroni, Barbara. "Adult Hypothyroidism." Griffith's 5-minute Clinical Consult. Dambro, Mark, ed. Philadelphia: Lippincott, Williams & Wilkins, 2000. 554-555.

Hypovitaminosis

Other names / synonyms: Single Vitamin Deficiency, Vitamin Deficiency

269.2

Definition

Hypovitaminosis refers to a range of health problems caused by vitamin deficiencies or necessary vitamins being unavailable for the normal body chemistry. The term hypovitaminosis can refer to a condition when a single vitamin is lacking or when there are multiple vitamin deficiencies.

Vitamin deficiencies can be caused by the inadequate intake of vitamins. This could occur as a result of poverty, fad diets, alcoholism, or the nausea and vomiting in pregnancy. Psychiatric disorders can result in malnutrition and vitamin deficiencies. Depression, schizophrenia, senility, Alzheimer's disease, and eating disorders such as bulimia and anorexia nervosa can all result in malnutrition.

The second cause of dietary vitamin deficiencies is when the actual vitamin intake is adequate but the vitamins are not absorbed by the body. This can be seen in different genetic diseases, cancer (malignancies), or infections. Some drugs can also interfere with vitamin absorption.

The third cause of vitamin deficiency occurs when the body develops an increased need for vitamins. This is normal during pregnancy and breast feeding (lactation). Increased physical activity, growth spurts, taking certain medications, and infections can increase the body's vitamin requirements.

There are no accurate and reliable sources of the extent of vitamin deficiency worldwide. Individuals in the poorer Third World countries and those living at the poverty level would be expected to experience a more frequent occurrence of vitamin deficiencies caused by malnutrition and improper diets. Any deaths that occur would be due to secondary diseases resulting from the vitamin deficiency.

Diagnosis

History: The diagnosis of a single, specific vitamin deficiency or multiple deficiencies is determined by obtaining information on the individual's dietary habits. Questions about the quantity of food and the types of foods in the diet should be asked. When the diet seems adequate, the individual may have a history of a disease that prevents the vitamins from being absorbed or a disease or condition that might increase the person's vitamin requirements.

Physical exam: Generally, in cases of malnutrition and vitamin deficiency, it is important to note whether the individual appears acutely or chronically ill. Some vitamin deficiencies take months or years to show their effects on the body, but the anemias that are linked to vitamin deficiencies take only weeks to evolve. The general appearance of the skin, hair, and mucous membranes like the mouth are noted. Wounds or burns and the healing status should be noted. The mental state should also be noted. Psychiatric disorders are common in B vitamin deficiencies.

Tests: Blood tests are almost always diagnostic for a particular vitamin deficiency. If the blood level of the vitamin itself cannot be measured, there are tests that will show characteristic responses such as blood clotting and changes in the red blood cell chemistry. Complete blood count (CBC), whole blood count, red blood cell count (RBC) should be done. Blood should be analyzed for decreased serum phosphate, decreased calcium, and increased alkaline phosphatase. Liver function tests should be done. A bone X-ray should be done to indicate bone malformations and disorders.

Treatment

Depending on the particular vitamin and the severity of the deficiency, the replacement of the vitamins is given by mouth, injections, intravenously, or by a combination of methods. The treatment of any secondary problems arising from the vitamin deficiency and lifestyle conditions that may have led to the malnutrition and deficiencies should be resolved.

Prognosis

The outcome is good provided that therapy is instituted to prevent recurrence of the problems of hypovitaminosis. Most forms of hypovitaminosis are easily and successfully treated with vitamin therapy.

Differential Diagnosis

The differential diagnoses that might be considered would depend on the particular vitamin deficiency. Cardiovascular diseases may present with similar signs and symptoms. Altered mental states may also show signs and symptoms that resemble some vitamin deficiencies.

Specialists

- Dietary Advisor
- Gastroenterologist
- Hematologist
- Internist
- Nephrologist
- Obstetrician
- Physical Therapist
- Psychologist
- Rheumatologist

Work Restrictions / Accommodations

There should be no special need for restrictions or accommodations with a successful treatment of vitamin deficiencies. Secondary diseases and illnesses that caused any vitamin deficiency may have different outcomes.

Comorbid Conditions

Pre-existing liver disease, kidney disease, stomach and intestinal disorders may worsen the effects of vitamin deficiency and may add to the likelihood of vitamin deficiency occurring.

Complications

Some effects of vitamin deficiencies cannot be reversed by adding the vitamin to the diet, especially if damage to nonregenerative tissue (e.g., cornea of the eye, nerve tissue, calcified bone) has occurred.

Factors Influencing Duration

If a vitamin deficiency is secondary to another disease, the length of disability will be based on the underlying condition. Age, physical condition, health status, and mental stature may influence the ability of the individual to undergo treatment and therapy.

Length of Disability

See specific vitamin deficiency to determine disability duration.

Failure to Recover

If an individual fails to recover within the maximum duration expectancy period, the reader may wish to reference the following questions to assist in better understanding the specifics of an individual's medical case.

Regarding diagnosis:

- Does the individual have a single or multiple vitamin deficiency?
- Does the individual have an inadequate intake of vitamins secondary to poverty, fad diets, alcoholism, or the nausea and vomiting in pregnancy? Psychiatric disorder? Senility? Alzheimer's disease?
- Does the individual have eating disorders such as bulimia or anorexia nervosa?
- Is the individual not able to absorb vitamins?
- Does the individual have an increased need for vitamins such as pregnancy and lactation, increased physical activity, growth spurts, taking certain medications, or infections?
- Does the individual appear acutely or chronically ill?
- Is the individual's general appearance of the skin, hair and mucous membranes normal?
- Does the individual have slow healing wounds?
- Is the individual's mental status normal or abnormal?
- Has the individual had blood level's for vitamins or tests to show the characteristic response to the deficiency? Did the individual have bone x-ray's done?
- Have conditions with similar symptoms been ruled out?

Regarding treatment:

- Is the individual being treated with oral, injectable or intravenous vitamin replacement?
- Has the individual addressed any correctable lifestyle conditions?
- Are any secondary conditions being treated?

Regarding prognosis:

- Is the individual's employer able to accommodate any necessary restrictions?
- Does the individual have any conditions that may affect ability to recover?
- Does the individual have any complications such as damage to nonregenerative tissue (e.g., cornea of the eye, nerve tissue, calcified bone)?

References

Vitamin B12 Deficiency. Med Help International. 1996. 14 Oct 2000 <http://www.medhelp.org/glossary/new/gls_4411.htm>.

Vitamins: B1, B12, E, C, D, K. Vitamins Plus. 01 Oct 2000. 15 Oct 2000. <http://www.vitaminsplus.com/library/vitamins/>.

Mahan, Kathleen L., and Sylvia Escott-Stump, eds. Krause's Food, Nutrition, and Diet Therapy, 10th ed. Philadelphia: W.B. Saunders Company, 2000.

Waldrop, Ron, MD. "Anorexia Nervosa." eMedicine.com 01 Oct 2000. 15 Oct 2000 <http://www.emedicine.com/emerg/topic34.htm>.

Hypovolemic Shock
785.59, 958.4

Definition

Shock may be defined as the state in which a profound and widespread reduction in the effective delivery of oxygen due to diminished blood volume leads first to reversible and then, if prolonged, to irreversible injury.

Hypovolemic shock is most often due to bleeding. The bleeding may be internal or external, acute or chronic. Acute external bleeding is commonly due to pre-existing but unrecognized conditions such as peptic ulcer disease or out-pouching of the large intestine (diverticula). Chronic internal bleeding can be caused by tumors (benign or malignant) of the gastrointestinal tract (GI) and rare diseases such as hereditary hemorrhage telangiectasia (Olser-Rendu-Weber disease) characterized by dilated, thin blood vessels in the skin and mucus membranes.

Hypovolemic shock is less often caused by a low blood volume due to loss of the non-red blood cell portion of blood called plasma. This may be the consequence of loss of body fluids from vomiting, diarrhea, burns, or excessive urination from water pills (diuretics). It may occasionally result from an unusual disorder known as diabetic insipidus. A reduction of plasma volume can also occur with inadequate fluid intake.

Diagnosis

History: The individual often reports visible blood loss due to an injury or vomiting of blood. However, when blood loss is internal, it may not be apparent. Black stool represents earlier bleeding in the GI tract. An individual may have a bruise over an injured site. Other individuals without blood loss may note diarrhea, vomiting, or thirst and report taking a diuretic for an unrelated condition.

Symptoms common to all causes of hypovolemic shock include a taste of sweetness, weakness, light-headedness, dizziness, and even loss of consciousness (syncope).

Physical exam: Individuals with hypovolemic shock have a blood pressure of 80/60 mm Hg or less and a heart rate of 100 beats per minute or more. Individuals with high blood pressure, however, may have a blood pressure above 80/60 when in hypovolemic shock. The skin is usually pale and cool and may display a bluish discoloration. The individual may be alert, confused, drowsy, or unconscious. Bruising and other evidence of trauma may be present.

Manifestation of the underlying disease process may also exist. For example, an individual with a ruptured ectopic pregnancy will have tenderness of the abdomen while an individual with hereditary hemorrhagic telangiectasia may have small, thin clusters of blood vessels in the skin or mouth.

Tests: The blood count (hematocrit) will be low when bleeding is the cause of hypovolemic shock and normal or high when fluid loss or inadequate fluid intake are the causative factors. Blood electrolytes (sodium, potassium, chlorides, bicarbonates) may also be abnormal when a fluid imbalance is present. Blood tests that assess kidney function (the ratio of urea nitrogen to creatinine) are often abnormal when other blood or fluid loss is the cause of hypovolemic shock. The ratio is elevated with the former and normal or decreased with the latter.

Measurement of the filling pressure (Wedge pressure) of the pumping chamber on the left side of the heart is often made to differentiate among the several causes of shock. Individuals with hypovolemic shock usually have a low wedge pressure whereas those with cardiogenic shock have elevated values.

Treatment

Hypovolemic shock is treated with intravenous (IV) fluids. Blood loss is replaced by blood. Nonblood fluid loss that accompanies vomiting and/or diarrhea or diuretic use is treated with nonblood volume expanders such as dextran and IV fluids. Individuals with hypovolemic shock due to fluid loss often have disturbances of the blood electrolytes (sodium, potassium, chlorides, and bicarbonates) that must be corrected.

When shock truly exists, hypovolemic shock must be differentiated from other causes of shock such as septic, neurogenic, anaphylactic, and cardiogenic shock. The differentiating diagnosis is made more difficult when two possible causes of shock coincide. For example, if an individual who chronically has a low blood count due to iron deficiency anemia develops a urinary tract infection with bacteria in the bloodstream (sepsis), the low blood count may lead to the (mis)diagnosis of hypovolemic shock when septic shock is the cause. Careful observation of the history, physical exam, and tests should permit identification of the correct cause(s) in most individuals.

Prognosis

Hypovolemic shock recognized early and treated promptly is associated with a good outcome. However, advanced stages of hypovolemic shock with a fluid loss of more than 25% of total body fluid is considered irreversible shock and usually associated with a poor outcome or death.

Differential Diagnosis

Sometimes shock may appear to exist when it does not. For example, the individual with "low" blood pressure but without other signs of shock may not be in shock. Shock requires evidence that a low blood pressure is causing reduced oxygen delivery to various organs of the body to warrant use of the term shock.

An individual with no measurable blood pressure may not be in shock. This occurs when a condition such as a dissecting aneurysm or arteriosclerosis blocks the artery to one or both arms resulting in no obtainable blood pressure or pulse with no evidence of shock.

Specialists

- Critical Care Specialist
- Emergency Medicine
- Traumatologist

Work Restrictions / Accommodations

An individual who fully recovers from hypovolemic shock with no complication of failure of a major organ may not require any work restrictions or accommodations. However, those individuals who sustain failure of an organ will need vocational and/or avocational restrictions and accommodations.

Comorbid Conditions

Age, arteriosclerosis, hypertension, stroke, myocardial infarction kidney disease, and peripheral vascular diseases are pre-existing conditions that can affect an individuals' ability to recover from hypovolemic shock.

Complications

Hypovolemic shock may be complicated by impaired function of any organ since all organs depend on an adequate blood supply and oxygen delivery for their functions. Therefore, an individual with hypovolemic shock may sustain a stroke, heart attack, liver failure, kidney failure, or gangrene of an extremity.

Factors Influencing Duration

The underlying cause of hypovolemic shock may affect disability. For example, an individual with a ruptured ectopic pregnancy may have no significant long-term disability because she is young and has a "one-time" acute illness. On the other hand, an older individual with hypovolemic shock due to a bleeding peptic ulcer may have more disability because of age and/or the need for medications, diet, or surgery to prevent recurrence.

Length of Disability

Duration depends on the underlying cause, severity of symptoms, response to treatment, and existence of complications. Disability may be permanent.

Duration in Days

Job Classification	Minimum	Optimum	Maximum
Sedentary work	7	14	28
Light work	7	14	28
Medium work	7	14	35
Heavy work	7	21	42
Very Heavy work	7	21	42

Failure to Recover

If an individual fails to recover within the maximum duration expectancy period, the reader may wish to reference the following questions to assist in better understanding the specifics of an individual's medical case.

Regarding diagnosis:

- Does the individual have any un-recognized bleeding such as a peptic ulcer or diverticula?
- Does the individual have blood loss secondary to a bleeding disorder?
- Has the individual lost body fluids from vomiting, diarrhea, burns or diuretic use?
- Does the individual have diabetes insipidus?
- Has the individual had inadequate fluid intake?
- Has the individual had an injury? Is there a bruise present?
- Does the individual have a taste of sweetness in the mouth?
- Do they report weakness, light-headedness, dizziness or syncope?
- On exam was their blood pressure 80/60 or less? Pulse rate 100 or more?
- Does the individual have hypertension?
- Is the skin pale, cool and cyanotic?
- Is the mental status altered? Is there any evidence of trauma?
- Have a hematocrit and electrolytes been done? Kidney function tests?
- Was the Wedge pressure measured?
- Have conditions with similar symptoms been ruled out?

Regarding treatment:

- Has the individual had IV fluid replacement - either blood or dextran and IV fluids?
- Have any electrolyte imbalances been corrected?

Regarding prognosis:

- Is the individual's employer able to accommodate any necessary restrictions?
- Does the individual have any conditions that may affect their ability to recover?
- Has the individual had any complications such as a stroke, heart attack, liver failure, kidney failure, or gangrene of an extremity?

References

Clochesy, John M., et al. Critical Care Nursing, 2nd ed. Philadelphia: W.B. Saunders Company, 1996.

Kolecki, Paul, and Carl Menckhoff, MD. "Hypovolemic Shock." eMedicine.com 30 Jan 2001. 22 Feb 2001 <http://www.emedicine.com/emerg/topic532.htm>.

Hysterectomy

Other names / synonyms: Excision of the Uterus, Hysterotomy with Bilateral Salpingo-Oophorectomy of the Uterus, Partial Hysterectomy, TAH-BSO, Total Abdominal Hysterectomy

68.3, 68.4, 68.5, 68.6, 68.7, 68.9

Definition

Hysterectomy is the surgical removal of the uterus. This procedure ends menstruation and the individual's ability to become pregnant.

A rarely performed procedure, called the partial hysterectomy, removes the upper part of the uterus but not the cervix. A total hysterectomy removes the entire uterus and cervix. The radical hysterectomy removes the uterus, cervix, upper part of the vagina, plus some surrounding tissue and lymph nodes. Radical hysterectomy is also performed for cancer of the cervix. A total hysterectomy with bilateral salpingo-oophorectomy involves removal of the uterus, cervix, fallopian tubes, and ovaries. Removal of the ovaries will initiate menopause.

Since 1980, this procedure has been the most common major operation performed on women. Approximately 670 per 100,000 women undergo an hysterectomy every year in the US. The procedure is less common in Europe, where only about 260 per 100,000 women undergo hysterectomy.

Reason for Procedure

Hysterectomy is indicated for the following emergency or urgent situations: cancer of the vagina, cervix, uterus, fallopian tubes, or ovaries; severe, uncontrollable bleeding; severe, uncontrollable infection; and procedures requiring the removal of the uterus in order to treat life-threatening problems affecting other organs.

Only after other treatments have been tried and failed can a hysterectomy be indicated in the following non-emergency situations: recurrent attacks of pelvic infection (i.e., bacterial infection that attacks the fallopian tubes and ovaries); widespread build-up of extra tissue that normally lines the uterus (endometriosis); large or excessive fibroid tumors in the muscle tissue of the uterus; loss of pelvic muscle support that is severe enough to interfere with bowel or bladder function (uterine prolapse); and vaginal and/or uterine bleeding extreme enough to cause anemia, that is uncontrolled by medication and hormones.

Description

Hysterectomy, a major surgical procedure, usually always requires hospitalization. Prior to surgery, a series of tests are performed including: a complete blood count, urinalysis, chest x-ray, and electrocardiogram (for individuals over the age of 35 years).

Hysterectomy is performed in the operating room under general anesthesia. Hysterectomies can be performed through an abdominal incision or through an incision inside the vagina. A vaginal incision is usually performed on individuals who also require bladder or vaginal repair. Both types of surgery take between 1-3 hours to perform. Occasionally a laparoscopically assisted vaginal hysterectomy (LAVH) is performed. This is a combined procedure requiring a small abdominal incision near the navel (through which an optical instrument is inserted) and a vaginal wall incision. After removal of the uterus and other structures (ovaries, tubes), the incision is closed with sutures or staples. Recovery time from these procedures is approximately 4-6 weeks.

Prognosis

Prognosis following an uncomplicated hysterectomy is good. Symptoms are usually relieved by the procedure, and a full return to normal activities can be expected.

If the hysterectomy was performed for cancer of the cervix or uterus, the prognosis depends upon the extent and severity of the cancer. Low grade cancer has a generally good prognosis, while high grade cancer with extensive spread has a poor prognosis.

If the individual has not previously undergone menopause, she is likely to experience symptoms associated with menopause. Depression often accompanies hysterectomy and may be a major factor in recovery. Some women feel they are less feminine, requiring psychological counseling or the help of a support group.

Specialists

- General Surgeon
- Gynecologist

Work Restrictions / Accommodations

Heavy lifting, prolonged standing, and strenuous physical activity will be restricted for a few weeks.

Comorbid Conditions

Conditions that could impact ability to recover and further lengthen disability include high blood pressure, obesity, heart conditions, and metastatic cancer.

Procedure Complications

Complications may include infection (e.g., bladder, kidney, incision), or bleeding. Urinary problems are possible after the procedure, such as varying degrees of incontinence. Injury to the bowels can occur, and this would require an operation to repair the injury. Another complication is abnormal blood clotting in the legs or pelvic veins (thrombophlebitis).

Factors Influencing Duration

Length of disability may be influenced by the individual's age, the type of hysterectomy (partial, total, radical), the approach (abdominal, vaginal, laparoscopic), or the presence of complications.

Length of Disability

Laparoscopic or vaginal.

Job Classification	Duration in Days		
	Minimum	Optimum	Maximum
Sedentary work	21	28	42
Light work	21	28	42
Medium work	28	42	56
Heavy work	28	56	70
Very Heavy work	28	70	84

Abdominal.

Job Classification	Duration in Days		
	Minimum	Optimum	Maximum
Sedentary work	28	42	56
Light work	28	42	56
Medium work	42	56	70
Heavy work	42	70	84
Very Heavy work	42	84	98

Radical.

Job Classification	Duration in Days		
	Minimum	Optimum	Maximum
Sedentary work	42	49	56
Light work	56	63	70
Medium work	70	77	84
Heavy work	70	84	98
Very Heavy work	70	84	98

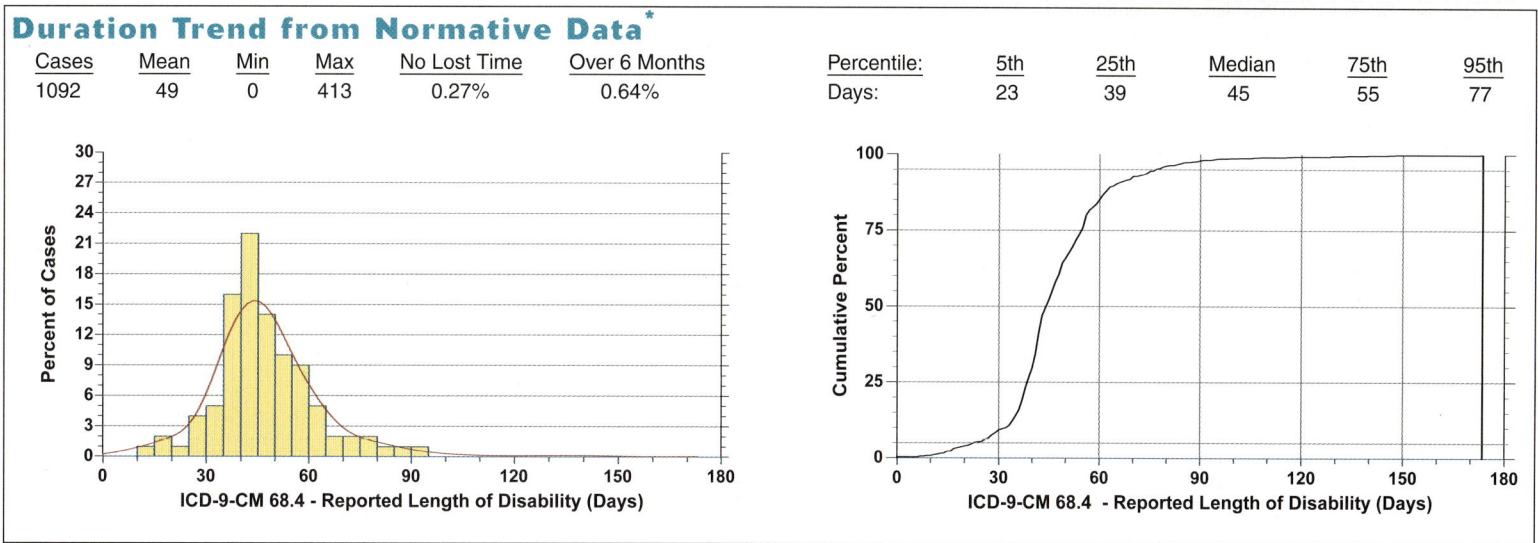

Duration Trend from Normative Data*

Cases	Mean	Min	Max	No Lost Time	Over 6 Months
1092	49	0	413	0.27%	0.64%

Percentile:	5th	25th	Median	75th	95th
Days:	23	39	45	55	77

ICD-9-CM 68.4 - Reported Length of Disability (Days)

* Differences may exist between the expected duration tables and the normative graphs. Duration tables provide expected recovery periods based on the type of work performed by the individual. The normative graphs reflect the actual observed experience of many individuals across the spectrum of physical conditions, in a variety of industries, and with varying levels of case management.

References

Hill, Edward, MD. "Gynecology." Current Surgical Diagnosis and Treatment. Way, Lawrence Norwalk: Appleton & Lange, 1991. 950-985.

Hysterectomy. drkoop.com. 1998. 25 Aug 2000 <http://www.drkoop.com/conditions/ency/article/002915.htm>.

Hysteria

Other names / synonyms: Conversion Disorder, Dissociative Disorder, Hysterical Reaction, Somatoform Disorder

300.1, 300.10

Definition

At one time, the term 'hysteria' was used to describe a situation in which, according to Freud, intense, unconscious memory is converted into a physical symptom such as paralysis or blindness. The hysterical symptoms were thought to result from a repressed painful memory, either a traumatic event or a psychological conflict, such as unwelcome sexual thoughts. Hysteria was not considered a psychosis because the individual's sense of reality was otherwise normal, without hallucinations or delusions.

Current diagnostic categories that include similar symptomatologies are those of conversion disorders or dissociative disorders. According to the DSM-IV-TR (Diagnostic and Statistical Manual of Mental Disorders, 4th Edition, Text Revision, published by the American Psychiatric Association), a conversion disorder is the presence of symptoms or deficits affecting voluntary motor or sensory function that suggest a neurological or other general medical condition. These symptoms or deficits are not intentionally produced, may cause clinically significant distress or impairment, and are not limited to pain or sexual dysfunction. Conversion disorder symptoms may include impaired coordination or balance, paralysis, difficulty swallowing, a sensation of a lump in the throat, double vision, blindness, deafness, loss of touch or pain sensitivity, or pseudoseizures. Dissociative disorders are described as a disruption in the usually integrated functions of consciousness, memory, identity, or perception which may be gradual, transient, or chronic. The individual may have episodes of inability to recall important personal information or recent events, find themselves suddenly and unexpectedly traveling away from home or work, have the perception of two or more distinct personality states, or have feelings of being detached from one's mental processes or body.

Somatization disorder and histrionic personality disorder are also psychiatric conditions in which psychological conflicts are transformed into physical symptoms. For more specific information, see Conversion Disorder.

References

Diagnostic and Statistical Manual of Mental Disorders, 4th ed. First, Michael B., ed. Washington, DC: American Psychiatric Association, 1994.

Idiopathic Thrombocytopenic Purpura

Other names / synonyms: Autoimmune Thrombocytopenic Purpura (Primary), Idiopathic Thrombocytopenia, Immune Thrombocytopenic Purpura, Primary Thrombocytopenia

286.9, 287.3

Definition

Idiopathic thrombocytopenic purpura (ITP) is a condition characterized by a low platelet count with no apparent underlying cause. This is in contrast to other occurrences of low platelet counts (thrombocytopenia), in which the deficiency can be attributed to an infection, disease, or drug.

Individuals with this condition have normal, functioning bone marrow, and no systemic illness. Nevertheless, the platelets are destroyed in the circulating blood by the body's own immune system (autoantibodies). Platelets play a vital role in forming blood clots and stopping bleeding. A reduction in the number of platelets causes a tendency to bleed, especially from the smaller blood vessels. The term "purpura" refers to the bruising and deposits of blood under the skin commonly seen in association with platelet deficiency.

There are two forms of idiopathic thrombocytopenic purpura (ITP). An acute form typically occurs in childhood. A chronic form, defined as lasting longer than 6 months, occurs in adults.

In the US, 66 adults per million develop the ITP each year. Most of these are between the ages of 20-50 years. The female to male ratio is 2.6 to one.

Diagnosis

History: Symptoms typically appear gradually. Individuals will report bruises on the skin, prolonged or heavy menstrual bleeding, nosebleeds, gum bleeding, gastrointestinal bleeding, or blood in their urine. Headache and dizziness may indicate a risk of brain hemorrhage. Often an individual has no symptoms and the condition is discovered unintentionally during a routine examination or while being checked for another medical condition.

Physical exam: The individual may present with small capillary hemorrhages (petechia) or larger bruises (ecchymoses) under the skin. Hemorrhagic blisters may be present in the mouth. The rest of the exam will be normal. An enlarged spleen is an unusual sign and, if present, points to another diagnosis.

Tests: A complete blood count (CBC) will show an abnormally low platelet count, but will otherwise be normal. A bone marrow aspiration and biopsy will reveal normal platelet production, in appearance and in number. Coagulation tests to check platelet function and to look for other clotting abnormalities include bleeding time, prothrombin time (PT), partial thromboplastin time (PTT), fibrinogen, platelet aggregation, and platelet antibody studies. Additional tests will be performed as needed to rule out other causes of thrombocytopenia, and may include liver function tests, and tests to identify infection such as HIV and Ehrlichiosis, and connective tissue disease, such as systemic lupus erythematosus.

Taking into account history, physical, CBC, and bone marrow findings, diagnosis of idiopathic thrombocytopenic purpura is made by excluding other possible causes of the low platelet count.

Treatment

Treatment depends on the platelet count and the presence of bleeding. Asymptomatic individuals need only observation and periodic monitoring of the platelet count. General caution, however, dictates that individuals with thrombocytopenia avoid invasive procedures or injury, if possible, and avoid any drug that may affect platelets, such as aspirin and other nonsteroidal anti-inflammatory drugs (NSAIDs). Treatment may be needed only when the individual has had a traumatic injury or is preparing for surgery.

Individuals with very low platelet counts or moderate counts plus bleeding should be treated with immunosuppressant glucocorticoid drugs until counts return to normal. At that time, the glucocorticoids should be gradually tapered off. Additional treatment cycles are often needed to maintain an adequate platelet count.

Individuals with severe bleeding are hospitalized and treated with intravenous glucocorticoids plus high-dose immune globulin (immune globulin increases platelet survival time). If the bleeding is life threatening, platelet transfusions are also given.

Surgical removal of the spleen (splenectomy) is beneficial for individuals who do not respond to steroid therapy or require unacceptably high doses to maintain adequate platelets. Although in ITP the spleen does not sequester platelets, it does produce the antibodies that attack the platelets. Removing the spleen removes the source of the destructive antibodies.

Prognosis

In adults, ITP is typically chronic. Only 5% of adults will have a spontaneous remission. Immunosuppressant glucocorticoid treatment usually reduces bleeding within 1 day and raises platelet counts within 1-3 weeks. Approximately 80% of individuals with ITP respond to this treatment, but most will relapse once the treatment has stopped and will require additional treatment cycles. Individuals who don't respond to glucocorticoid treatment or who require unacceptably high doses often will benefit from splenectomy. This surgical procedure brings about partial or complete remission in 80% of individuals.

Differential Diagnosis

Other conditions associated with low platelet counts include some viral infections, drug-induced thrombocytopenia, hypersplenism, myelodysplastic and lymphoproliferative disorders, pregnancy, systemic lupus erythematosus and other autoimmune and connective tissue diseases, thrombotic thrombocytopenic purpura, hemolytic-uremic syndrome (HUS), disseminated intravascular coagulation (DIC), posttransfusion reaction, aplastic anemia, and liver disease.

Specialists

- Emergency Medicine
- Hematologist
- Immunologist
- Rheumatologist
- Surgeon

Work Restrictions / Accommodations

Individuals who have significantly decreased platelet counts need a safe work environment, avoiding the risk of personal injury, which could trigger an acute bleed. Where indicated, protective gear, especially to the head, should be worn. Office work or sedentary work would probably be more appropriate than strenuous work involving heavy lifting or other physical exertion. The employer should be aware of the condition so that the appropriate level of care can be obtained quickly in the event of an on-the-job injury. Once the individual's platelet counts have returned to normal, no work restrictions should be needed. Time off will be needed if splenectomy or hospitalization is required.

Comorbid Conditions

Disability may be lengthened if other risk factors for bleeding are present, such as gastrointestinal bleeding, urologic disease, and high blood pressure. Approximately 10% of individuals with ITP have concurrent hemolytic anemia (Evan's syndrome). Pregnancy may limit the drugs available for safe treatment.

Complications

Complications from this disease include acute bleeding into any area of the body, including the brain (intracranial hemorrhage). In fact, intracranial hemorrhage is the main cause of death attributable to ITP, and occurs in 5% of individuals with the condition. Splenectomy carries the risk of infection.

Factors Influencing Duration

Length of disability may be influenced by severity of the disease, need for and response to treatment, whether splenectomy is performed, and presence of complications.

Length of Disability

Medical treatment.

Duration in Days

Job Classification	Minimum	Optimum	Maximum
Sedentary work	1	14	28
Light work	1	14	28
Medium work	7	21	42
Heavy work	14	28	56
Very Heavy work	14	28	56

Surgical treatment (splenectomy).

Duration in Days

Job Classification	Minimum	Optimum	Maximum
Sedentary work	14	21	28
Light work	14	21	28
Medium work	28	35	42
Heavy work	35	42	56
Very Heavy work	35	42	70

Failure to Recover

If an individual fails to recover within the maximum duration expectancy period, the reader may wish to reference the following questions to assist in better understanding the specifics of an individual's medical case.

Regarding diagnosis:

- Has an underlying cause of idiopathic thrombocytopenic purpura (ITP) been identified?
- Have conditions with similar symptoms been ruled out?
- Has individual experienced any complications related to the idiopathic thrombocytopenic purpura?
- Does individual have a coexisting condition that may impact recovery?
- If pregnant, are there drugs that the individual may safely use?

Regarding treatment:

- Are the individual's platelet counts periodically monitored?
- Is treatment currently being sought due to a traumatic injury or in preparation for surgery?
- If the bleeding was life threatening, were platelet transfusions also given?
- Has treatment sufficiently raised platelet count for this purpose? If not, what else can be done?
- Has the individual responded to immunosuppressant therapy?
- Are the doses required to maintain adequate platelet counts intolerable?

Regarding prognosis:

- If individual does not respond to glucocorticoid treatment or requires unacceptably high doses, is individual a candidate for a splenectomy?
- Is individual aware that he/she needs to avoid the risk of personal injury, which could trigger an acute bleed?
- Does the individual continue to participate in activities that are high risk for bodily injury, particularly to the head? If so, does the individual wear protective gear, such as a helmet?

References

Carey, Charles, Hans Lee, and Keith Woeltje. Washington Manual of Medical Therapeutics, 29th ed. Philadelphia: Lippincott-Raven, 1998.

Lee, Richard, et al. Wintrobe's Clinical Hematology, 10th ed. Baltimore: Lippincott Williams & Wilkins, Inc, 1999.

Impacted Tooth

Other names / synonyms: Embedded Teeth, Obstructed Tooth Eruption, Unemerged Tooth

520.6, 524, 524.3

Definition

Impacted tooth refers to a dental disorder that involves failure of a tooth to fully emerge through the gums. An impacted tooth remains embedded in soft gingival (gum) tissue or bone beyond its normal eruption time.

Because they are the last teeth to emerge, the most common teeth to become impacted are the third set of molars (the wisdom teeth), which normally emerge between 17 and 21 years of age. Impacted wisdom teeth are very common. They are often painless and cause no trouble; however, in some cases, the impacted tooth pushes on the next tooth and causes it to become misaligned, eventually causing the bite to become shifted.

The cause may be overcrowding, often because the jaw is too small to fit the third set of molars (the wisdom teeth). Consequently, teeth may become twisted, tilted, or displaced as they attempt to emerge, resulting in impacted teeth.

A partially emerged tooth can trap food, plaque, and other debris in the soft tissue around it, leading to inflammation and tenderness of the gums and unpleasant mouth odor (pericoronitis). For these reasons, surgical removal of the impacted wisdom tooth or teeth is usually recommended.

Some dentists advocate the removal of impacted third molars because of the increased incidence of cysts and tumors around impacted molars.

Impacted upper canine teeth are different. Since the upper canine teeth play a much more important role in biting and chewing than do wisdom teeth, upper canine teeth are not usually removed. They are, instead, trained into correct position via the use of orthodontic braces (orthodontic appliances).

Diagnosis

History: Symptomatic individuals with an impacted tooth may report pain and tenderness of the gums (gingiva), unpleasant taste when biting down on or near the area, visible gap where a tooth did not emerge, bad breath, redness and swelling of the gums around the impacted tooth, swollen lymph glands (occasionally), difficulty opening the mouth (occasionally), and prolonged headache or jaw ache.

Physical exam: Examination of the teeth by the dentist may show enlargement of the tissue where a tooth has not emerged or has emerged only partially. The impacted tooth may be pressing on adjacent teeth. The gums around the area may show signs of infection (such as redness, drainage, and tenderness). As gums swell over impacted wisdom teeth and then drain and tighten, the perception of the individual is that the tooth came in and then went back out again.

Tests: Dental x-rays confirm the presence of a tooth (or teeth) that has not emerged.

Treatment

The goal of treatment is to relieve irritation of the mouth caused by the impacted tooth. If the impacted tooth is not causing infection or inflammation, or is not affecting the alignment of the other teeth, no treatment may be necessary.

Over-the-counter pain medications (analgesics) may relieve discomfort. Warm salt water (one-half teaspoon of salt in one cup of warm water) or over-the-counter mouthwashes may be soothing to the gums.

Extraction (removal) of the tooth is the usual treatment for a symptomatic impacted tooth. This is often performed in the dentist's office with the individual under local anesthesia. If the tooth is deeply impacted or difficulty with extraction is expected, the dentist may refer the individual to an oral surgeon for tooth removal. Antibiotics may be required prior to tooth extraction if the area around the tooth is infected.

Prognosis

Impacted upper canine teeth are usually trained into correct position via the use of braces (orthodontic appliances). Treatment may effectively clear up the inflammation or infection of an impacted wisdom tooth. However, the tooth may require surgical removal (extraction) to prevent recurrence.

Impacted wisdom teeth that are causing symptoms are usually surgically removed (extracted). Symptoms are successfully resolved.

Differential Diagnosis

Differential diagnosis might include a chronically inflamed (ankylosed) tooth, or a tooth with failure of its eruption mechanism that has been mistaken for an impacted tooth. Also, a dental abscess may present with similar symptoms.

Specialists

- Dentist
- Oral Surgeon

Work Restrictions / Accommodations

Some additional time off may be required for complications, such as dry socket or infection.

Complementary and Alternative Therapies

Content is intended for awareness only. Treatments may or may not be effective. Scientific evidence may be lacking and some substances have potentially toxic effects. Dr. Presley Reed and the editors do not endorse the use of these therapies in the absence of consultation with a licensed medical professional.

Acupuncture - Individuals who received acupuncture reported longer pain-free duration times and experienced less pain intensity following surgical extractions of third molars.

Comorbid Conditions

Comorbid conditions that might influence the length of disability include medically compromising conditions, such as diabetes mellitus and human immunodeficiency virus (HIV infection). Also, individuals on medications that cause dry mouth are at higher risk for bacterial infections.

Complications

Complications of impacted wisdom teeth include recurrent infection of a partially buried tooth, abscess of the tooth/gums, malocclusion of the teeth, and chronic discomfort in the mouth.

About 25% of individuals with impacted teeth develop an infection called "dry socket," which is caused by improved clotting or loosening of the clot that forms after the tooth is removed. Because infection can reach the bone, dry socket can take quite some time to heal, requiring not only antibiotics but regular dressing changes. It is vital for the individual to diligently follow the dentist's aftercare instructions, keeping the mouth as clean as possible following extraction to prevent recurrence. Some individuals with heart conditions such as valvular disease, atrial fibrillation, and foreign bodies are at risk for infective endocarditis if treatment is begun without preventive antibiotic therapy.

Factors Influencing Duration

Swelling and bleeding after tooth extractions, and exposure of bone in the socket after a lower back tooth has been removed (dry socket) may prolong recovery.

Length of Disability

No disability is expected. Length of disability may be influenced by the severity of symptoms or the presence of complications. Most individuals will require a day of bed rest following the removal of an impacted tooth.

Surgical extraction.

Duration in Days

Job Classification	Minimum	Optimum	Maximum
Any work	0	1	3

Duration Trend from Normative Data*

Cases	Mean	Min	Max	No Lost Time	Over 6 Months
314	9	0	184	6.51%	0.33%

Percentile:	5th	25th	Median	75th	95th
Days:	1	4	7	11	19

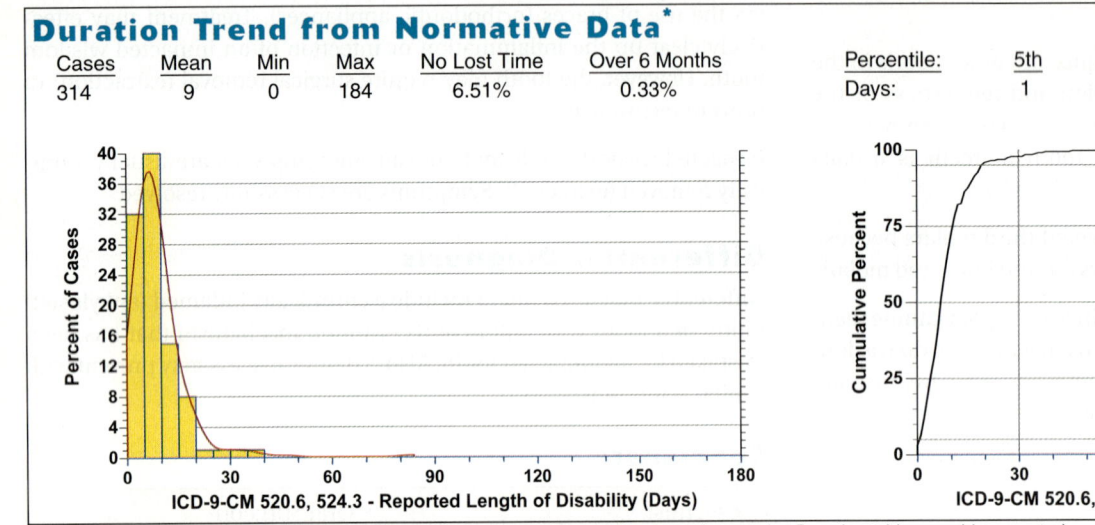
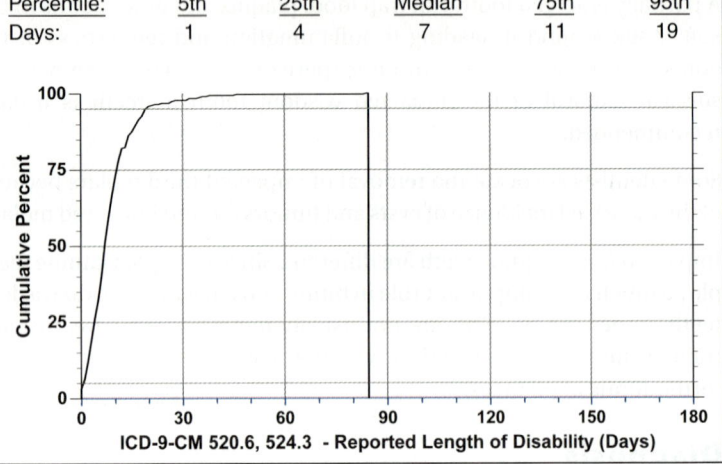

ICD-9-CM 520.6, 524.3 - Reported Length of Disability (Days)

* Differences may exist between the expected duration tables and the normative graphs. Duration tables provide expected recovery periods based on the type of work performed by the individual. The normative graphs reflect the actual observed experience of many individuals across the spectrum of physical conditions, in a variety of industries, and with varying levels of case management.

Failure to Recover

If an individual fails to recover within the maximum duration expectancy period, the reader may wish to reference the following questions to assist in better understanding the specifics of an individual's medical case.

Regarding diagnosis:

- Does the individual report pain and tenderness of the gums?
- Does the individual have bad breath (pericoronitis)?
- Does the individual complain of an unpleasant taste when biting down on or near the area?
- Does the individual report prolonged headache or jaw ache?
- Were x-rays done to reveal the presence of a tooth (or teeth) that has not emerged?
- Has the diagnosis of impacted tooth been confirmed?

Regarding treatment:

- If the impacted tooth is not causing infection or inflammation, or is not affecting the alignment of the other teeth, is treatment required?
- If no treatment is required for the tooth, but the individual has some discomfort, have over-the-counter pain medications (analgesics) and warm salt water rinses been tried?
- If the area around the tooth is infected, has an antibiotic been given? Has the individual been compliant with the medication regimen?
- Did the tooth require removal (extraction)?
- Was the tooth deeply impacted or was there any difficulty with extraction?
- If the upper canine teeth were impacted, were braces (orthodontic appliances) used to realign the teeth?

Regarding prognosis:

- Was (were) the impacted wisdom tooth (teeth) surgically removed (extracted)?
- Did symptoms completely resolve?
- Were braces required?
- Has the individual experienced recurrent infection of a partially buried tooth, abscess of the tooth/gums, malocclusion of the teeth, or chronic discomfort in the mouth?
- Has the individual developed the infection called "dry socket," caused by improved clotting or loosening of the clot that forms after the tooth is removed?
- If so, is the individual on an appropriate antibiotic and compliant with the medication regimen?
- Are regular dressing changes being done?
- Is the individual following directions explicitly regarding keeping the mouth as clean as possible following extraction?

References

Medline Plus Health Information - Impacted Tooth. Adam.com. 01 Jan 2000. 18 Jan 2001 <http://medlineplus.adam.com/ency/article/001057trt.htm>.

Impetigo
Other names / synonyms: Pyoderma
684

Definition

Impetigo is a superficial infection of the skin by Staphylococcus aureus and/or Streptococcus pyogenes bacteria. There are two forms of impetigo: bullous, and superficial or common. Bullous impetigo is caused by Staphylococcus aureus, and is characterized by thin-walled blisters that rupture and develop a thin, varnish-like crust. Superficial or common impetigo is caused by Streptococcus pyogenes alone or in combination with Staphylococcus aureus, and is characterized by thick, adherent, yellow crusts with a red border. The most likely regions to be affected are the face, scalp, and extremities.

Impetigo at a deeper level of skin, usually in an unexposed area (the legs), is called ecthyma. Poor hygiene and overcrowding are contributing factors. Impetigo affects primarily children and adolescents, but adults can be affected as well. It is more common in warm, humid climates.

Diagnosis

History: The individual may complain of an itchy, rapidly-spreading rash, or fluid-filled blisters. There may be a history of a minor breach in skin integrity such as a cut, insect bite, or herpes outbreak.

Physical exam: Individuals with common impetigo would have the typical small, multiple, red-rimmed collections of pus (pustules) with adherent dirty-yellow colored crust. Large, fluid-filled blisters that leave a thin crust would be present in individuals suffering from bullous impetigo. Some individuals may present with both types of lesions. Nearby lymph nodes may be swollen. The affected region may have evidence of pre-existing scabies, eczema, herpes, or lice infestation (pediculosis).

Tests: A microscopic examination (Gram stain) of a sample of the pus will confirm the infection. Bacterial cultures and antibiotic sensitivity testing may be performed.

Treatment

Topical or systemic antibiotics are used to treat this infection. The crusts may be gently removed after soaking the affected area in a warm antiseptic solution.

Prognosis

Impetigo is easily treated with antibiotics so it has an excellent prognosis. Left untreated, impetigo should spontaneously resolve in time.

Differential Diagnosis

Infection of hair follicles (folliculitis), erysipelas, shingles (herpes zoster), oral herpes (herpes labialis), blister (bullous) diseases, fungal infection (tinea), allergic contact dermatitis, or atopic dermatitis can resemble impetigo.

Specialists

- Dermatologist
- Infectious Disease Physician

Work Restrictions / Accommodations

Because impetigo is highly contagious, the individual should avoid direct contact with others until the infection has cleared. Maintaining moderate ambient temperature and humidity in the work place can help to reduce future infection.

Comorbid Conditions

Immune system-suppressing diseases, such as AIDS or certain cancers, can increase the length of disability.

Complications

Deeper infection of the skin is possible, forming a boil. Impetigo involving Staphylococcus aureus may progress to Staphylococcal scalded skin syndrome, characterized by large sheets of peeling skin; however, this syndrome is rarely seen in individuals over the age of 12 years. Uncommonly, Streptococcus infection can result in glomerulonephritis (an acute kidney disease), scarlet fever, hives (urticaria), and erythema multiforme.

Factors Influencing Duration

The severity of the infection and the appropriateness of the antibiotic may influence the length of disability.

Length of Disability

No disability is expected.

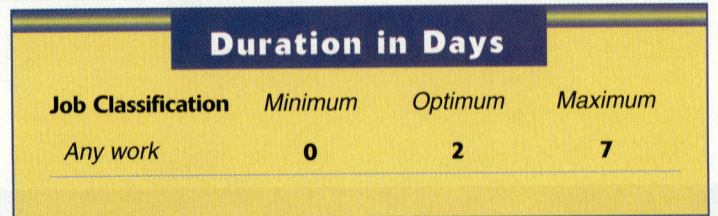

Job Classification	Minimum	Optimum	Maximum
Any work	0	2	7

Failure to Recover

If an individual fails to recover within the maximum duration expectancy period, the reader may wish to reference the following questions to assist in better understanding the specifics of an individual's medical case.

Regarding diagnosis:

- Does the individual have signs of impetigo, such as blisters, or lesions with thick yellow crusts and red borders?
- Are the lesions located on the face, scalp and/or extremities?
- Has there been a history of insect bites, herpes or skin lacerations?
- Are the physical findings consistent with the diagnosis of impetigo?
- Did a gram stain or culture identify the presence of Staphylococcus aureus or Streptococcus pyogenes?
- Have other conditions with similar symptoms been ruled out in the differential diagnosis?

Regarding treatment:

- Has the causative bacteria been subject to sensitivity testing to confirm that the appropriate antibiotic treatment was undertaken?
- If the symptoms persisted following antibiotic treatment, were the lesions recultured to determine if the bacteria are resistant to the current antibiotic therapy?
- Has the antibiotic been changed?

Regarding prognosis:

- Has the individual had this infection before?
- Does the individual have an underlying condition that may impact ability to recover?
- Did the individual complete the entire course of antibiotic?

References

Aly, Raza. "Staphylococcal Infections." Atlas of Infections of the Skin. Aly, Raza, and Howard Maibach, eds. New York: Churchill Livingstone, 1999. 115-122.

Aly, Raza. "Streptococcal Infections." Atlas of Infections of the Skin. Aly, Raza, and Howard Maibach, eds. New York: Churchill Livingstone, 1999. 123-131.

Anderson, Philip, and Kristin Malaker. "Most Common Skin Disorders." Managing Skin Diseases. Hiscock, Tim Baltimore, eds.: Williams & Wilkins, 1999. 90-95.

Malcolm, B. "Impetigo." Practitioner 242 (1998): 405.

Impingement Syndrome

Other names / synonyms: Rotator Cuff Impingement Syndrome, Subacromial Impingement Syndrome

726.2

Definition

Impingement syndrome occurs when the musculotendinous structure that provides strength and mobility to the shoulder joint (rotator cuff) rubs against the arch created by ligament and bone.

The shoulder is made up of three bones. The tendons that attach these three bones to four muscles in the shoulder area form the rotator cuff. The top of the shoulder blade is the acromion, and the area underneath is the subacromial space. A lubricating sac of tissue that protects the muscles and tendons as they move against each other is the bursa. Usually there is enough room between the acromion and rotator cuff so the tendons slide easily underneath the acromion as the arm is raised. However, when the space is made smaller either by changes in the shape of the shoulder blade (acromion), increased rigidity of the ligament, bone spurs, or swelling in the rotator cuff tissue, the rotator cuff is forced to rub against the arch. Impingement is thought to be a precursor to a rotator cuff tear; impingement can also cause the bursa to become inflamed, resulting in bursitis.

Age, repetitive overhead activity, shoulder looseness (laxity), sleeping with the shoulder abducted, previous injury, osteoarthritis, bone spurs (osteophytes), and anatomical abnormalities are all causative factors. Although swollen rotator cuff tendons can be the cause of the problem, they can also be the result of an impingement. Shoulder laxity that allows the head of the upper arm bone (humerus) to ride high in the shoulder joint will force the rotator cuff against the arch, resulting in impingement. Any changes in the shape of the acromion, especially bone spurs (osteophytes) or a beak-like shape, will increase the impingement symptoms. When shoulder ligaments are chronically inflamed with irritation from the rubbing of the rotator cuff, they lose some elasticity, which in turn can cause more irritation of the rotator cuff mechanism. This cycle of events also leads to an impingement syndrome.

Excluding impingement that results from repetitive motion, impingement syndrome more commonly develops after the age of 30. Individuals who are at risk of developing impingement syndrome include athletes (e.g., baseball players), assembly-line workers, warehouse workers, typists, data entry personnel, and others who perform repetitive work, especially with the arms raised above shoulder height. Conditions that predispose individuals to impingement syndrome include bone spurs, osteoarthritis, and shoulder injuries or degenerative disease.

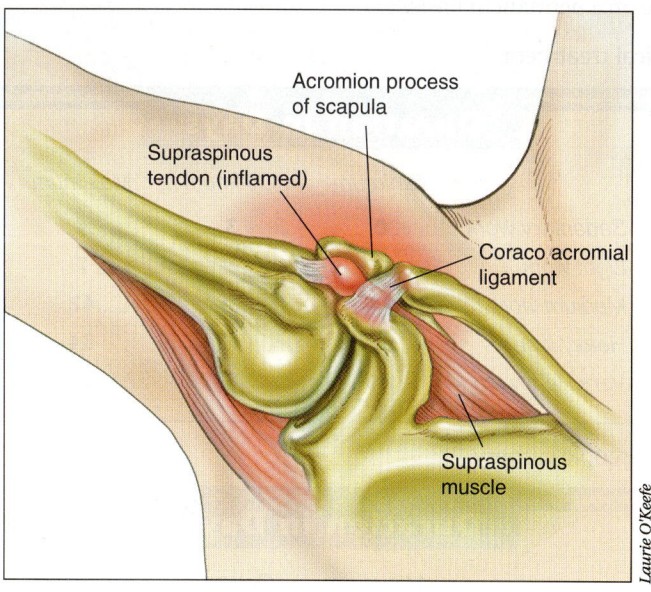

Diagnosis

History: The hallmark symptom of impingement syndrome is shoulder pain that may appear suddenly, such as after an injury; more often, however, onset is gradual and progressive. In early stages, individuals will experience pain only when the arm is held out from the side or in front of the body above shoulder level, and will be relieved with rest. There may be a "catching" sensation when the arm is lowered. As the impingement syndrome becomes more chronic, pain is felt most with activity, but will not be relieved with positional change or rest. Shoulder pain may be so severe that it prevents the individual from moving his or her shoulder. Pain is also felt at night, enough to interfere with sleep, particularly when the individual rolls onto the affected shoulder. There may be a clicking or popping sensation felt with arm motion. The individual may have an occupation that requires repetitive arm motions. Complaints of weakness or the inability to raise the arm may indicate that the rotator cuff tendons are actually torn.

Physical exam: Pain will be evident in individuals as they elevate their arm against downward force on the shoulder as applied by the physician (positive impingement sign or test). Range of motion testing will reveal limitations in certain aspects. Individuals may exhibit total relief of symptoms after injection of a local anesthetic into the subacromial space (injection test). Pressure to the subacromial region produces pain.

Tests: Routine shoulder x-rays, including special views of the acromial arch, are used to evaluate the shape of the arch and rule out other diagnoses. MRI examination, diagnostic ultrasound, or taking x-rays after injecting dye into the shoulder joint (arthrography) may be ordered to examine the integrity of the rotator cuff.

Treatment

In the early stages, impingement syndrome will resolve when the aggravating activity and any overhead work are avoided. Physical therapy modalities to increase shoulder stability and decrease inflammation may also be helpful. Application of ice can relieve pain. Medications to control pain and inflammation are usually prescribed. Injection of corticosteroid and anesthetic agents into the subacromial space is often part of the conservative treatment.

Surgical intervention is necessary when individuals fail to improve after several months of physical therapy and subacromial injections. The goal of surgery is to increase the size of the subacromial space and remove inflamed tissue. Reshaping the acromion (acromioplasty) combined with removing the subacromial bursae and cutting the coracoacromial ligament are common procedures. Removal (excision) of any bone spurs and inflamed rotator cuff tissue (debridement) may also be needed. This combination of procedures is often called a subacromial decompression. These procedures can be performed either through open surgery (arthrotomy) or arthroscopically. Typically, these are outpatient procedures.

Prognosis

The outcome for impingement syndrome is excellent. Most individuals are effectively treated by conservative methods. Only a very small percentage of individuals require subacromial decompression, which also has a favorable outcome. Recovery in more chronic situations is expected, but may be prolonged due to surgical intervention.

Differential Diagnosis

Painful arc syndrome, rotator cuff tear, rotator cuff tendonitis, bursitis, shoulder instability, thoracic outlet syndrome, calcific tendonitis, shoulder (acromioclavicular or glenohumeral) arthritis, rheumatoid arthritis, septic arthritis, gout, lyme disease, systemic lupus erythematosus, tumor, avascular necrosis, dislocating or subluxating shoulder, biceps tendon rupture, or cervical disc disease could present with similar findings.

Specialists

- Occupational Therapist
- Orthopedic Surgeon
- Physiatrist
- Physical Therapist

Rehabilitation

Rehabilitation of impingement syndrome may begin with goals to decrease pain and inflammation and reduce the pressure on irritated tendon and/or tissues. The physical therapist may use cold or warm treatments throughout the period of rehabilitation to control inflammation and pain. Heat treatments help reduce inflammation and pain. Forms of heat treatment used in the region of the shoulder joint include ultrasound that uses high frequency sound waves to produce heat that penetrates deep into the involved tissues. Electrostimulation is another technique that helps decrease pain by mildly producing an electrical response in the muscle around the joint.

Rehabilitation of impingement syndrome progresses with stretches that pull the head of the upper arm bone (humerus) downward. This reduces upward pressure placed on the tendons on the upper portion of the shoulder joint (impingement).

As pain subsides, strengthening exercises of specific shoulder muscles (rotator muscles) are emphasized. These initiate a natural downward glide as the individual lifts the arm upward at the side of the body (abduction). When strengthened and working properly, these muscles help reduce and prevent impingement syndrome.

Job requirements may need to be modified during the rehabilitation process until pain and swelling diminishes. For example, lifting objects overhead may need to be limited as well as repetitive pushing and pulling at or above chest height.

The physical therapist may need to make modifications for individuals with arthritis or other shoulder joint irritations. If the shoulder joint requires surgical repair, some restrictions may be placed on the progression of the range of motion and strengthening in certain movements. This varies depending on the degree of impingement or type of surgery performed.

Work Restrictions / Accommodations

The aggravating activities need to be avoided until symptoms have been relieved. During early treatment, the individual should not lift, carry, or push objects. Individuals should not use the arm above shoulder level. These restrictions may become permanent. An ergonometric evaluation of the work place may be necessary. Change in job duties, sharing or alternating tasks, reduced work rate, more frequent rest breaks, and limiting the time and frequency of repetitive activities are important accommodations. Work site modifications can include forearm rests for individuals who use computer keyboards frequently, headsets for those who answer telephones, and changing task performance such that repetitive activities can be done with the arms in a lower level of elevation.

Comorbid Conditions

Osteoarthritis, rheumatoid arthritis, advanced age, shoulder injuries (including a history of shoulder injury), shoulder instability, and shoulder degeneration can influence the length of disability.

Complications

Rotator cuff tear, biceps tendonitis, subacromial bursitis, frozen shoulder (adhesive capsulitis) could complicate impingement syndrome.

Factors Influencing Duration

The individual's age, occupation, dominant or nondominant arm affected, response to treatment, and compliance with treatment recommendations and rehabilitation programs would affect the disability period.

Length of Disability

Duration depends on job requirements and whether dominant or non-dominant arm is involved. Disability may be longer for individuals who perform repetitive actions and/or overhead work as part of their work duties. For individuals who have surgery, heavy work may be inappropriate on a permanent basis.

Medical treatment.

Duration in Days

Job Classification	Minimum	Optimum	Maximum
Sedentary work	0	3	4
Light work	0	3	7
Medium work	14	21	42
Heavy work	28	42	84
Very Heavy work	28	42	84

Arthroscopic surgery.

Duration in Days

Job Classification	Minimum	Optimum	Maximum
Sedentary work	7	10	21
Light work	7	10	21
Medium work	28	42	56
Heavy work	56	70	84
Very Heavy work	56	70	84

Surgical treatment (open).

Duration in Days

Job Classification	Minimum	Optimum	Maximum
Sedentary work	28	42	70
Light work	28	56	84
Medium work	42	84	140
Heavy work	70	84	140
Very Heavy work	70	84	140

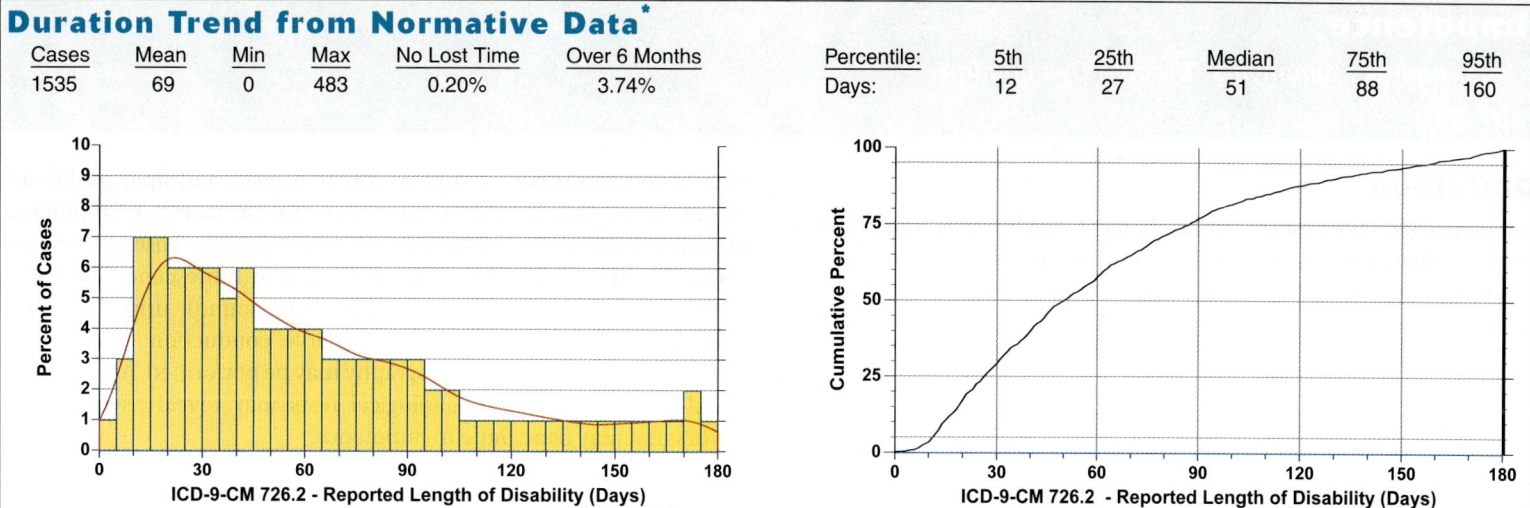

Failure to Recover

If an individual fails to recover within the maximum duration expectancy period, the reader may wish to reference the following questions to assist in better understanding the specifics of an individual's medical case.

Regarding diagnosis:

- Does the individual have any risk factors or predisposing conditions such as bone spurs, osteoarthritis, shoulder injuries, or degenerative disease?
- Did the shoulder pain appear suddenly or was the onset gradual and progressive?
- Was there pain following an injury?
- What symptoms does the individual have?
- What were the findings on physical exam?
- Has the individual received shoulder x-rays, MRI, ultrasound, or arthrography to establish the diagnosis?
- Have conditions with similar symptoms been ruled out?

Regarding treatment:

- Has the individual responded favorably to conservative treatment?
- Did it become necessary for the individual to have surgery? What type?

Regarding prognosis:

- Is recovery prolonged due to surgery?
- Is the individual active in physical therapy? In a home exercise program?
- Is the individual's employer able to accommodate necessary restrictions (for example, lifting objects overhead may need to be limited, as well as repetitive pushing and pulling at or above chest height)?
- Does the individual have osteoarthritis, rheumatoid arthritis, shoulder injuries, shoulder instability, or shoulder degeneration?
- Does the individual have complications such as Rotator cuff tear, biceps tendinitis, bursitis, or frozen shoulder?
- Is the affected shoulder on the individual dominant or nondominant side?

References

Anderson, Bruce. "Shoulder." Office Orthopedics for Primary Care: Diagnosis and Treatment. Philadelphia: W.B. Saunders Company, 1999. 13-47.

Cohen, Randolph, and Gerald Williams. "Impingement Syndrome and Rotator Cuff Disease as Repetitive Motion Disorders." Clinical Orthopaedics and Related Research 351 (1999): 95-101.

Fongemie, Allen, Daniel Buss, and Sharon Rolnick. "Management of Shoulder Impingement Syndrome and Rotator Cuff Tears." American Family Physician 57 4 (1998): 667-674.

Kessler, R.M. Management of Common Musculoskeletal Disorders: Physical Therapy Principles and Methods. Philadelphia: J.B. Lippincott Company, 1990.

Kisner, C., and Lynn Allen Colby. Therapeutic Exercise Foundations and Techniques. Philadelphia: F.A. Davis Company, 1990.

Morrison, David, Brad Greenbaum, and Andy Einhorn. "Shoulder Impingement." Orthopedic Clinics of North America 31 2 (2000): 285-293.

Impotence

Other names / synonyms: Erectile Dysfunction

607.84

Definition

Impotence (erectile dysfunction) is characterized by the failure to attain or maintain an erection sufficient to complete satisfactory intercourse. Ejaculation may or may not be affected. Impotence is classified as either primary or secondary. A man with primary impotence has never had successful intercourse with a partner but may achieve normal erections in other situations. A man with secondary impotence, despite current problems, has some history of success completing intercourse in the past. Over 80% of impotence is based on physical problems such as disease, injury, or drug side effects. Psychological problems including depression, anxiety, fatigue, boredom, stress, or various fears (including fear of failure, infection, or recurring heart problems) are another cause of impotence. Other causes include low levels of testosterone, arteriosclerosis, high blood pressure (hypertension), drug abuse (narcotics or stimulants), medications (blood pressure medication, anticholinergics, antihistamines, psychotherapeutic drugs, narcotics, estrogen), kidney failure, circulatory or heart failure, liver disease (from alcoholism), smoking (nicotine abuse), complications from urologic procedures (prostatectomy, orchiectomy, radiation therapy), vascular and back surgeries, trauma (disk or spinal cord injuries), endocrine disturbances (diabetes mellitus, hyperthyroidism, Addison's disease), zinc deficiency, neurologic injury, trauma, or disorders (multiple sclerosis, tumors, peripheral neuropathies), pernicious anemia, or urologic disorders (tight foreskin, Peyronie's disease), or penile implants or prostheses that are not functioning properly. Injury to or inflammation of the penis may also be a factor.

This disorder affects approximately 10 million American men. Impotence is not a natural part of aging, and although aging alone does not cause impotence, its incidence does increase with age. Fifty percent of all men experience at least temporary erectile dysfunction at some time. Approximately 5% of men aged 40 and older and approximately 15-25% of men aged 65 and older experience impotence.

Diagnosis

History: The failure to achieve or maintain an erection is the main physical complaint. Pertinent history includes prior difficulties, whether the onset was sudden or gradual, length of time difficulty has existed, the degree of dysfunction (chronic, occasional, or situational), the presence or absence of normal erections (such as in the morning, during the night, or with masturbation), the nature of difficulty (primary or secondary), difficulty urinating, changes in penile sensation, or psychological factors including stress, performance expectations, or change in sexual partners. An evaluation of aggravating factors such as medications, recent surgeries, the amount of alcohol or nicotine usually ingested, changes in emotional state, or physical problems is done.

Physical exam: During a thorough physical exam, the genitalia and secondary sexual characteristics are evaluated, as well as neurological, vascular, and endocrine status. Injury, scarring, or abnormalities of the genitals are noted. The prostate will also be palpated for abnormalities.

Tests: Blood tests may include checking the hormone levels of testosterone, gonadotropin, prolactin, follicle stimulating hormone, and luteinizing hormone. A complete blood count (CBC) including glucose levels, urinalysis, thyroid function tests, and lipid profile are useful. Tests that help determine the organic cause of impotence include the injection of vasoactive substances into the base of the penis, test of nighttime erections (nocturnal penile tumescence, or NPT), blood flow velocity (duplex or doppler ultrasound), urinary voiding studies (voiding cystourethrogram), nerve conduction tests (NCV), cavernosometry and cavernosography may be performed. Also psychosocial examination or psychological tests may reveal psychological factors that may contribute to impotence.

Treatment

Treatment depends on the cause of the impotence and may include behavior-oriented sex therapy, supplemental testosterone injections, use of a vacuum constriction device, injections of vasoactive medication into the penis (penile injection therapy), penile prosthetic devices surgically implanted in the penis (intraurethral therapy), and vascular reconstruction surgery (revascularization and venous ligation).

Drugs that may be prescribed for impotence include sildenafil citrate (marketed as Viagra). Other drugs that may be used for impotence, but which have not been proven scientifically effective, include alpha2-adrenergic blockers, dopamine and serotonin agonists, and some antidepressants.

Drugs such as peripheral vasodilators, some antihypertensive medications, and prostaglandin may be injected into the penis to enhance erection. Topical vasodilators may be rubbed on the surface of the penis to enhance erection.

Prostaglandin pellets (MUSE) may be inserted into the urethra to enhance erection.

If medication is causing or exacerbating the condition, the medication may be changed, stopped, or the dose altered. Arterial abnormalities may be helped by expanding the narrowed artery using an inflated balloon (balloon angiodilation), removing the lining of an artery narrowed by atherosclerosis (endarterectomy), or surgical repair of blood vessels (angioplasty). Hormones may be prescribed when the endocrine system is involved. For impotence caused by smoking, smoking must be discontinued; for impotence caused by liver disease, alcohol consumption must be stopped.

Prognosis

Treatment with medications, vacuum constriction devices, avoiding or altering aggravating factors, injection therapy, and intraurethral therapy and medications may or may not solve the problem. The individual may retain a strong sexual drive in spite of impotence and this can cause feelings of vulnerability and frustration. Impotence may persist due to underlying conditions. When this happens, surgery (penile implants, reconstructing arteries, and repairing veins) may be considered.

Differential Diagnosis

Other possibilities include loss of libido, loss of emission, retrograde ejaculation, loss of orgasm, premature ejaculation, hormonal disorders, endocrine disturbances, urologic disorders, neurologic disorders, side effects of medications, and prostate cancer.

Specialists

- Internist
- Psychiatrist
- Psychologist
- Urologist

Rehabilitation

Performing the Kegel exercise 3-5 times daily can help with the recovery. This exercise can be done while urinating on the toilet. The individual should contract the muscle until the urine flow is slowed or stopped and then release it. The individual should perform 5-10 contractions and hold each for 10 seconds.

Work Restrictions / Accommodations

There are no restrictions or accommodations associated with most treatment options. Surgery may result in restrictions on activity or lifting for a brief period. Emotional difficulties associated with impotence may result in depression in some men. Counseling and participation in support groups are recommended.

Complementary and Alternative Therapies

Content is intended for awareness only. Treatments may or may not be effective. Scientific evidence may be lacking and some substances have potentially toxic effects. Dr. Presley Reed and the editors do not endorse the use of these therapies in the absence of consultation with a licensed medical professional.

Phentolamine -	Vasomax, oral form may dilute blood vessels.
Apomorphine -	Sublingual tablets said to send signal in the brain to trigger an erection.
Pentoxifylline -	Said to improve oxygen delivery to the penis by reducing the stickiness of the red blood cells.
Dipyridamol -	Nitromed works by inhibiting phosphodiesterase-5.
Yohimbine -	May improve blood flow, which may result in an erection.
Ginkgo -	May improve blood flow and result in an erection.
ArginMax -	Is being marketed for improving sexual dysfunction and well-being. This product is supposed to release nitric oxide, which relaxes blood vessels.

Comorbid Conditions

Comorbid conditions include atherosclerosis, heart disease, high blood pressure (hypertension), emotional and psychological problems.

Complications

The presence of more than one causative factor will complicate treatment. A partner who will not participate in therapy will also hinder recovery. Accumulation of scar tissue within the penile shaft (Peyronie's disease) and sustained, painful, unwanted erection that occurs despite a lack of sexual stimulation (priapism) can be complicating.

Factors Influencing Duration

The method of treatment and the individual response to treatment will affect the length of disability. The age of the individual can also affect disability.

Length of Disability

No disability is associated with impotence.

Failure to Recover

If an individual fails to recover within the maximum duration expectancy period, the reader may wish to reference the following questions to assist in better understanding the specifics of an individual's medical case.

Regarding diagnosis:

- Are the clinical characteristics of either primary of secondary impotence present?
- Was a thorough physical and psychological exam done to detect organic or psychological components to the impotence?
- If the cause was uncertain, were appropriate diagnostic tests done to rule out other conditions with similar symptoms?
- Does the individual have any underlying situational events, physical problems or medication use that may have contributed to the problem?

Regarding treatment:

- Was the cause(s) of the impotence determined?
- Has the condition improved with conservative treatment interventions?
- Was drug therapy successful?
- Has the individual been compliant with lifestyle modifications such as weight management, smoking cessation, limiting alcohol, and eliminating certain medications?
- Did treatment options include use of a vacuum constriction device, penile injection therapy, intraurethral therapy, or revascularization and venous ligation?
- Would the individual benefit from consultation with an appropriate specialist (urologist, sex-therapist, psychologist)?

Regarding prognosis:

- Does the individual have any underlying physical or psychological conditions that may affect response to treatment and prognosis? Are more than one causative factors present? Have comorbid conditions been addressed in the treatment plan?
- If unresponsive to more conservative measures, is individual a candidate for a surgical implant?
- Is the individual and his partner receiving appropriate behavioral or psychological consultation?
- Because a partner who will not participate in therapy will also hinder recovery, does partner understand how important it is to be a willing and active participant in the treatment?

References

"Chapter 220: Erectile Dysfunction." Merck Manual of Diagnosis and Therapy, 17th ed. Beers, Mark H., and Robert Berkow, MD, eds. Whitehouse Station, NJ: Merck & Co. Inc., 1999. 21 July 2000 <http://www.merck.com/pubs/mmanual/section17/chapter220/220a.htm>.

Impotence. National Kidney and Urologic Diseases Information Clearinghouse. 01 Aug 2000. 21 Aug 2000 <http://www.niddk.nih.gov/health/urolog/pubs/impotnce/impotnce.htm>.

Incision and Drainage of Ischiorectal and/or Perirectal Abscess
Other names / synonyms: Anorectal Abscess, Ischiorectal Abscess, Perianal Abscess, Perirectal Abscess
48.81, 49.01

Definition
This surgical procedure is performed to drain a collection of pus (abscess) that has developed in the deeper fatty tissue on either side of the rectum (ischiorectal) or superficially around the rectum (perirectal).

The abscesses result from an infection of the anal crypt glands. Less commonly, they can occur from perianal skin infections, abrasions, trauma, or foreign bodies.

Up to 50% of perirectal abscesses result in a fistula due to tissue damage from the infection. Because fistulas are persistent, they must also be removed (fistulectomy) for healing to take place.

Simple drainage of the abscess results in cure for 50% of individuals. Men are more frequently affected by anorectal abscesses than women.

Reason for Procedure
An abscess in the rectal area is a collection of pus formed by an infection. Unless it is cut open and drained, the abscess may continue to enlarge or form tube-like passages due to tissue damage (fistulas). Draining an abscess removes the infected pus, relieves the painful pressure, and allows the healing process to begin.

Description
The depth of the abscess determines whether the procedure can be done under local or general anesthesia. The means by which the abscess is drained depends on the depth of the abscess. Superficial abscesses that are large and close to the skin may be drained as an outpatient either in an office setting or often in the emergency room. After a local anesthetic is injected over the abscess, an incision is made, opening the abscess and allowing the pus to drain. The cavity is irrigated and packed. The individual is then sent home with pain medication. Antibiotics are not necessary.

For deeper abscesses, the individual is taken to the operating room where the abscess is drained under general anesthesia. Once again, the cavity is irrigated and packed. The individual can go home after the procedure, usually the same or next day.

No further treatment is usually necessary as draining the pus cures the condition.

Prognosis
About 50% of individuals are cured after the drainage procedure. Another 50% will develop an anal fistula that is a tunnel from inside the anal canal to the outside skin. This fistula can be opened surgically (fistulectomy). Unfortunately, recurrence may be frequent after the development of an anorectal abscess.

Specialists
- Colorectal Surgeon
- Gastroenterologist
- General Surgeon
- Proctologist

Work Restrictions / Accommodations
The individual may need to avoid prolonged sitting. Special pillows can provide some relief when the individual must sit. Strenuous activity may need to be temporarily modified following surgery.

Comorbid Conditions
Diabetes mellitus, an immunocompromised state (HIV, cancer, or chemotherapy), or other infectious diseases may lengthen disability.

Procedure Complications
Complications from the procedure are few. Bleeding may occur or the infection may spread. It is rare if the anal sphincter becomes damaged, leading to anal incontinence.

Factors Influencing Duration
Length of disability may be influenced by the depth or extent of the abscess, presence of fistulas, response to treatment, job requirements, or any complications.

Sometimes individuals with diabetes may develop a rapidly spreading infection of the perirectal and perineal areas called Fournier's disease. This is a serious condition that must be treated with hospitalization and antibiotics. Surgery may be required.

Length of Disability

Duration in Days

Job Classification	Minimum	Optimum	Maximum
Any work	7	14	21

References

Russel, Thomas. "Anorectum." Current Surgical Diagnosis and Treatment. Way, Lawrence New York: Appleton & Lange, 1991. 681-699.

Schwartz, Seymour, MD. Principles of Surgery. New York: McGraw-Hill, 1999.

Incision of Skin and Subcutaneous Tissue, Drainage of Abscess or Cyst
Other names / synonyms: I&D, Incision and Drainage
86.0, 86.01, 86.04, 86.09

Definition

An incision of skin and subcutaneous tissue is the first surgical step performed in order to drain an abscess or cyst. An incision is a cut or a wound produced by cutting with a scalpel. The procedure is usually carried out under local anesthesia. An abscess is a cavity containing pus. Often abscesses are surrounded by reddened (inflamed) tissue. Abscesses of the skin are often due to staphylococcal bacteria. Abscesses may occur in other organs and tissues deeper in the body. A cyst is a closed sac containing fluid or semisolid material that is located under the skin. A common type of cyst is a sebaceous cyst (epidermal cyst), a benign cyst formed from the epidermis (the outermost layer of the skin) or the epithelium (cells lining surfaces of the body) of the hair follicle. Cysts may be unsightly or bothersome and can become infected.

Reason for Procedure

Cysts may be removed (excised) for many reasons. Removal of cysts may be recommended if the appearance has become unsightly, the cyst has become bothersome or painful, a cyst is recurrent, an infection has developed, a cyst is enlarging, or if there is foul-smelling discharge from the cyst. Abscesses are removed (incision and drainage) to provide treatment and healing when conservative treatments such as antibiotics and heat have been ineffective. Antibiotics cannot reach bacteria within an abscess or infected cyst. An abscess must be "ripe" prior to performing an incision and drainage. "Ripe" means that the abscess is localized, that there is freely flowing fluid inside the abscess (fluctuant), that it is tender, and that it is reddened (inflamed). An incision and drainage creates an open wound through which the infected fluid (pus) can freely drain.

Description

The area of the abscess or cyst is thoroughly cleansed with an antibacterial solution. Local anesthetic is given. For excision of a cyst, two slightly curved, intersecting, parallel incisions are made (elliptical) over the main portion of the cyst. Care is taken not to rupture the cyst. The incisions will be somewhat longer than the cyst, and the skin between the incisions will be removed intact with the cyst. The cyst and its covering skin can then be carefully lifted while gently cutting it away from the underlying tissue (dissecting). Any bleeding that occurred with removal is controlled (with pressure, cautery, or suturing). The skin is sutured together and a dressing is applied. For an abscess or an infected cyst, a stab incision is made down to the pus-filled cavity. The small stab incision is then enlarged to allow full drainage of the abscess. The tip of the forceps is introduced into the cavity and then the jaws of the instrument are opened to improve drainage; additionally, the cavity should be explored by finger to break down all small spaces. Samples of the pus can be obtained for identification of the bacteria responsible for the infection (culture). The contents can also be aspirated (suction) by a tube passed through the incision. After completely draining, the cavity is thoroughly irrigated. The cavity may be packed with gauze containing an antibacterial medication. The exterior wound should be kept open until the cavity heals from within. A dressing is placed over the area. Treatment with antibiotics is unnecessary unless there is evidence of spreading infection or unless the procedure was performed on the hand or face.

Prognosis

The predicted outcome is complete healing. Scarring may occur following surgical treatment of cysts and abscesses. Some incisions may heal with minimal or no scarring. The degree of scarring may vary depending to the size and severity of the original lesion, infection, and how well the edges of the incision were closed together (approximated). The degree of scarring following treatment of small abscesses (those treated before becoming large) is often much less than the scar resulting from larger abscesses that need packing and prolonged treatment.

Specialists

- Dermatologist
- General Surgeon

Work Restrictions / Accommodations

Adequate hygienic care of the surrounding skin is necessary to prevent infection. Sometimes dressings over the wound may be necessary for a prolonged period of time to protect the wound and to prevent contamination and infection. Employees may be restricted from returning to work areas that may be especially dirty. Alternative, temporary work duties may be needed during recovery. Time off from work may be necessary for recovery and healing of abscesses that have been packed open. Recovery time may be longer if the original abscess or cyst occurred in a location that is subject to stress and strain, such as in the area of a joint. Extra recovery time may be needed to allow adequate healing and return of tissue strength.

Comorbid Conditions

Comorbid conditions that may interfere with the procedure include bleeding disorders, decreased immune response (immunosuppression), or any severe underlying medical condition that may require treatment prior to the incision and drainage procedure.

Procedure Complications

Complications may include bleeding and spread of infection.

Factors Influencing Duration

Size, location, and cause of the abscess, as well as complications, may influence the length of disability.

Length of Disability

Duration depends on site.

Aspiration of superficial abscess.

Duration in Days

Job Classification	Minimum	Optimum	Maximum
Any work	1	2	7

References

Ely, John W. "Excision of a Sebaceous (Epidermal) Cyst." Saunders Manual of Medical Practice, 2nd ed. Rakel, Robert E., ed. Philadelphia: W.B. Saunders Company, 2000. 1267-1269.

Ise, Charleen. "Percutaneous Incision and Drainage of Abscess." Saunders Manual of Medical Practice, 2nd ed. Rakel, Robert E., ed. Philadelphia: W.B. Saunders Company, 2000. 1270-1272.

Infection
136.4, 136.5, 136.9

Definition

An infection is defined as the presence and growth of a microorganism that produces tissue damage. Such microorganisms are called pathogens. The pathogen can be bacterial, viral, or fungal in nature. The extent of infection varies depending on the number of microorganisms, their ability to cause illness (virulence), and the body's ability to defend against them. Tissue damage can occur directly or from substances produced by the organism (e.g., toxins and enzymes). Localized infections affect one particular tissue or area of the body while systemic infections affect the whole body.

Infections can be acquired in many different ways. Pathogens can be consumed (botulism, salmonella) or inhaled (influenza virus, tuberculosis). In addition, some pathogens acquire access to the body by penetrating the skin or mucous membranes (gonorrhea, HIV, bacterial conjunctivitis). Sometimes organisms not usually harmful move from a part of the body where they normally exist to another part of the body where they can cause damage. For example, the bacteria E. coli is a normal inhabitant of the intestinal tract but causes serious illness if ingested.

Many infections can be spread from individual to individual in several ways. Airborne pathogens are discharged into the air from the respiratory tract of an infected individual through coughing or sneezing. They may be inhaled or settle on another individual, clothing, walls, or floors and then transmitted by direct contact. Direct contact includes kissing and sharing utensils. Other pathogens can live on or in the bodies of individuals who do not experience symptoms but transmit the pathogens to others (carriers). Prenatal infection occurs when the mother passes an infection to her baby during pregnancy either through the placenta or from contact with maternal membranes. Infections can also spread through insect vectors (such as mosquitoes or ticks), animal carriers (by direct or indirect contact), on food (due to bacteria from the soil or from fertilizer), when soil enters the body through wounds (tetanus, gangrene), or through a contaminated water supply (typhoid, dysentery, or cholera).

Certain factors increase the risk of acquiring an infection including injury (trauma), surgery, defect in the body's natural defense system (immune compromise), and age. The very young and the elderly are at increased risk compared to the rest of the population.

Diagnosis

History: Symptoms of an infection vary greatly depending on the primary site of infection. For example, meningitis is associated with pain in the neck and involves difficulty turning and bending the head, while appendicitis is associated with pain in the lower abdomen, and involves nausea and vomiting. Symptoms of an upper respiratory infection may include headache, cough, and nasal discharge. Symptoms of a gastrointestinal infection may include nausea, vomiting, and diarrhea. The common cold is a systemic viral infection with symptoms may include fever, aching muscles (myalgias), and a vague feeling of discomfort or illness (malaise).

Physical exam: Physical examination findings depend on where the infection is located. When examined by touch (palpated), the area around a local infection may feel warm. Touching the area may elicit pain. In general, there may be redness, warmth, and/or tenderness of the affected area. Discharge from an abscess may be present. A systemic infection may not cause any specific physical abnormalities. Diagnosis may rely on history, symptoms, and testing.

Tests: A complete blood count (CBC) with differential or a sedimentation rate can indicate the presence of an infection irrespective of its site. Examining the stool for white blood cells may indicate an infectious process if it involves the gastrointestinal tract. A microbial culture of an infected site often identifies the organism responsible for the infection.

Based on the location of an infection, tests that assess the extent of the infection include chest x-ray, abdominal ultrasound, sinus films, CT, spinal tap, or MRI. Fluid from an infected site should be obtained whenever possible for culture and sensitivity, especially before antibiotics are started in order to optimize the opportunity for a positive culture. This may involve removal (aspiration) of the fluid with a needle and syringe.

1202   The Medical Disability Advisor—Fourth Edition

Treatment

Rest and adequate fluid intake are important factors in the recovery from any infection. Individuals with pain or muscle aches may need pain-relieving medicine (analgesics). Those with fever may require fever-reducing medicine (antipyretics). Other treatments vary depending on the responsible pathogen and the tissues or organ systems involved.

A bacterial infection is treated with an antibiotic. The specific antibiotic used is either chosen based on experience (empirically) or on the sensitivity of the organism to different antibiotics used in the bacteriology laboratory. If the infection has become walled-off (abscess), it is usually cut open (incised) and allowed to drain. Severe bacterial infections (e.g., meningitis) may require intravenous antibiotic administration.

A viral infection may or may not be treated with an antiviral medication. Viruses are more difficult than bacteria to combat with drugs because it is difficult to design drugs that kill the virus without also killing the cells they live in. Therefore, treatment of viral infections depends largely on relieving the symptoms while relying on the body's own defense system to eradicate the virus. If the individual has a defective immune system (immunocompromised), more aggressive therapy may be necessary.

Fungal infections are treated with antifungals based on the location of the infection. Skin and nail fungal infections are generally treated with antifungal creams or lotions applied to the skin. Antifungal drugs are also available in tablet, lozenge, suspension, vaginal suppositories, and injection forms. Fungal infections in immunocompromised individuals may require antifungal drugs administered intravenously (IV).

Prognosis

Infections are usually controlled by appropriate antibiotic therapy, however death can occur. Complications increase the risk of disability and death. The very young and the elderly are at increased risk of complications from infections. If the individual is immunocompromised, recovery is slower with an increased risk of death due to the underlying disease.

Differential Diagnosis

Many of the common symptoms of infection are actually symptoms of inflammation occurring in response to the microorganism. However, inflammation can (and often does) occur without infection. In addition, some allergic reactions share similar signs and symptoms with infection.

Specialists

- Infectious Disease Physician
- Internist

Work Restrictions / Accommodations

Accommodations may include additional sick leave to allow the individual to rest and prevent transmission to coworkers. Restrictions will vary depending on the nature of the infection and the job requirements of the individual. For example, a chef with an upper respiratory infection should not prepare food or a nurse with the flu should avoid patient contact.

In some cases, complications may result in permanent disability (e.g., gangrene resulting in amputation).

Comorbid Conditions

Chemotherapy, diabetes, hematologic disorder, and any disease resulting in a deficient immune system may lengthen disability.

Complications

Infection can cause death to body tissue (necrosis) requiring removal of tissue or amputation of that body part. Infections can create life-threatening diseases including but not limited to pneumonia, meningitis, encephalitis, botulism, tetanus, typhoid, and cholera. An infection can also spread beyond the local area of involvement and into the bloodstream causing a potentially fatal condition known as sepsis or bacteremia.

Factors Influencing Duration

The length of disability is based on the type of infection, any underlying disease or complications, and individual's response to treatment.

Length of Disability

Disability varies depending on the nature and severity of the infection, individual's response to treatment, and any complications. See specific infection for expected length of disability.

Failure to Recover

If an individual fails to recover within the maximum duration expectancy period, the reader may wish to reference the following questions to assist in better understanding the specifics of an individual's medical case.

Regarding diagnosis:

- Was the pathogen inhaled, ingested, skin or mucous membrane penetration, or movement from one part of the body to another?
- Was an insect vector or animal carrier involved? Was the water supply contaminated?
- Has the individual recently had an injury or surgery?
- Is the individual immunocompromised?
- Where is the individual's infection? What symptoms does the individual have?
- On exam, is the area tender to palpation? Is the area warm?
- Was the exam normal?
- Has the individual had a CBC with differential and sedimentation rate? Have a culture and sensitivity of the affected area been done?
- Depending on the location of the infection, has a chest x-ray been done? Ultrasound? Other x-rays? CT or MRI? Spinal tap?
- Have conditions with similar symptoms been ruled out?

Regarding treatment:

- Has the individual received rest, fluids, analgesics, and antipyretics, as needed?
- Is the infection bacterial? Has the individual been treated with the appropriate antibiotic?
- Is the infection viral? Has the individual received appropriate treatment?
- Is the infection fungal? Has the individual been treated with the appropriate antifungal medication?

Regarding prognosis:

- Can the individual's employer accommodate any necessary restrictions?
- Does the individual have any conditions that may affect ability to recover?
- Have any complications occurred such as necrosis, sepsis or bacteremia that may impact recovery?

References

Peterson, Johnny. "Bacterial Pathogenesis." Medical Microbiology. Baron, Samuel, ed. New York: Churchill Livingstone, 1991. 133-146.

Infertility, Female
628, 628.0, 628.2, 628.3, 628.4, 628.8, 628.9

Definition

Infertility is generally considered to be the failure to conceive a child after one year of unprotected sexual activity. About 6.1 million women in the US have difficulty conceiving and carrying a child to term, and about 2.1 million married couples in the US are infertile. Approximately one third of infertility cases can be traced to causes in the male, about one third to causes in the female, and the remaining cases to unidentifiable problems or conditions in each partner that interact to cause infertility.

Major causes of infertility in women include anatomic abnormalities of the reproductive tract; disorders of the cervix such as infection, laceration, tearing from previous childbirth or narrowing of the cervical opening for any reason; abnormal ovulation or irregular release of an egg (ovum) from the ovary; chemical changes in the cervical mucus, severe vaginitis, ovarian cysts, endometriosis, and tumors. Other causes include hormone dysfunction including diabetes, thyroid disorders, low levels of sex hormones or elevated prolactin. The lack of menstrual periods (amenorrhea) caused by strenuous exercise programs or psychiatric disorders such as bulimia or anorexia nervosa, chronic emotional stress, weight gain or weight loss cycles can also cause infertility. Cigarette or marijuana smoking, side effects of certain medications, including contraceptives, may also cause infertility.

Diagnosis

History: The individual will report failure to conceive. Women may have a history of past pelvic inflammatory disease or sexually transmitted diseases. Some may report abnormal menstrual patterns.

Physical exam: The physical exam may be normal. Evidence of vaginal infections, fibroid tumors, or ovarian cysts may be found.

Tests: Tests include complete blood count (CBC), HIV testing, urinalysis, cervical cultures, blood tests for syphilis, rubella antibody, thyroid function, sickle cell disease (in blacks), luteinizing hormone tests, serum progesterone level, follicle stimulating hormone level, prolactin level, histocompatibility antigen testing, ultrasound of the pelvis, hysterosalpingography, endometrial biopsy, laparoscopy, and genetic testing to rule out possible genetic causes of infertility. Cervical mucus will be tested. There will be semen analysis of the male partner.

Treatment

Treatment depends on the underlying cause, and may include hormone supplementation, antibiotics, fertility drugs, artificial insemination, surgery to correct blocked fallopian tubes, endometriosis, fibroids, genetic defects, or ovarian cysts. These problems are often evaluated and treated via laparoscopy.

Assisted Reproductive Technologies (ART) can also be used. In these cases, fertility drugs and other conventional treatment options are combined with high-tech procedures. ART procedures include in vitro fertilization (IVF), gamete intrafallopian transfer (GIFT), zygote intrafallopian transfer (ZIFT), intracytoplasmic sperm injection (ICSI), and donor egg or embryo IVF. The use of a surrogate mother is another ART method.

Prognosis

The chances of conceiving are good if the reason for the infertility can be found and treated. When the cause is unexplained, pregnancy occurs 34% of the time within 6 months and 76% of the time within 2 years of treatment. In vitro fertilization is successful 20-50% of the time; success rates of newer treatment options vary according to individual circumstances. Failure to impregnate can cause frustration, resentment, feelings of inadequacy, anger, guilt, and marital strain.

Differential Diagnosis

Other possible diagnoses include polycystic ovaries, pituitary microadenoma, hypothalamic amenorrhea, and other underlying medical problems such as diabetes or hypothyroidism.

Specialists

- Fertility Specialist
- Gynecologist
- Urologist

Work Restrictions / Accommodations

Work restrictions depend on the treatment method. There may be activity restrictions if surgery is done, and frequent trips to the doctor may be necessary for follow-up care. Infertility tests and treatments are numerous and often time-sensitive. Therefore, the employer should be considerate and provide flexibility with scheduling. If not, this might increase the individual's stress level and defeat the treatment goal. Heavy lifting or long periods of standing may need to be limited, depending on the surgical procedures performed.

Comorbid Conditions

Endometriosis, ovarian tumors, and uterine tumors may further lengthen disability. Psychiatric illnesses such as major depression, anorexia nervosa, or bulimia may also impact the individual's ability to recover.

Complications

The presence of infertility in both partners may complicate treatment. Various ethical and moral decisions may need to be made throughout the diagnostic and treatment phase. Infertility that is severe or prolonged over three years is more difficult to treat. Advancing age may introduce a sense of urgency about treatment and further complicate treatment.

Psychological complications such as grief and depression may also occur. The inability to conceive a child can be emotionally disturbing to both partners.

Factors Influencing Duration

The treatment of underlying causes of fertility and the individual's response can influence length of disability.

Length of Disability

Length of disability depends on job requirements and the type of treatment that is required. If surgical treatment is necessary, this may lengthen disability, depending on complications.

Medical treatment.

Duration in Days

Job Classification	Minimum	Optimum	Maximum
Any work	0	2	3

Surgical treatment.

Duration in Days

Job Classification	Minimum	Optimum	Maximum
Any work	1	3	7

Failure to Recover

If an individual fails to recover within the maximum duration expectancy period, the reader may wish to reference the following questions to assist in better understanding the specifics of an individual's medical case.

Regarding diagnosis:

- Has individual consulted the appropriate medical fertility specialists?
- Has individual had a thorough infertility work-up?
- Was the diagnosis of infertility confirmed?
- Does individual struggle with grief, depression, anorexia nervosa, or bulimia?
- Is the condition or its treatment complicated by factors such as advancing age, endometriosis, and ovarian or uterine tumors?

Regarding treatment:

- Were underlying physical conditions effectively resolved?
- Would individual and/or partner benefit from psychological counseling?
- Were all appropriate options considered? Which ones have been tried so far?
- What further options are individual and partner willing to try?
- Were other pertinent factors addressed such as exercise and weight gain, nutritional assessment, and psychotherapy or counseling if stress or other psychological factors are present?

Regarding prognosis:

- Is individual prepared to spend the time and finances to attempt fertility?
- Do individual and partner have a realistic grasp of the situation?
- Have they seriously considered adoption as a viable option?

References

Albo, Shana. Infertility Solutions: Natural Approaches. New York: Penguin Putnam, 2000.

Herman, Barry, MD, and Susan Perry, PhD. Infertility. Lycos Health with WebMD. 1997. 19 Jul 2000 <http://webmd.lycos.com/content/dmk/dmk_article_3961112>.

Infertility, Male
606, 606.9

Definition

Male infertility is generally recognized as the failure to impregnate after one year of unprotected sexual activity.

The most common reasons for infertility are abnormal sperm, poor sperm quality, or low sperm count. Abnormal sperm production may be categorized as less than 10 million sperm per cubic centimeter of semen (oligospermia), no sperm (azoospermia), low-quality sperm (dysspermia), or no ejaculation (aspermia).

Other factors causing infertility in men are malnutrition, genetic defects, chronic illness, structural abnormalities, environmental or workplace toxins, stress, fatigue, alcohol, tobacco or drug use, increased heat inside the scrotum, exposure to diethylstilbestrol, anabolic steroids, or prescription drugs that impair potency.

Infertility affects one in five couples in the US. About 30% of infertility problems originate with the man.

Diagnosis

History: The couple reports failure to conceive over a period of time. Individual may report prolonged fever or illness in the past 3 months, past surgery for varicocele, mumps orchitis, cryptorchidism, or testicular injury.

Physical exam: If there are any abnormalities such as varicocele in the testes or any prostate problems, these would be evident upon exam. The size of the testicles and the temperature of the scrotum are checked.

Tests: Sperm analysis is done. Lab tests include a complete blood count (CBC), urinalysis, blood testing for syphilis, rubella antibody, Tay-Sachs (if Jewish), sickle cell (if Black), thyroid function tests, and hormone levels. A testicular biopsy may be done. Ultrasound techniques may be used to detect tumors, cysts, abnormal blood flow, or varicoceles. An x-ray can reveal an obstruction (vasogram).

Treatment

Recent developments in reproductive medicine have made fertility possible for many men who are able to produce at least some sperm. There is no treatment for men who do not produce sperm.

Hormone therapy such as gonadotropin-releasing hormone (GnRH), estrogen, or testosterone may be used to increase fertility. Drugs such as alpha-adrenergic agonists or tricyclic antidepressants reduce acidity in the urine and can treat retrograde ejaculation.

Surgery to repair a varicocele (varicocelectomy) is a common procedure. Removal of the obstruction in the area of the ejaculatory ducts by excising or scraping the area can improve fertility in men.

Lifestyle changes that can help increase sperm count include avoiding cigarettes and drugs that affect sexual function, getting enough rest and moderate exercise, and following a healthy diet. To help prevent low sperm count, the individual should avoid hot baths, showers, and steam rooms, and wear loose clothing. In addition, any underlying cause should be treated. To avoid low sperm count per ejaculation, sexual intercourse should be limited to once every 2 to 3 days. Counseling may be given with regard to sexual technique that could enhance fertility.

Prognosis

In vitro fertilization is successful 14% of the time. It is difficult to predict which couples will eventually conceive.

The chances of conceiving are good if the reason for the infertility is found and treated. When the cause is unexplained, pregnancy occurs 34% of the time within 6 months, and 76% of the time within 2 years. This could be due to the fact that some couples need more time to conceive.

Failure to impregnate can cause frustration, resentment, a feeling of inadequacy, anger, guilt, and marital strife. The time and financial costs of fertility treatment may be a burden.

Differential Diagnosis

Other possible diagnoses include prostatitis, hypospadias, hypogonadism, endocrine disorders, varicocele, premature ejaculation, congenital genital abnormalities, retrograde ejaculation, neurologic dysfunction, cryptorchidism (failure of testes to descend from the abdomen), testicular cancer, sexually transmitted diseases, Kallmann's syndrome, and panhypopituitarism (pituitary gland fails to make almost all hormones).

Specialists

- Fertility Specialist
- Psychiatrist
- Urologist

Work Restrictions / Accommodations

Work restrictions may be needed if a varicocelectomy is required to repair a varicocele. Recovery takes about 6 days and most men cannot resume full activity for about 3 weeks.

Complementary and Alternative Therapies

Content is intended for awareness only. Treatments may or may not be effective. Scientific evidence may be lacking and some substances have potentially toxic effects. Dr. Presley Reed and the editors do not endorse the use of these therapies in the absence of consultation with a licensed medical professional.

Vitamin C - Said to improve the longevity and vitality of the sperm by helping the body absorb calcium, zinc, potassium, copper, and magnesium. Men with low levels of zinc should take supplements.

Vitamin E - Said to improve fertility in men with normal sperm count but there is evidence of excess free-oxygen radicals.

Comorbid Conditions

Comorbid conditions may include obesity, excessive exercise, stress, psychological conditions, malnutrition, chronic anemia, starvation, and kidney failure.

Complications

Infertility in both partners may complicate treatment. Severe infertility or infertility prolonged for over 3 years is more difficult to treat. Advancing age may introduce a sense of urgency about treatment.

Factors Influencing Duration

Available treatment options may result in different lengths of disability. An individual's response, mental health, and age can also contribute to the length of disability.

Length of Disability

No disability is expected.

Failure to Recover

If an individual fails to recover within the maximum duration expectancy period, the reader may wish to reference the following questions to assist in better understanding the specifics of an individual's medical case.

Regarding diagnosis:

- Has an underlying disorder been diagnosed?
- Did diagnostic tests include sperm analysis, blood tests and perhaps x-rays to rule out obstructive lesions?
- If the underlying cause is uncertain, have other possible diagnosis been considered or ruled out?
- Are coexisting conditions present that may contribute to reproductive dysfunction?
- Would the individual benefit from consultation with a specialist (fertility specialist, andrologist, psychiatrist, urologist)?

Regarding treatment:

- Was treatment appropriate to the underlying cause?
- Was individual instructed in lifestyle changes that can help increase sperm count, such as avoiding cigarettes and drugs that affect sexual function, getting enough rest and moderate exercise, and following a healthy diet?
- Was individual instructed to avoid situations that may lower sperm count, such as hot baths or showers, steam rooms, and tight clothing?
- Did individual and/or couple receive counseling with regard to sexual techniques that could enhance fertility?
- Would individual benefit from involvement in a stress management program?
- Were hormone injections effective in raising sperm counts?
- Was surgery required to correct anatomical deformities or obstructions? What is the expected outcome?

Regarding prognosis:

- Has adequate time elapsed for a response to treatment?
- Was the individual compliant with treatment recommendations or lifestyle modifications aimed at supporting reproductive health?
- Does the individual have any coexisting conditions (such as obesity, excessive exercise, stress, psychological conditions, malnutrition, chronic anemia, starvation, kidney failure) that may complicate treatment or impact prognosis? If so, have these conditions been addressed in the treatment plan?
- Has the condition persisted longer than 3 years?
- Because failure to impregnate can cause frustration, resentment, a feeling of inadequacy, anger, guilt, and marital strife, would individual and/or couple benefit from psychological counseling?
- If the time and financial costs of fertility treatment is a burden, has the possibility of adoption been discussed?

References

Getting Started. Resolve: The National Infertility Association. 31 Dec 1998. 07 July 2000 <http://www.resolve.org/started.htm>.

Werbach, Melvin, MD. "Conception Connections." Healthwell. 02 Aug 1999. 17 July 2000 <http://www.healthwell.com/hnbreakthroughs/feb99/sperm.cfm?path=hw&cond=104&mcat=30>.

Influenza

Other names / synonyms: Flu
487, 487.0, 487.1, 487.8

Definition

Influenza is an acute respiratory tract infectious disease caused by one of the influenza viruses. The symptoms, severity, and length of disability attributed to influenza are variable. Individuals often confuse the stomach flu with influenza. Influenza is a respiratory condition and stomach flu is a gastrointestinal condition.

Although most persons can benefit from annual immunization against influenza (annual flu shots), it is imperative that the people at highest risk receive the vaccination annually without fail. However, those people allergic to eggs should not receive annual flu shots because the vaccine is cultured in eggs. There are 3 types of influenza viruses: A, B, and C. Type A and B influenza usually occur during the flu season (November-April). Types A and B are more common and more serious forms and are associated with higher rate of hospitalization and death. Type C is a milder type of respiratory infection, which often does not have any symptoms. The influenza viruses (types A and B) mutate frequently, and so influenza vaccines are changed annually in anticipation of the expected predominate strain(s). Therefore, vaccines need to be taken every year.

The influenza virus is highly contagious. Spread occurs through airborne respiratory droplets. Influenza occurs more frequently and severely in smokers. It strikes hardest with the highest morbidity and mortality in the elderly in those with chronic medical conditions.

Individuals with asthma, chronic bronchitis, chronic obstructive pulmonary disease (COPD), emphysema, chronic heart disease, diabetes, severe anemia, and kidney dysfunction are prone to complications of influenza, as are individuals who are immunosuppressed.

Influenza is well known as a cause for epidemics in closed groups such as schools and nursing homes, as well as entire communities or whole countries. Occasionally, there are worldwide pandemics; the most recent pandemics occurred in 1957, 1968, and 1977; all began in Mainland China. Epidemics in temperate climates occur during the winter months; however, in tropical climates, they can occur at any time. Epidemics in the US occurred during the 1984-85, 1989-90, 1991-92, 1993-94 influenza seasons.

Infections with an influenza virus occur in about 1 of every 6 adults annually, with half seeking medical attention. About 1 in 1,500 persons with an underlying disease die from the complications of influenza. Each year, 20,000 Americans die because of influenza.

Diagnosis

History: Common to almost all cases of influenza are fever and systemic symptoms followed by upper and lower respiratory symptoms several days later. The systemic symptoms individuals may report include an abrupt onset of fever, chills, headache, muscle aches, joint pain, sore throat, runny nose, and fatigue. In some individuals, diarrhea, nausea, and vomiting may be reported. When the systemic symptoms somewhat subside, respiratory symptoms become dominant.

Physical exam: Upon examination, individuals may seem weary and tired. The skin may feel warm and there may be a fever of 101°F-104°F present. A runny nose may be evident. The mucous membrane of the throat may appear reddened. Lymph nodes may be slightly swollen.

Tests: A chest x-ray is indicated in individuals who are at high risk of developing pneumonia, such as individuals with chronic obstructive pulmonary disease (COPD), the elderly and the immunosuppressed, or in the individual with abnormalities detected on physical exam.

Treatment

Treatment is primarily symptomatic in most cases and includes rest, fluids, pain killers (analgesics), fever reducing medications (antipyretics), and cough suppressants, if necessary. Antibiotics are not warranted unless a bacterial infection is suspected. Over-exertion during symptomatic illness should be avoided.

Antiviral medications may be used to treat influenza A and B. They must be given within 48 hours of developing symptoms. Some may be used in the prevention of influenza, as well. They are available in pill, nasal spray, or inhaler forms. They prevent spread of influenza by blocking the virus from escaping the already infected cells.

Influenza illness and death caused can be prevented by yearly vaccination. The vaccine is effective against both influenza A and B strains. Influenza vaccine is recommended for people who are at high risk of developing complications due to influenza infection.

Prognosis

In healthy young and middle-aged adults, full recovery from influenza with no residual effects can be expected in a matter of days or weeks. In older adults and those with underlying pulmonary and cardiac disease, the outcome may leave them in a partially disabled condition by worsening their underlying chronic disease process.

The body can be so weakened by influenza that its defenses against bacteria are low. In influenza complicated by bacterial pneumonia, full recovery is expected in healthy young and middle-aged adults. Those who might contract the more serious primary viral influenza pneumonia are at risk of prolonged disability and, if hospitalized in respiratory failure, there is a mortality rate of 50%.

Differential Diagnosis

It may be difficult to distinguish a case of influenza from other upper and lower respiratory tract diseases, especially early and late in the flu season. Mycoplasma and chlamydial pneumonia may produce the same syndrome as well as a number of other viral and bacterial infections. Other conditions that may produce the same symptoms include the common cold, strep throat, acute or chronic bronchitis, allergic rhinitis, sinusitis, pneumonia, and asthma.

Specialists

- Infectious Disease Physician
- Pulmonologist
- Internist

Work Restrictions / Accommodations

Because of the ease with which influenza is transmitted, individuals should stay home until fever has dissipated or body temperature has returned to normal. Fever may last 2-5 days, individuals should stay home for 2 days after fever is gone.

Comorbid Conditions

Comorbid conditions may include stress, AIDS, cancer, diabetes, asthma, and certain genetic disorders, such as sickle-cell disease, cystic fibrosis, and Kartagener's syndrome.

Complications

Three types of pneumonia can occur as complications to influenza. They are viral, bacterial, and mixed viral and bacterial.

Influenza viral pneumonia occurs most frequently in individuals with underlying pulmonary or cardiac disease and in those who are immunosuppressed. It has a rapid, debilitating onset that can require hospitalization. If the pneumonia worsens, it can result in respiratory failure and death. The mortality rate is close to fifty percent.

Secondary bacterial pneumonia follows a different course. It affects mostly the drug abusers who use needles, hospitalized individuals, and those with chronic medical diseases. Generally, bacterial influenza can develop about 5 days after viral influenza. Bacterial pneumonia can be treated with antibiotics.

Mixed viral and bacterial pneumonia generally involves a milder form of viral pneumonia combined with a bacterial pneumonia. The condition will respond at least partially to antibiotic therapy.

Other non-pulmonary complications are rare in adults but can occur. A few of these are toxic shock syndrome, inflammation of the membrane enveloping the brain and spinal cord (meningitis), inflammation in the brain (encephalitis) and inflammation of the heart muscle or lining (carditis or pericarditis).

Factors Influencing Duration

Factors that might have an impact on the disability include age of individual, underlying chronic medical conditions, individual's immune response, severity of the symptoms, the type of influenza virus causing the infection, the number and severity of complications, compliance with medical treatment, the stage of illness at which medical intervention was begun, and the type of work to which the individual must return.

Length of Disability

Duration of disability depends on the nature of the job, job requirements, and the severity of influenza.

Duration in Days

Job Classification	Minimum	Optimum	Maximum
Any work	3	7	14

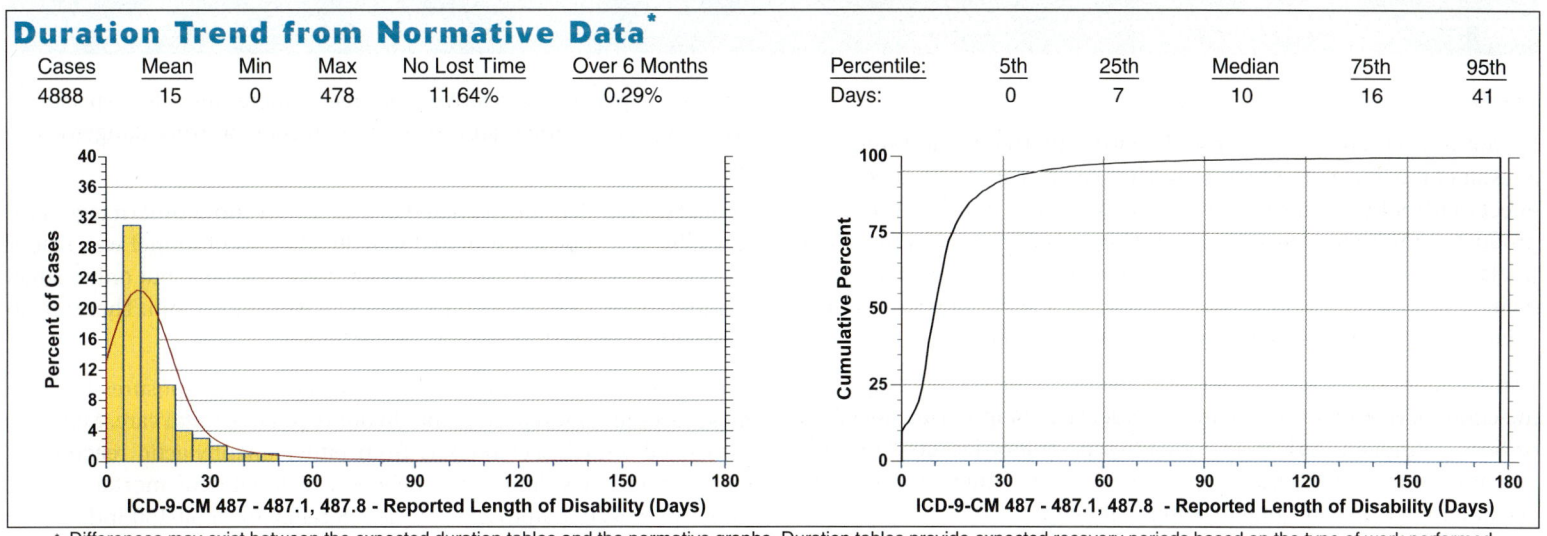

* Differences may exist between the expected duration tables and the normative graphs. Duration tables provide expected recovery periods based on the type of work performed by the individual. The normative graphs reflect the actual observed experience of many individuals across the spectrum of physical conditions, in a variety of industries, and with varying levels of case management.

Failure to Recover

If an individual fails to recover within the maximum duration expectancy period, the reader may wish to reference the following questions to assist in better understanding the specifics of an individual's medical case.

Regarding diagnosis:

- Did the individual have an influenza immunization this year?
- Does the individual have respiratory or GI symptoms?
- Is the individual a smoker?
- Does the individual have asthma, chronic bronchitis, COPD, emphysema, chronic heart disease, diabetes, severe anemia, kidney dysfunction or are immunosuppressed?
- Did the individual have an abrupt onset of fever, chills, headache, muscle aches, joint pain, sore throat, runny nose, and fatigue?
- Does the individual also report diarrhea, nausea, and vomiting?
- Have the respiratory symptoms become dominant?
- On exam did the individual have a fever of 101°F-104°F?
- Does the individual have a runny nose, red throat or swollen lymph nodes?
- Has the individual had a chest x-ray?
- Have conditions with similar symptoms been ruled out?
- Has the individual been seen by a specialist?

Regarding treatment:

- Is the individual receiving symptomatic treatment such as rest, fluids, analgesics, antipyretics, and cough suppressants, if necessary?
- Did the individual seek treatment within 48 hours of the onset of symptoms?
- Are they being treated with an antiviral medication?

Regarding prognosis:

- Does the individual have any conditions that may affect their ability to recover?
- Does the individual have any complications such as viral, bacterial or mixed viral and bacterial pneumonia resulting in respiratory failure and death? Does the individual have toxic shock syndrome, meningitis, encephalitis, carditis or pericarditis?

Influenza

References

Facts About Influenza For Adults. National Coalition for Adult Immunization. 01 Apr 2000. 21 August 2000 <http://www.nfid.org/factsheets/influadult.html>.

General Recommendations for Preventing Influenza Infection Among Travelers. Centers for Disease Control and Prevention. 10 Jul 2000. 21 August 2000 <http://www.cdc.gov/travel/feb99.htm>.

Influenza (Flu). American Lung Association. 2001. 21 Feb 2001 <http://www.lungusa.org/diseases/luninfluenz.html>.

The Common Cold. National Institute of Allergy and Infectious Diseases. 01 May 1998. 21 August 2000 <http://www.niaid.nih.gov/factsheets/cold.htm>.

Insect or Spider Bites and Stings

Other names / synonyms: Bee Sting, Spider Bite

989.5

Definition

Syndromes caused by insect or spider (arthropods) bites and stings are a result of the injected toxic venom. They can be caused by direct toxic effects and/or hypersensitivity to the venom, the organism, or their by-products, or from transmission of microorganisms carried by the insect (malaria, Lyme disease). Arthropods and insects that bite or sting include lice, bedbugs, fleas, mosquitoes, flies, ants, mites, ticks and spiders, wasps and bees (Hymenoptera), and scorpions.

Hymenoptera stings account for more deaths in the US than any other injections of venom (envenomation). Order Hymenoptera includes Apis or bees (European, African), vespids (wasps, yellow jackets, hornets), and ants. Ants sting 9.3 million people each year. Other Hymenoptera account for more than 1 million stings annually.

The reaction to a bite or sting may be local or systemic, and it can develop in a minute or up to several hours after the initial insult. Insect and spider toxins may cause local pain, swelling, skin inflammation (dermatitis), tissue necrosis, abdominal and vascular crises, cardiac problems (myocarditis), and shock. Allergic reactions are most commonly caused by bees, and include urticaria (hives), angioedema, breathing difficulties (bronchospasm and laryngeal swelling), and life-threatening anaphylactic shock. Arthropods and insects may be carriers for microorganisms that cause malaria, Lyme disease, and tick paralysis, Rocky Mountain spotted fever, west Nile virus.

Regional Poison Control Center reports show the following exposures to insect bites in 1998 (the last year for which information is available): ants/fire ants: 2,818; bee/wasp/hornet: 14,884; caterpillar: 2,704; centipede/millipede: 139; mosquito: 334; scorpion: 12,845; tick: 3,127; and other insects: 16,307. There was one death associated with the bee/wasp/hornet exposure. Reports of spider bite incidents include black widow spider: 2,452; brown recluse spider: 2,319; other spider: 9,253; and tarantulas: 256. One death was reported due the brown recluse spider and one due to another variety of spider.

Accurate, reliable worldwide data on scorpion envenomations do not exist. Many potentially dangerous scorpions inhabit the underdeveloped or developing world. Consequently, numerous envenomations go unreported, and true incidence is unknown. The highest reported mortality is in data from Mexico, with estimates as high as 1,000 deaths in one year. In the US, only 4 deaths were reported over an 11-year period. No deaths due to the Arizona bark scorpion (C exilicauda) have been reported in Arizona in over 30 years.

Outside the US, tarantulas can be found in Mexico, South America, the Caribbean, Africa, the Mediterranean, and Australia. While all North American species are relatively harmless, there are a few species in South America, Africa, and Australia that may be truly dangerous to humans.

Funnel web spiders are restricted to the eastern and southern regions of Australia. It has been estimated that 30-40 cases of funnel web spider bite occur each year in eastern and southern Australia, but only a small number (maybe 1 in 10) require treatment with antivenom. There are no international reports on widow spider bites.

Reliable statistics are not available for insect bite exposures because most cases are not reported and do not require hospital care. Mortality associated with insect bites is from either anaphylactic reaction or complications resulting from infection. Estimates of mortality from insect-provoked anaphylaxis in the US range from 50-150 individuals annually.

Only one fatality from a centipede bite has been reported worldwide. That incident was in the Philippines. Most species of centipedes are smaller and relatively innocuous. There have been no documented deaths from millipede exposures, and it is unlikely that such an exposure could be fatal, even to small children.

Diagnosis

History: The initial exposure may not be recognized in all cases. Symptoms usually develop within minutes to an hour and depend on the type of venom injected. After minor insect or spider bites and stings, the reaction is often localized to the site of the insult, with only symptoms of pain, swelling, itching, or burning. Individuals may report nausea, vomiting, diarrhea, cramps, dizziness, and breathing problems. The venom of the black widow spider causes severe abdominal pain, trunk and abdominal muscle spasm, and diffuse tingling (paresthesias). A scorpion sting causes pain, itching, tingling, and in severe cases, drowsiness, fainting (syncope), diminished vision, profuse sweating, muscle spasm, and convulsions.

Physical exam: The exam may reveal red, elevated patches of skin (urticaria or hives), swelling (angioedema), and blisters. There is local tissue destruction and possible necrosis after brown recluse spider bite, or a board-like abdomen after black widow spider bite. Swelling of the larynx, low or high blood pressure (hypo- or hypertension), rapid heartbeat (tachycardia), and irregular heartbeat (arrhythmia) may develop.

Tests: There are no specific laboratory tests for tarantula, centipede, millipede, insect, or bee/wasp/hornet bites and stings. Laboratory studies may help evaluate organ damage caused by reaction to bee/

wasp/hornet stings. A complete blood count (CBC) and blood chemistry may be of benefit as well. Brown recluse spider: Wound cultures and gram stain may be of value for local wounds. If signs of systemic toxicity are present, monitor the individual for evidence of deterioration of red blood cells (hemolysis), kidney (renal) failure, and disorder of blood coagulation (coagulopathy). Widow spiders: If the diagnosis is uncertain, laboratory studies to rule out an acute abdomen may be indicated (e.g., CBC, pregnancy test). The serum creatine phosphokinase (CPK) may be elevated.

Scorpion sting cases vary from those requiring no laboratory tests to scenarios requiring extensive hematologic, electrolyte, and respiratory analysis. A complete blood count (CBC), platelets, and coagulation parameters should be obtained as needed. Electrolytes, blood urea nitrogen (BUN), creatinine, and urinalysis may be considered. Renal failure may occur secondary to hemoglobin in the urine (hemoglobinuria) from hemolysis. Creatine phosphokinase (CPK) and urine myoglobin (a red iron-containing protein pigment in muscles that is similar to hemoglobin) may reveal destruction or degeneration of skeletal muscle (rhabdomyolysis) after severe muscle hyperactivity. Obtain arterial blood gases (ABGs) as indicated for respiratory distress. Obtain an electrocardiogram if indicated.

Treatment

Treatment includes gentle removal of a stinger (when present), ice, and topical hydrocortisone or oral antihistamines to reduce swelling, pain, and itching. Treatment of lice and fleas includes shampoos and creams containing insecticides. In the case of anaphylactic shock from bee/wasp/hornet or scorpion stings and spider bites, adrenergic receptor stimulators, antihistamines, antivenin, and hospitalization may be necessary.

Individuals with a history of hypersensitivity to any of these venoms are advised to carry a dosage of an injectable adrenergic receptor stimulator when there is a risk of exposure to the offending species.

Prognosis

The prognosis for a successful recovery is good following treatment for minor insect and spider bites and stings. However, anaphylactic reactions can be fatal in some cases. Prompt and appropriate treatment will lessen the chances for a fatal outcome.

While the vast majority of stings cause only minor problems, stings cause a significant number of deaths. Bee, wasp, and hornet stings may be fatal following an anaphylactic reaction to the sting. Most stings resolve with no residual complaints.

Although deaths have been attributed to presumed brown recluse envenomation, severe outcomes are rare. Typical cases involve only local, soft tissue destruction. Mortality from spider bites occurs mostly in very young children and the elderly.

Prognosis for recovery from scorpion stings is species dependent. Most individuals recover fully from Centruroides scorpion envenomation. The Centruroides species are found in the southern US, Mexico, Central America, and the Caribbean. C exilicauda is found in the southwestern US (primarily Arizona, and small parts of Texas, New Mexico, Nevada, and California) and Mexico.

Differential Diagnosis

Other diagnoses include dermatitis or allergic reaction to another allergen. The differential diagnosis for spider bites requires excluding various disorders that present with abdominal and vascular crises, tetanus, and lead poisoning. The clinical presentation of tick paralysis may suggest poliomyelitis, Guillain-Barré syndrome or other acutely developing neuropathies. If there is no history of an insect bite, anaphylactic shock may mimic different vascular, cardiac, or neurologic disorders.

Specialists

- Allergist
- Cardiologist
- Dermatologist
- Emergency Medicine
- Entomologist
- Internist
- Medical Toxicologist
- Occupational Medicine Physician
- Occupational Therapist
- Physical Therapist
- Pulmonologist

Work Restrictions / Accommodations

Depending on job requirements, the individual should wear adequate clothing and use chemical repellents as protection from insects and spiders. Those with a history of life-threatening reactions, if in constant contact with insects, may require desensitization, and should carry an injectable adrenergic receptor stimulator.

Complementary and Alternative Therapies

Content is intended for awareness only. Treatments may or may not be effective. Scientific evidence may be lacking and some substances have potentially toxic effects. Dr. Presley Reed and the editors do not endorse the use of these therapies in the absence of consultation with a licensed medical professional.

Hydrotherapy - Initially, ice placed over the site of the sting may reduce the pain. For wound healing, warm soaks and compresses may increase circulation to the area, promoting healing.

Comorbid Conditions

Pre-existing cardiovascular disease, pulmonary disease and disorders, skin hypersensitivity, allergies, and gastrointestinal disease may all worsen the effects of insect bites and stings.

Complications

Secondary infection may result from insect bites or stings. Symptoms of any disease transmitted by an insect bite may not be evident for days, weeks, or even longer.

Bee, wasp, hornet sting sites may become infected. Infection is more common in fire ant stings because they frequently are multiple; stings form a fluid filled growth (vesiculate) and then ulcerate, leaving itching (pruritic) open wounds. Anaphylaxis may occur in susceptible individuals from exposure to other insect-related material, including honey and treatment involving bee venom in certain diseases and disorders (apiotherapy). Myocardial infarction, kidney (renal) failure, and cerebral edema may occur after a bee sting. Peripheral nerve block may occur if sting is near the path of a nerve.

Scorpion stings may result in respiratory arrest, cardiac arrest, shock, seizures, or destruction or degeneration of skeletal muscle (rhabdomyolysis). Death may occur as result of the bite/sting of certain scorpion species found worldwide. Loss of a protein in the blood (defibrination), hemolysis, or inflammation of the pancreas (pancreatitis) may also result from bites of specific, individual species of scorpions.

Bites of widow spiders may result in respiratory difficulty with a worsening in the reactive airway. Spontaneous abortion or preterm labor may occur in pregnant women. A high blood pressure (hypertensive) emergency with or without associated seizures and acute myocardial infarction may also occur following the bite of widow spiders. There may also be destruction or degeneration of skeletal muscle (rhabdomyolysis).

Delayed skin grafting may be necessary after 4-6 weeks of standard therapy following the bite of a brown recluse spider. Losses of digits and amputations have been reported. Inflammation of conjunctiva and a round, gray swelling where each hair is embedded (ophthalmia nodosa) and inflammation of the uveal tract (panuveitis) can complicate eye exposure to tarantula hairs. Once the bite of a funnel web spider has been successfully treated with antivenom and recovered from the acute illness, further complications are unlikely.

Secondary infections and wound necrosis may result from centipede exposures. Conjunctivitis or corneal ulcerations can complicate eye exposures to exposure to millipedes.

Factors Influencing Duration

The type of arthropod or insect responsible, the site of insult, the number of stings or bites, and the individual's reaction to the venom will influence the length of disability. Age, physical condition, nutritional status and general health will influence the individual response to bites and stings and on their recovery.

Length of Disability

Minor non-venomous.

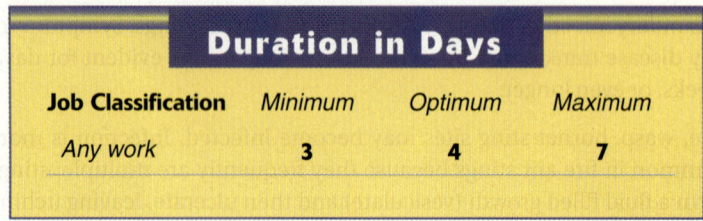

Duration in Days

Job Classification	Minimum	Optimum	Maximum
Any work	0	0	1

Poisonous spiders, scorpions.

Duration in Days

Job Classification	Minimum	Optimum	Maximum
Any work	3	4	7

Failure to Recover

If an individual fails to recover within the maximum duration expectancy period, the reader may wish to reference the following questions to assist in better understanding the specifics of an individual's medical case.

Regarding diagnosis:

- Does the individual have a recent history of an insect or spider bite or sting?
- Does the individual complain of local pain, swelling, skin inflammation, tissue necrosis, abdominal and vascular crises, myocarditis, or shock?
- Does the individual have urticaria, angioedema, dizziness, bronchospasm, laryngeal swelling, or life-threatening anaphylactic shock?
- Does the individual have severe abdominal pain, trunk and abdominal muscle spasm, and paresthesias?
- Does the individual have drowsiness, syncope, diminished vision, profuse sweating, muscle spasm, or convulsions?
- On physical did the individual have urticaria or hives, angioedema, blisters, tissue necrosis, a board-like abdomen, swelling of the larynx, hypo or hypertension, tachycardia, or arrhythmia?
- Has the individual had a CBC, complete chemistry panel, coagulation studies, arterial blood gasses if necessary, urine myoglobin, wound culture and ECG?
- Have conditions with similar symptoms been ruled out?

Regarding treatment:

- Has the individual had the stinger removed?
- Is the individual being treated with ice, topical hydrocortisone or oral antihistamines?
- If necessary has the individual been treated with medicated shampoo?
- Does the individual have anaphylactic shock?
- Has the individual been treated with adrenergic receptor stimulators, antihistamines, or antivenin?
- Was hospitalization necessary?
- Does the individual have a history of hypersensitivity to any venoms?
- Does the individual carry a dose of an injectable adrenergic receptor stimulator when there is a risk of exposure to the offending species?

Regarding prognosis:

- Is the individual's employer able to accommodate any necessary restrictions?
- Does the individual have any conditions that may affect their ability to recover?
- Does the individual have any complications such as secondary infection, any disease transmitted by an insect bite, site vesiculation with ulceration?
- Does the individual have anaphylaxis, hypertension, myocardial infarction, renal failure, or cerebral edema?
- Did a peripheral nerve block occur?
- If pregnant, did spontaneous abortion or preterm labor occur?

- Did the individual have respiratory arrest, cardiac arrest, shock, seizures, rhabdomyolysis, defibrination, hemolysis, or pancreatitis?
- Will reconstructive surgery be necessary?

References

"Chapter 308: Bites and Stings." Merck Manual of Diagnosis and Therapy, 17th ed. Beers, Mark H., and Robert Berkow, MD Whitehouse Station, NJ: Merck & Co., Inc., 1999. 29 Sept 2000 <http://www.merck.com/pubs/mmanual/section23/chapter308/308c.htm>.

Fernandez, Miguel C., and Nicolas Arredondo, MD. Insects Bites. eMedicine.com. 01 Aug 2000. 1 Oct 2000 <http://emedicine.com/emerg/topic62.htm>.

Insertion of Inflatable Penile Prosthesis
Other names / synonyms: Penile Implant, Penile Prosthetic Surgery
64.97

Definition

This procedure involves the implantation of an inflatable prosthesis into the penis.

The inflatable penile prosthesis is one of many options available to individuals with erectile dysfunction. There are many brands of penile prostheses available, including one-, two-, and three-piece designs.

The most common inflatable implants consist of paired cylinders, which are surgically inserted inside the penis and can be expanded using pressurized fluid. Tubes connect the cylinders to a fluid reservoir and pump, which also are surgically implanted. The individual can inflate the cylinders by pressing on the small pump, located under the skin in the scrotum. Inflatable implants can expand the length and width of the penis somewhat. They also leave the penis in a more natural state when not inflated than malleable rod implants.

Alternatives to penile implants include oral medications, urethral suppositories, intracorporeal injections, vacuum erection devices, and behavior modification.

In current practice, individuals undergoing insertion of an inflatable penile prosthesis have usually already tried and failed available medical treatments and vacuum devices.

This procedure is often used to treat impotence. Impotence can be defined as a total inability to achieve erection, an inconsistent ability to achieve erection, or a tendency to sustain only brief erections. Due to these variations in defining impotence, its incidence is difficult to estimate. It is believed that impotence affects between 10 and 15 million American men.

Approximately 20,000 to 30,000 penile prostheses are implanted annually in the US. The success rate, as judged by the individual's and their partner's satisfaction, runs between 85-90 percent.

Reason for Procedure

The inflatable penile prosthesis is one of many options available to individuals with erectile dysfunction. This procedure is often used to treat impotence. Impotence can be defined as a total inability to achieve erection, an inconsistent ability to achieve erection, or a tendency to sustain only brief erections.

Alternatives to penile implants include oral medications, urethral suppositories, intracorporeal injections, vacuum erection devices, and behavior modification.

In current practice, individuals undergoing insertion of an inflatable penile prosthesis have usually already tried and failed available medical treatments and vacuum devices.

The insertion of an inflatable penile prosthesis is the most common surgical method for treatment of impotence (erectile dysfunction) in men.

Damage to arteries, smooth muscles, and fibrous tissues, often as a result of disease, is the most common cause of impotence. Diseases including diabetes, kidney disease, chronic alcoholism, multiple sclerosis, atherosclerosis, and vascular disease account for about 70% of cases of impotence. Between 35-50% of men with diabetes experience impotence.

Surgery (e.g., prostate surgery) can injure nerves and arteries near the penis, causing impotence. Injury to the penis, spinal cord, prostate, bladder, and pelvis can lead to impotence by harming nerves, smooth muscles, arteries, and fibrous tissues of the corpora cavernosa.

Description

The procedure is performed in a hospital under local, epidural, spinal, or general anesthetic. The incision may be made in 1 of 3 places. The perineal approach is beneath the scrotum. The penoscrotal approach is at the base of the underside of the penis just above the scrotum. The incision may also be made above the penis in the pubic area (infrapubic incision). The spongy tissue of the penis is partially removed and the prosthesis put in its place. The reservoir and pump may be implanted in the lower pelvis and scrotal sac or self-contained within the cylinder itself. Antibiotics are given intravenously during the surgery. The incision is closed with sutures.

The average hospital stay is 3 to 7 days.

Prognosis

Complete recovery can be expected after allowing about 4 to 6 weeks for recovery from surgery. Penile sensations and sexual arousal should be at or near normal. A majority of individuals find that prosthetic erections are about a half-inch shorter than their former natural erections.

Specialists

- Urologist

Work Restrictions / Accommodations

Resumption of driving is usually permitted 1 week after surgery, but only if the individual is pain-free without medication. During the initial 2 weeks following surgery, the individual should not lift heavy objects (more than 10 pounds) and should not engage in any activity that involves abdominal straining (e.g., excessive stair climbing, squatting).

Comorbid Conditions

Existing conditions that may impact ability to recover and may further lengthen disability include fibrotic diseases of the penis (e.g., Peyronie's disease, tunica albuginea fibrosis, and cavernosal fibrosis).

Procedure Complications

Possible complications of the procedure include collection of blood in the incisional area (hematoma), surgical-wound infection, rejection of synthetic implants, erosion of skin or urethra, and mechanical failure of the implanted device.

Factors Influencing Duration

The presence of complications and the individual's response to the procedure will determine the length of disability.

Length of Disability

Duration in Days

Job Classification	Minimum	Optimum	Maximum
Any work	14	21	42

References

Inflatable Penile Prosthesis. The Mentor Corporation. 01 Jan 1997. 13 Jan 2001 <http://www.bcm.tmc.edu/urol/fertility/ipp.htm>.

Penile Prosthesis Implants. The Reed Centre. 01 Jan 1999. 13 Jan 2001 <http://www.penisdoctor.com/prosthesis.htm>.

Insomnia with Sleep Apnea

Other names / synonyms: Dysomnia, Dyssomnia, Mixed Sleep Apnea, Obstructive Sleep Apnea Syndrome, Sleep Disorder

780.51

Definition

Insomnia describes a disturbance in sleep that includes difficulty falling asleep or staying asleep. The term apnea means a pause in breathing. Poor-quality sleep results from problems falling asleep, waking frequently during the night with difficulty returning to sleep, waking too early in the morning, or sleep that does not refresh. Insomnia can be short-term (transient), off and on (intermittent), or constant (chronic). Individuals who experience sleep apnea stop breathing (apnea) several times during the night for short periods of time. True apnea occurs for 10 seconds or more, at least 5 times each hour. Often, during the periods of apnea, drops in blood oxygen levels cause the individual to wake suddenly. These frequent interruptions in sleep associated with sleep apnea are referred to as insomnia with sleep apnea.

Sleep apnea can affect anyone; however, obesity, cigarette smoking, alcohol ingestion, taking sedatives, sleeping on the back, male gender, and being over 40 years old are factors that increase one's risk of insomnia with sleep apnea. It is estimated that 12 million Americans suffer from sleep apnea.

Diagnosis

History: Recurrent low oxygen levels bring on sleep disturbances resulting in daytime symptoms including sleepiness, morning headache, and slowed mental activity. Individuals may report excessive yawning, dozing during the day, hand tremors, and an inability to concentrate. Bed partners may report that the individual has restless sleep and periodically stops breathing during sleep.

Physical exam: The physical exam may be normal or may reveal high blood pressure. The individual may appear sleepy during the exam. The back of the mouth and throat (oropharynx) is often narrowed by excessive soft tissue folds, large tonsils or adenoids, and a prominent tongue. There may be evidence of a nasal obstruction or poor nasal airflow. The individual may have a short, thick neck (bull neck). Obesity is evident in many individuals with sleep apnea.

Tests: A test that monitors multiple physiologic parameters during sleep (polysomnography) can help confirm the diagnosis of obstructive sleep apnea and determine the severity and frequency of episodes of low blood oxygen levels. In addition, monitoring the heart's electrical activity (electrocardiogram, or ECG), measuring blood oxygen levels (via oximetry or arterial blood gas), and measuring respiratory effort and airflow (pulmonary function tests) may be done.

Treatment

Multiple therapeutic approaches may have to be tried, although no one treatment can be considered a panacea. Individuals are encouraged to try sleeping on their sides or stomach. For obesity-related sleep apnea, weight reduction may reduce obstructive episodes, improve blood oxygenation, and reduce daytime drowsiness. Individuals are strictly instructed to avoid alcohol and sedative or hypnotic medications. Supplemental oxygen may help raise blood oxygen levels. Nasal continuous positive airway pressure (CPAP) or bi-level positive airway pressure (BiPAP) may be used in severe obstructive sleep apnea. Removable dental appliances may be used during sleep to prevent the upper airway from being obstructed by the tongue or other oral structures.

In the few individuals who have severe symptoms (such as heart or lung abnormalities) and fail to respond to the above measures, surgery may be recommended. If present, enlarged tonsils and/or adenoids will be removed. One procedure, uvulopalatopharyngoplasty, consists of removing the obstructing soft tissue in the back of the mouth and upper throat. For those with significant nasal deformities, nasal surgery may include realigning the nasal septum (nasal septoplasty), or decreasing the size of large nasal bones. Creating an airway opening in the neck (tracheostomy) is a surgical procedure that effectively bypasses the obstruction in the mouth and upper throat (oropharynx).

Prognosis

Treatments are generally successful in all but the most severe cases. Uvulopalatopharyngoplasty and nasal septoplasty are effective only 50% of the time in reducing apnea episodes. A tracheostomy is the most effective (radical) surgical procedure for obstructive sleep apnea, but carries adverse effects such as scar tissue formation, speech disturbances, and infection.

Differential Diagnosis

Other sleep disorders such as narcolepsy, nightmares, or psychiatric depression should be included in the differential diagnosis. Insomnia is a common symptom of menopause.

Specialists

- Cardiologist
- Internist
- Otolaryngologist
- Pulmonologist

Work Restrictions / Accommodations

Daytime sleepiness and poor concentration may interfere with the safe operation of vehicles and machinery. Job reassignment may be necessary and should be done on a case-by-case basis. Part attention should be given to those whose jobs require prolonged period of alertness, such as pilots, professional drivers, and surgeons.

Comorbid Conditions

Comorbid conditions of cardiac disease, hypothyroidism, and obstructive lung diseases may impact ability to recover and further lengthen disability.

Complications

Complications include cardiac rhythm abnormalities (e.g., sinus arrhythmias, extreme bradycardia, atrial flutter, ventricular tachycardia), high blood pressure (hypertension), heart attack, and stroke. The mortality rate from stroke and heart attack is significantly higher in individuals with obstructive sleep apnea than in the general population.

Factors Influencing Duration

The severity of the condition, type of treatment, response to treatment, the type of work performed, and the presence of psychiatric disturbances or complications may influence disability.

Length of Disability

Length of disability is dependent on the type of treatment required to relieve the sleep apnea. Even in the most severe cases, surgical treatment is generally effective at relieving apnea, insomnia, and the associated complications.

Medical treatment.

Duration in Days

Job Classification	Minimum	Optimum	Maximum
Any work	0	3	7

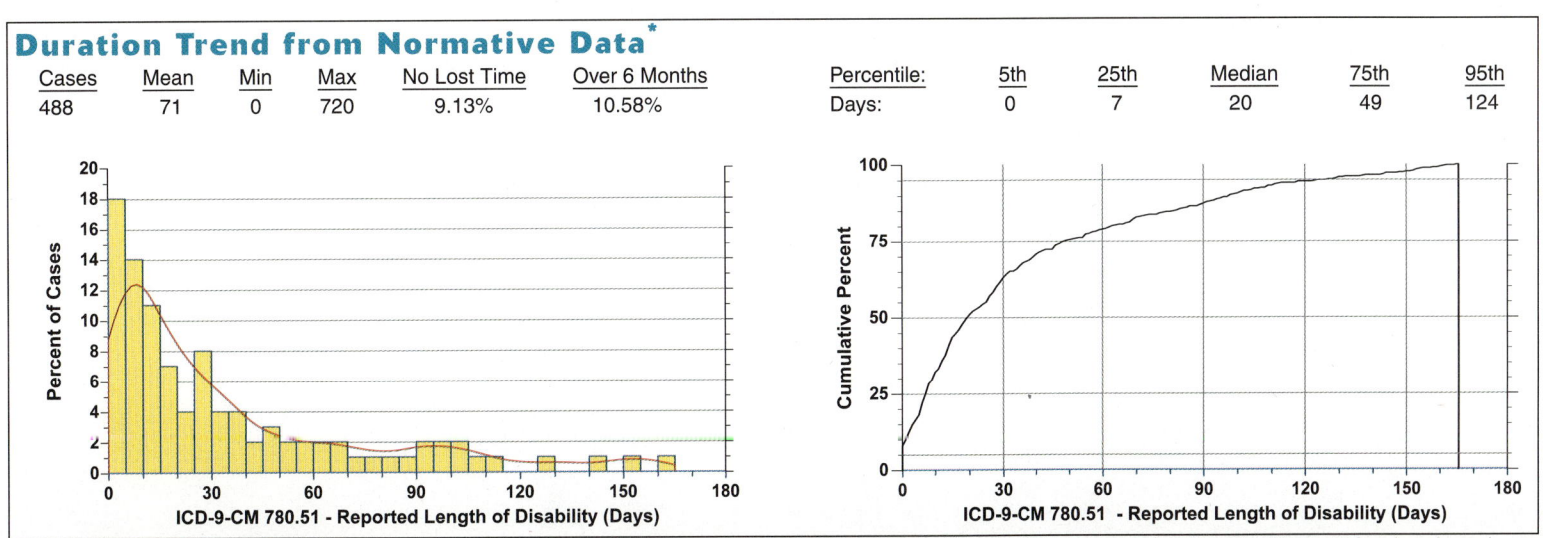

Duration Trend from Normative Data*

Cases	Mean	Min	Max	No Lost Time	Over 6 Months
488	71	0	720	9.13%	10.58%

Percentile:	5th	25th	Median	75th	95th
Days:	0	7	20	49	124

* Differences may exist between the expected duration tables and the normative graphs. Duration tables provide expected recovery periods based on the type of work performed by the individual. The normative graphs reflect the actual observed experience of many individuals across the spectrum of physical conditions, in a variety of industries, and with varying levels of case management.

Insomnia with Sleep Apnea

Failure to Recover

If an individual fails to recover within the maximum duration expectancy period, the reader may wish to reference the following questions to assist in better understanding the specifics of an individual's medical case.

Regarding diagnosis:

- Is insomnia accompanied by apnea that occurs for 10 seconds or more at least 5 times each hour?
- Is the individual obese? A smoker? Uses alcohol? Uses sedatives? Sleeps on their back?
- What is their gender? Age?
- Does the individual report daytime symptoms?
- Does their bed partner report restless sleep or that breathing stops during sleep?
- On exam did the individual appear sleepy?
- Were abnormalities found in the back of the mouth and throat?
- Does the individual have a short thick neck?
- Has the individual had a sleep study done?
- Have they had an ECG? Arterial blood gasses measured? Pulmonary function tests?
- Were conditions with similar symptoms ruled out?

Regarding treatment:

- Has the individual tried sleeping on their side?
- If obese, is the individual in a weight control program?
- Has the individual tried CPAP or BiPAP?
- Did the individual try removable dental appliances during sleep?
- Has the individual been compliant in avoiding alcohol, cigarettes, and sedatives or hypnotic medications?
- Did the individual have surgery? What procedure(s) was done?

Regarding prognosis:

- Is the individual's employer able to accommodate any necessary restrictions?
- Does the individual have any conditions that may affect their ability to recover?
- Does the individual have any complications such as arrhythmias? Hypertension? Heart attack or stroke?
- What type of work does the individual do?
- Has the individual had a psychiatric evaluation?

References

"Facts About Insomnia." National Institutes of Health. 01 Oct 1995. 1 Jan 2001 <http://www.nhlbi.nih.gov/health/public/sleep/insomnia.txt>.

Tierney, Lawrence M., J. Stephen McPhee, and Maxine A. Papadakis, eds. Current Medical Diagnosis and Treatment, 39th ed. New York: Lange Medical Books/McGraw-Hill, 2000.

Intermittent Explosive Disorder

Other names / synonyms: Aggressive Personality Disorder, Anger Attacks, Episodic Dyscontrol, Impulse Control Disorder, Rage Attacks

312.34

Definition

Intermittent explosive disorder is categorized as one of the impulse-control disorders by the DSM-IV-TR (Diagnostic and Statistical Manual of Mental Disorders, 4th Edition, Text Revision, published by the American Psychiatric Association). The primary feature is failure to resist an impulse, drive, or temptation to perform an act that is harmful to the individual or others. There is a pattern of aggressive episodes grossly out of proportion to any provocation or precipitating psychosocial stressor. These episodes frequently result in physical or verbal assaults or property destruction and are not related to other medical, psychiatric, or substance-related disorders. The individual may report feeling a sense of tension prior to the episode and immediately followed by a sense of relief and then feelings of remorse, regret, or embarrassment. This disorder may lead to occupational and relationship difficulties, accidents, hospitalizations, financial problems, or legal problems.

Intermittent explosive disorder may begin abruptly with usual age of onset from childhood to the early 20s. It is more common in men than women and may be more common among first-degree relatives of individuals with this disorder. Some women with the disorder have reported an increase in intermittent explosive symptoms before their menstrual cycle.

Diagnosis

History: The individual may give a childhood history of severe temper tantrums, impaired attention, hyperactivity, and other behavioral difficulties such as stealing or fire setting. The individual may report irritability, increased energy, or racing thoughts during the aggressive impulses and acts and rapid onset of fatigue and depression afterward. The episode is often followed by remorse, shame, or embarrassment. The aggressive episodes may be preceded with tingling, tremor, the feeling of a very fast heart rate (palpitations), chest tightness, head pressure, or hearing an echo. Individuals may also report having aggressive impulses that they resisted or acted out in a less assaultive way such as hitting a wall.

Physical exam: The exam may reveal signs of tension or anxiety such as pacing or clenched jaws or fists. Bruises or abrasions may occur if the individual has recently had a fight as a result of aggressive impulses.

Tests: There are no specific diagnostic tests but nonspecific changes may be noted in electroencephalogram (EEG), visual evoked potentials, or altered serotonin metabolism. Personality testing such as the Minnesota Multiphasic Personality Inventory may reveal difficulty with impulse control.

Treatment

The goal of treatment is to decrease or end the destructive episodes. Group and individual psychotherapy and pharmacotherapy are treatments of choice in various combinations. Self-help and anger-management groups may also be useful. Pharmacotherapy utilizes antianxiety agents and antidepressants to reduce symptoms of anxiety and depression. Tricyclic antidepressants, serotonin reuptake inhibitors, and mood stabilizers are often effective in controlling the explosive episodes. If the individual also has attention-deficit/hyperactivity disorder (ADHD), he or she may require a central nervous system stimulant to control the associated symptoms. Behavioral interventions play an important role in treatment.

Group therapy may be effective especially when individuals in the group have experienced similar disorders. Group therapy may help the individual identify, understand, and deal with underlying problems that result in aggressive behavior. Group situations can also help the individual learn how to improve interpersonal relationships and find more appropriate ways of expressing feelings.

Prognosis

There is little data on the course of this disorder. Some individuals have a chronic course and others a more episodic course. Many individuals experience some decrease in symptoms or a change in fixed patterns of thoughts, feelings, or behaviors that are causing difficulty over a period of time or after receiving treatment. In a recent study of 20 symptomatic individuals, 60% had a moderate response to serotonin reuptake inhibitors and 75% to mood stabilizers with a reduction in aggressive impulses and explosive acts.

Differential Diagnosis

Aggressive episodes can occur in many other mental or medical conditions such as delirium, dementia, brain injury, temporal lobe epilepsy, or brain tumor. Other psychiatric diagnoses with similar presentation include antisocial personality disorder, manic episode, dissociative disorder, paranoid schizophrenia, delirium, dementia, or substance intoxication or withdrawal. Malingering is a possibility to avoid legal consequences of the destructive behavior.

Specialists

- Advanced Practice Registered Nurse
- Neurologist
- Occupational Therapist
- Psychiatrist
- Psychologist

Work Restrictions / Accommodations

Tolerance for explosive rage is minimal in the workplace, particularly in light of concern for the safety of coworkers. Frequency of episodes has a direct bearing on employability. Job accommodations, when possible, should include a quiet, predictable low stress environment; work that is completed independent of coworkers; provisions for flexible breaks to control stress and anger levels; and flexibility in schedule to contact support system and attend treatment programs, meetings among the employer, supervisor, and job coach to explore sources of tension on the job, and any solutions or other accommodations.

Comorbid Conditions

Comorbid conditions that may affect recovery and lengthen disability include psychiatric disorders such as schizophrenia, major depression, anxiety disorder, ADHD, or substance abuse. Comorbidity with other psychiatric conditions is high. In a recent study of intermittent explosive disorder, 93% of individuals also had lifetime DSM-IV diagnoses of mood disorders. In addition, 48% had substance use, 48% anxiety disorders, 44% impulse-control disorders other than intermittent explosive disorder, and 22% had an eating disorder.

Complications

This disorder often results in repeated loss of employment, damage to personal relationships, divorce, social isolation, accidental injury, or confinement in prison. Substance abuse including alcohol is often associated with this disorder and can produce significant complications. Assaultive behavior poses an increased risk of premature death from suicide, accident, or homicide.

Factors Influencing Duration

An underlying, treatable condition such as alcohol or drug abuse can influence disability. The presence or absence of any underlying mental illness, individual's social support system, appropriateness of treatment choice, compliance with treatment, motivation to change, and adequacy of ongoing care can also affect length of disability. In general, unless a psychosis or severe physical illness is present, an already employed individual should be allowed to continue working especially if enrolled in or has completed a treatment program.

Many individuals respond to treatment and are able to learn to control their aggressive impulses. Individuals who are able to develop supportive relationships and make use of self-help groups are more likely to experience continued improvement in social and occupational functioning.

Length of Disability

This condition represents a life-long pattern of behavior. In most cases, no disability is expected.

Failure to Recover

If an individual fails to recover within the maximum duration expectancy period, the reader may wish to reference the following questions to assist in better understanding the specifics of an individual's medical case.

Regarding diagnosis:

- Does the individual's condition fit the criteria for intermittent explosive disorder?
- Has diagnosis been confirmed?
- Have psychological and medical disorders with similar symptoms been ruled out?

Regarding treatment:

- If the individual is not responding effectively to current medication, what other drug options are available?
- Is the individual currently involved in a therapy group?
- Does this group help individual identify, understand, and deal with underlying problems that result in aggressive behavior?
- Is the individual learning how to improve interpersonal relationships and find more appropriate ways of expressing feelings?
- Would the individual benefit from enrollment in a self-help or anger-management group?

Regarding prognosis:

- Does the individual have an underlying condition, such as substance abuse, that may impact recovery?
- Have underlying psychiatric conditions that tend to worsen prognosis been identified and treated appropriately?
- Has the individual been involved in the current form of treatment for over 6 weeks without a noticeable effect?
- Should treatment plan been reassessed?

References

Bars, D.R., et al. "Use of Visual Evoked-potential Studies and EEG Data to Classify Aggressive, Explosive Behavior of Youths." Psychiatric Services 52 1 (2001): 81-86.

Lanza, M.L. "Developing Psychodynamic Group Treatment Methods for Aggressive Male Inpatients." Issues in Mental Health Nursing 17 5 (1996): 409-425.

Internal Derangement of Knee
717, 717.9

Definition

An "internal derangement of the knee" is a traumatic or mechanical disorder of the knee involving the ligaments, capsule, menisci, or cartilage. It encompasses most intracapsular conditions other than the various forms of arthritis (arthritides) and tumors (neoplasms). Modern diagnostic methods, MRI and arthroscopy, now permit specific diagnoses.

See Meniscus Disorders, Patella Chondromalacia, and Sprains and Strains, Knee.

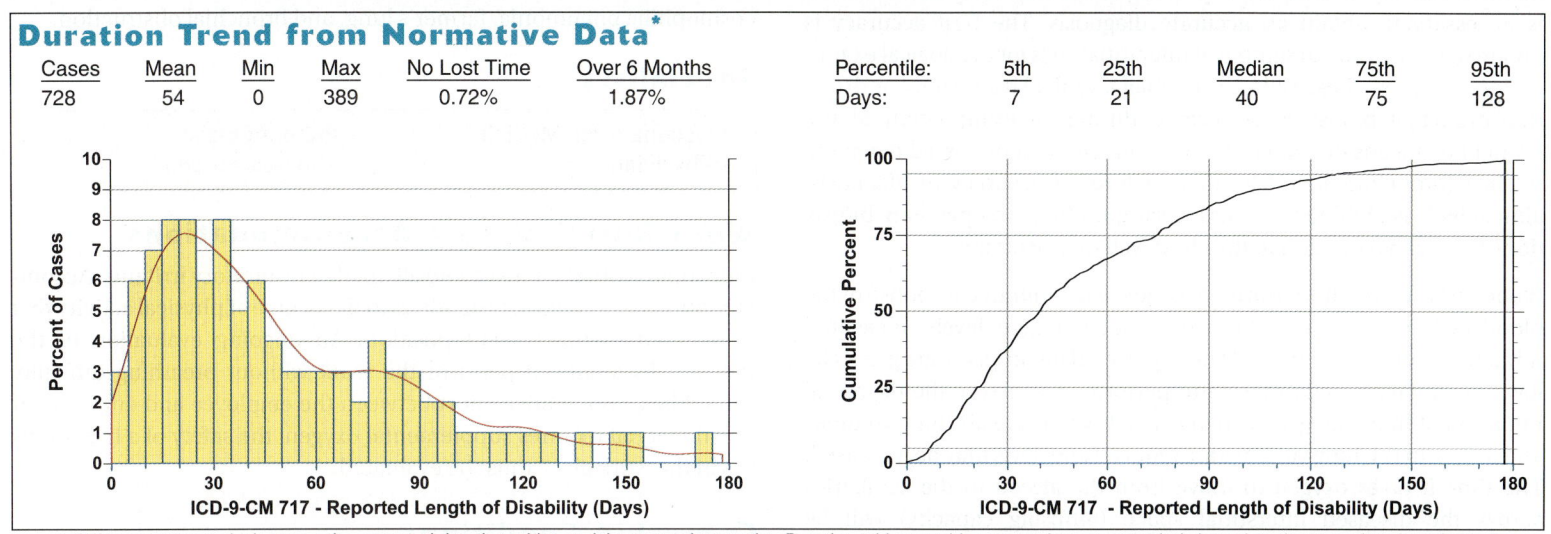

* Differences may exist between the expected duration tables and the normative graphs. Duration tables provide expected recovery periods based on the type of work performed by the individual. The normative graphs reflect the actual observed experience of many individuals across the spectrum of physical conditions, in a variety of industries, and with varying levels of case management.

Interstitial Pulmonary Fibrosis

Other names / synonyms: Cirrhosis of Lung, Fibrosing Alveolitis, Fibrotic Lung Disease, Idiopathic Pulmonary Fibrosis, Interstitial Lung Disorders, Pulmonary Fibrosis

515

Definition

Interstitial pulmonary fibrosis (IPF) is characterized by the replacement of normal lung tissue with fibrous tissue (fibrosis). It is one of over 150 different interstitial lung diseases. IPF is a stiffness or scarring of the tissue in between the air sacs (alveoli) and blood vessels of the lungs. This stiffness reduces the ability of the alveoli to expand and take in adequate amounts of oxygen, leading to shortness of breath and eventually respiratory failure. IPF is irreversible.

The disease may be of unknown cause (idiopathic), or it can be triggered by a severe viral infection. An inflammation in the air sacs of the lung leads to fluid leakage and cellular breakdown. Because the healing and cleanup processes of the lung are altered, there is destruction of the walls of the air sacs and the walls of small blood vessels (capillaries), resulting in widespread scarring. The chronic nature of the disease is caused by poor regulation of the clean-up cells of the lung (macrophages).

The known causes of IPF are numerous and include inorganic and organic dusts, gases, fumes, vapors, medications, radiation, and certain lung infections. Some occupational lung diseases (e.g., hypersensitivity pneumonitis, coal worker's pneumoconiosis, silicosis, and byssinosis) can lead to IPF.

Interstitial pulmonary fibrosis affects approximately 5 out of 100,000 individuals in the US. Individuals who smoke are at increased risk. Individuals over the age of 40 years are more frequently affected. IPF affects men more than women (at a ratio of 1.5:1).

Diagnosis

History: Shortness of breath is the hallmark symptom of IPF. It begins with breathlessness during exertion, which the individual may attribute to just being "out of shape." As the disease progresses, there is shortness of breath even at rest. Other symptoms may include fatigue, chronic dry cough, chest pain, decreased tolerance for activity, expectoration of blood or blood-stained sputum (hemoptysis), nonspecific muscle and joint pain, loss of appetite, and/or weight loss.

Most important to the diagnostic process is a detailed occupational history (even as far back as a summer job in high school) to try to determine the causative exposure. History should also include hobbies or recent viral illnesses.

Physical exam: On physical exam, the individual may appear in varying degrees of respiratory distress depending on the severity or stage of the disease. Symptoms may include rapid respirations and a bluish tint to the skin if blood oxygen levels are very low. Listening to the lungs through a stethoscope (auscultation) may reveal abnormal crackling sounds. The individual may have stunted growth of the fingertips called "clubbing." In the late stages of the disease, there may also be abnormal heart sounds associated with right-sided heart failure (cor pulmonale).

Tests: Chest x-ray is one of the first noninvasive tests ordered to begin to confirm the diagnosis of IPF. A classic pattern called "ground glass" may be detected. High-resolution computerized tomography (HRCT) can further reveal the presence and type of interstitial disease. HRCT can improve the accuracy of diagnosis from 33 to 46 percent. Because the medical management for IPF is prolonged and has many side effects, it is necessary to obtain an accurate diagnosis. The best accuracy is obtained with an actual sample of interstitial cells for cytological examination. To access these cells, a bronchial alveolar lavage (BAL) and/or a transbronchial biopsy is performed during an examination of the bronchi by means of a fiberoptic viewing instrument passed down the trachea (bronchoscopy). The highest level of accuracy of diagnosis, almost 95%, is obtained with tissue samples from an open lung biopsy done through an incision in the chest wall (thoracotomy).

Blood tests are usually performed to look at the immune response of the blood cells to the disease process. Blood oxygen levels, measured initially by pulse oximetry and later by arterial blood gases, are generally low. Pulmonary function tests are performed to assess the degree of impairment in the lung's mechanical ability to move air (lung volumes and flows). In IPF, lung volumes are reduced and flows may be increased. The time it takes oxygen to move from the alveoli to the capillaries across the diseased interstitial space (diffusing capacity) will be increased.

Treatment

anti-inflammatory drugs (corticosteroids) are the mainstay of treatment for interstitial pulmonary fibrosis. A favorable response occurs in less than 25% of individuals, however, and it is desirable to wean the individual to low-dose steroids after 6 months to a year. In individuals who are not responsive to corticosteroids, medication to suppress the action of the body's immune system (immunosuppression therapy) may be considered. Along with drug therapy, it is imperative that the individual quit smoking and be removed from any environment that might contain respiratory irritants. Due to impaired lung function, vaccinations against pneumococcal pneumonia and influenza are also important.

Some individuals may develop bronchoconstriction due to scarring around the airways. Drugs may be given to help widen airway passages (bronchodilators). Individuals often benefit greatly from supplemental oxygen therapy, especially during the day when they are active. In the late stages of the disease, the individual may require medication for the treatment of right heart failure.

In individuals who have end-stage IPF that is unresponsive to medical treatment, lung transplantation may be considered.

Prognosis

Individuals with IPF are rarely cured, and become increasingly disabled. The clinical course of IPF is progressive; median survival is 4 to 6 years after diagnosis. In good candidates, lung transplantation during end-stage IPF has yielded 1-year survival rates of 60-80 percent. The level of functioning that can be maintained with vigorous medical therapy is very individualized.

Differential Diagnosis

Once a tissue specimen is obtained for diagnosis, there is little doubt of the diagnosis. Up until that time, conditions with similar symptoms include similar interstitial lung diseases classified by the injurious agents that caused them (such as silicosis, pneumoconiosis, asbestosis), sarcoidosis (widespread granulomatous lesions in the lungs), allergic inflammation of the lungs (hypersensitivity pneumonitis), lung cancer, eosinophilic pneumonia, farmer's lung, and bronchial obstruction.

Specialists

- Occupational Medicine Physician
- Pulmonologist
- Thoracic Surgeon

Work Restrictions / Accommodations

Individuals with IPF must avoid all inhaled respiratory irritants. Accommodations may need to be made as to the degree of physical activity that is required in the current position. An ongoing evaluation of the individual's ability to perform the work without breathing difficulty should be a cooperative effort between the employee and employer. If the individual requires supplemental oxygen, the safety of a hazardous gas in the work place must be evaluated.

Comorbid Conditions

Existing conditions that may impact ability to recover and may further lengthen disability include obesity, nicotine abuse, tuberculosis, and cancer.

Complications

Possible complications of IPF include progressive respiratory failure, cor pulmonale, pulmonary embolism, pneumothorax, pneumonia, pulmonary hypertension, and bronchogenic carcinoma.

Factors Influencing Duration

Ultimately, disability for this disease may be permanent. In the years between diagnosis and permanent disability, there are factors that can influence both episodes of temporary disability and the speed with which an individual reaches permanent disability. These factors include age, underlying chronic medical conditions, the severity of the disease on diagnosis, the response to medical management and resultant side effects, individual compliance with medical management, the necessity for hospitalization or surgery, the present severity of the disease, the cause of the disease, and the type of work the individual must resume.

Length of Disability

Duration depends on underlying cause versus idiopathic. Disability may be permanent. Contact physician for additional information.

Failure to Recover

If an individual fails to recover within the maximum duration expectancy period, the reader may wish to reference the following questions to assist in better understanding the specifics of an individual's medical case.

Regarding diagnosis:

- In individual progressively short of breath?
- Has a tissue specimen confirmed the diagnosis of interstitial pulmonary fibrosis?

Regarding treatment:

- Has drug therapy been effective in relieving symptoms?
- What other options are available to individual?
- What has been done to remove respiratory irritants from individual's environment?
- Has individual been able to quit smoking? Would individual benefit from enrollment in a community stop smoking program?
- Would individual benefit from oxygen therapy?
- Would individual benefit from consultation with a specialist?
- Is individual a candidate for lung transplantation?

Regarding prognosis:

- Does individual have an underlying condition that may impact recovery?
- Has individual experienced any complications, including progressive respiratory failure, cor pulmonale, pulmonary embolism, pneumothorax, pneumonia, pulmonary hypertension, or bronchogenic carcinoma?

References

"Chapter 78: Idiopathic Interstitial Lung Diseases." Merck Manual of Diagnosis and Therapy, 17th ed. Beers, Mark H., and Robert Berkow, MD Whitehouse Station, NJ: Merck & Co., Inc., 1999. 3 Jan 2001 <http://www.merck.com/pubs/mmanual/section6/chapter78/78b.htm>.

Diffuse Interstitial Pulmonary Fibrosis. MEDLINEplus. 01 Jan 2000. 1 Jan 2001 <http://medlineplus.adam.com/ency/article/000128.htm>.

Intervertebral Disc Disorders
722, 722.1, 722.2, 722.3

Definition

The spinal column (or vertebral column) is made up of 24 moveable vertebrae (seven cervical vertebrae, twelve thoracic vertebrae, five lumbar vertebrae) and two fused sections (the sacrum and the coccyx). An intervertebral disc disorder refers to an abnormal protrusion or herniation of one of the discs that separate the vertebrae of the spine. The displaced nucleus of the disc may press against the spinal nerves or the spinal cord itself, causing changes in sensory, motor, and reflex function (radiculopathy). Disc disorders of the cervical, thoracic, and lumbar vertebrae are discussed separately.

See cervical disc disorders with and without myelopathy, thoracic disc disorders with and without myelopathy, and lumbar disc disorders with and without myelopathy for more information.

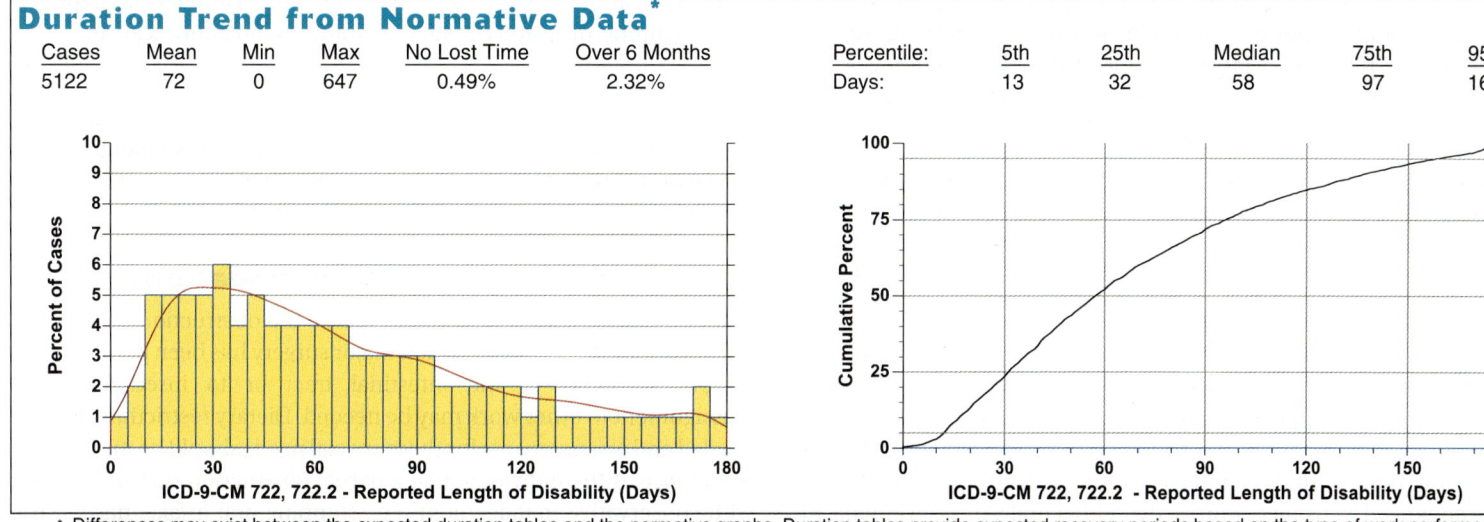

Duration Trend from Normative Data*

Cases	Mean	Min	Max	No Lost Time	Over 6 Months
5122	72	0	647	0.49%	2.32%

Percentile:	5th	25th	Median	75th	95th
Days:	13	32	58	97	161

* Differences may exist between the expected duration tables and the normative graphs. Duration tables provide expected recovery periods based on the type of work performed by the individual. The normative graphs reflect the actual observed experience of many individuals across the spectrum of physical conditions, in a variety of industries, and with varying levels of case management.

Intestinal Obstruction

Other names / synonyms: Bowel Obstruction, Intestinal Volvulus, Paralytic Ileus
560, 560.0, 560.1, 560.2, 560.3, 560.30, 560.31, 560.39, 560.8, 560.81, 560.9

Definition

An intestinal obstruction is a partial or complete blockage that results in the failure of the intestinal contents to pass through the bowel. Obstruction of the bowel can occur either from a non-mechanical obstruction or mechanical causes. The obstruction may occur anywhere in the small or large intestine.

Obstruction of the bowel due to paralysis of the bowel wall (paralytic ileus) is one of the causes of obstruction. The causes of paralytic ileus may include an infection within the abdominal cavity, decreased blood supply to the support structures in the abdomen, injury to the abdominal blood supply, after abdominal surgery, kidney or disease in the upper part of body (thorax), or disturbances in the metabolism (such as decreased potassium levels).

Mechanical obstruction occurs when movement of material through the intestines is physically blocked. The mechanical causes of obstruction are numerous and may include scar tissue that sometimes forms inside the abdomen after surgery (adhesions). Cancer is a second cause. Hernias in the groin can cause the intestine to become trapped and obstructed. Narrowing of the intestine (stenosis) can result in obstruction, as in Crohn's disease. In older individuals or in the bedridden, feces can become hard and obstruct the bowel (fecal impaction). Uncommonly, the intestine can twist on itself (volvulus) and become obstructed.

The incidence of intestinal obstruction is 1cases out of 1,000 people.

Diagnosis

History: Symptoms of a small intestinal obstruction include abdominal pain, nausea, and vomiting. The vomitus is usually greenish because of the presence of bile. With a large intestine obstruction, vomiting is less likely, but abdominal pain is still present. Bowel movements are infrequent or absent in both, as is the passing of gas.

Physical exam: The exam with a complete obstruction will show abdominal distention and tenderness. Listening to the abdomen may reveal characteristic bowel sounds of obstruction, such as high pitched "tinkling" or loud rushes of sound. Temperature is normal or slightly elevated.

Tests: Blood tests include a complete blood count (CBC), electrolytes, and prothrombin time. Serum chemistries, blood urea nitrogen (BUN), creatinine, lactate, urinalysis, and arterial blood gases (ABGs) should also be done. Plain x-rays of the abdomen may be normal early in an obstruction, but can show characteristic abnormalities later on. X-rays can be enhanced by using a contrast dye, either orally or as an enema, to confirm the obstruction. Sometimes CT scans are used, especially if a tumor is suspected.

Treatment

A partial obstruction is treated in the hospital by stopping oral intake of liquids and food, giving intravenous fluids, keeping the stomach empty through a stomach tube, or resting the bowel with a long intestinal tube. These methods are employed prior to surgery.

A complete small intestine obstruction will generally be treated by surgical exploration of the abdomen (laparotomy). The obstruction is relieved and any diseased intestine that might not survive is removed. Laparotomy also may be used to remove gallstones that entered the small intestine. Large intestine obstruction will require surgery, in which the lower colon and anus are bypassed (colostomy). Fecal impactions sometimes can be removed manually.

Prognosis

With proper diagnosis and early treatment of the obstruction, outcome is generally good. Complete obstructions managed successfully with nonoperative treatment have higher incidence of recurrence than those treated surgically. If the obstruction is secondary to cancer, the outcome is dependent on the cancer prognosis. There is a 2% mortality rate with uncomplicated small bowel obstruction, mostly in the elderly; the fatality rate is much higher if some of the small intestine has died. The overall mortality with large bowel obstruction is 20 percent.

Individuals who have colostomy are able to return to normal activities (the colostomy bags need to be emptied and changed routinely). Those with a temporary colostomy usually have a second surgery a few months later. This is to reattach the bowel and get rid of the colostomy. In these cases, bowel function often returns to normal.

Differential Diagnosis

Intestinal obstruction can be confused with acute gastroenteritis, acute pancreatitis, blockage of the arteries supplying the intestine, or pseudo-obstruction having the symptoms and signs of obstruction but without a mechanical blockage (this can be seen with scleroderma, hypothyroidism, lupus, drug abuse, radiation injury, or no known cause).

Specialists

- Gastroenterologist
- General Surgeon
- Hematologist
- Occupational Medicine Physician
- Physical Therapist

Work Restrictions / Accommodations

If abdominal surgery is required to relieve the obstruction, limitations on lifting may be necessary. When major surgery has been performed to remove segments of the intestinal tract or to insert bypasses, reassignment to other work may be needed. Dietary restrictions may be needed and arrangements for these special needs should be made in the work place. If the individual had a partial obstruction that was treated with conservative management (i.e., stopping oral intake, nasogastric tube), then the individual may be on a soft diet for a few days to weeks.

Comorbid Conditions

Liver disease, kidney disease, gastrointestinal disease, and stomach cancer may all worsen the effects of an obstruction. They may also adversely affect the outcome of treatment (the individual may not recover).

Complications

If treatment is delayed, dehydration and electrolyte imbalance can complicate treatment. The intestine can become perforated, sometimes through a pre-existing weak spot (diverticulum). Abdominal abscesses and wound rupturing and bursting may also occur. The intestine can become strangulated under some conditions and have its blood supply seriously reduced. The bowel can then develop gangrene and die, a very serious complication with a high fatality rate.

Factors Influencing Duration

The severity of symptoms, location and cause of the obstruction, and method of treatment influence the length of disability. Age, physical condition and status, and overall health will influence the individual's ability to undergo treatment and recover.

Length of Disability

If major portions of the gastrointestinal system have been removed, permanent disability may be the result.

Colon resection, open.

Job Classification	Minimum	Optimum	Maximum
Sedentary work	21	28	42
Light work	21	28	42
Medium work	28	35	56
Heavy work	35	42	56
Very Heavy work	42	42	56

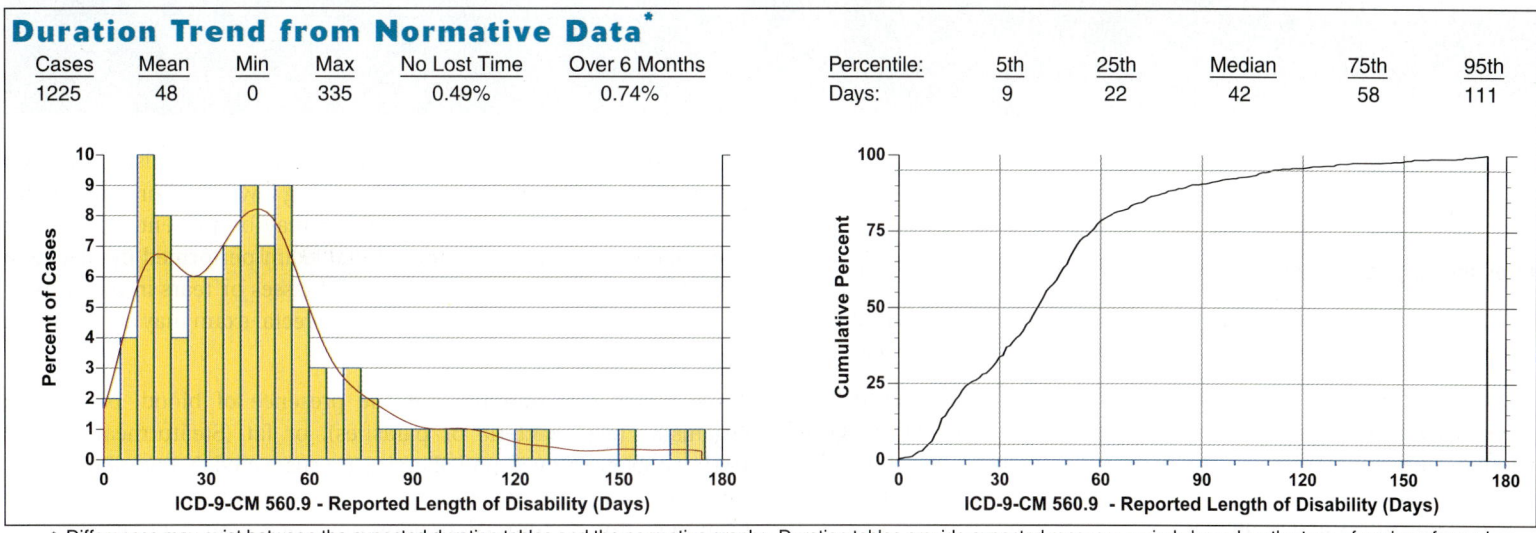

Duration Trend from Normative Data*

Cases	Mean	Min	Max	No Lost Time	Over 6 Months
1225	48	0	335	0.49%	0.74%

Percentile:	5th	25th	Median	75th	95th
Days:	9	22	42	58	111

* Differences may exist between the expected duration tables and the normative graphs. Duration tables provide expected recovery periods based on the type of work performed by the individual. The normative graphs reflect the actual observed experience of many individuals across the spectrum of physical conditions, in a variety of industries, and with varying levels of case management.

Failure to Recover

If an individual fails to recover within the maximum duration expectancy period, the reader may wish to reference the following questions to assist in better understanding the specifics of an individual's medical case.

Regarding diagnosis:

- Does individual complain of abdominal pain, nausea, and vomiting? Is the vomitus greenish in color (suggesting small intestine obstruction)?
- Does individual complain of abdominal pain without vomiting, suggesting a large intestine obstruction?
- Are bowel movements and passing gas infrequent or absent?
- Were a complete blood count (CBC), blood chemistries, prothrombin time, and arterial blood gases (ABGs) done?
- Were x-rays of the abdomen done? Did they reveal an obstruction, or may they have been taken before the obstruction could be seen?
- Was computed tomography (CT scan) done, especially if a tumor is suspected?

- Has the diagnosis of intestinal obstruction been confirmed?
- Has the cause of the obstruction been determined?
- Is the obstruction partial or complete?

Regarding treatment:

- For partial obstruction, was individual hospitalized to stop oral intake of liquids and food, to receive intravenous fluids, to keep the stomach empty through a stomach tube, or to rest the bowel with an intestinal tube? Was this treatment successful, or was surgery required?
- For complete small intestine obstruction, was surgical exploration of the abdomen (laparotomy) done and the obstruction relieved? Was any diseased intestine removed also?
- For large intestine obstruction, was surgical creation of an opening (stoma) onto the abdomen made for stool to pass, thereby bypassing the lower colon and anus (colostomy)?
- Is the colostomy expected to be temporary or permanent?
- Were medical and/or surgical interventions successful in relieving the obstruction?
- Were there any complications after surgery?

Intestinal Obstruction 1223

Regarding prognosis:

- Is this the first intestinal obstruction individual has had, or is this a recurrence?
- If the obstruction is secondary to cancer, was the obstruction able to be relieved?
- Has the cancer spread (metastasized) to other parts of the body?
- Did any surgical complications occur?
- Did individual experience dehydration or electrolyte imbalance complications?
- Did the intestine become perforated?
- Did the intestine become strangulated causing decreased blood flow and development of gangrene? If so, is individual expected to live?
- If individual has a colostomy, would psychological counseling be of benefit to cope with the impact of the changes in body image?

References

McCormick, III, J. MD, and Siri Sat Khalsa, MD. "Bowel Obstruction, Small from Emergency Medicine/Gastrointestinal." eMedicine.com. 24 Feb 2001. 24 Feb 2001 <http://emedicine.com/emerg/topic66.htm>.

Schwartz, Seymour, MD. Principles of Surgery. New York: McGraw-Hill, 1999.

Intestinal Upset

Other names / synonyms: Gastrointestinal Distress
564.0, 564.3, 564.4, 564.5, 564.8, 564.9

Definition

Intestinal upset is a term used to describe a variety of symptoms that arise from disturbances in the lower intestinal tract (either small intestine, large intestine, or both).

Intestinal upset is often associated with changes in intestinal motility and bowel habits that result in diarrhea, constipation, or rectal bleeding.

Lower intestinal disturbances that can cause intestinal upset include intestinal infections (bacterial, viral, or parasitic), food sensitivity or allergies, intestinal diseases such as inflammatory bowel disease (Crohn's or ulcerative colitis), intestinal masses, or lack of circulation to the intestine (intestinal ischemia).

Depending on the cause, the intestinal upset may occur as an isolated incident such as following an intestinal infection, or may be recurring with persistent discomfort. Intestinal upset associated with food sensitivities or inflammatory bowel diseases tends to be recurrent. Intestinal upset associated with masses or ischemia tends to be persistent. Due to the broad range of disturbances associated with intestinal upset, it is impossible to ascertain its exact prevalence and incidence.

Diagnosis

History: Individuals may complain of abdominal cramping, bloating, rumbling, gas, diarrhea, constipation, or rectal bleeding. They may describe their discomfort as continuous or intermittent. Those with intermittent intestinal upset may be able to pinpoint certain foods or conditions (e.g., stress) that seem to trigger their symptoms. Certain body positions may relieve discomfort or accentuate it. Some individuals may complain of fever, chills, nausea, vomiting, and the inability to eat as well.

Physical exam: Careful examination of the abdomen may reveal a localized mass, tenderness, or distention. Bowel sounds may be diminished or absent in the case of inflammation of the lining of the stomach (peritoneum) or bowel obstruction. Hyperactive, loud bowel sounds may be present in cases of acute infection or inflammatory bowel disease. Other findings associated with inflammatory bowel disease include inflamed joints (arthritis) or inflamed eyes (iritis). Prolonged diarrhea may result in dehydration causing low blood pressure, rapid heart rate, and low urine output. Fever may be present if there is a bacterial or parasitic infection. A rectal exam performed by placing a gloved finger in the rectum may reveal masses or tears in the anus or rectum. Fecal material obtained from the rectal exam may demonstrate frank blood.

Tests: Stools are examined for the presence of blood, pathogenic organisms (e.g., bacteria or parasites), or fat (Steatorrhea). Allergy testing may be done if food allergies are suspected. X-rays of the lower intestine using barium contrast may be taken. A lighted flexible scope examines the rectum (sigmoidoscopy) or colon (colonoscopy) to identify inflammatory conditions, masses, or obstructions. Masses found in these exams are biopsied to rule out cancer. An x-ray exam of the circulatory system of the bowel (mesenteric angiography) helps rule out ischemia of the bowel.

Treatment

Treatment is directed at reducing the intestinal upset and treating the underlying problem. The diet is generally restricted to bland, nonirritating foods. Inflammatory conditions may be treated with medications to slow intestinal motility and reduce cramping (antispasmodics). If dehydration from diarrhea is present, the individual may require intravenous fluids. Those with constipation may be treated with stool softeners, laxatives, enemas, and a high-fiber diet. Bacterial or parasitic infections are treated with appropriate antibiotics or antimicrobial medications. If food sensitivities or allergies are suspected, the offending foods are eliminated from the diet. Surgery may be performed to remove masses or ischemic bowel (exploratory laparotomy with excision of mass or bowel resection).

Prognosis

Outcomes vary based on the underlying cause of the intestinal upset. Many types of intestinal upset resolve spontaneously without treatment. When treatment is required, most individuals enjoy a full recovery within days. Those with colon or rectal cancer have a 5-year survival rate of 50% following bowel resection. Inflammatory bowel diseases tend to be chronic and often result in recurring episodes of debilitating intestinal upset.

Differential Diagnosis

A variety of conditions present with intestinal upset, and include bacterial, viral, or parasitic gastrointestinal (GI) infections, tumors, bowel ischemia, gallbladder inflammation, GI bleeding, inflammatory bowel disease, ingestion of toxic substances, GI gas (flatus), constipation, and immobile bowel (paralytic ileus).

Specialists

- Emergency Medicine
- Gastroenterologist
- General Surgeon
- Internist
- Oncologist
- Primary Care Provider

Work Restrictions / Accommodations

Work restrictions or accommodations vary according to the underlying cause of the intestinal upset and type of treatment necessary. Some individuals may need close access to restroom facilities. The individual's physician should be consulted for specific guidelines regarding work restrictions and accommodations.

Comorbid Conditions

Comorbid conditions of immune suppression, bleeding disorders, cancer, or malnutrition can impact ability to recover and further lengthen disability.

Complementary and Alternative Therapies

Content is intended for awareness only. Treatments may or may not be effective. Scientific evidence may be lacking and some substances have potentially toxic effects. Dr. Presley Reed and the editors do not endorse the use of these therapies in the absence of consultation with a licensed medical professional.

Friendly bacteria - Probiotic treatment with Lactobacillus plantarum may significantly reduce intestinal gas.

Flaxseed - May treat intestinal upset secondary to chronic constipation.

Herb therapy - Caraway, chamomile, dill, fennel, peppermint, spearmint, and turmeric may relieve intestinal upset by reducing intestinal gas production.

Complications

Bacterial and parasitic infections can cause severe diarrhea that can lead to significant dehydration and possible kidney failure, particularly in very young or elderly individuals. Prolonged or severe diarrhea can also cause loss of vital electrolytes (electrolyte imbalance) and contribute to a variety of physical disturbances including muscle cramping, neurological disturbances, and heart rhythm abnormalities particularly in elderly individuals. Ischemia to the bowel can cause bowel perforation and overwhelming systemic infection (sepsis).

Factors Influencing Duration

Factors that may influence length of disability include advanced age, underlying cause, severity of symptoms, and response to treatment.

Length of Disability

This is a vague diagnosis. No disability is expected. Contact physician to obtain a more specific diagnosis.

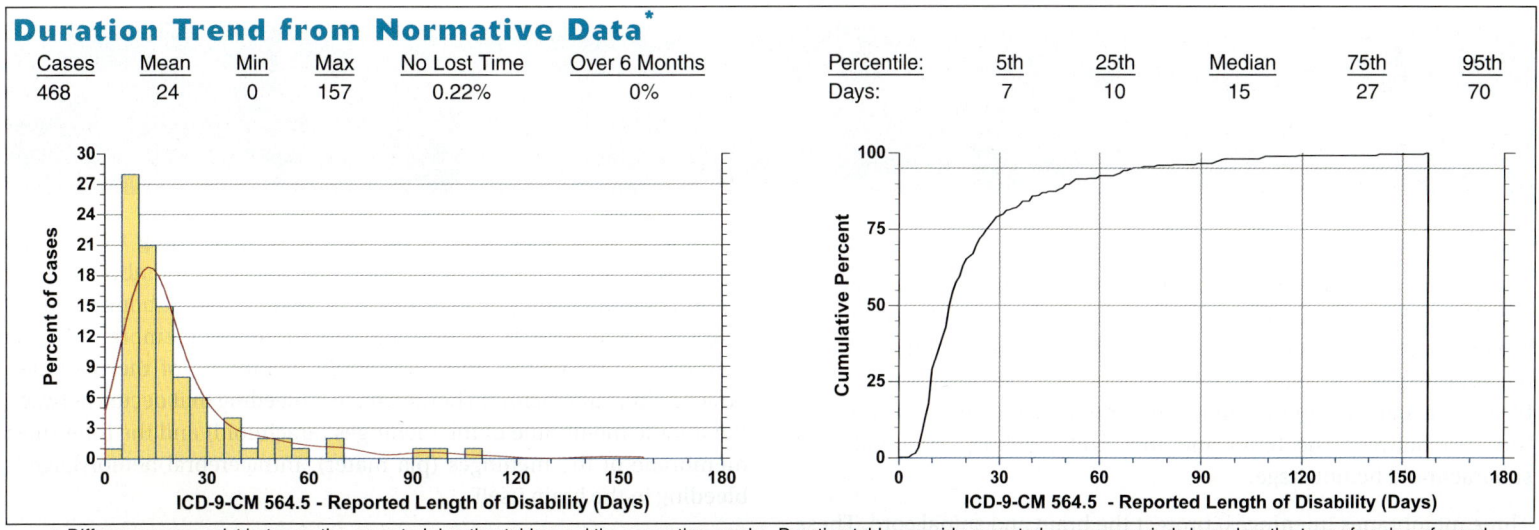

Duration Trend from Normative Data*

Cases	Mean	Min	Max	No Lost Time	Over 6 Months
468	24	0	157	0.22%	0%

Percentile:	5th	25th	Median	75th	95th
Days:	7	10	15	27	70

* Differences may exist between the expected duration tables and the normative graphs. Duration tables provide expected recovery periods based on the type of work performed by the individual. The normative graphs reflect the actual observed experience of many individuals across the spectrum of physical conditions, in a variety of industries, and with varying levels of case management.

Failure to Recover

If an individual fails to recover within the maximum duration expectancy period, the reader may wish to reference the following questions to assist in better understanding the specifics of an individual's medical case.

Regarding diagnosis:

- Does individual complain of abdominal cramping, bloating, gas, diarrhea, constipation, or rectal bleeding?
- Does individual have fever, chills, and diarrhea suggesting a possible infection?
- Does individual have a history of food allergies or inflammatory bowel disease?
- Is the discomfort continuous or intermittent?
- If the discomfort is intermittent, can individual pinpoint diet changes or conditions such as stress that seem to trigger the symptoms?
- Did the physician find a localized mass, tenderness, or distention of the abdomen?
- When listening with a stethoscope (auscultation), does the physician hear diminished or absent bowel sounds?
- Are hyperactive, loud bowel sounds present (with acute infection or inflammatory bowel disease)?
- Did a rectal exam reveal masses or tears in the anus or rectum?
- Have the stools been testing for blood, bacteria, parasites, and fat?
- Have lower GI x-rays been obtained?
- Have endoscopic exams been done to rule out inflammatory bowel disease, intestinal masses, or bleeding?
- Has allergy testing been done?
- Does a mesenteric angiography need to be done?

Regarding treatment:

- Has individual been placed on a bland diet or diet that eliminates offending foods?
- Has individual received supplemental fluids and electrolytes as appropriate?
- Have antibiotics or antimicrobials been ordered in the case of intestinal infections?
- Have medications to reduce gas and slow intestinal motility been tried?
- Has constipation been treated with laxatives, enemas, and fiber supplementation?
- Have tumors or masses been biopsied to rule out cancer?
- Have intestinal obstructions been surgically removed?

Regarding prognosis:

- Does individual have colon or rectal cancer or inflammatory bowel disease? Did individual require surgery for intestinal obstruction?
- Has a postsurgical infection developed?
- Did individual have severe diarrhea?
- Does individual have underlying conditions that may impact recovery?
- Has individual experienced complications?
- What complications have occurred and how will they be treated?
- What length of time is required to recover from the complication?

References

Current Medical Diagnosis and Treatment, 39th ed. Tierney, Lawrence M., Stephen J. McPhee, and Maxine Papadakis, eds. New York: Lange Medical Books/McGraw-Hill, 2000.

Intracranial Hemorrhage

Other names / synonyms: Epidural Hematoma, Epidural Hemorrhage, Hemorrhagic Stroke, Intracerebral Hemorrhage, Subarachnoid Hemorrhage, Subarachnoid Stroke, Subdural Hematoma, Subdural Hemorrhage

432.9

Definition

Intracranial hemorrhage is a medical emergency and is a result of bleeding within the skull cavity (cranium) that usually progresses rapidly and often results in permanent brain damage and death. All bleeding within the skull is called intracranial bleeding, whether the bleeding occurs within the brain itself (intracerebral hemorrhage) or in the area between the brain and the skull (epidural, subdural, and subarachnoid hemorrhage).

Three membranes (meninges) protect the brain and spinal cord. These are the tough outermost membrane (dura mater), the delicate middle membrane (arachnoid), and the innermost membrane lying next to the brain (pia mater). Bleeding within the skull is categorized according to where it occurs, i.e., between the layers of the protective membranes (meninges) or in and around the brain itself. Bleeding that occurs between the inner surface of the skull and the outer membrane of the meninges (dura mater) is called epidural hemorrhage. Subdural hemorrhage is bleeding that occurs between the outer membrane of the meninges (dura mater) and the middle membrane of the meninges (arachnoid). Subarachnoid hemorrhage is bleeding that occurs between the middle membrane of the meninges (arachnoid) and the innermost membrane of the meninges (pia mater). Intracerebral hemorrhage is bleeding in the brain itself.

Epidural hemorrhage is a life-threatening injury requiring immediate evaluation and treatment. This type of intracranial hemorrhage is caused by a blunt traumatic head injury (e.g., a motor vehicle accident, pedestrian accident, fall, assault, or sports injury) or a penetrating traumatic head injury (e.g., gunshot wound). The most common cause of traumatic head injury is motor vehicle accidents especially in teenagers and young adults, often as a result of alcohol and drug use. Falling is the second most common cause especially in older adults. Epidural hemorrhage is associated with a skull fracture that tears an artery or sometimes a vein. Blood collects quickly within the skull, taking up valuable space and putting pressure on the brain.

Subdural hemorrhage is also a life-threatening injury requiring immediate evaluation and treatment once symptoms develop. This type of intracranial hemorrhage is the result of a traumatic head injury that causes the brain to move around inside the skull (rotational injury) and become bruised (contused). The condition occurs most frequently in individuals with some degree of brain shrinkage (atrophy) such as chronic alcoholics and individuals over the age of 60. Bleeding is from a torn vein more often than a torn artery so blood collects more slowly within the skull. Because of the larger space in the skull surrounding the atrophied brain, slow bleeding can expand for days or weeks before the pool of blood is large enough to compress the brain and cause symptoms.

Subarachnoid hemorrhage is the most common type of bleeding following a traumatic head injury. Abrasions, bruises (contusions), and lacerations on the surface of the brain cause bleeding that seeps between the arachnoid and the pia mater that covers the brain. Subarachnoid hemorrhage is frequently due to the rupture of a weakened blood vessel in the brain (cerebral aneurysm). This defect in the vessel is described as an outpouching or ballooning present from birth or as the result of trauma. About 5% of the population has cerebral aneurysms. Ruptured aneurysms occur more frequently in women and in individuals with a history of cigarette smoking, high blood pressure (hypertension), and excessive alcohol consumption. Subarachnoid hemorrhage may also be caused by leakage from a faulty vascular formation in the brain (arteriovenous malformation) present from birth in 0.14% of the population, and occurs twice as often in men as women. Subarachnoid hemorrhage also accounts for 6% of strokes caused by spontaneous bleeding from a cerebral artery (hemorrhagic stroke), often as a result of hypertension, diabetes, and treatment with blood thinners (anticoagulant therapy). Hemorrhagic strokes account for 20% of all strokes.

Intracerebral hemorrhage is bleeding in or around the brain primarily due to hypertension, trauma that causes severe bruising of the brain, bleeding tumors, ruptured cerebral aneurysms, leaking arteriovenous malformations, and treatment with blood thinners (anticoagulant therapy). Intracerebral hemorrhage accounts for 14% of all strokes caused by spontaneous bleeding of a cerebral artery (hemorrhagic stroke). The most devastating intracerebral hemorrhages are those that occur in the back of the brain near the brain stem, which controls respiration and other vital functions. Blacks and Asians have a higher incidence of hemorrhagic stroke than whites.

Risk factors for intracranial hemorrhage include the black race, female gender, prior stroke, hypertension, excessive anticoagulation, and low weight. Intracranial hemorrhage occurs in about 1% of older adults on blood thinners following a heart attack.

Diagnosis

History: The individual with an intracranial hemorrhage is often unconscious or dazed or otherwise unable to give a complete medical history. The physician may need to rely on those who were with the individual when the event occurred as well as friends or family members to provide information about the individual's current and past medical conditions and diseases. In this case, the history may be inaccurate or incomplete for past injuries, illnesses, and surgical procedures and for current treatment for existing chronic diseases.

Many individuals with an epidural hemorrhage caused by an arterial tear become unconscious at the trauma scene then experience a brief period of consciousness referred to as a lucid interval. This is followed by a decrease in the level of consciousness. Other individuals never regain consciousness and others are awake but dazed. Symptoms include headache, vomiting, and seizures.

Individuals with a subdural hemorrhage report headache, drowsiness, confusion, and a decreasing level of consciousness. The individual may remember experiencing a bump on the head or some other head trauma in the recent past but frequently no obvious traumatic injury has occurred.

Symptoms of subarachnoid hemorrhage may include a sudden onset of severe headache, nausea, vomiting, stiff neck (nuchal rigidity), fainting, and sensitivity to light (photophobia). Occasionally, an individual may experience warning symptoms that indicate a cerebral aneurysm is leaking or about to rupture and include headache, weakness on one side of the body, numbness, tingling, speech disturbance, and double vision that does not go away. Some individuals with a ruptured cerebral aneurysm may complain of a severe headache and fall unconscious almost immediately. Others may experience a headache but remain conscious. Still others may become unconscious suddenly without a headache and without warning. Symptoms of arteriovenous malformations may include seizures and cognitive impairment.

Individuals with intracerebral hemorrhage may have a history of hypertension, diabetes, or treatment with anticoagulants. Symptoms of hemorrhage include headache, nausea, vomiting, progressive deterioration in consciousness, weakness or paralysis on one side (including face, arm, and leg), slurred speech, difficulty expressing themselves in words (expressive aphasia) or understanding speech (receptive aphasia), seizures, disturbances in eye movement, difficulty swallowing (dysphagia), or respiratory depression.

Physical exam: The mental status and level of consciousness in individuals with intracranial bleeding may range from drowsy and confused to comatose. Weakness or paralysis may be present on one side. The individual may be vomiting and seizure activity may be present. Speech may be disturbed. Intracranial pressure may be elevated with pupils unequal in size that react sluggishly to light. If the individual's neurological status is deteriorating rapidly, a quick diagnosis of the type of trauma or hemorrhage must be made based on the most prominent signs and symptoms so surgical intervention can proceed.

Tests: CT is the standard diagnostic tool to quickly determine the presence of skull fractures and bleeding within the skull. If the CT is negative for blood, lumbar puncture is performed to determine if blood is present in the cerebrospinal fluid (CSF). MRI is not used in the acute phase of injury but is useful after the initial 48 hours to assess the extent of injury to the brain. If a ruptured aneurysm is suspected, a complete vascular study (arteriography) of the carotid and cerebral arteries helps pinpoint the location of the ruptured aneurysm and also look for other aneurysms. Additional diagnostic tests may include an electrocardiogram (ECG), chest x-ray, urinalysis, and blood studies (complete blood count, prothrombin time, erythrocyte sedimentation rate [ESR], blood glucose, electrolytes, type and crossmatch). A diagnosis of subdural hemorrhage/hematoma may require additional tests because symptoms are similar to those of many other diseases and conditions.

Treatment

Immediate medical treatment for acute intracranial hemorrhages includes maintaining the airway; assisting respiration if needed; regulating body temperature, blood oxygen level, and blood pressure; establishing intravenous (IV) access to replace fluids and maintain a constant blood sugar level; controlling external bleeding; monitoring pressure within the brain (intracranial pressure); and stabilizing the cervical spine until cervical fracture is ruled out. Maintaining an acceptable intracranial pressure with corticosteroids and diuretics is mandatory so that further brain injury does not occur. Setting respiratory parameters so that breaths occur frequently and deeply (hyperventilation) decreases carbon dioxide levels, which lowers intracranial pressure. Once the individual's condition stabilizes, treatment focuses on maintaining the status quo and treating underlying medical conditions and diseases.

Epidural hemorrhage from a torn artery is a life-threatening injury that requires immediate evaluation and treatment. Immediate decompression of the brain is required through a burr hole procedure, craniectomy incision, or opening of the skull cavity (craniotomy). The collection of blood and clots is removed and active bleeding stopped.

Once a definitive diagnosis of subdural hemorrhage/hematoma is made, the brain is decompressed through a craniotomy procedure. The collected blood and clots are removed, the brain examined, and active bleeding stopped.

If the diagnosis is subarachnoid hemorrhage due to a ruptured cerebral aneurysm, surgical clipping of the aneurysm is performed through a craniotomy procedure as soon as the individual's neurological condition permits in order to prevent the rebleeding that frequently occurs approximately 2 weeks after the rupture. Until surgery, the individual is kept on absolute bed rest. Fluid balance and nutrition are maintained, narcotics given for headache relief, antiepileptic drugs for seizure control, and stool softeners to prevent constipation. The individual is instructed not to strain especially during bowel movements. If an arteriovenous malformation is accessible, a craniotomy may be performed and the malformation excised to prevent further bleeding. Narrowing of brain arteries (vasospasm) should be treated with calcium-channel blockers.

For individuals with an intracerebral hemorrhage, treatment is generally conservative and supportive and may include antiepileptic drugs for seizure control, antianxiety drugs, and medications to control blood pressure. If increased intracranial pressure cannot be controlled medically, an attempt may be made to evacuate an intracerebral hematoma through a craniotomy procedure, but this is often unsuccessful. Placing a shunt from the ventricular system in the brain to the abdominal cavity (ventriculoperitoneal shunt) helps decrease intracranial pressure by draining excess CSF when the ventricles are blocked or enlarged (hydrocephalus).

Prognosis

Survival following spontaneous bleeding within the brain itself (subarachnoid or intracerebral hemorrhage) is poor if the bleed is large or if the individual is already in a coma when arriving at the emergency room. For those who survive the initial hemorrhage, consciousness gradually returns as the blood is reabsorbed and neurologic function begins to return. Many individuals who experience this type of hemorrhage do make a reasonable recovery however 90% have some degree of permanent physical and mental disability.

Individuals who have burr hole, craniotomy, or craniectomy procedures to treat intracranial hemorrhage generally recover from surgery. Mortality from intracranial hemorrhage is related more to the severity of the brain trauma, the amount of brain swelling as a result of trauma, and how deep the individual's coma is at the time of arrival in the emergency room. In general, the deeper the coma at arrival in the emergency room, the worse the individual's chance of recovering without serious disability.

Some studies show a 90% mortality rate for epidural hemorrhage caused by arterial bleeding. Over half of the individuals admitted with gunshot wounds to the head alive upon arrival at a hospital eventually die because their initial injuries are so severe. Similarly, prognosis for individuals suffering a ruptured cerebral aneurysm is poor. Ten percent of individuals with a subarachnoid hemorrhage die immediately and 50% die within a month. Twenty to thirty percent of cerebral aneurysms rebleed in the 2 weeks following a rupture. If the aneurysm rebleeds, the mortality rate climbs to 75%. Prognosis depends on the severity of the injury to the brain, amount of brain swelling, and depth of coma when the individual arrives in the emergency room.

Individuals who survive intracranial hemorrhage may have seizures, permanent brain damage, and persistent problems with memory loss, dizziness, headache, anxiety, and difficulty concentrating.

Differential Diagnosis

Subdural hemorrhages must be differentiated from cerebrovascular disease, senile dementia, and other diseases with a dementia component. Spontaneous subarachnoid hemorrhage must be differentiated from cerebral contusion, ruptured cerebral aneurysm, subdural hematoma, bleeding from an arteriovenous malformation, brain abscess, brain tumor, epilepsy, delirium, and intoxication. Spontaneous intracerebral hemorrhage must be differentiated from brain tumors, ruptured cerebral aneurysms, and arteriovenous malformations.

Specialists

- Cardiologist
- Emergency Medicine
- Endocrinologist
- Internist
- Neurologist
- Neurosurgeon
- Ophthalmologist
- Otolaryngologist
- Radiologist

Rehabilitation

The type and duration of rehabilitation for individuals who have survived an intracranial hemorrhage are determined by the extent of brain injury and the rate of recovery of neurological function. Those with less severe brain injuries who are showing significant neurologic recovery can be transferred to a rehabilitation unit as soon as they can leave the acute care setting. Those with more severe brain injuries may require skilled nursing care at home or in a nursing home setting until they regain sufficient neurological function for a rehabilitation unit. Individuals in a coma require skilled nursing care, most likely in a nursing home setting.

Rehabilitative therapy focuses on restoring the functions required for activities of daily living as much as possible and may include speech, physical, occupational, and cognitive therapy. Individuals with damage to the nerves supplying the head and neck (cranial nerves) may require rehabilitation of hearing, swallowing, maintaining balance, and using the muscles of facial expression. Many individuals require psychological counseling to help them adjust to chronic pain or the loss of mental or physical function. Throughout the recovery and rehabilitation period, families need to be kept informed of their injured family member's progress and limitations. Most families benefit from the support of a social worker to help them work through the emotional, financial, and practical aspects of living with a loved one with a brain injury.

Work Restrictions / Accommodations

Many individuals who survive an intracranial hemorrhage are permanently disabled and unable to return to work. Others may return to work in another capacity or with significant restrictions and accommodations to their workplace. Individuals who have undergone a craniectomy have portions of their brains unprotected by bone and would risk severe injury if assigned to work in an environment containing moving equipment and similar hazards. Some individuals may suffer damage to the nerves supplying the head and neck (cranial nerves) because of the initial trauma, the bleeding itself, or surgical procedure required to stop the bleeding. They may experience a number of conditions including chronic pain, decreased sensation or paralysis in any of the structures above the neck, difficulty swallowing, hearing impairment, visual impairment, or balance disorders that require special restrictions of work duties. Many individuals recovering from intracranial hemorrhages have changes in their personalities that prevent them from fulfilling the responsibilities of their former positions.

Comorbid Conditions

Comorbid conditions that can affect the individual's ability to recover include obesity; a history of smoking, alcoholism, or drug abuse; and pre-existing diseases that affect any of the major body systems such as bleeding disorders, diabetes, chronic obstructive lung disease, chronic heart disease, and immunosuppressive diseases. Any pre-existing neurologic or psychiatric conditions may have their own impairments additive to those related to the intracranial hemorrhage. Bleeding disorders, heart conditions, and immunosuppressed states such as AIDS may complicate surgery or increase risk of operative morbidity.

Complications

Individuals with intracranial hemorrhage are at risk for developing seizures or increased intracranial pressure (ICP). Increased ICP is a life-threatening situation that results from bleeding within the skull, swelling of the brain, or an increase in the quantity of cerebrospinal fluid. Increasing ICP decreases the flow of blood and oxygen to the brain cells and eventually leads to permanent brain damage, coma, downward displacement (herniation) of the brain into the spinal canal, and death. Other complications include a second hemorrhage, wound infection, cranial nerve damage, leakage of cerebrospinal fluid into the ear or nasal passages (as a result of skull fractures), and coma.

Complications of epidural hemorrhage include epidural hematoma, an organized collection of blood clot. Complications of subdural hemorrhage include subdural hematoma. Subdural hematomas are classified according to how much time has passed between the injury and the onset of symptoms. Acute subdural hematomas occur within 4 days of trauma, subacute hematomas occur between 4 and 14 days, and chronic subdural hematomas occur after 14 days. Narrowing of the cerebral arteries near the site of rupture (vasospasm) is a complication of subarachnoid hemorrhage. Blood in the subarachnoid space can slow the normal flow of CSF and cause the small chambers within the brain containing CSF (ventricles) to enlarge. This condition is called hydrocephalus. A ventriculostomy may be required to drain dangerous amounts of CSF acutely, or in chronic phase, may require placement of a shunt draining the ventricle into the abdominal cavity (ventriculoperitoneal shunt).

Factors Influencing Duration

Factors influencing the length of disability include the number and severity of postoperative complications such as wound infection and adverse reaction to a general anesthetic, extent of the brain injury, individual's mental and emotional stability, access to rehabilitation facilities, and strength of the individual's support system.

Individuals who experience an intracranial hemorrhage as the result of a traumatic head injury often have other major internal and orthopedic injuries that are also life-threatening and affect their ability to recover. In some cases, the individual may recover fully from the head injury and be disabled by traumatic injuries to some other body system.

Length of Disability

Duration depends on type, severity and response to treatment. The individual with permanent brain damage caused by bleeding, infection, or increased intracranial pressure may have decreased cognitive ability and may not be able to perform tasks they could before surgery. In some cases, the impairment may be severe enough to require permanent disability. Individuals with paralysis or weakness, hearing or visual impairments, or speech difficulties may need retraining in order to return to work.

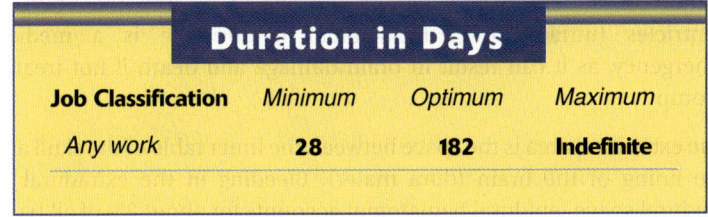

Duration in Days			
Job Classification	Minimum	Optimum	Maximum
Any work	28	182	Indefinite

Failure to Recover

If an individual fails to recover within the maximum duration expectancy period, the reader may wish to reference the following questions to assist in better understanding the specifics of an individual's medical case.

Regarding diagnosis:

- Has the diagnosis of intracranial hemorrhage been confirmed by CT?
- Are other tests needed such as MRI, lumbar puncture if the CT is inconclusive, or angiography if ruptured aneurysm is suspected?
- Has the location and source of the bleeding been confirmed?
- Are there any underlying conditions predisposing to intracranial hemorrhage?

Regarding treatment:

- Has appropriate supportive care, medical therapy, and surgery been instituted? Could the individual benefit from second opinion consultation concerning treatment?
- Does the individual have adequate access to rehabilitative services including physical, occupational, and speech therapy (existence of the services as well as transportation to the facilities offering the services)?
- Is the individual compliant with the prescribed treatment plan with regard to medication, nutrition, exercise, and therapy?
- Does the individual have a support system of family and friends who are well-informed about the individual's condition and limitations? Is additional education or support needed?

Regarding prognosis:

- Did the individual suffer permanent brain damage as the result of trauma, bleeding, infection, or increased intracranial pressure?
- Does the individual have unresolved difficulties associated with damage to a cranial nerve such as impaired balance, facial paralysis, or trouble swallowing or hearing?
- Has the individual recovered from the intracranial hemorrhage and neurosurgery but not from injuries to other body systems and organs that were sustained in the same traumatic event?
- Does the individual have pre-existing chronic diseases that are preventing recovery from the neurosurgical procedure?
- Has a brain tumor been ruled out?

References

Brass, L.M., et al. "Intracranial Hemorrhage Associated with Thrombolytic Therapy for Elderly Patients with Acute Myocardial Infarction." Stroke 31 8 (2000): 1802-1811.

Mattiello, J.A., and M. Munz. "Images in Clinical Medicine. Four Types of Acute Post-Traumatic Intracranial Hemorrhage." New England Journal of Medicine 344 8 (2000): 580.

Intracranial Hemorrhage, Closed
Other names / synonyms: ICH, Intracranial Bleed, Intracranial Hematoma
853.0, 854

Definition

An intracranial hemorrhage refers to bleeding within the brain. Closed intracranial hemorrhage refers to the fact that the skull cavity is not opened or penetrated by an external object or by a bone fragment in the case of skull fracture. Bleeding usually results from trauma either from a direct blow to the head or occurs during rapid deceleration (i.e., car crash) where the brain moves violently against the surface of the skull causing bruising and tearing of brain tissue. Bleeding may occur into the extradural, subdural, or subarachnoid spaces or into the brain or ventricles (intracerebral). Intracranial hemorrhage is a medical emergency, as it can result in brain damage and death if not treated promptly.

The extradural area is the space between the inner table of the skull and the lining of the brain (dura mater). Bleeding in the extradural or epidural space (epidural hematoma) accounts for about 2% of all types of head injury. About 85% of those with an extradural hematoma have also sustained a skull fracture. The most common site of the fracture is the temporal bone that lies just above the ear on either side of the head. This fracture can cause tearing of an artery (middle meningeal artery) and result in bleeding and blood clot (hematoma) formation. The bleeding is usually rapid and can cause a sudden increase in pressure in the brain. Left untreated, it can force the brain to move downward toward the spinal canal (herniate) and may result in further neurologic morbidity or even death.

The subdural area of the brain refers to the potential space between the outermost dura mater and the middle layer of the brain (arachnoid). Since this area normally adheres closely to the brain, any bleeding in this area causes immediate and direct pressure on the brain. Approximately 10-15% of head injury victims develop subdural bleeding and clots (hematoma). The bleeding can stem from torn arteries, causing rapid bleeding and sudden onset of symptoms, or from torn veins with slower bleeding and slower onset of symptoms.

When bleeding occurs beneath the arachnoid, it is referred to as subarachnoid hemorrhage. Though less common, subarachnoid hemorrhage can occur in severe head trauma. Ruptured brain aneurysms or arteriovenous malformations can also result in subarachnoid hemorrhage. Blood in the subarachnoid area usually causes generalized brain irritation.

Intracerebral bleeding refers to bleeding into the cerebral hemispheres of the brain. These areas of the brain are responsible for alertness, higher level thought processes, and intellectual behavior. Intracerebral bleeding occurs in 2-3% of head injury victims. The bleeding typically occurs in the frontal region (frontal lobe) or area above the ears (temporal lobes). This frontal region is primarily responsible for motor functions, insight, and higher intellectual activities. The temporal region is primarily responsible for memory, hearing, and interpretation of speech. Hemorrhagic strokes account for 20% of all strokes and are a frequent cause of intracerebral bleeding especially in individuals with high blood pressure (hypertension).

Those with (bruising) contusions and/or lacerations of the brain may suffer bleeding from any of these areas, singly or in combination. Bleeding may begin soon after the injury. In some cases, symptoms of intracranial bleeding may not become apparent until sufficient blood collects to displace the brain (space-occupying lesion). The rate of bleeding and the site of bleeding often dictate how quickly symptoms develop. Therefore, the interval between the onset of bleeding and onset of symptoms can range from a matter of hours to months.

Diagnosis

History: The clinical presentation varies based on the location, size, and rate of bleeding. History may reveal a recent motor vehicle accident, fall, or physical altercation. The individual, family member, or witness may report a loss of consciousness, breathing, or pulse. If alert, individual may have complaints of nausea, vomiting, headache, visual disturbances, sensitivity to light, or neck pain. Other symptoms may include muscle weakness, problems with walking or balance, problems with memory, confusion, irritability, or seizures. In addition, a past history of alcohol or drug use may be reported.

Physical exam: The initial physical exam of an unconscious individual should quickly assess adequacy of airway, breathing, pulse and blood pressure then followed by a more detailed neurological and physical exam. This includes an evaluation of level of consciousness, pupil response and vital signs, motor function, reflexes, and memory.

The level of consciousness is the most sensitive indicator of neurological function. Depending on the size and location of the intracranial hemorrhage, changes in the level of consciousness can range from mild lethargy to deep coma. The Glasgow Coma Scale (GCS) is an internationally recognized tool for evaluating level of consciousness and is used to predict outcome. A GCS score of 15 is normal. A GCS score of 3 is the lowest level and represents a deep coma state. The lower the score, the deeper the level of coma and the higher the morbidity and mortality. Vital signs are taken as a baseline and then monitored for changes throughout the recovery. A hallmark of imminent neurological crisis is a loss of the normal autoregulation of blood pressure and pulse called the Cushing reflex. This generally results in a sudden rise in blood pressure and a slowing of the pulse.

Breathing rate and pattern is also evaluated. Irregularities in breathing patterns may indicate pressure from the accumulated blood in any of the respiratory centers scattered throughout the brain.

Pupils are normally equal in size, round and briskly reactive to light. Bleeding may create pressure on the nerves leading to the pupils, producing changes in pupil size, shape, and reaction to light and movement. These changes can be correlated with the severity of bleeding. A sudden dilation of one pupil (anisocoria) is an ominous sign and indicates dangerously high pressures within the brain that requires immediate intervention.

Drooping of one side of the face is a classic sign indicating damage to the nerve pathways supplying facial muscles. Reflexes can be overactive (hyperreflexia). The head and neck may be bruised and swollen. Blood may be present in the ear and behind the eardrum (Battle's sign) or discoloration may occur under the eyes (raccoon's sign). Speech can be slurred or absent (aphasia). If damage has occurred to the frontal lobe behind the forehead, sense of smell may be impaired (anosmia). Signs of memory failure may be present.

Tests: Baseline lab tests include arterial blood gases, complete blood count, glucose, electrolytes, blood urea nitrogen and creatinine, and drug screen and ethanol (alcohol) levels. Skull x-rays may be ordered to rule out skull fractures. CT of the brain confirms the presence of hemorrhage as well as size and location. If CT reveals no blood, spinal tap (lumbar puncture) may be performed to determine if blood is present in the cerebrospinal fluid. MRI is not helpful immediately after the injury to diagnose bleeding but is useful after the initial 48 hours to assess extent of brain injury.

X-rays of the cerebral blood vessels (cerebral angiography) or MRA may be performed if aneurysms are suspected and in other clinically stable vascular disorders. A brain wave test (electroencephalogram or EEG) may be useful in some cases where seizures are noted and if the individual's exam and imaging are inconsistent with the clinical presentation.

Treatment

Initial management of any individual with head trauma focuses on stabilization of airway, breathing, and blood pressure. Increased pressure in the brain (intracranial pressure or ICP) following intracranial hemorrhage is a life-threatening emergency. Neurological status and ICP are usually monitored continuously until stable. Increased ICP may be treated with mechanical hyperventilation to reduce arterial carbon dioxide levels. This decreases blood flow to the brain and hence ICP. Barbiturates and/or diuretics may also help treat increased ICP.

If increased ICP is related to bleeding into the ventricles that may interfere with normal reabsorption and circulation of cerebrospinal fluid, a shunt may be placed from the ventricle to the abdominal cavity (ventriculoperitoneal shunt) to drain excess fluid and thereby reduce increased ICP. Clot formations such as epidural or subdural hematomas may require surgical removal (craniotomy with evacuation of hematoma). Any concurrent seizure activity is treated with anticonvulsant medications. Blood pressure, temperature, and respiratory status are carefully monitored. Mechanical ventilators, medications, fluids, and thermal blankets may be used as needed to maintain normal blood pressure, temperature, and respirations. Ruptured aneurysms may need surgical treatment (clipping) either immediately or when the individual is more stable. Subarachnoid hemorrhage is often associated with constriction of surrounding blood vessels (vasospasm) needing treatment with calcium-channel blockers.

Prognosis

Chances for recovery depend on the location of the bleeding, severity of brain injury associated with the bleeding, and level of consciousness when first seen as measured by the GCS score. Death rate is up to 90% in cases of epidural hemorrhage caused by arterial bleeding. Following rupture of a brain aneurysm, 10% of individuals die immediately and 50% die within a month. In the two weeks following aneurysm rupture, 20-30% of aneurysms rebleed and cause death in three-fourths of cases. Surgical removal of large hemorrhages in the subdural or epidural spaces (craniotomy with evacuation of hematoma) can be lifesaving and survivors often have full recoveries. However, surgical intervention for deep cerebral bleeding and clots (craniotomy with evacuation of hematoma) carries a high mortality rate and is rarely done. Consequently, individuals with deep cerebral bleeding can have profound neurological disabilities.

Recovery may take weeks to months. In adults, most recovery after severe intracranial bleeding occurs within the first 6 months. Smaller improvements may continue for perhaps as long as 2 years. Possible outcomes include memory loss, intellectual impairment, muscular weakness in an arm or leg, or slurred speech but patterns of recovery vary. The injury may be fatal in cases of damage to vital centers that regulate breathing and blood flow.

Differential Diagnosis

Metabolic disorders such as diabetes or hypothyroidism, meningitis, drug and alcohol abuse, or misuse of prescription drugs can share some symptoms with intracranial bleeding. Severe headache suggests intracranial bleeding or meningitis rather than metabolic cause. Meningitis is usually associated with high fever, unlike most forms of intracranial hemorrhage (other than subarachnoid hemorrhage) that can give rise to some temperature elevation. History of trauma is a helpful clue to traumatic brain injury.

Specialists

- Internist
- Neurologist
- Neurosurgeon
- Physiatrist
- Psychiatrist
- Pulmonologist

Rehabilitation

Any unspecified intracranial hemorrhage that has caused physical and mental deficits may need rehabilitation to facilitate recovery. A physiatrist may access the individual's degree of mental and functional disability and determine the rehabilitation plan. Most individuals with severe head injury (initial GCS less than or equal to 8) benefit from formal neurorehabilitation. Some individuals with major brain injury and significant mental and functional deficits may be referred to an inpatient rehabilitation facility. Those with less complicated injuries and deficits may benefit from outpatient rehabilitation that can include occupational, behavioral, physical, and speech therapy.

The overall objective for rehabilitation of individuals with traumatic brain injury including intracranial hemorrhage is to return them as quickly and as fully as possible to the mainstream of their lives. This requires achieving functional recovery and assisting the individual in coping with any remaining disabilities. Goal setting is necessary for effective use of time and resources when treating severe symptoms of intracranial hemorrhage. An organized treatment approach from a team of healthcare professionals is necessary for a complete treatment program that combines carryover during a variety of daily-related activities.

Treatment varies for each individual because specific problems after each head injury are unique.

Even when the individual becomes less comatose and more alert, confusion and easy distractibility may occur. Exercises to promote memory return and accomplishment of simple tasks may be helpful. Sequencing of activities from easy to more difficult includes teaching the individual to rise from a chair before instruction in proper walking patterns. Once the individual regains his or her thinking processes, rehabilitation then focuses on muscular strength, endurance, and flexibility. Muscle imbalance is corrected by traditional methods using techniques to help the muscles and nervous system work together. Individuals with damage to the nerves supplying the head and neck (cranial nerves) may require rehabilitation of hearing, swallowing, balance, and use of muscles of facial expression.

The final phase of rehabilitation following intracranial hemorrhage involves helping the individual return to work. Work restrictions or modifications may be needed for those with various levels of head trauma. Participants in the rehabilitation program include physical, occupational, speech, and recreational therapists and social workers.

Work Restrictions / Accommodations

In less severe injury, a worker may temporarily need shorter work hours or more frequent breaks. Time off from work for ongoing rehabilitation and treatment may be necessary. In severe cases, permanent physical and/or mental impairment may prevent individuals from performing previous duties and require adjustment in duties and expectations.

Comorbid Conditions

Advanced age, bleeding disorders, high blood pressure, smoking history, alcohol or drug abuse, and other concurrent illnesses or injuries may affect ability to recover and result in longer disability. Pre-existing neurologic or psychiatric conditions may have their own impairments additive to those related to the intracranial hemorrhage. Bleeding disorders, heart conditions, and immunosuppressed states such as AIDS may complicate surgery or increase risk of operative morbidity.

Complications

Individuals with intracranial hemorrhage are at risk for developing seizures or ICP. Increased ICP is a life-threatening emergency that results from bleeding within the skull cavity, brain swelling, or increased amount of cerebrospinal fluid. Increasing ICP decreases the flow of blood and oxygen to the brain cells, eventually leading to permanent brain damage, coma, downward displacement (herniation) of the brain toward the spinal canal where vital brain structures are easily compressed, and death. Other complications include rebleeding, damage to nerves supplying the head and neck (cranial nerves), and coma. Narrowing of cerebral arteries near the site of aneurysm or arteriovenous malformation rupture (vasospasm) can complicate subarachnoid hemorrhage. Blood in the subarachnoid space can obstruct absorption and recirculation of cerebrospinal fluid causing fluid-filled chambers within the brain (ventricles) to enlarge. This condition is called hydrocephalus and may require placement of a shunt draining the ventricle into the abdominal cavity (ventriculoperitoneal shunt).

Factors Influencing Duration

Type and severity of hemorrhage, response to treatment, residual neurological damage, and job requirements may impact disability.

Length of Disability

Disability may be permanent

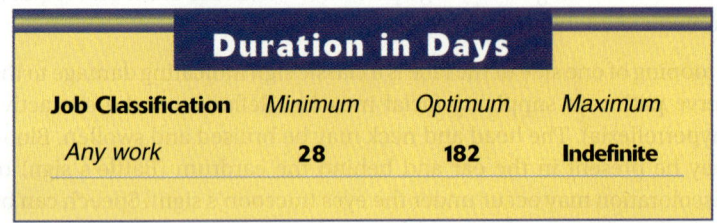

Duration in Days

Job Classification	Minimum	Optimum	Maximum
Any work	28	182	Indefinite

Failure to Recover

If an individual fails to recover within the maximum duration expectancy period, the reader may wish to reference the following questions to assist in better understanding the specifics of an individual's medical case.

Regarding diagnosis:

- Has individual had any trauma to the head or a deceleration injury?
- Did individual receive prompt treatment?
- Does individual or witness report a loss of consciousness, breathing, or pulse? Are there complaints of nausea, vomiting, headache, visual disturbances, sensitivity to light, or neck pain? Does

individual complain of muscle weakness, problems with walking or balance, problems with memory, confusion, irritability, or seizures?

- Is there a past history of alcohol or drug use?
- Is individual conscious or unconscious?
- What was individual's initial Glasgow Coma Scale (GCS) score?
- Were arterial blood gases, complete blood count, complete chemistry panel and drug screen, and ethanol levels done? Were skull x-rays, CT of the brain, spinal tap, and later a MRI performed? Was angiography or an EEG done?
- Have conditions with similar symptoms been ruled out?

Regarding treatment:

- Is individual hospitalized and being monitored in ICU?
- Has individual been treated with the appropriate medications such as barbiturates, diuretics, or calcium-channel blockers?
- Was a ventilator necessary? Was mechanical hyperventilation tried?
- Was a ventriculoperitoneal shunt necessary? Was surgical clipping needed?
- Was it necessary to do a craniotomy with evacuation of a hematoma?

Regarding prognosis:

- Is individual active in rehabilitation? Is a home exercise program in place?
- Can individual's employer accommodate any necessary restrictions?
- Does individual have any conditions that may affect ability to recover?
- Have any complications developed such as seizures, permanent brain damage, coma, and death? Did individual have rebleeding, damage to the cranial nerves, vasospasm, or hydrocephalus?

References

Brass, L.M., et al. "Intracranial Hemorrhage Associated with Thrombolytic Therapy for Elderly Patients with Acute Myocardial Infarction." Stroke 31 8 (2000): 1802-1811.

Machulda, M.M., and M.W. Haut. "Clinical Features of Chronic Subdural Hematoma: Neuropsychiatric and Neuropsychologic Changes in Patients with Chronic Subdural Hematoma." Neurosurgical Clinics of North America 11 3 (2000): 473-477.

Intravenous Pyelogram
Other names / synonyms: Excretory Urogram, Excretory Urography, IVP, LVP
87.73

Definition

An intravenous pyelogram (IVP) is an x-ray examination of the urinary system that is done after material that absorbs x-rays (contrast medium) is injected into the bloodstream. The contrast medium concentrates in the kidneys and a series of x-rays are taken at timed intervals as it travels through the kidneys, the tubes from the kidneys to the urinary bladder (ureters), and into the urinary bladder. The test enables the radiologist to examine the anatomy and functioning of the kidneys and urinary tract. It is done to evaluate infections in the bladder and kidneys, blood in the urine, flank pain (kidney stone), tumors, and to look for damage to the urinary tract after abdominal surgery.

IVP is used to demonstrate abnormalities in the urinary tract. Diseases that put an individual at risk for developing a renal abscess include polycystic renal disease, hemodialysis treatment, spinal cord injury, a deficient (compromised) immune system, diabetes mellitus, urinary tract obstruction, renal or ureteral mineral deposits (calculi), abnormal growth (neoplasm) in the kidney, genitourinary tuberculosis, renal transplantation, surgical trauma to the kidney, steroid administration, and chronic or recurrent urinary tract infection.

The incidence of renal abscess ranges from 1 to 10 cases per every 10,000 individuals. Most cases are a result of complications from a lower urinary tract infection. The condition affects men and women in equal proportion. Renal abscesses usually occur singly and in only one kidney (unilateral). Sixty-three percent of the time, the right kidney is affected.

Reason for Procedure

Intravenous pyelogram (IVP) is performed in order to visualize the kidneys, ureters, and urinary bladder. It is done to identify the cause of a variety of urinary tract complaints including frequent urination, blood in the urine (hematuria), or pain in the side or lower back (flank). IVP allows detection of kidney stones (urolithiasis), an enlarged prostate, internal injuries following an accident or trauma, damage to the urinary tract after an abdominal surgery, and tumors in the kidney, ureters, or urinary bladder.

Description

Intravenous pyelogram (IVP) is an outpatient procedure that is done in the x-ray department; it usually takes 1-2 hours.

After emptying the bladder, the individual is positioned on an x-ray table and a preliminary x-ray of the abdomen is taken. Then a contrast medium is injected into a vein in their arm. There may be a minor sting associated with injection of the contrast agent but no other pain is associated with this procedure. Some individuals report feeling a flush of heat, a metallic taste in the mouth, or a mild itching sensation following injection. These side effects usually disappear within a minute or two and are not harmful. If the itching persists or is accompanied by hives, it can be easily treated.

During the imaging process, the individual may be asked to turn from side to side and to hold several different positions so that views from several angles can be captured. As the contrast medium is processed by the kidneys, a series of images will be captured to determine the size of the kidneys, and to show the rest of the urinary tract as it begins to empty. Kidneys do not empty at the same rate, so x-ray images may begin between 30 minutes and 3-4 hours following injection of the contrast. However, once begun, the IVP usually takes about an hour. Near the end of the exam the individual may be asked to empty their bladder so that an additional x-ray can be taken as it drains to determine how well it empties.

The contrast medium used for IVP studies will not discolor the urine or cause any discomfort during urination. A physician should be informed if these conditions occur following the procedure as they may indicate some other ongoing problem.

Prognosis

With intravenous pyelogram, the kidneys, ureters, and urinary bladder will be visible on x-ray, and the shape of these structures will be clearly apparent. Abnormalities such as kidney stones (urolithiasis), prostate enlargement, internal injuries, and tumors in the kidney, ureters, or urinary bladder should also be visible.

Specialists

- Radiologist
- Urologist

Work Restrictions / Accommodations

There should not be any work restrictions or accommodations following intravenous pyelogram.

Comorbid Conditions

Allergies to shellfish or any previously used contrast material may impact an individual's ability to recover and further lengthen disability.

Procedure Complications

Complications that might result from intravenous pyelogram include itching, hives, swelling, nausea, vomiting, or difficulty in breathing, any of which may result from an allergic reaction to injection of contrast medium.

In rare cases, dehydration, shortness of breath, or swelling in the throat or other parts of the body may occur. These conditions should be treated promptly and the radiologist should be informed immediately.

Factors Influencing Duration

There should be no disability from the procedure itself, unless allergic reaction or dehydration develop. The underlying cause for the procedure might influence disability. Serious conditions such as kidney stones, internal injuries, and tumors in the urogenital tract may need to be treated immediately and further lengthen the time of disability.

Length of Disability

No disability is expected. Most individuals are able to return to work the day after the test unless there is an allergic reaction to intravenous injection of contrast medium.

References

Llach, F. Papper's Clinical Nephrology. Boston: Little, Brown and Company, 1993.

Loeb, S. Illustrated Guide to Diagnostic Tests. Springhouse, PA: Springhouse Corporation, 1994.

Intravenous Therapy
99.1

Definition

Intravenous (IV) therapy involves the administration of a therapeutic solution directly into a vein.

There are several delivery methods available, the choice of which depends on several factors including the purpose of therapy, the solution to be given, the medical diagnosis, the individual's age and medical history, and condition of the veins.

Intravenous therapy may be administered for short- or long-term purposes. Short-term IV therapy can be given through veins that are smaller and very close to the skin surface, such as in the hand, arm, leg, or foot. Longer-term IV therapy is generally given through larger, deeper veins (central veins); they are used for solutions that may cause damage to small veins, when large amounts of fluid may be needed, or to deliver high-calorie solutions that provide nutritional support (although some low-calorie nutritional solutions may be given through a peripheral IV). A surgically implanted vascular access device (hep lock) may be inserted under the skin when a central catheter is needed long-term.

Depending on the components of the solution, it can be given slowly (by IV infusion) or rapidly (by injection, "push," or "bolus"). IV solutions may be infused by gravity, or via mechanized delivery pump, and may be given on an intermittent or continuous basis.

Reason for Procedure

The most common reasons for intravenous (IV) therapy are to maintain or restore the fluid volume and electrolyte balance of the body, to infuse medications, to transfuse blood or blood components, and to administer high-calorie solutions that provide nutritional support (total parenteral nutrition, or TPN). IV therapy is commonly used to maintain fluid volume in individuals who are not allowed to eat or drink before or after medical or surgical procedures, or to restore the fluid volume level in individuals who may have become severely dehydrated (such as through vomiting or other illness). IV therapy is also used to administer certain drugs that cannot be taken by mouth because they will be destroyed by gastric juices, or are irritating or cannot be absorbed by the gastrointestinal tract. Commonly infused medications may include those used to fight infection (antibiotics), to dissolve blood clots (thrombolytics), to prevent blood clots (anticoagulants), anticancer medications (chemotherapy), heart and blood pressure medications, anticonvulsants, and pain medications. IV therapy is used to replace blood (or plasma) lost in an accident or during an operation. Nutritional supplements and electrolyte replacements may be given through infusion to maintain body fluids in individuals who are unable to eat or drink. Some types of catheters can also be used to withdraw blood for laboratory tests.

Description

Generally, an intravenous (IV) catheter must be placed before beginning IV therapy (in some situations, a medication may be injected directly into a vein using a needle and syringe without an intravenous catheter). A catheter is a thin, hollow, plastic tube that is introduced through the skin into a vein; several types of catheters are available. The technique for placing a catheter into a vein (venipuncture) varies depending on the vein to be used (peripheral or central) and on the type of catheter that will be used. Before placing the catheter, the solution, tubing, and delivery system are prepared. The catheters most commonly used for a peripheral IV have a fine needle inside the catheter; this is necessary for puncturing the skin and vein during placement. To place a peripheral catheter, a tourniquet is placed above the insertion site, filling the vein with blood; this makes it easier to find and enter. The site is cleansed with an antibacterial solution to prevent infection. A local anesthetic may be given just under the skin to ease any discomfort that may occur when inserting the catheter. The catheter is inserted through the skin and into the vein. After entry, the catheter is gently threaded into the vein and the tourniquet removed. The needle used for introduction is removed, and the IV tubing that is connected to the solution is attached to the catheter, allowing the solution to drip in. The catheter and tubing are securely taped in place.

Placement of a central catheter varies. Some types of central catheters used for long-term outpatient therapy (peripherally inserted central catheter, PICC lines) are placed by a physician or specially trained nurse. Central catheters may be placed in a large vein in the upper chest area (subclavian vein) or one located in the neck (internal jugular vein). There is some variation in technique depending on the type of catheter and the vein to be used. Generally, however, the individual is positioned very carefully, with the head and shoulders slightly lower than the body (Trendelenburg's position) so as to fill the veins with blood (dilate), and to help prevent introducing an air embolus. The skin is cleansed with a surgical scrub and small surgical drapes are placed around the site to help prevent infection. A needle and syringe are used to enter the vein. The syringe is then removed from the needle and a small guidewire is placed through the needle into the vein; afterwards the needle is removed leaving the guidewire in place. The catheter is inserted into the vein over the guidewire. The guidewire is removed and the IV tubing that is connected to the solution is attached to the catheter, allowing infusion to begin. A suture is often used to secure the catheter in place. A dressing is placed over the site and the tubing is taped to the skin. A plain solution is slowly infused until a chest x-ray confirms that the catheter is in the correct position, and that there has been no accidental injury to the lungs. After confirmation of placement, the desired solution at the appropriate rate can be administered.

Vascular access devices are placed by a surgeon through a small incision located in the chest area. This type of IV infusion device is usually placed during a surgical procedure using an x-ray machine (fluoroscopy) to guide placement. A small incision is made and the catheter is inserted into the vein (often the subclavian, jugular, or cephalic vein). A pocket is made in the subcutaneous tissue, through which the catheter is tunneled. The reservoir is then placed in the pocket and attached to the catheters. The reservoir and the catheters must be flushed with an anticoagulant solution to keep them from clotting closed. The incision is sutured closed and a dressing placed.

Prognosis

In most cases, intravenous (IV) therapy provides administration of fluids, total parental nutrition, blood transfusions, chemotherapy, and medications, successfully and without occurrence of complications (fluid overload, allergic reaction, electrolyte imbalance, injury to veins, extravasation). IV therapy can restore or maintain fluid volume status, maintain daily caloric and nutritional requirements, replace red blood cells and other blood components, treat cancer, and deliver medications.

Specialists

- Emergency Medicine
- General Surgeon
- Internist

Work Restrictions / Accommodations

The underlying reason for the intravenous therapy, rather than the therapy itself, will influence any work restrictions or special accommodations. Time off during the work shift may be needed for infusion of medications, and time off may be needed for medical appointments to assess the condition of, and care for, the catheter. Work restrictions may be needed if the work area may contaminate the IV site and cause infection. Work restrictions may also be needed to prevent dislodging or damage to the IV catheter.

Comorbid Conditions

Some individuals, especially the elderly and chronically ill, may have very small, crooked, or hard veins that make catheter insertion difficult. Individuals with certain heart conditions, heart failure or kidney failure may be especially prone to volume overload. Conditions in which there is compromised circulation or lymphatic drainage would add to disability time. Other comorbid conditions include infections, thrombophlebitis, diabetes. IV catheters that are not placed in extremities that have an arteriovenous fistula, graft, or shunt (used for hemodialysis).

Procedure Complications

There may be problems associated with the catheter such as kinking or other occlusion of the catheter itself, or developing a clot or an infection at the venous insertion site (phlebitis). The catheter may become dislodged from the vein, allowing medication and fluid to infuse into subcutaneous tissue (infiltration or extravasation), or air may be introduced into the vein (air embolism). Problems associated with the administration of medications include medication or allergic reaction. Heart rhythm abnormalities (cardiac arrhythmias) can occur if electrolyte solutions such as potassium are infused too rapidly. If too much fluid volume is given, an imbalance of components in the blood (electrolytes) or circulatory overload can result. With blood transfusions, a reaction may develop if there are incompatibilities of blood type. Finally, during administration of total parenteral nutrition, blood sugar may rise too high. During insertion of a central catheter, the lung may be nicked, causing air to leak from the lungs into the chest cavity (pneumothorax).

Factors Influencing Duration

The length of disability is dependent on the underlying condition. Some medications administered intravenously may have serious side effects.

Length of Disability

No disability is expected to result from this therapy. Disability may occur as a result of an underlying condition.

References

Hamilton, Sandra, et al. "Intravascular Therapy." Nursing Procedures, 3rd ed. Holmes, Nancy H Springhouse, PA: Springhouse Corporation, 2000. 272-341.

Stone, Eric B. "Starting an Intravenous Infusion: Adult and Infant." Saunders Manual of Medical Practice, 2nd ed. Rakel, Robert E., ed. Philadelphia: W.B. Saunders Company, 2000. 296-301.

Iontophoresis

Other names / synonyms: Transdermal Iontophoresis

99.27

Definition

Iontophoresis is a therapeutic method for delivering treatment (medications) into and through the skin through the use of electrical current. The method transfers ions (electrically charged particles) across the skin membrane. This technique can be used to test for the presence of medical conditions, such as cystic fibrosis. Iontophoresis is also used to deliver medications to a localized tissue area to treat medical conditions, such as painful feet (plantar fasciitis).

A variation of iontophoresis, electrochemotherapy, exposes cancerous tissues to short pulses of electricity during chemotherapy.

It has proven to be a beneficial treatment for many localized skin disorders such as nail diseases, Herpes lesions, psoriasis, eczematous, and cutaneous T-cell lymphoma. The method has also been reported useful for topical anesthesia to the skin prior to cut-down for artificial kidney dialysis, insertion of tracheotomy tubes, and infiltration of lidocaine into the skin prior to venipuncture. Treatment of various musculoskeletal disorders can be treated with iontophoresis using anti-inflammatory agents.

Reason for Procedure

Iontophoresis enhances the transdermal delivery of ionized drugs through the skin's outermost layer (stratum corneum). Iontophoresis is used to diagnose cystic fibrosis. Because the sodium and chloride concentration in sweat is higher than normal in individuals with cystic fibrosis, it is possible to use iontophoresis methods to obtain an accurate diagnosis.

Iontophoresis is also used to treat musculoskeletal disorders such as plantar fasciitis or heel pain. Recent research has shown the potential for iontophoresis methods to be used for the delivery of chemotherapy by exposing cancerous tissues to short pulses of electricity during chemotherapy. This enhances cell membrane permeability and may have antitumor effects.

Because iontophoresis acts quickly, it's also an effective method for numbing an I.V. injection site.

Description

Iontophoresis used as a method for testing involves the placement of a positive and a negative electrode applied to the thigh or arm. The positive electrode is covered with gauze that is saturated with a stimulating drug that induces sweating. The negative electrode is covered by gauze saturated with a bicarbonate solution. Following this, a low electrical current is generated to the test site. The current flows for approximately 5-12 minutes. The electrodes are removed, and the area is washed with distilled water.

Paper disks are then applied over the test site. These disks are covered with paraffin (a waxy substance obtained from petroleum), which allows for an airtight seal to eliminate evaporation of sweat. After 1 hour, the paraffin is removed. The paper disks are immediately placed in a weighing jar, and sent for sodium and chloride analysis/evaluation. Iontophoresis "sweat testing" takes approximately 90 minutes and is painless.

There are a number of techniques for applying medications via iontophoresis to treat inflammation conditions. Most techniques require preparing/cleaning the skin, applying the medication, and then applying an electrode to the skin. The electrode, which is attached to the appropriate machine, is then used to direct a low electrical current to the skin, causing the medication to be transferred to the selected site.

In some specialized procedures, which are used most frequently for medical research, a metal probe is inserted into the selected area, such as a cancerous tumor, medication is applied, and the electrical current is used to disperse the medication.

Prognosis

Iontophoresis adequately delivers medications for skin ailments, assists in the application of topical anesthesia, and treats inflammation of the muscles and joints.

Specialists

- Oncologist
- Podiatrist
- Rheumatologist
- Sports Medicine Physician

Work Restrictions / Accommodations

Restrictions and accommodations are not associated with this procedure. Any work accommodations are related to underlying medical conditions.

Comorbid Conditions

If being used for treatment of musculoskeletal disorders, other conditions, such as arthritis or sports injuries, may affect recovery time. Allergies to the medications being used or to the paper or adhesives used in the process may impact recovery time.

Procedure Complications

As when using any low-voltage direct-current device, iontophoresis has the potential to cause injuries through electrolysis, especially if equipment is not maintained or staff well-trained in its use. Although rare, burns or electric shocks may occur.

Factors Influencing Duration

No disability is expected as a result of testing or treatment unless complications occur.

Length of Disability

There is no disability associated with uncomplicated iontophoresis. Disability may occur as a result of an underlying condition.

References

Glass, L.F., et al. "Intralesional Bleomycin-mediated Electrochemotherapy in 20 Patients with Basalcell Carcinoma." Journal of the American Academy of Dermatology 37(4) (1997): 596-599.

Gudeman, S.D., et al. "Treatment of Plantar Fasciitis by Iontophoresis of 0.4% Dexamethasone. A Randomized, Double-blind, Placebo-controlled Study." American Journal of Sports Medicine. 25(3) (1997): 312-316.

Guy, R.H. "Iontophoresis - Recent Developments." Journal of Pharmacy and Pharmacology. 50(4) (1998): 371-374.

Japour, C.J., et al. "Management of Heel Pain Syndrome with Acetic Acid Iontophoresis." Journal of the American Podiatric Medical Association 89(5) (1999): 251-257.

Ravel, Richard. "Sweat Test for Screening." Clinical Laboratory Medicine: Clinical Applications Of Laboratory Data. Mosby-Year Book, Inc., 1995. 2 Feb 2001 <http://home.mdconsult.com/das/book/view/104?sid=32516272>.

Rosenstein, E.D. "Topical Agents in the Treatment of Rheumatic Disorders." Rheumatic Diseases Clinics of North America. 25(4) (1999): 899-918.

Iridectomy

Other names / synonyms: Optical Iridectomy, Peripheral Iridectomy, Sector Iridectomy, Total Iridectomy

12.14

Definition

An iridectomy is a surgical procedure to remove a piece of the colored part of the eye (the iris). The goal of this procedure is to improve the flow of the fluid within the eye (aqueous humor) and thereby reducing or preventing an increase in the internal eye pressure (intraocular pressure or IOP). This procedure is a treatment for the progressive disease called glaucoma.

There are several types of iridectomy. Total iridectomy removes the total iris. Peripheral iridectomy removes tissue from the outer edge of the iris (away from the pupil). Sector iridectomy removes a piece of iris from the edge of the pupil to the outer edge of the iris, producing a keyhole shaped pupil. Optical iridectomy creates an artificial pupil by removing tissue from the central iris.

Iridectomy is only useful in certain types of glaucoma (specifically narrow angle glaucoma). The causes of glaucoma are unknown, although a family link exists. Therefore, individuals with a family history of glaucoma are at an increased risk of developing glaucoma and subsequently requiring intervention.

While 3 million Americans and nearly 67 million individuals worldwide have glaucoma, iridectomy has become increasingly less common now that laser procedures accomplish the same goal.

Reason for Procedure

An iridectomy relieves pressure in the eye. This procedure is performed to prevent damage to the optic nerve and slow any related vision loss. It may be done in cases of sudden (acute) glaucoma. Individuals with long-term (chronic) glaucoma may benefit from this operation when other procedures (trabeculectomy or trabeculoplasty) have failed. This procedure may also be done to prevent pressure problems from occurring in the future (prophylactic treatment).

Description

Iridectomy is a surgical procedure usually performed under local anesthesia in an outpatient setting. In adults, general anesthesia is rarely used. Prior to surgery, individuals are given a medication to help relieve any anxiety related to the procedure. Injections around the eye numb it. With the aid of a surgical microscope, the surgeon removes a small piece of iris.

In a peripheral iridectomy, the iris tissue is removed from the outer edge of the iris away from the pupil. A sector iridectomy involves removal of a portion of the iris from the pupil to the outer edge of the iris. This results in a keyhole-shaped pupil. Some individuals may have a total iridectomy where the entire iris is removed. During an optical iridectomy, tissue is removed from the central portion of the iris, creating an artificial pupil.

Removal of iris tissue allows the aqueous humor to flow more freely thereby lowering or preventing an increase in the IOP.

Prognosis

Iridectomy is an effective method for relieving or preventing elevated eye pressure (IOP) in individuals with certain types of glaucoma. It should be noted that although iridectomy may completely relieve the elevated IOP, it couldn't reverse damage already done by glaucoma. Vision loss occurring prior to this procedure will not be restored. The progression of glaucoma may cease or slow down following this procedure.

Specialists

- Ophthalmologist

Work Restrictions / Accommodations

The individual's vision may be impaired for a period of time. The eye will be sensitive, requiring an individual to wear a visor or sunglasses when in strong light. These facts should be taken into consideration if the individual's work requires good eyesight. There may be restrictions on bending and lifting. Frequent breaks may be needed and individual may have to constantly use eyedrops.

Comorbid Conditions

Any condition that may impair healing such as diabetes or immune dysfunction would lengthen disability.

Procedure Complications

The primary complication of iridectomy is failure of the incision to close properly. Other possible complications that are common to most eye surgeries include bleeding (hyphema), inflammation, infection of the iris (iritis), abnormal blood vessel growth (neovascularization), loss of too much fluid causing flattening of the eye, worsening of cataracts, swelling of the clear, outer layer of the eye (cornea), and permanent worsening of underlying glaucoma. These complications can result in permanent vision loss. Iridectomy has a higher rate of failure if the eye has undergone previous surgeries. General anesthesia is rarely used in adults since it has been known to increase the risk of heart or breathing complications.

Factors Influencing Duration

Length of disability may be influenced by type of procedure, response to treatment, and the individual's job requirements. Eyesight may be temporarily affected. Bending and heavy lifting are not advised in the first month after surgery.

Length of Disability

Disability may be longer for individuals who perform heavy work or for those whose jobs require keen vision.

Laser.

Duration in Days

Job Classification	Minimum	Optimum	Maximum
Sedentary work	1	2	3
Light work	2	3	7
Medium work	3	7	14
Heavy work	3	7	14
Very Heavy work	3	7	14

Surgical treatment.

Duration in Days

Job Classification	Minimum	Optimum	Maximum
Sedentary work	7	9	14
Light work	7	9	14
Medium work	14	21	28
Heavy work	14	21	28
Very Heavy work	14	21	28

References

Surgery for Glaucoma. American Academy of Ophthalmology. 1996. 13 July 2000 <http://www.medem.com/search/article_display.cfm?path=n:&mstr=/ZZZJSNRNH4C.html&soc=AAO&srch_typ=NAV_SERCH>.

Iridotomy

Other names / synonyms: Iridotomy, Laser Iridotomy, Laser Peripheral Iridotomy, LPI
12.12

Definition

Laser peripheral iridotomy is a surgical treatment for glaucoma. As the name suggests, laser peripheral iridotomy involves the use of a laser to make a small hole in the colored part of the eye (iris). The object of this procedure is to improve the flow of fluid within the eye (aqueous humor) thereby reducing or preventing an increase in the internal eye pressure (intraocular pressure, IOP). This procedure is usually conducted in the doctor's office or eye clinic under local anesthetic. The procedure is complete in a matter of minutes, and the individual may go home soon after.

Laser peripheral iridotomy has become the treatment of choice for acute, angle-closure glaucoma. It is also used frequently used for individuals with narrow angle glaucoma. The causes of glaucoma are currently unknown; however, it does tend to run in families. Therefore individuals with a family history of glaucoma are at an increased risk for developing that disease, and thus at an increased risk for needing surgical intervention.

There are about 300,000 people in the US and nearly 7 million people worldwide who have the type of glaucoma who can be treated by laser peripheral iridotomy.

Reason for Procedure

Laser peripheral iridotomy is a surgical treatment for glaucoma. Individuals with glaucoma usually have abnormally high pressure in their eyes (intraocular pressure, or IOP), which causes damage to the optic nerve. Damage to the optic nerve causes a progressive loss of vision. Thus, one of the primary objectives of glaucoma treatment is lowering or stabilizing increased IOP.

There are different causes of high IOP, depending on the type of glaucoma. In acute angle closure glaucoma and in narrow angle glaucoma, the colored part of the eye (iris) is interfering with the flow of fluid (aqueous humor) between the front (anterior) and back (posterior) chambers of the eye. Laser peripheral iridotomy is currently the treatment of choice for acute, angle closure glaucoma. It is also commonly used to treat narrow angle glaucoma. Laser peripheral iridotomy involves using a laser to create an opening in the iris, thereby improving fluid flow. The result is reduced (or stabilized) IOP.

Description

Laser peripheral iridotomy is usually performed in the doctor's office or in an outpatient eye clinic. Local anesthesia is used, and the procedure is completed within a matter of minutes. Just before the procedure, the individual will be given eye drops to numb the eye. Then, with the aid of a special microscope, the doctor aims the laser at the iris. A bright flash of light, like a camera flash, is seen and the individual may feel a slight tingling sensation. At this point, the procedure is complete. Medicated eye drops may be prescribed to prevent inflammation.

Prognosis

Laser peripheral iridotomy is an effective method for treating elevated eye pressure due to certain types of glaucoma. Individuals who undergo this procedure may experience a reduction or stabilization of eye pressure. Vision loss occurring prior to this procedure will not be restored. Similarly, laser peripheral iridotomy will not cure the underlying disease, which may eventually progress, resulting in further loss of vision.

Specialists

• Ophthalmologist

Work Restrictions / Accommodations

Following laser peripheral iridotomy, the eye may be slightly irritated and vision may be slightly blurred. These effects are usually short-term, resolving within a day or two. Individuals are usually able to resume normal activity within 1-2 days after the procedure; however, eye drop medication may be required for several days to several weeks, thus accommodations for frequent breaks may be necessary. Frequent visits to the eye doctor to check eye pressure may be required for several weeks following the procedure. Restricted bending and/or heavy lifting may be advised, and alternative work assignments may be necessary for individuals who normally perform heavy work or whose jobs require frequent or prolonged bending.

Comorbid Conditions

There are no known comorbid conditions that would influence the length of disability following this procedure.

Procedure Complications

Laser surgery is generally safe; however, there are risks associated with any surgical procedure. Some individuals will experience an increase in internal eye pressure (intraocular pressure, or IOP) immediately after surgery. This elevation in IOP is usually short-term, resolving within a few weeks. Rarely, individuals will develop cataracts as a result of laser surgery. Other complications include inflammation (iritis), abnormal growth of blood vessels (neovascularization), bleeding (hyphema), or infection. Individuals who have had previous surgical procedures on the same eye have a higher risk of failure following this procedure.

Factors Influencing Duration

Individuals who have had previous surgical procedures on the same eye may experience a longer recovery period. Complications of this procedure may increase the length of disability. It is also important to understand that laser peripheral iridotomy cannot reverse vision loss that has already occurred. Thus, individuals with substantial vision loss may be permanently disabled. Similarly, if the underlying disease (i.e., glaucoma) progresses, eye pressure may increase requiring further treatment.

Length of Disability

Individuals who perform heavy work or whose jobs require frequent or prolonged bending may have a longer disability period. If the individual has experienced substantial vision loss, disability may be permanent.

Unilateral.

Duration in Days

Job Classification	Minimum	Optimum	Maximum
Sedentary work	1	3	7
Light work	1	3	7
Medium work	3	7	14
Heavy work	7	14	21
Very Heavy work	7	14	21

References

Learn About Glaucoma. Glaucoma Research Foundation. 3 Aug 2000 <http://www.glaucoma.org>.

Iritis

Other names / synonyms: Anterior Uveitis, Uveitis

364.0, 364.3

Definition

Iritis is an inflammation of the inner-colored part of the eye (iris). The condition may be caused by the body's immune response to a disease or an infection in other parts of the body (i.e., rheumatoid arthritis, tuberculosis, ulcerative colitis, syphilis, herpes simplex, shingles [herpes zoster], and psoriasis). When the immune system attacks molecules interpreted as foreign, certain vessels and cells in the eye may also be damaged. Other causes of iritis include cancer (malignancy), trauma (especially penetrating injuries), gout, and retinal detachment.

Iritis is the most common and usually the mildest type of inflammation found in the eye's uveal tract (uveitis). In addition to the iris, the uveal tract also contains the inner lining of the eye (choroid) and the set of muscles that enable the eye to focus (ciliary body).

Iritis is also known as anterior uveitis since it occurs in the anterior or front part of the eye. While iritis tends to be associated with immune disorders, uveitis in other parts of the eye may be linked to infection elsewhere in the body.

Iritis is most common in young or middle-aged adults. The disease tends to occur in only one eye (unilateral).

Diagnosis

History: Symptoms include a slight to moderate decrease in vision accompanied by swelling or redness in the white part of the eye (sclera). Individual may complain of seeing floating black spots (floaters). Moderate to severe eye pain is possible that can worsen by exposure to light (photophobia).

Physical exam: The eye's interior may be red or swollen with increased tearing. Material accumulated on the underside of the cornea may also be seen.

Tests: An ophthalmoscope and slitlamp exam may reveal redness in the eye along with a scarred, irregular pupil. This demonstrates a decreased response to light. An abnormal smoky or hazy flare may be illuminated in the eye's fluids. Pressure within the eye (intraocular pressure) should also be measured (tonometry). Other tests to identify underlying conditions include blood tests (erythrocyte sedimentation rate, VDRL, FTA-ABS), skin test (PPD), chest x-ray to rule out tuberculosis, and x-rays of the sacroiliac joints.

Treatment

Treatment should begin as soon as possible to prevent permanent damage. Eyedrops that dilate the pupils (mydriatics and cycloplegics) can ease pain and help sensitivity toward light. Corticosteroid eyedrops may diminish inflammation, but the individual will require close monitoring since the drug may increase interior eye pressure. In moderate to severe cases, a steroid may be injected into the outer layer of the eye (periocular steroid injection) or systemic steroids may be required. Underlying cause must also receive appropriate treatment.

Prognosis

Iritis (anterior uveitis) usually responds well but slowly to proper treatment. In most cases, there is no loss of vision. However, extreme or chronic cases may result in high eye pressure with accompanying nerve damage that creates permanent vision loss. If complications occur, the pupil may fail to react properly to light and vision will be decreased. Iritis often recurs even if treated promptly.

Differential Diagnosis

Conditions with similar symptoms include other types of uveitis (heterochromic uveitis, lens-induced uveitis, intermediate uveitis, and posterior uveitis), acute glaucoma, intraocular tumors, central nervous system lymphoma, retinal detachment, acute conjunctivitis, or trauma to the eye.

Specialists

- Ophthalmologist
- Rheumatologist

Work Restrictions / Accommodations

When necessary to the individual's work, visual acuity should be evaluated. Eyedrops may need to be applied frequently during the workday. Time may be needed for frequent eye exams until recovery is complete.

Comorbid Conditions

Coexisting conditions that may impact recovery and lengthen disability include AIDS or other immunodeficiency states (rheumatoid arthritis, ankylosing spondylitis, Reiter's syndrome, ulcerative colitis, lens-induced uveitis, sarcoidosis, Crohn's disease, or psoriasis), infections (syphilis, tuberculosis, herpes zoster, herpes simplex, or adenovirus), malignancy (retinoblastoma, leukemia, lymphoma, or malignant melanoma), retinal detachment, Fuchs' heterochromic iridocyclitis, gout, and glaucomatocyclitic crisis.

Complications

Iritis can rapidly damage the eye and result in long-term complications. The iris may permanently adhere to the cornea or lens (anterior or posterior synechiae). Severe or advanced iritis may result in clouding of the fluid in the front of the eye (aqueous humor), a blockage in fluid drainage (glaucoma), or a cloudy lens (cataract). Iritis may also cause swelling of the retina (macular edema) or retinal detachment.

Factors Influencing Duration

Length of disability may be influenced by the underlying cause, type of treatment, response to treatment, any complications, and recurrence of the iritis.

Length of Disability

Duration depends on severity, underlying cause, location of inflammation, response to treatment, and side effects of therapy.

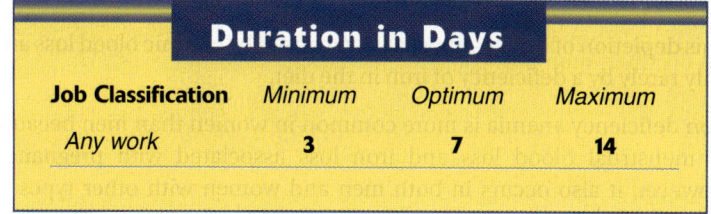

Duration in Days

Job Classification	Minimum	Optimum	Maximum
Any work	3	7	14

Failure to Recover

If an individual fails to recover within the maximum duration expectancy period, the reader may wish to reference the following questions to assist in better understanding the specifics of an individual's medical case.

Regarding diagnosis:

- Has diagnosis of iritis been confirmed?
- Could symptoms be related to another condition such as injury, retinal detachment, or a tumor?
- Have underlying causes (i.e., immune disorders or infections) been identified or ruled out?
- Is inflammation confined only to the anterior part of uveal tract? Is posterior also involved (posterior uveitis)?

Regarding treatment:

- What type of eyedrops has the individual used for treatment?
- Have topical corticosteroids been used?
- Were periocular steroid injections or systemic steroids required?
- Is the individual receiving treatment for underlying diseases such as immune disorders or infections?
- Has the use of eyedrop steroids caused side effects such as high pressure within the eye?

Regarding prognosis:

- Is inflammation confined only to anterior part of uveal tract?
- Is posterior also involved (posterior uveitis)?
- Aside from iritis, is the individual's overall health a factor in recovery time?

References

Gordon, Kilbourn III, and Barbara Blasko. Iritis and Uveitis. eMedicine.com. 10 Apr 2000. 28 June 2000 <http://www.emedicine.com/emerg/topic284.htm>.

Iron Deficiency Anemia
Other names / synonyms: Anemia
280, 280.0, 280.1, 280.8, 280.9

Definition

Iron deficiency anemia is the most common form of anemia (a low number of red blood cells in the circulation). In this condition, the amount of iron in the body is low and results in a decreased amount of hemoglobin, the oxygen-carrying component of red blood cells.

This depletion of iron is almost always caused by chronic blood loss and only rarely by a deficiency of iron in the diet.

Iron deficiency anemia is more common in women than men because of menstrual blood loss and iron loss associated with pregnancy. However, it also occurs in both men and women with other types of chronic bleeding such as gastrointestinal bleeding from ulcers, the presence of tumors, and use of medications such as aspirin and other nonsteroidal anti-inflammatory drugs (NSAIDs).

Diagnosis

History: Mild anemia usually has no symptoms and may be recognized only because of abnormal laboratory test results. Individuals with moderate to severe anemia may have symptoms such as fatigue, weakness, dizziness, shortness of breath, and decreased exercise capacity. If the anemia is from gastrointestinal bleeding, individuals may report black stools or bloody bowel movements. A desire to eat large amounts of ice (conditions known as pica for ice or pagophagia) is uncommon but considered to be a very specific symptom of iron deficiency.

Physical exam: Individuals with anemia may look pale (particularly the conjunctiva, tongue, palms, and nails), have chapped lips, brittle nails, or the whites of the eyes (sclerae) may look bluish, and the heart and respiratory rates may be elevated, even at rest.

Tests: A complete blood count (CBC) shows anemia with small red blood cells and a low hemoglobin concentration. A low serum ferritin level is a test of iron status and confirms the diagnosis. Although it is rarely needed, a bone marrow biopsy can also establish the diagnosis. Once a diagnosis of iron deficiency anemia is established, a variety of other tests may need to be done to locate the cause.

Treatment

Iron deficiency anemia is usually successfully treated with oral iron supplements. In rare cases when an individual cannot tolerate or absorb iron, the iron may be given through a vein (intravenously). Sometimes if the anemia is causing severe symptoms such as shortness of breath, severe dizziness, or chest pain, red blood cell transfusions may be necessary. In addition, the underlying cause of the anemia such as gastrointestinal bleeding must always be treated. A CBC is usually done around 6 weeks after treatment begins in order to reassess the condition.

Prognosis

Uncomplicated iron deficiency anemia is easily treated with oral iron supplements. Normalization of the CBC is seen in around 6 weeks. Correction of iron deficiency anemia due to a serious underlying problem such as gastrointestinal bleeding or a tumor is more difficult and depends on successful treatment of the underlying problem.

Differential Diagnosis

Iron deficiency anemia may be confused with noniron deficiency anemia that occurs with many chronic diseases such as kidney, inflammatory, or infectious diseases. Other less common anemias that may sometimes be mistaken for iron deficiency anemia are the thalassemias and autoimmune hemolytic anemias.

Specialists

- Gastroenterologist
- Hematologist
- Internist

Work Restrictions / Accommodations

Work may be temporarily interrupted by the occasional side effects of oral iron therapy (constipation, nausea, or heartburn) or by the need for intravenous iron therapy or red blood cell transfusions. If the individual has symptoms such as chest pain, shortness of breath, or dizziness, physical exertion at work may need to be reduced until the anemia is corrected.

Complementary and Alternative Therapies

Content is intended for awareness only. Treatments may or may not be effective. Scientific evidence may be lacking and some substances have potentially toxic effects. Dr. Presley Reed and the editors do not endorse the use of these therapies in the absence of consultation with a licensed medical professional.

Dietary modifications - If IDA is related to inadequate iron in diet, usually adding three portions of lean red meat (heme iron sources) per week, along with adequate consumption of all other essential vitamins and minerals, may help to correct anemia.

Comorbid Conditions

Malabsorption of iron, continued uncontrolled bleeding, or a complicated underlying cause may lengthen disability.

Complications

If iron deficiency anemia is severe, it can result in shortness of breath and fainting spells or in individuals with heart disease can cause chest pain (angina pectoris) or congestive heart failure.

Factors Influencing Duration

If the individual cannot tolerate oral iron and needs intravenous iron replacement or transfusions of red blood cells, there may be brief absences from work for these treatments. In addition, a serious underlying condition will influence the length of disability.

Length of Disability

Duration depends on severity and underlying cause. Unless the underlying cause of iron deficiency is complicated, recovery is usually complete.

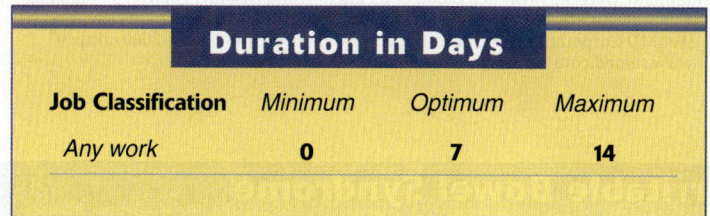

Duration in Days

Job Classification	Minimum	Optimum	Maximum
Any work	0	7	14

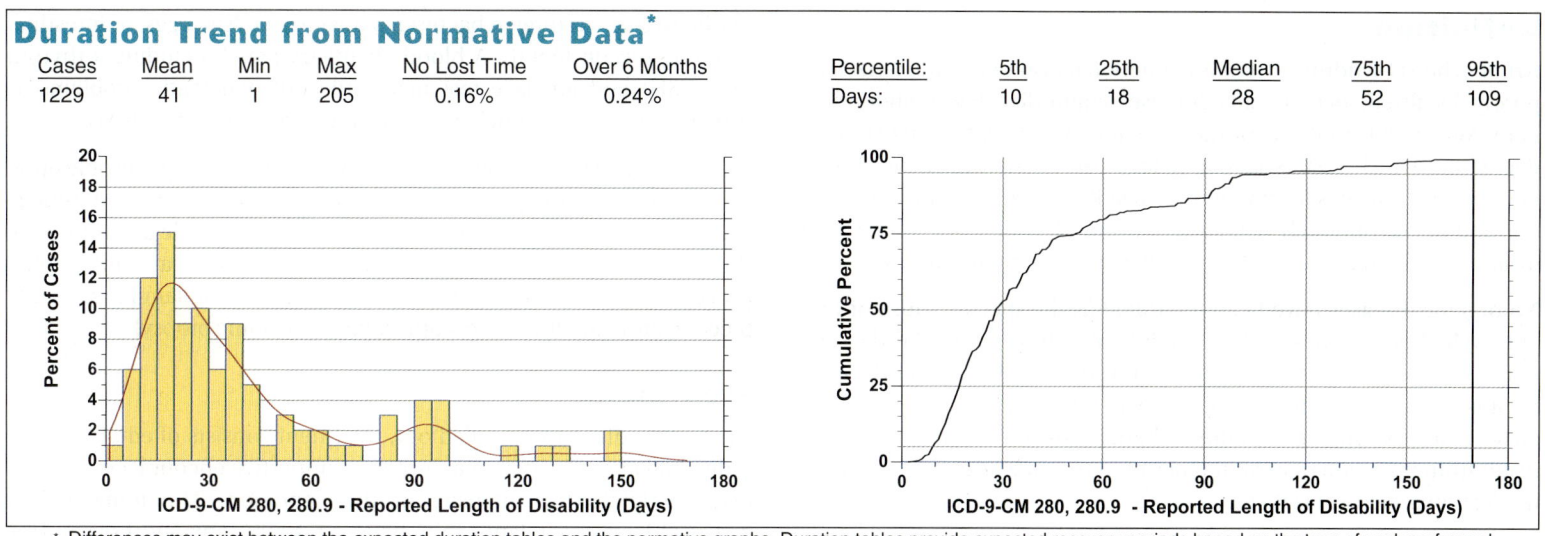

Duration Trend from Normative Data*

Cases	Mean	Min	Max	No Lost Time	Over 6 Months
1229	41	1	205	0.16%	0.24%

Percentile:	5th	25th	Median	75th	95th
Days:	10	18	28	52	109

* Differences may exist between the expected duration tables and the normative graphs. Duration tables provide expected recovery periods based on the type of work performed by the individual. The normative graphs reflect the actual observed experience of many individuals across the spectrum of physical conditions, in a variety of industries, and with varying levels of case management.

Failure to Recover

If an individual fails to recover within the maximum duration expectancy period, the reader may wish to reference the following questions to assist in better understanding the specifics of an individual's medical case.

Regarding diagnosis:

- Does the individual have chronic bleeding such as gastrointestinal bleeding from ulcers, the presence of tumors, and use of medications such as aspirin and other NSAIDs?
- Does the individual have a deficiency of iron in their diet?
- Was the individual's anemia discovered on a routine blood test?
- Does the individual report fatigue, weakness, dizziness, shortness of breath, and decreased exercise capacity? Black stools or bloody bowel movements?
- Does the individual report they a desire to eat large amounts of ice?
- On physical exam did the individual appear pale (particularly the conjunctiva, tongue, palms, and nails), have chapped lips, brittle nails, or a bluish look of the sclerae?
- Are the individual's heart and respiratory rates elevated, even at rest?

- Has the individual have a CBC and serum ferritin level?
- Was it necessary to do a bone marrow biopsy?
- Did the individual have other specific testing to determine the underlying cause?
- Have conditions with similar symptoms been ruled out?

Regarding treatment:

- Is the individual being treated with oral iron supplements? Intravenously?
- Was it necessary for the individual to have a red blood cell transfusion?
- Was a CBC repeated in 6 weeks from the start of treatment?
- Is the underlying condition being treated?

Regarding prognosis:

- Is the individual's employer able to accommodate any necessary restrictions?
- Does the individual have any conditions that may affect their ability to recover?
- Does the individual have any complications such as shortness of breath, fainting spells, angina pectoris or congestive heart failure?

References

Brittenham, Gary M., MD. "Red Blood Cell Function and Disorders of Iron Metabolism." Scientific American® Medicine Online Dale, D.C., and D.D. Federman New York: WebMD Corporation, 2000 Scientific American Medicine. 28 June 2000 <http://www.samed.com/sam/forms/index.htm>.

Pandit, S., T.K. Biswas, and P.K Debnath. "Chemical and Pharmacological Evaluation of Different Ayurvedic Preparations of Iron." Ethnopharmacology 65 2 (1999): 149-156.

Irritable Bowel Syndrome

Other names / synonyms: Adaptive Colitis, Cathartic Colitis, Functional Dyspepsia, Intestinal Neuroses, Irritable Bowel Disease, Irritable Colon, Laxative Colitis, LBS, Mucous Colitis, Nervous Indigestion, Spastic Colitis, Spastic Colon

564.1

Definition

Irritable bowel syndrome (IBS) is a functional disorder characterized by poorly localized, occasionally intense, cramp-like lower abdominal pain. Movement (motility) of the intestine may be either increased or decreased, which results in either loose stools (diarrhea) or constipation. Increased gas formation may result in bloating or distention of the abdomen. Although usually a chronic disorder, symptoms may disappear for long periods of time only to recur without warning.

No organic diseases have been identified as the specific cause of IBS, although abnormalities of the sigmoid colon (prediverticular disease) may be involved. IBS is sometimes considered a functional disorder because of its frequent association with psychiatric conditions like anxiety, depression, and inability to handle stress. However, it can also result from ingestion of certain types of foods such as coffee or milk or medications such as laxatives.

IBS may also be a symptom of another disease such as an inflamed bowel (diverticulitis), pouch formation in the sigmoid colon (diverticulosis), or colon cancer. Approximately 17% of adults have symptoms of IBS at some point during their lives. Women are affected more often than men with a 4 to 1 ratio. More prevalent in lower socioeconomic groups, IBS is equally common among blacks and whites in the US.

Diagnosis

History: Individuals may report abdominal pain, constipation, and/or diarrhea relieved by a bowel movement. The number or consistency of stools are usually different from what is normally experienced. Pain is often reported in more than one site in the abdomen or in different sites at different times. Individuals may also experience abdominal distention, bloating, and other nonintestinal symptoms such as headache, backache, fatigue, or urinary symptoms.

Physical exam: The exam may reveal an anxious but otherwise healthy individual. Although some distention and tenderness may be found, abdominal organs are not enlarged The diagnosis of IBS requires at least 3 months of continuous or recurring abdominal pain that is relieved with defecation, or associated with a change in the frequency or consistency of the stool.

Tests: No specific tests give a definitive diagnosis for IBS. Consequently, numerous diagnostic tests and procedures are performed in an effort to rule out other disease states. These tests may also help convince the individual that a more serious malady does not exist. A reasonable evaluation includes a complete blood count (CBC) and stool examination to rule out foreign bacteria, parasites, parasite eggs, or intestinal bleeding (occult blood). A blood chemistry panel including a thyroid test (TSH) and amylase test helps rule out pancreatic problems. A urinalysis is usually sufficient to rule out urinary tract problems.

Examination of the sigmoid colon (sigmoidoscopy) using a flexible optic instrument (endoscope) may reveal abnormal spasms and mucus within the large intestine. Other diagnostic tests include an endoscope (full colonoscopy) to visualize the entire colon, a radiographic procedure to visualize the colon (barium enema), or sampling a small piece of the colon for microscopic analysis (colonic biopsy).

Treatment

Once other diseases are ruled out, treatment consists of educating the individual and providing reassurance. Supportive encouragement may help moderate the intensity of the condition. The individual is instructed on the relationship between stress, anxiousness, and/or nervousness and IBS. Behavioral modification and relaxation techniques are often beneficial. Psychiatric consultation may be warranted for diagnosing or treating depression, chronic anxiety, or obsessive-compulsive disorders. Antidepressant drugs may be effective in some individuals with IBS.

The importance of regular hours, nourishing meals, adequate sleep, and recreational activities should be emphasized. The individual is encouraged to establish a regular bowel routine. Regular exercise to relieve stress and anxiety may help moderate symptoms of IBS. Any aerobic exercise such as walking, jogging, or swimming may be beneficial. It is important that the individual enjoys the exercise program so it will be done on a regular basis.

Certain foods may precipitate symptoms of IBS. In general, foods to be avoided include those that are gas-producing or irritating, nondigestible carbohydrates, milk and milk-products, caffeinated beverages, and alcohol. Increased fiber in the diet may help control the diarrhea or constipation associated with IBS by producing bulkier stools and reducing tension in the walls of the colon. Sources of dietary fiber include bran, whole wheat, and many fruits and vegetables. Individuals should be encouraged to drink 6 to 8 glasses of water a day to regulate stool consistency and frequency. When the IBS is related to chronic laxative abuse, bowel training may be necessary to correct the condition and alleviate symptoms.

Rest and heat applied to the abdomen may help alleviate cramping. In some cases, sedatives and anti-gas or anti-spasmodic drugs may also provide relief. Care must be taken to avoid dependence on these medications, however.

Prognosis

Individuals with IBS may experience intermittent or chronic symptoms throughout their lifetime. Symptoms that are usually more of an annoyance than a disability may be moderated with education, stress reduction, exercise, and dietary modifications.

Differential Diagnosis

Conditions with similar symptoms include depression, sagging of the rectum from its normal position (rectal prolapse), medication-induced constipation, inflammation of the bowel (diverticulitis), pouch formation in the sigmoid colon (diverticulosis), colon cancer, abnormal function of the thyroid gland (hypo- or hyperthyroidism), inflammatory bowel disease (colitis), milk (lactose) intolerance, intestinal parasites, and problems with absorption from the intestine (malabsorption).

Specialists

- Gastroenterologist
- Internist
- Psychiatrist

Work Restrictions / Accommodations

Work restrictions are not required, although ready access to toilet facilities may be necessary if diarrhea occurs.

Comorbid Conditions

Coexisting conditions that may further lengthen disability include chronically stressful or anxiety-producing situations. Untreated depression may also impact the ability to recover.

Complications

Hard stools, inflammation, and irritation from frequent loose stools may cause crack-like tears in the anus (anal fissures). Constipation may produce a sense of fullness along with nausea, belching, stomach distention, or abdominal discomfort. Long-term, untreated constipation may produce headache, dizziness (vertigo), generalized weakness and discomfort (malaise), loss of appetite (anorexia), or a bad taste in the mouth. Although rare, severe diarrhea can cause dehydration and subsequent chemical imbalances. Diarrhea may interfere with daily activities or prevent individuals from venturing far from toilet facilities, causing social isolation.

Factors Influencing Duration

Factors that may influence any disability include the severity of symptoms and the individual's response to suggested lifestyle modifications. Psychological stress, anxiety, ingestion of certain foods, and use of laxatives may also have a deleterious effect.

Length of Disability

Symptoms are rarely severe enough to warrant time off from work other than for doctor visit. In most cases, no disability is expected.

Duration in Days

Job Classification	Minimum	Optimum	Maximum
Any work	0	0	3

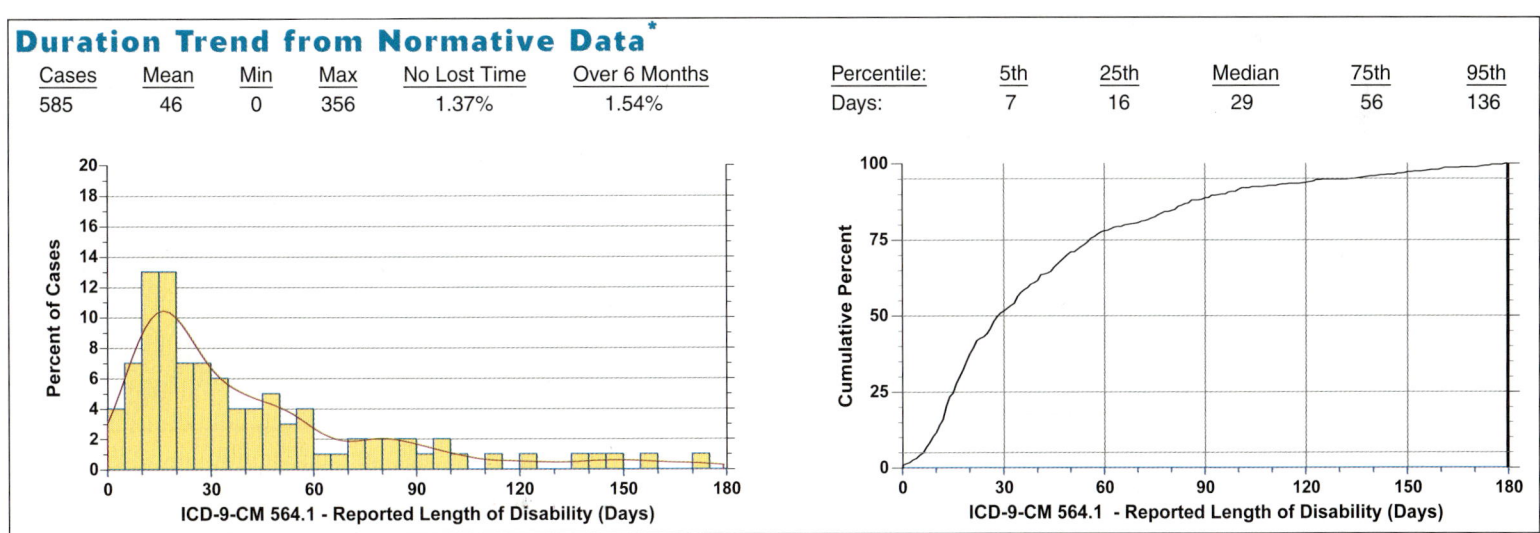

Failure to Recover

If an individual fails to recover within the maximum duration expectancy period, the reader may wish to reference the following questions to assist in better understanding the specifics of an individual's medical case.

Regarding diagnosis:

- Does the individual complain of poorly localized, occasionally intense, cramp-like lower abdominal pain?
- Does the individual report bloating or abdominal distension?
- Does the individual report abdominal pain, constipation, and/or diarrhea that is relieved by a bowel movement?

Irritable Bowel Syndrome

- Does the individual report that the number or consistency of stools is different from what is normally experienced?
- Does the individual also complain of headache, backache, fatigue, or urinary symptoms?
- Has the individual experienced symptoms for at least 3 month continually or recurring?
- Have the symptoms been absent for an extended period of time only to return?
- Does the individual have prediverticular disease, anxiety, depression, or inability to handle stress? Does the individual have diverticulitis or diverticulosis?
- Do the symptoms seem to be related to the ingestion of certain types of foods such as coffee or milk or medications such as laxatives?
- On physical exam, did the individual appear anxious but otherwise healthy?
- Did the individual have any abdominal distention and tenderness?
- Has the individual had a CBC, urinalysis, comprehensive stool testing, blood chemistry panel including a TSH and amylase test?
- Has the individual had a sigmoidoscopy, colonoscopy, barium enema, or a colon biopsy?
- Have conditions with similar symptoms been ruled out?

Regarding treatment:

- Has the individual received education about IBS and control of the condition?
- If necessary, has the individual sought psychiatric consultation?
- Has the individual addressed correctable causes of symptoms?
- Is the individual being treated with any medications?

Regarding prognosis:

- Does the individual exercise regularly?
- Is the individual's employer able to accommodate any necessary restrictions?
- Does the individual have any conditions that may affect their ability to recover?
- Does the individual have any complications such as anal fissures, headache, vertigo, malaise, anorexia, a bad taste in the mouth, or dehydration and subsequent chemical imbalances? Does the diarrhea may interfere with daily activities or prevent the individual from venturing far from toilet facilities, causing social isolation?

References

Bensoussan, A., et al. "Treatment of Irritable Bowel Syndrome with Chinese Herbal Medicine: A Randomized Controlled Trial." Journal of the American Medical Association 280 18 (1998): 1585-1589.

Diehl, D.L. "Acupuncture for Gastrointestinal and Hepatobiliary Disorders." Journal of Alternative and Complimentary Medicine 5 1 (1999): 27-45.

Leahy, A., et al. "Computerised Biofeedback Games: A New Method for Teaching Stress Management and Its Use in Irritable Bowel Syndrome." Journal of the Royal College of Physicians of London 32 6 (1998): 552-556.

Luckmann, Joan, and Karen C. Sorensen. Medical-Surgical Nursing. Philadelphia: W.B. Saunders Company, 1987.

Radnitz, C.L., and E.B. Blanchard. "Bowel Sound Biofeedback as a Treatment for Irritable Bowel Syndrome." Biofeedback and Self-Regulation 13 2 (1988): 169-179.

Talley, Nicholas J. "Treatment of the Irritable Bowel Syndrome." Therapy of Digestive Disorders. Wolfe, M. Michael, ed. Philadelphia: W.B. Saunders Company, 2000. 477-490.

Jacksonian Seizure

Other names / synonyms: Focal Seizure, March Seizure, Partial Motor Seizure, Sensory-Induced Epilepsy, Somatosensory Epilepsy

345.5

Definition

A Jacksonian seizure was first described by the English neurologist, Dr. John Hughlings Jackson in 1863 and is a type of seizure characterized by abnormal movements that begin in one group of muscles and progress to adjacent groups (motor seizure). These movements reflect the march of seizure activity through the motor cortex area of the brain. The seizures are transitory brain disturbances caused by abnormal electrical activity or discharging of the nerve cells that initially arise in the localized motor area of the cerebral cortex. These seizures or attacks are divided into two main types consisting of partial or focal seizures that originate in one area of the brain although they can spread to other areas of the brain and generalized seizures that involve the entire brain.

The causes of seizures may include a lesion of the frontal lobe of the brain, lack of oxygen resulting in tissue damage, or tissue damage due to brain tumors or strokes.

A partial (focal) seizure affects approximately 8 out of 100,000 individuals. The first seizures are usually seen in childhood or adolescence, although they may occur at any age. They can be a single episode or develop into a repeated, chronic condition (epilepsy). In most studies, the incidence of seizures in general is slightly higher in males than females, which may be related to the greater number of head injuries that occur among men.

Diagnosis

History: Jacksonian seizures are extremely varied. They may present with localized muscle twitching or contractions of the fingers of one hand, the face on one side, or one foot; and sometimes a series of these movements build up to a contraction. In some cases, the one-sided seizure is followed by a turning of the head and eyes to the side. In the classic Jacksonian form, the seizure spreads from the hand up the arm to the face and down the leg. If the first movement is in the foot, the seizure marches up the leg, down the arm, and to the face. Usually the seizure is fleeting and lasts between 20 and 30 seconds. There is no loss of awareness, alertness, or consciousness if the motor symptoms remain confined to one side of the brain. Partial motor attacks usually involve the limbs, face, or head and can cause speech problems. Seizures are often followed by a period of weakness or paralysis.

Physical exam: The physical and neurologic exam may be normal. The neurological exam includes tests of motor, reflex, and sensory function. Testing the cranial nerves may point to specifically affected areas of the brain. Abnormalities in movement (motor function) and reflexes may be detected on examination.

Tests: Electroencephalogram (EEG) is the most useful test in diagnosing Jacksonian motor seizures because these seizures have characteristic findings not only during the seizure but also between seizure episodes (the interictal phase). The EEG will show an abnormal brain wave pattern that signifies seizure (epileptiform) activity. In partial (focal) seizures, the discharging neural focus is in some area of the cerebral cortex. Simple partial seizures most often arise from the sensori-motor cortex. Jacksonian seizures, however, arise from the prerolandic gyrus area of the brain. Routine imaging tests such as MRI, computer-aided x-rays (computerized axial tomography or CAT scan), and possibly x-ray visualization of the blood vessels of the brain after injecting contrast dye (cerebral angiogram), can be used to detect brain lesions that may be responsible for the seizures.

Treatment

If brain imaging studies detect an operable lesion such as tumor or arteriovenous malformation (AVM), surgery to remove the tumor or malformation is indicated and will often eliminate or control seizures. Antiepileptic drugs (AEDs) effective in treating seizures that arise from one area of the brain (focal or partial seizures) are used to treat Jacksonian motor seizures. Broad-spectrum AEDs are used to treat partial seizures and seizures that spread to other areas of the brain (generalized seizures). They may also be used when convulsions occur. The AEDs can be used alone or in combinations. The goal of antiepileptic treatment is to reduce the frequency and severity of seizures and minimize side effects. Depending on the cause of the seizures, if no seizures occur over 1 to 2 years, the medication may be reduced and eventually stopped.

Prognosis

The outcome is difficult to predict, however, seizure control is possible with appropriate AED selection. The goal of treatment with AEDs is to optimize seizure control and minimize side effects. There is no cure for epilepsy, but some individuals with simple partial seizures may become seizure-free after a year of treatment with AEDs. Outcome also depends on whether the seizures evolve into generalized seizures, which are more difficult to treat and control. If the seizures are due to an operable brain lesion, surgical removal may eliminate the seizures or make them easier to control. If seizures are left uncontrolled, the seizures may worsen and develop into complex partial seizures resulting in loss of consciousness, or become generalized and spread to other areas of the brain.

Differential Diagnosis

Jacksonian seizures typically have a unique pattern easily recognized by EEG patterns. They are usually not mistaken for other seizure types.

Specialists

- Neurologist

Work Restrictions / Accommodations

An individual with epilepsy may be unfit for jobs that require operating machinery, motor vehicles, or working from heights. Special precautions should be taken for those individuals who are at risk for recurring seizures. These rules may be gradually relaxed if an individual remains seizure-free for one year. The Jacksonian seizure involves the involuntary contraction and relaxation of muscles (clonic movements) that may lead to falls and necessitate work accommodations to prevent injury.

Comorbid Conditions

Other neurological deficits such as cerebral palsy may impact the ability to recover and further lengthen disability.

Complications

Jacksonian motor seizures may worsen and evolve into generalized seizures that are more difficult to treat and control. AEDs have many unpleasant side effects, most of which affect the central nervous system. Some of these side effects include dizziness, headache, nausea, altered gait (ataxia), speech disorders, impaired concentration, rash, nervousness, drowsiness (somnolence), tremor, and double vision.

Factors Influencing Duration

Disability may be influenced by the frequency of seizures, response to treatment, and the side effects of medications. It may also depend on the individual's work environment and duties. Tasks that expose the individual or others to a risk in the event of a seizure such as driving are not be acceptable for an individual whose seizures are not well-controlled.

Length of Disability

With effective treatment and control of the seizures, there is no disability. The duration depends on whether seizures are controlled by AEDs and whether side-effects of medication interfere with job requirements.

Medical treatment.

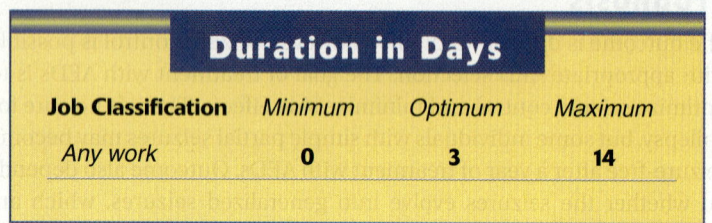

Duration in Days			
Job Classification	Minimum	Optimum	Maximum
Any work	0	3	14

Failure to Recover

If an individual fails to recover within the maximum duration expectancy period, the reader may wish to reference the following questions to assist in better understanding the specifics of an individual's medical case.

Regarding diagnosis:

- Does the individual have a history of a head injury, a lesion of the frontal lobe of the brain, lack of oxygen resulting in tissue damage, or tissue damage due to brain tumors or stroke?

- Does the individual report localized muscle twitching or contractions of the fingers of one hand, the face on one side, or one foot; or sometimes a series of these movements building up to a contraction?
- Does the individual have the classic Jacksonian form with the seizure spreading from the hand up the arm to the face and down the leg?
- How long does the seizure last?
- Does the individual remain alert, aware and conscious during the seizure?
- Does the individual have a period of weakness or paralysis after the seizure?
- Does the individual experience speech problems?
- Has the individual had a complete physical and neurological examination?
- Were abnormalities in motor function or reflexes detected?
- Has the individual had an EEG, CT scan, MRI, or cerebral angiogram?

Regarding treatment:

- Does the individual have an underlying cause of the seizures such as a tumor or AVM?
- Has it been corrected surgically?
- Is the individual being treated with anti-epileptic drugs?

Regarding prognosis:

- Is the individual's employer able to accommodate any necessary restrictions?
- Does the individual have any conditions that may affect their ability to recover?
- Does the individual have any complications such as the seizures worsening and evolving into generalized seizures or side effects from the anti-epileptic drugs such as dizziness, headache, nausea, ataxia, speech disorders, impaired concentration, rash, nervousness, drowsiness, tremor or double vision?

References

Adams R.D., M. Victor, and A.H. Ropper. Principles of Neurology. New York: McGraw Hill, 1997.

Rowland, L.P. Merritt's Textbook of Neurology. Philadelphia: Lea & Febiger, 1989.

Jaundice

Other names / synonyms: Cholestatic Jaundice, Hemolytic Jaundice, Icterus, Infectious Jaundice, Malignant Jaundice, Obstructive Jaundice

782.4

Definition

Jaundice is a physical sign characterized by a yellowish pigmentation of the skin, tissues, and certain body fluids. It results when excess amounts of bilirubin circulating in the bloodstream dissolve in the layer of fat just beneath the skin (subcutaneous fat).

Bilirubin is formed when the hemoglobin in the red blood cells breaks down. In normal circumstances, this form of bilirubin (unconjugated bilirubin) is converted by the liver into conjugated bilirubin that becomes a component of bile and is ultimately eliminated from the body in the feces. Jaundice can occur when there are elevated levels of either unconjugated bilirubin or conjugated bilirubin.

With the exception of normal newborn jaundice, all other jaundice is a symptom of overload or damage to the liver, or the inability to move bilirubin from the liver through the biliary tract to the intestines. For example, overproduction of bilirubin from the breakdown of red blood cells (after internal bleeding or in bleeding disorders) may present the liver with more bilirubin than it can conjugate. This results in an increase of unconjugated bilirubin and causes yellowing of the skin (hemolytic jaundice). Jaundice may occur in liver cancer (malignant jaundice) or infectious diseases (infectious jaundice) such as hepatitis or cirrhosis where the damaged or inflamed liver cells are unable to convert bilirubin to the conjugated form. Obstructive or cholestatic jaundice occurs when there is an obstruction to the flow of bilirubin from the liver to the intestines.

The exact incidence of jaundice is unknown, however, the most common types may be infectious (due to hepatitis) and obstructive.

Infectious jaundice due to hepatitis can result from a variety of causes such as bacterial or viral infections, infestation with parasites, chemicals (alcohol or drugs), toxins, or immune diseases. Some forms of infectious hepatitis are transmitted through blood products, eating contaminated food, sexual contact, and other unknown means.

The most common cause of obstructive jaundice is a common bile duct stone (choledocholithiasis). These are firm, stone-like structures that develop from accumulations of cholesterol, bile, and other matter and occur in about 15% of people with gallstones. The percentage also increases with age. Other causes of obstructive jaundice are cancer of the pancreas (representing about 2% of all cancers) or biliary tract (about 3% of all cancers).

Diagnosis

History: Individuals may report yellowing of the whites of the eyes (sclerae) and skin. Depending on the underlying cause of the jaundice, symptoms may also include abdominal pain, loss of appetite, nausea and vomiting, fever, chills, and itching. Because bilirubin is excreted through the kidneys, the urine may be dark.

Individuals should be questioned as to family history, use of drugs or alcohol, unprotected sexual activity, pre-existing metabolic disorders, recent receipt of blood or blood components, hepatitis, and prior surgery.

Physical exam: The exam may reveal yellow skin or eyes, elevated temperature, abdominal tenderness, abdominal mass, enlarged liver or spleen, fluid accumulation in the abdomen (ascites), enlarged breast in men (gynecomastia), decreased testicle size (testicular atrophy), dilated and irregular blood vessels (spider angioma), and surgical scar.

Tests: Diagnostic tests may include serum bilirubin, serum chemistries especially liver enzymes, prothrombin time, CT, abdominal ultrasound, endoscopic retrograde cholangiopancreatography (ERCP), percutaneous cholangiography, MRI, liver scan, and liver biopsy.

Treatment

Treatment varies based on the underlying cause of the jaundice. Treatment may include rest for recovery from an infection or dietary modifications (moderate protein, low fat, or high caloric intake) in order to promote liver health. If cholestatic liver disease is present, treatment may consist of cessation of alcohol, discontinuance of a drug, use of certain drugs (e.g., interferon), phlebotomy for hemochromatosis, and copper chelation. If primary biliary cirrhosis is present, treatment may include skin softeners and drug therapy.

If obstruction of the bile ducts (cholestatic jaundice) is the underlying cause of the jaundice, mechanical intervention may be required. In many cases, diagnosis and treatment can be performed at the same time by placing a lighted tube (endoscope) through the mouth and the upper intestinal tract into the pancreatic or bile ducts (ERCP). A similar procedure called percutaneous transhepatic cholangiography (PTC) passes the endoscope through a puncture in the skin. Special instruments can be placed through the endoscope and into the ducts in order to open the entry of the ducts into the bowel or stretch out narrow segments (papillotomy), remove or crush stones (stone extraction), take tissue samples (biopsy), or drain obstructed areas.

Treatments vary for hemolytic conditions that produce jaundice. Corticosteroids, folic acid, and sometimes iron supplements may be given. Blood transfusions may occasionally be required.

Jaundice occurring secondary to cancers is typically treated with surgery to remove the cancer tumor (tumor resection) then followed by anticancer drugs (chemotherapy) and/or the use of radiation to arrest cancer growth (radiation therapy).

Prognosis

Outcome depends on the cause. As the underlying condition improves, the jaundice will usually disappear. Individuals with jaundice secondary to cirrhosis may develop chronic renal or liver failure. Individuals with jaundice secondary to acute viral hepatitis may develop chronic active hepatitis.

ERCP is usually successful in removing stones that are often the source of obstructive jaundice, therefore, once the obstruction is relieved, the jaundice clears. Complications that may arise from ERCP, however, include pancreatitis in 5% of cases, and less commonly, inflammation of the bile duct (cholangitis) and bleeding or duodenal perforation.

Outcomes for jaundice secondary to cancers are less favorable. Cancers of the liver have a fair prognosis with a 5-year survival rate of up to 56% following tumor resection. Biliary tract or pancreatic cancers are associated with a poor prognosis with 5-year survival rates averaging between 2-5%.

Differential Diagnosis

Accumulation of red and orange food pigments in the bloodstream (lycopenemia and carotenemia) may cause symptoms similar to jaundice. As jaundice can arise from various diseases or disorders, a differential diagnosis must be done to identify the exact cause and appropriate treatment for jaundice.

Specialists

- Gastroenterologist
- General Surgeon
- Hematologist
- Internist

Work Restrictions / Accommodations

Individual may temporarily need job assignments that limit physical exertion and allow frequent rest periods.

Complementary and Alternative Therapies

Content is intended for awareness only. Treatments may or may not be effective. Scientific evidence may be lacking and some substances have potentially toxic effects. Dr. Presley Reed and the editors do not endorse the use of these therapies in the absence of consultation with a licensed medical professional.

Milk thistle - May have properties that protect the liver. Advertised as an herbal supplement for the treatment of inflammatory liver disorder secondary to hepatitis, cirrhosis, or alcoholic fatty liver (conditions associated with symptoms of jaundice).

Comorbid Conditions

Comorbid conditions of congestive heart failure, liver failure, kidney failure, cancer, or autoimmune diseases may impair the individual's response to treatment and contribute to a longer disability.

Complications

Jaundice is a physical sign of an underlying disease, consequently, no complications result from jaundice itself.

Factors Influencing Duration

Factors that might influence length of disability include age, mental illness, cause of the jaundice, severity and extent of underlying disease at presentation, complications, type of treatment, and response to treatment.

Length of Disability

Duration depends on underlying cause. Contact physician for additional information.

Failure to Recover

If an individual fails to recover within the maximum duration expectancy period, the reader may wish to reference the following questions to assist in better understanding the specifics of an individual's medical case.

Regarding diagnosis:

- Does individual have yellowing of the whites of the eyes (sclerae) and skin?
- Does individual have other symptoms such as abdominal pain, loss of appetite, nausea and vomiting, fever, chills, and itching?
- Is urine dark?
- Does individual have history of drug or alcohol use, unprotected sexual activity, pre-existing metabolic disorders, recent receipt of blood or blood components, hepatitis, and prior surgery?
- Is liver or spleen enlarged?
- Does physical exam reveal fluid accumulation in the abdomen (ascites), enlarged breast in men (gynecomastia), decreased testicle size (testicular atrophy), dilated and irregular blood vessels (spider angioma), and surgical scar?
- Does individual take any medications that are cleared by the liver and may contribute to liver toxicity (e.g., erythromycin, sulfa drugs, antidepressants, anticancer drugs, Aldomet, rifampin, steroids, chlorpropamide, tolbutamide, oral contraceptives, testosterone, or propylthiouracil)?
- Were diagnostic tests such as serum bilirubin, serum chemistries, prothrombin time, CT, abdominal ultrasound, endoscopic retrograde cholangiopancreatography (ERCP), percutaneous cholangiography, MRI, liver scan, and liver biopsy done to confirm diagnosis?

Regarding treatment:

- To promote liver health, did individual rest from an infection? Modify diet (moderate protein, low fat, or high caloric intake)?
- If cholestatic liver is present, did individual stop alcohol consumption and discontinue any drug use? Was phlebotomy performed for hemochromatosis? Copper chelation?
- Were skin softeners and drug therapy used if individual has primary biliary cirrhosis?
- Was mechanical intervention required if cholestatic jaundice is the underlying cause?
- Was endoscopy performed? Was it an ERCP or PTC? Were stones removed?
- For hemolytic conditions producing jaundice, were corticosteroids, folic acid, or iron supplements given? Was a blood transfusion required?

Regarding prognosis:

- Has the underlying condition improved? Did jaundice disappear?
- Did individual develop chronic renal or liver failure? Chronic active hepatitis?
- Have any complications developed from ERCP such as pancreatitis, inflammation of the bile duct (cholangitis), or bleeding or duodenal perforation?
- Does individual have any comorbid conditions such as congestive heart failure, liver failure, kidney failure, cancer, or autoimmune diseases that could impair the response to treatment?

References

Mahan, Kathleen L., and Sylvia Escott-Stump, eds. Krause's Food, Nutrition, and Diet Therapy, 10th ed. Philadelphia: W.B. Saunders Company, 2000.

Tierney, Lawrence M., Stephen J. McPhee, and Maxine A. Papadakis, eds. Current Medical Diagnosis and Treatment, 39th ed. New York: Lange Medical Books/McGraw-Hill, 2000.

Joint Disorders
719, 719.0, 719.9, 719.90, 719.91, 719.92, 719.93, 719.94, 719.95, 719.96, 719.97, 719.98, 719.99

Definition

Joint disorder is a general term describing any condition that involves any aspect of any joint.

A large number of diseases fall under the heading of joint disorder. A list compiled by the American College of Rheumatology contains more than 190 individual disorders that cause musculoskeletal pain and stiffness. Joint disorders are caused by infection, inflammation, chronic repetitive injury, injury, or degeneration.

Examples of joint disorders include osteoarthritis, systemic lupus erythematosus, ankylosing spondylitis, Behçet's syndrome, gout, infectious (septic) arthritis, rheumatoid arthritis, Felty's syndrome, and patella chondromalacia. Joint disorders may be associated with diseases such as regional enteritis or ulcerative colitis.

Joint pain (arthralgia) is a very common symptom that affects everyone at some point during life. More than 6% of the population of North America has some form of arthritis or rheumatism at some time. Chronic arthralgia afflicts women more often than men. The most common cause (arthritis) and less common causes (e.g., systemic lupus erythematosus) of arthralgia are between 2 and 10 times more prevalent in women than in men. The prevalence of joint disorders increases with age.

Diagnosis

History: Individuals will complain of joint pain with stiffness in one or more joints. The pain may be of sudden onset or may have gradually worsened over a period of weeks or months.

Physical exam: The individual may present with swelling, stiffness, and cracking, popping, or grinding (crepitation) with joint motion. On examination, tenderness, deformity, muscle spasm, and swelling may be evident. The joint may be locked into a nonfunctional position (contracture). The individual may have a fever.

Tests: Blood tests may include erythrocyte sedimentation rate (ESR), rheumatoid factor, and complete blood count (CBC). Plain x-rays would be taken. Bone scans, CT scans, and MRI are more sensitive methods to detect early disease. A sample of joint fluid may be removed for analysis including white blood cell count and laboratory cultures. Additional tests may be performed depending on the suspected diagnosis.

Treatment

Minimizing stress to the affected joints can help. This includes weight loss, avoidance of activities that produce a higher load across the joint, judicious rest, splinting, and use of assistive devices such as a cane for individuals with hip and knee disease. Other conservative treatment methods include heat, ice, exercise, analgesics, and anti-inflammatory agents, along with selective use of injectable steroid preparations. Infection is treated with antibacterial or antifungal agents, as applicable.

In cases when the pain becomes severe, symptoms are unresponsive to conservative measures, and joint dysfunction leads to the inability to perform activities of daily living, surgery (arthrotomy or arthroscopy) may be considered. Possible joint surgeries include removal of the joint membrane (synovectomy), bone fusion (arthrodesis), and joint reconstruction or replacement (arthroplasty).

Prognosis

The outcome depends on the underlying cause and can vary from complete resolution to permanent deformity with associated disability. Conservative measures may lead to resolution of some conditions but be ineffective for other conditions. In general, surgical treatment of joint disorders has a good outcome, but this also is dependent on the specific condition.

Differential Diagnosis

It is important when attempting to diagnose joint pain and arthritis to determine if the joint disorder is secondary to a different systemic disease. Pain caused by a bone fracture or muscular injury in the vicinity of a joint may appear to be localized to a joint.

Specialists

- Immunologist
- Infectious Disease Physician
- Orthopedic Surgeon
- Pain Specialist
- Physical Therapist
- Psychiatrist
- Psychologist
- Rheumatologist
- Sports Medicine Physician

Rehabilitation

Rehabilitation for joint disorders is area-specific and depends on the cause (etiology) of the joint disorder.

In general, physical modalities to reduce pain and swelling, physical/occupational therapy and education on joint-loading during activity are all part of any rehabilitation program involving the joints. More specific protocol depends on the nature of the joint disorder. Rehabilitation for disease states such as rheumatoid arthritis is typically more complex and involves a staged approach when implementing a rehabilitation program.

If an individual is experiencing an acute stage of rheumatoid arthritis, the individual is instructed to rest and use splints on the affected joint. If exercises are prescribed at all, they will be static and isometric (contraction of a muscle without joint movement).

Once the acute stage subsides, it is important to get the joint active through its full range of motion. During the subacute phase, active assisted range-of-motion exercises are implemented as tolerated. Topical heat can be used during exercise sessions to help increase blood flow. It is important not to over stretch the joint or increase intra-articular pressure or joint temperature. A pool routine in water that is slightly heated would be ideal during this stage even if the only exercises performed were walking with light arm swings. For example, the individual may wear a night splint on the wrist to help reduce access motion and the pull of gravity.

In addition, an occupational therapist may re-evaluate the individual's home environment. Environmental changes may include building up handles on anything the individual grips or elevating the toilet seat. Although subtle, each of these act to decrease joint stress on a daily basis.

Once the individual is out of the subacute phase, the inflammation response in the joints has decreased enough to start gentle stretching and more dynamic low-resistance isotonic exercises. Given the fragile status of the joint, a pool routine is very beneficial. Most therapists also educate the individual on joint mechanics and load so that during this chronic pain phase the individual can moderate exercise according to his/her pain level on a given day.

Work Restrictions / Accommodations

Work restrictions and accommodations are related to the underlying cause of joint disorder, the location of the affected joint, and if more than one joint is affected.

Complementary and Alternative Therapies

Content is intended for awareness only. Treatments may or may not be effective. Scientific evidence may be lacking and some substances have potentially toxic effects. Dr. Presley Reed and the editors do not endorse the use of these therapies in the absence of consultation with a licensed medical professional.

Acupuncture - May help in the treatment of painful joints. The mechanism of action is unknown.

Comorbid Conditions

Systemic disease (e.g., AIDS, cancer, diabetes), depression, and obesity may lengthen disability.

Complications

Complications are associated with the disease or condition that is causing the joint disorder. Possible complications include avascular necrosis, destruction of joint cartilage, joint dislocation, loss of joint function, and deformity.

Factors Influencing Duration

The specific factors will depend on the diagnosis. In general, the location of the joint disorder, number of joints affected, effectiveness of treatment, severity of pain, job demands, and presence of complications can influence the length of disability.

Length of Disability

This is a vague diagnosis. Contact physician for more information regarding site and underlying cause.

Failure to Recover

If an individual fails to recover within the maximum duration expectancy period, the reader may wish to reference the following questions to assist in better understanding the specifics of an individual's medical case.

Regarding diagnosis:

- What is the cause of the individual's joint disorder?
- Was the onset of the individual's pain sudden or gradual?
- What joints are involved?
- What other symptoms does the individual have?
- Does the individual have a fever?
- Does the individual present with swelling, stiffness, and cracking, popping, or grinding (crepitation) with joint motion?
- Is there tenderness, deformity, muscle spasm, and swelling?
- Has the individual had testing, such as erythrocyte sedimentation rate (ESR), rheumatoid factor, and CBC; x-rays, bone scans, CT scans, and MRI; joint fluid analysis performed to determine the diagnosis? What were the results?

Regarding treatment:

- If needed, is the individual on a weight loss program?
- Has the individual reduced the stress on the involved joints?
- Have conservative treatment options been tried?
- Is the individual taking the appropriate medications? Are they helpful?
- Did the individual have steroid injections?
- If the pain was secondary to infection were they treated with the appropriate medications?
- Will the individual require surgery, such as arthrotomy or arthroscopy?

Regarding prognosis:

- Is the individual in physical/occupational therapy?
- Does the individual have a home exercise program?

References

Goodgold, Joseph. Rehabilitation Medicine. St. Louis: The C.V. Mosby Group, 1988.

Kisner, Carolyn, and Lynn Allen Colby. "Principles of Treating Soft-tissue, Bony and Postsurgical Problems." Therapeutic Exercise: Foundations and Techniques. Philadelphia: F.A. Davis Company, 1990. 211-240.

Prentice, William. Rehabilitation Techniques in Sports Medicine. St. Louis: Mosby, 1994.

Salter, Robert. "Degenerative Disorders of Joints and Related Tissues." Textbook of Disorders and Injuries of the Musculoskeletal System. Salter, Robert, ed. Baltimore: Williams & Wilkins, 1999. 257-302.

Salter, Robert. "Inflammatory Disorders of Bones and Joints." Textbook of Disorders and Injuries of the Musculoskeletal System. Salter, Robert, ed. Baltimore: Williams & Wilkins, 1999. 207-255.

Wilson, J. Watson-Jones Fractures and Joint Injuries Volume 2. London: Churchill Livingstone, 1982.

Other names / synonyms: Idiopathic Multiple Pigmented Sarcoma, Kaposi Sarcoma, Multiple Idiopathic Hemorrhagic Sarcoma

176, 176.0, 176.1, 176.2, 176.3, 176.4, 176.5, 176.8, 176.9, M9140/3

Definition

Kaposi's sarcoma is a type of cancer characterized by red or purple raised areas or lesions appearing on the skin, mucous membranes, or swollen lymph nodes. Its cause is unknown.

Before the AIDS epidemic, Kaposi's sarcoma was known as a condition of men older than 60 and of Eastern European, Jewish, or Italian ancestry. Studies in Israel show an incidence for this "classic" form of about 18 per million in men and 6 per million in women. In classic Kaposi's sarcoma, the lesions appear mainly on the feet and legs and spread slowly. The disease sometimes infiltrates the soft tissue or bone, but in only 5-10% of cases spreads to the lymph nodes or other organs of the body. Today this "indolent" form of Kaposi's sarcoma accounts for less than 10% of cases.

Under conditions of immunosuppression such as occurs with AIDS, an aggressive form of Kaposi's sarcoma has become much more common. It eventually occurs in up to 25% of males with AIDS, although less than 3% of female AIDS sufferers develop it. The incidence of Kaposi's sarcoma among people with AIDS decreased from 4.1 per 100 person-years in 1990 to 0.7 per 100 person-years in 1998 as a result of the introduction of improved antiretroviral medications for AIDS.

Occasionally, the aggressive form of Kaposi's sarcoma is seen in transplant patients treated with drugs to prevent rejection of new organs.

In the AIDS-related form, the lesions first appear on the upper body or mucosa, including the lining of the eyelids (conjunctiva). Ophthalmic lesions occur in 20-24% of individuals with AIDS-related Kaposi's sarcoma, and are the first manifestation of the condition in 4-12%. The lesions spread rapidly on the skin and to the lymph nodes and other organs of the body, and cause both internal and external bleeding.

Diagnosis

History: Older men of Jewish or Italian background and without AIDS will generally report multiple purple or dark brown lesions on the legs and feet. Individuals with AIDS generally complain of pink, red, brown or purple lesions on the upper body or in the mouth, which may be painful and bleed. Gastrointestinal distress may indicate involvement of these organs.

Physical exam: Physical examination usually reveals enlarged lymph nodes and numerous lesions, ranging from small, slightly raised, reddish-blue nodules to large, firm nodules on and under the skin, in the mouth, on the hard and soft palate, the gums, and the external ear. In about one-quarter of individuals with AIDS-related Kaposi's sarcoma, the eyelids and mucous membranes around the eye are involved.

Tests: If the individual is not already known to be HIV-positive, a blood test to determine HIV status should be performed. Biopsy of one or more lesions will allow a definitive diagnosis. If involvement of internal organs is suspected, fiber-optic examination (endoscopy) or appropriate imaging studies should be made.

Treatment

Treatment depends on the type of Kaposi's sarcoma as well as the individual's age and general health. In the slowly spreading (indolent) form that appears in older men without AIDS, the lesions may be destroyed by exposing them to cold (cryotherapy), electrical current (electrocoagulation), or radiation (electron beam radiotherapy).

In AIDS-related Kaposi's sarcoma, chemotherapeutic drugs may be injected into the whole body or into the tumors themselves (intralesional chemotherapy). Surgical excision may be necessary if the lesions bleed excessively, are painful or interfere with function. For example, surgery is often necessary if lesions obstruct the gastrointestinal tract or if lesions on the eyelid obscure vision or prevent closing the eye.

Prognosis

Kaposi's sarcoma is managed rather than cured. However, individuals with the classical form of Kaposi's sarcoma generally have a good prognosis. As an indolent disease of older men, often it does not have an effect on length of life. Individuals with locally aggressive disease have a five-year survival rate of fifty percent.

Individuals with generalized aggressive disease, as in epidemic HIV-associated Kaposi's sarcoma, who do not also have a concurrent opportunistic infection, have a median survival rate of only about three years. However, in many cases of AIDS, Kaposi's sarcoma or its treatment have no affect on length of life because death is caused by opportunistic infections.

Differential Diagnosis

Other conditions with similar symptoms may include other skin cancers, including basal cell carcinoma, squamous cell carcinoma, and melanoma, vascular tumors such as hemangiomas and lymphangiomas, allergic reaction, and skin infections.

Specialists

- Dermatologist
- General Surgeon
- Infectious Disease Physician
- Oncologist
- Ophthalmologist
- Pathologist
- Radiation Oncologist

Work Restrictions / Accommodations

Individuals with classic, indolent Kaposi's sarcoma may require few accommodations other than periodic time off for outpatient therapies. Most individuals with AIDS-related Kaposi's sarcoma will require extended sick leave for treatment. Infection control protocols are important to observe should bleeding occur in the employment setting.

Comorbid Conditions

Immune deficiency, bleeding disorders, non-Hodgkin's lymphoma, and other cancers may lengthen disability.

Complications

Complications include coughing up blood (hemoptysis), gastrointestinal bleeding or obstruction, and the development of a metastatic lesion as a result of cancer cells traveling to other organs or areas of the body, such as the lungs or liver.

Factors Influencing Duration

Factors influencing the length of disability include the type and stage of disease at initial presentation, the presence of concurrent infection and overall general health, the type of treatment pursued, and the presence of complications.

Length of Disability

Duration of disability depends on the course of the disease and the job requirements. In many cases, disability with AIDS-related Kaposi's sarcoma may be permanent.

Failure to Recover

If an individual fails to recover within the maximum duration expectancy period, the reader may wish to reference the following questions to assist in better understanding the specifics of an individual's medical case.

Regarding diagnosis:

- Has diagnosis of Kaposi's sarcoma been confirmed through biopsy?
- Has the individual's HIV status been determined?
- Does the individual have a compromised immune system due to organ transplant or chemotherapy?
- To what extent has disease metastasized to other organs or body systems?

Regarding treatment:

- By which method has disease been treated so far: cryosurgery, electrocoagulation, radiation therapy, and/or chemotherapy?
- If unsuccessful, what further treatment or combination is being considered?
- Was surgery successful in reducing pain and bleeding or restoring function?
- What treatment options are now appropriate?

Regarding prognosis:

- Does individual have an indolent or aggressive type of Kaposi's sarcoma?
- Are opportunistic infections diagnosed and promptly treated?

References

"Kaposi's Sarcoma." Merck Manual of Diagnosis and Therapy, 17th ed. Beers, Mark H., and Robert Berkow, M.D., eds. Whitehouse Station, NJ: Merck & Co., Inc., 1999. 5 Jan 2001 <http://www.merck.com/pubs/manual/section10/chapter126/126f.htm>.

Tierney, Lawrence, Stephen McPhee, and Maxine Papadakis. Current Medical Diagnosis and Treatment. New York: McGraw-Hill, 2000.

Keloid
701.0, 701.4

Definition

A keloid is a raised, hard, thick, itchy scar on the skin.

A keloid occurs when tissue response is out of proportion to the amount of scar tissue needed for normal repair and healing. Because of a defective healing process, excess collagen forms at the site of a healing injury or surgical incision. Keloids may continue to enlarge over a period of time and become unsightly. Most eventually flatten out and stop itching.

Although keloids can occur anywhere on the body, the most common sites are the chest, upper back, and shoulder muscle (deltoid) areas. Keloids can also develop at the site of acne pustules. Although they generally occur secondary to a wound, they may arise spontaneously. A hereditary tendency to form keloids has been suggested. Keloids must be differentiated from a related condition called "hypertrophic scar." While a hypertrophic scar is a thick scar that remains within the borders of a wound, the keloid extends beyond the original wound borders.

Keloid formation is most common between the ages of ten and thirty. Blacks are more prone to keloids than are whites.

Diagnosis

History: Individuals may complain of itchy or painful scars at the site of a previous injury or surgical incision. Keloids may not cause any symptoms.

Physical exam: The exam may reveal an overgrowth of scar tissue at the site of an injury or surgical incision. The scar extends beyond the border of the wound. The keloid is smooth, shiny, and slightly pink in color.

Tests: Skin biopsy may be used to distinguish between a hypertrophic scar and a keloid.

Treatment

Injections of anti-inflammatory drugs (corticosteroids) directly into the keloid may cause some shrinkage and reduce the itchiness. Surgical removal of the keloid (keloid excision) consists of cutting the skin around the keloid and removing it as one piece, then sewing (suturing) the skin edges back together. Other treatment options include laser therapy, pressure devices, radiation, using extreme cold to destroy excessive tissue (cryosurgery) and chemotherapy.

Prognosis

No treatment option, or combination thereof, is particularly effective. Surgical removal is of little value because a new keloid almost always forms at the site. Most keloids eventually flatten and cease to be itchy, even without treatment. Nonsurgical treatments usually hasten this result. If successful, surgical treatment (keloid excision) will replace a keloid with a flat, painless scar.

Differential Diagnosis

Keloids are easily distinguishable from other types of skin changes, although some may resemble hypertrophic scars.

Specialists

- Dermatologist
- Plastic Surgeon

Work Restrictions / Accommodations

If an individual requires surgery, a short amount of time off may be required, depending on size of keloid and anatomic location.

Comorbid Conditions

Comorbid conditions include skin rash in the keloid area, burns or other scarring in the keloid area, peripheral vascular disease, and systemic lupus erythematosus.

Complications

There are no complications of untreated keloids. Treated keloids may recur.

Factors Influencing Duration

There are no factors influencing length of disability.

Length of Disability

Disability is not expected.

Failure to Recover

If an individual fails to recover within the maximum duration expectancy period, the reader may wish to reference the following questions to assist in better understanding the specifics of an individual's medical case.

Regarding diagnosis:

- Are symptoms consistent with a keloid?
- Has diagnosis of keloid been confirmed?
- Was a skin biopsy done to differentiate between a keloid and a hypertrophic scar?

Regarding treatment:

- Did the keloid resolve over time? If not, were interventions considered?
- Were anti-inflammatory drugs effective in resolving the keloid?
- Did treatment include more aggressive measures such as keloid excision, laser therapy, pressure devices, radiation, cryosurgery, or chemotherapy?

Regarding prognosis:

- Was treatment effective in resolving the keloid?
- Does the individual have any coexisting conditions, such as rash, burns or other scarring in the keloid area, peripheral vascular disease, or systemic lupus erythematosus, that may complicate treatment or impact recovery?
- Since most keloids eventually flatten and cease to be itchy, even without treatment, is further therapy indicated?

References

Rest, Ellen B., and Valda N. Kaye. "Tumors of Connective Tissue, Muscle, Fat, and Nerves." Principles and Practice of Dermatology, 2nd ed. Sams, W. Mitchell, and Peter J. Lynch, eds. New York: Churchill Livingstone, 1996. 291-299.

Keratectomy, Laser Photorefractive

Other names / synonyms: LASIK, PK, PRK

11.49

Definition

Laser vision correction primarily addresses common eyesight deficiencies such as nearsightedness or blurred distance vision (myopia) and farsightedness or blurred near vision (hyperopia). The procedure also is used to correct unfocused vision usually caused by an improperly shaped clear lens (astigmatism) found at the front of the eye (cornea). During procedures for all three of these major vision problems, an excimer laser producing ultraviolet light energy removes microscopically thin layers of eye tissue (ablation) to reshape the cornea and improve focus.

There are two major types of laser vision correction procedures. The most common is laser in situ keratomileusis (LASIK) where an eye surgeon cuts a thin flap into the cornea. No flap is cut in the second method, photorefractive keratectomy (PRK). LASIK and PRK have virtually replaced an earlier vision correction surgical procedure known as radial and astigmatic keratotomy (RK) that involved making spoke-like incisions into the cornea to flatten it as a means of reshaping the eye to improve focus.

Researchers are experimenting with laser vision correction to see if other types of vision deficiencies might also be addressed including loss of the eye's ability to accommodate both near and far vision (presbyopia). Almost half of all adults under age 40 require vision correction. This number increases to more than 90% after age 55 largely because of the onset of presbyopia. Heredity is linked to many vision deficiencies, while aging causes presbyopia.

Reason for Procedure

The recent invention of excimer lasers provides new options for vision correction through ultraviolet energy that can be precisely aimed at the cornea where microscopically thin layers of tissue are removed to reshape the eye and correct focus. Laser vision correction represents one of the first potentially permanent solutions for common vision deficiencies that occur when the eye's natural lenses (found in the cornea at the front of the eye and in the natural crystalline lens behind the cornea) fail to correctly focus light rays onto the retina located in the back of the eye. For the past few centuries, artificial lenses such as eyeglasses and, more recently, contact lenses were the only method of correcting vision errors related to improper focusing of light rays.

Description

Typically, with laser vision correction, only one eye is treated at a time with the second eye treated about a week later. However, both eyes sometimes are treated during the same day. The individual's eye is first evaluated through visual acuity tests and methods that map the contours of the eye's surface (topography). Previous prescriptions for eyeglasses and contact lenses may also be reviewed. Newly developed wavefront technology that provides three-dimensional imaging of the eye's features may also be used.

Laser vision correction procedures are usually performed in an eye surgery center on an outpatient basis. On the day of the procedure, topical anesthesia is provided via eyedrops. A mild sedative also may be given. A lid speculum or other device is used to prop open the individual's eyelids to prevent blinking during the procedure. A computer is used to adjust the laser to provide just the right power and dimensions customized for the individual's eye and prescription. With LASIK, the surgeon uses a specially developed instrument known as a microkeratome to cut a thin flap that remains attached by a hinge on the surface of the cornea on the outside of the eye. The flap then is lifted and a beam from the excimer laser is projected onto the eye's exposed surface where a tiny amount of tissue is removed to reshape the eye to improve focusing ability. The flap is then replaced over the wound, helping to protect the area and promote fast healing.

The same procedure is used in PRK except that no flap is cut into the eye and a shield or contact lens bandage is applied to protect the wound. Both procedures typically take no longer than a few minutes.

With PRK, eyedrops are likely to be prescribed for up to several months to help prevent infection and promote healing. Visual recovery and improvement typically begin about 1 day after a LASIK procedure and 3 days after a PRK procedure. With PRK, a follow-up examination is needed the next day and a return to work is possible in about 2 days. With LASIK, the individual may be able to return to work the following day but will still need a follow-up examination that day. It usually takes several months for the eye to stabilize enough for the final visual outcome to be fully measured.

Prognosis

Having received Food and Drug Administration approval in late 1995, laser vision correction procedures are very new and certain problems are still being worked out. Results often improve but may not completely correct vision deficiencies. Individuals with mild vision problems tend to have better results. Even with improved vision, some individuals may still require eyeglasses or contact lenses. In some cases, the procedure may need to be repeated to correct lingering vision problems.

Specialists

- Ophthalmologist

Work Restrictions / Accommodations

Time may need to be allotted for the individual to apply eyedrops during the day. The individual may require reassignment to tasks that do not require keen visual acuity if fluctuations in vision occur during healing.

Comorbid Conditions

Presbyopia will adversely affect an individual's ability to achieve full correction of eyesight. An age-related condition, presbyopia is the eye's inability to accommodate both near and far distance. Individuals with high degrees of nearsighted or farsighted vision (myopia or hyperopia) may be unable to achieve full correction of vision. Vision correction procedures typically are not given to individuals with pre-existing conditions or eye diseases that may seriously hamper results.

Procedure Complications

Individuals considered undercorrected may still need glasses or contact lenses for residual vision problems. Individuals who are overcorrected may experience an overall loss of vision since glasses or contact lenses may be unable to completely correct residual vision problems after a procedure. Older individuals who are nearsighted (blurred distance vision) may be corrected but find that they no longer have sharp near vision because of the eye's inability to accommodate both near and far vision (presbyopia). After a procedure, some individuals experience glare or halos from light sources especially at night. Infection is also possible. During healing, vision fluctuations may occur. Rare complications include bleeding, scarring, corneal inflammation (keratitis), or retinal detachment.

Factors Influencing Duration

The type of procedure done and the presence of complications may influence length of disability.

Length of Disability

Most individuals should be able to return to work within a day or two of a procedure.

Duration in Days

Job Classification	Minimum	Optimum	Maximum
Any work	1	2	3

References

Cornea and Laser Eye Institute. Laser Eye Surgery. Hackensack University Medical Center. 11 Jul 2000. 27 Jul 2000 <http://www.vision-institute.com>.

Lewis, Carol. "Laser Eye Surgery: Is It Worth Looking Into?" FDA Consumer 07 Jun 1999 27 Jul 2000 <http://www.fda.gov/fdac/features/1998/498_eye.html>.

Keratitis

Other names / synonyms: Acanthamoeba Keratitis, Bacterial Keratitis, Chlamydial Keratoconjunctivitis, Corneal Inflammation, Fungal Keratitis, Herpes Keratoconjunctivitis, Herpes Simplex Keratitis, Keratoconjunctivitis Sicca, Peripheral Ulcerative Keratitis, Superficial Punctate Keratitis, Viral Keratitis, Xerotic Keratitis

054.42, 370, 370.2, 370.5, 370.9

Definition

Keratitis is the inflammation of the clear layer at the front of the eye that surrounds the pupil (cornea).

There are several types and causes of keratitis. Superficial punctate keratitis can develop after a foreign object penetrates the tissue and bacteria or fungi pass into the cornea causing a deep infection and inflammation. Superficial punctate keratitis can also be caused by viral conjunctivitis, intense light or ultraviolet light (from snow or water glare, welding arcs and sunlamps), wearing contact lenses too long, medications, inability to close the lids (Bell's palsy), reaction to topical eye medications or preservatives, and allergies to cosmetics, airborne particles or pollutants, or other allergens. Superficial punctate keratitis rarely affects vision.

Other forms of keratitis can be more severe. Dendritic keratitis is due to an infection of herpes simplex type I virus. An infected cornea can scar and become severely damaged. Keratoconjunctivitis sicca (or dry eye syndrome) is the insufficient production of tears associated with aging. Other causes include the use of certain systemic and topical drugs, hereditary disorders, erythema multiforme (a type of hypersensitivity reaction), rheumatoid arthritis, and other autoimmune disorders (such as Sjögren's syndrome). Peripheral ulcerative keratitis is characterized by inflammation and ulceration of the cornea and often occurs in individuals with connective tissue disorders such as rheumatoid arthritis. Acanthamoeba keratitis is a serious infection that can occur in contact lenses wearers. Trachoma refers to a severe eye disorder caused by infection with the chlamydia bacteria. In xerotic keratitis, the cornea becomes dry and cloudy because of vitamin A deficiency and malnutrition.

Diagnosis

History: The individual may present with a history of eye pain, photophobia (light sensitivity), tearing (lacrimation), blurred vision, decreased visual acuity, or the sensation of a foreign body in the eye. Some individuals report recent eye trauma, viral infections elsewhere in their body, or blisters from cold sores or genital herpes.

Physical exam: Both the eye and the eyelid may be red and inflamed. There may be discharge in the affected eye, deposits on the cornea, and enlargement (dilation) of blood vessels. The cornea may appear hazy. Staining with fluorescein dye and use of a slitlamp may reveal ulcers or erosion of the cornea.

Tests: Diagnostic tests may include a vision test, corneal scrapings and culture (to determine the cause of infection), and Schirmer's test (to measure the amount of tears).

Treatment

Treatment depends on the cause and must begin without delay. Minor corneal infections are treated with antibacterial or antifungal eye drops. If the infection is more severe, oral antibiotics and steroid eye drops are given. A herpes simplex infection is treated with topical or oral antiviral medication. A cotton-tipped swab may help remove loose cells and deposits prior to therapy. Keratitis due to dry eyes is treated with artificial tears or ointment. If keratitis is due to contact lens overwear, antibiotic ointment is used and the lenses must not be worn until the condition resolves. The eye is generally not patched due to increased risk of serious infection. Keratitis from ultraviolet light exposure is treated with short-acting cycloplegic drops (to paralyze the ciliary muscle), antibiotic ointment, and eye patching for 24 hours.

The individual may need systemic analgesics. Vitamin A deficiency is treated with oral vitamin A supplements. Malnutrition is treated with improved diet and/or supplements. Severe cases that do not respond to treatment require a corneal transplant.

Prognosis

With early adequate treatment, many types of keratitis resolve with little or no scarring or loss of vision. Keratitis due to viral infection usually responds well to therapy. If the infection affects other parts of the eye, additional treatment may be necessary to clear the infection. Herpes simplex infection may decrease vision and ultimately require a corneal transplant. Injury due to welding arc exposure may persist. Over time, visual acuity may improve but some individuals can experience a permanent loss of vision. Keratitis due to overwear of contact lenses should heal fairly rapidly, however, a severe infection or ulceration may impair vision and require a corneal transplant. Surgical procedures may be necessary to correct problems associated with the inability to completely close the eyelids. Decreased vision may result from Sjögren's syndrome, congenital syphilis, and trachoma when not adequately treated.

Differential Diagnosis

Inflammation of the cornea can occur as a result of corneal abrasion, foreign body, or ulceration. Other eye conditions that may cause similar symptoms such as pain, photophobia, redness, and decreased vision include anterior uveitis, conjunctivitis, and acute glaucoma.

Specialists

- Ophthalmologist

Work Restrictions / Accommodations

Vision should be tested if it is an essential part of the individual's job. Excessive exposure to sunlight or ultraviolet light as well as stressful situations may need to be avoided to help prevent eye pain or the recurrence of herpes simplex. Individuals may need to regularly use artificial eye drops if keratitis is a result of chronic dry eye conditions.

Comorbid Conditions

Comorbid conditions that may affect keratitis include HIV, rheumatoid arthritis, Bell's palsy, and Sjögren's syndrome. Immunosuppressed individuals may experience recurrences of infection.

Complications

A corneal ulcer may develop as a complication of keratitis. Untreated infections may spread to other eye structures or permanently scar the cornea. Vision may be permanently impaired as a result of scarring.

Factors Influencing Duration

Length of disability may be influenced by the severity of symptoms, the underlying medical conditions causing the keratitis, type of treatment required (i.e., corneal transplant), response to treatment, complications, and recurrence of infection.

Length of Disability

Duration depends on underlying cause and whether one or both eyes are affected.

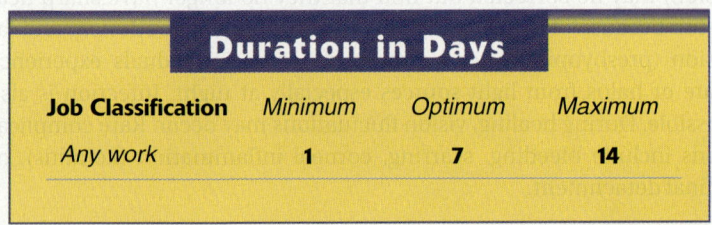

Duration in Days

Job Classification	Minimum	Optimum	Maximum
Any work	1	7	14

Failure to Recover

If an individual fails to recover within the maximum duration expectancy period, the reader may wish to reference the following questions to assist in better understanding the specifics of an individual's medical case.

Regarding diagnosis:

- Did individual report recent eye trauma?
- Does individual experience eye pain, photophobia (light sensitivity), tearing (lacrimation), blurred vision, decreased visual acuity, or the sensation of a foreign body in the eye?
- Was Schirmer's test performed to measure the amount of tears? Has visual acuity been tested? Have corneal scrapings and culture been obtained to confirm causative agent and identify best treatment plan?
- How severe are the symptoms?
- Was diagnosis of keratitis confirmed? What specific type of keratitis (or caused by what underlying condition) was diagnosed?

Regarding treatment:

- Were the underlying causes addressed in the treatment plan (i.e., overuse of contact lenses, infection, vitamin deficiency)?
- Was treatment prompt? Were ophthalmic or oral antibiotics or antifungal agents indicated for infection?
- Was eye dryness relieved with the use of artificial tears?

Regarding prognosis:

- Based on the underlying cause, what was the expected outcome?
- Did symptoms persist despite treatment?
- Were there any associated problems with visual acuity? Was a corneal transplant or other surgery indicated?
- Does individual have any existing conditions such as HIV, rheumatoid arthritis, Bell's palsy, or Sjögren's syndrome that may impact recovery and prognosis?

References

Chabra, Ashish. "Corneal Ulceration." Saunders Manual of Medical Practice, 2nd ed. Rakel, Robert E., ed. Philadelphia: W.B. Saunders Company, 2000. 110-111.

Riordan-Eva, Paul, and Daniel G. Vaughan. "Eye." Current Medical Diagnosis and Treatment 2000, 39th ed. Tierney, Lawrence M., Stephen J. McPhee, and Maxine A. Papadakis, eds. New York: Lange Medical Books/McGraw-Hill, 2000. 189-222.

Keratoconus

Other names / synonyms: KC

371.60, 371.61, 371.62

Definition

Keratoconus is a condition in which the clear, outermost layer of the front part of the eye (cornea) thins and becomes cone-shaped, distorting the physical appearance of the eye as well as interfering with vision. In a normal, healthy eye, the cornea is round and dome-shaped. The cornea's purpose is to protect the eye and to focus light so that one can see well. When the cornea thins and distorts into a cone-shape, it loses its ability to focus light correctly, resulting in significant vision loss.

Keratoconus is characterized by progressive thinning and distortion of the cornea occurring over 5-10 years, at which point the progression stops. The causes of keratoconus remain unknown. Most cases are diagnosed at puberty, although some cases will be diagnosed in individuals who are in their twenties. Keratoconus rarely appears after an individual has reached 30 years of age. Women are more commonly affected than men, and 13% have a family history of keratoconus. This condition affects approximately 1 in every 2,000 individuals in the general population. It is present in all parts of the US and throughout the world.

Diagnosis

History: The individual will complain of blurred and/or distorted vision. In general, vision changes are gradual, but some may report a sudden change. Those who report a sudden clouding of vision may have advanced disease and a complication called acute hydrops.

Physical exam: The cornea will appear thin, and its shape will be distorted. Scars may be present at the tip of the bulging cornea.

Tests: A test to measure the individual's ability to see clearly will be conducted. This test (a visual acuity test) involves reading letters, gradually decreasing in size, from a chart. Those with keratoconus will have decreased ability to see clearly. A test called corneal topography produces an image of the surface characteristics of the eye. This can help confirm the diagnosis and help the physician assess the severity of the disease.

Treatment

In the early stages of keratoconus, ordinary eyeglasses will correct the individual's vision. As the disease progresses, hard (gas permeable) contact lenses are needed to adequately correct vision. Because keratoconus tends to progress gradually over a period of several years, frequent, regular visits to the eye doctor are necessary to ensure that the glasses or contact lenses are the appropriate strength (prescription).

In about 20% of cases, a procedure called a corneal transplant will be required. A corneal transplant involves surgically removing the distorted cornea and replacing it with a healthy cornea from a donor.

Prognosis

Overall, the prognosis is very good. Use of eyeglasses or contact lenses is very effective in correcting the vision in most cases. In those cases where corneal transplant is indicated, the procedure is about 95% successful. Recurrence of keratoconus in the transplanted cornea can occur, but is very rare. Blindness is a remote possibility.

Differential Diagnosis

Many other conditions can affect an individual's ability to see clearly, including myopia, presbyopia, and astigmatism. Other diseases of the cornea should also be considered, such as corneal dystrophy and corneal erosion.

Specialists

- Ophthalmologist

Work Restrictions / Accommodations

Because individuals with keratoconus are more likely to get eye infections or eye injuries, protective eye wear may be indicated. In cases where glasses or contact lenses can't correct vision completely, those whose jobs require keen vision may need to be reassigned. If surgery is required, extended sick time may be required. For several weeks after surgery, flexibility to return for frequent eye exams may be necessary.

Comorbid Conditions

Individuals with other eye conditions that result in excessive eye rubbing (allergies, eczema) may have more severe symptoms and a longer period of disability.

Complications

Because the cornea is thin and distorted, the individual is more prone to eye injuries (scratches, for example) and eye infections. In advanced cases, a condition in which the fluid that normally fills the front part of the eye (aqueous humor) accumulates in the cornea (acute corneal hydrops) can occur, making vision difficult or impossible. Very rarely, permanent loss of vision can occur.

Factors Influencing Duration

The length of disability will be affected by the severity of symptoms and the individual's response to treatment. If surgery is required, the skill of the surgeon, the presence of procedure complications (such as rejection), recurrence of keratoconus, as well as the individual's recovery may all influence the length of disability.

Length of Disability

Disability duration for corneal transplant depends on individual's job requirements and may be incompatible with return to very heavy work. Very rarely, blindness and permanent disability may occur.

Medical treatment.

Duration in Days

Job Classification	Minimum	Optimum	Maximum
Sedentary work	1	3	7
Light work	1	3	7
Medium work	1	3	7
Heavy work	1	3	7
Very Heavy work	1	3	7

Surgical treatment.

Duration in Days

Job Classification	Minimum	Optimum	Maximum
Sedentary work	14	21	28
Light work	14	21	28
Medium work	28	35	42
Heavy work	42	56	Indefinite
Very Heavy work	42	56	Indefinite

Failure to Recover

If an individual fails to recover within the maximum duration expectancy period, the reader may wish to reference the following questions to assist in better understanding the specifics of an individual's medical case.

Regarding diagnosis:

- Does the individual complain of blurred and/or distorted vision?
- Were the changes gradual or sudden?
- On physical exam, did the cornea appear thin, and its shape distorted?
- Were scars present at the tip of the bulging cornea.
- Did the individual have a visual acuity test?
- Was a corneal topography done?
- Have conditions with similar symptoms been ruled out?

Regarding treatment:

- Do ordinary eyeglasses correct the individual's vision?
- Has it become necessary to use gas permeable contact lenses to correct vision?
- Does the individual require a corneal transplant?

Regarding prognosis:

- Is the individual's employer able to accommodate any necessary restrictions?
- Does the individual have any conditions that may affect their ability to recover?
- Has the individual had more eye injuries or infections?
- Does the individual have acute corneal hydrops?
- Does the individual have permanent loss of vision?

References

Herrin, Stan, ed. Is it or is it not keratoconus?. Review of Ophthalmology. 2000. 13 Nov 2000 <http://www.revophth.com/rph6kera.htm>.

Keratoconus. National Keratoconus Foundation. 2000. 9 Nov 2000 <http://www.nkcf.org/kerawhat.htm>.

Kidney Transplant
55.6, 55.69

Definition

Kidney transplantation is a surgical procedure in which an individual whose own kidneys have stopped functioning (chronic kidney failure) receives a new kidney (graft or donor kidney) to take over the task of cleansing the blood of waste materials. Graft kidneys may come from donors who are living or dead and who are related or unrelated to the recipient.

Important requirements for successful transplantation include a careful match between the recipient's and the donor's blood types and tissue types. When the graft kidney is from a living donor, it is most often from a close family member of the recipient such as a parent, child, brother, or sister. There is usually a better match of blood and tissue types with close family members and, as a result, a lower chance of rejection of the graft kidney.

Often recipients must wait until a suitable donor kidney is found, using dialysis treatments during the waiting period. When a donor kidney is finally found, time is usually short, and the operation must be performed within a few hours.

Reasons for chronic kidney failure include glomerular diseases, diabetes, polycystic kidneys, hypertensive nephrosclerosis, renovascular disease, congenital and metabolic disorders, tubular and interstitial diseases, rheumatoid disease, and neoplasms.

In 1999, over 12,000 kidney transplants, and nearly 1,000 kidney-pancreas transplants were performed in the US.

Reason for Procedure

Kidney transplantation is 1 of 3 common options for the treatment of chronic kidney failure. The remaining options include hemodialysis and peritoneal dialysis. In the US, kidney transplantation is the preferred option because it provides to an individual a healthy kidney that will function normally. The other options compensate for lack of kidney function through ongoing procedures that attempt to simulate kidney function, resulting in poorer outcome and greater expense over time.

Description

The donor and recipient operations are scheduled at the same time, usually in adjacent operating rooms. The left kidney is ordinarily taken as the donor kidney because it has the longer renal vein. The operation typically involves an incision from the donor's back, through the bed of the twelfth rib. Rarely, the operation enters through the donor's abdomen (anterior transperitoneal approach).

In the recipient, the operation involves an incision in the lower part of the abdomen and placement of the donor kidney there. This location is chosen instead of the location of the individual's original, failed kidney, because the operation is both simpler and quicker. Connections of the kidney artery and vein are made to corresponding blood vessels in the abdomen, and the tube that carries the urine (ureter) is connected to the individual's bladder. The operation takes about 3-4 hours.

Prognosis

Overall, 1-year survival for individuals following kidney transplant is approximately ninety-five percent. The 3-year survival rate is approximately 90%. Ten-year survival for individuals receiving a kidney from a matched sibling donor is nearly eighty percent, while 10-year survival for individuals receiving a cadaveric kidney is 44%.

The primary causes of mortality following kidney transplant include sepsis, coronary artery disease, neoplasia, and liver failure.

Specialists

- Cardiologist
- Dietary Advisor
- General Surgeon
- Nephrologist
- Oncologist
- Transplant Surgeon

Work Restrictions / Accommodations

Depending on the exertion level of the type of work, there are few restrictions and accommodations to be placed on returning to work. Heavy lifting may need to be restricted for a short period. Special accommodations, if required, may be identified by the recipient's physician.

Comorbid Conditions

Obesity, diabetes, and cardiovascular disease are risk factors for complications and mortality following kidney transplant surgery.

Contraindications to kidney transplantation include recent malignancy, active infection, HIV infection, uncontrolled psychiatric disorder, and active substance abuse. Advanced age is not a contraindication.

Procedure Complications

Most complications due to the surgery itself involve the urinary tract system, resulting in outcomes such as urine obstruction or leak, or constriction of the tube through which urine flows from the kidney to the bladder (ureter). Other complications include sexual impotence and hydrocele, bleeding or blood clots, infection (including sepsis), accumulation of lymph fluid (lymphocele), or narrowing of the renal artery (renal artery stenosis).

Graft rejection is a major concern following transplant. Acute rejection can take a matter of hours to days, and typically occurs within the first few months, or even later. Chronic rejection generally takes longer and is accompanied by steady loss of renal function. Rarely, hyperacute rejection may occur, in which the kidney is rejected within minutes to hours after transplantation, with irreversible damage to the graft kidney.

Anti-rejection drugs may cause side effects, such as anxiety, unwanted hair growth or hair loss, weight gain, increased blood sugar, trouble sleeping, mood swings, tremors, nausea or vomiting, diarrhea, and high blood pressure. These drugs also increase an individual's short- and long-term risk of certain malignancies, especially lymphoma.

Major causes of morbidity following kidney transplant are hypertension, cataracts, avascular necrosis, malignancy, urinary tract infection, pneumonia, steroid-induced diabetes mellitus, chronic hepatitis, peptic ulcer disease, diverticulitis, myocardial infarction, and cerebrovascular accident.

Factors Influencing Duration

In addition to complications associated with the surgery, the principle factor that may influence the length of disability is the onset of graft rejection. To prevent graft rejection, it is essential that individuals take anti-rejection drugs exactly as prescribed. Changes in doses or formulations without physician knowledge or monitoring may lessen the drugs' effectiveness, increasing the risk of rejection and disability. Office visits to check kidney function and check for possible rejection episodes occur on a regular basis.

Development of a common cause of morbidity following the transplant (hypertension, cataracts, avascular necrosis, malignancy, urinary tract infection, pneumonia, steroid-induced diabetes mellitus, chronic hepatitis, peptic ulcer disease, diverticulitis, myocardial infarction, and cerebrovascular accident) also produces or prolongs disability.

Length of Disability

For donor.

Duration in Days

Job Classification	Minimum	Optimum	Maximum
Sedentary work	7	21	35
Light work	7	28	35
Medium work	14	35	42
Heavy work	21	42	56
Very Heavy work	21	42	56

Recipient.

Duration in Days

Job Classification	Minimum	Optimum	Maximum
Sedentary work	28	42	56
Light work	28	42	56
Medium work	42	49	56
Heavy work	56	63	70
Very Heavy work	56	63	70

References

Breener, Barry. Brenner and Rector's The Kidney, 6th ed. Philadelphia: W.B. Saunders Company, 2000.

UNOS Transplant Patient Datasource: Statistics. United Network for Organ Sharing. 28 Jun 2000. 11 Jan 2001 <http://www.patients.unos.org/tpd/frm_stats_application.asp?org=Kl&tab1=&tab2=national&ctr=&>.

Knee Replacement, Total

Other names / synonyms: Knee Arthroplasty, TKR

81.54

Definition

Total knee replacement or knee arthroplasty is a surgical procedure in which the worn, damaged surfaces of the knee joint are replaced with metal and high-density plastic. Once the damaged bone or tissue is replaced and the joint moves smoothly, the pain usually goes away.

In order to understand the knee arthroplasty procedure, it is important to review a bit of the basic anatomy. Two bones form the knee joint. One is the femur, which is the thigh-bone, and the other is the tibia, which is the lower leg bone. The ends of the bones are lined with a tough, elastic tissue (cartilage) that keeps the bones from rubbing directly together. The supporting structures of these two bones are called the ligaments and capsule. There is a lining in the capsule that creates synovial fluid, which nourishes the cartilage, since it has no blood supply. The kneecap (patella) protects the joint and anchors the tendons, which together with the muscles stabilize the joint.

Over time, the cartilage that lines the ends of the bones wears away until the bones are touching and rubbing directly together. That's when the deformities and the extreme pain occur. The wearing away of the bone surfaces sheds cells, which are often referred to as debris. The debris causes irritation of the lining of the knee. For a time, this irritation can be treated conservatively with medications, and/or physical therapy, crutches, canes, walkers, or minor surgical procedures. When these treatments lose their effectiveness and when the deformities or pain become severe, reconstructive surgery becomes the recommended treatment.

Aging, injury, and disease all cause wear and tear on the knees. The most common reason for knee replacement is osteoarthritis. Osteoarthritis causes a gradual deterioration of the cartilage between the femur and tibia. Without the cartilage to serve as a cushion, the bones begin to rub directly together and to cause pain. Rheumatoid arthritis, an inflammation of the tissue around the joints, is another cause of knee deterioration. A third cause for knee replacement is post-traumatic arthritis, a form of arthritis that is caused by knee injury. The pain from post-traumatic arthritis sometimes is not manifested for many years after the injury. At risk for osteoarthritis and rheumatoid arthritis are individuals who have an inherited predisposition to the disease and individuals who are obese. At risk for post-traumatic arthritis are heavy laborers and athletes who engage in contact sports.

According to reports issued by the Centers for Disease Control and Prevention (CDC) in 1998, the number of total knee replacement procedures performed in the US was 266,000. Almost twice as many knee replacement procedures were performed on women as on men. Most of the replacements were performed on individuals in the 65-years-and-over age group in the south (81,000) and midwest (80,000) regions. The northeast and west regions reported almost equal lesser numbers.

Reason for Procedure

Pain relief from osteoarthritis and rheumatoid arthritis, injury to the knee, and restoration of knee function are the primary indications for total knee replacement. The decision to perform the procedure is not based on x-ray findings alone, which may, in fact, show extensive changes in the joint. The two main determining criteria are pain and loss of function.

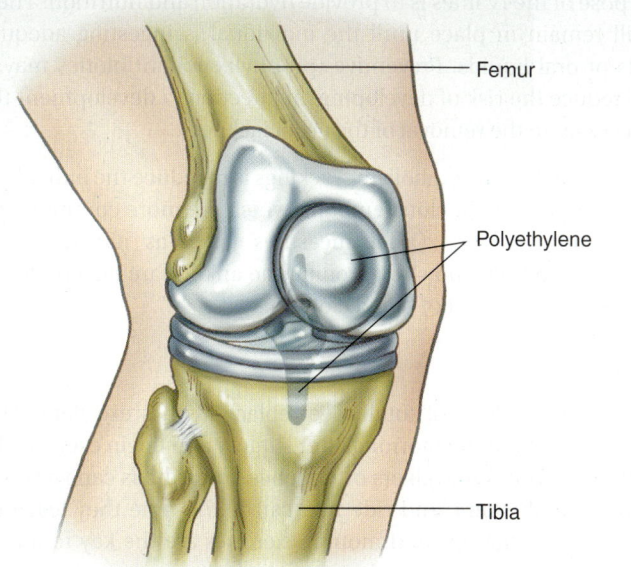

Until recently, knee replacement implants (prostheses) were affixed to the individual's bones with bone cement and were expected to function for 10-15 years. Because of this time constraint, recommendation for the knee arthroplasty procedure was often delayed until the individual was older. Technology has recently advanced to the point that we now have biological fixation of implants to the bone. The latest addition to this fixation process is the use of hydroxy apatite (a substance normally found in bone that promotes bone growth) into the prosthesis. Before the biological fixations, the problem of wear was cause for concern. Today, individuals are enjoying prostheses whose wear characteristics have dramatically improved.

Description

A total knee replacement is performed with the individual under general anesthesia. The orthopedic surgeon makes an incision over the affected knee. The knee cap (patella) is removed. The adjoining surfaces of the femur and tibia are shaved to eliminate any rough edges and to permit better adhesion of the metal and high-density plastic prosthesis. One metal part attaches to the bottom of the femur; a smaller metal part attaches to the top of the tibia with a rodlike part that inserts into the shaft of the bone. A high-density plastic "tray" on top of the metal rod provides a resting place for the metal cap and the end of the femur and acts as cartilage for the new joint. The new joint is anchored into place with bone cement or a biological fixation process.

The individual returns from what is usually a 2-hour surgery with a large dressing to the knee area, several IV lines in place, and wearing anti-embolism or pneumatic stockings. A small drainage tube positioned during surgery helps to drain excess fluids from the knee (joint) area. The individual's leg is placed into a mechanical device that bends (flexes) and straightens (extends) the knee at a pre-set rate and amount of flexion (continuous passive motion or CPM device). Gradually, the rate and amount of flexion is increased as tolerated by the individual. Orthopedists recommend that the leg be in the CPM device when the individual is in bed. The CPM device has been shown to speed recovery and to decrease post-operative pain, bleeding, and infection.

The purpose of the IV lines is to provide hydration and nutrition. The IV lines will remain in place until the individual is ingesting adequate amounts of oral liquids. Preventive (prophylactic) antibiotics may be given to reduce the risk of developing an infection (a development that could necessitate the removal of the artificial knee).

The purpose of the anti-embolism stockings is to reduce the individual's risk of developing blood clots (emboli), which are more common after lower extremity surgery. Other measures (such as moving about, walking and bending, and straightening the ankles) are encouraged to prevent the development of blood clots.

Prognosis

The short-term outlook of total knee replacement is excellent. Most individuals can stand the morning after surgery and begin exercise that day. With the support of walkers or crutches, individuals can walk with confidence, climb stairs, and ride in a car by the time they leave the hospital. Physical therapy and motion exercises are the key to a good result and these activities should continue for several months. Some swelling, aching, and numbing are normal during this time. Most individuals are able to return to their normal activities within 6 weeks after surgery.

The long-term outlook after total knee replacement is also very good, according to recent research findings. One group of findings suggests that individuals with well-performed knee replacements can expect a 98% chance that his or her knee replacement will be in place and functioning at 10 years, and a 94% chance at 20 years. Another group of findings suggests that the rate of failure over the first 20 years after the surgery is less than 1 percent. Individuals can influence these odds by maintaining an ideal weight, by exercising, by protecting against infection, and by avoiding impact sports.

Specialists

- Orthopedic Surgeon
- Physiatrist
- Physical Therapist

Rehabilitation

Individuals who undergo total knee replacement require both physical and occupational therapy. Occupational therapy is needed during an individual's hospitalization after surgery. Individuals learn how to dress, bathe, and cook for themselves safely without injuring the new knee joint. Occupational therapists may order equipment such as tub seats and long-handled sponges to help the individual accomplish these tasks.

Physical therapy begins in the hospital and continues on an outpatient basis. The first goal of physical therapy is to control pain.

The second goal of physical therapy is increasing the range of motion of the knee. Individuals learn to stretch the knee into flexion by sliding the heel up an exercise mat while using the other leg to help increase the amount of stretch. Individuals can stretch the knee into extension by placing their leg up on a footstool and placing a light weight on the thigh to provide a stretch. Therapists may also passively stretch the knee into flexion and extension. Therapists may perform and teach patellar mobilizations in which the kneecap is moved up and down and laterally to help increase knee motion.

The third goal of physical therapy is to increase knee and hip strength. Individuals perform isometric quadriceps sets in which the thigh muscles are contracted and held. Individuals perform knee extensions while in a seated position and hamstring curls in which the knee is bent while standing or while lying on their stomachs. Individuals also perform straight leg raises on their back, stomach, and side to strengthen the hip. Cuff weights may be added to increase resistance.

The final goal of physical therapy is to increase functional abilities. Physical therapists teach individuals how to walk using a walker or crutches. Individuals progress to walking with a cane and then walking without any assistance, as they are able. Individuals may walk on a treadmill to help normalize their gait pattern. Individuals learn to ascend and descend stairs while using crutches and are eventually progressed to negotiating stairs without assistance.

Work Restrictions / Accommodations

Restrictions at work include limited use of the knee, including kneeling, squatting, twisting, jumping, climbing, prolonged standing, and walking. Prolonged sitting is also to be avoided as swelling of the lower extremity is increased. These restrictions may become permanent.

Accommodations at work include the use of assistive devices for ambulation, frequent rest periods, and avoidance of at-risk activities. All of these accommodations are conducive to a more rapid return to full-time work.

Use of medications will require review of drug policies. Work release time for rehabilitation will be required.

Comorbid Conditions

Obesity may lengthen disability. Pre-existing conditions such as peripheral vascular disease, cardiopulmonary disease, arthritis, or disease in other lower extremity joints, hips, or other knee may also lengthen disability.

Procedure Complications

While blood clots of the leg veins (thrombophlebitis) are not rare, the occurrence of death from this malady has been almost totally eliminated with the use of support stockings, knee motion machines, and blood thinning medications (such as Coumadin and low molecular weight Heparin).

Infection in a total knee replacement can be a disaster. Like other complications, an infection is better avoided than treated. In some hospitals, all joint replacement surgery is performed in special laminar flow operating rooms designed to keep out dust, germs, and unclean air. The surgeons also wear full-body "space suits." These full-body suits, worn over normal scrubs, allow the surgeons to move and breathe without spreading germs, since an exhaust tube carries contaminated, dirty air out of the room. An infection rate of less than 0.5% in joint replacement surgeries is achievable in some hospitals.

Long-term complications, such as wear, stiffness, or loosening of prosthetic parts, relate as much to the individual's behavior as to surgical success. However, knees with prosthetic-part problems can usually be improved through subsequent surgery called revision surgery.

Factors Influencing Duration

Motivation, ability to participate in rehabilitation, underlying medical conditions, type of implants, and work requirements will influence disability periods. Results are better for individuals with osteoarthritis than for individuals with rheumatoid arthritis. Procedure complications may increase length of disability periods.

Length of Disability

Sedentary work and light work can be performed sooner if done sitting. In general, heavy and very heavy work is not appropriate after total knee replacement. The underlying disease process may also determine the disability.

Duration in Days

Job Classification	Minimum	Optimum	Maximum
Sedentary work	14	28	42
Light work	21	42	84
Medium work	84	112	Indefinite
Heavy work	Indefinite	Indefinite	Indefinite
Very Heavy work	Indefinite	Indefinite	Indefinite

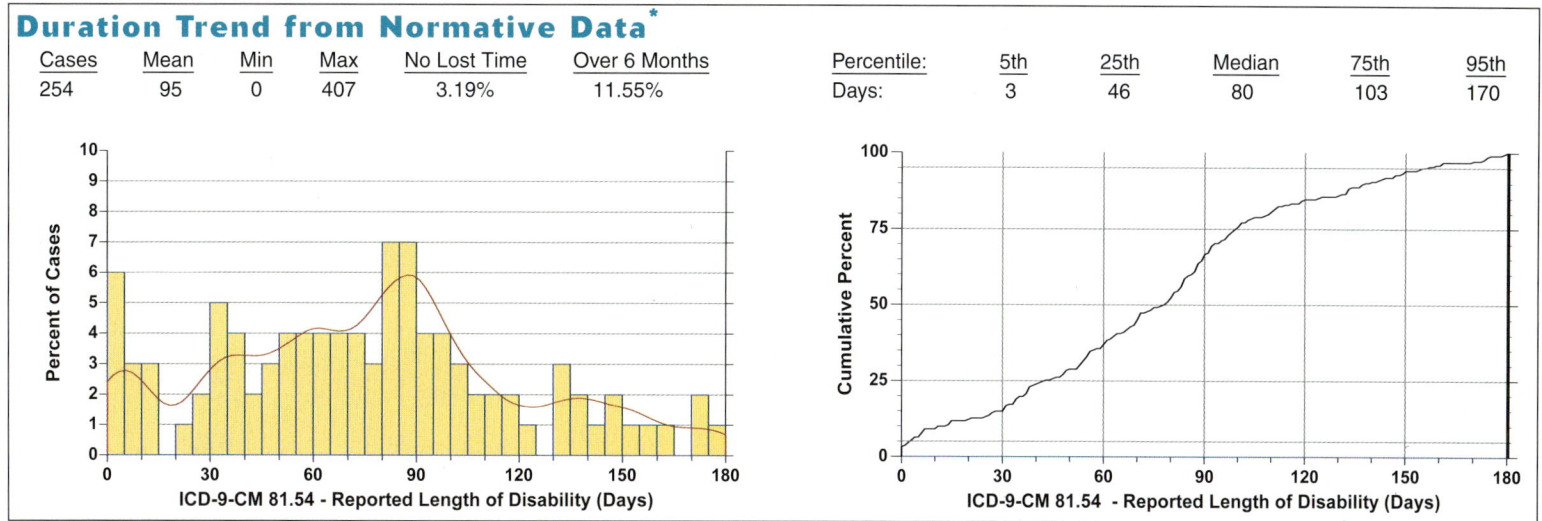

Duration Trend from Normative Data*

Cases	Mean	Min	Max	No Lost Time	Over 6 Months
254	95	0	407	3.19%	11.55%

Percentile:	5th	25th	Median	75th	95th
Days:	3	46	80	103	170

ICD-9-CM 81.54 - Reported Length of Disability (Days)

* Differences may exist between the expected duration tables and the normative graphs. Duration tables provide expected recovery periods based on the type of work performed by the individual. The normative graphs reflect the actual observed experience of many individuals across the spectrum of physical conditions, in a variety of industries, and with varying levels of case management.

References

Kisner, Carolyn, and Lynn Allen Colby. "The Knee." Therapeutic Exercise: Foundations and Techniques, 2nd ed. Philadelphia: F.A. Davis Company, 1990. 345-384.

Knee Joint Replacement. drkoop.com. 01 Jan 2000. 18 Oct 2000 <http://www.drkoop.com/conditions/ency/article/002974.htm>.

Knee Replacement. Knee1.com. 01 Dec 1999. 15 Dec 2000 <http://www.knee1.com/infoctr/new_procedures.cfm?bulletinid=18>.

Popovic, J.R., and L.J. Kozak. National Hospital Discharge Survey: Annual Summary, 1998. National Center for Health Statistics. 01 Sep 2000. 15 Nov 2000 <http://www.cdc.gov/nchs/data/sr13_148.pdf>.

Rakel, Robert E., and Edward T. Bope. Conn's Current Therapy 2000, 52nd ed. Philadelphia: W.B. Saunders Company, 2000 20 Feb 2001 <http://home.mdconsult.com/das/book/view/887?sid=34229418>.

Sharkey, Peter F. The Knee. Rothman Institute at Jefferson. 01 Dec 1998. 19 Oct 2000 <http://www.rothmaninstitute.com/joints/knee/>.

References

Knee Replacement. Post Graduate Medicine/The McGraw-Hill Companies. 01 Dec 1999. 20 Feb 2001 <http://www.postgradmed.com/issues/1999/12_99/pn_knee.htm>.

Peck, Brian. Total Knee Replacement. Arthritis Center of Connecticut. 01 Jan 2000. 15 Dec 2000 <http://www.arthritiscenter.com/html/total_knee_replacement.htm>.

Total Knee Replacement. Clinical Reference Systems 2000. 01 Jan 2000. 20 Feb 2001 <http://home.mdconsult.com/das/patient/view/2/1478.html/top?sid=34229422>.

Labyrinthitis

Other names / synonyms: Bacterial Labyrinthitis, Otitis Interna, Serous Labyrinthitis, Vestibulitis

386.3, 386.31, 386.32, 386.33, 386.34, 386.35

Definition

Labyrinthitis is an inflammation of the labyrinth, which contains a system of interlocking, fluid-filled sacs and tubes in the canals of the inner ear that help maintain balance and control eye movements (vestibular system). The semicircular canals of the labyrinth become inflamed, disrupting their function. This syndrome may affect specific areas of the inner ear including nerves that connect to the brain (neuronitis) or the spiral-shaped organ that responds to sound vibrations traveling through fluid (cochlea).

Two types of labyrinthitis have been identified: viral and bacterial. This condition may also follow allergy, cholesteatoma, or ingestion of toxic drugs. While symptoms are often the same, treatment differs depending on the cause of labyrinthitis. Ongoing (chronic) middle ear infections (otitis media) or upper respiratory infections (URI) are common causes that develop after bacteria invade the inner ear. Bacterial inflammation of the protective lining of the brain (bacterial meningitis) may also migrate to the inner ear. Injury or disorders such as a tear in the membrane between the middle and inner ear (perilymph fistula) may also result in bacterial labyrinthitis.

Viral labyrinthitis may originate from widespread (systemic) infections such as herpes or from diseases such as infectious mononucleosis, German measles (rubella), measles (rubeola), polio, influenza, and hepatitis. This condition is also associated with hearing loss that may accompany AIDS.

Labyrinthitis affects almost twice as many women as men and tends to develop during middle age. Other risk factors include prescription or nonprescription drugs (especially aspirin), stress, fatigue, and a history of allergy, smoking, or alcohol consumption.

Diagnosis

History: The individual may report symptoms of hearing loss in one ear, a sensation of dizziness or spinning (vertigo) particularly when turning over in bed, and a loss of balance, notably falling toward the affected side. A history of recent middle ear infections (otitis media), upper respiratory infection (URI), or injury to the area may also be described. A general feeling of illness (malaise), nausea and vomiting, and a sound like ringing in the ear (tinnitus) may be reported.

Physical exam: The physical exam may be normal or may show signs of an URI. A neurological exam may show abnormal involuntary eye movements (nystagmus). A tuning fork may be used to test for possible hearing loss. Various maneuvers involving specific movements of the head may be conducted to see if symptoms such as vertigo or nystagmus can be duplicated, helping to identify the disease. Changes in the individual's position also may cause onset of nausea and malaise.

Tests: Hearing testing (audiometry) and other studies may be needed to determine any underlying disorder. If the ear is draining, a sample may be sent to the lab to identify (culture) the specific microorganisms that may be causing the infection. Blood or urine cultures may also be evaluated. A chest x-ray or examination of cerebrospinal fluid (CSF) may also be necessary. In certain cases, examining the interior structures in head by magnetic resonance imaging (MRI) or CT scan may be required. A series of tests that measure eye movements (caloric stimulation test), dizziness associated with head movements, and responses to water circulating in the ear canal (electronystagmography) may be administered. Other tests may include an EEG or evoked auditory potential studies.

Treatment

Antibiotics are taken if labyrinthitis is due to a bacterial infection. Some antiviral medications may be useful if the condition is caused by viral infection. Antinausea drugs and sedatives or hypnotics are used to control symptoms and keep the individual calm and still during attacks of vertigo. The individual may need to rest in bed for several days. Individuals with chronic symptoms however may be encouraged to move around as much as possible to enable the brain to compensate for possible damage.

In extreme cases, surgical intervention may be required such as an incision in the eardrum to promote drainage of fluid (myringotomy) from the middle ear. A ventilation tube may also be inserted in the eardrum to equalize pressure in the ear. If permanent hearing loss occurs, a hearing aid may be required. Antihistamines may be given if the condition is allergy-related. Medication that blocks the action of the parasympathetic nervous system (anticholinergics) may also be given.

Prognosis

Spontaneous recovery is common within a few days to weeks however the condition may recur. A return to normal functioning depends on the speed and efficacy of treatment as well as the source of the condition. Severe symptoms of vertigo usually pass within a few days to a week but feelings of imbalance may persist for several weeks or even months, particularly with quick movements. In some cases, inflammation may cause severe damage within the labyrinth, resulting in permanent hearing loss. Even when permanent damage occurs, the brain may be able to adapt well enough to resolve symptoms in a period of days or months.

If insertion of a tube in the eardrum is required to correct the condition (myringotomy), the outcome is usually very good and complete healing occurs with improved hearing within a month. In rare cases, complications of the surgery may include bleeding, infection, or hearing loss.

Differential Diagnosis

Vertigo, trauma to the inner ear, cardiovascular disease, allergies, neurological disorders, Ménière's disease, and some psychological conditions such as panic attacks or other anxiety disorders produce similar symptoms. Other conditions that may be confused with labyrinthitis include migraine headache, stroke, multiple sclerosis, middle ear infection (otitis media), vestibular neuronitis, subarachnoid hemorrhage, brain stem tumor, and side effects from certain prescription and illegal drugs. Tobacco, alcohol, and caffeine use may also create similar symptoms.

Specialists

- Audiologist
- Infectious Disease Physician
- Internist
- Otolaryngologist

Rehabilitation

In some cases of labyrinthitis, individuals with permanent damage may be required to move around after initial onset of symptoms to encourage the brain to adapt and restore balance.

Work Restrictions / Accommodations

Hazardous activities should be avoided until one week after symptoms disappear. Depending on the nature of the individual's job, accommodations such as amplification may be necessary when permanent hearing loss occurs. If the individual experiences ongoing or recurrent symptoms such as dizziness, job tasks requiring good balance or sudden changes in position may need to be reevaluated. Continuing symptoms of dizziness may also mean that the individual is unable to drive. If the individual has had a tube inserted in the eardrum, care must be taken to ensure no water gets into the ear canal.

Comorbid Conditions

If the individual has another condition that prevents mobility, such as a leg or back injury, symptoms may persist since the brain sometimes requires motion to adapt and restore balance. Other diseases that weaken immunity, such as AIDS, may prolong infections, causing labyrinthitis and increase severity of the symptoms.

Complications

Labyrinthitis can result from or cause meningitis. The inflammation can spread into other ear areas or the brain (rarely). Permanent hearing loss is possible on the affected side. Individual can become injured or injure others during attacks of vertigo. Viral sources of labyrinthitis such as hepatitis may fail to resolve and cause ongoing symptoms.

Factors Influencing Duration

Length of disability is influenced by the underlying cause of the disease, timeliness of intervention, and severity of symptoms such as vertigo, abnormal involuntary eye movements (nystagmus), or ringing in the ears (tinnitus). If hearing loss occurs, the individual's response to treatment or need for hearing aids may determine ability to resume work tasks.

Length of Disability

The individual may be unable to perform tasks requiring good balance if recovery is incomplete or if symptoms recur.

Duration in Days

Job Classification	Minimum	Optimum	Maximum
Any work	3	7	14

Duration Trend from Normative Data*

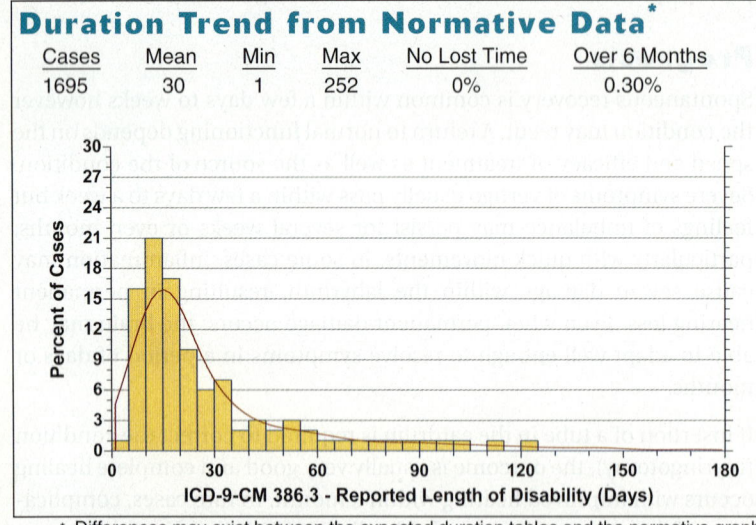

Cases	Mean	Min	Max	No Lost Time	Over 6 Months
1695	30	1	252	0%	0.30%

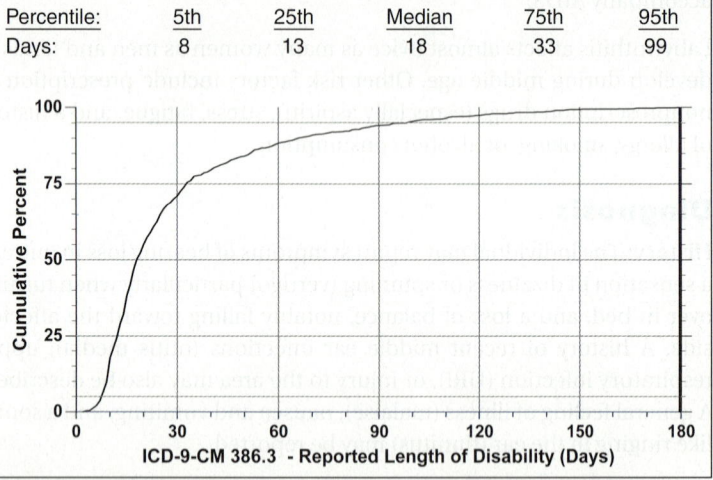

Percentile:	5th	25th	Median	75th	95th
Days:	8	13	18	33	99

ICD-9-CM 386.3 - Reported Length of Disability (Days)

* Differences may exist between the expected duration tables and the normative graphs. Duration tables provide expected recovery periods based on the type of work performed by the individual. The normative graphs reflect the actual observed experience of many individuals across the spectrum of physical conditions, in a variety of industries, and with varying levels of case management.

Failure to Recover

If an individual fails to recover within the maximum duration expectancy period, the reader may wish to reference the following questions to assist in better understanding the specifics of an individual's medical case.

Regarding diagnosis:

- What is the cause of individual's labyrinthitis? Viral or bacterial?
- Has individual suffered from allergy, cholesteatoma, ingestion of toxic drugs, chronic otitis media, URI, bacterial meningitis, or injury?
- Has individual had a recent viral illness?
- Does individual take aspirin?
- Are other risk factors such as, stress, fatigue, a history of allergy, smoking, or alcohol consumption, involved?
- Does individual have a hearing loss? Vertigo? Any other symptoms such as, malaise, nausea and vomiting, or tinnitus?

- Has individual received adequate testing (hearing, blood or urine cultures, x-ray, CT, MRI, caloric stimulation test, electronystagmography, EEG, or evoked auditory potential studies) to establish the diagnosis?
- Have conditions such as, vertigo, trauma to the inner ear, cardiovascular disease, allergies, neurological disorders, Ménière's disease, panic attacks or other anxiety disorders, migraine headache, stroke, multiple sclerosis, middle ear infection (otitis media), vestibular neuronitis, subarachnoid hemorrhage, brain stem tumor, and side effects from certain prescription and illegal drugs, been ruled out?
- Does individual use tobacco, alcohol, or caffeine?

Regarding treatment:

- Has individual received appropriate treatment such as, antibiotics, antiviral medications, antinausea drugs, sedatives, or hypnotics?
- Was surgery (myringotomy or ventilation tube) necessary?
- Has individual had a spontaneous recovery? Is this episode a recurrence?

Regarding prognosis:

- Are other conditions present such as, leg or back injury, or diseases that weaken immunity, that may impact recovery?
- If surgery was performed, did individual experience any complications?

References

Labyrinthitis and Neuronitis: Infections of the Inner Ear. The Vestibular Disorders Association (VEDA). 13 Jan 1996. 30 Oct 2000 <http://www.teleport.com/~veda/labyrin.html>.

Lacerations

Other names / synonyms: Cut, Wound

870, 870.0, 870.1, 870.2, 871, 871.0, 871.1, 871.4, 872, 872.0, 872.1, 873, 873.0, 874, 875, 876, 877, 878, 879, 880, 881, 882, 882.0, 883, 883.0, 883.2, 884, 890, 891, 892, 893, 894

Definition

A laceration is a cut that results in an opening or break of the outer layers of an organ. Lacerations can be shallow cuts or deep cuts into muscle and internal organs. A superficial laceration involves the upper skin layers only and is unlikely to involve any major blood vessels so light or heavy bleeding will probably cease within minutes. A deeper laceration may involve all the layers of the skin plus veins or arteries and can be rapidly fatal.

Causes of lacerations include personal violence, accidents at home and work, and motor vehicle crashes. In 1996, almost 11 million lacerations were treated in emergency rooms throughout the US. A 4-year study reported in 1998 found that 38% of the lacerations occurred on the head. Workers in the food industry and other individuals working with sharp instruments are at risk for lacerations that are both shallow and deep.

A study of bar staff in the UK found that 74% of 91 bar staff reported lacerations from broken glassware at work with 18% being lacerated more than ten times. Another study found that lacerations with bleeding made up 8% of the accidental skin injuries in Dutch cardiothoracic surgical teams.

The number of facial lacerations in individuals surviving motor vehicle crashes is fewer if a seatbelt is used. In a Tennessee study, 31% of 254 individuals using a seatbelt had facial lacerations compared with 76% of 290 individuals not wearing seatbelts.

Diagnosis

History: Individual has a history of recent injury or trauma involving something sharp. The sharp object can be anything from paper edges and broken glass to knives, opened cans, scissors, nails, farming tools, and building materials.

Physical exam: The exam may reveal a bleeding wound. The skin around the wound may be red, warm, and tender. The condition of the skin, nerves, tendons, blood vessels, bones, cartilage, muscles, and fascia of the involved area are examined for damage.

Tests: X-rays, CT, and MRI may be needed if deep lacerations have occurred.

Treatment

A superficial laceration is washed with sterile solution, its edges held together, and the wound dressed and bandaged. If bleeding continues, direct pressure is applied to the skin around it. Injections may be given against tetanus or hepatitis if the individual is at risk for these diseases.

A deeper skin laceration is treated with stitches after the individual is given local anesthesia. A deeper muscle laceration may be treated with as many as 100 stitches to repair blood vessels, tendons, and several layers of skin and muscle while the individual is under general anesthesia. A deep laceration involving internal organs and massive bleeding is treated as a surgical emergency in order to stop the individual from going into shock or bleeding to death.

Prognosis

The individual with minor superficial lacerations or deeper lacerations should be completely healed within two weeks. The individual with lacerations involving a sliced tendon may never regain use of the tendon. If profuse bleeding from internal organs and blood vessels resulted from lacerations, the individual may bleed to death before, during, or after emergency surgery to sew the wounds.

Specialists

- Emergency Medicine
- General Surgeon
- Hand Surgeon
- Orthopedic Surgeon
- Physiatrist
- Plastic Surgeon

Rehabilitation

Superficial lacerations require no rehabilitation. However, rehabilitation programs following deep/significant lacerations become important if muscles, tendons and other joint related structures are involved. If this is the case, loss of motion to that particular joint becomes a concern because of the possible scar tissue that may be present and because of any decrease in elasticity seen in the laceration site compared to normal skin tissue. The early stages of rehabilitation begin with, controlling pain, and swelling, avoiding infection and returning any loss of function.

Cold treatments after trauma from the laceration cause the blood vessels to become smaller helping to control excess bleeding and swelling of soft tissues. This is accomplished using cold packs with or without compression.

Once pain and swelling have subsided, rehabilitation then focuses on returning range of motion and strength to the affected joints at or near the area of the laceration. Flexibility to specific muscles is important to help the individual return to as normal functioning as possible.

Normally, therapy includes exercises consisting of range-of-motion, beginning with passive and progressing to active range-of-motion to regain and improve flexibility and joint mobility. Strengthening of the affected limb begins early in rehabilitation.

The final step is to incorporate activities helping the individual return to his or her previous work environment. This includes exercises that resemble work requirements and patient education to avoid injury. Modifications may need to be made by the physical therapist for those individuals who have experienced traumatic lacerations. Variations in rehabilitation will depend on the location of the laceration and whether surgery is required.

Work Restrictions / Accommodations

The individual with superficial lacerations can return to work immediately provided that the severity and location of the laceration does not interfere with work. An individual with cut tendons whose work involves either standing on the affected leg or performing manual labor with the affected hand may not be able to return to work.

Comorbid Conditions

Comorbid conditions that slow full recovery include hemophilia, diabetes, obesity, arthritis, and cancer.

Complications

The individual may be more seriously injured than first believed and may have internal bleeding injuries as well as superficial lacerations. In a car accident or work-related injury, an individual may be diagnosed with superficial lacerations and walk away only to die within a few hours of shock or internal injuries. Bacteria or other foreign bodies may contaminate the wound causing massive infections or serious disease. Individuals may become infected with the HIV virus after being lacerated with an instrument in contact with blood from another individual with HIV.

Factors Influencing Duration

The size of the injury, location (especially a dominant limb), depth, other injuries and diseases, and infection all influence the length of disability.

Length of Disability

Duration depends on site and severity. The length of disability may be one day for superficial lacerations or may be permanent if tendons and arteries were cut and the individual can no longer satisfy work requirements.

Minor.

Duration in Days

Job Classification	Minimum	Optimum	Maximum
Sedentary work	1	1	2
Light work	1	1	2
Medium work	1	1	2
Heavy work	1	1	2
Very Heavy work	1	1	2

Major.

Duration in Days

Job Classification	Minimum	Optimum	Maximum
Sedentary work	1	3	7
Light work	1	3	7
Medium work	1	3	14
Heavy work	1	3	28
Very Heavy work	1	3	28

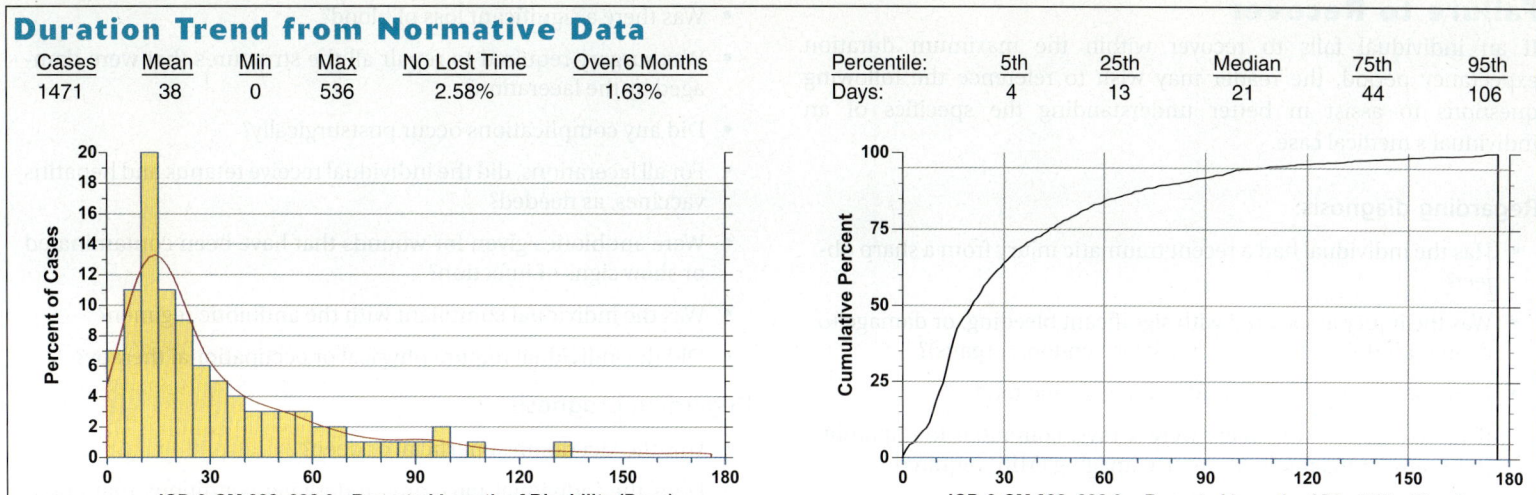

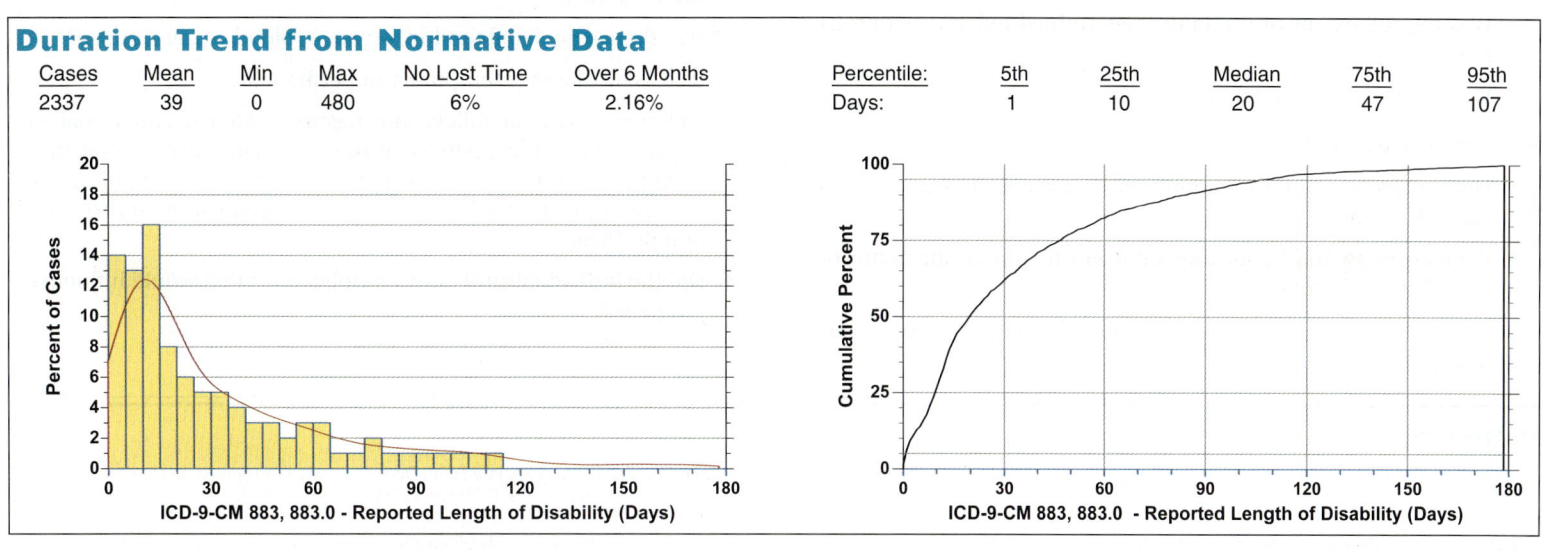

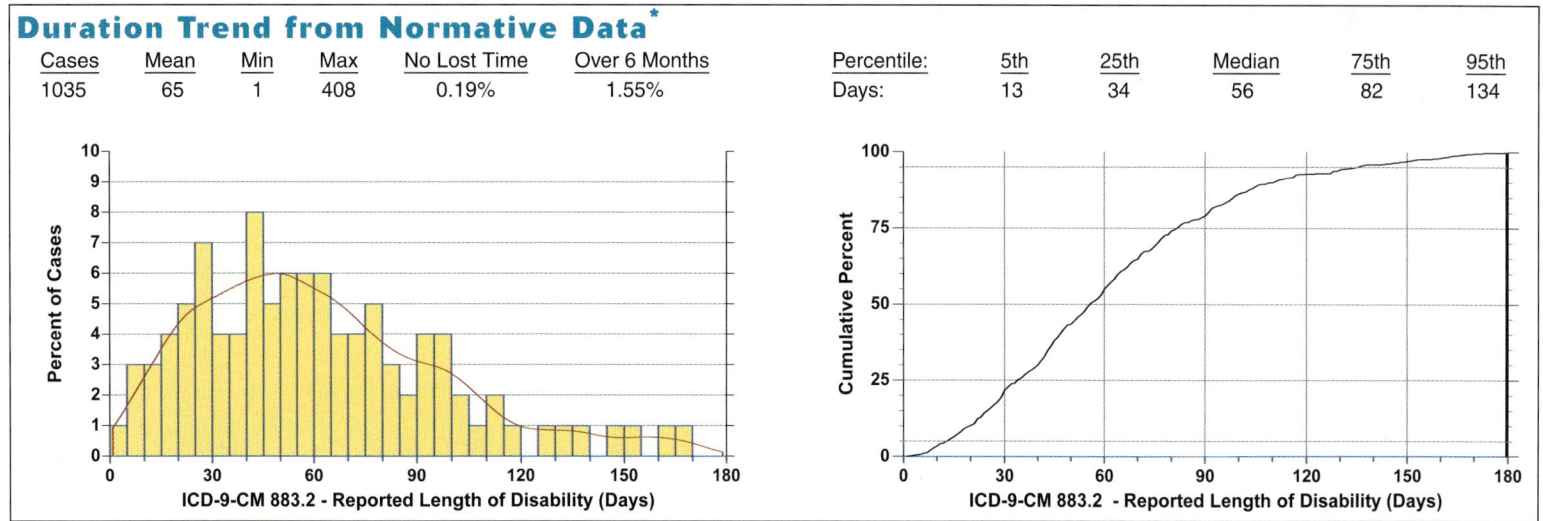

* Differences may exist between the expected duration tables and the normative graphs. Duration tables provide expected recovery periods based on the type of work performed by the individual. The normative graphs reflect the actual observed experience of many individuals across the spectrum of physical conditions, in a variety of industries, and with varying levels of case management.

Lacerations

Failure to Recover

If an individual fails to recover within the maximum duration expectancy period, the reader may wish to reference the following questions to assist in better understanding the specifics of an individual's medical case.

Regarding diagnosis:

- Has the individual had a recent traumatic injury from a sharp object?
- Was the injury associated with significant bleeding, or damage to deep underlying structures (muscles, tendons, organs)?
- Is the skin around the wound red, warm, and tender?
- If the laceration was deep, were x-rays, computed tomography (CT scan), or magnetic resonance imaging (MRI) required?
- Was the individual evaluated thoroughly and promptly following the traumatic event?
- Was the full extent of the injury determined quickly (within 24 hours)?
- Was there any additional injury?

Regarding treatment:

- How severe was the laceration and how promptly was medical care obtained?
- Were cleaning and bandaging sufficient treatment for minor or superficial laceration?
- If the laceration was deep, were tendons, blood vessels, or organs disrupted?
- Was there a significant loss of blood?
- Was surgery required to repair all the structures that were damaged by the laceration?
- Did any complications occur postsurgically?
- For all lacerations, did the individual receive tetanus and hepatitis vaccines, as needed?
- Were antibiotics given for wounds that have been contaminated or show signs of infection?
- Was the individual compliant with the antibiotic regimen?
- Did the individual require physical or occupational therapy?

Regarding prognosis:

- Was the laceration superficial or deep?
- Does the individual have any underlying conditions that could prolong recovery, such as a bleeding disorder or a depressed immune system?
- Was there associated tendon, organ, or blood vessel damage?
- If so, is the damage temporary or permanent?
- Did the individual follow any recommended occupational or physical therapy guidelines? If not, are there barriers that may prevent the individual from participating in the rehabilitation treatment (insurance limitations, lack of motivation, transportation problems)?
- Did the individual suffer any complications that would influence prognosis?

References

Kisner, C., and L. Colby. Therapeutic Exercise Foundations and Techniques. Philadelphia: F.A. Davis Company, 1990.

Kjaergard, H.K., J. Thiis, and N. Wiinberg. "Accidental Injuries and Blood Exposure to Cardiothoracic Surgical Teams." European Journal of Cardiothoracic Surgery 6 4 (1992): 215-217.

McLean, W., et al. "Risks Associated with Occupational Glass Injury in Bar Staff with Special Consideration of Hepatitis B Infection." Occupational Medicine (London) 47 3 (1997): 147-150.

Reath, D.B., et al. "Patterns of Maxillofacial Injuries in Restrained and Unrestrained Motor Vehicle Crash Victims." Journal of Trauma 29 (1989): 806-809.

Laminectomy or Laminotomy

Other names / synonyms: Foraminotomy, Lumbar Laminectomy, Rachiotomy, Spondylotomy

03.09

Definition

A laminectomy is a surgical procedure designed to relieve pressure on nerves or spinal cord in either the back or the neck. The procedure involves the complete removal of the back portion of the spinal vertebrae (lamina) and attached ligaments. A laminectomy is frequently confused with a laminotomy, which is the partial removal of the lamina and attached ligaments. Laminectomies and laminotomies are often performed in the course of a number of operations on the spinal canal such as removal of a ruptured disc.

During both procedures, the surgeon gains access to the spinal canal, spinal cord, and nerve roots to remove the source of the problem such as a slipped disc, bone spurs, or damaged or thickened ligaments.

Depending on where the laminectomy or laminotomy is performed, different terms are used to describe it. In the neck, the term is cervical laminectomy or laminotomy; in the chest, thoracic; in the lower spine, lumbar; and in the fused base of the spine (sacrum), sacral. Most of these procedures are performed in the cervical or lumbar regions.

According to reports issued by the Centers for Disease Control and Prevention (CDC) in 1998, the number of laminectomy procedures in the US was 137,000. Half were performed on men and half on women.

Reason for Procedure

There are two main reasons for performing a laminectomy or laminotomy. The first is to relieve pressure on the spinal cord or the nerves that branch from it. This pressure is often called nerve root compression or a "pinched nerve" and causes back and leg pain. Nerve root compression can result from different structural problems, either individually or in combination. These include a ruptured disc (also called slipped, herniated, or prolapsed disc), deterioration or "wear and tear" of multiple discs with bony spur formation and degenerative disc disease (also called spondylosis), or scar tissue. In a laminectomy procedure, the lamina has to be removed before the nerve root can be seen and the disc removed (discectomy).

The second reason for performing either of the two procedures is to allow access to the spinal cord to operate on the spinal cord itself. Examples of surgery requiring a laminectomy or laminotomy before the procedure can be completed include removing a slipped disc that is pressing on a nerve root, treating severe arthritis of the spine, and removing a tumor from the spinal cord. The choice of procedure depends on the location, level, and size of the disc herniation or other structural problem.

The success of discectomy in relieving back pain and symptoms involving the limbs depends heavily on patient selection. Normally, laminectomy/laminotomy and discectomy is only performed if there are signs of nerve root compression, which suggest that the individual's symptoms will improve when pressure on the nerve root is relieved. These signs include significant weakness, failure to improve on medication and physical therapy, MRI or CT evidence of a slipped disc compressing the nerve root, and EMG or nerve conduction velocity testing evidence of nerve root injury. Test results should be consistent with the side and location of the individual's pain and other symptoms.

Description

When laminectomies and laminotomies are performed, the individual is always under general anesthesia and positioned face-down on a well-padded laminectomy frame or spinal board. This keeps the individual's back in the correct degree of arch for the procedure. An incision is made in the middle of the back over the area of involvement. X-rays may be taken to confirm the correct location. The muscles underneath are spread apart to expose the laminae surrounding the spinal cord and to view the disc contents. A small amount of bone is clipped away using a bone cutter or air drill. More x-rays may be taken to confirm completion of the procedure.

The laminectomy procedure is often combined with the "foraminotomy" procedure. During a foraminotomy, the bony canal through which the nerves pass as they leave the spinal cord is widened. The foraminotomy, like the laminectomy procedure, relieves pressure on the nerves.

If a discectomy is performed, an operating microscope or special magnifying lenses may be used. Some of the ligament under the bone is removed and the nerve root is carefully moved. The ruptured disc is then found and removed from in front of the nerve root. The disc space may then be entered and additional loose disk material removed.

If enough bone is removed to cause weakening of the spine, the bone is strengthened with the installment of metal rods or bone grafts (fusion) from the hip bone (iliac crest).

At the end of the surgery, which normally takes approximately 2 hours, bleeding is controlled and the muscles and skin are sewn back into place. Stitches or staples are used to close the skin.

Prognosis

The predicted outcome of laminectomies and laminotomies is contingent on the history of the disorder, the extent of damage, number of vertebra involved, and location within the spinal column. Review of the literature suggests that between 25-75% of individuals improve following laminectomy, between 15-30% are unchanged, and between 5-50% worsen.

Improvement after laminectomy and laminotomy includes decreased acute and severe pain often with decreased pins-and-needles sensation (numbness) and weakness.

Specialists

- Neurosurgeon
- Orthopedic Surgeon

Rehabilitation

In rehabilitation for lumbar laminectomy, individuals learn to ambulate and negotiate stairs. Individuals perform leg-strengthening exercises such as heel slides, isometric glut sets (squeezing the buttocks together), standing knee bends, marching, and seated leg extensions. Individuals also perform arm-strengthening exercises such as biceps curls and arm raises. Therapists initially focus on pain control and the reduction of swelling. Hot packs and ultrasound decrease muscle spasm and reduce pain.

Increasing range of motion is the second objective of rehabilitation. Stretching exercises also maintain the reduction of spasm. Individuals perform lower trunk rotation stretches by lying on the back and moving their bent knees from one side to the other. Individuals increase forward bending by lying on the back and bringing the knees to the chest. Individuals increase back extension by lying on the stomach and pressing up onto their elbows while allowing their hips to remain on the mat. Individuals stretch the hamstring muscles by sitting, placing one foot on a low stool, and leaning forward.

Strengthening the muscles prevents future injury. Performing sit-ups strengthens the abdominal muscles. Pelvic tilts also strengthen the lower abdominal muscles. In this exercise, an individual lies on their back and flattens the low back against the exercise mat. Performing prone extension exercises strengthens the muscles of the back. In these exercises, individuals lift the upper body or both the upper body and legs from the exercise mat. Treadmill walking is performed to increase endurance and strength.

In rehabilitation for cervical laminectomy, individuals learn to actively move the neck into forward flexion, extension, side bending, and rotation within a pain-free range to increase motion. Individuals also perform isometric exercises. Chin tucks also strengthen the neck musculature. This exercise lengthens the spine by bringing the head straight back so that the chin is tucked into the neck. Postural muscles also may require strengthening after a prolonged period of neck immobilization.

Therapy also addresses correct posture and proper body mechanics. Individuals learn strategies for reaching and lifting that protect the back and neck.

Work Restrictions / Accommodations

Lifting, standing, and walking while at work may be restricted during the recovery period. For about 3 weeks after discharge, the time period an individual should remain in the sitting position is no longer than 15 to 30 minutes at a time.

The individual should be discouraged from lifting or participating in work activities that cause unusual movement and stress to the spine such as excessive bending, lifting, stooping, unassisted carrying and lifting, and overhead work. When the individual does return to physical activities, these should be performed with careful attention to proper body mechanics. Use of a lumbar support or belt may be helpful for repeated lifting.

Comorbid Conditions

Prior spinal or abdominal surgery, obesity, prior trauma or repetitive injury, and cigarette smoking may lengthen disability. Osteoarthritis and nerve and muscle damage may also lengthen disability.

Procedure Complications

A common complication of the laminectomy and laminotomy procedures is some degree of neck or back pain. Relief can be obtained with painkilling injections or tablets. Some oozing from the wound is also common but is not usually serious and settles spontaneously after a few days.

Infection of the wound is very uncommon, occurring in only 4% of cases, and can usually be treated with antibiotics. Surgery is sometimes required to treat severe infections with abscess formation by allowing them to drain. Some surgeons routinely give antibiotics before the procedures to help prevent the complication of postsurgery infection. Other complications with any type of general surgery include uncontrolled bleeding that requires blood transfusions, injury to blood vessels, or injury to the bowel, ureters, or other neighboring structures.

Another complication is neurologic injury that occurs when the spinal cord and spinal roots (exposed during the surgery) are damaged. This kind of damage occurs more frequently in thoracic and cervical laminectomy has caused paralysis, numbness, difficulties walking or moving around (ambulation), or bowel/bladder function. Fortunately, these complications are rare and occur in less than 1% of cases. If the nerve covering (dura) is torn, there may be leakage of spinal fluid that can lead to headache or infection.

As with any surgery requiring general anesthesia, unexpected complications of anesthesia may rarely occur such as allergic reaction, irregular heart rate (cardiac arrhythmia), drop in blood pressure (hypotension), muscular rigidity, and severe, sometimes fatal, temperature elevation (malignant hyperthermia). As the individual lies face down during the procedure and as the bone is cut, there is an increased risk of air embolism where an air bubble can enter a blood vessel and travel to a smaller blood vessel. This can cause blockage with stroke or loss of blood flow to the organ supplied by the affected vessel.

Factors Influencing Duration

Factors that may influence length of disability include type of laminectomy or laminotomy procedure, location within the spinal column, underlying cause of the disorder and its severity, additional procedures performed with laminectomy such as discectomy or fusion, occurrence of complications, individual's job requirements, ability to modify work activities, and compliance with treatment and rehabilitation. Assumes no persisting spinal cord or cauda equina deficit.

Length of Disability

The duration of disability is highly variable depending on whether the root compression is cervical, thoracic, lumbar, or sacral, whether the disorder involves the spinal cord, and if the individual's job classification is sedentary, light, medium, heavy, or very heavy work.

Duration in Days

Job Classification	Minimum	Optimum	Maximum
Sedentary work	21	35	91
Light work	28	42	119
Medium work	28	84	182
Heavy work	42	98	Indefinite
Very Heavy work	56	112	Indefinite

References

Goldman, Lee, J. Claude Bennett, and Russell L. Cecil. Cecil Textbook of Medicine, 21st ed. New York: W.B. Saunders Company, 1999 13 Feb 2001 <http://home.mdconsult.com/das/book/view/882?sid=33600792>.

Kisner, Carolyn, and Lynn Allen Colby. "The Spine: Treatment of Acute Problems." Therapeutic Exercise: Foundations and Techniques, 2nd ed. Philadelphia: F.A. Davis Company, 1990. 473-499.

Laminectomy. PPP Health Care. 01 Jan 1999. 19 Oct 2000 <http://www.ppphealthcare.com/html/health/laminect.htm>.

Laminectomy: Post-op and Recovery. Surgery101 and Amazon.com. 20 Sep 2000. 23 Oct 2000 <http://www.surgery101.com/extremities/laminectomy_post.htm>.

Laminectomy: Surgical Process. Surgery101 and Amazon.com. 20 Sep 2000. 23 Oct 2000 <http://www.surgery101.com/extremities/laminectomy_sp.htm>.

Lumbar discectomy. YourSurgery.com. 01 Jan 2000. 10 Jan 2001 <http://www.yoursurgery.com/data/Procedures/lumbar/p_lumbar.htm>.

Popovic, J.R., and L.J. Kozak. National Hospital Discharge Survey: annual Summary 1998. National Center for Health Statistics, Vital Health Stat 13(148). 2000. 31 Dec 1999. 23 Oct 2000 <http://www.cdc.gov/nchs/data/sr13_148.pdf>.

Saunders, H. Duane, and Robin Saunders. Evaluation, Treatment, and Prevention of Musculoskeletal Disorders. Chaska: The Saunders Group, 1993.

Laparoscopy
Other names / synonyms: Peritoneoscopy
54.21

Definition

Laparoscopy is an endoscopic technique that provides direct visualization of the abdominal (peritoneal) cavity, ovaries, outside of the fallopian tubes, and uterus by using a laparoscope. A laparoscope is an instrument similar to a miniature telescope with a fiber-optic system that illuminates the abdomen.

The abdomen is filled (insufflated) with carbon dioxide (CO_2) through a special needle that is inserted just below the navel. This gas helps to separate the organs inside the abdominal cavity, making it easier for the physician to view the reproductive organs during the procedure. The laparoscope is guided to examine the pelvic organs and surrounding tissues. If the surgeon finds abnormal growths or tissues, the area is biopsied. The sample is then sent to the lab for analysis. Surgery can also be performed through the laparoscope, such as removal of the appendix, gallbladder, spleen, or colon cancers.

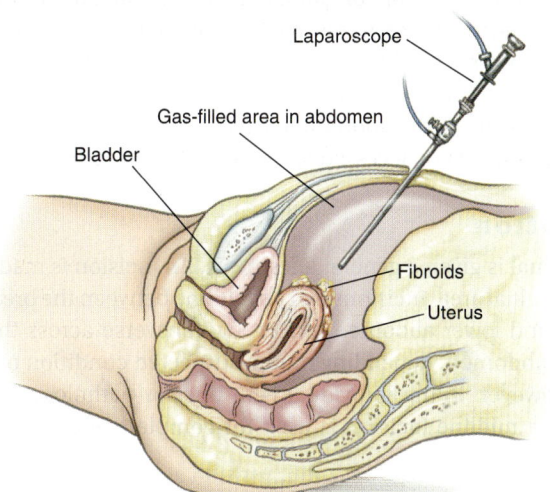

Reason for Procedure

A laparoscopy is indicated in any situation when inspection of the abdomen will help establish a diagnosis and in determining subsequent treatment. Individuals that must undergo this procedure should have a complete preoperative evaluation prior to having the surgery.

There are 2 types of laparoscopy: diagnostic and operative. A diagnostic laparoscopy is performed to determine the cause of abdominal or pelvic pain, and severe menstrual pain (dysmenorrhea). Often, the procedure is used to diagnose or rule out infertility.

An operative laparoscopy is necessary for several reasons, including the removal of ovarian cysts or the entire ovary, ectopic or tubal pregnancy, treatment of endometriosis, removal of abdominal or scar tissue (pelvic adhesions), uterine fibroids, and hysterectomy.

Laparoscopy is frequently used in the assessment of blunt or penetrating trauma, and as a follow-up after cancer surgery. It is rapidly becoming the most common surgical procedure for liver biopsy, gallstones, appendicitis, colon pathology, and many gynecological operations.

Description

Laparoscopy is performed under general anesthesia in the operating room. The laparoscope is introduced through a small incision in the navel, and the abdominal cavity is filled with carbon dioxide to lift the abdominal wall away from underlying organs.

The duration of the operation depends upon the procedure being performed, with a simple diagnostic laparoscopy usually taking about 10 to 15 minutes. Operative laparoscopy can take several hours, depending on the procedure. Photographs or a video recording of the procedure are taken to include in the medical record.

After the instruments have been removed and the carbon dioxide gas released, dissolving stitches are placed in each incision site. After complex surgery, a thin drain tube may be left in the abdominal wall for the first 24 hours.

Prognosis

The outcome depends on the severity of any disease that is discovered during the procedure. Generally, prognosis is good.

Specialists

• General Surgeon	• Gynecologist

Work Restrictions / Accommodations

Unless complications are present, no work restrictions or special accommodations are required.

Comorbid Conditions

A blood disorder such as anemia or the presence of cancerous tissues or lesions could impact the individual's ability to recover.

Procedure Complications

Complications are rare. However, the most common complications are cardiac and respiratory problems resulting from insufflation. Other complications include bleeding, tissue damage, and blood vessel damage. Injury to the intestines may occur. This would necessitate a surgical procedure to repair the injury. Since general anesthesia is required, this poses another possible complication.

Factors Influencing Duration

This is a diagnostic procedure; therefore, the underlying cause of the laparoscopy will influence the length of disability.

Length of Disability

See specific procedure or diagnosis for disability durations.

Diagnostic.

Duration in Days

Job Classification	Minimum	Optimum	Maximum
Sedentary work	1	2	3
Light work	2	3	4
Medium work	3	4	7
Heavy work	3	4	7
Very Heavy work	3	4	7

References

Laparoscopy. IVF.com. 01 Dec 2000. 17 Jan 2001 <http://www.ivf.com/laprscpy.html>.

Schwartz, Seymour, MD. *Principles of Surgery*. New York: McGraw-Hill, 1999.

Laparotomy

Other names / synonyms: Exploratory Abdominal Surgery, Exploratory Laparotomy

54.1, 54.11, 54.12, 54.19

Definition

A laparotomy is an exploratory surgical procedure performed by making an incision into the abdominal wall in order to view the internal organs. Although this is a common procedure, its use has declined in recent years due to improvements in noninvasive diagnostic procedures such as medical imaging and sonography.

Peritonitis is a common indicator of the need for a laparotomy. Peritonitis is the inflammation and infection of the internal lining (peritoneum) of the abdominal cavity. Symptoms of peritonitis include severe abdominal pain, abdominal distention, nausea and vomiting, absent or decreased bowel sounds, or signs of local or systemic infection. The exploratory laparotomy may be used to detect and remove the cause of acute peritonitis.

Laparotomy is also used to take samples of abdominal tumors in order to determine the stage of a cancer or diagnosis and repair internal organs damaged due to disease or trauma.

Reason for Procedure

A laparotomy is frequently performed as an exploratory procedure to assist in determining a cause of abdominal pain or peritonitis. An emergency laparotomy is performed when all other means of diagnosing a problem such as CT or ultrasound have been exhausted. Other reasons for laparotomy include making an accurate identification and/or removal of malignant or benign growths (neoplasms), correcting an ectopic pregnancy (a fertilized egg that is trapped in the fallopian tube), correcting twisted intestines (volvulus), taking samples (biopsies) of abdominal tissue or tumors in order to determine the stage of a cancer, draining infection, and stopping bleeding.

A laparotomy is performed when organs such as the appendix, intestine, esophagus, stomach, colon, or gallbladder are opened up or torn apart (perforated) due to disease or trauma. Gunshot or knife wounds to other parts of the body such as the flank or back should also be considered a risk for a cut or tear in the lining (peritoneum) that surrounds and protects the inside of the abdominal cavity. Peritoneal perforation can lead to peritonitis if not accessed and repaired via laparotomy.

Description

The individual is given a general anesthesia. An incision is made in the lower abdominal area. Incisions can be midline between the breastbone (sternum) and lower abdomen (pubis) or transverse across the lower part of the abdomen, depending on the suspected condition or area of trauma. However, in the individual with unclear pathology or diffuse symptoms, a midline incision is used for complete abdominal exploration.

The incision reaches down through the skin and muscle layers and is spread open so the abdominal cavity can be directly visualized. After the source of the problem is located and corrected using standard surgical procedures, the incision is closed with surgical thread (suture) or metal staples. If the stomach or intestines were affected, the individual may have a rubber or plastic tube inserted through the nose and esophagus into the stomach to drain the contents while the affected area heals. The individual usually requires several days of inpatient recovery depending on the extent of the damaged tissue and the underlying reason for the laparotomy.

Prognosis

The outcome following a laparotomy depends on the underlying reason for surgery, the individual's general health condition, extent of tissue damage, length of time the individual has had peritonitis (if present), age, obesity, loss of blood due to trauma and any other disorders such as emphysema or heart disease.

If peritonitis is caused by a quickly diagnosed ruptured appendix, the laparotomy becomes a method of performing an appendectomy and allowing access to treat the peritonitis in the abdominal cavity. In this situation, the outcome may be full recovery. An appendix that ruptured several days before the laparotomy however may result in a longer recovery time than a quickly diagnosed and treated ruptured appendix.

A laparotomy can successfully diagnose and identify the extent of late-stage cancer.

Specialists

- General Surgeon

Work Restrictions / Accommodations

No restrictions or special accommodations are necessary for healthy individuals resuming light to medium work. Resumption of heavy work and lifting should be delayed until healing is complete and medical clearance received.

Comorbid Conditions

Comorbid conditions include obesity, age, extreme loss of blood due to trauma and other medical conditions such as emphysema or heart disease.

Procedure Complications

Complications include allergy or abnormal responses to anesthesia, unintentional perforation of an organ, excessive bleeding, wound or systemic infection, or internal scarring and chronic pain. If peritonitis is present and not treated rapidly, it can lead to multisystem failure and death. Delayed laparotomy in the instance of trauma can lead to excessive or fatal bleeding.

Factors Influencing Duration

Recovery after laparotomy is determined by the age and general health of the individual, findings at the time of the procedure, and final diagnosis.

Length of Disability

Lengths of disability are for the procedure itself. Duration will be influenced by the underlying condition. For surgery of abdominal organs, see specific procedure.

Diagnostic.

Duration in Days

Job Classification	Minimum	Optimum	Maximum
Sedentary work	7	14	21
Light work	7	14	21
Medium work	14	21	28
Heavy work	21	42	70
Very Heavy work	21	56	70

References

"Acute Abdomen and Surgical Gastroenterology." The Merck Manual. Beers, Mark H., and Robert Berkow, eds. Whitehouse Station, NJ: Merck Research Laboratories, 1999. 257-269.

Barresi, Roberto. "Penetrating Abdominal Injury." Common Surgical Diseases: An Algorithmic Approach to Problem Solving. Millikan, Keith W., and Theodore J. Saclarides, eds. New York: Springer-Verlag, 1998. 70-74.

Laryngectomy
30.0

Definition

A laryngectomy is the surgical removal of the larynx. The larynx is the organ in the throat that contains the vocal cords (that enable speech), guards the airway into the lungs (trachea) during swallowing, and maintains a patent airway.

The larynx is divided into several different structures. In some cases, a partial laryngectomy may be performed, removing only the diseased portions (such as removing only one vocal cord) of the larynx. The ability to speak may remain following partial laryngectomy, although the voice may be altered. In most cases, the entire larynx is removed and a procedure to install an artificial airway (tracheostomy) may be performed simultaneously.

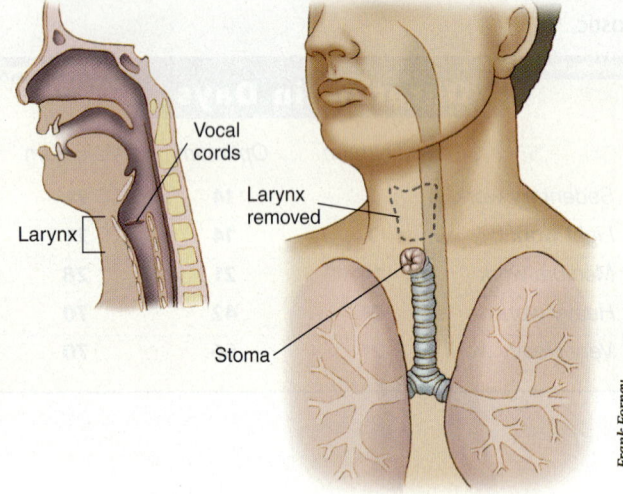

Reason for Procedure

A laryngectomy is performed when the individual has throat cancer, typically squamous cell carcinoma, which has not responded to radiation treatment.

Description

The individual is positioned on the operating table lying on the back with the neck extended. Anesthesia is by general anesthesia and a breathing tube (endotracheal tube). This tube will be replaced later in the procedure. The neck region is cleansed with a surgical scrub solution, and surgical drapes are positioned over the rest of the body. An incision is made and the area is exposed. Structures around the larynx (such as muscles, nerves, blood vessels, thyroid gland) are identified and separated from surrounding tissues. The endotracheal tube placed for anesthesia is removed so that an incision can be made into the trachea. A different breathing tube is placed into the lower part of the trachea. The surgeon then separates the larynx from the upper part of the airway (pharynx). The larynx and tumor can then be totally removed. A tube that will be used for feeding is inserted through the nose down through the back of the throat into the esophagus. The size (diameter) of the hole that has been made for breathing (tracheal stoma) is adjusted, and drains are placed into the wound. Either a tracheostomy or laryngectomy tube may be placed into the tracheal stoma to aid breathing and keep the airway open following surgery.

Prognosis

Complete removal of the malignancy is often the outcome of laryngectomy. The 5-year survival rate is 90% following surgical removal or radiation therapy of early-stage cancers that have not spread to nearby structures from the primary (original) site. The outcome of more advanced cancer and more extensive surgeries may vary and may include chemotherapy and radiation. The outcome for laryngectomy includes an open (patent) healed stoma, through which the individual can easily breathe and clear secretions from the lungs. To aid breathing, a laryngectomy or tracheostomy tube will be necessary for several months until the stoma is completely healed. In total laryngectomy, speech may be enabled by using air that has been held in the esophagus to speak (esophageal speech), surgical creation of a tracheoesophageal fistula (also known as tracheoesophageal puncture) which is placement of a one-way valve into an opening between the trachea and esophagus for speech, and use of a device that is held against the throat for speech (electric larynx).

Speech therapy is necessary for learning new methods of speaking. The individual may not be able to swallow food correctly until healing is completed. A tube placed through the nose, down the esophagus, and into the stomach (nasogastric tube) may be necessary for liquid tube feedings for several days or weeks. For laryngectomy without extensive surgery to the neck and esophagus (radical neck surgery), oral nutrition is often possible. Therapy may be necessary to ensure that food that is swallowed flows into the stomach and not into the lungs.

Specialists

- Otolaryngologist

Rehabilitation

Speech rehabilitation may be needed to learn alternative methods of speech, such as esophageal speech, use of an artificial larynx, and tracheoesophageal puncture. Esophageal speech is a technique for producing words by swallowing and holding air in the esophagus. With an artificial larynx, speech is produced by an electronic device held at the side of the neck or in the mouth. With a tracheoesophageal puncture, speech is enabled by placement of a voice button (a one-way valve) into a small puncture wound that is placed into the airway. Learning these techniques may be a lengthy process. Swallowing difficulties may occur with partial laryngectomy, requiring rehabilitation and therapy.

Work Restrictions / Accommodations

Time off from work will be needed for surgery, complete recovery, and rehabilitation. Further time off from work may be needed for further cancer treatments, such as chemotherapy and radiation therapy. Learning to care for the tracheostomy tube and tracheal stoma may require time off of work. Temporary accommodations may be necessary for individuals whose jobs require oral communication. Until the stoma is well healed, laryngectomy and tracheostomy tubes may require care during the workshift, requiring additional break time. With total laryngectomy and loss of voice, job reassignment may be needed either temporarily or permanently.

Comorbid Conditions

Coexisting conditions that may impact recovery and lengthen disability include lymph node metastasis and chronic obstructive pulmonary disease.

Procedure Complications

Several complications can occur with a laryngectomy including hemorrhage, airway obstruction (which may be due to tissue swelling or accumulation of secretions), infection, rupture of the carotid artery, fistula formation, narrowing of the tracheostomy (tracheostomy stenosis), and nerve injury. With partial laryngectomy, there may be difficulty swallowing with potential aspiration.

Factors Influencing Duration

The individual may require more time in the hospital if there are complications following surgery. A prolonged period of time may be needed for speech rehabilitation and if rehabilitation is needed for swallowing difficulties.

Length of Disability

Duration depends on extent of surgery (partial, complete, radical).

Duration in Days

Job Classification	Minimum	Optimum	Maximum
Sedentary work	7	14	28
Light work	7	21	28
Medium work	14	28	42
Heavy work	21	35	56
Very Heavy work	21	42	56

References

Jackler, Robert K., and Kaplan, Michael J. "Ear, Nose, and Throat." Current Medical Diagnosis and Treatment, 39th ed. Tierney, Lawrence M., Stephen J. McPhee, and Maxine A. Papadakis, eds. New York: Lange Medical Books/McGraw-Hill, 2000. 223-263.

Way L.W. Current Surgical Diagnosis and Treatment, 10th ed. Norwalk: Appleton & Lange, 1994.

Laryngitis

Other names / synonyms: Acute Laryngitis, Chronic Laryngitis, Edematous Laryngitis, Septic Laryngitis, Suppurative Laryngitis

464.0

Definition

Laryngitis is an inflammation or infection of the voice box (larynx) that causes swelling of the vocal cords. Laryngitis is characterized by hoarseness and a loss of voice, and may also cause pain in the laryngeal area during swallowing or speaking. Laryngitis may last only a few days (acute) or persist over a long period (chronic).

Acute laryngitis is most often caused by viral or bacterial infections in the upper respiratory tract. It may occur along with a common cold, bronchitis, flu, or pneumonia. Chronic laryngitis is most commonly caused by overuse or misuse of the voice (singing, screaming); chronic irritation by smoke, dust, or other airborne substances; excessive alcohol consumption; or the reflux of acid from the stomach. Less commonly, laryngitis may be secondary to allergies, direct trauma, or more serious conditions such as laryngeal polyps, a benign or malignant tumor, or laryngeal paralysis (Horner's Syndrome).

Laryngitis can affect individuals of any age and is equally common in men and women.

Diagnosis

History: Individuals may report hoarseness or loss of voice, soreness when clearing the throat or swallowing, and a dry, irritated cough. Fever may or may not be present.

Physical exam: The physician visually inspects the larynx using a mirror held against the back of the roof of the mouth. A viewing instrument (laryngoscope) may be passed down the throat in order to view the larynx directly (laryngoscopy) or to take a biopsy.

Tests: Tests are not required for the diagnosis of laryngitis. However, a throat culture may be taken to identify organisms responsible for a bacterial infection.

Treatment

Laryngitis is most often treated by resting the voice as much as possible, increasing fluid intake, using a humidifier, and avoiding common irritants (i.e., cigarette smoke and alcohol). Over-the-counter analgesics or throat lozenges may be used if soreness or throat pain are present. Antibiotics are prescribed only if a bacterial infection is present. Chronic laryngitis is treated differently depending on the cause. Symptoms persisting for longer than 2 weeks without relief from common treatment methods, or hoarseness accompanied by a lump in the neck or blood-tinged sputum, require medical attention for additional diagnostic evaluation.

Prognosis

Full recovery is expected.

Differential Diagnosis

The symptoms of laryngitis may occur in the presence of numerous respiratory infections such as influenza, pneumonia, or bronchitis. Laryngitis may also be a symptom of a malignant tumor or polyps on the vocal chords, paralysis of the vocal chords (such as Horner's syndrome), allergies, or trauma.

Specialists

- Otolaryngologist

Work Restrictions / Accommodations

The voice should be rested as much as possible. Inhaled irritants (such as smoke, dust, or pollution) and extremely cold air should be avoided.

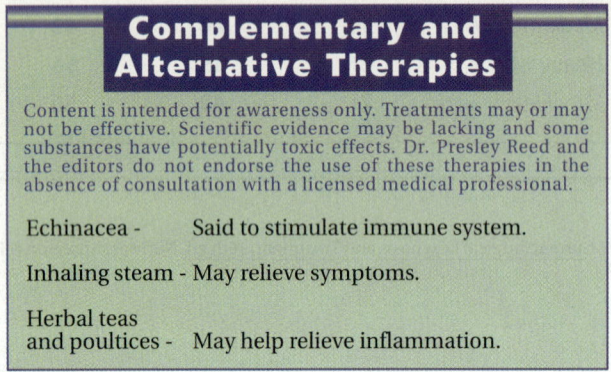

Complementary and Alternative Therapies

Content is intended for awareness only. Treatments may or may not be effective. Scientific evidence may be lacking and some substances have potentially toxic effects. Dr. Presley Reed and the editors do not endorse the use of these therapies in the absence of consultation with a licensed medical professional.

Echinacea - Said to stimulate immune system.

Inhaling steam - May relieve symptoms.

Herbal teas and poultices - May help relieve inflammation.

Comorbid Conditions

Underlying respiratory infections such as influenza, pneumonia, or bronchitis may prolong the condition. Malignant tumors or polyps on the vocal chords or paralysis of the vocal chords may also result in prolonged symptoms.

Complications

Rarely does severe respiratory distress develop that requires immediate medical intervention. Persistent laryngitis (more than 2 weeks) may be a symptom of a more serious underlying condition such as a tumor or cancer within the larynx or on the vocal cords.

Factors Influencing Duration

Situations resulting in persistent overuse or misuse of the voice may aggravate and prolong symptoms.

Length of Disability

Duration depends on the underlying cause and severity of inflammation.

Duration in Days

Job Classification	Minimum	Optimum	Maximum
Any work	0	1	3

Failure to Recover

If an individual fails to recover within the maximum duration expectancy period, the reader may wish to reference the following questions to assist in better understanding the specifics of an individual's medical case.

Regarding diagnosis:

- Was diagnosis of underlying condition such as, influenza, pneumonia, bronchitis, malignant tumor or polyps on the vocal chords, paralysis of the vocal chords (such as Horner's syndrome), allergies, or trauma, confirmed?
- Has a throat culture been performed to identify the causative agent?
- In the case of persistent laryngitis (more than 2 weeks), was laryngoscopy and/or biopsy performed to rule out benign or malignant tumors?

Regarding treatment:

- Is individual receiving appropriate treatment for an underlying viral or bacterial infection? Has individual complied with prescribed treatment?
- Have symptoms persisted longer than 2 weeks?
- Has a laryngoscopy and/or biopsy been performed to rule out benign or malignant tumors?
- Once identified, is underlying condition receiving appropriate treatment?

Regarding prognosis:

- How long has laryngitis been present?
- Has a laryngoscopy and/or biopsy been performed to rule out benign or malignant tumors?
- Is underlying condition responding to treatment?

References

Gaut, Andrew. Laryngitis. The Johns Hopkins Center for Laryngeal and Voice Disorders. 01 Aug 1997. 12 Jul 2000 <http://www.med.jhu.edu/voice/laryngitis.html>.

Laryngitis. PlanetRx.com. 01 Oct 1999. 2 Aug 2000 <http://www.planetrx.com/condition/cond_detail/info/67_introduction.html>.

Laryngoscopy
31.42

Definition

Laryngoscopy is a common procedure that enables detailed examination of the voice box (larynx) or windpipe (trachea) through use of a mirror, fiberoptic tubing, or other means.

There are two types of laryngoscopy. Indirect laryngoscopy involves holding a mirror against the very back of the mouth (palate) in order to view the vocal cords. Direct laryngoscopy may be done with a rigid, hollow tube (laryngoscope) passed down the throat via the mouth. A direct laryngoscopy may also be performed with a flexible, fiberoptic instrument (nasopharyngoscope) threaded through the nostril into the throat.

A laryngoscopy can help determine causes of symptoms such as choking, bleeding, difficulty swallowing, persistent hoarseness, and other conditions affecting the area of the voice box and/or windpipe. A direct laryngoscopy is used to obtain tissue samples or remove tumors or foreign bodies.

Reason for Procedure

Laryngoscopy is used both diagnostically and therapeutically. The procedure may be necessary when there is throat pain, presence of a foreign body, choking, bleeding (hemorrhage), difficulty swallowing, persistent hoarseness or other voice change, persistent harsh noise during respiration (stridor), or difficulty inhaling.

Indirect laryngoscopy can help detect inflammation of the epiglottis (epiglottiditis), inflammation of the larynx (laryngitis), benign or malignant (cancerous) tumors in the larynx, or reduced movement in the vocal cords.

Direct laryngoscopy is used when more intensive examination is needed or to obtain tissue samples for further laboratory testing (biopsy). The procedure can evaluate and remove a benign tumor, remove a foreign body, use in laser surgery, or introduce drugs directly into a specific area (i.e., treatment of paralyzed vocal cords).

Description

The individual receiving a direct laryngoscopy is typically seen on an outpatient basis. Several days before the procedure, preliminary tests such as x-rays and imaging of internal structures (CT) may be performed.

For less invasive procedures using flexible, fiberoptic tubing inserted through the nostril (nasopharyngoscope), the individual usually receives a local anesthetic sprayed and/or dripped into the throat both to numb the targeted area and control the natural gag reflex. An injection of anesthetic directly into the affected area may also be required. Use of more rigid tubing inserted directly into the throat through the mouth may require general anesthesia. Depending on the purpose of the procedure, a dye is used for staining to mark abnormal tissue. The procedure is usually completed in less than an hour.

During the procedure, the nasopharyngoscope is threaded through the nostril into the throat. This narrow, lighted magnifying device enables a closer look at an area of concern. Because the scope is flexible, it allows a better view farther down the throat than possible with other standard techniques. Cameras may also be attached to the end of a scope to provide better viewing.

A rigid laryngoscope may be used for procedures such as suctioning to remove abnormal tissue, manipulating internal structures, or obtaining a tissue sample (biopsy) for laboratory examination.

Depending on the type and purpose of the procedure, some individuals may need to stay in a hospital for overnight observation. Individuals who receive less invasive forms of laryngoscopy can usually return to work immediately. Others may require several days of recovery time.

Prognosis

Since a laryngoscopy is often a diagnostic procedure, the outcome depends on the condition requiring examination. An indirect laryngoscopy may help provide viewing of affected structures or function of vocal cords but could set off a gag reflex that makes examination difficult or impossible. Direct laryngoscopy provides opportunity for more detailed diagnosis and possibility for therapeutic procedures such as removal of abnormal tissue during the same procedure.

The outcome of a therapeutic procedure depends on the underlying condition. However, complete recovery can usually be expected if tissue removed during the procedure is not cancerous (benign).

Specialists

• Otolaryngologist	• Pulmonologist

Work Restrictions / Accommodations

The procedure itself typically should not warrant special accommodation although the individual may have an underlying condition such as cancer that may require consideration. Some individuals may require several days off from work to recover from more invasive or therapeutic procedures involving laryngoscopy. If the individual's speech is affected, assignment to duties that do not require vocal communication may be needed during recovery.

Comorbid Conditions

Individuals with breathing disorders such as inflammation of the upper airway (epiglottitis, supraglottitis) may experience severe symptoms that can prolong any hospital stay associated with the need for a laryngoscopy.

Procedure Complications

Complications are uncommon but may include coughing, gagging, temporary sneezing, and/or bleeding. Some individuals may react adversely to the anesthesia used in the procedure. Injury may occur to the mouth, nose, or throat.

Factors Influencing Duration

The underlying condition for which the procedure is required such as removal of a malignant (cancerous) tumor may determine whether the individual requires extended leave from work.

Length of Disability

In most cases, no disability is expected. Duration depends on type of anesthesia (local versus general) and underlying condition, if any.

References

Clinical Indicators: Laryngoscopy/Nasopharyngoscopy. American Academy of Otolaryngology-Head and Neck Surgery Inc. 2000. 20 Jan 2001 <http://www.entnet.org/indicators/laryngoscopy_nasopharyngoscopy.html>.

Levitan, Richard M. "Direct Laryngoscopy Imaging: Teaching and Research Applications." Hospital of the University of Pennsylvania. 1998. 21 Jan 2001 <http://www.gasnet.org/esia/1998/june/samart.html>.

Legionnaire's Disease
Other names / synonyms: Legionellosis, Legionnaire's Pneumonia
482.83, 482.84

Definition

Legionnaire's disease is an acute respiratory infection that causes a serious type of pneumonia; it is caused by the bacterium Legionella pneumophila that dwells in man-made and natural aquatic environments.

The bacteria have been isolated from diverse areas such as plumbing systems, air conditioners, humidifiers, hot tubs, whirlpools, ice machines, and potable water systems. An outbreak of serious pulmonary infections among individuals attending a convention of the American Legion in Philadelphia, Pennsylvania, during the US Bicentennial celebration in July 1976 prompted the description of Legionnaires' disease. A nonpneumonic variant caused by the same species is called Pontiac Fever, named for an outbreak of this disease that occurred in Pontiac, Michigan, in 1968.

Legionnaire's disease is not spread from person to person, but rather through contaminated water or ventilation systems. It is one of the most common types of community acquired pneumonia, and usually strikes smokers, the elderly, diabetics, and alcoholics, and individuals who receive ongoing ventilation, have cancer, lung problems, renal failure, a low resistance to disease, or who have suppressed immune systems.

Certain free-living amebic organisms in water are capable of supporting the intracellular growth of legionellae. Factors that are now known to enhance the growth of Legionella bacteria in man-made water environments include water temperatures between 25-42 degrees C, stagnant water, and water with scale and sediment.

Since the initial identification of it in 1976, Legionnaires' disease has become recognized as the most common cause of atypical pneumonia in hospitalized individuals, and the second most common cause of community acquired bacterial pneumonia. Passive reports received by the Center for Disease Control (CDC) indicate an incidence of 0.48 cases per 100,000 people. More active surveillance estimates upward of 20,000 cases annually in the US. Legionnaires' disease is more common in the summer, especially in August, and is slightly more prevalent in the northern US. Outbreaks have also been recognized throughout North America, Africa, Australia, Europe, and South America.

Males are affected more frequently than females. The middle-aged and elderly are at increased risk. Legionnaires' disease has a 25% mortality rate; older individuals have higher mortality rates.

Diagnosis

History: Classical presentation begins with an incubation period of 2-8 days; improvement begins in another 4-5 days. Individuals complain of high fever, shaking, chills, headaches, muscle aches and stiffness, chest pain, a dry cough, lethargy, weakness, and shortness of breath. As the disease progresses, individuals may complain of abdominal pain, diarrhea, and muscular discoordination (ataxia). Musculoskeletal symptoms include joint pain (arthralgia) and muscle pain (myalgia).

Physical exam: Physical findings include a high fever, rapid breathing (tachypnea), severe pneumonia, and altered mental status. Relatively slow pulse (bradycardia) may occur in up to 66% of individuals. The absence of inflammation of the upper respiratory tract is common and is a clinically useful indicator. Chest sounds may be normal or may reveal crackling (rales), a musical pitch (rhonchi), or signs of solid formations (consolidation). The individual may have blood-streaked sputum (hemoptysis). Inflammation of the covering of the heart (pericarditis) and inflammation of the inner portions of the heart (endocarditis) may be present. An enlarged liver (hepatomegaly) may be seen in rare cases. The neurological examination, or the individual's mental status, may be abnormal.

Tests: Laboratory tests may include chest x-ray and a non-contrast head computerized tomography (CT scan). Serologic (blood) testing for Legionella may include a complete blood count (CBC), including an electrolyte panel, blood urea nitrogen (BUN), and creatinine levels; the white blood cell count will be elevated (leukocytosis). A sedimentation rate may also be elevated. The urine and lung fluid will be examined for signs of the disease. Because the Legionella pneumophila bacteria does not show up in ordinary sputum cultures, a special sputum culture or stain test (sputum DFA-direct fluorescent antibody) will be necessary to identify it. Arterial blood gases may show low concentrations of oxygen, and liver function tests may be mildly elevated. Alkaline phosphatase and creatinine phosphokinase levels may be checked as well.

Treatment

Hospitalization is often required, during which time the individual is given intravenous (IV) antibiotics for several days. Some individuals require supplemental oxygen during this time, along with fluids and electrolyte replacement. After the individual stabilizes, oral antibiotic therapy must be continued for an additional 14-21 days. Antimicrobial therapy should be guided by practical experience, and comprehensively cover all likely pathogens.

Prognosis

Recovery is variable. Most individuals recover from Legionnaire's disease if it is diagnosed early enough. However, some outbreaks have had mortality rates between 15-25%. Some individuals experience rapid improvement, while others have a much more protracted course despite treatment. The mortality rate approaches 50% with hospital-acquired (nosocomial) infections. Death may occur in 10% of individuals with healthy immune systems who receive treatment, but rises to 80% among individuals with compromised immune systems who do not receive treatment.

Differential Diagnosis

Bronchitis, congestive heart failure, pulmonary edema, inflammation of the rib cartilages (costochondritis), gastroenteritis, HIV infection and AIDS, meningitis, increased fluid in the pleural space (pleural effusion), pneumonia from various causes, or prostatitis have similar symptoms. Adult respiratory distress syndrome (ARDS) and septic shock may also present with similar signs and symptoms.

Specialists

- Critical Care Specialist
- Pulmonologist
- Infectious Disease Physician

Work Restrictions / Accommodations

Relapses are not uncommon. Therefore, recovering individuals with physically demanding occupations should be careful to avoid over-exertion until they are fully recovered. Buildings in which they work should be examined and the water and ventilation systems modified, cleaned, and repaired.

Comorbid Conditions

Immune deficiency may lengthen disability. Those who take medications that suppress the immune system may have a greater disability.

Complications

Complications include lung abscess, respiratory failure, low blood pressure (hypotension), shock, and kidney failure. In addition, any underlying lung disease or immunological problems may make Legionnaire's disease more resistant to treatment. An acute, rapid, quickly worsening (fulminating), potentially fatal disease of skeletal muscle that entails destruction of muscle (rhabdomyolysis) is occasionally seen in Legionnaires' disease. This may be so severe as to cause renal failure. Dehydration, respiratory insufficiency, and inflammation of the inner portions of the heart (endocarditis) are also complications of the disease.

Factors Influencing Duration

If the individual is over 60, has poor underlying health, or has a compromised immune system, recovery time may be longer.

Length of Disability

Constant exposure to the organisms and the environment(s) in which they reside could lead to recurrences of the disease and a permanent state of disability.

Duration in Days

Job Classification	Minimum	Optimum	Maximum
Sedentary work	5	7	14
Light work	5	7	14
Medium work	5	10	21
Heavy work	7	10	28
Very Heavy work	7	14	35

Failure to Recover

If an individual fails to recover within the maximum duration expectancy period, the reader may wish to reference the following questions to assist in better understanding the specifics of an individual's medical case.

Regarding diagnosis:

- Has diagnosis of Legionnaire's disease been confirmed?
- Have conditions with similar symptoms been ruled out?
- Was there a positive history of pathogen exposure?
- Is the timing between exposure and clinical onset compatible with the known biologic facts about the illness?
- Is the clinical illness, including the history, physical examination, and laboratory findings, consistent with other case descriptions?
- Are the laboratory values and tests at or near the normal levels?
- Has individual experienced any complications such as lung abscess, respiratory failure, hypotension, shock, kidney failure, dehydration, respiratory insufficiency, or endocarditis?

Regarding treatment:

- Do symptoms persist despite treatment?
- Was culture and sensitivity done to identify the pathogen and determine the most effective antibiotic to use?
- Have antibiotic-resistant organisms been ruled out?

Regarding prognosis:

- Does individual have an underlying condition such as immune deficiency or underlying lung disease that may be impacting recovery?
- Does the individual smoke tobacco?
- Are there special attributes of the particular individual that make it more or less likely that he or she would be so affected?
- Because constant exposure to the organisms and the environment(s) in which they reside could lead to recurrences of the disease and a permanent state of disability, is there a positive history of exposure in the workplace?
- Could exposure be occurring in the home, the community, or in recreational activities?
- What can be done to prevent further exposure to pathogens?

References

Shiel, M.D., FACP, chief ed "Legionellosis." MedicineNet.com. 01 Nov 2000. 1 Jan 2001 <http://www.medicinenet.com/Script/Main/art.asp?li=MNI&ArticleKey=10790>.

Leukemia

Other names / synonyms: Acute Lymphocytic Leukemia, Acute Myelogenous Leukemia, Acute Myeloid Leukemia, Acute Nonlymphoblastic Leukemia, ALL, AML, ANLL, Chronic Granulocytic Leukemia, Chronic Lymphocytic Leukemia, Chronic Myelogenous Leukemia, Chronic Myeloid Leukemia, CLL, CML, Leukocytic Sarcoma, Lymphoid Leukemia

208, 208.0, 208.1, 208.10, 208.11, 208.2, 208.20, 208.8, 208.9

Definition

Leukemia is a type of cancer in which large numbers of white blood cells are produced.

Blood is made up of fluid called plasma and three types of cells that each have special functions: white blood cells (WBCs), red blood cells (RBCs), and platelets. WBCs help the body fight infections and other diseases; RBCs carry oxygen from the lungs to the body's tissues and take carbon dioxide from the tissues back to the lungs; and platelets help form blood clots that control bleeding. They are formed in the bone marrow, and new or immature blood cells are called blasts. Under normal conditions, blood cells are produced in an orderly, controlled way as the body needs them.

The leukemia white blood cells are abnormal. They usually look different from normal blood cells and do not function properly. Circulating blood contains five types of WBCs. These five types, however, arise from only two primary white blood cell lines. The myeloid line develops into neutrophils, eosinophils, basophils, and monocytes. The lymphoid line develops into lymphocytes. Leukemia involving the myeloid line is referred to as myelogenous leukemia. Leukemia involving the lymphoid line is referred to as lymphoid (lymphoblastic or lymphocytic) leukemia. These primary types are categorized according to the acuteness with which they develop, the course they take, and the type of WBC affected.

The four primary types of leukemia are acute myelogenous leukemia (AML), chronic myelogenous leukemia (CML), acute lymphoblastic leukemia (ALL), and chronic lymphocytic leukemia (CLL). In acute leukemia, the abnormal blood cells, either myeloblasts or lymphoblasts, remain very immature and cannot carry on their normal function (AML and ALL). Because their number increases rapidly, the disease worsens quickly. Abnormal production of mature lymphocytes results in a chronic leukemia called CLL. CML is unique among leukemias in that individuals usually stay in a chronic phase for many years before the disease progresses.

Risk factors for leukemia generally include exposure to chemical or environmental carcinogens such as benzene, petrochemicals, ionizing radiation, or previous chemotherapy. Individuals with certain chromosome abnormalities such as Down's syndrome are at an increased risk for developing leukemia. Most cases of leukemia develop, however, with no known link to a risk factor.

Leukemia is diagnosed in 8 to 10 individuals per 100,000 each year. AML accounts for 46% of leukemias, typically developing in adults between the ages of 30 and 60. CML primarily affects middle-aged adults and 14% of leukemias are diagnosed as CML. ALL accounts for 11% of leukemias.

CLL makes up 29% of leukemias, and is the most common type of leukemia in Western countries. It primarily affects middle-aged to elderly adults. Males are affected at twice the rate of females.

Diagnosis

History: In acute leukemia, symptoms appear and get worse quickly. Individuals with this disease go to their doctor because they feel sick. In chronic leukemia, symptoms may not appear for a long time and when they do appear, they are generally mild at first and worsen gradually. Chronic leukemia is generally discovered during a routine checkup before there are any symptoms. Symptoms may include fever, chills, and other flu-like symptoms; weakness and fatigue; frequent infections; generally feeling ill (malaise); loss of appetite; easy bleeding and bruising; swollen or bleeding gums; weight loss; shortness of breath; bone and joint pain; abdominal pain; and/or night sweats.

Physical exam: Individuals may present with enlarged and tender lymph nodes most often in the underarms, groin, or neck areas, an enlarged liver and/or spleen, large or pinpoint bruises, gum enlargement, tiny red spots (petechiae) under the skin, and fever. Individuals may appear pale if anemia has developed.

Tests: Although blood tests may reveal that an individual has leukemia, they may not show what type of leukemia it is. A complete blood count (CBC) with differential diagnoses will show abnormalities consistent with leukemia including the number, appearance, and maturity of WBCs. The hemoglobin, hematocrit, and platelet count may be decreased.

A sample of bone marrow is removed with a needle (bone marrow aspiration) and examined under the microscope. A bone marrow biopsy, performed with a larger needle, involves removing a small piece of bone and the bone marrow. Both the bone marrow aspiration and bone marrow biopsy are used to tell what type of leukemia the person has. If leukemia cells are found in the bone marrow sample, a spinal tap (lumbar puncture) is used to check for leukemia cells in the fluid that fills the spaces in and around the brain and spinal cord (cerebrospinal fluid). Chest x-rays can reveal signs of the disease in the chest. Special stains used on WBCs found in the peripheral blood and those in the bone marrow help identify and confirm the diagnosis.

Chromosome studies (cytogenetic studies) provide further information. A variety of acquired chromosome abnormalities are associated with the diagnosis and prognosis of leukemia. For example, up to 95% of individuals with CML have an exchange between chromosomes 9 and

22. This exchange produces the "Philadelphia chromosome." This finding helps in the diagnosis of CML.

Treatment

Treatment for leukemia is based on the type of leukemia diagnosed. Treatment is not the same for all individuals as it is based on certain features of the leukemia cells, the extent of the disease, and whether the leukemia has been treated before. It also depends on the individual's age, symptoms, and general health.

Acute leukemia needs to be treated immediately and typically more aggressively than chronic leukemia. Immediately after diagnosis, a first round of chemotherapy called induction therapy is given. The purpose of induction therapy is to destroy the leukemia cells and bring about remission. Once the individual is in remission, a second round of chemotherapy called consolidation therapy begins. Its purpose is to prolong remission and improve the chances of cure. Consolidation therapy is followed by maintenance chemotherapy. In ALL, intermittent maintenance therapy continues for at least 3 years. In AML, therapy typically continues for at least 1 year.

High-energy rays that damage the cancer cells and stop them from growing (radiation therapy) are used in conjunction with chemotherapy for some kinds of leukemia. Radiation may be directed to one specific area of the body where there is a collection of leukemia cells such as the spleen or testicles. Others may receive radiation directed to the whole body (total-body radiation). This is usually administered before a bone marrow transplant.

Bone marrow transplant (BMT) for individuals with acute leukemia may be performed after relapse or when efforts to achieve remission have failed. In acute lymphocytic leukemia, bone marrow transplant may be done during the first complete remission. The ideal marrow donor is a matched sibling. BMT using marrow from a matched sibling may be done for individuals with AML younger than 40. If this is not an option, the marrow may come from a matched unrelated donor. The marrow also may come from the individual after their leukemia-producing bone marrow is destroyed by chemotherapy and radiation therapy and then replaced by new healthy bone marrow. BMT using an individual's own marrow may be done for individuals younger than 55.

Biological therapy involves treatment with substances such as interferon that affect the immune system's response to cancer.

In chronic leukemias, treatment may be withheld in early stages unless required by symptoms or increased white counts. As CLL advances, it is treated with chemotherapy. In advanced cases, the spleen may receive radiation. BMT is typically not performed for CLL.

In the later stages of CML, treatment may include traditional chemotherapy or interferon.

Prognosis

The predicted outcome varies according to the type of leukemia. Adults with ALL have a 40% cure rate. In ALL, the presence of certain chromosome changes predicts a worse prognosis. BMT from a matched sibling donor can cure 20-40% of individuals who do not go into remission or who relapse after remission.

The average survival rate for an individual with CLL diagnosed at an early stage is 10 years. If diagnosed at a late stage, the average survival is 30 months.

AML has an 80% remission rate for adults younger than 55. The cure rate following BMT using a matched sibling donor is 60%. In AML, the presence of certain chromosome changes predicts a better prognosis.

Individuals with CML spend an average of 3 to 6 years in the chronic phase. When the disease finally progresses to an acute phase during which immature leukemic cells are seen in the peripheral blood (blast crisis), its course resembles that of acute leukemia. Individuals with the Philadelphia chromosome enjoy a survival rate 8 times greater than those without the chromosome marker. BMT using a matched sibling donor puts 50-60% of individuals into remission for 5 to 10 years if performed during the chronic phase. If performed during the acute phase, survival rates drop to 10 %.

In general, cure rates following BMT are lower if the marrow is from the individual or from a matched unrelated donor.

Differential Diagnosis

Many conditions also produce similar abnormalities of the peripheral blood and similar initial symptoms and include infectious mononucleosis, viral infection, multiple myeloma, lymphoma, myelodysplastic syndrome, infiltrative disease of the bone marrow, and aplastic anemia.

Specialists

- Hematologist
- Pathologist
- Psychiatrist
- Psychologist
- Radiation Oncologist

Work Restrictions / Accommodations

Individuals with acute leukemia are not able to work during their treatment. Individuals receiving outpatient chemotherapy or radiation therapy may require time off from work because of the side effects of the treatment. If they are able to work, individuals may require sedentary work due to fatigue. Individuals who receive a BMT cannot work for 6 to 12 months after treatment.

Comorbid Conditions

Any condition that compromises the general health of an individual such as diabetes or anemia may make it more difficult to withstand the rigors of chemotherapy, radiation, or BMT.

Complications

Complications of leukemia can include bleeding, infection, anemia, involvement of the central nervous system or other body sites, and secondary cancers. Chemotherapy and radiation therapy cause nausea, vomiting, diarrhea, bone marrow suppression, and immunosuppression. BMT carries an additional risk of early death due to complications including graft versus host disease.

Factors Influencing Duration

The length of disability is based on the type of leukemia, the treatment received, side effects of treatment, availability of a BMT donor, involvement of central nervous system and other body sites, the development of infections, the development of secondary cancers, individual's nutritional status, emotional or mental health, and individual's overall health.

Length of Disability

Duration depends on type, site, and stage. Disability may be permanent.

High-dose chemotherapy or alpha-interferon treatment.

Duration in Days

Job Classification	Minimum	Optimum	Maximum
Sedentary work	28	42	168
Light work	28	42	168
Medium work	28	42	168
Heavy work	42	84	Indefinite
Very Heavy work	42	84	Indefinite

Bone marrow transplant.

Duration in Days

Job Classification	Minimum	Optimum	Maximum
Sedentary work	84	112	168
Light work	84	112	168
Medium work	84	112	168
Heavy work	112	168	Indefinite
Very Heavy work	112	168	Indefinite

Failure to Recover

If an individual fails to recover within the maximum duration expectancy period, the reader may wish to reference the following questions to assist in better understanding the specifics of an individual's medical case.

Regarding diagnosis:

- Was the diagnosis confirmed?
- Were conditions such as, infectious mononucleosis, viral infection, multiple myeloma, lymphoma, myelodysplastic syndrome, infiltrative disease of the bone marrow, and aplastic anemia, ruled out?
- Which tests were used in diagnosis? Was bone marrow aspiration and biopsy performed?
- What type of leukemia does the individual have (acute myelogenous leukemia, chronic myelogenous leukemia, acute lymphoblastic leukemia, or chronic lymphocytic leukemia)?
- Have chromosome studies (cytogenetic studies) been performed to aid in diagnosis of chronic myelogenous leukemia (CML)?
- Does individual have underlying conditions such as, diabetes or anemia that may impact treatment, therapy, or recovery?

Regarding treatment:

- What type of leukemia does individual have?
- Has the individual received induction and consolidation therapy, and maintenance chemotherapy for treatment of diagnosed acute leukemia?
- Is the individual a candidate for a BMT?
- Does individual have a matching sibling donor?
- Does individual's age preclude using his/her own marrow? Has a matching unrelated donor been located?
- Has chemotherapy or spleen radiation been effective in reducing symptoms or increasing white counts for individuals with chronic leukemia?
- What treatment has individual received up to this point (traditional chemotherapy or alpha-interferon, or radiation of the spleen)?
- What other treatment options are available (BMT using an individual's own treated marrow or marrow from a matched sibling or HLA-matched unrelated donor)?

Regarding prognosis:

- What type of leukemia does individual have?
- At what stage in the disease was it diagnosed?
- Did individual receive a BMT?
- At what stage in the disease was the BMT performed?
- Is the individual's nutritional status being monitored? Is the individual prone to infections due to a low white count? What precaution is individual using against infection?

References

Applebaum, Frederick. "The Acute Leukemias." Cecil Textbook of Medicine, 21st ed. Goldman, Lee, and J. Claude Bennett, eds. Philadelphia: W.B. Saunders Company, 2000. 953-958.

Keating, Michael. "The Chronic Leukemias." Cecil Textbook of Medicine, 21st ed. Goldman, Lee, and J. Claude Bennett, eds. Philadelphia: W.B. Saunders Company, 2000. 944-953.

Ligation and Stripping of Varicose Veins

Other names / synonyms: High Ligation

38.5, 38.50, 38.51, 38.52, 38.53, 38.55, 38.57, 38.59

Definition

Ligation and stripping of varicose veins is performed in order to remove veins that have become damaged, enlarged, and twisted (varicose veins).

The enlarged veins are just under the skin and are easily seen. The leg is the most common site for varicose veins.

This vein disorder is very common. This disorder is often seen in women, especially with pregnancy, in those with a family history of varicose veins, and in individuals with weak-walled veins. Prolonged standing in one place does not cause varicose veins, but may intensify the disorder. Varicose veins are sometimes a result of blockage of the deep veins in the leg (deep venous thrombosis).

Reason for Procedure

Ligation and stripping of varicose veins is indicated for individuals with swelling and aching pain in the legs, which is worse with standing and relieved by elevating the legs. Ligation and stripping is also used to treat inflammation in the veins (superficial phlebitis), blood clotting in the veins (thrombophlebitis), bleeding from a broken varicose vein, or skin ulceration. Varicose veins may also be removed for cosmetic reasons.

Description

This procedure is usually performed on an outpatient basis, but requires the individual to be placed under general anesthesia.

The surgical removal of varicose veins is done through small incisions between the ankle and groin. The individual's varicose veins are located, tied off (ligated), and then severed. A flexible wire is used to strip out the main superficial leg vein (saphenous vein) from ankle to groin. The leg is then bandaged tightly to prevent bleeding.

Prognosis

Although varicose veins cannot be cured, greater than 85% of individuals who undergo surgery have good long-term benefits. Veins that are treated surgically will not develop varicosities; however, new varicose veins may appear.

Specialists

- General Surgeon
- Vascular Surgeon

Work Restrictions / Accommodations

The individual's legs will be bandaged for several weeks. Prolonged standing or sitting must be avoided during the recovery period. Elevation of legs while sitting will be required. Walking is encouraged for healing, but should not be done for prolonged periods. Activities that cause straining, such as pushing, pulling, and lifting, should be avoided during the recovery period.

Comorbid Conditions

Circulatory disorders, cardiovascular disorders, diabetes mellitus, and obesity may influence length of disability.

Procedure Complications

Postoperative infection, formation of blood clots (thrombi), and adverse reactions to general anesthesia or other medications might complicate this procedure.

Factors Influencing Duration

The extent of the condition and the presence of complications will influence the length of disability.

Length of Disability

Duration of disability may depend on job requirements. If the individual has a sedentary job and can keep the legs elevated, the disability may be shorter than if the individual has a job that requires prolonged standing or walking.

Duration in Days

Job Classification	Minimum	Optimum	Maximum
Sedentary work	7	14	21
Light work	7	14	21
Medium work	14	21	28
Heavy work	21	28	35
Very Heavy work	21	28	35

References

"Varicose Veins." Merck Manual of Diagnosis and Therapy, 17th ed. Beers, Mark H., and Robert Berkow, MD, eds. Whitehouse Station, NJ: Merck & Co., Inc, 1999 30 Dec 2000 <http://www.merck.com/pubs/mmanual/section16/chapter212/212h.htm>.

Medline Plus Health Information. "Varicose Vein Surgery." Medical Encyclopedia. 01 Jan 2000 19 Jan 2001 <http://medlineplus.adam.com/ency/article/002952.htm>.

Ligation of Esophageal Varices
42.91

Definition

Ligation of esophageal varices is an endoscopic surgical procedure in which an enlarged vein (a varix) in the wall of the lower esophagus is tied off (ligated) to prevent it from bleeding.

In esophageal varices, the veins deep in the lining of the esophagus (the submucosa) become swollen (dilated) and fragile. An esophageal varix occurs as a result of increased blood pressure in the portal vein of the liver (portal hypertension). The most common cause of portal hypertension is cirrhosis. In portal hypertension, blood passing from the intestines to the liver meets very high resistance in the portal vein. High resistance in the portal vein causes blood to be diverted into the veins of the walls of the esophagus and stomach. These veins are thin-walled, becoming twisted, fragile, and tend to balloon outward because of the pressure. The major problem with esophageal varices is the risk of bleeding and hemorrhage.

It is not yet known why esophageal varices begin bleeding. It may be due to spontaneous rupture, irritation from passing food, or inflammation of the esophagus (esophagitis) resulting in erosion of the mucous membrane.

Several factors are associated with an increased risk for bleeding. Factors include large size of varices, localized sites of hemorrhage within the wall of the blood vessel (red wales or cherry red spots), high hepatic vein pressure, and poor liver function with accumulation of fluid in the abdominal cavity (ascites), and yellow color to the skin and mucous membranes (jaundice). Also, many individuals with cirrhosis have underlying bleeding abnormalities.

Reason for Procedure

Ligation of an esophageal varix (varices is the pleural form of the word varix) is used to stop bleeding or prevent re-bleeding of esophageal varices.

Description

Ligation of esophageal varices is a procedure performed through a lighted fiber-optic tube (endoscopy). The viewing tube (endoscope) is passed through the mouth down the esophagus, which allows affected varices to be seen. A small suction chamber on the endoscope tip allows the varix to be pulled into a stretched band that will be used to "tie off" the varices. A trigger device is used to release the band around the varix base, causing subsequent death (necrosis) and scarring of the tissue. Banding is repeated every 1-2 weeks until the varices are gone or reduced in size. Often, from 4-6 treatments are needed.

The individual's condition is stabilized prior to endoscopy. Blood and intravenous fluids are given to replace losses. It may take 2 to 12 hours to stabilize some individuals prior to the procedure. In some cases, a breathing tube may be placed in the lungs (endotracheal intubation) to prevent aspiration of blood into the lungs during the procedure.

Ligation is used as an alternative to sclerotherapy (a procedure in which an irritant solution is injected into or next to the bleeding varix). The resulting scar tissue stops the bleeding.

Prognosis

The outcome of endoscopic ligation of esophageal varices is generally good. Ligation of esophageal varices stops the bleeding in 90% of cases. Without ligation, 70% of individuals will rebleed, but the risk of rebleeding is cut in half following ligation.

However, the outcome of individuals experiencing esophageal bleeding is poor. Bleeding from esophageal varices will stop spontaneously in 60-80% of individuals; unfortunately more than half will bleed again within one week. Although recurrent bleeding can sometimes be controlled with medications, the death rate associated with acute bleeding episodes ranges from 15-40%. Over 60% of these individuals die within 5 years.

Specialists

- Gastroenterologist
- General Surgeon

Work Restrictions / Accommodations

Because these individuals may be very ill, work restrictions and special accommodations are determined on an individual basis. Individuals may be permanently disabled as a result of liver disease.

Comorbid Conditions

Comorbid conditions may include conditions associated with bleeding abnormalities.

Procedure Complications

Complications associated with endoscopic ligation of esophageal varices include additional bleeding due to tearing additional varices, ulceration of the lining over varices, perforation of the esophagus, and aspiration of blood into the lungs. If treatment with a sclerosing agent is performed, the sclerosing agent may be spread into the pulmonary or systemic circulation.

There are many complications associated with the bleeding, including life-threatening loss of blood, coma (hepatic coma), and infection. Coma results from absorption of blood products from the stomach. Individuals who have cirrhosis are unable to adequately metabolize certain products found in blood, resulting in dysfunction of the brain (encephalopathy). Bleeding from more than one site is common. Rebleeding may occur, with the greatest risk of rebleeding occurring in the first 6 weeks.

Successful eradication of esophageal varices can lead to development of gastric varices. Unfortunately, gastric varices do not respond to treatment as successfully as esophageal varices.

Factors Influencing Duration

The length of disability will be influenced by the severity of the condition, the underlying cause (portal hypertension due to liver disease), or the presence of complications.

Length of Disability

The number of procedures necessary to obliterate or reduce the size of varices will affect the length of disability.

Duration in Days

Job Classification	Minimum	Optimum	Maximum
Sedentary work	14	28	56
Light work	28	42	70
Medium work	42	63	84
Heavy work	56	70	112
Very Heavy work	56	70	112

References

Friedman, Scott L. "Cirrhosis of the Liver and its Major Sequelae." Cecil Textbook of Medicine, 20th ed. Bennett, J. Claude, and Fred Plum, eds. Philadelphia: W.B. Saunders Company, 1996. 788-796.

Potts, John R., and William C. Chapman. "Liver." Essentials of General Surgery, 3rd ed. Lawrence, Peter F., ed. Philadelphia: Lippincott, Williams & Wilkins, 2000. 343-367.

Ligation of Spermatic Vein for Varicocele
Other names / synonyms: Varicocelectomy
63.1

Definition

This procedure involves the tying of the spermatic veins to treat a varicocele.

A varicocele is an abnormal distention of the veins surrounding the testes. It is caused by ineffective valves within the veins along the spermatic cord that suspends the testis. The abnormal valves obstruct normal blood flow, causing a back up of blood and enlargement (dilation) of the veins. They most often occur on the left side. They may be associated with pain, atrophy, and infertility.

Varicoceles occur in approximately 15-20% of the male population, and in 40% of infertile males.

Reason for Procedure

The most common reason for this procedure is to treat varicoceles that are associated with infertility. Although varicoceles are not usually symptomatic, they may be associated with significant pain or testicular atrophy. These problems can be treated with surgery.

Description

The procedure is usually performed in an outpatient setting using general, regional, or local anesthetic; however, many individuals prefer general anesthetic for comfort.

Approaches used are transinguinal, retroperitoneal, infrainguinal. The preferred approach is the transinguinal approach and involves an incision in the groin and ligation of the abnormal veins using optical magnification to correctly identify all contributory veins and the testicular arteries. The spermatic vein is cut and tied off (ligated). The retroperitoneal approach (where the incision is made through the abdomen) and the infrainguinal approach (where the incision is made through the base of the scrotum) are generally reserved for individuals who have already had an attempted varicocele or hernia repair and may have considerable scarring in the groin.

Prognosis

Ligation of spermatic vein for varicocele is an effective treatment for male subfertility. Following this procedure, approximately 66-70% of individuals have improved bulk semen parameters, and 40-60% of previously infertile males may establish a pregnancy. The first improvements in semen analysis are usually apparent 3 to 4 months after the procedure. The procedure is also effective in relieving pain and reducing testicular atrophy.

Specialists

- Urologist

Work Restrictions / Accommodations

Strenuous lifting and vigorous activity should be limited immediately following the procedure.

Comorbid Conditions

Comorbid conditions that may influence length of disability include obesity and chronic illnesses such as diabetes.

Procedure Complications

Postoperative complications that require prompt medical attention include wound infection indicated by fever and/or swelling, redness, pain, and draining at the incision site; and collection of blood at the incision site (hematoma). Other less serious complications may include bruising, discoloration, sensation of hardness, redness, and tenderness around the incision site; sore throat, headache; nausea; constipation; and general body ache as a result of the anesthetic and surgical procedure. Approximately 2-5% of individuals develop increased fluid around the testicle (hydrocele). Rare complications include injury to the testicle or vas deferens, which could lead to impaired fertility. The recurrence rate for varicoceles may be as high as 10%.

Factors Influencing Duration

Factors influencing length of disability include type of anesthesia used and the presence of complications.

Length of Disability

Duration in Days

Job Classification	Minimum	Optimum	Maximum
Sedentary work	7	9	14
Light work	7	9	14
Medium work	7	14	21
Heavy work	7	14	21
Very Heavy work	7	21	28

References

Kim, Edward. *Varicocele*. University of Tennessee Medical Center. 05 Dec 2000. 17 Jan 2001 <http://www.emedicine.com/>.

Varicocele Removal (Varicocelectomy). healthgate.com. 23 Feb 2000. 18 Jan 2001 <http://www.healthgate.com/choice/uic/cons/mdx-books/sym/surg166.shtml>.

Lipoma

Other names / synonyms: Adipoma, Adipose Tumor
214, 214.0, 214.1, 214.2, 214.3, 214.4, 214.8, 214.9, M8850/0

Definition

A lipoma is a noncancerous (benign) tumor composed of fat cells.

Lipomas may occur virtually anywhere there are fat cells, including the internal organs, but appear most often beneath the skin on the trunk, neck, back, thighs, and arms. They may occur singly or in groups.

The tendency to develop lipomas is probably inherited. The growth may also be triggered by a minor injury. Certain disorders cause multiple lipomas to develop, including diffuse congenital lipomatosis, benign symmetric lipomatosis, and familial multiple lipomatosis.

Lipomas usually occur in early adulthood in both sexes, but are more common in women.

Diagnosis

History: Most individuals report a lump under the skin that may have been present for several years; they increase in size very gradually. They may either develop initially, or grow larger when an individual gains weight; they do not, however, generally decrease in size with weight loss. They do not usually cause any discomfort.

Physical exam: Most lipomas are dome-shaped and a few centimeters in diameter. They can be felt under the skin as a smooth, rubbery growth. The skin above the lipoma is normal in appearance and can be moved back and forth over the nodule.

Tests: Usually no tests are required. If the individual's history or physical examination suggests the possibility of a malignant liposarcoma, microscopic examination of lipoma cells extracted via fine-needle aspiration (biopsy), and CT scans are indicated.

Treatment

Lipomas generally require no treatment unless they are large, painful, in an inconvenient spot, and/or unsightly. They may be removed by surgical excision or liposuction.

Prognosis

Recovery from removal of lipomas is generally uneventful. No fatalities have been reported with subcutaneous lipomas.

Differential Diagnosis

Conditions with similar symptoms may include liposarcoma or other malignant tumor, angiolipomas, sebaceous cyst, and hibernomas.

Specialists

- Dermatologist
- General Surgeon
- Internist
- Pathologist
- Plastic Surgeon

Work Restrictions / Accommodations

For subcutaneous lipomas, few work restrictions or accommodations are required. If the job involves significant exposure to dirt, and if the individual has had the lipoma surgically removed, temporary reassignment may be necessary in order to keep the area clean postoperatively. Lipomas in or near internal organs will require major surgery for removal; this may necessitate an extended work leave for the employee, the length of which will be dependent upon whether or not the job is strenuous in nature.

Comorbid Conditions

Obesity is a comorbid condition for lipomas.

Complications

Lipomas under the skin (subcutaneous) rarely cause complications, but large nodules may interfere with muscle function. If they develop in the bowel, lipomas can cause potentially serious obstructions.

Factors Influencing Duration

Factors include the type and location of the lipoma and the specifics of its removal. The length of disability may be affected by job requirements, especially the ability to keep the surgical area clean postoperatively. For internal lipomas requiring major surgery, length of disability will depend on how extensive the surgery was, whether any complications developed, and whether or not the job is strenuous.

Length of Disability

Duration depends on size and location of lipoma.

Surgical treatment.

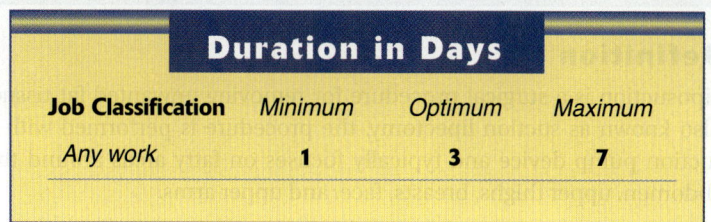

Duration in Days

Job Classification	Minimum	Optimum	Maximum
Any work	1	3	7

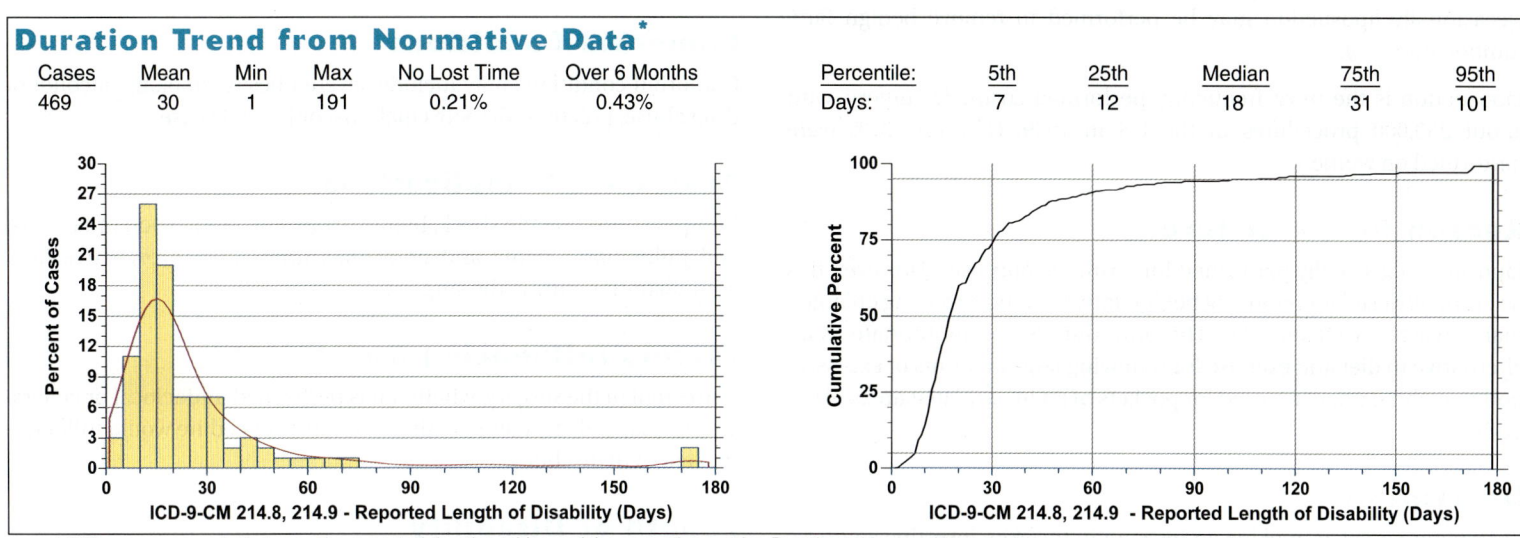

* Differences may exist between the expected duration tables and the normative graphs. Duration tables provide expected recovery periods based on the type of work performed by the individual. The normative graphs reflect the actual observed experience of many individuals across the spectrum of physical conditions, in a variety of industries, and with varying levels of case management.

Failure to Recover

If an individual fails to recover within the maximum duration expectancy period, the reader may wish to reference the following questions to assist in better understanding the specifics of an individual's medical case.

Regarding diagnosis:

- Does the individual have a family history of lipomas?
- Has the individual recently gained weight?
- Were conditions with similar symptoms, such as liposarcoma or other malignant tumor, angiolipomas, and hibernomas, ruled out?

Regarding treatment:

- Was it necessary to remove the lipoma(s)?

Regarding prognosis:

- Is the individual obese?
- Is the individual on a weight reduction program?
- Were the lipomas located in the bowel or other regions that necessitated major surgery?
- Did the individual have any complications?

References

Beers, Mark H., and Robert Berkow. The Merck Manual of Diagnosis and Therapy. Whitehouse Station, NJ: Merck & Co., Inc, 1999.

Lipomas. Healthgate.com. 23 Feb 2000. 1 Jan 2001 <http://www.healthgate.com/sym/sym281.shtml>.

Liposuction

Other names / synonyms: Reduction of Adipose Tissue, Suction Lipectomy, Tumescent Liposuction

86.83

Definition

Liposuction is a surgical procedure for removing unwanted fat tissue. Also known as suction lipectomy, the procedure is performed with a suction pump device and typically focuses on fatty areas around the abdomen, upper thighs, breasts, face, and upper arms.

Liposuction is generally performed for cosmetic regions, to remove specific areas of excess fat that remain despite diet and/or exercise. Occasionally liposuction may be performed to remove benign fatty tumors (lipomas).

Liposuction is the most frequently performed cosmetic surgery, with about 230,000 procedures in the US in 1999. Of these, 87% were performed on women.

Reason for Procedure

Liposuction is usually performed for cosmetic purposes. However, it is occasionally used for removing benign fatty tumors or treating enlarged male breasts (gynecomastia). The procedure is not appropriate as an alternative to diet and exercise for removing large amounts of excessive body weight. Rather, it is used for pockets of fat in particular areas of the body.

Description

Liposuction involves making an incision in the skin, inserting a narrow tube (cannula), and applying suction to remove fat. The most common method involves injecting a medicated solution before the fat is removed. The fluid is a saline solution with a local anesthetic and a vasoconstrictive drug to control bleeding. A newer technique involves a cannula that emits ultrasonic energy to liquify the fat. Depending on the technique used and the size of the area involved, the procedure may be done under local or general anesthetic, and in a hospital or outpatient setting.

Prognosis

In most cases, recovery is uneventful and the procedure results in an improved appearance. However, complications are possible, the most serious being shock from fluid loss, and pulmonary thromboembolism. The mortality rate is approximately one in five thousand.

Specialists

- Dermatologist
- Plastic Surgeon

Work Restrictions / Accommodations

Individuals whose work is physically demanding may benefit from more sedentary responsibilities during the first month after surgery.

Comorbid Conditions

Comorbid conditions may include severe obesity, smoking, alcohol or drug abuse, phlebitis, diabetes mellitus, or heart disease.

Procedure Complications

Complications include shock, hemorrhage, infection, blood or fat clots, and pulmonary edema and/or cardiac arrest due to excessive fluid administration during the surgery.

Factors Influencing Duration

The extent of the surgery, whether it is performed under local or general anesthesia, and any complications from the procedure would influence the length of disability.

Length of Disability

If the job is sedentary, the individual may be able to resume his or her regular duties within a few days. If the job is particularly strenuous, temporary reassignment may be necessary. Location and size of area involved may influence disability duration.

Duration in Days

Job Classification	Minimum	Optimum	Maximum
Any work	2	3	7

References

Gingrass, M.K. "Lipoplasty Complications and Their Prevention." Clinical Plastic Surgery 26 3 (1999): 341-354.

1999 Gender Distribution: Cosmetic Procedures National Clearinghouse of Plastic Surgery Statistics. American Society of Plastic Surgeons. 01 Jan 2000. 3 Feb 2001 <http://www.plasticsurgery.org/mediactr/99gender.htm>.

Lithotomy

Other names / synonyms: Open Lithotomy, Ureterolithotomy

55.01, 56.2, 57.19

Definition

Lithotomy is a surgical procedure in which a kidney stone (renal calculus) is removed from the urinary tract, which includes the kidney, the bladder, and the tube connecting the kidney and bladder (ureter).

Kidney stones are rock-like masses created when crystalline substances, such as calcium, are not excreted in the urine but, instead, build up along the wall of the kidney. Tiny stones can be washed out of the urinary tract without symptoms, but larger stones cause pain or inflammation as they pass through the kidneys, ureters, bladder, or urethra. Rarely, stones may be caused by infection (struvite stones), uric acid, or the amino acid, cystine.

Kidney stones are the third most frequent urinary tract disorders, affecting approximately 10% of Americans. Twice as many males as females, and 3 times as many whites as blacks are diagnosed with kidney stones. Open lithotomy is required in about 2% of those treated for kidney stones. Newer, noninvasive or less invasive procedures such as transurethral removal of the obstruction, shock wave lithotripsy, or percutaneous lithotomy are more commonly used. An advantage of lithotomy is that the surgeon is able to remove the stone fragments directly instead of relying on their natural passage from the kidney.

Reason for Procedure

Lithotomy is an option for cases of kidney stones where other approaches have failed or are contraindicated, the individual is very obese, the stone does not pass after a reasonable period of time and causes constant pain, the stone is too large to pass on its own or is caught in a difficult place, the stone has remained in the ureter for more than 4 weeks, the stone blocks the flow of urine, the stone causes ongoing urinary tract infection, the stone damages kidney tissue or causes constant bleeding, or the stone has grown larger (as seen on follow-up x-ray studies). The criteria is the same, whether the stone is located in the kidney or the ureter.

Lithotomy is the preferred approach for kidney transplant patients when there are structural abnormalities in the kidney or surrounding area, for drug-resistant cystine stones, which are usually resistant to shock wave therapy, or for complicated conditions involving stones that branch out within the body of the kidney (staghorn calculi).

Description

During an open lithotomy, an incision is made through the skin in the area between the back and side, or flank, and under the lowest rib. A small incision is then made in the kidney, ureter, or bladder, and an instrument called a nephroscope is used to locate and remove the stone. For large stones, an energy probe such as an ultrasonic device, a pneumatic drill-like device, or a special device (holmium laser lithotriptor) may be needed to break the stone into small pieces before removal. After removal, a small plastic or latex tube called a nephrostomy tube is inserted to allow drainage of urine while the area heals. The tissues under the skin are closed with large absorbable sutures, and the skin is closed with sutures or metal clips (staples) that are removed about 1 week after surgery.

Prognosis

Success rates for lithotomy have been reported to be about 98% for kidney stones and 88% for ureteral stones. There is a recurrence rate of new stone formation, even after successful stone removal or natural passing of a stone, in approximately 50% of cases.

Specialists

- Nephrologist
- Urologist

Work Restrictions / Accommodations

There are no specific accommodations required for individuals with a normal recovery.

Comorbid Conditions

Obesity, history of kidney transplant, or other chronic illness might impact ability to recover.

Procedure Complications

Complication rates, which are about 3%, include the usual anesthesia-related complications of allergic or abnormal response to anesthesia drugs or processes. Other complications include scarring, which usually does not impair kidney function, excessive bleeding after surgery, surgical site infection, imbalances in the fluid used to irrigate the area between the skin and kidney or ureter, collapsed lung, and injuries to areas outside the kidney but within the operative area, such as the abdomen or chest. A recent study reports that the holmium laser produces cyanide as a by-product of uric acid stone fragmentation, but no poisoning has been reported in any individual after this procedure.

Factors Influencing Duration

Surgical complications, such as antibiotic-resistant infections, may affect length of recovery, but usually do not lead to permanent disability.

Length of Disability

Percutaneous.

Duration in Days

Job Classification	Minimum	Optimum	Maximum
Sedentary work	1	2	7
Light work	1	2	7
Medium work	1	2	7
Heavy work	1	2	7
Very Heavy work	1	2	7

Bladder, open.

Duration in Days

Job Classification	Minimum	Optimum	Maximum
Sedentary work	7	14	21
Light work	14	17	21
Medium work	21	25	28
Heavy work	28	35	42
Very Heavy work	28	35	42

Open.

Duration in Days

Job Classification	Minimum	Optimum	Maximum
Sedentary work	14	21	28
Light work	14	21	28
Medium work	21	28	42
Heavy work	28	35	42
Very Heavy work	28	35	42

References

Kidney Stone Removal. HealthGate.com. 23 Feb 2000. 19 Jan 2001 <http://www.healthgate.com/sym/caps92.shtml>.

Munch, Larry C. "Renal Calculi." Conn's Current Therapy. Rakel, Robert E., ed. Philadelphia: W.B. Saunders Company, 2000. 712-715.

Lithotomy, Percutaneous

Other names / synonyms: Percutaneous Kidney Stone Surgery, Percutaneous Nephrolithotomy

55.03

Definition

Percutaneous lithotomy is a surgical procedure where a kidney stone (renal calculus) is removed from the urinary tract.

The urinary tract consists of the kidneys, the tubes connecting each kidney to the bladder (ureter), the bladder, and the tube leading from the bladder to the outside (urethra). Instead of cutting the kidney open (open lithotomy), percutaneous lithotomy uses a tiny, lighted microscope (endoscope) to examine the inside of an organ.

Kidney stones are rock-like masses created when crystalline substances such as calcium, are not excreted in the urine but instead build up along the wall of the kidney. Tiny stones can be washed out of the urinary tract without symptoms but larger stones cause pain or inflammation as they pass through the kidneys, ureters, bladder, or urethra. Stones are rarely caused by infection (struvite stones), uric acid, or the amino acid cystine.

Kidney stones are the third most frequent urinary tract disorders and affect approximately 10% of Americans. Twice as many males as females and three times as many whites as blacks are diagnosed with kidney stones.

Reason for Procedure

Percutaneous lithotomy is performed to remove kidney stones from the urinary tract and is done when the stone is very large or associated with an obstruction in the urinary tract. It is also performed when ultrasound waves are ineffective in breaking up the stone and allowing it to be washed out of the urinary tract (shock wave lithotripsy). Sometimes shock wave lithotripsy and percutaneous lithotomy are used together to treat large stones.

Description

A common approach to percutaneous lithotomy is to first locate the stone and then extract it. During the location procedure, the individual lies face down on a special table that allows radiology to locate the stone. Either local anesthesia or intravenous sedation may be used at this time.

Once the location of the stone is determined, a needle is placed through a tiny incision in the skin into the kidney or ureter and a small tube (catheter) inserted at the location of the stone. The individual is then anesthetized and small dilators (metal rods of various diameters) are used to gradually and progressively dilate the kidney opening or ureter. The stones are then removed by flushing fluid through the kidney or ureter. Large stones may first be fragmented using ultrasound waves prior to removal. A small rubber or plastic catheter is left in the ureter for several days to drain the urine and allow internal incisions to heal over them.

Prognosis

Success rates vary from 85-99% depending on the size and number of stones, comorbid conditions, and complications. Outcome for an uncomplicated kidney stone removal is usually a full recovery although some individuals may continue to develop stones if dietary and other modifications are not made. Solitary stones have almost a 100% success rate while stones in the body of the kidney (staghorn calculi) or the presence of multiple stones may recur (10% or cases).

Specialists

- Nephrologist
- Radiologist
- Urologist

Work Restrictions / Accommodations

The normal postsurgical no heavy lifting restriction may be in effect for a few weeks but, in general, there are no specific accommodations required for individuals with a normal recovery.

Comorbid Conditions

Anatomic abnormalities such as enlarged colon or the absence of the spleen following splenectomy, urinary tract infection, an uncontrolled bleeding condition, or severe obesity may influence length of disability.

Procedure Complications

Complications of this procedure may include unintentional puncture of the pleural cavity that may lead to a collapsed lung or damage to the colon or other organ near the kidney. Excessive bleeding or leakage of urine into the abdominal cavity may also occur.

Factors Influencing Duration

The underlying condition for which the procedure was performed or postsurgery complications may add to length of disability.

Length of Disability

Duration in Days

Job Classification	Minimum	Optimum	Maximum
Any work	1	2	7

References

Segura, Joseph W. "Percutaneous Lithotomy." <u>Glenn's Urologic Surgery</u>, 5th ed. Graham, Sam D. Jr., ed. Philadelphia: Lippincott-Raven Publishers, 1998. 947-955.

Lithotripsy, Extracorporeal Shock Wave

Other names / synonyms: Extracorporeal Shock Wave Lithotripsy
98.5, 98.51, 98.52, 98.59

Definition

Extracorporeal shock-wave lithotripsy (ESWL) is a noninvasive procedure that breaks apart kidney stones (renal calculi) or gallstones with shock waves generated outside of the body. The procedure requires no incisions, catheters, or special scopes. For kidney stones, ESWL shatters the calculi into particles small enough to be passed in the urine. Although ESWL is a noninvasive procedure, regional or general anesthesia is administered because the shock waves cause some pain when they enter the body.

The focused shock waves pass through fluids and tissues and converge on the stone, causing it to fragment. The entire procedure usually involves 300 to 2500 shock waves, and takes no longer than 1-2 hours. Lithotripsy permits a shorter hospitalization, and allows the individual to return to normal life activities without delay.

Reason for Procedure

ESWL is performed as a noninvasive alternative to surgery for the removal of kidney stones or gallstones. The procedure is especially useful for individuals that do not want to undergo traditional surgery, which is an invasive procedure and involves a longer period of recovery.

Lithotripsy is not appropriate for every individual with kidney stones. The individual's body structure may prohibit proper positioning in the tank of water in which the individual must be submerged. Other contraindications include calcium deposits in the arteries, obstruction to urine flow, which is depended upon to flush out the fragments, and exaggerated spinal curvature, which interferes with visualization of the stones upon x-ray.

Description

In most cases, individuals are admitted to the hospital the morning of treatment. An anesthetic will be administered and is based on the individual's choice and recommendation of an anesthesiologist. Most common are epidural or spinal anesthetics in which a small tube is placed in or near the spinal canal to give anesthetic directly to the nerves leading to the kidney or bladder and surrounding tissue. General anesthesia is also available, but rarely used. Sedatives are routinely given intravenously during the procedure to make the individual more comfortable.

The anesthetized individual is placed on a support platform, which is suspended overhead. The individual is secured with straps to prevent movement. A catheter is sometimes placed into the individual's urinary bladder after he or she has been anesthetized.

The individual is then positioned in the water bath with the head and shoulders out of the water, so that the stones are positioned at the highest energy point of the shock waves. Positioning is assisted with the use of 2 x-ray monitors. When positioning is complete, shock wave treatment is initiated. Approximately 300-2500 shock waves from the electrode are utilized. The urologist conducting the treatment monitors stone fragmentation using instruments called fluoroscopes. The individual is occasionally repositioned using fluoroscopes and the hydraulic suspension system.

The radiation received from the x-ray monitors is well below minimum toleration limits, and females are routinely checked for pregnancy.

Upon completion of treatment, the individual is removed from the water bath and sent to the recovery room until the anesthetic has worn off. Additional procedures might be done before or after the treatment, such as telescopic examination of the bladder (cystoscopy).

A follow-up examination is required after the procedure is completed to determine if the individual is pain-free and asymptomatic. Follow-up is usually recommended within 3-4 weeks of the ESWL procedure.

Prognosis

Stone pulverization occurs in about 99% of individuals selected for treatment. Approximately 85-90% become stone free. Approximately 10-15% of individuals have some residual stone fragments on x-rays taken 3 months after treatment. In most cases, the residual stones cause no symptoms.

Specialists

- Gastroenterologist
- General Surgeon
- Urologist

Work Restrictions / Accommodations

There are no work restrictions after recovery and return to work. However, the individual must attend one follow-up examination after the procedure.

Comorbid Conditions

Pregnancy, obesity, or the presence of a large number of stones may lengthen disability.

Procedure Complications

Blood-tinged urine is to be expected for a few days. Stone particles typically begin to pass during treatment and may continue to pass intermittently for several weeks. Most individuals experience very little discomfort. Pain is usually treated with appropriate painkilling medications.

Factors Influencing Duration

The length of disability depends on the success of the procedure and the presence of any complications. The procedure is normally done on an outpatient basis. If kidney or gallstones are recurrent, this is likely to influence length of disability.

Length of Disability

Duration depends on site (kidney, ureter, gallbladder, etc.) and on job requirements.

Duration in Days

Job Classification	Minimum	Optimum	Maximum
Any work	1	2	7

References

Extracorporeal Shock-Wave Lithotripsy (ESWL). Miller-Keane Medical Dictionary, 2000. 01 Dec 2000. 17 Jan 2001 <http://my.webmd.com/content/asset/miller_keane_19298>.

Schwartz, Seymour, MD. Principles of Surgery. New York: McGraw-Hill, 1999.

1296 The Medical Disability Advisor—Fourth Edition

Liver Biopsy

Other names / synonyms: Needle Aspiration Liver Biopsy, Percutaneous Liver Biopsy

50.11, 50.12

Definition

Liver biopsy is a diagnostic procedure in which a small sample of tissue is removed from the liver for laboratory examination. Samples are most often obtained from 3 different sites, since liver diseases may be patchy and not widespread (diffuse). These sites vary and are chosen based on the suspected sites of disease. Laboratory tests on the samples include culture for infectious agents, chemical analysis, and microscopic analysis.

Liver biopsy is the most definitive method of diagnosing liver diseases (cirrhosis and hepatitis). Liver biopsies are also helpful in the evaluation of acute hepatitis of unexplained cause, unexplained jaundice, unexplained hepatomegaly, unexplained abnormal liver chemistry, and in follow-up of individuals receiving long-term methotrexate therapy for rheumatoid arthritis or psoriatic arthritis.

Reason for Procedure

Liver biopsies are performed to diagnose or assess liver diseases (cirrhosis and different types of hepatitis). Biopsies can help to diagnose tumors or lymphomas (tumors of lymphatic tissue) that can spread throughout the body, affecting the liver as well as many other organs. Liver biopsies assist in determining the cause of fevers of unknown origin, and can determine if there are complications from liver transplant operations. In addition, a liver biopsy can provide important information on the effectiveness of treatment for liver diseases such as chronic active hepatitis.

Description

Two different liver biopsy techniques are commonly used: blind percutaneous technique and suction technique. Both techniques are usually done in the individual's hospital room. Prior to surgery, ultrasonography of the liver is sometimes done to outline the position and boundaries of the liver. Ultrasonography is also used during the procedure in some cases to guide the biopsy in the proper position.

The individual is placed lying on the back (supine position). The skin is cleaned with an antiseptic solution, then the biopsy site is draped with a sterile towel. The skin and deeper structures are then anesthetized with local anesthetic injection. A small skin incision is made. In the blind percutaneous procedure, the needle is inserted through the skin incision, punctures the liver, and is withdrawn. In the suction technique, the needle is inserted through the skin incision through a plastic tube (cannula), and suction is applied through the needle as it punctures the liver (allowing for a quicker biopsy). With both techniques, tissue is often taken from up to 3 different sites based on suspected area of pathology. When the biopsy is completed, the area is bandaged and the individual is kept on bed rest for 3 hours.

Prognosis

The procedure is successful in providing liver tissue specimens for examination. The vast majority of individuals undergoing liver biopsy recover fully from the procedure without complications. The incidence of major complications is less than three percent.

Specialists

- Gastroenterologist
- General Surgeon

Work Restrictions / Accommodations

Work restrictions or special accommodations are not usually associated with a liver biopsy procedure.

Comorbid Conditions

Comorbid conditions include obesity, heart diseases, and all types of liver diseases.

Procedure Complications

Complications of liver biopsy include pain at site of entry, hemorrhage, bile peritonitis, pneumothorax, severe apprehension, shock, bacteremia, sepsis, bile embolism, penetration of abdominal viscera, arteriovenous fistula, fractured needles, and death (resulting from hemorrhage or bile peritonitis).

Factors Influencing Duration

Length of disability may be influenced by the type of biopsy procedure performed, the presence of an underlying liver disease, or the presence of complications.

Length of Disability

Duration depends on underlying condition and complications.

Laparoscopic or percutaneous (needle).

Duration in Days

Job Classification	Minimum	Optimum	Maximum
Any work	1	2	3

References

Schiff, Eugene R., and Leon Schiff. "Needle Biopsy of the Liver." Diseases of the Liver, 7th ed. Schiff, Leon, and Eugene R. Schiff, eds. Philadelphia: Lippincott, 1993. 216-225.

Liver Disease
573.0, 573.3, 573.4, 573.8, 573.9

Definition
Liver disease refers to many conditions that affect the ability of the liver to function.

The principle diseases are scarring of the liver cells (cirrhosis) and inflammatory damage to liver cells (hepatitis). Cirrhosis is a chronic liver disease characterized by the progressive and irreversible destruction of liver tissue as a result of viral infection; chronic exposure to alcohol, drugs, or toxic substances; or in association with other diseases. As liver cells die, they are replaced with scar tissue. The overall incidence of cirrhosis in the US is 360 per 100,000 population, or approximately 900,000 total individuals. At least 30,000 people die from cirrhosis annually in the US. Most cases result from alcoholism, and the majority of cases involve middle-aged to elderly men. It occurs in about 20% of heavy drinkers.

Hepatitis refers to inflammatory disease of liver cells resulting from exposure to certain chemicals or from exposure to virus infections (hepatitis A, B, C, D, and E). Hepatitis A is an acute inflammation occurring soon after exposure, while hepatitis B, C, D, and E are more likely to be chronic, or lasting longer than 6 months. Hepatitis A is foodborne or waterborne, while the others are spread through exchange of body fluids (blood, semen).

Many infections of the liver itself can also occur, including those from viruses, fungi, bacteria, amoebae, protozoa, and worms (helminths). Numerous types of tumors can begin in the liver (primary tumors), including many cancerous tumors (malignant tumors). Cancer from other parts of the body (metastatic cancer) may spread to the liver. Rare, hereditary diseases of the biochemical functions of the liver (metabolic diseases) can occur, especially Wilson's disease (a disorder of copper metabolism), and alpha anti-trypsin deficiency (a disorder of protein metabolism). Other metabolic disorders of the whole body can affect the liver. These include sarcoidosis, hemochromatosis, cystic fibrosis, and amyloidosis. Two notable liver (hepatic) complications of pregnancy are "acute fatty liver of pregnancy" and "HELLP Syndrome" (Hemolysis, Elevated Liver enzymes, Low Platelets). Acute fatty liver of pregnancy affects 1 in 6,000 to 1 in 13,000 women, 14% of whom are carrying twin fetuses. The HELLP Syndrome affects older mothers who have had previous children (multipara) and in whom the pregnancy complications of eclampsia or preeclampsia are present.

Diagnosis
History: Family history, occupational and environmental exposures, contact with jaundiced individuals, recent vaccinations, drugs, medical treatment, episodes of jaundice, recent illness, drug use, transfusions, and tattooing may be reported. The individual's symptoms may include abdominal pain, yellowing of the skin (jaundice), fatigue, weakness, fever and chills, excessive alcohol use, weight loss, dark urine, itching, loss of appetite, and menstrual problems.

Physical exam: The exam may reveal pale skin; muscle loss; yellowing of the skin or white of the eye (scleral icterus); enlargement of the liver, spleen, and/or salivary gland behind the ear (parotid gland); decreased testicular size; bruising; redness of the palms (palmar erythema); clubbing of the fingers; and darkening of the skin (increase in pigmentation). Tenderness may be noted when touching (palpation) the edge of the liver (liver tip) through the abdominal skin, and fluid in the abdominal cavity (ascites) may be evident.

Tests: Blood tests may include measurement of key liver enzymes (alkaline phosphatase, AST, ALT, GGT, LDH), liver protein (bilirubin, albumin, fibrinogen), immunoglobulin levels, ammonia, clotting factors, blood lipids, total blood count, and hematocrit. In addition, MRI, diagnostic ultrasound, CT scan, or other similar methods of visualization may be performed. A liver biopsy, in which a small piece of liver tissue is removed and analyzed microscopically for evidence of inflammation, cirrhosis, and infection, may also be performed.

Treatment
The specific course of treatment recommended is dependent upon the type and underlying cause of the liver disease. In other words, a more specific diagnosis must be made. General treatment strategies for liver conditions may include dietary and vitamin supplementation, the administration of anti-inflammatory drugs, and in some severe cases, liver transplantation. Avoidance of alcohol and of chemicals that are toxic to the liver or that are metabolized by the liver is important. Antibiotic therapy is necessary for abscesses and infection, while anticancer chemotherapy may be useful for some tumors. Surgical resection of tumors is sometimes necessary.

Prognosis
The outcome is dependent upon the specific condition, the underlying cause and severity of the disease, and the presence or absence of complications. Outcomes may range from complete recovery to cirrhosis, cancer, liver and renal failure, and death.

Differential Diagnosis
Differential diagnoses include biliary disease, tumor, pancreatic cancer, primary hemochromatosis, metastatic cancer, abscesses, peritonitis, cystic fibrosis, protoporphyria, amyloidosis, and sarcoidosis.

Specialists
- Gastroenterologist
- Infectious Disease Physician
- Internist

Work Restrictions / Accommodations
Extended work leave, frequent rest periods, transfer to sedentary duties, or leave of absence may be needed and will require consideration on an individual, case-by-case basis. Individuals with hepatitis B should avoid jobs involving the possibility of blood contact, as this disease is contagious from blood exposure.

> **Complementary and Alternative Therapies**
>
> Content is intended for awareness only. Treatments may or may not be effective. Scientific evidence may be lacking and some substances have potentially toxic effects. Dr. Presley Reed and the editors do not endorse the use of these therapies in the absence of consultation with a licensed medical professional.
>
> Herb therapy – Silybum marianum (milk thistle) and Picrorrhiza kurroa may exert antioxidative, anti lipid peroxidative, antifibrotic, anti-inflammatory, immunomodulating, and liver regenerating effects.

Comorbid Conditions

Alcoholism or pancreatic cancer may lengthen disability.

Complications

Complications of liver disease are dependent upon the specific condition, underlying cause, and severity of the disease. Complications may include infection, fluid retention in the abdomen (ascites), blood flow impairment through the portal vein that serves the liver (portal hypertension), liver failure, bleeding, inflammation of the pancreas (pancreatitis), and neurologic damage (hepatic encephalopathy).

Factors Influencing Duration

Factors that would influence the length of disability include continued alcohol consumption, the individual's gender, the development of complications, compliance with treatment, the age and general health of the individual, and the severity of the disease or condition upon initial diagnosis.

Length of Disability

Vague diagnosis. A more specific diagnosis is required to determine specific disability duration.

Failure to Recover

If an individual fails to recover within the maximum duration expectancy period, the reader may wish to reference the following questions to assist in better understanding the specifics of an individual's medical case.

Regarding diagnosis:

- Does individual have a history of chronic exposure to alcohol and/or drugs? Occupational or environmental contact with toxic substances?
- Has individual received a recent blood transfusion?
- Has individual had a recent tattoo applied?
- Is there a history of viral infection, particularly of hepatitis A, B, C, D, or E? Does individual have a history of infections, metabolic disorders, or cancer that can affect the liver directly?
- Does individual report abdominal pain, yellowing of the skin (jaundice), fatigue, weakness, and/or fever and chills?
- Is there weight loss, dark urine, itching, loss of appetite, or menstrual problems?
- Were blood tests done to measure liver enzymes (alkaline phosphatase, AST, ALT, GGT, LDH) and proteins (bilirubin, albumin, fibrinogen)?
- Were immunoglobulin levels, ammonia, clotting factors, and blood lipids measured? Were MRI, ultrasound, or CT required? Was a tissue sample (biopsy) of the liver taken to identify inflammation, cirrhosis, and infection?
- Was a diagnosis of liver disease confirmed?

Regarding treatment:

- What type of liver disease does individual have and what is the underlying cause? How is the underlying cause being treated?
- Did general treatment include dietary and vitamin supplementation and the administration of anti-inflammatory drugs?
- Does individual understand the important of avoidance of alcohol and chemicals that are toxic to the liver?
- Would individual benefit from chemical dependency counseling?
- If abscesses and infection were present, were organism-specific antibiotics given?
- Was individual compliant with the medication regimen?
- Was surgical removal (resection) of a tumor required? If so, was the tumor removed completely?

Regarding prognosis:

- What type of liver disease does individual have?
- How severely was the liver damaged?
- Is the underlying cause under control? If not, what other treatment options are available?
- Has individual developed complications of liver disease such as infection, fluid retention in the abdomen (ascites), blood flow impairment through the portal vein that serves the liver (portal hypertension), liver failure, bleeding, inflammation of the pancreas (pancreatitis), or neurological damage (hepatic encephalopathy)?
- How will the complications be treated and what is expected outcome with treatment?

References

Luper, S. "A Review of Plants Used in the Treatment of Liver Disease: Part 1." Alternative Medicine Review 3 6 (1998): 410-421.

Weisiger, Richard A. "Laboratory Tests in Liver Disease." Cecil Textbook of Medicine, 20th ed, vol 1. Bennett, J. Claude, and Fred Plum Philadelphia: Williams & Wilkins, 1996. 759-762.

Loose Bodies, Knee

Other names / synonyms: Joint Mice

717.6, 718.1

Definition

Loose bodies are fragments of bone and/or cartilage that freely float in the joint space. Loose bodies may occur singly or in groups and typically affect only one joint.

Loose bodies may be considered either stable or unstable. Stable loose bodies are in a fixed position and are generally well tolerated by the individual. Unstable loose bodies are free to move about the joint and cause symptoms.

Loose bodies are classified into three types: fibrinous, cartilaginous, and osteocartilaginous. Fibrinous loose bodies result from bleeding within the joint or from the death of the tissue lining of joints (synovial membrane) associated with tuberculosis, osteoarthritis, and rheumatoid arthritis. Cartilaginous loose bodies are fragments of cartilage and are caused by injury (trauma) to the joint and osteoarthritis. Osteocartilaginous loose bodies are fragments of cartilage and bone caused by fractures, bone and cartilage inflammation (osteochondritis dissecans), osteoarthritis, and benign tumors of the synovial membrane (synovial chondromatosis). Cartilage is nourished by the fluid within the joint (synovial fluid) so loose bodies often increase in size and become smoother over time.

Individuals at risk of developing loose bodies in the knee include those who participate in sports and with a degenerative joint disease (e.g., arthritis or osteochondritis dissecans). Loose bodies are common and equally affect men and women.

Diagnosis

History: The most common symptoms include knee pain and swelling with intermittent locking or catching of the joint. The locking disappears spontaneously only to recur. Individuals may report hearing a grating sound (crepitus) with joint movement. Individuals may report that the joint intermittently "gives way" or "goes out," causing them to fall. There may be a history of osteoarthritis or injury that is significant in making an accurate diagnosis.

Physical exam: The exam may reveal tenderness, soft tissue swelling, or a grating sound in the affected joint. The affected joint may be locked (unable to fully extend). There may be evidence of fluid build-up (effusion) in the joint. The loose bodies are rarely felt by touch (palpation). A history of degenerative or post-traumatic arthritis may be significant and indicate further testing. The interior of the joint can be examined directly by arthroscopy and if indicated arthroscopic surgery may be performed at the same time.

Tests: Larger loose bodies are typically calcified and, thus, easy to see with a plain film x-ray of the affected joint. Loose bodies that are small or contain little or no bone may not be visible with an x-ray and are typically diagnosed using either a CT or arthrography. MRI may be useful in determining whether associated bone changes have occurred. Ultrasound scans may be performed.

Treatment

For small loose bodies, treatment may be directed at relief of symptoms. If pain and swelling are present, analgesics or nonsteroidal anti-inflammatory medications may be prescribed. In general, any loose body that is causing symptoms should be removed.

Large loose bodies may require removal by use of an arthroscope (arthroscopy). Some bodies may not be retrievable due to their position in the joint space and an instrument (mechanical burr or resector) may be used to break the loose body apart. Once it is in small pieces, it can be easily reabsorbed through the body's normal means of elimination (enzyme degradation). Very large loose bodies and those located in the back of the knee need to be removed by open surgery (arthrotomy). Large osteocartilaginous loose bodies can be realigned (reduced) and secured using pins or screws. In some cases, such as synovial chondromatosis, part of the synovium may be removed (partial synovectomy).

Prognosis

This is a self-limited condition that can be successfully treated. The symptoms caused by small loose bodies can be effectively controlled by analgesics and anti-inflammatory medications however more aggressive treatment (surgery) may be necessary. Most individuals who undergo a surgical procedure (arthroscopy, arthrotomy, synovectomy, or loose body pulverization) to treat loose bodies recover with good early results. Individuals with loose bodies in the knee are predisposed to developing osteoarthritis in the affected joint.

Differential Diagnosis

Differential diagnoses include arthritis, synovitis, tumor, torn meniscus, or a bony growth (exostosis).

Specialists

- Orthopedic Surgeon
- Physical Therapist
- Radiologist

Rehabilitation

The goals of rehabilitation for loose bodies of the knee before or after surgical removal are very similar to other rehabilitation of other knee problems and surgeries.

Once pain and swelling is controlled, the knee does not lock, and the physician advocates beginning movement of the knee, the physical therapist begins range-of-motion exercises.

Muscles are then strengthened initially with isometric exercises, as these require that the muscles around the knee joint contract with no movement taking place at the joint. Strengthening is progressed to exercises with weighted resistance. Leg raises may be taught. Ankle weights may be used for resistance as the muscles strengthen. Individuals may perform hamstring curls

Resisted exercises and balance exercises may be added at this time. At this point, the individual is encouraged to walk and may be allowed to return to light work.

The individual's reinstatement to work is addressed in specific exercises prescribed by the physical therapist as these activities are now directed toward work requirements. Modifications may need to be made by the physical therapist for those individuals with arthritis or other joint irritations. If the joint resulted in torn cartilage (meniscus), it becomes important to minimize excessive forces on the joint until adequate muscle strength can protect the joint. Rehabilitation of the knee joint with loose bodies varies depending on whether surgery was required.

Work Restrictions / Accommodations

Prior to surgical treatment, the knee may suddenly give out causing the individual to fall. The individual may therefore need to work in an area away from dangerous machinery or other hazards. The individual may need crutches or a walking cane temporarily so work site rearrangement may be required. Standing, squatting, kneeling, crawling, and walking may need to be limited temporarily. Operating a motor vehicle or other machinery that requires use of the feet may be restricted temporarily.

Comorbid Conditions

Obesity and arthritis may influence the length of disability. If the loose body was formed by a traumatic event, other concurrent injuries (e.g., fractures and damage to ligaments or cartilage) may influence the length of disability.

Complications

Severe pain and swelling and potential damage to the surface of the joint (post-traumatic arthritis) or synovial lining of the joint cavity are possible complications. Long-term inflammation of the synovium (synovitis) can occur.

Factors Influencing Duration

Factors include the number of loose bodies, affected joint, and location of the loose body within the joint, underlying cause, type of treatment, and the individual's job requirements.

Length of Disability

Duration may be shorter for individuals with sedentary jobs.

Arthroscopic.

Duration in Days

Job Classification	Minimum	Optimum	Maximum
Sedentary work	14	21	21
Light work	21	35	42
Medium work	28	35	42
Heavy work	35	42	56
Very Heavy work	35	42	56

Failure to Recover

If an individual fails to recover within the maximum duration expectancy period, the reader may wish to reference the following questions to assist in better understanding the specifics of an individual's medical case.

Regarding diagnosis:

- Does individual have stable or unstable loose bodies in the knee?
- Is the individual active in sports?
- Is there a history of degenerative joint disease?
- Does the individual have a history of knee pain following exercise, episodes of the knee giving way, and/or recurrent knee effusion?
- Does the individual have crepitus?
- Has the individual received adequate testing to establish the diagnosis?
- Have conditions with similar symptoms been ruled out?

Regarding treatment:

- Was symptomatic treatment effective?
- Was it necessary to perform surgery?
- Has physical therapy been prescribed?

Regarding prognosis:

- How severe are symptoms? Are they incapacitating?
- Are any conditions present that could affect recovery?
- Has individual developed any complications?
- Can the individual perform normal activities of daily life?
- Is the individual involved in physical therapy?

References

Bentley, George. "Affections of the Knee Joint." Mercer's Orthopaedic Surgery. Duthie, Robert, and George Bentley, eds. London: Arnold, 1996. 1125-1192.

Malone, Terry R., Thomas McPoil, and Arthur J. Nitz. Orthopedic and Sports Physical Therapy. St. Louis: Mosby, 1997.

Low Back Pain

Other names / synonyms: Low Back Syndrome, Lumbago, Lumbosacral Pain

724.2

Definition

Low back pain is a symptom, not a specific disease. Low back pain is discomfort in the lumbosacral area of the back that may or may not radiate to the legs, hips, and buttocks. The pain may be due to a variety of causes, and as many as 90% of all individuals may never receive a clear diagnosis for the cause of the pain. A small percentage may have a serious disease unrelated to the back.

Although low back pain may be caused by medical conditions, such as infection or cancer, the vast majority of low back pain cases are attributed to mechanical or musculoskeletal conditions. These conditions include lumbosacral muscle and ligament sprains and strains; disorders of the intervertebral discs and associated joints, such as general degeneration (spondylosis) and arthritis, degeneration that narrows the space through which spinal nerves pass (spinal stenosis), and displacement (herniation of a disc); and disorders of the vertebral body, such as slippage (spondylolisthesis), fracture, or postural deformities, such as scoliosis. This section will focus on mechanical and musculoskeletal conditions that cause low back pain.

Low back pain ranks second only to upper respiratory infections as a cause of loss of work. The direct cost is estimated to be 30 billion dollars annually in the US.

In a British study of 1455 adults, one third reported no lifetime low back pain. Average lifetime prevalence was 59%. A 4% population incidence rate was reported. The likelihood of having had low back pain increased significantly with age.

Diagnosis

History: Individuals may complain of stiffness, local tenderness, generalized discomfort, and weakness of the lower back. Pain that radiates to the leg may indicate nerve involvement, or reflect refereed pain from myofascial, sacroiliac, or facet involvement.

Most episodes have no apparent cause. The history should focus on when and under what circumstances the pain began. Information should be gathered regarding a possible precipitating incident such as a fall or an episode of heavy lifting. Questions should be asked regarding the pain: Has it worsened? Are there any activities that aggravate or diminish it? Is it intermittent? Is it worse at a particular time of the day? Has the quality of the pain changed?

Perhaps one of the most important questions is whether this is the first episode of this particular type of pain. With over 80% of adults having experienced low back pain, a complaint that this episode of pain is different from prior episodes or more persistent might be cause for more extensive testing.

Physical exam: Individuals are examined in 3 positions: lying flat, sitting, and standing. The exam includes visual inspection for obvious asymmetry, deformities, or accentuated spinal curves. Posture, gait, and range of motion are evaluated. Neurological examination assesses reflexes, muscle strength, sensation, and gait. Palpation along the spine, muscles, and tendon insertions can reveal areas of localized tenderness. Examination of the circulation in the lower extremities is important to exclude vascular causes of leg pain.

Tests: In many cases, testing is not needed for simple low back pain. When testing is required, the type and amount is determined by the severity and chronicity of the pain and history of trauma or signs or symptoms (frequently called "red flags") suggesting the possibility of serious disease like spinal infection or tumor. To be diagnostic, test results must be closely correlated to symptoms.

Plain x-rays show most fractures and deformities (like scoliosis, spondylolisthesis) and may show more advanced spinal infections or tumors. Other than these conditions, the aging changes and/or anomalies visible on x-ray do not generally correlate with the individual's symptoms.

Bone scans, MRIs, and CT scans are used to rule out infection or tumor if musculoskeletal pain is not the obvious diagnosis. In general, in the absence of specific symptoms or signs to suggest fracture, infection, or tumor, no imaging studies or tests are indicated. If tumor or infection is suspected, blood and urine tests will generally be performed.

Provocative tests, such as discography or analgesic injections, are extremely controversial tests believe by proponents to help identify whether or not a specific disc is the source of pain. Neurological testing may include electromyography (EMG) and nerve conduction studies. Blood tests to rule out inflammation and infections may be required.

Treatment

Pain without an underlying diagnosis is treated conservatively with tolerable activity and reassurance. Simple analgesics may be appropriate. Muscle relaxants are frequently prescribed; however, their effectiveness is due to their sedative action. Use of light support corsets may help with the pain.

Spinal manipulation may decrease the pain, especially in the first 4-6 weeks from the pain onset.

Prognosis

Individuals suffering from uncomplicated back pain usually recover from the acute episode, though recurrence is common. Ninety percent of episodes resolve in a few weeks.

Differential Diagnosis

A variety of medical conditions can cause low back pain. Physical conditions include benign and malignant tumors; infection, such as osteomyelitis; inflammatory conditions, such as ankylosing spondylitis, rheumatoid arthritis, and fibromyalgia; vascular abnormalities, such as aortic aneurysm; visceral disease, such as kidney, pancreatic, or pelvic disease; and metabolic bone disease, such as osteoporosis.

Specialists

- Chiropractor
- Internist
- Neurologist
- Occupational Medicine Physician
- Orthopedic Surgeon
- Physiatrist
- Physical Therapist
- Primary Care Provider
- Rheumatologist
- Sports Medicine Physician

Rehabilitation

Physical therapy modalities may decrease pain. Aerobic activity, especially walking, should be encouraged as part of reassurance that normal activity is usually helpful for recovery from low back pain episodes.

A flexibility program may be initiated during physical therapy. The individual may be instructed in several McKenzie extension (half pushups) or, less frequently, Williams' flexion exercises (lying on the back and bringing knees to the chest). Education for proper lifting of heavy objects is important in the rehabilitation of the lumbar spine and to prepare the individual for returning to work.

Aerobic exercise is a popular form of treatment for low back rehabilitation with the basis for these exercise programs including the release of the body's own pain relievers (endorphins). Other activities that do not place excess stress on the lower back are walking short distances, using a stationary bike, and swimming. The exercises in a low back exercise program are designed to start slowly and to gradually build up speed and duration.

Spinal manipulation following the onset of low back pain may decrease the pain.

Return to work may be facilitated by "work conditioning" (specific exercises to improve strength, flexibility, and endurance required for the job in question), by the availability of modified work programs, and perhaps by a work site visit by a health professional who can evaluate the work site and job in question, looking for potential job modifications, alternative placement, and educating the supervisor and human resource manager about the individual's condition.

Work Restrictions / Accommodations

Heavy or unassisted lifting, repetitive rotation of the back, carrying or pushing heavy objects, overhead work, and prolonged sitting are to be avoided early on. Prolonged standing should be evaluated for aggravation of the pain. Rest periods are an important part of both treatment and prevention. Wearing a lumbosacral support for both treatment may be recommended by some healthcare providers for some individuals. Use of medication while working necessitates review of safety issues and drug testing policies.

Comorbid Conditions

Any condition that stresses the back may influence recovery. Obesity strains the back, as does a greater than one inch difference in leg lengths, and pregnancy. Congenital and developmental abnormalities, such as vertebral fusion, scoliosis, and spondylolisthesis may affect the back and duration of pain. Osteoporosis weakens the vertebrae, leaving them vulnerable to repeated fracture.

Complications

Low back pain due to simple muscle or ligament sprain or strain does not result in real medical complications. Lower back problems that involve the vertebral discs carry the risk of nerve root impingement. Five percent of episodes of acute back pain become chronic back pain with varying degrees of disability.

Factors Influencing Duration

Factors include occupation, age, and conditioning of the individual. Any conditions affecting the spine could prolong recovery. The individual's need and ability to obtain secondary gains from the pain could lengthen disability time. Psychological assessment is crucial in cases with prolonged disability and no obvious specific spinal disorder.

Length of Disability

Vague diagnosis for purposes of determining disability duration. Contact physician to obtain more specific information.

Nonspecific treatment.

Duration in Days

Job Classification	Minimum	Optimum	Maximum
Sedentary work	0	1	14
Light work	0	3	14
Medium work	1	14	56
Heavy work	3	28	84
Very Heavy work	3	42	84

Duration Trend from Normative Data*

Cases	Mean	Min	Max	No Lost Time	Over 6 Months		Percentile:	5th	25th	Median	75th	95th
31,1174	56	0	521	0.58%	1.94%		Days:	8	17	36	78	148

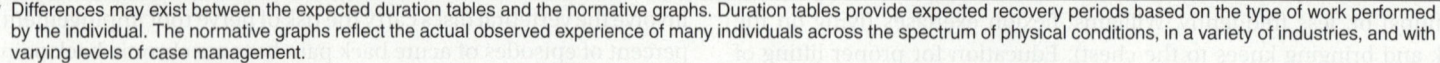

ICD-9-CM 724.2 - Reported Length of Disability (Days)

* Differences may exist between the expected duration tables and the normative graphs. Duration tables provide expected recovery periods based on the type of work performed by the individual. The normative graphs reflect the actual observed experience of many individuals across the spectrum of physical conditions, in a variety of industries, and with varying levels of case management.

Failure to Recover

If an individual fails to recover within the maximum duration expectancy period, the reader may wish to reference the following questions to assist in better understanding the specifics of an individual's medical case.

Regarding diagnosis:

- Have infection and cancer been ruled out in the individual?
- Does the individual's pain radiate to either leg?
- Did the individual have a fall or a near fall?
- Is this the individual's first episode of pain or is it recurrent?
- Was adequate testing done on the individual to establish the diagnosis?
- Has an MRI been obtained?
- Have conditions with similar symptoms been ruled out?
- Has a second opinion been obtained from an appropriate specialist?

Regarding treatment:

- How did the individual respond to conservative treatment?
- Was it necessary for the individual to have surgery?

Regarding prognosis:

- Is the individual actively participating in physical therapy and a home exercise program?
- Has work conditioning been tried? Was pain behavior noted during work conditioning?
- Has a work site visit occurred to negotiate a modified duty return to work compromise?
- Has a functional capacity assessment been done to have a general idea of activity tolerances?
- Is the individual involved in any hobbies or other activities that can strain the back? If overweight, is the individual enrolled and participating in a weight loss program?
- Is the individual experiencing secondary gains from low back pain?
- Is the individual experiencing stressful situations that may be intensifying his or her pain? Has a psychological assessment been obtained?

References

Hellmann, David, and John Stone. "Arthritis and Musculoskeletal Disorders." Current Medical Diagnosis and Treatment. Tierney, Lawrence, Steven McPhee, and Maxine Papadakis, eds. New York: Lange Medical Books/McGraw-Hill, 2000. 807-859.

Kessler, R.M. Management of Common Musculoskeletal Disorders: Physical Therapy Principles and Methods. Philadelphia: J.B. Lippincott Company, 1990.

Nordenson, Nancy. "Differential Diagnosis in the Low Back." Courtroom Medicine - The Low Back, Vol. 2. Gelfand, Leo, Raoul Magaña, and R. Merliss, eds. New York: Matthew Bender & Company, Inc, 2000. 30-1 to 30-93.

Waxman, R., A. Tennant, and P. Helliwell. "A Prospective Follow-up Study of Low Back Pain in the Community." Spine 25 16 (2000): 2085-2090.

Lower Gastrointestinal Series
Other names / synonyms: Barium Enema, Lower GI Series
87.64

Definition

A lower gastrointestinal series is a test that allows visualization of the large intestine.

X-rays of the large intestine (colon) are taken after rectal instillation (enema) of a radiopaque contrast medium (barium). The barium allows the general outline of the colon to be visible on the x-rays, and this is called a single contrast barium enema. A more detailed examination of the colon can be done if air is introduced after the barium is expelled. This procedure is called an air contrast or double contrast barium enema. Either type of lower GI series is typically done as an outpatient procedure.

A lower gastrointestinal series is typically done to detect cancer of the lower bowel. Cancer of the rectum accounts for about 30% of the 133,500 colorectal cancer cases that occur annually. Men are affected by rectal cancer slightly more than women and most cases occur after age 50. Rectal cancer may be both hereditary and related to diet. Experimental studies and dietary histories indicate that diets high in fat and red meat may be related to the incidence of rectal cancer. Alcohol consumption has been implicated as well. Other diseases of the colon such as familial polyposis, inflammatory bowel disease, chronic ulcerative colitis, villous adenoma, Crohn's disease, and prior large bowel cancers increase the risk of colon or rectal cancer. Colorectal cancer is the second most common visceral cancer in the US, and approximately 55,000 people die from this disease each year. The incidence of the disease among Americans is approximately 5% and the long-term survival rate is only about thirty-five percent.

Reason for Procedure

A lower gastrointestinal series is done to visualize the large intestine. The procedure may be performed in response to a change in the pattern of bowel movements, unexplained lower abdominal pain, or blood in the stool. A lower gastrointestinal series can help in the diagnosis of colon cancer, polyps, diverticulitis, Crohn's disease, ulcerative colitis, or other inflammatory bowel diseases by allowing visualization of these abnormalities on x-ray or by fluoroscopy.

Description

Either type of lower GI series is typically done as an outpatient procedure. Warm water enemas may be administered. The test may be done in a physician's office or a hospital radiology department. The individual will be asked to lie on his/her side while a well-lubricated enema tube is inserted gently into the rectum. Radiopaque contrast medium (barium) is then instilled into the colon and a balloon at the tip of the enema tube may be inflated to help keep the barium inside. The flow of barium from the tube into the colon can be monitored on a screen that looks like a television monitor (x-ray fluoroscope). The individual will be asked to move to different positions and the table may be tipped slightly to get different views while x-ray pictures are taken. Also, the individual may be asked to hold his/her breath and be still at certain times during x-ray exposure.

The enema tube will be removed after the pictures are taken and the individual will be given a bedpan or helped to the toilet. The individual will then expel as much of the barium as possible and 1-2 additional x-rays may be taken after the barium is expelled. If a double-contrast (also called an air-contrast) examination is being done, the enema tube will be reinserted and a small amount of air will be gently introduced into the colon. More x-ray pictures are then taken, which can give a more detailed picture of the colon. The enema tube is removed.

Prognosis

With single-contrast barium enema, the colon will be filled with barium and the shape of the colon will be clearly apparent. With double-contrast barium enema, the colon will be uniformly distended with air and a thin layer of barium will provide excellent visualization of the details of the inner lining (mucosa) of the gut. X-rays from this procedure can help in diagnosing and determining the appropriate treatment for bowel cancer; inflammatory diseases such as diverticulitis, ulcerative colitis, and granulomatous colitis; intestinal polyps; structural changes in the intestine such as intussusception, telescoping of the bowel, and sigmoid volvulus and torsion; gastroenteritis; irritable colon; vascular injury due to blood vessel (arterial) occlusion; and certain cases of appendicitis.

Specialists

- Gastroenterologist
- Radiation Oncologist

Work Restrictions / Accommodations

There should be minimal work restrictions after this test. The individual may require ready access to bathroom facilities for 24 hours following the procedure.

Comorbid Conditions

Existing conditions that may impact an individual's ability to recover and further lengthen disability include severe hemorrhoids, partial or complete rectal prolapse, any inflammatory bowel disease, or constipation.

Procedure Complications

Complications that might result from lower gastrointestinal series include constipation or diarrhea, bloating, cramping, nausea or vomiting, lower abdominal pain, tightness in the chest or troubled breathing, or wheezing.

Factors Influencing Duration

There may be increased disability if soreness in the rectum, colon irritation, or perforation has occurred during the procedure. If any suspicious cancer-like masses are seen during lower gastrointestinal series, further tests and treatments may be required.

Length of Disability

No disability is expected. Most individuals are able to return to work the day after the test.

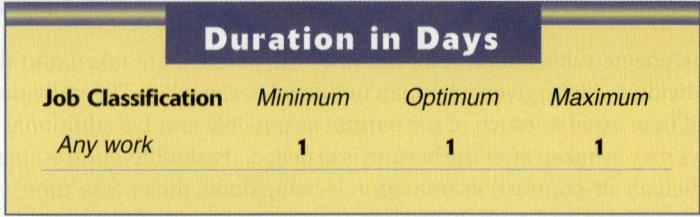

Job Classification	Minimum	Optimum	Maximum
Any work	1	1	1

References

LeMone, P., and K.M. Burke. Medical-Surgical Nursing. Upper Saddle River, NJ: Prentice Hall Health, 2000.

Loeb, S. Illustrated Guide to Diagnostic Tests. Springhouse, PA: Springhouse Corporation, 1993.

Phillips, M. "Barium Enema (BE), Single Contrast." Manual of Radiology. Eng, J, ed. Philadelphia: Lippencott-Raven Publishers, 1997. 253.

Phillips, M. "Barium Enema (BE), Double Contrast." Manual of Radiology. Eng, J, ed. Philadelphia: Lippencott-Raven Publishers, 1993. 251-252.

Ludwig's Angina

Other names / synonyms: Cellulitis and Abscess of Oral Soft Tissues, Cellulitis of the Neck, Neck Infection, Sublingual Infection, Submandibular Space Infection

528.3

Definition

Ludwig's angina is a serious infection and inflammation of the connective and cellular tissue (cellulitis) occurring in the area under the tongue (sublingual) and the jawbone (submandibular).

The most common cause in adults, associated with 80% of cases, is the spread of a dental infection, especially from the second or third lower molars. Other infections in the mouth or throat may also cause Ludwig's angina. The condition may arise as a complication arising from tongue piercing. In drug abusers, it can be caused by injections into the jugular vein.

It is a rare condition, and the incidence has decreased further since the widespread use of antibiotics.

Diagnosis

History: Pain in the area of the affected tooth is frequently the first symptom. The jaw feels tender and moving the tongue may be extremely painful. Difficulty opening the mouth, speaking, and swallowing may be present, resulting in drooling and problems with breathing. Individuals will report difficulty eating and drinking.

Physical exam: Inflammation under the floor of the mouth will create redness and swelling. As the infection spreads and moves toward the back of the mouth, it may cause the tongue to be displaced upward and backward. If the larynx is swollen, breathing will have a high-pitched sound (stridor). Often the individual is dehydrated as a result of lack of drinking and eating.

Tests: CT scan or x-ray examination may be performed to determine the degree of swelling and the likelihood of airway obstruction. Fluid from the tissues may be cultured to identify the pathogen involved.

Treatment

Hospitalization is usually required because of the importance of monitoring the airway. High doses of antibiotics are used to treat the infection. Incision and drainage of the infection may be required. Teeth involved in the infection may need to be extracted. Tracheotomy will be required if the airway is obstructed.

Prognosis

The goal of treatment is first to keep the airway open to prevent asphyxiation, and then to eradicate the infection. Appropriate treatment (antibiotics) will usually produce a cure of this illness, although because of the asphyxiation danger, mortality is ten percent.

However, for about 80% of individuals, incision and drainage will be necessary in conjunction with antibiotics in order to result in complete cure. For half of the individuals, the condition will be resolved with antibiotics and tracheostomy.

Differential Diagnosis

Other, less localized infections in the mouth or upper neck could resemble Ludwig's angina.

Specialists

- Infectious Disease Physician
- Otolaryngologist
- Oral Surgeon

Work Restrictions / Accommodations

This acute illness is not compatible with work.

Comorbid Conditions

Comorbid conditions might include immune suppression, respiratory disorders, and temporomandibular joint syndrome.

1306 The Medical Disability Advisor—Fourth Edition

Complications

Complications that may occur include pneumonia, lung abscess, and bacterial infection of the blood (blood poisoning, or septicemia). The swelling may block the airway, making an emergency tracheotomy necessary.

Factors Influencing Duration

Factors include underlying cause, complications, type of treatment, and the individual's response to treatment.

Length of Disability

Duration of the disability depends on job requirements.

Duration in Days

Job Classification	Minimum	Optimum	Maximum
Any work	7	9	14

Failure to Recover

If an individual fails to recover within the maximum duration expectancy period, the reader may wish to reference the following questions to assist in better understanding the specifics of an individual's medical case.

Regarding diagnosis:

- Does the individual have pain with tongue movement and trouble opening the mouth?
- Does the individual drool or have problems with breathing?
- Has a CT scan and/or x-ray examination confirmed the diagnosis?
- Has the origin of the infection been established and dealt with?
- Has the specific pathogen been identified by culturing fluid from the tissues?
- Were conditions with similar symptoms ruled out ruled out?

Regarding treatment:

- Was the individual hospitalized?
- Was the individual given high doses of antibiotics?
- Was it necessary to extract the affected teeth?
- Was a tracheotomy needed?

Regarding prognosis:

- This acute illness is not compatible with work. When able to return to work, is the individual's employer able to accommodate any necessary restrictions?
- Does the individual have any conditions that may affect their ability to recover?
- Did the individual have any complications such as pneumonia, lung abscess, and blood poisoning, or septicemia?

References

"Head and Neck Abscesses." Merck Manual of Diagnosis and Therapy, 17th ed. Beers, Mark H., and Robert Berkow, MD, eds. Whitehouse Station, NJ: Merck & Co., Inc, 1999 5 Jan 2001 <http://www.merck.com/pubs/mmanual/section13/chapter155/155d.htm>.

Beasley, D.J., and R.G. Amedee. "Deep Neck Space Infections." J La State Med Soc 147 5 (1995): 181-184.

De Bast, Y., et al. "Ludwig's Angina." Rev Med Brux 21 3 (2000): 137-141.

Fritsch, D.E., and D.G. Klein. "Ludwig's Angina." Heart Lung 21 1 (1992): 39-46.

Kurien, M., et al. "Ludwig's Angina." Clinical Otolaryngology 22 3 (1997): 263-265.

Perkins, C.S., J. Meisner, and J.M. Harrison. "A Complication of Tongue-piercing." British Dental Journal 182 4 (1997): 147-148.

Spitalnic, S.J., and Sucov, A. "Ludwig's Angina: Case Report and Review." Journal of Emergency Medicine 13 4 (1995): 499-503.

Tierney, Lawrence, Stephen McPhee, and Maxine Papadakis. Current Medical Diagnosis and Treatment. New York: McGraw-Hill, 2000.

Lumbar Disc Disorder with Myelopathy

Other names / synonyms: Lumbar Disc Displacement with Myelopathy, Lumbar Spinal Cord Compression

722.6, 722.73, 724.9

Definition

Lumbar disc displacement refers to an abnormal protrusion or herniation of a disc that separates the vertebrae in the lower back or lumbar area of the spine. The lumbar area of the spine contains five vertebrae (L1-L5). The most common areas of disc herniation are between L4 and L5 and between L5 and the first sacral vertebra (S1). Since the spinal cord ends at L1 or at the L1-2 disc (varies), only herniations of L1-2 can cause spinal cord compression or myelopathy. Herniations of L2-3 through L5-S1 can cause radiculopathy (one nerve root) or cauda equina syndrome (many nerve roots compressed).

A "high" lumbar disc disorder with myelopathy is a rare situation. The most common risk factor is degeneration due to aging. Other risk factors include obesity and diabetes.

For L1-2 herniations with myelopathy, refer to Thoracic Disc Disorder with Myelopathy, since L1-2 herniations behave like lower thoracic herniations. For L2-3 through L5-S1 herniations, refer to the section on Displacement, Lumbar Intervertebral Disc Without Myelopathy.

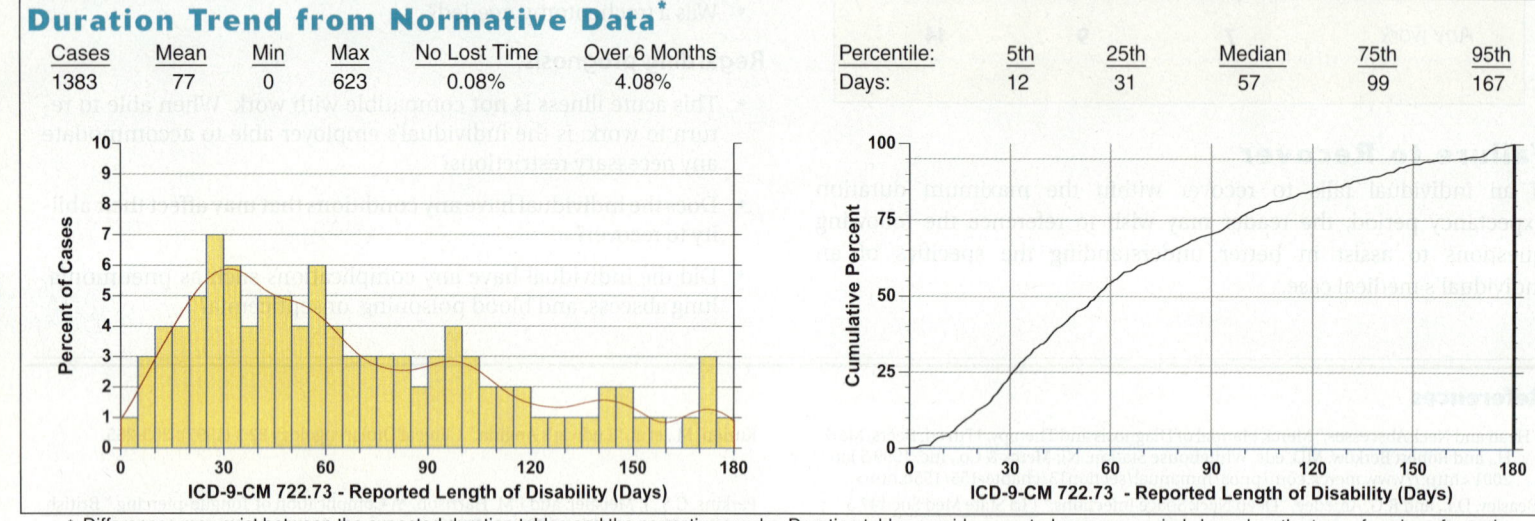

Duration Trend from Normative Data*

Cases	Mean	Min	Max	No Lost Time	Over 6 Months
1383	77	0	623	0.08%	4.08%

Percentile:	5th	25th	Median	75th	95th
Days:	12	31	57	99	167

* Differences may exist between the expected duration tables and the normative graphs. Duration tables provide expected recovery periods based on the type of work performed by the individual. The normative graphs reflect the actual observed experience of many individuals across the spectrum of physical conditions, in a variety of industries, and with varying levels of case management.

References

Berger, Joseph, and Stephen Ryan. "Medical Myelopathies." The Spine. Herkowitz, H.N., et al Philadelphia: W.B. Saunders Company, 1999. 1413-1428.

Golub, Benjamin, Richard Rovit, and Henry Mankin. "Cervical and Lumbar Disc Disease: A Review." Bulletin on the Rheumatic Diseases 21 (1971): 635-642.

Hardy, Russell Jr. Lumbar Disc Disease. New York: Raven Press, 1993.

Kessler, R.M. Management of Common Musculoskeletal Disorders: Physical Therapy Principles and Methods. Philadelphia: J.B. Lippincott Company, 1990.

Porterfield, J.A. Mechanical Low Back Pain Perspectives in Functional Anatomy. Philadelphia: W.B. Saunders Company, 1991.

Scully, Rosemary M., and Marylou R. Barnes. Physical Therapy. Philadelphia: J.B. Lippincott Company, 1989.

Wisneski, Ronald, et al. "Lumbar Disc Disease." The Spine. Herkowitz, H.N., et al Philadelphia: W.B. Saunders Company, 1999. 613-673.

Lumbar Puncture

Other names / synonyms: Cerebrospinal Fluid Examination, CSF, CSF Examination, LC, LP, Spinal Puncture, Spinal Tap
03.31

Definition

A lumbar puncture involves the insertion of a hollow needle into the spinal canal, specifically into the subarachnoid space. The needle is inserted in the lower back, usually between the fourth and fifth lumbar vertebrae. It is performed using local anesthesia, and can be done as an outpatient procedure. In general, the most common reasons for a lumbar puncture are to collect cerebrospinal fluid (CSF) or to administer medications.

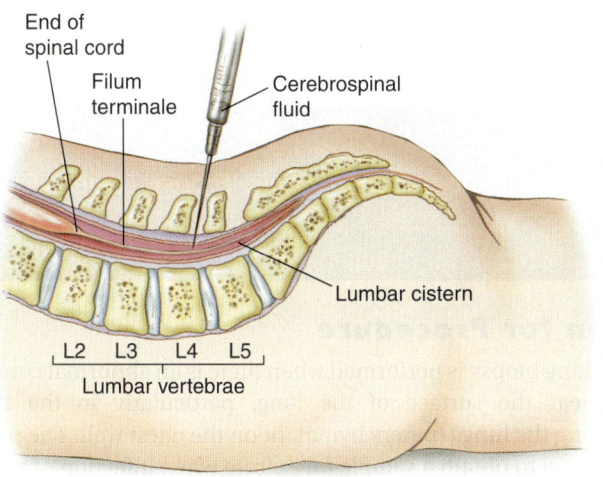

Reason for Procedure

Lumbar puncture may be used as a diagnostic tool or to administer treatment. Lumbar puncture may be done to collect a sample of the liquid that cushions the brain and spinal cord (cerebrospinal fluid, CSF), measure the pressure inside the spinal column, administer medications, or administer contrast material for radiographic visualization for certain tests.

Cerebrospinal fluid is collected and analyzed in order to help diagnose a number of different diseases and conditions, including subarachnoid hemorrhage, infections (such as meningitis or encephalitis), Guillain-Barré syndrome, polio, certain cancers (such as leukemia and lymphoma), and multiple sclerosis. A lumbar puncture is also used to measure the pressure of the CSF inside the spinal column. Certain medications, such as anesthesia for surgery, pain medications, antibiotics, or cancer drugs may be administered directly into the spinal canal using a lumbar puncture.

Description

During a lumbar puncture, the individual lies on his or her side with the knees drawn up to the abdomen and the forehead bent towards the knees. This position allows for maximum separation of the vertebrae in the lower back, allowing the needle to be inserted more easily. A local anesthetic is injected into the skin near where the needle will be inserted to numb the area. The needle is then inserted through the lower back and into the spinal canal. Depending on the reason for the procedure, a small sample of CSF may be extracted (which takes about 5 minutes), and the needle will be removed. If the purpose of the lumbar puncture is to administer medication, the needle will be left in place, and tubes will be attached through which the medication can enter the spinal canal. If a myelography is to be performed, contrast material will be injected through the needle. If the pressure of the CSF is being measured, a device called a manometer is attached to the lumbar puncture needle. Following the procedure, a bandage will be applied to the puncture site, and the individual will be required to remain in a reclining position for some time (anywhere from 15 minutes to several hours). If a CSF sample has been taken, the body naturally replaces the amount lost in about 1 hour. The individual should not engage in strenuous activities for 24 hours following the procedure.

Prognosis

The majority of individuals who undergo lumbar puncture have no complications from the procedure and experience a full recovery in 1-2 days. In individuals who experience headache, bed rest, increased fluid intake, and pain medication normally relieve symptoms within 1 week.

Specialists

- Anesthesiologist
- Emergency Medicine
- Neurologist

Work Restrictions / Accommodations

Individuals who undergo lumbar puncture are advised to rest and avoid all strenuous activity for the first 24 hours following the procedure. Most individuals will experience no complications and may then return to normal activities. However, work restrictions and accommodations are usually based on the underlying condition for which the LP was done, as well as on the severity of any complications that might occur.

Comorbid Conditions

Bleeding in the epidural or subarachnoid space can occur if the individual has a clotting deficiency or is on anticoagulant medication. A skin infection near the lumbar puncture site can spread to the epidural or subarachnoid spaces.

Procedure Complications

The most common complication following lumbar puncture is headache, which occurs in 10-30% of individuals within 1-3 days, and may last 2-7 days. The headache, sometimes referred to as a "spinal headache," is treated with bed rest, increased fluid intake, and over-the-counter analgesics (such as ibuprofen). In less than 1% of individuals, the spinal headache may become severe due to CSF leakage. In such cases, some physicians recommend a "blood patch," a procedure in which a small quantity of the individual's own blood is injected into the epidural space to "patch" or block the hole in the dura for evaluation and/or to cause the injection site to heal or clot more quickly and stop the leakage. Some individuals experience discomfort or a short period of mild to moderate pain during a lumbar puncture. Other less common complications include bleeding into the spinal canal, brain herniation (in individuals with increased intracranial pressure), accidental damage to the spinal cord (particularly if the individual moves during the procedure), hypersensitivity to the anesthetic used, infection, and pain or tingling in the back or leg.

Factors Influencing Duration

There is no disability associated with the lumbar puncture itself. The underlying condition for which the lumbar puncture was indicated may influence the length of disability. In addition, any complications will influence length of disability; a post-puncture headache may last up to two weeks.

Length of Disability

Disability from the lumbar puncture itself is not expected. Post-procedural headache occurs in 30% of cases, usually lasts four days, but may last up to two weeks.

Duration in Days

Job Classification	Minimum	Optimum	Maximum
Any work	1	2	4

References

CSF Collection. drkoop.com. 2000. 25 Oct 2000 <http://www.drkoop.com/conditions/ency/article/003428.htm>.

Reis, Carlos Eduardo. Lumbar Puncture. Noticias Medicas Diarias. 2000. 25 Oct 2000 <http://www.medstudents.com.br/proced/lumbpunc.htm>.

Lung Biopsy

Other names / synonyms: Aspiration Biopsy, Brush Biopsy, CT-Guided Biopsy, Endoscopic Biopsy, Open Biopsy, Percutaneous Biopsy, VATS, Video-Assisted Lung Biopsy

33.26, 33.27, 33.28

Definition

A lung biopsy is a procedure that involves obtaining a tissue specimen from the lungs for microscopic analysis to establish a precise diagnosis. There are 2 types of lung biopsies. A needle lung biopsy or percutaneous lung biopsy is performed by passing a biopsy needle through the skin into the lung. An open lung biopsy is performed via a surgical incision in the chest. When the microscopic analysis involves lung tissue, it is referred to as a histology. When the analysis involves cells from the lung, it is referred to as a cytology.

According to reports issued by the Centers for Disease Control and Prevention (CDC) in 1998, the number of needle lung biopsy procedures performed in the US was 46,000. More of the procedures (25,000) were performed on men than on women (20,000). A majority of the needle lung biopsies were performed on individuals aged 65 and over. A smaller number were performed on individuals aged forty-five to sixty-four. No needle lung biopsies were reported for the 15-44 age group. The southern region of the US reported the most (21,000 needle lung biopsies), with the Midwest, West, and Northeast regions reporting fewer (between 8,000 and 9,000 procedures).

The numbers reported for the open lung biopsies were considerably lower (17,000). As in needle lung biopsies, more open lung biopsies were performed on men (9,000) than on women (7,000-8,000). The numbers for these procedures were derived from discharges from short-stay, non-Federal hospitals.

A needle lung biopsy should not be performed if other tests indicate the presence of enlarged alveoli associated with emphysema (bullae), cysts, blood coagulation disorder of any type, insufficient blood oxygenation (hypoxia), pulmonary hypertension, enlargement of the right ventricle secondary to pulmonary hypertension that results from primary lung diseases (cor pulmonale, a type of heart failure).

An open lung biopsy should not be performed if the individual has pre-existing lung disease.

Reason for Procedure

A needle lung biopsy is performed when there is an abnormal condition that is near the surface of the lung, particularly in the tissues surrounding the lungs (parenchyma), or on the chest wall. The test can be performed to obtain a sample for culture when infection of the lung is suspected and cultures have not identified the cause of the infection. The needle lung biopsy procedure is used to diagnose pneumonia, lung cancer, spread of cancer throughout the body (carcinosis), lymphoma, and tuberculosis.

An open lung biopsy or video-assisted biopsy is performed to determine whether a tumor is benign or malignant. If a lung tumor is found to be malignant, biopsies of surrounding tissue and lymph nodes are often performed to determine whether the cancer has spread (metastasized). These types of lung biopsy is usually performed after other methods have been inconclusive.

Description

The needle lung biopsy is performed in a clinic on an outpatient basis. Often, a CT scanner will be used to precisely locate the tissue in question. The skin is scrubbed and a local anesthetic is injected. A small (about 1/8-inch) incision is made in the skin, and the biopsy needle, which is attached to a syringe, is inserted into the abnormal tissue, tumor, or lung tissue. The biopsy needle has either a cutting tip or an aspiration tip. The cutting tip facilitates removal of small sample of the suspected lesion while the aspiration tip is equipped to "suck" cells from the lesion.

After a sample of lung tissue is obtained, pressure is applied over the site of the biopsy to stop bleeding; then, a bandage is applied. The procedure usually takes from 30 to 60 minutes; laboratory analysis usually takes a few days.

The video-assisted lung biopsy (VATS, or video-assisted thoracic surgery) is performed in a hospital under general anesthesia. In the operating room, a camera is inserted into the chest cavity through a small incision. One or two more small incisions are made for the insertion of instruments. A small piece of lung tissue is removed. Usually a chest tube is left in the chest for a couple of days to prevent lung collapse.

The open lung biopsy procedure is done in a hospital operating room with the individual under general anesthesia. The skin is cleansed; the chest cavity is surgically opened; a small sample of lung tissue is removed. The incision is closed with stitches. Some surgeons leave a chest tube in place; one end inside the lung and the other protruding through the closed incision for 1 to 2 days to prevent the lung from collapsing.

Video-assisted or open lung biopsy is used when a needle lung biopsy is not appropriate, or when it is likely that the organ or tumor will require removal. Prompt analysis of the biopsy sample enables the diseased area to be removed immediately.

Prognosis

Lung biopsies generally provide reliable results in treatment, examination, and diagnosis when performed on easily accessible tumors. Needle biopsies are not as reliable as open lung biopsies when performed on deeper or obscured tumors.

Abnormal results indicate the following possibilities: bacterial, viral, or fungal lung infection (for example, cytomegalovirus), pneumonia, cancerous cells, immunoglobulin deposits (IgG, or rarely IgA) in the lung alveolar basement membranes (indicating immune disorders).

Specialists

- Infectious Disease Physician
- Pulmonologist
- Thoracic Surgeon

Work Restrictions / Accommodations

Moderate-to-heavy physical activity may need to be modified while the individual recovers from the lung biopsy procedure. The duration of the restriction would be greater for an individual who had undergone an open lung biopsy than for an individual who has undergone a needle lung biopsy. Accommodations would need to be made to ensure that the individual would not breathe dust or fumes.

Comorbid Conditions

Obesity and cigarette smoking may lengthen disability. Residual lung function may also lengthen disability.

Procedure Complications

Complications of the needle lung biopsy procedure include a collapse of the lung, which is due to an abrupt change in the intrapleural pressure within the chest cavity (pneumothorax), bleeding within the space between the layers of membrane that surround the lungs (plural cavity), and blockage of an artery by an air bubble (air embolism).

Complications of open lung biopsy or video-assisted biopsy include excessive bleeding (hemorrhage), infection, pneumothorax, air embolism, reactions to general anesthesia, or the creation of an abnormal opening (fistula) between the lungs and their surrounding membranes.

Factors Influencing Duration

Length of disability is influenced by the underlying condition.

Length of Disability

Needle (percutaneous).

Duration in Days

Job Classification	Minimum	Optimum	Maximum
Sedentary work	2	3	4
Light work	2	3	4
Medium work	2	4	7
Heavy work	2	4	7
Very Heavy work	2	4	7

Open.

Duration in Days

Job Classification	Minimum	Optimum	Maximum
Sedentary work	21	28	35
Light work	21	28	35
Medium work	21	28	35
Heavy work	28	35	42
Very Heavy work	28	35	42

References

Lung Needle Biopsy. Catholic Healthcare West. 01 Jan 1999. 01 Jan 2001 <http://your.chwhealth.com/mhc/top/003860.cfm>.

Lung Needle Biopsy. U.S. National Library of Medicine. 01 Jan 2000. 01 Jan 2001 <http://medlineplus.adam.com/ency/article/003860ris.htm>.

Open Lung Biopsy. Catholic Healthcare West. 01 Jan 1999. 01 Jan 2001 <http://your.chwhealth.org/mhc/top/003861.cfm>.

Schwartz, Seymour, MD. Principles of Surgery. New York: McGraw-Hill, 1999.

Lung Collapse

Other names / synonyms: Atelectasis, Middle Lobe Syndrome, Pneumothorax

518.0

Definition

Lung collapse is the term to describe the collapse of part or all of a lung caused by blockage of the larger or smaller air passages (bronchi or bronchioles), very shallow breathing, or accumulation of air in the pleural space.

When air passages in a lung become blocked, the air already in the lung cannot be breathed out and instead is absorbed into the blood. Being unable to take in any more air, the lung loses its elasticity and a part or all of it collapses. Blood passing through the collapsed lung or the collapsed area can no longer absorb oxygen or dispose of carbon dioxide.

Blockage of the bronchi or the bronchioles may be caused by the following conditions: accumulation of thick mucus plugs due to infection (chronic bronchitis) or disease (cystic fibrosis), difficulty dispersing mucus following abdominal or chest surgery (due to painful coughing), a complication of general anesthesia, or a spasm in the bronchial tubes (asthma). Blockage may also be caused from an inhaled foreign object or a tumor in the lung that presses on the bronchus. Middle lobe syndrome is a chronic form of collapsed lung caused by enlarged lymph glands pressing on the middle lobe bronchus.

Another cause of a collapsed lung is accumulation of air in the space between the chest wall and lung (pneumothorax). This can be due to fractured ribs, a chest injury, or a penetrating wound that perforates the outer covering of the lung. The pneumothorax can also be spontaneous and usually occurs in young males.

According to reports issued by the Centers for Disease Control and Prevention (CDC) in 1998, the number of diagnoses for lung collapse in the US was 336,000. Slightly more women were diagnosed with lung collapse than men. The majority of diagnoses occurred from age 65 and over. The South and Midwest regions reported the most diagnoses. The numbers for these diagnoses were derived from discharges from short-stay, non-Federal hospitals.

Diagnosis

History: Individuals may report sudden chest pain (especially when severe and one-sided upon inhalation), shortness of breath, chest tightness, easy fatigue, dizziness, rapid heart beat, fever, and bluish color of the skin caused by lack of oxygen. Many individuals report these symptoms began during rest or sleep.

Physical exam: Stethoscope examination with careful listening to breath sounds (auscultation) reveals decreased breath sounds on the side of the body of the affected lung.

Tests: A chest x-ray reveals reduced lung size and/or the presence of air outside of the lung. If performed, blood tests show changes in oxygen and carbon dioxide (arterial blood gases) levels in the blood. Sometimes a CT is helpful in determining the cause of lung collapse. Bronchoscopy involving the insertion of a bronchoscope into the lung through the mouth is useful to inspect the interior of the trachea-bronchial tree, take specimens for biopsy and culture, and remove foreign bodies.

Treatment

The objective of treatment is to remove the obstruction from the lung air passages and/or evacuate air from the pleural space, allowing the lung to reexpand.

When collapse is caused by an accumulation of mucus, treatment may include chest clapping, deep breathing, coughing, and postural drainage (technique using gravity to assist in drainage). Treatment may also include antibiotics and increased fluid intake. If mechanical obstruction is suspected, the first measures are forced coughing, suctioning, and respiratory or physical therapy. If there is no relief, then fiberoptic bronchoscopy (lighted viewing instrument passed down the trachea into the bronchi) helps identify and remove the obstruction. Heavy secretions can be suctioned at the time of bronchoscopy. If a foreign body is present, it can be removed at this time as well. It is rare that surgery is required to extract foreign objects.

The placement of a chest tube between the ribs into the pleural space allows the evacuation of air from the pleural space. With the chest tube left in place, the lung may take several days to reexpand. Hospitalization is required for chest tube management. Pain relievers and antibiotics are prescribed while increased fluid intake is encouraged.

Surgery may be indicated to prevent recurrent episodes. Surgical removal of the affected area (resection) is used when the collapse is chronic due to recurrent respiratory infections or a tumor. Tumors may also be treated with radiation or chemotherapy. Laser therapy is effective in reducing obstruction in selected cases.

In the case of unresectable tumors, sometimes stents are placed to hold the airways open to prevent lung collapse.

Prognosis

The prognosis following treatment for lung collapse is generally good. In some cases, the collapsed lung may resolve spontaneously. However, up to 50% of afflicted individuals have a recurrence.

When the obstruction (usually a mucus plug or inhaled foreign object) causing the collapse is noncancerous (benign), the obstruction may be removed surgically or nonsurgically. After the removal, the collapsed lung usually returns gradually to its normal, inflated state. However, some residual scarring or damage may result.

If the obstruction is caused by a malignant tumor, appropriate treatment for cancer (e.g., surgery, chemotherapy, radiation) is prescribed. Prognosis depends on the extent of spread of the cancer (metastasis).

In an adult, a collapsed lung is not usually life-threatening because unaffected parts of the lung (or, if the whole lung is collapsed, the other lung) expand to compensate for the loss of function in the collapsed area.

Differential Diagnosis

One condition with symptoms similar to lung collapse is pneumothorax. Lung collapse occurs in both conditions (pneumothorax and lung collapse). The distinction between the two is the cause of the collapse. Causes of lung collapse are secretions that plug the airway, foreign objects in the airway, and pressure by tumor. In pneumothorax, an abnormal collection of air or gas inside the pleural space (pneumothorax) causes the lung to partially or completely collapse. The abrupt, abnormal collection of air occurs after chest penetration (trauma) and spontaneous lung rupture.

Specialists

- General Surgeon
- Internist
- Pulmonologist
- Thoracic Surgeon

Rehabilitation

The cause of the lung collapse determines the rehabilitation required. The frequency and duration of rehabilitations may be contingent on the extent of the lung collapse at diagnosis. Collapse due to problems with secretions or mucus is handled with continued emphasis on breathing exercises and strategies for bringing up secretions (chest clapping, postural drainage). Nutritional and physical rehabilitation may be required after treatment for lung cancer.

Work Restrictions / Accommodations

Following recovery, special restrictions or accommodations are not usually required at the individual's workplace. Work restrictions must be determined on an individual basis if the individual returns to work before all symptoms have improved.

Comorbid Conditions

Comorbid conditions include cigarette smoking, obesity, diabetes, AIDS, chronic obstructive lung diseases (emphysema and bronchiectasis), or the use of drugs that depress alertness or conscious (sedatives, barbiturates, tranquilizers), or alcohol.

Complications

Possible complications of lung collapse include pneumonia (develops rapidly after partial lung collapse), lung abscess, permanent lung scars, and subsequent recurrent collapse of lung tissue.

Factors Influencing Duration

Duration of disability depends on the underlying cause of the collapsed lung, whether the collapse was partial or complete, severity of symptoms, type of treatment, individual's response to treatment, or any complications.

Length of Disability

Duration depends on size, cause, and condition of other lung. Recurrence may cause lengthy disability and may require surgery.

Closed thoracostomy with chest tube.

Duration in Days

Job Classification	Minimum	Optimum	Maximum
Sedentary work	3	14	28
Light work	3	14	28
Medium work	3	21	42
Heavy work	7	21	42
Very Heavy work	7	21	42

Failure to Recover

If an individual fails to recover within the maximum duration expectancy period, the reader may wish to reference the following questions to assist in better understanding the specifics of an individual's medical case.

Regarding diagnosis:

- Does the individual have a history of accumulation of thick mucous plugs in the lungs such as in chronic bronchitis or cystic fibrosis?
- Does the individual have a history of asthma?
- Has the individual undergone recent abdominal or chest surgery?
- Did the individual inhale a foreign object?
- Is there a tumor in the lung that is pressing on the bronchus?
- Has the individual recently had trauma to the chest?
- Does the individual report sudden chest pain especially severe and one-sided upon inhalation?
- Does the individual complain of shortness of breath, chest tightness, easy fatigue, dizziness, rapid heartbeat, fever, and bluish color of the skin?
- Does the individual report that the symptoms began during rest or sleep?
- Was a chest x-ray done? Did it reveal reduced lung size and/or the presence of air outside the lung?
- Were changes in oxygen and carbon dioxide levels in the blood measured (arterial blood gases or ABGs)?
- Were CT or bronchoscopy done?
- Was the diagnosis of lung collapse confirmed?

Regarding treatment:

- If collapse was caused by an accumulation of mucus, did the individual receive chest clapping, deep breathing, coughing, and postural drainage?
- Were antibiotics or pain medications required? If so, was the individual compliant with the medication regimen?
- Is the individual increasing fluid intake?
- If mechanical obstruction caused collapse, were forced coughing, suctioning, and respiratory or physical therapy done?

- If there was no relief, was fiberoptic bronchoscopy done?
- Was the obstruction removed or suctioned?
- Was the individual hospitalized for chest tube placement to reexpand the lung?
- Was surgery required to prevent recurrent episodes if collapse is chronic due to recurrent respiratory infections or a tumor?
- If due to a tumor, is treatment with radiation or chemotherapy also recommended?
- If the tumor cannot be removed (resected), is placement of a stent to hold the airways open recommended?

Regarding prognosis:

- Is this the first collapsed lung the individual has had or is this a recurrence?
- If surgical removal was required, is there residual scarring or lung damage? If so, how extensive is the scarring and what type of damage occurred?
- If a malignant tumor caused the collapse, has the cancer spread (metastasized)? To what extent?
- Has the individual developed complications such as pneumonia or lung abscess? If so, how was the complication treated and what was outcome?

References

Atelectasis. WebMD Health. 01 Jan 1999. 05 Nov 2000 <http://my.webmd.com/content/asset/adam_disease_atelectasis>.

National Hospital Discharge Survey: Annual Summary 1998. Centers for Disease Control and Prevention (CDC). 01 Dec 2000. 23 Oct 2000 <http://www.cdc.gov/nchs/data/sr13_148.pdf>.

Pneumothorax. Catholic Healthcare West. 01 Jan 1999. 03 Nov 2000 <http://your.chwhealth.org/mhc/top/000087.cfm>.

Schwartz, Seymour, MD. Principles of Surgery. New York: McGraw-Hill, 1999.

Lung Excision

Other names / synonyms: Lobectomy, Partial Lobectomy, Pneumonectomy, Segmental Resection, Total Lobectomy, Wedge Resection

32.29, 32.3, 32.4

Definition

Lung excision is the surgical removal (excision) of all or part of the lung. Pneumonectomy is excision of the entire lung. Lobectomy is excision of one or more sections (lobes) of the lung. Segmental resection is removal of one or more sections (segment) of a lobe. Wedge resection is excision of a triangular portion of a lung across more than one segment.

Occupational exposure to asbestos and radioactive emissions from radon in uranium mines can cause lung cancer.

Lung disease is the number three killer in the US and responsible for 1 in 7 deaths. More than 30 million Americans are now living with chronic lung disease. Emphysema affects 1.8 million Americans with almost 44% reporting that the disease limits their daily activities. Lung cancer is the single largest cause of death from cancer among both men and women in the US and accounts for more than 1 to 4 cancer deaths nationally. Lung cancer is the second most common cancer found in black or white men, following prostate cancer. It is the second most common cancer in white women, following breast cancer, and the third most common cancer in black women, following breast and colorectal cancer. Lung cancer generally occurs in individuals between the ages of 50 and 70.

Cigarette smoking is the leading cause of lung cancer and chronic obstructive lung disease including emphysema. The risk of lung cancer for male cigarette smokers is more than 2,000% higher than among male nonsmokers. For women, the risks are approximately 1,200% greater. Nonsmokers who live or work with smokers experience a 30-50% elevated risk for lung cancer.

Reason for Procedure

Excision of the entire lung (pneumonectomy) is most commonly performed to remove cancer originating in the lung (primary lung cancer) that cannot be removed with a lobectomy, segmental resection, or wedge resection. Other diseases and conditions treated with pneumonectomy include chronic dilation of the airways within the lung as a result of infection (chronic bronchiectasis) and multiple abscesses of the lung. Before a decision is made to remove a lung, pulmonary function tests are performed on the remaining lung to ensure it is healthy enough to cope with increased demands.

Excision of one or more sections or lobes of the lung (lobectomy) is most commonly performed to remove cancer that has spread from another organ (metastatic cancer) but is confined to a particular lobe. Other diseases and conditions treated with lobectomy include bronchiectasis, giant blisters (blebs or bullae) associated with bullous emphysema, noncancerous (benign) tumors confined to the lobe, fungal infections, and congenital abnormalities.

Segmental resection is most commonly performed to remove lung tissue damaged by bronchiectasis or chronic inflammation. During a segmental resection, only the segment of lung containing the diseased tissue is removed. Healthy segments are preserved.

Wedge resection is most commonly performed to remove small, benign primary lung tumors, to treat localized inflammatory disease, and remove tissue for biopsy.

Description

Pneumonectomy, lobectomy, segmental resection, and wedge resection procedures approach the lungs from the side through a thoracotomy incision. In some cases, the surgeon may choose to approach the lungs from the front through the breastbone (median sternotomy incision) but this is much less common.

For a thoracotomy, the individual is at first positioned on the back (supine position) and secured to the table with a safety belt across the upper thighs. Monitoring equipment is secured (temperature probe, ECG leads, and a pulse oximeter finger cot to measure the level of oxygen in the blood). Intravenous lines are inserted for administration of fluids, medications, and blood during and after surgery. A special line to monitor arterial blood gases (oxygen and carbon dioxide) may be inserted. General anesthesia is induced and a breathing tube (endotracheal tube) is placed through the mouth and into the windpipe (trachea) to maintain an airway during surgery.

After being anesthetized, the individual is repositioned onto the nonoperable side (lateral or semilateral position). Arms are secured and bony prominences (hip, ankle, elbow, shoulder) are padded to prevent pressure sores. A catheter may be inserted into the spine to deliver pain medication postoperatively (epidural analgesia). Compression stockings may be applied to keep an even flow of blood moving through the legs during surgery and prevent formation of clots. A urinary catheter may be inserted into the bladder with the tubing hooked to a drainage bag in order to monitor kidney (renal) function during surgery. A nasogastric tube may be passed through the nose and into the stomach to drain accumulated stomach secretions. A conduction pad may be secured on the thigh to prevent burns when blood vessels are cauterized with the electrocautery machine.

The surgical area is washed (prepped) with an antibacterial solution including the entire rib cage on the surgical side from the middle of the back to the middle of the chest and stomach and from the neck to below the hip. The individual is covered with sterile, moisture-proof surgical drapes, leaving the surgical area exposed (the entire rib cage on the surgical side). The head portion of the drape is lifted off the individual's face and fastened to a canopy so that the entire head and neck are protected from the surgical field but exposed to the anesthesiologist. A sterile plastic adhesive drape is placed over the exposed surgical field.

The individual's skin, underlying tissue, and muscle are cut (incised) usually between the fourth and fifth ribs. A rib may be removed to provide a better view. The ribs are separated with a rib retractor. The retractor is slowly cranked open, separating the ribs and exposing the diseased lung. The surgeon uses scissors to open the membrane that surrounds the lung (the pleura) and gently peels it away from the lung.

For a pneumonectomy, all branches of the main blood vessels entering and leaving the lung (pulmonary artery and vein) are clamped, tied twice with nonabsorbable suture, and cut in two (divided). The main air tube (bronchus) going from the windpipe (trachea) to the diseased lung is clamped and divided. The lung is removed from the chest. A piece of pleura may be used to cover the bronchus stump. The bronchus stump is then closed with nonabsorbable suture. The chest cavity is irrigated with sterile salt water (saline) to check for leaks in the bronchus stump and to clear the chest of old blood. Bleeding is controlled with sutures and electrocautery.

A lobectomy is performed in a similar way. The bronchus is clamped and divided above the lobe or lobes to be removed. The bronchus stump is closed previously described. The edges of the remaining lung are sutured together and the lung reinflated. The chest cavity is irrigated with saline to check for leaks in the suture line of the remaining lung and to clear the chest of old blood. At this time, the surgeon also assesses the degree of expansion the remaining lung can provide. Bleeding is controlled with sutures and electrocautery.

A segmental resection procedure is performed much like a lobectomy with only a segment of a lobe being removed rather than the whole lobe. Blood vessels supplying the segment are clamped and tied with nonabsorbable suture and divided. The segment of bronchus supplying the segment is clamped, divided, and closed in the usual manner. The edges of lung are sutured together and bleeding is controlled. A wedge resection is very similar to a segmental resection but the portion of lung removed comes from more than one lobe segment.

Chest tubes are not inserted after pneumonectomy. Following pneumonectomy, the chest cavity is allowed to fill with air and fluid. The levels are monitored with just enough pressure placed on the heart and other lung to keep them in their normal space without obstructing them or letting them drift to the empty side. Chest tubes are inserted after lobectomy, segmental resection, and wedge resection. Chest tubes are inserted through the skin and into the space around the lung (the pleural space). The other ends of the chest tubes are attached to sealed drainage systems that allow blood to drain from the heart cavity while not allowing air back in. The tubes are secured to the skin with sutures.

During closure, the muscle and each layer of tissue are closed with surgical sutures. The skin is closed with sutures and the suture line covered with a thin layer of sterile gauze and secured with tape. The individual may transfer directly to the intensive care unit for recovery from anesthesia rather than the recovery room.

Wedge resection can now be performed using a scope much like a laparoscopic procedure. This is called a video-assisted thoracoscopic surgery (VATS). It is set up much the same as a standard wedge resection except three small incisions are made in the chest wall. A chest tube is often left in place for a few hours. This procedure works best when only a small amount of tissue needs to be removed.

Prognosis

Prognosis following partial removal of a lung depends on the underlying disease or condition requiring surgery. Individuals with diseased lungs from emphysema, infection, or other conditions have reduced lung capacity before surgery. Removing part of the lung reduces this capacity even more. In general, the less of a lung removed, the better the outcome in terms of returning to work and performing activities of daily living.

Prognosis following pneumonectomy for lung cancer is poor. If lung cancer is found early before it has spread to lymph nodes or other organs, the 5-year survival rate following surgery is 42%. However, the 5-year survival rate for all stages of lung cancer combined is 14%.

Specialists

| • Pulmonologist | • Thoracic Surgeon |

Rehabilitation

Individuals who undergo the excision of one or more lobes of the lungs require occupational, physical, and respiratory therapy after surgery.

Respiratory therapy addresses the increase of lung capacity and a decreased risk for the buildup of lung secretions. Respiratory therapists teach individuals pursed lip breathing to increase the airflow to the lungs. Individuals may also use an incentive spirometer. This is a device that measures and displays the amount of air inspired to help motivate individuals to take deeper breaths. Individuals also learn to produce an effective cough through techniques such as huffing where air is breathed out forcefully while the mouth is open.

Physical therapy addresses decreased endurance, strength, and range of motion. Individuals learn to stretch the shoulder and chest muscles on the side of the removed lung to help normalize posture. Individuals perform strengthening exercises of the arms and legs to improve overall endurance. In addition to strengthening the arms and legs, the muscles of the upper back are strengthened through exercises such as shoulder blade squeezes to promote normal posture. Individuals also strengthen the diaphragm by lying on the back and performing abdominal breathing exercises. These exercises can be made more difficult by placing weights or a book on the abdomen to provide resistance. Individuals may perform aerobic activity such as walking on a treadmill or riding a stationary bicycle to further increase endurance. Individuals learn to rate the amount of energy they expend by utilizing a rating of perceived exertion scale. This is a numbered scale that rates exercises.

Work Restrictions / Accommodations

Hours of work may be gradually increased over the next several weeks until individual is working a full day, if possible. Many individuals who have had all or part of a lung removed may experience some degree of shortness of breath even without exertion. These individuals most likely require work restrictions and accommodations that help conserve energy and reduce the requirement for oxygen.

Other medical problems or permanent disabilities because of underlying medical conditions such as diabetes, chronic renal failure requiring dialysis, or chronic heart disease or postoperative complications may also require work restrictions and accommodations.

Comorbid Conditions

Pre-existing diseases that affect any of the major body systems such as high blood pressure, chronic kidney (renal) disease, bleeding disorders, diabetes mellitus, chronic obstructive lung disease, chronic heart disease, and immunosuppressive diseases affect length of disability. Other comorbid conditions that influence length of disability include a history of smoking or exposure to secondhand smoke, occupational exposure to asbestos and radioactive emissions from radon in uranium mines, and obesity.

Procedure Complications

Complications following lung surgery include collapsed lung (atelectasis), heart rhythm disturbances, air leakage from the bronchial stump (pneumothorax), hemorrhage, shifting of organs and tissue into the space formerly filled by the removed lung or lobe (mediastinal shift), lung infection (pneumonia), accumulation of excess fluid in the space formerly filled by the removed lung or lobe (pleural effusion), respiratory insufficiency, respiratory failure, and death.

A ruptured bronchial stump requires immediate surgery, as does hemorrhage caused by slippage of a suture from one of the major pulmonary blood vessels that were cut and sutured during lung surgery.

Factors Influencing Duration

Stage of the disease when first diagnosed, individual's age and general health, and type of tumor and its growth rate are factors that influence disability. Previous lung surgery also affects disability.

Following lung surgery, disability factors include the number and severity of postoperative complications (i.e., wound infections, bleeding, pneumonia, respiratory insufficiency, or an adverse reaction to a general anesthetic), amount of blood loss during surgery and postoperatively, number of blood transfusions required, individual's nutritional status and mental and emotional stability, access to rehabilitation facilities, and strength of the individual's support system.

Length of Disability

Durations reflect recovery period from uncomplicated surgery, not for the underlying cause. Disability may be permanent if the individual's lung capacity is seriously limited due to the amount of lung removed and/or the underlying disease.

Partial lobectomy.

Duration in Days

Job Classification	Minimum	Optimum	Maximum
Sedentary work	21	28	56
Light work	21	28	56
Medium work	28	42	70
Heavy work	42	56	Indefinite
Very Heavy work	42	Indefinite	Indefinite

Total lobectomy.

Duration in Days

Job Classification	Minimum	Optimum	Maximum
Sedentary work	56	84	Indefinite
Light work	56	84	Indefinite
Medium work	56	84	Indefinite
Heavy work	Indefinite	Indefinite	Indefinite
Very Heavy work	Indefinite	Indefinite	Indefinite

References

Kisner, Carolyn, and Lynn Allen Colby. "Chest Physical Therapy." Therapeutic Exercise: Foundations and Techniques, 2nd ed. Philadelphia: F.A. Davis Company, 1990. 57-61.

Watchie, Joanne. Cardiopulmonary Physical Therapy. Philadelphia: W.B. Saunders Company, 1995.

Lupus Erythematosus, Systemic

Other names / synonyms: Lupus

695.4, 710.0, 710.9

Definition

Systemic lupus erythematosus (SLE) is an ongoing (chronic) inflammatory disease primarily affecting connective tissue of the skin, joints, kidneys, nervous system, and mucous membranes. Damage accompanying symptoms occurs when the body's immune system malfunctions and attacks healthy tissue.

The hallmark symptom of SLE is the characteristic red, blotchy, butterfly-shaped rash over the cheeks and bridge of the nose. Systemic lupus erythematosus is a serious and potentially fatal condition that can disrupt any organ system in the body. The disease is characterized by periods when symptoms lessen or disappear without a known cause (spontaneous remissions) and periods when symptoms return or flare (relapses).

SLE's exact cause is unknown. Its prevalence is influenced by many factors, including gender, race, and heredity. About 85% of those diagnosed with lupus are women. Sex hormones appear to play some role since most cases develop during the childbearing years. In the US, black and Asian women appear to be at increased risk. Other family members often have SLE or other connective tissue disorders or are considered at increased risk. While individuals considered at risk may have no symptoms, they often carry and pass on through heredity the antibodies that attack body tissue (autoantibodies).

More people have lupus than AIDS, cerebral palsy, multiple sclerosis, sickle cell anemia and cystic fibrosis combined. Most are between the ages of 20 and 40 years old. About 1 in 2,000 people are thought to have SLE.

Diagnosis

History: Severity of symptoms varies in different individuals and within the same individual over time. Joint and muscle pain are often the earliest symptoms of SLE. Most individuals will complain of a skin rash at some time, particularly after exposure to sunlight. The characteristic red, blotchy, butterfly-shaped rash over the cheeks and bridge of the nose occurs in about half of cases. While temporary hair loss may occur, there is no scarring and the hair grows back between attacks. The individual may complain of fingers turning from white to blue and finally red during exposure to cold or periods of stress (Raynaud's syndrome). Anxiety and depression may also be reported, accompanying stress and the uncertainty over having a chronic, potentially serious disease. Visual disturbances may occur, including over-sensitivity to light (photophobia) or blurred vision. Other symptoms include fever, weight loss, loss of appetite (anorexia), abdominal pain, headaches (muscle tension or migraine), or a general feeling of ill health (malaise).

Physical exam: Individuals with SLE may present with butterfly facial rash, ulcers in the mouth, hair loss, and red, swollen painful joints. If more systems are involved, symptoms are related to inflammation in the involved organs. Common findings include inflammation of the lining of the lungs (pleurisy) and inflammation of the membrane surrounding the heart (pericarditis). Scattered abdominal tenderness may be due to inflammation of the membrane lining the abdominal cavity, unrelated to infection (sterile peritonitis). High blood pressure (hypertension) and ankle swelling (peripheral edema) are the most common indications of kidney involvement (renal disease).

Tests: No one test can determine lupus. Anemia detected on a complete blood cell count (CBC) may be caused by chronic inflammation, renal disease, or destruction of red blood cells (hemolysis). Increased urea nitrogen or creatinine on a blood chemistry, or an abnormal urinary sediment indicates kidney involvement. Blood tests used to detect specific antibodies include ANA (antinuclear antibody test), the anti-DNA antibody test, the anti-Sm antibody test, and complement levels. Removal of tissue for microscopic examination (skin biopsy) can also detect antibodies that occur when the disease is active. X-rays of painful joints, muscle testing through electromyography (EMG), and microscopic examination of fluid withdrawn from the joints may be done to rule out other disease processes.

Treatment

There is no cure for SLE. Treatment is aimed at reducing inflammation and relieving symptoms. Any drug that may have triggered the condition should be withdrawn, if possible. Individuals whose symptoms are made worse by sunlight should avoid exposure to sunlight and should use sunscreen. The skin rash can often be effectively treated with antimalarial drugs. Inflammation of the joints related to the disease (lupus arthritis) is treated with nonsteroidal anti-inflammatory (NSAID) drugs or antimalarial drugs. Disease-caused muscle inflammation (lupus myositis) may be treated with corticosteroids and an effective exercise program. Other anti-inflammatory (corticosteroid) drugs may be prescribed for fever, pleurisy, pericarditis, and neurological symptoms. Anti-cancer (cytotoxic) drugs are reserved for serious systemic involvement, especially when corticosteroids have been tried but are ineffective. If kidneys fail, mechanical support (dialysis) may be required. Psychological needs must be addressed through counseling or other support.

Prognosis

The outlook for individuals with SLE has improved dramatically. However, about half of all individuals with lupus experience kidney involvement, which can lead to life-threatening conditions. The 10-year survival rate is now eighty to ninety percent. Factors aiding this improved prognosis include a more accurate diagnosis, faster and more effective treatment, availability of dialysis for treatment of kidney failure, and more availability of antibiotics effective in treating infectious complications. In most individuals, the illness pursues a mild, ongoing (chronic) course, occasionally interrupted by relapses of disease activity. For many, the disease may affect only a few organs.

Differential Diagnosis

Infections that mimic SLE include syphilis, Epstein-Barr virus, cytomegalovirus, HIV, Lyme borreliosis, tuberculosis, vasculitis, hepatitis, and subacute bacterial endocarditis. The early stages of other connective tissue diseases (scleroderma, rheumatoid arthritis) can be confused with SLE. Fibromyalgia syndrome and malignancies such as lymphomas can also have similar symptoms.

Individuals using certain medication may develop a lupus-like syndrome. The drugs most frequently responsible are for high blood pressure (anti-hypertensives), irregular heart rhythms (cardiac depressants), and tuberculosis (tuberculostatics). Symptoms of drug-induced lupus are generally milder, affect men and women equally, and fade when the drug is discontinued.

Specialists

- Dermatologist
- Nephrologist
- Neurologist
- Psychiatrist
- Psychologist
- Rheumatologist

Work Restrictions / Accommodations

Restrictions and accommodations are determined by the severity of symptoms and the particular organ or system involved. Flexibility and adaptability are necessary because there can be periods of remission and flare-ups. Individuals with lupus may require protection from sunlight, such as sunscreens and hats.

Complementary and Alternative Therapies

Content is intended for awareness only. Treatments may or may not be effective. Scientific evidence may be lacking and some substances have potentially toxic effects. Dr. Presley Reed and the editors do not endorse the use of these therapies in the absence of consultation with a licensed medical professional.

Glucosamine - This synthetic version of a natural substance (glycosaminoglycans) that builds cartilage may provide at least some pain relief and increased range-of-motion in individuals suffering from arthritis, which often is a symptom of SLE.

Comorbid Conditions

Other disorders with potentially severe effects on the organs such as kidney disease, hepatitis and/or multiple sclerosis likely will affect the length of disability.

Complications

Possible complications include serious impairment of vital organs such as lungs, heart, brain, or kidneys. Infections that occur due to an impaired physical state (opportunistic infections) are a leading cause of death. Treatment with antimalarial drugs can have side effects such as damage to the back inner portion of the eye where focusing occurs (retina). Corticosteroid treatment also may have side effects such as facial swelling or high blood pressure (hypertension). Other infections such as colds or influenza may worsen symptoms.

Factors Influencing Duration

Length of disability may be influenced by the severity of the symptoms and the organs involved. Treatment, particularly prolonged corticosteroid therapy, may produce side effects that can also cause disability.

Length of Disability

The individual's ability to continue long-term tasks may be hampered because of cycles of remission and relapse. Each individual case is highly variable. Remissions and exacerbations are common. Some individuals have symptoms so severe and continuous they can be considered life-threatening, with accompanying permanent disability.

Duration in Days

Job Classification	Minimum	Optimum	Maximum
Sedentary work	0	14	28
Light work	0	14	28
Medium work	0	21	42
Heavy work	0	28	56
Very Heavy work	0	28	56

Failure to Recover

If an individual fails to recover within the maximum duration expectancy period, the reader may wish to reference the following questions to assist in better understanding the specifics of an individual's medical case.

Regarding diagnosis:

- Has diagnosis of systemic lupus erythematosus been confirmed (SLE)? Where diagnosis is uncertain, have other conditions with similar symptoms been ruled out?
- Is there a family history of SLE or other connective tissue disorders?
- Does individual report spontaneous remissions and relapses?
- Has individual experienced complications, such as impairment of vital organs (lungs, heart, brain, or kidneys), opportunistic infections, retinal damage, or hypertension that may impact recovery?

Regarding treatment:

- As there is no cure, has treatment been aimed at reducing inflammation and relieving symptoms?
- If symptoms are made worse by sunlight, is individual avoiding exposure to sunlight? Does individual use sunscreen?
- If the condition was triggered by a drug, has that drug been withdrawn? Is there another drug that could be used instead?
- Have antimalarial drugs been effective against skin rash?
- Was an appropriate exercise program recommended? Is individual complying with exercise plan?
- If corticosteroids were ineffective against a serious systemic involvement, is the use of cytotoxic drugs indicated?
- Has individual experienced kidney failure? If dialysis was necessary, are kidneys functional again?
- Are individual's psychological needs being met through counseling or other support?

Regarding prognosis:

- If symptoms persist despite treatment, does diagnosis need to be revisited?
- Does individual have access to factors indicating an improved prognosis such as faster and more effective treatment, availability of dialysis for treatment of kidney failure, and more availability of antibiotics effective in treating infectious complications?
- Does individual have an underlying condition, such as kidney disease, hepatitis or multiple sclerosis, that may complicate treatment and impact recovery?

References

Job Accommodation Network. Accommodating People With Lupus. U.S. Department of Labor Office of Disability. 25 Jan 2001. 02 Feb 2001 <http://www.jan.wvu.edu/media/Lupus.html>.

Parker, Lisa S. Systemic Lupus Erythematosus. Library of the National Medical Society. 28 Aug 2000. 27 Dec 2000. <http://www.medical-library.org/journals/secure/rheumatology_81100/systemic_lupus_erythematosus.htm>.

Lyme Disease
Other names / synonyms: Lyme Arthritis
088.81, 088.9

Definition

Lyme disease is a bacterial infection caused by Borrelia burgdorferi. It is spread by a bite from an infected tick. The tick (Ixodes species) requires a blood meal and feeds primarily on white-tail deer and white-footed mice. After ingesting bacteria in the blood from infected animals, they become infected and then spread the bacteria to the next animal that they bite. The ticks also feed on human blood.

Approximately 30% of individuals who have Lyme disease have been exposed to ticks or have been bitten by a mature tick. Although a full-grown tick is only one half the size of a pencil eraser, most bites are from immature ticks (nymphs), which are only about the size of a poppy seed.

The many signs and symptoms of Lyme disease mimic other diseases making it difficult to diagnose. The disease may have three stages, so symptoms of advanced disease can take months or even years to develop.

Adults who are at highest risk for infection are between 30-49 years old, and those who work outdoors or participate in outdoor recreation are more likely to become infected.

More than 15,000 cases of Lyme disease are reported each year. About 90% of cases are concentrated in three main geographic areas: the coastal and wooded regions of the Northeast, upper Middle-West, and Pacific Coast. The disease is not limited to rural settings, however, and is becoming increasingly common in suburban areas. Lyme disease is also found in Europe, particularly the Netherlands, Switzerland, Croatia, and parts of Italy.

Diagnosis

History: Symptoms vary depending upon the stage of the disease and the length of time since exposure. Early symptoms may arise within 2-30 days; symptoms of heart, brain, or joint disease may appear several weeks or months after exposure. The disease may become chronic (tertiary stage) at any time within two years of the initial infection. Individuals sometimes do not seek treatment until the later stages develop because symptoms are variable, mimic symptoms from other diseases, and may appear at different times.

The individual may initially see a flat or slightly raised red dot at the site of the tick bite. Over several days this will gradually expand to several inches across; it is called erythema migrans. Sometimes the reddened area has a characteristic "bulls-eye" appearance with a red center, pale circular ring, then another reddened area. This is called target erythema migrans. In about half of all cases, additional smaller red areas form. Flu-like symptoms such as fever, chills, extreme fatigue or lethargy, headache, itching, intermittent muscle pain, and a mild neck stiffness usually develop next. If untreated, the symptoms of the first stage may disappear after a few weeks, making diagnosis difficult.

A second stage (secondary Lyme disease) may develop after a few weeks or months, and can involve the bones and muscles (musculoskeletal system), nervous system, and/or heart. The most common symptom in this stage is joint pain, which occurs in 60% of cases. Intermittent or temporary joint pains are often followed by more intense pain and swelling of the knees and other large joints. Lasting weeks to months, these episodes of joint inflammation may be followed by periods during which symptoms lessen or disappear (remission). If left untreated, however, these joint symptoms can lead to persistent symptoms and disability. Neurologic symptoms at this stage may include constant headache, stiff neck, facial droop (facial nerve palsy) involving one (unilateral) or both (bilateral) sides of the face, muscle paralysis, and pain and weakness in the extremities and trunk. Heart problems resulting from disturbances in the heart's ability to contract (cardiac contractility), can cause the individual to feel dizzy, lightheaded, or as if they will faint (syncope).

The third (chronic, or tertiary Lyme disease) stage begins months to years after the initial tick bite. This stage is dominated by musculoskeletal and nervous system disorders. Pain in the large joints is more persistent and frequent, often lasting more than a year without remission. Impaired memory, difficulty concentrating, sleep disorders, and unusual or strange behavior are common complaints. Pain in the spine is often accompanied by tingling or shooting pains in the extremities.

Physical exam: Individuals may not seek treatment until later stages, as symptoms are variable and may appear at different times. In the early stage, a small, red, flat, or slightly raised skin lesion surrounded by a round, bulls-eye-like red rash with a pale center may be present. The rash will increase in size, then fade, and may reappear at another site. The area does not itch but may feel warm to the touch. Additional smaller red, round rashes may appear at other body sites. Symptoms of heart, joint, or brain disease will become apparent within several weeks or months. Heart abnormalities may include irregular heartbeat (arrhythmias) due to heart block. Joint inflammation usually does not correspond in size or amount to same joint on opposite sides of the body; the knee joint is most frequently involved. Exam may reveal impaired memory and difficulty concentrating, diminished touch sensation, stiff neck or back, and facial droop.

Tests: The diagnosis of Lyme disease can be confirmed by testing the blood for antibodies to the bacteria causing the disease. Test results may be variable results depending on the stage of the disease and the individual's immune response. Infected individuals may not show antibodies during the first stage of the disease. In later stages, most individuals have antibodies. Routine laboratory tests are helpful by excluding other diseases that can mimic Lyme disease. The electrocardiogram (EKG) can show variable degrees of heart block. Skeletal x-rays can show joint damage and erosive changes due to chronic inflammation.

Treatment

Antibiotics are prescribed based on the disease stage and symptoms. They can be taken for as long as 21 days to treat early stage infections, or for a month or more when treating chronic inflammation. Over-the-counter pain relievers may reduce fever and inflammation. In more advanced disease stages, severe joint pain and inflammation may require treatment with nonsteroidal anti-inflammatory drugs or corticosteroids.

A temporary pacemaker may be needed for severe heart block. Since the heart block is temporary (transient), a permanent pacemaker is rarely required. Chronic joint inflammation that is resistant (refractory) to treatment may eventually require removal of the inflamed membrane lining the joint (arthroscopic synovectomy).

Prognosis

In some cases, the infection subsides spontaneously. If diagnosed in the early stages and treated promptly with antibiotics, response to treatment and prognosis is very good. With appropriate antibiotic therapy, the rash should begin to fade within a week. Later stages of the disease can take weeks or months to respond and can recur despite therapy. Individuals with later-stage disease may require long-term follow-up.

The outcome of untreated disease is difficult to predict. Occasionally, the infections subside with no lasting effects, but more often untreated infections progress to chronic arthritis, resulting in partial or permanent disability. The prognosis for neurologic or cardiac complications varies with the severity of infection and response to treatment.

Differential Diagnosis

Other bacterial infections may invade joints causing infectious arthritis similar to that found in early Lyme disease. Other viral, bacterial, and fungal causes of meningitis or encephalitis may have symptoms similar to the neurological complications of Lyme disease, or may cause inflammatory skin rashes resembling Lyme disease.

Specialists

- Cardiologist
- Dermatologist
- Infectious Disease Physician
- Neurologist
- Occupational Medicine Physician
- Orthopedic Surgeon
- Primary Care Provider
- Rheumatologist

Rehabilitation

Individuals who contract Lyme disease may require physical and occupational therapy. The frequency and duration of therapy varies and is contingent upon the symptoms exhibited.

Individuals who experience infectious arthritis associated with Lyme disease require physical or occupational therapy as either discipline addresses arthritis symptoms.

Individuals who experience cardiac symptoms in association with Lyme disease may require both physical and occupational therapy. Physical therapists provide individuals with basic strengthening exercises for the arms and legs and instruct individuals in aerobic exercise such as treadmill walking.

For those individuals who experience neurological impairment in association with Lyme disease, physical, occupational, and psychological therapy may be necessary. Both physical and occupational therapy address decreased balance, strength, and range of motion.

Occupational therapy further addresses any difficulty with activities of daily living. Individuals learn strategies for dressing, bathing, and meal preparation that are geared toward their particular functional limitations.

Work Restrictions / Accommodations

There are no restrictions for early stage disease, but accommodations may be required for neurological or arthritic damage due to chronic stage disease. The type and extent of accommodations will depend upon the nature and severity of symptoms. Partial or intermittent disability may be expected if the disease is allowed to progress.

Complications

Even with antibiotic therapy, the recurrence of infectious arthritis or development of chronic arthritis in untreated infections may complicate the disease. Chronic arthritis may lead to joint stiffness and limitations in movement. Cardiac complications might include arrhythmias or severe heart block. Serious neurologic disorders (such as meningitis or encephalitis), and demyelinating disorders (similar to multiple sclerosis) have been associated with Lyme disease and can lead to permanent impairment and death.

Factors Influencing Duration

The length of disability will be influenced by the severity of symptoms, stage at which the disease is diagnosed and treated, and the presence of any neurologic or cardiac complications.

Length of Disability

Duration in Days

Job Classification	Minimum	Optimum	Maximum
Sedentary work	1	7	14
Light work	1	7	14
Medium work	1	14	21
Heavy work	1	21	28
Very Heavy work	1	21	28

Failure to Recover

If an individual fails to recover within the maximum duration expectancy period, the reader may wish to reference the following questions to assist in better understanding the specifics of an individual's medical case.

Regarding diagnosis:

- Has diagnosis of Lyme disease been confirmed?
- Has the individual experienced any complications, such as infectious arthritis, cardiac complications, serious neurologic disorders (such as meningitis or encephalitis), and demyelinating disorders (similar to multiple sclerosis)?
- Does the individual have an underlying condition that may impact recovery?
- Is the individual pregnant?

Regarding treatment:

- Was the individual compliant with antibiotic therapy, especially if long-term therapy was required?
- If individual did not take antibiotics faithfully due to side effects from medication, can an alternative antibiotic be used instead?
- Have medications such as nonsteroidal anti-inflammatory drugs or corticosteroids, been effective in relieving joint pain? If not, what other options are available?
- Is individual a candidate for a pacemaker if a severe heart block is present? If not, at what point would this option be considered?

Regarding prognosis:

- At what stage in the disease was it first diagnosed?
- Did individual receive prompt and appropriate treatment for that stage of illness?
- Have symptoms persisted despite treatment or is this episode a recurrence of the initial infection?
- How long was the antibiotic therapy regimen?
- Was individual compliant in taking prescribed medication?
- Would individual benefit from extended therapy or change in antibiotics?
- Is residual neurologic or cardiac impairment present? To what extent does impairment impact function?
- How disabling is condition at present?
- Would individual benefit from re-evaluation by infectious disease specialist or orthopedic surgeon?

References

Heuther, Sue E., and Melva Kravitz. "Structure, Function, and Disorders of the Integument." Pathophysiology. McCance, Kathryn L., and Sue E. Heuther, eds. St. Louis: Mosby, 1994. 1512-1560.

O'Sullivan, Susan B. "Motor Control Assessment." Physical Rehabilitation: Assessment and Treatment. O'Sullivan, Susan B., and Thomas J. Schmitz, eds. Philadelphia: F.A. Davis Company, 1994. 111-132.

Rahn, Daniel W., and Michael W. Felz. "Lyme Disease Update." Postgraduate Medicine 103 5 (1998): 51-64.

Seltzer, Elyse G., et al. "Long-term Outcomes of Persons with Lyme Disease." Journal of the American Medical Association 283 5 (2000): 609-615.

Shen, Harry, MD, and Cheryl Solimini. Living with Arthritis. New York: Plume, 1993.

Steere, Allen C. "Diagnosis and Treatment of Lyme Disease." Advances in Rheumatology 81 1 (1997): 179-194.

Lymphadenitis and Lymphadenopathy

Other names / synonyms: Adenitis, Adenopathy, Cervical Adenitis, Lymph Follicular Hypertrophy, Lymph Gland Infection, Lymphadenitis, Lymphadenopathy, Swollen Lymph Glands

289.1, 289.2, 289.3

Definition

Lymphadenitis and lymphadenopathy are terms that refer to abnormal, swollen lymph nodes (lymph nodes greater than 1 cm in diameter). The lymph nodes (glands) in the human body are small, rounded masses of tissue that cluster in certain areas of the human body, especially in the neck (cervical), arm pits (axillary), above the groin (inguinal), and near various organs and large blood vessels. The lymphatic drainage system collects lymph from all parts of the body and returns it to the blood. As part of the immune system, lymph nodes filter lymph fluid and its many white blood cells fight to keep organisms, especially bacteria, from entering the bloodstream.

Lymphadenitis is the term used to describe lymph nodes that are enlarged and inflamed because of infection due to bacteria, viruses, fungi or other organisms; infections that develop within the nodes; or from circulating cancer cells. The location of the affected nodes is usually associated with the site of the underlying infection, tumor, or inflammation; when infection occurs, the lymph node(s) and the area adjacent to the infection become swollen and inflamed. The enlarged node(s) tend to be tender to the touch and mobile, meaning that each individual node moves freely when touched. Lymphadenitis is a noncancerous condition.

The term "lymphadenopathy" refers to lymph nodes that are abnormal either in size, consistency, or number; enlargement is due to infection, inflammation or other reasons, such as cancer. The enlarged nodes tend to be firm, rubbery, and nontender to the touch.

Some of the causes of lymphadenitis and lymphadenopathy are obvious, as in the case of the individual who presents with a sore throat, tender lymph nodes in the neck area (cervical nodes), and a positive strep test. In other cases, the etiology is less clear, as in the case of the individual who only presents with symptoms of swollen lymph nodes in the groin (inguinal nodes). Such presentation often raises the specter of serious illnesses like Castleman's disease, lymphomatoid granulomatosis, cancer of the lymphatic system (lymphoma), acquired immunodeficiency syndrome (AIDS), or cancer that has spread from some other primary source (metastatic cancer). Etiology has also been associated with exposure to industrial chemicals or certain anti-seizure medications that have been associated with enlarged nodes. In addition some drugs--such as cephalosporins, penicillins, or sulfonamides--have been associated with enlarged nodes and other symptoms, including fever and rash, that may resemble Hodgkin's disease.

Of the nearly 600 lymph nodes throughout the body, only a few are normally detectable by physician's examination and manipulation (palpation). Most often, lymph node abnormality (adenopathy) indicates a benign, self-limited disease. For persons under the age of 30, the cause is benign in 80% of cases; over age 50, the rate of benign disease falls to 40 percent. This indicates that age is a risk factor for affliction with malignant illnesses that present initially as lymphadenopathy.

Reports issued by the Centers for Disease Control and Prevention (CDC) in 1998 revealed about 36,000 cases of lymphadenopathy and 9,000 cases of lymphadenitis in the US. For lymphadenitis, the reported cases were almost equally divided between males and females. Reported lymphadenopathy cases were also equally divided between men and women, were most prominent in the group aged 45-64 years old, and seemed to cluster in the Southern region of the US.

Diagnosis

Differentiating between "localized" and "generalized" presentations of lymphadenitis and lymphadenopathy is important in formulating a diagnosis. In the localized presentation, nodes are enlarged or otherwise abnormal in only one area, such as the cervical area. In generalized presentation, nodes are enlarged or otherwise abnormal in two or more non-contiguous areas. Approximately three-fourths of individuals will present with the localized (usually less serious) condition, while one-fourth will present with the generalized (often serious) condition.

History: Individuals with lymphadenitis will generally complain of one area where enlarged lymph nodes are tender to the touch. They may also report an acute streptococcal or staphylococcal infection such as from an insect or animal bite or sting. A careful history may identify a readily diagnosable cause such as upper respiratory tract infection (UTI), pharyngitis, periodontal disease, conjunctivitis, recent immunization, or dermatitis. By contrast, an individual with lymphoadenopathy will report an area or areas with enlarged lymph nodes that are firm, rubbery, but which may not be tender. Accompanying symptoms for both lymphadenitis and lymphadenopathy include fever, weight loss, fatigue, and night sweats. The individual may mention recent travel, occupational exposures, high-risk sexual behavior, intravenous drug use, and the use of medications known to specifically cause lymphadenopathy.

Physical exam: Physicians usually examine the area of concern by touch (palpation) to evaluate 5 node characteristics: size, pain/tenderness, consistency, matting, and location. Nodes are generally considered normal if they are up to 1 cm in diameter. When a node increases in size, its capsule stretches and causes pain. Stony-hard nodes are typically a sign of cancer. Very firm rubbery nodes suggest lymphoma. Softer nodes are the result of infections or inflammatory conditions. Nodes that are matted feel connected and seem to move as a unit. The anatomic locations of the nodes can be helpful in narrowing a differential diagnosis. For example, cat scratch disease and infectious mononucleosis typically cause swollen lymph nodes in the cervical area.

Individuals with lymphadenitis typically present with one area containing nodes that are tender, swollen, mobile, and enlarged (3 cm in diameter); the overlying skin may feel warm and appear red (erythematous).

People with lymphadenopathy will have one or more areas where the nodes are swollen and enlarged. These nodes will feel firm and rubbery or stony hard, will be clumped or matted, and may or may not be painful.

Tests: While the cause of infection or disease is often easily diagnosed by x-rays of the lymphatic system (lymphangiography), a lymph node aspiration, culture, or open/closed biopsy may be necessary. Blood tests are useful in identifying Epstein-Barr virus, mononucleosis and hepatitis, and certain bacterial infections where abnormality in the lymph nodes is a symptom.

Treatment

Treatment for both lymphadenitis and lymphadenopathy should begin promptly once a diagnosis is made for two reasons: First, because etiology, even though not readily apparent, could be serious (e.g., lymphoma, AIDS); and second, because the etiology could be a rapidly spreading infection (e.g., sepsis) that could be fatal after only a few hours in the blood stream. However, in persons with unexplained localized lymphadenopathy and a reassuring clinical picture, a 3-4 week period of observation is appropriate before a biopsy is necessary.

Treatment usually consists of antibiotics to control bacterial infection and anti-inflammatory medications to help reduce inflammation and swelling. Aspirin may be recommended as a fever-reducing (antipyretic) medication. When the cause of swollen lymph nodes is viral, treatment is usually not required. When swollen nodes cause tissue degeneration, infection, and the formation of a localized collection of pus buried within the nodes (abscess), surgical drainage of abscesses may be required.

In persons with localized lymphadenopathy and a worrisome clinical picture or those with generalized lymphadenopathy, further diagnostic evaluation will include a biopsy before determining etiology.

Prognosis

For lymphadenitis, prompt treatment with antibiotics often results in complete recovery, with symptoms controlled within a few days. The outcome can be complicated by abscess formation and cellulitis, and can become negative if the individual is diagnosed with sepsis.

For lymphadenopathy, the outcome is not good when the etiology of generalized lymphadenopathy is found to be a malignant or systemic disease, such as lymphoma, AIDS, or leukemia. When the etiology of generalized or local lymphadenopathy is due to environmental substances, medications, or drugs, the prognosis is good because the nodes will return to their normal size after the toxic substance, medication, or drug is removed from the individual's environment.

Differential Diagnosis

Swollen lymph nodes are a common finding in a number of medical conditions, including lymphoma, HIV infection, mononucleosis, and toxoplasmosis.

Differential diagnoses for lymphadenopathy might include lymphoma, non-Hodgkin's lymphoma, Epstein-Barr virus, Cytomegalovirus, Cat-scratch disease, tuberculosis lymphadenitis, Secondary syphilis, Hepatitis B, Lymphogranuloma venereum, Chancroid, Lupus erythematosus, Rheumatoid arthritis, Leukemia, Sarcoidosis, Kawasaki disease, and pelvic and head-and-neck malignancies.

Specialists

- General Surgeon
- Infectious Disease Physician
- Internist

Work Restrictions / Accommodations

Restriction of work activities (usually temporary) may be indicated depending on the degree of weakness, the general ill health experienced, and degree of recovery expected. If the individual is especially fatigued, he or she may need less strenuous or part-time work. If the individual experiences pain, he or she may benefit from aggravating movements or positions. Accommodations at work may temporarily include an allotment of time and space for quiet rest periods.

Comorbid Conditions

Comorbid conditions include conditions such as obesity, diabetes, and AIDS.

Complications

Complications of lymphadenitis and lymphadenopathy include localized formations of pus and tissue degeneration (abscesses); inflammations of deep, subcutaneous tissue (cellulitis); and a systemic, invasive, bacterial infection of the bloodstream (sepsis). Sepsis has been shown to be fatal for 30-50% of sufferers and is of particular concern when individuals have not received prompt treatment.

Factors Influencing Duration

Length of disability depends upon the etiology of symptoms, the disease process diagnosed, and treatment options. Factors that influence the length of disability for lymphangitis include the type of infectious agent, how promptly the infectious agent was discovered, and effectiveness of treatment. Length of disability for lymphadenopathy varies considerably depending upon the disorder diagnosed, the type of treatment necessary, effectiveness of treatment and prognosis.

Length of Disability

Length of disability depends on the underlying cause of the condition.

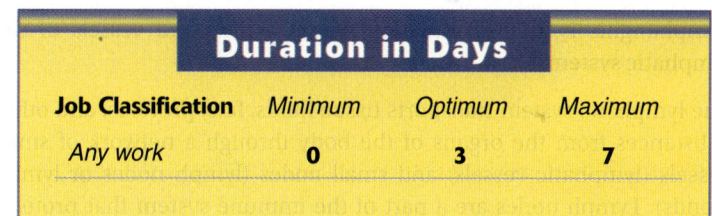

Job Classification	Minimum	Optimum	Maximum
Any work	0	3	7

Failure to Recover

If an individual fails to recover within the maximum duration expectancy period, the reader may wish to reference the following questions to assist in better understanding the specifics of an individual's medical case.

Regarding diagnosis:

- Has underlying cause of condition been identified and confirmed?
- Is condition due to infection as a result of bacteria, viruses, fungi, or other organisms?
- Are conditions present, such as the following: lymphoma, HIV infection, mononucleosis, toxoplasmosis, non-Hodgkin's lymphoma, Epstein-Barr virus, cytomegalovirus, cat-scratch disease, tuberculosis lymphadenitis, secondary syphilis, hepatitis B, lym-

phogranuloma venereum, chancroid, lupus erythematosus, rheumatoid arthritis, leukemia, sarcoidosis, Kawasaki disease, and pelvic and head-and-neck malignancies?
- Is it being effectively resolved or managed?
- Has individual experienced any complications such as abscesses, cellulitis, or sepsis?

Regarding treatment:
- If treatment was delayed, what was the criteria?
- Did the individual undergo a period of observation if clinical signs were reassuring?
- Is a biopsy now appropriate?
- Has infection and inflammation been effectively resolved?
- Has a culture and sensitivity been done to determine the most effective antibiotic to be used?
- Was causative agent antibiotic-resistant?
- If condition has persisted past what is expected for viral resolution, does diagnosis need to be revisited?

- If infected nodes caused an abscess, was surgical drainage required? Was surgical drainage effective?

Regarding prognosis:
- Is delayed recovery due to complication by abscess formation, cellulitis, or sepsis?
- If treatment has not been as effective as expected, has a culture and sensitivity been done to determine the most effective antibiotic to be used?
- Have antibiotic-resistant organisms been ruled-out?
- Is the etiology of generalized lymphadenopathy a malignant or systemic disease, such as lymphoma, AIDS, or leukemia?
- What is prognosis for the underlying condition?
- Is underlying cause due to environmental substances, medications, or drugs that can be avoided?
- Can alternate medications be used instead?
- Would protective clothing or change in occupational environment be beneficial?

References

Ferrer, Robert. Lymphadenopathy: Differntial Diagnosis and Evaluation. University of Texas Health Sciences Center at San Antonio. 15 Oct 1998. 22 Aug 2000 <http://www.aafp.org/afp/981015ap/ferrer.html>.

Rosen, Peter. Emergency Medicine: Concepts and Clinical Practice, 4th ed. St. Louis: Mosby Year-Book, Inc, 1998 10 Mar 2001 <http://home.mdconsult.com/das/book/view/624?sid=35999613>.

Lymphangitis
Other names / synonyms: Acute and Subacute Lymphangitis, Chronic Lymphangitis, Lymph Gland Infection
457.2

Definition

Lymphangitis is an inflammation of the glands and vessels of the lymphatic system.

The lymphatic system transports tissue fluids, fats, proteins, and other substances from the organs of the body through a network of small vessels (lymphatic vessels) and small nodes (lymph nodes or lymph glands). Lymph nodes are a part of the immune system that protects against infections, inflammation, and cancer. They produce white blood cells to help the body fight off foreign substances, and also sift out foreign substances, such as bacteria or cancer cells.

The usual cause of lymphangitis is bacteria, most often streptococci or staphylococci, which enter the body through a wound, a scrape (abrasion), or an insect or animal bite. The infection may cause abscesses to form and cellulitis to develop. The infection may progress rapidly, often in a matter of hours, and can lead to an infection in the blood (sepsis) and death if not treated promptly.

Risk factors for lymphangitis may include working with animals, or working with tools and equipment, particularly if they are rusty.

Diagnosis

History: The individual may complain of red streaks beginning at the site of the wound that lead to the groin or armpit, throbbing pain along the area of the wound, fever (between 100-104 degrees F), chills, loss of appetite, unintentional weight loss, headache, muscle aches, and a general ill feeling (malaise).

Physical exam: The most prominent symptom of lymphangitis is red steaks that extend from the wound, usually located on the arm or leg, toward the lymph nodes. Lymph nodes in the armpit (axillary), neck (cervical), or groin (inguinal) may be enlarged and tender. There may be swelling at the site of the wound. Chills, fever, and a rapid pulse rate may be noted.

Tests: A complete blood count (CBC) should be done to determine if the white blood cell count is elevated (leukocytosis). Wound cultures need to be done only if the wound is open and pus is present. Blood cultures should be done if there is suspicion that the infection is progressing.

Treatment

Lymphangitis may spread within hours, and spreading to the bloodstream may be fatal; treatment should commence promptly. The source of the infection should be determined and treated with antibiotics. Analgesics may be prescribed for pain and anti-inflammatory medications may help reduce the inflammation and swelling. Warm moist compresses should be applied to the localized infection to reduce inflammation and pain, the affected area should be elevated if possible to reduce swelling, and the affected area should be immobilized to decrease pain and the spread of infection. Incision and drainage from an abscess may be required, but this should be done only when it is clear that the abscess is associated with the site of initial infection.

Prognosis

Without prompt treatment, the infection may lead to an infection in the bloodstream (sepsis) and even death. Prompt treatment with antibiotics offers a complete recovery within a few days.

Differential Diagnosis

The most common differential diagnosis is thrombophlebitis (inflammation of a vein obstructed with a blood clot).

Specialists

- Infectious Disease Physician
- Internist

Work Restrictions / Accommodations

Elevation and the application of warm compresses to the affected limb may be required. If the individual does not have a sedentary job, sufficient time and a private area to appropriately treat the affected limb will need to be provided.

Comorbid Conditions

Underlying conditions such as diabetes mellitus may lengthen disability.

Complications

Complications of lymphangitis include the spread of infection through the bloodstream (sepsis), which can be fatal. Abscess formation and inflammation of the skin (cellulitis) are other complications of lymphangitis.

Factors Influencing Duration

Length of disability might be influenced by the individual's age, the extent of infection, and the response to antibiotic treatment.

Length of Disability

Duration in Days

Job Classification	Minimum	Optimum	Maximum
Sedentary work	2	3	14
Light work	3	4	14
Medium work	7	9	14
Heavy work	7	9	14
Very Heavy work	7	9	14

Failure to Recover

If an individual fails to recover within the maximum duration expectancy period, the reader may wish to reference the following questions to assist in better understanding the specifics of an individual's medical case.

Regarding diagnosis:

- Did the individual have a history that would place him/her at risk for developing lymphangitis (i.e., a scrape; an insect or animal bite)?
- Are there red streaks extending from the wound to the local lymph node(s) that might include lymph nodes in the armpit (axillary), neck (cervical), or groin (inguinal)? Are these lymph nodes enlarged and tender?
- Is there swelling at the site of the wound?
- Is there a fever or rapid pulse?
- Has a recent complete blood count (CBC) been done to determine if the white blood cell count is elevated (leukocytosis)?
- Is there an open wound open or wound exudate? If so, have wound cultures been done?

Regarding treatment:

- Was referral to an infectious disease specialist considered?
- Was surgical excision and drainage indicated?
- Did the symptoms persist after treatment with antibiotics? If so, was a repeat culture and sensitivity done to determine appropriate antibiotic therapy?

Regarding prognosis:

- Did the individual have a full recovery?
- Did the individual suffer any complications that may have impacted recovery and prognosis?

References

Berkow, Robert E. The Merck Manual of Medical Information - home ed. Merck & Co., Inc., 1995. 1 Jan 2001 <http://www.merck.com/pubs/mmanual_home/sec17/174.htm>.

Magnetic Resonance Imaging

Other names / synonyms: MRI, Nuclear Magnetic Resonance Imaging

88.91, 88.92, 88.93, 88.94, 88.95, 88.97

Definition

Magnetic resonance imaging (MRI) is a noninvasive diagnostic technique that provides detailed cross-sectional images of organs and structures without the use of x-rays or other radiation.

Each part of the body, on a cellular level, responds differently when exposed to a magnetic field. Therefore, when an individual is surrounded by a magnetic field, a computer can measure the way in which the different parts of the body respond to the magnetic field, resulting in detailed images that can be used for diagnosis of various medical conditions.

MRI is particularly suited to imaging soft tissues. It can assess organ function, reveal degenerative changes in body structures, and may be used in evaluating the suitability of organs for transplant. Also, unlike Computed Tomography (CT) scans, in which the slices are cross-sectional, MRI can produce slices in any direction throughout the body.

MRI is commonly used to reveal tumors throughout the body, examine joints and soft tissues, or evaluate cardiac or brain function.

Reason for Procedure

MRI can be used to reveal tumors throughout the body, indicating their precise location and extent. It can also be used to produce detailed images of the internal structure of the brain, spinal cord, eye, and ear and is useful for examining joints and soft tissues, particularly in the knee and shoulder.

In addition to imaging solid structures, MRI protocols have been developed for highlighting fluid flow, allowing investigation of blood vessels (MRI angiography). Evaluation of cardiac function is becoming practical. Some facilities are acquiring the capability for very rapid imaging studies (cine MRI), permitting the study of movements throughout the cardiac cycle.

Although images produced by MRI and those produced by CT scanning are similar in many ways, MRI generally gives a much greater contrast between normal and abnormal tissues. MRI is a valuable diagnostic tool and has a role in selected cases where other techniques are unreliable. For example, dense breast tissue (as in young women) makes mammography difficult to read. So does scarring, or the presence of silicone implants. In such circumstances, if the woman is at high risk for breast cancer, MRI may be preferable to mammography.

Description

In MRI, the individual is placed inside a hollow, magnetic tube. The body is then exposed to short, pulsated radio waves. In a magnetic field, hydrogen molecules in the body line up parallel to each other. When knocked out of alignment by the strong pulse of radio waves, hydrogen nuclei produce a detectable radio signal as they fall back into alignment. Magnetic coils in the machine detect these signals. They are changed by a computer into an image based on the strength of the signal produced by the different types of tissue. Because the concentration of hydrogen varies in different soft tissues (muscle, fat, fibrous tissue), MRI can differentiate between them. Tissues that contain little or no hydrogen (such as bone) appear as darker images. Also, unlike CT scan (in which the slices are cross-sectional), MRI can produce slices in any direction throughout the body.

In some cases, the contrast of MRI images can be enhanced by means of paramagnetic contrast agents. (A paramagnetic substance is one that can be temporarily magnetized by placing it in a magnetic field.) The contrast agent, injected into a vein, is taken up selectively by tissues with more blood vessels. During the MRI procedure, these tissues emit radio waves more readily, increasing the image contrast.

For the individual, most MRI procedures involve lying on a moveable table, which is inserted into the opening of the magnet. While confining, the opening is not overly constrictive. Mild sedation is available for individuals uncomfortable in this position (claustrophobic), as are view mirrors, music, and voice communication with the attending technologists. The procedure may take as little as a few minutes or up to an hour, and is characterized by the various rapid, tapping sounds of the MRI scanner acquiring the image. Other than these sounds, the individual feels nothing, and merely has to lie still until the attendants complete the procedure. There are some newer models of MRI scanners, called open MRI scanners, which are less claustrophobic than the normal scanner, but are also not always able to provide the detailed images as are provided by traditional scanners.

Prognosis

MRI imaging provides excellent images for diagnostic purposes. However, it requires a certain level of cooperation from the individual being scanned, which precludes some individuals from having this test performed. Individuals with dementia, agitation, or psychosis may not be able to lie still long enough for the MRI to be performed.

Specialists

- Radiologist

Work Restrictions / Accommodations

No restrictions or accommodations are anticipated as a result of this procedure.

Comorbid Conditions

Individuals who are unable to lie still, such as those with severe agitation or dementia, may not be able to tolerate the testing procedure. Individuals with severe obesity or other physical abnormalities that prevent their ability to fit within the scanner may be prohibited from receiving an MRI scan.

Procedure Complications

Some individuals may experience anxiety while having the MRI scan performed. Those individuals who have cardiac pacemakers, metal clips that have been applied to blood vessels to prevent blood clot complications (ferromagnetic aneurysm clips, intrauterine metallic implants, or other metal implants) are contraindicated for MRI scans and may suffer complications if they do undergo MRI scans, since the scanner may interfere with the proper functioning of the ferromagnetic device. Another possible complication is allergy or abnormal reaction to the contrast medium that may be used during some MRI procedures.

Factors Influencing Duration

There are no factors associated with this procedure that would influence disability.

Length of Disability

No disability is expected for this procedure. Disability may occur as a result of an underlying condition.

References

Beers, Mark H., and Robert Berkow, eds. "Diagnostic Cardiovascular Procedures." The Merck Manual. Beers, Mark H., and Robert Berkow, eds. Whitehouse Station, NJ: Merck Research Laboratories, 1999. 1611-1629.

Wilson, Michael A., Jesus A. Bianco, and Donald J. Stallman. "Tumor." Textbook of Nuclear Medicine. Wilson, Michael A., ed. Philadelphia: Lippincott-Raven, 1998. 211-238.

Malaise

Other names / synonyms: Asthenia
780.7, 780.79

Definition

Malaise is a feeling of weakness, fatigue, or discomfort usually associated with an illness.

Malaise may be experienced in several diseases including most acute viral disorders, HIV-associated infections, Lyme disease, chronic fatigue syndrome and fibromyalgia.

Medications such as interferons (used in immune therapy) or GM-CSF (used in neutropenic individuals with HIV infection) may cause malaise in some individuals. Chronic exposure to allergens may cause malaise in susceptible individuals. Malaise can be associated with depression and other psychological conditions.

Diagnosis

History: Individual may report muscle pain, body discomfort, fever, headache, lethargy, altered mental status, fatigue, sore throat, chest discomfort, nonproductive cough, joint pain, memory impairment, and unrefreshing sleep.

Physical exam: The exam may reveal a low-grade fever, redness in the throat, swollen glands, low pulse and blood pressure.

Tests: Blood tests (CBC, sedimentation rate) should be done to rule out infection, anemia, and other conditions.

Treatment

Treatment for malaise should be directed toward treating the underlying conditions with rest, fluids, and analgesics.

Prognosis

Outcome is directly related to the underlying cause and treatment. Malaise is a predominant symptom of chronic fatigue syndrome, with headache, pain, low energy, and depression, and generally improves with treatment.

Differential Diagnosis

Other possibilities may include fatigue, depression, stress, and side effects of certain medications.

Specialists

- Infectious Disease Physician
- Internist
- Neurologist
- Primary Care Provider
- Psychiatrist
- Psychologist
- Pulmonologist

Rehabilitation

Individuals experiencing malaise, or generalized fatigue, may require physical and occupational therapy if symptoms persist. The frequency and duration of the therapy depends on the underlying cause of the malaise. In general, occupational therapy addresses any fatigue that may occur during activities of daily living.

Physical therapy addresses decreased endurance, strength, and range of motion. Individuals learn to perform stretching and strengthening exercises of the arms and legs to improve overall endurance.

Work Restrictions / Accommodations

A less stressful work environment may help the individual. Work hours may need to be altered to reduce individual's discomfort. Taking extra breaks during the day can also be helpful.

Complementary and Alternative Therapies

Content is intended for awareness only. Treatments may or may not be effective. Scientific evidence may be lacking and some substances have potentially toxic effects. Dr. Presley Reed and the editors do not endorse the use of these therapies in the absence of consultation with a licensed medical professional.

Acupuncture -	Can provide certain symptom relief.
Massage -	May help promote stress relief and relaxation.
Accupressure -	May help calm and balance emotions.
Hypnotherapy -	May promote relaxation, anxiety reduction, and help relieve certain symptoms.

Comorbid Conditions

Comorbid conditions may include stress and alcoholism.

Complications

Emotional stress, medications, presence of other medical conditions, and psychological status of the individual are possible complications.

Factors Influencing Duration

Factors that influence length of disability may include the individual's response to treatment, underlying causes, diet, caffeine intake, and mental health of the individual.

Length of Disability

Vague diagnosis (discomfort with weakness or fatigue). Malaise is symptom usually associated with an illness. Contact physician for additional information to determine disability duration.

Duration in Days

Job Classification	Minimum	Optimum	Maximum
Any work	0	1	3

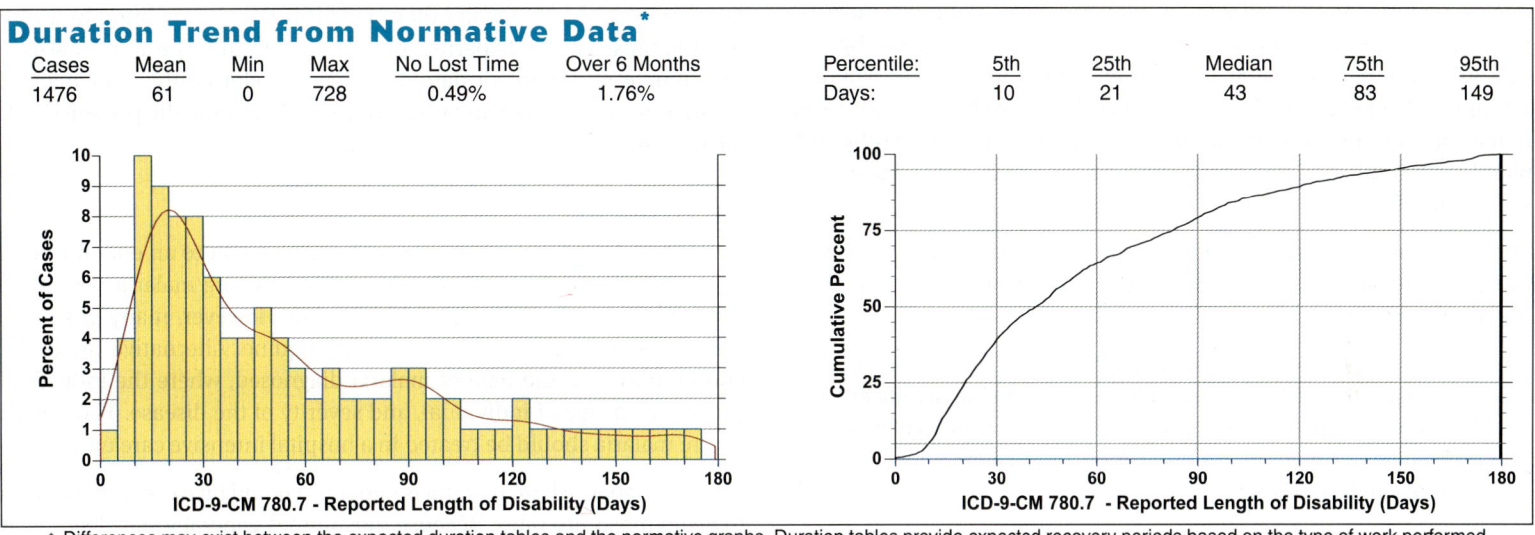

Duration Trend from Normative Data*

Cases	Mean	Min	Max	No Lost Time	Over 6 Months
1476	61	0	728	0.49%	1.76%

Percentile:	5th	25th	Median	75th	95th
Days:	10	21	43	83	149

ICD-9-CM 780.7 - Reported Length of Disability (Days)

* Differences may exist between the expected duration tables and the normative graphs. Duration tables provide expected recovery periods based on the type of work performed by the individual. The normative graphs reflect the actual observed experience of many individuals across the spectrum of physical conditions, in a variety of industries, and with varying levels of case management.

Failure to Recover

If an individual fails to recover within the maximum duration expectancy period, the reader may wish to reference the following questions to assist in better understanding the specifics of an individual's medical case.

Regarding diagnosis:

- Since malaise is considered a symptom and not, in and of itself, a disease, has underlying condition been identified? Are more diagnostic tests needed to confirm the condition?
- Is emotional stress, medication, or coexisting medical or psychological conditions complicating diagnosis and treatment of the underlying condition?

Regarding treatment:

- Once identified, is the underlying condition(s) responding to treatment? Is malaise decreasing as underlying condition resolves?
- If caused by medications, can medication type or dose be changed?
- If malaise persists despite treatment, or because of a necessary treatment, what palliative measures can be instituted?

Regarding prognosis:

- If underlying cause has not yet been determined, are further diagnostic studies planned?
- How is individual dealing with the psychological and emotional stress of malaise?
- Would individual benefit from psychological counseling?

References

Fauci, Anthony, Joseph Martin, and Eugene Braunwald. Harrison's Principles of Internal Medicine. New York: McGraw-Hill, 1998.

Guccione, Andrew A. "Functional Assessment." Physical Rehabilitation: Assessment and Evaluation. O'Sullivan, Susan B, and Thomas J. Schmitz, eds. Philadelphia:F.A. Davis Company, 1994. 193-208.

Kisner, Carolyn, and Lynn Allen Colby. Therapeutic Exercise: Foundations and Techniques, 2nd ed. Philadelphia: F.A. Davis Company, 1990.

Lundstrom, J.O. "Mosquito-Borne Viruses in Western Europe: A Review." Journal of Vector Ecology 24 1 (1999): 1-39.

Malaria

Other names / synonyms: Biduoterian Fever, Blackwater Fever, Falciparum Malaria, Quartan Malaria, Tertian Malaria Plasmodium

084, 084.0, 084.1, 084.2, 084.3, 084.4, 084.5, 084.6, 084.7, 084.8, 084.9

Definition

Malaria is an infection caused by one of several minute protozoan parasites known as Plasmodium. The disease is transmitted through the Anopheles mosquito and if a mosquito bites an infected individual, the insect too becomes infected. The parasite grows in the mosquito and is transmitted to other individuals when that mosquito bites a human and injects material from her salivary glands, which contains malarial parasites called sporozoites. Once injected into the blood by the mosquito, the parasite circulates before settling in the liver where it multiplies. After about 12 days, each liver cell is so packed with parasites that it ruptures, releasing them into the bloodstream to infect other red blood cells and simultaneously releasing a toxin that causes the symptoms of malaria.

The four species of Plasmodium that can cause malaria are P. vivax, P. ovale, P. falciparum, and P. malariae. Each species causes slightly differing symptoms.

The most serious type of malaria is P. falciparum malaria. It can become quickly fatal as the parasites multiply rapidly causing significant red blood cell destruction (hemolysis) amongst cells at all levels of maturity. The other types of malaria are less serious and cause a low grade of malaria that can last for years.

Besides mosquito bites, malaria can be transmitted through an infected blood transfusion, the use of contaminated needles, or from mother to fetus during pregnancy. It is not directly contagious from individual to individual.

Over 500 million individuals are exposed to endemic malaria and more than 200 million individuals in the world are infected with malaria. It is estimated that 2.5 million deaths annually are a result of malaria, 1 million being children. The disease is rare in the US and most temperate climates. It is found widely in tropical or subtropical areas where it is a major health problem and presents a risk for travelers. Residents in areas where malaria is endemic develop some immunity to the disease.

Diagnosis

History: Individuals who suspect malaria should see a physician immediately and be sure to mention that they have traveled to an area where malaria is common. Individuals may report flu-like symptoms including periodic fever and chills, sweating, headache, nausea, vomiting, muscle aches, and diarrhea. Symptoms also include periodic attacks of chills and fever accompanied by tiredness (malaise) and headache. Individuals may also report mental confusion and convulsions. Symptoms may appear 8 days to 4 months after being bitten by an infected mosquito but can take much longer. Symptoms are often cyclical, occurring every 48 to 72 hours. This replicates the life cycle of the parasite.

Physical exam: The exam can reveal an enlarged spleen or liver. Jaundice may also be present. Severe malaria from P. falciparum may cause jaundice, renal failure, hypoglycemia, severe anemia, high fever (hyperpyrexia), and coma.

Tests: Blood samples are examined microscopically for the presence of parasites. Because the number of parasites in the blood varies depending on the life cycle stage of the parasite, blood samples are best collected when the individual's temperature is rising and may need to be taken every few hours in order to identify the plasmodium. In severe malaria caused by P. falciparum, blood tests may indicate abnormal liver function tests, hemolytic jaundice, low platelet count, and marked anemia. Serology tests can also be done to determine the presence of P. falciparum.

Treatment

Antimalarial drugs taken prior to and during a visit to an endemic area can reduce the risk of an individual in contracting malaria. The most common antimalarial drug is chloroquine. However, many strains of malaria have become resistant to chloroquine. Alternative drugs are chosen based on the type of malaria diagnosed, where the individual was infected, age of individual, and severity of the disease. Those with severe malaria should be treated in a hospital intensive care unit (ICU).

Visitors to areas where malaria is endemic should take every precaution to avoid mosquito bites. Because mosquitoes generally start feeding at dusk, wearing fully protective clothing and using insect high DEET (15%) mosquito repellent at those times is particularly critical. Covering beds with netting is another essential precaution.

Prognosis

The outcome depends on the type of malaria contracted. Uncomplicated malaria usually subsides with proper treatment. Without treatment, P. vivax and P. ovale infections can continue to cause relapses for up to 5 years. Infections with P. malariae can last longer.

Infections with P. falciparum cause cerebral malaria resulting in mental confusion, convulsions, and coma. This prognosis is worse and without treatment death can occur as quickly as within 24 hours.

Differential Diagnosis

Malaria may mimic other fever-producing diseases including influenza, yellow fever, typhoid fever, tuberculosis, babesiosis, and meningitis, as well as urinary tract infection, liver abscess, or hepatitis.

Specialists

- Hematologist
- Hepatologist
- Infectious Disease Physician
- Internist

Work Restrictions / Accommodations

After recovery, the individual may experience extended periods of weakness that may restrict the ability to perform strenuous work or require additional breaks.

Comorbid Conditions

Individuals with immune deficiencies may be at greater risk of developing a more serious form of malaria.

Complications

Complications associated with P. falciparum include severe anemia, pulmonary edema, kidney failure, jaundice, renal failure, decreased blood sugar (hypoglycemia), and irregular heart beats (arrhythmia). P. Falciparum malaria can also block small blood vessels depriving some tissues of oxygen. P. Vivax and P. ovale can become dormant in the liver causing relapses several months to years after initial infection. Chronic infection can result in immunological disorders.

Factors Influencing Duration

Disability is influenced by the type of malaria contracted as well as the severity of the disease. If the disease affects any organs such as the kidneys, liver, heart, or brain, the disability is protracted.

Length of Disability

Acute febrile, not latent.

Duration in Days

Job Classification	Minimum	Optimum	Maximum
Sedentary work	5	7	14
Light work	5	7	14
Medium work	5	7	14
Heavy work	5	10	21
Very Heavy work	5	10	21

Failure to Recover

If an individual fails to recover within the maximum duration expectancy period, the reader may wish to reference the following questions to assist in better understanding the specifics of an individual's medical case.

Regarding diagnosis:

- Has individual recently traveled to tropical or subtropical areas and been bitten by mosquitoes?
- Has individual recently received a blood transfusion?
- Has individual used contaminated needles?
- Does individual report flu-like symptoms including periodic fever and chills, sweating, headache, nausea, vomiting, muscle aches, and diarrhea?
- Does individual report mental confusion and convulsions?
- Do the symptoms cycle every 48 to 72 hours?
- Were blood samples examined microscopically for the presence of parasites?
- Has a diagnosis of malaria been confirmed?

Regarding treatment:

- Was the strain of Plasmodium that caused the malaria susceptible to chloroquine?
- If not, what alternative drug(s) was chosen based on the type of malaria diagnosed, where individual was infected, age of individual, and severity of the disease?
- Did individual require hospitalization?
- Has individual responded to drug therapy? If not, what other treatment options are available?

Regarding prognosis:

- What strain of Plasmodium caused the malaria?
- Was treatment administered for 2 to 4 weeks? Was individual compliant with medication regimen?
- Is this an initial episode of malaria or could this be a relapse?
- What other treatment options are available for this strain of Plasmodium?
- Have complications occurred such as immunological disorders?
- If P. falciparum caused malaria, has individual developed anemia, pulmonary edema, kidney failure, jaundice, renal failure, decreased blood sugar (hypoglycemia), or irregular heart beats (arrhythmia)? If so, how will these be treated and what is the expected outcome with treatment?

References

Brooks, George F., Janet S. Butel, and Stephen A. Morse. Medical Microbiology. Stamford: Appleton & Lange, 1998.

Male Climacteric

Other names / synonyms: Andropause, Hypogonadism, Male Menopause

608.89

Definition

Male climacteric (male menopause) refers to various symptoms exhibited by some men with advancing age.

Although unproved as a pathological entity, male climacteric may be associated with a decrease in the secretion of the male sex hormone, testosterone. Decreased secretion of testosterone occurs normally as a function of age (~1% decrease per year between the ages of 40 and 70). This phenomenon generally happens to some degree in all men as they get older. Forty percent of men 40 years or older experience the symptoms associated with male climacteric that occur randomly throughout the aging male population.

Little information on the worldwide prevalence of male climacteric is available. Most data on this condition are obtained from individuals in the US. Higher prevalence may occur, however, in the US and be associated with certain factors of western culture that may contribute to male climacteric. These include excessive alcohol consumption, obesity, smoking, high blood pressure (hypertension), certain prescription and over-the-counter medications, poor diet, lack of exercise, poor circulation, and psychological problems. If there is a relationship between testosterone level and the appearance of male climacteric, it may be important to note that only 20% of men between the ages of 60 and 80 have levels of testosterone below the normal limits.

Diagnosis

History: Individuals may complain of fatigue, sleep disturbances, depression, headaches, and decreased sexual drive. Other symptoms include anxiety, lethargy, mood swings, increased irritability, insomnia, difficulty attaining and sustaining an erection (impotence or erectile dysfunction), and memory impairment.

Physical exam: The exam will be normal for that of an elderly male.

Tests: The blood level of testosterone can be measured using radioimmunoassay (RIA).

Treatment

Testosterone replacement therapy (TRT) may effectively lessen symptoms of fatigue, depression, and headaches and often improves sex drive.

Testosterone is administered by patches, subcutaneous pellets, creams, gels, or by intramuscular injection on a weekly or biweekly basis for an indefinite period of time.

Psychological counseling may also be necessary to relieve symptoms of depression, anxiety, and doubt. If there is an accompanying persistent problem attaining and maintaining an erection rigid enough for sexual intercourse (impotence or erectile dysfunction), a phosphodiesterase inhibitor (Viagra) may be prescribed or surgery (penile implants or inflatable prostheses) performed.

Prognosis

TRT may lessen many of the symptoms resulting from a decreased testosterone level. This treatment however, may cause liver damage. Individual may also have an increased risk for developing prostate cancer when using TRT.

Differential Diagnosis

Conditions with similar symptoms include hardening of the arteries (atherosclerosis), diabetes mellitus, chronic alcohol liver damage, cancer, and prostate disorders. Disorders of the testes or pituitary gland (acquired hypogonadotropic hypogonadism) can result in low levels of testosterone. Use of certain drugs (alcohol, potassium-sparing diuretics, antifungals, androgens) can decrease the level of testosterone even more markedly than increasing age. Decreased testosterone may also be the result of surgical removal of the testes (orchiectomy) for testicular cancer or the treatment of prostate cancer and certain bone cancers.

Specialists

- Endocrinologist
- Psychiatrist
- Psychologist
- Urologist

Rehabilitation

Rehabilitation professionals help in decreasing the impact of the reduction of muscle and bone mass as seen in male climacteric. Forms of moderate exercise include jogging, bicycling, swimming, and weight-lifting.

Work Restrictions / Accommodations

Aside from complications of liver damage or the development of prostate cancer as a result of TRT, there are no work restrictions or accommodations associated with this condition.

Comorbid Conditions

Existing conditions that may lengthen the disability include obesity, alcoholism, and advanced age.

Complications

Complications of aging include reduced muscle and bone mass, impaired formation of blood components (hematopoiesis), and reduced mental capabilities (cognitive function).

Factors Influencing Duration

Severity of symptoms, the presence of underlying disease, method of treatment, response to treatment, and complications of treatment may influence the length of disability.

Length of Disability

Disability is not usually associated with this condition.

Failure to Recover

If an individual fails to recover within the maximum duration expectancy period, the reader may wish to reference the following questions to assist in better understanding the specifics of an individual's medical case.

Regarding diagnosis:

- Were conditions with similar symptoms such as atherosclerosis, diabetes mellitus, chronic alcohol liver damage, cancer, and prostate disorders considered in the differential diagnosis?
- Was diagnosis of male climacteric confirmed?
- Is an underlying condition (i.e., use of alcohol, potassium-sparing diuretics, antifungals or androgens) causing decreased levels of testosterone?
- Have disorders of the testes or pituitary glands been ruled out?

Regarding treatment:

- Is TRT the appropriate treatment? Is the dose of testosterone appropriate? Has the treatment been effective in reducing symptoms of hot flashes, fatigue, depression or headaches?
- Does the individual experience impotence? Are other interventions warranted, such as treatment with a phosphodiesterase inhibitor or placement of prosthesis?
- Is individual experiencing depression? Would individual benefit from psychological counseling?

Regarding prognosis:

- Have physical symptoms been effectively relieved with pharmacological treatment with TRT or a phosphodiesterase inhibitor? If not, what other treatment options are available to individual?
- Would the individual benefit from placement of a prosthesis or implant?
- Would individual benefit from psychological counseling to relieve psychological symptoms such as depression?

References

Kisner, C., and L. Colby. Therapeutic Exercise Foundations and Techniques. Philadelphia: F.A. Davis, 1990.

Lund, B.C., K.A. Bever-Stille, and P.J. Perry. "Testosterone and Andropause: The Feasibility of Testosterone Replacement Therapy in Elderly Men." Pharmacotherapy 19 8 (1999): 951-956.

Sternbach, H. "Age-associated Testosterone Decline in Men: Clinical Issues for Psychiatry." American Journal of Psychiatry 155 10 (1998): 1310-1318.

Winters, S.J. "Current Status of Testosterone Replacement Therapy in Men." Archives of Family Medicine 8 3 (1999): 257-263.

Mallory-Weiss Syndrome
Other names / synonyms: Mallory-Weiss Tear
530.7

Definition

Mallory-Weiss syndrome is the term for a tear (laceration) of the inner lining (mucous membrane) of the esophagus where it connects to the stomach (gastroesophageal junction).

Most of the tears are located on the stomach (gastric) side of the junction, although 10-20% will involve the esophagus. Ten to twenty percent of individuals with Mallory-Weiss syndrome will have two or more tears at the gastroesophageal junction.

Mallory-Weiss tears may result in massive bleeding (hemorrhage), and in 30-50% of individuals diagnosed with this condition, the tears are a result of repeated vomiting or retching. Other risk factors include alcoholism, stomach problems (gastritis, dyspepsia), heavy lifting or any action that increases abdominal pressure (e.g., coughing or straining during bowel movements), protrusion of abdominal organs through a weak area in the abdominal wall (hernia), or severe hiccuping.

Mallory-Weiss syndrome is a rare condition; however, it accounts for 5-15% of all cases of bleeding that occur in the upper gastrointestinal tract. The incidence is higher in men than in women at a ratio of approximately three-to-one. Mallory-Weiss syndrome has an overall mortality rate of 3-8 percent.

Diagnosis

History: The individual may report a history of repeated retching, vomiting, or straining. Ninety percent of individuals will report bright red blood in their vomit (hematemesis) and some will describe black, tarry stools (melena) that result from blood passing through the intestine. Other individuals may report bright red blood in their stool (hematochezia). Light-headedness followed by brief lapses in consciousness (syncope) may also be reported.

Physical exam: Finger manipulation (palpation) of the upper abdomen may reveal tenderness. The individual may appear to be dehydrated.

Tests: Visualization of the esophagus and upper region of the stomach to identify the location and size of the tear(s) can be done using a flexible fiber-optic microscope (endoscope). A complete blood count (CBC) may be done to test for low hemoglobin in the blood stream (anemia), and a test for hemoglobin in the stool (fecal occult blood test or FOBT) may further verify esophageal bleeding.

Treatment

Bleeding from Mallory-Weiss tears is sometimes left untreated because it often stops spontaneously. However, individuals who are actively bleeding during examination of the esophagus with a flexible fiber-optic microscope (endoscopy) are usually treated using techniques that are designed to control the bleeding (hemostatic techniques). Techniques that may be used to control bleeding include electrical discharge at the site of bleeding (endoscopic electrocoagulation), injection of a coagulating agent directly into the bleeding site (endoscopic sclerotherapy), and exposure of the blood to a high energy light beam (laser photocoagulation).

Bleeding may also be controlled by stopping the flow of blood in the ruptured vessels using a blocking agent such as gelatin sponge (angiotherapy with transcatheter embolization). A final possibility is to inject a chemical (vasopressin) directly into the bleeding vessel (systemic arterial infusion), which causes it to constrict and the blood flow to stop.

Individuals are advised to avoid consumption of alcohol and irritating foods for a short period of time following endoscopic treatment for Mallory-Weiss syndrome.

Prognosis

Seventy-five to ninety percent of individuals who have only intermittent bleeding and are left untreated will stop bleeding and heal spontaneously. Recurrence of the bleeding rarely occurs in such cases. Actively bleeding tears can be treated successfully using any of the three hemostatic techniques with success rates nearing 100 percent. Blocking the bleeding vessel with a gelatin sponge (angiotherapy with transcatheter embolization) will be successful approximately 80% of the time. Injection of an agent (vasopressin) directly into the bleeding vessel (systemic arterial infusion) has been found to control bleeding from Mallory-Weiss tears 71% of the time.

Differential Diagnosis

Conditions that present with similar symptoms as Mallory-Weiss syndrome include peptic ulcer, inflammation of the stomach (gastritis) or esophagus (esophagitis), rupture of the esophagus (Boerhaave's syndrome), bleeding from enlarged veins in the esophagus (esophageal varices), or stomach cancer.

Specialists

- Gastroenterologist
- Internist

Work Restrictions / Accommodations

Alcohol intake should be curtailed. Restrictions on any activity that increases intra-abdominal pressure (such as lifting, climbing, and strenuous physical activity) should be expected following treatment for Mallory-Weiss syndrome.

Comorbid Conditions

Existing conditions that may impact an individual's ability to recover and further lengthen disability include alcoholism, diabetes, and an increased venous pressure in the liver circulation (portal hypertension).

Complications

Possible complications of Mallory-Weiss syndrome include bleeding from the site of the tear. If left unchecked, loss of blood may result in low hemoglobin in the blood stream (anemia). Severe and uncontrolled bleeding may ultimately cause low-blood pressure (hypotension), life-threatening organ dysfunction (shock), and death.

Factors Influencing Duration

Factors that might influence the length of disability include continuation of the underlying cause for the onset of the Mallory-Weiss tears. Continued vomiting, retching, or abdominal straining may have this effect.

Length of Disability

The expected length of disability following treatment for Mallory-Weiss tears depends upon the requirements of the job. Heavy physical labor, climbing, or straining that increases intra-abdominal pressure may have to be curtailed until recovery is complete.

Medical treatment for single episode without surgery.

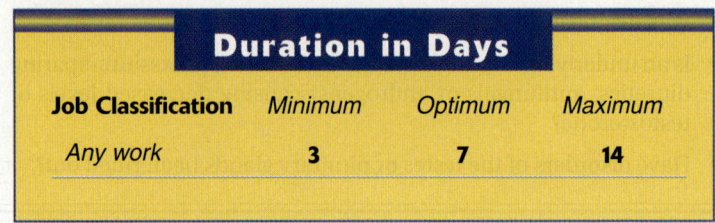

Job Classification	Minimum	Optimum	Maximum
Any work	3	7	14

Failure to Recover

If an individual fails to recover within the maximum duration expectancy period, the reader may wish to reference the following questions to assist in better understanding the specifics of an individual's medical case.

Regarding diagnosis:

- Did the individual present with a complaint of a severe vomiting episode or bloody emesis?
- Was the diagnosis confirmed with an upper GI series or endoscopy?
- If the diagnosis was uncertain were other conditions with similar symptoms ruled out (i.e., peptic ulcer, gastritis or esophagitis, Boerhaave's syndrome, esophageal varices, and stomach cancer)?
- Did the individual receive urgent consultation by an appropriate specialist (gastroenterologist, general surgeon)?

Regarding treatment:

- Did the individual receive prompt control of the bleeding using endoscopic electrocoagulation, sclerotherapy or laser photocoagulation?
- If not, were other methods used to control bleeding (i.e., angiographic embolization)?
- Did the individual experience severe blood loss or hypotensive shock? If so, was the fluid loss treated appropriately with rapid intravenous fluid administration and/or transfusion?
- Has the individual been instructed to avoid alcohol or other gastric irritants until healed? Have they been compliant with the instructions?
- Would individual benefit from enrollment in an alcohol dependency program?

Regarding prognosis:

- Did the individual have a delay in treatment that might impact severity of symptoms and prognosis?
- Has the individual experienced re-bleeding? If so, was the individual re-evaluated by a gastroenterologist?
- Does individual have an underlying condition that may impact recovery, such as alcoholism, diabetes, liver disease or portal hypertension?
- Did the individual experience any complications such as organ dysfunction secondary to the blood loss? If so, how will this impact the recovery and prognosis?

References

Fan, K.D., et al. "Acute Upper Gastrointestinal Bleeding in Chang Gung Memorial Hospital: Comparison Between 1980 and 1989." Chang-Keng i Hsueh Tsa Chih 16 3 (1993): 182-187.

LeMone, P., and K.M. Burke. Medical-Surgical Nursing. Upper Saddle River, NJ: Prentice Hall Health, 2000.

Lichtenstein, D.R. "Nonvariceal Upper Gastrointestinal Hemorrhage." Therapy of Digestive Disorders. Wolfe, M.M Philadelphia: W.B. Saunders Company, 2000. 127-152.

Peterson, W.L., and L. Laine. "Gastrointestinal Bleeding." Gastrointestinal Disease. Sleisenger, M.H., and J.S. Fordtran, eds. Philadelphia: W.B. Saunders Company, 1993. 162-192.

Malunion and Nonunion of Fracture
733.8, 733.81, 733.82

Definition

A malunion is a broken (fractured) bone that has healed in an imperfect position. A nonunion is a fracture that has failed to heal after several months.

In malunion, the bone could have healed at a crooked angle, could be rotated on itself, or the fractured ends could be overlapped causing bone shortening.

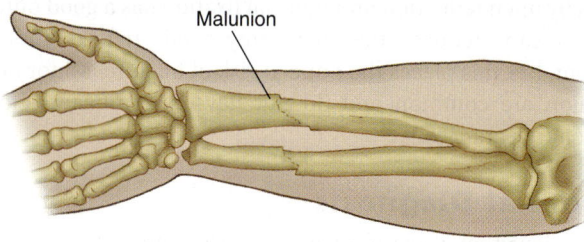
Malunion

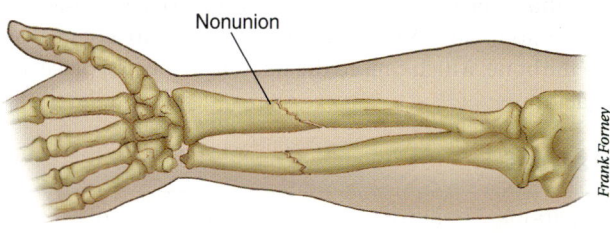
Nonunion

Nonunion may be caused by several different factors. The broken ends of bone might be separated too much (overdistraction), which can occur if excess traction weight was applied. There could have been too much motion at the fracture site, either from inadequate immobilization after the injury or from having a cast removed prematurely. There could have been muscle or other tissue caught between the fracture fragments. The presence of infection at the fracture site can prevent healing. There could be poor blood supply at the fracture site. A disease of bone itself could be present (e.g., bone cancer). Diabetes can cause nonunion as can corticosteroids or malnutrition.

There are 2 types of nonunions: fibrous nonunion and false joint (pseudarthrosis). Fibrous nonunion refers to fractures that have healed with fibrous tissue, not bone. Pseudarthrosis refers to nonunions in which continuous movement of the fracture fragments led to the development of a false joint.

Individuals at risk for malunion are those who have inadequate immobilization of the fracture or premature removal of the cast or other immobilizer. Individuals who had a severe trauma, refracture, or large displacement between fracture fragments and those whose bone was broken into many pieces (comminuted) are at an increased risk of nonunion. Also, diabetics and individuals who are malnourished or taking corticosteroids have a higher risk of nonunion. Nonunion occurs in approximately 5-10% of the 6 million fractures that occur in North America each year. Malunion occurs in many fractures, although only to a slight degree that causes little or no functional difficulties.

Diagnosis

History: History is of a fracture that may or may not have been treated by a physician. The individual may report pain, instability, or deformity at the site of a previously broken bone.

Physical exam: The exam reveals the deformity of a malunion and the instability of a nonunion. Touching with the hands (palpation) may reveal tenderness.

Tests: Plain x-rays demonstrate the fracture malunion or nonunion. At times, CT scan, MRI, or bone scan may be indicated.

Treatment

Nonunions with little separation of fracture fragments may be successfully treated without surgery by electromagnetic bone stimulators. However, most malunions and nonunions require open surgery to realign the fracture fragments (open reduction) and stabilize the fracture by use of metal plates, rods, screws, and/or wires (internal fixation).

Treatment of nonunion is complemented with a bone graft that is obtained from the individual (autogenous graft), from another individual (allograft, homogenous graft), or from an animal (heterogenous graft). Treatment of pseudarthrosis involves removal (resection) of the false joint tissue prior to placement of the bone graft.

Malunion is treated by breaking (dividing) the malunion followed by reduction and internal fixation. Alternatively, the bony deformity from a malunion may be excised (osteotomy), however, this approach weakens the bone. Infection will require surgical removal of any infected bone or tissue, followed by intensive antibiotic treatment.

In some instances, nonunion causes only slight problems, such as certain fractures of a wrist bone (scaphoid), and the condition is left untreated. Likewise, malunion may be left untreated if it causes little or no functional difficulties, such as malunion of the collarbone (clavicle).

Prognosis

Bone grafting is usually a successful treatment of nonunion, especially in the long bones of the body. Electrical bone stimulators have a limited success rate and treatment takes several months. Treatment of malunion by open reduction and internal fixation has a good outcome. Osteotomy can reduce the deformity and relieve functional impairment, but this places the bone at risk of fracture. Minor degrees of malunion are common and do not have a significant effect on function or appearance.

Differential Diagnosis

There may be other diseases that cause deformities, such as gout, rheumatoid arthritis, or nutritional deficiencies during childhood, but these conditions have quite a different history. Delayed union may be mistaken for nonunion. A nonunion could be due to a bone disease or cancer in the bone, which caused the fracture in the first place (a pathological fracture).

Specialists

- Occupational Therapist
- Orthopedic Surgeon
- Physical Therapist

Rehabilitation

In cases of nonunion or malunion fractures, physical therapy often becomes involved in the fitting of bone stimulators. These units are electrical stimulation devices that may be used to stimulate bone growth.

If immobilization is required by use of a cast, passive and active range-of-motion exercises of the affected joint and muscles begin as soon as the bone has healed properly and the cast is removed. Exercise to the affected joint called range of motion is generally started and performed, as tolerated. This is often initiated in a warm whirlpool or in conjunction with another form of heat treatment and continued until all the movement is restored.

Range-of-motion exercises begin with passive range of motion. This is then progressed to the individual performing some of the motion/effort along with the help of the therapist (active assist range of motion). As the individual improves with increased motion of the joint, the next step of progression is active range of motion (the individual performs all the motion independently).

In this early phase of strengthening, isometric exercises begin with muscles around the involved joint contracting yet no movement takes place at the joint.

The next phase of rehabilitation involves movement at the joint called isotonic exercise. An example of this type of rehabilitation exercise is strengthening with weights and elastic bands. As the resistance is lifted or pulled throughout the range of motion, the muscle shortens and lengthens. Strength training of this type also includes weight equipment/machines. The amount of resistance is determined by increasing the weight to a point where the individual's final repetition of each set is difficult but obtainable.

The physical therapist may need to make modifications depending on the extent of the fracture and for individuals with arthritis or other joint irritations.

Work Restrictions / Accommodations

The restrictions and accommodations would be related to the specific fracture and the severity of the malunion or nonunion. If surgical correction is necessary, work may be modified temporarily to avoid use of the affected limb.

Comorbid Conditions

Obesity, bone cancer, cardiovascular disease, rheumatoid arthritis, osteoarthritis, and osteoporosis may influence the length of disability.

Complications

A malunion can result in a functional impairment with limited mobility. Malunion in a finger can interfere with the use of other fingers. There can be nerve damage, especially with an elbow fracture. A malunion in a leg can result in an abnormal gait. Any malunion can put increased stresses on other joints causing pain and/or accelerated wear. Major degrees of malunion can cause impairment in function and significant deformity and can lead to degenerative arthritis. A nonunion can be painless, but the fracture will be unstable and the bone not as strong.

Factors Influencing Duration

Disability will be influenced by the location and severity of the malunion or nonunion.

Length of Disability

Duration depends on the bone involved and whether the fracture is a malunion or nonunion. Contact physician for additional information.

Failure to Recover

If an individual fails to recover within the maximum duration expectancy period, the reader may wish to reference the following questions to assist in better understanding the specifics of an individual's medical case.

Regarding diagnosis:

- Does the individual have a fractured bone that has healed in an imperfect position (malunion) or fracture that has failed to heal after several months (nonunion)?
- Does the individual have any of risk factors (over distraction, poor blood supply at site of fracture, diabetes)?

- Does the individual report pain, instability, or deformity at the site of a previous fracture?
- What symptoms does the individual have?
- What findings were present on exam?
- Has the individual received x-rays, CT scan, MRI, or bone scan to confirm the diagnosis?
- Have conditions with similar symptoms been ruled out?

Regarding treatment:
- Did the individual have open reduction or internal fixation?
- Was a bone graft done?

Regarding prognosis:
- Is the individual active in physical therapy? In a home exercise program?
- Is the individual's employer able to accommodate necessary restrictions such as work modification?
- Does the individual have any of these conditions, such as obesity, bone cancer, cardiovascular disease, rheumatoid arthritis, osteoarthritis that could influence the length of disability?
- Does the individual have any complications such as nerve damage, abnormal gait, or degenerative arthritis?

References
Adams, John, and David Hamblen. "Complications of Fractures." Outline of Fractures: Including Joint Injuries. Edinburgh: Churchill Livingstone, 1999. 52-73.

Kessler, R.M. Management of Common Musculoskeletal Disorders: Physical Therapy Principles and Methods. Philadelphia: J.B. Lippincott Company, 1990.

Kisner, C., and L. Colby. Therapeutic Exercise Foundations and Techniques. Philadelphia: F.A. Davis Company, 1990.

Salter, Robert. "Fractures and Joint Injuries: General Features." Textbook of Disorders and Injuries of the Musculoskeletal System. Baltimore: Williams & Wilkins, 1999. 417-497.

Mammography
Other names / synonyms: Mammogram
87.36, 87.37

Definition

Mammography is an x-ray technique used to visualize the interior tissue of the breast. It is a procedure used to screen for, diagnose, and monitor breast disease.

Women who have a higher risk of developing breast cancer require more frequent mammograms, including those with a family history of breast cancer, genetic alterations (which may make them prone to breast cancer), or noncancerous (benign) breast disease. Other women who are at risk of developing breast cancer are those who are greater than 50 years old (especially if overweight), consume alcohol, began menstruating before 12 years of age, went through menopause after 55 years of age, had their first child after 30 years of age, or have no biological children. Men who have had radiation exposure and those who have Klinefelter's syndrome are at an increased risk of developing breast cancer.

A baseline mammogram should be obtained for all women between the ages of 35-40 so that it may be compared to those obtained later. Women aged 40 and older should have a screening mammogram every 1-2 years. However, women who are at a higher risk of developing breast cancer usually begin mammogram screening at an earlier age.

In the US, more than 180,000 individuals are diagnosed with breast cancer each year, fewer than 1,500 of which are men. The incidence of breast cancer varies for different age groups; for instance, approximately 150 per 100,000 women in their 40s will be diagnosed with breast cancer each year. Forty million mammograms are performed in the US each year.

Reason for Procedure

Mammography is most frequently used as a screening device for the detection of breast cancer at an early stage. It may be used as a screening device in men who are at a high risk of developing breast cancer. Mammography is also used for women and men to diagnose or monitor breast disease. The images produced by mammography provide visual comparisons and/or differentiations between scar tissue, cysts, abscesses, and tumors, and determines the degree of spread of an existing tumor (cancer staging).

Although a mammogram can identify an abnormality in breast tissue, further testing is required to determine whether or not the abnormality is cancerous (malignant). Diagnostic ultrasound may be used as an additional diagnostic tool, but a sample (biopsy) of the suspected tissue would need to be analyzed to confirm the diagnosis.

Description

Mammography is performed on an outpatient basis without anesthesia. It causes only brief, mild discomfort. The individual stands or sits at the mammography unit, and his or her bare breast is placed on a platform (detector plate). A plate (compression paddle) is lowered to flatten the breast slightly to allow optimal visualization. The x-rays pass down through the breast and the resulting image is recorded either on x-ray film (film mammography) or a computer (digital mammography). Images may be taken from more than one angle by adjusting the breast and the angle of the mammography unit. Two images (craniocaudal and mediolateral oblique) are usually taken from each breast during a screening or diagnostic mammogram. Additional images may be taken should an abnormality be detected. Individuals who are experiencing nipple discharge may have a ductogram performed to highlight the milk duct and assist in the visualization of a mass. For this procedure, a fine plastic tube is inserted into a milk duct at the nipple and a small amount of an x-ray contrast medium is injected. The mammogram is then performed as usual. Mammograms are evaluated by a radiologist.

Prognosis

Mammography is a simple procedure that has no ill effect on the individual. The individual is able to return to normal activities immediately. The vast majority of masses detected by mammography are benign. For a variety of reasons, cancerous masses are occasionally missed (false positive) on a mammogram.

Specialists

- General Surgeon
- Gynecologist
- Oncologist
- Radiologist

Work Restrictions / Accommodations

There are no work restrictions or accommodations associated with mammography; however, if a mammogram is poor (e.g., blurry, bad angle, or inadequate breast compression), the individual may need additional time off to have the procedure repeated.

Comorbid Conditions

There is no disability associated with mammography.

Procedure Complications

Although the radiation exposure is negligible, approximately 1 out of 10,000 individuals will develop radiation-related breast cancer 10 or more years following mammography.

Factors Influencing Duration

Disability is not associated with mammography.

Length of Disability

No disability is expected for this procedure. Disability may occur as a result of an underlying condition.

References

Feig, Stephen. The Radiologic Clinics of North America: Breast Imaging. Philadelphia: W.B. Saunders Company, 2000.

Runowicz, Carolyn. "Benign Breast Disease and Screening for Malignant Tumors." Textbook of Gynecology. Copeland, Larry, and John Jarrell, eds. Philadelphia: W.B. Saunders Company, 2000. 1107-1130.

Mammoplasty, Augmentation

Other names / synonyms: Augmentation Mammaplasty, Breast Augmentation

85.5, 85.50, 85.51, 85.52, 85.53, 85.54

Definition

Breast augmentation or augmentation mammoplasty is a procedure in which mammary implants are either placed beneath the breast tissue or beneath the muscle of the chest wall in an effort to increase the size of or reconstruct the breast. Implants consist of a silicone bag filled with either silicone gel, saline (salt water), air, or some combination of these.

Augmentation mammoplasty may be performed as a reconstructive procedure after surgery for breast cancer. It may also be performed as a cosmetic procedure, either because the woman desires larger breasts or because of a difference in size or shape between the 2 breasts.

Although about 1 million women in the US alone have silicone-filled implants, there is concern about the risks of silicone leaks. Therefore, the FDA currently approves their use only in special cases, such as for post-mastectomy reconstruction, congenital breast deformities, women who cannot use saline implants, and women involved in research studies. Approximately 100,000 women receive saline implants every year.

Reason for Procedure

A breast augmentation procedure is performed either to increase the size of the breasts for cosmetic reasons or to reconstruct a breast following complete or partial removal during treatment for breast cancer.

Description

The procedure may be performed in a hospital or outpatient setting, under local or general anesthesia. An incision is made, most often under the breast but alternatively through the nipple or in the armpit. The breast tissue is brought forward to create a pocket in which the implant is inserted, and the incision is closed with sutures or surgical clips.

Prognosis

Most women recover well from the surgery; recuperation time is about 2 weeks.

Specialists

- Plastic Surgeon

Work Restrictions / Accommodations

Following recuperation, possible work restrictions and accommodations include temporary transfer from duties involving lifting or strenuous physical activity.

Comorbid Conditions

Comorbid conditions may include obesity, smoking, substance abuse, bleeding disorders, and immune system disorders.

Procedure Complications

Potential surgical complications include bleeding or infection. Longer-term complications may include development of painful, hardened scar tissue, and rupture or displacement of the implants. If a woman chooses to have the implant removed without replacing it, the result may be cosmetic problems such as dimpling or puckering of the skin.

Factors Influencing Duration

Factors that might influence the length of disability include the development of complications and the individual's type of work, including the frequency and degree of physical activity.

Length of Disability

The duration of the disability depends on the type of surgery performed (e.g., whether placed in front or behind pectorals and extent of muscle incision) and job requirements. Disability may be longer for jobs that are very strenuous; for example, those involving heavy lifting.

Duration in Days

Job Classification	Minimum	Optimum	Maximum
Sedentary work	3	7	10
Light work	3	7	10
Medium work	7	14	21
Heavy work	14	21	28
Very Heavy work	21	28	35

References

Papanastiou, Stephanos, and Judy Evans. "Postoperative Analgesia in Augmentation Mammaplasty." Plastic and Reconstructive Surgery 105 (2000): 1241.

Spear, Scott L., Mohamed Elmaraghy, and Christoher Hess. "Textured-surface Saline-filled Silicone Breast Implants for Augmentation Mammaplasty." Plastic and Reconstructive Surgery 105 (2000): 1542-1552.

Manic Disorder, Recurrent

Other names / synonyms: Recurrent Hypomanic Psychosis, Recurrent Mania

296.1

Definition

This diagnosis describes those who have recurrent manic episodes, characterized by an elevated (euphoric) mood and self-image. The individual is filled with ideas and overflowing with energy. Behavior is dramatic, expansive, and usually overactive. Behavior may also be impulsive, intruding on other people's lives, or alienating to friends, family, and co-workers. Because of an inflated sense of self-worth (grandiosity), there is often lack of insight into how harmful the mania is to relationships. Mood can be unstable and irritable. If opposed, the individual may even become hostile.

Manic episodes usually have a rapid onset, building suddenly over a few days, and last a few weeks to several months. They are often preceded by difficulty sleeping. Impaired sense of reality (psychotic features) can be seen during mania, such as seeing visions, hearing voices (hallucinations), or fixation upon untrue beliefs (delusions). The psychosis is usually consistent with the individual's sense of extraordinary well being. Grandiose delusions are common, such as the individual believing he is a genius or of noble birth.

Although usually beginning in the early twenties, the onset of mania ranges from adolescence to over age 50. The manic episodes usually appear after some psychologically stressful event. Recurrent mania occurs in 5% of individuals with bipolar affective disorder. Recurrent mania disorder is not the diagnosis if the manic episode are caused by a medical disorder (such as hyperthyroidism), use of antidepressant medication, or drug abuse. In a large Swiss study, prevalence up to age 35 was 2.8%.

Diagnosis

History: History is of recurrent manic episodes characterized by a persistently elevated or irritable mood for at least one week. During the episode, at least three of the following symptoms must be seen: inflated opinion of self (grandiosity), requiring drastically less sleep than usual, excessive talking, racing thoughts, distractibility, increased goal-directed activity, and indulging excessively in pleasurable activities that can have undesirable consequences (such as buying sprees or sexual binges). The manic episode leads to a marked impairment of relationships or work performance, and may even endanger the person or others.

Physical exam: The exam does not contribute to making this diagnosis. Observation of the individual's orientation, dress, mannerisms, behavior, and content of speech may provide essential clues to diagnose the illness.

Tests: Tests do not establish the diagnosis.

Treatment

Because mania is a medical and social emergency, many physicians feel that hospitalization to stabilize medication and maintain the individual's safety is the most effective form of treatment.

Mania is due to an imbalance in the brain chemicals called neurotransmitters. Lithium or divalproex sodium adjusts brain chemicals, stabilizing moods, and controlling highs and lows. When taken regularly, lithium helps prevent mania from recurring.

Because lithium may take 4 to 14 days to take effect, another faster-acting drug such as haloperidol may be given at the same time. Because haloperidol can cause unpleasant side effects, a smaller amount may be given in combination with a benzodiazepine. This can enhance the antimanic effects while reducing side effects. Anticonvulsants and calcium channel-blockers can also be used as mood stabilizers.

Prognosis

Without treatment, manic episodes can be expected to recur.

Many individuals with mild forms of mania are extremely successful because of their high energy level and enthusiasm. Eventually, however, the associated psychosis erodes social support and effective functioning.

Lithium can effectively reduce mania symptoms. Proper treatment will vastly improve the level of functioning and can usually restore the individual to their "old self." Many individuals require long-term, even lifelong, maintenance treatment, which significantly decreases the likelihood of recurrences. Not realizing the harm that mania can cause, however, individuals often refuse to take anti-mania medication or refuse to continue treatment because they feel more powerful and effective when manic.

Also, because lithium takes 4 to 10 days to be effective, other faster-acting drugs may be given at the same time. Unfortunately these drugs can have unpleasant side effects. Individual may stop taking medication to avoid these side effects. Fortunately, a smaller amount of the antimanic drug can be given in combination with a benzodiazepine, which enhances the antimanic effects while reducing unpleasant side effects.

Differential Diagnosis

Psychiatric illnesses with similar symptoms include delusional disorder, paranoid schizophrenia, or other bipolar affective illness. Cocaine or amphetamine abuse, and medical conditions such as hyperthyroidism may also mimic the symptoms of recurrent mania.

Specialists

- Psychiatrist
- Psychologist

Work Restrictions / Accommodations

Schedule may need to incorporate flex-time, a part-time position, or job sharing, and break time according to individual needs rather than a fixed schedule. Other accommodations may include creating a flexible schedule for therapy appointments, and allowing workers to phone professionals during the workday and meet with employer, supervisor, or job coach to explore other alternatives. The individual's work may need to be more closely supervised due to a lack of judgment or insight when a manic episode is developing. Night shifts or rotating shifts may increase the severity of manic episodes.

Comorbid Conditions

Coexisting conditions that may affect recovery and lengthen disability include alcohol and substance abuse, underlying neurological conditions such as multiple sclerosis, suicidal tendencies, and personality disorders.

Complications

Suicide or accidental injury are the most serious complications. Alcohol and drug abuse, common in this disorder, may contribute to symptoms associated with poor judgment. Other complications of manic episodes may include physical exhaustion, accidental injury, ruined personal relationships and finances, irregular employment or other work-related problems, and failure to attend to proper nutrition and self-care. Not realizing the harm that mania can cause, these individuals often refuse to take anti-mania medication or refuse to continue treatment because they feel more powerful and effective when manic.

In extreme cases, mental and physical activity is so frenzied that mood and behavior merge into a senseless agitation called delirious mania. Immediate treatment is vital because the individual may die of sheer physical exhaustion. Hospitalization may also be needed to protect the individual and his/her family from ruinous financial or sexual behavior.

Factors Influencing Duration

Poor compliance with medication or concurrent drug or alcohol abuse may prolong disability.

Length of Disability

Maximum disability duration includes hospitalization.

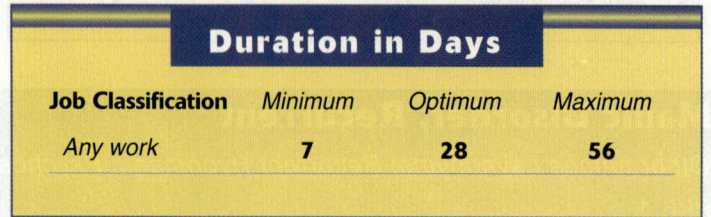

Job Classification	Minimum	Optimum	Maximum
Any work	7	28	56

Failure to Recover

If an individual fails to recover within the maximum duration expectancy period, the reader may wish to reference the following questions to assist in better understanding the specifics of an individual's medical case.

Regarding diagnosis:

- Has diagnosis of recurrent manic disorder been confirmed?
- Does the individual's behavior meet the diagnostic criteria?
- Although they share characteristic symptoms, does individual experience manic or hypomanic episodes?
- Have other conditions with similar symptoms been ruled out?
- Is the individual unaware of or denying that anything is wrong with his/her mental state or behavior?
- Has physician obtained a reliable report from a family member or associate who has ample opportunity to observe individual?
- Have all underlying physical diseases been ruled out that may be causing the mania?

Regarding treatment:

- Because mania is a medical and social emergency, would individual benefit from hospitalization to stabilize medication and maintain the individual's safety? Should treatment thereafter be inpatient or outpatient?
- Is the individual taking lithium or divalproex sodium?
- Is the individual on maintenance therapy?
- How often are the mania episodes recurring? How long do they last?

- Is the individual being treated with haloperidol? Are side effects present? Is physician considering combining haloperidol with a benzodiazepine?
- Does the individual continue to exhibit overactive or highly physical behavior?
- Is the individual taking medication as prescribed? If unwilling to take the medication, is it because the individual enjoys how a manic episode feels?
- Is there someone else available who could administer or monitor the medication regime?

Regarding prognosis:

- Since the individual may require long-term, even lifelong maintenance treatment, is individual willing and reliable in medication regime? Is there someone else who can help monitor and ensure the individual remains on medication as prescribed?

- Do manic episodes appear associated with psychosocial stressors?
- How does the individual deal with current stresses? How were major stresses dealt with in the past? If healthy and adaptive methods were used in the past, are they currently being used?
- What is happening outside of work that may be contributing to or worsening the problems experienced at work?
- Does the individual have a personal accepting support system in place? What are his/her social supports? Family? Friends? Church or other community affiliations? Are these resources being utilized?

References

Angst, J. "The Emerging Epidemiology of Hypomania and Bipolar II Disorder." Journal of Affective Disorders 50 2-3 (1998): 143-151.

Keck P.E., Jr., et al. "Outcome and Comorbidity in First Compared with Multiple Episode Mania." Journal of Nervous Mental Disability 183 5 (1995): 320-324.

Marijuana Dependence/Abuse

Other names / synonyms: Marijuana Abuse, Marijuana Addiction, Marijuana Dependence

304.3, 304.31, 304.32, 304.33, 305.2

Definition

Marijuana dependence usually develops over an extended period of time with use that gradually increases in frequency and amount. Marijuana or cannabis is made from the dried leaves, tops, and stems of the Cannabis sativa plant. Hallucinogenic substances (cannabinoids) are derived from the Cannabis sativa plant and include marijuana and hashish. Hashish is derived from the dried, resinous exudate that seeps from the plant. Marijuana is usually smoked in the form of loosely rolled cigarettes or in pipes but may also be taken orally in the form of food or tea. The effects of marijuana last 2 to 4 hours when smoked and 5 to 12 hours when taken orally.

Diagnosis is based on criteria listed in the DSM-IV-TR (Diagnostic and Statistical Manual of Mental Disorders, 4th Edition, Text Revision, published by the American Psychiatric Association). A destructive pattern of cannabis use must be evident that can lead to significant social, occupational, or medical impairment. Three or more of the following diagnostic criteria are exhibited in worst case scenarios for cannabis use: need for gradually increased amounts of cannabis to achieve the desired effect; diminished effects with continued use of the same amount of cannabis; persistent unsuccessful attempts to quit or control use; a great deal of time spent in activities related to the use of or recovery from the use of cannabis; social, occupational, recreational, or relational activities given up for the sake of cannabis use; and continued cannabis use despite knowledge of recurrent physical or psychological problems related to its use.

Individuals with a history of conduct disorder in childhood/adolescence and/or antisocial personality disorder are at risk to develop cannabis dependency. Individuals intoxicated from marijuana exhibit impaired motor coordination and social withdrawal. Individuals experience euphoria, decreased anxiety, a sensation of slowed time, and impaired judgment. Individuals may consider themselves more insightful or knowledgeable when intoxicated however both memory and concentration are impaired. Long-term use can lead to mild forms of depression, anxiety, irritability, physical and mental lethargy, or the inability to feel pleasure during activities that are normally pleasurable (anhedonia).

Marijuana and its active ingredient THC can be used for treating nausea, vomiting, chronic pain, and glaucoma. Marijuana can also be used as an antianxiety agent, muscle relaxant, appetite stimulant, and anticonvulsant.

Surveys show that at least one-third of the US population or about 65 to 70 million have at least tried using marijuana with individuals under 35 reporting most frequent usage. An estimated 5% of individuals report marijuana abuse or dependence at some time during their lifetime. About 2-3% use marijuana daily or nearly daily.

Diagnosis

History: History includes information about the pattern of past use as well as regular use in the most recent 12-month period. Symptoms reported while using marijuana may include a dreamy state of consciousness; altered sense of time, color, and spatial perceptions; and a high feeling of relaxed well-being. With increased marijuana use, the individual may report changes in cognitive functioning (memory and recall deficits or decreased speed of learning), psychological functioning (anxiety, panic attacks, or mood disorders), behavioral functioning (legal, financial, or relational issues), and/or physiological functioning (weight gain, sinusitis, bronchitis, or chronic cough). Both an individual and a family history for any substance abuse/dependence and other psychiatric disorders or treatments should be obtained.

Physical exam: Individuals may present with reddening of the lining of the eye (conjunctival injection), increased heart rate (tachycardia), dry mouth, increased appetite, or impaired motor coordination. Objective symptoms may also include increased blood pressure, decreased intraocular eye pressure, loss of coordination (ataxia), sinusitis, bronchitis, emphysema, or pulmonary dysplasia. Psychiatric examination may reveal schizophrenic symptoms or panic reactions.

Tests: A polydrug screen, preferably urine, can generally identify cannabinoid metabolites. However, these metabolites can be seen up to 4 weeks after use so the test cannot establish current use or intoxication. A urine polydrug screen should be ordered to detect whether the individual is using drugs other than marijuana and should always be confirmed by a second test since a positive test may result in serious consequences for the individual. Blood tests may show decreased levels of testosterone and luteinizing hormone. Acute cannabinoid use causes diffuse slowing of background activity as seen on an electroencephalogram (EEG) with rapid eye movement (REM) suppression. Pulmonary function tests may show decreased measures of lung function.

Treatment

According to the DSM-IV-TR, substance abuse recovery occurs in four phases: an acute phase that focuses on alleviating symptoms of withdrawal, a one-month period of abstinence during which the individual focuses on changing behaviors, an early remission phase that can last up to 12 months, and a sustained remission phase that lasts as long as the individual abstains from cannabis use or from meeting the criteria for substance or cannabis dependence.

Cannabis withdrawal symptoms rarely require inpatient monitoring or pharmacological treatment. These symptoms can include irritability, anxious mood, mild tremor, sweating, or insomnia. In severe cases of cannabis-induced anxiety or panic, antianxiety drugs may be used. Antipsychotic drugs are occasionally needed to treat protracted cannabis-induced psychosis. If cannabis was used to alleviate symptoms of depression or anxiety, appropriate antidepressants or antianxiety drugs should be considered as substitution therapy. Detoxification is not necessary.

Treatment for the one-month abstinence and early remission phases may include education on physical, emotional, and mental aspects of addiction and recovery, identification of stressors and stress management skills, improved coping skills, assertiveness training, relaxation training, and lifestyle management changes. When drug abuse is a symptom of chronic anxiety, depression, or feelings of anxiety rather than being the primary problem, psychotherapy may be helpful. Psychotherapy should focus on the reasons for the drug abuse. Family therapy is often indicated. Behavior therapy teaches ways other than drug abuse to reduce anxiety.

In addition to professional treatment, many individuals are referred to self-help groups like Narcotics Anonymous (NA) or Rational Recovery. The long-term support that self-help groups provide can be crucial in preventing relapse.

Prognosis

Dependency usually develops over an extended period of time, sometimes years, with gradual increasing amounts and frequency of use. The most reliable predictor of treatment outcome regardless of treatment strategy is the individual's readiness to change. Recovery is not an easy process and first, second, or later episodes may be followed by relapse. Cycling one or more times from recovery back through relapse to dependence or abuse is common. Outpatient therapy and counseling are becoming more common and help enable the individual to continue working.

Many individuals who seek treatment for excessive, prolonged use of marijuana respond to treatment and remain in remission from cannabis dependence especially when adequate social support systems are in place. However, a significant number of individuals experience at least one relapse after treatment. Some individuals never seek treatment and/or never stop usage. Support groups (e.g., Alcoholics Anonymous, Narcotics Anonymous, or Rational Recovery), family support, and social support all contribute to the individual's success in recovery.

Differential Diagnosis

The individual using cannabis may be suffering from a psychiatric disorder such as panic, anxiety, or bipolar disorder along with the substance abuse disorder. If substance abuse predates the onset of affective symptoms, then primary substance abuse with a secondary mood disorder is diagnosed.

Specialists

- Advanced Practice Registered Nurse
- Occupational Therapist
- Psychiatrist
- Psychologist

Work Restrictions / Accommodations

In more serious cases, temporary work accommodations may include reducing or eliminating activities where the safety of self or others is contingent upon a constant and/or high level of alertness, such as driving a motor vehicle, operating complex machinery, or handling dangerous chemicals; introducing the individual to new or stressful situations gradually under individually appropriate supervision; allowing some flexibility in scheduling to attend therapy appointments (which normally should occur during the employee's personal time); promoting planned, proactive management of identified problem areas; and offering timely feedback on job performance issues. It will be helpful if accommodations are documented in a written plan designed to promote timely and safe transition back to full work productivity.

Exposure to situations where substances of abuse are available such as pharmacies or establishments that serve alcohol should be avoided.

Comorbid Conditions

Comorbid conditions that may affect recovery and lengthen disability include any psychiatric disorders such as schizophrenia or antisocial personality disorder and the abuse of or dependence on tobacco, alcohol, or other substances. Studies show the most common polydrug combination to be alcohol, cocaine, and marijuana.

The combination of a psychiatric illness with substance abuse (dual diagnosis) can complicate the treatment of both the chemical dependency and the psychiatric illness. Up to 90% of the individuals diagnosed with a clinical psychiatric disorder also report a substance use disorder sometime in their lifetime. In addition, approximately one-third of those hospitalized for psychiatric disorders manifest coexisting nonnicotine substance use disorders.

Complications

Paradoxical anxiety, panic, and paranoid reactions to acute intoxication have been reported. Long-term effects of using marijuana include decreased testosterone levels for men that can result in a lower sperm count and increased testosterone levels for women that can possibly affect reproductive functioning. Regular marijuana use can lead to chronic weight gain, a slightly weakened immune system, or respiratory problems such as sinusitis, pharyngitis, bronchitis, emphysema, and abnormal lung tissue cells (pulmonary dysplasia).

Factors Influencing Duration

Length of disability is influenced by the duration and severity of cannabis dependence, presence or absence of chronic physical consequences of cannabis use, any underlying mental illness, other substance abuse, the individual's social support system, appropriateness of treatment choice, compliance with treatment, and adequacy of ongoing care.

Length of Disability

Although most individuals are eventually able to abstain from marijuana use, there are other individuals who become chronically dependent.

Detoxification and counseling.

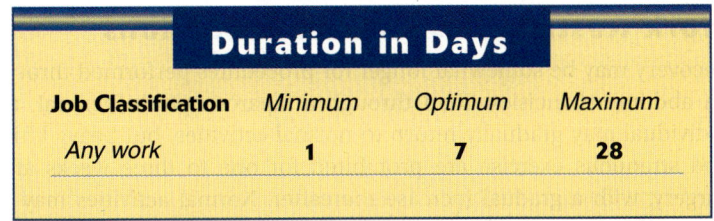

	Duration in Days		
Job Classification	Minimum	Optimum	Maximum
Any work	1	7	28

Failure to Recover

If an individual fails to recover within the maximum duration expectancy period, the reader may wish to reference the following questions to assist in better understanding the specifics of an individual's medical case.

Regarding diagnosis:

- Was a comprehensive assessment, including detailed history of past and present substance use, general medical and psychiatric history, prior psychiatric treatments with outcomes, and family and social history, completed on this individual? If not, what areas were omitted?
- Would this missing information affect the current treatment plan?
- What changes should now be made?
- Have all underlying medical disorders been identified?
- Have underlying psychiatric disorders been identified?

Regarding treatment:

- Because marijuana can often be used intermittently without causing noticeable social or psychologic dysfunction or addiction, what brought this individual to treatment in the first place?
- Is treatment aimed at behavioral and psychotherapies plus regular attendance at a support group such as Narcotics Anonymous?
- If marijuana abuse were a symptom of underlying depression or anxiety rather than the primary problem, would anxiolytics or antidepressants be helpful?

Regarding prognosis:

- Is the individual currently involved in a support group (Narcotics or Alcoholics Anonymous)?
- What other support system does individual have in place? Family? Friends? Social? Is the individual receiving the external support and motivation necessary to continue in treatment beyond the initial stages?
- Because addicts need to think about developing new relationships and rebuilding their lives, does the individual have the needed tools, skills, and encouragement to move ahead with his/her life?

References

"Cannabis (Marijuana) Dependence." Merck Manual of Diagnosis and Therapy, 17th ed. Beers, Mark H., and Robert Berkow, MD, eds. Whitehouse Station, NJ: Merck & Co., Inc., 1999. 03 Jan 2001 <http://www.merck.com/pubs/mmanual/section15/chapter195/195e.htm>.

Long, Philip W., MD. Cannabis Dependence: Treatment. Internet Mental Health. 1990. 03 Jan 2001 <http://www.mentalhealth.com/rx/p23-sb03.html>.

Marshall-Marchetti Operation

Other names / synonyms: Bladder Neck Suspension, Marshall-Marchetti-Krantz Procedure, Vesicourethropexy

59.5, 59.79

Definition

The Marshall-Marchetti operation is performed to relieve stress urinary incontinence in women. There are many terms for this type of procedure, including bladder neck suspension and vesicourethropexy (vesico means bladder, and urethropexy means surgical fixation of the urethra).

In this surgical procedure, the lower part of the bladder that connects to the urethra (bladder neck) and urethra are raised and repositioned higher in the pelvis so that the muscles of the pelvic floor can squeeze more effectively, thus helping the individual have more control over urination and less leakage from the bladder. Sutures applied between the bladder and nearby structures or tissues hold the bladder in a more functional position. There are several types of procedures performed to resuspend the bladder and urethra. There are multiple procedures that have been developed to control female stress incontinence similar to the Marshall-Marchetti procedure. The Burch procedure is such a procedure.

Reason for Procedure

This procedure is performed to treat a type of urinary incontinence called "stress incontinence." Stress incontinence refers to the inability to control urine leakage when pressure from the abdomen places extra pressure on the bladder. It is caused by the weakening of tissues that support the urethra and bladder, which allows the bladder neck and urethra to shift into an abnormal position in the pelvis. When the bladder neck and urethra are positioned abnormally, surrounding muscles are unable to apply enough pressure on the urethra to prevent the passage of urine when extra pressure is placed on the bladder. Abdominal pressure increases pressure on the bladder during normal activities such as sneezing, coughing, laughing, physical activity, and even, sometimes, by simply changing position.

In women, the tissues and muscles that support the bladder and urethra most often become weakened by pregnancy and vaginal delivery as well as following menopause when the beneficial effects of estrogen are no longer present.

Description

The procedure is performed through an incision in the abdomen (an open procedure). An incision is made low across the abdomen (suprapubic). The surgeon opens up the area around the bladder and urethra, separates the bladder and urethra from surrounding structures, lifts the vagina upward, and places sutures through tissue in the wall of the vagina alongside the urethra suturing the tissue to the symphysis pubis to provide support for the urethra. Skin is closed and a dressing is applied. A packing may be placed in the vagina to be removed in the next day or two. Urine will be drained by a catheter placed in the bladder during surgery. The catheter that is placed in the bladder may be inserted either through the urethra (Foley catheter), or it may be inserted into the bladder through a tiny incision made through the abdominal wall (suprapubic catheter).

The procedure may also be performed laparoscopically. The laparoscope is a lighted tube used for viewing the inside of the abdomen and pelvis. Instead of being performed through an incision in the abdomen, the procedure is performed through the laparoscope. Three or four small puncture wounds are placed in the abdomen, and all instruments needed for the procedure are inserted through the puncture wounds.

Prognosis

The outcome is variable. Five years after surgery, there is a good outcome in about 50% of women. These women are able to urinate (void) normally and are not affected by stress incontinence. The best chance of a good outcome occurs after the first surgery to relieve stress incontinence. Also, abdominal procedures in which the bladder neck is stabilized provide the best chance of a good outcome. Vaginal procedures may continue to allow bladder neck movement, which may result in continued incontinence. Finally, the outcome is poorer in women who have very low pressure in the urethra (found with urodynamic testing) prior to surgery.

Specialists

- Gynecologist
- Urologist

Work Restrictions / Accommodations

Recovery may be somewhat longer for procedures performed through an abdominal incision than through a laparoscope. In general, the individual may gradually return to normal activities, but heavy lifting and strenuous exercise are prohibited for one to three weeks after surgery, with a gradual increase thereafter. Normal activities may be resumed in six weeks. Development of complications such as infection may increase recovery time. Some individuals may go home with a catheter remaining in the bladder and attached to a leg bag. A longer recovery period may be needed, or if the individual returns to work with a catheter, work restrictions and accommodations may be needed to provide care to the catheter.

Comorbid Conditions

Comorbid conditions include diabetes and obesity. These conditions may increase the risk of infection and affect wound healing. The presence of other types of urinary incontinence (such as overflow, urge, functional incontinence) may affect outcome.

Procedure Complications

Complications can include injury or perforation of the bladder, urethra, bowel or rectum. Hemorrhage can also occur. During the procedure, complications from anesthesia can occur. Sometimes the individual may experience chronic inflammation and pain of the pubic bone (pubic symphysis). Another complication is incomplete emptying of the bladder during urination, resulting in the accumulation of urine in the bladder (urinary retention). Urinary retention may lead to another type of incontinence, known as overflow incontinence. In some cases, stress incontinence continues to occur.

Factors Influencing Duration

Factors that may influence length of disability include any post-surgery complications such as infection, hemorrhage, urinary retention, chronic inflammation and pain of the pubic bone area (pubic symphysis).

Length of Disability

Duration in Days

Job Classification	Minimum	Optimum	Maximum
Sedentary work	42	49	56
Light work	42	49	56
Medium work	42	49	70
Heavy work	56	63	84
Very Heavy work	56	63	112

References

Benson, J. Thomas. "Urinary Incontinence." Textbook of Gynecology, 2nd ed. Copeland, Larry J., and John F. Jarrell Philadelphia: W.B. Saunders Company, 2000. 1055-1076.

Nagle, Gratia M. "Genitourinary Surgery." Alexander's Care of the Patient in Surgery. Meeker, Margaret H., and Jane C. Rothrock St. Louis: Mosby, 1999. 501-598.

Mastectomy
Other names / synonyms: Breast Excision, Lumpectomy
85.23, 85.34, 85.36, 85.4, 85.41, 85.42, 85.43, 85.44, 85.45, 85.46, 85.47, 85.48

Definition

A mastectomy is a surgical operation to remove breast tissue and, in some cases, connecting lymph node and structural tissue. The type of mastectomy performed depends upon the tumor size, its location, the type of cancer, whether the cancer has spread to the lymph nodes, and personal wishes.

Mastectomies are usually performed as a treatment for breast cancer. The incidence of the procedure declined from 78.8 to 61.5 per 100,000 between 1988 and 1995, reflecting the trend toward performing breast-conserving surgery ("lumpectomy") as an alternative. The mastectomy procedure may or may not be coupled with reconstructive surgery.

Reason for Procedure

This procedure is used to treat breast cancer or lesions that may develop into breast cancer. It is indicated in individuals who have a collagen vascular disease, such as rheumatoid arthritis or systemic lupus erythematosus, in cases where the breast cancer is located in the central portion of the breast, in individuals with more than one tumor, and as a preventative measure for high-risk individuals.

Description

A lumpectomy removes the cancerous lump and its surrounding tissue. While the cancer is removed, most of the breast tissue is spared. A segmental or partial mastectomy is another type of breast-sparing surgery. In this procedure, the lump and surrounding tissue are removed.

The modified radical mastectomy removes the breast. The modified radical mastectomy is used for large tumors greater than 5 centimeters, in cases where reconstruction and regional control cannot be accomplished by other breast conserving procedures, and for women who do not desire a breast conserving procedure.

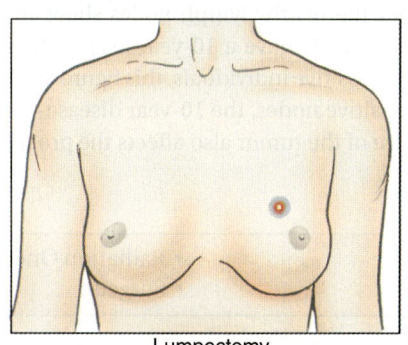
Lumpectomy

Modified radical mastectomy

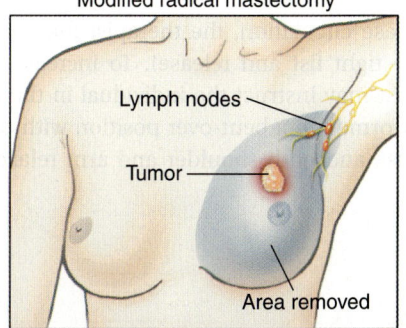
Radical mastectomy

The radical mastectomy removes the breast, armpit (axillary) lymph nodes, overlying skin, nipple, areola, and the chest wall muscle (pectoralis major muscle). Although in the past, this procedure was commonly performed, it is seldom performed today due to the associated disfigurement, the diminished arm mobility, and arm swelling (lymphedema).

The subcutaneous mastectomy removes some of the breast tissue, leaving everything else intact. This is not a treatment for breast cancer and is performed only as a preventative or prophylactic measure in persons who are deemed at high risk for the development of this disease.

Prognosis

Most women recover well from mastectomy. The extent of postsurgical discomfort and disability depends on the type of mastectomy. The most disabling surgery, radical mastectomy, is rarely performed today. However, even with modified radical mastectomy, many women experience some discomfort and swelling in the upper arm on the affected side, especially if a large number of lymph nodes were removed.

The risk of developing a new primary cancer in the remaining breast after a mastectomy (reflecting the fact that an initial cancer is indicative of belonging to a higher risk group) is about 0.5-1.0% per year. The risk of recurrence of the original cancer in the form of spreading (metastasis) to other areas of the body depends on the stage of the cancer at the time it was diagnosed and treated. The most predictive factor in determining this risk is whether the nearby lymph nodes show any sign of cancer. Node-negative individuals have a 10-year disease-free survival rate of over 70%. For node-positive individuals, this figure drops to 25%. If there are more than 4 positive nodes, the 10-year disease-free survival rate is about 15%. The size of the tumor also affects the prognosis.

Specialists

- Oncologist
- Pathologist
- Radiation Oncologist
- Surgeon

Rehabilitation

Although there has been some argument as to its effectiveness, rehabilitation therapy following a mastectomy has proven beneficial for some individuals. Therapy can begin once the individual has physician approval.

Focus of therapy should be on improving arm circulation and shoulder mobility, preventing postural deformities and muscle tension, and gaining shoulder strength. There are also special considerations for individuals who have had the lymph nodes removed in order to prevent lymphedema.

In order to increase circulation, the therapist may begin with hand-clasps (making a tight fist and release). To increase mobility in the shoulder, therapist may instruct the individual in the pendulum. The pendulum is performed in a bent-over position with the affected-side arm hanging loose and both shoulder and arm relaxed. Keeping the shoulder and arm relaxed and using body motion, the individual swings the arm forward and back, side-to-side, and circles in both directions.

Individuals may be instructed in the clasp, reach, and spread for a chest and shoulder stretch. The individual sits with hands clasped together and slowly raises hands toward the top of the head. When the incision begins to pull, the individual stops and holds the position while breathing deeply. When the pulling stops, the hands come down slowly. The individual may eventually progress to putting hands behind head to back of neck, keeping the head straight, and then progress to spreading elbows apart.

Performing the wall climb will also stretch the shoulder. The therapist instructs the individual to face a wall with feet slightly apart and about a foot away from the wall. Both hands are placed on the wall. The individuals slowly walk the fingers up the wall until incisional pulling occurs. At this point, the individual stops and holds the position a few seconds and then slowly walks the fingers down the wall.

Exaggerated deep breathing exercises can be performed to ease the feeling of tightness in the chest and to fully expand the lungs.

In order to prevent lymphedema, the extremity should be elevated above the level of the heart while sleeping and as often as possible during the day. As the individual progresses, he/she can advance to strengthening exercises such as closed chain pushups against a wall, and lightweight exercises such as lateral raises (lying on stomach, raise arm outward, keeping elbow straight and palm down), external rotation (lie on side and rotate arm outward, keeping lower arm perpendicular to floor and elbow tucked in at side), and rows (with elbows at side, pinch scapulas together and slowly bring elbows backwards with forearm parallel to ground).

Work Restrictions / Accommodations

Following recuperation, possible work restrictions and accommodations include temporary transfer from duties involving strenuous physical activity. While resuming daily activities as soon as possible is desirable, vigorous exercise should be avoided for about 6 weeks.

Comorbid Conditions

Comorbid conditions might include obesity, immune suppression, and bleeding disorders.

Procedure Complications

Complications might include postoperative infection, arm pain and swelling, and emotional problems such as grief, depression, anxiety, and body-image issues.

Factors Influencing Duration

Factors that might influence the length of disability include the development of complications, the extent and spread of the disease, the surgical procedure performed, whether the operation was also coupled with reconstructive surgery, and the age and general health of the individual.

Length of Disability

Duration of the disability depends on job requirements. For all procedures, durations reflect recovery from procedure only. For a lumpectomy, partial or segmental mastectomy, duration depends on amount of tissue removed (size of incision and type of anesthesia - local versus general).

Lumpectomy, segmental, or partial mastectomy.

Job Classification	Duration in Days		
	Minimum	Optimum	Maximum
Sedentary work	1	3	14
Light work	1	3	14
Medium work	1	3	14
Heavy work	3	7	21
Very Heavy work	3	7	21

Radical or modified radical mastectomy.

Job Classification	Duration in Days		
	Minimum	Optimum	Maximum
Sedentary work	21	28	42
Light work	28	35	42
Medium work	42	49	56
Heavy work	56	63	84
Very Heavy work	56	63	84

References

"Breast Cancer." Merck Manual of Diagnosis and Therapy, 17th ed. Beers, Mark H., and Robert Berkow, MD, eds. Whitehouse Station, NJ: Merck & Co., Inc., 1999. 25 Jan 2001 <http://www.merck.com/pubs/mmanual/section18/chapter242/242c.htm>.

Wingo, P.A., et al. "Patterns of Inpatient Surgeries for the Top Four Cancers in the United States, National Hospital Discharge Survey, 1988-95." Cancer Causes Control 11 6 (2000): 497-512.

Mastoidectomy

Other names / synonyms: Modified Radical Mastoidectomy, Simple Mastoidectomy, Tympanoplasty Radical Mastoidectomy

20.4, 20.41, 20.42, 20.49

Definition

A mastoidectomy is the surgical removal of all or part of the mastoid bone at the side of the skull directly behind the ear.

A mastoidectomy is done to treat the effects of the spread of an infection into the various parts of the mastoid process from the middle ear. The mastoid process consists of several porous or honeycomb-like areas and is part of the temporal bone that lies behind the ear. Mastoiditis is an inflammation of any part of this structure. Inflammation is due to an infection. However, mastoiditis is almost always a result of acute or chronic ear infection (otitis media). At one time, mastoiditis was a very serious and dangerous disease. Due to the use of antibiotics it is now quite uncommon. Before antibiotics, mastoiditis was one of the leading causes of death in children. Mastoiditis is a relatively uncommon disorder, although it can occur in adults.

Occasionally an active infection may cause the skin of the ear canal to grow through a hole in eardrum. A skin-lined cyst called a cholesteatoma may be formed when the infection passes into the middle ear and the mastoid bone. These may come about because of chronic otitis media. When these conditions occur, it may become necessary to undertake an operation called a radical mastoidectomy. Several operations of varying scope and intensity may be necessary over a long period of time to fully remove infections and their effects. The initial operation is a mastoidectomy with tympanoplasty. The final stage of this sequence of operations may be the radical mastoid obliteration operation. When this becomes necessary, improvement or restoration of hearing is not a consideration.

Reason for Procedure

A revision mastoidectomy operation may be used to get rid of any discharge from a mastoid cavity defect that has been created and, if possible, to improve the hearing. A modified radical mastoidectomy may be necessary to get rid of infection in individuals who have a very resistant infection or who have infections in an only hearing ear. Finally, a mastoid obliteration operation may be needed to get rid of any mastoid infection and to obliterate or fill any created mastoid cavity. Hearing improvement is not usually considered in the two latter operations.

Description

A mastoidectomy is usually done under general anesthesia.

Entry is made through the ear canal or from behind the ear. In a simple mastoidectomy, infected bone cells are removed. The eardrum is cut to drain the middle ear. Antibiotics are then put in the ear.

In a radical procedure, the eardrum and most middle ear structures are removed. After surgery a hearing aid may be used. In a modified radical procedure, the eardrum and the middle ear structures are saved.

The incision is closed with sutures, and a dressing is applied.

Prognosis

The outcome is generally excellent for infection control, although additional surgery is occasionally needed to address new pockets of infection or provide refinements in hearing once infection has been cleared. Useful hearing is often achievable. Complete healing may require three or four months.

Specialists

- Anesthesiologist
- Audiologist
- General Surgeon
- Infectious Disease Physician
- Occupational Therapist
- Otolaryngologist
- Otologist
- Physical Therapist
- Speech Pathologist

Work Restrictions / Accommodations

Heavy lifting or work that requires exertion should be restricted since it may damage the supporting structure of the inner ear and slow healing. Since the individual may be dizzy for several days following the procedure, they should be advised not to pilot or fly in an airplane or drive a car until dizziness and/or vertigo has completely disappeared. When a radical mastoidectomy has been performed this condition may last for several months.

Comorbid Conditions

Infections in other parts of the system, heart disease and pulmonary diseases and disorders may lengthen the recovery period and slow healing.

Procedure Complications

Complications are rare, but may include nerve damage to the face, dizziness, hearing impairment, taste disturbances, and infection.

Factors Influencing Duration

The use of antibiotics greatly reduces the risk of post-operative infection. Allergic reactions to antibiotics may limit their use and would lengthen disability.

Length of Disability

Duration in Days

Job Classification	Minimum	Optimum	Maximum
Sedentary work	14	21	28
Light work	14	21	28
Medium work	14	21	28
Heavy work	21	28	42
Very Heavy work	21	35	42

References

Loury, Mark, MD. Mastoidectomy. Hendrickson, Gail RN, BS, reviewer. 15 Oct 1999. 2 Jan 2001 <http://www.healthanswers.com/centers/body/overview.asp?id=bone+muscle+joint&filename=887.htm>.

Rowe, Lee, MD. "Otolaryngology." Current Surgical Diagnosis and Treatment. Way, Lawrence, ed. Norwalk: Appleton & Lange, 1991. 843-872.

Mastoiditis

Other names / synonyms: Mastoid Empyema

383, 383.0, 383.1, 383.9

Definition

Mastoiditis is a serious complication that occurs following inadequate treatment of an acute middle ear infection (otitis media). The prevalence of mastoiditis has decreased with the advent of a wide variety of antibiotics. It is now a relatively uncommon and much less dangerous (but still serious) disorder that occurs when medical treatment has not been sought for an acute middle ear infection or when treatment has failed to eliminate the infection.

The infections spread from the affected middle ear to a projection of the temporal bone located behind the ear (the mastoid process) through hollow spaces of various sizes and shapes (mastoid cells) connecting the two areas. Causes of failed treatment for acute middle ear infection that lead to mastoiditis include poor compliance with antibiotic therapy, the presence of an antibiotic-resistant organism, or a weakened immune system that cannot fight infection adequately. The most common organisms (pathogens) causing mastoiditis are Streptococcus pneumoniae, Haemophilus influenzae, and Streptococcus pyogenes.

Chronic mastoiditis is a serious infection that can destroy the mastoid bone and the structures of the middle ear and lead to a number of intracranial complications, some of them life-threatening.

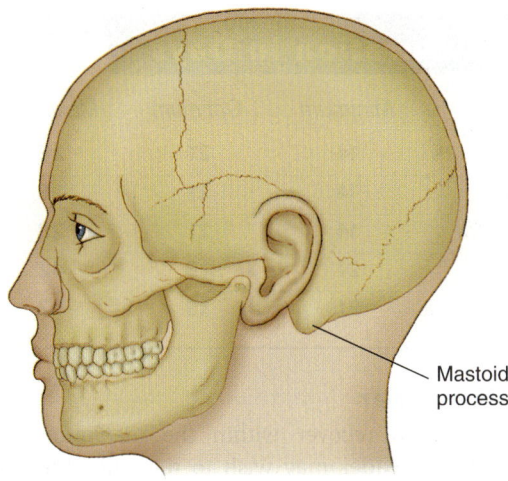

Frank Forney

Diagnosis

History: The individual with acute mastoiditis usually relates a recent history of severe pain behind the ear (retroauricular), high fever, recent history of middle ear infection, decrease in hearing, a purulent drainage from the ear, ringing in the ear, and dizziness.

Physical exam: The exam reveals tenderness, redness (erythema), and swelling over the mastoid area behind the ear. If the eardrum is perforated, purulent drainage from the middle ear may be present in the ear canal. If the infection is very severe, neurological symptoms may be present (signs of increased intracranial pressure, facial paralysis, or meningitis). When examined through a microscope, the eardrum associated with mastoiditis may be perforated, scarred, or completely eroded and drainage from the middle ear may be present in the ear canal.

Tests: A sample of the purulent ear drainage is sent to the laboratory for culture and sensitivity testing to determine the organism and best category of antibiotics for use in treating the infection. MRI or CT may reveal temporal bone destruction, absence of the bones (ossicles) of the middle ear, or a cyst-like mass (cholesteatoma) in the ear canal or mastoid area. If neurological symptoms are present, MRI or CT may reveal inflammation of the lining of the brain and spinal cord (meningitis). Audiometric studies may be performed to test the diminished degree of transmission of sound waves through the ossicles of the middle ear (conductive hearing loss).

Treatment

The goal of treatment for mastoiditis is to clear the middle ear, mastoid cells, and mastoid bone of infection before permanent damage occurs or serious intracranial complications arise. Because of the high incidence of intracranial complications in individuals with acute mastoiditis, prompt admission to the hospital is usually required in order to administer intravenous antibiotic therapy and perform surgical drainage of the infection through an incision (myringotomy) in the eardrum (tympanic membrane) or mastoidectomy, depending on the extent of disease.

When persistent purulent discharge is found despite antibiotic therapy and surgical drainage, chronic mastoiditis should be suspected. Chronic mastoiditis requires urgent surgical intervention, i.e., surgical drainage and evacuation of the infection and removal of the mastoid process (mastoidectomy). The extent of surgery required depends on the extent of destruction caused by the infection. Surgery is followed by a prolonged course of antibiotic therapy, 4 to 6 weeks or longer.

When the infection is completely resolved, surgery (myringoplasty or tympanoplasty) is usually required to repair any residual perforation in the eardrum.

Prognosis

Outcome is generally good following antibiotic therapy and surgical treatment of mastoiditis. Infection is usually eliminated in individuals who are otherwise healthy. Treatment of mastoiditis in individuals with weakened immune systems (immunosuppression) is more difficult and may require extensive surgery and treatment with several different antibiotics before the infection resolves. In any case, full recovery is dependent on completion of a full course of antibiotic therapy. Disruption in antibiotic therapy before the prescription is completed can result in a recurrence of the infection and contributes to the growth of antibiotic-resistant organisms.

Surgical procedures for treatment of mastoiditis (myringotomy and mastoidectomy) should result in the removal of infection from the middle ear and mastoid area. The structures of the middle ear are preserved as much as possible.

Differential Diagnosis

Other diagnoses could be middle ear trauma, middle ear tumor (neoplasm), or chronic suppurative otitis media that has not progressed to mastoiditis.

Specialists

- Audiologist
- Infectious Disease Physician
- Neurologist
- Neurosurgeon
- Otolaryngologist
- Primary Care Provider
- Radiologist

Rehabilitation

Rehabilitation is generally not required for this condition except in the case of hearing loss or facial nerve paralysis. Individuals with permanent conductive hearing loss or facial nerve paralysis may require vocational or occupational therapy to help them prepare for a different job.

Work Restrictions / Accommodations

Work restrictions and accommodations for individuals with acute or chronic mastoiditis are related to the degree of hearing loss the individual experiences. Because the structures of the middle ear are often destroyed by the infection or surgical intervention, individuals with chronic mastoiditis may experience long-term or permanent hearing loss. This may require a long-term or permanent accommodation in the workplace and the use of hearing aids. Balance disorders can result from ear infections and may require work restrictions for the safety of the individual and coworkers. Persistent facial paralysis or palsy may also require accommodations if the individual's job requires distinct speech.

Comorbid Conditions

Comorbid conditions include chronic pulmonary or cardiovascular diseases that increase an individual's risk during surgical procedures requiring a general anesthetic, and diseases and conditions that increase the likelihood of surgical wound infection such as obesity, AIDS, and diabetes. Diseases, conditions, and medications that weaken immune systems (immunosuppression) also influence the length of disability. Some of these include chronic diseases like HIV/AIDS, cancer, or leukemia; chemotherapy for treatment of cancer; and antirejection drug therapy following organ transplantation.

Complications

If treatment of acute or chronic mastoiditis fails, the infection can spread to other areas of the head and neck and cause serious, even life-threatening complications such as meningitis, subdural infection, brain abscess, infection of the petrous bone (petrous apicitis) situated between the inner and middle ear, infection of the temporal bone (osteomyelitis), facial paralysis caused by inflammation of the facial nerve, and facial palsy caused by chronic pressure on the facial nerve. Thrombosis of the sigmoid sinus can lead to sepsis and increased intracranial pressure and must be treated with intravenous antibiotics or surgical drainage, and may even require tying off the internal jugular vein in the neck. Permanent hearing loss can be a complication of chronic mastoiditis or a consequence of the mastoidectomy procedure.

Factors Influencing Duration

Factors influencing the length of disability include the general health and fitness of the individual before being diagnosed with mastoiditis, evidence of pre-existing diseases affecting any of the major body systems, the general ability to fight infection, any antibiotic-resistant organisms, poor compliance with taking the full course of antibiotic therapy, diagnosis of an acute complication requiring surgery, and working or living in a smoke-filled environment.

Length of Disability

Length of disability can vary depending on the severity of the infection, the infection's response to treatment, success of surgical intervention, and occurrence of complications involving the neurological system.

Medical treatment.

Duration in Days

Job Classification	Minimum	Optimum	Maximum
Sedentary work	7	14	21
Light work	7	14	21
Medium work	7	14	21
Heavy work	7	14	21
Very Heavy work	7	14	21

Surgical treatment (mastoidectomy).

Duration in Days

Job Classification	Minimum	Optimum	Maximum
Sedentary work	14	21	28
Light work	14	21	28
Medium work	14	21	28
Heavy work	21	28	42
Very Heavy work	21	35	42

Failure to Recover

If an individual fails to recover within the maximum duration expectancy period, the reader may wish to reference the following questions to assist in better understanding the specifics of an individual's medical case.

Regarding diagnosis:

- Does individual report a recent history of severe pain behind the ear and high fever? Has individual had a middle ear infection recently? Was there a decrease in hearing, tinnitus, or dizziness?
- Has drainage from the ear occurred?
- On physical exam, were tenderness, erythema, and swelling over the mastoid area observed? Is purulent drainage present? Facial paralysis? Meningitis?
- Is the eardrum perforated, scarred, or completely eroded?
- Is drainage from the middle ear present in the ear canal?
- Has individual had a culture and sensitivity done on the drainage? Was CT or MRI performed? Were audiometric studies done?

- Were conditions with similar symptoms ruled out?

Regarding treatment:
- Was individual admitted to the hospital for intravenous antibiotic therapy?
- Has surgical drainage of the area been done?
- Has individual developed chronic mastoiditis? Is this being treated with surgical drainage and a prolonged course of antibiotics?
- Does individual need additional surgery to repair a residual perforation?

Regarding prognosis:
- Can individual's employer accommodate any necessary restrictions?
- Does individual have any conditions that may affect ability to recover?
- Have any complications developed such as the infection spreading to other areas of the head and neck? Facial paralysis? Thrombosis of the sigmoid sinus? Hearing loss?

References

Bailey, Byron, et al. Head and Neck Surgery - Otolaryngology. Philadelphia: J.B. Lippincott Company, 1993.

Tierney, Lawrence M., Stephen J. McPhee, and Maxine A. Papadakis, eds. Current Medical Diagnosis and Treatment. New York: McGraw-Hill, 2000.

Meckel's Diverticulum
Other names / synonyms: Meckel's Diverticulosis
751.0

Definition

Meckel's diverticulum is a saclike outpouching of the wall of the small intestine. A small, hollow, wide-mouthed pouch protrudes in an area of within 100 centimeters of where the large intestine (colon) and the small intestine (ileum) meet (ileocecal valve). Most diverticula pouches are between one and ten centimeters in size.

The abnormality begins during pregnancy when the duct leading from the naval to the small intestine in the fetus fails to decrease in size (atrophy) and close, forming a pouch (diverticulum). Meckel's diverticulum is a fairly common birth defect that is noticed incidentally in about 2% of adult individuals undergoing abdominal surgery for other reasons.

Meckel's diverticulum is 2 to 3 times more prevalent in males than in females and has no symptoms (asymptomatic) in about 90% of cases. There are usually no symptoms unless the diverticulum is affected by infection, obstruction, or ulceration.

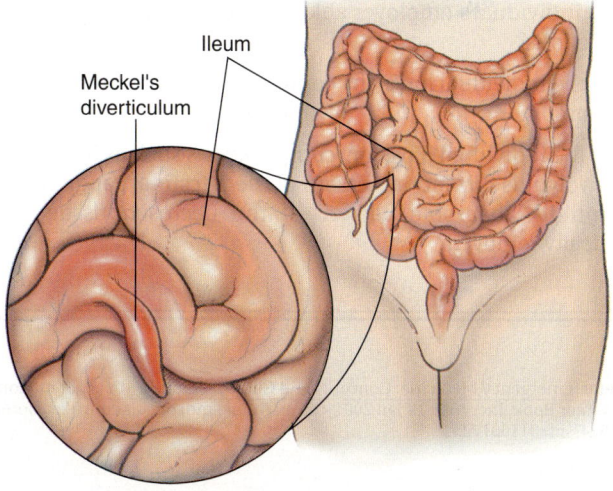

Diagnosis

History: Symptoms of Meckel's diverticulum include painless bleeding, poorly localized abdominal pain, tiredness, and weakness. Intestinal obstruction can cause abdominal distention, cramps, and vomiting.

Physical exam: When the physician presses and massages the individual's abdomen (palpates), he or she notes tenderness in the middle of the abdomen (medial abdominal tenderness). Since the symptoms of Meckel's diverticulum so starkly resemble the symptoms of appendicitis, the only way to obtain a clear diagnosis in many cases is through surgery where the abdomen can be open for inspection.

Tests: If the situation is not so acute that surgery is needed as an emergency, the best way to diagnose the disorder is with a nuclear scan. A radioactive isotope injected into the bloodstream will accumulate at sites of bleeding or in stomach tissue. If a piece of stomach tissue or a pool of blood shows up in the lower intestine, Meckel's diverticulum is indicated.

Another, less effective way to diagnose the disorder is the small bowel barium x-ray. Only occasionally can a diverticulum be seen on this type of x-ray.

Almost one-third of Meckel's diverticulum cases present as intestinal obstruction, and one-third present with inflammation or as an abnormal opening (fistula) in the abdominal wall.

Treatment

The treatment of choice for Meckel's diverticulum that is symptomatic is surgical removal (diverticulectomy), which can be performed without completely dividing the intestine. Asymptomatic diverticula found incidentally during exploratory abdominal surgery (laparotomy) in older individuals need not be removed if they are small. Most will never cause problems and the risk of surgical complications outweighs the benefit of removal of the abnormality.

Prognosis

Normal bowel function is retained and complete recovery is expected without complications if the diverticula or a small section of intestine is removed. Surgical removal of more than the diverticula or a small section of the intestine may be followed by compromised bowel function (temporary) and a delay in the healing process.

Differential Diagnosis

Other conditions that present with similar symptoms are appendicitis, small bowel lesion leading to intussusception, inflammatory bowel disease, and intestinal duplication cyst containing gastric mucosa.

Most individuals are asymptomatic and are diagnosed only incidentally on laparotomy for other conditions. The list of conditions producing abdominal pain of rectal bleeding is long. Intestinal obstruction, intussusception, appendicitis, pelvic inflammatory disease, volvulus, intestinal polyp, and anal fissure should all be considered in the differential diagnosis.

Specialists

- Gastroenterologist

Work Restrictions / Accommodations

Individuals may resume normal activities and workload after recuperation from surgery. Asymptomatic individuals may require no restrictions or accommodations.

Comorbid Conditions

Comorbid conditions that might influence the length of disability include obesity or excessive thinness, allergy to treatment medication, and chronic diseases, such as diabetes mellitus, heart disease, and osteoporosis.

Complications

Meckel's diverticulum can cause the small intestine (ileum) to telescope (intussusception) or twist upon itself (volvulus formation). Bleeding, which began painlessly, can become sudden and severe, making a blood transfusion necessary. Intestinal obstruction can lead to twisting (torsion) of the intestine, tissue death from loss of blood supply (gangrene), and infection by anaerobic bacteria if the dead (necrosed) tissue is not surgically removed. Surgery may involve only the diverticula, but if the adjacent small intestine is ulcerated, surgery to repair the small intestine (ileal resection) would be required. These surgeries are complex, with postoperative complications occurring in approximately 6% of cases.

Factors Influencing Duration

The number and severity of symptoms and frequency of occurrence may influence the length of disability. Occupational situations requiring repetitive loading and bending of the spine would increase the likelihood of periods of disability from pain.

Length of Disability

Surgical treatment.

Duration in Days

Job Classification	Minimum	Optimum	Maximum
Sedentary work	3	7	10
Light work	3	7	10
Medium work	3	14	21
Heavy work	7	21	28
Very Heavy work	7	21	35

Failure to Recover

If an individual fails to recover within the maximum duration expectancy period, the reader may wish to reference the following questions to assist in better understanding the specifics of an individual's medical case.

Regarding diagnosis:

- Has the diverticulum become affected by infection, obstruction, or ulceration?
- Does the individual have painless bleeding, poorly localized abdominal pain, tiredness or weakness?
- Does the individual have abdominal distention, cramps, and vomiting?
- Upon palpation, does the physician note medial abdominal tenderness?
- Did surgery become necessary to make the diagnosis?
- Did the individual have a nuclear scan?
- Have conditions with similar symptoms been ruled out?

Regarding treatment:

- Did the individual undergo a diverticulectomy?

Regarding prognosis:

- Is the individual's employer able to accommodate any necessary restrictions?
- Does the individual have any conditions that may affect ability to recover?
- Does the individual have any complications such as intussusception, volvulus formation, torsion of the intestine, gangrene or infection by anaerobic bacteria if the necrosed tissue is not surgically removed?

References

Gastroenterology: Meckel's Diverticulum. Vanderbilt University Medical Center. 16 Jul 1998. 18 Jan 2001 <http://www.mc.vanderbilt.edu/peds/pidl/gi/meckel.htm>.

Rosen, Peter. Emergency Medicine: Concepts and Clinical Practice, 4th ed. Saint Louis: Mosby-Year Book, Inc, 1998 18 Jan 2001 <http://home.mdconsult.com/das/book/view/624?sid=31100772>.

Méničre's Disease

Other names / synonyms: Méničre's Syndrome

386.0, 386.00, 386.01, 386.02, 386.03, 386.04

Definition

Méničre's disease is a recurrent (episodic) disease typically characterized by hearing loss, pressure in the ear, ringing in the ear (tinnitus), and a sensation of spinning or movement (vertigo). Accumulations of excessive fluid (endolymph) in the inner ear are thought to cause most attacks.

Sudden, unprovoked attacks of vertigo accompanying the disease may cause vomiting and loss of balance. Each episode can last from minutes to days although most symptoms resolve within a few hours. If Méničre's disease is untreated or unresolved, symptoms may recur over a period of years and create hearing loss. As the disease progresses, tinnitus may become as constant and debilitating as vertigo. Vertigo often ceases if permanent hearing loss develops in the affected ear.

Accumulation of endolymph in the inner ear stretches the membranes that divide the inner ear, causing hearing to decrease and tinnitus to increase. Severely stretched membranes may rupture, mixing two types of fluid, one rich in sodium and the other rich in potassium. Mixture of these two types of fluid is thought to bring on the vertigo. Direct causes of the disease are often unknown although the condition may be linked to factors such as injury, autoimmune disorders, genetics, or metabolic processes. Symptoms of Méničre's disease may resolve with treatment of underlying conditions such as allergies, syphilis, viral infections, and abnormal connections between inner and middle ear channels (perilymphatic fistula).

Méničre's disease usually affects one ear at onset with 25-50% of afflicted individuals eventually developing the condition in both ears (bilateral). The first attack generally occurs between ages 30 and 60. The disease may affect about 0.2% of the US population, similar to prevalence in other industrialized nations such as Great Britain and Italy. World prevalence rates vary depending on criteria used to confirm the diagnosis of Méničre's disease.

Diagnosis

History: In the initial stages of Méničre's disease, the individual may first complain of fullness in the ear and/or tinnitus followed by vertigo. The symptoms may range in severity from a brief episode of impaired balance to an intense, extended illusion of spinning that can last several hours. The individual may also describe tinnitus as the sound of roaring or buzzing in the ear. Symptoms typically subside completely after the attack however the individual may report a continuing sense of unsteadiness. The individual may report fatigue after an episode. The attacks may occur at any time and waken the individual from sleep. Tinnitus may be the chief complaint in later stages of the disease. Hearing loss has been reported. In rare cases as the disease progresses, attacks may cause falls.

Physical exam: The exam is generally normal.

Tests: Hearing (audiometry) tests may be conducted to identify the extent and type of auditory losses associated with Méničre's disease. The pattern of hearing loss is described as a low frequency upsloping hearing loss of neural type. Test results in combination with other symptoms may help confirm the diagnosis. More detailed analysis includes measurements of the function of the auditory nerve (transtympanic electrocochleography) and other interior structures. Balance test (electronystagmography) measures balance (vestibular) function of the inner ear. Brain stem-evoked response audiometry helps pinpoint the location within the nervous system of the hearing problem. Blood tests (serology) or imaging of internal structures of the body (MRI) may be conducted to rule out other possible causes of symptoms such as infections or metabolic disorders.

Treatment

Medications such as those aimed at reducing fluids in the body (diuretics) are usually given to help relieve fluctuations of fluids in the inner ear. A low-salt diet helps avoid fluid retention in the body. Other medications may be prescribed to relieve symptoms of vertigo and accompanying nausea and vomiting. The individual may be advised to avoid consumption of caffeine, nicotine, and alcohol that can cause symptoms to worsen. Regular exercise may promote good circulation within the inner ear. Sedatives may be prescribed to relieve severe anxiety caused by serious attacks. In some instances, oral steroids help relieve underlying autoimmune disorders that may cause Méničre's disease. Antibiotics may also be needed to treat possible underlying infections. As a way of relieving symptoms, certain antibiotics are administered and carefully controlled so the balance portion of the inner ear is disrupted while hearing is preserved.

Medical treatment fails to control the frequency and severity of attacks for fewer than 10% of individuals with Méničre's disease. In these cases and as a last resort, several surgical procedures are available. The pressure within the inner ear may be relieved through establishment of an opening with or without an artificially constructed passageway (endolymphatic sac decompression, endolymphatic shunt surgery, or cochleosacculotomy). Sometimes the nerve controlling balance is cut (vestibular nerve section) to relieve symptoms. One method involves placing a toxic substance within the inner ear to eliminate balance functions and resolve vertigo (gentamicin perfusion). When hearing loss is severe or complete in the affected ear and vertigo is disabling, a procedure may be used to destroy function of the inner ear (labyrinthectomy, vestibular neurectomy) but only in the most extreme cases.

Prognosis

For most individuals, the disorder is primarily an inconvenience. Attacks are sporadic, sometimes occurring months or years apart. The disease often resolves on its own though the prognosis may depend on other underlying conditions such as autoimmune disorders. For a few individuals, Méničre's disease can cause total deafness. When the condition is unresolved, vertigo and accompanying nausea can be frequent and debilitating. Disability issues may be significant in certain cases.

In extreme cases when surgical options are used, success rates are about 80-95% for relief of pressure within the inner ear and other symptoms (endolymphatic sac surgery, endolymphatic shunt surgery, cochleosacculotomy). Compared to individuals with vertigo alone, individuals with Méničre's disease causing vertigo tend to have more favorable results from a procedure used to restore balance through cutting the nerve controlling the function (vestibular nerve section). Relief is obtained in 85-99% of these cases. Permanent hearing loss may result however as a complication of surgical procedures. In a few cases, surgical intervention actually improves hearing ability.

In cases where hearing loss has already occurred, surgical interventions aimed at eliminating symptoms such as vertigo by disabling or destroying inner ear function (gentamicin perfusion, labyrinthectomy, vestibular neurectomy) are 85-95% successful. Most individuals with Ménière's disease have normal life expectancies.

Differential Diagnosis

Acoustic neuroma, cerebellar pontine angle tumor, vestibular neuronitis, head trauma, perilymphatic fistula, ischemic vertigo, and acute labyrinthitis are other possible diagnoses. Inner or middle ear infections (otitis) may produce similar symptoms and can result from influenza, measles, mumps, cytomegalovirus, or varicella zoster. Similar symptoms are also found with autoimmune diseases such as rheumatoid arthritis, Cogan's syndrome, Wegener's granulomatosis, scleroderma, allergies, ulcerative colitis, Sjögren's syndrome, and systemic lupus erythematosus. Other diseases producing similar symptoms are multiple sclerosis, hypothyroidism, hyperglycemia, syphilis, and severe headaches (migraine).

Specialists

- Audiologist
- Otolaryngologist
- Neurologist

Rehabilitation

While rehabilitation is not generally indicated in this disorder, individuals with frequent bouts of vertigo may benefit from a few physical or occupational therapy sessions to discuss safety issues pertaining to balance, strategies for optimal positioning, and remaining stationary for greater relief.

Work Restrictions / Accommodations

Severity of vertigo and the extent of hearing loss should be considered in possible work situations. In unresolved cases of Ménière's disease, tasks requiring keen hearing or good physical balance may need to be reassigned. As an example, individuals who climb ladders or operate heavy equipment may be unable to continue fulfilling these duties. Some individuals may be unable to continue tasks that involve driving. Workers who must continually change positions such as aerobics instructors may be severely affected. Individuals with hearing impairment may require accommodations such as telephone adaptations, interpreters, visual aids, video captions, hearing aids, or amplification at workstations.

Complementary and Alternative Therapies

Content is intended for awareness only. Treatments may or may not be effective. Scientific evidence may be lacking and some substances have potentially toxic effects. Dr. Presley Reed and the editors do not endorse the use of these therapies in the absence of consultation with a licensed medical professional.

Ginger -	May relieve vertigo.
Gingko -	May relieve vertigo and improve blood flow to the ear.
Low-salt diet -	May decrease fluid retention in the inner ear.
Celery seed -	May relieve dizziness.
Supplements -	Calcium, magnesium, and potassium may balance the harmful effect of increased salt.
Pumpkin seeds -	May relieve dizziness.

Comorbid Conditions

Immune disorders related to genetic factors may both cause and prolong symptoms of Ménière's disease. Individuals addicted to nicotine have constricted blood vessels affecting flow to the inner ear that reduces the ability to recover. Other diseases affecting the inner ear, the brain stem, or associated nerve pathways may worsen disability associated with Ménière's.

Complications

Untreated or unresolved Ménière's disease may result in permanent hearing loss and chronic ringing in the ear (tinnitus). If surgery is needed, individuals may experience hearing loss as a complication of the procedure. Even when more severe symptoms are resolved, the individual may experience an ongoing feeling of unsteadiness for an indefinite time period. Some individuals with Ménière's disease experience severe, often debilitating headaches (migraine). Once Ménière's disease occurs in one ear, the chance of the other ear being affected is significant.

Factors Influencing Duration

Severity of symptoms and frequency of attacks may influence recovery time. Individual response to treatment will also determine length of disability. If surgical intervention is required, additional recovery time may be required. In some cases, the individual's symptoms may continue indefinitely. Some individuals experience permanent hearing loss.

Length of Disability

If permanent or partial deafness occurs, individuals may be unable to perform tasks requiring keen hearing. Individuals with ongoing symptoms of vertigo may be unable to operate heavy equipment or climb ladders.

Medical treatment.

Duration in Days

Job Classification	Minimum	Optimum	Maximum
Sedentary work	0	2	3
Light work	0	2	3
Medium work	0	2	3
Heavy work	0	3	7
Very Heavy work	0	3	7

Failure to Recover

If an individual fails to recover within the maximum duration expectancy period, the reader may wish to reference the following questions to assist in better understanding the specifics of an individual's medical case.

Regarding diagnosis:

- Does the individual have hearing loss, pressure in the ear, tinnitus, and spinning or vertigo? Are one or both ears affected?
- Has the individual had a hearing test? ENG? Brainstem evoke response? MRI?
- Has the individual had any blood tests?
- Have conditions with similar symptoms been ruled out?

Regarding treatment:

- Is the individual on diuretic therapy? Have sedative been prescribed?
- Is the individual following a low-salt diet, and avoiding caffeine and nicotine?
- Has surgery been necessary?

Regarding prognosis:

- Has the individual received training in safety issues, etc.?
- Is the individual's employer able to accommodate any necessary restrictions?
- Does the individual have any conditions that may affect their ability to recover?
- Does the individual have any complications such as hearing loss as a complication of the surgical procedure, an ongoing feeling of unsteadiness for an indefinite time period, or severe migraine headaches?

References

Duke, James A. The Green Pharmacy. Emmaus, PA: Rodale Press, Inc, 1996.

Levenson, Mark J. Ménière's Disease. Ear Surgery Information Center. 01 Jan 2000. 10 Jan 2001 <http://www.earsurgery.org/meniere.html>.

Meningioma

Other names / synonyms: Neoplasm of Meninges

192.1, 198.4, 237.5, 237.6

Definition

A meningioma is a tumor, generally benign, that originates in the fibrous tissue that protects the brain and spinal cord (meninges). The cause of meningiomas is unknown but 40-80% of afflicted individuals seem to have genetic material missing from chromosome 22. Although most occur in the area surrounding the brain, there are rare spinal meningiomas. Meningioma tumors usually occur singly, although multiple meningiomas may occur.

Meningiomas are characterized by slow growth and typically are present for years before any symptoms occur. Approximately 2% of routine autopsies reveal the presence of undiagnosed brain tumors and most of these are less than 2 cm in diameter. Symptoms of meningiomas generally result from compression of brain structures but tumors may also invade bone and cause localized thickening (hyperostosis).

Meningiomas can become cancerous. The distinction between malignant and nonmalignant tumors is less important in the brain than other parts of the body. The spread of both malignant and nonmalignant brain tumors is generally confined to the central nervous system (CNS) although malignant tumors tend to grow faster.

Meningiomas account for 15-20% of all brain tumors and occur in 2.7 per 100,000 individuals. They are most often diagnosed between the ages of 40 and 60, although they can appear in childhood. Meningiomas occur twice as often in women than men, the only type of brain tumor where this is true.

Diagnosis

History: The individual may complain of seizures, recent onset of persistent headaches, and vomiting. Depending on the location of the meningioma, focal neurological deficits may include symptoms such as gait problems, numbness, vision disturbances, or protrusion of the eye (exophthalmos). A family history of meningiomas, peripheral neurofibromatosis (van Recklinghausen's disease), or basal cell nevus syndrome (Gorlin syndrome) may also be reported.

Physical exam: The exam may be normal. Occasionally, individuals may develop enlargement of the head due to fluid accumulation within the skull (hydrocephalus).

Tests: A complete neurological workup using MRI and CT should be performed. Chest x-rays and other tests are performed as necessary to determine whether the tumor is secondary to a primary cancer elsewhere that has spread (metastasized) to the brain.

Treatment

If possible, surgical removal of the meningioma is the treatment of choice. However, in some cases, the tumor or some portion of it cannot be removed with an acceptable level of risk because of its size or location. In other cases, the removal of a small accidentally discovered asymptomatic meningioma might be postponed because the risk from the surgery is greater than the risk from the tumor. In this circumstance, periodic clinical evaluation with MRI is important to monitor tumor growth. Even after total tumor removal, recurrence rates are 10-20% over 10 years. In cases where residual tumor remains even after resection, recurrence rates are as high as 30-50%. Radiation therapy (stereotactic radiosurgery) may be used for recurrent or malignant meningiomas or for those that cannot be totally removed. It is used to target treatment to only the tumor and avoid treating normal brain tissue. There are generally no side effects to this type of treatment.

Prognosis

Most meningiomas can be removed safely and completely with an operative mortality rate of 0.5%, a 5-year survival rate greater than 90%, and a 10-20% recurrence rate. Approximately 1 in 3 individuals are left with residual tumor after surgery. The 5-year recurrence rate for malignant meningioma is 33%.

Differential Diagnosis

Other conditions with similar symptoms may include meningitis, benign intracranial hypertension, other types of brain tumors, and metastatic cancer originating elsewhere in the body (especially lung cancer, breast cancer, and malignant melanoma).

Specialists

- Neurologist
- Neurosurgeon
- Pathologist
- Radiation Oncologist

Work Restrictions / Accommodations

After treatment, the prospect for return to work is generally good but eventual recurrence is a possibility. Individuals who only require surgery may return to their normal duties after an appropriate recuperation period. If radiation is required, additional leave from work may be needed.

Comorbid Conditions

Comorbid conditions include other neurological problems such as Alzheimer's disease or seizure disorders and debilitating medical conditions such as advanced cardiovascular disease that would preclude surgery to remove the meningioma.

Complications

Possible complications depend on the size and location of the meningioma and include seizures, loss of vision, and urinary incontinence. The pressure of the tumor may cause inflammation of the optic nerve (papilledema) and result in blindness.

Factors Influencing Duration

Factors affecting disability include the type and location of the meningioma and type of treatment required.

Length of Disability

Duration depends on size, location, and type. Disability may be permanent if the meningioma cannot be adequately treated because of its size or position.

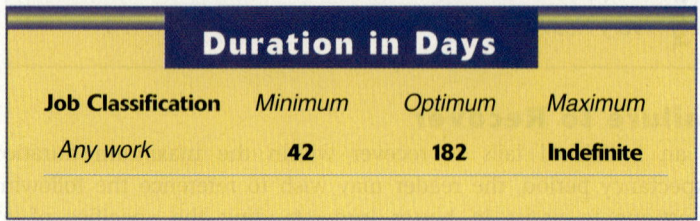

Duration in Days

Job Classification	Minimum	Optimum	Maximum
Any work	42	182	Indefinite

Failure to Recover

If an individual fails to recover within the maximum duration expectancy period, the reader may wish to reference the following questions to assist in better understanding the specifics of an individual's medical case.

Regarding diagnosis:

- Has the individual complained of seizures, recent onset of severe headaches, or vomiting?
- Does the individual have any problems walking?
- Has the individual noticed any numbness, vision disturbances, or protrusion of the eyes?
- Does the individual have a family history of meningiomas, van Recklinghausen's disease, or Gorlin syndrome?
- Is there evidence of hydrocephalus?
- Has the individual had a complete neurological work up including CT and MRI?
- Has metastatic carcinoma been ruled out?
- Have conditions with similar symptoms such as meningitis, benign intracranial hypertension, other types of brain tumors, and metastatic cancer been ruled out?

Regarding treatment:

- Has the tumor been surgically removed?
- Is the individual experiencing a recurrence of the tumor?
- Will the individual have periodic evaluation with MRI to monitor changes in the tumor?

Regarding prognosis:
- Does the individual have any conditions such as Alzheimer's disease, seizure disorder, or cardiovascular disease that could impact recovery?
- Did the individual have any complications such as seizures, loss of vision, urinary incontinence, or inflammation of the optic nerve (papilledema) that could lengthen disability?

References

Beers, Mark H., and Robert Berkow. "CNS Neoplasms: Intracranial Neoplasms." The Merck Manual of Diagnosis and Therapy. Beers, Mark H., and Robert Berkow, eds. Whitehouse Station, NJ: Merck & Co., 1999. 14-177.

Preston-Martin, S., et al. "An International Case-control Study of Adult Glioma and Meningioma: The Role of Head Trauma." International Journal of Epidemiology 27 (1998): 579-586.

Meningitis, Bacterial

Other names / synonyms: Acute Bacterial Meningitis, Meningococcal Meningitis, Subacute Meningitis
320, 320.1, 320.2, 320.3, 320.8, 320.82, 320.9, 321, 321.1, 321.2, 322, 322.9

Definition

Bacterial meningitis is an inflammation of the membranes that cover the brain and spinal cord (meninges) that is caused by bacteria. In most cases, the bacteria spread to the meninges through the bloodstream from an area of infection elsewhere in the body, especially from the respiratory tract.

Although it may occur in healthy individuals, bacterial meningitis usually afflicts those with significant underlying diseases such as sickle cell anemia, alcoholism, cirrhosis, and concurrent infections of the ears, paranasal sinuses, lungs, or cardiac valves. A viral infection of the upper respiratory tract may predispose an individual to bacterial meningitis by allowing bacteria already present in the respiratory tract to enter the bloodstream and invade the meninges.

Due to the vaccination of children to particular bacteria called Haemophilus influenzae type b, bacterial meningitis has become predominantly a disease of adults. The incidence of bacterial meningitis is 2-3 per 100,000. The bacteria S. pneumoniae accounts for about 40-60% of adult cases of bacterial meningitis. In many cases, bacterial meningitis is secondary to bacteremic pneumococcal pneumonia. One bacterial strain (meningococcus) spreads quickly within relatively confined environments such as boarding schools or military bases and can cause local epidemics. This type of meningitis is considered to be a medical emergency as it can be lethal in hours if not diagnosed and treated promptly.

Bacterial meningitis affects up to 5,000 people in the US every year. Meningococcal meningitis is endemic in parts of Africa, India, and other developing nations. There are periodic epidemics in the so-called sub-Saharan "meningitis belt," as well as among religious pilgrims traveling to Saudi Arabia for the Haj.

Diagnosis

History: The duration of symptoms before individuals seek medical help varies from less than 24 hours to more than 1 week. Initially, symptoms of a viral respiratory tract infection such as sore throat, runny nose, nasal congestion, and general aches and pains occur. The symptoms then progress to those most commonly found in bacterial meningitis: headache, fever, and stiff neck (apparent in 90% of persons). Symptoms may deteriorate rapidly or over several days to a week. Deterioration is evident if the individual demonstrates confusion, irritability, drowsiness, seizures, and coma. In meningococcal meningitis, the symptoms develop rapidly. Adults may become desperately ill within 24 hours. Tuberculosis meningitis progresses much more slowly. The individual may be sick for several weeks before the typical meningitis symptoms develop. Individuals may report recent vaccination against pneumonia, meningitis, influenza, mumps, or chickenpox. Individuals may report recent contact with someone who has meningitis or travel to an area where hygiene conditions are poor and/or a meningitis outbreak occurred.

Physical exam: An involuntary flexion of the knees (positive Brudzinski's sign) may be evident when the neck is abruptly flexed (neck bending towards chest) with the individual lying on his back. Attempts to extend the knee from the flexed-thigh position are met with pain and reflex contraction (positive Kernig's sign).

Tests: Lumbar puncture is performed. The cerebrospinal fluid is analyzed for increased pressure, protein, white blood cells (leukocytes), and bacteria. The fluid is cultured. Search for an infectious source may also include cultures of blood, nose, and throat (nasopharynx), respiratory secretions, urine, and any skin lesion. Laboratory analysis of the blood usually includes a complete blood cell count (CBC) and glucose level. X-rays of the skull may show evidence of sinus or mastoid infection or skull fracture.

Treatment

Bacterial meningitis is treated with medications that fight infection (antibiotics). The specific antibiotic used depends on the type of bacteria causing the infection. The antibiotics will often be given directly into the vein (intravenously). Medications may also be given to reduce pain (analgesics), fever (antipyretics), and to prevent or stop seizures. If the individual is unconscious, nutrients are given intravenously. Depending on the length and severity of the disease, the treatment is usually given in the hospital setting.

Prognosis

Prognosis depends on the causative organism and the severity of the illness. In most cases, recovery is possible with prompt and appropriate treatment. In some cases, brain damage may occur. Statistically, mortality is about 10-15% from meningococcal meningitis. Mortality is higher, typically 20-30%, from meningitis caused by other organisms.

About 30% of individuals with pneumococcal meningitis have moderate to severe residual problems including dementia, seizures, hearing loss, and difficulty walking. About 20% have mild problems, such as dizziness, impaired memory, and headaches.

Differential Diagnosis

Differential diagnoses include subarachnoid hemorrhage, bacterial endocarditis, malignant hypertension, lead poisoning, porphyria, migraine, viral encephalitis, cerebral abscesses, cerebral tumor, and subdural hematoma.

Specialists

- Infectious Disease Physician
- Neurologist

Work Restrictions / Accommodations

Restrictions or accommodations depend on the individual's work responsibilities. Physical weakness may be a factor. Strenuous activities may need to be modified temporarily or permanently. Frequent breaks or rest periods may need to be built into the individual's work schedule. If there is difficulty walking, ramps may need to be installed as needed, and access to an elevator made available. If dizziness remains a problem, jobs that require driving a car or operating machinery may need to be curtailed and vocational counseling offered. If there is hearing loss, special equipment may need to be purchased to enhance the individual's ability to hear, or duties may need to be reevaluated.

Comorbid Conditions

Alcoholism, diabetes, and conditions that weaken the immune system such as cancer or HIV infection may lengthen disability.

Complications

Possible complications include seizures, shock, deafness, dehydration, and death. Fluid leaking into the membrane covering the brain (subdural effusion) can cause swelling in the brain (cerebral edema, hydrocephalus). A localized infection (cerebral abscess) can form in the brain.

Factors Influencing Duration

Length of disability may be influenced by the organism responsible, the severity of the illness, the individual's response to treatment, age, underlying conditions, or the presence of complications. Factors associated with higher mortality include advanced age (over 60), onset of seizures during the first 24 hours after infection, and coma on hospital admission.

Length of Disability

Duration depends on cause and severity. Length of disability will depend on any residual effects. Weakness may cause a reduction in manual labor duties. Hearing loss may require equipment to enhance hearing or speech therapy. Disability may be permanent.

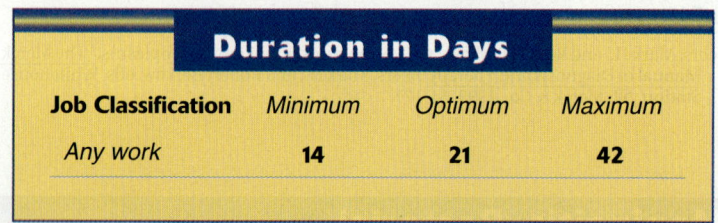

Duration in Days

Job Classification	Minimum	Optimum	Maximum
Any work	14	21	42

Failure to Recover

If an individual fails to recover within the maximum duration expectancy period, the reader may wish to reference the following questions to assist in better understanding the specifics of an individual's medical case.

Regarding diagnosis:

- Has diagnosis of bacterial meningitis been confirmed?
- Have conditions with similar symptoms been ruled out?
- Has source of infection been identified?
- Has individual experienced any complications related to the meningitis?
- Does individual have a coexisting condition that may impact recovery?

Regarding treatment:

- Do symptoms persist despite treatment?
- Was culture and sensitivity done to identify causative organisms and determine the most effective antibiotic to use?
- Were antibiotic-resistant organisms ruled out?

Regarding prognosis:

- Do symptoms persist despite treatment?
- Does diagnosis need to be revisited?
- Would individual benefit from evaluation by an infectious disease specialist?
- Did individual experience residual impairment?
- If impairment is physical, would individual benefit from physical therapy?
- Would individual be able to return to present occupation if appropriate accommodations could be made? If not, is vocational retraining warranted?

References

Hirschmann, J.V., MD. "Bacterial Infections of the Central Nervous System." Scientific American® Medicine Online Dale, D.C., and D.D. Federman New York: WebMD Corporation, 2000 Scientific American Medicine. 04 Sept 2000 <http://www.samed.com/sam/forms/index/htm>.

Meningitis Overview. InteliHealth. 09 Aug 2000. 4 Sept 2000 <http://www.intelihealth.com/IH/ihtIH?t=9630&p=~br,IHW|~st,24479|~r,WSIHW000|~b,*|>.

Meningitis, Chronic
Other names / synonyms: Chronic Aseptic Meningitis, Chronic Meningitis, Chronic Septic Meningitis
322.2

Definition

Meningitis is an inflammation of the three layers of membranes that cover the brain and spinal cord (meninges). In most cases, meningitis is an acute illness, however, it can also develop into a long-term or chronic form. Chronic meningitis most often occurs when slow-growing organisms such as bacteria or fungi gain access to the meninges via the bloodstream from another part of the body. This disease develops over weeks, sometimes months, and occasionally years. Meningitis is usually classified as chronic if symptoms are present for 4 weeks or longer.

Chronic meningitis may be due to noninfectious causes (chronic aseptic meningitis) such as cancer, chemicals used in diagnostic tests, inflammatory illnesses such as lupus, or an allergic (hypersensitivity) reaction to certain medications especially ibuprofen, Isotamine, or Cipro. It may also be due to lepromatous, rickettsial or tuberculous infections.

Individuals at special risk for chronic meningitis caused by infectious organisms (chronic septic meningitis) are those whose immune system is weakened by drugs or diseases such as AIDS, diabetes, cancer, connective tissue diseases, sarcoidosis, or alcoholism. Organisms causing chronic septic meningitis may include fungi, yeast, cryptococcus, tuberculous bacteria, amoeba, syphilis, and HIV.

In the US, the incidence of bacterial meningitis is 2 to 3 per 100,000. Meningococcal meningitis is endemic in parts of Africa, India, and other developing nations. Periodic epidemics occur in the sub-Saharan "meningitis belt" as well as among religious pilgrims traveling to Saudi Arabia.

Diagnosis

History: Symptoms evolve slowly over a period of at least 4 weeks, sometimes months, and even (rarely) years. The individual may complain of fever, persistent headache, pain in the neck or back, neck stiffness, personality changes, clumsiness, fatigue, weakness or paralysis of the extremities, double vision (diplopia), and decreased vision or hearing. The individual may report a history of recent vaccination against pneumonia, meningitis, influenza, mumps, or chickenpox. Individual may report recent contact with someone with meningitis or have traveled to an area where hygiene conditions are poor and/or a meningitis outbreak occurred.

Physical exam: The exam may reveal fever, changes in level of mental alertness, and lethargy.

Tests: Signs of meningeal irritation may be present, but are not typically found in chronic meningitis.

It is important to distinguish between chronic meningitis and recurrent meningitis. In recurrent meningitis, attacks of meningitis are separated by periods where the individual is free of symptoms and has normal cerebrospinal fluid (CSF). In chronic meningitis, the individual is not symptom-free and the CSF is not normal. Examination of the CSF is the most important test in the diagnosis of chronic meningitis. It may be necessary to insert a needle into the area surrounding the spinal cord (lumbar puncture) to obtain large volumes of CSF. The CSF should be examined under the microscope for fungi, yeast, bacteria, and cancer cells (neoplasms) and cultured for bacteria and fungi. The fluid is also tested for syphilis and polymerase chain reaction that may help identify infectious organisms difficult to culture.

A careful search should be made for evidence of infection outside the brain and spinal cord (central nervous system). This may require culture and/or examinations of stomach (gastric) washings, bone marrow tests, and liver biopsy specimens.

Treatment

Treatment depends on the nature of the causative agent. Medication to fight specific problems such as syphilis, tuberculosis, and bacterial and fungal infections is prescribed depending on the cause or causes. These medications may be given intravenously or by injecting them directly into the CSF, usually through a plastic shunt inserted into the fluid-filled chambers within the brain (ventricles) attached to a reservoir on the skull (Ommaya reservoir). In aseptic meningitis, steroids may be given to reduce inflammation although their use is somewhat controversial. Supportive measures may be required especially if a specific cause cannot be found. Supportive measures include medications to reduce pain (analgesics), lessen fever (antipyretics), and prevent or stop seizures (anticonvulsants) and nutrients given intravenously if the individual is unconscious or unable to take in adequate nourishment. Depending on the length and severity of the disease, treatment is usually done in the hospital setting. Since the individual may have worked for a considerable period of time until becoming seriously ill, the possibility that he/she may have passed the infection on to others in the workplace must be considered. Employees should be examined and given preventive treatment as recommended by the employer's medical advisor or employee's physician.

Prognosis

Chronic meningitis is a serious, potentially life-threatening disease. The death rate in meningitis is about 10-15% with treatment. Without treatment, it is often fatal. Individuals with severe neurologic impairment on presentation or with extremely rapid onset of illness even if treated immediately have a 50-90% mortality and even higher morbidity.

With treatment, some permanent residual damage may occur causing hearing and speech difficulties, memory problems, and persistent weakness of the extremities. Recovery may also be complete without residual damage. Factors that are linked to poor prognosis and/or permanent damage include age, length of time between development of symptoms and treatment, and any simultaneous infections or chronic illnesses.

Differential Diagnosis

Differential diagnoses that share symptoms with chronic meningitis include bacterial endocarditis, malignant hypertension, lead poisoning, porphyria, migraine, viral encephalitis, cerebral abscesses, cerebral tumor, viral meningitis, and subdural hematoma.

Specialists

- Infectious Disease Physician
- Neurologist
- Physiatrist

Rehabilitation

Individuals with chronic meningitis may experience a variety of symptoms due to enlargement of the ventricular system within the brain (hydrocephalus), inflammation, or the underlying causes of meningitis such as tuberculosis or cancer. In addition to any therapy that may be necessary due to the cause of the meningitis, occupational, physical, speech, and psychological therapy may all be appropriate depending on the resultant neurological symptoms.

Occupational therapy addresses self-care strategies. Individuals may require speech therapy if a difficulty in speech production (dysarthria) or an inability to speak or understand speech (aphasia) occurs. A computer may also be used where a computer-generated voice "speaks" as the individual types what it is he or she wants to vocalize.

If impairments persist, individuals may require psychological counseling to deal with feelings about loss of physical function and help them remain motivated in rehabilitation.

Work Restrictions / Accommodations

If permanent weakness occurs, the physical setting may need to be adapted. The environment may need to be wheelchair-accessible. Alternatives to stairs such as ramps and elevators must be available. If job performance requires significant physical labor, duties may need to be curtailed temporarily or even permanently, requiring vocational counseling. The ability to perform duties must be assessed in terms of job requirements and physical capabilities. Use of assistive devices to help move and lift equipment, files, and boxes are helpful. If speech, hearing, and communication are limited, efforts must be made to accommodate the hearing-impaired individual and duties may need to be adjusted.

Comorbid Conditions

Alcoholism, diabetes, and conditions that weaken the immune system such as cancer or HIV infection may lengthen disability. Underlying conditions such as cancer or tuberculosis are associated with their own impairments additive to those of chronic meningitis.

Complications

Complications include enlargement of the fluid-filled ventricles within the brain (chronic communicating hydrocephalus), seizures, shock, deafness, neurologic impairments, dehydration, pericardial effusion, hemolytic anemia, coma, and death. Fluid leaking into the membrane covering the brain (subdural effusion) can cause swelling in the brain (cerebral edema, hydrocephalus). A localized infection (cerebral abscess) can form in the brain. If a shunt is needed for treatment of hydrocephalus or chronic administration of antibiotics, the shunt itself can become a source of infection and further complicate management. Steroid treatment may result in numerous complications including gastrointestinal bleeding, ulcers, osteoporosis, increased susceptibility to infections, Cushing's syndrome, and steroid psychosis. Chronic use of antibiotics can cause kidney or liver damage.

Factors Influencing Duration

Length of disability is influenced by the responsible organism, severity of the illness, individual's response to treatment, age, underlying conditions (particularly those that weaken the immune system), medications that might weaken the immune system, or any complications.

Length of Disability

Length of disability depends on any residual effects. Weakness may cause a reduction in manual labor duties. Hearing loss may require equipment to enhance hearing or speech therapy. Communication skills may be impaired, requiring speech therapy. Chronic meningitis may result in permanent disability or death.

Duration in Days

Job Classification	Minimum	Optimum	Maximum
Any work	42	182	Indefinite

Failure to Recover

If an individual fails to recover within the maximum duration expectancy period, the reader may wish to reference the following questions to assist in better understanding the specifics of an individual's medical case.

Regarding diagnosis:

- Was individual recently vaccinated against pneumonia, meningitis, influenza, mumps, or chickenpox?
- Has individual had contact with someone with meningitis? Travel to an area where hygiene conditions are poor and/or a meningitis outbreak occurred?
- Was surgery recently performed on the face or head that might provide a route of entry of infectious organisms?
- Are attacks of meningitis separated by periods where individual is free of symptoms and has a normal cerebrospinal fluid (CSF), suggesting recurrent meningitis rather than chronic meningitis?
- Was a careful search made for evidence of infection outside the brain and spinal cord (central nervous system) with culture and/or examinations of stomach (gastric) washings, bone marrow tests, and liver biopsy specimens? Should a brain or meningeal biopsy be considered?
- Are symptoms similar to acute bacterial meningitis but evolving slowly over a period of at least 4 weeks, sometimes months, and even (rarely) years?
- Was diagnosis of chronic meningitis confirmed?

Regarding treatment:

- Was culture and sensitivity done to identify causative organisms and determine the most effective drug therapy?
- Were antibiotic-resistant organisms ruled out?
- If hydrocephalus is present and/or if antibiotics need to be given into the spinal fluid for long periods of time, should shunt placement with Ommaya reservoir be considered?
- If the cause is not infectious, should steroid treatment be considered?

- Are any complications of steroid treatment, antibiotic treatment, and shunt placement being managed appropriately?

Regarding prognosis:

- Is individual over 60?
- Is individual taking medications that weaken the immune system?

- Does individual have a coexisting condition that may complicate treatment or impact recovery?
- Is there residual damage to the brain or other organs?
- Is individual permanently disabled or is vocational training indicated?
- Is individual's immune system weakened from cancer, HIV, or other conditions or medications?

References

Boss, Barbara J. "Alterations of Neurologic Function." Pathophysiology. McCance, Kathryn L, and Sue E. Heuther, eds. St. Louis: Mosby, 1994. 527-586.

Meningitis Overview. IntelliHealth. 09 Aug 2000. 04 Sep 2000 <http://www.intelihealth.com/IH/ihtIH/WSWCT000/331/10302.html>.

Meniscectomy and Meniscus Repair
Other names / synonyms: Cartilage Surgery, Meniscus Shaving, Partial Meniscectomy
80.6, 81.47

Definition

Meniscectomy is the surgical removal or repair of a C-shaped band of cartilage in the knee (knee meniscus). The meniscus forms a buffer between bones, serves as a shock absorber, assists in lubrication of the joint, and limits the joint's flexion, extension, and rotation. Twisting or hyperflexion of the joint is the most common cause of meniscal tears. The location and type of tear determine how much of the meniscus needs to be removed. The entire meniscus is rarely removed these days since the advent of arthroscopic surgery. In arthroscopic surgery, the surgeon uses a viewing scope (arthroscope) to view the joint and diagnose the problem, and other special tools to perform surgery through small incisions or portals.

Exercise aficionados and athletes who participate in contact sports are at risk for meniscal tears. Although use of proper technique when exercising or playing sports is emphasized, many causes of meniscus tears may not be preventable. A sign of meniscus injury is typically a "pop" noted at the time of injury. Joint tenderness, knee pain, and recurrent knee catching may follow.

According to reports issued by the Centers for Disease Control and Prevention (CDC) in 1998, the number of meniscectomy and meniscus repair procedures in the US was 473,000: 247,000 were performed on men, and 226,000 on women. Most individuals undergoing meniscectomies were in the 15 to 44 age group (197,000), 176,000 in the 45 to 64 age group, and 91,000 in the 65 and over age group. The number of meniscectomies performed in the south region of the US (192,000) surpassed those performed in the Northeast, Midwest, and western regions. Numbers for these procedures are based on discharges from short-stay, non-Federal hospitals.

Specialists

- Orthopedic Surgeon
- Physiatrist
- Physical Therapist

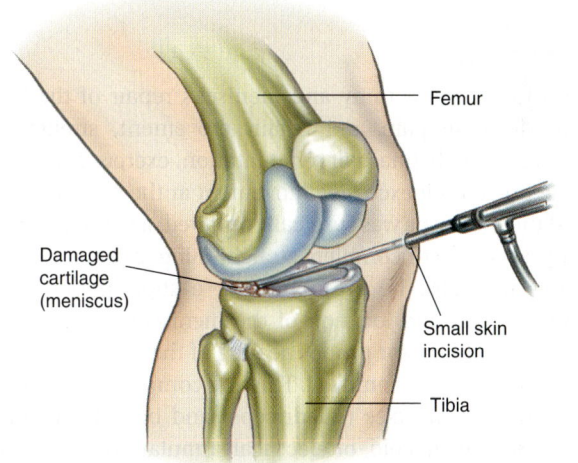

Reason for Procedure

The meniscectomy procedure is used to remove injured or damaged cartilage from the knee joint. The procedure is also used to relieve symptoms (joint tenderness, knee pain, and recurrent knee catching). In contrast to partial meniscus excision, meniscus repair may slow down the inevitable post-traumatic arthritis that follows a meniscus tear, and also provide protection to the knee ligaments. The goal of a meniscectomy is to relieve symptoms.

Description

In an arthroscopic meniscectomy or meniscus repair, after the individual is anesthetized, the surgeon puts an arthroscope that is about the thickness of a pencil, and one or two tools into the knee joint through small incisions (cuts or portals). Fluid is injected into the knee to expand the joint so the structures and cartilage can be seen. The surgeon first examines the knee to find any tears or other damage.

Tears along the inner curve of the meniscus especially those that are of the ragged, degenerative type, are most commonly treated by removing the damaged part of the meniscus. Tears near the outer rim of the meniscus where the blood supply is located may be repaired with stitches (sutures). Any resulting pieces of cartilage are removed. Injured ligaments are sewn together. The surgery concludes by removing the arthroscope and tools and closing the small openings with stitches.

In a conventional meniscectomy or meniscus repair, after the individual is anesthetized, the affected area is approached by an incision into the knee joint. As in the arthroscopy procedure, the knee is examined for tears or other damage. Tears along the inner curve of the meniscus especially those that are of the ragged, degenerative type, are most commonly treated by removing the damaged part of the meniscus. Tears near the outer rim of the meniscus where the blood supply is located are repaired with stitches (sutures). Any resulting pieces of cartilage are removed via forceps or suction. Injured ligaments are sewn together. The surgery concludes with the closure of the skin with sutures or clips that can usually be removed about 1 week after surgery.

Prognosis

Predicted outcome of a meniscectomy procedure is good. Most individuals who undergo meniscectomy can expect significant improvement without complications. About 6-12 weeks should be allowed for recovery from surgery.

Rehabilitation

Rehabilitation for meniscectomy and meniscus repair of the knee is important to decrease pain and regain movement, strength, and stability. During the early phase of rehabilitation, exercises to promote strength while preventing excessive movement at the joint surface are introduced. If the meniscus was surgically repaired, a special brace may be used that prevents both complete straightening and bending of the knee. Crutches may also be prescribed for a short period of time depending on the size and location of the meniscus tear. Promoting knee stability is important for proper healing of the meniscus whether the cartilage was repaired or removed. This is accomplished by strengthening the front thigh muscles (quadriceps) and back thigh muscles (hamstrings). Use of heat, cold, or electrical stimulation may be added to address initial pain.

Once pain and swelling are controlled and the physician recommends beginning movement of the knee, the physical therapist starts range of motion. If the meniscus was repaired instead of removed, the physician may advise the individual to avoid any excessive rotation or compression at the joint surface. This allows proper healing of the cartilage before any aggressive strengthening begins. Individuals start with passive range-of-motion exercises and then progress to exercises where they perform some of the effort in bending and straightening of the knee joint along with the help of the therapist (active assist range of motion).

As the individual improves with increased motion of the knee joint, the next step is active range of motion where the individual performs all the motion independently. This can be initiated in a warm whirlpool or in conjunction with another form of heat treatment and continued until all movement is restored.

Isometric exercises are often instructed initially for strengthening. These demand that the muscles around the knee joint contract with no movement taking place at the joint. An example of an isometric exercise for the knee region is the quad set. Another example of an isometric exercise for the knee joint is the hamstring set.

Strengthening is progressed to exercises with weighted resistance. For example, leg raises may be performed. Ankle weights may be used for resistance as the muscles strengthen from this exercise. Hamstring curls may be performed.

Resisted exercises with ankle weights or machines under the supervision of the therapist are then performed. Balance exercises may be added at this time.

At this point, the individual is encouraged to walk and may be allowed to return to light work. For the individual who has undergone surgical removal or repair of the meniscus within the knee joint, this phase may not be reached for several weeks longer. The individual's reinstatement to work is addressed in specific exercises prescribed by the physical therapist as these activities are now directed toward work requirements. Modifications may need to be made by the physical therapist for those individuals with arthritis or other joint irritations.

Work Restrictions / Accommodations

Strenuous activities should be restricted for several weeks. Other restrictions include no kneeling, squatting, crawling, climbing, or prolonged standing during the early phase of recovery. Use of crutches and a knee brace will affect agility. Frequent rest periods with facilities that allow the individual to elevate the lower extremity may enable earlier return to work.

Some individuals may have permanent restrictions on kneeling, jumping, and squatting based on findings during surgery. Use of medications for pain and swelling may require review of any drug policies.

Comorbid Conditions

Obesity may lengthen disability. Pre-existing or coexisting conditions such as osteoarthritis, knee ligament injury, inflammation of the inner lining of a joint cavity (synovitis), and scar tissue build-up inside the knee joint (arthrofibrosis) are known to lengthen disability.

Procedure Complications

Complications of meniscus repair may include nerve or blood vessel damage, bleeding, infection, stiffening of the knee joint (arthrofibrosis), and failure of the procedure.

Complete meniscectomy may increase the rate of degenerative changes to the articular surface and often leads to increased instability of the knee. In addition, blood vessels and nerves around the knee may be injured that cause numbness or weakness in the leg below the knee. Besides the usual surgical complications of anesthesia, chronic pain, infection, and bleeding, the individual may experience the formation of blood clots within a deep-lying vein (deep vein thrombosis) and changes in sensation around the incision.

Osteoarthritis, knee ligament injury, loose bodies, synovitis, and arthrofibrosis may complicate both meniscus repair and complete meniscectomy. Some individuals develop a postsurgical inflammation aggravated by physical therapy that slows recovery. It is important to note that having the procedure performed arthroscopically does not automatically mean recovery will be short and/or easy.

Factors Influencing Duration

Type of procedure, occurrence of complications, the individual's job requirements, ability to modify work activities, and compliance with rehabilitation may affect duration of disability.

Length of Disability

Duration depends on job requirements. Individuals who sit while at work may return sooner than those who stand.

Open meniscectomy.

Duration in Days

Job Classification	Minimum	Optimum	Maximum
Sedentary work	7	14	43
Light work	7	14	49
Medium work	14	21	56
Heavy work	21	42	84
Very Heavy work	28	42	126

Arthroscopic meniscectomy.

Duration in Days

Job Classification	Minimum	Optimum	Maximum
Sedentary work	7	14	28
Light work	14	21	35
Medium work	21	35	56
Heavy work	35	42	84
Very Heavy work	35	56	126

Meniscus repair.

Duration in Days

Job Classification	Minimum	Optimum	Maximum
Sedentary work	7	10	42
Light work	14	21	84
Medium work	28	35	91
Heavy work	42	84	140
Very Heavy work	56	91	182

Duration Trend from Normative Data*

Cases	Mean	Min	Max	No Lost Time	Over 6 Months
414	65	0	533	0.73%	8.23%

Percentile:	5th	25th	Median	75th	95th
Days:	9	20	39	61	118

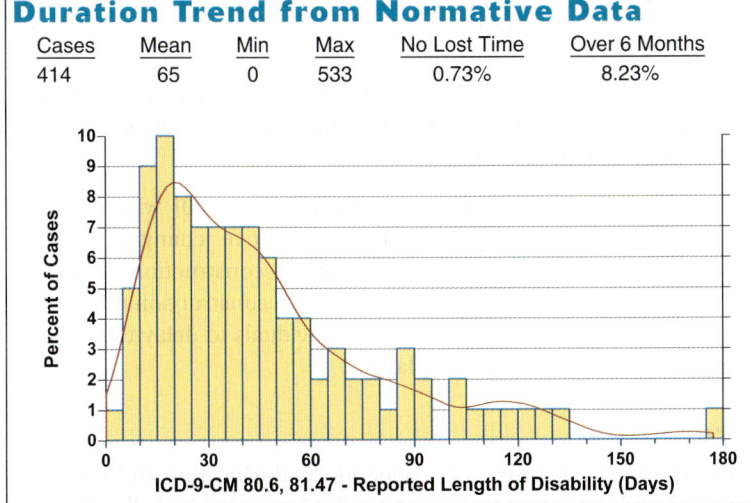
ICD-9-CM 80.6, 81.47 - Reported Length of Disability (Days)

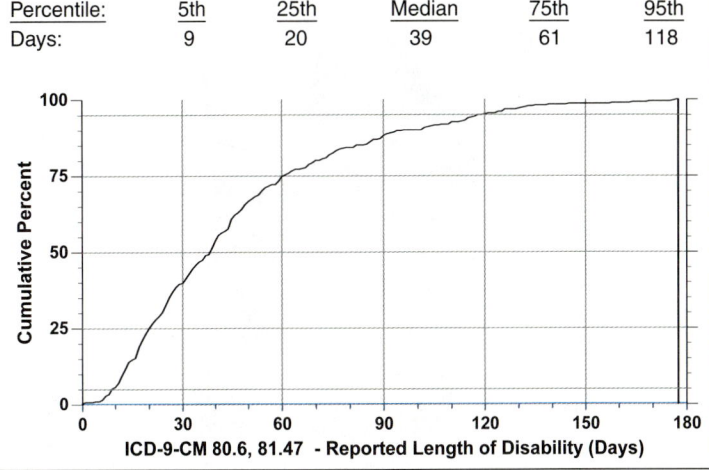
ICD-9-CM 80.6, 81.47 - Reported Length of Disability (Days)

* Differences may exist between the expected duration tables and the normative graphs. Duration tables provide expected recovery periods based on the type of work performed by the individual. The normative graphs reflect the actual observed experience of many individuals across the spectrum of physical conditions, in a variety of industries, and with varying levels of case management.

References

Arthroscopic Surgery. 25 Oct 2000 <http://www.ibjd.com/arthrosc.html>.

Meniscus Tears. Methodist Hospitals of Dallas. 18 Oct 2000 <http://mhd.drkoop.com/conditions/ency/article/001071.htm>.

Meniscus Disorders, Knee

Other names / synonyms: Injured Knee Cartilage, Meniscal Injury, Meniscus Lesion

717.0, 717.1, 717.2, 717.3, 717.4, 717.5, 836.0, 836.1, 836.2

Definition

Knee meniscus disorders involve the medial meniscus or lateral meniscus. These are two pads of cartilage in the knee between the joint surfaces of the femur and tibia (femoral and tibial condyles). Menisci serve as shock absorbers. The most common disorder is a tear of the meniscus. The medial meniscus is more commonly torn than the lateral. Tears are classified according to location, shape, size, and stability. The major classes of tears include the vertical longitudinal, oblique (often called parrot-beaked), degenerative, transverse, horizontal, or complex (involving multiple tears). Oblique and vertical longitudinal tears are the most common.

Individuals with a previous knee injury, leg length difference, an abnormally shaped (discoid) meniscus, cysts (pockets of thick liquid) of the meniscus, tight, weak muscles, or who walk on the insides of the feet (gross pronation) are at risk for knee injuries. In young individuals, tears are usually caused by trauma especially involving a twisting of the knee. In older individuals, there may be a gradual degeneration of the meniscus with no one causative event.

Knee injury is the second most common work-related accident. More than 3 million Americans have knee injuries each year and the meniscus is the most commonly injured part of the knee. Disorders of the lateral meniscus occur more often in women. Meniscus injuries are more frequent in young to middle-aged adults as opposed to other age groups. Meniscus tears most commonly occur to individuals in their 20s or over the age of 60.

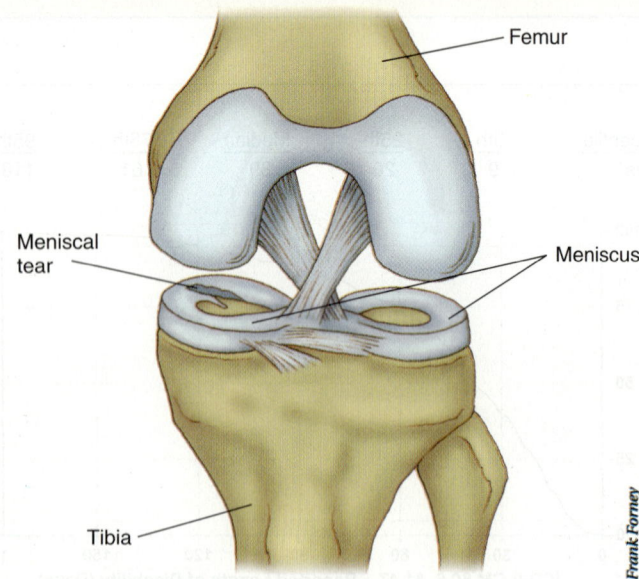

Diagnosis

History: In young individuals, there is usually a history of trauma. The individual may recall feeling a popping or snapping sensation when the trauma occurred. In older individuals, the trauma may be nonspecific such as repeated squatting or kneeling. The individual may complain of knee pain, swelling, limited range of motion, and a clicking sound. Locking (inability to straighten the knee) or buckling (sudden giving way of the knee) may occur.

Physical exam: The exam may reveal tenderness over the medial or lateral joint line of the knee. There may be evidence of fluid build-up (effusion) in the joint. Squatting may cause pain. Apley's compression and distraction test and McMurray's flexion test that involve applying rotational and axial compression forces to the knee will be positive.

Tests: Plain x-rays are not diagnostic, but rule out fracture and most loose bodies. MRI is a non-invasive method of evaluating the condition of the menisci. Individuals who cannot undergo MRI testing may be evaluated by an arthrogram (x-rays taken after dye is injected into the joint) or CT arthrogram. The interior of the joint can be examined directly by arthroscopy and, if indicated, arthroscopic surgery may be performed at the same time.

Treatment

Smaller meniscal tears with mild tolerable symptoms may be treated with rehabilitative exercise, activity modification, and analgesics, as some of these individuals are not willing to undergo surgery. More symptomatic meniscus injuries are treated surgically. Some meniscus tears can be repaired by suturing or by scraping (abrasion) to stimulate blood vessel growth. The possibility of repair must be determined by the surgeon at the time of surgery. Meniscus repair is generally reserved for younger individuals. Most tears require removal of the damaged part of the meniscus (partial meniscectomy). Because removal of the entire meniscus (complete or total meniscectomy) leads to bone remodeling and cartilage degeneration, it is avoided whenever possible.

Meniscectomy is done most commonly by arthroscopy but may also be done by open operation (arthrotomy). Arthroscopy has the advantage of producing less pain and a quicker recovery. However, arthroscopic meniscectomy is occasionally difficult depending on the type and location of the tear and the presence of adhesions. In these cases when the entire meniscus must be removed, open surgery may be preferable to avoid damaging the articular surfaces.

Young individuals (between the ages of 20 and 40) who require a complete meniscectomy or have degenerative changes following meniscectomy are candidates for meniscal reconstruction (transplantation) through use of graft tissue. Meniscal reconstruction may also be performed in middle-aged or elderly individuals to delay the need for total knee replacement (arthroplasty).

Prognosis

The outcome of meniscectomy depends on the location and severity of the tear and the repair technique used. Most individuals however can return to previous activities including athletics. Meniscus injury may predispose the individual to develop osteoarthritis in the involved knee. Progressive joint deterioration occurs following partial or complete meniscectomy. Long-term outcome of meniscal reconstruction is unknown.

Differential Diagnosis

Arthritis, ligament injuries, patellofemoral problems, tendon inflammation (tendinitis), fracture, and articular conditions can have similar symptoms. Degenerative and inflammatory conditions of the knee can also present with similar symptoms.

Specialists

- Orthopedic Surgeon
- Physiatrist
- Physical Therapist
- Sports Medicine Physician

Rehabilitation

Individuals with a meniscus disorder usually require outpatient physical therapy. Physical therapy progression is dictated by postoperative considerations such as immobilization, weight bearing, and range-of-motion restrictions that may be imposed by the surgeon according to the repair technique used. In general, physical therapy focuses on controlling pain, restoring range of motion, increasing strength, and improving functional activities. The ultimate goal of therapy is discharge to an independent home exercise program.

Rehabilitation for meniscectomy and meniscus repair of the knee is important to decrease pain and regain movement, strength, and stability. During the early phase of rehabilitation, exercises to promote strength while preventing excessive movement at the joint surface are introduced. If the meniscus was surgically repaired, a special brace may be used that prevents both complete straightening and bending of the knee. Crutches may also be prescribed for a short period of time depending on the size and location of the meniscus tear. Promoting knee stability is important for proper healing of the meniscus whether the cartilage was repaired or removed. This is accomplished by strengthening the front thigh muscles (quadriceps) and back thigh muscles (hamstrings). Use of heat, cold, or electrical stimulation may be added to address initial pain.

Once pain and swelling are controlled and the physician recommends beginning movement of the knee, the physical therapist starts range of motion. If the meniscus was repaired instead of removed, the physician may advise the individual to avoid any excessive rotation or compression at the joint surface. This allows proper healing of the cartilage before any aggressive strengthening begins. Individuals start with passive range-of-motion exercises and then progress to exercises where they perform some of the effort in bending and straightening of the knee joint along with the help of the therapist (active assist range of motion).

As the individual improves with increased motion of the knee joint, the next step is active range of motion where the individual performs all the motion independently. This can be initiated in a warm whirlpool or in conjunction with another form of heat treatment and continued until all movement is restored.

Isometric exercises are often instructed initially for strengthening. These demand that the muscles around the knee joint contract with no movement taking place at the joint. An example of an isometric exercise for the knee region is the quad set. Another example of an isometric exercise for the knee joint is the hamstring set.

Strengthening is progressed to exercises with weighted resistance. For example, leg raises may be performed. Ankle weights may be used for resistance as the muscles strengthen from this exercise. Hamstring curls may be performed.

Resisted exercises with ankle weights or machines under the supervision of the therapist are then performed. Balance exercises may be added at this time.

At this point, the individual is encouraged to walk and may be allowed to return to light work. For the individual who has undergone surgical removal or repair of the meniscus within the knee joint, this phase may not be reached for several weeks longer. The individual's reinstatement to work is addressed in specific exercises prescribed by the physical therapist as these activities are now directed toward work requirements. Modifications may need to be made by the physical therapist for those individuals with arthritis or other joint irritations.

Work Restrictions / Accommodations

The individual may need to use crutches or a walking cane temporarily. Standing and walking may need to be limited temporarily. Squatting, kneeling, and crawling may need to be limited permanently.

Comorbid Conditions

Coexisting ligamentous instability, arthritis, obesity, and diabetes may increase the length of disability.

Complications

The trauma that led to a meniscal tear may also have caused torn knee ligaments. Elderly individuals may have other degenerative changes of the knee.

Factors Influencing Duration

Length of disability is influenced by the severity of symptoms, region of meniscal tear, presence of underlying joint disease (osteoarthritis, rheumatoid arthritis), and type of surgery. Sustaining multiple injuries to the knee lengthens disability. The individual may return to work sooner if job is performed in a seated position.

Length of Disability

Duration depends on job requirements. Individuals who sit while they work may return sooner than those who stand. Meniscal tears treated nonoperatively usually interfere with heavy work.

Medical treatment.

Duration in Days

Job Classification	Minimum	Optimum	Maximum
Sedentary work	7	7	14
Light work	7	14	21
Medium work	14	28	42
Heavy work	28	35	91
Very Heavy work	28	42	91

Surgical treatment by open meniscectomy.

Duration in Days

Job Classification	Minimum	Optimum	Maximum
Sedentary work	7	14	42
Light work	7	14	49
Medium work	14	21	56
Heavy work	21	42	84
Very Heavy work	28	42	126

Surgical treatment by arthroscopic meniscectomy.

Duration in Days

Job Classification	Minimum	Optimum	Maximum
Sedentary work	7	14	28
Light work	14	21	35
Medium work	21	35	56
Heavy work	35	42	84
Very Heavy work	35	56	126

Surgical treatment by meniscus repair.

Duration in Days

Job Classification	Minimum	Optimum	Maximum
Sedentary work	7	10	42
Light work	14	21	84
Medium work	28	35	91
Heavy work	42	84	140
Very Heavy work	56	91	182

Duration Trend from Normative Data

Cases	Mean	Min	Max	No Lost Time	Over 6 Months
2483	55	0	414	0.53%	1.70%

Percentile:	5th	25th	Median	75th	95th
Days:	10	21	39	72	143

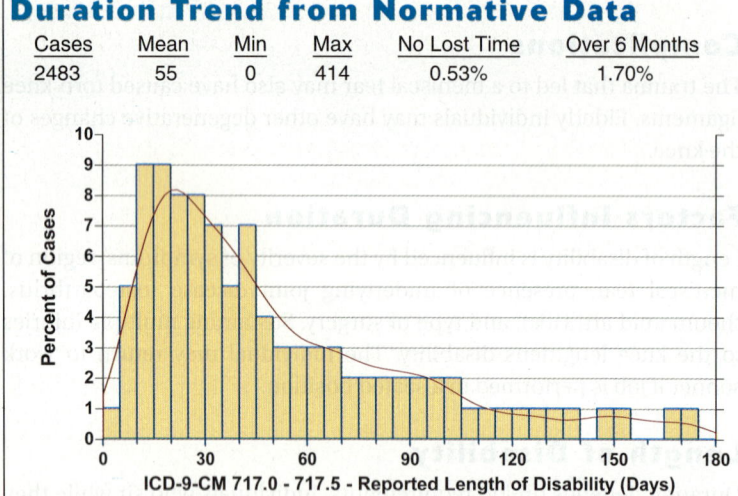
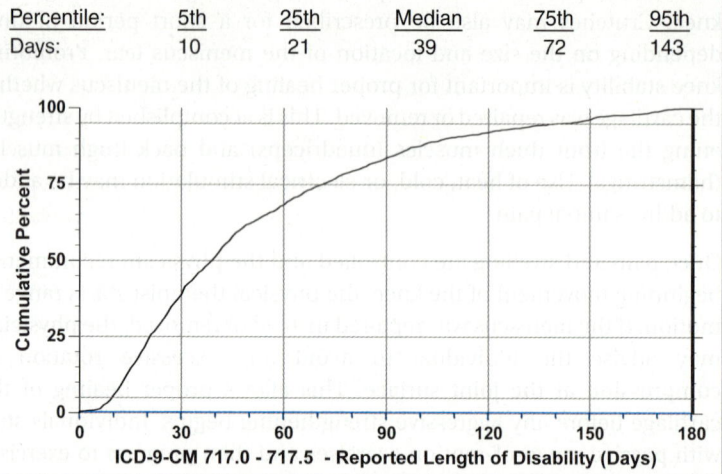

Duration Trend from Normative Data*

Cases	Mean	Min	Max	No Lost Time	Over 6 Months
15779	56	0	495	0.10%	1.62%

Percentile:	5th	25th	Median	75th	95th
Days:	13	25	42	69	135

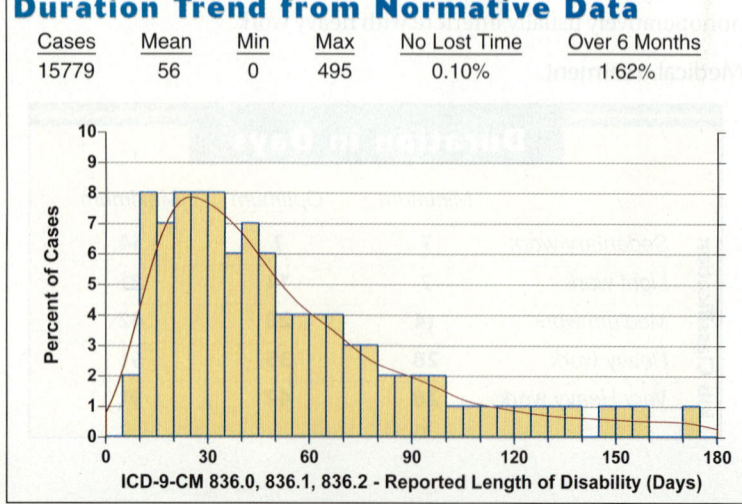
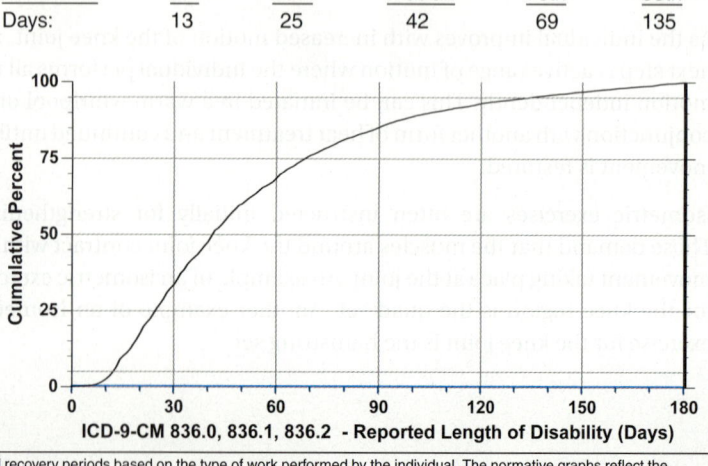

* Differences may exist between the expected duration tables and the normative graphs. Duration tables provide expected recovery periods based on the type of work performed by the individual. The normative graphs reflect the actual observed experience of many individuals across the spectrum of physical conditions, in a variety of industries, and with varying levels of case management.

Failure to Recover

If an individual fails to recover within the maximum duration expectancy period, the reader may wish to reference the following questions to assist in better understanding the specifics of an individual's medical case.

Regarding diagnosis:

- Does the individual have a history of trauma, especially twisting of the knee?
- Did the individual feel a popping or snapping sensation when the trauma occurred?
- Does repeated squatting or kneeling cause pain?
- Is the knee swollen with limited range of motion?
- Were x-rays done to rule out a fracture?
- Was an MRI done to confirm the diagnosis? If not, was an arthrogram done?
- Was the meniscus examined directly by arthroscopy?
- Was arthroscopic surgery done at the same time?

Regarding treatment:

- Did the surgeon miss small tears during arthroscopic surgery?
- Is the individual motivated to comply with the rehabilitation regimen?
- Has the individual demonstrated an increase in range of motion at each physical therapy session?
- If arthroscopic surgery was performed, would arthrotomy be more effective?
- Is the individual a candidate for meniscal reconstruction?

Regarding prognosis:

- What is the extent and location of the meniscal tear?
- Was the rupture located in a region of the meniscus with no blood supply (avascular)? If so, was a fibrin clot used to facilitate healing?
- Has physical therapy been effective?
- Is the individual prolonging rehabilitation out of fear of sustaining another knee injury?
- Are the knee ligaments torn?
- Is there evidence of joint deterioration?

References

Kisner, Carolyn, and Lynn Allen Colby. "The Knee." Therapeutic Exercise: Foundations and Techniques, 2nd ed Philadelphia: F.A. Davis Company, 1990. 345-384.

Magee, David J. "Knee." Orthopedic Physical Assessment. Biblis, Margaret M., ed. Philadelphia: W.B. Saunders Company, 1992. 372-447.

Maitra, Ranjan, Mark Miller, and Darren Johnson. "Meniscal Reconstruction Part II: Outcome, Potential Complications, and Future Directions." The American Journal of Orthopedics 28 (1999): 280-286.

Maitra, Ranjan, Mark Miller, and Darren Johnson. "Meniscal Reconstruction Part I: Indications, Techniques, and Graft Considerations." The American Journal of Orthopedics 28 (1999): 213-218.

Messner, Karola, and Jizong Gao. "The Menisci of the Knee Joint. Anatomical and Functional Characteristics, and a Rationale for Clinical Treatment." Journal of Anatomy 193 (1998): 161-178.

Polkinghorn, B.S. "Conservative Treatment of Torn Medial Meniscus Via Mechanical Force, Manually Assisted Short Lever Chiropractic Adjusting Procedures." Journal of Manipulative and Physiological Therapeutics 17 7 (1994): 474-484.

Stone, Jeffrey, and Freddie Fu. "The Knee." Principles of Orthopaedic Practice. Dee, Roger, et al., eds. New York: McGraw-Hill, 1997. 895-905.

Wallace, Lynn, Robert Mangine, and Terry Malone. "The Knee." Orthopedic and Sports Physical Therapy. Malone, Terry, Thomas McPoil, and Arthur Nitz, eds. St. Louis: Mosby, 1997. 295-325.

Menopause

Other names / synonyms: Change of Life, Climacteric

256.3, 627.2, 627.8, 627.9

Definition

Menopause occurs when egg production (ovulation) ceases, ending the possibility of pregnancy, and menstruation becomes less frequent and eventually stops. In some individuals, menstruation stops suddenly. In most women, menstruation tapers off, in both quantity and length of flow. Often, the interval between menstrual periods changes, becoming more closely or more widely spaced. This irregularity may last for 2-3 years until menstruation ultimately ends.

Menopause normally occurs between the ages of 40-55 years, with an average age of onset of 51 years.

A decrease in estrogen and progesterone production is associated with menopause. The symptoms of menopause are caused by these changes in estrogen and progesterone levels. A gradual decrease of estrogen (as seen in natural menopause) allows the body to slowly adjust to the hormone change. In some individuals, the estrogen level decreases suddenly, causing more severe symptoms. This sudden decrease in estrogen is also seen when the ovaries are surgically removed (surgical menopause).

Diagnosis

History: Individuals may present with symptoms that include hot flashes and skin flushing, mood changes, decreased sex drive (libido), irregular menstrual periods, and vaginal dryness. Other symptoms may include disturbed sleep patterns, headaches, joint pain, and heart palpitations.

Physical exam: On physical exam changes (thinning) in the vaginal lining caused by changes in estrogen levels may be noted.

Tests: Blood and urine tests may be used to check hormone and reproductive steroid levels (e.g., estrogen, progesterone, plasma estradiol, estrone, and FSH).

Treatment

Generally, natural menopause requires no treatment. Surgical menopause may require estrogen replacement therapy (ERT). All postmenopausal women do not need to be treated with ERT. Each individual should discuss the benefits and risks of ERT with her physician. Many physicians recommend ERT to reduce the symptoms of menopause, decrease vaginal drying, and help prevent postmenopausal osteoporosis. ERT has many side effects including vaginal bleeding, nausea, vomiting, breast tenderness, uterine cramps, and abdominal bloating. Some physicians try to reduce the side effects of ERT by titrating to the lowest effective dose of ERT, or adding progesterone or testosterone to ERT.

Some women may not be able to take estrogen if they have had certain types of breast cancer, other cancers, or blood clots. Other medication may be substituted instead, such as beta-blockers and calcium supplements. Bone resorption inhibitors prevent bone loss but do not alleviate hot flashes. Severe psychological symptoms may warrant treatment with antidepressant medication.

Prognosis

While symptoms of menopause may last only a month or persist for several years, most women experience menopause without long-term problems. Many woman report an increase in energy and self-confidence after menopause. Some women may experience a loss in bone mass of 2-5% per year for the 5 years following menopause.

Many studies have been done to assess the effects of estrogen treatment. The results of these studies are conflicting. Estrogen does seem to reduce the severity of hot flashes and vaginal dryness and help prevent osteoporosis. The effect of estrogen on preventing heart disease is disputed.

Differential Diagnosis

Other conditions that may mimic the symptoms of menopause include pituitary gland dysfunction, anxiety, depression, and uterine cancer.

Specialists

- Endocrinologist
- Gynecologist
- Internist
- Psychiatrist
- Psychologist

Work Restrictions / Accommodations

No general work restrictions or accommodations apply, but specific cases may have unique needs. Sleep deprivation may create issues around concentration. Working with machinery may need to be assessed.

Comorbid Conditions

Underlying psychiatric/psychological conditions may lengthen disability.

Complications

The hormonal changes (primarily decreased estrogen levels) associated with menopause increase the long-term risk for developing osteoporosis and also increase the long-term risk of cardiovascular disease.

Estrogen protects against heart disease in many ways. Estrogen reduces the individual's total cholesterol level, raises the "good" high-density lipoprotein HDL cholesterol level, and lowers the "bad" low-density lipoprotein cholesterol level. Once a woman's body is no longer producing estrogen, her risk of heart attack slowly increases.

Factors Influencing Duration

The individual's overall state of physical or mental health prior to experiencing menopause may influence the length of disability. Other factors that may affect length of disability include severity of symptoms, especially sleep disturbances.

Length of Disability

In most cases, no disability is expected. Duration depends on severity of symptoms.

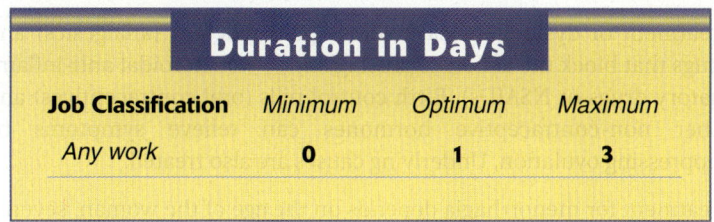

Duration in Days			
Job Classification	Minimum	Optimum	Maximum
Any work	0	1	3

Failure to Recover

If an individual fails to recover within the maximum duration expectancy period, the reader may wish to reference the following questions to assist in better understanding the specifics of an individual's medical case.

Regarding diagnosis:

- Does the individual have natural or surgical menopause?
- Does the individual present with hot flashes and skin flushing, mood changes, decreased libido, irregular menstrual periods, and vaginal dryness?
- Does the individual also report disturbed sleep patterns, headaches, joint pain, and heart palpitations?
- On physical exam was thinning in the vaginal lining noted?
- Did the individual have blood and urine tests to check hormone and reproductive steroid levels?
- Have conditions with similar symptoms been ruled out?

Regarding treatment:

- Has the individual discussed estrogen replacement therapy (ERT) with her physician?
- Is the individual being treated with ERT?
- Is it necessary for the individual to consider other treatment such as beta-blockers, calcium supplements or bone resorption inhibitors?
- If necessary has the individual sought psychiatric counseling? Is she using antidepressants?

Regarding prognosis:

- Is the individual's employer able to accommodate any necessary restrictions?
- Does the individual have any conditions that may affect their ability to recover?
- Does the individual have any complications such as osteoporosis or cardiovascular disease? Does the individual have any side effect of ERT such as vaginal bleeding, nausea, vomiting, breast tenderness, uterine cramps, or abdominal bloating?

References

Menopause. drkoop.com. 1998. 25 Aug 2000 <http://www.drkoop.com/conditions/ency/article/000894.htm>.

Tierney, Lawrence M., Stephen J. McPhee, and Maxine Papadakis, eds. Current Medical Diagnosis and Treatment, 39th ed. New York: Lange Medical Books/McGraw-Hill, 2000.

Menstrual Disorders

Other names / synonyms: Amenorrhea, Dysmenorrhea, Menorrhagia, Metrorrhagia
625.2, 625.3, 625.9, 626.0, 626.1, 626.2, 626.4, 626.5, 626.6, 626.9

Definition

Menstrual disorders are irregularities or abnormalities of the menstrual cycle including the absence of menstrual periods (amenorrhea), discomfort associated with the menstrual period (dysmenorrhea), excess blood loss with the menstrual period (menorrhagia), and abnormal bleeding (metrorrhagia).

Amenorrhea may occur as a result of many conditions. Failure to start menstruating by the age of sixteen is one type of amenorrhea (primary). Amenorrhea that occurs in a woman who has menstruated regularly in the past (secondary) is more typical. Pregnancy and menopause are very common causes. Other causes include hormone imbalances, ovarian disorders, Polycystic ovarian disease, endocrine disorders (diabetes, thyroid abnormality, and Cushing's syndrome), genetic abnormalities, emotional stress, depression, obesity, excessive or rapid weight loss, reduced caloric intake, including self-starvation (anorexia nervosa), systemic diseases (syphilis, tuberculosis, nephritis), or drugs. About 80% of women with polycystic ovarian disease have amenorrhea. Menstrual periods may cease temporarily after a woman stops taking birth control pills. Although this temporary amenorrhea usually only lasts 6 to 8 weeks, it is possible to persist for a year or more.

Dysmenorrhea refers to pain or discomfort during or just before a menstrual period. Approximately 30-80% of menstruating women experience this disorder. Dysmenorrhea is associated with the hormone prostaglandin released during the menstrual period, but the exact cause is uncertain. Dysmenorrhea can also be caused by underlying conditions such as an ectopic pregnancy or miscarriage, ovarian cysts, an intrauterine device (IUD) used for contraception, growth of endometrial tissue outside of the uterus (endometriosis), postoperative adhesions, bacterial infection of the uterus and fallopian tubes (pelvic inflammatory disease), fibroid tumors in the uterus (uterine leiomyoma), an obstructed cervix, or congenital malformation.

Menorrhagia is the excessive loss of blood during a menstrual period. Excessive loss of blood may be due to the period lasting more than 7 days and/or blood loss greater than 80 milliliters. It is usually due to an imbalance between the hormones estrogen and progesterone, but can also be caused by any disorder that affects the uterus including fibroid tumors, polyps, an intrauterine device (IUD) used for contraception, or a pelvic infection. Sometimes no physical cause can be found. Polyps occur in about 10% of all women. Fibroids are diagnosed in about 20-30% of all women.

Metrorrhagia is uterine bleeding that is irregular in pattern and in the amount of blood lost. It is caused by a hormonal imbalance, stress or travel, unsuspected pregnancy, early miscarriage, gynecologic disorders, or cancer (uterine, ovarian, or cervical).

Diagnosis

History: Amenorrhea (primary and secondary) is the absence of menstrual periods. Some causes may be ruled out through the individual's history.

In dysmenorrhea, symptoms include cramping labor-like pain in the lower abdomen that starts just prior to or at the time the menstrual period begins. Pain may come and go in waves. Individual may also report nausea, vomiting, and a dull, lower backache. Approximately 10% of women have symptoms severe enough to interfere with their work or leisure activities. In secondary dysmenorrhea, pain begins several days before and lasts throughout the menstrual period. Dysmenorrhea can be preceded by premenstrual syndrome (bloating, irritability, and depression).

A woman normally loses about 2 fluid ounces (60 milliliters) of blood during an average menstrual period. During menorrhagia, a woman may lose 3 ounces (90 milliliters) or more. Menorrhagia can be a regular occurrence or rare event.

Metrorrhagia means a deviation from the normal menstrual pattern. Variations may include the intervals between periods, duration of the bleeding, or amount of blood lost.

Physical exam: A pelvic exam is needed to rule out congenital abnormalities, pregnancy, and ovary disorders for amenorrhea.

For dysmenorrhea, a bimanual pelvic exam rules out uterine tenderness or enlarged ovaries.

For menorrhagia and metrorrhagia, the rate of bleeding is assessed. Pelvic exam may reveal increased size of the uterus that may indicate the presence of uterine polyps. Pelvic exam may reveal absence of the uterus or ovaries, indicative of congenital abnormalities.

Tests: For amenorrhea, blood tests measure hormone levels. A laparoscopy (tiny microscope inserted into the abdomen) enables visual inspection of reproductive organs to detect abnormalities. CT or MRI of pituitary should be done if fasting prolactin is markedly elevated. Ultrasound scanning of abdomen and pelvis can rule out tumor of adrenal gland or ovary.

Diagnostic tests for dysmenorrhea, menorrhagia, and metrorrhagia may include pregnancy test, Pap smear, or urine and cervical cultures. An endometrial biopsy, ultrasound, or laparoscopy may be considered. Treatment of secondary dysmenorrhea depends on the cause, so it is essential that the underlying condition be accurately identified. Conditions that must be ruled out include endometriosis pelvic inflammatory disease and fibroid tumors of the uterus. Other tests for menorrhagia and metrorrhagia may include a complete blood count (CBC) and endocrine testing to rule out underlying conditions. A transvaginal ultrasound may be done to assess endometrial thickness. A D&C (dilation and curettage) may be performed to investigate the cause of the bleeding.

Treatment

Treatment is focused on the cause of the disorder and any underlying disorders.

Treatment of amenorrhea includes correction of hormonal imbalances and induction of ovulation. Weight problems, overexercise, and anorexia nervosa need to be addressed due to the long-term threat to the woman's health.

Treatment of dysmenorrhea includes pain relievers (analgesics) and drugs that block the action of prostaglandin (nonsteroidal anti-inflammatory drugs or NSAIDs). Birth control pills (oral contraceptives) and other non-contraceptive hormones can relieve symptoms by suppressing ovulation. Underlying causes are also treated.

Treatment for menorrhagia depends on the age of the woman, severity of the bleeding, whether or not she wants children in the future, and any underlying medical condition. Hormone medications (estrogen, progesterone) can be used to reduce the bleeding. If an IUD is the cause, it can be removed. A D & C, in which the endometrium lining is scraped away, may be beneficial if the lining has thickened and is causing excessive bleeding. The endometrial lining can also be thinned (endometrial ablation) using laser or electrocautery. If the condition is severe or does not respond to treatment, the uterus may be surgically removed (hysterectomy).

Metrorrhagia may be treated with hormones such as those in birth control pills (oral contraceptives). If bleeding becomes profuse (hemorrhage), bed rest and/or hospitalization may be required.

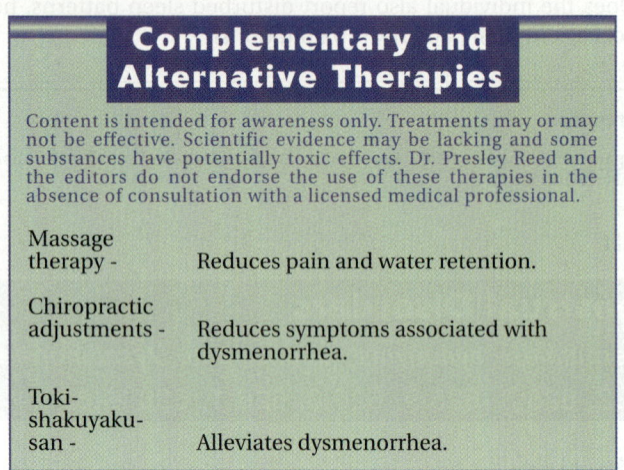

Complementary and Alternative Therapies

Content is intended for awareness only. Treatments may or may not be effective. Scientific evidence may be lacking and some substances have potentially toxic effects. Dr. Presley Reed and the editors do not endorse the use of these therapies in the absence of consultation with a licensed medical professional.

Massage therapy -	Reduces pain and water retention.
Chiropractic adjustments -	Reduces symptoms associated with dysmenorrhea.
Toki-shakuyaku-san -	Alleviates dysmenorrhea.

Prognosis

The predicted outcome depends on the underlying cause of the menstrual disorder. The outcome may be normal menopause in women experiencing amenorrhea. Amenorrhea due to genetic abnormalities (absent ovaries for example) may not respond to therapy and replacement hormones may be necessary. The predicted outcome of amenorrhea due to pregnancy is delivery of a healthy infant. Some women with amenorrhea choose not to receive treatment if underlying cause is not a health threat.

The predicted outcome of dysmenorrhea, menorrhagia, and metrorrhagia again depend on the underlying conditions. Dysmenorrhea due to hormone imbalances and prostaglandin production may respond well to medical treatment. The outcome of endometriosis may also be good with treatment and reduction of the endometriosis. The outcome of pelvic inflammatory disease may vary. Infection generally resolves with antibiotic therapy. Unfortunately, some cases of pelvic inflammatory disease result in scarring of the fallopian tubes, resulting in infertility. The outcome of fibroids is usually good. The predicted outcome of cancers of the reproductive tract varies with the type, stage of disease, and response to treatment.

The outcome of a D & C procedure is generally good. The outcome of endometrial ablation is also generally good.

Differential Diagnosis

Menstruation disorders may also be abnormalities in the thyroid, pituitary, or adrenal glands.

Specialists

- Endocrinologist
- Genetics Specialist
- Gynecologist
- Pathologist
- Surgeon

Work Restrictions / Accommodations

In general, physical activity may need to be reduced or limited when symptoms are present. Specific restriction or accommodations depend on underlying cause and resulting treatment. Women with amenorrhea due to regular, heavy physical exercise and associated lean body mass may need to reduce the activity and increase the portion of body fat for ovulation in order for regular menstrual cycles to resume. Pregnancy, diagnostic, and therapeutic procedures may require time off from work. The necessary amount of time off depends on the extent of the procedure. Diagnostic laparoscopy may only require a few days for recovery but abdominal hysterectomy may require 6 to 8 weeks off from work.

Comorbid Conditions

Comorbid conditions may include medical conditions that affect the overall health of the woman such as renal failure and hemodialysis.

Complications

In general, any complications are related to the underlying condition. Complications of amenorrhea relate to the underlying condition including endocrine disorder, hormonal imbalance, congenital abnormalities of the reproductive tract, emotional disorders, and ovarian tumor or cyst. Prolonged amenorrhea may result in osteoporosis even in younger women.

Menorrhagia complications can include anemia.

Factors Influencing Duration

The severity of and duration of symptoms, underlying cause, duration and frequency of bleeding, treatment, and individual's job requirements affect the length of disability. For amenorrhea, no disability is expected.

Length of Disability

For secondary dysmenorrhea, duration depends on the underlying cause

Primary dysmenorrhea or menorrhagia.

Duration in Days

Job Classification	Minimum	Optimum	Maximum
Any work	0	3	7

Metrorrhagia.

Duration in Days

Job Classification	Minimum	Optimum	Maximum
Any work	0	7	14

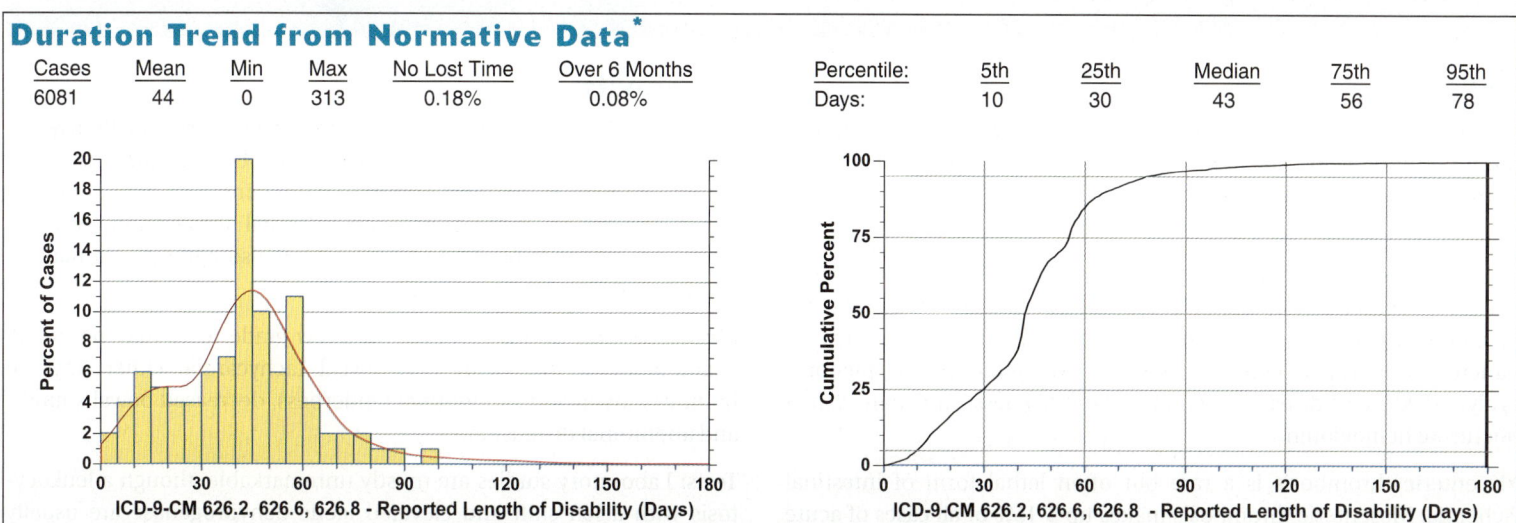

Duration Trend from Normative Data*

Cases	Mean	Min	Max	No Lost Time	Over 6 Months
6081	44	0	313	0.18%	0.08%

Percentile:	5th	25th	Median	75th	95th
Days:	10	30	43	56	78

ICD-9-CM 626.2, 626.6, 626.8 - Reported Length of Disability (Days)

* Differences may exist between the expected duration tables and the normative graphs. Duration tables provide expected recovery periods based on the type of work performed by the individual. The normative graphs reflect the actual observed experience of many individuals across the spectrum of physical conditions, in a variety of industries, and with varying levels of case management.

Menstrual Disorders

Failure to Recover

If an individual fails to recover within the maximum duration expectancy period, the reader may wish to reference the following questions to assist in better understanding the specifics of an individual's medical case.

Regarding diagnosis:

- Does individual have symptoms of dysmenorrhea such as cramping labor-like pain in the lower abdomen that starts just prior to or at the time the menstrual period begins? Pain that comes and goes in waves? Nausea, vomiting, and a dull, lower backache?
- Does individual have primary or secondary dysmenorrhea?
- Does individual lose 3 ounces or more of blood during an average menstrual period?
- Was diagnosis of the specific menstrual disorder confirmed through pelvic exam and diagnostic testing (i.e., pregnancy test, Pap smear, or urine and cervical cultures)?
- Were conditions such as congenital abnormalities, pregnancy, and ovary disorders ruled out? Endometriosis pelvic inflammatory disease or fibroid tumors of the uterus?
- What type of menstrual disorder does individual have? Amenorrhea, dysmenorrhea, menorrhagia, or metrorrhagia?

Regarding treatment:

- Was underlying condition identified? Is it responding to treatment?
- Has treatment included not only correcting the hormonal imbalance but also making pertinent lifestyle modifications?
- Do symptoms warrant a more aggressive treatment such as endometrial ablation or hysterectomy?
- Was hospitalization required?
- If underlying cause was cancer, was it caught before it metastasized?

Regarding prognosis:

- Is underlying condition responding to treatment?
- Is the disorder expected to reoccur?
- Does individual have a coexisting condition that may complicate treatment or impact recovery?
- Has individual experienced complications related to the menstrual disorder such as endocrine disorder, hormonal imbalance, congenital abnormalities of the reproductive tract, emotional disorders, ovarian tumor or cyst, or anemia?
- If symptoms persist despite treatment, would individual benefit from consultation with a specialist (gynecologist, endocrinologist)?

References

Baase, Carol A. "Amenorrhea." Saunders Manual of Medical Practice, 2nd ed. Rakel, Robert E., ed. Philadelphia: W.B. Saunders Company, 2000. 514-516.

Barrow, Ann, Clinical Director. Professional's Guide to Signs and Symptoms. Springhouse, PA: Springhouse, PA, 2000.

Hernandez-reif, M., A. Martinez, and T. Field. "Premenstrual Symptoms are Relieved by Massage Therapy." Journal of Psychosomatic Obstetrics and Gynecology 21 1 (2000): 9-15.

Kotani, N., T. Oyama, and I. Sakai. "Analgesic Effect of a Herbal Medicine for the Treatment of Primary Dysmenorrhea - A Double-blind Study." American Journal of Chinese Medicine 25 2 (1997): 205-212.

Paul, Stephen. "Dysmenorrhea." Saunders Manual of Medical Practice, 2nd ed. Rakel, Robert E., ed. Philadelphia: W.B. Saunders Company, 2000. 510-514.

Walsh, M.J., and B.I. Polus. "A Randomized, Placebo-controlled Clinical Trial on the Efficacy of Chiropractic Therapy on Premenstrual Syndrome." Journal of Manipulative and Physiological Therapeutics 22 9 (1999): 582-585.

Mesenteric Thrombosis

Other names / synonyms: Mesenteric Venous Thrombosis, MVT

557, 557.0

Definition

Mesenteric thrombosis refers to a blood clot that blocks off (occludes) the mesenteric vein, which is located in the tissue that connects the intestine to the back of the abdominal wall.

Individuals who have undergone previous abdominal surgery and individuals who suffer from hyper-coagulable states are at increased risk for mesenteric thrombosis. Other predisposing factors include use of estrogen-containing oral contraceptives; inflammation, such as pancreatitis; portal hypertension; enlargement of the spleen (splenomegaly); sickle cell disease; decompression sickness; and paroxysmal nocturnal hemoglobin.

Mesenteric thrombosis is a rare but often lethal form of intestinal ischemia. Mesenteric thrombosis makes up 5-15% of all cases of acute mesenteric ischemia. While the true prevalence is unknown, the incidence of symptomatic mesenteric thrombosis is reported to be 2 per 100,000 individuals.

Diagnosis

History: Individuals with mesenteric thrombosis are usually asymptomatic until the onset of late complications. Once symptoms begin, abdominal pain is the most common complaint. The pain is usually vague and slowly progressive, with eventual localization over the affected segment of bowel. Individuals may also complain of nausea, vomiting, diarrhea, and anorexia.

Physical exam: Upon examination, a low grade fever may be noted. Examination of the heart may reveal tachycardia. Other physical findings may include abdominal tenderness, decreased bowel sounds, and abdominal distension.

Tests: Laboratory studies are mostly unremarkable, though a leukocytosis with a left shift and elevated lactic dehydrogenase are usually present. X-rays, MRI, and CT scan may be performed. Among these, CT scans are the most accurate (90% and better) in diagnosing mesenteric thrombosis.

Treatment

Nonsurgical management of mesenteric thrombosis includes administration of intravenous fluids, nasogastric decompression, and anticoagulation with heparin.

If signs of peritonitis or intestinal infarction are present, surgical intervention (thrombectomy) is indicated. During the operation, only nonviable tissue is removed. Following surgery, the individual is placed on anticoagulation therapy (warfarin sodium) for 6 months.

Prophylactic antibiotics are recommended for both surgical and nonsurgical management of the condition.

Prognosis

Mesenteric thrombosis frequently causes severe morbidity, and the mortality rate of mesenteric thrombosis varies greatly from 20-80% among published studies for both surgical and nonsurgical treatment. Even though there has been a slight improvement in survival over the past 20 years, the recurrence rate remains high, and long-term prognosis poor.

Differential Diagnosis

Other conditions that present with similar symptomatology include Crohn's disease, cecal diverticulitis, perforated cecal carcinoma, mesenteric adenitis, and pelvic inflammatory disease.

Specialists

- Gastroenterologist
- Internist
- Surgeon

Work Restrictions / Accommodations

During the early course of the condition, most individuals are asymptomatic and require no work accommodations. In time, mesenteric thrombosis can be a catastrophic event that significantly affects the body's ability to absorb nutrients, and the individual may need to receive nutrition intravenously at home (parenteral nutrition); therefore, disability may be permanent.

Comorbid Conditions

Existing conditions that may impact ability to recover and may further lengthen disability include obesity, hypertension, hypercoagulability, and polycythemia vera.

Complications

Possible complications of this condition include gastrointestinal hemorrhage, portal hypertension, and ascites.

Factors Influencing Duration

Factors that might influence the length of disability include the individual's age and general health, the duration and severity of disease, the specific treatment provided, the individual's response to treatment, and the development of complications.

Length of Disability

Duration reflects recovery from surgical procedure only. Disability may be permanent.

Surgical treatment.

Duration in Days

Job Classification	Minimum	Optimum	Maximum
Sedentary work	14	21	28
Light work	14	21	28
Medium work	28	35	42
Heavy work	91	119	182
Very Heavy work	91	119	182

Failure to Recover

If an individual fails to recover within the maximum duration expectancy period, the reader may wish to reference the following questions to assist in better understanding the specifics of an individual's medical case.

Regarding diagnosis:

- Has the individual received adequate diagnostic testing to establish the diagnosis of mesenteric thrombosis?
- Have conditions with similar symptoms been ruled out?
- Did individual experience any complications associated with mesenteric thrombosis, such as gastrointestinal hemorrhage, portal hypertension, or ascites?

Regarding treatment:

- Did the individual respond favorably to nonsurgical treatment?
- Was surgery indicated due to signs of peritonitis or intestinal infarction?
- Following surgery, was individual placed on anticoagulation therapy for 6 months?
- If mesenteric thrombosis has significantly affected the body's ability to absorb nutrients, can individual receive nutrition intravenously at home?

Regarding prognosis:

- Has mesenteric thrombosis persisted or recurred despite treatment?
- Does individual have a coexisting condition that may complicate treatment or impact recovery?

References

Blood Disorders: Mesenteric Venous Thrombosis. Fitness Culture. 1999. 3 Jan 2001 <http://www.fitnessculture.com/disease/blood/mesenteric.htm>.

Mesenteric Venous Thrombosis. MedScape. 1999. 3 Jan 2001 <http://www.medscape.com/SMA/SMJ/1999/v92.n06/smj9206.02.hass-01.html>.

Metal Fume Fever

Other names / synonyms: Brass Chills, Brassfounder's Ague, Foundry Fever, Monday Fever, Smelter Chills, Welder's Ague, Zinc Chill

985.9

Definition

Metal fume fever is an elusive industrial disease that has been known to exist for at least 170 years. Metal fume fever is seen primarily in welders who perform soldering, brazing, cutting, metalizing, forging, melting, and casting operations utilizing elements of zinc, copper, iron, and other metals. Scrap metal cutters are at risk for metal fume fever, also. Although metal fume fever can occur following exposure to several metal oxide fumes, zinc oxide is the most frequent cause of the syndrome. Currently, the arc welding of steel galvanized with zinc coating is the most common source of exposure.

Approximately 1500-2000 cases of metal fume fever are reported each year in the US, which represents an underestimate of the actual number of cases. The underestimate is due to the resilient nature of the work population and the tendency for workers at risk to avoid seeking medical attention for their symptoms and to accept the transient discomfort associated with the syndrome. It is estimated that greater than 40% of welders 30 years of age or older have experienced metal fume fever at some point during their careers. Over the last several decades, the incidence of metal fume fever has been reduced considerably due to improved engineering controls and respiratory protection devices; however, significant occupational exposures to freshly formed metal oxide fumes still occur in the US and other countries. Regional Poison Control Centers reported 1,136 exposures due to metal fume fever in 1998.

Diagnosis

History: The clinical signs of metal fume fever typically appear within 4-8 hours after exposure. Workers normally present in the later afternoon or early evening hours with a number of nonspecific complaints. Normally, individuals complain of a sweet or metallic taste in the mouth, as well as a distorted taste for foods and cigarettes. Fever, chills, nausea, headache, fatigue, chest and/or abdominal discomfort, muscle aches, and joint pains may also occur between 8-12 hours after exposure.

Individuals also commonly complain of a constricted, dry or irritated throat sensation that may give rise to hoarseness and coughing. The diagnosis of metal fume fever can be difficult, due to the nonspecific nature of the individual's complaints and the fact that the symptoms themselves resemble a number of other common illnesses. The diagnosis is based primarily on a history of exposure to metal oxide fumes.

Physical exam: Findings vary among individuals exposed, and depend primarily upon the stage in the course of the syndrome during which evaluation occurs. Individuals can present with or without pulmonary findings of wheezing or crackles in the lungs upon examination with a stethoscope.

Tests: A complete blood count (CBC) may be done. An increased white blood cell count may develop 2-5 hours after exposure occurs. Pulmonary function testing may reveal a decrease in forced expiratory volume in one second (FEV1), and forced vital capacity (FVC) in individuals who experience an asthma-like response to metal fumes. Chest x-ray findings are normally unremarkable. Urine and blood plasma zinc and other metal levels may also be elevated after exposure to zinc oxide and other metal fumes.

Treatment

Treatment of metal fume fever consists of symptomatic therapy, which includes removal from the exposure itself, bedrest, oral hydration, and medications to treat fever (such as aspirin or ibuprofen); intravenous steroids may be required in severe cases as well as inhaled bronchodilators for wheezing. Oxygen therapy for managing hypoxemia may be required.

Although restricting the worker from the workplace setting in which exposure occurs is the most effective strategy for the prevention of metal fume fever, it is not a realistic long-term solution for either the worker or the employer. Prevention of exposure at the engineering control or personnel protection level must be utilized.

Prognosis

Complete recovery usually occurs within 12-24 hours of removal from the exposure, without any lasting effects. The next morning, the majority of the afflicted worker's symptoms are gone, appetite returns, and he or she is able to return to work, despite feeling slightly "hung over" from the experience of the previous 24 hours.

Symptoms often recur upon re-exposure. Prognosis is positive as long as the individual stays away from the offending agent.

Workers who have experienced previous episodes of zinc oxide or other metal fume exposure are also prone to repeat attacks of metal fume fever, particularly if they have not been exposed in the previous few days. Hence, the term "Monday fever," which refers to the development of tolerance after frequent repeated exposures, with loss of tolerance over the weekend exposure hiatus.

Differential Diagnosis

When respiratory symptoms are prominent, metal fume fever may be confused with acute bronchitis. Organic dust toxicity syndrome and polymer fever also share similar clinical features with metal fume fever, but the history of exposure differs among the three. Asthma may present with similar symptoms and signs. Respiratory irritation and difficulties from other chemicals, allergens, and metal compounds may present with similar signs and symptoms.

Specialists

- Medical Toxicologist
- Occupational Medicine Physician

Work Restrictions / Accommodations

Prevention of metal fume fever occurrence is paramount in the complete management of the disease. Prevention involves a number of direct interventional strategies in the workplace environment, the most important of which involves improved engineering controls. Reduced fume exposure concentrations can be achieved by increasing the general room ventilation, as well as by installing permanent overhead exhaust hoods. Portable exhaust collection systems can also help to remove metal oxide fumes that are being generated by the welding process; in addition, fume extractors built into welding equipment are also extremely helpful engineering controls.

Personal protective equipment such as positive pressure air supply respirators and eye and skin protective wear should also be utilized at all times when performing welding duties. The current 8-hour Threshold Limit Value (TLV) of 5 milligrams per cubic meter and 15-minute short-term exposure limit (STEL) of 10 milligrams per cubic meter have been established to prevent adverse health effects secondary to exposure to zinc oxide fumes. However, various industry and case reports have indicated that metal fume fever symptoms can occur in individuals exposed to limits below the current TLV. Therefore, instituting an aggressive prevention strategy is crucial, in order to minimize adverse health effects in the occupational setting.

It is not necessary to restrict workers from return to welding operations immediately after full recovery from an episode of metal fume fever as long as engineering or personal protection controls have been implemented.

The Occupational Safety and Health Administration (OSHA), The National Institute of Occupational Safety and Health (NIOSH), and The American Conference of Governmental Industrial Hygienists (ACGIH) have established TLVs, recommended exposure limits (REL), and permissible exposure limits (PEL) values to protect workers from exposure to hazardous levels of the metals and their oxides. (See the toxic effects of other metals elsewhere in this volume).

Prevention at the engineering control level, in combination with education of the workforce at risk, have been shown to be the most effective secondary prevention strategy that is instrumental in reducing the number of metal fume fever cases overall.

Comorbid Conditions

Welders who smoke may be at greater risk of health impairment than welders who do not smoke. Pre-existing asthma and lung disease may worsen the effects of metal fume fever.

Factors Influencing Duration

Asthma, or other pre-existing lung diseases, may lengthen recovery period and lengthen disability.

Length of Disability

Absorbed dose is the primary determinant of severity of toxic effects, and therefore severity and duration of disability. Absorbed dose is dependent on environmental levels, routes of exposure (skin contact, inhalation, ingestion) and duration of exposure. Contact physician for additional information.

Other factors influencing disability include pre-existing disease, age, pregnancy and allergy, all of which affect individual susceptibility to the toxic effect of chemical exposures. Psychological and emotional factors may also play a role in the extent and duration of disability. In some cases, there may be residual permanent disability despite prompt diagnosis and appropriate treatment.

Failure to Recover

If an individual fails to recover within the maximum duration expectancy period, the reader may wish to reference the following questions to assist in better understanding the specifics of an individual's medical case.

Regarding diagnosis:

- Has diagnosis of metal fume fever been confirmed?
- Is there a positive history of the suspected metals exposure in the workplace?
- Is the clinical illness, including the history, physical examination, and laboratory findings, consistent with other case descriptions?
- Is the timing between exposure and clinical onset compatible with the known biologic facts about the hazard?
- Does individual appear to develop tolerance after frequent repeated exposures, with loss of tolerance over the weekend exposure hiatus?
- Does individual have an underlying condition that may impact recovery?

Regarding treatment:

- If symptoms persist despite treatment, does diagnosis need to be revisited?
- Are there special attributes of this particular individual that make it more or less likely that he or she would be so affected?
- Are adequate preventive measures employed at the engineering control level?

Regarding prognosis:

- Are adequate preventive measures in place?
- Has the individual recently worked in another organization where the suspected metals exposure is higher?
- Are there alternative ways of constructing the case that better fit the available facts?

References

Agency for Toxic Substances and Disease Registry. Case Studies in Environmental Medicine: Arsenic, Beryllium, Cadmium, Cholinesterase Inhibitors, Lead, Mercury. US Department of Health and Human Services, 1993.

Occupational Medicine. LaDou, J., ed. Norwalk, CT: Appleton and Lange, 1990.

Proctor and Hughes' Chemical Hazards of the Workplace, 3rd edition. Hathaway, G.J., et al., eds. New York: Van Nostrand Reinhold, 1991.

Metatarsalgia
726.70

Definition

Metatarsalgia is a nonspecific term referring to pain on the sole (plantar surface) or the ball of the foot (metatarsal heads). It is not a specific clinical entity, rather it is a symptom of many conditions.

Metatarsalgia may be due to irritation of bone, tendon, muscle, joint, or nerve. Conditions causing metatarsalgia include fracture, stress fracture, bursitis, plantar displaced metatarsal, capsulitis, arthritis, infection, neuroma, flat foot, cavus foot, tendinitis, periostitis, hammertoe, Freiberg's infraction, congenital metatarsal deformity, plantar fat pad atrophy, neuropathy, trauma, neoplasm, foreign body, and circulatory insufficiency.

The incidence and prevalence varies depending on the causative condition. One of the most common causes, hammertoe, occurs in 1 in 100 whites and 1 in 33 blacks aged 15-30 years, but increases to 1 in 15 and 1 in 5, respectively in individuals over 30 years of age. The incidence of another common cause, metatarsal stress fracture, has not been studied in the general population but comprises 10% of all athletic injuries and 15% of all running injuries, with the second and third metatarsals most commonly involved.

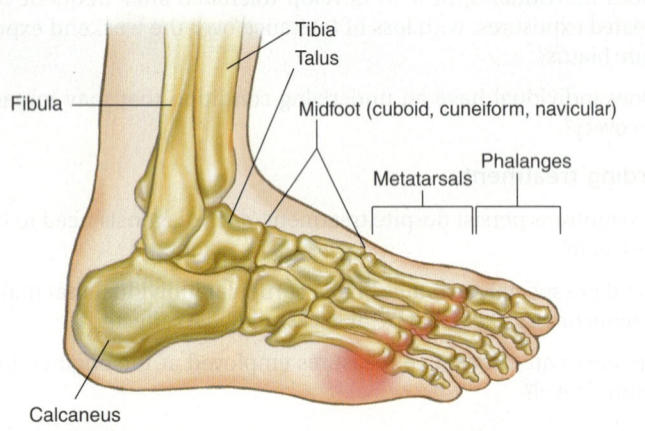

Diagnosis

History: The individual may relate pain on the sole of the foot in the metatarsal head area. One or several metatarsal heads may be painful. The pain may be described as sharp, shooting, burning, cramping, or aching. Depending on the causative condition, the pain may radiate into the toes or into the arch and leg. The pain may be worsened or improved with footwear, depending on the diagnosis.

Physical exam: Pressing (palpating) the metatarsal heads may elicit pain. There may also be pain when the joint between the toe and metatarsal (metatarsophalangeal joint) is moved. Squeezing the forefoot with one hand and pushing on the sole of the forefoot (Mulder's sign) will elicit pain in cases of neuroma. Slight swelling (edema) on the top (dorsum) of the foot may be noticed in cases of metatarsal stress fracture. A layer of thickened skin (callus, tyloma, hyperkeratosis) may be present beneath the metatarsal head due to friction or pressure.

Tests: X-rays will rule out fractures and arthritis. Blood tests will rule out underlying systemic conditions. Bone scans are useful in diagnosing stress fractures, infections, and tumors. MRI is useful in assessing some soft tissue pathologies.

Treatment

Treatment is determined by diagnosing the causative condition. In some cases, transferring the pressure away from the forefoot is helpful, and is accomplished with strappings or prescription insoles (orthotics). In cases caused by fat pad atrophy, periostitis, or other shock-related problems, soft insoles may be helpful. Stress fractures are treated with immobilization with strapping, casting, a fracture brace, and/or crutches. Neuromas, capsulitis, and bursitis are treated with corticosteroid injections. Metatarsalgia from all causes other than fracture or stress fracture may respond to physical therapy.

Surgery is indicated for severe or resistant cases of neuroma, plantar displaced metatarsal, Freiberg's infraction, or hammertoe. Neuromas are treated with surgical removal (neurectomy). Plantar displaced metatarsals are treated with cutting and repositioning the metatarsal bone (metatarsal osteotomy). Hammertoes are surgically treated (arthroplasty), while Freiberg's infraction is treated with surgical removal of the metatarsal head (metatarsal head resection).

Prognosis

The outcome varies depending on the cause of the metatarsalgia. However, the majority of individuals obtain complete symptomatic relief with treatment (conservative or surgical) of the causative condition.

Differential Diagnosis

Connective tissue diseases such as fibromyalgia, Reiter's syndrome, and rheumatoid arthritis can cause symptoms in the metatarsal head area.

Specialists

- Orthopedic Surgeon
- Podiatrist

Rehabilitation

Some conditions causing metatarsalgia are successfully treated with physical therapy. Such therapy includes hydrotherapy, ultrasound, electrical stimulation, corrective stretches and exercises. Electrostimulation combined with cold treatment may be a technique used to relax muscles at the region as well as to help decrease pain and inflammation of metatarsal bones and associated ligaments.

Treatments in the form of heat may be used to help relieve foot/joint pain and stiffness and increase blood flow to this region of the foot. Ultrasound, in which high frequency sound waves producing heat penetrates deep into the involved joints and muscles of the forefoot region, may be used. Iontophoresis is another treatment in the rehabilitation of metatarsalgia.

When pain and swelling have been greatly reduced, the physical therapist may perform stretching exercises to help restore full motion to the affected foot and ankle joints.

Occupational therapy may become involved in the rehabilitation process if there is a need for foot inserts (orthotics). Soft felt material called metatarsal pads may be placed in the individual's shoes. These may help reduce pressure on the painful metatarsal bone during weight-bearing activities.

Once minimal discomfort is present with stretching, strengthening of this aspect of the foot and ankle may begin with isotonic exercises. An example of this type of rehabilitation exercise is strengthening with weights and elastic bands. Strength training of this type may also include weight equipment/machines.

Work Restrictions / Accommodations

Individuals whose work requires walking or standing may need to be temporarily assigned to sedentary work. Individuals recovering from surgery may need to use crutches, walker, or cast. Individuals with stress fractures may have a cast and/or crutches.

Comorbid Conditions

Conditions that can worsen the metatarsalgia or delay recovery include obesity, diabetes mellitus, and peripheral vascular disease.

Complications

Complications of metatarsalgia include compensatory changes that result from walking differently to relieve the pain. This can lead to contractures of the toes, eventually resulting in crooked toes (hammertoes), as well as chronic muscle pains in the calf muscles of the leg.

Factors Influencing Duration

The job requirements, severity of pain, and whether surgery is required will influence the length of disability.

Length of Disability

Medical treatment.

Duration in Days

Job Classification	Minimum	Optimum	Maximum
Sedentary work	0	3	7
Light work	0	5	14
Medium work	0	7	28
Heavy work	0	14	35
Very Heavy work	0	21	42

Failure to Recover

If an individual fails to recover within the maximum duration expectancy period, the reader may wish to reference the following questions to assist in better understanding the specifics of an individual's medical case.

Regarding diagnosis:

- Does the individual have irritation of bone, tendon, muscle, joint, or nerve?
- Does the individual have a fracture, stress fracture, bursitis, plantar displaced metatarsal, capsulitis, arthritis or infection? Neuroma, flat feet, cavus foot, tendinitis, periostitis, hammertoe, Freiberg's infraction or congenital metatarsal deformity? Plantar fat pad atrophy, neuropathy, trauma, neoplasm, foreign body or circulatory insufficiency?
- Does the individual have pain on the sole of the foot in the metatarsal head area?
- Is the pain sharp, shooting, burning, cramping, or aching?
- Does the pain radiate into the toes or into the arch and leg?
- Is the pain worsened or improved with footwear?
- When the physician palpated the metatarsal heads, did it elicit pain?
- Is there pain when the metatarsophalangeal joint is moved?
- Does squeezing the forefoot with one hand and pushing on the sole of the forefoot elicit pain?
- Is there edema on the dorsum of the foot?
- Is there a callus, tyloma, or hyperkeratosis present beneath the metatarsal head?
- Did the individual have x-rays, bone scan, MRI and blood tests?
- Have conditions with similar symptoms been ruled out?

Regarding treatment:

- What is the causative condition?
- Was transferring the pressure away from the forefoot helpful?
- Were soft insoles helpful?
- Was immobilization needed?
- Did the individual have corticosteroid injections?
- Was physical therapy helpful?
- Was surgery necessary?

Regarding prognosis:

- Is the individual active in physical therapy?
- Does the individual have any conditions that could affect recovery?
- Does the individual have compensatory changes from walking differently?
- Has individual developed a hammertoe?
- Does individual have chronic muscle pains in the calf muscles of the leg?

References

Kessler, R.M. Management of Common Musculoskeletal Disorders: Physical Therapy Principles and Methods. Philadelphia: J.B. Lippincott Company, 1990.

Trepal, Michael J. Preferred Practice Guidelines: Central Metatarsalgia. Park Ridge, IL: American College of Foot and Ankle Surgeons, 1991.

Metatarsus Primus Varus
754.52

Definition

Metatarsus primus varus is a congenital, structural abnormality of the foot in which the first metatarsal (metatarsus primus) or the metatarsal that connects to the big toe is not parallel to the other four metatarsals but deviates away from the rest of the foot (varus deviation). As this occurs, the side of the first metatarsal head is subject to shoe pressure and becomes enlarged and inflamed. This is known as a bunion deformity and metatarsus primus varus is the most common cause of bunion deformity. As the first metatarsal moves medially, the big toe joint (metatarsophalangeal joint) buckles, and the big toe (hallux) drifts toward the second toe. This combination of metatarsus primus varus and the lateral drift of the big toe is known as the clinical condition of hallux abducto valgus. See Bunion for more information.

Migraine Headache

Other names / synonyms: Classical Migraine Headache, Common Migraine Headache, Migraine Headache with Aura, Migraine Headache Without Aura

346, 346.0, 346.1, 346.8, 346.9

Definition

Migraine is a type of headache characterized by narrowing (constriction) of blood vessels in the brain followed by painful dilation and inflammation of the same blood vessels. It is described as a "sick headache," not only because there may be nausea and vomiting, but also because the individual typically feels completely disabled throughout the duration of the headache. The pain is moderate to severe, throbbing or pulsating, and usually localized to one side of the head. Migraines can last from hours to days, and may also be associated with sensitivity to light and sound. The headaches can be preceded by an aura or warning symptoms related to the blood vessel narrowing and may include visual disturbances, limb numbness, tingling, or hyperactivity.

Coexisting medical conditions such as seizures, sleep disorders, high blood pressure, and depression may be related to migraine. Migraines can be triggered or made worse by certain foods (chocolate, aged cheeses, peanuts, red wine, food additives [MSG, nitrates]), alcohol, insufficient sleep, stress, and hormonal changes associated with the menstrual cycle.

Migraines are more common in women than men, affecting 18% of women and 6% of men in the US. Migraine usually begins in adolescence or early adulthood, peaking at ages 30 to 45. The cause is not fully understood although it may be hereditary, as family history is often positive for incidence of migraine.

Diagnosis

History: Individuals may report symptoms associated with the headache such as nausea, vomiting, pale skin, feeling faint, or sensitivity to light (photophobia) and sound (sonophobia). Duration, location, pulsating quality, intensity, presence of aura, and frequency of headaches should be noted. Visual symptoms account for more than half of symptoms that may be associated with the aura, including bright spots resembling stars, sparks, geometric patterns, or lightning bolts (fortification spectra). When the bright spots disappear, blind spots or decreased vision may follow. Other symptoms associated with the aura may include numbness especially of the hand and lower face. Weakness, clumsiness, or speech disturbances are less common. The aura usually lasts about 30 minutes followed by a brief period of normalcy before the headache begins.

Some individuals may report behavioral changes before or after attacks including depression, anxiety, irritability, excitability, or increased or decreased sexual appetite. Identification of possible triggers is also helpful in distinguishing migraine from headache caused by other disorders such as a brain tumor. An essential component of diagnosis is to obtain a detailed history of previous headaches and an investigation of family history.

Physical exam: The exam may reveal abnormalities such as recent head or neck trauma and muscle spasms that can help establish diagnosis and select treatment. Neurological examination includes evaluation of brain and nerve function, sensory discrimination, reflexes, strength, coordination, and cognitive abilities. Eye examination may reveal neurologic disease, diabetes, high blood pressure (hypertension), and other coexisting medical conditions.

Tests: Tests are performed if there are other suspected causes of headache like a brain tumor or aneurysm. Radiographic studies, such as CT or MRI, may reveal such brain abnormalities that can mimic migraine. If history suggests seizures, an EEG may help diagnose epilepsy that may coexist with migraine. These cases are rare, and therefore the tests are not routinely done unless warranted by history and physical examination findings. Laboratory tests may also be done if an organic condition is suspected.

Treatment

During an acute episode, it may help the individual to rest in a quiet, darkened room. Acute episodes may be treated with medications once the headache has begun. The three main classes of drugs available to treat acute migraine are triptans, ergotamines, and painkillers such as naproxen sodium, acetaminophen, aspirin, and ibuprofen. Painkillers can relieve mild to moderate migraine. The newer COX-2 inhibitors may also be used to avoid gastrointestinal side effects seen with nonsteroidal anti-inflammatory drugs (NSAIDS). Combination painkillers that contain caffeine may be helpful.

Once the headache is underway, treatment usually requires a vasoconstrictor such as an ergot alkaloid to stop the attack. These medications are most helpful if given during the aura. A new type of vasoconstrictor is now available, and pain relief may begin within a few minutes of taking it by mouth or injection. If nausea and vomiting occur, medication may have to be administered under the tongue, by injection, or rectally. Migraine attacks that are severe, prolonged, or unresponsive to self-administered medications may have to be treated in the doctor's office or emergency room.

Prevention of migraine is an important part of treatment. Avoiding precipitating factors may decrease the frequency of acute episodes. If episodes occur more than 2 or 3 times a month, a variety of drugs can be taken for prevention including beta-blockers, anticonvulsants, tricyclic antidepressants, calcium antagonists, methysergide, and selective serotonin re-uptake inhibitors (SSRIs). The individual may have to try several different drugs, one at a time, before the headaches are brought under control. Naproxen sodium has also been used for short-term prevention of migraine, especially menstrual migraine. Drug combinations may be used for individuals that do not respond to a single therapy. Beta-blockers and antidepressants may be used together. Once an effective drug or combination is found, it should be continued for at least 6 months and then gradually tapered off after the disappearance of headaches. Acute medication may be occasionally used with preventive medication if breakthrough headaches occur, e.g., menstrual migraine.

Prognosis

Occasionally migraine headaches may spontaneously disappear especially as individuals reach middle age. Self-care is very important, and the migraine sufferer can increase the chance of successful outcome by taking medications as directed by the doctor and modifying lifestyle factors such as diet, exercise, avoidance of migraine triggers, stress control, and proper rest. Any changes in headache frequency or severity should be communicated to the doctor and adjustments in treatment made to improve outcome.

Differential Diagnosis

Other headaches like tension-type, sinus headache, cluster headache, chronic daily headache, and rebound headaches may be confused with migraine. Brain tumors, aneurysms, or other structural causes of headache are relatively rare and should be ruled out by appropriate tests.

Specialists

- Neurologist

Work Restrictions / Accommodations

Often the migraine sufferer may not be able to work or perform job responsibilities during a migraine headache episode. Heavy physical activity may also be limited. Providing a dark, quiet room where the individual can rest until the attack passes may be helpful.

Comorbid Conditions

Comorbid conditions that may be related to migraine and to each other include asthma, depression, hypertension, stroke, chronic fatigue syndrome, Raynaud's syndrome, epilepsy (seizures), anxiety or mood disorders, and sleep disorders. These medical conditions may be due to changes in brain chemicals such as serotonin. It is important to diagnose comorbid conditions to successfully manage migraine. In some cases, the condition can make the migraine worse or limit treatment options. Other causes of headache such as headaches or neck injury following an accident (post-traumatic headache) may make migraine headaches more frequent or severe.

Complications

Migraine sufferers are more prone to develop tension-type headaches that result in mixed headache syndrome. Excessive use of painkillers may cause rebound headaches when the drug's effects wear off, and episodic headaches may be transformed into chronic daily headaches. Coexisting medical conditions may complicate the disorder by limiting treatment options. Many medications used to treat headaches affect the cardiovascular system. The relative risk of thrombotic stroke may be up to twice as high in women with migraine or even four times as high in women under the age of 45. Stroke risk in migraine sufferers is further increased by smoking or the use of birth control pills. Migraine may also be associated with epilepsy or depression.

Complementary and Alternative Therapies

Content is intended for awareness only. Treatments may or may not be effective. Scientific evidence may be lacking and some substances have potentially toxic effects. Dr. Presley Reed and the editors do not endorse the use of these therapies in the absence of consultation with a licensed medical professional.

Acupuncture -	May help with migraine, pain management, and other inflammatory conditions.
Chiropractic therapy -	Manipulation of the spine may benefit some individuals with migraine if they also have spinal or musculoskeletal abnormalities.
Relaxation techniques -	May help to reduce muscle tension and alleviate the symptoms of migraine.
Stress management -	Teaches migraine sufferers skills that may be used to control responses to a wide range of situations that can trigger and prolong headaches.
Biofeedback -	May improve control of the body's senses.
Cognitive therapy -	Provides individuals with coping skills that may be used in situations that trigger headaches.
Magnesium and riboflavin -	Have been used with varying degrees of success as preventative agents for migraine.
Feverfew -	May help as an anti-inflammatory and relaxant.
Hypnosis -	May help some migraine sufferers with self-coping skills through altered pain perception.
Massage -	May aid in relaxation and improve muscle tone by alleviating stress and muscle tension, important precipitating factors of headaches.

Factors Influencing Duration

Length of disability depends on the severity, frequency, and duration of migraine headaches, and the response to treatment.

Length of Disability

Disability often corresponds to the duration of the headache (several hours to three days). Duration of disability depends on proper diagnosis and individualized treatment plan. Individuals with high stress jobs or who perform heavy physical work may need more time to see progress in migraine management.

Single episode.

Duration in Days

Job Classification	Minimum	Optimum	Maximum
Any work	0	1	3

Notes

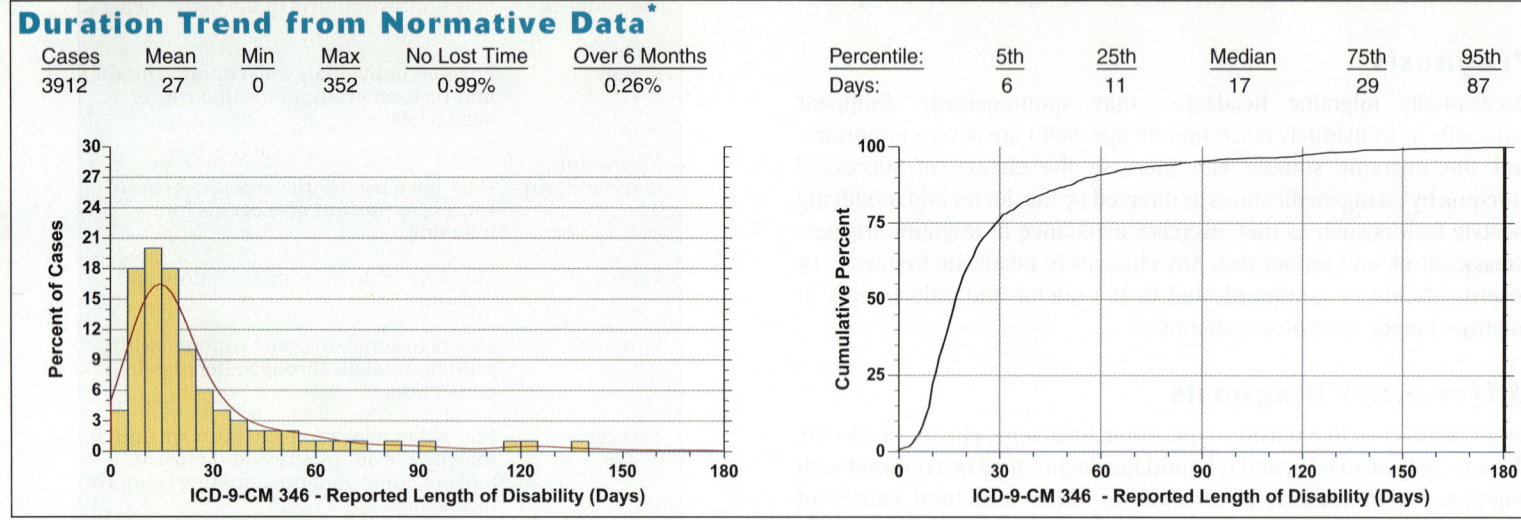

Duration Trend from Normative Data*

Cases	Mean	Min	Max	No Lost Time	Over 6 Months
3912	27	0	352	0.99%	0.26%

Percentile:	5th	25th	Median	75th	95th
Days:	6	11	17	29	87

* Differences may exist between the expected duration tables and the normative graphs. Duration tables provide expected recovery periods based on the type of work performed by the individual. The normative graphs reflect the actual observed experience of many individuals across the spectrum of physical conditions, in a variety of industries, and with varying levels of case management.

Failure to Recover

If an individual fails to recover within the maximum duration expectancy period, the reader may wish to reference the following questions to assist in better understanding the specifics of an individual's medical case.

Regarding diagnosis:

- Has diagnosis of migraine been confirmed?
- Have other conditions with similar symptoms been ruled out?
- Has individual experienced complications related to migraine headaches, such as mixed headache syndrome, rebound headaches from excessive use of painkillers, chronic daily headaches, or thrombotic stroke?
- Does individual have a coexisting condition that may limit treatment options or impact recovery?

Regarding treatment:

- Does individual require medical intervention for most episodes of migraine headaches?
- Is a change in medication or combination therapy warranted?
- Would individual benefit from self-administered medication?
- Have headache triggers (certain foods, alcohol, insufficient sleep, stress, hormonal changes associated with the menstrual cycle) been identified and eliminated, if possible?
- Is individual on prevention therapy?
- Would a combination-drug prevention therapy be more effective?

Regarding prognosis:

- Is individual compliant with prescribed treatment plan?
- Does individual self-administer medication during aura phase whenever possible? Has individual modified lifestyle factors that may trigger migraine episodes? Does individual communicate changes in headache frequency or severity to the doctor so that treatment adjustments can be made?

References

American Headache Society: Migraine and Coexisting Conditions. American Headache Society. 2000. 25/05/2000 <http://ahsnet.org/resources/migraine.php>.

American Headache Society: Headache Facts. American Headache Society. 2000. 25/05/2000 <http://ahsnet.org/resources/headachefacts.php>.

Gallagher, R. Michael. "Headache Evaluation and Diagnosis." JAOA 98 4 (1998): S1-S4.

Godfrey Meisler, Jodi. "Toward Optimal Health: The Experts Respond to Migraine." Journal of Women's Health and Gender-Based Medicine 8 6 (1999): 739-744.

Hoffman, David. The Complete Holistic Herbal. New York: Barnes & Noble, Inc, 1996.

Office Practice of Neurology. Samuels, Martin A., and Steven Feske, eds. New York: Churchill Livingstone, 1996.

Miscarriage

Other names / synonyms: Spontaneous Abortion
634, 634.7, 634.9, 634.90, 634.92

Definition

A miscarriage or spontaneous abortion is a pregnancy loss that occurs prior to 20 weeks, before the fetus is able to survive outside the woman's uterus. Most miscarriages occur in the first 12 weeks of pregnancy (first trimester). A miscarriage is a naturally occurring and involuntary event. It should not be confused with an elective or induced abortion, which is a planned surgical procedure.

There are 3 types of miscarriage or spontaneous abortion. A complete abortion occurs when all the contents of the uterus are expelled through the vagina. An incomplete abortion occurs when some of the fetus or placenta remains in the uterus, while a missed abortion occurs when the fetus has died but remains in the uterus.

Three or more miscarriages in a row may be called "repeated miscarriage" or "habitual abortion." This condition occurs in less than 1% of all pregnancies. Often, the reason for repeated miscarriage is unknown. It is possible for each miscarriage to have a different cause.

Abnormalities of the uterus cause 15-30% of repeated miscarriages. Some women are born with a uterus that is too small or abnormally shaped. Fifty to sixty percent are caused by abnormalities of the fertilized egg, usually a chromosomal defect. Others develop noncancerous uterine tumors (fibroids) or have scars in the uterus from past surgery. These abnormalities can limit space for the growing fetus or interfere with the blood supply to the uterus. A weakened (incompetent) cervix can lead to miscarriage, usually between 16-18 weeks of pregnancy. Drug or alcohol abuse and exposure to environmental or industrial toxins increase the risk of miscarriage.

When endocrine glands secrete too much or too little of certain hormones, the risk of miscarriage increases. Low levels of the hormone progesterone, which is crucial to an early pregnancy, are believed to cause between 15-60% of losses that occur prior to 10 weeks of pregnancy.

Immunity problems may also cause a miscarriage. Some women may produce antibodies (called autoantibodies) that can attack their own tissues, causing a variety of health problems. Studies suggest that the presence of these autoantibodies may cause between 5-15% of repeat miscarriages. Research also suggests that other immune system problems may cause a woman's body to reject her fetus as foreign tissue.

Acute and chronic infections, certain symptomless infections of the genital tract, and the necessity of abdominal surgery during pregnancy have also been shown to cause miscarriages. A woman with certain systemic diseases, including diabetes, thyroid problems, cardiac and renovascular (kidney) problems, malnutrition, and women who smoke have increased risk of miscarriage.

The risk of miscarriage increases as the woman gets older. While women 20-30 years old miscarry 15-20% of the time, women over 42 have a miscarriage rate of 40%. Approximately 15-20% of all known pregnancies end in spontaneous abortion. Percentages are approximate since a miscarriage may occur before the woman realizes she is pregnant.

Specialists

- Gynecologist
- Obstetrician

Diagnosis

History: Women may report vaginal bleeding, cramping, and the passing of any large clots or tissue. There may also be a gush of fluid from the rupture of the amniotic sac. A foul-smelling or cloudy vaginal discharge may also be reported. The woman may not know that she is pregnant.

Physical exam: A miscarriage is confirmed if the pelvic exam reveals tissue protruding through an open cervix, or if the cervix is found to be dilated and open, indicating imminent expulsion of tissue. A missed abortion can be detected by the disappearance of pregnancy signs, except that menstrual periods will not have resumed.

Tests: A pregnancy test should be done. Blood tests that measure quantitative levels of human chorionic gonadotropin (HCG) may be done and then repeated in several days to see if the level is increasing or decreasing. If the passed tissue is recovered, laboratory analysis can determine if it is of fetal origin. A complete blood count (CBC) will be done if the degree of blood loss needs to be determined. A white blood count (WBC) with differential can be used to rule out potential infection. In some instances, an ultrasound can also be used to confirm fetal death.

If there is "repeated miscarriage" (3 or more miscarriages in a row), evaluation may include genetic studies, tests to rule out chronic infections or hormonal dysfunction, and x-ray imaging of the uterus and fallopian tubes (hysterosalpingography).

Treatment

With an uncomplicated, complete abortion (in which all fetal tissue is passed out of the uterus), no unusual medical treatment is required. Follow-up care is necessary to check for infection or excessive blood loss. Severe bleeding (hemorrhage) might require a blood transfusion and hospitalization.

An incomplete or missed abortion, in which some of the fetal tissue remains in the uterus, may require removal by D&C (dilation and curettage or suction curettage). If this is not done, the tissue remaining inside the uterus can cause an infection or delayed bleeding. The D&C is usually done under general anesthesia at the outpatient department of a hospital or clinic. Cases that develop infection require treatment with antibiotics. Severe bleeding may require a blood transfusion and hospitalization. Women who have repeated miscarriage need special tests to determine the reason and should see a specialist familiar with the care of such cases.

Rh-negative women are given Rh(D) immune globulin to prevent future Rh complications. Psychological treatment such as counseling or psychotherapy may be indicated for help in coping with the loss of the pregnancy. Some women may also benefit from attending support groups with other women that have experienced a miscarriage.

Prognosis

Complete physical recovery is expected. The majority of women who miscarry can eventually carry a baby to full term.

Differential Diagnosis

Other possibilities include an ectopic pregnancy, hydatidiform mole, or a protruding uterine fibroid or cervical polyp.

Work Restrictions / Accommodations

Work responsibilities may need to be largely sedentary at first. Heavy work, especially involving heavy lifting, may be restricted throughout the period of disability. Long periods of standing may need to be avoided at first. Most women with uncomplicated miscarriages can return to full time sedentary to modified duty work within 7 to 14 days.

Comorbid Conditions

A diagnosis of anemia or other blood disorder may impact the individual's ability to recover. An individual with pre-existing depression or other mood disturbances may further lengthen disability.

Complications

Complications might include infection, severe bleeding, or complications from a D&C and/or blood transfusion. Anemia may occur due to severe blood loss or hemorrhage. Psychological depression may slow overall physical recovery.

Factors Influencing Duration

Abortions that are incomplete, missed, or those resulting in infection or hemorrhage will require a longer period of disability than will an uncomplicated abortion. Severe depression or grief reaction due to pregnancy loss may impact length of disability.

Length of Disability

Duration depends on job requirements and whether or not the miscarriage was complete. For uncomplicated, complete abortion, disability begins after hospital discharge.

Uncomplicated, complete abortion, first trimester.

Duration in Days

Job Classification	Minimum	Optimum	Maximum
Any work	1	3	7

Second or third trimester.

Duration in Days

Job Classification	Minimum	Optimum	Maximum
Any work	7	14	28

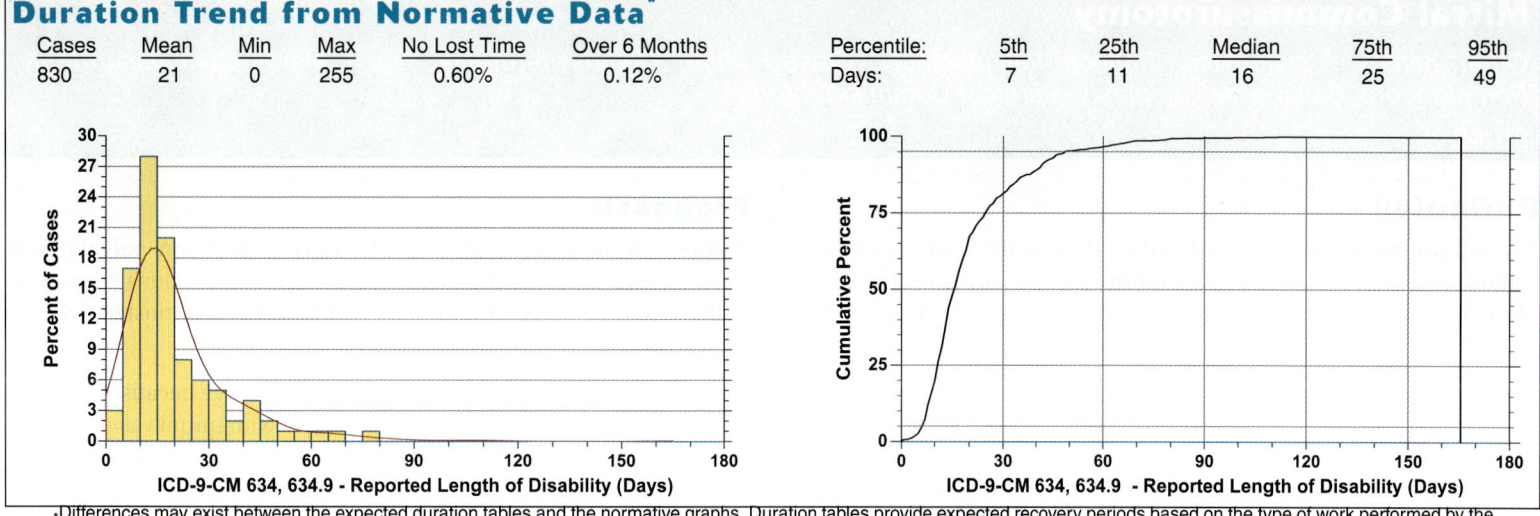

Failure to Recover

If an individual fails to recover within the maximum duration expectancy period, the reader may wish to reference the following questions to assist in better understanding the specifics of an individual's medical case.

Regarding diagnosis:

- Has the woman had a complete, incomplete or missed spontaneous abortion or miscarriage?
- Has the woman had previous miscarriages? What is her age?
- Does the woman have risk factors such as acute and chronic infections, certain symptomless infections of the genital tract, or the necessity of abdominal surgery during pregnancy?
- Does the woman have diabetes, thyroid problems, cardiac or renal disease, malnutrition, or smoke?
- Does the woman report vaginal bleeding, cramping, or passing large clots or tissue?
- Did the woman report a gush of fluid?
- Does the woman complain of a foul-smelling or cloudy vaginal discharge?
- On pelvic exam did the physician find tissue protruding through an open cervix or an open and dilated cervix?
- Has the woman had a blood or urine pregnancy test?
- Was laboratory analysis of any passed tissue done?
- Did the woman have a CBC with WBC differential?
- Was it necessary for the woman to have an ultrasound?
- Were genetic studies, tests to rule out chronic infections or hormonal dysfunction, or hysterosalpingography indicated?
- Have conditions with similar symptoms been ruled out?

Regarding treatment:

- Did the woman have an uncomplicated complete miscarriage? Did she follow-up with her physician as scheduled?
- Did the woman require hospitalization or a blood transfusion? Antibiotics?
- Did the woman have an incomplete or missed miscarriage?
- Was it necessary for the woman to have a D&C?
- Was it necessary to induce labor?
- Is the woman Rh negative? Was she given Rh(D) immune globulin?
- If necessary, did the woman seek psychiatric counseling? Attend a support group?

Regarding prognosis:

- Is the woman's employer able to accommodate any necessary restrictions?
- Does the woman have any conditions that may affect her ability to recover?
- Does the woman have any complications such as infection, severe bleeding, or complications from a D&C and/or blood transfusion? Does she have anemia? Does she have depression?

References

Rosenthal, M. Sara. The Gynecological Sourcebook. New York: NTC/Contemporary, 1999.

Tierney, Lawrence M., Stephen J. McPhee, and Maxine A. Papadakis, eds. Current Medical Diagnosis and Treatment, 39th ed. New York: Lange Medical Books/McGraw-Hill, 2000.

Mitral Commissurotomy

Other names / synonyms: Balloon Valvuloplasty, Closed Mitral Commissurotomy, Open Mitral Commissurotomy, Percutaneous Balloon Valvuloplasty, Surgical Commissurotomy

35.12

Definition

A mitral commissurotomy is a procedure done in the cardiac catheterization laboratory or surgical suite to correct severe narrowing (stenosis) of the mitral valve that directs the flow of blood on the left side of the heart. The procedure physically separates the fused flaps of the mitral valve restoring the opening to a more normal size and allowing blood to pass more easily.

Mitral stenosis is a condition where the flaps of the mitral valve fuse together, usually due to a much earlier attack of rheumatic fever. This condition creates an abnormal narrowing of the mitral valve causing the atrial portion of the left side of the heart to work harder in forcing blood through the narrowed valve into the left ventricle that pumps blood to the body. Although not generally a life-threatening condition, left-sided (and eventually right-sided) heart failure may develop from mitral stenosis.

Mitral stenosis develops in about 40% of individuals with rheumatic heart disease.

Reason for Procedure

Mitral commissurotomy is recommended for treatment of mitral stenosis and to prevent pulmonary hypertension and heart failure.

Mitral commissurotomy is usually considered only if the potential effects of the malfunctioning valve on the heart and general health are severe enough to pose a threat to the individual. Over time, the increased workload on the heart associated with mitral stenosis can result in heart failure, elevated pulmonary pressures (pulmonary hypertension) that cause respiratory failure, and irregular heart rhythms (arrhythmias).

The mechanism of improvement following commissurotomy is related to the successful opening of mitral valve flaps (commissures) that have become fused by scarring related to previous rheumatic fever. The decrease in pressure gradient and increased mitral valve area after commissurotomy result in the improvement of clinical symptoms.

Description

The two approaches to mitral commissurotomy are closed mitral commissurotomy performed as a cardiac catheterization procedure, and open commissurotomy, which is a major, open surgical procedure. In a closed mitral commissurotomy, a specially designed balloon (Inoue balloon) or mechanical dilator is directed through a cardiac catheter into the mitral valve to split the fused flaps. This is a is a technically challenging procedure. The open or surgical commissurotomy accesses the mitral valve via a surgical opening in the chest. The surgeon can physically release the fused flaps of the stenosed mitral valve with a finger or mechanical probe. The open procedure allows for direct visualization of the mitral valve and provides the opportunity to correct other valvular defects such as removing blood clots or calcium deposits on or around the valve.

Prognosis

Recovery from either balloon valvuloplasty or open valvuloplasty (commissurotomy) is dependent on pre-existing conditions. In general, both procedures carry low mortality (less than 1%) and most individuals have full recovery.

However, these procedures are considered palliative because they only temporarily relieve complications associated with mitral valve stenosis. At some point, most individuals will require a repeat commissurotomy or a mitral valve replacement for recurrent mitral valve stenosis. Individuals with pliable, noncalcified valves and minimal fusion have the best immediate and long-term outcome from commissurotomy. The surgeon's skill and experience is also a major determinant of outcome. For this reason, this procedure should be done at major centers with good immediate and long-term results on a large population. In large reported surgical series, the five-year complication-free survival rate is usually better than 80% in individuals with more favorable mitral valves before surgery. Age, severity of stenosis, and heart and lung function before surgery also influence outcome.

Specialists

- Cardiologist
- Cardiovascular Surgeon

Rehabilitation

Most individuals may be encouraged to participate in a cardiac rehabilitation program to ensure an uncomplicated and full recovery from this procedure. Cardiac rehabilitation incorporates outpatient physical and occupational therapy. Cardiac rehabilitation centers offer EKG monitoring of all participants during the exercise sessions. Individuals learn to self-monitor their pulse and to rate the amount of energy they expend by utilizing a rating of perceived exertion scale. Individuals also perform aerobic exercise such as treadmill walking or stationary bicycling. Initial activities may include limited walking, range-of-motion, and treadmill exercises. These exercises should be performed independently two to three times per day for 5-20 minutes per session. Eventually, more frequent walks, walk-jog, biking, and arm ergometer exercises may be encouraged. Exercise becomes more strenuous as permitted by an individual's physician with a goal of attaining 75-85% maximum intensity while walking, jogging, biking, swimming, performing calisthenics, and/or weight training. Eventually, individuals should perform an exercise program independently with sessions occurring three to five times per week for 30-60 minutes per session.

Occupational therapy addresses any fatigue or shortness of breath that may occur during activities of daily living. Individuals learn to utilize equipment such as a shower chair to decrease the energy expended during bathing, or a long-handled sponge to decrease the amount arm activity necessary for bathing. (Excessive arm activity is more taxing on the heart and can lead to fatigue).

Comorbid Conditions

Comorbid conditions limiting or delaying full functional recovery include poor cardiac performance such as heart failure, pulmonary hypertension, or heart rhythm disturbances.

Procedure Complications

Complications of balloon mitral valvuloplasty include the leaking of blood backward through the widened mitral valve (mitral regurgitation) and clots on the valve that can travel through the bloodstream and cause strokes (thromboembolism). Although death is rare (1-3%), it can occur as a result of heart wall tears (cardiac perforation) or cardiac tamponade. In cardiac tamponade, bleeding occurs between the heart and the sac that covers it (pericardium) and prevents the heart from beating.

Surgical commissurotomy uses cardiopulmonary bypass and carries complications associated with it in addition to complications related to the procedure. Although the mortality rate associated with cardiac surgery is low, systemic changes following cardiopulmonary bypass may contribute to complications such as dehydration and shock, bleeding, heart rhythm disturbances, congestive heart failure, infection, and mental changes. Heart rhythm disturbances may require additional treatment with antiarrhythmic medications. A leaking mitral valve (mitral regurgitation) and heart failure must be treated surgically with a mitral valve replacement.

Factors Influencing Duration

Length of disability may be influenced by pre-existing medical conditions or postsurgical complications such as heart rhythm disturbances, heart perforation, bleeding, clot formation, or infection.

Length of Disability

Following a balloon valvuloplasty, individuals usually have a short hospital stay with prompt recovery and return to work. Open valvuloplasty is an open-heart surgical procedure requiring a longer hospital stay (5 to 7 days) and a more lengthy recovery.

The return to pre-procedure functional capacity for balloon valvuloplasty should be similar to other uncomplicated cardiac catheterization procedures.

Following an open mitral valvuloplasty (commissurotomy), the length of disability is similar to that of any uncomplicated open-heart procedure.

Disability may be permanent for heavy and very heavy work.

Open.

Duration in Days

Job Classification	Minimum	Optimum	Maximum
Sedentary work	28	42	56
Light work	28	42	56
Medium work	56	70	84
Heavy work	84	98	112
Very Heavy work	84	98	112

References

Clochesy, John M., et al. Critical Care Nursing, 2nd ed. Philadelphia: W.B. Saunders Company, 1996.

Reyes V.P., et al. "Percutaneous Balloon Valvuloplasty Compared with Open Surgical Commissurotomy for Mitral Stenosis." New England Journal of Medicine 331 (1994): 961-967.

Mitral Insufficiency
Other names / synonyms: Mitral Regurgitation
394.1, 394.2, 396.3, 424.0

Definition

Mitral insufficiency (MI) is a condition characterized by the reverse flow of blood from the primary pumping chamber of the heart (left ventricle) to the pumping receiving chamber (left atrium) of the heart. The mitral valve is located between the left upper chamber of the heart (the left atrium) and the left lower chamber of the heart (left ventricle). When the blood flows out of the lungs, it enters the left atrium, flows through the mitral valve into the left ventricle, and from there it is pumped into the main artery of the body, the aorta.

MI has a number of causes that have changed over the past 40 years. Early in the 20th century, acute rheumatic fever was the predominant cause. Today, mitral valve prolapse and insufficiency due to hardening of the coronary arteries (coronary arteriosclerosis) have become the leading causes. Other less common causes include infection of the valve (bacterial endocarditis), an enlarged, poorly contracting heart due to a variety of causes (cardiomyopathy), ruptures of the supporting structures of the valve (chordae tendineae), and ruptured papillary muscles.

Other causes of MI include connective tissue disorders, cardiac trauma, radiation therapy, and congenital abnormalities. Considering all causes, MI is the most frequent cardiac valvular abnormality.

MI predominantly occurs in males because of the increasing prevalence of arteriosclerosis. Mitral insufficiency affects approximately 5 out of 10,000 individuals.

Diagnosis

History: Common symptoms include shortness of breath with activity (dyspnea with exertion) or when lying down (orthopnea) and fatigue. Rapid irregular heart beating (atrial fibrillation) may also occur.

Physical exam: MI produces murmurs audible with the stethoscope. It occurs when the left ventricle contracts, pumping blood backwards across the mitral valve into the left atrium. Other murmurs may coexist when rheumatic heart disease is the cause. The heart rhythm may be irregular due to atrial fibrillation.

Tests: An electrocardiograms (ECG), chest x-ray, and echocardiogram are done initially and at periodical intervals thereafter depending on the severity of the MI. Each test may show enlargement of the left ventricle and/or left atrium. The chest x-ray and echocardiogram also provide information about how the heart is coping with the insufficient valve including the presence or absence of heart fatigue.

In the case of mitral valve prolapsed (MVP), echocardiogram may demonstrate prolapse in the absence of a murmur and in the presence of a normal ECG and chest x-ray. MVP may or may not be associated with mitral insufficiency.

Treatment

Individuals with mild MI require no treatment other than antibiotics before dental work or other procedures that may allow bacteria in the mouth or other organ to enter the bloodstream. This can result in a serious cardiac complication known as bacterial endocarditis.

Individuals with more severe degrees of MI causing dyspnea with exertion and fatigue are usually treated with medications to remove excess fluid (diuretics), strengthen the heart's contraction (digitalis), and/or decrease the work of the heart (vasodilators). Medications that thin out the blood (anticoagulants) are used to prevent blood from clotting in the enlarged, fibrillary, left atrium.

In more advanced cases, mitral reconstruction or replacement is usually done. Surgery is generally elective but emergent valve replacement surgery is sometimes necessary for conditions such as ruptured chordae tendineae.

Prognosis

Outcome is good with mild degrees of MI. Longevity may be normal in the absence of bacterial endocarditis.

If surgery is necessary, operative mortality is 5-7% when surgery is done electively. Age, associated coronary arteriosclerosis, and more severe cases of MI increase the operative risk. Long-term survival is approximately 75% at 5 years and 60% at 10 years. Survivors usually show significant symptomatic improvement.

Differential Diagnosis

Other cardiac conditions causing a heart murmur may be mistaken for MI. However, when appropriate laboratory tests are done, the cause of the murmur is generally clarified.

Specialists

- Cardiologist
- Cardiovascular Surgeon

Work Restrictions / Accommodations

No work restrictions or accommodations are necessary for individuals without symptoms. For those experiencing dyspnea with exertion and/or fatigue, reassignment to a less strenuous position may be necessary. Individuals taking blood thinners may need reassignment if their job involves an increases risk of injury.

Comorbid Conditions

Existing conditions that may impact recovery include other heart disease, respiratory disease, age, and obesity.

Complications

The primary complications of MI are congestive heart failure, atrial fibrillation, and occasionally bacterial endocarditis.

Factors Influencing Duration

Factors that may affect length of disability include age, response to treatment, severity of symptoms, and general state of health.

Length of Disability

Duration of disability depends on job requirements, amount of physical labor involved in individual's job, and strength and severity of symptoms. Following surgery, individuals are anticoagulated. Disability may be permanent.

Medical treatment.

Duration in Days

Job Classification	Minimum	Optimum	Maximum
Sedentary work	1	14	42
Light work	1	14	42
Medium work	1	28	56
Heavy work	1	28	56
Very Heavy work	1	28	56

Surgical treatment.

Duration in Days

Job Classification	Minimum	Optimum	Maximum
Sedentary work	28	42	56
Light work	28	42	56
Medium work	56	70	84
Heavy work	Indefinite	Indefinite	Indefinite
Very Heavy work	Indefinite	Indefinite	Indefinite

Failure to Recover

If an individual fails to recover within the maximum duration expectancy period, the reader may wish to reference the following questions to assist in better understanding the specifics of an individual's medical case.

Regarding diagnosis:

- Does the individual have a history of rheumatic fever, coronary arteriosclerosis, bacterial endocarditis, cardiomyopathy, or chordae tendineae?
- Does the individual have dyspnea with exertion or when lying down? Fatigue?
- Do they have atrial fibrillation?
- With auscultation is a murmur audible? Is the heart rhythm irregular?
- Has the individual had an ECG, chest x-ray and echocardiogram? Are the tests repeated periodically?
- Have conditions with similar symptoms been ruled out?

Regarding treatment:

- Does the individual have mild mitral insufficiency? Does the individual take antibiotics prior to any dental work or other procedures where bacteria may enter the bloodstream?
- Does the individual have more severe mitral insufficiency? Is the individual on medications such as diuretics, digitalis, vasodilators and anticoagulants?
- Is valve replacement a consideration?

Regarding prognosis:

- Is the individual's employer able to accommodate and necessary restrictions?
- Does the individual have any conditions that may affect ability to recover?
- Does the individual have any complications of mitral insufficiency such as congestive heart failure, atrial fibrillation or bacterial endocarditis?

References

Holmes, Nancy, H., managing ed. Handbook of Diseases. Springhouse, PA: Springhouse Corporation, 2000.

Mitral Regurgitation; Acute. Drkoop.com. 2000. 14 August 2000 <http://www.drkoop.com/conditions/ency/article/000177.htm>.

Mitral Stenosis
394.0, 396.1

Definition

Mitral stenosis refers to narrowing of the mitral valve resulting in obstruction to blood flow from the receiving chamber on the left side of the heart (left atrium) to the pumping chamber (left ventricle).

It is caused by acute rheumatic fever (ARF) during childhood that leaves the valve damaged and deformed predisposing it to scarring and narrowing (stenosis) later in life. ARF is caused by a streptococcus infection. The incidence of ARF decreased to a low level in the 1960s and 1970s and is associated with a reduction in the incidence of mitral stenosis in the 1980s and 1990s.

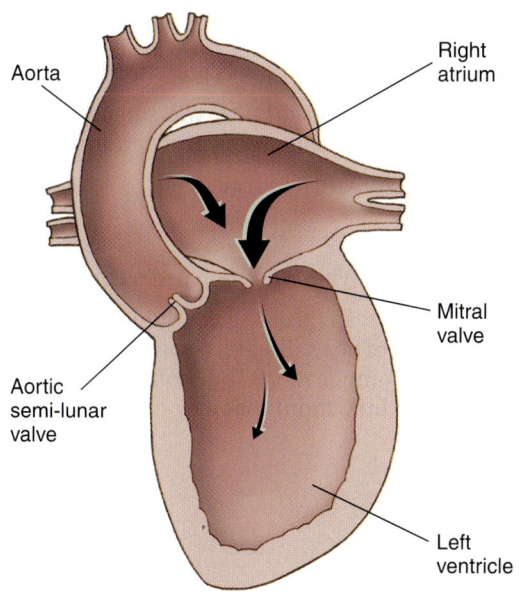

Diagnosis

History: Even though ARF precedes mitral stenosis by 20 to 30 years, a history of ARF is only recognized in 40% of individuals. After 20 to 30 years of feeling well, the individual gradually develops shortness of breath with ordinary activities. Alternatively, abrupt episodes of shortness of breath during sleep (acute pulmonary edema) occur at the onset of the irregular heart rhythm. Atrial fibrillation may be the first symptom that the individual notices.

Physical exam: The heart rhythm may be irregular (atrial fibrillation). There may be distension of the neck veins and sounds in the lungs (rales) indicative of congestion. A murmur during the filling phase of the heart's cycle (diastole) is always present but may be difficult to hear in overweight individuals or large-breasted women.

Tests: The electrocardiogram (ECG) may show atrial fibrillation. A chest x-ray usually shows evidence of enlargement of the filling chamber on the left side of the heart (left atrium). An echocardiogram is often done and shows limited motion of the mitral valve. The echocardiogram is usually abnormal even when the chest x-ray and ECG are not.

Treatment

Medications that remove excess fluid from the body (diuretics) are often given. Digitalis may be given to slow atrial fibrillation. Blood thinners (e.g., warfarin) are given especially if atrial fibrillation is present because of the increasing risk of blood clotting in the enlarged left atrium. If a small piece of the blood clot breaks off and is carried by the bloodstream to another organ, significant adverse consequences can occur. The blood clot is known as an embolism. If the embolism travels to the brain, the individual may suffer a stroke.

Digitalis, diuretics, and blood thinners are designed to treat or prevent complications of mitral stenosis. The only effective treatment for the narrowed valve itself is surgery (mitral commissurotomy). This may be done as a closed procedure where the surgeon's index finger is inserted into the beating heart to open the narrowed valve, or it may be done as an open procedure where the valve is directly visualized by the surgeon while the individual is in the heart-lung machine. Alternatively, in some older individuals with a heavily calcified valve, replacement of the valve with a prosthetic valve may be done.

Prognosis

The results of mitral commissurotomy (closed or open) are good. Operations mortality is 1%, surviving after 10 years is 95%, and reparations for recurrent valve narrowing is about 1% per year. Valve replacement carries a higher operative mortality (up to 5%) and is associated with the morbidity related to prostheses.

Differential Diagnosis

There are a few rare causes of mitral valve obstruction due to other processes such as a left atrial myoma, carcinoid, heart diseases, and methyl sergide therapy.

Specialists

- Cardiologist
- Cardiothoracic Surgeon

Work Restrictions / Accommodations

Successful surgery usually allows the individual to resume vocational and avocational activities. Large restrictions are necessary, however, for symptomatic individuals with mitral stenosis who do not have surgery. Anticoagulant therapy (blood thinners) is needed if atrial fibrillation is present. Use of anticoagulants may prevent individuals from optional types of work that involve possible injury.

Comorbid Conditions

Cigarette smoking, obesity, and coexisting unrelated heart disease might affect recovery.

Complications

Abrupt fluid collection in the lungs may occur causing marked shortness of breath (acute pulmonary edema). Atrial fibrillation presents in the majority of cases of mitral stenosis. Blood clots (emboli) to various organs often break off. A clot can form within the heart due to obstruction to flow caused by the mitral stenosis and the atrial fibrillation.

Factors Influencing Duration

The presence or absence of atrial fibrillation, success of surgery, and need for medications postoperatively may affect disability.

Length of Disability

For individuals with medical treatment, duration depends on severity of symptoms. Disability may be permanent for heavy and very heavy work.

Medical treatment.

Duration in Days

Job Classification	Minimum	Optimum	Maximum
Sedentary work	0	14	42
Light work	0	14	42
Medium work	0	28	56
Heavy work	0	28	56
Very Heavy work	0	28	56

Surgical treatment (valvuloplasty, balloon).

Duration in Days

Job Classification	Minimum	Optimum	Maximum
Sedentary work	7	9	14
Light work	7	9	14
Medium work	14	21	28
Heavy work	14	21	28
Very Heavy work	21	28	35

Failure to Recover

If an individual fails to recover within the maximum duration expectancy period, the reader may wish to reference the following questions to assist in better understanding the specifics of an individual's medical case.

Regarding diagnosis:

- Does the individual have a clinical history and presentation consistent with the diagnosis of mitral stenosis?
- Has the individual ever had rheumatic fever?
- Was a diastolic heart murmur noted?
- Was the diagnosis confirmed with an echocardiogram?
- If the diagnosis was uncertain, were other causes of heart murmur ruled out? Would the individual benefit from consultation with a specialist (cardiologist, cardiac surgeon)?

Regarding treatment:

- Were medications such as diuretics, vasodilating drugs, digitalis, or blood thinners, prescribed?
- Is the individual taking medications as prescribed?
- Did symptoms persist or worsen? If so, was surgery (mitral commissurotomy or valve replacement surgery) performed?
- Was a closed or open surgery performed?

Regarding prognosis:

- Was surgery performed? What was the expected outcome?
- Did the individual have any existing conditions (advanced age, associated conditions of heart disease, respiratory disease, diabetes, and obesity) or complications (pulmonary edema, embolic stroke, or myocardial infarction) that may have impacted ability to recover?

References

Mitral Valve Disease." The Merck Manual of Diagnosis and Therapy. Beers, Mark, and Robert Berkow, eds. "Medical Services, USMEDSA, USHH, 1999. 1 Jan 2001 <http://www.merck.com/pubs/mmanual/section16/chapter207/207b.htm>.

DeBakey, Michael, and Antonio Gotto. The New Living Heart. Holbrook, MA: Adams Media Corporation, 1997.

Mitral Valve Prolapse

Other names / synonyms: Ballooning Mitral Cusp, Barlow Syndrome, Barlow's Syndrome, Billroth I Procedure, Floppy Valve, Myxomatous Mitral Valve

424.0

Definition

Mitral valve prolapse is a common and highly variable syndrome associated with a disorder of the heart's mitral valve. It is characterized by excessive tissue in the valve's flaps (leaflets) that results in abnormal or exaggerated movement of a flap of the valve. This movement allows for blood to flow backward through the valve (mitral regurgitation). The most common cause of mitral valve prolapse is a collagen-like growth (myxomatous changes) on the leaflets. These changes are often idiopathic, but may occur in conjunction with connective tissue disorders such as Marfan syndrome, Duchenne muscular dystrophy, or cardiomyopathy.

Mitral valve prolapse is found more commonly in women. Some individuals may have chest wall deformities. One-tenth of mitral valve prolapse cases are found in otherwise healthy individuals between the ages of fourteen and thirty. Most cases of mitral valve prolapse are asymptomatic and are found incidentally on physical exam.

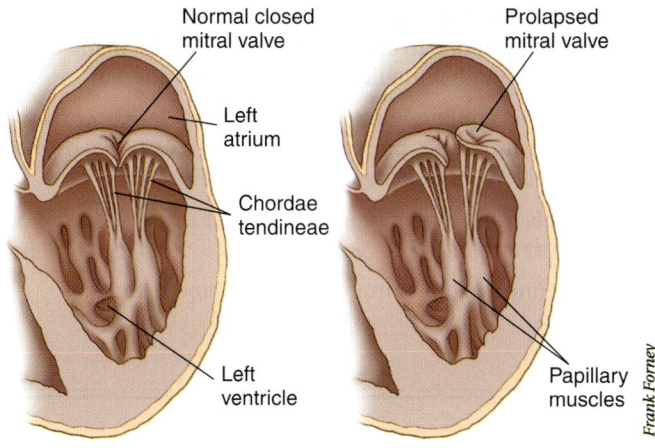

Diagnosis

History: Some individuals have no symptoms at all. Others complain of chest pain, shortness of breath, lightheadedness, fainting, fatigue, and irregular heartbeat (palpitations). Palpitations are often correlated with heart rhythm disturbances. Emotional stress may aggravate symptoms.

Physical exam: Listening to the heart will reveal heart sounds and blood flow patterns that are typical of mitral valve prolapse (mid-systolic clicks and late systolic murmur). The sounds are accentuated when the individual stands.

Tests: Tests may include an electrocardiogram and an echocardiogram. Rarely, cardiac catheterization is done to assess the degree of mitral regurgitation.

Treatment

Individuals who are found to have an irregular or fast heartbeat (arrhythmias or tachycardia) or chest pain are often treated with beta-blocker drugs. When typical symptoms are not present with the tachycardia, the doctor may suggest anti-arrhythmic therapy to help regulate the heart rhythm. Individuals who have a systolic murmur (mitral regurgitation) are at a higher risk for infections of the heart lining (endocarditis), and should be given antibiotics before dental, genitourinary, gastrointestinal, and upper respiratory procedures or surgeries to minimize their risks of infection.

Mitral valve prolapse rarely requires surgical treatment. However, mitral valve replacement may be warranted for refractory heart rhythm disturbances, severe mitral regurgitation or incapacitating pain. In older individuals, males require surgical intervention more often than females. Approximately 2 in 100 individuals over age 60 may require valve replacement.

Behavior modification programs for smoking or alcohol cessation may be recommended for appropriate individuals.

Prognosis

This is a relatively benign disorder. Most individuals will go through life without any symptoms or complications. A very small percentage (about 2%) may require valve replacement if mitral regurgitation becomes a serious problem.

Cerebral emboli (associated with increased platelet coagulant activity) are rare. Sudden death (less than 1%) may occur, usually in individuals who presented with a heart murmur and click.

Differential Diagnosis

Papillary muscle infarction or dysfunction, rheumatic heart disease, and infective endocarditis can all cause mitral insufficiency, a finding with mitral prolapse.

Specialists

| • Cardiologist | • Cardiovascular Surgeon |

Work Restrictions / Accommodations

If the individual is symptomatic, severe stressful activity should be reduced. Individuals with definite clicks and murmurs are sometimes advised to avoid competitive sports or activities that require maximum effort, but such a recommendation is controversial.

Comorbid Conditions

Alcohol, caffeine, or cigarette use may aggravate symptoms and prolong disability. Atrial myxomas, coronary artery disease, or cardiac dysrhythmias are common comorbid conditions that may prolong disability. Endocarditis or cerebral emboli are less common, but may also lengthen disability.

Complications

Bacterial endocarditis may develop in individuals with mitral valve prolapse. There may be a connection between this disorder and stroke. When the valve is especially thickened, the individual is at a higher risk for these complications. On rare occasions, mitral valve prolapse may progress to mitral regurgitation, which can precipitate congestive heart failure.

Factors Influencing Duration

Most individuals with this disorder will not require surgery or other aggressive treatment; therefore, disability time should be minimal or nonexistent, unless surgery is involved. Any disability time is a function of complications (mitral regurgitation, endocarditis, or arrhythmias). Disability depends on severity of symptoms, presence of complications, and treatment method.

Length of Disability

There is no disability expected without complications.

Medical treatment.

Duration in Days

Job Classification	Minimum	Optimum	Maximum
Sedentary work	0	14	42
Light work	0	14	42
Medium work	0	28	56
Heavy work	0	28	56
Very Heavy work	0	28	56

Failure to Recover

If an individual fails to recover within the maximum duration expectancy period, the reader may wish to reference the following questions to assist in better understanding the specifics of an individual's medical case.

Regarding diagnosis:

- Is individual a female? Is she under 30 years of age?
- Does individual have any chest wall deformities?
- Does individual complain of chest pain, shortness of breath, lightheadedness, fainting, fatigue, and irregular heartbeat (palpitations), or was this an incidental finding during a physical exam? Is individual experiencing emotional stress?
- Did the physician hear a distinct click or murmur of the heartbeats when listening with a stethoscope (auscultation)?
- Were electrocardiogram (ECG) and echocardiogram done?
- Has a diagnosis of mitral valve prolapse been confirmed?

Regarding treatment:

- If individual has an irregular or fast heartbeat (arrhythmias or tachycardia) or chest pain, are beta-blocker drugs being used?
- If individual has a systolic murmur (mitral regurgitation), are antibiotics given before dental, genitourinary, gastrointestinal, and upper respiratory procedures or surgeries?
- If individual has heart rhythm disturbances that cannot be controlled, severe mitral regurgitation, or incapacitating pain, would individual benefit from mitral valve replacement surgery?
- Would individual benefit from smoking or alcohol cessation programs, if appropriate?

Regarding prognosis:

- Is individual currently receiving beta-blocker or other antiarrhythmic medications to control symptoms? If the medication is ineffective, what other medications can be considered?
- If individual has undergone recent surgery or dental work, were prophylactic antibiotics prescribed and taken as ordered? If not, has individual developed bacterial endocarditis?
- How will this infection be treated and what is the expected outcome with treatment?
- Does individual require mitral valve replacement surgery?

References

Clochesy, John M., et al, eds. Critical Care Nursing, 2nd ed. Philadelphia: W.B. Saunders Company, 1996.

Tierney, Lawrence M., Stephen J. McPhee, and Maxine A. Papdakis, eds. Current Medical Diagnosis and Treatment, 39th ed. New York: Lang Medical Books/McGraw-Hill, 2000.

Mononucleosis

Other names / synonyms: Glandular Fever, Infectious Mononucleosis, Kissing Disease

075

Definition

Mononucleosis is a contagious disease that is caused by the Epstein-Barr virus (EBV) related to herpes simplex.

Kissing, coughing, and sneezing are common ways of spreading infectious mononucleosis. The disease usually develops several weeks to 2 months after exposure to the virus, which spreads primarily through exchanges of saliva. Sharing contaminated eating utensils is another common way of transmitting the disease, which is widespread at college campuses, public schools, and military bases.

As many as 3% of all college students in the US are thought to have the disease. Healthy individuals once exposed to the virus are carriers of the disease, which is considered difficult to prevent. Immunity often results after infection, although in rare cases the disease may recur periodically. Since most older adults already have been exposed to the virus, mononucleosis is considered contagious primarily among younger age groups.

Mononucleosis is so widespread that about 95% of adults in the US are thought to have been infected. Many individuals are unaware of the infection because symptoms often are non-existent to very mild. In developing countries, almost 100% of young children are afflicted with mononucleosis. Infections tend to occur later in developed countries, affecting primarily individuals of ages fifteen to thirty.

Diagnosis

History: The individual typically reports a general feeling of illness (malaise) at onset. Symptoms slowly become more specific, and may develop into fever, jaundice, sore throat, fatigue, and loss of appetite. White patches may develop at the back of the throat. Lymph nodes may be swollen in the neck and under the armpits. Less common symptoms include persistent muscle aches, joint pain, chills, and nausea. The individual may also report exposure to a person infected with the disease. Most symptoms usually last from 2-4 weeks, but fatigue and malaise can linger for months. An individual with an extreme or advanced case of mononucleosis may also complain of pain in the left upper part of the abdomen, faintness, difficulty breathing, a rapid heart rate, and abnormal bleeding indicating the spleen has ruptured.

Physical exam: The exam may show enlarged tonsils, presence of strep throat (pharyngitis), and enlarged lymph nodes in the neck or elsewhere in the body (lymphadenopathy). An enlarged spleen (splenomegaly) or liver (hepatomegaly) may be detected. The individual may complain of tenderness when pressure is applied over the spleen or liver. Jaundice or a rash are occasionally seen. Fever may be as high as 102 degrees. A sore throat (palatal petechiae), swollen eye (periorbital edema), or scarlet fever may be detected.

Tests: A complete blood count (CBC) may be performed. A white blood cell count (WBC) may show elevated levels peaking between 10,000-20,000 during the second or third week after infection. A high percentage of abnormal white blood cells (lymphocytes) also indicates presence of the disease. Liver function tests (LFTs) may also show abnormal function through increased bile pigment (serum bilirubin) and somewhat elevated levels of certain enzymes (serum transaminases and alkaline phosphatase). A positive Monospot blood test indicating the presence of antibodies to EBV is usually the best way of detecting short-term (acute) infectious mononucleosis. The best indicator of mononucleosis is the presence of IgM antibody to EBV viral capsid antigen, usually apparent when the infection is most active. In ongoing (chronic) or recurring cases of mononucleosis, antibodies needed to confirm the diagnosis may be absent. A throat culture to detect microorganisms related to the disease may also be indicated.

Treatment

Since no specific treatment exists for mononucleosis, options for medical intervention are usually limited. Individuals may be advised to rest, although there is no evidence that extended rest shortens the duration of mononucleosis. Nonsteroidal anti-inflammatory drugs (NSAIDs) may be used to reduce fever. Aspirin should be avoided. If an enlarged spleen is suspected, contact sports and strenuous activities may be curtailed because of the possibility of rupture. Other activities are reduced in accordance with the symptoms. Good hygiene also is recommended.

Drugs that suppress immune responses (corticosteroids) are sometimes used for treating complications such as preventing the throat from swelling and blocking the airway. However, some experts advise against use of steroids because of potential side effects such as an association with development of encephalitis or myocarditis. Other researchers recommend use of steroids for severe central nervous system involvement (e.g., Guillain-Barré syndrome), serious anemia, or low blood platelets. Antiviral agents may inhibit replication of EBV, but have not been shown to directly affect duration of the disease. Antibiotics may be used to treat secondary bacterial infections. While no specific treatment may be indicated for liver inflammation, the individual should be advised to avoid alcohol to prevent a worsening of symptoms. If splenic rupture occurs as a complication, the condition may be life threatening and the spleen may need to be surgically removed (splenectomy).

Prognosis

The prognosis for uncomplicated mononucleosis is very good. Symptoms usually last no longer than a month, and most individuals will recover completely within 6 months. The incidence and duration of complications depend upon the severity of the initial EBV infection and how quickly it is diagnosed. Individuals with immune disorders may have greater difficulty recovering from the disease and any accompanying complications. Chronic or recurrent mononucleosis is rare. In other rare cases, fatalities occur when the spleen ruptures or liver failure is involved. Death occurs in 1 of about 3,000 mononucleosis cases.

Differential Diagnosis

Other viral and parasitic diseases can resemble acute mononucleosis. These agents include cytomegalovirus, various hepatitis viruses, adenovirus, Q Fever, and Toxoplasma gondii. Other similar conditions include malignancies, rubella, AIDS, and diphtheria. If the illness lasts longer than 6 months, other chronic diseases may be indicated.

Specialists

- Infectious Disease Physician
- Primary Care Provider

Work Restrictions / Accommodations

Depending on the severity of symptoms, work activities may need to be curtailed or restricted until the individual, who usually suffers fatigue, is completely recovered. If the liver, spleen, or kidneys are involved, care should be exercised in lifting heavy objects or bending to grasp and carry objects. Strenuous activity such as contact sports should be strictly avoided because of the possibility of rupturing the spleen. Most people can resume normal activities within 3-4 weeks.

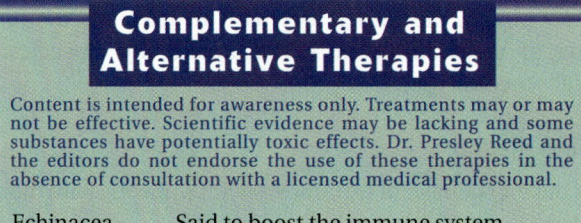

Complementary and Alternative Therapies

Content is intended for awareness only. Treatments may or may not be effective. Scientific evidence may be lacking and some substances have potentially toxic effects. Dr. Presley Reed and the editors do not endorse the use of these therapies in the absence of consultation with a licensed medical professional.

Echinacea - Said to boost the immune system.

Comorbid Conditions

In rare instances, mononucleosis can recur in an individual. Usually, the latent virus is reactivated when the body's immunity is suppressed. This can occur as a result of other infectious illnesses, steroid therapy, leukemia, radiation therapy, or generalized malignancy. Individuals with AIDS may develop tongue lesions (oral hairy leukoplakia) associated with EBV.

Complications

Possible blood disorders include anemia and selectively reduced white cell counts. Neurological disorders may manifest as seizures, psychosis, cranial nerve palsies, encephalitis, and central nervous system inflammation. Spatial distortion (metamorphopsia) may also occur. Interstitial pneumonia or airway obstruction may develop. When the virus invades the blood, inflammation may occur in other organs such as the heart, spleen, liver, parotid glands, kidneys, and pancreas.

In rare instances, mononucleosis can recur in an individual. Usually, the latent virus is reactivated when the body's immunity is suppressed. This can occur as a result of other infectious illnesses, steroid therapy, leukemia, radiation therapy, or generalized malignancy. In rare cases, symptoms may continue beyond 6 months leading to a condition called chronic mononucleosis. Other serious complications related to EBV include nasopharyngeal carcinoma and Burkitt's lymphoma. Individuals with AIDS may develop tongue lesions (oral hairy leukoplakia) associated with EBV. In rare cases, a ruptured spleen may develop and become fatal. Another rare but sometimes fatal consequence of mononucleosis is liver disease and failure (fulminant hepatitis).

Factors Influencing Duration

The infection's severity and possible complications will influence length of disability. Individuals with pre-existing immune disorders likely will need longer recovery time.

Length of Disability

Rarely, chronic mononucleosis may develop resulting in prolonged disability

Duration in Days

Job Classification	Minimum	Optimum	Maximum
Any work	7	14	28

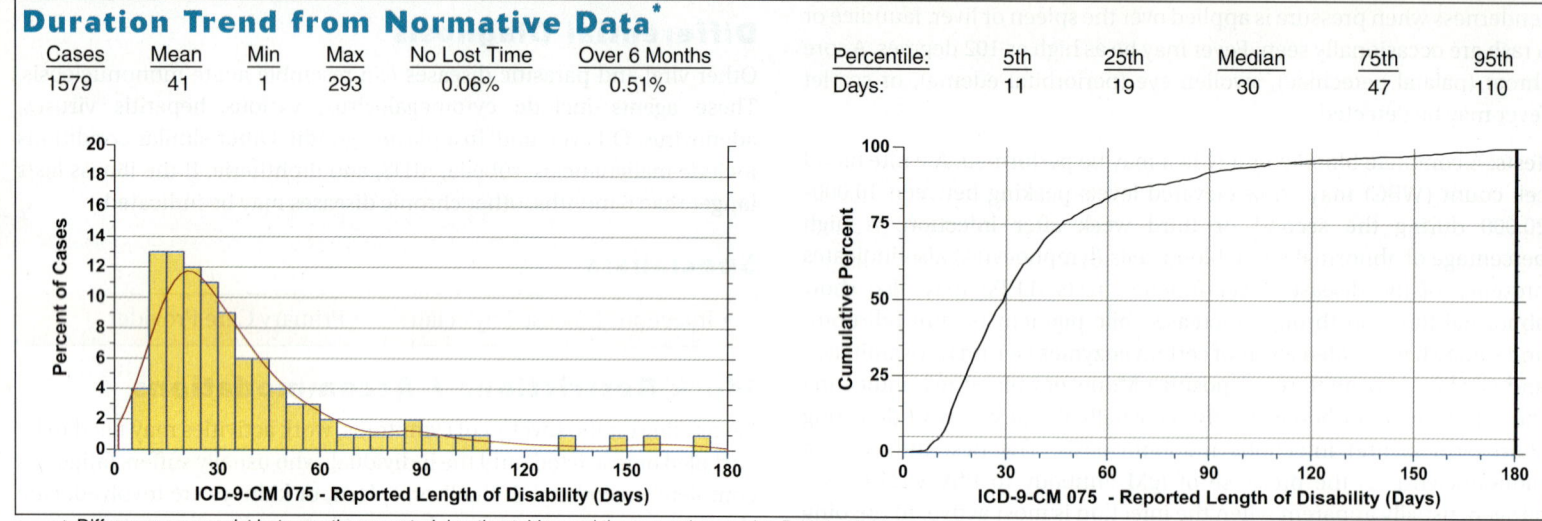

Failure to Recover

If an individual fails to recover within the maximum duration expectancy period, the reader may wish to reference the following questions to assist in better understanding the specifics of an individual's medical case.

Regarding diagnosis:

- Has the individual had exposure to with someone with mononucleosis?
- Did the individual report malaise?
- Did the individual develop fever, sore throat, loss of appetite and jaundice?
- Were the lymph nodes swollen in the neck and under the armpits?
- Does the individual complain of left-sided abdominal pain? Faintness? Difficulty breathing? Rapid heart rate? Abnormal bleeding?
- On physical exam were the tonsils enlarged? Pharyngitis? Lymphadenopathy?
- Were splenomegaly or hepatomegaly detected? Were they tender to palpation?
- Was jaundice or a rash seen? Fever?
- Has the individual had a CBC and liver function tests? Monospot test? Throat culture?
- Have conditions with similar symptoms been ruled out?

Regarding treatment:

- Was the individual advised to rest?
- Were NSAIDs may be used to reduce fever?
- Were corticosteroids used to treat complications?
- Were anti-viral agents used?
- Were there any secondary bacterial infections? Were they treated with antibiotics?
- Was the individual advised to avoid alcohol?
- Did splenectomy become necessary?

Regarding prognosis:

- Is the individual's employer able to accommodate any necessary restrictions?
- Is the individual also following these restrictions at home and play?
- Does the individual have any conditions that may affect the ability to recover?
- Has the individual had recurrent mononucleosis?
- Has the individual had complications such as nasopharyngeal carcinoma? Burkitt's lymphoma? Fulminant hepatitis? Ruptured spleen?

References

Laval, Judith D. "Infectious Mononucleosis." Journal of the National Medical Society 24 Apr 2000 6. Library of the National Medical Society. 1 Jan 2001 <http://www.medical-library.org>.

Morton's Neuroma
Other names / synonyms: Morton's Neuralgia
355.6

Definition

Morton's neuroma is a form of foot disease caused by a falling arch and pressure on the branches of the plantar nerve in the sole of the foot. The increased pressure results in a tumor or growth of nerve cells and nerve fibers on the nerve of the foot called a neuroma. The neuroma causes pain and tenderness in the metatarsal bones of the foot (metatarsalgia). The growth is usually caused by mechanical irritation and increased pressure on the bones of the foot during walking and standing. The plantar nerve becomes compressed and the chronic pressure leads to the formation of the neuroma.

This disease affects individuals between the ages of 30 and 80. Women are most often affected possibly because of shoe type worn.

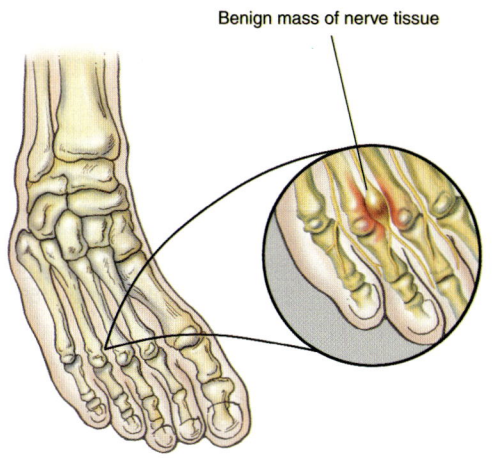

Diagnosis

History: History includes pain on the ball (plantar area) of the foot during walking or prolonged standing. The pain can be quite severe and incapacitating. Individuals may stop walking, remove their shoes, and rub their feet. The pain may radiate to the toes in some cases and subside after resting. Numbness in the toes may be reported.

Physical exam: Structural abnormalities of the foot may be evident. Pain occurs when pressure is applied to any of the five metatarsal bones of the foot.

Tests: Plain x-rays (radiographs) may reveal bony abnormalities of the metatarsus, but typically are not useful in diagnosing neuroma. Bone scans are more definitive and can detect the neuroma. Testing of touch sensation using a monofilament may reveal neuropathy. Nerve conduction studies are not useful in this diagnosis.

Treatment

Complete excision of the neuroma is usually the best treatment for most cases, however not all neuromas lend themselves to this procedure. In all cases, properly fitted and corrective footwear is recommended to prevent compression of the metatarsals and plantar nerve. The neuroma can be injected with a local anesthetic and/or steroidal preparation to relieve pain.

Prognosis

Most individuals have near complete recovery from surgical removal of the neuroma with little residual discomfort in the forefoot. Injection of pain-relieving medication is usually effective for temporary relief. Most individuals recover from the symptoms of pain and any distortion of touch sensation.

Differential Diagnosis

Pain in the front of the foot may be a result of a disease in the joints between the foot and toes (metatarsal-phalangeal) such as synovitis, rheumatoid arthritis, or degenerative arthritis. Another source may cause pain such as degenerative lumbar disc disease, tarsal tunnel syndrome, or diabetic peripheral nerve disease (neuropathy). There may be other painful lesions in the plantar part of the foot such as calluses and warts, synovial cysts, soft tissue tumor, or tumor of the metatarsal bone. Pain may originate from the bone itself, a stress fracture (march fracture), Freiberg-Kohler disease, Morton's syndrome, and Deutschländer's disease.

Specialists

- Orthopedic Surgeon
- Podiatrist

Rehabilitation

The individual's sports and work shoes are evaluated for improper support and narrow toe width. Suggestions for shoe choice include wider shoes with lower heels to alleviate metatarsal (ball of the foot) pressure. For sports shoes, 1/2 to 3/4 of an inch of additional room should be allowed between the big toe and the end of the shoe. This space accommodates any foot swelling and forward movement of the foot during exercise, especially running.

The individual may also be fitted with orthotics to help control excessive foot pronation during the heel strike phase of gait motion. The goal of orthotics is to shift pressure from the forefoot to the arch and provide extra stabilization during pronation phases of walking and running. Modality treatment such as ice therapy may also be prescribed along with ultrasound. As pain lessens, the individual may participate in whirlpool treatments where strengthening exercises are performed for the ankle and foot.

A physical therapist may help in initial scar management that includes cross-frictional massage. Active and passive toe mobilization also begins.

The individual does not need extensive physical therapy in order to return to work. If the individual's occupation requires continual standing or foot movement, the individual should take frequent breaks. If pain and foot weakness persist, added exercise therapy may be prescribed to resolve muscle imbalances around the ankle and foot.

Work Restrictions / Accommodations

Walking and standing is limited due to severe pain. If surgery is performed, this limitation may last 3 to 6 weeks postoperatively. The individual may need to wear corrective footwear during recovery.

Comorbid Conditions

Obesity, diabetes, and peripheral neuropathy may impact the ability to recover and further lengthen disability.

Complications

A complication of Morton's neuroma may be the development of abnormal gait due to continuous pain and pressure. Distortion of sensation (dysesthesia) in the foot with the neuroma may also occur. The neuroma and accompanying pain may recur following surgery.

Factors Influencing Duration

Factors that influence disability includes response to surgical treatment and willingness to wear properly fitted and corrective footwear.

Length of Disability

The length of disability depends on severity of the pain and surgical outcome.

Medical treatment.

Duration in Days

Job Classification	Minimum	Optimum	Maximum
Sedentary work	0	7	14
Light work	0	7	14
Medium work	0	10	28
Heavy work	0	14	28
Very Heavy work	0	14	28

Surgical treatment.

Duration in Days

Job Classification	Minimum	Optimum	Maximum
Sedentary work	1	7	21
Light work	3	14	21
Medium work	3	21	28
Heavy work	7	28	35
Very Heavy work	7	28	42

Duration Trend from Normative Data*

Cases	Mean	Min	Max	No Lost Time	Over 6 Months
1721	46	3	276	0%	0.23%

Percentile:	5th	25th	Median	75th	95th
Days:	13	24	38	58	106

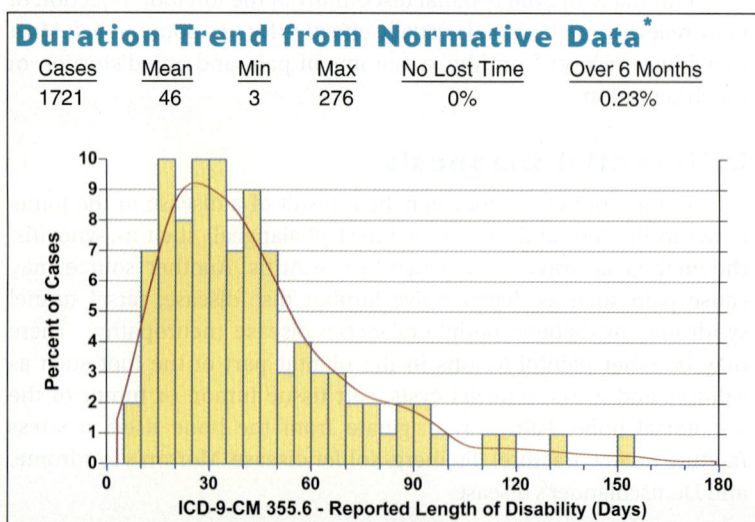

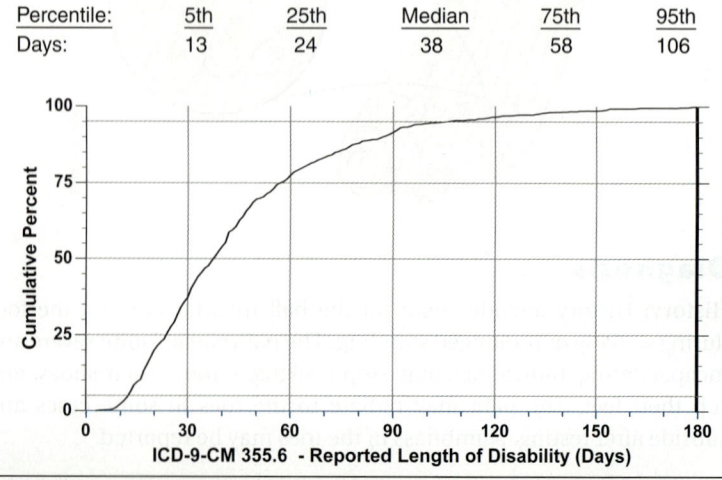

* Differences may exist between the expected duration tables and the normative graphs. Duration tables provide expected recovery periods based on the type of work performed by the individual. The normative graphs reflect the actual observed experience of many individuals across the spectrum of physical conditions, in a variety of industries, and with varying levels of case management.

Failure to Recover

If an individual fails to recover within the maximum duration expectancy period, the reader may wish to reference the following questions to assist in better understanding the specifics of an individual's medical case.

Regarding diagnosis:

- Did the individual present with severe pain in the ball of the foot?
- Was the diagnosis of neuroma confirmed with a bone scan?
- Did the physical exam and diagnostic work up rule out other forms of neuropathy or forefoot pain such as arthritis, synovitis, stress fractures, etc?

Regarding treatment:

- Was an injection of local anesthetic and/or corticosteroids effective in relieving pain? Would further injections be beneficial?
- Was surgical excision of the neuroma indicated?
- Has the individual been compliant with wearing well-fitting shoes?
- Would individual benefit from a prosthetic insert?

Regarding prognosis:

- Does individual's pain persist despite treatment?
- Is individual a candidate for surgical removal of neuroma?
- Were preventative measures instituted such as properly fitted and corrective footwear?
- Does the individual have other conditions such as obesity, diabetes, and peripheral neuropathy that may impact recovery and prognosis?
- Did the individual experience any associated complications such as gain abnormalities, recurrence of pain or altered sensation that could impact prognosis?

References

Adams, Raymond D., Maurice Victor, and Allan H. Ropeer. Principles of Neurology, 6th ed. New York: McGraw Hill, 1997.

Brantingham, J.W., W.R. Snyder, and T. Michaud. "Morton's Neuroma." Journal of Manipulative and Physiological Therapeutics 14 5 (1991): 317-322.

Kotte, Frederic, and Justus Lehmann. Krusen's Handbook of Physical Medicine and Rehabilitation. Philadelphia: W.B. Saunders Company, 1990.

Scully, Rosemary, and Marylou Barnes. Physical Therapy. Philadelphia: J.B. Lippincott Company, 1989.

Motion Sickness

Other names / synonyms: Car Sick, Motor Sickness, Sea Sickness

994.6

Definition

Motion sickness is a motion-induced syndrome that occurs on ships, submarines, aircraft, in automobiles, trains, amusement park rides, spacecrafts, and with the use of virtual reality devices. Symptoms can range from mild discomfort to a more severe condition marked by extreme exhaustion and powerlessness (prostration) from continual vomiting and associated dehydration.

The discomfort is caused because the brain receives conflicting information from the sensory organ receptors (visual vestibular and body proprioceptors). The inner ear (the vestibular system) experiences acceleration forces that are not confirmed by visual references. An example is reading a book while riding in an automobile. The reader's visual reference (the book) is not moving (or moving minimally) relative to the reader; therefore the reader perceives him/herself as stable in space based on visual input. However, the vestibular input, in response to bumpy roads, hills, or cornering is that of variable movement. This mismatch of sensory information somehow gives rise to the release of a brain chemical agent (neurotransmitter) that stimulates the nearby vomiting center.

The development of symptoms follows a sequence that varies with intensity of stimulus and individual susceptibility: initially, discomfort around the upper abdomen; next, nausea and increased malaise; finally, vomiting. At the same time, sweating can develop along with rapid worsening of symptoms (avalanche syndrome) such as increased salivation, body warmth, lightheadedness, and apathy.

Some individuals are more motion sensitive and so have a greater susceptibility to motion sickness. However, motion sickness occurs in all populations, and with equal frequency in both males and females. It peaks between ages 3-12, with a gradual decrease thereafter. Most individuals adapt to motion over time. Once adaptation takes place, the symptoms of motion sickness abate. Some adapt quickly (within minutes or hours), while others take days to weeks to adapt. About 5% of individuals do not adapt and remain symptomatic as long as the stimulus persists.

Diagnosis

History: Individuals may complain of fatigue, nausea, dizziness, sweating, headache, abdominal discomfort, and/or vomiting during travel. Individuals often relate a previous experience of motion sickness. Those with previous history of motion sickness may complain of anticipatory anxiety, nausea, and vomiting before air travel.

Physical exam: The individual will appear completely healthy when not in motion. With motion the individual may appear flushed or pale, and may have cool, moist skin. Other symptoms may include increased salivation, lightheadedness, hyperventilation, sighing and yawning, headache, tightness around the forehead, drowsiness, lethargy, somnolence, panic or confusion, hyperactive bowel and gastric sounds (flatulence and belching), and associated vomiting.

Tests: There are no specific tests for motion sickness. Examination of the ear canal using a lighted scope (otoscope) can be done to rule out ear infections. CT scan or MRI of the head will rule out brain or inner ear masses.

Treatment

In most cases, motion sickness completely resolves once the journey is over, leaving no ill effects. There are several measures that are effective in preventing motion sickness in most individuals.

Being rested and in good health before the journey helps prevent motion sickness. Other preventive measures include selecting an area in the vehicle, boat, or plane where motion is minimized (i.e., in the middle of a boat, over the wing in airplanes, front seat of a car). Staying seated with the back and head supported helps to minimize unnecessary head movements. Selecting an area near a window can provide a stable visual reference and can help the individual fix visually on the horizon or a stable external object. Fresh air, removing noxious stimuli, and improved ventilation will help: open a window, stay on the ship's top deck, open the airplane's overhead air vent. Eating a small, low-fat meal prior to departure, helps to settle the stomach. Avoid reading, smoking and drinking alcohol. Engaging in distracting activities will help, including driving and controlling the vehicle.

Medications can be used to either prevent or treat motion sickness. Oral antihistamines, sometimes in combination with stimulants, may be given 1-2 hours before departure.

If motion sickness does occur, intramuscular injections or rectal suppositories of antihistamine or antiemetic (antinausea) medications may be given.

Prognosis

Most individuals adapt to motion over time; with adaptation, symptoms disappear. In most cases, symptoms of motion sickness are well controlled when preventive measures are taken and medications are administered. Therefore, the outcome is good in all but rare cases where motion sickness persists for more than a week, due to prolonged periods in motion such as on boats at sea. In such cases, severe dehydration and debilitation can occur.

Differential Diagnosis

Other possibilities include chronic inner ear disease, tumors, and anxiety.

Specialists

- Emergency Medicine
- Internist
- Otorhinolaryngologist
- Primary Care Provider

Work Restrictions / Accommodations

For some individuals, limiting or restricting travel may be an option. Motion sickness may disqualify an individual for certain occupations. Even with treatment, some individuals may require alternative modes of travel (i.e., car vs. plane). Medications used to prevent or treat motion sickness may impair alertness and performance. These individuals should avoid critical decision-making, or operating machinery or vehicles while taking medication.

Complementary and Alternative Therapies

Content is intended for awareness only. Treatments may or may not be effective. Scientific evidence may be lacking and some substances have potentially toxic effects. Dr. Presley Reed and the editors do not endorse the use of these therapies in the absence of consultation with a licensed medical professional.

Acupuncture/ acupressure - May relieve nausea, including nausea of motion sickness.

Behavior modification - Individual is taught various techniques for coping with a situation. Behavior modification been used with some success in the Navy for management of motion sickness in pilots and seamen.

Herbal therapy - Ginger products are widely touted as providing prophylaxis for the nausea and vomiting of motion sickness. Studies have yielded variable results. Ginger is on the FDA's GRAS (generally recognized as safe) list and seldom causes any side effects.

Comorbid Conditions

Comorbid conditions of inner ear disturbances, brain tumors, or anxiety may impact ability to recover from motion sickness and may possibly lengthen disability.

Complications

Prolonged, severe motion sickness and associated nausea can lead to dehydration and prostration.

Length of Disability

Duration in Days

Job Classification	Minimum	Optimum	Maximum
Any work	0	0	1

Failure to Recover

If an individual fails to recover within the maximum duration expectancy period, the reader may wish to reference the following questions to assist in better understanding the specifics of an individual's medical case.

Regarding diagnosis:

- Has diagnosis of motion sickness been confirmed?
- Has individual been evaluated for disturbances in the inner ear or brain tumors?
- Has anxiety been evaluated and treated?
- Is there an underlying condition or factors (inner ear disturbances, brain tumors, tobacco smoke and unpleasant odors, over-consumption of alcohol, overeating and rich foods, stuffy rooms, and reading during travel) that may be impacting recovery?

Regarding treatment:

- Does motion sickness persist despite taking measures such as, being rested and in good health prior to the journey; selecting an area in the vehicle; staying seated with back and head supported minimizes unnecessary head movements; sitting near a window to provide a stable visual reference; fresh air, removing noxious stimuli, and improved ventilation will help; eating a small, low-fat meal prior to departure to settle the stomach; avoiding reading, smoking and drinking alcohol; and engaging in distracting activities?
- Have medications been effective in preventing or treating motion sickness?
- Were oral antihistamines taken as prescribed prior to departure?

Regarding prognosis:

- If travel is necessary, but symptoms, accompanied by severe dehydration and debilitation, persist despite medication and preventive measures, can a change be made in mode of transportation?
- When motion sickness is associated with excessive anxiety, would individual benefit from counseling?
- Would individual benefit from enrollment in a support group?

References

Tierney, Lawrence M., et al. Current Medical Diagnosis and Treatment, 39th ed. New York: Lange Medical Books/McGraw-Hill, 2000.

Virtual Naval Hospital. Department of the Navy. 01 Jan 2000. 10 Oct 2000 <http://www.vnh.org/GMO/01Contents.html>.

Multiple Chemical Sensitivity Syndrome

Other names / synonyms: 20th Century Syndrome, Allergic Toxemia, Chemical AIDS, Chemically Induced Immune Dysfunction, Environmental Hypersensitivity, Environmental Illness, Total Allergy Syndrome, Total Immune Disorder Syndrome

995.3

Definition

Considerable controversy continues to surround the cause (etiology), definition, diagnosis and treatment of persons with this disorder.

There is no single term or universally accepted case definition for persons with this disorder. One definition of Multiple Chemical Sensitivity (MCS) is an acquired disorder characterized by recurrent symptoms, referable to multiple organ symptoms, occurring in response to demonstrable exposure to many chemically unrelated compounds at doses far below those established in the general population to cause harmful effects and for which no single widely accepted test of physiologic function can be shown to correlate with symptoms. Despite variation in definitions, all agree that persons with a diagnosis of MCS list multiple symptoms referable to multiple body systems, with little consistency among persons.

The person with MCS typically reports symptoms after exposure to common environmental substances such as perfumes, food additives, fabrics, food, exhaust fumes, new carpets, copy machines, preservatives, household cleaners and pesticides. Reported symptoms include: neurologic symptoms (headaches, mental confusion, memory loss, irritability, mood swings, inability to concentrate, drowsiness), dermatologic symptoms (skin irritation, rashes), musculoskeletal symptoms (muscle and joint pain), respiratory symptoms (throat irritation, runny or stuffy nose) genital/urinary symptoms (vaginal burning, frequent urination), ocular symptoms (watery eyes) and gastrointestinal symptoms (constipation, diarrhea, nausea). Symptoms are reported for hours to days or weeks, with typical "reactions" reported after these common exposures. A person with MCS will often have identified a variety of substances that result in symptoms and will have initiated an avoidance regimen. Self-limitation in work and social activities include: driving, shopping, wearing certain types of clothing or entering office buildings or other work places. Persons with MCS do not have concurrent occupational or environmental conditions such as asthma or contact dermatitis.

The cause of MCS is unknown. Based on available evidence to date there is no convincing evidence that MCS is an immunologic disorder, a respiratory disorder or an olfactory-limbic disorder. Mental and behavioral factors appear to play a role in symptom production, including work stress and conflict and secondary gain from the sick role. Many persons with MCS have psychiatric disorders (affective or anxiety disorders, psychoses or somatoform disorders), which predate the onset of their MCS. Although some argue that mental and behavioral disorders are caused by MCS rather than mental and behavioral disorders causing MCS, it is certain that mental and behavioral disorders play a prominent role in this syndrome.

Diagnosis

History: The person with MCS typically reports symptoms after exposure to common environmental substances, some of which are noted in the section Definition above. Reported symptoms include: neurologic, dermatologic, musculoskeletal, genital/urinary, respiratory, ocular and gastrointestinal as noted in the section Discussion above. Persons with this history are predominately women in the 30-40 year age range.

Physical examination: The physical examination is normal.

Tests: There is no test(s) that confirms the diagnosis of MCS. Routine laboratory testing is reserved for ruling out other medical conditions.

Based on available evidence to date, the following tests have no role in diagnosing MCS: hair testing for heavy metals, provocation-neutralization testing, chemical and food challenges, immunologic testing, inhalant challenges, serologic testing for Epstein-Barr virus antibodies, autoantibodies or blood testing for organic hydrocarbon and pesticides.

In the absence of other concurrent medical conditions suggested by history, physical examination or routine laboratory testing, the diagnosis of MCS is based on the person's self-report.

Treatment

Although it is not clear whether psychologic symptoms are the cause of MCS or whether they merely accompany the diagnosis, cognitive and behavioral interventions may be useful in the treatment of MCS; for example, relaxation techniques, breath-control exercises and a structured plan to increase overall physical and social activity. Medication treatment is reserved for specific symptoms indicative of depression or anxiety.

The following therapies have not been validated through adequately designed controlled trials, may have unwanted side effects, may serve to reinforce counterproductive behaviors and are not recommended for the treatment of MCS: elimination or rotary diversified diets, vitamin therapy, antifungal and antiviral agents, thyroid hormone supplement, chemical detoxification through exercise and heat stress, intra- or subcutaneous neutralization and avoidance of low level irritants.

Prognosis

The prognosis for persons with this disorder is unknown because there are no scientifically valid outcome studies upon which to base an opinion regarding prognosis.

Differential Diagnosis

The differential diagnosis includes other medical conditions which would account for the reported symptoms including: major depressive disorder (MDD), preoccupation with physical discomfort (somatoform disorder), bipolar disorder, schizophrenia, delusional disorders, seasonal affective disorder (SAD), obsessive-compulsive disorder, Cushing syndrome, dementia, sleeping disorders (sleep apnea), breathing disorders (hypoxia, hypercapnia), myalgic encephalomyelitis, Lyme disease, Addison's disease, hypothyroidism, hyperthyroidism, diabetes mellitus, hepatitis B, hepatitis C, alcohol or substance abuse, AIDS, tuberculosis, anemia, endocarditis, rheumatoid arthritis, systemic lupus erythematosus, endocrine disorders, neuromuscular disorders, malignancy, metabolic/nutritional disorder, and immune or inflammatory disease.

Specialists

• Internist	• Primary Care Provider
• Occupational Medicine Physician	• Psychiatrist
	• Psychologist

Work Restrictions / Accommodations

Persons with this disorder have no identifiable objective medical basis for their symptoms; that is, persons with this disorder report symptoms but have normal physical examinations and normal findings on diagnostic testing. Consequently, there is no objective medical basis upon which to predicate work restrictions or accommodations.

Comorbid Conditions

Many persons with MCS have psychiatric disorders (affective or anxiety disorders, psychoses or somatoform disorders), which predate the onset of MCS.

Complications

Complications can arise from treatment (i.e., unwanted side effects or reinforcement of counterproductive behaviors) or from the person's behavior (i.e., self-limitation of activities of daily living).

Factors Influencing Duration

The factors influencing duration of disability are unknown because there are no scientifically valid studies that have determined the factors influencing duration of disability in this disorder.

Length of Disability

Although individuals with this disorder self limit their work and social activities, there may be no objective medical basis for disability. This is a controversial diagnosis. Contact physician for more information.

Failure to Recover

If an individual fails to recover within the maximum duration expectancy period, the reader may wish to reference the following questions to assist in better understanding the specifics of an individual's medical case.

Regarding diagnosis:

- Have alternative diagnoses been investigated?

Regarding treatment:

- Have nonproven treatments resulted in unwanted side effects?
- Have treatment methods reinforced counterproductive behaviors?
- Have cognitive and behavioral interventions been employed?

Regarding prognosis:

- Have psychosocial factors, i.e., family and workplace dynamics, been considered?

References

Estes, E.H., Jr., et al. "Clinical Ecology." JAMA 268 (1992):3465-3467.

Editorial. "Conclusions and Recommendations of a Workshop on Multiple Chemical Sensitivities (MCS)." Reg Toxicol and Pharmacol. 24.95 (1996):S188-S189.

Multiple Myeloma

Other names / synonyms: Multiple Myelomatosis, Plasma Cell Myeloma

203, 203.0, 203.00

Definition

Multiple myeloma is a malignant (cancerous) condition characterized by the uncontrolled reproduction and dysfunction of the plasma cells in the bone marrow. Plasma cells are white blood cells that respond to an invading organism (viral or bacterial) by producing antibodies against it. Antibodies are made of a protein called immunoglobulin of which there are several types. In multiple myeloma, the abundance of plasma cells overproduce a single type of immunoglobulin or portions of immunoglobulin called light or heavy chains. In contrast, other types of immunoglobulin are underproduced.

As healthy bone marrow is replaced by malignant plasma cells, there is a reduced production of red blood cells, platelets, and granulocytes. This can result in anemia, recurrent infection, or a bleeding tendency. When the plasma cell tumors expand within the bone, the bone tissue is destroyed resulting in fractures and spinal cord compression.

Little is known about the cause of multiple myeloma. Theories suggest that a virus or exposure to herbicides or radiation may be the cause. It may also be a genetic disease. Individuals with immune systems that react against the body's own tissues (autoimmune diseases) are more often affected with multiple myeloma.

Multiple myeloma usually occurs in older individuals with peak incidence at age 69. It is rare before the age of 40. The incidence of multiple myeloma is 4 cases per 100,000 individuals. The incidence in blacks is twice that of whites.

Diagnosis

History: Individuals may report pain in the bones especially the vertebrae, pelvis, ribs, and skull. If the vertebrae are affected, they may collapse and compress nerves causing numbness or paralysis. Individual may have a history of recurrent bacterial infections. Anemia symptoms can include increased fatigue and shortness of breath upon exertion. Nausea, confusion, frequent urination (polyuria), and constipation may be present due to increased calcium level in the blood (hypercalcemia) or pending renal failure.

Physical exam: Complete physical exam may reveal paleness, tenderness with pressure over an involved bone, and, on rare occasions, soft tissue masses. Cardiac examination can show an abnormal heart beat due to anemia, excessive amount of potassium in the blood (hyperkalemia), or amyloid heart disease. Neurologic exam may give evidence of nerve disorder (neuropathy) or spinal cord compression. Carpal tunnel syndrome may be present in the upper extremities. Enlargement of the liver or spleen may also occur.

Tests: A complete blood count (CBC) indicates decreased red blood cells (anemia) and other cell count discrepancies. Blood chemistry tests identify excess immunoglobulin and free immunoglobulin chains and can detect abnormally high levels of calcium (hypercalcemia) from bone breakdown. Free chains can also be detected in the urine. These chains are called Bence Jones proteins. Serum electrophoresis identifies the overproduced immunoglobulins and free chains. A bone marrow aspiration and biopsy show large amounts of plasma cells. Chromosome studies may reveal acquired chromosome abnormalities that may help with the prognosis.

Treatment

Treatment should be withheld until differential diagnoses are ruled out. Therapy for multiple myeloma includes simultaneous treatment of the disease and complications related to the disease. Treatment of the disease consists of anticancer drugs (chemotherapy) for at least one year to reduce the number of abnormal plasma cells. Radiation therapy is frequently given to areas of diseased bone for relieving pain and helping prevent fractures.

Anemia is treated with blood transfusions and medication to stimulate red cell production. Infections are treated with antibiotics. Skeletal damage may be prevented by monthly infusion of a drug that protects against skeletal complications.

Treatment of associated complications may include blood transfusions to correct anemia and antibiotics to combat infections. Hypercalcemia and renal failure are treated with a combination of increased fluid intake, hormones produced by the adrenal glands (glucocorticoids), and chemotherapy. Pain relievers (analgesics) are often needed. Bone marrow transplantation may be performed in younger individuals. Transplanted marrow may be the individual's own treated marrow (autologous transplant) or from a matched sibling donor (allogeneic transplant).

Prognosis

With treatment, the median survival time after diagnosis is 30 to 36 months. The outcome is better for individuals diagnosed with few, if any, symptoms. These individuals have a median survival of 10 years. Forty percent of individuals receiving a bone marrow transplant with their own marrow (autologous transplant) achieve regrowth of healthy bone marrow and experience a median post-transplant survival of 41 months. Thirty-six percent of individuals receiving marrow from a matched sibling donor (allogeneic transplant) achieve regrowth of healthy donor marrow. Transplant-related mortality in autologous transplants is 7% and in allogeneic transplants, 25-40%. Almost all individuals eventually relapse. Fewer than 5% survive longer than 10 years.

Differential Diagnosis

Similar symptoms can arise from benign conditions that involve chronic inflammation. These conditions are referred to as monoclonal gammopathy of undetermined significance (MGUS). Other diseases with a similar appearance include chronic lymphocytic leukemia, non-Hodgkin's lymphoma, primary amyloidosis, metastatic carcinoma, bone neoplasms, and macroglobulinemia.

Specialists

- Cardiologist
- Hematologist
- Nephrologist
- Oncologist
- Orthopedist
- Radiation Oncologist
- Surgeon

Work Restrictions / Accommodations

Due to pain and weakness, sedentary work and a shortened work schedule may be necessary.

Comorbid Conditions

Any condition that exacerbates the incidence of infection, skeletal damage, anemia, or immune weakness influences length of disability. Examples include diabetes, immune disorders, or blood diseases.

Complications

Complications include increased risk of infection, destruction of bone tissue that may result in fractures, spinal cord compression with possible neurological impairment, kidney damage or failure due to increased levels of calcium released during bone destruction and excess immunoglobulin in the blood, and anemia or bleeding disorders.

A condition where a substance containing protein and starch accumulates in tissues and organs (amyloidosis) occurs in approximately 15% of individuals with multiple myeloma.

Factors Influencing Duration

Length of disability is determined by the severity of symptoms, stage of disease, advanced age, complications of the disease, and response to treatment.

Length of Disability

Duration depends on stage and severity of symptoms. Disability may be permanent. Contact physician for additional information.

Failure to Recover

If an individual fails to recover within the maximum duration expectancy period, the reader may wish to reference the following questions to assist in better understanding the specifics of an individual's medical case.

Regarding diagnosis:

- Does individual have pain in the bones, especially the vertebrae, pelvis, ribs, and skull?
- Does individual have history of recurrent bacterial infections?
- Does individual show symptoms such as nausea, confusion, frequent urination (polyuria), and constipation?
- Were other conditions with similar symptoms such as MGUS, chronic lymphocytic leukemia, non-Hodgkin's lymphoma, primary amyloidosis, metastatic carcinoma, bone neoplasms, and macroglobulinemia ruled out?
- Did CBC show anemia? Were blood chemistry tests performed? What were the results?
- Has diagnosis of multiple myeloma been confirmed?

Regarding treatment:

- Has chemotherapy been effective in slowing progression of the disease?
- Has radiation therapy helped managed pain?
- Are complications such as anemia or infections being effectively treated with blood transfusions and antibiotics, respectively?
- Is individual a candidate for bone marrow transplant? Does individual have a matched sibling donor?
- Is skeletal damage being prevented?
- Are hypercalcemia and renal failure being treated with increased fluid intake, glucocorticoids, and chemotherapy?

Regarding prognosis:

- Has treatment been effective in slowing progression of the disease?
- Have complications been avoided or responded to treatment?
- Is pain being adequately managed?
- Did any complications occur such as increased risk of infection, destruction of bone tissue, spinal cord compression with possible neurological impairment, kidney damage or failure due to increased levels of calcium released during bone destruction and excess immunoglobulin in the blood, and anemia or bleeding disorders?
- Does individual have an underlying condition (other chronic disease such as diabetes, heart disease, kidney disease or lung disease) that may impact recovery?
- Would individual benefit from psychological counseling or enrollment in a multiple myeloma support group?

References

Ferri, Fred. Ferri's Clinical Advisor. St. Louis: Mosby, 2000.

Kyle, Robert. "Plasma Cell Disorders." Cecil Textbook of Medicine, 21st ed. Goldman, Lee, and J. Claude Bennett, eds. Philadelphia: W.B. Saunders Company, 2000. 977-987.

Multiple Sclerosis

Other names / synonyms: Disseminated Multiple Sclerosis, Disseminated Sclerosis, MS

Definition

Multiple sclerosis (MS) is a slowly progressive, lifelong chronic disease of the central nervous system. It is the most common cause of neurologic disability in young adults. In MS, local areas of the fatty substance that surrounds and insulates nerve cell fibers in the brain and spinal cord (myelin) are destroyed. This demyelination can cause slowed or blocked nerve impulse conduction and occurs in random patches (plaques) at any site where "white matter" (nerves encased in myelin) occurs. New evidence suggests that nerve fiber loss may provide an explanation for some of the neurologic deficits experienced by many persons with MS.

Although the exact cause of MS is unknown, many believe it to be a condition in which the body's defense system reacts against its own tissue (autoimmune disease). Such attacks may be linked to unknown environmental triggers such as viruses. There seems to be a genetic factor as well, as first degree relatives (parents, children and siblings) of those with MS have a 1-3% chance of getting the disease.

Since it is 5 times more common in temperate zones (such as the northern US, Canada, and Europe) than in the tropics, environment may also play a part. Living the first 15 years or more in a high risk area seems to increase the risk, suggesting that environmental factors acquired during this early period of life may be responsible for a susceptible person later developing the disease. MS generally occurs in persons between 20-40 years of age. In high-risk areas, the incidence is about 1:1000 people. Women outnumber men at a ratio of 2:1; the gender ratio is more balanced among those who develop symptoms at a later age. Whites are afflicted more than twice as often as other races. MS is essentially unknown among Eskimos, Gypsies, and Bantus, and rare among Native North and South Americans and Asian people.

Diagnosis

History: Because it can disrupt function in any area of the central nervous system (CNS), symptoms are varied, numerous, and of differing severity and duration. Approximately 50% of individuals will present with visual problems (including blurred or double vision, red-green color distortion, loss of vision in one eye, or optic nerve inflammation called optic neuritis). Other common symptoms include severe fatigue, muscle weakness in extremities, numbness, tingling and loss of sensation (paresthesias), unsteady or abnormal limb movements and positioning, loss of coordination, loss of balance or equilibrium, prominent gait, impaired dexterity, urinary problems, disturbed speech patterns, mental disturbances, impaired thermal sensation, muscle stiffness and spasms, tremor, and dizziness.

Cognitive problems with attention span, concentration, memory, and judgment may be noted at any time during the course of the disease. Depression is common, and over the course of the disease 5-10% of the individuals with MS will develop overt psychiatric disorders such as manic-depression (bipolar) or paranoia. Symptoms can last from several days to weeks.

MS can be characterized by a series of attacks followed by a period during which the symptoms of the disease lessen or disappear (complete or partial remission). After a period of stability, the next attack may not occur for several years and recur with new symptoms. In some persons, the disease progresses by gradual clinical decline with no distinct periods of remission. In females, relapses are common in the first 2-3 months following pregnancy. Diagnosis is often a considerable challenge because of the potential for an infinite array of signs and symptoms. After exclusion of all other causes, criteria for diagnosis must include at least two neurologic events separated in time by at least a month, occurring in more than one location within the central nervous system.

Physical exam: Physical findings are variable depending on which region of the central nervous system (CNS) is involved. Clumsiness, muscle weakness, and unsteady gait may be due to damage to the white matter in the brain. When the inflammation occurs in the portion of the brain involved with vision, the eye's pupillary response to light is often diminished. Involuntary movements of the eye (nystagmus) may be present. Inflammation of the spinal cord can cause extremity weakness or stiffness (spasticity). Urinary incontinence indicates that the nerve fibers to the bladder may be involved. Heat may cause symptoms to temporarily worsen. In later stages bladder and bowel control may be lost.

Tests: There is no specific diagnostic test for MS, but the accuracy of the diagnosis can be improved with several indicators. A spinal tap to obtain a sample of cerebrospinal fluid may be used to confirm the presence of an inflammatory lesion or to rule out other possible CNS diseases or infections. Recording nerve responses to various visual or auditory stimuli (evoked potentials) are routinely employed; absence of response or an abnormality in response is useful in detecting and localizing lesions in the CNS. Laboratory studies used to rule out other types of diseases include a complete blood count (CBC), serum glucose and serum electrolyte levels, blood clotting ability (coagulation studies), and urinalysis. Study of brain waves (EEG, or electroencephalogram) is abnormal in about one-third of the individuals who have MS. Two types of magnetic resonance imaging (T1 MRI and T2 MRI) are used to both diagnose and monitor the disease. They can also be helpful in excluding other CNS disorders, and can be more sensitive and specific in diagnosing MS than other imaging studies. The T2 MRI can identify the presence of MS lesions, while the T1 MRI with a pre-scan injection of gadolinium distinguishes new lesions from old ones. MRI findings often support a preliminary diagnosis (50% will progress to clinically definite MS within 2 years); however, 5% of suspected individuals with normal MRI findings will similarly progress to MS. Periodic testing and close monitoring, generally for years, is necessary.

Treatment

Search for a cure is still in progress. Treatment is designed to deal with acute exacerbations, modify the disease process, lessen the symptoms, and improve day-to-day lifestyle. Treatment is directed at modifying the course of the disease and primarily includes the use of anti-inflammatory (corticosteroids or beta-interferon) medications, procedures such as plasmapheresis that interfere with or suppress the body's immune response (immunosuppressants), or a combination of corticosteroid and immunosuppressant drugs. MS symptoms can be treated with drugs to address muscle weakness and spasticity, physical therapy to strengthen weakened muscles, and occupational therapy to teach individuals how to deal with stress both in the workplace and at home. Treatment also targets bladder, bowel, and sexual dysfunction, and pain management. One of the most difficult aspects for the individual with MS is the sense of uncertainty about the course of the disease. Psychiatric or psychological counseling may be necessary to provide support.

Prognosis

MS may progress rapidly, disabling the person by early adulthood or causing death within months of onset. However, the majority of young individuals with MS (70%) has a virtually normal life expectancy and can lead active and productive lives for years. The course of the disease and the rate of disability does, however, vary considerably from person to person. Some persons may have periods of acute exacerbation with prolonged full or partial remissions. While most individuals at least partially recover from the first attack, others gradually become more disabled, bedridden, and incontinent by early mid-life. A small group of individuals suffer gross disability within the first year. Although MS is not in itself fatal, those who are severely disabled may die from the complications of being bedridden or from recurrent infections.

Differential Diagnosis

Conditions with similar symptoms include tumors and infections of the central nervous system. Specific considerations might include amyotrophic lateral sclerosis (Lou Gehrig's Disease), brain stem tumors, pernicious anemia, spinal cord tumors, Guillain-Barré syndrome, Bell's Palsy, stroke, Parkinson's Disease, spinal cord injuries, syphilis, epilepsy, tick-borne disease, trigeminal neuralgia, systemic lupus erythematosus, chronic fatigue syndrome, and ruptured disk.

Specialists

- Internist
- Neurologist
- Occupational Therapist
- Ophthalmologist
- Physiatrist
- Physical Therapist
- Psychiatrist
- Psychologist
- Speech Therapist
- Urologist

Rehabilitation

Individuals with the diagnosis of multiple sclerosis require a range of rehabilitation services due to the chronic and often progressive nature of the disease. The frequency and duration of rehabilitation is contingent upon the increasing severity of the symptoms. Because this disease is chronic, individuals will require rehabilitation at regular intervals throughout their lives.

Occupational therapy addresses any difficulty with activities of daily living. Individuals learn strategies for dressing, bathing, and meal preparation that are geared toward their particular functional limitations. For example, an individual with decreased grip strength may benefit from thicker-handled eating utensils, while an individual with decreased standing balance may require a tub bench to facilitate bathing. Because there is a large component of fatigue associated with this disease, individuals learn energy conservation techniques, in which activities of daily living such as meal preparation are broken up into smaller components thereby making tasks more manageable. Individuals also learn strategies to complete tasks during the portion of the day that their energy level is highest.

Both physical and occupational therapy address decreased balance, strength, and range of motion. Speech therapy may be required for improved speech and eating. Individuals may require a consultation with a rehabilitation nurse and/or nutritionist who specializes in multiple sclerosis treatment if bowel and bladder function are compromised.

Individuals may benefit from ongoing consultation with a psychologist or psychiatrist to cope with the loss of functional and physical abilities and with any depression that may occur.

Work Restrictions / Accommodations

In advanced cases of MS, the individual may require handicapped, ADA-compliant, accessible facilities. Other restrictions and accommodations will depend on the nature of the employment, and nature and severity of symptoms. The individual may require frequent rest periods or changes in work hours, start times, and length of the work day because of fatigue. Visual disturbances may also impact the ability to perform certain activities.

Comorbid Conditions

Comorbid conditions include obesity and pre-existing mental illness or physical disability.

Complications

Complications include those related to symptoms such as extreme fatigue, deteriorating general health, urinary incontinence or frequent urinary tract infections, constipation or bowel incontinence, skin ulceration, painful muscle spasms and stiffness, paralysis, and depression or other mental health problems. Although MS is not in itself fatal, those who are severely disabled may die from the complications of being bedridden, including recurrent infections such as pneumonia, blood clot in the lungs (pulmonary embolism), infected open areas of the skin, and suicide.

Factors Influencing Duration

Factors that influence disability include response to treatment, the severity and frequency of symptoms and exacerbations, the degree of recovery from exacerbations, and any pre-existing mental or physical problems.

Length of Disability

The length of disability will depend on the severity and frequency of symptoms, the frequency of exacerbations, and the degree of recovery from prior episodes. The individual's specific work duties and requirements will also impact the length of disability. Disability may be permanent. Contact physician for additional information.

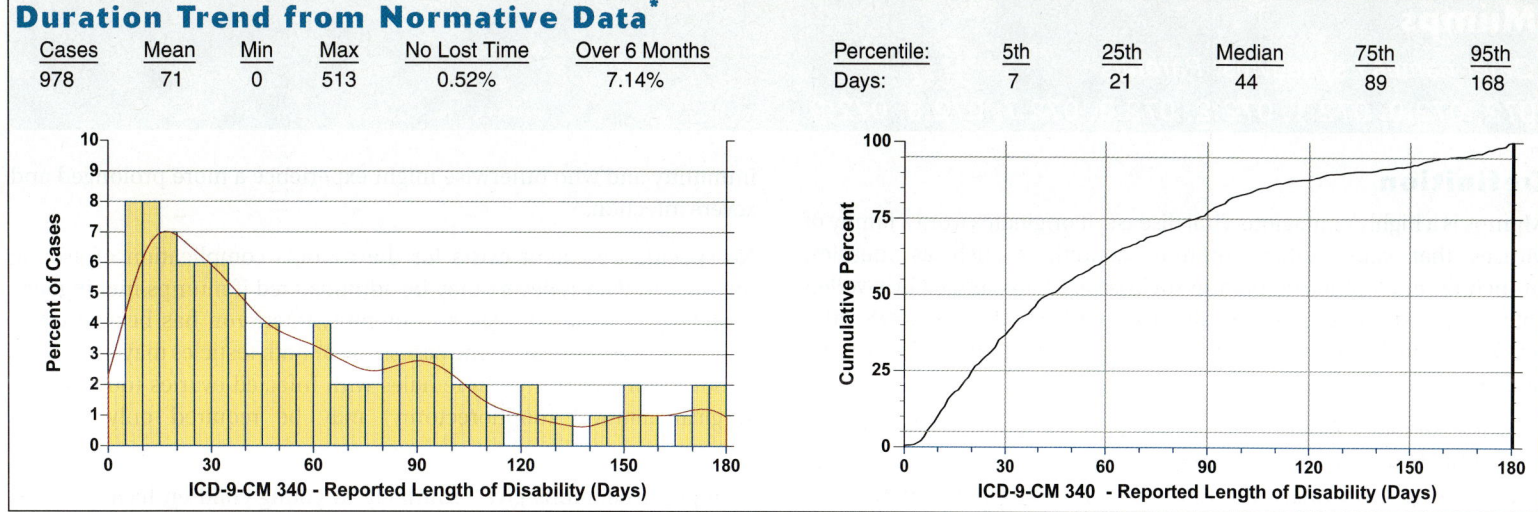

Failure to Recover

If an individual fails to recover within the maximum duration expectancy period, the reader may wish to reference the following questions to assist in better understanding the specifics of an individual's medical case.

Regarding diagnosis:

- Did the individual present with symptoms consistent with the diagnosis of MS?
- Does the individual have a history or risk factors for development of MS (such as living in a temperate climate, age or family history)?
- Were appropriate diagnostic tests done to rule out other conditions and establish the diagnosis of MS?
- Has the individual received consultation with the appropriate specialists?

Regarding treatment:

- Were anti-inflammatory and immunosuppressant agents prescribed?
- Is individual taking medication as prescribed?
- Has individual received physical, occupational, and/or speech therapy as indicated to help with activities of daily living?
- Is individual receiving appropriate psychiatric and/or psychological counseling?

Regarding prognosis:

- Based on the severity and frequency of symptoms what is the expected course of the disease?
- Is there complete or partial recovery after an exacerbation?
- Has the individual had good response to the present treatment? If not, are more aggressive interventions been considered?
- Is the individual severely disabled or bedridden?
- Has the individual experienced any complications of immobility that may impact prognosis? Have these complications been addressed in the treatment plan?

References

Anderson, Kenneth N., revision ed. Mosby's Medical, Nursing, and Allied Health Dictionary. St. Louis: Mosby, 1998.

Holmes, Nancy H., managing ed. Handbook of Diseases, 2nd ed. Springhouse, PA: Springhouse Corporation, 2000.

Lazoff, Marjorie, MD. Multiple Sclerosis. eMedicine.com. 12 Feb 2001. 24 Feb 2001 <http://www.emedicine.com/emerg/topic321.htm>.

Maleskey, Gale. Nature's Medicines. Emmaus, PA: Rodale Press, 1999.

O'Sullivan, Susan B. "Multiple Sclerosis." Physical Rehabilitation: Assessment and Treatment. O'Sullivan, Susan B., and Thomas J. Schmitz, eds. Philadelphia: F.A. Davis Company, 1994. 451-471.

Tierney, Lawrence M., Stephen J. McPhee, and Maxine A. Papadakis, eds. Current Medical Diagnosis and Treatment, 39th ed. New York: Lange Medical Books/McGraw-Hill, 2000.

Mumps

Other names / synonyms: Parotitis

072, 072.0, 072.1, 072.2, 072.3, 072.7, 072.8, 072.9

Definition

Mumps is a highly contagious viral disease. It originates from a family of viruses that cause other common conditions such as measles, bronchitis, and influenza (paramyxoviruses). Characterized by swollen salivary glands (parotids), the disease manifests 2 to 3 weeks after exposure and is contagious for a week preceding and following the appearance of symptoms.

The disease tends to occur in late winter or early spring. The virus is spread by direct contact or through the airborne droplets of coughing and sneezing. Individuals who have had a previous infection or vaccination are usually immune. While more commonly associated with children, mumps can infect individuals of all ages.

Mumps occurs worldwide, but prevalence has dropped dramatically in many countries where immunization is required. Prior to US vaccination programs in 1964, 212,000 cases of mumps were reported. In 1999, the number was reduced to 352 cases. Other countries with widespread immunization programs report similar reductions. Mumps vaccine is routinely used in 92% of developed countries but only in 24% of developing countries. Outbreaks and epidemics are common in countries without required immunization. In Poland where immunization is available only on a volunteer basis, a prevalence of 216 cases per 100,000 was reported in 1997, doubling the rate from the previous year.

Diagnosis

History: The individual usually has a history of exposure to someone who has been infected. Mumps is usually preceded by fever and general ill health (malaise). Symptoms include swelling and pain in the salivary glands especially in the parotid glands overlying the jaw. Twenty percent of infected adult males report swelling of at least one testicle (orchitis). Headache and neck pain are sometimes reported. In cases involving meningitis, the individual may complain of high fever, sensitivity to light (photophobia), and nausea. Symptoms are absent in about a third of those infected.

Physical exam: Swelling and tenderness are usually present in the parotid salivary glands. Pain on neck flexion is noted in cases of infection in areas near the brain and spinal cord (aseptic meningitis).

Tests: Diagnosis is confirmed through detection of the mumps IgM antibody in blood tests (serology) or through isolation and identification of the mumps virus (culture).

Treatment

While no effective therapy exists for an active infection, mumps usually resolves in a few days. A nonaspirin pain reliever (acetaminophen) may be administered to relieve pain and fever. Passive immunization in the form of mumps-specific antibodies help individuals with deficient immunity and who otherwise might experience a more prolonged and severe infection.

No specific treatment exists for the mumps complication of aseptic meningitis. Pain-relievers may be administered if mumps meningoencephalitis develops. In cases of orchitis, interferon has been used to relieve symptoms. In extreme cases, one or both testicles may need to be removed (orchiectomy). In females with infected ovaries (oophoritis), surgical removal (oophorectomy) may be required only in rare instances.

Mumps vaccinations given routinely to young children have reduced incidence of the disease by 95% in the US. Susceptible adults with normal immune systems can also benefit from the vaccine. The vaccine should not be given to individuals with suppressed immunity. In countries with active immunization programs, complications are rare.

Prognosis

Prognosis for mumps is excellent. Without complications, complete recovery should occur within 2 weeks from the appearance of symptoms. Individuals are then usually immune to the disease.

The outcome for complications of mumps depends on the affected tissue, extent of the infection, and immune status of the individual. Aseptic meningitis usually resolves on its own in about a week. Most individuals fully recover from mumps meningoencephalitis with recovery time dependent on the severity of symptoms. Individuals undergoing surgical treatment typically recover from orchitis in several days and oophoritis in about 2 weeks, depending on the extent and type of procedures.

Differential Diagnosis

Conditions with similar symptoms include staph infection in the parotid gland, Epstein-Barr virus (EBV), cytomegalovirus infections, and mononucleosis caused by EBV. Noninfectious causes of parotid gland enlargement are diabetes, malnutrition, and sarcoidosis. A tumor, cyst, or parotid duct obstruction can cause one-sided parotid enlargement. Other viral infections of the brain can occur that appear similar to mumps encephalitis.

Specialists

- Infectious Disease Physician
- Primary Care Provider
- Neurologist

Work Restrictions / Accommodations

Because it is a contagious disease, individuals with mumps should not be in the workplace. Risk of contagion usually ceases about a week after symptoms first appear. Work restrictions or accommodations are not usually associated with uncomplicated recovery from mumps infections.

Complementary and Alternative Therapies

Content is intended for awareness only. Treatments may or may not be effective. Scientific evidence may be lacking and some substances have potentially toxic effects. Dr. Presley Reed and the editors do not endorse the use of these therapies in the absence of consultation with a licensed medical professional.

Acupuncture -	Pressure on the Pingjian point may have a therapeutic affect on mumps.
Scrotum support -	May provide comfort for testicular swelling.

Comorbid Conditions

Mumps may be prolonged or made more severe by immune deficiency associated with AIDS, leukemia, lymphoma, generalized malignancy, steroid therapy, chemotherapy, or other infections.

Complications

Infection in areas near the brain and spinal cord is a common complication of mumps. The infection becomes more serious when it spreads into the brain (mumps meningoencephalitis). Infection can also spread to the ovaries (oophoritis), testicles (orchitis), breasts, kidneys, and pancreas (pancreatitis). Sterility, deafness, prolonged arthritis, and (sometimes) death have been reported. Swelling of the brain (encephalitis) may also occur. Miscarriage is possible if a woman is infected during the first 3 months of pregnancy. An individual can develop complications from mumps without demonstrating the primary symptoms of the disease.

Factors Influencing Duration

Length of disability is influenced more by the contagious nature of mumps than the symptoms of the disease. A simple mumps infection should be quarantined for 7 to 10 days after symptoms appear. The individual's immune status and the severity of the disease will influence the duration of disability, especially if the brain, spinal cord, or pancreas is affected.

Length of Disability

In most uncomplicated cases of mumps, the individual should fully recover. If the brain, spinal cord or pancreas are involved, the disability may be extended or require special accommodations after the individual returns to work.

Duration in Days

Job Classification	Minimum	Optimum	Maximum
Any work	7	10	14

Failure to Recover

If an individual fails to recover within the maximum duration expectancy period, the reader may wish to reference the following questions to assist in better understanding the specifics of an individual's medical case.

Regarding diagnosis:

- Has the individual had recent exposure to another person with mumps?
- Did the individual experience fever, malaise, and swollen parotid glands?
- Has diagnosis of mumps been confirmed by serology or culture?
- Have other viral infections been ruled out?
- Was a noninfectious cause of parotid gland enlargement such as diabetes, malnutrition, sarcoidosis, tumor, cyst or parotid duct obstruction considered in the differential diagnosis?

Regarding treatment:

- Did the infection resolve spontaneously?
- If appropriate, was individual given passive immunization?
- Was interferon or surgical intervention required to treat orchitis?

Regarding prognosis:

- Did adequate time elapse for complete recovery (2 weeks)?
- If the symptoms persisted, was the individual re-evaluated by a physician?
- Has the individual developed complications related to mumps such as encephalitis, meningoencephalitis, oophoritis, orchitis, pancreatitis, sterility, deafness, or prolonged arthritis?
- Does the individual have any conditions that could impact recovery (i.e., AIDS, leukemia, lymphoma, generalized malignancy, steroid therapy, chemotherapy, or other infections)?

References

Facts About Mumps for Adults. National Coalition for Adult Immunization. 01 Apr 2000. 27 Sept 2000 <http://www.nfid.org/factsheets/mumpsadult.html>.

Song, G.Y. "1000 Cases of Mumps Treated with Ear Needling on Pingjian Point (MA-T2)." Journal of Traditional Chinese Medicine 9 1 (1989): 14.

Muscle Injury

Other names / synonyms: Avulsions, Bruises, Detached Injury, Strains

ICD-9 Depends on Site

Definition

Any muscle in the body may be damaged or injured. The various types of muscle injuries are categorized as strains, bruises (contusions), detached injuries (avulsions), and exercise-induced injury or delayed-onset soreness. The thigh and the back muscles are the most commonly injured. Athletes are at a particularly high risk for muscle injuries caused by overstretching, sudden muscle contraction (weight lifting), or rapid changes in speed or direction (sprinting, tennis).

Individuals who are inflexible or fail to warm up sufficiently prior to engaging in physical activity have an increased risk for muscle strains. Muscle strains are classified as mild, moderate, or severe. Mild strains refer to slightly pulled muscle without tearing of muscle or tendon fibers. Moderate strains involve tearing of fibers that result in diminished strength, and severe strains are a rupture of a tendon-bone attachment with separation of muscle fibers. Severe strains may require surgical repair.

Muscle contusions are also classified as mild, moderate, or severe. Contusions refer to injuries that do not involve a break in the skin but cause damage to muscle fibers and other soft tissues. Blood seeps out of damaged small blood vessels into the surrounding tissue forming black-and-blue marks beneath the skin (ecchymosis). After injury, gravity may pull the blood downward so that the black-and-blue "bruise" may be far from the contusion site. Blood can form (hematoma) within the muscle. Muscle contusions frequently occur in athletes participating in contact sports like football, hockey, and boxing.

Tearing or ripping the muscle away from an attachment point (avulsions) is usually caused by an intense force or dynamic overload. Avulsion injuries most frequently occur in the groin and upper connections of the hamstring muscles. Individuals with rapid growth, stress fractures, overdeveloped muscles in combination with an immature skeletal system, or weakened bones (osteoporosis) are at risk for avulsion injuries.

Exercise-induced injuries and delayed-onset soreness occur when stress applied to a muscle exceeds the tolerance level of the muscle and muscle attachments. Viral infection, performance of a new activity, or excessive away-from-center (eccentric) work can predispose an individual to this type of injury.

Muscle strains are common injuries, and in any year 6% of the population of the US experience one of these strains. Each year, contusions are reported in 5% of the US population. Exercise-induced injuries and delayed-onset soreness are also very common. In the US, approximately 165,000 work-related contusion injuries occur every year; 799,000 work-related muscle strains lead to time away from work.

Diagnosis

History: Symptoms of a muscle strain include swelling, constant pain or pain with muscle use, and muscle weakness or loss of muscle function. Muscle contusion symptoms include pain, swelling, and local skin discoloration. A muscle avulsion usually causes severe pain, swelling, and loss of function in the affected limb. An exercise-induced injury may result in swelling, joint stiffness, pain, and usually a decrease or loss of muscle function 1 to 2 days after exercising. Delayed-onset soreness refers to muscle pain, weakness, and a decreased range of motion occurring 1 to 3 days following the performance of a new exercise. Headaches or dizziness (vertigo) may also be present if neck muscles are injured.

Physical exam: The exam may reveal swelling, muscle tenderness, ecchymosis, and hard areas in the affected muscle. Specific "trigger points" of pain may be present. Movement may be decreased with the individual guarding the affected muscle.

Tests: Plain x-rays, CT, MRI, nerve conduction tests, or electromyography (EMG) may be done to determine the extent of the injury and rule out bone fractures.

Treatment

Mild strains, exercise-induced injuries, delayed-onset soreness, and most contusions are treated by resting the affected muscle, applying ice, initially, or heat, later, compression, and the use of pain relievers (analgesics) or muscle relaxants. Open injuries are treated with surgical cleansing (débridement), repair, and antibiotic therapy. Muscle tears may also require surgery to realign (reapproximate) the torn edges. Avulsions require surgery to reattach the muscle to the tendon. Traction, a cervical collar, splints, crutches, or a cane may be prescribed. Corticosteroids, in rare circumstances, may be given to reduce inflammation especially in chronic conditions. When recovery is complete, gradual strengthening of the muscle is important.

Prognosis

Most contusions resolve completely without residual symptoms within a few weeks. Delayed-onset soreness resolves within a few days. Mild strains heal in 2 to 10 days, moderate strains in 10 days to 6 weeks, and severe strains in 6 to 10 weeks. Avulsions usually require 6 to 10 weeks to heal. A longer recovery period (6 to 10 weeks) is also necessary for any muscle injury requiring surgical repair.

Differential Diagnosis

Conditions with similar symptoms include bone fractures, cerebral palsy, fibromyalgia, rheumatism, hypotonia, hypertonia, spasticity, rigidity, spastic or hysterical paralysis, muscle fatigue, muscular dystrophies, myasthenia gravis, lumbar disc syndrome, and whiplash.

Specialists

- Orthopedic Surgeon
- Physiatrist
- Physical Therapist

Rehabilitation

Rehabilitation of a muscle injury depends on the type, location, and extent of the injury. For example, muscles can be strained by excessive stretching or forced contracture. They can also be torn and need surgical repair. Each muscle performs a different function and responds differently to injury as well as treatment. Consequently, rehabilitation protocol for a strain is different than that of a tear.

A classic example of a muscle strain is a groin strain. Rehabilitation from a groin strain usually requires progressive stretching and bilateral muscle strength balancing. Gentle stretching and adduction and flexion exercises without resistance can start after initial pain and swelling subsides. Stair climbing and cycling exercises begin when the individual tolerates the activity. Once range of motion for the injured leg comes within 10 degrees of the noninjured leg, more advanced stretches and strength training are integrated into therapy. Strength training that stresses adductor and hip flexor muscles continues until the muscle strength proportions between and within both legs are balanced.

Rehabilitation from surgical repair of a muscle is more complicated than that of a muscle strain since the formation of scar tissue disrupts the muscle regeneration process. More stages in rehabilitation are needed to ensure proper muscle function, biomechanically as well as biochemically. When a muscle is torn and/or surgically repaired, scar tissue forms. One goal of rehabilitation is to prevent adhesions or scar tissue from forming. The individual undergoes cross-friction massage and range-of-motion exercises to keep scar formation to a minimum.

Because of limited motion, a repaired muscle may lose up to 50% of its muscle strength. The phases of rehabilitation follow pain and swelling (edema) management, passive and active range of motion to the affected area, light resistance and coordination of the limb, and functional retraining. Therapy protocol differs in that the prescribed exercises are limb-and degree-of-injury specific.

The first part of therapy is to control edema and pain. If the muscles of the hand are affected, the hand should be held overhead with the individual performing light fist motions to increase blood flow. If repair was done to the leg area, the leg should be elevated higher than the heart while individual is in a reclined position.

During the range of motion phase of therapy, the individual engages in exercises that help increase limb movement.

Once pain and swelling subside, the individual performs more resistive exercises. The goal in this stage is to build muscle strength and flexibility of the affected area. An individual may participate in more functional activities such as riding a stationary bike at low resistance or starting to grip objects. Alternative methods of therapy during this stage may include a whirlpool or full aqua therapy.

One major aspect of therapy is to regain muscle balance in the affected limb. For example, building muscles of the wrist and fingers (including the thumb) is crucial for proper hand function. Muscle imbalances cause uneven loading to the limb while individual performs tasks thus causing further injury. The functional phase combines several different techniques such as using a balancing platform to build lower body reaction.

Work Restrictions / Accommodations

Repetitive motion, strenuous activities, or movement of the affected limb may be restricted. For leg injuries, crutches or a cane may be required or a brace may need to be worn over the affected muscle or limb. Muscle injuries in a lower limb may affect the individual's ability to walk, stand, or sit for extended periods of time. The individual with upper limb muscle injury may be temporarily unable to lift and carry heavy or bulky objects, operate equipment, or perform other tasks requiring the use of both hands. Muscle injury in the dominant arm or hand may affect fine motor skills such as those needed to write legibly, type well, or work in a laboratory. Depending on work duties, the individual may need to be temporarily reassigned. Training on proper lifting and movement is helpful.

Complementary and Alternative Therapies

Content is intended for awareness only. Treatments may or may not be effective. Scientific evidence may be lacking and some substances have potentially toxic effects. Dr. Presley Reed and the editors do not endorse the use of these therapies in the absence of consultation with a licensed medical professional.

Contrast baths -	Alternate application of hot and cold is said to improve circulation.
Electrical stimulation -	May stimulate healing.
Arnica -	Used externally, it may help to relieve pain, bruising, and swelling.
Witch hazel -	Used externally, this may act as an anti-inflammatory.
Ice -	May help control bleeding (bruising) and numb pain.
Therapeutic massage -	After healing takes place, gentle massage may increase circulation and prevent soft tissues from adhering to bones, tendons, or ligaments.
Ultrasound -	Said to stimulate cell healing.
Whirlpool -	Said to improve circulation and stimulate healing

Comorbid Conditions

Coexisting conditions that may impact recovery include obesity, bleeding disorders (e.g., hemophilia), fibromyalgia, poor nutrition, osteoporosis, and other injuries such as a fracture or laceration.

Complications

Resumption of strenuous physical activity before the muscle has healed completely can lead to reinjury. A muscle may be so extensively damaged that it must be removed. Hematomas within the muscle prolong recovery time and delay return of function. Pressure on the muscle from swelling or bleeding can result in compartment syndrome, causing permanent muscle and nerve damage. Disintegration of muscle (rhabdomyolysis) can occur. In a condition known as myositis ossificans, damaged muscle converts into a bone-like substance (ossification) that causes disfigurement and impaired muscle function.

Factors Influencing Duration

Length of disability may be influenced by the location of injured muscle, type of muscle injury, severity of injury, type of treatment, response to treatment, and any coexisting injuries (laceration, fracture) or complications.

Length of Disability

Duration depends on location of muscle injury, severity, job requirements, and whether accommodations can be made for an individual with a muscle injury.

Groin strain.

Duration in Days

Job Classification	Minimum	Optimum	Maximum
Sedentary work	0	3	7
Light work	0	3	7
Medium work	3	7	14
Heavy work	7	10	21
Very Heavy work	7	10	21

Quadriceps or hamstring in the thigh.

Duration in Days

Job Classification	Minimum	Optimum	Maximum
Sedentary work	1	3	7
Light work	3	7	14
Medium work	7	14	28
Heavy work	14	28	56
Very Heavy work	28	56	112

Failure to Recover

If an individual fails to recover within the maximum duration expectancy period, the reader may wish to reference the following questions to assist in better understanding the specifics of an individual's medical case.

Regarding diagnosis:

- Has muscle injury been confirmed?
- Has type of injury been identified?
- Did individual experience any complications such as reinjury; damage so extensive that muscle must be removed; compartment syndrome causing permanent muscle and nerve damage; disintegration (rhabdomyolysis) of muscle; and a condition known as myositis ossificans in which damaged muscle converts into a bone-like substance (ossification) causes disfigurement and impaired muscle function?
- Does individual have an underlying condition that may impact recovery?

Regarding treatment:

- Has individual overused the injured muscle?
- Is individual following the plan of treatment?
- Was surgery required to repair a muscle tear?
- Was individual treated with corticosteroids?

Regarding prognosis:

- How severe are the persisting symptoms? Are they incapacitating?
- Can the individual perform normal activities of daily life?
- Would individual benefit from muscle conditioning or additional physical therapy?
- Has the individual injured this same muscle before?
- Did the individual resume strenuous physical activity before the muscle was completely healed?
- Have X-rays, MRI, or other scans been used to detect muscle tears, avulsions, fractures, or complicating conditions?

References

Bonfiglio, Richard, L. Anita Cone, and Francis Lagattuta. "Pathophysiology of Soft Tissue Injuries." Soft Tissue Injuries: Diagnosis and Treatment. Windsor, Robert, and Dennis Lox, eds. Philadelphia: Hanley & Belfus, Inc, 1998. 1-11.

Lagattuta, Francis, Terry Nicola, and Lawrence Frank. "Soft Tissue Injuries of the Lower Limbs." Soft Tissue Injuries: Diagnosis and Treatment. Windsor, Robert, and Dennis Lox, eds. Philadelphia: Hanley & Belfus, Inc, 1998. 105-128.

Muscle Spasm

Other names / synonyms: Muscle Cramp

728.85

Definition

A muscle spasm is the sudden, uncontrollable cramp (contraction) of one or more muscles.

Individuals who fail to properly stretch or condition muscles may experience cramping during or following extensive exercise. Wearing of poorly fitted or elevated shoes also commonly leads to cramping of foot muscles. Muscle spasms may also result from excess sweating (dehydration) or a prolonged period of sitting, standing or lying in an uncomfortable position. The condition also commonly occurs during pregnancy.

Muscle spasms, specifically spasticity, may be signs of more serious disorders affecting the central nervous system such as spastic cerebral palsy (CP), upper motor neuron diseases, or a stroke. Many diseases, medications or other factors may cause muscle spasms. In some cases, the contractions may have no identifiable cause.

Almost everyone will experience some form of a muscle cramp in his/her lifetime, often associated with unusual physical exertion.

Diagnosis

History: The individual may complain of contractions and sudden pain in a muscle, with symptoms that worsen with movement. The muscle contractions may come and go. The individual may report unusual physical exertion or prolonged sitting, standing, or reclining in an uncomfortable position prior to onset.

Physical exam: The exam may reveal muscles that are visibly contracted while feeling hard and tense to the touch. The individual may favor the muscle and lean to one side. When movement is attempted in the affected area, decreased movement and accompanying visible discomfort may be observed.

Tests: Blood tests (serology) for the presence of dissolved salts (electrolytes) may be indicated if cramps are recurrent, possibly associated with dehydration or other factors. If an underlying disease is suspected, other appropriate tests such as those assessing motor function may be necessary.

Treatment

Warm, moist heat or ice packs may be applied to the area. Oral pain relievers (analgesics) and muscle relaxants may be prescribed. Massage and gradual stretching of the muscle can be helpful. The individual may be advised to warm up muscles before exercising and to drink fluids before and during exercise. If muscle spasms are caused by an underlying disease or disorder, treatments may include chemical deadening of nerves (chemodenervation) through injection of medication such as botulinum toxin. Other conditions causing muscle spasms may be helped through electrical stimulation of nerves in affected areas (TENS, or Transcutaneous Electric Nerve Stimulation).

Prognosis

In most cases, spasms are relatively mild and the muscle typically will recover on its own within a matter of minutes. Pain and soreness might linger, but likely will resolve within several days. If an underlying disease or disorder is present, the outcome could vary considerably. Some conditions such as spastic cerebral palsy may cause ongoing (chronic) muscle spasms.

Differential Diagnosis

Other possibilities are muscle strain or twitches, heat exhaustion, hemifacial spasm, hardening of the arteries (ischemic claudication), and rare metabolic diseases of the muscle.

Specialists

- Neurologist
- Orthopedist
- Physiatrist
- Rheumatologist

Rehabilitation

Individuals with muscle spasm may require outpatient physical therapy. The goals of physical therapy are reduction of pain and spasm and the prevention of further injury.

The reduction of pain and spasm can be achieved in a variety of ways. Basic instruction for muscle spasm reduction includes intermittent use of a heating pad or ice pack, e.g., 15-minutes at time, followed by stretching of the affected muscle. Individuals learn that to prevent the pain and muscle spasm from increasing that they must stretch diligently. For persistent muscle spasm, therapists may passively stretch the affected muscles. Therapists may also utilize massage to eliminate spasm. Ultrasound, which uses high-frequency sound waves to provide deep heating, may also be used to break up muscle spasm.

Work Restrictions / Accommodations

If the condition persists, activities requiring lifting or excessive physical exertion may be restricted. The individual may require special physical conditioning, or might need to be reassigned to other tasks if an underlying disease is the cause of spasms. If tasks require considerable physical endurance and exertion, plenty of fluids should be provided at the work site to prevent dehydration and possible recurrence of muscle spasms.

Complementary and Alternative Therapies

Content is intended for awareness only. Treatments may or may not be effective. Scientific evidence may be lacking and some substances have potentially toxic effects. Dr. Presley Reed and the editors do not endorse the use of these therapies in the absence of consultation with a licensed medical professional.

Fluid replacement - Adequate fluid intake can help prevent muscle spasms accompanying dehydration during or following moderate to strenuous physical activity. The American College of Sports Medicine recommends drinking about 17 ounces of fluid 2 hours prior to activity and at regular intervals during physical exertion. Fluids containing carbohydrates and/or electrolytes are recommended if exertion lasts longer than 1 hour.

Comorbid Conditions

Muscle spasms may be more frequent or pronounced in individuals with poor physical conditioning. Underlying diseases or factors such as obesity also may hamper adequate physical conditioning.

Complications

Muscle tearing or other injury will complicate the treatment of cramps. The existence of an underlying disease such as a stroke or spastic cerebral palsy may cause ongoing (chronic) spasticity. Neurological injury can also result in recurrent or persistent spasticity such as seen in paraplegics or quadriplegics.

Factors Influencing Duration

Individuals in poor physical condition may be more prone to experience muscle spasms associated with tasks requiring physical exertion such as lifting or straining. Muscles could be re-injured, lengthening disability time.

Length of Disability

Duration in Days

Job Classification	Minimum	Optimum	Maximum
Sedentary work	0	1	2
Light work	0	1	2
Medium work	1	1	2
Heavy work	1	1	3
Very Heavy work	1	1	3

Failure to Recover

If an individual fails to recover within the maximum duration expectancy period, the reader may wish to reference the following questions to assist in better understanding the specifics of an individual's medical case.

Regarding diagnosis:

- Did individual experience a sudden muscle spasm and pain following unusual or prolonged physical exertion?
- Was muscle tension or favoring the affected muscle noted during the physical exam?
- Were diagnostic tests done to rule out electrolyte imbalances or other conditions (i.e., muscle tears or strain, muscle twitches, heat exhaustion, hemifacial spasm, claudication)?

Regarding treatment:

- Was the individual treated appropriately with rest, ice and analgesics?
- Did the individual receive instruction about proper warm-up and cool down to prevent recurrent spasm?
- Has the individual been compliant with treatment recommendations?

Regarding prognosis:

- Did the condition resolve with appropriate relaxation and massage of the muscle, or has individual continued to experience spasms?
- Has the individual been tested for a possible underlying disease or condition that may be causing the spasms?
- Was the muscle spasm associated with any complications such as muscle tearing or other injury to the affected area?

References

Hayes, Karen W. Manual for Physical Agents. Norwalk: Appleton & Lange, 1993.

Tappan, Frances M. Healing Massage Techniques. Norwalk: Appleton & Lange, 1988.

Myalgia and Myositis

Other names / synonyms: Muscle Ache, Muscle Pain

729, 729.1

Definition

Myalgia means muscle pain. The pain may be localized, as in a muscle strain or crushing injury, or generalized with an underlying disease such as a viral infection. Myositis means muscle inflammation. Myositis can cause muscle pain, weakness, or both.

Diseases that may cause myalgia and/or myositis include viruses such as HIV, influenza, Epstein-Barr, herpes simplex, or poliomyelitis. Bacterial infections causing similar symptoms include strep throat, Lyme disease and tetanus. Fungi causing histoplasmosis and parasites associated with malaria, toxoplasmosis and trichinosis also can create symptoms that include myalgia and/or myositis. Other conditions that may produce similar symptoms include vaccinations against various diseases (immunizations) and medications such as anticonvulsants, antibiotics, anticancer agents, cholesterol-lowering agents, and diuretics. Abuse of substances such as alcohol, amphetamines, cocaine and narcotics also may cause symptoms. Poisons including strychnine and snake, insect or spider bites may create related symptoms. Exposure to toxic chemicals and other environmental factors such as ultraviolet light also may be linked to symptoms. Deficiencies in vitamin C and B-complex, as well as mineral and electrolyte deficiencies involving calcium, magnesium, phosphorus, potassium or sodium can cause myalgia. The condition can also result from certain endocrine and metabolic disorders such as hypothyroidism, hyperthyroidism, Addison's disease, hypoparathyroidism, diabetes mellitus, metastatic neoplasm, and diabetic neuropathy. Eosinophilia-myalgia with accompanying severe or chronic muscle pain results from ingestion of a contaminated dietary supplement known as L-tryptophan.

Myalgia and myositis also are commonly linked to connective tissue diseases (collagen vascular diseases), which can include disorders such as rheumatoid arthritis, systemic lupus erythematosus, polymyositis, dermatomyositis and polymyalgia. In central nervous system disorders, myalgia may be related to involuntary muscle movement (spasticity) that may accompany multiple sclerosis, amyotrophic lateral sclerosis, and spinal cord injuries. Muscle pain also can accompany rigidity caused by Parkinson's disease. Fibromyalgia and myofascial pain syndrome also involve chronic muscle pain.

Other conditions in which myalgia and/or myositis may be present include a disease of unknown cause that can cause widespread inflammation or growths (sarcoidosis). Swelling that compromises circulation and nerve function (compartment syndrome) also can cause symptoms. Other possible causes of myalgia and/or myositis are certain inherited metabolic disorders and muscle pain with no apparent physical basis (psychogenic myalgia). Individuals diagnosed with myositis may have underlying conditions such as pneumonia or other lung diseases.

Since myalgia and myositis are symptoms rather than disorders, specific incidence is unknown. About 15% of the US population annually consults physicians regarding discomfort or pain in skeletal muscles.

Diagnosis

History: The individual may report trauma, an insect bite, or drug ingestion that preceded muscle pain or weakness. Individuals may describe symptoms occurring virtually anywhere in the body, with severity of pain ranging from dull or aching to cramping and discomfort that may include stiffness or weakness. Other symptoms may include fever, chills, sweats, and weight loss. The individual may experience neurological symptoms such as numbness, tremor, visual disturbances, or ringing in the ears. Depression, sleep disturbances, fatigue, or rash may be reported. Respiratory, cardiac, or gastrointestinal symptoms sometimes accompany the condition.

Physical exam: To help identify possible underlying causes, the individual should be asked to describe whether onset was gradual or sudden and whether symptoms are constant or intermittent. The exact location of pain or discomfort should be noted. Stiffness or weakness may be evident in the individual's gait, posture, and coordination. Wasting (atrophy), enlargement (hypertrophy), or permanent shortening (contracture) of the muscles may also be evident. Muscle tone (natural tension) and strength are assessed through range-of-motion and resistance exercises. Examination by touching (palpation) may reveal tenderness or abnormal muscle tension (spasm). Joint disease can be ruled out with examination of joints for swelling, redness, accumulations of fluid (effusion), localized tenderness, increased temperature, and mobility.

Tests: Blood tests detect inflammation and rule out underlying conditions. These may include a complete blood count (CBC) and measurement of the speed of sedimentation of red blood cells (ESR, or erythrocyte sedimentation rate). Various tests to detect presence of specific antibodies in the blood may be needed to identify underlying diseases. Tests may also be administered to evaluate levels of electrolytes, hormones, and various other chemistries (calcium, phosphate, serum enzymes) to help determine presence of injury or breakdown in muscle tissue. A urine test (urinalysis) assists diagnosis of muscle disorders. Electromyography (EMG) and nerve conduction studies (NCS) measure the electrical activity and proper functioning of muscles. X-ray, CT, and bone scans can diagnose bone and joint disorders, differentiating them from muscle disorders. A muscle biopsy may be needed to identify inherited metabolic disorders, connective tissue disease, eosinophilia-myalgia, sarcoidosis, trichinosis, and possible toxic agents. Other imaging tests including MRI and ultrasonography can detect any inflammation.

Treatment

Treatment depends on the specific diagnosis. Nonspecific myalgias due to overexertion, systemic viral infection, or immunization can usually be relieved by over-the-counter pain medicines (analgesics). Other types of treatment are highly dependent on the underlying cause of muscle pain or inflammation. Passive stretching, heat, or massage may provide temporary relief. Ultrasound, nerve stimulation (transcutaneous electrical nerve stimulation, or T.E.N.S. unit), and application of deep pressure to tender or trigger points are useful in some types of myalgia such as fibromyalgia. Individuals with myositis may be treated with steroids or drugs suppressing immune responses to reduce inflammation.

Prognosis

Since myalgia and myositis are symptoms of an underlying condition, the expected outcome depends on the specific diagnosis. Nonspecific myalgia due to overexertion or immunization is usually mild and self-limited. Myalgia accompanying widespread (systemic) infection usually resolves along with the underlying condition. However, if ongoing (chronic) diseases such as multiple sclerosis or diabetes mellitus are the underlying cause, symptoms may continue indefinitely.

Differential Diagnosis

Rheumatoid arthritis, osteoarthritis, and other diseases or injuries affecting joints display symptoms similar to myalgia. Conditions that mimic muscle inflammation or that manifest as a form of myositis include trichinosis, tuberculous pyomyositis, Lyme myositis, influenza myositis, viral myositis, toxoplasma myositis, trypanosomiasis, osteomyelitis, dermatomyositis, polymyositis, neuromuscular complications accompanying AIDS, and paraneoplastic neuropathy. Other conditions with symptoms similar to myalgia or myositis include cellulitis, deep vein thrombosis, wasting syndrome, and hematoma.

Specialists

- Internist
- Orthopedic Surgeon
- Physiatrist

Work Restrictions / Accommodations

Brief limitations on physical activity may be necessary due to muscle pain, stiffness, weakness, or fatigue. The nature and duration of the limitations depend on the specific diagnosis, affected muscles, and severity of symptoms. Workplace accommodations may include avoidance of tasks that require physical strength or stress certain affected muscles. Time off may be required for rest and recovery from underlying conditions such as an infection or disease. If the underlying condition causing symptoms is ongoing (chronic), the individual may require permanent assignment to less physically demanding activities.

Complementary and Alternative Therapies

Content is intended for awareness only. Treatments may or may not be effective. Scientific evidence may be lacking and some substances have potentially toxic effects. Dr. Presley Reed and the editors do not endorse the use of these therapies in the absence of consultation with a licensed medical professional.

Nutritional therapy— Lack of vitamins C and B-complex and/or minerals including calcium, magnesium, phosphorus, potassium, or sodium may be related to some forms of myalgia.

Comorbid Conditions

Many conditions display symptoms similar to those of myalgia or myositis including ongoing (chronic) diseases such as AIDS or diabetes mellitus. Recovery may be hampered if the individual has a disability that restricts or prevents exercise therapy, which may be beneficial in the treatment of certain types of myalgia. Individuals who are addicted to substances such as certain drugs or alcohol are less likely to find relief from symptoms.

Complications

Complications may accompany the many underlying diseases or conditions causing symptoms. Some diseases may be ongoing (chronic) or degenerative, such as multiple sclerosis or Parkinson's disease. Serious, underlying injuries like those involving the spinal cord can create chronic symptoms. An undetected underlying disease such as diabetes mellitus or hypothyroidism usually causes chronic symptoms unless appropriate treatments are initiated.

Factors Influencing Duration

Symptoms may be related to ongoing (chronic) conditions such as multiple sclerosis or AIDS. Depending on the reasons for the condition, some individuals may not be able to return to work as quickly as others. Disability depends on the type of duties involved.

Length of Disability

Duration depends on cause and diagnosis. Length of disability depends on the specific diagnosis of the condition causing symptoms. Nonspecific myalgia due to overexertion or immunization usually resolves in 1 to 2 days. Myalgia following immunization for yellow fever may last 2 to 3 weeks.

Duration in Days

Job Classification	Minimum	Optimum	Maximum
Sedentary work	0	3	7
Light work	0	3	7
Medium work	1	3	7
Heavy work	1	3	7
Very Heavy work	1	3	7

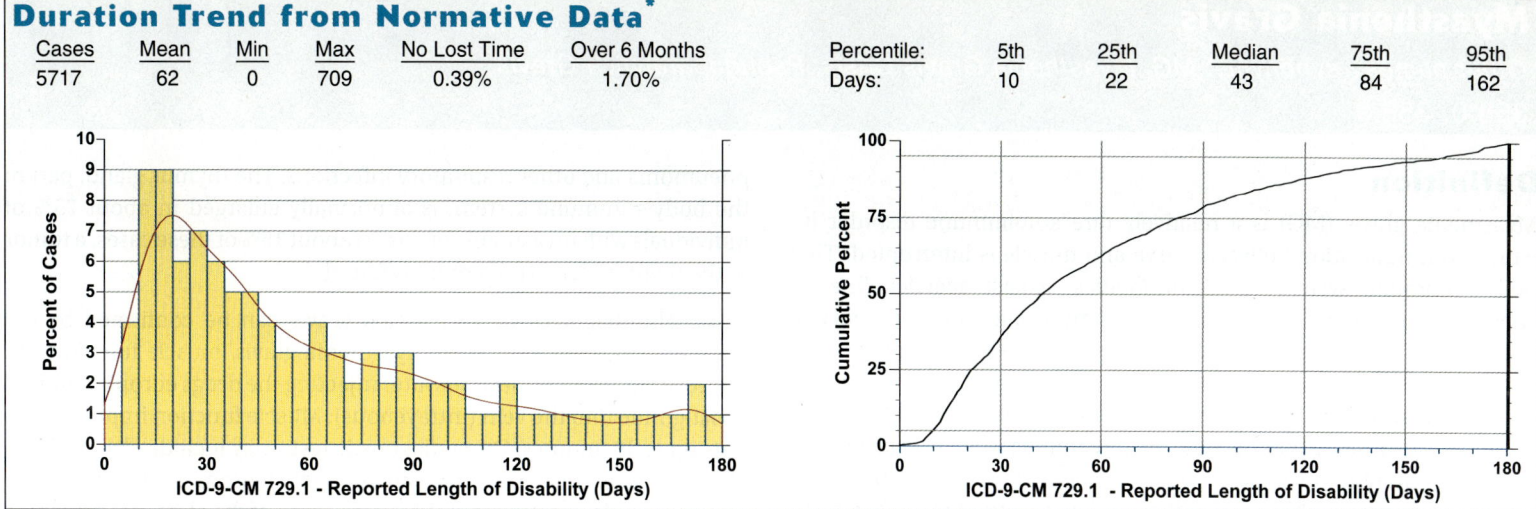

Failure to Recover

If an individual fails to recover within the maximum duration expectancy period, the reader may wish to reference the following questions to assist in better understanding the specifics of an individual's medical case.

Regarding diagnosis:

- Is the underlying condition causing the myalgia and myositis known?
- Does the individual have any viral illnesses?
- Has the individual had any recent trauma?
- Does the individual have any bacterial, fungal, or parasitic illnesses?
- Has the individual recently had any vaccinations?
- Are they on any medications with a side effect of myalgia and myositis?
- Do they abuse alcohol or drugs such as amphetamines, cocaine, or narcotics?
- Have they recently been exposed to any poisons? Toxic chemicals? Ultraviolet light?
- Do they have any vitamin or mineral deficiencies? Any metabolic disorders?
- Have they ingested L-tryptophan?
- Does the individual have any collagen vascular diseases? Central nervous system disorders? Parkinson's disease? Fibromyalgia? Myofascial pain syndrome? Sarcoidosis? Psychogenic myalgia?
- How does the individual describe pain or weakness (fever, chills, sweats, or weight loss)?
- Does the individual report any numbness, tremor, visual disturbances, ringing in the ears, depression, sleep disturbances, fatigue, or rash?
- Are there respiratory, cardiac, or gastrointestinal symptoms?
- Was the onset of the symptoms gradual or sudden? Are they constant or intermittent?
- Were any abnormalities noted in the individual's gait, posture, or coordination?
- Is there any atrophy, hypertrophy, or contracture of the muscles? Is strength normal? Was there any muscle tenderness to palpation? Joint tenderness?
- Has the individual had blood tests and urinalysis? EMG? Nerve conduction studies? X-rays? CT scan? Bone scan? MRI? Ultrasound?
- Have conditions with similar symptoms been ruled out?

Regarding treatment:

- Has the underlying condition been determined?
- Is it being treated?

Regarding prognosis:

- Is the individual's employer able to accommodate any necessary restrictions?
- Does the individual have any conditions that could affect ability to recover?
- Does the individual have any complications?

References

Andreoli, Thomas, MD, et al. Cecil Essentials of Medicine. Philadelphia: W.B. Saunders Company, 1997.

Zafar, Mohammed J. Infectious Myositis. eMedicine.com. 18 Jul 2000. 1 Jan 2001 <http://www.emedicine.com>.

Myasthenia Gravis

Other names / synonyms: MG, Myasthenia Gravis Crisis, Pseudoparalytica Gravis

358.0, 358.9

Definition

Myasthenia gravis (MG) is a relatively rare autoimmune disorder in which communication between nerve and muscle is interrupted. The body's immune system forms antibodies against acetylcholine, a substance that is needed for proper communication between nerves and muscles. Receptors in the muscles responsible for picking up and correctly interpreting nerve impulses are destroyed. Consequently, affected muscles fail to respond or respond only weakly to nerve impulses. The disease may become life threatening when it weakens the respiratory system (myasthenic crisis). MG is a chronic condition that follows an unpredictable course of periodic exacerbations and remissions.

The cause of MG is unknown. There is, however, a genetic predisposition to autoimmune diseases in women and in individuals with certain substances(antigens) that cause the formation of antibodies. The disease has also occassionally been triggered by a drug reaction or has been associated with organ transplantation. Because antibodies circulate in the blood stream, mothers with myasthenia gravis may pass the disease through their placenta to the unborn child (neonatal myasthenia). Although the infant may then be born with muscle weakness, it disappears within a few weeks after birth.

MG affects 1 in 25,000 people at any age, but incidence peaks between 20-40 years of age. It is 3 times more common in women than in men in this age group. After age 40, the gender incidence is similar. There is, however, a slight male predominance in the older adult peak (older than 50 years). Remissions occur in about 25% of individuals.

Diagnosis

History: Myasthenia gravis (MG) is characterized by chronic fatigue and muscle weakness, especially in the face and throat. The onset of symptoms is usually gradual, with drooping of the upper eyelids (ptosis), double vision (diplopia), and weakness of the facial muscles. The weakness may then extend to other muscles, particularly the respiratory muscles. Muscular exertion, stress, and infection may aggravate symptoms, which typically vary over the course of the day.

In early stages of the disease, there may be no other symptoms. Typically, myasthenic muscles are strongest in the morning but weaken throughout the day, especially after exercise. Short rest periods may temporarily restore muscle function. As the disease progresses, symptoms may eventually include difficulty chewing, swallowing, and talking; difficulty handling objects or doing tasks with the hands and arms; and difficulty standing or walking.

Physical exam: The exam may reveal weak eye closure, drooping eyelids, double vision, slack facial muscles, and a blank facial expression. Muscle fatigue improves with rest. The individual may have difficulty chewing and swallowing. Because the gag reflex is often absent, there is a risk for inhalation (aspiration) of food, liquid, or saliva causing the individual to choke. The voice may have a nasal quality. Neck muscles may be too weak to hold up the head, causing it to fall onto the chest when the individual is seated. Weakened respiratory muscles may make breathing difficult, making the individual prone to pneumonia and other respiratory infections. The thymus gland, part of the body's immune system, is abnormally enlarged in about 75% of individuals with myasthenia gravis. In about 15% of these cases, a tumor of the thymus gland (thymoma) is found.

Tests: The diagnosis of myasthenia gravis can be confirmed by the Tensilon Challenge test. With myasthenia gravis, muscle function will improve within 30-60 seconds after injecting the drugs edrophonium or neostigmine into the vein (intravenous). Muscle function improvement lasts up to 30 minutes. Other diagnostic tests may include electrophysiologic tests to assess the transmission of neuromuscular messages. Through an electromyogram (EMG), a record of the electrical activity of muscles can show changes in response to nerve stimulation. A blood test can detect antibodies to acetylcholine (the chemical which transmits messages between nerve and muscle cells). A special x-ray, using a computer to record various views and measurements of the thymus (CT scan), may be done to rule out a tumor of the thymus gland (thymoma), especially in individuals over 40 years of age.

Treatment

In myasthenia gravis (MG), treatment is aimed at relieving symptoms. Anticholinesterase drugs counteract fatigue and muscle weakness, and allow about 80% of normal muscle function. These types of drugs may need to be taken as often as every 3-4 hours by mouth or injection. Unfortunately, these medications become less effective as the disease worsens. During acute relapses, treatment may also include anti-inflammatory drugs (such as corticosteroids) and drugs that suppress the immune system (such as azathioprine).

Individuals with tumors of the thymus (thymomas) require removal of the thymus gland (thymectomy).

Acute MG exacerbations causing severe respiratory difficulty (myasthenic crisis) may require critical emergency treatment. This may include an incision made into the trachea or "windpipe" (tracheotomy) so that the individual can breathe. Saliva from the mouth may need to be suctioned in order to prevent choking, and the anticholinesterase drugs will have to be given by injection.

A process called plasmapheresis may be recommended when drugs don't bring relief, during a myasthenic crisis, or to prepare an individual for surgery. In plasmapheresis, blood is progressively removed from the body, cleansed of toxic substances (in this case the offending antibodies), and then returned to the body. Although a slow process, taking several hours, the individual usually improves markedly for weeks to months thereafter. Plasmapheresis can be repeated at regular intervals.

Prognosis

Although there is no cure for myasthenia gravis (MG), drug treatment has improved prognosis and allowed individuals to lead relatively normal lives with a nearly normal life expectancy. Approximately 25% of individuals, however, experience a spontaneous remission in which all symptoms permanently disappear.

In general, the outcome is dependent on the rapidity of the disease progression and the effectiveness of medications. As more and more muscles become weakened, some muscles may eventually lose function entirely. Impaired muscle strength can result in aspiration, respiratory complication, falls, and death.

Approximately 10% of individuals with myasthenia gravis develop the life-threatening complication of myasthenic crisis. Outcome is then influenced by whether or not they required a tracheotomy, and whether it is temporary or permanent. If temporary, the opening is allowed to close and the individual will return to breathing through the nose. If permanent, the individual will continue to breathe through this opening in the throat (trachea). Care must be taken to guard against infection of the opening.

Surgical removal of the thymus gland leads to a remission in approximately 80% of the cases. Since the thymus helps the body's immune system to recognize and combat infection, special care must now be taken to avoid infection. Medical attention must be sought immediately if signs of infection develop.

Differential Diagnosis

Conditions with similar presentations include acute respiratory distress syndrome, amyotrophic lateral sclerosis, botulism, Brown-Sequard syndrome, Guillain-Barré syndrome, Lambert-Eaton myasthenic syndrome, hypothyroidism, tetanus, tick-borne diseases, and Wernicke's encephalopathy.

Specialists

- Neurologist
- Physiatrist
- Psychiatrist
- Psychologist
- Rheumatologist

Rehabilitation

Although there is no cure for myasthenia gravis, rehabilitation alone or in combination with other forms of treatment can relieve symptoms for many individuals. Because myasthenia gravis often causes muscle weakness in the arms or legs, physical therapy is beneficial for long-term restoration of muscle strength.

Strengthening exercises help the individual remain as functional as possible. If significant weakness is present, active assist exercises may be necessary in which the individual generates some of the effort along with the help of the therapist. When improvement is noted and the exercises are well-tolerated, active range-of-motion exercises are introduced. Resistance is then added to each exercise by the use of an elastic band or light weights.

In myasthenia gravis, good days alternate with bad, and the physical therapist should modify the rehabilitation program accordingly. The rehabilitation program will also vary as the intensity and progression of the exercise depends on the stage of the individual's disease and his or her overall health.

Occupational therapy may help the individual adapt to new ways of performing specific domestic and occupational tasks. Speech therapy may be used as facial and throat muscles become weak or if the individual needs to be trained to speak by forcing air in and out of the esophagus (esophageal speech) following a permanent opening in the throat or "windpipe" (tracheotomy).

Work Restrictions / Accommodations

Work restrictions and special accommodations are determined on an individual basis according to severity of symptoms. The individual may need to be placed in a job that requires less physical strength and mobility. If job performance requires physical strength for physical labor, the individual may reach a point when it is no longer possible to work due to muscle weakness. A job that requires public speaking may be in jeopardy if facial and throat muscles are affected resulting in speech difficulties. As muscle weakness advances, environmental work alterations may be necessary to be ADA-compliant, and to make sure that the work place is accessible.

Comorbid Conditions

Coexisting conditions that may impact recovery include obesity, rheumatoid arthritis, lupus erythematosus, thyrotoxicosis, infections, pregnancy, and physical or emotional stress.

Complications

Possible complications of the disease include pneumonia as a result of aspiration of saliva, food, or liquids; choking as a result of inability to swallow or manage oral secretions; and increased risk of falls as a result of muscle weakness in the legs. If the respiratory muscles become too weak, the individual may lose the ability to breathe without assistance (myasthenic crisis). Excessive physical or emotional stress may trigger a crisis.

Factors Influencing Duration

Length of disability might be influenced by the individual's age, the severity of symptoms, the type of treatment, response to treatment, frequency of exacerbations, and residual impairments.

Length of Disability

Length of disability may be influenced by job requirements for individuals who perform physical labor or public speaking duties, by the degree and severity of fatigue, and by which muscle groups are affected by the disease. Duration depends on severity and response to treatment. Return to heavy work is unlikely.

Medical treatment.

Duration in Days

Job Classification	Minimum	Optimum	Maximum
Sedentary work	4	28	56
Light work	4	28	56
Medium work	14	56	84
Heavy work	56	84	Indefinite
Very Heavy work	56	84	Indefinite

Surgical treatment (thymectomy).

Duration in Days

Job Classification	Minimum	Optimum	Maximum
Sedentary work	14	21	28
Light work	14	21	28
Medium work	28	28	56
Heavy work	42	42	84
Very Heavy work	42	70	112

Failure to Recover

If an individual fails to recover within the maximum duration expectancy period, the reader may wish to reference the following questions to assist in better understanding the specifics of an individual's medical case.

Regarding diagnosis:

- Does the individual have chronic fatigue?
- Muscle weakness especially in the face and throat? Does it extend to the respiratory muscles?
- Has the individual noticed they are stronger in the morning? Does rest restore strength?
- Do they have difficulty chewing, swallowing, or talking? Is the gag reflex absent?
- Do they have difficulty using their arms, hands, or legs?
- On physical exam were weak eye closure, drooping eyelids, double vision, slack facial muscles, and a blank facial expression noted?
- Is the individual able to hold the head up?
- Is the voice nasal-sounding?
- Is the thymus gland enlarged? Is there a tumor?
- Has the individual had a tension challenge test? EMG? CT scan? Acetylcholine antibody test?
- Have conditions with similar symptoms been ruled out?

Regarding treatment:

- Is the individual being treated with anticholinesterase drugs?
- For acute relapses have corticosteroids and immunosuppressant drugs been used?
- Was a thymectomy performed?
- Has plasmapheresis been conducted as needed?

Regarding prognosis:

- Is the individual active in rehabilitation? Do they have a home exercise program? Have they sought psychological intervention?
- Is the individual's employer able to accommodate any necessary restrictions?
- Does the individual have any conditions that may affect their ability to recover?
- Has the individual had any complications such as pneumonia? Choking? Frequent falls?
- Have they had a myasthenic crisis?

References

Anderson, Kenneth N., revision ed. Mosby's Medical, Nursing, and Allied Health Dictionary. St. Louis: Mosby, 1998.

Beekman, R., and H.J. Oosterhuis. "Use of Alternative Treatments by Patients with Myasthenia Gravis." Ned Tijdschr Geneeskd 138 6 (1994): 294-296.

Holmes, Nancy H., managing ed. Handbook of Diseases. Springhouse, PA: Springhouse Corporation, 2000.

Newton, Edward, MD. Myasthenia Gravis. eMedicine.com. 12 Feb 2001. 12 Feb 2001 <http://www.emedicine.com/emerg/topic325.htm>.

Scully, Rosemary M., and Marylou R. Barnes. Physical Therapy. Philadelphia: J.B. Lippincott Company, 1989.

Umphred, Darcy A. Neurological Rehabilitation. St. Louis: The C.V. Mosby Company, 1990.

Mycosis Fungoides

Other names / synonyms: CTCL, Cutaneous T-cell Lymphoma, MF, Sézary Syndrome, SS
202.1, M9700/3

Definition

Mycosis fungoides (MF) is a type of cancer (lymphoma) of the immune system characterized by the development of red, itchy skin sores (lesions) that eventually involve the lymph nodes.

The uncontrolled growth of certain white blood cells (T lymphocytes) causes MF to appear in the skin. Sézary syndrome (SS) is an advanced form of MF characterized by severe generalized itching and redness (erythema) of the skin.

Mycosis fungoides develops slowly over the course of several years and many individuals with MF have a long history of other skin disorders. There are four stages of the disease each characterized by bright red or brown raised, scaly areas on 10% or more of the skin. These lesions itch and have a tendency to form open sores. The more advanced stages of the disease produce swollen lymph nodes in addition to redness over most of the skin along with peeling, scaling, and intense itching. The disease may eventually spread to the lungs, liver, or other organs.

Red skin and large numbers of tumor cells found in the blood indicate the advanced form of the disease known as Sézary syndrome.

The cause of MF is unknown although certain viral infections (including human T-cell lymphotropic virus-I/II and human herpes viruses) may put an individual at risk. Other risk factors may include chromosomal abnormalities, overexpression of cancer-causing genes (oncogenes), environmental toxins (i.e., chromium, mercury, aromatic hydrocarbons, plastics, cosmetics, and hair dyes), certain bacteria (Staphylococcus aureus), and naturally occurring regulatory molecules (i.e., cytokines, growth factors). MF and SS are the most frequent lymphomas involving the skin.

Over the past few years, the incidence of this disease appears to be an increasing in the US with over 1,000 new cases a year reported. MF is typically a disease of middle-aged adults with an average age of about 50. It is not uncommon, however, for adults younger than 50 to be diagnosed with this condition. There is a 2 to 1 incidence ratio of blacks to whites and a 2.2 to 1 ratio of men to women with this disorder.

Diagnosis

History: Individuals usually complain of patches of scaling and itching (pruritic) skin. If the disease is more advanced, well-differentiated areas (plaques) on the skin that are red and inflamed (erythematous) may occur. Some individuals may report skin overgrowth (keratoses) and cracking (fissuring) of the skin on the palms of the hands and soles of feet. Plaques may also appear as open sores (ulcers) on the skin. The individual's history should include details of previous skin disorders, how long lesions have been present, whether lesions have undergone any change, if lesions are associated with itching or breaks in the skin surface, if they worsen with changes in temperature or are helped by moisturizers.

Physical exam: Depending on the stage of the disease at initial presentation, the physical examination may reveal areas of redness, ulcerations, and enlarged lymph nodes, liver (hepatomegaly), or spleen (splenomegaly). For accurate staging, the physical examination should indicate the number and type (patch, plaque, tumor, erythroderma) of lesions and their distribution, percent of skin involved, number and sites of enlarged lymph nodes, and whether the liver or spleen is enlarged.

Tests: Diagnosis of mycosis fungoides may be extremely difficult. It may require taking skin samples (biopsies) and special (immunohistochemical) staining of these samples over a number of years before a diagnosis can be made accurately. Chest x-ray, CT, and MRI may help determine if the disease has spread to internal organs. A blood smear can identify the cancerous blood cells (Sézary lymphocytes) associated with Sézary syndrome.

Treatment

Treatment depends on the stage of the disease. Cortisone ointments may be applied to the skin (topically) to alleviate some of the symptoms of mild mycosis fungoides. Exposure to high-energy electron beams (radiation therapy) can be used locally or for treating the entire skin (total skin electron beam radiation or TSEB). Cancer-fighting drugs (chemotherapy) may be applied directly to the skin (topical chemotherapy), given orally, or by injection. Chemotherapy plus ultraviolet radiation therapy (photochemotherapy) may also be used. This treatment requires two to three office visits per week of 10 to 15 minutes each. In addition, drugs that enhance the immune system may help boost the individual's response to the cancer (immunotherapy).

Prognosis

The prognosis is dependent on the type and extent of disease at initial presentation. Individuals with early stage disease treated with topical ointments or radiation therapy have variable positive response rates ranging from 30-98%. At least one treatment (TSEB) may bring about a disappearance of symptoms (remission) that lasts for up to 10 years. Treatment response using chemotherapy or photochemotherapy is highly variable. Reportedly, 38-83% of cases show complete remission for at least 3 to 4 years. Immunotherapy produces disappearance of symptoms (i.e., complete response) less than 10% of the time.

Individuals whose disease has progressed to Sézary syndrome are rarely cured and usually die of infection or the effects of progressive lymphoma.

Differential Diagnosis

Conditions that present with similar symptoms as mycosis fungoides include Hodgkin's disease, adult T-cell leukemia/lymphoma, primary cutaneous lymphomas, Jessner's infiltrate, and actinic reticuloid disease.

Specialists

- Dermatologist
- Oncologist
- Pathologist
- Radiation Oncologist

Rehabilitation

A general exercise program may be beneficial to any individual undergoing radiation and/or chemotherapy treatments. Frequent walks, walk-jog, biking, and arm ergometer exercises should be encouraged. The walking program aims toward a goal of 2 miles in less than 60 minutes. Eventually, as the individual regains vitality, exercise may become more strenuous with a goal of attaining 75-85% maximum intensity while walking, jogging, biking, swimming, performing calisthenics, and/or weight training.

Work Restrictions / Accommodations

Extended work leave for treatment and recuperation may be required. Once individuals have returned to work, they may require work accommodations to allow them to attend several physician visits a week for continued treatment. Individuals may be weakened from chronic itching and the effects of chronic chemotherapy.

Comorbid Conditions

Existing conditions that may impact individual's ability to recover and further lengthen disability include diseases that produce a deficiency of the immune system or other secondary infections (e.g., HIV infection, AIDS).

Complications

Complications of mycosis fungoides are related to the stage of the disease and include ulceration, infection, and bleeding. Mycosis fungoides may also spread to other organ systems including the liver, spleen, lungs, and lymph system and if not treated, can result in mortality.

Factors Influencing Duration

The extent or stage of the disease at initial diagnosis, treatment regimen required, and development of complications may influence length of disability.

Length of Disability

Duration depends on the stage of the disease. Individuals treated using radiation and chemotherapy may need extensive recovery time and more sedentary work until recovery is complete. Disability may be permanent for individuals whose disease has spread (metastasized) into other organ systems.

Duration in Days

Job Classification	Minimum	Optimum	Maximum
Sedentary work	10	28	182
Light work	10	28	182
Medium work	14	28	182
Heavy work	28	63	Indefinite
Very Heavy work	28	91	Indefinite

Failure to Recover

If an individual fails to recover within the maximum duration expectancy period, the reader may wish to reference the following questions to assist in better understanding the specifics of an individual's medical case.

Regarding diagnosis:

- Does individual have a long history of skin disorders? History of infections caused by human T-cell lymphotropic virus-I/II or human herpes viruses?
- Does individual have chromosomal abnormalities or an overexpression of cancer-causing genes (oncogenes)?
- Was individual exposed to environmental toxins such as chromium, mercury, aromatic hydrocarbons, plastics, cosmetics, or hair dyes?
- Has individual had an infection caused by the bacteria Staphylococcus aureus?
- Does individual complain of patches of skin that are scaling and itching (pruritic) or of well-differentiated areas (plaques) on the skin that are red and inflamed (erythematous)?
- Does individual report skin overgrowth (keratoses) and cracking (fissuring) of the skin on the palms of the hands and soles of feet?
- How long were the skin lesions present and have they undergone any change? Do the lesions worsen with changes in temperature? Does application of moisturizers help?
- Were skin samples (biopsies) and special (immunohistochemical) staining of these samples done over a number of years?
- Were chest x-ray, CT, and MRI done to determine if the disease has spread to internal organs?
- Was a blood smear used to identify the cancerous blood cells (Sézary lymphocytes) associated with Sézary syndrome?
- Was the diagnosis of mycosis fungoides confirmed?

Regarding treatment:

- Was mild disease treated with cortisone ointments to alleviate some of the symptoms?
- Was radiation therapy used either locally or over the entire skin (total skin electron beam radiation or TSEB)?
- Were anticancer drugs (chemotherapy) applied directly to the skin (topical chemotherapy), given orally, or via injection? Was ultraviolet radiation therapy (photochemotherapy) used in addition to chemotherapy?
- Were drugs given to enhance the immune system (immunotherapy) in an attempt to increase individual's ability to respond to the cancer? Was treatment successful?

Regarding prognosis:

- What was the extent of disease at the time of diagnosis?
- Did treatment begin at an early stage of the disease?
- If combination treatments were not used, would individual benefit from them now?
- Has the disease progressed to Sézary syndrome?
- Have complications developed such as ulceration, infection, or bleeding?
- Has the disease spread to other organ systems such as the liver, spleen, lungs, and lymph? If so, what treatment can be done and what is the expected outcome with treatment?

References

Diamandidou, E., P.R. Cohen, and R. Kurzrock. "Mycosis Fungoides and Sézary Syndrome." Blood 88 7 (1996): 2385-2409.

LeMone, P., and K.M. Burke. Medical-Surgical Nursing. Upper Saddle River, NJ: Prentice Hall Health, 2000.

Myelography

Other names / synonyms: Myelogram

87.21

Definition

Myelography is a special x-ray that allows for visualization of the spinal canal; it outlines the spinal cord, spinal nerve roots, and surrounding membranes (meninges). A dye is injected into the spinal canal through a needle inserted between vertebrae (lumbar puncture). Dye is injected and then the area is x-rayed. A myelogram is used as a tool to determine the cause of pain in the back, neck, arms, or legs.

For more detailed visualization, computed tomography (CT scan) may be done.

Because magnetic resonance imaging (MRI) is now considered the imaging method of choice for visualizing the spinal cord and canal, myelography is not done as frequently as it once was. It is now employed primarily for individuals who cannot have an MRI, such as those with claustrophobia or a metal implant, or when MRI results are inconclusive.

Reason for Procedure

Myelography is used to diagnose conditions such as herniated discs, spinal cord or nerve root compression caused by rough bony protrusions (bone spur), herniated disc, filling defect caused by scar tissue, tumors or cysts, degenerative conditions of the spine, spinal nerve injury, or arteriovenous malformations. It is typically done when surgery is being considered, not only to confirm the diagnosis, but also to determine the exact location of the abnormality.

Description

With the individual lying down, a needle is inserted through two vertebrae (lumbar puncture). A small amount of cerebrospinal fluid is removed and replaced with an equal volume of dye. The individual's body is positioned at an angle so that the dye is able to circulate throughout the spinal canal. The movement of the dye is watched with a machine called a fluoroscope. The movement of the dye will reveal an obstruction or other abnormality. Appropriate x-ray pictures are taken. If CT pictures will also be taken, several hours are typically allowed to pass before the beginning the CT procedure to ensure full circulation and penetration of the dye.

The individual is often instructed to remain lying in bed for several hours, up to 24 hours if headache is present. The head may need to remain in a specific position depending on the type of dye used. During this period, the individual must be closely supervised.

Prognosis

Before the CT scan and MRI, myelography was the gold standard for detecting structural abnormalities in individuals with low back pain. It is not, however, sensitive to detecting all abnormalities. CT scans and MRIs, unless contraindicated, have now replaced myelography in routine use.

Specialists

- Neurosurgeon
- Orthopedic Surgeon
- Radiologist

Work Restrictions / Accommodations

The individual may need a day or two after the procedure to rest, especially if any complications developed, such as a headache. More time may be needed for more serious complications. Lifting is discouraged for 48 hours to permit the puncture to seal; normal activity may be resumed after this period.

Comorbid Conditions

Individuals with increased intracranial pressure, infection near the injection site, or bleeding tendency are at higher risk for complications and generally should not undergo the procedure. Individuals with a potential dye allergy or a history of dye allergy should either forego having the procedure or be premedicated with corticosteroids or antihistamines prior to the procedure to minimize or prevent an allergic reaction.

Procedure Complications

The most common complications include a severe headache, nausea, and vomiting. Irritation of the membranes (meningeal irritation) or change in the cerebrospinal fluid pressure after spinal tap may cause the development of a headache, fever, nausea, dizziness, stiff neck, shoulders or back, and a sensitivity or aversion to light (photophobia). An infection of the membranes (meningitis), herniation of the brain, or seizures may also develop. Some individuals have an allergic reaction to the dye used, ranging from mild to life-threatening. Rarely, hypovolemic collapse and shock have been reported.

Factors Influencing Duration

The underlying condition for which the procedure was performed and the development of complications will influence the length of disability. Post myelography headaches may prolong disability by a few days.

Length of Disability

Duration in Days

Job Classification	Minimum	Optimum	Maximum
Any work	1	2	4

References

Goetz, Christopher, and Eric Pappert. Textbook of Clinical Neurology, 1st ed. Philadelphia: W.B. Saunders Company, 1999.

Pagana, Kathleen, and Timothy Pagana. Mosby's Manual of Diagnostic and Laboratory Tests. St. Louis: Mosby, 1998.

Myelopathy

Other names / synonyms: Spinal Cord Dysfunction, Spinal Cord Injury

336.1, 336.8, 336.9, 952.02

Definition

Myelopathy refers to either a dysfunction of the long tracts of the spinal cord or, more generally, any disease or disorder that affects the spinal cord.

Myelopathy may be caused by spinal cord trauma (fracture or dislocation of the vertebrae), herniated disc (intervertebral disc disorder with myelopathy), osteoarthritis of the spine (spondylosis), or a space-occupying lesion such as a tumor. A syndrome that results from compression of one side of the spinal cord, above the tenth thoracic vertebrae and is characterized by spastic paralysis on the body's injured side and loss of postural sense and the senses of pain and heat on the other side of the body (Brown-Sequard's syndrome) may also be a type of myelopathy. Additional causes include viral infections, immune reactions, or insufficient blood flow through the blood vessels in the spinal cord. It may occur as a complication of loss of nerve sheath tissue (demyelination) or as a complication of reactions to smallpox, measles, or chickenpox vaccinations.

In general, a disease or injury resulting in a myelopathy can begin at any time of life and affects males and females in equal numbers. The level of the spinal cord lesion determines the extent of functional loss. There is no specific information on incidence of myelopathy obtainable. However, information on some common causes of myelopathy is available. There are approximately 7,800 spinal cord injuries in the US each year and at least 100 new cases of spinal cord tumors. A variety of tumors may cause spinal cord compression. Primary spinal tumors are relatively rare in the adult with an incidence of 1,800 to 2,000 per year in the US.

Diagnosis

History: Symptoms of myelopathy vary depending on the cause, the severity of the cause, and whether the problem causing myelopathy is acute or chronic. In the case of a spinal cord tumor, compression, or trauma there may be pain (that may also radiate down the arms or legs), loss of sensation or movement, and/or contractures on one or both or alternate sides of the body. If the cause is osteoarthritis, there may be complaints of pain and tenderness, warmth over the area with movement, weakness, and possible spinal deformity. Infections (as a cause) may produce fever, redness, swelling, and increased tenderness. If the individual suffers from Brown-Sequard's syndrome, there may be spastic paralysis on the body's injured side and loss of postural sense and the senses of pain and heat on the other side of the body.

Physical exam: A standard neurologic exam may reveal disease involving the spinal nerve root (cervical radiculopathy) or leg spasticity. The individual will be tested for reflexes (which may be overactive or reduced depending on the cause) and loss of or alterations in sensation over the body. Voluntary movement may be diminished. There may be paralysis and/or diminished sensation over various parts of the body.

Tests: Diagnostic testing depends on the history and physical examination findings. X-rays, bone scan, computerized analysis of multiple x-rays (CT) or a magnetic field study (MRI) of the spinal cord may detect lesions in or near the spinal cord. Laboratory tests may be indicated to rule out other causes (such as vitamin B_{12} deficiency or heavy metal poisoning). An elevated white blood cell count suggests infection (meningitis or osteomyelitis of the spine). An elevated erythrocyte sedimentation rate of the blood (ESR) may be a sign of inflammation, infection, or tumor. A lumbar puncture may be done to obtain cerebrospinal fluid (CFS) for laboratory tests if meningitis or multiple sclerosis is suspected. Other diagnostic tests may include biopsies of bone or soft tissue, and culture of blood or cerebrospinal fluid.

Treatment

Treatment depends on the cause of myelopathy. For fracture or dislocated vertebrae, pain medications (analgesics), traction, immobilization for several weeks, and rehabilitation therapy (physical, occupational, and vocational) may be needed. Surgery to correct spinal deformity may include removal of part of the vertebra(e) and/or fusion of the fractured vertebrae. Analgesics, medications to reduce inflammation (steroids), and possibly physical therapy may be used to treat arthritic problems. Infections require medications to reduce the infection (antibiotics), to reduce fever (antipyretics), and possibly anti-inflammatory drugs (steroids) to reduce existing inflammation. Myelopathy caused by compression of the spinal cord may require surgery to remove a tumor or a herniated disc (laminectomy).

Prognosis

Outcome depends on the cause of the myelopathy and any permanent neurological damage. Traction and immobilization of the spinal column may lead to complete recovery if no residual damage has been done to the spinal cord. Complete recovery is also possible in cases of infection. Chronic conditions such as arthritis and osteoporosis cause variable outcomes ranging from no further progression of problems, or continual progression resulting in deformed spinal column and decreased mobility, to the point of needing assistive devices such as a cane or a wheelchair. Spinal cord injury or cord compression may result in permanent residual damage, including loss of sensation over various parts of the body as well as a loss of voluntary movement in extremities. Recovery after a tumor removal depends on any residual damage if the tumor is cancer, and if the cancer has spread. Recovery after removal of a herniated disc (laminectomy) is often excellent as long as no damage is done to the cord during surgery or as a result of compression.

Differential Diagnosis

A differential diagnosis depends on the particular history and physical findings presented by the suspected myelopathy. Trauma and infection must be included in the diagnostic possibilities.

Specialists

- Neurologist
- Neurosurgeon
- Physiatrist

Work Restrictions / Accommodations

Restrictions and accommodations would most likely result if there is permanent damage to the spinal cord following trauma, surgery, or due to lengthy compression of the cord. If mobility is lost, the work environment needs to be wheelchair accessible. If loss of movement affects upper extremities, equipment such as telephones and computers may need to be adapted. Vocational counseling may be necessary.

Comorbid Conditions

Comorbid conditions that impact on recovery include obesity and conditions such as arthritis that might hamper mobility and strength.

Complications

Complications as a result of myelopathy may be addiction to pain medication, permanent loss of sensation and/or voluntary movement, and spinal deformities.

Factors Influencing Duration

Length of disability depends on the specific diagnosis, the location and completeness of the lesion, the severity of the lesion, the severity of the symptoms, whether it is acute or chronic, and the severity of functional loss. The disability could be transient or permanent, and would depend on the cause of the myelopathy and any treatment options.

Length of Disability

Duration of disability depends on the cause, type, and extent of loss of movement and sensation, and the individual's response to treatment. Disability may be permanent. A more specific diagnosis is required to determine disability duration.

Failure to Recover

If an individual fails to recover within the maximum duration expectancy period, the reader may wish to reference the following questions to assist in better understanding the specifics of an individual's medical case.

Regarding diagnosis:

- Has individual had spinal cord trauma, herniated disc, osteoarthritis of the spine, or a tumor? Were there any viral infections, immune reactions, or insufficient blood flow through the blood vessels in the spinal cord?
- Does individual have any demyelination?
- Does pain radiate to any extremities? Is there pain and tenderness with warmth over the area? Does pain occur with movement, weakness, or possible spinal deformity?
- On exam, was radiculopathy or spasticity noted? Were reflexes and sensation normal or abnormal? Was any paralysis noted?
- Has individual had x-rays, bone scan, CT, or MRI of the spinal cord? Were laboratory tests done? Lumbar puncture? Were biopsies of bone or soft tissue performed?
- Have conditions with similar symptoms been ruled out?

Regarding treatment:

- Does individual have a fracture or dislocated vertebrae? Is it being treated with analgesics, traction, and immobilization?
- Does individual have an arthritic problem? Is it being treated with analgesics or steroids?
- Is there an infection? Is it being treated with antibiotics?
- Does individual have compression of the spinal cord? Was surgery necessary?

Regarding prognosis:

- Is individual active in rehabilitation? Is a home exercise program in place?
- Can individual's employer accommodate any necessary restrictions?
- Does individual have any conditions that may affect ability to recover?
- Has individual become addicted to pain medication? Are there any other complications such as loss of sensation or voluntary movements? Spinal deformities?

References

Anderson, Kenneth N., revision ed. Mosby's Medical, Nursing, and Allied Health Dictionary. St. Louis: Mosby, 1998.

Myelophthisic Anemia

Other names / synonyms: Leukoerythroblastic Anemia, Leukoerythroblastosis, Myelopathic Anemia, Secondary Myelofibrosis

285.8

Definition

Myelophthisic anemia is a type of bone marrow failure caused by the invasion or replacement of normal bone marrow tissue by abnormal tissue. The reduction of normal bone marrow tissue limits the production of blood cells (red blood cells, white blood cells, and platelets). This causes a decrease in the number of mature blood cells in the peripheral blood and an increase in the immature blood cells. Severe anemia is the result of the decreased number of red blood cells and subsequent decreased oxygen-carrying capacity of the blood. Low numbers of platelets can result in bleeding, and low numbers of white blood cells can leave an individual vulnerable to infection.

Metastatic cancer is the most common abnormal tissue to invade the bone marrow. The cancer spreads to the marrow from another location such as the breast, prostate, lung, or thyroid. Other causes of bone marrow invasion include lymphoproliferative malignancies (e.g., lymphoma), fungal infections, lipid disorders (e.g., Gaucher's or Niemann-Pick disease), and tumors (granulomas) of tuberculosis.

In the US, less than 10% of individuals with metastatic cancer develop myelophthisic anemia. Those who do are typically in an advanced stage of cancer. The incidence of myelophthisic anemia is higher in geographic areas where access to medical care is limited.

Diagnosis

History: Symptoms include weakness, dizziness, drowsiness, a vague feeling of discomfort or illness (malaise), chest pain, the sensation of a rapid or intense heartbeat (palpitations), and shortness of breath. There may be fever and evidence of infection. The individual will typically have a history that points to an underlying disease such as advanced cancer or tuberculosis. Additional symptoms are usually specific for the underlying disease.

Physical exam: On exam paleness (pallor) of skin, fingernail beds, and mucous membranes, and an increased heart rate (tachycardia) may be present. Bruises and bleeding under the skin (petechiae) may be evident. Additional physical signs reflect the underlying disease.

Tests: A complete blood count (CBC) will show a significant decrease in the number of red blood cells (anemia), white blood cells (leukopenia), and platelets (thrombocytopenia). One type of cell may exhibit a more significant decrease than the other types, or all cell types may be significantly decreased (pancytopenia). Microscopic examination of a peripheral blood smear will show an increase in the number of immature red and white blood cells, and platelets. The red blood cells have a characteristic teardrop shape (poikilocytosis). Aspiration of bone marrow may be unsuccessful due to the fibrotic nature of the invaded marrow tissue. Microscopic examination of a bone marrow biopsy will reveal and identify the invasive tissue. Additional tests may be needed (i.e., tuberculosis or lipid storage disorders) to confirm the diagnosis.

Treatment

Treatment is aimed at the underlying disease causing the marrow tissue invasion. When caused by infection (i.e., tuberculosis or fungal), the myelophthisic anemia usually corrects itself once the infection is successfully treated. When caused by a malignant process, chemotherapy specific to the type of malignancy is indicated. During treatment of the underlying disease, the individual may need blood transfusions to boost blood counts to safe levels and antibiotics to prevent infection. If the spleen is enlarged, surgical removal (splenectomy) may be necessary. Some individuals with low levels of the hormone erythropoietin (EPO) that stimulates bone marrow to produce blood cells may benefit from EPO supplementation.

Prognosis

Prognosis depends on the underlying cause. When caused by a treatable underlying condition such as a fungal infection or tuberculosis, the anemia is corrected when the underlying condition is treated. In many cases, however, the underlying cause may not respond to treatment. For example, this is the case when the invasive tissue is metastatic cancer, an endstage cancer that is usually fatal.

Differential Diagnosis

Conditions with similar symptoms include aplastic anemia, leukemia, myelodysplasia, and myelofibrosis.

Specialists

- Hematologist
- Oncologist
- Infectious Disease Physician

Work Restrictions / Accommodations

Work responsibilities may need to be primarily sedentary due to weakness and fatigue. Exposure to individuals with infection should be limited. The underlying cause of the condition will dictate further restrictions or accommodations.

Individuals with significantly decreased platelet counts need a safe work environment in order to avoid the risk of personal injury that could trigger acute bleeding. Where indicated, protective gear, especially to the head, should be worn. Office work or sedentary work would probably be more appropriate than strenuous work involving heavy lifting or other physical exertion. The employer should be aware of the condition so that the appropriate level of care can be obtained quickly in the event of an on-the-job injury.

Comorbid Conditions

Myelophthisic anemia may be exacerbated by comorbid conditions that also affect the bone marrow such as AIDS, specific viral infections, or the use of certain toxic drugs.

Complications

Complications include infection, hemorrhage, tissue damage (hypoxia), and death due to inadequate oxygen levels in the blood. If the platelet count of an individual drops to a dangerously low level, severe, even life-threatening bleeding can occur, particularly inside the brain (intracranial hemorrhage). Splenectomy carries the risk of infection.

Factors Influencing Duration

Factors that may influence length of disability include severity of the condition, the underlying medical condition causing the anemia, any complications, access to medical care, and response to treatment.

Length of Disability

Duration depends on underlying cause. Disability may be permanent.

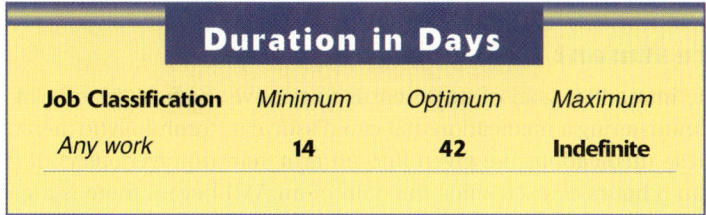

Duration in Days

Job Classification	Minimum	Optimum	Maximum
Any work	14	42	Indefinite

Failure to Recover

If an individual fails to recover within the maximum duration expectancy period, the reader may wish to reference the following questions to assist in better understanding the specifics of an individual's medical case.

Regarding diagnosis:

- Does individual have weakness, dizziness, drowsiness, a vague feeling of discomfort or illness (malaise), chest pain, the sensation of a rapid or intense heartbeat (palpitations), and shortness of breath? Fever or evidence of infection?
- Does individual have a history that points to an underlying disease such as advanced cancer or tuberculosis?
- On exam, does individual have paleness (pallor) of skin, fingernail beds, and mucous membranes and an increased heart rate (tachycardia)? Are bruises and bleeding under the skin (petechiae) evident?
- Was a complete blood count (CBC) done? Did results show a significant decrease in the number of red blood cells (anemia), white blood cells (leukopenia), and platelets (thrombocytopenia)?
- Was microscopic examination of a peripheral blood smear done? Did it show an increase in the number of immature red and white blood cells, and platelets? Do the red blood cells have a characteristic teardrop shape (poikilocytosis)?
- Was the underlying condition identified?
- Were other causes of marrow invasion ruled out?

Regarding treatment:

- Was the underlying condition treated, i.e., infection, chemotherapy for malignancy, or surgery for spleen enlargement? If not, what other treatment options are available?
- Are blood counts kept at safe levels by regular monitoring and periodic transfusions?

Regarding prognosis:

- Has the underlying condition responded favorably to treatment? If not, what other treatment options are available?
- Are efforts concerning individual's environment being made to prevent infection and injury? Does individual have access to emergency medical care?
- Has individual experienced any complications that may impact recovery?

References

Besa, Emmanuel, and Ulrich Woermann. Myelophthisic Anemia. eMedicine.com. 04 Apr 2000. 29 Aug 2000 <http://www.emedicine.com/MED/topic1562.htm>.

Rosen, Peter, et al. Emergency Medicine: Concepts and Clinical Practice, 4th ed. St. Louis: Mosby, 1998.

Myocardial Infarction, Acute

Other names / synonyms: Coronary, Coronary Occlusion, Coronary Thrombosis, Heart Attack, MI

410, 410.0, 410.1, 410.2, 410.3, 410.4, 410.5, 410.6, 410.7, 410.8, 410.9

Definition

Acute myocardial infarction (AMI) is widely known as a heart attack and results in damage, usually permanent, to a portion of the heart's wall. An AMI is caused by the sudden formation of a small blood clot (thrombus) on a cholesterol build-up (plaque) that has developed slowly over years within a coronary artery. They are often preceded by pain in the chest with exertion (effort angina) for weeks, months, or years.

The major risk factors for an AMI are the same as for cholesterol deposits in other arteries. The cholesterol deposits cause hardening of the arteries (arteriosclerosis). Atherosclerosis is a form of arteriosclerosis characterized by fatty (lipid) deposits in the arterial wall. The major risk factors for atherosclerosis and AMI include cigarette smoking, high blood pressure (hypertension), high blood cholesterol level, diabetes and heredity. Stress and lack of exercise are considered minor risk factors for atherosclerosis. Stress and heavy exertion are considered even less important in the actual precipitation of an AMI because most AMIs occur during sleep or in the early morning hours when stress and exertion are minimal. The occasional occurrence, however, of an AMI during strenuous exercise contributes to the misperception that exercise causes heart attacks.

Atherosclerosis causes more than 95% of AMIs. Other much less common causes are an overactive thyroid gland (hyperthyroidism), extremely low blood pressure (shock), very low blood count (anemia), and thick blood (polycythemia).

AMI is the most common cause of death in the US. It occurs in 750,000 individuals a year with an in-hospital mortality rate of 6%.

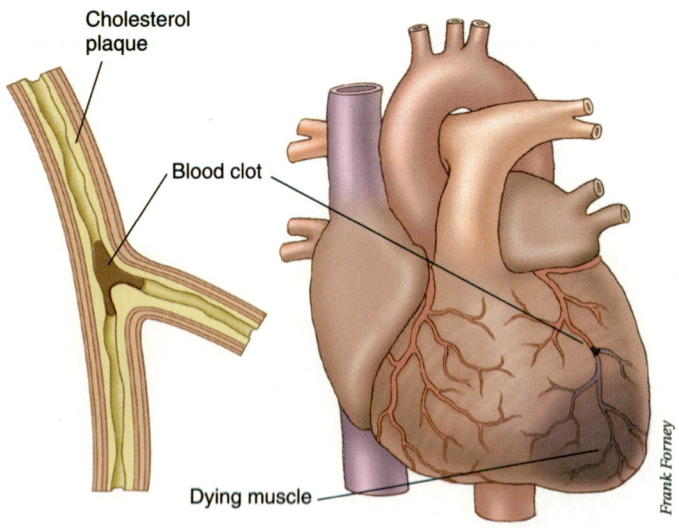

Diagnosis

History: Pain is almost always in the center of the chest under the breastbone. It may radiate into the arm, back, neck, or jaw. Individuals usually describe the pain as heavy, constricting, achy, or burning but not usually sharp. Pain rarely, if ever, radiates below the navel. Sweating, shortness of breath, nausea, and vomiting often accompany the pain.

Physical exam: The individual may be sweaty, pale, and grimacing in pain. The heart rate may be increased and blood pressure decreased. The heart rhythm may be regular or irregular (arrhythmia). A heart murmur and "crackles" in the lungs (rales) may present.

Tests: Tests include an electrocardiogram (ECG) and measurements of enzymes normally present in the heart (cardiac enzymes) but not in the blood. If an AMI is present, results of one or both of these tests will be abnormal. An echocardiogram is often done to evaluate the function of the heart. Other less widely available tests include CT and nuclear magnetic resonance (NMR).

Treatment

The immediate goal of treatment is to remove the fresh blood clot by administering a medication that can dissolve it (thrombolytic therapy). These medications are given into an arm vein (intravenously). If less than 6 hours elapsed since the pain of an AMI began, there is a good chance (more than 80%) that the clot can be dissolved. The chances decrease to about 50% if 6 to 12 hours have gone by. After 12 hours, clot-dissolving drugs are usually not given.

A very effective alternative to clot-dissolving drugs for opening up blocked arteries is balloon angioplasty. However, the procedure requires a heart catheterization laboratory and specialized personnel not available in many hospitals.

Any of a number of drugs known collectively as beta-blockers are frequently given intravenously early after an AMI in addition to clot-dissolving drugs. These drugs also help limit the size of an AMI and improve survival. Another group of drugs known as angiotensin converting enzyme (ACE) inhibitors used soon after an AMI help improve long-term survival.

Other drugs given include painkillers (analgesics) like morphine, nitroglycerin, antiarrhythmic drugs for a variety of irregular heart rhythms, medications to increase or decrease blood pressure, diuretics to increase urine output and remove excess fluid from the lungs (congestive heart failure, pulmonary edema), and drugs to dilate veins and arteries in the arms and legs (periphery).

At the time of discharge, individuals with an AMI are placed on aspirin to thin out the blood and reduce the chances of another heart attack. Many individuals are also discharged on a beta-blocker and an ACE inhibitor to further decrease the likelihood of another AMI. If the blood cholesterol level is above 200 mg/dl, individual may be given a drug to lower cholesterol.

Prognosis

In general, predicted outcome of an AMI is good with 90-95% of individuals leaving the hospital. Death is largely due to mechanical complications of the AMI. Arrhythmias are a much less frequent cause of death.

A low-level treadmill stress test is often done just before discharge to help assess long-term prognosis, need for medication to treat exertional chest pain (effort angina), and for further procedures to improve blood flow to the AMI region (revascularization procedures). These procedures include balloon angioplasty, stents, and coronary bypass surgery. The treadmill study also helps decide how long an individual should be off work and what accommodations are needed.

Differential Diagnosis

Other conditions with similar symptoms include pericarditis, esophageal spasm, peptic ulcer disease, reflux esophagitis, dissecting aneurysm, and pulmonary embolism.

Specialists

- Cardiologist
- Critical Care Specialist

Rehabilitation

Cardiac rehabilitation can be very helpful in prevention and recovery of cardiac disorders and disease. With a specifically designed exercise program set at a level considered safe for that individual, those who have experienced heart failure can improve their fitness levels substantially. Rehabilitation following a myocardial infarction is progressed in phases.

Phase one often begins in the hospital and provides low levels of exercise to prevent the hazards of bed rest, reduces episodes of low blood pressure when changing positions (orthostatic hypotension), and maintains overall mobility of the body. Exercise may begin in the coronary care unit of a hospital with low-level exercise having the individual on the back (supine position). The individual progresses with exercises to sitting and eventually to standing. Progressive walking (ambulating) and eventually stair climbing are an important part of the individual's exercise program while hospitalized. Intensity is gradually increased until discharge from the hospital.

Phase two goals are to improve functional capacity by increasing physical endurance and promoting return to activity. This is done in an outpatient setting such as a rehabilitation center. Individuals typically are attached to an electrocardiograph (ECG) monitor that records the continuous electrical activity of the heart muscle. A physical therapist keeps a daily log of the individual's blood pressure, heart rate, and cardiac rhythm.

Phase three continues in an outpatient setting such as a rehabilitation center. Depending on the individual's condition, this phase may last for several months. Individuals may stay involved with an outpatient program for up to a year to accomplish all of their goals while still at modified work duty. Eventually, the level of exercise increases with the addition of recreational activities such as swimming and outdoor hiking. Light jogging at approximately 5 miles per hour (mph) and cycling at approximately 12 mph are appropriate as long as the individual tolerates the rehabilitation program well. Modifications may need to be made in order to meet the needs of individuals who have had surgery or with other medical conditions.

Work Restrictions / Accommodations

Individuals with a relatively uncomplicated AMI, who have passed a low-level treadmill test before discharge, and whose work entails nonstrenuous activity can usually return to full-time work without restrictions within 2 to 4 weeks. Individuals with work involving more strenuous activity or who have developed complications usually require a longer time off before returning to work or may be reassigned to a less strenuous job. The predischarge treadmill test helps make the decision.

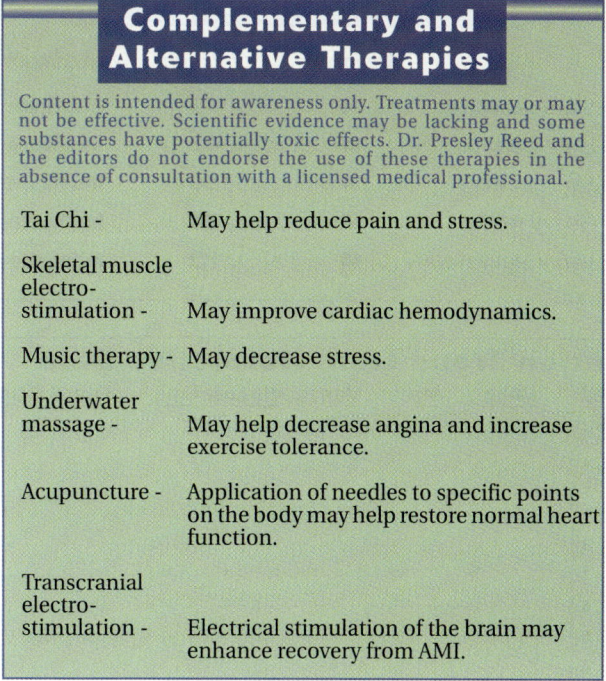

Complementary and Alternative Therapies

Content is intended for awareness only. Treatments may or may not be effective. Scientific evidence may be lacking and some substances have potentially toxic effects. Dr. Presley Reed and the editors do not endorse the use of these therapies in the absence of consultation with a licensed medical professional.

Tai Chi -	May help reduce pain and stress.
Skeletal muscle electro-stimulation -	May improve cardiac hemodynamics.
Music therapy -	May decrease stress.
Underwater massage -	May help decrease angina and increase exercise tolerance.
Acupuncture -	Application of needles to specific points on the body may help restore normal heart function.
Transcranial electro-stimulation -	Electrical stimulation of the brain may enhance recovery from AMI.

Comorbid Conditions

Comorbid conditions include peripheral vascular disease, diabetes, lung disease, stroke, renal disease, and obesity.

Complications

Fast and/or irregular heart beating (arrhythmias) occur often after an AMI. Some arrhythmias such as premature ventricular contractions (PVCs) are so frequent that they may be considered part of the AMI rather than a complication of it. Slow heat beating (bradycardia) is less common than arrhythmias and requires treatment to speed it up using a drug called atropine or by inserting an electronic pacemaker.

There are several mechanical complications of AMI. These include rupture of a valve, rupture of the wall between the two pumping chambers (ventricular septal defect), and rupture of the wall of the heart (cardiac rupture). Treatment is usually urgent surgery.

Another complication is either recurrent or persistent chest pain. Persistent chest pain for several days after an AMI frequently occurs. It may be due to either an inflammation of the surface of the heart (pericarditis) or inadequate oxygen reaching the heart (angina).

Factors Influencing Duration

Factors that may lengthen disability include individuals over the age of 60, those with larger or more complicated AMIs, individuals with poor results on predischarge low-level treadmill study, and those on multiple medications.

Myocardial Infarction, Acute

Length of Disability

The length of disability may depend on the physical and emotional requirements of the job. Disability may be permanent.

Duration in Days

Job Classification	Minimum	Optimum	Maximum
Sedentary work	14	42	Indefinite
Light work	14	42	Indefinite
Medium work	14	56	Indefinite
Heavy work	14	84	Indefinite
Very Heavy work	14	112	Indefinite

Duration Trend from Normative Data*

Cases	Mean	Min	Max	No Lost Time	Over 6 Months
6600	63	0	560	0.39%	1.11%

Percentile:	5th	25th	Median	75th	95th
Days:	12	31	53	83	141

ICD-9-CM 410, 410.9 - Reported Length of Disability (Days)

* Differences may exist between the expected duration tables and the normative graphs. Duration tables provide expected recovery periods based on the type of work performed by the individual. The normative graphs reflect the actual observed experience of many individuals across the spectrum of physical conditions, in a variety of industries, and with varying levels of case management.

Failure to Recover

If an individual fails to recover within the maximum duration expectancy period, the reader may wish to reference the following questions to assist in better understanding the specifics of an individual's medical case.

Regarding diagnosis:

- Was the diagnosis confirmed by serial cardiac enzyme tests and/or an ECG? Was the individual seen by a cardiologist?
- Did individual experience complications from the AMI?
- Does individual have an underlying condition that may impact recovery? Is this condition being effectively treated?

Regarding treatment:

- Did the individual receive prompt treatment with a clot-dissolving medication or an urgent coronary angioplasty?
- Were appropriate medications given to improve long-term survival?
- Were there significant complications of the AMI?
- Were the complications appropriately treated?
- Is the individual taking more than the usual aspirin, beta-blocker, ACE inhibitor, and/or cholesterol-lowering drugs? If so, why?

Regarding prognosis:

- Was a low-level predischarge treadmill study done?
- Is individual a candidate for revascularization procedures such as balloon angioplasty, stents, or coronary bypass surgery?
- Was individual enrolled in a comprehensive cardiac rehabilitation program?

References

Chen, K.M., and M. Snyder. "A Research-based Use of Tai Chi/Movement Therapy as a Nursing Intervention." Journal of Holistic Nursing 17 3 (1999): 267-279.

Davydova, O.B., et al. "Submerged Hydromassage as a Method for the Rehabilitation of Myocardial Infarct Patients at the Polyclinic Stage." Voprosy Kurortologii, Fizioterapii Lechebnoi, and Fizicheskoi Kultury 6 (1994): 3-6.

Scully, Rosemary M., and Marylou R. Barnes. Physical Therapy. Philadelphia: J.B. Lippincott Company, 1989.

Smith, F.W., Jr. "Acupuncture for Cardiovascular Disorders." Problems in Veterinary Medicine 4 1 (1992): 125-131.

References (Continued)

Golikov, A.P., et al. "Effects of Transcranial Electrostimulation of the Opioid Systems on Reparative Processes in Patients with Myocardial Infarction." Kardiologiia 29 12 (1989): 45-48.

Hochman, Judith S., and Bernard J. Gersh. "Acute Myocardial Infarction." Textbook of Cardiovascular Medicine. Topol, Eric J., ed. Philadelphia: Lippincott-Raven Publishers, 1998. 437-480.

Kisner, C., and L. Colby. Therapeutic Exercise Foundations and Techniques. Philadelphia: F.A. Davis Company, 1990.

Luckmann, Joan, and Karen C. Sorensen. "Nursing People Experiencing Coronary Artery Disease." Medical-Surgical Nursing. Kay, Dudley, ed. Philadelphia: W.B. Saunders Company, 1987. 927-947.

Stempien-Otero, April, and Douglas W. Weaver. "Post-myocardial Infarction Management." Textbook of Cardiovascular Medicine. Topol, Eric J., ed. Philadelphia: Lippincott-Raven Publishers, 1998. 481-502.

Sumin, A.N., et al. "Pilot Experience with Skeletal Muscle Electrostimulation in Rehabilitation of Patients with Complicated Myocardial Infarction." Terapevticheskii Arkhiv 71 12 (1999): 18-20.

van Dixhoorn, J.J., and H.J. Duivenvoorden. "Effect of Relaxation Therapy on Cardiac Events After Myocardial Infarction: A 5-year Follow-up Study." Journal of Cardiopulmonary Rehabilitation 19 3 (1999): 178-185.

White, J.M. "Effects of Relaxing Music on Cardiac Autonomic Balance and Anxiety After Acute Myocardial Infarction." American Journal of Critical Care 8 4 (1999): 220-230.

Myocardial Perfusion Scan
Other names / synonyms: Myocardial Perfusion Imaging
92.05

Definition

A myocardial perfusion scan is a radiological diagnostic procedure in which a radioactive compound is injected into a vein (intravenously). The flow of the radioactive compound in the bloodstream is imaged as it passes through the heart (coronary) circulation and is taken up by the heart muscle (myocardium). Delivery of the radioactive compound to the myocardium depends on blood flow, therefore areas of blood flow deficiency, and subsequently oxygen deficiency (ischemia), appear as defects.

Approximately 2.5 million individuals undergo myocardial perfusion scans each year in the US.

Reason for Procedure

This procedure is performed to evaluate the heart muscle (myocardium) and identify the location of myocardial infarcts, areas of ischemia, coronary artery disease (CAD), and congenital diseases. This procedure is also used to demonstrate abnormal myocardial blood flow, and assist in the diagnosis of cardiac metastases or granulomas.

Description

The radioactive compound is injected intravenously. With the individual lying down, a special camera that detects radioactivity is positioned over the heart. The camera is connected to a computer that translates the detected radioactivity into an image of the heart. Important measurements of blood flow, such as ventricular ejection fraction, can also be made during the procedure.

The exam can be done at rest or during an exercise or pharmacologic cardiac stress test. When this technique is used during a stress test, a scan is obtained immediately after the stress test; a second scan is done several hours later.

Prognosis

Myocardial perfusion scanning effectively detects areas of decreased blood flow in the heart, thereby assisting in the diagnosis of heart disease.

Specialists

- Cardiologist
- Nuclear Medicine Physician

Work Restrictions / Accommodations

Restrictions will be based on cardiac damage. Cardiac arrhythmias and abnormalities in blood pressure or symptoms occurring with strenuous exercise are taken into consideration.

Comorbid Conditions

Pregnant women should not undergo this procedure because of fetal exposure to radioactive material.

Procedure Complications

The test may provoke angina, leg fatigue, and muscle aches.

Factors Influencing Duration

The underlying cause and reason for the scan will determine the length of the disability.

Length of Disability

This diagnostic test does not produce disability.

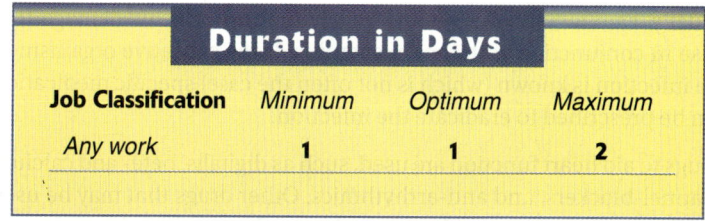

Job Classification	Minimum	Optimum	Maximum
Any work	1	1	2

Duration in Days

References

Braunwald, Eugene. Heart Disease: A Textbook of Cardiovascular Medicine, 5th ed. Philadelphia: W.B. Saunders Company, 1997.

Goldman, Lee, and J. Claude Bennett. Cecil Textbook of Medicine, 21st ed. Philadelphia: W.B. Saunders Company, 2000.

Pagana, Kathleen, and Timothy Pagana. Mosby's Manual of Diagnostic and Laboratory Tests. St. Louis: Mosby, 1998.

Zaret, Barry L., MD, senior ed. Myocardial Perfusion Scan. The Yale University School of Medicine Patient's Guide to Medical Tests. 01 Jan 1997. 31 Jan 2001 <http://my.webmd.com/content/asset/yale_lab_tests_test_name_myocardial_perfusion_scan.html>.

Myocarditis, Acute

Other names / synonyms: Interstitial Myocarditis, Subacute Myocarditis
032.82, 036.43, 074.23, 130.3, 391.2, 422, 422.90

Definition

Acute myocarditis is an inflammation of the heart muscle, most often caused by the body's response to an infection with fever. The infectious organism triggers release of proteins that are normally found only in the heart muscle. While trying to eliminate the virus, the body's immune system attacks these proteins, which cause significant injury and inflammation to the heart muscle.

Individuals at risk for developing myocarditis have experienced an infection caused by a bacterium, virus, parasite, rickettsia, or fungus. Diseases caused by some of these organisms are rheumatic fever, trichomoniasis, influenza, and diphtheria. In cooler climates, the virus that most often causes myocarditis is coxsackievirus B, but in South and Central America, it is most often caused by the transmission of the parasite Trypanosoma cruzi via an insect (Chagas disease). Rarely, myocarditis may be caused by an adverse reaction to prescription drugs or illicit drugs (such as cocaine), or to radiation therapy for treatment of cancer.

Diagnosis

History: Individuals most often have a history of an infection with fever, although they may not recall or realize that it occurred. Flu-like symptoms often bring them to a physician with complaints of weakness, fatigue, and shortness of breath with activity, often indicating some degree of heart failure.

Physical exam: The heart rate is increased. Listening to the heart and lungs can reveal an irregular or "galloping" heart rhythm and evidence of fluid in the lungs (pulmonary edema).

Tests: Chest x-ray, Doppler electrocardiogram, and an echocardiogram. A endomyocardial biopsy may also be suggested.

Treatment

Usually, care focuses on treating any symptoms of heart damage that arise in conjunction with the myocarditis. If the causative organism of the infection is known (which is not often the case) specific medication can be prescribed to eradicate the infection.

Drugs to aid heart function are used, such as digitalis, beta- and calcium channel-blockers, and anti-arrhythmics. Other drugs that may be used are diuretics, corticosteroids, and anti-coagulants.

Rest, sleep, and avoidance of stress are necessary, but physical exercise, based on limitations of symptoms, may be beneficial.

Some individuals may have such serious damage to the heart that heart transplant must be considered.

Prognosis

In some individuals, the microorganism is successfully treated, and damage to the heart is minimal. Because heart damage has often been done by the time symptoms are noted, progression to heart failure can occur. Untreated, the disease can cure itself spontaneously or lead to sudden congestive heart failure and death. Even with treatment, many individuals do not survive severe myocarditis.

Differential Diagnosis

Valvular or congenital heart disease, cardiomyopathy, and ischemic heart disease can present with similar symptoms.

Specialists

- Cardiologist
- Infectious Disease Physician

Work Restrictions / Accommodations

Restrictions and accommodations are not necessary with complete recovery. An individual who is still recovering may slowly return to regular duties. Follow-up doctor visits are frequently needed. For individuals with severe heart damage, a permanent leave may be required.

Comorbid Conditions

Underlying cardiac disease, immune deficiency, or severe viral disease may lengthen disability.

Complications

Complications of myocarditis can include progression to dilated cardiomyopathy, heart failure, and death.

Factors Influencing Duration

Most individuals with myocarditis are advised to avoid exercise and strenuous activity until their electrocardiogram readings return to normal. Some individuals may require extensive hospitalization until their condition stabilizes. When bedrest is called for, recovery depends on the severity of the inflammation. The age of the individual and the response to treatment may also determine length of disability.

Length of Disability

Duration depends on job demands, severity, underlying cause, and response to treatment. Disability may be permanent if heart damage is severe.

Duration in Days

Job Classification	Minimum	Optimum	Maximum
Sedentary work	7	28	84
Light work	7	28	84
Medium work	14	42	112
Heavy work	14	42	112
Very Heavy work	21	56	168

Failure to Recover

If an individual fails to recover within the maximum duration expectancy period, the reader may wish to reference the following questions to assist in better understanding the specifics of an individual's medical case.

Regarding diagnosis:

- Has the individual recently been infected by a bacterium, virus, parasite, rickettsia, or fungus, causing diseases such as rheumatic fever, trichomoniasis, influenza, or diphtheria?
- Has the individual recently been in South or Central America, and been bitten by an insect causing transmission of the parasite Trypanosoma cruzi (Chagas disease)?
- Does the individual recall a recent infection accompanied by fever?
- Did flu-like symptoms, such as weakness, fatigue, or shortness of breath with activity, cause them to seek medical attention?
- Were chest x-ray, electrocardiogram (ECG), and echocardiogram done?
- Was an endomyocardial biopsy required?
- Was the diagnosis of acute myocarditis confirmed?

Regarding treatment:

- Was the individual treated with antibiotics?
- If so, was the individual absolutely compliant with the antibiotic regimen?
- Were drugs to aid heart function used, such as digitalis, beta- and calcium channel-blockers, and anti-arrhythmics?
- Were other drugs used, such as diuretics, corticosteroids, and anticoagulants?
- Was the individual instructed on getting enough rest and sleep and avoiding stress?
- Was physical exercise, based on limitations of symptoms, prescribed?
- Is the individual compliant with all medication and treatment regimens?
- If serious damage to the heart was done, is a heart transplant being considered?
- If so, has the individual been placed on a heart transplant list?

Regarding prognosis:

- Did the condition respond favorably to treatment?
- Was the diagnosis made in time to prevent heart damage?
- If not, how extensive is the damage to the heart?
- Are there underlying disorders that are compromising heart function?
- Have complications occurred, such as progression to dilated cardiomyopathy or heart failure?
- If these complications have occurred, what is the individual's chance for survival?
- Is this individual a candidate for heart transplant?

References

About Cardiovascular Disease. Center for Disease Control. 28 Jul 2000. 14 Nov 2000 <http://www.cdc.gov/hccdphp/cvd/aboutcardio.htm>.

Beers, Mark, and Robert Berkow, eds. "Cardiomyopathy." The Merck Manual of Diagnosis and Therapy. Medical Services, USMEDSA, USHH, 1999. 15 Nov 2000 <http://www.merck.com/pubs/mmanual/section16/chapter203/203b.htm>.

Comprehensive Risk Reduction for Patients with Coronary and Other Vascular Disease. American Heart Association. 1999. 14 Nov 2000 <http://www.Americanheart.org/scientific/statements/1995/hguide2.html>.

DeBakey, Michael, and Antonio Gotto. The New Living Heart. Holbrook, MA: Adams Media Corporation, 1997.

Myomectomy, Uterine

Other names / synonyms: Uterine Fibroidectomy

68.29

Definition

Myomectomy is the surgical removal of uterine fibroids while preserving the uterus. Uterine fibroids (leiomyofibromas) are benign tumors of the uterine muscle. Fibroids are classified by location in the uterus; those that grow into the uterine cavity are called submucous fibroids, those located in the uterine wall are called mural fibroids, and those that protrude outside the uterine wall are called subserous fibroids.

Several approaches are available for myomectomy, including endoscopy, vaginal incision (colpotomy), abdominal incision (laparoscopic myomectomy), and myomectomy performed through the woman's cervical canal, which does not involve abdominal incisions (hysteroscopic myomectomy).

Uterine fibroids are extremely common; approximately 25% of all women over the age of 35 years have fibroids. Fibroids are even more common among black women. Approximately 250,000 operations are performed annually in the US for fibroid tumors; of these, 75% are hysterectomies and 25% are myomectomies.

Reason for Procedure

Uterine fibroids often cause no symptoms at all, in which case the fibroids require no treatment. However, in some cases uterine fibroids cause infertility, miscarriage, pelvic pain, excessive bleeding, abdominal distension, and urinary and gastrointestinal problems. When symptomatic, uterine fibroids require treatment.

Uterine fibroids can be treated medically (with drugs that interfere with the production of gonadotropins) or surgically (myomectomy or hysterectomy). Because a myomectomy removes just the tumors and not the entire uterus, myomectomy is indicated when the individual wishes to retain the ability to have children (fertility). A myomectomy permits shorter hospital stays, shorter recovery time, less bleeding, and less scar tissue formation (adhesions) than a hysterectomy.

Description

Depending on the location of the fibroids, myomectomy can be accomplished by either an abdominal or vaginal approach. In the presence of large fibroids in the uterine wall (mural) or bulging out of the uterus (subserosal), an abdominal approach is normally used. Performed under general anesthesia, the laparotomy involves an incision into the abdominal cavity. The tumors, which have previously been identified by ultrasound, are removed, and the incision sewn up. In laparoscopy, a viewing instrument (laparoscope) is inserted into the abdomen through a small incision in the abdominal wall. This device allows small surgical instruments to be passed through the scope for removal of the tumors. Typically, a laparoscopy requires a smaller incision, fewer complications, and a shorter recovery time than a laparotomy. If the fibroids causing symptoms are bulging into the uterine cavity (submucous), a vaginal approach is normally used. An operating telescope is inserted into the uterus via the vagina, and the fibroids are identified and removed.

Critical to the success of the myomectomy procedure is the reconstruction of the uterus after fibroid removal. Each defect created in the uterine wall must be carefully repaired to eliminate possible sites for infection and bleeding. If the uterus is not optimally reconstructed, it may rupture during subsequent pregnancy or delivery.

Prognosis

Myomectomy is a safe and effective alternative to hysterectomy. The successful myomectomy should result in resolution of all symptoms related to fibroids. While myomectomy is usually successful, fibroids may recur.

Specialists

- Gynecologist

Work Restrictions / Accommodations

Some strenuous physical activity (e.g., lifting) may need to be temporarily modified or eliminated.

Following laparoscopic myomectomy, individuals return to their daily routines in 2-3 days and to full activities (including exercise and sex) within 7 days.

Hysteroscopic myomectomy is usually performed on an outpatient basis, and requires a 2-3 day recovery period at home before resumption of full activity.

Comorbid Conditions

About 1 in 200 women with fibroids is found to have a malignant tumor of the uterus (sarcoma) at the time of myomectomy. The presence of sarcoma may impact the ability to recover and affect length of disability.

Procedure Complications

The primary complications that may arise from uterine myomectomy include postoperative bleeding and infection. In some cases, excessive bleeding may necessitate hysterectomy. The risk of excessive bleeding increases if there are many large fibroids in different areas of the uterus that require numerous incisions.

A poorly reconstructed uterus could rupture during future pregnancy or delivery.

Factors Influencing Duration

Length of disability may be influenced by the type of myomectomy procedure performed (laparoscopic vs. laparotomy vs. hysteroscopic), the size, location, and number of myomas removed, or the presence of complications (excessive bleeding or postoperative infection).

Length of Disability

Laparoscopic.

Job Classification	Duration in Days		
	Minimum	Optimum	Maximum
Sedentary work	3	7	21
Light work	3	7	21
Medium work	7	14	28
Heavy work	7	21	35
Very Heavy work	14	21	35

Vaginal.

Job Classification	Duration in Days		
	Minimum	Optimum	Maximum
Sedentary work	21	28	42
Light work	21	28	42
Medium work	28	42	56
Heavy work	28	56	70
Very Heavy work	28	70	84

References

Alternatives to Hysterectomy: Uterine Fibroids, Myomectomy. Toaff, Michael E., MD, MSc. 2000. 25 Aug 2000 <http://www.netreach.net/~hysterectomyedu/myomecto.htm>.

Myopia
Other names / synonyms: Nearsightedness
367.1

Definition

Myopia (nearsightedness) is the condition in which images focus in front of the light-sensitive retina rather then directly on the retina. This results in distant objects being blurry while those nearby are focused.

Myopia is a type of refractive (ametropic) error. It is caused by an abnormally long eyeball from front to back (axial myopia), or by a cornea or lens that is more powerful than normal (curvature or refractive myopia).

Estimates on the number of people who have myopia tend to vary. About 10% of young army recruits have myopia, but these are very healthy young men. A study of the general population in Sweden revealed that almost 40% of people had some degree of myopia, ranging in severity from low to high myopia. Finally, a survey of eye clinicians in England revealed that about 20% of all eyeglass prescriptions were written for people with myopia.

It usually begins about during the grade school years and gradually worsens until about the mid-twenties. Most cases of myopia in this age group are known as physiologic or school myopia, and are probably the result of an inherited predisposition combined with excessive close work that is necessary during the school years. Very little change in myopia occurs after age thirty. Myopia tends to be genetic.

Some individuals develop pathological myopia. This type of myopia is an inherited trait, but it is believed that environment also plays a role. Pathological myopia is characterized by enlargement of the eyeball with lengthening of the posterior part of the eyeball. Visual acuity, due to the degree of myopia, may be quite poor. The condition is associated with a high incidence of degenerative changes to the retina, retinal detachment, glaucoma, and development of a defect of the eye inside the cornea (staphyloma). Pathological myopia affects about 2-3% of all people. It is also one of the leading causes of blindness in the US.

Diagnosis

History: The individual will report the inability to focus on distant objects while having no problem with focusing on nearby objects.

Physical exam: The individual with myopia will have improved vision when visualizing the eye chart or distant objects through a card with a pinpoint-sized hole.

Tests: A visual acuity test and refraction exam will determine which lens (diopter) will correct the vision.

Treatment

Eyeglasses, contact lenses with a concave, or minus spectacle will be prescribed. Surgical correction (radial keratotomy) is also an option. Accuracy of correction with eyeglasses or contact lenses is greater than with radial keratotomy, and effects of the lenses is totally reversible with a new prescription.

In radial keratotomy, tiny radial incisions are made in the outer edges of the cornea, causing the eye to become "flattened," improving visual acuity. Radial keratotomy can dramatically improve vision, often to near perfect 20/20 visual acuity. But correction is not perfect. Because it is a surgical procedure, the effects are not reversible. The vast majority of people are very happy with their results.

Currently there are 2 other procedures available to correct myopia, including photorefractive keratectomy (PRK) and laser in situ keratomileusis (LASIK). In PRK, a specialized laser is used to flatten the cornea. In LASIK, a special laser is also used, but a tiny flap is made by a small incision in the cornea, and the laser is directed to the bed underneath the cornea, resulting once again in flattening of the cornea and improvement of visual acuity.

There is currently no proven method to treat pathological myopia. Individuals with pathological myopia have an increased risk for retinal detachment, glaucoma and a defect of the eye inside the cornea (staphyloma development). It is recommended that the increased ocular pressure associated with glaucoma be treated. Conservative measures such as avoidance of eye rubbing, trauma, Valsalva maneuver, corticosteroids, and regular use of aspirin are recommended. Unfortunately, degenerative pathological myopia is a common cause of legal blindness.

Prognosis

Vision can usually be corrected to normal (20/20) or near normal with glasses or contact lenses. Radial keratotomy has a less predictable outcome. Overall results with PRK are acceptable. PRK may result in a small amount of corneal scarring. There is less scarring with LASIK and there may be less pain associated with the procedure than with PRK. Problems with astigmatism and residual refractive errors may occur with the LASIK procedure. LASIK, however, may be used to treat more significant degrees of myopia. Pathological myopia may result in blindness.

Differential Diagnosis

Most eye diseases can cause blurred vision.

Specialists

- Ophthalmologist

Work Restrictions / Accommodations

Individual vision may need to be tested if this is an important aspect of the job. Those who wear contact lenses may be more sensitive to dust or fumes. If eye protection is required while on the job, some individuals may need prescription eye protection, either safety glasses or goggles, for correction of myopia. Radial keratotomy can weaken the eye. Individuals who have had radial keratotomy should always wear eye protection to protect their eyes from blunt trauma.

Comorbid Conditions

Comorbid conditions can include other refractory errors of the eye, such as an eye condition in which light rays can't be focused because the curve of the cornea is not equal in all planes, resulting in blurred vision (astigmatism); and changes in visual acuity that occur with advancing age, due to a loss of elasticity of the lens (presbyopia).

Complications

When the vision continues to worsen from axial myopia past the usual time that myopia stabilizes, the condition is known as pathological myopia. The back layer of the eye becomes very thin, which can cause retinal tears or detachment. Glaucoma and development of staphyloma occur. Pathological myopia is a common cause of legal blindness.

Factors Influencing Duration

Individual tolerance and adjustment to glasses or contact lenses, the practitioner's ability to prescribe a lens that will correct vision, and the quality of the glasses or lenses will affect length of disability.

Length of Disability

In most instances, no disability is expected.

Medical treatment.

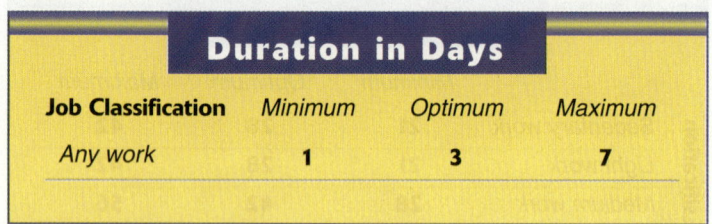

Job Classification	Minimum	Optimum	Maximum
Any work	1	3	7

Failure to Recover

If an individual fails to recover within the maximum duration expectancy period, the reader may wish to reference the following questions to assist in better understanding the specifics of an individual's medical case.

Regarding diagnosis:

- Does individual report that they can't focus on things in the distance?
- Are they able to focus on things that are close?
- Was their vision improved when looking thru a pinpoint-sized hole?
- Have they had a visual acuity test? A refraction?
- Have conditions with similar symptoms been ruled out?

Regarding treatment:

- Were eyeglasses, contact lenses with a concave, or minus spectacle prescribed?
- Were radial keratotomy, PRK, or LASIK offered as options?
- Does individual have glaucoma? Is it being treated?
- Was it recommended that individual avoid eye rubbing and trauma?

Regarding prognosis:

- Is individual's employer able to accommodate any necessary restrictions?
- Does individual have any conditions that may affect their ability to recover?
- Has individual developed the complication of pathological myopia? Staphyloma?
- Have they had a retinal detachment?

References

Abad, Juan Carlos, and Dimitri T. Azar. "Introduction to Refractive Surgery." Ophthalmology. Yanoff, Myron, and Jay S. Duker, eds. London: Mosby, 1999. 3.1.1-3.1.12.

Hardten, David R. "Excimer Laser Photorefractive Keratectomy." Ophthalmology. Yanoff, Myron, and Jay S. Duker, eds. London: Mosby, 1999. 3.4.1-3.4.18.

Miller, David. "Epidemiology of Refractive Errors." Ophthalmology. Yanoff, Myron, and Jay S. Duker, eds. London: Mosby, 1999. 2.8.1-2.8.2.

Palay, David A. "Corneal Abnormalities." Ophthalmology for the Primary Care Physician. Palay, David A., and Jay H. Krachmer, eds. St. Louis: Mosby, 1997. 68-79.

Pruett, Ronald C. "Degenerative Myopia." Ophthalmology. Yanoff, Myron, and Jay S. Duker, eds. London: Mosby, 1999. 8.29.1-8.29.4.

Slade, Stephen G., and John F. Doane. "LASIK - Laser In Situ Keratomileusis." Ophthalmology. Yanoff, Myron, and Jay S. Duker, eds. London: Mosby, 1999. 3.6.1-3.6.8.

Solley, Wayne A., and G. Broocker. "General Eye Exam." Ophthalmology for the Primary Care Physician. Palay, David A., and Jay H. Krachmer, eds. St. Louis: Mosby, 1997. 1-21.

Zabriskie, Norman A., and Randall J. Olson. "Occupational Eye Disorders." Environmental and Occupational Medicine, 3rd ed. Rom, William N., ed. Philadelphia: Lippincott-Raven, 1998. 743-754.

Myotomy of Esophagus

Other names / synonyms: Division of Esophagus, Endosurgical Myotomy, Heller Myotomy, Long Myotomy

42.7

Definition

A myotomy refers to cutting into a muscle down to the level below the mucous membrane (submucosa).

Conditions that may be treated with myotomy include esophageal motility disorders such as difficulty swallowing (dysphagia) and failure of the esophageal muscles to relax (achalasia). The walls of the esophagus consist of strong muscle fibers arranged in bundles, some circular and others longitudinal. When contractions of the muscles cause spasms that are not relieved by medication, it may be necessary to make an incision through all the muscle layers in order to weaken them and relieve the spasms. Diffuse esophageal spasm, where the muscles of the esophagus strongly contract, can produce similar symptoms as achalasia. It typically causes more chest pain, and can be adequately treated with myotomy as well. Spasm of the lower esophageal sphincter can cause symptoms of dysphagia (difficulty swallowing). It can be treated with a localized myotomy.

Esophageal motility disorders can be diagnosed with 24-hour outpatient esophageal motility monitoring.

Reason for Procedure

Esophageal myotomy is used to treat the severe swallowing problems and chest pain of diffuse esophageal spasm when it has failed to respond to medical treatment. The procedure may also be used to treat failure of the esophageal muscles to relax (achalasia). When the sphincter between esophagus and stomach fails to relax enough to allow food to enter the stomach (lower esophageal sphincter spasm) and has not responded to dilation or botulism toxin injection, a myotomy may be performed.

A myotomy may need to be done as part of the repair procedure of a perforation that occurred during esophageal dilation. When an abnormal pouching in the esophagus (esophageal diverticulum) is caused by the failure of the sphincter at the entrance of the esophagus to relax during swallowing, an esophageal myotomy may be used to weaken the sphincter and prevent recurrence.

Description

Esophageal myotomy is performed in the operating room under general anesthesia. It may be done using several different approaches. It may be an open procedure where an incision is made on the chest; or it may be done with an instrument inserted through an incision in the chest wall (thoracoscopy) or through an incision in the abdominal wall (laparoscopy). In a limited myotomy, the muscles of the esophagus are cut, starting at the aortic arch and ending at the junction where the esophagus enters the stomach (esophageal sphincter). Occasionally, it may be necessary to extend the myotomy past the sphincter and into the stomach (long myotomy). The muscles of the upper third of the esophagus may also need to be cut if presurgery testing establishes their involvement, but usually this is not necessary. For lower esophageal sphincter spasm, a localized myotomy of only the sphincter muscles may be performed.

Immediately after the procedure, the individual stays in the hospital for several days. A tube inserted through the nose into the stomach (nasogastric tube) stays in place while the esophagus heals. An x-ray then is taken while the individual swallows barium (barium swallow). This is to confirm that the esophagus is intact.

Prognosis

Esophageal myotomy is successful in about 95% of cases. Five-year success rates are at 95%, declining to about 70% at 10, 15, and 20 years. Surgical mortality is extremely rare, and the safety of the procedure is excellent. Some individuals experience mild dysphagia even after the procedure, but this is usually minimal.

Specialists

- Gastroenterologist
- General Surgeon
- Thoracic Surgeon

Work Restrictions / Accommodations

Individuals treated with an open or thoracoscopic myotomy may require extended work leave. A soft diet is necessary in some individuals after the procedure.

Comorbid Conditions

Conditions that impair an individual's ability to heal, such as diabetes or an immune disorder, may prolong an individual's recovery.

Procedure Complications

Surgical complications can include bleeding or wound infection. Perforation of the esophagus is a rare complication.

Factors Influencing Duration

Length of disability may be influenced by the specific disorder necessitating the procedure, extent, and severity of the disorder, method of procedure, or the presence of complications.

Length of Disability

Laparoscopy.

Duration in Days

Job Classification	Minimum	Optimum	Maximum
Sedentary work	7	9	14
Light work	7	9	14
Medium work	7	9	14
Heavy work	7	9	14
Very Heavy work	7	9	14

Open myotomy.

Duration in Days

Job Classification	Minimum	Optimum	Maximum
Sedentary work	14	21	48
Light work	14	21	48
Medium work	14	21	48
Heavy work	21	48	56
Very Heavy work	21	48	56

References

Pellegrini, Carlos, and Lawrence Way. "Esophagus and Diaphragm." Current Surgical Diagnosis and Treatment. Way, Lawrence, ed. Norwalk: Appleton & Lange, 1991. 400-429.

Schwartz, Seymour, MD. Principles of Surgery. New York: McGraw-Hill, 1999.

Myringotomy

Other names / synonyms: PE Tube Placement, Tube Placement
20.0, 20.01, 20.09, 20.6

Definition

Myringotomy is an incision of the eardrum (tympanic membrane) often needed to relieve pressure caused by fluid buildup in the internal, air-filled cavity (middle ear). A myringotomy is the most common surgical procedure used on or in the ear.

The procedure is commonly performed to help restore hearing and relieve pain following ear infections (otitis media) that may be accompanied by fluid buildup that medications alone cannot resolve.

While the procedure is far more common in children, adults also may develop conditions that require it.

Reason for Procedure

Myringotomy is performed to treat residual problems following ear infections. Ear infections even when resolved often leave behind fluids that can build in the middle ear cavity. If these fluids persist for longer than several months, they can cause hearing loss and other symptoms such as loss of balance and severe pain.

Without intervention such as a myringotomy, individuals with an ongoing (chronic) condition are considered at risk to have spontaneous rupture of the eardrum and future hearing impairment. Intervention may also be necessary to prevent spread of infection to other areas of the head. In rare cases, the procedure may also be considered for ongoing (chronic) episodes of discomfort from unequal ear pressure between the outside and internal ear cavity (barotrauma) caused by factors such as flying, deep sea diving, allergies, and congestion.

Description

A myringotomy is usually performed on an outpatient basis under either local or general anesthesia. Oral antibiotics may be prescribed immediately before and after the procedure to help resolve or prevent infection. A small cut (incision) is made in the eardrum (tympanic membrane), which alone may be enough to resolve the condition. In some cases, the incision may need to be followed with insertion of a small, hollow tube (ventilation tube) to assist with fluid drainage and help achieve equalized air pressure within the internal cavity (middle ear). The tube may be left in the eardrum from 6 months to a year. During this time, individuals need to be very careful to prevent water from entering the ear through the tube that can cause fluid buildup accompanied by infection.

The procedure is generally considered mild and the individual should resume work and other activities within a few days.

Prognosis

A myringotomy is generally considered a mild, simple procedure that often resolves the underlying condition. In some individuals, however, a myringotomy may fail to cure damage to the eardrum severe enough to produce permanent hearing loss. However, it is likely that the procedure will provide pain relief.

Specialists

- Otolaryngologist
- Otologist

Work Restrictions / Accommodations

In rare instances, individuals may experience permanent hearing loss that could lead to needed accommodations such as amplification or hearing aids at work. The individual may also experience problems with balance that makes it necessary to reassign work tasks that do not require standing or fine motor skills. Time off for doctor appointments may be necessary.

Comorbid Conditions

Individuals who have developed resistance to antibiotic treatments may have ongoing (chronic) ear infections that can result in repeated surgeries. Diabetes and immune disorders increase the frequency and severity of infections.

Procedure Complications

Complications are very rare but if present usually involve infection requiring antibiotic treatment. Improper healing of the eardrum may require surgical correction. Scarring as a result of the procedure may lead to permanent hearing loss. Individuals may also experience an allergic reaction to anesthetic used during the procedure.

Factors Influencing Duration

The severity of the underlying condition, any complications, and the individual's compliance with postoperative instructions may influence length of disability. The individual receiving treatment in a timely manner is less likely to experience ongoing (chronic) problems that would require repetition of the procedure.

Length of Disability

Disability may be permanent for individuals who lose their hearing and perform tasks that require keen hearing ability.

Duration in Days

Job Classification	Minimum	Optimum	Maximum
Any work	1	1	3

References

National Institute on Deafness and Other Communication Disorders. Otitis Media (Ear Infection). National Institutes of Health. 2000. 21 Jan 2001 <http://www.nidcd.nih.gov/health/pubs_hb/otitism.htm#treated>.

Narcissistic Personality Disorder
301.81

Definition

Individuals with narcissistic personality disorder possess a heightened sense of self-importance and grandiose feelings that they are unique in some way. These individuals overvalue their personal worth, direct their affections toward themselves rather than others, and expect others to recognize their unique value. Narcissistic personalities are often viewed by others as arrogant, pompous, snobbish, and highly conceited. They believe and behave as if they are above the conventions and ethics of their culture.

While interacting with others, narcissists range from being interpersonally exploitative (in milder variants) to shameless in their disregard for others (in more severe variations). They may exploit others to enhance themselves or indulge their own desires. They often feel entitled to express themselves in ways denied to others. Individuals who live or work with narcissists often feel taken advantage of or used.

Narcissists' relationships are fragile since they refuse to obey conventional rules of relating to others and have little or no ability to show empathy. They may use shaming in a relationship as a means of control. They may resort to lies or fabrications to maintain or redeem their illusions of self-worth. Certain narcissistic individuals may see themselves as admirable, extra-special, wonderful, and superior. The term narcissistic comes from the story of Narcissus who saw his reflection in a clear pond and fell in love with himself.

Diagnosis

History: Narcissistic personality disorder often presents together or in combination with another personality disorder such as borderline, histrionic, antisocial, or passive-aggressive. The psychiatric interview and mental status examination are the main tools leading to diagnosis of this disorder.

According to the DSM-IV, a pervasive pattern of grandiosity (in fantasy or behavior), need for admiration, and lack of empathy beginning by early adulthood and present in a variety of contexts is characteristic of the narcissistic personality. Five or more of the DSM-IV criteria need to be met for this diagnosis. These criteria are grandiose sense of self-importance (e.g., exaggerates achievements and talents, expects to be recognized as superior without commensurate achievements); preoccupation with fantasies of unlimited success, power, brilliance, beauty, or ideal love; belief that he or she is "special" and unique and can only be understood by, or should associate with, other special or high-status people (or institutions); need for excessive admiration; sense of entitlement (unreasonable expectations of especially favorable treatment or automatic compliance with his or her expectations); interpersonal exploitation (takes advantage of others to achieve his or her own ends); lack of empathy and unwillingness to recognize or identify with the feelings and needs of others; envy of others, or belief that others are envious of him or her; and arrogant, haughty behaviors or attitudes.

Individuals with narcissistic personality disorder may handle the aging process poorly as they value beauty, strength, and youthful attributes. They have a tendency to frequently seek cosmetic surgery especially when it is not necessary. Family history may reveal an emotionally distant parent who tried to mold the individual according to the parent's needs. Individuals with narcissistic personality disorder often have trouble forming intimate relationships and are overly sensitive to criticism and disapproval.

Physical exam: The exam is not particularly useful in diagnosing this disorder. Observation of the individual's orientation, dress, mannerisms, behavior, and content of speech provide essential clues in diagnosing this illness.

Tests: In conjunction with the individual's history, a variety of psychological tests can be done that help identify and classify personality disorders.

Treatment

Psychotherapy is usually not helpful in the treatment of narcissistic personality disorder because of the individual's inability to renounce his or her narcissism. The psychoanalytic approach may be effective in changing the individual's behavior. Pharmacotherapy can help alleviate symptoms of depression that frequently accompanies this disorder. Mood-stabilizing agents may be helpful for mood swings and antidepressants for depression.

Hospitalization may be needed for individuals who are impulsive or self-destructive, or with poor reality-testing. These stays should be brief with treatment specific to the particular symptom involved. Long-term residential treatment may be needed for individuals with poor motivation for outpatient treatment, unstable relationships, chronic destructive behavior, or a chaotic lifestyle. In this situation, individual psychotherapy, family involvement, and a specialized residential environment can provide needed support while psychotherapy tries to solve conflicts. The individual is often contemptuous of the physician, which can make treatment more difficult. Goals for group therapy include helping the individual acknowledge others as separate individuals with their own needs.

Prognosis

Outcome depends on the individual's willingness to renounce narcissism and seek treatment. The course of this disorder is chronic and difficult to treat.

Differential Diagnosis

Four other common psychiatric disorders may be associated with the narcissistic personality disorder. Dysthymia or depressive neurosis is less severe than a major depressive disorder and may result when a narcissistic individual cannot live up to his or her inflated self-image. Major depression can occur but is seldom seen in narcissists. Acute anxiety reactions can occur when the individual is confronted or challenged with realities of incompetence. Prolonged anxiety episodes are not as common. Somatoform disorders such as hypochondriacal symptoms can occur as a way of excusing or explaining defeats or failures. Paranoid disorders, unwillingness to accept facts when presented about their inadequacy or incompetence, and delusions of persecution may evolve.

Other psychiatric conditions that share some common features with narcissistic personality disorder include histrionic, antisocial, borderline, obsessive-compulsive, schizotypal, or paranoid personality disorder; manic or hypomanic episodes; personality change due to a general medical condition; or symptoms secondary to chronic substance use.

Specialists

- Psychiatrist
- Psychologist

Work Restrictions / Accommodations

Work restrictions or accommodations are necessary only infrequently, for the most serious cases. In these instances, time-limited restrictions and work accommodations should be individually determined based on the characteristics of the individual's response to the disorder, the functional requirements of the job and work environment, and the flexibility of the job and work site. The purpose of the restrictions/accommodations is to help maintain the worker's capacity to remain at the workplace without a work disruption or to promote timely and safe transition back to full work productivity.

Comorbid Conditions

Alcohol abuse or drug use, or the presence of another psychiatric illness may lengthen disability.

Complications

Any experience narcissistic individuals may have that results in a blow to their self-esteem can have significant behavioral consequences. A term used in psychiatry called "narcissistic injury" describes it as a blow to their god-like perception of themselves. These injuries may include the severing of a relationship with the partner having an affair, loss of job, or being turned down for a job.

Factors Influencing Duration

Influences from their interpersonal relationships and job, if unstable, affect length of disability. Loss or rejection even if resulting from their own behavior creates further stress and more dysfunctional behavior that lengthens disability.

Length of Disability

This condition represents a life-long pattern of behavior. In most cases, no disability is expected.

Failure to Recover

If an individual fails to recover within the maximum duration expectancy period, the reader may wish to reference the following questions to assist in better understanding the specifics of an individual's medical case.

Regarding diagnosis:

- Does individual's behavior fit the criteria for narcissistic personality disorder? Has diagnosis been confirmed?
- Have other personality disorders with similar symptoms been ruled out?

Regarding treatment:

- If individual is impulsive, self-destructive, or exhibits poor reality testing, would he/she benefit from hospitalized? If hospitalized, was inpatient treatment brief and targeted toward the specific symptom involved?
- If the individual is poorly motivated for outpatient treatment, has fragile object relationships, chronically acts-out in a destructive manner or has a chaotic lifestyle, is a residential treatment program indicated?
- Has health care team been able to establish a trust rapport with individual? If not, what can be done to foster a trusting relationship?
- Instead of focusing on the crisis symptoms, is the therapist helping individual rebuild a functional self-image?
- If not already involved in group therapy, would this be a beneficial adjunct to the current treatment plan?

Regarding prognosis:

- Are expectations and treatment goals realistic?
- Does the individual appear to be building a healthy self-image?
- Is the individual learning effective coping skills, or does he/she still rely on self-defeating behavior?

References

Hannig, Paul. The Narcissistic Personality Disorder: A Profile. Sense Media. 2000. 21 Oct 2000 <http://sensemedia.net:8080/dml/Odyssey/NPD.htm>.

Long, Philip W., MD. Narcissistic Personality Disorder. Internet Mental Health. 01 Jan 2000. 21 Oct 2000 <http://www.mentalhealth.com/rx/p23-pe07.html>.

Narcolepsy
Other names / synonyms: Sleep Epilepsy

Definition
Narcolepsy is a sleep disorder with irrepressible, involuntary sleep episodes during usual waking hours. It is characterized by excessive daytime sleepiness, disturbed nighttime (nocturnal) sleep, and sudden weakness or loss of muscle tone without loss of consciousness (cataplexy). While these cataplectic attacks may last from a few seconds to more than an hour, the frequency varies greatly from daily episodes to attacks occurring years apart.

Some individuals with narcolepsy also experience sleep paralysis, a sensation of being unable to move, and vivid, terrifying hallucinations (hypnagogic hallucinations). Both the paralysis and hallucinations occur at the onset and at the end of sleep. In addition, narcolepsy is sometimes associated with another condition called sleep apnea where a sleeping individual repeatedly stops breathing.

Narcolepsy is a chronic, lifelong disorder that can be mildly inconvenient or severely disabling. Hazardous activities such as driving a car become dangerous to self and others.

Narcolepsy affects over 100,000 individuals in the US. It may be genetic, as it tends to occur in close relatives such as siblings. Narcolepsy is difficult to diagnose because all individuals do not experience all the characteristic symptoms. Men and women are affected equally. It is interesting to note that in the white and Japanese population, narcolepsy is 100% associated with the HLA-DR2 antigen detected in tissue typing. Symptoms of narcolepsy can begin at any age but usually have a gradual onset between the ages of 15 and 35. It is fully established by age 25, but becomes less severe in old age.

Diagnosis
History: Symptoms and signs include excessive daytime drowsiness with recurring episodes of uncontrolled sleep during usual waking hours. Sleep paralysis and vivid hallucinatory dreams may occur at sleep onset. Seventy-five to eighty percent of individuals report sudden weakness or loss of muscle tone while awake (cataplectic attacks). First-degree relatives (parent and child, siblings) of known narcoleptics have at least a hundred-fold higher incidence of narcolepsy than the general population.

Physical exam: Aside from observing the individual during an actual episode of narcolepsy, there are no physical findings associated with this disorder.

Tests: Testing at a sleep disorder clinic is the most accurate way to confirm a diagnosis of narcolepsy. Various tests conducted include an analysis of the electrical activity of the brain (electroencephalogram or EEG), a record of eye movements during sleep (electroculogram or EOG), and a record of muscle activity (electromyogram or EMG). Rapid eye movement sleep (REM) recorded by the EOG along with the multiple sleep latency test (MSLT) can distinguish the rapid onset of REM sleep seen in narcolepsy. REM sleep (sleep associated with dreaming) has a quicker onset in individuals with narcolepsy.

Treatment
Treatment is symptomatic. Stimulant drugs are used to control drowsiness and sleep attacks. Treatment of cataplexy, hypnagogic hallucinations, and sleep paralysis requires tricyclic antidepressant drugs known to suppress REM sleep activity. Structured daytime napping can be part of the behavior modification used with drug therapy. Narcolepsy support groups can be helpful as well.

Prognosis
Narcolepsy is a lifelong disorder that can be mildly inconvenient or severely disabling. Treatment is directed at controlling or reducing the number of sleep attacks and associated symptoms. The condition becomes less severe with old age.

Differential Diagnosis
Atonic seizures are very similar to the cataplectic attacks of narcolepsy. Unlike narcolepsy, however, the individual having an atonic seizure loses consciousness.

Specialists
- Neurologist
- Psychologist
- Sleep Disorder Specialist

Work Restrictions / Accommodations
Due to sudden periods of uncontrolled drowsiness or sleep attacks, individuals may not be able to work in positions where safety is a concern. Job requirements may need to be modified depending on the effectiveness of treatment in controlling attacks. Work that requires the operation of dangerous machinery or performing physical labor may be difficult, if not impossible. Duties involving significant social interaction or verbal presentation skills may be in jeopardy if attacks cannot be controlled.

Comorbid Conditions
Comorbid conditions that may impact the ability to recovery include seizure disorders and mental illness.

Complications
Narcolepsy has physical and social ramifications that can be debilitating or life-threatening. Hazardous activities such as driving a car become dangerous to self and others. Fulfilling job requirements and social interactions may be extremely difficult due to unexpected attacks.

Factors Influencing Duration
Length of disability may be influenced by severity of symptoms, frequency of attacks, response to treatment, exposure to hazards (e.g., working at heights and around heavy equipment), and the individual's coping skills.

Length of Disability

Job Classification	Minimum	Optimum	Maximum
Any work	1	5	14

Duration in Days

Failure to Recover

If an individual fails to recover within the maximum duration expectancy period, the reader may wish to reference the following questions to assist in better understanding the specifics of an individual's medical case.

Regarding diagnosis:

- Does the individual experience excessive daytime drowsiness with recurring episodes of uncontrolled sleep?
- Do sleep paralysis and vivid hallucinatory dreams occur at sleep onset?
- Does the individual report sudden weakness or loss of muscle tone while awake?
- Has the individual undergone testing at a sleep disorder clinic with electroencephalogram or EEG, electroculogram or EOG, and electromyogram or EMG?
- Did the tests confirm the diagnosis?

Regarding treatment:

- Were stimulant medications prescribed? Do they help counteract the drowsiness and sleep attacks?
- Were tricyclic antidepressants prescribed? Do they suppress the episodes of cataplexy, hypnagogic hallucinations, and sleep paralysis?
- Is the individual taking medications exactly as prescribed by the doctor?
- Is individual receiving behavior modification in addition to drug therapy? What are the results? Does the individual participate in a support group?

Regarding prognosis:

- To what extent do symptoms interfere with daily activities? Does the individual have unrealistic expectations concerning abilities or limitations? How old is the individual?
- Does the individual perform hazardous activities that could be dangerous to self and others? Can the employer make accommodations that will allow the individual to work safely?
- Is individual receiving the appropriate emotional support? Would additional counseling be beneficial?

References

Chokroverty, Sudhansu, MD. "Narcolepsy." XIII Disorders of Sleep. Scientific American® Medicine Online Dale, D.C., and D.D. Federman New York: WebMD Corporation, 2000 Scientific American Medicine. 02 July 2000 <http://www.samed.com/sam/forms/index/htm>.

Mosby's Medical, Nursing and Allied Health Dictionary. Anderson, Kenneth N., revision ed. St. Louis: Mosby, 1998.

Nasal Polypectomy

Other names / synonyms: Nasal Polyps Removal
21.31

Definition

A nasal polypectomy is the surgical removal of polyps (abnormal tissue growths) that are located in the nasal passages. In healthy individuals, this is a minor outpatient procedure done under local anesthetic. If polyps recur, it may be necessary to remove polyps from the deeper ethmoid, sphenoid, and maxillary sinus linings to provide longer-lasting relief. This type of surgery requires a general anesthetic.

The polyps originate near the ethmoid sinuses (located at the top of the nose on both sides of the nasal cavity) and grow into the open areas of the nasal cavity. Large polyps can obstruct the airway and block drainage from the sinuses. Sinus infections can result from fluid accumulating in the blocked sinuses.

Caused by an overproduction of fluid in the mucous membranes, polyps are seen with asthma, allergic rhinitis (hay fever), vasomotor rhinitis (may be caused by emotional upset and sexual arousal), and certain kinds of drug use, chronic sinus infections, and cystic fibrosis. About 1 out of 4 people with cystic fibrosis have nasal polyps. Frequently, no specific cause can be found.

Nasal polyps are seen in individuals of all ages. They are present in approximately 2% of the population. There is at least a 2:1 male to female predominance. The frequency of nasal polyps increases with age, reaching a peak in individuals 50 years and older. Nasal polyps are not a disease, but a physical finding with a number of causes and associated conditions. Most commonly, 25-30% of individuals with nasal polyps have asthma, while approximately 12% have aspirin intolerance.

Reason for Procedure

A polypectomy is performed to remove nasal polyps. Nasal polyps are removed to restore normal breathing. Nasal polyps are commonly associated with allergy and particularly aspirin sensitivity, and can cause nasal obstruction and loss of the sense of smell. In addition, a small percentage of nasal polyps contain cancerous or precancerous cells. By removing the polyps, the individual's risk is reduced accordingly.

Description

Surgery for nasal polyps is usually done as an outpatient in an ambulatory surgery center where individuals go home the same day as surgery. The range of surgical treatment encompasses a variety of procedures ranging from snare and forceps removal of a polyp (polypectomy) under local anesthesia to functional endoscopic sinus surgery (ESS). A flexible endoscope may be used in the ESS. Either a local anesthesia by topical application or a local anesthesia by injection is used.

The nose is held open with a nasal speculum. The polyps are located, clamped, and removed with a wire loop. Bleeding is controlled with electrocautery. Petroleum jelly and gauze may be applied to the surgical area to prevent bleeding. The doctor will remove this dressing, usually 3 to 4 days after surgery.

Prognosis

Medical treatment may be effective in relieving signs and symptoms. Surgical removal usually allows easier breathing through the nose and improves sinus drainage and sense of smell. The individual may expect complete healing without complications.

Recurrences may be due to an underlying systemic disease or condition. Most recurrences may be successfully treated with medications without resorting to an additional surgical procedure if they are detected early.

Specialists

- Otolaryngologist

Work Restrictions / Accommodations

The individual should require no special accommodations when returning to work after surgery.

Comorbid Conditions

High blood pressure is a possible comorbid condition.

Procedure Complications

There may be excessive bleeding and surgical-wound infection. Nasal polyps may recur if an underlying allergy or infection is not controlled.

Factors Influencing Duration

If the individual is an asthmatic, or has had recurrent problems with nasal polyps, it may be necessary to perform a more complicated surgical procedure, with increased hospital and recuperation time.

Length of Disability

Duration in Days

Job Classification	Minimum	Optimum	Maximum
Any work	1	2	7

References

Berkow, Robert, MD, ed. The Merck Manual of Diagnosis and Therapy, 16th ed. Rathway: Merck Research Laboratories, 1992.

Nasal Polyps. HealthAnswers.com. 01 Dec 2000. 2 Jan 2001 <http://www.healthanswers.com/centers/body/overview.asp?id=nose+and+sinuses&filename=2327.htm/>.

Nasal Airway Surgery and Surgical Instructions. MedicineNet, Inc. 01 Nov 2000. 5 Jan 2001 <http://www.medicinenet.com/Script/Main/art.asp?li=MNI&ArticleKey=6248>.

NASAL POLYPS REMOVAL (Nasal Polypectomy). Healthgate.com. 23 Feb 2000. 5 Jan 2001 <http://search1.healthgate.com/sym/surg113.shtml>.

Nasal Polyps
Other names / synonyms: Nasal Polyposis, Nasal Polypus
471, 471.0, 471.9

Definition

Nasal polyps occur when the mucous membrane lining the inside of the nose becomes swollen and distends into the nasal cavity, creating protuberances.

The polyps appear as small, pearly grapes, and can appear as a single polyp or in clusters. Although harmless, they often obstruct the nasal passages.

Polyps are usually present with asthma, hayfever (allergic rhinitis), vasomotor rhinitis (may be caused by emotional upset and sexual arousal), and certain kinds of drug use, chronic sinus infections, and cystic fibrosis.

Estimated prevalence ranges from 0.2-1% of the population, although some studies suggest up to 20% of individuals may develop nasal polyps during their lifetime. In addition, about 1 out of 4 people with cystic fibrosis have nasal polyps.

Diagnosis

History: Symptoms may include nasal blockage, stuffed nose, and decreased sense of smell. Some individuals may have a clear nasal discharge and sneezing. Some individuals may complain of sinus pressure and severe headaches.

Physical exam: Nasal examination with an instrument that enlarges the opening of the nose for inspection (nasal speculum) reveals a grayish grape-like mass within the nasal cavity. Occasionally, shining a light up the nostrils can reveal the polyps while using a mirror, though most polyps are not easily seen.

Tests: A nasal smear may show an increase in eosinophils (a type of white blood cell).

Treatment

Medical treatment with a nasal steroid spray or a short course of oral corticosteroids is usually effective and causes the polyps to shrink or disappear. Surgery to remove the polyps (polypectomy) and infected material is recommended if the medical treatment is unsuccessful.

Surgery for nasal polyps is usually done on an outpatient basis with the use of a local anesthetic.

Prognosis

Treatment can be effective in relieving signs and symptoms. Surgical removal usually allows easier breathing through the nose, and improves sinus drainage and the sense of smell. The predicted outcome depends largely on the amount and size of nasal polyps that are present. Recurrence of nasal polyps is possible if the condition is not effectively treated.

Differential Diagnosis

A malignant tumor of the nasal or sinus mucosa may present in a similar manner.

Specialists

- Allergist
- Otolaryngologist

Work Restrictions / Accommodations

Individuals may need to avoid dust, chemicals, allergens, or strong odors that might aggravate the polyps.

Complementary and Alternative Therapies

Content is intended for awareness only. Treatments may or may not be effective. Scientific evidence may be lacking and some substances have potentially toxic effects. Dr. Presley Reed and the editors do not endorse the use of these therapies in the absence of consultation with a licensed medical professional.

Oral gold therapy - May reduce the need for corticosteroids by its effect on the immune system.

Electro-acupuncture - May improve sense of smell (olfactory function), mucociliary transport, and local immunity.

Comorbid Conditions

Allergies, seasonal hayfever, or aspirin sensitivity may lengthen disability. A diagnosis of cancer in the nasal cavity would also lengthen disability.

Complications

Nasal polyps may recur if an underlying allergy or infection is not controlled. A sinus infection can also result from nasal polyps.

Factors Influencing Duration

There is no disability caused by nasal polyps alone. The treatment approach and the individual's response to treatment may influence disability.

Length of Disability

Medical treatment.

Duration in Days

Job Classification	Minimum	Optimum	Maximum
Any work	1	1	2

Surgical treatment (nasal polypectomy).

Duration in Days

Job Classification	Minimum	Optimum	Maximum
Any work	1	2	7

Failure to Recover

If an individual fails to recover within the maximum duration expectancy period, the reader may wish to reference the following questions to assist in better understanding the specifics of an individual's medical case.

Regarding diagnosis:

- Does the individual have any risk factors?
- What symptoms does the individual have?
- What was found on physical exam?
- Have conditions with similar symptoms been ruled out?

Regarding treatment:

- Did the individual respond to conservative treatment?
- Was surgery necessary?

Regarding prognosis:

- Is the individual's employer able to accommodate avoidance of dust, chemicals, allergens, or strong odors that might aggravate the polyps?
- Does the individual follow the restrictions away from work as well?
- Does the individual have allergies, seasonal hayfever, or aspirin sensitivity, or a diagnosis of cancer in the nasal cavity?

References

Nasal Polyps. National Library of Medicine. 01 Nov 2000. 18 Jan 2001 <http://medlineplus.adam.com/ency/article/001641.htm>.

Tierney, Lawrence, Stephen McPhee, and Maxine Papadakis. Current Medical Diagnosis and Treatment. New York: McGraw-Hill, 2000.

Nasal Septum Perforation

Other names / synonyms: Perforated Nasal Septum

478.1

Definition

Nasal septal perforation refers to a hole that has eroded in the central partition between the nostrils. Repeated injury to the septum or conditions that affect the tissue in this area can result in perforation.

Nasal septal perforation has numerous causes including cocaine abuse, septal surgery, trauma, habitual nose picking, syphilis, tuberculosis, or Wegner's granulomatosis (a rare condition affecting the respiratory tract).

Septal perforation is not a common condition, and there is no age group prevalence.

Diagnosis

History: Individual may complain of new or recurrent nose bleeding that is spontaneous or caused by a specific incident. It can be severe or mild. Excess nasal crusting and dryness of the nasal passages is possible. Some perforations can result in an annoying nasal whistling sound that causes the individual to seek treatment. An underlying disease may cause other symptoms to manifest.

Physical exam: The exam may reveal nasal septal perforation, tissue that develops on the surface of an open wound during the healing process (granulations), and crusting.

Tests: Laboratory evaluation for anemia and toxicology may be indicated. Typical tests include urinalysis (drug screening to rule out cocaine use), CBC, ESR, ANCA (to rule out granulomatous diseases), and VDRL (to rule out syphilis).

A CT may be used to examine the sinuses if a granulomatous disease is suspected. A chest x-ray may help to diagnose tuberculosis or sarcoidosis. Cultures and biopsy of the septal tissue may be helpful.

Treatment

Generally, the perforated nasal septum heals with correction of the underlying cause. Habitual nose picking should be eliminated. Proper treatment of granulomatous diseases with corticosteroids enables healing. If an infectious disease such as tuberculosis or syphilis is the cause, proper treatment should be sought. Perforation due to cocaine abuse necessitates drug rehabilitation and counseling.

Septal perforations are surgically repaired only if complicated by persistent nosebleeds, crusting that causes nasal obstruction, or, rarely, a whistling sound produced by air passing through the perforation. Smaller perforations are more easily repaired surgically. Mucosal flap closure is the most common method of repairing a septal perforation. This involves creating a small flap out of the skin on the inside of the nose to cover the hole. Large perforations are often not repaired and some are even enlarged to reduce the symptoms of the perforation.

Prognosis

The perforated nasal septum usually heals with correction of the underlying cause such as treatment of granulomatous disease or infectious disease. Removal of the chronic irritation from cocaine abuse allows the septum to heal. Surgical repair with mucosal flap closure yields better results with smaller perforations. Large perforations may not be repaired and may never heal.

Individuals recovering from surgery may find breathing through the nose difficult for a while until the swelling subsides. Forceful nose blowing and insertion of objects or fingers into the nose should be avoided.

Differential Diagnosis

Other conditions that may present with nose bleeding include hypertension, bleeding disorders (hemophilia, Von Willebrand's disease), trauma, nose picking, or a tumor. Conditions with excessive crusting include sinus infections or tumors. A deviated septum may resemble a perforated septum and cause the same annoying nasal whistle and dryness.

Specialists

- Internist

Work Restrictions / Accommodations

Work restrictions and accommodations are not usually associated with this condition. Individuals whose jobs require large amounts of talking such as sales reps or telephone operators may find their job difficult after surgery due to the nasal quality of the voice. This should resolve quickly.

Comorbid Conditions

Any condition that impairs healing of tissues such as diabetes, immune disorders, and collagen-vascular disease can impact individual's recovery.

Complications

Persistent and profuse nosebleeds may complicate nasal septum perforation.

Factors Influencing Duration

Length of disability may be influenced by the severity of the perforation, the underlying cause, response to treatment, or any complications. Nasal infections after surgery can impair healing. Continued cocaine abuse or habitual nose picking also lengthens disability.

Length of Disability

Surgical treatment.

Duration in Days

Job Classification	Minimum	Optimum	Maximum
Sedentary work	3	10	14
Light work	3	10	14
Medium work	3	14	21
Heavy work	7	14	21
Very Heavy work	7	14	21

Failure to Recover

If an individual fails to recover within the maximum duration expectancy period, the reader may wish to reference the following questions to assist in better understanding the specifics of an individual's medical case.

Regarding diagnosis:

- Does the individual have a history that places them at risk for perforated septum (trauma to nasal septum, cocaine use, or underlying conditions of tuberculosis, granulomatosis, etc.)?
- Did the individual present with symptoms such as new or recurrent nosebleeds, nasal crusting, and nasal whistling?
- Did the physical exam confirm the diagnosis?
- Was the underlying cause of the perforation determined?
- Were other conditions with similar symptoms or associated conditions (bleeding disorders, hypertension, nasal tumor or trauma) ruled out?

Regarding treatment:

- Was treatment appropriately directed at correcting the underlying cause (eliminated habitual nose picking or cocaine use, treating underlying granuloma)?
- Did the perforation warrant surgical intervention?

Regarding prognosis:

- Does the individual have an underlying condition such as diabetes, immune disorders, and collagen-vascular disease that may impair healing and prolong recovery?
- Does the individual continue to have persistent and profuse nosebleeds? If so, has the individual been compliant with treatment recommendations?
- If cocaine abuse is a problem, has behavioral counseling been considered?

References

Cheney, Mack, MD. Facial Surgery, Plastic and Reconstructive. Baltimore: Williams & Wilkins, 1997.

Tierney, Lawrence, Stephen McPhee, and Maxine Papadakis. Current Medical Diagnosis and Treatment. New York: McGraw-Hill, 2000.

Nasogastric Intubation

Other names / synonyms: Gastric Decompression, NG Tube, NG Tube Placement
96.07

Definition

Nasogastric intubation is the placement of a tube into the stomach through the nose.

Several types of NG tubes composed of different materials and varying diameters are available. Feeding may be accomplished through the tube or the stomach contents may be removed by suction for therapeutic reasons. Medications can also be administered through the tube for an individual unable to swallow.

A NG tube may be used in hospitalized individuals or individuals in home care. Tubes may be placed for either short- or long-term use. In some situations, the tube is inserted through the mouth rather than the nose (oral gastric intubation). Once in place (whether inserted through the nose or mouth), a NG tube is generally well tolerated.

Reason for Procedure

NG tubes may be used for diagnostic purposes such as to withdraw (aspirate) a sample of gastric contents, assess gastrointestinal (GI) bleeding, measure volume of stomach contents, and measure the acidity of gastric contents. NG tubes may be used for several therapeutic reasons. A NG tube may be placed in surgery in order keep the stomach empty (decompressed) until the normal functioning (peristalsis) of the GI tract returns. It may be used during emergency treatment of over doses and GI conditions including GI hemorrhage, loss of intestinal movement (paralytic ileus) with accumulation of gastric liquids, gastric outlet obstruction and trauma.

To decompress the GI tract, the tube remains in place with intermittent or constant suction to aspirate the gastric contents and decompress gaseous buildup. A NG tube may also be used in the hospital room or in a home care situation to administer medications to individuals no longer able to swallow safely. Placement of a NG tube is also performed for administration of liquid feedings (enteral feeding, tube feeding) both in the inpatient and outpatient setting.

Description

The procedure is performed with the individual sitting up. The head and neck are bent slightly forward. If there is an injury or an orthopedic condition of the spine at the neck, the tube is placed without using flexion. A local anesthetic gel can be placed in the nostril used for tube placement. The tube is then inserted through the nostril into the back of the throat. Once in the stomach, proper tube placement is verified by removing stomach contents through it, introducing air into the stomach while listening over the stomach with a stethoscope, or taking an x-ray to confirm its position. When properly positioned, the tubing is taped to the nose to prevent pulling and dislodgment.

Prognosis

The predicted outcome depends on purpose of tube placement. When a NG tube is placed to provide gastric decompression, the predicted outcome is adequate removal of air and gastric contents and relief from vomiting. Other outcomes of decompression include adequate removal of blood and other gastric contents, return of normal bowel function and motility, relief of paralytic ileus, and removal of an overdose. The outcome of a NG tube placed to administer feedings is adequate nutrition and an increase or maintenance of body weight.

Specialists

- Emergency Medicine
- Gastroenterologist
- Internist
- Primary Care Provider
- Radiologist
- Registered Nurse
- Surgeon

Work Restrictions / Accommodations

No work restrictions or special accommodations are generally necessary after NG tube is removed. Individuals receiving outpatient NG feedings are often debilitated and home care services are generally needed.

Comorbid Conditions

Comorbid conditions may include any medical condition that can complicate or impair recovery from surgery. Leak of gastric contents into the abdominal cavity following bowel obstruction, GI surgery, or traumatic injury can result in life-threatening infection (peritonitis). Other comorbid conditions that may impact placement of a NG tube for feeding purposes include any medical condition that results in severe debilitation and weakness. Many conditions may be responsible for debilitation and weakness including a terminal illness such as cancer or progressive medical conditions such as multiple sclerosis or dementia. Individuals with thin, fragile skin or who are malnourished may be at increased risk of skin breakdown of the nostril.

Procedure Complications

In general, a NG tube is inserted without difficulty however several complications may occur. A nosebleed (epistaxis) may be induced as the tube is inserted through the nose. The tube may be inadvertently introduced into the trachea resulting in coughing, choking, and difficulty talking. Inadvertent placement of certain tubes (those with weighted tips or metal stylets) into the trachea may cause injury to the lung. Puncture (perforation) of the esophagus may also occur. Gastric contents may be introduced into the lungs causing injury and inflammation.

If a NG tube is used for feeding, the liquid feeding solution may go into the lungs and result in aspiration pneumonia. When tubes are left in the same nostril for a prolonged period of time, the skin and tissue of the nostril may breakdown (ulcerate) due to pressure of the tube. The tissue lining the stomach (gastric mucosa) may become eroded and perforate if a NG tube is connected to suction to provide decompression. Inflammation of the nasal sinuses (sinusitis) and the esophagus (esophagitis) may also occur. There may be an imbalance of electrolytes in the blood following the removal of a large volume of gastric fluid.

Factors Influencing Duration

The underlying cause for which the procedure was performed and any complications related to the tube's insertion may influence the length of disability.

Length of Disability

No disability is expected for this procedure. Disability may occur as a result of an underlying condition.

References

Harper, Michael B. "Nasogastric Intubation." Saunders Manual of Medical Practice, 2nd ed. Rakel, Robert E., ed. Philadelphia: W.B. Saunders Company, 2000. 404-406.

Shollenberger, Daniele, Marian Spirk, and Cynthia C. Small. "Gastrointestinal Care." Nursing Procedures, 3rd ed. Holmes, Nancy H., ed. Springhouse, PA: Springhouse Corporation, 2000. 530-581.

Nausea

Other names / synonyms: Queasiness

787.0, 787.02

Definition

Nausea is usually described as queasy, unpleasant sensations in the stomach leading to the urge to vomit.

The nervous system mechanism that produces the symptom of nausea is believed to be the same as that for vomiting. Various stimuli can activate this nervous system mechanism, such as disturbances in the balance center in the inner ear and irritation or pressure on the nerve endings in the stomach. Once stimulated, messages are sent to the brain to the region that controls the vomiting reflex. In addition, a wide variety of disturbances in the brain including concussion or other head injury, brain infections (encephalitis or meningitis), tumors, or migraine headaches can disturb the brain's vomiting reflex and cause nausea and/or vomiting. It is believed that nausea results when there is mild stimulation of this nervous system mechanism, while vomiting occurs with more intense stimulation of this nervous system mechanism.

Nausea is often a symptom of various disorders that may be relatively minor or quite severe. For example, nausea may be the manifestation of pregnancy, motion sickness, food allergies, food poisoning, alcohol or drugs, side effects of radiation therapy (radiation sickness) or medications, over-eating, obstruction of the intestinal tract, inflammation of the liver (hepatitis), heart attack (myocardial infarction), internal problems such as appendicitis, viruses (stomach flu), kidney failure, increased brain pressure (increased intracranial pressure), poor gastric motility (gastroparesis). At times, tumors, particularly those in the brain, intestinal tract, gallbladder, or liver, cause nausea.

Side effects from medications are one of the most common causes of nausea and vomiting. In addition, nausea occurs in 50-90% of all pregnancies. Less common is the nausea due to gastroparesis, which affects nearly 25% of diabetics. With the exception of pregnancy, the underlying causes of nausea are equally prevalent in both genders and every ethnic group.

Diagnosis

History: Individuals may complain of lack of appetite or an unsettled feeling in their stomach. They may be able to correlate factors that bring on the unsettled feeling or relieve the feeling. Along with feelings of nausea, they may report associated symptoms such as fever, dizziness, feeling cold and clammy, cramps, diarrhea, sweating (diaphoresis), and vomiting. The individual may report a recent, unintended weight loss. They may provide information about medication use, alcohol use, or other exposures or trauma that could have possibly precipitated the nausea. Women of childbearing age may report a delay in the onset of their menstrual cycle.

Physical exam: The exam is directed at assessing the acuteness and severity of the problem as well as uncovering additional symptoms that may be clues as to the cause. The individual is evaluated for acute weight loss and dehydration, and the presence of blood in the vomitus. The abdomen is examined for abdominal pain, abnormal bowel sounds, and distention. Vital signs are taken to determine the presence of fever, rapid pulse, or low blood pressure, which may be indicative of infection, heart attack, or inflammatory conditions. An examination of the eyes, ears, and balance may provide clues about inner ear problems or brain dysfunction. The individual should also be examined for the presence of severe headache and stiff neck, and for signs of lethargy, confusion, decreased alertness, or marked irritability, which would also indicate problems with the brain. The presence of yellow skin (jaundice) or liver enlargement may suggest nausea associated with liver dysfunction.

Tests: Laboratory testing includes blood or urine tests to rule out pregnancy, gastrointestinal x-ray studies (barium enema, upper gastrointestinal, esophagogastroduodenoscopy), stool testing, and diagnostic testing for inner ear function and balance, and head injury (CT scan, MRI).

Treatment

Sudden onset of nausea is usually associated with infection (especially of the GI tract, or stomach flu), ingestion of toxins (food poisoning), food intolerance, motion sickness, medications, pregnancy, head injury, brain infection, or gastrointestinal inflammation. On the other hand, chronic nausea is suggestive of a partial mechanical obstruction of the intestinal tract, brain tumor, poor stomach motility (gastroparesis), and metabolic, endocrine, or psychogenic disturbance.

Lying down can often help. Antinausea (antiemetic) medications, taken orally or by skin patch, may be used to provide short-term relief from nausea resulting from medications, motion sickness, inner ear disturbances or gastroenteritis. Nausea from pregnancy is usually managed by taking small, frequent meals and avoiding foods that trigger symptoms. Surgery may be indicated for gallbladder disease (cholecystectomy or common bile duct exploration), appendicitis, or obstructions of the intestinal tract (exploratory laparotomy with bowel resection). Small, frequent meals that are low in fat and fiber and careful timing of insulin are often helpful for those with poor gastric motility (gastroparesis) associated with diabetes. Occasionally, medications to increase gastric motility may be prescribed for these individuals. Diseases of equilibrium and chronic inflammatory conditions of the gastrointestinal tract (ulcer, heartburn, colitis) may require long-term treatment with medications and dietary modifications. Underlying metabolic or endocrine disturbances may be corrected with appropriate medications. Often any nausea associated with such disturbances disappears with proper medical intervention. Blood tests including blood cultures and scans such as CT and MRI may help determine problems with the brain. Psychogenic sources of nausea are best treated with psychological counseling and behavior modification.

Prognosis

Nausea associated with motion sickness usually responds well to antiemetics and tends to completely resolve shortly after the travel has ended (i.e., when the individual gets back on stable ground). Inner ear disturbances or gastroenteritis respond well to medications (decongestants and/or antibiotics). The nausea associated with these disturbances is usually well managed with antiemetics, and disappears when the underlying problem is resolved.

Nausea secondary to drug side effects is well managed with antiemetics and usually disappears when the offending drug is discontinued.

Nausea secondary to diseases of the gallbladder or intestinal obstructions usually resolves when the inflammation or obstruction is treated. Typically, nausea from pregnancy has no serious consequences and disappears spontaneously by the third or fourth month of pregnancy. Nausea due to problems with the brain such as infections or head injury takes longer to resolve, but symptoms may be controlled with antiemetics.

Prolonged nausea can lead to malnutrition and weight loss.

Differential Diagnosis

Dyspepsia, which refers to a whole host of upper abdominal discomforts including pain, fullness, bloating, belching, heartburn, and indigestion present similar symptoms and should be included in the differential diagnosis.

Specialists

- Emergency Medicine
- Endocrinologist
- Gastroenterologist
- General Surgeon
- Internist
- Oncologist
- Primary Care Provider
- Radiation Therapist
- Radiologist

Work Restrictions / Accommodations

Work restrictions and accommodations will vary with the cause of the nausea.

Complementary and Alternative Therapies

Content is intended for awareness only. Treatments may or may not be effective. Scientific evidence may be lacking and some substances have potentially toxic effects. Dr. Presley Reed and the editors do not endorse the use of these therapies in the absence of consultation with a licensed medical professional.

Acupressure - May prove an effective, harmless way to control nausea.

Diet modification - Sipping fluids such as ginger ale or cola, and sucking on ice chips may help relieve nausea and replace fluids lost by vomiting. As nausea subsides, add apple juice, bouillon, or gelatin. Progress to the "BRAT" diet (bananas, rice, applesauce, and toast) as tolerated. Avoid oily foods, dairy products, smoking cigarettes, and alcohol until back to normal. Avoid aspirin or other medications that can upset the stomach.

Comorbid Conditions

Comorbid conditions of terminal cancer, diabetes, severe head injury, liver failure, or kidney failure may impact the ability to recover and further lengthen disability.

Complications

Nausea is usually accompanied by a rapid pulse (tachycardia) and can result in abnormal heart rhythms in those with heart disease. In addition, chronic conditions of nausea may result in poor dietary intake, malnutrition, and various deficiency states. If nausea is associated with vomiting, more severe complications such as fluid and electrolyte depletion, dehydration, aspiration of stomach contents (aspiration pneumonia), and tearing of the esophagus or stomach lining can occur.

Factors Influencing Duration

The length of disability is influenced by the underlying cause of the nausea.

Length of Disability

Vague diagnosis. Additional information required regarding a specific diagnosis to determine disability duration.

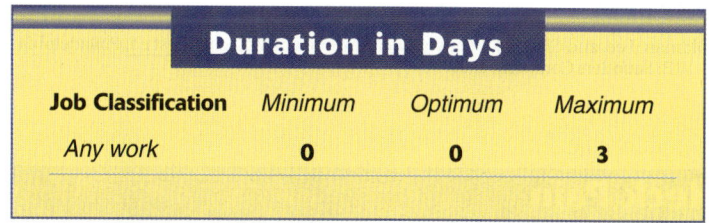

Duration in Days			
Job Classification	Minimum	Optimum	Maximum
Any work	0	0	3

Failure to Recover

If an individual fails to recover within the maximum duration expectancy period, the reader may wish to reference the following questions to assist in better understanding the specifics of an individual's medical case.

Regarding diagnosis:

- Does individual have disturbances in the balance center in the inner ear and irritation or pressure on the nerve endings in the stomach?
- Does individual have a concussion or other head injury, encephalitis, meningitis, tumors, or migraine headaches?
- Is individual pregnant, have motion sickness, food allergies, food poisoning, radiation sickness, overeating, obstruction of the intestinal tract, hepatitis, or heart attack?
- Were there any side effects from medications or alcohol?
- Does individual have internal problems such as appendicitis, stomach flu, kidney failure, increased intracranial pressure, or poor gastric motility?
- Are there any tumors in the brain, intestinal tract, gallbladder, or liver?
- Does individual complain of lack of appetite or an unsettled feeling in their stomach? Are fever, dizziness, feeling cold and clammy, cramps, diarrhea, diaphoresis, and vomiting present?
- Did a recent, unintended weight loss occur? Late menstrual cycle?
- On exam, is there evidence of dehydration, blood in the vomitus, abdominal pain, abnormal bowel sounds, or distention? Jaundice?
- Were vital signs normal or abnormal? Eyes? Ears?
- Does individual have a severe headache, stiff neck, lethargy, confusion, decreased alertness, or marked irritability?
- Were blood or urine tests done to rule out pregnancy? Barium enema? Upper GI series or esophagogastroduodenoscopy? Stool testing? CT or MRI?
- Have conditions with similar symptoms been ruled out?

Regarding treatment:

- Has individual been given antinausea medications?
- What is the underlying condition? Is it being treated?
- If necessary, was individual instructed regarding dietary modifications?
- If necessary, is individual being treated by an appropriate mental health professional?

Regarding prognosis:

- Can individual's employer accommodate any necessary restrictions?
- Does individual have any conditions that may affect ability to recover?
- Have any complications occurred such as tachycardia, arrhythmia's, malnutrition, fluid and electrolyte depletion, dehydration, aspiration pneumonia, or tearing of the esophagus or stomach lining?

References

Goldman, Lee, and Claude J. Bennett. Cecil Textbook of Medicine, 21st ed. Philadelphia: W.B. Saunders Company, 2000.

Tierney, Lawrence M., Stephen J. McPhee, and Maxine A. Papadakis, eds. Current Medical Diagnosis and Treatment, 39th ed. New York: Lange Medical Books/McGraw-Hill, 2000.

Neck Pain

Other names / synonyms: Cervical Pain, Cervicalgia
723.1

Definition

Neck pain is a symptom, not a disease or injury diagnosis. Neck pain can be caused by a disease or direct injury to the neck or be the result of an injury or disease elsewhere in the body. When not attributable to a more serious and definite cause, neck pain is often called cervicalgia.

Causes of neck pain include musculoskeletal conditions, neurological conditions, systemic conditions (osteoarthritis), rheumatoid-related conditions (Lyme disease, fibromyalgia), and psychological conditions.

Neck pain is considered chronic when it has continued for at least 6 months. An example of chronic neck pain is cervical zygapophyseal pain that often follows a whiplash.

As in low back pain, neck pain may be caused by, or significantly affected by, psychosocial factors.

It is estimated that chronic neck pain affects approximately 15% of the general population. Occurring equally in men and women, the incidence of neck pain increases with age.

Diagnosis

History: Individuals often complain of stiffness or pain in the neck region. The pain may be affected by neck motion. Complaints of pain, weakness, or numbness in the arms, or symptoms affecting the legs or abdomen should lead to another diagnosis.

Physical exam: Feeling for points of tenderness (palpation), testing range of motion (ROM), and a complete neurological exam are necessary.

Tests: Plain x-rays are used to evaluate the cervical spine if trauma has occurred, where instability is suspected, or if the symptoms have persisted for 30 days. When indicated, more extensive testing may include a CT and/or MRI, EMG, nerve conduction, and laboratory studies.

Treatment

Treatment for neck (cervical) pain varies with the source of the discomfort.

Treatment of an acute neck strain usually includes pain medication and modification of activity by avoiding painful movements and positions. If the neck muscles are extremely painful, a soft collar worn for a day or two can help relieve neck pain. The collar provides support for the spine, reduces mobility, and may reduce pain and irritation. Depending on the severity of the pain, the collar may be worn at all times or only at night.

Manipulation of the neck may help to decrease neck pain, particularly in the first 4-6 weeks after the onset of the neck pain.

Persistent or chronic pain can often be effectively controlled through participation at a pain management clinic.

Prognosis

With time, neck pain usually resolves. Treatment may make the individual more comfortable, but does not hasten recovery. Individuals must be made aware of any symptoms indicating a progressive disease.

Differential Diagnosis

Neck pain could indicate problems such as infection or tumor, fractures of the vertebrae, osteoarthritis, cervical spondylosis, degenerative disc disease, rheumatoid arthritis, and fibromyalgia. The individual may interpret symptoms from problems in the chest and shoulder as neck pain.

Specialists

- Chiropractor
- Internist
- Neurologist
- Occupational Medicine Physician
- Occupational Therapist
- Orthopedic Surgeon
- Physiatrist
- Physical Therapist
- Psychiatrist
- Psychologist
- Rheumatologist
- Sports Medicine Physician

Rehabilitation

Rehabilitation for cervical pain varies with the source of the discomfort. Therapy for acute neck pain from an injury is managed by decreasing pain and inflammation if present. The goal of therapy is to have the individual regain mobility in the neck region and strength in the muscles that may have been affected.

The early introduction of movement is important and should be explored before presuming the individual requires rest, bracing, immobilization, medication, or other anti-inflammatory procedures. This applies to all musculoskeletal conditions.

The therapist may initially use treatments involving cold or heat to control muscle pain and spasm in the neck muscles. Methods of cold treatment include cold packs applied to the neck region before or after exercises. Heat treatments are helpful to reduce inflammation and pain, and are beneficial prior to stretching of the neck muscles. Forms of heat treatment include ultrasound using high frequency sound waves to produce heat that penetrate deep into the involved muscles.

Electrostimulation combined with heat or cold treatment is another technique used in physical therapy to relax muscles around the dislocated joint. TENS is a form of electrical stimulation. An electrical impulse, predetermined by the physical therapist, produces a high frequency tingling sensation blocking pain at that level of the spine.

Traction is another popular form of rehabilitation for tight or inflexible neck muscles as well as various cervical disc disorders. Whether the therapist applies it mechanically or manually, traction produces a separation of joint surfaces of the cervical spine to help reduce the disc displacement and decompress any structures causing associated pain. This device is attached to the head and distracts the cervical spine that helps relieve tight muscles and decreases the pressure on any irritated and compressed nerve. The therapist may also give instructions in the use of a home traction unit.

Soft tissue mobilization and joint mobilization techniques are used by a physical therapist experienced in manual therapy to help improve neck mobility. This is a hands-on approach and provides increased elasticity of the muscles, thereby improving flexibility. Joint mobilization is important for increasing the movement at each spinal level that results in overall cervical spine motion.

ROM exercises are introduced in order to diminish pain and regain neck mobility. Range of motion for the neck normally may include retraction, forward, side bending, rotation, and extension and are instructed with caution by the therapist.

Once the neck pain decreases and range of motion is restored, strengthening of the neck, shoulder girdle, and trunk becomes important in the rehabilitation process. Isometric resistance helps strengthen the muscles of the neck without moving the neck through the range of motion. These exercises help improve stability around the displaced cervical disc. The individual places the palm of one hand on the forehead and temple region and applies resistance with the hand while trying to press into the hand without moving it. This position is held 6 to 10 seconds for 5 to 10 repetitions or as tolerated.

Strengthening of muscles related to cervical complaints includes the broad muscles of the back and shoulder girdle (lat dorsi, middle trapezius, lower trapezius) as well as the deep neck flexors. Resistance machines are rarely required for rehabilitation of intrinsic neck muscles. Examples of muscles potentially affected from a cervical disc disorder are those located between the trapezius, the deltoid, and virtually any of the other muscles of the arms, hands, and fingers. These nerves are responsible for sending messages to and from the brain and pass through the spinal column at the neck region. Strengthening of the upper extremities begins slowly and endurance is increased using low resistance and high repetitions. The focus then moves to strengthening by employing fewer repetitions and heavier resistance.

Therapists may need to make modifications for those individuals with other muscle or joint pain near or at the cervical spine, especially if there is an indication of a herniated cervical intervertebral disc. In this instance, some restrictions may be placed on the progression of the range of motion and strengthening with close monitoring of symptoms.

Work Restrictions / Accommodations

Working with the neck flexed or extended should be avoided. Careful attention must be paid to the proper position of chairs, table heights, and computer keyboards (ergonomics). Repetitive activities of the neck may increase symptoms. Heavy lifting and carrying should be avoided as it may aggravate symptoms. Lifting overhead may need to be restricted.

Complementary and Alternative Therapies

Content is intended for awareness only. Treatments may or may not be effective. Scientific evidence may be lacking and some substances have potentially toxic effects. Dr. Presley Reed and the editors do not endorse the use of these therapies in the absence of consultation with a licensed medical professional.

Chiropractic manipulation -	May aid in pain relief and may increase mobility (effective when continued for up to 4 weeks).
Acupuncture -	May aid in pain relief.
Electro-magnetic therapy -	May reduce neck pain.

Comorbid Conditions

Coexisting conditions that may impact recovery include cervical fractures, musculoskeletal disorders, and degenerative disorders such as osteoarthritis, other disorders like lumbar or thoracic spine pain, poor spinal posture, obesity, and injuries that prevent participation in physical therapy.

Complications

Neck pain due to damaged nerves or cervical discs, or from conditions such as rheumatoid arthritis or spondylosis, would change the diagnosis.

Factors Influencing Duration

Factors that might influence the length of disability include severity of symptoms, mode of treatment, response to treatment, the presence of an underlying condition such as a degenerative disc disease, and the requirements of the individual's job.

Length of Disability

Specific diagnosis is required to determine length of disability.

Nonspecific treatment.

Duration in Days

Job Classification	Minimum	Optimum	Maximum
Sedentary work	1	1	14
Light work	1	3	14
Medium work	1	7	42
Heavy work	3	7	56
Very Heavy work	3	14	56

Duration Trend from Normative Data*

Cases	Mean	Min	Max	No Lost Time	Over 6 Months
16383	41	0	723	0.21%	0.39%

Percentile:	5th	25th	Median	75th	95th
Days:	7	14	26	53	125

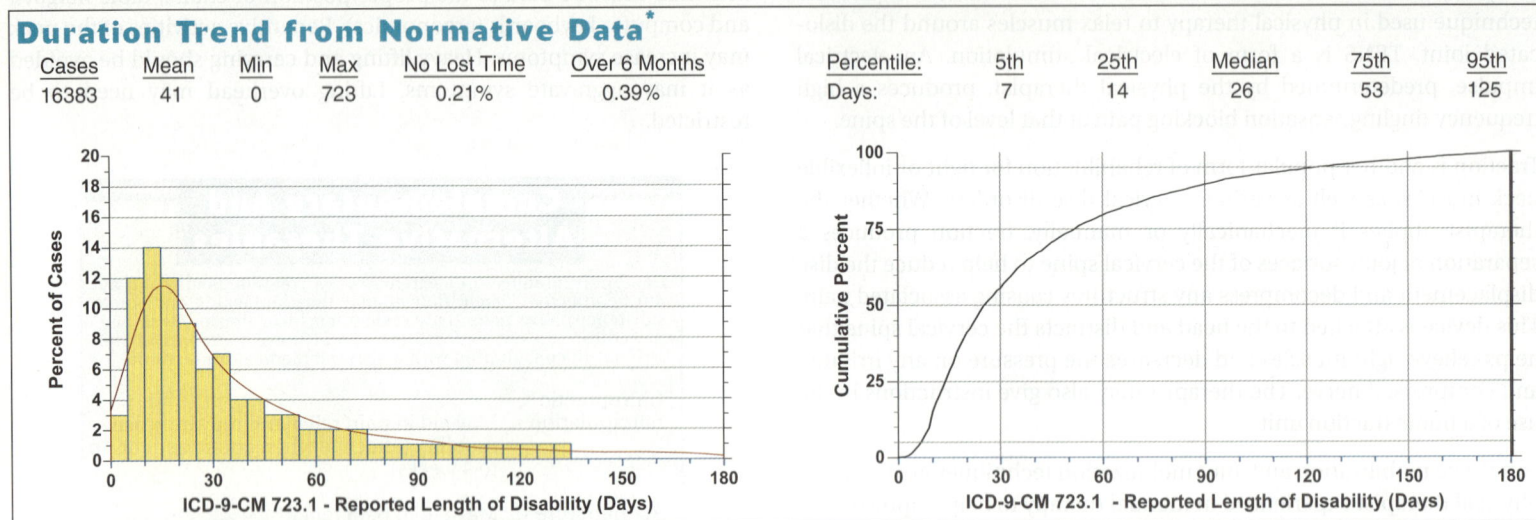

* Differences may exist between the expected duration tables and the normative graphs. Duration tables provide expected recovery periods based on the type of work performed by the individual. The normative graphs reflect the actual observed experience of many individuals across the spectrum of physical conditions, in a variety of industries, and with varying levels of case management.

Failure to Recover

If an individual fails to recover within the maximum duration expectancy period, the reader may wish to reference the following questions to assist in better understanding the specifics of an individual's medical case.

Regarding diagnosis:

- Does individual have any other diagnosed diseases or disorders?
- Were other causes of the symptoms ruled out by MRI and neurological tests?
- Has a second opinion with an appropriate specialist been obtained?

Regarding treatment:

- Did the individual follow the prescribed therapy including activity modification, ice, and heat?
- Did the individual complete the recommended course in physical therapy? Did the individual show any improvement during physical therapy?
- Were pain behaviors noted during therapy?
- Is the individual inappropriately using a soft collar for more than a few days (pain behavior)?
- Did the individual use a home traction unit, and if so, did it help?
- Did the use of TENS provide any relief?
- Did the individual rely on alternative therapies that delayed treatment?
- Did range-of-motion exercises help individual regain neck mobility? Were isometric resistance exercises effective in strengthening the muscles of the neck?
- If individual has other muscle or joint pain near or at the cervical spine (e.g., a herniated cervical intervertebral disc), were modifications made by the physical therapist?

Regarding prognosis:

- Does individual continue to gain mobility and strength in the neck region?
- Would individual benefit from being enrolled in a pain management clinic?
- Has individual been instructed in these signs and symptoms?

References

Cassidy, J.D., et al. "Effect of Eliminating Compensation for Pain and Suffering on the Outcome of Insurance Claims for Whiplash Injury." New England Journal of Medicine 342 16 (2000): 1179-1186.

Hartigan, C., L. Miller, and S.C. Liewehr. "Rehabilitation of Acute and Subacute Low Back and Neck Pain in the Work-injured Patient." Orthopedic Clinics of North America 27 4 (1996): 841-860.

Kessler, R.M. Management of Common Musculoskeletal Disorders: Physical Therapy Principles and Methods. Philadelphia: J.B. Lippincott Company, 1990.

Kisner, C., and L. Colby. Therapeutic Exercise Foundations and Techniques. Philadelphia: F.A. Davis Company, 1990.

Malone, Terry R., Thomas McPoil, and Arthur J. Nitz. Orthopedic and Sports Physical Therapy. St. Louis: Mosby, 1997.

Smith, L.A., et al. "Teasing Apart Quality and Validity in Systematic Reviews: An Example From Acupuncture Trials in Chronic Neck and Back Pain." Pain 86 1-2 (2000): 119-132.

Nephrectomy

Other names / synonyms: Excision of Kidney, Partial Nephrectomy, Radical Nephrectomy, Simple Nephrectomy

55.4, 55.5

Definition

Nephrectomy is the surgical removal of a kidney. The three basic groups of nephrectomies are simple, partial, and radical. Simple nephrectomy removes the kidney with a small section of the tube that connects the kidney to the bladder (ureter). In a partial nephrectomy, only the portion of the kidney harboring the pathology is removed. A radical nephrectomy removes the kidney, surrounding fat, fascia, lymph nodes, and two-thirds of the ureter. The operations can be done with incisions through the side (flank), back (dorsal), or abdomen.

Nephrectomies are primarily performed for cancers of the kidney. They are also performed for severe hereditary deformities of the kidney or any type of acquired condition that damages the kidney and impairs its function. When a kidney is removed, the remaining healthy kidney enlarges and takes over the function of the removed kidney. If both kidneys are removed, kidney function is done artificially for the remainder of life with a machine (dialysis) unless a healthy kidney can be transplanted into the individual.

The majority of nephrectomies are performed for the treatment of renal cell carcinoma. This is a type of kidney cancer that accounts for 2.3% of all cancer deaths in men and 1.6% in women in the US. The cancer is twice as common in men and tends to affect individuals age 55 to 60. It is more common in Scandinavians and whites in North America than in Asians or Africans. The incidence of renal cell carcinoma is 7.5 per 100,000 individuals. There are 27,600 cases reported annually in the US with 11,300 individuals dying from the condition.

The other frequent indication for nephrectomy is the donation of a kidney by a healthy individual for a kidney transplant. There are 45,000 kidney transplants performed annually in the US and 93% use donor kidneys from healthy individuals (the other 7% use cadaver kidneys).

Reason for Procedure

Simple nephrectomy is performed for severe enlargement of the kidney due to obstruction (chronic hydronephrosis); an underdeveloped, poorly functioning kidney (hypoplasia); diseased kidney causing severe high blood pressure (renovascular hypertension); large, obstructive kidney stones (calculi); and donation of a kidney for a transplant. Partial nephrectomy is performed for small tumors of the kidney, both benign and malignant. Radical nephrectomy is performed for cancer of the kidney (renal cell carcinoma) and renal pelvis.

Description

Nephrectomies are done as inpatient procedures. Because of the numerous surgical approaches and their specific risks and complications, careful preoperative evaluation and planning is necessary. The surgical approach chosen varies with specific considerations of each individual. All approaches are done with general anesthesia.

The four basic surgical approaches for nephrectomy are extraperitoneal flank, dorsal lumbotomy, abdominal, and thoracoabdominal. In all procedures, a skin incision is made. The deeper structures such as fascia and muscle are then cut and moved (retracted). In the abdominal and thoracoabdominal incisions, the abdominal organs (viscera) must be moved out of the way (retracted) to expose the kidney. In the flank approach, the eleventh or twelfth rib must be removed to expose the kidney. Once the kidney is exposed, the connective tissue that encloses it (Gerota's fascia) is cut (incised) to expose the kidney. However, this is never done if the nephrectomy is being performed to remove a renal cancer. The artery and vein to the kidney (renal artery and vein) are then identified, clamped, and cut. Sutures are used to tie off these vessels. The ureter is then identified and clamped, cut, and sutured. The kidney is removed and sent to the laboratory for examination (pathologic examination). Any fascial tissue or cut muscles are then repaired with suturing. The skin incision is also sutured. A plastic tube or rubber drain is inserted into the wound through a separate stab incision to allow drainage from the wound and prevent hematoma formation. A dressing is applied.

In the partial nephrectomy procedure, only the diseased portion of kidney is removed. In the radical nephrectomy, the entire kidney is removed along with surrounding fat, fascia, lymph nodes, and two-thirds of the ureter. This procedure is more extensive than a simple nephrectomy. The extraperitoneal flank position involves placing the individual on his/her side with the middle of the table elevated. This position is particularly useful for the obese individual but cannot be used for individuals with scoliosis or cardiorespiratory problems. The incision is located over the rib and the rib is removed.

The dorsal lumbotomy approach is done with the individual lying face down (prone) with the incision done on the back. This approach has the advantages of not having to cut muscle or remove a rib. It is useful for removing small kidneys and both (bilateral) kidneys.

The abdominal approach is done with the individual on his/her back (supine position). It involves an incision over the abdomen and moving (retraction) of the abdominal organs. Its advantage is better exposure of the portion of the kidney known as the renal pedicle but has more potential complications especially those common in abdominal surgery (ileus, adhesions).

The thoracoabdominal approach involves a long incision on the chest and abdomen with the individual in a supine position. This incision is useful for radical nephrectomy. It has all of the disadvantages of the abdominal approach and can result in pulmonary complications such as pneumothorax and atelectasis.

Prognosis

Recently, the removal of a kidney has been accomplished by performing a laparoscopic procedure. This is a new technique for renal surgery and offers much promise to diminish the morbidity of the classical approaches to the kidney. Because this procedure removes the diseased kidney, most individuals obtain a complete cure. However, the prognosis after a nephrectomy for kidney cancer is dependent on whether the cancer has already spread to distant organs.

Specialists

- General Surgeon

Work Restrictions / Accommodations

Heavy lifting, pushing, and pulling may need to be restricted. Individuals need time off to recuperate from the surgery.

Comorbid Conditions

Obesity, poor nutritional status, debilitation, and heart disease may lengthen recovery.

Procedure Complications

Complications of nephrectomy include infection, excessive bleeding (hemorrhage), urinary fistula formation, renal insufficiency, ileus, pneumothorax, pneumonia, cerebrovascular accident, pulmonary embolism, atelectasis, and adhesions.

Factors Influencing Duration

The reason for the surgery, type of surgery, and any complications may influence the length of disability.

Length of Disability

Simple.

Duration in Days

Job Classification	Minimum	Optimum	Maximum
Sedentary work	7	21	35
Light work	7	28	35
Medium work	14	35	42
Heavy work	21	42	56
Very Heavy work	21	42	56

Radical.

Duration in Days

Job Classification	Minimum	Optimum	Maximum
Sedentary work	14	28	42
Light work	14	28	56
Medium work	21	35	56
Heavy work	28	42	70
Very Heavy work	28	42	70

References

Novick, Andrew C., and Steven B. Streem. "Surgery of the Kidney." Campbell's Urology, 6th ed, vol 3. Walsh, Patrick C., et al., eds. Philadelphia: W.B. Saunders Company, 1992. 2413-2500.

Nephritis, Interstitial

Other names / synonyms: Balkan Nephropathy, Papillary Necrosis, Pyelonephritis

583.89

Definition

Interstitial nephritis is an inflammation of the connective tissue of the kidney. There is little or no involvement of the filtering units of the kidneys (glomeruli).

Acute interstitial nephritis is most often caused by the reaction to a drug. Drugs that are risk factors for development of this condition include antibiotics, diuretics, and nonsteroidal anti-inflammatory drugs (NSAIDs). Other risk factors for acute interstitial nephritis may include systemic infections (streptococcus, diphtheria, leprosy, syphilis), primary kidney infections, and immune disorders (systemic lupus erythematosus, necrotizing vasculitis).

Risk factors for ongoing (chronic) interstitial nephritis include chronic urinary tract obstruction, abuse of pain relievers (analgesics), a drug used to treat psychiatric illnesses (lithium), abnormal concentrations of substances normally present in the kidney (uric acid, calcium oxalate, calcium, potassium), chronic bacterial kidney infections (pyelonephritis), persistent or progressive acute interstitial nephritis, immune disorders (systemic lupus erythematosus, necrotizing vasculitis), cancers (leukemia, lymphoma), abnormal proteins (amyloid, multiple myeloma), diabetes, sickle cell anemia, and exposure to environmental agents (lead, cadmium).

Interstitial nephritis is uncommon and it occurs in about 4 out of 100,000 individuals. The disorder is more severe and more likely to involve chronic or permanent kidney damage in the elderly. A rare form of interstitial nephritis (Balkan nephropathy) occurs in a specific area of the Balkans, where 20% of individuals are affected. An unidentified environmental toxin is generally thought to be the most likely cause of this condition.

Diagnosis

History: In acute interstitial nephritis, the individual may report a sudden decrease in kidney function after taking a new medication, or a recent bacterial or viral infection. Symptoms characteristic of an allergic reaction are common, including fever and skin rash. Pain in the side (flank) may occur, and blood may be present in the urine (hematuria). Individuals with chronic interstitial nephritis may have a history of chronic analgesic abuse, prolonged immunosuppressant (cyclosporine) therapy, or occupational exposure to lead or cadmium.

Physical exam: The physical exam in both acute and chronic interstitial nephritis may be normal. Occasionally, individuals with acute interstitial nephritis may have a rash or flank pain.

Tests: Urinalysis may reveal blood (hematuria), increased protein (proteinuria), pus (pyuria) and increased white blood cells. High-frequency sound waves (ultrasound) or x-rays of the urinary tract wherein the radiopaque dye has been injected up into the kidneys from the ureters (retrograde pyelography) may be used to rule out other conditions such as renal lesions, obstructions, or tumors. If the diagnosis is unclear, a small sample of tissue surgically removed for microscopic examination (kidney biopsy) may be indicated.

Treatment

If the acute interstitial nephritis is due to a specific drug, the drug may be discontinued, changed, or the dosage modified. Antibiotics are used if the condition is due to infection. Both acute and chronic interstitial nephritis may be treated with anti-inflammatory drugs (corticosteroids). Toxic materials may be removed from the blood by passing it through a filter (dialysis) and this may be used to treat reduced kidney function, and to restore fluid and electrolyte balance.

Prognosis

Outcome is dependent on the cause or type of the nephritis. Most individuals with acute interstitial nephritis recover completely. Individuals with prolonged and severe acute interstitial nephritis may progress to renal failure.

While most individuals with chronic interstitial nephritis will recover some function with treatment, a few of the individuals will progress to chronic renal failure. Recovery from renal failure in individuals with chronic interstitial nephritis is rare.

Individuals with interstitial nephritis associated with analgesic abuse will recover some kidney function if the drug is stopped. If it is not stopped, progression to renal failure will occur.

Differential Diagnosis

Conditions that present with similar symptoms include tumors, diabetes, renal tuberculosis, and disease that results from obstruction of the urinary tract (chronic obstructive uropathy).

Specialists

- Neurologist
- Urologist

Work Restrictions / Accommodations

Extended leave of absence may be required. Upon returning to work, part-time hours may need to be considered for a short period, and periodic rest breaks will need to be scheduled.

Complementary and Alternative Therapies

Content is intended for awareness only. Treatments may or may not be effective. Scientific evidence may be lacking and some substances have potentially toxic effects. Dr. Presley Reed and the editors do not endorse the use of these therapies in the absence of consultation with a licensed medical professional.

Laser radiation -	Treatment with laser beam may decrease kidney inflammation and stimulate the immune system.
Iodobromine baths -	Kidney and urinary function may improve after bathing in Iodobromine.
Acupuncture -	Application of needles to certain points on the body may enhance renal function, and promote recovery and remission of interstitial nephritis.

Comorbid Conditions

Existing conditions that may impact an individual's ability to recover and further lengthen disability include other kidney diseases that affect the function of the renal interstitium (e.g., lupus nephritis, Sjögren's syndrome, mixed cryoglobulinemia, crescentic glomerulonephritis, IgA nephropathy, Wegener's granulomatosis), or diseases that affect the cardiovascular system (e.g., congestive heart failure, hypertension), immune system (e.g., systemic lupus erythematosus, or SLE), or metabolic state (e.g., diabetes mellitus, thyrotoxicosis).

Complications

Complications include renal failure, tissue death in certain areas of the kidney (papillary necrosis), gouty arthritis, increased risk of atherosclerotic diseases (especially coronary artery disease), narrowing or constricting (stenosis) of the renal artery, sodium and fluid retention, metabolic acidosis, cancer (transitional cell carcinoma), and nephrotic syndrome.

Factors Influencing Duration

Length of disability may be influenced by the underlying cause of the condition, the extent and severity of disease at initial presentation, effectiveness of treatment, the age of the individual, and the presence of high blood pressure or complications.

Length of Disability

The duration of disability depends on cause, severity, response to treatment, and the job requirements. Individuals who are receiving dialysis may need to be reassigned to sedentary duties on the days of treatment.

Acute.

Duration in Days

Job Classification	Minimum	Optimum	Maximum
Any work	0	3	14

Chronic.

Duration in Days

Job Classification	Minimum	Optimum	Maximum
Any work	0	7	21

Failure to Recover

If an individual fails to recover within the maximum duration expectancy period, the reader may wish to reference the following questions to assist in better understanding the specifics of an individual's medical case.

Regarding diagnosis:

- Did individual notice decreased kidney function?
- Did they have a recent bacterial or viral infection? Did they have any skin symptoms?
- Did they have flank pain or blood in the urine?
- Has individual abused analgesics?
- Is individual on prolonged immunosuppressant therapy?
- Was individual exposed to lead or cadmium?
- Did individual receive appropriate testing to confirm the diagnosis?
- Were conditions such as tumors, diabetes, renal tuberculosis, and chronic obstructive uropathy ruled out?

Regarding treatment:

- What was the underlying cause? Was it corrected?
- Was it necessary for individual to be on dialysis?

Regarding prognosis:

- Can individual's employer accommodate part-time work?
- Does individual have any conditions such as lupus nephritis, Sjögren's syndrome, mixed cryoglobulinemia, crescentic glomerulonephritis, IgA nephropathy, Wegener's granulomatosis, congestive heart failure, hypertension, systemic lupus erythematosus, diabetes mellitus, or thyrotoxicosis?
- Did individual have any complications such as renal failure, tissue death in areas of the kidney (papillary necrosis), gouty arthritis, increased risk of coronary artery disease, stenosis of the renal artery, sodium and fluid retention, metabolic acidosis, cancer (transitional cell carcinoma), or nephrotic syndrome?

References

Darenkov, A.F., et al. "Acupuncture in the Combined Treatment of Pyelonephritis." Urologiia i Nefrologiia 2 (1993): 10-12.

LeMone, P., and K.M. Burke. Medical-Surgical Nursing. Upper Saddle River, NJ: Prentice Hall Health, 2000.

Llach, F. Papper's Clinical Nephrology. Boston: Little, Brown and Company, 1993.

Nesterov, N.I., et al. "The Use of Laser Radiation and Sinusoidal Modulated Currents in the Therapy of Patients with Chronic Calculous Pyelonephritis." Voprosy Kurortologii, Fizioterapii i Lechebnoi Fizicheskoi Kultury 4 (1999): 24-25.

Nesterov, N.I., et al. "The Use of Interference Currents and Iodobromine Baths in the Therapy of Patients with Chronic Nonobstructive Pyelonephritis." Voprosy Kurortologii, Fizioterapii i Lechebnoi Fizicheskoi Kultury 5 (1996): 19-22.

Nesterov, N.I., et al. "The Combined Therapy of Patients with Chronic Nonspecific Pyelonephritis Using Interference Currents and Radon Procedures." Voprosy Kurortologii, Fizioterapii i Lechebnoi Fizicheskoi Kultury 6 (1999): 21-24.

Nephropexy

Other names / synonyms: Laparoscopic Nephropexy

55.7

Definition

Nephropexy is the surgical correction of a condition known as floating or dropped kidney (nephroptosis or hypermobile kidney).

Nephroptosis is present if the kidney drops approximately 2 inches when the individual is standing. It is usually present at birth, occurs more frequently in thin women and on the right side, and is rarely symptomatic or requires treatment. Symptoms such as flank pain, abdominal pain, or nausea are thought to occur because of restriction of blood flow to the kidney or an obstruction of urinary flow due to the kidney's abnormal position.

Nephropexy is only performed if symptoms persist after less invasive procedures are tried such as placement of a ureteral stent for blocking leakage of urine. A stent is a catheter placed within the ureter (tube connecting the kidney to the bladder) that keeps the ureter open after obstruction or surgery. It is as if you placed a straw inside the ureter. A skin incision to perform a nephropexy is no longer necessary since the laparoscopic approach has fewer risks.

Reason for Procedure

If a floating kidney is believed to cause symptoms such as flank pain, lower abdominal pain, or chronic urinary tract infection, laparoscopic nephropexy may be considered.

Description

During laparoscopic nephropexy, an instrument using fiberoptic lighting and a tiny camera is inserted through a small incision into the abdominal cavity. The cavity is filled with CO_2 gas to make the organs easier to see and manipulate. Other instruments such as incisors or sutures are inserted through another small incision. The surgeon can directly observe the operative area by looking through the laparoscope or by using a camera and monitoring system. The kidney is then cut (dissected) from its current position, moved into the correct position, and sewn (sutured) into place. Sutures are placed under the skin to close the small incisions.

Prognosis

The usual outcome for an uncomplicated nephropexy is full recovery and relief from symptoms.

Specialists

- Nephrologist
- Urologist

Work Restrictions / Accommodations

There are no specific accommodations required for individuals with a normal recovery. Work requiring heavy lifting may need to be restricted or modified until recovery is complete.

Comorbid Conditions

Obesity, history of kidney transplant, or other chronic illness can impact ability to recover.

Procedure Complications

Complications include allergic or abnormal response to anesthesia drugs, scarring (usually does not impair kidney function), excessive bleeding after surgery, surgical site infection, or injuries to areas outside the kidney but within the operative area. The bowel can be perforated, which would necessitate a surgical procedure to repair the injury. It is rare for the floating kidney (nephroptosis) to reoccur and can usually be prevented by careful suturing technique (how the kidney is sewn into place) during the surgical procedure.

Factors Influencing Duration

Surgical complications such as antibiotic-resistant infections may affect length of recovery but usually do not lead to permanent disability. The age of the individual, any superimposed chronic disease, and complications may influence length of disability.

Length of Disability

Duration depends on diagnosis. Durations reflect recovery time for procedure only.

Duration in Days

Job Classification	Minimum	Optimum	Maximum
Sedentary work	3	7	14
Light work	3	7	14
Medium work	7	10	21
Heavy work	7	14	28
Very Heavy work	7	14	28

References

Adams, John B. "Laparoscopic Retroperitoneal Renal Procedures." Glenn's Urologic Surgery, 5th ed. Graham, Sam D., Jr., ed. Philadelphia: Lippincott-Raven Publishers, 1998. 1043-1049.

Fornara, P. Doehn, and D. Jocham. The Technique of Laparoscopic Nephropexy. Italian Urological Association. 09 Jan 2000. 19 Jan 2001 <http://www.siu.it/eng/acta/articles/volume13_3/acta99mayjun3.html>.

Nephrotic Syndrome
581, 581.0, 581.1, 581.2, 581.3, 581.8, 581.9

Definition

Nephrotic syndrome is a condition characterized by very high levels of protein in the urine (proteinuria), low levels of protein in the blood (hypoalbuminemia), swelling (edema), fat in the urine (lipiduria), and high levels of cholesterol in the blood (hypercholesterolemia). Nephrotic syndrome occurs when renal structures in the kidney (glomeruli) become damaged. Normally, glomeruli filter waste and excess water from the blood to create urine, which travels from the kidney to the bladder.

There are many causes of nephrotic syndrome. The most common cause in adults is kidney disease. Other diseases associated with nephrotic syndrome include diabetes mellitus, a condition in which an abnormal protein collects in the tissues and organs (amyloidosis), and an inflammatory autoimmune disease (systemic lupus erythematosus). High blood pressure (hypertension), cancer, toxic exposure to heavy metals, reactions to carbon tetrachloride, poison ivy, snake venom or other toxins, and adverse drug reactions can also cause nephrotic syndrome. Infections with various bacteria, hepatitis C and other viruses, or other microorganisms are also linked to nephrotic syndrome. Other risk factors include addiction to heroin or other drugs, suppressed or compromised immune system, use of medications that are toxic to the kidneys (nephrotoxic), chronic abuse of pain medications, pregnancy, congestive heart failure, and vesicoureteral reflux. Finally, there are many cases of nephrotic syndrome in which the cause cannot be identified (idiopathic).

Nephrotic syndrome occurs in very young children (1.5-6 years old) and in adults of all ages. Men and women are affected equally, and there does not appear to be any race-related increased risk. The incidence in adults is 3 out of every 100,000 people. In affected individuals, there may be a protein in the blood affecting the ability of the glomeruli to selectively filter out waste. This glomerular permeability factor can cross the placenta, so that a baby born to a woman with nephrotic syndrome may have the same condition for a few days. Persistence of glomerular permeability factor in the blood of a individual with nephrotic syndrome may cause the disease to recur after kidney transplant.

Diagnosis

History: Symptoms include persistent, worsening swelling (edema). In the early stages, edema might be most noticeable in the legs and feet after standing for long periods. It may also be quite noticeable around the eyes when the individual first wakes up (dependent position). Later, edema may be constantly present. A bloated or tight feeling in the abdomen may be present as a result of fluid build-up in the abdomen (ascites). Individuals may also complain of shortness of breath or loss of appetite. Other symptoms include blood in the urine, change in urinary frequency or consistency, and the appearance of foam in the toilet after urinating (caused by the high protein content of the urine). Some individuals also report weight gain related to fluid retention.

Physical exam: The exam may reveal marked edema in legs and face. Exertion may cause shortness of breath (dyspnea) due to fluid retention in the chest (pleural effusion, pulmonary edema). High blood pressure (hypertension) is often noted. The blood pressure may fall abnormally when the individual sits or stands up after lying down (orthostatic hypotension). The skin may have a streaked or banded appearance (striae), and the fingernails may develop white lines. Eye examination with an ophthalmoscope (funduscopic examination) often reveals abnormally shiny retinae.

Tests: The physician usually orders a standard urinalysis as well as a 24-hour urine collection. The standard urinalysis shows abnormal levels of protein, sugar (glucose), blood, amino acids, fats, potassium and sodium, and the urine may appear foamy. Microscopic examination of the urine reveals clumps of various blood cells. Microscopic examination of urine sediment suggests kidney diseases. Kidney (renal) function can be determined by evaluation of a 24-hour urine collection. Blood tests show decreased levels of albumin (hypoalbuminemia), excessive fat (hyperlipidemia) and cholesterol (hypercholesterolemia). Other blood chemistries (sodium, calcium, potassium) are useful and may be abnormal.

In cases where the suspected cause is kidney disease, a sample of kidney tissue may be removed for microscopic examination (kidney biopsy), which helps determine the type of kidney disease and the extent of kidney damage.

Treatment

Treatment depends on the underlying condition causing the nephrotic syndrome. However, some therapies are common to nephrotic syndrome regardless of the underlying cause. Dietary changes may include a low-sodium, low-fat diet, with increased protein. Nutritional supplements (especially vitamin D and iron) are often prescribed. Individuals who have diabetes or who are overweight may be instructed to reduce caloric intake. If the blood protein level is particularly low, protein may need to be given intravenously. Drugs that increase urination (diuretics) are given to reduce swelling (edema). High blood pressure (hypertension) may be treated with pressure-reducing (antihypertensive) medication. If the kidneys are inflamed, anti-inflammatory medications (corticosteroids) are given. Medication to reduce protein in the urine (ACE inhibitors) may also be prescribed. If nephrotic syndrome fails to respond to these treatments, cyclosporin A may be helpful in some individuals. A recent report describes improvement of uncontrolled nephrotic syndrome by blocking blood flow to the renal arteries (renal ethanol embolization).

Individuals with nephrotic syndrome are often given vaccines against certain lung infections (pneumonia, viral influenza, bacterial influenza) because nephrotic syndrome appears to diminish the body's natural immunity. Individuals are also instructed to report illnesses promptly to the physician, so treatment can begin immediately.

Prognosis

The prognosis varies considerably depending on the underlying cause of nephrotic syndrome. If the underlying cause has been identified and is treatable, the prognosis is excellent, and the individual can expect complete resolution of symptoms. Elderly individuals are more likely to have a poor outcome.

If the underlying cause is not treatable, such as with many types of kidney disease, the prognosis is poor. Symptoms may be controlled with medication. Some individuals will experience a period of time during which symptoms lessen or disappear (remission). However, relapses after remission are common. If kidney failure develops, regular kidney dialysis and/or a kidney transplant may prolong life.

Differential Diagnosis

Conditions with similar symptoms include congestive heart disease, diabetes, collagen vascular disease such as systemic lupus erythematosus or scleroderma, and cancer. Generalized edema is common in congestive heart failure, and ascites or leg edema may accompany cancer of the abdominal organs if lymph drainage is obstructed by tumor. Diabetes and collagen vascular disease are associated with proteinuria in early stages, and with kidney damage or failure as the conditions get worse.

Specialists

- Cardiologist
- Endocrinologist
- Hematologist
- Immunologist
- Infectious Disease Physician
- Medical Toxicologist
- Oncologist
- Pulmonologist

Work Restrictions / Accommodations

Restrictions and accommodations vary considerably depending on the underlying cause of nephrotic syndrome, the severity of symptoms, and the individual's job requirements. Extended sick leave or a leave of absence may be required while the individual recovers. Jobs that are physically demanding or require prolonged standing should be avoided, and reassignment to a sedentary, slow-paced position may be helpful. Due to the increased risk of infection, individuals whose jobs require close contact with others (nurse, physician, school teacher, daycare worker, etc.) should be avoided. Depending on the underlying cause, these restrictions may be permanent. Individuals with severe kidney disease may be permanently disabled.

Comorbid Conditions

Individuals with a suppressed or compromised immune system; obese individuals; or those with diabetes mellitus, cancer, chronic infection such as hepatitis C, or collagen vascular diseases may have a longer period of disability.

Complications

Complications include progression to end-stage kidney (renal) disease, renal failure, increased risk of coronary artery disease and heart attacks, blood clots (thrombosis), increased risk of infections, and decreased levels of adrenocortical or thyroid hormones.

Factors Influencing Duration

Disability may be influenced by the severity and extent of disease, the underlying cause, the response to therapy, and the presence of complications.

Length of Disability

The length of disability depends on the underlying cause and response to treatment. Some individuals can expect complete recovery; others may progress to permanent disability.

Duration in Days

Job Classification	Minimum	Optimum	Maximum
Sedentary work	14	28	42
Light work	14	28	42
Medium work	28	42	56
Heavy work	28	42	56
Very Heavy work	28	42	56

Failure to Recover

If an individual fails to recover within the maximum duration expectancy period, the reader may wish to reference the following questions to assist in better understanding the specifics of an individual's medical case.

Regarding diagnosis:

- Has the diagnosis of nephrotic syndrome been confirmed?
- Has testing included 24-hour urine collection and analysis and appropriate blood tests?
- Have other conditions with similar symptoms been eliminated as possibilities? Has the underlying cause been determined?
- If kidney disease is suspected as the underlying cause, has kidney biopsy been done?

Regarding treatment:

- If the underlying cause has been identified, can it be treated? If so, is it being treated?
- Have other treatments or medications been considered?
- Would the individual benefit from a second-opinion consultation to assist in management?
- Is the individual compliant with diet and medication regime?
- Is he/she dependent on kidney dialysis?
- Has a kidney transplant been considered?

Regarding prognosis:

- Are complications present?
- Does the individual have comorbid conditions needing specific treatment?
- Has the individual developed end-stage kidney disease?
- Is the individual elderly?

References

Holt, P., and J. Swinnen. "Bilateral Femoral Artery Thrombosis in Nephrotic Syndrome." New Zealand Medical Journal 113 1123 (2000): 521.

Nephrotic Syndrome in Adults. National Kidney and Urologic Diseases Information Clearinghouse. 01 Jun 2000. 1 Jan 2001 <http://www.niddk.nih.gov/health/kidney/summary/nephsynd/nephsynd.htm>.

Nephrotomy

Other names / synonyms: Abdominal Nephrotomy, Anatrophic Nephrotomy, Lumbar Nephrotomy, Nephrolithotomy

55.01

Definition

A nephrotomy is a surgical procedure in which a kidney stone (renal calculus), cyst, or other damaged tissue is removed from the kidney.

Kidney stones are rock-like masses created when crystalline substances, such as calcium, are not excreted in the urine but, instead, build up along the wall of the kidney. Tiny stones can be washed out of the urinary tract without symptoms, but larger stones cause pain or inflammation as they pass through the kidneys, ureters, bladder, and urethra. Rarely, stones may be caused by infection (struvite stones), uric acid, or the amino acid, cystine.

Kidney stones is the third most frequent urinary tract disorder, affecting approximately 10% of Americans. Open lithotomy accounts for only about 2% of the treatments used for kidney stones. Newer, noninvasive or less invasive procedures such as transurethral removal of the obstruction, shock wave lithotripsy, or percutaneous lithotomy are more commonly used. An advantage of lithotomy is that the surgeon is able to remove the stone fragments directly instead of relying on their natural passage from the kidney.

Reason for Procedure

Nephrotomy is a surgical option for cases of stone removal where other approaches have failed. Nephrotomy is also performed when the individual is very obese.

If the stone does not pass after a reasonable period of time (about a month) and causes constant pain or if the stone is too large to pass on its own or is caught in a difficult place, nephrotomy may be performed.

Other reasons for nephrotomy include blocked flow of urine by a stone, urinary tract infection as a result of the stone, damaged kidney tissue, or constant bleeding.

If the stone has grown larger, if there are structural abnormalities in the kidney or surrounding area, in individuals with drug-resistant cystine stones, if there are conditions involving stones that branch out within the body of the kidney (staghorn calculi), a nephrotomy may be performed.

Description

During a nephrotomy, an incision is made through the skin in the area between the back and side and under the lowest rib (flank area), the abdomen, or the loin. A small incision is then made into the kidney and an instrument called a nephroscope is used to locate and remove the stone. For large stones, a type of energy probe such as an ultrasonic device, a pneumatic drill-like device, or a special device (holmium laser lithotriptor), may be needed to break the stone into small pieces before removal. After removal, a small plastic or latex tube called a nephrostomy tube is inserted to allow drainage of urine while the area heals. The tissues under the skin are closed with large absorbable sutures and the skin is closed with sutures or metal clips (staples) that are removed about 1 week after surgery.

Prognosis

Outcome for an uncomplicated kidney stone removal is usually a full recovery, although some individuals may continue to develop stones if dietary and other modifications are not made. Solitary stones have almost a 100% success rate, while stones in the body of the kidney (staghorn calculi) or the presence of multiple stones may result in up to 10% recurrence of the stones. Outcome after removal of cysts or tissue damaged by lack of blood flow depends upon the severity of the underlying kidney disease.

Specialists

- General Surgeon
- Nephrologist
- Urologist

Work Restrictions / Accommodations

There are no specific accommodations required for individuals with a normal recovery. Heavy lifting and strenuous activity should be avoided for 3-6 weeks.

Comorbid Conditions

Obesity, history of kidney transplant, or other chronic illness might impact ability to recover.

Procedure Complications

Complications include the usual anesthesia-related complications including allergic or abnormal response to anesthesia drugs. Other complications include scarring, which usually does not impair kidney function, excessive bleeding after surgery, surgical site infection, imbalances in the fluid used to irrigate the area between the skin and kidney, collapsed lung, or injuries to areas outside the kidney but within the operative area, such as the abdomen or chest. A recent study reports that the holmium laser produces cyanide as a by-product of uric acid stone fragmentation, but no poisoning has as yet been reported in any individual after this procedure.

Factors Influencing Duration

Surgical complications, such as antibiotic-resistant infections, may affect length of recovery, but usually do not lead to permanent disability. The age of the individual, any superimposed chronic disease, and complications may influence length of disability.

Length of Disability

Job Classification	Duration in Days		
	Minimum	Optimum	Maximum
Sedentary work	14	21	28
Light work	14	21	28
Medium work	21	28	42
Heavy work	28	35	42
Very Heavy work	28	35	42

References

Fitzpatrick, John M. "Pyelolithotomy." Glenn's Urologic Surgery, 5th ed. Graham, Sam D. Jr., ed. Philadelphia: Lippincott-Raven Publishers, 1998. 155-161.

Kranzfelder, Kathy, and Toni Dove. Kidney Stones in Adults. National Institute of Diabetes and Digestive and Kidney Diseases (NIDDK). 02 Jan 2001. 19 Jan 2001 <http://www.niddk.nih.gov/health/kidney/pubs/stonadul/stonadul.htm>.

Nerve Conduction Studies
Other names / synonyms: Nerve Conduction Velocity Test, Stimulation Myelographic Study
89.15

Definition

Nerve conduction studies measure electrical conduction along peripheral nerves, which are bundles of thread-like fibers that connect the central nervous system (brain and spinal cord) to the rest of the body. Stimulation of a nerve generates an electrical impulse (current), which travels along the nerve fibers, similar to a pulse of current traveling along a telephone cable. Sensory nerves carry incoming messages from sensory receptors to the spinal cord and brain. Motor nerves carry outgoing messages from the brain and spinal cord to the muscles.

Results from these studies provide information about abnormalities in the nerves supplying a particular muscle, or in the area where the nerve connects to the spinal cord. A nerve conduction test reflects the status of the "best" surviving nerve fibers and may remain normal if even a few fibers are unaffected by a disease process; thus, a normal test result can occur despite extensive nerve damage. However, the test is useful in revealing abnormalities limited to a particular nerve (focal nerve injury or entrapment), to a nerve root where it connects to the spinal cord (radiculopathy), or generalized to multiple nerves (neuropathy).

Nerve conduction velocity testing is frequently accompanied by electromyography (EMG) which measures electrical activity in the muscle, and which can therefore give more information about diseases affecting the muscle (myopathies) as well as diseases affecting the nerves supplying the muscles tested.

Reason for Procedure

Nerve conduction studies are used to diagnose nerve damage or destruction, whether generalized as in alcoholic, diabetic, or other peripheral neuropathy, or localized as in compression to or stretch injury to nerve roots (radiculopathy). Nerve compression problems, such as carpal tunnel syndrome (compression of the median nerve in the wrist) or brachial plexus syndrome (compression of the nerves coming from the neck into the arm) may also lead to abnormal test results. Nerve conduction studies evaluate the functioning of the peripheral nerves in order to determine sensory or motor dysfunction. For example, compression of the median nerve may occur near either the wrist (as in carpal tunnel syndrome) or the elbow. In nerve compression syndromes, sensory conduction is usually affected first. Motor conduction may not be affected until the disorder has progressed to a more advanced stage.

Although this type of testing allows for the detection of peripheral nerve injury or disease, nerve conduction studies alone do not diagnose the cause of dysfunction. Nerve conduction studies are often done in conjunction with electromyography (EMG), which records the electrical activity of the muscles. EMG is more helpful in diagnosing muscle disease (myopathy) or neuromuscular conditions such as muscular dystrophy, amyotrophic lateral sclerosis (Lou Gehrig's disease), myasthenia gravis, and other disorders.

Description

There is no pre-test preparation necessary, although the individual being tested may be asked to refrain from using cigarettes, caffeine, sedatives, painkillers, or other neurologic or psychiatric medications on the day of the test.

In nerve conduction studies, electrodes (thin metal discs) are placed on the skin and a mild electrical impulse, initiated at one location, travels along the nerve and is recorded by another electrode at a different location. A device called an oscilloscope is used to measure the time it takes from initiation of nerve stimulation to the nerve response. The distance between electrodes and the time it takes for electrical impulses to travel between electrodes are used to calculate the nerve conduction velocity. The height (amplitude) of the impulse may also be diminished, reflecting a decreased number of functioning nerve fibers. In addition to measuring the amplitude, the oscilloscope can also reveal the shape of the impulse, which may have diagnostic value as well. Both sensory and motor conduction can be measured, but not all nerve disorders result in slowed conduction. In nerve compression syndromes, conduction velocity is abnormally slow where the nerve is being compressed. By measuring conduction velocities over different segments of the nerve, it is possible to determine the site of compression. The measured velocity is compared to a normal range of values for that nerve segment. It may also be helpful to compare the affected and unaffected sides. H reflexes and F waves are additional test parameters that give more information about the nerve root (radiculopathy).

Prognosis

After the nerve conduction study is performed, a neurologist or other physician interprets the test results, giving information about diagnostic possibilities, or the need for further tests such as evoked potential studies or electromyography. Although nerve conduction velocity varies for different nerves and between individuals of different sex, age, and height, an abnormally slow conduction can help in the diagnosis of nerve injury or disease. Certain test results, such as those suggesting nerve entrapment as in carpal tunnel syndrome, may lead to consideration of surgery or other specific treatment. The outcome depends upon any underlying conditions, not on the nerve conduction test itself.

Specialists

- Neurologist
- Neurophysiologist
- Physiatrist

Work Restrictions / Accommodations

Work accommodations or restrictions are based on any underlying disease or condition, not on the nerve conduction test itself, as this is a harmless procedure.

Comorbid Conditions

If the nerve conduction study includes electromyography, which uses a needle electrode to pierce the skin and stimulate a muscle cell, there could be complications of pain, skin infection, or bleeding. Individuals with compromised immune system or blood clotting ability may be more likely to suffer complications related to infection or bleeding. However, disability is affected by any underlying condition, rather than by the test itself.

Procedure Complications

There are no side effects from nerve conduction studies, which use external electrodes (thin metal discs), except for the possible complication of a skin sensitivity to the paste used to attach the electrodes to the skin. If the nerve conduction study includes electromyography, in which a needle electrode pierces the skin in order to stimulate a muscle cell, then there can be complications of pain, skin infection, bruising or bleeding.

Factors Influencing Duration

No disability is expected to result from nerve conduction studies. Disability relates to the underlying disorder.

Length of Disability

No disability is expected for this procedure. Disability may occur as a result of an underlying condition.

References

Buschbacher, R.M. "Median Nerve Motor Conduction to the Abductor Pollicis Brevis." *American Journal of Physical Medicine and Rehabilitation* 78 6 (1999): S1-8.

Nerve Conduction Test. WebMD, Inc. 1999. 12 Jan 2001 <http://health.excite.com/content/asset/adam_test_ncv#why_the_test_is_performed>.

Nerve Injury

Other names / synonyms: Nerve Transection, Nerve Trauma
957, 957.9

Definition

Nerve injury includes total and partial transection of the nerve from cutting and shear, and crush injuries.

Nerve injury may complicate accidents, altercations, or other acute trauma, or it may develop more slowly from gradual compression due to repetitive movements, as in carpal tunnel syndrome, or due to sustained positions, as in radial nerve palsy. It may occur during or after surgery because of traction or casting putting pressure on a nerve, or because of incidental injury to a nerve located in the operative field.

There are 5 different grades of nerve injury classified by the degree of pathological change to the nerve with grade I being minimal injury and grade V being complete disruption. When a motor nerve is injured, there is loss of function of the muscle(s) that the nerve supplies (innervates), a sensory nerve injury usually results in pain or numbness. The closer the nerve injury to its origin in the spinal cord, the less chance of recovery.

Diagnosis

History: The individual may complain of pain, lack of sensation (hypoesthesia) or weakness of an extremity after trauma. Sometimes, no specific trauma is revealed.

Physical exam: General physical examination may reveal associated injuries. A standard neurology exam may show some of the degree of involvement, with confirmation of the complaints noted above. Peripheral nerve testing should include tests of light touch, pain, temperature, and vibration sensation. Other sensory tests include the ability to distinguish 2 pinpricks applied closely together (2-point discrimination) and the ability to appreciate small movements of the joint (joint position sense). Motor testing includes tests of strength of muscles supplied by the affected nerve. In nerve injuries related to entrapment or compression, lightly tapping over the nerve where it is compressed may cause a painful or tingling sensation. In carpal tunnel syndrome, for example, tapping over the median nerve at the wrist elicits pain in the fingers (Tinel's sign). Reflexes are typically depressed or absent in affected muscle groups.

Tests: Electromyogram (EMG) helps differentiate between grade I and higher grades of injury (II-V). A nerve conduction study, done by stimulating the nerve using an electrical stimulus on the skin and measuring the nerve response, indicates which motor and sensory nerves are affected. These tests become abnormal 2-3 weeks after the injury. A single test cannot distinguish between the lesions that will demonstrate eventual recovery (II, III) and those that are less likely (IV, V), but repeated tests can show whether improvement is occurring over time. Somatosensory evoked potentials are abnormal immediately after nerve injury, making this a useful test for monitoring nerve function during surgery that might compromise the nerve.

The skin surrounding the nerve may be examined using a magnifying lens or light scope (ophthalmoscope) to examine for patterns of sweating. This test, called a "sweat test," can indicate if the nerve fibers controlling sweating and blood vessel dilation (parasympathetic nerves) are affected.

Treatment

The treatment timing of open wound nerve injuries is critical. The wound is explored, and if a clean cut of the nerve is found, the proximal and distal nerve ends are matched and brought together (microneurosurgical repair, neurorrhaphy) can be carried out.

The repair might be done at a later date; the timing of nerve repair is dictated by the nature of the nerve injury and may be performed after the wound has healed, when some of the swelling and scarring has resolved. Delayed repairs usually require nerve grafting using a piece of another nerve to connect across the injured area.

In a closed injury (crush or shear), there is no indication for immediate surgery. The degree of nerve injury should be diagnosed as soon as possible. The individual is periodically examined over a 3-month period. During this period, gentle active motion of the involved extremity keeps the joints and soft tissue supple. If by 3 months there is some clinical or electrical evidence of recovery, the individual's course is followed. On the other hand, there is no clinical or electrical (EMG) evidence of return of function at 3 months, the nerve is explored and tested. If the test indicates any activity across the injury, then corrective nerve surgery is performed. If there is no activity, the injured area is cut out (excised) and grafted.

Prognosis

With grade I and II injuries, eventually, full recovery is expected. With grade III, scarring will result in a less than perfect reinnervation with an extremely variable pattern. There is no recovery from grade IV and V nerve injuries. Outcome also depends on the location and territory supplied by the injured nerve, and on whether there is overlap in function with neighboring nerves that are not injured. In some cases, these nerves may be able to take over some functions of the injured nerves.

Differential Diagnosis

Motor and sensory nerve dysfunction can be from ALS, MS, DM, poisoning, and other causes of peripheral neuropathy.

Specialists

- Neurologist
- Neurosurgeon

Work Restrictions / Accommodations

The extent of injury, associated motor and sensory disability, and type of work will dictate the type of work restrictions or accommodations necessary. For example, those with injuries to the nerves supplying the hand and wrist may have residual weakness or loss of sensation and coordination in the affected hand that may make it impossible to operate hand controls or equipment.

Complications

Open wounds may be complicated by wound infection and systemic infection (sepsis). Immobility (contractures) of joints around the affected nerve may complicate motor nerve injury. Loss of sensation may lead to accidental burns or other injuries. Growths of scar or nerve connective tissue (neuromas) may appear around injured nerves.

Factors Influencing Duration

Elderly individuals have poorer outcomes with surgical nerve repair. The severity of associated injuries to bones, blood vessels, muscles, and tendons may influence functional outcome and contribute to disability.

Length of Disability

Length of disability varies considerably. Duration depends on site and severity. Disability may be permanent for grade IV and V nerve injuries. Disability depends on specific job duties and specific nerves injured. For example, a pianist with slight injury to a nerve supplying a single finger may be totally and permanently disabled. Disability is not only related to grade of nerve injury, but also to specific loss of function related to job requirements.

Failure to Recover

If an individual fails to recover within the maximum duration expectancy period, the reader may wish to reference the following questions to assist in better understanding the specifics of an individual's medical case.

Regarding diagnosis:

- Does the individual have a history of trauma, surgery, or repetitive task-type injury to the affected area?
- Does the individual have complaints of pain, lack of sensation, increased sensitivity, or unpleasant sensation to the affected area?
- Did the diagnostic work-up include a neuro-sensory exam of the affected area?
- Has the nerve injury been identified and quantified using an electromyelogram?
- Were additional diagnostic studies, such as MRI, done to rule out blood clot, foreign body, or other mass that could be interfering with nerve function and repair?

Regarding treatment:

- Has surgical repair been considered? Should it be immediate or delayed?
- Are associated injuries and underlying conditions being treated appropriately?
- Might the individual benefit from second opinion consultation to consider management strategies? Has the individual been receiving physical and occupational therapy?

Regarding prognosis:

- Based on the severity of the symptoms, treatment received and the general health of the individual, what was the expected outcome?
- Was there a prolonged time between the initial injury and the surgical repair?
- Did the individual suffer any complications such as wound infection following surgery that could impact recovery and prognosis?
- Has the individual suffered associated muscle wasting or muscle contracture that could impact recovery and prognosis?

References

Braunwald, Eugene, et al, eds. Harrison's Principles of Internal Medicine, 11th ed. New York: McGraw-Hill Book Company, 1987.

Campbell, Willis C. Campbell's Operative Orthopaedics, Volume 4, 9th ed. New York: Mosby, Inc, 1998.

Candal-Couto, J.J., et al. "The Below Elbow Cast: A Cause of Median and Radial Nerve Injury After Coronary Bypass Surgery." Injury 32 1 (2001): 78-79.

Feinstein, Alice, ed. Healing with Vitamins. Emmaus, PA: Rodale Press, Inc, 1996.

Galloway, E.B., et al. "Role of Topical Steroids in Reducing Dysfunction After Nerve Injury." Laryngoscope 110 11 (2000): 1907-1910.

Gottlieb, Bill, ed. New Choices in Natural Healing. Emmaus, PA: Rodale Press, Inc, 1995.

Rochkind, S., and M. Alon. "Microsurgical Management of Old Injuries of the Peripheral Nerve and Brachial Plexus." Journal of Reconstructive Microsurgery 16 7 (2000): 541-546.

Sawyer, R.J., et al. "Peripheral Nerve Injuries Associated with Anesthesia." Anaesthesia 55 10 (2000): 980-991.

Nervous Breakdown
Other names / synonyms: Acute Stress Reaction, Mental Breakdown
300.9

Definition

Nervous or mental breakdown refers to a sudden deterioration in mental and emotional function brought on by severe stress. Beyond this most general connotation, the term lacks clinical specificity and is no longer in professional use. As there are many medical and psychiatric conditions that could fit this description, it is therefore not an appropriate or sufficiently specific diagnosis for the purposes of a disability claim.

Some of the more common psychiatric causes of "mental breakdown" include schizophrenia, depression, acute stress disorder, post-traumatic stress disorder, and bipolar mood disorder. Nonpsychiatric causes commonly include glandular and metabolic disturbances (especially of the thyroid and adrenal glands), infections, lupus, various cancers, a wide variety of neurological diseases such as stroke, multiple sclerosis, vasculitis, encephalitis, and Parkinson's disease as well as side effects from various prescription and over-the-counter medications.

This is a vague diagnosis. Contact physician for additional information.

Nervous Fatigue
Other names / synonyms: Nervous Exhaustion, Psychophysiological Asthenic Reactions
300.5

Definition

Nervous fatigue or neurasthenia is a psychological disorder characterized by chronic fatigue and weakness, loss of memory, and generalized aches and pains, formerly thought to result from exhaustion of the nervous system. However, the diagnosis is no longer in scientific use nor is it recognized in the Diagnostic and Statistical Manual of Mental Disorders, Text Revision (DSM-IV-TR). Most of the symptoms previously classified under nervous fatigue now fall under the categories of anxiety, mood, or somatoform disorders. Some medical historians consider neurasthenia to be the diagnostic predecessor of Chronic Fatigue Syndrome (CFS). For more information on the physical symptoms of nervous fatigue, refer to the Chronic Fatigue Syndrome diagnosis.

Nervousness

Other names / synonyms: Anxiety, Anxiousness

799.2

Definition

Nervousness is an unpleasant emotional state ranging from mild uneasiness to intense anxiety. Although a certain amount of anxiety is normal, serving to improve performance, nervousness becomes a problem when it starts to inhibit thought and disrupt normal activities of daily life.

Nervousness is a normal reaction to real or perceived threat. Although there may be no obvious threat, nervousness may reflect a feeling of being challenged or threatened or a sense of impending doom. A common example is the feeling of "butterflies in the stomach" before giving a speech or competing in a sports event. Once the event is completed or the perceived threat is eliminated, the symptoms disappear. Brief episodes of nervousness are normal emotions, experienced by everyone at some time in their life.

However, persistent nervousness may be associated with side effects of medications or other underlying conditions. It is prevalent in both sexes and in all ethnic groups. Common conditions associated with the symptoms of nervousness include actual danger, physical or emotional stress, grief (from loss of a loved one or even one's job), side effects from caffeine, cold remedies, decongestants, bronchodilators, thyroid supplements, or withdrawal from drugs. Nervous restlessness, tension, or irritability may also be a physical symptom resulting from an underlying medical condition or endocrine imbalance, such as hyperthyroidism or menopause.

Diagnosis

History: Individuals may complain of disturbances in sleep, eating, and drinking patterns. Individuals may describe feelings of restlessness, apprehension, irritability or inability to relax, which may be associated with other symptoms such as fatigue, headaches, pain, muscle tension, sweating, blushing, nausea, diarrhea, frequent urination, rapid breathing, difficulty breathing, or a pounding or irregular heart rhythm. They may report a recent event, such family or work issues, or a traumatic experience, that may have triggered their symptoms. They may describe circumstances that make their symptoms worse or those that make their symptoms better.

Physical exam: Physical exam may reveal abnormal behaviors may include restlessness, pacing, rapid (pressured) speech, stuttering, stereotyped jerking movements or gestures (tics), or inappropriate giggling or silence. The exam may reveal muscle tension as the cause of headaches, neck spasms, and back pain. There may be excessive blushing or sweating, pale skin, hand tremors, an overly firm or weak handshake, or an inability to relax. When the nervous state is being caused by an underlying medical condition, such as an endocrine imbalance, other physical symptoms such as rapid heart and respiratory rate, fever, or weight loss may be noted. If the nervousness is not accompanied by other physical signs and symptoms, a psychological cause may be suspected. A referral for psychiatric evaluation may be necessary.

Tests: Diagnostic tests may include lab studies to rule out medical causes of the nervousness. This may include a complete blood count, thyroid panel, chemistry panel, and possibly an electrocardiogram. If there are no obvious causes for the nervousness, psychological testing may be done to rule out an underlying psychiatric disorder.

Treatment

Treatment is most effective when there is an identifiable and justified reason for the nervousness. Psychotherapy may help to identify the real cause of the anxiety. Otherwise, treatment usually includes reassurance and counseling. Occasionally, antianxiety drugs may be necessary to relieve symptoms. When nervousness is the symptom of an underlying medical condition, such as an endocrine imbalance, treatment is targeted at the underlying cause.

Prognosis

Treatment is most effective when there is an identifiable and justified reason for the stress. Nervousness is often manageable and disappears when the underlying cause is treated or eliminated. In general, the nervousness associated with endocrine disturbances responds well to medical treatment of the underlying condition. Occasionally, nervousness associated with underlying psychological disturbances may be prolonged or incapacitating, requiring treatment with medication and ongoing psychotherapy.

Differential Diagnosis

Other possibilities include reaction to drugs or medication, psychiatric illness, or medical condition, such as hyperthyroidism or other endocrine imbalance, mitral valve prolapse or other heart condition, or neurological disorder.

Specialists

- Endocrinologist
- Internist
- Neurologist
- Psychiatrist
- Psychologist

Rehabilitation

There are no specific rehabilitation recommendations for individuals with symptoms of nervousness.

Work Restrictions / Accommodations

If nervousness is inhibiting performance of normal work duties, individuals may need to be transferred to a less stressful situation. Allowing breaks may improve coping ability. Some nervous individuals may prefer working in a more structured environment with closer supervision, whereas others may do better working independently.

Comorbid Conditions

Substance abuse, psychiatric illness such as phobias, and medical conditions such as heart, endocrine, or neurological conditions may lengthen disability.

Complementary and Alternative Therapies

Content is intended for awareness only. Treatments may or may not be effective. Scientific evidence may be lacking and some substances have potentially toxic effects. Dr. Presley Reed and the editors do not endorse the use of these therapies in the absence of consultation with a licensed medical professional.

Acupressure -	May help calm and balance emotion.
Aromatherapy -	May promote calmness and sense of well-being.
Biofeedback -	May reduce rapid heart rate, rapid breathing associated with nervousness.
Dietary modification -	Alcohol, caffeine, and concentrated sugars should be avoided, as they tend to increase anxiety.
Exercise -	Regular exercise may help to relieve stress and anxiety.
Reflexology -	May help relieve anxiety.
Relaxation therapy -	May relieve tension.

Complications

Nervousness may result from another psychological disorder, such as hypochondriasis, depression, or an anxiety disorder. Because the symptoms of nervousness mimic the symptoms of many other diseases, the sense of impending doom may lead the individual to seek numerous unnecessary medical consultations and treatments, including surgery.

Factors Influencing Duration

Factors influencing length of disability include severity of symptoms, response to treatment, overall mental health, and the underlying cause of the condition.

Length of Disability

Disability is not usually associated with this condition. This is a vague diagnosis. Contact physician for specific diagnosis.

Failure to Recover

If an individual fails to recover within the maximum duration expectancy period, the reader may wish to reference the following questions to assist in better understanding the specifics of an individual's medical case.

Regarding diagnosis:

- Has the individual had lab tests to rule out an underlying endocrine disorder? Have cardiac or neurological evaluations ruled out heart conditions or neurodegenerative disease?
- Has the individual sought numerous unnecessary medical consultations and treatments, including surgery?
- Does individual have an underlying condition, such as substance abuse, general medical condition, or psychological disorder that may impact recovery? How is this condition being addressed?

Regarding treatment:

- If caused by a medical or psychological disorder, is underlying condition responding to treatment?
- Has individual had a psychiatric evaluation? Is psychotherapy or counseling warranted?
- Would individual benefit from anti-anxiety drug therapy?
- Has individual tried eliminating substances or medications, such as caffeine or cold medications, that may contribute to the nervousness?
- Would other lifestyle modifications, such as regular exercise, be beneficial?

Regarding prognosis:

- Was an identifiable and justified reason for the stress identified? Was nervousness relieved when stressful situation was managed or eliminated?
- If related to a medical condition, does nervousness seem to be resolving with treatment of medical condition?
- Since nervousness associated with underlying psychological disturbances may be prolonged or incapacitating, would individual benefit from medication and ongoing psychotherapy?

References

Duke, James A. The Green Pharmacy. Emmaus, PA: Rodale Press, Inc, 1997.

Tierney, Lawrence M., Stephen J. McPhee, and Maxine A. Papadakis, eds. Current Medical Diagnosis and Treatment, 39th ed. New York: Lange Medical Books/McGraw-Hill, 2000.

Neuralgia, Neuritis, and Radiculitis

Other names / synonyms: Neuropathy, Radiculopathy

729.2

Definition

Neuropathy is inflammation or degeneration of the nerves outside the brain or spinal cord (peripheral nerves). "Neuritis" is a term used loosely to describe symptoms of pain or numbness without degeneration of the nerve (without objective signs of nerve dysfunction).

Actually, neuritis should be reserved for conditions in which actual inflammation of a nerve occurs, like optic neuritis seen in multiple sclerosis.

The peripheral nerves are responsible for both sensation and movement; therefore, damage to these nerves may result in pain, changes in sensation or loss of motion (paralysis). Pain caused by nerve injury is called "neuralgia." Many disease states such as diabetes, toxic exposure, alcoholism, vitamin B_{12} deficiency, poor nutritional states, and infections may include neuropathy as a sign or neuralgia as a symptom.

Radiculitis is a nonspecific term used loosely to describe pain or numbness in the distribution of a single spinal nerve root, but without objective signs of neurologic dysfunction.

This is a vague diagnosis. Contact physician for additional information on the specific diagnosis and corresponding treatment.

Neuralgic Amyotrophy

Other names / synonyms: Idiopathic Brachial Neuritis, Parsonage-Aldren-Turner Syndrome

353.5

Definition

Neuralgic amyotrophy, a type of brachial plexus neuropathy, is a disorder characterized by sudden pain and muscle weakness in the upper limbs with possible muscular wasting or atrophy, and involves the network of lower cervical and upper thoracic nerves supplying the upper extremities (brachial plexus).

It begins as an ache in and around the shoulder, at the root of the neck or base of the skull. The pain rapidly becomes more severe and is followed by rapid development of muscular weakness and sensory and reflex impairment. Neuralgic amyotrophy may develop abruptly in an otherwise healthy individual.

The cause of neuralgic amyotrophy is largely unknown. It may be a complication of an infection, an injection of vaccine or antibiotic, trauma, childbirth, surgical procedures of any type, or the use of heroin.

Nearly all cases are seen in adults ranging from 20-65 years of age with males being slightly more susceptible than females. The incidence rate is difficult to predict due to its obscure nature and unknown cause. Approximately 50% of individuals report a preceding illness or injury.

Diagnosis

History: The individual usually reports severe pain beginning in the shoulder area that is aggravated by movement. Within 3-10 days, muscle weakness develops and is followed by sensory and reflex impairment. Symptoms may be reported in one arm (unilateral) but may affect both (bilateral). Certain muscles in the arm such as the triceps or biceps may become partially or totally paralyzed. Motor nerve function becomes impaired in 7-10 days. The individual may report a preceding illness, trauma, or vaccination.

Physical exam: Physical and neurological examinations reveal decreased sensory function of the shoulder and arm and decreased reflexes. In some cases the biceps and triceps reflex is abolished.

Tests: A test that records the electrical activity of the muscles (electromyography or EMG) can isolate the muscle site(s) that are affected. EMG findings may suggest a lesion of the peripheral nerves of the shoulder and upper arm. A spinal tap may be done to test for protein in the cerebrospinal fluid, which may be slightly increased in some cases of neuralgic amyotrophy.

Treatment

Treatment consists of maintaining arm function and physical therapy exercises. The pain usually subsides with the onset of weakness. Through rehabilitation, recovery of paralysis and restoration of senses is usually complete in about 6-12 weeks, but sometimes not for a year or longer.

Prognosis

Recovery may occur within a few weeks or may take up to 2 years or longer. In most cases the pain subsides in 3-10 days, but may last for weeks. Recovery of paralysis and sensory reflexes usually occurs in 6-12 weeks, but may take up to a year or longer. In 5-10% of cases, there is residual weakness and wasting of the affected muscles. A similar percentage has had a recurrence. The majority of individuals will eventually recover full strength of the affected arm.

Differential Diagnosis

Conditions with similar symptoms include compression of a cervical nerve by a herniated disc (spondylosis), a ruptured disc, rotator cuff syndrome, or bursitis, neuropathy of the scapular nerve, or cancer that has spread (metastasized) from the breast or lung. Brachial neuropathy may develop as a complication of radiation therapy for breast cancer.

Specialists

- Neurologist

Rehabilitation

Individuals with the diagnosis of neuralgic amyotrophy may require outpatient physical therapy. Individuals should continue with a home exercise program after discharge from formal therapy, as the symptoms may not completely resolve for several months.

The primary goal of therapy is to reduce pain and swelling. Individuals may use hot packs to painful or stiff upper extremity joints prior to exercise to decrease pain and promote muscle relaxation. Ice packs may be applied after exercise. Additionally, a T.E.N.S. (transcutaneous electrical nerve stimulation) unit may be utilized.

Therapy also focuses on increasing the range of motion of any restricted joints in the arm. Therapists may stretch the shoulder, elbow, wrist, and hand to facilitate increased range of motion. Therapists encourage individuals to use the arm as much as possible during daily activities to reduce the chance of further loss of range of motion. Individuals learn to stretch the affected joints in the arm. The actual stretches performed are determined by which joints in the upper extremity have restriction of motion.

The final goal of therapy is to increase the strength of any muscles that were affected. The actual exercises performed are determined by the extent of muscle weakness. For example, if the biceps muscle is weak, an individual performs biceps curls in which the elbow is flexed and then straightened. Individuals may use light hand weights to add resistance to an exercise.

Work Restrictions / Accommodations

Pain and muscle weakness affects the ability of the individual to perform highly physical work. If paralysis is present, the individual will be further limited. If the individual recovers fully from the paralysis, and in the absence of residual muscle weakness, return to moderately physical work is possible.

Comorbid Conditions

Other conditions such as bursitis or inflammation of the shoulder due to sports injury or trauma may affect the ability of the individual to recover and lengthen disability.

Complications

The shoulder may become locked in one position, requiring extensive rehabilitation. In rare cases, paralysis of the arm from a lesion of the brachial plexus may develop.

Factors Influencing Duration

The length of disability may be affected by the severity of pain, muscle weakness and paralysis (if present), whether the dominant side is affected, and the nature of the individual's work.

Length of Disability

Duration depends on whether the dominant or non-dominant side is affected. The expected length of disability may be a few weeks up to 2 years.

Duration in Days

Job Classification	Minimum	Optimum	Maximum
Sedentary work	1	28	56
Light work	1	28	56
Medium work	28	56	84
Heavy work	56	112	168
Very Heavy work	56	112	168

Failure to Recover

If an individual fails to recover within the maximum duration expectancy period, the reader may wish to reference the following questions to assist in better understanding the specifics of an individual's medical case.

Regarding diagnosis:

- Does individual report severe pain beginning in the shoulder that is aggravated by movement?
- Has muscle weakness developed?
- Have sensory and reflex impairment occurred?
- Are both arms affected?
- Have the triceps or biceps muscles become partially or totally paralyzed?
- Does individual may report a preceding illness, trauma, or vaccination?
- Does the physician note decreased sensory function of the shoulder and arm?
- Are reflexes decreased?
- Has electrical activity of the muscles (electromyography or EMG) been tested?
- Has a spinal tap (lumbar puncture) been done to test for protein in the cerebrospinal fluid?

Regarding treatment:

- Has treatment maintained arm function?
- Has individual been compliant with the physical therapy regimen?
- Has pain been relieved?

Regarding prognosis:

- Does individual have residual weakness or wasting of the muscles?
- Has individual experienced a recurrence of the disorder?
- Is individual expected to recover full strength in the affected arm?
- Has individual developed a locked shoulder?
- If so, what type of rehabilitation is required and how long is it expected to continue? Has individual developed paralysis of the arm?
- What other neuropathies may be present that may complicate the outcome?

References

Adams, Raymond D., Maurice Victor, and Allan H. Ropper. Principles of Neurology, 6th ed. New York: McGraw Hill, 1997.

Kisner, Carolyn, and Lynn Allen Colby. "The Shoulder and Shoulder Girdle." Therapeutic Exercise: Foundations and Techniques, 2nd ed. Philadelphia: F.A. Davis Company, 1990. 241-271.

Neurocirculatory Asthenia

Other names / synonyms: Cardiac Neurosis, Da Costa's Syndrome, Effort Syndrome, Hyperkinetic Heart Syndrome, Irritable Heart, Soldier's Heart

306.2

Definition

Neurocirculatory asthenia or DaCosta's syndrome is a condition characterized by shortness of breath, fatigue, rapid pulse, and irregular or pounding heartbeats (palpitations). It occurs mostly with exertion and is not due to physical disease of the heart, but is associated with exhaustion and may have a psychological basis. In psychiatry, there is a tendency to view this disorder as a form of anxiety disorder yet it does not appear in the DSM-IV-TR. It has classically been described in soldiers exposed to combat, and is now thought to overlap with post-traumatic stress disorder and/or chronic fatigue syndrome.

Risk factors are basically the same as for any chronic anxiety condition. Specific causes are not known, however, a stressful life situation may be a risk factor.

Symptoms of neurocirculatory asthenia usually start in adolescence or the early twenties but may also present in middle age. The condition is twice as common in women than men, and tends to be chronic with recurrent acute exacerbations.

Diagnosis

History: The psychiatric interview, mental status exam, and neurologic exam are needed for diagnosis of this disorder. The established diagnostic criteria for neurocirculatory asthenia include respiratory complaints such as the inability to take a deep breath, a smothering sensation upon taking a breath, a choking sensation, the feeling of being short of breath (dyspnea), the sensation of a racing heart (palpitations) and/or a pulse rate of over 100 beats per minute (tachycardia), chest pain or discomfort, undue fatigue or limitation of activities, excessive sweating, insomnia, irritability, and feelings of nervousness, dizziness, faintness, or discomfort in crowds.

Physical exam: On physical exam, an increased respiratory rate of greater than 24 breaths per minute or shallow respirations or sighing respirations may be evident. Pulse may be irregular or rapid.

Tests: Psychological tests such as the Minnesota Multiphasic Personality Inventory and their interpretation can be helpful. Cardiac evaluation may be needed to exclude physical diseases with similar symptoms such as mitral valve prolapse.

Treatment

The treatment of neurocirculatory asthenia is challenging since many individuals may receive secondary gain of attention and sympathy for their symptoms, and tend to seek help from medical specialists rather than psychiatrists. Psychotherapy may be useful and focuses on feelings of anxiety and explores ways to decrease anxiety levels. Medication therapy focuses on the symptoms of anxiety that may be controlled with beta-blockers or antianxiety agents, and fatigue that may indicate a need for stimulants. Stimulants may worsen symptoms of anxiety, however, and should be avoided if possible.

Prognosis

The expected outcome for neurocirculatory asthenia is guarded, particularly if it is chronic. Treatment is difficult and the individual most often avoids psychiatric help insisting there is an organic reason for the symptoms. The outcome can be positive if the individual accepts treatment aimed toward relieving the symptoms of anxiety such as medication or psychotherapy.

Differential Diagnosis

Other conditions with similar presentation include anxiety disorders, somatization disorders, factitious illness with physical symptoms, and substance abuse/dependence disorders. Often the individual will go through exhaustive medical workups to determine the cause of the symptoms.

A bona fide cardiac or other medical condition may be the cause of the symptoms or may exist concurrently with the disorder. Personality disorders should also be considered. The chief complaint is often weakness and symptoms associated with the respiratory and cardiovascular systems. Sometimes it is difficult to distinguish early schizophrenia from the asthenic reaction. The schizophrenic may have similar physical complaints and eventually becomes delusional. The asthenic lacks the listless apathy and indifference to external circumstances usually manifested by the schizophrenic. Thiamin deficiency may produce an asthenic reaction syndrome characterized by generalized feelings of weakness, fatigability, poor appetite, poor sleep, various somatic complaints, and subjective difficulties in concentration and memory. Mitral valve prolapse can cause similar cardiac symptoms. Chronic fatigue syndrome may be associated with fatigue, exhaustion, and cardiac or breathing symptoms.

Specialists

- Internist
- Licensed Clinical Social Worker
- Psychiatrist
- Psychologist

Rehabilitation

In addition to psychotherapy and pharmacotherapy treatments, occupational therapy may be helpful. Supportive therapies such as expressive therapies (i.e., art, music, or dance therapy) or relaxation techniques may be helpful to certain individuals. Physical therapy addresses relaxation through use of breathing relaxation techniques.

Mild exercises such as calisthenics incorporated and supervised by rehabilitation professionals can also be helpful in decreasing anxiety and promoting relaxation. Physical and occupational therapists often use biofeedback techniques to help reduce anxiety. Biofeedback machines allow individuals to experience any changes in their heart rate through the use of sight and/or sounds. The therapist can then address specific exercises that help individuals control their heart rate and anxiety.

Since medication therapy is one of the primary treatments for individuals with neurocirculatory asthenia, rehabilitation may need to be modified in accordance to any side effects from medication.

Work Restrictions / Accommodations

Accommodations may include modifying identifiable work situations that provoke symptoms of fatigue, dizziness, or muscle weakness; decreasing workplace stimulants such as noise, cigarette smoke, or noxious chemicals; introducing the individual to stressful situations gradually under close supervision and support; providing flexibility with work schedule to accommodate medical or psychiatric appointments; allowing break time according to individual's needs rather than a fixed schedule; arranging for meetings among the employer, supervisor, and job coach to discuss other possibilities; temporarily adjusting highly stressful activities such as operating machinery; and modifying the work space to reduce noise or visual distractions.

Comorbid Conditions

Coexisting psychiatric illness, personality disorders, substance abuse/dependence, or the presence of a cardiac or respiratory illness will influence the length of disability.

Complications

The coexistence of other psychiatric disorders involving mood, anxiety, personality, and substance abuse or dependence may cause complications.

Factors Influencing Duration

Specific job duties, response to treatment, and coexisting conditions may influence duration of disability.

Length of Disability

Vague diagnosis. No disability expected. Duration of disability depends on response to medications and psychotherapy and the presence of other psychiatric disorders.

Failure to Recover

If an individual fails to recover within the maximum duration expectancy period, the reader may wish to reference the following questions to assist in better understanding the specifics of an individual's medical case.

Regarding diagnosis:

- Does the individual have shortness of breath, fatigue, rapid pulse, and palpitations?
- Has the individual previously been diagnosed with post-traumatic stress disorder and/or chronic fatigue syndrome?
- Have physical disorders been ruled out as the cause of symptoms?
- Has diagnosis of neurocirculatory asthenia been confirmed?
- Does individual have an underlying condition such as psychiatric illness, personality disorders, substance abuse/dependence, or the presence of a cardiac or respiratory illness that may impact recovery?

Regarding treatment:

- Is the individual willing to seek help from both medical specialists and psychiatrists?
- Is individual taking medication as prescribed? Are the side effects from medication preventing use or benefit from that particular medication?
- Would individual benefit from more frequent therapeutic encounters?

Regarding prognosis:

- If symptoms have persisted despite medication, is individual now willing to explore psychotherapy?
- What are the individual's expectations?

References

Braunwald, Eugene. Heart Disease: A Textbook of Cardiovascular Medicine, 5th ed. Orlando: W.B. Saunders Company, 1997 3 Nov 2000 <http://home.mdconsult.com/das/book/view/242?sid=25387514>.

Duke, James A. The Green Pharmacy. Emmaus, PA: Rodale Press, Inc, 1997.

Frances, A., J.P. Docherty, and D.A. Kakn. Healing With Vitamins. Emmaus, PA: Rodale Press, Inc, 1996.

Frances, Allen. Diagnostic and Statistical Manual of Mental Disorders: 4th ed, text revision. Weatherford: American Psychiatric Association, 2000.

Gottlieb, Bill, ed. New Choices in Natural Healing. Emmaus, PA: Rodale Press, Inc, 1995.

Hall, Laura Lee. "Making the ADA Work for People with Psychiatric Disabilities." Mental Disorder, Work Disability, and the Law. Bonnie, Richard J., and John Monahan, eds. Chicago: The University of Chicago Press, 1997. 241-280.

Kisner, C., and L. Colby. Therapeutic Exercise Foundations and Techniques. Philadelphia: F.A. Davis Company, 1990.

Sonino, N., et al. "Life Events and Neurocirculatory Asthenia: A Controlled Study." Journal of Internal Medicine 244 6 (1998): 523-528.

Neurofibromatosis

Other names / synonyms: BAN, Bilateral Acoustic Neurofibromatosis, Central Bilateral Acoustic NF, NF, NF1, NF2, Peripheral NF, Von Recklinghausen's Disease

237.7, 237.70, 237.71, 237.72, M9540/1

Definition

Neurofibromatosis (also called NF) is an inherited condition that is characterized by the growth of various-sized tumors on nerves that lie outside the brain and spinal cord (peripheral nerves). There are 2 well-known forms of NF, and these are NF1 and NF2.

NF1, also called von Recklinghausen NF or Peripheral NF, is the most common form of NF. NF1 affects nerves throughout the body, and occasionally tumors may develop in the brain, on nerves leading away from the brain (cranial nerves), or on the spinal cord. NF1 is associated with numerous, soft fibrous swellings (neurofibromas) that grow from nerves in the skin, brain and spinal cord (central nervous system), muscles, and bone. Individuals with NF1 often develop severe physical disfigurement as the disease progresses.

NF2, also called Bilateral Acoustic Neurofibromatosis (BAN) or Central Bilateral Acoustic NF, is a rare type of NF that is characterized by multiple tumors on the cranial and spinal nerves, and by other lesions of the brain and spinal cord. The hallmark of NF2 is tumor growth (schwannoma) on the nerves to the ears (auditory or eighth cranial nerve). Unlike NF1, NF2 is not associated with extreme physical alterations.

Neurofibromatosis is usually an inherited condition and individuals with a family history of NF are at risk for developing the condition. NF may also occur as a result of random mutation of a gene, and this occurs in 50% of all cases. NF1 is one of the most common inherited genetic disorders, and it occurs in 1 of every 4,000 individuals. NF2 is much more rare and it occurs in 1 of every 40,000 individuals.

Diagnosis

History: Individuals with NF1 usually report pale, coffee-colored patches (cafe-au-lait spots) on the skin of their trunk and pelvis, and they may report tumors on their skin (dermal tumors). Other complaints may include headaches, severe itching, gastrointestinal pain or chronic constipation, seizures, and vision abnormalities. Individuals with NF2 usually complain of a ringing in the ears (tinnitus) and deafness. They may report that they are able to use a telephone only with one ear. Also, they may complain of vision and memory problems, weakness in their facial muscles, skin tumors, and an inability to maintain their balance.

Physical exam: For both NF1 and NF2, manipulation of the skin by touch (palpation) usually reveals moveable, small, solid lumps (nodules) on or under the skin. The skin nodules may be unsightly. In some cases, there may be an underlying bony abnormality and abnormal freckling in the armpit (axillary) area. Coffee-colored (cafe-au-lait) spots on the skin of the trunk and pelvis are common in individuals with NF1. Individuals with NF1 may also exhibit abnormal curvature of the spine (scoliosis); high blood pressure (hypertension); abnormal height, weight, and head circumference; an abnormal shape (asymmetry) of the face; and nodules in the eye (Lisch nodules).

Tests: Genetic testing for the mutations associated with either NF1 or NF2 are not currently recommended. Low-energy radio waves (magnetic resonance imaging, or MRI) may be useful in identifying complications resulting from tumor growth that is associated with NF1 and NF2. Individuals with NF2 should have their hearing checked (audiology test) on a routine basis.

Treatment

There is no cure for either NF1 or NF2. Surgical removal of the tumors (neurofibromas) that are associated with NF1 and NF2 may be necessary when they start to cause complications in other organ systems. Plastic surgery may be a useful treatment to correct the disfigurement that is often associated with NF1. Physical and sensory defects that are associated with NF1 and NF2 may produce social adjustment problems. Speech and general appearance along with hearing and visual acuity can be adversely affected. As the disease progresses, ongoing treatment should include interaction with a clinical social worker and a vocational counselor. The clinical social worker can help the individual mobilize his or her resources to cope with the disease. The social worker may also serve as an advocate for the individual when dealing with the medical establishment and other agencies. A vocational counselor can be of assistance when problems arise in the individual's relationship with his or her work.

Prognosis

Neurofibromatosis is a progressive and unpredictable disease that is associated with a variety of clinical outcomes and problems. In general, the life expectancy of individuals with neurofibromatosis is reduced, oftentimes as a result of complications of the disease itself. Surgical removal of neurofibromas is necessary only when they cause complications in other organ systems. The outcome for individuals with successful surgical removal of neurofibromas is a 10-year survival rate of 50-90%. For acoustic neurofibromas (most often associated with NF2), the predicted outcome may result in loss of hearing or facial palsy 30-40% of the time.

Differential Diagnosis

Conditions that present with similar symptoms as NF1 include NF2, McCune-Albright syndrome, LEOPARD syndrome, Bannayan-Riley-Ruvalcaba syndrome, multiple endocrine neoplasia syndrome type 2B, Klippel-Trenaunay-Weber syndrome, multiple lipomatosis, congenital generalized fibromatosis, juvenile hyaline fibromatosis, multiple intra-dermal nevi, and Proteus syndrome. Conditions that present with similar symptoms as NF2 are rare and generally include only NF1.

Specialists

- Licensed Clinical Social Worker
- Neurologist
- Neurosurgeon
- Oncologist

Work Restrictions / Accommodations

Work restrictions and accommodations may include considerations for hearing or visual impairment. Also, the individual's general health and well being may suffer as the disease progresses, and work responsibilities may need to be modified accordingly. If the disease should progress to the severe stage, it may severely compromise the individual's ability to function. In this case, disability can be permanent.

Comorbid Conditions

A condition that may impact an individual's disability is diabetes.

Complications

Tumors (neurofibromas) that occur in the central nervous system may cause vision and hearing impairment, and onset of seizures (epilepsy). Hearing deficit is most commonly associated with NF2 as a result of tumor (schwannoma) growth on the auditory nerves. Individuals with either type of NF are more prone to cancers of the nerves that are not contained within the brain or spinal cord (peripheral nerves), brain tumors (meningiomas, gliomas, optic nerve gliomas), abnormal bone growths (cysts), abnormal adrenal gland cells (pheochromocytoma), abnormal curvature of the spine (scoliosis), and fluid accumulation in the brain (obstructive hydrocephalus).

Factors Influencing Duration

The length of disability depends upon the severity of symptoms and whether or not surgery is required. Older individuals may be expected to have longer recovery times following surgery that requires general anesthesia.

Length of Disability

Duration depends on location and grade of tumor(s). Heavy labor may have to be restricted for a period of days to weeks following surgical removal of associated tumors. If the disease progresses to a severe stage, any sort of work may become difficult or impossible, and disability may become permanent.

Surgical treatment.

Duration in Days

Job Classification	Minimum	Optimum	Maximum
Any work	28	182	Indefinite

Failure to Recover

If an individual fails to recover within the maximum duration expectancy period, the reader may wish to reference the following questions to assist in better understanding the specifics of an individual's medical case.

Regarding diagnosis:
- What symptoms does the individual have?
- What were the findings on physical exam?
- Has the individual received appropriate diagnostic testing to establish the diagnosis?
- Have any conditions with similar symptoms been ruled out?

Regarding treatment:
- Has the individual received appropriate treatment?
- Is there a clinical social worker and vocational counselor on the team?

Regarding prognosis:
- Is the individual's employer able to accommodate any necessary restrictions?
- Does the individual have diabetes, any systemic disease of the cardiovascular system, or any other neurological disorder?
- Does the individual have any complications, such as cancers of the peripheral nerves, meningiomas, gliomas, optic nerve gliomas, bone cysts, pheochromocytoma, scoliosis, or obstructive hydrocephalus?

References

Friedman, J.M. "Evaluation and Management." Neurofibromatosis. Phenotype, Natural History, and Pathogenesis. Friedman, J.M., et al., eds. Baltimore: The Johns Hopkins University Press, 1999. 87-109.

MacCollin, M. "Clinical Aspects." Neurofibromatosis. Phenotype, Natural History, and Pathogenesis. Friedman, J.M., et al., eds. Baltimore: The Johns Hopkins University Press, 1999. 299-326.

Neurogenic Bladder

Other names / synonyms: Neuropathic Bladder

596.54

Definition

Nerves carry messages from the bladder to the brain letting the brain know when the bladder is full, and from the brain to the bladder muscles telling them either to tighten or release. A neurogenic bladder is a disorder in which the nerves that carry these messages and control the bladder malfunction; this interferes with bladder control and/or the awareness of a full bladder.

The symptoms of neurogenic bladder depend on the function of the specific nerves that are damaged. In some cases, nerves signaling that the bladder is full fail to work properly, resulting in a flaccid, distended bladder that constantly leaks small amounts of urine (hypotonic neurogenic bladder). In other individuals, the nerves that control emptying of the bladder cause it to contract and empty involuntarily (spastic neurogenic bladder). Yet another problem may be that the bladder muscles do not get the message that it is time to let go, so the bladder remains full. In such cases, the bladder becomes too full and urine may back up into the kidneys, causing extra pressure and damage to the small blood vessels in the kidney. Urine that remains in the bladder too long may also cause an infection to develop in the bladder or the tubes that carry the urine from the kidney to the bladder (ureters).

The nerve malfunction may be congenital, or it may be caused by trauma to the brain or spinal cord. Diseases that are risk factors for neurogenic bladder include diabetes, multiple sclerosis, amyotrophic lateral sclerosis (ALS, or Lou Gehrig's disease), and syphilis. Strokes, brain and spinal cord tumors, ruptured intervertebral discs, acute infections, surgical errors, and heavy metal poisoning can also cause nerve damage resulting in a neurogenic bladder.

Overall, the inability to control urination (incontinence) affects more than 8% of the adult population, and is more prevalent among women.

Diagnosis

History: The individual with a hypotonic bladder usually complains of constantly leaking urine. Individuals with a spastic bladder may be unable to void completely, have urinary retention, or inadvertently void after a strong, sudden urge (urge incontinence).

Physical exam: A neurogenic bladder that fails to completely empty will result in a distended bladder that can be felt (palpated). Most other causes are generally not detected on physical exam. However, signs of reduced anal sphincter control may also be evident.

Tests: A urinalysis will usually be necessary to rule out possible bladder infection. A number of tests may be ordered to assess bladder capacity and function, and include x-rays of the bladder, urethra, and overall urinary tract after the introduction of a radiopaque substance (cystography, urethrography, or urography); ultrasound imaging; examination of the bladder and urethra using a fiber-optic instrument (cystourethroscopy); measurement of bladder size and reaction to pressure (cystometrography); measurement of urine flow rates (urodynamic assessment); and tests of muscular reaction to electrical stimulation (electromyography). To diagnose underlying problems in the brain or spinal cord, x-rays of the skull and spine, and an electroencephalogram (EEG) may be performed.

Treatment

Treatment of neurogenic bladder depends upon the cause of nerve damage and the resultant type of voiding dysfunction. Involuntary bladder contractions and lack of sphincter muscle coordination are treated with drugs to improve bladder control, to prevent muscle spasms (antispasmodics), and to block certain nerve impulses (anticholinergics and alpha-sympathetic blockers). Some clinicians have tried electrical stimulation of the bladder, sacral nerves, or spinal cord and results are certainly promising. Appropriate management includes monitoring for urinary tract infection and kidney disease, and encouraging the individual to drink sufficient fluids, limit calcium intake, and change position frequently. Individuals are encouraged to walk, if possible.

With a hypotonic bladder and in some cases of a spastic bladder, the individual must have a flexible tube inserted through the urethra into the bladder to drain it of urine (catheterized) and avoid overdistention. This may be done intermittently preferably by the individual and is then called self-catheterization. In some cases, continuous catheterization is necessary.

If the condition cannot be managed satisfactorily by conservative means, surgery may be necessary. If the sphincter muscle is the main problem, an artificial sphincter can be implanted. Urine flow may also be diverted; the bladder can be opened through the abdominal wall (cutaneous vesicostomy) with urine flowing into an external appliance, or diverted into an intestinal conduit.

Prognosis

Complete recovery is uncommon, so the goal is to manage the effects of a neurogenic bladder. However, appropriate therapy and careful management can often produce satisfactory results. In individuals with mild cases, drug treatment complemented by incontinence pads will provide enough relief for the individual to have a relatively normal lifestyle. Often, however, catheterization is required. If the individual is able and motivated to learn to perform intermittent self-catheterization, this will generally yield a better quality of life, fewer complications, and less disability than continuous catheterization.

Differential Diagnosis

Prostate enlargement, urinary tract infection, and obstructive disorders of the urinary tract can produce symptoms similar to those of neurogenic bladder.

Specialists

- Nephrologist
- Neurologist
- Urologist

Work Restrictions / Accommodations

The individual may require time off for frequent doctor visits that are necessary for regular monitoring, and to avoid the possibility of infection or other complications. On the job, the individual may need longer than usual breaks and a suitable restroom facility in order to deal with such hygiene tasks as changing incontinence pads or emptying and cleaning an external appliance. Individuals with such an appliance or who wear a catheter may need to be reassigned if their ordinary work is physically strenuous. Those who perform intermittent catheterization may require a flexible work schedule.

Comorbid Conditions

Comorbid conditions include senile dementia and immune suppression.

Complications

Potential complications of neurogenic bladder include kidney damage due to urine backup (reflux) from an overextended bladder. Eventually, kidney insufficiency may result in a toxic condition in which waste products remain in the blood (uremia). Urine retention may also lead to infections of the bladder, ureters, and kidneys (cystitis, pyelonephritis), and stones (calculi) developing in the urinary tract.

Factors Influencing Duration

Individuals with neurogenic bladder can be expected to require lifelong treatment, with varying intermittent periods of disability.

Length of Disability

Duration depends on the underlying cause. Contact physician for additional information.

Failure to Recover

If an individual fails to recover within the maximum duration expectancy period, the reader may wish to reference the following questions to assist in better understanding the specifics of an individual's medical case.

Regarding diagnosis:

- Is the individual's nerve malfunction congenital?
- Due to trauma to the brain?
- Due to trauma to the spinal cord?
- Is it secondary to other diseases such as diabetes, multiple sclerosis, amyotrophic lateral sclerosis, or syphilis?
- Has the individual had a stroke?
- Does the individual have a brain or spinal cord tumor?
- Do they have a ruptured intervertebral disc?
- Do they have an acute infection?
- Was there a surgical procedure where an error may have occurred?
- Has there been exposure to heavy metals?
- Does the individual leak urine all the time or do they inadvertently urinate after a strong sudden urge?
- Is a distended bladder felt with palpation?
- Does the individual have reduced anal sphincter control?
- Have appropriate diagnostic tests been performed to characterize the specific cause of neurogenic bladder, so that appropriate treatment can be provided?
- Have conditions with similar symptoms been ruled out?

Regarding treatment:

- Has the individual been treated with the appropriate drugs to improve bladder control, prevent muscle spasms, and block certain nerve impulses?
- Is the individual complying with instructions including diet and fluid intake?
- Is the individual being monitored for infection and kidney involvement?
- Has the individual been trained in self-catheterization?
- Did the individual have surgery?

Regarding prognosis:

- Does the individual have senile dementia or immune suppression?
- Is the individual's employer able to make accommodations for the individual's situation?
- Has the individual had any complications?

References

Beers, Mark H., and Robert Berkow. The Merck Manual of Diagnosis and Therapy. Whitehouse Station, NJ: Merck & Co., Inc, 1999.

Neurogenic Bladder. National Institute of Diabetes and Digestive and Kidney Diseases. 23 Sep 1998. 2 Jan 2001 <http://www.niddk.nih.gov/health/urolog/summary/neuro/>.

Neuropathy of Ulnar Nerve (Entrapment)

Other names / synonyms: Cubital Tunnel Syndrome, Ulnar Neuritis, Ulnar Neuropathy

354.2

Definition

Neuropathy is pain and decreased function of the ulnar nerve when the nerve becomes constricted (entrapped) or compressed along its route from the neck to the hand. The nerve must travel through a tunnel at the elbow and canal in the wrist, both potential sites for entrapment and irritation. The ulnar nerve is responsible for muscle function in the hand and sensation along the ring and small fingers.

The nerve can become constricted (entrapped) at the elbow or wrist from swelling caused by direct pressure over the nerve tunnel/canal. In the elbow, this tunnel is along the back and inside (medial border) of the elbow (cubital tunnel.) The nerve may also slide out of this groove or tunnel when the elbow is bent (flexed) causing irritation and swelling (neuritis, neuropathy).

Common causes for ulnar entrapment at the elbow (cubital tunnel syndrome) include activities that require repeated bending of the elbow. This includes driving, sleeping, keyboarding, weightlifting and pitching a baseball. Driving can place added insult to the elbow from direct pressure as well as frequent bending.

In the wrist, the ulnar nerve and artery pass through a very small boney canal (Guyon's canal). A direct blow over this area, on the palm, or near the wrist will cause inflammation and compression of the nerve. Compression and inflammation can also be the result of repetitive trauma such as using a hammer. Pressure on the nerve can also come from a cyst (ganglion) in the canal.

Fractures or dislocations in the elbow or wrist may cause entrapment of the nerve. At the elbow, particularly, the nerve may be dislodged from the canal.

Diagnosis

History: Individuals with compression in the elbow will complain of numbness, tingling or pain in the ring and small fingers. These symptoms (paresthesias) are worse with increased activity or use of the elbow. As the neuropathy progresses, weakness and loss of coordination become apparent. The pain may awaken the individual at night.

In the wrist, nerve compression leads to some loss of sensation but more pronounced change in strength and grip. The hand along the small finger side (ulnar side) may be less fleshy (atrophied) and can be held like a claw.

Physical exam: Joint range of motion is tested as well as muscle strength. Tingling along the nerve may be noted by the individual when the physician taps the nerve with a percussion hammer (positive Tinel's sign). The ulnar nerve may be felt at the elbow and found to slide out of the tunnel (sublux) over the medial condyle when the elbow is bent (flexed). Decreased strength in pinching the thumb to index finger may be noted (positive Frommet's sign). The nerve is also tested by bending the elbow fully with the wrist in a neutral position. This test is positive for entrapment if tingling in the ring and small fingers begins in less than 60 seconds.

If symptoms are originating from the wrist, Tinel's sign will be positive here, not at the elbow. Flexion of the elbow will not increase symptoms in the hand. Changes in sensation in the ring and small fingers will be noted along with atrophy of the ulnar edge of the hand around the intrinsic muscles. Deformity of the hand comes in late stages of the syndrome and is more common with nerve destruction than with entrapment.

Tests: Electromyographic and nerve conduction studies establish nerve function. X-rays may be done to determine if abnormal anatomy is contributing to nerve compression.

Treatment

Ulnar neuropathy at the elbow and wrist is treated conservatively with splinting, cushioning or padding the area, and limiting elbow flexion or stopping the activity causing pressure over the nerve. Local injections of corticosteroids can be helpful in decreasing inflammation of the nerve.

Enlarging the tunnel (surgical decompression) of the tunnel is recommended if conservative treatment is not successful or the symptoms progressively worsen. In the elbow, it may also be necessary to reposition the ulnar nerve (ulnar nerve transposition) to prevent it from slipping (subluxating) and/or to relieve direct pressure on the nerve when the elbow is resting on a hard surface. In the wrist, the canal is enlarged to relief pressure on the nerve (surgical decompression) by cutting the overlying ligament. An elbow or wrist splint will be required for several weeks after surgery.

Some cases of neuropathy resolve spontaneously.

Prognosis

Early recognition of the neuropathy along with either medical or surgical treatment (decompression and/or transposition) provides good to excellent relief of weakness and changes in sensation, allowing for return to normal function.

Transfer of the ulnar nerve (ulnar nerve transposition) relieves pressure on the nerve and prevents it from sliding over the medial epicondyle. This procedure has good to excellent results in most individuals.

Differential Diagnosis

Cervical disc disease, thoracic outlet syndrome, carpal tunnel syndrome, epicondylitis, and elbow sprain may present symptoms similar to ulnar neuropathy.

Specialists

- Hand Surgeon
- Hand Therapist
- Neurologist
- Neurosurgeon
- Occupational Therapist
- Orthopedic Surgeon
- Physiatrist

Rehabilitation

Individuals with the diagnosis of ulnar neuropathy may require outpatient therapy. The individual should be seen by either an occupational therapist or a physical therapist who is a certified hand therapist.

Individuals will require therapy regardless of whether conservative treatment or surgery is indicated.

Therapy first addresses pain control and the reduction of swelling. Individuals learn taught to position the hand so that it rests above the elbow on a pillow to decrease swelling in the hand. Additionally, individuals learn that straightening the elbow decreases stress on the ulnar nerve and thereby decreases pain. Hot packs and hot paraffin wax decrease joint stiffness prior to therapy. Therapists perform scar massage to promote healing and scar mobility over any surgical site. Ice packs decrease pain and swelling after exercise and should be applied for fifteen minutes. Individuals may require nerve desensitization techniques in which different textures such as cotton and burlap are rubbed over the palm of the hand opposite the thumb as well as the last two fingers.

Therapists teach stretching techniques to increase range of motion at the hand. Therapists passively stretch the wrist and fingers to increase flexion and extension and perform interphalangeal joint mobilizations on the last two fingers to increase persistent lack of finger extension. Individuals also learn techniques called nerve glides, which are a series of positions the neck, shoulder, elbow, wrist and hand are placed in to help decrease nerve entrapment. Individuals stretch their fingers by using their non-injured hand to straighten the last two digits. Finger and thumb opposition is restored by touching the thumb to each finger. Individuals may also wear a custom-made splint to decrease the risk of flexion contracture in the last two fingers.

Strengthening exercises are necessary to restore function and to prevent re-injury. Individuals squeeze therapy putty to restore hand strength. The muscles of the fingers should be strengthened by pinching therapy putty between the fingers, or by placing a rubber band around two fingers at a time and spreading them apart. Individuals learn functional grasp exercises such as holding a ball, grabbing a handle and picking up cylindrical objects such as a can, which emphasize strengthening the muscles that power the last two fingers.

Work Restrictions / Accommodations

Restricted use of the wrist or elbow is required with both conservative treatment and in the early post-operative phase if surgical intervention is necessary. Ergonomic evaluation of the work area is important to identify contributing risk factors, such as keyboards that are too high, driving, holding a telephone for repeated or extended periods of time. Eliminating these risk factors may allow for early return to work, at least in a limited capacity. Some individuals may not be able to return to aggravating activities such as using a hammer.

Comorbid Conditions

Inflammatory diseases, diabetes, peripheral neuropathy, cervical disc disease, and fractures or dislocations of the elbow and/or wrist would impact recovery.

Complications

Failure to treat the neuropathy could result in permanent nerve damage, resulting in loss of function of the hand and wrist.

Factors Influencing Duration

Inability to modify job requirements would greatly affect disability, as would severity of symptoms, response to conservative treatment, and subsequent need for surgery.

Length of Disability

Disability may be prolonged or permanent if job requirements cannot allow for changes in position of the elbow or wrist, even after surgery.

Surgical treatment.

Duration in Days

Job Classification	Minimum	Optimum	Maximum
Sedentary work	7	21	42
Light work	7	28	42
Medium work	28	56	Indefinite
Heavy work	28	98	Indefinite
Very Heavy work	42	98	Indefinite

Failure to Recover

If an individual fails to recover within the maximum duration expectancy period, the reader may wish to reference the following questions to assist in better understanding the specifics of an individual's medical case.

Regarding diagnosis:

- Does the individual frequently perform activities that require repeated bending of the elbow, such as driving, sleeping, keyboarding, weightlifting and pitching a baseball?
- Has the individual experienced recent trauma to the wrist or palm?
- Has there been a recent fracture or dislocation of the elbow or wrist?
- Does the individual perform activities that cause repetitive trauma, such as using a hammer?
- Does the individual complain of numbness and tingling or pain in the ring and small fingers?
- Do the symptoms worsen with increased activity or use of the elbow?
- Does the individual complain of weakness and loss of coordination in the arm or a decrease in grip strength?
- Does the pain awaken the individual when sleeping?
- Were electromyographic and nerve conduction studies done?
- Were x-rays done to determine if abnormal anatomy is contributing to nerve compression?
- Was a diagnosis of ulnar nerve neuropathy confirmed?

Regarding treatment:

- Were elbow and wrist splinted and cushioned or padded?
- Was elbow flexion restricted? Was the activity that caused pressure over the nerve stopped?
- Were injections of corticosteroids required to decrease nerve inflammation?

- Did splinting, restricting activity, and administering medication effectively resolve the neuropathy?
- If symptoms worsened, did the individual require surgical decompression of the nerve tunnel?
- If the elbow was affected, was it necessary to reposition the ulnar nerve (ulnar nerve transposition)?
- Did any postsurgical complications occur?

Regarding prognosis:

- Was medical treatment sufficient to resolve the condition or was surgical treatment necessary?
- Did the individual restrict activities and wear splints exactly as directed?
- Does post-treatment nerve pain interfere with the individual's daily activities?
- Has permanent nerve damage, resulting in loss of function of the hand and wrist, occurred?
- Is any treatment available to treat the nerve damage and/or restore hand and wrist function?

References

"Ulnar Nerve Dysfunction." adam.com. 1999. 11 Jan 2001 <http://my.webmd.com/content/asset/adam_disease_neuropathy-ulnar_nerve>.

Magee, David J. "Forearm, Wrist, and Hand." Orthopedic Physical Assessment. Biblis, Margaret M., ed. Philadelphia: W.B. Saunders Company, 1992. 168-215.

Neurotic Disorders

Other names / synonyms: Neuroses, Neurosis
300, 300.0, 300.00, 300.01, 300.02, 300.9

Definition

In contrast to the psychotic disorders, which are characterized by hearing voices or seeing visions (auditory or visual hallucinations), fixed but false beliefs (delusions), or bizarre or unusual behaviors, neuroses are characterized by anxiety and distress over some circumstance. The traditional view is that neurotic symptoms are due to an unconscious psychological conflict that is unacceptable to the individual's self-concept. If the conflict were acknowledged, it would threaten some aspect of the individual's psychological life and, therefore, a defense mechanism keeps the deeper conflict from entering awareness. However, the term "neurosis" or "neurotic disorder" is no longer in common use for psychiatric diagnosis. The DSM-IV-TR (Diagnostic and Statistical Manual of Mental Disorders, 4th Edition, Text Revision, published by the American Psychiatric Association) instead identifies specific diagnostic groups, such as the Anxiety Disorders, Dissociative Disorders, Mood Disorders, or Somatoform Disorders.

The Anxiety Disorders include disorders with symptoms such as panic attack, a sudden onset of intense apprehension or terror, often associated with symptoms like shortness of breath, racing heart rate (palpitations), chest pain, or smothering sensations; agoraphobia, anxiety in situations from which escape is difficult, such as being in a crowd, traveling in a car or train, or being on a bridge or elevator; unreasonable fears (phobias) of specific types, such as animal, blood, or weather-related phobias; or obsessive-compulsive behavior, in which repetitive thoughts and behaviors become time-intensive and intrusive in one's life.

Adjustment Disorders include anxiety symptoms that occur in response to an identified stressful condition or event (stressor), while Dissociative Disorders are characterized by distress or impairment associated with the inability to recall important personal information, usually of a traumatic nature. Mood Disorders include symptoms of major depression and bipolar disorder, in which an individual may cycle between manic and depressive moods to an extreme that can impair normal functioning. The Somatoform Disorders are a diagnostic category including many of what were formerly termed neurotic symptoms. These disorders are characterized by physical symptoms that suggest a general medical condition but which are not explained by a medical condition. They include somatization disorder, formerly known as Briquet's syndrome, in which the individual has a combination of pain, gastrointestinal, sexual, and pseudoneurological symptoms; conversion disorder, involving unexplained symptoms or deficits affecting voluntary motor or sensory function, such as being temporarily blind or paralyzed; or hypochondriasis, the preoccupation with the fear of having a disease.

As a group, the neurotic disorders are the most common psychiatric diagnoses, accounting for more than half of all psychiatric cases seen in primary care. They may result in significant costs to society from missed work as well as from direct healthcare costs. Generalized anxiety disorder may affect up to 5% of the general population; phobias up to 8%, and somatization disorder up to 18%.

Length of Disability

Duration in Days

Job Classification	Minimum	Optimum	Maximum
Any work	7	14	28

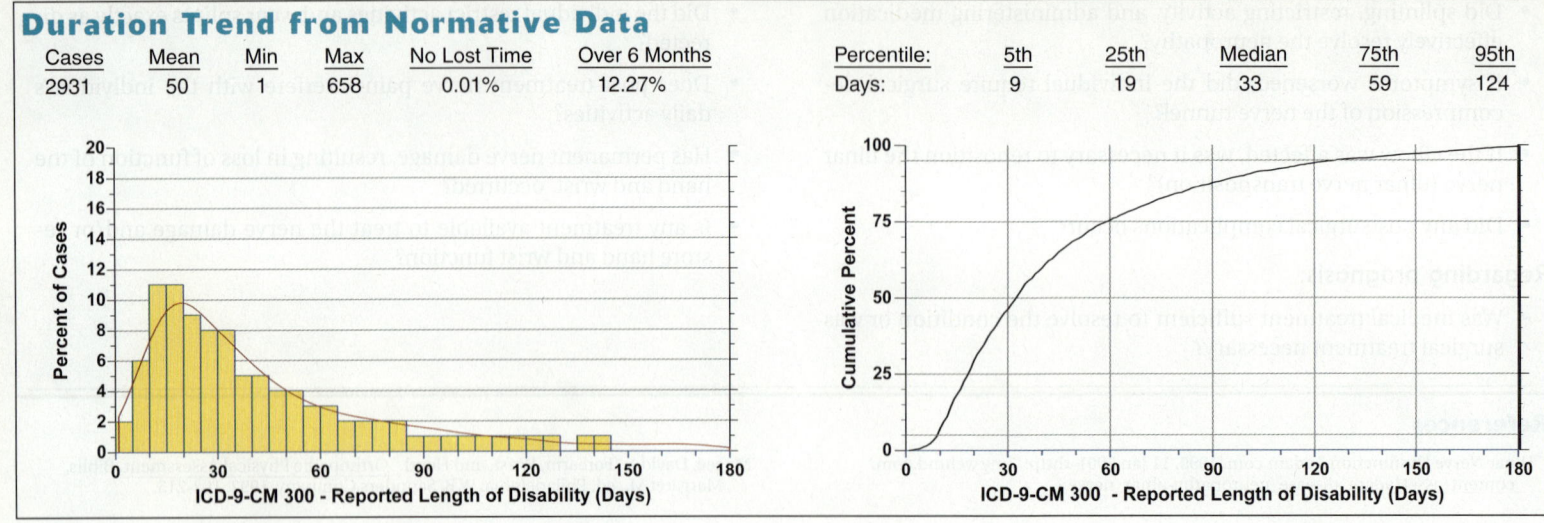

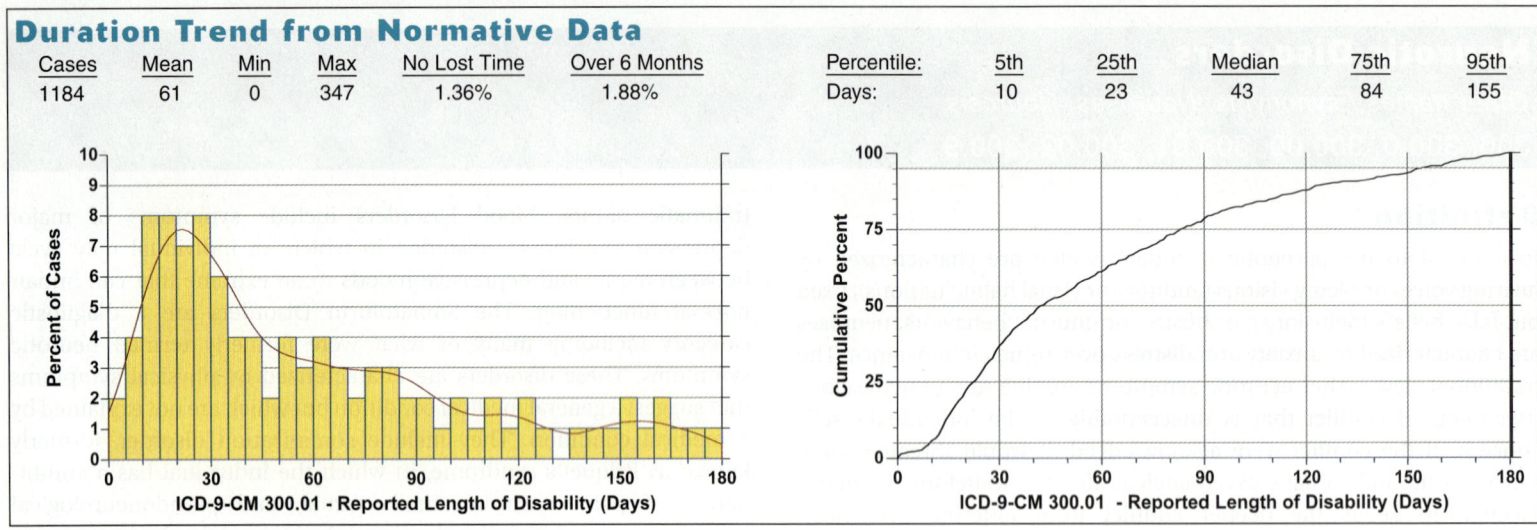

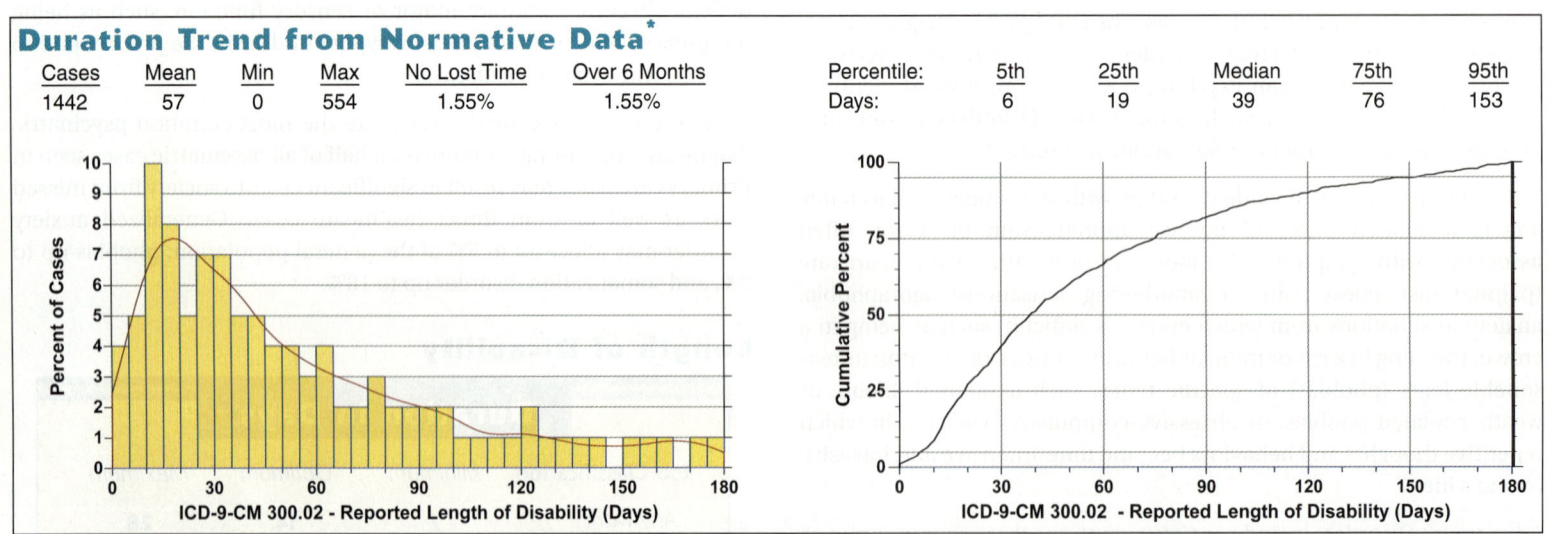

* Differences may exist between the expected duration tables and the normative graphs. Duration tables provide expected recovery periods based on the type of work performed by the individual. The normative graphs reflect the actual observed experience of many individuals across the spectrum of physical conditions, in a variety of industries, and with varying levels of case management.

References

Frances, Allen. Diagnostic and Statistical Manual of Mental Disorders: 4th ed, text revision. Washington, DC: American Psychiatric Association, 2000.

Green, Ben. Neurotic Disorders and Somatization. Priory Bookshop. 01 Jan 2000. 12/11/2000 <http://www.priory.com/neuro.htm>.

Thomas, Clayton L. Taber's Cyclopedic Medical Dictionary, 18th ed. Philadelphia: F.A. Davis Company, 1997.

Neutropenia
Other names / synonyms: Agranulocytosis, Chronic Idiopathic Neutropenia, Granulocytopenia
288.0

Definition

Neutropenia is an abrupt, abnormal decrease in a certain type of white blood cells (leucocytes) called neutrophils that are manufactured in the soft tissue center (marrow) of most bones. Neutrophils play an essential role in fighting bacterial infections by surrounding and destroying invading bacteria (phagocytosis). Neutropenia occurs when the bone marrow does not manufacture enough neutrophils or when neutrophils are destroyed too rapidly.

Causes for the disorder vary. Some individuals are borne with the disorder; it can also develop after a viral infection, or it can be the side effect of a drug or exposure to certain poisons. In other individuals, the disorder develops after treatment with anticancer drugs (chemotherapy). According to the Neutropenia Support Association Incorporated, as many as one in three individuals who receive chemotherapy become neutropenic. This is because the chemotherapeutic drugs act mainly on quickly-dividing cells; because it cannot distinguish between the cells of a growing cancerous tumor and normal cells, such as neutrophils, which also divide quickly, both cancerous cells and neutrophils are killed by the chemotherapy.

Besides the type of neutropenia caused by chemotherapy, there are several rare types of neutropenia. Chronic congenital neutropenia is an inherited type of neutropenia that affects children more often than adults. Cyclic neutropenia occurs in both children and adults and tends to recur every three weeks, lasting three to six days each time. Chronic idiopathic neutropenia, appears to have no clearly known cause, but may result in repeated infections that can be life-threatening.

According to reports issued by the Centers for Disease Control and Prevention (CDC) in 1998, the number of neutropenia cases diagnosed in the US was approximately 247,000. Neutropenia generally affects females slightly more than males.

Diagnosis

History: Many individuals report chills and high fever, symptoms typically associated with infection. Other symptoms may include generalized fatigue; urinary tract infections; ear infections; skin, gum, and mouth sores (ulcers); infection and inflammation of tissues that surround and support the teeth (periodontitis); decreased appetite (anorexia); loose bowel movements (diarrhea); cough and sore throat; abscesses and boils, particularly in the rectal area; recurrent superficial infections; or pneumonia. In some cases, no symptoms are apparent.

Physical exam: The physician will look for boils, abscesses, or sores on the skin, in the mouth, and on other mucous membranes. The examination also consists of pressing and manipulating (palpation) lymph nodes areas (such as the neck, armpits, and groin) to search for abnormal and swollen lymph nodes that may be tender to the touch. Abdominal palpation sometimes reveals an enlarged spleen (splenomegaly).

Tests: A complete blood count (CBC) with a differential that shows a low neutrophil count (absolute neutrophil count - ANC), of 1000 or less, indicates neutropenia. An individual with an ANC of less than 500 cells per cubic centimeter is considered severely neutropenic.

Additional information regarding the cause and indicated treatment is often obtained by laboratory tests such as Vitamin B_{12} and folate level assessment, autoimmune titers (ANA and RA), liver and kidney function tests (LFTs and KFTs), and a bone marrow biopsy with culture.

Treatment

Treatment of neutropenia depends on its cause. Most individuals with neutropenia develop fever and are treated with antibiotics; if the infection is severe the individual will be hospitalized and antibiotics administered intravenously (IV). New drugs called blood cell growth factors (granulocyte colony stimulating factors) may be given to stimulate the growth of neutrophils in the bone marrow. Two nerve cell growth factors, gCSF and gmCSF, have been shown to shorten the duration of neutropenia caused by chemotherapy and to correct the condition if it is caused by other medications. Bone marrow transplant, with bone marrow obtained from donors (allogeneic bone marrow transplants), is another treatment option for those individuals who have been matched with bone marrow donors.

Prognosis

The outcome depends on whether the neutropenia was caused by chemotherapy, was inherited (chronic congenital neutropenia), is cyclic, or is chronic idiopathic neutropenia. Neutropenia caused by chemotherapy can be fatal. When accompanied by fever (febrile neutropenia), which is any temperature over 100.5 degrees Fahrenheit, it is a medical emergency and must be dealt with immediately.

The outcome for chronic congenital neutropenia is favorable as most afflicted individuals outgrow it. In cases where it is left untreated, this type of neutropenia has been associated with loss of teeth due to gum infections and the side effects of antibiotic treatment.

The outcome for cyclic neutropenia is usually good because this form of neutropenia is generally benign. In about 10% of cases, afflicted individuals die from infection. When death does occur, it is most often because of pneumonia and peritoneal sepsis. Symptoms tend to recur with less intensity as the individual ages.

The outcome for chronic idiopathic neutropenia is usually unfavorable because the recurring infections (characteristic of this type of neutropenia) are treated repeatedly with antibiotics; repeated antibiotic treatment causes the bacteria to become resistant to them, at which point the disease becomes life threatening.

Differential Diagnosis

Conditions with symptoms similar to those of neutropenia include viral hepatitis, rheumatoid arthritis, leukemia, myelofibrosis, polycythemia vera, vitamin B_{12} or folate deficiency, myelodysplastic syndrome, malnutrition, sepsis, or AIDS.

Specialists

- Hematologist
- Oncologist
- Rheumatologist

Work Restrictions / Accommodations

Individuals with neutropenia must avoid contact with anyone who is ill or who has a cold or other infection. They must also avoid situations where they may receive bruises, breaks, or cuts to the skin. Individuals who are fatigued may require more sedentary work until they regain their normal strength and stamina. Depending on the severity of the neutropenia the individual may be advised to avoid the workplace. An alternative strategy would be to make arrangements for the individual to work from home (telecommute) for a time.

Comorbid Conditions

Chronic liver disease, HIV infection, tuberculosis, or leukemia may lengthen disability.

Complications

Neutropenia can be complicated by repeated infections, a serious infection such as pneumonia, an infection that spreads through the tissue (cellulitis), or an infection of the bloodstream (sepsis).

Just as neutropenia can be complicated by other conditions, neutropenia can complicate treatment for cancer when individuals develop this condition following the administration of chemotherapy. In such instances, physicians may have to delay chemotherapy treatments or reduce the dose strength of the chemotherapy drug. Clinical studies have shown that for certain diseases where the dose is reduced or the treatment cycle prolonged, treated individuals have lower cure rates than if they had been able to receive the full dose of the anticancer drug on schedule. Fortunately, administration of the blood cell growth factors (gCSF and gmCSF) has been shown to reduce the incidence of fever, infection, hospital admissions, and help individuals receiving chemotherapy take the full dose of drugs on schedule.

Factors Influencing Duration

Factors that might influence length of disability include the underlying cause of the neutropenia, the type of treatment, and the effectiveness of the treatment.

Length of Disability

Length of disability depends on the underlying cause of the neutropenia (such as chemotherapy, diseases such as leukemia, and causative drugs) as well as the treatment and its efficacy. Disability from neutropenia itself is rarely permanent but if left untreated, the condition may precipitate disability from repeated minor infections or severe, life-threatening infections.

Failure to Recover

If an individual fails to recover within the maximum duration expectancy period, the reader may wish to reference the following questions to assist in better understanding the specifics of an individual's medical case.

Regarding diagnosis:

- Does the individual have a clinical history of a viral infection, malnutrition or recent medications use (particularly cancer chemotherapy)?
- Does the individual have HIV infection?
- Did the individual present with symptoms suggestive of neutropenia, such as fever, chills, fatigue and inflammatory changes of the skin or mucous membranes (i.e., stomatitis, gingivitis, boils, abscesses)?
- Were the findings from the physical exam such as enlarged and tender lymph nodes, skin lesions or ulcerations that are suggestive of neutropenia?
- Was neutropenia (neutrophil count of 1000/µL or less) confirmed with a complete blood count?
- Was the underlying cause of the neutropenia determined (i.e., drugs or cancer chemotherapy, HIV, infection, leukemia, malnutrition)?
- Would the individual benefit from consultation with appropriate specialists (hematologist, internal medicine specialist, oncologist, infectious disease specialist)?
- If the diagnosis was uncertain, were other conditions with similar symptoms ruled out in the differential diagnosis?

Regarding treatment:

- Was the treatment appropriate for the diagnosis? Did it take into consideration the individual's medical and family history and other medical conditions and allergies?
- Were appropriate antimicrobial agents administered as necessary?
- If the acute neutropenia is suspected to be drug-induced, were appropriate drugs eliminated?
- If splenomegaly and severe neutropenia (< 500/µL) was present, was splenectomy considered as a treatment alternative?
- Was there evidence of bone marrow suppression? If so, was a bone marrow transplant considered?
- Was administration of myeloid growth factors (G-CSF and GM-CSF) considered?

Regarding prognosis:

- Was the individual severely neutropenic?
- Based on the underlying cause and the severity of the neutropenia, what was the expected outcome?
- Was the infection controlled promptly with antimicrobial therapy and supportive care? Did the individual suffer a serious infection (sepsis, pneumonia, cellulitis) that may have impacted recovery and prognosis?
- Does the individual have any debilitating underlying conditions, (HIV, tuberculosis, liver disease or leukemia) that could impact recovery and prognosis?

References

"Hematology and Oncology." Merck Manual of Diagnosis and Therapy, 17th ed. Beers, Mark H., and Robert Berkow, MD, eds. Whitehouse Station, NJ: Merck & Co., Inc., 1999. 1Mar 2001 <http://www.merck.com/pubs/mmanual/section11/chapter135/135a.htm>.

Goldman, Lee, and J. Claude Bennett. Cecil Textbook of Medicine, 21st ed. Philadelphia: W.B. Saunders Company, 2000 07 Mar 2001 <http://home.mdconsult.com/das/book/view/882?sid=35783047>.

Kisner, C., and L. Colby. Therapeutic Exercise Foundations and Techniques. Philadelphia: F.A. Davis Company, 1990.

Neutropenia. Imaginis Corporation. 10 Nov 2000. 07 Mar 2001 <http://www.imaginis.com/breasthealth/neutropenia.asp>.

Popovic, J. R., and L.J. Kozak. National Hospital Discharge Survey: Annual Summary. National Center for Health Statistics. 01 Jan 2000. 25 Sept 2000 <http://www.cdc.gov/nchs/data/sr13_148,pdf>.

Rosen, Peter. Emergency Medicine: Concepts and Clinical Practice, 4th ed. Mosby Year-Book, Inc: St. Louis, 1998 07 Mar 2001 <http://home.mdconsult.com/das/book/view/624?sid=35783047>.

Nicotine Dependence

Other names / synonyms: Cigarette Addiction, Smokeless Tobacco Addiction, Smokeless Tobacco Dependence, Smoking Addiction, Tobacco Addiction

305.1

Definition

Nicotine is a widely used addictive compound found naturally in tobacco (cigarettes, cigars, chewing tobacco) and now available in pharmaceutical preparations such as gum, skin patches, and nasal spray. Some would consider nicotine among the most addictive drugs known, and no matter which form is used, there is potential for dependence. Cigarette smoking is the most addictive method of using nicotine. Dependence occurs when an individual uses nicotine in a maladaptive way that includes the need for increased amounts of substance to achieve the desired effect (tolerance); spending a great deal of time obtaining or using nicotine, such as chain-smoking; using the substance in larger amounts or for longer periods of time than intended; a persistent, unsuccessful attempt to control or stop using nicotine; continued use despite of physical or psychological problems. The case for nicotine's huge addictive potential becomes even more compelling when one considers that initial exposure typically leads to nausea and dizziness. Unlike alcohol or cocaine, there is little, if any, pleasurable sensation or psychological relief initially. After habitual use, sensations of improved concentration and mood and decreased anger may be reported.

Despite full knowledge of the harmful physical effects and a strong desire not to become addicted, casual use may evolve into dependence. Most smokers develop dependence within a few years of daily smoking. Nicotine is frequently used early in the morning or after long periods without use because individuals are seeking to avoid the unpleasant symptoms of withdrawal, such as depression, insomnia, irritability, or restlessness. Only 1/3 of self-quitters remain abstinent for 2 days, and fewer than 5% are able to quit successfully on any given attempt, although half quit eventually after multiple attempts. Factors leading to addiction include that the effect of nicotine is almost instantaneous, as it reaches the brain within 10 seconds after inhalation, and the dose and frequency are easily controlled by the smoker.

Nicotine use is decreasing in industrialized nations but increasing in developing nations. The incidence of use is slightly higher in males than females in the US, but in other nations males are 8 times as likely as females to use nicotine. Blacks have been shown to have higher nicotine blood levels for a given number of cigarettes than other racial groups, which may lead to greater difficulty in quitting. It is estimated that 25% of individuals in the US have nicotine dependence, with 80-90% of regular users developing dependence. A 1996 survey reported that 65% of adolescents had used nicotine/tobacco at least once. Nicotine use usually begins in early adolescence, with 95% of those who continue to use after age 20 becoming dependent. The risk for smoking is 3 times higher for first-degree relatives of users, although specific genetic factors are unknown.

Diagnosis

Diagnosis is based on criteria listed in the DSM-IV-TR (Diagnostic and Statistical Manual of Mental Disorders, 4th Edition, Text Revision, published by the American Psychiatric Association). There is a destructive pattern of nicotine use, leading to significant social, occupational, or medical impairment. There must be 3 or more of the following when the nicotine use was at its worst: nicotine tolerance; nicotine withdrawal symptoms; greater use of nicotine than intended; unsuccessful efforts to cut down or control nicotine use; a great deal of time spent in using nicotine; reduction in social, occupational, or recreational activities because of nicotine; and continued use despite knowing that nicotine causes significant problems. Nicotine tolerance is defined as the need for markedly increased amounts of nicotine to achieve intoxication, or markedly diminished effect with continued use of the same amount of nicotine. Nicotine withdrawal symptoms include 2 or more of the following developing within several hours to a few days of reduction in heavy or prolonged nicotine use: sweating or rapid pulse; increased hand shaking (tremor); insomnia; nausea or vomiting; physical agitation; anxiety; grand mal seizures; or transiently seeing, feeling, or hearing things that aren't there (visual, tactile, or auditory hallucinations or illusions). Nicotine withdrawal symptoms may also be diagnosed if nicotine is taken to relieve or avoid withdrawal symptoms.

History: The diagnosis of nicotine dependence is made on the basis of history. Almost by definition, any use of tobacco products constitutes abuse. The individual may report difficulty stopping use, smoking or using soon after awakening, using when ill, or using more in the afternoon. The individual may report withdrawal symptoms if they have stopped use within the past 96 hours of depression, insomnia, irritability, anxiety, difficulty concentrating, restlessness, or increased appetite.

Physical exam: The exam may reveal a dry or productive cough, decreased heart rate, weight gain, excessive skin wrinkling, or tobacco stains on the fingers. If the individual has had prolonged use for many years, they may show evidence of chronic obstructive pulmonary disease or complications of existing cardiovascular disease.

Tests: Routine urine toxicology tests can detect nicotine use. Continued smoking can be inferred from elevated levels of carbon monoxide in the blood. Pulmonary function tests may be used to assess lung damage. Blood tests may show decreased levels of catecholamines and cortisol or increased mean corpuscular volume (MCV) of the red blood cells. Electrocardiogram (ECG) and chest x-ray may show the effects of chronic smoking on the heart and lungs.

Treatment

The goal of treatment is abstinence. Because it is difficult for many individuals to quit on their first attempt, various strategies should be used in combination, with as much outside support as possible. Although some people are able to quit "cold turkey," the presence of uncomfortable withdrawal symptoms commonly causes relapse within 48 hours. Nicotine replacement therapies (nicotine gum, the transdermal patch, nasal spray, and inhaler) relieve withdrawal symptoms while providing users with lower overall nicotine levels than they received with tobacco. The individual is not likely to become dependent on these replacements since they do not produce the pleasurable effects of tobacco products. They are also safer as they do not contain the carcinogens and gases associated with tobacco smoke. All are considered equally effective. Although the main treatment focus has been nicotine replacement, there is now available a non-nicotine prescription drug. An antidepressant called bupropion contains no nicotine, can be taken in pill form, and has been demonstrated to be helpful to some individuals. This atypical antidepressant has been shown to double quit rates, and is usually begun 1 week prior to the quit date and taken for several weeks thereafter. It is effective in those without symptoms of depression. Its most common side effect is dry mouth.

Behavioral interventions play an important role in treatment. Treatment approaches include hypnosis, acupuncture, aversive conditioning, psychotherapy, medications, and tobacco substitutes, to name a few. Key recovery factors involve avoiding smokers and smoking environments, support from family and friends, and learning coping skills for both short- and long-term prevention of relapse. Smokers must not only learn behavioral and cognitive tools to prevent relapse, but must also be ready to apply those skills in a crisis. Smoking cessation programs are available in clinics, numerous community and public health settings, and by telephone and in written formats as well.

Prognosis

Those who are motivated and make persistent efforts to quit using nicotine have a good chance of success. Once abstinent, the risk for heart disease and cancers will decline with time and may even return to normal. More advanced pulmonary problems such as chronic bronchitis and emphysema can be slowed down or arrested, and early damage may be reversible. About 80% of those who use tobacco express a desire to quit, and 35% per year attempt to quit, with about 5% being able to quit unaided on the first attempt. For those seeking treatment to help quit, less than 25% are able to quit at their first attempt, but up to 45% are able to quit eventually, after several attempts and relapses. Smoking has been called the most important preventable cause of death and disease. It causes 20% of all deaths in the US, and 45% of smokers die of a tobacco-induced disorder.

Differential Diagnosis

Other substance-abuse disorders may mimic nicotine dependence, such as caffeine intoxication; anxiety, mood, or sleep disorders; or medication-induced muscle jitteriness or restlessness (akathisia).

Specialists

- Advanced Practice Registered Nurse
- Internist
- Occupational Therapist
- Psychiatrist
- Psychologist
- Pulmonologist

Work Restrictions / Accommodations

Many workplaces and public buildings are now smoke-free. It is the decision of the employer whether or not to provide smoking areas. Employers who encourage a smoke-free environment may be able to encourage employees to quit and remain off tobacco. Specific accommodations may include modifying specific environments that trigger memories or the desire to smoke, providing education and/or smoking-cessation courses, and providing stress-management and relaxation courses.

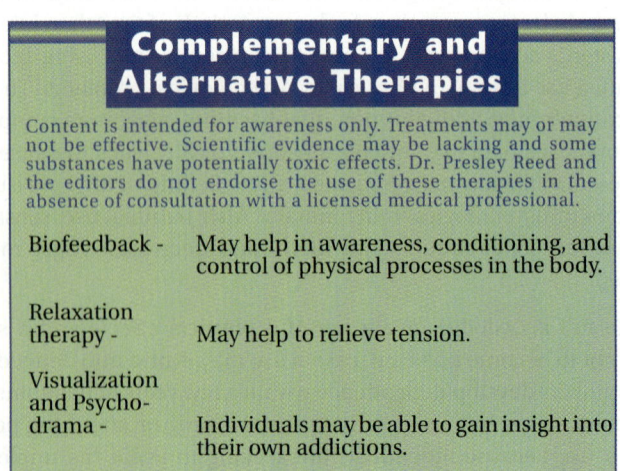

Complementary and Alternative Therapies

Content is intended for awareness only. Treatments may or may not be effective. Scientific evidence may be lacking and some substances have potentially toxic effects. Dr. Presley Reed and the editors do not endorse the use of these therapies in the absence of consultation with a licensed medical professional.

Biofeedback -	May help in awareness, conditioning, and control of physical processes in the body.
Relaxation therapy -	May help to relieve tension.
Visualization and Psychodrama -	Individuals may be able to gain insight into their own addictions.

Comorbid Conditions

Coexisting conditions that may affect recovery and lengthen disability include alcohol and other substance abuse (particularly marijuana and cocaine dependence), and psychiatric disorders such as major depression, schizophrenia, and anxiety disorders. Smokers with a past or present history of anxiety, depression, or schizophrenia are less likely to quit. Those with current problems related to alcohol abuse or dependence are unlikely to stop smoking unless their alcohol problem resolves.

Nicotine dependence and withdrawal complications can also jeopardize cancer and heart disease treatment. Women who smoke during pregnancy are at a greater risk for miscarriage (spontaneous abortion) in the first trimester, premature delivery, and lower-birth-weight infants. Nicotine concentrates in the breast milk and amniotic fluid, and readily crosses the placenta where it concentrates in the fetal blood. Nicotine concentrations in the fetus can be as much as 15% higher than maternal levels. Another ingredient of tobacco smoke, carbon monoxide, has been shown to inhibit the release of oxygen into fetal tissues. The combination of these factors may account for the developmental delays commonly seen in the fetuses and infants of smoking mothers.

Complications

Lung cancer, mouth cancers, chronic obstructive pulmonary disease, emphysema, ulcers, and heart disease are some of the major illnesses resulting from exposure to tobacco products. Smokers are also believed to be more susceptible to minor respiratory illness such as viral infection, and may be at higher risk for other types of cancer. Both asthma and allergies are exacerbated by exposure to smoke. Maternal and fetal complications may also occur in pregnant women who use tobacco products. Approximately 55-90% of individuals with mental disorders smoke, and tobacco use may be more common in those with mood, anxiety, and other substance-abuse disorders than in the general population. Cigarette smoking increases the metabolism of many medications. Stopping smoking can therefore increase the blood levels of these medications and other substances, sometimes to a clinically significant degree.

Factors Influencing Duration

Mild physical discomfort, cravings, sleep disturbance, drowsiness, and irritability usually occur during withdrawal, which lasts 4-5 days, but there is no significant disability associated with nicotine addiction. Disability is attributable to the type and severity of associated physical illness. The number of cigarettes or tobacco products used daily, the nicotine yield of the product, and the number of years of use can affect the ability to quit as well as the severity of physical/medical consequences.

Length of Disability

In most cases, no disability is expected. Tobacco use in itself is not a disability, but prolonged use may increase the risk of lung and cardiovascular diseases that could lead to disability. Therefore, length of disability is related to the severity of other physical and medical conditions, which may be exacerbated if the individual is unable to quit using tobacco products.

Duration in Days

Job Classification	Minimum	Optimum	Maximum
Any work	1	1	2

Failure to Recover

If an individual fails to recover within the maximum duration expectancy period, the reader may wish to reference the following questions to assist in better understanding the specifics of an individual's medical case.

Regarding diagnosis:

- Because a comprehensive assessment is essential when developing the treatment plan, did the individual's evaluation include detailed history of past and present substance use, including a persistent desire to quit or unsuccessful efforts made to control the amount used, family and social history, general medical and/or psychiatric history and examination, and physical exam to assess any associated serious medical complications? If not, what areas were omitted?
- Would this information affect the current treatment plan? If so, what changes could be made?
- Have conditions with similar symptoms been ruled out?

Regarding treatment:

- Is the individual on nicotine replacement therapy?
- If not satisfied with one product, does the individual realize that there are several equally effective alternatives?
- If other nicotine replacement products have been unsuccessful, would the individual be willing to try a non-nicotine prescription drug?
- Since behavioral interventions play an important role in treatment, does the individual's current treatment include behavioral therapy?
- Has individual learned behavioral and cognitive tools to prevent a relapse?
- Are both short and long-term coping skills a major focus of the therapeutic regime? Is the individual ready to apply those skills in a crisis?
- Is the individual uncomfortable in a clinic-based, formal smoking-cessation program? Would the individual be willing to change to a different format such as community or public health settings, or telephone, or written format?

Regarding prognosis:

- Since studies have shown it to be the most effective approach, is the individual involved is a combination of both behavioral therapy and drug therapy?
- Does the individual participate in a group therapy program for additional support?

References

Duke, James A. The Green Pharmacy. Emmaus, PA: Rodale Press, Inc, 1997.
Frances, Allen. Diagnostic and Statistical Manual of Mental Disorders: 4th ed, text revision. Washington, DC: American Psychiatric Association, 2000.
Gottlieb, Bill, ed. New Choices in Natural Healing. Emmaus, PA: Rodale Press, Inc, 1995.
Nicotine Dependence. American Psychiatric Association. 01 Jan 2000. 09 Jan 2001 <http://www.psych.org/clin_res/pg_nicotine_1.cfm>.

Non-Hodgkin's Lymphoma

Other names / synonyms: Burkitt's Lymphoma, Diffuse Large Cell Lymphoma, Diffuse Small Cleaved Cell Lymphoma, Follicular Mixed Small Cleaved and Large Cell Lymphoma, Follicular Predominantly Large Cell Lymphoma, Follicular Small Cleaved Cell Lymphoma, Large Cell Immunoblastic Lymphoma, Lymphoblastic Lymphoma, Lymphoblastoma, Small and Large Cell Lymphoma, Small Lymphocytic Lymphoma, Small Noncleaved Cell Lymphoma

200.2, 202.8

Definition

Non-Hodgkin's lymphoma (NHL) is a type of cancer within the lymphatic system.

The lymphatic system is a connective network of glands and vessels that circulate a clear, plasma-like fluid (lymph) throughout the body. NHL occurs when certain cell types (B or T lymphocytes) within the lymphatic tissues multiply uncontrollably and destroy the normal structure of the vessels within the lymph system. NHL tends to spread (metastasize) quickly and invade other organs such as the spleen and liver.

Some types of NHL involve unusual areas such as the bones, the central nervous system, and the digestive (gastrointestinal) tract. Cancers that are classified as NHL are sub-categorized into one of at least fifteen different types of deadly growths (malignant neoplasms) that may occur within the lymph system. The distinctions between these different categories of NHL are based upon the type of cell from which the cancer originated and their rate of growth. In general terms, NHL is classified as high grade (highly aggressive), intermediate grade, or low grade (indolent).

Risk factors for NHL include infection with certain viruses including the Epstein-Barr virus (EBV). The Epstein-Barr virus is frequently found in tumors taken from individuals with non-Hodgkin's lymphoma and individuals who test positive for EBV show a two- to three-fold increased risk of developing NHL. Another viral risk factor is the human immunodeficiency virus (HIV), which appears to increase the risk of NHL by about 60-fold. Notably, HIV does not appear to actually cause NHL. However, the immunosuppression associated with HIV appears to be a major risk factor for NHL. A final viral risk factor is the human T-cell lymphotropic virus type I (HTLV-1) which is associated with development of a type of NHL called adult T-cell lymphoma (ATL). HTLV-1 carriers have a 2-5% lifetime risk of developing ATL.

A number of different occupations, including anesthesiology, carpentry, chemistry, construction, engineering, farming, fishing, forestry, leather work, mechanics, metal working, road transport working, rubber working, sales and clerical work, vinyl chloride work, and food industry occupations have been linked to NHL risk. However, most of these associations are weak or inconsistent, and further studies are needed to confirm these findings. Other risk factors may include exposure to pesticides, hair dyes, or certain prescription medications. There is no evidence that either smoking tobacco or alcohol consumption play any major role in development of NHL.

Generally, NHL has a higher incidence in more developed countries. The worldwide incidence rate of NHL ranges from 3.7 to 14.0 per 100,000 individuals. Notably, the age-adjusted incidence rates in 20 countries (including the United States) increased by about 50% or more in both men and women between 1968 and 1987. Currently, in the United States, the incidence rate for NHL is 15.1 per 100,000 people for both men and women combined. The incidence of NHL in the US is increasing at a rate of 3% per year among women and 4% per year among men. Overall in the US, the incidence of NHL has increased more than 73% between 1973 and 1991. NHL occurs generally in individuals after 24 years of age although the incidence increases dramatically in the elderly. The highest rates of incidence occur after 60 years of age.

Diagnosis

History: Individuals usually report a painless or slightly tender, swollen lymph node in the neck or inner thigh (ilioinguinal) region. Other symptoms may include unexplained fever and/or night sweats. Gastrointestinal involvement can cause the individual to experience abdominal cramping or bloody diarrhea. Obstruction of the tube that carries urine from the kidney (ureter) may produce pain in the flank area.

Physical exam: Enlarged lymph nodes, nearly always in the neck or armpit but occasionally in the groin, are usually noted during physical examination. Enlargement of both the spleen (splenomegaly) and liver (hepatomegaly) may be noticed during finger or hand manipulation (palpation) of the abdomen.

Tests: Definite diagnosis of NHL requires taking a sample of tissue (biopsy) from an enlarged lymph node. Other tests may include a routine x-ray (chest radiographic examination), which could reveal a mass in the middle of the chest (mediastinal mass). Computer-aided x-ray analysis (computerized tomography), low-frequency radio waves (magnetic resonance imaging or MRI), or exploratory surgery into the abdomen (laparotomy) may aid in determining the spread of the disease. A sample of bone marrow (bone marrow biopsy) may reveal the extent of bone involvement. X-ray imaging of the lymph glands and lymphatic vessels after injection of a contrast dye (lymphangiography) may be done to determine the extent of lymph node involvement. Blood analysis can be run (serum alkaline phosphatase test) to determine the extent of liver involvement and high frequency sound waves (ultrasound) may be used to determine liver enlargement. A complete blood count (CBC) will provide information regarding the number of white blood cells (leukocytes) and platelets in the blood stream, both of which are usually elevated. Other blood tests may include serum albumin level, serum lactate dehydrogenase, and serum Beta-2 microglobulin level. A hemoglobin level test may reveal a low concentration of hemoglobin in the red blood cells (anemia). A test to identify a generalized inflammatory condition (erythrocyte sedimentation rate or ESR) may be done, and it is usually elevated in individuals with NHL.

Treatment

Treatment will vary, depending upon the type of NHL and the extent of the disease. Low grade types (including small lymphocytic, follicular small cleaved cell, and follicular mixed small cleaved and large cell lymphomas) are usually treated using one (single-agent) or more (combination) chemotherapeutic agents. Administration of nonspecific drugs that may enhance the immune system (interferon; interleukin-2) have not proven effective. Alternatively, treatment may include administration of radioactive antibodies that are specific for cancer cells (antibody-delivered therapy). Intermediate grade NHL (including follicular predominantly large cell, diffuse small cleaved cell, diffuse small and large cell, and diffuse large cell lymphomas) are systemic diseases when diagnosed and combination chemotherapy is the mainstay of treatment.

New therapeutic approaches include removal of a portion of the affected individual's bone marrow and storing it while chemotherapy or radiation treatment are administered to destroy cancerous cells (autologous bone marrow transplantation or autologous BMT). Later, the stored bone marrow is injected back into the individual and it becomes part of the individual's bone marrow (engraftment) with a return (hopefully) to normal function.

High grade NHL (including immunoblastic large cell lymphoma, lymphoblastic lymphoma, and small noncleaved cell lymphomas such as Burkitt's lymphoma) have been treated in a number of ways. Conventional multi-drug chemotherapy and radiation treatments are the best option, and autologous BMT has also been used.

Prognosis

Survival rates in adults are widely variable and usually depend upon the type of NHL, the extent of the disease, and the age of the individual. Older people with NHL generally have shorter survival times than do younger people. Most recurrences of the disease occur in the first two or three years after diagnosis, and these often are effectively treated with chemotherapy. Low-grade NHL that is treated with conventional chemotherapy invariably shows disease progression in 50-90% of individuals and overall survival times average from 30 to 50 months after finishing treatment. Complete remission of low-grade NHL may occur in only 10-20% of individuals with this condition. However, initial results using antibody delivery of radioactive treatment (antibody-delivered therapy) are promising and in one study, 84% of individuals with low-grade NHL showed complete remission. Individuals with intermediate NHL that is in its early stages show a strong response to chemotherapy treatment with an overall survival rate of 73% five years after treatment. This figure drops to 26% overall survival rate at 5 years if the disease is more advanced. Individuals with intermediate NHL in an advanced stage may benefit from autologous bone marrow transplantation (autologous BMT). Results are not conclusive, however, at least one study reported 74% of individuals with intermediate NHL who received autologous BMT showed progression-free survival at 40 months following treatment. Individuals with advanced NHL such as Burkitt's lymphoma who receive extensive chemotherapy in combination with radiation treatment will show a cure rate of 90% or greater if their disease is limited. Individuals with more extensive Burkitt's lymphoma may be expected to show a cure rate of 80-90%. Other forms of advanced NHL do not have such a good prognosis and survival at 4 years following treatment may be as low as 45%.

Differential Diagnosis

Conditions that present with symptoms similar to non-Hodgkin's lymphoma include Hodgkin's disease or other lymphomas, non-cancerous growth or tumor, mononucleosis, HIV infection, lupus, and tuberculosis.

Specialists

- General Surgeon
- Hematologist
- Oncologist
- Pain Specialist
- Psychiatrist
- Psychologist
- Radiation Oncologist

Work Restrictions / Accommodations

Individuals with Hodgkin's disease will experience high levels of fatigue with normal levels of physical exertion. Chemotherapy and radiation therapy can cause additional weakness and fatigue. Work responsibilities may need to be modified and heavy physical labor curtailed until recovery is complete.

Complementary and Alternative Therapies

Content is intended for awareness only. Treatments may or may not be effective. Scientific evidence may be lacking and some substances have potentially toxic effects. Dr. Presley Reed and the editors do not endorse the use of these therapies in the absence of consultation with a licensed medical professional.

Massage therapy -	May help with relaxation and well-being.
Acupuncture -	Needles inserted into certain points on the body may help to alleviate pain from non-Hodgkin's lymphoma.

Comorbid Conditions

Conditions that may impact an individual's ability to recover from non-Hodgkin's lymphoma include prior liver disease, heart disease, or any systemic disease such as diabetes.

Complications

Complications of non-Hodgkin's lymphoma can include several emergency situations that may result from the condition. These include lymph node enlargement or fluid accumulation in various organs to the point where there is airway obstruction, obstruction of the major vein that returns blood to the heart (superior vena caval obstruction), compression of the heart (pericardial tamponade), spinal cord compression, obstruction of the bile duct (extrahepatic biliary obstruction), or pressure on nerves in the head or periphery (cranial and peripheral neuropathies).

Complications of radiation treatment for NHL include development of secondary cancers such as acute nonlymphocytic leukemia, radiation-induced carcinomas and sarcomas, and Hodgkin's disease. Also, radiation therapy to the neck region may result in an underactive thyroid (hypothyroidism) several years after treatment is complete.

Chemotherapy treatments often result in acute (but reversible) toxicity leading to nausea, vomiting, and neurologic disorders. Infections may occur as a result of depression of the immune system by chemotherapy treatment or as a result of the NHL itself. Other complications of chemotherapy may include heart or lung disorders, and female infertility.

Finally, psychological problems may occur in individuals with grossly enlarged lymph nodes. Such changes may produce problems with the affected individual's body image, self-esteem, and interpersonal relationships.

Factors Influencing Duration

Individuals older than 50 years tend to have more advanced disease and do less well in response to combination chemotherapy and irradiation than do younger individuals. The length of disability depends upon the stage of the disease when it is first detected, methods and complexity of treatment, and the individual's response to treatment. Disability may result from the adverse effects of radiation or chemotherapy and not only from the disease itself.

Length of Disability

Duration depends on stage, severity of symptoms, dose and type of chemotherapy. Durations reflect recovery period for treatment. Heavy physical labor is usually restricted for weeks to months following surgery, chemotherapy, and/or radiation therapy treatments. Disability may be permanent.

Chemotherapy.

Duration in Days

Job Classification	Minimum	Optimum	Maximum
Sedentary work	7	14	28
Light work	7	14	28
Medium work	7	14	28
Heavy work	7	14	28
Very Heavy work	7	14	28

High dose chemotherapy and autologous bone marrow transplant.

Duration in Days

Job Classification	Minimum	Optimum	Maximum
Sedentary work	28	42	56
Light work	42	56	70
Medium work	56	70	84
Heavy work	70	84	112
Very Heavy work	70	98	112

Failure to Recover

If an individual fails to recover within the maximum duration expectancy period, the reader may wish to reference the following questions to assist in better understanding the specifics of an individual's medical case.

Regarding diagnosis:

- Does the individual have a history of Epstein-Barr virus (EBV) or human immunodeficiency virus (HIV)?
- Does the individual have human T-cell lymphotropic virus type I (HTLV-1)?
- Does the individual report a painless or slightly tender, swollen lymph node in the neck or inner thigh (ilioinguinal) region?
- Has the individual experienced unexplained fever and/or night sweats?
- Does the individual report experience abdominal cramping or bloody diarrhea?
- Does the individual note pain on the right or left side of the mid-back (flank)?
- Was a sample of tissue (biopsy) from an enlarged lymph node taken to make a definitive diagnosis?
- Were other tests required, such as x-ray of the chest, computed tomography (CT scan), or magnetic resonance imaging (MRI)?
- Was surgery into the abdomen (laparotomy) required to determine the spread (metastasis) of the disease?
- Was a bone marrow biopsy obtained to reveal the extent of bone involvement or a lymphangiography done to determine the extent of lymph node involvement?
- Were complete blood count (CBC), serum alkaline phosphatase, serum albumin, serum lactate dehydrogenase, and serum Beta-2 microglobulin levels drawn?
- Was the diagnosis of non-Hodgkin's lymphoma confirmed? Is it high-, intermediate-, or low-grade NHL?
- Has the disease spread (metastasized) into other organ systems?

Regarding treatment:

- What is the type of NHL and extent of the disease?
- If low-grade NHL, was one (single-agent) or more than one (combination) chemotherapeutic agent used?
- Did the individual receive radioactive antibodies (antibody-delivered therapy)?
- If intermediate grade NHL, was combination chemotherapy used?
- If high grade NHL, did the individual receive multi-drug chemotherapy and radiation treatments?
- Were these treatments successful?
- If not, is the individual a candidate for autologous bone marrow transplantation?

Regarding prognosis:

- What is the type of NHL, extent of the disease, and age of the individual?
- Is this an initial diagnosis or a recurrence?
- Has the individual experienced complications from the disease, such as lymph node enlargement that compresses or obstructs vital organs and/or nerves?
- Has the individual experienced complications associated with radiation therapy, such as radiation-induced secondary cancer or hypothyroidism?
- Has toxicity from chemotherapy treatments occurred resulting in nausea, vomiting, neurologic disorders, and/or suppressing the immune system?
- What is the treatment plan for the complication and what is the expected outcome after treatment?
- Has the individual experienced grossly enlarged lymph nodes that alter appearance? Would the individual benefit from psychological counseling to cope with body image changes and the impact of the disease?

References

Brown-Saltzman, K. "Replenishing the Spirit by Meditative Prayer and Guided Imagery." Seminars in Oncology Nursing 13 4 (1997): 255-259.

Gaidano, G., and R. Dalla-Favera. "The Biology of High-grade Non-Hodgkin's Lymphoma." The Lymphomas. Canellos, G.P., T.A. Lister, and J.L. Sklar, eds. Philadelphia: W.B. Saunders Company, 1998. 353-367.

Jaffe, E.S., and K. Mueller-Hermelink. "Relationship Between Hodgkin's Disease and Non-Hodgkin's Lymphomas." Hodgkin's Disease. Mauch, P.M., et al., eds. Philadelphia: Lippincott, Williams & Wilkins, 1999. 181-193.

LeMone, P., and K.M. Burke. Medical-Surgical Nursing. Upper Saddle River, NJ: Prentice Hall Health, 2000.

Lin, A.Y., and M.A. Tucker. "Epidemiology of Hodgkin's Disease and Non-Hodgkin's Lymphoma." The Lymphomas. Canellos, G.P., T.A. Lister, and J.L. Sklar, eds. Philadelphia: W.B. Saunders Company, 1998. 43-61.

Zutter, M.M., and S.J. Korsmeyer. "The Biology of Low-grade Malignant Lymphoma." The Lymphomas. Canellos, G.P., T.A. Lister, and J.L. Sklar, eds. Philadelphia: W.B. Saunders Company, 1998. 337-351.

Nosebleed
Other names / synonyms: Epistaxis
784.7

Definition

Epistaxis is the medical term for a nosebleed. The blood is lost from the mucous membrane lining of the nose and usually comes from only one nostril. Bleeding may occur toward the front of the nose (anterior epistaxis) or much farther up inside the nose (posterior epistaxis).

Common causes of epistaxis include trauma (direct blow to the nose, nose picking, foreign bodies, forceful nose blowing, and wiping the nose), dry mucous membrane or fragile nasal blood vessels, or deviated nasal septum (wall between nostrils is out of alignment causing one side to become blocked and inflamed). Epistaxis can also be the result of a cold or other infection, alcohol use, or blood thinning (anticoagulation) medication. Chemical irritation may cause nosebleeds. Nosebleeds occur more frequently when environmental humidity is low (i.e., in colder climates in the winter months).

Recurrent epistaxis can be a symptom of high blood pressure (hypertension), a bleeding disorder (coagulation disorder, anemias, leukemia, idiopathic thrombocytopenia purpura, polycythemia vera, and disseminated intravascular coagulation), or a tumor of the nose or sinuses. A nosebleed can occur with allergic rhinitis and during pregnancy (rhinitis of pregnancy).

About 11% of Americans experience at least one nosebleed in their lifetime. Men are more often affected than women. Epistaxis is less common in healthy, young adults but occurs more frequently and with more serious effects in elderly individuals.

Diagnosis

History: Individuals report an episode of bleeding out through the nose (anterior epistaxis) or down through the mouth (posterior epistaxis). Swallowed blood may be coughed up. Individuals or family members should report the approximate amount of blood loss and on which side of the nose bleeding first began. Individuals may also have a history of taking blood thinning medications (e.g., aspirin and nonsteroidal anti-inflammatory drugs [NSAIDs]). Individuals may report a history of previous nosebleeds, easy bruising and bleeding, bleeding after surgery, hypertension, or liver disease.

Physical exam: In active epistaxis, examination of the nose reveals blood in a nostril or down the back of the throat (posterior pharynx). Posterior bleeding is more likely due to an arterial bleed. The individual is examined for signs of trauma and focuses on signs of low fluid volume (hypovolemia) due to excessive blood loss (dizziness, loss of conscious).

The pulse, respiratory rate, and blood pressure are checked. While not actively bleeding, nasal examination may still reveal vascular changes in the mucous membrane lining, ulcerations, small tissue growths (polyps), structural deformities (septal, turbinate), or tumors. The nose may also be completely normal upon examination.

Tests: A complete blood count (CBC) and hematocrit may be performed to rule out anemia or a condition in which the immune system reacts against the body's own tissues (autoimmune disease). Hematocrit measurement may however not accurately reflect blood loss if significant volume replacement is needed. A platelet count is usually obtained. Coagulation disorders may be ruled out through tests that evaluate bleeding and clotting times including prothrombin time and partial thromboplastin time.

Rhinoscopy refers to the magnified examination of the nose using a lighted instrument (rhinoscope). Anterior rhinoscopy is done by looking inward through the nostrils. A posterior rhinoscopy is an examination from the inside looking out into the opening between the nasal cavity and the top of the throat (posterior nares). It is usually performed using a small mirror placed in the passageway connecting the nasal cavity to the upper section of the throat (nasopharynx).

Treatment

The goal of treatment is to stop the bleeding and prevent recurrences. For anterior bleeding, direct pressure is applied to the bleeding site by squeezing the nostrils against the septum. If the bleeding doesn't stop with 15 minutes of direct pressure, the site of the bleed must be identified. Procedures used to visualize the bleeding site include examination through the nostrils (anterior rhinoscopy) and use of an illuminated instrument (nasal endoscopy). Solutions may be used that cause vasoconstriction or stop the bleeding of the blood vessels in the nose. If necessary, the bleeding site may be cauterized by electric cautery. Local anesthetic is used.

When pressure or cauterization is unable to control the bleeding, it may be necessary to pack the nasal passages. Both anterior and posterior bleeding can be packed. Packing may be performed with long strips of gauze or nasal tampons or sponges. When packing is placed, antibiotic coverage is necessary to prevent sinusitis and toxic shock syndrome. Analgesics may also be prescribed, if needed.

Cautery is not recommended if bleeding is due to bleeding abnormalities as the cautery itself may cause bleeding. In this case, petrolatum gauze packing is applied. If recurrent bleeding is from a deviated septum, surgical correction (septoplasty) may be required. Anterior nasal packing is left in place for 2 to 3 days and then removed by the physician in an office procedure.

Posterior bleeding is more difficult to control and can be life-threatening. These bleeds are usually due to underlying medical conditions such as high blood pressure or bleeding disorders. A surgical posterior rhinoscopy performed by a specialist in the field of ear, nose, and throat (otolaryngologist) may be necessary to identify the bleeding site. Nasal endoscopy may also be used to identify the bleeding site.

Procedures to control the bleeding of posterior bleeding include injection of vasoconstrictive medications, packing, placement of a catheter in the nose to provide pressure, balloon devices (similar to that of a catheter but specially made for placement in the posterior nose), cautery, or binding or tying off of associated nasal arteries (ligation). A neuroradiologist may also perform a procedure where clotting material is injected into an arterial bleeder in the nose that occludes the artery at the bleeding site (angiographic procedure called angiographic embolization). In extreme cases, bleeding may have to be controlled with surgical correction. Packing is uncomfortable and often pain and sedative medications are given during the procedure. Antibiotics and analgesics are prescribed while the packing is in place. Angiography may be necessary if surgical packing has not been successful for stopping the nosebleed.

If treatment included posterior packing, the individual is usually hospitalized for observation of cardiac arrhythmias, respiratory failure, and hypoxia. Oxygen may be necessary for treatment of the hypoxia.

Prognosis

A complete recovery is expected. Prevention of recurrent epistaxis when it is a symptom of an underlying condition depends on correction or maintenance of the predisposing factor.

Differential Diagnosis

Epistaxis may be the symptom of bleeding disorders such as inherited disorders (von Willebrand's disease and hereditary hemorrhagic telangiectasia, also known as Osler-Weber-Rendu syndrome) or granulomatous disease. Nasal bleeding is also a result of other bleeding disorders such as hemophilia, liver failure, vitamin K deficiency, abnormally low numbers of platelets (idiopathic thrombocytopenia purpura), leukemia, increased number of red blood cells (polycythemia vera), and a life-threatening bleeding disorder occurring as a result of severe disease or injury (disseminated intravascular coagulation). Epistaxis may also be the initial symptom of a nasal or nasopharyngeal malignancy.

Specialists

- Emergency Medicine
- Hematologist
- Internist
- Otolaryngologist

Work Restrictions / Accommodations

Restrictions or accommodations depend on the cause of the nosebleed and the risk of triggering additional nosebleeds due to the type of work activities performed or the work environment. Individuals may need to avoid excessively dry and/or cold environments. Individuals with posterior nasal packs may have significant work restrictions depending on the job activity.

Comorbid Conditions

Hypertension or clotting disorders may lengthen disability.

Complications

Predisposing factors (bleeding disorders, high blood pressure, chronic inflammation, metabolic disorders, and structural deformities) may make bleeding more difficult to control and can be life-threatening. Appropriate treatment is necessary to stop the bleeding.

Posterior bleeding is more often arterial and severe. Posterior bleeding is more likely to be associated with underlying medical conditions including hypertension, atherosclerosis, and bleeding abnormalities. These conditions occur more frequently in the elderly.

If packing is placed (either anterior or posterior), sinusitis or toxic shock (very rare) may occur. There is a risk of stroke with embolization procedures.

There is an increased risk of arrhythmias, respiratory problems, and hypoxia (low blood oxygen) with posterior packing.

Enemas and cathartics may be needed to evacuate swallowed blood from the gastrointestinal tract in individuals with liver disease. The absorption of byproducts from the breakdown of blood can lead to coma in individuals with liver disease.

Factors Influencing Duration

Length of disability depends on the severity of the epistaxis, underlying condition, treatment required, and any complications secondary to necessary treatment.

Length of Disability

Duration depends on cause. No disability is expected unless excessive blood loss or individual is hypertensive.

Failure to Recover

If an individual fails to recover within the maximum duration expectancy period, the reader may wish to reference the following questions to assist in better understanding the specifics of an individual's medical case.

Regarding diagnosis:

- Was there bleeding through the anterior epistaxis or the posterior epistaxis?
- Was blood in a nostril or going down the back of the throat (more often indicative of an arterial bleed)?
- Did the individual cough up blood?
- Did the individual note how much blood was lost and from which nostril the bleeding started?
- Has the individual experienced trauma to the nose such as a direct blow to the nose, nose picking, foreign bodies, or forceful nose blowing?
- Does the individual use alcohol or have a cold or other infection?
- Has the individual been taking blood-thinning medications (e.g., aspirin and nonsteroidal anti-inflammatory drugs [NSAIDs])?

- Has the individual been exposed to an environment that is low in humidity?
- Is there a history of nosebleeds or of easy bruising and bleeding? If so, does the individual have hypertension or liver disease?
- Were signs of trauma visible? Has the individual been dizzy or lost consciousness?
- Were the pulse, respiratory rate, and blood pressure abnormal?
- Were there vascular changes in the mucous membrane lining, ulcerations, polyps, structural deformities, or tumors present on examination?
- Was the nose completely normal upon examination?
- Was a CBC and hematocrit performed (to rule out anemia or an autoimmune disease)?
- Was a platelet count obtained?
- Were prothrombin time and partial thromboplastin time obtained?
- Was rhinoscopy performed?

Regarding treatment:

- Did bleeding stop after 15 minutes of direct pressure? If not, was cauterization required? Did the nasal passages require packing? If so, is the individual on antibiotics and analgesics?
- Did the individual require septoplasty?
- Was posterior bleeding controlled? If not, what treatments were administered? Vasoconstrictive medication, packing, catheter placement?
- Was cauterization or ligation required?

Regarding prognosis:

- Has the bleeding recurred?
- Is the individual being treated for underlying conditions such as hypertension, liver disease, bleeding disorders, structural deformities, and metabolic disorders?
- How severe and frequent are their nosebleeds?
- Was packing successful?
- Has the individual experienced any complications? If so, what was the complication and how will it be treated?
- What is the expected outcome of this complication?

References

Alvi, Aijaz, and Nedra Joyner-Triplett. "Acute Epistaxis." Post Graduate Medicine 99 5 (1996): 83-91, 95-96.

McGlashan, J.A., et al. "A Comparative Study of Calcium Sodium Alginate (Kaltostat) and Bismuth Tribromophenate (Xeroform) Packing in the Management of Epistaxis." Journal of Laryngology and Otology 106 12 (1992): 1067-1071.

Nystagmus

Other names / synonyms: Ocular Ataxia
379.5, 379.51, 379.52, 379.53, 379.55, 379.56

Definition

Nystagmus is an uncontrollable (involuntary), rapid, rhythmic movement of the eyes. The movement may be from side to side, up and down, or in a circular motion. It may be pendular (where the eyes have undulating movements of equal speed and amplitude) or jerky (where the eyes move more slowly in one direction and then quickly return to the original position). Many people with nystagmus have a "null point." This is an angle of gaze where eye movement is reduced and vision improved. In some cases, the position of the null point causes the individual to have a head tilt (anomalous head posture or AHP). There are approximately 45 different types of nystagmus.

Nystagmus may appear in early childhood or infancy (congenital nystagmus) or later in life (acquired nystagmus). Acquired nystagmus may be a symptom of another medical condition such as stroke, multiple sclerosis, brain tumor, meningitis, or head injury. Nystagmus can also be caused by chemical agents such as barbiturates or other sedatives, anticonvulsants, and alcohol. Nystagmus is neither infectious nor contagious.

Diagnosis

History: Nystagmus can be an inherited condition, but in many cases there is no family history of the disorder. Any initial presentation of nystagmus after 6 years of age should be considered acquired nystagmus and secondary to an active disease process. Individuals with acquired nystagmus usually report recent onset of signs and symptoms such as the perception that stationary objects are moving (oscillopsia), dizziness, or ringing in the ears (tinnitus).

Physical exam: On physical examp, characteristic rapid eye movements are observed and tilting of the head (AHP) may be observed. Visual acuity decreases and the visual field diminishes.

Tests: Several tests are used to diagnose or rule out different types of nystagmus. Command movements test fast eye movement refixation where the individual looks in various directions when instructed. Pursuit system tests involve the individual keeping the head still and attempting to follow a target with the eyes as it moves to various positions. Optokinetic nystagmus (OKN) is a normal, reflexive response that allows an individual to follow moving images while keeping the head steady. OKN testing helps diagnose congenital nystagmus and can indicate whether the ocular motor pathway is intact.

The "Doll's head test" or oculocephalic maneuver assesses whether the part of the brainstem involved in transmitting eye movements is still intact. This test uses a passive and brisk rotation of the head. Rotational testing evaluates the vestibulo-ocular reflex, which ensures that images stay steady as the head and body move. Caloric testing is used on the vestibular system and evaluates the reflexive movement of the eyes when warm water or ice water is poured into one ear at a time. Neuroimaging testing is done such as MRI or CT with contrast if acquired nystagmus is thought to involve the eighth cranial nerve or its brainstem pathways. If drug toxicity is suspected, medication blood levels and testing for illegal drug use may be indicated.

Treatment

There is no cure for nystagmus but treatment may be indicated for the underlying cause. For example, brainstem tumors may require surgery. Nystagmus caused by drug toxicity may resolve when medication dose is reduced or the drug discontinued. Several treatments can help improve visual acuity, improve the appearance of the condition, or reduce nystagmus. These treatments include corrective lenses, prisms, and surgery.

It is important to correct existing refractive errors and try to optimize vision. Both eye glasses and contact lenses can help correct reduced visual acuity. Because contact lenses move with the eyes, they allow the eye to focus through the optical center of the lens at all times and are therefore more effective than glasses at correcting vision if a null point exists. In addition, the sensation caused by the small movements of the contact lenses on the eye have been shown in some studies to help reduce nystagmus.

Prisms may be used when an individual has problems with work or driving. In these cases, the prisms eliminate AHP and improve visual acuity. The prisms are generally placed with the apex toward the null point of each eye, thus moving the eyes into the primary position. The use of prisms is limited to individuals with binocular vision. Among the disadvantages of prisms are the increased weight of prism glasses and the awkward appearance.

Surgery can be performed to correct AHP by directing the eyes toward the head shift. This shifts the null point into the straight ahead position. The surgery involves lengthening and weakening the four horizontal muscles around the eye. Another surgical procedure shortens the outer horizontal muscle (lateral recti) in order to induce convergence, which dampens the nystagmus. This procedure can only be performed on individuals with binocular vision. Complications of surgery include overcorrection of the AHP, double vision, and difficulty moving the eyes in certain directions.

Prognosis

Congenital nystagmus tends to persist throughout an individual's life, whereas nystagmus secondary to viral labyrinthitis or drug toxicity resolves along with the underlying problem. Nystagmus is not painful and does not lead to total blindness. Quality of life may be affected by the persistent reduction in depth perception, decreased reading speed, and periods of oscillopsia. Most individuals with nystagmus are capable of leading productive, independent lives.

Differential Diagnosis

Conditions with similar symptoms to nystagmus include macrosquare wave jerks, ocular dysmetria, ocular flutter, opsoclonus, and saccadic intrusions.

Specialists

- Neuro-ophthalmologist
- Ophthalmologist
- Neurologist

Work Restrictions / Accommodations

Individuals with nystagmus usually cannot get a driver's license. Those with a constant head tilt may experience physical discomfort or neck pain, and seating position accommodations should be made to provide the individual with the best angle of vision when looking at blackboards or screens. The option of large print material should be made available. Computer screens should be adjusted for brightness, character size, and angle. Most individuals with nystagmus benefit from good task lighting. When balance problems accompany nystagmus, working at heights or under conditions that require agility and stability should be avoided.

Comorbid Conditions

Numerous comorbid conditions may influence the degree of disability including underlying eye problems that are unrelated to nystagmus, vestibular disorders, and other neurologic conditions.

Complications

The inability to hold a steady gaze almost always results in some loss of visual acuity. The perception that stationary objects are moving (oscillopsia) and the loss of depth perception can cause individuals with nystagmus to lose their balance or appear clumsy. Nystagmus that comes on suddenly such as with a viral infection of the labyrinth responsible for maintaining balance (viral labyrinthitis), is often associated with nausea and vomiting.

Factors Influencing Duration

In individuals with nystagmus, visual acuity varies throughout the day. Emotional and physical factors such as tiredness, stress, tension, nervousness, or unfamiliar surroundings tend to decrease visual acuity temporarily.

Length of Disability

Duration depends the underlying cause of nystagmus. Physical ability may be limited, but visual loss may be permanent. This condition is usually permanent unless it is secondary to a treatable or temporary cause such as viral labyrinthitis or drug toxicity. Durations shown represent disability as it relates to time to confirm diagnosis.

Duration in Days

Job Classification	Minimum	Optimum	Maximum
Any work	1	3	7

Failure to Recover

If an individual fails to recover within the maximum duration expectancy period, the reader may wish to reference the following questions to assist in better understanding the specifics of an individual's medical case.

Regarding diagnosis:

- Does the individual have congenital or acquired nystagmus?
- Has the individual had a stroke or brain tumor?
- Does the individual have multiple sclerosis? Have meningitis? A head injury?
- Does the individual use barbiturates, sedatives, anticonvulsants or alcohol?
- What age was the individual at the onset of their nystagmus?
- What active disease process is it secondary to?
- Does the individual report the perception that stationary objects are moving?
- Do they have dizziness or ringing in their ears?
- Does the individual tilt their head. Do they have reduced visual acuity?
- Has the individual had command movements, pursuit system tests and optokinetic nystagmus testing done?
- Have conditions with similar symptoms been ruled out been ruled out?

Regarding treatment:

- Has the individual had treatment for the underlying cause?
- Has the individual had a complete vision examination?
- Are they using contact lenses? Is the individual a candidate for prisms?
- Is the individual a surgical candidate?

Regarding prognosis:

- Is the individual's employer able to accommodate any necessary restrictions?
- Does the individual have any conditions that may affect their ability to recover?
- Does the individual easily lose their balance or appear clumsy?
- Does the individual understand the effect that tiredness, stress, tension, nervousness or unfamiliar surroundings can have on their visual acuity?

References

General Information About Nystagmus. American Nystagmus Network. 16 Apr 2000. 23 May 2000 <http://www.nystagmus.org/aboutn.html>.

Treatments and Ongoing Research. Nystagmus Network UK. 31 Jul 1999. 23 May 2000 <http://www.btinternet.com/~lynest/nystag01.htm>.

Obesity, Simple

Other names / synonyms: Adiposity, Corpulence, Overweight

278, 278.0, 278.00, 278.01

Definition

Obesity is an increase in body weight beyond the limitation of skeletal and physical requirements as the result of an excessive accumulation of fat in the body.

Most commonly, obesity occurs when energy intake (calories) exceeds energy use. Obesity can also occur with disturbances in body hormones or as a result of certain genetic conditions. What causes the imbalance between energy intake and energy use remains unclear.

Simple obesity differs from morbid obesity. Morbidly obese individuals have a body weight that accelerates to two, three, or more times the ideal weight and includes the state reached when the degree of obesity begins to interfere with normal physiological functions such as breathing.

Evidence suggests obesity often has more than one cause. Genetic, environmental, psychological, and other factors may play a part.

Obesity tends to run in families, which suggests a genetic cause. However, family members not only share genes but also diet and lifestyle habits that may contribute to obesity. An individual's environment includes lifestyle behaviors such as what he or she eats and the amount of activity expended. Americans tend to have high-fat diets, often putting taste and convenience ahead of nutritional content when choosing meals. Most Americans do not get enough exercise.

Many individuals eat in response to negative emotions such as boredom, sadness, or anger. While most overweight individuals have no more psychological disturbance than normal-weight individuals, about 30% of those seeking treatment for serious weight problems have difficulties with binge eating. Research is showing that binge eaters have more difficulty losing weight and keeping the weight off than individuals without binge eating problems.

Some rare illnesses can cause obesity and include hypothyroidism, Cushing's syndrome, depression, and certain neurologic problems. Certain drugs such as steroids and some antidepressants may cause excessive weight gain.

The prevalence of obesity (defined as a body mass index [BMI] of over 30) in the US has risen dramatically over the past few years. According to one study, prevalence increased from 12% in 1991 to nearly 18% in 1998. The study was based on individuals reporting their own height and weight so these statistics may actually be too low. In fact, other studies reported that more than half of American adults are overweight (BMI over 25). Obesity has increased in every state in both men and women across all age groups and in every ethnic group. The greatest increases occurred in young adults, those with some college education, and Hispanics (11.6% to 20.8%). Regionally, the prevalence of obesity ranges from 31.9% in the Mid-Atlantic States to 67.2% in the South Atlantic region. The World Health Organization now considers obesity to be a global epidemic and a public health problem as more nations become westernized. Globally, an estimated 250 million adults are now obese and many more are overweight.

Diagnosis

History: Obese individuals are frequently conscious of being overweight. Complaints may include shortness of breath (dyspnea); fatigue; joint pains in the hips, knees, and ankles; and a general dissatisfaction with state of health. Family history may point to diabetes or include obesity.

Physical exam: The exam includes measuring height and weight (BMI) as well as waist and hip ratio. Skinfold measurements taken by skinfold calipers are measured at various locations on the individual's body. Another part of the physical exam is a method for measuring body fat called the Body Mass Index (BMI). It is derived by dividing an individual's weight in kilograms by his or her height in meters squared (BMI = $kg/m2$). Multiplying an individual's weight in pounds by 703 and then dividing it twice by individual's height in inches can also compute BMI. For example, a woman who weighs 150 pounds and is 68 inches tall has a BMI of 22.8. The result is graded on a scale to indicate levels of body fat. Federal guidelines define overweight as a BMI of 25 to 29.9 and obesity as a BMI of 30 or greater. Individuals with a BMI greater than 40 are considered morbidly obese.

To compute an individual's waist and hip ratio, divide the waist measurement (measured at narrowest point) by the hip measurement (measured at fullest point). Women with waist-to-hip ratios of more than 0.8 or men with waist-to-hip ratios of more than 1.0 are "apples" (because of their apple shape). Apples are at considerably greater health risk because of their fat distribution than are "pears."

Tests: Blood sugar (glucose) at various times including after fasting or ingestion of glucose (glucose tolerance tests) are used to evaluate diabetes. Blood tests may also reveal high cholesterol, high fats, (hyperlipidemia), and elevated uric acid levels (hyperuricemia). TSH should be measured to exclude thyroid deficiency.

Treatment

The five medically accepted treatment modalities currently available are diet modification, exercise, behavior modification, drug therapy, and surgery. All these modalities, alone or in combination, are capable of inducing weight loss sufficient to produce significant health benefits in many obese individuals. Unfortunately, health benefits are not maintained if weight is regained. With the exception of surgery, it is difficult to adhere to these modalities in a manner sufficient to maintain long-term weight loss.

Calorie restriction has remained the cornerstone for the treatment of obesity. The standard dietary recommendations for losing weight include reducing calorie intake by 500 to 1,000 calories a day and having a fat intake of no more than 30% of total calories. Saturated fats should be avoided.

The addition of an exercise program to diet modification results in more weight loss than dieting alone and seems especially helpful in maintaining weight loss and preserving lean body mass. Although vigorous workouts do not immediately burn great numbers of calories, the metabolism remains elevated after exercise. The more strenuous the exercise, the longer the metabolism continues to burn calories before returning to its resting level. Although the calories lost during the postexercise period are not high, over time they may count significantly for maintaining a healthy weight. Included in any regimen should be resistance or strength training performed 2 or 3 times a week. Even moderate regular exercise helps improve insulin sensitivity and in turn helps prevent heart disease and diabetes. Exercising regularly is critical. Exercise improves psychological well-being and replaces sedentary habits that usually lead to snacking. Exercise may even act as a mild appetite suppressant.

Behavior modification for obesity refers to a set of principles and techniques designed to modify eating habits and physical activity. It is most helpful for mildly to moderately obese individuals. One frequently used form of behavior modification called cognitive-behavioral therapy is very useful in preventing relapse after initial weight loss.

Surgery is considered the treatment of choice for well-informed and motivated severely or morbidly obese adults (more than 180% overweight or whose BMI is greater than 40) who have failed to respond to medical weight control. Surgery may also be considered for those with less severe obesity (BMI between 35 and 40) afflicted with disabling joint disease, pulmonary insufficiency, hypertension, or diabetes mellitus. The two main surgical procedures used to achieve weight loss are the gastric bypass and the lap band.

Prognosis

If an individual strictly follows a sensible diet and exercise program and loses the needed number of pounds, the prognosis is excellent provided the individual continues with the program or with a maintenance program based on the original program. Research shows that most individuals who successfully achieve their weight loss goals return to pretreatment weight within 5 years.

The ability of most individuals to maintain weight loss is portrayed in two recent studies. In the first study, Kaiser Permanente tested 190 individuals, each who had lost 100 pounds. At follow-up 18 months after completing a program that followed a VLCD, half the individuals regained 50% of their weight loss. The second study from Finland showed that fewer than 6% of overweight individuals can lose weight and keep it off with any diet.

For untreated obesity, the prognosis is poor and tends to progress.

Differential Diagnosis

Other disorders that could masquerade as obesity are hormonal disorders such as a deficiency in thyroid activity (hypothyroidism), Cushing's syndrome, and tumors of the adrenal or pituitary glands. Genetic disorders such as Down's syndrome, severe familial obesity, and severe familial high cholesterol (hyperlipidemia) may also have similar symptoms.

Specialists

- Dietary Advisor
- Endocrinologist
- Internist
- Neurologist
- Psychiatrist
- Psychologist

Work Restrictions / Accommodations

Some obese individuals, especially those who are morbidly obese, may no longer be able to perform their duties efficiently since obesity tends to tire them out more easily. Weight-related conditions and diseases may also occur. Accommodations may include the possibility of a more sedentary position or one that incorporates limited exertion. A position that involves walking and moving around may also be beneficial since it engages the individual in exercise while working.

Individuals may need additional time away from work for appointments with the physician, dietitian, or personal trainer. A flextime arrangement may be a consideration for the individual whose weight reduction plan includes regular visits to a fitness club.

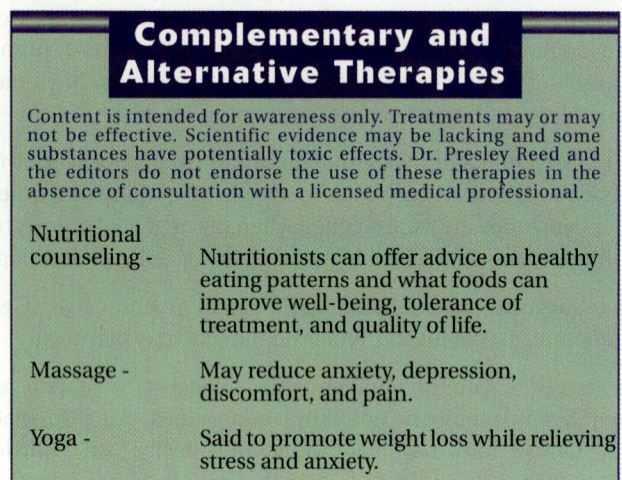

Complementary and Alternative Therapies

Content is intended for awareness only. Treatments may or may not be effective. Scientific evidence may be lacking and some substances have potentially toxic effects. Dr. Presley Reed and the editors do not endorse the use of these therapies in the absence of consultation with a licensed medical professional.

Nutritional counseling - Nutritionists can offer advice on healthy eating patterns and what foods can improve well-being, tolerance of treatment, and quality of life.

Massage - May reduce anxiety, depression, discomfort, and pain.

Yoga - Said to promote weight loss while relieving stress and anxiety.

Comorbid Conditions

High blood pressure (hypertension), diabetes, and arthritis can lengthen disability.

Complications

Obesity is associated with a number of complications detrimental to health and quality of life. Included are the individual's continued inability to lose weight, degenerative joint disease, diabetes, high blood pressure, arthritis, predisposition to cancer (type varies for men and women), gum disease, gallstones, reproductive and hormonal problems, lung diseases, stoppage of breathing during sleep (sleep apnea) and other sleep disorders, binge eating and other eating disorders, and emotional and social problems.

From a mortality perspective, complications of obesity are associated with death. Recent estimates attribute 280,000 deaths a year in the US to obesity, making it second to cigarette smoking as a cause of death.

Very-low-calorie diets (VLCDs) are associated with transient fatigue, hair loss, dizziness, and other symptoms. More serious adverse events associated with periods of severe caloric restriction include the development of gallstones and acute gallbladder disease. The risk for cardiac arrhythmias and death was eliminated with a supplementation diet of high quality protein, minerals, and electrolytes.

Factors Influencing Duration

Factors that may influence length of disability include type of job and compliance with treatment protocol.

Length of Disability

Obesity is seldom disabling unless it becomes morbid obesity.

Failure to Recover

If an individual fails to recover within the maximum duration expectancy period, the reader may wish to reference the following questions to assist in better understanding the specifics of an individual's medical case.

Regarding diagnosis:

- Does individual have a genetic predisposition to obesity?
- Does individual have a history of hypothyroidism, Cushing's syndrome, depression, or certain neurological problems?
- Is individual taking drugs that may cause weight gain such as steroids or certain antidepressants?
- What does individual eat? Is individual active?
- Does individual eat in response to negative emotions such as boredom, sadness, or anger?
- Is individual a binge eater?
- Is individual very conscious of being overweight?
- Does individual complain of shortness of breath (dyspnea); fatigue; joint pains in the hips, knees, and ankles; or a general dissatisfaction with state of health?
- Was individual's body mass index (BMI) measured? Was it 30 or greater?
- Was blood sugar (glucose) measured at various times including after a fast or ingestion of glucose (glucose tolerance tests)?
- Were blood tests taken to measure fats (lipids) uric acid levels?
- Was a diagnosis of obesity confirmed?

Regarding treatment:

- Was caloric intake reduced by about 500 to 1,000 calories per day?
- Was fat intake kept to no more than 30% of total calories per day? Does individual avoid saturated fats?
- Is individual involved in an exercise program that promotes the recommended amount of physical activity?
- Would individual benefit from enrollment in a community exercise or weight-loss program?
- Did individual maintain weight loss? Was individual compliant with treatment regimen? What could be done to increase compliance?
- Would a behavior modification program be beneficial?
- Did individual more than 180% overweight or with a BMI greater than 40 have surgery?
- What surgical procedure was performed? Gastric bypass or the lap band? How effective was the procedure?

Regarding prognosis:

- Has individual depended on diet alone to lose weight?
- Does individual understand the importance of keeping an exercise regimen?
- How successful was individual in keeping weight off?
- How much is obesity impacting individual's health?
- Is individual a candidate for a more stringent, multidisciplinary weight-loss program or for surgical intervention?
- Do the benefits of surgery outweigh the risks?
- If weight does not decrease, can individual still perform daily activities?

References

Obesity and Being Overweight. Nidus Information Services, Inc. 01 Dec 1999. 06 Nov 2000 <http://www.mdconsult.com>.

"Obesity:" The Merck Manual of Diagnosis and Therapy. Beers, Mark H. MD, and Robert Berkow, MD, *eds* Merck and Co, Inc. 1999. 06 Nov 2000 < http://www.merck.com/pubs/mmanual/section1/chapter5/5a.htm >.

Oeser, D. Obesity Part I. Epidemiology, Etiology and Pathophysiology, and Nonpharmacotherapeutic Treatments. The Internet Journal of Academic Physician Assistants. 1997. 06 Nov 2000 < http://www.ispub.com/journals/IJAPA/Vol1N2/obesity1.html >.

Understanding Adult Obesity. National Institute of Diabetes and Digestive and Kidney Diseases. 09 Feb 1998. 06 Nov 2000 < http://www.niddk.nih.gov/health/nutrit/pubs/unders.htm >.

Obsessive-Compulsive Disorder

Other names / synonyms: Obsession-Compulsion Personality Disorder, Obsessive-Compulsive Anxiety Disorder

300.3

Definition

Obsessive-compulsive disorder is an anxiety disorder characterized by persistent, intrusive, and inappropriate thoughts (obsessions) along with ritualistic, repetitive behaviors (compulsions). These disturbing thoughts and behaviors occupy more than one hour each day and can cause significant interference in a individual's normal routine, occupational or academic functioning, social activities, or relationships. Common obsessions are fear of contamination by germs or dirt, imagining having harmed self or others, imagining losing control of aggressive urges, intrusive sexual thoughts or urges, excessive religious or moral doubt, forbidden thoughts, a need to have things "just so," or a need to tell, ask, or confess. Common compulsions are washing, repeating, checking, touching, counting, ordering/arranging, hoarding, or praying. Some behaviors, such as gambling, drinking, or sexual activity are termed "compulsive." However, in these cases, the behavior is experienced as pleasurable and is not done to defend against an obsession, so would not be considered obsessive compulsive disorder.

Obsessive-compulsive disorder is usually first recognized in early adulthood, but can start in childhood, with males developing symptoms earlier than females.

Diagnosis

History: A diagnosis is based on criteria listed in the DSM-IV-TR (Diagnostic Statistical Manual, 4th Edition, Text Revision, published by the American Psychiatric Association). Obsessions occur when an individual experiences recurrent and persistent thoughts, impulses, or images that are intrusive and inappropriate, which are not simply excessive worries about real-life problems, and which the individual attempts to suppress with another thought or action. Compulsions occur when an individual performs repetitive behaviors (e.g., hand washing, ordering, or checking) that the individual feels driven to perform in response to an obsession or according to rules that must be applied rigidly, and which are aimed at preventing or reducing distress and are not connected in a realistic way with what they are designed to neutralize. Other criteria are that the obsessions or compulsions are usually recognized by the individual as excessive or unreasonable, cause marked distress, take more than one hour per day, significantly interfere with an individual's normal routine, are recognized as a product of the individual's own mind, and are not due to the effects of drug abuse, medication, or a general medical condition.

Physical exam: A physical exam might show things such as raw, chapped hands from repeated hand washing, or the individual might be observed performing ritualistic actions such as checking and rechecking the position of one's chair.

Tests: There are no diagnostic tests for this disorder. However, PET scans used in the research of obsessive-compulsive disorder may show abnormal metabolism in certain sections of the brain.

Treatment

Medication therapy, combined with cognitive-behavioral therapy, is the most successful treatment. The most effective group of drugs for treating obsessive-compulsive disorder is the serotonin-specific reuptake inhibitor (SSRI) antidepressant group. These medications increase the level of serotonin, a neurochemical messenger, in the brain. The most effective, nondrug type of therapy is cognitive behavior therapy, which helps the individual learn to change his or her thoughts and feelings by first changing their behavior through the techniques of exposure and response prevention.

The exposure technique is based on the fact that anxiety tends to decrease after repeated exposure to a feared thought or situation. Thus, an individual with obsessions about germs is told to stay in contact with "germy" objects (e.g., handling money) until their anxiety is gone. In response prevention, the individual with excessive worries about germs must not only stay in contact with "germy things," but must also refrain from ritualized washing.

Family therapy might be useful since this disorder is quite stressful to family members. It may be helpful for family members to understand the characteristics of the disorder and the way in which it is most effectively treated. The individual may meet with their psychiatrist or psychologist one or more times a week at the beginning of treatment and then gradually spread out the appointments until a maintenance level of once every 3-6 months is reached. Group therapy might also be a useful and cost-effective way to provide cognitive behavioral treatment.

Prognosis

About 20% of individuals improve significantly with treatment, half have some improvement, and the rest stay the same or become more disturbed. Approximately 15% show a gradually progressive deterioration in functioning. Outcome is worse when individuals don't realize their obsessions and/or compulsions are not reality-based.

Differential Diagnosis

Other disorders that may resemble obsessive-compulsive disorder are phobias, generalized anxiety disorder, delusional disorders, eating disorders, sexual disorders, obsessive-compulsive personality disorders, or Tourette's syndrome.

Specialists

- Psychiatrist

Work Restrictions / Accommodations

Work accommodations may include modifying identifiable work situations that provoke symptoms of anxiety; by decreasing workplace stimulants such as noise, cigarette smoke, or noxious chemicals; introducing the individual to stressful situations gradually under close supervision and support; providing flexibility with work schedule to accommodate medical or psychiatric appointments (which normally should occur during the employee's personal time); allowing break time according to individual needs rather than a fixed schedule; and temporarily adjusting highly stressful activities.

Comorbid Conditions

Depression may coexist with obsessive-compulsive disorder.

Complications

Suicide could be a risk for those who develop major depression along with obsessive-compulsive disorder. Tics or secondary complications, such as skin problems from continuous hand-washing, may occur. About half of individuals with Tourette's disorder have coexisting OCD; however, only 5% of OCD patients have Tourette's disorder.

Factors Influencing Duration

Response to treatment, type of job responsibilities, and the individual's insight into their obsessive-compulsive disorder could influence the length of disability.

Length of Disability

In most cases, no disability is expected. Duration depends upon response to medications and psychotherapy and the presence of other psychiatric disorders. While the condition is chronic, there may be exacerbations that require hospitalization or intensive outpatient treatment. Severe obsessive-compulsive disorder can be quite disabling.

Duration in Days

Job Classification	Minimum	Optimum	Maximum
Any work	7	14	28

Failure to Recover

If an individual fails to recover within the maximum duration expectancy period, the reader may wish to reference the following questions to assist in better understanding the specifics of an individual's medical case.

Regarding diagnosis:

- Does individual's behavior meet the criteria for obsessive-compulsive disorder?
- Has diagnosis been confirmed?
- Have physiological effects of substance abuse or medication been ruled out?
- Have underlying neurological and general medical conditions been ruled out?

Regarding treatment:

- Has individual's treatment included a combination of both behavioral therapy and drug therapy?
- What type of medication is individual currently taking?
- If one SRI was not effective, would another SRI give a better response?
- Would individual benefit from the use of an SRI as the primary medication and one of a variety of medications as an augmenter?
- Does individual's behavioral therapy include exposure and response prevention?
- Do repeated exposures to the situations or people that trigger the obsessions help the individual forego the usual ritual while diminishing the anxiety and discomfort?
- Does the individual's behavioral therapy include "exposure and response" prevention? Would addition of this type of approach be beneficial?
- Is the individual currently involved in a therapy group?
- Are coexisting or resultant psychological conditions, such as depression or anxiety, being appropriately treated?

Regarding prognosis:

- Is a coexisting depression interfering with treatment?
- Is the therapist trained and experienced in this form of therapy?
- Is the individual highly motivated and faithful in completing homework assignments?
- Is the family cooperative?

References

"Expert Consensus Treatment Guidelines for Obsessive-compulsive Disorder: A Guide for Patients and Families." The Expert Consensus Guideline Series. 1997. 17-Oct-2000 <http://www.psychguides.com/oche.html>.

Ellingrod, Vicki. "Obsessive Compulsive Disorder Pharmacotherapy." Clinical Psychopharmacology Seminar 2000 (1999): 1-6. 17-Oct-2000 <http://www.vh.org/Misc/Outline.html>.

Frances, Allen. Diagnostic and Statistical Manual of Mental Disorders: 4th ed, text revision. Washington, DC: American Psychiatric Association, 2000.

Post, Doug. "Obsessive Compulsive Disorder." Clinician Reviews 10(7) (2000): 122-123.

Obsessive-Compulsive Personality Disorder
301.4

Definition

An individual with obsessive-compulsive personality disorder is characterized as being emotionally constricted, persevering, indecisive, stubborn, and orderly.

There is a pervasive pattern of perfectionism and inflexibility. These individuals are preoccupied with rules, regulations, orderliness, neatness, details, and the achievement of perfection. Individuals with this disorder appear very formal and serious, usually lack a sense of humor, and may have restricted ability to show warm and tender feelings. They may appear stubborn, possessive, stingy, uncreative, and unimaginative. Almost the slightest disruption in their daily routine promotes anxiety sometimes to the point of panic attacks. These individuals are preoccupied with trivial details and rules and do not appreciate changes in routine. Obsessive-compulsive personalities frequently are found in vocations that value accuracy, orderliness, and moral rectitude more than warmth and sociability.

Individuals with obsessive-compulsive personality disorder commonly have a stable marriage and occupational success, yet usually have few friends. They have difficulty relaxing and enjoying life. These individuals appear serious most of the time. It is difficult for them to take vacations, admit pleasure, or display emotions. Much of their time is spent in organizing, making lists, or keeping notebooks and mental notes in an attempt to keep their lives neat and orderly.

This disorder typically begins by early adulthood. It is more common among men, although the exact prevalence is unknown.

Diagnosis

History: As with all personality disorders, the psychiatric interview and mental status exam are the most useful diagnostic tools. According to the DSM-IV, the obsessive-compulsive disorder presents a pervasive pattern of preoccupation with orderliness, perfectionism, and mental and interpersonal control at the expense of flexibility, openness, and efficiency. It begins by early adulthood and presents in a variety of contexts.

The obsessive-compulsive personality displays four or more of the following: preoccupation with details, rules, lists, order, organization, or schedules to the extent that the major point of the activity is lost; perfectionism interfering with task completion (unable to complete a project because his or her own overly strict standards are not met); excessive devotion to work and productivity to the exclusion of leisure activities and friendships (not accounted for by obvious economic necessity); being overly conscientious, scrupulous, and inflexible about matters of morality, ethics, or values (not accounted for by cultural or religious identification); inability to discard worn out or worthless objects even when they have no sentimental value; reluctance to delegate tasks or to work with others unless they submit to exactly his or her way of doing things; miserly spending style toward both self and others (money is viewed as something to be hoarded for future catastrophes); or rigidity and stubbornness.

In the psychiatric interview, individuals with obsessive-compulsive personalities may present with conventional and meticulous dress. Their posture may be unusually stiff, hair unusually neat, mood serious, and speech monotone. They may give very detailed and accurate historical accounts and are prone to lengthy monologues.

Physical exam: The exam is usually not helpful in the diagnosis of this disorder.

Tests: Psychological testing can help identify and classify personality disorders in conjunction with the history obtained in the psychiatric interview and information obtained during the mental status exam.

Treatment

In general, individuals with obsessive-compulsive personalities recognize that they have problems unlike those with other personality disorders. These individuals know they suffer from their inflexibility and realize they do not permit themselves to have good feelings. Individual psychotherapy may be helpful but treatment is difficult since these individuals tend to see the world as "all-or-nothing" or "black-or-white."

Therapy should focus on current feelings and situations with goals to provide short-term symptom relief, support existing coping mechanisms, and teach new coping mechanisms. Excessive time should not be spent on examining the psychological basis of the condition since the personality is resistant to change. Treatment is often a long and complex process. Struggles for control should be avoided as individuals may distance themselves from their feelings by attacking the credentials of the therapist. Group therapy and behavior therapy may offer certain advantages, but cognitive therapy is rarely helpful in this disorder. These individuals are likely to point out other people's shortcomings and may become ostracized by the group. Because these individuals often lack insight into their emotions, writing down feelings in a journal as soon as they become apparent may be helpful.

Pharmacotherapy is usually not needed in uncomplicated cases but may be utilized to treat coexisting or resultant depression and anxiety. The use of benzodiazepine to reduce anxiety or tricyclic antidepressants to reduce depression may be indicated. Selective serotonin reuptake inhibitors may be helpful if obsessive-compulsive signs and symptoms persist. Hospitalization is rarely needed.

Prognosis

During the course of obsessive-compulsive personality disorder, the incidence of symptomatic episodes is unpredictable and variable. Obsessions and compulsions may evolve from time to time as in other major depression and psychosomatic disorders. Treatment is often a long process for these individuals. Therapy often helps individuals deal with conflicts and symptoms in the short-term but rarely has much effect on the underlying personality disorder.

Differential Diagnosis

It is not uncommon for an individual to meet the DSM-IV criteria for more than one personality disorder. Other personality disorders that may resemble obsessive-compulsive personality disorder include obsessive-compulsive disorder, narcissistic personality disorder, antisocial personality disorder, schizoid personality disorder, and personality change due to a general medical condition. Associated and sometimes coexistent psychiatric disorders such as substance abuse, schizophrenia, somatoform disorder, dissociative disorder, anxiety, and depressive disorders can be included in the differential diagnoses.

Specialists

- Licensed Clinical Social Worker
- Psychiatrist
- Psychologist

Work Restrictions / Accommodations

Time-limited work restrictions and accommodations should be individually determined based on the characteristics of the individual's response to the disorder, the functional requirements of the job and work environment, and the flexibility of the job and work site. The purpose of the restrictions/accommodations is to help maintain the worker's capacity to remain at the workplace without a work disruption and to promote timely and safe transition back to full work productivity.

Comorbid Conditions

Alcohol abuse or drug use or the presence of another psychiatric illness may lengthen disability.

Complications

Complications occur with the coexistence of another mental disorder such as an anxiety disorder, mood disorder, or substance abuse or dependence. Other complications may include a change in financial, occupational, or marital status related to personality conflicts.

Factors Influencing Duration

Important factors influencing the length of disability are the progress and effectiveness of psychotherapy and pharmacotherapy and the individual's willingness to cooperate with therapy. The coexistence of other psychiatric diagnoses such as Axis I disorders or substance abuse and the severity of the personality disorder are also factors. The current influence of life circumstances such as relationships, legal, financial, and occupational problems may influence the length of disability.

Length of Disability

This condition represents a life-long pattern of behavior. In most cases, no disability is expected.

Failure to Recover

If an individual fails to recover within the maximum duration expectancy period, the reader may wish to reference the following questions to assist in better understanding the specifics of an individual's medical case.

Regarding diagnosis:

- Does the individual fit criteria for obsessive-compulsive personality disorder?
- Has diagnosis been confirmed?
- Have other underlying medical and psychiatric disorders been ruled out?

Regarding treatment:

- Has the individual established a trusting, therapeutic rapport with the physician/therapist? If not, what can be done to foster this relationship?
- Has the individual been provided with a detailed and clearly presented account of the disease process and treatment options?
- Since trust is necessary for an effective therapeutic relationship, has individual been given documentary evidence in the form of specific laboratory test results (ECG, x-rays, actual reports from literature)?
- Is the individual able to participate as an informed partner in the healing process?
- Is the individual on an effective drug therapy program?
- Have ritual and anxiety levels become intolerable? Would removal from the external environmental and stresses lessen symptoms to a more tolerable level?
- Would the individual benefit from brief inpatient treatment?
- Is the therapist experienced with and able to handle the intricacies of obsessive-compulsive personality disorders?
- In what type of therapy is the individual currently involved?
- Has therapy included desensitization techniques, flooding techniques, saturation therapy, and/or thought-stopping techniques? What other options would be appropriate at this point?
- Is individual involved in a group therapy session? Would this be a good adjunct to present therapy?
- Is individual's family involved in therapy or treatment plan? Can this be implemented?

Regarding prognosis:

- Is individual able to moderate or control obsessive-compulsive personality disorder traits?
- Would extended or additional therapy be beneficial at this time?

References

Long, Phillip W., MD. Obsessive-compulsive Personality Disorder. Internet Mental Health. 1999. 16 Aug 2000 <http://www.mentalhealth.com/fr20.html>.

Treatment: Obsessive-compulsive Personality Disorder. Mental Health Net. 1996. 10/16/2000 <http://mentalhelp.net/disorders/sx26t.htm>.

Occupational Asthma

Other names / synonyms: Asthma, Occupational Exposure Asthma

505

Definition

Occupational asthma is a breathing disorder caused by inhaling irritating substances in a particular occupational environment, and not to stimuli encountered outside of the workplace. It is characterized by wheezing, chest tightness, shortness of breath, and a dry cough; the symptoms tend to worsen as the work week progresses, and lessen or completely resolve on weekends or during vacations. It can occur for the first time in a person who has been previously healthy, or pre-existing asthma can be aggravated by work place exposures. A wide array of substances can trigger occupational asthma, including dust, pollen, chemical fumes, gasses, animal proteins, tobacco, synthetic dyes, etc. Even substances that are not normally considered harmful or dangerous can be responsible if the individual is exposed to high levels over long periods of time (e.g., flour can trigger symptoms in a professional baker).

There are three mechanisms responsible for the development of occupational asthma. The first involves direct contact, allergic, and/or pharmacologic mechanisms. Exposure to a high concentration of irritants that directly provoke occupational asthma without any period of latency include chemicals such as hydrochloric acid, sulfur dioxide, ammonia, etc. This is often referred to as Reactive Airways Dysfunction Syndrome (RADS). Workers who already have asthma or some other respiratory disorder are particularly affected by these types of irritants. Secondly, allergies can develop only after a latent period of long-term exposure (months to years) to a work-related substance, which then causes occupational asthma to develop. Examples of irritants that provoke a long-term exposure allergic-type occupational asthma to develop include food products, animal proteins, plastics, rubber, resins, enzymes, latex, etc. The third cause of this condition results when aerosolized particles of certain substances are inhaled and result in an accumulation of a naturally occurring chemical in the body. For example, insecticides used in agricultural work can cause a buildup of a chemical called acetylcholine, which causes airway muscles to constrict, resulting in asthma.

Individuals who smoke are at a greater risk of developing occupational asthma, as does a person with a family history of asthma or allergy. Certain professions also hold higher risks: highest incidence rates are among plastics workers, printers, metal workers, bakers, millers, farmers, grain elevator workers, laboratory workers, drug manufacturers, and detergent manufacturers. Occupational asthma affects anyone of working age, from the young adult to those of retirement age.

Occupational asthma has become the most common cause of newly diagnosed cases of occupational lung disease in developed countries. Asthma in general affects 1 out of 20 people, and occupational asthma represents up to 15% of those cases. Experts believe the number of cases is higher than reported, because many cases are misdiagnosed as bronchitis. In addition, many workers do not make the association between their symptoms and their work environment, especially if symptoms persist after work hours, or if co-workers are not similarly affected (some individuals are more sensitive to irritants than others).

Diagnosis

History: Common symptoms include wheezing, shortness of breath, a feeling of tightness in the chest, hives (urticaria), and coughing. Often, wheezing or coughing at night are the only symptoms. Other symptoms may include sneezing, inflammation of the nose (rhinitis) that manifests as an itchy, blocked, reddened, or runny nose, and watery, itchy, or glazed eyes. The individual may relate a pattern of exposure and symptoms that connect the condition with the workplace; however, this relationship is not always initially clear and may not be reported.

Physical exam: Breath sounds may reveal wheezing unless the symptoms resolve prior to the examination. The diagnosis of occupational asthma is largely based on history, exposure patterns, and tests.

Tests: Pulmonary function tests (PFTs), which measure the efficiency of lung function (including lung volume, total lung capacity, and residual volume), are often performed. If an allergic response to an irritant is suspected, a patch test may be performed; this involves placing small amounts of the suspected irritant directly onto the skin and watching for a reaction. During a bronchial provocation test, the individual inhales a small amount of the suspected irritant and the response is measured. A chest x-ray and blood tests may be recommended to rule out other causes of breathing difficulty.

Treatment

The most important aspect of treatment is preventing additional exposure to the irritating agent. Continued exposure will lead to more severe and persistent symptoms. In some industries, where exposure cannot be eliminated (for example, flour cannot be eliminated from the environment of a professional baker), the individual's job and responsibilities will need to be changed. To control symptoms, medications that open the airways (bronchodilators) are often prescribed. In more severe cases, anti-inflammatory/anti-allergic medicines (corticosteroids) may be required to suppress the immune response.

Prognosis

If exposure to the irritating agent is eliminated, the outcome is excellent. Full recovery is likely. However, with repeated exposure, symptoms will become more severe and persistent. The outcome in these cases is less optimistic. In very rare, severe cases, death may occur.

Differential Diagnosis

The following conditions produce symptoms similar to asthma: foreign body aspiration, cystic fibrosis, viral respiratory infection, epiglottitis, bronchopulmonary aspergillosis, tuberculosis, hyperventilation syndrome, mitral valve prolapse, habitual coughing, recurrent pulmonary emboli, congestive heart failure, chronic obstructive pulmonary disease, and hypersensitivity pneumonitis.

Specialists

- Allergist
- Occupational Medicine Physician
- Pulmonologist

Work Restrictions / Accommodations

Eliminating exposure to the offending irritant is critical to the individual's recovery. If protective measures cannot be put into place, reassignment to another position within the company where exposure will be avoided may be necessary. If exposure cannot be controlled, the individual may need to change jobs entirely.

Comorbid Conditions

Presence of other respiratory diseases may result in more severe symptoms and a longer recovery period.

Complications

Occupational asthma does not usually involve any complications. In very severe cases, however, respiratory distress and death could occur.

Factors Influencing Duration

Individuals who smoke are likely to have a longer recovery period. The development of complications or the presence of severe symptoms may also lengthen the recovery period.

Length of Disability

Prolonged disability is not expected with occupational asthma, as the symptoms generally respond well to treatment. Disability may be permanent if exposure to the offending agent cannot be avoided in the workplace.

Acute attack.

Duration in Days

Job Classification	Minimum	Optimum	Maximum
Any work	1	3	7

Failure to Recover

If an individual fails to recover within the maximum duration expectancy period, the reader may wish to reference the following questions to assist in better understanding the specifics of an individual's medical case.

Regarding diagnosis:

- Have other conditions with similar symptoms been eliminated (foreign body aspiration, cystic fibrosis, viral respiratory infection, epiglottitis, bronchopulmonary aspergillosis, tuberculosis, hyperventilation syndrome, mitral valve prolapse, habitual cough, recurrent pulmonary emboli, congestive heart failure, chronic obstructive pulmonary disease, and hypersensitivity pneumonitis)?
- Does individual have any underlying conditions, such as other respiratory diseases, that may impact recovery?
- Has individual experienced any episodes of respiratory distress?
- If objective evidence is scant or absent, have psychological causes been considered?

Regarding treatment:

- Has individual been able to avoid contact with or exposure to the irritating substance?
- Has changing jobs been considered?
- Is the individual being treated with medications, such as bronchodilators or corticosteroids? If so, is the individual compliant with the usage instructions provided by the physician?

Regarding prognosis:

- Has the individual been able to avoid contact with or exposure to the irritating substance?
- Has changing jobs been considered?

References

Morgan, W.K.C. "Occupational Lung Diseases." The Merck Manual of Medical Information. Berkow, Robert, et al New York: Pocket Books, 1997. 195-201.

Occupational Asthma. American Academy of Asthma, Allergy & Immunology. 16 Oct 2000 <http://www.aaaai.org/public/publicedmat/tips/occupationalasthma.stm>.

Occupational Therapy
Other names / synonyms: OT
93.83

Definition

Occupational therapy is the rehabilitation process that helps individuals perform their daily activities despite any illness, disability, or injury.

Occupational therapy is used to help individuals with medical impairment(s) adapt to the impairment(s) to regain optimal function and to modify the environment to reestablish participation in desired activities. Occupational therapy interventions focus on the individual within the context of his or her environment, addressing activities that are meaningful to the individual. Individuals receive occupational therapy after surgeries such as total hip replacement to learn how to dress and bathe using tools such as a long-handled shoehorn or sponge to help protect the new hip. Individuals receive occupational therapy after illnesses such as heart attacks or pulmonary disease to learn how to perform their daily activities without becoming tired. Individuals receive occupational therapy after injury or surgery to the hand, such as carpal tunnel syndrome or carpal tunnel release, to maximize function in the injured hand by regaining dexterity and strength. In short, occupational therapy enables individuals who suffer from any illness or injury to engage in all of the meaningful activities in their lives. These activities are divided into three categories: activities of daily living, work and productive activities, and play or leisure activities.

Activities of daily living are tasks such as grooming, dressing, bathing, mobility, eating, and communication. Relearning these essential skills decreases dependence on others. Tasks focus on the use of orthotic or prosthetic devices and the adaptation of the individual's physical environment.

Work and productive activities include home management activities such as cooking, money management, and job-related activities such as pursuing a career and job performance. Productivity and employability training focuses on what skills the person needs to hold to be successful at a job. Work performance skills, grooming, how to get along with others, punctuality, following instructions, social conduct, use of proper body mechanics, and work habits may also be taught.

Because occupational therapy focuses on the whole person, attention must be given to what activities the individual uses for enjoyment. Individuals are taught about and engage in specific leisure activities, but also learn how participation in leisure activities contributes to their overall health and well being.

Reason for Procedure

Individuals receive occupational therapy if they are unable to meet their life goals, fulfill their social roles, or participate fully in their lives due to physical or mental impairments. Occupational therapy addresses the timely return to both personal tasks such as household management and professional tasks that are found within one's current job. Injuries such as carpal tunnel syndrome, surgery such as total hip replacement, diseases such as Multiple Sclerosis, and mental impairments such as those due to a traumatic brain injury are examples of conditions treated by occupational therapists.

Individuals who engage in occupational therapy do so to help them adjust to a progressive illness such as Multiple Sclerosis by utilizing tools such as writing implements with thicker shafts to adapt to decreased grip strength or braces for the arms and hands to support areas of decreased strength. Individuals may also undergo occupational therapy to help strengthen the arms and hands due to any fracture, nerve injury, or disease process such as arthritis. Individuals learn exercises to increase dexterity and grip strength and to increase range of motion in the joint of the arm and hand.

Description

Occupational therapists evaluate physical and mental function and an individual's ability to perform the tasks that he or she must perform each day. The specific therapeutic measures employed take into account the individual's needs and interests. Following interviews, observation-specific tests, and physical measurements (used to establish a baseline), a program of specific goal-oriented activities and instruction is designed for the individual. Occupational therapists evaluate range of motion, strength, sensation, balance, fine motor coordination, and cognition to determine where deficits may lie. In addition, occupational therapists evaluate home and work environment to enable accessibility and safety in these areas. Therapy is conducted either on an individual basis or as part of group therapy.

Occupational therapists may provide general exercises for strengthening and stretching any injured joints. Occupational therapists may have individuals perform exercises to improve fine motor coordination such as removing pegs from a pegboard. Individuals who have altered sensation in an area of the body may undergo desensitization techniques, such as having different stimuli such as cotton balls, ice cubes, and sandpaper rubbed over the affected area. Individuals may engage in practice of activities of daily living, such as dressing or bathing and may utilize adaptive equipment such as a dressing stick or tub bench to assist. Individuals may learn strategies for home management such as planning household tasks to decrease the amount of energy that is expended, or cooking dinner by sitting on a high stool to compensate for decreased balance. Individuals may learn adaptive strategies for work such as using an ergonomic keyboard to prevent carpal tunnel syndrome or arranging a workspace to accommodate a wheelchair. Individuals may learn community mobility such as maneuvering a wheelchair in a store. Individuals may learn to compensate for cognitive deficits by writing down any instructions they need to remember, practicing tasks such as making change, or writing notes to remind themselves of important tasks such as locking the door or turning off the oven.

Prognosis

Therapeutic outcomes vary depending upon the individual's diagnosis, the severity of the diagnosis, the individual's motivation, social support, and comorbid conditions. Therapeutic outcomes are generally good for individuals without acute impairments (e.g., rotator cuff injury). Those persons with severe or multiple deficits may see marginal improvement during therapy. In some cases, spontaneous recovery may continue to occur well after therapy is complete.

In general, individuals who receive occupational therapy achieve faster recovery than those individuals who do not participate in rehabilitation. For individuals with complicated diagnoses such as stroke or spinal cord injury, rehabilitation is crucial if any recovery of function is to be attained. Most individuals can expect to engage in most of the activities that they participated in prior to disability either independently or through the use of adaptive equipment.

Specialists

- Licensed Clinical Social Worker
- Occupational Therapist
- Physical Therapist
- Psychiatrist

Work Restrictions / Accommodations

Many persons treated with occupational therapy continue to work. If the occupational therapy requires the use of hand splints, a person whose job requires extensive hand use may require temporary reassignment to other duties. Work restrictions and accommodations will need to be tailored to the individual's disability. The occupational therapist may need to visit the work site before making recommendations on accommodations or alternate job placement.

Comorbid Conditions

An individual's level of health prior to the injury significantly determines the length of time taken to recover. Conditions such as obesity, diabetes mellitus, and hypertension may adversely impact rehabilitation.

Procedure Complications

Individuals may experience muscle pain due to exertion. Individuals may also experience pain due to over-exertion from being progressed too quickly.

Factors Influencing Duration

Because there is no disability associated with the occupational therapy itself, the only factors influencing the length of disability involve the underlying condition that prompted therapy. These factors will require evaluation on an individual, case-by-case basis. Insurance limitations and the employer's ability to accommodate the worker may influence length of disability.

Length of Disability

No disability is expected to result from this therapy. Disability may occur as a result of an underlying condition.

References

Neistadt, Maureen E., and Elizabeth Blesedell Crepeau. Occupational Therapy. Philadelphia: Lippincott, 1998.

Trombly, Catherine A, ed. Occupational Therapy for Physical Dysfunction. Baltimore: Williams & Wilkins, 1995.

Oophorectomy

Other names / synonyms: Excision of Ovary, Ovariectomy
65.3, 65.5, 65.51, 65.52

Definition

Oophorectomy, sometimes referred to as ovariectomy, is the surgical removal of an ovary or part of an ovary (unilateral oophorectomy), or both ovaries (bilateral oophorectomy). In women under the age of 40, an attempt is made whenever possible to preserve ovarian function by performing only a unilateral oophorectomy.

In 1997, there were 13,000 bilateral oophorectomies performed in the US. The procedure was almost equally divided between 2 groups of women: 15 to 44 and 45 to 64 years of age.

Of the 20,000 unilateral oophorectomies reported, two-thirds were performed on women between 15 and 44 years of age.

Reason for Procedure

Oophorectomies are done to treat ovarian cancer, breast cancer, endometriosis, or benign tumors (fibromas or teratomas). The procedure may be necessary when an ovarian cyst does not respond to surgical removal (resection). Both ovaries may be removed during the surgical removal of the uterus (hysterectomy), particularly if there is an underlying disease that has spread from the uterus to the ovaries. Healthy ovaries may also be removed as a preventive (prophylactic) measure to reduce the risk of ovarian cancer in high-risk women. Oophorectomy may be performed on women with breast cancer when physicians believe that a reduction in the amount of hormones produced by the ovaries (estrogens) might slow the growth of the cancer. The ovaries, along with the fallopian tubes, may also be removed as a treatment for endometriosis, pelvic inflammatory disease (PID), or an ectopic pregnancy.

Description

The oophorectomy is performed in a hospital or outpatient clinic under local or general anesthesia. Laparoscopy, the most common method used to perform an oophorectomy, begins with a tiny incision in the abdomen either in or near the naval. The surgeon inserts a slender, lighted, telescope-like viewing instrument (laparoscope) through the incision. A second small incision is made just above the pubic hair line, through which a probe is inserted and the ovaries are removed.

Another, often-used method, the minilaparotomy, involves making an incision about 2 inches long in the lower abdomen; it relies upon direct visualization and removal through the single incision.

A third, less common method called a laparotomy, requires an larger, 2 to 5 inch abdominal incision. Decisions regarding the most appropriate method depend on the woman's weight, number of prior lower abdominal surgeries, heart and lung disease history, and other considerations.

Prognosis

The predicted outcome after oophorectomy depends on the reason for the procedure (i.e., removal of cyst, tumor, abscess, ectopic pregnancy, or treatment of ovarian or breast cancers, endometriosis, and pelvic inflammatory disease), whether the method was a laparoscopy, minilaparotomy, or laparotomy, and whether the procedure was unilateral or bilateral. Generally, most individuals recover without problems after any of the 3 surgical methods. Individuals who have a laparoscopy recover more quickly and with fewer problems.

Specialists

- Gynecologist
- Obstetrician

Work Restrictions / Accommodations

Extended sick leave may be necessary, depending on whether the procedure was a laparoscopy, minilaparotomy, or laparotomy. The length of sick leave will be contingent on the age of the woman, surgical complications, resulting diagnoses, and prognosis. An individual required to do strenuous physical activities and lifting at work may need to have the job modified temporarily. Allowances may also need to be made for rest periods, shorter work hours, and/or fewer work days per week. Additional sick leave may be necessary if postsurgery treatment includes chemotherapy and radiation.

Comorbid Conditions

Comorbid conditions that might influence length of disability are obesity, previous abdominal surgeries, heart and lung conditions, and allergy to pain medications.

Procedure Complications

As with any procedure performed under general anesthesia, the individual's reaction to the anesthesia drugs, and breathing difficulties pose possible problems. Some individuals experience complications with the surgery itself, such as bleeding or infection. On rare occasions, the bowel or blood vessels may be injured during surgery, requiring additional surgical repair.

Longer-term complications occur when ovaries are removed prior to menopause. When unilateral oophorectomy is used to treat premenopausal women, normal hormone production continues in the remaining ovary. However, when bilateral oophorectomy is used to treat premenopausal women, normal hormone production is halted, causing acute menopause, a condition often requiring hormone replacement therapy (HRT). Because the estrogen levels of premenopausal women are higher than those of postmenopausal women, premenopausal women require a much higher dose of estrogen or hormone replacement than women who enter menopause naturally.

Factors Influencing Duration

Most individuals who are treated with laparoscopies are able to return to work or to resume previous activities with only minor restrictions; they may need to refrain from strenuous exercise or heavy lifting for up to 2 weeks. Individuals treated with more invasive procedures (minilaparotomies and laparotomies) usually require a longer leave of absence from work and more stringent restrictions.

Length of Disability

Laparoscopic.

Duration in Days

Job Classification	Minimum	Optimum	Maximum
Sedentary work	3	7	21
Light work	3	7	21
Medium work	7	14	28
Heavy work	7	21	35
Very Heavy work	14	21	35

Open surgery.

Duration in Days

Job Classification	Minimum	Optimum	Maximum
Sedentary work	28	42	56
Light work	28	42	56
Medium work	42	56	70
Heavy work	42	70	84
Very Heavy work	42	84	98

References

Simon, Harvey, and Carol Peckham. Ovarian Cancer. Nidus Scientific Publications. 01 Dec 1999. 1 Jan 2001 <http://www.well-connected.com>.

Langston, Amelia MD, et al. Ovarian Cancer Risk: A Guide to Understanding. Seattle: National Cancer Institute, 2000.

Oophorectomy, Bilateral

Other names / synonyms: Bilateral Excision of Ovary, Bilateral Ovariectomy

65.5

Definition

Bilateral oophorectomy is the surgical removal of both ovaries. It is a fairly common procedure that is performed on either menopausal or postmenopausal women, particularly when the uterus is being surgically removed (hysterectomy). Removing both ovaries is avoided whenever possible in women of child-bearing age in order to retain fertility and maintain the source of important hormones (e.g., estrogen).

A bilateral oophorectomy is commonly done to treat ovarian or uterine cancer. Women at a higher risk of ovarian cancer include women who are older than 50 years old and who have gone through menopause, those who have taken fertility drugs, those who have never been pregnant (nulliparous), those with a family history of ovarian cancer, women who have never taken oral contraceptives, women who have used talc/genital powder, women with a history of breast cancer, and women who began menarche early or went through menopause late. In the US, approximately 25,000 new cases of ovarian cancer and 14,000 ovarian cancer-related deaths occur each year. One out of every 57 women (1.8%) will develop ovarian cancer in her lifetime.

Reason for Procedure

Bilateral oophorectomy is performed on women with uterine or ovarian cancer. It is also performed when the blood supply to the ovaries is compromised and when the ovaries have severe involvement by fluid-filled sacs (cysts), tumors, infection, scar tissue (adhesions), or endometriosis. In postmenopausal women, bilateral oophorectomy is routinely performed during hysterectomy. The ovaries may also be removed to eliminate estrogen in women who have estrogen-responsive breast cancer. For women who are at a high risk of developing ovarian cancer, apparently healthy ovaries may be removed as a measure to prevent ovarian cancer (prophylactic oophorectomy).

Description

This procedure may be performed by traditional open-abdominal surgery (laparotomy) or by laparoscopy, in which a small wand-like instrument (laparoscope) is inserted into the abdominal (peritoneal) cavity to visualize the ovaries.

Laparotomy is indicated when the ovaries need to be removed intact, as in the case of cancer. It is also indicated for individuals who have internal scar tissue (adhesions) because of the increased risk of cutting the intestines, or for individuals who are obese. Laparoscopy is indicated for noncancerous conditions.

The ovaries may also be removed through an incision in the vaginal wall (colpotomy). Colpotomy allows the ovaries to be removed intact and is less traumatic than laparotomy.

The method chosen can also depend upon the expertise of the surgeon; laparoscopy and colpotomy are more technically difficult. Generally, laparoscopy and colpotomy are performed on an outpatient basis, while the individual is hospitalized for a laparotomy.

All bilateral oophorectomies are performed under general anesthesia. For laparoscopy, the abdominal cavity is inflated with carbon dioxide gas (pneumoperitoneum) to allow visualization within the abdomen, provide an open work space, and reduce the incidence of certain complications (e.g., cutting the intestines). The gas is put into the abdominal cavity through a needle (Veress needle). One or more small incisions are made into the abdominal cavity and needle-like tubes (trocar) are inserted. Once the laparoscope is inserted through a trocar, the abdominal cavity can be viewed on a video screen. Small instruments, which are either attached to the laparoscope or inserted through the trocar, are used to perform the surgery. For laparotomy, a large incision is made to open the abdomen and expose the ovaries. For colpotomy, the ovary is approached through an incision in the vaginal wall.

There are 3 different methods for cutting the attachments that secure the ovary in the pelvis: the ligature method (which uses loops of catgut, cotton, or wire to tie off supportive ligaments), an automatic stapling method (which staples off the supportive ligaments), and the bipolar coagulation method (which destroys or cauterizes the supportive tissue). The ligaments are then cut and bleeding is controlled by electric current (coagulation) or laser. The ovary is freed after all supportive structures have been cut. With laparoscopy, the ovary is cut into pieces that are small enough to be removed through the trocar. Any incisions made during the procedure are closed with stitches (sutures). Antibiotics and analgesics are generally prescribed prophylactically.

Prognosis

Regardless of the surgical procedure, ovaries can be removed without complications. Most individuals recover from a laparoscopy within a week and from a laparotomy within 4-6 weeks.

Specialists

- General Surgeon
- Gynecologist
- Oncologist

Work Restrictions / Accommodations

Strenuous physical activities (e.g., heavy lifting, walking long distances, going up and down stairs, carrying heavy objects) may need to be temporarily restricted following oophorectomy. Even normal activities may cause fatigue, so frequent rest breaks may be necessary. Women who underwent laparotomy may be temporarily unable to drive a car or other motor vehicles.

Comorbid Conditions

Obesity and general debility can increase the length of disability.

Procedure Complications

Improper placement of the Veress needle can result in gas being introduced into the wrong cavity (emphysema), which can cause breathing difficulty and sometimes a collapsed lung (pneumothorax). The Veress needle or trocar can cut major abdominal or pelvic blood vessels, or injure the intestines, bladder, or tubes leading from the kidneys to the bladder (ureters). The ureters may be cut when the ovaries are being excised. Rarely, the intestine may protrude out of the incisions (herniate). Bleeding (hemorrhage), infection, and blood clots (thromboembolism) are complications of any gynecologic surgical procedure. Abdominal surgery can lead to formation of internal scar tissue (adhesions), which can cause pain, constriction of the intestines, and infertility. Failure to remove the entire ovary can result in ovarian remnant syndrome. Without hormone replacement, long-term complications associated with bilateral oophorectomy include reduction in bone density (osteoporosis), heart disease, and diabetes.

Factors Influencing Duration

Length of disability may be influenced by the underlying reason for the surgery, bleeding, or other complications.

Length of Disability

Laparoscopic.

Duration in Days

Job Classification	Minimum	Optimum	Maximum
Sedentary work	3	7	21
Light work	3	7	21
Medium work	7	14	28
Heavy work	7	21	35
Very Heavy work	14	21	35

Open surgery.

Duration in Days

Job Classification	Minimum	Optimum	Maximum
Sedentary work	28	42	56
Light work	28	42	56
Medium work	42	56	70
Heavy work	42	70	84
Very Heavy work	42	84	98

References

Langston, Amelia MD, et al. Ovarian Cancer Risk: A Guide to Understanding. Seattle: National Cancer Institute, 2000.

Levine, Ronald. "Operative Laparoscopy." Te Linde's Operative Gynecology Updates 1 3 (1997): 1-13.

Namnoum, Anne, and Ana Murphy. "Diagnostic and Operative Laparoscopy." Te Linde's Operative Gynecology. Rock, John, and John Thompson, eds. Philadelphia: Lippincott-Raven, 1997. 389-413.

Sanfilippo, Joseph, and John Rock. "Surgery for Benign Disease of the Ovary." Te Linde's Operative Gynecology. Rock, John, and John Thompson, eds. Philadelphia: Lippincott-Raven, 1997. 625-644.

Open Wound

Other names / synonyms: Abrasion, Avulsion Injury, Cut, Laceration, Puncture Wound, Stab Wound

870, 870.1, 870.2, 870.3, 870.4, 870.8, 870.9, 871, 871.0, 871.2, 871.3, 871.4, 871.5, 871.6, 871.7, 871.9, 872, 872.0, 872.02, 872.1, 872.6, 872.69, 872.7, 872.8, 872.9, 873, 873.0, 873.1, 873.2, 873.39, 873.4, 873.43, 873.44, 873.49, 873.5, 873.59, 873.6, 873.60, 873.7, 873.8, 873.9, 874, 874.8, 874.9, 875, 876, 877, 878, 879, 879.0, 879.1, 879.6, 879.8, 880, 881, 882, 882.0, 882.2, 883, 883.0, 883.1, 883.2, 884, 890, 891, 892, 893, 894

Definition

An open wound is any injury resulting in the breaking of the skin. Wounds are classified as open wounds if the protective skin layer is damaged, exposing underlying tissue to the outside air. Even surgical wounds are considered open wounds until they are physically closed with stitches (sutures) or form a scar.

Open wounds can occur as a result of a physical act or injury, not a disease. Causes include direct trauma such as a fall, assault with a weapon, vehicular accident, exposure to extreme heat or cold (burn or frostbite), animal bite, or puncture wound from stepping on an object such as a nail or piece of wood. Wounds may result from medical interventions such as surgery or the injection or insertion of intravenous devices.

There are six basic types of open wounds, based on how the skin is broken. These include abrasions, amputations, avulsions, incisions, lacerations, and punctures. An abrasion is caused when the skin is rubbed or scraped off. Traumatic amputation is the nonsurgical removal of a finger, toe, hand, foot, arm, leg, or ear from the body. An avulsion is an injury where the skin is torn completely away from a body part or is left hanging as a flap. A cut (incision) is a wound made by a sharp cutting instrument such as a knife, scalpel, razor, or broken glass. A lacerations is a wound in which the skin is torn rather than cut. Wounds made by nails, needles, wire, knives, and bullets are usually classified as punctures. They have ragged, irregular edges and torn tissue underneath. Many wounds are a combination of two or more of these types. The two main concerns with these injuries are bleeding and infection.

Open wounds may be further categorized according to the area of the body involved. For example, an open wound to the hand is a wound involving any structure in the hand with the exception of the fingers (digits). These wounds may involve just the skin surface or extend into the tendons, ligaments, nerves, or major blood vessels of the hand. Open wounds to the hand and/or finger are rarely life-threatening, but these injuries represent over 10% of on-the-job injuries. When an open wound of the hand or finger involves bones, joints, nerves, or major blood vessels, there is the risk of chronic pain, deformity, and dysfunction. Because hand and finger function are integrally involved in many tasks, deformity and dysfunction of these body parts can have a tremendous impact on work performance.

An open wound to the knee is any open wound on the surface of the knee or extending into the knee joint. An open wound to the leg refers to any open wound to any part of the leg from the hip to the ankle. Open wounds can be only a minor break wound at the skin surface or can extend into deeper structures such as ligaments, bone, muscle, nerves or blood vessels.

Individuals of any age or gender are at risk of sustaining an open wound. Traumatic injuries, however, are most common in those younger than age 45. Open wounds secondary to gunshot or stab injuries are more common in males.

Diagnosis

History: Individuals may give a history of recent direct trauma to the area in question (i.e., hand, finger, or foot), often with bleeding from the involved site. Some individuals may report exposure of the wound to dirt or other contaminants such as manure or rust. History should include information on how much time elapsed between receiving the wound and getting medical attention; pre-existing conditions that could affect wound healing such as smoking, diabetes, vascular disease, or medication use; and the most recent date of tetanus injection.

Physical exam: Physical exam reveals an open wound involving a particular body part, such as hand, finger, or foot. The wound is explored to evaluate involvement of tendons, ligaments and nerves. Profuse bleeding or bleeding that spurts from the wound may indicate involvement of major blood vessels. Large amounts of blood loss may lead to early signs of shock such as decreased level of consciousness, rapid pulse, and low blood pressure. The area around the wound is tender to touch and may be swollen. Redness (erythema), warmth and color change suggests infection.

Obvious deformity of an extremity (hand, foot, or lower leg) suggests fractures of underlying bone (open fractures). Damage to the nerves and/or tendons may cause altered sensation or extremity weakness. Injuries to the hand, finger, foot, or leg may be associated with loss of tissue, parts of fingers or toes, or even complete loss of limbs. The wound edges may be jagged or pale or appear as a fine line. The wound may extend into deep tissue and contain pieces of foreign debris, such as glass, wood, or gravel.

Tests: Blood tests (complete blood count) may be needed to monitor signs of blood loss and infection. X-rays help to detect fractures or the presence of foreign bodies. X-rays of the blood vessels (arteriograms) are done if vascular injury is suspected. Nerve conduction studies or evoked potentials may reveal associated nerve injury.

Treatment

The primary goal of open wound management is to restore optimal function to the involved area by prompt and thorough repair of injured tissue to minimize the risk of infection and deformity. Initial treatment consists of controlling the bleeding, treating for shock, and thoroughly cleansing the wound to reduce the risk of infection. Local or regional anesthesia may be necessary to evaluate a wound and to control bleeding (hemostasis) before repair can begin. Some anesthetic agents containing epinephrine may be used for both its anesthetic and hemostasis properties.

Once bleeding is controlled and the individual stabilizes, wound care begins. The treatment approach is the same whether the wound involves the hand, finger, leg, knee, or foot. Any open wound extending into deep surrounding structures such as bone, blood vessels, or nerves requires specific interventions. Open wounds associated with a fracture of nearby bones (open fractures) require urgent surgery (open reduction and internal fixation of open fracture) to stabilize the fracture and close the wound. Open wounds extending to tendons, nerves, and major blood vessels (lying in close proximity to joints and bones of the hand, feet, and ankle) typically require prompt surgical repair (repair and/or reconstruction of tendon, nerve, or vessel). Amputations and some avulsion wounds usually require urgent plastic surgery to reattach amputated parts (reimplantation) or to graft skin on wounds with large amounts of skin and tissue loss (avulsion wounds). In some circumstances, severe wounds to the hands or feet may necessitate amputation of any digits not salvageable.

Less extensive abrasions, lacerations, and puncture wounds are generally treated by cleansing the wound with saline or mild antiseptic solution through use of a high-pressure irrigating device (syringe or water Pik). Any remaining foreign matter is removed, and the ragged or unhealthy tissue is trimmed with sterile scissors or a scalpel. Most wounds are then closed using stitches, surgical tape (Steri-Strips), staples, or a combination of these.

Wounds with a high risk of infection (puncture wounds to the foot, human and animal bites) or wounds 12 to 24 hours old are left open and then closed with stitches, if needed, in 5 to 7 days. In larger wounds which are more than 24 hours old, the area is cleansed, débrided and then packed with wet to dry dressings. The wound is then either allowed to heal naturally, allowing scar formation, or it may be closed surgically in 5-7 days.

The repaired wounds are covered with an antibiotic ointment and appropriate bandage. A tetanus shot (tetanus toxoid) may be given if over 10 years has passed since the individual's last booster shot, or if there is a question about when the individual was last vaccinated. If the individual has never been immunized against tetanus, human tetanus immune globulin may be given.

Wounds that extend over bending joints, such as the fingers, hand, or ankle, are sometimes splinted to prevent pulling on the wound edges. Wounds are rechecked for signs of infection, which usually develops within 48 hours. Oral antibiotics may be prescribed to treat or prevent infection.

Prognosis

In general, open wounds that are treated promptly and appropriately have good outcomes. However, the extent of the wound, the involvement of surrounding structures, and the type of treatment required also influence outcome. Wounds involving extensive tissue loss, amputation, or damage to blood vessels, nerves, or tendons may lead to sensory loss, deformity, and disability. Surgical repair of partial or complete amputation of a finger (replantation) is up to 90% successful. Surgical vascular repair generally has a good outcome. However, surgical repair and reconstruction of completely severed nerves is often associated with some degree of sensory or functional loss.

Differential Diagnosis

The history and clinical presentation of an open wound make the diagnosis straight forward.

Specialists

- Emergency Medicine
- General Surgeon
- Infectious Disease Physician
- Neurosurgeon
- Orthopedic Surgeon
- Plastic Surgeon
- Vascular Surgeon

Rehabilitation

Specific physical therapy interventions depend on the extent and type of the open wound. Most open wounds may benefit from hydrotherapy (water therapy) to help remove unhealthy tissue as well as physical removal of dead tissue (debridement). Electrical stimulation with direct current may also be used to facilitate good wound healing. Loss of strength or mobility resulting from wounds of the hand, finger, ankle or leg may benefit from range of motion exercises to restore mobility of affected joints, strength training and functional mobility exercises. Following limb amputation, physical and/or occupational therapy assists with artificial limb (prosthesis) fitting and training. Both therapy disciplines train individuals in the use of mobility aids such as walkers and functional aids such as thick-handled utensils. These therapies are usually conducted up to three times a week until wound healing is complete and optimal physical function is restored.

Work Restrictions / Accommodations

Work restrictions and/or accommodations will be influenced by the severity of the wound. Until the wound is fully healed, most individuals need modified duty jobs that do not expose the wound to moisture or undue strain. The severity of the wound and associated loss of function due to nerve injury, tendon injury, fracture, or amputation dictates the type of work accommodations needed. For example, individuals with wounds to the hand or fingers and associated dysfunction or deformity may require reassignment to jobs not requiring manual dexterity. Individuals with wounds to the feet, ankles, or legs may need to be reassigned to jobs not requiring excessive standing, walking, or lifting. Accommodations must be made on an individual basis according to the nature and extent of the disability.

Comorbid Conditions

Comorbid conditions of diabetes, immune suppression, peripheral vascular disease, bleeding disorders, smoking and malnutrition may delay wound healing and prolong recovery.

Complications

Complications associated with open wounds may include infection, cellulitis, deformity, overgrowth of scar tissue (keloid formation), gangrene which may require amputation, bleeding (wound hemorrhage), overwhelming systemic infection (sepsis), and tetanus, a potentially fatal infection of the nervous system). Open wounds involving vascular injury may result in decreased circulation (ischemia) and tissue death (necrosis) that require amputation of affected parts. Wounds involving nerve injury may be complicated by temporary or permanent loss of sensation or function of the affected body part. Trauma not involving direct nerve injury may lead to delayed involvement of the nervous system (reflex sympathetic dystrophy).

Complementary and Alternative Therapies

Content is intended for awareness only. Treatments may or may not be effective. Scientific evidence may be lacking and some substances have potentially toxic effects. Dr. Presley Reed and the editors do not endorse the use of these therapies in the absence of consultation with a licensed medical professional.

Gotu kola -	Contains ascitic acid, which may promote connective tissue development.
Vitamins A and C -	May enhance or accelerate wound healing in skin ulcers and other wounds.
Zinc -	May enhance wound healing, especially in individuals who are deficient in this mineral.
Aloe -	May treat superficial cuts but not deep wounds.
Arnica -	May disinfect cuts and other wounds when applied externally.
Bioflavonoids -	Said to help maintain blood vessel strength and control inflammation.
Calendula -	Used externally, may reduce inflammation and promote wound healing.
Clove -	Used externally as an antiseptic, it may promote wound healing and relieve pain.
Comfrey -	Used externally, it may promote wound healing.
Echinacea -	Said to stimulate immune system and promote healing.
Enzymes (proteases) -	Said to play a key role in protein metabolism and may promote wound healing.
Garlic -	Used internally or externally, it may help to fight injection.
Goldenseal -	Used externally as an antiseptic, it may help to promote wound healing.
Horsebalm -	Used externally, this may act as an antiseptic to promote wound healing.
Iron -	Said to play a key role in collagen formation needed to repair skin and soft tissue wounds.
Marsh mallow -	Used externally, it may help to soothe wounds.
Teatree oil -	Used externally, it may act as an antiseptic for burns, cuts, and abrasions.
Vitamin E -	May reduce inflammation and enhance wound healing and skin repair.
Vitamin K -	May enhance blood clotting and reduce bleeding associated with wounds.

Factors Influencing Duration

The severity of the wound and the degree of muscle, nerve, blood vessel, tendon and bone injury influence the length of disability.

Length of Disability

Duration depends on site, severity, and presence of complications. Contact physician for additional information.

Finger or hand without complication.

Duration in Days

Job Classification	Minimum	Optimum	Maximum
Sedentary work	1	1	7
Light work	1	1	7
Medium work	1	2	14
Heavy work	1	3	14
Very Heavy work	1	3	14

Foot.

Duration in Days

Job Classification	Minimum	Optimum	Maximum
Sedentary work	1	3	7
Light work	1	3	7
Medium work	1	7	14
Heavy work	1	7	28
Very Heavy work	1	7	28

Finger with compplication or tendon involvement.

Duration in Days

Job Classification	Minimum	Optimum	Maximum
Sedentary work	3	7	14
Light work	7	14	21
Medium work	7	21	42
Heavy work	7	21	56
Very Heavy work	7	21	56

Hand with complication or tendon involvement.

Duration in Days

Job Classification	Minimum	Optimum	Maximum
Sedentary work	3	14	28
Light work	7	14	28
Medium work	7	28	56
Heavy work	21	56	84
Very Heavy work	21	56	84

Duration Trend from Normative Data

Cases	Mean	Min	Max	No Lost Time	Over 6 Months
1471	38	0	536	2.58%	1.63%

Percentile:	5th	25th	Median	75th	95th
Days:	4	13	21	44	106

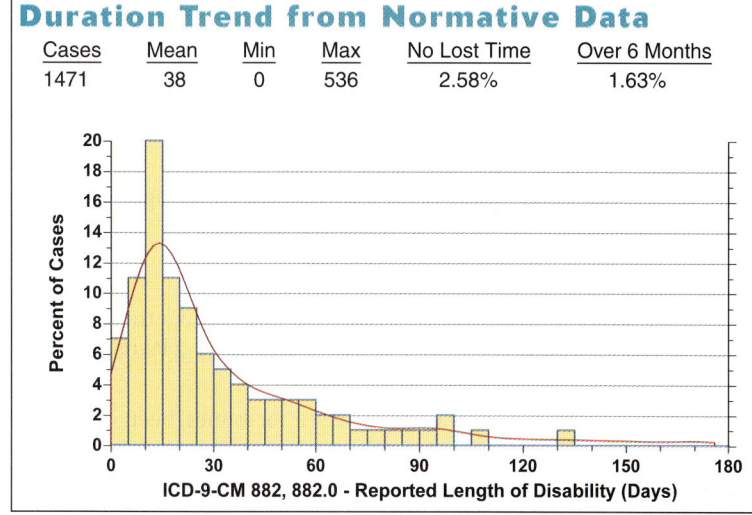

ICD-9-CM 882, 882.0 - Reported Length of Disability (Days)

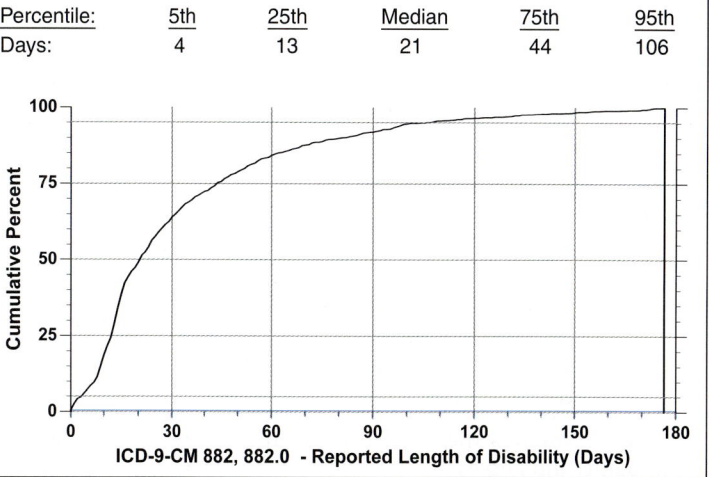

ICD-9-CM 882, 882.0 - Reported Length of Disability (Days)

Open Wound 1507

Duration Trend from Normative Data

Cases	Mean	Min	Max	No Lost Time	Over 6 Months		Percentile:	5th	25th	Median	75th	95th
2337	39	0	480	6%	2.16%		Days:	1	10	20	47	107

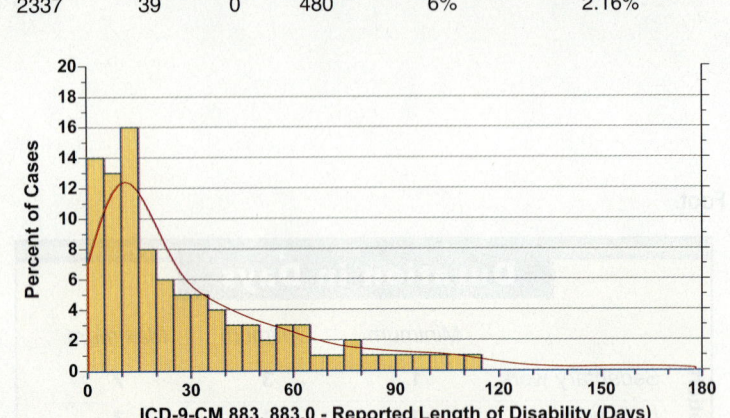
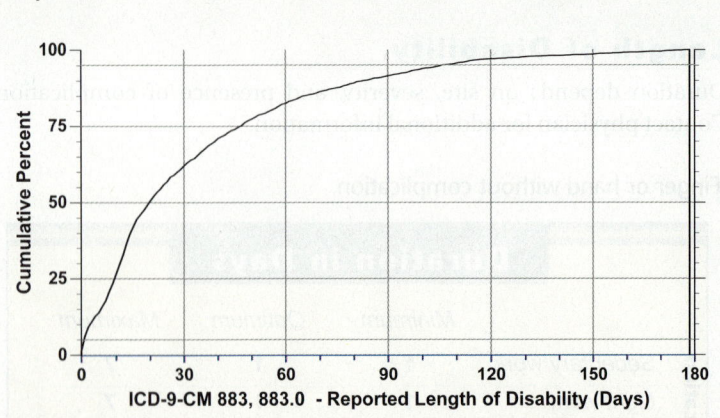

Duration Trend from Normative Data*

Cases	Mean	Min	Max	No Lost Time	Over 6 Months		Percentile:	5th	25th	Median	75th	95th
1035	65	1	408	0.19%	1.55%		Days:	13	34	56	82	134

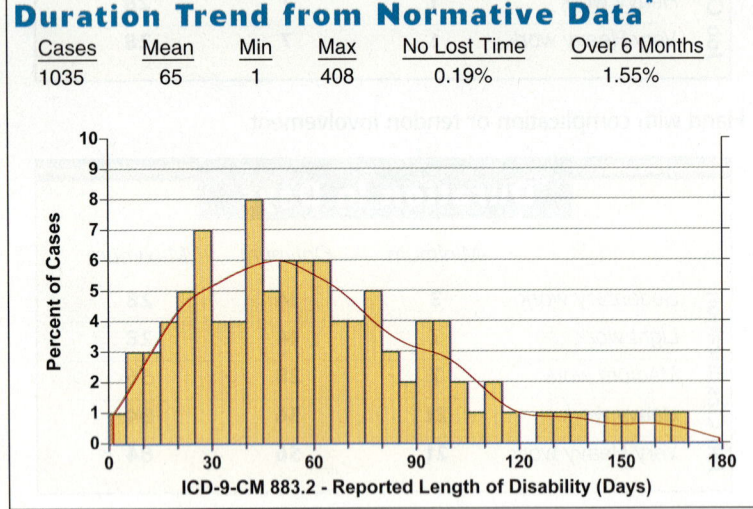
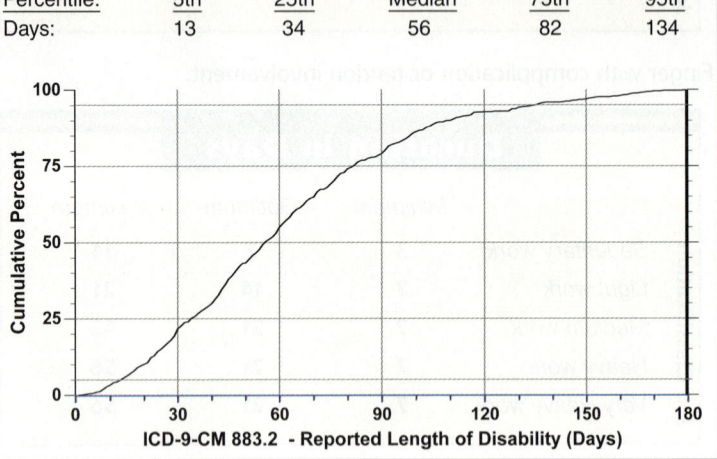

* Differences may exist between the expected duration tables and the normative graphs. Duration tables provide expected recovery periods based on the type of work performed by the individual. The normative graphs reflect the actual observed experience of many individuals across the spectrum of physical conditions, in a variety of industries, and with varying levels of case management.

Failure to Recover

If an individual fails to recover within the maximum duration expectancy period, the reader may wish to reference the following questions to assist in better understanding the specifics of an individual's medical case.

Regarding diagnosis:

- How did individual acquire the open wound? Is it an abrasion, amputation, avulsion, incision, laceration, or puncture? Has it become infected? Has it bled?
- Where is the wound? Has it been contaminated?
- When did individual last have a tetanus injection?
- Was the wound explored to evaluate involvement of tendons, ligaments, and nerves?
- Is the wound bleeding profusely or spurting blood?
- Does individual have a decreased level of consciousness, rapid pulse, or low blood pressure?
- Is the area around the wound tender to touch and swollen? Is there altered sensation?
- Are erythema and warmth present? Are there any obvious deformities?
- Has individual had a CBC and x-ray? Was an arteriogram done? Nerve conduction studies? Evoke potentials?

Regarding treatment:

- Initially did individual's treatment consist of controlling the bleeding, treating for shock, and thoroughly cleansing the wound?
- Have injured nerves, tendons, arteries, or bones been treated? Was surgery necessary?
- Was amputation necessary?
- Was the wound closed with stitches, Steri-Strips, or staples? Was it necessary to leave the wound open? Will reconstructive surgery be needed?
- Does individual have a prescription for antibiotics?

Regarding prognosis:

- If necessary, is individual active in physical therapy? Is a home exercise program in place?
- Can individual's employer accommodate any necessary restrictions?
- Does individual have any conditions that may affect ability to recover?
- Have any complications occurred such as infection, cellulitis, deformity, keloid formation, gangrene, bleeding, sepsis, tetanus, ischemia, necrosis, temporary or permanent loss of sensation, or function of the affected body part? Does individual have reflex sympathetic dystrophy?

References

Bucci, Luke R. Nutrition Applied to Injury Rehabilitation and Sports Medicine. Boca Raton: BRC Press, Inc, 1994.

Hayes, Karen W. "Direct Current." Manual for Physical Agents. Hayes, Karen W., ed. Norwalk: Appleton & Lange, 1993. 125-130.

Open Wound, Back
876

Definition

An open wound to the back refers to any break in the skin of the back. The back includes any area from the shoulders down to the pelvis. Wounds are classified as open wounds if the protective skin layer is damaged and exposes underlying tissue to the outside air.

An open wound can cause serious internal and external bleeding. In addition, since the protection of the skin has been penetrated, the wound is easily contaminated and may become infected.

The majority of open wounds to the back are due to stab wounds from assaults (knife wounds) or becoming accidentally impaled by a sharp object. Other causes of open wounds of the back include gunshot wounds, direct trauma such as falls, vehicle accidents, or exposure to extreme heat or cold (burns or frostbite). Individuals in occupations such as construction, law enforcement, or the military may be at greater risk of sustaining open wounds to the back.

Open wounds to the back are most common in young adult males.

Diagnosis

History: Individuals may report direct trauma to the back area coupled with a history of bleeding from the site. If conscious, individual may complain of chest pain, shortness of breath, or dizziness.

Some individuals may have exposed the wound to dirt or other contaminants such as manure or rust. Information may be ascertained as to how much time elapsed between receiving the wound and getting medical attention. They may report pre-existing conditions that could affect wound healing such as smoking, diabetes, vascular disease, or certain medications. The date of last tetanus injection is helpful.

Physical exam: Since open wounds to the back may be associated with significant blood loss or severe life-threatening injuries to the lung or spinal cord, diagnostic workup and treatment is usually done simultaneously. A sharp object may be protruding from the wound. There may be signs of shock such as low blood pressure (hypotension), cool skin, and rapid pulse. Breathing may be labored and noisy or absent. The trachea may be deviated to one side because of a collapsed lung (pneumothorax). Respirations may be rapid (tachypnea) and the skin may appear blue (cyanosis). If the wound has penetrated the spinal cord, the individual may display loss of sensation or motor function below the level of the wound. Other findings can include blood pooled beneath the skin (hematoma).

Tests: Arterial blood gases or pulse oximetry determines adequacy of oxygenation. Hemoglobin and hematocrit levels are checked for evidence of significant blood loss. A chest x-ray determines extent of the injury. CT of the upper torso shows if the wound extends into the chest cavity or spinal cord. An electrocardiogram (ECG) may be done to detect heart rhythm disturbances.

Treatment

Treatment consists of prompt control of bleeding and thorough repair of injured tissue in order to minimize risk of infection and loss of function. Applying pressure with a sterile dressing usually controls bleeding. Intravenous fluids may be given to treat any symptoms of shock. If the lung is penetrated, a tube is placed in the chest (thoracostomy) to drain blood (hemothorax) or expand a collapsed lung (pneumothorax). Extensive wounds such as burns or blast-type wounds from explosions or guns may require surgical wound exploration and removal of foreign debris, foreign bodies, bone fragments, and unhealthy or dead (necrotic) tissue (debridement). Wounds that damage the vertebrae and or spinal cord may require surgical stabilization of any vertebral fractures (spinal fusion) or the placement of an external vest (body brace or Jewett brace) to stabilize the fracture.

Less extensive wounds to the back such as abrasions, lacerations, and puncture wounds are treated by using scissors to clip the hair surrounding the wound, cleaning the wound with saline or mild antiseptic solution using a high-pressure irrigating device (syringe or water Pik), removing any remaining foreign matter, and trimming the ragged or unhealthy tissue with sterile scissors or a scalpel. Most wounds are then closed using stitches, surgical tape (Steri-Strips), staples, or a combination.

Prognosis

The outcome of an open wound to the back varies according to the extent and severity of the injury, damage to internal organs or the spinal cord, and the promptness of emergency intervention. Superficial back wounds are rarely associated with serious complications and generally have a good outcome. Even those wounds that penetrate deeply and cause lung injury have an excellent outcome with prompt emergency treatment and thoracostomy, as appropriate. If the wound penetrates and damages the spinal cord, there may be partial or complete loss of sensation or motor function (partial paralysis or hemiplegia) below the level of the injury resulting in permanent disability.

Differential Diagnosis

There are no other conditions that present with similar symptoms.

Specialists

- Emergency Medicine
- General Surgeon
- Internist
- Neurosurgeon
- Occupational Therapist
- Physiatrist
- Physical Therapist
- Primary Care Provider
- Pulmonologist
- Respiratory Therapist

Work Restrictions / Accommodations

Work restrictions and accommodations vary according to the location and extent of injury sustained from the wound. Individuals with wounds that only penetrate the skin surface should avoid conditions that expose the wound to moisture, pressure, or contamination. Individuals with wounds that extend into the lungs may need modified duty and avoid heavy lifting until the wound heals. Those with spinal cord involvement need work accommodations according to the degree of physical disability. The individual's physician and therapists can provide exact specifications regarding restrictions and accommodations in these cases.

Complementary and Alternative Therapies

Content is intended for awareness only. Treatments may or may not be effective. Scientific evidence may be lacking and some substances have potentially toxic effects. Dr. Presley Reed and the editors do not endorse the use of these therapies in the absence of consultation with a licensed medical professional.

Vitamin C -	Involved in immune function. Said to make collagen for wound repair.
Vitamin A -	Involved in immune function. May stimulate regrowth of tissue (epithelialization).
Vitamin E -	May reduce inflammation and aid in skin repair.
Zinc -	Said to accelerate wound healing.

Comorbid Conditions

Comorbid conditions of diabetes, bleeding disorders, immune suppression, peripheral vascular disease, and malnutrition may impact ability to recover and further lengthen disability.

Complications

Possible complications of open wounds to the back include infection, hemorrhagic shock, and death (from uncontrolled hemorrhage or overwhelming infection).

Factors Influencing Duration

The age of the individual, extent and location of injury, and response to treatment may influence disability.

Length of Disability

Duration depends on site, severity, presence of complications, and nature of internal injuries, if any. Disability may be permanent. Contact physician for additional information.

Failure to Recover

If an individual fails to recover within the maximum duration expectancy period, the reader may wish to reference the following questions to assist in better understanding the specifics of an individual's medical case.

Regarding diagnosis:

- Does the individual have serious internal and external bleeding?
- Has the wound become contaminated?
- What was the cause of the individual's wound? Stabbing, gunshot, fall, vehicle accident, burn, or frostbite? Was the individual conscious?
- Did the individual have any chest pain, shortness of breath, or dizziness?
- How much time elapsed between receiving the wound and getting medical attention?
- When did individual last have a tetanus booster?
- Does the individual smoke or have diabetes, vascular disease, or take medications that might delay healing?
- Does the individual display signs of shock?
- Were other parts of the body also injured? To what extent?
- What were the individual's vital signs?
- Did individual have loss of sensation or motor function below the level of the wound?
- Were appropriate diagnostic tests done such as blood, chest x-ray, CT, and ECG?

Regarding treatment:

- Did the individual receive appropriate and timely treatment for all the injuries?
- Was bleeding stopped with application of direct pressure?
- Was the wound explored to determine the extent of injury?
- Was the wound thoroughly cleaned and then débrided if necessary?
- Did the wound extend into the chest cavity or spinal cord?
- Did the individual have an abrasion, laceration, or puncture?
- How was the wound closed? With ster-strips or staples or both?

Regarding prognosis:

- Does the individual have any conditions such as diabetes, bleeding disorders, immune suppression, peripheral vascular disease, and malnutrition that may impact ability to recover and further lengthen disability?
- Did any complications arise such as infection, hemorrhagic shock, or death?

References

Clochesy, John M., et al. Critical Care Nursing, 2nd ed. Philadelphia: W.B. Saunders Company, 1996.

Open Wound, Chest

Other names / synonyms: Chest Injury, Penetrating Chest Injury, Penetrating Chest Wound, Penetrating Thoracic Injury, Penetrating Thoracic Wound

875

Definition

An open chest wound refers to any wound in the chest wall that enters the lung cavity (pleural space).

About 70% of open wounds to the chest penetrate the chest cavity and often result in serious, life-threatening injury to the lungs, blood vessels, heart and upper abdominal organs.

Open chest wounds are most commonly associated with violence and are the result of stab wounds and gunshot wounds. In these cases, the injuries to the chest occur most often in the home environment and are often associated with domestic or social disputes. However, open chest wounds are also associated with accidental injury by nails, objects thrown from machinery, and industrial explosions.

Consequently, persons at risk for open chest wounds include those who handle weapons, such as law enforcement officers military personnel, hunters, or criminals. Construction workers, farmers, gardeners and factory workers whose work involves power machinery, compressors or explosives may also be at risk of sustaining open chest wounds. Open chest wounds are most prevalent among young, adult males.

Diagnosis

History: If conscious, the individual may complain of chest pain, shortness of breath, or dizziness. The individual or bystanders may report a recent accident, such as a fall and impalement with a sharp object or assault with a sharp object (e.g., knife) or gun.

Physical exam: On physical exam, breathing may be labored and noisy or absent. Bluish-colored skin (cyanosis) and rapid respirations are hallmarks of inadequate oxygenation. Distended neck veins, distant heart sounds and low blood pressure are indicative of blood in the sac around the heart (cardiac tamponade). Complete absence of blood pressure and pulse is suggestive of open wound to the heart and or great vessels and associated hemorrhagic shock. Other findings may include the presence of blood clots beneath the skin (hematoma) or crackling sound when the skin surface is touched (crepitus). The trachea may be deviated to one side in the presence of a collapsed lung (pneumothorax).

Tests: Arterial blood gases or pulse oximetry is done to determine adequacy of oxygenation. A hemoglobin and hematocrit will be checked to detect evidence of significant blood loss. A chest x-ray will be done to determine extent of chest injury. A computed tomography (CT) scan or magnetic resonance imaging (MRI) of the chest may be needed to identify injuries to structure within the chest cavity. An electrocardiogram (ECG) will be done to detect disturbances on the heart rhythm.

Treatment

Superficial chest wall injuries (those that don't penetrate the chest cavity) may be thoroughly cleaned, nonviable tissue and debris removed (debridement) and the wound closed with stitches. If no evidence of hemo- or pneumothorax is seen on chest x-ray in 6 hours, and individuals are otherwise asymptomatic, they may be discharged.

In serious injuries, the first step is to ensure an adequate airway. An artificial airway (endotracheal intubation) may be necessary. Supplemental oxygen is administered. Intravenous fluid and blood may be administered to help maintain an adequate blood pressure if there is evidence of shock or excessive bleeding. A tube may be placed in the stomach (nasogastric tube) to decompress and drain excess stomach contents, and a bladder catheter may be necessary to drain and monitor urine output. Impaled or embedded objects are left in place until the individual has a stable blood pressure. These objects are then removed in the operating room (removal of foreign body).

Chest tubes (thoracostomy) may be inserted to drain blood (hemothorax), fluid, or air (pneumothorax) and allow full expansion of the lungs. The tube is placed between the ribs and into the space between the inner lining and the outer lining of the lung (pleural space). If cardiac tamponade is suspected, a needle attached to a catheter is carefully inserted into the heart sac (pericardium) to drain blood (pericardiocentesis).

Those with penetrating injuries to the heart, great vessels, major airways (trachea or bronchi) or esophagus, or those who have ongoing bleeding will require surgical exploration of the chest (thoracotomy) to repair any injuries. Approximately, 30% of all penetrating chest wounds require thoracotomies. All individuals will require ongoing monitoring in the intensive care until stable.

Prognosis

Outcomes for chest wounds vary according to the extent and severity of the injury and the promptness of emergency intervention. Superficial chest wounds are rarely associated with serious complications and generally have a good outcome. Even those wounds that penetrate the chest cavity and cause lung injury have an excellent outcome with prompt emergency treatment and thoracostomy or thoracotomy (as appropriate). Most superficial and penetrating chest injuries are discharged from the hospital, fully recovered.

However, penetrating injuries to the heart or great vessels are associated with poorer outcomes due to hemorrhagic shock and cardiopulmonary arrest. These cases have a mortality rate ranging from fifty to eighty percent. Those who have a blood pressure and pulse at the time of initial treatment fair better than those with no blood pressure or pulse at the time of treatment.

Differential Diagnosis

There are no other possible diagnoses.

Specialists

- Cardiologist
- Emergency Medicine
- General Surgeon
- Internist
- Pulmonologist
- Thoracic Surgeon

Work Restrictions / Accommodations

Depending on the severity and extent of injury, individuals may need to have activity restricted.

In general, those with superficial injuries to the chest wall can return to work with no restrictions. However, those whose injuries penetrated the chest wall may need to be assigned modified duty and should avoid exposure to airborne irritants until the wound is thoroughly healed. Individuals who had critical injuries to the heart or great vessels may need further work accommodations depending on the extent of their physical disability. Specific restrictions should be dictated by the individual's physician.

Comorbid Conditions

Pre-existing conditions of diabetes, cardiovascular disease, pulmonary disease, immune suppression or bleeding disorders may impact ability to recover and further lengthen disability.

Complications

Complications include hemorrhage, infection, and cardiac or respiratory arrest.

Often, the injury results in leakage of air into the space between the lung lining (pleura) and chest (pleural space) causing a collapsed lung (pneumothorax) and hemorrhage into the chest cavity (hemothorax). Sudden collapse of the lung (pneumothorax) causes impaired breathing and oxygenation (respiratory failure) and can shift the heart and great vessels (tension pneumothorax) causing impairment of heart function and circulation.

Factors Influencing Duration

Factors that might influence disability include extent of injury, severity of symptoms (i.e., whether there is shock) and response to treatment.

Length of Disability

Duration depends on severity and nature of internal injuries, if any. Fifty to eighty percent of individuals with wounds that penetrate the heart or great vessels die. Disability may be permanent.

Failure to Recover

If an individual fails to recover within the maximum duration expectancy period, the reader may wish to reference the following questions to assist in better understanding the specifics of an individual's medical case.

Regarding diagnosis:

- Is the individual's wound associated with violence such as a stab or gunshot wound?
- Is the individual's wound associated with accidental injury by nails, objects thrown from machinery, or industrial explosions?
- Does the individual's work put them at increased risk for an open chest wound?
- Is the individual conscious? Does the individual complain of chest pain, shortness of breath, or dizziness?
- Does the individual or bystanders report a recent accident, such as a fall and impalement with a sharp object or assault with a sharp object (e.g., knife) or gun?
- On exam are respirations labored, rapid, noisy or absent? Is the individual cyanotic?
- Does the individual have distended neck veins, distant heart sounds or hypotension? Does the individual have a hematoma or crepitus? Does the individual have a pneumothorax?
- Has the individual had arterial blood gasses or pulse oximetry? Have a hemoglobin and hematocrit been done?
- Has the individual had a chest x-ray, CT or MRI of the chest? ECG?

Regarding treatment:

- Was the individual's injury superficial? Was it thoroughly cleaned and débrided and closed with sutures if needed?
- Did the individual have endotracheal intubation done?
- Did the individual receive oxygen, intravenous fluid and blood? Was a nasogastric tube inserted? Bladder catheter?
- Was a chest tube necessary? Pericardiocentesis?
- If necessary were any foreign bodies removed surgically?
- If necessary was a thoracotomy done to repair any injuries?

Regarding prognosis:

- Is the individual's employer able to accommodate any necessary restrictions?
- Does the individual have any conditions that may affect ability to recover?
- Does the individual have any complications such as hemorrhage, infection, and cardiac or respiratory arrest?
- Does the individual have a pneumothorax or hemothorax?

References

Bone, Roger C., ed. Pulmonary and Critical Care Medicine. Philadelphia: Mosby-Year Book, Inc, 1998.

Sabiston, David C., and H. Kim Lyerly. Textbook of Surgery, 15th ed. Philadelphia: W.B. Saunders Company, 1997.

Open-Chest Cardiac Massage
37.91

Definition

Open-chest cardiac massage is an emergency procedure for managing a heart that is not beating or beating infectively (cardiac arrest). It is done in conjunction with the administration of drugs directly into the heart or into a peripheral vein and the use of direct electrical defibrillation if the rhythm is ventricular fibrillation.

Reason for Procedure

Open-chest cardiac massage is usually done when the chest is already open in an individual undergoing surgery whose heart stops beating effectively. On occasion, if a cardiac arrest occurs a few hours or days after chest surgery, the chest is reopened to institute open-chest cardiac massage.

The cause of the cardiopulmonary arrest is usually an intraoperative event such as an unexpected effect of an anesthetic, massive hemorrhage, a pulmonary embolus, high potassium, or reaction to drug or an air embolus.

Description

The heart is compressed with one or both hands (preferably both) at a rate of 60 to 70 times a minute. The massage is briefly interrupted after each fifth compression to allow inflation of the lungs. Lungs are easily inflatable through a tube inserted before the surgery. More than one individual rotates in performing the compressions due to hand fatigue. At the same time, drugs are administered directly into the heart or intravenously. One or more attempts are made to defibrillate the heart with sterile paddles applied directly to the heart. The amount of electrical energy delivered via the paddles is much less than the amount delivered when the paddles are placed on the chest wall to deliver the electrical shock. If the cardiac arrest occurs in the recovery room or later in the surgical ward, the chest is reopened through the original incision.

Prognosis

Open-chest cardiac massage is an emergency, life-saving procedure. Success means that the individual lives through the arrest. Failure means death.

Specialists

- Anesthesiologist
- Cardiologist
- Critical Care Specialist
- Thoracic Surgeon

Work Restrictions / Accommodations

Work restrictions and accommodations depend on the degree of cardiac and neurologic damage (if any) caused by procedure. Lifting restrictions are necessary for up to 6 or 8 weeks.

Comorbid Conditions

Coronary artery atherosclerosis, obesity, heart failure, and underlying lung disease may lengthen disability.

Procedure Complications

Open-chest cardiac massage may be complicated by perforation of the heart. This may occur if the individual has had a recent heart attack. Other complications include an air or embolus to the brain and laceration of the liver or lung. Other possible delayed complications include a heart attack or brain damage.

Factors Influencing Duration

Length of disability may be influenced by the effectiveness of the procedure and any complications. Open-chest cardiac massage is usually performed on an individual already in the hospital for a presumably serious open-chest surgical procedure. In addition to whatever recovery time is customary for the surgery itself, it is possible that the attending physician will want to have the individual stay under close electronic monitoring to guard against a recurrence of cardiac arrest.

Length of Disability

Duration in Days

Job Classification	Minimum	Optimum	Maximum
Sedentary work	14	42	56
Light work	14	42	56
Medium work	28	70	84
Heavy work	63	98	112
Very Heavy work	84	98	112

References

Meeker, Margaret, and Jane Rothrock. Alexander's Care of the Patient in Surgery. St. Louis: Mosby, 1999.

Operations on Muscle, Tendon, and Fascia of Hand
82.99

Definition
Given the number of muscles, tendons, ligaments, and nerves that allow the complex movements and dexterity of the human hand, the variety of surgical interventions that are possible is extremely broad. Any of the muscles, tendons structures may be injured or affected by disease either alone or in combination with each other. Surgery to treat these various conditions should be investigated by the specific named procedure.

Reason for Procedure
Operations on the hand are performed to restore function and appearance of the hand or to remove a blood clot, tumor, cyst, or foreign body from the hand.

Description
Surgical procedures to the hand may be either minor or complex. Local, regional or general anesthesia may be required. Procedures are done in physicians' offices, outpatient settings or as inpatients. Arthroscopic and microscopic assisted procedures are common in the hand and wrist.

Prognosis
Outcome is dependent on the severity of the injury/disease and the procedure. Each case would need to be evaluated individually.

Specialists
- Hand Surgeon
- Orthopedic Surgeon

Rehabilitation
Return to function after a hand operation involving the muscles, tendons, and fascia of the hand is best achieved through specialized therapy performed by a certified hand rehabilitation specialist. Careful analyses of the initial trauma as well as the corrective procedures are a determinant in creating an effective therapy schedule. However, the therapy schedule is not rigidly set. Progress is determined by the individual's functional improvement.

Hand structures involved and the type of operation performed will determine the type and duration of immobilization. Type of immobilization in turn influences the amount of early motion the individual is able to achieve. For example, if damage is to the flexor mechanism of the hand, a splint might be worn with the involved fingers placed in dynamic traction by an elastic thread attached from the finger nails to the outer splint. This mechanism helps take pressure off the healing flexor structures while the hand is not in motion. Light tension is achieved, however, when the individual extends the fingers.

A conservative amount of tension should be applied to the healing structures during therapy sessions, especially during the first weeks post surgery. Most tendon operation failures occur when the tendon ruptures or fails to adhere to the bone. As therapy progresses, the integrity of the hand structures should be functionally evaluated to minimize the risk of re-injury. Additionally, scar management is crucial to restoring appropriate biomechanical function during and after therapy. A program for scar management is initiated once sutures or the cast is removed.

The individual may be fitted with a smaller blocking cast once proper healing is evident. The quality of curling the fingers (tendon gliding) or muscle movement determines whether therapy progresses. For example, if the individual shows signs of tendon rupture such as no response of the tendon while performing gliding exercises, no further therapy is conducted until the primary physician has re-evaluated the tendon. Once approved, active range of motion exercises are added to the therapy routine.

The goal of work therapy is to improve handgrip strength and sustained use of the hand. An example of this type work therapy is screwing pegs of varying lengths into a board. Wood working exercises may include sanding with the hand in either a flat or gripped position. It is important to exercise joints at different angles to continue to functionally retrain the hand to move correctly. As this phase of therapy progresses, putty of graded resistance may be used to facilitate hand strength.

When resistive exercises are started, the individual should be tested for muscle weakness. Muscle weakness such as impairment in extending the fingers (extensor lag) will become apparent as exercises become more advanced. Specific exercises like rolling a can affixed with cloth across a Velcro board by placing a partially formed fist on the can and uncurling the fingers toward the can (extension) can help to strengthen the hand in extension. As well as muscle strength, exercises in this phase of therapy should emphasize both hand and wrist movements. Wrist curls in different planes of motion as well as manipulating functional tools such as a screwdriver or hammer are examples of movements performed during this phase. The individual is expected to engage in a home routine that includes picking up objects and sustained gripping (gripping an object for a period of time). The home routine will also include an upper body routine that aims at increasing arm, chest, and upper back strength.

Return to work is dependent on the amount of functional recovery. If the individual experiences a major trauma to the hand such as a crushing injury, the dexterity of the hand may not improve significantly enough to return to the same type of job.

Work Restrictions / Accommodations
Restrictions and accommodations include temporary transfer to a position that does not involve lifting, gripping, manual dexterity or extensive use of the hand. Large bulky dressings, splints or external fixation devices are often worn for several weeks. These appliances must be kept clean and dry. The device may also cause of safety hazard from the risk of being caught in equipment used by the worker.

Extended disability or time away from work shifts for physical/occupational therapy is critical for optimum recovery.

In some cases, work duties may need to be permanently changed or alterations made to allow the individual with a permanent disability to continue to perform the duties of his or her position.

Procedure Complications

Complications of hand surgery include infection, skin sloughing, skin and muscle contracture, failure to relieve symptoms, nerve or vessel damage. Loss of dexterity may be a result of the surgical procedure.

Factors Influencing Duration

Factors include the type of disease or injury, the location, extent, and severity of disease or injury, the treatment provided, the development of complications, and the job requirements or physical activity level of the individual. In some cases, disability may be permanent.

Length of Disability

Duration depends on the specific procedure performed.

References

Guidelines Tendon Surgery Therapy. e-Hand.com. 15 Mar 2000. 05 July 2000 <http://www.e-Hand.com/thr/thr064.htm>.

Meals, Roy A. "The Wrist and Hand." Turek's Orthopaedics, Principles and Their Application, 5th ed. Turek S.L., and J.A. Buckwalter, MD, eds. Philadelphia: Lippincott-Raven, 1994. 417-442.

Opioid Type Dependence
Other names / synonyms: Codeine Dependency, Heroin Addiction, Pain Medication Abuse, Pain Medication Addiction
304.0, 304.00, 304.01, 304.02, 304.03

Definition

Opioid type dependence is defined as dependence upon the class of natural or synthetic drugs that include morphine, codeine, or heroin.

Opioids are generally prescribed as pain management medications, antidiarrheal agents, or cough suppressants and, when used regularly, cause symptoms of drowsiness, slurred speech, constricted pupil size, and attention or memory impairment. Dependence reflects prolonged use of opioid substances for non-medical purposes or, if a medical purpose is present, use occurs in amounts or frequencies greater than needed for pain management.

Individuals who have developed an opioid dependence have a history of regular, frequently daily, use over a period of time, with withdrawal symptoms occurring within 6-12 hours of the last dose. Withdrawal symptoms include depression, nausea, vomiting, diarrhea, muscle aches, excessive tearing of the eye or nose, pupillary dilation, yawning, fever, or insomnia.

Heroin is a commonly misused drug of this class and is usually taken by injection or, occasionally, smoked or inhaled. Those individuals who are dependent upon prescribed opioids, usually pain management medications, will frequently either illegally purchase the drug or obtain prescriptions by faking or exaggerating illnesses or by receiving prescriptions from a number of different physicians, most of whom are not aware of duplicate opioid prescriptions.

Although the use of prescribed pain medications can be a risk for opioid dependency, only a small minority (between 1-5%) of individuals who are prescribed opiates for medical reasons develop opiate abuse or dependency. The male/female dependency ratio is 1.5/1 for non-heroin opioids and 3:1 for heroin. Approximately 0.7% of the Unites States population is estimated to have an opioid dependence at some time in their lives, with an increase in the late-adolescence age group use from 1.3% in 1990 to 2% in 1997.

Diagnosis

A diagnosis is based on criteria listed in the DSM-IV-TR (Diagnostic and Statistical Manual of Mental Disorders, 4th Edition, Text Revision, published by the American Psychiatric Association).

History: Diagnosis depends upon the individual demonstrating at least three or more of the criteria at any time in the same 12-month period. Criteria include a need for markedly increased amounts of drug to achieve intoxication; diminished effects with continued use of the same amount of drug; symptoms of withdrawal, such as, tremors, increased blood pressure or heart rate, cravings, sweating, diarrhea, or fever; persistent unsuccessful attempts to quit or control drug intake; a great deal of time spent in activities related to the use of or recovery from the use of drugs; social, occupational, recreational, or relational activities given up for the sake of drug use; continued drug use despite knowledge of recurrent physical or psychological problems related to its use.

Individuals who are in withdrawal complain of muscle cramps, nausea, anxiety, insomnia; depressed mood, and/or drug cravings.

Physical exam: Signs of opiate abuse differ significantly depending on whether the individual presents with opiate dependence, overdose, or withdrawal. Opiate dependence is manifested by pinpoint pupils, slowed speech and movement, euphoria, and/or weight loss. Drug overdose is indicated by slow, shallow respirations, unconsciousness, pinpoint-sized pupils, and skin that is cold, moist, and bluish in color. Observable signs of heroin withdrawal include restlessness, vomiting, runny nose, sweating, diarrhea, fever, or yawning. Needle tracks or scars may be evident, usually in the arms, hands, feet, or groin areas. Most withdrawal symptoms resolve within a week, but some, such as anxiety or insomnia, can last for weeks to months.

Tests: Urine toxicology tests for heroin remain positive for up to 36 hours after the last dose. Screening tests for HIV (human immunodeficiency virus) and hepatitis A, B, and C are important. The intravenous-drug abuser population represents a very high risk for each of these diseases.

Treatment

Abstinence is the treatment goal. Treatment services may include individual psychotherapy, family therapy, drug education, and relaxation training and are usually conducted in an outpatient setting. Inpatient hospitalization may be necessary if the individual is suicidal or is having severe withdrawal symptoms during detoxification. Treatment may include education on physical, emotional, and mental aspects of addiction and recovery, identification of stressors and stress management skills, improved coping skills, assertiveness training, and relaxation training. Ongoing structured self-help programs such as Narcotics Anonymous and Rational Recovery are recommended as an adjunct to treatment services. Regular but random drug screens should be part of the treatment process. Some heroin-dependent individuals enroll in medically supervised methadone-maintenance programs, in which methadone is substituted for heroin and then gradually decreased until the individual achieves abstinence.

A longer acting opioid called L-alpha-acetyl-methadol (LAMM) has been used for maintenance treatment. The use of buprenorphine and naltrexone are being investigated as other pharmacologic means or relapse prevention.

One approach to heroin treatment is called Ultra Rapid Opioid Detox (UROD), which involves the use of opiate antagonists and general anesthesia to allow individuals to be safely detoxed within a few hours. This technique greatly shortens the time of detoxification, avoids the pain and other discomforts of withdrawal, allows sooner entry into the rehabilitation phase of a recovery program, minimizes time lost from work and family, and helps to decrease the relatively high number of individuals who leave conventional detoxification programs prematurely. However, it is a high-risk procedure, requiring careful medical monitoring. Even though the success rate of this 1-2 day detoxification process is high, the actual measure of success is whether the individual remains abstinent over a period of time, usually after involvement with traditional outpatient addiction treatment programs.

Withdrawal symptoms, which occur for up to 7 days, may require medication management for symptoms such as nausea, diarrhea, or anxiety.

Prognosis

There are a significant number of individuals who respond to treatment and stay in remission. However, there are individuals who experience periods of relapse, in which they begin opioid use/abuse after a period of remission, and again meet the criteria for substance dependence. There are other individuals who are never able to abstain from use and who do not experience any periods of remission.

Outcome is improved if the individual seeks treatment early in the disease process and has adequate social support systems in place. Many individuals experience at least one relapse after treatment and some individuals never seek treatment. Although relapses can be a common part of the recovery process, about 20-30% of individuals with opioid dependence do achieve long-term abstinence.

Differential Diagnosis

The individual using opioids may be suffering from a psychiatric disorder along with the substance abuse disorder. Some types of opioid dependence may begin or be continued as a form of self-medication to treat anxiety, depression, or other psychiatric disorders. The most prevalent forms of psychiatric disorders found in those with substance abuse problems are affective disorders, antisocial personality disorder, and alcoholism.

Specialists

- Advanced Practice Registered Nurse
- Psychiatrist
- Psychologist

Rehabilitation

In addition to substance abuse treatment and support groups, occupational therapy could assist the individual to develop communication skills, identify and match personal skills and work habits to the work place, and learn how non-substance-related participation in leisure activities contributes to overall health and well being. Physical conditioning may be needed to address deconditioning that occurs due to inactivity during the period of addition and early recovery. Supportive therapies, such as expressive therapies (art, music, or dance therapy), relaxation techniques, or breath therapy might be helpful in decreasing stress levels that some individuals perceive put them at risk for relapse.

Work Restrictions / Accommodations

Many employers have systems in place for individuals recovering from substance dependence disorders to return to work under special contracts or conditions. These conditions may provide guidelines for testing blood and urine levels of identified substances and provide work performance and substance abuse treatment guidelines for the recovering individual. Opiate use should not be tolerated at the workplace because employees who use on the job endanger their safety and that of their coworkers and often create a negative work environment.

In general, time-limited temporary work accommodations may include reducing or eliminating activities where the safety of self or others is contingent upon a constant and/or high level of alertness, such as driving a motor vehicle, operating complex machinery, or handling dangerous chemicals; introducing the individual to new or stressful situations gradually under individually appropriate supervision; allowing some flexibility in scheduling to attend therapy appointments (which normally should occur during the employee's personal time); promoting planned, proactive management of identified problem areas; and offering timely feedback on job performance issues. It will be helpful if accommodations are documented in a written plan designed to promote timely and safe transition back to full work productivity.

Complementary and Alternative Therapies

Content is intended for awareness only. Treatments may or may not be effective. Scientific evidence may be lacking and some substances have potentially toxic effects. Dr. Presley Reed and the editors do not endorse the use of these therapies in the absence of consultation with a licensed medical professional.

Acupuncture -	Can decrease cravings, reduce withdrawal symptoms, relieve tension and help relax.
Biofeedback -	May help in the awareness, conditioning, and control of physical processes in the body.
Visualization and Psycho-drama -	Individuals may be able to gain insight into their own addictions.

Comorbid Conditions

Conditions that may impact recovery and lengthen disability include the presence of psychiatric disorders (such as schizophrenia, major depression, anxiety disorder), and the abuse or dependence on tobacco, alcohol or other substances. Skin infections (cellulitis), hepatitis, HIV (human immunodeficiency virus), tuberculosis, and infection of the lining of the heart (endocarditis) occur frequently in the intravenous-drug-abusing population.

Complications

Many opiate-dependent individuals also abuse alcohol, cocaine, antianxiety agents, sedatives, and/or other psychoactive substances and may become dependent on these as well. Users who inject the drug risk not only overdosing, but also infections such as skin abscesses, infections of the heart lining and valves (endocarditis), inflammation of the membranes of the spinal cord or brain (meningitis), tuberculosis, hepatitis, or acquired immune deficiency syndrome (AIDS) from sharing needles with others.

Regular use can lead to dry mouth, visual impairment, constipation, male sexual erectile dysfunction, or female disturbances in menses. Mortality rates resulting from complications are as high as 2% per year and usually result from overdose, accidents, injuries, AIDS or other medical complications.

Factors Influencing Duration

It has been demonstrated that the most reliable predictor of treatment outcome, regardless of treatment strategy, is the individual's readiness to change. The severity of the abuse/dependence, early intervention, the success of the treatment program, appropriate individual-treatment matching, and any physical complications may influence the length of disability as well. A stable history of employment is also a major predictor of permanent abstinence.

Length of Disability

Once dependence develops, it may continue over a period of many years, with frequent periods of abstinence. There are a significant number of individuals who respond to treatment, with up to 30% achieving long-term abstinence. It is fairly common for opiate dependence to decrease after age 40, although there are many individuals who remain dependent for 50 years or longer. There are some, however, who are never able to abstain from opioid use and who do not experience any periods of remission.

Non-hospital detoxification and counseling are becoming more common and most outpatient programs enable the individual to continue working.

Uncomplicated.

Duration in Days

Job Classification	Minimum	Optimum	Maximum
Any work	7	28	42

Failure to Recover

If an individual fails to recover within the maximum duration expectancy period, the reader may wish to reference the following questions to assist in better understanding the specifics of an individual's medical case.

Regarding diagnosis:

- Did the individual's evaluation include a detailed history of past and present substance use, a general medical and psychiatric history and examination; history of any/all prior psychiatric treatments with outcomes; a family and social history; screening of blood, breath or urine for abused substances; and other laboratory tests to help confirm the presence or absence of comorbid conditions frequently associated with substance use disorders? If not, what areas were omitted?

- Would this information impact current treatment plan? If so, what changes can be made?

- Have underlying medical, and particularly psychiatric, disorders been ruled out?

Regarding treatment:

- Does the individual require maintenance with opioid agonists?

- Because the concurrent use of or withdrawal from other substances can complicate treatment of opioid withdrawal, has other substance use been identified and appropriately addressed?

- Is the effectiveness of agonist drug therapy limited by lack of compliance and low treatment retention?

- Would the individual benefit from change to an alternative drug treatment strategy?

- Was choice of treatment based on the individual's preferences, the medical issues to be addressed, associated psychiatric disorders, and the individual's past response to various forms of treatment?

- Has treatment approach been matched to the particular needs of the individual?

- Would the individual benefit from a behavioral therapy approach that uses a voucher-based system to give positive rewards for staying in treatment and remaining cocaine free (contingency management)?

- Does current treatment program include cognitive behavioral interventions?

- Does the individual's life and social interactions focus predominantly on substance use?

- Does the individual lack sufficient social and vocational skills and drug-free social supports to maintain abstinence in an outpatient setting?

- If the individual does not meet clinical criteria for hospitalization, would he/she benefit from admission to a residential treatment program?

- Have underlying psychiatric disorders been addressed?

Regarding prognosis:
- Was individual treated with 3 or more months of residential treatment that is associated with a better long-term outcome?
- Is individual currently involved in a support group such as Narcotics or Alcoholics Anonymous?
- Does support group provide the external support and motivation to continue in treatment beyond the initial stage of detoxification?
- Besides just kicking the habit, is individual receiving necessary tools, skills, and encouragement to move ahead with his/her life?

References

Frances, Allen. Diagnostic and Statistical Manual of Mental Disorders: 4th ed, text revision. Washington, DC: American Psychiatric Association, 2000.

Hall, Laura Lee. "Making the ADA Work for People with Psychiatric Disabilities." Mental Disorder, Work Disability, and the Law. Bonnie, Richard J., and John Monahan, eds. Chicago: The University of Chicago Press, 1997. 241-280.

Optic Atrophy
377.1, 377.10

Definition

Optic atrophy is a shrinking or wasting (degeneration) of nerve fibers that carry impulses for the sense of sight (optic nerve fibers). Optic atrophy is a sign of chronic optic nerve disease.

Recent research has uncovered various hereditary factors that may be directly linked to development of optic atrophy, which, in some cases, may occur equally in both males and females in successive generations. In some of those cases, about half of family members carrying the genetic trait develop the condition. The most common inherited form of optic atrophy, Leber's Hereditary Optic Neuropathy (LHON), causes vision loss primarily in young men between 26 to 45 years of age. Prevalence depends on how inherited genetic factors combine. Also, some individuals who have the same genetic makeup do not develop optic atrophy, indicating that other unknown factors are involved in the disease's progression. Some individuals with LHON also experience spontaneous remission, apparently independent of any therapy.

Many other conditions may cause optic atrophy through blood vessel changes that result in a decreased blood supply, or inflammation to the optic nerve (optic neuritis). Swelling of the optic nerve at the point where it enters the eyeball (papilledema) also leads to optic atrophy. Pressure on the optic nerve also may be caused by aneurysm (anterior circle of Willis), bone deformation (osteitis deformans), tumor, or thyroid eye disease. Other causes include inflammation or damage to cells of the retina (retinal disease), metabolic diseases (such as diabetes), neurological diseases, hydrocephalus, meningitis, direct injury to the optic nerve, and excessive fluid pressure within the eye (glaucoma). Certain toxic substances may also damage the optic nerve (toxic amblyopia), including excessive alcohol consumption, vitamin deficiency, smoking, reaction to certain antibiotics and blood pressure drugs, or exposure to toxic chemicals. Individuals with a genetic propensity toward developing optic atrophy are also believed to be affected by toxic substances.

Optic atrophy originating from various underlying conditions is the most common cause of vision loss in individuals aged 50 and older.

Diagnosis

History: Symptoms include slow visual changes that will have occurred over weeks or months. In certain cases of hereditary disease, vision loss might be sudden. Changes in visual function may include a loss of visual sharpness (blurred vision) and perception (acuity), a loss in central vision, and a decrease in color vision. Headaches may be reported, along with dizziness and sensitivity to light (photophobia). Both eyes may be affected. The macula is the part of the retina responsible for central vision and sharp focus. If the nerve fibers of the macula are involved, the ability to define images in the center of the visual field will be compromised; peripheral vision, however, will usually remain unimpaired.

Physical exam: The exam may reveal a loss of pupil response (constriction) to light. An exam with an illuminated instrument that magnifies the eye's interior (ophthalmoscopy) may reveal paleness in the area of the retina where the optic nerve enters (optic disc), indicating loss of or damage to nerve fibers. This area may be covered by tissue with irregular and indistinct margins.

Tests: Vision testing may include evaluation of visual sharpness and perception (visual acuity), measurement of the area of visual perception while looking straight ahead (visual field test), and evaluation of color vision. Diagnostic testing may be done to identify the underlying disease causing optic atrophy (such as diabetes, glaucoma, toxic amblyopia). A test that detects and identifies specific genes (polymerase chain reaction) may be indicated if no other underlying cause can be found, or if a family history of optic atrophy is reported.

Treatment

Once the nerve fibers in the optic nerve are lost they never heal or grow back. The best defense is an early diagnosis; if the cause can be found and corrected, further damage can be prevented. Therefore, although there is currently no effective treatment, the condition usually stabilizes and some useful vision can be retained. Because optic atrophy results from another medical condition, treatment targets the underlying cause of the atrophy. In a few cases, full vision may dramatically return with appropriate treatment of the underlying cause. Some researchers recommend use of decompression chambers associated with deep sea divers (hyperbaric oxygen therapy) to deliver pure oxygen at high pressure to optic nerve cells to promote normal function.

Prognosis

Generally, severe damage to the optic nerve will cause permanent vision loss and possible blindness. The prognosis for recovery of vision is good if the underlying cause of the condition involves pressure applied to the optic nerve, such as the presence of a tumor, and if the problem is resolved quickly. Other causes such as vascular and degenerative diseases, trauma, or toxins generally create permanent damage. Outcomes from hereditary factors tend to be unpredictable, ranging from severe impairment to complete remission.

Differential Diagnosis

Conditions that have similar symptoms or that may cause optic atrophy include diabetes, glaucoma, tumor, age-related macular degeneration, optic nerve trauma, optic neuritis, retinitis, thyroiditis, toxic amblyopia, Tay-Sachs disease, neurological disorders, osteitis deformans, papilledema, aneurysm, and multiple sclerosis.

Specialists

- Neurologist
- Ophthalmologist

Work Restrictions / Accommodations

Depending on the extent of visual loss, the individual may need enhancements to perform work tasks, such as large and high contrast print, magnification tools, and greatly increased illumination. The individual may be unable to perform tasks requiring keen visual acuity or color perception.

Complementary and Alternative Therapies

Content is intended for awareness only. Treatments may or may not be effective. Scientific evidence may be lacking and some substances have potentially toxic effects. Dr. Presley Reed and the editors do not endorse the use of these therapies in the absence of consultation with a licensed medical professional.

Hyperbaric oxygen therapy - Some studies indicate that delivery of pure oxygen at high pressure to optic nerve cells may promote normal function.

Antioxidants - Vitamins A, C, and E may help regenerate nerve cells.

Comorbid Conditions

Specific combinations of certain mutated genes that are associated with inherited forms of optic atrophy may increase the severity of the condition. Optic atrophy often is a symptom of other ongoing (chronic), sometimes incurable diseases such as diabetes, multiple sclerosis, or macular degeneration.

Complications

The condition may be complicated by the presence of more than one underlying cause of the atrophy. A delay in seeking treatment may limit the amount of vision that can be restored. Excessive use of toxins such as alcohol and tobacco may increase its severity in individuals with genetic propensity for developing optic atrophy.

Factors Influencing Duration

Length of disability may be influenced by the underlying cause of the atrophy, the amount of time that elapsed before seeking treatment, method of treatment, response to treatment, or the development of complications. In some cases, irreversible blindness may occur.

Length of Disability

The specific type of visual loss may influence the individual's ability to perform certain tasks requiring visual acuity or color perception. Permanent, complete, or partial blindness might result. Disability may be permanent for some jobs.

Failure to Recover

If an individual fails to recover within the maximum duration expectancy period, the reader may wish to reference the following questions to assist in better understanding the specifics of an individual's medical case.

Regarding diagnosis:

- Has diagnosis of optic atrophy been confirmed?
- Has vision testing included visual acuity, visual field test, and evaluation of color vision?
- Has diagnostic testing been done to identify the underlying cause of the optic atrophy?
- Has individual experienced any complications?
- Does individual have an underlying condition that may impact the course of the optic atrophy?

Regarding treatment:

- Did the individual promptly seek treatment when vision loss became apparent?
- Has the optic nerve sustained permanent damage?
- Have underlying causes been identified?
- Are underlying conditions receiving, and responding to, appropriate treatment?
- Would the individual benefit from hyperbaric oxygen therapy?

Regarding prognosis:

- Has underlying cause been identified?
- Has underlying cause been resolved or controlled through appropriate treatment?
- Has there been any visual improvement following treatment of underlying cause?
- To what extent was optic nerve damaged?
- What is the degree of vision loss?
- How disabling is the vision loss?
- Does the individual have access to appropriate visual aides?
- Has the individual received assistance/training in regards to psychological and physical adaptation to the visual loss?

References

Leber's Hereditary Optic Neuropathy (LHON). International Foundation for Optic Nerve Disease. 01 Jan 2000. 1 Jan 2001 <http://www.ifond.org>.

Optic Neuritis
377.3, 377.30, 377.32, 377.39

Definition

Optic neuritis is an inflammation of the optic nerve causing sudden loss of a portion of central vision, sometimes accompanied by painful eye movements.

Various diseases may cause the condition, especially those such as multiple sclerosis (MS) associated with loss of the optic nerve's protective fatty tissue (myelin) sheath. Viral infections, sinus infections, or inflammation located elsewhere in the body may cause the condition. Other causes of optic neuritis are decreased blood supply or injury to the optic nerve, tumors, cancer, and nutritional and metabolic disorders. Exposure to toxic chemicals such as lead may also cause the condition. A common form of optic neuritis, retrobulbar neuritis, is associated with development of multiple sclerosis (MS), especially in women.

Optic neuritis affects individuals between 20 and 40 years old. More than 75% of those affected are women, and 85% are white. From 1 to 6 new cases of optic neuritis per 100,000 occur annually in the US. A recent study found that about 30% of individuals with optic neuritis are at risk of developing MS within 5 years of diagnosis.

Diagnosis

History: Individuals may complain of eye pain that worsens with movement. Eyes may be tender when touched. Visual defects occurring over the first few hours gradually increase during the next several days. Blind gaps in vision (scotomas) are commonly reported visual defects. Individuals may also report loss of color perception. Vision loss usually occurs during a period of several days, and may be mild or significant.

Physical exam: On examination, pupil response to light may be slowed. Upon ophthalmoscopic examination, the optic nerve may at first appear normal. Follow-up exams may reveal that the edge of the optic disc has become blurry and, finally, swollen as the disease progresses. Small areas of bleeding (hemorrhages) near the optic nerve may be detected. In retrobulbar neuritis, the nerve inflammation occurs far enough behind the point in the retina where the optic nerve enters the eyeball (optic disc) that early changes are not evident even upon examination using an illuminated instrument that magnifies the eye's interior (ophthalmoscopy).

Tests: Vision tests may include evaluation of visual acuity and of total visual field. With the high prevalence of MS associated with optic neuritis, a measurement of anatomical structures (magnetic resonance imaging) may be performed to identify white lesions associated with loss of the optic nerve's protective sheath of fatty tissue (demyelination). This evidence is a strong indicator of MS.

Treatment

Anti-inflammatory drugs (steroids) may be given intravenously. Although treatment with steroids may aid the return of vision, they seem to have little effect on the long-term outcome of the inflammatory process. Recent studies indicate that use of oral steroids alone increases the risk that optic neuritis will recur.

A form of optic neuritis found in the portion of the optic nerve behind the eyeball (retrobulbar neuritis), commonly associated with development of MS, generally resolves on its own or with early administration of intravenous steroids. Studies are now being conducted to determine if treatment with interferon will reduce risk of developing MS after diagnosis of optic neuritis.

Prognosis

Simple optic neuritis usually resolves without treatment within 1-3 months. Full recovery occurs in 65% of all cases. Some cases, however, result in small vision defects. Other cases progress into wasting or degeneration of the optic nerve (optic atrophy) and may result in permanent blindness. Each recurrence produces further visual loss, and may eventually lead to optic nerve atrophy that results in permanent blindness. If caused by poor circulation, optic neuritis will often not improve. Optic neuritis could indicate that MS will develop within 5 years. However, MS that develops in association with optic neuritis usually is a milder form.

Differential Diagnosis

Conditions with similar symptoms or that might produce optic neuritis include papilledema, lupus erythematosus, sinusitis, toxic amblyopia, multiple sclerosis, Leber's Hereditary Optic Neuropathy (LHON), optic atrophy, diabetes mellitus, vitamin B deficiency, glaucoma, tumor, age-related macular degeneration, trauma to the optic nerve, retinitis, thyroiditis, Tay-Sachs disease, neurological disorders, osteitis deformans, and aneurysm.

Specialists

- Neurologist
- Ophthalmologist

Work Restrictions / Accommodations

During a recovery period that may last several months, the individual with vision defects may be unable to perform tasks requiring keen visual acuity. Permanent vision loss may require accommodation such as larger and high-contrast print. Significant increase in illumination may be required at work stations. If vision loss is permanent, the individual may require reassignment to different tasks that do not require keen visual acuity.

Complementary and Alternative Therapies

Content is intended for awareness only. Treatments may or may not be effective. Scientific evidence may be lacking and some substances have potentially toxic effects. Dr. Presley Reed and the editors do not endorse the use of these therapies in the absence of consultation with a licensed medical professional.

Vitamin B -	May assist in nerve regeneration.
Chinese acupuncture -	May improve nerve conduction.
Electrical stimulation -	Stimulation to the spinal cord may improve nerve conduction.

Comorbid Conditions

A rare disorder called Devic disease may cause loss of fatty tissue around the optic nerve, leading to optic neuritis, and creating a poor prognosis for recovery from the condition. Sjögren's syndrome, causing dry eyes, may also cause and lengthen symptoms of optic neuritis.

Complications

Use of oral steroids may cause the condition to recur, thus increasing chances of permanent vision loss. In severe cases, inflammation may spread to a large portion of the optic nerve to temporarily cause complete blindness. Neuromyelitis optica, a complication of MS, involves deterioration of both optic nerves and the spinal cord.

Factors Influencing Duration

Length of disability may be influenced by the severity of symptoms, the underlying cause of the inflammation, response to treatment, and the extent of temporary or permanent visual impairment. If MS is the cause of the symptom, long-term or permanent disability is possible.

Length of Disability

If the individual experiences permanent vision loss, even mild disability may require reassignment if job tasks require keen visual acuity and color perception.

Failure to Recover

If an individual fails to recover within the maximum duration expectancy period, the reader may wish to reference the following questions to assist in better understanding the specifics of an individual's medical case.

Regarding diagnosis:

- Has diagnosis of optic neuritis been confirmed?
- Has the individual experienced any complications?
- Does individual have an underlying condition that may impact recovery?

Regarding treatment:

- Did treatment involve just oral steroids, or were they given in combination with IV steroids?
- Is current condition an initial episode or a recurrence of optic neuritis?
- Has the individual been tested for the presence of multiple sclerosis?
- Have IV steroids administration helped to resolve retrobulbar neuritis?

Regarding prognosis:

- Has the individual's vision loss failed to resolve, continuing beyond a period of several months?
- Does diagnosis need to be revisited?
- Is current condition an initial episode or a recurrence of optic neuritis?
- Did treatment include IV steroids?

References

Graham, Ken, and Joseph Rizzo. "A Review of Optic Neuritis." Digital Journal of Ophthalmology (1995): 5. 1 Jan 2001 <http://www.djo.harvard.edu>.

Huang, S.Y., and Y.C. Zeng. "Clinical Observation on Treatment of Disorders of the Optic Nerve by Acupuncture." Journal of Traditional Chinese Medicine 5 3 (1985): 187-190.

Optic Neuritis
377.3, 377.30, 377.32, 377.39

Definition

Optic neuritis is an inflammation of the optic nerve causing sudden loss of a portion of central vision, sometimes accompanied by painful eye movements.

Various diseases may cause the condition, especially those such as multiple sclerosis (MS) associated with loss of the optic nerve's protective fatty tissue (myelin) sheath. Viral infections, sinus infections, or inflammation located elsewhere in the body may cause the condition. Other causes of optic neuritis are decreased blood supply or injury to the optic nerve, tumors, cancer, and nutritional and metabolic disorders. Exposure to toxic chemicals such as lead may also cause the condition. A common form of optic neuritis, retrobulbar neuritis, is associated with development of multiple sclerosis (MS), especially in women.

Optic neuritis affects individuals between 20 and 40 years old. More than 75% of those affected are women, and 85% are white. From 1 to 6 new cases of optic neuritis per 100,000 occur annually in the US. A recent study found that about 30% of individuals with optic neuritis are at risk of developing MS within 5 years of diagnosis.

Diagnosis

History: Individuals may complain of eye pain that worsens with movement. Eyes may be tender when touched. Visual defects occurring over the first few hours gradually increase during the next several days. Blind gaps in vision (scotomas) are commonly reported visual defects. Individuals may also report loss of color perception. Vision loss usually occurs during a period of several days, and may be mild or significant.

Physical exam: On examination, pupil response to light may be slowed. Upon ophthalmoscopic examination, the optic nerve may at first appear normal. Follow-up exams may reveal that the edge of the optic disc has become blurry and, finally, swollen as the disease progresses. Small areas of bleeding (hemorrhages) near the optic nerve may be detected. In retrobulbar neuritis, the nerve inflammation occurs far enough behind the point in the retina where the optic nerve enters the eyeball (optic disc) that early changes are not evident even upon examination using an illuminated instrument that magnifies the eye's interior (ophthalmoscopy).

Tests: Vision tests may include evaluation of visual acuity and of total visual field. With the high prevalence of MS associated with optic neuritis, a measurement of anatomical structures (magnetic resonance imaging) may be performed to identify white lesions associated with loss of the optic nerve's protective sheath of fatty tissue (demyelination). This evidence is a strong indicator of MS.

Treatment

Anti-inflammatory drugs (steroids) may be given intravenously. Although treatment with steroids may aid the return of vision, they seem to have little effect on the long-term outcome of the inflammatory process. Recent studies indicate that use of oral steroids alone increases the risk that optic neuritis will recur.

A form of optic neuritis found in the portion of the optic nerve behind the eyeball (retrobulbar neuritis), commonly associated with development of MS, generally resolves on its own or with early administration of intravenous steroids. Studies are now being conducted to determine if treatment with interferon will reduce risk of developing MS after diagnosis of optic neuritis.

Prognosis

Simple optic neuritis usually resolves without treatment within 1-3 months. Full recovery occurs in 65% of all cases. Some cases, however, result in small vision defects. Other cases progress into wasting or degeneration of the optic nerve (optic atrophy) and may result in permanent blindness. Each recurrence produces further visual loss, and may eventually lead to optic nerve atrophy that results in permanent blindness. If caused by poor circulation, optic neuritis will often not improve. Optic neuritis could indicate that MS will develop within 5 years. However, MS that develops in association with optic neuritis usually is a milder form.

Differential Diagnosis

Conditions with similar symptoms or that might produce optic neuritis include papilledema, lupus erythematosus, sinusitis, toxic amblyopia, multiple sclerosis, Leber's Hereditary Optic Neuropathy (LHON), optic atrophy, diabetes mellitus, vitamin B deficiency, glaucoma, tumor, age-related macular degeneration, trauma to the optic nerve, retinitis, thyroiditis, Tay-Sachs disease, neurological disorders, osteitis deformans, and aneurysm.

Specialists

- Neurologist
- Ophthalmologist

Work Restrictions / Accommodations

During a recovery period that may last several months, the individual with vision defects may be unable to perform tasks requiring keen visual acuity. Permanent vision loss may require accommodation such as larger and high-contrast print. Significant increase in illumination may be required at work stations. If vision loss is permanent, the individual may require reassignment to different tasks that do not require keen visual acuity.

Complementary and Alternative Therapies

Content is intended for awareness only. Treatments may or may not be effective. Scientific evidence may be lacking and some substances have potentially toxic effects. Dr. Presley Reed and the editors do not endorse the use of these therapies in the absence of consultation with a licensed medical professional.

Vitamin B -	May assist in nerve regeneration.
Chinese acupuncture -	May improve nerve conduction.
Electrical stimulation -	Stimulation to the spinal cord may improve nerve conduction.

Comorbid Conditions

A rare disorder called Devic disease may cause loss of fatty tissue around the optic nerve, leading to optic neuritis, and creating a poor prognosis for recovery from the condition. Sjögren's syndrome, causing dry eyes, may also cause and lengthen symptoms of optic neuritis.

Complications

Use of oral steroids may cause the condition to recur, thus increasing chances of permanent vision loss. In severe cases, inflammation may spread to a large portion of the optic nerve to temporarily cause complete blindness. Neuromyelitis optica, a complication of MS, involves deterioration of both optic nerves and the spinal cord.

Factors Influencing Duration

Length of disability may be influenced by the severity of symptoms, the underlying cause of the inflammation, response to treatment, and the extent of temporary or permanent visual impairment. If MS is the cause of the symptom, long-term or permanent disability is possible.

Length of Disability

If the individual experiences permanent vision loss, even mild disability may require reassignment if job tasks require keen visual acuity and color perception.

Failure to Recover

If an individual fails to recover within the maximum duration expectancy period, the reader may wish to reference the following questions to assist in better understanding the specifics of an individual's medical case.

Regarding diagnosis:

- Has diagnosis of optic neuritis been confirmed?
- Has the individual experienced any complications?
- Does individual have an underlying condition that may impact recovery?

Regarding treatment:

- Did treatment involve just oral steroids, or were they given in combination with IV steroids?
- Is current condition an initial episode or a recurrence of optic neuritis?
- Has the individual been tested for the presence of multiple sclerosis?
- Have IV steroids administration helped to resolve retrobulbar neuritis?

Regarding prognosis:

- Has the individual's vision loss failed to resolve, continuing beyond a period of several months?
- Does diagnosis need to be revisited?
- Is current condition an initial episode or a recurrence of optic neuritis?
- Did treatment include IV steroids?

References

Graham, Ken, and Joseph Rizzo. "A Review of Optic Neuritis." Digital Journal of Ophthalmology (1995): 5. 1 Jan 2001 <http://www.djo.harvard.edu>.

Huang, S.Y., and Y.C. Zeng. "Clinical Observation on Treatment of Disorders of the Optic Nerve by Acupuncture." Journal of Traditional Chinese Medicine 5 3 (1985): 187-190.

Orchiectomy

Other names / synonyms: Castration, Excision of Testis, Gonadectomy, Male Castration, Orchidectomy

62.8

Definition

Orchiectomy is the surgical removal of one or both testicles.

Removal of one or both testicles may be necessary due to illness (tumor of the testicle or prostate), injury (twisting of the testicle), or developmental problems such as an undescended testicle.

The average annual incidence of prostate cancer in the US is approximately 23 cases per 100,000 men under age 65 and 884 cases per 100,000 men age 65 and older. Testicular cancer occurs in 4.2 per 100,000 males. Torsion (twisting of the testicle) most frequently occurs in males age 25 or younger with incidence in this population of approximately 1 to 4,000. Undescended testicles (cryptorchidism) occurs in about 3% of the male population.

Reason for Procedure

One testicle may be removed (unilateral orchiectomy) if a tumor of the testicle is present, the testicle is twisted (torsion), or it is undescended (cryptorchidism).

Removal of both testicles (bilateral orchiectomy) may be necessary for the treatment of prostate cancer.

Because prostate cancer depends on male sex hormones for its growth, orchiectomy is often effective in reducing the growth of prostate cancer (androgen ablation). In the same manner, orchiectomy may also be effective in controlling the symptoms of secondary tumors that have spread (metastasized) to the bones. A bilateral orchiectomy may be performed for the treatment of major trauma (e.g., gunshot wound to the scrotum).

Description

The procedure is performed under either spinal, epidural, or general anesthesia as mutually agreed upon by individual and physician. An incision is made into either the inguinal area or the scrotum. The blood vessels and nerves leading to the testicle are located, isolated, and cut free. The testicle is then excised from the surrounding soft tissue and removed. The skin is then closed with absorbable sutures.

An ice pack is applied to the affected area as needed to prevent excessive swelling (edema) for the first 24 hours postoperatively. A heating pad, heat lamp, or warm compresses may help relieve incisional pain beginning 24 hours after surgery.

Prognosis

Individuals should expect complete healing from the procedure without complications. Three weeks should be allowed for complete healing.

Specialists

- General Surgeon
- Urologist
- Oncologist

Work Restrictions / Accommodations

To assist recovery and aid the individual's well-being, daily activities including work should be resumed as soon as possible. Lifting and strenuous activity may need to be restricted for up to 6 weeks. Temporary transfer to sedentary duties may be required. Driving should be avoided until 2 weeks after surgery.

Comorbid Conditions

Existing conditions that may impact ability to recover and further lengthen disability include cancers of the genitourinary system and chronic urinary tract infections.

Procedure Complications

Complications are rarely a problem but may include wound infection, inguinal skin numbness from injury to the genitofemoral nerve, collection of blood in the incisional area (hematoma), and standard anesthetic risks.

Factors Influencing Duration

Length of disability may be influenced by the underlying condition for which the procedure was done, age of individual, or any complications.

Length of Disability

Duration in Days

Job Classification	Minimum	Optimum	Maximum
Sedentary work	3	7	14
Light work	3	7	21
Medium work	7	14	21
Heavy work	7	14	21
Very Heavy work	7	14	21

References

Kinkade, Scott. "Testicular Cancer." American Family Physicians. 01 May 1999. 05 Jan 2001 <http://www.aafp.org/afp/990501ap/2539.html>.

Orchiectomy. Health Square. 2000. 12 Jan 2001 <http://www.healthsquare.com/mc/fgmc0817.htm>.

Prostate Cancer: FAQs. CoMed Communications, Inc. 11 Jul 1995. 05 Jan 2001 <http://www.comed.com/Prostate/Faqs.html#PhysIncidence>.

Testicle Removal (Orchiectomy). HealthGate Data Group. 23 Feb 2000. 12 Jan 2001 <http://www.healthgate.com/choice/uic/cons/mdx-books/sym/surg152.shtml>.

Orchitis

Other names / synonyms: Inflammation of the Testis, Testicular Inflammation

604.0

Definition

Orchitis is the inflammation of one or both of the testicles. If the sperm ducts (epididymis) are also involved, the condition is called epididymoorchitis.

Epididymoorchitis may be caused by a bacterial infection after prostate surgery, instrument examination of the urinary tract (cystoscopy), or urinary tract infections (UTI). Less common causes of orchitis are tuberculosis, syphilis, and a condition believed to be caused by the body developing an autoimmune reaction to its own spermatozoa (granulomatous orchitis). Orchitis is considered a sexually transmitted disease when the organisms that cause gonorrhea or chlamydia are involved.

Mumps is the most common viral cause of orchitis. Orchitis is seen in 20-35% of men with mumps, and in 10% of cases, the condition is in both testicles (bilateral).

Diagnosis

History: Mumps orchitis occurs about 3 to 4 days after the salivary (parotid) gland swells (parotitis) as characteristically seen with mumps. The individual may report severe pain and swelling of the scrotum or a tender swollen "heavy feeling" in the testicle on the affected side, testicular pain that may be aggravated by bowel movement or straining, pain and swelling in the entire groin area on the affected side, fever, chills, nausea, vomiting, pain with intercourse or ejaculation, and profound weakness. Bacterial epididymoorchitis has similar symptoms but is preceded by a history of surgery, infection, or instrument examinations. The swelling is rapid and either one (unilateral) or both (bilateral) of the testicles may double in size in 3 to 4 hours. Individuals may also report symptoms of painful urination (dysuria), a discharge from the penis, blood in the semen, and cloudy urine (pyuria).

Physical exam: Fever associated with mumps orchitis and bacterial epididymoorchitis may be very high. The testicle and scrotal sac is swollen, warm, tender to the touch, and the scrotal skin may appear reddish. Often the sperm ducts (epididymis) and testes cannot be distinguished by palpation because of glandular enlargement. A pocket of fluid (hydrocele) may form within the scrotum. Lymph nodes in the groin area (inguinal) may be tender and enlarged on the affected side. Rectal exam may reveal an enlarged and/or tender prostate gland.

Tests: A microscopic urine test (urinalysis) and urine culture (clean catch) should be done if infection of the urinary tract is suspected. Blood chemistries, and a complete blood count (CBC) to check for elevation of white blood cells (leukocytosis) may also be done. Tests for chlamydia and gonorrhea should be done.

Treatment

Bed rest is necessary during the acute phase. Scrotal elevation for support and ice pack applications may provide some symptomatic relief. Pain medication (analgesics) may be taken. A local anesthetic may be injected into the spermatic cord in cases of severe pain that is unrelieved by other methods. Antibiotics should be given if the inflammation is due to a bacterial infection while corticosteroids are usually prescribed for granulomatous orchitis. Because it is a viral infection, antibiotics are of no value in mumps orchitis. In the case of gonorrhea or chlamydia, sexual partners must also be treated.

Surgery to remove one or both testicles (orchidectomy) may be necessary if the swelling is severe enough to compromise blood circulation.

Application of ice to the swollen scrotum aids healing in the early phase of the condition. Afterward, local heat may afford comfort to the inflamed area. Support of the testicles using a towel placed under the scrotum or an athletic supporter may be helpful.

Prognosis

Complete recovery from orchitis is expected within about a week. However, bilateral orchitis may result in irreversible damage to the testicles and their ability to produce sperm, resulting in sterility. Permanent testicular atrophy may develop within several months to several years after mumps orchitis. If orchidectomy is necessary, the individual will be sterile and hormonal supplementation to replace the male sex hormone (testosterone replacement therapy) is required.

Differential Diagnosis

The later stages of epididymitis and torsion of the spermatic cord may have symptoms similar to those of orchitis. Granulomatous orchitis is easily confused with testicular tumors. Bleeding (hemorrhage) into the testicles as a result of minor trauma may also be confused with orchitis.

Specialists

- Fertility Specialist
- Urologist

Work Restrictions / Accommodations

Heavy lifting or other physical activities should be restricted at work until recovery is complete.

Comorbid Conditions

Untreated syphilis may further lengthen the disability.

Complications

In most cases, mumps orchitis causes shrinkage (atrophy) of the testicles. This results in a decreased ability to produce sperm. In about 30% of testicles with orchitis, there is a low sperm count and possible sterility. Fever and scrotal pain after the acute illness phase may indicate the development of a scrotal abscess that will require hospitalization and possible surgical drainage. In rare cases, bacterial epididymoorchitis may progress to tissue death (gangrene) in men over 50.

Factors Influencing Duration

The underlying cause of the disease, individual's response to treatment, job requirements, age, and severity of the inflammation all contribute to the length of disability. Complications and surgery prolong the period of disability.

Length of Disability

Approximately one week of bed rest is required in the acute phase of orchitis.

Duration in Days

Job Classification	Minimum	Optimum	Maximum
Sedentary work	3	7	14
Light work	3	7	14
Medium work	7	14	21
Heavy work	14	17	21
Very Heavy work	14	17	21

Failure to Recover

If an individual fails to recover within the maximum duration expectancy period, the reader may wish to reference the following questions to assist in better understanding the specifics of an individual's medical case.

Regarding diagnosis:

- Does individual have severe pain and swelling of the scrotum or a tender swollen "heavy feeling" in the testicle on the affected side, testicular pain that may be aggravated by bowel movement or straining, pain and swelling in the entire groin area on the affected side, fever, chills, nausea, vomiting, pain with intercourse or ejaculation, and profound weakness?
- Does individual have a history of surgery, infection, or instrument examinations?
- Is swelling rapid? Has either one or both of the testicles doubled in size in 3 to 4 hours? Is there painful urination (dysuria), a discharge from the penis, blood in the semen, and cloudy urine (pyuria)?
- Does individual have a high fever? Is the testicle or scrotal sac warm, tender to the touch with the scrotal skin reddish in appearance? Has a pocket of fluid (hydrocele) formed within the scrotum? Does rectal exam reveal an enlarged and/or tender prostate gland?
- Was a microscopic urine test (urinalysis) and urine culture (clean catch) done if infection is suspected? Were blood tests done to check for elevation of white blood cells (leukocytosis)? Tests for chlamydia and gonorrhea?
- Was the diagnosis of orchitis confirmed? Were tumor or torsion ruled out?

Regarding treatment:

- Has individual received appropriate drug therapy?
- Were measures such as bed rest, analgesics, heat, or support for the scrotum effective in providing relief of symptoms?
- Was surgery required? If an orchidectomy was necessary, is individual on hormonal replacement therapy?

Regarding prognosis:

- Has the individual adhered to the prescribed drug therapy, bed rest, and avoidance of physical exertion for an appropriate period of time?
- Does individual understand the possibility of sterility? Would counseling be beneficial? Were underlying conditions identified and appropriately treated?

References

Holtgrewe, H. Logan. "Transurethral Resection of the Prostate." Prostatic Diseases. Lepor, Herbert, ed. Philadelphia: W.B. Saunders Company, 2000. 232-245.

Nistal, M., and R. Paniagua. Testicular and Epididymal Pathology. New York: Thieme-Stratton Inc, 1984.

Organic Psychosis

Other names / synonyms: Delirium, Metabolic Encephalopathy, Organic Brain Syndrome, Organic Brain Syndrome with Psychotic Features, Organic Mental Syndrome, Organic Psychosis, Senile Organic Psychosis

290, 290.1, 291, 291.0, 291.2, 291.3, 291.4, 291.9, 292, 293, 294, 294.0, 294.9

Definition

Organic psychosis refers to a wide group of psychological and behavioral abnormalities thought to be secondary to a disturbance in brain structure or function although the specific cause is unknown. It was formerly known as organic brain syndrome. These abnormalities in brain function may be temporary or permanent. An organic cause is suspected when there is no indication of a clearly defined psychiatric or "inorganic" cause such as a mood disorder. However, as more is understood about derangement in the brain chemistry underlying psychiatric disorders, the distinction between organic and inorganic processes has become increasingly unclear.

The syndrome can appear as delirium and dementia with major impairment of intellectual functions such as orientation, memory, thinking, and speech. There may be loss of memory (amnesia), hearing voices or seeing visions (hallucinations), fixed but untrue beliefs (delusions), or mood and personality changes. Judgment and impulse control are altered. Restlessness, sluggishness, or groping, unproductive movements may also occur. Fearfulness is a common emotional disturbance in this disorder and can lead to running away or aggressive behavior. Sleep is usually disturbed with insomnia, drowsiness, or stupor. In all cases, impairment of social and occupational functioning is severe.

Organic brain syndromes can occur at any age.

Diagnosis

History: Individual may have a history of a major disturbance in thinking, emotions, behavior, and/or level of consciousness. Observation of the individual's orientation, dress, mannerisms, behavior, and content of speech provide essential signs for diagnosing this illness.

Physical exam: The exam may reveal decreased level of consciousness, stupor, agitation, restlessness, responding to hallucinations, or neurological abnormalities such as tremor or other abnormal movement pattern.

Tests: To rule out more specific causes of these findings, tests are done including blood chemistries and cell count, drug and alcohol screen, brain CT or MRI, toxicological screen, electroencephalogram (EEG), and spinal tap (lumbar puncture), if indicated. These tests are negative or nondiagnostic in unspecified organic psychosis. Experimental studies looking at brain function such as PET or SPECT scans are considered more of a research tool than help in diagnosing this syndrome.

Treatment

Once specific, treatable causes are ruled out, treatment is directed at maintaining safety for the individual and for others. It can involve antipsychotic, antianxiety, or antidepressant medication and confinement. Observation and testing, if indicated, should continue in hopes of clarifying the diagnosis and lead to more specific treatment. When dementia (disturbances in thinking and memory) is prominent, cholinergic agonists should be considered. In central nervous system disease, aggressiveness and rage states can be reduced with lipophilic beta-blockers.

Visiting nurses, homemakers, and adult protective services may be helpful in maintaining the individual at home. Counseling may help the family cope with problems involved in keeping the individual at home as long as possible. When family is no longer able to care for the individual, substitute home care, board and care, or convalescent home care may be helpful. Setting should include familiar people and objects, light at night, and a simple schedule.

Prognosis

The course and outcome are extremely variable. There can be lucid intervals between disturbances. If the cause is transient such as unsuspected drug overdose or withdrawal, the disorder will totally clear within a few days. If it is caused by a progressive condition such as Alzheimer's disease, the individual never recovers. Efforts to clarify the diagnosis should be ongoing as a specific diagnosis will help predict the outcome and may even lead to treatment that could improve or reverse the condition.

Differential Diagnosis

Other psychiatric conditions that may resemble organic psychosis include schizophrenia, major depression, manic episode, or malingering. Other neurological conditions with some features suggesting organic psychosis include dementia of the Alzheimer's type or other degenerative dementia, delirium, metabolic encephalopathy secondary to drug or alcohol abuse, derangement in blood chemistries or hormonal levels, infection such as meningitis or encephalitis, widespread inflammation of blood vessels in the brain (cerebral vasculitis), or spread of tumor cells into the cerebrospinal fluid bathing the brain (carcinomatous meningitis).

Specialists

- Endocrinologist
- Internist
- Neurologist
- Psychiatrist
- Psychologist

Work Restrictions / Accommodations

It is unlikely that the individual with organic brain syndrome is able to maintain competitive employment.

Comorbid Conditions

Current alcohol abuse or drug use or the presence of a personality disorder may lengthen disability.

Complications

The individual may become injured falling out of bed, wander, get lost, or be unable to take care of basic nutritional and hygienic needs. Other possible complications include susceptibility to infections, severe depression, suicide, or injury to others.

Factors Influencing Duration

Discovery of an underlying, treatable cause may lead to improvement or recovery.

Length of Disability

Duration depends on the underlying cause and the individual's response to treatment. Duration assumes this condition is not permanent.

Alcoholic, drug, or transient organic psychosis.

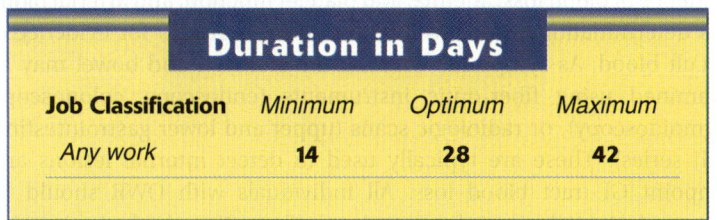

Job Classification	Minimum	Optimum	Maximum
Any work	14	28	42

Failure to Recover

If an individual fails to recover within the maximum duration expectancy period, the reader may wish to reference the following questions to assist in better understanding the specifics of an individual's medical case.

Regarding diagnosis:

- Has diagnosis of organic psychosis been confirmed?
- Did evaluation include a comprehensive physical examination (including a search for neurologic abnormalities, infection, or hypoxia), laboratory tests (including a toxicologic screen), and a lumbar puncture for cerebrospinal fluid analysis?
- Did diagnostic tests include electroencephalography, CT, MRI, PET, and SPECT?
- Has organic psychosis, which is caused by structural brain changes, been differentiated from functional psychiatric illness?

Regarding treatment:

- Has a primary brain disease or underlying medical disorder been identified?
- Is the individual receiving appropriate treatment to resolve or control underlying condition(s)?
- Has the physician explored the option of using drugs to increase cholinergic activity?
- If condition is due to a central nervous system disease, would the individual benefit from the use of lipophilic beta-blockers to reduce aggressiveness and rage?
- Is the individual receiving proper care in an appropriate setting?
- Has the family received the counseling and support necessary to cope with problems involved in keeping the individual at home for as long as possible?
- As the family becomes unable to care for individual, have appropriate arrangements been made for substitute home care, board and care, or convalescent home care?

Regarding prognosis:

- Has the individual responded to treatment of underlying medical condition?
- If underlying condition was reversible, to what extent has mental functioning been recovered?
- Because medication (particularly sedatives) may further impair thinking abilities and contribute to overall problems, could unnecessary medications be discontinued?
- Have impulsive behavior, poor judgment, and deterioration in the total behavior of the individual made major rearrangement of lifestyle necessary?
- What input has the physician given individual and family in this regard?
- Does individual exhibit both the organic effects due to brain damage and psychological reactions to the deficits?
- Do impulsive behavior, depression, and suicide attempts pose a threat to individual's safety? Would individual benefit from closer observation, monitoring, or confinement?

References

Purdie, F.R., B. Honigman, and P. Rosen. "Acute Organic Brain Syndrome: A Review of 100 Cases." Annals of Emergency Medicine 10 9 (1981): 455-461.

Tierney, L.M. Jr., S.J. McPhee, and M.A. Papadakis. Current Medical Diagnosis and Treatment. Stamford: Appleton & Lange, 1997.

Osler-Weber-Rendu Disease

Other names / synonyms: Familial Hemorrhagic Telangiectasia, Hereditary Hemorrhagic Telangiectasia, Osler-Rendu Disease, Osler-Weber-Rendu Syndrome

448.0

Definition

Osler-Weber-Rendu Syndrome (OWR), also called hereditary hemorrhagic telangiectasia (HHT), is an inherited circulation disorder. This disease involves the wide distribution throughout the cardiovascular system of permanently dilated small blood vessels (telangiectasia) that cause focal red lesions usually in the skin or mucous membranes; defects that affect both the arteries and veins (arteriovenous malformations); and sacs that are formed by dilated artery or vein walls (aneurysms).

The disorder impedes the development of tiny capillaries which route arterial blood into the veins for its trip back to the heart in a small percentage of the blood vessels. Instead, the affected arteries connect directly to the veins. Because of the difference in arterial and venous blood pressure, ruptures tend to occur where the arteries and veins join, resulting in bleeding into the skin, mucous membranes, or internal organs. In the 19th century, the condition was usually mistaken for a bleeding (blood clotting) disorder similar to hemophilia.

OWR occurs in about 1-2 in 10,000 individuals, affecting all racial and ethnic groups and both sexes. It is a genetic (chromosomal) disorder. Some cases are so mild that they may never be diagnosed; about 20% of cases occur in individuals with no known family history. Symptoms of the disorder often first appear in childhood as recurrent nosebleeds due to ruptures in the mucous membranes that result in bleeding. Red lesions on the skin (telangiectasia) eventually appear on almost all affected individuals, usually first becoming evident between the ages of 30 to 40 years.

Neurologic complications have been observed in 8-12% of reported cases; approximately 15% have pulmonary A-V fistulas. Longevity is not inevitably reduced among those with OWR, nor is the quality of life necessarily impaired. Fewer than 10% ultimately die of complications directly attributable to the trait.

Diagnosis

History: OWR is usually recognized as a triad, including red lesions on the skin or mucous membranes (telangiectasia), recurrent nosebleeds (epistaxis), and a family history of the disorder. However, because of the variability in location, type, and number of randomly distributed vascular formations, the affected person may be asymptomatic, or present at any age with a wide range of clinical manifestations. It is most often initially diagnosed when an individual complains of frequent nosebleeds. The individual may also have begun to notice telangiectasias characteristic of the disorder, although often this does not develop until much later. Occasionally, the individual may report spitting up blood, or black or bloody stools, indicating internal bleeding. The individual may also report recurrent hemorrhaging precipitated by spontaneous or minor trauma.

Physical exam: The exam reveals small red to violet lesions (telangiectasia) most often visible on the ears, scalp, hands, arms, feet, face, and under the nails. These lesions bleed easily, may be flat or raised, and turn white (blanch) on pressure. Spider-like lesions may appear sometime after age thirty.

Tests: Diagnostic tests should include complete blood count (CBC) for evidence of blood loss, anemia, and platelet function, and arterial blood gas determinations; stools will be tested (Hemoccult) for evidence of occult blood. As symptoms warrant, the stomach and bowel may be examined using fiber-optic instruments (endoscopy, colonoscopy, sigmoidoscopy), or radiologic scans (upper and lower gastrointestinal [GI] series). These are typically used to detect internal lesions and pinpoint GI tract blood loss. All individuals with OWR should be screened upon diagnosis for vascular malformations in the brain using magnetic resonance imaging (MRI). In addition, the individual should be screened for lung circulatory abnormalities (pulmonary A-V fistula); this should include at least one heart/lung screening using ultrasound (echocardiography), chest x-ray, or CT. Brain and lung screenings are important because complications in these areas can cause serious damage without any warning.

Treatment

Aspirin and other medications that impair the ability of blood to stop bleeding (hemostasis) are contraindicated. Visible and/or accessible lesions are treated with local applications of pressure and topical vasoconstricting agents to stop bleeding (hemostatics). They may also be treated with laser coagulation therapy. Individuals should be protected from trauma and unnecessary bleeding. Individuals should be instructed how to treat minor bleeding episodes, and how to recognize major episodes that require immediate medical treatment. The frequency of nosebleeds may be reduced by using a home humidifier and lubricating the lining of the nose. If this is not effective, laser therapy generally gives good results with less risk of damage to the lining of the nose than electric or chemical cautery. For intractable cases, surgical replacement of the lining of the nose with a skin graft (septal dermoplasty) may be considered. Other surgical treatments include cryosurgery, arterial ligation, irradiation, and subcutaneous resection.

Gastrointestinal bleeding is generally not treated unless it is copious enough to cause iron deficiency in the blood (anemia). In such cases, oral or injectable iron or folate supplements are prescribed. If iron supplementation does not correct the anemia, it may be necessary to deal with the GI bleeding directly using endoscopic laser therapy. Hormone therapy with oral estrogen-progesterone combination medications has also been helpful in some individuals.

Vascular abnormalities detected in the lungs or brain should be treated before they cause problems. Depending upon their size, structure, and location of the vessel in question, the vessel may need to be blocked off (embolization) by inserting a catheter through the groin, surgically excising the abnormality, or using targeted radiation (stereotactic radiosurgery).

Periodic blood transfusions may be necessary to restore blood volume in cases of acute hemorrhage; these individuals should receive hepatitis B vaccine as a precaution.

Prognosis

This is a lifelong condition. With proper management, individuals should experience only periodic periods of disability related to specific bleeding episodes or the development of complications. The disease is generally manageable with proper medical treatment and regular follow-up. Longevity is not necessarily reduced, nor quality of life necessarily impaired. About 10% of individuals with OWR are believed to die of complications related to the disease.

Differential Diagnosis

Other diagnoses with similar symptoms may include scleroderma, purpura, Ehlers-Danlos syndrome, autoerythrocyte sensitization, petechiae, scurvy, gastrointestinal ulcer or tumor, and bone marrow disorder.

Specialists

- Cardiologist
- Dermatologist
- Gastroenterologist
- Hematologist
- Hepatologist
- Internist
- Neurologist

Work Restrictions / Accommodations

In mild cases, no work accommodations may be necessary. If the individual is having trouble with nosebleeds, or subcutaneous bleeding, assignment to sedentary duties where there is little associated chance of trauma may be appropriate. Work accommodations may also include frequent rest periods to relieve extreme fatigue related to iron-deficiency anemia. If the individual is experiencing this complication and works in an occupation generally associated with high stress and long hours, such as a surgeon or physician's assistant, a part-time schedule or other accommodations may be required in order to allow the individual to continue to work.

Comorbid Conditions

Comorbid conditions include clotting disorders, arteriosclerosis, or other disorders requiring blood thinners.

Complications

Complications that may be associated with this condition include anemia from gastrointestinal bleeding, lung hemorrhage, hemorrhage in the brain (hemorrhagic stroke), cerebral abscess or embolism, and enlarged liver (hepatomegaly). Bluish skin coloring (cyanosis), shortness of breath upon exertion, and clubbed fingers result from oxygen deficiency due to vascular abnormalities in the lungs.

Factors Influencing Duration

Factors include the frequency and severity of blood loss, the degree of internal lesions and bleeding, the effect on the individual's outward appearance, and the development of complications.

Length of Disability

Duration of disability depends on job requirements. In the case of a particularly strenuous job where the individual cannot be adequately protected from trauma, disability may be permanent.

Duration in Days

Job Classification	Minimum	Optimum	Maximum
Sedentary work	3	5	10
Light work	3	5	10
Medium work	3	5	10
Heavy work	5	7	15
Very Heavy work	5	7	15

Failure to Recover

If an individual fails to recover within the maximum duration expectancy period, the reader may wish to reference the following questions to assist in better understanding the specifics of an individual's medical case.

Regarding diagnosis:

- Has the individual had any neurological complications? Pulmonary complications? Does the individual have the "triad" (red lesions on the skin or mucous membranes, recurrent nosebleeds, and a family history of the disorder)?
- Was telangiectasia present on physical exam?
- Has the individual had the appropriate blood tests?
- Has the individual's stool been tested for occult blood?
- Were the stomach and bowel appropriately examined?
- Has the individual been screened for brain and lung complications?
- Have conditions with similar symptoms been ruled out?

Regarding treatment:

- Does the individual avoid the use of aspirin and other medications that impair the ability of the blood to clot?
- Is it time to consider more aggressive treatment?
- Has the individual been instructed on ways to prevent some symptoms (avoiding trauma, using a humidifier, lubricating nostrils)?
- Has the individual been instructed how to treat minor bleeding episodes and how to recognize major episodes that require immediate medical treatment?
- Is the individual experiencing anemia from gastrointestinal bleeding?
- Is the individual receiving iron and/or folate supplements?
- Is gastrointestinal bleeding under control, or are more aggressive treatments such as endoscopic laser required?

- Have the vascular abnormalities in the brain or lungs been treated?
- Has it been necessary for the individual to have blood transfusions?
- Have they completed the Hepatitis B vaccinations?

Regarding prognosis:
- Is the individual's employer able to accommodate any needed restrictions?
- Does the individual have any conditions such as clotting disorders, arteriosclerosis, or other disorders requiring blood thinners?
- Has the individual had any complications? To what extent?

References

Hereditary Hemorrhagic Telangiectasia. Vanderbilt Medical Center. 16 Jun 1998. 2 Jan 2001 <http://www.mc.vanderbilt.edu/peds/pidl/genetic/oslerweb.htm>.

Osteoarthritis

Other names / synonyms: Arthrosis, Atrophic Arthritis, Degenerative Joint Disease, Hypertrophic Arthritis, Osteoarthrosis

715, 715.0, 715.00, 715.1, 715.10, 715.11, 715.12, 715.13, 715.14, 715.15, 715.16, 715.17, 715.18, 715.19, 715.2, 715.20, 715.21, 715.22, 715.23, 715.24, 715.25, 715.26, 715.27, 715.28, 715.29, 715.3, 715.30, 715.31, 715.32, 715.33, 715.34, 715.35, 715.36, 715.37, 715.38, 715.39, 715.8, 715.9

Definition

Osteoarthritis is the most common joint disorder. Loss of cartilage and overgrowth of bone within the affected joint can lead to pain and joint deformity. The disease may affect one or more joints and is the primary cause of disability among adults.

Osteoarthritis usually begins with painless changes in components of the joint cartilage such as collagen and the substances that provide the cartilage's resilience (proteoglycans). As the cartilage starts to erode, particles irritate the joint lining (synovium) causing stiffness and swelling. Tiny cavities form in the bone marrow beneath the cartilage, weakening the bone. Bone overgrowths at joint edges can produce bumps (osteophytes) causing pain and interference with normal joint function. Instead of being smooth and slippery, the cartilage eventually becomes so rough and pitted that the joint no longer moves smoothly. The bone, joint capsule, tissue lining the joint (synovial tissue), tendons, and cartilage are all eventually affected.

Primary osteoarthritis affects joints without any known cause, primarily the joints of the finger, hip, knee, big toe, and the cervical and lumbar spine. The hip and knee are particularly vulnerable to osteoarthritis because of their weight-bearing function. A variation called erosive osteoarthritis affects multiple small joints of the hand, particularly in middle-aged and elderly women.

Secondary osteoarthritis occurs as the result of trauma to a joint. It can also be caused by a congenital joint disease, an infection, or by a neurologic, metabolic, or endocrine disease. Secondary osteoarthritis may affect any joint.

Osteoarthritis should not be confused with rheumatoid diseases, such as rheumatoid arthritis. Rheumatoid diseases are systemic diseases that can affect the entire body, including the joints. In contrast, osteoarthritis is limited only to the joints.

Although it is the most common joint disease, little is known about what actually causes osteoarthritis. Often thought of as an inevitable part of aging, osteoarthritis is, in fact, not caused by the simple wear and tear that occurs with aging. Risk factors for developing osteoarthritis include being overweight, participation in high impact or competitive combat sports such as football, and activities that require frequent bending or carrying heavy loads. Genetics and bone density also seem to play a role in the development of osteoarthritis.

Symptoms of osteoarthritis typically begin to appear after the age of 40 years. Although the disease is diagnosed in only 2-6% of the population, by the age of 40 most individuals have x-ray evidence of osteoarthritis.

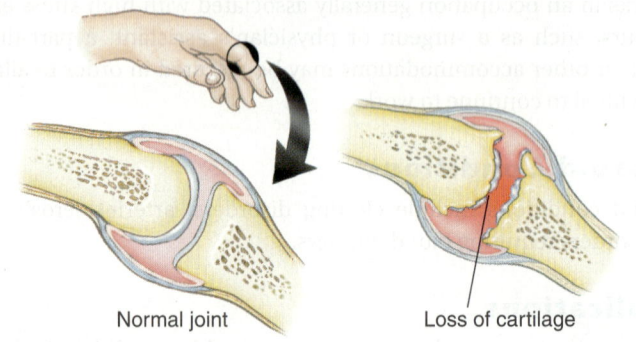

Normal joint — Loss of cartilage

Laurie O'Keefe

Diagnosis

History: Symptoms of osteoarthritis develop gradually. In the early stages, the only complaint may be morning stiffness that resolves within 30 minutes after starting activity. As the disease progresses, joints become swollen and painful. The pain worsens with increased activity and weight-bearing throughout the day, and is relieved with rest. Range of motion may be limited. Stiffness becomes more intense. Certain movements produce a grating, grinding, or catching sensation. Some joints such as the knee may become unstable due to stretching of the ligaments that surround and support the joint. The hip loses its range of motion and becomes stiffer and painful. Symptoms of osteoarthritis in the hip may sometimes be felt in the groin or the knee. Back pain is the most common symptom of osteoarthritis of the spine. When osteoarthritis occurs in the neck or lower back, bone overgrowth can press on the nerves causing pain, numbness, and weakness in an arm or leg.

Physical exam: In the early stages, few or no signs may be seen on physical examination. As the disease progresses, deformity and contractures may develop. Joints may be warm to the touch and swollen from increased synovial fluid or bone overgrowth. Nodular swellings (Heberden's or Bouchard's nodes) may be felt or seen on the fingers. Knees may bend either inward or outward or may seem flexed in a fixed state. Affected joints may be tender to the touch. Active and passive range of motion may cause pain.

Tests: X-rays of the affected joint show narrowing of the joint space, bony growths (spurs or osteophytes), bone cysts, and lipping at the joint surface. The signs visible on x-ray may not however, correlate with the individual's symptoms. For example, the x-ray signs may be severe while the individual's symptoms are mild.

Laboratory tests are done only to rule out another diagnosis. Erythrocyte sedimentation rate, complete blood count (CBC), and antinuclear antibody test are performed if an inflammatory process is suspected. Examination of joint fluid may be performed to rule out infection, gout, or rheumatoid arthritis.

Treatment

Treatment is aimed at controlling pain and inflammation while maintaining mobility. Primary treatment options include exercise and medication. The treatment plan is based on several factors and includes the extent of joint involvement, the number and sites of involved joints, the nature of the individual's pain symptoms, other health problems, the individual's age, and lifestyle issues such as occupation and typical everyday activities.

The goal of exercise in treating and managing osteoarthritis is to keep the cartilage healthy, maintain range of motion, and strengthen tendons and muscles to enable them to absorb stress placed on the joints. Exercises may include range-of-motion, strengthening (isotonic, isokinetic, and isometric), postural, and stretching exercises.

Physical therapy may also include heat treatments (warm baths, dipping the hand into hot paraffin mixed with mineral oil), massage, and traction. When the neck is affected, deep heat treatment using high-frequency current (diathermy) or ultrasound may be helpful.

Because they provide only short-term relief, drugs are the least important aspect of the total treatment plan. Pain relievers (analgesics) may be taken to reduce pain. Nonsteroidal anti-inflammatory drugs (NSAIDs) are used to reduce inflammation. In addition, local corticosteroid injection may occasionally be given to reduce inflammation. Injections of sodium hyaluronate (viscosupplementation), a natural ingredient of joint fluid, may be given to lubricate the joint. This helps reduce pain and improve function, particularly of the knee joint. COX-2 inhibitors are a group of newer drugs that reduce pain and inflammation with fewer side effects. Topical analgesic creams may also be used. Muscle relaxants may be given if muscles are strained while compensating for the affected joint.

During severe episodes, supportive devices such as canes, braces, or shoe inserts may be needed to lessen stress on the joint and assist mobility. Exercise should not be discontinued but may need to be modified during periods when supportive devices are required.

Surgical options should be considered in cases of advanced osteoarthritis or when all other treatments have failed to bring relief. Surgical cutting and realignment of bone (osteotomy) increases movement and helps redistribute weight evenly on the joint. This may be done at the knee or hip. Arthrodesis surgically fixes the joint in a permanent position. The hip or knee joint is commonly replaced with an artificial joint (arthroplasty). Joint replacement is usually very successful in improving motion and function and dramatically decreasing the pain.

Prognosis

The outcome of osteoarthritis is unpredictable. Individuals with osteoarthritis often experience periods of time when symptoms are mild and periods when they are more severe. Although the disease typically progresses, it can stabilize or even reverse.

Outcome generally depends on which joints are involved and the extent of joint degeneration. The disease may cause long-term pain and significantly limit activity, especially when knees, hips, or cervical spine is involved.

Differential Diagnosis

Rheumatoid diseases (such as rheumatoid arthritis, ankylosing spondylitis, pseudogout, and psoriatic arthritis) also involve the joints. Although the difference between rheumatoid disease and osteoarthritis is usually clear, in some cases, rheumatoid diseases must be carefully ruled out.

Other conditions that affect joints and may mimic osteoarthritis include bursitis, tendonitis, radicular spine pain, pigmented villonodular synovitis, and conditions that affect cartilage such as osteochondritis dissecans and osteochondromatosis. Conditions that affect bone (i.e., osteonecrosis, Paget's disease, and osteoporotic fractures) may cause similar symptoms. In the spine, joint pain may be caused by cancer that has spread to the spine (metastatic neoplasia), osteoporosis, multiple myeloma, and other bone diseases.

Specialists

- Occupational Therapist
- Orthopedic Surgeon
- Physiatrist
- Physical Therapist
- Rheumatologist

Rehabilitation

Individuals with osteoarthritis may require physical or occupational therapy. Therapists often instruct individuals in the use of heat to decrease joint stiffness and pain. Therapists instruct in stretching and strengthening exercises for the affected joints. Individuals learn to perform these exercises independently to help reduce impairment due to arthritis. Individuals also perform low-impact aerobic exercise such as walking or swimming to increase strength and endurance and decrease fatigue. Individuals unable to perform exercises because of pain may benefit from an aquatic therapy program in a heated pool. Aquatic exercise provides resistant exercise that reduces the stress through an individual's joints due to the buoyant properties of water.

Occupational therapy may need to address activities of daily living such as bathing and dressing. Individuals learn to conserve their joints during dressing by first laying out their clothes and then sitting down to dress. For those individuals with arthritis in the fingers, wrist, and hand, occupational therapists may order adaptive equipment such as jar-openers and elastic shoelaces that help decrease stress in these joints during daily activities.

Work Restrictions / Accommodations

Modifications may be necessary during weight-bearing activities or where a joint is overused or repetitively stressed. When hips or lower extremities are involved, limited stair climbing, squatting, and kneeling are advised. Additional rest periods may be needed. Accommodations must be made for supportive devices such as canes, braces, stools, or wheelchairs. Use of medication to control pain and swelling will require review of safety issues and drug policies. Occupational therapy referral for work area evaluation can be beneficial.

Complementary and Alternative Therapies

Content is intended for awareness only. Treatments may or may not be effective. Scientific evidence may be lacking and some substances have potentially toxic effects. Dr. Presley Reed and the editors do not endorse the use of these therapies in the absence of consultation with a licensed medical professional.

Acupuncture -	May reduce pain and restore mobility to affected joints.
Chondroitin sulfate -	May enhance repair of cartilage and minimize further degeneration. Ongoing research continues with some controversial outcomes.
Glucosamine -	May help prevent or postpone the onset of arthritis. Often used together with chondroitin sulfate.
Therapeutic touch -	May relieve tension.
Massage -	May relieve pain and increase mobility.
Hydrotherapy -	Swimming or using flotation devices may take weight off joints, increase flexibility, and reduce pain.
Hypnotherapy -	Said to promote relaxation and reduce the anxiety and depression accompanying the condition.
Reflexology -	May relieve pain and inflammation when directed to reflex areas related to affected joints.
Shiatsu -	May help to relieve pain and stiffness.
Yoga -	Said to increase mobility and relieve stress by promoting relaxation.

Comorbid Conditions

Obesity increases stress on weight-bearing joints (hips and knees), making osteoarthritis worse and lengthening disability. Conditions that precipitated secondary osteoarthritis produce their own symptoms and may lengthen disability. Concurrent rheumatoid conditions may also lengthen disability.

Complications

A bone overgrowth (osteophyte) pressing on nerves in the cervical or lumbar vertebrae (spondylosis) can cause spinal nerve compression (radiculopathy) and dysfunction of the spinal cord (myelopathy). Compression of blood vessels supplying the back of the brain can result in vision problems, vertigo, nausea, and vomiting. Osteophytes pressing on the esophagus can make swallowing difficult. Infection or increased inflammation of an affected joint can complicate the course and treatment plan.

It is important to note that while the disease is diagnosed by x-ray findings, the symptoms of pain, swelling, and stiffness may not correlate well with the findings. For example, an individual's knee films may exhibit large spurs, narrow joint space, and loose bodies floating in the joint. While this would indicate a longstanding problem, the individual may have had only mild symptoms or no symptoms at all. The individual may have sought medical care only after a seemingly insignificant injury or prolonged activity aggravated the symptoms. Such scenarios can greatly complicate cases related to cause and effect settlements.

Factors Influencing Duration

Rest and exercise must be balanced. Too much rest will weaken muscles surrounding the affected joint. This places further stress on the joint and causes additional pain and instability. Repetitive activities at home or on the job that place stress on the affected joint or cause overuse of the affected joint may lengthen disability. Depression or other emotional reaction possibly triggered by pain and limitation of movement and function can make it more difficult to cope or overcome symptoms of osteoarthritis.

Length of Disability

Disability may range from days (with an acute episode) to permanent disability, depending on the joint affected, severity and extent of the arthritis, results of treatment, and the individual's work duties. Disability may be permanent.

Nonoperative treatment.

Duration in Days

Job Classification	Minimum	Optimum	Maximum
Sedentary work	0	14	Indefinite
Light work	0	14	Indefinite
Medium work	1	21	Indefinite
Heavy work	7	28	Indefinite
Very Heavy work	7	28	Indefinite

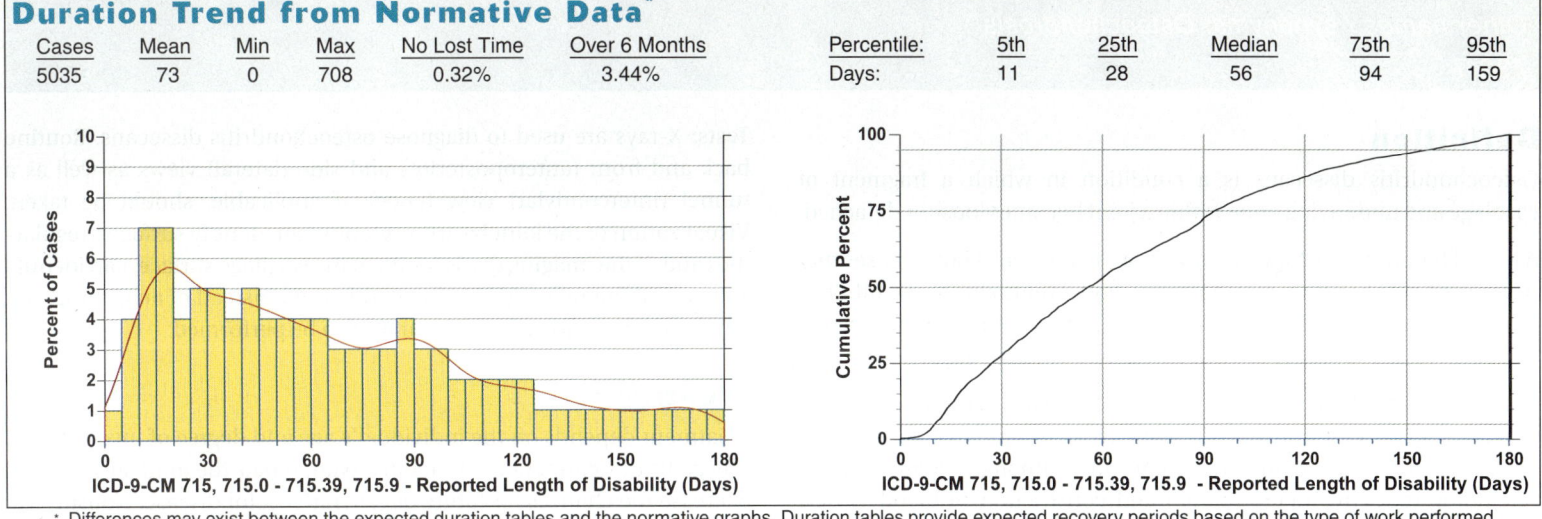

Failure to Recover

If an individual fails to recover within the maximum duration expectancy period, the reader may wish to reference the following questions to assist in better understanding the specifics of an individual's medical case.

Regarding diagnosis:

- Has the individual experienced progressive joint stiffness, pain and loss of motion?
- Did the physical exam reveal one or more inflamed, stiff, deformed joints?
- Was the diagnosis confirmed with diagnostic x-rays?
- Were other conditions with similar symptoms ruled out (i.e., bursitis, tendonitis, radicular spine pain, pigmented villonodular synovitis, osteochondritis dissecans, osteochondromatosis osteonecrosis, Paget's disease, osteoporotic fractures)?
- Is osteoarthritis primary or secondary? If secondary, how are underlying conditions being addressed?

Regarding treatment:

- Have pain and inflammation been effectively controlled with anti-inflammatory medications? If side effects are present, is there an alternative medication that could be prescribed?
- Has the individual been instructed about maintaining an appropriate body weight and getting regular physical exercise?
- Is the individual following a prescribed exercise plan that includes range-of-motion, strengthening, and stretching exercises?
- Would the individual benefit from consultation with a physical and/or occupational therapist?
- If the conservative treatments have been ineffective, is surgical intervention warranted?
- If overweight, has individual been referred to a weight loss program?

Regarding prognosis:

- To what extent is function impaired?
- Have work and home activities been modified in order to reduce weight-bearing action and repetitive movement stress on affected joint?
- Has individual experienced any complications, such as spondylosis or infection that may impact recovery?
- Does the individual feel helpless or depressed in regard to coping with the pain?
- Would the individual benefit from attending a chronic pain management program?
- Would the individual benefit from counseling or enrollment in a support group?

References

Beers, Mark, and Robert Berkow. The Merck Manual, 17th ed. Whitehouse Station, NJ: Merck Research Laboratories, 1999.

Ferri, Fred. Ferri's Clinical Advisor. St. Louis: Mosby, 2000.

Hellmann, David, and John Stone. "Arthritis and Musculoskeletal Disorders." Current Medical Diagnosis and Treatment. Tierney, Lawrence, Stephen McPhee, and Maxine Papadakis, eds. New York: Lange Medical Books/McGraw-Hill, 2000. 807-859.

Kee, S. "Osteoarthritis: Manageable Scourge of Aging." Nurs Clin North Am 35 1 (2000): 199-208.

Shen, Harry, MD, and Cheryl Solimini. Living with Arthritis. New York: Plume, 1993.

Wise, Christopher. "Osteoarthritis." Dale, D.C., and Daniel D. Federman, MD New York: WebMD Corporation, 2000 Scientific American Medicine. 11 July 2000 <http://www.samed.com/sam/forms/index.htm>.

Osteochondritis Dissecans

Other names / synonyms: Osteochondrosis

732.7

Definition

Osteochondritis dissecans is a condition in which a fragment of cartilage and underlying bone within a joint becomes loose or detached.

A lack of blood supply (devascularization) to an area of bone causes that portion of the bone to die (necrosis) and eventually break off. The fragment may be in a fixed location (stable) or it may be loosely attached or detached (unstable). A detached fragment is called a loose body.

Osteochondritis dissecans is most commonly found in the knee but may also occur in the elbow, ankle, hip, hand, wrist, or shoulder. The cause of osteochondritis dissecans is unknown, although joint trauma (including repetitive microtrauma) and constriction of blood vessels (ischemia) have been implicated. It has been proposed that many factors play a role in the development of osteochondritis dissecans. Osteochondritis dissecans can be aggravated by relatively minor trauma to a joint resulting in further loosening or the detachment of the fragment.

Osteochondritis dissecans that involves a significant part of the weight bearing surface and has become completely detached is a serious problem, especially in younger individuals. There are 30 to 60 cases of osteochondritis dissecans per 100,000 individuals. The condition usually presents itself when an individual is between 10 to 30 years of age, however, it can present at an older age. It is rare in individuals older than 50 years of age. Between 30-40% of the individuals affected by osteochondritis dissecans have the condition in the joints of both sides (bilateral). Osteochondritis dissecans affects men more frequently than women; the knee is affected three times more often in men than in women.

Osteochondritis dissecans of the elbow or shoulder is usually in the dominant arm. Individuals with a history of joint injury and those who frequently participate in strenuous sports or perform repetitive activities that put the joint under stress are at an increased risk of developing osteochondritis dissecans. Athletes in baseball, gymnastics, wrestling, tennis, weight lifting, cheerleading, football, golf, shot put, and shooting are at an increased risk of developing osteochondritis dissecans of the elbow.

Diagnosis

History: The individual may complain of gradually worsening pain in one or more joints (arthralgia). Pain worsens with movement of the joint(s) and is usually relieved by rest. A grating and grinding sensation (crepitus) caused by joint movement may be reported. He or she may report that the affected joint periodically becomes locked or that joint movement is limited. The individual with an affected knee may also report a catching or giving way on bending or straightening the knee (as when going up and down steps).

Physical exam: Exam findings may be minimal. Bending the joint would be painful. Minor joint swelling (effusion) may be present. There may be evidence of muscle wasting (atrophy) due to disuse of the affected joint. The chief physical finding is the presence of crepitus upon movement of the joint. The individual with an affected knee may walk with his or her foot turned outward (externally rotated) in an effort to relieve pain.

Tests: X-rays are used to diagnose osteochondritis dissecans. Routine back and front (anteroposterior) and side (lateral) views as well as a tunnel (intercondylar) view (knee), if applicable, should be taken. Visualization of the joint by arthrography can identify surface irregularities and, if the imaging dye is found in the cartilage surface, can identify a detached fragment. MRI is frequently used instead of an arthrogram. CT, bone scan, and arthroscopy may also be performed.

Treatment

Treatment depends on the individual's age and degree of involvement. The goals of treatment are to reduce pain, repair the joint surface, and decrease the chances for future degenerative joint disease. Nonsurgical management consists of immobilization for one to two weeks, following which normal activities are permitted but rapid or strenuous use of the affected joint is avoided for six to twelve weeks. Analgesics may be used as needed.

Surgical treatment is performed as an open procedure (arthrotomy) or by arthroscopy. Arthroscopy is frequently used because it can serve as both a diagnostic and therapeutic tool. Arthrotomy is required for large fragments and joint replacements (arthroplasty). Indications for surgery include failed nonsurgical treatment, joint pain, impairment of joint function, unstable fragments, and the presence of a fragment that is larger than one centimeter in diameter. Surgical options include drilling through the fragment and into the bone to promote new blood vessel growth; fixation of the fragment with pins, screws, or wires; removal (excision) of the fragment; or bone grafting.

Prognosis

The prognosis depends on the size and stability of the fragment and the location of the affected joint. In young adults with stable fragments, nonsurgical management has a good outcome. Surgical management of osteochondritis dissecans usually has a good early outcome, regardless of the surgical method employed. Bone grafting is especially successful. Small residual craters, especially those at the edge of a weight-bearing surface and those in or near the middle of the head of the bone (intercondylar notch) cause little if any disability. Larger craters will eventually cause some disability, usually from degenerative arthritis.

Differential Diagnosis

Loose bodies, torn meniscus, arthritis, and injuries or degeneration of cartilage and ligaments can cause signs and symptoms similar to those of osteochondritis dissecans.

Specialists

- Orthopedist
- Physical Therapist
- Sports Medicine Physician

Rehabilitation

The type of rehabilitation for osteochondritis dissecans depends on the specific joint affected. In general, physical therapy is aimed at restoring normal flexibility and strength and decreasing pain. This may be achieved through stretches and isometric strengthening exercises.

Work Restrictions / Accommodations

Work restrictions and accommodations are related to the location of the affected joint and number of affected joints. Strenuous use of any affected joint needs to be avoided for six to twelve weeks. If the osteochondritis dissecans is in the knee or hip, limited standing, walking, stooping, and climbing can be expected. If the fragment is in the elbow or shoulder, restrictions will be placed on repetitive motion, lifting, and carrying.

Comorbid Conditions

Osteoarthritis, rheumatoid arthritis, obesity, and the presence of any other joint disorder or injury may influence the length of disability.

Complications

Because a weight-bearing surface is involved, osteoarthritis may develop. Osteoarthritis is a chronic disease especially involving weight-bearing joints characterized by destruction of surface cartilage, and overgrowth of bone with spur formation, which results in impaired function. Disuse of an affected limb may lead to muscle atrophy.

Factors Influencing Duration

The size and stability of the fragment, location of the affected joint, number of affected joints, age of the individual, and compliance with the activity restrictions will affect disability.

Length of Disability

Arthroscopic. For fragments less than 2 centimeters.

Duration in Days

Job Classification	Minimum	Optimum	Maximum
Sedentary work	1	7	14
Light work	3	14	28
Medium work	7	14	42
Heavy work	7	28	56
Very Heavy work	7	28	56

Open. For fragments greater than 2 centimeters.

Duration in Days

Job Classification	Minimum	Optimum	Maximum
Sedentary work	7	14	28
Light work	14	21	42
Medium work	14	21	56
Heavy work	21	42	70
Very Heavy work	28	42	84

Failure to Recover

If an individual fails to recover within the maximum duration expectancy period, the reader may wish to reference the following questions to assist in better understanding the specifics of an individual's medical case.

Regarding diagnosis:

- Has diagnosis of osteochondritis been confirmed?
- Does individual have a coexisting condition that may impact recovery?

Regarding treatment:

- Has individual been compliant with prescribed treatment plan?
- If not, what can be done to increase compliance?
- Was repair by arthrotomy or arthroscopy?
- Was procedure considered successful?
- What additional therapy may now be appropriate?
- Did individual receive physical therapy?
- Would individual benefit from additional or extended therapy?

Regarding prognosis:

- Was a bone scan performed?
- Was the affected joint immobilized for more than two weeks?
- Is the individual still experiencing pain?
- How severe are the symptoms? Are they incapacitating?
- Can the individual perform the normal activities of daily life?

References

Apley, A. Graham, and Louis Solomon. "Osteonecrosis and Osteochondritis." Concise System of Orthopaedics and Fractures. Oxford: Butterworth-Heinemann Ltd, 1994. 42-48.

Peterson, Robert, Felix Savoie, and Larry Field. "Osteochondritis Dissecans of the Elbow." AAOS Instructional Course Lectures 48 (1999): 393-398.

Osteoma

Other names / synonyms: Benign Bone Tumor, Exostosis

213, 213.0, 213.1, 213.2, 213.3, 213.4, 213.5, 213.6, 213.7, 213.8, 213.9, M9180/0

Definition

An osteoma is a small, non-cancerous (benign), slow-growing tumor that is composed of abnormally dense, but otherwise normal bone.

Osteomas may form in response to trauma, infection, an invading tumor such as a meningioma, or a soft tissue lesion adjacent to the bone such as a hemangioma or lipoma.

Osteomas are sometimes found in association with other diseases, such as intestinal polyps, fibromatous lesions of the connective tissue, or epidermal cysts as in Gardner's syndrome. Although osteomas typically occur singly, multiple osteomas may occur in Gardner's syndrome, a disease characterized by multiple internal polyps and other non-malignant tumors. The most common sites for tumor development are the skull and facial bones; osteomas that form in the long bones or spine are uncommon in adults.

Osteomas occur in all age groups but most commonly develop between the ages of 30 and 60 years. Overall, osteomas occur more frequently in women than men (3:1). Certain types of osteomas (such as osteoid osteoma) occur most often in young adults and children (ages 5 to 25) and are more common in males than females. The overall occurrence of osteoma is rare. Osteomas are the most frequent benign tumors of the paranasal sinuses, and the incidence varies from 0.01 to 0.43% of individuals.

Diagnosis

History: The individual may complain of pain, often in the area of a protruding bone mass. In the long bone, the individual may have noticed a mass or lesion that enlarged gradually. Individuals with osteoma of the sinus region may complain of headache, facial swelling (edema), runny nose (rhinorrhea) and sinusitis. Symptoms may result from deformity or nerve pressure, but often the individual experiences no symptoms at all.

Physical exam: The exam may reveal the area containing an osteoma as a visible mass that is noticeable to the touch (palpable).

Tests: To confirm the diagnosis, x-rays of the area are taken. Using the x-ray, a physician can exclude other tumors because the mass is very dense and attached to the bone cortex. It will be clear that the underlying bone is not involved and that there is no unmineralized soft tissue. A CT may be needed to delineate the margins of the tumor.

Treatment

Osteomas are only treated if they cause symptoms. Nonprescription nonsteroidal anti-inflammatory drugs or aspirin are often all that is needed to control pain. If the individual is symptomatic, or if the diagnosis is in doubt, surgery may be performed to remove the mass (excision). A new surgical technique (radiofrequency ablation; RFA) is now being performed on some individuals with osteoid osteoma; this procedure is less invasive than traditional surgical excision.

Prognosis

Some individuals experience a spontaneous regression of their osteoma over an extended period of time (3 to 7 years). Most osteomas, however, do not regress, but because growth is slow, the individual may experience a very good outcome for several years using pain medication alone. Prognosis is also very good with surgical removal (excision) of the mass, and most individuals recover completely. Radiofrequency ablation also has very good outcomes, but some individuals experience a recurrence, and about 10% will require a second procedure.

Differential Diagnosis

Differential diagnoses include tuberous sclerosis, parosteal osteosarcoma, and enostosis.

Specialists

- Dentist
- Oncologist
- Orthopedic Surgeon
- Otolaryngologist
- Radiologist

Work Restrictions / Accommodations

Work leave for surgery and recuperation may be necessary. Individuals with osteoma in the leg are advised to avoid vigorous physical activity, such as running or jumping, for 3 months.

Comorbid Conditions

Comorbid conditions that may influence length of disability include obesity (in cases of long bone or spinal osteomas) and the presence of Gardner's syndrome.

Complications

Complications associated with the development of an osteoma often depend on the location of the tumor and may include the obstruction of one or more sinus cavities and the inhibition of normal dental formation or tongue movement.

Factors Influencing Duration

Factors that may influence length of disability include age, the site of the osteoma, and the extent of the surgery required to remove it.

Length of Disability

Duration depends on size, location, and treatment. Contact physician for specific case information.

Failure to Recover

If an individual fails to recover within the maximum duration expectancy period, the reader may wish to reference the following questions to assist in better understanding the specifics of an individual's medical case.

Regarding diagnosis:

- Is individual complaining of pain or soreness, either related to a swelling on a bone or to headaches?
- Has diagnosis of osteoma been confirmed through x-rays?

Regarding treatment:

- If osteomas are now causing symptoms, or if medication is not effective in controlling pain, is individual now a candidate for surgical intervention?
- Would individual be a candidate for radiofrequency ablation?
- Was surgery required?
- Did surgery confirm the diagnosis of osteomas?

Regarding prognosis:

- Is the osteoma located in an area so that the symptoms impair function?
- Is this an initial osteoma or a recurrence of a previous one? Is surgical excision now being considered?
- How effective is medication in controlling pain?
- Did individual experience any complications associated with the generally successful removal of the mass?
- Is there a situation present that may impact recovery?

References

Giant Osteoma of the Maxillary Sinus. Case Report. Universidade Federal de São Paulo - Escola Paulista de Medicina. 09 June 2000. 11 Jan 2001 <http://www.sborl.com.br/revista664e/html/body_materia10.htm>.

Osteoid Osteoma Treatment. Massachusetts General Hospital. 2000. 09 Jan 2001 <http://www.mgh.harvard.edu/mghimaging/Osteoid_Osteoma_Site/NewFiles/FAQs.html>.

Osteoma. 28 May 2000. 02 Jan 2001 <http://www.bonetumor.org/page12.html>.

Osteoma. Wheeless' Textbook of Orthopaedics. 2000. 02 Jan 2001 <http://www.medmedia.com/o6/90.htm>.

Osteomyelitis
Other names / synonyms: Bone Infection
730.0, 730.1, 730.2

Definition

Osteomyelitis is a serious infection of bone, bone marrow, and surrounding soft tissue. The disease may be either recent (acute) or long term (chronic); acute cases may become chronic (or recurrent) if treatment is delayed or unsuccessful. The most common cause of osteomyelitis is bacteria (including the tuberculosis bacterium) or fungi. Often the original site of the infection is elsewhere in the body, but it will spread to the bone via the bloodstream. The bone may also become predisposed to infection if there has been recent minor trauma resulting in a blood clot.

In acute osteomyelitis, bacteria lodge in bones where circulation is sluggish. The bacteria then multiply, causing bone destruction. That destruction is the result of increased pressure as well as the body's response to the infection; the resulting creation of pus causes a bone abscess. Because the abscess deprives the bone of its blood supply, the bone will die (necrosis). As the disease progresses, areas of good bone may become isolated by the infection and areas of necrotic bone.

These necrotic areas of bone form islands or segments that remain infected (sequestra), becoming a source of recurrent infections and, often, draining wounds (sinus tracts). The infection can also spread to other areas of the body. This pattern of recurring infection or failure of the bone to heal is termed chronic osteomyelitis. When some areas of the bone die, circulation throughout the bone stops.

Osteomyelitis may be differentiated based on how the organisms enter the bone (route of infection). They may enter directly through the bloodstream (hematogenous osteomyelitis), through an open wound (direct infection), or in rare cases, from soft tissue infections near the bone (contiguous focus). Hematogenous osteomyelitis usually originates in the respiratory tract, gastrointestinal tract, skin, or urinary tract. Hematogenous osteomyelitis is more commonly found in those over age 50.

In cases of direct infection, the organism is introduced into the bone during surgery, from a compound or open fracture, from a contaminated wound over exposed bone, or from a foreign object penetrating the skin and bone. Hardware or prosthetic implants may carry infection into a bone, which later develop infections and become pockets where bacteria multiply rapidly (focus of infection). Because the metal is not affected by circulating blood, antibiotics may not have any effect on that type of infection.

Infection may spread from a soft tissue injury (contiguous focus) as a result of trauma, pressure ulcers, or burns. The bone itself is not initially injured, but the infection spreads through the layers of soft tissues around the bone.

The target bones are primarily the spine and pelvis; children most often have their long bones affected. Individuals who are at an increased risk of developing osteomyelitis include the elderly, those with chronic granulomatosus disease, sickle cell disease, diabetes, or AIDS, those who have suffered recent trauma, and those who use intravenous drugs or are on hemodialysis. Osteomyelitis is rare in the US and occurs in 2 out of every 10,000 individuals. Men are twice as likely than women to develop osteomyelitis.

Diagnosis

History: In individuals with acute osteomyelitis, the main complaint is pain in the bone or bone tenderness, localized swelling and warmth, and perhaps redness of the area. The individual may avoid using, or have a reduced ability to use the affected body part. In acute cases, individuals may report a generalized feeling of illness (malaise), loss of appetite, fatigue, nausea, and fever. There may be a history of recent trauma, surgery, or infection of another organ (i.e., lungs, bladder). Individuals with chronic osteomyelitis will have a history of an acute episode (if it was recognized initially), and often have a recurrence of pus draining out through the skin, pain, and swelling. They may also have generalized complaints of fever, loss of appetite, and fatigue. Additional symptoms may include excessive sweating (diaphoresis), chills, and low back pain. These individuals may have an underlying immune system disease or peripheral vascular disease. Individuals must be questioned about IV drug abuse.

Physical exam: An examination will reveal local pain and tenderness. Redness over the area (erythema), swelling (edema), draining wounds, draining sinuses, or chronic skin ulcers may also be evident. Fever, signs of dehydration, or other signs of blood infection (sepsis) may be evident.

Tests: Blood tests include a complete blood count (CBC) and erythrocyte sedimentation rate (ESR). Samples of blood and wound drainage (or samples taken directly from the infected bone or sinus tract) may be cultured to identify the causative organism and determine antibiotic (or antifungal) sensitivities. Other possible tests include needle aspiration within the vertebral space for culture, tuberculin skin test, open bone biopsy, Doppler studies in cases of peripheral vascular disease, plain x-rays, bone scan (most specific is gallium), CT, and MRI.

Treatment

The treatment goal is to eliminate the infection and prevent the development of a chronic infection. Because early treatment is critical, high-dose antibiotic intravenous (IV) therapy is usually started immediately, before test results are known. Antibiotics can be changed later depending upon results of cultures. Hospitalization is necessary, at least during the early stages of treatment. The IV antibiotics continue for 3-4 weeks and may be followed with oral treatment for several months. Analgesics are prescribed as needed. Wound care, if applicable, may include removal of dying or dead tissue (debridement) and frequent dressing changes. Bed rest and immobilization of the infected body part are essential. If improvement is not evident after 24 hours of antibiotic treatment, surgery to relieve pressure in the bone (surgical decompression) by drilling into the bone and removing pus will be done. Open spaces left by the removed bone will be filled with bone graft, or left with packing material in to promote regrowth of new bone tissue. If a prosthetic implant or hardware is suspected as the cause, the device may be removed; the infection should be eradicated before a replacement device is inserted.

Chronic osteomyelitis will require surgical removal of the sequestra (sequestrectomy) and surrounding tissue, followed by antibiotic therapy. In severe cases, amputation may be necessary. Dehydration, protein deficiency, and anemia caused by draining wounds require nutritional supplementation. Education is very important to insure compliance with long-term therapy. Home care services are necessary for IV medication administration and wound care.

Prognosis

Acute episodes have a good prognosis, although complications can occur in as many as 25% of cases. Surgical decompression or sequestrectomy can provide the means to obtain a specimen for culture, provide pain relief, resolve the infection, and prevent necrosis of additional bone. Amputation can eradicate the infection but will cause varying degrees of disability depending on the body part removed, and extent of removal. Delayed or inadequate treatment may lead to chronic osteomyelitis, which can be inactive for several years, with a flare-up occurring as long as 20 to 30 years later. Chronic cases often have a poor outcome. Treatment failure occurs for 20% of all cases of osteomyelitis.

Differential Diagnosis

Acute septic arthritis, tenosynovitis, rheumatic fever, cellulitis, tumor, compression fracture of spine, chronic skin ulcer (decubitus), gas gangrene, local trauma to bone or soft tissues, and arthritis of spine are other possibilities.

Specialists

- Infectious Disease Physician
- Orthopedic Surgeon

Rehabilitation

The type of rehabilitation for osteomyelitis depends on the location of the infected bone and the underlying cause of infection. In general, rehabilitation is aimed at restoring normal range of motion, flexibility, strength, and endurance. The goal of rehabilitation for progressive osteomyelitis is to maintain function and enhance mobility.

Physical therapy helps maintain flexibility and strength and relieves the pain associated with muscular weakness and immobility. Active range of motion involves the individual performing joint motion independently. Passive range of motion means the therapist moves the involved joint(s) with no effort from the individual.

Strengthening is typically accomplished via resistance provided by an elastic band or light weights (isotonic exercise). In the event of muscle weakness to the legs, balance exercises are beneficial and include side stepping and walking with the eyes closed with and without assistance. As strength continues to progress, endurance becomes a focus in the individual's rehabilitation program for osteomyelitis. Aerobic exercises that increase cardiovascular fitness are emphasized and include walking briskly, running, jogging, swimming, climbing stairs, or bicycling. The American Heart Association recommends 30 to 60 minutes of aerobic activity 3 or 4 times a week.

Learning how to avoid injury is another important intervention in the rehabilitation of progressive osteomyelitis. Occupational therapy helps individuals arrange their homes and organize their lives in ways that support their physical and mental well-being. Activities are also provided to relieve the mental boredom of inactivity. Devices and techniques that help the individual communicate are invaluable in maintaining peace of mind. The rehabilitation program varies among individuals with progressive osteomyelitis as the intensity and progression of the exercise depends on the stage of the disease and individual's overall health.

Work Restrictions / Accommodations

Individuals may be able to receive intravenous (IV) therapy at work if a clean space that permits privacy, equipment to handle infusion, and refrigeration of medication can be made available. Home health nursing may be brought to the workplace to assist in this treatment plan. Frequent rest periods to relieve fatigue and supplement nourishment may be necessary. Depending on the affected bone, weight lifting or motion restriction may be necessary. Other restrictions and accommodations would be related to the specific body part involved.

Comorbid Conditions

Conditions that are associated with a disabled immune system (e.g., organ transplantation, AIDS, cancer), diabetes, obesity, general debility, tuberculosis, bone fracture, cardiovascular disease, diseases causing impaired circulation (e.g., arteriosclerosis), and other injuries (e.g., fractures, lacerations) sustained during the traumatic event may influence the length of disability.

Complications

An acute condition can become chronic. Soft tissue abscess formation, septic arthritis, spreading of a localized infection, chronic drainage, toxic shock syndrome, joint contracture, and amputation could all result from acute or chronic osteomyelitis. Bone resorption can weaken bone and lead to fractures. Osteomyelitis of the spine can be complicated by paraplegia or inflammation of the membranes that surround the spinal cord and brain (meningitis). Untreated or inadequately treated osteomyelitis can lead to blood poisoning (septicemia), which can be fatal.

Factors Influencing Duration

The location of the infection, effectiveness of treatment, severity of pain, and availability of home intravenous (IV) therapy will influence the length of disability. The development of complications (particularly those requiring surgery) would greatly increase the disability period, perhaps to a permanent status. Osteomyelitis frequently requires lengthy hospitalizations.

Length of Disability

Duration depends upon site, acute versus chronic form, predisposing factors, infectious agent, severity of disease, type of treatment, and job demands. Contact physician for more nformation.

Failure to Recover

If an individual fails to recover within the maximum duration expectancy period, the reader may wish to reference the following questions to assist in better understanding the specifics of an individual's medical case.

Regarding diagnosis:

- Has diagnosis of osteomyelitis been confirmed?
- Was the causative organism identified?
- Were antibiotic (or antifungal) sensitivities determined?
- Has individual experienced complications related to the osteomyelitis?
- Does individual have an underlying condition (disorders associated with a disabled immune system (organ transplantation, AIDS, cancer), diabetes, obesity, general debility, tuberculosis, cardiovascular disease, and other fractures or lacerations sustained during the traumatic event) that may impact recovery?

Regarding treatment:

- Was treatment with broad-spectrum antibiotic initiated immediately once osteomyelitis was suspected?
- Was the causative organism identified?
- Were antibiotic (or antifungal) sensitivities determined?
- Have antibiotic-resistant organisms been ruled out?
- Did the initial therapy consist of oral antibiotics?
- Was antibiotic therapy discontinued before 3 to 4 weeks of treatment was completed?
- Was surgical decompression required?
- Is the osteomyelitis associated with some type of fixation device (screw, plate, prosthesis)? Has the device been removed?
- Have home care services been employed to provide necessary intravenous medication administration and wound care?
- Has individual received the education and support services necessary to insure compliance with long-term therapy?

Regarding prognosis:

- Did osteomyelitis result from a bone fracture? Has permanent bone damage occurred?
- If the osteomyelitis is associated with some type of fixation device (screw, plate, prosthesis), has the device been removed? How does this affect function?
- Is the osteomyelitis considered chronic ?

References

Kisner, C., and L. Colby. Therapeutic Exercise Foundations and Techniques. Philadelphia: F.A. Davis Company, 1990.

Tsukayama, Dean. "Pathophysiology of Posttraumatic Osteomyelitis." Clinical Orthopaedics and Related Research 360 (1999): 22-29.

Osteoporosis

Other names / synonyms: Brittle Bone Disease

733.0, 733.00, 733.01, 733.03

Definition

Osteoporosis is a condition in which the bones become porous, resulting from a change in the normal and ongoing metabolic process of bone reabsorption and formation. When more bone substance is reabsorbed than rebuilt, the density or amount of the bone decreases. The bone material that remains is biochemically normal, but overall the bone is weakened and more brittle because of lack of bone mass, which increases risk of fractures.

Osteoporosis may be regional, such as in a fractured and casted lower extremity upon which there has been no weightbearing for 6-12 weeks (disuse osteoporosis). More typically osteoporosis is generalized (throughout the body). It may be primary, from an unknown cause, or secondary, related to an underlying disease process. Primary osteoporosis, or involutional osteoporosis, is a disease of the elderly, especially elderly women. Age-related osteoporosis can be separated into two types: Type I occurs after menopause or in men with testosterone deficiency, and tends to be associated with fractures in the forearm near the wrist and in the vertebrae. Type II is associated with normal aging and occurs after age 60 to 70, and tends to be associated with hip and pelvic fractures.

Common causes of osteoporosis are decrease in estrogen production, alcohol and cigarette use, poor nutrition, inactivity and immobilization (disuse) or overactivity, and long term use of corticosteroids to treat another disease such as asthma or rheumatoid arthritis. There is also evidence of a genetic component that increases the risk of osteoporosis. Diseases of the thyroid gland and intestine that affect absorption of calcium and vitamins can contribute to osteoporosis. Other diseases associated with osteoporosis include systemic inflammatory diseases, endocrine diseases including diabetes, and chronic obstructive pulmonary disease. Other medications that can cause osteoporosis include methotrexate, heparin, diuretics, and anticonvulsants.

Osteoporosis is the most common metabolic bone disease and leads to approximately 1.3 million fractures per year. Osteoporosis affects women of all ages, most severely those over age 60, and predominately those who are postmenopausal, petite, thin, fair-skinned white, or Asian. Men and women can both be affected by metabolic changes as they age, leading to age-related osteoporosis.

Even younger women are now recognized as having decreased bone density, and they should be included in preventive treatment programs aimed at identifying individuals at risk and correcting the problem long before any fractures occur. Peak bone mass in both sexes is in the mid-thirties, followed by a plateau during which rates of bone formation and resorption are approximately equal, then a period of net bone loss of about 0.3 to 0.5% per year. After menopause, bone loss increases 10-fold in women, so that bone may be lost at the rate of 3-5% per year.

In women, 15% have osteoporosis at age 50, 30% at age 70, and 40% at age 80. Overall, one in three women, and one in 12 men, will be affected at some stage in their lives.

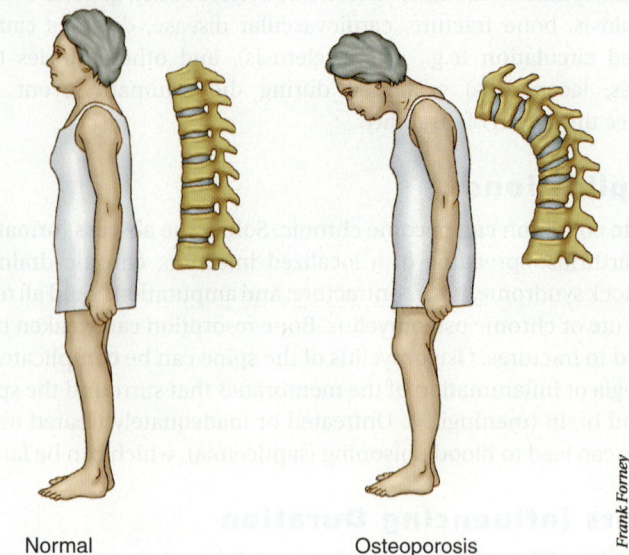

Normal / Osteoporosis

Frank Forney

Diagnosis

History: Most commonly, the disease is not discovered until a fracture occurs, or it may be an incidental finding during evaluation for another problem. Fractures may occur suddenly after a fall, sudden movement, lifting, jumping, or even minor events such as bumping the rib cage or coughing. Individuals present with pain, a change in body height if the spine is involved, weakness, and stiffness. Individuals should be questioned about a family history of osteoporosis, underlying metabolic disease, history of steroid use, alcohol and cigarette use, and nutritional status.

Physical exam: If the vertebrae are involved, there may be midline back pain with an increase in the thoracic curve (kyphosis). Exaggerated upper spine curve or thoracic kyphosis is called dowager's hump. There may be a loss of height or change in the ratio of upper body to lower body height. If there is an acute fracture of the hip or wrist, deformity, pain, tenderness over the fracture, decreased motion, and swelling will be obvious.

Tests: Laboratory tests are done to rule out other disease processes, as most blood tests involving calcium and bone function studies are normal in primary osteoporosis. Plain x-rays are normal in early osteoporosis, but in advanced involutional osteoporosis, the vertebral bodies can appear abnormal. X-rays are used to evaluate possible fractures. Special radiographic studies to measure bone density are ordered when the episode of the fracture has resolved, or in screening examinations. The most specific is dual-energy x-ray absorptiometry (DEXA), measuring the density of the spine, hip, wrist, and total skeleton. The dose of radiation is low and the examination does not require much time. Biochemical markers of bone turnover, measured with blood tests, reflect bone formation or bone resorption. These tests can be made before and during treatment to help monitor treatment response, but are not helpful in diagnosis.

Treatment

In individuals who are known to have many risk factors, prevention is the best treatment. Preventive measures may include use of estrogen, nutritional guidance with use of vitamins or other supplements, maintaining a proper balance between activity and over-activity, which could negatively affect estrogen production, and avoiding medications that are known to affect bone metabolism. Once the diagnosis has been made, treatment may include estrogen supplements, nutritional supplements, increase in weight-bearing activity, treatment of any underlying metabolic disease, and nonsteroidal anti-inflammatory medications for pain control.

New treatments for osteoporosis in postmenopausal women include the bisphosphonates (such as alendronate or Fosamax), drugs that alter the bone resorption rate, thereby increasing bone mass density (BMD) and reducing the risk of fracture. In type II osteoporosis, sodium fluoride, androgens, and parathormone injections may stimulate new bone formation, but there may be significant side effects including increased bone pain and liver damage. Sodium fluoride is still considered experimental, as there is some concern about the quality of bone being formed. Raloxifene or Evista, a selective estrogen-receptor modulator, may offer the benefits of estrogen without the increased risk of breast and uterine cancer. Calcitonin therapy, now available as a nasal spray (Miacalcin), also results in an increase in bone mineral density and offers some pain-relieving (analgesic) effect. Calcium and vitamin D are being used because many individuals are on diets low in calcium, and lack of exposure to sunlight causes some individuals to become deficient in vitamin D. Both calcium and vitamin D are needed for normal bone formation. Treatment of fractures that result from osteoporosis may be difficult because of altered bone healing and secondary complications, especially with hip fractures. Wrist fractures are often not manipulated because of the risk of further damage. Compression fractures of the spine may be treated with a corset or supporting brace and limited bed rest. Vertebroplasty involves injection of bone cement into the fractured vertebral body to stabilize it and reduce pain. Sometimes the injection is preceded by inflation of a balloon within the compressed vertebra in an attempt to elevate it back to its normal height. Individual education should include decreasing risk factors and creating a safe environment to reduce the chance of falls.

Prognosis

There is no single treatment or cure for osteoporosis, although new drug therapies are now available that may slow the process and increase bone density. Increased bone density reduces the occurrence of pain and risk of fracture. The effect of these therapies on osteoporosis is to cut the risk of fractures in half. Prevention is critical in those individuals who are at high risk. Recovery from fractures in individuals with osteoporosis can be slow and fraught with complications, leading to a poor outcome. The outcome of individuals with secondary osteoporosis depends on management of the underlying cause.

Differential Diagnosis

Osteomalacia, metastatic cancer involving the bone, and Paget's disease can mimic primary osteoporosis. Secondary causes to be ruled out are malignancies, hyperparathyroidism, malabsorption syndromes, poor nutrition, and immobilization.

Specialists

- Endocrinologist
- Internist
- Orthopedic Surgeon
- Physiatrist

Rehabilitation

Individuals with osteoporosis may benefit from outpatient physical therapy. The main goals of physical therapy are to stretch any tightened muscle structures, strengthen any weakened muscles, improve balance, and educate individuals about osteoporosis.

Individuals learn to stretch any tight muscles to improve posture. The neck, chest, and abdominal muscles are commonly shortened. Individuals stretch the neck by tilting the head from side to side, turning it, and looking up and down. The chest muscles can be stretched by standing in a corner, placing the arms on each wall, and leaning into the corner. Individuals stretch the abdominal muscles by lying on their backs and reaching their arms overhead.

Individuals should also strengthen any weak muscles to improve posture and support brittle bones. Common areas of weakness are the neck, the upper and low back, abdomen, and legs. The neck can be strengthened by performing chin tucks where the neck is retracted so the chin flattens against the neck. The upper back can be strengthened by shoulder blade pinches where the shoulder blades are squeezed together. Individuals strengthen the lower back by performing isometric back extension where seated posture is exaggerated and the back presses into the back of a chair. Pelvic tilts strengthen the abdominal muscles where the supine individual presses the low back into the floor or exercise mat. A full lower extremity program includes straight leg raises, bridging exercises, seated knee extensions, and standing heel raises.

Individuals may need to improve their balance since their standing posture tends to assume a forward bent position and in this position, the center of gravity shifts and can cause loss of balance. Individuals may perform balance exercises in the parallel bars such as heel-to-toe walking or standing on one foot. Individuals may also be taught how to walk with a cane or walker if there is a history of falling.

To prevent the occurrence of pathological fractures, individuals learn proper body mechanics. They learn to avoid twisting or excessive forward bending of the spine, e.g., sitting on a stool to reach into lower cupboards or walking closer to objects to be lifted instead of reaching for them. Individuals learn that weight-bearing exercise and lifting light dumbbells increase bone density, which can slow the progression of osteoporosis. A nutritionist may be consulted if individuals find it difficult to consume enough dietary calcium.

Work Restrictions / Accommodations

Work restrictions include precautions to prevent fracture, such as decreased or absent load-bearing activity, repetitive bending, and lifting. Accommodations should allow for rest periods. Providing a safe work environment will help to prevent falls. Individuals recovering from hip fracture may need crutches, canes, or wheelchairs, and a work space to accommodate such devices. Evaluation of safety issues concerned with the use of pain medications will be necessary.

Once significant osteoporosis is recognized, heavy and very heavy work are usually prohibited.

Comorbid Conditions

Recovery may be delayed by any conditions that cause low estrogen levels or nutritional deficiencies, particularly of vitamin D and calcium. Malabsorption syndromes may prevent adequate absorption of both vitamin D and calcium. Lack of exposure to sunlight can also result in vitamin D deficiency. Any factors which delay fracture healing or any associated bony deformities can increase the length of time required for adequate healing of fractures, thereby lengthening disability. Underlying metabolic disorders require management to prevent increased osteoporosis. Treatment of metastatic disease with radiation could increase osteoporosis, as could immobilization in the treatment of fractures. Factors that increase the risk of falls and, hence, fractures, include poor coordination or vision, weakness, confusion, and use of sedating medications. These factors are especially common in the elderly.

Complications

Fractures are the most common complication of osteoporosis, with associated problems of pain, immobility, and loss of function. Most individuals with osteoporotic fractures will have additional fractures within the first few years. Risk of death within 1 year is significantly increased after a hip fracture, usually because of complications. Decreased respiratory capacity or gastrointestinal function may result from changes in posture. Progressive loss of height of the vertebrae usually affects mostly the front (anterior) surface, leading to the characteristic round shoulders and stooped posture known as dowager's hump, which can make breathing difficult. Vertebral changes in the lower spine can weaken the abdominal muscles, producing a protuberant abdomen that can lead to constipation or other digestive complaints. Fear of ambulation or activity, complications from surgery, and side effects of medications could also complicate the disease and its treatment.

Factors Influencing Duration

Treatment of fractures, underlying causes that require management, and job requirements will affect the disability period. There may be no disability for individuals with osteoporosis without fracture, but other individuals may have repeated fractures and ongoing disability. Treatment of fractures and any underlying disease could create a disability period ranging from several days to permanent disability. Poor physical functioning is related to increased number of fractures and delayed recovery. Fractures in younger individuals generally heal faster.

Length of Disability

Disability in individuals with osteoporosis may be permanent for heavy or very heavy work, particularly with compression fractures of the spine. Length of disability is influenced most by fracture healing ability and job demands. Contact physician for more information.

Duration in Days

Job Classification	Minimum	Optimum	Maximum
Sedentary work	0	14	112
Light work	0	14	112
Medium work	3	21	Indefinite
Heavy work	84	140	Indefinite
Very Heavy work	84	140	Indefinite

Failure to Recover

If an individual fails to recover within the maximum duration expectancy period, the reader may wish to reference the following questions to assist in better understanding the specifics of an individual's medical case.

Regarding diagnosis:

- Does the individual have a history of risk factors?
- Has the individual had adequate testing to confirm the diagnosis?
- Have conditions such as osteomalacia, metastatic cancer involving the bone, and Paget's disease, and secondary causes such as malignancies, hyperparathyroidism, malabsorption syndromes, poor nutrition, and immobilization been ruled out?

Regarding treatment:

- Is the individual compliant with the treatment program?
- Is the individual receiving proper treatment?
- Has the individual received education in prevention and decreasing risk factors?

Regarding prognosis:

- Does the individual exercise as recommended by the physician?
- Does the individual practice proper body mechanics?
- Has the individual consulted with a nutritionist?
- Is the individual's employer able to accommodate any necessary restrictions?
- Does the individual have any conditions that might delay recovery?
- Does the individual have any complications?

References

Kleerekoper, Michael. "Osteoporosis: A Four-article Symposium." Postgraduate Medicine 104 4 (1998): 51-114.

Levinson, Wendy, and Diane Altkorn. "Primary Prevention of Postmenopausal Osteoporosis." Journal of the American Medical Association 280 21 (1998): 1821-1822.

Shen, Harry, MD, and Cheryl Solimini. Living with Arthritis. New York: Plume, 1993.

Wood, Alastair. "Treatment of Postmenopausal Osteoporosis." New England Journal of Medicine 338 11 (1998): 736-746.

Otitis Externa, Infective

Other names / synonyms: Otorrhea, Swimmer's Ear

380.1, 380.10, 380.11, 380.12, 380.13, 380.14, 380.15, 380.16

Definition

Infective otitis externa is an inflammation of the skin of the external ear canal and the folds of skin and cartilage that make up the visible part of the ear (auricle or pinna). The infection is usually caused by bacteria (pseudomonas aeruginosa or proteus vulgaris) but can also be caused by fungus (aspergillus or candida albicans) especially in warm, moist climates. Chronic otitis externa is occasionally caused by dermatitis such as seborrhea, eczema, or psoriasis. It is also known as "swimmer's ear" as it can result from prolonged exposure to freshwater.

External otitis most commonly occurs in young adults.

Diagnosis

History: Individuals with infective otitis externa complain of moderate to severe external ear pain sometimes disproportionate to the infection's severity. Pressing directly in front of the ear is especially painful. Clenching the teeth, opening the mouth, or chewing may also increase pain. The individual often reports recent exposure to water or mechanical trauma to the ear canal (scratching with a sharp object or cotton applicator). Fever may or may not be present. Swelling of the ear canal blocks hearing and may cause dizziness. In chronic external otitis, itching rather than pain is the chief symptom.

Physical exam: An examination of the external ear canal with an otoscope reveals redness (erythema) and swelling (edema). A purulent, foul-smelling discharge (otorrhea) is often present. Movement (manipulation) of the ear is usually painful. Pain on movement of the external ear structures distinguishes otitis externa from middle ear infection. If the canal skin is very swollen, it may be impossible to visualize the eardrum with an otoscope. When visualized, however, the eardrum is found to move normally. Tender lymph nodes in front of or behind the external ear (periauricular lymphadenopathy) are usually present.

Tests: A sample of the discharge may be submitted to the laboratory for culture and sensitivity testing. A culture identifies the organism (pathogen) causing the infection. Sensitivity indicates the most appropriate antibiotic for treatment.

Treatment

Pain can initially be eased with pain medication and warm moist compresses applied to the area. Debris is gently removed from the ear canal. Eardrops prescribed may contain both an aminoglycoside antibiotic to treat the infection and a corticosteroid to reduce inflammation. If swelling prevents entry of the drops, a cotton ear-wick is inserted into the swollen ear canal to absorb the drops and deliver medication to the area most in need of treatment. If fever persists or regional inflammation (cellulitis) develops, oral antibiotics are prescribed. If the culture identified fungus as the cause of infection, antifungal drops are prescribed instead of antibiotics. While the condition is healing, the ear must be protected from moisture and further scratching of the ear canal.

Prognosis

With proper treatment, the individual with acute otitis externa should notice improvement within 48 hours. Chronic otitis externa does not have a predictable outcome and may recur.

Differential Diagnosis

Drainage from the external ear canal can also be caused by seborrhea, psoriasis, acute and chronic otitis media, basal cell carcinoma, boils (furunculosis), and the presence of a foreign body in the ear.

Specialists

- Audiologist
- Dermatologist
- Infectious Disease Physician
- Otolaryngologist

Rehabilitation

Individuals with decreased balance as a result of infective otitis externa may require a consultation session with a physical therapist. The physical therapist can provide gait instruction with the use of a cane or walker and may suggest other safety measures such as grab bars in the shower.

Work Restrictions / Accommodations

Because of the severe ear pain and the need to keep the ear canal as dry as possible, an individual with infective otitis externa should not wear clothing or protective gear that covers the ear. Because hearing is reduced in the affected ear, temporary reassignment to a position not requiring frequent phone calls may be necessary. Exposure of the ear canal to water or extremely humid conditions should be avoided during the healing process. Exposure to chemical environments that emit fumes and vapors also delay the healing process. Individuals with chronic otitis externa may need to indefinitely avoid warm, moist environments and water exposure.

Complementary and Alternative Therapies

Content is intended for awareness only. Treatments may or may not be effective. Scientific evidence may be lacking and some substances have potentially toxic effects. Dr. Presley Reed and the editors do not endorse the use of these therapies in the absence of consultation with a licensed medical professional.

Acetic acid and Burow's solution -	The antimicrobial activity in this 13% aluminum acetate solution, when used as eardrops, may treat as well as prevent otitis externa.

Comorbid Conditions

Comorbid diseases that might influence the length of disability include underlying medical conditions (diabetes or HIV/AIDS) and a weakened immune system (immunosuppression). Severe chronic otitis externa may reflect underlying diabetes, underactive thyroid, or kidney infection.

Complications

The condition may become recurrent especially if caused by a fungus and the individual remains in a humid environment. Persistent otitis externa in diabetic or immunocompromised individuals may evolve into osteomyelitis of the skull base (malignant external otitis). This condition is characterized by a foul-smelling discharge from the ear, deep ear pain (otalgia), and progressive paralysis of certain cranial nerves. Severe chronic otitis externa may reflect underlying diabetes, underactive thyroid, or kidney infection.

Factors Influencing Duration

Factors that may influence the length of disability include the individual's general state of health, pre-existing diseases affecting major body systems (e.g., diabetes, HIV/AIDS, leukemia, or cancer), functional immune system, type and virulence of infection, presence of antibiotic-resistant organisms, response to treatment, compliance with treatment regimen, complications requiring surgery, and working or living in a humid environment.

Length of Disability

In most cases, no disability is expected.

Duration in Days

Job Classification	Minimum	Optimum	Maximum
Any work	0	1	3

Failure to Recover

If an individual fails to recover within the maximum duration expectancy period, the reader may wish to reference the following questions to assist in better understanding the specifics of an individual's medical case.

Regarding diagnosis:

- Does individual complain of moderate to severe external ear pain sometimes disproportionate to the infection's severity? If front of ear is pressed, is it painful? Does clenching the teeth, opening the mouth, or chewing increase pain?
- Was individual recently exposed to water or mechanical trauma to the ear canal (scratching with a sharp object or cotton applicator)?
- Does swelling of the ear canal block hearing? If so, does it cause dizziness?
- Is itching present rather than pain?
- On exam, was ear canal red (erythema) and swollen (edema)? Was a purulent, foul-smelling discharge (otorrhea) present?
- Was diagnosis of infective otitis externa confirmed? Was source of infection identified?

Regarding treatment:

- Was a culture and sensitivity done to identify the organism and determine the most effective antibiotics and/or antifungal drops?
- Were eardrops prescribed containing both an aminoglycoside antibiotic to treat the infection and a corticosteroid to reduce inflammation? Did swelling prevent entry of drops? If so, was medication administered with a cotton ear-wick?
- Are eardrops used at room temperature to decrease dizziness during application?
- Did fever persist or regional inflammation (cellulitis) develop? If so, were oral antibiotics given?
- Did individual protect ear from moisture and further scratching of the ear canal?

Regarding prognosis:

- Has individual experienced complications that may impact recovery?
- Does individual have an underlying condition that may impact recovery?
- Is the climate or workplace environment dry in order to be conducive to healing?
- Is individual applying the eardrops correctly? Is individual using good, clean technique when applying the eardrops so that the organisms causing the infection are not introduced back into the bottle of drops?

References

Hannley, M.T., J.C. Denneny III, and S.S. Holzer. "Use of Ototopical Antibiotics in Treating 3 Common Ear Diseases." Otolaryngology Head and Neck Surgery 122 6 (2000): 934-940.

Lewis, Sharon, Margaret Heitkemper, and Shannon Dirksen. Medical-Surgical Nursing. St. Louis: Mosby, 2000.

Thorp, M.A., J. Kruger, and S. Oliver. "The Antibacterial Activity of Acetic Acid and Burow's Solution as Topical Otological Preparations." Journal of Laryngology and Otology 112 10 (1998): 925-928.

Tierney, Lawrence M., Stephen McPhee, and Maxine Papadakis. Current Medical Diagnosis & Treatment. New York: McGraw-Hill, 2000.

Otitis Media

Other names / synonyms: Acute Middle Ear Disease, Allergic Otitis Media, Chronic Middle Ear Disease, Ear Infection, Middle Ear Infection, Nonsuppurative Otitis Media, Secretory Otitis Media, Serous Otitis Media

381, 381.00, 381.01, 382, 382.0, 382.00, 382.9

Definition

Otitis media is an inflammation of the lining of the middle ear canal (mucosa), eardrum (tympanic membrane), and the associated structures such as the small bones of the ear (ossicles) and the tube that connects it to the throat (eustachian tube). Because fluid buildup behind the eardrum can cause poor transmission of sound waves, otitis media may be associated with some degree of conductive hearing loss.

Different forms of acute otitis media (serous, secretory, and suppurative or purulent) are based on the severity of the infection and the involvement of different parts of the ear. In serous otitis media, the hearing or pressure equalization tube (eustachian tube) that extends between the eardrum and the back of the throat (nasopharynx) fails to open and close as it should. Continuous or intermittent pressure changes cause fluid to build up behind the eardrum, resulting in conductive hearing loss. Acute serous otitis media usually follows an upper respiratory infection or trauma to the ear and is sometimes associated with an allergy or enlarged adenoids.

In secretory otitis media, the lining of the middle ear canal (mucosa) changes and releases (secretes) fluid that is thicker than normal. Acute secretory otitis media also follows an upper respiratory infection. Serous and secretory otitis media are the usual forms of the disease seen in individuals with acquired immunodeficiency syndrome (AIDS).

Suppurative otitis media is usually caused by a viral upper respiratory tract infection that causes swelling (edema) in the eustachian tube and an accumulation of fluid and mucus behind the eardrum. Caused by pus-producing bacteria introduced into the middle ear from the nasopharynx, the most common organisms (pathogens) are Streptococcus pneumoniae, Haemophilus influenzae, and Streptococcus pyogenes.

Otitis media of less than 3 weeks duration (acute) is one of the most common infections of childhood but is also seen in adults. Recurrent acute otitis media becomes chronic when it persists for longer than 3 months and when accompanied by changes in the lining of the middle ear. Growth of new tissue (granulation tissue) may extend into the middle ear. Often the result of untreated ear infections, this disease is considered more dangerous because the slow, chronic effects can result in permanent damage. Chronic otitis media may not be noticed or cause enough discomfort to warrant immediate action until it is well-established.

Individuals at increased risk for otitis media are those on chemotherapy, antirejection drugs following organ transplantation, or who have weakened immune systems (immunosuppression) or chronic diseases like HIV/AIDS or leukemia. Individuals with upper respiratory infections who scuba dive or fly in an airplane may also develop otitis media caused by persistent negative middle ear pressure. Chronic otitis media is more common in adults with recurrent childhood acute otitis.

Diagnosis

History: Individuals with acute otitis media may complain of moderate to severe ear pain (otalgia), pain behind the ear, fever, decreased hearing, fluid drainage from the ear, dizziness, or a sense of fullness in the ear (aural pressure).

Individuals with chronic otitis media often report a history of recurrent acute otitis media, long-term decreased hearing, and a chronically draining ear. Pain does not usually accompany chronic otitis media unless the individual has an upper respiratory infection.

Physical exam: Physical findings will vary depending on the type of infection present. When examined through an otoscope, the eardrum associated with acute otitis media is red (erythema) with slow or absent mobility. Painful blisters (bullae) are occasionally present on the eardrum, or the drum will bulge outward because of the severe infection behind it. Without medical intervention, bulging eardrums may eventually rupture and fluid will drain from the ear canal. This event brings an immediate decrease in the level of pain. A recent perforation in the eardrum may be seen as well as scarring from previously healed perforations. If the eardrum is perforated, drainage from the middle ear may be present in the ear canal. If the infection is very severe, neurological symptoms may also be present (signs of increased intracranial pressure, facial paralysis, or meningitis).

When examined through an otoscope, the eardrum associated with chronic otitis media may be perforated or scarred, and drainage from the middle ear will be present in the ear canal.

Tests: Fluid drawn from behind the eardrum with a needle and syringe (tympanocentesis) may be sent to the laboratory for culture and sensitivity testing. This identifies the causative organism and determines the appropriate antibiotic to use in treating the infection. Audiometric studies may be performed to test the degree of conductive hearing loss. Tympanometry can be used to measure the middle ear pressure and mobility of the eardrum (tympanic membrane.) A MRI or CT may be ordered if chronic otitis media is suspected. The temporal bone may reveal bone destruction, an absence of ossicles, or the presence of a cholesteatoma mass. If neurological symptoms are present, a MRI or CT may reveal inflammation of the lining of the brain and spinal cord (meninges).

Treatment

Treatment of acute otitis media focuses on clearing the middle ear of infection. Acute otitis media is initially treated with a broad-spectrum antibiotic, pending the results of culture and sensitivity testing. If necessary, more specific antibiotic therapy may be ordered depending on what organism is causing the infection. Standard medical therapy for acute otitis media includes prescribing antibiotics for 10 to 14 days.

Recurrent acute otitis media may be managed with long-term antibiotic prevention for 1 to 3 months. If this regimen fails to control the infection, insertion of ventilating tubes into the eardrum through a surgical drainage incision (myringotomy) may be required. Eardrums rupturing spontaneously usually heal by themselves.

Persistent perforation frequently evolves into chronic otitis media.

Persistent serous otitis media may be treated with a course of oral corticosteroids and antibiotics, separately or in combination. Placement of a ventilating tube (tympanostomy tube) through a myringotomy incision in the eardrum may restore hearing and alleviate the sense of fullness in the ear. In adults, this is usually an office procedure.

A myringotomy for acute middle ear infections is reserved for individuals with severe ear pain or complications such as inflammation or infection of the mastoid process of the temporal bone (mastoiditis) or the lining of the brain and spinal cord (meningitis), involvement of the facial nerve, or signs of brain abscess.

Treatment of chronic otitis media requires the regular removal of infected debris from the middle ear through the perforation (an outpatient procedure), use of earplugs to protect against water exposure, and topical antibiotic drops for treatment of ear drainage. Surgery (myringoplasty or tympanoplasty) is usually required to repair the perforation or remove a cholesteatoma (cyst-like mass) that eventually grows in the middle ear, mastoid process, or mastoid region, and erodes bone and invades the middle ear structures.

Prognosis

Most individuals with acute otitis media improve after 48 hours on antibiotic therapy and may be symptom-free after several days. However, full recovery is dependent on the individual's compliance with a complete course of antibiotic therapy regardless of how well the individual feels after a few doses. Disruption in antibiotic therapy before the prescription is completed can result in a recurrence of the infection, and may contribute to the growth of antibiotic-resistant organisms. Outcomes for chronic otitis media are less predictable and outpatient treatment tends to be ongoing. At some point, surgery is often required to reconstruct the perforated eardrum (tympanoplasty), clear the mastoid air cells of infection (mastoidectomy), and remove the growth of excess tissue in the ear canal (removal of cholesteatoma).

Differential Diagnosis

Since serous otitis media is not common in adults, individuals with persistent serous otitis media on one side (unilateral) should be examined for nasopharyngeal cancer (carcinoma). Other diagnoses could be middle ear trauma, middle ear tumor (neoplasm), and otic barotrauma (an inability to equalize the barometric stress exerted on the middle ear by air travel, rapid altitudinal change, or underwater diving).

Specialists

- Audiologist
- Neurologist
- Neurosurgeon
- Otolaryngologist
- Radiologist

Rehabilitation

Because the middle and inner ear not only allow an individual to hear but also contribute to balance, rehabilitation is important if any problems with steadiness and equilibrium (center of gravity) occur. Once the initial inflammation or infection of otitis media resolves, individuals may need a physical therapist trained in vestibular rehabilitation to help regain any loss of balance. The physical therapist begins by evaluating the individual to determine if the balance problem is a result of an inner ear dysfunction or from other areas such as the brain's center for balance. Once this is determined, the therapist establishes a plan of care. Much of the therapy focuses on balance exercises that challenge the individual's balance with and without the help of visual and sensory stimulus.

Individuals with permanent conductive hearing loss may require vocational or occupational therapy to help prepare them for a different job. Amplification (use of hearing aids) may be required depending on the severity of the hearing loss.

Work Restrictions / Accommodations

Work restrictions and accommodations for individuals with acute or chronic otitis media are related to the degree of hearing loss. Because hearing loss caused by acute otitis media is usually temporary, accommodations are usually temporary. Hearing will most often return to normal levels when the infection clears, the normal pressure resumes in the eustachian tube, and the fluid behind the eardrum is absorbed. This may take a few weeks. Hearing loss associated with chronic otitis media is more long-term and may be permanent requiring a long-term or permanent accommodation in the workplace, in addition to the use of hearing aids. Balance disorders resulting from ear infections may require work restrictions for the safety of the individual and co-workers.

Complementary and Alternative Therapies

Content is intended for awareness only. Treatments may or may not be effective. Scientific evidence may be lacking and some substances have potentially toxic effects. Dr. Presley Reed and the editors do not endorse the use of these therapies in the absence of consultation with a licensed medical professional.

Kampo-medicine - Sairei-to may resolve inflammation and immune response associated with secretory otitis media.

Borneol-walnut oil - A concentration of 20% of this oil may provide therapeutic and nontoxic reactions in treating purulent otitis media.

Comorbid Conditions

Comorbid conditions that may influence the length of disability include chemotherapy, antirejection drugs following organ transplantation, weakened immune systems (immunosuppression), chronic diseases like HIV/AIDS or leukemia, and conditions that increase the likelihood of surgical wound infection (such as obesity, AIDS, and diabetes). Chronic pulmonary or cardiovascular diseases increase an individual's risk during surgical procedures that require general anesthetic.

Complications

If treatment of acute or chronic otitis media fails, the infection can spread to other areas of the head and neck causing serious, even life-threatening complications. Acute suppurative mastoiditis requires surgical drainage. Infection of the petrous bone (petrous apicitis) situated between the inner and middle ear, requires prolonged antibiotic therapy and surgical drainage. Infection of the skull base (osteomyelitis) requires antibiotic therapy and possible surgical debridement of the infected bone. Facial paralysis caused by inflammation of the facial nerve requires drainage of the middle ear and intravenous antibiotic therapy. Facial palsy caused by chronic pressure on the facial nerve requires steroid and antibiotic therapy, a myringotomy, and occasionally more aggressive surgical correction of the underlying disease (removal of cholesteatoma or mastoidectomy).

Complications involving the nervous system are particularly dangerous. Thrombosis of the sigmoid sinus can lead to sepsis and increased intracranial pressure. Treatment for this includes administration of intravenous antibiotics based on culture and sensitivity testing, surgical drainage, or tying off the internal jugular vein in the neck. Central nervous system infections include epidural abscess, brain abscess, and meningitis.

Permanent hearing loss can be a complication of chronic otitis media.

Factors Influencing Duration

Factors that may influence the length of disability include general state of health, pre-existing diseases affecting major body systems (such as diabetes, HIV/AIDS, leukemia, or cancer), functional immune system, type and virulence of infection, presence of antibiotic-resistant organisms, response to treatment, compliance with treatment regimen, complications requiring surgery, and working or living in a smoke-filled environment.

Length of Disability

The duration of disability depends on the acute versus chronic form and severity of otitis media, and the individual's job requirements.

Duration in Days

Job Classification	Minimum	Optimum	Maximum
Any work	0	3	7

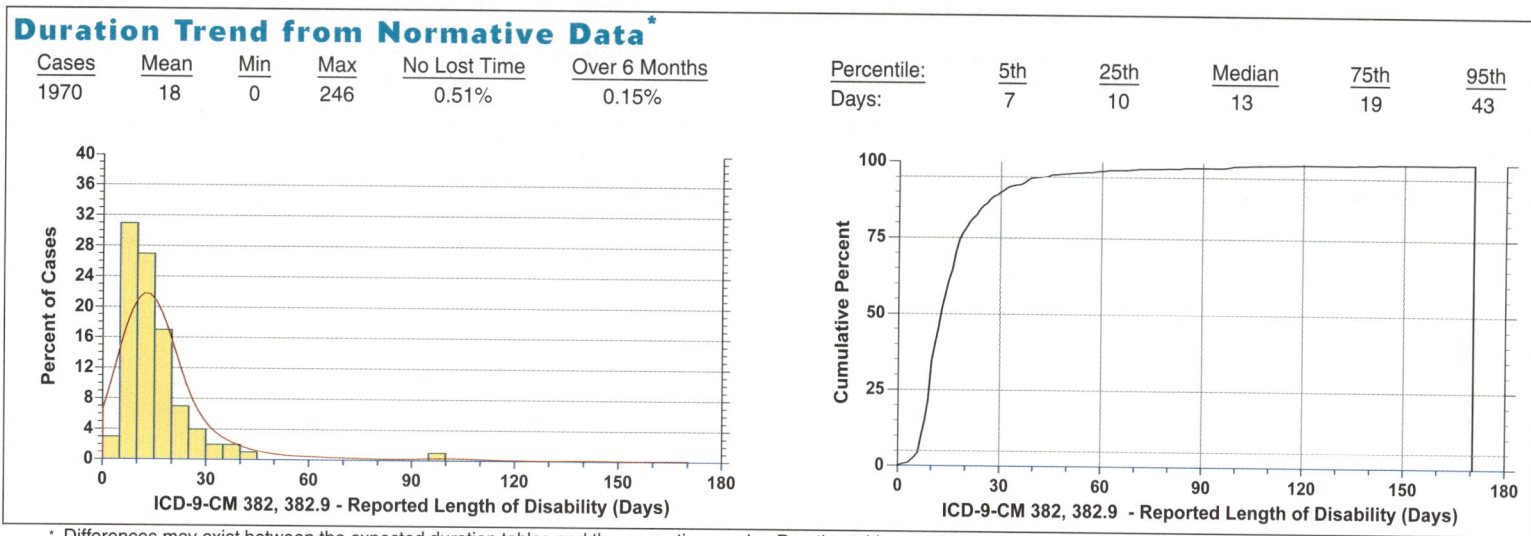

* Differences may exist between the expected duration tables and the normative graphs. Duration tables provide expected recovery periods based on the type of work performed by the individual. The normative graphs reflect the actual observed experience of many individuals across the spectrum of physical conditions, in a variety of industries, and with varying levels of case management.

Failure to Recover

If an individual fails to recover within the maximum duration expectancy period, the reader may wish to reference the following questions to assist in better understanding the specifics of an individual's medical case.

Regarding diagnosis:

- Has individual recently had an upper respiratory tract infection?
- Does individual have a history of allergies or enlarged adenoids? History of recurrent acute otitis media, long-term decreased hearing, and a chronically draining ear?
- Has individual recently experienced trauma to the ear?
- Does individual have a suppressed immune system?
- Does individual participate in activities that cause negative middle ear pressure such as scuba diving or flying?
- Does individual complain of moderate to severe ear pain (otalgia), pain behind the ear, fever, decreased hearing, fluid drainage from the ear, dizziness, or a sense of fullness in the ear (aural pressure)?
- Was a culture done of fluid drawn from behind the eardrum with a needle and syringe (tympanocentesis)?
- What was the causative organism of the otitis?
- Were audiometric studies performed to determine the degree of conductive hearing loss?
- Did tympanometry measure the middle ear pressure and mobility of the eardrum (tympanic membrane)? Was MRI or CT done if chronic otitis media was suspected?
- Was the diagnosis of acute or chronic otitis media confirmed?

Regarding treatment:

- Was acute otitis media treated initially with a broad-spectrum antibiotic? Did the antibiotic need to be changed when the organism was identified? Was individual compliant with the antibiotic regimen?
- Was recurrent acute otitis media managed with long-term antibiotic prevention?
- If that regimen failed, did individual require insertion of ventilating tubes into the eardrum through a surgical drainage incision (myringotomy)?

- Was persistent serous otitis media treated with oral corticosteroids and antibiotics, separately or in combination?
- Was placement of a ventilating tube (tympanostomy tube) through a myringotomy incision in the eardrum required to restore hearing and alleviate the sense of fullness in the ear?
- Was chronic otitis media treated with removal of infected debris from the middle ear and antibiotic drops?
- Was surgery (myringoplasty or tympanoplasty) required to repair perforation or remove a cyst-like mass (cholesteatoma) in the middle ear?

Regarding prognosis:

- Is this an acute or recurrent infection?
- Was the reason for recurrent infection established?
- Has antibiotic sensitivity test indicated a better option or effective combination?
- Is there lack of compliance with antibiotic regimen? What is being done to ensure compliance?
- Are underlying medical conditions impacting the ability to recovery?
- Have complications developed such as thrombosis of the sigmoid sinus, sepsis, or increased intracranial pressure?
- Have central nervous system infections developed such as epidural abscess, brain abscess, or meningitis? Does individual have permanent hearing loss?
- What treatment is available for complications and what is the expected outcome with treatment?

References

Cavanaugh, Bonita. Nurses Manual of Laboratory and Diagnostic Tests. Philadelphia: F.A. Davis Company, 1999.

Friese, K.H., S. Kruse, and R. Ludtke. "The Homeopathic Treatment of Otitis Media in Children - Comparisons with Conventional Therapy." International Journal of Clinical Pharmacology 35 7 (1997): 296-301.

Ikeda, K., and T. Takasaka. "Treatment of Secretory Otitis Media with Kampo Medicine." Archives of Otorhinolaryngology 245 4 (1988): 234-236.

Lewis, Sharon, Margaret Heitkemper, and Shannon Dirksen. Medical-Surgical Nursing. St. Louis: Mosby, 2000.

Liu, S.L. "Therapeutic Effects of Borneol-Walnut Oil in the Treatment of Purulent Otitis Media." Chung Hsi I Chieh Ho Tsa Chih 10 2 (1990): 93-95.

Murdy, A. "Controversies Concerning Acute Otitis Media." Archives of Pediatry 6 12 (1999): 1338-1344.

Scully, Rosemary. M., and Marylou R. Barnes. Physical Therapy. Philadelphia: J.B. Lippincott Company, 1989.

Tierney, Lawrence M., Stephen McPhee, and Maxine Papadakis. Current Medical Diagnosis and Treatment. New York: McGraw-Hill, 2000.

Otosclerosis
387, 387.9

Definition

Otosclerosis is a disease marked most often by abnormal bone growth in the middle ear. This growth results in decreased vibration and poor transmission of sound waves through the external ear canal to the ear bones (ossicles) of the middle ear causing a conductive hearing loss. The poor transmission of sound waves may also occur in the inner ear or in the hearing nerves and results in a sensori-neural hearing loss. A mixture of both types of hearing loss may sometimes occur. Otosclerosis causes bilateral (occurring in both ears) hearing loss in 80-90% of individuals and usually progresses more rapidly on one side than the other.

Otosclerosis is marked by the formation of spongy bone (otospongiosis) especially in the front and back of the footplate of the ear bone called the stapes. Over time, these lesions interfere with the ability of the auditory bones of the middle ear (incus, malleus, and stapes) to transfer sound vibrations to the inner ear. The most common form of otosclerosis develops when the footplate of the stapes becomes attached (fixed) to an opening in the inner wall of the middle ear (the oval window). This causes immobility (stapedial ankylosis) and results in a conductive hearing loss. The spread of otosclerosis to the inner ear (cochlear otosclerosis) results in a sensori-neural hearing impairment.

Although there is a familial tendency, the cause of otosclerosis is unknown. While the condition can be treated, there is no cure. Otosclerosis begins in the early teens or twenties and is the most common cause of hearing loss in young adults. Twice as many women than men are affected, and the condition may worsen during pregnancy. The disease is more prevalent among Europeans and North Americans of European descent and occurs only half as often in the black population. Otosclerosis affects approximately 10% of the general population. Only 1% of these individuals, however, show clinical evidence of significant hearing impairment.

Diagnosis

History: Individuals with otosclerosis usually report a progressive loss of hearing over a period of many years. Some individuals with otosclerosis are unaware they have the disease until hearing loss becomes so severe that communication is difficult. Some individuals will report ringing in the ears (tinnitus) or that hearing is better in noisy environments than quiet areas. If the otosclerosis spreads to the balance center of the inner ear, an individual may report episodes of unsteadiness.

Physical exam: A positive family history of otosclerosis is found in about 60% of individuals with otosclerosis. Otoscopic examination of the ear may reveal a reddish blush of the eardrum (tympanum or tympanic membrane). This condition is called Schwartze's sign and is related to vascular and bony changes within the middle ear. A hearing examination using a tuning fork (Rinne or Weber test) will help identify conductive hearing loss.

Tests: Audiometry testing is the primary tool for diagnosing otosclerosis as it reveals the extent of hearing loss and identifies conductive hearing loss. The individual's ability to discriminate speech is usually excellent, but variable degrees of sensori-neural hearing loss may be evident. Individuals reporting balance disturbances may require vestibular testing. A CAT scan or head x-ray may be useful in assessing the condition of the ossicles, cochlea, and vestibular organs, and distinguish otosclerosis from other causes of hearing loss.

Treatment

Otosclerosis usually progresses slowly so the condition may not require treatment until hearing loss is significant. Some individuals with otosclerosis may prefer a hearing aid (amplification) for a trial period before considering surgical intervention, since surgery for otosclerosis is usually elective. Surgery (stapedectomy), however, is the preferred form of treatment in almost all cases of otosclerosis. This procedure usually restores at least partial hearing in individuals with otosclerosis involving the stapes and can significantly improve the individual's quality of life. The procedure is performed first in the ear with the most significant hearing loss and then on the other ear, 6 months to 1 year later. During this waiting period, hearing loss in the second ear can usually be effectively managed with amplification.

During a total stapedectomy, the stapes is freed from the opening in the inner wall of the middle ear (oval window) and replaced with other tissue or a wire prosthesis. In some cases, a laser may be used to make a hole in the stapes to allow placement of the prosthesis. Following surgery, precautions must be taken to prevent disruption of the prosthesis. The individual may be advised to avoid nose blowing, lifting, or straining for 6 weeks, and to sneeze with the mouth open. Airline travel is restricted for about 2 weeks, and water in the ear should be avoided until the ear is healed. If surgical repair is not successful and results in hearing loss, treatment consists of developing skills for coping with deafness and includes hearing aids, visual clues, or other technology.

Candidates not suitable for surgery (e.g., individuals with cochlear otosclerosis or persistent, serious balance disorders) can be treated medically. Pharmacological treatment to relieve symptoms associated with balance disorder (possible nausea and vomiting) might include antihistamines, anticholinergics, and sedative-hypnotics (the individual should be warned that these drugs can cause drowsiness). Some evidence suggests that permanent sensori-neural hearing loss associated with cochlear otosclerosis may be stabilized by treatment with oral sodium fluoride over prolonged periods of time, along with vitamin D and calcium therapy. These individuals will also benefit from the use of amplification.

Prognosis

Without a stapedectomy, the individual's hearing loss will progress until middle age (45 to 50 years) and then stabilize. Ninety percent of individuals who have had a stapedectomy will experience a significant improvement in hearing postoperatively, and may often enjoy near normal hearing. Improvement in hearing may be apparent within 3 weeks following surgery. Maximum hearing is obtained in approximately 4 months. Following successful surgery, tinnitus is reduced or eliminated in about 50% of individuals. Ten percent of individuals experience no improvement in hearing postoperatively, and 3% will suffer persistent, profound sensori-neural hearing loss.

Even after a successful stapedectomy, persistent or progressive conductive hearing loss can occur years later due to loosening of the prosthesis and other causes.

Differential Diagnosis

Diseases or conditions resembling otosclerosis include any that cause conductive, sensori-neural, or mixed hearing loss. These include head trauma, chronic otitis media with or without the formation of cholesteatoma, middle ear effusion, congenital fixation of the stapes or malleus (although this is usually diagnosed in childhood), tympanosclerosis, tumors (neoplasms) of the middle ear or external auditory canal, Paget's disease, and osteogenesis imperfecta.

Specialists

- Audiologist
- Otolaryngologist
- Psychiatrist
- Psychologist
- Radiologist

Rehabilitation

Individuals with mild to moderate otosclerosis may require consultation with a speech therapist. The frequency and duration of speech therapy is contingent upon the degree of hearing loss. Individuals may be able to function with the use of hearing aids. Speech therapists also teach lip reading for improved communication. Speech therapists provide suggestions for coping with hearing loss such as eliminating environmental background noise with the use of carpeting, drapes, and upholstered furniture to absorb noise, and by eliminating extraneous background noise such as the radio when communication is necessary. Individuals with severe otosclerosis require a stapedectomy that restores hearing in most cases.

Individuals with persistent balance disorders may benefit from an exercise program designed to take advantage of the brain's tendency to eventually adapt (habituate) to the repetition of a specific stimulus that causes an individual's sensation of rotation or movement of themselves or their surroundings (vertigo and vestibular rehabilitation). Individuals visit the physical therapist or occupational therapist during an initial period and also exercise daily at home. Adaptation may take days or months and requires the individual's willingness to move around despite sensations of imbalance or vertigo. Although sitting or lying with the head perfectly still may feel more comfortable, this immobility can prolong or even prevent the adaptation process and should be avoided.

Traditional physical therapy addresses secondary symptoms associated with inactivity that accompany persistent balance disorders. These symptoms include decreased strength, loss of range of motion, and increased tension particularly in the cervical and shoulder region that can lead to muscle fatigue and headaches.

Work Restrictions / Accommodations

Work restrictions and accommodations may be required for individuals who continue to experience balance disturbances or persistent hearing loss following recovery from a stapedectomy (for their own protection as well as the safety of others). Individuals with hearing loss (temporary or permanent) might require vocational or occupational therapy to help them prepare for a different job. Amplification may be required depending on the severity of the hearing loss. Physical therapy may be required for individuals with balance disorders. Persistent facial paralysis or palsy may also require accommodations if the individual's job requires distinct speech.

Comorbid Conditions

Comorbid conditions that may influence the length of disability for individuals with otosclerosis include chronic pulmonary or cardiovascular diseases (increase individual's risk during surgical procedures requiring sedation or a general anesthetic), and diseases and conditions that increase the likelihood of surgical wound infection (i.e., obesity, AIDS, and diabetes).

Complications

Complications related to otosclerosis are primarily surgical complications following stapedectomy. These can include tympanic membrane perforation (requiring additional surgery), persistent conductive hearing loss (result of middle ear effusion, a loose prosthesis, or a displaced prostheses), sensori-neural hearing loss, cochlear deafness, alterations in taste, dryness of the mouth due to potential injury to the chorda tympani nerve, temporary or persistent balance disorders, persistent tinnitus, facial nerve palsy, facial nerve paralysis (uncommon), perilymph fistula (due to incomplete closure of the oval window), and nystagmus.

Individuals receiving fluoride therapy may experience gastrointestinal irritation (nausea and vomiting) that usually responds to adjustment in dosage.

Acute otitis media in the postoperative period is a rare but very serious condition that threatens hearing in the operated ear. Middle ear infection can quickly involve the inner ear, and in rare cases, lead to meningitis.

Individuals with permanent profound hearing loss following surgery or other complication may become depressed.

Factors Influencing Duration

Factors influencing the length of disability for otosclerosis include the general health and fitness of the individual before surgery, evidence of pre-existing diseases affecting any of the major body systems that might interfere with the healing process (e.g., diabetes, HIV/AIDS, or leukemia), individual's general ability to heal, compliance with postoperative orders, and whether or not the individual experiences any degree of depression following permanent hearing loss.

Length of Disability

Duration may be reduced if stapes removal and reconstruction are performed using microsurgical techniques. Disability may be influenced by surgical complications.

Surgical treatment.

Duration in Days

Job Classification	Minimum	Optimum	Maximum
Sedentary work	7	14	28
Light work	7	14	28
Medium work	7	21	42
Heavy work	7	21	42
Very Heavy work	7	21	42

Failure to Recover

If an individual fails to recover within the maximum duration expectancy period, the reader may wish to reference the following questions to assist in better understanding the specifics of an individual's medical case.

Regarding diagnosis:

- Does the individual report a gradual bilateral hearing loss over several years with one side progressing more rapidly? Does the individual report communication difficulty?
- Does the individual report tinnitus or unsteadiness?
- Does the individual have a familial tendency for otosclerosis?
- On exam did the physician find a reddish blush of the eardrum?
- Has the individual had audiometric testing?
- Has the individual had a CT scan, MRI and vestibular testing?
- Have conditions with similar symptoms been ruled out?

Regarding treatment:

- Has the individual used a hearing aid?
- Is the individual a candidate for stapedectomy?
- Has the individual elected to have a stapedectomy done?
- Is the individual taking precautions to prevent disruption of the prosthesis?
- If surgery was unsuccessful, is the individual developing skills for coping with deafness?
- Is the individual also being treated with antihistamines, anticholinergics, or sedative-hypnotics or fluoride therapy?

Regarding prognosis:

- Is the individual active in speech and vestibular rehabilitation?
- Does the individual have a home exercise program?
- Is the individual's employer able to accommodate any necessary restrictions?
- Does the individual have any conditions that may affect their ability to recover?
- Does the individual have any complications such as nausea and vomiting, tympanic membrane perforation, persistent conductive hearing loss, sensori-neural hearing loss, cochlear deafness, alterations in taste, dryness of the mouth, temporary or persistent balance disorders, persistent tinnitus, facial nerve palsy, facial nerve paralysis, perilymph fistula or nystagmus? Does the individual have any postoperative infections? Has the individual become depressed?

References

Lewis, Sharon, Margaret Heitkemper, and Shannon Dirksen. Medical-Surgical Nursing. St. Louis: Mosby, 2000.

Tierney, Lawrence, Stephen McPhee, and Maxine Papadakis. Current Medical Diagnosis and Treatment. New York: McGraw-Hill, 2000.

Ovarian Cyst, Benign

Other names / synonyms: Adnexal Mass, Corpus Albicans Cyst, Corpus Luteum Cyst, Follicular Cysts, Functional Ovarian Cysts, Physiological Ovarian Cysts, Serous Cyst of Ovary, Simple Cyst of Ovary

620.0, 620.1, 620.2

Definition

An ovarian cyst is a sac filled with a collection of fluid or semi-solid material that forms on the ovary. These cysts (functional cysts) are relatively common and can develop at any time, most often during childbearing years. In women who are menopausal and no longer having periods, functional cysts should not develop.

As part of the normal menstrual cycle, the ovary releases an egg (ovum). This ovum develops within a sac or pouch-like depression (follicle), which then appears as a bulge on the surface of the ovary. When the follicle bursts open, the ovum is released; the ovarian follicle then collapses. Blood within the follicle clots and, under the influence of the luteinizing hormones, the remaining cells of the follicle become the corpus luteum. The corpus luteum secretes estrogen and progesterone for the next 7-8 days in preparation for fertilization and pregnancy. If pregnancy occurs, the corpus luteum continues to produce hormones until the placenta develops. If pregnancy does not occur, the corpus luteum deteriorates, becoming the corpus albicans; it eventually disappears. Follicular cysts occur when the ovarian follicle fails to rupture and release the ovum. These cysts continue to secrete estrogen instead of being reabsorbed, and the fluid within the follicle persists, forming a cyst. Follicular cysts usually resolve during the next 2 menstrual periods without treatment.

A corpus luteum cyst is formed when the ovarian follicle ruptures but fails to deteriorate. These cysts, filled with either serous fluid or blood, continue to produce progesterone. They, also, may disappear during the next two menstrual periods.

Serous cysts, also known as cystomas, usually form from the surface tissue of the ovary. Serous cysts may develop into ovarian cancer. They also have the potential of growing so large that the abdomen may distend.

Another type of ovarian cyst, theca-lutein cysts, may develop as a result of excessive levels of the hormone HCG (human chorionic gonadotropin). When the hormone level drops, the cysts usually shrink. Such cysts may be found in women who take infertility drugs to stimulate the ovaries as part of their infertility treatment. Theca-lutein cysts may also be found in association with tumors that produce excess amounts of chorionic gonadotropin (hydatidiform mole, choriocarcinoma).

Ovarian cysts occur in 30% of females with regular menses, 50% of females with irregular menses, and 6% of postmenopausal females. Approximately 5% of functional cysts may actually be the beginning of a malignant tumor. Ovarian cancer is more common among women over the age of 50.

Diagnosis

History: Individuals may report symptoms such as abnormal bleeding (shortened or lengthened cycles), absent or irregular menses, constant dull aching pelvic pain, pain when moving, pain shortly after beginning or ending menses (dysmenorrhea), nausea and/or vomiting, or breast tenderness. Pain during sexual intercourse (dyspareunia) may be related to a ruptured cyst. Sudden onset of severe pain or intermittent severe pain, usually associated with nausea and vomiting, is suggestive of the cyst twisting on the stem by which it is attached to the ovary (ovarian torsion).

Physical exam: A complete physical exam should be performed to search for signs of infection or tumor (neoplasm). Ovarian cysts may be discovered by pressing down on the abdomen with hand (palpating the abdomen) or bimanual pelvic exam (during pelvic exam, one hand is on top of the abdomen; the ovary is pressed between the hands to evaluate its size and shape).

Tests: Tests should include a blood test (human chorionic gonadotropin or HCG) to rule out pregnancy. An ultrasound, or a thin, lighted microscope (laparoscope) inserted into the abdominal cavity for a visual examination (laparoscopy), may be necessary to confirm the diagnosis, and to determine the size and position of the cyst. A chorionic gonadotropin titer blood test may reveal extremely high levels of chorionic gonadotropin hormone if a theca-lutein cyst is present; a blood test for FSH can determine the level of the follicle stimulating hormone; a blood test for LH will determine the level of the luteinizing hormone.

Treatment

Most ovarian (functional) cysts do not require treatment, and usually disappear in about 60 days. Oral contraceptives are sometimes prescribed to suppress the hormones that may be causing the cyst to grow, to help re-establish normal cycles, and to reduce cyst size. The individual may be examined after her next menstrual period to see if the cyst has resolved. Discontinuation of gonadotropin therapy, given for infertility, may also cause cysts to spontaneously disappear as the many follicles then begin to mature. It may, however, take several months for them to resolve.

Depending on the size of the cyst and how it appears on the ultrasound, for diagnostic purposes a laparoscope can be inserted into the abdomen through a small surgical opening (exploratory laparoscopy). If the cyst is small, it can be removed through the laparoscope. If there appears to be more than one cyst, if the ultrasound indicates the cyst is solid rather than fluid-filled, or if the cyst is larger than 8 centimeters, a larger abdominal cut (laparotomy) is made to remove either the cyst or the entire ovary (oophorectomy).

Any cyst that enlarges or persists longer than 60 days probably is not a functional cyst, and surgery is required to rule out other causes of the symptoms. If a cyst becomes twisted on its stem (torsion) and shuts off its blood supply, or ruptures and causes severe bleeding, a laparoscopy or laparotomy is usually necessary. Any postmenopausal ovarian enlargement should be investigated promptly regardless of its size.

Prognosis

A complete recovery can be expected. Most cysts resolve spontaneously within 60 days without treatment. Medication or surgery (laparotomy) effectively treats those cysts that do not resolve spontaneously.

Differential Diagnosis

Other conditions with similar presentation that need to be ruled out include: acute appendicitis, bowel obstruction, diverticular disease, inflammatory bowel syndrome, ovarian torsion, pelvic inflammatory disease (PID), ectopic pregnancy, renal calculi, ovarian abscess, distention of the fallopian tube by clear fluid (hydrosalpinx), and ovarian cancer.

Specialists

- General Surgeon
- Gynecologist

Work Restrictions / Accommodations

Time off may need to be allotted for follow-up doctor visits. Heavy lifting may be restricted if surgery was necessary.

Comorbid Conditions

Endometriosis would impact ability to recover and further lengthen disability.

Complications

A small percent of cysts may be cancerous (malignant). Complications that generally require emergency surgery include twisting (torsion) of the cyst on its stem and rupture that results in severe bleeding (hemorrhage). If surgical removal of the entire ovary (oophorectomy) is performed, infertility may result. Enlargement of the cyst or a cyst that persists longer than 60 days may complicate the condition.

Factors Influencing Duration

The need for surgery and hospitalization may influence the length of disability.

Length of Disability

Length of disability is dependent on whether surgery (hospitalization) is required.

Medical treatment.

Duration in Days

Job Classification	Minimum	Optimum	Maximum
Sedentary work	0	3	14
Light work	0	3	14
Medium work	0	3	14
Heavy work	0	3	14
Very Heavy work	0	3	14

Surgical treatment. Laparoscopic resection of ovarian cyst (cystectomy).

Duration in Days

Job Classification	Minimum	Optimum	Maximum
Sedentary work	3	7	21
Light work	3	7	21
Medium work	7	14	28
Heavy work	7	21	35
Very Heavy work	14	21	35

Surgical treatment. Oophorectomy or abdominal hysterectomy.

Duration in Days

Job Classification	Minimum	Optimum	Maximum
Sedentary work	28	42	56
Light work	28	42	56
Medium work	42	56	70
Heavy work	42	70	84
Very Heavy work	42	84	98

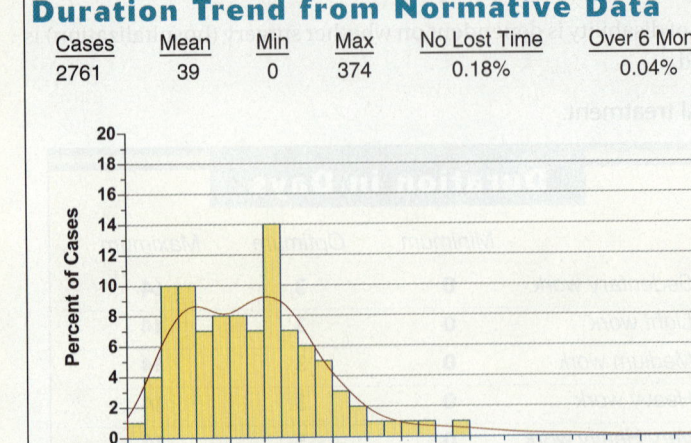
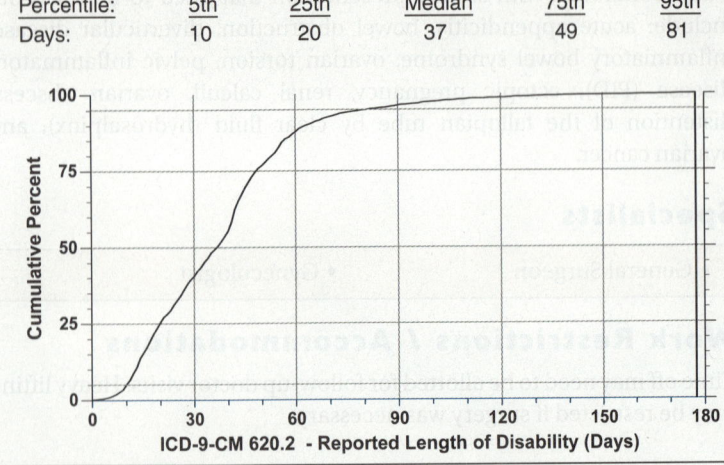

*Differences may exist between the expected duration tables and the normative graphs. Duration tables provide expected recovery periods based on the type of work performed by the individual. The normative graphs reflect the actual observed experience of many individuals across the spectrum of physical conditions, in a variety of industries, and with varying levels of case management.

Failure to Recover

If an individual fails to recover within the maximum duration expectancy period, the reader may wish to reference the following questions to assist in better understanding the specifics of an individual's medical case.

Regarding diagnosis:

- Is the woman of childbearing age?
- Did the woman experience symptoms consistent with the diagnosis of an ovarian cyst, such as abnormal bleeding, absent or irregular menses, pelvic pain, dysmenorrhea, pain during sexual intercourse or nausea and vomiting?
- Did the woman have symptoms of a ruptured cyst or ovarian torsion?
- Was a mass noted during the pelvic exam?
- Was a complete physical exam done?
- Was a CBC and HCG done?
- Was there evidence of a follicular cyst, such as elevated FSH levels?
- Was the diagnosis confirmed using laparoscopy?
- Were other conditions considered in the differential diagnosis (acute appendicitis, bowel obstruction, diverticular disease, inflammatory bowel syndrome, ovarian torsion, pelvic inflammatory disease (PID), ectopic pregnancy, renal calculi, ovarian abscess, distention of the fallopian tube by clear fluid (hydrosalpinx), and ovarian cancer)?

Regarding treatment:

- Were follow-up exams performed?
- Did the cyst resolve or shrink in size?
- Were oral contraceptives tried?
- Was surgery indicated? If so, was malignancy or torsion detected?

Regarding prognosis:

- Did the cyst resolve without treatment?
- Was medication or surgical intervention indicated and effective?
- Did the individual have any associated conditions or complications, such as endometriosis, malignancy, torsion associated with bleeding, and infertility, that may impact recovery?

References

Crayford, T.J., et al. "Benign Ovarian Cysts and Ovarian Cancer: A Cohort Study with Implications for Screening." Lancet 355 9209 (2000): 1060-1063.

Goldman, Lee, and J. Claude Bennett. Cecil Textbook of Medicine, 21st ed. Philadelphia: W.B. Saunders Company, 2000.

Ovarian Cyst, Resection of

Other names / synonyms: Ovarian Cystectomy

65.2

Definition

A resection of an ovarian cyst is the surgical removal of an abnormal fluid-filled sac (cyst) within ovarian tissue.

Eggs within the ovary are surrounded by specialized cells that assist in the process of egg maturation and release (ovulation). The egg with its surrounding cells is called an ovarian follicle, and cysts that developed from ovarian follicles are called follicular cysts. The follicular remnant after release of an egg (corpus luteum) can also develop into a cyst (corpus luteum cyst). For some reason, the cells of the follicle or corpus luteum produce excess fluid, which often creates cysts. Ovarian cysts can develop from uterine tissue (endometrial cyst) that has been transplanted onto the ovary (endometriosis).

Ovarian cysts are very common and are most prevalent in women of child-bearing age. Most ovarian cysts are noncancerous (benign) and resolve on their own.

Reason for Procedure

Resection of an ovarian cyst is done to remove symptomatic noncancerous (benign) cysts of the ovary that do not resolve with time, do not respond to treatment, or cause heavy bleeding. Resection, as opposed to ovary removal (oophorectomy), is usually done in younger women who wish to retain their ability to have children. It allows for shortened hospital stays and shorter recuperation time.

Description

This procedure is usually done by inserting a small wand-like instrument (laparoscope) into the abdominal (peritoneal) cavity to visualize the ovaries (laparoscopy).

Ovarian cysts may also be removed by traditional open surgery (laparotomy). Although not a standard procedure, ovarian cysts may be removed by approaching the ovary through an incision in the vaginal wall in a procedure called a colpotomy. Colpotomy is less traumatic than laparoscopy and greatly reduces the risk that the contents of the cyst will spill into the abdominal cavity.

The method used largely depends upon the expertise of the surgeon and the size of the cyst. A laparoscopy is more technically difficult, but reduces the incidence of certain complications (e.g., cutting the intestines). A laparotomy would be indicated for individuals with a very large cyst, internal scar tissue (adhesions) which increases the risk of cutting the intestines, and for individuals who are obese. In general, laparoscopy and colpotomy are performed on an outpatient basis and laparotomy is performed as an inpatient procedure; all are done under general anesthesia.

For laparoscopy, the abdominal cavity is inflated with carbon dioxide gas (pneumoperitoneum) to allow visualization within the abdomen and provide an open work space. Gas is introduced into the abdominal cavity through a needle (Veress needle). One or more small incisions are made into the abdominal cavity and needle-like tubes (trocar) are inserted. Once the laparoscope is inserted through a trocar, the abdominal cavity can be viewed on a video screen. Small instruments, either attached to the laparoscope or inserted through other trocars, are used to perform the surgery.

For laparotomy, a large incision is made into the abdomen to expose the ovary. With colpotomy, the incision is made into the vaginal wall. The cyst may be drained prior to removal, and along with its shell (capsule) it is gently peeled away from the ovarian tissue. Bleeding may need to be controlled by electric current (coagulation) or laser. At the discretion of the surgeon, the ovarian incision may be stitched (sutured) closed or left open. Before suturing the abdomen closed, the abdominal cavity is washed to remove any cyst contents that might have spilled.

The excised cyst is examined microscopically to make sure it is noncancerous (benign).

Prognosis

Regardless of the surgical procedure, most cysts can be completely removed (excised) without complications, and a thorough recovery can be expected.

Women are encouraged to resume normal activities and perform mild exercise (e.g., walking) as soon as they are able.

Specialists

- Gynecologist
- Pathologist
- Radiologist

Work Restrictions / Accommodations

Strenuous physical activities (e.g., heavy lifting, walking long distances, going up and down stairs, carrying heavy objects) may need to be temporarily restricted following ovarian cyst resection. Even normal activities may cause fatigue, so frequent rest breaks may be necessary. Women who have a laparotomy may be temporarily unable to drive a car or other motor vehicle.

Comorbid Conditions

Obesity and general debility can increase the length of disability.

Procedure Complications

Improper placement of the Veress needle can result in gas being introduced into the wrong cavity, which, if it enters into the pleural cavity can cause breathing difficulty (dyspnea) and, rarely, a collapsed lung (pneumothorax). The Veress needle or trocar can cut major abdominal or pelvic blood vessels, or injure the intestines, bladder, or tubes leading from the kidneys to the bladder (ureters). Rarely, the intestine may protrude out of the incisions (herniate). Bleeding (hemorrhage), infection, and blood clots (thromboembolism) are complications of any gynecological surgical procedure. Abdominal surgery can lead to formation of internal scar tissue (adhesions), which can cause pain, constriction of the intestines, and infertility.

Factors Influencing Duration

Length of disability may be influenced by the type of surgery performed and the development of complications. Women who have a laparoscopy may have a shorter disability than those who have a laparotomy.

Length of Disability

Disability may be longer if the strenuous activity is required.

Laparoscopic.

Duration in Days

Job Classification	Minimum	Optimum	Maximum
Sedentary work	5	7	14
Light work	5	7	14
Medium work	7	10	21
Heavy work	7	21	21
Very Heavy work	14	21	21

Open surgery.

Duration in Days

Job Classification	Minimum	Optimum	Maximum
Sedentary work	28	42	56
Light work	28	42	56
Medium work	42	56	70
Heavy work	42	70	84
Very Heavy work	42	84	98

References

Adelson, Mark, and Katherine Adelson. "Miscellaneous Benign Disorders of the Upper Genital Tract." Textbook of Gynecology. Copeland, Larry, and John Jarrell, eds. Philadelphia: W.B. Saunders Company, 2000. 723-739.

Levine, Ronald. "Operative Laparoscopy." Te Linde's Operative Gynecology Updates 1 3 (1997): 1-13.

Namnoum, Anne, and Ana Murphy. "Diagnostic and Operative Laparoscopy." Te Linde's Operative Gynecology. Rock, John, and John Thompson, eds. Philadelphia: Lippincott-Raven, 1997. 389-413.

Namnoum, Sanfilippo, and John Rock. "Surgery for Benign Disease of the Ovary." Te Linde's Operative Gynecology. Rock, John, and John Thompson, eds. Philadelphia: Lippincott-Raven, 1997. 625-644.

Paget's Disease of Bone

Other names / synonyms: Osteitis Deformans

731.0

Definition

Paget's disease is an ongoing (chronic) disorder that results in enlarged and deformed bones. Normally, the body maintains a healthy balance between the cells that break down bone tissue and those that rebuild it. That balance is disturbed in Paget's disease, causing bones to weaken, thicken, and become deformed. The bones most commonly affected are the hip bone (pelvis), skull, collar bone (clavicle), vertebrae, and the bones of the thighs and lower legs (lower extremities). The changes in the skull brought about by the disease have been associated with a distortion of the facial bones, producing a lion-like appearance (leontiasis) and with loose teeth. Ultimately, the individual is plagued with bone pain, arthritis, and fractures.

In individuals with Paget's disease of the bone, the condition of the skeleton is characterized by rapid, chaotic bone resorption followed by equally chaotic and excessive bone formation. Such disease activity leads to enlarged but weakened and highly vascularized bone that is painful, easily deformed, and subject to fractures with minimal trauma. Cranial and vertebral involvement can also cause neurologic deficits.

Theories about causes for Paget's disease abound, but none have been proven. One theory holds that the disease may be caused by a "slow virus" infection that is sometimes present for many years before symptoms appear. Another theory holds that the cause may be hereditary, since the disease often appears in more than one family member.

Paget's disease is rarely diagnosed in individuals under 40 years of age. Men and women are affected equally. Prevalence of Paget's disease ranges from 1.5 to 8%, depending on age and country of residence. Prevalence of familial Paget's disease (where more than one family member has the disease) ranges from 10 to 40% in different parts of the world. Because early diagnosis and treatment are important after age 40, siblings and children of someone with Paget's disease may wish to have an alkaline phosphatase blood test every 2 or 3 years. Alkaline phosphatase is a chemical (enzyme) that is produced by bone cells and that is over-produced by Pagetic bone. An elevated level of alkaline phosphatase indicates abnormal bone cell activity, which can suggest Paget's disease.

Diagnosis

History: In mild cases of Paget's disease of the bone, there may be few or no symptoms. However, bone or skeletal pain, the most common symptom, can occur in any bone affected by Paget's disease, and often localizes to areas adjacent to the joints. Other forms of pain include headaches, radicular pain (sciatica), muscular pain, and osteoarthritic pain. Hearing loss may occur when Paget's disease affects the skull. Pressure on nerves may also occur when the skull or spine is affected. Hip pain may occur when the hipbone (pelvis) or thigh bone (femur) is involved. Individuals may also complain of arthritis, which may be due to damage to the cartilage of joints adjacent to the affected bone.

Physical exam: The exam may reveal hearing loss (when Paget's disease affects the skull), pressure on the nerves (when the disease affects the skull or spine), increased head size, bowing of the long bones in the legs, curvature of the spine (scoliosis), and damage to cartilage in the joints.

Tests: Diagnostic procedures for Paget's disease may include x-ray studies, blood tests (especially the bone-specific alkaline phosphatase test), and bone scans. The bones of individuals that have Paget's disease have a characteristic appearance on x-ray tests; thickened and porous areas in certain bones are apparent. The blood tests reveal an elevated level of the enzyme associated bone cell formation (alkaline phosphatase). Bone scans are useful in determining the extent and activity of the condition. If a bone scan suggests Paget's disease, the affected bone(s) should be x-rayed to confirm the diagnosis.

Treatment

If the afflicted individual presents without symptoms, no treatment is necessary. Specific treatment for Paget's disease of the bone is determined by the physician based on the individual's overall health and medical history, the extent of the disease, the individual's tolerance for specific medications, procedures, or therapies, expectations for the course of the disease, and the individual's opinion and preference.

Treatment may include painkillers (analgesics) and anti-inflammatory medications (to help relieve painful symptoms), calcium (1000-1500 mg daily), vitamin D (400 units daily), and hormones (to promote growth and repair of thinning, brittle bones, or osteoporosis), and physical therapy and exercise (to maintain skeletal health, avoid weight gain, and maintain joint mobility).

The hormone calcitonin and other drugs (e.g., etidronate disodium and mithramycin) control resorption of bone, reduce alkaline phosphatase levels, promote normal bone formation, and relieve bone pain.

Surgery may be recommended to remedy 3 major complications of Paget's disease, which are fractures, severe degenerative arthritis, and bone deformity. Surgery may enable fractures to heal in a better position. If disability is severe (severe degenerative arthritis), and medication and physical therapy are no longer helpful, joint replacement of the hips and knees may be considered. Finally, cutting and realignment of Pagetic bone (osteotomy) may help painful, weight-bearing joints, especially the knees.

The goal of treatment is to normalize Paget's disease activity (which involves rapid, chaotic bone resorption followed by equally chaotic and excessive bone formation) for a prolonged period of time. Some of the new bisphosphonates have been shown to accomplish this in a large percentage of individuals afflicted with the disease.

Prognosis

The course of Paget's disease varies greatly and may range from completely stable to rapid progression. In general, symptoms progress slowly in affected bones, and there is usually no spread to normal bones. The outlook is generally good, particularly if treatment is given before major changes have occurred.

Treatment can control Paget's disease and lessen symptoms, but it is not a cure. When untreated, Paget's disease will continue to progress slowly and weaken the individual as complications (such as fractures, severe deformities [arthritis], head enlargement, neurologic deficits, and visual impairment) become more apparent. Death can result from heart failure, paralysis, or bone cancer, which tends to develop in bone areas that have been affected by the disease.

Differential Diagnosis

Another possible diagnosis is osteoarthritis. Paget's disease can cause osteoarthritis when Pagetic bones become enlarged, causing the joint surfaces to undergo excessive wear and tear. Osteoarthritis is a common source of pain in Paget's disease, but the disease itself also causes bone pain. In many individuals, pain may be due to a combination of Paget's disease and arthritis.

Specialists

- Endocrinologist
- Internist
- Orthopedic Surgeon
- Otolaryngologist
- Physiatrist
- Rheumatologist

Rehabilitation

Individuals with Paget's disease may benefit from physical and occupational therapy to strengthen and conserve the joints. In general, physical therapists teach individuals pain control techniques and establish a gentle, strengthening program that the individual should perform daily. Individuals use heating pads to decrease joint stiffness and pain and apply heat for 15 minutes as needed for pain control. Therapists instruct in stretching and strengthening exercises for the affected joints. Individuals learn to perform these exercises independently to help reduce impairment due to arthritis. Individuals also perform low-impact aerobic exercise such as walking to increase strength and endurance and decrease fatigue.

Individuals unable to perform exercises due to pain may benefit from an aquatic therapy program in a heated pool. Aquatic exercise provides resistant exercise while reducing the stress through an individual's joints because of the buoyant properties of water. Individuals may also be taught to use assistive devices such as a cane or walker to decrease stress through the legs. Physical therapists may collaborate with orthotists to provide bracing systems that support affected joints.

Occupational therapists address activities of daily living such as dressing and bathing. Individuals may require a consultation with a speech therapist if hearing is affected.

Work Restrictions / Accommodations

Restrictions would include elimination of any work activities that would impose mechanical stress on affected bones, such as carrying, loading, and unpacking boxes and files and lifting and pushing heavy objects (to reduce the chance of fractures and other complications).

Accommodations would involve allowances for time away from work to take part in an exercise program that would help to maintain skeletal health, avoid weight gain, and maintain joint mobility.

Comorbid Conditions

Comorbid conditions that might influence the length of disability include obesity, osteoporosis, arthritis, allergy to treatment medications, and chronic illnesses, such as heart disease and diabetes.

Complications

There are generally 3 major complications of Paget's disease for which surgery may be recommended. The first is a fracture in Pagetic bone. Surgical repair of Pagetic fractures may allow the fracture to heal in better position.

The second complication occurs when the individual develops severe degenerative arthritis. If medication and physical therapy are no longer helpful, and if disability is severe, surgery may be considered as an option.

The third situation involves bone deformity, especially of the tibia. The surgical cutting and realignment of a Pagetic bone (osteotomy) may help painful weight-bearing joints, especially the knees.

Other complications include head enlargement, carpal/tarsal tunnel syndromes, neurologic deficits, deafness, visual impairment, congestive heart failure (high output), kidney stones (renal calculi), and a rare form of bone cancer (osteogenic sarcoma). Medical therapy prior to surgery helps to decrease bleeding and other complications during surgery.

Factors Influencing Duration

The individual's job requirement may determine disability. Replacement of diseased bone requires surgery and will lengthen disability.

Length of Disability

In some cases, disability may be permanent. In cases requiring surgical correction, see specific procedure for length of disability.

Medical treatment.

Duration in Days

Job Classification	Minimum	Optimum	Maximum
Sedentary work	0	14	28
Light work	1	14	28
Medium work	28	42	Indefinite
Heavy work	Indefinite	Indefinite	Indefinite
Very Heavy work	Indefinite	Indefinite	Indefinite

Failure to Recover

If an individual fails to recover within the maximum duration expectancy period, the reader may wish to reference the following questions to assist in better understanding the specifics of an individual's medical case.

Regarding diagnosis:

- Does the individual have bone pain?
- Which of the individual's bones are involved?
- What is the individual's age?
- Is the individual's disease mild or severe?
- Was there evidence of nerve pressure, damage to cartilage or bone deformity noted on the physical exam?
- Were diagnostic x-rays done to confirm the diagnosis?
- Was the possibility of osteoarthritis ruled out?

Regarding treatment:

- Has conservative therapy with anti-inflammatory drugs and analgesics been effective at relieving symptoms?
- Have calcium supplements, hormones and physical therapy been prescribed?
- Has the individual been compliant with treatment recommendations?
- Are the symptoms severe enough to warrant surgical intervention?

Regarding prognosis:

- Is the individual active in physical therapy? Does the individual have a home exercise program?
- Are occupational and speech therapists part of the treatment team?
- Has the employer been able to make appropriate work accommodations so the individual can return to work safely?
- Does the individual have any underlying conditions such as obesity, osteoporosis, arthritis, chronic illnesses or medication allergies that may impact recovery?
- Has the individual experienced any complications such as carpal/tarsal tunnel syndrome, neurological impairment, visual or hearing deficits, CHF, kidney stones or bone cancer that may impact recovery?

References

Bone Disorders. Methodist Health Care System (Houston, Texas). 01 Jan 2000. 1 Jan 2001 <http://www.methodisthealth.com/bone/pagets.htm>.

Mourad, Leona A. "Alterations of Musculoskeletal Function." Pathophysiology. McCance, Kathryn L., and Sue E. Heuther, eds. St. Louis: Mosby-Year Book, 1994. 1434-1481.

Paget's Disease of Breast

Other names / synonyms: Cancer of the Nipple, Paget's Disease of the Nipple

174, 174.0

Definition

Paget's disease of the breast is an uncommon condition of the nipple and surrounding tissue (areola) that is nearly always associated with an underlying breast cancer (greater than 97% of the cases).

The underlying breast cancer is usually extensive; however, in 10% of the cases it is localized to the nipple and nearby tissue. Rarely, there is no apparent underlying breast cancer. Paget's disease of the breast is believed to occur when invasive or breast cancer of the milk ducts (intraductal cancer) spreads through the milk ducts to the nipple.

There are no risk factors that are specific for Paget's disease of the breast. Women who have a higher risk of developing breast cancer include those with a family history of breast cancer, genetic alterations which may make them prone to breast cancer, or noncancerous (benign) breast disease. Also at risk are women who are greater than 50 years old (especially if overweight), consume alcohol, began menstruating before 12 years of age, went through menopause after 55 years of age, had their first child after 30 years of age, or have no biological children. Men who have had radiation exposure and those who have Klinefelter's syndrome are at an increased risk of developing breast cancer.

In the US, approximately 180,000 women are diagnosed with breast cancer each year. Paget's disease of the breast represents approximately 2% of all breast cancers. It afflicts both men and women; however, breast cancer is rare in men. The average age of women with Paget's disease of the breast is 62 years and of men is 69 years.

Diagnosis

History: The individual may complain of redness, scaling, and flaking of the nipple skin. The individual may also report nipple tingling, itching (pruritus), oversensitivity (hypersensitivity), burning, or pain. Alternatively, the individual may report a painless, nonitchy rash in the nipple area. The individual with involvement of the areola would most likely report that the skin problem originated at the nipple and then spread out to include the areola.

Physical exam: The nipple may have an eczema-like (eczematoid) rash with irritation, crusting, and scaling. In addition, a small sore or erosion that does not heal may be present. The nipple may be discharging blood and/or pus. The areola may also be involved. Touching the breast with the hands (palpation) may reveal a mass.

Tests: A scraping of the nipple (exfoliative or scrape cytology) or a smear of the discharge from the nipple or sore may be obtained for microscopic analysis. A sample of nipple tissue may be taken (punch biopsy, superficial epidermal shave biopsy, or wedge incisional biopsy) for microscopic analysis. Mammography, MRI, ultrasound scanning, and breast biopsy may be performed.

Treatment

Paget's disease of the breast is treated with the same treatment options as other breast cancers including breast removal (mastectomy), chemotherapy, and/or radiation therapy. The treatment plan chosen depends on many factors including the size of the cancerous tissue and whether or not the cancer has spread.

Individuals with Paget's disease that is confined to the nipple and areola are usually treated with breast conservation methods. In these cases, just the nipple and areola (nipple areolar complex) would be surgically removed (excised). Mastectomy would be performed on cases in which cancer has spread throughout the breast. Chemotherapy may be used before and/or after surgery. Postoperative radiation therapy may or may not be utilized.

Prognosis

Paget's disease of the breast has an excellent prognosis. For cancer that is localized to the nipple and surrounding tissue, excision of the nipple-areolar complex has a good success rate, especially when used in combination with radiation therapy. If the cancer is confined to the nipple-areolar complex, the incidence of spreading (metastasis) to the lymph nodes is about 5 percent. If Paget's disease is associated with cancer throughout the breast, the chance of metastasis rises, and the prospect of a cure by surgery or other treatment declines. Recurrence of breast cancer is common, even when a mastectomy was performed. Approximately 44,000 women and 400 men in the US die from breast cancer each year.

Differential Diagnosis

Contact dermatitis, eczema, postradiation dermatitis, or bacterial infection have similar signs and symptoms.

Specialists

- General Surgeon
- Oncologist
- Physical Therapist
- Plastic Surgeon
- Psychiatrist
- Psychologist

Rehabilitation

Rehabilitation for Paget's disease of the breast may be indicated if surgical treatment is necessary for removal of breast tissue. This is the case especially if a larger or more aggressive tumor required extensive surgery. For example, if a mastectomy is required, physical therapy is utilized after the surgery to control swelling and restore range of motion, and mobility to the joints of the upper extremities.

Focus of therapy should be on improving arm circulation and shoulder mobility, preventing postural deformities and muscle tension, and gaining shoulder strength. There are also special considerations for individuals who have had the lymph nodes removed in order to prevent lymphedema.

In order to increase circulation, the therapist may begin with hand-clasps (making a tight fist and release). To increase mobility in the shoulder, therapist may instruct the individual in the pendulum. The pendulum is performed in a bent-over position with the affected-side arm hanging loose and both shoulder and arm relaxed. Keeping the shoulder and arm relaxed and using body motion, the individual swings the arm forward and back, side-to-side, and circles in both directions.

Individuals may be instructed in the clasp, reach, and spread for a chest and shoulder stretch. The individual sits with hands clasped together and slowly raises hands toward the top of the head. When the incision begins to pull, the individual stops and holds the position while breathing deeply. When the pulling stops, the hands come down slowly. The individual may eventually progress to putting hands behind head to back of neck, keeping the head straight, and then progress to spreading elbows apart.

Performing the wall climb will also stretch the shoulder. The therapist instructs the individual to face a wall with feet slightly apart and about a foot away from the wall. Both hands are placed on the wall. The individuals slowly walk the fingers up the wall until incisional pulling occurs. At this point, the individual stops and holds the position a few seconds and then slowly walks the fingers down the wall. Exaggerated deep breathing exercises can be performed to ease the feeling of tightness in the chest and to fully expand the lungs.

Rehabilitation programs will also depend on the prognosis, the size of the tumor, and whether it is invasive or has spread to the lymph nodes.

Work Restrictions / Accommodations

During the surgical recovery period, work responsibilities may need to be largely sedentary with no lifting or overhead work. Individuals undergoing chemotherapy and/or radiation therapy need considerable accommodations due to frequent medical appointments and the possibility of potentially incapacitating side effects (e.g., nausea, fatigue) of the treatments. A change in job duties, working part-time, working from home, a flexible work schedule, and frequent breaks may allow the individual to return to work sooner. Use of analgesics and other medications can affect dexterity and alertness. Drug testing policies will need to be evaluated.

Comorbid Conditions

Depression, anemia, and conditions associated with reduced immune system functioning (e.g., AIDS, leukemia, organ transplantation) may influence the length of disability.

Complications

Breast cancer can spread (metastasize) to other areas, especially bone. Cancer is associated with an increased risk of developing blood clots (thrombus).

Factors Influencing Duration

Factors influencing the length of disability include the type and stage of disease at initial presentation, the presence of concurrent infection, overall general health, the type of treatment utilized, the presence of complications, and whether breast reconstruction is performed.

Length of Disability

Duration of the disability depends on job requirements. For all procedures, durations reflect recovery from procedure only. For a lumpectomy, partial or segmental mastectomy, duration depends on amount of tissue removed (size of incision and type of anesthesia - local versus general). For radical mastectomy, duration depends on whether dominant or non-dominant arm is affected and extent of surgery.

Lumpectomy, segmental, or partial mastectomy.

Job Classification	Minimum	Optimum	Maximum
Sedentary work	1	3	14
Light work	1	3	14
Medium work	1	3	14
Heavy work	3	7	21
Very Heavy work	3	7	21

Radical or modified radical mastectomy.

Job Classification	Minimum	Optimum	Maximum
Sedentary work	21	28	42
Light work	28	35	42
Medium work	42	49	56
Heavy work	56	63	84
Very Heavy work	56	63	84

Failure to Recover

If an individual fails to recover within the maximum duration expectancy period, the reader may wish to reference the following questions to assist in better understanding the specifics of an individual's medical case.

Regarding diagnosis:

- Does the individual have underlying breast cancer?
- Does the woman have any risk factor's such as a family history of breast cancer, age over 50 years, obesity, onset of menses before age 12, menopause after age 55, had their first child after age 30 or have no biological children?
- Does the man have risk factors such as, radiation exposure or Klinefelter's syndrome?
- Does the individual complain of redness, scaling, and flaking of the nipple skin?
- Does the individual also report nipple tingling, pruritus, hypersensitivity, burning, or pain? Does the individual report a painless, nonitchy rash in the nipple area?
- Does the individual indicate that the skin problem started at the nipple and then spread?
- On exam, does the individual have an eczema-like rash with irritation, crusting, and scaling? Is an unhealed sore present?
- Is there bloody or purulent discharge from the nipple?
- Is there a mass palpable in the breast?
- Has the individual had exfoliative or scrape cytology testing?
- Has the individual had a smear of the discharge from the nipple examined?
- Has the individual had a biopsy of the affected area?
- Has the individual had a mammogram, MRI, or ultrasound done
- Have conditions with similar symptoms been ruled out?

Regarding treatment:

- Has the individual been treated with surgery to remove the nipple and areolar area, mastectomy, chemotherapy and/or radiation therapy?

Regarding prognosis:

- Is the individual active in physical therapy?
- Does the individual have a home exercise program?
- Is the individual's employer able to accommodate any necessary restrictions?
- Does the individual have any conditions that may affect ability to recover?
- Does the individual have any complications such as metastasis or blood clots?

References

Bassett, Lawrence, Reza Jahan, and Yao Fu. "Invasive Malignancies." Diagnosis of Diseases of the Breast. Bassett, Lawrence, et al., eds. Philadelphia: W.B. Saunders Company, 1997. 461-500.

Dow, Karen, and Barbara Kalinowski. "Nursing Care in Patient Management and Quality of Life." Diseases of the Breast. Harris, Jay, ed. Philadelphia: Lippincott Williams & Wilkins, 2000. 985-999.

Gerber, Lynn, and Elizabeth Augustine. "Rehabilitation Management: Restoring Fitness and Return to Functional Activity." Diseases of the Breast. Harris, Jay, ed. Philadelphia: Lippincott Williams & Wilkins, 2000. 1001-1007.

Kaelin, Carolyn. "Paget's Disease." Diseases of the Breast. Harris, Jay, ed. Philadelphia: Lippincott Williams & Wilkins, 2000. 677-682.

Kisner, C., and L. Colby. Therapeutic Exercise Foundations and Techniques. Philadelphia: F.A. Davis Company, 1990.

Lagios, Michael, and David Page. "In Situ Carcinomas of the Breast: Ductal Carcinoma In Situ, Paget's Disease, Lobular Carcinoma In Situ." The Breast: Comprehensive Management of Benign and Malignant Diseases. Bland, Kirby, and Edward Copeland, eds. Philadelphia: W.B. Saunders Company, 1998. 261-283.

Mullins, Diane. "Epithelial Neoplasms and Dermatological Disorders." The Breast: Comprehensive Management of Benign and Malignant Diseases. Bland, Kirby, and Edward Copeland, eds. Philadelphia: W.B. Saunders Company, 1998. 323-338.

Tierney, Lawrence, Stephen McPhee, and Maxine Papadakis. Current Medical Diagnosis and Treatment. New York: McGraw-Hill, 2000.

Pain in Limb
729.5

Definition
Pain in limb is a term used to describe discomfort affecting any part of a limb or extremity (such as an elbow) or the entire limb (arm or leg). The term is general in nature and could be used to describe pain that arises from various etiologies. The pain may arise from the skin, nerves, muscles, bones, joints, or even the brain (in psychogenic or phantom pain). Typically, the term "pain in the limb" would be used to describe a person's symptoms until a definitive diagnosis is made (such as broken arm, tendonitis, peripheral neuropathy, etc.).

Diagnosis
History: The individual will complain of discomfort in all or part of an extremity. Individuals may use other descriptive terms such as burning, throbbing, aching, or stabbing, to further explain the type of discomfort they are experiencing. They may provide additional information such as how the pain began, exactly where the pain is, and the factors that increase or relieve the pain. They may report a history of an injury, strain, or trauma that preceded the onset of pain.

Physical exam: The physical exam may reveal tender spots, obvious deformities, redness, warmth or coolness, or swelling at the affected site. Range of motion in the affected limb may be limited, and the limb may be weaker in strength than other limbs. The affected site may also demonstrate alterations in sensation (numbness, tingling).

Tests: X-rays, CT scans, and MRI tests may be done to detect abnormalities in the bone, joint, or tissue. X-ray exams of the arteries within the limb (arteriogram) may reveal the presence of blood clots (thrombi) or weakened blood vessels (aneurysms). Tests to detect nerve damage (nerve conduction velocity studies) or evaluate the electrical condition in muscles (electromyography) may be done. Blood tests may be done to check for arthritis and other diseases that affect the entire body (systemic disease).

Treatment
Treatment depends upon the limb affected and the diagnosis made. The treatment will vary according to the underlying cause.

Prognosis
The prognosis depends on the underlying cause and treatment thereof, and can range between full recovery and complete disability.

Differential Diagnosis
Pain in the limb is a descriptive term for a symptom that could result from a variety of disorders that should be considered in the differential diagnosis. These include sprains, strains, fractures, bruises, lacerations, contusions, crush or burn injuries, dislocation or compression, skin conditions, connective tissue diseases such as arthritis or lupus erythematosus, infections, crystal-induced conditions such as gout, benign or malignant tumors, neurological disorders, bone and cartilage disorders, rheumatism, joint problems, hand or foot disorders, spine or pelvic disorders, systemic diseases such as multiple sclerosis, AIDS, and hysteria or other mental disorders.

Specialists
- Dermatologist
- Emergency Medicine
- Infectious Disease Physician
- Internist
- Neurologist
- Oncologist
- Orthopedist
- Pain Specialist
- Physiatrist
- Primary Care Provider
- Psychiatrist
- Psychologist
- Rheumatologist

Work Restrictions / Accommodations
Depending of the nature of the pain and the degree of disability present, restrictions may include either limited or no use of the affected limb.

Comorbid Conditions
Comorbid chronic conditions such as diabetes, thoracic outlet syndrome, peripheral vascular disease, arthritis, immune suppression, autoimmune disorders, cancer, or mental illness may impact ability to recover and further lengthen disability.

Complications
Complex regional pain syndrome (reflex sympathetic dystrophy, or RSD) may be a complication. Chronic pain may be accompanied by issues of dependence and depression. In cases in which pain persists but no cause is identified with objective testing, psychosocial factors (somatization) may be involved.

Factors Influencing Duration
The cause, its treatment, and the individual's response to treatment will determine the length of disability.

Length of Disability
Duration depends on the specific diagnosis.

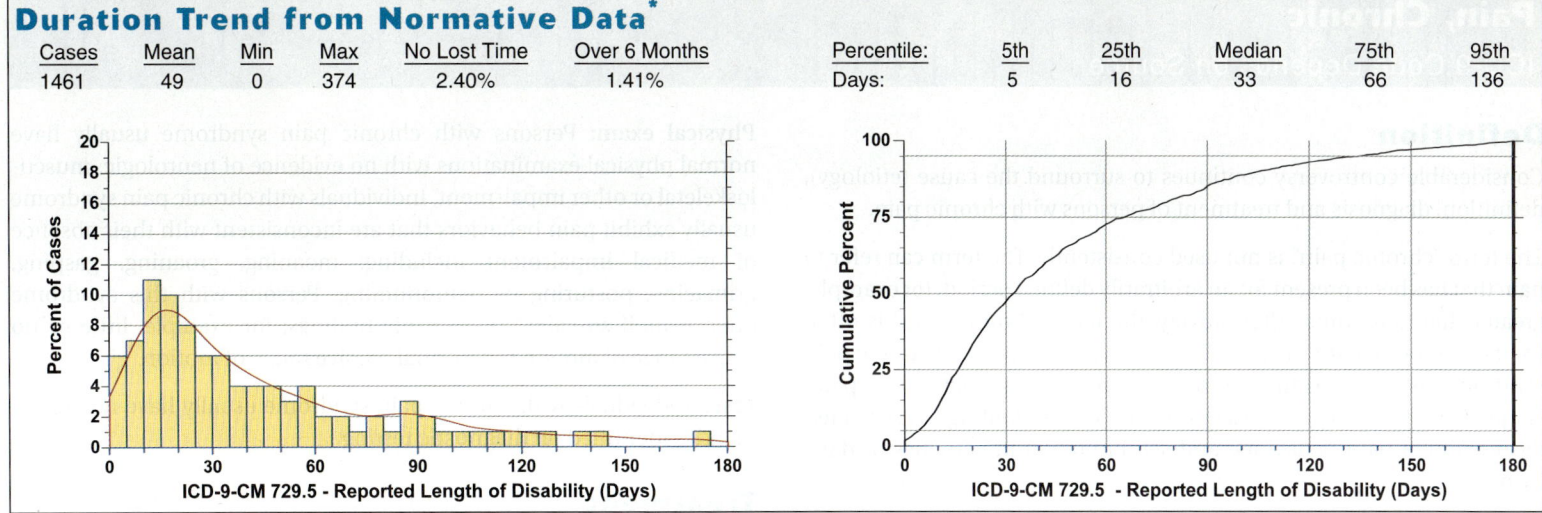

Failure to Recover

If an individual fails to recover within the maximum duration expectancy period, the reader may wish to reference the following questions to assist in better understanding the specifics of an individual's medical case.

Regarding diagnosis:

- Is pain in limb being used as a temporary diagnosis until a more exact one can be made?
- Did the exam reveal any tender spots, deformities, redness, warmth, coolness, or swelling at the affected site?
- Were range of motion and strength affected?
- Is there any numbness or tingling?
- Has the individual received x-rays, a CT scan, MRI, arteriogram, nerve conduction studies, or electromyography to definitively diagnose the underlying problem?
- If no obvious reason for the pain could be determined, was the individual seen by a mental health practitioner to rule out psychogenic causes for pain?

Regarding treatment:

- Have appropriate interventions been used to treat the underlying problem (such as splinting for fractures, etc.)?

Regarding prognosis:

- Can the individual's employer accommodate any needed restrictions?
- Does the individual have any chronic comorbid conditions, such as cancer, autoimmune disorders, etc., that may impact recovery?
- Has the individual received mental health intervention, as appropriate?
- Has the individual been referred to a pain clinic?
- Has the individual had a complete psychiatric evaluation?

References

Tierney, Lawrence M., Stephen J. McPhee, and Maxine Papadakis, eds. Current Medical Diagnosis and Treatment, 39th ed. New York: Lange Medical Books/McGraw-Hill, 2000.

Pain, Chronic
ICD-9 Code Depends on Source

Definition

Considerable controversy continues to surround the cause (etiology), definition, diagnosis and treatment of persons with chronic pain.

The term "chronic pain" is not used consistently. The term can refer to pain that has been present for an arbitrarily defined period, for example, greater than 6 months. Alternatively, the term "chronic pain" is often used as a synonym for the term "chronic pain syndrome." Chronic pain syndrome is a descriptive term used to indicate persistent pain, subjective symptoms in excess of objective findings, associated dysfunctional pain behaviors, and self limitation in activities of daily living.

Chronic pain syndrome is not the same as acute pain or recurrent acute pain. Acute pain is due to actual or pending tissue damage. Its duration is short and its psychosocial consequences are minimal. A person's perception of acute pain and behavior following the onset of acute pain are commensurate with the inciting event. Acute pain resolves as healing occurs. Acute pain is common, occurring for example with fractured bones, skin lacerations, sprains and other similar events. Recurrent, acute pain refers to episodic pain associated with chronic conditions such as trigeminal neuralgia or rheumatoid arthritis.

Chronic pain syndrome refers to persistent pain which usually has no identifiable source and which is associated with abnormal illness behaviors including: pain-related behaviors (moaning, groaning, gasping, grimacing, posturing, pantomiming) grossly disproportional to any underlying cause, substance abuse involving prescription and nonprescription drugs and alcohol, self-imposed prolonged excessive disuse, self-limitation of social and recreational activities, and a self-perception of total occupational disability absent objective signs of medical impairment.

Chronic pain syndrome should be considered if a person does not respond to appropriate medical care within a reasonable time frame or if the person's pain behavior greatly exceeds the usual response to a specific disorder.

Diagnosis

History: Individuals with chronic pain syndrome describe persistent pain with subjective symptoms disproportionate to their objective findings. Individuals with chronic pain syndrome often have a history of prescription or nonprescription drug abuse, alcohol abuse, treatment by multiple medical professionals, extensive diagnostic testing and treatment and self-limitations in personal and occupational activities of daily living.

Physical exam: Persons with chronic pain syndrome usually have normal physical examinations with no evidence of neurologic, musculoskeletal or other impairment. Individuals with chronic pain syndrome usually exhibit pain behaviors that are inconsistent with their absence of medical impairment including: moaning, groaning, gasping, grimacing, posturing or pantomiming. Persons with this syndrome often exhibit so-called nonorganic findings; for example, little or no active range of motion but normal passive range of motion.

Tests: Individuals with chronic pain syndrome usually have no abnormalities identified on diagnostic testing.

Treatment

In persons with chronic pain syndrome, the focus of treatment should be on management rather than cure. The goals should be clearly defined and articulated. Goals include an increase in functional capacity and a decrease in dependencies on medication and medical providers. Abnormal illness behavior usually can be diminished. Return to the work force is highly desirable but depends on many variables including: character traits, personality, ethnic and cultural background, the presence of support systems, motivation and satisfaction with the job held before the event that gave rise to the chronic pain syndrome. Effective management is based upon rehabilitation, behavior modification and cognitive therapy.

Prognosis

The prognosis for individuals with chronic pain syndrome has not been adequately defined in scientifically valid outcome studies. However, individuals fitting the criteria for chronic pain syndrome likely have a poor prognosis.

Differential Diagnosis

The differential diagnosis includes mental and behavioral disorders (for example, depression, somatoform disorders, factitious disorders), unconscious symptom exaggeration and malingering.

Specialists

- Pain Specialist
- Psychiatrist
- Psychologist

Rehabilitation

Rehabilitation should include mobilization, stretching and strengthening exercises.

Work Restrictions / Accommodations

Although individuals with chronic pain syndrome self-limit their occupational activities, there is usually no objective medical basis for work restrictions or accommodations. Furthermore, medical doctor prescribed work restrictions or accommodations can reinforce the individual's self-perception of incapacity, thereby prolonging the duration of this syndrome.

Complementary and Alternative Therapies

Content is intended for awareness only. Treatments may or may not be effective. Scientific evidence may be lacking and some substances have potentially toxic effects. Dr. Presley Reed and the editors do not endorse the use of these therapies in the absence of consultation with a licensed medical professional.

Acupuncture -	May help manage pain.
Biofeedback -	May help manage pain.
Massage -	May help manage pain.
Meditation -	May help manage pain.
Music therapy -	May help manage pain.

Comorbid Conditions

Comorbid conditions include mental and behavioral disorders including depression.

Complications

Complications are usually related to the secondary gain factors which reinforce chronic pain syndrome including: a life structured around disability, treatment by multiple medical professionals, extensive diagnostic testing and treatment, treatment with prescription narcotic medication and other addictive drugs, relief from occupational activities, attention and support of spouse and family, and financial compensation.

Factors Influencing Duration

Although persons with chronic pain syndrome usually have no objective medical impairment, their self-perception of incapacity depends on many variables including: character traits, personality, ethnic and cultural background, the presence of support systems, motivation and satisfaction with the job held before the event that gave rise to the chronic pain syndrome.

Length of Disability

Duration depends on specific diagnosis. Contact physician for more information.

Failure to Recover

If an individual fails to recover within the maximum duration expectancy period, the reader may wish to reference the following questions to assist in better understanding the specifics of an individual's medical case.

Regarding diagnosis:
- How was the diagnosis of chronic pain syndrome established?
- Have alternative explanations for the person's symptoms been investigated?
- Have mental and behavioral disorders been ruled out?
- Is this a somatoform disorder?
- Is this a factitious disorder?
- Is this malingering?

Regarding treatment:
- Has mobilization, stretching and strengthening been employed?
- Has behavioral modification including operant conditioning and relaxation therapy been employed?
- Has cognitive therapy been employed?
- Has treatment reinforced the presence of chronic pain syndrome (treatment by multiple medical professionals, extensive diagnostic testing and treatment, treatment with narcotic medication and other addictive drugs)?

Regarding prognosis:
- Have psychosocial factors, i.e., family and workplace dynamics been considered?

References

Ensalada, L.H. "The Importance of Illness Behavior in Disability Management." Occupational Medicine State of the Art Reviews: Risk and Disability Evaluation in the Workplace. Randolph, D.C., and M.I. Ranavaya, eds Philadelphia: Hanley & Belfus, October/December 2000.

Tollson CD, ed. Handbook of Pain Management, Second edition, Baltimore:Williams & Wilkins, 1994.

Palpitations
785.1

Definition

Palpitations refer to forceful or rapid beating of the heart. Palpitations may be caused by a variety of cardiac disorders associated with a sudden change of heart rhythm or rate. Palpitations are most often due to either "skipped beats" or a short-lived rapid beating of the heart known as paroxysmal atrial tachycardia (PAT).

Palpitations may also occur in individuals with no heart disease or only a mild heart disorder. Absent or minimal heart disease is frequently the case. Palpitations may also be associated with anxiety, excitement, nervousness, strong exertion, or certain substances or medications. At times, individuals with palpitations have no underlying organic cause, but instead are overly sensitive to normal heart actions. In such cases, palpitations are commonly noticed just before going to sleep or when resting quietly.

Palpitations are very common making it difficult to obtain prevalence and incidence information.

Diagnosis

History: A history of an abrupt onset and termination of an attack of "fast heart beating" that is "regular as a clock" suggests PAT. A history of irregular, rapid heart beating suggests atrial fibrillation. History of skipped beats or thumping infers premature atrial or ventricular contractions. Since a variety of excesses can cause palpitations, history of heavy cigarette smoking, caffeine or alcohol consumption, lack of sleep, and cocaine or amphetamine use should be noted.

The individual may report a sensation of skipping, fluttering, pounding, or racing heartbeats. Individual may complain of shortness of breath (dyspnea), tingling of the hands and around the mouth, and light-headedness, weakness, and chest pain. Chest pain, light-headedness, and weakness can be indicative of low blood pressure from poor heart function and may also signal other serious underlying heart disease.

Physical exam: The exam is aimed at differentiating between pathologic and physiologic palpitations. It involves a careful evaluation of heart rate, heart rhythm, and blood pressure. A rapid or irregular heart rate may indicate heart rhythm disturbances, aortic regurgitation, or hyperthyroid conditions. If the palpations are just a sensation, the heart rate and rhythm are likely to be normal. Listening to the heart and lungs (auscultation) is done to determine if there are abnormal heart sounds or evidence of lung congestion that may be associated with congestive heart failure.

If actual palpitations occur during examination, the pulse will be fast or irregular. If no palpitations occur during examination, a heart murmur may be present that infers an underlying cause.

Tests: An electrocardiogram (ECG) in the absence of palpitations may be normal or show a variety of changes due to enlargement of a heart chamber or an old heart attack (myocardial infarction). An unusual, but important cause of some arrhythmias causing palpitations is the Wolf-Parkinson-White syndrome. An ultrasound recording (echocardiogram) may be done to look for evidence of mitral valve prolapse. An ambulatory ECG recording (Holter monitoring) or transtelephonic transmission of the ECG is often done in an attempt to document the type of arrhythmia causing palpitations.

Lab tests may include lipid panels, thyroid hormone levels, chemistry panels, and cardiac enzymes to rule out coronary artery disease, myocardial infarction, and thyroid disease. Lab tests to evaluate drug levels may be needed for those on digitalis or thyroid replacement therapy.

Treatment

Treatment depends on the cause of the palpitations. In many individuals, no apparent cause for the palpitations is evident even after repeated Holter recordings and transtelephonic ECG transmissions.

Calming, emotional reassurance can be quite helpful when the palpitations are secondary to a heightened sensation rather than a physical cause. Modification of lifestyle including limiting caffeine and alcohol intake may be effective in reducing palpitations.

Antiarrhythmic medications and, on occasion, sending an electrical current through the heart to safely correct an irregular heart rhythm (cardioversion) may be used to slow excessively fast heart rates. Antihypertensive medications may be necessary if the individual has high blood pressure.

In some individuals with premature contractions, exercise reduces or abolishes them.

Prognosis

Outcome varies considerably with the underlying cause of the palpitations. Anxiety disorders are often brief and respond well to behavior modification and medications. Those with heart rhythm disturbances or thyroid disorders generally respond well to medications. Palpitations due to PAT or premature ventricular contractions (PVCs) usually diminish with time. Even if they do not, palpitations do not usually affect survival. An exception may be those individuals with frequent, multifocal PVCs that lead to ventricular tachycardia.

Differential Diagnosis

Other possible conditions include anxiety, malingering, thyroid disease, heart murmur, or a preoccupation with one's heart.

Specialists

- Cardiologist
- Emergency Medicine
- Endocrinologist
- Internist
- Psychologist

Rehabilitation

Individuals with heart palpitations due to serious underlying medical conditions should attend outpatient physical and occupational therapy at a clinic specializing in cardiac rehabilitation, 3 times a week for 8 to 12 weeks. Heart palpitations are associated with abnormal heart rhythms that can decrease the amount of blood the heart can pump and amount of work it can perform.

Cardiac rehabilitation centers offer ECG monitoring of all participants during the exercise sessions. Individuals learn to self-monitor their pulse and rate the amount of energy they expend by utilizing a rating of perceived exertion scale. This is a numbered scale that rates exercises from "very, very light" to "very, very hard." Individuals use this scale and their pulse to stay within safe exercise parameters predetermined by their physicians.

Individuals attend physical therapy to learn basic conditioning and stretching exercises. Aerobic exercise is performed such as treadmill walking or stationary bicycling. Occupational therapy addresses any fatigue or shortness of breath that may occur during activities of daily living. Individuals learn to utilize equipment such as a shower chair to decrease the energy expended during bathing or a long-handled sponge to decrease the amount of arm activity necessary for bathing. (Excessive arm activity is more taxing on the heart and can lead to fatigue.) Occupational therapists may teach energy conservation techniques where activities of daily living such as meal preparation are broken into smaller components that make tasks more manageable.

Work Restrictions / Accommodations

No work restrictions or accommodations are necessary for most individuals with palpitations. If dizziness or syncope is associated with palpitations in those responsible for the well-being of others (i.e., bus drivers), reassignment may be warranted.

Comorbid Conditions

Mitral valve prolapse and Wolf-Parkinson-White syndrome may be associated with palpitations.

Complications

If palpitations are caused by an arrhythmia with some duration, dizziness or a loss of consciousness (syncope) may result. The specific type of arrhythmia may have its own complications. In general, however, palpitations are not associated with significant complications.

Factors Influencing Duration

Disability varies with the underlying cause, course of treatment, and individual's response to treatment.

Length of Disability

Vague diagnosis. Duration depends on underlying cause.

Failure to Recover

If an individual fails to recover within the maximum duration expectancy period, the reader may wish to reference the following questions to assist in better understanding the specifics of an individual's medical case.

Regarding diagnosis:

- Has the underlying cause of palpitations been identified (i.e., caffeine, certain medications, fatigue, anxiety, underlying heart disturbance)?
- Does the individual display symptoms of anxiety such as nervousness, sleep disturbances, or fatigue?
- Does the individual have a rapid heart rate (over 100 beats/minute) while at rest? Does the individual complain of chest pain?
- Has the individual had a chemistry panel, cardiac isoenzymes, thyroid panel, and electrocardiogram (ECG)?
- Does the individual display signs of congestive heart failure such as low blood pressure, swelling of feet and legs, or shortness of breath?

Regarding treatment:

- Have modifications in lifestyle including limiting caffeine and alcohol intake been effective in reducing palpitations?
- Has treatment of underlying conditions (arrhythmias, congestive heart failure, thyroid disorders) effectively controlled rapid heart rate?
- Has treatment been appropriate according to underlying condition? Were antiarrhythmic medications indicated? Was cardioversion indicated?
- If not effective, what alternative therapy is available?
- Is surgery indicated to correct an underlying disorder (i.e., valvular heart disease)?

Regarding prognosis:

- Have palpitations resolved with appropriate treatment? If not, what else could be going on? Should diagnosis be revisited?
- Would individual benefit from additional counseling or change in medication or medication dosage?

References

Clochesy, John M., et al. Critical Care Nursing, 2nd ed. Philadelphia: W.B. Saunders Company, 1996.

Watchie, Joanne. Cardiopulmonary Physical Therapy. Philadelphia: W.B. Saunders Company, 1995.

Pancreatectomy

Other names / synonyms: Distal Pancreatectomy, Excision of Pancreas, Partial Pancreatectomy, Total Pancreatectomy, Whipple Procedure

52.5, 52.51, 52.52, 52.53, 52.59, 52.6

Definition

Pancreatectomy is the surgical removal of a part or the entire pancreas.

Removal of the entire pancreas (total pancreatectomy) takes out the whole pancreas, part of the small intestine, part of the stomach, the bile duct, gallbladder, spleen, and most of the lymph nodes in the area. Organs other than the pancreas may be preserved when the procedure is performed for a benign (noncancerous) disease.

Removal of part of the pancreas (subtotal or partial pancreatectomy) is performed whenever possible. This procedure leaves a portion of the pancreas so digestive juices are still secreted into the intestine and hormones (insulin, glucagon) into the bloodstream.

Diseases that obstruct the pancreatic duct may require partial pancreatectomy. This involves removal of the narrow end of the pancreas lying near the spleen (tail of the pancreas) and surgically linking the duct into the small intestine (distal pancreatectomy). Partial pancreatectomy may also be performed for diseases located in the broad end of the pancreas situated in a loop of the small intestine (head of the pancreas). This procedure may necessitate removal of the head of the pancreas, part of the small intestine, and some of the tissues around it (Whipple procedure).

The primary disease that puts an individual at risk for pancreatectomy is pancreatic cancer. Other risk factors include inflammation of the pancreas (pancreatitis), pancreatic trauma, pancreatic cysts, and cancer of the stomach or large intestine that has infiltrated (metastasized) into the pancreatic tail.

Pancreatectomy is the only treatment option for pancreatic cancer and it is estimated that 29,000 new cases of this disease occur in the US each year. Pancreatic cancer is more common in individuals age 50 to 70. Incidence is 30% higher in men than women. Pancreatic cancer occurs 65% more often in blacks than whites.

Reason for Procedure

Pancreatectomy is performed to remove part or all of the pancreas and surrounding diseased organs. The most common reasons for the procedure include localized pancreatic cancer, acute or chronic inflammation of the pancreas (pancreatitis) that does not respond to medical treatment, cancer of the small chamber formed by the union of the common bile duct and pancreatic duct (ampulla of Vater), pancreatic trauma, pancreatic cysts, and cancer of the stomach or large intestine that has metastasized into the pancreatic tail. A pancreatectomy may also be done to treat hormone-secreting tumors (insulinomas).

Description

Pancreatectomy is a major surgical procedure requiring a hospital stay.

The procedure is performed with general anesthesia. It involves making an incision across and through the upper abdominal wall to expose the pancreas and other abdominal organs, as needed. The procedure requires that a part or the entire pancreas be removed (resected) surgically. In addition to the entire pancreas, total pancreatectomy may also involve removal of part of the small intestine and stomach, the bile duct, gallbladder, spleen, and most of the lymph nodes in the area. Blood vessels (arteries, veins) and other ducts (lymphatics, pancreatic and bile ducts) are tied off as the pancreas and other organs are removed. The intestines are reconnected although the anatomy may be altered by the procedure. The skin is closed with sutures or staples.

The individual stays in the hospital for an average of 16 days.

Prognosis

The predicted outcome for individuals treated for pancreatic cancer using partial or total pancreatectomy is very poor with a cure rate of 1% over 5 years following diagnosis and treatment. Individuals with acute or chronic inflammation of the pancreas (pancreatitis) treated with partial or total pancreatectomy have an operative mortality of 4% and 10%, respectively. Pain relief is experienced initially in about 80% of individuals with pancreatitis receiving this treatment. Other conditions treated using partial pancreatectomy (i.e., pancreatic trauma or cysts and insulinoma) have a postoperative mortality rate ranging from 5-22%.

Specialists

- Gastroenterologist
- General Surgeon

Work Restrictions / Accommodations

Individuals require more sedentary work for a period of time due to weakness and fatigue following surgery. Medium to heavy-duty responsibilities should be postponed.

Comorbid Conditions

Existing conditions that may impact the ability to recover and further lengthen disability include prolonged malnutrition, digestive disorders such as Crohn's disease or colitis, and systemic diseases such as diabetes.

Procedure Complications

Complications of pancreatectomy may include bleeding (hemorrhage), general organ failure (hypovolemic shock), kidney-liver (hepatorenal) failure, postoperative infection of the incision wound, infection of the abdominal cavity (sepsis), inability to digest food properly, and inability to control blood sugar levels (diabetes).

Factors Influencing Duration

Factors that may influence length of disability following pancreatectomy include age of individual, amount and location of pancreatic tissue removed, any concurrent infections and overall general health, and other complicating diseases.

Length of Disability

Depends on extent of resection and head versus tail of pancreas. Individuals who are cured may require more sedentary work until recovery from surgery is complete. Disability may be permanent when total pancreatectomy is performed.

Subtotal.

Job Classification	Duration in Days		
	Minimum	Optimum	Maximum
Sedentary work	28	42	56
Light work	28	42	56
Medium work	42	56	70
Heavy work	56	70	84
Very Heavy work	56	70	84

Total.

Job Classification	Duration in Days		
	Minimum	Optimum	Maximum
Sedentary work	42	56	70
Light work	42	56	70
Medium work	56	70	84
Heavy work	70	84	112
Very Heavy work	70	84	112

References

Trede, M. "Left Hemipancreatectomy." Surgery of the Pancreas. Trede, M., and D.C. Carter, eds. New York: Churchill Livingstone, 1997. 517-520.

Trede, M., and D.C. Carter. "The Surgical Options for Pancreatic Cancer." Surgery of the Pancreas. Trede, M., and D.C. Carter, eds. New York: Churchill Livingstone, 1997. 471-481.

Pancreatic Pseudocyst
577.2

Definition

A pancreatic pseudocyst is a collection of enzyme-rich pancreatic fluid and tissue debris arising within areas of diseased pancreatic tissue or an obstructed pancreatic duct. In contrast to true cysts, the fluid in pseudocysts is not surrounded by a wall of tissue (epithelium), but instead tissue debris forms a wall-like structure that encapsulates the fluid. Hence, the name is pseudocyst rather than cyst.

Pseudocyst formation occurs in 10-15% of individuals with acute pancreatitis. In addition, pseudocyst formation increases in frequency in those with severe and protracted attacks of pancreatitis. In 10% of cases, pseudocysts are associated with trauma.

The exact incidence and prevalence of pancreatic pseudocysts is uncertain. However, since the pseudocyst formation is strongly associated with pancreatitis, one can extrapolate from data on pancreatitis. For example, gallstones and alcohol abuse are etiologic factors in 60.0-86.8% of cases of acute pancreatitis. In addition, men are affected 5 to 10 times more frequently than women. So one could assume that pancreatic pseudocysts are more common in men than women and have a higher incidence in those who have history of gallstones or alcohol abuse.

Diagnosis

History: Though abdominal pain is the chief complaint of pancreatic pseudocysts, the individual may also complain of the symptoms of pancreatitis, which include upper abdominal pain (which may radiate to the back, groin, or shoulder), sweating, nausea, vomiting and weakness, loss of appetite, weight loss, gas, and constipation.

Physical exam: Most pseudocysts are found when the individual is being seen for acute pancreatitis. Physical findings may include a tender, distended abdomen, fever, clammy skin, irregular heartbeat, low blood pressure, and a lack of bowel sounds, indicating that digestion has been halted. A large pseudocyst may be detected as a firm mass felt (palpated) in the left or middle upper abdomen.

Tests: Tests may include complete blood count (CBC), serum electrolyte study, serum amylase, serum lipase, and endoscopic pancreatography. Pseudocysts may be evident with CT scan, ultrasound, or angiography.

Treatment

Approaches to the treatment of pseudocysts vary. Most pseudocysts, even large ones, usually resolve spontaneously and may not require surgery. As a result, most cases are monitored closely with frequent CT scans and left untreated if the cyst does not grow or begin to create symptoms.

However, if symptoms are associated with the pseudocyst (pain, fever, etc.) or if the pseudocyst appears to be growing, it must be treated by surgical excision and drainage, drainage with a needle through the skin (percutaneously), or drained by using a lighted scope (endoscopically). Older pseudocysts (greater than 6 weeks) may be surgically connected (anastomosed) for drainage through the stomach (cystogastrostomy) or small intestine (cystoduodenostomy or cystojejunostomy).

Prognosis

Small pseudocysts often are self-limiting. Prognosis depends on whether the cyst is infected and whether drainage or surgery has been required. Needle aspiration of noninfected cysts has a success rate of roughly 50-75%, while aspiration of infected cysts is less successful (about 40-50%).

The overall mortality rate ranges from 14-60%, and is higher if complicated by cyst hemorrhage or rupture. When hemorrhage and rupture occur together, there is a mortality rate of over 60 percent.

Differential Diagnosis

Many symptoms of acute pancreatitis are identical to those of a perforated duodenal ulcer, intestinal obstruction, leaking aortic aneurysm, and acute vascular insufficiency or thrombosis.

Specialists

- Emergency Medicine
- Gastroenterologist
- General Surgeon
- Internist

Work Restrictions / Accommodations

Frequent breaks or a shorter workday may be needed until the individual regains full strength and stamina following a prolonged illness.

Comorbid Conditions

Comorbid conditions such as diabetes, immune suppression, bleeding disorders, and liver or kidney dysfunction may impact ability to recover and further lengthen disability.

Complications

Pancreatic pseudocysts may abscess, hemorrhage, or rupture, causing shock and requiring immediate treatment. Bleeding from a pseudocyst occurs in 2-7% of cases. Pseudocysts rupture in 10-20% of cases.

Factors Influencing Duration

The individual's age, severity of symptoms, underlying disease, method of treatment, and response to treatment affect length of disability.

Length of Disability

Surgical treatment.

Duration in Days

Job Classification	Minimum	Optimum	Maximum
Sedentary work	14	28	42
Light work	14	28	42
Medium work	21	42	56
Heavy work	28	56	70
Very Heavy work	28	56	70

Failure to Recover

If an individual fails to recover within the maximum duration expectancy period, the reader may wish to reference the following questions to assist in better understanding the specifics of an individual's medical case.

Regarding diagnosis:

- Does the individual have any risk factors?
- What symptoms does the individual have?
- What were the findings on physical exam?
- Has the individual received appropriate diagnostic testing to establish the diagnosis?
- Have these conditions with similar symptoms been ruled out?

Regarding treatment:

- Has the individual received appropriate treatment? Was surgery necessary?

Regarding prognosis:

- Is the individual's employer able to accommodate any necessary restrictions?
- Does the individual have any complications?

References

Burdick, J. Stephen. "Diseases of the Pancreas." Gastroenterology. Dale, D.C., and Daniel D. Federman, MD New York: WebMD Corporation, 2000 Scientific American Medicine. 7 Dec 2000 <http://www.samed.com/sam/forms/index.htm>.

Pancreaticoduodenectomy

Other names / synonyms: Whipple Pancreatoduodenectomy, Whipple Procedure

52.7

Definition

Pancreaticoduodenectomy (also called a Whipple procedure) refers to the surgical removal of the head of the pancreas. It is the only way to treat an individual with pancreatic cancer. In order to completely remove a tumor in the head of the pancreas, it is necessary to remove it along with part of the small intestine (duodenum), the gallbladder, the end of the common bile duct, and sometimes part of the stomach. The lymph nodes that surround these organs are also removed. The middle part of the small intestine (jejunum) is then attached to the remaining parts of the pancreas and bile duct so pancreatic secretions (digestive enzymes) and bile still flow into the intestinal tract.

Diseases that put an individual at risk for needing pancreaticoduodenectomy are pancreatic cancer, tumor of the bile duct, inflammation of the pancreas (pancreatitis), chronic pancreatitis, pancreatic trauma, and pancreatic cysts.

There are an estimated 29,000 new cases of pancreatic cancer in the US each year. Pancreatic cancer is more common in individuals who are 50-70 years of age, and the incidence is higher in men than women. It occurs 65% more often in blacks than whites.

Reason for Procedure

Pancreaticoduodenectomy is performed to remove diseased pancreatic tissue and to relieve the severe pain produced by these diseases.

Pancreaticoduodenectomy is used to treat localized pancreatic cancer, acute or chronic inflammation of the pancreas (pancreatitis) that does not respond to medical treatment, hormone-secreting tumors (insulinomas), cancer of the small chamber formed by the union of the common bile duct and pancreatic duct (ampulla of Vater), pancreatic trauma, and pancreatic cysts.

Description

Pancreaticoduodenectomy is a major surgical procedure that requires hospitalization.

This surgical procedure is performed under general anesthesia; a urinary catheter is usually inserted to facilitate bladder elimination.

An incision is made across and through the upper abdominal wall (wide transverse subcostal approach) to expose the pancreas and other abdominal organs as needed. Most commonly, the head of the pancreas and varying amounts of its neck and body, the gallbladder, the end of the common bile duct, and the upper part of the small intestine (duodenum and proximal 10 centimeters of the jejunum) are removed. Sometimes part of the stomach (distal third with the right half of the greater omentum), and the lymph nodes that surround the pancreas and small intestine (peripancreatic and hepatoduodenal lymph nodes) will also be removed. Blood vessels (arteries, veins) and lymphatic ducts are tied off as these tissues are removed. The portion of pancreas remaining will then be connected to the small intestine and the remaining bile duct so that the pancreatic duct secretions and bile can empty into the intestinal tract (pancreatojejunostomy). Temporary abdominal drains (Jackson-Pratt and Volker drains) may be put in. Abdominal sutures and drains will be removed on an outpatient basis 2-3 weeks after surgery.

Prognosis

The average mortality rate immediately following pancreaticoduodenectomy is approximately 18%. Morbidity is also common. The postoperative complication producing the most problems is breakdown of the surgical connection (anastomosis) between the small intestine and the pancreas. This occurs in 17% of cases, and is fatal nearly 30% of the time.

The average mortality rate 5 years after surgery for individuals who undergo pancreaticoduodenectomy is 10-20 percent.

Specialists

- Gastroenterologist
- General Surgeon

Work Restrictions / Accommodations

Individuals will require more sedentary work for a period of time due to weakness and fatigue following surgery; medium to heavy-duty responsibilities should be postponed.

Comorbid Conditions

Existing conditions that may impact the ability to recover and further lengthen the disability include prolonged malnutrition, digestive disorders such as Crohn's disease or colitis, and systemic diseases such as diabetes.

Procedure Complications

Complications of pancreaticoduodenectomy may include leakage from the pancreatic duct, abdominal pain, bleeding (hemorrhage), creation of an abnormal channel out of the bile duct (biliary fistula), decreased blood flow to the abdominal tissues (mesenteric ischemia), development of pockets of infection (abscess) within the liver or abdomen, fluid accumulation in the intestine (chylous ascites), puncture of the stomach (gastric perforation), and twisting of the small intestine (jejunal torsion).

The pancreas may become inflamed (acute pancreatitis). An abnormal channel may form through the pancreatic duct (pancreatic fistula) in nearly 2% of cases. Death rarely occurs from either of the later 2 complications.

Factors Influencing Duration

Factors that might influence the length of disability following pancreaticoduodenectomy include the age of the individual, the amount and location of pancreatic tissue removed, the presence of concurrent infections, overall general health, and the presence of other complicating diseases.

Length of Disability

Duration depends on extent of resection and job requirements. Duration reflects recovery period for the procedure only, not for the underlying medical condition. Disability may be permanent. Individuals will be hospitalized for at least 2 weeks and possibly longer. Subsequent recuperation time at home will also be required. Upon return to work, the individual may only be able to perform modified duty with sedentary requirements until recovery is complete. Disability may be permanent.

Duration in Days

Job Classification	Minimum	Optimum	Maximum
Sedentary work	42	56	70
Light work	42	56	70
Medium work	56	70	84
Heavy work	70	84	112
Very Heavy work	70	84	112

References

"Whipple Procedure." Dept. of Surgery-Beth Israel Deaconess Medical Center 20 Feb 2001 <http://www.bidmc.harvard.edu/surgery/general/indexWhippleprocedure.html>.

Trede, M., and D.C. Carter. "The Complications of Pancreatoduodenectomy and Their Management." Surgery of the Pancreas. Trede, M., and D.C. Carter, eds. New York: Churchill Livingstone, 1997. 675-691.

Notes

Pancreaticojejunostomy

Other names / synonyms: Modified Puestow Procedure

52.96

Definition

Pancreaticojejunostomy is a surgical procedure where the duct that permits drainage of digestive juices (pancreatic enzymes) from the pancreas (pancreatic duct) is opened and reconnected to the small intestine (jejunum).

The procedure involves opening the pancreatic duct lengthwise and cutting the midportion of the small intestine (jejunum) into two sections. The pancreas with its opened duct is then inserted and stitched into the lower section of the jejunum. The upper section of the jejunum is reattached to its lower section at a point below the pancreas. The pancreatic digestive enzymes can then travel through the section of jejunum where the pancreas is attached and into the small intestine.

Pancreaticojejunostomy is most often used as a treatment for individuals with an inflamed pancreas (chronic pancreatitis). Chronic pancreatitis often causes the common bile duct and/or the pancreatic duct to become obstructed by mineral deposits (calculi), resulting in ongoing and severe pain intense pain. In the US, the most common risk factor for chronic pancreatitis is alcoholism. Other causes may include a hereditary predisposition and obstruction of the pancreatic duct resulting from duct narrowing or pancreatic cancer. On rare occasions, an episode of severe acute pancreatitis makes the pancreatic duct so narrow that chronic pancreatitis results. In many cases, the cause of chronic pancreatitis is not known.

Chronic pancreatitis accounts for 122,000 outpatient visits and 20,000 inpatient hospitalizations in the US each year. Overall incidence is 2 in every 10,000 individuals and occurs more often in men than women.

Reason for Procedure

Pancreaticojejunostomy is performed to improve drainage through the pancreatic duct and help relieve the pain of chronic pancreatitis. Other diseases that may be treated using pancreaticojejunostomy include pancreatic cancer, foreign bodies (e.g., parasitic worms) obstructing the pancreatic duct, pancreatic cysts, or trauma causing obstruction of the pancreatic duct.

Description

Pancreaticojejunostomy is a major surgical procedure requiring a hospital stay.

The procedure is performed under general anesthesia. The pancreaticojejunostomy surgical procedure involves making an incision across and through the upper abdominal wall (upper midline or transverse incision) to completely expose the pancreas and other abdominal organs (laparotomy). The pancreatic duct is exposed and opened lengthwise and the small intestine (jejunum) is cut into two sections. The pancreas with its opened duct is then inserted and stitched into the lower section of the jejunum. The upper section of the jejunum is reattached to its lower section (anastomosis) at a point below the pancreas and the abdomen is then closed. Bleeding (hemorrhage) is controlled during this procedure by tying off blood vessels (arteries, veins), as needed. A urinary catheter may be inserted to facilitate bladder elimination.

Following surgery, the individual is transferred from the operating suite to the postanesthesia care unit (PACU) and stay there until awakening and condition stabilizes. At this point, the individual is transferred to a room and monitored routinely by nursing staff. Postoperative medications (opioid analgesics) and nonsteroidal anti-inflammatory drugs (NSAIDS) are administered at regular intervals to alleviate pain. The nasogastric tube is removed that evening or the morning after surgery. Individual stays in the hospital for 16 days (on average) until able to move (ambulate) on his/her own, diet returns to normal, and it is clear there are no other postoperative complications. Abdominal sutures are removed 2 to 3 weeks after surgery on an outpatient basis.

Prognosis

Pancreaticojejunostomy has an operative mortality of approximately 4%. Chances of complete or substantial relief of pain at five years after surgery are about 70%.

Twenty-two percent of individuals require that the surgery be redone due to complications resulting from the initial operation. The incidence of late mortality (months to years following surgery) may be as high as 39% and is influenced by the number of individuals continuing to abuse alcohol. The average time before death in individuals who continue to drink heavily following pancreaticojejunostomy is about 6 years.

Specialists

- Gastroenterologist
- General Surgeon

Work Restrictions / Accommodations

Individuals require more sedentary work for a period of time due to weakness and fatigue following surgery. Medium to heavy-duty responsibilities should be postponed. Individuals may need sedentary duties until fully recovered.

Comorbid Conditions

Existing conditions that may impact the ability to recover and further lengthen disability include prolonged malnutrition, digestive disorders such as Crohn's disease or colitis, pancreatic cancer, and systemic diseases such as diabetes.

Procedure Complications

Complications of pancreaticojejunostomy may include bleeding (hemorrhage), general organ failure (hypovolemic shock), kidney-liver (hepatorenal) failure, postoperative infection of the incision wound, infection of the abdominal cavity (sepsis), and inability to digest food properly. A substantial portion (25%) of individuals treated with pancreaticojejunostomy develops insulin-dependent diabetes.

Factors Influencing Duration

Factors that may influence the length of disability following pancreaticojejunostomy include age of the individual, any concurrent infections, overall general health, and other complicating diseases.

Length of Disability

Duration reflects recovery period for the procedure only, not for the underlying medical condition. The duration of disability depends on the requirements of the job. Upon return to work, individual may only be able to perform modified duty with sedentary requirements until recovery is complete. Disability may be permanent.

Duration in Days

Job Classification	Minimum	Optimum	Maximum
Sedentary work	28	42	56
Light work	28	42	56
Medium work	42	56	70
Heavy work	56	70	84
Very Heavy work	56	70	84

References

Carter, D.C., and K.R. Palmer. "Drainage Procedures in Chronic Pancreatitis." *Surgery of the Pancreas*. Trede, M., and D.C. Carter, eds. New York: Churchill Livingstone, 1997. 329-346.

Forsmark, C.E., and P.P. Toskes. "Treatment of Chronic Pancreatitis." *Therapy of Digestive Disorders*. Wolfe, M.M., ed. Philadelphia: W.B. Saunders Company, 2000. 235-245.

Pancreatitis

Other names / synonyms: Acute Pancreatitis, Chronic Pancreatitis, Pancreatic Inflammation
577, 577.0, 577.1, 577.2, 577.8, 577.9

Definition

Acute pancreatitis is an inflammation of the pancreas that usually resolves without permanent damage to the organ.

Acute pancreatitis is caused by alcohol consumption in approximately 80% of cases. The remaining 20% are caused by drugs, infection, surgical complications, blunt and penetrating trauma, hereditary predisposition, obstruction of the pancreatic duct due to pancreatic cancer or gallstone formation, structural abnormalities, or excessive calcium or fats in the blood. One risk factor for pancreatitis is high levels of triglycerides in the blood (hypertriglyceridemia).

Chronic pancreatitis indicates that damage persists even after the causative agent (usually alcohol) is removed. Recurrent attacks can lead to progressive deterioration of the pancreatic structure and function.

The incidence of pancreatitis is 4 to 100,000 for Native Americans, 5.7 to 100,000 for whites, and 20.7 to 100,000 for blacks. The disorder is most common between the ages of 35 and 64.

Diagnosis

History: Individuals with acute pancreatitis almost always have severe abdominal pain (95% of cases) and tenderness. The pain usually does not reach its peak for 30 minutes to several hours and may last for hours to days. It is usually very severe and often leaves an individual writhing even after medication. Eighty-five percent of individuals report nausea, vomiting, and weight loss. Individuals with chronic pancreatitis also have abdominal pain that is usually dull rather than sharp. A characteristic feature is radiation of the pain directly through to the back and instant aggravation of the pain after eating. Pain in chronic pancreatitis may continue, diminish, or disappear completely.

Physical exam: Individuals with acute pancreatitis have low-grade fevers in 60% of cases and pulse rate of 100 to 140 beats per minute with low blood pressure in 40% of cases. Respiration is shallow and rapid. Abdominal tenderness is common and bowel sounds are often decreased or absent. The physical exam is less useful in chronic pancreatitis because the intensity of the symptoms varies widely and often the individual sees the doctor between episodes.

Tests: Blood tests for infection and pancreatic function are complete blood count, blood glucose, BUN, creatinine and electrolytes, serum amylase and lipase, and serum bilirubin. CT helps in the visualization of the pancreas. X-rays and ultrasound may also be useful.

Treatment

Treatment for acute and mild pancreatitis is aimed only at nutritional support and maintaining blood chemical balance using intravenous (IV) fluids with careful monitoring until the inflammation subsides. No food is taken by mouth during the episode and IV nutrition must be provided if pancreatitis lasts more than a few days. If the acute pancreatitis is severe, treatment takes place in an intensive care unit of the hospital. In addition, a nasogastric suction tube (to counteract vomiting) and oxygen ventilation are used.

Treatment of chronic pancreatitis is directed at the control of pain and replacement of pancreatic enzymes that aid in the absorption of food. Control of pain begins with the avoidance of alcohol. Analgesics, enzyme therapy, and, sometimes, endoscopic therapy are then given to relieve obstructions.

If all medical measures have failed to relieve pain, surgery to remove the damaged tissue is considered. No single procedure is ideal for all individuals. One-third of individuals obtain long-lasting relief of pain from duct drainage procedures. Procedures that combine resection and duct drainage have a long-term success rate in the 80% range. Two methods for pancreatic head resection, which preserve the anatomy of the stomach, duodenum, and bile duct, represent an advance in surgical therapy for chronic pancreatitis. Total pancreatectomy with islet autotransplantation is a procedure that may be appropriate in selected individuals. Thoracoscopic splanchnicectomy is a new, minimally invasive procedure still in evaluation that may become a valuable method when the only indication for surgery is intractable pain.

Prognosis

In mild pancreatitis where the inflammation is confined to the organ itself, the prognosis is excellent. The condition usually leaves no permanent damage and mortality is less than 5%. Severe acute pancreatitis may result in hemorrhage or damage to other organs and mortality is 10-50% or higher.

In chronic pancreatitis, recurrent attacks tend to become progressively more severe, especially if the individual is not compliant with recommendations to avoid alcohol and modify diet.

Surgical intervention is associated with an overall mortality rate of less than 2% and offers good results in terms of improving quality of life. However, as a result of surgery, individuals will require pancreatic enzyme supplementation and many become insulin-dependent diabetics. Individuals who underwent resection for chronic pancreatitis have significantly lower scores on a quality of life questionnaire in physical and psychological domains than healthy controls. Common problems are weight loss, abdominal pain, fatigue, foul stools, and diabetes.

Differential Diagnosis

Acute pancreatitis must be distinguished from other acute abdominal conditions such as kidney stones, gallstones, abdominal aneurysm, intestinal obstruction, gastroenteritis, peritonitis, ectopic pregnancy, appendicitis, or a perforated gastric or duodenal ulcer. With chronic pancreatitis, other possibilities include hepatitis and pancreatic cancer.

Specialists

- Gastroenterologist
- General Surgeon

Work Restrictions / Accommodations

Individuals may need to transfer to modified duty or switch to part-time work. Heavy lifting restrictions may be necessary for a minimum of 6 weeks.

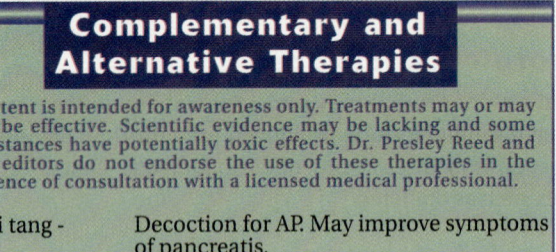

Complementary and Alternative Therapies

Content is intended for awareness only. Treatments may or may not be effective. Scientific evidence may be lacking and some substances have potentially toxic effects. Dr. Presley Reed and the editors do not endorse the use of these therapies in the absence of consultation with a licensed medical professional.

Liyi tang - Decoction for AP. May improve symptoms of pancreatis.

Comorbid Conditions

Comorbid conditions include alcoholism, biliary tract disease, and hypertriglyceridemia.

Complications

Acute pancreatitis may be complicated by infections from pancreatic fluid collections, pancreatic fluids collecting in the abdominal cavity (ascites), death of pancreatic tissue (necrosis), and cysts forming channels (fistulas) to other body organs. Chronic pancreatitis is complicated in up to 25% of cases with a collection of pancreatic juice outside the normal boundaries of the system (pseudocyst). Other possible complications are splenic vein blood clots (thrombosis) and an excessive loss of fats in the feces (steatorrhea). In intractable cases, circulating toxins may cause systemic failure.

Factors Influencing Duration

Degree of severity, whether the treatment is medical or surgical, presence of complications, and the ability of the individual to abstain from alcohol affect the length of disability.

Length of Disability

With medical treatment, the duration of disability depends on job requirements, severity of the condition, and whether the individual is compliant with doctors' recommendations. With surgical treatment, duration depends on extent of resection and head versus tail of pancreas.

Medical treatment.

Duration in Days

Job Classification	Minimum	Optimum	Maximum
Sedentary work	7	14	28
Light work	7	14	28
Medium work	14	21	42
Heavy work	14	21	42
Very Heavy work	14	28	56

Pancreatectomy (subtotal).

Duration in Days

Job Classification	Minimum	Optimum	Maximum
Sedentary work	28	42	56
Light work	28	42	56
Medium work	42	56	70
Heavy work	56	70	84
Very Heavy work	56	70	84

Duration Trend from Normative Data*

Cases	Mean	Min	Max	No Lost Time	Over 6 Months
1124	41	0	365	0.27%	0.80%

Percentile:	5th	25th	Median	75th	95th
Days:	9	15	27	53	114

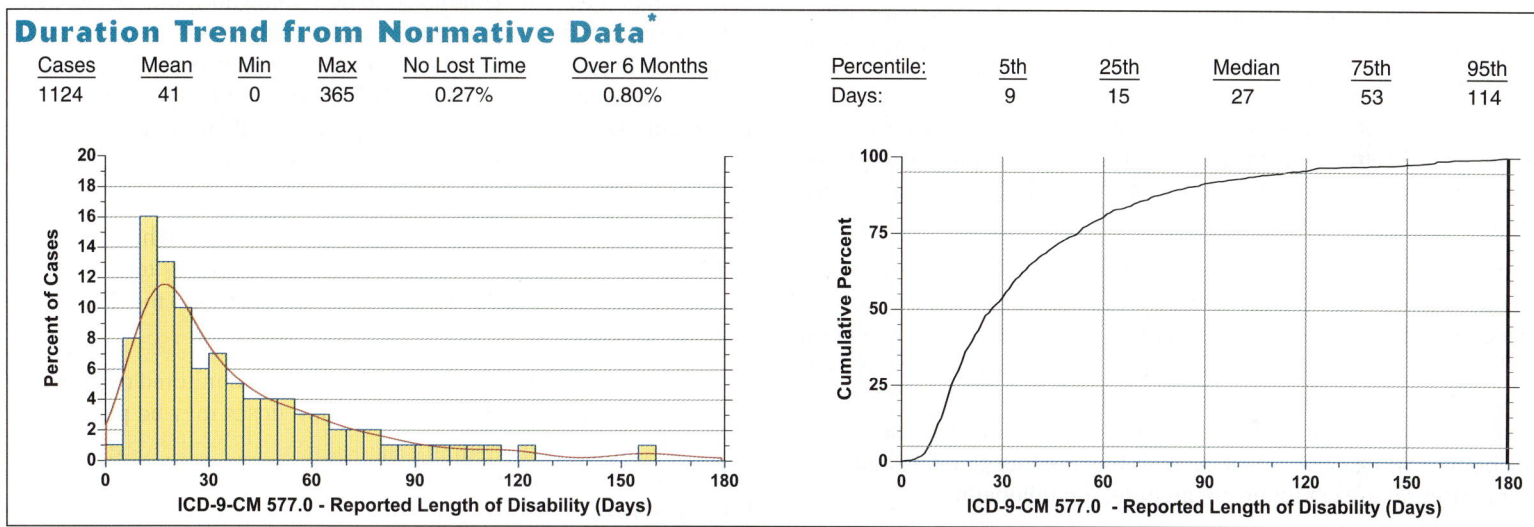

* Differences may exist between the expected duration tables and the normative graphs. Duration tables provide expected recovery periods based on the type of work performed by the individual. The normative graphs reflect the actual observed experience of many individuals across the spectrum of physical conditions, in a variety of industries, and with varying levels of case management.

Failure to Recover

If an individual fails to recover within the maximum duration expectancy period, the reader may wish to reference the following questions to assist in better understanding the specifics of an individual's medical case.

Regarding diagnosis:

- Does individual have severe abdominal pain and tenderness? Low-grade fever, elevated pulse rate, low blood pressure, or shallow respiration?
- Does individual report nausea, vomiting, and weight loss?
- Is the abdominal pain dull rather than sharp?
- Has individual received adequate blood testing to establish the diagnosis?
- Were conditions with similar symptoms ruled out?

Regarding treatment:

- If treated for acute and mild pancreatitis, is individual following treatment until inflammation subsides? If acute pancreatitis is severe, was hospitalization required? Was nasogastric suction tube and oxygen ventilation used?
- If treated for chronic pancreatitis, is individual avoiding alcohol? Was endoscopy needed? Analgesics or enzyme therapy?
- Was surgery necessary? What procedure was performed? Duct drainage? Pancreatic head resection? Total pancreatectomy or Thoracoscopic splanchnicectomy?

Regarding prognosis:

- Did individual become an insulin-dependent diabetic?
- Does individual have any comorbid conditions that may impact recovery?
- Did complications occur that could impact recovery and lengthen disability?

References

American Gastroenterological Association. "Medical Position Statement: Treatment of Pain in Chronic Pancreatitis." Gastroenterology 115 (1998): 763-764.

Beers, Mark H., and Robert Berkow. The Merck Manual of Diagnosis and Therapy. Whitehouse Station, NJ: Merck & Co., Inc, 1999.

Bell, R.H. "Surgical Options in the Patient with Chronic Pancreatitis." Current Gastroenterology Report 2 2 (2000): 146-151.

Chen, Q., and J. Lu. "Treatment of Acute Pancreatitis with Liyi Tang - A Report of 50 Cases." Journal of Traditional Chinese Medicine 17 4 (1997): 250-252.

Chowdury, P., et al. "Response of Rat Exocrine Pancreas to High-fat and High-carbohydrate Diets." Proceedings of the Society for Experimental Biology and Medicine 223 3 (2000): 310-315.

Huang, J.J., C.J. Yeo, and T.A. Sohn. "Quality of Life and Outcomes After Pancreaticoduodenectomy." Annals of Surgery 231 6 (2000): 890-898.

Khoury, Gattas. "Pancreatitis." Emergency Medicine: An On-line Medical Reference. Adler, Jonathan, et al., eds. 2000. 999.

Sohn, T.A., et al. "Quality of Life and Long-term Survival After Surgery for Chronic Pancreatitis." Journal of Gastrointestinal Surgery 4 4 (2000): 355-365.

Panhypopituitarism
Other names / synonyms: Hypopituitarism, Hypopituitarism Syndrome, Pituitary Cachexia, Simmond's Disease, Simmond's Syndrome

253.2

Definition

Panhypopituitarism is a condition where the gland at the base of the brain (pituitary gland) fails to produce adequate levels of all hormones that it normally produces.

The pituitary gland is a small pea-sized gland located at the base of the brain. In a healthy individual, the pituitary gland produces several hormones essential for controlling many of the body's functions. Lack of these hormones will negatively affect many body systems.

Causes of panhypopituitarism include lesions or tumors of the pituitary gland (pituitary adenomas, pituitary tumors), birth defects, stroke, bleeding into the pituitary gland (pituitary apoplexy), surgical removal of the pituitary gland (hypophysectomy), diseases such as sarcoidosis or histiocytosis X, inflammation of the pituitary gland (hypophysitis), irradiation, accidental or surgical trauma, and disease of the portion of the brain (hypothalamus) that controls the pituitary gland. In addition, some cases may occur for no apparent reason (idiopathic).

Panhypopituitarism is a rare condition. Men and women are affected equally. Pregnancy and delivery increase the risk of developing inflammation of the pituitary gland; hemorrhage during delivery can also lead to panhypopituitarism. While panhypopituitarism can occur at any age, it is more difficult to diagnose in the elderly.

Diagnosis

History: Individuals may complain of headache, lethargy, cold intolerance, loss of appetite, abdominal pain, vision problems, loss of strength and weakness, loss of arm pit (axillary) or pubic hair, decrease in breast size, loss of sex drive (libido), impotence, infertility, or menstrual problems. New mothers may report a lack of breast milk.

Physical exam: Physical findings may include decreased blood pressure (hypotension), decreased heart rate (bradycardia), premature wrinkling, pale complexion (pallor), thinning of the lips, delayed deep tendon reflexes, and absent pubic, scalp, and axillary hair. In men, findings may include a small prostate and soft testicles.

Tests: Lab tests vary depending on the individual's symptoms. In general, blood tests are conducted to determine hormone levels. CT or MRI of the pituitary gland may also be performed. Special tests to determine the ability to smell may be conducted. If visual problems are reported, a test to measure the field of vision is conducted. Cortisol level is particularly critical, since if it is very low, it could be fatal.

Treatment

Treatment consists of medication to replace the deficient hormones. If a pituitary tumor is responsible for the disorder, surgery to remove the tumor is necessary. Individuals are encouraged to wear a medical identification bracelet.

Individuals with panhypopituitarism should be monitored regularly for hormone levels. Adjustment to medication doses may be periodically required.

Prognosis

With hormone replacement, individual may expect recovery of almost all the lost endocrine functions. In cases where surgery is indicated (removal of a pituitary tumor), the procedure should result in resolution of symptoms. In some cases, medical treatment (hormone replacement) may still be necessary following surgery in order to achieve a complete resolution of symptoms.

Differential Diagnosis

Conditions with similar symptoms include primary hypothyroidism, Addison's disease, anorexia nervosa, chronic liver disease, primary hypogonadism, myotonia dystrophica, and primary psychosis.

Specialists

- Endocrinologist
- Gynecologist
- Urologist

Work Restrictions / Accommodations

Work restrictions and accommodations are not usually associated with this condition. If surgery is required, extended sick leave may be required while the individual recovers from the procedure. Flexibility in the work schedule may be necessary to allow for regular visits to the physician.

Comorbid Conditions

Pregnancy may prolong the recovery period.

Complications

Progressive loss of vision resulting in blindness can occur. Because the pituitary gland controls the adrenal glands, panhypopituitarism can result in a lack of adrenal hormones. A life-threatening condition called adrenal crisis can occur and requires immediate intravenous corticosteroid administration to prevent death.

Factors Influencing Duration

Length of disability may be influenced by the severity and extent of hormonal insufficiency and what hormones are insufficient. Need for surgery and any complications also influence the length of disability.

Length of Disability

In most cases, complete recovery is expected. Complications such as blindness may lead to permanent disability.

Duration in Days

Job Classification	Minimum	Optimum	Maximum
Any work	3	7	28

Failure to Recover

If an individual fails to recover within the maximum duration expectancy period, the reader may wish to reference the following questions to assist in better understanding the specifics of an individual's medical case.

Regarding diagnosis:

- Does individual have a history of lesions or tumors of the pituitary gland?
- Is there a history of surgical removal of the pituitary gland (hypophysectomy) or inflammation of the pituitary gland (hypophysitis)? History of sarcoidosis, histiocytosis X, irradiation, or accidental or surgical trauma to the portion of the brain (hypothalamus) that controls the pituitary gland?
- Does individual have a birth (congenital) defect affecting the pituitary gland?
- Does individual complain of headache, lethargy, cold intolerance, loss of appetite, abdominal pain, vision problems, or loss of strength? Loss of arm pit (axillary) or pubic hair, decrease in breast size, loss of sex drive (libido), impotence, infertility, or menstrual problems?
- If individual is a new mother, does she report lack of breast milk?
- Were blood tests done to determine hormone levels? CT or MRI of the pituitary gland? Were tests to determine ability to smell conducted?
- Was the diagnosis of panhypopituitarism confirmed?

Regarding treatment:

- Was medication given to replace the deficient hormones?
- How often is individual evaluated to monitor hormone levels?
- Is medication adjustment required?
- Was a high calorie, high protein diet prescribed?
- Does individual participate in regular physical activity, as prescribed?
- If a pituitary tumor is responsible for the disorder, is surgery to remove the tumor necessary? Did surgery resolve symptoms or is hormone replacement still required?
- Does individual wear a medical identification bracelet for this condition?

Regarding prognosis:

- Was all or almost all of the lost endocrine function successfully replaced with hormone treatment?
- Is individual compliant with taking hormone replacements, as prescribed?
- Was surgery required for removal of a pituitary tumor? Did any postsurgical complications occur?
- Has individual experienced progressive loss of vision resulting in blindness? Adrenal crisis? If so, did individual receive immediate intravenous corticosteroid administration to prevent death?
- Does individual have underlying medical conditions that would prolong recovery? If so, how are these conditions being treated and what is expected outcome with treatment?

References

Young, William. "Hypopituitarism." Griffith's 5-minute Clinical Consult. Dambro, Mark, ed. Philadelphia: Lippincott, Williams & Wilkins, 2000. 550-551.

Panic Disorder

Other names / synonyms: Panic Attacks

300.01

Definition

Panic disorder is characterized by sudden and unpredictable panic attacks. Panic attacks are brief episodes of intense fear, a sense of impending disaster, and bodily sensations including rapid heart rate, breathlessness, and dizziness. The attack comes "out of the blue," peaks in 10 minutes, and usually lasts less than 1 hour.

Panic disorder is present in 1-3% of individuals at some time in their lives. Age at onset is usually between the late teens and mid-30s. Women are 2 to 3 times as likely than men to have panic disorder. Individuals with a close relative with panic disorder are up to 8 times more likely than the general population to develop the disorder.

Diagnosis

History: Individual has history of recurrent panic attacks that include at least four of the following: a pounding heart or rapid heart rate, sweating, trembling or shaking, shortness of breath or sensations of suffocating, feeling of choking, chest pain, nausea or abdominal distress, dizziness or faintness, feelings of unreality (derealization) or being detached from oneself (depersonalization), fear of losing control or going crazy, fear of dying, numbness or tingling sensations (paresthesias), and chills or hot flushes. Onset of the attack is sudden with symptoms reaching a peak in 10 minutes or less. For at least a month after one or more of the attacks, there is worry about having another attack, worry about the implication of the attack or its consequences (such as losing control, having a heart attack, or going crazy), or a significant change in behavior related to the attacks.

To meet DMS-IV diagnostic criteria, the panic attacks must not be due to the direct effects of a drug or other substance or to a general medical condition such as hyperthyroidism. The panic attacks must not be a part of or better explained by another disorder such as social phobia or other phobia, obsessive-compulsive disorder, post-traumatic stress disorder, or separation anxiety disorder.

Physical exam: Although the physical exam does not typically contribute to this diagnosis, if performed during a panic attack, the examination may reveal a rapid heart rate and elevated blood pressure.

Tests: Psychological tests can be consistent with this disorder but do not prove the diagnosis.

Treatment

Panic disorder is treated with both panic-focused cognitive behavioral therapy and drug therapy. Because individuals with panic disorder have an intense fear of abandonment, it is essential to establish and maintain a good therapeutic relationship with a single therapist who will continue to be available to the individual. The goal of cognitive therapy is to suggest that panic is a misinterpretation of body sensations and that the danger is not as extreme as perceived. Other psychotherapy may be considered but should be supplemented with or replaced with cognitive behavioral therapy if no significant improvement occurs within 6 to 8 weeks.

Relaxation training and progressive muscle relaxation may be helpful along with training in breath control. Drug therapy is usually with a potent benzodiazepine or a selective serotonin reuptake inhibitor (SSRI) type of antidepressant. Supportive psychotherapy is provided, as needed. Outpatient therapy is usually sufficient and hospitalization is rarely needed in the absence of comorbid depression or substance abuse. The acute phase of treatment with either cognitive behavioral therapy or medication usually lasts about 12 weeks then tapers off with periodic treatment thereafter.

Prognosis

Outcome is variable. The panic attacks may come and go over the years. Most individuals are able to live normal lives with only 10-20% becoming significantly impaired.

Differential Diagnosis

Some medical conditions can create anxiety such as an overactive thyroid (hyperthyroidism), a seizure disorder, low blood sugar (hypoglycemia), mitral valve prolapse, or a rapid heart rhythm (i.e., supraventricular tachycardia). Substance abuse with stimulants such as cocaine or amphetamines can precipitate a panic attack. Other anxiety disorders such as phobias or separation anxiety disorder can feature sudden anxiety.

Specialists

- Psychiatrist
- Psychologist

Work Restrictions / Accommodations

Time-limited restrictions and work accommodations should be individually determined based on the characteristics of the individual's response to the disorder, the functional requirements of the job and work environment, and the flexibility of the job and work site. The purpose of the restrictions/accommodations is to help maintain the worker's capacity to remain at the workplace without a work disruption or to promote timely and safe transition back to full work productivity.

Complementary and Alternative Therapies

Content is intended for awareness only. Treatments may or may not be effective. Scientific evidence may be lacking and some substances have potentially toxic effects. Dr. Presley Reed and the editors do not endorse the use of these therapies in the absence of consultation with a licensed medical professional.

Biofeedback - May aid in lowering stress.

Diaphragmatic breathing exercises - May help to reduces stress, promote relaxation, and counteract hyperventilation.

Comorbid Conditions

Coexisting conditions that most often affect recovery and lengthen disability are agoraphobia, general anxiety disorders, depression, and substance abuse. Major depression occurs in as many as 50-60% of individuals with panic disorder. It is also estimated that up to 30% of those with panic disorder use alcohol and 17% use drugs (such as cocaine and marijuana) in unsuccessful attempts to relieve the distress caused by their condition. In addition, about 25% of these individuals also have obsessive-compulsive disorder.

Panic disorder often coexists with hypochondriasis, irritable bowel syndrome, mitral valve prolapse, and unexplained medical problems such as chest pain that is not associated with a heart attack or chronic fatigue. Current alcohol abuse or drug use or the presence of a personality disorder or mood disorder may lengthen disability. Concomitant cardiovascular, pulmonary, neurologic, gastrointestinal, endocrinologic, or gastrointestinal disorders may intensify symptoms.

Complications

Fear of a panic attack in public (agoraphobia) may cause the individual to stay at home, resulting in the loss of employment or relationships. Individuals may become convinced they have an undiagnosed life-threatening disease or are going crazy, which can limit their activities even further. Major depressive disorder occurs at some point in half the individuals with this disorder. Alcohol and substance abuse also occur, as can suicide attempts.

Factors Influencing Duration

Length of disability may be influenced by the severity of the symptoms, response to treatment, and any complications such as a coexisting personality disorder or substance abuse.

Length of Disability

Disability is usually transient, lasting the duration of the panic attack.

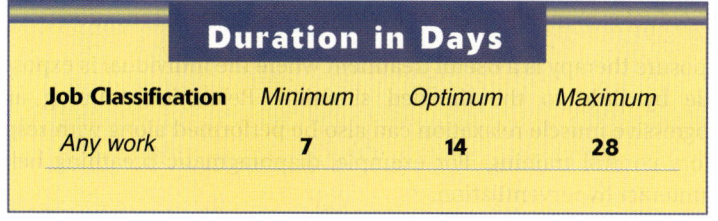

Job Classification	Minimum	Optimum	Maximum
Any work	7	14	28

Duration in Days

Failure to Recover

If an individual fails to recover within the maximum duration expectancy period, the reader may wish to reference the following questions to assist in better understanding the specifics of an individual's medical case.

Regarding diagnosis:

- Does the individual's condition fit the criteria for panic disorder?
- Has the diagnosis been confirmed?
- Have all cardiovascular, endocrine, respiratory and neurological disorders that can cause similar symptoms been ruled out?

Regarding treatment:

- If the individual is not responding effectively to current medication, what other medication options are available?
- Is therapist trained and experienced in cognitive-behavioral therapy?
- Has the individual learned to recognize early thoughts and feelings in the panic cycle?
- Has the individual learned to eliminate thought patterns that contribute to panic behavior?
- Does therapy incorporate interceptive exposure? Through repeated, controlled exposure experiences, has the individual learned to cope effectively with sensations that bring on a panic attack?
- Has the individual learned relaxation techniques to reduce anxiety and stress leading to a panic attack?
- Would the individual benefit from psychodynamic therapy in order to uncover underlying emotional conflicts?

Regarding prognosis:

- Has the individual been involved in the current form of treatment for over 6 weeks without a noticeable effect?
- Has the treatment plan been reassessed?
- Would the individual benefit from extended therapy?
- Are coexisting conditions such as substance abuse (both intoxication and withdrawal states) or depression interfering with treatment? Are these conditions being appropriately addressed?
- Does the individual have a functional support system?
- Besides family and one-on-one therapy support, is individual currently involved in a therapy group?

References

Anxiety Disorders - Panic Disorder. National Institute of Mental Health. 1997. 17 July 2000 <http://www.nimh.nih.gov/anxiety/anxiety/panic/index.htm>.

Disease Definition, Natural History, and Epidemiology: Panic Disorder. American Psychiatric Association. 01 Jan 2000. 10 Oct 2000 <http://www.psych.org/clin_res/pg_panic_2.cfm>.

Panic Disorder with Agoraphobia

Other names / synonyms: Fear of Open Spaces

300.21

Definition

Agoraphobia is the fear of being alone in any place or situation from which escape might be difficult or embarrassing or where help may be unavailable should the need arise. Most individuals with agoraphobia develop the disorder after first suffering from one or more spontaneous panic attacks. Panic disorder with agoraphobia is characterized by recurrent, unexpected panic attacks brought on by being in an open place usually one that is unfamiliar. This is followed by persistent concern about having another attack, worries about the consequences of the attacks, or a behavioral change related to the attacks. A panic attack is the sudden onset of feelings in the absence of real danger of intense apprehension, fearfulness, terror, or a sense of impending doom.

Symptoms include shortness of breath, the feeling that the heart is racing or pounding (palpitations), chills or hot flushes, chest pain or discomfort, choking or smothering sensations, or fear of losing control or "going crazy." Panic attacks occur suddenly, build quickly in intensity, and frequently dissipate within 15 to 60 minutes. Panic attacks with agoraphobia include feelings of anxiety about being in places or situations where escape is difficult such as alone outside the home, standing in line, or traveling in a bus, or where help in unavailable in the instance of a panic attack. Examples of feared situations are being in a stadium, shopping mall, or other crowded situation.

The incidence of panic attack is approximately 1-2% of the population but can be up to 10% in those hospitalized for mental disorders or 60% of those in cardiology clinics. About one-third of individuals diagnosed with panic disorder also have agoraphobia. Age of onset is usually between adolescence and the mid-30s.

Diagnosis

History: Individual reports a history of recurrent panic attacks that includes at least four of the following: a pounding heart, sweating, trembling, shortness of breath or suffocating, choking, chest pain, nausea, dizziness, feelings of unreality, fear of going crazy, fear of dying, numbness, or chills. Onset of the attack is sudden with symptoms peaking in 10 minutes or less. There is chronic worry about having another attack or that the attacks indicate a serious medical or mental disease. Agoraphobia is the additional fear about being in a public place and experiencing a panic attack with the belief that help would be unavailable and escape from this situation difficult or embarrassing. The fear leads to consistently avoiding those situations.

Individuals may be able to expose themselves to the situation with difficulty if accompanied by someone they trust. The panic attacks are judged not directly due to drug abuse, a medical condition (i.e., an overactive thyroid gland), or side effects of medication. The panic is not explained by other anxiety disorders such as a specific or social phobia, obsessive-compulsive disorder, post-traumatic stress disorder, or separation anxiety disorder.

Physical exam: The exam if performed during a panic attack can demonstrate a rapid heart rate and elevated blood pressure. Observation of the individual's orientation, dress, mannerisms, behavior, and content of speech may provide signs helpful in diagnosis.

Tests: Tests do not help establish this diagnosis although personality tests such as the Minnesota Multiphasic Personality Inventory may indicate anxiety and specific fears. Anxiety scales may be useful in determining response to treatment.

Treatment

Panic disorder with agoraphobia is treated with both drug therapy and cognitive-behavioral therapy. Medications can control the panic experienced during phobic situations as well as the anxiety aroused by anticipation of the situation and usually include the administration of a serotonin-specific reuptake inhibitor (SSRI) along with some use of a benzodiazepine. Tricyclic antidepressants are occasionally prescribed. Safety and effectiveness plus the personal needs and preferences of the individual determine what drug is used.

The goal of cognitive therapy is to suggest that panic is a misinterpretation of body sensations and that the danger is not as extreme as perceived. Cognitive-behavioral therapy teaches the individual effective ways to reduce anxiety and view fearful situations differently. It is estimated that appropriate treatment by an experienced professional can reduce or prevent panic attacks in 70-90% of cases. Individuals with panic disorder are often unaware of the distortions in their thinking that can cause the fear cycles. Cognitive-behavioral therapy can help individuals recognize their earliest thoughts and feelings in the panic cycle, eliminate thought patterns contributing to symptoms, and change their behavior. Cognitive-behavioral therapy may also involve "interoceptive exposure" where the individual is encouraged to artificially bring on the symptoms experienced during a panic attack. The individual is then taught to cope effectively with these sensations.

Exposure therapy is a useful treatment where the individual is exposed little by little to the dreaded situation. Relaxation training and progressive muscle relaxation can also be performed along with respiratory control training. For example, diaphragmatic breathing helps counteract hyperventilation.

Many therapists include homework and specific readings (bibliotherapy) for the individual to do between sessions. Since the individual may only spend a few sessions in one-on-one contact with a therapist, this method allows the individual to continue to work on his or her own with the aid of a printed manual.

Psychodynamic treatment refers to another "talk therapy" where the therapist and individual work together to uncover underlying emotional conflicts. Although this type of therapy may help relieve the stress that contributes to panic attacks, there is no scientific evidence this form of therapy by itself is effective in overcoming panic disorder or agoraphobia. However, if a panic disorder occurs along with another emotional disturbance, psychodynamic therapy may be a helpful addition to the overall treatment plan.

Therapy groups can also be beneficial. In weekly meetings, the group discusses progress, exchanges encouragement, and receives guidance from the therapist.

Prognosis

Outcome is variable. The panic attacks may come and go over the years. The agoraphobia may subside if the panic attacks subside but not necessarily. Although many individuals show significant progress after a few weeks of therapy, cognitive-behavioral therapy generally requires at least 8 to 12 weeks. However, some individuals may need longer to learn and implement skills. Some studies show that after 6 to 10 years in tertiary care settings, 30% of individuals have no symptoms, 40% are improved but have some symptoms, and 20-30% have the same or slightly worsened symptoms.

Differential Diagnosis

Other possibilities are agoraphobia without a history of panic disorder, anxiety disorder due to a medical condition, substance-induced anxiety disorder, social phobia, specific phobia, obsessive-compulsive disorder, hyperventilation syndrome, separation anxiety disorder, and delusional disorder. Medical causes include an underactive or overactive thyroid gland, inner ear problems, cardiac conditions, or seizure disorders. Intoxication with central nervous system stimulants (cocaine, amphetamines, caffeine) or alcohol withdrawal can precipitate panic attacks.

Specialists

- Advanced Practice Registered Nurse
- Internist
- Occupational Therapist
- Physical Therapist
- Psychiatrist
- Psychologist

Work Restrictions / Accommodations

Temporary work accommodations may include reducing or eliminating activities where the safety of self or others is contingent upon a constant and/or high level of alertness, such as driving a motor vehicle, operating complex machinery, or handling dangerous chemicals; introducing the individual to new or stressful situations gradually under individually appropriate supervision; allowing some flexibility in scheduling to attend therapy appointments (which normally should occur during the employee's personal time); promoting planned, proactive management of identified problem areas; and offering timely feedback on job performance issues. It will be helpful if accommodations are documented in a written plan designed to promote timely and safe transition back to full work productivity. Situations and settings bringing on feelings of agoraphobia should be avoided if possible.

Comorbid Conditions

Coexisting conditions that most often affect recovery and lengthen disability are depression and substance abuse. Major depression occurs in as many as 50-60% of individuals with panic disorder. It is also estimated that as many as 30% of individuals with panic disorder use alcohol and 17% use drugs such as cocaine and marijuana in unsuccessful attempts to relieve the distress caused by their condition. About 25% of these individuals also have obsessive-compulsive disorder. Panic disorder also often coexists with social and specific phobias, generalized anxiety disorder, hypochondriasis, irritable bowel syndrome, mitral valve prolapse, and unexplained medical problems such as chest pain not associated with a heart attack or chronic fatigue.

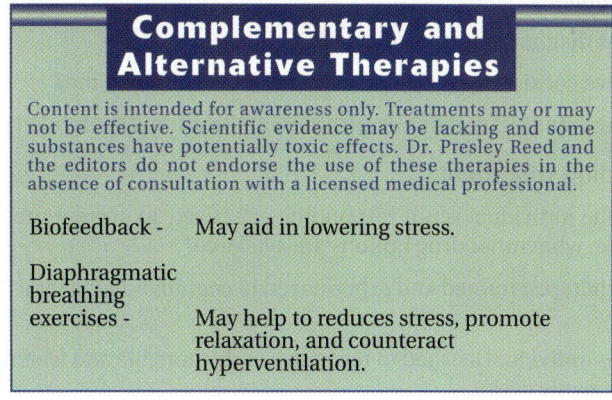

Complementary and Alternative Therapies

Content is intended for awareness only. Treatments may or may not be effective. Scientific evidence may be lacking and some substances have potentially toxic effects. Dr. Presley Reed and the editors do not endorse the use of these therapies in the absence of consultation with a licensed medical professional.

Biofeedback - May aid in lowering stress.

Diaphragmatic breathing exercises - May help to reduces stress, promote relaxation, and counteract hyperventilation.

Complications

Staying at home can often result in a loss of most relationships and employment. Some individuals may become convinced they are going crazy and so limit their activities even further. Approximately 20% of individuals with panic disorder attempt suicide.

Factors Influencing Duration

Length of disability is influenced by the duration and severity of the panic attacks and agoraphobia, any underlying mental illness, other substance abuse, the individual's social support system, appropriateness of treatment choice, response to medications, compliance with treatment, and adequacy of ongoing care.

Length of Disability

Maximum duration includes hospitalization. Agoraphobia can be disabling for work outside the home. In severe cases, it may be totally disabling. Untreated panic disorder may resolve gradually or the individual may have intermittent attacks for many years. Medication treatment for anxiety can have an immediate effect but may not address underlying issues that can trigger panic attacks. Approximately 70-90% of panic attacks can be reduced or prevented with treatment.

Duration in Days

Job Classification	Minimum	Optimum	Maximum
Any work	7	14	42

Failure to Recover

If an individual fails to recover within the maximum duration expectancy period, the reader may wish to reference the following questions to assist in better understanding the specifics of an individual's medical case.

Regarding diagnosis:

- Does the individual fit the criteria for panic disorder with agoraphobia?
- Has diagnosis been confirmed?
- Have coexisting psychological disorders been ruled out?
- Have medical conditions with similar symptoms been ruled out?

Regarding treatment:

- If the individual is not responding effectively to current medication, what other drug options are available?
- Is therapist trained and experienced in cognitive-behavioral therapy?
- Has individual learned to recognize early thoughts and feelings in the panic cycle?
- Has individual learned to eliminate thought patterns that contribute to panic behavior?
- Does therapy incorporate interceptive exposure? Through repeated, controlled exposure experiences, has individual learned to cope effectively with sensations that bring on a panic attack?
- Does the individual's current therapy program include in vivo or real-life exposure therapy?
- Is the therapist willing and able to go to the individual's home to conduct sessions?
- Has individual learned relaxation techniques to reduce anxiety and stress leading to a panic attack?
- Would individual benefit from psychodynamic therapy in order to uncover underlying emotional conflicts?

Regarding prognosis:

- Has the individual been involved in the current form of treatment for over 6 weeks without a noticeable effect? Has the treatment plan been reassessed?
- Would the individual benefit from extended therapy?
- Are coexisting conditions such as substance abuse (both intoxication and withdrawal states) or depression interfering with treatment? Are these conditions being appropriately addressed?
- Does individual have a functional support system?
- Besides family and one-on-one therapy support, is individual currently involved in a therapy group?

References

Allen, Francis. Diagnostic and Statistical Manual of Mental Disorders, 4th ed, text revision. Washington, DC: American Psychiatric Association, 2000.

Anxiety Disorders - Panic Disorder Treatment and Referral. National Institute of Mental Health. 01 Oct 1998. 17 Jul 2000 <http://www.nimh.nih.gov/anxiety/pdtr.cfm#pand6>.

Duke, James A. The Green Pharmacy. Emmaus, PA: Rodale Press, Inc, 1997.

Gottlieb, Bill, ed. New Choices in Natural Healing. Englewood: Rodale Press, Inc, 1995.

Paracentesis

Other names / synonyms: Abdominal Tap
54.91

Definition

Paracentesis is a minor surgical procedure where a large needle is used to withdraw fluid from the abdominal cavity for diagnostic purposes or for the removal of excess fluid.

Various conditions can lead to the collection of fluid within the abdominal cavity, which will then cause abnormal pressure on the organs in that area and may cause pain or discomfort for the individual. Liver failure is a common cause of the collection of serous fluid (ascites) in the abdominal cavity. Depending on the location and cause, paracentesis may be performed in from 5% to approximately 25% of cases.

Reason for Procedure

Paracentesis is performed to obtain fluid for diagnostic purposes, instill medication directly into a cavity, or remove excess serous fluid (ascites). Diagnostic tests done on the fluid obtained may indicate internal bleeding; infection; presence of cancer, appendicitis, or cirrhosis; or indicators of abnormalities in the pancreas, kidneys, heart, or intestine.

Description

Paracentesis can be done on an inpatient or outpatient basis. The puncture site is cleansed and shaved, if necessary, and a local anesthetic applied. A large needle (tap needle) is inserted 1 to 2 inches into the abdomen. If necessary, a small incision is made to help insert the needle. The fluid is then withdrawn through the needle into a syringe or drained through a tube depending on the amount removed. Needle is removed, the incision (if there is one) is closed with a few sutures, and a dressing applied to the puncture site. In this situation, paracentesis is done to remove excess ascitic fluid in order to relieve distention, weight gain, anorexia, and nausea. As much as 2 quarts of fluid may be removed in some instances.

Prognosis

The outcome for a paracentesis in removing excess ascitic fluid is usually an immediate decrease in symptoms. However, the long-term outcome depends on any underlying medical conditions. In some instances, the individual has a chronic condition such as cirrhosis that requires more than one paracentesis over a period of time.

Specialists

- Gastroenterologist
- Surgeon

Work Restrictions / Accommodations

Accommodations are based on any underlying disease or condition, and not the procedure itself.

Comorbid Conditions

Recovery from paracentesis may be affected by obesity.

Procedure Complications

Excessive bleeding or leakage of the ascitic fluid around the needle is a possible complication. If a large amount of ascitic fluid is withdrawn, lowered blood pressure and dizziness or lightheadedness may occur but should resolve within a few hours. Small risks include allergy to the local anesthetic agent used, infection, or the needle puncturing the bowel, bladder, or a blood vessel in the abdomen.

Factors Influencing Duration

Age of the individual, any superimposed chronic disease, and possible complications may influence length of disability.

Length of Disability

Duration depends on diagnosis. Durations reflect recovery time for procedure only.

Duration in Days

Job Classification	Minimum	Optimum	Maximum
Any work	0	5	10

References

"Diagnostic and Therapeutic Gastrointestinal Procedures." The Merck Manual. Beers, Mark H., and Robert Berkow, eds. Whitehouse Station, NJ: Merck Research Laboratories, 1999. 223-227.

Current Medical Diagnosis and Treatment 2001. Tierney, Lawrence M. Jr., Stephen J. McPhee, and Maxine A. Papadakis, eds. New York: Lange Medical Books/McGraw-Hill, 2001.

Gines, Pere, Vicente Arroyo, and Juan Rodes. "Renal Complications." Schiff's Diseases of the Liver, 8th ed. Schiff, Eugene R., Michael F. Sorrell, and Willis C. Maddrey, eds. Philadelphia: Lippincott-Raven Publishers, 1999. 453-464.

Lipsky, Martin S., and Marna R. Sternbach. "Evaluation and Initial Management of Patients with Ascites." American Academy of Family Physicians. 15 Sep 1996. 19 Jan 2001 <http://aafp.com/afp/091596/abs_8.html>.

Paralysis, Paraplegia, and Quadriplegia
344.0, 344.00, 344.01, 344.02, 344.03, 344.04, 344.09, 344.1, 344.9

Definition

Paralysis is a loss or impairment of motor function in a part of the body due to a lesion of the neural or muscular mechanism. When applied to motor function, paralysis is the loss of voluntary movement. Paraplegia refers to weakness or paralysis of both legs and the lower part of the body. Quadriplegia or tetraplegia refers to weakness or paralysis of all four extremities.

Paralysis is caused by an interruption of one or more motor pathways at any point from the cerebrum to the muscle fiber. The paralysis may result in a partial or complete loss of function and may be temporary or permanent. Complete paralysis indicates a total loss of function below the level of the injury. Incomplete paralysis indicates that the individual has some motor function below the injury level. If all of the peripheral motor nerve fibers supplying a muscle are interrupted, all voluntary, postural, and reflex movements are lost. The muscle becomes loose and soft and does not resist passive stretching, a condition known as flaccidity. Muscle tone appears to be reduced (hypotonia or atonia), and there is atrophy of the muscles. If this effect only occurs in a portion of motor fibers supplying the muscle, the result is partial paralysis. In partial paralysis, there is less atrophy, and the tendon reflex will be reduced and not completely lost. The paralysis may be spastic where the affected muscles are stiff and movements are awkward as a result of damage to the upper motor neuron system (brain or spinal cord).

Paralysis occurs more frequently in males between 16-30 years of age. Motor vehicle accidents are the main cause of injury leading to paralysis followed by acts of violence, falls, and other causes.

In paraplegia, paralysis of the legs may occur with diseases of the spinal cord, nerve roots, or peripheral nerves. In acute spinal cord diseases, the paralysis or weakness affects all muscles below a given level and often loss of sensation to pain and temperature can occur. In bilateral disease of the spinal cord, there is loss of bladder and bowel function. There are both acute and chronic forms of paraplegia. The most common cause of acute paraplegia is spinal cord trauma, usually associated with fracture-dislocation of the spine. Other causes are obstruction (thrombosis) of the spinal artery, occlusion of aortic branches due to an aneurysm, or hemorrhage into the spinal cord (hematomyelia) due to a blood vessel (vascular) malformation. Brain hemorrhage from bleeding diseases or anti-coagulant therapy with agents such as warfarin can cause an acute or subacute paraplegia.

In adults, multiple sclerosis is the most common cause of chronic spinal paraplegia. Other conditions that may cause chronic paraplegia include vitamin B_{12} deficiency, protruded cervical disc and cervical spondylosis, syphilitic meningomyelitis, brain abscess and other infections, motor system disease, syringomyelia, and degenerative disease of the spinal cord of unknown cause. Paraplegia occurs less often than paralysis of one side of the body (hemiplegia).

Quadriplegia may result from disease of the peripheral nerves, muscles, or myoneural junctions, gray matter of the spinal cord, brainstem, or cerebrum. The lesion typically occurs in the cervical area of the spinal cord. Depending on the location in the cervical area, the paralysis of the arms may be flaccid and areflexic in type and that of the legs is spastic. Compression of the cervical spinal cord segments may occur with rheumatoid arthritis. This form of paralysis is not as common as paralysis on one side of the body (hemiplegia). The incidence of quadriplegia is difficult to predict due to the various underlying causes of the paralysis.

Diagnosis

History: In paralysis, individuals may report a history of traumatic injury, brain tumor or abscess, or infection. The individual may report weakness of muscles in the limbs, loss of sensation, muscle stiffness, muscle rigidity, or muscle looseness (flaccidity).

Individuals with paraplegia may report a history of a traumatic injury, brain tumor, or diseases of the spinal cord, nerve roots or peripheral nerves. The individual may report weakness of the muscles of both lower extremities, loss of pain and temperature sensation below a particular level, and loss of position and vibratory sense.

Quadriplegic individuals may report weakness of the muscles of all four extremities. Flaccidity of the arms and spasticity of the legs are typical patterns of paralysis. The individual may also experience pain in the neck and shoulders, numbness of the hands, and staggering gait and postural imbalance (ataxia).

Physical exam: The neurological exam may reveal spinal cord damage and localize the level of injury in individuals with paralysis. Spastic movement and increased tendon reflexes may be evident. Peripheral nerve damage is indicated by muscle wasting (atrophy) and weakness with reduced tendon reflexes. Affected muscles may reveal involuntary contraction or twitching of groups of muscle fibers (fasciculation).

In individuals who are paraplegic, the neurological exam may reveal spinal cord damage and localize the level of injury. The bladder and sphincter muscles may be affected and result in loss of bladder and rectal function. Sensory loss is more prominent in the distal segments of the limbs.

In quadriplegia, the neurological exam may reveal brain damage or lesions of the cervical spinal cord. In diplegia, the legs are more affected than the arms. There may be dislocation of spinal cord segments, especially in the presence of rheumatoid arthritis. In individuals with triplegia, the exam may reveal spastic weakness of one limb followed by involvement of the other limbs in a "round the clock" pattern. Loss of pain and temperature sensation may be observed.

Tests: For paralysis, paraplegia, and quadriplegia, diagnostic tests include x-rays, CT scan, or MRI. The diagnostic tests may reveal a spinal cord injury or tumor in individuals with paralysis; lesions of the spinal cord or an extrinsic mass that narrows the spinal canal in individuals with paraplegia; and lesions of the cervical spinal cord in individuals with quadriplegia. Electromyography tests the electrical activity of the muscles. A lumbar puncture (spinal tap) may be performed to rule out infection and it often demonstrates a dynamic block and increase in cerebrospinal fluid protein.

Treatment

Paralysis Treatment depends upon the type, location, and extent of the paralysis. The primary consideration in treatment of spinal cord injury (trauma) is to immobilize the spine. If the damage is due to compression of the spinal column, surgery may relieve pressure. If there is a blockage in the column due to a tumor, chemotherapy and radiation may be indicated. Infections are treated with antibiotics. In cases of temporary paralysis, physical therapy is used to retrain and strengthen muscles and joints so that some degree of mobility is possible after recovery. If there is complete loss of function, supportive measures such as physical therapy to prevent joints from becoming locked and contracted and avoidance of complications from prolonged immobility (pressure ulcers, blood clots, urinary tract infections, constipation) should be instituted.

Paraplegia Treatment depends on the cause of the paraplegia. If it is due to spinal cord injury, then immobilization of the spine is of primary importance. Surgery can relieve pressure if present. Less common causes such as thrombosis may require administration of thrombolytic agents. Infections should be treated with appropriate antibiotics. If there is a tumor causing spinal cord compression, surgery may relieve the pressure.

Quadriplegia Treatment depends on the cause of the quadriplegia. If it is due to spinal cord injury, then immobilization of the spine is of primary importance. Surgery can relieve pressure if present. Less common causes such as thrombosis may require administration of thrombolytic agents. Infections should be treated with appropriate antibiotics. If there is a tumor causing spinal cord compression, surgery may relieve the pressure. There will be no recovery from spinal cord transection.

Prognosis

Paralysis Paralysis from spinal cord injury may be temporary, and partial function may be regained as the swelling subsides. Improvement can begin as early as three weeks after the initial injury, and after one year the level of functioning usually stabilizes at 1-2 levels below the injury site. Surgery to remove tumors in the spinal cord can relieve pain and pressure and improve neurological deficits.

Paraplegia Decompression of the spinal cord or nerve roots and spinal stabilization results in improvement in pain, neurological deficits and walking (ambulatory) ability. Identification of the individual's symptoms allows for appropriate surgical intervention with favorable results. Recent evidence suggests that the life expectancy of those with spinal cord injuries is improving. Regardless of total life expectancy, individuals can expect to spend about six of their remaining years in poor health, most likely toward the end of life. Those with paraplegia usually become less independent over time resulting in a lower life expectancy. The prescription of treatment systems including mobile standing devices and orthoses to enable individuals with spinal lesions to walk is widely practiced and can provide relief from secondary medical complications and improvement in quality of life.

Quadriplegia Decompression of the spinal cord or nerve roots and spinal stabilization results in improvement in pain, neurological deficits, and walking (ambulatory) ability. Identification of the individual's symptoms allows for appropriate surgical intervention with favorable results. Recent evidence suggests that the life expectancy of those with spinal cord injuries is improving. Regardless of total life expectancy, individuals can expect to spend about six of their remaining years in poor health, most likely toward the end of life. Those with quadriplegia have a high expectation of independence over time resulting in a longer life expectancy. The prescription of treatment systems including mobile standing devices and orthoses to enable individuals with spinal lesions to walk is widely practiced and can provide relief from secondary medical complications and improvement in quality of life.

Differential Diagnosis

Paralysis The diagnosis of paralysis is evident but should be distinguished from general weakness of muscles. Fatigue and similar symptoms may be manifestations of systemic illnesses such as anemia, malignant tumor, or acute infection. Pseudoweakness can occur in individuals who have a gait disorder, peripheral neuropathy, or difficulty raising one or both arms because of bursitis, not limb weakness. Examination findings will reveal these circumstances.

Paraplegia The diagnosis of paraplegia is evident but should be distinguished from paralytic poliomyelitis and acute polyneuritis (Guillain-Barré). Other conditions that may produce the same effects as paraplegia include vitamin B_{12} deficiency, protruded cervical disc and cervical spondylosis, syphilitic meningomyelitis, brain abscess and other infections, motor system disease, syringomyelia, and degenerative disease of the spinal column.

Quadriplegia The diagnosis of quadriplegia is evident but should be distinguished from repeated cerebral accidents, which may lead to bilateral hemiplegia.

Specialists

- Neurologist
- Neurosurgeon
- Oncologist
- Orthopedic Surgeon
- Physiatrist

Rehabilitation

If an individual becomes a quadriplegic, either through illness or trauma, there is a lengthy rehabilitation process involved. Therapy goals in the hospital focus on prevention of further illness.

Respiratory therapy includes deep breathing exercises and chest percussions are performed by the therapist to keep the lungs clear of mucus. Respiratory therapists routinely assess individuals on ventilators to determine continued need for assisted breathing.

Physical therapists establish a routine for changing an individual's position in bed to prevent skin breakdown. Physical therapists teach an individual's family members to be consistent with this routine. They stretch all of an individual's joints to maintain flexibility.

Occupational therapists assess an individual's potential for self-care. Both occupational and physical therapists focus on increasing sitting tolerance and sitting balance. Psychologists and psychiatrists are a crucial link in the rehabilitation process, helping to focus individuals on attainable goals and treating the depression that occurs after spinal cord injury.

Once individuals are medically stable, individuals are transferred to a rehabilitation hospital for several months. Therapy lasts for several hours each day. Special equipment can increase the independence of individuals with spinal cord injuries. Physical and occupational therapists order wheelchairs with a seat cushion system that maintains correct posture and sitting balance. Adaptive equipment is ordered, such as utensils with thick handles to allow for better grasp.

Mobility is the goal of physical therapy. Physical therapists teach individuals and their families strategies for rolling, transferring to and from the bed, the wheelchair, the shower, and the car. Wheelchair mobility is a key component to regaining independence. Individuals who have fractures of one of the first four cervical vertebrae learn to utilize a mouth control system to propel the wheelchair. Other individuals learn to use a joystick control. As wheelchair skills progress, individuals learn to maneuver their wheelchairs outside and to perform activities such as shopping. Slight changes in position, made while sitting in a wheelchair, are taught to prevent skin breakdown.

Achieving independence in self-care is the primary goal of occupational therapists. Occupational therapists teach dressing, grooming, and feeding techniques to individuals with cervical fractures of C5 and below. Individuals with fractures above C5 cannot perform self-care.

Both disciplines develop a flexibility program for all joints and teach this program to family members. Individuals learn to perform strengthening exercises for any arm muscles that have movement.

Speech therapists work on communicating strategies for those who are ventilator dependent and increasing the volume of speech for all individuals.

Individuals with fractures of C5 and below are discharged to outpatient occupational and physical therapy to further address functional gains. Individuals with fractures of C4 and higher may be eligible for in-home physical and occupational therapy. These individuals will not be independent in transferring or self-care. In-home therapy should focus on reinforcing family care of the individual.

If an individual becomes a paraplegic, either through illness or injury, a lengthy rehabilitation is involved. While in the hospital, physical therapy focuses on frequently changing an individual's position in bed to prevent skin breakdown, and teaching an individual's family members to comply with the turning schedule. Physical therapists also begin stretching all of the individual's joints to maintain flexibility.

Occupational therapists teach self-care strategies at this time. Both occupational and physical therapists will attempt to increase sitting tolerance and sitting balance. Respiratory therapists teach deep breathing exercises and perform chest percussions to keep the lungs clear of mucus. Psychologists and psychiatrists are a crucial link in the rehabilitation process through treatment of the depression that occurs after spinal cord injury. Additionally, they work to help individuals set attainable goals.

Once individuals are medically stable, they may be transferred to a rehabilitation hospital for several months. Therapy lasts for several hours each day. Physical and occupational therapists may order equipment that will enable individuals to be as independent as possible. A wheelchair with a seat cushion system that supports correct posture is the most important piece of equipment. Additional equipment such as a sliding board is also ordered. This board allows for safer transfer from the wheelchair to other seating surfaces.

Occupational therapists teach dressing, grooming, and food preparation techniques to individuals. They make suggestions for changing the home environment to allow for independent self-care.

Both occupational and physical therapists stretch all joints to maintain flexibility and provide strengthening exercises for any muscles that have movement. Therapists provide a home exercise program based on these exercises that must be followed to maintain function. Therapists also emphasize pressure reliefs, which are changes in position made while sitting, to prevent skin breakdown.

Outpatient physical therapy may be warranted to maximize functional gains and to reinforce the mobility techniques learned in rehabilitation.

Individuals cleared by their physicians to drive can be assessed for car adaptations and driving school at outpatient physical therapy.

Work Restrictions / Accommodations

Paralysis Wheelchair accessibility is required. Additional accommodations depend on the degree of paralysis and job requirements. Extremes in temperature and highly stressful activities should be avoided.

Paraplegia Wheelchair accessibility is required. Additional accommodations include handicap facilities for individuals using mobile walking devices or orthoses for the ability to maneuver adequately.

Quadriplegia Wheelchair accessibility is required. Additional accommodations include handicap facilities for individuals using mobile walking devices or orthoses for the ability to maneuver adequately.

Comorbid Conditions

Paralysis Obesity, diabetes, diabetic neuropathy, and degenerative diseases of the nervous system such as multiple sclerosis can complicate the condition and impact the ability to recover and further lengthen disability.

Paraplegia Obesity, diabetes, diabetic neuropathy, and degenerative diseases of the nervous system such as multiple sclerosis can impact the ability to recover and further lengthen disability.

Quadriplegia Obesity, diabetes, diabetic neuropathy, and degenerative diseases of the nervous system such as multiple sclerosis can impact the ability to recover and further lengthen disability.

Complications

Paralysis Joints may become locked in both temporary and permanent paralysis. Complications from permanent paralysis due to prolonged immobility include limb deformities, bed sores (pressure ulcers), blood clots (deep vein thrombosis), fluctuating blood pressure and body temperature, osteoporosis, respiratory and urinary tract infections, and constipation. Psychological stress due to loss of body functions most often results in depression.

Paraplegia Complications include respiratory infections (pneumonia, atelectasis), coronary heart disease, autonomic dysreflexia, urinary tract infections, kidney stones, kidney and liver insufficiency, gallstones, constipation, bed sores (pressure ulcers), and osteoporosis. Chronic severe pain and spasm may also complicate paraplegia. Extreme physical inactivity may cause elevation in blood lipids (cholesterol) resulting in an increased risk for cardiovascular diseases. Psychological stress due to loss of body functions most often causes depression.

Quadriplegia Complications include respiratory infections (pneumonia, atelectasis), coronary heart disease, autonomic dysreflexia, urinary tract infections, kidney stones, kidney and liver insufficiency, gallstones, constipation, bed sores (pressure ulcers), and osteoporosis. Chronic severe pain and spasm may also complicate quadriplegia. Extreme physical inactivity may cause elevation in blood lipids (cholesterol and triglycerides) resulting in an increased risk for cardiovascular diseases. Psychological stress due to loss of body functions most often causes depression.

Factors Influencing Duration

Paralysis Length of disability will be determined by the underlying diagnosis, whether the paralysis is temporary or permanent, the extent of paralysis (monoplegia, hemiplegia, paraplegia, quadriplegia), and the body parts affected.

Paraplegia Length of disability will be determined by the cause (acute spinal cord injury, spinal cord lesions), whether there is restoration of function following spinal decompression and stabilization, and if there is any underlying illness that preceded the condition (infection, tumor).

Quadriplegia Length of disability will be determined by the cause (acute spinal cord injury, cervical lesion), whether there is restoration of function following spinal decompression and stabilization, and if there is any underlying illness that preceded the condition (infection, tumor).

Length of Disability

Disability varies since each spinal cord injury is unique. Disability may be permanent. Contact physician for additional case information.

Paralysis The disability may be permanent if there is no recovery from the paralysis. In cases where there is partial recovery, there may be improvement within three weeks after injury, but rehabilitation will take longer depending on degree of paralysis and body parts involved.

Paraplegia The disability is most likely permanent; however, there may be some improvement after surgical intervention (spinal cord decompression) and spinal stabilization. Orthoses and standing mobility devices may improve the ability to walk and increase the likelihood of return to work.

Quadriplegia The disability is most likely permanent; however, there may be some improvement after surgical intervention (spinal cord decompression) and spinal stabilization. Orthoses and standing mobility devices may improve the ability to walk and increase the likelihood of return to work.

Duration in Days

Job Classification	Minimum	Optimum	Maximum
Sedentary work	119	182	Indefinite
Light work	Indefinite	Indefinite	Indefinite
Medium work	Indefinite	Indefinite	Indefinite
Heavy work	Indefinite	Indefinite	Indefinite
Very Heavy work	Indefinite	Indefinite	Indefinite

Failure to Recover

If an individual fails to recover within the maximum duration expectancy period, the reader may wish to reference the following questions to assist in better understanding the specifics of an individual's medical case.

Regarding diagnosis:

- Was paralysis distinguished from general muscle weakness or complications of other systemic illnesses?
- Was paraplegia distinguished from paralytic poliomyelitis and acute polyneuritis?
- Was quadriplegia distinguished from paralytic poliomyelitis and acute polyneuritis?

- Has individual experienced any complications from permanent paralysis due to prolonged immobility such as, limb deformities, pressure ulcers, deep vein thrombosis, fluctuating blood pressure and body temperature, osteoporosis, respiratory and urinary tract infections, and constipation?
- Has individual experienced any complications from paraplegia such as, respiratory infections (pneumonia, atelectasis), coronary heart disease, autonomic dysreflexia, urinary tract infections, kidney stones, kidney and liver insufficiency, gallstones, constipation, pressure ulcers, and osteoporosis, chronic severe pain and spasm? Has individual experienced complications of quadriplegia such as respiratory infections (pneumonia, atelectasis), coronary heart disease, autonomic dysreflexia, urinary tract infections, kidney stones, kidney and liver insufficiency, gallstones, constipation, bed sores (pressure ulcers), and osteoporosis, chronic severe pain and spasm?
- Were other pre-existing illnesses (obesity, diabetes, diabetic neuropathy, and degenerative diseases of the nervous system) identified and treated?

Regarding treatment:

- If there is a blockage in the column due to a tumor, is chemotherapy and radiation indicated?
- Is surgery indicated due to compression of the spinal column?
- Have infections been treated with antibiotics?
- Has culture and sensitivity been performed to determine the most effective antibiotic therapy?
- Have antibiotic-resistant organisms been identified or ruled-out?

- Did individual receive prompt, appropriate treatment?
- Has there been sufficient rehabilitation, such as physical therapy, for the individual?
- Has individual experienced pressure ulcers, blood clots, urinary tract infections, and/or constipation as a result of immobility?
- Were thrombolytic agents administered as appropriate? Was treatment effective in relieving thrombosis?
- Were other pre-existing illnesses (obesity, diabetes, diabetic neuropathy, and degenerative diseases of the nervous system) identified and treated?
- Has cardiovascular risk been monitored with cholesterol and triglyceride testing?
- Would individual benefit from psychological evaluation and counseling?

Regarding prognosis:

- Is individual receiving sufficient rehabilitation?
- Is progressive improvement evident or has it stabilized?
- If more conservative treatment has failed, is individual now a candidate for surgical intervention, such as, decompression of the spinal cord or nerve roots, and spinal stabilization?
- Is individual enrolled in a comprehensive rehabilitation program?
- Does he/she have access to appropriate orthotic devices?
- Does individual have realistic expectations?
- Would individual benefit from psychological evaluation and counseling?

References

Adams, Raymond D., Maurice Victor, and Allan H. Ropeer. Principles of Neurology, 6th ed. New York: McGraw Hill, 1997.

Somers, Martha Freeman. Spinal Cord Injury. Norwalk: Appleton & Lange, 1992.

Paranoid Personality Disorder
301.0

Definition

The central feature of individuals with paranoid personality disorder is their unjustified mistrust and suspicion of other people in general. Paranoid individuals are rigid, angry, and have an urgent need to be self-sufficient. Their demeanor tends to be cold, sullen, humorless, and quick tempered. They tend to blame their problems on others and are unable to accept their own faults and weaknesses. Individuals with this personality disorder have a knack for pointing out other's subtle faults with great accuracy. The essential hallmark of paranoid personality disorder is a pervasive and unwarranted tendency to interpret other people's actions as deliberately demeaning or threatening. Paranoid individuals frequently, without justification, question the loyalty or trustworthiness of friends, family, and associates.

In the workplace, they tend to be jealous of co-workers, guarded, and loners, often isolating themselves from others. They react with anger even to constructive criticism, would much rather work alone, and tend to be quarrelsome and abrasive. It is common for them to turn a small issue or problem into a catastrophic issue. They often feel mistreated, overlooked, and picked on by their superiors. Co-workers may become exasperated and angry toward them.

The disorder is more common in men than women, and occurs in about 0.5-2.5% of the population. It does not appear to run in families. The disorder is more common in minority groups, immigrants, the deaf, or relatives of schizophrenics.

Diagnosis

History: The diagnosis is based on criteria set forth in the Diagnostic and Statistical Manual IV, Text Revision (DSM-IV-TR). An individual with paranoid personality has a pervasive distrust and suspiciousness of others, interpreting their motives as malevolent. The disorder begins by early adulthood and is present in a variety of contexts. To justify the diagnosis, individuals must have four of the following seven behaviors, or personality traits: suspects without sufficient basis that others are exploiting, harming, or deceiving him or her; is preoccupied with unjustified doubts about the loyalty or trustworthiness of friends or associates; is reluctant to confide in others because of unwarranted fear that the information will be used maliciously against him or her; reads hidden demeaning or threatening meanings into benign remarks or events; persistently bears grudges, or is unforgiving of insults, injuries, or slights; perceives attacks on his or her character or reputation that are not apparent to others, and is quick to react angrily or to counterattack; or has recurrent unjustified suspicions regarding the fidelity of their spouse or sexual partner.

For a diagnosis of paranoid personality disorder to be made, these behaviors cannot occur exclusively during the course of schizophrenia, a mood disorder with psychotic features, or another psychotic disorder, nor can they be due to the direct physiological effects of a general medical condition.

Inquiries as to drug and alcohol use are warranted, but this area must be broached carefully so as not to provoke hostility and jeopardize any rapport that may have been established.

Physical exam: There are no findings on the physical exam that contribute to this diagnosis.

Tests: Psychological tests such as the Minnesota Multiphasic Personality Inventory (MMPI) that can be used to help identify and classify personality disorders; however, they are rarely needed by an experienced clinician. The interpretation of these tests can only be used in conjunction with the history and would not be used in isolation to make a final diagnosis of paranoid personality disorder.

Treatment

The two primary approaches to treating this disorder are psychotherapy and medications (pharmacotherapy). As medications are likely to be received with suspicion, the treatment of choice is usually psychotherapy, but this depends on the individual's specific behaviors and willingness to participate in treatment. Antianxiety drugs may be helpful for brief crisis management, and antipsychotics might be needed briefly for severe agitation or for thinking bordering on delusional. Supportive psychotherapy is the treatment of choice, but excessive interpretation by the therapist of deep conflicts should be avoided initially, as trust and tolerance of intimacy are difficult to establish. The therapist should be professional, straightforward, and not overly warm. When behavior becomes threatening, limits must be set gently but realistically, without humiliating or frightening the individual. Group therapy and behavior therapies are usually not helpful in paranoid personality disorder.

Prognosis

Currently, there are no systematic, reliable long-term studies to predict outcome. However, the disorder is life long and may be a precursor to schizophrenia or other psychiatric disorders. Occupational and marital problems are common in paranoid personality disorder, as are financial and legal problems to a lesser extent. Proper treatment may allow better quality of life, unless there is poor compliance with treatment recommendations.

Differential Diagnosis

Paranoid personality disorder often exists in combination with other personality disorders, such as paranoid-narcissistic, paranoid-antisocial, or paranoid-compulsive personality disorders. Differential diagnosis may also include a persecutory type of delusional disorder, paranoid schizophrenia, mood disorder with psychotic features, personality change due to a general medical condition, substance abuse disorders, paranoid traits secondary to physical handicaps, and other personality disorders.

Specialists

- Licensed Clinical Social Worker
- Psychiatrist
- Psychologist

Work Restrictions / Accommodations

Accommodations might include allowing the employee to work alone or in a small group, creating a private workspace, limiting contact with a large or unfamiliar group of people, and assigning a tolerant and understanding supervisor. Frequent cyclical shift changes (days to swing to graveyard and back to days) may lead to disturbances of the sleep-wake cycle, which could worsen symptoms.

Comorbid Conditions

Alcohol abuse, drug use, or the presence of another psychiatric disorder may lengthen disability.

Complications

Any change or increase in stress can create complications, especially if occupational, financial, or legal problems or personal relationships are involved. The paranoid personality exaggerates even minimal problems. Examples of stress involving the workplace are a change of supervisor, moving to another workspace, change in work hours, and/or a shift change.

Substance abuse is often the individual's way of coping with the distress. Self-medication can lead to abuse and dependence. Alcoholism, which is often associated with this disorder, leads to a vicious cycle of paranoid perceptions becoming reality, as it leads to estrangement from family members, co-workers, and friends. The presence of another personality disorder may also complicate treatment.

Factors Influencing Duration

The progress and effectiveness of the psychotherapy and the individual's willingness to participate in therapy will influence length of disability. Other factors might include the coexistence of other psychiatric diagnoses, especially substance abuse. The current status of life stressors such as marital, legal, or financial problems can affect duration of disability.

Length of Disability

This condition represents a life-long pattern of behavior. In most cases, no disability is expected.

Failure to Recover

If an individual fails to recover within the maximum duration expectancy period, the reader may wish to reference the following questions to assist in better understanding the specifics of an individual's medical case.

Regarding diagnosis:

- Does individual fit the criteria for paranoid personality?
- Has the diagnosis been confirmed?
- Are the individual's symptoms due to another psychological disorder?
- Have medical conditions with similar symptoms been ruled out?

Regarding treatment:

- Was anti-anxiety medication beneficial for crisis management?
- If individual experienced severe agitation or borderline delusional thinking, was antipsychotic medication indicated?
- Was drug therapy perceived with suspicion?
- Did drug therapy actually interfere with treatment?
- Has the individual been able to trust the therapist? If not, what can be done to improve rapport?
- Although delusional accusations must be dealt with realistically, was this accomplished without humiliating the individual?
- Could behavioral therapy and/or role-playing be used to diminish suspiciousness and improve socialization skills?

Regarding prognosis:

- Are the paranoid traits of the individual persistent, inflexible, and causing significant dysfunction and distress?
- Is social or occupational function impaired?
- How does the individual cope with stress?
- Does the individual have an effective, trusting support group?
- Would the individual benefit from additional treatment or treatment alternatives?

References

American Psychiatric Association, eds. Diagnostic and Statistical Manual of Mental Disorders IV, Text Revision. Washington, DC: American Psychiatric Association, 1999.

Long, Phillip W. Paranoid Personality Disorder. Internet Mental Health. 1996. 16 Aug 2000 <http://www.mentalhealth.com/fr20.html>.

Paraovarian Cyst
752.11

Definition

A paraovarian cyst is a closed, fluid-filled sac that grows beside or near the ovary and fallopian tube, but is never attached to them. It is usually located on the broad ligament between the uterus and the ovary, and is usually found on only one side (unilateral) of the uterus. It is thought to develop from embryological vestiges (Wolffian structures), the external covering of the Fallopian tubes (tubal epithelium), or the smooth serous membrane that lines the cavity of the abdomen (peritoneum). Paraovarian cysts are usually very small (ranging in size from 2 to 20 cm). These cysts have little clinical significance, occurring asymptomatically as incidental findings during other pelvic examinations and surgeries. Most often, they are diagnosed as benign ovarian cysts or as fluid-filled distentions of the fallopian tube (hydrosalpinx).

Although known for their small size, paraovarian cysts can sometimes grow larger, especially during pregnancies. Unlike the small cysts, the larger cysts are usually symptomatic. Depending on their size and location, large paraovarian cysts can put pressure on the bladder or bowel, and cause pelvic pain or pain during sexual intercourse (dyspareunia).

Paraovarian cysts are relatively common and account for 10% of all pelvic masses. The smaller cysts are most commonly found in middle-aged women (in the 30-40 years of age group), and are often indistinguishable from simple ovarian cysts. Larger paraovarian cysts tend to develop in younger women, quite often during a pregnancy, at which time they have a tendency to grow rapidly.

Diagnosis

History: Many individuals with small paraovarian cysts report no symptoms. However, individuals with larger paraovarian cysts frequently complain of pelvic pain, usually on one side (unilateral), irregular periods, abnormal uterine bleeding, and pain during sexual intercourse (dyspareunia).

Physical exam: Paraovarian cysts may be discovered when the physician presses with his or her hands on the abdomen (abdominal palpation), or when he or she inserts one hand into the vagina and presses with the other on the top of the abdomen (bimanual pelvic exam).

Tests: Both an ultrasound scan and a visual exam (using a thin, lighted microscope inserted into the abdomen, or a laparoscopy) are used to confirm the diagnosis, size, and location of a paraovarian cyst.

Treatment

Most paraovarian cysts that remain small and asymptomatic do not require treatment; sometimes they disappear on their own. Surgical removal of the cyst (laparoscopic cystectomy) is usually indicated for young girls who have not reached puberty, those with an ovarian mass, and for postmenopausal women. A laparoscopic cystectomy enables the surgeon to insert a tiny scope into the abdomen to determine whether more extensive surgery is needed. Sometimes, it is possible to remove the cyst during the laparoscopic procedure.

However, if the cyst is larger than 4 inches (10 cm), is complex, increasing in size, persists after several months, is solid, dense, and irregularly shaped, or is infected, bleeding or ruptured, more invasive surgery (cystectomy) may be required. Such cysts pose a problem if they put pressure on pelvic structures, thus risking damaging them, and cause pelvic pain or pain during sexual intercourse (dyspareunia).

Prognosis

In instances where the individual is not pregnant, a complete recovery can be expected; surgical removal of the cyst is curative and no recurrence is expected. In instances where the individual is pregnant, a complete recovery can be expected if surgery to remove the cyst is performed between 14 to 20 weeks gestation (particularly if it is very large, low in the pelvis, and not movable).

Differential Diagnosis

Conditions with similar symptoms include ovarian cyst, fluid-filled distention of the fallopian tube (hydrosalpinx), and turbo-ovarian abscess.

Specialists

- General Surgeon
- Gynecologist

Work Restrictions / Accommodations

Possible work restrictions and accommodations include time off from work allotted for follow-up doctor appointments. More frequent examinations may be necessary if the individual is pregnant. If surgery is necessary, heavy lifting may need to be restricted temporarily.

Comorbid Conditions

Comorbid conditions that might influence the length of disability include obesity and diabetes.

Complications

Complications that arise from paraovarian cyst include infection, bleeding, and rupture of the cyst; the rupture or bursting of a cyst is a medical emergency.

In pregnant women, the cyst causes the enlarging uterus to be pushed up, out, and to the opposite side of the pelvic region. Such repositioning may cause the period of gestation to be overestimated, and abnormal intrauterine fetal positioning. During labor, abnormal uterine and fetal positions can make delivery difficult (dystocia). In the absence of timely intervention, damage to important pelvic structures may lead to intrauterine fetal death and life-threatening complications for the mother, such as rupture of the uterus. Additionally, the cyst may rupture due to compression by the uterus and the fetus.

Other less common complications include internal cystic bleeding (intracystic hemorrhage), and the formation of pus and its discharge (suppuration) from the cyst.

Factors Influencing Duration

The need for surgery and hospitalization may influence the length of disability.

Length of Disability

For individuals who have undergone surgery, the length of disability is determined by the type of surgery, the individual's recovery, and development of complications.

Laproscropic cystectomy.

Duration in Days

Job Classification	Minimum	Optimum	Maximum
Sedentary work	3	7	21
Light work	3	7	21
Medium work	7	14	28
Heavy work	7	21	35
Very Heavy work	14	21	35

Failure to Recover

If an individual fails to recover within the maximum duration expectancy period, the reader may wish to reference the following questions to assist in better understanding the specifics of an individual's medical case.

Regarding diagnosis:

- Has diagnosis of paraovarian cyst been confirmed with a laparoscopy or ultrasound?
- If the diagnosis was uncertain, were other conditions with similar symptoms such as ovarian cyst, hydrosalpinx, and turbo-ovarian abscess ruled out?
- Has the individual experienced symptoms associated with a large paraovarian cyst such as bladder or bowel pressure, pelvic pain, or pain with intercourse?

Regarding treatment:

- Was treatment unnecessary? If so, did the individual receive periodic reevaluation to detect any changes in the ovarian cyst that would warrant treatment?
- Was cyst removed laparoscopically, or was more invasive surgery involved?
- Was emergency surgery indicated due to cyst rupture and bleeding?
- Were any complications associated with the procedure itself, such as bleeding or infection?
- Did cyst cause any damage to associated structures?
- Have associated structural damage and/or complications been addressed in the treatment plan?
- What will be the impact on recovery?

Regarding prognosis:

- Was the treatment delayed due to pregnancy (beyond 20 weeks)?
- Did the individual suffer any complications with fetal positioning and delivery due to the size and location of the cyst?
- Did the individual suffer any other complications associated with the cyst such as bleeding, infection or rupture?

References

Barloon, T.J. "Paraovarian and Paratubal Cysts: Preoperative Diagnosis Using Transabdominal and Transvaginal Sonography." Journal of Clinical Ultrasound 24 3 (1996): 117-122. 25 Feb 2001 <http://home.mdconsult.com/ >.

Spero, Kenneth. Paraovarian Cyst. Indiana University School of Medicine - Radiology Department. 28 Nov 2000. 12 Dec 2000 <http://www.indyrad.iupui.edu/public/lectures/ovarian/sld019.htm>.

Paresthesia

Other names / synonyms: Numbness and Tingling, Pins and Needles, Sensation Disturbance
782.0

Definition

Paresthesia is a symptom not a disease that refers to abnormal sensations occurring without any apparent cause (spontaneously). Paresthesias are often described as tingling, pins and needles, prickling, electric, burning, vibrating, buzzing, or crawling. Paresthesias have also been described as "the limb falling asleep" (due to brief compression of the sciatic, peroneal, or ulnar nerves). They often occur due to compression of peripheral nerves or an abnormality along the peripheral or central nervous systems.

Paresthesia can occur with many different diseases including carpal tunnel syndrome, cervical and lumbosacral radiculopathy, restless leg syndrome, diabetic neuropathy, vitamin B_{12} deficiency, and alcoholic polyneuropathy. Less common causes of paresthesias include cancer, human immunodeficiency virus (HIV), hypocalcemia, malabsorption, multiple sclerosis, Guillain-Barré syndrome, hypocalcemia, and use of certain medications (isoniazid, vincristine, diuretics, and nonsteroidal anti-inflammatory drugs [NSAIDs]).

Paresthesia affects men and women equally. The incidence of paresthesia varies with the underlying cause.

Diagnosis

History: Individuals complain of sensations of tingling, pins and needles, prickling, electric, burning, vibrating, buzzing, crawling, or of "a limb falling asleep." Individuals may report the presence of other symptoms such as pain, numbness, weakness, stiffness, or clumsiness. Important information obtained from the history includes location of the paresthesia, how long paresthesia has been present, and if the paresthesia worsens in any one position or by a specific activity.

Physical exam: The exam may reveal decreased sensation over the involved area. Tinel's sign is elicited by tapping an entrapped nerve that increases distal paresthesias. Tinel's sign may be present with carpal tunnel and cubital tunnel syndromes. Phalen's sign is elicited by flexion of the wrist that increases median nerve paresthesia. Phalen's sign may be present with carpal tunnel syndrome. Physical examination may also reveal presence of nerve root pain (radiculopathy) that is due to compression of the spinal column with decreased strength, sensation, and reflexes in the affected nerve root. Individuals with diabetic neuropathy may reveal bilateral loss of sensation to pain, touch, temperature, and proprioception. Many paresthesia manifestations occur with multiple sclerosis. Physical examination of individuals with Guillain-Barré syndrome may reveal increasing paralysis and hyporeflexia.

Tests: Electromyography (EMG) and nerve conduction tests can rule out nerve dysfunction. A vitamin B_{12} level below 200 pg/ml indicates vitamin B_{12} deficiency. The calcium level may also be abnormal. In restless legs syndrome, a polysomnography can demonstrate periodic movements during sleep. An MRI may be used for diagnosis of multiple sclerosis. A spinal tap is used to obtain cerebrospinal fluid samples for diagnosis of Guillain-Barré and multiple sclerosis. Abnormally elevated liver function tests and an elevated mean corpuscular volume may reveal alcohol abuse.

Treatment

Treatment for paresthesia is based on the underlying cause of the symptom. For example, carpal tunnel syndrome is treated with wrist splints, anti-inflammatory medications, or surgical decompression. Cubital tunnel syndrome is treated with splinting or surgical decompression. Compression of a nerve in the lower leg (the peroneal nerve) may be relieved by not crossing the legs. Radiculopathies are treated by avoiding activities that increase pain, following physical therapy, taking NSAIDs, limited bed rest, and surgery when relief is not obtained through previous therapies. Diabetic neuropathy is treated by more tightly controlling blood sugar levels. Vitamin B_{12} deficiency is treated with supplementation. Guillain-Barré syndrome is treated with plasmapheresis. Multiple sclerosis is treated with corticosteroid medications, interferon beta-1a and beta-1b, and glatiramer acetate.

Prognosis

Outcome is based on the underlying condition. Many individuals with mild carpal tunnel syndrome do well with conservative treatment. It may take several weeks to months for improvement to become apparent. There is marked improvement following surgical treatment for carpal tunnel. Some individuals may continue to have symptoms of carpal tunnel following surgery. The outcome of compression of a nerve in the lower leg (the peroneal nerve) is generally good. Time of recovery may vary from days to months. Outcome of radiculopathies may vary. Diabetic neuropathy may be disabling. Neuropathy due to vitamin B_{12} deficiency is treatable with vitamin B_{12} supplementation. The outcome following Guillain-Barré syndrome is variable and recovery slow. Guillain-Barré may recur. Multiple sclerosis may become disabling.

Differential Diagnosis

As a symptom not a diagnosis, paresthesia is associated with many conditions including entrapment neuropathies (carpal tunnel, cubital tunnel, peroneal neuropathy), cervical or lumbar radiculopathy, restless legs syndrome, diabetic neuropathy, vitamin B_{12} deficiency, alcoholic neuropathy, multiple sclerosis, Guillain-Barré syndrome, medication side effect, hypocalcemia, carcinomatous neuropathy (with breast and lung cancers), and human immunodeficiency virus infection (HIV).

Specialists

- Endocrinologist
- Neurologist
- Orthopedist
- Primary Care Provider
- Surgeon

Work Restrictions / Accommodations

Accommodations may include work environment design to avoid self-injury. Individuals with carpal tunnel syndrome and other nerve entrapment syndromes may need to avoid activities that exacerbate symptoms. Ergonomic keyboards and reconfiguring the work area may be necessary to help keep the wrist in proper alignment. Individuals with cervical or lumbar radiculopathy may also require work restrictions and accommodations to prevent exacerbation of symptoms and underlying condition. These individuals are often unable to lift and bear weight. Individuals with paresthesias due to diabetic neuropathy may need to regularly monitor their blood sugar and take insulin.

Comorbid Conditions

Comorbid conditions may include arthritis.

Complications

The condition of paresthesia is complicated by the primary or underlying disease causing its occurrence. For example, individuals with paresthesias can have difficulty with ambulation or grasping items in their hands when a particular extremity is affected.

Factors Influencing Duration

Length of disability is based on the primary disease not the paresthesia. However, paresthesia can complicate the primary disease and influence the length of disability.

Length of Disability

Length of disability is based on the underlying condition.

Failure to Recover

If an individual fails to recover within the maximum duration expectancy period, the reader may wish to reference the following questions to assist in better understanding the specifics of an individual's medical case.

Regarding diagnosis:

- Does individual have a history of carpal tunnel syndrome, neck (cervical) or lower back (lumbosacral) problems, restless leg syndrome, diabetic neuropathy, vitamin B_{12} deficiency (pernicious anemia), or alcoholism?
- Does individual have a history of cancer, human immunodeficiency virus (HIV), hypocalcemia, malabsorption, multiple sclerosis, or Guillain-Barré syndrome?
- Are there sensations of a limb falling asleep, tingling, pins and needles, prickling, electric, burning, vibrating, buzzing, or crawling?
- Does individual report pain, numbness, weakness, stiffness, or clumsiness?

- Where are these sensations located and how long have they been present?
- Does the paresthesia worsen or improve with position change or with a specific activity?
- Was electromyography (EMG) done to rule out nerve dysfunction?
- Were vitamin B_{12} and calcium levels obtained? Any abnormalities?
- If restless leg syndrome was suspected, was polysomnography done?
- If suspicion of multiple sclerosis, was MRI taken?
- Did a spinal tap (lumbar puncture) rule out Guillain-Barré syndrome and multiple sclerosis?
- Was blood tested to determine if liver function levels were elevated? Is there alcohol abuse?
- Was the underlying cause for the paresthesia diagnosed?

Regarding treatment:

- Has the underlying cause been identified and confirmed?
- If carpal tunnel syndrome is the cause, have wrist splints, anti-inflammatory medications, or surgical decompression been used? Did this relieve the paresthesia?
- If vitamin B_{12} or calcium deficiency is the cause, has individual received vitamin B_{12} and calcium supplementation?
- If individual has Guillain-Barré syndrome, has plasmapheresis been done?
- Has multiple sclerosis been treated with corticosteroid medications, interferon beta-1a and beta-1b, and glatiramer acetate?
- If individual has diabetes, is blood sugar adequately controlled?
- Would individual benefit from an alcohol cessation program, as appropriate?

Regarding prognosis:

- What is the underlying condition causing the paresthesia? Is underlying condition under control? If not, what other treatments are available? Is individual compliant with all medication and treatment regimens for the underlying condition?
- Could there be another condition or reason for the paresthesia?
- Given enough time to heal, is it likely the paresthesia will resolve?
- Have any complications occurred as a result of the underlying disorder? If so, what are they and what is expected outcome with treatment?

References

McKenna, James P. "Paresthesias." Saunders Manual of Medical Practice, 2nd ed. Rakel, Robert E., ed. Philadelphia: W.B. Saunders Company, 2000. 1323-1325.

Zalski, Andrew H. "Guillain-Barre Syndrome." Saunders Manual of Medical Practice, 2nd ed. Rakel, Robert E., ed. Philadelphia: W.B. Saunders Company, 2000. 1396-1398.

Parkinson's Disease

Other names / synonyms: Idiopathic Parkinson's, Paralysis Agitans, Parkinsonism, Shaking Palsy

332, 332.0, 332.1

Definition

Parkinson's disease is a gradual loss of nerve cells in a part of the brain that controls movement. These nerve cells normally communicate with each other using a chemical called dopamine. In Parkinson's disease, dopamine decreases in the brain as the nerve cells that use it die out, and as a result, the individual exhibits shaking (tremor), slowness, stiffness, balance problems, and other symptoms.

Parkinson's disease begins in midlife with peak age of onset at 55 to 65 years. The cause is unknown, but both hereditary (genetic) and environmental factors may be involved. Abnormalities in three different genes have been found in familial Parkinson's disease. Living in rural areas, drinking well water, and pesticide exposure are associated with increased risk of Parkinson's disease, while drinking coffee and smoking cigarettes may decrease risk.

Parkinson's disease affects 1 to 1.5 million Americans or 1% of the population over age 55. Male to female ratio is 3 to 2. This disease affects an equal numbers of whites and blacks living in the same geographic area.

Diagnosis

History: Parkinsonian symptoms may develop slowly which can make diagnosis more difficult. Early symptoms are often related to muscle rigidity and include slowness of movements (bradykinesia) and vague heaviness, stiffness, or aching in the limbs. Tremor or rhythmic shaking usually begins in one hand but later may involve all limbs. As the disease progresses, the individual develops a stooped posture, has difficulty maintaining balance, getting up from a seated position, or beginning to walk. The individual walks with small, shuffling steps, experiences loss of the normal automatic arm swing, unsteadiness on turning, difficulty in stopping, and has a tendency to fall.

Some individuals may report dementia but this usually occurs in the later stages. The individual may experience depression that may occur prior to physical symptoms. Some individuals may report feelings of indifference, lack of assertiveness, difficulty making decisions, or self-centeredness. Temperamental or demanding behaviors are also characteristic. Sleep disturbances may include daytime drowsiness, frequent napping, a rigidity that makes it difficult to turn in bed, or jerking movements of the body or legs that disrupt sleep. Disruption in the autonomic nervous system that controls bodily functions may lead to constipation, sexual or bladder dysfunction, or drop in blood pressure upon standing with associated dizziness or light-headedness.

Physical exam: Voluntary and emotional facial movements are limited and slow and include an expressionless face, decreased eye blinking, and a blank stare (masked facies). Speech is monotonous and of low volume (hypophonia), and eventually the individual becomes difficult or impossible to understand. Drooling, decreased swallowing, increased sweating, and dandruff or oily skin may indicate abnormalities in the autonomic nervous system controlling bodily functions. Strength is normal, but rigidity and slowness in starting movement limit both voluntary and spontaneous tasks. Rigidity may initially be confined to one limb but eventually involves most muscles. At first the muscles exhibit only a slight stiffness on movement which then progresses to a ratchet-like jerking (cogwheeling). Handwriting becomes smaller and shaky (micrographia).

The characteristic Parkinsonian tremor is described as "pill-rolling" because it looks as if the individual rolls a pill between the thumb and index finger at a speed of 4 to 5 movements per second. The tremor later spreads and involves the wrist and then the entire limb. It is worse at rest and improves or disappears with movement.

Tests: There are no specific diagnostic tests for Parkinson's disease. Medical tests, including brain MRI, should be done to eliminate other causes of disease. A response to medication that increases brain dopamine supports the diagnosis.

Treatment

Although there is no cure for Parkinson's disease, drugs, surgery, and rehabilitation may provide significant symptomatic relief. Sinemet has long been the mainstay of antiparkinsonian drug treatment. It contains levodopa that increases brain dopamine levels, and carbidopa that interferes with the peripheral action of dopamine before it reaches the brain, thereby decreasing side effects. Sinemet improves all the major features of Parkinson's disease but does not stop its progression. Over half the individuals taking Sinemet eventually experience the "on-off" effect or fluctuations in their response to the drug, the "wearing-off" effect with shorter duration of action of each dose, and side effects that include uncontrollable twisting or flailing movements.

Other drugs that may be helpful either alone or in combination include those that mimic the action of dopamine (dopamine agonists), monoamine oxidase inhibitors, and catechol-O-methyl transferase (COMT) inhibitors that cause dopamine to remain in the brain longer. A large study published in May 2000 found fewer side effects with Requip than with Sinemet, suggesting that it should now become the first line of treatment for many individuals.

Surgical treatment may be helpful in selected individuals unresponsive to medication or who develop intolerable adverse drug reactions or "on-off" effect. The surgery involves the destruction of brain tissue (ablative surgery) in areas called the thalamus or globus pallidus, which are involved in movement control (thalamotomy or pallidotomy). Deep brain stimulation and fetal or genetically engineered brain cell transplantation are being investigated as alternate approaches. In deep brain stimulation, an electrode is implanted deep in the brain in the subthalamic nucleus, and is controlled by the individual with an on/off magnetic device. In cell transplantation, fetal brain cells from a pig or human embryo are placed into the areas of the brain controlling movement where they increase dopamine levels.

Prognosis

Although symptoms of Parkinson's disease can be relieved or controlled, there is no cure and most individuals will continue to deteriorate. However, individuals differ considerably in how severely they are affected and in the rate of progression. Many individuals with late onset have relatively mild symptoms that do not interfere with their lives. As symptoms progress, individuals may notice impairment on both sides of the body, although the first side involved usually remains more severely impaired. Some individuals eventually become completely dependent and wheelchair-bound. In advanced Parkinson's disease, walking and balance become more difficult, leading to falls. "Wearing-off" effect with decreased duration of effect from Sinemet, and "on-off" effect with fluctuating uncontrolled movements alternating with slow and decreased movements, both limit function. Accompanying dementia may be a significant cause of disability. Life expectancy is not significantly reduced unless onset is under the age of 50.

In a recent study from Argentina, surgery (pallidotomy) that removed part of a brain structure involved in movement control (globus pallidus) gave excellent results in 30% of individuals, good results in 46%, and fair results in 23%. No individuals died from this surgery and side effects were relatively minor. In a recent study from Toronto, surgery (thalamotomy) that removed part of the thalamus (another structure involved in movement control) sometimes had to be repeated to be effective, but eventually reduced or abolished tremor in about three-fourths of individuals.

Differential Diagnosis

Idiopathic Parkinson's disease with no known underlying cause accounts for 75% of all cases of Parkinsonism. Secondary Parkinsonism, where Parkinsonian signs and symptoms are caused by some other underlying condition, includes drug-induced Parkinsonism, Wilson's disease or hepatolenticular degeneration, vascular Parkinsonism secondary to stroke, Creutzfeldt-Jakob disease, dementia pugilistica or "punch-drunk" syndrome caused by repeated head trauma, diffuse Lewy body disease, and spinocerebellar ataxia type 3 (Machado-Joseph disease).

The "Parkinson's-plus" syndromes are diseases in which brain cells die in multiple areas of the brain including those areas responsible for the findings in Parkinson's disease. The Parkinson's plus syndromes are associated with other neurologic symptoms such as dementia, autonomic nervous system dysfunction, and abnormalities involving the cranial nerves that supply the head and neck or the cerebellum and help control movement. These syndromes include progressive supranuclear palsy, cortical basal ganglia degeneration, and multiple system atrophy (including striatonigral degeneration, olivopontocerebellar atrophy, and Shy-Drager syndrome).

Specialists

- Neurologist

Rehabilitation

Individuals with Parkinson's disease may require physical, occupational, speech, and psychological therapy.

All therapies should educate individuals and their caregivers about both the disease process and the need to engage in a regular exercise routine. Individuals learn to perform their routine during periods when their medication allows maximum function rather than when it is wearing off. Individuals may take exercise classes designed specifically for those with Parkinson's disease. Exercise requiring mild to moderate exertion such as walking, aquatic exercise, stretching, yoga, or Tai Chi has been shown to decrease disability.

Speech therapy may be useful to improve voice volume and intelligibility or to evaluate swallowing ability so that diet can be modified, as needed. Speech therapy may be required to strengthen the muscles of the face for improved speech and swallowing.

Because individuals experience weakness and stiffness with resultant decreased function in all joints, a comprehensive stretching program is critical in order to maintain range of motion in the joints. Occupational and physical therapists instruct individuals and their family members how to safely stretch the arms and legs. Individuals also learn to perform range-of-motion exercises of all body parts, e.g., trunk rotation to promote normal gait and reverse shoulder rolls to promote normal posture. For individuals with discomfort associated with stiffness and rigidity, massage and modalities such as heat and ultrasound may help.

Individuals also learn a strengthening program in occupational and physical therapy that allows the arms and legs to maintain functional abilities. Individuals perform arm exercises such as elbow extensions using light hand weights that strengthen the muscles used with crutches or a walker. Bridging exercises may be performed where the individual lies on the back with the knees bent and lifts the buttocks up from the bed. This promotes the ability to get out of a chair. Shoulder blade squeezes also help promote better posture.

Parkinson's disease may result in impaired coordination. Individuals perform fine motor coordination exercises in occupational therapy such as picking up pegs and placing them in a pegboard or may work on practical coordination exercises such as fastening buttons or practicing signatures. Individuals work on gross motor coordination in physical therapy such as kicking a soccer ball rolled toward them or throwing beanbags at a target. Performing alternating movements may also be difficult so individuals work on alternating tasks such as playing catch or pouring water from one cup to another.

Physical and occupational therapists instruct individuals on sitting and standing balance. Sitting balance can be improved if the individual sits on a therapy ball while attempting to reach for objects placed at various distances. Physical therapists may focus on standing balance in order to preserve the ability to walk. Individuals perform exercises in a set of parallel bars such as walking heel-to-toe to help improve standing balance.

The main focus of physical and occupational therapy is to maximize functional capabilities. Occupational therapists teach individuals skills such as getting in and out of the shower, dressing, and meal preparation. Physical therapists teach skills such as getting in and out of bed, walking, turning safely while walking, and rolling in bed.

A psychologist or psychiatrist can help individuals and their families adjust to the stresses of a debilitating illness.

Work Restrictions / Accommodations

Because physical abilities vary between individuals, work restrictions and accommodations must be evaluated on a case-by-case basis. Slowness of movement may limit driving, standing up from a chair, walking, and turning. Balance problems may limit crawling, stooping, kneeling, and working at heights. Decreased fine motor control and tremor may cause difficulties with writing, keyboard operation, or manipulation of small objects. Soft, monotonous speech may impair communication skills. Dementia, depression, and personality change may interfere with judgment, memory, and interpersonal skills. Visual problems may hinder reading or sorting tasks. Urinary urgency may cause frequent interruptions. Accommodations may include grab-bars or railings, well-lit work areas without clutter or scatter rugs, and good color contrast between safety devices and surrounding areas and between the floor and stairs. Use of a cane or walker may be helpful.

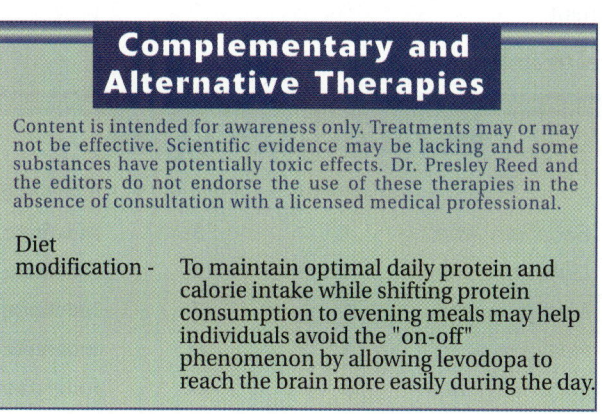

Complementary and Alternative Therapies

Content is intended for awareness only. Treatments may or may not be effective. Scientific evidence may be lacking and some substances have potentially toxic effects. Dr. Presley Reed and the editors do not endorse the use of these therapies in the absence of consultation with a licensed medical professional.

Diet modification - To maintain optimal daily protein and calorie intake while shifting protein consumption to evening meals may help individuals avoid the "on-off" phenomenon by allowing levodopa to reach the brain more easily during the day.

Comorbid Conditions

Any comorbid condition that limits mobility or independence would lengthen disability due to Parkinson's disease. These conditions include arthritis, injury, stroke, other neurological disorders, dementia or psychiatric disease, or general health conditions that cause chronic disability such as heart failure, obesity, diabetes mellitus, or kidney disease.

Complications

Dementia occurs in up to 30% of individuals with Parkinson's disease especially those with symptoms of decreased movement and rigidity, and is often preceded by depression or drug-induced hallucinations. Depression is seen in 40-50% of individuals and may even precede Parkinsonian symptoms in 20% of these cases. It may be accompanied by anxiety, panic attacks, loss of energy and initiative, or loss of pleasure in normally enjoyable activities. Balance difficulty can cause falls or self-injury. Difficulty swallowing and decreased gastric motility may lead to complications of weight loss, depletion of body fluids (dehydration), or pneumonia caused by mouth contents entering the airway (aspiration pneumonia). Sensory problems in Parkinson's disease may include decreased sense of smell, abnormal color vision, and blurred vision related to decreased visual contrast sensitivity. Stiffness and difficulty with movement may eventually cause deconditioning, joint immobility (contractures), or accelerated arthritis.

Factors Influencing Duration

The extent and length of disability vary depending on the severity of symptoms, the rapidity of deterioration, response to treatment, the extent of associated conditions such as dementia, depression, or visual dysfunction, and the demands of the individual's occupation. Parkinson's disease is typically associated with continued deterioration. Recovery is not expected, although some improvement may be shown with treatment. Initially, there may be some acute periods of disability while medications are adjusted or surgery is performed. Once the individual is incapacitated or disabled despite optimal therapeutic intervention, disability should be considered permanent.

Length of Disability

Duration depends on severity of symptoms and response to treatment. Durations reflect recovery from procedure only. Disability may be permanent.

Medical treatment.

Duration in Days

Job Classification	Minimum	Optimum	Maximum
Sedentary work	1	3	Indefinite
Light work	1	3	Indefinite
Medium work	1	7	Indefinite
Heavy work	1	21	Indefinite
Very Heavy work	1	21	Indefinite

Surgical treatment (thalamotomy).

Duration in Days

Job Classification	Minimum	Optimum	Maximum
Sedentary work	14	21	28
Light work	14	21	56
Medium work	28	35	84
Heavy work	56	70	112
Very Heavy work	56	70	140

Surgical treatment (adrenal tissue implant or transplant).

Duration in Days

Job Classification	Minimum	Optimum	Maximum
Sedentary work	28	42	56
Light work	28	42	56
Medium work	42	63	84
Heavy work	70	84	Indefinite
Very Heavy work	70	84	Indefinite

Failure to Recover

If an individual fails to recover within the maximum duration expectancy period, the reader may wish to reference the following questions to assist in better understanding the specifics of an individual's medical case.

Regarding diagnosis:

- Was the diagnosis suspected based on the presenting symptoms and clinical presentation?
- Were other conditions with similar symptoms such as Wilson's disease, striatonigral degeneration, essential tremor, Creutzfeldt-Jakob disease, Huntington's disease, Shy-Drager syndrome, progressive supranuclear palsy, cortical basal ganglionic degeneration, stroke, and hydrocephalus ruled out?
- Has a positive response to a trial of dopaminergic medication supported the diagnosis of Parkinson's disease?
- Because the prognosis and treatment differ significantly, it is important to differentiate between idiopathic Parkinson's disease, secondary Parkinsonism, and the "Parkinson's-plus" syndromes. Has distinction been made?
- Would individual benefit from consultation with a specialist?

Regarding treatment:

- Are individual's symptoms being effectively controlled by medication?
- Has individual begun to experience the "on-off" or "wearing-off" effects? Would individual benefit from use of an alternate medication or combination of medications?
- Is individual a candidate for surgical intervention?

Regarding prognosis:

- At what age was individual diagnosed with Parkinson's disease?
- To what extent do symptoms impair function?
- Would the individual benefit from physical therapy?
- Has home health or other assistance with activities of daily living been considered?
- Does the individual have an underlying condition such as arthritis, injury, stroke, other neurological disorders, dementia or psychiatric disease, heart failure, obesity, diabetes mellitus, or kidney disease that could impact prognosis?
- Has the individual experienced any complications that could impact prognosis such as weight loss, dehydration or pneumonia? If so, have these conditions been addressed in the treatment plan?
- What support system does individual have in place? Would individual benefit from psychological counseling or enrollment in a community support group?

References

"Parkinson's Disease and Basal Ganglia Movement Disorders." Dale, D.C., and Daniel D. Federman, MD, eds. New York: WebMD Corporation, 2000 Scientific American Medicine. <http://www.samed.com/sam/forms/index.htm>.

Herrera, E.J., et al. "Posteroventral Pallidotomy in Parkinson's Disease." Acta Neurochir (Wien) 142 2 (2000): 169-175.

Linhares, M.N., and R.R. Tasker. "Microelectrode-guided Thalamotomy for Parkinson's Disease." Neurosurgery 46 2 (2000): 390-395.

Lister, Marilyn J., ed. Contemporary Management of Motor Control Problems. Fairfax: Foundation for Physical Therapy, 1991.

Mesher, R. MD. "Winning the Fight Against Parkinson's Disease with Richard A. Mesher, MD." WebMD Corporation. 03 Feb 2000. 23 May 2000 <http://my.webmd.com/content/article/1707.50143>.

O'Sullivan, Susan B. "Parkinson's Disease." Physical Rehabilitation: Assessment and Treatment. O'Sullivan, Susan B., and Thomas J. Schmitz, eds. Philadelphia: F.A. Davis Company, 1994. 473-490.

Rascol, O., et al. "A Five-year Study of the Incidence of Dyskinesia in Patients with Early Parkinson's Disease Who Were Treated With Ropinirole or Levodopa." New England Journal of Medicine 342 20 (2000): 1484-1491.

Ross, G. Webster, et al. "Association of Coffee and Caffeine Intake with the Risk of Parkinson Disease." Journal of the American Medical Association 283 20 (2000): 2674-2679.

Sarno, Martha Taylor. "Neurogenic Disorders of Speech and Language." Physical Rehabilitation: Assessment and Treatment. O'Sullivan, Susan B., and Thomas J. Schmitz, eds. Philadelphia: F.A. Davis Company, 1994. 633-654.

What Methods of Treatment are Available for Persons with Parkinson's Disease?. National Parkinson Foundation, Inc. 03 Mar 2000. 23 May 2000 <http://www.parkinson.org/treament.htm>.

Passive-Aggressive Personality Disorder
Other names / synonyms: Negative Personality Disorder
301.84

Definition

The catchword for this personality disorder is "ambivalence." Persons with this disorder have been referred to as "negativistic personalities" because of their underlying aggression, which is expressed passively. Individuals with this disorder display covert obstructionism, procrastination, stubbornness, and inefficiency. They tend to be constantly complaining, sulky, pessimistic, and unaccommodating. They find themselves in dependent relationships, yet resist demands for adequate performance, find excuses for delays, and find fault with those on whom they depend. They usually lack assertiveness by failing to express their needs and wishes directly, and they often fail to ask needed questions to discover what is expected of them. They are generally pessimistic about the future, and lack self-confidence. In relationships, they often get others to do their errands and chores, and tend to dampen everyone's spirits.

Individuals with passive-aggressive personality disorder may be irritable or even agitated, with low frustration tolerance and vacillating moods changing in rapid succession. They seem fidgety and impatient with others, and their moods of excitement and cheerfulness are usually short-lived. They often feel discontented, mistreated, cheated, and unappreciated, and tend to see themselves as victims of circumstance. While they are often aware of solutions to their problems, they are unwilling to implement them. They resent being criticized, but often find fault with those in authority.

Diagnosis

History: The psychiatric interview and mental status exam are the primary tools used to diagnose passive-aggressive personality disorder. Diagnostic criteria utilizing the DSM-IV require a pervasive pattern of negativistic attitudes and passive resistance to demands for adequate performance, beginning by early adulthood and present in a variety of contexts, with 4 or more of the following: resists fulfilling routine social and occupational tasks; complains of being misunderstood and unappreciated by others; is sullen and argumentative; unreasonably criticizes and scorns authority; expresses envy and resentment toward those apparently more fortunate; voices exaggerated and persistent complaints of personal misfortune; alternates between hostile defiance and contrition. The diagnosis cannot be made if the behavior occurs exclusively during major depressive episodes, or if it is better accounted for by dysthymic disorder.

Physical exam: Is not helpful in diagnosing this disorder. Observation of the individual's orientation, dress, mannerisms, behavior, and content of speech may be helpful.

Tests: There are a variety of psychological tests that can be utilized to help identify and classify personality disorders. The interpretation of these tests by a professional is used in conjunction with the history.

Treatment

Individuals with passive-aggressive personality disorder tend to do well with an individual or a one-to-one supportive psychotherapy or psychoanalytic approach. Good outcomes have been reported. Therapy is difficult, usually lasting longer than 1 year, and utilizes gentle confrontation about the individual's behavior and the consequences of their behavior.

When clinical depression is present, antidepressants should be used. Benzodiazepines or antianxiety drugs may be used when anxiety is present.

Prognosis

Prognosis is fairly good for those who are willing to seek and accept supportive psychotherapy. Personality disorders tend to persist long-term, but may burn out with therapy or as they are modified by life experiences.

Differential Diagnosis

Differential diagnosis for passive-aggressive personality disorder includes other personality disorders, especially histrionic and borderline personality disorder. The passive-aggressive personality is more dramatic, openly aggressive, and more emotional than the histrionic or borderline personality. Prolonged and generalized anxiety disorders or psychosomatic disorders may coexist with passive-aggressive personality. These individuals openly display their discomfort as a means of upsetting others or soliciting the attention and support of others, and tend to use physical complaints as a disguise for hostile impulses of anger and resentment. If they are aware of this manipulative behavior, this could warrant the diagnosis of a factitious disorder when imaginary physical symptoms arise. Affective disorders such as dysthymia, cyclothymia, and major depression have been associated with this personality disorder.

Specialists

- Licensed Clinical Social Worker
- Psychiatrist
- Psychologist

Work Restrictions / Accommodations

These individuals require stability, and need to work in an environment where there is little change. Changes in shift, work site, co-workers or team members should be avoided. Individually appropriate, close supervision is recommended.

Comorbid Conditions

Coexisting conditions that may affect recovery and lengthen disability include alcohol or substance abuse, or the presence of another psychiatric disorder such as depression. In addition, passive-aggressive behavior often occurs in individuals with borderline, histrionic, paranoid, dependent, antisocial, and avoidant personality disorders.

Complications

Passive-aggressives tend to be in a state of turmoil and discontentment. Complications occur when there is a perceived or real lack of stability in the individual's life. This instability can occur in any area of life such as social, occupational, legal, spiritual, or financial. Complications may occur when there is continued support of their behavior and their demands, without confrontation. To confront them can be equally harmful and is usually viewed as rejection. Rejection is often internalized and the individual will often have suicidal thoughts or ideation. Coexisting personality disorders, substance abuse, and other psychiatric disorders may also complicate the course, progress, and outcome.

Factors Influencing Duration

The progress and effectiveness of the psychotherapy and the individual's level of functioning all affect length of disability. Instability associated with failure of support systems will lengthen their disability. Substance abuse, suicidal gestures, and coexisting depression and anxiety can prolong recovery.

Length of Disability

This condition represents a life-long pattern of behavior. In most cases, no disability is expected.

Failure to Recover

If an individual fails to recover within the maximum duration expectancy period, the reader may wish to reference the following questions to assist in better understanding the specifics of an individual's medical case.

Regarding diagnosis:

- Does the individual fit criteria for passive-aggressive personality disorder?
- Has the diagnosis been confirmed?
- Does the individual's behavior appear to be separate from other psychological disorders, such as dysthymic or a major depressive episode?
- Have underlying medical conditions and substance abuse been ruled out?

Regarding treatment:

- Is the individual currently on medication?
- If depression and/or anxiety are also present, would medication be a beneficial adjunct to the treatment regimen?
- In what type of psychotherapy is the individual currently involved?
- Is the individual receptive to gentle confrontation about his/her behavior and the consequences of such behavior?

Regarding prognosis:

- To what degree does the passive-aggressive behavior still interfere with social or occupational function?
- Does the individual's work environment involve shift changes, moving from one work site to another, or frequent change of co-workers/team members?
- Can anything be done to provide more stabilization in the individual's work and/or social environment?
- Are coexisting personality traits, substance abuse, or other psychiatric disorders complicating the course, progress, and outcome of this disorder? Are these disorders being appropriately addressed?

References

First, Michael B., ed. Diagnostic and Statistical Manual of Mental Disorders, 4th ed. Washington DC: American Psychiatric Association, 1994.

Hendrickson, Gail RN, BS. "Passive-aggressive Personality Disorder." Discoveryhealth.com. 08 Jul 2000. 10 Oct 2000 <http://health.discovery.com/diseasesandcond/encyclopedia/700.html>.

Patella Chondromalacia

Other names / synonyms: Anterior Knee Pain, Patellofemoral Syndrome

717.7

Definition

Chondromalacia patella is a condition in which the cartilage of the kneecap (patella) becomes worn from age or damaged from injury. In a healthy knee, the undersurface of the patella is covered with articular cartilage that is smooth and slick. This surface allows the patella to slide easily in the groove of the femur as the knee bends and straightens (flexes, extends). With chondromalacia patella, the surface of the patella becomes thin and rough. Symptoms are caused by the rough, ragged surface rubbing against the femur. Areas of cartilage can erode away, leading to the onset of osteoarthritis.

Chondromalacia patella can develop as a result of the normal wear and tear on the knee and the degeneration that accompanies the aging process. Some individuals are born with natural anatomic variations that make them more prone to develop chondromalacia patella. Certain sports (such as football, soccer, running, sailing, and fencing) are more commonly associated with chondromalacia patella. Chondromalacia may also be caused by trauma, such as a twisting injury in which the patella is pulled out of the femoral groove and the cartilage surface is bruised, scratched, or chipped.

The incidence of chondromalacia patella is approximately 2 out of 10,000 individuals. It tends to occur more often in young adults than older individuals, and more often in women than in men.

Diagnosis

History: Individuals may complain of knee pain with walking, running, squatting, or descending stairs or hills; however, knee pain is not always present, and is not an indicator of the severity of chondromalacia patella. The individual may report a feeling of grating, catching, or locking with motion. Some individuals will have a sensation that the knee is giving out. Some individuals report pain after sitting with the knee bent for long periods of time (movies, plane trips, etc.).

Physical exam: Chondromalacia patella may be evaluated by placing manual pressure on the patella while the individual contracts the quadriceps muscle (Clarke's sign or also known as the quadriceps inhibition test). Pain during this examination is a positive indicator of chondromalacia patella. A crackling sound in the knee (crepitus) is often noticeable with passive range-of-motion (PROM), and active range-of-motion (AROM) against resistance is usually painful. Patellar alignment may be evaluated by measurement of the Q-angle (quadriceps angle). An easy lateral dislocation (subluxation) of the patella may be noticed (genu valgum).

Tests: Routine knee x-rays should include special patella views to evaluate the patella position in the femoral groove. MRI or CT scans can be used to evaluate the articular surface in difficult cases, but these tests are not routinely ordered.

Treatment

Conservative treatment involves rest and avoidance of activities that aggravate the condition, such as squatting, climbing or descending stairs, kneeling, lunging, sitting with knees bent, and shifting gears in a vehicle. Use of anti-inflammatory medication and cold therapy can provide relief of pain and swelling. A patella stabilizing brace may be recommended as both treatment and prevention in some cases. Taping or bandaging of the affected knee may provide some pain relief, but do not facilitate healing of the injury.

Physical therapy to increase quadriceps strength and decrease swelling and pain are very helpful. Patient education is an important part of treatment, because chondromalacia patella is a chronic condition, and compliance with treatment is key to successful management.

For severe cases in which symptoms do not respond to conservative treatment within 6 months, arthroscopic surgery may be recommended to smooth (debride) the undersurface of the patella. This procedure involves shaving of the damaged cartilage down to the normal cartilage underneath. In more severe cases, the damaged cartilage may be removed (chondrectomy). If the problem is aggravated by malalignment of the patella, various surgical procedures can be performed to realign the patella and relieve pressure on the cartilage surface (such as tightening of the medial capsule of the knee and lateral release to relieve excessive tightness of the lateral capsule). In very severe cases, part or all of the patella may be removed (partial or full patellectomy) and a patellar prosthesis may be inserted. The Maquet procedure involves frontal (anterior) displacement of the tibial tubercle (at the lower leg bone) and insertion of a bony block to decrease the force on the patella.

A surgical procedure may be performed in which small holes are drilled through the damaged cartilage to facilitate growth of healthy tissue up from the layers underneath; however, this technique has not yet been widely used and proven effective in a large population.

Prognosis

Although chondromalacia patella is a chronic situation, acute symptoms usually resolve with rest and a period of avoidance of aggravating activities. Most individuals recover fully with conservative treatment, but may experience subsequent recurrences.

In severe cases in which surgery is required, outcome depends on the severity of the cartilage damage and the type of surgery performed. Individuals who undergo a full patellectomy usually experience persistent weakness and shrinking (atrophy) of the quadriceps muscle. Individuals who undergo insertion of a patellar prosthesis may eventually experience wearing of the opposing articular surface, causing further symptoms. The outcomes for the Maquet procedure and chondrectomy vary, and can depend on the individual's overall health, the health of the bones and knee joint, and the physician's familiarity with the procedures.

Differential Diagnosis

Other possible diagnoses are peripatellar tendinitis or bursitis, osteoarthritis, osteochondritis dissecans, recurrent patella subluxation, fat pad syndrome, and patellar malalignment syndrome.

Specialists

- Orthopedic Surgeon
- Orthopedist
- Physiatrist
- Sports Medicine Physician

Rehabilitation

Rehabilitation of patella chondromalacia focuses on decreasing the amount of compression on the undersurface of the kneecap (patella). If pain and inflammation is present, the physical therapist may apply an anti-inflammatory agent to the kneecap region using ultrasound. If pain is intense, preventing mobility of the knee, the therapist may initially need to use electrical stimulation in conjunction with a cold pack for intense knee pain.

Once pain has decreased and the individual is ready to progress with the rehabilitation program, quadriceps stretches become a vital part of the recovery program. Specific strengthening exercises are also important. Isometric exercises are often taught initially for strengthening, requiring that the muscles around the knee contract without movement occurring at the joint. An example of an isometric exercise for the knee region is the quad set.

Straight leg raises are used in rehabilitation. The individual sits on a flat surface with the involved knee straight and the uninvolved knee in a flexed or bent position, while the involved leg is raised to height of the opposite knee. Ankle weights are used for resistance as the muscles strengthen from this exercise. The use of a stationary bicycle may also be recommended.

Modifications may need to be made by the physical therapist for those individuals who have patella chondromalacia. Generally speaking, rehabilitation of the knee will vary depending on the reasons producing the excess of pressure on the undersurface of the patella, and whether surgery was performed prior to the rehabilitation.

Work Restrictions / Accommodations

Individuals whose job requirements include frequent or prolonged periods of walking, descending stairs, or squatting may need to restrict or eliminate these activities until symptoms subside or during recovery from surgery. Individuals should be given frequent rest breaks to avoid prolonged sitting until pain subsides. Depending upon the type of surgery performed, the individual may be treated as an outpatient and may return to work within a few days, or, with more involved surgeries, the individual may require 1-2 nights in the hospital and a more extended break from work.

Comorbid Conditions

Other problems in the knee (such as ligament strains or tears) or any other condition (such as obesity) that interferes with the individual's ability to follow an appropriate exercise program may hinder response to conservative treatment and therefore lengthen recovery.

Complications

The most common complication is discomfort. Other possible complications that could develop include patella malalignment, recurrent patella subluxation, dislocation, or osteoarthritis.

Complementary and Alternative Therapies

Content is intended for awareness only. Treatments may or may not be effective. Scientific evidence may be lacking and some substances have potentially toxic effects. Dr. Presley Reed and the editors do not endorse the use of these therapies in the absence of consultation with a licensed medical professional.

Arch supports -	OTC or custom-molded arch supports are designed to "center" bio mechanic forces and reduce pronation.
McConnell Taping -	Biofeedback technique in which the tape pulls kneecap inward to help re-establish normal tracking.
Nonimpact conditioning -	Exercise on stationary bike or swimming may help re-establish normal tracking.

Factors Influencing Duration

The main factors influencing the length of disability are the severity of symptoms and severity of cartilage damage. In milder cases, the ability to modify work requirements and compliance with a physical therapy program should serve to shorten the length of disability. More severe cartilage damage and symptoms that do not respond to conservative treatment are indications for surgery, leading to longer periods of disability. The length of disability following surgery depends upon which surgery is performed. Return to work after arthroscopic surgery may be sooner if work is done sitting rather than standing.

Length of Disability

Moderate and severe patella chondromalacia may not be compatible with heavy or very heavy work.

Medical treatment.

Duration in Days

Job Classification	Minimum	Optimum	Maximum
Sedentary work	1	3	7
Light work	1	3	7
Medium work	1	7	14
Heavy work	7	21	56
Very Heavy work	7	21	56

Surgical treatment, arthroscopic.

Duration in Days

Job Classification	Minimum	Optimum	Maximum
Sedentary work	1	3	7
Light work	3	7	14
Medium work	7	14	21
Heavy work	14	28	56
Very Heavy work	14	28	56

Surgical treatment, open.

Job Classification	Duration in Days		
	Minimum	Optimum	Maximum
Sedentary work	7	7	14
Light work	7	14	21
Medium work	14	28	42
Heavy work	28	35	91
Very Heavy work	28	42	91

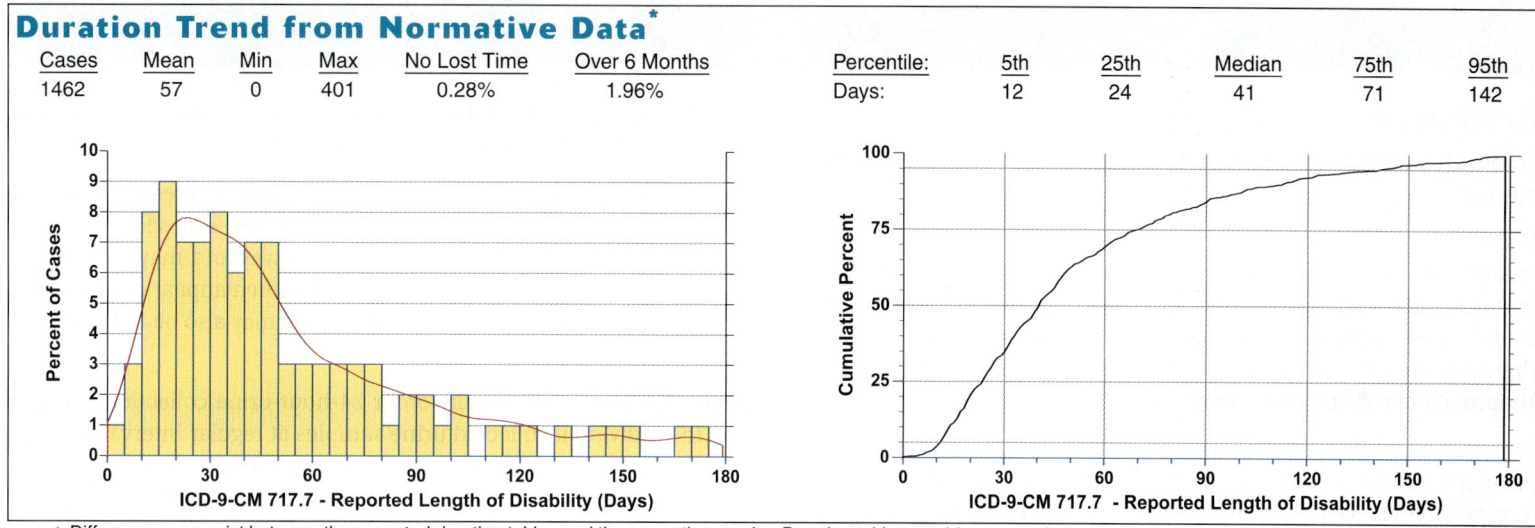

Duration Trend from Normative Data*

Cases	Mean	Min	Max	No Lost Time	Over 6 Months
1462	57	0	401	0.28%	1.96%

Percentile:	5th	25th	Median	75th	95th
Days:	12	24	41	71	142

* Differences may exist between the expected duration tables and the normative graphs. Duration tables provide expected recovery periods based on the type of work performed by the individual. The normative graphs reflect the actual observed experience of many individuals across the spectrum of physical conditions, in a variety of industries, and with varying levels of case management.

Failure to Recover

If an individual fails to recover within the maximum duration expectancy period, the reader may wish to reference the following questions to assist in better understanding the specifics of an individual's medical case.

Regarding diagnosis:

- Has diagnosis of patella chondromalacia been confirmed?
- Has an x-ray or CT scan been done to assess patellar alignment?
- Has a bone scan been done to rule out other diagnoses?
- Has individual experienced any complications such as patella malalignment, recurrent patella subluxation, dislocation, or osteoarthritis?
- Does individual have an underlying condition that may impact recovery?

Regarding treatment:

- Were conservative methods effective in resolving symptoms?
- Did individual receive sufficient physical therapy?
- Is the individual following an exercise program to strengthen the quadriceps muscle?
- Have other family members or care givers been educated when needed to help individual comply with treatment plan?
- Has a 6-month period of conservative therapy been unsuccessful?
- Was surgical intervention required?
- What procedure was performed?

Regarding prognosis:

- Has a 6-month period of conservative therapy been unsuccessful? If not, could symptoms be expected to resolve with additional time and therapy?
- Did surgical procedure achieve expected results?
- Have symptoms recurred?
- Have other problems occurred as a result of the procedure?
- What further treatment options are available?

References

A Patient's Guide to Knee Problems. Orthogate. 13 Sep 1998. 18 Oct 2000 <http://patient.orthogate.org/knee/patella/patella.html>.

Chondromalacia Patellae. drkoop.com. 2000. 18 Oct 2000 <http://www.drkoop.com/conditions/ency/article/000452.htm>.

Malone, Terry R., Thomas McPoil, and Arthur J. Nitz. Orthopedic and Sports Physical Therapy. St. Louis: Mosby, 1997.

Patella (Chondromalacia). The Center for Orthopaedics and Sports Medicine. 03 Jun 1999. 18 Oct 2000 <http://www.arthroscopy.com/sp05032.htm>.

References (Continued)

Ferrari, Rachele. Chondromalacia Patella. Curtin University of Technology. 29 May 2000. 18 Oct 2000 <http://www.curtin.edu.au:80/curtin/dept/physio/podiatry/encyclopedia/chondro/chondro.html>.

Kessler, R.M. Management of Common Musculoskeletal Disorders: Physical Therapy Principles and Methods. Philadelphia: J.B. Lippincott Company, 1990.

Southmayd, W. Sports Health :The Complete Book of Athletic Injuries. New York: Putnam Publishing Group, 1981.

Walker, Kristen Xan. A Common Cause of Knee Pain in Sports: Chondromalacia Patella. University of Oregon. 2000. 18 Oct 2000 <http://www.veggie.org/run/chondromalacia/>.

Pellagra

Other names / synonyms: Cereal Pellagra, Niacin Deficiency, Nicotinamide Deficiency, Nicotinic Acid Deficiency, Vitamin B$_3$ Deficiency

265.2

Definition

Pellagra is a nutritional disorder caused by a lack of niacin, an essential nutrient.

Niacin (also called nicotinamide, nicotinic acid, or Vitamin B$_3$) is required for normal metabolism and for the manufacture of certain hormones like insulin, cortisone, and the sex hormones. Niacin is also necessary for proper functioning of the nervous system. Pellagra is characterized by diarrhea, inflammation of the skin (dermatitis), and abnormal mental function (dementia).

Pellagra results when the diet contains inadequate amounts of niacin or inadequate amounts of tryptophan-containing proteins (the body uses tryptophan to make niacin). Good sources of niacin include meats, fish, legumes, and certain nuts. Diets that lack protein and rely on corn as the staple food tend to contain inadequate amounts of tryptophan and niacin and results in pellagra. Pellagra can also result when the body fails to absorb niacin from the diet as in chronic gastrointestinal disorders, cirrhosis of the liver, or in a rare hereditary condition called Hartnup's Disease. A rare form of niacin deficiency occurs with certain cancers (carcinoid syndrome).

Pellagra was a widespread condition until its cause was identified in the 1930s. Since then, the wide availability of vitamin-enriched foods has virtually eliminated this disease from all industrialized countries (e.g., Europe, North America). A notable exception to this is found in individuals with chronic alcoholism whose poor dietary habits put them at increased risk for niacin deficiency. Similarly, individuals who are grossly malnourished or with severe eating disorders (i.e., anorexia nervosa, bulimia nervosa) also remain at risk.

Pellagra continues to be a problem in countries where malnutrition is prevalent and/or the diet staple is corn such as Africa, India, and areas of China. The exact incidence of this condition is not known. Pellagra can occur at any age. Men and women are at equal risk.

Diagnosis

History: Individuals may complain of a loss of appetite (anorexia), nausea, and/or vomiting. Diarrhea is common and may be bloody. Individuals may report abdominal pain. Women may report abnormal menstrual cycles (dysmenorrhea). Tiredness (fatigue) and difficulty sleeping (insomnia) are also common complaints. The individual (or a family member) may report behavior changes, nervousness (anxiety), memory problems and/or confusion, or hallucinations. Questioning the individual or a family member on the individual's typical diet will usually reveal an inadequately balanced diet with a lack of protein and, in most cases, a high reliance on corn products.

Physical exam: A characteristic feature of pellagra is a red rash (dermatitis) that resembles sunburn and worsens when exposed to sunlight (photosensitive). The redness does not go away and may turn brown and scaly over time. The mouth and tongue often appear bright scarlet red and may be tender. In women, the vagina may also be inflamed and tender.

Tests: The doctor will usually order 24-hour urine collection. For this test, the individual collected urine samples at regular intervals over an entire 24-hour period. These samples are then evaluated for niacin by-products. The levels of these by-products will help determine whether a niacin deficiency is present. Blood samples may also be taken for analysis.

Treatment

Initially, treatment consists of high doses of niacinamide, a form of niacin. This supplement may be given as an oral medication or administered intravenously. Usually, supplements of other B-vitamins are also given, as many individuals with pellagra also have low levels of B$_1$, B$_2$, B$_6$, and pantothenic acid.

In addition to vitamin supplements, the individual's diet must be changed for complete recovery and prevention of recurrence. The physician will discuss proper nutrition, healthy foods, and the importance of a balanced diet. The individual will be instructed on how to change his/her eating habits to ensure proper nutrition.

In cases where an underlying illness is causing or contributing to pellagra, treatment of that underlying condition is essential for recovery.

Specialists

- Dermatologist
- Dietary Advisor
- Gastroenterologist
- Gynecologist
- Internist
- Neurologist

Prognosis

The prognosis for individuals with pellagra is excellent. Niacin supplements and a nutritionally balanced diet are very effective treatments and result in a complete resolution of symptoms in most cases.

When an underlying illness is present, treatment of that condition will affect the outcome of pellagra. For example, if a chronic alcoholic doesn't stop drinking, the poor eating habits that led to pellagra are not likely to change and the nutritional disorder will recur or worsen.

Untreated, pellagra is a progressive disorder and death will result within 4- to 5 years.

Differential Diagnosis

The signs and symptoms of pellagra are common to many other conditions. Severe sunburn can cause reddening of the skin and nausea and vomiting. Bacterial, viral, or parasitic infections of the gastrointestinal system can cause bloody diarrhea, abdominal pain, nausea, vomiting, and fatigue. A red tongue is an early sign of scarlet fever. Mental changes can be seen in a variety of neurological disorders.

Work Restrictions / Accommodations

In severe cases, the individual may need to be hospitalized for intravenous nutritional supplements and may require sick leave. Once treated, individuals with pellagra do not require accommodation or work restrictions. Untreated individuals will experience a gradual decline in physical and mental ability eventually resulting in permanent disability and death.

Comorbid Conditions

The following conditions may increase an individual's need for niacin, and as such they may prolong the recovery and disability time: cancer, diabetes mellitus, chronic diarrhea, prolonged fever, prolonged infection, intestinal problems, liver disease, mouth or throat sores, overactive thyroid (hyperthyroidism), diseases of the pancreas, stomach ulcers, prolonged stress, or surgical removal of the stomach.

The following conditions may affect the use of niacin or niacinamide: bleeding problems, diabetes mellitus, glaucoma, gout, liver disease, low blood pressure, or stomach ulcers.

Complications

Complications are not expected with pellagra.

Factors Influencing Duration

The severity of the disease when diagnosed and the individual's willingness and ability to follow the diet instructions determine the length of disability.

Length of Disability

Duration depends on severity. Untreated disease will progress to eventual death.

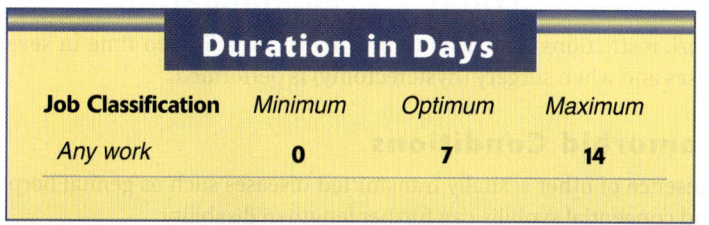

Job Classification	Minimum	Optimum	Maximum
Any work	0	7	14

Duration in Days

Failure to Recover

If an individual fails to recover within the maximum duration expectancy period, the reader may wish to reference the following questions to assist in better understanding the specifics of an individual's medical case.

Regarding diagnosis:

- Does individual have diarrhea, dermatitis, and dementia?
- Is individual's diet lacking in niacin and tryptophan-containing proteins?
- Does individual have chronic gastrointestinal disorders, cirrhosis of the liver, or Hartnup's Disease? Carcinoid syndrome?
- Does individual have chronic alcoholism with poor dietary habits? Does individual's diet have a high reliance on corn products?
- Does individual have anorexia nervosa or bulimia nervosa?
- Does individual complain of anorexia, nausea, and/or vomiting? Bloody diarrhea? Does individual report abdominal pain? Dysmenorrhea? Fatigue and insomnia?
- Has individual or a family member reported behavior changes, anxiety, memory problems and/or confusion, or hallucinations?
- Does individual have dermatitis that resembles sunburn and is photosensitive? Has it turned brown and scaly over time?
- What color is the individual's mouth and tongue? Bright scarlet red? Are they tender?
- Is the vagina inflamed and tender?
- Has individual had blood tests and a 24-hour urine test?
- Have conditions with similar symptoms been ruled out?

Regarding treatment:

- Has individual been treated with high doses of niacinamide orally or intravenously? Have supplements of other B-vitamins been given?
- Has individual completely changed diet to facilitate complete recovery and prevent a recurrence?
- Is individual compliant with the treatment regime?

Regarding prognosis:

- Can individual's employer accommodate any necessary restrictions?
- Does individual have any conditions that may affect ability to recover?

References

"Vitamins and Minerals." The Merck Manual of Medical Information. Berkow, Robert, Mark Beers, and Andrew Fletcher, eds. New York: Pocket Books, 2000. 713-728.

IntelliHealth. "Niacin." USP DI, Advice for the Patient. II 26 May 1995 06 Dec 2000 <http://www.intelihealth.com/IH/ihtIH?d=dmtUSPV2&c=222807&p=~br,IHW|~st,9339|~r,WSIHW000|~b,*|>.

Pelvic Inflammatory Disease

Other names / synonyms: PID

614.3, 614.4, 614.5, 614.6, 614.7, 614.9

Definition

Pelvic inflammatory disease (PID) is an infection of the upper female genital tract caused by bacterial infection. It is an inflammatory condition of the female pelvic organs.

The disease can manifest as any combination of infection of the ovary, fallopian tube, or uterus (oophoritis, salpingitis, and endometritis respectively), tubo-ovarian abscess, and pelvic peritonitis. It is a common and serious sexually transmitted disease.

Women using an intrauterine device (IUD) for birth control have a higher rate of PID. Most often it is caused by sexually transmitted infections of Chlamydia trachomatis, Neisseria gonorrhoeae, or both, although it may be caused by bacteria that are normally found in the vagina. The infection can spread throughout the fallopian tubes and cause inflammation, scarring, and obstruction.

Approximately 10% of women in the US will develop PID during their reproductive years, and a significant number will have complications from the infection.

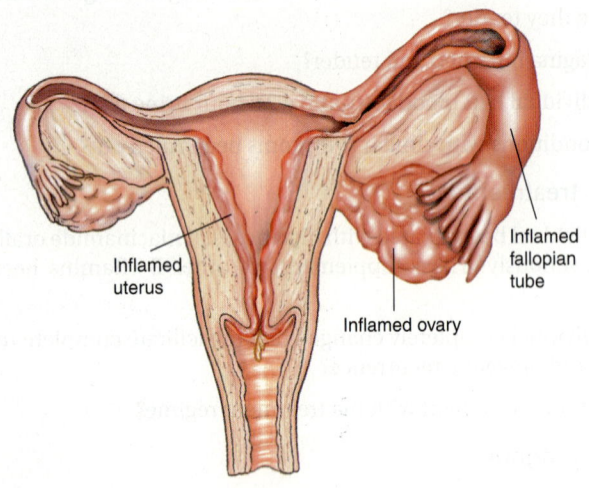

Diagnosis

History: Symptoms include fever, foul-smelling vaginal discharge, pain in the lower abdomen, pain with sexual intercourse (dyspareunia), abnormal uterine bleeding, and tenderness or pain in the uterus, affected ovary, or fallopian tube upon bimanual pelvic examination. Some cases occur without symptoms (asymptomatic) and others have mild or nonspecific symptoms. Severe PID is usually very painful.

Physical exam: The uterus, ovary, or fallopian tube can be enlarged or tender on bimanual pelvic examination. An oral temperature of >38.3 degrees C (101 degrees F) is indicative of infection along with the other signs of lower abdominal tenderness and abnormal vaginal discharge.

Tests: Swabs from the vagina and cervix are cultured to identify the infecting microorganism. A complete blood count to detect an elevated white blood cell count in the presence of infection may be done. A microscopic examination of the tissues (histologic exam) on endometrial biopsy to test for evidence of endometritis may be performed.

Transvaginal sonography or other imaging studies may be done to show thickened fluid-filled tubes with or without free pelvic fluid or tubo-ovarian disease. Laparoscopic examination may also reveal abnormalities consistent with PID.

Treatment

Treatment with oral antibiotics that are affective against a broad range of microorganisms, including Neisseria Gonorrhoeae and Chlamydia trachomatis should be started immediately. Follow-up care should be available within 72 hours to evaluate response to treatment.

Hospitalization of individuals with PID is recommended in a few instances, such as pregnancy, surgical emergencies that cannot be excluded (appendicitis), no clinical response to oral antimicrobial therapy, inability to follow or tolerate the oral antibiotic regimen, severe illness with high fever or nausea and/or vomiting, presence of tubo-ovarian abscess, and a weakened immune system. Besides antibiotic therapy, bed rest and surgical drainage of an abscess may be required.

In severe cases of PID, surgical removal of the uterus (hysterectomy) may be necessary to prevent fatal blood infection (septicemia). If the cause is by gonococci or chlamydiae, the woman's sexual partners are also treated with antibiotics. Removal of a IUD is usually done if it appears to be contributing to the infection.

Prognosis

A favorable outcome depends on prompt diagnosis and treatment with broad-spectrum antibiotics. With chronic, recurring PID, each episode increases the chance of infertility, tubal scarring and obstruction leading to tubal pregnancy, and abscesses of the ovaries, fallopian tubes, and other pelvic areas.

Differential Diagnosis

Other possibilities include appendicitis, ectopic pregnancy, ovarian cysts, endometriosis, diverticulitis, or ulcerative colitis.

Specialists

- General Surgeon
- Gynecologist
- Infectious Disease Physician

Work Restrictions / Accommodations

Work restrictions may need to be applied for a limited time in severe cases and when surgery (hysterectomy) is performed.

Comorbid Conditions

Presence of other sexually transmitted diseases such as genital herpes and congential syphilis can further lengthen disability.

Complications

Complications of PID include infertility, scarring or obstruction of the fallopian tubes, chronic pelvic pain, tubal pregnancy, and spontaneous abortion. Infertility occurs in approximately 20% of women who have had PID due to scarring and blockage of the fallopian tube. Many women with blocked fallopian tubes may never have had symptoms since chlamydial infections can silently invade the fallopian tubes. A woman with PID has a much high risk of a tubal pregnancy because the fertilized egg cannot pass through the blocked fallopian tubes. Untreated, PID can result in chronic pelvic pain in about 20% of individuals.

Factors Influencing Duration

Factors that might influence the length of disability include severity of the infection, job demands, and if surgery was performed. Laparoscopic surgery will usually have a shorter disability than surgery to remove the uterus, ovary, and/or fallopian tube(s).

Length of Disability

Duration depends on severity and acute versus chronic form.

Medical treatment.

Duration in Days

Job Classification	Minimum	Optimum	Maximum
Sedentary work	3	7	14
Light work	3	7	14
Medium work	3	7	14
Heavy work	3	7	14
Very Heavy work	3	7	14

Salpingo-oophorectomy, laparoscopic.

Duration in Days

Job Classification	Minimum	Optimum	Maximum
Sedentary work	3	7	21
Light work	3	7	21
Medium work	7	14	28
Heavy work	7	21	35
Very Heavy work	14	21	35

Percutaneous or transvaginal aspiration.

Duration in Days

Job Classification	Minimum	Optimum	Maximum
Sedentary work	3	7	14
Light work	3	7	14
Medium work	3	7	14
Heavy work	7	14	14
Very Heavy work	7	14	14

Salpingo-oophorectomy, open.

Duration in Days

Job Classification	Minimum	Optimum	Maximum
Sedentary work	28	42	56
Light work	28	42	56
Medium work	42	56	70
Heavy work	42	70	84
Very Heavy work	42	84	98

Duration Trend from Normative Data*

Cases	Mean	Min	Max	No Lost Time	Over 6 Months
904	40	0	188	0.22%	0.11%

Percentile:	5th	25th	Median	75th	95th
Days:	10	18	36	52	96

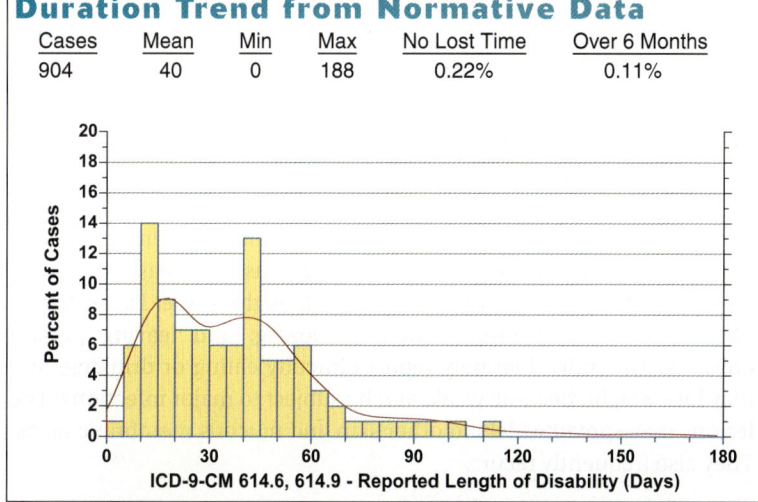
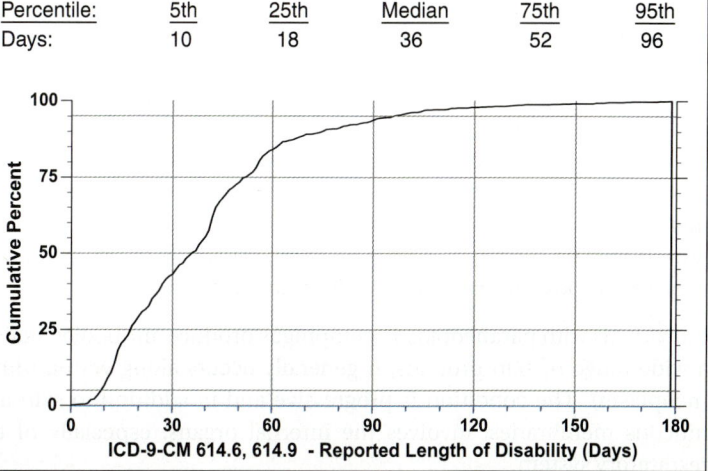

ICD-9-CM 614.6, 614.9 - Reported Length of Disability (Days)

* Differences may exist between the expected duration tables and the normative graphs. Duration tables provide expected recovery periods based on the type of work performed by the individual. The normative graphs reflect the actual observed experience of many individuals across the spectrum of physical conditions, in a variety of industries, and with varying levels of case management.

Pelvic Inflammatory Disease

Failure to Recover

If an individual fails to recover within the maximum duration expectancy period, the reader may wish to reference the following questions to assist in better understanding the specifics of an individual's medical case.

Regarding diagnosis:

- Is the woman sexually active?
- Does she use an IUD for contraception?
- Did the individual present with symptoms and clinical findings consistent with the diagnosis of PID?
- Was an endometrial culture done?
- If the clinical evidence was inconclusive were appropriate additional diagnostic tests done to confirm the diagnosis (ESR, C-reactive protein, endometrial biopsy, ultrasound or laparoscope)?
- If the diagnosis was uncertain, were other conditions with similar symptoms ruled out?
- Was a pregnancy test done?
- Was abdominal ultrasound, culdocentesis or laparoscopy done?

Regarding treatment:

- Was the individual treated promptly with broad-spectrum oral antibiotics?
- Was the individual re-examined within 72 hours to determine response to treatment?
- Was hospitalization indicated?
- Was the individual placed on parenteral antibiotics?
- Did symptoms subside in 72 hours?
- Was surgical intervention indicated?

Regarding prognosis:

- Did the woman receive prompt and appropriate treatment?
- Did the woman experience any complications that may influence prognosis and length of disability?
- Did the woman have any comorbid conditions that may have impacted ability to recover?
- Were these conditions addressed appropriately in the treatment plan?

References

Miller, Karl E., and J. Christopher Graves. "Update on the Prevention and Treatment of Sexually Transmitted Diseases." American Family Physician 10 5 (15 Jan 2000): 11. 12 Dec 2000 <http://www.aafp.org/afp/20000115/379.html>.

Woodward, Carol PharmD, and Melanie A. Fisher, MD. "Drug Treatment of Common STDs: Part II. Vaginal Infections, Pelvic Inflammatory Disease and Genital Warts." American Family Physician 8 3 (15 Oct 1999): 11. 07 Dec 2000 <http://www.aafp.org/afp/991015ap/1716.html>.

Pemphigus
694.4

Definition

Pemphigus is an uncommon, severe disease in which blisters (bullae) arise from apparently normal skin or mucous membrane. It is an autoimmune disease caused by the action of antibodies against certain of the body's proteins and adhesion substances in the skin and mucous membranes (autoantibodies), resulting in the failure of cells to adhere to each other. These antibodies produce a reaction that leads to the separation of epidermal cells. The exact cause of autoantibody development is unknown.

There are three major types of the disease: pemphigus vulgaris, paraneoplastic pemphigus, and pemphigus foliaceus. The most common form, pemphigus vulgaris, usually develops between 30 and 50 years of age, and manifests as painful oral ulcerations on the back (posterior) of the cheeks (buccal mucosa) and gums. The disease is chronic and progressive, but in many individuals remains limited to the mucous membranes. With pemphigus foliaceus, blisters develop only on the skin. It may be caused by a drug reaction, especially to Penicillin, and may also be possibly caused by environmental agents.

Individuals with paraneoplastic pemphigus produce antibodies against a wide range of skin proteins; it generally occurs along with a tumor (neoplasm). The condition is progressive and in addition to skin and mucous membranes, involves the internal organs, especially of the respiratory system.

In the United States, pemphigus is relatively uncommon. Although certain populations have a greater genetic predisposition to the condition, it occurs almost exclusively in middle-aged or older people of all races and ethnic groups. In one study, 2% of normal subjects from the US and Japan had Pemphigus foliaceus autoantibodies to skin proteins. Countries such as Brazil and Mexico, where there may be an environmental cause of the disease, have a higher incidence rate. Pemphigus vulgaris has been observed in 18.3% of individuals studied in Mexico; in Brazil, the prevalence of autoantibodies of Pemphigus foliaceus is high (19-55%) among individuals who live in areas where the disease is common. Pemphigus foliaceus autoantibodies to skin proteins are more prevalent in individuals of Indian origin compared with white northern Europeans.

Diagnosis

History: The individual reports painful skin lesions including blisters or ulcers in the mouth, head, neck, and scalp, and as the disease progresses on the trunk and curves of the body, such as the spine. Large, fragile blisters spread and break, draining, oozing, and leaving painful erosions. The individual may report difficulty eating or drinking, and may lose weight, become weak, and be subject to major infections. The lesions may spread widely to other skin and mucous membrane areas. They also frequently recur.

Physical exam: Blisters and erosion on normal-appearing skin, large red patches, and sometimes crusting and excessive granulation (healing) tissue may be evident. Mucous membrane erosion may be found in the mouth, throat, head, neck, and inside body curves.

Tests: Pemphigus antibodies can be detected in the blood and biopsy tissue by immunofluorescence (IIF) testing. A newly developed, more specific blood test called enzyme-linked immunosorbent assay (ELISA) detects pemphigus antibodies. When the surface of uninvolved skin is rubbed with a swab or the finger, the skin separates easily (Nikolsky's sign). Test of a smear from the base of a blister (Tzanck test), or a skin biopsy will show intracellular disruption (acantholysis).

Treatment

Treatment is aimed at reducing symptoms and preventing complications. Systemic therapy with a combination of corticosteroids and other medications to suppress the immune system (immunosuppressive agents) is aimed at reducing the levels of autoantibodies. In pemphigus foliaceus, the treatment is the same but usually less aggressive. Individuals with paraneoplastic pemphigus are treated with combination therapy of steroids and an antibiotic (cyclosporine) to alleviate symptoms. Treatment of the tumor (neoplasm) does not appear to alter the progression of the condition. In some cases, treatment with only immunosuppressive agents such as high doses of prednisone alone may control the disease. In resistant cases, removing plasma from the individual's blood and reinfusing the other formed elements into the circulation (plasmapheresis) has been used to remove the autoantibodies from the blood. The administration of intravenous (IV) fluids, electrolytes, and proteins may be required. Mouth ulcers may necessitate IV feedings, and anesthetic mouth lozenges may reduce the pain of mild mouth ulcers. Soothing or drying lotions and wet dressings may be helpful in treating ulcers and blisters.

Prognosis

If not treated, pemphigus vulgaris is usually fatal within 2 months to 5 years, generally because of complications; generalized infection is the most frequent cause of death. Pemphigus vulgaris can be a chronic, progressive, and often fatal disease. However, the prognosis of this disease has recently changed from almost universal fatality to a controllable condition with a return to near normal life due to the combination treatment of steroids and immunosuppressive medications. The mortality rate in individuals with pemphigus vulgaris can be as high as 10%, with sepsis (infection of the blood) being the complication most frequently causing death.

The outcome in individuals with pemphigus foliaceus is better than individuals with pemphigus vulgaris.

In individuals with paraneoplastic pemphigus, death usually occurs within 2 years due to its progressive nature, the presence of a tumor (neoplasm), and the involvement of internal organs.

Differential Diagnosis

Impetigo, cutaneous lupus erythematosus, and erythema multiforme may have similar symptoms. Pemphigoid, a bullous disease resembling pemphigus, is distinguished by thicker walled blisters arising from erythematous or urticarial lesions. Oral lesions are uncommon in pemphigoid, and spontaneous remission occasionally occurs after several years.

Specialists

- Dermatologist
- Oncologist

Work Restrictions / Accommodations

Exposure of the skin and mucous membranes to sun, heat, and the combination of sweat and friction may cause the disease to worsen. The individual with pemphigus vulgaris or pemphigus foliaceus may be able to return to work only in a limited capacity, and should avoid lifting heavy objects.

Comorbid Conditions

Other skin diseases that produce similar lesions such as erythema multiforme and infectious diseases such as acquired immunodeficiency syndrome (AIDS) may further lengthen disability.

Complications

Complications include secondary bacterial, viral or fungal infections, side effects of systemic medications, spread of infection through the bloodstream (sepsis), excessive loss of body fluids (dehydration), loss/disturbance of electrolyte balance, tumors (neoplasms), weight loss, and weakness.

Factors Influencing Duration

The severity and extent of the disease, complications, and effectiveness of the treatment will influence the length of the disability.

Length of Disability

The disability may be permanent for individuals with severe pemphigus vulgaris or paraneoplastic pemphigus. Those individuals with pemphigus foliaceus or a less severe case of pemphigus vulgaris may be able to return to work in a limited capacity with restrictions on heavy moving, or heat or sun exposure.

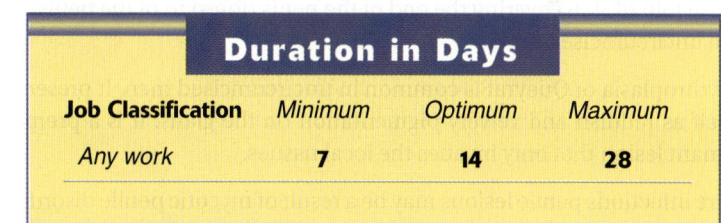

Duration in Days

Job Classification	Minimum	Optimum	Maximum
Any work	7	14	28

Failure to Recover

If an individual fails to recover within the maximum duration expectancy period, the reader may wish to reference the following questions to assist in better understanding the specifics of an individual's medical case.

Regarding diagnosis:

- Did the individual present with painful skin lesions including blisters or ulcers in the mouth, head, neck, and scalp or other areas of the body?
- Was the diagnosis confirmed with blood tests for presence of autoantibodies?
- Did a skin biopsy show intracellular disruption (acantholysis)?
- If the diagnosis was uncertain were other conditions with similar symptoms ruled out?

Regarding treatment:

- Was combination therapy with both steroids and immunosuppressive medications or in severe cases plasmapheresis aimed at reducing the antibodies?
- Were special considerations given to the prevention and treatment of other autoimmune or immune deficiency diseases that could affect the outcome?

Regarding prognosis:

- Does the individual have other skin or infectious diseases that could impact recovery? If so, are these conditions being addressed in the treatment plan?
- Did the individual suffer any complications such as secondary bacterial, viral or fungal infections, or associated neoplasms that could impact prognosis?

References

Harman K.E., et al. "A Study of Desmoglein 1 Autoantibodies in Pemphigus Vulgaris: Racial Differences in Frequency and the Association with a More Severe Phenotype." British Journal of Dermatology 143 2 (2000): 343-348.

Ramirez-Amador, V.A., L. Esquivel-Pedraza, and R. Orozco-Topete. "Frequency of Oral Conditions in a Dermatology Clinic." International Journal of Dermatology 39 7 (2000): 501-505.

Penis Disorders

Other names / synonyms: Balanitis Xerotica Obliterans, Balanoposthitis, Cancer of the Penis, Condyloma Acuminatum, Epispadias, Erythroplasia, Hypospadias, Impotence of an Organic Origin, Infectious Penile Lesions, Paraphimosis, Peyronie's Disease, Phimosis, Vascular Disorders

607, 607.1, 607.2, 607.3, 607.8

Definition

Disorders that affect the penis include balanitis xerotica obliterans, balanoposthitis, erythroplasia, infectious penile lesions, phimosis, paraphimosis, hypospadias, epispadias, vascular disorders, Peyronie's disease, impotence of an organic origin, Condyloma acuminatum, cancer of the penis, and other conditions such as fibrosis, ulcers, and warts.

Balanitis xerotica obliterans results from chronic inflammation of the head of the penis (glans). It is a blanched area near the tip of the penis, which surrounds and often constricts the urinary passage (meatus).

Balanoposthitis is caused by bacterial and yeast infections beneath the loose fold of skin covering the end of the penis (foreskin of the penis) of the uncircumcised male.

Erythroplasia of Queyrat is common in uncircumcised men. It presents itself as reddish and velvety pigmentation on the glans. It is a premalignant lesion that only invades the local tissues.

Rare infectious penile lesions may be a result of mycotic penile disorder, herpes zoster, and TB.

Phimosis is the most common form of the penile malformations. It refers to an abnormally tight foreskin that prevents it from being drawn back over the head of the penis. It can make urination difficult and erection painful. Phimosis prevents proper cleaning of the glans, leading to balanitis. It is also associated with an increased risk of penile cancer.

Paraphimosis often occurs as a complication of phimosis. Although the foreskin retracts at erection, it is too tight to move back over the glans. The penis becomes constricted, causing painful swelling of the glans. It is a medical emergency because of the potential for the gangrenous glans. Paraphimosis may cause urine retention.

Hypospadias occurs when the urethra opens on the inferior (ventral) surface of the penis.

Epispadias occurs when the urethral opening is on the dorsal surface of the penis. This condition is rare.

Vascular disorders of the penis include the obstruction of a blood vessel by a foreign substance (embolism) or blood clot (thrombosis), a localized swelling and mass of blood caused by a broken blood vessel (hematoma), or excessive bleeding (hemorrhage).

In Peyronie's disease, strands of dense, fibrous tissue form within the penis. This fibrosis can interfere with intercourse by causing the penis to curve during erection, or by preventing erection past the area of fibrosis. It can also cause impotence. When examined, the fibrous areas have a gritty, bulky feel to them.

Painful and prolonged erection of the penis (priapism) is a dangerous condition that requires emergency treatment. It occurs when blood fails to drain from the spongy tissue of the penis, keeping the penis erect. Causes of priapism include damage to the nerves that control blood supply to the penis, a blood disease that causes partial clotting of blood in the penis (leukemia, sickle cell anemia), testosterone replacement, or an infection or inflammation that may block the normal outflow of blood from the penis (prostatitis, urethritis).

Condyloma acuminatum is a viral infection that may be spread by venereal disease. The infection is caused by the human papillomavirus (HPV) type 6 or 11. The lesions may be single or multiple and occur in the inner surface of the prepuce.

Cancer of the penis is rare and is more common in uncircumcised men who practice poor hygiene.

In the US, balanitis xerotica obliterans affects about 11% of adult men who are seen in urology clinics. The incidence of phimosis and paraphimosis is about 1% in males older than 16 years.

Diagnosis

History: The individual may report pain in the flaccid penis that is usually caused by inflammation (balanitis, phimosis), ulceration (balanoposthitis), swelling (vascular disorders), or the painful swelling when the glans is constricted by paraphimosis. In an erect penis, pain may be due to the painful curvature of the penis in Peyronie's disease, or to the prolonged painful erection of priapism. Some individuals may notice warts (condyloma acuminatum) on the penis that are soft, flat, and usually not itchy. Redness and velvety pigmentation may be associated with erythroplasia. Urinary incontinence may be present due to hypospadias or epispadias.

Physical exam: The exam may reveal red (erythroplasia), moist inflammation of the glans (balanitis, phimosis), or ulcerated areas (balanoposthitis). Swelling is associated with vascular disorders or paraphimosis. In Peyronie's disease, the fibrous areas have a gritty, bulky feel. Warts are soft and flat, and may be difficult to distinguish visually (condyloma acuminatum). The foreskin is retracted to evaluate phimosis or paraphimosis. The dorsal (back) of the penile shaft is felt (palpated) for plaques of Peyronie's disease, and the ventral (front) surface for evidence of urethral tumors.

Tests: Culture may be necessary to identify the organism responsible for the balanitis inflammation or for ulcerated areas. To detect warts, the penis can be wrapped in a vinegar solution (acetic acid). Warts absorb solution at a different rate than surrounding skin, making them easily visible. Vascular function may be tested by injecting papaverine and phentolamine into the penis to create an erection. Ultrasound may be performed to identify arterial abnormalities. These tests may be done to diagnose any of the penile disorders.

Treatment

Balanitis may be treated by a topical anti-inflammatory or antifungal cream, and appropriate antibiotic therapy against the agent causing the infection. If constriction has occurred, the opening of the penis may need to be surgically enlarged (meatotomy). Removing the foreskin (circumcision) will cure phimosis, paraphimosis, and prevent recurrence of balanitis when caused by an irritating foreskin. Circumcision also reduces the risk of cancer.

Treatment of priapism may involve spinal anesthesia or withdrawal of blood from the penis through a wide-bore needle. Treatment of underlying causes, such as sickle cell disease, may be effective. Several drugs, such as antidepressants, antipsychotics, alpha-adrenergic blockers, antidiabetic agents, certain antihypertensive and anticoagulant drugs, and corticosteroids may be used to reduce priapism.

Antiviral agents may lessen the symptoms of herpes ulcers but will not cure the disease. Recurrence is expected since once the virus enters the body, it stays there for the rest of the individual's life. Gonorrhea and syphilis are effectively treated with appropriate antibiotic therapy. Genital warts may be removed by electrocauterization, laser, use of cold (cryotherapy), surgery (varicectomy), or by the application of an acid solution (podophyllin).

Peyronie's disease may improve without treatment. Local injections of anti-inflammatory medications (corticosteroids) or calcium channel blockers are sometimes effective. If the condition persists, the thickened area can be surgically removed and replaced with a graft of normal tissue (plication).

Phimosis and paraphimosis require surgical circumcision. A preliminary dorsal slit may be required.

In epispadias, bladder outlet reconstruction is required to achieve urinary control.

In hypospadias, functional and cosmetic correction may be needed. A neourethra may be constructed using penile shaft skin or foreskin.

Specialists

- Dermatologist
- Internist
- Psychiatrist
- Urologist

Prognosis

Most disorders of the penis can be cured or improved through medication or surgical correction if done promptly and properly. Warts tend to recur; however, circumcision may prevent recurrence. The plication procedure for Peyronie's disease may result in more scarring, making the problem worse. Viral infections may return since once the virus enters the individual's body, it will stay there for the rest of the individual's life. Priapism treatment with drugs or creation of fistula is usually successful. Prognosis for epispadias and hypospadias is usually favorable with plastic surgery.

Differential Diagnosis

Other possibilities include congenital deformities, cancer, psychological impotence, impotence, Bowen's disease, syphilis, or genital infection and inflammation.

Work Restrictions / Accommodations

Work restrictions and accommodations are dependent upon the type of disorder, method of treatment, individual's responsiveness, and individual's job responsibilities.

Comorbid Conditions

Comorbid conditions include emotional and mental disturbances, impotence, and kidney problems.

Complications

Complications include an increased risk of cancer with phimosis, permanent damage to the penis with vascular disorders or priapism, impotence with Peyronie's disease, risk of transmission to another sexual partner with herpes, gonorrhea, syphilis, or genital warts, infertility, urine retention, urinary incontinence, and sexual dysfunction.

Factors Influencing Duration

Length of disability may be influenced by type of disorder, method of treatment, individual's job responsibilities, individual's response to treatment, age, or the presence of complications.

Length of Disability

This is a vague diagnosis. Specific diagnosis is required to determine disability duration.

Failure to Recover

If an individual fails to recover within the maximum duration expectancy period, the reader may wish to reference the following questions to assist in better understanding the specifics of an individual's medical case.

Regarding diagnosis:

- Does individual have a history of any penile disorders?
- Does individual report pain in the flaccid penis and redness of the glans, suggesting inflammation (balanitis and phimosis)?
- Is there any ulceration (balanoposthitis)?
- Does individual complain of tight foreskin that makes urination difficult and erection painful (phimosis)? Does individual report painful swelling of the glans after erection (paraphimosis)? Is erection painful, suggesting Peyronie's disease or priapism?
- Are there warts (condyloma acuminatum) on the penis that are soft, flat, and do not itch? Was the penis wrapped in an acetic acid solution to make warts easily visible?
- Is there urinary incontinence possibly due to hypospadias or epispadias?
- Was a culture taken to identify the organism responsible for the ulceration?
- Was vascular function tested after injection of papaverine and phentolamine into the penis to create an erection?
- Was ultrasound done to identify arterial abnormalities?

Regarding treatment:

- What disorder was diagnosed?
- Was balanitis treated with anti-inflammatory or antifungal cream and appropriate antibiotic therapy?
- If constriction occurred, was the opening of the penis surgically enlarged (meatotomy)?
- Was phimosis or paraphimosis resolved by removing the foreskin (circumcision)?
- Did individual require withdrawal of blood from the penis through a wide-bore needle to treat priapism?
- Were underlying causes such as sickle cell disease identified and treated?
- Does individual require medications such as antidepressants, antipsychotics, alpha-adrenergic blockers, antidiabetic agents, certain antihypertensive and anticoagulant drugs, and corticosteroids to reduce priapism?
- Were genital warts removed by electrocauterization, laser, cryotherapy, varicectomy, or by application of an acid solution (podophyllin)?
- Were antiviral agents given to lessen the symptoms of herpes ulcers?
- Were gonorrhea and syphilis treated with appropriate antibiotic therapy?
- If individual has Peyronie's disease, were corticosteroids or calcium-channel blockers required or did it resolve without treatment? If Peyronie's disease persists, will the thickened area be surgically removed and replaced with a graft of normal tissue (plication)?
- For epispadias, was bladder outlet reconstruction done to achieve urinary control?
- For hypospadias, were functional and cosmetic corrections required? Was construction of a neourethra using penile shaft skin or foreskin done?

Regarding prognosis:

- Was medication or surgical correction done promptly and properly?
- Have medications been taken exactly as prescribed?
- Is this a recurrence of a viral infection such as with genital warts?
- Does individual continue to have sexual partners who have not been treated for herpes or gonorrhea?
- Did any complications arise as a result of surgery?
- If individual has phimosis, did cancer develop?
- Has permanent damage to the penis occurred as a result of vascular disorders?
- Has individual developed impotence particularly with Peyronie's disease? Has individual developed infertility, urine retention, urinary incontinence, or sexual dysfunction?
- Would individual benefit from psychological counseling to cope with the impact of the disorder?

References

"Chapter 164: Sexually Transmitted Diseases." Merck Manual of Diagnosis and Therapy, 17th ed. Beers, Mark H., and Robert Berkow, MD, eds. Whitehouse Station, NJ: Merck & Co. Inc., 1999. 21 Jul 2000 <http://www.merck.com/pubs/mmanual/section13/chapter164/164a.htm>.

"Disorders of the Penis." Merck Manual of Diagnosis and Therapy, 17th ed. Beers, Mark H., and Robert Berkow, MD, eds. Whitehouse Station, NJ: Merck & Co. Inc., 1999. 21 Jul 2000 <http://www.merck.com/pubs/mmanual/section17/chapter219/219b.htm>.

Pathology of the Penis. Male Genital Tract Pathology. UVA Health Sciences Center. University of Virginia, School of Medicine. 05 Oct 2000. 23 Feb 2001 <http://www.med.virginia.edu/med-ed/path/gu/penis3.html>.

Steidle, Chris, MD. Peyronie's Disease. National Institute of Health. 01 May 2000. 28 Jul 2000 <http://207.106.34.40/impotent/chris/peyronie.htm>.

Peptic Ulcer Disease

Other names / synonyms: Duodenal Ulcer, Gastric Ulcer, Gastroduodenal Ulcer

533, 533.0, 533.1, 533.2, 533.3, 533.4, 533.5, 533.6, 533.7, 533.9

Definition

Peptic ulcer disease is a raw area (erosion) of the lining of the intestinal tract. Cells in the lining of the intestinal tract secrete protective mucus. Glands in the lining of the stomach secrete acid and pepsin to help break down food for digestion. Without the protective mucus, the acid and pepsin would quickly eat away the stomach and the first part of the small intestine connected directly to the stomach (duodenum). When damaging influences overcome this protective mucus in the stomach or duodenal lining, the tissue in the stomach becomes eroded and an ulcer forms.

Peptic ulcers are typically found in the lower half of the stomach or the first part of the duodenum. Ulcers of the lower esophagus occur when there is a reflux of acid from the stomach. Although rare, ulcers may occur in the lower part of the small intestine (jejunum or ileum) when a large amount of gastric acid is produced in the stomach (Zollinger-Ellison syndrome).

The primary causative factors for peptic ulcer disease include the presence of a certain bacterium (H. pylori) in the stomach and the smoking of tobacco. Other causes include increased secretion of acid and the enzyme pepsin by the stomach, reduced production of protective stomach mucus, and intake of medications that aggravate the stomach lining such as aspirin or nonsteroidal anti-inflammatory drugs (NSAIDs). Individuals with deficient immune systems (immunodeficiency) are at risk to contract infections (cytomegalovirus, tuberculosis, or syphilis) that can create ulcers. Some individuals may have a genetic predisposition toward development of peptic ulcer disease. There is no evidence that psychological stress or excessive alcohol intake are causative factors, although they may aggravate an existing ulcer.

Peptic ulcers most commonly occur between the ages of 30 and 55. Overall, 9% of women and 12% of men will acquire this disease some time in their lives. There are 500,000 new cases with 4 million recurrences annually.

Diagnosis

History: Individuals with peptic ulcer disease usually report a gnawing, hunger-like pain in the upper middle abdomen that fluctuates in intensity especially when the stomach is empty. Antacids and eating may relieve the pain or sometimes make it worse. Other symptoms may include heartburn, a sour taste in the mouth, nausea, blood in the stool making it a black tarry color (melena), vomiting of blood, weakness, fatigue, belching, bloating, or weight loss. No symptoms may be reported in some cases.

Physical exam: Finger manipulation (palpation) of the abdomen may reveal tenderness over the stomach (epigastric) area. Paleness (pallor) occurs in about 25% of cases due to low hemoglobin in the blood (anemia) caused by chronic blood loss.

Tests: X-rays may be taken using barium as the contrast medium (upper gastrointestinal series). This is an effective screening test for detecting a peptic ulcer. A flexible, lighted fiberoptic microscope passed down the esophagus (upper endoscopy) enables the physician to view the stomach lining and also obtain a tissue sample (biopsy) of the visualized gastric ulcer. The presence of H. pylori can be identified from such a biopsy. Multiple biopsies from the margins of the ulcer are required to rule out cancer (malignancy). A test done on a stool sample (guaiac test) shows positive when blood is present in the stool. Other tests may include a complete blood count (CBC) to rule out anemia and tests to determine if a certain hormone is causing excess stomach acid secretion (fasting serum gastrin test, gastric secretory test).

Treatment

Smoking and intake of NSAIDs and aspirin should be discontinued if possible. Treatment may include drugs that inhibit or block acid secretions (proton pump inhibitors, histamine receptor antagonists) or medications (such as sucralfate) that form a protective coating on the mucosal surface of the stomach. Antacids may be used to alleviate the symptoms of peptic ulcer. All H. pylori-associated ulcers are treated with a combination of antisecretory agents and antibacterial agents. The best therapy for eradication of H. pylori appears to be a triple therapy regimen consisting of a proton pump inhibitor and two antibiotic drugs. Three antibiotics plus an antisecretory agent (quadruple therapy) may be used if triple therapy is ineffective. Other associated infections (tuberculosis or syphilis) will require appropriate antibiotic therapy. Ulcers resistant to treatment (refractory) may require surgery.

Surgical intervention may include removal of the portion of stomach or duodenum where the ulcer is located (ulcer excision), cutting the vagus nerve fibers that control the production of digestive acid (vagotomy), repair of the valve between the stomach and small intestine (pyloroplasty), or surgical removal of a portion of the stomach (gastrectomy). If bleeding from the ulcer is substantial, a blood transfusion may be necessary.

Prognosis

In more than two-thirds of all cases, drug therapy effectively promotes healing within 6 to 8 weeks from the start of treatment. In the remaining third, long-term drug therapy is usually required. If drug therapy is not effective, ulcer excision generally produces good to excellent results in up to 90% of individuals. The mortality rate for this procedure is very low (<1%).

Vagotomy reduces acid output by 40-50% and possibly lessens the requirements for antisecretory drug therapy an average of 38%. Vagotomy can never eliminate the need for these drugs, however, and individuals with peptic ulcer will always require them to some degree. Ulcer recurrence is 10-20% of cases following vagotomy. It should be noted that vagotomy can make subsequent gastrectomy more difficult and may increase acid reflux into the esophagus (esophageal reflux). This procedure, therefore, is not routinely used to treat individuals with peptic ulcer.

In general, gastrectomy is used to treat only those individuals not able to take antisecretory medication. There may be some degree of postoperative morbidity following gastrectomy (including weight loss, cramping, or diarrhea). Mortality resulting from this procedure ranges from 2.4-5.6%. Gastrectomy is sometimes used in combination with vagotomy, and ulcer recurrence is rare (1%) after this treatment. When pyloroplasty is used to repair the valve between the stomach and small intestine, it is effective 50-80% of the time. If pyloroplasty is used in combination with vagotomy, the results are generally positive.

Specialists

- Gastroenterologist
- General Surgeon

Differential Diagnosis

Conditions that present with similar symptoms to peptic ulcer disease include stomach cancer, biliary tract disease, irritable bowel syndrome, hiatal hernia, pancreatic tumor (Zollinger-Ellison syndrome), inflammation of the pancreas (pancreatitis), low blood flow to the gastrointestinal tract (gastrointestinal vascular insufficiency), and bleeding from the esophagus (bleeding esophageal varices).

Rehabilitation

Regular physical activity on a daily basis is recommended to relieve stress that may exacerbate peptic ulcer. Aerobic exercise such as walking, jogging, or swimming (30 to 45 minutes per session) is usually beneficial.

Work Restrictions / Accommodations

There are no work restrictions for individuals with mild or moderate peptic ulcer disease. Individuals with anemia as a result of bleeding from a peptic ulcer will need light or sedentary duty for up to 3 weeks until blood counts return to normal. If treatment includes surgery, individuals may need light to sedentary work for 2 to 4 weeks until recovery is complete.

Complementary and Alternative Therapies

Content is intended for awareness only. Treatments may or may not be effective. Scientific evidence may be lacking and some substances have potentially toxic effects. Dr. Presley Reed and the editors do not endorse the use of these therapies in the absence of consultation with a licensed medical professional.

Sangre de grado - An Amazonian herbal medicine. May be beneficial in treatment of peptic ulcers.

Yuyang powder - A Chinese herbal medicine (YYP) may be beneficial in treatment of peptic ulcers.

Acupuncture - May decrease hyperacidity in the stomach.

Biofeedback - Teaches stress control techniques.

Nigerian traditional medicines - Extracts of certain medicinal plants from Nigeria may have anti-ulcer activity.

Comorbid Conditions

Existing conditions that may affect an individual's ability to recover from peptic ulcer disease include inflammation of the duodenum (duodenitis) or stomach (gastritis). Reinfection with H. pylori may cause recurrence of the peptic ulcer and further lengthen disability.

Complications

Complications may include chronic blood loss that can result in low hemoglobin in the bloodstream (iron deficiency anemia). The wall of the digestive tract may also develop a hole (perforation) that allows blood, partially digested food, and hydrochloric acid into the abdominal cavity. Leaking digestive juices can cause inflammation of the abdominal lining (peritonitis) that produces sudden, severe pain and requires emergency hospital admission. Chronic ulcers may cause extensive scarring and result in narrowing of the outlet between the stomach and the duodenum (pyloric stenosis) that can obstruct the passage of food.

Factors Influencing Duration

Factors that may influence length of disability include the severity of the disease, the presence of H. pylori at presentation, effectiveness of drug therapy, and whether or not surgery is required.

Length of Disability

Duration depends on severity of symptoms and response to treatment. Individuals with mild to moderate cases of peptic ulcer may have only minimal disability time. The length of disability from peptic ulcer disease, however, is often dependent on the severity of the ulcer and whether chronic blood loss has produced anemia. Disability may be longer (weeks) for individuals with this condition.

Medical treatment.

Duration in Days

Job Classification	Minimum	Optimum	Maximum
Sedentary work	3	7	10
Light work	3	7	10
Medium work	3	7	10
Heavy work	3	7	10
Very Heavy work	3	7	10

Surgical treatment (vagotomy).

Duration in Days

Job Classification	Minimum	Optimum	Maximum
Sedentary work	7	14	21
Light work	14	21	21
Medium work	14	28	35
Heavy work	14	28	35
Very Heavy work	14	28	35

Surgical treatment (partial gastrectomy with or without vagotomy).

Job Classification	Minimum	Optimum	Maximum
Sedentary work	28	35	42
Light work	28	35	42
Medium work	42	49	56
Heavy work	42	49	56
Very Heavy work	42	49	56

Failure to Recover

If an individual fails to recover within the maximum duration expectancy period, the reader may wish to reference the following questions to assist in better understanding the specifics of an individual's medical case.

Regarding diagnosis:

- Was the diagnosis of peptic ulcer confirmed with diagnostic x-rays or endoscopy?
- Has a gastric biopsy revealed H. pylori infection in the stomach?
- If the diagnosis was uncertain were other conditions with similar symptoms ruled out (e.g., stomach cancer, biliary tract disease, irritable bowel syndrome, hiatal hernia, pancreatic tumor, pancreatitis, gastrointestinal vascular insufficiency, and bleeding esophageal varices)?
- Has there been any evidence of upper gastrointestinal bleeding?
- Was anemia detected on a complete blood count?

Regarding treatment:

- Has individual been advised to quit smoking? Would individual benefit from enrollment in a smoking cessation program?
- Has the individual limited the intake of NSAIDs and aspirin?
- Has drug treatment been effective? Are appropriate drugs included in treatment regimen? Would additional or different medication be more appropriate now?
- Is H. pylori infection being treated as appropriate with antisecretory agents and antibacterial agents (triple therapy)? If triple therapy has not proven effective, is quadruple therapy being considered?
- Was surgery required? On what basis was the specific procedure chosen?
- Has the individual experienced any anemia secondary to the ulcer? If so, has this been addressed in the treatment plan?

Regarding prognosis:

- Is long-term therapy warranted?
- Has the individual been compliant with treatment recommendations?
- Has individual experienced any complications, such as anemia, gastric perforation, pyloric stenosis or peritonitis that could impact recovery and prognosis?
- Does individual have an underlying condition that may impact recovery such as duodenitis or gastritis?
- Is individual now a candidate for surgical intervention?
- If individual was treated by vagotomy, what were extenuating circumstances?
- Has individual given up smoking? Would individual benefit from enrollment in a smoking cessation program?
- Has individual limited the intake of NSAIDs and aspirin? Are other alternatives available?

References

Akah, P.A., et al. "Evaluation of Nigerian Traditional Medicines: II. Effects of Some Nigerian Folk Remedies on Peptic Ulcer." Journal of Ethnopharmacology 62 2 (1998): 123-127.

Organ, A.N. "The Effect of Acupuncture on the Gastric Acid-forming Function in Patients with Duodenal Peptic Ulcer." Voprosy Kurortologii, Fizioterapii i Lechebnoi Fizicheskoi Kultury 5 (1999): 12-14.

Pericardiectomy

Other names / synonyms: Pericardectomy

37.31

Definition

Pericardiectomy is the surgical removal of all or part of the pericardium, the membranous sac that holds the heart in place. Surgery is performed through an incision on the front or side of the chest. In most cases, the entire pericardium is removed (radical pericardiectomy).

The most common reason for pericardiectomy is when a rind of thick scar tissue forms around the heart causing compromise of cardiac function (constrictive pericarditis). This is most often the result of a viral infection of the pericardium.

Pericardiectomy can also be performed for recurrent fluid filling the pericardial sac (pericardial effusion) usually occurring in individuals with cancer.

Viral pericarditis is more frequent in young adults and only rarely progresses to constrictive pericarditis.

Reason for Procedure

Pericardiectomy is usually the treatment of choice for chronic constrictive pericarditis, a condition where the pericardium becomes scarred, thickened, and contracts, interfering with the heart's action.

Description

Pericardiectomy is an invasive surgical procedure performed in the operating room under general anesthesia. An incision is made either on the front of the chest (median sternotomy) or on the side (anterolateral thoracotomy). The thick scar tissue surrounding the heart is then removed. The heart-lung machine is on standby in case significant bleeding occurs. Several days in the hospital are required to recover from this procedure.

Prognosis

Pericardiectomy is an invasive procedure that has significant risk. Operative death rate is between 5-10% although the risk is worth the procedure due to the serious nature of constrictive pericarditis. About 15% of individuals must be put on the heart-lung machine during the procedure.

The results of the procedure are generally excellent with between 75-95% of individuals receiving long-term benefit from pericardiectomy for constrictive pericarditis.

Pericardiectomy for cancerous pericardial effusions is also typically met with good success although the seriousness of the underlying disease impacts survival.

Recovery from pericardiectomy involves healing of the painful chest incision and maintaining good lung function that may be impaired due to the pain of deep breathing.

Specialists

- Cardiologist
- Cardiovascular Surgeon

Rehabilitation

Strenuous exercise should be avoided for 3 to 4 weeks while the incision heals. Deep breathing and coughing exercises should be performed several times a day for several weeks. Early return to light exercise (walking, stationary bike) is also beneficial in healing and maintaining good lung function.

Work Restrictions / Accommodations

Strenuous physical activity may need to be replaced by sedentary work responsibilities.

Comorbid Conditions

Any condition that impairs wound healing such as diabetes and immune disorders can lengthen disability. Underlying pulmonary disease such as emphysema or chronic obstructive pulmonary disease can lengthen disability by impairing or compromising good lung function.

Procedure Complications

Operative complications of pericardiectomy include excessive bleeding, injury to nerves or blood vessels, cardiac injury, or even death. Postoperative infections such as wound infections or mediastinitis may result.

Factors Influencing Duration

Length of disability may be influenced by the individual's response to treatment, age of individual, severity or duration of the disease, extent of cardiac injury, or any complications.

Length of Disability

Duration in Days

Job Classification	Minimum	Optimum	Maximum
Sedentary work	14	21	28
Light work	14	21	28
Medium work	28	35	42
Heavy work	42	49	56
Very Heavy work	42	49	56

References

Magilligan, Donald, MD, and Daniel Ullyot, MD. "The Heart: I. Acquired Diseases." Current Surgical Diagnosis and Treatment. Way, Lawrence, ed. Norwalk: Appleton & Lange, 1991. 349-373.

Schwartz, Seymour, MD. Principles of Surgery. New York: McGraw-Hill, 1999.

Pericarditis, Acute

Other names / synonyms: Acute Pericarditis, Dressler's Syndrome, Neoplastic Pericarditis, Nonrheumatic Pericarditis, Pericardectomy Syndrome, Pericardial Inflammation, Radiation Pericarditis, Tuberculosis Pericarditis, Uremic Pericarditis, Viral Pericarditis

420, 420.90, 420.91, 420.99

Definition

Pericarditis is an inflammation of the sac-like structure that surrounds and confines the heart (pericardium or pericardial sac). Acute inflammation of the pericardium may be due to an infectious process or systemic diseases, (autoimmune syndromes, uremia) tumors, radiation therapy, drugs toxicity, or bleeding into the pericardium (hemopericardium).

Pericarditis most often affects men aged 20-50, usually following respiratory infections. It occurs in approximately 1 out of 1,000 individuals.

Acute pericarditis may also be an early consequence of heart attacks. About 10-15% of those who have heart attacks will develop pericarditis.

Diagnosis

History: In most individuals, chest pain is usually present and can be severe. The individual may mistake it for a heart attack. The pain is sharp and worsens by breathing in or coughing. Others may have a steady pain, originating in the center of the chest, and radiating to the arms. In almost all cases, pain is relieved markedly when the individual sits up and leans forward. Pain is usually absent in pericarditis caused by chronic kidney failure (uremic pericarditis), cancer, or after radiation therapy.

Physical exam: Fever may be present when the pericarditis is caused by an infection. The most important physical sign is scratching or squeaking heart sounds (pericardial friction rub) heard with a stethoscope, which changes with different positions.

Tests: Usual tests include blood work, a urine analysis, chest x-rays, an electrocardiogram, echocardiogram, and CT or MRI. Endomyocardial biopsy may be done in pericarditis thought to be associated with cancer.

Treatment

Treatment is focused on relieving the acute symptoms and treating any underlying cause of the problem. The inflammation is often treated with anti-inflammatory agents such as aspirin, indomethacin, or other non-steroidal anti-inflammatory agents. Corticosteroids may be used if pain and inflammation is unresponsive to the standard anti-inflammatory drugs.

If the inflammatory condition is secondary to bacterial infection or tuberculosis, antibiotic or antituberculin drugs will be added as appropriate. If source of inflammation is drug induced, then the offending drug will be discontinued.

Sometimes, fluid accumulates around the heart restricting its movement (cardiac tamponade). It may be necessary to use a needle to remove fluids and relieve excess pressure (pericardiocentesis). In persistent cases of fluid accumulation, typically with tumors or kidney disease, it may be necessary to surgically remove part of the pericardium (pericardiectomy) to allow for continuous drainage.

Prognosis

Pericarditis may be life threatening if left untreated. However, most cases of acute pericarditis that are treated heal promptly. There may be recurrences in the first few weeks or months.

Surgical removal of the pericardium (pericardiectomy) to treat a chronically stiffened pericardium (chronic constrictive pericarditis) has a mortality rate approaching 40% when there is associated severe heart failure.

Removing excess fluid from around the heart (pericardiocentesis) can be a lifesaving measure. However, complications of this procedure include accidental puncture of cardiac vessels, the lung, or the liver. Therefore, this procedure is usually reserved for individuals who have large accumulations of fluid and associated shock (severe cardiac dysfunction).

Differential Diagnosis

The symptoms of acute pericarditis can mimic a heart attack (particularly in middle-aged men). It may be the first visible sign of an important underlying problem such as lupus erythematosus, tuberculosis, or cancer.

Specialists

- Cardiologist

Rehabilitation

Rehabilitation for acute pericarditis can include treatment to relieve symptoms of pain as well as exercises to improve strength and endurance. Initially and when appropriate, physical therapists may choose to use moist heat in the form of hot packs over the chest to relieve pain. Once the acute symptoms have subsided, individuals are encouraged to resume normal activities gradually. A prescribed exercise program can be very helpful in the rehabilitation of acute pericarditis along with other cardiac disorders and disease.

A physical therapist knowledgeable in cardiac rehabilitation will design an individualized exercise program considered safe for each individual's physical stamina. The greatest benefit to the heart occurs as the muscles improve their efficiency in the use of oxygen, which reduces the need for the heart to pump as much blood. While such exercise doesn't appear to improve the condition of the heart itself, the increased fitness level reduces the total workload of the heart. The related increase in endurance should also translate into a generally more active lifestyle. Endurance or aerobic routines, such as running, brisk walking, cycling, or swimming increase the strength and efficiency of the muscles of the heart.

The American Heart Association recommends 30 to 60 minutes of aerobic activity 3 to 4 times a week. The physical therapist should make sure that the individual in rehabilitation allows his or her heart rate to slowly return to normal after conditioning exercises. The physical therapist will also watch closely for any shortness of breath and rapid heartbeat, coughing up blood, and unexplained excessive weight loss. Because of the various degrees and effects of acute pericarditis, modifications may need to be made for those individuals who are taking various medications or are experiencing other conditions resulting from the pericarditis.

Work Restrictions / Accommodations

Individuals will be able to return to work more quickly after treatment if they are assigned lighter duties.

Comorbid Conditions

Tuberculosis, renal failure, cancer, heart attack, or autoimmune disorders (lupus erythematosus or rheumatoid arthritis) are all comorbid conditions that can precipitate pericarditis and prolong the disability. Advanced age, recurrent or chronic pericarditis, and congestive heart failure are conditions that could prolong disability as well.

Complications

Acute pericarditis may be accompanied by fluid buildup (effusion) in the pericardial sac. When the fluid accumulates, it can constrict the heart, obstructing blood flow into the chambers of the heart, and reduce blood flow out of the heart (cardiac tamponade). Tamponade may occur within minutes after cardiac trauma or rupture causing shock and occasionally death, but it usually develops over time.

In rare occasions, acute pericarditis recurs chronically, and sometimes leads to stiffening of the pericardial sac that can impair heart movement and result in heart failure (chronic constrictive pericarditis).

Factors Influencing Duration

Duration will be increased if drainage is required to remove excess fluid around the pericardium (pericardiocentesis), or if pericardium needs to be surgically removed (pericardiectomy). The duration of pericardiocentesis, and therefore the length of disability, varies. Bloody fluid accumulations secondary to a pericarditis following a heart attack may dissipate quickly and necessitate only a brief period of drainage (1 to 2 days). Persistent accumulations of excess fluid, which may occur in those with cancer or kidney failure, requires prolonged drainage (a week or more) and longer disability. If pericardiectomy is performed, the length of disability might be 2 to 3 weeks longer.

Length of Disability

Medical treatment.

Duration in Days

Job Classification	Minimum	Optimum	Maximum
Sedentary work	7	14	28
Light work	7	14	28
Medium work	7	21	42
Heavy work	7	21	42
Very Heavy work	7	28	56

Failure to Recover

If an individual fails to recover within the maximum duration expectancy period, the reader may wish to reference the following questions to assist in better understanding the specifics of an individual's medical case.

Regarding diagnosis:

- Has individual recently had a respiratory infection or any other infections?
- Does individual have an autoimmune disorder?
- Does individual have a history of tumors?
- Has individual undergone recent radiation therapy?
- Has individual recently had a heart attack (myocardial infarction)?
- Does individual complain of severe chest pain? Is the pain worsened by breathing in or coughing and relieved markedly by sitting up and leaning forward?
- Is fever present?
- Does the physician hear scratching or squeaking heart sounds (pericardial friction rub) with a stethoscope (auscultation)?
- Were a complete blood count (CBC) and blood chemistries done? Were chest x-rays, electrocardiogram (ECG), echocardiogram, CT or MRI performed? If cancer was suspected was endomyocardial biopsy done?
- Was the diagnosis of pericarditis confirmed?

Regarding treatment:

- Were nonsteroidal anti-inflammatory (NSAIDs) administered? If pain and inflammation did not respond to the anti-inflammatory drugs, were corticosteroids administered?
- If the condition is secondary to bacterial infection or tuberculosis, were antibiotic or antituberculin drugs added?
- Has individual been compliant with all medication regimens?
- Did fluid accumulate around the heart restricting its movement (cardiac tamponade)? Was it necessary to remove the fluid using a needle (pericardiocentesis)? If fluid accumulates persistently, is surgical removal of part of the pericardium (pericardiectomy) required to allow for continuous drainage?

Regarding prognosis:

- Was pericarditis treated promptly? If not, is individual in a life-threatening situation?
- Is this an initial diagnosis or a recurrence?
- Does individual have any underlying heart or other conditions that could prolong recovery?
- Did complications from pericardiectomy or pericardiocentesis occur such as accidental puncture of cardiac vessels, the lung, or liver? If so, what is the treatment plan for these complications and expected outcome after treatment?

References

"Chapter 209: Pericardial Diseases." The Merck Manual of Diagnosis and Therapy. 1999 21 Jun 2000 <http://www.merck.com/pubs/mmanual/section16/chapter209/209b.htm>.

Scully, Rosemary M., and Marylou R. Barnes. Physical Therapy. Philadelphia: J.B. Lippincott Company, 1989.

Pericarditis, Chronic Constrictive

Other names / synonyms: Concato's Disease

423.2

Definition

Chronic constrictive pericarditis is a condition characterized by thickening of the normally very thin covering over the surface of the heart called the pericardium. This thickening encases the heart like a cast, impeding its ability to fill with blood. Consequently blood pools in the venous system where it leaks out into the surrounding tissues causing swelling of the legs and abdomen.

Tuberculosis, radiation therapy, and malignancy can cause chronic constrictive pericarditis, but, in most cases, the cause is unknown (idiopathic).

Chronic constrictive pericarditis is an uncommon condition affecting males and females equally over age 40.

Diagnosis

History: The individual often does not recall having acute pericarditis since symptoms are similar to a common cold. Individuals in midlife develop shortness of breath and fatigue with ordinary activities. The individual may report initially losing weight and looking gaunt then followed by gaining more weight than was lost with the abdomen becoming swollen.

Physical exam: Blood pressure is usually normal and the pulse may be irregular due to atrial fibrillation. The neck veins are generally enlarged. A fluid-filled, enlarged abdomen (ascites) and swelling (edema) of the ankles is often visible.

Tests: An electrocardiogram (ECG) often shows an irregular rhythm due to atrial fibrillation. A chest x-ray discloses a normal-sized or minimally enlarged heart in many cases and a ring of calcium around the heart. An echocardiogram may show thickening or calcification of the pericardium.

Cardiac catheterization helps distinguish chronic constrictive pericarditis from conditions that may mimic it.

Treatment

Bed rest, salt restriction, and diuretics are most often used to treat individuals with chronic constrictive pericarditis. Steroids may be given to decrease inflammation, and nonsteroidal anti-inflammatory drugs (NSAIDS) or aspirin may also be given.

Surgery to remove the thickened pericardium (pericardiectomy) is usually performed. The operative mortality is 10-15%, and reoperations to control bleeding are common. Complete removal of the thickened pericardium is usually not possible. As a result, the individual often has incomplete relief of signs and symptoms.

Prognosis

The long-term outcome may vary from complete relief of symptoms to little effect. The outcome correlates with the ease and extent of pericardial removal.

The prognosis is very good for those treated with bed rest, salt restriction, and medications to eliminate excess fluid (diuretic) and decrease inflammation (NSAIDS, steroids, and aspirin).

Surgery to remove the thickened pericardium (pericardiectomy) generally yields a positive prognosis with an operative mortality of 10-15%. Complete removal of the thickened pericardium is usually not possible. As a result, the individual often has incomplete relief of signs and symptoms.

Differential Diagnosis

Chronic constrictive pericarditis should be distinguished from restrictive cardiomyopathy. Cardiac and echocardiography usually show this distinction but sometimes exploration of the chest is needed to visibly inspect the heart. Tricuspid valve insufficiency and right infarction may also mimic chronic constrictive pericarditis. Cirrhosis of the liver is a noncardiac cause of ascites and edema that resembles chronic constrictive pericarditis.

Specialists

- Cardiologist
- Cardiothoracic Surgeon

Work Restrictions / Accommodations

Individuals engaged in cognitive work or a job requiring minimal physical activity can resume their vocations. Those performing more strenuous work may need to be reassigned to other responsibilities. Time off for follow-up medical appointments also may be required.

Comorbid Conditions

Obesity, cigarette smoking, and coronary and/or peripheral atherosclerosis may affect disability.

Complications

Complications of pericarditis include atrial fibrillation and its consequences.

Factors Influencing Duration

Severity of symptoms, age of the individual, and response to treatment may all influence length of disability.

Length of Disability

The length of disability depends on job requirements and type of treatment. Disability may be permanent.

Medical treatment.

Duration in Days

Job Classification	Minimum	Optimum	Maximum
Sedentary work	7	14	28
Light work	7	14	28
Medium work	7	21	42
Heavy work	7	21	42
Very Heavy work	7	28	56

Pericardiectomy.

Duration in Days

Job Classification	Minimum	Optimum	Maximum
Sedentary work	14	21	28
Light work	14	21	28
Medium work	28	35	42
Heavy work	42	49	56
Very Heavy work	42	49	56

Failure to Recover

If an individual fails to recover within the maximum duration expectancy period, the reader may wish to reference the following questions to assist in better understanding the specifics of an individual's medical case.

Regarding diagnosis:

- Did the individual present with symptoms (a slow progression of dyspnea, fatigue, and weakness) and clinical findings (edema, hepatic enlargement, ascites, jugular vein distention, and often atrial fibrillation) consistent with chronic constrictive cardiomyopathy?
- Was the diagnosis confirmed with an echocardiogram, CT scan, or MRI?
- If the diagnosis was uncertain, were other conditions with similar symptoms ruled out?
- Would the individual benefit from consultation with a specialist (cardiologist, cardiac surgeon)?

Regarding treatment:

- Was the individual treated with bedrest, salt-restriction, and diuretics?
- Did the symptoms persist?
- Was surgery (removal of the pericardium) required?

Regarding prognosis:

- Has advanced age, bleeding disorders, pulmonary disease, renal failure, or malignancy impacted ability to recover?
- What was the underlying cause?
- Was surgery required? What was the expected outcome?
- Did the individual experience any complications that may have lengthened disability?

References

About Cardiovascular Disease. Center for Disease Control. 28 Jul 2000. 1 Jan 2001 <http://www.cdc.gov/hccdphp/cvd/aboutcardio.htm>.

DeBakey, Michael, and Antonio Gotto. The New Living Heart. Holbrook, MA: Adams Media Corporation, 1997.

Perineorrhaphy
71.71

Definition

Perineorrhaphy is the use of stitches (sutures) to repair the perineum, which is the region between the birth canal (vagina) and anus.

Although perineorrhaphy refers to any repair of the perineum, the procedure is most frequently performed after vaginal childbirth to repair a tear or surgical cut (episiotomy). Episiotomy is the most frequent surgical procedure performed on women in the US, and is estimated to be used in 63% of deliveries. Therefore, perineorrhaphy is also a very common procedure.

Reason for Procedure

Perineorrhaphy repairs cuts or tears in the perineum that may occur during the delivery of a baby. This procedure reinforces the partition between the rectum and the vagina, and returns the size of the vaginal opening (introitus) to normal. Perineorrhaphy is also performed for other perineal surgeries including the repair of a rectocele (in which the rectum balloons into the vagina) or perineal trauma.

Description

Perineorrhaphy is usually performed in a hospital or birthing center. A local or regional anesthetic is used. The cut tissues are realigned and sutured together using catgut or a synthetic suture material. More than one layer of sutures may be utilized, depending on the depth of the cut or tear. Depending on the suture material used, the sutures may either be removed or dissolve after about 10 days. Analgesics and antibiotics would be prescribed as needed.

Prognosis

Perineorrhaphy has a good outcome. Complications are uncommon.

Specialists

- Certified Nurse Midwife
- Obstetrician
- Gynecologist

Rehabilitation

Individuals may be taught Kegel exercises by a physical therapist to increase the strength of the pelvic floor muscles that may have been weakened or injured during childbirth. In these exercises, the woman tightens the muscles in the pelvic floor as if she were attempting to stop the flow of urine. Exercises are initially performed while lying on the back and then progressed to a sitting position. Each exercise is held for 5 seconds for 10 repetitions.

Work Restrictions / Accommodations

Strenuous physical activities may need to be modified temporarily. Time off for follow-up doctor visits may be necessary.

Comorbid Conditions

Bleeding disorders (e.g., hemophilia), obesity, and postpartum depression may influence the length of disability.

Procedure Complications

Complications associated with perineorrhaphy include excessive pain, swelling, bruising (hematoma), infection that may become walled off (abscess), scar tissue, and painful sexual intercourse (dyspareunia).

Factors Influencing Duration

Length of disability may be influenced by the development of complications and the reason for the procedure. However, disability beyond the normal time frame associated with vaginal delivery is not expected with this procedure.

Length of Disability

No disability is expected for this procedure. Disability may occur as a result of an underlying condition.

References

Addison, W. Allen, and M. Chrystie Timmons. "Abdominal Sacral Colpopexy for the Treatment of Vaginal Vault Prolapse with Enterocele." Te Linde's Operative Gynecology. Rock, John, and John Thompson, eds. Philadelphia: Lippincott-Raven, 1997. 1030-1059.

Bo, K. PhD, and T. Talseth, MD. "Long-term Effect of Pelvic Floor Muscle Exercise 5 Years After Cessation of Organized Training." Obstetrics and Gynecology 87 2 (1996): 261-271.

Dunbar, Anne, MS PT. "Exercise Rx: Is There a Standard for Pelvic Floor Muscle Strengthening." Journal of Obstetric and Gynecological Physical Therapy 20 4 (1996): 10-12.

Kisner, Carolyn, and Lynn Allen Colby. "Principles of Exercise for the Obstetric Patient." Therapeutic Exercise: Foundations and Techniques, 2nd ed. Philadelphia: F.A. Davis Company, 1990. 547-573.

Nichols, David, and Clyde Randall. "Posterior Colporrhaphy and Perineorrhaphy." Vaginal Surgery. Mitchell, Charles, ed. Baltimore: Williams & Wilkins, 1996. 257-289.

Penalver, M. "Should Sacrospinous Ligament Fixation for the Management of Pelvic Support Defects be Part of a Residency Program Procedure? The University of Miami Experience." American Journal of Obstetric Gynecology 2 178 (1998): 326-329. 6 March 2001 <http://www.ncbi.nlm.nih.gov/entrez/query.fcgi?cmd=Retrieve&db=PubMed&list_uids=9500494&dopt=Abstract>.

Periodontitis

Other names / synonyms: Dental Abscess, Gum Disease, Periapical Abscess, Pyorrhea Alveolaris

523.3, 523.4

Definition

Periodontitis is a disease that affects the gums, ligaments, and bones supporting the teeth.

The disease is a complication of untreated gingivitis, which is an inflammation of the gums caused by bacterial plaque deposits on the teeth. As periodontitis progresses, the gums recede and small ulcerous pockets form between the tooth and the gumline where plaque deposits continue to accumulate and, in turn, cause further recession of the gumline and deepening of the pockets. Ultimately, these pockets penetrate to the roots of the teeth where supporting tissues are slowly destroyed. The teeth may become loose and eventually may need to be removed (extracted).

Two major predisposing factors for the development of periodontitis are poor care of the mouth and teeth (poor oral hygiene) and increasing age. Most cases of the disease are diagnosed after age 35. Other risk factors include smoking, diabetes mellitus, thyroid conditions, and poor diet. Hormonal effects such as those found in puberty, menstruation, and pregnancy have also been associated with the disorder, as have various genetic disorders such as Down's syndrome and agranulocytosis. In rare cases, periodontitis may be associated with defective dental fillings or structural defects in the mouth.

The American Dental Association estimates gingival bleeding occurs in nearly 45% of working age adults in the US, gingival recession in over 50%, and severe destruction due to periodontal disease in almost 25%.

Diagnosis

History: Because little pain occurs with periodontitis unless there is an accompanying abscess, the usual symptoms of the disorder are bleeding of the gums during tooth brushing and bad breath (halitosis). Bad breath is caused by food particles being trapped in the pockets. The individual may also notice a gradual receding of the gumline.

Physical exam: Upon examination, the dentist may find, soft, swollen, red-purple gums that bleed easily on irritation. Deposits of plaque and calculus may be visible at the base of the teeth with enlarged pockets in the gums. The gums are usually painless or mildly tender unless a tooth abscess is also present. Teeth may be loose and gums receded. Peridental pocket measurements (usually greater than 3 mm in depth) provide information about the extent of the disease.

Tests: No test is needed to diagnose periodontitis although x-rays help determine the extent of any periodontal destruction.

Treatment

Treatment for individuals in the early stages of the disease consists of a thorough professional cleaning to remove plaque from the tooth surfaces and a cutting away of diseased tissue from the pockets around the teeth (subgingival curettage). Treatment for individuals in advanced stages of the disease may include a correction or reshaping of soft tissue (gingiva) around the teeth (gingivectomy or gingivoplasty). Flap surgery may be necessary and involves lifting away the gums from the teeth, repairing the damaged bone, and replacing the gum in its proper position.

In cases where periodontitis is due to structural problems of the mouth or has progressed to the point where it has significantly damaged the underlying structure, extensive bone surgery may be required. When the problem is due to uneven tooth surfaces, occlusal adjustment may be recommended to reshape the chewing and biting surfaces of the teeth.

Other treatment options include using antibiotics or chemical irrigation to control bacterial growth. Some dentists have reported favorable results after putting antibiotic fibers into the pockets between the teeth and gums to control infection and encourage healing.

Following treatment, individuals who smoke are usually urged to quit. All individuals are encouraged to practice good dental hygiene by brushing and flossing regularly and having teeth cleaned professionally for plaque removal. Some individuals may be advised to use special dental cleaning tools as well.

Prognosis

In general, the earlier periodontitis develops or the more advanced it is when diagnosed, the more chronic a problem it is likely to be. Gingivitis is usually reversible after cleaning the teeth and removal of diseased tissue. The problem may not recur provided that the individual practices good oral hygiene thereafter. Unlike gingivitis, serious cases of periodontitis are liable to recur and the individual may require extensive care for the remainder of his or her life.

Differential Diagnosis

Gingivitis or gingival abscess may present with similar symptoms.

Specialists

- Dentist
- Periodontist
- Oral Surgeon

Work Restrictions / Accommodations

The individual with chronic periodontitis may benefit from having access to a lavatory for brushing and flossing teeth after lunch and snacks.

Complementary and Alternative Therapies

Content is intended for awareness only. Treatments may or may not be effective. Scientific evidence may be lacking and some substances have potentially toxic effects. Dr. Presley Reed and the editors do not endorse the use of these therapies in the absence of consultation with a licensed medical professional.

Vitamin C - May improve gum condition.

Warm salt water - Gargling with warm salt water may be soothing to the gums.

Comorbid Conditions

Comorbid conditions that may influence length of disability after treatment for gingivitis include medically compromising conditions such as diabetes mellitus and human immunodeficiency virus (HIV) infection. Individuals on medications that cause dry mouth are also at higher risk for bacterial infections.

Complications

Certain medications for high blood pressure (hypertension) and epilepsy can cause gums to swell. If periodontal disease has progressed to the point where it damages the underlying support structure of the teeth, extensive reconstructive surgery may be recommended.

Factors Influencing Duration

Factors that may influence length of disability include method of treatment and response to treatment. Surgical treatment requires some at-home recovery time.

Length of Disability

Gingivectomy.

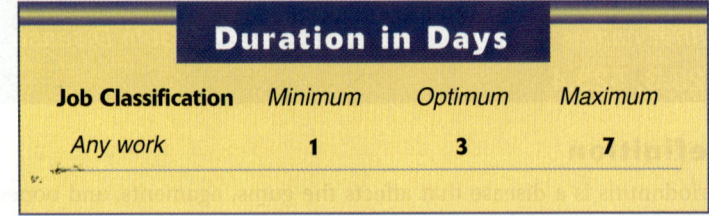

Job Classification	Minimum	Optimum	Maximum
Any work	1	3	7

Failure to Recover

If an individual fails to recover within the maximum duration expectancy period, the reader may wish to reference the following questions to assist in better understanding the specifics of an individual's medical case.

Regarding diagnosis:

- Has diagnosis of periodontitis been confirmed by dental examination?
- Have x-rays been done to determine the extent of periodontal destruction?

Regarding treatment:

- Has conservative treatment with thorough cleaning been effective in resolving the periodontitis?
- Are more aggressive interventions, such as gingivectomy or gingivoplasty, being considered?
- Is structural repair or correction indicated?
- Is individual compliant with dental hygiene regimen?
- What can be done to enhance compliance?

Regarding prognosis:

- If symptoms persist despite treatment, are other treatment options being considered (i.e., gingivectomy or gingivoplasty)?
- Does individual understand the importance of diligent oral hygiene and frequent dental follow-up?
- Does individual have an underlying condition (such as immune suppression or bleeding disorder) that may impact recovery?

References

"Chapter 106. Teeth and Periodontium Topics." Merck Manual of Diagnosis and Therapy, 17th ed. Beers, Mark H., and Robert Berkow, MD, eds. Whitehouse Station, NJ: Merck & Co., Inc, 1999 21 Jan 2001 <http://www.merck.com/pubs/mmanual/section9/chapter106/106f.htm>.

Mandell, Gerald, E., Bennett Gordon, and Douglas Dolin. Principles and Practice of Infectious Diseases, 5th ed. New York: Churchill Livingstone, 2000. 21 Jan 2001 <http://home.mdconsult.com/das/book/view/883?sid=31251659>.

McLeod, D.E. "The Effectiveness of Periodontal Treatment as Measured by Tooth Loss." Journal of the American Dental Association 128 3 (1997): 316-324.

McLeod, D.E. "Tooth Loss Due to Periodontal Abscess: A Retrospective Study." Journal of Periodontology 68 10 (1997): 963-966.

Peripheral Neuropathy
Other names / synonyms: Distal Sensorimotor Neuropathy, Peripheral Neuritis, Proximal Motor Polyneuropathy
356.8, 356.9

Definition

Peripheral neuropathy is a condition caused by damage to nerves in the peripheral nervous system. The peripheral nervous system consists of nerves that connect the brain and spinal cord (central nervous system) to the rest of the body (muscles, glands, and internal organs).

Most neuropathies are caused by damage or irritation to the conducting fibers of the nerves (nerve axons) or to the fatty insulating substance protecting the nerve (myelin sheaths). Nerve axons may suffer a thinning, patchy, or complete loss of their myelin sheath that results in slowed or a complete block of electrical impulses.

Degenerative changes in one or more nerves can be the result of an injury, dietary deficiency, metabolic upset, poisoning, inflammation from a viral infection, a condition in which the immune system mistakenly reacts against the body's own tissues (autoimmune disorder), or an inherited disease. The most common causes of peripheral neuropathy are diabetes and alcoholism.

Neuropathies are classified according to the site, extent, and distribution of damage. Distal neuropathy starts with damage to the end of a nerve farthest from the brain or spinal cord. Damage to a single nerve is called mononeuropathy or (mononeuritis), and damage to several nerves is called polyneuropathy (or polyneuritis). Neuropathies can also be described according to their underlying cause such as diabetic neuropathy or alcohol neuropathy.

The incidence varies with the specific type of neuropathy.

Diagnosis

History: Individuals with peripheral neuropathy usually report three types of symptoms: changes in sensation, changes in movement, and/or changes in bodily functions (autonomic changes). The most common sensation changes are tingling and numbness in the hands and feet. Changes in movement may include muscle weakness, lack of muscle control, muscle atrophy, and pain. Autonomic changes may include blurred vision, decreased or absent sweating (anhidrosis), dizziness or fainting when standing (orthostatic hypotension), nausea or vomiting after meals, urinary incontinence, and impotence (in males).

Physical exam: Characteristic physical findings include weakness and wasting in affected areas of the body with a loss of tendon reflexes. The skin may be sweaty or dry, hot or cold, pale or flushed. Sores (lesions) may erupt. Neurologic and muscular examination may reveal abnormalities in movement, sensation, and organ function.

Tests: Electromyography (a recording of electrical activity in the muscles), nerve conduction tests, and nerve biopsies may be performed to determine the extent of nerve damage. The suspected cause of the neuropathy (as determined by history and symptoms) determines necessary testing such as blood tests, x-rays, or other procedures.

Treatment

Treatment is directed toward the underlying cause. Treatment may include control of blood sugar levels, abstinence from alcohol, and nutritional supplements. When neuropathy is caused by compression of a neighboring anatomic structure, surgical release or decompression may be necessary.

Over-the-counter analgesics or prescription pain medications may be needed to control pain (neuralgia). Inflammation may be treated with a short course of steroids. Transcutaneous electrical nerve stimulation (TENS) is also effective in reducing pain. Antiepileptic drugs are often useful in controlling the burning and/or shooting pains characteristic of neuropathy.

Prognosis

Full recovery from peripheral neuropathy may be possible if the underlying cause can be identified and successfully treated before nerve cell bodies are destroyed.

In some cases, partial or complete loss of movement, function, or sensation may result in disability. Nerve pain may be extremely uncomfortable and persist for a prolonged period. In some cases, the neuropathy may cause life-threatening symptoms such as rapid heartbeats (arrhythmias) or difficulty in breathing or swallowing.

Differential Diagnosis

Conditions that present with similar symptoms include cytomegalovirus (CMV) myelitis, vacuolar myelopathy, and herpes infections.

Specialists

- Neurologist
- Neurosurgeon
- Physiatrist

Rehabilitation

Rehabilitation of peripheral neuropathy depends on its cause. If the peripheral neuropathy is a result of a compressed nerve, immobilizing the affected area often relieves the symptoms. For example, the physical or occupational therapist may fabricate a wrist splint to relieve pressure on a nerve located within the wrist region.

The physical therapist uses techniques to help reduce the inflammation that is causing pressure on a nerve resulting in peripheral neuropathy. For example, ultrasound uses high frequency sound waves to produce heat for penetrating deep into the involved region. This treatment is used with or without an anti-inflammatory medication prescribed by a physician. Massage techniques affect the central nervous system and are used in rehabilitation to treat peripheral neuropathy by temporarily relieving pain. Physical therapy also uses massage to improve circulation of the limbs affected by this condition.

Improved circulation to the legs and feet and relief from pain can be achieved through a general exercise program created by the physical therapist. Strengthening exercises in addition to education with regard to the importance of activity address muscle weakness. If exercises are tolerated well, resistance is added to each exercise. The amount of resistance is determined at the point when the individual's final repetition is difficult yet obtainable. Balance exercises such as side stepping and walking with the eyes closed with and without assistance address any loss of balance and coordination from peripheral neuropathy. Vocational therapy and occupational therapy may be recommended to promote self-care and independence. Wheelchairs, braces, and splints may be necessary to improve mobility or the ability to use an affected extremity.

The rehabilitation program varies for individuals with peripheral neuropathy just as the intensity and progression of the exercise depend on the stage of the disease and overall health of the individual. If a chronic disease such as diabetes is causing the peripheral neuropathy, controlling the disease may not eliminate the neuropathy but may play a key role in managing it.

Work Restrictions / Accommodations

Work restrictions and/or special accommodations depend on the site, extent, and distribution of nerve damage and must be determined on an individual basis. Lack of muscle control or decreased sensation may increase the risk of falls or other injury. Safety measures include hand railings and removal of obstacles. Safety measures for individuals experiencing lack of sensation may include adequate lighting and protective shoes. Individuals susceptible to nerve injury at pressure points need to avoid positions that result in prolonged pressure on these areas (e.g., kneeling, crossing the legs, or leaning on elbows). Wheelchairs, braces, and splints may be necessary to improve mobility or increase the ability to use an affected extremity.

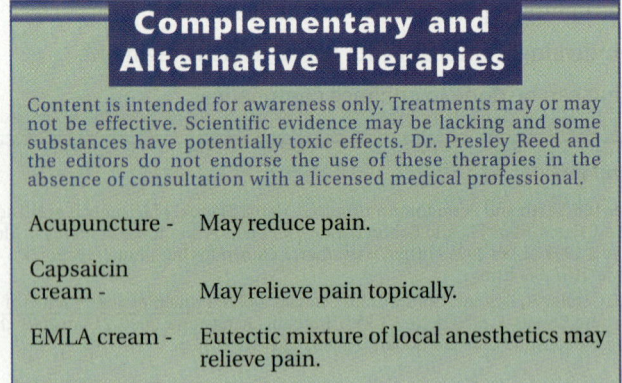

Complementary and Alternative Therapies

Content is intended for awareness only. Treatments may or may not be effective. Scientific evidence may be lacking and some substances have potentially toxic effects. Dr. Presley Reed and the editors do not endorse the use of these therapies in the absence of consultation with a licensed medical professional.

Acupuncture -	May reduce pain.
Capsaicin cream -	May relieve pain topically.
EMLA cream -	Eutectic mixture of local anesthetics may relieve pain.

Comorbid Conditions

Coexisting bedsores (decubitus ulcers), traumatic arthropathy, pathologic fractures, uncontrolled diabetes mellitus, or alcoholism may lengthen disability.

Complications

If the cell bodies of the damaged nerves have been destroyed, functional loss (sensory loss or muscle weakness) may become permanent. Complications are commonly associated with diabetic, amyloid, and hereditary sensory neuropathies. Other neuropathies may result in heightening of the arch of the foot (pes cavus), backward and lateral curvature of the spine (kyphoscoliosis), and loss of hair or ulceration in the affected area. X-ray examination may reveal loss of bone density, pathologic fractures, or joint disease (neuropathic arthropathy).

Factors Influencing Duration

Length of disability depends on the success of identifying and treating the underlying cause, location of the nerve damage, severity of the symptoms, and the amount of functional loss (sensory loss and/or muscle weakness).

Length of Disability

Disability duration varies considerably depending on the extent of nerve degeneration. Contact physician for additional information.

Failure to Recover

If an individual fails to recover within the maximum duration expectancy period, the reader may wish to reference the following questions to assist in better understanding the specifics of an individual's medical case.

Regarding diagnosis:

- Has cause of peripheral neuropathy been confirmed (uncontrolled diabetes, alcoholism, active herpes infection)?
- Have nerve conduction tests been performed? Have nerve biopsies been taken? Are biopsies consistent with neuropathy or myelopathy?

- What is the extent of neuropathy? Have nerve cell bodies been damaged? Will function be permanently affected?

Regarding treatment:

- Is the underlying cause being effectively treated or controlled? By what standards?
- Does treatment plan include nutritional supplements?
- Has individual been able to abstain from alcohol?
- Are analgesics helping to relieve the pain?
- Are steroids included in the treatment plan?
- Would individual benefit from the use of a TENS device?
- Was physical therapy prescribed for the individual? Is the individual compliant with physical therapy program?
- If neuropathy was caused by compression of a neighboring anatomic structure, was surgical release or decompression effective in relieving symptoms?

Regarding prognosis:

- Has underlying cause been identified and successfully treated before nerve cell bodies were destroyed? If diabetic, is the individual maintaining normal blood sugar levels?
- If neuropathy is alcohol-induced, is the individual abstaining from alcohol? Would individual benefit from enrollment in a community program or support group?
- Is neuropathy permanent?
- Did neuropathy result in partial or complete loss of movement, function, or sensation?
- How severe are the symptoms? To what extent is the disability?
- Depending on the site, extent, and distribution of nerve damage, would work accommodations allow the individual to continue in same occupational duties?

References

Bromberg, M. "Nondiabetic Peripheral Neuropathies." Comparative Therapeutics 24 11/12 (1998): 545-552.

Illa, I. "Diagnosis and Management of Diabetic Peripheral Neuropathy." European Neurology 41 suppl 1 (1999): 3-7.

Morgenlander, J. "Recognizing Peripheral Neuropathy. How to read the clues to an underlying cause." Postgraduate Medicine 102 3 (1997): 71-2, 75, 80.

O'Brien, S., M. Schwedler, and M. Kerstein. "Peripheral Neuropathies in Diabetes." Surgical Clinics of North America 78 3 (1998): 393-408.

Poncelet, A. "An algorithm for the evaluation of peripheral neuropathy." American Family Physician 15 Feb 1998 23 Jun 2000 <http://www.aafp.org/afp/980215ap/poncelet.html>.

Simple Facts Sheets: Peripheral Neuropathy. AIDS Treatment Data Network. 18 Jun 1999. 23 Jun 2000 <http://www.aidsinfonyc.org/network/simple/neurop.html>.

Thomas, P. "Diabetic Peripheral Neuropathies: Their cost to patient and society and the value of knowledge of risk factors for development of interventions." European Neurology 41 suppl 1 (1999): 35-43.

Umphred, Darcy A. Neurological Rehabilitation. St. Louis: The C.V. Mosby Company, 1990.

Vaillancourt, P., and H. Langevin. "Painful Peripheral Neuropathies." Medical Clinics of North America 83 3 (1999): 627-642.

Younger, D., G. Rosoklija, and A. Hays. "Diabetic Peripheral Neuropathy." Seminars in Neurology 18 1 (1998): 95-104.

Peripheral Thrombosis

Other names / synonyms: Deep Vein Thrombosis, Peripheral Arterial Thrombosis, Venous Thrombosis
444.22

Definition

Peripheral thrombosis, a complication of peripheral vascular disease, is the development of a blood clot (thrombus) in a vein (venous thrombosis or deep vein thrombosis) or artery (arterial thrombosis) in the pelvis or legs.

A thrombus is blood clot composed of different factors found in the blood. It forms in a blood vessel and causes obstruction of blood flow through the vessel, usually at a site that has been narrowed by atherosclerosis, as well as in grafts that have surgically replaced diseased vessels. Atherosclerosis (arteriosclerosis) clogs and narrows blood vessels, either veins or arteries, as deposits of yellowing plaques containing cholesterol and lipids form in the vessel lining. If a thrombus detaches from the vein or artery, the formation is then called an embolism. Emboli pass through the blood stream to the heart, lungs, brain, or other vital organs and cause obstruction of blood flow to those organs, resulting in stroke and organ damage.

Peripheral venous thrombosis is more common than peripheral arterial thrombosis because blood flows more slowly in veins, allowing a thrombus to form more easily. Venous thrombosis usually develops as a complication of inflammation in the vein (thrombophlebitis) during prolonged bed rest after surgery or in chronic illnesses. Venous thrombosis can also be the result of injury to the vein. Arterial thrombosis develops as a direct result of atherosclerosis, and is also caused by infection or injury.

Acute deep vein thrombosis occurs in 800,000 individuals each year. Risk factors for peripheral thrombosis (venous or arterial) include cigarette smoking, diabetes mellitus, increased fats in the blood (hyperlipidemia), high blood pressure (hypertension), age older than 60 years, obesity, a family history of premature atherosclerosis, and a condition called hyperhomocystinemia, in which blood levels of homocysteine are elevated. Use of estrogen or birth control pills increases risk of deep venous thrombosis. At least 30% of individuals with peripheral arterial thrombosis have a blood coagulation disorder in which blood clots more quickly than normal. These clotting disorders may accompany cancer, pregnancy, increased red blood cell count (polycythemia), or dehydration.

Diagnosis

History: The individual with peripheral arterial thrombosis experiences pain, burning and tingling (paresthesia), and motor weakness below the site of the vascular blockage. The individual with peripheral venous thrombosis experiences a feeling of heaviness in the limb below the obstruction, as well as pain, swelling, and possibly chills and fever. Individuals with peripheral thrombosis may report a history of cigarette smoking, diabetes mellitus, high blood pressure (hypertension), and use of estrogen or birth control pills.

Physical exam: In individuals with peripheral arterial thrombosis, pulses below the obstruction may be absent or faint. Skin below the obstruction may feel cold and look pale or blue/grey (cyanotic). Areas of the skin may appear dead or dying (gangrenous) and may have an unpleasant odor. In individuals with peripheral venous thrombosis, the skin over and below the obstruction may be red, pale, or blue/grey (cyanotic), depending on how severe the obstruction is. The extremity may be swollen (edematous) and the individual may have a fever.

Tests: Doppler ultrasonography is a noninvasive test that can identify obstructed vessels. X-ray of the arteries after injection of dye (arteriography) is an invasive test that can identify the location of severe obstruction of blood flow in the limb (ischemia), and can distinguish a thrombus from an arterial embolism. Veins can be studied further with tests including impedance plethysmography, radionuclide phlebography, and venogram.

Treatment

Individuals with a peripheral thrombosis are admitted to the hospital and observed closely. Treatment for peripheral arterial thrombosis includes administration of intravenous (IV) blood thinners (anticoagulation therapy), and/or administration of products to dissolve the thrombus (urokinase or recombinant human tissue plasminogen activator). The purpose of both of these treatments is to get rid of the thrombus and restore blood flow.

Treatment for peripheral venous thrombosis includes bedrest with the leg elevated and application of heat to the affected area. If the thrombosis is in a deep vein, the limb must be immobilized to prevent a clot from becoming an embolism and obstructing blood flow to a vital organ. Occasionally, surgery is performed and veins in which thrombi have formed are tied off. Postoperatively, other veins take over and circulation returns to normal. Supportive pharmacological treatment can include aggressive lipid-lowering therapy to reduce the progression of atherosclerosis in peripheral vessels; cholesterol-lowering therapy to reduce the risk of heart attacks in individuals with atherosclerosis in the coronary arteries; control of blood pressure with antihypertensive drugs; control of blood glucose level with insulin; vasodilator and antithrombotic prostaglandins to reduce likelihood of thrombosis; and pain medication. Other treatment includes prevention of skin ulcers and foot infections that can occur when circulation to a limb is reduced, including application of moisturizers (being careful not to massage the area and dislodge the thrombus); placement of cotton wicks between the toes to reduce moisture and skin breakdown; placement of sheepskin beneath the heel to prevent pressure sores; and maintenance of a warm environment to prevent vasoconstriction of the blood vessels.

If the thrombus fails to dissolve and the survival of the affected limb is threatened, circulation must be improved by surgically removing the thrombus or by replacing the diseased portion of the vessel with a vessel taken from another part of the individual's body (autograft) or with a Dacron graft. Procedures that may be performed include intra-abdominal aortoiliac reconstruction, axillobifemoral bypass, femoro-femoral bypass, and infrainguinal bypass. If all measures fail to restore circulation to the affected limb, and if tissue death has occurred, amputation of the limb above the blockage may be required.

Preventive measures in situations increasing risk for peripheral embolus may be helpful, such as use of low-dose heparin (blood thinner) or elasticized stockings (compression stockings) after orthopedic surgery or during prolonged bedrest. Placement of a Greenfield or other filter in the large vein draining the lower body (inferior vena cava) may prevent thromboemboli from the legs from traveling to the heart and lungs, resulting in pulmonary embolus.

Prognosis

Recovery from a peripheral venous or arterial thrombosis is good if the thrombus dissolves without releasing an embolism and before cells die in the tissue below the obstruction. If an embolism is released, it can travel to the site of a vital organ and obstruct blood flow to that organ. This is often a life-threatening complication requiring emergency medical and/or surgical treatment. Outcome of these complications can be permanent disability or death.

Treatment of acute arterial thrombosis by administration of products to dissolve the thrombus (thrombolytic therapy) is successful 50-80% of the time. Because of the length of time it takes to dissolve the thrombus, however, 5% of these individuals will require amputation. Prognosis is often poor in individuals who require limb amputation, not necessarily because of the amputation, but because of the extent of underlying disease, which contributed to formation of a thrombus. Seventy to eighty-five percent of the surgical grafts that are used to replace diseased blood vessels are still open 5 years after surgery.

In a large prospective study of 1719 individuals with deep vein thrombosis or blood clot in the lung (pulmonary embolus), recurrence rates were 8% at 3 months, 10% at 6 months, 13% at 1 year, and 30% at 10 years. Individuals with peripheral arterial disease who also have IgG anticardiolipin antibody have a higher risk of overall mortality and of mortality related to cardiovascular disease.

Differential Diagnosis

A diagnosis of peripheral thrombosis must be differentiated from embolism, traumatic injury to a vein or artery, popliteal artery entrapment, thromboangiitis obliterans, and peripheral artery aneurysm. Isolated symptoms seen in peripheral thrombosis may be seen in other disorders. For example, leg pain, temperature changes, skin changes and swelling can be seen in regional complex pain syndrome (reflex sympathetic dystrophy). Leg swelling with changes in skin color and temperature can be seen in congestive heart failure.

Specialists

- Emergency Medicine
- Internist
- Radiologist
- Vascular Surgeon

Rehabilitation

Individuals with peripheral vascular disease require a supervised exercise training program that is focused on walking with enough intensity to improve circulation in the legs. Individuals who have had amputations need physical therapy to help them adapt to walking on a prosthesis, and to improve their balance. Individuals experiencing grief over loss of a limb may benefit from counseling or other activities that provide emotional support.

Work Restrictions / Accommodations

Individuals who have had a leg amputated must expend between 10-65% more energy to walk with a prosthesis, compared to an individual who has use of both legs. These individuals may also have problems with balance. Both of these conditions may require workplace restrictions and accommodations for the safety and well-being of the individual. Individuals with peripheral vascular disease may benefit from an exercise facility/program within the workplace.

Comorbid Conditions

Comorbid conditions influencing the length of disability for individuals with a peripheral thrombosis include obesity, smoking, pre-existing chronic diseases that are associated with the development of atherosclerosis, such as diabetes, peripheral vascular disease, hyperlipidemia, hypertension, and cardiovascular diseases. Anticardiolipin antibodies are common in individuals with peripheral arterial disease, and are associated with increased risk of overall mortality and of mortality related to heart disease. Atrial fibrillation is an important risk factor for peripheral arterial thromboembolic disease. Diseases that predispose to a hypercoagulable state, such as cancer, also increase risk of peripheral venous thrombosis, and the morbidity of the two conditions is additive.

Complications

Complications include blood clots (emboli) that travel to the heart, lungs, or brain and gangrene (necrosis) of the limb below the obstruction. Legs affected by blood clot are more prone to infection and injury. Individuals requiring amputation of a limb may experience a range of emotions, including anger, sadness and depression.

Factors Influencing Duration

Factors influencing the length of disability include surgical complications that can delay recovery, cigarette smoking, a high fat diet and a sedentary lifestyle. Occupations requiring walking, standing and heavy labor are more likely to be affected than sedentary occupations.

Length of Disability

Duration depends on the type of thrombus (arterial or venous), the presence of emboli, and the type of treatment (medical or surgical). Disability can range from a few weeks to several months, depending on how quickly circulation is restored to the affected limb, the number and severity of complications, the progression of coexisting chronic diseases, and the individual's ability to adapt to life with a prosthesis, if necessary. Disability may be permanent.

Failure to Recover

If an individual fails to recover within the maximum duration expectancy period, the reader may wish to reference the following questions to assist in better understanding the specifics of an individual's medical case.

Regarding diagnosis:

- Has the individual provided the physician with an adequate medical history, including information about past injuries to the leg, smoking history, use of birth control pills or other medications increasing thrombotic risk, chronic conditions such as cancer, high blood pressure, hyperlipidemia or other risk factors for peripheral thrombosis?
- Has the diagnosis been confirmed by Doppler ultrasound, arteriography, plethysmography, venography, or other tests to identify the existence and location of an obstructed blood vessel?

Regarding treatment:

- Has the individual been treated with anticoagulants or thrombolysis?
- Have other specialists been consulted to treat coexisting chronic diseases that might complicate or prolong recovery?
- Has a vascular surgeon been consulted to evaluate the options for surgical treatment?
- Is good skin care being provided to the affected limb in order to prevent infection?
- Has physical therapy been provided to help the individual adapt to use of a prosthesis?
- Has psychological support been provided to help the individual cope with the emotional aspects of losing a limb?

Regarding prognosis:

- Does the individual have risk factors associated with poor outcome, such as advanced age or presence of anticardiolipin antibodies?
- Is there evidence of recurrence?

References

de Graaff, J.C., et al. "The Diagnosis of Deep Venous Thrombosis Using Laser Doppler Skin Perfusion Measurements." Microvasc. Res. 61 1 (2001): 49-55.

Deep Vein Thrombosis. Washington University. 01 Jan 2000. 12 March 2001 <http://faculty:washington.edu/momus/PB/deepvein.htm>.

Duke, James A. The Green Pharmacy. Emmaus, PA: Rodale Press, Inc, 1997.

Feinstein, Alice, ed. Healing with Vitamins. Emmaus, PA: Rodale Press, Inc, 1996.

Frost, L., et al. "Incident Thromboembolism in the Aorta and the Renal, Mesenteric, Pelvic, and Extremity Arteries After Discharge From the Hospital with a Diagnosis of Atrial Fibrillation." Archives of Internal Medicine 161 2 (2001): 272-276.

Nenci, G.G., and A. Minciotti. "Low Molecular Weight Heparins for Arterial Thrombosis." Vascular Medicine 5 4 (2000): 251-258.

Nichollis, S.C. "Peripheral Arterial Embolization: Doppler Ultrasound Scan Diagnosis." Journal of Vascular Surgery 31 4 (2000): 811-814.

Puisieux, F., et al. "Association Between Anticardiolipin Antibodies and Mortality in Patients with Peripheral Arterial Disease." American Journal of Medicine 109 8 (2000): 635-641.

Schweizer, J., et al. "Short- and Long-term Results of Abciximab Versus Aspirin in Conjunction with Thrombolysis for Patients with Peripheral Occlusive Arterial Disease and Arterial Thrombosis." Angiology 51 11 (2000): 913-923.

Tierney, Lawrence, Stephen McPhee, and Maxine Papadakis. Current Medical Diagnosis and Treatment. New York: McGraw-Hill, 2000.

Peripheral Vascular Disease

Other names / synonyms: Claudication, Intermittent Claudication, Peripheral Arterial Disease, Peripheral Arterial Insufficiency, Peripheral Arteriosclerosis, Peripheral Atherosclerosis

443.9

Definition

Peripheral vascular disease (PVD) is a condition in which the arteries or veins carrying blood to or from the arms or legs become narrow or clogged. The feet and legs may be more affected than the hands and arms. The most common symptom is leg cramps or pain that becomes worse with walking or other activity, and better with rest (claudication). Other symptoms may include leg numbness, tingling, or weakness. The feet may be cold or discolored, with loss of hair.

Disruption of circulation in the peripheral veins can be caused by failure of blood to move sufficiently quickly through the veins (venous stasis), or overly active blood clotting (hypercoagulability). It can be a result of immobility or prolonged inactivity, trauma or serious injury, orthopedic surgery, aging, or dehydration. The most common cause of narrowing of the peripheral arteries is atherosclerosis, which used to be called "hardening of the arteries." Atherosclerosis develops gradually as cholesterol and scar tissue build up, forming a substance called plaque that clogs the blood vessels. Other causes of narrowed arteries include trauma, spasm of the smooth muscles in artery walls, and structural defects in the arteries that are present at birth.

Peripheral vascular disease (PVD) affects about 1 in 20 individuals over age 50, or about 8 million in the US. It is slightly more common in men than women. Risk factors include smoking, diabetes, obesity, sedentary lifestyle, high blood pressure, high cholesterol, and family history of heart or vascular disease.

Diagnosis

History: The most common symptom of peripheral vascular disease of the lower extremities that individuals report is leg pain, particularly when walking or exercising, which disappears after a few minutes rest (claudication). Other symptoms of peripheral vascular disease of the lower extremities include numbness and tingling in the legs, feet, or toes; coldness in the lower legs and feet; loss of hair on the feet or legs; discoloration or cold feeling in the legs and feet; and ulcers or sores on the legs and feet that don't heal properly.

Physical exam: Abnormal or reduced pulse in the feet (pedal pulses), murmur (bruit) over the large artery in the groin (femoral artery) or in arteries in the lower abdomen (iliac arteries), prolonged venous filling time, and unilaterally cool limbs are associated with peripheral vascular disease. Observations of the effect of hanging the affected leg over the side of the bed on an individual's pain (the Buerger test) and warm knees are predictive of the extent of vascular disease.

Tests: Doppler ultrasound may identify reduced blood flow to a specific area and locate any obstruction to venous flow. Plethysmography helps view areas of decreased circulation around the affected area. Phlebography involves injection of dye visualized on x-ray (radiopaque) into the veins, which shows areas of decreased or diverted blood flow. Arteriography involves injection of radiopaque contrast dye into the artery, to look at the diameter of the arteries, areas of plaque or blood clots, and diversion of blood to alternate vessels. Treadmill walking can quantify the amount of effort expended before pain occurs, and can be useful to monitor response to treatment.

Treatment

In some cases, PVD can be successfully controlled by certain lifestyle changes, such as exercise programs and dieting to lose weight and lower blood cholesterol. The single most important thing an individual can do to slow PVD is to stop smoking. When lifestyle changes alone are not enough to control the symptoms of PVD, there are a number of treatment options, including: opening up the blockage in the blood vessel by inserting a very small balloon attached to a thin tube (catheter) into the vessel through a small nick in the skin (angioplasty); administration of clot-dissolving drugs through a catheter directly into the clot (thrombolytic therapy); a vein graft from another part of the body or a graft made from artificial material to create a detour around the blocked artery (bypass grafts); and insertion of a balloon catheter into the affected artery above the clot, which when inflated and pulled back brings the clot with it (thrombectomy). Medications that thin the blood (anticoagulants) or affect platelets involved in blood clotting (such as aspirin) may be helpful.

Prognosis

Overall, with treatment (thrombolytic therapy, angioplasty, bypass grafts, or thrombectomy), the prognosis is reasonably favorable; without treatment limb loss may be imminent. The prognosis does vary somewhat depending on the specific type and cause of disease and the stage at which it is first diagnosed. Treatment to bypass an obstructed vessel is generally not very helpful if atherosclerosis also affects smaller arteries beyond the site of blockage. As atherosclerosis underlying PVD is typically a progressive condition, it tends to recur and PVD tends to worsen following treatment unless there are significant lifestyle changes, including stopping smoking.

Differential Diagnosis

Conditions with similar symptoms include vasculitis, Raynaud's disease, and Buerger's disease. Difficulty walking, cramping leg pain, and other symptoms involving the legs may be seen in spinal stenosis, cauda equina syndrome, lumbar radiculopathy, and peripheral neuropathy.

Specialists

- Cardiologist
- Cardiovascular Surgeon
- Internist
- Physiatrist
- Radiologist

Rehabilitation

Rehabilitation of peripheral vascular disease focuses on increasing the exercise capacity of the individual. However, individuals with this disease have a lowered aerobic capacity when exercising the arms or legs. Because of this, aerobic activity for these individuals cannot be maintained for long periods of time. Short periods and intervals of intense exercise for 10-20 seconds, followed by lower levels of activity, are usually achievable goals set in the rehabilitation program. Activities include walking, stationary biking, or pool activities. This activity continues under the supervision of a physical therapist or other trained professional in rehabilitation.

Upper extremity exercises in conjunction with leg exercises serve as good rehabilitation to improve overall endurance. This can be accomplished with the use of an exercise bike with reciprocal moving handlebars. Jogging, if comfortable for the individual, helps to establish collateral blood flow to the legs and heart. Realistic goals should be set with regard to time, frequency, and distance of all exercises. Buerger-Allen exercises may also be recommended, in which the individual begins by lying flat in bed with legs elevated above the heart level for 2 minutes or until blanching takes place, then exercising the feet until the legs are pink, then lying flat for 5 minutes.

Work Restrictions / Accommodations

Work accommodations that may be required include postural and positional changes to accommodate the affected limbs and promote better circulation. If the individual performs a desk job, short routine walks should be scheduled to promote lower limb circulation. Strenuous physical activity or walking long distances may need to be limited in accordance with medical recommendations.

Complementary and Alternative Therapies

Content is intended for awareness only. Treatments may or may not be effective. Scientific evidence may be lacking and some substances have potentially toxic effects. Dr. Presley Reed and the editors do not endorse the use of these therapies in the absence of consultation with a licensed medical professional.

Folic acid -	Decreases homocysteine, which may contribute to atherosclerosis formation.
Gingko -	Increases blood flow. May be helpful in circulatory disorders.
Alfalfa -	Appears to decrease serum cholesterol.
Black cohosh -	Dilates blood vessels. May lower cholesterol. Overdose may cause nervous system disturbances.
Capsicum -	Said to have pain relieving properties.
Ginseng -	Appears to lower cholesterol. Diabetics should use ginseng with caution because of the hypoglycemic effects.

Dietary supplements:

Vitamin C -	Antioxidant. May help prevent atherosclerosis.
Vitamin E -	May help prevent atherosclerosis. May improve blood flow through clogged arteries.
Zinc -	May help prevent atherosclerosis.

Comorbid Conditions

Other cardiovascular diseases, diabetes mellitus, obesity, vasculitis, or smoking may lengthen disability.

Complications

When venous blood flow is impeded, blood and bacteria may accumulate, leading to the formation of leg ulcers. Decreased venous flow results in increased venous pressure, promoting varicose veins that can become inflamed and clotted (thrombophlebitis). Interrupted blood flow to the peripheral arteries can lead to inadequate delivery of oxygen to the tissues and, consequently, to tissue death and gangrene, which may require leg amputation in 3-6% of cases. Clots in the veins or arteries can break off and travel to other vessels, causing stroke or blood clots in the lungs (pulmonary embolism).

Factors Influencing Duration

Individual response to treatment and the extent of vascular involvement affect the duration of disability.

Length of Disability

Duration depends on specific diagnosis and treatment.

Duration in Days

Job Classification	Minimum	Optimum	Maximum
Sedentary work	7	14	28
Light work	7	14	28
Medium work	7	21	42
Heavy work	7	28	Indefinite
Very Heavy work	7	28	Indefinite

Failure to Recover

If an individual fails to recover within the maximum duration expectancy period, the reader may wish to reference the following questions to assist in better understanding the specifics of an individual's medical case.

Regarding diagnosis:

- Does individual complain of claudication with activity?
- Does individual have leg numbness, tingling, or weakness? Are the lower legs and feet cold or discolored with loss of hair?
- Does individual have sores that do not heal properly?
- Does individual have venous stasis or hypercoagulability? Does individual have diabetes, obesity, sedentary lifestyle, high blood pressure, high cholesterol, and family history of heart or vascular disease? Does individual smoke?
- On exam, were reduced pedal pulses, a bruit over the femoral artery or iliac arteries, prolonged venous filling time, and unilaterally cool limbs evident?
- Were Doppler ultrasound, plethysmography, phlebography, arteriography or treadmill walking performed?
- Have conditions with similar symptoms been ruled out?

Regarding treatment:

- Has individual addressed correctable lifestyle activities such as diet, weight loss, lowering blood cholesterol, and cessation of smoking?
- Was an angioplasty necessary? Was thrombolytic therapy done? Was a bypass graft or thrombectomy performed?
- Is individual on anticoagulant medication?

Regarding prognosis:

- Is individual active in physical therapy?
- Can individual's employer accommodate any necessary restrictions?
- Does individual have any conditions that may affect ability to recover?
- Have any complications occurred such as leg ulcers, thrombophlebitis, or gangrene and amputation? Did individual have a pulmonary embolism?

References

DerMarderosian, Ara, ed. The Review of Natural Products. St. Louis: Facts and Comparisons, 2000.

Feinstein, Alice, ed. Healing With Vitamins. Emmaus: Rodale Press, Inc, 1996.

Peripheral Vascular Disease. Society of Cardiovascular & Interventional Radiology. 2000. 05 Aug 2000 <http://www.scvir.org/patient/pci/page10.htm>.

Peripheral Vascular Disease. Hall-Garcia Cardiology Associates. 01 May 2000. 13 Aug 2000 <http://www.hgcardio.com/periph.htm>.

Peripheral Vascular Disease. Clayton College and State University. 2000. 13 Aug 2000 <http://healthsci.clayton.edu/sanner/notespvd.htm>.

Scully, Rosemary M., and Marylou R. Barnes. Physical Therapy. Philadelphia: J.B. Lippincott Company, 1989.

Peritonitis

Other names / synonyms: Dialysis-Associated Peritonitis, Inflammation of the Peritoneum, Secondary Peritonitis, Spontaneous Peritonitis

567, 567.1, 567.8, 567.9

Definition

Peritonitis is an acute or chronic inflammation of the membrane (peritoneum) that lines the wall of the abdomen and covers the abdominal organs.

Peritonitis is caused by an invasion of bacteria or foreign matter following rupture of an internal organ, an infection in the bloodstream, an infection originating elsewhere in the body, by a penetrating injury to the abdominal wall, or an accidental contamination during surgery.

There are 3 types of peritonitis: spontaneous peritonitis, secondary peritonitis, and dialysis-associated peritonitis.

Risk factors for spontaneous peritonitis include liver disease (cirrhosis) caused by alcoholism or other liver conditions, a group of kidney diseases (nephrotic syndrome), peptic ulcer disease, appendicitis, and diverticulitis. Risk factors for secondary peritonitis include a perforation in the gastrointestinal tract (e.g., perforated bowel or ruptured appendix), and severe chemical reactions from bile or pancreatic enzymes as a result of injury to, or perforation of, the intestine or biliary tract. The most common cause of secondary peritonitis, seen in 60-80% of all cases, is the perforation of a large organ in 1 of the 3 body cavities (viscus).

The risk factor for dialysis-associated peritonitis occurs when bacteria (most commonly pneumococci and staphylococci) are introduced into the peritoneum by the dialysis procedure.

The incidence of this condition is about 2 per 1 million persons per year. In adults, up to 30% of all individuals hospitalized with cirrhosis, or for a condition in which serous fluid accumulates in the abdominal cavity (ascites), develop spontaneous peritonitis. Although peritonitis can affect individuals of any age, spontaneous peritonitis is rare in children.

Diagnosis

History: The individual will present with complaints of abdominal pain, abdominal distension, fever, and excessive thirst. The individual may also complain of low urine output and an inability to pass gas or feces. Many individuals will complain of a specific area of tenderness that they are able to touch or point out (point tenderness). Additional symptoms include nausea and vomiting, joint pain, and chills.

Physical exam: Physical examination will reveal abdominal pain to the touch (upon palpation), rebound tenderness, abdominal rigidity, increased heart rate (tachycardia), low blood pressure (hypotension), fever, decreased bowel sounds, an accumulation of fluid in the abdomen (ascites), and decreased respirations. Those with dialysis-associated peritonitis will have cloudy dialysis fluid.

Tests: Laboratory tests will include complete blood count (CBC) with differential; blood culture; peritoneal fluid culture, chemical analysis, and cell studies (cytology); urinalysis; and urine culture. Other diagnostic procedures may include chest and abdominal x-rays, and an ultrasound or CT scan of the abdomen and pelvis. Sometimes a surgical procedure called a exploratory laparotomy may be done.

Treatment

The individual is usually hospitalized for treatment. Treatment depends on the underlying cause of the peritonitis. Surgery is sometimes necessary to remove (e.g., infected bowel, abscess, inflamed appendix) or repair (e.g., perforated ulcer) the source(s) of infection. Either intravenous or intraperitoneal antibiotics will be given to control infection. Intravenous fluids will be given to control dehydration. A nasogastric (NG) tube will be placed to decompress the stomach, and narcotics and sedatives will be given to keep the individual comfortable and calm.

Prognosis

For dialysis-associated peritonitis, most individuals recover uneventfully with either intraperitoneal or intravenous antibiotics.

For spontaneous and secondary peritonitis, regardless of treatment modality, the outcome depends on the underlying cause of the disease and the duration of symptoms before treatment was implemented. Complete recovery can occur, but in some cases the disease can be lethal. Up to one-half of individuals with spontaneous peritonitis will die from the acute illness; one-quarter will suffer from recurrences.

Peritonitis carries with it a mortality rate of between 3-60%.

Differential Diagnosis

Other conditions that present with similar symptoms include constipation/fecal impaction, appendicitis, perforated ulcer, sickle cell anemia, herpes zoster, diabetic ketoacidosis, tabes dorsalis, porphyria, familial Mediterranean fever, lead poisoning, systemic lupus, or uremia.

Specialists

- Cardiologist
- Gastroenterologist
- General Surgeon
- Gynecologist
- Infectious Disease Physician
- Nephrologist
- Pulmonologist

Work Restrictions / Accommodations

If the individual underwent surgery, heavy lifting should be eliminated for a minimum of 6 weeks.

Comorbid Conditions

Existing conditions that could impact ability to recover and further lengthen disability include alcoholism, cirrhosis, hepatitis, malnutrition, and leukocytosis.

Complications

Possible complications that may arise include development of abdominal abscesses, intestinal obstruction from scar tissue, secondary organ failure, septic shock, intraperitoneal adhesions, hepatorenal syndrome, recurrent peritonitis, catheter tract infection (in those individuals with dialysis-associated peritonitis), and hepatic encephalopathy.

Factors Influencing Duration

Factors that might influence the length of disability include the underlying condition causing peritonitis, the individual's age, duration of disease prior to treatment, type of treatment, response to treatment, job requirements, and possible complications.

Length of Disability

Surgical treatment.

Duration in Days

Job Classification	Minimum	Optimum	Maximum
Sedentary work	14	28	56
Light work	14	28	56
Medium work	21	42	70
Heavy work	28	56	70
Very Heavy work	28	56	70

Failure to Recover

If an individual fails to recover within the maximum duration expectancy period, the reader may wish to reference the following questions to assist in better understanding the specifics of an individual's medical case.

Regarding diagnosis:

- Did the individual complain of abdominal pain, abdominal distension, or excessive thirst?
- Does the individual have a medical history (i.e., peptic ulcer disease, recent gastrointestinal surgery, cirrhosis, or peritoneal dialysis, etc.) that may place him/her at increased risk for developing peritonitis?
- Was abdomen rigid? Was there abdominal guarding?
- Was a peritoneal tap done? Was a peritoneal culture positive?
- Did an ultrasound or CT of the abdomen demonstrate findings consistent with the diagnosis of peritonitis? Were blood cultures positive?
- Was culture of dialysis fluid (if appropriate) positive?
- If the diagnosis was uncertain, were other possible conditions ruled out (i.e., constipation/fecal impaction, appendicitis, perforated ulcer)?

Regarding treatment:

- Was the individual given intravenous or intraperitoneal antibiotics?
- Did the individual require surgery? If so, what was found in the surgical exploration?

Regarding prognosis:

- What was the expected outcome?
- Did the individual have any complications (abscess formation, adhesions, sepsis, multisystem organ failure, etc) that would impact recovery?
- Does the individual have any underlying conditions that could impact ability to recover (cirrhosis, malnutrition, immune suppression, etc.)?

References

Peritonitis; Dialysis Associated. medelineplus. 01 Jan 2000. 1 Jan 2001 <http://medlineplus.adam.com/ency/article/000652.htm>.

Peritonitis; Secondary. medlineplus. 01 Jan 2000. 1 Jan 2001 <http://medlineplus.adam.com/ency/article/000651.htm>.

Peritonitis; Spontaneous. medlineplus. 01 Jan 2000. 1 Jan 2001 <http://medlineplus.adam.com/ency/article/000648.htm>.

Beers, Mark H., and Robert Berkow. The Merck Manual of Diagnosis and Therapy. Whitehouse Station, NJ: Merck and Co, Inc., 1999

Pernicious Anemia

Other names / synonyms: Addison's Pernicious Anemia, Vitamin B_{12} Deficiency Anemia

281.0

Definition

Pernicious anemia is a form of anemia resulting from the body's inability to absorb vitamin B_{12}, which is essential for the production of red blood cells. Vitamin B_{12} is not made in the body in sufficient amounts so must be absorbed from foods such as meat and eggs. In pernicious anemia, the inability to absorb vitamin B_{12} is due to an absence of a protein normally made in the stomach called intrinsic factor. It is more common in individuals with other autoimmune glandular deficiencies such as hypothyroidism, Type I diabetes mellitus, and celiac sprue.

Pernicious anemia occurs most often in older individuals, those of northern European descent, and blacks. It is also seen in anyone who has had a large part of the stomach removed, which results in a loss of the cells that make intrinsic factor.

Diagnosis

History: Pernicious anemia, like other anemias, may have nonspecific symptoms such as fatigue, dizziness, shortness of breath, and decreased exercise capacity. Symptoms specific to pernicious anemia include a smooth, sore tongue (glossitis), numbness and tingling of the hands and feet (neuropathy), weakness, trouble with coordination and balance (ataxia), memory disturbances, and depression.

Physical exam: Specific physical features of pernicious anemia include a smooth, "beefy red" tongue, an abnormal "broad-based" gait, imbalance, and a loss of vibration and position sense. Nonspecific features of the anemia may include pale skin and rapid respiratory and heart rates even at rest.

Tests: A complete blood count (CBC) shows low numbers of large red blood cells (macrocytic anemia) and sometimes low numbers of platelets and large white blood cells. The level of vitamin B_{12} in the blood is low, while blood levels of methylmalonic acid and homocysteine are usually high. Antibodies against the stomach cells (parietal cells) that make the intrinsic factor are almost always present. A bone marrow biopsy may be done if the diagnosis is in doubt and will show large numbers of large, immature red blood cells (megaloblastic erythroid hyperplasia). If vitamin B_{12} deficiency is documented but the reason for it is not clear, a Schilling test may also be done.

Treatment

Treatment of pernicious anemia is with regular injections of vitamin B_{12}. This is a lifelong treatment because the absorption defect itself cannot be corrected.

Prognosis

If diagnosed early, most individuals see a rapid improvement in symptoms once treatment begins. However, neurologic symptoms may take months to improve or they may progress and become permanent if the disease remains untreated for a long period of time.

Differential Diagnosis

Folic acid deficiency, malabsorption syndromes, hypothyroidism, excessive alcohol intake, and many drugs including anticonvulsants, methotrexate, and various cancer chemotherapy drugs can all produce a macrocytic anemia. Leukemia may also result in bone marrow biopsy findings similar to those in pernicious anemia.

Specialists

- Gastroenterologist
- Hematologist
- Neurologist

Work Restrictions / Accommodations

Individuals with pernicious anemia may require a reduction in physical activity until the condition is adequately treated. If neurologic complications occur, individuals may require more sedentary work.

Comorbid Conditions

Pancreatic insufficiency or any associated autoimmune disorders may lengthen disability.

Complications

There is an increased risk of developing stomach polyps and stomach cancer with pernicious anemia. It is also associated with other autoimmune disorders such as thyroid disease, adrenal gland insufficiency, and loss of skin pigment (vitiligo). Nonspecific complications of severe anemia include chest pain (angina pectoris) and congestive heart failure, especially in individuals with heart disease.

Factors Influencing Duration

The presence of neurologic problems, psychiatric symptoms, or autoimmune disorders can lengthen the period of disability. Initially, the individual requires sufficient time off to receive weekly vitamin B_{12} injections usually for about 6 weeks, then proceeds to once a month.

Length of Disability

Duration depends on severity of anemia. In most cases, no disability is expected. Disability may be permanent if neurologic disturbances do not resolve and the job requires significant physical activity or activities that require normal balance and gait.

Without complications.

Duration in Days

Job Classification	Minimum	Optimum	Maximum
Any work	3	7	14

Failure to Recover

If an individual fails to recover within the maximum duration expectancy period, the reader may wish to reference the following questions to assist in better understanding the specifics of an individual's medical case.

Regarding diagnosis:

- Does the individual have a history that would place them at risk for developing pernicious anemia? What is the individual's ethnic background? Has the individual had a large part of the stomach removed?
- Were appropriate diagnostic test done (CBC, serum B_{12} levels, bone marrow biopsy or Schilling test) to confirm the diagnosis and underlying cause?
- Have other conditions been ruled out (e.g., Folic acid deficiency, malabsorption syndromes, and drug effects including anticonvulsants, methotrexate, and various cancer chemotherapy drugs)?

Regarding treatment:

- Is the individual compliant with the treatment of B_{12} injections, if appropriate?
- Have appropriate drugs been eliminated as indicated?
- Have underlying malabsorption syndromes been addressed in the treatment plan?

Regarding prognosis:

- Does the individual have any existing conditions that could impact recovery such as pancreatic disease or autoimmune conditions?
- Have appropriate accommodations been made so the individual can return safely to work? Has the individual had any neurological complications? If so, have they been reassigned to sedentary work?
- Has the individual been trained to watch for symptoms of other conditions that could develop (i.e., stomach polyps, cancer, thyroid disease or renal insufficiency?

References

"Anemia: Production Deficits." Dale, D.C., and Daniel D. Federman, MD New York: WebMD Corporation, 2000 Scientific American Medicine. 01 Jan 2001 <http://www.samed.com/sam/forms/index.htm>.

Merenstein, A., and M. Schenkman. "Pernicious Anemia: The Disease and Physical Therapy Management. A Case Report." Physical Therapy 64 7 (1984): 1076-1077.

Petit Mal Epilepsy

Other names / synonyms: Absence Seizures, Absence Spells, Generalized Nonconvulsive Epilepsy, Minor Epilepsy

345.0

Definition

Typical petit mal seizures are extremely short in duration, lasting only a few seconds. Petit mal seizures appear as staring episodes or "absence spells." During one of these seizures, speech and activity cease. An individual experiencing a petit mal seizure may stop talking in mid-sentence, then complete the sentence one to several seconds later. Individuals fall if standing or walking at the onset of one of these seizures. The seizures may range from infrequent to quite frequent (many times per hour).

Atypical petit mal seizures start more slowly, are longer in duration, and may be associated with more noticeable muscle activity than typical petit mal seizures. Individuals usually have no memory of the seizure.

A cause for typical petit mal seizures is usually not identified. Typical petit mal seizures are not associated with other neurologic disorders, while atypical petit mal seizures may or may not be associated with other neurologic disorders.

Petit mal seizures occur in 2 out of 1,000 individuals. They are most common in those under 20 years of age.

Diagnosis

History: Individuals report symptoms of a typical petit mal seizure that include muscle activity changes (lack of movement, minor facial twitches, fluttering of the eyelids, lip smacking, and chewing motions) and consciousness changes (staring, lack of awareness of surroundings, sudden halt in speech or movement). Symptoms of atypical petit mal seizures include muscle activity changes (no muscle movement, slumping or loss of posture, loss of muscle tone, and falling) and consciousness changes (staring, lack of awareness of surroundings, sudden halt in speech or movement, and hand fumbling).

Physical exam: A complete physical and neurological examination usually reveals no abnormal findings, although individuals with atypical seizures may have some neurologic abnormalities.

Tests: A recording of the abnormal electrical activity of the brain during the seizures by electroencephalogram (EEG) may show changes typical of petit mal seizures. Atypical petit mal seizures have a different EEG pattern. Laboratory tests, x-rays, CT, or MRI may be used to rule out other causes of seizure.

Treatment

Goals of treatment include maximizing learning ability and preventing progression to more serious types of seizures. Treatment of any identifiable causes may decrease the number of seizures or eliminate seizures entirely.

Seizures may be eliminated or minimized by treatment with antiseizure (anticonvulsant) medications. Response to anticonvulsants varies widely with individuals. Changes in medication and dosage are made frequently in an effort to find a long-term medication and adjust the dose (titrate) of that medication to optimal blood levels.

Individuals who experience petit mal seizures should get proper rest every night (too little sleep is a major trigger for seizures) and should avoid smoking, alcohol, and caffeine.

Prognosis

Petit mal seizures are usually effectively controlled by medication. In some individuals, petit mal seizures may stop spontaneously, continue indefinitely, or may progress to grand mal seizures.

Individuals who go through a typical petit mal seizure experience a full recovery with no associated confusion. Most individuals with petit mal seizures lead a reasonably normal life with minimal activity restrictions.

Differential Diagnosis

Seizures can be associated with many types of conditions including head injury, brain infections (e.g., encephalitis and meningitis), brain tumor, stroke, drug intoxication, and withdrawal from alcohol, narcotics, cocaine, tranquilizers, and sleeping pills. Absence attacks can also be mimicked by attention deficit disorder.

Specialists

- Neurologist
- Neurosurgeon

Work Restrictions / Accommodations

Individuals with recurrent seizures may be restricted from driving or operating potentially dangerous machinery. Individuals taking medications that cause drowsiness may face the same restrictions. Special precautions (e.g., high railings or safety harnesses) should be taken for individuals working at heights.

Comorbid Conditions

Individuals with atypical petit mal seizures may have an underlying neurologic problem (congenital brain abnormalities, complications from kidney disease, liver disease, or brain injury) that causes the seizures.

Complications

Complications arising from petit mal seizures may include learning disabilities, injury from fall, injury caused by a seizure while driving or operating machinery, a type of petit mal seizure that lasts for several hours (absence status epilepticus), and progression to generalized tonic-clonic seizures (grand mal seizures). Hyperventilation (rapid breathing) may trigger seizures in some individuals.

Factors Influencing Duration

Disability may be influenced by the frequency of seizures or difficulty finding effective drugs the individual can tolerate. Injuries from falls or accidents suffered during a seizure may increase disability time. Progression to generalized tonic-clonic seizures may also increase disability time.

Length of Disability

With effective treatment and control of the seizures, there may be no disability. The length of disability would be the time necessary to stabilize medications. Duration of disability depends on job requirements.

Medical treatment.

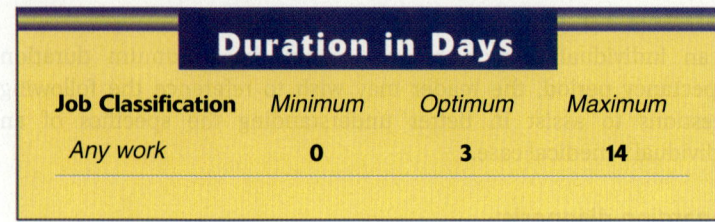

Duration in Days

Job Classification	Minimum	Optimum	Maximum
Any work	0	3	14

Failure to Recover

If an individual fails to recover within the maximum duration expectancy period, the reader may wish to reference the following questions to assist in better understanding the specifics of an individual's medical case.

Regarding diagnosis:

- Does the individual have short periods where he or she seems "absent?" Were these episodes reported by the family or the individual? How frequently do these occur?
- Is the neurologic examination normal?
- Has an EEG demonstrated abnormal brain wave activity? Has CT or MRI been done to rule out structural causes of seizures?
- Has the individual had a complete work-up, including psychiatric evaluation, to rule out other conditions with similar symptoms (i.e., head injury, brain infections, brain tumor, stroke, drug intoxication, and withdrawal from alcohol, narcotics, cocaine, tranquilizers, and sleeping pills)?

Regarding treatment:

- Has treatment with anticonvulsants lessened or stopped seizure activity?
- Does the individual get proper rest every night?
- Is the individual avoiding the use of alcohol, tobacco, and caffeine?
- Has there been progression to generalized tonic-clonic seizures? If so, has this condition been addressed in the treatment plan? Have adjustments been made in the medication?

Regarding prognosis:

- Has it been necessary to restrict the individual from driving or operating potentially dangerous machinery? Is the individual's employer able to accommodate these restrictions?

1632 The Medical Disability Advisor—Fourth Edition

- Does the individual have any underlying conditions that contribute to seizures (e.g., congenital brain abnormalities, complications from kidney disease, liver disease, or brain injury) been addressed in the treatment plan?

- Has the individual experienced any associated complications that could impact recovery and prognosis (learning disabilities, seizure-related trauma, status epilepticus, or grand mal seizures)?

References

Myslobodsky, Michael S., and Allan F. Mirsky. Elements of Petit Mal Epilepsy. Portland, OR: Book News, Inc, 1998.

Beers, Mark H., and Robert Berkow. The Merck Manual of Diagnosis and Therapy. Whitehouse Station, NJ: Merck and Co, Inc., 1999

Pharyngitis, Acute

Other names / synonyms: Infective Pharyngitis, Pneumococcal Pharyngitis, Sore Throat, Staphylococcal Pharyngitis, Suppurative Pharyngitis

462

Definition

Acute pharyngitis is a painful inflammation of the throat (pharynx).

Acute pharyngitis is most often caused by a viral infection (in 40-60% of cases), but can also be caused by bacteria (5-40%), most commonly group A Streptococcus (known as strep throat). Viral pharyngitis is often associated with the common cold or influenza. It may also be an early feature of mononucleosis. Pharyngitis can also be caused by swallowing substances that burn, irritate, or scratch the lining of the throat. Smoking or excess alcohol consumption can aggravate pharyngitis.

Acute pharyngitis is a common illness. The average adult in the US will experience streptococcal pharyngitis about once every 8 years, and will experience upper respiratory infections (which include pharyngitis) about twice a year. The incidence of acute pharyngitis is higher internationally, primarily due to higher rates of resistance of bacterial pharyngitis to antibiotics. Streptococcal pharyngitis is most prevalent in late fall through early spring.

Diagnosis

History: The individual may complain of a sore throat of varying duration, difficulty with or discomfort on swallowing, and slight fever. In addition, the individual may also report neck pain, nasal discharge, nasal congestion, joint stiffness, headache, and breath odor. In severe cases, the soft palate and throat may swell, making breathing and swallowing difficult.

Physical exam: Upon examination, the throat will appear red, raw, and inflamed. Tender or swollen lymph nodes in the neck may be noted. It is not possible to accurately and reliably distinguish between viral and bacterial pharyngitis on the basis of clinical signs alone; however, streptococcal pharyngitis is often associated with tonsillar swelling, swollen anterior cervical lymph nodes, a fever greater than 100.4 degrees Fahrenheit, and no cough.

Tests: A throat swab culture will be performed to determine whether the pharyngitis is bacterial and to identify the specific bacteria. A streptococcal screen or rapid antigen test may be done to identify Group A streptococcal infections.

Treatment

Viral pharyngitis usually clears up on its own without medication. Treatment is directed toward pain relief, and may include over-the-counter analgesics, such as ibuprofen or acetaminophen. The individual may gargle with warm salt water several times a day. Antibiotics are not useful in the treatment of viral pharyngitis.

If throat culture reveals a bacterial infection, treatment generally consists of a course of antibiotics. The most commonly prescribed antibiotic for bacterial pharyngitis is penicillin. In individuals who are sensitive to penicillin or who have a particularly resistant infection, other forms of antibiotic may be prescribed.

Prognosis

The prognosis is excellent for most cases. Most individuals are fully recovered within 10 days, often without any treatment. Viral pharyngitis, in particular, usually clears up on its own. Bacterial pharyngitis responds very well to appropriate antibiotic treatment.

Differential Diagnosis

Conditions that may present with similar symptoms include candidiasis, diphtheria, adult epiglottitis, gonorrhea, herpes simplex, mononucleosis, peritonsillar abscess, pneumonia, retropharyngeal abscess, rheumatic fever, allergic rhinitis with postnasal drip, airway obstruction, gastroesophageal reflux disease (GERD), and peritonsillar cellulitis.

Specialists

- Infectious Disease Physician
- Internist
- Otolaryngologist
- Primary Care Provider

Work Restrictions / Accommodations

Work restrictions or accommodations are not usually necessary for an individual with acute pharyngitis due to viral infection. Contact with co-workers should be minimized during the first few days of a bacterial infection to limit spread of the infection to others.

Comorbid Conditions

Comorbid conditions that may influence ability to recover include any conditions that compromise the individual's immune system (e.g., AIDS).

Complications

Untreated streptococcal throat infections may lead to a serious inflammation in the kidneys (glomerulonephritis), rheumatic fever, peritonsillar abscess, toxic shock syndrome, and airway obstruction due to swelling of the larynx. Other complications include sinusitis, ear infections, epiglottitis, mastoiditis, pneumonia, and recurrence due to bacterial resistance or failure to complete the full course of antibiotics.

Factors Influencing Duration

Length of disability is variable and may be influenced by the underlying infectious organism (viral versus bacterial), the response to treatment, or the presence of complications.

Length of Disability

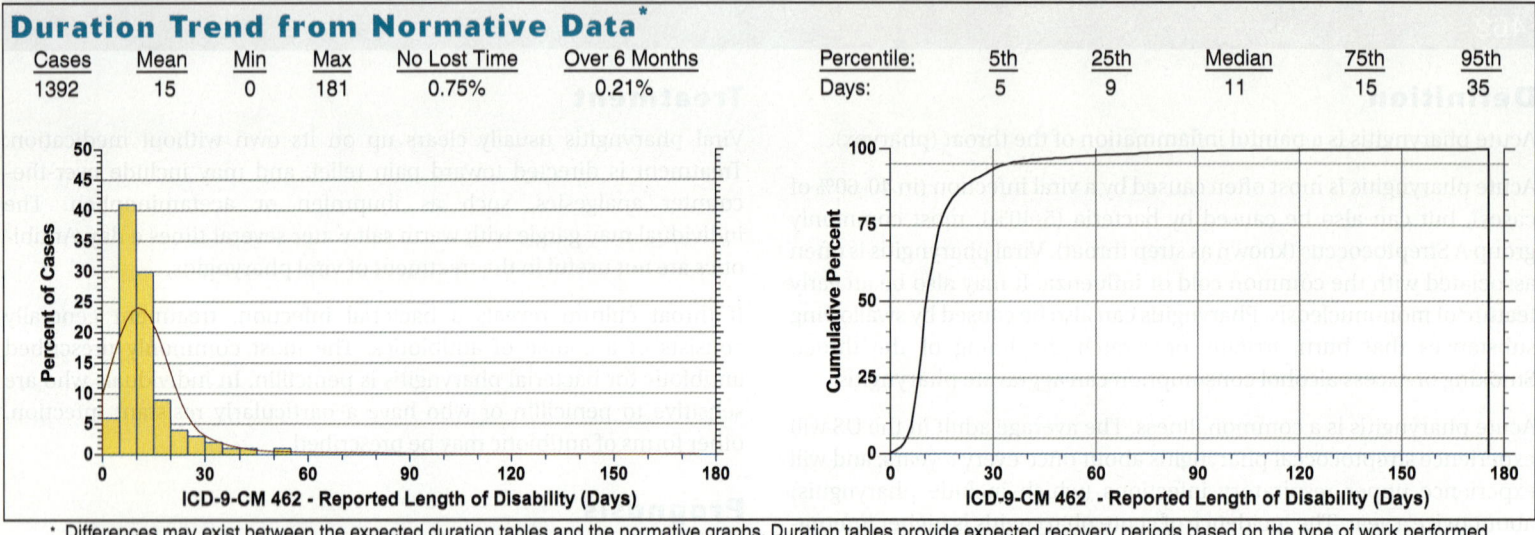

* Differences may exist between the expected duration tables and the normative graphs. Duration tables provide expected recovery periods based on the type of work performed by the individual. The normative graphs reflect the actual observed experience of many individuals across the spectrum of physical conditions, in a variety of industries, and with varying levels of case management.

Failure to Recover

If an individual fails to recover within the maximum duration expectancy period, the reader may wish to reference the following questions to assist in better understanding the specifics of an individual's medical case.

Regarding diagnosis:

- Did individual experience symptoms associated with acute pharyngitis?
- Was there a history of an infectious exposure, or ingestion of an irritant?
- Did individual have physical findings consistent with the diagnosis of strep throat? If so, was a throat culture or rapid antigen test done to confirm the diagnosis?
- If the diagnosis was uncertain, were other conditions with similar symptoms ruled out?

Regarding treatment:

- Were symptoms relieved with conservative measures?
- Has individual been compliant with treatment recommendations?
- Were appropriate antibiotics administered as indicated for bacterial infections?

Regarding prognosis:

- If individual was not recovering as expected, were neck or chest x-rays performed to rule out epiglottitis or airway compromise and pneumonia?
- Did individual take the entire course of antibiotics (for bacterial pharyngitis) exactly as prescribed?
- If bacterial pharyngitis was present, was the infection resistant to certain antibiotics?
- Is individual immunocompromised?
- Was any streptococcal infection treated promptly and appropriately? If not, has individual suffered any secondary inflammation resulting from lack of treatment such as serious inflammation in the kidneys (glomerulonephritis), rheumatic fever, peritonsillar abscess, toxic shock syndrome, or airway obstruction due to swelling of the larynx? Have these secondary conditions been addressed in the treatment plan?

> **Complementary and Alternative Therapies**
>
> Content is intended for awareness only. Treatments may or may not be effective. Scientific evidence may be lacking and some substances have potentially toxic effects. Dr. Presley Reed and the editors do not endorse the use of these therapies in the absence of consultation with a licensed medical professional.
>
> Antiseptic or antibacterial lozenges, sprays, mouthwashes, and gargles - May relieve sore throat pain.

References

"Guideline for the Diagnosis and Treatment of Acute Pharyngitis." The Alberta Clinical Practice Guidelines Program. 01 Jul 1999. 01 Jan 2001 <http://www.amda.ab.ca/cpg/catalogue/documents/infectious_diseases/pharyngitis/pharyngitis_guideline.html>.

Beers, Mark H., and Robert Berkow. The Merck Manual of Diagnosis and Therapy. Whitehouse Station, NJ: Merck and Co, Inc., 1999

Phencyclidine Abuse

Other names / synonyms: Angel Dust Abuse, PCP Abuse, Phencyclidine Addiction, Phencyclidine Dependence

305.3, 305.9

Definition

The phencyclidines (a group of drugs with pain-killing [analgesic], numbing [anesthetic], and hallucinogenic properties) include phencyclidine (PCP, Sernylan), ketamine, and others. PCP is mainly used in veterinary medicine, but has become popular as an illegally obtained recreational drug. These drugs can be taken orally, smoked, or injected intravenously, and produce a sensory deprivation syndrome by affecting the central nervous system. Small doses create a feeling of euphoria, while larger doses may cause irrational rages and violent actions (suicide, mutilation, assault, or homicide), convulsions (seizures), psychosis, coma, or death. Phencyclidine abuse occurs when an individual uses one or more of the these substances in a maladaptive way that includes a need for increased amounts of substance to achieve the desired effect (tolerance), using the substance in larger amounts or for longer periods of time than intended; a persistent, unsuccessful attempt to control use of the substance; giving up important activities in order to use the substance; continued use in spite of physical, emotional, occupational, legal, or relational difficulties related to phencyclidine use. Phencyclidine intoxication includes behavioral symptoms (such as belligerence, impulsiveness, unpredictability, or impaired judgment) and clinical symptoms (such as increased blood pressure or heart rate, uncoordinated muscle movements, or excessively sensitive hearing). There are currently no strongly established symptoms of withdrawal for phencyclidines. These behavioral symptoms may be related to disturbances in 2 brain chemicals, dopamine and serotonin. Males between 20-40 years are twice as likely as females of the same age to use phencyclidines, with about 3% of those of either gender over age 12 having ever used these drugs, and with the highest recent use (0.7%) being in the 12-17 year age range. Ethnic minorities are twice as likely to use these drugs, and three-fourths of phencyclidine-related emergency room visits are by males.

Diagnosis

Diagnosis is based on criteria listed in the DSM-IV-TR (Diagnostic and Statistical Manual of Mental Disorders, 4th Edition, Text Revision, published by the American Psychiatric Association). Phencyclidine abuse occurs when use of the drug is maladaptive in the following ways: There is a need for increased amounts of substance to achieve the desired effect (tolerance); use in larger amounts or for longer periods of time than intended; a persistent, unsuccessful attempt to control use; giving up important activities in order to continue use; or continued use in spite of physical, emotional, occupational, legal, or relational difficulties related to phencyclidine use; or the pattern of use during the past 12 months has caused a decline in interpersonal, occupational, and social functioning.

History: Since there may be no dramatic physical effects when the drug is withdrawn, the history is of great importance in establishing this diagnosis. Violence, agitation, and bizarre behaviors such as confused wandering may lead to multiple emergency room visits or legal and relationship problems. The individual may complain of visual or hearing disturbances or illusions.

Physical exam: If intoxicated when examined, the individual may exhibit fast, jerky sideways movements of the eyeballs (nystagmus), increased blood pressure or heart rate, significantly increased or decreased body temperature, decreased sensitivity to pain, hypersensitive hearing (hyperacusis), uncoordinated muscle movements, muscle rigidity, seizures, or coma. Other physical signs of chronic use might be evidence of injuries from accidents, fights, or falls. Needle tracks, hepatitis, HIV, or bacterial endocarditis might be present in individuals who inject phencyclidines intravenously.

Tests: Phencyclidines can be detected in the urine of those acutely intoxicated and may be detected for several weeks after use, since these drugs are fat-soluble. Muscle damage from falls and fights might show increased enzyme levels of CPK or SCOT. Hair analysis during active use detects PCP and its breakdown products (metabolites). If seizures occur, electroencephalogram (EEG) may be indicated.

Treatment

Abstinence is the treatment goal. Fatigue, restlessness, and depression may occur several days after quitting the drug. Although antidepressant medications can be helpful in combating the depressive symptoms, severely depressed individuals may become suicidal. For this reason, chronic users may need to be hospitalized during drug withdrawal. For individuals who experience delusions or hallucinations, antipsychotic medications such as haloperidol or chlorpromazine may be given to calm and relieve distress. Individuals in this condition often benefit from psychiatric hospitalization. Buspirone may be effective later in the withdrawal process.

In general, phencyclidine recovery can be described as occurring in 4 phases. Although there are no formally recognized withdrawal symptoms, there is usually a detoxification phase of a few days. During the second phase of abstinence, lasting about a month, the individual focuses on changing his or her behaviors. The early remission phase can last up to 12 months, and the sustained remission phase lasts as long as the individual abstains from phencyclidine use. The most effective treatments for phencyclidine dependence appear to be cognitive behavioral therapy and addiction education and support groups. These interventions are designed to help modify the individual's thinking, expectancies, and behaviors, and to increase coping skills for various life stressors. Early treatment, following detoxification, which usually occurs in an outpatient setting, may include education on physical, emotional, and mental aspects of addiction and recovery, identification of stressors and stress management skills, improved coping skills, assertiveness training, relaxation training, or individual or family psychotherapy. Ongoing structured self-help programs such as Narcotics Anonymous and Rational Recovery are recommended as an adjunct to treatment services. Regular but random drug screens may be part of the treatment process.

It should also be understood that relapse may occur, and may even be part of the recovery process. Medication therapy may include dopamine antagonists and/or antidepressants, as indicated by psychiatric or clinical evaluation. The only clearly accepted factors indicating need for inpatient substance abuse treatment are severe depression or psychotic symptoms lasting beyond 1-3 days after abstinence or repeated outpatient failures. Therefore, hospitalization may be necessary if the individual is violent towards others, suicidal, or is having severe withdrawal symptoms during detoxification.

Prognosis

Many individuals respond to treatment and stay in remission from substance abuse for many years. However, some individuals experience periods of relapse, in which they begin using phencyclidine after a period of remission, and again meet the criteria for substance abuse. There are other individuals who are never able to abstain from substance use/abuse and who do not experience any periods of remission. Individuals who are able to develop new relationships, and who consistently make use of self-help groups, are more likely to experience continued abstinence and achieve improvement in social and occupational functioning.

Factors usually associated with a more favorable outcome include a good occupational history, a group of supportive family and friends, older age of first use, motivation to change, lack of a criminal or antisocial lifestyle, and good psychosocial adjustment.

Overdose can cause coma and death.

Differential Diagnosis

Other substance abuse disorders, such as cocaine or amphetamine abuse, might appear similar, or the individual might abuse several substances, which makes it difficult to pinpoint behaviors specific to one substance. The individual might have a psychiatric disorder (bipolar disorder, major depressive disorder, schizophrenia) or a personality disorder (antisocial personality disorder, conduct disorder) that could present with similar behaviors at times. Neurological disorders such as brain injury, stroke, or metabolic encephalopathy could be associated with similar symptoms such as seizures, coma, hallucination, poor coordination, and/or muscle rigidity.

Specialists

- Advanced Practice Registered Nurse
- Cardiologist
- Neurologist
- Occupational Therapist
- Physical Therapist
- Psychiatrist
- Psychologist

Rehabilitation

In addition to substance abuse treatment and support groups, physical therapy might be helpful if the individual has chronic problems with gait and balance and if the individual has become deconditioned due to inactivity during period of addiction and early recovery. Occupational therapy could assist the individual to develop communication skills, identify and match personal skills and work habits to the work place, and learn how participation in leisure activities unrelated to drug use contributes to overall health and well being.

Work Restrictions / Accommodations

Many employers have systems in place for individuals recovering from alcohol dependence disorders to return to work under special contracts or conditions. These conditions may provide guidelines for random testing of blood and urine levels of identified substances and provide work performance and substance abuse treatment guidelines for the recovering individual.

Temporary work accommodations may include reducing or eliminating activities where the safety of self or others is contingent upon a constant and/or high level of alertness, such as driving motor vehicles, operating complex machinery, or handling dangerous chemicals; introducing the individual to new or stressful situations gradually under individually appropriate supervision; allowing some flexibility in scheduling to attend therapy appointments (which normally should occur during employee's personal time); promoting planned, proactive management of identified problem areas; and offering timely feedback on job performance issues. It will be helpful if accommodations are documented in a written plan designed to promote timely and safe transition back to full work productivity.

If the individual has medical complications of phencyclidine abuse, such as cardiac, liver, or nervous system damage, he/she may need to be restricted to sedentary type activities.

Comorbid Conditions

Coexisting conditions that may affect recovery and lengthen disability include the abuse of or dependence on alcohol or other substances, the presence of psychiatric illnesses such as bipolar disorder or schizophrenia, infection with hepatitis B or C or HIV, or heart, nervous system or kidney complications. The combination of a psychiatric illness with substance abuse (dual diagnosis) can complicate the treatment of both the chemical dependency as well as the psychiatric illness. Up to 90% of the individuals diagnosed with a clinical psychiatric disorder also report a substance use disorder during their lifetime. Approximately 1/3 of hospitalized psychiatric individuals have coexisting substance use disorders not involving nicotine.

Complications

Other psychiatric illnesses may complicate treatment of the phencyclidine abuse, while the substance use disorder complicates treatment of the other illness (dual diagnosis). About one-half of those with bipolar mood (affective) disorder or schizophrenia are thought to have drug or alcohol problems. Those with posttraumatic stress disorder may have substance abuse rates as high as 80%. The individual may experience psychological problems including disinhibition, anxiety, rage, aggression, panic, or flashbacks. Medical problems may include fever (hyperthermia), increased heart rate (tachycardia), increased blood pressure (hypertension), or seizures. Intravenous use may lead to skin infections, bacterial endocarditis, HIV, or hepatitis. Respiratory problems might include bronchospasm, periods of not breathing (apnea), or aspiration during coma. Kidney (renal) impairment is seen in about 2% of those seeking emergency care.

Factors Influencing Duration

Length of disability is influenced by the duration and severity of phencyclidine abuse, presence or absence of organ damage, any underlying mental illness, other substance abuse, the individual's social support system, appropriateness of treatment choice, compliance with treatment, motivation to change, and adequacy of ongoing care.

Length of Disability

Maximum duration includes hospitalization. After an initial detoxification period of a few days, which usually does not require hospitalization, the individual is usually ready to return to work, as long as accommodations are made for continued participation in a treatment program.

Duration in Days

Job Classification	Minimum	Optimum	Maximum
Any work	7	14	28

Failure to Recover

If an individual fails to recover within the maximum duration expectancy period, the reader may wish to reference the following questions to assist in better understanding the specifics of an individual's medical case.

Regarding diagnosis:

- Did the individual's evaluation include detailed history of past and present substance use, including its effects on cognitive, psychological, behavioral, and physiologic functioning; general medical and psychiatric history and examination; history of prior psychiatric treatments with outcomes; family and social history; screening of blood, breath, or urine for abused substances; and other laboratory tests to help confirm the presence or absence of comorbid conditions frequently associated with substance use disorders. If not, what areas were omitted?

- Would this information affect the current treatment plan? What changes should be made?

- Have all underlying medical and psychiatric disorders been identified or ruled out?

Regarding treatment:

- Since phencyclidine abuse may lead to irrational or violent behavior and multiple emergency room visits before the individual is ready to seek treatment for substance abuse, what brought individual to treatment this time?

- Does treatment include detoxification, behavioral therapies, and regular attendance at support groups such as Narcotics Anonymous or Rational Recovery?

- Has this individual experienced any psychotic symptoms?

- Was drug therapy effective?

- Would individual benefit from psychiatric hospitalization?

- Is individual involved in a cognitive behavioral therapy program?

- Does this therapy appear to be helping to modify the individual's thinking, expectancies, and behaviors, and increase coping skills for various life stressors?

- Does individual's treatment plan consider all underlying psychiatric or general medical conditions, gender-related factors (including the possibility of pregnancy), social and living environment, cultural factors, and family characteristics? If current treatment plan does not take these factors into consideration, what changes could be made to better meet this individual's needs?

- Is the individual currently in a period of high relapse risk, such as the early stages of treatment, periods of transition to less intensive levels of care, or the first year after completion of active treatment? Is an intensive monitoring system for substance use in place during these periods of high relapse risk?

- Are the individual's needs being effectively met?

Regarding prognosis:

- Is the individual currently involved in a support group such as Narcotics Anonymous or Rational Recovery?

- Does the individual participate in a formal support group that provides the external support and motivation to continue in treatment beyond the initial stage of detoxification?

- What other support systems does individual have in place? Family? Friends?

- Is the individual improving in social and occupational functioning?

- Does the individual have the necessary tools, skills, and encouragement to move ahead with his or her life?

References

Fishbein, D.H., Y. Nakahara, et al. "Female PCP-using Jail Detainees: Proneness to Violence and Gender Differences." Addictive Behavior 21 2 (1996): 155-172.

Giannini, A.J., R.H. Loiselle, et al. "Behavioral Response to Buspirone in Cocaine and Phencyclidine Withdrawal." Journal of Substance Abuse Treatment 10 6 (1993): 523-527.

Pheochromocytoma

Other names / synonyms: Paraganglioma, Pheochromoblastoma, Tumor of the Adrenal Medulla

227.0, M8700/0

Definition

Pheochromocytoma is a tumor of the adrenal gland that causes excess release of two hormones, epinephrine and norepinephrine that regulate heartbeat and blood pressure. Although most pheochromocytomas are noncancerous (benign), their excessive production of the two hormones (catecholamines) causes high blood pressure (hypertension) and increased cardiac output, putting a severe strain on the heart, if not diagnosed and treated. Thirteen percent of pheochromocytomas are cancerous (malignant).

The tumor may be single or multiple and usually develops in the center or core (medulla) of one or both adrenal glands. Sometimes, the tumors occur outside the adrenal gland, usually within the abdomen (along the carotid artery or in the wall of the urinary bladder).

Pheochromocytomas may occur at any age, but they occur most frequently in young to mid-adult life individuals and slightly more often in women than in men. A typical clinical feature of pheochromocytoma is a sudden attack of symptoms (paroxysm). The paroxysm may become frequent but sporadic, and may increase in frequency, duration, and severity. The tumors have been associated with various neurologic disorders and with the cancerous condition, medullary carcinoma of the thyroid.

According to reports issued by the Centers for Disease Control and Prevention (CDC) in 1998, 22,000 cases of pheochromocytoma were diagnosed in the United States. More than twice as many cases (16,000) were diagnosed in women than in men (6,000).

Diagnosis

History: Symptomatic individuals almost always have sustained or intermittent high blood pressure (hypertension) and most often present with headache, heart palpitations, and excessive, inappropriate perspiration. A recent study revealed that the absence of all three of these symptoms in individuals who presented with hypertension virtually ensured that pheochromocytoma was absent.

Less commonly encountered symptoms include nervousness and anxiety, tremor, extreme paleness of complexion (pallor), nausea, weakness, exhaustion, fatigue, chest or abdominal pains, visual disturbances, decreased blood pressure with changes in position (orthostatic hypotension), and weight loss.

In up to 50% of individuals with pheochromocytoma, the symptoms (which are due to the high levels of the two hormones, epinephrine and norepinephrine) occur suddenly in an outburst (paroxysm).

Physical exam: Elevated blood pressure (hypertension), rapid heart rate, and orthostatic hypotension may be noted during a physical examination.

Tests: Tests include an adrenal biopsy that shows pheochromocytoma, adrenal medullary imaging (MIBG scintiscan) that shows tumors, an magnetic resonance imaging (MRI) scan of the abdomen that shows adrenal mass, an abdominal computed tomography (CT) scan that shows adrenal mass, tests that measure level of adrenal hormones in urine (urine metanephrine and urine catecholamines), a glucose test, and a blood test that measures levels of catecholamines.

Treatment

The treatment for pheochromocytoma is removal of the tumor by surgery. Continuous monitoring of all vital signs is necessary in the postoperative period in an intensive care unit. Stabilization of the individual's vital signs with medication prior to surgery is important and may require hospitalization. In the case of an inoperable tumor, management with medication is necessary. Radiation therapy or chemotherapy have not been shown to be effective in destroying the tumor.

Prognosis

In individuals with benign tumors, the five-year survival rate after surgery is 95% with a recurrence rate of less than ten percent. Hormone secretion levels of norepinephrine and epinephrine return to normal after surgery.

In individuals with malignant tumors, the 5-year survival after surgery is less than 50%.

Differential Diagnosis

Differential diagnosis may include excessive production of the thyroid hormone (thyrotoxicosis) and acute intracranial disturbances (subarachnoid hemorrhage) that cause or simulate catecholamine excess. (Catecholamine is a neurotransmitter-like substance.)

Also, certain drugs have been associated with pheochromocytoma symptoms. Examples include self-administered epinephrine or isoproterenol (especially when self-administered), abrupt withdrawal from clonidine (which can provoke a sympathoadrenal discharge with "rebound" blood pressure elevation), and MAO inhibitors, which may lead to hypertensive crises if ingested with foods rich in tyramine. MAO inhibitors are used to treat depression.

Specialists

- Endocrinologist
- General Surgeon

Work Restrictions / Accommodations

Extended work leave for recovery from surgery and recuperation may be required. After recuperation from surgery, chemotherapy, and radiation therapy, return to normal work can be expected for individuals with benign tumors. For individuals with malignant tumors, return to work may be delayed. Some individuals may not return to work.

Comorbid Conditions

Comorbid conditions that might influence the length of disability include obesity, diabetes mellitus, and heart disease.

Complications

Potential complications associated with the development of pheochromocytoma include severe high blood pressure (hypertension), heart problems, cardiac arrest, and diabetes mellitus.

Factors Influencing Duration

Factors that might influence length of disability include the type of tumor (benign or malignant), the extent of surgery necessary to remove the tumor, and the development of complications.

Length of Disability

Surgical treatment and chemotherapy.

Job Classification	Minimum	Optimum	Maximum
Sedentary work	28	42	56
Light work	28	42	56
Medium work	28	42	84
Heavy work	42	49	168
Very Heavy work	42	49	168

Duration in Days

Failure to Recover

If an individual fails to recover within the maximum duration expectancy period, the reader may wish to reference the following questions to assist in better understanding the specifics of an individual's medical case.

Regarding diagnosis:

- Did the individual present with a history of hypertension and headaches?
- Was an adrenal mass detected with abdominal ultrasound, CT or MRI?
- Was the diagnosis confirmed with an adrenal gland biopsy?
- If the diagnosis was uncertain were other conditions with similar symptoms considered (i.e., primary or essential hypertension, drug effect, thyrotoxicosis, intracranial disorders)?
- Would the individual benefit from consultation with an endocrinologist?

Regarding treatment:

- Was surgery indicated? Have hormone secretion levels of norepinephrine and epinephrine returned to normal after surgery?
- If the mass was inaccessible, was medication therapy effective at controlling symptoms?

Regarding prognosis:

- Did the symptoms persist despite treatment? If so, has the individual been re-evaluated to rule out the possibility of recurrence?
- Was malignancy detected? What was the expected outcome?
- Did the individual have any postoperative complications such as hypertensive crisis, cardiac arrest or heart disease that could impact recovery and prognosis?
- Does individual have underlying conditions such as cancer, neurological disorders, or heart disease that may impact recovery?

References

Endocrinology - Pheochromocytoma. Vanderbilt University Medical Center. 16 Jun 1998. 21 Jan 2001 <http://www.mc.vanderbilt.edu/peds/pidl/endocr/pheochr.htm>.

Wilson, Jean D. Williams Textbook of Endocrinology, 9th ed. Philadelphia: W.B. Saunders Company, 1998 21 Jan 2001 <http://home.mdconsult.com/ >.

Phobias, Specific

Other names / synonyms: Acrophobia, Claustrophobia, Isolated Phobia, Simple Phobia, Specific Phobia

300.29

Definition

Individuals with specific phobias have unwarranted and intense fears of specific objects or situations. The most common phobias are of animals (zoophobia), blood (hemophobia), heights (acrophobia), travel by airplane (aerophobia), being closed in (claustrophobia), and thunderstorms (keraunophobia). Others include spiders (arachnophobia), strangers (xenophobia), and crowds (agoraphobia).

The anxiety produced by exposure to one of these objects or situations may be a panic attack or more generalized anxiety, but it is always directed at something specific. Individuals with this disorder also worry about what they might do (i.e., faint, panic, or lose control) if they have to confront the feared stimulus. The symptoms often get worse when the individual is closer to the source of their fear. Individuals with specific phobias involving blood, injury, or injection often faint because of a "vasovagal response" associated with reduced heart rate and blood pressure.

Adolescents and adults may acknowledge that their fears are unrealistic, but remain fearful nonetheless. The fear usually leads to avoiding the situation, but it may sometimes be endured with great discomfort. The fear and avoidance may lead to significant distress or impairment in personal, social, or occupational functioning. The phobia might have developed after a first-hand experience of being injured, or after witnessing another person become injured.

Fear is usually not of the object itself, but to the imagined harmful consequences resulting from contact with the object. For example, those with a snake phobia are afraid of being bitten, while those with claustrophobia are afraid of suffocation or of being trapped forever.

Among the general population, specific phobia is one of the most frequently reported of the anxiety disorders. Approximately 10% of adults in the US have suffered, to some degree, from a specific phobia, although they may not always meet criteria for clinical diagnosis. While fear of animals, heights, or water usually begins in childhood, onset is usually in the late teens or early twenties. More women than men have specific phobias.

This diagnosis is not made if symptoms are part of another mental disturbance such as panic disorder, posttraumatic stress disorder, or obsessive-compulsive disorder.

Diagnosis

History: According to the Diagnostic and Statistical Manual of Mental Disorders IV, Text Revision (DSM-IV-TR), the following criteria are necessary for this diagnosis to be made: The individual experiences a persistent and unreasonable fear, provoked by a specific situation or object. The fear stimulus almost always immediately provokes an anxiety response. The fear is out of proportion and unreasonable, and the individual realizes this. The individual either avoids the fear stimulus or endures it with severe anxiety or stress. Either there is marked distress about the fear, or the fear markedly impairs personal, social, academic, or occupational functioning. The symptoms are not better explained by another anxiety or mental disorder. For those younger than 18, the phobia must be present for at least 6 months.

Physical exam: The physical exam, if done at the time of a phobic response to needle injections, can show a very slow heart rate and low blood pressure (vasovagal reaction).

Tests: Tests are not diagnostic for this disorder, although projection tests such as the Rorschach or Thematic Apperception Test, or personality inventories such as the Minnesota Multiphasic Personality Inventory, may assist in diagnosis.

Treatment

The treatment of choice is exposure therapy to the feared object or situation, which is also known as systematic desensitization. This therapy is for those who are truly committed to change. It involves specific objectives and strategies, and could begin just by imagining contact with the source of fear, proceeding to real life contact. Exposure is usually gradually increased, but can also be done suddenly ("flooding"). Exposure therapy is done individually or as a group. As expected, the treatment plan depends on the individual's specific phobia. For example, a claustrophobic person may need to practice being in a confined space, while an individual who is afraid of animals may be asked to own a pet during the course of therapy. Insight-oriented psychotherapy is used less frequently. Beta-blocking drugs may be useful in the treatment of anxiety symptoms associated with specific phobia. If the phobic symptoms include panic attacks, antianxiety medication and serotonin-specific reuptake inhibitors (SSRI), or tricyclic antidepressants may be used.

Prognosis

Even with proper treatment, only one of five phobias that begin in childhood and extend into adulthood resolve completely.

Differential Diagnosis

Other possible diagnoses include social phobia, panic disorder, posttraumatic stress disorder, acute stress disorder, obsessive-compulsive disorder, separation anxiety disorder, hypochondriasis, Tourette's syndrome, or a psychotic disorder.

Specialists

- Licensed Clinical Social Worker
- Psychiatrist
- Psychologist

Work Restrictions / Accommodations

Time-limited restrictions and work accommodations should be individually determined based on the characteristics of the individual's response to the disorder, the functional requirements of the job and work environment, and the flexibility of the job and work site. The purpose of the restrictions/accommodations is to help maintain the worker's capacity to remain at the workplace without a work disruption or to promote timely and safe transition back to full work productivity. Specific accommodations may vary depending on the phobia, such as avoiding cramped work environments in individuals with claustrophobia, or dealing with the public in individuals with xenophobia.

Comorbid Conditions

The presence of a personality disorder or other psychiatric illness might further lengthen disability.

Complications

With fear of needles, medical and dental health may be neglected due to avoidance of necessary care. Suicidal thoughts are more common in individuals with specific phobias than in the general population, but actual suicide attempts suggest another accompanying psychiatric disorder. There can be impairments in personal, social, academic, or occupational functioning, and the individual may be unaware that this is due to the phobia. The presence of a personality disorder may also complicate this disorder.

Factors Influencing Duration

The length of disability may be affected by the severity and nature of the phobia, length of time the individual has suffered from the phobia, age of onset, and presence or absence of financial and social support systems.

Length of Disability

This condition should not be disabling unless the phobic object or situation is encountered at work. Length of disability depends upon how the phobia affects the individual's work or social life. Most individuals do not seek help unless work life is adversely affected. Most individuals avoid situations that would put them in contact with the feared object or situation, so disability is not an issue.

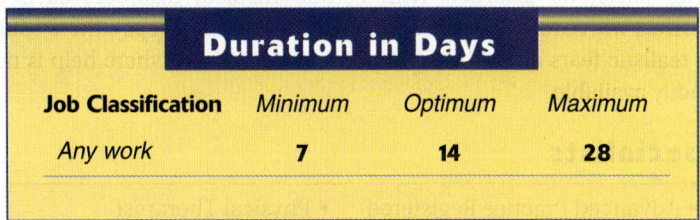

Job Classification	Minimum	Optimum	Maximum
Any work	7	14	28

Failure to Recover

If an individual fails to recover within the maximum duration expectancy period, the reader may wish to reference the following questions to assist in better understanding the specifics of an individual's medical case.

Regarding diagnosis:

- Does the individual fit the criteria of specific phobia?
- Has the diagnosis been confirmed?
- If the individual does not recognize that the fear is excessive or unreasonable, could the individual have a delusional disorder instead?

Regarding treatment:

- Has current therapy helped individual confront and overcome his/her fear?
- Is the therapist trained in cognitive-behavioral therapy?
- Is the therapist experienced in working with individuals with phobias?
- Has the individual been taught skills needed for other social situations?
- Is the individual involved in behavioral group therapy as well as individual therapy?

Regarding prognosis:

- If current therapy does not appear to be effective, what changes can be made?
- Is the individual's ability to function greatly impaired?
- Since specific phobias do not usually interfere with daily life or cause as much distress as most other anxiety disorders, should diagnosis be reviewed?

References

Anxiety Disorders - Phobias. National Institute of Mental Health. 10 Jul 2000. 11 July 2000 <http://www.nimh.nih.gov/anxiety/anxiety/phobia/index.htm>.

Let's Talk Facts About Phobias. American Psychiatric Association. 1999. 11 July 2000 <http://www.psych.org/public_info/phobias.cfm>.

Morrison, James. DSM-IV Made Easy. New York: Guilford, 1995.

Allen, Francis. Diagnostic and Statistical Manual of Mental Disorders, 4th ed, text revision. Washington, DC: American Psychiatric Association, 2000.

Phobic Disorders

Other names / synonyms: Simple Phobias, Specific Phobias
300.2

Definition

Phobias are intense, excessive, irrational fears provoked by a situation or object. The fear response may include all the symptoms of extreme anxiety including panic (a pounding heartbeat, sweating, shortness of breath, and a sense of impending doom). Fear may be experienced just by the anticipation of coming in contact with the source of fear. The individual will make every effort to avoid the feared situation or object due to the discomfort associated with it. This can interfere with daily routines, job functioning, or social life. Individual realizes these fears are unreasonable but feels unable to control them or his or her emotions. The intensity of the feelings may increase as the feared object approaches and decrease as the object leaves, or may vary from time to time.

There are several subtypes of specific phobias including the fear of animals or insects (animal type); fear of storms, heights, or water (natural environment type); fear of blood, injections, the sight of a bodily injury, or other medical procedure (blood-injection-injury type); fear of heights (acrophobia); fear of enclosed spaces (claustrophobia); fear of another specific situation such as tunnels, bridges, stairs, or flying in airplanes (situational type); fear of being watched or humiliated while doing something in front of others (social phobia); or fear of choking, loud sounds, or falling down when not next to walls (other type). Cultural differences can affect the content of phobias such as the fear of magic or spirits in some cultures.

Women are twice as likely as men to experience phobias. Approximately 75-90% of individuals with animal and environmental-type phobias are female and 55-70% of individuals with blood-injection-injury phobias are female. Prevalence of phobias in the population ranges from 5-11% depending on the type of survey. Phobias are the most common psychiatric illness among women of all ages and the second most common illness among men older than age 25.

Diagnosis

History: The individual has a history of persistent, excessive, or unreasonable fear triggered by a specific object or situation (e.g., flying, heights, animals or insects, or seeing blood). The fear appears immediately on contact with the dreaded circumstance and can occur even with imagined contact. Associated feelings may include panic, dread, horror, or terror. The individual realizes that the fear is excessive or unreasonable and goes beyond the actual threat of danger. Reactions to the fear are automatic and uncontrollable, taking over the individual's thoughts. They may include rapid heartbeat, shortness of breath, trembling, and an overwhelming desire to flee the situation. Phobias result in the individual making great efforts to avoid the phobic situation.

There can be subtle or obvious impairment in the personal, social, academic, or occupational life. The individual may report that job promotions are held back due to fear of flying or that social activities are restricted by fears of crowded places.

Specific phobias frequently coexist with other psychiatric disorders for which an individual seeks treatment. Individuals with blood-injection-injury type phobia may report episodes of fainting (vasovagal response) when having blood specimens drawn or receiving injections.

Physical exam: The exam can document changes in respiratory and heart rates when the feared situation is imagined or encountered.

Tests: Tests do not contribute to these diagnoses although personality tests such as the Minnesota Multiphasic Personality Inventory may provide content concerning specific sources of phobia and symptoms of anxiety.

Treatment

Phobias are usually treated with behavioral therapy gradually exposing the individual to the feared situation. Antianxiety medication, beta-blockers, and serotonin-specific reuptake inhibitor antidepressants are frequently given. The goals of cognitive therapy are to suggest that the danger is not as extreme as perceived, and to teach the individual effective ways to reduce anxiety and view fearful situations differently.

Relaxation training, progressive muscle relaxation, and respiratory control training may be done. Many therapists include homework and specific readings (bibliotherapy) for the individual to do between sessions. Since the individual may only spend a few sessions in one-on-one contact with a therapist, this method allows the individual to continue to work on his or her own with the aid of a printed manual.

Psychodynamic treatment refers to another "talk therapy" where the therapist and individual work together to uncover underlying emotional conflicts. Although this type of therapy may help relieve the stress that contributes to panic attacks, there is no scientific evidence this form of therapy by itself is effective in overcoming panic disorder or agoraphobia. However, if a phobic disorder occurs along with another emotional disturbance, psychodynamic therapy may be a helpful addition to the overall treatment plan. Therapy groups can also be helpful.

Prognosis

Many of the specific phobias first appear in childhood and may disappear in adulthood. Only about 20% of phobias that persist in adulthood disappear without treatment and only 12-30% of individuals with phobias seek treatment. Fortunately, phobias are very treatable. Many individuals who seek treatment completely overcome their fears for life. Studies from the National Institute of Mental Health report a 90% success rate when using cognitive therapy and a behavioral therapy group.

Differential Diagnosis

Other possibilities are acute stress disorder, post-traumatic stress disorder, generalized anxiety disorder, avoidant personality disorder, obsessive-compulsive disorder, hypochondriasis, schizophrenia, or other psychotic disorder. With certain medical disorders such as diarrhea with Crohn's disease or convulsions with epilepsy, there could be realistic fears about being in public in situations where help is not readily available.

Specialists

- Advanced Practice Registered Nurse
- Internist
- Occupational Therapist
- Physical Therapist
- Psychiatrist
- Psychologist

Work Restrictions / Accommodations

Time-limited restrictions and work accommodations should be individually determined based on the characteristics of the individual's response to the disorder, the functional requirements of the job and work environment, and the flexibility of the job and work site. The purpose of the restrictions/accommodations is to help maintain the worker's capacity to remain at the workplace without a work disruption or to promote timely and safe transition back to full work productivity. Specific accommodations may vary depending on the phobia, such as avoiding cramped work environments in individuals with claustrophobia, or dealing with the public in individuals with xenophobia.

Comorbid Conditions

Coexisting conditions that most often affect recovery and lengthen disability are depression and substance abuse. Rates of occurrence with other disorders range from 50-80%. Other coexisting conditions that may affect recovery and lengthen disability include panic disorder and agoraphobia. Medical conditions often occurring with phobic disorders include peptic ulcer, hypertension, skin rashes, tooth grinding, hemorrhoids, headaches, muscle aches, and heart disease.

Complications

Limitation and impairment in personal, social, academic, or occupational functioning can result from avoidance of fearful situations. A major depressive disorder can be a complication.

Factors Influencing Duration

Substance abuse, underlying mental illness, individual's social support system, appropriateness of treatment choice, response to medications, compliance with treatment, and adequacy of ongoing care can influence disability. Disability will be influenced by the individual's motivation to resolve the phobia if it involves work-related triggers such as flying or public speaking.

Length of Disability

Phobias are seldom disabling except when associated with workplace or other disorder. Most individuals do not seek help unless work life is adversely affected; therefore, length of disability depends on how the phobia affects the individual's work or social life. Most individuals avoid employment that would put them in contact with the feared object or situation so disability is usually not a factor.

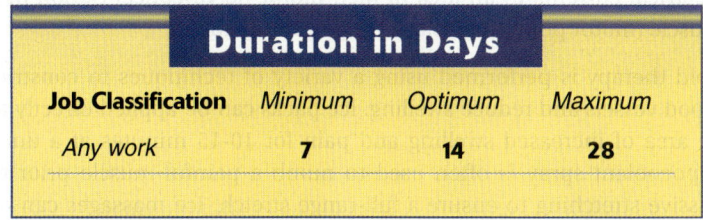

Job Classification	Minimum	Optimum	Maximum
Any work	7	14	28

Failure to Recover

If an individual fails to recover within the maximum duration expectancy period, the reader may wish to reference the following questions to assist in better understanding the specifics of an individual's medical case.

Regarding diagnosis:

- Does the individual fit the criteria for phobia?
- Has a diagnosis of phobic disorder been confirmed?
- If the individual does not recognize that the fear is excessive or unreasonable, could it be a delusional disorder instead?
- Have other psychological disorders been ruled out?
- Have medical disorders with similar symptoms been ruled out?

Regarding treatment:

- Does the phobia interfere with daily living and create extreme disability?
- Would the individual benefit from antidepressant drug therapy?
- Is the therapist trained in cognitive-behavioral therapy?
- Does the therapist have experience working with phobias?
- Is the individual involved in a therapy that helps confront the object of fear and overcome it?
- Has the individual been taught skills needed for other social situations?

Regarding prognosis:

- Do symptoms persist despite treatment?
- Is the individual's ability to function greatly impaired?
- Is the individual involved in a combination of cognitive and behavioral therapy? Group as well as individual?
- If current therapy does not appear to be effective, what changes can be made?
- Should diagnosis be revisited?

References

Allen, Francis. Diagnostic and Statistical Manual of Mental Disorders, 4th ed, text revision. Washington, DC: American Psychiatric Association, 2000.

Let's Talk Facts About Phobias. American Psychiatric Association. 1999. 11 July 2000 <http://www.psych.org/public_info/phobias.cfm>.

Physical Therapy

Other names / synonyms: Physical Medicine, Physical Rehabilitation, Physiotherapy, PT, Therapeutic Exercise

93.0, 93.01, 93.02, 93.03, 93.04, 93.05, 93.06, 93.07, 93.09, 93.1, 93.11, 93.12, 93.13, 93.14, 93.15, 93.16, 93.17, 93.18, 93.19, 93.2, 93.21, 93.22, 93.23, 93.24, 93.25, 93.26, 93.27, 93.28, 93.29, 93.3, 93.31, 93.32, 93.33, 93.34, 93.35, 93.36, 93.37, 93.38

Definition

Physical therapy is the profession concerned with the evaluation, treatment, and prevention of physical disabilities caused by disease or injury. This medical discipline is used as a conservative measure prior to, in conjunction with, or following other treatment options such as medicines or surgery. Physical therapy is practiced in hospitals, rehabilitation centers, private offices of physical therapists, extended-care facilities, home health agencies, special diagnostic clinics in outpatient treatment centers, academic institutions, fitness and wellness centers, and research centers.

Physical therapy as a profession has been recognized in the US for 75 years. The profession's main focus at that time was the rehabilitation of individuals from diseases such as polio. Since that time, physical therapy has branched out from traditional areas such as orthopedics and neurology into areas such as women's health, ergonomics, and cardiopulmonary disease. Physical therapy is practiced throughout the world, with teams of visiting therapists from Europe and the US traveling to developing nations to provide instruction on therapeutic techniques as well as equipment such as crutches and prosthetic limbs.

Physical therapy uses a wide variety of techniques ranging from soft tissue massage to acupressure to help restore and improve flexibility of muscles, tendons, and joints. Physical therapy also uses various forms of techniques for soft tissue healing such as hydrotherapy, electrical stimulation, application of cold and the application of heat through the use of shortwave diathermy, microwave, and ultrasound. Therapeutic exercise is an important part of physical therapy, helping to strengthen muscles and joints weakened by disease and injury.

Reason for Procedure

The goal of physical therapy is to enhance human movement and function and to assess, prevent, and treat movement dysfunction and physical disability. Many individuals are advised to obtain physical therapy services while recovering from surgery, accidents, and illnesses. Physical therapy can help improve mobility in the older individuals when effects of disease are coupled with a decrease in physical activity. It is used successfully to prevent abnormal scarring and loss of movement from potential sources of musculoskeletal dysfunction that also are associated with pain, edema, weakness, fatigue, and tissue degeneration.

Physical therapy is used in treating burn victims to preserve normal joint motion. It is used in spinal cord injuries to optimize function and strength of paralyzed or weak limbs and with stroke victims to help them relearn ordinary life skills. Cancer patients use physical therapy to build strength and relieve discomfort. Therapeutic exercise prescribed by a physical therapist is believed to enhance traditional medical and surgical treatment. For example, individuals undergoing heart surgery are found to recover more quickly when exercise is included in their recovery regimen.

Description

In general, physical therapy begins with a referral from a physician with a specific diagnosis and, often, particular treatments are recommended. On the first visit, the physical therapist will conduct an evaluation assessing the individual's medical history, range of motion, strength, neurological involvement, and functional level. The therapist and the individual treated make both short-term and long-term goals. Next, a plan of care is written up by the therapist and discussed with the individual. From that point on the therapist will decide (if not already noted by the physician) how frequent and for what period of time the individual will be seen in physical therapy.

If pain and swelling are included in the individual's diagnosis, then procedures such as electrical stimulation, cryotherapy, and ultrasound may be used. Once pain and swelling have subsided, the therapy will progress with focus placed on returning range of motion and strength. The final step is to incorporate activities helping the individual return to home or their previous work environment. A home program will be started at the time of the evaluation with gradual progression in difficulty up to the date of discharge. Patient education is also an important aspect of the physical therapy program.

Specific manual and mechanical therapeutic techniques are employed by the physical therapist as determined by the diagnosis and the symptoms.

Massage therapy is a manual method of treatment helping restore movement and function of muscles and joints by improving circulation and eliminating metabolic toxins that are stored within muscles. In this technique, the therapist rubs the individual's muscles with massage lotion, first using broad, light strokes and then focusing on specific points of tightness or tenderness with deeper, more concentrated pressure. Treatment time can vary from 2 minutes for cross-friction massage to up to 1 hour for intensive massage therapy.

Acupressure is a manual technique that consists of pressing specific points on the body to relieve pain and promote balance among the physiological systems. Different acupressure points correspond to different areas of the body. For example, applying pressure to the area between the thumb and forefinger decreases headache.

Hydrotherapy utilizes whirlpools or Hubbard tanks to allow individuals to exercise in a warm, buoyant, gravity-eliminated environment. Individuals engaging in hydrotherapy are supported by the water and experience less stress through the joints, and therefore less pain. However, the water also provides resistance, which can lead to increased muscle strength.

Electrical stimulation utilizes electrical currents passing through surface electrodes for pain control (TENS) or muscle reeducation (NMES). TENS utilizes low-level electrical currents to block the pain message before it is perceived by the brain. NMES applies stronger electrical currents to an area of high motor nerve concentration in a muscle (motor point) to elicit a muscle contraction.

Cold therapy is performed using a variety of techniques to constrict blood vessels and reduce swelling. Ice packs can be applied directly to an area of increased swelling and pain for 10-15 minutes at a time. Vapocoolant spray is often used to numb a painful muscle prior to passive stretching to ensure a full-range stretch. Ice massages can be performed on a sprained ligament or strained tendon to numb the area before cross-friction massage is performed.

Heat treatment is used to increase the extensibility of soft tissues, enhance blood flow, increase function of the tissue cells, and help relieve pain. Ultrasound therapy is a technique that converts electrical energy into mechanical sound waves that provide heat to deeper muscle, tendons, ligaments, and bone. Diathermy is a form of heat treatment in which deep heating of tissues is accomplished by the use of high-frequency electrical current. Fluidotherapy utilizes dry heat from cellulose particles that are circulated by a stream of continuous air. This technique is useful for heating body parts with irregular surface area, such as the hand. Paraffin is often used for heating uneven surface of the body such as the hands. It consists of a paraffin-melted wax and mineral oil that is heated to 125 degrees F.

Prognosis

Outcome varies with diagnosis, severity of impairment, motivation, social support, and co morbidity. Some individuals may not return to their prior level of function due to the underlying condition and inability to successfully treat the condition. Such conditions may include progressive illnesses such as Parkinson's disease; however, with adaptive equipment, individuals can expect to participate in their prior activities to some degree.

Outcomes of specific therapeutic procedures may vary among individuals. Massage therapy has been shown to decrease muscle tightness, increase the flexibility of muscles and tendons, and promote healing to ligaments. Acupressure may provide relief from pain as a result of pressure applied to specific points on the body.

Individuals who have pain in muscles and bones experience a positive outcome and reduction in pain from heat treatment (ultrasound, diathermy, fluidotherapy, paraffin treatment).

Electrical stimulation has been shown to decrease pain via surface electrodes (TENS mode). Muscle strength has been shown to increase (NMES mode) through electrical impulses delivered to a muscle during therapy to aid in muscle contraction during therapeutic exercise.

Cold therapy has been shown to be effective in decreasing pain and swelling in an injured area.

Hydrotherapy has been shown to promote increased range of motion and strength while decreasing stress through the body.

Specialists

- Physical Therapist

Work Restrictions / Accommodations

Work restrictions would depend on the disorder being treated. The employee will need time off for visits to the physical therapist.

Upon returning to work, the physician and therapist may advise the individual to begin work at 4 hours a day and then slowly progress to a full workday. If lifting is a job requirement, the physician may prescribe weight restrictions as long as the individual is following proper lifting techniques as instructed by the physical therapist.

Comorbid Conditions

Individuals with circulatory disorders and or cardiac and pulmonary conditions may need special attention when receiving physical therapy. This is especially the case when various forms of exercise are used.

Procedure Complications

Some individuals may experience muscle soreness and/or fatigue when flexibility and/or strengthening exercises have begun. Symptoms usually subside with or without modifications made to the treatment plan.

Factors Influencing Duration

There is no disability associated with the different physical therapy modalities, only with the disorders being treated.

Length of Disability

No disability is expected to result from this therapy. Disability may occur as a result of an underlying condition.

References

Guccione, Andrew A. Geriatric Physical Therapy. St. Louis: Mosby, 1993.

Scully, Rosemary M., and Marylou R. Barnes. Physical Therapy. Philadelphia: J.B. Lippincott Company, 1989.

Pilonidal Cyst
Other names / synonyms: Jeep Rider's Disease, Nest of Hair Disease, Pilonidal Disease
685, 685.0, 685.1

Definition

A cyst is a closed sac that contains a liquid or semisolid material. Pilonidal cysts contain hairs and are usually located at the bottom of the spine (sacrococcygeal pilonidal cyst) between the buttocks (gluteal cleft). Although usually harmless, pilonidal cysts can become infected by bacteria and walled off to form an abscess. A draining channel (sinus) or an abnormal tube-like passage (fistula) may also develop. The disease has been referred to as "Jeep rider's" disease because so many US Army soldiers were diagnosed with the problem during World War II.

Pilonidal cysts are now considered to be an acquired condition involving midline pits in the gluteal cleft, which are actually enlarged hair follicles in the skin. Gravity and motion of the gluteal folds create a vacuum that pulls on the follicle, allowing bacteria and debris (it is close to the anus) to enter into this area, producing local inflammation. The resulting swelling (edema) occludes the mouth of the follicle, which then continues to expand, rupturing into the underlying area of fatty tissue. Keratin (the principal component of hair) and pus finally escape, setting into motion a foreign body reaction that produces acute and chronic abscesses, and sometimes fistulas. Risk factors associated with the development of pilonidal cysts include obesity, repeated local trauma, sedentary occupation and lifestyle, and a family history of the disease. Pilonidal cysts most frequently affect hairy, white males between 18-30 years of age.

Each year, 26 out of 100,000 individuals will acquire the condition. Men are 2-3 times more likely than women to develop pilonidal cysts. Pilonidal cysts are predominantly found in whites, rarely occur among blacks, and are almost nonexistent in Asians.

Diagnosis

History: A pilonidal cyst generally produces no symptoms until it becomes infected. Many do not seek medical attention until experiencing progressive tenderness after physical activity or a period of prolonged sitting, such as occurs during a long drive. When infected, individuals may report local pain, tenderness, and swelling. The individual may also have chills, fever, headache, flatulence, and generalized discomfort (malaise). The cyst may suddenly drain pus (purulent material).

Physical exam: A cyst, looking like a swollen area or nodule, which feels warm and is tender to touch, would be apparent along the midline of the lower spine approximately 1-2 inches above the anal opening. Channels (sinuses) and openings 2-5 centimeters in length may be seen in chronic or recurrent disease. Foul-smelling drainage may be coming from the lesion, and a tuft of fine hair may protrude from the cyst. A manual anorectal examination may be performed to detect fistulas or other defects. If any defect is detected by the manual exam, a short, tubular instrument (anoscope) will be utilized to view the rectum (anoscopy).

Tests: Laboratory culture of the pus may be performed to identify the bacteria responsible for the infection.

Treatment

Asymptomatic pilonidal cysts require only observation and information on improving hygiene practices, including keeping the area shaved. Several surgical methods to treat a pilonidal cyst are employed at the discretion of the surgeon. Treatment of the acute abscess consists of surgically incising and draining the abscess or sinus and packing it.

Acute exacerbations of chronic or recurring disease are treated by removing (excising) the cyst and surrounding tissue; the wound may be left either open or closed. Using a skin graft or skin flap to close the wound are other treatment possibilities; however, these methods are not done as much any more because of the high incidence of graft or flap failure. Incision with marsupialization is a lengthy surgical procedure in which the cyst is incised and stitched (sutured) so as to form a pouch instead of a closed sac. Incising and scrapping (curettage) may be performed in the office, so it is gaining in popularity. Analgesics and antibiotics are used as needed, but antibiotics are not necessary in the majority of cases and should not be the primary mode of treatment.

Prognosis

The outcome depends upon the surgical method employed; however, in general most procedures have a favorable outcome. Conservative treatment can be effective in minor pilonidal disease. An excision procedure that involves leaving an open wound produces satisfactory results, but has a prolonged healing time and recurrence is common. Excision leaving a closed wound heals within 2 weeks but, again, recurrence is fairly common. Excision and wound closure using a skin graft or flap may result in lengthy healing time, and has a high incidence of graft or flap failure. The incision with marsupialization has a 97% success rate. Incision and curettage of the wound has a 100% success rate.

Differential Diagnosis

Abscess, anorectal fistula, hidradenitis suppurativa, syphilis, tuberculosis, simple carbuncle or furuncle, and osteomyelitis are differential diagnoses for pilonidal cyst.

Specialists

- Colorectal Surgeon
- General Surgeon
- Infectious Disease Physician

Work Restrictions / Accommodations

A pilonidal cyst may affect the individual's ability to walk, stand, or sit for extended periods of time, so temporary accommodations may be necessary. Operation of a car or other vehicle may temporarily be affected. Depending on work duties, the individual may need to be temporarily reassigned.

Comorbid Conditions

Immune system-suppressing diseases, such as AIDS or certain cancers, can increase the length of disability by making the individual more prone to infection. Diabetes can prolong wound healing time.

Complications

Pilonidal cysts may progress to form extensive sinus tracts and fistulas. Individuals who have suffered from pilonidal cyst for a long period of time (20 years, on average) are at risk of developing aggressive squamous cell carcinoma at the affected site. Other complications include recurrence, infection, and abscess.

Factors Influencing Duration

The length of disability is dependent on the extent of sinus tract formation, surgical method employed, and development of complications following surgery.

Length of Disability

Duration depends on job requirements.

Incision and drainage.

Duration in Days

Job Classification	Minimum	Optimum	Maximum
Sedentary work	7	14	21
Light work	7	14	21
Medium work	7	14	21
Heavy work	7	14	21
Very Heavy work	7	14	21

Surgical excision.

Duration in Days

Job Classification	Minimum	Optimum	Maximum
Sedentary work	7	21	42
Light work	7	21	42
Medium work	7	28	56
Heavy work	7	28	56
Very Heavy work	7	28	56

Failure to Recover

If an individual fails to recover within the maximum duration expectancy period, the reader may wish to reference the following questions to assist in better understanding the specifics of an individual's medical case.

Regarding diagnosis:

- Is individual a young hairy male? Obese? Family history of the disease?
- Does individual have a sedentary lifestyle?
- Has individual had repeated local trauma?
- Has it become infected?
- Does individual report local pain, tenderness, and swelling?
- Does individual have chills, fever, headache, or malaise?
- Has the cyst drained purulent material?
- On exam, is the cyst located about 1-2 inches above the anus?
- Are channels and openings apparent?
- Is purulent drainage present?
- Is there a tuft of hair present?
- Was a manual anorectal exam done? Anoscopy?
- Have a culture and sensitivity of the pus been done?
- Have conditions with similar symptoms been ruled out?

Regarding treatment:

- Is the cyst asymptomatic?
- Is it being observed?
- Has individual received information on improving hygiene practices?
- Were antibiotics necessary?
- Did surgery become necessary?

Regarding prognosis:

- Is individual's employer able to accommodate any necessary restrictions?
- Does individual have any conditions that may affect their ability to recover?
- Has individual suffered from the pilonidal cyst for a very long time?
- Have they developed the complication of an aggressive squamous cell carcinoma at the site?
- Do they have recurrent infections or abscess?

References

Barnett, Jeffrey. "Anorectal Diseases." Textbook of Gastroenterology. Yamada Tadataka, ed. Philadelphia: Lippincott, Williams & Wilkins, 1999. 2083-2106.

da Silva, Jose. "Pilonidal Cyst: Cause and Treatment." Diseases of the Colon and Rectum 43 8 (2000): 1146-1156.

Pineal Gland Neoplasm
Other names / synonyms: Choriocarcinoma, Embryonal Carcinoma, Endodermal Sinus Tumor, Germ Cell Tumor, Germinoma, Pinealoma, Pineoblastoma, Pineocytoma, Teratoma
194.4, 198.89, 234.8, 237.1

Definition

Pineal gland neoplasm is a type of cancer that originates in or near the pineal gland. The pineal gland is a cone-shaped structure located in the brain that secretes the hormone melatonin.

Secretion of melatonin from the pineal gland is affected by light input through the eyes. During the day, when an individual's eyes are open and seeing light, melatonin secretion from the pineal is reduced. At night, when the eyes are closed and no light is entering the eye, melatonin secretion is high. Although light input affects normal functioning of the pineal gland, it is not known to be a factor in development of pineal gland cancer.

Classification of pineal gland tumors is complicated but can be grouped generally as either germ cell tumors (includes germinomas, choriocarcinomas, embryonal carcinomas, endodermal sinus tumors, and teratomas) or pinealomas (includes pineocytomas and pineoblastomas). Eighty percent of pineal gland tumors are of the germ cell type. Of these, 65% are germinomas and 18% teratomas. The other three subtypes of germ cell tumors constitute the remaining 17%. Notably, many germ cell tumors are a mixture of the five subtypes so the cancer cannot be classified as one or the other. For example, the combination of a teratoma and an embryonal carcinoma is called a teratocarcinoma. Among the pinealoma type of pineal gland neoplasms, pineocytomas are more harmless (benign) than pineoblastomas, which are always deadly (malignant).

Currently, there are no known environmental or dietary risk factors for pineal gland neoplasms. However, the incidence may be influenced by geography or race, age, and gender. Frequency of this condition is higher in Asian countries (i.e., Japan) than in Western nations (i.e., US). In the US, pineal gland neoplasms account for about 1% of all primary brain tumors although this figure increases to about 6% for individuals under the age of 19. Pineal tumors primarily affect young adults although they may occur at any age. No significant difference in age distribution occurs between different subtypes of pineal gland neoplasms except for teratoma, which tends to occur in individuals age 18 or younger.

The overall incidence of these tumors shows a strong male predominance with a male to female ratio of 4.3 to 1 in the US. Notably, the incidence of pineal neoplasms does not correlate with pregnancy in women. The high incidence in males appears to be strongly influenced by hormones rather than a direct genetic influence.

Diagnosis

History: Many of the early symptoms of pineal gland neoplasms are related to increased pressure in the head (intracranial pressure) caused by the tumor. Individuals may complain of headaches, nausea, vomiting, sudden mood changes, loss of coordination or hearing, increased urination, sleepiness (somnolence), and continual thirst.

Physical exam: The exam of the eyes reveals dilated pupils that respond sluggishly to light (accommodation reflex is present) and upward gaze palsy.

Tests: MRI is the test of choice for identifying tumors in the pineal region. This test can confirm the presence of a mass in the area of the pineal gland and an abnormal accumulation of brain fluid (cerebrospinal fluid) in the brain ventricles (hydrocephalus). CT may also be helpful. X-rays can help visualize weak areas of the cerebral vessels (aneurism) following injection of a radiopaque dye (angiography). In the absence of intracranial pressure, a sample of cerebrospinal fluid is taken from the spinal canal using a needle and syringe (spinal tap). The spinal fluid and blood are then tested for markers of pineal gland tumors such as alpha-fetoprotein (AFP) and human chorionic gonadotropin (hCG) that may be elevated as a result of pineal gland germinomas.

Treatment

Abnormal accumulation of cerebrospinal fluid in the brain ventricles (hydrocephalus) may be relieved through draining (shunting) some of the fluid away (hydroventricular decompression). Surgery (posterior fossa supracerebellar subtentorial or occipital-transtentorial approach) can then be done to either remove (excise) the tumor or obtain a sample (biopsy) of it for analysis. If surgery is not possible, a guided (stereotaxic) biopsy needle can obtain a sample of tissue from the tumor. Tumor analysis is important because it determines the type of treatment to be used. Radiation therapy should be used to treat all deadly (malignant) germ cell tumors and pinealomas. The spine should be irradiated if the tumor has started to spread (seed) into the spinal cord. Harmless (benign) pinealomas that can be completely removed do not require radiation treatment. Anticancer drugs (chemotherapy) are generally used only for tumors that have spread (metastasized). Malignant pinealomas are usually treated with both chemotherapy and radiation therapy.

Prognosis

The 5-year survival rate for individuals with germ cell tumors is 75-80%. The 10-year survival rate is 69% when treated with a combination of surgery and radiation therapy. Individuals with malignant nongerminomatous germ cell tumors (i.e., choriocarcinomas, embryonal carcinomas, endodermal sinus tumors, and teratomas) receiving this treatment rarely survive more than 2 years. Teratomas that are not well-developed (immature) have a slightly better outcome with a 25% survival rate at 5 years following treatment. Individuals treated with surgery and radiation therapy for pineocytoma have a 5-year survival rate of approximately 75% but the outcome for pineoblastoma is somewhat worse than this. In general, chemotherapy is not an effective treatment for any type of pineal gland neoplasm.

Differential Diagnosis

Conditions with similar symptoms include benign tumors of the pineal gland, hemangioblastomas, medulloblastomas, and astrocytomas of the cerebellum, all of which may cause hydrocephalus and increased intracranial pressure.

Specialists

- Neurologist
- Neurosurgeon
- Oncologist
- Radiation Therapist

Work Restrictions / Accommodations

Individuals may experience changes in ability to concentrate and a weakening of mental capabilities for a period of time until recovery and rehabilitation are complete. Stressful jobs that require a high degree of concentration such as accounting, software programing, lawyering, or technical writing may not be possible and accommodations may be needed before the individual can return to such work. Accommodations may include reassignment to a less mentally demanding position. Physically demanding work may also be impossible as a result of radiation and/or chemotherapy treatments. In this case, reassignment to light physical duty or a desk job may be required.

Comorbid Conditions

Comorbid conditions that may impact an individual's ability to recover from pineal gland neoplasm include any systemic diseases such as diabetes.

Complications

Complications of pineal gland neoplasms include hydrocephaly and secondary neurological effects it may cause including headaches, nausea, vomiting, sudden mood changes, loss of coordination or hearing, increased urination, sleepiness (somnolence), continual thirst, weight gain, and body temperature fluctuations.

Factors Influencing Duration

Factors that may influence disability include extent of the surgery and how well radiation therapy is tolerated. Older individuals do not do as well in response to surgery, chemotherapy, and irradiation as younger individuals. Individuals who have had brain surgery are at high risk for infection due to multiple invasive lines that are usually needed. Manifestation of infection severely increases length of disability. The individual's response to surgery and radiation treatments with attendant loss of hair and physical and mental capabilities also contribute to the length of disability.

Length of Disability

The duration of disability may depend on the requirements of the job. Disability may be permanent.

Radiation therapy and shunt.

Duration in Days

Job Classification	Minimum	Optimum	Maximum
Sedentary work	28	42	56
Light work	28	42	56
Medium work	42	56	84
Heavy work	42	56	84
Very Heavy work	42	56	84

Surgical treatment.

Duration in Days

Job Classification	Minimum	Optimum	Maximum
Sedentary work	28	56	84
Light work	28	56	84
Medium work	28	56	98
Heavy work	28	70	112
Very Heavy work	28	84	112

Failure to Recover

If an individual fails to recover within the maximum duration expectancy period, the reader may wish to reference the following questions to assist in better understanding the specifics of an individual's medical case.

Regarding diagnosis:

- Is individual a young adult male? Of Asian ethnicity?
- Does individual complain of headaches, nausea, vomiting, sudden mood changes, loss of coordination or hearing, increased urination, sleepiness (somnolence), and continual thirst?
- Has individual lost the ability to gaze upward?
- Was MRI done to identify tumor in the pineal region? CT and angiography?
- Was a sample of cerebrospinal fluid taken to test for markers of pineal gland tumors such as alpha-fetoprotein (AFP) and human chorionic gonadotropin (hCG)? Were these values elevated?
- Was a diagnosis of pineal gland tumor confirmed?

Regarding treatment:

- Was tumor classified as a germ cell or pinealoma?
- Was radiation therapy used for germ cell tumors and malignant pinealomas? Were malignant pinealomas also treated with chemotherapy?
- Did individual require surgery (superior fossa supracerebellar subtentorial or occipital-transtentorial approach) to completely remove a benign pinealoma? Was it successful? Were there any postsurgical complications?
- Were anticancer drugs (chemotherapy) used for metastasized tumors? Did tumor respond?
- If tumor spread (seeded) into the spinal cord, was the spinal cord irradiated? Was it successful?

Regarding prognosis:

- Was the tumor benign or malignant?
- Did individual undergo chemotherapy, radiation therapy, and/or surgery? Did complications occur as a result of treatment? If so, what were they?
- Are other treatment options available?
- Would individual benefit from participating in an experimental protocol?
- Have other neurological complications of pineal gland in addition to the initial symptoms developed? If so, what are they and how will they be treated?
- How will the effects of the tumor and additional treatment affect daily activities of individual?
- Has the malignancy spread to the spinal cord?

References

Greenberg, H.S., W.F. Chandler, and H.M. Sandler. Brain Tumors. New York: Oxford University Press, 1999.

Nishi, T., et al. "Treatment of Cancer Using Pulsed Electric Field in Combination with Chemotherapeutic Agents or Genes." Human Cell 10 1 (1997): 81-86.

Pityriasis Rosea
696.3

Definition

Pityriasis rosea is a mild, acute inflammatory disease of the skin, characterized by a pink rash on the trunk, arms, and legs. The rash may also appear on the neck, and rarely on the face.

The rash usually first appears as a large, pink patch (which may be scaly in texture) on the chest or back. This first patch is called the herald patch or the mother patch. One to two weeks after the appearance of the mother patch, more pink patches will appear. These new patches are often smaller than the mother patch, and they follow lines of cleavage of the skin, thus forming the rough outline of a Christmas tree on the back. Like the mother patch, they are pink, often scaly, and oval. After a period of 2-10 weeks, the rash disappears on its own (spontaneously). Rarely, pityriasis rosea may be localized to a specific region of the skin.

The cause of this disease is unknown. It is not caused by a fungus, bacteria, or allergy. Some scientists have suggested it might be caused by a virus, but this has not been proven. Based on antibody studies, human herpesvirus-6 and human herpesvirus-7 may be involved in some individuals. It is similar to rashes caused by infections (infectious exanthems) in that household contacts of individuals with the condition are at increased risk; there is a seasonal tendency for it to occur in the spring, fall, or winter; and there is a low rate of recurrence. Other scientists suggest this disease might be caused when an individual's immune system attacks its own tissues (autoimmune disease), but this theory has not been proven either. Drug-induced pityriasis rosea may be caused by bismuth, barbiturates, captopril, gold, or other drugs. Individuals with dandruff or other skin conditions, such as atopy, seborrheic dermatitis, and acne vulgaris, have increased risk of pityriasis rosea.

Pityriasis rosea usually affects adolescents and young adults, with the peak age of onset between 10 and 35 years of age. However, individuals of any age can be affected. There does not appear to be a strong hereditary link, as fewer than 5% of individuals report a family history of this condition. Pityriasis occurs equally in men and women, and equally among various races. It is a relatively common disease, estimated to affect 0.13% of men and 0.14% of women. Approximately 0.3-3.0% of individuals attending dermatology clinics have this condition.

Diagnosis

History: Rash is often the only symptom, with itching (pruritus) in 75% of cases. Itching is usually mild and rarely severe. Rarely, individuals complain of feeling generally ill (malaise), fever, headache, and fatigue.

Physical exam: The rash consists of rosy pink, oval patches (lesions), with fine scales in the middle and loose scales around the border of each lesion. The first lesion to appear (herald patch) is usually 2-6 cm in diameter, but the subsequent (and more numerous) lesions are smaller, about 1-2 cm in diameter. These secondary lesions are symmetrical, and follow lines of skin cleavage, typically making a Christmas tree pattern on the back. The rash most commonly appears on the torso, arms and legs, less frequently on the neck, and rarely on the face. In atypical pityriasis rosea, which occurs in about one-fifth of individuals, the herald patch may be missing or may blend into the secondary lesions. There may be associated mouth (oral) lesions.

Tests: The diagnosis is usually based on the physical examination and the individual's symptoms. However, blood tests may be conducted to rule out other conditions, such as autoimmune disease or syphilis. Often, the physician will perform a potassium hydroxide (KOH) test to distinguish pityriasis rosea from another skin condition called ringworm (tinea corporis). Skin biopsy may be needed to confirm the diagnosis.

Treatment

Pityriasis rosea will go away (resolve) on its own (spontaneously) without treatment. The skin should be kept clean to avoid infection. Artificial and natural sunlight seem to help clear up the rash, but this approach should be used with caution due to the potentially harmful effects of ultraviolet light, such as sunburn and skin cancer. Many doctors prefer to let the rash go away naturally over time. Itching may be relieved by lukewarm oatmeal baths, or by itch-relieving medication (anti-pruritics, antihistamines, steroids) applied directly to the skin (topically) or taken by mouth (orally). A recent study showed that oral erythromycin was effective in three-fourths of individuals.

Prognosis

Pityriasis rosea gradually resolves over 1-14 weeks (usually 2-6 weeks). Complete recovery is expected, and recurrence is rare (less than 3%).

Differential Diagnosis

Other possibilities are seborrhea, eczema, psoriasis, parapsoriasis, pityriasis alba, secondary syphilis, erythema multiforme, fungal infection, acute viral rashes, and drug reactions.

Specialists

- Dermatologist

Work Restrictions / Accommodations

Most individuals will not require restrictions or accommodations. Because sweating will aggravate itching, strenuous activity or working outdoors in warm temperatures should be avoided until the rash clears. Chemicals that may not normally be irritating (soap, for example), might irritate the rash of an individual with this condition. Thus, protective clothing may be required if the job requires contact with such chemicals. Certain medications (antihistamines) that may be prescribed to relieve itching can also cause drowsiness. Individuals using these medications should avoid operating heavy machinery, driving, or performing work where alertness is required.

Comorbid Conditions

Individuals with other skin disorders or those with a compromised immune system may experience a longer recovery period. Associated viral infections or autoimmune conditions may be associated with their own disability.

Complications

Pityriasis rosea is generally uncomplicated. However, secondary infection of the skin lesions can occur.

Factors Influencing Duration

The length of disability varies depending on the severity of the individual's symptoms, response to treatment if any is indicated, and the natural course of this condition. If the individual develops a secondary infection, the period of disability will be longer.

Length of Disability

Pityriasis rosea typically resolves without treatment.

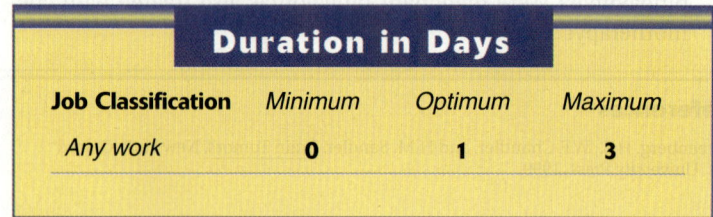

Duration in Days				
Job Classification	Minimum	Optimum	Maximum
Any work	0	1	3

Failure to Recover

If an individual fails to recover within the maximum duration expectancy period, the reader may wish to reference the following questions to assist in better understanding the specifics of an individual's medical case.

Regarding diagnosis:

- Has the diagnosis of pityriasis rosea been confirmed?
- Have other conditions been excluded, such as syphilis or ringworm?
- Is fungal scrape, serologic test for syphilis, or skin biopsy needed to confirm the diagnosis?

Regarding treatment:

- Is treatment with oral or topical medication needed for itching, inflammation, or secondary infection?
- In rare cases not responding to treatment, should a trial of erythromycin be considered?

Regarding prognosis:

- Are underlying conditions, such as unrelated skin problems or immunosuppression, delaying recovery?

References

Berkow, Robert, Mark Beers, and Andrew Fletcher. The Merck Manual of Medical Information. New York: Pocket Books, 1997.

Kosuge, H., et al. "Epidemiological Study of Human Herpesvirus-6 and Human Herpesvirus-7 in Pityriasis Rosea." British Journal of Dermatology 143 4 (2000): 795-798.

Lichenstein, Richard. Pityriasis Rosea. eMedicine.com. 14 Jan 2001. 7 Mar 2001 <http://www.emedicine.com/emerg/topic426.htm>.

Wolfrey, Jeffrey. "Pityriasis Rosea." Griffith's 5-minute Clinical Consult. Dambro, Mark, ed. Philadelphia: Lippincott, Williams & Wilkins, 2000. 818-819.

Placenta Accreta
666.0, 667, 667.0, 667.1

Definition

Placenta accreta is an abnormal attachment of part or all of the placenta to the uterine wall. It is caused by the partial or complete absence of the thin lining (decidua basalis) that separates the placenta from the uterine muscle (myometrium).

If this lining is missing or damaged, the chorionic villi of the placenta attaches directly onto the uterine muscle. This causes a serious problem at the time the placenta is delivered. Because of its firm attachment, the placenta may not separate from the uterus, causing significant bleeding.

Placenta accreta is positively associated with increased parity, advanced maternal age, previous placenta previa and prior uterine surgery.

Although many cases are not reported, placenta accreta may occur in approximately 1 in every 2,500 pregnancies in the US.

Diagnosis

History: Incomplete separation of the placenta occurs at delivery. Massive bleeding (hemorrhage) is the most significant symptom.

Physical exam: On exam placental fragments may be felt inside the uterus. Inspection of the placenta already removed reveals damaged or missing portions.

Tests: Women at risk for placenta accreta should be screened by ultrasound examination, or the ultrasonic technique for detecting anatomic details called color-flow Doppler studies. Magnetic resonance imaging (MRI) is not used to establish a diagnosis of placenta accreta, but can be used to confirm or rule out the condition when ultrasound results are uncertain.

Treatment

Managing placenta accreta requires controlling hemorrhaging; removing the placenta that has adhered to the uterine wall is very difficult and can result in blood loss. If the diagnosis is made before labor begins, the delivery should be scheduled so that adequate blood replacements (blood for transfusion) are available. In cases of severe bleeding, control of bleeding while avoiding a hysterectomy is done by selectively occluding (embolizing) pelvic blood vessels with embolizing agents such as vasoconstrictors, absorbable gelatin sponge, microfibrillar collagen, polyvinyl alcohol, or silicone beads, and balloon occlusion of the aorta or lower abdominal region (hypogastric) vessels. In the majority of cases, a hysterectomy is required.

Prognosis

Placenta accreta is the most common indication for birth-related hysterectomy. The mortality rate from postpartum hemorrhage, the most significant complication of placenta accreta, is approximately 7 percent. If the individual becomes pregnant again, there is a high risk of recurrence of placenta accreta.

Differential Diagnosis

Placenta previa, a condition in which the placenta implants abnormally in the uterus so that it covers the internal opening of the uterine cervix, may also be diagnosed.

Specialists

- Gynecologist
- Obstetrician

Work Restrictions / Accommodations

Following cesarean and/or hysterectomy, particularly an abdominal hysterectomy, heavy lifting, excessive standing, climbing, bending, kneeling, stooping, and squatting may need to be restricted.

Comorbid Conditions

If the individual has other forms of uterine scarring, the ability to recover may be further lengthened.

Complications

Complications include massive bleeding (postpartum hemorrhage), perforation of the uterus, uterine prolapse, infection, and death.

Factors Influencing Duration

The age of the woman, development of complications, and whether a hysterectomy was done will influence the length of disability.

Length of Disability

An immediate hysterectomy may be performed. Return to work can be expected but may be delayed if very heavy physical work is required.

Hysterectomy, vaginal approach.

Duration in Days

Job Classification	Minimum	Optimum	Maximum
Sedentary work	21	28	42
Light work	21	28	42
Medium work	28	42	56
Heavy work	28	56	70
Very Heavy work	28	70	84

Hysterectomy, abdominal approach.

Duration in Days

Job Classification	Minimum	Optimum	Maximum
Sedentary work	28	42	56
Light work	28	42	56
Medium work	42	56	70
Heavy work	42	70	84
Very Heavy work	42	84	98

Failure to Recover

If an individual fails to recover within the maximum duration expectancy period, the reader may wish to reference the following questions to assist in better understanding the specifics of an individual's medical case.

Regarding diagnosis:
- Is the placenta attached directly to the uterine muscle?
- Has individual had previous cesarean deliveries?
- Has she had previous uterine surgery?
- Is individual over 35 years of age?
- Has she given birth 7 or more times?
- Did hemorrhage occur at delivery?
- On exam of the placenta, were there damaged or missing portions? Were placental fragments felt inside the uterus?
- Did individual have ultrasound done? Color-flow Doppler studies? MRI? Blood test for alpha-fetoprotein?
- Have conditions with similar symptoms been ruled out?

Regarding treatment:
- Was the diagnosis made prior to delivery? Was delivery scheduled?
- Were they able to control bleeding?
- Was it necessary to do a hysterectomy?

Regarding prognosis:
- Is individual's employer able to accommodate any necessary restrictions?
- Does individual have any conditions that may affect their ability to recover?
- Does individual have any complications such as perforation of the uterus? Uterine prolapse? Infection?

References

Mulvihill, Kimberly, MD. "Placenta Accreta." Oxygen. 08 Oct 1998 20 Feb 2001 <http://thriveonline.oxygen.com/medical/womensdoc/womensdoc.10-08-98.html>.

Beers, Mark H., and Robert Berkow. The Merck Manual of Diagnosis and Therapy. Whitehouse Station, NJ: Merck and Co, Inc., 1999

Placenta Previa

Other names / synonyms: Low-Lying Placenta

641.1, 641.11, 641.13

Definition

Placenta previa occurs when the organ joining the fetus to the uterus (placenta) is attached so low in the uterus that it partially or totally blocks the opening of the uterus (cervix). The condition varies in severity depending on how close the placenta is to the cervix.

Individuals who are pregnant with multiple gestations are more likely to develop placenta previa, although it's not clear why. However, most individuals who develop the condition have no apparent risk factors.

Incidence of placenta previa at the time of delivery varies widely. Risk factors that increase the incidence of placenta previa include advancing age, having had previous pregnancy terminations and/or cesarean sections, a previous diagnosis of placenta previa, increasing parity, smoking and cocaine use.

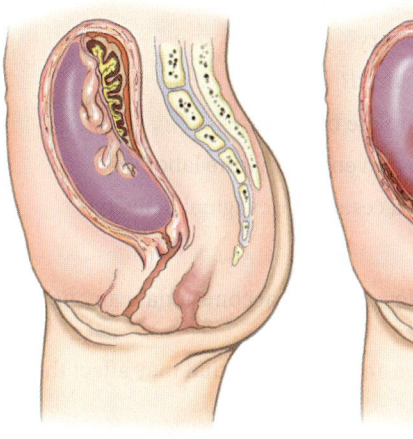
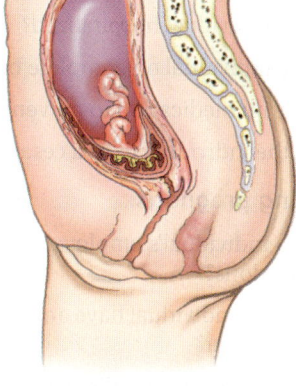

Normal | Placenta previa

Laurie O'Keefe

Diagnosis

History: Painless second or third trimester bleeding (hemorrhage) is the primary sign of placenta previa. Although there may be some spotting of blood early in the pregnancy, the first episode of hemorrhage usually begins sometime after the 28th week of pregnancy. Caused by placental tissue separating from the uterus, the bleeding is sudden, painless, and profuse. There may be some cramping.

Physical exam: The uterus is usually soft, relaxed, and non-tender. A vaginal or pelvic exam is not done as it may cause more bleeding. Most cases of placenta previa turn up during routine ultrasound exams.

Tests: Ultrasound is used to view the placement of the placenta in the uterus.

Specialists

• Obstetrician	• Perinatologist

Treatment

The treatment depends on the amount of bleeding, how far along the pregnancy is, the ability of the fetus to survive, how much the placenta covers the cervix, and whether or not labor has begun. Hospitalization is mandatory until it is certain the condition of the mother and fetus is stable. Major blood loss is replaced by transfusions.

Medication can be given to prevent premature labor and to prolong pregnancy until at least 36 weeks. After the 36th week of pregnancy, 75% of the cases are brought to early delivery to reduce further risks to the mother and fetus.

Cesarean section is the delivery method used in most cases as it presents the least risk to the mother and fetus. Vaginal delivery is only used if the placental placement is high enough in the uterus and the fetus is presenting headfirst (cephalic presentation) or if there is no chance of the fetus surviving.

Prognosis

For the mother, with transfusions, antibiotics, and cesarean section delivery, the outcome is excellent. There is a 10% death rate for the fetus. However, this may be greatly reduced by early intervention and aggressive care both before and after birth.

Differential Diagnosis

Premature separation of the placenta (abruptio placentae) can be mistaken for placenta previa.

Work Restrictions / Accommodations

If hospitalization or complete bed rest is necessary, the individual will be unable to work. If the individual is physically able to work, work responsibilities must be sedentary with frequent work breaks. Following a cesarean delivery, heavy lifting and prolonged standing will temporarily be restricted.

Comorbid Conditions

Anemia or other blood disorders may lengthen disability.

Complications

The mother risks excessive bleeding (hemorrhage), shock, and death. The fetus may suffer blood loss (hemorrhage) due to tearing of the placenta or birth injury. A diagnosis of anemia or other blood disorder may cause further complications.

Factors Influencing Duration

The severity of hemorrhage will influence the length of disability. If the fetus dies, a period of psychological adjustment and grieving is expected.

Length of Disability

Length of disability depends on stage of pregnancy, severity of bleeding, and any other complications. With hemorrhage, the durations do not include labor and delivery or Cesarean Section. Disability may be permanent.

Without hemorrhage.

Duration in Days

Job Classification	Minimum	Optimum	Maximum
Sedentary work	1	1	1
Light work	1	1	1
Medium work	1	14	28
Heavy work	1	28	56
Very Heavy work	1	28	56

With hemorrhage.

Duration in Days

Job Classification	Minimum	Optimum	Maximum
Sedentary work	14	56	112
Light work	14	56	112
Medium work	14	56	112
Heavy work	14	56	112
Very Heavy work	14	56	112

Failure to Recover

If an individual fails to recover within the maximum duration expectancy period, the reader may wish to reference the following questions to assist in better understanding the specifics of an individual's medical case.

Regarding diagnosis:

- Has the individual had a previous placenta previa?
- Has she had previous pregnancies? Cesarean delivery?
- Over 35 years of age?
- After the 28th week of pregnancy did she experience sudden, profuse, and painless bleeding? Any cramping?
- On exam is the uterus soft, relaxed, and non-tender?
- Was placenta previa diagnosed on a routine ultrasound?
- Have conditions with similar symptoms been ruled out?

Regarding treatment:

- How far along in the pregnancy is the individual?
- Have they been able to control the bleeding?
- Were transfusions necessary?
- Is the individual hospitalized?
- Is the individual on complete bed rest?
- Is she on medication to prevent premature labor?
- Did the individual have a cesarean or vaginal delivery?

Regarding prognosis:

- Is the individual's employer able to accommodate any necessary restrictions?
- Does the individual have any conditions that may affect the ability to recover?
- Were there any complications such as hemorrhage or shock?
- Did the fetus die?
- If necessary, has the individual obtained counseling to assist with the grief process?

References

Bakshi, S., and B.A. Meyer. "Indications For and Outcomes of Emergency Postpartum Hysterectomy. A Five-year Review." Journal of Reproductive Medicine 45 9 (2000): 733-737.

Neilson, J.P. "Interventions for Suspected Placenta Previa." Cochrane Database System Review 2 (2000): CD001998.

Plantar Fasciitis
728.71

Definition

Plantar fasciitis is an irritation or inflammation of the plantar fascia, or fibrous band on the sole of the foot that extends from the bottom of the heel bone (calcaneus) to the base of the toes. It acts like a thick rubber band on the bottom arch of the foot. The inflammation results from mechanical strain (traumatic fasciitis) or from abnormalities of foot structure (biomechanical plantar fasciitis).

Pain may occur along the entire course of the plantar fascia because of microtears along that band. It may be inflamed at its point of attachment into the calcaneus, or along the inside edge of the arch (medial band plantar fasciitis), middle of the arch (central band plantar fasciitis), or outer edge of the arch (lateral band plantar fasciitis).

The condition is most common in several sub-groups of people including runners and other athletes, people whose jobs require a lot of walking or standing, and among those who have put on weight, either by dietary habits or pregnancy. Some cases of plantar fasciitis are the result of a biomechanical fault that causes abnormal pronation. Plantar fasciitis is the most common cause of pain in the sole of the heel (plantar surface) and in the arch of the foot (90%). Plantar fasciitis is common in both men and women; most individuals (76%) are between 40-70 years of age. Although both feet may be involved (bilateral), most cases involve only one foot (unilateral). It takes about 6 months for 75% of people to recover from this condition; 98% seem to have improved by 12 months.

Diagnosis

History: The individual may complain of pain under the heel or in the arch. The pain usually occurs when arising from bed or after being seated, and improves with walking. The pain is worse when the individual is barefooted, and is improved with shoes.

Physical exam: The examiner may elicit pain when touching (palpating) the heel or arch. Bending the foot toward the shin (ankle dorsiflexion) may increase the pain.

Tests: X-rays may be negative or show increased soft tissue density of the plantar fascia and/or a bone spur on the sole portion of the heel bone (plantar calcaneal tuberosity). A bone scan may show increased activity in the heel.

Treatment

Plantar fasciitis usually responds to conservative (nonsurgical) treatment. Well over 95% of individuals obtain complete relief without surgery. Treatment may consist of ice packs, Achilles tendon stretching exercises, heel pads or heel cups, over-the-counter arch supports, prescription arch supports (orthotics), heel lift if due to limb length inequality, physical therapy, anti-inflammatory medications, injections of corticosteroid medication into the heel area, full foot taping, night splints, casting, or crutches. Sometimes a splint is worn at night to stretch out the plantar fascia. Weight loss is essential if the individual is obese.

Although conservative treatment is effective, it can often take several weeks or even months for the pain to resolve. Some type of shoe insert (heel pad or cup, arch support, or orthotic) is usually necessary after treatment to prevent recurrence.

Surgery is required in cases of severe plantar fasciitis that do not respond after a lengthy period of conservative treatment (1-5%). Considerable controversy exists regarding whether to operate on these individuals, and which of several procedures to use. Some surgeons advocate cutting the tight fascia to relieve the tension (Schön procedure; Baxter procedure), while others resect the heel spur and detach the plantar fascia (DuVries procedure). Recently, some surgeons have performed a plantar fascia release (plantar fasciotomy) through an endoscope (endoscopic plantar fasciotomy; Barrett procedure) with a 97% success rate.

Prognosis

The pain in most cases is relieved completely. Some individuals will need to wear orthotics permanently to prevent symptom recurrence. Most individuals treated surgically obtain reduction (50-80% reduction), but not resolution, of pain.

Differential Diagnosis

Other conditions causing heel pain include gout, rheumatoid arthritis, Reiter's syndrome, psoriatic arthritis, calcaneal stress fracture, and tarsal tunnel syndrome (tibial nerve compression at the ankle).

Specialists

- Orthopedic Surgeon
- Physiatrist
- Podiatrist
- Rheumatologist

Rehabilitation

Individuals with plantar fasciitis may attend physical therapy and receive treatment for pain control, stretching plantar fascia, and strengthening. They may also be referred to a pedorthotist to correct any biomechanical causes of this condition.

Pain control can be addressed in a variety of ways. Individuals learn to apply a heating pad to the sole of the foot for 15 minutes prior to the physical therapy session. The therapist may initiate ice massage, followed by cross friction massage to the sole of the foot. To perform self-massage, the individual can sit in a chair, place a golf ball under the sole of the foot, and then move the foot forward and backward to roll the golf ball along the sole. Ultrasound, which is the use of high frequency sound waves to promote deep heating, may be applied to the sole of the foot. Individuals learn to apply ice to the sole of the foot for 10 minutes after any exercise. The use of a heel lift in the shoe can alleviate stress on the plantar fascia, and decrease pain.

Restoration of muscle flexibility is important to prevent recurrence of plantar fasciitis. A common cause of this condition is tight calf muscles. The individual learns to stretch the calf by standing on the edge of a stair with the heels hanging over the edge, and slowly lowering the heels downward. Another common cause of plantar fasciitis is tightness in the muscles that turn the foot out (into eversion). To stretch these muscles, the individual sits in a chair, places the ankle on the affected side on the opposite thigh, then grasps the outer foot and slowly pulls it up so the foot turns inward (into inversion).

Muscle strengthening helps correct any strength imbalances that can contribute to this condition. Individuals use elastic tubing to provide resistance for leg muscles as the toes point down (plantarflexion) and the foot turns inward and outward (inversion and eversion). Towel scrunches strengthen the foot muscles; the individual curls the toes around a towel placed flat on the floor.

Individuals may be referred to a pedorthotist or podiatrist for corrective shoe inserts. These inserts (or orthotics) help to normalize walking and running by placing the foot in a neutral position. Individuals with exceptionally high arches should be fitted for inserts that cushion the arch. Those who are flat-footed should be fitted for inserts that provide more rigid arch support.

Work Restrictions / Accommodations

Any restrictions or accommodations depend on the severity of the condition. Standing and walking may need to be restricted. If casting or crutches are used either as a primary treatment or postoperatively, the individual will need to limit ambulation and must be allowed to elevate the foot. If orthotics are used, the individual must be allowed to wear enclosed shoes (such as nursing shoes, or work boots) that will accommodate the orthotics.

Complementary and Alternative Therapies

Content is intended for awareness only. Treatments may or may not be effective. Scientific evidence may be lacking and some substances have potentially toxic effects. Dr. Presley Reed and the editors do not endorse the use of these therapies in the absence of consultation with a licensed medical professional.

Arch support -	Weight redistribution with arch support, heel pads, or arch strapping may help resolve symptoms.
Ice massage -	May provide pain relief.
Ultrasound therapy -	May help relieve symptoms.

Comorbid Conditions

Arthritis of the foot may lengthen disability.

Complications

Painful heel spurs may develop from the chronic tension of the plantar fascia on the calcaneus.

Factors Influencing Duration

Compliance with recommended treatment and activity restrictions, job demands (especially standing and walking requirements), and response to treatment affect the duration of disability.

Length of Disability

Medical treatment.

Duration in Days

Job Classification	Minimum	Optimum	Maximum
Sedentary work	0	3	7
Light work	0	3	7
Medium work	1	7	10
Heavy work	3	10	14
Very Heavy work	3	10	14

Surgical treatment.

Duration in Days

Job Classification	Minimum	Optimum	Maximum
Sedentary work	1	7	14
Light work	7	14	21
Medium work	14	21	28
Heavy work	21	28	42
Very Heavy work	21	28	42

Duration Trend from Normative Data*

Cases	Mean	Min	Max	No Lost Time	Over 6 Months
1541	57	2	509	0%	1.27%

Percentile:	5th	25th	Median	75th	95th
Days:	12	26	43	73	146

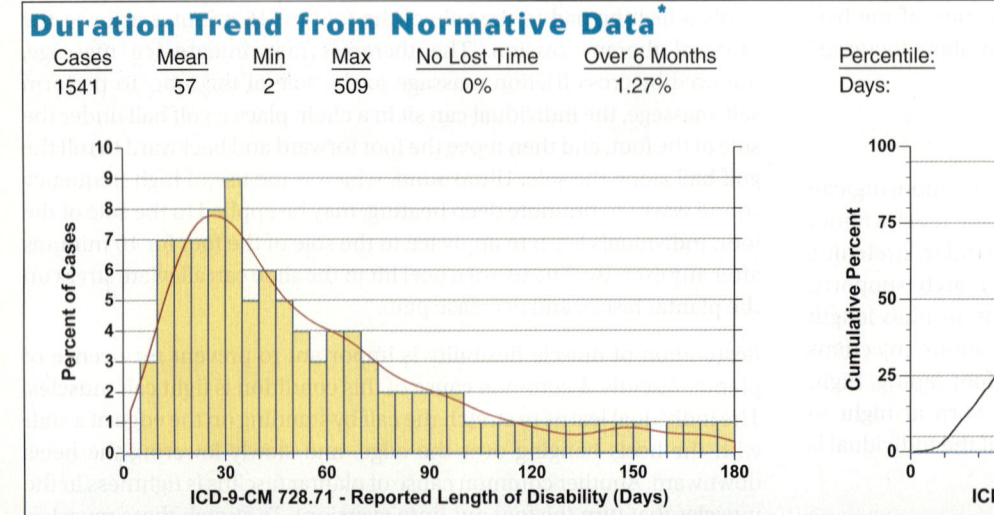

* Differences may exist between the expected duration tables and the normative graphs. Duration tables provide expected recovery periods based on the type of work performed by the individual. The normative graphs reflect the actual observed experience of many individuals across the spectrum of physical conditions, in a variety of industries, and with varying levels of case management.

Failure to Recover

If an individual fails to recover within the maximum duration expectancy period, the reader may wish to reference the following questions to assist in better understanding the specifics of an individual's medical case.

Regarding diagnosis:

- Has diagnosis of plantar fasciitis been confirmed? Has a bone scan ruled out a stress fracture of the calcaneus?
- Does individual have an underlying condition such as painful heel spurs, obesity, or arthritis that could impact recovery?

Regarding treatment:

- Do symptoms persist despite treatment? Has enough time elapsed for pain to resolve?
- If unable to lose weight on his/her own, would individual benefit from enrollment in a community weight loss program?
- Is individual a candidate for surgical intervention? By which procedure? Based on what criteria?

Regarding prognosis:

- Has enough time elapsed to evaluate effectiveness of treatment?
- Would individual benefit from consultation with a podiatrist regarding the entire weight distribution in that foot?
- Is individual compliant with preventive measures, such as wearing some type of shoe insert, heel pad or cup, arch support, or orthotic?
- Is individual realistic about prognosis expectations?

References

Barrett, Stephen L., DPM, and Robert O'Malley, DPM. "Plantar Fasciitis and Other Causes of Heel Pain." American Academy of Family Physicians. 15 Apr 1999. 14 Feb 2001 <http://www.aafp.org/afp/990415ap/2200.html>.

Magee, David J. "Lower Leg, Ankle, and Foot." Orthopedic Physical Assessment. Biblis, Margaret M., ed. Philadelphia: W.B. Saunders Company, 1992. 448-515.

Pleural Biopsy

Other names / synonyms: Biopsy by Pleural Needle, Biopsy of the Open Pleura, Needle Biopsy, Thoracoscopic Biopsy
34.24

Definition

A pleural biopsy is a diagnostic procedure in which a sample of the membrane that lines the chest cavity (pleura) is obtained for further examination.

The biopsy sample can be obtained in several ways. In a needle biopsy, a needle is inserted into the pleura and a sample of tissue or cells is removed for examination. Another method of obtaining a pleural biopsy sample is through thoracoscopy. In this procedure, a tiny, lighted instrument (thoracoscope) is inserted between the ribs and into the pleura. An attachment on the thoracoscope is used to take a sample. If a needle biopsy or thoracoscopic biopsy does not provide sufficient information to make a diagnosis, an open pleural biopsy is performed. A small opening between the ribs is made (thoracotomy) so that a tissue sample may be obtained.

Persons suspected of having tuberculosis, lung cancer, cancers that have spread to other parts of the body, abnormal growths, parasitic infections, viral infections, or fungal infections may be candidates for pleural biopsies. According to National Center for Health Statistics reports, there were 18,361 cases of tuberculosis reported for a disease rate of 6.8 per 1 million population in 1998, the last year for which cumulative data are available. During the same reporting period there were 37.0 deaths per 100,000 population due to malignant neoplasms in the trachea, bronchus, and lung. Most of those were in the age group over 75 years of age. There were 54.2 cases per 100,000 population of cancer associated with the lungs reported for the same period.

Reason for Procedure

A pleural biopsy is performed to diagnose a disease, determine the cause of excessive fluids within the pleura, or further investigate a suspicion of cancer (malignancy). An open biopsy is used when a larger sample is needed. It is done when there are no bodily fluids in the pleura or when the doctor needs a direct view of the lungs and the pleura. A needle biopsy may be used to detect cancerous and noncancerous growths. Viral, fungal, or parasitic diseases are detectable by these means.

Description

The open pleural biopsy is performed in a hospital and a general anesthetic is used. A tube (endotracheal tube) is passed through the nose or mouth so that an airway may be maintained during the procedure. An incision is made in the chest after that. A sample of the tissue is removed from the lung membrane (pleura) under the physician's observation. The incision is closed using stitches when the sample has been taken.

The needle pleural biopsy is done on an outpatient basis. A trip to the hospital isn't necessary. The procedure is done while the individual is sitting up. Skin at the site of the biopsy is cleansed and a local anesthetic applied. The needle is inserted through the skin. The needle is rotated and tissue samples withdrawn. A bandage is then applied to the site.

Prognosis

The outcome from the needle biopsy procedure is generally good. However, results of pleural biopsies may show the presence of cancer, tuberculosis, a viral or fungal disease, or a parasitic disease. It may also reveal the presence of other abnormal growths (neoplasms).

Specialists

- Pulmonologist
- Thoracic Surgeon

Work Restrictions / Accommodations

Work restrictions or accommodations depend upon the individual's job requirements. Strenuous activity and heavy lifting may be temporarily restricted.

Comorbid Conditions

Comorbid conditions that might affect the length of disability include respiratory diseases, allergies, and gastrointestinal disease.

Procedure Complications

There is a slight chance of excessive loss of blood or injury to the lung and a slight chance of a lung collapsing as a result of the procedures.

Factors Influencing Duration

Length of disability may be influenced by the underlying condition for which the pleural biopsy was performed or by the presence of complications.

Length of Disability

The length of disability will depend upon the diseases, disorders, and nature of any growths discovered during the procedures.

Needle or thoracoscopy.

Duration in Days

Job Classification	Minimum	Optimum	Maximum
Sedentary work	2	4	7
Light work	2	4	7
Medium work	2	4	7
Heavy work	2	4	7
Very Heavy work	2	4	7

Open (thoracotomy).

Duration in Days

Job Classification	Minimum	Optimum	Maximum
Sedentary work	21	28	35
Light work	21	28	35
Medium work	21	28	35
Heavy work	28	35	42
Very Heavy work	28	35	42

References

"Open Pleural Biopsy." Medline Plus Health Information. 1.0, 1999 26 Sep 2000 1 Jan 2001 <http://medlineplus.adam.com/ency/article/003863.htm>.

Beers, Mark H., and Robert Berkow. The Merck Manual of Diagnosis and Therapy. Whitehouse Station, NJ: Merck and Co, Inc., 1999

Pleurisy

Other names / synonyms: Acute Pleuritis, Pleural Inflammation, Pleuritis

511, 511.0, 511.1, 511.9

Definition

Pleurisy is inflammation of the membrane that covers the lungs and lines the inside of the chest cavity (pleura). Pleurisy is a symptom of another underlying condition and is characterized by sharp chest pain (pleurodynia) that is worse when breathing in (inspiration), coughing, or with chest movement.

The pleura has two layers, the inner and outer membranes, that are very thin and close together. A small amount of fluid is normally present between the layers, which acts as a lubricant, so when the lungs inflate and deflate during breathing the surfaces glide easily over each other. When the pleura is roughened by inflammation, the membranes rub against each other causing pain, and a chest sound that ranges from a faint squeak to a loud creak (friction rub) is heard with a stethoscope (auscultation).

Depending on its cause, pleurisy can occur either with (pleural effusion) or without (dry pleurisy) an accumulation of fluid. Pleurisy with pleural effusion is more common and is associated with less pain because the fluid accumulation keeps the pleural membranes separated, helping to minimize rubbing. However, pleural effusion can cause pressure on the lungs leading to breathing problems (respiratory distress) or possibly lung collapse. Large accumulations of fluid also compromise breathing and may cause coughing, shortness of breath with rapid breathing (tachypnea), bluish skin from lack of oxygen (cyanosis), and retractions.

Many conditions can cause pleurisy, including bacterial (pneumonia or tuberculosis) or viral lung infections. Other diseases that cause pleurisy include immune disorders (e.g., rheumatoid arthritis, systemic lupus erythematosus, sarcoidosis), lung cancer, inflammation of the pancreas (pancreatitis), certain liver diseases (cirrhosis), heart failure, kidney failure, or rheumatic fever. A blood clot in the lung (pulmonary embolism) can cause pleurisy, as can inhaling a substance called asbestos. Injury such as from a rib fracture, collapsed lung, or rupture of the tube that connects the mouth to the stomach (esophagus) may also result in pleurisy. Reactions to certain drugs (generally drugs used to treat the above conditions) may also be responsible for developing this condition.

Pleurisy used to be a common illness. However, since the development of antibiotics and modern treatment of diseases, it has become much less common. Because this condition is the result of such a wide array of other conditions, the exact incidence is unknown. Pleurisy affects men and women of all ages, and is more common in those with the conditions mentioned above.

Diagnosis

History: Symptoms include a sharp, stabbing chest pain that is usually worse with coughing, deep breathing, or when breathing in (inhale or inspiration). The pain may be focused in one area (localized) or it may spread to the shoulder and/or back. In rare cases, the individual will complain of a constant, dull ache. Individuals may report that holding their breath or pressing on their chest provides pain relief. Some individuals will also complain of shortness of breath. A recent or current respiratory illness with symptoms of cough, fever, and a general ill feeling (malaise) may be evident.

Physical exam: The exam may reveal rapid, shallow breathing. Often, the individual is bent over toward the side of the pain. Listening to breath sounds with a stethoscope (auscultation) may reveal a rough squeaky or creaking sound (friction rub) over the area of pain that accompanies inspiration and expiration, and decreased breath sounds. In severe cases, the individual may have a bluish color to the complexion (cyanosis) due to a lack of oxygen. Chest sounds that may be heard with a stethoscope (auscultation) include a crackling sound (rales) if pneumonia is present, or a continuous low-pitched snore-like sound (rhonchi) if pneumonia or bronchitis are present.

Tests: Specific tests will vary depending on the suspected cause of the individual's pleurisy. A chest x-ray may be taken to look for signs of accumulated fluid (pleural effusion), pneumonia, tuberculosis, pulmonary embolism, lung cancer, a fractured rib, or other physical injury. Blood samples may be tested to help diagnose pneumonia, rheumatic fever, pulmonary embolism, or other diseases. A CT scan (computed tomography) or an ultrasound may be used to help confirm and/or pinpoint the location of fluid buildup. When fluid is present, a sample may be collected and analyzed to help determine the underlying cause (thoracentesis). This involves inserting a needle through the chest wall into the pleural space and collecting fluid. When fluid is not present, and the cause of pleurisy is unclear, a sample of the pleural tissue (pleural biopsy) can be obtained and analyzed under a microscope. A complete blood count (CBC) with differential can help determine the presence of a bacterial versus viral infection.

Treatment

The initial treatment is usually aimed at relieving the individual's pain by prescribing pain killers (analgesics) and medication to reduce inflammation (anti-inflammatories). Lying on the painful side may also provide some relief.

If a significant amount of fluid has accumulated, this fluid may need to be drained by a procedure called thoracentesis. A needle will be inserted through the chest wall into the pleural space and the excess fluid will be extracted. In severe cases, a chest tube may need to be surgically inserted and remain in place for several days so that fluid can drain.

Further treatment is aimed at treating the underlying precipitating disease. Bacterial infections are treated with appropriate antibiotics; viral infections usually run their course without medications.

Prognosis

The prognosis for pleurisy is linked to the seriousness of the underlying cause. For instance, if the underlying cause is a bacterial lung infection, treatment with antibiotics and symptomatic relief of pain will usually provide full recovery. On the other hand, if the underlying cause is lung cancer, the prognosis may range from poor to grim, depending on the location of the tumor and whether or not the cancer has spread to other parts of the body.

Differential Diagnosis

Conditions with similar symptoms include pleural effusion, empyema, mesothelioma, tuberculosis, lupus erythematosus, or pulmonary embolism.

Specialists

- Infectious Disease Physician
- Pulmonologist
- Internist
- Primary Care Provider

Work Restrictions / Accommodations

Work restrictions and accommodations will vary depending on the severity of the individual's symptoms and his/her job requirements. In general, activities requiring significant amounts of bending or reaching should be avoided. Jobs that are physically demanding or require significant activity may be difficult due to decreased lung capacity. In these cases, temporary reassignment to a more sedentary position would be helpful. Frequent breaks may also be required.

Comorbid Conditions

The presence of other lung disease, a suppressed or compromised immune system and obesity may lengthen the period of disability.

Complications

Possible complications might include inflammation of the membranous sac enclosing the heart (pericarditis), pus in the pleural cavity (empyema), or collapse (atelectasis) of the lung.

Factors Influencing Duration

Length of disability may be influenced by the severity of symptoms, the underlying cause of the pleurisy, response to treatment, and the development of complications.

Length of Disability

Duration depends on cause. Individuals whose jobs require heavy work or prolonged physical activity may experience a longer period of disability. In some cases, disability may be permanent.

Duration in Days

Job Classification	Minimum	Optimum	Maximum
Sedentary work	3	7	14
Light work	3	7	14
Medium work	5	7	21
Heavy work	5	7	21
Very Heavy work	7	7	21

Failure to Recover

If an individual fails to recover within the maximum duration expectancy period, the reader may wish to reference the following questions to assist in better understanding the specifics of an individual's medical case.

Regarding diagnosis:

- Did the individual have any medical history that could possibly contribute to the development of pleurisy (lung infection, tuberculosis, cancer, systemic lupus erythematosus, sarcoidosis, etc)?
- Did the individual present with symptoms of sharp, stabbing chest pain that is usually worse with coughing, deep breathing, or on inspiration?
- Did the physical exam reveal any characteristic findings such as tachypnea, pleural pain, cyanosis, pleural friction rub, or rales and rhonchi?
- Were specific diagnostic tests such as a chest x-ray, CT scan of the chest, or thoracentesis done to determine the underlying problem and/or detect the presence of an infectious process?
- Was the individual referred to an appropriate specialist (pulmonologist, oncologist)?
- If the diagnosis was uncertain, were other conditions with similar symptoms (empyema, pleural effusion, pulmonary embolus, etc) ruled out?

Regarding treatment:

- Were analgesics and anti-inflammatories prescribed?
- Was thoracentesis to drain accumulated fluid indicated?
- Was antimicrobial therapy indicated for underlying pulmonary infection?

Regarding prognosis:

- Based on the age, general health and underlying cause of the pleurisy, what was the expected outcome?
- Does the individual have any comorbid conditions that could impact recovery and prognosis, such as cancer, chronic lung disease, immune suppression, etc? If so, were these conditions addressed in the treatment plan?
- Did the individual suffer any associated complications that could prolong disability?

References

"Pleurisy." Intelihealth. 29 Jan 2000 13 Dec 2000 <http://www.intelihealth.com/IH/ihtprint/WSIHW000/9339/23663.html?k=baseprint>.

Beers, Mark H., and Robert Berkow. The Merck Manual of Diagnosis and Therapy. Whitehouse Station, NJ: Merck and Co, Inc., 1999

Pleurodynia

Other names / synonyms: Bornholm Disease, Devil's Grip, Epidemic Benign Dry Pleurisy, Epidemic Myalgia, Sylvest's Disease

786.52

Definition

Pleurodynia is a viral illness in which either the muscles between the ribs or the nerves located in that region become inflamed, causing sharp pain and tenderness made worse by moving, breathing, coughing, or sneezing. It most often results from Coxsackie virus infections and occasionally as a result of ECHO virus infections. The name, pleurodynia (pleura, side; odyne, pain), refers merely to the characteristic rib pain (intercostals), but does not connote disease of the lung lining (pleura).

The illness occurs in young adults most commonly, although it can occur at any age. In epidemics, disease is observed in adults of both genders. Pleurodynia is characterized by the abrupt onset of fever and sharp pain over the lower ribs or upper abdomen, which sometimes radiates to the back, shoulders, or abdomen.

Transmission is primarily from person to person, and multiple family members may be attacked almost simultaneously or in rapid succession at intervals of 2-5 days.

Pleurodynia was first recognized in the early 1900s in Scandinavian countries. Recently, epidemics and sporadic cases have been reported in many parts of the world. The majority of the illnesses occur in the summer and early fall.

Diagnosis

History: The illness is sometimes preceded by a few days of headache, muscle ache, sore throat, fatigue, and loss of appetite. However, these associated symptoms may not occur until after the onset of the chest pain. Individuals may report sharp pain over the lower ribs and abdomen.

Physical exam: Localized tenderness may be revealed upon physical examination. During episodes of severe pain, the individual may sweat profusely and appear acutely ill and apprehensive. Often there are associated findings of fever, sore throat and muscle spasms.

Tests: The diagnosis is made clinically on the basis of the classical symptom complex and a normal chest x-ray study. To rule out cardiac causes of chest pain, an EKG and cardiac isoenzymes are usually ordered. Other tests such as viral cultures of throat swabs, stool, or pleural fluid, muscle biopsy, or complete blood count may be done to confirm the diagnosis.

Treatment

Treatment of pleurodynia is symptomatic. Episodes of pain can usually be controlled with mild analgesics, but narcotic analgesics are sometimes used in severe episodes of pain. Heat applied to affected muscles may also be useful. Bed rest and consumption of fluids is usually recommended until the acute illness resolves, which is usually within 3-7 days.

Prognosis

Pleurodynia is a self-limiting disease (like a flu virus), that runs its course, without treatment, in 3-7 days. Most individuals recover fully. However, relapses can occur.

Differential Diagnosis

Differential diagnoses include heart attack (myocardial infarction), inflammation of the lining covering the lungs (pleurisy), and localized accumulation of pus in the lung cavity associated with either tuberculosis or pneumonia (empyema).

Specialists

- Anesthesiologist
- Cardiologist
- Emergency Medicine
- Internist
- Neurologist
- Pulmonologist

Work Restrictions / Accommodations

During the acute phase of the illness, bed rest and infection control measures (i.e., handwashing, limiting contact with others) to prevent transmission of the illness is usually recommended. Once recovered from the illness, most individuals can return to work with no restrictions or accommodations.

Complementary and Alternative Therapies

Content is intended for awareness only. Treatments may or may not be effective. Scientific evidence may be lacking and some substances have potentially toxic effects. Dr. Presley Reed and the editors do not endorse the use of these therapies in the absence of consultation with a licensed medical professional.

Heat therapy - Heat applied to affected muscles may help to relieve discomfort.

Comorbid Conditions

Comorbid conditions of chronic pulmonary disease or immune suppression (i.e., AIDS) may impact ability to recover and further lengthen disability.

Complications

Complications rarely occur; however, when seen, they may include relapse, inflammation of the lining covering the lungs (pleurisy), inflammation of the lining of the brain (meningitis), inflammation of the heart muscle (myocarditis), hepatitis, and inflammation of the testicle (orchitis).

Factors Influencing Duration

Factors that may result in disability include the severity of pain, the development of complications, and the possibility of relapse. No long-term disability is usually associated with this disease.

Length of Disability

In most cases, no disability is expected.

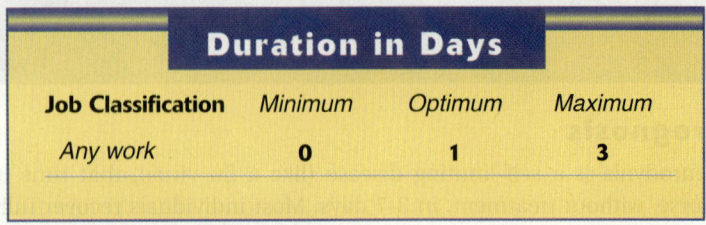

Job Classification	Minimum	Optimum	Maximum
Any work	0	1	3

Failure to Recover

If an individual fails to recover within the maximum duration expectancy period, the reader may wish to reference the following questions to assist in better understanding the specifics of an individual's medical case.

Regarding diagnosis:

- Has diagnosis of pleurodynia been confirmed?
- Have cardiac causes been ruled out with EKG or testing of cardiac isoenzymes?
- Has individual experienced a complication that may impact recovery?
- Does the individual have coexisting chronic pulmonary disease or immune suppression?

Regarding treatment:

- Have symptoms persisted despite treatment?
- Does diagnosis need to be revisited?

Regarding prognosis:

- Is there evidence of relapse?
- Have symptoms persisted beyond expected duration?
- Does diagnosis need to be revisited?
- Would individual benefit from consultation with a specialist (cardiologist, pulmonologist, neurologist)?

References

Goldman, Lee, and J. Claude Bennett. Cecil Textbook of Medicine, 21st ed. Philadelphia: W.B. Saunders Company, 2000.

Tierney, Lawrence M., Stephen J. McPhee, and Maxine A. Papadakis, eds. Current Medical Diagnosis and Treatment, 39th ed. New York: Lange Medical Books/McGraw-Hill, 2000.

Pneumoconiosis
500, 502, 505

Definition

Pneumoconiosis is the medical term for a group of chronic lung diseases caused by inhalation of dust particles. It is usually caused by prolonged environmental or occupational exposure such as the inhalation of coal dust in coal miners. The effects the various types of dust particles have on the lungs depend on the size of the particles inhaled, their shape, and the chemical reactivity that they may possess.

There are three categories of pneumoconiosis. Simple pneumoconiosis is caused by the inhalation of nonirritating dust that settles in the lungs. Examples of this type of pneumoconiosis include inhalation of iron (siderosis), tin (stannosis), coal (black lung, coal miner's pneumoconiosis), or barium (baritosis) dusts. The individual may not report any symptoms or impaired lung function for some time; however, deposits will show up on an x-ray and symptoms such as chronic bronchitis or emphysema can develop later.

Another category of pneumoconiosis involves inhalation of irritating dusts. Examples of irritating dusts include silica (silicosis), asbestos (asbestosis), beryllium (berylliosis), and aluminum (aluminosis). When these dusts are inhaled, they cause inflammation, lung tissue damage, and scarring.

The third category of pneumoconiosis results from inhaling organic dusts such as cotton, flax, or hemp fibers (byssinosis, brown lung disease), sugar cane residue (bagassosis), hay, grains, castor beans, western red cedar wood, or mushrooms. When these types of dust are inhaled, they provoke an allergic reaction in some individuals (even those who did not previously have allergies). This category of pneumoconiosis is often called occupational asthma.

Pneumoconiosis primarily affects workers over age 50. The risk of developing the disease is directly related to the amount of dust inhaled over the years. While smoking does not increase the prevalence of this disease, it may have an additive detrimental effect on lung function. Each year about 1,700 new cases of pneumoconiosis are diagnosed in the US, causing about 1,000 premature deaths. The incidence of new cases is now decreasing due to the enforcement of maximum permitted industrial dust levels and by the use of protective masks and clothing.

For more detailed information on the specific types of pneumoconiosis, please refer to: aluminosis, asbestosis, bagassosis, baritosis, berylliosis, black lung, brown lung disease, byssinosis, coal miner's pneumoconiosis, occupational asthma, siderosis, silicosis, and stannosis.

References

Berkow, Robert, Mark Beers, and Andrew Fletcher, ed. "Occupational Lung Diseases." The Merck Manual of Medical Information. Berkow, Robert, Mark Beers, and Andrew Fletcher New York: Pocket Books, 1997. 195-201.

Pneumocystis Carinii Pneumonia

Other names / synonyms: PCP

136.3

Definition

Pneumocystis carinii pneumonia (PCP) is a lung infection caused by a fungus, which, in the past, was mistaken for a protozoan parasite. The P. carinii microorganism that causes the pneumonia is found in the lungs of both animals and humans, though it is not ordinarily considered a disease-causing agent (pathogen) in healthy individuals. PCP instead occurs almost exclusively in individuals with weakened immune systems.

The disease is thought to spread primarily by air, but might also be transmitted person to person. The period between exposure to the agent and development of symptoms (incubation period) is between 4-8 weeks. Most people are exposed at an early age, but those with healthy immune systems ward off the disease.

Individuals with immune disorders, particularly those with AIDS (acquired immune deficiency syndrome), are considered at high risk for development of PCP. As many as 85% of individuals with AIDS in some studies were diagnosed with this disease. However, recent preventive antibiotic therapy programs (prophylaxis) have dropped the prevalence of PCP in the more than 730,000 AIDS-infected individuals in the US to about 20%. Reported prevalence of PCP is much lower outside the US among the approximately 33.6 million AIDS-infected individuals worldwide. But some researchers believe the disease likely is present but undetected in developing countries where medical intervention is lacking. Untreated PCP is a leading cause of death for AIDS-infected individuals. Recent preventive treatments have dropped the mortality rate from PCP for AIDS-infected individuals in the US from about 32% to 14%. Because immune systems are compromised, individuals who survive PCP are likely to have repeated infections. Some studies suggest that recurrence is due to different strains of the microorganism causing the disease.

Other groups at risk for PCP are individuals with organ transplants requiring drugs to suppress immunity. The disease also is found in individuals with cancer. Up to 10% of individuals with other immune disorders are thought to have PCP.

Diagnosis

History: Individuals in early stages of the disease typically complain of shortness of breath (dyspnea), fever, rapid breathing (tachypnea), bluish skin (cyanosis) from lack of oxygen, joint pain, and a dry nonproductive cough. If the disease has progressed, the individual may be unable to breathe properly without extra oxygen being supplied.

Physical exam: PCP may produce extremely variable symptoms. Individuals may have increased heart rate (tachycardia), rapid breathing (tachypnea), and abnormal chest sounds (rales or crackles). Many individuals will show signs of weight loss.

Tests: Analysis of cells (flow cytometry) may detect lower than normal levels of immune system boosters (CD4+ T lymphocytes), indicating vulnerability to infection. Blood tests (serology) may indicate malnourishment. Chest x-rays may appear abnormal. Occasionally, a computerized tomography (CT) scan of the chest is performed. Lung function and blood gases revealing oxygen content may also be measured. The diagnosis is confirmed when the infection-causing microorganism is identified after microscopic examination of sputum (phlegm) from the lungs. The sample is obtained when the individual coughs or when a tube is inserted into the lungs (bronchoscopy). A bronchial or open lung biopsy in some cases may also be conducted to obtain tissue for microscopic examination.

Treatment

Antibiotics given orally, intravenously or in aerosol form are used as a preventive measure or to control the disease in individuals with immune disorders. Oxygen is required in advanced stages of the disease. Corticosteroids may also be used to address inflammatory responses associated with the disease.

Prognosis

Untreated Pneumocystis carinii pneumonia results in death. When respiratory failure occurs as a result of damage to lungs, chances of survival are low. Because of the various medical conditions associated with AIDS, it's difficult to assess survivor rates for those with this disease even when PCP has been treated. PCP often recurs, which increases the chance for complications and possible death. When those with weakened immune systems are given preventive antibiotic treatment, risks of serious or prolonged illness from PCP are greatly reduced.

Differential Diagnosis

Symptoms are similar in any of several dozen types of pneumonia. Bronchitis or other bacterial or viral infections are also capable of producing similar symptoms. Emphysema, allergies, asthma, and various other lung diseases also may resemble PCP.

Specialists

- Gastroenterologist
- Immunologist
- Infectious Disease Physician
- Internist
- Neurologist
- Pathologist
- Primary Care Provider
- Pulmonologist

Work Restrictions / Accommodations

Most individuals who are infected with PCP require extended sick leave unless the disease is addressed in its early stages. Since PCP almost always infects individuals with immune disorders and various related medical conditions, work restrictions and accommodations will require consideration on an individual, case-by-case basis.

Comorbid Conditions

Coexisting conditions that may impact recovery include immune deficient disorders, particularly AIDS (acquired immune deficiency syndrome).

Other groups at risk for PCP are individuals with organ transplants requiring drugs to suppress immunity. The disease also is found in individuals with cancer. Up to 10% of individuals with other immune disorders are thought to have PCP.

Smoking increases risk of lung-related complications. Allergies or intolerance to medications also might extend recovery time.

Complications

Various lung complications may develop, including spontaneous lung collapse (pneumothorax), bronchopleural fistula, pneumatocele, and subcutaneous emphysema. Some individuals have adverse or allergic reactions to medications.

Factors Influencing Duration

The severity of the disease, response to treatment, complications, and the presence of other illnesses might influence length of disability.

Length of Disability

Duration depends on comorbid conditions such as impaired immune system. Disability may be permanent. Individuals infected with PCP are likely to have recurrences of the disease.

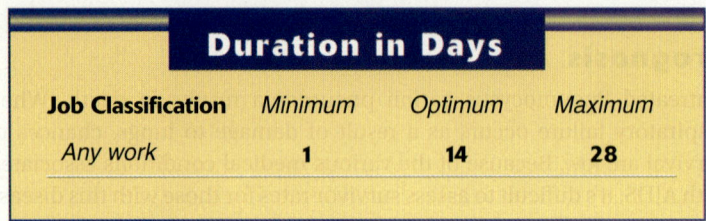

Duration in Days

Job Classification	Minimum	Optimum	Maximum
Any work	1	14	28

Failure to Recover

If an individual fails to recover within the maximum duration expectancy period, the reader may wish to reference the following questions to assist in better understanding the specifics of an individual's medical case.

Regarding diagnosis:

- Does individual have an immune disorder?
- Is individual on immunosuppressant drugs secondary to an organ transplant?
- Does individual have cancer?
- Does individual have dyspnea, fever, tachypnea, cyanosis, joint pain, or a dry nonproductive cough?
- Does the individual have tachycardia? Weight loss?
- Is individual on supplemental oxygen?
- Has individual had flow cytometry, blood tests, chest x-rays, and a CT scan of the chest? Were lung function and blood gases measured?
- Has sputum been examined microscopically?
- Was it necessary to do a bronchial or open lung biopsy?
- Have conditions with similar symptoms been ruled out?

Regarding treatment:

- Has individual received antibiotics orally, intravenously, or in aerosol form?
- Was oxygen required?
- Were corticosteroids also used?

Regarding prognosis:

- Is individual's employer able to accommodate any necessary restrictions?
- Does individual have any conditions that may affect ability to recover?
- Has individual addressed correctable risk factors?
- Has individual had any complications such as pneumothorax bronchopleural fistula? Pneumatocele? Subcutaneous emphysema? Allergic reactions to any of the drugs?

References

Leoung, Gifford S. Pneumocystis Carinii Pneumonia. The AIDS Knowledge Base. 01 Jun 1998. 01 Jan 2001 <http://hivinsite.ucsf.edu/akb/1997/06pcp/index.html#A>.

Pneumonectomy

Other names / synonyms: Lung Removal, Removal of Lung, Total Lung Excision

32.5

Definition

A pneumonectomy is the surgical removal of an entire lung, primarily for the treatment of lung cancer. Before a decision is made to remove a cancerous lung, pulmonary function tests are performed on the lung that will remain to ensure it is healthy enough to cope with the increased demands to be placed on it.

Lung cancer is the single largest cause of death from cancer among both men and women in the US, and accounts for more than 1 in every 4 cancer deaths nationally. Cigarette smoking is the leading cause of lung cancer. The risk of lung cancer for male cigarette smokers is more than 2,000% higher than among male nonsmokers; for women, the risks are approximately 1,200% greater. Nonsmokers who live or work with smokers experience a 30-50% elevated risk for lung cancer. Occupational exposure to asbestos and radioactive emissions from radon in uranium mines are other causes of lung cancer.

Lung cancer is the second most common cancer found in men following prostate cancer. It is the second most common cancer in women following breast cancer and colorectal cancer. Lung cancer generally occurs in individuals between the 50-70 years of age.

Reason for Procedure

Pneumonectomy is most commonly performed to treat lung cancer that cannot be removed with a lobectomy or lung resection. Types of lung cancer include squamous cell carcinoma, adenocarcinoma, small cell carcinoma, large cell carcinoma, and malignant mesothelioma (caused by occupational exposure to asbestos). Other diseases and conditions treated with pneumonectomy include chronic bronchiectasis and multiple abscesses of the lung.

Description

To perform a pneumonectomy, the surgeon usually approaches the lungs from the side through a thoracotomy incision. In some cases, the surgeon may choose to approach the lungs from the front through the breastbone (median sternotomy incision), but this approach is much less common.

For a thoracotomy approach, the individual is at first positioned on the back (supine position), and secured to the table with a safety belt across the upper thighs. Monitoring equipment is secured (temperature probe, ECG leads, and a pulse oximeter finger cot to measure the level of oxygen in the blood). Intravenous lines are inserted for administration of fluids, medications, and blood during and after surgery. A special line to monitor arterial blood gases (oxygen and carbon dioxide) is also inserted. General anesthesia is induced and a breathing tube (endotracheal tube) is placed through the mouth and into the windpipe (trachea), in order to maintain an airway.

After being anesthetized, the individual is repositioned onto the non-operable side (lateral or semi-lateral position). (In some cases, the surgeon may decide to divide the breastbone with a saw to provide better access to the lungs. In this case, the individual remains positioned on the back.) Arms are secured and bony prominences (hip, ankle, elbow, etc.) are padded to prevent pressure sores. A catheter may be inserted into the spine to be used for the delivery of pain medication postoperatively (epidural analgesia). Compression stockings may be applied to keep an even flow of blood moving through the legs during surgery, and prevent clot formation. A urinary catheter is inserted into the bladder and the tubing is hooked to a drainage bag in order to monitor kidney (renal) function during surgery. A nasogastric tube may be passed through the nose and into the stomach to drain accumulated stomach secretions. A conduction pad may be secured on the thigh to prevent burns when blood vessels are cauterized with the electrocautery machine. The surgical area is washed (prepped) with an antibacterial solution, including the entire rib cage on the surgical side, from the middle of the back to the middle of the chest and stomach, and from the neck to below the hip). The individual is covered with sterile, moisture-proof surgical drapes, leaving the surgical area exposed (the entire rib cage on the surgical side). The head portion of the drape is lifted off of the individual's face and fastened to a canopy so that the entire head and neck is protected from the surgical field but exposed to the anesthesiologist. A sterile plastic adhesive drape is placed over the exposed surgical field.

The individual's skin, underlying tissue, and muscle is cut (incised), usually between the fourth and fifth ribs. A rib may be removed to provide a better view. The ribs are separated with a rib retractor. The retractor is slowly cranked open, separating the ribs and exposing the diseased lung. The surgeon uses scissors to open the membrane that surrounds the lung (the pleura) and gently peel it away from the lung. All the branches of the main blood vessels entering and leaving the lung (pulmonary artery and vein) are clamped, tied twice with nonabsorbable suture, and divided. The main air tube (bronchus) going from the windpipe (trachea) to the diseased lung is clamped and divided. The lung is removed from the chest. A piece of pleura may be used to cover the bronchus stump. The bronchus stump is then closed with nonabsorbable suture. The chest cavity is irrigated with sterile salt water (saline) to check for leaks in the bronchus stump, and to clear the chest of old blood. Bleeding is controlled with sutures and electrocautery.

Chest tubes are not inserted after pneumonectomy, although they are inserted after other surgical procedures on the lung. Following pneumonectomy, the chest cavity is allowed to fill with air and fluid. The levels are monitored so that they put just enough pressure on the heart and other lung to keep them in their normal space, without obstructing them or letting them drift to the empty side. During closure, the muscle and each layer of tissue is closed with surgical sutures. The skin is closed with sutures and the suture line is covered with a thin layer of sterile gauze and secured with tape. The individual may transfer directly to the Intensive Care Unit for recovery from anesthesia rather than transferring to the Recovery Room.

Prognosis

Prognosis following pneumonectomy for lung cancer is poor. If lung cancer is found early before it has spread to lymph nodes or other organs, the 5-year survival rate following surgery is 42%. However, the 5-year survival rate for all stages of lung cancer combined is 14%.

Following pneumonectomy, an individual may be able to return to work. As the disease progresses, however, the individual may become permanently disabled.

Specialists

- Thoracic Surgeon

Rehabilitation

Individuals who undergo pneumonectomy may require occupational, physical, and respiratory therapy after surgery.

Respiratory therapy addresses increasing lung capacity and decreasing the risk for the buildup of lung secretions. Respiratory therapists teach individuals pursed lip breathing to increase the airflow to the lungs. Individuals may also use an incentive spirometer, which is a device that measures and displays the amount of air inspired to help motivate individuals to take deeper breaths. Individuals also learn to produce an effective cough through techniques such as huffing, in which air is breathed out forcefully while the mouth is open. Individuals also learn positions to relieve shortness of breath such as leaning forward while sitting, with the arms resting on the thighs.

Occupational therapy addresses any fatigue or shortness of breath that may occur during activities of daily living. Occupational therapists may teach energy conservation techniques, in which activities of daily living are broken up into smaller components, thereby making tasks more manageable.

Physical therapy addresses decreased endurance, strength, and range of motion. Individuals learn to stretch the shoulder and chest muscles on the side of the removed lung to help normalize posture. Individuals perform strengthening exercises of the arms and legs to improve overall endurance. In addition to strengthening the arms and legs, the muscles of the upper back are strengthened through exercises, such as shoulder blade squeezes to promote normal posture. Individuals also strengthen the diaphragm by lying on the back and performing abdominal breathing exercises. Individuals may perform aerobic activity such as walking on a treadmill or riding a stationary bicycle to further increase endurance. Individuals learn to rate the amount of energy they expend by utilizing a rating of perceived exertion scale. This is a numbered scale that rates exercises from "very, very light" to "very, very hard." Individuals use this scale to stay within safe exercise parameters that have been predetermined by their physicians.

Work Restrictions / Accommodations

Individuals who have had a pneumonectomy without experiencing serious postoperative complications or disabilities may be able to return to work part time 6-10 weeks after surgery. Hours of work may be gradually increased over the next several weeks until the individual is working a full day, if that is possible. Individuals with chronic lung disease will most likely require work restrictions and accommodations that aid in conserving energy and reducing the load on the remaining lung. Most individuals with only one lung will experience some degree of shortness of breath even without exertion. Oxygen capacity of the lung is decreased and, therefore, individuals will not be able to do heavy work.

Other medical problems or permanent disabilities because of underlying medical conditions (such as diabetes, chronic renal failure requiring dialysis, chronic heart disease) or postoperative complications may also require work restrictions and accommodations.

Comorbid Conditions

Pre-existing diseases that affect any of the major body systems, such as high blood pressure, chronic kidney (renal) disease, bleeding disorders, diabetes mellitus, chronic obstructive lung disease, chronic heart disease, and immunosuppressive diseases; a history of smoking or exposure to secondhand smoke; occupational exposure to asbestos and radioactive emissions from radon in uranium mines; or obesity are possible comorbid conditions.

Procedure Complications

Complications following pneumonectomy include collapsed lung (atelectasis), heart rhythm disturbances, air leakage from the bronchial stump (pneumothorax), hemorrhage, shifting of organs and tissue into the empty chest cavity (mediastinal shift), lung infection (pneumonia), accumulation of excess fluid in the empty chest cavity (pleural effusion), respiratory insufficiency, respiratory failure, and death.

A ruptured bronchial stump requires immediate surgery, as does hemorrhage caused by slippage of a suture from one of the major pulmonary blood vessels that were cut and sutured during the pneumectomy.

Factors Influencing Duration

Factors influencing the length of disability include the stage of the disease when first diagnosed, the individual's age and general health, and the type of tumor and its growth rate. Previous lung surgery may influence disability. Following pneumonectomy, the number and severity of postoperative complications (such as wound infection, bleeding, pneumonia, respiratory insufficiency, or an adverse reaction to a general anesthetic), the amount of blood loss during surgery and postoperatively, the number of blood transfusions required, the individual's nutritional status and mental and emotional stability, access to rehabilitation facilities, and the strength of the individual's support system are other factors that influence disability.

Length of Disability

Expected length of disability ranges from 6-14 weeks following uncomplicated pneumonectomy. Disability may be permanent if the individual's remaining lung cannot provide sufficient oxygen to permit activity, or if the underlying cancer has spread to other vital organs.

Duration in Days

Job Classification	Minimum	Optimum	Maximum
Sedentary work	56	84	Indefinite
Light work	56	84	Indefinite
Medium work	56	84	Indefinite
Heavy work	Indefinite	Indefinite	Indefinite
Very Heavy work	Indefinite	Indefinite	Indefinite

References

Kisner, Carolyn, and Lynn Allen Colby. "Chest Physical Therapy." Therapeutic Exercise: Foundations and Techniques, 2nd ed. Philadelphia: F.A. Davis Company, 1990. 57-61.

Watchie, Joanne. Cardiopulmonary Physical Therapy. Philadelphia: W.B. Saunders Company, 1995.

Pneumonia

Other names / synonyms: Atypical Pneumonia, Bacterial Pneumonia, Bronchopneumonia, Eaton's Pneumonia, Lobar Pneumonia, Nonbacterial Pneumonia, Pneumonitis, Primary Atypical Pneumonia, Viral Pneumonia, Walking Pneumonia

480, 481, 482, 482.0, 482.1, 482.2, 482.3, 482.4, 482.8, 482.9, 483, 484, 485, 486, 507, 507.0

Definition

Pneumonia is a general term used for an infection of the lungs. This infection can be caused by a variety of microorganisms and results in an inflammatory reaction within the small air spaces of the lung (alveoli). The alveoli fill with fluid and white blood cells, interfering with the lung's ability to receive oxygen. This process can occur gradually or quickly, depending on the potency of the infecting organism and the ability of the body's immune system to fight off the infection. Pneumonia can be mild enough to be cured with oral antibiotics and a few days rest, or severe enough to require hospitalization in an intensive care unit. Death may occur as a result of respiratory failure.

Several classification systems are used to define the types of pneumonias. One system classifies pneumonia by its anatomic location within the lungs. If the pneumonia involves all or most of the alveoli in just one lobe of the lung, it may be called lobar pneumonia. If the pneumonia starts in the bronchi and bronchioles (airways) and then spreads to patches of tissue in one or both lungs, it may be called bronchopneumonia. Interstitial pneumonia is pneumonia located in the space around the alveoli (interstitial tissue).

Another classification system is based on whether the symptoms are typical pneumonia or atypical pneumonia. Pneumonia may also be classified by its place of origin. Pneumonia acquired in a hospital setting is referred to as nosocomial pneumonia, while pneumonia acquired in the community is referred to as community-acquired pneumonia. Aspiration pneumonia refers to pneumonia caused by accidental inhalation of vomit or other liquid.

Although each of these classifications supplies some helpful information about the characteristics of an individual's pneumonia, the most important classification is the one based on the organisms causing the infection. For example, pneumonia can be referred to as viral, pneumococcal, staphylococcal, or Klebsiella pneumonia according to the infecting agent.

Viral infections make up about one-half of all cases of pneumonia. Most often caused by influenza viruses, viral pneumonia can also be caused by the chickenpox virus or by adenovirus (a group of related viruses that cause respiratory tract infections). Other viruses that can cause pneumonia include varicella, adenovirus, and cytomegalovirus (CMV). Because a virus causes viral pneumonia rather than a bacterium, it does not generally respond well to antibiotics.

Bacterial pneumonia is more common among adults. The four routes by which bacteria can enter the lungs are inhalation from the surrounding air, through the bloodstream from an infection elsewhere within the body, contact with nearby infected sites, or by inhalation (aspiration) of organisms already growing in the individual's mouth or throat. The most common causes of bacterial pneumonia include Streptococcus pneumoniae (also called pneumococcus), Haemophilus influenzae, Legionella pneumophila, Klebsiella pneumoniae, Staphylococcus aureus, Pseudomonas species, and Escherichia coli.

Many types of fungi and yeast, as well as protozoa, mycoplasma, and Chlamydia psittaci (a bacteria-like microorganism transmitted by birds) can cause pneumonia. Another organism, Pneumocystis carinii, is of particular concern because it causes pneumonia in individuals with compromised immune systems, particularly HIV-infected individuals.

Pneumonitis is a term that also refers to inflammation of the lungs. It may be due to infection, an allergic reaction (caused by inhalation of dust containing animal or plant material), exposure to radiation, accidental inhalation of vomit or other liquid (aspiration pneumonia), or as a rare side effect of certain drugs (acebutolol, azathioprine).

Because pneumonia tends to occur when pathogenic agents overwhelm the defenses that normally protect the lower respiratory tract, a recent illness such as influenza can lead to pneumonia. Other risk factors include individuals over the age of 60, malnutrition, smoking, alcoholism, and drug addiction. Pneumonia can also occur if an individual's immune system has been compromised by chronic medical conditions such as cystic fibrosis, congestive heart failure, chronic obstructive pulmonary (lung) disease, cancer, diabetes, cirrhosis of the liver, or kidney failure, acquired immunodeficiency syndrome (AIDS), chemotherapy, and corticosteroid therapy can also compromise the immune system.

The incidence of certain types of pneumonia tends to peak at different times during the year. Bacterial and viral pneumonia tend to peak in the winter months, and pneumonia caused by Mycoplasma pneumonia and Legionella in the summer and fall.

Pneumonia is the sixth leading cause of death in the US and the fourth leading cause of death among the elderly. Every year in the US, 2 million individuals develop pneumonia and 40,000 to 70,000 of these die. It is estimated that each year over 1 million cases of community-acquired pneumonia are severe enough to require hospitalization. These infections are usually viral or bacterial in origin, with rare instances of fungal or parasitic infection. Over 275,000 individuals per year are diagnosed with hospital-acquired (nosocomial) pneumonia with a very high mortality rate.

Diagnosis

History: Typical symptoms of pneumonia include sudden onset, shortness of breath, fever, chills, headache, and muscle pain (myalgia). A cough may produce yellow-green sputum and occasionally blood. Chest pain is worse when inhaling because of inflammation in the membranes lining the lungs and chest cavity (pleurisy).

Symptoms of viral and atypical pneumonia are different in that chills are not accompanied by fever, and the cough is dry and nonproductive (no mucus is coughed up). Flu-like symptoms include headache, muscle pain, and weakness. Within 12 to 36 hours, breathlessness may increase accompanied by a worsening cough that now produces a small amount of mucus. Typical respiratory symptoms may be masked in the elderly and in individuals taking corticosteroids or aspirin. These individuals may instead present with confusion, lethargy, and an elevated respiratory rate.

To assist in identifying less common infectious organisms, the medical history should include a complete history of the illness (including nonrespiratory symptoms such as rash, diarrhea, nausea, and mental status), and a history of the individual's occupation, hobbies, pets, and recent travel. To aid in diagnosis, the individual should also provide any history of alcoholism, swallowing difficulties, or decreased mental alertness, all of which can cause inhalation of food or liquid into the lungs (aspiration pneumonia).

Physical exam: On physical exam, breathing may be labored, using accessory muscles in the neck, chest, and abdomen. In severe pneumonia, the individual may exhibit a respiratory rate above 30 breaths per minute (tachypnea). Listening through a stethoscope (auscultation) may reveal abnormal breath sounds that indicate fluid in the lungs (rales or crackles) or areas lacking air exchange (consolidative breath sounds).

Tests: A chest x-ray can establish the diagnosis of pneumonia, determine the extent of lung infection, and track the progression of the disease. A complete blood count (CBC) is routinely obtained, but viral pneumonias do not produce the high white cell count generally associated with bacterial pneumonia. Blood oxygen level is measured by arterial blood gases or oximetry and is often low.

Cultures of blood or sputum samples can identify the infecting microorganism. A gram stain can provide clues to the physician about the identity of the infecting microorganism and appropriate antibiotics even before cultures are completed. Antibiotic sensitivity is used to identify appropriate drug therapy. In mild to moderate pneumonia, cultures and sensitivity may not be performed unless the individual does not respond to treatment.

Routine cultures detect only bacteria. Special viral cultures must be ordered to detect viruses. Often these cultures are not practical since it takes weeks for the virus to grow. Serology studies can identify some microorganisms by looking for the development of antibodies to that microorganism in an individual's blood.

Examination of the main airways of the lungs by using a flexible, fiberoptic scope (bronchoscopy) or surgical removal of lung tissue for microscopic examination (open lung biopsy) may be required when analyzing very difficult cases or pneumonia that occurs in immunocompromised individuals.

Treatment

Antibiotics are the primary treatment for most cases of pneumonia. In mild to moderate cases, oral antibiotics are given for the most likely infecting organism. If an individual does not begin to respond to the selected antibiotic therapy in 2 to 3 days, cultures and antibiotic sensitivity tests may be performed to positively identify the causative organism and select the best antibiotics with which to treat it. Growing resistance of microorganisms to antibiotics makes it increasingly difficult to predict which antibiotic will be effective without confirmatory antibiotic sensitivity tests.

Supportive therapy includes increased fluid intake (hydration) and agents to thin and mobilize secretions (mucolytic and mucokinetic agents), medication to widen the airways in the lungs (bronchodilators), cough suppressants, and medication to reduce fever (antipyretics) and pain (analgesics).

Viral pneumonia most often caused by influenza viruses, does not respond effectively to antibiotic therapy unless a secondary bacterial infection develops in the lungs. Although antiviral agents are available to work against several specific viruses (influenza A, varicella), there is no effective drug treatment for most viral pneumonias. General treatment measures include adequate fluid intake and analgesics for chest pain. Oxygen is administered only if the individual becomes oxygen-deprived (hypoxic).

Individuals with severe pneumonia often require hospitalization to provide extra oxygen, respiratory therapy, intravenous antibiotics, and intravenous fluids. Individuals with multiple risk factors indicating poor outcome from pneumonia (i.e., those with chronic underlying medical conditions) may also be hospitalized for closer observation.

Pneumonia caused by the influenza virus can be prevented with an annual influenza vaccine. There is also a vaccine against the Streptococcus pneumoniae bacteria. One dose of the pneumococcal vaccine offers lifetime protection. Some experts, however, recommend a booster after 6 years. These vaccines are recommended for seniors (over 65 years), residents of long-term care facilities, and individuals with underlying chronic disease or compromised immune systems. Neither vaccine offers complete protection, however. Although unlikely, an immunized individual can still develop pneumonia.

Prognosis

Outcome for any individual diagnosed with pneumonia is variable and will depend on the overall health and immune competence of the individual, the virulence of the organism causing the pneumonia, and the effectiveness of the prescribed treatment. Most cases of mild to moderate pneumonia respond well to oral antibiotic therapy. However, elderly or debilitated individuals may fail to respond to treatment and consequently, more and more of their lung tissue becomes affected. Death may occur as a result of respiratory failure.

Community-acquired pneumonia requiring hospitalization has a mortality rate of approximately 14%. Where hospitalization is not required, the mortality rate is 1%. Nosocomial pneumonia, the most deadly of nosocomial infections, has a mortality rate of 20-50%.

Lung damage caused by pneumonia can result in chronic respiratory diseases later in life.

Differential Diagnosis

Conditions with similar symptoms include bronchitis, chronic obstructive pulmonary disease (COPD), pulmonary embolism, asthma, bronchiectasis, tuberculosis, cancer, congestive heart failure, and AIDS. Adult respiratory distress syndrome (ARDS) is a noninfectious, extremely serious lung disease similar to pneumonia.

Specialists

- Infectious Disease Physician
- Pulmonologist
- Internist

Rehabilitation

Physical and respiratory therapy when applied appropriately and in conjunction with antibiotics can be an important aspect of the overall treatment in rehabilitating individuals with pneumonia. Physical therapy improves ventilation using breathing exercises localized to the area of involvement followed by a gradual strengthening program.

When hospitalized, the physical therapist and/or respiratory therapist help the individual cough in order to mobilize secretions and clear the airway by having the individual lie in a position that allows for the most effective drainage of secretions. The individual may lie on his or her side with the affected side upward and the head slightly lower than the chest. In addition to proper positioning, the physical therapist uses percussion and vibration techniques to the affected areas to help "shake loose" mucous and secretions. The therapist performs chest percussion with the hands in a cupped position, mildly striking repeatedly over the area of the lung affected by pneumonia.

Once the symptoms of pneumonia subside and breathing becomes easier, focus is then placed on strength and endurance by incorporating aerobic-type activity into the rehabilitation program. By building endurance, the individual increases the ability to work and the resistance to fatigue. A physical therapist experienced in cardiac and pulmonary rehabilitation keeps a daily log of the individual's blood pressure, heart rate, and cardiac rhythm. As endurance increases without symptoms of shortness of breath, the individual begins active upper and lower extremity exercises using very light resistance in addition to light aerobic activities such as brisk walking and low-resistance biking.

The individual with pneumonia is told that the exercise program can be a lengthy process in order to obtain the maximum benefit of increased pulmonary stamina. Through an exercise program, the negative cardiovascular and pulmonary effects of pneumonia can be reversed.

Because most pulmonary disorders are managed with medication, it is important that individuals with pneumonia tell the rehabilitation personnel what medications they are taking as many of these drugs alter the acute and chronic response to exercise.

Work Restrictions / Accommodations

Work restrictions are determined on an individual basis. Individuals may need to avoid inhaled irritants such as dust, fumes, cigarette smoke, and cold. Strenuous activity may need to be temporarily avoided. Longer, more frequent rest breaks may be required until physical stamina returns.

Complementary and Alternative Therapies

Content is intended for awareness only. Treatments may or may not be effective. Scientific evidence may be lacking and some substances have potentially toxic effects. Dr. Presley Reed and the editors do not endorse the use of these therapies in the absence of consultation with a licensed medical professional.

Bakumondo-to - May be a good antitussive agent for pneumonia associated with a dry cough resistant to other antitussives.

Comorbid Conditions

Disability may be lengthened by a deficient or suppressed immune system, nicotine abuse, or the presence of an industrial lung disease.

Complications

Viral infection can progress into a bacterial infection. Pneumonia can cause fluid to accumulate in the space between the lung and the chest wall (pleural effusion). This fluid can then become infected (empyema) and spread the infection to the bloodstream (sepsis). As a result, other tissues may become infected including joints (arthritis), membranes lining the brain and spinal cord (meningitis), the brain itself (encephalitis), the heart (endocarditis or pericarditis), or the kidneys (nephritis). Septic shock is a severe complication and occurs when multiplying bacteria release toxins into the bloodstream. Other serious complications include respiratory failure or the development of an abscess in the lung. Individuals with chronic medical conditions such as diabetes, heart disease, kidney disease, or lung disease often experience a worsening of their medical condition during pneumonia.

Factors Influencing Duration

Length of disability may be influenced by the age of the individual, general state of health, underlying chronic medical conditions, severity of the pneumonia, complications, immune competence, type of organism causing the pneumonia, susceptibility of the organism to prescribed treatment, individual's compliance with treatment, and cigarette smoking.

Length of Disability

Viral and lobar pneumonia.

Duration in Days

Job Classification	Minimum	Optimum	Maximum
Sedentary work	7	14	21
Light work	7	14	21
Medium work	7	14	21
Heavy work	7	14	21
Very Heavy work	7	14	21

Bronchopneumonia.

Duration in Days

Job Classification	Minimum	Optimum	Maximum
Sedentary work	7	14	21
Light work	7	14	21
Medium work	7	14	28
Heavy work	7	14	35
Very Heavy work	7	14	35

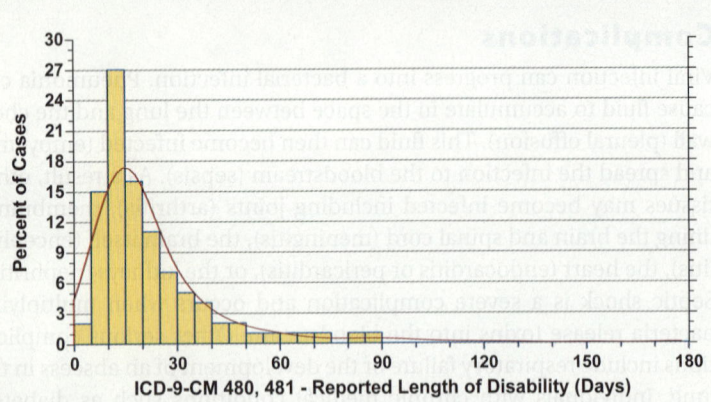
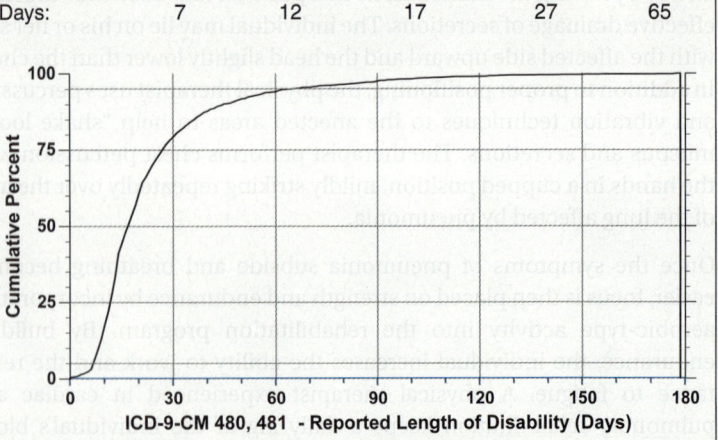
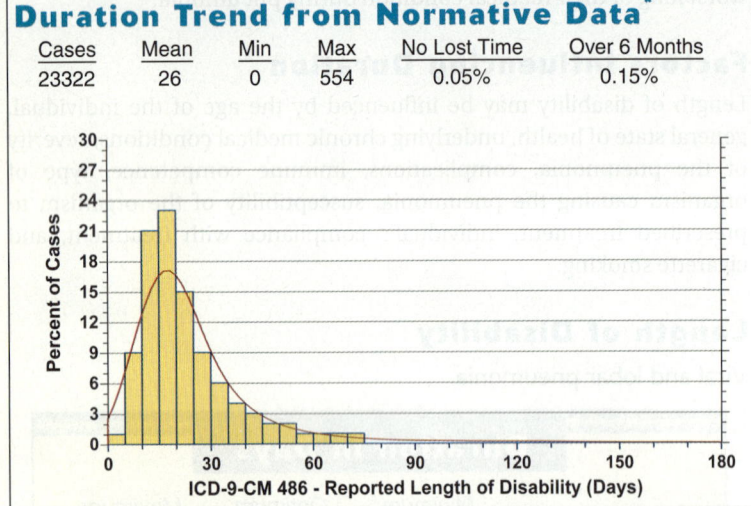
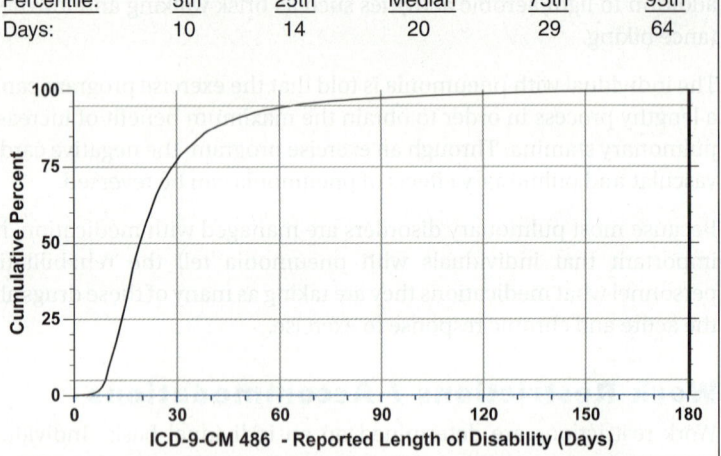

* Differences may exist between the expected duration tables and the normative graphs. Duration tables provide expected recovery periods based on the type of work performed by the individual. The normative graphs reflect the actual observed experience of many individuals across the spectrum of physical conditions, in a variety of industries, and with varying levels of case management.

Failure to Recover

If an individual fails to recover within the maximum duration expectancy period, the reader may wish to reference the following questions to assist in better understanding the specifics of an individual's medical case.

Regarding diagnosis:

- Has individual had a recent history of flu-like symptoms?
- Were abnormal breath sounds noted on physical exam?
- Was the diagnosis of pneumonia confirmed with a chest x-ray and/or positive sputum cultures?
- Were cultures and sensitivity tests of sputum and/or blood done to help identify the causative organism and appropriate antimicrobial treatment?
- Was the underlying cause bacterial, fungal, or viral?
- Has individual had the appropriate influenzae vaccinations?
- Did individual have a bronchoscopy? Open lung biopsy?
- Were other conditions with similar symptoms such as bronchitis, COPD, asthma, PE, bronchiectasis, tuberculosis, cancer, CHF, ARDS ruled out?

Regarding treatment:

- Did individual receive appropriate supportive care, i.e., respiratory care, fluids, antipyretics, or analgesics?
- Did individual receive appropriate antimicrobial treatment? Has individual responded favorably to prescribed treatment?
- Were the symptoms severe enough to warrant hospitalization?
- Was individual counseled regarding influenza vaccination for future prevention?

Regarding prognosis:

- Was individual compliant with the treatment recommendations?
- Has adequate time elapsed for complete recovery?
- If the symptoms persisted despite treatment, was a repeat culture and sensitivity done to rule out the possibility of antibiotic resistant bacteria or a secondary infection?
- Was individual reexamined to rule out the possibility of complications?

- Does individual have any existing conditions (advanced age, immune suppression, chronic lung disease, or other chronic illness) that could impact recovery and prognosis? If so, are these conditions being addressed in the treatment plan?
- Has individual suffered any associated conditions or complications that may influence recovery and prognosis (i.e., pleural effusion, empyema, septic shock, respiratory failure)?
- What work or environmental factors impact individual's recovery or prolong disability? Does individual smoke? If so, was he or she referred to a smoking cessation program?

References

Ferri, Fred. Ferri's Clinical Advisor. St. Louis: Mosby, 2000.

Kisner, C., and L. Colby. Therapeutic Exercise Foundations and Techniques. Philadelphia: F.A. Davis Company, 1990.

Mizushima, Y., A. Hirata, and T. Hori. "Antitussive Effect of Herbal Medicine Bakumondo-to: A Case Report." American Journal of Chinese Medicine 24 3-4 (1996): 321-325.

Scully, Rosemary M., and Marylou R. Barnes. Physical Therapy. Philadelphia: J.B. Lippincott Company, 1989.

Pneumothorax

Other names / synonyms: Aeropleura, Aerothorax, Collapse of the Lung, Lung Collapse, Pneumatothorax, Spontaneous Pneumothorax, Tension Pneumothorax

512, 512.0, 512.8, 860.0, 860.1

Definition

Pneumothorax is a condition in which air or gas has entered the pleural cavity (space between the two layers of pleura lining the outside of the lungs and the inside of the chest wall). This collection of air can expand the normally closed pleural space, drive up pleural pressure, and result in a partial or complete collapse of the lung. This air usually enters the pleural space through a hole in the lung or chest wall. There are several causes for development of a pneumothorax.

A spontaneous pneumothorax is typically caused by rupture of small air-filled sacs in the lungs called blebs; they are usually located at the apex of the lung. Symptoms of a spontaneous pneumothorax usually begin without warning in persons who were thought to be otherwise healthy; cigarette smoking and family history are the most common risk factors for developing spontaneous pneumothorax in these individuals. It occurs most commonly in tall, thin men between the ages of 20 and 40; it is believed that the increased length of the chest may contribute to bleb formation in the lungs. About 20,000 new cases of spontaneous pneumothorax are diagnosed each year in the US.

Traumatic pneumothorax results from a blunt or penetrating injury to the chest. For example, trauma from a car accident or a stab wound can allow air into the pleural space, causing the lung to collapse. Pneumothorax also can occur when the lung or chest wall is damaged during a medical procedure.

In tension pneumothorax, air accumulates inside the pleural space with each inspiration causing excessive pressure to build. This not only collapses the nearby lung but also puts abnormal pressure on the heart and great vessels, reducing cardiac output (outflow of blood from the heart). Tension pneumothorax most commonly occurs in individuals who are receiving mechanical ventilation (in which a machine "breathes" for the individual) or who have undergone cardiopulmonary resuscitation.

Pneumothorax related to menses is a rare form of pneumothorax that occurs in otherwise healthy women during menstruation. Symptoms develop within 48 hours of menstrual flow.

Pneumothorax may be a complication of underlying lung diseases such as asthma, lung cancer, tuberculosis, whooping cough (pertussis), or chronic obstructive pulmonary disease (COPD). It may also occur in individuals with cystic fibrosis or AIDS. Pneumothorax affects 9 out of 100,000 individuals a year.

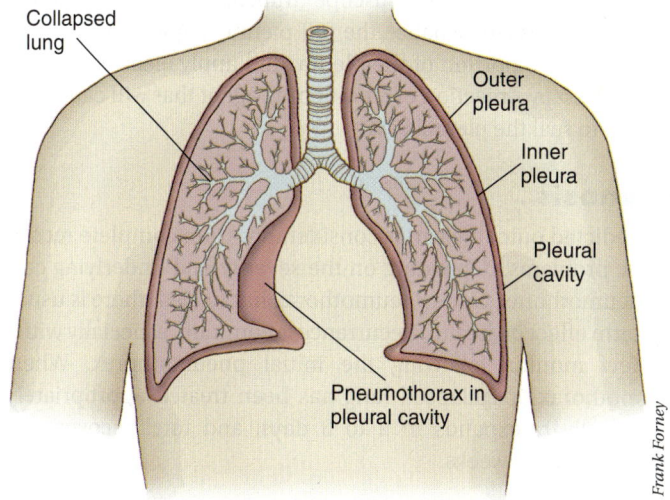

Frank Forney

Diagnosis

History: Symptoms may include a sudden onset of sharp chest pain, shortness of breath (dyspnea), easy fatigue, and occasionally, a dry, hacking cough, painful breathing, and chest tightness. The degree of breathlessness is proportional to the size of the pneumothorax. Symptoms tend to be less severe in a slowly developing pneumothorax, and may actually subside as the body adjusts to the altered physiological state.

Physical exam: With a small collection of air, there may be no detectable signs other than diminished voice and breath sounds. With a large or tension pneumothorax, breath sounds are markedly depressed or absent, heart rate will be rapid, and a lack of oxygen may result in a bluish tinge to the skin (cyanosis). Additional symptoms may include nasal flaring, anxiety, stress, and abdominal pain.

Tests: Characteristic chest x-rays usually show the presence of air outside the lung itself. A small pneumothorax may be overlooked on inhalation and will be obvious only on exhalation. Chest x-rays may also detect some underlying lung disease. CT scans can be used for critical care individuals with complicated pleural spaces or pre-existing multiple chest tubes. Tests of lung volume and capacity (pulmonary function tests), and arterial blood gas (ABG) tests may be performed when the individual is stable. An electrocardiogram (ECG) may be used to assess cardiac affects.

Treatment

The objective of treatment is to remove the gas or air from the pleural space, allowing the lung to re-expand. A small pneumothorax in a healthy adult requires no treatment, as the air will usually reabsorb in a few days. A larger pneumothorax, or a small one associated with lung disease, usually requires treatment. In a small pneumothorax, air can be withdrawn from the pleural cavity through a needle and syringe. Treatment of a large pneumothorax usually requires hospitalization and involves removing air from the pleural space with a suction tube (tube thoracostomy) inserted through the chest wall. The tube may need to stay in place for several days. If the opening (fistula) is large and persistent, surgical repair of the fistula or surgical removal of the involved lung (pneumonectomy) segment may be required.

Treatment of a pneumothorax associated with an underlying lung disease is often more difficult and requires more definitive therapy. Although these individuals may be poor surgical candidates, the surgeon can now use a thoracoscope (thin, lighted instrument inserted between the ribs) to visualize the full pleura, staple or resect a blister (bleb), remove a portion of the pleura, and apply electrocautery, laser, or sclerotherapy (injection of a hardening agent that will cause internal scarring) to seal the pleural cavity.

Prognosis

The predicted outcome varies considerably, from complete recovery to chronic problems, depending on the severity and underlying cause of the pneumothorax. Once pneumothorax has healed, there is usually no long-term effect on health. Recurrence is common, especially within the first few months following the initial pneumothorax. When the pneumothorax or collapsed lung has been treated appropriately, the lung usually re-expands in 2 to 3 days, and total recovery can be expected in 1 to 2 weeks.

A spontaneous pneumothorax has a 30% chance of recurrence, usually on the same side; 50% of individuals who have one spontaneous pneumothorax will have another.

Removing air from the pleural cavity is generally successfully whether accomplished via needle and syringe (small pneumothorax) or tube thoracostomy (large pneumothorax).

Pneumonectomy is a serious procedure; however, most of these surgeries are success. The eventual outcome of the surgery itself depends upon additional treatment, which is usually uneventful.

After the pneumothorax has healed, there is usually no long-term effect on the individual's health. Recurrence is common within the first few months. A spontaneous pneumothorax may happen more than once in over 50% of the cases. To avoid recurrence, the individual should discontinue smoking, and avoid high altitudes, scuba diving, or flying in unpressurized aircraft.

Differential Diagnosis

Conditions with similar symptoms include emphysema, lung abscess, and herniation of the stomach or intestines through the diaphragm. Asthma, chronic obstructive pulmonary disease (COPD), rib fractures, congestive heart failure, pulmonary edema, inflammation of the esophagus (esophagitis), pulmonary embolism, aspiration pneumonia, acute respiratory distress syndrome, angina, and adult respiratory distress syndrome (ARDS) may present with similar signs and symptoms.

Specialists

- Critical Care Specialist
- Emergency Medicine
- Pulmonologist
- Thoracic Surgeon

Work Restrictions / Accommodations

Work restrictions and accommodations are not usually associated with this condition. However, should exertions lead to increased efforts to breathe, a pneumothorax could recur. In such cases, the individual should be restricted from strenuous and heavy work until all danger of recurrence has passed.

Comorbid Conditions

Pre-existing pulmonary disease could lengthen any disability period.

Complications

If there is continual air leakage, the pneumothorax may become progressively larger. This can result in a tension pneumothorax, a condition in which air is allowed to enter but not escape the pleural space. A tension pneumothorax is a medical emergency as it may cause a life-threatening compression of the heart.

Factors Influencing Duration

Length of disability may be influenced by the severity of the symptoms, response to treatment, pre-existing lung disease, the presence of complications, and whether or not the individual smokes cigarettes.

Length of Disability

Duration depends on size, cause, and condition of other lung. Recurrence may cause lengthy disability and surgery.

Closed thoracostomy with chest tube.

Duration in Days

Job Classification	Minimum	Optimum	Maximum
Sedentary work	3	14	28
Light work	3	14	28
Medium work	3	21	42
Heavy work	7	21	42
Very Heavy work	7	21	42

Open thoracotomy.

Duration in Days

Job Classification	Minimum	Optimum	Maximum
Sedentary work	21	28	35
Light work	21	28	35
Medium work	21	28	35
Heavy work	28	35	42
Very Heavy work	28	35	42

Failure to Recover

If an individual fails to recover within the maximum duration expectancy period, the reader may wish to reference the following questions to assist in better understanding the specifics of an individual's medical case.

Regarding diagnosis:

- Is there a history of injury to the chest and lungs?
- Did the individual have a sudden onset of sharp chest pain and shortness of breath? How severe?
- Is the individual a smoker? What is the individual's gender? Is the individual tall and thin?
- Has the individual undergone CPR? Are they on a respirator?
- Does the individual have any underlying condition that places him/her at risk for developing a pneumothorax such as asthma, COPD, lung cancer, AIDS or cystic fibrosis?
- Did the individual have chest x-ray's that included inspiration and expiration views?
- Was the diagnosis confirmed with a chest x-ray? If so, does it show residual or recurrent pneumothorax?
- Were pulmonary function tests, arterial blood gasses and ECG done later?
- Were other conditions with similar symptoms ruled out (e.g., Asthma, chronic obstructive pulmonary disease and emphysema, rib fractures, congestive heart failure and pulmonary edema, inflammation of the esophagus (esophagitis), pulmonary embolism, aspiration pneumonia, acute respiratory distress syndrome, angina, and adult respiratory distress syndrome)?

Regarding treatment:

- Was placement of a thoracostomy tube or needle decompression warranted?
- Was a repeat chest x-ray done to monitor resolution of the pneumothorax?
- If the pneumothorax persisted or worsened despite treatment was placement of additional chest tubes tried?
- Was surgery indicated?
- Were underlying conditions addressed appropriately in the treatment plan?
- Was this episode a recurrence or the initial episode?

Regarding prognosis:

- Does the individual have any underlying conditions such as chronic lung disease, asthma, AIDS, heart disease or cancer that could impact recovery and prognosis?
- Did the individual experience any complications such as spontaneous pneumothorax and/or cardiopulmonary arrest, which could impact recovery and prognosis?

References

"Pneumothorax." Medline Plus Health Information. 1.0, 1999 26 Sep 2000 14 Dec 2000 <http://medlineplus.adam.com/ency/article/000087.htm>.

"Pneumothorax." InteliHealth, Inc. 29 Jan 2000. 19 Dec 2000 <http://www.intelihealth.com/IH/ihtIH?t=23665&p=~br,IHW|~st,24479|~r,WSIHW000|~b,*|>.

Chang, A.K., MD, and Erik D. Barton, MD, MS. "Pneumothorax, Iatrogenic, Spontaneous and Pneumomediastinum." eMedicine.com. 01 Oct 2000. 19 Dec 2000 <http://emedicine.com/emerg/topic469_pr.htm>.

Staton, G.W. Jr., and R.H. Ingram, Jr. "Disorders of the Pleura, Hila, and Mediastinum." Dale, D.C., and Daniel D. Federman, MD New York: WebMD Corporation, 2000 Scientific American Medicine. 19 Dec 2000 <http://www.samed.com/sam/forms/index.htm>.

Poison Ivy, Oak, Sumac, or Other Plant Dermatitis

Other names / synonyms: Rhus Dermatitis
692.6

Definition

Plant dermatitis is an allergic contact dermatitis, which is a skin inflammation caused by direct contact with any of a number of toxic plants especially poison ivy, poison oak, or poison sumac. Other plants that induce allergic contact dermatitis include cashew nut tree, mango tree and fruit, Brazilian pepper tree, Japanese lacquer tree, Indian marking nut tree, Hawaiian Kahili tree flower, Ginkgo tree, tulip bulbs, and certain members of the sunflower and onion families.

Allergic reactions occur when an individual's immune system becomes sensitized to a substance (sensitization phase) and then reacts when again exposed to that substance (elicitation phase). In the case of plant dermatitis, individuals are sensitive to certain chemicals produced by the plant. The immune response occurs in the skin and leads to the characteristic rash. The rash appears soon after direct contact with toxic plants, contact with contaminated clothing or pets, or inhalation of the smoke produced by burning toxic plants.

Half of the population of the US reacts to poison ivy. Sensitivity to toxic plants appears to be hereditary so individuals with a family history of plant dermatitis may be at an increased risk of developing plant dermatitis. Individuals who recreate outdoors, horticulturists, florists, grocers, agricultural workers, foresters, forest fire fighters, and other outdoor workers are at an increased risk of developing plant dermatitis. Poison ivy and poison oak are the primary causes of dermatitis in outdoor workers.

Plant dermatitis affects 36% of US agricultural workers at least once a year. Eight percent of florists have hand dermatitis at any given time, 30% during any year, and a 46% career incidence. Ten percent of lost-time injuries for foresters are due to plant dermatitis.

Diagnosis

History: Signs of plant dermatitis usually include red, swollen, or itchy areas on the skin. Blisters, weeping, and crusting may also be present. The individual may report a previous reaction to a particular suspected substance. The individual with plant dermatitis often reports working or recreating outdoors. Plant dermatitis usually occurs on exposed skin of the legs and arms. Air transfer of the plant allergens can lead to extensive dermatitis on the face and other exposed areas.

Physical exam: The early stages of plant dermatitis typically present as reddened (erythematous) and swollen (edematous) skin followed by development of small and large blisters (vesicles and bullae, respectively). The blisters may ooze and then crust over with scab formation. Plant dermatitis is commonly seen as streaks or lines of blisters on the arms or legs.

Tests: Tests are usually not required. Patch testing may be performed in difficult cases where the causative agent is unknown.

Treatment

Treatment consists primarily of identifying the offending agent and avoiding it. Clothing worn by the individual when he or she contracted plant dermatitis should be washed to remove residual toxic chemicals. Within the first hour following exposure to a toxic plant, gently washing the skin with a mild soap can remove some of the allergenic chemicals. Medications include application of topical corticosteroid cream before blisters appear, oral antihistamines to reduce itching (pruritus), and astringent lotions to resolve blisters. Oral corticosteroids may be required for severe cases and those involving the genitals or face. Cool, wet compresses of Burrow's solution or cool oatmeal baths can provide relief. Blisters may be opened with scissors (debridement).

Prognosis

Plant dermatitis usually resolves within 10 to 14 days provided the offending plant is identified and avoided. Dermatitis caused by contact with toxic plants is usually not harmful although it is unpleasant. Anaphylaxis and angioedema are potentially fatal conditions that can occur if extremely hypersensitive individuals are exposed to the allergen.

Differential Diagnosis

Contact dermatitis caused by other agents and exanthems (e.g., measles, scarlet fever, or rubella) may present with similar symptoms.

Specialists

- Dermatologist
- Primary Care Provider

Work Restrictions / Accommodations

Pressure or friction of the affected area should be avoided therefore use of personal protective equipment (e.g., respirator, gloves) may be affected temporarily. Contact with the allergenic plant should be avoided. In cases where the allergenic plant cannot be avoided, individuals at risk of exposure (e.g., work outdoors, in greenhouses, or florist shops) need to wear protective equipment (e.g., gloves or long sleeves) when working with or around the allergenic plant. Care must be taken to ensure the protective equipment or clothing that came in contact with the allergenic plant is disposed of or washed. In cases where these preventive measures are ineffective and plant exposure cannot be avoided, reassignment of duties may be required.

Comorbid Conditions

Immune system-suppressing diseases such as AIDS or certain cancers can increase the length of disability by making the individual more prone to infection.

Complications

Scratching may lead to bacterial secondary infection. Inflammation of blood vessels (vasculitis) and involvement of other organs may complicate allergic contact dermatitis. A life-threatening generalized hypersensitivity reaction (anaphylaxis) characterized by hives (urticaria), itching, angioedema, and breathing difficulties can occur in individuals with allergic contact dermatitis.

Factors Influencing Duration

The length of disability is dependent on the location and extent of the dermatitis.

Length of Disability

In most cases, no disability is expected. When necessary, length of disability depends on job requirements. Use of personal protective equipment may be affected and can affect disability.

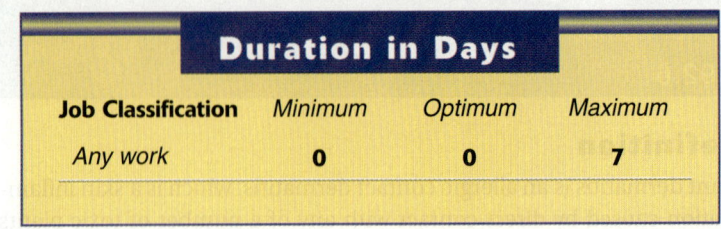

Job Classification	Minimum	Optimum	Maximum
Any work	0	0	7

Failure to Recover

If an individual fails to recover within the maximum duration expectancy period, the reader may wish to reference the following questions to assist in better understanding the specifics of an individual's medical case.

Regarding diagnosis:

- Was individual exposed to poison ivy, oak, or sumac? Any other plants?
- Does the individual have a family history of plant dermatitis?
- Does the individual spend much time outdoors?
- Does the individual have a pet that may be carrying the allergic agent in their coat?
- Does individual exhibit symptoms of plant dermatitis, such as inflamed, itching, possibly blistered areas of skin?
- Have conditions with similar symptoms been ruled out (e.g., measles, scarlet fever, or rubella)?

Regarding treatment:

- Did the individual wash his or her clothing following exposure to the toxic plant? Did the individual wash his or her pet?
- Was the offending plant identified?
- Were topical corticosteroids and oral antihistamines prescribed to treat the itching? Were they effective in reducing the symptoms?
- If not, were oral corticosteroids tried?
- Have cool compresses and oatmeal baths been tried to provide symptomatic relief?
- Was the skin condition severe enough to warrant debridement?

Regarding prognosis:

- Does the individual have any immune suppressing condition such as AIDS or cancer that could increase the risk of infection?
- Has the individual experienced any complicating skin infections that could impact recovery? If so, has the infection been addressed in the treatment plan?
- Was the condition complicated by anaphylaxis?

References

Anderson, Philip, and Kristin Malaker. "Most Common Skin Disorders." Managing Skin Diseases. Hiscock, Tim, ed. Baltimore: Williams & Wilkins, 1999. 35-120.

Hall, John. "Dermatologic Allergy." Sauer's Manual of Skin Diseases. Hall, John, ed. Philadelphia: Lippincott, Williams & Wilkins, 2000. 66-90.

Liao, S.J. "Acupuncture for Poison Ivy Contact Dermatitis. A Clinical Case Report." Acupuncture and Electrotherapy Research 13 1 (1988): 31-39.

McGovern, Thomas, and Theodore Barkely. "Botanical Dermatology." International Journal of Dermatology 37 (1998): 321-334.

Poisoning

Other names / synonyms: Overdosage, Substance Intoxication, Toxic Effects of a Substance

905, 909, 929.5, 958, 960-989.5

Definition

Poisoning is defined as injury or impairment of organ function or death by any substance capable of producing adverse effects. Poisoning can be acute or chronic. A poison can have local and systemic effects. Poisons can be divided into those intended for human use (foods and their additives, pharmaceuticals, toiletries, and cosmetics) and those that are not (household products, industrial chemicals, and agricultural products). Overdose refers to excessive amounts of the former and any amount of the latter.

Exposure can be from ingestion, inhalation, or absorption through the skin or mucous membranes. Poisoning can also occur from bites, stings, and injection of venom from insects, sea creatures (jellyfish, man-o'-war, and other fish) and arachnids (spiders, scorpions).

Poison may be taken accidentally or for the purpose of committing suicide. The individual may suffer unexpected complications after intentional drug abuse. The individual may suffer accidental poisoning from acute or chronic exposure in the workplace.

Poisoning occurs from acute or chronic ingestion of common substances such as aspirin, acetaminophen, and ibuprofen. Chronic poisoning occurs most commonly in elderly persons who regularly take large doses of aspirin (e.g., for osteoarthritis) or in whom renal insufficiency develops.

Drug overdose and poisoning are leading causes of emergency department visits and hospital admissions in the US, accounting for more than 250,000 emergency department visits and 7,000 deaths each year.

Diagnosis

History: Any individual presenting with multisystem disorders should be suspected of poisoning or overdosage.

The history of exposure to poison may or may not be present. The individual can be asymptomatic, or complain of generally feeling ill (malaise). Individual may report vomiting, diarrhea, blood in stool, difficulty breathing, weakness, irritability, or dizziness.

The most common initial manifestation of aspirin (salicylate) poisoning is hyperventilation. Early signs of acetaminophen overdose are often asymptomatic, with mild nausea, vomiting, profuse sweating (diaphoresis), pale complexion, and beginning signs of diminished urine output. Ibuprofen overdose is usually characterized by GI upset and dizziness.

Physical exam: The exam can reveal skin irritation, different levels of central and peripheral nervous system impairment and depression, pale blue skin due to lack of oxygen (cyanosis), tachycardia, and coma.

In aspirin (salicylate) poisoning, arterial blood gases usually reveal respiratory alkalosis and underlying metabolic decrease in alkalinity of the blood and tissues (acidosis). Other findings include ringing in the ears (tinnitus), confusion, and lethargy. Individuals with severe intoxication may experience coma, seizures, elevated temperature (hyperthermia), pulmonary edema, and circulatory collapse.

Later acetaminophen symptoms (at 24-48 hours) include nausea and protracted vomiting, upper right quadrant pain, jaundice, coagulation defects, decreased blood sugar (hypoglycemia), disease of the brain (encephalopathy), liver failure, kidney (renal) failure, possible disease of the heart muscle (myocardiopathy).

Tests: Types of tests depend on the type of poisoning suspected. A salicylate or acetaminophen level may be obtained if indicated. Other laboratory tests include an arterial blood gas; serum sodium, potassium, and bicarbonate; BUN; blood glucose; urine pH and specific gravity. Determinations of serum salicylate should be followed serially during therapy.

In any individual with altered mental status, computed tomography (CT) of the head and lumbar puncture should be considered.

Treatment

If asymptomatic, an individual should have the substance removed from the eye, skin, or gastrointestinal tract, and should be observed for potential development of symptoms. In addition to the above, the therapy for a symptomatic individual usually consists of emergency management with resuscitation and ventilation, use of antidotes, elimination of the absorbed substance (hemodialysis), and supportive therapy.

Once poison has been absorbed through the gastrointestinal tract, skin, or lungs, it can quickly spread throughout the body. Most poisons are eventually detoxified by the liver or excreted in the urine. The goal of treatment is to accelerate detoxification and elimination of poison while simultaneously trying to reverse their toxic effects. Intravenous fluids are given to keep the individual well hydrated and maintain urine output. Mild acids or bases can be added to these fluids to increase the amount of poison excreted through the urine. Chelation therapy (using chemicals that bind to certain poisons) may be used to neutralize and eliminate certain poisons. Poisons not readily neutralized or eliminated from the blood may need to be removed through dialysis. When available, a specific antidote is given as quickly as possible. Respiration may need to be ventilator-assisted. Kidney failure may require dialysis. Cerebral edema requires specific management.

Early gastric emptying may be accomplished by inducing vomiting within 30 minutes of ingestion, unless the mental status of the individual prevents this. If the individual presents too late to induce vomiting, gastric lavage or activated charcoal should be administered by mouth or by a tube introduced through the nose into the stomach. Adequate hydration and maintenance of kidney (renal) function is imperative. Arterial blood gases, serum potassium, and urine pH should be monitored often. Hemodialysis may be required, especially if the individual has impaired kidney (renal) function.

Prognosis

The outcome depends on the type of the poison, duration of exposure, individual sensitivity, severity of any organ system impairment, and the effectiveness of the treatment. Prognosis is good when treatment begins early and there are no underlying gastrointestinal problems, such as ulcers, or complications such as liver or kidney damage.

Differential Diagnosis

Whenever an individual with suspected poisoning or drug overdose is evaluated, the possibility that other illnesses are mimicking or complicating the presentation should always be considered. These illnesses include: head trauma, organic brain syndrome, myocardial infarction, cerebrovascular accident, meningitis, sepsis, metabolic abnormalities (hypoglycemia, hyponatremia, hypoxemia), influenza, allergy, pneumonia, gastroenteritis, and underlying liver disease.

Specialists

- Emergency Medicine
- Gastroenterologist
- Internist
- Medical Toxicologist
- Nephrologist
- Occupational Medicine Physician
- Poison Control Center Personnel
- Psychologist

Work Restrictions / Accommodations

Work restrictions or accommodations depend on the poisoning agent and the outcome. No work restrictions may be recommended in the case of uneventful treatment and recovery.

Comorbid Conditions

Impairment of the lung, liver, or kidney can slow elimination of toxic agents. Therefore, underlying disease of any of these organ systems can impact ability to recover and further lengthen disability.

Complications

Poisoning can have permanent injury after acute or chronic exposures with damage to the central nervous system, liver, and kidneys, the most common.

Factors Influencing Duration

The type and amount of the poisoning agent, when the treatment was instituted, the nature and severity of organ system impairments, and the presence of complications will affect the length of disability.

Length of Disability

This is a vague diagnosis. Contact physician to obtain additional information.

Failure to Recover

If an individual fails to recover within the maximum duration expectancy period, the reader may wish to reference the following questions to assist in better understanding the specifics of an individual's medical case.

Regarding diagnosis:

- Did the individual have a history of exposure to a poisonous or toxic substance?
- Did the individual present with symptoms consistent with poisoning or overdose? Has a diagnosis of a specific substance overdose/poisoning been confirmed?

- How was detection of toxic levels of substance in blood or tissue conducted?
- Is there a positive history of exposure to this toxic substance in the workplace? Could the exposure be occurring outside the workplace (i.e., in the home, in the community, or in recreational activities)?
- Has the individual recently worked in another organization where exposure to this substance is higher?
- If the diagnosis is uncertain, have other conditions with similar symptoms been ruled out?
- Is there pre-existing dysfunction of lung, liver, or kidney slowing elimination of toxic agents?
- Have underlying medical conditions been identified or ruled out?
- Are liver or kidney abnormalities, or gastrointestinal disorders evident?
- Has psychiatric evaluation been performed?

Regarding treatment:

- How soon after exposure was appropriate treatment initiated?
- Would individual benefit from additional or continued therapy?
- Did the individual experience any complications associated with the poisoning? If so, was appropriate intervention for the complications addressed in the treatment plan?
- Would the individual benefit from consultation with a specialist (medical toxicologist, nephrologist, poison-control center, gastroenterologist, psychological counselor)?
- If there is evidence of purposeful self-overdose, is individual receiving appropriate psychiatric counseling?
- If accidental overdose, has individual received proper education/clarification?

Regarding prognosis:

- What was the expected outcome?
- Did the individual suffer any permanent damage to the brain, kidneys, or liver?
- Has the source of the toxicity been identified and removed?

References

Beers, Mark H., MD, and Robert Berkow, MD, eds. "Chapter 307: Poisoning." Merck Manual of Diagnosis and Therapy, 17th ed. Rahway, NJ: Merck & Co, Inc, 1999 01 June 2000 <http://www.merck.com/pubs/mmanual/section23/chapter307/307a.htm>.

Paul, M., ed. Occupational and Environmental Reproductive Hazards: A Guide for Clinicians. Baltimore: Williams & Wilkins, 1993.

Poisoning, Iron
964.0

Definition

Iron poisoning occurs when an individual has a blood iron level of greater than 100 milligrams/DL. Any of a large number of organic or inorganic iron (usually ferrous) compounds are used for the treatment of hypochromic anemias (caused by iron deficiency). Iron poisonings may be acute or chronic. Acute poisoning occurs primarily in children or in suicide attempts by adults, and can be fatal.

Chronic iron poisoning occurs when an individual is given iron therapy in excessive amounts or for too long, receives repeated blood transfusions, or has iron overload disease (hemochromatosis).

Diagnosis

History: The individual may present with vomiting, diarrhea, and abdominal pain. A careful history will usually indicate the ingestion of large amounts of iron supplements. If an individual has iron overload disease (hemochromatosis) general weakness and fatigue associated with cirrhotic liver disease may be present.

Physical exam: Acute iron poisoning may be classified into four distinct stages. In Stage 1 nausea and diarrhea and abdominal pain and gastric bleeding are characteristic. The individual may be in shock and this initial phase can be fatal. In Stage 2 the individual appears to recover, but low blood pressure (hypotension), metabolic acidosis, and coagulopathy may be present in this stage. In Stage 3, metabolic acidosis, elevated liver enzymes and bilirubin (liver failure) are commonly seen, with a disease affecting blood coagulation (coagulopathy) and failure of other organs, such as the heart and kidneys. In stage 4, there is recovery, but scarring of the GI tract may be experienced a few weeks after a severe poisoning.

Tests: For individuals in shock, ICU management with appropriate testing is indicated. A plain x-ray of the abdomen (kidney-ureter-bladder [KUB] view) may reveal x-ray visible (radiopaque) iron tablets.

Treatment

In acute cases, symptoms should be treated as they appear. Use of a specific complexing agent administered intravenously is a treatment for iron overdose and intoxication may be needed (Deferoxamine is the drug of choice). Intravenous fluids may be necessary in individuals where blood volume is lowered (hypovolemic). Supplemental oxygen may be needed. Ingested iron may be removed with activated charcoal, nasogastric tube, washing out the stomach (gastric lavage), or use of a complexing agent to react with iron and any co-ingested metals. Aggressive hydration may be used where iron complexes have been formed to aid in the urinary elimination of the complex. Whole-bowel irrigation may be needed in individuals where x-ray (KUB) indicates the presence of iron materials.

Prognosis

There may be fatalities in the early stage of large iron ingestion. Individuals are expected to recover where prompt and appropriate treatment has been done. Asymptomatic individuals with a blood serum iron level less than 300-350 micrograms per deciliter may be considered recovered. However, there may be long-term disabilities and effects on other body organs when there has been a significant iron overload or overdose. Individuals with persistent symptoms and high serum iron levels may need lengthy hospitalization.

Differential Diagnosis

Infections due to bacteria, gastroenteritis, or hemochromatosis may present with similar signs and symptoms. Mushroom poisoning, poisoning from other medications, alcohol, diabetic ketoacidosis, mercury or arsenic poisoning, and pesticide poisoning may also present with similar signs and symptoms.

Specialists

- Cardiologist
- Emergency Medicine
- Gastroenterologist
- Hematologist
- Hepatologist
- Medical Toxicologist
- Nephrologist
- Occupational Therapist
- Physical Therapist

Work Restrictions / Accommodations

There should be no work restrictions following complete recovery from iron intoxication.

Comorbid Conditions

Iron is the second most common overdose in pregnancy. Pre-existing liver, kidney, and gastrointestinal disease may worsen the effects of iron overdose and ingestion.

Complications

Iron in large quantities is corrosive to the gastrointestinal tract, causes nausea and vomiting, and may cause bloody vomiting and gastric or duodenal perforation. Shock may result from volume loss and fluid shifts, as well as from iron-induced peripheral vasodilatation. In addition, free iron is toxic to cells (cytotoxic), and coma, convulsion, adult respiratory distress syndrome (ARDS), cardiogenic shock, central nervous system (CNS) depression, metabolic acidosis, coagulopathy, and liver failure may develop from excessive, acute systemic absorption. Stricture may be a late complication. Overloads of iron can also damage the pancreas, leading in some cases to diabetes or to hemochromatosis a genetic disorder susceptible to iron overload.

Factors Influencing Duration

Age, physical condition, health status, and job requirements may affect the individual's ability to recover and may influence length and level of disability.

Length of Disability

In most cases, no disability is expected. Duration depends on the amount and time of presentation and complications. Chronic hemochromatosis (cirrhotic liver disease) may be permanently disabling.

Medical treatment.

Duration in Days

Job Classification	Minimum	Optimum	Maximum
Any work	0	1	7

Failure to Recover

If an individual fails to recover within the maximum duration expectancy period, the reader may wish to reference the following questions to assist in better understanding the specifics of an individual's medical case.

Regarding diagnosis:

- Has the individual been receiving iron therapy?
- Has the individual received repeated blood transfusions?
- Does the individual have chronic alcoholism?
- Does the individual have hemochromatosis?
- Is the individual's iron level 100 milligrams or more?
- Does the individual have vomiting, diarrhea, and abdominal pain?
- Does the individual have general weakness and fatigue?
- On physical exam were nausea and diarrhea and abdominal pain present?
- Does the individual have gastric bleeding or shock?
- Does the individual have hypotension, metabolic acidosis or coagulopathy?
- Does the individual have elevated liver enzymes and bilirubin?
- Does the individual have scarring of the GI tract?
- Did the individual have steady-state blood serum iron levels done at least 4 hours after ingestion?
- Were glucose levels done? CBC? Arterial blood gases? Blood pH? Coagulation studies? Prothrombin time? Liver and kidney function tests? Electrolytes? Lipase and amylase levels? A pregnancy test? Blood typed and cross-matched? KUB x-ray?

Regarding treatment:

- Has the individual been treated with Deferoxamine? Was gastric lavage done?
- Has the individual been aggressively rehydrated?
- Is the individual receiving symptomatic treatment as symptoms appear?
- Was whole-bowel irrigation needed?

Regarding prognosis:

- Is the individual's employer able to accommodate any necessary restrictions?
- Does the individual have any conditions that could affect their ability to recover?

- Does the individual have any complications such as liver tissue damage, heart dysfunction, cardiogenic shock, central nervous system depression, coma, convulsion, anemia, adult respiratory distress syndrome, gastrointestinal perforation, or narrowing of the intestine?
- Does the individual have coagulopathy? Does the individual have damage to the pancreas, leading in some cases to diabetes?

References

Beers, Mark H, MD, and Robert Berkow, MD, eds. Merck Manual of Diagnosis and Therapy, 17th ed. Rahway, NJ: Merck & Co., Inc, 1999 30 Sept 2000 <http://merck.com/pubs/mmanual>.

New Center Treats Victims of Chronic Iron Poisoning. Hemochromatosis Center @ UPMC Presbyterian. 10 Nov 1998. 12 Jan 2001 <http://www.post-gazette.com/healthscience/19981110hemo1.asp>.

Poisoning, Vitamin B

Other names / synonyms: B_1: (Thiamine) Poisoning, B_{12}: (Cobalamin) Poisoning, B_2: (Riboflavin) Poisoning, B_3: (Niacin) Poisoning, B_6: (Pyridoxine) Poisoning, B_9: (Folic Acid) Poisoning, Cobalamin Poisoning, Cyanocobalamin Poisoning, Folic Acid Poisoning, Niacin Poisoning, Nicotinamide Poisoning, Nicotinic Acid Poisoning, Pyridoxine Poisoning, Riboflavin Poisoning, Thiamine Poisoning

270, 964.1

Definition

Vitamin B poisoning occurs as a result of taking high potency vitamin supplements. Most nutrient toxicities do not occur because of dietary intakes of foods.

The vitamin B complex refers to several water soluble vitamins, pantothenic acid, biotin, thiamine (Vitamin B_1), riboflavin (vitamin B_2), niacin (vitamin B_3), pyridoxine (vitamin B_6), folic acid (vitamin B_9), and cyanocobalamin (vitamin B_{12}) that are traditionally grouped together because of loose similarities in their properties, their distribution in food, and their overlapping physiological functions as coenzymes.

Morbidity and mortality are rare from pure vitamins. One study of acute or chronic overdoses, with more than 40,000 exposures, reported 1 death and 8 major adverse outcomes, mainly from niacin and pyridoxine.

Diagnosis

History: Nonspecific symptoms, such as nausea, vomiting, diarrhea, and rash are common with any acute or chronic vitamin overdose. Vitamin-caused symptoms may be secondary to those caused by additives (such as mannitol), colorings, or binders, although those symptoms are not usually severe.

The individual with suspected megavitamin overdose of vitamin B_1 may present with signs of anaphylactic shock including difficulty breathing (dyspnea), weakness, fainting, itching, and hives, or they may appear ready to fall asleep (drowsiness). The individual who has overdosed on vitamin B_2 may have dark yellow-orange urine. The individual may complain of flushed skin 20 to 30 minutes after taking too much vitamin B_3, along with abdominal cramps, lightheadedness, headache, fainting, or sweating. Numbness in hands and feet causing clumsiness may be experienced due to vitamin B_6 overdose; loss of appetite (anorexia), flatulence, and abdominal distention may be from high doses of folic acid (vitamin B_9).

Physical exam: Vitamin B_2, B_{12}, and folate effects may be minimal and nonspecific. Signs of B_1 (thiamine) toxicity may include: rapid heart beat (tachycardia), low blood pressure (hypotension), irregular heartbeat (cardiac dysrhythmias), headache, shock (anaphylaxis), dilated blood vessels (vasodilation), weakness, and convulsions.

The observed acute toxicity effects of vitamin B_3 (niacin, nicotinic acid) overdosage include flushing, itching (pruritus), wheezing, blood vessel expansion (vasodilation), increased intracranial blood flow, and headache. Chronic toxicity effects include heart rhythm disturbances, jaundice, abnormal liver function tests, and a rare skin disease characterized by gray-black warty patches (acanthosis nigricans).

Pyridoxine (vitamin B_6) overdose findings range from normal central nervous system (CNS) functions to uncoordinated muscle movements (ataxia). There may be a decrease in or loss of reflexes, and sensory confusion. Observed effects may include rapid breathing (tachypnea), sensory neuropathies such as burning pains and prickling or tingling of the skin (paresthesia), clumsiness, paralysis, and numbness around the mouth (perioral numbness). Abdominal distention may be due to folic acid (vitamin B_9) toxicity.

Tests: Urinalysis may be done to determine color: excreted vitamin B_2 (riboflavin) turns the urine yellow/orange. A complete blood count (CBC) may show an increase in the red blood cell hemoglobin level. For vitamin B_3 (niacin) toxicity, liver function tests (LFTs) should be done. Uric acid may be elevated leading to gouty arthritis; the glucose level is occasionally elevated. With vitamin B_6 toxicity, a lumbar puncture may be used to rule out other causes if the person shows signs of peripheral neuropathy. A reduced number of red blood cells may ultimately reveal that vitamin B_{12} has failed to be properly absorbed, leading to pernicious anemia. A measure of electrolytes should be done if there has been severe vomiting or diarrhea.

Treatment

High dosages of vitamin supplements should be immediately discontinued. Symptoms are treated supportively as they occur, but all ingestions require the person be given copious amounts of fluids to drink (rehydrated), particularly if there has been vomiting or diarrhea. In cases of significant ingestions, intravenous (IV) fluids may need to be administered. The stomach may be washed out (gastric lavage) if there have been other materials swallowed along with the vitamins; this should only be done if less than one hour has elapsed after they have been taken. Activated charcoal may be given for acute overdoses of vitamins. Medicines to relieve vomiting and diarrhea are helpful where needed.

Prognosis

Outcome of treatment for vitamin B overdosage is excellent. In rare cases, susceptible individuals (those with some other disease process or who are in poor physical condition) may need to be observed for a brief period for lowered calcium levels, kidney or liver dysfunctions, and any electrocardiogram (EKG) changes. Complete recovery from toxic conditions with little or no lasting effects usually occurs if the individual stops taking excessive doses of vitamin B. Fatalities are very uncommon.

Differential Diagnosis

Threatened abortion, fish poisoning, dermatitis, fluoride poisoning, migraine headache, hypercalcemia, excess parathyroid hormone (hyperparathyroidism), inflammation of bone and cartilage attached to the shinbone in adolescent males (Osgood-Schlatter Disease), gastroenteritis, gastrointestinal bleeding, concussion reactions from a blow to the head (post-concussive syndrome), or iron toxicity may all present with similar signs and symptoms.

Specialists

- Allergist
- Cardiologist
- Dermatologist
- Dietary Advisor
- Emergency Medicine
- Gastroenterologist
- Hematologist
- Hepatologist
- Nephrologist
- Obstetrician
- Pulmonologist
- Respiratory Therapist

Work Restrictions / Accommodations

Following appropriate treatment, accommodations or restrictions should not be necessary in most cases of vitamin megadose and overdosage.

Comorbid Conditions

Allergies to any of the B vitamins, including B_{12} given by injection, may worsen the effects of megadoses of these vitamins. Pregnancy may worsen the effects of megadoses of some B vitamins (B_2, B_6). Individuals with liver or kidney disease or failure may experience worsened effects from vitamin B_1, B_2, and B_3. Individuals with an active peptic ulcer, diabetes, gout, or gallbladder disease may also experience worsened effects from vitamin B_3. Intestinal problems, liver disease, an overactive thyroid, and Parkinson's disease may worsen the effects of vitamin B_6 in some individuals. Individuals who take anticonvulsant medication, have anemia or who have a decrease in number and increase in size and hemoglobin content of the red blood cells (pernicious anemia) may have worsened effects from vitamin B_9 (folic acid). Folic acid will make the blood appear normal, but neurological problems may progress and be irreversible. Hereditary optic nerve atrophy (Leber's disease) and gout may worsen the effects of megadoses of Vitamin B_{12}.

Complications

High dosages of vitamin B_3 over long periods may cause liver damage or aggravate a stomach ulcer. Vitamin B_6 toxicity occurs when doses more than 50-500 times the Recommended Daily Allowance (RDA) are taken over months or years; it can cause temporary or permanent nerve damage. Prolonged use of high doses of vitamin B_9 can produce damaging crystals in the kidney (renal calculus or kidney stones).

Factors Influencing Duration

Age, physical condition, and nutritional status will influence recovery and have an effect on any disability.

Length of Disability

In most cases, no disability is expected.

Medical treatment.

Duration in Days

Job Classification	Minimum	Optimum	Maximum
Any work	0	1	3

Failure to Recover

If an individual fails to recover within the maximum duration expectancy period, the reader may wish to reference the following questions to assist in better understanding the specifics of an individual's medical case.

Regarding diagnosis:

- Does individual take high potency vitamin supplements?
- Does individual complain of nausea, vomiting, diarrhea, or rash?
- Does individual have dyspnea, weakness, fainting, itching, hives, or drowsiness? Is the urine dark yellow-orange? Does individual have flushed skin, abdominal cramps, lightheadedness, headache, fainting, or sweating? Is there numbness in hands and feet that causes clumsiness?
- Does individual have anorexia, flatulence, or abdominal distention? Did physical exam show tachycardia, hypotension, cardiac dysrhythmias, headache, anaphylaxis, vasodilation, weakness, or convulsions?
- Were a urinalysis, CBC, liver function tests, and chemistry panel performed? If signs of peripheral neuropathy were present, was a lumbar puncture done?

Regarding treatment:

- Have the high dosages of vitamin supplements been immediately discontinued?
- Has individual been rehydrated?
- Are individual's symptoms being treated supportively as they appear?
- Has individual received medicines to relieve vomiting and diarrhea, if needed?

Regarding prognosis:

- Can individual's employer accommodate any necessary restrictions?
- Does individual have any conditions that may affect ability to recover?
- Have any complications occurred such as liver damage, aggravated stomach ulcer, or kidney stones? Is there any nerve damage?

References

Hardman, J.G., and L.E. Lilmbird, eds. Goodman and Gilman's The Pharmacological Basis of Therapeutics, 9th ed. New York: McGraw-Hill, 1996.

"Vitamin B6 Deficiency and Dependency." The Merck Manual of Diagnosis and Therapy, 17th ed. Beers, Mark H, MD, and Robert Berkow, MD, eds. Whitehouse Station, N.J.: Merck and Co, Inc. 1999. <http://www.merck.com/pubs/mmanual/section1/chapter3/3m.htm>

Poisoning, Vitamin K
Other names / synonyms: Menadione, Menaquinone, Phylloquinone
964.3

Definition

There is no generally established level that indicates poisoning from vitamin K, because toxic response levels vary widely among individuals.

Vitamin K is required for the liver synthesis of four of the blood's coagulation factors: prothrombin, and factors VII, IX, and X. Vitamin K is somewhat unique because it has both fat- and water-soluble forms. One form, K-1 or phylloquinone, is found in many plants and animals; K-2, or menaquinone, is manufactured by microorganisms such as bacteria in the intestinal tract of many animals. K-3 (menadione) is a synthetic version with the basic structure of the naturally occurring vitamins, but is biologically twice as active; this version is soluble in boiling water.

In either fat- or water-soluble forms, Vitamin K is effective in raising prothrombin levels and controlling hemorrhage in newborns. Newborns do not have the bacteria form of the vitamin and are often given injections of Vitamin K to prevent hemorrhaging. An alternative to giving newborns injections is having the mother take oral supplements during the last few days of pregnancy and giving them orally to the child after birth. Vitamin K is now believed necessary for the formation and maintenance of healthy bones. Individuals undergoing surgery may be given vitamin K injections before or after surgery to prevent excess bleeding.

Most nutrient toxicities don't occur from dietary intakes of foods. Vitamin toxicities usually come from taking high potency vitamin supplements. High doses of supplements may lead to a certain type of anemia, brain damage, and liver damage. Much of the data on adverse health effects from taking large amounts of a vitamin or mineral pertain to acute rather than chronic use. Pregnant women should avoid excessive doses of vitamin K, and breast-feeding mothers should not take megadoses of vitamin K.

Individuals on blood thinners (anticoagulants) should avoid multivitamin pills containing vitamin K because it will cancel out the effects of the medication, and will result in blood clot formation.

In rare instances, the intravenous (IV) administration of vitamin K has been associated with severe reactions resembling anaphylaxis (but occurring even in individuals without previous exposure to the drug), resulting in shock, cardiac or respiratory arrest, and death.

Diagnosis

History: There will be a history of large oral doses of vitamin K or recent injections of the vitamin. The individual may be flushed in the face, have an upset stomach, and nausea, vomiting, or a rash. There may be redness, pain, or swelling where vitamin K has been injected. The skin may also be itchy.

Physical exam: Examination may reveal flushing, sweating, low blood pressure (hypotension), a weak pulse, or a bluish tinge to the skin (cyanosis). Reactions resembling anaphylaxis or anaphylactic shock, such as itching of the scalp and tongue, flushing of the skin of the whole body, difficulty breathing (dyspnea), a sudden drop in blood pressure, unconsciousness, and a severe headache may be reported. Excessive destruction of red blood cells (hemolytic anemia), and excess of reddish-yellow pigment that occurs when bile and blood build up in the bloodstream (hyperbilirubinemia) may be present.

Tests: Prothrombin time should be determined if the individual is on oral anticoagulants. A complete blood count (CBC) including red blood count (RBC) should be done to detect red blood cell destruction. Blood should also be tested for an increased level of bilirubin. Serum prothrombin levels and vitamin K levels should be determined.

Treatment

Administration of excessive or large doses of vitamin K should be discontinued immediately. Symptoms and effects are treated as they occur. Cardiovascular support and observation should be provided where heart functions have been altered. Treatment should mainly consist of supportive measures.

Prognosis

The chances for an uneventful recovery are excellent when appropriate and prompt treatment is undertaken. A worst case could result in brain or liver damage, jaundice, or the destruction of red blood cells.

Differential Diagnosis

Gastroenterological diseases, and reaction to prescription and over-the-counter drugs or to chemicals may present with similar signs and symptoms.

Specialists

- Cardiologist
- Emergency Medicine
- Gastroenterologist
- Hematologist
- Medical Toxicologist
- Occupational Therapist
- Physical Therapist
- Pulmonologist

Work Restrictions / Accommodations

There are no particular restrictions or accommodations that need to be taken in the workplace environment. Individuals should inform doctors of increased vitamin K usage prior to any surgery, including dental surgery.

Comorbid Conditions

Liver disease may worsen the effects of large doses of vitamin K. Individuals with an inherited condition that results in a deficiency in an enzyme (glucose-6-phosphate dehydrogenase, or G6PD deficiency) may have adverse reactions to vitamin K. Individuals with cystic fibrosis, prolonged diarrhea, prolonged intestinal problems, or who take certain other medications may have adverse reactions to vitamin K as well. Allergies may worsen the effects of vitamin K.

Complications

Like vitamins A, D, and E, vitamin K is fat soluble, which means that it can be stored in the body and that it's possible to overdose on supplements.

Factors Influencing Duration

Age, physical condition, nutritional status, severity of reaction, to the vitamin toxicity, and job requirements will influence recovery and have an effect on any disability.

Length of Disability

In most cases, no disability is expected.

Medical treatment.

Duration in Days

Job Classification	Minimum	Optimum	Maximum
Any work	0	1	3

Failure to Recover

If an individual fails to recover within the maximum duration expectancy period, the reader may wish to reference the following questions to assist in better understanding the specifics of an individual's medical case.

Regarding diagnosis:

- Has a toxic level of vitamin K been confirmed?
- Is there a positive history of vitamin K usage?
- Is the clinical illness, including the history, physical examination, and laboratory findings, consistent with other case descriptions?
- Are the laboratory values consistent with a toxic level of vitamin K and are they at or near the normal value?
- Is the timing between exposure and clinical onset compatible with the known biologic facts about the hazard?
- Is the exposure dose within the range of doses believed to cause effects such as anaphylaxis shock, cardiac or respiratory arrest, and death?
- Has individual experienced any complications?
- Does individual have an underlying condition (liver disease, cystic fibrosis, prolonged diarrhea, prolonged intestinal problems, or allergies) that may impact recovery?

Regarding treatment:

- Have all sources of vitamin K been discontinued?
- Have all medications that the individual takes, especially vitamin combinations and supplements, been reviewed? Has individual been instructed to read ingredient labels before taking supplements?
- Did individual receive prompt and appropriate treatment?

Regarding prognosis:

- Is individual aware that vitamin combinations and supplements may contain vitamin K?
- Could vitamin K dosages be occurring outside the home, in the community, or in other locations?
- Are there special attributes of the particular individual that make it more or less likely that he or she would be so affected?
- Are there alternative ways of constructing the case that better fit the available facts?
- Where there remains significant uncertainty about the cause, how important is it to be certain?

References

"Vitamin K Poisoning." Merck Manual of Diagnosis and Therapy, 17th ed. Beers, Mark H., MD, and Robert Berkow, MD, eds. Whitehouse Station, NJ: Merck & Co., Inc, 1999. 29 Sept 2000 < http://www.merck.com/pubs/mmanual/section1/chapter3/3i.htm >.

Vitamin and Mineral Toxicities in Adults. University of Nebraska Cooperative Extension Service. 01 Jan 2000. 2 Oct 2000 <http://www.ianr.unl.edu/pubs/browse.htm>.

Polio
045, 045.1, 045.2, 045.9

Definition

Poliomyelitis (polio) is an infectious disease, caused by a virus, which affects the entire body including the muscles and nerves. Polio is a communicable disease that is transmitted by direct person-to-person contact, contact with infected nose or mouth secretions, or by contact with infected feces. It enters through the mouth and nose and multiplies in the throat and intestinal tract; it is then absorbed by and spread via the blood and lymph system. Average incubation time is 7-14 days.

There are 2 basic patterns of polio infection: minor (subclinical), and major (nonparalytic or paralytic). Minor forms of the disease are by far the most common (95%), and these individuals may show no symptoms at all (asymptomatic). When symptoms are present, however, they generally include fever, sore throat, general ill feeling (malaise), tiredness (fatigue), headache, vomiting, stiffness of the neck and back, and pain in the limbs.

The more serious forms (nonparalytic and paralytic) primarily affect the central nervous system; symptoms are most often seen in the legs, but can extend to involve any muscle in the body, and can cause paralysis or death. Although paralysis occurs in less than 1% of infections, the involvement of respiratory muscles can lead to life-threatening respiratory failure.

Polio is largely a disease of young children; infection in adulthood is very rare. Children 5 years and younger (particularly those under 3) are at the highest risk for infection. Other risk factors include lack of immunization, poor hygiene, poverty, unsanitary living conditions, or travel to a high-risk area or area experiencing a recent outbreak.

While there is no treatment for polio, there is an effective vaccine. Due to the wide availability of this vaccine, polio has nearly been eradicated from the world. In fact, the World Health Organization (WHO) reports only 7,094 cases of polio worldwide in 1999. When an estimated number of unreported cases are factored into that number, the WHO estimates the total worldwide incidence to be less than 20,000 cases. Given a world population in excess of 6 billion people, 20,000 cases represents an incidence rate of 3 people per million.

The Americas have been certified polio-free since 1994, and polio has been virtually eliminated from the WHO European and Western Pacific regions (including China). There are, however, unexpected breakouts from time to time even in areas of the world considered free of the disease. Most recently (2000) an area of France identified the virus in its sewer system; it was eventually traced to viral escape from a biomedical laboratory. Today, polio is mostly confined to parts of sub-Saharan Africa and the Indian sub-continent. WHO plans to eliminate the vaccine once it declares polio eradicated, which it hopes to do by 2005.

Because polio has been virtually eliminated from the vast majority of the world and when it does occur it primarily affects young children, this disease is not likely to be encountered as a medical disability diagnosis.

Diagnosis

History: Symptoms depend on the severity of disease. Symptoms of a mild case of polio may include fever, headache, sore throat, vomiting, or loss of appetite. In a more severe form of the illness, symptoms of meningitis (inflammation of the coverings of the brain and spinal cord) appear. These may include fever, severe headache, pain and stiffness in the neck or back, and muscle aches or spasms with possible widespread muscle twitching. This condition may rapidly progress to include extensive paralysis, especially involving the legs and lower trunk. If the infection spreads to the brain stem (lowest part of the brain), the individual may experience difficulty in or become unable to swallow, speak, or breathe.

Physical exam: The exam may reveal fever, stiffness of neck or back, and weak, asymmetrical paralysis of legs or arms. An acute feverish illness combined with muscle paralysis is so characteristic of polio that it usually enables an immediate diagnosis.

Tests: The polio virus can be isolated from a throat culture, stool culture, or from cerebrospinal fluid taken by a puncture of the spinal canal with a needle in order to withdraw cerebrospinal fluid for diagnostic purposes (lumbar puncture).

Treatment

There is no effective drug cure for polio, so treatment is supportive. Analgesics (pain relievers) help relieve muscle pain. Paralysis of the respiratory muscles may require an opening made in the windpipe in order to insert a breathing tube (tracheostomy), and breathing may need to be maintained by mechanical ventilation. Paralysis of the lower body interferes with normal bladder function, requiring catheterization. Physical therapy is essential to prevent muscle damage and to help retain muscle function.

Prognosis

Most individuals recover completely from nonparalytic polio. Of those who suffer paralysis, more than half eventually make a full recovery. A small percentage of individuals are left with minor muscle weakness or severe disability. Less than 10% die of the disease, and those who do are usually adults who suffered severe brain stem damage. A small number of individuals who experienced extensive polio paralysis as children may have a recurrence of muscle pain and weakness years later (post-poliomyelitis syndrome).

Differential Diagnosis

Other possibilities include Guillain Barré, meningitis, other paralytic diseases, hysteria, neuropathy of diphtheria, tic paralysis, osteomyelitis, encephalitis, and postinfectious polyneuropathy.

Specialists

- Infectious Disease Physician
- Internist
- Neurologist
- Physical Therapist
- Pulmonologist

Work Restrictions / Accommodations

Individuals whose job responsibilities require heavy lifting or physical activity may need to be transferred to sedentary duties. Extended work leave or leave of absence may be required.

Comorbid Conditions

Any concurrent illness affecting the immune system may lengthen disability.

Complications

Complications include paralysis, respiratory failure, pneumonia, pulmonary edema, blood clot to the lungs (pulmonary embolism), inflammation of the heart muscle (myocarditis), hemorrhage, paralysis of the intestines (paralytic ileus), and urinary tract infections.

Factors Influencing Duration

Factors include the severity and extent of motor dysfunction and the presence of complications.

Length of Disability

Disability may be permanent.

Acute.

Duration in Days

Job Classification	Minimum	Optimum	Maximum
Sedentary work	84	168	Indefinite
Light work	84	168	Indefinite
Medium work	168	Indefinite	Indefinite
Heavy work	168	Indefinite	Indefinite
Very Heavy work	168	Indefinite	Indefinite

Failure to Recover

If an individual fails to recover within the maximum duration expectancy period, the reader may wish to reference the following questions to assist in better understanding the specifics of an individual's medical case.

Regarding diagnosis:

- Has diagnosis of polio been confirmed?
- Is this an episode of postpoliomyelitis syndrome rather than an initial occurrence?
- Has the individual experienced any complications that may impact recovery?

Regarding treatment:

- How extensive is the paralysis?
- What body systems are affected?
- Has the individual received physical therapy as part of the rehabilitative process? Is function returning?

Regarding prognosis:

- Is the paralysis still resolving? How much more function is individual expected to regain?
- To what extent does residual impairment impact function?
- What accommodations would need to be made in order for individual to return to occupational duties?

References

Poliomyelitis: Fact Sheet N 114. World Health Organization. 01 Sep 2000. 02 Jan 2001 <http://www.who.int/inf-fs/en/fact114.html>.

Shelton, Mark. "Poliomyelitis." Griffith's 5-minute Clinical Consult. Dambro, Mark, ed. Philadelphia: Lippincott, Williams & Wilkins, 2000. 836-837.

Polyarteritis Nodosa

Other names / synonyms: Disseminated Periarteritis, Infectious Periarteritis, Necrotizing Angitis, Periarteritis Nodosa

446, 446.0

Definition

Polyarteritis nodosa is an immune-mediated disorder that is characterized by inflammation and destruction of small and medium-size arteries in many organ systems.

The inflammation can result in obstruction of the vessels that reduces the supply of blood reaching the affected area. The skin, intestines, kidney, liver, and heart are at greatest risk.

Polyarteritis nodosa is an uncommon disease, with age of onset usually between 40 and 60 years. The cause is unknown. The disease is associated with hepatitis B and C, lupus, and rheumatoid arthritis. The disease is more common in intravenous drug abusers than in the general population.

Diagnosis

History: The majority of individuals will have nonspecific symptoms of generally feeling ill (malaise), fatigue, weight loss, headache, and abdominal pain. Joint and muscle pain, particularly in the calves, is a common complaint. Difficulty breathing and wheezing can be a symptom of non-classical polyarteritis nodosa. The general nature of these symptoms can make diagnosis difficult until late in the disease when symptoms of extreme high blood pressure, acute abdomen (surgical emergency), stroke, kidney failure, or nerve damage are reported.

Physical exam: Physical findings are nonspecific. Hypertension may be present. Skin abnormalities are observed in many individuals, the most frequent of which is bluish mottled skin of the legs and hands (livedo reticularis). The arteries of the retina may show changes. There may be wheezing heard in the lungs.

Tests: Blood tests are abnormal but not specific to this disease. Abnormalities include anemia (low red cell count), elevated white blood cell count, elevated platelet count, and elevated sedimentation rate. Urinalysis typically shows protein and red blood cells and casts. Surgical removal of a piece of affected tissue (biopsy) and microscopic examination can make a definitive diagnosis when the inflammatory changes are seen in the arteries. Examination of arteries by x-rays (angiography) can reveal characteristic changes in the kidney, liver, or intestine.

Treatment

No cure exists for polyarteritis nodosa. Initial treatment is high doses of steroids, with gradual tapering of the dose after response is observed. In more severe cases, a drug may be added that suppresses the body's immune response. These drugs may need to be continued to maintain remission.

Prognosis

Corticosteroid therapy usually results in decreased severity or disappearance of the symptoms, but impaired kidney function or nerve damage can persist. Currently, the 5-year survival rate is 50-90%, depending on the treatment given. Cause of death is usually kidney failure. Without treatment, 5-year survival is 5-10 percent.

Differential Diagnosis

The symptoms of polyarteritis are fairly nonspecific and include weakness, malaise, muscle pain, headache, abdominal pain, and weight loss. The list of syndromes presenting with similar symptoms is quite large, but this constellation of symptoms is also seen in viral illnesses such as influenza, gastroenteritis, and hepatitis. Other immune-mediated disorders also can have similar symptoms, disorders such as Wegener's granulomatosis, polymyalgia rheumatica, giant cell arteritis, inflammatory bowel disease, rheumatoid arthritis, or lupus. Chronic infectious diseases, such as tuberculosis, can also present with similar symptoms.

Inflammation of the arteries is much more specific. Other disorders that also involve inflammation of the arteries are lupus, rheumatoid arthritis, rheumatic fever, serum sickness, or bacterial sepsis.

Specialists

- Cardiologist
- Dermatologist
- Gastroenterologist
- Neurologist
- Rheumatologist

Work Restrictions / Accommodations

Because the symptoms vary depending on stage of the disease, work accommodations should be considered individually. For most individuals, early stage symptoms are manageable. Few, if any, restrictions may be required.

Comorbid Conditions

Underlying vascular or renal disease could impact the individual's recovery. Conditions such as diabetes or renal insufficiency could lengthen disability.

Complications

Kidney involvement occurs eventually in more than 80% of cases. Inflammation of the gallbladder (cholecystitis) and appendix (appendicitis) can occur. Cardiac disorders such as inflammation of the heart muscle (myocarditis), its covering membrane (pericarditis), or rhythm disturbances occur in the late stages of the disease. The most frequent causes of death are gastrointestinal hemorrhage and perforation, congestive heart failure, kidney failure, and infections. There can be complications from drug therapy because it suppresses the immune system. The individual has a higher risk of developing an infection or cancer.

Factors Influencing Duration

Polyarteritis nodosa is a progressive disease. The rate of progression and degree of disability are dependent on different factors, including the promptness of diagnosis and appropriateness of treatment. Factors indicating a prolonged disability are an age greater than 50 years and involvement of the heart, kidneys, or intestinal tract.

Length of Disability

Permanent disability is a possibility, as this is a condition that is managed, not cured. Relapse is common.

Duration in Days			
Job Classification	Minimum	Optimum	Maximum
Any work	7	28	Indefinite

Failure to Recover

If an individual fails to recover within the maximum duration expectancy period, the reader may wish to reference the following questions to assist in better understanding the specifics of an individual's medical case.

Regarding diagnosis:

- Does the individual have Hepatitis B or C? Lupus? Rheumatoid arthritis?
- Is the individual an IV-drug user?
- Does the individual have nonspecific symptoms of malaise, fatigue, weight loss, headache, and abdominal pain? Do they have muscle pain in the calves?
- Does the individual have difficulty breathing or wheezing?
- Has the individual developed acute abdomen (surgical emergency)?
- Has the individual had a stroke, kidney failure, or nerve damage?
- Was the blood pressure elevated on exam?
- Were skin abnormalities noted, such as livedo reticularis?
- Were there changes in the retinal arteries?
- On auscultation was there wheezing in the lungs?
- Did the individual have a CBC and urinalysis?
- Were affected arteries biopsied?
- Was angiography done of affected organs?
- Have conditions with similar symptoms been ruled out?

Regarding treatment:

- Was the individual initially treated with high doses of steroids? Tapered later?
- Were immunosuppression drugs added?
- Is there kidney or nerve damage from long-term use of the drugs?

Regarding prognosis:

- If necessary, is the individual's employer able to accommodate restrictions?
- Does the individual have any conditions that may affect ability to recover?
- Does the individual have any cardiac involvement?
- Have they had multiple infections? Developed cancer?

References

Andreoli, Thomas, MD, et al. Cecil Essentials of Medicine. Philadelphia: W.B. Saunders Company, 1997.

Tierney, Lawrence, Stephen McPhee, and Maxine Papadakis. Current Medical Diagnosis and Treatment. New York: McGraw-Hill, 2000.

Polycystic Ovary Syndrome

Other names / synonyms: Stein-Leventhal Syndrome
256.4

Definition

Polycystic ovary syndrome is a hormone (endocrine) disorder that affects women.

It is characterized by lack of ovulation, menstrual abnormalities such as absence of menstruation (amenorrhea), infertility, enlarged ovaries, obesity, blood cholesterol (lipid) abnormalities, and elevated levels of hormones that increase male characteristics (androgens). Increased levels of luteinizing hormone (LH) and decreased levels of follicle stimulating hormone (FSH) also occurs. Estrogen production is found not to occur in the normal cycle pattern. The syndrome is the most frequent cause of anovulatory infertility. Usually there is no well-defined cause of the androgen excess.

The underlying defect in polycystic ovary syndrome is unknown, but there is growing evidence that key features include insulin resistance, male characteristic (androgen) excess, and abnormal hormone dynamics that stimulate the function of the ovaries.

Polycystic ovary syndrome is one of the most common hormone (endocrine) disorders, affecting approximately 6% of women of reproductive age in the US. The syndrome has an initial onset in the prepubertal years and is progressive.

Diagnosis

History: Women may complain of a number of symptoms including obesity, excessive hairiness (hirsutism), menstrual irregularities (amenorrhea and/or dysfunctional uterine bleeding), acne, and anovulation (lack of ovulation), and infertility. Most women with the syndrome experience the onset of their menstrual period (menarche) at a normal age but have irregular menstrual periods that gradually become abnormal, often leading to amenorrhea.

Physical exam: Approximately 70% of women will present with growth of coarse hair in the sideburn area, chin, upper lip, chest, lower abdominal midline, and thigh, and upper-body obesity with the waist being higher in diameter than the hip (waist-to-hip ratio of greater than

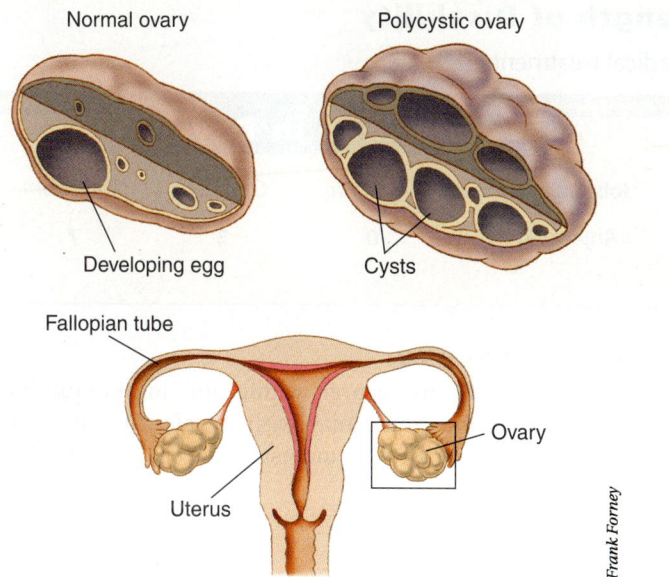

0.85). Presence of a skin condition in which there is abnormal darkening and thickening of the skin in the neck, groin or armpit (acanthosis nigricans) may be evident in the individual with insulin resistance. Ovarian enlargement, possibly detectable upon pelvic examination, may be present in one ovary, both ovaries, or absent.

Tests: Blood tests are performed to detect elevated hormone levels such as testosterone, androstenedione, luteinizing hormone (LH), estradiol, estrone, follicle-stimulating hormone (FSH), and fasting insulin. A test for a protein called sex hormone-binding globulin may be done to detect reduced levels typically found in this syndrome. An LH-to-FSH ratio of 3:1 is considered diagnostic of the syndrome. Ultrasound of the ovaries and/or insertion of a viewing instrument through a small incision in the abdomen to examine the ovaries (laparoscopy) may reveal multiple follicles in the ovaries that resemble a "pearl necklace" on examination but is not needed to make the diagnosis. A urine pregnancy test to detect human chorionic gonadotropin (hCG) should be done to exclude pregnancy in any woman of reproductive age who has menstrual irregularities or amenorrhea. In the absence of pregnancy, hCG is low or absent in woman with polycystic ovary syndrome. Prolactin levels are usually done to rule out pituitary gland disorders. Fasting glucose and blood cholesterol profile are also routinely done.

Treatment

Treatment is directed at the symptoms of the disorder. Few treatment approaches have improved all aspects of the syndrome, however the goals of treatment should include maintaining a normal uterine lining (endometrium), reducing the actions of the androgen hormones on the tissues, reducing insulin resistance (when present), and correcting anovulation.

The individual's desire for fertility is an important consideration, because the available treatments, especially those used to induce ovulation, have their own complications. Medications used in women who do not wish to become pregnant and are not at risk for pregnancy include medroxyprogesterone or norethindrone. Low-dose oral contraceptives are another choice in individuals who do not desire pregnancy. This treatment offers normalization of menstrual cycles, prevention of certain cancers, and treatment of hirsutism and acne. Antiandrogens may be combined with oral contraceptives for the treatment of hirsutism.

Gonadotropin-releasing hormone (GnRH) such as leuprolide should be reserved for use in women who do not respond to combination hormonal therapy or cannot tolerate oral contraceptive pills. Ovulation-inducing agents are used in women who desire pregnancy. Clomiphene citrate is the drug of choice for ovulation stimulation. Women who do not respond to clomiphene may be treated with human menopausal gonadotropins such as follitropin alpha (Gonal-F). This therapy has achieved pregnancy rates of 58-82% but the risks from ovarian hyperstimulation and multiple pregnancies are of concern.

Treatment with insulin-sensitizing agent such as metformin has been shown to improve insulin sensitivity and decrease blood LH and free testosterone levels. Metformin also restores menstrual cycles in 68-95% of women treated for at least 4 to 6 months. Recent successes with ovulation-inducing agents have decreased the use of surgery (ovarian wedge resection). Newer surgical techniques such as ovarian drilling may provide temporary results and do not address the underlying hormone disturbances in individuals with polycystic ovary syndrome. A significant percentage of women who undergo ovarian cautery or laser vaporization via laparoscopic techniques have spontaneous restoration of ovulation. However, complications from the surgery, including adhesion formation, tend to outweigh the benefits of surgical procedures. Behavior modifications, including weight reduction, diet, and exercise, are recommended for all women with polycystic ovary syndrome.

Prognosis

Treatment with medications along with behavior modifications (weight reduction, diet, exercise) is usually successful at managing symptoms and restoring hormonal balance and ovulation. If medication is ineffective, surgery to remove the diseases part of the ovaries (wedge resection) has been found to be successful.

Differential Diagnosis

Rapid fluctuations in weight or extreme physical exertion with normal follicle-stimulating hormone (FSH) and luteinizing hormone (LH) levels, eating disorders with low FSH and LH levels, premature ovarian failure with high FSH and LH levels, use of certain medications (i.e., progestational agents), tumors of the pituitary (pituitary adenoma) with elevated prolactin levels, or hyperthyroidism or hypothyroidism can all produce anovulation in the reproductive years. Other possible causes of androgen excess and menstrual irregularities include conditions during pregnancy, such as cancer of the ovarian lutein cells (luteoma) and a hyperactive luteal body formed from an ovarian follicle that has discharged an ovum (egg), also called corpus luteum. Hereditary cancer of the adrenal glands (congenital adrenal hyperplasia) and Cushing's disease results in abnormal hormone levels.

Specialists

- Endocrinologist
- Gynecologist
- General Surgeon

Work Restrictions / Accommodations

Restrictions or accommodations are usually not required.

Complementary and Alternative Therapies

Content is intended for awareness only. Treatments may or may not be effective. Scientific evidence may be lacking and some substances have potentially toxic effects. Dr. Presley Reed and the editors do not endorse the use of these therapies in the absence of consultation with a licensed medical professional.

Diet modification -	In obese women, weight reduction may help lower the conversion of androgens to estrone, and may help to restore ovulation.
Regular exercise -	A decrease in body fat, with resulting lowered conversion of androgen to estrone, may help restore ovulation.

Comorbid Conditions

Obesity, insulin resistance (diabetes), and high blood pressure (hypertension) will impact the ability to recover and further lengthen disability.

Complications

Untreated polycystic ovary syndrome is a progressive disorder that continues until the time of menopause. Some studies suggest that women with the syndrome are at increased risk for cardiovascular disease. The syndrome is associated with blood cholesterol (lipid) abnormalities. Long-term effects of abnormal estrogen levels place women with the syndrome at considerable risk for endometrial cancer, endometrial hyperplasia, and, possibly, breast cancer. The risk of endometrial cancer is three times higher in women with the syndrome than in normal women. Some studies have shown that there is a three to four times increased risk of breast cancer in the postmenopausal years.

Factors Influencing Duration

If surgery is necessary, the individual will need to take sufficient time for post-operative recovery.

Length of Disability

Medical treatment.

Duration in Days

Job Classification	Minimum	Optimum	Maximum
Any work	0	3	7

Failure to Recover

If an individual fails to recover within the maximum duration expectancy period, the reader may wish to reference the following questions to assist in better understanding the specifics of an individual's medical case.

Regarding diagnosis:

- Has diagnosis of polycystic ovary syndrome confirmed?
- Were other conditions producing anovulation ruled out?
- Does individual have an underlying condition that may impact recovery?

Regarding treatment:

- Was combination hormonal therapy effective in relieving symptoms?
- If drug therapy was not effective in relieving symptoms, is individual a candidate for surgical intervention?
- What type of procedure is being considered?
- Has individual been compliant with behavior modification regimen?
- What can be done to increase compliance?

Regarding prognosis:

- Has drug therapy and behavior modification been successful in managing symptoms while restoring hormonal balance and ovulation? Are other medication options or combinations available?
- Would individual benefit from surgical intervention?
- Would benefits of surgical procedure outweigh the risk of complications?

References

Huneter, Melissa H., and James J. Sterrett. "Polycystic Ovary Syndrome: It's Not Just Infertility." American Family Physician 10 5 (2000): 15.

Tierney, Lawrence M. Jr., Stephen J. McPhee, and Maxine Papadakis. Current Medical Diagnosis and Treatment, 36th ed. Stamford: Appleton & Lange, 1997.

Polycythemia Vera

Other names / synonyms: Erythremia, Hyperglobulinemia, Myeloproliferative Disorders, Polycythemia Rubra, Primary Polycythemia, Waldenström's Disease

238.4, 238.7

Definition

Polycythemia vera is an acquired disorder of bone marrow that causes an overproduction of red blood cells, The overproduction of red blood cells results in increased volume of the blood (hypervolemia) and thickening of the blood (hyperviscosity), both of which impair its usual rapid flow through the blood vessels to the brain, heart, gastrointestinal tract, and other tissues. The hyperviscosity of the blood and the increase in platelets result in a high potential for clot formation (thromboembolism) that can result in heart attack (myocardial ischemia) and stroke.

The cause of polycythemia vera is unknown. One theory suggests that it may be an acquired (rather than inherited) mutation in a subset or clone of normal bone marrow cells called stem cells, leading to excessive production of blood cells. These stem cells may be abnormally sensitive to growth factors involved in blood cell production. Another theory suggests a link to radiation exposure.

Polycythemia vera is associated with three to five times greater risk of peptic ulcer disease and increased risk for acute myelogenous leukemia that develops in about 2-15% of individuals with polycythemia vera 8 or more years after diagnosis. About 10% of individuals progress to a "spent" phase 2 to 13 years after diagnosis. The spent phase is characterized by fibrous degeneration (fibrosis) of the bone marrow, abnormal elevation of white blood cell count (leukocytosis), and massive enlargement of the spleen (splenomegaly).

Polycythemia vera is a rare disorder occurring at a rate of 1 in 100,000 individuals. Risk factors are unknown, but incidence is highest in individuals of Jewish ancestry. About 60% of the individuals diagnosed with polycythemia vera are males. Average age at diagnosis is from age 50 to 60 and incidence increases with age.

Diagnosis

History: Onset of polycythemia vera is frequently gradual without marked symptoms (insidious). Afflicted individuals may complain of headache, dizziness, a sensation of spinning or movement (vertigo), itchiness (pruritus) especially after warm or hot showers, reddish discoloration of the face (facial plethora), shortness of breath, breathing difficulty when lying down, and symptoms of blood clot formation (thrombosis) and vein inflammation (phlebitis).

Other symptoms include abdominal fullness and feeling full after eating a small amount of food (early satiety). These symptoms are associated with enlargement of the spleen (splenomegaly).

Physical exam: The exam may reveal a flushed, red appearance of the face (facial plethora), high blood pressure (hypertension), and an enlargement of the spleen (splenomegaly) typically discovered when the physician presses on the individual's abdomen (abdominal palpation). Seventy-five percent of afflicted individuals have splenomegaly, while 30% have liver enlargement (hepatomegaly).

Tests: The most characteristic laboratory feature of polycythemia vera is an elevated red blood cell count (hematocrit) of greater than 55-65%. White blood cell counts greater than 12,000 (leukocytosis) occur in about 60-80% of individuals, and platelet counts greater than 400,000 (thrombocytosis) in about 50-70%. Elevated levels of leukocyte alkaline phosphatase and vitamin B_{12} (both related to the high white blood cell count) are found in 70% of individuals. Bone marrow biopsy confirms the diagnosis of polycythemia vera.

Treatment

The objective of treatment is to reduce the thickness (viscosity) of the blood due to increased red blood cell mass and prevent bleeding (hemorrhage) and blood clots (thrombosis). Withdrawal of blood (phlebotomy or venesection) is used to treat the disorder when red blood cells are primarily affected. In the phlebotomy process, one unit (pint) of blood is removed weekly until the red blood cell count (hematocrit) is less than 45%, then repeated, as needed.

If red blood cells, white cells, and platelets are all increased, anticancer drugs (chemotherapy) or intravenous radioactive phosphorous may be administered to control the overproduction of cells in the bone marrow. Hydroxyurea is one of the drugs frequently used and may possibly increase the risk of developing leukemia. Newer therapeutic agents include interferon alpha and anagrelide. The use of antiplatelet therapy such as aspirin is controversial because it is associated with gastric bleeding.

Prognosis

Polycythemia vera is a potentially fatal disease. Untreated, most individuals with polycythemia vera die within months of vascular complications. However, maintenance of the red blood cell mass at or near normal using phlebotomy, chemotherapy, or radioactive phosphorous allows for long-term survival (10 to 15 years).

About 2% of individuals treated with phlebotomy and 15% treated with chemotherapy eventually develop acute leukemia. About 5% die from complications of myeloid metaplasia and 15% die from other cancers (neoplasms). The major causes of death in individuals with polycythemia vera are blood clots (thrombosis) and stroke.

Differential Diagnosis

A diagnosis of polycythemia vera is quite likely when there is a clinical picture of elevated red blood cell count (hematocrit), spleen enlargement (splenomegaly), increased number of platelets (thrombocytosis), and increased number of white blood cells (leukocytosis). However, polycythemia vera must be distinguished from other causes of increased red blood cells (erythrocytosis) such as secondary and relative erythrocytosis. Secondary erythrocytosis is an expanded red blood cell mass in response to increased levels of erythropoietin, a hormone that regulates red blood cell production in the bone marrow. Causes include conditions that decrease availability of oxygen, such as lung disease. In relative erythrocytosis, the red blood cell mass increases due to reduced plasma volume rather than to increased red blood cell mass. Chronic myelogenous leukemia also has symptoms similar to those of polycythemia vera.

Specialists

- Hematologist
- Oncologist

Work Restrictions / Accommodations

Individuals with polycythemia vera may not be able to work while recovering from complications such as stroke, thrombosis, gout, and peptic ulcer disease. Individuals receiving outpatient chemotherapy and intravenous radioactive phosphorous may require more sedentary work due to fatigue, weakness, and dizziness. Time off from work may be needed for phlebotomy and other treatment appointments.

Comorbid Conditions

Comorbid conditions that may influence length of disability include other blood disorders (i.e., hemophilia, thrombotic states, or leukemia), obesity, allergy to treatment medications, and chronic illnesses such as heart disease and diabetes.

Complications

Complications of polycythemia vera include blood clots (thrombosis) that lead to stroke or heart damage due to an occluded artery (heart attack), peptic ulcer disease, gastric bleeding, recurrent arthritis caused by deposits of uric acid in the joints (gout or hyperuricemia), and accumulation of fluid in the lungs due to inefficient pumping of the heart (heart failure).

Over time, polycythemia vera may convert to a condition where bone marrow is replaced with fibrous tissue (myelofibrosis) or to a type of leukemia characterized by the spread of immature white blood cells called granular leukocytes (chronic myelogenous leukemia).

Factors Influencing Duration

Length of disability is determined by the phase at which the disease was diagnosed and severity of symptoms.

Length of Disability

Disability may be permanent.

Medical treatment.

Duration in Days

Job Classification	Minimum	Optimum	Maximum
Any work	14	84	Indefinite

Failure to Recover

If an individual fails to recover within the maximum duration expectancy period, the reader may wish to reference the following questions to assist in better understanding the specifics of an individual's medical case.

Regarding diagnosis:

- Does individual have a history of blood clots (thrombosis), heart attack (myocardial infarction), or stroke? History of stomach (peptic) ulcer disease?
- Although onset of polycythemia vera is gradual and without marked symptoms, does individual complain of headache, dizziness, or a sensation of spinning (vertigo)?
- Are there complaints of itchiness (pruritus) especially after warm or hot showers?
- Does individual note reddish discoloration of the face (facial plethora), shortness of breath, or breathing difficulty when lying down? Is there abdominal fullness and feeling full after eating a small amount of food (early satiety)?
- On exam, was high blood pressure (hypertension) and an enlargement of the spleen (splenomegaly) noted?
- Did a complete blood count (CBC) reveal elevated red blood cell (hematocrit)?
- Were levels of leukocyte alkaline phosphatase and vitamin B_{12} elevated?
- Was a sample of tissue (biopsy) taken from the bone marrow to confirm diagnosis of polycythemia vera?

Regarding treatment:

- Has individual undergone blood withdrawal (phlebotomy or venesection) if red blood cells are primarily affected? If so, has the red blood cell count (hematocrit) decreased to less than 45%? If not, how many more blood withdrawals are anticipated for the hematocrit to decrease to less than 45%?
- If red blood cells, white cells, and platelets are all increased, were anticancer drugs (chemotherapy) or intravenous radioactive phosphorous administered?
- If the drug hydroxyurea is used, how much is individual's risk of developing leukemia increased?
- Is individual a candidate for newer therapeutic agents such as interferon alpha and anagrelide?
- How effective is treatment in controlling the disorder?

Regarding prognosis:

- Although polycythemia vera is a fatal disease, what is the expected survival rate for this individual with maintenance of the red blood cell mass at or near normal by phlebotomy, chemotherapy, or radioactive phosphorous?
- Has individual developed acute leukemia or other types of cancer?
- Have complications developed such as blood clots (thrombosis), heart attack (myocardial infarction), stroke, or heart failure? Has individual developed stomach (peptic) ulcer disease or gastric bleeding?

- Has arthritis caused by deposits of uric acid in the joints (gout or hyperuricemia) occurred?
- Has polycythemia vera converted to the condition where bone marrow is replaced with fibrous tissue (myelofibrosis)?
- If complications have developed, what is the treatment and what are expected outcomes with treatment?

References

Brodmann, S., et al. "Myeloproliferative Disorders: Complications, Survival, and Causes of Death." Annals of Hematology 79 6 (2000): 312-318.

Ridell, B., et al. "Incidence of Chronic Myeloproliferative Disorders in the City of Goteborg, Sweden 1983-1992." European Journal of Haematology 65 4 (2000): 267-271.

Polymyalgia Rheumatica
725

Definition

Polymyalgia rheumatica is an inflammatory disorder that causes muscle and large joint (shoulder, hip, and neck) pain and stiffness.

Inflammation of the bursa (bursitis), synovial membrane (synovitis), and tendon sheath (tenosynovitis) of the hip and shoulder are characteristic of polymyalgia rheumatica. The cause is unknown, and there is no apparent defect of muscle or joints. There may be an immunological basis and/or an autoimmune component to the disease process. The disorder may be triggered by an infection. There is a strong association between polymyalgia rheumatica and temporal arteritis, although the reasons for this are unknown.

Polymyalgia rheumatica affects primarily whites and is rare in other races. It appears to be more common in northern latitudes and occurs more frequently in individuals with a northern European ancestry. Polymyalgia rheumatica is found in the middle aged and older individuals; 85% of the cases are in individuals older than 60 years. It is two times more common in women than in men. In the United States, polymyalgia rheumatica has a yearly incidence of 12 to 68 cases per 100,000 individuals over the age of 50 years. It has a prevalence of 0.5% in individuals older than 50 years.

Diagnosis

History: The individual may complain of pain and stiffness in the thighs, hip, upper arms, shoulders, upper torso, and neck that began abruptly or developed over a long period of time. The stiffness is pronounced in the morning and after periods of inactivity. The individual may complain of difficulty rising from bed and the stiffness lasting for up to an hour. Pain is usually on both sides (bilateral). The individual often complains of fatigue and an inability to perform normal daily activities. Other symptoms that are frequently associated with polymyalgia rheumatica include weight loss, loss of appetite (anorexia), depression, night sweats, sleep disturbance, general ill feeling (malaise), and low-grade fever. The individual may report that he or she has pain on the sides of the head, especially when chewing (temporal arteritis).

Physical exam: The hip, shoulder, and neck joints and the affected muscles would be tender to the touch (palpation). There may be swelling in the knees, wrists, and possibly the joints of the hand. Fever may be present.

Tests: A variety of blood tests would be performed including erythrocyte sedimentation rate (ESR), C-reactive protein (CRP), CBC, liver function, thyroid function, and von Willebrand factor. An elevated ESR and/or CRP is highly characteristic of polymyalgia rheumatica.

Treatment

There is no cure for polymyalgia rheumatica and treatment is aimed at relieving symptoms. Initial treatment consists of a low to moderate dose of an oral corticosteroid. Symptoms are often relieved within two to three days, after which the dose is tapered down to a low maintenance dose. NSAIDs may be used in conjunction with the maintenance dose of corticosteroid. Corticosteroid therapy may need to be maintained for two or more years. More than 90% of the individuals respond well to corticosteroid therapy. Other treatment options include methotrexate or injections of corticosteroid (intramuscular or intravenous). Alendronate may be prescribed to prevent corticosteroid-induced bone mass loss (osteoporosis).

Prognosis

Polymyalgia rheumatica is not a life-threatening illness, however, it can cause substantial disability. The course of the illness is self-limited, usually running from one to eleven years. In most cases, corticosteroid treatment produces a dramatic improvement of symptoms within two to three days.

Differential Diagnosis

Fibromyalgia, cervical spondylosis, rheumatoid arthritis, multiple myeloma, lymphoma, leukemia, bone disease (e.g., osteomyelitis), Parkinsonism, miliary tuberculosis, endocarditis, dermatomyositis, polymyositis, neoplastic disease, and hypothyroidism can produce signs and symptoms that mimic polymyalgia rheumatica.

Specialists

- Immunologist
- Physical Therapist
- Rheumatologist

Rehabilitation

Individuals with polymyalgia rheumatica may benefit from physical therapy by establishing a home exercise program to reduce stiffness, strengthen muscles, and relieve pain. In addition, therapy encourages weight-bearing exercises to reduce the risk of osteoporosis that may be caused by prolonged steroid use.

Physical therapists develop both an active stretching and gentle strengthening program that the individual can perform on a routine basis. Individuals learn to stretch any area of tightness and perform strengthening exercises of all joints of the upper and lower back. Because this is a chronic condition, individuals learn pain control techniques they can perform at home such as the use of heating pads or visualization techniques. For individuals with acute pain, aquatic exercise or massage and passive stretching may be warranted. A lifetime program of walking, aquatic exercise, stretching exercises, and other physical fitness programs should be initiated prior to discharge from physical therapy.

Occupational therapy may also be necessary to address activities of daily living.

Work Restrictions / Accommodations

Work restrictions and accommodations would vary depending on the severity of the symptoms and the effectiveness of treatment. No accommodations should be necessary for individuals who are being effectively treated. Individuals who are not effectively treated may be suffering from sleep deprivation, which could severely affect motor skills and thought processes. Pain, stiffness, and sleep deprivation could affect the individual's ability to operate machinery, perform tasks that require a great deal of concentration, drive a motor vehicle, and perform tasks that involve fine motor skills. Pain and stiffness worsen with inactivity so the individual would need to walk around and stretch on a regular basis.

Comorbid Conditions

Rheumatoid arthritis, temporal arteritis, depression, obesity, and spine disorders (e.g., spondylitis, radiculopathy) are possible comorbid conditions.

Complications

Temporal arteritis (also called giant cell arteritis) occurs in up to 30% of the individuals with polymyalgia rheumatica. Pain may inhibit the use of muscles, which can lead to muscle wasting (atrophy).

Factors Influencing Duration

The response to treatment and development of complications can affect the length of disability.

Length of Disability

Duration in Days

Job Classification	Minimum	Optimum	Maximum
Sedentary work	0	7	14
Light work	3	7	14
Medium work	7	14	28
Heavy work	7	14	28
Very Heavy work	14	21	35

Failure to Recover

If an individual fails to recover within the maximum duration expectancy period, the reader may wish to reference the following questions to assist in better understanding the specifics of an individual's medical case.

Regarding diagnosis:

- Does the individual complain of pain and stiffness in the thighs, hip, upper arms, shoulders, upper torso, and neck that began abruptly or developed over a long period of time?
- Did the physical exam reveal joint swelling and/or associated fever?
- Were characteristic findings of elevated ESR and C-reactive protein noted?
- Were other conditions with similar symptoms considered in the differential diagnosis (e.g., fibromyalgia, cervical spondylosis, rheumatoid arthritis, multiple myeloma, lymphoma, leukemia, osteomyelitis, Parkinsonism, miliary tuberculosis, endocarditis, dermatomyositis, polymyositis, neoplastic disease, and hypothyroidism)?

Regarding treatment:

- Were symptoms relieved with conservative treatment such as oral corticosteroids and analgesics? If not, were more aggressive intervention such as injections of methotrexate or corticosteroids considered?

Regarding prognosis:

- Did the individual have physical therapy? Does the individual have a home exercise program?
- If necessary, is the individual active in counseling or a support group?
- Has the individual's employer made appropriate accommodations to allow a safe return to work?
- Did the individual suffer any associated conditions or complications such as muscle wasting or temporal arteritis that could impact recovery and prognosis?
- Does the individual have an existing condition such as rheumatoid arthritis, depression, obesity or spine deformities that could impact recovery and prognosis?

References

Cush, John, and Arthur Kavanaugh. "Rheumatic Diseases." <u>Rheumatology Diagnosis and Therapeutics.</u> Baltimore: Williams & Wilkins, 1999. 147-387.

Matsen, Frederick, III, MD, ed. "Polymyalgia Rheumatica." The University of Washington Orthopedics and Sports Medicine 22 Jan 2001 28 Jan 2001 <http://www.orthop.washington.edu/bonejoint/tzzzzzzz1_1.html>.

Porphyria

Other names / synonyms: Acute Intermittent Porphyria, Congenital Erythropoietic Porphyria, Erythropoietic Protoporphyria, Hereditary Coproporphyria, Hereditary Coproporphyria, Porphyria Cutanea Tarda, Proporphyria, Variegate Porphyria

277.0, 277.1, 277.2, 277.3

Definition

Porphyrias are a group of disorders caused by abnormalities in the production of the oxygen-carrying molecule of blood called heme. This results in an overproduction of substances called porphyrins that can be toxic to body tissues. In the body, heme is produced primarily in the red blood cells of the bone marrow or in the liver. The three main groups of porphyrias are those mostly involving the bone marrow (erythropoietic), the liver (hepatic), or those that involve both. Most porphyrias are inherited in an autosomal dominant pattern. This means that about half the children born to affected individuals will inherit the disease.

Attacks that involve both the nervous system and the abdominal organs (neurovisceral attacks) are a major feature of some types of porphyria. These attacks may be caused by exposure to medications, alcohol, anesthesia, or other triggering factors.

The acute hepatic porphyrias arranged in order from most common to least common in North America are acute intermittent porphyria, variegate porphyria, hereditary coproporphyria, and ALAD deficiency. These are all characterized by neurovisceral attacks and other symptoms depending on the type. Porphyria cutanea tarda also involves the liver but is not associated with acute attacks. It is the most common of all porphyrias, more often seen in men than women, and is familial in 4/5 of cases.

The erythropoietic porphyrias include congenital erythropoietic porphyria or Günther's disease (extremely rare) and erythropoietic protoporphyria. Erythropoietic protoporphyria involves a defect in liver cells and is autosomal dominant.

A 1999 study of acute intermittent porphyria found that about 1 in 125,000 individuals in Argentina were affected with this disease with women to men ratio of 7:3. Individuals carrying the gene may be more common than those with symptoms of the disease. Recent population studies suggest that 1 in 2,000 individuals may carry the acute intermittent porphyria gene.

Diagnosis

History: Acute intermittent porphyria, variegate porphyria, and hereditary coproporphyria are all inherited porphyrias characterized by recurrent attacks involving both the nervous system and gastrointestinal organs (neurovisceral attacks) and followed by long periods without attacks. Individuals may report attacks associated with abdominal pain, cramps, constipation, nausea, vomiting, anxiety, and disturbed behavior. Skin changes such as a rash becoming evident with sun exposure (photosensitivity) can also be seen in variegate porphyria and hereditary coproporphyria. Individuals with porphyria cutanea tarda report photosensitivity of the skin but no neurovisceral attacks.

Individuals may report acute attacks of porphyria brought on by taking various drugs (birth control pills and other estrogen-containing compounds, phenytoin, barbiturates, tetracycline, or certain anesthetics), alcohol, menstrual cycles, malnutrition, surgery, and other coexisting illnesses. Family history and history of medication, and drug and alcohol use are essential in evaluation.

Physical exam: Physical findings depend on the type of porphyria. During attacks of acute intermittent porphyria, variegate porphyria, or hereditary coproporphyria, symptoms may occur such as high blood pressure, restlessness, sweating, abnormal reflexes, and muscle weakness. Variegate porphyria and hereditary coproporphyria may also exhibit blistering skin lesions. With porphyria cutanea tarda, blistering skin lesions or ulcers may occur usually in sun-exposed areas, and sometimes there is residual thickening and scarring of the skin. A decrease in sensation, reflexes, or strength in the feet or hands may suggest peripheral neuropathy.

Tests: Blood, urine, and stool is tested for abnormal levels of porphyrins and their precursors (porphobilinogen, aminolevulinic acid, uroporphyrin, coproporphyrin, protoporphyrin). Blood is also tested for the specific enzyme abnormality responsible for the abnormal heme production.

Treatment

In general, porphyrias are treated using preventive measures such as avoiding precipitating factors (sunlight and drugs) and supportive therapy such as relief of pain and nausea. Screening family members is recommended as they are at high risk and genetic counseling should be conducted.

Attacks of acute intermittent porphyria, variegate porphyria, and hereditary coproporphyria often require hospitalization. In this setting, the individual receives intravenous fluids containing sugar, injected drugs to relieve pain, and obtains treatment for complications such as seizures, severely elevated blood pressure (hypertension), rapid heartbeat (tachycardia), and problems with breathing (respiratory failure). Artificial respiration and tube feeding may be needed in severe attacks. Intravenous therapy with heme products (hematin, heme albumin, or heme arginate) may be used to halt the attack if supportive therapy is not enough. Women who have recurrent attacks related to their menstrual cycles may use heme products on a regular basis.

Because porphyria cutanea tarda is usually associated with excess iron, the primary treatment is the depletion of iron by repeated blood removal through a vein (phlebotomy). This can be done on an outpatient basis. Chloroquine, deferoxamine, and beta-carotene can also be used.

Prognosis

With appropriate preventive measures and treatment, individuals usually have a normal life span. Hospitalizations may be intermittent and are usually brief. Without appropriate treatment, however, individuals may die during an acute attack. Although prompt use of hematin usually reverses attacks of acute intermittent porphyria before paralysis occurs, hematin therapy is less effective, and prognosis is poor when full support and continuous respiratory assistance are needed.

Individuals with porphyria cutanea tarda usually go into remission in about a year after repeated removal of small amounts of blood (phlebotomy). Ill effects have not been associated with variegate porphyria where either repeated phlebotomy of small amounts of blood or a single phlebotomy of a larger amount of blood has been performed.

Differential Diagnosis

Conditions with similar symptoms include lead poisoning, pseudoporphyria from nonsteroidal anti-inflammatory medications, an inherited metabolic disorder called hereditary tyrosinemia, and chronic liver disease.

Specialists

- Hematologist
- Neurologist
- Psychiatrist

Rehabilitation

Rehabilitation for porphyria depends on the residual effects of the condition. However, the general goal of rehabilitation for individuals afflicted by weakness from the disease is to improve function and enhance mobility. If joint stiffness occurs, range-of-motion (ROM) exercises begin with passive ROM exercises where the therapist moves the body part without effort initiated by the individual. Active assist ROM exercises are then initiated where the individual performs some of the motion/effort with the help of the therapist. As the individual improves with increased motion of the joint, active ROM exercises are introduced where the individual performs all the motion independently.

Strengthening progresses with isometric exercises where the muscles around the involved joint or limb joint contract without any movement taking place.

Isotonic exercises begin the next phase of rehabilitation and involve joint movement. Strength is improved using weights and elastic bands. As the resistance is lifted or pulled throughout the range of motion, the muscle shortens and lengthens. Strength training of this type may also utilize weight equipment and machines. The amount of resistance is determined by increasing the weight to a point where the individual's final repetition of each set is difficult yet obtainable. The physical therapist may need to modify this regime for those individuals taking medication for porphyria or with arthritis or other joint irritations.

Work Restrictions / Accommodations

Individuals with a history of seizures need a safe environment. Those with photosensitivity need to avoid sunlight by working indoors or using protective cotton clothing. Sunscreens do not protect the skin of porphyric individuals. Conditions that could further damage fragile skin should also be avoided such as putting pressure on bony prominences or exposure to cleaning solutions and other chemicals. Individuals should wear a Medic-Alert disc or other identification that tells healthcare providers of their condition in case of an accident or an attack at work. Regular meal times should be scheduled to avoid attacks precipitated by fasting.

Comorbid Conditions

Infections, seizures, or any medical illness may exacerbate porphyria as may treatments for these conditions.

Complications

Depending on the type of porphyria, complications may occur from peripheral neuropathy associated with muscle weakness, kidney dysfunction, scarring of the skin, corneal damage, loss of digits, and skin infections. Acute attacks may be complicated by seizures, respiratory failure, difficulty swallowing, hypertension, and tachycardia.

Complications of acute intermittent porphyria may include psychiatric disturbance or seizures related to an abnormality in the part of the brain called the hypothalamus. This abnormality causes sodium depletion in the syndrome or inappropriate secretion of antidiuretic hormone (SIADH). Involvement of the nerves supplying the head and neck (cranial nerves) may cause thickened speech, difficulty swallowing, and aspiration pneumonia due to mouth secretions entering the airway. Peripheral neuropathy causes pain and weakness. Involvement of the nerves supplying the ribs and diaphragm may lead to respiratory failure. Involvement of the nerves controlling bodily functions (autonomic nerves) may cause abdominal pain, hypertension, tachycardia, intestinal paralysis, or diarrhea.

In erythropoietic protoporphyria, protoporphyrin is deposited in the liver. This usually results in only mild abnormalities of liver function and rarely does cirrhosis or death from liver failure occur. Gallstones may also be present. About half the affected individuals have a mild form of anemia.

Factors Influencing Duration

Scarring of the skin, established neuropathy with associated muscle weakness, poor response to treatment, and other medical illnesses requiring treatments known to exacerbate porphyria, influence the length of disability.

Length of Disability

Disability from porphyria is highly variable. Acute attacks typically settle rapidly. In some cases, disability may be permanent. Duration depends on the form of porphyria and any complications. Contact physician for additional information.

Failure to Recover

If an individual fails to recover within the maximum duration expectancy period, the reader may wish to reference the following questions to assist in better understanding the specifics of an individual's medical case.

Regarding diagnosis:

- Does the individual have symptoms and history that are characteristic of a porphyria?
- Was a thorough investigation of the family history, medication history and drug and alcohol use done in the initial evaluation?
- Would the individual benefit by consultation with a specialist?
- Was the diagnosis confirmed by elevated porphyrin levels in the blood, urine or stool?
- If the diagnosis was uncertain, were other conditions with similar symptoms ruled out?

Regarding treatment:

- Have probable triggering factors been identified?
- Has the individual been compliant with preventive measures?
- Was supportive care given to relieve associated symptoms?
- Was hospitalization required?
- Were family members screened for the disorder and counseled as appropriate?

Regarding prognosis:

- Was appropriate treatment received?
- Did the individual have pre-existing conditions that may have influenced ability to recover and length of disability?
- Did the individual suffer any complications that may have influenced ability to recover?

References

De Siervi, A., M.V. Rossetti, and V.E. Parera. "Acute Intermittent Porphyria: Biochemical and Clinical Analysis in the Argentinean Population." Clin Chim Acta 288 1-2 (1999): 63-71.

Harper, P., T. Hybinette, and S. Thunell. "Large Phlebotomy in Variegate Porphyria." Journal of Internal Medicine 242 3 (1997): 255-259.

Portal Systemic Shunt

Other names / synonyms: Distal Splenorenal Shunt, DSRS, End-to-Side Portacaval Shunt, Nonselective Shunt, Portacaval Shunt, Portal Vein to Vena Cava Shunt, Portosystemic Shunt, Selective Shunt, Side-to-Side Portacaval Shunt, Splenorenal Shunt

39.1

Definition

A portal systemic shunt is a surgical operation done to redirect blood flow in cases of elevated blood pressure in the portal vein of the liver (portal hypertension). This process of redirecting blood flow is done to decrease the pressure in the portal vein.

In portal hypertension, the pressure in the portal vein (largest vein of the liver) is forced backwards into all the smaller veins leading to the liver such as the veins of the stomach, esophagus, and intestines. The veins then dilate and become fragile under the increased pressure and are susceptible to bleeding. Dilated veins in the esophagus are called esophageal varices. Dilated veins in the stomach are called gastric varices. Portal hypertension may lead to recurrent life-threatening bleeding from esophageal or gastric varices.

Several shunt procedures are available. The nonselective shunt redirects the entire portal blood flow. The selective shunt separates the portal circulation into a stomach and spleen circuit and an upper intestinal circuit that continues to perfuse the liver. The transvenous intrahepatic portosystemic shunt (TIPS) is a nonsurgical procedure done in the x-ray department. A catheter is directed through a vein into the liver where it connects the portal system to the systemic venous system and decreases portal venous pressure.

The incidence of portal hypertension is 1 out of 10,000 individuals. Portal hypertension is commonly associated with cirrhosis where scar tissue formation in the liver blocks blood flow. Approximately 50-80% of all cirrhosis is caused by alcohol abuse.

Besides cirrhosis, portal hypertension may result from mechanical obstruction within the hepatic veins. This may be caused by chronic right-sided heart failure (cor pulmonale) and tricuspid regurgitation, as well as obstructing lesions of the hepatic veins and inferior vena cava. These latter conditions and the symptoms they produce are termed Budd-Chiari syndrome. Predisposing conditions for Budd-Chiari syndrome include abnormal blood clotting (hypercoagulable states), tumor invasion into the liver (hepatic) vein or inferior vena cava, and membranous obstruction of the inferior vena cava (webs). Inferior vena cava webs are observed most commonly in South and East Asia and may be due to nutritional factors. Sometimes blood clots in the vein of the spleen (splenic vein thrombosis) or liver (portal vein thrombosis) can cause portal hypertension. These conditions are associated with cancer or abnormal blood clotting (hypercoagulable states).

Reason for Procedure

Portal systemic shunt treats individuals with portal hypertension. The shunt procedure is primarily used to treat individuals with dilated veins in the esophagus (esophageal varices) that continue to bleed despite treatment with other methods such as sclerotherapy or drug therapy. While the procedure is generally done to reduce the risk of bleeding associated with portal hypertension, a portal systemic shunt also seems to help reduce fluid accumulation in the abdomen (ascites) associated with portal hypertension.

The type of shunt selected is based on the individual's general condition and risk of bleeding.

Description

Both selective and nonselective shunt surgeries are performed using general anesthesia. The surgeon makes a long incision in the right upper abdomen. The portal vein underneath the liver is located.

In a nonselective shunt procedure, the portal vein is tied off near the liver. The remaining section of the portal vein is then joined to another large vein in the abdomen, either the inferior vena cava or a vein leading to the spleen or kidney. This redirects the blood in the portal vein around the diseased liver and essentially reduces the amount of pressure in the portal vein.

In a selective shunt, only a branch of the portal vein is tied off. This branch is then joined to another large vein in the abdomen. This type of shunt redirects only a portion of the blood from the portal vein allowing some portal blood to still circulate to the liver. The pressure in the portal vein is reduced as a result of directing some of the portal blood away from the liver.

The abdominal muscle and tissue is closed with stitches. The skin surface is closed with small surgical staples. There may be a small, temporary drain inserted near the abdominal wound to drain any accumulated fluid or blood.

The TIPS is a minimally invasive treatment done in the x-ray department under local anesthesia. A long flexible tube (catheter) is inserted into a large vein in the neck (jugular vein). Using x-ray guidance (fluoroscopy), a needle is directed through this catheter into the portal vein. A metal tube (stent) is then positioned between the portal vein and the hepatic vein. The stent serves to redirect blood from the high-pressure portal vein to the low-pressure hepatic vein. This effectively reduces the pressure in the portal vein and reduces the risk of bleeding from dilated veins.

Prognosis

Regardless of the type of shunt performed, the procedure is not curative. However, these procedures are generally successful at reducing pressure within the portal vein and the risk of bleeding from esophageal or gastric varices. In addition, these procedures help reduce fluid accumulation in the abdomen (ascites). However, the procedures are associated with a high rate of morbidity and mortality due to neurological depression (encephalopathy) and deterioration of liver function. The mortality associated with an emergency portal systemic shunt ranges from 25-50%. The rate of severe complications is only 1-2% when a TIPS procedure is done. TIPS can control acute bleeding in over 90% of individuals actively bleeding from gastric or esophageal varices.

Specialists

- Gastroenterologist
- General Surgeon
- Radiologist
- Vascular Surgeon

Work Restrictions / Accommodations

An extended leave of absence may be needed for rest and recuperation following the procedure.

Comorbid Conditions

Comorbid conditions of cancer, heart disease, renal failure, or neurological dysfunction may impact ability to recover and further lengthen disability.

Procedure Complications

Complications associated with surgical shunt procedures include bleeding, heart failure, respiratory failure, infection, and neurological depression secondary to anesthesia administration.

Procedural complications occur in less than 10% of TIPS procedures. Severe life-threatening bleeding has been reported in 1-2% of cases as a result of puncture of the liver. Other major complications include x-ray contrast-induced renal failure, heart failure, dislodged stent (stent migration), infection, and inadvertent puncture of the gallbladder or other organs adjacent to the liver.

Factors Influencing Duration

Factors that may influence the length of disability include the presence of fluid in the abdomen (ascites) or alcoholic liver disease and the type of shunt operation performed.

Length of Disability

Durations reflect recovery from procedure only. Disability may be permanent.

Duration in Days

Job Classification	Minimum	Optimum	Maximum
Sedentary work	56	63	70
Light work	70	77	84
Medium work	84	98	112
Heavy work	112	126	182
Very Heavy work	112	126	182

References

McQuaid, Kenneth R. "Alimentary Tract." Current Medical Diagnosis and Treatment, 39th ed. Tierney, Lawrence M., Stephen J. McPhee, and Maxine A. Papadakis, eds. New York: Lange Medical Books/McGraw-Hill, 2000. 553-655.

Smith, Susan L. "Patients with Liver Dysfunction." Critical Care Nursing, 2nd ed. Clochesy, John M., et al., eds. Philadelphia: W.B. Saunders Company, 1996. 2048-1083.

Post Polio Syndrome

Other names / synonyms: PPS

138

Definition

Post polio syndrome (PPS) is a condition characterized by progressive muscle weakness, tiredness (fatigue), muscle and joint pain, and gradual loss of muscle function (muscular atrophy). PPS strikes individuals who have survived a previous infection with the polio virus (paralytic poliomyelitis).

To understand PPS, it is helpful to understand a little bit about the individual's previous polio virus infection. A small percentage of people infected with the polio virus experience varying degrees damage to the nerves that control muscle movement (motor neurons). Damage to these nerves results in varying degrees of impaired muscle movement and/or paralysis. These individuals are said to have paralytic poliomyelitis. The nerves that survive this attack take over and provide nerve function to the damaged muscle fibers, providing a period of recovery that can last for many years. In PPS, these surviving nerves begin to lose function, resulting in the characteristic symptoms described above. The severity of PPS depends on the severity of the individual's initial polio infection; more severe PPS is related to more severe initial infections.

There are more than 1.63 million survivors of paralytic poliomyelitis, with about 640,000 in the United States. Of those survivors, estimates of the number of individuals who will develop PPS vary between 20-60%. Symptoms of PPS tend to occur 30-40 years after the initial polio attack, but cases have been reported in which PPS was diagnosed as few as 8 or as many as 71 years later. Additional risk factors include age and severity of symptoms during the initial paralytic attack, with older individuals who suffered more severe symptoms at greater risk. Risk also increases as the length of the stability period increases.

Since the development of the polio vaccine, the incidence of polio has been dramatically reduced to only a handful of new cases each year. Thus, it is reasonable to expect that the incidence of PPS will also dramatically decrease over the course of the next few years.

Diagnosis

History: Individuals will report a history of diminished muscle function and/or paralysis associated with a previous infection with the polio virus (i.e., a history of paralytic poliomyelitis). Post polio syndrome (PPS) is characterized by tiredness (fatigue), which occurs in about 90% of cases. In addition to an overall sense of fatigue, individuals may complain of a lack of physical endurance (muscle fatigue), muscle pain, joint pain, and new muscle weakness. Less common symptoms include speech disturbances (dysarthria), difficulty swallowing (dysphagia), muscle cramps, intolerance to the cold environments and muscle twitches.

Physical exam: The initial physical exam is often unremarkable. Signs of PPS are common to many other medical conditions. When the individual's history suggests PPS, the physician will often systematically rule out other causes of the reported symptoms. Once other illness have been ruled out, the physician will likely schedule regular check-up examinations with the individual. Over time, a gradual decrease in muscle strength will be noted. Photographs may be taken so that the physician can compare the size of various muscles (particularly muscles of the arms and legs) over time.

Tests: Routine blood tests are often normal. Certain enzymes that indicate muscle function may be abnormal in some cases. Antibodies to the polio virus may be elevated. The physician may order regularly scheduled computed tomography (CT) scans or magnetic resonance imaging (MRI) scans of affected muscle groups to document gradual changes in muscle size.

Treatment

At the present time, there is no cure for post polio syndrome (PPS), nor can it be prevented. Treatment is aimed at managing the various symptoms. A physical, occupational and/or speech therapist may be consulted to educate the individual on proper exercise techniques that can improve mobility, increase endurance, and combat loss of muscle strength. Both resistance/strength training exercises and aerobic exercises are important for management of PPS. The individual will also be encouraged to rest frequently to minimize fatigue. Overweight individuals will be encouraged to lose weight, and will be instructed on proper nutrition and healthy eating patterns. If assistance devices (wheelchairs, canes, crutches, etc.) are required, the individual will receive training on their use. Medication may be prescribed to relive pain (analgesics, anti-inflammatories).

Prognosis

Post polio syndrome (PPS) is a slowly progressive condition marked by long periods of stability. Lifestyle adjustments are common. As symptoms progress, individuals will experience increasing difficulty with daily tasks such as climbing stairs, driving, cooking, cleaning, bathing, etc. Assistive devices such as canes, walkers, wheelchairs, etc. may be required. Occupational changes may become necessary, particularly if the current job requires physical strength or endurance.

In most cases, PPS is not life-threatening. However, rare cases can be fatal, and these usually involve severe impairment to the muscles that control breathing and/or swallowing.

Differential Diagnosis

Several other conditions share signs and symptoms with post polio syndrome (PPS). The following diagnoses should be ruled out when making a diagnosis of PPS: degenerative arthritis, fibromyalgia, radiculopathy, multiple sclerosis, chronic fatigue syndrome, compression peripheral neuropathies, acquired primary myopathy, amyotrophic lateral sclerosis, progressive muscular atrophy, and multifocal motor neuropathy disease of peripheral nerves.

Specialists

- Dietary Advisor
- Infectious Disease Physician
- Occupational Therapist
- Orthopedic Surgeon
- Physiatrist
- Physical Therapist
- Speech Therapist

Rehabilitation

Individuals with post polio syndrome (PPS) often require physical, occupational and/or speech therapy, depending on their particular symptoms.

Physical therapy generally consists of regular, moderate exercise that does not exhaust the individual. The goal of this type of therapy is to increase muscle strength, maintain muscle mass, minimize loss of muscle function, and increase endurance. In general, the physical therapist will prescribe a regimen that consists of regular strength training exercise. The individual will be trained to recognize the symptoms of fatigue, and to stop exercising when such symptoms are noted. The specific exercises will vary depending on the particular muscle involved and the extent of existing damage to that muscle. In severely impaired muscles, exercise may be limited to range-of-motion exercises to maintain flexibility.

Occupational therapy may be required to help the individual adjust to progressive disability. The particulars of this type of therapy will vary with the individual and his/her symptoms as well as his/her work and home environments.

Speech therapy may be indicated for those with difficulty swallowing and/or speaking. Again, the details of such therapy will vary depending on the extent of impairment.

Work Restrictions / Accommodations

Individuals with post polio syndrome (PPS) may require time off for regularly scheduled doctor's appointments. In the early stages of PPS, work restrictions may not be required, particularly if the job is sedentary in nature. As symptoms progress, increasing restrictions may become necessary. Increasing fatigue may require frequent breaks, a shortened workday, a shortened work week, and/or longer vacation periods. Jobs requiring physical strength, prolonged physical activity or prolonged exposure to cold environments may become impossible, and the individual may require reassignment to increasingly sedentary positions. Difficulty speaking may necessitate a job change for certain individuals (e.g., telephone customer service representatives, telemarketers, teachers, etc.). Those with jobs requiring physical dexterity (e.g., surgeons, typists, craftsmen, etc.), or those requiring physical mobility (professional athletes, delivery people, etc.) may be permanently disabled. Accommodations to the workstation, break room, restroom, etc. may be necessary for individuals requiring use of a wheelchair.

Comorbid Conditions

Obesity or the presence of another degenerative condition of the musculoskeletal system may hinder recovery and lengthen the period of disability. Depression may also delay recovery, particularly if the individual is not motivated to follow the exercise and/or dietary regimen suggested by the physician.

Complications

Post polio syndrome is generally uncomplicated.

Factors Influencing Duration

Disability will be progressive and permanent. However, progression is slow, and is marked by long periods of stability. Disability will be influenced by the individual's symptoms, job demands, the affected muscles, and the willingness of the individual to follow the treatment regimen.

Length of Disability

Disability may be progressive and permanent.

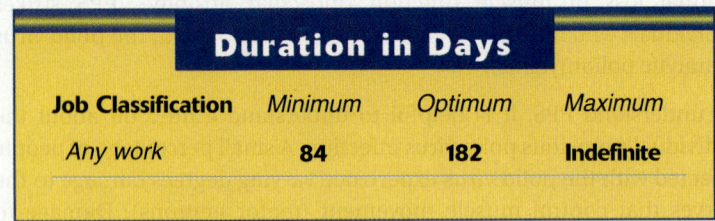

Job Classification	Minimum	Optimum	Maximum
Any work	84	182	Indefinite

Failure to Recover

If an individual fails to recover within the maximum duration expectancy period, the reader may wish to reference the following questions to assist in better understanding the specifics of an individual's medical case.

Regarding diagnosis:

- Was diagnosis of post polio syndrome confirmed?
- Was there a previous history of paralytic poliomyelitis?
- Were conditions such as degenerative arthritis, fibromyalgia, radiculopathy, multiple sclerosis, chronic fatigue syndrome, compression peripheral neuropathies, acquired primary myopathy, amyotrophic lateral sclerosis, progressive muscular atrophy, or multifocal motor neuropathy disease of peripheral nerves ruled out?
- Were symptoms such as fatigue, lack of physical endurance, muscle and joint pain, new muscle weakness, speech disturbances, difficulty swallowing, muscle cramps and twitches, or cold intolerance exhibited by individual?

Regarding treatment:

- Is individual following the physician's instructions regarding rest, exercise, dietary guidelines, weight loss (if applicable), and medication?
- Was individual referred for physical, occupational and/or speech therapy?
- Was individual given assistance devices such as, wheelchair, cane, or crutches?

Regarding prognosis:

- Were therapy, weight reduction and medication effective in improving mobility, increasing endurance, and combating loss of muscle strength?
- How seriously affected is individual's ability to swallow and breathe?
- Is individual depressed? Is depression being treated?
- Have occupational changes been made to accommodate changes in strength and mobility?

References

Cashman, Neil R., MD. Post Polio Syndrome Fact Sheet. Gazette International Networking Institute Coordinator of International Polio Network. 11 Dec 2000 <http://www.post-polio.org/task/news.html>.

Spector, Sidney, and Kumaraswamy Sivakumar. "The Post-polio Syndrome: Current Concepts and Treatment." Infections in Medicine 14 6 (1997): 10 pgs. 7 Dec 2000 <http://www.medscape.com/SCP/IIM/1997/v14.n06/m3101.spector/m3101.spector.html>.

Postconcussion Syndrome

Other names / synonyms: Closed Head Injury Syndrome, Mild Brain Injury, Postconcussional Syndrome, Postconcussive Syndrome

310.2

Definition

Postconcussion or postconcussive syndrome, first described by Strauss and Savitsky in 1934, is characterized by impairments in memory, attention, and concentration (cognition); emotional state (affect); and behavior following a closed head injury. In a closed head injury, there is no penetration of the skull, but trauma results in the brain knocking against the hard inner surface of the skull. The closed head injury itself may be accompanied by loss of consciousness, loss of memory of the trauma and for events immediately following (posttraumatic amnesia), and possibly posttraumatic seizure disorder. Postconcussive syndrome usually follows mild head injury, in which loss or alteration in consciousness lasts less than 20 minutes. Cognitive symptoms include poor concentration, attentional deficits, and impaired memory. Affective symptoms may include irritability, anxiety, depression, or fluctuation in mood (emotional lability). Physical symptoms can include fatigue, headaches, vertigo, or an intolerance of noise (sonophobia) and bright lights (photophobia). Occasionally, there will be visual or hearing impairments or a loss of the sense of smell (anosmia), which may affect appetite.

Diagnosis

History: A diagnosis is based on criteria listed in the DSM-IV-TR (Diagnostic and Statistical Manual of Mental Disorders, 4th Edition, Text Revision, published by the American Psychiatric Association. The individual will exhibit some impairment in attention, concentration, shifting focus of attention, and performing simultaneous cognitive tasks, memory, learning, or recall of information. Three or more of the following occur after the trauma, and last at least 3 months: becoming fatigued easily; disordered sleep; headache; vertigo or dizziness; irritability or aggression on little or no provocation; anxiety, depression, or mood swings (affective lability); changes in personality, such as social or sexual inappropriateness; apathy or lack of spontaneity. The impairment represents a significant decline from pre-trauma functioning and causes significant difficulty with school or occupational performance. Postconcussion disorder is not considered if the individual has post-head trauma dementia.

Physical exam: A general physical and neurological examination will determine if other disorders are causing the symptoms. Physical impairments that may be observed include loss of sense of smell (anosmia), slowed movement or speech (psychomotor retardation), impaired gait on specialized tests such as standing with feet together and eyes closed (Romberg) or walking a straight line (tandem gait), or other subtle neurological findings.

Tests: Include skull x-rays, brain CT scan or MRI, and psychological tests. Electroencephalogram (EEG) may be indicated if seizures are suspected.

Treatment

There are various treatment options, depending on the nature of the trauma and associated symptoms. Medication therapy may be helpful for specific areas of concern such as sleep disturbances, depression, anxiety, headaches, or seizures. Psychotherapy, specifically the behavioral approaches, are helpful, depending upon the individual's level of cognitive impairment. Substance abuse treatment may also be indicated.

Prognosis

In most cases of mild-to-moderate head injury, the symptoms clear up in 6-12 months. However, some individuals may experience symptoms for several years and may never be completely back to normal. Residual impairment and changes in mood (excitement or depression) are common. Depending on the severity of the injury, there may be residual cognitive impairment or seizures.

Differential Diagnosis

Cerebral contusion, factitious disorder, and malingering may also need to be considered. Individuals with somatization disorder may show similar behavioral or somatic symptoms, but do not have an identifiable head injury or measurable impairment in cognitive functioning.

Specialists

- Neurologist
- Neuropsychologist
- Occupational Therapist
- Psychiatrist
- Psychologist

Rehabilitation

In addition to psychotherapy and pharmacotherapy treatments, occupational therapy may be helpful. Occupational therapy could help the individual to develop communication skills, identify and match personal skills and work habits to the work place, and learn how participation in leisure activities contributes to overall health and well being. In the first weeks or months after the head trauma, physical therapy may be useful to increase balance and coordination that may have been affected by the injury. Cognitive rehabilitation may help the individual cope with memory or concentration problems through strategies such as making lists, or learning new information presented in writing as well as verbally.

Work Restrictions / Accommodations

Accommodations may include modifying the work space to decrease noise and visual distractions; introducing the individual to new or stressful situations gradually under appropriate supervision and support; providing written instructions and new information in small steps; allowing break time according to individual needs rather than a fixed schedule; limiting physical tasks that involve stooping, sneezing, physical exertion, noise, and excitement; adjusting or eliminating highly stressful activities; providing sensitivity training for co-workers; providing praise and positive reinforcement. Individuals with seizures should not work at heights, drive, or operate heavy machinery. Persistent memory problems may require reassignment of job duties, or even result in total disability. Avoiding work environments where there is loud noise or bright lights may help decrease headaches.

Comorbid Conditions

Substance abuse and other psychiatric illness may lengthen disability. Because of the changes in physical and cognitive functioning, some individuals may develop a depressive disorder. Post-traumatic seizures, post-traumatic headache, and post-traumatic cognitive impairment are all comorbid complications that can lengthen disability.

Complications

Complications may be caused by psychosocial factors. Substance abuse and major depression may occur, and require treatment in their own right. Impairments in memory, vision, hearing, and sense of smell that may have resulted from the head trauma can also complicate recovery. Seizures (post-traumatic epilepsy), persistent headaches (post-traumatic headache), or specific neurological impairments may also occur.

Factors Influencing Duration

Factors influencing length of disability include the individual's psychological makeup and secondary gain, such as financial gain related to litigation, increased attention from friends and family, and avoidance of work or other responsibilities. Some orthopedic and neurological complications may be present, depending upon the severity and circumstances of the trauma.

Length of Disability

The length of disability is highly variable and dependent upon the nature of the head trauma and associated symptoms, response to medications and psychotherapy, the presence of substance abuse or other psychiatric disorders, the presence of other physical complications of the closed head injury, and the presence of a supportive emotional network.

Duration depends on severity of manifestations (headache to total and permanent disability). Although symptoms following a mild-to-moderate head injury may clear up in 6-12 months, some individuals exhibit symptoms for years after the injury. Disability may be permanent.

Duration in Days

Job Classification	Minimum	Optimum	Maximum
Any work	1	14	Indefinite

Failure to Recover

If an individual fails to recover within the maximum duration expectancy period, the reader may wish to reference the following questions to assist in better understanding the specifics of an individual's medical case.

Regarding diagnosis:

- Has the diagnosis of postconcussive syndrome been confirmed?
- Is there evidence of neurological problems following head trauma, such as seizures or memory problems?
- Is additional testing warranted?
- Does the individual have a coexisting medical or psychological condition that may impact recovery?
- Have changes in physical and cognitive functioning resulted in a depressive disorder?

Regarding treatment:

- Has drug therapy been effective for specific areas of concern such as sleep disturbances, depression, anxiety, headaches, or seizures?
- Is the individual taking medication as prescribed? Are side effects interfering with use or benefit from that particular medication?
- Could other medication options be used instead?
- Are post-traumatic seizures and/or post-traumatic headaches being properly addressed?
- Depending on the level of cognitive impairment, would the individual benefit from more frequent or a different type of therapeutic encounters?
- As coexisting substance abuse may complicate treatment and delay recovery, would the individual benefit from enrollment in a substance abuse treatment program?

Regarding prognosis:
- Do symptoms persist despite treatment?
- Does cognitive impairment persist?
- Would cognitive or vocational rehabilitation be beneficial?
- Would the individual benefit from additional psychotherapy or enrollment in a support group?
- Are other factors prolonging disability, such as financial gain related to litigation, or secondary gain related to increased attention from family and friends?

References

Erlanger, D.M., et al. "Neuropsychology of Sports-related Head Injury: Dementia Pugilistica to Postconcussion Syndrome." Clinical Neuropsychologist 13 2 (1999): 193-209.

Frances, A., J.P. Docherty, and D.A. Kakn. Healing with Vitamins. Emmaus, PA: Rodale Press, Inc, 1996.

Frances, Allen. Diagnostic and Statistical Manual of Mental Disorders: 4th ed, text revision. Washington, DC: American Psychiatric Association, 2000.

Hall, Laura Lee. "Making the ADA Work for People with Psychiatric Disabilities." Mental Disorder, Work Disability, and the Law. Bonnie, Richard J., and John Monahan, eds. Chicago: The University of Chicago Press, 1997. 241-280.

Margulies, S. "The Postconcussion Syndrome After Mild Head Trauma: Part II." Journal of Clinical Psychiatry 7 6 (2000): 495-499.

Margulies, S. "The Postconcussion Syndrome After Mild Head Trauma: Is Brain Damage Overdiagnosed? Part I." Journal of Clinical Neuroscience 7 5 (2000): 400-408.

Miller, Laurence. Shocks to the System: Psychotherapy of Traumatic Disability Syndromes. New York: W.W. Norton & Company, 1998.

O'Brien, Gregory, and Beth Cheesebrough. "Traumatic Brain Damage." Developmental Disability and Behaviour. Gillberg, Christopher, and Gregory O'Brien, eds. Cambridge: Cambridge University Press, 2000. 64-76.

Santalucia, P., and E. Feldmann. "Concussion and Head Injury." Med Health R.I 83 6 (2000): 173-177.

Yates, William R. "Psychiatric Conditions." Head Injury and Postconcussive Syndrome. Rizzo, Matthew, and Daniel Tranel, eds. New York: Churchill Livingstone, 1996. 305-320.

Post-Laminectomy Syndrome
Other names / synonyms: Failed Back Surgery Syndrome, Failed Back Syndrome
722.8, 722.80, 722.81, 722.82, 722.83

Definition

Post-laminectomy syndrome refers to symptoms not relieved by back surgery or that recur after surgery. It is used to describe almost any bad result following any type of disc surgery. Laminectomy is removal of the lamina of a vertebra. Even though "partial laminotomy" and not laminectomy is done at the time of most open disc excision (discectomy) operations, the historic term "laminectomy" is frequently misapplied to the operation.

The causes of poor results or "failed back surgery syndrome" include poor patient selection (operating when nerve compression did not exist), nerve root injury at the time of surgery, operating too late in time (beyond 6 months of leg pain), disc space or epidural space infection, unrecognized lateral stenosis or instability, arachnoiditis, and reherniation. Rarely is it determined that the first surgery was done by mistake on the wrong side or at the wrong level (malpractice). Sometimes the surgery corrected the mechanical spinal problem but psychosocial factors may be involved in maintaining the chronic pain.

More than 200,000 "laminectomies" (discectomies) are performed in the US each year. The prevalence and incidence of post-laminectomy syndrome are not precisely known. The yearly incidence of laminectomy failure is estimated between 25,000 and 50,000.

Diagnosis

History: The medical history of individuals with this syndrome varies considerably; however, all the individuals recently underwent back surgery and are still experiencing low back pain and or leg pain (sciatica).

Physical exam: The exam may include a complete neurovascular and musculoskeletal exam to rule out all other possible causes of symptoms.

Tests: The tests include flexion and extension x-rays of the spine to help determine whether the pain is from documented instability (rare). MRI and CT/myelography may both be performed to evaluate for persisting nerve compression, discitis, etc. Lab studies include blood work to detect infection (WBC, ESR). If an infection is suspected, a bone scan (nuclear imaging bone scan) may be ordered. Nerve conduction and EMG studies evaluate nerve root pain. Both psychological evaluation and a second surgical opinion should be obtained before spinal surgery is repeated.

Treatment

The true cause of the "failed" surgery must be determined so appropriate treatment can be provided. Conservative back pain treatment is usually tried first and consists of oral medications (analgesics, nonsteroidal anti-inflammatory drugs [NSAIDs], antidepressants, muscle relaxants and anti convulsants), physical therapy, and exercise. Anesthetics or steroids may be injected directly into the affected area of the back. Chronic opioids (narcotics) may be prescribed but while they may decrease pain, they less frequently impact disability.

Repeat surgical decompression (discectomy, vertebral fusion, and/or additional laminectomy) is only occasionally indicated when a clear-cut diagnosis is established. Individuals with recurrent back pain without any apparent cause may benefit from psychotherapy and treatment by a pain specialist.

Prognosis

The outcome is extremely variable but can range from complete relief to worsening of symptoms. Some individuals may experience pain for the rest of their lives. While first back operations yield good or excellent results in 80-90% of individuals, second operations in those with poor results from first surgeries yield good results in only 40-50% of cases. Results are even worse for third or fourth operations. Multiple surgeries on older individuals often have poorer outcomes. Unresolved psychosocial factors (e.g., marital or sexual problems, job dissatisfaction) may delay or prevent recovery.

Differential Diagnosis

Tumor, arthritis, osteomyelitis, osteoporosis, degenerative disc disease, neurological disease, fracture of the spine, infection, spinal stenosis, cauda equina syndrome, and inflammatory disease may present with similar symptoms. Psychosocial and environmental factors may be involved.

Specialists

- Neurosurgeon
- Occupational Therapist
- Orthopedic Surgeon
- Pain Specialist
- Physiatrist
- Physical Therapist
- Psychiatrist
- Psychologist
- Spine Surgeon

Rehabilitation

Outpatient physical therapy is rarely helpful, as the individual has already "failed" the usual outpatient therapy that followed the first back operation. Comprehensive multidisciplinary assessment at a tertiary or multi-disciplinary pain/rehab clinic will usually be necessary. Potentially surgically treatable structural causes (like unrecognized instability or lateral recess stenosis or disc space infection) will be sought, but uncommonly found.

Some individuals with the post laminectomy syndrome improve with the combination of physical rehabilitation (active exercise), which is facilitated by having a peer group of fellow back sufferers with which to exercise, and cognitive and behavioral treatment of associated mental disorders and psychosocial stressors. Chronic pain units utilize this combination of treatments most frequently.

If these measures fail, options are limited. Spinal cord stimulation with an implantable, battery powered unit that stimulates the spinal cord with electricity, somewhat like what a cardiac pacemaker does for the heart, may be tried. Only about half of the individuals will respond to spinal cord stimulation, and, generally, with only a 50% or less decrease in pain.

For some, the only option is whether or not to use chronic opioids (narcotics), either orally, or from an implanted pump, which delivers the narcotic directly to the spine/spinal cord or nerves while remaining disabled.

Work Restrictions / Accommodations

Individuals with this diagnosis rarely return to work. If successfully treated by additional surgery, or multidisciplinary rehabilitation, they usually return to sedentary, light or medium work.

Comorbid Conditions

Comorbid conditions that may increase length of disability include arthritis, cardiopulmonary disease, obesity, diabetes, cancer, depression, other mental disorders and psychosocial stressors, and general debility.

Complications

Post-laminectomy syndrome may be complicated by infection, surgical trauma, or bleeding. If there is poor healing after a bone fusion, recovery is more complicated.

Factors Influencing Duration

Duration depends on source of pain, underlying cause, and method of treatment. The type and amount of surgery and rehabilitation required have an effect on disability time. Permanent disability is a possibility for individuals in certain job situations. Psychosocial factors have a significant impact on disability.

Length of Disability

Duration depends on job requirements and severity of pain. Disability may be permanent.

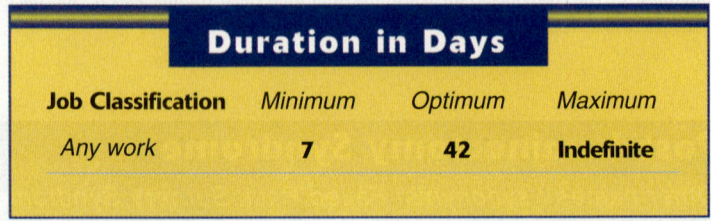

Job Classification	Minimum	Optimum	Maximum
Any work	7	42	Indefinite

Failure to Recover

If an individual fails to recover within the maximum duration expectancy period, the reader may wish to reference the following questions to assist in better understanding the specifics of an individual's medical case.

Regarding diagnosis:

- Is the location of the pain as before surgery or is it in a different location?
- Have postoperative MRI CT/myelography, EMG, and sedimentation rate studies suggested a surgically treatable cause?
- Has the individual had a complete psychiatric evaluation to rule out psychosocial factors?
- What were the results of the neurovascular and musculoskeletal exams?
- Has the individual been referred to a clinical psychologist for a complete psychological evaluation including testing (Minnesota Multiphasic Personality Inventory)?
- Has the individual had a second surgical opinion?
- Has a functional assessment been performed to identify approximate activity tolerances?
- Have conditions such as tumor, arthritis, osteomyelitis, osteoporosis, muscle spasm and other conditions with similar symptoms been ruled out?
- Is impending litigation regarding the condition causing the individual to exaggerate symptoms? Does the individual exaggerate symptoms in order to avoid work?

Regarding treatment:

- Has the true cause of the failed surgery been determined?
- What has the individual's response to conservative treatment (analgesics, NSAIDs, antidepressants, muscle relaxants, physical therapy, and exercise)?
- Did the individual have additional surgery? Was it done in stages?
- Was electrical stimulation tried to stimulate bone healing in the case of a failed fusion?
- Is the individual active in psychotherapy?
- Did the original surgery fail?
- Is evaluation at a multidisciplinary pain center indicated?
- Has the individual consulted with a pain specialist?

Regarding prognosis:

- How severe are the symptoms? Are they incapacitating? Can the individual perform the normal activities of daily life?
- Has the individual undergone multiple back surgeries?
- Did the individual organize their work area ergonomically?
- Is the individual's employer able to accommodate the needed restrictions?
- Does the individual have any comorbid conditions that could increase length of disability?

References

Chapman, Michael. "Degenerative Disorders of the Lumbar and Thoracic Spine." Principles of Orthopaedic Practice. Dee, Roger, et al., eds. New York: McGraw-Hill, 1997. 1315-1350.

Lapointe, J.S. "Imaging of the Spine and Spinal Cord." Spinal Cord Disease: Basic Science, Diagnosis and Management. Critchley, Edmund, and Andrew Eisen, eds. London: Springer-Verlag, 1996. 117-143.

Postmenopausal Bleeding
627.1

Definition

Postmenopausal bleeding is vaginal bleeding that occurs six months or more after menstrual function stops. This differentiates it from the irregular, infrequent periods (oligomenorrhea) that occur around the time of menopause, which can last between 1 to 2 years.

There are many conditions that cause postmenopausal bleeding; abnormal vaginal bleeding is a common complaint among women. In general, postmenopausal vaginal bleeding is caused by a hormonal disturbance or lesion in either the cervix or uterine lining (endometrium). The most common causes of upper reproductive system bleeding relate to the wasting or shrinkage of the endometrium following menopause (atrophic endometrium), rapid reproduction of endometrial cells (endometrial proliferation), overgrowth of the endometrium (hyperplasia), endometrial or cervical cancer, uterine tumors, and using estrogen replacement therapy without adding progestin. The most common cause of lower reproductive tract postmenopausal bleeding is inflammation and drying of the vagina associated with menopause and loss of estrogen (atrophic vaginitis); this can be the cause of short term bleeding that occurs after intercourse. Other causes of postmenopausal bleeding include lesions and cracks on the vulva, trauma, growths protruding inside the uterus (endometrial polyps), cervical ulcers caused by prolapse of the uterus, estrogen-secreting tumors in other parts of the body, and bleeding abnormalities.

Fifteen percent of postmenopausal bleeding is due to endometrial cancer or its precursors; uterine hyperplasia can be a precursor to cancer.

Diagnosis

History: A detailed history as to how long bleeding has existed, including frequency, length, and quantity of bleeding should be provided to the physician. The woman may report individual episodes of spotting, or she may report days or months of profuse bleeding. Pain may or may not be reported. The woman may report a history of conditions affecting the thyroid, kidneys, or liver. She may report a history of bleeding or easy bruising. Medications taken, especially estrogens or steroids, should be disclosed.

Physical exam: The results of physical and pelvic examination will depend on the underlying cause of the postmenopausal bleeding. Examination of the vulva, vagina, and uterus both by visual and palpation exam may reveal signs of atrophy, and areas of bleeding, ulcers, or tumors. A sample of vaginal fluid may be obtained for examination under the microscope and may indicate low estrogen effect. Examination of the cervix may reveal polyps or other lesions. A uterus that is larger than normal may be indicative of the presence of fibroids or polyps.

Tests: The tests ordered depend on the suspected underlying cause, and can include complete blood count (CBC) and platelet count. Cytologic smears from the vagina may be obtained. A Pap smear and biopsy of the cervix will be obtained. Tests performed to identify abnormalities of the uterus may include endometrial biopsy, and dilation and curettage (D & C). Hysteroscopy may reveal the presence of uterine polyps, atrophy, endometrial hyperplasia, or cancer. Imaging examinations that may be performed include a pelvic sonogram, vaginal probe (transvaginal) ultrasonography to measure the thickness of the endometrium, the injection of liquid into the uterus prior to inserting a vaginal probe (saline infusion sonogram - SIS) to more clearly identify structural abnormalities, CT scan, MRI, or hysterosalpingography.

Treatment

Treatment of postmenopausal bleeding depends on the cause. Postmenopausal bleeding due to bleeding from the vagina or vulva can be treated with local application of estrogen (hormone replacement therapy-HRT). Removal of tissue from the inside of uterus (aspiration curettage) may be all that is necessary to relieve postmenopausal bleeding. Removal of polyps (polypectomy) will correct bleeding associated with their presence. Cyclic progestin administration for three months may be given for treatment of overgrowth of the endometrium (simple endometrial hyperplasia). At completion of progestin therapy, a repeat D&C or endometrial biopsy will be performed to verify absence of hyperplasia. Then oral HRT with progestin may be given; most women who are on HRT, taking estrogen along with progesterone, may experience monthly withdrawal bleeding; this is a normal side effect that does not require treatment.

Hysterectomy may be necessary to treat endometrial hyperplasia with atypical cells, cancer of the uterus (endometrial), uterine fibroids, and bleeding that does not resolve with treatment (refractory) causing anemia due to chronic blood loss. Cancer of the uterus or cervix may require treatment with anti-cancer medications (chemotherapy).

Prognosis

Outcome depends on the cause of the bleeding, and can range from complete cure to death from cancer. A simple dilation and curettage (D & C) aspiration may completely stop postmenopausal bleeding. Polypectomy will relieve any bleeding associated with the presence of polyps. Endometrial hyperplasia is usually resolved by administering progestin for three months. Estrogen replacement therapy (HRT) with progestin usually prevents additional abnormal postmenopausal bleeding. A hysterectomy will permanently cure endometrial hyperplasia with atypical cells, uterine fibroids, bleeding, and anemia. The outcome of a hysterectomy, as treatment of cancer of the endometrium (uterus) or cervix, depends on the extent of tumor spread. The outcome of endometrial and cervical cancers that are diagnosed early is very good.

Differential Diagnosis

Other possible diagnoses include atrophic vaginitis, atrophic endometrium, endometrial polyps or hyperplasia, cancer of the reproductive organs, and blood dyscrasias.

Specialists

- Gynecologist
- Oncologist

Work Restrictions / Accommodations

Time off from work may be needed for tests, and for diagnostic and therapeutic procedures. Work restrictions may be needed if surgery is required. A hysterectomy due to cancer is usually performed through an abdominal incision. Recovery time following hysterectomy may be between six to eight weeks. If chemotherapy is needed, additional time away from work will be necessary, not only for the therapy itself, but for side effects and individual response to the medication.

Comorbid Conditions

Prolonged use of estrogen replacement therapy (HRT) that is not combined with progestin increases the risk of endometrial hyperplasia and endometrial cancer in women who have not had a hysterectomy.

Complications

Profuse bleeding can cause anemia. Endometrial hyperplasia in which atypical cells are found progresses to endometrial cancer in 23% of women, whereas hyperplasia in which no atypical cells are identified progresses to cancer in only 2% of women. Cancer, both endometrial and cervical, can spread to other areas of the body.

Factors Influencing Duration

Factors include the underlying cause, its treatment, complications, job demands, and the response to treatment.

Length of Disability

Medical treatment.

Duration in Days

Job Classification	Minimum	Optimum	Maximum
Sedentary work	0	2	5
Light work	0	2	5
Medium work	0	2	5
Heavy work	0	2	5
Very Heavy work	0	2	5

With D&C.

Duration in Days

Job Classification	Minimum	Optimum	Maximum
Sedentary work	2	3	7
Light work	2	3	7
Medium work	3	4	7
Heavy work	3	4	7
Very Heavy work	3	4	7

Failure to Recover

If an individual fails to recover within the maximum duration expectancy period, the reader may wish to reference the following questions to assist in better understanding the specifics of an individual's medical case.

Regarding Diagnosis:

- Does the history of postmenopausal bleeding involve individual episodes of spotting, or was the bleeding profuse, lasting days or months?
- Was there any pain reported?
- Did the woman report a history of other conditions such as thyroid, kidneys, or liver?
- Was there a history of bleeding or easy bruising?
- Has the woman been taking anticoagulants, estrogens or steroids?
- Did examination of the vulva and vagina reveal areas of bleeding, ulcers, or tumors?
- Did an unstained wet mount in saline and potassium hydroxide reveal the presence of white blood cells, infection-causing organisms, basal epithelial cells (that indicate low estrogen effect)?
- Did examination of the cervix reveal polyps or other lesions? normal (may be indicative of the presence of fibroids)?
- Did examination of the uterus reveal a uterus that is larger than

- Did a CBC and platelet count reveal any abnormalities that may contribute to spontaneous bleeding?
- Did the Pap smear or biopsy of the cervix reveal abnormalities?
- Were other diagnostic procedures performed such as biopsy, dilation and curettage (D & C), or hysteroscopy? What did they reveal?
- Were imaging examinations performed such as a pelvic sonogram, transvaginal ultrasonography, CT scan, MRI scan, or hysterosalpingography? What did they reveal?

Regarding treatment:
- Was aspiration curettage performed for treatment of postmenopausal bleeding?
- Was polypectomy performed?
- Was progestin given to treat simple endometrial hyperplasia? Was it effective?
- Was hysterectomy performed for treatment of endometrial hyperplasia (with atypical cells), cancer of the endometrium, uterine fibroids, anemia or bleeding that didn't resolve with treatment?
- Was chemotherapy given for treatment of cancer of the endometrium or cervix?

Regarding prognosis:
- Based on the age, general health and underlying cause of the bleeding, what was the expected outcome?
- Did the individual have any pre-existing conditions that could impact recovery and prognosis? If so, have these conditions been addressed in the treatment plan?
- Did the individual suffer any complications (anemia, etc) that could prolong disability?

References

Adelson, Mark D., and Katherine L. Adelson. "Miscellaneous Benign Disorders of the Upper Genital Tract." Textbook of Gynecology, 2nd ed. Copeland, Larry J., ed. Philadelphia: W.B. Saunders Company, 2000. 723-739.

Beebe, Diane K. "Abnormal Vaginal Bleeding." Saunders Manual of Medical Practice, 2nd ed. Rakel, Robert E., ed. Philadelphia: W.B. Saunders Company, 2000. 516-518.

Davidson, Tish. "Postmenopausal Bleeding." Blue Cross and Blue Shield of Massachusetts. 2000. 20 Feb 2001 <http://www.ahealthyme.com/article/gale/100083895>.

Dawood, M. Yusoff. "Menopause." Textbook of Gynecology, 2nd ed. Copeland, Larry J., ed. Philadelphia: W.B. Saunders Company, 2000. 603-629.

MacKay, H. Trent. "Gynecology." Current Medical Diagnosis and Treatment, 39th ed. Tierney, Lawrence, M., Stephen J. McPhee, and Maxine A. Papadakis, eds. New York: Lange Medical Books/McGraw-Hill, 2000. 723-757.

Morrow, Paul C., and John P. Curtin. "Etiology and Detection of Gynecologic Cancer." Synopsis of Gynecologic Oncology, 5th ed. New York: Churchill Livingstone, 1998. 1-15.

Postpartum Mastitis
Other names / synonyms: Puerperal Mastitis
675, 675.0, 675.2, 675.8, 675.9

Definition

Postpartum mastitis (puerperal mastitis) is an infection in the breast, generally in a woman who is breastfeeding.

Nipples may become cracked or fissured with breastfeeding, especially during the first few days. The pressure on nipple tissue from the infant's sucking, increased moisture on the nipple, improper infant positioning during breast feeding, not completely emptying the breast of milk, and the frequency of breast feeding can all contribute to sore nipples that become cracked and fissured. The new mother will also have a lowered resistance to illness. Then, commonly, the mother's breast becomes infected from a strain of bacteria passed into a milk duct from the mouth, nose, or throat of her infant. Bacteria responsible for most cases of postpartum mastitis are the staphylococci bacteria.

About 1 in 20 nursing mothers develop postpartum mastitis; non-nursing mothers can also develop this condition. Women who are nursing for the first time are most often affected. In most cases, only one breast is affected. Postpartum mastitis usually develops 2-3 weeks after delivery (postpartum) but may occur up to 3 months later.

Diagnosis

History: Mastitis leaves the woman feeling as if she has come down with the flu. She will complain of a hard, warm, red, tender area on the breast and swelling of the affected milk duct. She may recall having a sore, cracked nipple and breast engorgement prior to the development of symptoms. The woman may report chills, fever (101-102 degrees F), fatigue, and a feeling of general illness (malaise).

Physical exam: The exam may reveal signs of infection and inflammation (cellulitis) such as redness, tenderness, local warmth, and fever. The nipple may have fissures. The lymph glands in the armpit near the breast may be swollen and tender. There may also be systemic signs of infection such an increased pulse. Often other areas may also show evidence of infection (earaches, sinusitis, conjunctivitis, etc.).

Tests: A culture is done to identify the presence and type of bacteria. A complete blood count (CBC) may show increased white blood cells, and a sedimentation rate (ESR) may be elevated; both are indicators of general inflammation.

Treatment

When caught in the early stages, oral antibiotics will be prescribed. The most commonly prescribed antibiotics are safe for babies. Anti-inflammatory drugs may be given to control pain and fever. Although painful, breastfeeding should continue to keep the milk supply flowing, thus avoiding the risk of further blockage. To completely empty the breast of milk, any milk that remains after each feeding should be expressed by hand or by the use of a mechanical suction device. Bed rest and applying warm or cold compresses may be recommended. Firm breast support (brassieres) and pillows may be used to support the breast. When the condition is in an advanced stage, the hard mass (abscess) will be cut open to drain (incision and drainage); in this eventuality, nursing must be stopped.

Prognosis

The outcome of mastitis is usually good. When caught early, mastitis is usually controlled within 24 to 48 hours, after which the woman will begin to feel better. If treatment is delayed, an abscess will develop. About 10% of women with mastitis develop an abscess. If an abscess occurs, surgical drainage (requiring general anesthesia) is necessary. Although the incision will initially be packed open, it generally heals without problems. An antibiotic-resistant infection may be spread to other areas of the body, and to other members of the family.

Differential Diagnosis

Breast cancer is a possible diagnosis.

Specialists

- Gynecologist
- Obstetrician
- Primary Care Provider
- Surgeon

Work Restrictions / Accommodations

While at work, time and privacy may be needed to empty the breast (by breast pump) periodically. Heavy lifting and reaching above shoulder level should be restricted temporarily.

Comorbid Conditions

A comorbid condition is engorgement, which usually precedes development of mastitis.

Complications

If allowed to advance, postpartum mastitis will become a breast abscess. An antibiotic-resistant infection may be spread to other parts of the body and may lead to sepsis.

Factors Influencing Duration

The occurrence of complications, such as an abscess or infection with an antibiotic resistant bacterium, and the response to treatment will determine length of disability.

Length of Disability

In most cases, no disability is expected.

Duration in Days

Job Classification	Minimum	Optimum	Maximum
Sedentary work	1	3	7
Light work	1	3	7
Medium work	1	3	7
Heavy work	1	3	14
Very Heavy work	1	3	14

Failure to Recover

If an individual fails to recover within the maximum duration expectancy period, the reader may wish to reference the following questions to assist in better understanding the specifics of an individual's medical case.

Regarding diagnosis:

- Has individual been trained on proper positioning of the infant during breast-feeding?
- Does individual completely empty the breast at each feeding?
- Did the woman note a hard, red, tender spot on the breast?
- Was there a sore, cracked nipple, or breast engorgement prior to the development of the breast lump?
- Did the woman report chills, fever, and a feeling of general malaise?
- Is individual's breast warm, red, and tender?
- Does individual have a fever?
- Are the lymph nodes in the armpit near the breast swollen and tender?
- Has a culture been done?
- Did individual have a CBC ESR? What were the results?
- Has breast cancer been ruled out?

Regarding treatment:

- Was the mastitis diagnosed early?
- Has individual responded to oral antibiotics?
- Was individual instructed to continue breast-feeding?
- Have warm or cold compresses been helpful?
- Is individual using a brassiere with firm support?
- Was it necessary to surgically drain the abscess?

Regarding prognosis:

- Is the individual's employer able make the necessary accommodations?
- Was engorgement present?
- Did individual have any complications?

References

Bowman, Marjorie A., and Marcia B. Szewczyk. "Diseases of the Breast." Family Medicine. Rudy, David R., and Kurt, eds. Kurowski Baltimore: Williams & Wilkins, 1997. 341-349.

Cantu, Darlene N., and Sarah Whitaker. "Maternal-neonatal Care." Nursing Procedures, 3rd ed. Holmes, Nancy H., ed. Springhouse, PA: Springhouse Corporation, 2000. 692-745.

Crombleholme, William R. "Obstetrics." Current Medical Diagnosis and Treatment, 39th ed. Tierney, Lawrence M., Stephen J. McPhee, and Maxine A. Papadakis, eds. New York: Lange Medical Books/McGraw-Hill, 2000. 758-782.

Cunningham, Gary F., et al. "Infection and Disorders of the Puerperium." Williams Obstetrics, 20th ed. Cunningham, F. Gary, et al., eds. Appleton & Lange, 1997. 547-567.

Runowicz, Carolyn D. "Benign Breast Disease and Screening for Malignant Tumors." Textbook of Gynecology, 2nd ed. Copeland, Larry J., ed. Philadelphia: W.B. Saunders Company, 2000. 1107-1130.

Williams, Rebecca. "Breast-feeding." Saunders Manual of Medical Practice, 2nd ed. Rakel, Robert E., ed. Philadelphia: W.B. Saunders Company, 2000. 648-650.

Posttraumatic Stress Disorder

Other names / synonyms: Chronic Post-Traumatic Stress, Extreme Stress Response, PTSD

309.81

Definition

Posttraumatic stress disorder (PTSD) occurs when an individual is exposed to an extremely traumatic, usually life-threatening stressor such as military combat or a violent personal assault. This traumatic event is outside the individual's normal realm of experience and overwhelms the individual's usual psychological defenses. In PTSD, the memory of the trauma is repeatedly experienced in ways that are nearly as distressing as the original trauma.

Symptoms include being constantly anxious and alert because danger is imagined everywhere (hypervigilance), irritability, sleep disturbance, inability to concentrate, impaired ability to express emotion, self-destructive and impulsive behavior, and the sensation of losing awareness of self and not remembering what one has done or said for extended periods of time (dissociative symptoms). Individual may have physical complaints such as indigestion, headaches, and fatigue. They may have feelings of ineffectiveness, shame, despair, or hopelessness and feel permanently damaged. Individuals can experience a loss of previously sustained beliefs and be socially withdrawn or have impaired relationships with others.

It is not known why some individuals develop PTSD while others sharing the same experience do not. For example, of all Vietnam War veterans, only a fraction of the combatants exposed to horrifying events developed PTSD. The same is true across a wide spectrum of survivors of violence or violent situations whether accident victims, battered spouses, hostages, or prisoners of war. Personality factors can promote either emotional resilience after a trauma or predispose the individual to significant impairment. The prevailing belief is that every individual however well-adjusted has a point of tolerance that, if exceeded, will result in PTSD. For example, wounded veterans have five times the likelihood of later developing PTSD than their uninjured comrades. Of all identified risk factors for PTSD, the most important is believed to be the lack of a supportive network of friends and family. Cultural aspects such as the belief that it is dishonorable to reveal instances of torture may affect an individual's willingness to seek help for PTSD symptoms.

Most estimates of overall lifetime prevalence are five to ten percent. In groups at risk (combatants, victims of natural disasters or criminal violence), prevalence ranges from thirty to sixty percent. Women have a 2 to 3 times higher risk of developing PTSD than men. Based on the National Comorbidity Survey Report published in 1995, estimated lifetime prevalence of PTSD among adult Americans is 7.8% (10.4% for women and 5% for men). The prevalence rates are low compared with the proportion of adults having experienced at least one major traumatic event (60.7% for men and 51.2% for women). The traumatic events most often associated with PTSD in men are rape, combat exposure, childhood neglect, and childhood physical abuse. In women, traumatic events most likely to precede PTSD are rape, sexual molestation, physical attack, being threatened with a weapon, and childhood physical abuse.

Diagnosis

History: Diagnosis is based on criteria listed in the DSM-IV-TR (Diagnostic and Statistical Manual of Mental Disorders, 4th Edition, Text Revision, published by the American Psychiatric Association). The history, psychiatric interview, and mental status exam of an individual who has experienced or witnessed a traumatic event are used to establish whether the individual's response or behavior meets the diagnostic criteria from the DSM-IV-TR. The event must have involved threatened or actual death, serious injury, or threat to physical integrity with the individual's response being intense fear, helplessness, or horror.

Persistent avoidance of stimuli associated with the trauma should include three or more of the following: efforts to avoid thoughts, feelings, or conversations associated with the trauma; efforts to avoid activities, places, or people that arouse recollections of the trauma; inability to recall an important aspect of the trauma; markedly diminished interest or participation in significant activities; feeling of detachment or estrangement from others; inability to relate emotionally to others (restricted range of affect or warmth towards others); and sense of foreshortened future with the individual not expecting to have a career, marriage, children, or normal life span.

At least two or more of the following symptoms occur with PTSD: difficulty falling or staying asleep, irritability or outbursts of anger, difficulty concentrating, hypervigilance, or exaggerated startle response. These symptoms were not present before the trauma and result in a significant decline in social or occupational functioning. The symptoms must persist for 1 month to support the diagnosis of PTSD. If the symptoms do not appear until 6 months after the original event, it is considered PTSD with delayed onset. In this case, a second, lesser traumatic event may have added to and reinforced the original trauma.

Sufferers of PTSD must show evidence of preoccupation with the original trauma. This may take any of several forms such as recurrent nightmares or frequently feeling as if the event was happening again or just about to happen. In the most dramatic case, the event is vividly reexperienced as a flashback that completely replaces normal awareness (a form of dissociation). More typically, this preoccupation is in the form of intrusive memories and thoughts that constantly compete with normal attention and are triggered by cues that remind the individual of the trauma. Bodily signs of anxiety may accompany these cues. As a result, performance of even simple tasks such as freeway driving may become impossible. In an effort to ward off painful memories and feelings, victims of PTSD begin to avoid situations that remind them of the trauma. They may pretend the trauma never happened (denial). In attempting to forget the trauma, important pieces are sometimes missing (repression). As the severity of PTSD increases, this process becomes more generalized.

Physical exam: The exam may reveal signs of a physical trauma like burn scars or an increased rate of somatic complaints.

Tests: Evidence of impaired attention and concentration may be present or the range of expressed emotion or affect may be considerably reduced. Individual may lack reception to humor. Psychological testing can be helpful in substantiating the diagnosis but cannot be used as the sole diagnostic tool. A few tests are designed specifically to detect PTSD but these are limited to combat veterans. Increased arousal may be measured through studies of autonomic functioning such as heart rate, electromyography, or sweat gland activity.

Treatment

In general, treatment consists of individual and group psychotherapy. Retelling of the event is encouraged especially in groups composed of fellow trauma victims. PTSD and other anxiety disorders are frequently treated by desensitization and related techniques. Desensitization includes the exposure technique based on the fact that anxiety tends to decrease after repeated exposure to a feared thought or situation. Medication therapy is frequently used and consists primarily of antidepressants and sedatives. Occasionally tranquilizers may be used but should be done so cautiously and only after a thorough assessment for possible alcohol and/or drug abuse.

The best treatment is preventive in nature. The most successful treatment interventions are those implemented immediately after a civilian disaster or war zone trauma. This treatment is referred to as critical incident stress debriefing. Every effort should be made to develop the individual's social support network. Unfortunately, many individuals in the early phases of PTSD will assume their symptoms will resolve with time so do not seek attention until much later when the symptoms are more entrenched.

Prognosis

Outcomes vary greatly. Most individuals subjected to an experience outside the normal realm of human experience never become symptomatic. Complete recovery occurs within 3 months in about 50% of the cases of PTSD while others have symptoms lasting longer than 12 months after the trauma. Some individuals improve but when under a new stress may have a period of recurring PTSD symptoms. A subset of individuals with PTSD develop a lifelong illness marked by exacerbations and remissions that makes it extremely difficult to maintain employment or close relationships.

Differential Diagnosis

Acute stress disorder has the same symptoms as PSTD but with shorter duration. Symptoms of PTSD overlap with those of other syndromes including other anxiety disorders, depressive disorders, and obsessive-compulsive disorder. Although substance abuse is a frequent complication of PTSD, substance abuse may be the primary problem instead. Alcoholics and heavy drug abusers often overemphasize the role of a distant trauma as the cause of their problems and use it to justify their habits. Careful studies failed to demonstrate this association and note only a tendency to blame external causes. Various personality disorders can also resemble PTSD with borderline personality disorder having the closest resemblance to PTSD. Some therapists consider borderline personality disorder a form of PTSD where the traumatic event(s) occurred in childhood. Psychosis with hallucinations can also resemble PTSD.

What distinguishes PTSD from other psychiatric disorders is the appearance of symptoms in response to a definite catastrophic event with a subsequent decline in function. Overactivity of the thyroid gland (hyperthyroidism) or adrenal gland (pheochromocytoma) can mimic the high level of arousal seen in PTSD. Malingering is another possibility if a financial or legal advantage exists in having the diagnosis of PTSD. Although the diagnostic criteria for PTSD are quite explicit, it can be a difficult diagnosis to establish in practice.

Specialists

- Advanced Practice Registered Nurse
- Licensed Clinical Social Worker
- Occupational Therapist
- Psychiatrist
- Psychologist

Work Restrictions / Accommodations

Work accommodations may include modifying specific environments that trigger memories or reactions of the original stressor, introducing the individual to new or stressful situations gradually under close supervision and support, providing some flexibility in scheduling for medical therapy appointments, allowing work-at-home or job-sharing opportunities, providing conflict-resolution mechanisms, providing guidelines for feedback on problem areas and proactive management of problem areas, and reducing or eliminating activities where safety of self and/or others is contingent upon constant and/or high levels of alertness (driving or operating machinery).

Comorbid Conditions

Depression, substance abuse and addiction, or borderline personality disorder may lengthen disability.

Complications

Significant disruption of relationships is a common complication with high rates of unemployment and divorce. This may be the result of irritability, isolation, anger, and compromised coping skills in general. A number of other psychiatric syndromes may appear. Substance abuse and major depression are among the more serious of these and require treatment. These individuals are at particularly high risk for suicide. Other psychiatric complications include generalized anxiety and panic attacks.

Factors Influencing Duration

Factors that negatively influence outcome and lengthen disability include previous trauma, poor or marginal levels of functioning before the diagnosis of PTSD, previous or current substance abuse, lack of a support system, reluctance to get appropriate treatment, and the persistence of denial regarding the event or its consequences. Failure to settle litigation issues promptly and decisively can also delay recovery.

Length of Disability

Duration of disability depends on response to medications and psychotherapy, any other psychiatric disorders, and a supportive emotional network.

Chronic.

Duration in Days

Job Classification	Minimum	Optimum	Maximum
Any work	7	28	56

Failure to Recover

If an individual fails to recover within the maximum duration expectancy period, the reader may wish to reference the following questions to assist in better understanding the specifics of an individual's medical case.

Regarding diagnosis:

- Does the individual meet all the criteria for PTSD?
- Has diagnosis been confirmed?
- Have other psychiatric disorders or underlying medical conditions been ruled out?

Regarding treatment:

- Based on the fact that anxiety tends to decrease after repeated exposure to a feared thought or situation (desensitization), has the individual been encouraged to retell experience, especially in groups composed of fellow trauma victims?
- Would the individual benefit from more frequent therapeutic encounters or additional types of therapy?
- Has the individual taken antidepressants and/or sedatives as prescribed? Have side effects prevented the individual from using or benefiting from that particular medication?

Regarding prognosis:

- Although individual showed initial improvement, has a new stress triggered a period of recurring PTSD symptoms?
- Has a subsequent trauma intensified the effects of the initial event?
- How are current stresses being dealt with?
- How were major stresses dealt with in the past? If healthy and adaptive methods were used in the past, are they being used currently?
- If coping methods are maladaptive, such as with drug or alcohol abuse, to what extent are these conditions causing additional problems?
- Who are the individual's social supports? Family? Friends? Church or other community affiliations? Are these being utilized?
- What is happening at work or outside of work that may be contributing to the problem?
- Are there incentives not to improve such as ongoing litigation, social security, or disability insurance?

References

Ethnocultural Aspects of Post-traumatic Stress Disorders: Issues, Research and Application. Marsella, A.J., et al., eds. Washington: American Psychological Association, 1996.

Friedman, Matthew J. Post-traumatic Stress Disorder: An Overview. National Center for PTSD. 12 Jun 2000. 17 Jan 2001 <http://www.ncptsd.org/facts/general/fs_overview.html>.

Pott's Disease

Other names / synonyms: Spondylodiscitis, Tuberculosis of the Spine, Tuberculous Spondylitis
015, 015.0, 737.4

Definition

Pott's disease is a form of tuberculosis that affects the thoracic or lumbar spine. Caused by the bacteria Mycobacterium tuberculosis, which is transmitted by airborne droplets, Pott's disease accounts for approximately 2% of all cases of tuberculosis. The infection may occur in conjunction with tuberculosis of the lung, or years later as a reactivation of the disease. Progressive destruction of the spine can cause an abnormal curvature of the spine. If untreated, the infection can lead to paraplegia.

Although Pott's disease can affect people of any age, it is most common in children and the elderly. Recently, however, scientists and doctors have noticed an increase in the number of cases of tuberculosis, even in countries where the disease had become quite rare. The increased number of cases of active tuberculosis infection is due in part to the number of individuals with compromised immune systems (such as HIV infection); it has also increased among ethnic minorities. Between 20-33% of the world's population is infected with tuberculosis. Because Pott's disease is a type of tuberculosis infection, as the incidence rate for tuberculosis increases, it is reasonable to expect an increase in Pott's disease.

Besides age and a compromised immune system, poverty is also a risk factor. This is because exposure occurs by sharing common airspace with infectious persons. Poor and minority communities, that more intensely share living spaces, are less likely to take advantage of available tuberculosis vaccine.

Diagnosis

History: Mycobacterium tuberculosis is a slow growing organism. History may include a prior diagnosis of tuberculosis, living in an area of widespread tuberculosis infection, or exposure to a person with active tuberculosis. Symptoms in the spinal region may include swelling, back pain, or stiffness that is usually worse at night. Although any joint may be involved, the hips or knees are most commonly affected, followed by ankles, elbows, wrists, and shoulders.

Physical exam: The exam may show localized tenderness over the spine; pain may precede x-ray changes by weeks to months. As the disease progresses, abnormal curvature in the spine may develop. Deformities may include a humpback (kyphoscoliosis) or a side-to-side curvature (scoliosis). Abscesses may be present in adjacent tissues. Collapse of the spinal vertebrae may cause spinal cord and nerve compression.

Tests: The tests may include a skin reactivity test for M. tuberculosis, or detection of the organism from joint fluid, pus, or tissue samples. A biopsy may also be taken of the bony lesion or a regional lymph node. Plain x-ray may show degeneration of vertebrae or narrowing of the disk spaces. A CT scan can demonstrate the degree of soft tissue infection surrounding the spinal cord. A chest x-ray or sputum smear and culture may show evidence of lung infection with M. tuberculosis.

Treatment

Pott's disease is treated with multiple antibiotics. Because of the rise of resistant organisms, recommended treatment includes the use of a 4-drug regimen. In addition, treatment must be maintained for at least 2 months and often for as long as 6 to 8 months. Immunodeficient individuals may require lifelong drug therapy to keep the infection from recurring. Although immobilization with a splint or cast may be effective, surgery (spinal fusion, rod placement) may ultimately be needed to correct abnormal curvature of spine or loss of bone mass. Bed rest and relief of spinal cord pressure may be indicated.

Prognosis

Prognosis is variable. Some individuals will recover completely, particularly if the infection is treated promptly and aggressively. Advanced disease may leave the individual with long-term disability even after the bacterial infection is cured. Those requiring long-term suppressive therapy may develop recurrences if drug therapy is not maintained. Spinal fusion may be effective in relieving discomfort, depending on the severity of symptoms. Surgery will not, however, treat the underlying disease.

Differential Diagnosis

Conditions with similar symptoms include other infections, rheumatoid arthritis, gout, osseous dysplasia, and metastatic tumors of the spine.

Specialists

- Infectious Disease Physician
- Neurologist
- Occupational Therapist
- Orthopedic Surgeon
- Physiatrist
- Pulmonologist

Work Restrictions / Accommodations

Individuals must be restricted from work for 10 to 14 days when respiratory tuberculosis is concurrently present. Accommodations may be required for recovery from surgery or as a result of permanent locomotor disability. It may be necessary to reassign the individual to a more sedentary position. Heavy lifting, prolonged bending, and strenuous exercise will be restricted. If paralysis occurs, accommodations such as wheelchair access, specially equipped bathroom facilities, etc. may be necessary.

Comorbid Conditions

Coexisting conditions that may impact recovery include obesity, the individual's age, and immune deficiency conditions.

Complications

Antibiotic-resistant strains of bacteria pose complications for the treatment of spinal tuberculosis. Without effective therapy, bone and joint destruction may occur. Abscesses may spread into adjacent soft tissues, forming sinuses. Collapse of spinal vertebrae may cause spinal cord and nerve compression.

Paraplegia, or paralysis of the lower body, is the most serious complication of spinal tuberculosis. Immunodeficiency contributes to a more rapid progression of the infection.

Factors Influencing Duration

Length of disability might be influenced by the severity of the symptoms, extent of the infection, prompt and appropriate treatment, response to treatment, the age of the individual, and the presence of a concurrent immune deficiency condition.

Length of Disability

The length of disability will vary depending on whether or not surgery is performed or if there is concurrent lung involvement. Complications or severe cases of Pott's disease may leave the individual permanently impaired. Those who perform heavy work may also experience a longer (or permanent) disability. With severe complications of Pott's disease, disability may be permanent.

With respiratory infection.

Duration in Days

Job Classification	Minimum	Optimum	Maximum
Sedentary work	10	21	84
Light work	10	28	84
Medium work	10	42	84
Heavy work	10	Indefinite	Indefinite
Very Heavy work	10	Indefinite	Indefinite

Failure to Recover

If an individual fails to recover within the maximum duration expectancy period, the reader may wish to reference the following questions to assist in better understanding the specifics of an individual's medical case.

Regarding diagnosis:

- How old is the individual? Does individual live at the poverty level?
- Is individual's immune system compromised?
- Has individual had tuberculosis in the past? Currently?
- Does individual complain of swelling, back pain, or stiffness that is worse at night? Are any other joints involved?
- On exam, was localized tenderness over the spine present? Does individual have kyphoscoliosis or scoliosis? Are there any abscesses present in adjacent tissues?
- Does individual have spinal cord and nerve compression?
- Has individual had a skin test for TB? Have joint fluid, pus, or tissue samples been tested for the presence of M. tuberculosis? Sputum smear and culture?
- Has individual had a plain x-ray of the affected area? CT?
- Have conditions with similar symptoms been ruled out?

Regarding treatment:

- Is individual being treated with the four-drug regimen?
- Is culture confirmation with antibiotic sensitivities available?
- Was surgery necessary to correct spinal deformities?

Regarding prognosis:

- Can individual's employer accommodate any necessary restrictions?
- Does individual have any conditions that may affect ability to recover?
- Have any complications occurred such as antibiotic-resistant strains of bacteria, bone and joint destruction, abscesses, collapse of spinal vertebrae with spinal cord and nerve compression? Does individual have paraplegia or paralysis of the lower body?

References

Mader, Jon, and William Wallace. "Bone, Joint, and Necrotizing Soft Tissue Infections." Medical Microbiology. Baron, Samuel, ed. New York: Churchill Livingstone, 1991. 1233-1242.

Preeclampsia and Eclampsia

Other names / synonyms: Toxemia of Pregnancy
642.0, 642.1, 642.2, 642.3, 642.4, 642.5, 642.6, 642.7, 642.9

Definition

Preeclampsia is a serious metabolic disturbance (toxemia) of pregnancy that usually occurs during the second half of pregnancy. Preeclampsia is characterized by high blood pressure (hypertension), swelling (edema), and high amounts of protein in the urine (proteinuria).

Preeclampsia is more common with first pregnancies, in women with high blood pressure, and with a family history of the condition. The risk of preeclampsia increases in teenagers and women over 40. The greatest risk factor for both preeclampsia and eclampsia is a maternal age of less than 20. Other risk factors include obesity, diabetes, and kidney disease. HELLP Syndrome is a severe type of preeclampsia named from symptoms associated with the condition (hemolysis, elevated liver enzymes, and low platelets).

The cause of preeclampsia is unknown. Some theories on the cause of preeclampsia include immune system dysfunction, genetic factors, placental abnormalities or premature placental detachment from the uterine wall, and low antitoxic protective mechanisms due to low protein (albumin) levels in the blood.

Eclampsia is a more severe form of preeclampsia and is characterized by one or more convulsions (seizures) not associated with epilepsy, brain hemorrhage, or coma. It can occur before, during, or after childbirth. Risk factors for eclampsia include age of the mother, number of previous births, and pre-existing medical or neurological complications. Women at greatest risk are those not receiving adequate prenatal care.

Preeclampsia and eclampsia are among the leading causes of maternal death in the US. Data on pregnancies from the National Hospital Discharge Survey between 1979 and 1986 show that 26 out of 1,000 births were complicated by preeclampsia and 0.56 out of 1,000 births by eclampsia. While the rate of mild preeclampsia remained constant over the study period, the rate of severe preeclampsia increased sharply and the rate of eclampsia declined by 36%.

Diagnosis

History: Individuals with preeclampsia report swelling of the hands, face, and ankles upon arising in the morning, weight gain in excess of 2 pounds per week, or particularly sudden weight gain over 1 to 2 days. Other symptoms may include severe headache, rapid heartbeat, dizziness, nausea, ringing or buzzing in the ears, double or blurred vision, irritability, drowsiness, vomiting, abdominal pain, and decrease in urinary output.

Eclampsia includes symptoms of preeclampsia and the addition of seizures. Before the onset of a seizure, there may be a severe headache, confusion, blurred vision, or upper abdominal pain. The seizures consist of violent, rhythmic, jerking movements of the limbs. Breathing may be difficult due to the constriction of the muscles of the voice box (larynx). Coma may follow.

Physical exam: Monitoring of blood pressure, swelling, and protein in the urine should be done at each doctor's visit. Hypertension (high blood pressure) is the most important standard for judging preeclampsia. Mild preeclampsia involves borderline hypertension. Any significant increase during the second trimester is a warning signal.

Edema (fluid retention) is not relieved even with bed rest. However, edema is not always present in preeclampsia or eclampsia. The abdominal pain in severe eclampsia is caused by an enlarged liver and can be detected by pressing on the abdomen with the hand (palpation). Examination of the eyes (ophthalmic exam) may show the arteries of the eyes in spasm, causing the blurred vision.

Tests: No single test can diagnose preeclampsia. A urinalysis may reveal proteinuria. In severe preeclampsia, blood tests may reveal elevated levels of hemoglobin and hematocrit, or elevated uric acid and serum creatinine. Alkaline phosphatase may increase 2 to 3 times the normal level due to liver injury, liver function tests and coagulation tests may be abnormal; platelet count may decrease.

Treatment

Early detection is the key to treatment and involves careful monitoring of both mother and baby. Preeclampsia and eclampsia do not usually respond to diuretics or a low-salt diet. Blood pressure may be decreased through bed rest or medication. In some cases, hospitalization may be necessary. Recent studies suggest that taking aspirin or extra calcium may reduce the risk of preeclampsia in high-risk individuals. Lying on the left side while resting increases uterine flow and takes weight off the large blood vessels. Some doctors may treat with magnesium sulfate during labor and for a few days after delivery to help prevent eclampsia.

When preterm preeclampsia does not resolve, the individual is usually hospitalized. If preeclampsia still persists and worsens, the baby may be delivered prematurely. If HELLP syndrome is diagnosed, immediate delivery is recommended. The treatment for preeclampsia is delivery.

Treatment for eclampsia is usually more aggressive. Anticonvulsants and antihypertensive drugs may be given to control seizures and reduce high blood pressure. As soon as the mother is stable, labor is induced or the baby delivered by cesarean section. Following delivery, the mother is closely monitored for further signs of eclampsia. Twenty-five percent of eclampsia cases occur 2 to 4 days after delivery. Treatment is the same as prior to delivery.

Prognosis

Most women with preeclampsia deliver healthy babies. When chronic hypertension is not a factor, 97% of the mothers' blood pressure returns to normal within a week. Protein in the urine is usually resolved within 6 weeks. Preeclampsia does not usually cause permanent damage or adversely affect the long-term health of the mother. Maternal death is rare.

Eclampsia is a significant complication of pregnancy with a high potential for maternal death. When it occurs before delivery, the risk is even greater. Onset of eclampsia at less than or equal to 32 weeks gestation is very dangerous to both the mother and baby. With optimum care, however, the survival rate can be as high as 98%.

Differential Diagnosis

Preeclampsia and eclampsia can mimic other conditions including chronic hypertension, chronic kidney (renal) disease, diseases of the gallbladder and pancreas, idiopathic or thrombotic thrombocytopenic purpura, hemolytic uremic syndrome, and seizure disorders.

Specialists

- Gynecologist
- Obstetrician
- Perinatologist

Work Restrictions / Accommodations

In cases where a cesarean section was performed, heavy lifting and other appropriate work restrictions may apply.

Comorbid Conditions

Comorbid conditions that may further lengthen disability include chronic hypertension, diabetes, renal disease, collagen-vascular and autoimmune disorders, gestational trophoblastic disease, and obesity.

Complications

Complications of preeclampsia and eclampsia for the woman include the breakdown of red blood cells (hemolysis), impaired blood clotting ability, liver damage, and renal failure. Additional complications from seizures may include bleeding in the brain (cerebral hemorrhage), brain damage due to lack of oxygen (hypoxic encephalopathy), and pneumonia caused by inhaling foreign matter into the lungs (aspiration pneumonia).

Early emergency delivery may cause complications for both mother and premature infant. Placenta malfunction can cause low birth weight and other deficiencies for the baby. Babies born to women with preeclampsia are up to 5 times more likely to experience health problems.

One-third to one-half of babies fails to survive eclampsia. This is usually due to lack of oxygen in the uterus (uteroplacental insufficiency).

Factors Influencing Duration

The length of disability may be influenced by the severity of the condition, length of time to stabilize the condition, whether delivery was induced or by cesarean section, whether eclampsia occurred before, during, or after birth, and the condition of the infant.

Length of Disability

Duration depends on week of pregnancy when diagnosis is made. Bedrest may be required until delivery.

Medical treatment. High-risk pregnancy.

Duration in Days

Job Classification	Minimum	Optimum	Maximum
Any work	7	28	56

Failure to Recover

If an individual fails to recover within the maximum duration expectancy period, the reader may wish to reference the following questions to assist in better understanding the specifics of an individual's medical case.

Regarding diagnosis:

- Did the individual experience a mild or severe case of preeclampsia? Eclampsia?
- Did eclampsia occur before, during, or after delivery? Was appropriate treatment available immediately?
- If infant was delivered early, how early? By induced labor or cesarean section?
- Did infant suffer any complications from premature birth? Low birth weight? Physical impairments?

Regarding treatment:

- How long did it take to stabilize mother's condition? Was bed rest prolonged? Was hospitalization necessary?
- How long was the mother hospitalized? Infant?
- Is individual on antihypertension therapy? With what results?

Regarding prognosis:

- Has mother's blood pressure returned to the safe range?
- Does she have regular checkups scheduled and keeps faithfully to these appointments?
- Did blood pressure return to normal by the 6-week checkup?
- Is underlying cause being investigated?
- What is the condition of the infant? Are special treatments or care required?

References

Caritis, Steve, et al. "Predictors of Pre-eclampsia in Women at High Risk." American Journal of Obstetrics and Gynecology 179 4 (1998): 946-951.

Dekker, Gustaaf A., Sibai, and M. Baha. "Etiology and Pathogenesis of Preeclampsia: Current Concepts." American Journal of Obstetrics and Gynecology 179 5 (1998): 1359-1375.

Katz, V.L., R. Farmer, and J.A. Kuller. "Preeclampsia and Eclampsia: Toward a New Paradigm." American Journal of Obstetrics and Gynecology 182 6 (2000): 1292-1298.

Mattar, Farid, Sibai, and M. Baha. "Eclampsia VII. Risk Factors for Maternal Morbidity." American Journal of Obstetrics and Gynecology 182 2 (2000): 307-312.

Pregnancy Complications
646.9

Definition

During pregnancy, a broad range of complications may occur. Pregnancy is the condition of having a developing embryo or fetus in the body, which occurs as a result of the union of an ovum and spermatozoon. The length of pregnancy averages 270 days from fertilization, but may be counted from the first day of menses prior to conception, approximately 284 days.

The growth and development of the fetus is affected by the mother's age at the time of pregnancy, nutritional status, habits (diet, drug use, alcohol consumption, or cigarette smoking), medical conditions, and prenatal care. A pregnancy with complications may be affected by pre-existing disease conditions of the mother. Disease conditions that are secondary to the pregnancy may present during the gestational period or the pregnancy may terminate. The mother may also have a history of a complicated pregnancy and/or other risk factors.

The diagnosis of pregnancy complications is vague. Contact physician to obtain more specific information on the nature of the complication of pregnancy. Specific complications of pregnancy are discussed separately. See Abruptio Placentae, Anemia Complicating Pregnancy, Cardiovascular Disease in Pregnancy, Ectopic Pregnancy, Gestational Diabetes, Hydatidiform Mole, Hyperemesis Gravidarum, Miscarriage, Placenta Accreta, Preeclampsia and Eclampsia, Multiple Gestation Pregnancy, Premature Labor, Premature Rupture of Membranes, Rh Incompatibility and Threatened Abortion for specific information on disability duration.

Pregnancy, Multiple Gestation

Other names / synonyms: Multiple Pregnancy, Quadruplets, Triplets, Twins

651, 651.0, 651.00, 651.1, 651.10, 651.2, 651.20, 651.3

Definition

Multiple gestation refers to a pregnancy in which 2 or more fetuses are present in the womb. Multiple pregnancy can occur when 2 or more eggs (ova) are released from the ovary and fertilized at the same time, or if a single fertilized egg divides at an early stage of development.

It is important to diagnose a multiple pregnancy early in the pregnancy to ensure proper care of the mother and fetuses. Multiple pregnancies frequently involve premature labor and delivery. The average length of a single gestation pregnancy is 39 weeks. The average length of multiple gestation pregnancies is 35 weeks for twins, 33 weeks for triplets, and 29 weeks for quadruplets.

A multiple gestation occurs in about 1-2% of all pregnancies in the general population. However, the use of fertility drugs and high-tech procedures (e.g., in vitro fertilization) is making multiple gestations more common. Multiple pregnancies usually produce twins. Twins occur once in about 90 pregnancies, triplets occur about once in 8,000 pregnancies, and one in about 73,000 pregnancies results in quadruplets. Approximately 95,000 twin births, 4,000 triplet births, and 900 higher order births occur annually in the US.

Diagnosis

History: General symptoms of pregnancy may include absence of menstrual periods, nausea and vomiting, breast tenderness and tingling, increased frequency of urination, breast enlargement, abdominal enlargement, increased pressure on pelvic bone, backache, constipation, painful hemorrhoids, or varicose veins. Symptoms of a multiple gestation are not necessarily exaggerated. Medical history may include a family history of twins, a history of fertility drugs, or in vitro fertilization.

Physical exam: Besides the usual signs of pregnancy (breast enlargement, bluish color and softening of the cervix) physical exam may reveal more than one heart beat. In addition, the weight gain may be greater, and uterine size greater than expected by date.

Tests: A urine or blood pregnancy test confirms the pregnancy. As late as the late 1970s, half of all twin pregnancies were undiagnosed until labor began. Today, the diagnosis is made safely and accurately by using a combination of ultrasound examination and an alpha-fetoprotein blood test. Ultrasound scanning can reveal multiple fetal parts or the outline of more than one fetus.

Routine pregnancy monitoring is similar to that of a singleton pregnancy and may include the following **tests:** complete blood count (CBC), serum iron, BhCG, alpha-fetoprotein, glucose tolerance test, tests for syphilis and rubella, antibody tests, blood group and Rh tests, atypical antibody screen, HBsAg, and/or HIV. Regular urinalysis provides early detection of infection.

Treatment

As with a single gestation pregnancy, the woman should attend regular prenatal visits. Prenatal visits may be scheduled more often than for women carrying a single fetus. Frequent monitoring allows early detection and treatment of complications.

Individual should be instructed in diet and nutrition. Vitamin and iron supplements are usually prescribed. Instruction also includes avoidance of harmful substances (tobacco, alcohol, recreational drugs), which prescription and over-the-counter medications to avoid, abstinence from strenuous activities (especially heavy lifting), and weight control. The individual is instructed to take frequent rest periods after the 24th week of pregnancy. If complications occur, bedrest may be advised.

Prognosis

Premature labor occurs in 43% of twin pregnancies, 88% of triplet pregnancies, and 97% of quadruplet pregnancies. Babies who are delivered early may not be fully developed and are usually of low birth weight, putting them at risk for developing other medical complications.

While outcomes are variable, multiple pregnancies involving twins usually result in the birth of 2 healthy infants. Multiple pregnancies involving more than 2 fetuses have an increased incidence of premature labor and delivery. With adequate prenatal care and constantly improving neonatal care, delivery can still result in healthy infants.

Differential Diagnosis

Conditions with similar symptoms include single pregnancy with inaccurate dates, excessive accumulation of amniotic fluid (polyhydramnios), gestational trophoblastic disease (hydatidiform mole), abdominal tumor, or uterine myomas.

Specialists

- Gynecologist
- Obstetrician
- Perinatologist

Work Restrictions / Accommodations

Obstetricians recommend that individuals with multiple gestation pregnancies rest more, especially during weeks 20 through 30 of gestation. Individuals may require a 2-hour rest period in the afternoon and 8 full hours of sleep every night. Individuals carrying triplets or more may need to reduce their physical activity and stop working by the 20th week of gestation. In many cases, shortened work hours or earlier pre-term leave may be required. As with any pregnancy, strenuous work, heavy lifting, and prolonged periods of standing should be avoided.

Comorbid Conditions

Coexisting conditions that may impact recovery or lengthen disability include elevated blood pressure, diabetes mellitus, deep vein thrombosis, high-risk pregnancy, or prior cesarean section.

Complications

Complications of multiple pregnancy include abnormal placenta implantation, spontaneous abortion (miscarriage), premature labor and delivery, low birth weight infants, birth defects, and increased risk of fetal death. Complications affecting the mother's health include severe nausea and vomiting (hyperemesis gravidarum), severe anemia, gestational diabetes, pregnancy-induced hypertension or pre-eclampsia (toxemia), an increase in urinary tract infections, ineffective (hypotonic) uterine contractions, a longer latent stage of labor, and vaginal/uterine hemorrhage. In addition, complications due to pre-existing medical and surgical conditions may occur.

Factors Influencing Duration

Length of disability may be influenced by the mother's age, pre-existing medical or surgical conditions, type of delivery (vaginal or cesarean section), or the presence of complications (vaginal/uterine hemorrhage, infection). Bedrest is sometimes required for the duration of the pregnancy.

Length of Disability

Durations reflect postpartum recovery.

Without complications. High-risk pregnancy.

Job Classification	Minimum	Optimum	Maximum
Any work	28	42	56

Duration in Days

Failure to Recover

If an individual fails to recover within the maximum duration expectancy period, the reader may wish to reference the following questions to assist in better understanding the specifics of an individual's medical case.

Regarding diagnosis:

- Was multiple gestation confirmed? By what method (ultrasound examination and an alpha-fetoprotein blood test)?
- How many fetuses?
- How was mother's general health prior to pregnancy?
- Anemia?
- Recent pregnancy?
- Does individual have an underlying condition, such as hypertension, diabetes mellitus, deep vein thrombosis, prior high-risk pregnancies, prior cesarean section, and a history of preeclampsia, eclampsia, hypotonic uterine contractions, or miscarriage, that may impact pregnancy and recovery?
- Have there been pregnancy related complications such as hyperemesis gravidarum, severe anemia, gestational diabetes, pregnancy-induced hypertension or pre-eclampsia (toxemia), an increase in urinary tract infections, ineffective uterine contractions, a longer latent stage of labor, and vaginal/uterine hemorrhage?

Regarding treatment:

- Is individual scheduled for (and attending) frequent prenatal appointments?
- Is individual regularly monitored (lab, blood pressure, fetal distress test) for potential problems?
- Have complications been caught early? Treated appropriately?
- Was individual adequately instructed in nutrition guidelines and supplements?
- Is individual able to obtain adequate nutrition? If not, has individual been directed to a community resource that can assist?
- Does individual understand the reason for and importance in avoiding harmful substances (tobacco, alcohol, certain prescription and over-the-counter medication)?
- Is individual compliant with treatment regimen? If not, what can be done to increase compliance?
- Is this pregnancy at risk?
- Is multifetal pregnancy reduction being considered?

Regarding prognosis:

- Is individual keeping scheduled prenatal appointments? If not, why not?
- What can be done to enable attendance or improve compliance?
- Have complications been caught early and treated appropriately?

References

Fact Sheet: Multiple Gestation and Multifetal Pregnancy Reduction. American Society for Reproductive Medicine. 1998. 25 Aug 2000 <http://www.americaninfertility.org/asrm/mulitple.html>.

Pregnancy, Normal
650, V22, V22.0, V22.1, V22.2

Definition

Pregnancy is the condition of having a developing embryo or fetus in the body, which occurs as a result of the union of an ovum and spermatozoon. Pregnancy can occur anytime after a female begins menstrual function (menarche) until she reaches menopause. However, most pregnancies occur between the age of 15-40 years. There is an increased risk of complications in pregnancies before the age of 15 years and after the age of 35.

The first indication of a pregnancy is a missed period. Laboratory tests or home test kits check for human chorionic gonadotropin (HCG) produced by the placenta. With confirmation of the pregnancy, the physician, with information from the mother, can determine an approximate date of birth. The length of pregnancy averages 270 days from fertilization, but may be counted from the first day of menses prior to conception, approximately 284 days.

The growth and development of the fetus is affected by the mother's nutritional status, habits (diet, drug use, alcohol consumption, or cigarette smoking), medical conditions, age at time of pregnancy, and prenatal care.

Diagnosis

History: Most women miss a menstrual period before they suspect pregnancy. Other early symptoms may include tender, swollen breasts; frequent urination; fatigue; nausea and vomiting; and blurred vision.

Physical exam: The exam may reveal enlargement of breasts or abdomen, bluish color (cyanosis) of the vagina, and softening of the uterus and cervix. At 10 to 12 weeks, fetal heart tones can be heard.

Tests: Pregnancy can be confirmed through laboratory tests or home test kits that check for human chorionic gonadotropin (HCG) produced by the placenta. Other initial testing may be done to screen for problems that may threaten the health of the mother and fetus. These include: urinalysis, complete blood count (CBC), hemoglobin and hematocrit, syphilis screening, rubella (German measles) antibodies, blood group and Rh type, and screening for antibodies to blood group antigens. Individuals at risk receive a glucose tolerance test (to screen for a predisposition for diabetes), hepatitis B, and HIV tests. Cervical cultures may be done to rule out infection.

Ultrasound, performed to find answers to specific questions, may not be used in every pregnancy. When used, ultrasound may reveal the age of the baby, abnormal physical development, location of the placenta (to make sure it is in the right place), and possible complications. Ultrasound can be done at any time, but it is most useful during the second trimester, between weeks sixteen and twenty.

Although not required, a maternal serum alpha-fetoprotein test, or AFP test, is recommended. Usually performed 15 to 20 weeks after the last menstrual period, the test measures how much AFP is in the mother's blood. AFP is a protein made by the baby's liver. A small amount of the baby's AFP also enters the mother's blood. If the baby's spinal cord has not developed correctly, however, more AFP may leak into the mother's bloodstream.

Amniocentesis is a procedure used to evaluate conditions such as elevated AFP, advanced maternal age, or possible genetic abnormalities. It is usually performed 15 to 20 weeks after the last menstrual period, but can be performed earlier. The test analyzes cells in the amniotic fluid to identify four types of problems: chromosomal problems (e.g., Downs syndrome), problems within the genes (e.g., genetic disease like cystic fibrosis), abnormally high level of AFP in the amniotic fluid (e.g., spina bifida, anencephaly or other spinal abnormalities), or to determine if the baby's lungs are mature enough to survive outside the uterus.

Chorionic villus sampling may be used instead of amniocentesis unless a test specifically requires amniotic fluid. Also used to diagnose disorders in the fetus, the advantage of chorionic villus sampling is that its results are available much earlier in the pregnancy than are those of amniocentesis.

If the mother is black, a test for sickle cell anemia may be ordered. Jewish mothers of eastern European ancestry and French Canadians should be tested for the Tay-Sachs gene.

Treatment

Regular prenatal visits to a physician or maternity clinic are essential for a healthy, safe pregnancy, delivery, and postpartum period.

For an uncomplicated pregnancy, visits are usually scheduled every 4 weeks during the first and second trimester, and every 2 to 3 weeks during the third trimester. At week 36, visits should be increased to weekly until delivery.

At each prenatal visit, blood pressure, weight, fundal height, and fetal heart rate will be measured and recorded. Urine is tested for abnormal amounts of glucose and albumin (urinalysis).

Each individual should receive counseling or information regarding proper nutrition, exercise, sexual activity, work activity, use of tobacco, alcohol and drug restrictions. Prenatal vitamins are usually prescribed. Childbirth classes, breast-feeding instruction, and family planning should be offered.

Prognosis

The large majority of individuals will deliver a healthy child and proceed to a complete recovery.

Differential Diagnosis

Other conditions that present similarly to pregnancy include cervical lesions, ovarian tumors, or myomas.

Specialists

- Certified Nurse Midwife
- Gynecologist
- Obstetrician
- Primary Care Provider

Rehabilitation

During pregnancy, women can continue to exercise and derive health benefits from mild to moderate exercise routines. Regular exercise is preferable. Exercise during and after pregnancy has many benefits, such as stress reduction, decrease in weight gain, it helps the body to adjust to postural changes, prevents low back strains, helps to maintain pre-pregnancy fitness level, and helps body to return to prepregnant state more quickly.

Rehabilitation or exercise during pregnancy can be initiated as long as there are not any medical or pregnancy complications. If a specific exercise causes pain or discomfort, it should be discontinued and alternative exercise should be used.

According to the American College of Obstetrics and Gynecology (ACOG), how much a pregnant woman can exert herself during exercise should be measured by perceived exertion - she can push herself as much or as little as she is comfortable. The heart rate guideline is usually a maximum of 140 beats per minute. For a woman who is a regular exerciser or athlete, 140 bpm may be low. This is where perceived exertion comes into play. For a woman who hasn't exercised much, 140 bpm may be too high and beginning an exercise program during pregnancy isn't recommended.

Although exercise during pregnancy is relatively safe, there are things that need to be avoided or at least modified. A pregnant woman should avoid holding her breath during exercise (Valsalva maneuver) as it restricts oxygen to the placenta. Exercising while lying on the back (supine position) after the first trimester is not recommended because it decreases the cardiac output to the fetus. Excessive stretching should be avoided as the already present looseness in the joints may increase susceptibility to injury. Activities, such as skiing or horseback riding, in which loss of balance could be detrimental in maternal or fetal well being, should be avoided as well.

A total body workout twice a week should be sufficient. A workout could include squats, leg lifts, assisted pull-ups, dumbbell or cable rows, shoulder press or modified pushup, biceps curls, triceps extensions and light abdominal work. Special attention should be paid to strengthening the lower back and pelvic floor muscles (Kegel exercises). In addition to the strength training, a cardiovascular workout of either walking or riding a bicycle 3 times weekly is also recommended. As stated previously, prenatal exercise should be kept at a mild to moderate level.

Work Restrictions / Accommodations

Exposure to toxic substances in the workplace needs to be avoided because of the potential harm to the fetus. If complications occur, transfer to a sedentary job, elimination of strenuous work (especially heavy lifting), elevation of legs during the day, shortened work hours, and extended leave may be required.

Comorbid Conditions

Comorbid conditions include diabetes mellitus, deep vein thrombosis, underlying cardiovascular disease, anemia, lupus, asthma, AIDS, heart disease, herpes, high blood pressure, acute fatty liver, infection, thyroid problems, tuberculosis, and urinary tract infection.

Complications

Complications from pregnancy range from minor to life threatening. They include excessive nausea and vomiting (hyperemesis gravidarum), preeclampsia, eclampsia, constipation, various varicose veins, tumors of the uterus (gestational trophoblastic diseases such as hydatidiform mole and choriocarcinoma), third trimester bleeding, placenta previa, Rh sensitization, and premature labor.

HELLP Syndrome is a severe type of preeclampsia. Its name comes from symptoms associated with the condition: Hemolysis, Elevated Liver enzymes, and Low Platelets. If an individual has HELLP, immediate delivery is recommended.

In addition, complications due to pre-existing medical conditions (anemia, lupus, asthma, AIDS, diabetes, heart disease, herpes, high blood pressure, acute fatty liver, infection, thyroid problems, tuberculosis, and urinary tract infection) may occur. Complications from surgical conditions (appendicitis, breast cancer, gallstones, and ovarian tumors) may also occur.

Although asymptomatic, up to 30% of women carry the Group B Strep (GBS) bacteria in their vagina. In 2-3 births out of every 1,000, however, it can develop into an active infection in either the mother or the baby. If there are signs of infection, including a fever and bad-smelling amniotic fluid, the baby and mother will be tested. Antibiotics given before birth have a good chance of preventing infection in the baby. Infection can be very dangerous to the baby. If an infected baby gets sick just after birth, up to 1 in 5 can die. If the infected baby gets sick a week or later after birth, pneumonia or meningitis may develop.

Factors Influencing Duration

Factors influencing length of disability include mother's age at delivery; pre-existing medical or surgical conditions; episiotomy or cesarean section; and the presence of postpartum infection, mastitis, or other complications. Postpartum depression can interfere with return to work. Workplace maternity leave policies may also be a consideration.

Length of Disability

Durations are based on societal norms and not on physiological recovery times.

Uncomplicated pregnancy. Normal vaginal delivery.

Duration in Days

Job Classification	Minimum	Optimum	Maximum
Any work	28	42	42

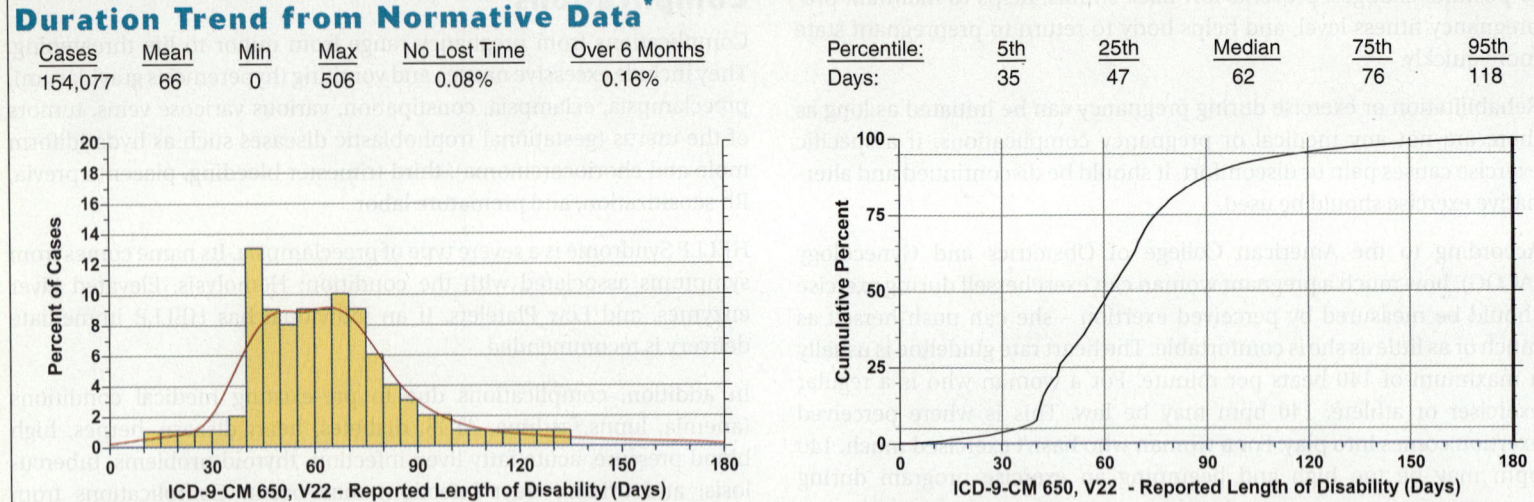

Failure to Recover

If an individual fails to recover within the maximum duration expectancy period, the reader may wish to reference the following questions to assist in better understanding the specifics of an individual's medical case.

Regarding diagnosis:

- What is the mother's age?
- Does the individual report tender, swollen breasts; frequent urination; fatigue; nausea and vomiting; or blurred vision?
- Does physical exam reveal enlargement of breasts or abdomen, cyanosis of the vagina, and softening of the uterus and cervix?
- Are fetal heart tones heard?
- Has the individual had a pregnancy test?
- Has the individual had a urinalysis, CBC, syphilis screening, rubella antibodies, blood group and Rh type, and screening for antibodies to blood group antigens?
- Has the individual had a glucose tolerance test, hepatitis B, and HIV tests?
- Has the individual had a cervical culture? AFP? Amniocentesis? Chorionic villus sampling? Ultrasound? Sickle cell anemia tests? Tay-Sachs gene test?
- Have conditions with similar symptoms been ruled out?

Regarding treatment:

- Does the woman see her physician regularly?
- Is the mother taking pre-natal vitamins?
- Has the mother received the appropriate pre-natal teaching? Has she incorporated this into her daily routine?

Regarding prognosis:

- Is the mother exercising as directed by her physician?
- Is the individual's employer able to accommodate any necessary restrictions?
- Does the mother have any conditions that may affect her ability to recover?
- Has the individual had any complications such as hyperemesis gravidarum, preeclampsia, eclampsia, constipation, various varicose veins, tumors of the uterus, third trimester bleeding, placenta previa, Rh sensitization, premature labor or HELLP Syndrome?
- Did the mother have a cesarean section?
- Does the mother have post-partum depression?

References

"Women and Exercise." American College of Obstetricians and Gynecologists ACOG Technical Bulletin 173 (1992).

Beers, Mark H., and Robert Berkow, eds. The Merck Manual of Diagnosis and Therapy. Whitehouse Station, NJ: Merck and Co, Inc. 1999.

Kelsey, Moira, ed. American College of Sports Medicine's Resource Manual for Guidelines for Exercise Testing and Prescription, 3rd ed. Baltimore: Williams & Wilkins, 1998.

Pauls, Julie A., and Katherine L. Reed. Quick Reference to Physical Therapy. Gaithersburg, MD: Aspen, 1996.

Prenatal Health Guidelines for Normal Pregnancy. CareFirst. 2000. 25 Aug 2000 <http://www.carefirst.com/pages/providers/nca/pregnant.htm>.

Roitman, Jeffrey, ed. ACSM's Resource Manual for Guidelines for Exercise Testing and Prescription, 3rd ed. Baltimore: Williams & Wilkins, 1998.

Premature Beats

Other names / synonyms: APCS, Arrhythmia, Atrial Premature Complexes, Dysrhythmia, Ventricular Premature Complexes

427.6

Definition

Premature beats are a type of disturbance in the normal heartbeat that result from altered electrical impulse patterns in the heart (arrhythmia). The arrhythmia in premature beats manifests as an early beat that originates in either the atria or ventricles.

Premature ventricular contractions (PVCs) are the most common type of premature beat. They can occur in healthy individuals or in those with disease states. Disorders that are commonly associated with PVCs are ischemic, hypertensive, valvular, and congenital heart disease, cardiomyopathy, myocarditis, low potassium (hypokalemia), acidity of the blood (acidosis), coronary artery disease (CAD), and hypermetabolic states. PVCs can be a side effect of antiarrhythmic drugs, sympathomimetic drugs (notably cold and sinus medications), cardiac catheterization, exercise, anxiety or stress, and excessive caffeine, tobacco, and alcohol.

Premature atrial contractions (PACs) can occur in individuals with normal or diseased hearts. They may be associated with stress, fatigue, alcohol, smoking, CAD, heart failure, pulmonary congestion, and pulmonary hypertension. They can also occur from the same drugs/substances that cause PVCs.

PACs are linked with paroxysmal supraventricular tachycardia and atrial fibrillation, and may accompany heart attack (myocardial infarction) or congestive heart failure.

Premature beats occur occasionally in otherwise healthy individuals, and these usually are of minimal or no consequence. However, the prevalence of premature beats increases with age, and more than 100 PACs or PVCs per 24 hours have been shown to occur in at least 17% of a population of healthy individuals age 60 or older.

Diagnosis

History: Individuals who have arrhythmias may have no other symptoms. PVCs can cause a feeling of fullness and discomfort in the neck or chest that has been described as a "thumping." Fatigue, weakness, shortness of breath (dyspnea), and chest discomfort occur with frequent PVCs. Symptoms of PVCs are recognized during quiet periods and at rest, and disappear with exertion. Individuals may describe the symptoms as "fluttering" and a missed beat.

Physical exam: Distinctive physical signs of PACs include wave patterns in the neck veins, and an unusual pause and sound when listening to the heart with a stethoscope. PVCs also produce unusual wave and rhythm patterns.

Tests: An electrocardiogram (ECG) will confirm the diagnosis if the individual actually experiences either of these arrhythmias while being tested. Otherwise, there are no other tests for this disorder.

Treatment

There is often no treatment for atrial and ventricular premature beats other than requiring that the individual avoids alcohol, caffeine, nicotine, and/or prescription drugs that may trigger onset of arrhythmias. Drugs that slightly accelerate the heart rate usually alleviate the arrhythmia if it occurs persistently or frequently. Antiarrhythmic drugs that suppress PVCs are usually not given unless the individual has experienced an acute myocardial infarction.

Prognosis

Most individuals with premature beats live a normal life unless there is significant underlying heart disease.

Differential Diagnosis

A left or right bundle branch block or other aberrantly conducted PACs can simulate PVCs. Atrial fibrillation, sinus arrhythmia, secondary atrioventricular block, and PVCs are considered in the differential diagnoses of PACs. PVCs may occur as a result of anxiety or stress and could be manifested during a panic attack. Holter monitors on well-conditioned runners have demonstrated frequent high-grade atrial and ventricular arrhythmias suggesting that such variations in heart rhythm are a normal phenomenon.

Specialists

- Cardiologist

Work Restrictions / Accommodations

Work restrictions and accommodations are not necessary for this condition.

Comorbid Conditions

Increased stress resulting from psychiatric disorders or overuse of stimulants (diet drugs, caffeine) may lengthen disability.

Complications

Underlying heart disease and the symptoms that are related to this condition may complicate arrhythmias.

Factors Influencing Duration

Complications from underlying disease states could influence the length of disability.

Length of Disability

This is a vague diagnosis. Duration of disability depends on the underlying condition.

Failure to Recover

If an individual fails to recover within the maximum duration expectancy period, the reader may wish to reference the following questions to assist in better understanding the specifics of an individual's medical case.

Regarding diagnosis:

- Did the individual describe symptoms such as fluttering in the chest characteristic of a premature beat?
- Does the individual have any underlying heart or lung conditions or electrolyte disturbances that may be associated with a premature beat?
- Was an irregular pulse or irregular heart sounds noted on the physical exam?
- Were additional studies such as serum electrolytes, oxygen saturation tests, cardiac isoenzymes, cardiac cauterization, treadmill test, and cardiac ultrasound performed to determine an underlying cause?

- Was the individual referred to an appropriate specialist (i.e., cardiologist, internist, or pulmonologist)?
- Have other dysrhythmias such as sinus arrhythmia, sinoatrial block, atrial fibrillation, or atrioventricular blocks been considered in the differential diagnosis?

Regarding treatment:

- Was the individual instructed to avoid cardiac stimulants such as alcohol, caffeine, nicotine, and some over-the-counter or prescription drugs? Did the individual follow the recommendations?

Regarding prognosis:

- Does the individual have any conditions that may impact recovery and prognosis?
- Did the individual suffer any complications such as increased frequency of premature beats or disturbances in cardiac output associated with the premature beats that may impact recovery and prognosis?

References

Benson, H., S. Alexander, and C.L. Feldman. "Decreased Premature Ventricular Contractions Through Use of the Relaxation Response in Patients with Stable Ischaemic Heart Disease." Lancet 2 7931 (1975): 380-382.

Pantano, J.A., and R.J. Oriel. "Prevalence and Nature of Cardiac Arrhythmias in Apparently Normal Well-trained Runners." American Heart Journal 104 4 Pt 1 (1982): 762-768.

Premature Labor

Other names / synonyms: Early Onset of Delivery, Early or Threatened Labor, Preterm Labor, Threatened Premature Labor

644, 644.0, 644.03, 644.1, 644.2

Definition

Premature or preterm labor refers to the onset of labor contractions before 37 weeks of gestation. As opposed to the irregular nature of false labor contractions, premature labor contractions occur every 10 minutes and last at least 30 seconds. In addition, either cervical dilation or thinning (effacement) of the cervix is present.

Although the exact cause is usually unknown, many factors have been associated with premature labor. Maternal factors include elevated blood pressure; nonexistent or poor prenatal care; inadequate or excessive weight gain; pre-existing medical conditions (such as diabetes, heart problems); infections (systemic, vaginal, urinary tract, amnionitis); anemia; preeclampsia; short interval between pregnancies; premature rupture of membranes; previous preterm labor; cervical incompetence; Rh-negative mother with an Rh-positive fetus (isoimmunization); multiple pregnancies, especially for women who have given birth 7 or more times (grand multiparity); overdistended uterus (polyhydramnios, multiple gestation); history of infertility; surgical complications; uterine anomalies; fibroids; retained IUD; trauma; alcohol or drug use; and cigarette smoking. The risk of premature labor is greatest in women under 15 or older than 35. Fetal factors include birth defects (congenital anomalies) and intrauterine death.

Premature labor is a complication in approximately 10% of all pregnancies. It is associated with increased infant illness (morbidity) and death (mortality).

Diagnosis

History: Symptoms of premature labor may include frequent contractions (more than 4 per hour), cramping, pelvic pressure, excessive vaginal discharge, and backache or low back pain. Premature rupture of membranes often occurs with the onset of premature labor.

Physical exam: The woman may present with contractions, cervical dilation (>2 centimeters), cervical thinning (effacement) exceeding 50%, ruptured membranes, or a change in cervical dilation, or effacement as noted in serial examinations.

Tests: Nitrazine paper testing may be performed in order to rule out ruptured membranes. In cases associated with hemorrhage, laboratory tests may include complete blood count (CBC) with differential and hematologic workup (hematocrit, hemoglobin, serum chemistries, prothrombin time, partial thromboplastin time). Electrolytes and serum glucose testing are done in cases requiring suppression of contractions (tocolysis). A urine culture and sensitivity may be done to rule out urinary tract infection. Ultrasound scanning is used to determine fetal size, position, and placental location. An amniocentesis may be performed to obtain fluid for assessing fetal maturity. A fibronectin test is used to predict premature labor during the 7 days following the test.

Specialists

- Gynecologist
- Neonatologist
- Obstetrician
- Perinatologist

Treatment

Treatment depends on whether or not the labor is allowed to continue. Critical factors in this decision include gestational age, fetal maturity, and the amount of dilation and effacement of the cervix.

Standard treatment to prolong gestation usually involves bed rest with the individual lying on the left side (left lateral decubitus position). This treatment alone is effective in 50% of cases. Treatment also includes sedation, increased fluid intake (hydration), antibiotics, fetal heart rate monitoring, uterine monitoring, and antenatal steroids (to accelerate lung maturation). With this regimen, up to 80% of pregnancies can be continued for at least 2 more weeks.

In more urgent situations, labor can often be stopped with drugs (pharmacologic intervention). Uterine contractions can be inhibited (tocolysis) with beta-mimetic adrenergic agents, magnesium sulfate, prostaglandin synthetase inhibitors, and calcium channel blockers. If the labor can be stopped, the individual may have the cervix bound (cervical cerclage). If the labor cannot be stopped, the individual is transferred to a hospital with a neonatal intensive care unit. Internal fetal monitoring is done to determine the most effective mode of delivery.

Prognosis

Approximately 50% of cases of premature labor can be successfully treated with bed rest alone. The addition of sedation, hydration, and steroid therapy can prolong gestation for another 2 weeks in another 30% of cases. About 20% of cases will require the administration of drugs to try to stop the labor. If labor cannot be stopped, a premature infant will be delivered.

Differential Diagnosis

"False labor" (Braxton Hicks contractions) is a series of painless uterine contractions that usually occur every 10 to 20 minutes. These contractions occur more frequently as pregnancy nears completion. Even though Braxton Hicks contractions are often misinterpreted as labor pains, they are not actually true labor contractions as they are not associated with cervical change.

Work Restrictions / Accommodations

Risk factors for premature labor include standing for periods greater than 4 hours without a break, lifting weights greater than 12 kg more than 50 times per week, working more than 36 hours per week or more than 10 hours per shift, and high stress.

Possible work restrictions and accommodations may include extended leave, or placement on short-term disability. If the individual is allowed to return to work, shortened work hours, increased rest breaks, and transfer to sedentary duties may be required.

Comorbid Conditions

Coexisting conditions that may impact recovery include nonexistent or poor prenatal care; inadequate or excessive weight gain; pre-existing medical conditions (such as diabetes, circulatory and cardiovascular disorders); infections (systemic, vaginal, urinary tract, amnionitis); anemia; preeclampsia; premature rupture of membranes; cervical incompetence; Rh-negative mother with an Rh-positive fetus (isoimmunization); multiple pregnancies, especially women who have given birth 7 or more times (grand multiparity); overdistended uterus (polyhydramnios, multiple gestation); uterine anomalies; fibroids; retained IUD; or trauma.

Complications

Complications include maternal infection and hemorrhage and increased morbidity and mortality of the premature infant.

Factors Influencing Duration

Length of disability may be influenced by how far along the pregnancy has progressed, methods used to stop the premature labor, response to treatment, and presence of bleeding or infection.

Length of Disability

High risk pregnancy. Bedrest may be required until delivery. Contact physician for additional information.

Duration Trend from Normative Data*

Cases	Mean	Min	Max	No Lost Time	Over 6 Months
5435	90	0	588	0.11%	0.65%

Percentile:	5th	25th	Median	75th	95th
Days:	22	62	90	115	155

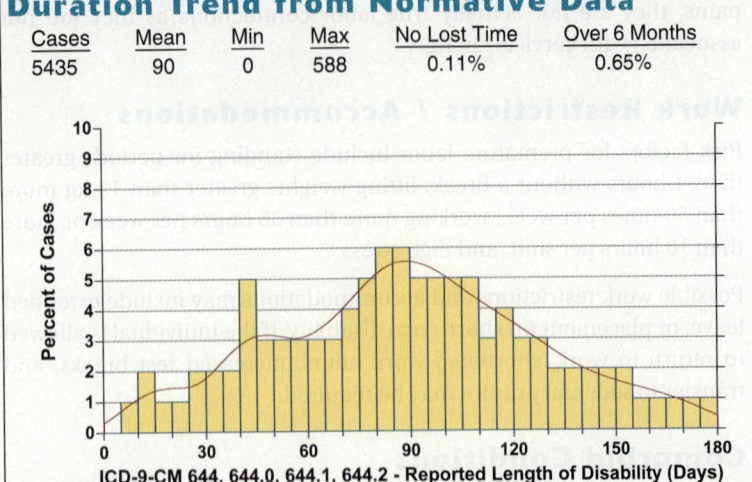
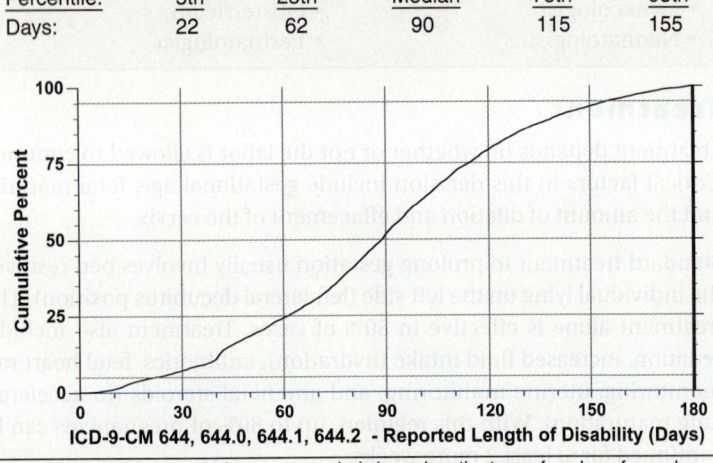

ICD-9-CM 644, 644.0, 644.1, 644.2 - Reported Length of Disability (Days)

* Differences may exist between the expected duration tables and the normative graphs. Duration tables provide expected recovery periods based on the type of work performed by the individual. The normative graphs reflect the actual observed experience of many individuals across the spectrum of physical conditions, in a variety of industries, and with varying levels of case management.

Failure to Recover

If an individual fails to recover within the maximum duration expectancy period, the reader may wish to reference the following questions to assist in better understanding the specifics of an individual's medical case.

Regarding diagnosis:

- Has diagnosis of premature labor been confirmed?
- What underlying conditions may have caused contractions to begin?

Regarding treatment:

- Did treatment include bed rest with the woman lying on the left side (left lateral decubitus position)?
- Did regimen include sedation, increased hydration, antibiotics, fetal heart rate monitoring, uterine monitoring, and antenatal steroids to accelerate lung maturation?
- If the situation was more urgent, were drugs able to stop the uterine contractions?
- If the labor could not be stopped, was individual transferred to a hospital with a neonatal intensive care unit?
- Was internal fetal monitoring done to determine the most effective mode of delivery?

Regarding prognosis:

- Did individual respond to treatment? Was premature labor stopped?
- If the labor could not be stopped, was there a premature delivery?
- Was individual transferred to a hospital with a neonatal intensive care unit?
- Did mother or infant experience any complications that may impact recovery?

References

Premature Labor (PTL). Core Obstetrics Reference Archive. 27 Apr 2000. 25 Aug 2000 <http://192.215.104.222/obgyn/cobra/cobra/TEXT/PROTOCOL/ptl.htm>.

Gabbe, Steven G., Jennifer R. Niebyl, and Joe L. Simpson. Obstetrics - Normal and Problem Pregnancies, 3rd ed. New York: Churchill Livingstone, Inc, 1996.

Premature Rupture of Membranes

Other names / synonyms: Amniorrhexis, PROM
658, 658.0, 658.1, 658.13, 658.2

Definition

Premature rupture of membranes (PROM) refers to breaking of the sac that surrounds a fetus (amniotic sac) and, therefore, leakage of fluid from that sac in pregnancy. Leakage from the amniotic sac is further referred to as PROM when the leakage begins at least 1 hour prior to the onset of labor at any stage of pregnancy. (The word premature in PROM refers to rupture before labor, rather than to fetal prematurity.)

Studies have suggested several risk factors associated with a higher risk of PROM. Genital tract infection, recent intercourse, low socioeconomic status, poor nutrition, smoking, multiple gestation, and bleeding in pregnancy have all been linked to an increased chance of preterm or term PROM.

PROM is the precipitating event in one third of all preterm deliveries. Three percent of all pregnancies are affected by premature rupture of membranes (PROM).

Diagnosis

History: The woman will report a rush of clear, yellow or green fluid that escapes uncontrollably from the vaginal opening and then may continue to leak slowly. She may mention that she did not experience any labor pains prior to the rupture of membranes.

Physical exam: Instead of a digital exam of the cervix (which might lead to infection) a sterile speculum exam will be done. The doctor may see fluid escaping from the uterine opening (cervix). The cervical opening may be only partially open (dilated) and not sufficiently thin (effaced) in a woman who is not near the time of labor and delivery. The closer to the time of delivery (within 24 to 48 hours) the cervical opening will be fully open (dilated) and thin (effacement).

Tests: The amniotic fluid will be tested by Nitrazine pH paper, measured for levels of fibronectin or smeared on a glass slide to look for a fern-like pattern when dried. This will confirm rupture of membranes. Amniotic fluid may also be gathered, perhaps by amniocentesis, to test the maturity of the fetal lungs, if rupture occurs prior to the due date. Internal or external fetal monitoring is done to examine fetal heart rate in comparison to any contractions of the uterus, and to measure the strength and length of any contractions. An ultrasound evaluation for amniotic fluid volume should be performed in all cases of confirmed preterm PROM to determine fetal presentation and to estimate fetal weight and gestational age.

Treatment

Once the diagnosis of PROM is established, the treatment will depend on several factors: length of pregnancy (gestational age) and maturity of fetus, whether active labor is present, presence or absence of infection, and degree of fetal well-being or distress. If the fetus is at term and appears developmentally mature, and if there are no signs of fetal distress (decreased fetal heart rate or fetal movement) or infection (fever), the woman may be monitored closely (either in the hospital or at home) to allow for labor to begin spontaneously. If the woman spontaneously begins effective labor and delivery expected or unavoidable, the safest type of delivery (vaginal vs. caesarean) for both woman and fetus will be implemented.

If labor does not begin spontaneously (within 24 hours), if there are signs of fetal distress (such as decreased fetal movement) or if the women develops a fever, labor may be induced to facilitate prompt delivery and minimize complications of fetal distress or infection. If the induction fails (failed induction), to produce adequate cervical dilation and effective labor, a caesarean delivery will be done.

If the fetus is premature and not fully developed, close monitoring for signs of fetal distress or infection is done either in the hospital or occasionally on an outpatient basis. Bedrest may be recommended to reduce the risk of premature labor. Magnesium sulfate or beta-adrenergic drugs may be infused to stop or delay premature labor. Corticosteroid injections may be given to the woman if the fetal lungs are not yet mature enough for delivery. Intravenous antibiotics may be given if intrauterine infection is suspected. Once the fetus has developed sufficiently, or the fetus is at term, delivery will proceed.

Prognosis

In 10-15% of the PROM cases, the fetus is at or near term, and there are normal, uncomplicated deliveries. Infants delivered prematurely often have underdeveloped organs (i.e., lungs), and hospitalization and intensive care may be necessary until adequate growth and organ development takes place. When PROM is associated with fetal prematurity, there is significant fetal morbidity and mortality.

Differential Diagnosis

Leakage of fluid from the membranes, rather than a full rupture, is a possibility. Leakage of urine or liquefaction of cervical mucus may be confused with ruptured membranes as may be a vaginal infection.

Specialists

- Neonatologist
- Perinatologist
- Obstetrician

Work Restrictions / Accommodations

Restrictions and accommodations are not associated with this condition. Individuals may resume normal duties postpartum.

Comorbid Conditions

Comorbid conditions of anemia, asthma, autoimmune disorders, hepatitis, high blood pressure, heart disease, diabetes, immune suppression, bleeding disorders, thyroid disorders, seizure disorders, or eclampsia may impact ability to recover and further lengthen disability.

Complications

Infection may invade the uterus and fetus through the opening in the membranes. Stress may cause the fetus to expel stool into the amniotic fluid that may then enter its lungs upon delivery. Compression of the umbilical cord may interfere with oxygen delivery to the fetus causing fetal distress. The fetus may be born prematurely.

Factors Influencing Duration

Fetal maturity at the time of rupture of membranes will help determine the time and type of delivery. Those with ruptures occurring well before term may be associated with a prolonged period of disability prior to delivery. Those requiring caesarean deliveries will have a prolonged hospital stay and recovery. Complications such as infection in the mother or infant, or premature delivery may be associated with a prolonged recovery.

Length of Disability

Expected length of disability varies according to the type of delivery involved and complications. Durations are based on societal norms and not on physiological recovery times. Those who are preterm may have longer disabilities if placed on bedrest until delivery. Individuals who require caesarean deliveries may have a longer hospitalization, longer physical recovery due to the surgery, and longer disability.

With normal vaginal delivery.

Duration in Days

Job Classification	Minimum	Optimum	Maximum
Any work	28	42	42

Failure to Recover

If an individual fails to recover within the maximum duration expectancy period, the reader may wish to reference the following questions to assist in better understanding the specifics of an individual's medical case.

Regarding diagnosis:

- Has premature rupture of membranes been confirmed?

Regarding treatment:

- Did treatment take into consideration gestational age and maturity of fetus, whether active labor was present, presence or absence of infection, and degree of fetal well-being or distress?
- If the fetus was at term and developmentally mature, and if there are no signs of fetal distress or infection, was labor allowed to begin spontaneously? Were any complications encountered?
- If the woman spontaneously began strong labor, with delivery expected or unavoidable, was delivery by vaginal or caesarean delivery? Were any complications encountered?
- If labor was induced due to signs of fetal distress or maternal infection, were any complications encountered?
- Was premature labor successfully prevented? If not, did infant experience any complications?

Regarding prognosis:

- What was the gestational age and maturity of fetus upon delivery?
- If delivery was premature, were complications encountered? Have complications responded to treatment?

References

Gabbe, Steven G., Jennifer R. Niebyl, and Joe L. Simpson. Obstetrics - Normal and Problem Pregnancies, 3rd ed. New York: Churchill Livingstone, Inc, 1996.

Tierney, Lawrence M., Stephen J. McPhee, and Maxine A. Papadakis, eds. Current Medical Diagnosis and Treatment, 39th ed. New York: Lange Medical Books/McGraw-Hill, 2000.

Premenstrual Syndrome
Other names / synonyms: Menstrual Migraine, Menstrual Molimen, PMS
625.4

Definition

Premenstrual syndrome (PMS) refers to a group of menstrually related disorders and symptoms that occur 1-2 weeks before the start of menstruation and subside after menstruation begins. No single cause has been identified for PMS, but it is related to when the ovary produces an ovum or egg (ovulation). Other theories include chemical changes in the brain, such as changes in serotonin levels, as seen with depression. Changing hormone levels during the menstrual cycle may also play a role in PMS. Low levels of vitamins and minerals, such as magnesium, manganese and vitamin E, have been found in women with PMS. Eating an excess of salty foods may cause fluid retention and aggravate PMS symptoms. Caffeine and stress may also affect irritability, a symptom of PMS.

In the US, PMS is estimated to occur in up to 40% of women of reproductive age, with 5% of these women having severe symptoms. PMS is a highly prevalent and common disorder affecting women of reproductive age in many other countries. Studies in Scandinavian and Asian countries have shown incidence rates similar to those found in the US.

Diagnosis

History: Individuals may report nervous tension, irritability, weight gain, swelling (edema), headache, affective disorder characterized by depression and anguish (dysphoria), confusion and memory problems (cognitive disturbances), alterations in appetite, and various types of pain.

Physical exam: A physical exam is not usually helpful to this diagnosis.

Tests: There are no diagnostic tests for PMS. Thyroid disorders are common in women of reproductive age, and measurement of thyroid hormone levels may be useful. Other laboratory tests should only be considered as suggested by history and physical examination findings.

Treatment

Treatment of PMS is based on symptoms. Oral contraceptives, diuretics, and antidepressants have been used to relieve symptoms. Cognitive therapy may help individuals cope with stress. Nutritional supplementation has varying success in improving symptoms. Weight gain, bloating, and swelling due to fluid retention may be relieved by reducing salt in the diet. Some relief is also reported from the use of calcium and magnesium supplements. If this is not helpful, a "water pill" (diuretic) may be needed to relieve fluid retention.

Breast tenderness may be lessened by the use of a support bra, reduction in caffeine, and the use of vitamin B_6 or oral contraceptives.

Regular daily exercise has been shown to help relieve symptoms of depression, tension, anxiety, fatigue, and irritability. Exercise also increases the release of a group of substances formed within the brain that relieve pain (endorphins).

Women experiencing sleep disturbances with PMS generally fall asleep easily, but awaken in the middle of the night. A mild antidepressant may prove effective.

Headaches, backaches, and lower abdominal cramps can usually be relieved with pain medication (analgesics).

Many women report improvement from changes in their diet. Guidelines include increasing complex carbohydrates (whole grains, fruits, vegetables, potatoes, and pasta), while decreasing sugar, artificial sweeteners, salt, caffeine, and alcohol. Avoiding sugar and salt can lessen bloating and fluid retention. Reducing caffeine (including intake of coffee, tea, cola, and chocolate) can improve anxiety, irritability, nervousness, and insomnia. Reducing protein may also be helpful. Eating 6 small balanced meals instead of 3 large ones is also recommended.

While stress does not cause PMS, it may intensify the symptoms. Relaxation techniques and exercise may help to relieve anxiety and tension.

The selective serotonin reuptake inhibitors (SSRIs) have recently been tried as a short duration treatment with each menstrual cycle and appear to be helpful.

Prognosis

PMS symptoms usually resolve with the onset of the menstrual period. If symptoms persist longer, another diagnosis should be considered.

Differential Diagnosis

Other possibilities include thyroid abnormality, major depression, migraine headache, or anxiety disorder.

Specialists

- Gynecologist
- Psychiatrist
- Psychologist

Work Restrictions / Accommodations

No work restrictions apply to this diagnosis. Working with heavy machinery during this time may be challenging for some individuals and needs to be assessed on a case-by-case basis.

Complementary and Alternative Therapies

Content is intended for awareness only. Treatments may or may not be effective. Scientific evidence may be lacking and some substances have potentially toxic effects. Dr. Presley Reed and the editors do not endorse the use of these therapies in the absence of consultation with a licensed medical professional.

Chaste tree - May help balance hormones and relieve anxiety and depression.

Dandelion - May reduce bloating (acts as a diuretic).

Vitamin B_6 - Mood swings, fluid retention, cravings, fatigue and breast tenderness may be a result of a vitamin B deficiency.

Magnesium - May address mood swings, bloating, food cravings and fatigue.

Comorbid Conditions

Underlying psychiatric/psychological condition may lengthen disability.

Complications

Individuals with more severe symptoms may need additional medical intervention. Women experiencing sleep disturbances with PMS generally fall asleep easily, but awaken in the middle of the night. Sleeping pills can cause physical dependence. Severe emotional symptoms can disrupt work and social relationships.

Factors Influencing Duration

The overall health of the individual, job demands, and severity of symptoms will determine if disability is required.

Length of Disability

In most cases, no disability is expected.

Duration in Days

Job Classification	Minimum	Optimum	Maximum
Any work	0	0	1

Failure to Recover

If an individual fails to recover within the maximum duration expectancy period, the reader may wish to reference the following questions to assist in better understanding the specifics of an individual's medical case.

Regarding diagnosis:

- Has the woman experienced symptoms that are consistent with the diagnosis of PMS?
- Is the woman between 25 and 40 years of age?
- Do the symptoms arise approximately 1-2 weeks before menstruation and subside after menstruation begins?
- Have other conditions that with similar symptoms been ruled out?

Regarding treatment:

- Was treatment directed at reducing possible triggers and relief of symptoms? Was individual asked to keep a diary to determine a pattern of triggers and symptoms? Were any patterns for the PMS detected?
- Were specific measures done to reduce suspected triggers?
- Was individual instructed in lifestyle modifications that include good nutrition, proper sleep, avoidance of excess salt, caffeine or alcohol, regular exercise, and stress reduction?
- Was individual compliant with treatment recommendations?
- Were symptoms severe or persistent enough to warrant treatment with medication?
- Have mild diuretics or analgesics relieved symptoms of bloating and pain?
- Were antianxiety or antidepressant medications effective against associated symptoms?

Regarding prognosis:

- Do symptoms persist despite treatment?
- Has individual been compliant with recommended lifestyle changes and medication? If not, what can be done to enhance compliance?
- Are symptoms so severe that they interfere with work performance or social relationships? Is more aggressive treatment an option?
- Does individual have a coexisting condition that may complicate treatment or impact recovery?
- If underlying psychiatric/psychological component is present, has individual been referred for counseling?

References

Daugherty, J.E. "Treatment Strategies for Premenstrual Syndrome." *American Family Physician* 10 1 (1998): 23-24.

Hoffman, David. *Holistic Herbal.* New York: Barnes & Noble, 1996.

Prinzmetal's Angina
Other names / synonyms: Variant Angina, Vasospastic Angina
413.1

Definition

Prinzmetal's variant angina or variant angina is an unusual syndrome of cardiac pain (angina) that typically occurs at rest. It is not brought on by exertion (effort angina) and is associated with characteristic changes of the electrocardiogram (ECG) involving the ST-segments.

Variant angina is due to constriction (spasm) of a coronary artery. Spasm causes a temporary, dramatic reduction of the diameter of a coronary artery resulting in oxygen deprivation of the heart muscle (myocardial ischemia). This may lead to chest pain (angina), irregular heart beating (arrhythmias), a heart attack (acute myocardial infarction), or sudden death.

Variant angina is much less common than classic effort angina and constitutes less than 1% of all cases of angina. Variant angina tends to occur in younger individuals ages 20 to 50, and is equally common in men and women.

Diagnosis

History: Individuals typically report pain at rest in the center of the chest that sometimes radiates to the arms, neck, or shoulders. Pain with exertion is unusual. Characteristically, pain occurs between midnight and six in the morning. It usually resolves spontaneously, but tends to recur many times during the night. Pain is very responsive to nitroglycerin.

Physical exam: The blood pressure and heart rate may be elevated during pain. A transient arrhythmia and/or a heart murmur may also be present but disappear when the pain resolves.

Tests: The hallmark of Prinzmetal's angina is ST-segment elevation on the ECG during pain. In addition, there may be a wide variety of transient arrhythmias. Ambulatory ECG monitoring (Holter monitoring) often shows episodes of ST-segment deviation even in the absence of pain. Treadmill testing is usually well tolerated and not associated with ST-segment depression typical of effort angina.

Treatment

Nitroglycerin (NTG) under the tongue (sublingual) or swallowed (orally) usually promptly abolishes attacks of variant angina. Larger doses of NTG taken orally or applied to the skin as an ointment (topically) often prevent attacks in ambulatory individuals. Intravenous NTG is used in hospitalized individuals who have frequent attacks.

Calcium-channel blockers are another class of medications often given instead of or in addition to NTG preparations to dilate arteries. Beta-blockers are used widely for the treatment of effort angina and are not helpful in variant angina but may actually aggravate it.

Revascularization (coronary bypass or angioplasty) is not recommended for Prinzmetal's angina since symptoms due to coronary spasm usually persist or recur after these procedures. However, in those individuals with significant coronary artery disease, revascularization may help relieve symptoms.

Prognosis

Variant angina has a cyclical course. The first 3 to 6 months are characterized by frequent episodes of nocturnal pain. After that, it often enters a quiescent phase. The quiescent phase may last indefinitely, or be punctuated by one or more recurrences of activity. Over time, the illness tends to "burn out."

An AMI occurs during the initial phase in about 5% of individuals. Death occurs in 1 percent. The 5-year survival is good at about 95 percent.

Differential Diagnosis

Unstable angina due to coronary atherosclerosis may mimic variant angina. Esophageal spasm produces similar pain that may be relieved by NTG.

Specialists

- Cardiologist

Rehabilitation

The goal of rehabilitation for Prinzmetal's angina is to design a physical conditioning program for the individual that increases the amount of activity yet limits the onset of symptoms of this form of angina. Individuals must first be able to identify and communicate the symptoms as true angina pain. The physical therapist and/or other healthcare personnel knowledgeable in treating various forms of angina use a scale to rank anginal symptoms that helps determine the amount and intensity of exercise prescribed. This scaling helps individuals grade and communicate to the physical therapist their angina symptoms during exercise.

The exercise session for individuals with angina begins with a prolonged warm-up period. Proper breathing while exercising is critical. Rehabilitation begins with low intensity exercise such as mild calisthenics, including marching in place and raising both arms overhead. Walking (ambulating) with continuous monitoring for 2 to 5 minutes and progressing to 15 to 20 minutes while symptom-free is also part of the program. As endurance improves without symptoms of angina, the use of a stationary bicycle beginning at very light resistance for 3 minutes is performed under supervision and eventually increased by 15- to 30-second intervals. Exercises progress with time and intensity and vary from individual to individual. However, as the individual continues to improve, work-type activities are incorporated into the rehabilitation regimen to address endurance needed for return to work.

This related increase in endurance also translates into a generally more active lifestyle. Endurance or aerobic routines such as running, brisk walking, cycling, or swimming is the ultimate goal, as it increases the strength and efficiency of the heart because of uninterrupted blood flow. Since individuals experience varying degrees and effects of Prinzmetal's angina, modifications may be needed for those individuals taking medication or with other resulting conditions.

Work Restrictions / Accommodations

Individuals with variant angina usually require no work restrictions or accommodations. However, those individuals engaged in occupations that expose them or others to a significant chance of serious injury (e.g., bus drivers) are often reassigned to other duties during the active phase of the illness when life-threatening arrhythmias may occur.

Comorbid Conditions

Individuals with variant angina may have other associated disorders due to vasospasm, such as Raynaud's phenomenon or migraine headaches, which may lengthen disability.

Complications

During pain, life-threatening arrhythmias may occur. These arrhythmias include ventricular tachycardia, ventricular fibrillation, and heart block. A fatal, or more often nonfatal, acute myocardial infarction (AMI) may also occur.

Factors Influencing Duration

Factors that may influence the length of disability include the presence of underlying diseases such as coronary artery disease, cigarette smoking, severe stress, potential need for revascularization surgery, and development of complications. Duration depends primarily on individual's response to treatment.

Length of Disability

If significant CAD is also present, the length of disability is usually that of the CAD.

Coronary artery spasm without significant coronary artery disease.

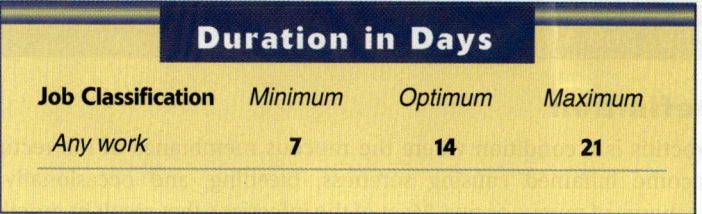

Job Classification	Minimum	Optimum	Maximum
Any work	7	14	21

Failure to Recover

If an individual fails to recover within the maximum duration expectancy period, the reader may wish to reference the following questions to assist in better understanding the specifics of an individual's medical case.

Regarding diagnosis:

- Did the individual present with a clinical history and physical findings consistent with the diagnosis of Prinzmetal's angina?
- Were cardiac isoenzymes and a 12-lead ECG done? Were characteristic ECG changes noted during pain?
- If the diagnosis was uncertain, were other conditions with similar findings ruled out?
- Would the individual benefit from consultation with a cardiologist?

Regarding treatment:

- Was the chest pain relieved with treatment?
- Would individual benefit from nutritional counseling in order to comply with a low-fat, low-cholesterol diet?
- Would individual benefit from enrollment in a community weight management program?
- If individual is unable to quit smoking, has he/she been referred to a smoking cessation program?
- Is individual participating in a regular exercise program?

Regarding prognosis:

- Do symptoms persist despite treatment?
- Has individual been compliant with treatment and lifestyle recommendations? If not, what can be done to enhance compliance?
- Was the Prinzmetal's angina complicated by a myocardial infarction, arrhythmias, or cardiac arrest?
- Does individual have coexisting medical conditions that may complicate treatment or impact recovery?

References

Braunwald, Eugene. Heart Disease: A Textbook of Cardiovascular Medicine, 5th ed. Philadelphia: W.B. Saunders Company, 1997.

Scully, Rosemary M., and Marylou R. Barnes. Physical Therapy. Philadelphia: J.B. Lippincott Company, 1989.

Proctitis
569, 569.49, 569.8

Definition

Proctitis is a condition where the mucous membranes of the rectum become inflamed causing soreness, bleeding, and occasionally a discharge of mucus or pus. Most of the infections that result in proctitis are sexually transmitted and include herpes, syphilis, gonorrhea, chlamydia, or cytomegalovirus.

Male homosexual behavior, specifically receptive anal intercourse, is the major risk factor for infection-related proctitis. Nonsexually transmitted infections causing proctitis are seen less frequently than sexually transmitted proctitis. Autoimmune proctitis is associated with diseases such as ulcerative colitis or Crohn's disease.

Proctitis may be caused by radiation treatment for cancers in the lower abdomen or pelvic region. About 1 in 5 individuals who receive a total dose greater than 5000 rads develop proctitis within two years of completion of radiotherapy. There is no known way to prevent this other than to limit the amount of radiation. Proctitis is often the dose-limiting consideration in radiotherapy for pelvic cancers. Proctitis may also be caused by infections.

As a result of male homosexual behavior, the prevalence of proctitis is higher in men than women and primarily affects adults.

Diagnosis

History: Individuals with proctitis may complain of itching, constipation, a feeling of rectal fullness, left-sided abdominal pain, passage of mucus through the rectum, rectal bleeding, and pain in the rectal area. Some individuals with proctitis may have no symptoms and can spread the infection unknowingly.

Physical exam: The rectal mucosa appears red and irritated with blisters and small ulcers. Lymph nodes in the groin may be tender.

Tests: Stool smears for bacterial, viral, or fungal pathogens should be performed. A complete blood count is used to determine whether blood loss is a problem. Proctoidoscopy, sigmoidoscopy, or colonoscopy may be indicated to determine the extent of the condition. In some cases, x-ray, ultrasound, or MRI imaging may be helpful.

Treatment

If the proctitis is bacterial in origin, antibiotics are necessary. Herpetic proctitis can be treated with antiviral agents. If the inflammation is caused by Crohn's disease or ulcerative colitis, the drug 5-aminosalicylic acid (5ASA) or corticosteroids may be applied directly to the area or taken in pill form. Mild radiation proctitis is generally treated with topical application of corticosteroids or nonsteroidal anti-inflammatory medications in the form of enemas, foam, or suppositories. Sitz baths can provide relief from symptoms. Surgical treatment such as a diverting colostomy may be required in severe cases where medical treatment is unsuccessful.

Prognosis

The long-term prognosis for proctitis depends on its cause and severity. Mild radiation proctitis generally resolves with topical treatment. While most bacterial forms of proctitis respond to antibiotics, some may be more persistent. For example, treatment failure occurs in as many as 35% of individuals with rectal gonorrhea.

If no treatment is given or the treatment is unsuccessful, the condition may extend to the colon. Surgery including removal of the colon is indicated for some serious forms of ulcerative colitis.

Differential Diagnosis

Proctitis should be distinguished from diverticulitis, foreign body in the rectum, HIV/AIDS or other sexually transmitted disease, and inflammatory bowel disease.

Specialists

- Gastroenterologist
- Proctologist

Work Restrictions / Accommodations

An individual with very mild proctitis may possibly be accommodated in an employment setting if he or she can work in a comfortable position (some individuals may be more comfortable standing) and if convenient access to restroom facilities is provided. Severe or chronic proctitis is generally disabling because of pain, fatigue, and the frequent urgent necessity to pass diarrhea, blood, and mucus.

Comorbid Conditions

Comorbid conditions include compromised immune status and pelvic or abdominal cancer.

Complications

Potential complications include chronic bleeding, the development of tears or constrictions in the tissue, ulcers, abscesses, anemia, rectovaginal fistula (women), and anal fistula (men and women).

Factors Influencing Duration

In infection-related proctitis, factors that may influence disability include compliance with doctor's recommendations for treatment and prevention of reinfection. In radiation proctitis, a major issue may be the underlying cause for the radiotherapy itself.

Length of Disability

Duration depends on the cause and severity, the physical demands of the job, and availability of sanitary facilities.

Duration in Days

Job Classification	Minimum	Optimum	Maximum
Any work	0	3	10

Failure to Recover

If an individual fails to recover within the maximum duration expectancy period, the reader may wish to reference the following questions to assist in better understanding the specifics of an individual's medical case.

Regarding diagnosis:

- Does individual have soreness, bleeding, or discharge of mucus or pus in the rectum?
- Does individual have a sexually transmitted infection?
- Does the individual engage in sexual practices that place them at risk for the condition (e.g., anal intercourse)?
- Have conditions with similar symptoms, such as diverticulitis, foreign body, inflammatory bowel disease, HIV/AIDS been ruled out?
- Does the individual have either ulcerative colitis or Crohn's disease, which may be associated with the development of proctitis?
- Has the individual had pelvic radiation treatment in the past 2 years?
- Does individual complain of itching, constipation, or other symptoms related to proctitis?
- Has the individual had adequate testing to establish the diagnosis (e.g., proctoscopy, sigmoidoscopy, or colonoscopy, ultrasound or MRI)?

Regarding treatment:

- What is the underlying cause of the proctitis? Has the individual been treated with the appropriate medications (antivirals or anti-inflammatories)?
- Have sitz baths been recommended for symptoms relief?
- Is surgery necessary to correct the condition?

Regarding prognosis:

- Does the individual have any conditions such as immune suppression or pelvic or abdominal cancer that may impact recovery?
- Has the individual experienced any complications such as bleeding, ulcers, abscesses, or fistulae that could impact recovery and prognosis?

References

Beers, Mark H., and Robert Berkow. The Merck Manual of Diagnosis and Treatment. Whitehouse Station, NJ: Merck & Co., Inc, 1999.

Zimmerman, F.B., and H.J. Feldmann. "Radiation Proctitis: Clinical and Pathological Manifestations, Therapy and Prophylaxis of Acute and Late Injurious Effects of Radiation on the Rectal Mucosa." Strahlenther Onkol 174 Suppl III (1998): 85-89.

Prostatectomy

Other names / synonyms: Radical Prostatectomy, TURP

60.2, 60.3, 60.4, 60.62

Definition

A prostatectomy is a surgical procedure used to remove part or all of the prostate gland due to enlargement or disease. The prostatectomy has no other purpose than to remove all or part of the prostate gland.

There are two major approaches in a prostatectomy. A transurethral prostatectomy (TURP) is performed for partial removal of the prostrate and a radical prostatectomy is complete prostate removal.

TURP is performed for benign prostatic hypertrophy (BPH), a condition where the prostate gland is enlarged and presses in on the tube that leads from the bladder to the end of the penis (urethra), interfering with urine flow.

Complete prostate removal (radical prostatectomy) is usually done for a diagnosis of prostate cancer that occurs in approximately 10% of males.

BPH occurs in 50% of men ages 51 to 60 and 90% of men over 80 with an overall, age-adjusted incidence of 15% in the US.

Reason for Procedure

A prostatectomy is performed when an enlarged prostate (prostatic hypertrophy) obstructs the flow of urine from the bladder through the urethra, leading to difficulty emptying the bladder or urinary tract infections. A prostatectomy may also be performed to remove tissue damaged by chronic inflammation of the prostate (prostatitis) and to treat cancer of the prostate.

A TURP is performed in the instance of a benign (noncancerous) enlarged prostate. If cancer is suspected, then a radical prostatectomy is required.

Description

TURP is used when cancer is not suspected but the enlarged prostate gland needs to be reduced in size. No abdominal incision is made so this procedure usually permits a shorter hospital stay. Under general or spinal anesthesia, a viewing instrument (resectoscope) is passed up the urethra until the prostate can be seen. A heated wire loop, laser, or other cutting instrument is inserted through the resectoscope and used to cut away as much of the prostate tissue as possible. These pieces of tissue are washed out through the resectoscope. An electrode is passed up through the tube and seals off any bleeding vessels (cauterization). When the resectoscope is withdrawn, a rubber tube (catheter) is passed through the urethra into the bladder. The catheter is left in place for several days to drain urine from the bladder and allow blood to be washed out while the tissues heal.

If the prostate gland is very enlarged or if cancer is suspected, prostatectomy is performed via an incision made in the perineal area (retropubic) or the area adjacent to the pubic bone (suprapubic). Under general anesthesia, an incision is made exposing the bladder and prostate gland. The capsule containing the gland is opened and the prostate tissue removed. Bleeding vessels are cauterized, a tube is inserted into the empty capsule to drain fluid and blood, and the abdomen is stitched closed. A catheter is passed up through the urethra to drain urine from the bladder. The drainage tube and catheter are left in place for about a week.

Prognosis

If a radical prostatectomy is performed because of prostate cancer and the tumor is contained within the prostatic capsule, nearly 90% of individuals have undetectable prostate-specific antigen (PSA) tests, a good indication that the cancer was completely removed. Outcomes are less effective if the cancer has spread to surrounding tissues or the lymph system. Approximately 90% of individuals who undergo TURP have a significant relief of symptoms.

Specialists

- Urologist

Work Restrictions / Accommodations

Heavy lifting or straining should be avoided for several weeks after surgery. Extended work leave or a temporary transfer to sedentary duties may be necessary depending on the underlying reason for the prostatectomy.

Comorbid Conditions

For radical prostatectomy, comorbid conditions include obesity or the presence of bladder cancer or other cancer that has spread.

Procedure Complications

Complications of a TURP include excessive bleeding and transurethral resection (TUR) syndrome. The TUR syndrome is a condition resulting from excessive absorption of irrigation fluids that leads to confusion, nausea, vomiting, high blood pressure, slowed heart rate, and visual disturbances. TUR syndrome occurs in about 2% of the TURP cases. Other complications include bladder perforation, failure to urinate, blood clots in the urethra, infection, scarring of the urethra, chronic incontinence, or impotence.

Complications of radical prostatectomy include allergy or abnormal reaction to anesthetic agents, excessive bleeding, wound infection, urinary tract infection, and perforation of the bladder or rectum. Chronic incontinence occurs in about 10% of cases while the incidence of impotence ranges from 10-40% depending on age of individual, extent of surgery, and other underlying medical conditions.

Factors Influencing Duration

Length of disability may be influenced by type of surgery performed or any complications. The most common disability following prostatectomy for benign conditions is urinary incontinence. Disability related to radical prostatectomy performed for reasons of prostate cancer depends on the underlying medical condition.

Length of Disability

Length of disability depends on surgical complications and underlying medical conditions. There is usually no permanent disability associated with uncomplicated TURP. Durations reflect recovery period for procedure only, not from underlying medical condition.

Transurethral approach.

Duration in Days

Job Classification	Minimum	Optimum	Maximum
Sedentary work	7	9	14
Light work	7	9	14
Medium work	14	16	21
Heavy work	21	24	28
Very Heavy work	21	24	28

Retropubic, suprapubic, or perineal approaches.

Duration in Days

Job Classification	Minimum	Optimum	Maximum
Sedentary work	14	21	28
Light work	14	21	28
Medium work	21	35	42
Heavy work	28	42	56
Very Heavy work	28	42	56

Radical.

Duration in Days

Job Classification	Minimum	Optimum	Maximum
Sedentary work	21	42	84
Light work	21	42	84
Medium work	42	63	105
Heavy work	42	84	126
Very Heavy work	42	84	126

References

Eastham, James A., and Peter T. Scardino. "Radical Prostatectomy." Campbell's Urology, 7th ed. Walsh, Patrick C., et al., eds. Philadelphia: W.B. Saunders Company, 1998. 2547-2564.

Santarosa, Richard P., Alexis E. Te, and Steven A. Kaplan. "Transurethral Resection, Incision, and Ablation of the Prostate." Glenn's Urologic Surgery, 5th ed. Graham, Dan S., Jr., ed. Philadelphia: Lippincott-Raven Publishers, 1998. 921-932.

Prostatic Hypertrophy

Other names / synonyms: Benign Adenoma of the Prostate, BPH, Hyperplasia of Prostate, Prostate Enlargement, Prostate Fibroma, Prostate Myoma, Prostatic Hyperplasia, Prostatic Obstruction, Prostatomegaly

Definition

Prostatic hypertrophy is a non life threatening (benign) enlargement of the prostate gland.

As the prostate enlarges, it gradually compresses and distorts the tube (urethra) that carries urine from the bladder. Consequently, the flow of urine is obstructed and the bladder muscle becomes overdeveloped in an attempt to force flow during urination. The bladder is eventually unable to expel all the urine, which causes it to become distended and unable to empty completely (urinary retention). The result may be abdominal pain and only a limited ability to pass urine. Overflow of small amounts of urine from the bladder may result in an inability to control urination (incontinence), or the bladder may become overactive resulting in the need to urinate frequently.

The exact cause of prostatic hypertrophy is unknown but may be related to hormonal changes associated with aging. Prostatic hypertrophy usually affects men over 50 and prevalence is consistent regardless of ethnicity. By the age of 50 to 60, it is estimated that 80% of men will have had some degree of prostatic hypertrophy. The incidence increases to over 95% in men over 70.

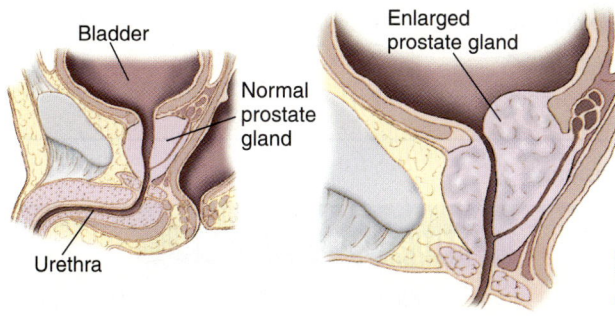

Diagnosis

History: Individuals with prostatic hypertrophy report a decrease in the force and diameter (caliber) of the urine stream, difficulty starting urination (hesitancy), the need to urinate frequently at night (nocturia), disruption of the urinary stream (intermittency), a feeling of incomplete bladder emptying, increasing desire to urinate (urgency), involuntary loss of urine (incontinence), bladder pain when not urinating, pain associated with urination (dysuria), and incomplete emptying of the bladder that creates the need to urinate frequently.

Physical exam: An enlarged prostate can be detected using a gloved finger inserted into the rectum (digital rectal exam). The lower abdomen can be examined by pressing with hands (palpation) to determine if the bladder is distended.

Tests: Urinalysis and microscopic examination of the urine is performed to rule out infection. Blood chemistry tests including blood urea nitrogen (BUN) and creatinine are used to measure kidney function. A prostate-specific antigen (PSA) test rules out prostate cancer. High frequency sound waves (ultrasound scanning), x-rays of the kidneys using radiopaque dye (pyelography), and recording the strength of urine flow (uroflowmetry) may be performed to give additional information about the severity of the obstruction and to rule out other defects in the urinary system.

Treatment

Prostate enlargement that produces only mild symptoms does not require treatment.

If symptoms are more severe, treatment to reduce the size of the prostate may include drugs (alpha-1 and alpha-2 blockers) or anti male sex hormone (antiandrogen) medication.

Surgical options to remove prostatic tissue include transurethral resection of the prostate (TURP), transurethral incision of the prostate (TUIP), open prostatectomy, transurethral ultrasound-guided laser prostatectomy (TULIP), or transurethral needle ablation (TUNA). Transurethral balloon dilation of the prostate (TUBD) involves the use of a balloon catheter to dilate the prostate under pressure. Devices (stents) may also be inserted that hold the urethra open and allow urine to flow more easily.

If bladder inflammation (cystitis) is involved, treatment is directed toward controlling the infection with antibiotics. Urine retention may be relieved by catheterization of the urethra until the prostate enlargement can be corrected. A urethral catheter may need to be kept in place permanently if the individual is unable to undergo surgery due to advanced age or ill health.

Prognosis

Alpha-blocking drugs effectively improve urine flow rates. Approximately 50% of individuals in clinical studies and 75% overall show some degree of improvement with this medication. Individuals taking antiandrogen medication also show general improvement in urinary flow rates. Surgical treatment of prostatic hypertrophy effectively reduces voiding problems in 80-90% of individuals 1 year after surgery. This percentage decreases to 60-75% with 5 years after surgery, and approximately 5% of individuals will require a repeat surgical intervention within this time frame.

Differential Diagnosis

Conditions that present with similar symptoms include cancers of the prostate or bladder, urethral stricture, bladder neck contractures, bladder stones (calculi), or neurologic disease.

Specialists

- Urologist

Rehabilitation

Certain exercises can be performed to help the individual regain urinary control following surgical intervention. After the second or third postoperative day, the individual learns to breath normally while contracting stomach (abdominal) and buttocks (gluteal and perineal) muscles 12 to 25 times every hour. Another helpful exercise is to squeeze the rectal sphincter tensely while relaxing other body muscles.

Work Restrictions / Accommodations

Frequent work breaks may be needed and easy access to restroom facilities are usually required. Strenuous physical activity may need to be modified temporarily if surgical intervention is necessary.

Comorbid Conditions

Existing conditions that may impact the ability to recover and further lengthen disability include obesity and a family history of prostate enlargement.

Complications

Complications that may arise include inflammation of the bladder (cystitis) or kidney (pyelonephritis), formation of a cyst in the kidney due to urine retention (hydronephrosis), and possible formation of kidney stones (renal calculi) from stagnant urine.

Factors Influencing Duration

Length of disability may be influenced by age, the amount of prostate enlargement, method of treatment, effectiveness of treatment, or any other complications. Other factors that may influence length of disability include smoking and certain medications that enhance the symptoms of prostate hypertrophy.

Length of Disability

No disability is expected for medical treatment alone. The duration of disability from prostatic hypertrophy is dependent on the severity of the condition and whether surgery is needed to correct it. Recovery time may take weeks when surgical intervention is necessary. Strenuous physical labor may not be possible during recovery. However, disability is not permanent and the individual will eventually return to work in full capacity.

For prostactectomy, durations reflect recovery period for procedure only, not from underlying medical condition. For transurethral balloon dilation, duration depends on type of anesthesia.

Medical treatment.

Job Classification	Minimum	Optimum	Maximum
Sedentary work	0	0	1
Light work	0	0	1
Medium work	0	0	1
Heavy work	1	1	2
Very Heavy work	1	1	2

Orchiectomy.

Job Classification	Minimum	Optimum	Maximum
Sedentary work	3	7	14
Light work	3	7	21
Medium work	7	14	21
Heavy work	7	14	21
Very Heavy work	7	14	21

Laser incision.

Job Classification	Minimum	Optimum	Maximum
Sedentary work	1	2	3
Light work	1	2	3
Medium work	1	2	3
Heavy work	1	2	3
Very Heavy work	1	2	3

Prostatectomy. Transurethral approach.

Job Classification	Minimum	Optimum	Maximum
Sedentary work	7	9	14
Light work	7	9	14
Medium work	14	16	21
Heavy work	21	24	28
Very Heavy work	21	24	28

Prostatectomy (retropubic, suprapubic, or perineal approaches).

Duration in Days

Job Classification	Minimum	Optimum	Maximum
Sedentary work	14	21	28
Light work	14	21	28
Medium work	21	35	42
Heavy work	28	42	56
Very Heavy work	28	42	56

Transurethral incision of bladder neck and prostate.

Duration in Days

Job Classification	Minimum	Optimum	Maximum
Sedentary work	3	7	9
Light work	3	7	9
Medium work	3	7	9
Heavy work	3	7	9
Very Heavy work	3	7	9

Transurethral balloon dilation.

Duration in Days

Job Classification	Minimum	Optimum	Maximum
Sedentary work	1	3	7
Light work	1	3	7
Medium work	1	3	7
Heavy work	1	3	7
Very Heavy work	1	3	7

Prostatic stent.

Duration in Days

Job Classification	Minimum	Optimum	Maximum
Sedentary work	3	7	9
Light work	3	7	9
Medium work	3	7	9
Heavy work	3	7	9
Very Heavy work	3	7	9

Duration Trend from Normative Data*

Cases	Mean	Min	Max	No Lost Time	Over 6 Months
698	41	0	326	0.76%	0.15%

Percentile:	5th	25th	Median	75th	95th
Days:	10	21	34	51	94

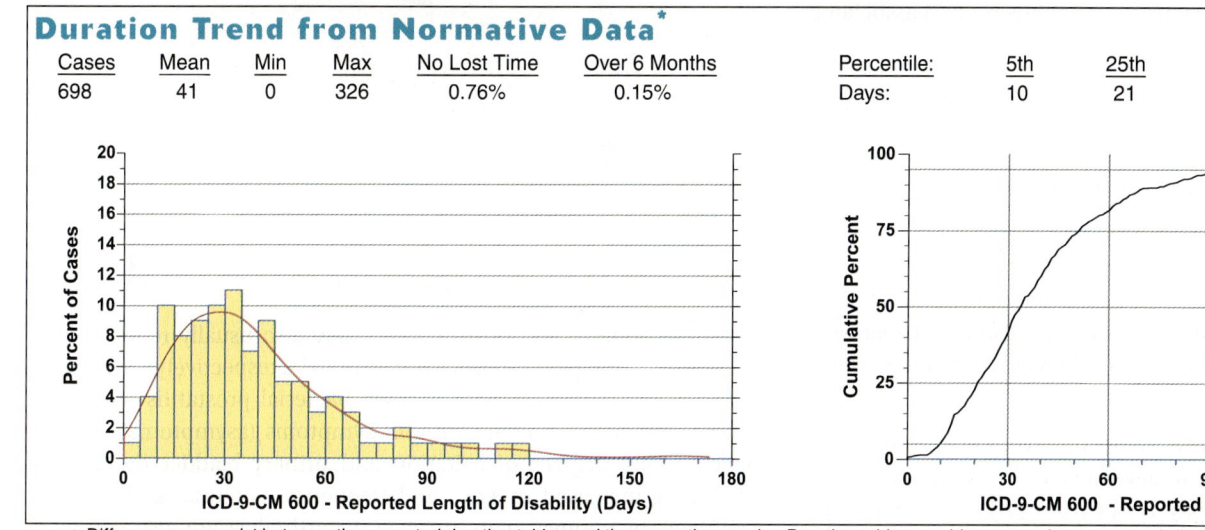

* Differences may exist between the expected duration tables and the normative graphs. Duration tables provide expected recovery periods based on the type of work performed by the individual. The normative graphs reflect the actual observed experience of many individuals across the spectrum of physical conditions, in a variety of industries, and with varying levels of case management.

Failure to Recover

If an individual fails to recover within the maximum duration expectancy period, the reader may wish to reference the following questions to assist in better understanding the specifics of an individual's medical case.

Regarding diagnosis:

- Did the individual present with symptoms consistent with prostatic hypertrophy?
- Was the diagnosis confirmed with a digital rectal exam?
- Were associated urinary tract infections ruled out with urine cultures and urinalysis?
- Were other conditions with similar symptoms ruled out?
- Would the individual benefit by consultation with a urologist?

Regarding Treatment:

- For what reasons did the individual's condition warrant treatment?
- Were medications prescribed to shrink the prostate?
- Did the symptoms persist despite treatment? If so, were alternative medications or dosage adjustments tried?
- Was surgical intervention required?
- Did the individual participate in a bladder training program?

Prostatic Hypertrophy 1733

- Did individual experience any complications associated with condition or its treatment that may impact recovery?

Regarding prognosis:

- What was the expected outcome from type of treatment received?

- Does individual have a coexisting condition that may complicate treatment or impact recovery?

References

Ernst, E. "Herbal Medications for Common Ailments in the Elderly." Drugs and Aging 15 6 (1999): 423-428.

Partin, Alan W. "Etiology of Benign Prostatic Hyperplasia." Prostatic Diseases. Lepor, Herbert, ed. Philadelphia: W.B. Saunders Company, 2000. 95-105.

Prostatitis

Other names / synonyms: Prostate Gland Inflammation
601, 601.0, 601.1, 601.2, 601.3, 601.8, 601.9

Definition

Prostatitis refers to inflammation of a secretory gland (prostate) in the male reproductive system. The types of prostatitis are acute bacterial, chronic bacterial, and nonbacterial.

Acute bacterial prostatitis is an acute infection of the prostate that is caused by certain types of bacteria (gram-negative aerobes). This condition is usually associated with inflammation of the urinary bladder (cystitis) and an inability to completely void the urinary bladder (acute urinary retention). Acute bacterial prostatitis is often associated with lower urinary tract infections (UTI).

Chronic bacterial prostatitis is also caused by gram-negative aerobes and, possibly, gram-positive bacteria. The inflammatory reaction in chronic prostatitis is less intense than in acute prostatitis, and the individual may be without symptoms (asymptomatic).

In either acute or chronic prostatitis, bacterial infection of the prostate may occur from the tube (urethra) by which urine is excreted from the urinary bladder, or it can be caused by a sexually transmitted disease (gonorrhea, chlamydia). Bacterial infection may also occur following anal intercourse, or it can be the result of tuberculosis that has spread through the bloodstream.

Nonbacterial prostatitis has similar signs and symptoms of bacterial prostatitis except that UTI almost never occurs in the nonbacterial form. Nonbacterial prostatitis may result from physical (neuromuscular) injury or an abnormal response of the immune system (autoimmune disease). It is unclear at this time whether either of these factors actually causes nonbacterial prostatitis; the origin of this condition remains a mystery.

Prostatitis frequently affects elderly men with enlarged prostates or individuals who have a bladder catheter. In many cases, however, the cause of prostatitis may be uncertain. Acute episodes have a sudden, rapid onset, while chronic prostatitis appears gradually and is more common. Prostatitis usually affects men between the ages of 30-50, and it accounts for 25% of physician visits made by males in the US.

Diagnosis

History: Individuals with acute bacterial prostatitis will report chills, low back and pubic area (perineal) pain, the urge to urinate frequently at night (nocturia), painful urination (dysuria), and a variable, slow urine

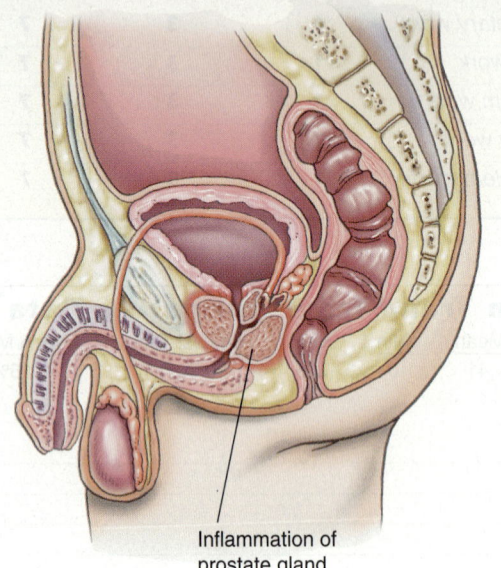

Inflammation of prostate gland

Laurie O'Keefe

stream (bladder outlet obstruction). They also usually report diffuse muscle and joint pain (myalgia and arthralgia, respectively). Symptoms reported by individuals with chronic bacterial prostatitis are inconsistent. Although some are without symptoms (asymptomatic), most have varying degrees of irritation and urinary bladder dysfunction (including increased urgency and frequency, nocturia, and dysuria). Low back or perineal pain, myalgia, or arthralgia are also common. Individuals with nonbacterial prostatitis will report symptoms similar to either the acute or chronic bacterial forms of the disease.

Physical exam: Insertion of a gloved finger into the rectum to feel the prostate (rectal palpation) will reveal a tender, swollen prostate gland that is firm and warm to the touch in individuals with acute bacterial prostatitis. The inflammation may affect all or only part of the prostate. In individuals with chronic bacterial prostatitis, the prostate may feel normal or firm in certain places by rectal palpation. Palpation may also reveal a grating feeling (crepitation) if large prostatic stones (calculi) are present. Examination of individuals with nonbacterial prostatitis will reveal symptoms similar to those of acute or chronic bacterial forms of the disease.

Tests: For all types of prostatitis, a complete blood count (CBC) with a white blood cell differential may be performed to identify signs of infection. Also, urinalysis and a urine culture can be performed to identify white blood cells, red blood cells, or bacteria in the urine (pyuria, hematuria, or bacilluria, respectively). A culture of the prostatic secretion that is obtained after massaging the prostate gland may also be performed. X-rays can be taken to identify the presence of complicating factors such as prostatic enlargement or stones (calculi) in the prostate. For chronic bacterial infections only, a flexible fiber-optic viewing scope can be inserted into the tube (urethra) that drains urine from the bladder (urethroscopy) to identify the presence of complicating factors such as prostate gland enlargement, blockage of the urethra (urethral stricture), or kidney (renal) infection.

Treatment

Antibiotics are used to eliminate acute bacterial prostatitis. Also, for individuals who are unable to completely void their bladder of urine because of extreme urethral inflammation, a drainage line (punch suprapubic tube) may be inserted that allows the bladder to empty. This procedure will require hospitalization because of the risk of infection (sepsis). For chronic bacterial prostatitis, ongoing antibiotic therapy may be required and this can be individualized to meet the person's needs and drug tolerance.

Surgical intervention (prostatovesiculectomy) may be used to treat individuals who do not respond to drug therapy. Nonbacterial prostatitis will not respond to antibiotics and treatment is directed toward control of symptoms by administering pain-relievers; anti-inflammatory, anticholinergic, or alpha-blocking drugs; stool softeners; and warm sitz baths.

Prognosis

Individuals with acute bacterial prostatitis usually respond dramatically to antibiotic drug therapy and most will not progress to chronic bacterial prostatitis using this treatment. It may take 4-5 weeks to eliminate the bacterial infection even though the symptoms of prostatitis may disappear more rapidly. Similarly, antibiotic therapy works extremely well for treatment of chronic bacterial prostatitis. For those individuals with chronic bacterial prostatitis who do not respond to drug therapy, surgical intervention (prostatovesiculectomy) to remove infected tissue is curative provided all the prostate tissue that contains bacteria is eliminated. Symptomatic relief of nonbacterial prostatitis can usually be achieved by the liberal use of warm sitz baths. However, the cause of nonbacterial prostatitis is unknown, and prevention and cure are not possible at this time.

Differential Diagnosis

Conditions that present with symptoms similar to prostatitis include enlargement of the prostate gland (benign prostatic hypertrophy) and cancer of the prostate.

Specialists

- Urologist

Work Restrictions / Accommodations

Certain work-related activities such as driving or operating machinery may be restricted if the individual is taking narcotic pain relievers. In this case, work should be strictly sedentary. A period of recovery will be necessary if the individual was treated using surgery (prostatovesiculectomy).

Complementary and Alternative Therapies

Content is intended for awareness only. Treatments may or may not be effective. Scientific evidence may be lacking and some substances have potentially toxic effects. Dr. Presley Reed and the editors do not endorse the use of these therapies in the absence of consultation with a licensed medical professional.

Acupuncture - Insertion of needles into certain points on the body may help relieve symptoms of prostatitis.

Comorbid Conditions

Conditions that may impact the ability to recover and further lengthen disability from prostatitis include the presence of untreated sexually transmitted diseases or benign prostatic hypertrophy.

Complications

The inflammation may spread causing a similar (inflammatory) response in the epididymis (epididymitis), urethra (urethritis), or the ureters and urinary bladder (cystitis). Prostatitis may lead to abnormal fluid collection within the prostate (prostatic abscess).

Factors Influencing Duration

Length of disability may be influenced by the severity of the inflammation and the response of the prostate to drug treatment. Older individuals may require a longer recovery time if surgery was used as a treatment.

Length of Disability

The duration of disability depends upon the response to medication that is prescribed and the requirements of the job.

Duration in Days

Job Classification	Minimum	Optimum	Maximum
Any work	1	3	10

Failure to Recover

If an individual fails to recover within the maximum duration expectancy period, the reader may wish to reference the following questions to assist in better understanding the specifics of an individual's medical case.

Regarding diagnosis:

- Did the individual present with symptoms such as chills, low back and pubic area (perineal) pain, the urge to urinate frequently at night (nocturia), painful urination (dysuria), and a variable, slow urine stream (bladder outlet obstruction).
- Was diagnosis of prostatitis confirmed with a digital rectal exam and culture?
- If the diagnosis was uncertain were other conditions with similar symptoms ruled out?

Regarding treatment:

- Has a sensitivity test been done to determine the most effective antibiotic and to rule out antibiotic-resistant organisms?
- If the prostatitis was nonbacterial in origin, did the treatment involve administration of anti-inflammatories, anticholinergics or alpha-blockers, stool softeners and sitz baths?
- Was the appropriate antibiotic therapy prescribed?
- Was surgical intervention required? Did individual experience any complications due to the procedure?

Regarding prognosis:

- Have symptoms resolved?
- Has individual been retested to ensure that infection is resolved?
- If symptoms persisted, was surgical intervention to remove infected tissue considered?
- Has individual experienced any complications, such as epididymitis, urethritis, cystitis or prostatic abscess that would impact recovery and prognosis?
- Does individual have an underlying condition (i.e., sexually transmitted diseases or prostatic hypertrophy) that may impact recovery?

References

Alternative Treatment. Prostate Health. 2000. 12 Jan 2001 <http://www.prostatehealth.com/altFS.htm>.

Iunda, I.F., et al. "Urethral Electrothermal Stimulation in Treating Patients with Chronic Non-gonococcal Urethroprostatitis." Vrachebnoe Delo 3 (1990): 21-22.

Pruritus Ani
698.0

Definition

Pruritus ani is severe itching (pruritus) of the skin around the anus.

Pruritus ani can be caused by many things including pinworms (parasites), bacterial infections, diet, yeast infections (candidiasis), and reactions to oral antibiotics. Pruritus ani may result from systemic conditions associated with generalized pruritus or from skin diseases associated with pruritus. The systemic conditions include uremia, anemia, cancer of lung or breast, liver diseases, lymphoma, leukemia, polycythemia vera, diabetes mellitus, and AIDS. The skin diseases include dry skin (xerosis), parasite infections (scabies), a condition causing an intensely itchy patch of bumps (lichen simplex chronicus), heat rash (miliaria), fungal infections, an inflammation between folds of skin caused by warmth mixed with moisture (intertrigo), and several inflammatory skin conditions (psoriasis, lichen planus, and pityriasis rosea). It may also be caused by irritating substances coming in contact with the skin (contact dermatitis) such as diarrhea, colon or vaginal secretions, or detergents that remain in underclothing.

Trauma or injury to the anal area, a defective anal muscle (incompetent anal sphincter), an abnormal opening (fistula), and hemorrhoids are often associated with pruritus ani. Other contributing factors may be either poor hygiene or too vigorous cleaning of the area. Some cases are due to psychological factors.

Pruritus ani is a common condition.

Diagnosis

History: There may be no other symptoms than severe itching of the anal area. Individuals may report that the itching seems to be particularly noticeable at night during sleep. Skin changes may or may not be seen.

Physical exam: The exam may reveal any of the following: red, irritated skin, bumps, an unusual thickening or softening of the skin, and scratches or breaks in the skin from scratching. Hemorrhoids, fistula, or evidence of an incompetent anal sphincter may also be present. A gynecological exam can rule out any underlying disease process, such as vaginitis.

Tests: Blood glucose levels, blood nitrogen levels, liver (hepatic) functions, analysis of feces, and a skin biopsy may be performed. An examination of the inside of the rectum and lower colon is done using a viewing tube inserted through the anus (proctocolonoscopy). Because there are so many possible causes of pruritus ani, it is very important that it is diagnosed and treated accurately.

Treatment

To be effective, treatment must match the cause. Parasites or bacterial infections can be treated with medication. Underlying disease processes (such as diabetes mellitus) need treatment. Injuries, fistulas, and hemorrhoids need to be medically addressed. Allergic reactions can be avoided by changing soaps or detergents, or by additional rinsing of clothes after washing to remove soap residue. Diet changes include avoiding spices, coffee, tea, cola, beer, chocolate, tomatoes, and citrus fruits. Poor hygiene needs to be corrected. On the other hand, too vigorous cleansing needs to be modified by stopping the use of over-the-counter preparations, cleaning pads, and solutions. Use of a blow dryer on the perineum may be used. Water, alone, may be adequate hygiene for over-sensitive skin. A sitz bath is often very effective. In some cases, the use of a mild corticosteroid cream is effective. Oral antihistamines can relieve the itching. Individual should be reexamined again in two to three weeks to evaluate effectiveness of treatment.

Prognosis

If the cause can be determined and effectively treated, pruritus ani can be eliminated. Symptoms can be lessened or eliminated in idiopathic cases with topical corticosteroid creams or oral antihistamines.

Differential Diagnosis

Hemorrhoids, fistula, fissures, tumors of the anorectum, infections, contact dermatitis, psoriasis, Bowen's disease or Paget's disease are other possibilities.

Specialists

- Dermatologist
- Gastroenterologist
- Gynecologist
- Proctologist

Work Restrictions / Accommodations

No general work restrictions or accommodations apply to this condition.

Complementary and Alternative Therapies

Content is intended for awareness only. Treatments may or may not be effective. Scientific evidence may be lacking and some substances have potentially toxic effects. Dr. Presley Reed and the editors do not endorse the use of these therapies in the absence of consultation with a licensed medical professional.

Thyme tea or verbena -	Compresses applied directly to the itchy anal area may decrease itching.
Herb therapy -	Massaging the itchy area with a dilute solution of chamomile, aspic, cedarwood, or niaouli may decrease itching.
"Rescue Remedy" -	This is an herbal remedy that is taken internally as a drink. It is made from equal amounts of essences of cherry plum, rock rose, impatiens, clematis, and star of Bethlehem, all mixed into brandy. This may decrease itching.

Comorbid Conditions

Comorbid conditions include skin allergies and inability to tolerate antihistamines.

Complications

Severe excoriation, ulceration and secondary infection of the perineum are complications.

Factors Influencing Duration

If procedures are performed to correct associated factors (hemorrhoids, anal fistula, incompetent anal sphincter). Infections resistant to medications would also lengthen the disability, as would cases of pruritus ani due to psychological problems that were not diagnosed or effectively treated.

Length of Disability

In most cases, no disability is expected.

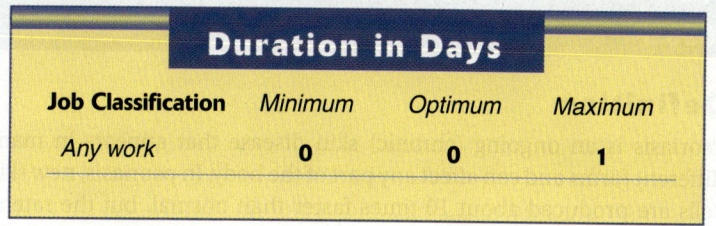

Duration in Days

Job Classification	Minimum	Optimum	Maximum
Any work	0	0	1

Failure to Recover

If an individual fails to recover within the maximum duration expectancy period, the reader may wish to reference the following questions to assist in better understanding the specifics of an individual's medical case.

Regarding diagnosis:

- Does the individual complain of severe itching of the anal area?
- Does the itching seem worse at night during sleep?
- Does the physician note red, irritated skin, bumps, an unusual thickening or softening of the skin, and scratches or breaks in the skin from scratching on exam?
- Does the physician note hemorrhoids or evidence of an incompetent anal sphincter after exam of the anus and rectum with a gloved finger?
- Have blood tests, analysis of feces, and a skin biopsy been done?
- Has proctocolonoscopy been done?
- Has the diagnosis been confirmed? If not, what else can be done to make the diagnosis?

Regarding treatment:

- Has the underlying cause been identified and is it being adequately treated?
- Has the individual been instructed to watch certain intake of foods?
- Have hygiene issues, whether inadequate or too vigorous, been addressed?
- Does the individual use corticosteroid cream and/or antihistamines? Is the individual compliant with these medications?
- Has the individual returned to be re-examined?

Regarding prognosis:

- Has treatment been effective? If not, is there an underlying cause that has not been identified?
- Has the individual made all changes required, such as hygiene, diet, and medication?
- Has the individual developed complications of this condition?
- If so, how will they be treated and what is the expected outcome with treatment?

References

Kantor, Gary R. "Pruritis." Principles and Practice of Dermatology, 2nd ed. Sams, W. Mitchell, and Peter J. Lynch, eds. New York: Churchill Livingstone, 1996. 881-885.

Psoriasis

Other names / synonyms: Eruptive Psoriasis, Plaque Psoriasis

696.1

Definition

Psoriasis is an ongoing (chronic) skin disease that appears in many different forms and can affect any part of the body. In psoriasis, new skin cells are produced about 10 times faster than normal, but the rate at which old cells are shed remains unchanged. As a result, the live cells stack up, becoming thickened patches covered by the dead, flaking skin.

The most common type of psoriasis is called plaque psoriasis. This form of psoriasis is characterized by raised, thickened patches of red skin, covered with silvery-white scales. These patches (plaques) generally begin as little red bumps that gradually grow larger and eventually develop scales. These patches become itchy and irritated. While any part of the body can be affected, the elbows, knees, groin, genitals, arms, legs, scalp, and nails are the most common sites. If the nails are affected, they will generally be pitted or thickened. Usually, the same place on both sides of the body will be affected.

Pustular psoriasis is characterized by pus-like blisters. Erythrodermic psoriasis is characterized by intense redness and swelling of a large part of the skin surface. Guttate psoriasis, usually affecting children and young adults, is characterized by small drop-like lesions. Inverse psoriasis, more common in older adults, is characterized by smooth red lesions in the folds of the skin, generally in the groin, armpits, buttocks, genitals, and under the breasts.

Although the exact cause of psoriasis is unknown, heredity is a factor as two-thirds of the individuals with psoriasis have a close family member who is also affected. Individual or family history of allergy is also associated with psoriasis. Other risk factors include local injury, local irritation, infection, hormonal changes, physical or emotional stress, sudden withdrawal of certain medications (steroids), alcohol use, and obesity.

Individuals between the ages of 16-22 and those between the ages of 57-60 have the highest incidence of this condition, although psoriasis can develop at any age. Whites are more commonly affected than other races; men and women are affected equally. Psoriasis affects 1-3% of the population, with about 150,000 new cases diagnosed each year.

Diagnosis

History: The signs and symptoms of psoriasis will come and go, with varying degrees of severity. Most individuals have stable, slowly growing patches (plaques) of scaly, thickened skin. The patches may be itchy or sore. Attempts to remove the scales may cause pinpoint bleeding (Auspitz sign). Seven to ten percent of individuals will complain of joint stiffness (psoriatic arthritis). Some will report a history of skin injury 1-2 weeks prior to the development of the skin lesions. Some individuals will report a sore throat (generally associated with guttate psoriasis).

Physical exam: Findings will vary depending on the form of psoriasis. Plaque psoriasis is the most common form, and is characterized by red, raised, thickened patches of skin, covered with silvery-white scales. Any part of the body may be affected, but the elbows, knees, groin, genitals, arms, legs, scalp, and nails are the most common sites. If nails are affected, they may be pitted or thickened, and may also be only loosely attached to the nail bed. Hair loss in the affected area may be noted.

Pustular psoriasis will appear as pus-like blisters, which may be localized to the palms or soles. Guttate psoriasis, usually in children and young adults, is characterized by small, drop-like, scaly spots. These spots occur all over the body, but are most concentrated on the trunk. Erythrodermic psoriasis is characterized by intense redness and swelling of large areas of the body. Inverse psoriasis, seen mostly in older adults, involves smooth, red lesions in the folds of the skin, particularly beneath the breasts, the groin, genitals, buttocks, and armpits.

Tests: If a certain diagnosis cannot be made from the history and physical exam, further testing would include a skin scraping examined under a microscope to check for other causes of the rash. If necessary, a skin biopsy will show the characteristic changes of psoriasis. Since 10-20% of the cases are associated with arthritis, blood tests for other diseases that can cause arthritis are usually done.

Treatment

Currently, there is no cure for psoriasis. Treatment will vary depending on the individual's age, lifestyle, health, symptoms, and severity of disease. Frequent visits to the dermatologist's office may be necessary.

Mild episodes of psoriasis may be helped by exposure to sunlight or an ultraviolet lamp (actinotherapy). Moisturizing creams and lotions loosen scales and help control itching. In addition, medications to be applied to the skin may also be prescribed. Medications include steroids, vitamin A derivatives, vitamin D derivatives, coal tar, or medication that sensitizes the skin to the effects of sunlight (photosensitizers).

Moderate-to-severe episodes are usually treated with an ointment that contains coal tar combined with ultraviolet light. This treatment, the Goeckerman treatment, when applied daily over a period of a month, can produce remissions of one year or longer.

If the psoriasis fails to respond to these treatments, then a type of phototherapy (PUVA) is used. It involves drugs taken by mouth before strong ultraviolet light (UVA) is directed at the lesions. When repeated 2-3 times a week, the psoriasis clears in 90% of the individuals within 2 months.

In severe cases, oral psoriasis medication (antipsoriatic) or prescription oral vitamin A-related drugs may be prescribed.

Arthritis symptoms can be alleviated with medications that reduce inflammation (nonsteroidal anti-inflammatory medications).

Prognosis

Psoriasis is considered a chronic condition, with no permanent cure. However, individual episodes can be relieved with appropriate treatment. While the signs and symptoms of psoriasis can be terribly bothersome and cosmetically unappealing, most cases of psoriasis do not represent serious medical conditions. However, one type, erythrodermic psoriasis, can be life-threatening.

Differential Diagnosis

Several conditions share signs or symptoms with psoriasis and should be considered when making this diagnosis. These include seborrheic dermatitis, impetigo, Candidiasis, onychomycosis, pityriasis rosea, pityriasis rubra pilaris, tinea corporis, squamous cell carcinoma, secondary and tertiary syphilis, cutaneous lupus erythematosus, eczema, lichen planus, localized scratch dermatitis (lichen simplex chronicus), mycosis fungoides, Reiter's disease, subcorneal pustulosis, and pustular eruptions.

Specialists

- Dermatologist
- Rheumatologist

Work Restrictions / Accommodations

Work restrictions and accommodations will depend on location and extent of condition, the severity of symptoms, and the nature of the job. Lesions on limbs, knees, elbows, palms, or soles may prohibit certain types of work, or limit an individual's ability to perform certain duties.

Individuals with psoriatic arthritis may have difficulty with tasks requiring flexibility and/or dexterity. If the job requires these types of tasks (such as professional musicians, typists, cashiers, bank tellers, etc.) a change in jobs may be required.

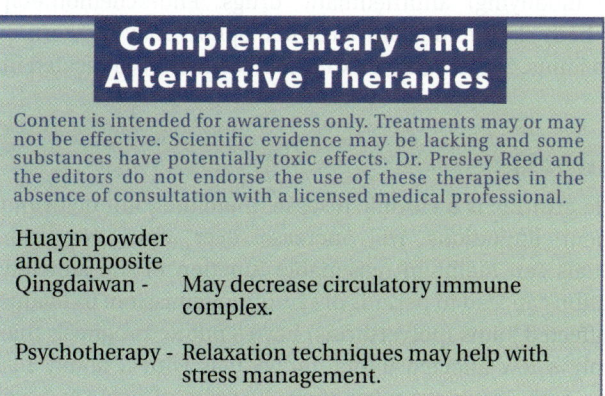

Complementary and Alternative Therapies

Content is intended for awareness only. Treatments may or may not be effective. Scientific evidence may be lacking and some substances have potentially toxic effects. Dr. Presley Reed and the editors do not endorse the use of these therapies in the absence of consultation with a licensed medical professional.

Huayin powder and composite Qingdaiwan - May decrease circulatory immune complex.

Psychotherapy - Relaxation techniques may help with stress management.

Comorbid Conditions

Individuals with restricted mobility may not be able to apply medications to the affected areas, which may result in longer disability.

Complications

Psoriasis can be accompanied by painful swelling and stiffness of the joints (psoriatic arthritis).

Factors Influencing Duration

Disability depends on the severity of symptoms, location of the lesions, and extent of disease. Psoriatic arthritis can also increase the length of disability.

Length of Disability

Duration in Days

Job Classification	Minimum	Optimum	Maximum
Any work	0	0	5

Failure to Recover

If an individual fails to recover within the maximum duration expectancy period, the reader may wish to reference the following questions to assist in better understanding the specifics of an individual's medical case.

Regarding diagnosis:

- Does individual have any risk factors (such as a family history of psoriasis, local injury or inflammation, stress, hormonal changes, alcohol or steroid use)?
- Did individual present with symptoms such as intermittent outbreaks of the red, scaly, thickened skin, particularly on the elbows, knees, groin, arms, legs, scalp, nails?
- Did the physical exam reveal red, scaly, or pustular lesions on the breasts, elbows, knees, groin, genitals, arms, legs, scalp, buttocks, or armpits?
- Was the diagnosis confirmed with a skin biopsy?
- Did the diagnostic work-up include blood tests to detect the associated finding of arthritis?
- If the diagnosis was uncertain, were other conditions with similar symptoms (seborrheic dermatitis, impetigo, Candidiasis, onychomycosis, pityriasis rosea, pityriasis rubra pilaris, tinea corporis, squamous cell carcinoma, secondary and tertiary syphilis, cutaneous lupus erythematosus, eczema, lichen planus, localized scratch dermatitis [lichen simplex chronicus], mycosis fungoides, Reiter's disease, subcorneal pustulosis, and pustular eruptions) considered in the differential diagnosis?

Regarding treatment:

- Has individual responded favorably to phototherapy? If not, were topical medications and moisturizing creams tried?
- Did individual warrant treatment with oral antipsoriatic or vitamin A-related drugs?
- Were symptoms of arthritic pain managed with NSAIDs?

Regarding prognosis:

- Have necessary work accommodations been made so individual can return to work safely?
- Has individual been compliant with treatment recommendations? If not, are physical restrictions impairing the ability to apply topical treatments?
- Does individual have any underlying conditions or associated complications that may impact recovery and prognosis?

References

Jaster, Paul. "Psoriasis." *Griffith's 5-minute Clinical Consult.* Dambro, Mark, ed. Philadelphia: Lippincott, Williams & Wilkins, 2000. 890-891.

What is Psoriasis? American Academy of Dermatology. 01 Jan 2000. 01 Jan 2001 <http://www.skincarephysicians.com/psoriasisnet/whatis.htm>.

Walsh, D. "Using Aromatherapy in the Management of Psoriasis." *Nursing Standards* 11 13-15 (1996): 53-56.

Yang, L.P., X.F. Jiang, and Y.B. Guang. "Clinical Observation on Fumigation and Inhalation of Huayin Powder in Treating Psoriasis." *Chung Kuo Chung Hsi I Chieh HoTsa Chih* 16 11 (1996): 655-657.

Psoriatic Arthritis
696.0

Definition

Psoriatic arthritis is an autoimmune arthritic disease marked by inflammation of the ligaments, tendons, fascia, and joint capsule (enthesitis).

Psoriatic arthritis is characterized by greater involvement of the joints of the upper limbs, especially the hands. Small joints of the feet, and large joints of the legs, such as hips, knees, and ankles, may be also involved. Most commonly, psoriatic arthritis affects fewer than 5 joints. Unlike other types of arthritis, psoriatic arthritis usually has an asymmetric distribution. Psoriatic arthritis is broken down into the following 5 subtypes: arthritis affecting the small joints of toes and fingers, asymmetrical arthritis of the extremities, symmetrical arthritis that resembles rheumatoid arthritis, deforming and destructive arthritis (arthritis mutilans), and arthritis of the spine and sacroiliac joints (psoriatic spondylitis).

Psoriasis is the second most common cause of arthritis with osteoarthritis being first. Approximately 6-10% of individuals with psoriasis develop psoriatic arthritis. The cause of psoriatic arthritis is unknown but genetic, immunologic, and environmental factors (infection, trauma) are considered to be important components.

In contrast to rheumatoid arthritis, psoriatic arthritis shows no gender preference. Psoriatic arthritis usually presents itself when an individual is between 35-45 years of age. Sixty percent of individuals with psoriatic arthritis have pre-existing skin psoriasis, 15% develop skin and arthritic psoriasis simultaneously, and 25% have psoriatic arthritis before skin involvement.

Diagnosis

History: Psoriasis is usually present. There may be a family history of psoriatic arthritis. The individual may complain of pain, stiffness, and swelling of certain joints, usually the small joints of the hand and feet. Other complaints may include acne, back pain, and chest pain. Reports of fever, fatigue, and anorexia are rare. Symptoms may be more extreme depending upon the climate (humid or cold).

Physical exam: Swelling, and in severe, chronic cases, deformity of the joints, especially those of the fingers, can be observed. "Sausage digits" (dactylitis) of the hands and feet are common in individuals with psoriatic arthritis. Affected joints often have a purplish discoloration. Loss of fluid (effusion) from the joint may be detected. Nails of the affected digits may be pitted or crumbling. Characteristic psoriatic lesions may be seen on the skin.

Tests: No currently recognized laboratory findings are diagnostic of psoriatic arthritis. Blood tests may include erythrocyte sedimentation rate, hemoglobin, rheumatoid factor, C-reactive protein, uric acid, human leukocyte antigen (HLA) typing, and autoantibodies. A sample of joint fluid may be analyzed. X-ray and CT scanning are required for diagnosis. An eye examination may be performed to detect psoriatic changes to the eyes.

Treatment

Treatment includes NSAIDs, corticosteroids, and slow-reacting (or disease modifying) antirheumatic drugs. Photochemotherapy can benefit both skin lesions and arthritis. Splints may be worn over the affected joints. Surgery (hip or knee replacement) is indicated in severe cases.

Prognosis

Psoriatic arthritis is a chronic disease, therefore joint deformities and movement limitations will increase over time. However, most individuals can maintain reasonable function of the afflicted joints. Medication can lead to periods of symptom remission. Individuals with many affected joints (polyarthritis) have a poorer prognosis than those with only a few affected joints. Individuals with a family history of arthritis, early onset (younger than 20 years of age), or severe skin psoriasis have a poor prognosis. Approximately 40% of individuals develop inflammatory arthritis of the back (spondyloarthropathy), which is usually more advanced in men than in women. Up to 16% of individuals progress to a severe stage characterized by joint disintegration (lysis) or immobility (ankylosis). Individuals with psoriatic arthritis have an increased risk for death as compared to the general population (standardized mortality ratio of 1.62).

Differential Diagnosis

The clinical features of psoriatic arthritis strongly resemble those of rheumatoid arthritis, rheumatoid arthritis of the spine (ankylosing spondylitis), Reiter's disease, vertebral inflammation (spondylitis) associated with ulcerative colitis or Crohn's disease, and arthritis associated with infection by the AIDS virus (HIV).

Specialists

- Orthopedic Surgeon
- Rheumatologist

Rehabilitation

Physical therapy plays a role in the management of arthritis; however, it may not be able to change disease outcome. Physical therapy is an ongoing process that is directed at improving joint function and includes passive range of motion exercises daily, and isometric and isotonic exercises every other day. Thirty minutes of low-impact exercise (swimming, walking, bicycling, etc.) on most days of the week is recommended. The individual would be instructed on how to continue these exercises at home.

Work Restrictions / Accommodations

Individuals are advised to avoid tasks that are potentially injurious including those that cause extreme joint stress and repetitive micro-injury. Work place modifications depend upon the location of the affected joints. Special attention must be paid to orthotics to improve weight-bearing patterns.

Comorbid Conditions

Obesity, osteoporosis, and AIDS may increase the length of disability.

Complications

Development of severe destructive arthritis may complicate psoriatic arthritis. Side effects (liver and lung damage) of drugs used in the treatment of psoriatic arthritis can complicate psoriatic arthritis.

Factors Influencing Duration

The severity of the condition, location and number of afflicted joints, effectiveness of treatment, and job demands will influence the length of disability.

Length of Disability

Duration depends upon job requirements; disability may be permanent for individuals who perform very heavy work.

Single episode.

Duration in Days

Job Classification	Minimum	Optimum	Maximum
Sedentary work	1	2	3
Light work	1	2	3
Medium work	3	5	7
Heavy work	3	5	10
Very Heavy work	3	5	10

Failure to Recover

If an individual fails to recover within the maximum duration expectancy period, the reader may wish to reference the following questions to assist in better understanding the specifics of an individual's medical case.

Regarding diagnosis:
- Does the individual have any risk factors for psoriasis?
- What other symptoms are present?
- Does the individual have psoriasis?
- Were swelling, deformity of the joints, or other symptoms characteristic of psoriasis present on physical exam?
- Has the individual received the appropriate testing?
- Have conditions with similar symptoms been ruled out?

Regarding treatment:
- Has the individual responded favorably to medications?
- Has surgery become necessary?

Regarding prognosis:
- Has the individual been instructed in physical therapy?
- Has individual incorporated them into their home exercise program?
- Is the individual's employer able to accommodate these restrictions?
- Does the individual follow the restrictions at home as well?
- Is the individual obese?
- Does the individual have any underlying conditions such as AIDS or osteoporosis that may affect recovery?
- If needed is the individual in counseling with an appropriate mental health provider?
- Does the individual have any complications?

References

FitzGerald, Oliver, and Kane, David. "Clinical, Immunopathogenic, and Therapeutic Aspects of Psoriatic Arthritis." Current Opinion in Rheumatology 9 (1997): 295-301.

Gladman, Dafna. "Psoriatic Arthritis." Rheumatologic Disease Clinics of North America 24 (1998): 829-844.

Kramer, N. "Why I Would Not Recommend Complementary or Alternative Therapies: A Physician's Perspective." Rheumatologic Disease Clinics of North America 25 4 (1999): 833-43,vii.

McGonagle, Dennis, Phillip Conaghan, and Paul Emery. "Psoriatic Arthritis." Arthritis and Rheumatism 42 6 (1999): 1080-1086.

Pitzalis, C. "Skin and Joint Disease in Psoriatic Arthritis: What is the Link?" British Journal of Rheumaology 37 5 (1998): 480-482.

Wilke, William. "Psoriatic Arthritis." Handbook of Psoriasis. Camisa, Charles Malden, ed.: Blackwell Science, Inc, 1998. 275-292.

Psychoanalysis

Other names / synonyms: Freudian Analysis, Psychoanalytic Psychotherapy

94.31

Definition

Psychoanalysis is an intensive, long-term psychotherapeutic process derived from the insights and writings of Sigmund Freud, his associates, and contemporaries. The goal of psychoanalysis is to achieve an understanding of repressed childhood memories and feelings, and of how these memories and feelings negatively affect adult reality. Psychoanalysis traces these unconscious factors back to their origins in the early parent/child relationship, demonstrates how the factors affect current relationships and patterns of behavior, shows how the factors change and develop over time, and, as a result, helps the individual to deal better with the current realities of life.

Four major concepts of the psychoanalytic process are free association, recall and interpretation of dreams, transference, and resistance. Free association occurs when an individual relates, to the analyst, all thoughts, feelings, and desires that come to mind, without holding anything back, and then works with the analyst to interpret this long-repressed material and its relation to current reality. Dream interpretation involves the recall and discussion of dreams, which are considered to be an outlet for unconscious desires and feelings in symbolic form. Transference occurs when an individual unconsciously applies to the analyst attitudes or feelings the individual had for a parent or other significant person from the past. The analyst then helps the individual to recognize these transferred feelings and work through or resolve inner conflicts and anxieties related to these transferred feelings or desires. Resistance (the individual's reluctance to talk about certain desires, feelings, or situations) is seen as a sign of painful material that must be dealt with in order for the individual to resolve their issues.

Reason for Procedure

The individual undergoing psychoanalysis hopes to gain greater self-understanding, relief from anxiety, and improved interpersonal relationships. Some of the symptoms that can be addressed by psychoanalysis are depression, anxiety, sexual incapacitates, physical symptoms without an obvious underlying physical cause (somatization), compulsions, repetitive thoughts, self-destructive behavior patterns, or eating disorders. Individuals who are experiencing auditory or visual hallucinations (psychosis) or who are in an emotional or psychological crisis, are generally not considered to be appropriate candidates for psychoanalysis.

Description

Psychoanalysis is performed by specially trained psychiatrists, psychologists, or therapists. However, as the designation "psychoanalyst" is not protected by law, and even an untrained person may use the title, it is important to know the practitioner's credentials before beginning treatment. The individual undergoing psychoanalysis usually attends sessions with the analyst up to 4 to 5 times weekly for a lengthy period of time, sometimes several years, in order to work though the insights gained and to observe the impact these insights have on daily life and relationships. The individual talks about anything and everything that comes to his or her consciousness, slowly becoming aware of difficult emotions, conflicts, and patterns of behavior. The analyst helps clarify these insights for the individual, who refines, corrects, rejects, and adds further thoughts and feelings, attempting to modify troublesome life patterns and symptoms. In order to encourage expression of thoughts and feelings, the individual undergoing analysis usually lies on a couch or sits comfortably during a session while the analyst is positioned behind the individual in order to decrease any distractions to the individual's ability to speak freely.

Prognosis

Most individuals who undergo the psychoanalysis experience gain an unusual understanding of problematic patterns of thoughts or behavior, relationship difficulties, and sense of self. Actual behavioral change and therapeutic success is difficult to document.

Specialists

- Psychiatrist
- Psychologist

Work Restrictions / Accommodations

Work restrictions and accommodations are related to the specific disorders. A flexible work schedule may be helpful, but most psychoanalysis sessions should be scheduled during the individual's personal time.

Comorbid Conditions

Alcohol abuse or drug use or the presence of more than one psychiatric illness may lengthen disability. Psychoanalysis in and of itself should not be associated with any disability.

Procedure Complications

Some individuals may feel that an immediate problem or crisis is being neglected in order to focus on long-term insight and change. Uncovering repressed conflicts or reliving painful emotional traumas may cause the individual to decompensate for a period of time, during which there may be increased depression or anxiety, or decreased ability to function.

Factors Influencing Duration

Length of disability is influenced by the duration and severity of any underlying mental illness, substance abuse or dependency, the individual's social support system, and compliance with scheduled psychotherapy sessions.

Length of Disability

No disability is expected to result from this therapy. Disability may occur as a result of an underlying condition.

References

About Psychoanalysis. American Psychoanalytic Association. 20 Jan 2000. 18 Nov 2000 <http://www.apsa.org/pubinfo/about.htm>.

Grunbaum, Adolf. "A Century of Psychoanalysis: Critical Retrospect and Prospect." University of Pittsburgh's Newsletter of its Center for West European Studies. 1998 Feb 1999 18 Nov 2000 <http://www.pol-it.com//ital/9grunb-i.htm>.

Psychopharmacotherapy
Other names / synonyms: Psychotropic Drug Therapy, Psychotropic Medication Therapy
94.25

Definition

Psychopharmacotherapy is the use of medications in the treatment of psychiatric disorders. These medications are frequently referred to as psychoactive or psychotropic medications. The medications used in psychopharmacotherapy are usually prescription medications, but these medications may occasionally be supplemented by alternative medicine therapy, such as herbal medications or nutritional supplements.

Most psychoactive/psychotropic medications are developed for the treatment of psychiatric disorders such as depression or schizophrenia. However, some medications developed for other purposes have been found to be helpful in psychiatric disorders. For instance, anticonvulsant medications, developed for the treatment of seizure disorders, have also been found to be helpful in managing bipolar mood disorders.

There are 5 major classifications of therapeutic psychoactive/psychotropic medications commonly used in the treatment of psychiatric disorders. Antipsychotic drugs (neuroleptics or major tranquilizers) help manage psychotic symptoms such as agitation, hearing or seeing things that aren't there (hallucinations), false beliefs (delusions), and disorganized thinking. They also calm and sedate the individual, but slow thought processes and motor activity. Anxiolytic sedatives decrease levels of anxiety and agitation. Antimanic agents decrease levels of agitation, increased motor and mental activity, and delusions seen in mania. Antidepressants reduce depression and improve mood. As psychostimulants increase levels of alertness, they are useful in attention deficit disorder and similar conditions.

Psychopharmacotherapy may be used alone or in conjunction with talk therapy (psychotherapy) to help reduce the negative symptoms of anxiety, depression, mania, psychosis, and other psychiatric disorders. A 1995 survey of psychoanalysts in training showed that they had prescribed medication to 20% of their patients in the preceding 5 years, and that 30% of their patients were taking psychoactive medications.

Reason for Procedure

Psychiatric drugs are most commonly used to treat anxiety, depression, mania, psychosis, or attention deficit hyperactivity disorder (ADHD).

Psychopharmacotherapy is designed to ease the symptoms of mental distress, either by correcting a biochemical imbalance or by giving the individual more energy to address the underlying conflicts that produced the symptoms. Psychopharmacotherapy can be life-saving in situations of suicidal depression or manic-depression. Medications may be used to improve or stabilize moods, decrease or suppress hallucinations and thought disorders, calm anxiety or agitation, improve memory, increase energy and alertness, and moderate hyperactivity.

Description

Medications must be prescribed by a psychiatrist or other licensed physician. Any individual receiving medications should be followed by a physician to ensure that the medication is having the desired effect and that there are no unmanageable side effects. Most psychotropic medications are administered by mouth, but some can be given by injection into a muscle. The duration of effect depends on the type of medication it is. Antianxiety and antipsychotic medications can have an effect within a few minutes or a few hours, while some antidepressants may not reach their full effect for several weeks. Dosages or changes in medication schedules may be necessary, depending upon the individual's response.

The administration of some medications, such as the mood stabilizer lithium or the antipsychotic Clozaril, must include regular blood tests to check for potentially life-threatening side effects. In many instances, an individual may need more than one psychotropic medication to achieve the desired effect. The method of how to select and combine psychotropic medications for optimum effect is usually monitored best by an appropriately trained psychiatrist. When the individual is also receiving psychotherapy, medications are sometimes prescribed by the analyst or therapist, if he or she is a physician. However, it is preferable in some cases for medications to be administered and monitored by another psychiatrist not involved in the talk therapy. Individuals receiving psychopharmacotherapy usually do so on an outpatient basis, unless their symptoms, such as psychosis or suicide tendencies, are severe enough to require hospitalization.

Prognosis

Many individuals achieve full recovery from their symptoms with the administration of appropriate medications. In some instances, such as acute depression, medications can be discontinued after a period of time and will not need to be reinstated as long as the individual's symptoms are absent. In other instances, such as bipolar disorder or schizophrenia, medication therapy may need to be continued for as long as symptoms are present, which may be life long.

Specialists

- Advanced Practice Registered Nurse
- Psychiatrist
- Psychologist

Work Restrictions / Accommodations

Any work modification will be based on the specific psychiatric illness, as well as any side effects of drug treatment. Depending upon the underlying disorder, work accommodations may include modifying the work space to decrease noise and visual distractions; introducing the individual to new or stressful situations gradually under appropriate supervision and support; providing flexibility in work schedule for medical or psychiatric appointments; allowing break time according to individual needs rather than a fixed schedule; providing praise and positive reinforcement; and reducing or eliminating activities requiring constant and high levels of alertness, such as driving or operating machinery.

Comorbid Conditions

Alcohol abuse or drug use or the presence of another psychiatric illness may lengthen disability. Coexistence of more than one type of psychiatric illness may necessitate use of more than one type of medication, which may complicate drug therapy because of medication interactions. Medical illness, such as liver damage or kidney failure, may interfere with breakdown (metabolism) and elimination (excretion) of psychoactive drugs, requiring decreased dosage, use of different medications, or careful monitoring for side effects. Chronic medical conditions may require the use of medications, which may also create adverse interactions with psychoactive drugs. Neurologic conditions such as Parkinson's disease may be aggravated by the use of antipsychotic medications.

Procedure Complications

All medications have potential side effects, ranging from fairly mild effects, such as indigestion, nausea or dry mouth, to severe allergic reactions or potentially serious effects such as depressed bone marrow cell production. Some undesirable effects of psychotropic medications are related to the mechanism of action of the drug. For example, antipsychotic drugs produce their calming effect by slowing thought processes and motor activity. Antidepressants may bring out manic tendencies in individuals with bipolar disorder. Side effects vary among individuals, and many side effects subside within the first few weeks of taking the medication.

The administration of some medications, such as the mood stabilizer lithium or the antipsychotic Clozaril, must include regular blood tests to check for potentially life-threatening side effects. When an individual receives prescription medications from a pharmacy, the medication is usually accompanied by written instructions which include a list of commonly encountered side effects as well as potentially severe side effects for that medication.

Complications may be avoided to some extent by not prescribing multiple medications at once (polypharmacy), by not exceeding the dose of the antipsychotic needed to control symptoms, and by an appropriate dosage schedule. Any physician prescribing psychoactive drugs should be aware of all other medications taken by the individual, as well as use of alcohol, recreational drugs, and supplements, and should actively communicate with other medical providers. Alcohol and recreational drug use should be discouraged, and may require withdrawal of psychopharmacotherapy if they are not discontinued.

Some psychotherapists feel that administration of psychoactive drugs may interfere with the psychoanalytic process. In some cases, this problem can be resolved by having a separate psychiatrist prescribe and monitor medications. However, in some cases, relief of anxiety, depression, or other psychiatric symptoms by psychoactive drugs may interfere with the individual's motivation to address underlying psychiatric conflicts.

Factors Influencing Duration

The specific psychiatric illness and its severity, along with any complications of treatment, will influence disability. All psychiatric drugs cause mild, unwanted side effects such as dry mouth or drowsiness. Adjustment to these effects usually occurs within a few days. The duration of the illness can affect disability as well; a longstanding, chronic psychiatric illness may have more disability than an acute illness. Response to drugs varies between different ethnic populations because of inherited (genetic) differences in how these drugs are broken down (metabolized).

Length of Disability

Disability will vary with the specific psychiatric illness. Changes in medication or dosage may require some adjustment to side effects. No disability is expected after appropriate medication and dosage have been determined.

Duration in Days

Job Classification	Minimum	Optimum	Maximum
Any work	1	7	14

References

Bailey, K.P. "Basic Principles of Psychopharmacologic Treatment for Advanced Practice Psychiatric Nurses with Prescriptive Authority." *Journal of Psychosocial Nursing and Mental Health Services* 37 4 (1999): 31-38.

Janicak, Philip G., et al. *Principles and Practice of Psychopharmacotherapy.* Philadelphia: Lippincott Williams & Wilkins, 2001.

Psychosexual Disorders

Other names / synonyms: Gender Identity Disorder, Paraphilia, Sexual Dysfunction

302, 302.2, 302.3, 302.6, 302.7, 302.70, 302.8, 302.9

Definition

This category includes sexual dysfunctions, sexual perversions (paraphilias), and gender identity disorders. Sexual dysfunction is characterized as a disturbance of sexual desire, arousal, or orgasm; sexual pain; or difficulties with sexual performance related to a medical condition, medication, or substance abuse.

Sexual perversions involve strong and recurrent sexual desire for unusual situations or objects. Examples are displaying one's genitals (exhibitionism); sexual desire for children (pedophilia), nonconsenting adults (sexual sadism), or objects (fetishism); observing other people unclothed or engaged in sexual activities (voyeurism); rubbing against someone or something for purposes of sexual stimulation (frottage or frotteurism); and cross-dressing (transvestic fetishism). In gender identity disorder, individuals are uncomfortable with their gender, and believe they should really be of the opposite gender and should live as such, which frequently leads them to have sex-change operations.

The sexual disorder may be present since the beginning of the individual's sexual functioning or may appear after initial normal functioning. It may be due primarily to psychological factors, a medical condition and the medications used to treat it, or to substance abuse.

Medical conditions resulting in sexual dysfunction include endometriosis, vaginal or urinary infections, lack of vaginal lubrication due to menopause or lactation, pelvic adhesions, radical pelvic surgery and/or radiation, spinal cord injury, cauda equina syndrome, diabetes, hypothyroidism, and multiple sclerosis.

Medications causing sexual dysfunction include antidepressants (especially serotonin-specific reuptake inhibitors), antipsychotic drugs, lithium, beta-blockers, anticholinergic drugs, antihistamines, antianxiety drugs, and barbiturates. Abuse of alcohol, opioids, or hallucinogens can also result in sexual dysfunction.

Diagnosis

History: History varies with the specific sexual disorder. DSM-IV criteria for sexual perversions require that unusual or bizarre imagery or acts are necessary for sexual excitement, are insistently or involuntarily repetitive, and interfere to varying degrees with the capacity for mutually affectionate sexual activity.

Physical exam: The exam may reveal a medical cause of sexual dysfunction but is not helpful in the sexual perversions. Observation of an individual's orientation, dress, mannerisms, behavior, and content of speech provide essential signs to diagnose the illness.

Tests: Tests may include endocrine studies for both men and women. A test for erections (penile tumescence) may be done for sexual perversion while individual views images of sexual obsession or done at night to check for erectile failure. Ultrasound studies may also be performed to measure genital blood flow.

Treatment

Once the medical causes underlying sexual dysfunctions are identified and treated, sex therapy may be helpful if the individual is involved in a relationship. Both members of the relationship are treated simultaneously. Sex therapy may be combined with supportive psychotherapy either individually or with the couple. Behavioral therapy may also involve desensitization and assertiveness training. Hypnotherapy may be helpful and focuses on the distressing symptoms. Group therapy can help support those with guilt, shame, or anxiety concerning a sexual problem. Medical treatment for erectile failure includes penile injections or surgical prostheses. For reduced desire or arousal, hormone therapy including androgens may be prescribed.

Androgen blockers can be useful for sexual perversions such as pedophilia or exhibitionism. The serotonin-specific reuptake inhibitors (SSRIs) are used for sexual perversions including voyeurism, exhibitionism, pedophilia, frotteurism, and for rapists. Estrogen, progesterone, and antiandrogens are given for compulsive sexual behavior in men. Behavior therapy is also used in sexual perversions and cognitive therapy addresses self-beliefs that lead to deviant behavior. Peer groups such as Sex Addicts Anonymous can be helpful. Psychodynamic psychotherapy and psychoanalysis are not usually effective.

Gender identity disorders can be treated with hormone therapy and sex change surgery to help the individual physically resemble the opposite sex. This is generally done only after rigorous psychological evaluation.

Prognosis

Outcome depends on the specific sexual disorder, but the disorders generally worsen when the amount of stress increases in an individual's life. Most sexual perversions are lifelong.

Differential Diagnosis

Sexual dysfunction may be the result of a major depressive episode, personality disorder, or a disturbed relationship with the sexual partner. A specific phobia may be a contributing factor. Gender identity conflicts may accompany schizophrenia or borderline personality disorder. Gender identity disorder may also be confused with endocrine or genetic abnormalities where individuals have ambiguous genitalia and share characteristics of both male and female organs. Individuals with antisocial personality disorder may commit acts of rape, pedophilia, or sexual sadism as a manifestation of that disorder rather than as an isolated sexual perversion.

Specialists

- Gynecologist
- Internist
- Psychiatrist
- Psychologist
- Urologist

Work Restrictions / Accommodations

Work modifications are usually not relevant unless specific issues exist with underlying medical condition.

Comorbid Conditions

Coexisting conditions that may affect recovery and lengthen disability include alcohol and drug abuse or another psychiatric disorder such as depression, phobias, mood disorders, and personality disorders. Sexual dysfunction is often associated with an underlying medical condition or the medication used to treat that condition.

Complications

Sexual dysfunctions can result in a failed relationship and subsequent depression. Sexual perversions may lead to arrest, criminal conviction, and loss of the individual's job or marriage (approximately one-half of individuals with sexual perversions are married). Surgery or hormonal treatments used in gender identity disorders may lead to complications or side effects.

Factors Influencing Duration

If the sexual disorder is due to a medical condition or substance abuse, the ability to treat the underlying condition influences the length of disability. Most treatment consists of outpatient appointments that should not affect ability to stay on a normal work schedule.

Length of Disability

This condition should not result in disability.

Failure to Recover

If an individual fails to recover within the maximum duration expectancy period, the reader may wish to reference the following questions to assist in better understanding the specifics of an individual's medical case.

Regarding diagnosis:
- Does the individual fit the criteria for a psychosexual disorder?
- Has diagnosis been confirmed?
- In sexual dysfunction, have underlying medical conditions or substance abuse been ruled out?

Regarding treatment:
- If sexual dysfunction was caused by a coexisting medical condition or substance abuse, has it improved with treatment of the underlying condition?
- If caused by a necessary medication, what other treatment options are available?
- Has treatment for sexual dysfunction included medical options for erectile failure, hormone therapy for reduced desire or arousal, and behavioral or sex therapy?
- Has hypnotherapy been used to focus on distressing symptoms?
- Has group therapy proved to be supportive if individual is experiencing guilt, shame or anxiety about a sexual problem?
- Have medications helped curtail inappropriate behaviors?
- Did behavior or cognitive therapy effectively address the individual's beliefs that led to the sexually inappropriate behavior?

Regarding prognosis:
- What life stressors is the individual dealing with at present?
- Because sexual perversions are life-long and generally worsen when stress increases in the individual's life, what stress reduction skills has the individual been taught?
- Would individual benefit from involvement in a peer group such as Sex Addicts Anonymous?

References

"Psychosexual Disorders." Merck Manual of Diagnosis and Therapy, 17th ed. Beers, Mark H., and Robert Berkow, MD Whitehouse Station, NJ: Merck & Co., Inc., 1999. 10 Oct 2000 <http://www.merck.com/pubs/mmanual/section15/chapter192/192a.htm>.

First, Michael B., ed. Diagnostic and Statistical Manual of Mental Disorders. 4th ed. Washington, DC: American Psychiatric Association, 1994.

Psychotherapy, Group

Other names / synonyms: Group Therapy, Therapist-Guided Support Group

94.44

Definition

Group psychotherapy is a procedure or technique used for the treatment of emotional disorders such as depression, anxiety, or post-traumatic stress disorders or behavioral disorders such as conduct disorders or substance abuse. One or two therapists guide a group that is typically limited to 10-12 individuals. Psychological changes in the group members are facilitated by their interaction with each other and the therapist(s).

Some therapy groups have specific themes or commonalities among members such as recovery from substance abuse, management of panic attacks, or grief recovery. The therapist selects other groups based on knowledge of each individual's emotional or developmental issues. The group acts as a miniature version of society. What happens in the group is similar to how an individual's strengths, weaknesses, and interpersonal interactions play out in the world. Sooner or later, each individual's characteristic difficulties in relating to others such as anger, arrogance, or impatience come out in full view before the group.

Receiving feedback from both the therapist and fellow group members allows the individual to identify his or her troublesome interpersonal behavior, express feelings associated with the behavior, and get a more objective view of the behavior and its effect on others. The intent is for the individual to gain insight into how they behave with others and how this behavior is related to personal issues, thus allowing the individual to identify and practice behavioral and relational changes.

Therapeutic factors identified as occurring in group therapy include feeling accepted by other members of the group (acceptance), experiencing that the group is working toward a common goal (cohesiveness), correction of distortions in interpersonal relationships (validation and reality testing), having the chance to work through old family and interpersonal conflicts (a corrective family and interpersonal experience), learning what another individual experiences and feels (empathy), and becoming hopeful from the example of others (inspiration).

Reason for Procedure

Group therapy is used to treat a wide variety of psychological disorders with the goal of symptom relief. A more ambitious aim may also be modification of personality or behavior change such as seen in an eating disorder or staying at home out of fear (agoraphobia). Group psychotherapy is often as effective as individual psychotherapy. It is currently being used for groups with the same medical condition such as breast cancer or heart attack to improve the quality of life and extend length of survival.

Description

Group psychotherapy generally treats 10 to 12 individuals at the same time and is facilitated by 1 or 2 therapists. Meetings are usually held weekly at 1 to 2 hours per meeting and may be time-limited (e.g., lasting 12 sessions). The therapist screens individuals to determine suitability for group therapy. Individuals agreeing to group psychotherapy should have the motivation to change and be able to perform the group tasks. Tasks include regular attendance, agreeing on the therapeutic goals, being committed to the work of therapy, listening respectfully to others without inappropriate interruptions, and keeping confidential about what others say during a group session.

Most groups go through several developmental stages including a formative stage, a period of initial resistance to change and feedback from therapists or peers, the development of a feeling of cohesiveness among group members, emergence of solutions and the ability of the group to achieve its goals, and a period of closure.

The therapist initially introduces group members and rules of interaction, maintains time limits, identifies issues that need to be pursued either in the group or individually, and provides general direction. As the group matures, the therapist may take a less directive role, allowing individuals to accept leadership roles, as appropriate. Several group therapy models can be used depending on the purpose of the group. In general, however, each individual has an opportunity to present his or her feelings or issues for a short period each session. From time to time, individuals have a longer period during the sessions for more intense focus on personal issues and behaviors.

Techniques include the identification, expression, and release of feelings; feedback (objective observations or shared feelings) about an individual's perceptions, behavior, or issues; role-playing of difficult anticipated encounters with significant others; or structured group exercises to identify specific feelings or issues.

Prognosis

Most group members experience some decrease in symptoms such as social anxiety, an improved ability to interact with others, or increased awareness of how their behavior affects others.

Specialists

- Psychiatrist
- Psychologist

Work Restrictions / Accommodations

Work restrictions and accommodations are related to the specific disorders. A flexible work schedule may be helpful, but most psychoanalysis sessions should be scheduled during the individual's personal time.

Comorbid Conditions

Alcohol abuse or drug use or another psychiatric illness can lengthen disability.

Procedure Complications

Some individuals may not have reached clinical stability to function in a group setting or have a level of tolerance for group feedback.

Factors Influencing Duration

Length of disability is influenced by the duration and severity of any underlying mental illness, substance abuse or dependency, the individual's social support system, and therapy group participation.

Length of Disability

No disability is expected to result from this therapy. Disability may occur as a result of an underlying condition.

References

Fehr, S.S. Introduction to Group Therapy: A Practical Guide. New York: Haworth Press, 1999.

Frances, Allen. Diagnostic and Statistical Manual of Mental Disorders: 4th ed, text revision. Washington, DC: American Psychiatric Association, 2000.

Rutan, S.J., and N.W. Stone. Psychodynamic Group Psychotherapy, 3rd ed. New York: Guilford Press, 2000.

Spitz, H.I., and S.T. Spitz. A Pragmatic Approach to Group Psychotherapy. Philadelphia: Brunner/Mazel, 1999.

Psychotherapy, Individual

Other names / synonyms: Analytical Therapy, Behavior Therapy, Cognitive Therapy, Cognitive-Behavioral Therapy, Freudian Therapy, Gestalt Theoretical Psychotherapy, Interpersonal Therapy, Jungian Therapy, Person-Centered Therapy, Psychoanalytic (Freudian) Therapy, Psychoanalytic Therapy, Rational-Emotive Therapy, Solution-Focused Brief Therapy, Talk Therapy

94.3

Definition

Psychotherapy is a general term covering many psychological treatment methods all taking place primarily through interaction with a trained therapist. With individual psychotherapy, the verbal interaction is between two individuals, the therapist and the individual seeking help. These two work together to identify and address the individual's problems with the expectation of making a positive change. The change is directed at characteristically fixed patterns of thought, feeling, or behavior that are causing difficulties.

The psychotherapist listens to what the individual has to say and tries to understand its meaning. A therapeutic alliance is developed with the two working together in a cooperative manner. The therapist has specific expertise in using communication and relationship in a helpful way usually based on a particular theory of personality and human behavior. These theories form the basis, goals, and techniques used in therapy. An individual's problem and treatment are usually linked to a particular theory as seen in cognitive therapy, cognitive-behavioral therapy, rational-emotive therapy, behavior therapy, person-centered therapy, interpersonal therapy, psychodynamic therapy, and others. Unfortunately, it is often not predictable which kind of therapy is most helpful for which individual experiencing which kind of disorder.

All forms of psychotherapy have some common therapeutic factors. The individual should view the therapist as someone who can help and can be trusted. Psychotherapy also provides a safe place for experiencing any and all emotions, provides new information and new meanings for seemingly unrelated symptoms and events, and creates the conditions to maximize success. In the process, symptoms may be relieved and unproductive patterns of behavior changed.

Reason for Procedure

The purpose of individual psychotherapy is to treat emotional, behavioral, or mental dysfunction, remove negative symptoms such as anxiety or depression, modify or reverse problem behaviors, help the individual cope with situational crises such as bereavement, pain, or prolonged medical illnesses, improve the individual's relationships, manage conflict, or enhance positive personality growth and development. There are a number of therapeutic approaches and techniques but all of them try to establish a relationship between the therapist and the individual who seeks to unlearn old or maladaptive patterns, gain insight, and learn more effective patterns of thinking and behavior.

Some approaches such as psychodynamic psychotherapy attempt to remove underlying personality conflicts. Others such as cognitive or behavior therapy focus more on direct removal of negative symptoms including depression, anxiety, obsessive-compulsive behavior, low self-esteem, marital conflicts, or substance abuse. Solution-focused brief therapy focuses on helping individuals construct solutions rather than solve problems.

Description

Individual psychotherapy is usually performed by a psychiatrist, psychoanalyst, clinical psychologist, or licensed mental health professional. The goals of therapy may include simple emotional support; insight into sources of thoughts, feelings, perceptions, or behaviors; relief of symptoms such as anxiety or depression; stress management; behavioral changes; or crisis intervention. Psychotherapy sessions can be short-term (4 to 6 sessions), intermediate (up to 6 months), or long-term (6 months to several years) and can occur several times a week, weekly, biweekly, or on an as-needed basis. Each session lasts about 50 minutes and is conducted by the therapist with a single individual.

During the initial period (usually the first session), the therapist attempts to establish rapport, assess the individual's needs, and determine therapeutic goals in cooperation with the individual. In an accepting, nonjudgmental atmosphere, the individual is encouraged to talk about feelings, fears and anxieties, relationship issues, problematic behaviors, or disturbing thoughts. The therapist listens and provides comment and feedback based on training and experience. The therapist guides the individual to a deeper insight and understanding of his or her thoughts, feelings, and behaviors and explores methods of self-acceptance or ways to make needed and desired changes.

There are a variety of therapeutic techniques under an umbrella of several major categories that include psychoanalysis, psychodynamic psychotherapy, cognitive psychotherapy, behavioral psychotherapy, marital or family psychotherapy, and brief psychotherapy. Psychoanalysis is derived from the works of Sigmund Freud and is a long-term approach taking several years where the goal is to help an individual recall, understand, and re-experience childhood conflicts in a way that allows insight and modification of destructive thoughts, feelings, or behaviors.

The psychodynamic psychotherapies draw on principles of psychoanalysis but focus on helping an individual modulate negative emotions. Rather than focusing on deep insight and change, they help maintain an acceptable level of functioning in a climate of unconditional acceptance and support. Cognitive psychotherapy focuses on the direct removal of negative symptoms such as anxiety and depression. By promoting discovery of irrational beliefs or thinking patterns related to negative feelings or behaviors, cognitive psychotherapy helps the individual develop methods to alter these negative patterns of thought or behavior.

The behavioral therapies are derived from learning theory. Through a variety of techniques such as desensitization and biofeedback, they focus on eliminating disruptive behavior patterns and substituting appropriate behaviors. Desensitization gradually exposes individuals to anxiety-provoking situations (phobias) until their anxiety decreases or disappears. A biofeedback session uses specialized equipment to help the individual realize how negative thoughts and feelings affect body processes such as heart rate or skin temperature.

In marital/family therapy, psychological symptoms of individual family members are thought to be expressions of disturbances in the social system of the family. The therapeutic goal is to focus on current issues and achieve improvement in relationship conflicts, communication patterns, emotional boundary management, and role-relationships. Brief psychotherapy is any type of therapeutic approach designed to bring about change in a short period of time, usually less than 20 therapy sessions.

Prognosis

Most individuals experience some decrease in symptoms or a change in fixed patterns of thought, feeling, or behavior that are causing difficulties. A number of studies have shown psychotherapy to be as effective as pharmacotherapy in many conditions. The ability of the individual and therapist to form a close therapeutic alliance is associated with better outcome, particularly in depression. A combination of psychotherapy and psychopharmacology has been documented as having the greatest effect for treating certain illnesses. With psychoanalysis, self-rating measures of symptom distress and morale are more likely to improve than self-rating measures of social relations.

Specialists

- Psychiatrist
- Psychologist

Work Restrictions / Accommodations

Work restrictions and accommodations are related to the specific disorders. A flexible work schedule may be helpful, but most psychoanalysis sessions should be scheduled during the individual's personal time.

Comorbid Conditions

Alcohol abuse or drug use or another psychiatric illness may lengthen disability.

Procedure Complications

Some individuals may not respond positively to a particular type of therapy or may be unable to develop an effective therapeutic relationship with the therapist.

Factors Influencing Duration

Length of disability is influenced by the duration and severity of any underlying mental illness, substance abuse or dependency, the individual's social support system, motivation to change, and compliance with scheduled psychotherapy sessions.

Length of Disability

No disability is expected to result from this therapy. Disability may occur as a result of an underlying condition.

References

Arnold, E.G., B.A. Farber, and J.D. Geller. "Changes in Patients' Self-representation Over the Course of Psychotherapy." Journal of American Academic Psychoanalysis 28 3 (2000): 449-466.

Gatchel, Robert J., and Ennis C. Turk. Psychological Approaches to Pain Management. New York: The Guilford Press, 1996.

Psychotic Disorder, Brief
Other names / synonyms: Brief Reactive Psychosis
298.8

Definition

Brief psychotic disorder is a short-term break from reality, or an acute episode of psychotic symptoms lasting more than a day but less than one month. The symptoms may or may not affect daily functioning, and may include fixed but false beliefs (delusions), hearing voices or seeing things that aren't there (hallucinations), disorganized speech, or seriously disorganized behavior. Confusion and mood shifts may also be present. The person may be screaming or silent, behavior or dress may be outlandish, and memory of recent events may be impaired. However, there is complete recovery after the episode to the pre-existing mental state.

The essential feature of brief psychotic disorder is the sudden onset of psychotic symptoms, sometimes but not always shortly after one or more events that would cause marked distress for most individuals. Examples of these events include wartime combat, an auto accident, or death of a loved one, which was previously termed a "brief reactive psychosis." Individuals who experience mental illness following pregnancy and delivery (postpartum psychosis) may also be given this diagnosis.

Onset of this condition usually occurs in individuals who are in their late twenties or early thirties. A pre-existing personality disorder such as histrionic, paranoid, or schizotypal personality disorder may make an individual more likely to have a brief psychotic disorder. This diagnosis is not made if a major mood disorder, schizoaffective disorder, or schizophrenia is present. It is not due to the effects of substance or alcohol abuse or a medical condition such as head injury. Although brief psychotic disorder is a rare condition, exact prevalence is difficult to estimate since the disorder is brief in duration.

Diagnosis

History: To decide whether a stressful event has caused a psychotic episode, it may be necessary for a mental health professional to interview a spouse, relative, or friend to learn about the individual's past history and the chronological relationship between the stressful event and the onset of symptoms. Warning signs reported by the family may include changes in eating or sleeping habits, energy level, or weight; confusion, inability to make decisions; hallucinations, delusions, ideas that do not connect or make sense; repetitive actions; hours of immobility; and strange statements and behaviors. They may stop socializing or going to work, and may be inattentive to personal hygiene.

When obtaining the individual's history, a mental health professional may notice false beliefs (delusions), hearing voices or seeing things that aren't there (hallucinations), disorganized speech, or severely disorganized behavior. Associated symptoms may include a learning problem, decreased activity (hypoactivity), elated (euphoric) or depressed mood, sexual dysfunction, or hyperactivity.

According to the DSM-IV, the following criteria must be satisfied to make the diagnosis. One or more of the following symptoms must be present: delusions, hallucinations, disorganized speech, or grossly disorganized behavior or severely withdrawn, immobile behavior (catatonia). If the symptom is a culturally sanctioned response, it cannot be included. Duration of the episode must be at least 1 day but less than 1 month, with eventual full return to premorbid level of functioning. The disturbance is not better explained by a mood disorder with psychotic features, schizoaffective disorder, or schizophrenia, and is not due to the direct physiological effects of a drug or medication or a general medical condition. The disorder can be specified as being with marked stressor(s) (if a major crisis precipitated the symptoms), without marked stressor(s), or with postpartum onset, if it began within 4 weeks of delivering a baby.

Physical exam: The exam does not contribute much to this diagnosis. However, observation of the individual's dress, mannerisms, behavior, and content of speech may provide helpful signs to diagnose the illness, such as evidence of poor hygiene, total lack of voluntary motion (catatonia), hyperactivity, lack of emotional reaction, or inappropriate emotional reaction, such as laughing at bad news.

Tests: Laboratory tests such as blood tests and urinalysis are needed to rule out substance intoxication or acute medical condition.

Treatment

Hospitalization is usually indicated, for psychiatric evaluation as well as for the protection of the individual and others. If the person's behavior is problematic, an antipsychotic medication or benzodiazepine may be employed. Shock therapy (electroconvulsive therapy) may be needed if medications fail to bring the individual back to reality. After the acute episode has subsided, psychotherapy or group therapy is useful to address a personality abnormality and any loss of self-esteem due to the psychotic symptoms. Support groups and family education may be helpful, while alcohol and recreational drugs should be avoided.

Prognosis

Recovery of mental functioning occurs within one month, without major psychiatric disturbances in the future. This quick recovery is inherent in the diagnosis.

Differential Diagnosis

Other possibilities are psychosis due to substance abuse, a medical condition, or delirium. If symptoms persist past one month, the diagnosis must be changed because a quick recovery is inherent in the diagnosis of brief psychotic disorder. The diagnosis may be changed to schizophrenia, schizophreniform disorder, schizoaffective disorder, mood disorder with psychotic features, or delusional disorder. Factitious disorder and malingering are other possible diagnoses.

Specialists

- Licensed Clinical Social Worker
- Psychiatrist
- Psychologist

Work Restrictions / Accommodations

Temporary work accommodations may include reducing or eliminating activities where the safety of self or others is contingent upon a constant and/or high level of alertness, such as driving a motor vehicle, operating complex machinery, or handling dangerous chemicals; introducing the individual to new or stressful situations gradually under individually appropriate supervision; allowing some flexibility in scheduling to attend therapy appointments (which normally should occur during the employee's personal time); promoting planned, proactive management of identified problem areas; and offering timely feedback on job performance issues. It will be helpful if accommodations are documented in a written plan designed to promote timely and safe transition back to full work productivity.

Comorbid Conditions

Coexisting conditions that may affect recovery include current alcohol and substance use, unresolved life-stressors, and the presence of a personality disorder. If symptoms persist past one month, the diagnosis must be changed because a quick recovery is inherent in the diagnosis of brief psychotic disorder.

Complications

The presence of a personality disorder or another psychiatric illness may complicate this disorder. There is a higher risk of accidental death or suicide for younger individuals primarily in the first year after the episode.

Factors Influencing Duration

A prompt recovery is likely with good mental and social functioning prior to the disorder, short duration of symptoms, and having no schizophrenic relatives.

Length of Disability

Duration is brief and inherent to this diagnosis.

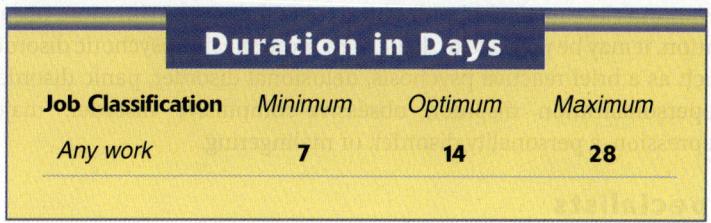

Job Classification	Minimum	Optimum	Maximum
Any work	7	14	28

Failure to Recover

If an individual fails to recover within the maximum duration expectancy period, the reader may wish to reference the following questions to assist in better understanding the specifics of an individual's medical case.

Regarding diagnosis:

- If symptoms have lingered longer than a month, does diagnosis need to be revisited?
- Have conditions with similar symptoms been ruled out?
- Was diagnosis revised if a major mood disorder, schizoaffective disorder, or schizophrenia was present or if symptoms are due to alcohol and substance abuse or other medical conditions (such as head injury)?

Regarding treatment:

- Since hospitalization is usually recommended for psychiatric evaluation as well as for the protection of individual and others, was individual hospitalized? If not, why not?
- Does the individual pose a threat to self or others?
- Are suicidal tendencies present?
- Are the individual's nutritional and hygienic needs being met?
- Would the individual benefit from hospitalization at this time?
- After the acute episode subsided, was the individual engaged in any counseling or therapy?
- Would individual benefit from psychotherapy to address the loss of self-esteem resulting from the psychotic episode?

Regarding prognosis:

- If symptoms have persisted (recovery of mental functioning should occur within one month with no further major psychiatric disturbances) does individual need further evaluation and a revised diagnosis?

References

American Psychiatric Association, eds. Diagnostic and Statistical Manual of Mental Disorders IV, text revision. Washington, DC: American Psychiatric Association, 1999.

First, M.B., et al, eds. Diagnostic and Statistical Manual of Mental Disorders 4th ed. Washington, DC: American Psychiatric Association, 1994.

Psychotic Disorder, Unspecified
Other names / synonyms: Atypical Psychosis, Psychosis
298.9

Definition

In a psychotic disorder, perception and understanding of reality is severely impaired. Symptoms may include fixed but untrue beliefs (delusions), seeing visions or hearing voices (hallucinations), confusion, disorganized speech, exaggerated or diminished emotions, or bizarre behavior. Level of functioning may be severely impaired with social withdrawal and inability to attend to work, relationships, or even basic personal care. Individual generally have little awareness of the mental abnormalities associated with their illness.

An unspecific psychotic disorder occurs when the psychotic symptoms though present do not meet all the diagnostic criteria for a specific psychotic disorder such as schizophrenia. It may be impossible to identify a specific psychotic disorder due to insufficient information or contradictory findings.

Psychotic symptoms are described as positive or negative. Positive symptoms are delusions, hallucinations, bizarre behaviors, and thought broadcasting where the individual believes others can supernaturally influence his or her thoughts or vice versa. Negative symptoms refer to a reduction or loss of normal functions such as restriction and flattening of emotions, severely reduced speech or thought, and lack of interest in goal-directed activities.

A delusion is a firm belief that others cannot verify. The delusional individual clings to the belief despite evidence to the contrary. A common type of delusion involves thoughts of persecution such as being spied upon or conspired against. There may also be delusions of grandeur where individuals believe they have extraordinary powers, are on a special mission, or think they are someone important such as Jesus Christ. The delusion is termed bizarre if it is not based on ordinary life experiences. An example is of aliens controlling an individual's body and/or thoughts.

Hallucinations are sensory perceptions that no one else can detect and can involve the sense of sight, touch, hearing, smell, or taste. Hearing voices is the most frequent hallucination in psychosis. The hallucinations occur when the individual is awake.

Disorganized thoughts (loosening of associations) are characterized by jumping from one topic to another. Grossly disorganized behavior can result in neglect of personal appearance and hygiene, proper nutrition, and other tasks of living. The individual may dress inappropriately and act unpredictably such as shouting or swearing in public. At the other behavioral extreme is catatonia where the individual becomes withdrawn, immobile, and unaware of the surrounding world.

Emotional flatness may include an unresponsive face and little eye contact with another individual. Emotions may be inappropriate for the situation such as laughing at a situation no one else finds amusing or crying for any apparent reason. Unexplained fear, anger, or sadness may also be present. Abnormal movements can include continuous pacing, rocking, facial grimacing, or rigid immobility in strange postures.

Diagnosis

History: A psychotic episode can involve any combination of delusions, hallucinations, abnormal speech, bizarre or highly disorganized behavior, emotions that are flat or inappropriate, or lack of any purposeful and productive activity.

In an unspecified psychotic disorder, however, the symptoms do not meet criteria for any other specific psychotic disorder. This may be due to inadequate or contradictory information. Examples include psychotic symptoms lasting less than a month but not yet resolved so does not yet meet the criteria for a Brief Psychotic disorder, persistent auditory hallucinations without any other symptoms, persistent nonbizzare delusion with overlapping mood episodes, or when a psychotic disorder appears to be present but has not yet been determined and may in fact be the result of a general medical condition or substance.

Physical exam: Exam findings do not establish the diagnosis. Observation of the individual's orientation, dress, mannerisms, behavior, and content of speech provide essential signs that may help diagnose the illness.

Tests: Tests are not helpful in establishing this diagnosis but are used to rule out disorders that might be confused with acute psychosis such as infections, substance abuse, and other metabolic causes of delirium.

Treatment

Psychiatric hospitalization may be needed to observe individuals and protect them from their own loss of reality, judgment, and impulse control. Antipsychotic medication may be given along with any appropriate psychotherapy. In certain situations, group therapy or electroconvulsive therapy might be helpful. With continued observation, it may be possible to reach a more specific diagnosis and initiate appropriate treatment.

Prognosis

Outcome is unclear given this nonspecific diagnosis. With continued observation, it may be possible to reach a more specific diagnosis and allow for appropriate treatment and more prognostic information.

Differential Diagnosis

Medical causes of psychotic symptoms include temporal lobe epilepsy, brain tumor, stroke, an endocrine or metabolic disturbance, a severe vitamin (thiamine) deficiency, infection such as neurosyphilis or encephalitis, autoimmune disease such as systemic lupus erythematosus, or toxic heavy metal poisoning. Drug intoxication with stimulants, hallucinogens, or anticholinergic drugs can also cause psychotic symptoms as can alcohol or barbiturate withdrawal. With more observation, it may be possible to diagnose a more specific psychotic disorder such as a brief reactive psychosis, delusional disorder, panic disorder, depersonalization disorder, obsessive-compulsive disorder, major depression, a personality disorder, or malingering.

Specialists

- Psychiatrist
- Psychologist

Work Restrictions / Accommodations

Temporary work accommodations may include reducing or eliminating activities where the safety of self or others is contingent upon a constant and/or high level of alertness, such as driving a motor vehicle, operating complex machinery, or handling dangerous chemicals; introducing the individual to new or stressful situations gradually under individually appropriate supervision; allowing some flexibility in scheduling to attend therapy appointments (which normally should occur during the employee's personal time); promoting planned, proactive management of identified problem areas; and offering timely feedback on job performance issues. It will be helpful if accommodations are documented in a written plan designed to promote timely and safe transition back to full work productivity.

Comorbid Conditions

Coexisting conditions that may affect recovery and lengthen disability include adults with fetal alcohol syndrome or fetal alcohol effects, alcohol or substance abuse, HIV infection, other medical condition, or the presence of a personality or anxiety disorder or other psychiatric condition.

Complications

Accidental injuries, suicide, or homicide can occur during a psychotic episode. Loss of relationships or employment is common.

Factors Influencing Duration

Length of disability may be influenced by type and severity of symptoms and response to treatment. If a specific psychiatric or medical diagnosis eventually emerges, the final diagnosis will determine disability.

Length of Disability

This is a vague diagnosis. Contact physician to obtain a more specific diagnosis.

Failure to Recover

If an individual fails to recover within the maximum duration expectancy period, the reader may wish to reference the following questions to assist in better understanding the specifics of an individual's medical case.

Regarding diagnosis:

- Do psychotic symptoms still not meet criteria for any specific psychotic disorder?
- If more information has become available since the initial evaluation, has the physician determined if the disorder is primary, due to a general medical condition, or substance-induced?

Regarding treatment:

- If the underlying or contributing condition has been identified, how is it being treated?
- Are psychotic symptoms resolving?
- Were antipsychotic medications or psychotherapy utilized? How effectively?
- Because suicide and even homicide is possible during a psychotic episode, is psychiatric hospitalization needed to protect individual from his or her own loss of reality, judgment, or impulse control?
- Would additional or a prolonged confinement be beneficial to monitor behavior and medication regime?

Regarding prognosis:

- Has any more information become available that may direct the physician to a specific diagnosis?

References

Famy C., A.P. Streissguth, and A.S. Unis. "Mental Illness in Adults with Fetal Alcohol Syndrome or Fetal Alcohol Effects." American Journal of Psychiatry 155 4 (1998): 552-554.

Ho, A.P., et al. "Achieving Effective Treatment of Patients with Chronic Psychotic Illness and Comorbid Substance Dependence." American Journal of Psychiatry 156 11 (1999): 1765-1770.

Pterygium
372.4, 372.5

Definition

A pterygium is a triangular growth of fleshy tissue on the mucous membrane covering the surface of the white of the eye (bulbar conjunctiva). Thought to be caused primarily by excessive exposure to sunlight and harmful ultraviolet (UV) radiation, the nonmalignant tumor or mass typically appears first at the inside (nasal) corner of the eye. In some cases, a pterygium spreads onto the transparent covering over the eye (cornea), resulting in a warped optical surface and distorted vision (irregular astigmatism).

The growths (pterygia) often occur in both eyes (bilateral), and may take years to fully develop. Although rare in children, pytergia may be linked to hereditary factors. Excessive exposure to sunlight and irritants such as dusty, sandy, windblown areas may contribute to development of the condition; it is also associated with cataracts. An untreated pterygium could cause blindness by blocking light to the back of the eye (retina) where images are processed.

Pterygia are linked to individuals who work many hours outdoors in tropical climates or "sunbelt" areas. In the southern US, an estimated 5-9% of residents develop the condition; in countries near the equator, about 10% of residents are affected. Pterygia are rare in countries such as England and France, where climates are milder. Wearing sunglasses with UV protection when outdoors may help stop or slow development of the condition.

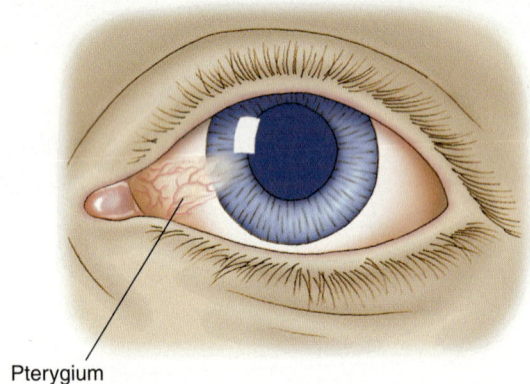
Pterygium

Diagnosis

History: The individual may report painless growths on one or both eyes. The condition may have been present for years without symptoms and spread slowly, ultimately causing distorted vision, discomfort from inflammation, and irritation. A foreign body sensation may be felt, and the eyes may seem dryer than usual. The individual may also report a history of excessive exposure to sunlight or dust particles.

Physical exam: A yellowish, fleshy tissue mass will be seen on the outer layer of the eye (sclera), growing toward the transparent surface of the eye's colored center (cornea). The sclera and outer protective membrane of the eye (conjunctiva) may be red from irritation and inflammation.

Tests: A visual acuity exam may be performed to see if vision is affected.

Treatment

In many cases, a mild pterygium presents mostly a cosmetic concern. The individual may have no symptoms or other ill effects, so periodic observation may be the only action warranted. In cases of mild irritation, artificial tears may be used for moisture, and eye protection such as sunglasses that block UV rays should be worn. Even in mild cases, however, follow-up is recommended to monitor a possible transformation from benign into malignant or cancerous tissue (neoplasm).

In cases where the growth is unsightly or vision is threatened as it encroaches on the pupillary area, the pterygium may be removed surgically (excision). Because of the risk of complications, experts differ about whether a mild pterygium should be excised.

A newer office procedure for removing pterygia involves excising the growth followed by grafting a small amount of nearby healthy conjunctiva tissue (conjunctival autograft) to promote healing and permanent recovery. In another method, graft human tissue recovered after cesarean sections (preserved human amniotic membrane tissue, or PHAMT) may be used. A topical antibiotic and steroid ointment will be applied after the procedure.

Prognosis

In the past, pterygia tended to recur even after surgical removal. But newer surgical techniques appear to have greatly decreased recurrence rates with some studies reporting better than 90% success at resolving the condition. In extreme cases, permanent vision loss or blindness might result. Mild cases of pterygia have no symptoms so may not require intervention.

Differential Diagnosis

A pinguecula is another type of fleshy eye growth, more yellow in appearance.

Specialists

- Ophthalmologist

Work Restrictions / Accommodations

Protective eyewear may be needed to shield the individual from sunlight, sand, dust, and wind. If the individual has experienced permanent loss of vision, office environment accommodations such as larger and high contrast print, or increased illumination may be necessary. In extreme cases, the individual may experience blindness or permanently reduced vision requiring reassignment to tasks that do not require keen visual acuity.

Comorbid Conditions

Individuals with pterygium may also have cataracts, which require additional treatment. Individuals who have had prolonged, unprotected exposure to the sun and ultraviolet radiation are likely to have more severe forms of pterygium.

Complications

A pterygium that is allowed to cover the cornea may produce distorted vision (irregular astigmatism), possibly leading to blindness when light is blocked to the back of the eye (retina) where visual processing takes place. The eye's affected area may become dehydrated, causing a dry depression to develop (dellen) that may reduce visual acuity. Cataracts sometimes are found in association with pterygia. Possible cancerous tissue (neoplasm) may develop. Conjunctival hemorrhage sometimes occurs. Scarring, swelling in the area of the graft (graft edema), corneal ulcer, necrosis, hematomas, epithelial cysts, or Tenon's granulomas may develop after surgery. The pytegium may also recur following its removal.

Factors Influencing Duration

The severity of the condition, the individual's response to recommended treatment, and the presence of complications will affect length of disability. Since a pterygium sometimes is associated with development of cataracts, this condition might also need to be treated. Use of proper eye protection might reduce the severity and the long-term effects of a pterygium.

Length of Disability

No disability is expected for medical treatment.

Surgical treatment.

Duration in Days

Job Classification	Minimum	Optimum	Maximum
Any work	1	3	7

Failure to Recover

If an individual fails to recover within the maximum duration expectancy period, the reader may wish to reference the following questions to assist in better understanding the specifics of an individual's medical case.

Regarding diagnosis:

- Has diagnosis of pterygium been confirmed?
- Has individual experienced any complications?
- Has the individual experienced recurrences of pterygium?
- Does individual have any underlying conditions that may impact recovery?

Regarding treatment:

- Is there any indication that tissue may be malignant?
- On what basis was surgical intervention decided? Was a graft used?

Regarding prognosis:

- If results were not as successful as expected, what are the extenuating circumstances?
- Has pterygia recurred?
- Has vision been decreased as a result of the pterygia? To what extent? Is vision loss permanent?
- Are additional treatment options being considered?

References

Sua, Alex S., et al. "High Frequency Radiosurgery Enables Safe, Easy, Bloodless Conjunctival Autograft." Ocular Surgery News May (2000): 3. 01 Jan 2001 <http://slackinc.com/eye/osn>.

Pulmonary Edema

Other names / synonyms: Hypostatic Pneumonia, Lung Water, Passive Pneumonia, Pulmonary Congestion, Wet Lung

506.1, 514, 518.4

Definition

Pulmonary edema refers to an accumulation of fluid in the lungs. The air sacs (alveoli) of the lungs become waterlogged, making it difficult to breathe.

Pulmonary edema is most commonly associated with various causes of heart failure. When the left side of the heart fails to empty completely with each contraction, or has difficulty accepting blood returning from the lungs, the retained blood creates a back pressure. As fluid backs up into the veins of the lungs, the lung circulation system becomes congested. Increased pressure in these veins forces fluid out of the vein into the lung alveoli, thus interfering with the exchange of oxygen and carbon dioxide in the alveoli. It also interferes with the ability of the lymph system to drain excess fluid and alters fluid balances, leading to excess fluid build-up in the lungs.

Occasionally, pulmonary edema is the first sign of heart disease. It is often a complication of a heart attack (myocardial infarction). Pulmonary edema can also occur following mitral or aortic valve disease, lung and heart bypass surgery, stroke, bacterial or viral infections, renal failure, near-drowning, head trauma, or as the result of inhaled toxins, vasoactive substances (histamines, kinins), uremia, aspiration and radiation pneumonia, smoke inhalation, adult respiratory distress syndrome (ARDS), subacute bacterial endocarditis, pulmonary vein stenosis, lymphatic insufficiency, central nervous system (CNS) trauma, eclampsia, and cocaine or heroin abuse. Pulmonary edema can also develop as a complication of improperly-performed intubation, or the rapid administration of blood, plasma, serum albumin, intravenous fluids, or intravenous narcotics. Many cases of pulmonary edema occur in otherwise healthy individuals who exert themselves at high altitudes to which they are unaccustomed.

Pulmonary edema occurs in about 1-2% of the general population. Between the ages of 40 and 75 years, males are affected more than females. After the age of 75 years, males and females are affected equally. The incidence of pulmonary edema increases with age and may affect about 10% of the population over the age of 75 years.

Diagnosis

History: Acute pulmonary edema is one of the most common medical emergencies and very life threatening; intervention must be made as soon as diagnosis is suspected. The clinical signs and symptoms can start as a primary manifestation of certain pathology or as an evolution of an already existing disease. Symptoms include difficulty breathing (dyspnea), rapid breathing (tachypnea) or shortness of breath, anxiety, restlessness, excessive sweating, and coughing up pink, frothy sputum. The individual may report feeling like they are "drowning" or that they cannot get enough air.

Physical exam: Physical findings include cold extremities either with or without a pale complexion or bluish skin coloration (cyanosis), engorged neck veins, rapid heartbeat (tachycardia), elevated blood pressure (hypertension), wheezing, swelling (edema) in the hands and feet, nasal flaring and the extensive use of accessory muscles just to breathe, temporary episodes of no breathing (apnea), and profuse sweating (diaphoresis). Listening to the chest with a stethoscope (auscultation) may reveal crackles in the lungs (moist rales) with or without wheezing, and abnormal heart sounds.

Tests: A chest x-ray, echocardiogram (in which ultrasound is used to detect structural or functional abnormalities of the heart), and heart catheterization (procedure in which a tiny catheter is introduced into the heart in order to diagnose and assess its condition) may aid in the diagnosis of pulmonary edema. Other tests that should be done include a complete blood count (CBC) with differential, BUN, creatinine, and serum protein concentrates; a urinalysis (UA); and, arterial blood gases (ABGs) - it will have a low oxygen concentration and high carbon dioxide concentration.

Treatment

Because it is a medical emergency individuals will require immediate hospitalization and emergency treatment. First, 100% oxygen will be delivered by mask or tube through the nose into the trachea (endotracheal tube - ETT) with mechanical ventilation to ensure sufficient oxygenation. The person will be instructed to sit up in bed with their legs dangling to make respiration easier and decrease venous return. A brief history, physical exam, and laboratory tests will be done to establish the underlying cause of the pulmonary edema, so that it can be treated with specific measures. These may include heart-regulating drugs, fast-acting diuretics to eliminate excess body fluid, morphine to relieve anxiety and pain, and bronchodilating drugs to widen airways in the lungs. The individual must be continuously monitored until the condition returns to normal. Post-hospitalization measures often include a low-sodium diet, regular exercise, avoiding smoking, and regular follow-up exams to monitor progress.

Prognosis

The outcome of pulmonary edema depends largely on the underlying cause. Untreated, pulmonary edema can lead to respiratory arrest and death. Pulmonary edema that is not heart related (non-cardiogenic) generally responds well to treatment, while cardiogenic pulmonary edema has a variable mortality rate.

Differential Diagnosis

Other conditions that present with similar symptoms include adult respiratory distress syndrome (ARDS), anaphylaxis, bronchitis, chronic obstructive pulmonary disease (COPD), emphysema, pericarditis, cardiac tamponade, pneumonia, pulmonary embolism, septic shock, and venous air embolism.

Specialists

- Cardiologist
- Critical Care Specialist
- Internist
- Pulmonologist

Work Restrictions / Accommodations

An underlying heart condition may necessitate changing job duties to ones with less physically demanding or emotionally stressful responsibilities. Because pulmonary edema can be an occupational hazard of exposure to chemical gasses (eg, phosgene), individuals should take precautions that include working in well-ventilated areas, wearing masks, reading hazardous material warnings, and following OSHA guidelines for handling and working with hazardous materials.

Comorbid Conditions

Existing conditions that may impact ability to recover and may further lengthen disability include underlying heart conditions or irregular heart rhythms, obesity, emphysema, and chronic obstructive pulmonary disease.

Complications

Possible complications of pulmonary edema include acute heart attack (myocardial infarction - MI), cardiogenic shock, arrhythmias, electrolyte disturbances, mesenteric insufficiency, protein enteropathy, digitalis intoxication, respiratory arrest, and death.

Factors Influencing Duration

Length of disability may be influenced by the underlying cause of the edema, the severity of symptoms, response to and method of treatment, the development of complications, and underlying medical conditions.

Length of Disability

Disability may be permanent. Duration depends on underlying cause.

Duration in Days

Job Classification	Minimum	Optimum	Maximum
Sedentary work	7	14	21
Light work	7	14	21
Medium work	7	14	21
Heavy work	14	21	28
Very Heavy work	14	21	28

Failure to Recover

If an individual fails to recover within the maximum duration expectancy period, the reader may wish to reference the following questions to assist in better understanding the specifics of an individual's medical case.

Regarding diagnosis:

- Does the individual have a history that places them at risk of developing pulmonary edema, such as heart failure, recent heart attack or heart surgery, valvular heart disease, renal failure, etc?
- Did the individual have the characteristic symptoms of pulmonary edema, such as (dyspnea), rapid breathing (tachypnea) or shortness of breath, anxiety, restlessness, excessive sweating, and coughing up pink, frothy sputum?
- Did a chest x-ray and/or pulmonary artery pressure measurements confirm the diagnosis of pulmonary edema?

Regarding treatment:

- Did the individual receive immediate life-support interventions (ECG monitoring, airway assistance, oxygenation and ventilation)?
- Were appropriate medications administered (such as diuretics, morphine)?
- Did the individual receive ongoing intensive care and monitoring?
- Was the underlying cause of the condition detected and addressed in the treatment plan?

Regarding prognosis:

- Based on the individual's age, general health and underlying cause of the pulmonary edema, what was the expected outcome?
- Does the individual have any underlying conditions (heart failure, kidney failure, chronic lung disease, etc) that may impact recovery and prognosis? If so, is this condition(s) being addressed in the treatment plan? Has the individual received consultation from appropriate specialists (cardiologist, pulmonologist, nephrologist)?
- Did the individual suffer any complications that could delay recovery or impact prognosis (cardiac arrest, etc)?

References

Grossman, S., and David Brown. "Congestive Heart Failure and Pulmonary Edema." eMedicine.com. 2000. 28 Dec 2001 <http://emedicine.com/emerg/topic108_pr.htm>.

Bone, Roger. Pulmonary and Critical Care Medicine. St. Louis: Mosby, 1998.

Pulmonary Function Tests

Other names / synonyms: FEV1, FVC, Lung Function Tests, MMEF, PFT, PFTS

89.37, 89.38

Definition

Pulmonary function tests are a series of tests that evaluate the lungs' function.

There are many types of pulmonary function tests. The most common are the peak expiratory flow rate (PEFR), forced vital capacity (FVC), forced expiratory volume in one second (FEV1), maximum voluntary ventilation (MVV), total lung capacity (TLC), and residual volume (RV). The tests either measure airflow rates, lung volumes, or the ability of the lungs to move oxygen into and remove carbon dioxide from the blood.

The primary test that measures airflow rate is the peak expiratory flow rate (PEFR). PEFR measures the maximal airflow rate during forced inhalation after taking a deep breath.

The primary tests that measure lung volumes include forced vital capacity (FVC), forced expiratory volume in 1 second (FEV1), maximum voluntary ventilation (MVV), total lung capacity (TLC), and residual volume (RV). FVC measures the total amount of air that can be forcefully expelled from the lungs after taking a deep breath. FEV1 measures the amount of air that can be forcefully expelled in the first second after taking a deep breath. MVV measures the maximum volume of air that an individual can breathe in and out in 1 minute. The maximum amount of air that an individual's lungs can hold is measured by TLC, and the amount of air left in the lungs after forced expiration is measured by RV.

The arterial blood gas test indicates how efficiently the lungs move oxygen into and remove carbon dioxide from the blood by measuring the level of those gases in the blood. A variation of this test, pulse oximetry, is a noninvasive test that measures the percentage of oxygenation in the blood.

Pulmonary function tests are used widely for diagnosis and management of the many individuals with lung disease (for example, the more than 14 million individuals with bronchitis, the more than 14 million with asthma, and the approximately 2 million with emphysema in the US alone). In addition, the tests are commonly included in routine health examinations in respiratory, occupational, and sports medicine, as well as in public health screening.

Reason for Procedure

Pulmonary function tests measure the extent and level of respiratory impairment in an individual, help to diagnose lung diseases such as pulmonary fibrosis, asthma, bronchitis, and emphysema, and evaluate response to therapy for lung conditions.

Description

With the exception of arterial blood gases, pulmonary function tests are typically performed using a procedure called spirometry. The individual breathes through a tube that is connected to a machine called a spirometer. The machine records the volume moved. A similar machine, a peak flow meter, may be used to measure PEFR. If airflow appears to be obstructed, the test may be repeated after administration of an inhaled bronchodilator (bronchoprovocation testing). These tests require that the individual be in a cognitive state such that he or she is able to understand and fulfill the test directions, and is also able to inhale and exhale deeply without being limited by pain.

The arterial blood gas test is performed on blood that has been drawn from an artery using a syringe.

The pulse oximetry test uses sensors placed on a fingertip or earlobe. The sensors are connected to a machine, called an oximeter, that measures the oxygen saturation of the blood.

Prognosis

When variation among testing protocols and compliance of individuals being tested is minimized through the use of standardized methodology, pulmonary function tests yield valid and dependable results.

Pulmonary function tests are the most definitive tests for assessing pulmonary function and for managing individuals with lung disease.

Specialists

- Pulmonologist

Work Restrictions / Accommodations

Restrictions and accommodations are not associated with this procedure.

Comorbid Conditions

Comorbid conditions include recent heart attack or unstable heart disease, pneumothorax, or active tuberculosis.

Procedure Complications

Individuals may become light-headed or may faint during the test. In individuals with asthma, the tests may trigger an episode that requires immediate treatment. Individuals with severe lung disease may become exhausted by the testing.

Factors Influencing Duration

An unstable heart or lung condition could influence length of disability.

Length of Disability

No disability is expected for this procedure. Disability may occur as a result of an underlying condition.

References

American Thoracic Society. "Lung Function Testing: Selection of Reference Values and Interpretative Standards." American Review of Respiratory Diseases 144 (1991): 1202-1218.

Pagana, Kathleen, and Timothy Pagana. Mosby's Manual of Diagnostic and Laboratory Tests. St. Louis: Mosby, 1998.

Puncture Wound
870.0, 870.3, 870.4, 871.5, 871.6, 871.7

Definition

Puncture wounds are caused by objects that penetrate the skin and underlying tissue or structures. Wounds made by nails, needles, wire, knives, and bullets are normally punctures. Small puncture wounds usually do not bleed freely; however, large puncture wounds may cause severe internal bleeding. The possibility of infection is great in all puncture wounds, especially if the object that caused the puncture is contaminated. Perforation (through and through) is a variation of a puncture wound, which results when a penetrating object enters, passes through, and exits the body. An example of a through-and-through puncture wound is a gunshot wound that enters the chest and exits the back.

Carpenters, healthcare workers, law enforcement agents, or anyone who handles sharp objects is at risk of sustaining puncture wounds.

Diagnosis

History: The individual may give a history of recent injury.

Physical exam: The physical exam reveals a hole. The surrounding skin may be red, warm, and tender. The condition of the skin, nerves, tendons, blood vessels, bones, cartilage, muscles, and fascia of the involved area must be examined for damage.

Tests: X-rays of the site may be taken if bone injury is suspected or if foreign objects are deeply embedded. Puncture wounds may require an exploratory operation of the abdominal cavity (laparotomy) or the chest cavity (thoracotomy).

Treatment

The wound is cleaned. Foreign matter and dead tissue are removed (débrided). The wound is irrigated with saline, antiseptic, or an antibiotic solution.

Damage to blood vessels, nerves, or bones often necessitates repair by specialized surgical techniques, such as microsurgery.

A tetanus shot (tetanus toxoid, TD) may be given preferably within 24 hours if it has been over 5 years since the individual's last booster shot, or if there is a question about when the individual was last vaccinated. If the individual has never been immunized against tetanus, human tetanus immune globulin may be given. The tetanus immunization series should be given for those who have never had the "tetanus diptheria" series.

If there is obvious contamination, the wound may need to be surgically opened and cleaned. The wound is then irrigated with an antiseptic solution, filled with layers of sterile gauze (packed), and covered with a bandage for 4-5 days. A surgical drain may be temporarily inserted to permit fluid drainage from the wound. If, after this time, there is no sign of infection, the wound may be left open and allowed to heal on its own.

Prognosis

Puncture wounds usually heal with minimal scarring and without any lasting effects.

Differential Diagnosis

Conditions with similar symptoms include incised wound or laceration.

Specialists

- Emergency Medicine

Work Restrictions / Accommodations

Restrictions and accommodations depend on the site of the wound and severity. Personal protection equipment may be required to protect against infection.

Complementary and Alternative Therapies

Content is intended for awareness only. Treatments may or may not be effective. Scientific evidence may be lacking and some substances have potentially toxic effects. Dr. Presley Reed and the editors do not endorse the use of these therapies in the absence of consultation with a licensed medical professional.

Hydrotherapy - Warm immersion soaks, using plain warm water or warm water with Epsom salt or table salt (4 tablespoons to 1 quart of water), may help relieve pain and swelling.

Comorbid Conditions

Bleeding disorders, immunosuppression, and diabetes are comorbid conditions that would influence disability.

Complications

Approximately 10-15% of puncture wounds result in infection of the underlying tissue. These infections can take the form of cellulitis, abscess formation, or inflammation of the underlying bone (osteomyelitis).

Factors Influencing Duration

Length of disability may be influenced by the severity of the wound, the site of the wound, the method of treatment, or the presence of complications.

Length of Disability

Most simple puncture wounds are not associated with disability. Duration depends on site, severity, depth of puncture wound, and presence of complications. Contact physician for additional information.

Failure to Recover

If an individual fails to recover within the maximum duration expectancy period, the reader may wish to reference the following questions to assist in better understanding the specifics of an individual's medical case.

Regarding diagnosis:

- Has puncture wound injury been confirmed?
- Were other types of injuries with similar symptoms, such as incision or laceration wound, ruled out?
- If bone injury is suspected or foreign objects was deeply embedded, was surgical exploration of the abdominal cavity (laparotomy) or the chest cavity (thoracotomy) required?
- Has individual experienced complications such as cellulitis, abscess formation, or osteomyelitis that may impact recovery?

Regarding treatment:

- If there was obvious contamination, did the wound need to be surgically opened and cleaned (débridement)?
- Did wound repair require specialized surgical techniques (microsurgery) to repair damage to blood vessels, nerves, or bones?
- If infection occurred, did it respond to antibiotic therapy? Was culture and sensitivity performed to identify the infective organism and determine the most effective antibiotic?
- Were antibiotic-resistant organisms ruled out?
- If the individual has never been immunized against tetanus, was human tetanus immune globulin given? If it has been over 5 years since the individual's last booster shot, or if there is a question about when the individual was last vaccinated, was a tetanus shot given?

Regarding prognosis:

- If healing was delayed, what were the extenuating circumstances?
- If complications occurred, did they respond to treatment?
- Will further treatment or procedures be required?
- Does individual have a coexisting condition, such as diabetes, bleeding disorders, or immunosuppression that may complicate treatment or impact recovery?

References

Tierney, Lawrence M., Stephen J. McPhee, and Maxine A. Papadakis, eds. Current Medical Diagnosis and Treatment, 39th ed. New York: Lange Medical Books/McGraw-Hill, 2000.

Purpura Simplex

Other names / synonyms: Capillaritis, Easy Bruising Syndrome, Gougerot-Blum Purpura, Lichen Aureus, Majocchi's Purpura, Nonthrombocytopenic Purpura, Schamberg's Purpura

287, 287.2, 287.4

Definition

Purpura simplex is the most common blood vessel disorder (vascular disorder). It is characterized by easy bruising and deposits of blood under the skin (purpura). Blood leaking out of fragile capillaries can leave tiny red dots (petechiae) or large bruises primarily on the thighs, buttocks, and upper arms.

There is no known cause for most cases of purpura simplex, but medications may induce purpura in about one-sixth of cases. It is not associated with clotting or platelet abnormalities or any systemic illness. Individuals with purpura simplex are not at increased risk of internal bleeding or excessive bleeding during surgery or following an injury.

Purpura simplex primarily affects healthy, middle-aged women and is also frequently seen with aging, as capillary fragility increases. The bruising may increase during menstruation.

Diagnosis

History: Individuals typically have no history of abnormal bleeding. Individuals report red dots or areas of bruising primarily on the thighs, buttocks, and upper arms.

Physical exam: Small capillary hemorrhages (petechiae) and larger areas of bruising (ecchymoses) under the skin are evident. Ecchymoses smaller than 6 centimeters do not indicate a serious condition. The petechiae and ecchymoses are not painful and do not disappear or turn white (blanch) under pressure. Bruising is typically not seen on the ankles or lower legs. The individual is otherwise healthy and there is no evidence of systemic illness.

Tests: Results of laboratory tests including platelet count, platelet function tests, and bleeding time are normal. Skin biopsy is usually unnecessary, but if affected areas of skin are examined microscopically, there is inflammation and bleeding without breakdown (fibrinoid necrosis) of blood vessels.

Treatment

Purpura simplex is not a disease. Treatment is not necessary or available. The individual should be reassured and advised to avoid aspirin and other medications that can increase purpura, such as nonsteroidal anti-inflammatory drugs (NSAIDs), diuretics, meprobamate, and ampicillin. If taking medication that interferes with platelet function or connective tissue integrity, the dose should be reduced or the drug discontinued, if possible.

Prognosis

Though the individual may find the areas of bruising unsightly, it is not a serious condition and is self-limiting. In a retrospective study of 174 individuals, about two-thirds who were seen in follow-up had eventual resolution of bruising.

Differential Diagnosis

Differential diagnoses include other conditions that cause petechiae or larger areas of bruising (ecchymoses) under the skin. These include senile purpura, Cushing's syndrome, scurvy, use of certain drugs, platelet abnormalities, amyloidosis, or certain infections such as Rocky Mountain spotted fever. Disorders of blood clotting (coagulation) may present with similar bruising, but are also associated with bleeding internally or from body openings. These include hemophilia and thrombocytopenic purpura, as well as different forms of cancer and autoimmune diseases that may be associated with decreased platelets or clotting factors.

Specialists

- Dermatologist
- Hematologist
- Internist

Work Restrictions / Accommodations

Since individuals with purpura simplex do not have increased risk of internal bleeding or bleeding following injury, work restrictions are not needed. Individuals may wish to wear clothing that covers the areas of bruising. In certain occupations such as modeling, visible bruising may create a disability.

Comorbid Conditions

Purpura simplex may be secondary to certain medications, such as NSAIDs, aspirin, or diuretics. Conditions requiring use of these drugs, such as arthritis, heart disease, or edema, may limit recovery from purpura simplex. Conversely, the individual with purpura simplex secondary to these medications is more likely to be disabled by the underlying conditions than by the purpura.

Complications

There are no complications associated with purpura simplex.

Factors Influencing Duration

Purpura simplex is typically not associated with disability. Job duties such as modeling, where appearance is important and skin is exposed, could create temporary or even permanent disability for these specific occupations.

Length of Disability

No disability is associated with this condition.

Complementary and Alternative Therapies

Content is intended for awareness only. Treatments may or may not be effective. Scientific evidence may be lacking and some substances have potentially toxic effects. Dr. Presley Reed and the editors do not endorse the use of these therapies in the absence of consultation with a licensed medical professional.

Arnica -	Used externally, may help relieve pain and treat bruises.
Bioflavonoids -	Said to repair and build capillary walls.
Bromelain -	May inhibit formation of prostaglandin E2 involved in inflammation and stimulate production of anti-inflammatory prostaglandin E1, promoting more rapid healing of bruises.
Comfrey -	Used externally, may help to relieve inflammation and bruising.
Vitamin Therapy -	Vitamins A, C, E, K and zinc may help repair and build skin tissue and capillary walls.
Gotu kola -	Used externally, may stimulate regeneration of skin cells and underlying tissue.
Herb therapy -	Helichrysum, hyssop, and lavender may be used externally to reduce swelling, control bleeding under the skin, and fight inflammation.
Parsley -	Used externally, may help to heal bruises.
Grape seed -	Said to increase vitamin C levels in body and strengthen capillaries.
St. John's wort -	Used externally, this may treat bruises.
Yarrow -	Used externally, said to reduce swelling, control bleeding under the skin, and fight inflammation.

Failure to Recover

If an individual fails to recover within the maximum duration expectancy period, the reader may wish to reference the following questions to assist in better understanding the specifics of an individual's medical case.

Regarding diagnosis:

- Has the diagnosis been confirmed?
- Have more serious reasons for the bruising been ruled out?
- Have platelet or clotting element disorders been ruled out with appropriate blood tests?
- Is the individual taking aspirin, NSAIDs, or any drug that interferes with platelet function or connective tissue integrity?
- Is skin biopsy needed to confirm diagnosis or rule out more serious conditions?

Regarding treatment:

- If purpura is drug-induced, can the offending drug be discontinued or reduced in dosage?
- Do other drugs need to be substituted to treat the underlying condition?
- Have alternative therapies for bruising been considered?

Regarding prognosis:

- If symptoms persist or worsen, should diagnosis be reconsidered, remembering that purpura simplex is usually benign and self-limiting?

References

Berkow, Robert, and Mark Beers. The Merck Manual of Diagnosis and Therapy, 17th ed. Whitehouse Station, NJ: Merck Research Laboratories, 1999.

Gottlieb, Bill, ed. New Choices in Natural Healing. Emmaus, PA: Rodale Press, Inc, 1995.

Pyelonephritis, Acute
Other names / synonyms: Acute Kidney Infection, Acute Pyelitis, Upper Urinary Tract Infection
590, 590.1, 590.8, 590.80, 590.9

Definition

Acute pyelonephritis is one of the most common renal diseases. It is an infection of the kidney including the renal pelvis.

Acute pyelonephritis results most commonly from the spread of an infection in the lower parts of the urinary tract (the urethra and bladder), up through the tubes (ureters) that connect the bladder to the kidneys. In many cases, urinary tract infections are caused by bacteria that have spread to the urinary tract from the colon. Bacteria most often responsible for acute pyelonephritis include Escherichia coli (responsible for 80% of infections), Proteus, Klebsiella, Staphylococcus saprophyticus, and Enterococcus. Acute pyelonephritis may also be caused by catheterization or bladder surgery, from a blood infection such as sepsis or endocarditis, or rarely from lymphatic infection. Difficulty emptying the bladder (neurogenic bladder) or urinary tract obstruction or stricture increase risk of acute pyelonephritis. Congenital weakness of a juncture between the bladder and ureter (vesicoureteral junction) may lead to vesicoureteral reflux, in which urine backs up from the bladder into the ureters and kidneys, predisposing to acute pyelonephritis.

This condition affects females much more than males because females have a shorter urethra with closer proximity to the vagina and rectum, allowing bacteria greater access. Females also lack an antibacterial secretion produced in males. Disease incidence is approximately 3-7 per 10,000 people, and increases with age or immunosuppression. Sexually active and pregnant women, diabetics, and persons with other renal diseases are at the greatest risk of developing this condition.

Diagnosis

History: The individual may report symptoms that develop rapidly over a few hours or days. Symptoms may include high fever (101 to 104 degrees F or higher) and shaking chills; pain in the flank or lower back, particularly on the right side; increased frequency of urination; pain (dysuria) and burning sensation when urinating; getting up to urinate at night (nocturia); nausea and vomiting; loss of appetite (anorexia); and general fatigue. The urine may appear bloody or cloudy with a fishy odor. Some individuals may note only diffuse abdominal pain with nausea, vomiting, and diarrhea. The elderly may experience only altered mental state or vague abdominal pain.

Physical exam: The exam may reveal generalized muscle tenderness as well as pain and tenderness when pressure is applied to the sides of the abdomen or flank (costovertebral angle tenderness). Fever and other symptoms may also be confirmed during a physical examination.

Tests: A sample of urine collected in midstream should be cultured to determine number and species of bacteria present. The isolated bacteria will be exposed to a battery of antibiotics and the sensitivity will be reported to the physician to aid in treatment. The urine sediment is examined microscopically for red blood cells (hematuria) and pus (white blood cells) in the urine (pyuria). Other routine urine tests determine whether it is abnormally concentrated or dilute. A blood culture may reveal the presence of bacteria in the blood. In some cases, a kidney x-ray (intravenous pyelogram), CT scan, or renal ultrasound may be indicated. CT and ultrasound studies are particularly useful when the diagnosis is unclear or the condition is complicated, or when there is an underlying condition predisposing to pyelonephritis. X-ray of the kidney may reveal kidney stones (calculi), tumors, or cysts in the kidney or urinary tract. Kidneys may also appear asymmetrical, indicating severe inflammation. In some cases, urine specimens from the ureter may be obtained for culture through an invasive ureteral catheterization procedure. Other tests may include voiding cystourethrogram or kidney (renal) biopsy. A recent study showed that CT is more accurate than (99m) Tc-DMSA scintigraphy in diagnosing acute pyelonephritis.

Treatment

Since acute pyelonephritis is typically due to a urinary tract infection and treatment is with antibiotics. Whenever possible, the type of bacteria causing the infection should be identified. Antibiotics are prescribed which are specific for that organism. The urine culture and sensitivity promotes the correct choice of antibiotic. If the organism is not identified, a broad-spectrum antibiotic is prescribed. Bacteria are usually eliminated from the urine within 2-3 days of treatment, but antibiotics are continued for a course of 7 to 14 days to make certain the infection has been eradicated. A follow-up culture is obtained if symptoms remain after antibiotic treatment is completed. Urologic consultation, ultrasound, x-ray studies of the urinary tract (intravenous pyelogram), or cystoscopy may be recommended in women who have had 2 recurrent episodes of acute pyelonephritis and in men following a single episode of pyelonephritis.

Treatment may be as outpatient or as an inpatient. Hospitalization may be recommended for males, the elderly, individuals with underlying medical conditions such as diabetes or pregnancy, and individuals with known genitourinary tract abnormalities. Inability to maintain oral intake of fluids or medications and severe illness with high fever, severe pain, or altered mental status may necessitate hospitalization. Initial treatment for the first 8-12 hours may be performed in an emergency setting. During this time, fluids and antibiotics are administered directly into a vein (intravenous), the first 1-2 doses of antibiotics are given, medications to treat nausea may be given, and the physician reevaluates the individual. If the individual is responding well, treatment can be continued as an outpatient.

In addition to antibiotics, an analgesic for pain relief and antipyretic medication for fever reduction are also often prescribed. The individual is also instructed to force fluids in an effort to clear out the bacterial infection. In some cases, an acid-ash diet may be recommended to prevent kidney stone formation. Individuals experiencing infection as a result of obstruction or vesicoureteral reflux are typically less responsive to antibiotic treatment. In these cases, surgery may be necessary to relieve the obstruction by insertion of a nephrostomy tube or transurethral stone extraction, for example, or to correct a structural problem.

Prognosis

With proper treatment and follow-up care, most individuals recover quickly and completely, and extensive permanent damage is rare. Individuals with coexisting renal disease and older age are at risk of developing of severe disease and complications. Without treatment, symptoms may disappear. However, residual infection usually remains and symptoms are likely to recur, possibly with greater severity.

Differential Diagnosis

Differential diagnoses include pelvic inflammatory disease, kidney stone (nephrolithiasis), acute appendicitis, acute gallbladder inflammation (cholecystitis), pancreatitis, and diverticulitis. In men, the differential diagnosis may also include epididymitis and acute prostatitis.

Specialists

- Internist
- Nephrologist
- Primary Care Provider
- Urologist

Work Restrictions / Accommodations

Usually, no work restrictions and accommodations are required upon recovery.

Comorbid Conditions

Comorbid conditions that may lengthen disability by complicating recovery and predisposing to recurrence include pregnancy, diabetes, older age, hydronephrosis, kidney stone, or ureteral obstruction. Diseases affecting the immune system, such as AIDS, may slow healing. Chronic illness, smoking, obesity, or alcohol abuse may hinder response to treatment and prolong infection.

Complications

Complications that may be associated with acute pyelonephritis include kidney (renal) damage or failure, localized infection (abscess), overwhelming generalized infection (sepsis), and shock. Diabetics may develop a life-threatening form of nephritis called emphysematous pyelonephritis, in which kidney tissues are distended by gases given off by the organism, producing the infection. Repeated pyelonephritis, combined with underlying structural or functional abnormalities of the kidneys, may lead to kidney scarring and shrinkage (chronic pyelonephritis).

Factors Influencing Duration

Factors that might influence length of disability include older age and general health, job requirements, infection with drug-resistant organisms, and drug allergies that prevent use of appropriate antibiotics.

Length of Disability

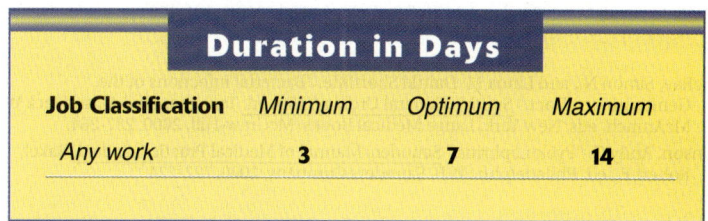

Job Classification	Minimum	Optimum	Maximum
Any work	3	7	14

Failure to Recover

If an individual fails to recover within the maximum duration expectancy period, the reader may wish to reference the following questions to assist in better understanding the specifics of an individual's medical case.

Regarding diagnosis:

- Did history suggest acute pyelonephritis?
- Did symptoms develop rapidly over a few hours or days?
- Was there a high fever (102 degrees F or higher) and shaking chills, pain in the flank, particularly in the lower back on the right side?
- Were there urinary symptoms such as increased frequency of urination, pain and a burning sensation upon urination?
- Were there complaints of nausea and vomiting, decreased appetite (anorexia), and general fatigue?
- Was there blood in the urine?
- Was the urine cloudy, blood-tinged, or foul smelling with a fishy odor?
- Did physical examination suggest acute pyelonephritis because of flank or abdominal tenderness, generalized muscle tenderness, fever, or other typical signs?
- Did urinalysis reveal red or white blood cells or a positive gram stain?
- Was urine or blood culture positive for bacteria?
- If symptoms did not improve or worsened within 48 to 72 hours, was a kidney x-ray (intravenous pyelogram) or renal ultrasound performed?
- Were abnormalities revealed with x-ray or ultrasound (kidney stones or calculi, tumors, or cysts) in the kidney or urinary tract?
- Did the kidneys appear asymmetrical, indicating severe inflammation?
- Was ureteral catheterization performed to obtain urine specimens from the ureter?

- Did ureteral urine culture reveal bacteria?
- Are additional tests needed, such as voiding cystourethrogram, abdominal CT, or kidney biopsy?

Regarding treatment:

- Is the infection being treated with appropriate antibiotics?
- Are drug-resistant organisms or drug allergies complicating treatment?
- Is fluid intake adequate?
- Is hospitalization needed for intravenous fluids and/or antibiotics?

- Are any complications being treated appropriately?

Regarding prognosis:

- Did the infection resolve with antibiotic treatment?
- Did the symptoms recur after completion of antibiotics?
- Have there been other episodes of pyelonephritis?
- Did complications occur such as renal damage, abscess, papillary necrosis, sepsis?
- Did emphysematous pyelonephritis occur in a diabetic?

References

Majd, M., et al. "Acute Pyelonephritis." Radiology 218 1 (2001): 101-108.

McRae, Simon N., and Linda M. Dairiki Shortliffe. "Bacterial Infections of the Genitourinary Tract." Smith's General Urology, 15th ed. Tanagho, Emil A., and Jack W. McAninch, eds. New York: Lange Medical Books/McGraw-Hill, 2000. 237-264.

Pinson, Andy G. "Pyelonephritis." Saunders Manual of Medical Practice, 2nd ed. Rakel, Robert E., ed. Philadelphia: W.B. Saunders Company, 2000. 722-724.

Presti, Joseph C., Marshall L. Stoller, and Peter R. Carroll. "Urology." Current Medical Diagnosis and Treatment, 39th ed. Tierney, Lawrence M., Stephen J. McPhee, and Maxine A. Papadakis, eds. New York: Lange Medical Books/McGraw-Hill, 2000. 917-958.

Roca-Tey, R., et al. "Acute Pyelonephritis. Study of 153 Cases." Nefrologia 20 4 (2000): 373-374.

Sandler, C.M., E.S. Amis, and L.R. Bigongiari. "Imaging in Acute Pyelonephritis. American College of Radiology Appropriateness Criteria." Radiology 215 Suppl (2000): 677-681.

Pyelonephritis, Chronic

Other names / synonyms: Chronic Pyelitis, Chronic Pyonephrosis, Pyelonephritic Scarring
590, 590.0

Definition

Unlike acute pyelonephritis, in which there is bacterial infection of the kidney, chronic pyelonephritis is a kidney condition that develops over time due to damage of kidney tissue. Infection may play a role, but the underlying disorder involves abnormality in the urinary tract. Chronic pyelonephritis is characterized by scarring and shrunken volume (atrophy) of the kidneys. It results in decreased ability of the kidneys to function (renal insufficiency).

In adults, it is caused by recurrent or persistent infection of the kidney, combined with an underlying structural or functional kidney abnormality. Abnormalities that increase the risk of chronic pyelonephritis with repeated urinary tract infections include diabetes, kidney stones (calculi), use of certain analgesics, and urinary tract obstruction. Infection alone rarely leads to chronic pyelonephritis and loss of kidney function.

Chronic pyelonephritis can develop without infection. Individuals with an abnormality of the junction between the ureter and bladder (vesicoureteral junction) in childhood may develop chronic pyelonephritis. Abnormality of the vesicoureteral junction, a congenital condition in which the juncture between the ureters and bladder is weak, allows urine to flow backward from the bladder to the ureter and up into the kidney. Severe reflux alone can lead to kidney scarring, even in the absence of other factors known to cause kidney scarring. The scarring of the kidneys associated with vesicoureteral reflux is similar to that seen with repeated infection combined with underlying structural abnormality. Some authorities theorize that kidney scarring due to reflux of urine (reflux nephropathy) may be an autoimmune process. Other noninfectious conditions that may scar the kidneys similarly to

vesicoureteral reflux are long-standing high blood pressure (hypertension) and use of certain analgesics.

This chronic condition may develop over a period of years, and affects women more frequently than men.

Diagnosis

History: Symptoms reported may vary, depending on whether or not infection is present. Individuals without infection may not have symptoms (asymptomatic) until they reach the later stages of chronic pyelonephritis with chronic kidney failure. Symptoms may be nonspecific, including high blood pressure (hypertension) and signs of kidney failure such as itching (pruritus), generalized malaise, feeling tired (lassitude), forgetfulness, easy fatigability, nausea, and loss of sexual drive (libido). If infection is present, the individual may complain of symptoms similar to those of acute pyelonephritis, with rapid development of symptoms over the course of a few hours or days. Individuals may report a high fever (101 to 104°F or higher) and shaking chills, pain in the flank, particularly in the lower back on the right side, increased frequency of urination, pain and a burning sensation upon urination (dysuria), nausea and vomiting, decreased appetite (anorexia) and general fatigue. The urine may appear cloudy or blood-tinged with a fishy odor. Some individuals may note only diffuse abdominal pain with nausea, vomiting, and diarrhea. When asked, the individual may report a history of unexplained fevers and bed-wetting during childhood.

Physical exam: In the absence of acute infection, the physical examination may be essentially normal. With infection, physical exam may reveal generalized muscle tenderness and pain and tenderness when pressure is applied to the sides of the abdomen (flank or costovertebral angle tenderness). Fever, high blood pressure, and other symptoms may be confirmed during physical examination.

Tests: If a urinary tract and/or kidney infection is suspected, a sample of urine collected in midstream should be cultured to determine the number and species of bacteria present. Sensitivities (to antibiotics) will be obtained. The urine sediment is microscopically examined for red blood cells or pus in the urine (hematuria or pyuria). Urinalysis may reveal protein in the urine (proteinuria, albuminuria) and whether the urine is abnormally concentrated or dilute. Laboratory testing may reveal decreased kidney functioning, with increased blood urea nitrogen (BUN) and creatinine. A 24-hour urine collection helps quantitate kidney function. Urine and blood cultures may reveal the presence of bacteria in the urine or blood. An x-ray of the kidney may reveal kidney stones (calculi), tumors, or cysts in the kidney or urinary tract. Kidney x-ray using dye injection that concentrates in the urine (intravenous pyelogram) helps visualize the kidneys and urinary tract. Kidneys may appear asymmetrical, indicating severe inflammation. In some cases, an abdominal CT scan or renal ultrasound may be indicated, especially in individuals with an unclear diagnosis or who have complicated conditions. In some cases, urine specimens from the ureter may be obtained for culture through an invasive ureteral catheterization procedure.

If a non-infectious cause is suspected, a kidney x-ray (intravenous pyelogram) or renal ultrasound procedure may be indicated. The kidneys may have an irregular outline and appear smaller than normal. If only one kidney is affected, the other kidney may be larger due to hypertrophy. An x-ray of the kidney may reveal kidney stones (calculi), tumors, or cysts in the kidneys or urinary tract. Kidney (renal) biopsy may be recommended in some cases to rule out other potential causes for the inflammation.

Treatment

Treatment is directed at eradicating infection if present, and at correcting underlying causes. If a urinary tract infection is the cause, antibiotics are the first line of therapy. Whenever possible, the type of bacteria causing the infection should be identified and antibiotics specific for that organism are then prescribed. A follow-up culture of the urine may be obtained one week after the end of drug therapy. It may be necessary to continue long-term antibiotic therapy for up to three to six months.

Underlying structural abnormalities are corrected wherever possible. Surgery may be necessary to remove obstruction or to repair a stricture.

A variety of surgical procedures may be performed, depending on the underlying cause of the obstruction or stricture. It may be necessary to repair the pelvis of the kidney (pyeloplasty) due to an obstruction of the ureteropelvic junction. Kidney stones may be removed through an open incision or through a transurethral approach using cystoscopy and a stone-basketing procedure. Surgical treatment of vesicoureteral reflux may involve repair of congenital abnormalities that lead to vesicoureteral reflux as a complication, or surgical treatment may involve a variety of procedures designed to correct the vesicoureteral reflux condition itself (reimplantation of ureters). Removal of a kidney (nephrectomy) may be recommended in cases in which only one kidney is severely affected (unilateral).

Other types of medical treatment may be necessary. Medications may be prescribed to control hypertension. If kidney failure has occurred, medications, diet changes, and dialysis may be necessary.

Prognosis

Provided that adequate treatment is given promptly and the disease is not allowed to progress to renal failure, the predicted outcome is generally quite good. Most individuals develop some renal scarring and atrophy of the kidney. Individuals with only one kidney affected have a normal life expectancy, while those with both kidneys affected have a slightly reduced life expectancy. Antibiotic treatment for infection and antihypertensive therapy for high blood pressure are usually effective. The outcome following the various surgical procedures (pyeloplasty, stone removal, and nephrectomy) is usually good.

Differential Diagnosis

Differential diagnoses include chronic interstitial nephritis, renal tumor, and other diseases affecting the kidney.

Specialists

- Nephrologist
- Urologist

Work Restrictions / Accommodations

Work restrictions and accommodations are not generally needed for chronic pyelonephritis. Time off from work may be necessary for doctor's appointments. If acute pyelonephritis has developed, time off from work until symptoms have resolved may be needed. Surgical treatment may necessitate time off from work for hospitalization and postoperative recovery.

Complementary and Alternative Therapies

Content is intended for awareness only. Treatments may or may not be effective. Scientific evidence may be lacking and some substances have potentially toxic effects. Dr. Presley Reed and the editors do not endorse the use of these therapies in the absence of consultation with a licensed medical professional.

Bearberry -	Contains arbutin, which may act as a diuretic and antibiotic.
Birch -	Contains flavonoids, and may act as a diuretic.
Blueberry -	May slow growth of bacteria in urinary tract. May help acidify urine, which enables some antibiotics to work better.
Buchu -	May act as a diuretic, decrease kidney inflammation. May act as an antiseptic.
Herb therapy -	Cornsilk, cypress, dandelion, fennel seed, goldenrod, lovage, stinging nettle may act as diuretics.
Couchgrass (quackgrass) -	May treat urinary tract inflammation and stones.
Cranberry -	May slow growth of bacteria in urinary tract. May help acidify urine, which enables some antibiotics to work better.
Echinacea -	Said to boost immune system.
Marsh mallow -	May soothe painful or burning urination.
Parsley -	May slow growth of bacteria in urinary tract. Said to help acidify urine, which enables some antibiotics to work better.
Vitamin C -	May slow growth of bacteria in urinary tract. It may acidify urine, which enables some antibiotics to work better.
Yogurt -	May help prevent urinary tract infections.

Comorbid Conditions

A comorbid condition lengthening disability is pre-existing kidney insufficiency or failure from any cause. Conditions that predispose to chronic pyelonephritis, such as chronic urinary tract infection, kidney stones, or vesicoureteral reflux, are associated with their own morbidity that would further lengthen disability. If surgical treatment is needed, immunosuppression, bleeding disorder, or any chronic illness could increase morbidity related to surgery.

Complications

Complications include recurrent infection with resistant bacteria, the possibility of continued renal damage leading ultimately to renal failure, and intractable high blood pressure (hypertension).

Factors Influencing Duration

Factors that may influence the length of disability include kidney stones or other obstruction or stricture, diabetes mellitus, hypertension, excessive use of phenacetin-containing analgesics, underlying renal disease or renal failure, drug-resistant organisms, and an individual's age and general health. More time for rest and recuperation may be required in cases necessitating surgery.

Length of Disability

The amount of recovery time may vary with the type of procedure, results, complications, and job requirements.

Medical treatment.

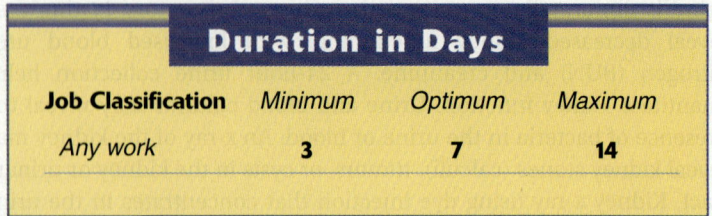

Duration in Days

Job Classification	Minimum	Optimum	Maximum
Any work	3	7	14

Failure to Recover

If an individual fails to recover within the maximum duration expectancy period, the reader may wish to reference the following questions to assist in better understanding the specifics of an individual's medical case.

Regarding diagnosis:

- Is the history and examination consistent with chronic pyelonephritis?
- Is there blood or pus in the urine, or is it cloudy with a fishy odor?
- Does the history suggest that renal failure is present because of high blood pressure (hypertension), itching (pruritus), feeling poorly (malaise), feeling tired (lassitude)?
- Did urinalysis reveal abnormalities associated such as the presence of white blood cells, protein, or a positive gram stain?
- Did urine or blood culture reveal bacteria?
- Should a kidney x-ray (intravenous pyelogram), renal ultrasound, or abdominal CT be performed?
- Do these tests reveal kidney stones or calculi, tumors, or cysts in the kidney or urinary tract?
- Do the kidneys appear asymmetrical, indicating severe inflammation?
- Was ureteral catheterization performed to obtain urine specimens from the ureter? Did ureteral urine culture reveal bacteria?
- Does blood testing reveal elevated blood urea nitrogen (BUN) or creatinine suggesting renal insufficiency or failure?
- Is kidney biopsy indicated to evaluate any underlying cause?

Regarding treatment:

- Did the infection respond to antibiotics?
- Was obstruction relieved?
- Were kidney stones removed? Did kidney stones reoccur?
- Was surgical correction of a vesicoureteral abnormality successful?
- Was a nephrectomy performed?
- Did complications occur with surgery?

Regarding prognosis:

- Did infection resolve with antibiotic treatment?
- Did symptoms recur after completion of antibiotics?
- Have there been multiple episodes of pyelonephritis?
- Did infection result in complications such as renal damage, abscess, papillary necrosis, sepsis?
- Has kidney function been impaired?

References

Amend, William J.C., and Flavio G. Vincenti. "Chronic Renal Failure and Dialysis." Smith's General Urology, 15th ed. Tanagho, Emil A., and Jack W. McAninch, eds. New York: Lange Medical Books/McGraw-Hill, 2000. 610-613.

Duke, James A. The Green Pharmacy. Emmaus, PA: Rodale Press, Inc, 1997.

Feinstein, Alice, ed. Healing with Vitamins. Emmaus, PA: Rodale Press, Inc, 1996.

Kunin, Calvin M. "Urinary Tract Infections and Pyelonephritis." Cecil Textbook of Medicine, 20th ed. Bennett, J. Claude, and Fred Plum, eds. Philadelphia: W.B. Saunders Company, 1996. 602-605.

McRae, Simon N., and Linda M. Dairiki Shortliffe. "Bacterial Infections of the Genitourinary Tract." Smith's General Urology, 15th ed. Tanagho, Emil A., and Jack W. McAninch, eds. New York: Lange Medical Books/McGraw-Hill, 2000. 237-264.

Presti, Joseph, et al. "Urology." Current Medical Diagnosis and Treatment, 39th ed. Tierney, Lawrence M., Stephen J. McPhee, and Maxine Papadakis, eds. New York: Lange Medical Books/McGraw-Hill, 2000. 917-958.

Ross, J.H. "Urinary Tract Infections: 2000 Update." American Family Physician 62 8 (2000): 177-184.

Tanagho, Emil A. "Vesicoureteral Reflux." Smith's General Urology, 15th ed. Tanagho, Emil A., and Jack W. McAninch, eds. New York: Lange Medical Books/McGraw-Hill, 2000. 221-236.

Pyloric Stenosis, Acquired (Adult) Hypertrophic

Other names / synonyms: Acquired Hypertrophic, Acquired Hypertrophic Pyloric Stenosis, Adult Hypertrophic Pyloric Stenosis, AHPS, Pyloric Constriction, Pyloric Obstruction, Pyloric Stenosis

537.0

Definition

Adult or acquired hypertrophic pyloric stenosis (AHPS) is a disorder that occurs when the opening (pylorus) between the stomach and the first part of the small intestine (duodenum) becomes partially or completely blocked because the pyloric muscle (muscularis propria) has increased in size (hypertrophy) and its cells have abnormally multiplied (hyperplasia) resulting in inflammation, swelling (edema), and mononuclear cell infiltration. Primary or idiopathic AHPS can occur without any apparent cause. Secondary AHPS results from other problems in the gastrointestinal tract. The terms "acquired" and "adult" are used when describing this disorder to differentiate it from the more common congenital or infantile hypertrophic pyloric stenosis (IHPS).

AHPS is uncommon and was not recognized as a distinct disorder until 1930. Conditions that may put an individual at risk for secondary AHPS include prolonged pylorospasm, pyloric ulcer, hiatal hernia, inflammation of the stomach (gastritis), gallbladder disease, and stomach cancer (gastric carcinoma). Some researchers suggest that having the infantile condition may predispose an individual to primary AHPS later in life. IHPS occurs in approximately 5 per 1,000 male infants and 1 per 1,000 female infants, and is most common in whites (2.4 per 1,000 live births vs. 1.8 in Hispanics, 0.7 in blacks, and 0.6 in Asians).

Diagnosis

History: Individuals often do not report any symptoms, but when symptoms do occur, they may be episodic or persistent. Many individuals with obstruction have a long history of peptic ulcers, pylorospasms, or other stomach (gastric) problems. The individual often reports weight loss, a feeling of fullness after just beginning to eat (early satiety), loss of appetite (anorexia), gradual increase of upper abdominal pain that occurs over weeks to months, nausea, and frequent vomiting.

Physical exam: The upper abdomen may be tender and the individual may be dehydrated. There is generally no mass in AHPS that can be felt from outside the abdomen.

Tests: Blood and urine analyses are important establishing the individual's electrolyte balance and extent of dehydration. X-rays taken after barium has been swallowed (a barium swallow) may reveal an elongated and thickened pylorus and a markedly increased stomach emptying time. An internal examination of the stomach and upper area of the small intestine using a flexible fiber optic instrument (endoscopy) is generally performed.

Treatment

Treatment for AHPS is surgical. The condition is structural and medications are not effective except as needed for underlying gastrointestinal conditions such as ulcer. If the individual experiences swelling and spasms, initial treatment usually involves passing a tube through the nose into the stomach (NG, or nasogastric tube) to remove its contents (nasogastric suctioning). This may be done for several days until the symptoms subside. Once improvement is noted, surgery is performed to remove the pylorus (partial gastrectomy).

Prognosis

Symptoms of AHPS generally resolve after partial gastrectomy. The long-term outcome, however, depends on the treatment of any underlying gastrointestinal disorder. Increased size (hypertrophy) as a result of ulcer scarring or other conditions may recur unless these problems are corrected.

Differential Diagnosis

Scarring and inflammation from ingestion of caustic agents can mimic pyloric stenosis. An obstruction caused by a tumor may also produce similar symptoms.

Specialists

- General Surgeon

Work Restrictions / Accommodations

Individuals requiring surgery may need to be assigned lighter duties on return to work.

Comorbid Conditions

Pre-existing conditions include gastrointestinal disorders such as ulcer, hiatus hernia, gallbladder disease, or cancer.

Complications

AHPS is often a secondary condition. Ulcer, hernia, gallbladder disease, or cancer may also be present.

Factors Influencing Duration

The length of disability may be increased by surgical infection or other complications, and the need to treat underlying gastrointestinal disorders.

Length of Disability

Duration of disability depends on job requirements. Disability is likely to be longer for those jobs with physical demands such as heavy lifting.

Partial gastrectomy.

Duration in Days

Job Classification	Minimum	Optimum	Maximum
Sedentary work	28	35	42
Light work	28	35	42
Medium work	42	49	56
Heavy work	42	49	56
Very Heavy work	42	49	56

Failure to Recover

If an individual fails to recover within the maximum duration expectancy period, the reader may wish to reference the following questions to assist in better understanding the specifics of an individual's medical case.

Regarding diagnosis:

- Has diagnosis of acquired hypertrophic pyloric stenosis been confirmed?
- Have other conditions with similar symptoms been ruled out?
- Has individual experienced any complications associated with hypertrophic pyloric stenosis that may impact recovery?

Regarding treatment:

- Since partial gastrectomy is usually the treatment of choice for AHPS, if surgery was not done, what are the extenuating circumstances?
- Did surgery effectively relieve symptoms?
- Did individual experience any surgical complications such as infection?
- Are complications responding to treatment?
- Is the individual following doctors' orders for postsurgical recovery?

Regarding prognosis:

- Do symptoms persist despite treatment?
- Has hypertrophy recurred as a result of uncorrected ulcer scarring or other condition?
- Does individual have coexisting conditions, such as ulcer, hiatus hernia, gallbladder disease, or cancer of the stomach, duodenum, or pancreas that may complicate treatment or impact recovery? Are these conditions being adequately addressed in the overall treatment plan?

References

Graadt van Roggen, J.F., and J.H. van Krieken. "Adult Hypertrophic Pyloric Stenosis: Case Report and Review." Journal of Clinical Pathology 51 6 (1998): 479-480.

Keet, A.D. The Pyloric Sphincteric Cylinder in Health and Disease. Berlin: Springer-Verlag, 1993 19 Oct 2000 <http://med.plig.org/>.

Pyloroplasty

Other names / synonyms: Pyloric Stenosis Repair, Pyloromyotomy

44.2

Definition

Pyloroplasty is a surgical procedure performed to widen or reconstruct the opening between the stomach and the small intestine to allow for normal movement of food and fluid.

The opening between the stomach and small intestine is called the pylorus. The pylorus, or pyloric canal, is a short canal primarily made of muscle. In some cases, the canal narrows, interfering with the movement of food and fluids to the stomach. The causes of a narrowing canal include pyloric stenosis or gastric outlet obstruction.

In addition, some surgical procedures (vagotomy or gastrectomy) performed to manage severe peptic ulcers or the complications associated with peptic ulcers (bleeding, perforation) alter the flow of contents from the stomach to the small intestine. A pyloroplasty may be done with these procedures to reconstruct the pyloric canal and facilitate more normal flow of stomach contents to the small intestine. About 5% of those with peptic ulcer disease develop perforations or severe bleeding that requires surgical intervention (vagotomy and pyloroplasty). Gastric outlet obstruction occurs in about 2% of individuals with peptic ulcer disease.

Reason for Procedure

Indications for a pyloroplasty include pyloric stenosis and gastric outlet obstruction. Pyloroplasty is performed to remove the effects of the scar tissue from ulcer disease in the pyloric ring to relieve spasm and permit rapid emptying of the stomach. It is also commonly done in conjunction with other surgical procedures (vagotomy, partial gastrectomy) in the management of perforated or bleeding peptic ulcers. The procedure reconstructs (plasty) the pyloric canal to provide more normal movement of food and fluid from the stomach to the small intestine.

Description

A pyloroplasty is done under general anesthesia. A small cut (incision) is made in the upper right side of the abdomen. The incision is extended through some of the muscle layers and down to the pylorus. The surgeon then makes a cut through the pylorus muscle. The muscle is then sewn back together providing a wider opening of the canal. The abdominal muscles are closed with stitches and the skin incision is closed with stitches, clips, or staples.

In the treatment of pyloric stenosis resulting from an ulcer, the pyloroplasty is usually done in combination with another procedure called a vagotomy. This procedure cuts the nerve that causes the stomach to make stomach acid. This is done to reduce excess stomach acid and the risk of future ulcers.

Prognosis

In general, the procedure is generally effective at reconstructing the pyloric canal so that food and fluid moves more normally from the stomach to the small intestine. Full recovery is common when the procedure is performed on individuals who are good physical condition who do not have underlying chronic conditions such as cancer. There may be a greater risk of procedure complications and poorer outcome when done under emergency circumstances (such as a massively bleeding ulcer).

Specialists

- General Surgeon

Work Restrictions / Accommodations

No work restrictions or special accommodations are required after an individual has made a complete recovery from pyloroplasty.

Comorbid Conditions

Comorbid conditions of diabetes, immune suppression, liver disease, bleeding disorders, heart disease, chronic lung disease, or obesity may impact ability to recover and further lengthen disability.

Procedure Complications

Complications of this procedure include bleeding, infection, and accidental puncture (perforation) of the stomach. This procedure, as well as any surgery in the abdomen can result in the development of scar tissue (adhesion) around the intestines, which can cause blockage of the intestines. These adhesions can occur many years after the pyloroplasty, and may necessitate additional surgery. As with any procedure done with general anesthesia, there is the risk of anesthesia such as reactions to the anesthetic agent or problems with heart rate, blood pressure, or breathing.

Factors Influencing Duration

Factors that might influence disability include advanced age, severity of symptoms (i.e., massive bleeding), underlying cause (i.e., perforated gastric ulcer), or if the surgery was done as an emergency procedure or in conjunction with other gastric surgeries (vagotomy, gastrectomy).

Length of Disability

Open surgery.

Duration in Days

Job Classification	Minimum	Optimum	Maximum
Sedentary work	14	21	28
Light work	21	28	35
Medium work	28	35	42
Heavy work	28	42	56
Very Heavy work	28	42	56

References

Tierney, Lawrence M., Stephen J. McPhee, and Maxine A. Papadakis, eds. Current Medical Diagnosis and Treatment, 39th ed. New York: Lange Medical Books/McGraw-Hill, 2000.

Pylorospasm
Other names / synonyms: Pyloric Stricture, Pyloric Valve Spasm
537.81

Definition

Pylorospasm occurs when the opening between the stomach and small intestine (pylorus) exhibits spasmodic contractions that prevent food from entering the small intestine (duodenum) from the stomach.

The condition may result from abnormal nerve activity (neurogenic), or it may be secondary to other disease states such as peptic ulcer or diabetes. Occasionally, pylorospasm has been attributed to food allergies or intolerance to certain foodstuffs but this association is difficult to prove. Obstruction from the stomach into the small intestine due to pylorospasm occurs in only 2% of individuals with peptic ulcer.

Diagnosis

History: The individual may complain of vomiting or nausea after meals. Pain in the upper-central (epigastric) region of the stomach is typical and this may be on-going or occur only occasionally. Heartburn (acid reflux) and regurgitation of stomach contents is common.

Physical exam: There may be diminished appetite (anorexia) and weight loss. If vomiting has been persistent, the individual may be lethargic and appear disoriented, and their urine could be dark and concentrated. The upper portion of the abdomen may be distended if the stomach is full. Laboratory tests might show mildly low sodium (hyponatremia), moderately low potassium (hypokalemia), and very low chloride (hypochloremia) in the blood. Serum bicarbonate will be increased.

Tests: Screening for pylorospasm is usually done using ultrasound (ultrasonography). Barium contrast radiography or the saline load test may reveal delayed emptying of the stomach. The DTPA test utilizes a radioactive marker to measure gastric emptying.

Treatment

Immediate effects of pylorospasm such as gastric distention and dehydration are typically treated using nasogastric suction in conjunction with restoration of fluid and electrolytes. Medication with anti-cholinergic drugs will often resolve the pyloric valve spasms. Also, stretching of the pylorus with a balloon (endoscopic balloon dilation) may be used to relieve the constriction. Individuals who do not respond to these treatments may require the vagus nerve to be cut surgically using highly selective vagotomy (HSV).

Prognosis

About half of the individuals who suffer from blockage due to pylorospasm will respond to treatment using anti-cholinergic drugs within several days. Others may respond to either balloon dilation of the pyloric valve (pyloroplasty) or surgical intervention to cut the vagus nerve (highly selective vagotomy or HSV). Pyloroplasty is variably effective and has been reported to relieve pylorospasm 50-80% of the time. However, all reports indicate that pyloroplasty, in combination with HSV, enhances emptying of stomach contents and these procedures in combination generally produce long-term relief.

Differential Diagnosis

Conditions that present with similar symptoms include pyloric stenosis, peptic ulcer, cholecystitis, appendicitis, irritable bowel syndrome (IBS), or stomach cancer.

Specialists

- Abdominal Surgeon
- Gastroenterologist
- Internist

Rehabilitation

If abdominal surgery is required for the condition of pylorospasm, postoperative breathing exercises may be necessary to prevent pulmonary complications.

Breathing outward (exhaling) into a device that measures the force of breathing outward (spirometer) is an example of a breathing exercise. The individual may learn several coughing exercises with the same intended goal. Specific exercises may be performed to reduce postoperative pain and speed recovery including progressive relaxation and deep breathing techniques. All of these are performed several times per day until pain from inhalation/exhalation is less noticeable.

Ankle pumps performed by elevating the feet and repeatedly moving them forward and backward helps increase circulation and prepare the individual for walking. Heel slides are often instructed with the individual sitting on a flat surface with both knees straight (long sitting) and sliding the heel of the affected limb toward the buttock. Leg raises are used to strengthen the quadriceps and are described as the individual long sitting with the uninvolved knee in a flexed or bent position while the involved leg is raised to the height of the opposite knee.

Training and exercises related to walking (gait training) are an important component in rehabilitation for the postoperative individual. The final step of the rehabilitation program is to incorporate activities that will help the individual return to the home and work environment. This may include exercises that resemble activities in the home and/or workplace. Modifications may need to be made by the physical therapist for those individuals with pylorospasm. Variations in rehabilitation will depend on the extent and residual effects of the disease and whether surgery was required.

Work Restrictions / Accommodations

The individual may be limited to modified duty with lifting restrictions upon return to work after undergoing surgery.

Comorbid Conditions

Existing conditions that may affect the individual's ability to recover include pyloric ulcer disease, stomach cancer, and inflammation of the stomach (gastritis), any of which can lead to enlargement (hypertrophy) of the circular pyloric muscle.

Complications

Complications may include dehydration, weight loss, anemia, and obstructive jaundice. Muscle cramps, twitching, and convulsions may occur on rare occasions.

Factors Influencing Duration

The severity of the symptoms and response to treatment will influence the length of disability. Disability will be prolonged if surgical intervention is required.

Length of Disability

Duration of disability depends on underlying cause and the treatment that is required. If surgical treatment is needed, length of disability will be increased. Also, if surgery was performed, the individual may be restricted from heavy lifting until recovery is complete.

Medical treatment.

Duration in Days

Job Classification	Minimum	Optimum	Maximum
Any work	0	5	10

Failure to Recover

If an individual fails to recover within the maximum duration expectancy period, the reader may wish to reference the following questions to assist in better understanding the specifics of an individual's medical case.

Regarding diagnosis:

- Does the individual have symptoms consistent with the diagnosis of pylorospasm?
- Did the physical exam and diagnostic workup reveal clinical findings consistent with the diagnosis of pylorospasm?
- Did an abdominal ultrasound or DPTA test show evidence of delayed gastric emptying?
- Does the individual have a history of peptic ulcer disease or diabetes mellitus?
- If the diagnosis was uncertain, were other diagnostic tests done to rule out conditions with similar symptoms?
- Would the individual benefit from consultation with a gastroenterologist?

Regarding treatment:

- Were symptoms relieved with gastric decompression and anticholinergic medications?
- If individual did not respond to these treatments, are more aggressive interventions being considered, such as endoscopic pyloric dilatation or as a last resort, highly selective vagotomy (HSV)?
- Did the individual suffer any complications that may affect recovery? If so, are these complications being effectively addressed?

Regarding prognosis:

- Do symptoms persist despite treatment?
- Does individual have a coexisting condition, such as pyloric ulcer disease, stomach cancer, or gastritis that may complicate treatment or impact recovery? Are these conditions being addressed as part of the overall treatment plan?

References

Davenport, Horace W. <u>Physiology of the Digestive Tract</u>. Chicago: Year Book Medical Publishers, Inc, 1982.

Scully, Rosemary M., and Marylou Barnes. <u>Physical Therapy</u>. Philadelphia: J.B. Lippincott Company, 1989.

Pyuria

Other names / synonyms: Bacteriuria, Pus in the Urine
599.0

Definition

Pyuria is the presence of pus in the urine. Pus consists mainly of white blood cells (leukocytes) and their remains. Pyuria is not a diagnosis in itself, rather, it is a laboratory finding in many diseases, most commonly urinary tract infections. Pyuria may also be found in the absence of infection and is frequently asymptomatic. Its cause in such cases is unclear. Almost half of chronically incontinent nursing home patients exhibit asymptomatic pyuria. In the absence of infection, asymptomatic pyuria does not require treatment.

Diagnosis

History: Pyuria itself may have no symptoms. The individual may seek medical attention because of cloudy and foul-smelling urine or symptoms of urinary tract infection such as a frequent urgent need to urinate or discomfort on urination.

Physical exam: Physical findings in pyuria depend on the underlying cause of the condition. Bladder infection (cystitis) is usually diagnosed from the individual's history in combination with urine culture, but in general, there are no abnormal findings on physical examination. Infections involving the upper urinary tract such as those involving the ureters and kidneys (pyelonephritis) may result in fever, tenderness and enlargement of the kidney.

Tests: Pyuria is detected by urinalysis. Urine culture is performed to determine whether bacterial infection is the underlying cause. Pyuria may also be found in the absence of infection and is frequently asymptomatic. Its cause in such cases is unclear.

Treatment

Treatment, if any, depends on the underlying disease. Asymptomatic pyuria in the absence of infection (sterile pyuria) does not require treatment. Urinary tract infections are treated with antibiotics.

Prognosis

The probable outcome depends on the underlying cause of the pyuria. Asymptomatic pyuria may disappear spontaneously or remain without causing problems. Urinary tract infections generally clear up promptly when treated with antibiotics. They can resolve without antibiotic therapy, but not as quickly, and recurrence and/or complications are more likely.

Differential Diagnosis

Cloudy urine can also be the result of precipitated salts in less acidic (alkaline) urine or could represent blood in the urine (hematuria). Diet and drugs can be the cause of foul-smelling urine.

Specialists

- Nephrologist
- Urologist
- Primary Care Provider

Work Restrictions / Accommodations

Asymptomatic pyuria requires no restrictions or accommodations. In cases of pyuria due to urinary tract infection, necessary accommodations may include frequent restroom breaks.

Complementary and Alternative Therapies

Content is intended for awareness only. Treatments may or may not be effective. Scientific evidence may be lacking and some substances have potentially toxic effects. Dr. Presley Reed and the editors do not endorse the use of these therapies in the absence of consultation with a licensed medical professional.

Cranberry juice - Said to inhibit bacterial adherence to cells lining the urinary tract reducing influx of white blood cells by 50% in elderly women. Acidifies urine diminishing ability of bacteria to multiply.

Hydration - In absence of infection or other underlying cause, increased fluids may flush urinary tract.

Comorbid Conditions

Comorbid conditions include incontinence or structural abnormalities of the urinary tract.

Complications

Potential complications depend on the underlying condition causing the pyuria. In cases of bladder infection, possible complications include progression of the infection to the upper urinary tract (ureters and kidneys).

Factors Influencing Duration

The individual's response to and compliance with treatment of the underlying condition can influence length of disability. Any complications of the causative disease will be a factor.

Length of Disability

Duration depends on site of infection. See underlying diagnosis to determine disability duration.

Failure to Recover

If an individual fails to recover within the maximum duration expectancy period, the reader may wish to reference the following questions to assist in better understanding the specifics of an individual's medical case.

Regarding diagnosis:

- Has the underlying cause of the pyuria been identified?
- Has a urine culture been performed to determine whether a bacterial infection is present?
- Was specimen properly collected? Has contamination been ruled out?

Regarding treatment:

- Since treatment, if any, depends on the underlying disease, has an underlying disease been identified?
- Have urinalysis and culture ruled out the possibility of infection? When in doubt, have diagnostic tests been repeated?
- Has culture and sensitivity been performed to identify the causative organism and to determine the most effective antibiotic to use? Have antibiotic-resistant organisms been ruled out?

Regarding prognosis:

- If symptoms recur or persist despite treatment, have diagnostic tests been repeated?
- Was initial infection unresolved?
- Have antibiotic-resistant organisms been ruled out?
- If an underlying cause is finally identified, what changes will this make in treatment plan?
- Would individual benefit from evaluation by a specialist (urologist, internist, or nephrologist)?

References

Beers, Mark H., and Robert Berkow. The Merck Manual of Diagnosis and Therapy. Whitehouse Station, NJ: Merck & Co., Inc, 1999.

Ouslander, J.G., et al. "Pyuria Among Chronically Incontinent but Otherwise Asymptomatic Nursing Home Residents." Journal of the American Geriatrics Society 44 4 (1996): 420-423.

Rabies

Other names / synonyms: Hydrophobia

071

Definition

Rabies is a viral infection that affects the brain (central nervous system), causing convulsions and paralysis. Once symptoms develop, rabies is almost always fatal in humans. Primarily affecting animals, rabies can be transmitted to a human through the bite or saliva of an infected dog, bat, skunk, or other wild animal. Virus in the infected saliva travels from the wound, along nerve pathways, to the brain where it causes inflammation. Another recently identified though extremely rare method of transmission is thought to be inhalation of the airborne virus associated with bats in caves. This theory is disputed by bat conservationists.

Once an individual is infected, the incubation period prior to development of symptoms may last weeks or years depending on the type of virus. However, symptoms usually occur within 3 months.

An estimated 50,000 cases of human rabies are reported worldwide each year, with about 35,000 of them resulting in death. The highest incidence of rabies is in India, where more than half of cases occur. Most infections are caused by a bite from a rabid dog. In the US, fewer than 5 rabies cases occur annually. This is the result of intensive dog vaccination programs and prompt medical attention to animal bites. US rabies cases are now more commonly associated with bats. Because almost 100% of individuals who develop symptoms die, rabies has one of the highest fatality rates of any infectious disease. Individuals at risk of exposure to rabies include travelers visiting countries where animal rabies vaccination programs are not aggressively pursued. Travelers are advised to consider pre-exposure vaccination when traveling to high risk areas.

Diagnosis

History: Painful burning may occur at the site of the bite. Other early symptoms include sore throat, low-grade fever, dizziness, headache, loss of appetite, nausea, vomiting, or diarrhea. These flu-like symptoms are followed by double vision, anxiety, confusion, increased sensitivity to light (photophobia), muscle spasms, seizures, and disorientation. Eye and facial muscles may become paralyzed. The individual may have an intense thirst, but attempts at drinking cause violent, painful spasms in the throat (laryngeal spasms). The resultant refusal to drink has caused the term hydrophobia (fear of water) to be associated with rabies. Hallucinations may also be reported. The individual may become comatose.

Physical exam: A painful wound, fever, dilated or irregular pupils, increased tears and perspiration, and low blood pressure may be evident. The individual may be drooling large amounts of thick saliva. Altered mental state may include agitation, combativeness, and mental confusion. Increased deep tendon reflexes may be present accompanied by tremors, seizures, or paralysis.

Tests: Establishing a diagnosis of rabies prior to onset of symptoms is difficult. Saliva may be tested (culture) for presence of the virus. Early diagnosis can sometimes be made from fluorescent antibody testing of organic tissue taken from the individual's brain or back of the neck (biopsy). A swab or slide may be placed against the eye's cornea to obtain antigen material (corneal impression). After the onset of symptoms, tests may be performed on both the blood and the cerebrospinal fluid (serology). The cerebrospinal fluid will not confirm rabies (nonspecific). However, a puncture of the spinal canal with a needle (lumbar puncture) may be performed to withdraw cerebrospinal fluid for diagnostic purposes aimed at ruling out other causes of the individual's mental status.

Treatment

Treatment must be initiated prior to the development of symptoms. The individual and clinician should thoroughly clean any bite wound with soap and water to remove contaminated body fluids as soon as possible, possibly helping to stop the spread of infection. An antiviral agent should be used to irrigate the wound at high pressure. During medical treatment, the wound should not be sutured. If there is any risk of rabies, the individual is given antibodies against the rabies virus (human rabies immune globulin). A series of rabies vaccine injections should be given over the next several weeks. Injections no longer are given in the abdomen due to improved vaccine. Antibiotics also might be prescribed to reduce chance of infection from the animal bite.

Meanwhile, every attempt is made to capture the biting animal. If the animal appears to be rabid, it is killed so that its brain tissue can be microscopically examined for the presence of rabies virus. If the dead animal has no evidence of rabies antibodies, or if the captured animal remains symptom-free for at least five days, the individual can stop treatment. However, the absence of the rabies antibodies does not exclude the presence of rabies.

If symptoms appear, the individual may be given sedative drugs (antiseizure, neuroleptic) and pain relievers (analgesics). Aggressive support care is aimed at maintaining breathing and cardiac function. However, survival is rare. Therefore, the main emphasis must be on preventing the disease.

Prognosis

Rabies can almost always be prevented if immunization is given within 2 days of the bite. With each additional day that passes, the chances of prevention decrease. However, immunization can still be effective even when given weeks or months following a bite.

Once symptoms have appeared, survival is rare. Coma and death occur 3-20 days after the onset of symptoms. Human death from rabies in the US is extremely rare because of aggressive animal control and vaccination programs.

Differential Diagnosis

Conditions with similar symptoms include treatable viral encephalitis, hysterical reaction, Guillain-Barré syndrome, poliomyelitis, and drug overdose.

Work Restrictions / Accommodations

During the observation and preventive immunization period, extended sick leave may be required. If rabies develops, there are no work restrictions and accommodations as the disease is uniformly fatal.

Comorbid Conditions

The onset of rabies symptoms causes death to occur so rapidly that pre-existing conditions tend to be of no consequence.

Specialists

- Infectious Disease Physician
- Neurologist

Complications

Complications include increased pressure within the skull (intracranial pressure), irregular heartbeats (cardiac arrhythmia), seizures, respiratory failure, acute renal failure, congestive heart failure, gastrointestinal hemorrhage, and coma. In some cases, paralysis occurs at the early onset of symptoms.

Factors Influencing Duration

Once rabies develops, there are no significant factors that might influence length of disability. The individual typically dies.

Length of Disability

Individuals who experience rabies symptoms almost always die within 3 weeks. The individual bitten by a suspected rabid animal but who has not developed symptoms may require time off from work to undergo a series of vaccinations aimed at preventing the spread of infection. Disability may be permanent.

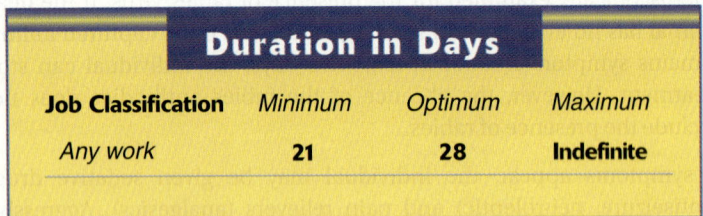

Duration in Days

Job Classification	Minimum	Optimum	Maximum
Any work	21	28	Indefinite

Failure to Recover

If an individual fails to recover within the maximum duration expectancy period, the reader may wish to reference the following questions to assist in better understanding the specifics of an individual's medical case.

Regarding diagnosis:

- Did the individual have painful burning at the site of the bite?
- Did the individual have flu-like symptoms followed by double vision, anxiety, confusion, photophobia, muscle spasms, seizures, and disorientation?
- Did paralysis in the eye and facial muscles occur?
- Has the individual been intensely thirsty?
- Has the individual had hallucinations?
- On physical exam, was a painful wound, fever, abnormal pupil response, increased tears and perspiration, or low blood pressure present?
- Was drooling noted?
- Was the mental status altered?
- Did the individual have increased deep tendon reflexes, tremors, seizures, or paralysis?
- Did the individual have adequate testing (saliva, serology of blood and cerebrospinal fluid, lumbar puncture) to determine the diagnosis?
- Were conditions such as viral encephalitis, hysterical reaction, Guillain-Barré syndrome, poliomyelitis, and drug overdose ruled out?

Regarding treatment:

- Was the wound thoroughly cleaned promptly?
- Did the individual receive human rabies immune globulin?
- Did the individual receive the series of rabies vaccine over several weeks?
- Did the individual receive antibiotics?
- Was the biting animal captured? Did it have rabies?
- When was rabies immunization started?

Regarding prognosis:

- Has rabies developed?

References

Noah, D.L., et al. "Epidemiology of Human Rabies in the United States, 1980 to 1996." Annals of Internal Medicine June 1998: 922-930. 1 Jan 2001 <http://www.acponline.org/journals/annals/01jun98/rabies.htm>.

Radial Keratotomy

Other names / synonyms: Radial Keratotomy, RK

11.75

Definition

Radial keratotomy (RK) is a surgical procedure used to reduce nearsightedness (myopia), a condition where individuals cannot see distant images well. Myopia tends to run in families, so those with a family history of myopia are at greater risk for developing this disorder. RK is an outpatient surgery that is generally performed under local anesthesia and usually completed in less than 30 minutes. In addition to local anesthesia, most individuals are given a medication to help them relax. RK is an elective procedure and not medically necessary.

The object of RK is to change the curvature of the clear, outer covering of the eye (cornea). By changing the curvature of the cornea, light is focused more directly on the back part of the eye (retina), reducing myopia and in some cases, eliminating it.

Several hundred thousand people have had RK since 1978 when it was introduced in the US. Approximately 250,000 RK procedures are performed each year in the US, up from 30,000 in 1990.

Reason for Procedure

RK is performed to improve the vision of myopic individuals and eliminate the need for glasses or contact lenses. However, this procedure does not always make this possible.

It is important to note that not all myopic individuals are good candidates for RK. The surgeon must consider several factors including the degree of myopia, other physical characteristics of the eye, and any underlying eye disease or systemic disease.

Description

RK is an outpatient surgical procedure generally completed within 30 minutes. Shortly before the procedure, the individual is often given a medication to help relax him/her. Eyedrops are instilled to numb the eye.

The surgeon then marks the portion of the cornea where the individual can see (optical zone) so that no cuts are made in this area. The surgeon measures the thickness of the cornea to determine how deep to make the incisions. The surgeon changes the shape of the cornea with the aid of a surgical microscope making a series of small corneal incisions with a fine, calibrated diamond blade. The incisions are arranged in a spoke-like (radial) pattern. The number of incisions varies depending on the degree of myopia and the individual characteristics of the eye. The natural biology of the eye will cause the areas around the incisions to steepen, thereby flattening the center of the cornea (the optical zone). This flattening allows light to be focused more precisely on the retina, improving the vision of the individual.

As the anesthesia wears off, the individual may experience some pain. If pain is noted, the surgeon prescribes eye drops and/or systemic medication to alleviate discomfort. The eye may be red and sensitive to light for a few days. The individual may feel a gritty sensation in the eye as well. These symptoms generally resolve within a few days. Eyedrop medication is given to protect against infection as the cornea heals and these drops may be required for several weeks.

Prognosis

Results of RK surgery vary considerably among individuals. To understand the outcomes, it is necessary to understand the standards of visual acuity where 20/20 vision is considered normal vision. When the bottom number is higher (20/40 or 20/200), individuals are less able to see at a distance. When the bottom number is lower (20/15 or 20/10) individuals can see "better" than 20/20.

Some individuals (approximately 53%) achieve complete success and experience postoperative vision of 20/20 or better without correction (the use of glasses or contact lenses). Approximately 85% of individuals achieve moderate success with postoperative vision of 20/40 or better without correction. The standard for obtaining a driver's license in most states is 20/40. A small minority (2-3%) of individuals experience postoperative vision of 20/200 or worse without correction. Additional procedures may be required to refine an unsatisfactory outcome.

Individuals with complications (particularly severe infection) may experience permanent loss of vision.

Specialists

- Ophthalmologist

Work Restrictions / Accommodations

Vision may fluctuate particularly during the first several months following the procedure. Individuals whose jobs require keen vision may need alternative duties during this period. Eyedrop medications are required for up to 3 weeks following surgery so individuals may require regular breaks to allow for application of these medications. Those individuals requiring prescription pain medications may need to avoid driving or using heavy machinery. Due to the compromised cornea, care should be taken to protect the eye from injury and foreign objects such as excessive dust or dirt, metal chips, or shavings.

Comorbid Conditions

Individuals with an underlying eye disease such as dry eye may require a longer recovery period.

Procedure Complications

Following RK, the eye heals slowly. Delayed corneal healing is associated with side effects such as fluctuating vision (especially during the first few months after surgery), a weakened cornea more susceptible to rupture if hit directly, infection, difficulty fitting contact lenses, glare or starburst around lights, and temporary pain. In addition to delayed corneal healing, RK is associated with rare complications that include development of cataracts, persistent pain, serious infection, traumatic rupture of an incision, and loss of vision.

Factors Influencing Duration

Side effects or complications such as prolonged pain, infection, ruptured incision, or corneal rupture may lengthen the disability period.

Length of Disability

Duration of disability depends on the individual's job requirements. Those who perform close work or require keen vision may experience a longer recovery period.

Duration in Days

Job Classification	Minimum	Optimum	Maximum
Any work	1	3	7

References

Radial and Astigmatic Keratotomy (RK & AK). American Academy of Ophthalmology. 15 Oct 1997. 13 Jul 2000 <http://www.medem.com/search/article_display.cfm?path=n:&mstr=/ZZZ7EZX727C.html&soc=AAO&srch_typ=NAV_SERCH>.

Segal, Marian. "Not a Cure-all: Eye Surgery Helps Some See Better." U.S. Food and Drug Administration 01 Dec 1996 10 Aug 2000 <http://www.fda.gov/fdac/features/695_rk.html>.

Radial Styloid Tenosynovitis

Other names / synonyms: De Quervain's Tenosynovitis, De Quervain's Disease, Stenosing Tenosynovitis of First Extensor Compartment

727.04, 727.64

Definition

Radial styloid tenosynovitis occurs when the tendons that move the thumb become inflamed and swollen (tenosynovitis) most commonly from irritation of repetitive gripping and twisting motion.

Two of the tendons involved with moving the thumb pass over the end of the radius (radial styloid) at the wrist. Normally, they slide through a canal (extensor retinaculum) without difficulty. Motion of the thumb and wrist become painful and difficult as the enlarged tendons pass through the canal.

The most common cause of the tenosynovitis is repetitive grip with the thumb against the fingers while the wrist is moved toward the palm (flexed) and toward the little finger side of the hand (ulnarly deviated) as in lifting or twisting. The problem is very similar to trigger finger.

Individuals who use repeated gripping and twisting motions of their hand and wrist, such as chefs or cooks, check-out clerks, and carpenters, seem to be more susceptible to this condition.

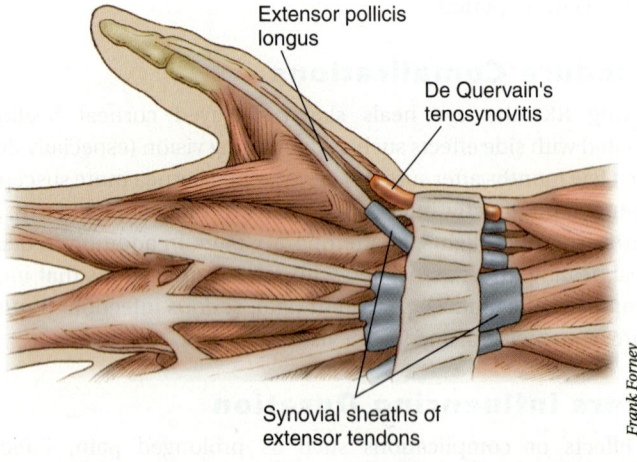

Extensor pollicis longus
De Quervain's tenosynovitis
Synovial sheaths of extensor tendons

Frank Forney

Diagnosis

History: Individuals complain of pain with thumb motion. There may be a visible swelling or a lump on the thumb side of the wrist and at times a catching or snapping sensation. Individuals may complain of inability to grip.

Physical exam: The exam reveal pains along the thumb side of the wrist (tip of radial styloid) aggravated with motion. Pain is made worse with stretching of the thumb while it is bent (Finkelstein test). Swelling or fullness may be felt over the tendon.

Tests: There are no invasive tests required and x-rays will appear normal.

Treatment

Stopping the aggravating activity may be the only treatment necessary. Immobilization of the thumb with a protective splint or cast may be necessary to provide rest for the tendons, which decreases the inflammatory response. Injection of corticosteroid and an anesthetic provides relief in more difficult cases. If conservative measures fail, surgery may be necessary to decrease pressure over the tendon (tenosynovectomy).

Physical and occupational therapy modalities to decrease inflammation and adaptive splints may be recommended.

Prognosis

Most individuals will recover with rest or injections. Pain may decrease quickly, while swelling is slower to resolve. Those who require surgery (tenosynovectomy) can expect recovery from symptoms. Permanent impairment after surgery is rare unless nerve injury occurs.

Differential Diagnosis

Trigger thumb (stenosing tenosynovitis) and osteoarthritis of the wrist are other possible diagnoses.

Specialists

- Hand Surgeon
- Hand Therapist
- Neurosurgeon
- Occupational Therapist
- Orthopedic Surgeon

Rehabilitation

Rehabilitation of radial styloid tenosynovitis begins with the goals of decreasing pain and inflammation as well as addressing the cause of the inflammation and the restoration of mobility and strength to the wrist region. Heat treatments can be helpful to reduce inflammation and pain. Forms of heat treatment used in the region of the wrist region include ultrasound and electrical stimulation. Iontophoresis is another treatment in the rehabilitation of radial styloid tenosynovitis. This technique uses a small electric current to drive anti-inflammatory medication of the same electrical charge into the painful muscle tissues.

As pain subsides, stretching and strengthening exercises of specific wrist and elbow muscles are emphasized. All motions of the wrist are emphasized and strengthened. Bending the wrist by bringing the palm side of the hand to the same of the wrist is called wrist flexion. Opposite motion of the wrist (wrist extension) is also performed. Ulnar deviation is accomplished as the individual brings his or her little finger side of the hand as close to the forearm on that same side as possible. The opposite direction of motion is called radial deviation and is accomplished when the individual brings his or her thumb side of the hand to that same side of the forearm.

The therapist may perform each range of motion exercise with the individual in a resting position such as sitting or lying down depending on patient comfort and therapist preference. Strengthening exercises progress with resistance from a relatively light weight and/or elastic band.

Job requirements may need to be modified during the rehabilitation process until pain and swelling diminishes. For example, lifting objects that stress the wrist and elbow joints may need to be limited despite the amount of force needed to accomplish the task. An occupational therapist may fabricate a specific splint for the individual to help immobilize and protect the region of tenosynovitis.

As the initial pain and swelling subsides and motion becomes pain free, the rehabilitation process may warrant less direct observation and guidance of a physical therapist. The individual at this point will then progress to an independent exercise program.

Modifications may need to be made by the physical therapist for those individuals who have arthritis or other wrist/elbow joint irritations. If the wrist joint requires surgical repair, some restrictions may be placed on the progression of the range of motion and strengthening in certain movements. This varies depending on the degree or type of surgery that was performed.

Work Restrictions / Accommodations

Work restrictions include no use of affected thumb, restricted lifting, gripping and twisting during early stages of treatment. Individuals may need to wear protective splinting for aggravating activities.

Complementary and Alternative Therapies

Content is intended for awareness only. Treatments may or may not be effective. Scientific evidence may be lacking and some substances have potentially toxic effects. Dr. Presley Reed and the editors do not endorse the use of these therapies in the absence of consultation with a licensed medical professional.

Magnet therapy - Application of magnets over the painful area may relieve pain and may be tried before surgery.

Comorbid Conditions

Comorbid conditions include any chronic inflammatory disease.

Complications

Previous injury that altered the anatomy of the wrist would make treatment more difficult. Corticosteroid injections may cause changes in skin color and cannot be repeated more than one or two times.

Factors Influencing Duration

Dominant hand use, job requirements, ability to avoid aggravating activity, tolerance to immobilizing devices (splints), and complications of treatment would all affect length of disability.

Length of Disability

Duration depends on whether dominant or non-dominant hand is involved, the individual's job requirement for thumb and wrist movement, and the severity of symptoms. Some individuals may not be able to return to the same job unless tasks can be modified.

Medical treatment (including corticosteroid injection).

Duration in Days

Job Classification	Minimum	Optimum	Maximum
Sedentary work	0	7	14
Light work	1	7	14
Medium work	3	7	14
Heavy work	3	7	14
Very Heavy work	3	7	14

Surgical treatment.

Duration in Days

Job Classification	Minimum	Optimum	Maximum
Sedentary work	1	14	21
Light work	3	14	21
Medium work	7	21	42
Heavy work	21	28	56
Very Heavy work	21	28	56

Failure to Recover

If an individual fails to recover within the maximum duration expectancy period, the reader may wish to reference the following questions to assist in better understanding the specifics of an individual's medical case.

Regarding diagnosis:

- Has diagnosis of radial styloid tenosynovitis been confirmed?
- Does individual have an underlying condition that may impact recovery?

Regarding treatment:

- Do symptoms persist despite avoidance of aggravating motion?
- If conservative measures failed to provide symptom relief, is individual now a candidate for surgical intervention?
- Has individual been involved in a comprehensive rehabilitation program?
- Has individual and/or job requirements been evaluated by an occupational therapist?
- Are assistive devices warranted and available?

Regarding prognosis:

- Has adequate time passed to allow conservative measures to resolve symptoms?
- Has individual been involved in a comprehensive rehabilitation program?
- Is individual now a candidate for surgical intervention?
- Has protective splinting been provided?
- Would individual benefit from reassignment or vocational re-

References

Anderson, Bruce C. Office Orthopedics for Primary Care, 2nd ed. Kersey, Ray, ed. Philadelphia: W.B. Saunders Company, 1999.

Kessler, R.M. Management of Common Musculoskeletal Disorders: Physical Therapy Principles and Methods. Philadelphia: J.B. Lippincott Company, 1990.

Kisner, C., and L. Colby. Therapeutic Exercise Foundations and Techniques. Philadelphia: F.A. Davis Company, 1990.

Skinner, J.B., and Harry B. Skinner. Current Diagnosis and Treatment in Orthopedics. Norwalk: Appleton & Lange, 1995.

Radiation Therapy
92.2, 92.21, 92.22, 92.23, 92.24, 92.26

Definition

Radiation therapy is the use of high-energy (ionizing) radiation for medical treatment, usually cancer. Radiation is effective against cancer cells because the radiation damages or breaks the cellular DNA and causes the cell to die. DNA is vital to the cell because it carries all genetic information and instructions. The radiation as it passes through the diseased tissue destroys or slows the growth of abnormal cells. About half of all individuals who undergo treatment for cancer receive radiation therapy.

Radiation therapy may be used as the only type of treatment in cancers such as Hodgkin's disease. Radiation therapy may also be used as an adjuvant therapy. Adjuvant radiation therapy is treatment given in addition to other treatments, such as surgery/chemotherapy to prevent recurrence of the cancer. Radiation may be given both before (neoadjuvant) and after surgical treatment. Radiation therapy can be combined with chemotherapy and in such cases both the radiation therapy and the chemotherapy may have to be reduced. A reduction in doses decreases the risk of side effects and complications.

Reason for Procedure

Radiation therapy is given to sterilize an area of cancer cells, control pain, and stop bleeding.

Furthermore, after a cancerous tumor (malignancy) is surgically removed, radiation may be used to destroy any remaining tumor cells in the area. Radiation therapy can be given prior to surgery to shrink the size of the tumor. Radiation therapy can also have an advantage over surgery by preserving more function or having a more cosmetic result.

Noncancerous (benign) conditions may also be treated with radiation therapy when the benefits of destroying diseased tissue far outweigh the risk of radiation damage to healthy skin. For example, an overactive thyroid gland can be treated with radiation in a liquid form. This radioactive iodine concentrates in the thyroid gland and destroys the overactive part of the gland.

Radiation therapy can also be done for relief of pain from cancer that is too far advanced to be curable. For example, reducing the size of a tumor can relieve pressure from a tumor on the esophagus that inhibits swallowing. It can relieve pain caused by bone cancer or relieve headaches or paralysis caused by a brain tumor.

Description

Radiation therapy is carefully planned. The dose of radiation to be given is determined. The dose is usually divided into several small doses that are given over a period of time. The dose and time schedule varies depending on the type of cancer. The area of the body to be radiated also varies depending on type and location of cancer.

Radiation therapy can be given by an external beam or by implanting radioactive material in the cancerous growth. Other methods include intraoperative radiotherapy, total body irradiation, and radiation surgery. Not all radiation therapy facilities, however, have all these capabilities.

External beam is the most common type of radiation therapy where the radiation is aimed at the cancer from a source outside the body. The beam penetrates through the skin to reach deeper tissues. Another method uses electrons produced by a machine called a linear accelerator.

Implant methods (brachytherapy or seeding) use radioactive material that is placed in or very close to the tumor. These sources may be described as either interstitial or intracavitary. The interstitial method

places the radioactive matter directly into the tumor, i.e., into the prostate gland. The intracavitary method places the sealed radioactive source in a body cavity close to the tumor such as in the cervical canal.

If the tumor is deep within the body, radiation therapy can be given at the time of surgery (intraoperative radiotherapy) so that surrounding organs can be moved out of the way. This allows a larger single dose to be delivered directly to the tumor without damaging surrounding normal tissues. Due to complexity and expense, this method is only used in special cases.

Total body irradiation is used in certain cases such as when an individual is preparing for bone marrow transplantation. Radiation can be given in higher doses than normal because the bone marrow will be replaced.

Other radiation treatment methods include neutron and proton therapy and the use of heavy ions and pions. These treatments are used primarily in specialized radiation oncology centers.

Prognosis

The outcome of radiation therapy varies widely with type of cancer treated, degree of spread of the tumor(s), type of radiation therapy administered, and location of cancer. Radiation therapy can provide curative treatment for individuals with limited Hodgkin's disease, skin tumors, laryngeal cancer confined to the vocal cords, and early-stage breast cancer after lumpectomy. The outcome of radiation therapy used as an adjuvant therapy to prevent spread of cancer is often good. Palliative radiation therapy does not cure the cancer but can improve the quality of life temporarily.

Specialists

- Radiation Oncologist

Work Restrictions / Accommodations

Work restrictions and accommodations depend on what side effects are present and their severity. Many individuals can work while receiving radiation therapy. Others find they need more rest than usual and are limited by fatigue. These workers may temporarily require more sedentary work. Individuals may need to work a reduced number of hours on a part-time schedule or work at home.

Comorbid Conditions

There are a number of comorbid conditions that may increase the risk associated with radiation therapy. Age is a comorbid condition that increases the risk of toxicity to radiation. Smoking may increase the risk of developing lung cancer following radiation therapy. Systemic lupus may increase the risk of complications associated with radiation therapy. Previous abdominal surgeries (laparotomies) may increase the risk of small bowel obstruction in individuals receiving whole abdominal radiation. Any chronic condition will impair recovery such as heart disease, lung disease, or diabetes.

Procedure Complications

Several complications may result from radiation therapy. Complications and their severity depend on several factors including the dose of radiation and tissues radiated. Many tissues of the body are affected. Some tissues are more resistant to the effects of radiation therapy than others. Tissues that rapidly divide such as bone marrow and the cells that line the intestinal tract are very sensitive to the effects of radiation therapy. Complications may occur within the first 6 months of therapy (acute effects), the second 6 months (subacute effects), or years later (late effects).

Radiation therapy to the skin may cause complications such as redness (erythema), peeling (desquamation), hair loss, and itching (pruritus). Radiation to the gastrointestinal tract may produce a number of complications depending on the area radiated. Complications can include loss of appetite (anorexia), mouth dryness (xerostomia), inflammation of the mucous membranes of the mouth (mucositis), mouth and throat pain, nausea, vomiting, abdominal pain, diarrhea, and rectal pain and bleeding.

Radiation to the liver may cause radiation hepatitis with symptoms such as a general feeling of ill health (malaise), fever, right-sided upper abdominal quadrant pain, and fluid accumulation in the abdominal cavity (ascites). Radiation to the lungs may cause radiation pneumonitis. Symptoms can include difficulty breathing (dyspnea), fever, chest pain, and a cough. Permanent damage to lung tissues (fibrosis) can occur. Radiation to the heart may cause pericarditis. Symptoms of pericarditis include pain and difficulty breathing. The heart may be severely damaged by radiation therapy.

Radiation to the bladder and kidneys can result in radiation cystitis. Symptoms include painful or difficult urination (dysuria), frequency, urgency, excessive nighttime urination (nocturia), and blood in the urine (hematuria). The ovaries and testes may be affected, often resulting in infertility. Radiation to the brain may cause death of brain cells (necrosis). Symptoms of brain necrosis are similar to symptoms of recurrence of the brain tumor. Radiation to the spinal cord may result in shock-like sensations going from the back to the extremities (Lhermitte's sign). Radiation myelopathy may also develop with spinal cord radiation. Symptoms can include sensations of numbness, prickling or tingling (paresthesias) and loss of control over muscular movement, bowel, and bladder function. Finally, cancer may develop several years after treatment by radiation therapy.

Factors Influencing Duration

The type and stage of the cancer itself is the most important in determining length of disability. The side effects of radiation therapy are also a factor in determining disability, as they vary depending on the treatment dose, part of the body treated, and general health of individual.

Length of Disability

Duration depends on underlying cause for which the procedure is performed and response to treatment. Contact physician for additional information.

References

Chao, K.S., et al. "Fundamentals of Patient Management." Radiation Oncology Management Decisions. Philadelphia: Lippincott - Raven, 1999. 1-13.

Markman, Maurie. "Principles of Radiation Oncology." Basic Cancer Medicine. Philadelphia: W.B. Saunders Company, 1997. 16-17.

Rieger, Paula Trahan, and Carmen P. Escalante. "Complications of Cancer Treatment." Primary Care Oncology. Boyer, Kathryn L., et al., eds. Philadelphia: W.B. Saunders Company, 1999. 353-373.

Salmon, Sydney E., and Joseph R. Bertino. "Principles of Cancer Therapy." Cecil Textbook of Medicine, 20th ed. Bennett, J. Claude, and Fred Plum, eds. Philadelphia: W.B. Saunders Company, 1996. 1036-1049.

Radiodermatitis
692.82

Definition

Radiodermatitis is an inflammation of the skin caused by radiation.

Radiodermatitis can result from over-exposure to diagnostic x-rays, from exposure to radiation therapy used to treat numerous diseases and disorders, and from occupational hazard exposure to workers in the nuclear energy industry. Although the dermatitis usually occurs many years after exposure, it can be more immediate after heavy radiation exposure.

Most individuals who develop the condition are middle-aged to older adults who had x-ray therapy for acne or scalp fungus infection (tinea capitis) many years ago (this treatment is no longer used for these conditions).

Because most cases of radiodermatitis were caused by superficial x-ray therapy for skin conditions, a treatment no longer used for several years now, the number of new cases of radiodermatitis is continually decreasing.

Diagnosis

History: Symptoms of radiodermatitis include a sunburn-like reddening of the skin, followed by skin breakdown (ulceration) or sloughing of the skin (desquamation and denudation). Symptoms can appear immediately or they may suddenly appear a long time after the exposure. The individual will relate a history of x-ray exposure, usually many years previously. This exposure could be occupational or therapeutic.

Physical exam: Examination of affected skin reveals reddened skin, possibly with ulcerations and skin loss.

Tests: Punch biopsy of affected skin will confirm the diagnosis.

Treatment

anti-inflammatory (corticosteroid) creams or lotions are prescribed to reduce the inflammation in the skin. A short course of oral anti-inflammatory medication (nonsteroidal or steroidal) may be used in severe cases. Ulcers are treated with removal of dead tissue (debridement), followed by daily dressing changes with saline, antibiotic creams, or topical medications to dissolve dead tissue (enzyme creams).

Skin cancers developing in radiodermatitis areas are treated with complete removal of the tumor (wide excision) or with specialized skin surgery (Moh's surgery). Avoidance of sunlight (ultraviolet) exposure to affected areas is important.

Plastic surgery may be necessary to correct large or slow-to-heal ulcers.

Prognosis

The effects of radiation depend on the dose received and the duration of exposure. Healing, although slow even with treatment, is expected to be complete. Even if the individual develops skin cancers, these are successfully removed surgically and the individual will recover fully.

Differential Diagnosis

Other possibilities include erythema multiforme, solar keratosis, cellulitis, ulcers of various etiologies, stasis dermatitis, and benign and malignant skin tumors.

Specialists

- Dermatologist
- General Surgeon

Work Restrictions / Accommodations

Depending on site, extent, and treatment of radiodermatitis, some specific work restrictions may apply. Individuals should avoid ultraviolet (sunlight) exposure on the involved area. If surgery is necessary for ulceration or skin cancers, the individual may need some time off until recovery is complete. Drug policies need to be reviewed in individuals who take postoperative pain medication. Individuals with radiodermatitis should avoid x-ray (radiation) exposure.

Complementary and Alternative Therapies

Content is intended for awareness only. Treatments may or may not be effective. Scientific evidence may be lacking and some substances have potentially toxic effects. Dr. Presley Reed and the editors do not endorse the use of these therapies in the absence of consultation with a licensed medical professional.

Aloe vera - Said to have an antibacterial and antifungal effect.

Vitamin E - Said to have antioxidant effects that produce decreased healing time for laser injury to skin.

Comorbid Conditions

Comorbid conditions that may lengthen disability include peripheral vascular disease and diabetes.

Complications

Since skin is the body's defense against infection, the loss of skin increases the risk of infection at the burn site.

Although the incidence is unknown, many individuals with radiodermatitis develop skin cancers (basal cell carcinoma and squamous cell carcinoma) in affected areas.

Factors Influencing Duration

Length of disability depends on the site and extent of the radiodermatitis. Infection or surgery to correct an ulceration may also increase length of disability. Development of skin cancer in the radiodermatitis site would necessitate surgery, further lengthening disability.

Length of Disability

Duration depends on degree and duration of exposure.

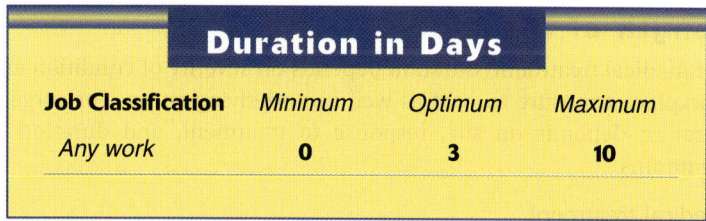

Job Classification	Minimum	Optimum	Maximum
Any work	0	3	10

Failure to Recover

If an individual fails to recover within the maximum duration expectancy period, the reader may wish to reference the following questions to assist in better understanding the specifics of an individual's medical case.

Regarding diagnosis:
- What symptoms does individual have?
- What were the physical findings?
- Has individual received appropriate testing to establish the diagnosis?
- Have conditions with similar symptoms been ruled out?

Regarding treatment:
- Has individual received appropriate treatment?

Regarding prognosis:
- Is individual's employer able to accommodate any necessary restrictions? Does individual also follow these restrictions when at home or play?
- Does individual have peripheral vascular disease or diabetes?
- Does individual have any complications?

References

Klein, A.D., and N.S. Penneys. "Aloe Vera." Journal of the American Academy of Dermatology 18 4 Pt 1 (1988): 714-720.

Thomas, Julian M. "Premalignant and Malignant Epithelial Tumors." Principles and Practice of Practice of Dermatology, 2nd ed. Sams, W. Mitchell, and Peter J. Lynch, eds. New York: Churchill Livingstone, 1996. 225-239.

Raynaud's Phenomenon
Other names / synonyms: Paroxysmal Digital Cyanosis Syndrome, Raynaud's Syndrome, Vibration White-Finger
443.0

Definition

Raynaud's phenomenon is a circulatory disorder in which the blood flow to the fingers and toes is temporarily diminished. The small blood vessels (arterioles) supplying finger and toes contract suddenly, often upon exposure to cold or stress. The fingers, usually on both hands, are affected more often than the toes. The thumb is not usually involved.

Although the exact cause for the blood vessel constriction (vasoconstriction) is unknown, there are several theories. The blood vessel constriction may be due to increased nervous system stimulation to the vessel walls.

Raynaud's phenomenon is associated with a known underlying disorder that may have serious long-term consequences. When symptoms occur from no known cause, it is called Raynaud's disease.

Raynaud's is a recognized occupational disorder of individuals who use pneumatic drills, chain saws, or other vibrating hand tools and machinery. This disorder is also seen in occupations involving repeated finger trauma, such as typing and playing the piano. Because it is often associated with connective tissue diseases such as rheumatoid arthritis, scleroderma, and systemic lupus erythematosus, vasoconstriction may be the result of an antigen-antibody immune response. Other possible causes include arterial diseases such as Buerger's disease, atherosclerosis, embolism, and thrombosis. Certain drugs (beta-blocker, ergotamine, vasoconstrictor, and nicotine from cigarette smoking or chewing tobacco) are also associated with Raynaud's phenomenon. The disorder may occur secondary to frostbite, leading to a theory that the vessel walls may be intrinsically hyperreactive to cold. Individuals in occupations in which they are exposed to cold, such as meat processing, are also prone to the disorder.

Raynaud's may affect as much as 5-10% of the population, with 75% of those affected being women. Women generally develop the disorder between the ages of 15-40; men tend to develop it later in life.

Diagnosis

History: Individuals may report that, upon exposure to cold or stress, fingers or toes turn white, become bluish in color (cyanosis) and then, with heat or warmth, become red. Pain, tingling, numbness, or burning often occurs in the affected fingers or toes. Symptoms usually begin at the tips of the fingers and toes and gradually spread to involve more of the digits. Episodes may last from minutes to hours, but are not generally severe enough to result in tissue loss from lack of circulation. Diagnosis is based in part on the individual's history, including the recurrence of symptoms for at least 2 years.

Physical exam: Severe or chronic cases may display shiny, tight skin, with ulcers on the fingertips. Tissue death (gangrene) is present only in the most severe of cases.

Tests: Response of the peripheral circulation to cold can be tested using comparison of readings from multiple blood pressure cuffs (plethysmography).

Treatment

Symptoms are generally relieved by warmth. Besides protecting the body (especially hands and feet) from cold, treatment is directed at the underlying disorder. The use of vibrating machinery or tools should be discontinued or minimized. Cigarette smoking, chewing tobacco, and emotional stress should be avoided. If symptoms are the result of medications, the drugs may need to be changed or discontinued. Vasodilator drugs, which relax the walls of the blood vessels, may be used in individuals with unusually severe symptoms. In cases where ulcers develop in spite of other treatments, excision of nerves controlling the contraction response (sympathectomy) may be used in an effort to improve blood flow to the skin.

Prognosis

The prognosis is favorable provided the individual complies with instructions about keeping warm and avoiding aggravating factors such as prolonged vibration and nicotine. Few cases are so severe as to require radical treatment for ulceration or amputation for gangrene.

Differential Diagnosis

Conditions with similar symptoms include diabetes, thyroid disease, neuropathy, autoimmune disease, carpal tunnel syndrome, or chronic arterial occlusive disease. Certain medications such as those used to treat hypertension or asthma can also diminish peripheral circulation.

Specialists

- Cardiovascular Surgeon
- Internist
- Neurologist

Work Restrictions / Accommodations

Work restrictions and accommodations may include monitoring the temperature of indoor/outdoor work areas and avoiding or minimizing the use of vibrating tools and machinery. Protective measures should be taken such as wearing warm clothing, using coated tool handles, and using anti-vibration gloves.

Complementary and Alternative Therapies

Content is intended for awareness only. Treatments may or may not be effective. Scientific evidence may be lacking and some substances have potentially toxic effects. Dr. Presley Reed and the editors do not endorse the use of these therapies in the absence of consultation with a licensed medical professional.

Biofeedback - Biofeedback may help decrease the severity and frequency of Raynaud's phenomenon in some individuals.

Comorbid Conditions

Comorbid conditions include heart and lung problems and other conditions that impede oxygenation of the extremities.

Complications

The walls of the arteries may gradually thicken and permanently reduce blood flow, which may lead to painful ulcerations or tissue death (gangrene) at the tips of the affected digits. Rarely, amputation may be required due to gangrene.

Factors Influencing Duration

Length of disability might be influenced by the severity of symptoms or the presence of complications. Length of disability might be influenced by continued exposure to cold temperatures or emotional stress, continued smoking or tobacco chewing, or the continued use of vibrating tools and machinery.

Length of Disability

For medical treatment, duration depends on severity of condition and workplace exposure to cold as well as underlying cause. For surgery, duration depends on site, response to treatment, and duration of symptoms.

Medical treatment.

Duration in Days

Job Classification	Minimum	Optimum	Maximum
Sedentary work	1	3	7
Light work	1	3	7
Medium work	1	3	7
Heavy work	1	3	7
Very Heavy work	1	3	7

Sympathectomy (ganglionectomy).

Duration in Days

Job Classification	Minimum	Optimum	Maximum
Sedentary work	1	3	14
Light work	1	3	14
Medium work	7	14	21
Heavy work	14	21	28
Very Heavy work	14	28	41

Failure to Recover

If an individual fails to recover within the maximum duration expectancy period, the reader may wish to reference the following questions to assist in better understanding the specifics of an individual's medical case.

Regarding diagnosis:

- Has diagnosis of Raynaud's phenomenon been confirmed?
- Have other causes for the poor circulation to the extremities been ruled out?
- Has the underlying condition causing the Raynaud's phenomenon been identified?

- Has individual experienced any complications related to the Raynaud's phenomenon?

Regarding treatment:

- If the underlying condition causing the Raynaud's phenomenon has been identified, is it being effectively treated?
- Does individual's occupation require the use of vibrating machinery or tools?
- Is individual abstaining from the use of nicotine?
- Is individual utilizing adequate protection from cold temperatures?

- Would individual benefit from a stress management program?

Regarding prognosis:

- Do work accommodations include monitoring the temperature of indoor/outdoor work areas and the wearing of warm, protective clothing?
- Can the use of vibrating tools and machinery be avoided or minimized through the use of coated tool handles and anti-vibration gloves?
- Would individual benefit from enrollment in a community smoking cessation program?

References

Beers, Mark H., and Robert Berkow. The Merck Manual of Diagnosis and Therapy. Whitehouse Station, NJ: Merck & Co., Inc, 1999.

Raynaud's Phenomenon. MedicineNet.Com. 26 Jul 2000. 18 Jan 2001 <http://www.medicinenet.com/Script/Main/Art.asp?li=MNI&ArticleKey=463>.

Rectal Polyps

Other names / synonyms: Adenomatous Polyps, Hamartoma Polyps, Hyperplastic Polyps, Polypoid Disease

569.0, 569.1

Definition

Rectal polyps are well-defined projections that grow from the mucous membrane that lines the wall of the lower intestine (rectum).

Polyps may grow singly or in groups, and they may grow on stalks (pedunculated) or they can have a broad, flat base (sessile). They range in size from 1-2 millimeters to greater than 10 centimeters.

There are 3 major groups of rectal polyps and the groups are classified according to their tissue-type (histology). The 3 groups of rectal polyps are adenomas (67%), hyperplastic polyps (11%), and a miscellaneous group (22%), which includes mucosal polyps (made of normal mucosa), inflammatory polyps, juvenile polyps, hamartomas, and a variety of nonmucosal lesions. Adenomas are unique among polyps in that only they are known to be direct precursors of cancer (carcinoma).

Risk factors for rectal polyps may include a high fat and calorie, low-fiber diet, obesity, cigarette smoking, alcohol consumption, liver disease (cirrhosis), chronic inflammatory bowel disease (ulcerative colitis, Crohn's disease), and any condition in which the immune system is compromised (immunodeficiency).

Adenomas occur in up to 40% of the adult population in Western countries and they are slightly more frequent in men than in women. They are uncommon before age 40, although prevalence increases with age. Twenty-five percent of all individuals will have adenoma(s) at age 50, and 60% will have them at age 80. The frequency of hyperplastic polyps also increases with age, and their prevalence has been reported to be as high as 80% in older individuals.

Diagnosis

History: Individuals will occasionally complain of abdominal pain, diarrhea, or rectal bleeding. More commonly, there are no signs or symptoms, and rectal polyps are detected during routine screening for rectal cancer.

Physical exam: The exam is usually normal. A gloved finger inserted into the rectum (digital rectal examination) may reveal rectal polyps, but cannot confirm the diagnosis.

Tests: Tests include examination of the inside of the rectum using a flexible, fiber-optic viewing instrument (colonoscopy). Also, small samples of polyp tissue (biopsy) may be taken during colonoscopy for microscopic examination. X-rays of the rectum can be taken following injection of a contrast medium into the bowel (barium enema) in order to further visualize the polyps. Blood in the stool can be identified using a fecal occult blood test (FOBT), which may be used as a screening test for rectal polyps or cancer.

Treatment

The preferred treatment for rectal polyps is to remove them during colonoscopy (colonoscopic polypectomy). The specific technique for polyp removal during colonoscopy (hot biopsy technique, snare excision with electrocautery, piecemeal snare excision) depends upon polyp size and configuration, experience and expertise of the physician, and the equipment that is available for the procedure. Surgical removal (excision) of polyps by cutting out a section (resection) of the rectum is recommended for individuals with polyps that cannot be removed completely during colonoscopy. Depending upon the extent of the surgical resection, the individual may require an artificial opening (stoma) through the abdominal wall for the purpose of bowel elimination (colostomy).

Prognosis

Most rectal polyps are removed without incidence and serious complications occur in less than 0.2% of sigmoidoscopy procedures. Following removal, rectal polyps will recur 40% of the time. Individuals with adenomas have a 1-15 chance of developing rectal cancer within 15 years of diagnosis. Approximately one-third of polyps that are removed from the rectum will be cancerous. Following surgical treatment, a colostomy may produce psychological problems and, as a result, individuals may become anxious and depressed. Individuals with a colostomy usually should avoid odor- and gas-forming foods, and they must learn proper colostomy irrigation technique. Good skin and stoma care are important in preventing infection of the colostomy.

Differential Diagnosis

Conditions that present with similar symptoms as rectal polyps may include colorectal cancer (carcinoma), diverticular disease, fecal impactions (constipation), bleeding from internal hemorrhoids, or infectious bowel disorders.

Specialists

- Gastroenterologist
- Surgeon

Rehabilitation

A regular exercise routine may be useful in reducing the risk of recurrence of rectal polyps. Aerobic exercise such as walking, jogging, or swimming (30-45 minutes per session) is usually beneficial.

Work Restrictions / Accommodations

No workplace restrictions should be necessary for individuals who are treated using colonoscopy for rectal polyps. If surgery was used as a treatment, heavy physical labor may have to be restricted until recovery is complete. Workplace accommodations should include easy access to restroom facilities if the individual has a colostomy.

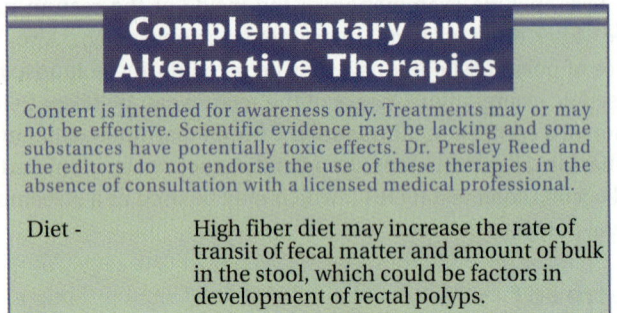

Complementary and Alternative Therapies

Content is intended for awareness only. Treatments may or may not be effective. Scientific evidence may be lacking and some substances have potentially toxic effects. Dr. Presley Reed and the editors do not endorse the use of these therapies in the absence of consultation with a licensed medical professional.

Diet - High fiber diet may increase the rate of transit of fecal matter and amount of bulk in the stool, which could be factors in development of rectal polyps.

Comorbid Conditions

Existing conditions that may impact an individual's ability to recover and further lengthen their disability include obesity, alcoholism, and diseases that compromise the immune system such as acquired immune deficiency syndrome (AIDS).

Complications

Rectal polyps may develop into cancer.

Factors Influencing Duration

Factors that might influence the length of disability include the size and number of polyps that are removed, whether sedation or general analgesia was required during polyp removal, whether surgery to remove part of the rectum was part of the treatment, and whether the individual was fitted with a colostomy during the surgical procedure.

Length of Disability

Endoscopic removal (sigmoidoscopy or colonoscopy).

Duration in Days

Job Classification	Minimum	Optimum	Maximum
Sedentary work	0	2	3
Light work	0	2	3
Medium work	0	2	3
Heavy work	0	2	3
Very Heavy work	0	2	3

Surgical resection of polyps or polypectomy.

Duration in Days

Job Classification	Minimum	Optimum	Maximum
Sedentary work	10	14	21
Light work	10	14	21
Medium work	14	21	28
Heavy work	14	35	42
Very Heavy work	14	42	56

Failure to Recover

If an individual fails to recover within the maximum duration expectancy period, the reader may wish to reference the following questions to assist in better understanding the specifics of an individual's medical case.

Regarding diagnosis:

- Has diagnosis of rectal polyps been confirmed?
- If diagnosis was uncertain, was a colonoscopy exam used to confirm the diagnosis and rule out other conditions with similar symptoms?
- Were x-rays of the rectum taken to further visualize the polyps?
- Was biopsy of polyp tissue used to determine the type of polyp?
- Did a fecal occult blood test (FOBT) reveal unseen blood in the stool?

Regarding treatment:

- Were polyps removed during colonoscopy?
- If not, will the individual need to undergo a resection in order to remove them?
- Did the individual require a colostomy during the surgery?
- What is the anticipated recovery time after surgery?
- Because psychological issues can be associated with a colostomy, would individual benefit from counseling?

Regarding prognosis:

- Were the polyps removed successfully?
- Was the polyp cancerous?
- Did postsurgical complications occur, such as severe bleeding or infection?

- Were complications effectively treated? What is the expected outcome after treatment?
- If colostomy was necessary, have psychological issues been resolved through counseling?
- Because polyps recur about 40% of the time, has individual been instructed in lifestyle modifications which may reduce the risk or polyps?
- Has individual complied with recommendations to lower fat and calories and increase fiber in the diet? Would individual benefit from consultation with a nutritionist?
- If individual has not been able to reduce weight, would he/she benefit from enrollment in a community weight loss program?
- Has individual been able to abstain from alcohol and tobacco use? would individual benefit from enrollment in community programs or support group?

References

Goodman, A.A. "Polypoid Diseases." Colon and Rectal Surgery. Corman, M.L., ed. Philadelphia: Lippincott-Raven, 1998. 566-624.

Schroy III, P.C. "Polyps, Adenocarcinomas, and Other Intestinal Tumors." Therapy of Digestive Disorders. Wolfe, M.M., ed. Philadelphia: W.B. Saunders Company, 2000. 645-673.

Rectal Prolapse
Other names / synonyms: Procidentia
569.1

Definition

Rectal prolapse refers to protrusion of the lower end of the large bowel (rectum) through the anal opening (anal orifice). Prolapse of the rectum may be classified as either incomplete (partial) or complete.

Incomplete rectal prolapse (also called rectal mucosal prolapse) occurs when only the inner tissue layer (mucosa) of the rectum protrudes through the anus. In complete rectal prolapse, the full thickness of the rectal wall protrudes through the anus.

The cause of rectal prolapse is not thoroughly understood, however, there are several factors that may put an individual at risk for developing this condition. These include poor bowel habits (especially constipation), neurological disease (cauda equina lesion; spinal cord injury; senility), female gender, women who have never given birth to a viable infant (nulliparity), a weak internal anal sphincter (patulous anus), certain surgical procedures (hemorrhoidectomy; fistulectomy; abdominoanal pull-through), and various anatomical abnormalities (deep pouch of Douglas; diastasis of levator ani muscle; lack of fixation of the rectum to the sacrum; intussusception secondary to a colonic lesion). Also, a disproportionately large percentage of individuals with rectal prolapse have a background of psychiatric illness or some other condition requiring institutionalization. Thus, mental illness may be considered as a risk factor for development of this condition.

In adults, nearly 90% of individuals with rectal prolapse are women and the female: male ratio is 7:1. The condition is not uncommon in middle-aged females and the incidence increases with increasing age. The peak incidence occurs in the sixth decade of life in females. In men, there is an even age distribution with respect to occurrence of rectal prolapse.

Diagnosis

History: Individuals with rectal prolapse will usually report that their rectum can be seen protruding from their anus. Other complaints may include difficulty in bowel regulation (fecal incontinence), a feeling of incomplete evacuation following a bowel movement, discomfort in the region near the anus (perianal region), persistent spasms of the rectum accompanied by the desire to defecate (tenesmus), mucus discharge from the anus, and rectal bleeding.

Physical exam: Complete rectal prolapse is dramatic and unmistakable in its appearance as a large red mass with circular (concentric) folds protruding from the anus. As much as 10 centimeters of rectum may be seen to protrude from the anal opening. Examination using a gloved hand will reveal a lax anal sphincter with impaired sensitivity around the anus. The prolapsed rectum should be felt between the thumb and forefinger and the thickness of the tissue may help to differentiate complete from incomplete rectal prolapse. In cases where the rectum is not visible and diagnosis is difficult, the prolapsed rectum may be visualized by having the individual sit on the toilet and bear down. Note that having the individual lie face-down with their knees drawn toward their chest (prone jackknife position) is the least effective way of evaluating rectal prolapse.

Tests: A flexible fiber-optic microscope (endoscope) can be inserted through the anus and into the rectum to examine the rectal mucosa (flexible sigmoidoscopy) and colon (colonoscopy). Contrast medium may be injected into the rectum (barium enema) and x-rays taken to detect any abnormal growths (neoplasms) in the lower intestine. Also, nontoxic radiopaque medium may be injected into the lower bowel and images recorded with a movie camera on a fluorescent screen (cineradiography). This test allows movement of the rectum to be examined and it is most useful when the diagnosis of rectal prolapse is suspected but not confirmed by physical examination. Other tests include anal manometry and anal electromyogram (EMG) to quantify the extent of anal sphincter impairment. Finally, the rate of movement of a radiopaque substance through the bowel (colonic transit study) can be useful to identify individuals with unusually severe constipation that may be associated with rectal prolapse.

Treatment

Incomplete rectal prolapse may be treated non-operatively by injecting a chemical (sclerosing agent) into the tissues around the rectum that causes fibrosis and fixation of the rectum. Training to correct poor bowel habits and to coordinate the musculature of the pelvic floor during defecation may also be part of treatment. Complete rectal prolapse can be treated only by surgery and there are essentially three major categories of surgical procedures for correction of this condition. These are surgery to narrow the anal opening (encirclement procedure); surgery to suspend and fix the rectum to the back (sacrum) so that it can no longer protrude through the anus (abdominal procedure); and surgery to remove part of the rectum so that prolapse does not occur (perineal procedure).

Prognosis

The outcome for incomplete rectal prolapse is generally positive when it is treated using non-operative procedures. Injection of a sclerosing agent and bowel habit training are usually successful and form the backbone of initial therapy for this condition.

For treatment of complete rectal prolapse, surgery to narrow the anal opening (encirclement procedure) has a number of disadvantages including breakage or erosion of the material used to narrow the anus (25% of cases) and fecal impaction (10% of cases). It is usually necessary to repeat encirclement procedures in approximately 25% of all cases as a result of these complications. Surgery to stabilize the rectum so it does not protrude through the anus (abdominal procedure) has relatively low recurrence rates (0-10% of cases). Average recurrence rate is 4.5% for all abdominal procedures. Another problem that may be associated with abdominal surgical procedures include fecal impaction and/or abnormal closing of the rectum (rectal stricture), which occurs in 8% of all cases.

Surgery to remove part of the rectum so that prolapse does not occur (perineal procedure) has been reported to have a variable recurrence rate (0-50%). However, recent technical advances have decreased the recurrence rate to less than 20% on a consistent basis.

Differential Diagnosis

Conditions that present with similar symptoms as rectal prolapse include hemorrhoids, infolding of one segment of the intestine into another (intussusception), growth of a rectal mass (rectocele), and internal or occult rectal prolapse.

Specialists

- Abdominal Surgeon
- Gastroenterologist

Rehabilitation

Training to correct poor bowel habits and to coordinate the musculature of the pelvic floor during defecation may be part of rehabilitation therapy. If surgery was used as a treatment, intermittent positive pressure breathing exercises may be necessary to prevent pulmonary complications that can result from general anesthesia. Also, certain exercises may be performed to reduce post-operative pain and speed recovery, including progressive relaxation and deep breathing techniques. These may be performed several times per day until pain from inhalation/exhalation is less noticeable. Ankle flexes, knee bends, and crossed-leg muscle contractions (all while lying on the back) will help to increase circulation and make walking easier. These are especially valuable during the first 48 hours after surgery. Individuals may continue with these exercises until recovery from surgery is complete and pain is no longer noticeable while walking or breathing.

Work Restrictions / Accommodations

Individuals with incomplete rectal prolapse generally will not require any restrictions or accommodations in order for them to successfully recover and return to work in full capacity. Following surgical treatment for complete rectal prolapse, individuals may need up to several weeks of recovery before returning to work. At that time, heavy physical labor (lifting, climbing, etc.) may have to be restricted until recovery is complete

Complementary and Alternative Therapies

Content is intended for awareness only. Treatments may or may not be effective. Scientific evidence may be lacking and some substances have potentially toxic effects. Dr. Presley Reed and the editors do not endorse the use of these therapies in the absence of consultation with a licensed medical professional.

Biofeedback - Information regarding anal sensation and pressure may help control rectal prolapse.

Acupuncture - Inserting needles into certain points on the body may alleviate symptoms associated with rectal prolapse.

Comorbid Conditions

Disability from rectal prolapse may be influenced by any condition that increases abdominal straining such as chronic constipation or persistent coughing. Obesity may impact an individual's ability to recover and further lengthen their disability. For both incomplete and complete rectal prolapse, mental health may influence disability, as there appears to be a high incidence of these conditions among individuals who have psychiatric problems or who are institutionalized.

Complications

Complications of rectal prolapse include a progressive worsening of the condition, appearing first after defecation and later becoming present continuously. At this point, the rectum cannot be pushed back up into the anus (irreducible). Other complications may include rectal tissue death (gangrene), development of sores (ulcers) in the rectum, and rupture of the rectum. In rare cases, the rectum may become pinched off (strangulated), which restricts blood flow to the tissue. The overall rate of complications (including bleeding, formation of abscess in the pelvis, and obstruction of the small intestine) following abdominal procedures is approximately seventeen percent.

Factors Influencing Duration

For complete rectal prolapse, advanced age may lengthen disability because older individuals tend to heal more slowly and progress at a slower rate following surgery. Also, heavy, physical labor may have to be restricted following surgical treatment until recovery is complete.

Length of Disability

The length of disability for individuals with incomplete rectal prolapse should be minimal and a return to full job responsibilities can probably occur within a day or two following treatment. Individuals who are treated surgically for complete rectal prolapse will require longer recovery times and recurrence of this condition is not uncommon.

Incomplete prolaspe.

Duration in Days

Job Classification	Minimum	Optimum	Maximum
Sedentary work	1	3	7
Light work	1	3	7
Medium work	3	7	14
Heavy work	3	7	14
Very Heavy work	3	7	14

Surgical treatment.

Duration in Days

Job Classification	Minimum	Optimum	Maximum
Sedentary work	7	14	21
Light work	7	14	21
Medium work	14	21	28
Heavy work	14	28	35
Very Heavy work	21	35	42

Failure to Recover

If an individual fails to recover within the maximum duration expectancy period, the reader may wish to reference the following questions to assist in better understanding the specifics of an individual's medical case.

Regarding diagnosis:

- Does the individual have a medical history that may increase the risk for developing rectal prolapse (constipations, spinal cord injury, rectal surgery, etc.)?
- Did the individual have symptoms such as fecal incontinence, rectal spasms, tenesmus, or bleeding or mucus discharge from the anus?
- On physical exam, did the physician find a large red mass with circular (concentric) folds protruding from the anus?
- During exam using a gloved finger, did the physician note a lax anal sphincter with impaired sensitivity around the anus?
- If the prolapse was not visible, did the physician have the individual sit on the toilet and bear down? Was the prolapse visual then?
- Was the diagnosis confirmed by history and physical exam?
- Were other diagnostic studies (sigmoidoscopy, anal manometry, etc) needed to confirm the diagnosis?
- If the diagnosis was uncertain, were other conditions with similar symptoms ruled out (i.e., hemorrhoids, intussusception, rectal mass (rectocele)?

Regarding treatment:

- Did the individual experience an incomplete or complete prolapse?
- If incomplete, did the individual undergo sclerotherapy treatment? Was it successful?
- Has the individual been instructed on proper bowel habits and how to better control muscles during defecation?
- If a complete prolapse occurred, was surgical intervention warranted? Was it successful?

Regarding prognosis:

- Based on the type of treatment required, was adequate time allowed for complete recovery?
- Has the individual been able to follow treatment recommendations (bowel habits, etc)?
- Has the condition worsened despite treatment?
- Has a surgical procedure or alternative surgical procedure been considered?
- Did the individual suffer any complications (i.e., irreducible prolapse, or ulcers or necrosis) that may impact response to treatment or recovery? Have these complications been addressed in the treatment plan?
- Does the individual have any underlying conditions such as obesity or psychiatric disturbances that may impact ability to recover?

References

Hamalainen, K.J., et al. "Biofeedback Therapy in Rectal Prolapse Patients." Diseases of the Colon and Rectum 39 3 (1996): 262-265.

Ludwig, K.A. "Management of Colorectal-anal Dysfunction." Obstetrics and Gynecology Clinics of North America 25 4 (1998): 923-944.

Rectal Ulcer

Other names / synonyms: Solitary Rectal Ulcer Syndrome, SRUS, Ulcer of Anus

569.41, 569.42

Definition

A rectal ulcer is an area of the rectal wall that is red (erythema) or has an open sore (ulceration). The condition is sometimes referred to as solitary rectal ulcer syndrome (SRUS), although the lesions are not necessarily solitary.

Multiple isolated areas on the wall of the rectum may be affected. A primary risk factor for developing rectal ulcers includes a condition in which the lower end of the rectum protrudes through the anal orifice (rectal prolapse). Other risk factors may include constipation and straining during bowel movements, deficient blood flow (ischemia) to the rectum, direct trauma as a result of inserting a finger (rectal digitation) or other foreign object into the rectum, anal intercourse, and abnormal toileting behavior due to psychological problems. Certain systemic diseases (oral ulceration, erythema nodosum, sacroiliitis) may also increase the risk for developing rectal ulcers.

Rectal ulcers are rare and there is a general lack of awareness of this condition. The incidence is estimated at 1 in 100,000 individuals per year. Approximately 26% of individuals with a rectal ulcer are misdiagnosed. The condition affects men and women in approximately equal proportions, and it can develop at any age. The majority of individuals with rectal ulcer are between 20-35 years old; 25% of individuals with this condition are over 60 years old.

Diagnosis

History: Individuals with rectal ulcers will usually report rectal bleeding, which is the hallmark of this condition. Passing mucus, abdominal cramps, painful (but involuntary) straining while passing only small amounts of fecal material (tenesmus), constipation, diarrhea, and painful spasms of the anus (proctalgia fugax) may also be reported. The individual may also report a sense of anal obstruction. Pain is often localized to the region around the anus (perineum) or the lower back (sacral area), and is usually described as dull, continuous, and unrelieved or unchanged by defecation.

Physical exam: A gloved finger inserted into the anus (digital rectal exam) may reveal tenderness and bleeding. Also, a localized area of tissue firmness or hardness (induration) may be felt during the rectal exam.

Tests: The diagnosis of rectal ulcers can usually be made by examining the inner wall of the rectum using a flexible, fiberoptic viewing instrument (sigmoidoscopy). Open sores (ulcerations) will be seen on the rectal wall approximately 57% of the time; bulging, nonulcerated tissue (polypoids) are responsible for the problem 25% of the time, and inflammation (hyperemic mucosa) may be present in localized area(s) 18% of the time. A tissue sample (biopsy) of the lesion for microscopic examination will be taken during a sigmoidoscopy. High frequency sound waves (transrectal and endoanal ultrasonography) may also be used to visualize the rectum. Barium thickened to the consistency of stool may be introduced into the rectum; evacuation of the barium will then be monitored via fluoroscopy and videotaped (video defecography) to assess any abnormal muscle control in the lower bowel. Physiological studies (anal canal electro-sensory threshold, rectal distention threshold, resting anal manometry, anal squeeze pressure manometry) may also be performed.

Treatment

Treatment will be either conservative or surgical. Conservative treatment may include local application of a drug (human fibrin sealant) to stimulate cell (fibroblast) and blood vessel (vascular) growth; taking stool softeners; assessment of any relevant psychological factors; and encouragement to stop taking laxatives, suppositories, and enemas.

Surgical treatments may include stitching (suturing) the ulcerated areas closed, or removing (local excision) the area with rectal ulcers. If rectal prolapse has occurred, the portion of the rectal mucosa that has prolapsed may be removed (prolapsectomy) or repaired (encirclement, abdominal, or perineal procedures).

Alternatively, the entire section of the rectum containing the ulcer may be removed (resection). For some individuals who are surgically treated, a temporary or permanent opening (stoma) may need to be surgically created to permit defection (colostomy).

Prognosis

There is no specific cure for rectal ulcers. Symptoms may be improved by either conservative treatment or surgery, but it is uncommon for tissues to completely return to normal. Topical application of human fibrin sealant has been found to stimulate tissue regeneration in ulcerated areas.

A combination of taking stool softeners, increasing fiber intake once the ulcers have healed, and discontinuing straining while defecating, will result in successful healing for virtually all individuals within weeks; these ulcers tend to remain healed for longer than one year. Stool softeners and/or increased fiber intake in combination with discontinuing straining while defecating will improve symptoms 66% of the time; this results in 38% of individuals healing.

Surgical excision or suturing closed the ulcerated region, in combination with correcting rectal prolapse, produces symptomatic cure in 56-80% of cases. Surgical resection of a segment of the rectum in combination with correcting rectal prolapse has somewhat poorer results.

Differential Diagnosis

Conditions that present with similar symptoms include rectal tumor, ulcerative proctitis, ulcerative colitis, Crohn's disease, nonspecific inflammatory bowel disease, and villous adenoma.

Specialists

- Gastroenterologist
- Proctologist
- Surgeon

Work Restrictions / Accommodations

No workplace restrictions should be necessary for individuals who are treated conservatively for rectal ulcers. If surgery has been performed, heavy physical labor may have to be restricted until recovery is complete. Workplace accommodations should also include easy access to restroom facilities if the individual has a colostomy. Heavy work may have to be restricted.

Complementary and Alternative Therapies

Content is intended for awareness only. Treatments may or may not be effective. Scientific evidence may be lacking and some substances have potentially toxic effects. Dr. Presley Reed and the editors do not endorse the use of these therapies in the absence of consultation with a licensed medical professional.

Biofeedback	Behavioral training may help to minimize bowel straining.
Acupuncture	Insertion of needles at certain points on the body may relieve constipation and reduce straining.
Abdominal wall (colonic) massage	Propulsive abdominal wall massage may decrease transit time through the colon and reduce constipation.
Baduanjin	Ancient Chinese exercises that may be effective for constipation.

Comorbid Conditions

Existing conditions that may impact an individual's ability to recover and further lengthen disability include rectal prolapse, rectal stricture, or any condition that increases abdominal straining such as chronic constipation or persistent coughing.

Complications

Complications of rectal ulcer may include excessive rectal bleeding (hemorrhage), extreme disturbance of bowel function, formation of an abscess, or formation of a hole (perforation) through the rectal wall beneath the ulcer.

Factors Influencing Duration

The severity of symptoms and the individual's response to treatment will influence the length of disability. Mental health may also be a factor as rectal ulcer may be more common in individuals with psychological problems. Older individuals who are treated surgically may require a longer time of disability. Disability is generally not permanent although heavy work may have to be restricted following surgical treatment.

Length of Disability

Surgical treatment.

Duration in Days

Job Classification	Minimum	Optimum	Maximum
Any work	7	14	21

Failure to Recover

If an individual fails to recover within the maximum duration expectancy period, the reader may wish to reference the following questions to assist in better understanding the specifics of an individual's medical case.

Regarding diagnosis:

- Was diagnosis of rectal ulcer confirmed? If diagnosis was uncertain, was it confirmed through sigmoidoscopy, transrectal or endoanal ultrasonography, or barium enema?
- Were physiological studies (anal canal electro-sensory threshold, rectal distention threshold, resting anal manometry, anal squeeze pressure manometry) performed to evaluate anal function?
- Has individual experienced any complications (such as hemorrhage, disturbed bowel function, or rectal wall perforation) related to the rectal ulcer?

Regarding treatment:

- Has individual complied with prescribed treatment plan?
- Has individual increased dietary fiber intake? Would individual benefit from a nutrition consult?
- Have psychological factors been resolved? Is psychological counseling warranted?
- Has individual stopped the use of laxatives, suppositories, and enemas?
- If conservative treatment wasn't effective, was surgical intervention necessary?
- If colostomy was required, is it permanent or temporary?

Regarding prognosis:

- Has persisted despite treatment?
- Has ulcer recurred?
- Is individual now a candidate for surgical intervention?
- If surgical intervention has not resolved symptoms, what further treatment is now being considered?
- Does individual have a coexisting condition (rectal prolapse, rectal stricture, chronic constipation, or any condition that increases abdominal straining such as persistent coughing) that may complicate treatment or impact recovery?

References

Corman, M.L. Colon and Rectal Surgery. Philadelphia: Lippincott-Raven Publishers, 1998.

Earnest, D.L., and L.J. Hixson. "Other Diseases of the Colon and Rectum." Gastrointestinal Diseases. Pathophysiology/Diagnosis/Management. Sleisenger, M.H., and J.S. Fordtran, eds. Philadelphia: W.B. Saunders Company, 1993. 1537-1570.

LeMone, P., and K.M. Burke. Medical-Surgical Nursing. Upper Saddle River, NJ: Prentice Hall Health, 2000.

Vaizey, C.J., et al. "Solitary Rectal Ulcer Syndrome." The British Journal of Surgery 85 12 (1998): 1617-1623.

Reduction Mammoplasty

Other names / synonyms: Breast Reduction, Reduction Mammaplasty

85.31, 85.32

Definition

A reduction mammoplasty or breast reduction is a surgical procedure designed to decrease the size of one or both breasts. It involves removing excess tissue and the skin overlying it. In most cases, it also involves reconstruction of the shape of the breast.

Reduction mammoplasty may be done as a cosmetic procedure to improve the appearance of overly large breasts and provide an easier fit in clothing. It may also be done to relieve problems caused by extremely large breasts such as difficulty in breathing; poor posture; neck, back, and shoulder pain; numbing in the arms; difficulty in running and other physical activities; irritation in the folds of the skin; and shoulder grooves from bra straps. Occasionally, reduction mammoplasty may be performed to more closely match a breast reconstructed after mastectomy.

Reason for Procedure

A reduction mammoplasty is used to relieve certain problems associated with large or sagging breasts or the disproportionate size of one breast in comparison to the other. Abnormally large breast size (mammary hypertrophy) is associated with chronic back, shoulder, and neck pain, painful shoulder grooves from bra straps, slumped shoulders, and the development of a hunchback spine curvature (kyphosis). Additionally, the procedure may be used to relieve symptoms such as shortness of breath (dyspnea), nerve compression affecting the hand and arm, and a poor self-image.

Description

The procedure may be performed in 2 basic ways. Removing the nipple and replacing it in a new position after the excess tissue has been excised (breast reduction with transposition of the nipple as a full thickness graft) is usually performed in elderly women to limit anesthesia time, in heavy women with pronounced sagging (ptosis), in women who require massive reduction (breast weighing greater than 1,500 grams), and in women who have had previous breast procedures. In most case, however, the nipple remains attached to a bridge of tissue while the rest of the work is done around it (breast reduction with transposition of the nipple elevated on a pedicle). Both procedures involve pre- and postoperative mammograms to screen for cancer, and are performed under general anesthesia involving a breathing tube (endotracheal anesthesia). In any breast reduction procedure, the single most important step is the proper selection of the new nipple site.

Prognosis

In most cases, women recover well from the surgery and experience an enhanced health status and quality of life, including relief of discomfort related to heavy breasts, improved posture, and choice of clothing.

Specialists

- Plastic Surgeon

Work Restrictions / Accommodations

Restrictions may include lifting, pushing, pulling, and reaching. Temporary transfer to duties requiring less physical activity may be required.

Comorbid Conditions

Comorbid conditions include obesity, smoking, substance abuse, immune suppression, and bleeding disorders.

Procedure Complications

Possible complications include postsurgical infection, bleeding, discoloration of the edges of the skin as the incision heals, and the development of small cysts filled with blood and serum (seromas) under the skin.

Factors Influencing Duration

Factors that may influence the length of disability include the development of complications, pre-existing medical or surgical conditions, and stress.

Length of Disability

Duration of the disability depends on the job requirements. Disability may be longer for strenuous jobs such as those involving heavy lifting.

Duration in Days

Job Classification	Minimum	Optimum	Maximum
Sedentary work	5	7	10
Light work	5	7	10
Medium work	7	14	21
Heavy work	10	21	28
Very Heavy work	10	28	35

References

Blomqvist, L., A. Eriksson, and Y. Brandberg. "Reduction Mammaplasty Provides Long-term Improvement in Health Status and Quality of Life." Plastic and Reconstructive Surgery 106 5 (2000): 991-997.

Zubowski, R., et al. "Relationship of Obesity and Specimen Weight to Complications in Reduction Mammaplasty." Plastic and Reconstructive Surgery 106 5 (2000): 998-1003.

Reduction of Fracture or Dislocation

Other names / synonyms: Manipulative Reduction

78.10, 78.6, 78.60, 79, 79.02, 79.03, 79.04, 79.06, 79.07, 79.08, 79.09, 79.13, 79.14, 79.23, 79.24, 79.26, 79.27, 79.33, 79.34, 79.36, 79.37, 79.71, 79.72, 79.74, 79.76, 79.77, 79.84, 79.87

Definition

Replacing a bone or bones to their normal position after a fracture or dislocation is called a reduction. The goals of a reduction are to restore position (alignment and rotation) and length to the bone or joint. In the case of a fracture, it is also important for the bone ends to meet correctly (apposition).

When a bone breaks, blood forms a clot (hematoma) around the ends of the fragments. The tough outer sheath of the bone (periosteum) is usually intact on one side of the fracture, forming a hinge between the fragments. The muscles that are attached to the bone contract or shorten during the early period after a fracture, actually holding the fragments out of position.

A closed reduction is accomplished by applying traction across the fracture to relax and lengthen the muscles, and then manipulating the bone fragments back into position, with the help of the hinge created by the bone sheath. Although many fractures are reduced using local or regional anesthesia, some individuals must be given general anesthesia in the operating room in order to provide pain control and muscle relaxation.

An open reduction involves the same concepts but is done as a surgical procedure to provide better pain control (analgesia) and visualization of the fracture. Open reductions are also necessary if the fracture is through the skin (compound) or there are open wounds that must be cleaned and repaired. Sometimes fractures that are initially reduced as a closed procedure need to be reduced again as an open procedure and then stabilized with hardware to maintain correct position (open reduction, internal fixation).

If the bones in a joint are intact but out of position (dislocated), a closed reduction is usually attempted first. Traction is applied to overcome muscle spasm and regain muscle length, and the bone will often slip back into place (closed reduction). There are times when pressure must also be applied to guide the bones into correct position (manipulative reduction). Muscle spasm is often difficult to overcome without pain control (analgesia) and/or sedation, including the use of general anesthesia in the operating room. The longer a joint is dislocated, the more difficult it is to reduce, due to muscle spasm. Fractures and dislocations often occur at the same time, and both problems must be addressed.

Spontaneous reductions can occur, in which the individual is able to relax the area and the bones slip back into position, commonly in the shoulder. Individuals can also do self-reduction by learning maneuvers that allow the joints to spontaneously reduce. This sometimes happens in shoulder dislocations and patella dislocations. Reductions are maintained with immobilization and rest. Both rest and immobilization can be obtained with devices ranging from slings to casts, and traction to internal or external fixation.

Multiple sets of x-rays may be needed to monitor the progress of healing after reductions of fractures and/or dislocations.

The need for a fracture reduction or reduction of a dislocation is not gender or age specific, but rather dependent on the severity of the injury. Care must be taken not to overlook the need for correct restoration of bone and joint position (reduction) to ensure complete return of function. Seemingly minor injuries to toes and fingers for example can be debilitating if not managed correctly.

Reason for Procedure

Reductions are performed to restore anatomical position of bones and soft tissue after a fracture or dislocation. This promotes normal function after the fractured bone heals and/or the supporting tissue heals in a dislocation. Attention is given to the nerve and blood supply in the injured area as they can be damaged during the injury or during reduction. Treatment of the fracture or dislocation may involve repair of these structures as well.

Description

In a closed fracture reduction, after examination of the skin and circulation, an x-ray is taken to determine the current position of the fracture fragments. Often an x-ray of the opposite or uninjured side is also taken and used as a guide during the reduction.

Local or regional anesthesia may be used to control pain and to promote muscle relaxation. Pressure is applied by the physician above and below the fracture, often with assistance by a person or device to maintain traction on the muscles around the fracture. First, the fragments are bent in the direction of the fracture and then lifted into correct position. Position is first maintained manually while function and restoration of circulation is checked. A cast or splint is then used to hold the bone fragments in correct position. A final x-ray confirms position of the fragments, and if alignment is not correct, the procedure may be repeated or the individual is scheduled for an open reduction with possible fixation of the fragments. Repeat x-rays and changes of the cast are sometimes done over the next several weeks because the reduction may move out of position (slip) or the bone may begin to heal incorrectly. Initially a splint or half cast may be used to avoid problems with swelling. A full cast is applied after 7-10 days. Closed reductions are most often done in the emergency room, physician's office or outpatient surgical setting.

An open reduction or open reduction with internal fixation (ORIF) is done when a closed reduction is not possible or when the fracture is complicated by an open wound. This is a surgical procedure performed in the operating room either as an in-patient or outpatient. An incision is made over the fracture, wounds are cleaned and the fracture position is corrected with pressure. Sometimes the reduced position is maintained with orthopedic hardware such as screws, plates and rods, placed through or around the fracture fragments. An external fixator device may be used to maintain position. The fixator is composed of pins or rods through the skin and bone and then attached to a long hinged bar on the outside of the skin. This device can allow for early motion of the joints above and/or below the fracture. It is always eventually removed, often in the physician's office, while internal hardware may be left in place. If internal hardware is to be removed, another surgical procedure is required.

In the reduction of dislocations, x-rays are done first to confirm position of the bones and to rule out a fracture combined with the dislocation. If there is only a dislocation, medication is given to control pain and relax the muscles around the dislocation. Gentle stretch or traction is then applied to the muscles, and the bones either slip into position or are eased into place with pressure from the physician's hands. These techniques can be done in the emergency room or doctor's office. Sometimes, it is necessary to take the individual to the operating room for general anesthesia to obtain enough muscle relaxation to manipulate the bones into correct position. Slings or braces are used to rest the joint after reduction. If the reduction is not maintained, surgery may be required to tighten or strengthen surrounding tissue (open reduction.) There may be instances where fixation is used to maintain the corrected position. This is called an open reduction with internal fixation (ORIF), but this term is more commonly used for fracture fixation.

Prognosis

The outcome of either type of reduction depends on the type of injury and treatment involved in maintaining the reduction and healing of the bone and supporting tissue (joint capsule, tendons, ligaments and muscles.) Generally speaking, fractures and dislocations can be repositioned (reduced.) This is not always a simple, straightforward procedure. The process may involve many attempts over several weeks. Any complication of nerves or blood vessels will delay healing and may contribute to a poor outcome.

Some fractures and dislocations naturally are at greater risk for complications and failure or repeated injury with less than optimum outcome. For example, the injury may affect blood and nerve supply to the bone fragments, which delays healing. Some bones, such as those in the wrist and hip have a poor blood supply to begin with and historically do not heal well. Individuals with loose tissue (laxity) have a higher incidence of recurrent dislocation, as do those with anatomical variations such as tilted kneecaps (patella.) Joints that remain dislocated for a long period of time have a less successful outcome.

Specialists

- Occupational Therapist
- Orthopedic Surgeon
- Physiatrist
- Physical Therapist

Rehabilitation

Rehabilitation goals after reduction and healing are to restore function, regain strength and to relieve pain. The time and techniques involved are dependent upon the type of injury, treatment used, and stability of the fracture/dislocation.

Once the dislocation or fracture has been reduced, the physical therapist may utilize various treatments to decrease pain. Physical therapy utilizing cold or warm treatments can help control inflammation during the rehabilitation process by decreasing the amount of blood flow as well as offering relief of pain. A form of heat treatment includes ultrasound that uses high frequency sound waves producing heat that penetrates deep into the involved muscles. Electrical stimulation is another technique used in physical therapy to help decrease pain by mildly producing an electrical response in the muscle around the joint. Electrical stimulation is often used in conjunction with cold and heat treatments.

Range of motion exercises may then begin. When an individual achieves full range of motion, has a minimal swelling, and can perform simple tasks such as dressing and grooming using the involved joint without pain, a strengthening program may be initiated. In the early phase of strengthening, isometric exercises may be introduced

Isotonic exercises such as strengthening with weights may be initiated. Strength training of this type may also include weight equipment/machines, elastic bands, or calisthenics as long as there is resistance against the involved joint and muscles.

Work Restrictions / Accommodations

Work restrictions are variable. Restrictions may not be necessary, or a reduction could require that work involving the injured part be temporarily eliminated from the individual's responsibilities. In some situations, surgery to stabilize a joint that could sustain repeated dislocation may be avoided or delayed by permanently stopping the at-risk activities.

Comorbid Conditions

Underlying conditions that alter tissue strength would complicate recovery from a fracture or dislocation. Smoking, obesity, diabetes, renal disease, neurological disease, inflammatory conditions would also complicate recovery.

Procedure Complications

Complications of reductions of fractures and dislocations include failure to obtain reduction, nerve or blood vessel damage and puncture of the skin, and reflex sympathetic dystropy. Any complication of nerves or blood vessels will delay healing and may contribute to a poor outcome.

Factors Influencing Duration

Type of injury, type of reduction, need for surgery, work requirements, extremity involved, and dominant use of injured area will affect disability. Fractures heal less quickly as an individual ages. Some dislocations are more prone to repeat injury in younger individuals.

Length of Disability

Some dislocations, especially shoulders and kneecaps (patella) are more prone to repeat injury. Some fractures are slower to heal and/or more likely to change position (slip) requiring more extensive care. Those individuals with sedentary work requirements could possibly return to work more quickly if they can prevent swelling in the injured area. Those with lower extremity injuries may have difficulty both with sitting too long and moving or standing too much. Assistive devices for ambulation may restrict some workers from being able to perform their usual activities.

For metacarpal and hand/finger fractures, duration depends on whether dominant or non-dominant extremity is involved.

Knee dislocations with vascular complications may result in leg amputation. In knee dislocation, residual instability and/or complications frequently preclude heavy or very heavy work.

For ankle fracture, sedentary and light durations assume duties may be performed seated.

For tibial fractures, durations for sedentary and light work reflect cast/brace on. For medium, heavy, and very heavy work, durations reflect out of cast/brace.

Dislocation, ankle (closed or open with or without internal fixation).

Duration in Days

Job Classification	Minimum	Optimum	Maximum
Sedentary work	1	7	14
Light work	7	14	28
Medium work	21	42	70
Heavy work	70	77	84
Very Heavy work	84	98	112

Dislocation, elbow (closed).

Duration in Days

Job Classification	Minimum	Optimum	Maximum
Sedentary work	7	10	14
Light work	7	14	28
Medium work	14	28	42
Heavy work	14	42	56
Very Heavy work	14	56	91

Dislocation, hand or finger (closed).

Duration in Days

Job Classification	Minimum	Optimum	Maximum
Sedentary work	1	3	7
Light work	1	3	7
Medium work	1	3	14
Heavy work	1	3	21
Very Heavy work	1	3	28

Reduction of Fracture or Dislocation

Dislocation, hand or finger (open).

Duration in Days

Job Classification	Minimum	Optimum	Maximum
Sedentary work	14	42	70
Light work	28	42	84
Medium work	42	56	84
Heavy work	42	56	84
Very Heavy work	42	56	84

Dislocation, knee (closed).

Duration in Days

Job Classification	Minimum	Optimum	Maximum
Sedentary work	7	14	28
Light work	14	21	42
Medium work	119	182	224
Heavy work	161	224	273
Very Heavy work	182	273	Indefinite

Dislocation, shoulder (closed). Medical treatment for first-time dislocation.

Duration in Days

Job Classification	Minimum	Optimum	Maximum
Sedentary work	7	14	28
Light work	21	28	56
Medium work	21	28	56
Heavy work	35	42	84
Very Heavy work	35	63	91

Fracture, ankle (closed). See also fracture, ankle for information on other fractures of ankle.

Duration in Days

Job Classification	Minimum	Optimum	Maximum
Sedentary work	1	7	14
Light work	7	14	28
Medium work	21	42	70
Heavy work	70	77	84
Very Heavy work	84	98	112

Fracture, ankle (open). With or without internal fixation. See also fracture, ankle for information on other fractures of ankle.

Duration in Days

Job Classification	Minimum	Optimum	Maximum
Sedentary work	14	28	42
Light work	56	70	84
Medium work	70	84	98
Heavy work	84	98	112
Very Heavy work	84	98	112

Fracture, calcaneus (closed). See also fracture, calcaneus for information on specific calcaneal fractures.

Duration in Days

Job Classification	Minimum	Optimum	Maximum
Sedentary work	14	21	28
Light work	42	56	70
Medium work	84	98	112
Heavy work	112	140	168
Very Heavy work	168	168	252

Fracture, clavicle (closed).

Duration in Days

Job Classification	Minimum	Optimum	Maximum
Sedentary work	7	14	28
Light work	14	28	42
Medium work	21	56	84
Heavy work	42	84	112
Very Heavy work	42	84	182

Fracture, distal radius (closed).

Duration in Days

Job Classification	Minimum	Optimum	Maximum
Sedentary work	3	7	21
Light work	7	14	91
Medium work	63	91	147
Heavy work	119	182	238
Very Heavy work	119	182	273

Fracture, fibula (closed or open.)

Job Classification	Duration in Days		
	Minimum	Optimum	Maximum
Sedentary work	1	7	14
Light work	7	14	28
Medium work	21	42	70
Heavy work	70	77	84
Very Heavy work	84	98	112

Fracture, fibula (open with internal fixation).

Job Classification	Duration in Days		
	Minimum	Optimum	Maximum
Sedentary work	14	28	42
Light work	56	70	84
Medium work	70	84	98
Heavy work	84	98	112
Very Heavy work	84	98	112

Fracture, metacarpal bone(s) (closed).

Job Classification	Duration in Days		
	Minimum	Optimum	Maximum
Sedentary work	1	7	28
Light work	7	14	28
Medium work	14	21	42
Heavy work	21	28	84
Very Heavy work	28	42	112

Fracture, metacarpal bone(s) (closed with internal fixation).

Job Classification	Duration in Days		
	Minimum	Optimum	Maximum
Sedentary work	1	7	42
Light work	7	14	42
Medium work	21	28	56
Heavy work	28	42	70
Very Heavy work	28	42	112

Fracture, metacarpal bone(s) (open).

Job Classification	Duration in Days		
	Minimum	Optimum	Maximum
Sedentary work	1	7	42
Light work	7	14	42
Medium work	21	28	56
Heavy work	28	42	70
Very Heavy work	28	42	112

Fracture, metacarpal bone(s) (open with internal fixation).

Job Classification	Duration in Days		
	Minimum	Optimum	Maximum
Sedentary work	7	14	28
Light work	7	14	28
Medium work	14	28	42
Heavy work	14	42	84
Very Heavy work	28	42	112

Fracture, metatarsal bone(s) (closed). See also fracture, metatarsal for information on specific foot fractures.

Job Classification	Duration in Days		
	Minimum	Optimum	Maximum
Sedentary work	1	7	14
Light work	7	14	28
Medium work	28	42	70
Heavy work	56	70	84
Very Heavy work	56	70	112

Fracture, phalanges of hand (closed or closed with internal fixation, or open).

Job Classification	Duration in Days		
	Minimum	Optimum	Maximum
Sedentary work	1	3	42
Light work	1	3	42
Medium work	14	21	56
Heavy work	28	42	70
Very Heavy work	28	42	112

Fracture, phalanges of hand (open with internal fixation).

Duration in Days

Job Classification	Minimum	Optimum	Maximum
Sedentary work	3	7	42
Light work	3	7	42
Medium work	21	28	56
Heavy work	28	42	70
Very Heavy work	28	42	112

Fracture, tibia (closed, with internal fixation, or open).

Duration in Days

Job Classification	Minimum	Optimum	Maximum
Sedentary work	14	28	84
Light work	28	42	182
Medium work	119	182	224
Heavy work	161	224	273
Very Heavy work	182	273	Indefinite

Fracture, rib (closed).

Duration in Days

Job Classification	Minimum	Optimum	Maximum
Sedentary work	3	14	21
Light work	7	21	28
Medium work	14	28	42
Heavy work	21	42	56
Very Heavy work	21	42	70

Fracture, toe (closed).

Duration in Days

Job Classification	Minimum	Optimum	Maximum
Sedentary work	1	3	14
Light work	3	7	21
Medium work	14	21	28
Heavy work	28	35	42
Very Heavy work	28	35	42

References

Browne, Patrick. Basic Facts of Fractures. Boston: Blackwell Scientific Publications, 1983.

Malone, Terry R., Thomas McPoil, and Arthur J. Nitz. Orthopedic and Sports Physical Therapy. St. Louis: Mosby, 1997.

Rehabilitation Therapy

Other names / synonyms: Cognitive Therapy, Occupational Therapy, Physical Therapy, Recreational Therapy, Speech Therapy, Vocational Rehabilitation

93.8, 93.81, 93.82, 93.89

Definition

Rehabilitation therapy is comprised of various treatments aimed to increase functional capacity, prevent further loss of function, and maintain or improve quality of life for individuals living with physical illnesses or conditions. The desired outcome is to become independent in as many activities of daily living as possible, including self treatment, work and family responsibilities. There are many different types of rehabilitation therapy, including Occupational, Physical, Speech, Cognitive/Psychological, and Social Services therapy.

Musculoskeletal therapists should utilize work and self-care tasks to help individuals regain functional abilities and to prevent further disability and help individuals regain functional mobility, strength, and range of motion. Speech therapists promote effective communication and swallowing. Respiratory therapists work to increase the volume of inspired air, maintain clear lungs, and decrease respiratory distress. Social workers facilitate rehabilitation through the careful planning of discharge from the hospital or rehabilitation center to ensure that individuals have proper environmental support for recovery. Psychologists and psychiatrists help to decrease depression, maintain motivation, and set realistic expectations for recovery.

Rehabilitation therapy may be used pre-operatively, as in the case of preparing an individual for a total joint replacement. Rehabilitation may also be used post-operatively, to teach individuals how to use an artificial limb or prosthesis, or to assist recovery from a total hip replacement. Therapy may help with rehabilitation after an acute condition such as stroke, or in more chronic conditions such as arthritis. Due to the chronic nature of many diagnoses, therapy interventions should involve family members in the coordination of care to maximize an individual's functional gains.

Rehabilitation therapy may be conducted on an inpatient basis in an acute care hospital, or on an outpatient basis. Rehabilitation specialists may also come to the homes of individuals who are temporarily homebound after undergoing surgery, or who have experienced an exacerbation of a disease. Residential rehabilitation centers focus on providing new skills or re-teaching skills to individuals to enable them to become productive members of their family and community.

Reason for Procedure

Rehabilitation therapy is designed to assist individuals in the recovery from a disease process or surgical procedure. Individuals attend therapy sessions that are tailored to their functional limitations and geared toward independence in self-care. Once functional limitations are identified, the disability level of an individual is reduced through mobility training, activities of daily living training, general conditioning, and vocational counseling. The ultimate goal is to help individuals resume independent participation in work and family life.

Description

Rehabilitation should be the basis and goal of all best practice techniques. Sometimes, a physician, social worker, or case manager may refer individuals for specialized rehabilitation services as outpatients, in the home, or as inpatients at a specialized rehabilitation center. During prescreening or after referral, an individual is evaluated to assess the individual's physical and cognitive ability, the overall degree of disability, and the indications for specific types of therapy. A team of appropriate rehabilitation specialists then develops a comprehensive program tailored to the individual's needs. Minor orthopedic conditions such as ankle sprain may only require physical therapy, while spinal cord injury requires a complete team of rehabilitation specialists.

Musculoskeletal therapists may help an individual to adapt work and home activities by ordering equipment such as elastic shoelaces, bathtub benches, ergonomic computer keyboards, teaching individuals to conserve energy while performing activities of daily living.

Physical therapists help the individual regain functional mobility, strength and range of motion through activities such as balance training, ambulation training, and exercise programs to stretch and strengthen affected areas of the body. Physical therapists may also order equipment such as wheelchairs and canes to promote mobility. Their focus is primarily on the legs and lower body.

Speech therapists promote effective communication by strengthening the muscles associated with the production of speech, and by teaching correct lip and tongue positioning to increase articulation. For those individuals who are unable to communicate vocally, speech therapists may order devices such as communication boards or computers that "speak" for individuals, or they may teach sign language. Speech therapists also promote the ability to chew and swallow food through the use of different food textures and exercises designed to promote salivation, sucking, and the "gag" reflex.

Cognitive therapists use mental exercises to improve return of function following head injury, encephalitis, or other nonprogressive neurological condition affecting memory, language skills, reasoning, and other thinking skills. They teach strategies to help cope with deficits in these areas, such as making lists or taking notes to help remember things.

Respiratory therapists teach breathing exercises and perform chest percussions in which the chest wall is clapped by the therapist's hands to decrease chest congestion and increase the volume of inspired air.

Social workers address the needs of individuals and their caregivers to ensure that adaptive equipment (hospital beds, wheelchairs), environmental support (community-based meal preparation programs), and spiritual support (support groups) are in place before discharge.

Recreational therapists facilitate return to the community by observing and assisting individuals in activities such as games, social get-togethers, and community visits to the mall or the theatre.

Psychologists and psychiatrists provide counseling to individuals who face loss of function following disability. Vocational counselors work with individuals to prepare individuals for their return to work and redirect individuals to alternative employment if physical impairment prevents return to their original occupation. Vocational rehabilitation evaluates and retrains individuals for job skills that will be needed in modified or new employment positions.

Prognosis

Therapeutic outcome varies depending on diagnosis, severity of impairment, motivation, social support, and comorbid conditions. Therapeutic outcomes are generally good for individuals with acute, self-limited impairments, such as simple sprains, or for more chronic but mild impairments such as rotator cuff injury. Individuals with severe or multiple deficits may see only marginal improvement during therapy. In some cases, spontaneous recovery may continue to occur well after therapy is complete.

In general, rehabilitation therapy allows faster recovery than is expected in the absence of rehabilitation. Rehabilitation principles (activity, mastery of physical skills, independence in self-care, restriction-elimination of passive therapy) should be explored early for acute musculoskeletal cases to prevent the need for such services in chronics who require the deployment of greater resources. For individuals with complicated diagnoses such as stroke or spinal cord injury, rehabilitation is crucial to any recovery of function. Depending on the injury, many individuals return to most of their customary activities either independently or by using adaptive equipment.

Specialists

- Chiropractor
- Neurologist
- Occupational Therapist
- Oncologist
- Orthopedic Surgeon
- Physiatrist
- Physical Therapist
- Psychiatrist
- Pulmonologist
- Respiratory Therapist
- Vocational Rehabilitation Counselor

Work Restrictions / Accommodations

Work restrictions or accommodations are generally determined by the underlying condition, and not by the rehabilitation therapy itself. If outpatient therapy continues once the individual returns to work, time off or flexible scheduling may be needed.

Comorbid Conditions

The individual's level of health before injury significantly affects recovery. Comorbid conditions that may adversely affect rehabilitation include obesity, diabetes mellitus, and hypertension.

Procedure Complications

If exercises are too difficult based on the individual's level of function, injury could complicate physical therapy. Poorly-fitting or inappropriate orthotics, wheelchairs, or other adaptive equipment may lead to pressure sores or other injury. Inappropriate lifting or other physical restrictions could lead to injury in vocational rehabilitation. Depression may complicate rehabilitation of any type, once the individual confronts his/her degree of disability and acknowledges his/her limitations. However, this can be avoided by ongoing counseling, support, and encouragement. Recovery may be hindered by lack of family or social support, or by litigation, Workers' Compensation claims, or other situations fostering the sick role. Learning difficulties (as seen following stroke or head injury) may hinder progress in rehabilitation due to poor follow-through with instructions.

Factors Influencing Duration

Because there is no disability associated with the rehabilitation therapy itself, the only factors influencing the length of disability involve the underlying condition that prompted therapy. These factors will require evaluation on an individual, case-by-case basis. The employer's ability to accommodate the worker may influence length of disability.

Length of Disability

No disability is expected to result from this therapy. Disability may occur as a result of an underlying condition.

References

Craemer, John. Virtual Reality Helping to Treat Muscle and Skeletal Problems. Johns Hopkins School of Medicine. 22 Feb 2000. 5 May 2000 <http://hopkins.med.jhu.edu/NewsMedia/press/1996/FEBRUARY/199602.HTM>.

Pierson, Frank M. Principles and Techniques of Patient Care. Philadelphia: W.B. Saunders Company, 1994.

Reiter's Syndrome
Other names / synonyms: Reactive Arthritis, Reiter's Disease, Reiter's Urethritis
099.3

Definition

Reiter's syndrome is an inflammatory complication arising from a previous infection. The syndrome is a group of symptoms that includes inflammation of the urethra (urethritis), inflammation of the eye (conjunctivitis), skin lesions, and arthritis.

Most cases of Reiter's occur within days or weeks of a sexually transmitted chlamydia infection. However, dysenteric infections caused by salmonella, yersinia, or Campylobacter can also lead to Reiter's syndrome. Reiter's syndrome itself is not contagious.

Reiter's is a rare disease occurring in 3.5 individuals per 100,000 in the US. Because it is rare, information regarding worldwide prevalence is not available. Men between the ages of 20 and 40 are the most likely to develop Reiter's syndrome. It is thought that susceptibility to Reiter's syndrome is an inherited genetic trait. Reiter's syndrome associated with dysentery occurs equally in men and women, while Reiter's associated with sexually transmitted disease occurs most commonly in men.

Diagnosis

History: Individuals may report initial symptoms of burning or stinging with urination, a constant urge to urinate, and discharge may be seen from the urethra. This may be followed by fever, and redness, pain, and discharge from the eye. Pain in the joints then occurs over the next several weeks, typically in the hip, knee, ankle, and lower back. Painless ulcers can occur in the mouth and a skin rash may develop that resembles psoriasis. Individuals may report a history of dysentery or sexually transmitted disease.

Physical exam: The exam may reveal inflammation of the eye, skin lesions, inflammation of the urethra, a tender prostate in men, and an inflamed cervix in women. Joints may be swollen and tender.

Tests: Tests are not typically used to make a diagnosis, but joint x-rays and a blood test for the genetic marker HLA-B27 may be performed. Cultures may be done on urethral discharge or joint fluid to identify any infectious agent. A special culture should be performed for chlamydia since this organism is often difficult to grow and diagnose, and is associated with Reiter's.

Treatment

The syndrome itself is not treatable; however, specific symptoms can be treated. Conjunctivitis and skin sores typically resolve without treatment. If an active infection is present, it can be treated with antibiotics.

Nonsteroidal anti-inflammatories (NSAIDs) as well as corticosteroids are used to treat arthritis associated with Reiter's syndrome. Sometimes simple bed rest can reduce pain and inflammation caused by arthritis associated with Reiter's syndrome.

Severe symptoms of Reiter's are treated with immunosuppressive medicines.

Prevention and appropriate treatment of sexually transmitted disease and dysentery may prevent Reiter's syndrome.

Prognosis

For most individuals, symptoms of Reiter's syndrome resolve fully in 6 months without treatment. Underlying infections resolve with antibiotic treatment. About 20% of individuals will experience chronic but mild arthritis that continues beyond 6 months. A few individuals will have recurrent symptoms that include back pain and arthritis. Rarely will individuals experience severe, deforming, long-term arthritis.

Differential Diagnosis

Gonorrhea, rheumatoid arthritis, inflammatory bowel disease, rheumatic fever, ankylosing spondylitis, and psoriasis present similar to Reiter's syndrome.

Specialists

- Cardiologist
- Dermatologist
- Infectious Disease Physician
- Internist
- Orthopedic Surgeon
- Rheumatologist

Rehabilitation

Individuals with arthritis associated with Reiter's syndrome may require physical or occupational therapy. Therapists instruct individuals in the use of heating pads to decrease joint stiffness and pain. Therapists instruct in gentle stretching and strengthening exercises for the affected joints. Individuals learn to perform these exercises independently to help reduce impairment due to arthritis. Individuals also perform low-impact aerobic exercise such as walking or swimming in order to increase strength and endurance and decrease fatigue. Physical therapists can order assistive devices for walking such as a cane or walker that decrease stress through the legs. For those individuals with arthritis in the fingers, wrist, and hand, occupational therapists can order adaptive equipment like jar-openers and elastic shoelaces to reduce the stress these joints experience in daily activities.

Individuals with heart rhythm or heart valve disturbances associated with Reiter's disease should attend outpatient physical and occupational therapy at a clinic specializing in cardiac rehabilitation. Cardiac rehabilitation centers offer electrocardiogram (EKG) monitoring of all participants during the exercise sessions. Additionally, individuals learn to self-monitor their pulse and perceived exertion so they can perform exercise within safe parameters. Individuals attend physical therapy to learn basic conditioning and stretching exercises. Individuals also perform aerobic exercise such as treadmill walking or stationary bicycling.

Occupational therapy addresses any fatigue or shortness of breath that may occur during activities of daily living.

Complementary and Alternative Therapies

Content is intended for awareness only. Treatments may or may not be effective. Scientific evidence may be lacking and some substances have potentially toxic effects. Dr. Presley Reed and the editors do not endorse the use of these therapies in the absence of consultation with a licensed medical professional.

Acupuncture -	May reduce pain and restore mobility to affected joints.
Hydrotherapy -	Swimming may take the weight off joints and help increase flexibility while reducing pain. Soaking in a warm bath may reduce pain by relaxing stiff muscles and joints.
Massage -	While massage should never be used on a joint that is inflamed, swollen, or extremely painful, massaging the area around the affected joint may relieve pain and increase mobility.

Work Restrictions / Accommodations

If arthritic joint pain is severe, certain accommodations may be necessary. For example, if the job requires lifting or strenuous work, these duties may need to be removed.

Comorbid Conditions

There are no known comorbid conditions.

Complications

In rare cases, aortic insufficiency and irregular heartbeats may occur.

Factors Influencing Duration

Disability is influenced by the severity and duration of the arthritis. Recurrent episodes will result in greater disability with time.

Length of Disability

Recurrent episodes will require progressively longer durations of disability. Permanent disability may develop in some individuals.

Duration in Days

Job Classification	Minimum	Optimum	Maximum
Sedentary work	1	7	14
Light work	1	7	14
Medium work	1	7	14
Heavy work	1	10	Indefinite
Very Heavy work	1	10	Indefinite

Failure to Recover

If an individual fails to recover within the maximum duration expectancy period, the reader may wish to reference the following questions to assist in better understanding the specifics of an individual's medical case.

Regarding diagnosis:

- Did individual present with symptoms of irritation to the urethra, eyes, and skin? Did associated joint pain occur?
- Have diagnostic tests been done to identify underlying infection or to rule out other conditions with similar symptoms such as gonorrhea, rheumatoid arthritis, inflammatory bowel disease, rheumatic fever, ankylosing spondylitis, and psoriasis?
- Has diagnosis of Reiter's syndrome been confirmed based on the physical exam and history?

Regarding treatment:

- Were specific symptoms treated as indicated with bed rest and anti-inflammatory agents?
- Were anti-inflammatory and immunosuppressive medications effective in resolving pain and inflammation?
- Was an active infection present?
- Was culture and sensitivity done to identify causative organism and determine the most effective antibiotic to use?

Regarding prognosis:

- Has a 6-month time period passed without resolution of symptoms?
- Are symptoms persisting or is this a recurrence of Reiter's syndrome? If symptoms persist, should diagnosis be revisited?
- Would individual benefit from consultation with specialist such as an infectious disease specialist, rheumatologist, orthopedic surgeon, cardiologist, or dermatologist?
- Have any complications developed as a result of Reiter's syndrome (joint and bone damage or cardiac abnormalities)? If so, are these conditions being addressed in the treatment plan?

References

Guccione, Andrew A. "Functional Assessment." Physical Rehabilitation: Assessment and Treatment. O'Sullivan, Susan B., and Thomas J. Schmitz, eds. Philadelphia: F.A. Davis Company, 1994. 193-208.

Tierney, L.M., S.J. McPhee, and M.A. Papadakis. Current Medical Diagnosis and Treatment. Stamford: Appleton & Lange, 1998.

Renal Dialysis

Other names / synonyms: Artificial Kidney Machine, CAPD, Continuous Ambulatory Peritoneal Dialysis, Dialysis, Hemodialysis, Kidney Dialysis, Peritoneal Dialysis

39.95

Definition

Renal dialysis is a method of artificially removing waste products and excess fluid from the blood when the kidneys are unable to do so (renal failure). The two forms of dialysis are hemodialysis and peritoneal dialysis.

In hemodialysis, blood cycles through a kidney machine. In peritoneal dialysis, fluid is cycled into and out of the abdomen using the individual's own abdominal membrane (peritoneum) as a filter.

In acute renal failure, dialysis is carried out intensively over a period of days or weeks until the kidneys work normally again. Chronic renal failure may require hemodialysis several times a week for the rest of the individual's life or until a kidney becomes available for transplant.

Acute renal failure may be caused from a disease, toxic drugs, surgery, trauma, reduction of blood flow to the kidneys, or obstruction of urine flow. Acute renal failure occurs in 5% of all hospital admissions and in 30% of all intensive care unit admissions.

Chronic renal failure may be caused by factors present at birth (congenital), a defect of the immune system (immunological), infectious diseases, high blood pressure (hypertension), or trauma to the kidneys. Over 50% of chronic renal failure cases are due to diabetes mellitus. Hypertension and inflammatory conditions of the kidney (glomerulonephritis) or urinary tract make up another 30-40% of the cases of chronic renal failure. Approximately one-sixth of chronic renal failure cases are from unknown causes. Due to the wide range of conditions that lead to renal failure, it is difficult to ascertain the exact prevalence of the disorder.

Approximately 260,000 individuals receive dialysis therapy. Of these, about 30,000 receive peritoneal dialysis and the rest are on hemodialysis.

Reason for Procedure

Renal dialysis is a method of artificially removing waste products and excess fluid from the blood when the kidneys are unable to do so (renal failure).

Healthy kidneys filter approximately 150 liters of blood daily. From this blood, the kidneys reabsorb important elements such as sodium, potassium, calcium, amino acids, glucose, and water. In turn, the kidneys excrete waste products such as excess minerals, toxins, and drugs in the form of urine. In damaged kidneys, this process may fail, either suddenly (acute renal failure) or gradually (chronic renal failure). Wastes begin to accumulate in the blood causing harmful or even life-threatening effects. Dialysis removes wastes and excess fluid from the body when the kidneys cannot perform this function.

Description

Hemodialysis may be done in the hospital or a dialysis clinic. A few individuals have technicians perform hemodialysis at home using a portable dialysis machine. Approximately 5% of individuals undergoing dialysis in the US perform the procedure themselves with a home kidney dialysis machine.

Prior to the first hemodialysis procedure, a surgical procedure is done to join an artery to a vein. This is called an insertion of an external shunt or arteriovenous fistula. The shunt or fistula provides a readily accessible site for directing the individual's blood to and from the dialysis machine. The shunt or fistula is left in place for each subsequent dialysis procedure. A small dose of anticoagulant (heparin) may be instilled into the shunt between dialysis procedures to prevent blood clots from forming and obstructing the shunt.

The procedure requires no anesthesia. A needle connected to the shunt passes blood from the individual through plastic tubes into the machine. The machine consists of many layers of special membrane. This membrane separates the blood from a fluid called dialysate. Wastes, toxic molecules, and excess fluid pass from the blood through the membrane and into dialysate. Which is then discarded. The purified blood is returned to the individual. Each dialysis session lasts 2 to 6 hours. The individual's heart rate, blood pressure, and respirations are monitored throughout the procedure. Blood chemistries may be drawn before, during, and after the procedure to monitor response to treatment.

Although peritoneal dialysis is usually performed in the hospital, an increasing number of individuals now carry out the dialysis themselves at home through continuous ambulatory peritoneal dialysis. Continuous ambulatory dialysis is a portable self-dialysis technique that allows an individual to have control over his or her own care. It requires no medical equipment and usually little assistance.

Prior to the first dialysis procedure, a surgical procedure is done that inserts a flexible catheter through a small incision in the abdomen into the abdominal cavity. This procedure is called insertion of a peritoneal catheter. The catheter is left in place indefinitely. The peritoneum is a smooth piece of tissue covering the abdominal contents like an apron. The peritoneum serves as a filter in the dialysis procedure. A special fluid solution (dialysate) is instilled via the peritoneal catheter into the abdominal cavity. The dialysate remains in the abdominal cavity for a prescribed period of time (approximately 30 to 60 minutes). The dialysate attracts excess fluid, electrolytes, and some toxins from the blood vessels in the peritoneum. The dialysate and the excess fluid, electrolytes, and toxins are then allowed to flow out of the peritoneal catheter into a collection bag. The individual is usually weighed prior to and following the procedure. A record is kept of the amount of fluid instilled and the amount withdrawn.

Prognosis

Outcome with dialysis procedures is dependent on the underlying disease process and physical condition of the individual. Acute renal failure is often reversible while chronic renal failure is not. In general, those undergoing dialysis therapy have an average life expectancy of 4 years although many survive as long as 25 years on dialysis therapy.

Specialists

- Nephrologist

Work Restrictions / Accommodations

Individuals on either form of renal dialysis should be restricted from any work such as lifting heavy objects or wearing restrictive belts or harnesses that could dislodge or contaminate an indwelling catheter or shunt.

Individuals on continuous ambulatory dialysis may require an additional break for approximately 1 hour to perform a dialysis exchange during the day. Special accommodations may be needed to perform the dialysis procedure at work. The procedure should be performed in a clean environment. Accommodations should be made that allow the individual to be seated and hang the sealed dialysis bag during the procedure.

Comorbid Conditions

Comorbid conditions that may impact ability to recover and further lengthen disability include bleeding disorders, immune suppression, heart disease, and chronic lung disease.

Procedure Complications

Complications of the hemodialysis procedure include dehydration, bleeding, and loss of electrolytes. Complications associated with the hemodialysis shunt are infection, blood clot (thrombosis), and weakening of the shunt arterial wall (aneurysm). Common complications of peritoneal dialysis are infection and inflammation of the abdominal covering (peritonitis).

Factors Influencing Duration

Length of disability may be influenced by the underlying cause of the kidney failure, effectiveness of dialysis, or any complications. If restrictions are not accommodated due to the lack of clean protected environment, the duration may differ greatly.

Length of Disability

Duration depends on underlying condition for which the procedure is performed. Hemodialysis treatments are most often carried out three times weekly with treatments lasting three to five hours each time. With peritoneal dialysis, treatments can often be managed with no period of disability.

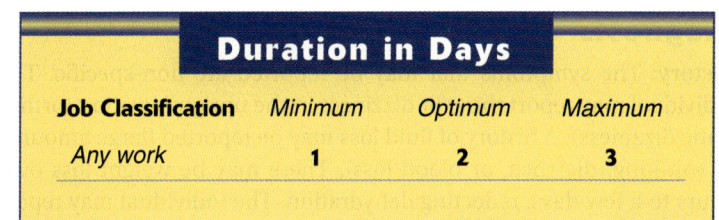

Duration in Days

Job Classification	Minimum	Optimum	Maximum
Any work	1	2	3

References

Clochesy, John M., et al. <u>Critical Care Nursing, 2nd ed.</u> Philadelphia: W.B. Saunders Company, 1996.

Renal Failure, Acute

Other names / synonyms: ARF, Postrenal Azotemia, Prerenal Azotemia, Renal Failure, Renal Insufficiency

584, 584.5, 584.6, 584.7, 584.8, 584.9, 586

Definition

Acute renal failure is a sudden (developing over the course of a few days) and severe decrease in the function of the kidneys.

There are many causes of acute renal failure. It can occur in individuals who have normal kidney function or in individuals with chronic kidney disease that was previously stable.

Acute renal failure can occur due to underlying conditions that occur before the kidneys begin the filtering process (prerenal). Some prerenal causes include inadequate blood flow to the kidneys, acute blood loss, low blood pressure, severe heart failure, dehydration, uncontrolled diabetes, diuretics, burns, severe liver disease, and an overwhelming infection.

Acute renal failure may arise from the kidneys themselves (renal causes). Renal causes include inflammatory disease of the filtering units of the kidney (such as acute glomerulonephritis), autoimmune disease (systemic lupus erythematosus), and damage to the kidney from either drugs, toxins (chemicals as well as x-ray contrast dyes), or allergic reactions.

Acute renal failure may also arise from conditions that affect drainage of urine from the urinary tract after urine leaves the kidneys (postrenal failure). Causes of postrenal failure can include obstruction anywhere in the urinary drainage system, kidney stones, scar tissue, surgical error, cancer, or benign prostate enlargement.

Nearly 5% of all hospitalized individuals develop acute renal failure.

Diagnosis

History: The symptoms that may be reported are non-specific. The individual may report thirst or dizziness in the upright position (orthostatic dizziness). A history of fluid loss may be reported (large amounts of vomiting, diarrhea, or blood loss). There may be weight loss over hours to a few days, reflecting dehydration. The individual may report nausea, vomiting, anorexia, lethargy, confusion, headache, or even a seizure. A metallic taste in the mouth may be reported. Shortness of breath, difficulty breathing on exertion, chest pain (from pericarditis), or swelling in the feet and ankles may be observed by the individual. The individual may note easy bruising or bleeding. The individual may note low urine production. There may be pain at the side of the back (flank pain), blood in the urine, or foamy urine. The individual may report drug use or exposure to toxins, as well as recent surgery, trauma, or hospitalization.

Physical exam: Signs of dehydration may be evident. The skin may not return easily to its normal position when pulled up (decreased skin turgor). The veins in the neck may be "collapsed" due to dehydration with inadequate fluid to keep them full and plump. The mucous membranes of the mouth may be very dry. Evaluation of blood pressures (while lying, sitting, and standing) and heart rate may reveal orthostatic changes, again indicative of dehydration.

Tests: The tests may include laboratory testing of the blood and urine, measurement of the central venous pressure, a fluid challenge test, ultrasound, renal scanning, and a renal biopsy. A complete blood count (CBC) may reveal blood loss. Electrolytes such as the potassium level may be abnormal. Blood testing may also reveal reduced bicarbonate. The blood urea nitrogen (BUN) and creatinine may be elevated. If the BUN is more than ten times the creatinine, a pre-renal cause should be suspected. The blood may also be tested for antibodies and other components that indicate an autoimmune or inflammatory process. Routine urinalysis may reveal abnormalities such as an abnormal acid level (an abnormal pH), abnormal concentration of solids and water (the specific gravity), the presence of protein or blood in the urine, or the presence of glucose or ketones in the urine. All urine produced for a 24-hour period may be collected. The volume of a 24-hour urine collection may be abnormally high or low, and there may be abnormalities in the amount of electrolytes excreted. Additional diagnostic tests may include ultrasound, which may reveal structural abnormalities in the urinary tract, or abnormalities in the size of the kidneys. A renal scan (using injection of a radiopaque dye) may also be performed, which can reveal kidney functioning and shape. A fluid challenge test may be performed, in which one to two liters (1,000 to 2,000 cubic centimeters, or about two to four quarts) of fluid are infused into a vein.

Treatment

Initial treatment is directed at immediately correcting the fluid balance and reducing the amount of excess electrolytes and waste products in the blood. To correct the fluid balance, either medication may be given to force the kidneys to excrete fluid (diuretics), or fluid volume may be given through an intravenous line to correct dehydration. Fluids may include saline, blood, or albumin. Medications may be given to help the heart pump blood more easily. Factors that would further injure the kidneys are avoided (for example, x-ray studies using a radiopaque contrast dye are avoided due to the damaging effects of the dye).

Treatment of the underlying cause may include antibiotics for infection, immunosuppressant medications to treat autoimmune and inflammatory conditions. Obstruction of the flow of urine is corrected. Dietary changes are initiated to reduce the workload of the kidneys. A diet that is low in protein (protein increases the work of the kidneys), potassium, and sodium is introduced.

If kidney function has decreased to the point of becoming life threatening, treatment (hemodialysis) to decrease the amount of excess fluid and waste products is begun.

Prognosis

It may be difficult initially to determine the long-term prognosis. The early diagnosis of acute renal failure is important for a successful recovery. Acute renal failure is reversible if the underlying cause is corrected in a timely manner, and if permanent, irreversible kidney damage has not already occurred. Most cases of acute renal failure due to dehydration resolve in 7 to 14 days. However, older individuals are at increased risk of developing permanent kidney damage as a result of acute renal failure due to dehydration.

In general, the mortality rate for acute renal failure is about 20-40%, and in cases occurring following surgical procedures, the mortality rate is about seventy percent. The most common causes of death associated with renal failure include infection, fluid and electrolyte imbalances, and worsening of the underlying disease. Mortality is greater with advanced age, with severe underlying medical conditions, or with failure of many different organs of the body (multisystem organ failure).

Differential Diagnosis

Chronic renal failure may have been present before the onset of acute renal failure.

Specialists

- Internist
- Nephrologist
- Urologist

Work Restrictions / Accommodations

The underlying cause of the acute renal failure will influence any work restrictions or special accommodations. Many individuals experiencing acute renal failure, especially those with severe failure, will be hospitalized for treatment and complete diagnosis. Time off from work will be necessary until the kidney failure resolves, and then, more time may be needed for home recovery. Accommodations for a worker undergoing dialysis treatment may include additional leave from work and/or flex time to accommodate treatment days. Activity is allowed as the individual can tolerate.

Comorbid Conditions

Comorbid conditions may include diabetes mellitus and high blood pressure.

Complications

Many complications can arise as a result of acute renal failure. Many of the complications of acute renal failure are closely related to the underlying cause and its associated complications. Generalized infection (sepsis), lung infection, urinary tract infection, multiple organ failure, and cardiac failure may occur either before or after the onset of acute renal failure. Complications that are directly related to renal failure may include cardiac arrhythmias due to abnormal levels of potassium in the blood as well as respiratory problems (pulmonary edema) and congestive heart failure due to excess fluid volume. Acute renal failure may progress to chronic renal failure depending on the underlying cause and whether permanent irreversible damage to the kidneys has already occurred.

Factors Influencing Duration

Most major improvements occur within the first few weeks of the recovery phase. It may take several months for the individual to return to normal activities. The underlying cause of acute renal failure, the required treatment (such as dialysis), and response to treatment, may effect the recovery period. In some cases, chronic renal failure may develop and affect the length of disability.

Length of Disability

Duration depends on underlying cause. Disability may be permanent.

Duration in Days

Job Classification	Minimum	Optimum	Maximum
Sedentary work	14	28	42
Light work	14	28	42
Medium work	28	42	56
Heavy work	28	42	56
Very Heavy work	28	42	56

Failure to Recover

If an individual fails to recover within the maximum duration expectancy period, the reader may wish to reference the following questions to assist in better understanding the specifics of an individual's medical case.

Regarding diagnosis:

- Has the individual received adequate diagnostic testing to establish diagnosis of acute renal failure?
- Were other conditions with similar symptoms ruled out?
- Has cause of renal failure been identified?
- Has individual experienced any complications related to the renal failure, such as cardiac arrhythmias, pulmonary edema or congestive heart failure?

Regarding treatment:

- Did initial treatment effectively correct fluid balance and reduce the amount of excess electrolytes and waste products in the blood?
- Is underlying cause of the renal failure responding to treatment?
- Has individual complied with diet modification that includes low protein, sodium and potassium? Would individual benefit from a nutrition consult?
- If kidney function was decreased to the point of life threatening, was hemodialysis begun? Will repeat hemodialysis be necessary?
- Did individual experience any complications related to the hemodialysis?

Regarding prognosis:

- Has permanent irreversible damage already occurred to the kidneys?
- Is acute renal failure progressing towards chronic renal failure?
- Does individual have a coexisting condition, such as diabetes mellitus or hypertension that may complicate treatment or impact recovery?

References

Amend, William J.C., and Flavio G. Vincenti. "Oliguria; Acute Renal Failure." Smith's General Urology, 15th ed. Tanagho, Emil A., and Jack W. McAninch, eds. New York: Lange Medical Books/McGraw-Hill, 2000. 605-609.

Watnick, Suzanne, and Gail Morrison. "Kidney." Current Medical Diagnosis and Treatment, 39th ed. Tierney, Lawrence, M., Stephen J. McPhee, and Maxine A. Papadakis, eds. New York: Lange Medical Books/McGraw-Hill, 2000. 886-916.

Renal Failure, Chronic

Other names / synonyms: Chronic Kidney Failure, Chronic Renal Insufficiency, End-Stage Renal Disease, Renal Insufficiency

585, 586

Definition

Chronic renal failure refers to gradually reduced functioning of the kidneys that is irreversible and progressive, and lasts longer than 3 months.

Chronic renal failure results in the accumulation of fluid and waste products in the blood (uremia) such as uric acid, creatinine, and other nitrogen end-products of protein and amino acid metabolism (azotemia).

Chronic renal failure that is mild is called chronic renal insufficiency; chronic renal failure that requires dialysis or a kidney transplant for survival is called end-stage renal disease.

Chronic renal failure may result from any disease that causes progressive and gradual damage to and destruction of the internal structures of the kidneys. Diabetes and high blood pressure (hypertension) are the 2 leading causes of end-stage renal disease in the US. Kidney damage may occur as a result of conditions directly affecting the kidney, such as damage to the filtration units (glomerulonephritis), inflammation of the renal pelvis where urine is collected in the kidney (pyelonephritis), underdevelopment of the kidney (congenital hypoplasia), cysts scattered throughout both kidneys (polycystic kidney disease), kidney scarring from chronic reflux (reflux nephropathy), obstruction causing a change in the urinary tract (obstructive uropathy), kidney stones, and kidney infection. Kidney damage can also occur as a result of abnormal conditions elsewhere in the body (secondary renal failure). In addition to diabetes and hypertension, secondary conditions can include a type of metabolic abnormality in which deposits occur in organs and tissues (amyloidosis), chronic inflammatory diseases (systemic lupus erythematosus), HIV, a form of cancer that is characterized by infiltration of bone and bone marrow by myeloma cells that form multiple tumor masses (multiple myeloma), obstruction in the urinary tract causing back-up of urine and pressure within the kidneys, and cancer. Chronic renal failure can also result from ingestion of substances that are toxic to the kidneys.

In the US, 200,000 individuals require dialysis for end-stage renal disease; there are 72,000 individuals who are alive with functioning kidney transplants.

Diagnosis

History: Progression of this disease may be so gradual that symptoms are not obvious until kidney function is down to one-tenth of normal. Individuals may initially report nonspecific symptoms such as nausea and vomiting, fatigue, itching (pruritus), headaches, forgetfulness, unintentional weight loss, and malaise. They may also report symptoms that include loss of appetite (anorexia), decreased exercise tolerance, difficulty breathing, chest pain, problems with taste, mood changes, and sleep disturbances. Some individuals may report a family history of kidney disease. Later symptoms include increased or decreased urinary output, increased nocturnal urination (nocturia), excessive thirst, easy bruising or bleeding, and blood in stool or vomitus.

Physical exam: The exam may reveal dry, brittle, and pale yellow- or brown-toned skin (sallow complexion), an ammonia odor on the breath, hair loss, nail changes, a rapid heartbeat, heart murmur, loss of sensation in the hands or feet, altered mental status (drowsy and lethargic, or agitated and confused), brownish discoloration of the tongue, muscle twitching or cramping, and hand flapping when the arms are extended (asterixis). It may also reveal accumulation of fluid in the tissues (edema), increased blood pressure (hypertension), fluid in the abdominal cavity (ascites), congestive heart failure, and a pericardial effusion. Physical examination may also reveal enlarged kidneys when the abdomen is felt with the fingertips (palpated); abnormal heart or lung sounds may be heard with a stethoscope (auscultation). An eye examination may reveal abnormalities associated with hypertension, diabetes, or other metabolic conditions. A neurologic exam may show changes in several of the peripheral nerves (polyneuropathy).

Tests: Tests may include laboratory testing of the blood and urine, diagnostic imaging, and a kidney biopsy. A complete blood count (CBC) may reveal anemia. The electrolyte levels of potassium, sodium, calcium, phosphate, and magnesium may be abnormal. Blood chemistry and arterial blood gas testing may also reveal reduced bicarbonate and metabolic acidosis. The blood urea nitrogen (BUN) and creatinine may be elevated. The parathyroid hormone level may be abnormal. Routine urinalysis may reveal abnormalities such as an abnormal acid level (an abnormal pH), abnormal concentration of solids and water (the specific gravity), the presence of protein or blood in the urine, or the presence of glucose or ketones in the urine. All urine produced for a 24-hour period may be collected. Additional diagnostic tests may include ultrasound, which may reveal structural abnormalities in the urinary tract, or abnormalities in the size of the kidneys. A renal scan (using injection of a radiopaque dye) may also be performed, which can reveal kidney functioning and shape. A renal biopsy may reveal changes in the kidney tissues that are associated with chronic renal failure. Other tests may include a renal or abdominal x-ray, CT scan, or MRI.

Treatment

There is no cure for chronic renal failure, but lifelong treatment may control symptoms. Therefore, treatment is focused on controlling the individual's particular symptoms, minimizing complications, and slowing the progression of the disease. Aggravating factors (volume depletion, drugs, obstruction, infections, high blood pressure, and metabolic abnormalities) are usually treated immediately to prevent worsening of the underlying renal failure. Infections and marked blood pressure elevations are treated with drugs.

Treatment is conservative until kidney function becomes severely affected. Initial treatment may involve a diet that is low in protein (protein increases the work of the kidneys), potassium, and phosphorus. The sodium intake is balanced to meet the needs of the individual. Bicarbonate may be given to control an increased acid level (metabolic acidosis). If anemia is severe, medications may be given to increase the iron level within the red blood cells, and blood transfusion may be required. The calcium and phosphorus levels in the blood are carefully monitored, and phosphate-retaining antacids, calcium, and vitamin D may be given to maintain the proper balance. Fluid intake may be restricted to equal the amount of urine that is produced.

When kidney function has decreased to the point of becoming life threatening, treatment to decrease the amount of excess fluid and waste products (dialysis) is begun. The 2 methods of dialysis are hemodialysis and peritoneal dialysis. In hemodialysis, a machine is used to pump blood through a dialysis membrane that filters water, electrolytes, and waste products from the blood. In peritoneal dialysis, fluid is infused into the membrane that lines the abdominopelvic walls (peritoneal cavity), where it filters the excess water, electrolytes, and waste products from the body.

A kidney transplant may eventually be necessary.

Prognosis

End-stage renal disease is the usual outcome. The rate of progression to end-stage disease depends on the nature of the kidney disease, level of kidney function, age, gender, the presence of complications, underlying medical conditions, type of treatment, and response to treatment. When treated by dialysis, well over half the individuals with end-stage renal failure are able to lead comparatively normal lives for more than 5 years. Unfortunately, some individuals become permanently disabled due to the presence of comorbid conditions, and due to complications associated with chronic renal failure or treatment. A successful kidney transplant improves the prognosis. The outcome of chronic renal failure without dialysis or transplantation is death.

Differential Diagnosis

There may be an episode of acute renal failure complicating a mild case of chronic renal failure.

Specialists

- Internist
- Nephrologist
- Urologist

Work Restrictions / Accommodations

Possible work restrictions and accommodations include transfer from duties that require heavy lifting or long periods of standing; increased rest periods, shortened workday, or extended work leave may be necessary. If undergoing dialysis, treatment is generally needed 3 days a week; often, dialysis appointments are scheduled around work schedules, but flexibility is necessary. Heavy lifting cannot be done and restrictive clothing cannot be worn over arms in which there is a surgical connection made between an artery and a vein (arteriovenous fistula or graft) used during hemodialysis. Medical appointments are needed for follow-up and evaluation of hemodialysis vascular access sites, or for evaluation of the peritoneal catheter needed for peritoneal dialysis. Time off from work may be necessary for hospital procedures required to maintain vascular access patency. Individuals who undergo a kidney transplant may need several weeks off from work for surgery and recovery. For several months after the transplant, extra precautions to prevent infection are necessary because of the medications that must be taken to preserve the transplant.

Complementary and Alternative Therapies

Content is intended for awareness only. Treatments may or may not be effective. Scientific evidence may be lacking and some substances have potentially toxic effects. Dr. Presley Reed and the editors do not endorse the use of these therapies in the absence of consultation with a licensed medical professional.

Diet modification - Diet should be low in protein, potassium, and phosphorus. Sodium intake is balanced to meet the needs of the individual. Fluid intake may be restricted to equal the amount of urine that is produced.

Comorbid Conditions

Comorbid conditions may include any condition worsening damage to the kidneys, such as diabetes mellitus and high blood pressure.

Complications

Chronic renal failure results in a large number of complications. Electrolyte levels may either rise or fall to life-threatening levels. The electrolyte potassium must be kept within the normal range for proper functioning of the heart; abnormal potassium levels may result in abnormal heart rhythms. The ability to produce red blood cells is decreased, resulting in anemia. Bleeding abnormalities may develop resulting in nosebleeds, excessive menstrual flow, and easy bruising. Skeletal changes (osteodystrophy) can occur as a result of an elevated phosphate level and an increase in the parathyroid hormone. The parathyroid gland may become hyperactive due to decreased calcium intake and a reduction in vitamin D. Cardiovascular abnormalities include accelerated atherosclerosis, high blood pressure (hypertension), and inflammation of the membrane of the heart (pericarditis). Gastrointestinal problems include nausea and vomiting, problems with taste, and weight loss. Muscle weakness and muscle wasting are common. Diabetics may lose their vision if undergoing hemodialysis. Individuals are also more susceptible to urinary tract infections (UTIs) and to developing kidney stones.

Factors Influencing Duration

Factors influencing length of disability include any underlying medical conditions including high blood pressure (hypertension), diabetes, and/or cardiac problems, the amount of kidney function remaining, whether undergoing dialysis, age, gender, and the development of complications. Although some amount of disability is permanent, dialysis has made it possible for individuals who have chronic renal failure to maintain some degree of independence. Loss of vision may increase the length of disability in diabetics.

Length of Disability

Duration depends on underlying cause and complications. May require periodic absence for dialysis. Disability may be permanent.

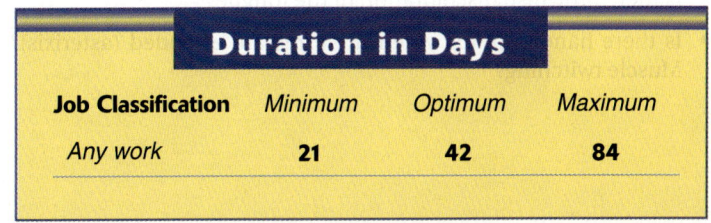

Duration in Days

Job Classification	Minimum	Optimum	Maximum
Any work	21	42	84

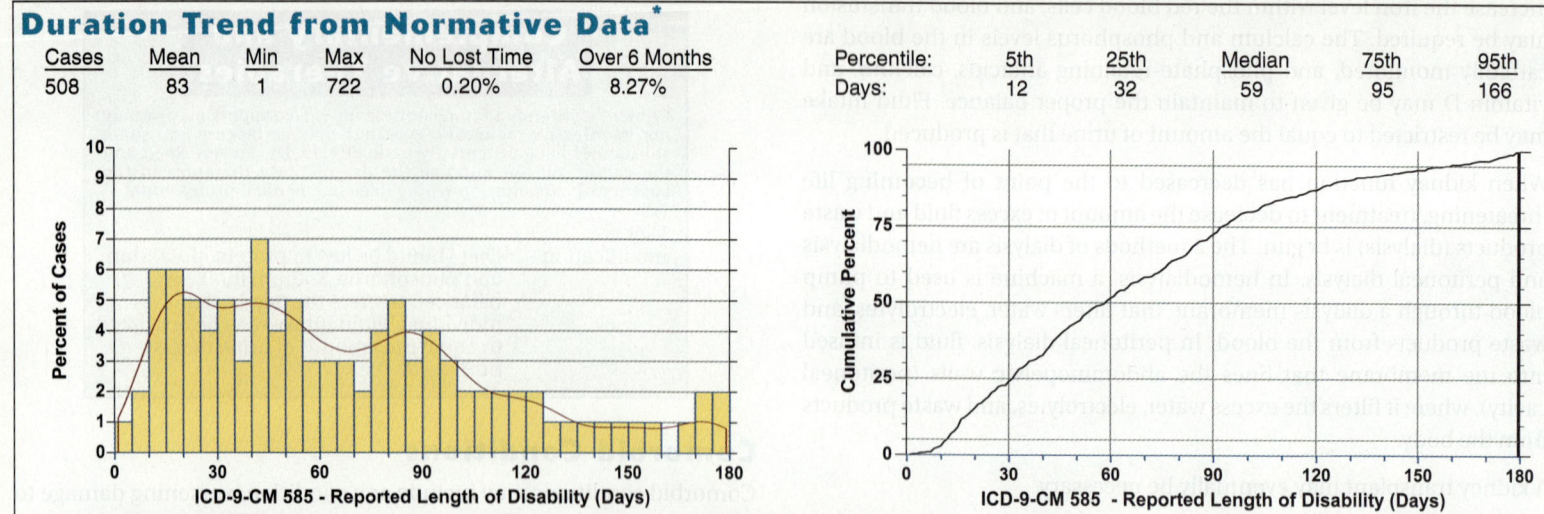

Failure to Recover

If an individual fails to recover within the maximum duration expectancy period, the reader may wish to reference the following questions to assist in better understanding the specifics of an individual's medical case.

Regarding diagnosis:

- Does individual have diabetes or hypertension? Glomerulonephritis or pyelonephritis? Congenital hypoplasia? Polycystic kidney disease? Reflux nephropathy? Obstructive uropathy? Kidney stones? Kidney infection? Amyloidosis?
- Does individual have systemic lupus erythematosus? HIV? Multiple myeloma?
- Have they ingested any substances that are toxic to the kidneys?
- Does individual report nausea and vomiting, fatigue, pruritus, headaches, forgetfulness, unintentional weight loss, or malaise?
- Does individual also report anorexia, decreased exercise tolerance, dyspnea, chest pain, problems with taste, mood changes, or sleep disturbances? Family history of kidney disease?
- Has individual noticed either an increase or a decrease in their urinary output?
- Does individual report excessive thirst? Easy bruising or bleeding? Blood in stool or vomitus?
- On exam, is their skin dry, brittle, and pale yellow or brown-toned?
- Is there an ammonia odor on the breath? Hair loss? Nail changes?
- Does individual have a rapid heartbeat, heart murmur, or loss of sensations in the hands or feet?
- Is individual's mental status altered? Were there changes in the peripheral nerves?
- Is there brownish discoloration of the tongue?
- Is there hand flapping when the arms are extended (asterixis)? Muscle twitching?
- Was edema or hypertension present? Ascites? Congestive heart failure? Pericardial effusion?
- Has individual had blood and urine testing? Did the blood tests include electrolytes, kidney function tests, and parathyroid hormone tests?
- Was a 24-hour urine done? Intravenous pyelogram? Kidney biopsy?
- Did individual have abdominal and kidney x-rays? Ultrasound? CT scan? MRI?
- Have conditions with similar symptoms been ruled out?

Regarding treatment:

- Have volume depletion, drugs, obstruction, infections, high blood pressure, and metabolic abnormalities been treated?
- Is individual on a low protein diet? Is sodium intake balanced for individual?
- Is metabolic acidosis being treated? Has fluid intake been restricted?
- Is individual on iron supplements? Have transfusions been necessary?
- Does individual see their physician frequently to monitor the disease?
- Are phosphate-retaining antacids, calcium, and vitamin D being given?
- Has dialysis become necessary? Is individual a candidate for a kidney transplant?

Regarding prognosis:

- Is individual's employer able to accommodate any necessary restrictions?
- Does individual have any conditions that may affect their ability to recover?
- Has individual had any complications such as bleeding disorders? Electrolyte imbalance? Pericarditis? Skeletal changes?

References

Amend, William J.C., and Flavio G. Vincenti. "Chronic Renal Failure and Dialysis." Smith's General Urology, 15th ed. Tanagho, Emil A., and Jack W. McAninch, eds. New York: Lange Medical Books/McGraw-Hill, 2000. 610-613.

Fischbach, Frances. "Urine Studies." A Manual of Laboratory and Diagnostic Tests, 6th ed. Walz, Nicole, ed. Philadelphia: Lippincott, 2000. 170-279.

Renal Vein Thrombosis
Other names / synonyms: Clot in the Renal Vein, Occlusion of the Renal Vein, RVT
453.3

Definition

Renal vein thrombosis (RVT) is a blood clot that develops in the vein draining the kidney.

The condition may be acute or chronic and affect one or both kidneys. Acute cases can cause extensive damage to the kidneys and result in potentially fatal loss of blood flow to the kidney (renal infarction). Chronic cases are generally less severe and the gradual pace of disease progression often allows for the development of collateral circulation that may help preserve at least partial renal function. When both kidneys are involved, the prognosis is poor.

Causes of RVT include obstruction of blood flow through the renal vein by a tumor (hypernephromas), obstruction of blood flow through the inferior vena cava by a blood clot resulting from abdominal trauma, congestive heart failure, and periarteritis. Other causes include pregnancy and the use of oral contraceptives.

Chronic cases of RVT are often complications of diseases affecting the blood-filtering component of the kidney (the glomerulus) known as glomerulopathic diseases. Individuals with systemic lupus erythematosus, renal cell carcinoma, antithrombin III deficiency, or substance P deficiency have an increased risk of developing RVT.

The incidence of RVT in the general population is difficult to establish. Studies have shown a high degree of variability of RVT among individuals with nephrotic syndrome with incidences ranging anywhere from 5-62%. There is no known race or sex predilection for RVT. A predilection for age only shown as related to age-related risk for glomerular disease.

Diagnosis

History: Individuals with chronic RVT usually have no symptoms and the disorder goes undetected. Individuals with gradual onset of RVT may experience diminished urine volume. Individuals with acute RVT may experience pain in the side between the ribs and hips. These individuals may also complain of fever, blood in the urine, and decreased urine output.

Physical exam: The exam may reveal tenderness in the stomach (epigastric) region, peripheral swelling, and fever in those individuals experiencing rapid disease onset. A vessel blockage with clot involvement usually produces hemorrhage and death of tissue that may be revealed during physical examination. Individuals with bilateral obstruction or disease affecting both kidneys may have high blood pressure (hypertension) and enlarged, easily felt (palpable) kidneys.

Tests: Blood and urine specimens are collected. Urine tests provide an indication of how well the kidneys are functioning. Episodes of acute onset may be suggested by blood or sugar in the urine. Gradual disease onset may be indicated by the presence of protein in the urine.

If the disease is acute, ultrasonography may reveal an enlarged kidney. A diagnostic procedure called intravenous pyelography (IVP) may also reveal enlarged kidneys and diminished excretory function. Renal arteriography procedures may be used to determine the location and extent of blood clot formation and blood flow restriction or obstruction.

Treatment

Most individuals are treated with medications. Anticoagulants prevent new clot formation, thrombolytics dissolve an existing clot, and corticosteroids reduce inflammation.

Although surgery to remove the blood clot(s) (thrombectomy) may be effective if performed within approximately 24 hours of thrombosis, surgery is rarely used because the blood clots often extend into the small veins where they cannot be removed. In cases where there is extensive bleeding, the kidney may be removed (nephrectomy). Individuals with abrupt disease onset may have extensive renal damage and develop nephrotic syndrome as a result. These individuals require treatment for renal failure in the form of dialysis and possible kidney transplantation.

To reduce peripheral swelling, a diuretic drug may be prescribed. In addition, certain dietary restrictions are recommended to control blood pressure such as reducing the amount of sodium and potassium ingested. Renal function must be monitored regularly.

Prognosis

When treated properly, RVT usually resolves over time without permanent injury to the kidney. Any negative prognosis of RVT is usually related to pulmonary embolic events. When both kidneys are involved, the prognosis is poor. Acute cases can cause extensive damage to the kidneys and result in potentially fatal renal infarction.

Individuals may develop hypertension that if left untreated, may develop into a serious and potentially fatal form of hypertension called malignant hypertension.

Differential Diagnosis

Other conditions with similar symptoms include advanced cardiovascular disease, renal cell carcinoma, renal colic, pulmonary embolism from lower extremities, renal papillary necrosis, renal infarction, loin pain hematuria syndrome, hydronephrosis, glomerulonephritis, nephrotic syndrome, or renal failure.

Specialists

- Endocrinologist
- General Surgeon
- Nephrologist
- Urologist

Work Restrictions / Accommodations

The individual may require time off from work to have blood pressure and kidney function regularly monitored and treated.

Comorbid Conditions

Existing conditions that may impact ability to recover and further lengthen disability include obesity, hypertension, glomerulosclerosis, hypernephroma, or lymphoma or other metastatic neoplasms.

Complications

Possible complications that may develop as a result of renal vein thrombosis include pulmonary emboli, recurrent thromboembolic phenomena, nephrotic syndrome, accelerated cardiovascular disease with malignant hypertension, glomerulonephritis, metastasis from renal cell carcinoma, and chronic renal failure.

Individuals with renal vein thrombosis may have hypertension because blood pressure is controlled in part by hormonally mediating the flow of blood through the kidney.

Factors Influencing Duration

Factors that can influence length of disability include individual's age and general health, overall implementation of lifestyle modifications, extent of renal vascular damage and systemic vascular disease, specific treatment provided, individual's response to treatment, and development of complications.

Length of Disability

Duration depends on underlying condition. For surgical treatment, duration depends on whether acute or chronic, bilateral or unilateral, and underlying condition. Disability may be permanent.

Medical treatment.

Duration in Days

Job Classification	Minimum	Optimum	Maximum
Sedentary work	21	28	42
Light work	21	28	42
Medium work	28	42	56
Heavy work	28	42	63
Very Heavy work	28	42	63

Surgical treatment.

Duration in Days

Job Classification	Minimum	Optimum	Maximum
Sedentary work	14	21	28
Light work	14	21	28
Medium work	28	35	42
Heavy work	91	119	182
Very Heavy work	91	119	182

Failure to Recover

If an individual fails to recover within the maximum duration expectancy period, the reader may wish to reference the following questions to assist in better understanding the specifics of an individual's medical case.

Regarding diagnosis:

- Are one or both kidneys involved?
- Is the condition acute or chronic?
- Does individual have a hypernephromas, a blood clot from abdominal trauma, congestive heart failure, or periarteritis? Is individual pregnant? Use oral contraceptives?
- Does individual have glomerulopathic disease, systemic lupus erythematosus, renal cell carcinoma, antithrombin III deficiency, or substance P deficiency?
- Is there pain in the side between the ribs and hips, fever, blood in the urine, and decreased urine output?
- Did the physical exam reveal tenderness in the epigastric region, peripheral swelling, and fever?
- Does individual have hypertension and easily palpable kidneys?
- Were blood and urine tests performed? Was an IVP done? Renal arteriography?
- Have conditions with similar symptoms been ruled out?

Regarding treatment:

- Has individual been treated with anticoagulants, thrombolytics, and corticosteroids?
- Is individual on a diuretic?
- Are any dietary restrictions needed?
- Was a thrombectomy necessary?
- Was a nephrectomy performed?
- Is individual on dialysis?
- Is individual a candidate for a kidney transplant?
- Does individual see physician regularly to monitor renal function?

Regarding prognosis:
- Can individual's employer accommodate any necessary restrictions?
- Does individual have any conditions that may affect ability to recover?
- Have any complications occurred such as hypertension, pulmonary emboli, recurrent thromboembolic phenomena, nephrotic syndrome, accelerated cardiovascular disease with malignant hypertension, glomerulonephritis, metastasis from renal cell carcinoma, or chronic renal failure?

References

"Chapter 125: Blood Vessel Disorders of the Kidneys." Merck Manual of Diagnosis and Therapy, 17th ed. Beers, Mark H., and Robert Berkow, MD, eds. Whitehouse Station, NJ: Merck & Co., Inc., 1999. 05 Jan 2001 <http://www.merck.com/pubs/mmanual_home/sec11/125.htm>.

Routecki, G., and Lewis Schwing, MD. "Renal Vein Thrombosis." eMedicine.com. 15 Dec 2000. 05 Jan 2001 <http://emedicine.com/med/topic2005.htm>.

Renovascular Hypertension
Other names / synonyms: Chronic Renal Artery Stenosis, Renal High Blood Pressure, Renal Vascular Hypertension
405, 405.91

Definition

Renovascular hypertension is a rise in high blood pressure that results from narrowing (stenosis) of one or both branches of the artery supplying a kidney (renal artery). The stenosis may affect the renal artery of one or both kidneys (unilateral or bilateral disease). Stenosis reduces blood flow to the kidney. This in turn decreases the amount of oxygen within kidney tissue (renal ischemia).

The decreased blood supply and decreased oxygen levels stimulate the kidney to release the hormone renin. Renin is one of several hormones that can cause peripheral blood vessels to constrict (vasoconstriction). This vasoconstriction leads to high blood pressure (hypertension).

In approximately 70% of cases, the stenosis and subsequent decreased blood flow are caused by the build-up of fatty deposits or plaque along vessel walls (atherosclerotic disease). The remaining 30% of cases are caused by fibromuscular disease of the renal artery wall.

Individuals at high risk for renal hypertension include those with high amounts of cholesterol in the blood (hyperlipidemia), severe high blood pressure, atherosclerotic disease of other blood vessels, particularly of the vessels in the legs, a family history of the disease, and diabetes. The incidence is also higher in individuals who smoke.

Renovascular hypertension occurs in 0.2-5% of individuals with high blood pressure. It is most common in those with severe high blood pressure. Approximately 43% of whites and 7-18% of blacks with the most severe type of high blood pressure (called malignant high blood pressure) develop renovascular hypertension. Individuals with renovascular hypertension often are younger than 20 years or older than 50 years. Fibromuscular disease typically occurs in women under the age of 50 years.

Diagnosis

History: Individuals may complain of headache, anxiety, the sensation of the heart pounding (palpitations), a rapid heartbeat (tachycardia), light-headedness, mental sluggishness, and decreased tolerance to temperatures. If the onset is acute, the individual may have abdominal or flank pain, nausea, vomiting, or fever. Alternately, the individual may report few or no symptoms. Previous high blood pressure that has been stable may abruptly accelerate. Another indicator may be high blood pressure that has not responded to hypertensive medication.

Physical exam: High blood pressure (hypertension) may be the only indication of renovascular hypertension revealed in a physical examination. Changes in the retina (hypertensive retinopathy) may be seen. An abnormal sound may be heard when listening to the abdomen with a stethoscope (abdominal bruit).

Tests: Several diagnostic procedures are used to test for renovascular hypertension. The diagnostic challenge is to find evidence of both renal stenosis and renal ischemia. Blood tests can demonstrate impaired renal function. These tests include BUN, creatinine, potassium, and plasma renin activity. Urinalysis may show blood or protein in the urine.

The captopril test involves the injection of captopril, followed by measurement of renin in the blood. Individuals with renovascular hypertension will show a rise in renin, while those with hypertension unrelated to renovascular disease (essential hypertension) will not. This test has a high percentage of false-positive results, particularly among blacks.

Radioisotope renography involves the injection of a radioisotope followed by an imaging procedure to monitor the movement of the radioisotope through the kidney. This procedure can provide information regarding the size of the kidneys, the glomerular filtration rate (GFR), and blood flow. A variation of this procedure is called captopril renography. The procedure is done before and again after injection of captopril. In renovascular hypertension, the test demonstrates a reduction in renal function. As in the captopril test, this test is less accurate in blacks.

Renal vein renin determination measures blood levels of renin in the right and left renal veins. These levels are then compared with that of the inferior vena cava. Increased renin levels indicate that the cause of the hypertension is kidney-related.

Duplex Doppler scanning utilizes ultrasound to measure the speed of blood flow through the kidney. Other procedures that allow imaging of the kidney include magnetic resonance angiography (MRA) following injection of a dye into the renal arteries, and computed tomography (CT) following injection of a contrast agent.

Renal arteriography is reserved for individuals who are high-risk for renovascular hypertension. This is because the procedure is invasive. The procedure takes place in the hospital on an outpatient basis. A catheter is inserted into the renal artery. A dye is then injected through the catheter into the artery. X-ray pictures are taken as the dye circulates throughout the kidney.

Treatment

Renovascular hypertension is treated with drugs, surgical revascularization, or angioplasty. In both surgical revascularization and angioplasty, adequate blood supply to the affected kidney is restored. The type of treatment selected depends on the cause of the hypertension and the individual's risk factors regarding surgery. Generally, however, returning adequate blood supply by revascularization or angioplasty is preferred to medication.

Surgical revascularization involves removing the narrowed portion of artery and replacing it with a healthy section of a blood vessel removed from another body site. Angioplasty involves the insertion of a catheter into the affected renal artery. On one end of the catheter is a deflated balloon. When the catheter reaches the narrowed portion of the artery, the balloon is inflated. This action opens up the artery. A hollow tube called a stent is usually inserted into the widened artery to help keep it open.

Fibromuscular disease is typically treated by angioplasty. Advanced kidney disease due to low oxygen supply (ischemic nephropathy) is treated either with surgical revascularization or angioplasty.

Renovascular hypertension caused by atherosclerosis is less effectively treated by surgical revascularization or angiography. This is because hypertension unrelated to renovascular disease (essential hypertension) may also be present in these individuals, atherosclerosis may be present in other vessels and will likely return to the renal arteries, and clumps (emboli) of cholesterol may be released during the surgery and may subsequently block a vessel.

Individuals with atherosclerosis and those who are poor candidates for revascularization or angioplasty receive ongoing drug therapy using angiotensin-converting enzyme (ACE) inhibitors and calcium channel blockers.

Prognosis

Untreated atherosclerotic renovascular hypertension will likely progress to a greater degree of stenosis within 2 years. Typically, it progresses at a rate of 7% per year. It is also likely to become bilateral, impair renal function, and develop into ischemic nephropathy, pulmonary edema, or congestive heart failure. Pulmonary edema and congestive heart failure are more likely with bilateral disease.

Atherosclerotic renovascular hypertension treated with revascularization surgery or angioplasty has a cure rate of 22%, improvement rate of 57%, and failure rate of 21%. Return of stenosis has been reported in up to 25% of individuals after 1 year, and in up to 82% after 5 years. Likelihood of cure or improvement is greater with unilateral disease.

Individuals with fibromuscular disease who undergo angioplasty experience a 58% cure rate, 35% improvement rate, and 7% failure rate. Rates are comparable with surgical revascularization. Most of these individuals remain free of stenosis up to 5 years after the angioplasty.

Long-term drug therapy is used for individuals who are not good candidates for surgery or angioplasty. Renovascular hypertension, however, is difficult to control with drug therapy. In some individuals, kidney function continues to decline in spite of drug therapy. ACE inhibitors also may cause a deterioration in kidney function. Individuals taking an ACE inhibitor should be monitored closely.

Differential Diagnosis

Differential diagnoses include advanced cardiovascular disease, essential hypertension tumor/malignancy, hydronephrosis, glomerulonephritis, portal hypertension, nephrotic syndrome, renal failure, or aortic atherosclerotic plaque encroaching upon the renal artery. Renovascular hypertension may be a symptom of Takayasu arteritis, a disease that causes narrowing (stenosis) of the aorta and other major arteries, including the renal arteries.

Specialists

- Cardiologist
- Nephrologist

Rehabilitation

Because renovascular hypertension can be an emergency requiring hospital treatment, rehabilitation for this form of hypertension begins after the underlying cause has been identified and treated. As with rehabilitation for other forms of hypertension, an exercise program developed by a healthcare professional is important and focuses on aerobic exercise proven optimal for reducing blood pressure.

Rhythmic forms of moderate exercise are used in the rehabilitation for most forms of hypertension such as jogging, bicycling, and swimming. The benefits come from the expansion of the blood vessels in the working muscles. This decreases the total resistance in blood vessels throughout the body and enhances blood flow. If rehabilitation is done at a cardiac center, an electrocardiograph attached to the individual is used to record the continuous electrical activity of the heart muscle. A physical therapist experienced in cardiac rehabilitation keeps a daily log of the individual's blood pressure, heart rate, and cardiac rhythm.

Throughout the course of rehabilitation for renovascular hypertension, patient and family education becomes necessary to establish a program the individual can continue once discharged from the care of the rehabilitation professional. If the individual enjoys exercising with machines, common units are that are recommended are the treadmill, NordicTrack, rowing machine, stair stepper, and the bicycle.

A 6-month exercise program contributes to a decrease in the resistance of blood flow within of the body. This results in a subsequent decrease in blood pressure. Because most individuals with hypertension are managed with medication, it is important that the therapist has a medication history for each individual as many of these drugs alter the acute and chronic response to exercise.

Work Restrictions / Accommodations

Temporary work restrictions may be required after surgical revascularization or angioplasty. Additionally, lifestyle changes may require less stress. The individual, therefore, may require work accommodations and/or reassignment to duties that are less stressful.

Comorbid Conditions

Diabetes and essential hypertension, independent of renovascular disease, complicate treatment and lengthen disability.

Complications

Complications that may be associated with renovascular hypertension include congestive heart failure, myocardial infarction, cerebrovascular accident (stroke), pulmonary edema, and renal failure.

Factors Influencing Duration

Factors include the individual's age, lifestyle modifications, the extent of renovascular damage and systemic vascular disease, presence of bilateral disease, the specific treatments instituted, the individual's response to treatment, and the development of complications.

Length of Disability

Disability duration depends on type of treatment (medical or surgical). Duration for individuals following surgical treatment depends on procedure, location, and extent of stenosis or occlusion.

Medical treatment.

Duration in Days

Job Classification	Minimum	Optimum	Maximum
Sedentary work	1	7	14
Light work	3	7	14
Medium work	3	14	28
Heavy work	7	21	35
Very Heavy work	7	21	35

Failure to Recover

If an individual fails to recover within the maximum duration expectancy period, the reader may wish to reference the following questions to assist in better understanding the specifics of an individual's medical case.

Regarding diagnosis:

- Does individual have a history of elevated cholesterol in the blood (hyperlipidemia), severe high blood pressure (malignant hypertension), fibromuscular disease, and/or diabetes mellitus? Is there a family history of any of these disorders or of renovascular hypertension?
- Does individual smoke cigarettes?
- Does individual complain of headache, anxiety, heart irregularity or pounding (palpitations), a rapid heartbeat (tachycardia), lightheadedness, mental sluggishness, and decreased tolerance to temperatures?
- Has blood pressure been controlled with properly taken medication? Has individual's controlled high blood pressure suddenly elevated?
- Were blood tests done such as blood urea nitrogen (BUN), creatinine, potassium, and plasma renin activity? Was the captopril test done followed by measurement of renin in the blood? Did rennin elevate suggesting renovascular hypertension? Is it fairly certain that these results were not false-positive results, particularly if individual is black?
- Was radioisotope renography or captopril renography done? Were ultrasound, magnetic resonance angiography (MRA), or CT required? Was renal arteriography performed if individual was deemed at high-risk for renovascular hypertension?
- Was the diagnosis of renovascular hypertension confirmed?

Regarding treatment:

- Did treatment require surgical revascularization or angioplasty with stent placement?
- Did any complications develop after surgery?
- If individual has atherosclerosis or is a poor candidate for revascularization or angioplasty, were angiotensin-converting enzyme (ACE) inhibitors and calcium-channel blockers used? Is the medication improving the renovascular hypertension?
- Are underlying disorders such as diabetes, hypertension, and increased cholesterol responding to treatment? Is individual compliant with all medication and treatment regimens as prescribed?

Regarding prognosis:

- Does the condition affect one (unilateral) or both (bilateral) renal arteries?
- Is this the initial diagnosis or have the arteries become obstructed again (restenosed)?
- If surgery or angioplasty was done, did any complications arise after the procedures?
- If individual is taking an angiotensin-converting enzyme (ACE) inhibitor, has this caused a decline in kidney function?
- Does individual diligently comply with all medication and treatment regimens?
- Have any complications developed such as congestive heart failure, heart attack (myocardial infarction), cerebrovascular accident (stroke), pulmonary edema, or renal failure? If so, what are they and what is expected outcome with treatment?

References

Ferri, Fred. Ferri's Clinical Advisor. St. Louis: Mosby, 2000.

Kisne, Carolyn MSPT, and Lynn Allen Colby, MSPT. Therapeutic Exercise: Foundations and Techniques. Philadelphia: F.A. Davis Company, 1990.

Pickering, Thomas, and Jon Blumenfeld. "Renovascular Hypertension and Ischemic Nephropathy." Brenner and Rector's The Kidney, 6th ed. Brenner, Barry, ed. Philadelphia: W.B. Saunders Company, 2000. 2007-2029.

Tierney, Lawrence, Stephen McPhee, and Maxine Papadakis. Current Medical Diagnosis and Treatment, 39th ed. New York: Lange Medical Books/McGraw-Hill, 2000.

Repair of Cerebral Aneurysm

Other names / synonyms: Brain Aneurysm Clipping, Brain Aneurysm Repair, Cerebral Aneursym Clipping, Intracranial Aneurysm Clipping, Intracranial Aneurysm Repair

39.51

Definition

Surgical repair of an aneurysm within the skull (cerebral or intracranial aneurysm) is referred to as clipping. An aneurysm is an abnormal ballooning of a weakened artery. Inside the skull cavity, aneurysms typically develop at the base of the brain. When the aneurysm bursts or ruptures, it bleeds into the brain tissue, into the space between the brain and the tissue covering it (subarachnoid hemorrhage) and into chambers (ventricles) within the brain filled with cerebrospinal fluid. About half of individuals with a ruptured aneurism die, and about half of the survivors have permanent brain damage.

Genetics plays a role in the development of aneurysms, which are often due to a malformation of blood vessels that is present at birth (congenital). They are often associated with other congenital conditions elsewhere in the body, such as polycystic kidney disease and a narrowing (coarctation) of the aorta. They are also associated with connective tissue disease such as fibromuscular dysplasia. Some types of aneurysms (mycotic aneurysms) are thought to result from an infection of the heart (endocarditis).

Most aneurysms are sac or berry aneurysms, which are good candidates for clipping because they are usually relatively small, round, and well defined. Others, because of their unusual shape and stiff walls (fusiform aneurysms) or location, are difficult to clip.

A ruptured aneurysm is the most common cause of subarachnoid hemorrhage, occurring in 10 individuals out of every 100,000, or about 15,000 Americans each year. The majority occurs in individuals between 40-65 years of age. Ruptured aneurysms are more common in women than in men. More than 14,000 clipping procedures are performed each year.

Reason for Procedure

After an aneurysm ruptures, if death does not occur immediately from the hemorrhage, normal blood clotting mechanisms typically stop the initial bleeding. The risk is high, however, that bleeding will begin again. Repair, or clipping, of the aneurysm is the surest way to remove the possibility that the aneurysm will rebleed.

Sometimes an aneurysm is discovered by chance, while checking for some other condition, as it is estimated that between 1-5% of Americans have unruptured brain aneurysms, many of which never cause symptoms. In this case, the decision to repair the aneurysm is usually made based on the size of the aneurysm and the age of the individual. As the risk of rupture is 1 in 100 each year, surgery is most advantageous in younger individuals who will live longer, and therefore will have a higher risk of rupture during their lifetime. Half of individuals with a ruptured aneurysm die, and half of the survivors are left with permanent brain damage. Typically, aneurysms smaller than 5 mm are followed carefully. Clipping is considered for those between 5-10 mm, and is performed as soon as possible for those larger than 10 mm.

Description

Ideally, clipping is performed before the aneurysm ruptures. Up to half of individuals have warning signs before a complete rupture. For example, they may experience an extreme sudden headache or a stiff neck. Computed tomography (CT) imaging, MRI, or angiography performed at this time can detect the aneurysm, and the need for surgery can be assessed before damage is done. If not detected early, the aneurysm is clipped after rupture.

Clipping is performed in the hospital. Before surgery, every effort is made to prevent rupture or rebleeding of the aneurysm. The individual is given a mild sedative and kept in a quiet room. A stool softener reduces straining and decreases risk of bleeding. The individual is monitored for signs of seizures and changes in blood pressure. Precautions are also taken against decreased blood flow to the brain from narrowing of arteries near the aneurysm at the base of the brain (vasospasm), which often follows bleeding from a ruptured aneurysm (subarachnoid hemorrhage).

The exact location of the aneurysm is identified using x-ray images inside the skull (cerebral angiography). Because it is common to have more than one aneurysm, the entire area, including the right and left carotid arteries, should be checked for additional aneurysms.

With the individual under general anesthesia, the skull is surgically opened (craniotomy) in the vicinity of the aneurysm. A clip is placed at the base of the aneurysm, at the point where it balloons out from the blood vessel. The clip removes the aneurysm from blood circulation by physically blocking blood from entering it. Some physicians recommend checking the placement of the clip and its effectiveness with another angiography at this time.

Experts don't agree on the best timing for the clipping procedure after aneurysm rupture. Generally, it is accepted that the procedure should be performed within the first 3 days after bleeding or after 10-14 days following bleeding. The reason for this timing is the need to prevent rebleeding by operating as soon as possible (rebleeding is most likely to occur in the first 2 weeks), yet to avoid operating during an episode of vasospasm (this is most likely to occur on days 3-10). Some experts believe that individuals who are not in coma should have the procedure at 24-36 hours after the onset of bleeding.

After surgery, the individual in monitored in intensive care. Medical treatments are continued to reduce the risk of rebleeding and vasospasm. The condition of the blood vessels inside the skull should be monitored daily using ultrasound imaging (transcranial Doppler examination). The individual should be kept well hydrated and have blood pressure maintained at a slightly high level. Appropriate treatment should be started if any sign of vasospasm develops.

1812   *The Medical Disability Advisor—Fourth Edition*

Prognosis

The mortality rate for aneurysm rupture (subarachnoid hemorrhage) is 50-60%, and about half of survivors are left with permanent brain damage. Half of those who die do so before reaching the hospital. Clipping performed before the aneurysm ruptures removes the risk of subarachnoid hemorrhage from future rupture of that aneurysm. Even after rupture, successful clipping removes the risk of rebleeding. Each episode of rebleeding has a mortality rate of 40-50%. If the clipping procedure fails, the risk of rupture or rebleeding remains.

The outcome of clipping is less successful if, during surgery, arteries narrow (vasospasm) near the aneurysm at the base of the brain. Stroke or death is more likely in this scenario. Overall, death rate from clipping of unruptured aneurysms ranges from 0-7%, and the complication rate from 4-15%. However, surgical centers performing more than 10 aneurysm surgeries per year have less than half the death rate of centers rarely performing aneurysm surgery (5% vs. 11%). In individuals who have already had a ruptured aneurysm, the rate of new aneurysm formation is 1-2% per year.

Specialists

- Neurosurgeon

Work Restrictions / Accommodations

Neurological impairment following the burst aneurysm or the clipping procedure may require a change of job or some of the duties associated with a particular job. To reduce the risk of future rupture or bleeding, job duties may need to be modified to reduce physical and emotional stress and overexertion. Many individuals are permanently disabled after aneurysm rupture.

Comorbid Conditions

Approximately 33% of individuals with one aneurysm have additional aneurysms and other blood vessel malformations that could result in future bleeding episodes.

Subarachnoid hemorrhage is a significant cause of maternal death during pregnancy, especially in the third trimester. In a pregnant woman, either clipping or delivery should occur as soon as possible after the aneurysm is detected or ruptured in order to reduce the risk of rebleeding. Clipping is typically successful, with no difference in prognosis due to the pregnancy.

Other neurological or vascular conditions could complicate recovery and lengthen disability following aneurysm clipping.

Procedure Complications

Approximately 50% of individuals with bleeding from a ruptured aneurysm (subarachnoid hemorrhage) develop narrowing of the arteries near the aneurysm at the base of the brain (vasospasm) following the bleeding or clipping procedure. Of these individuals, 15-20% will die. Stroke or rebleeding may complicate aneurysm clipping.

Surgery always carries the risks of infection. Anesthesia carries the risks of breathing trouble, pneumonia from fluids entering the airway (aspiration pneumonia), and reaction to anesthetics.

Factors Influencing Duration

Length of disability may be influenced by the type and location of aneurysm, extent of procedure required, presence of underlying medical conditions, and complications. The amount of hemorrhage and subsequent neurologic damage also influence length of disability.

Length of Disability

Disability may be permanent.

Duration in Days

Job Classification	Minimum	Optimum	Maximum
Sedentary work	42	56	Indefinite
Light work	42	56	Indefinite
Medium work	56	70	Indefinite
Heavy work	70	84	Indefinite
Very Heavy work	70	84	Indefinite

References

Barclay, Laurie. "American Heart Association Issues Brain Aneurysm Guidelines." WebMD 27 Oct 2000 01 Nov 2000 <http://www.webmd.com>.

Beers, Mark, MD, and Robert Berkow, MD, eds. The Merck Manual, 17th ed. Whitehouse Station, NJ: Merck Research Laboratories, 1999.

Goetz, Christopher. Textbook of Clinical Neurology. W.B. Saunders Company: Philadelphia, 1999.

National Center for Health Statistics. Detailed Diagnoses and Procedures, National Hospital Discharge Survey, 1997. Hyattsville: U.S. Department of Health and Human Services, 1997.

Pikus, H.J., and R.C. Heros. "Surgical Treatment of Internal Carotid and Posterior Communicating Artery Aneurysms." Neurosurgical Clinic of North America 9 4 (1998): 785-795.

Pulsinelli, William. "Hemorrhagic Cerebrovascular Disease." Cecil Textbook of Medicine, 21st ed. Goldman, Lee, and J. Claude Bennett, eds. Philadelphia: W.B. Saunders Company, 2000. 2109-2115.

Samson, D., et al. "Current Results of the Surgical Management of Aneurysms of the Basilar Apex." Neurosurgery 44 4 (1999): 697-702.

Zager, E.L. "Surgical Treatment of Intracranial Aneurysms." Neuroimaging Clinic of North America 7 4 (1997): 763-782.

Repair, Anterior Cruciate Ligament

Other names / synonyms: ACL Reattachment, ACL Reconstruction

81.45

Definition

Anterior cruciate ligament (ACL) repair is a reconstruction procedure that is used to repair the ACL after it has been torn, stretched, or dislocated from the bone attachments that form the knee. Unlike other injuries in other bodily tissues, the ACL does not heal or repair itself.

The ACL is a powerful ligament extending from the top-front surface of the shinbone (tibia) to the bottom-rear surface of the thigh bone (femur). The ligament prevents instability in the front of the knee joint (anterior instability).

ACL injury can occur when an individual comes to a quick stop (sudden deceleration); suddenly changes direction while running, pivoting, or landing from a jump; and overextending the knee joint in either direction. ACL injury occurs in 4 out of 1,000 individuals. Prevention includes hamstring strengthening exercises and the use of proper techniques when playing sports or exercising. However, many cases of ACL injury are not preventable.

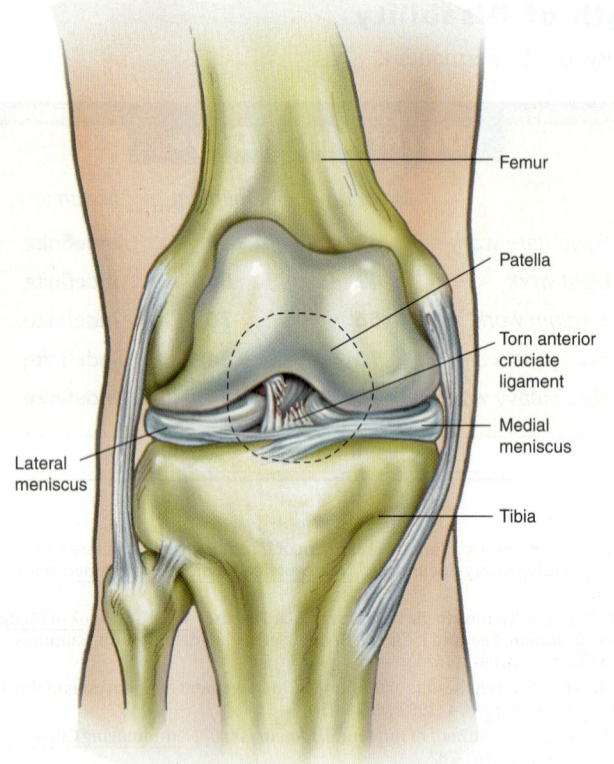

Reason for Procedure

The purpose of the anterior cruciate ligament (ACL) reconstruction procedure is to restore stability to the knee joint and to slow the progression of degenerative arthritis. Another reason for the procedure is to prevent serious damage to the knee. An untreated, torn ACL can over time cause muscles to atrophy and the knee joint to become dysfunctional. One case study revealed that after 11 years, an individual with a torn ACL in spite of rehabilitation (which included wearing of braces) found that his knee was severely damaged.

Description

There are different methods by which an anterior cruciate ligament (ACL) can be reconstructed.

One method involves using the patellar tendon, which connects the kneecap (patella) to the shin bone (tibia). The middle third of the tendon and a small portion of the bone on either end is "harvested" and used as the new ACL. This procedure is called a patellar tendon autograft because the individual's own tissue is used.

Reconstruction of the ACL begins with a small incision in the individual's leg where small tunnels are drilled in the bone. Next, the new or harvested ACL is brought through the tunnels and secured with a staple-and-buckle system.

Another autograft method of ACL reconstruction uses the individual's hamstring tendons (semitendinosus-gracilis), which connect muscles in the back of the thigh to the lower leg. A small portion of these 2 tendons is removed through a small incision in the individual's leg and looped to form a strong, new ACL.

The third method of ACL reconstruction uses an allograft, meaning that the graft comes from a source other than the individual's body. A donated Achilles tendon (from a cadaver) is an example.

The ACL reconstruction procedure is frequently performed on an outpatient basis. Rehabilitation after an ACL reconstruction procedure can be difficult and time-consuming, but it is critical for a successful outcome. Various styles of braces can be used during recovery from ACL surgery and for activity during the first 1-2 years following surgery. The decision to use braces and the amount of activity allowed is based on the knee's stability, surgeon preference, and the individual's compliance.

Prognosis

In general, conservative treatment has a variable long-term prognosis. For individuals who are sedentary, nonoperative treatment of mild instability may result in little improvement in the way of symptoms and only mildly increased onset and progression of osteoarthritis.

For individuals with major instability and for individuals with heavier use of the knee at work or recreationally, short term symptoms and function and long term arthritis are improved by ACL reconstruction.

Specialists

- Orthopedic Surgeon
- Physiatrist
- Physical Therapist

Rehabilitation

Physical therapy is recommended for successful recovery from surgical repair of the anterior cruciate ligament, and requires months of hard work in rehabilitation. Rehabilitation following anterior cruciate ligament repair follows a structured process beginning immediately after the surgical repair and ending with the individual returning to work and other activities.

Initially in phase one, the physical therapist uses various methods to decrease postoperative pain. The physician may request very gradual weight-bearing immediately after the anterior cruciate ligament repair. A rehabilitation brace, also called a postoperative brace, is used immediately after surgical repair in an effort to put the joint at rest and help protect it, while still allowing appropriate but limited motion. This form of bracing is available in 2 particular types: a straight immobilizer and a hinged brace. Straight immobilizers are made of foam with 2 metal rods down the side that are secured with Velcro and prevent all motion. The hinged brace allows range of motion to be set by tightening a screw control.

Once pain and swelling is controlled, range of motion is started in rehabilitation and performed as tolerated. This is often initiated in a warm whirlpool or in conjunction with another form of heat treatment and continued until all the movement is restored. This phase continues with isometric exercises such as the quadriceps set. By the end of this phase, crutch walking should be easily tolerated using a 3-point walking pattern with instructions from the physical therapist.

Phase two usually begins at the end of immobilization, when swelling is controlled, and pain is minimal. Goals of rehabilitation are to achieve full and pain-free motion of the knee joint along with strengthening of both the quadriceps and hamstring muscle groups. Exercises are done to strengthen all muscles in the leg. Leg raises may be used to strengthen the quadriceps Ankle weights may be used for resistance as the muscles strengthen from this exercise. Hamstring curls may be introduced.

Phase three is considered the intermediate stage of rehabilitation. The criteria for beginning phase three is no swelling and minimal to no pain and almost full range of motion. The individual at this point is encouraged to walk and may be allowed to return to light work. For some individuals, this phase may not be reached for several months longer. More intense exercising is instructed in this phase with increased resistance cycling popular at this time.

Phase three of knee joint rehabilitation may also use isokinetic machines in which the speed of the knee motion is set by the physical therapist. Resisted exercises with ankle weights or machines under supervision of the therapist may be used. Balance exercises are added at this time

In phase four, the isokinetic exercises are now increased. Weight resistance is initiated by the physical therapist. This may include leg curls, leg press, and half knee squats. Stationary biking may be added. At the completion of phase four of the rehabilitation for anterior cruciate ligament repair, the individual must have full range of motion, no symptoms, functional stability, and the involved limb demonstrating no more than 10% deficit of strength compared to the uninvolved leg.

Phase five is the individual's reinstatement to work as exercise is now directed toward work requirements. At the onset of returning to work, the physician may prescribe a functional brace to be worn as the individual returns to work, training, or competition. Generally speaking, rehabilitation of the anterior cruciate ligament will vary depending on the type of surgery that was performed, where the graft was harvested, and whether any associated supporting ligament and cartilage was also injured and repaired.

Modifications may need to be made by the physical therapist for those who have arthritis or other joint irritations.

Work Restrictions / Accommodations

Limited weight-bearing, use of a knee brace, and rest periods for elevation of the leg would be expected at work during the early stages of recovery. Long-term use of a protective knee brace may be recommended. Individuals should refrain from squatting, jumping, and torque activities.

Comorbid Conditions

Obesity and recent or chronic illness may lengthen disability. Also, pre-existing conditions, such as osteoarthritis, knee ligament injury, and inflammation of the inner lining of a joint cavity (synovitis) have been known to lengthen disability.

Procedure Complications

Complications include injuries associated with other structures in the knee, such as crescent-shaped disks of fibrocartilage attached to the superior articular surface of the tibia (menisci), fractures, and osteoarthritis.

Surgical complications include infection, stiffness of the joint (lexity), scar tissue build-up inside the knee joint (arthrofibrosis), vein inflammation (phlebitis), and complex regional pain syndrome (RPS).

Poor placement of the graft can cause impingement and require reoperation ("notch plasty").

Graft materials have also been associated with complications. Most complications occur with the use of donor tissue (allograft). One such complication occurs when the donor individual's tissue does not genetically match the tissue of the recipient individual. This condition, which is referred to as graft-versus-host disease (GVHD), can be life-threatening because the attack on the recipient individual's organs and tissues impairs their ability to function. A second complication occurs when the recipient individual's immune system destroys the donor individual's tissue in a process called graft rejection.

Other complications include infection, bleeding, and posttransplant immunodeficiency. Additionally, there may be side effects associated with the immunosuppressive drugs given to help prevent graft rejection.

Factors Influencing Duration

Work requirements, complications, and inability to follow a rehabilitation program will affect length of disability. Associated injuries and treatment will also affect the duration of disability.

Length of Disability

Individual must not be subject to stress activities across the joint. If job duties can be performed while sitting, duration may be shorter.

Arthroscopic reattachment and reconstruction.

Job Classification	Duration in Days		
	Minimum	Optimum	Maximum
Sedentary work	21	35	70
Light work	21	63	98
Medium work	182	273	Indefinite
Heavy work	182	273	Indefinite
Very Heavy work	182	273	Indefinite

References

Anterior Cruciate Ligament (ACL) Injury. National Library of Science. 01 Jan 2000. 07 Mar 2001 <http://medlineplus.adam.com/ency/article/001074.htm>.

Popovic, J.R., and Lozak, L.J. National Hospital Discharge Survey: Annual Summary, 1998. National Center for Health. 01 Jan 2000. 23 Oct 2000 <http://www.cdc.gov/nchs/data/sr13_148.pdf>.

Repair, Hammertoe
77.56

Definition

Hammertoe repair is a surgical procedure to correct a deformity (hammertoe) caused by tendons to the involved toe becoming too tight (contracted). This causes the joint to be excessively bent (flexed). The deformity can also result in painful corns and callus formation on the boney prominences.

This condition usually develops in adult life and occurs much more frequently in women. Hammertoe deformity is related to pressure on the toe from poorly fitting shoes but the exact physiological cause is unknown.

Reason for Procedure

The procedure is performed to correct a hammertoe, a deformity where one or more toes are bent up at the first joint of the toe. Surgery is done when conservative measures such as stretching, injections of corticosteroids, and trimming corns and calluses have failed and the deformity is rigid.

Description

Surgery is scheduled on an outpatient basis under regional or general anesthesia.

There are two techniques for correcting a hammertoe deformity. If the deformity is rigid, a section bone is removed in the toe at the site of the deformity (osteotomy.) The toe is then immobilized internally with a pin for several weeks. The end of the pin may extend beyond the tip of the toe and will be removed at a later date. Dissolvable pins are also sometimes used. The joint between the toe and the foot (the metatarsal phalangeal joint) may require osteotomy as well.

In a second technique, a tendon is transferred from the underside of the toe to the upper side (flexor to extensor). This corrects the deformity by changing the direction of pull by the tendon. Both procedures may be combined to treat the deformity.

A soft dressing is used for immobilization along with a postoperative shoe for 4 weeks. Weight bearing is restricted in both procedures.

Prognosis

Full correction of the deformity can be expected although recovery is often slow and pain may continue for several weeks.

Specialists

- Orthopedic Surgeon
- Podiatrist

Work Restrictions / Accommodations

Standing, stair climbing, and walking may need to temporarily be limited. Special shoes with a somewhat stiffer sole are often required during recovery. Rest periods to elevate the lower leg are necessary during early recovery.

Comorbid Conditions

Conditions that affect circulation to the lower extremities complicate recovery from foot surgery. Obesity, diabetes, inflammatory conditions, and smoking can impair healing.

Procedure Complications

Infection, skin sloughing, and failure to correct the deformity can result from the procedure. If the second toe is involved, initial correction may be changed with pressure from the great toe, with the second toe drifting to the outside (molding).

Factors Influencing Duration

Postoperative complications prolong disability. Multiple procedures involving the foot or procedures done on both feet at the same time can lengthen disability.

Length of Disability

Individuals who need to stand, climb, or squat will have a longer disability period. Crutches, canes, and special shoes may interfere with some job requirements and add to the length of disability.

Duration in Days

Job Classification	Minimum	Optimum	Maximum
Sedentary work	3	7	14
Light work	7	21	21
Medium work	14	21	28
Heavy work	28	35	42
Very Heavy work	28	35	49

References

Mercier, Lonnie R. Practical Orthopedics. Manning, Stephanie St. Louis: Mosby Year Book, Inc, 1995.

Repair, Tendon Laceration of Hand
82.41, 82.42, 82.43, 82.44, 82.45

Definition

Repair of a tendon that has been cut (lacerated) or torn is a surgical procedure often requiring the skill of a hand surgeon and specialized equipment. The goal is to restore length, strength, and function to the damaged tendon. Tendon repair(s) may be associated with other procedures in the hand.

Athletes lifting heavy objects and workers using cutting tools are most likely to pull the tendon away from the bone or cut (lacerate) the tendon. A tendon injury may also be part of crush injury.

Reason for Procedure

Tendon repair is performed when tendons in the hand are frayed, cut, torn, or pulled apart (ruptured.) Tendon function is an integral part of hand mechanics and essential for normal function as the tendon links the muscles controlling hand motion to the bones in the hand.

Tendons are often quite long in the hand, extending from the fingertips to beyond the wrist and attaching to muscles in the forearm. There are tendons to control bending (flexion) and straightening (extension) of all parts of the hand and fingers.

Description

Most repairs must be done in the operating room and not the emergency room or physician's office. Surgical repair is most often an outpatient procedure unless complicated by infection or massive injuries to the extremity.

Lacerated tendons often withdraw (contract) toward the forearm when damaged much like a rubber band that has been stretched and then snaps. This requires exploring the normal course of the tendon and often creates a long incision to restore tendon length and position. Once the incision is made, the ends of the tendon are located and the tendon is stretched to its original position or attachment. Not only must the tendon be repaired, but often times the sheath and pulley systems must also be repaired. Suturing techniques are intricate using very fine material and magnification for improved visualization. To maintain tendon length and prevent contractures, splints and outriggers may be used. Outriggers are devices attached through the fingernails to rubber bands that pull against the natural tendency of the tendon to retract again, causing contractures. The repairs are delicate and require progressing periods of rest and early guarded mobilization for optimum healing.

After the wounds are closed, a soft compressive dressing is applied and then a protective splint. A cast may be worn over the dressing instead of a splint.

Prognosis

Outcome is dependent on the cause of the tendon rupture, length of time from injury, and treatment required. If the damaged tendon can be restored to its normal length with adequate strength, good function should return. Involvement of more than one tendon or injury to other parts of the hand decreases the likelihood of a successful outcome.

If normal tendon function cannot be completely restored or if there are concomitant injuries to the joints, manual dexterity could be compromised. Tendons do not heal as well as other body tissues so recovery is more guarded in extensive or more complicated cases. Late tendon repair is not very successful and sometimes not even possible.

Rehabilitation

Recovery from hand tendon repair is an intricate process. Tendons may be part of the mechanism of opening the hand (extension) or closing it (flexion). Careful analyses of the initial trauma as well as the corrective procedures are a determinant in creating an effective therapy schedule.

However, the therapy schedule is not rigidly set. Progress is determined by the individual's functional improvement.

The tendons involved and type of operation performed determine the type and duration of immobilization. Type of immobilization, in turn, influences the amount of early motion the individual can achieve. For example, if damage is to the flexor mechanism of the hand, a splint might be worn with the involved fingers placed in dynamic traction by an elastic thread attached from the fingernails to the outer splint. This mechanism helps take pressure off the healing flexor structures while the hand is not in motion. Light tension is achieved, however, when the individual extends the fingers. Early mobilization of the fingers within the cast also helps reduce the adhesion formation that can limit motion and slow the progress of therapy.

A conservative amount of tension should be applied to the healing tendons during therapy sessions especially during the first weeks postsurgery. Most tendon operation failures occur when the tendon ruptures or fails to adhere to the bone. As therapy progresses, the integrity of the hand structures should be functionally evaluated to minimize the risk of reinjury. In addition, scar management is crucial to restoring appropriate biomechanical function during and after therapy. A program for scar management is initiated once sutures or the cast is removed.

Individual may be fitted with a smaller blocking cast once proper healing occurs. The quality of curling the fingers (tendon gliding) or muscle movement determines whether therapy progresses. For example, if the individual shows signs of tendon rupture such as no tendon while performing gliding exercises, no further therapy is conducted until the primary physician has reevaluated the tendon.

Once approved, active range-of-motion exercises are added to the therapy routine. For example, individual starts with the hand at full extension and then the four fingers without the thumb bend to form a tabletop. The individual progresses to a work therapy program once performance on gliding exercises suggests return of proper hand mechanics.

The goal of work therapy is to improve handgrip strength and sustained use of the hand. Screwing pegs of varying lengths into a board is one exercise is an example of a work therapy exercise. Other woodworking exercises may include sanding with the hand in either a flat or gripped position.

When resistive exercises begin, the individual should be tested for muscle weakness. Muscle weakness such as impairment in extending the fingers (extensor lag) becomes apparent as exercises become more advanced. Specific exercises include rolling a can affixed with cloth across a Velcro board by placing a partially formed fist on the can and uncurling the fingers toward the can (extension). This helps strengthen the hand in extension.

In addition to increasing muscle strength, exercises in this phase of therapy emphasize both hand and wrist movements. Performing wrist curls in different planes of motion and manipulating functional tools such as a screwdriver or hammer are examples of movements performed during this phase. The individual is expected to engage in a home routine that includes picking up objects and gripping an object for a period of time (sustained gripping). The home routine also includes an upper body routine that aims at increasing arm, chest, and upper back strength.

Return to work is dependent on the amount of functional recovery of the tendon. In some cases, the dexterity of the hand may not improve significantly enough to return to the same type of job. In this case, an occupational therapist specializing in hand rehabilitation may assess work-related tasks to determine if the individual can return to his/her current occupation. The work environment may need modification. It may be necessary for the individual to continue some form of exercise to maintain the functional ability of the hand.

Specialists

- Hand Surgeon
- Plastic Surgeon
- Orthopedic Surgeon

Work Restrictions / Accommodations

During initial recovery phase, individuals should not use the injured hand. Increasing use of the hand depends on healing progress and tolerance of the repair to stress. Individuals are often required to spend several hours in therapy sessions per week and wear complicated splints when not in therapy. Use of medications to control pain and swelling may require review of drug policies. Surgery on the dominant hand makes limited work capacity difficult.

Comorbid Conditions

Any underlying condition that affects tendon strength and integrity would impact recovery from surgery. This includes inflammatory diseases, peripheral vascular disease, diabetes, neurological disease, and smoking.

Procedure Complications

Possible complications of this procedure include adhesions or scar formation around the healing tendon that result in decreased function, rupture of the repair, infection, skin sloughing, and nerve and vessel damage. Sometimes the severity of tendon damage is missed. This creates long-term disability from what was thought to be a rather insignificant injury.

Factors Influencing Duration

Dominant hand involvement, work requirements, complications of the injury or surgery, and compliance with rehabilitation program influence disability. Disability time is variable depending on the tendon(s) involved.

Length of Disability

In general, extensor tendon injuries have a much shorter disability duration compared to flexor tendon injuries. If one-handed work is available, individuals may be able to return to work sooner. It may not be possible for the individual to return to job requirements that involve intricate dexterity, strength, or endurance of the hand. Complicated cases may have permanent disability.

Duration in Days

Job Classification	Minimum	Optimum	Maximum
Sedentary work	42	56	98
Light work	56	70	98
Medium work	70	84	98
Heavy work	70	84	98
Very Heavy work	70	84	98

References

Bednar, M., and T. Light. "Hand Surgery." Current Diagnosis and Treatment in Orthopedics. Skinner, J.B., and Harry B. Skinner, eds. Norwalk: Appleton & Lange, 1995. 468-479.

Stanley, Barbara, and Susan Tribuzi. Concepts in Hand Rehabilitation. Philadelphia: F.A. Davis Company, 1992.

Repetitive Strain Injury
727.2

Definition

Repetitive strain injuries (RSI), also known as cumulative trauma disorders (CTD), are commonly reported occupational illnesses. Small but cumulative tissue damage results from repeated and sustained tasks. There is usually no acute injury involved with the onset of symptoms, which include pain, weakness, and loss of function. All cases have in common the overuse of muscle tendon units. The terms RIS and CTD are often used in discriminantly and it is preferable to have a specific anatomic distinction for a painful disorder.

Job requirements most likely to produce the syndrome include repetition, high force, awkward joint position, direct pressure, vibration, cold temperatures and prolonged constrained posture. Work related risk factors can be unsatisfied by inadequate work-rest cycles, excessive work pace or duration, unaccustomed work and lack of task variability, machine paced work.

Individual risk factors such as deconditioning and increased body mass index (BMI) are also involved in the syndrome. Some studies show that individual risk factors coupled with work-related issues (ergonomic and psychosocial) contribute to the onset of repetitive strain injuries. Behavioral issues such as job dissatisfaction or conflict in the workplace may be confounding factors in interpreting complaints attributed to RSI.

For specific injury, see carpal tunnel syndrome, De Quervain's syndrome, radial styloid tenosynovitis, epicondylitis, trigger finger, Raynaud's phenomenon, low back pain, lumbar disc disease, tension neck syndrome, and knee bursitis.

Resection of Gastric or Duodenal Ulcer Site

Other names / synonyms: Antrectomy, Gastrectomy, Partial Excision of Gastric Ulcer Site, Pyloroplasty, Subtotal Gastrectomy, Vagotomy
43.4, 43.6

Definition

Resection of a gastric or duodenal ulcer site (peptic ulcer) is the surgical removal of damaged ulcerated tissue.

Peptic ulcers are lesions of the gastrointestinal tract that destroy the inner lining of the gastrointestinal tract (mucosa). The most common peptic ulcer sites are the first few centimeters of the duodenum (duodenal ulcer) or the lesser curvature of the stomach (gastric ulcer).

Surgical treatment of peptic ulcers is reserved for those ulcers that do not respond to medical therapy. Due to advances in the medical management of peptic ulcer disease, less than 10% of ulcers fail to respond to medical therapy and require surgical intervention.

There are about 500,000 new cases of peptic ulcers each year in the US. They occur in about 10% of the adult population. They are 5 times more common in the duodenum than in the stomach. Peptic ulcers are slightly more common in men than women. Ulcers in the duodenum are most common in ages 30 to 55, while gastric ulcers are more common between 55 to 70 years of age. Ulcers are more common in smokers and in individuals who used nonsteroidal anti-inflammatory drugs (NSAIDs) on a chronic basis. The role of emotional stress in the development of ulcers is uncertain. Other conditions that play a role in the development of peptic ulcers are chronic stomach infection with bacteria called Heliobacter pylori and gastric acid hypersecretion states, such as Zollinger-Ellison syndrome. It is believed that 70-75% of duodenal ulcers are associated with H. pylori infections.

Reason for Procedure

The procedure is most often performed on an emergency basis to stop bleeding from the ulcer site or for ulcer perforation with peritonitis. Peritonitis occurs when contents of the gastrointestinal tract leak into the sterile environment of the abdomen causing a serious life-threatening infection.

Local resection alone of an ulcer almost invariably leads to recurrence. Consequently, a wider resection of the stomach and, sometimes, duodenal tissue (partial gastrectomy) is usually done. Likewise, the procedure is often combined with transection of the vagus nerve (vagotomy) and excision of scar tissue and widening of the opening between the stomach and duodenum (pyloroplasty).

Specialists

- Gastroenterologist
- General Surgeon

Description

General anesthesia is administered. A tube may be inserted to drain the bladder (urinary catheter) and one to drain the stomach contents (nasogastric tube). The surgeon creates an incision that runs midline from the ribcage to the lower abdomen. After locating the injured or diseased area of the stomach, the surgeon will use a stapling device to section off the healthy stomach from the diseased stomach. A small section of the injured tissue will be sent to the laboratory for biopsy to rule out gastric cancer. If necessary, the free end of the stomach will be joined to a healthy segment of the small intestine. One or more small drains may be placed at the surgical site to allow for drainage of blood and fluid. The abdominal wound is closed in layers. The final skin layer will be closed with a small stapling device.

Prognosis

In peptic ulcers with significant bleeding, an emergency gastrectomy is generally successful in controlling bleeding. Approximately 5-10% of the individuals will have recurrence of ulcers.

Work Restrictions / Accommodations

Depending on the extent of surgery done and the presence of digestive disturbances, some individuals may need accommodations to take frequent small meals, (i.e., frequent short breaks).

Ulcers may recur. Although the role of emotional stress in ulcer development is uncertain, some individuals may benefit by reassignment to a less stressful job.

Comorbid Conditions

Comorbid conditions of immune suppression and bleeding disorders may impact ability to recover and further lengthen disability.

Procedure Complications

The most common complications from the procedure include wound infection, leaking at the site where the stomach is joined to the intestine (anastomosis), lung congestion (atelectasis), and bleeding. Less common complications include shock (from bleeding) or cardiac arrest. Late complications include recurrent ulcers, diarrhea (from sugar and carbohydrate intolerance), and iron deficiency anemia. As many as 30% of individuals have significant problems with digestion, including weight loss, bloating, anemia, low blood sugar, vomiting, and diarrhea (dumping syndrome).

Factors Influencing Duration

Length of disability may be influenced by the underlying condition, the extent of the presence of post-gastrectomy syndromes (side effects after gastric surgery), or the presence of surgical complications.

Length of Disability

Duration in Days

Job Classification	Minimum	Optimum	Maximum
Sedentary work	28	35	42
Light work	28	35	42
Medium work	42	49	56
Heavy work	42	49	56
Very Heavy work	42	49	56

References

Goldman, Lee, and J. Claude Bennett. Cecil Textbook of Medicine, 21st ed. Philadelphia: W.B. Saunders Company, 2000.

Respiratory Failure

Other names / synonyms: Extrapulmonary Respiration Failure, Respiratory Distress

518.81, 799.1

Definition

Respiratory failure is a general term used to describe the respiratory system's inability to effectively exchange carbon dioxide and oxygen. It may be due to the impairment of gas exchange in the lungs (oxygenation failure) or to obstruction of the free flow of air into the lungs (ventilation). Although both problems can occur simultaneously, it is more common for only one type of failure to occur at a time.

Almost any condition that affects breathing or the lungs can lead to respiratory failure. The cause can be classified as outside the lungs (extrapulmonary) or within the lungs (intrapulmonary). Extrapulmonary causes include disorders that affect the brain (trauma or drug overdose), spinal cord, neuromuscular system (myasthenia gravis, muscular dystrophy, polio, Guillain Barré syndrome, polymyositis, stoke, or amyotrophic lateral sclerosis), thorax (massive obesity or trauma), and abnormality of lung tissue or upper airways (pulmonary fibrosis, fibrosing alveolitis, widespread tumors, radiation, sarcoidosis, or burns).

Intrapulmonary causes include disorders that affect the lower airways (chronic obstructive pulmonary disease, emphysema, bronchiectasis, cystic fibrosis, asthma, bronchiolitis, bronchitis, or inhaled particles), the pulmonary circulation (pulmonary embolism or congenital disorders), or the gas exchange across the alveolar-capillary membrane (respiratory distress syndrome, inhalation of toxic gases, or near drowning).

Diagnosis

History: Symptoms may include shortness of breath (dyspnea), cough, bluish discoloration of the skin (cyanosis), restlessness, anxiety, confusion, headache, and generalized fatigue. Respiratory rate may be increased or less commonly, decreased.

Physical exam: Examination of the interior of the eye (using an ophthalmoscope) may reveal swelling of the optic nerve. Listening through a stethoscope (auscultation) may reveal abnormal breath sounds, irregular heart sounds, and lack of bowel sounds. Pressing with hands on the abdomen (palpation) may reveal abdominal tenderness and pain in the kidney area. A neurological exam may indicate impaired sensory and motor function.

Tests: Laboratory tests include arterial blood gases to measure oxygen and carbon dioxide levels in the blood. Chest x-rays, blood chemistry and hematology tests, sputum cultures, and pulmonary function tests may be done to determine underlying cause of the respiratory failure.

Treatment

Treatment is aimed at eliminating the underlying cause, promoting adequate gas exchange, and preventing multiple organ damage due to impaired oxygen.

If respiratory failure is due to obstruction of airflow, the cause must be removed. Treatment may include forced coughing, suctioning, and respiratory or physical therapy. If there is no relief, a flexible light source with camera (fiberoptic bronchoscopy) is passed down the trachea and into the bronchi to identify and remove the obstruction.

Supplemental oxygen therapy may be necessary to improve oxygenation. Many individuals can use noninvasive ventilation such as a nasal mask. In severe cases, however, invasive interventions may be required. An oral or nasal tube is inserted (intubation) in order to more efficiently deliver a carefully controlled amount of oxygen. The use of positive pressure mechanical ventilation may be necessary. Medications to treat or prevent infections (antibiotics), facilitate removal of secretions (expectorants), and dilate airways (bronchodilators) may also be beneficial. Sedation is necessary in many individuals to relieve restlessness and anxiety.

Prognosis

If respiratory failure is due to an airway obstruction, removal of the obstruction usually restores effective ventilation. When due to a lung disorder, outcome depends on the underlying cause.

Differential Diagnosis

Conditions with similar symptoms include pulmonary edema, atelectasis, respiratory distress syndrome, and hypoxia due to ischemia (reduced blood flow to a tissue) or severe anemia (reduced oxygen-carrying capacity of the blood).

Specialists

- Critical Care Specialist
- Pulmonologist

Rehabilitation

Individuals with respiratory failure require occupational, physical, and respiratory therapy. The exact therapy and frequency depends on the degree of respiratory failure.

Respiratory therapy addresses increasing the lung capacity and decreasing the risk for the buildup of lung secretions. Respiratory therapists teach individuals pursed lip breathing to increase the airflow to the lungs. Individuals may also use a device that measures and displays the amount of air inspired (incentive spirometer) to help motivate individuals to take deeper breaths. Individuals also learn to produce an effective cough through techniques such as huffing where air is forcefully breathed out while the mouth is open. Individuals also learn positions that relieve shortness of breath such as leaning forward while sitting with the arms resting on the thighs.

Occupational therapy addresses any fatigue or shortness of breath that may occur during activities of daily living. Individuals learn to utilize equipment such as a shower chair to decrease the energy expended during bathing or a long-handled sponge to decrease the amount of forward bending. Occupational therapists may teach energy conservation techniques where activities of daily living such as meal preparation are broken up into smaller components that make tasks more manageable.

Physical therapy addresses decreased endurance, strength, and range of motion. Individuals learn to stretch the shoulder and chest muscles to promote normal posture that in turn improves respiration. Individuals perform strengthening exercises of the arms and legs to improve overall endurance. In addition to strengthening the arms and legs, the muscles of the upper back are strengthened through exercises such as shoulder blade squeezes that promote normal posture. Individuals also strengthen the diaphragm by lying on the back and performing abdominal breathing exercises. These exercises can be made more difficult by placing weights or a book on the abdomen to provide resistance. Individuals may perform aerobic activities such as walking on a treadmill or riding a stationary bicycle to further increase endurance. Individuals learn to rate the amount of energy they expend by utilizing a rating of perceived exertion scale.

Work Restrictions / Accommodations

Work restrictions or accommodations must be determined on an individual basis depending on job requirements.

Comorbid Conditions

The underlying disease leading to the respiratory failure may impact recovery and lengthen disability. These conditions include bronchitis, emphysema, bronchiectasis, cystic fibrosis, asthma, bronchiolitis, myasthenia gravis, muscular dystrophy, polio, Guillain Barré syndrome, polymyositis, stroke, amyotrophic lateral sclerosis, spinal cord injury, acute respiratory distress syndrome, pulmonary fibrosis, fibrosing alveolitis, widespread tumors, radiation, sarcoidosis, burns, kyphoscoliosis, and chest wounds.

Complications

Respiratory failure may cause an inadequate supply of oxygen to the tissues (hypoxia). Hypoxia in the heart muscle causes chest pain (angina pectoris). Hypoxia of the brain may initially cause confusion, dizziness, and incoordination but if the condition persists, it can progress to unconsciousness and death. Severe hypoxia may lead to complete absence of oxygen in a tissue (anoxia). If prolonged, anoxia may result in tissue death.

Individuals on ventilators are at risk for deep vein thrombosis, pulmonary embolism, gastritis and ulcers, decubitus ulcers, and nosocomial infections. The ventilator itself introduces risk for damage to the lung (barotrauma), acute respiratory alkalosis, hypotension, and ventilator-associated pneumonia.

Factors Influencing Duration

Severity of symptoms, underlying cause of the condition, effectiveness of treatment, or any complications can influence length of disability.

Length of Disability

Duration depends on underlying cause. Contact physician to obtain additional information on this vague diagnosis.

Failure to Recover

If an individual fails to recover within the maximum duration expectancy period, the reader may wish to reference the following questions to assist in better understanding the specifics of an individual's medical case.

Regarding diagnosis:

- Does individual have a history of neuromuscular system disorders such as myasthenia gravis, muscular dystrophy, polio, Guillain-Barré syndrome, polymyositis, or amyotrophic lateral sclerosis? History of pulmonary disorders such as pulmonary fibrosis, chronic obstructive pulmonary disease, emphysema, bronchiectasis, cystic fibrosis, asthma, bronchiolitis, bronchitis, or pulmonary embolism?
- Has individual experienced drug overdose, inhalation of toxic gases, near drowning, or burns?
- Does individual complain of shortness of breath (dyspnea), cough, bluish discoloration of the skin (cyanosis), restlessness, anxiety, confusion, headache, and generalized fatigue?
- Were arterial blood gases (ABGs) performed? Were chest x-ray, blood chemistry, sputum culture, and pulmonary function tests done?
- Was the underlying cause of the respiratory failure determined?

Regarding treatment:

- How was obstruction of airflow corrected?
- Did individual require fiberoptic bronchoscopy to identify and remove the obstruction?
- Did individual receive oxygen via a nasal cannula or was intubation required?
- Was the use of positive pressure mechanical ventilation required?
- Were medications to treat or prevent infections (antibiotics), facilitate removal of secretions (expectorants), and dilate airways (bronchodilators) used?
- Was sedation required to relieve restlessness and anxiety?
- Were respiratory, physical, and/or occupational therapy recommended?
- Did treatment restore adequate air exchange?

Regarding prognosis:

- Did individual obtain prompt treatment for respiratory failure?
- What was the underlying cause for respiratory failure and how was it treated? Is additional treatment required to adequately control the underlying cause?
- Has individual participated in respiratory, occupational, and/or physical therapy as prescribed?
- Has the lack of oxygen affected other organs such as the heart or brain? If so, how severely were these organs damaged?
- If individual required mechanical ventilation, have complications occurred such as deep vein thrombosis, pulmonary embolism, gastritis and ulcers, decubitus ulcers, or infections?

- Did the ventilator cause damage to the lung (barotrauma), acute respiratory alkalosis, hypotension, or ventilator-associated pneumonia?
- Have complications occurred as a result of respiratory failure or treatment? How will complications be treated and what is the expected outcome with treatment?
- How will individual's daily activities be affected?

References

Beers, Mark, and Robert Berkow. The Merck Manual, 17th ed. Whitehouse Station, NJ: Merck Research Laboratories, 1999.

Watchie, Joanne. Cardiopulmonary Physical Therapy. Philadelphia: W.B. Saunders Company, 1995.

Retinal Detachment
361, 361.8, 361.9

Definition

Retinal detachment involves the separation of the light-sensitive transparent membrane at the inner back area of the eyeball (retina) from the supporting layers below that contain nourishing blood vessels (choroid). A break, tear, or hole in the retina where images are processed usually precedes detachment.

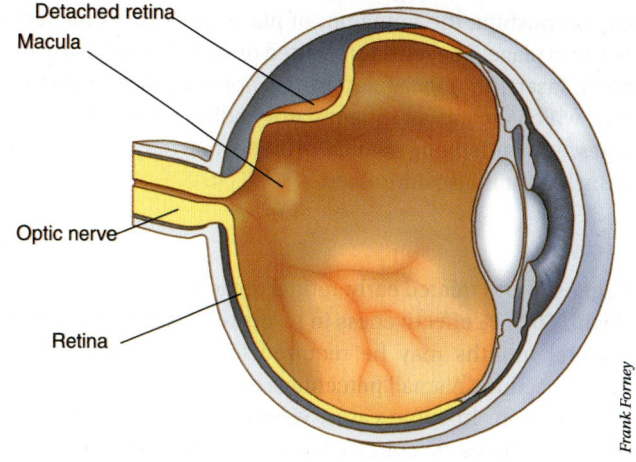

The retina may be weakened by trauma or injury, natural degeneration from aging, as part of a disease process or inflammatory disorder, a tumor, a strain caused by contracting strands in the gel-like substance that fills the eye's main cavity (vitreous humor), or spontaneously. Following a tear, clear fluid (vitreous fluid) leaks under the separated area and lifts it until detachment is complete. Visual deterioration is immediately apparent. Since retinal cells die if separated too long from nutrients provided by the choroid, treatment must begin as soon as possible to restore and preserve vision. In addition, bleeding from small blood vessels (hemorrhage) may cloud the vitreous fluid. Central vision becomes affected if the macula or central part of the retina becomes detached.

Poor distance vision (nearsightedness or myopia) is a strong risk factor. This condition is found in about half of all cases of retinal detachment worldwide. Most cases of retinal detachment occur spontaneously. Prior cataract removal is a factor almost half the time. Trauma or injury accounts for up to 20% of all cases particularly among younger age groups. Other risk factors include previous retinal detachment in either eye, family member with a detachment, tear in the retina (retinal tears), weakened spot in the retina, retinal eye diseases, diabetes mellitus, tumors, leukemia, sickle cell disease, and cardiovascular disease including high blood pressure (hypertension).

About 1 in 15,000 individuals in the US experience retinal detachment. The condition typically is found in middle-aged or older individuals. Men are at higher risk than women. Whites and individuals of Jewish ancestry are considered at higher risk of developing retinal detachment.

Diagnosis

History: Retinal detachment is usually painless. Symptoms are almost exclusively visual beginning as sudden flashes of bright lights (photopsia) seen at the edge of the field of vision (peripheral vision). This is accompanied by seeing dark, floating cobweb-like shapes (floaters) or translucent specks of various shapes. Flashes are caused by the stimulation of light-sensitive cells as the tear occurs. Floaters are caused by the release of blood or pigment into the vitreous gel. Flashes may occur once then return hours, days, or weeks later. They are seen with eye movement when the room lighting is dim. A wavy sensation may also be experienced in the visual field (metamorphopsia). One or both eyes may have symptoms but usually only one eye is affected at a time.

Symptoms do not always occur. The individual may be unaware of the detachment until vision becomes blurred or a shadow or black drape obscures part of the visual field in one eye. Symptoms appear opposite to the area of detachment. If the lower part of the retina is detached, the drape descends from the top. In an upper detachment, the drape ascends from the bottom. In a left detachment, the drape enters from the right. In a right detachment, the drape enters from the left.

Physical exam: The pupil is widely dilated with eyedrops (mydriatics) and the retina is examined with an illuminated instrument that magnifies the eye's interior (ophthalmoscopy) while gentle pressure is applied to the eyeball to bring all parts of the retina into view. A microscopic examination with a slit lamp (biomicroscopy) may also be conducted. A tear or detachment in the retina can then be clearly seen.

Tests: If a cataract or other lens cloudiness (opacity) prevents a visual view of the retina, high frequency sound waves (ultrasound) are employed to detect any tears or detachment. Visual acuity and an intraocular pressure test (tonography) are usually performed to determine the extent of vision loss and check for increased pressure within the eye. Additional tests may include the refraction test, color defectiveness determination, muscle integrity evaluation, pupillary reflex response, retinal photography, fluorescein angiography, and electroretinogram (measurement of the electrical response of the retina to light stimuli).

Treatment

Immediate treatment is needed to preserve sight. Once detachment has occurred, it may not be possible to restore normal central vision. Laser surgery can be used to seal the tears or holes in the retina that generally precede detachment.

Treatment is aimed at reattaching and sealing the detached portion of the retina to the choroid layer of the eye (retinal detachment surgery). The procedure may vary depending on the extent and type of detachment, but generally involves a series of steps that start with returning the retina to the back of the eye through injection of a gas bubble (pneumatic retinopexy). A soft silicone rubber sponge may then be sewn in place on the outside of the layer of eye (sclera) overlying the detachment (scleral buckling). This indents the sclera, reabsorbs the fluid that was pushing the retina out of place, and causes the retina to settle back into place. The retina is secured or sealed through use of heat (diathermy), laser (photocoagulation), or application of extreme cold (cryopexy), which creates an inflammatory adhesiveness in the underlying tissues. Any underlying medical problem that may have caused the retinal detachment is also addressed.

Prognosis

When diagnosed and treated early, retinal detachment can be surgically repaired with 60-95% effectiveness in terms of restoring original visual acuity. Several months may be required for visual acuity to return following a procedure. A small percentage of individuals will need more than one operation. In some cases, vision may be worse following a procedure and glasses or contact lenses may be required to restore acuity.

In some cases, the retina can never be reattached. If treatment is delayed until the center section of the retina (macula) is affected, the individual will always have blurring in the central visual area and lens magnification will be required to aid vision particularly when reading. Lack of treatment will result in retinal shrinkage and blindness in the affected eye. Retinal detachment can recur 6 to 8 weeks after the first detachment was repaired. One study indicated a 15% rate of detachment recurrence following a first reattachment procedure. Overlooked breaks or tears in the retina not repaired during the first procedure are the main cause for recurrence. About 15% of individuals with retinal detachment in one eye will experience the condition in the other eye (bilateral). Individuals who have had bilateral cataract extraction and developed a retinal detachment have almost a 30% chance of experiencing the condition in the other eye.

Differential Diagnosis

Conditions with similar symptoms include tumor, hemorrhage, cataract, migraine headaches, corneal opacities, uveitis, retinal vein occlusion, posterior vitreous detachment, ocular toxoplasmosis, ocular toxocariasis, ocular histoplasmosis, cytomegalovirus retinitis, myopia, coloboma, Stickler's syndrome, pars planitis, retinal ischemia, Marfan's syndrome, choroiditis, retinitis, sickle cell disease, age-related macular degeneration, chorioretinopathy, and diabetic retinopathy.

Specialists

- Ophthalmologist

Work Restrictions / Accommodations

Following retinal injury and reattachment, the individual must be allowed sufficient time off for frequent eye examinations to evaluate recovery and monitor the eyes for reoccurrence. Vision should also be evaluated and work duties temporarily changed if clear vision in both eyes is vital to the individual's work or safety. If permanent partial visual loss occurs, the individual may need accommodation such as large and high-contrast print or extra illumination at workstations. Additional accommodations are need if blindness results.

Comorbid Conditions

Retinal detachments are associated with trauma to the eye, myopia, proliferative diabetic retinopathy, and proliferative vitreoretinopathy.

Complications

If treatment is delayed, a partial retinal detachment may progress until the entire retina is lifted. When this happens, it may be impossible to restore normal vision. Other complications can include bleeding into the center of the eye (vitreous hemorrhage), inflammation, and infection. Loss of light and depth perception also may occur. Some retinal detachments may require additional treatment and some may never be resolved.

Factors Influencing Duration

The underlying cause of the detachment, method of treatment chosen, success of the repair, and individual's response to treatment may influence length of disability. Length of recovery can be affected by the presence of complications including inflammation, bleeding, infection, or the recurrence of a detachment.

Length of Disability

Individuals may be at risk to experience a retinal detachment in the second eye. Those with permanent vision loss may be unable to perform duties that require keen visual acuity.

Retinal detachment repair. Laser coagulation.

Job Classification	Minimum	Optimum	Maximum
Sedentary work	3	4	7
Light work	3	4	7
Medium work	3	4	14
Heavy work	3	14	28
Very Heavy work	3	14	28

Duration in Days

Surgical repair.

Duration in Days

Job Classification	Minimum	Optimum	Maximum
Sedentary work	3	7	14
Light work	3	7	14
Medium work	3	14	28
Heavy work	3	14	28
Very Heavy work	3	14	28

Failure to Recover

If an individual fails to recover within the maximum duration expectancy period, the reader may wish to reference the following questions to assist in better understanding the specifics of an individual's medical case.

Regarding diagnosis:

- Does individual have symptoms consistent with diagnosis of retinal attachment, such as flashes of bright light, floaters or wavy sensation in the visual field?
- Has diagnosis of retinal detachment been confirmed?
- Was confirmation through ophthalmoscopy and slit lamp?
- If a cataract or other lens opacity prevented a visual view of the retina, was ultrasound used?
- Was a visual acuity test and tonography performed to determine the extent of vision loss and check for increased pressure within the eye?

Regarding treatment:

- Did the individual seek and receive treatment promptly after the first signs of visual deterioration?
- Was intervention aimed at reattaching and sealing the detached portion of the retina to the choroid layer of the eye?
- Were underlying medical problems that may have caused the retinal detachment also addressed?

Regarding prognosis:

- Did individual receive prompt diagnosis and appropriate, timely treatment? Were efforts to reattach the retina successful?
- Was full visual acuity restored after procedures were undertaken to correct the condition?
- Has the individual experienced complications such as hemorrhage, inflammation, or infection that may impact recovery and prognosis?
- Was there recurrence of retinal detachment?
- Is there evidence that a break or tear in the retina may have been overlooked during the first surgical intervention?
- Has individual been provided with the glasses or contact lenses necessary to compensate for decreased visual capacity?
- Does individual have an underlying condition that may impact recovery?

References

Dellone-Larkin, Gregory, and Cecelia A. Dellone, MD. Retinal Detachment. Salomone, Joseph A., III, ed. eMedicine.com. 09 Feb 2001. 20 Feb 2001 <http://www.emedicine.com/emerg/topic504.htm>.

Liu, Y. "Effect of Chinese Medicines on the Subretinal Fluid Absorption After Operation for Retinal Detachment." Yen Ko Hsueh Pao 11 1 (1995): 41-43.

Retinal Detachment Repair

Other names / synonyms: Cryoretinopexy, Cryotherapy, Photocoagulation, Pneumatic Retinopexy, Retinal Attachment, Retinal Attachment by Cryotherapy, Scleral Buckle, Scleral Buckling

14.4, 14.41, 14.49, 14.5, 14.51, 14.52, 14.53, 14.54, 14.55, 14.59

Definition

Repairing a detached retina is a two-step process that first involves bringing the light-sensitive area at the back of the eye (the retina) back into direct contact with the tissue layer that nourishes it (the choroid). The retina is then reattached to the choroid, using one of several procedures. The treatment chosen by the eye doctor will depend on the severity and complexity of the tear or detachment.

If the retina has torn but has not become detached, or if the detachment is small and uncomplicated, a laser is used to make small burns around the tear. This type of laser procedure is called laser photocoagulation.

If fluid has leaked under the retina, the fluid may prevent the retina from settling against the choroid. In such cases, the fluid must be drained. Often, draining the fluid is sufficient to allow the retina to fall back into place.

In some cases, a bubble of air is injected into the eye. The bubble pushes the retina back into place. This is called pneumatic retinopexy.

A common treatment for retinal detachment is a procedure commonly referred to as a scleral buckle. This procedure involves surgical placement of a silicone implant or a silicone band around the outside of the tear.

Cryotherapy, a procedure using extreme cold to freeze the area around the tear to cause scarring and subsequent reattachment of the retina, is also effective.

Severe cases may require a procedure in which all or a portion of the gel-like fluid (vitreous humor) is removed from the back part of the eye (posterior chamber). This procedure is called a vitrectomy.

Retinal detachment will affect approximately 1 out of every 10,000 people each year. It can occur at any age, although it is more common in middle-aged and older people. Severe nearsightedness, family history, and prior cataract surgery are known risk factors. More men than women (at a ration of 3:2) experience retinal detachment. Individuals with other eye problems such as posterior vitreal detachment, glaucoma, vitreoretinal tufts, meridional folds or a lattice degeneration are also at an increased risk of retinal detachment. Trauma, particularly blunt trauma to the head, can cause a retinal detachment.

Reason for Procedure

Retinal detachment repair is indicated when the light-sensitive portion of the eye (retina) becomes disconnected from the wall of the eye. When the retina is not in contact with the wall of the eye, loss of vision may result. Prompt treatment--retinal detachment repair--is necessary to preserve eyesight.

Description

There are several procedures that can be used to repair a detached retina.

The least invasive procedure is called laser photocoagulation, which does not require anesthesia or a surgical incision and is conducted in the ophthalmologist's office. The ophthalmologist will aim a laser beam into the back of the eye and will make small burns around the area of the tear or detachment. The burns cause scarring, which seals the edges of the tear and prevents fluid from leaking under the retina. The procedure is over within a matter of minutes, and the individual can resume normal activity shortly after this procedure.

Surgical procedures are generally conducted under general anesthesia, although local anesthesia can be used in some cases. An overnight hospital stay may be recommended, although most individuals can go home soon after the procedure. Once the individual is anesthetized, the surgeon will make a small incision. If fluid has collected under the retina, it will be drained. For pneumatic retinopexy, gas will be injected through the incision into the back part of the eye. For cryotherapy, a probe will be used to deliver extreme cold to the area around the retinal detachment or tear. If the surgeon decides to perform a scleral buckle procedure, either a band of silicone will be placed around the eyeball or a small silicone implant will be fastened to the outside of the eye, in the area of the detachment. The silicone implant or band provides pressure, pushing the wall of the eye onto the retina from the outside. In all of these cases, the goal is to get the retina to settle back into its normal position, up against the choroid. If this has been achieved, the surgeon will stitch the incision closed, completing the procedure.

If vitrectomy is required, the surgeon will remove the gel-like substance (vitreous humor) from the back part of the eye. If necessary, the removed vitreous will be replaced with a mixture of gasses or with liquid silicone. The surgeon will then stitch the incision closed, completing the procedure.

Following the above procedures, individuals are usually able to resume normal activity within a short period (generally a day or two). If a gas bubble was used, it may be necessary to keep the head raised. Medication is usually limited to eyedrop medicines to prevent inflammation and infection. Some individuals may require pain killers for the first day or two following repair of a retinal detachment.

Prognosis

Retinal detachment repair is successful in preserving vision in over 90% of cases. A second treatment may be required in 10-30% of cases, depending on the nature and severity of the detachment. Approximately 40% of individuals will achieve excellent vision. Others will achieve varying degrees of reading or navigational vision. A small percentage will not achieve reattachment of the retina, resulting in blindness. If the condition remains untreated, blindness can result.

If the retina is reattached, vision will be restored to some extent, and blindness will be prevented. However, the degree of restored vision will vary significantly, depending on several factors. The longer a detachment is left untreated, the less vision is recovered. Fibrous growths on the retina are also related to a poor visual outcome.

Specialists

- Ophthalmologist

Work Restrictions / Accommodations

Following retinal reattachment, the individual may require time to attend frequent eye examinations to evaluate recovery and watch for the reoccurrence of a retinal detachment. Bending, lifting, and strenuous activity may be restricted for several weeks, and, if required by the individual's job, reassignment may be necessary. Vision will be impaired for several weeks, so driving may need to be restricted as well. Vision should also be evaluated. Work duties may need to be temporarily changed if clear vision in both eyes is essential to the individual's work or safety. As the eye heals, eye protection may be required. Some individuals may require certain head positioning if a gas bubble was used to repair the detachment.

Comorbid Conditions

Uncontrolled glaucoma may prolong disability.

Procedure Complications

The initial procedure may fail, or the retina may spontaneously detach several weeks following an apparently successful reattachment. Prolonged inflammation, infection, or bleeding may also occur and prolong recovery.

Factors Influencing Duration

The individual response to the procedure, need for repeat treatment, or the presence of localized inflammation, infection, or bleeding could delay healing and extend the length of disability.

Length of Disability

The length of disability will vary depending on the procedure used, and the individual's job requirements. Individuals who perform heavy work or whose jobs require frequent or prolonged bending or lifting may experience a longer disability. If keen vision is necessary, disability may be prolonged. If blindness or severely impaired vision results from the retinal detachment, disability may be permanent.

Laser coagulation.

Job Classification	Minimum	Optimum	Maximum
Sedentary work	3	4	7
Light work	3	4	7
Medium work	3	4	14
Heavy work	3	14	28
Very Heavy work	3	14	28

Surgical repair.

Job Classification	Minimum	Optimum	Maximum
Sedentary work	3	7	14
Light work	3	7	14
Medium work	3	14	28
Heavy work	3	14	28
Very Heavy work	3	14	28

References

Allinson, Richard. "Retinal Detachment." Griffith's 5-minute Clinical Consult. Dambro, Mark, ed. Philadelphia: Lippincott, Williams & Wilkins, 2000. 936-937.

Vitreo Retinal Eye Surgery. Healthy Eye. 5 Sep 2000 <http://www.healthyeye.co.za/Retinal_Detachment/retinal_detachment.html>.

Retinal Vascular Occlusion

Other names / synonyms: Retinal Artery Occlusion, Retinal Vein Occlusion
362.3, 362.32, 362.35

Definition

Retinal vascular occlusion is a blockage of the blood supply through a retinal artery or vein that leads to the light sensitive membrane in the back of the eye where images are processed (retina). This blockage, which generally occurs in one eye, may lead to various symptoms, including sudden onset of blurred or distorted vision. The blockage may be due to a blood clot (thrombosis), fragments of atherosclerotic plaque, or foreign material brought to the site by blood currents such as a fat globule, or an air or gas bubble (embolism).

The occlusion, which primarily occurs in individuals 50 or older, is often caused by conditions such as inflammation of the arteries (cranial arteritis, temporal arteritis), increased stickiness or cohesion of blood molecules (viscosity), or increased red blood cell (hematocrit) count. A recent study found that half of all retinal vein occlusions that occur in arterial branches are associated with high blood pressure (hypertension). In addition, both central and branch retinal vein occlusions are linked to cardiovascular disease, diabetes mellitus, and glaucoma. Other conditions which are related to and may cause retinal vascular occlusion include atherosclerosis, systemic lupus erythematosus, diabetic retinopathy, chronic uveitis, coagulation disorders, hyperlipidemia, surgical removal of intraocular lenses previously implanted during cataract procedures, cocaine use, and complications of the surgical removal of tissue from the eye's interior (vitrectomy).

Diagnosis

History: Symptoms may vary, with either subtle or obvious changes or distortions in vision. The individual may report a painless, sudden, blurring or loss of vision in the upper or lower half of the visual field. Complete blindness may develop in the affected eye. Other symptoms can include a vague haziness or loss of perception. Regression may be gradual, lasting days or weeks. The individual may also report underlying hypertension or cardiovascular disease.

Physical exam: A microscopic examination of the eye under illumination (slit lamp or biomicroscope) will be performed. The front third of the eyeball (anterior segment) usually appears normal. The extent of damage in the back interior portion (posterior segment) depends on whether the entire central retinal artery or one of its branches is blocked; the degree of loss is, related, in part, to the location of the occlusion. The pupil of the affected eye may be partially dilated and respond to light very sluggishly. Pupillary response may quicken when light is shone into the unaffected eye.

With retinal artery occlusion, findings often include a pale retina with a cherry-red spot over the center of the retina (macula). The retina may be opaque and the optic disc may appear very pale. Retinal vein occlusion may demonstrate distended and convoluted veins, along with congestion and swelling in the eye's interior region including the retina. Retinal hemorrhages may also be evident.

Tests: A visual acuity test may be performed to ascertain the degree of visual loss. A dye may be injected and examined under illumination to determine effects on blood circulation (fluorescein angiography). Measurements of the retina's reaction to light stimulation (electroretinogram) may help determine the extent of damage. Other tests that may be done include color perception determination, muscle integrity evaluation, intraocular pressure testing (tonometry), analysis of the eye's internal structures through use of high frequency sound waves (ultrasonography), and a record of the action currents that visual or light stimuli produces in the retina (electroretinogram).

Treatment

With central retinal arterial occlusion, treatment must be immediate to remove the blockage even though results are often unsatisfactory. The eye may be massaged to encourage movements of the blockage; this may help reduce damage to the retina. A needle may be used to drain (aspirate) eye fluid. Aspirin may be given to thin the blood thus encouraging circulation; anticoagulants may be given to prevent further clot formation or the spread of clots, which could cause a stroke. An attempt to lower intraocular pressure can be made by trying to clear the artery; this can be done by pressing on the eye at intervals with the heel of the hand. Other treatments to lower eye pressure, such as with medications, may be done later. The individual may need to breathe into a paper bag, thus increasing the carbon dioxide concentration and possibly dilating the retinal blood vessels. This may allow the occlusion to move further down the vessel, thereby reducing the area of the retina that is affected. If a hemorrhage in the eye is reabsorbed, vision may improve.

Treating this condition must also include managing any underlying causes. Hypertension can be treated with medication. Because a central retinal vein occlusion often is caused by glaucoma and high intraocular pressure, specific medication for this is essential, although vision loss often cannot be restored in these cases. Minimal success has been reported using an artificially constructed passageway (shunt) between the retina and nearby layer of the eye containing blood vessels and nutrients (choroid) to restore vision. Laser treatment to create new fluid passages (photocoagulation) may be done, but is more successful when the treatment is done on occlusions in vein branches.

If the individual experiences permanent vision loss, referral to an appropriate agency dealing with blindness may be appropriate.

Prognosis

The prognosis for retinal vascular occlusion varies depending on the location and severity of the blockage, and the underlying condition causing the problem. It can range from complete recovery without treatment, to permanent partial loss of vision, to blindness. If intervention is delayed, retinal artery occlusion nearly always causes a decrease in part or all of the visual field. Usually only about 10% of individuals who have retinal vascular occlusion benefit from treatment, even when it is administered promptly. If treatment has not been initiated within 24 hours from onset, no treatment will be considered effective.

The individual also is at risk for developing glaucoma in the affected eye due to the overgrowth of new blood vessels in the retina or iris. If elevated blood pressure (hypertension) or elevated eye pressure (glaucoma) is not controlled, the individual continues to be at risk for complications of retinal vein occlusions or related disorders.

Differential Diagnosis

Glaucoma, hypertension, diabetes mellitus, coagulation disorders, atherosclerosis, hyperlipidemia, sustained pressure on the eye, and carotid occlusive disease are possible diagnoses.

Specialists

- Ophthalmologist

Work Restrictions / Accommodations

This condition can have many varying degrees of visual changes, so the individual will need to be carefully evaluated in relation to work assignments. If job duties require keen visual acuity, the individual may need to be reassigned to other tasks.

If permanent loss of vision occurs, accommodations such as large and high contrast print, and appropriate illumination may be needed. The individual may need to be referred to agencies dealing in visual disability, where special training and other visual aids can be given.

Comorbid Conditions

Individuals with abnormal blood coagulation or perfusion are more likely to develop complications. Cardiovascular disease may impact recovery and disability requirements.

Complications

Retinal tissue damage from the obstruction of circulation, with resultant permanent loss of vision, can occur after only 20 minutes of oxygen deprivation. Retinal bleeding (hemorrhage) is also possible.

Factors Influencing Duration

The degree, type, and location of visual loss, the development of complications, treatment of underlying conditions, and the individual's response to loss of vision will affect the extent and length of disability.

Length of Disability

If permanent loss of vision has occurred, the individual will generally be unable to perform tasks requiring keen visual acuity.

Failure to Recover

If an individual fails to recover within the maximum duration expectancy period, the reader may wish to reference the following questions to assist in better understanding the specifics of an individual's medical case.

Regarding diagnosis:

- Does the individual complain of a sudden onset of blurred or distorted vision in the upper or lower half of the visual field?
- Does the individual have cranial arteritis, temporal arteritis, increased stickiness or cohesion of blood molecules (viscosity), or increased hematocrit count?
- Does the individual have hypertension?
- Does the individual have cardiovascular disease, diabetes mellitus, glaucoma, systemic lupus erythematosus, chronic uveitis, coagulation disorders, hyperlipidemia, surgical removal of intraocular lenses previously implanted during cataract procedures, cocaine use, or complications of vitrectomy?

- Did the individual have a slit lamp examination? Is the pupil partially dilated? Does it respond to light sluggishly?
- Is the individual's retina pale with a cherry-red spot over the macula? Are there distended and convoluted veins, along with congestion and swelling in the eye's interior region including the retina? Are retinal hemorrhages evident?
- Did the individual have a visual acuity and color perception test? Was fluorescein angiography done? Electroretinogram? Tonometry? Ultrasound?
- Have conditions with similar symptoms been ruled out

Regarding treatment:
- Was the individual's eye massaged to encourage movement of the blockage? Was aspiration done? Was aspirin given?
- Is the individual on anticoagulant therapy?
- Was intraocular pressure decreased?
- Was hyperventilation tried?
- Are any underlying conditions being treated?

Regarding prognosis:
- Is the individual's employer able to accommodate any necessary restrictions?
- Does the individual have any conditions that may affect ability to recover?
- If necessary has the individual been referred to an agency that deals with low vision or blindness?
- Does the individual have any complications such as permanent loss of vision can or retinal bleeding?

References

Cameron, J. Douglas, and Edwin H. Ryan, Jr., MD. "Retinal Vascular Occlusive Disease." The Medical Journal of Allina 6 1 (1997): 6. 19 Oct 2000 <http://www.mercy-unity.com/Allina_Journal/Winter1997/cameron.html>.

Guttman, Cheryl. "Make CRVO, BRVO a Healthy Wake-up Call for Patients." Ophthalmology Times 01 May 1998 2. Electric Library. 19 Oct 2000 <http://www.elibrary.com>.

Retinitis Pigmentosa
Other names / synonyms: Acquired Retinal Pigmentation, RP
362.1, 362.42, 362.65, 362.74

Definition

Retinitis pigmentosa is a general name given to a group of often hereditary diseases that cause degeneration of light-sensitive nerve cells lining the back inner portion of the eye (retina), where images are processed and sent to the brain. As the disease progresses, cells that convert light to electrical impulses (rods) typically are affected first to create loss of night or low light vision. Rods also help provide a wider (peripheral) field of vision. As these cells deteriorate, peripheral vision may deteriorate until the individual is left with only straight-ahead or "tunnel vision."

Other cells concentrated in the center of the retina (macula) that help provide detailed color vision (cones) may also slowly lose function, resulting in central blurred vision lacking color perception. In one form of retinitis pigmentosa, the cones are the first to deteriorate to cause loss of central vision and color perception. A form of retinitis pigmentosa known as Usher's syndrome also causes nerve damage creating deafness.

Retinitis pigmentosa is linked to other inherited syndromes including Bardet-Biedl (includes physical abnormalities), Bassen-Kornzweig (includes progressive neurological degeneration), choroideremia (causes degeneration of a blood vessel layer of the eye (choroid)), Refsum (includes widespread neurological conditions), gyrate atrophy associated with an amino acid disorder, and Leber congenital amaurosis (causes low retinal function at birth).

While new research may hold promise for therapies for retinitis pigmentosa, the condition generally is considered untreatable. Vision will continue to deteriorate, many times leading to blindness. The usual rate of vision loss is from 5-20% in individuals with retinitis pigmentosa until blindness occurs. About 1 of every 3,000 individuals has the disease. Approximately 1 in 80 individuals is estimated to be a carrier of genetic material that could be passed along and at times manifested in future generations. In about half of cases of retinitis pigmentosa, a genetic connection cannot be pinpointed.

Diagnosis

History: In most cases, individuals first will report progressive loss of night vision (nyctalopia). The field of vision may decrease gradually until only central sight is preserved. Central sight and color perception may then begin to deteriorate. In a few cases, the individual may first lose central sight and color perception. The individual may report a family history of retinitis pigmentosa. The slow process of vision deterioration may take place over a period of years.

Physical exam: An examination with an illuminated instrument that magnifies the eye's interior (ophthalmoscopy) may reveal mottling of the retina and a characteristic "bone-spicule" formation. The retinal arteries will appear narrowed and the optic disc may have a waxy, yellow appearance. Nearsightedness (myopia) is usually present.

Tests: The individual may be given tests to determine visual acuity (visual acuity test), visual field (visual field test), and adaptation to darkness (dark adaptometry). Electrical activity within the retina along with reaction to changes in light will be measured (electroretinogram, electro-oculogram).

Treatment

No known treatment has been conclusively proven to slow the course of retinitis pigmentosa, although research is being done in the area of vitamin supplementation and transplants of healthy fetal human retina or other potentially beneficial tissue. Vitamin A and lutein supplementation may slow progression of the disease.

Some researchers have reported positive results with the use of decompression chambers associated with deep sea divers (Hyperbaric Oxygen Therapy) that deliver pure oxygen at high pressure to cells within the retina. While the therapy may help preserve or stimulate existing, undamaged areas within the retina, there is no evidence of improvement of visual acuity that already has been lost.

Dark sunglasses, low vision aids, and image intensifiers may be used. Night vision devices may be helpful. Lenses with yellow filters are thought to help increase the individual's ability to see contrast. Surgery to correct associated complications such as cataract formation (cataract extraction, intraocular lens implantation) may be performed. Referrals for genetic counseling and to agencies that provide services to the visually impaired may be beneficial.

Complementary and Alternative Therapies

Content is intended for awareness only. Treatments may or may not be effective. Scientific evidence may be lacking and some substances have potentially toxic effects. Dr. Presley Reed and the editors do not endorse the use of these therapies in the absence of consultation with a licensed medical professional.

Hyperbaric oxygen therapy - Delivery of pure oxygen at high pressure may help preserve or stimulate existing undamaged areas within the retina. There is, however, no evidence of improvement in visual acuity that already has been lost.

Nutritional Therapy - Lutein and vitamin A may help stop progression of the disease.

Prognosis

While legal blindness almost always results, many individuals retain at least some residual vision. Individuals who have inherited other conditions along with retinitis pigmentosa may experience a variety of other potentially disabling complications, including neurological disorders. Cataracts that commonly occur with retinitis pigmentosa generally can be removed successfully, followed by implantation of an artificial lens. While the surgery can restore eyesight lost because of cataracts, it does not have a direct bearing on vision loss related to retinitis pigmentosa.

Differential Diagnosis

The condition may also be age-related macular degeneration, myopia, syphilis, rubella, chloroquine toxicity, chorioretinitis, eye injury, vascular occlusion, or retinal detachment. Similar symptoms also may be produced by the presence of cytomegalovirus, toxoplasmosis, and tumors.

Specialists

- Ophthalmologist

Work Restrictions / Accommodations

The extent and type of vision loss will need to be evaluated in relationship to the individual's work requirements. In some cases, the individual may be unable to drive or work at night. If the individual works outdoors, dark sunglasses may need to be worn. Other individuals may require yellow-filtered lenses to increase vision contrast. Enhancements such as magnification or large print and contrast accommodation may be required, along with appropriate illumination at workstations. Closed-circuit television readers may be needed.

Comorbid Conditions

Individuals with both cataracts and retinitis pigmentosa may experience even more loss of contrast vision.

Complications

Individuals who have both cataracts and retinitis pigmentosa tend to lose more ability to see contrast. Glaucoma may result from the condition. Swelling of the retina (cystoid macular edema) may cause complications. Retinal detachment may occur following efforts to transplant healthy tissue.

Factors Influencing Duration

How fast the disease progresses along with the extent of vision limitations will determine how long the individual will be able to perform work tasks, particularly those requiring keen visual acuity. Referrals to agencies for the visually impaired may impact the degree of disability. While the eye may be physically stable after the initial occurrence, the disease typically creates continuing vision loss.

Length of Disability

In the absence of proven effective therapies for retinitis pigmentosa, the individual likely will experience progressive loss of vision function and may eventually need reassignment to other duties if work tasks require keen visual acuity.

Failure to Recover

If an individual fails to recover within the maximum duration expectancy period, the reader may wish to reference the following questions to assist in better understanding the specifics of an individual's medical case.

Regarding diagnosis:

- Does individual complain of progressive loss of night vision? Does individual have tunnel vision? Blurred central vision?
- Does individual have any inherited syndromes including Bardet-Biedl, Bassen-Kornzweig, choroideremia, Refsum, gyrate atrophy associated with an amino acid disorder, and Leber congenital amaurosis?

1830 *The Medical Disability Advisor—Fourth Edition*

- Is there a family history of retinitis pigmentosa?
- On examination, was the retina mottled? Did it have bone-spicule formation?
- Are the retinal arteries narrowed?
- Does the optic disc have a waxy, yellow appearance? Is myopia present?
- Has individual had visual acuity and visual field tests?
- Was dark adaptometry testing done? Electroretinogram and electro-oculogram?
- Have conditions with similar symptoms been ruled out?

Regarding treatment:

- Is individual being treated with vitamin and lutein supplements?

- Was hyperbaric oxygen therapy tried?
- Does individual use dark sunglasses, low vision aids, and image intensifiers? Night vision devices? Lenses with yellow filters?
- Was surgery necessary to correct associated complications?
- Has individual been referred to agencies that provide services to the visually impaired?

Regarding prognosis:

- Can individual's employer accommodate any necessary restrictions?
- Does individual have any conditions that may affect ability to recover?
- Have any complications occurred such as glaucoma, cystoid macular edema, or retinal detachment?

References

Retinal Degenerative Diseases. Retina International. 2000. 19 Oct 2000 <http://www.retina-international.org>.

Rh Incompatibility

Other names / synonyms: Hemolytic Disease of the Newborn, Hydrops Fetalis, Kernicterus, Rhesus Isoimmunization, Rh-Induced Hemolytic Disease of the Newborn

652.2, 656, 656.1

Definition

Rh incompatibility is a difference in the blood type of a pregnant woman and that of her developing baby, causing anti-Rh antibodies to develop, and resulting in a serious, sometimes life-threatening reaction in the fetus or infant. The term Rh refers to the type of a group of molecules on the surface of the red blood cells that are unique to that person. Within this blood group, Rh0(D) is the one that usually causes incompatibility problems. If red blood cells have Rh0(D) molecules, the blood is Rh-positive; if they do not, the blood is Rh-negative.

Problems develop when the mother has Rh-negative blood and the fetus has Rh-positive blood (inherited from a father who has Rh-positive blood). Should red blood cells from the fetal circulation leak into the maternal circulation, particularly late in pregnancy or during delivery, her system will not tolerate the presence of these Rh-positive cells. This causes her immune system to treat the Rh-positive fetal cells as if they were a foreign protein or substance, and make antibodies against them. These anti-Rh-positive antibodies move through the placenta into the fetus destroying the red blood cells of the fetus and causing them to rupture (hemolyze).

The ruptured red blood cells create an increase in the waste product bilirubin (hyperbilirubinemia), which can be toxic to the infant's brain. A more serious concern is a life-threatening condition in which the red blood cell destruction results in severe anemia, heart failure, and generalized edema. This can occur in the fetus before birth (erythroblastosis fetalis), or in the infant immediately following birth (erythroblastosis neonatorum).

During a first pregnancy, the fetus or newborn rarely has problems because no significant contact occurs between the fetus' and mother's blood until delivery. However, with each subsequent pregnancy, the mother becomes more sensitized to Rh-positive blood, produces antibodies earlier, and creates greater risk for the fetus or infant.

Approximately, 15% of the white population and smaller fractions of other races are Rh-negative. Screening for these blood type incompatibilities is part of standard prenatal care. Preventative immunization of those at risk has been so effective that only 1 out of 27 Rh-positive babies born by Rh-negative women develops side effects related to incompatibility. Aside from pregnancy, rare cases of Rh incompatibility have been reported in individuals who have received a transfusion of incompatible blood.

Diagnosis

History: Rh incompatibility may cause symptoms that range from very mild to death of the newborn. A pregnant woman may give a history of a previous pregnancy, miscarriage, and/or abortion.

Physical exam: There are no signs or symptoms in the mother who has Rh-negative blood. Therefore, the physical exam is usually normal for pregnancy.

Tests: A woman's blood group is identified at her first prenatal visit. Individuals with Rh-negative blood are tested for the presence of Rh antibodies at this and subsequent visits. Additional tests may include indirect Coombs test and antibody titer. The fetal blood type and blood count may be tested by taking a sample from the umbilical cord (fetal cord blood). An amniocentesis may be performed to obtain fluid for assessing the degree of fetal hemolysis and determining fetal bilirubin level.

After birth, a Kleihauer test, hematocrit, mean corpuscular volume, ABO blood typing, Rh group, serum bilirubin level, and direct Coombs test may be done on the baby.

Treatment

Treatment is initially aimed at preventing any reaction to blood type incompatibility. An Rh-negative woman in her first pregnancy (desensitized) is given an injection of Rh(D) immune globulin (RhoGAM) at 28 weeks. This injection inactivates any of the baby's blood cells that enter the mother before she becomes sensitized to them. At birth, if the infant is Rh-positive, the mother is given RhoGAM again.

RhoGAM is also given to women after a miscarriage, abortion, amniocentesis, or any other procedure that might result in exposure of the mother to fetal blood cells. It is also given if antepartum (before the delivery) hemorrhage occurs.

If the pregnant female is sensitized from a previous pregnancy, ultrasound and periodic analysis of amniotic fluid is done to monitor the status of the fetus. If necessary, the fetus is given an intrauterine transfusion to correct blood abnormalities. If the fetus is severely affected, labor may be induced and the baby promptly delivered.

In the rare case where incompatible blood is transfused (Rh-negative blood given to Rh-positive recipient, or vice versa), the transfusion is promptly stopped. The individual is monitored for worsening signs and symptoms (fever, chills, backache, etc.). Generally, symptoms subside once the transfusion is stopped.

Prognosis

Preventatively treating Rh-negative mothers with RhoGAM effectively prevents Rh incompatibility in most cases. The risk of fetal-neonatal Rh incompatibility is approximately 6 per 10,000 births; the risk of fetal-neonatal death is less than 2%.

For those who do not receive prophylactic treatment, the risk of fetal-neonatal Rh incompatibility rises to 6 per 1000 births, and the risk of fetal-neonatal death to 25%.

Differential Diagnosis

A reaction to another blood type incompatibility is possible and may present in a similar manner.

Specialists

- Gynecologist
- Neonatologist
- Obstetrician
- Perinatologist

Work Restrictions / Accommodations

Generally, there are no work restrictions or accommodations for the mother upon return to work. However, in those who received an intrauterine transfusion, strenuous activity and heavy lifting may be temporarily restricted.

Comorbid Conditions

Comorbid conditions of eclampsia, diabetes, bleeding disorders, or heart disease may impact the ability of the mother to recover following delivery where there has been a case of Rh incompatibility.

In cases of transfusion-related Rh incompatibility, comorbid conditions of kidney dysfunction or heart disease may impact ability to recover and may further lengthen disability.

Complications

Complications include rupture of red blood cells (hemolysis) in the fetus or newborn, elevated blood bilirubin (hyperbilirubinemia), erythroblastosis fetalis, or erythroblastosis neonatorum.

Reactions following transfusion with incompatible blood may be complicated by acute kidney failure.

Factors Influencing Duration

This condition primarily affects the fetus and newborn. Disability is as for a normal pregnancy at 32 to 34 weeks. However, should the fetus die while in the uterus, the duration of disability may be influenced.

In rare cases of transfusion-related incompatibility, the possible complication of kidney dysfunction may influence length of disability.

Length of Disability

Durations do not reflect pregnancy and delivery.

Medical treatment with intrauterine transfusion.

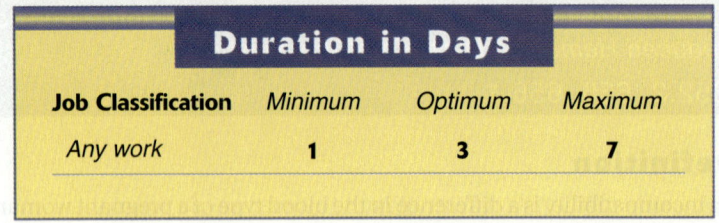

Job Classification	Minimum	Optimum	Maximum
Any work	1	3	7

Failure to Recover

If an individual fails to recover within the maximum duration expectancy period, the reader may wish to reference the following questions to assist in better understanding the specifics of an individual's medical case.

Regarding diagnosis:

- Does the mother have Rh-negative blood? Is the fetus Rh-positive?
- Has individual received a transfusion with incompatible blood?
- Does individual have a history of previous pregnancy? Miscarriage? Abortion?
- Has the mother been screened for Rh incompatibility?
- Was it necessary to obtain a fetal blood sample?
- Was an amniocentesis done?
- After birth, was a Kleihauer test, hematocrit, mean corpuscular volume, ABO blood typing, Rh group, serum bilirubin level, and direct Coombs test done?
- Have conditions with similar symptoms been ruled out?

Regarding treatment:

- Is this individual's first pregnancy?
- Has individual been given RhoGAM at 28 weeks of pregnancy? Did she receive it again at birth if the infant is Rh-positive?
- Was RhoGAM also given to the woman after a miscarriage, abortion, or amniocentesis?
- Was it also given if antepartum hemorrhage occurred?
- Is the pregnant female sensitized from a previous pregnancy?
- Have ultrasound and periodic analysis of amniotic fluid been done?
- Was it necessary to give the fetus an intrauterine transfusion?
- Did it become necessary to induce labor?
- If the reaction was due to a transfusion, was it immediately stopped?

Regarding prognosis:

- Is individual's employer able to accommodate any necessary restrictions?
- Does individual have any conditions that could affect their ability to recover?
- Was individual monitored for signs of kidney dysfunction?

References

Tierney, Lawrence M., Stephen J. McPhee, and Maxine A. Papadakis, eds. Current Medical Diagnosis and Treatment, 39th ed. New York: Lange Medical Books/McGraw-Hill, 2000.

Rheumatic Fever, Acute
Other names / synonyms: Rheumatic Heart Disease, Rheumatic Heart Fever
390, 391

Definition

Rheumatic fever is a disease causing inflammation in various tissues throughout the body. It generally occurs in young adults following a throat infection with group A Streptococcus bacteria. The bacteria in the affected tissues do not cause it; instead the bacteria appear to trigger an autoimmune reaction where the body's immune system mistakenly attacks its own tissues. Individuals with rheumatic fever will experience non-crippling joint inflammation. The central nervous system may also be affected.

Rheumatic fever is rare in most developed countries although it was reported to be on the rise again in the US. A small minority of individuals appears to have a genetic predisposition for the development of acute rheumatic fever.

Diagnosis

History: Individuals will have a history of streptococcal throat infection. A week or two after the infection, individuals may report initial symptoms of rheumatic fever which include fever, joint pain, loss of appetite, weakness, shortness of breath, and inflammation and swelling that affect the large joints such as the knees, elbows, ankles, and wrists. Symptoms may develop in one joint while the inflammation in another joint recedes, or several joints may be affected simultaneously. Individuals may report a transient pink rash with slightly raised edges on the stomach, chest, and back (erythema marginatum). The rash is usually crescent-shaped with a clear center (chicken-wire rash). Pea-sized nodules located under the skin may develop over tendons, joints, and bony prominences. Damage to the heart does not always occur, however when it does, the damage is insidious and symptoms may not develop until years later.

Physical exam: The exam may reveal red, swollen joints and pea-sized nodules beneath the skin (often over bony prominences). Symptoms of heart muscle inflammation (carditis) include a rapid heartbeat (tachycardia) that persists during sleep and increases markedly with slight activity. Irregular heartbeat (arrhythmias), changing quality of heart sounds, and heart murmurs may also be evident.

Damage to the heart may not be apparent until years later. The most common and serious symptom related to rheumatic fever is thickening and scarring of the heart valves causing them to narrow (stenosis) or become leaky (insufficiency). These changes are permanent and usually become progressively worse so that heart valve surgery may be necessary.

Tests: There are no specific tests for rheumatic fever. Diagnosis relies on the Duckett Jones criteria, i.e., the presence of two or more major clinical manifestations or one major manifestation plus two or more minor features.

Throat swabs may be cultured for group A streptococcus. Blood tests may reveal serological changes indicating a recent streptococcal infection (antistreptolysin O and antistreptokinase titers). The elevation of one particular blood test (erythrocyte sedimentation rate or ESR) is a useful way of following rheumatic activity.

An enlarged heart (cardiomegaly) may be detected using ultrasound to visualize internal cardiac structures (echocardiography). Changes in the electrical activity of the heart can be recorded using an electrocardiogram (ECG).

Treatment

Individuals with fever or active joint inflammation are treated with bed rest until the clinical syndrome has subsided (no fever, normal pulse rate, normal ESR, normal white blood cell count). If carditis occurs, it usually appears within 2 to 3 weeks of disease onset therefore close observation is needed during this initial period. Residual streptococcal infections are treated with penicillin even if the culture of nasal or throat swabs no longer reveals an infection. High-dose aspirin (salicylate) therapy is used to control joint pain and inflammation. Any subsequent streptococcal infection that develops should be treated promptly.

If carditis occurs, the individual should be hospitalized and 4 weeks of bed rest is usually recommended. Corticosteroids may be given to minimize heart damage. If these are ineffective, drugs may be used that enhance urine output (diuretics) or pumping ability of the heart (digitalis).

Recurrences of rheumatic fever are most common when cardiac damage is present, but may be prevented with continued administration of penicillin until the age of 20 or for 5 years after the last attack. The potential to develop antibiotic resistance should be considered when administering penicillin chronically as a preventive agent (prophylactically). Nevertheless, recent studies show that streptococcal infections remain highly sensitive to penicillin and therefore it remains the drug of choice for treatment of rheumatic fever. If the individual is allergic to penicillin, erythromycin or clindamycin may be used.

Prognosis

Prognosis depends on how much the heart has been affected and whether recurrences can be avoided. Heart inflammation may resolve with no permanent effects or rheumatic fever can lead to other problems later in life (even in the absence of recurrences). There may be permanent scarring of one or more valves which can result in stenosis or backward flow of blood into the heart (regurgitation or insufficiency). The progression of valve degeneration is usually slow and individuals may not notice any symptoms until many years after having had rheumatic fever. Eventually, valve function can become seriously compromised and surgery may be required to repair or replace the damaged heart valve(s). In rare instances, the heart muscle itself becomes over-inflamed and death from heart failure can occur.

Differential Diagnosis

Conditions with similar symptoms include rheumatoid arthritis, pyogenic arthritis, bacterial endocarditis, systemic lupus erythematosus, atrial myxoma, sickle cell crisis, viral myocarditis, dermatomyositis, influenza, Reiter's disease, osteomyelitis, and Lyme disease.

Specialists

- Cardiologist
- Internist
- Infectious Disease Physician

Rehabilitation

Individuals with valve disease or who require valve replacement as a result of rheumatic fever require rehabilitation to address weakness and functional deficits. A rehabilitation program comprised of both physical and occupational therapy at a cardiac rehabilitation clinic can return individuals to their previous physical status and activities.

A physical therapist knowledgeable in cardiac rehabilitation will design an individualized exercise program considered safe for the individual's physical stamina. ECG monitoring is usually performed during the initial exercise sessions. Once the ECG demonstrates that the heart responds appropriately to exercise, individuals learn to self-monitor their pulse and rate the amount of energy they expend by utilizing a rating of perceived exertion scale.

Individuals perform aerobic exercise such as treadmill walking or stationary bicycling. The aerobic exercise helps the heart muscle improve its efficiency in the use of oxygen, which reduces the need for the heart to pump as much blood. This increased fitness level in turn reduces the total workload of the heart. The related increase in endurance allows for individuals to resume their prior activity level.

Occupational therapy addresses any fatigue or shortness of breath that may occur during activities of daily living. Occupational and physical therapists also stress the importance of taking responsibility for improving the health of the heart. Individuals are taught that cardiac rehabilitation does not end once therapy ends, but is an ongoing process that allows the individual to enjoy a more active lifestyle. When appropriate, individuals should participate in 30 to 60 minutes of aerobic activity independently 3 or 4 times per week to promote continued cardiovascular endurance and strength.

Work Restrictions / Accommodations

Work restrictions and accommodations require consideration on a case-by-case basis. Strenuous activity may need to be temporarily modified until physical stamina returns.

Comorbid Conditions

Comorbid conditions that may impact an individual's ability to recover and further lengthen disability following acute rheumatic fever include malnutrition, greater exposure to bacterial infections, and fewer resources for medical and dental care. Certain individuals may be genetically predisposed to the disease. Pre-existing valvular heart disease may exacerbate the long-term deleterious effects that rheumatic fever can have on heart valves.

Complications

More than 50% of those who suffer acute rheumatic fever with carditis will later (after 10 to 20 years) develop chronic rheumatic heart disease that predominantly affects the mitral and aortic valves.

A very serious and potentially lethal complication of rheumatic heart disease is subacute bacterial endocarditis. This condition is caused by infection of the damaged heart valves by streptococcus (other than group A) or enterococcus, an organism commonly found in the gastrointestinal and urinary tracts. In most cases of subacute bacterial endocarditis, the source of the infection cannot be identified. However, streptococcus bacteria are normally present in the mouth and may invade the bloodstream as a result of minor tissue damage that occurs with tooth cleaning and brushing. The bacteria can then circulate in the bloodstream to the heart where they cause disease. For this reason, many individuals with rheumatic heart disease are placed on preventative (prophylactic) antibiotics indefinitely and must take antibiotics before dental procedures or surgery.

Other complications of rheumatic heart disease include arrhythmia, inflammation of the sac enclosing the heart (pericarditis), chronic lung inflammation (rheumatic pneumonitis), and congestive heart failure.

Factors Influencing Duration

The extent of the disease, severity of the symptoms, response to treatment, and the presence of chronic rheumatic heart disease may influence length of disability.

Length of Disability

Duration of disability may depend on physical demands of the job and the degree of structural damage to the heart. If there is heart involvement, duration depends on development of permanent heart damage. If valvular damage is extensive, physically demanding work may not be possible until surgery is performed to replace the valves. Disability may be permanent.

Without heart involvement.

Job Classification	Duration in Days Minimum	Optimum	Maximum
Sedentary work	14	21	28
Light work	14	21	28
Medium work	28	42	56
Heavy work	42	63	84
Very Heavy work	42	63	84

With heart involvement.

Job Classification	Duration in Days Minimum	Optimum	Maximum
Sedentary work	56	70	84
Light work	56	70	84
Medium work	84	98	112
Heavy work	112	140	Indefinite
Very Heavy work	112	140	Indefinite

Failure to Recover

If an individual fails to recover within the maximum duration expectancy period, the reader may wish to reference the following questions to assist in better understanding the specifics of an individual's medical case.

Regarding diagnosis:

- Did individual report a recent streptococcal throat infection?
- Did individual have onset of fever, joint pain, loss of appetite, weakness, shortness of breath, and inflammation and swelling that affect the large joints such as the knees, elbows, ankles, and wrists 1 to 2 weeks after the throat infection?
- Does individual have a transient rash?
- Has individual developed pea-sized nodules located under the skin over tendons, joints, and bony prominences?
- Has individual developed heart damage? Does individual have tachycardia that persists during sleep and increases markedly with slight activity? Were arrhythmias, changing quality of heart sounds, or heart murmurs evident?
- Does individual meet the Duckett Jones criteria?
- Has individual had a throat culture, serology testing for streptococcus, ECG, and echocardiogram?
- Have conditions with similar symptoms been ruled out?

Regarding treatment:

- Was individual treated with bed rest until the clinical syndrome subsided?
- Was a residual streptococcal infection treated with penicillin, erythromycin, or clindamycin?
- Is individual on high-dose aspirin therapy?
- Does individual know that all subsequent streptococcal infections need to be treated promptly?
- Has individual developed carditis? Was individual hospitalized?
- Were corticosteroids given? Diuretics? Digitalis?

Regarding prognosis:

- Is individual active in cardiac rehabilitation? Does individual have a home exercise program?
- Can individual's employer accommodate any necessary restrictions?
- Does individual have any conditions that may affect ability to recover?
- Does individual have any complications such as subacute bacterial endocarditis, arrhythmia, pericarditis, rheumatic pneumonitis, or congestive heart failure?
- Does individual use prophylactic antibiotics prior to dental work or surgery?

References

Kellermann, Jan J. "Rehabilitation of Patients with Coronary Heart Disease." Progress in Cardiovascular Diseases 17 4 (1975): 303-328.

Taranta, Angelo, and Milton Markowitz. Rheumatic Fever. Boston: Kluwer Academic Publishers, 1989.

Rheumatic Heart Disease, Chronic

Other names / synonyms: Inactive Rheumatic Fever, Rheumatic Carditis

398, 398.9

Definition

Rheumatic heart disease (RHD) is the long-term consequence of acute rheumatic fever during childhood. Acute rheumatic fever (ARF) damages one or more valves within the heart. As the initial damage (inflammation) subsides, it is succeeded by the formation of scar tissue which leaves the valve(s) either too narrow (stenotic) or too "leaky" (insufficient). This permanent scarring of the valve(s) is referred to as rheumatic heart disease.

There are four valves, two on each side of the heart. The two on the right side are called the tricuspid and pulmonic valves and the two on the left are the mitral and aortic valves. Right-sided valves are affected less often with less serious consequences than those on the left.

How an individual feels and fares over the years depends on how the right and left pumping chambers (ventricles) handle the increased workload imposed by the stenotic and/or insufficient valve(s). Mitral insufficiency is the most common valvular abnormality.

The prevalence of both ARF and RHD has decreased in the US. It is estimated that there are now 3 cases of RHD per 1,000 individuals. However, among the tropical and subtropical countries of Asia, South America, and Africa, the prevalence remains high. The incidence remains high in lower economic ethnic groups in the US.

Diagnosis

History: A heart murmur(s) during the childhood episode of ARF may persist into adult life or may develop years later even if no murmur(s) were present during ARF. Many individuals are not aware they had ARF as a child. Shortness of breath (dyspnea) and easy fatigability are the two most frequent symptoms of RHD. Chest pain with exertion (angina) and an irregular beating of the heart's upper chambers (atrial fibrillation) may also occur.

Physical exam: One or more heart murmurs are evident upon physical examination. Prominence of the veins in the neck and "crackles" in the lungs (rales) audible with a stethoscope may also exist. Swollen feet and ankles (edema) may be present due to congestive heart failure. Fast and/or irregular heart beating due to atrial fibrillation often accompanies murmurs of mitral stenosis or mitral insufficiency.

Tests: An electrocardiogram, chest x-ray, and echocardiogram are done initially and repeated over time to follow the natural or treated history of RHD. Additional and more detailed information is frequently obtained by cardiac catheterization.

Treatment

Arrhythmias and congestive heart failure (CHF) due to RHD are treated with medications, if possible. The medication(s) may need to be continued for life. If medications fail to control arrhythmias and/or CHF, surgery may be performed. In the case of atrial fibrillation (AF), this may involve inserting a permanent pacemaker. In the case of CHF, surgery may involve repairing a damaged valve(s) without replacing it or replacing it with an artificial (prosthetic) valve. In individuals under age 35, oral penicillin to prevent recurrences of ARF (prophylactic penicillin) is recommended.

Specialists

- Cardiologist
- Cardiothoracic Surgeon

Prognosis

Outcome is related to which valve is involved, severity of the abnormality, the presence or absence of complications, and whether or not surgery was performed.

Differential Diagnosis

Other possibilities include valve damage from congenital deformity, other infections (bacterial endocarditis), and viral infection.

Work Restrictions / Accommodations

Work restrictions and/or accommodations are largely related to the presence and severity of CHF, if present. If valve surgery is necessary, certain work restrictions and accommodations such as sedentary work may also be required.

Comorbid Conditions

Any heart condition or condition that weakens the immune system and predisposes the individual to infection will lengthen disability.

Complications

The two most frequent complications of RHD are AF and CHF. Another complication known as bacterial endocarditis is due to infection of a valve by bacteria transmitted through the bloodstream from the mouth or genitor-urinary tract. Bacterial endocarditis is easily preventable with appropriate antibiotic therapy. If valve replacement is necessary, complications related to an artificial (prosthetic) valve may ensue.

Factors Influencing Duration

Factors influencing the length of disability include severity of the valvular disease and which valve is involved, presence of recurrent bouts of infection, presence of pulmonary hypertension, adequacy of the individual's immune response to streptococcal infection, virulence of the infecting streptococcal strain, and heart failure.

Length of Disability

Duration varies depending on the severity of the valvular change and on which valve is involved. Duration depends on whether permanent heart damage develops. Disability may be permanent.

Duration in Days

Job Classification	Minimum	Optimum	Maximum
Sedentary work	56	70	84
Light work	56	70	84
Medium work	84	98	112
Heavy work	112	140	Indefinite
Very Heavy work	112	140	Indefinite

Failure to Recover

If an individual fails to recover within the maximum duration expectancy period, the reader may wish to reference the following questions to assist in better understanding the specifics of an individual's medical case.

Regarding diagnosis:

- Did the individual have ARF as a child?
- Does the individual note shortness of breath or easy fatigability?
- Was a heart murmur noted in the physical exam?
- Is there chest pain or an irregular heart beat?
- Is atrial fibrillation, mitral stenosis, or mitral insufficiency present?
- Are rales present?
- Are veins in the neck prominent? Is there edema of the feet and ankles?
- Was the diagnosis confirmed with cardiac ultrasound?
- Has an ECG, chest x-ray, and/or echocardiogram been obtained?
- Is cardiac catheterization required?

Regarding treatment:

- Does the individual take medication to control arrhythmia or CHF? Is the individual compliant with the medication regimen?
- Would the individual benefit from different medication?
- Does the individual require valve repair or replacement for CHF?
- Does the individual take prophylactic penicillin?

Regarding prognosis:

- Based on the valve involved, the severity of symptoms and the general health of the individual, what was the expected outcome?
- Is the individual a candidate for valve replacement surgery?
- Has the individual any associated conditions such as atrial fibrillation or congestive heart failure that may impact recovery and prognosis?
- Has the individual developed endocarditis? If so, how is the infection responding to antibiotic therapy?
- If valve replacement was required, has the individual developed any complications after surgery, such as bleeding, arrhythmia, or heart failure?
- Are any associated conditions or complications being addressed in the treatment plan?

References

Cotran, Ramzi, Vinay Kumar, and Tucker Collins. Robbins Pathologic Basis of Disease, 6th ed. Philadelphia: W. B. Saunders, 1999.

Tierney, Lawrence, Stephen McPhee, and Maxine Papadakis. Current Medical Diagnosis and Treatment, 39th ed. New York: Lange Medical Books/McGraw-Hill, 2000.

Rheumatism
729.0

Definition

Rheumatism is a general term that includes inflammation, degeneration, or metabolic derangement of the connective tissue structures of the body especially the muscles, joints, and related structures such as the bursae, tendons, and fibrous tissue. This term is occasionally used as a "non-specific diagnosis" while tests are performed to establish a specific diagnosis.

See specific rheumatic disease for more detailed information.

Rheumatoid Arthritis

Other names / synonyms: Chronic Inflammatory Arthritis, Proliferative Arthritis, RA, Systemic Arthritis
710.2, 714.0, 714.1

Definition

Rheumatoid arthritis (RA) is a chronic, systemic inflammatory disease primarily affecting the thin membrane that surrounds joints and tendon sheaths (synovial tissue).

The synovial tissue becomes thickened (pannus) and grows to cover the joint surface, tendons, ligaments and joint capsule. This process leads to tissue injury marked by swelling, redness, heat, and pain (inflammation) and can lead to joint destruction, torn tendons, and deformity. The disease primarily involves the small joints in the hands and feet, the large joints, or both. RA is usually symmetrical such as involvement of both hands.

Since RA is a systemic disease, other organs may be affected. The eyes sometimes become dry with burning and develop a sensitivity to light (Sjögren's syndrome). The spleen can become enlarged (Felty's syndrome). RA may also involve the lung and/or heart.

RA affects about 1% of the adult population and is two to three times more common in women than men. The highest incidence occurs during the middle years of life but can strike any age group. Genetic makeup plays a role in susceptibility to RA and many genes may be implicated in this disease (polygenic).

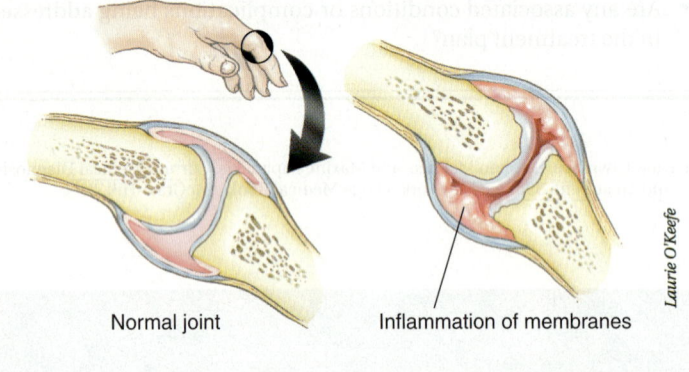

Normal joint — Inflammation of membranes

Laurie O'Keefe

Diagnosis

History: The onset of RA is usually gradual but can sometimes be abrupt. Symptoms may include stiff joints, nodules under the skin, and dry, sensitive eyes. Individuals complain of fatigue, loss of appetite, and weakness. There may be a family history of rheumatoid arthritis.

Physical exam: The exam may reveal joint swelling with warmth and decreased range of motion. Joints may be deformed if disease has progressed. Subcutaneous nodules occur in about 30% of cases. Other systemic manifestations include mild fever, anorexia, weight loss, and muscular weakness.

Tests: Lab tests include serum rheumatoid factor (positive in about 70% of RA cases), erythrocyte sedimentation rate (ESR, detects inflammation in the body and is elevated in 90% of RA cases), complete blood count (CBC), and antinuclear antibody (ANA). Synovial fluid analysis is an additional test for the diagnosis of RA. X-rays are used to evaluate joint space, erosive activity, effusion, and osteoporosis.

Treatment

There is no cure for RA and remissions as well as flare-ups (exacerbations) of the disease are common. Optimal management involves rest, drug therapy, physical therapy, and surgery to remove synovial tissue (synovectomy) or joints (arthroplasty). Regular rest is prescribed but complete bed rest may be indicated during more active painful stages of severe disease.

Drugs are used for pain management (analgesia), to control inflammation, and for immunosuppression. However, all drugs currently prescribed for RA have potential serious side effects. Salicylate and nonsteroidal anti-inflammatory drugs (NSAIDs) provide important symptomatic relief but do not alter the long-term course of the disease. Joint injections of corticosteroids may be helpful for acute flare-ups. Slow acting and potentially disease modifying drugs include gold compounds, penicillamine, hydroxychloroquine, and sulfasalazine and are often most effective when used in combination. Immunosuppressive drugs such as methotrexate are prescribed for the management of more severe, active RA.

The medical therapy of RA was influenced strongly during the past decade by the recognition that many individuals develop joint damage within the first year of the disease. This observation motivated rheumatologists to initiate disease-modifying antirheumatic drugs (DMARDs) early in the disease course. Three new drugs were recently approved for the treatment of RA. Celecoxib is a selective cyclooxygenase-2 inhibitor and has similar effectiveness as conventional NSAIDs. Treatment with leflunomide, an inhibitor of pyrimidine synthesis, produces significant clinical improvement in 50-60% of individuals with RA and delays radiologic progression of disease. Etanercept (Enbrel) inhibits tumor necrosis factor (TNF) and provides rapid and sustained improvement.

Splinting inflamed joints may decrease synovitis, prevent deformity, and improve limb function. As the disease progresses, arthroscopic surgery may be necessary to relieve pain by attempting to restore joint function or remove the synovial tissue to slow the disease. Removal of the joints (arthroplasty) with prosthetic replacement may be indicated if joint damage severely limits function.

Prognosis

RA is a progressive disease. Affected joints can eventually become grossly deformed and lose function, tendons can rupture, and bone destroyed. There is no cure for RA. Remission and exacerbations of the disease are common. The goal is to manage the symptoms and slow the destructive process. Up to 75% of individuals with RA improve symptomatically with treatment.

Differential Diagnosis

Conditions with similar symptoms to RA include Sjögren's syndrome, sarcoidosis, polymyositis, osteoarthritis, seronegative spondyloarthropathy, vasculitis, gout, pseudogout, inflammatory bowel disease, hypersensitivity reactions, Reiter's syndrome, Behçet's syndrome, psoriatic arthritis, systemic lupus erythematosus, lyme disease, scleroderma, chronic infection, ankylosing spondylitis, Whipple's disease, mixed connective tissue disease, infective arthritis, polymyalgia rheumatica, thyroid disease, and amyloidosis.

Specialists

- Physiatrist
- Rheumatologist

Rehabilitation

Initial goals in the rehabilitation of rheumatoid arthritis are to protect the involved joint with rest. This may involve immobilizing the joint with the use of a splint or sling.

At this stage of the rehabilitation process, the physical therapist may use several techniques to help decrease pain and swelling before beginning any exercise program.

Superficial heat can be applied using hot packs or, for uneven body surfaces such as the fingers or hand, melted paraffin wax and mineral oil can be used. For example, if the hand and fingers are affected, the entire hand is dipped into a heated container of paraffin wax 8 to 12 times. The wax coated hand and digits are then covered with a plastic bag, and a towel for insulation for 20 to 30 minutes.

Transcutaneous electrical nerve stimulation (TENS) may also be used and consists of a device resembling a small transistor radio connected via wires to 2 or 4 small pads called electrodes. These electrodes have a sticky substance on one side that is placed on the skin in the region of the pain. An electrical impulse predetermined by the therapist produces a high frequency tingling sensation that blocks pain in the region of the painful joint.

Work Restrictions / Accommodations

Restrictions and accommodations depend on the joints involved. Individuals must be able to stop activity with onset of pain, fatigue, or increased swelling. Periodic rest breaks are necessary even if symptoms are quiet. Individuals should avoid stooping, lifting, and standing for long periods with a change in position every 20 to 30 minutes. Individuals should avoid heavy lifting and high grip force. Adaptive devices should be used to avoid tight gripping or pinching. Evaluation of safety issues with assistive devices and lessened mobility are necessary. Use of medications requires review of drug policies.

Comorbid Conditions

Comorbid conditions include obesity (adds pressure on affected joints), diabetes (may interfere with medications prescribed for RA), osteoporosis (contributes to fatigue and weakness of joints), and osteoarthritis (contributes to fatigue and weakness of joints).

Complications

Due to the systemic nature of the disease, multiple organ systems may be affected such as the eyes (dryness), lungs (pleurisy and nodules), blood (anemia), blood vessels (vasculitis), and nerves and muscles (neuritis). Depression, fatigue, and weight loss are also possible complications of RA.

Factors Influencing Duration

Individual's age, rate of disease progression, joint involvement, system involvement, and reaction to treatment affect the length of disability. Individuals with RA may have difficulty with jobs that require constant physical work or where they are very sedentary.

Length of Disability

Persistent rheumatoid arthritis usually precludes moderate and heavy work. During the early stages of the disease, disability is limited to brief periods but as the disease progresses, disability becomes permanent. Persisting RA in multiple joints with functional consequences is sometimes considered a total disability.

Medical treatment.

Duration in Days

Job Classification	Minimum	Optimum	Maximum
Sedentary work	7	28	84
Light work	7	28	84
Medium work	14	56	112
Heavy work	Indefinite	Indefinite	Indefinite
Very Heavy work	Indefinite	Indefinite	Indefinite

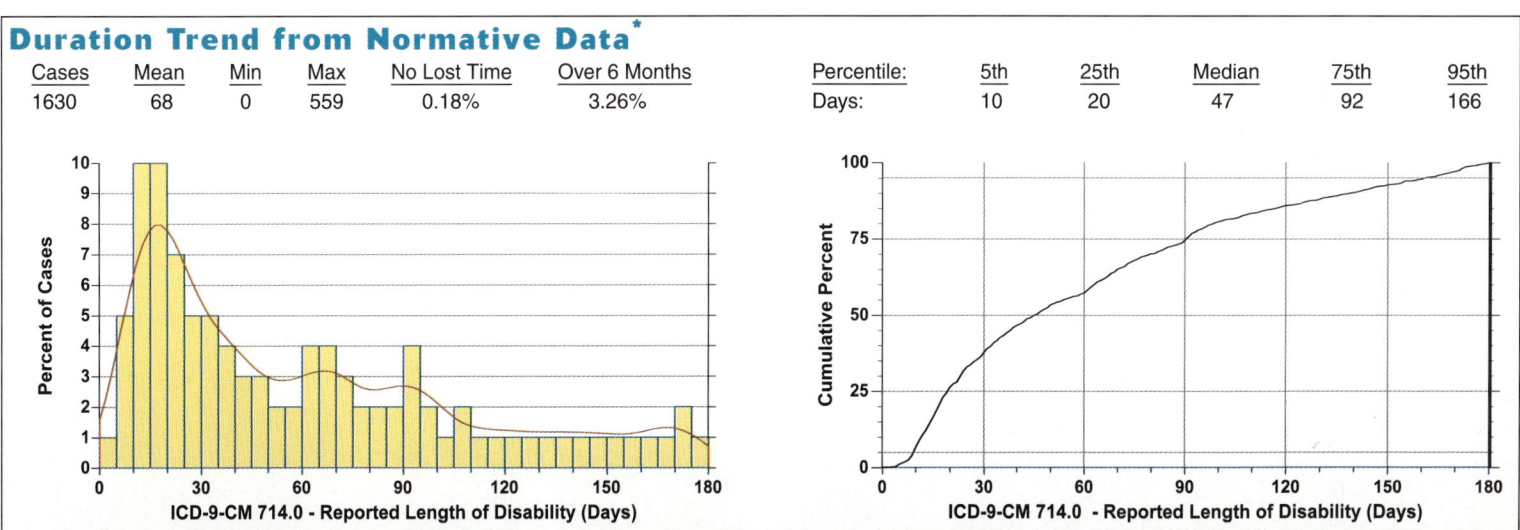

Duration Trend from Normative Data*

Cases	Mean	Min	Max	No Lost Time	Over 6 Months
1630	68	0	559	0.18%	3.26%

Percentile:	5th	25th	Median	75th	95th
Days:	10	20	47	92	166

ICD-9-CM 714.0 - Reported Length of Disability (Days)

* Differences may exist between the expected duration tables and the normative graphs. Duration tables provide expected recovery periods based on the type of work performed by the individual. The normative graphs reflect the actual observed experience of many individuals across the spectrum of physical conditions, in a variety of industries, and with varying levels of case management.

Rheumatoid Arthritis 1839

Failure to Recover

If an individual fails to recover within the maximum duration expectancy period, the reader may wish to reference the following questions to assist in better understanding the specifics of an individual's medical case.

Regarding diagnosis:

- Does individual have symptoms consistent with diagnosis of RA (stiff joints, nodules under the skin, and dry, sensitive eyes, fatigue, loss of appetite, and weakness)?
- Does the individual have a family history of RA?
- Has diagnosis of RA been confirmed through lab tests, synovial fluid analysis, and/or x-rays?
- Have conditions with similar symptoms of RA been ruled out (Sjögren's syndrome, sarcoidosis, polymyositis, osteoarthritis, seronegative spondyloarthropathy, vasculitis, gout, pseudogout, inflammatory bowel disease, hypersensitivity reactions, Reiter's syndrome, Behçet's syndrome, psoriatic arthritis, systemic lupus erythematosus, lyme disease, scleroderma, chronic infection, ankylosing spondylitis, Whipple's disease, mixed connective tissue disease, infective arthritis, polymyalgia rheumatica, thyroid disease, and amyloidosis)?

Regarding treatment:

- Is the individual enrolled in a comprehensive treatment plan that involves rest, medications to control pain and inflammation, physical therapy?
- Is the individual taking medication as prescribed?
- If the individual is experiencing side effects, are alternate drug options available?
- Have conservative measures been effective at reducing the symptoms and maintaining strength and mobility? If not, has surgery been considered?

Regarding prognosis:

- Based on the severity of the disease and the general health of the individual what was the expected outcome?
- Has individual experienced any associated conditions or complications (eye dryness, pleurisy, anemia, vasculitis, neuritis, depression, fatigue or weight loss) that could impact recovery and prognosis?
- Does individual have any underlying conditions (diabetes mellitus, osteoporosis or osteoarthritis) that may impact recovery?

References

Beers, Mark, and Robert Berkow. The Merck Manual of Diagnosis and Therapy, 17th ed. Rahway: Merck Research Laboratories, 1999 12 Jun 2000 <http://www.merck.com/pubs/mmanual/section5/chapter50/50a.htm>.

Cleland, James. "Dietary n-3 Fatty Acids and Therapy for Rheumatoid Arthritis." Seminars in Arthritis and Rheumatism 2 (1997): 85-97.

Healing Path: Arthritis Overview: Supplements Recommended for Arthritis. WholeHealthMD. 01 Jan 2000. 17 Jun 2000 <http://www.wholehealthmd.com/hc/arthritis/supplements/0,1788,,00.html>.

Rheumatic Disease and Arthritis. National Institute of Arthritis and Musculoskeletal and Skin Diseases Information Clearinghouse. 04 Jun 2000. 18 Jun 2000 <http://www.healingwell.com/arthritis/library/info2.htm>.

Rheumatoid Arthritis. Planet RX.com. 01 Jan 1999. 16 Jun 2000 <http://www.planetrx.com/condition/cond_detail/info/81_introduction.html>.

Scully, Rosemary M., and Marylou R. Barnes. Physical Therapy. Philadelphia: J.B. Lippincott Company, 1989.

St. Clair, E.W. "Therapy of Rheumatoid Arthritis: New Developments and Trends." Current Rheumatology Reports 1 2 (1999): 149-156.

Zeylstra, Hein. "The Phytotherapeutic Approach to Rheumatoid Arthritis." British Journal of Phytotherapy 2 1 (1991): 15-20.

Rhinoplasty

Other names / synonyms: Nose Surgery, Plastic Surgery on the Nose

21.8, 21.83, 21.84, 21.85, 21.86, 21.87

Definition

Rhinoplasty is plastic surgery to reshape the nose. Rhinoplasty can reduce or increase the size of the nose, change the shape of the tip or the bridge, narrow the span of the nostrils, or change the angle between the nose and upper lip. It may also correct a birth defect or injury or help relieve some breathing problems.

Rhinoplasty corrects external structural problems in the nose that arise from injury, illness, or heredity. The procedure can involve re-breaking nasal bones, trimming the cartilage, and sometimes borrowing cartilage from other parts of the individual's body.

Rhinoplasty is one of the most common of all plastic surgery procedures. National Clearinghouse of Plastic Surgery Statistics reports that in 1999, there were 46,596 nose reshaping (rhinoplasty) procedures performed. There were 11,831 males and 34,761 females included in that number.

Reason for Procedure

The nose is the most often-fractured bone in the body. Rhinoplasty is performed on adults and is medically necessary to correct breathing problems, open blocked nasal passages and correct other complications caused by a fracture or, occasionally, illness. Rhinoplasty is also frequently performed as an elective surgery by individuals who wish to change the appearance of their nose.

Description

Depending on the complexity of the procedure, rhinoplasty is done either as an outpatient procedure under local anesthesia, or an in-hospital procedure under general anesthesia.

The nostril is held open with a speculum, an instrument for exposing the inner surfaces of the nose. An incision is made in the nose. The bone or cartilage is fractured, trimmed, and molded into the desired shape. The mucous membrane is closed with fine sutures, which usually can be removed about 10 days after surgery. Bandages are applied. For some procedures, petroleum-jelly-coated packing gauze or plastic splints are used to hold the septum in place during healing (up to a week).

Prognosis

The individual may expect complete healing without complications. They should allow about 3 weeks for recovery from surgery.

Specialists

- Otolaryngologist
- Plastic Surgeon

Work Restrictions / Accommodations

To help recovery and aid well being, individuals should be encouraged to resume daily activities, including work, as soon as they are able. For 1-2 weeks after the individual's return to work, heavy lifting, bending, and strenuous activity must be avoided. Individuals with outdoor occupations will need to be careful to avoid sunburn for at least 8 weeks following surgery. All individuals will need occasional time off in the months after surgery for follow-up visits with their surgeons.

Individuals who wear glasses must tape their glasses to their foreheads or rest them on their cheeks for at least 6 weeks after surgery while the nose continues to heal, a factor that could prove to be a serious hindrance to the individual with a relatively active job.

Socio-psychological counseling and support group therapy may be needed where the surgery has not resulted in meeting the individual's expectations. Vigorous exercise should be avoided for 3 weeks after surgery. Driving can be resumed 1 week after returning home.

Comorbid Conditions

Obesity, smoking, poor nutrition, excess alcohol consumption, and recent or chronic illnesses could worsen the effects of surgery. Use of drugs such as antihypertensives, muscle relaxants, tranquilizers, sleeping pills, insulin, sedatives, beta-adrenergic blockers, or cortisone may make surgery riskier. Use of mind-altering drugs, including narcotics, psychedelics, hallucinogens, marijuana, sedatives, hypnotics, or cocaine may make the procedure and surgery more difficult, lengthen recovery time, and interfere with the individual's ability to understand instructions.

Procedure Complications

There may be excessive bleeding and surgical-wound infection, which is rare. There may also be discomfort and pain caused by the gauze packing. Recurrence of airway obstruction could also occur.

Factors Influencing Duration

Length of disability may be influenced by complications, particularly if a second surgical procedure is done to correct additional deformities found during the rhinoplasty.

Length of Disability

Duration depends on local versus general anesthesia.

Duration in Days

Job Classification	Minimum	Optimum	Maximum
Sedentary work	3	7	14
Light work	3	7	14
Medium work	7	14	21
Heavy work	7	14	21
Very Heavy work	7	14	21

References

Cheney, Mack, MD. Facial Surgery, Plastic and Reconstructive. Baltimore: Williams & Wilkins, 1997.

Plastic Surgery Information Service. American Society of Plastic Surgeons. 01 Nov 2000. 1 Jan 2001 <http://www.plasticsurgery.org/>.

Rhinoscleroma
040.1

Definition

Rhinoscleroma is a chronic, progressive infection of the upper airways (nose, nasal cavities, and nasopharynx) caused by infection from the bacteria Klebsiella rhinoscleromatis. Hard growths (granulomas) result from chronic inflammation of the nasal mucous membranes. The end stage is marked deformity of the nasal passages from extensive fibrosis (tumors composed of fully developed connective tissue) with scarring or tissue erosion. This is an airborne disease and is minimally contagious, yet it is spread by person-to-person transmission. Rhinoscleroma is an opportunistic infection; so one risk factor is immunodeficiency.

Most cases occur in developing countries, especially Central and South America, Egypt, and Eastern Europe because of crowded, unsanitary living conditions. Recent immigration patterns have led to an increasing number of cases in the US. Two-thirds of cases are hospital-acquired (nosocomial); it occurs most often in young to middle-aged adults.

Diagnosis

History: The individual will usually report a history of nasal airway obstruction or persistent nasal discharge. Because symptoms are similar to the common cold, diagnosis may initially be delayed. The individual may also report the onset of, or worsening of snoring. A painless mass may be present in the nose. This mass may initially be the size of a small pea, but can enlarge and eventually obstruct the entire nasal passage. History should include information on individual's birthplace and residence, as the condition is most often seen in immigrants from developing countries where the disease is common (endemic).

Physical exam: Physical findings will depend on the stage of the disease. On examination of the nasal passages, the physician may notice crusting or an unusual amount of blood (hyperemia) in nasal mucous membranes. Occasionally, bony destruction or narrowing and deformity of the nasal septum may be noticed on x-ray. The painless growth is hard and nodular with no tendency towards ulceration.

Tests: Microscopic examination of biopsied tissue, along with a culture to identify the infectious organism, is necessary for definitive diagnosis. A small, lighted magnification instrument used to examine the inside of a body cavity (endoscope) may be inserted into the nasal passages to detect the presence of additional growths. A CT scan or MRI can also be used to locate additional growths.

Treatment

Antibiotic drugs are used to treat the bacterial infection. An endoscope may be used to widen the passageway (dilation), and the growth can be removed by laser excision or surgery (rhinoplasty). It is important to remove the entire growth to prevent recurrence. It is also important to repair and reconstruct the nasal passages and septum after removing the granuloma to restore proper nasal breathing.

Prognosis

Although treatment with rhinoplasty is usually effective in removing the obstructive growths, individuals may still have some residual deformity or irregularity in the internal contour of the nose. This may result in continued difficulty with nasal breathing, and may possibly result in snoring.

Differential Diagnosis

Conditions with similar symptoms include leprosy (Hansen's disease), paracoccidioidomycosis, blastomycosis, sarcoidosis, histoplasmosis, basal cell carcinoma, Wegener's granulomatosis, and mucocutaneous leishmaniasis.

Specialists

- Infectious Disease Physician
- Otolaryngologist

Work Restrictions / Accommodations

Extended sick leave may be required. Strenuous physical activities may need to be modified temporarily following surgery.

Comorbid Conditions

Any underlying disease, such as diabetes mellitus or AIDS, may lengthen disability. Immunosuppressed individuals, especially those with AIDS, are at greater risk for developing rhinoscleroma.

Complications

Possible complications from rhinoscleroma include laryngeal or tracheal obstruction, constriction or narrowing (stenosis) of the airway passages, recurrence of airway obstruction, hemorrhage during or following surgery, internal scarring, or irregularities in the internal contour of the nose.

Factors Influencing Duration

Length of disability may be influenced by the extent and severity of the disease, type of treatment required, the effectiveness of treatment, or by any complications.

Length of Disability

Duration in Days

Job Classification	Minimum	Optimum	Maximum
Any work	3	7	14

Failure to Recover

If an individual fails to recover within the maximum duration expectancy period, the reader may wish to reference the following questions to assist in better understanding the specifics of an individual's medical case.

Regarding diagnosis:

- Did the individual present with symptoms of a chronic upper respiratory infection or inflammation?
- Was nasal crusting or deformity of the nasal septum noted in the physical exam?
- Has diagnosis of rhinoscleroma been confirmed with tissue biopsy and nasal culture?
- Were other conditions with similar symptoms (leprosy, paracoccidioidomycosis, blastomycosis, sarcoidosis, histoplasmosis, basal cell carcinoma, Wegener's granulomatosis, and mucocutaneous leishmaniasis) considered in the differential diagnosis?

Regarding treatment:

- Were appropriate antibiotics prescribed to treat the bacterial infection?
- If symptoms persist despite treatment, was culture and sensitivity done to determine the most effective antibiotic to use?
- Was treatment successful in restoring proper nasal breathing? If not, are other measures such as endoscopic treatment or surgery being considered?

Regarding prognosis:

- Is individual still experiencing difficulty with nasal breathing? Have additional treatments such as rhinoplasty been considered?
- Has the individual experienced any complications such as laryngeal or tracheal obstruction, stenosis of the airway passages, recurrence of airway obstruction, hemorrhage, internal scarring or internal nasal deformity that may impact recovery and prognosis?
- Does the individual have any existing condition such as diabetes, immune suppression or chronic respiratory condition that may impact recovery and prognosis?

References

Andraca, R., R.S. Edson, and E.B. Kern. "Rhinoscleroma: A Growing concern in the United States?" Mayo Clinic Proceedings 68 12 (1993): 1151-1157.

Eisenstein, Barry I. "Enterobacteriaceae." Principles and Practice of Infectious Diseases, 4th ed, vol 2. Mandell, Gerald L., John E. Bennett, and Raphael Dolin, ed. New York: Churchill Livingstone, 1995. 1964-1980.

Rib Resection

Other names / synonyms: Obtaining Bone Graft, Removal of Rib

77.91

Definition

A rib resection is the surgical removal of a segment of rib or ribs. Resection may be necessary to treat fractures that are at risk for damaging lung tissue, remove sections of rib damaged by diseases such as cancer. A rib resection may also be performed as part of the treatment for thoracic outlet syndrome. Resection is commonly part of surgical procedures requiring access to the chest (thoracic) cavity.

Reason for Procedure

A rib resection is usually performed to gain access to organs in the chest cavity, to the kidney, or to use the rib as a bone graft in some other part of the body. A rib resection may also be done to drain an abscess between the diaphragm and liver (subphrenic abscess). Other indications are for cancer or for noncancerous conditions that change the shape or damage the rib, thus causing pain. In the case of thoracic outlet syndrome, the first rib may be removed, as may a cervical rib if one is present. It is also done in the course of correcting a chest wall deformity called pectus excavatum.

Description

Rib resection or removal is done in the operating room under general anesthesia. The placement of the surgical incision will depend not only on the location of the rib to be cut or removed, but also on the nature of any accompanying procedure. Although the resection may be a relatively minor procedure if done alone, the associated procedures may be extremely complicated.

Resection is accomplished through a skin incision, dissecting down to the involved rib and then cutting the rib section free with surgical instruments designed for cutting bone (osteotomes and rongeurs). Bone wax may be necessary over the ends of the exposed bone to control bleeding. The wound is closed over a drain if necessary and a chest tube may need to be inserted to facilitate re-inflation of the lung.

Ribs are attached to the spine and the upper ribs also attach to the breastbone (sternum). For this reason, rib sections used for bone grafting are most easily obtained from the lowest rib, which remains free floating in the front.

Prognosis

Rib resection is most often very successful in itself. The underlying or associated problem, however, may not have as successful an outcome.

Specialists

- General Surgeon
- Orthopedic Surgeon
- Thoracic Surgeon
- Vascular Surgeon

Rehabilitation

A rib resection may require rehabilitation in the event additional structures including muscles and ligaments associated with the rib are also affected. Rehabilitation is also indicated if the individual's pulmonary status has changed following the rib resection. At the onset of the rehabilitation following the resection, the physical therapist may apply treatments utilizing ice or heat to minimize swelling and pain. Electrostimulation combined with heat or cold treatment is another technique used in physical therapy to relax muscles around the resection site. Transcutaneous electrical nerve stimulation (T.E.N.S.) is a form of electrostimulation in which an electrical impulse, predetermined by the physical therapist, produces a high frequency tingling sensation blocking pain.

Once pain and swelling have been reduced, the physical therapist performs stretching exercises to help restore full motion to any affected joint and/or upper limb. If the individual experiences a decrease in shoulder motion because of tight muscles attaching to the rib, stretching exercises are beneficial and consist of the physical therapist moving the arm while no effort is provided by the individual.

Modifications may need to be made by the physical therapist for those individuals with severely affected range of motion to any joints near the rib resection. Modifications may also be needed in the event the rib resection has resulted in the complication of pneumonia or any other pulmonary disorder. Physical therapy addresses this possible complication by increasing ventilation with breathing exercises localized to the area of involvement followed by a gradual strengthening program. Until the rib is fully healed and shoulder/trunk motion has returned, the individual should refrain from heavy lifting or contact sports.

Work Restrictions / Accommodations

Work involving strenuous use of the arm on the side of the surgery may need to be temporarily avoided. Underlying conditions/diseases would have to be considered in evaluating work restrictions.

Comorbid Conditions

Any condition affecting the lungs, heart, chest, pulmonary function, bone healing or bleeding disorders could complicate recovery from a rib resection.

Procedure Complications

The risk of complication would vary if the resection was performed as an isolated procedure or associated with other procedures. Unintentional collapse of a lung, nerve damage, fracture along the rib in other locations, perforation of the diaphragm, infection and pneumonia could be complications of an isolated procedure.

Factors Influencing Duration

Factors that may influence the length of disability include the reason for the procedure and the location and length of rib removed. Because the underlying lung may be collapsed during surgery, a chest tube is often used to re-expand the lung, and would stay in place for several days after the operation.

Length of Disability

Length of disability will be greatly affected by the underlying reason for the surgery. Job requirements for upper body strength and agility may be restricted as so many upper body muscles either attach to or pass over the ribs.

Duration in Days

Job Classification	Minimum	Optimum	Maximum
Sedentary work	21	28	42
Light work	21	28	42
Medium work	28	35	56
Heavy work	28	42	84
Very Heavy work	35	42	84

References

Hagler, D., and G. Traver. "Respiratory System." Mosby's Clinical Nursing. Thompson, June St. Louis: Mosby-Year Book, Inc, 1997. 121-190.

Schwartz, Seymour, MD. Principles of Surgery. New York: McGraw-Hill, 1999.

Rocky Mountain Spotted Fever

Other names / synonyms: Rocky Mountain Fever, Spotted Fever, Tick Fever, Tick Typhus
082, 082.0, 082.8, 082.9, 083

Definition

Rocky Mountain Spotted Fever is an acute infectious disease caused in the western US by a bacterium called Rickettsia rickettsi. Other ticks transmit the infection in the southern US, and in Central and South America. Ticks infected with Rickettsia rickettsi transmit the infection to humans, either through a direct bite, or during removal of an infected tick from another person or animal. This infection is characterized by persistent fever, head and muscle aches, and a spotted skin rash.

Rocky Mountain Spotted Fever is a serious illness, with about 600 new cases reported each year in the US. Despite the name, most cases occur in the southeastern states. Ticks infected with this bacterium are found throughout the country, and in all states except Maine, Alaska, and Hawaii. Peak incidence is from May to September, but can occur at any time of the year if the weather is warm. Men are more likely to be infected than women, because men engage in more outdoor activities. For this same reason, about two thirds of reported cases are in children; young adults are more frequently affected although the infection can occur in individuals of any age. Besides outdoor activity in warm months, contact with dogs will increase one's risk of infection.

Rocky Mountain Spotted Fever is theoretically completely curable if treated early and appropriately. For reasons that are unclear, symptoms of the disease are more severe in men, and men have a higher mortality than women. The elderly also are at risk for higher mortality and more severe disease.

Diagnosis

History: Individuals may report a tick bite, recent hiking activities, or travel to an endemic area. Symptoms appearing 2-14 days after the tick bite include persistent high fever, severe headache, muscle pain, chills, and extreme exhaustion (prostration). In some cases nausea and vomiting, restlessness, insomnia, and irritability will be reported. Less frequently, abdominal pain, joint pain, cough, confusion, or stupor are reported. Two to six days following the onset of symptoms, small pink spots appear on the wrists and ankles. This non-tender rash then spreads to the palms of the hands and soles of the feet, before spreading over the rest of the body. As blood vessels bleed beneath the skin, the rash darkens and develops bruised-looking areas called petechiae. Additional symptoms that may be associated with Rocky Mountain Spotted Fever include excessive thirst, hallucinations, diarrhea, loss of appetite, and abnormal sensitivity to light (photophobia).

Physical exam: Individuals may present with a fever that can be as high as 106 degrees Fahrenheit, conjunctivitis, and the characteristic rash. Pressing with hands (palpation) on the abdomen may reveal tenderness, and an enlarged spleen (and occasionally an enlarged liver). In severe cases, the individual may look very ill. Drowsiness or sluggishness (lethargy), mental confusion and disorientation, stupor, seizures, and coma may be evident.

Tests: Before the rash appears, Rocky Mountain Spotted Fever resembles several other infections, making diagnosis very difficult. Blood tests reveal a low level of sodium, and may be done to rule out other conditions such as thrombocytopenia. Urine tests may detect the presence of blood or protein. During the acute phase of the illness, diagnosis can be made by isolating the Rickettsiae through skin biopsies. By the second week, blood tests that confirm the diagnosis will reveal a rise in antibody titer that can be detected by specific complement fixation test, immun-ofluorescent antibody (IFA), and microscopic latex agglutination tests.

Treatment

Individuals with mild disease may be treated on an outpatient basis, but must be told to watch for the signs and symptoms of progression or complications. Moderately or severely ill individuals should be hospitalized, and are treated with oral or intravenous (IV) antibiotic drug therapy. If the lungs become involved, oxygen therapy and/or assisted ventilation might be necessary. Blood transfusions may also be necessary in cases where anemia develops.

Prognosis

With proper treatment, the illness usually subsides after about 2 weeks; there is usually complete recovery. In severe or complicated cases, the recovery period will be longer, and holds the possibility of neurological damage. Death will occur in approximately 4% of individuals who receive treatment; untreated cases are associated with a higher mortality rate of 20-25 percent.

Differential Diagnosis

Conditions with similar symptoms include measles, typhoid fever, viral or bacterial meningitis, viral encephalitis, meningococcemia, toxic shock syndrome, typhus, rickettsialpox, ehrlichiosis, Lyme disease, relapsing fever, rubella, secondary syphilis, leptospirosis, idiopathic thrombocytopenia purpura (ITP), thrombotic thrombocytopenia, and infectious mononucleosis.

Specialists

- Cardiologist
- Dermatologist
- Gastroenterologist
- Hematologist
- Hepatologist
- Infectious Disease Physician
- Nephrologist
- Neurologist
- Ophthalmologist
- Psychiatrist

Work Restrictions / Accommodations

Extended sick leave may be required. Specific work restrictions or accommodations depend on the individual's job requirements. Strenuous activity may need to be modified until physical stamina returns.

Comorbid Conditions

A compromised immune system may delay recovery.

Complications

Complications may include encephalopathy, pneumonia, heart, lung or kidney failure, hemorrhage, inflammation of the heart (myocarditis), pulmonary edema, tissue death (gangrene), vascular damage to brain, lungs, or heart, and swelling or inflammation of the optic nerve (papilledema) where it enters the eyeball.

Factors Influencing Duration

Length of disability may be influenced by the individual's age, delay in diagnosis or treatment, the presence of complications, and the severity of the disease. In addition, because men tend to experience the disease more severely, they may experience a longer period of disability.

Length of Disability

Individuals usually recover completely within 2 weeks of infection. Severe or complicated disease may take longer to resolve. In rare cases, permanent disability may occur. Death, although rare, may occur.

Duration in Days

Job Classification	Minimum	Optimum	Maximum
Sedentary work	14	28	42
Light work	14	28	42
Medium work	14	28	42
Heavy work	21	42	63
Very Heavy work	21	42	63

Failure to Recover

If an individual fails to recover within the maximum duration expectancy period, the reader may wish to reference the following questions to assist in better understanding the specifics of an individual's medical case.

Regarding diagnosis:

- Has the diagnosis of Rocky Mountain Spotted Fever been confirmed?
- Have conditions with similar symptoms been ruled out?

Regarding treatment:

- Was antibiotic therapy started promptly?
- Was culture and sensitivity done to determine the most effective antibiotic to use?
- Has the individual been compliant with the treatment regimen?
- What can be done to increase compliance?
- During treatment, has individual experienced any complications such as inadequate blood circulation or fluid accumulation in the lungs or brain?
- Have complications responded to treatment?

Regarding prognosis:

- Has illness extended beyond 2 weeks?
- Do symptoms persist despite treatment?
- Did individual complete entire course of drug therapy?
- Did individual follow physician's instructions regarding bed rest and/or restricted activity?
- Would individual benefit from evaluation by an infectious disease specialist?
- If case was severe or complicated, did neurological damage occur?
- Would individual benefit from involvement in a rehabilitation program?
- Does individual have any underlying conditions that may impact recovery?
- Has individual experienced any complications related to the infection?

References

Fine, Douglas, and Ronald Greenfield. "Rocky Mountain Spotted Fever." Griffith's 5-minute Clinical Consult. Dambro, Mark, ed. Philadelphia: Lippincott, Williams & Wilkins, 2000. 954-955.

Walker, David. "Rickettsiae." Medical Microbiology. Baron, Samuel New York: Churchill Livingstone, 1991. 517-532.

Root Canal Therapy
Other names / synonyms: Endodontics, Root Canal Treatment
23.70

Definition

Root canal therapy is treatment for a tooth in which the innermost chamber (pulp) has been abscessed or has become infected (pulpitis). The treatment consists of removing the abscessed or infected pulp and filling the inside areas (the pulp chamber and root canals) with a nonreactive (inert) filling material and a sealer cement.

In short, root canal therapy involves cleaning and sealing the inside of the tooth. The goal is to prevent the pulp canal spaces from serving as a haven for the growth of bacteria.

Causes for a root canal include an abscessed or infected tooth that causes great pain. If left untreated, the infection will spread, causing the bone around the tooth to degenerate, and the tooth may ultimately fall out. The only other treatment alternative is extraction of the tooth, which may cause surrounding teeth to shift crookedly (resulting in a bad bite), unless an expensive implant or bridge is installed to replace the extracted tooth. Without question, it is in the individual's best interest to strive to keep his or her original teeth.

Root canal therapy has become a common dental procedure; more than 14 million procedures are performed every year in the US, with a 95% success rate, according to the American Association of Endodontists.

Reason for Procedure

The most common reason to perform a root canal is to treat a dental abscess. A dental abscess occurs when nerve tissue within the canals of a tooth becomes infected or inflamed. If the infection is left untreated, it may ultimately lead to removal of the tooth.

By removing infected tissue from the interior of the tooth, the root is preserved, thereby enabling the tooth to remain in the mouth.

Description

Root canal therapy is performed in 2 visits and is done by a general dentist or by a dentist who specializes in inside-the-tooth (endodontic) procedures (endodontist).

At the first visit, the dentist administers local anesthesia, removes any tooth decay, makes an opening though the natural crown of the tooth into the pulp chamber, uses small files to clean out the debris and bacteria from the canals, fills the canal spaces with a nonreactive filling material (gutta percha) and a sealer cement to prevent bacteria from entering the tooth in the future, and puts a temporary filling into place.

At the second visit, the dentist seals each canal with filling material and puts a permanent filling on the chewing surface of the tooth. Most often, the dentist will recommend a crown to protect the tooth from breaking, since a tooth treated with root canal therapy is no longer vital, is more brittle, and may break more easily.

Prognosis

More than 95% of root canal therapies are successful. However, sometimes a case needs to be redone due to diseased canal offshoots that went unnoticed or the fracturing of a canal filing instrument, both of which rarely occur. Occasionally, a root canal therapy will fail altogether, marked by a return of pain.

Specialists

| • Dentist | • Endontist |

Work Restrictions / Accommodations

There are no work restrictions or special accommodations required.

Comorbid Conditions

Comorbid conditions that might influence the length of disability after root canal therapy include medically compromising conditions, such as diabetes mellitus and human immunodeficiency virus (HIV) infection. Also, individuals on medications that cause dry mouth are at higher risk for bacterial infections.

Procedure Complications

An abscess can persist, even after a root canal has been performed. A new infection may result if the procedure is performed improperly.

Factors Influencing Duration

A factor that might influence the length of disability is an abscess that persists even after root canal therapy has been performed. In such a case, the individual's dentist may refer him or her to a specialist skilled in performing a surgical procedure to remove the diseased tissues from the tip of the root and to reseal it with another filling.

Other factors include infections and other problems that might occur after the procedure, such as bleeding or swelling.

Length of Disability

Job Classification	Minimum	Optimum	Maximum
Any work	0	1	2

Duration in Days

References

MD Consult L.L.C. - Root Canal Treatment. Clinical Reference Systems 2000. 01 Jan 2000. 19 Jan 2001 <http://home.mdconsult.com/ >.

Rosen, Peter. Emergency Medicine: Concepts and Clinical Practice, 4th ed. Saint Louis: Mosby-Year Book, Inc, 1998 19 Jan 2001 <http://home.mdconsult.com/ >.

Rotator Cuff Repair
83.63

Definition

Rotator cuff repair is defined as surgically restoring the integrity of a torn rotator cuff mechanism in the shoulder. This involves smoothing (debriding) the ragged edges of the torn tendon and suturing the tissue edges together. Often, the end of the tendon must be reattached to the upper arm (humeral head) as well. If the hole created by the tear is too large and/or the tissue too stiff to be pulled together again, a graft may be necessary to cover the humeral head. To provide adequate space and decrease friction, the undersurface of the acromion may be removed and the coracoacromial ligament cut. These added procedures (acromioplasty, coracoacromial ligament release, acromionectomy) enlarge the arch under which the rotator cuff passes during arm motion.

Tears of the rotator cuff occur either suddenly (acute) during an injury to the shoulder or over time from progressive wearing on the tendon. Acute injuries are most common in young adults while more chronic wear and tear changes are seen in older individuals. In an acute injury, tension greater than the cuff can tolerate cause it to tear such as when lifting heavy objects overhead. More chronic tears are brought on by repetitive activities (wear and tear changes) such as lifting or throwing. Diabetes, gout, and the inflammatory diseases are often underlying causes of rotator cuff tear.

Repair of the rotator cuff is most often done fairly quickly after acute injuries in young adults and after conservative treatment has failed in older individuals. The procedure is often a combined arthroscopic and open (arthrotomy) procedure, depending on the type of tear/repair and surgeon preference. Rotator cuff repairs are done in outpatient settings as well as inpatient procedures under regional or general anesthesia.

Reason for Procedure

The goal of a rotator cuff repair is to restore arm and shoulder motion and alleviate pain. Rotator cuff repair enables the rotator cuff tendons to work together to move the arm in many directions as intended. Loss of integrity of the group affects arm motion and function and creates pain that can be debilitating. Repair of a rotator cuff tear can also slow the process of degenerative (osteoarthritis) arthritis.

Description

If the procedure is done using arthroscopic assistance, several small holes are made around the shoulder to insert the arthroscope and other surgical instruments. The torn rotator cuff is examined, then a decision is made about the type of repair required. Some tears can be repaired using arthroscopic techniques alone utilizing specially designed equipment to reattach the torn cuff edges to the arm bone (humerus).

Other usually more chronic tears require a more extensive open repair. An open repair involves an incision along the top and front of the shoulder to gain access to the entire cuff mechanism. It may be possible to stretch the existing tissue back together and secure it to the humerus with staples, wire, or sutures. This technique requires that a tunnel be drilled in the top of the humeral head providing an attachment area for the reconstructed tendon. In other situations, a tissue graft is used to repair the hole in the rotator cuff and suture it in place.

After surgery, the arm is placed in a restrictive sling strapped across the waist, oftentimes holding a small bolster of pillow to maintain correct tension on the repair. The sling is worn about 6 weeks.

Rotator cuff repair is done under anesthesia. It also requires extensive rehabilitation for optimum recovery.

Prognosis

In those individuals with acute injury and repair and those without complications, return to normal function is often gained in 6 to 12 months. Complete restoration of shoulder function may not be possible especially in those with more chronic tears. Relief of pain and regaining of some function is often the goal. Recovery from surgery is often very slow, limited by pain and the need for extensive rehabilitation.

Specialists

- Orthopedic Surgeon
- Physiatrist
- Physical Therapist

Rehabilitation

Individuals who undergo surgical repair of a torn rotator cuff tendon may undergo physical therapy. Initial recovery from surgery or the time before aggressive therapy can begin is somewhere between 4 to 6 weeks.

Immediately postsurgery, individuals learn to perform active motion of the wrist and hand to decrease swelling and maintain motion.

A physical therapist performs passive range-of-motion exercises in flexion, abduction, and external rotation. Therapists stretch the shoulder within a pain-free zone to avoid excessive stretching of the newly attached tendon.

Individuals can begin active abduction of the shoulder from a 90-degree position approximately 4 to 6 weeks after surgery. Once able to do this, abduction can be attempted with the arm at the side as a starting position. Strengthening exercises are taught once active abduction against gravity is achieved. Initially, individuals perform isometric exercises where they manually resist the shoulder as it moves into flexion, abduction, internal rotation, external rotation, and extension. Once normal range of motion is restored, individuals may progress to using resistive elastic tubing as the shoulder is moved into each of these directions.

Work Restrictions / Accommodations

Individuals should not use the affected arm for 6 weeks although very limited use of the hand is often permitted. Immediately postoperative, the individual has a sling that holds the arm close to the body.

Progressing activity should be based on the type of repair and surgeon preference. Long-term restrictions of limited overhead work, lifting, carrying, and repetitive activities may follow the recovery period.

Comorbid Conditions

Any neurological condition affecting shoulder motion and strength would impact recovery as well. Instability of the shoulder from injury to the joint capsule (sprain) can complicate recovery if untreated.

Procedure Complications

Complications from a rotator cuff repair include failed repair, nerve or vessel damage in the shoulder area, infection, adhesive capsulitis, and decreased shoulder motion and/or strength.

Factors Influencing Duration

Use of affected dominant arm, work requirements for overhead activity, heavy lifting, type of repair, age of individual, and response to rehabilitation affect the disability period. Return to work depends greatly on achieving rehabilitation goals of function, strength, and endurance.

Length of Disability

Some individuals may not be able to return to heavy or overhead work. Chronic situations may result in permanent disability to protect the repair.

Arthroscopic.

Duration in Days

Job Classification	Minimum	Optimum	Maximum
Sedentary work	7	10	21
Light work	7	10	21
Medium work	28	42	56
Heavy work	56	70	84
Very Heavy work	56	70	84

Open surgery.

Duration in Days

Job Classification	Minimum	Optimum	Maximum
Sedentary work	28	42	70
Light work	28	56	84
Medium work	42	84	140
Heavy work	70	84	140
Very Heavy work	70	84	140

Duration Trend from Normative Data*

Cases	Mean	Min	Max	No Lost Time	Over 6 Months
210	76	0	413	4.39%	9.27%

Percentile:	5th	25th	Median	75th	95th
Days:	1	19	44	88	154

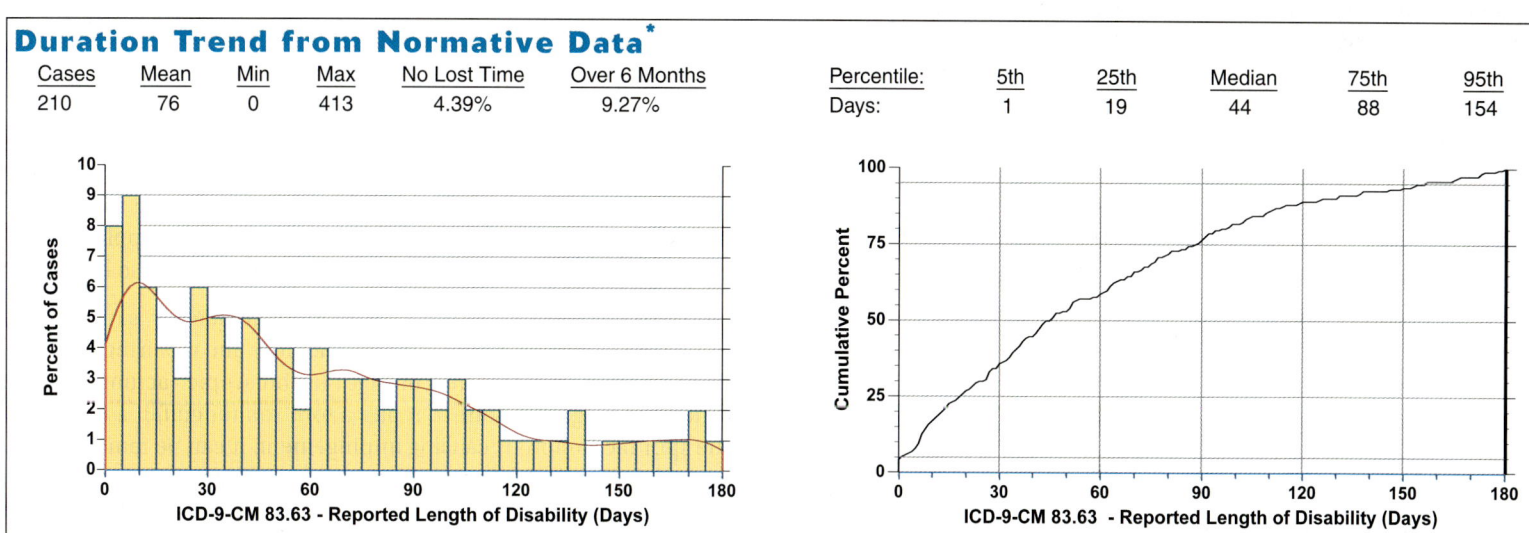

* Differences may exist between the expected duration tables and the normative graphs. Duration tables provide expected recovery periods based on the type of work performed by the individual. The normative graphs reflect the actual observed experience of many individuals across the spectrum of physical conditions, in a variety of industries, and with varying levels of case management.

Rotator Cuff Repair

References

Kisner, Carolyn, and Lynn Allen Colby. "The Shoulder and Shoulder Girdle." Therapeutic Exercise: Foundations and Techniques, 2nd ed. Philadelphia: F.A. Davis Company, 1990. 241-271.

Miniaci, A., and P. Dowdy. "Rotator Cuff Disorders." Shoulder Injuries in Athletes. Hawkins, Richard J.J., and Gary W. Misamore, ed. New York: Churchill Livingstone, 1996. 103-111.

Rotator Cuff Syndrome
Other names / synonyms: Painful Arc Syndrome, Rotator Cuff Impingement Syndrome
726.1, 726.10, 726.11

Definition

The rotator cuff syndrome is a shoulder disorder most frequently diagnosed only in workers whose work involves constantly raising their upper arms more than 30 degrees over the horizontal. This syndrome is defined as a chronic pain syndrome originating from the rotator cuff in the shoulder. Irritation to the muscles and tendons can be caused by pressure against the bone (acromion) at the top of the shoulder blade as the arm is raised or from repeated motion against the ligament across the shoulder joint (impingement syndrome or painful arc syndrome).

Rotator cuff impingement syndrome is divided into three stages of severity. In stage I, edema and/or hemorrhage occurs and is found mostly in individuals under age twenty-five. Stage I is frequently associated with an overuse injury, and is reversible or can progress to Stage II. Stage II is more advanced and mostly occurs in individuals between twenty-five and forty. Evident pathologic changes show fibrosis as well as irreversible tendon changes. Stage III mostly occurs in individuals over 50, and frequently involves a tendon rupture or tear. Stage III is largely a process of attrition and the culmination of fibrosis and tendinosis present for many years.

Workers at risk for rotator cuff syndrome are those required to constantly move heavy weights over their heads such as welders, plate workers, and slaughterhouse workers. A study of more than 1,500 slaughterhouse workers in Denmark over a period of 13 years found that almost 6% of current workers and more than 7% of former workers had impingement syndrome. This syndrome has also been reported in sewing machine operators. Rotator cuff impingement syndrome makes up about 40% of time and costs of disability caused by work-related shoulder disorders.

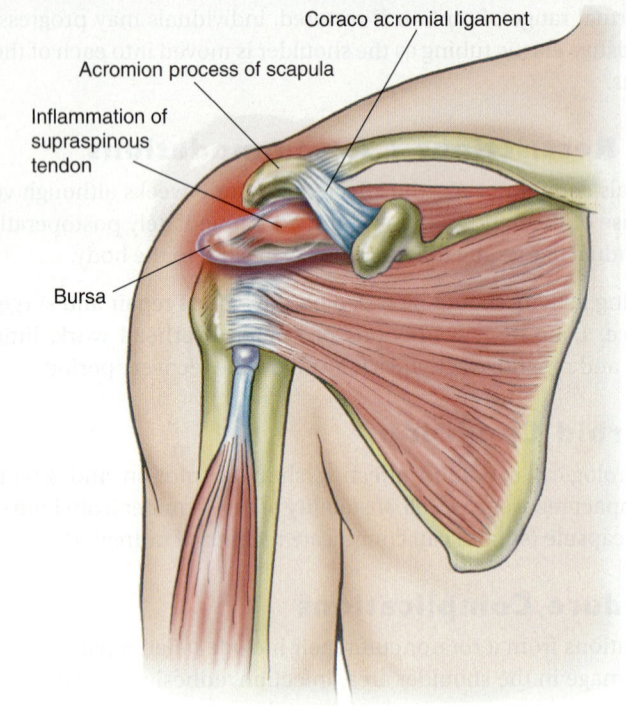

Diagnosis

History: The individual frequently reports aching pain in the shoulder or on the outside upper arm. The pain worsens when the arm is lifted overhead and at night. Other symptoms may include weakness and loss of motion. The onset of symptoms is often gradual.

Physical exam: The individual's arm is rotated to determine the source of pain. The pain is more intense at some rotations or when pressure is applied and can disappear at other rotations.

Tests: MRI detects soft tissue abnormalities in the shoulder and is the definitive diagnostic test for rotator cuff syndrome. X-rays rule out calcifying bone and joint diseases. Ultrasonography, MRI, and arthrography rule out rotator cuff tears. Other diagnostic tests for rotator cuff syndrome are bone scintigraphy and CT.

Treatment

Conservative treatment is the initial method for minor impingement or rotator cuff tendonitis. The goals of conservative treatment are to decrease pain and restore normal shoulder function. Activities causing the pain should be slowly resumed only when the pain is gone. Sometimes a cortisone injection into the space above the rotator cuff tendon is helpful to relieve swelling and inflammation. Application of ice to the tender area 3 to 4 times a day for 15 minutes is also helpful.

Chronic rotator cuff syndrome with impingement is satisfactorily treated with surgically cutting into the shoulder and repairing the bone and/or tendon and/or the muscle (arthroscopic acromioplasty). Rotator cuff surgery is done to repair a torn rotator cuff. If a thickened bone spur (acromion) is causing impingement, it can be removed with a burr. The main goals of surgery are pain relief, improved strength, and increased functioning.

Prognosis

Some individuals whose rotator cuff syndrome was caused by repetitive over-shoulder lifting may recover completely if the repetitive work is stopped and nonsurgical treatment is followed exactly. An otherwise healthy individual with a minor rotator cuff impingement is expected to recover full use of his/her arm after rotator cuff surgery. The final outcome often depends on the willingness and ability of an individual to participate actively in postoperative physical therapy. The reported success rate for torn rotator cuffs is between 85-95% following surgery. In many individuals who resume overhead work or the activity that initially caused the problem, recurrent episodes may continue despite appropriate acute treatment. These individuals need to alter their work activities.

Differential Diagnosis

Other with similar symptoms of rotator cuff syndrome include referred shoulder pain from a problem with the nerves in the neck, adhesive capsulitis, fractures and dislocations, thoracic outlet syndrome, degenerative arthritis of the acromioclavicular joint, tumors, pain from poor posture, tendon rupture, and suprascapular nerve entrapment.

Specialists

- Orthopedic Surgeon
- Physiatrist
- Physical Therapist
- Rheumatologist
- Sports Medicine Physician

Rehabilitation

Individuals with rotator cuff syndrome may benefit from physical therapy and/or occupational therapy. Therapy focuses on pain reduction, increasing strength and range of motion, and addresses underlying causes of tendonitis.

The first focus of therapy is the reduction of pain and swelling. During this phase, individuals learn to use heat for 15 minutes prior to exercise to help increase muscle flexibility and decrease pain. Individuals also learn to use ice packs for 10 minutes after exercise and as needed to control pain and swelling. Individuals also learn to identify and avoid any activities that may have led to the rotator cuff tear such as repetitive overhead activities like painting or an athletic injury such as pitching or swimming.

The second focus of therapy is to increase range of motion at the shoulder. Therapists may perform passive range-of-motion exercises and joint mobilization exercises. Therapists stretch the shoulder into overhead reaching (flexion), reaching out to the side (abduction), backward reaching (extension), and into rotation (internal and external). Individuals learn self-assisted shoulder exercises for flexion, abduction, internal rotation, external rotation, and extension by holding a cane or broomstick and using the non-affected arm to stretch the other shoulder. Individuals may also increase shoulder motion by using overhead pulleys so that by pulling down with the non-affected arm the shoulder with the tear is stretched.

The third focus of therapy is to increase strength and correct muscle imbalances. Initially, individuals perform isometric exercises in which they manually resist the shoulder as it moves into flexion, abduction, internal rotation, external rotation, and extension. Once normal range of motion is restored, individuals may progress to using resistive elastic tubing as the shoulder is moved into each of these directions. Once full strength is established, dynamic strengthening such as playing catch with a medicine ball and performing push-ups can begin.

The final focus of therapy is to correct any postural deficits that may have predisposed the individual to tendinitis. Individuals stretch out the chest muscles by standing in a corner with one forearm on each wall and leaning inwards. Individuals may also perform reverse shoulder rolls to further promote normalized posture. Individuals strengthen the neck by performing chin tucks, in which the neck is retracted so that the chin is flattened against the neck. Individuals strengthen the upper back by performing shoulder blade pinches, in which the shoulder blades are squeezed together; this can be made more difficult by holding elastic tubing to add some resistance.

Work Restrictions / Accommodations

The individual should stop overhead work, repetitive lifting, and carrying. Physical therapy may be needed for some months until the pain is gone and the individual regains the use of his/her shoulder.

Comorbid Conditions

Comorbid conditions include obesity, diabetes, cardiovascular disease, tendon tears, and adhesive capsulitis.

Complications

The main complication of rotator cuff syndrome is when rotator cuff tears are undiagnosed and the individual is in great pain. This pain and other symptoms persist until the rotator cuff is repaired surgically. Another complication comes from inadequate treatment. If the shoulder is immobilized in a sling, the individual can develop frozen shoulder, also known as adhesive capsulitis. Conditions such as a rotator cuff tear or impingement syndrome may eventually lead to adhesive capsulitis. These conditions usually result in a decrease in shoulder motion and lead to the loss of mobility and scarring.

Factors Influencing Duration

Factors that may influence disability include the age and overall health of the individual and whether modifications can be made to the individual's daily duties (especially avoidance of overhead work).

Length of Disability

Duration depends on the severity of symptoms, on whether one or both shoulders is affected, whether the dominant or non-dominant arm is involved, whether the individual can be assigned a job where full mobility of one shoulder is not needed, and whether the job can be performed adequately while the individual takes pain relievers.

Heavy work is often inappropriate on a permanent basis if rotator cuff surgery has been performed.

Medical treatment.

Duration in Days

Job Classification	Minimum	Optimum	Maximum
Sedentary work	1	3	4
Light work	1	3	7
Medium work	14	21	42
Heavy work	28	42	84
Very Heavy work	28	42	84

Arthroscopic surgery.

Duration in Days

Job Classification	Minimum	Optimum	Maximum
Sedentary work	7	10	21
Light work	7	10	21
Medium work	28	42	56
Heavy work	56	70	84
Very Heavy work	56	70	84

Surgical treatment (open).

Duration in Days

Job Classification	Minimum	Optimum	Maximum
Sedentary work	28	42	70
Light work	28	56	84
Medium work	42	84	140
Heavy work	70	84	140
Very Heavy work	70	84	140

Duration Trend from Normative Data*

Cases	Mean	Min	Max	No Lost Time	Over 6 Months
1117	76	0	563	0.81%	7.88%

Percentile:	5th	25th	Median	75th	95th
Days:	9	24	47	87	151

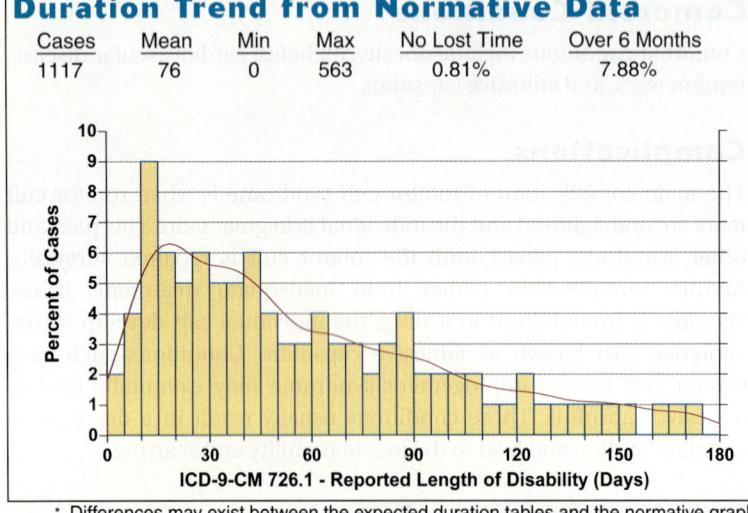
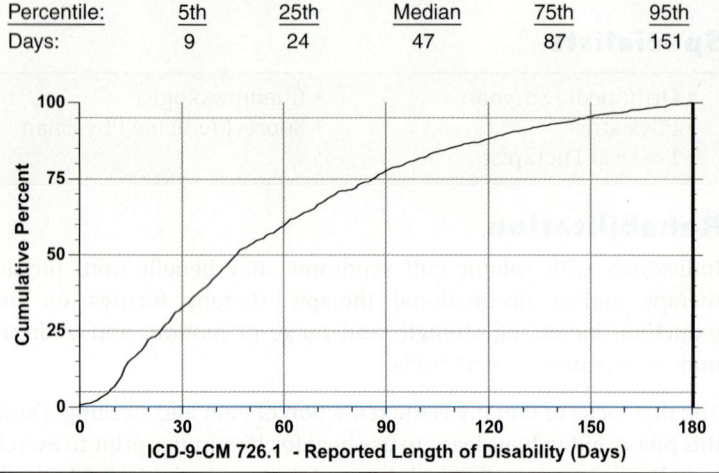

ICD-9-CM 726.1 - Reported Length of Disability (Days)

* Differences may exist between the expected duration tables and the normative graphs. Duration tables provide expected recovery periods based on the type of work performed by the individual. The normative graphs reflect the actual observed experience of many individuals across the spectrum of physical conditions, in a variety of industries, and with varying levels of case management.

Failure to Recover

If an individual fails to recover within the maximum duration expectancy period, the reader may wish to reference the following questions to assist in better understanding the specifics of an individual's medical case.

Regarding diagnosis:

- Does individual have symptoms of rotator cuff syndrome such as aching pain in the shoulder?
- Does individual have an occupation that requires lifting heavy weights overhead?
- Was source of pain located?
- Has individual had adequate testing to establish the diagnosis?
- Have conditions with similar symptoms been ruled out?

Regarding treatment:

- Did individual respond to conservative treatment?
- Was a cortisone injection given?
- Was surgery necessary? Was it successful?

Regarding prognosis:

- Has individual stopped overhead work, repetitive lifting, and carrying?
- Has individual actively participated in their physical therapy?
- Does individual have a home exercise program?
- Does individual have any conditions that may affect recovery?
- Did any complications arise?

References

Andersen, J.H., O. Gaardboe-Poulsen, E.M. Jensen. "The Rotator Cuff Syndrome - A Frequent Disease Caused by Loading." Ugeskr Laeger 151 37 (1989): 2352-2355.

Kessler, Randolph M., and Darlene Hertling. "The Shoulder and Shoulder Girdle." Management of Common Musculoskeletal Disorders. Philadelphia: J.B. Lippincott Company, 1990. 169-204.

Kisner, Carolyn, and Lynn Allen Colby. "The Shoulder and Shoulder Girdle." Therapeutic Exercise: Foundations and Techniques, 2nd ed. Philadelphia: F.A. Davis Company, 1990. 241-271.

Magee, David J. "Shoulder." Orthopedic Physical Assessment. Biblis, Margaret M., ed. Philadelphia: W.B. Saunders Company, 1992. 90-142.

Rotator Cuff Tear
718.01, 727.61, 840.4

Definition

Rotator cuff tear occurs when the tendons that form the rotator cuff weaken and tear.

The rotator cuff is comprised of four muscles and their tendon attachments that wrap over the upper arm (humeral head) in the shoulder. These tendons come under stress from repeated activities that require lifting and rotating the arm. Any abnormalities of the shoulder joint can aggravate the stress, especially looseness (laxity), pinching under the arch formed by the shoulder blade and the collarbone (impingement syndrome), and bursitis. As the tendons become irritated, they become inflamed and eventfully weaken and may tear.

Tears are described as either partial thickness tears or complete rupture, depending on the amount of tissue damage. Partial tears do not go all the way through the cuff, although there may be a fairly large surface area involved. Complete tears demonstrate a hole in the cuff with partial or total loss of tendon function. The size of tear ranges from small to massive, depending on the size of the hole created and how much of the humeral head is exposed.

Tears are classified as acute or chronic related to the onset. Acute tears are the result of forceful injury to the shoulder, straining the tendon beyond its limits, which causes a tear. Chronic tears come for repetitive wear and tear to the cuff mechanism.

Although rotator cuff tears can affect young adults, typically as the result of a trauma, they are most often found in individuals over 40 years of age. Individuals at a higher risk of sustaining a rotator cuff tear include those who perform overhead work (e.g., warehouse workers, laborers, carpenters, construction workers), certain athletes (e.g., swimmers, tennis players, baseball players), and those who have impingement syndrome, instability of the glenohumeral joint, or inborn (congenital) abnormalities of the shoulder. Men are two times more likely than women to sustain rotator cuff tears. Approximately one half of all individuals over the age of 60 years and one quarter of individuals between 40 and 60 years of age have tears of the rotator cuff, most of which produce no symptoms (asymptomatic).

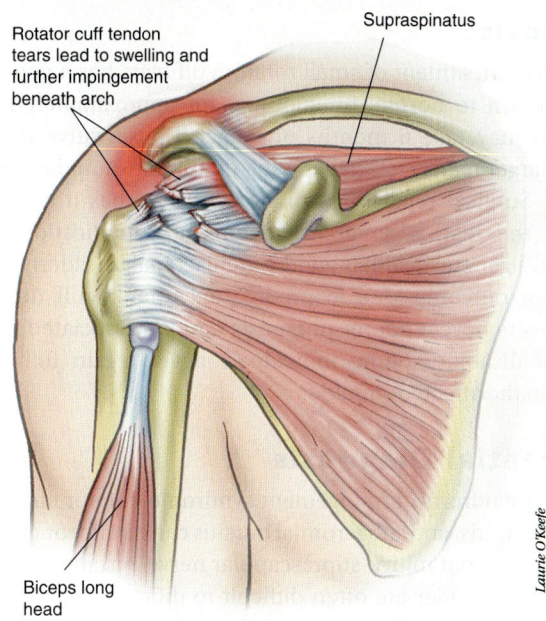

Diagnosis

History: Most individuals with acute tears will describe a fall or attempt to break a fall by grabbing a rail. Those with a chronic tear will describe increasing pain and a difficulty using the shoulder. Individuals will complain of increasing shoulder pain with activity and pain at night with inability to sleep on the affected shoulder. They may complain of shoulder weakness and the inability or limited ability to raise (abduct) their arm. The individual may report that he or she has impingement syndrome.

Physical exam: Range of shoulder motion is tested by asking individuals to raise their arm away from their side toward the ear (abduction). A tear is indicated with inability to perform this maneuver. If assisted to this position (passive abduction) there is a lack of endurance holding the position. Touching (palpation) over the top of the shoulder into the deltoid will produce pain. There may be wasting (atrophy) of the cuff muscles with fairly good range-of-motion (ROM) by substitution of other shoulder muscles. There are numerous other active and passive shoulder physical examination tests; each is specific for different muscle groups and function of the shoulder. The non affected shoulder is examined first to establish a normal baseline.

Tests: Plain x-rays are not diagnostic for rotator cuff tears but will show abnormalities in the bone, shoulder structure, and inflammation and calcification of the shoulder bursa (calcific tendonitis). Arthrography, MRI, or combined arthro tomogram CT scan are the tests used most often to define a tear. Ultrasonography is used in many facilities, although differentiating a partial and full thickness tear may not be as accurate as with the other tests. Diagnostic arthroscopy is occasionally done to evaluate the rotator cuff and shoulder mechanics.

Treatment

The goals of treatment are pain relief and improved shoulder function. Partial tears that do not cause dramatic or progressive shoulder weakness are treated conservatively with rest, ice, NSAIDs, and, possibly local anesthetic-corticosteroid injection into the subacromial space. Physical therapy modalities are used to increase cuff strength, stabilize the shoulder blade (scapula), increase motion, and decrease pain and inflammation. Use of heat on an inflamed or torn tendon may increase pain and worsen the situation. While nonoperative treatment will not repair the tear, it often achieves the goals of pain relief and partial restoration of function.

Complete tears and any tear that causes marked pain or weakness and interferes with daily activities in younger adults are treated with a surgical repair, either arthroscopically or with open surgery (open rotator cuff repair). Partial tears are sometimes cleaned (débrided) arthroscopically to remove the inflamed tissue and ragged edges of the tear. Rotator cuff surgery may be performed under regional or general anesthesia. Treatment in older individuals is based on overall health, weakness of the shoulder joint, pain, and the ability to function. Surgery is done to repair the tear when there are marked changes in these parameters. Otherwise, a complete tear in an elderly individual is treated conservatively, or with simpler procedures such as arthroscopic debridement and subacromial decompression. Massive tears may be inoperable and would also be treated nonoperatively.

Prognosis

Conservative treatment of small rotator cuff tears has a good outcome (with a return to normal functioning) for approximately half of the cases, but may take 6 months or longer. Conservative treatment of chronic, larger tears, especially in the dominant shoulder, have a poor outcome. Surgical repair of a rotator cuff tear has a good outcome provided the tear is small, there are no complications, and the individual's general health is good. Surgical repair in elderly individuals has a poor outcome, due to pre-existing rotator cuff degeneration. Massive tears have a poorer prognosis and are associated with a high degree of disability. Some individuals never regain full motion or strength in the affected shoulder.

Differential Diagnosis

Painful arc syndrome, impingement syndrome, rotator cuff tendonitis, biceps tendonitis, and subacromial bursitis can mimic rotator cuff tears. Cervical nerve root injury, suprascapular nerve entrapment, and instability of the shoulder are often difficult to differentiate from a rotator cuff tear.

Specialists

- Orthopedic Surgeon
- Physiatrist
- Sports Medicine Physician

Rehabilitation

Individuals with rotator cuff tears may require physical therapy and/or occupational therapy. Individual treatment plans may vary contingent on physician protocol.

The first focus of therapy is the reduction of pain and swelling. During this phase, individuals use heat prior to exercise to help increase muscle flexibility and decrease pain. Individuals also use ice packs after exercise and as needed to control pain and swelling. Individuals learn to identify and avoid any activities that may have led to the rotator cuff tear such as repetitive overhead activities like painting or an athletic injury such as pitching or swimming.

The second focus of therapy is to increase range of motion at the shoulder with passive range-of-motion and joint mobilization exercises. Therapists stretch the shoulder into overhead reaching (flexion), reaching out to the side (abduction), backward reaching (extension), and into rotation (internal and external). Individuals learn self-assisted shoulder exercises for flexion, abduction, internal rotation, external rotation, and extension by holding a cane or broomstick and using the nonaffected arm to stretch the other shoulder. Individuals may also increase shoulder motion by using overhead pulleys so that by pulling down with the nonaffected arm, the shoulder with the tear is stretched.

The third focus of therapy is to increase strength and correct muscle imbalances. Initially, individuals perform isometric exercises where they manually resist the shoulder as it moves into flexion, abduction, internal rotation, external rotation, and extension. Once normal range of motion is restored, individuals may progress to using resistive elastic tubing as the shoulder is moved in each of these directions. Once full strength is established, dynamic strengthening such as playing catch with a medicine ball and performing pushups can begin.

The final focus of therapy is to correct any postural deficits that may have predisposed the individual to a tear. Individuals stretch out the chest muscles by standing in a corner with one forearm on each wall and leaning inward. Individuals may also perform reverse shoulder rolls to further promote normalized posture. Individuals strengthen the neck by performing chin tucks where the neck is retracted so that the chin is flattened against the neck. Individuals strengthen the upper back by performing shoulder blade pinches (shoulder blades are squeezed together). This can be made more difficult by holding elastic tubing to add some resistance.

Work Restrictions / Accommodations

No use or limited use of the affected shoulder may apply. Arm use above shoulder level should be avoided. The arm and hand can be used at the individual's side for activities that do not require lifting, pushing, or carrying. These restrictions may become permanent. An ergonometric evaluation of the work place may be necessary. Change in job duties, sharing or alternating tasks, reduced work rate, more frequent rest breaks, and limiting the time and frequency of repetitive activities are important accommodations. Work site modifications can include forearm rests for individuals who use computer keyboards frequently, headsets for those who answer telephones, and alterations such that repetitive activities are performed with the arms in a lower level of elevation.

Recovery from surgical repair is the most restrictive, with no use of the arm and shoulder for two months and with gradual increase in allowed activities. Use of sling will affect manual dexterity. Some individuals will never regain full range-of-motion or strength in the affected arm which, depending on the job duties, and may require a permanent reassignment of duties, which may necessitate retraining. Use of analgesics and other medications can affect dexterity and alertness. Use of these medications may require review of drug policies.

Comorbid Conditions

Shoulder dislocation (and other shoulder injuries), tendonitis, osteoarthritis, rheumatoid arthritis, diabetes, gout, osteoporosis, and general debility can influence the length of disability.

Complications

Post-traumatic arthritis of the shoulder, rheumatoid arthritis, impingement syndrome, osteoporosis of the humeral head, chronic inflammation of the subacromial bursa, nerve injury, frozen shoulder (adhesive capsulitis), and poor shoulder motion are possible complications.

Factors Influencing Duration

The size of the tear, individual's age, occupation, overall health, dominant side involvement, need for surgery, and success of rehabilitation would affect the length of disability. There may be permanent disability regarding certain activities. The larger the tear, the more likely that permanent weakness will result, and, therefore, heavy and very heavy work may no longer be possible.

Length of Disability

Disability may be permanent for individuals who do heavy work or repetitive overhead work.

Medical treatment and arthroscopic treatment.

Duration in Days

Job Classification	Minimum	Optimum	Maximum
Sedentary work	7	10	21
Light work	7	10	21
Medium work	28	42	56
Heavy work	56	70	84
Very Heavy work	56	70	84

Surgical treatment, open.

Duration in Days

Job Classification	Minimum	Optimum	Maximum
Sedentary work	28	42	70
Light work	28	56	84
Medium work	42	84	140
Heavy work	70	84	140
Very Heavy work	70	84	140

Failure to Recover

If an individual fails to recover within the maximum duration expectancy period, the reader may wish to reference the following questions to assist in better understanding the specifics of an individual's medical case.

Regarding diagnosis:

- Does the individual have any risk factors for a rotator cuff tear (those who perform overhead work, certain athletes, those who have impingement syndrome, instability of the glenohumeral joint, or congenital abnormalities of the shoulder)?
- Did the individual fall?
- Did the individual experience associated shoulder weakness or inability to raise his/her arm?
- Did the individual have any positive findings on exam, such as pain in the deltoid, muscle atrophy or impairment of range of motion?
- Has the individual received adequate testing to establish the diagnosis (i.e., MRI, CT scan, arthroscopy)?
- If the diagnosis was uncertain were other conditions with similar symptoms been ruled out (i.e., painful arc syndrome, impingement syndrome, rotator cuff tendinitis, biceps tendinitis, and subacromial bursitis)?

Regarding treatment:

- Has the individual responded favorably to conservative treatment of rest, ice, NSAIDs, and physical therapy? If not, have steroid injections been tried?
- Did it become necessary to repair the tear surgically?

Regarding prognosis:

- Is the individual active in physical therapy? Does the individual have a home exercise program?
- Is the individual's employer able to accommodate necessary restrictions?
- Is the affected shoulder the dominant or non-dominant side?
- Does the individual have any of other conditions such as shoulder dislocation or other shoulder injuries, osteoarthritis, rheumatoid arthritis, diabetes, gout, osteoporosis that could impact recovery?
- Has the individual experienced any complications that could impact recovery and prognosis?

References

Arroyo, Julian, and Evan Flatow. "Management of Rotator Cuff Disease: Intact and Repairable Cuff." Disorders of the Shoulder: Diagnosis and Management. Iannotti, Joseph, and Gerald Williams, eds. Philadelphia: Lippincott, Williams & Wilkins, 1999. 31-56.

Gerber, Christian. "Massive Rotator Cuff Tears." Disorders of the Shoulder: Diagnosis and Management. Iannotti, Joseph, and Gerald Williams, eds. Philadelphia: Lippincott, Williams & Wilkins, 1999. 57-92.

Kisner, Carolyn, and Lynn Allen Colby. "The Shoulder and Shoulder Girdle." Therapeutic Exercise: Foundations and Techniques, 2nd ed. Philadelphia: F.A. Davis Company, 1990. 241-271.

Magee, David J. "Shoulder." Orthopedic Physical Assessment. Biblis, Margaret M., ed. Philadelphia: W.B. Saunders Company, 1992. 90-142.

Sher, Jerry. "Anatomy, Biomechanics, and Pathophysiology of Rotator Cuff Disease." Disorders of the Shoulder: Diagnosis and Management. Iannotti, Joseph, and Gerald Williams, eds. Philadelphia: Lippincott, Williams & Wilkins, 1999. 3-29.

Woodward, Thomas, and Thomas Best. "The Painful Shoulder: Part II. Acute and Chronic Disorders." American Family Physician 61 11 (2000): 3291-300.

Rubella

Other names / synonyms: German Measles, Three-Day Measles
056, 056.0, 056.7, 056.8, 056.9, 647.5, 771.0

Definition

Rubella, or German measles, is a mild viral disease. While primarily a childhood condition, 75% of individuals with rubella infections are between the ages of 15-44 years.

Rubella is moderately contagious and is spread by respiratory droplets during coughing, sneezing, and talking. Once infected, the individual has lifelong immunity to the disease. The most important aspect of rubella is the high incidence of birth defects (up to 65% of infants) if the mother is infected during the first 2 trimesters of her pregnancy. This syndrome of birth defects is called congenital rubella syndrome, and can result in spontaneous abortion (miscarriage), abnormally small head (microcephaly), mental retardation, congenital heart defects, cataracts, blindness, and hearing impairment.

Due to effective immunization programs, rubella is seen infrequently in the US. The incidence declined 99% between 1969 (57,686 cases) and 1999 (128 cases), for a US prevalence of 0.1 per 100,000 people; men accounted for 55.6% of cases reported. Hispanics and individuals who are natives of foreign countries are at a higher risk as they generally have no opportunity for routine vaccination, or gain exposure from individuals who travel to countries where rubella vaccinations are not available. Individuals with immune system impairment (those with AIDS, autoimmune diseases, or on chemotherapy) are also at greater risk for acquiring rubella.

Occasionally small outbreaks of rubella occur in the US, particularly in prisons, in work places with foreign-born individuals who are contagious, and among those who refuse immunization for religious or philosophical reasons.

The worldwide incidence of rubella is also decreasing; however, as 78 countries (97% of industrialized countries, 36% of those with economies-in-transition, and 28% of developing countries) now have immunization programs. In areas without immunization, rubella epidemics occur every 4-7 years.

Diagnosis

History: The disease is usually mild and may even go unnoticed. History often includes contact with another person ill with rubella. Children can have few symptoms, but adults may experience warning symptoms (prodrome symptoms) that include a rash with skin redness or inflammation, low grade fever, joint aches, headache, loss of appetite, general discomfort (malaise), a runny nose, and loss of interest in personal care. The rash usually begins on the face, neck, and torso, and progresses down the body to the arms and legs. It lasts between 3-5 days. Minor joint and muscle aches may last from 1-14 days. Rare complications such as severe joint pain and arthritis are more common in adult women.

Physical exam: The exam may reveal a faint rash, low-grade fever, and enlarged and tender lymph nodes behind the ears and at the back and sides of the neck. Redness of the eyes (conjunctivitis) is usually present. An enlarged spleen is infrequently palpated. Sometimes, purple spots (petechiae) called "Forchheimer spots" will be seen on the soft palate.

Tests: Blood tests (rubella serology) may confirm early rubella infections. As the immune system mounts a response to the virus, virus-specific antibodies appear. A nasal or throat swab may be taken for a viral culture.

Treatment

There is no treatment for rubella that will change the progression of the infection. Symptoms can be treated with over-the-counter medications to relieve the fever, headache, or muscle and joint aches. Individuals are contagious and should be quarantined for about a week after symptoms appear, especially if they work with at-risk individuals (those with altered immunity or non-immune women of childbearing age).

The most effective way to reduce the spread of rubella infections is to implement vaccination programs, particularly among children. Many states require children to be immunized before entering public school. Healthy young adults can also be vaccinated effectively. Because of the high risk of serious complications from congenital infection of the fetus, women who anticipate bearing children should be tested for their susceptibility to rubella infection. If they show susceptibility, women should be vaccinated at least 3 months before they anticipate becoming pregnant (if already pregnant, vaccination must not be done). If a woman becomes pregnant while experiencing a rubella infection or is infected with rubella during the first 2 trimesters of pregnancy, she should seek immediate medical attention to monitor the developmental progress of the fetus.

Prognosis

The prognosis for rubella is generally excellent. In otherwise healthy individuals, rubella infections clear within 2-3 weeks, resulting in lifelong immunity against the virus. Treatment of symptoms such as headache and muscle pain (myalgia) with analgesic medications helps the individual become more comfortable during the self-limiting course of the disease; the individual then recovers completely. Rubella infection or inadvertent vaccination of pregnant mothers is generally not an immediate risk to the mother, but can lead to fetal death or severe birth defects.

Differential Diagnosis

Other possibilities include a mild measles infection, scarlet fever, roseola, toxoplasmosis, infectious mononucleosis, erythema infectiosum, and other viral infections.

Specialists

- Infectious Disease Physician
- Internist
- Obstetrician

Work Restrictions / Accommodations

Because it is often difficult to determine who is at-risk, people with rubella should be isolated from other individuals for at least 1 week after the initial symptoms appear. Extended restrictions or accommodations will not be required after the overt symptoms of infection disappear.

Comorbid Conditions

Individuals with deficient immunity (such as leukemia, lymphoma, generalized cancer, AIDS) or who are undergoing steroid treatment or chemotherapy may experience more serious disease if infected with rubella. These persons should not receive the rubella vaccine. The rubella vaccination itself can cause a transient viral infection in the blood (viremia), especially in women over age 25 years. Up to 40% of such women may experience this.

Complications

The most serious complication of rubella infection occurs if a woman is infected during the first 2 trimesters of pregnancy; if this happens, serious birth defects can occur. Congenital rubella syndrome may result in the baby being born with mental retardation, congenital heart defects, cataracts, blindness, or hearing impairment. If infection occurs in the first 2 months of pregnancy, the risk of this syndrome or of spontaneous abortion is 20-50 percent. There is a small risk of the syndrome if the woman receives the vaccine too close to becoming pregnant, or early in the pregnancy.

Very rarely, rubella causes inflammation of the brain (encephalitis) or results in blood clotting abnormalities. Persons with deficient immunity (for example, leukemia, lymphoma, generalized cancer, AIDS) or who are undergoing steroid treatment or chemotherapy may experience more serious disease if infected with rubella. These persons should not receive the rubella vaccine. The rubella vaccination itself can cause a transient viral infection in the blood (viremia); up to 40% of women over age 25 may develop this.

Factors Influencing Duration

After the quarantine period, up to a week of disability may be required. The length of extended disability for complications of rubella infection will depend upon the nature and severity of the symptoms. The immune status of the person at the time of rubella infection will affect the development of complications and alter the length of disability. Diabetic individuals and those with depressed immunity (those on chemotherapy or with AIDS) may have more severe infections and require longer disability. Pregnant women who become infected with rubella may need a longer period of disability, particularly if they experience difficulties with their pregnancy or if their child is born with congenital rubella syndrome.

Length of Disability

An individual who is contagious should not be in the workplace.

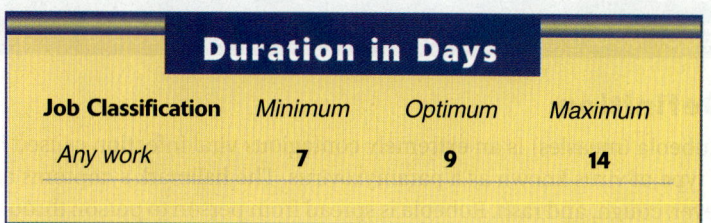

Job Classification	Minimum	Optimum	Maximum
Any work	7	9	14

Failure to Recover

If an individual fails to recover within the maximum duration expectancy period, the reader may wish to reference the following questions to assist in better understanding the specifics of an individual's medical case.

Regarding diagnosis:

- Has the individual had contact with someone with rubella?
- Does the individual have a rash?
- Did the rash start on the face, neck, and torso, and then spread to the rest of the body?
- Does the individual have a low-grade fever, joint aches, or headache?
- Does the individual have loss of appetite, malaise, runny nose, and loss of interest in personal care?
- On exam, were enlarged lymph nodes present?
- Does the individual have conjunctivitis?
- Was the spleen palpable? Was petechia present on the soft palate?
- Was rubella serology done? Antibody testing?
- Have conditions with similar symptoms been ruled out?

Regarding treatment:

- Did individual respond to conservative treatment?

Regarding prognosis:

- Was the individual isolated from other individuals who may be at risk?
- Does the individual have any conditions that may affect ability to recover?
- Is individual in the first or second trimester of pregnancy?

References

Brunell, Philip A. "Rubella." Cecil Textbook of Medicine, 20th ed, vol 2. Bennett, J. Claude, and Fred Plum, eds. Philadelphia: W.B. Saunders Company, 1996. 1761-1762.

Gershon, Anne A. "Rubella virus." Principles and Practice of Infectious Diseases, 4th ed, vol 2. Mandell, Gerald L., John E. Bennett, and Raphael Dolin, eds. New York: Churchill Livingstone, 1995. 1459-1465.

Rubeola

Other names / synonyms: Hard Measles, Measles, Nine-Day Measles, Red Measles

055, 055.0, 055.1, 055.2, 055.7, 055.8, 055.9

Definition

Rubeola (measles) is an extremely contagious viral infection caused by a type of virus known as a paramyxovirus. The hallmark symptoms are fever, cough, and rash. Rubeola is spread from person to person through airborne droplets of moisture that enter the air as the infected person coughs or sneezes. After infection, the virus incubates for 7-14 days before symptoms emerge. The individual is contagious 2-4 days before the rash appears, and remains contagious until the rash disappears. Although measles is primarily a disease of children, adults who are infected have a more severe disease. Infection results in life-long immunity.

Rubeola was once a very common disease, occurring in epidemics every 2-3 years. Widespread immunization in developed countries has resulted in a significant decrease in the number of cases reported each year. Because proof of immunization is required before a child can attend school, there are now only several thousand cases reported annually in the US. In 1996, only 488 cases were reported in the US. Most cases in the US may now be imported from other countries. Prevention is important because measles can have rare but serious complications. Approximately 90% of susceptible individuals who are exposed to the virus actually contract the disease.

Diagnosis

History: The first symptoms to appear, usually 9-11 days after exposure to the virus, generally include high fever, a hacking cough, profuse nasal discharge (coryza), and red eyes (conjunctivitis). After 3-5 days, a mildly itchy, red rash appears. Usually starting on the face or neck, the rash spreads downward, covering the whole body. Patches of rash sometimes join to produce larger blotchy areas, especially above the shoulders. Individuals may also report diarrhea, muscle soreness, general malaise, sensitivity to light (photophobia), vomiting, and abdominal pain. The rash begins to fade and the symptoms subside after 3-5 days.

Physical exam: The exam usually reveals rash, tiny bluish-white spots inside the mouth (Koplik spots), fever, and swollen lymph nodes. Upon questioning, the individual or the individual's parent may be able to confirm prior exposure to an infected individual.

Tests: Are not generally necessary for a diagnosis of rubeola. The signs and symptoms of this disease are quite characteristic, and are usually sufficient for diagnosis. However, in rare, atypical cases, blood tests during acute illness and after recovery (acute and convalescent serum), hemagglutination inhibition, or enzyme-linked immunosorbent assay (ELISA) for detection of measles antibodies can be used to confirm diagnosis. Secretions from the nose can be stained and examined under the microscope, and may reveal characteristic cells (multinucleated giant cells).

Treatment

Treatment consists of bedrest and increased fluid intake. Other treatments are aimed at reducing symptoms. If the individual is sensitive to light, it may be necessary to keep them in a dark room. Drugs to reduce fever (antipyretics) and reduce pain (analgesics) may be given. Antibiotics are not indicated unless needed to treat a secondary bacterial infection. Pregnant women exposed to rubeola are at higher risk of stillbirth, and immunocompromised individuals are at high risk of complications from rubeola. These individuals should therefore be given injections of immunoglobulin into the muscle after exposure to prevent the disease. In the US, individuals are immunized with measles, mumps, and rubella (MMR) vaccine before the age of two.

Prognosis

The vast majority of individuals will recover completely. Among the rare cases of encephalitis, about half will suffer permanent brain damage, and approximately 20% will die.

Differential Diagnosis

Several other diseases are associated with signs and symptoms that are similar to those associated with rubeola. These diseases include rubella (German measles), secondary syphilis, scarlet fever, Kawasaki's disease, toxic shock syndrome, varicella virus, Rocky Mountain spotted fever, infectious mononucleosis, secondary syphilis, and drug reactions.

Specialists

- Dermatologist
- Infectious Disease Physician
- Internist
- Neurologist

Work Restrictions / Accommodations

Bedrest is an important aspect of recovery. Because the recovery period can be long, extended sick leave may be required. Return to work prior to complete recovery is not advised. In the infectious phase, individuals should stay home to avoid spread of the disease.

Comorbid Conditions

Malnutrition and/or a compromised immune system may delay recovery or increase the risk of complications.

Complications

Rubeola is usually uncomplicated and not serious. Individuals who are malnourished or immunocompromised are the most likely candidates for complications. Severe lung and neurologic complications occur in up to 80% of immunocompromised individuals with cancer or AIDS, and death related to these complications occurs in 40-70% of the afflicted. Infection with the measles virus may also suppress the immune response, which could cause reactivation of inactive (latent) infection such as tuberculosis. The most common complications are middle ear infections (otitis media) and chest infections (pneumonia), which usually occur 2-3 days after the rash appears. Individuals infected with rubeola are particularly susceptible to additional infection with bacteria called streptococci. Blood platelet levels may drop to abnormally low levels (thrombocytopenia), resulting in a tendency to bruise and bleed easily, but this is rare. Hemorrhagic measles, also called black measles, is a severe form of measles characterized by a dark colored rash that is due to increased blood flow to the skin. Other complications may include inflammation of portions of the eye known as the conjunctiva and cornea (keratoconjunctivitis), or a temporary inflammation of the liver (hepatitis). Young adults who were inadequately immunized may develop an allergic reaction to the measles virus. This reaction is called measles syndrome and can be severe. Inflammation of the brain (encephalitis) occurs in one of 1:2000 measles cases, and 10-20% of those cases are fatal. The seizures and coma that follow may lead to mental deterioration, imbalance when walking (ataxia), or death. Seizures are common with measles, however, and are not necessarily related to encephalitis.

Rarely (about one in a million), a progressive brain disorder (subacute sclerosing panencephalitis) may develop months to years after the acute illness. Subacute sclerosing panencephalitis (characterized by seizures, muscle jerking, and mental deterioration) is not treatable and is usually fatal.

Measles during pregnancy results in stillbirth in about one-fifth of cases.

Factors Influencing Duration

Severity of the illness is related to an increased recovery period. Adults tend to experience severe symptoms and thus may recover more slowly. Complications such as pneumonia or thrombocytopenia may lengthen recovery, and encephalitis can result in permanent disability.

Length of Disability

Duration in Days

Job Classification	Minimum	Optimum	Maximum
Sedentary work	10	14	28
Light work	10	14	28
Medium work	10	14	28
Heavy work	14	21	42
Very Heavy work	14	28	42

Failure to Recover

If an individual fails to recover within the maximum duration expectancy period, the reader may wish to reference the following questions to assist in better understanding the specifics of an individual's medical case.

Regarding diagnosis:

- Did the individual have past immunization against rubeola?
- Was there a recent history of exposure to the rubeola virus?
- Did the individual present with symptoms of fever, cough and a skin rash?
- Has the diagnosis of rubeola been confirmed (usually by a blood test)?
- Have other diseases with similar symptoms been ruled out (e.g., rubella, secondary syphilis, scarlet fever, Kawasaki's disease, toxic shock syndrome, varicella virus, Rocky Mountain spotted fever, infectious mononucleosis, secondary syphilis, and drug reactions)?

Regarding treatment:

- Was conservative treatment with bedrest, fluids and antipyretics effective in reducing symptoms?
- Was immunoglobulin administered to exposed individuals who have high-risk of severe measles (pregnant or immunocompromised)?

Regarding prognosis:

- Did the individual suffer complications of rubeola infection that may be delaying or preventing recovery (e.g., pneumonia, thrombocytopenia, or encephalitis)?
- Is the individual obeying the doctor's orders (especially those related to rest and fluid intake)?
- Does the individual have conditions such as pregnancy or immune suppression that could prolong recovery?

References

Enders, Gisela. "Paramyxoviruses." Medical Microbiology. Baron, Samuel, ed. New York: Churchill Livingstone, 1991. 769-784.

Watson, Wendy. "Viral Infections." The Merck Manual of Medical Information. Berkow, Robert, ed. New York: Pocket Books, 1999. 1380-1383.

Rupture of Spleen, Traumatic
Other names / synonyms: Splenic Rupture
865, 865.0, 865.00, 865.01, 865.02, 865.09, 865.1, 865.10, 865.11, 865.12, 865.19

Definition

A ruptured spleen occurs when the organ or its blood supply has been interrupted by either a traumatic impact to the upper left abdomen or by a spontaneous event. Spleens can rupture by penetrating trauma, nonpenetrating trauma, operative trauma, or can rupture spontaneously.

The spleen is the most common intra-abdominal organ injured in blunt trauma (often associated with automobile accidents or body-contact sports), and is frequently injured in penetrating abdominal injury. Splenic ruptures can occur acutely (such as after an automobile accident) or may develop a delayed rupture from a very slow bleed. Surgeons classify splenic ruptures relative to the amount of injury to the organ with Class I having the least amount of damage and Class V with the worst.

Conditions that cause splenic enlargement (splenomegaly) such as lymphoma or mononucleosis make the spleen more fragile and susceptible to spontaneous rupture. The spleen is vulnerable to injury during operative procedures in the upper abdomen. Operations on the stomach, esophageal hiatus, vagus nerves, pancreas, left kidney and adrenal gland, and transverse and descending colon carry risk of splenic injury.

Mortality rates for splenic injury range from 10-20%, and are often due to associated injury to other organs.

Diagnosis

History: Individuals may report blunt upper abdominal trauma such as from a steering wheel during an automobile accident or the handlebars of a bicycle. In some cases, individuals may report penetrating trauma (knife or gunshot wound) to the left chest or upper abdomen. They may complain of abdominal or chest pain. At times, individuals also complain of left shoulder or neck pain. They may report feelings of lightheadedness or dizziness.

Physical exam: The diagnosis and clinical course of an isolated splenic injury is variable. Rupture of the protective outer layer of the spleen (splenic capsule) may cause significant bleeding into the abdomen and result in associated signs of abdominal distention and hemorrhagic shock. More commonly, injuries to the body of the spleen that do not disrupt major vessels cause an initial blood loss of about 500 ml that ceases spontaneously without signs of abdominal distention or shock. These types of injuries, however, have the potential to rupture at a time remote from the injury and account for the phenomenon of delayed rupture of the spleen. Consequently, these injuries must be monitored carefully.

Splenic injury resulting in blood in the abdomen produces characteristic signs and symptoms. Generalized left upper abdominal pain occurs in approximately one-third of those with splenic injury. Palpation to the left upper abdomen may cause referred pain to the tip of the left shoulder (Kehr's sign) that suggests splenic injury. Palpable rib fractures may be felt on the left side. Any penetrating (gunshot or knife) wounds to the abdomen or chest are potential sources of splenic injury and are promptly evaluated by emergency exploratory surgery.

Signs of hemorrhagic shock such as increased pulse, decreased blood pressure, sudden drop in blood pressure when positioned upright from a supine position (orthostatic hypotension), and cool skin may be associated with more significant acute injuries. In such circumstances, an emergency exploratory abdominal surgery (laparotomy) should be performed to confirm the diagnosis.

Tests: Tests may include a complete blood count (CBC) to determine presence and degree of blood loss. Individuals with splenic trauma usually have hemoglobin/hematocrit values that are 10-30% below normal. A needle sampling of the peritoneal fluid or diagnostic peritoneal lavage looks for evidence of bleeding, and continues to be an important adjunct to the diagnosis of abdominal injuries including injuries to the spleen.

In general, a CT of the abdomen may reveal the presence and approximate quantity of hemorrhage of the spleen and other adjacent structures. Ultrasound studies of the spleen are being used with greater frequency to detect evidence of free blood and splenic trauma. In the case of a delayed rupture, x-rays of the splenic vessels (splenic arteriograms) are usually taken.

Treatment

Of prime importance in the management of an individual with a ruptured spleen is treatment for shock. Depending on the mechanism of injury, management will vary. Those with sustained multiple injuries may need emergency interventions to maintain their airway and provide ventilation. Any injuries including a ruptured spleen associated with low blood pressure and rapid pulse (shock) need to be treated with rapid fluid replacement and possibly blood transfusion. If shock is severe, a large vein is often catheterized (central vein, internal carotid, brachial, or femoral vein) to rapidly administer large volumes of fluid. Individuals with signs of hemorrhagic shock are treated with a laparotomy to identify and control the source(s) of bleeding.

Treatment for a ruptured spleen in stable individuals is controversial. In the past, the individual was closely watched and the decision to perform surgery based on the serial hemoglobin and hematocrit counts and the severity of the rupture. Those with significant bleeding and associated shock were routinely treated with a laparotomy and removal of the entire spleen (splenectomy).

In recent years, there is greater interest in preserving the spleen because of its important role in immunity. Consequently, partial splenectomy or splenic repairs are being done with greater frequency and success. If surgery is the treatment, two-thirds of individuals will have their spleen repaired and one-third will have it removed. Immunizations against pneumococcal, meningococcal, and Haemophilus influenza organisms are recommended prior to splenic operations to protect the individual from postsplenectomy infections and sepsis. These immunizations are generally repeated every 5 years following splenic surgery to extend the protection.

Nonoperative management of splenic trauma is less common due to the potential for missing concomitant abdominal injuries. Likewise, nonoperative management may require significant transfusions that increase the risk of transfusion-related illnesses. A delayed rupture poses an additional problem for those treated nonoperatively. Delayed ruptures of the spleen typically occur within 2 weeks in approximately 15-30% of those treated nonoperatively. Individuals managed nonoperatively require close monitoring for a period of up to 2 weeks. In addition, hospital time is usually longer for nonoperative management (13 to 16 days) compared with operative management (7 days).

The laparoscopic approach to splenectomy is now regarded by some as preferable to open splenectomy for individuals with bleeding disorders due to its efficacy and reduction in morbidity and mortality.

Prognosis

Outcomes for both nonoperative and operative management of splenic ruptures are Good when treatment is received promptly.

Differential Diagnosis

Other possible diagnoses include ruptured left kidney, pancreatitis, and a possible lacerated liver.

Specialists

- General Surgeon
- Traumatologist

Work Restrictions / Accommodations

If individual receives surgery, once back at work, assignment of light sedentary duties may be needed until the surgical site fully heals or medical clearance is obtained from the surgeon. Those who have had a laparoscopic splenectomy may return to work and usual activities sooner, often within a week. If individuals are medically observed, they may need light sedentary duty for 1 to 3 weeks after return to work based on the severity of the splenic rupture.

Comorbid Conditions

Comorbid conditions that may lengthen recovery and disability include obesity, diabetes, and cardiovascular or pulmonary disease. Other injuries sustained during the traumatic injury of the spleen may also influence rate of recovery and disability.

Complications

Hemorrhagic shock is a common complication of a ruptured spleen along with complications such as intra-abdominal infection, shock-related bleeding disorder (disseminated intravascular coagulopathy), and infiltrative lung conditions (shock lung or adult respiratory distress syndrome).

Factors Influencing Duration

The factors that influence disability include severity of the injury to the spleen, type of surgery done, and whether the individual had any other medical conditions such as anemia, bleeding disorders, or lymphoma.

Length of Disability

Surgical treatment. Splenectomy.

Duration in Days

Job Classification	Minimum	Optimum	Maximum
Sedentary work	14	21	28
Light work	14	21	28
Medium work	28	35	42
Heavy work	35	42	56
Very Heavy work	35	42	70

Failure to Recover

If an individual fails to recover within the maximum duration expectancy period, the reader may wish to reference the following questions to assist in better understanding the specifics of an individual's medical case.

Regarding diagnosis:

- Has individual experienced recent blunt trauma (from a steering wheel, bicycle handlebars, or from participating in body-contact sports) or penetrating trauma (gunshot or knife wound)?
- Does individual have a history of an enlarged spleen (splenomegaly)?
- Has individual undergone recent surgery that may have caused splenic rupture?
- Is individual experiencing bleeding into the abdomen? Was bleeding severe enough to cause hemorrhagic shock?
- Is individual experiencing a delayed rupture from a previous injury?
- Does individual demonstrate signs of a bleeding disorder such as prolonged bleeding or bleeding from gums, wounds, or urinary tract?
- Was a recent CBC done to rule out infection or hemorrhage? Was a chest x-ray taken to rule out lung complications? Does peritoneal fluid, CT scan, or ultrasound reveal the presence of bleeding?
- If this is a delayed rupture, was a recent splenic arteriogram obtained?

Regarding treatment:

- Were emergency interventions required to maintain airway and replace fluids including possible blood transfusions?
- If signs of hemorrhagic shock, was a laparotomy done to identify and control the source(s) of bleeding?
- Was surgery required for repair or partial removal of the spleen (partial splenectomy)?
- Did individual receive appropriate vaccinations prior to surgery such as pneumococcal, meningococcal, and Haemophilus influenzae type b conjugate vaccines?

Regarding prognosis:

- Did individual receive nonoperative treatment or require surgical intervention?
- Could individual have a delayed rupture?
- Did individual experience hemorrhagic shock? Did individual develop shock-related bleeding disorder (disseminated intravascular coagulopathy or DIC)?
- Have postsurgical complications arisen, particularly infection?
- Did individual develop lung problems?
- What is the treatment plan for the complication and what is the expected outcome of this treatment?

References

Clochesy, John M., et al. Critical Care Nursing, 2nd ed. Philadelphia: W.B. Saunders Company, 1996.

Ruptured Biceps Tendon (Traumatic and Nontraumatic)
840.8

Definition

Ruptured biceps tendon is the condition where the fibrous attachment (tendon) for the biceps muscle is torn.

There are three biceps tendons, two at the shoulder (proximal tendons or the long head and short head of biceps tendons) and one at the elbow (distal biceps tendon).

Ruptures can be complete or partial although partial ruptures are rare. Distal ruptures are more disabling because they result in the complete loss of biceps muscle function. A rupture that occurs at the junction between tendon and bone is called an avulsion and is the most common type of tendon rupture. Rupture at the junction between tendon and muscle (musculotendinous junction) and within the tendon is very rare.

The cause of the majority of biceps tendon ruptures is a single traumatic incident that usually involves lifting a heavy weight while the elbow is bent at a 90-degree angle. Rupture is also caused by falling on an outstretched arm or certain sporting activities such as pitching a baseball. Nontraumatic or chronic rupture refers to spontaneous ruptures in the absence of a traumatic event that usually occurs in elderly individuals with advanced tendon degeneration. Individuals with degenerative changes of the biceps tendon, shoulder impingement syndrome, laborers, athletes, and weight lifters (especially those who use anabolic steroids) are at a higher risk of sustaining a ruptured biceps tendon. Weight lifters who use anabolic steroids are at an increased risk of sustaining a rupture at the musculotendinous junction or within the tendon.

Biceps tendon rupture is an extremely uncommon event. Ninety-six percent of biceps tendon ruptures occur in the long head of the biceps tendon, 3% in the distal biceps tendon, and 1% in the short head of the biceps tendon. The majority (80%) of biceps tendon ruptures involve the right arm. Biceps tendon rupture usually affects men between the ages of 21 and 70.

Diagnosis

History: The individual may report feeling a tearing or popping sensation followed by a sudden, sharp pain in the upper arm. Individuals may report having lifted a heavy object, suffered a fall, or participated in a sporting event. A few individuals may complain of forearm pain. Following the episode of severe pain, the individual may feel upper arm discomfort or complete pain relief. Difficulty using the arm and arm weakness may be reported. Grip strength may be decreased and individual may have difficulty opening doors or using a screwdriver. There may be a history of shoulder pain. Individuals with a partial rupture may report constant pain and arm weakness.

Physical exam: The upper arm may be swollen. Bending the elbow may reveal a lump sometimes called a "Popeye muscle" that is either too far up due to rupture of the distal tendon or too far down due to rupture of a proximal tendon. If a lump is not readily apparent, the physician may perform Ludington's test where both arms are placed on the head and the contours of both upper arms compared. The muscle defect is usually felt by touch (palpable). If it is not palpable, then a partial rupture may have occurred. The upper arm and possibly the inner elbow (antecubital fossa) may be tender to the touch. There may be black-and-blue marks beneath the skin (ecchymosis) of the upper arm.

Tests: Diagnostic tests are not usually necessary for complete biceps tendon ruptures. The diagnosis of a partial rupture may include plain x-rays, arthrography, ultrasound, or MRI.

Treatment

Partial ruptures may be treated nonsurgically or surgically. Surgical treatment involves either reimplanting the torn section of the tendon to bone (tenodesis) or cutting the tendon to produce a complete tear and treating as for an avulsion. Avulsion of the long head of the biceps tendon is usually treated nonsurgically because the injury causes only minor functional changes. However, certain young, active individuals may not tolerate any loss of function and request that a tenodesis be performed. Avulsion of the distal biceps tendon is treated by tenodesis with the use of a metal stitch (suture) anchor.

Rupture of the musculotendinous junction or rupture within the body of the tendon is treated surgically (tendinoplasty) by a ligament augmentation device or a simple folding or tucking (plication) method. Following surgery, the arm is maintained in a bent position for 4 to 5 days. Nonsurgical treatment of any biceps tendon rupture consists of nonsteroidal anti-inflammatory drugs (NSAIDs) and ice for the first 2 days then followed by heat.

Prognosis

Conservative treatment of partial or proximal biceps tendon ruptures has a good outcome. Reimplantation of the partially ruptured tendon to bone has a poor success rate. Cutting the tendon and treating it as an avulsion produces a good outcome.

Tenodesis of either proximal or distal biceps tendon avulsion injuries has an excellent outcome and restoration of normal arm strength is common. Rupture at the musculotendinous junction or within the tendon has a poor outcome. Simple plication of the tendon is not reliable. Use of a ligament augmentation device has a slightly better outcome but is still associated with an incomplete recovery. Nonsurgical treatment of long head of the biceps tendon ruptures has a good outcome with minimal loss of strength and no loss of mobility.

Differential Diagnosis

A complete biceps tendon rupture is unmistakable and a differential diagnosis is not needed. Partial rupture may have signs and symptoms in common with bursitis, bicipital tendonitis, muscle injury, tendinosis, shoulder injuries (e.g., rotator cuff tear), and impingement syndrome.

Specialists

- Orthopedic Surgeon
- Physiatrist

Rehabilitation

Basic goals in the rehabilitation of a ruptured biceps tendon is to control postoperative pain and swelling (if surgery was required) followed by regaining full motion, flexibility, strength, and endurance of the muscle/joint structures involved. The final result is aimed at returning the individual to full function for work and recreational activities with minimal risk of reinjury.

Heat treatments are helpful to reduce inflammation and pain and once appropriate, are beneficial to mildly stretch the affected muscles. Forms of heat treatment include ultrasound that uses high frequency sound waves to produce heat that penetrates deep into the involved muscles. Electrical stimulation combined with heat or cold treatment is another technique that relaxes irritated muscles in spasm.

Once movement is allowed, passive motion of the elbow is permitted only as tolerated by the individual. Range-of-motion exercises begin with the therapist bending and straightening the elbow (flexion and extension).

Other important movements of the elbow that are vital to restore are supination and pronation. Supination is movement that occurs when the elbow is bent at 90 degrees beginning with the palm of the hand facing down. The hand is then rotated to a position with the palm facing upward. Pronation is the opposite movement of supination and occurs when the palm is rotated back to a position of facing down.

This type of exercise then progresses to the individual performing some of the effort in bending and straightening of the elbow joint along with the help of the therapist.

Active range of motion follows. This can be initiated in a warm whirlpool or in conjunction with another form of heat treatment and continued until all movement is restored.

The instruction of isometric strengthening exercises begins early in the phase of elbow strengthening. Isometric exercise demands that the muscles around the elbow joint contract yet no movement takes place at the joint. An example of an isometric exercise for the elbow joint is having the individual push a hand upward against the other hand or other immovable object. Supination and pronation are also strengthened isometrically in this manner.

Once both range of motion and isometric exercises are tolerated, the individual progresses to isotonic strengthening involving movement at and around the elbow joint. An example of this type of rehabilitation exercise is strengthening with weights using weight equipment/machines and elastic bands.

After rehabilitation therapy, the individual is instructed in the performance of the exercises at home. Modifications may need to be made by the physical therapist for those with arthritis or other elbow/shoulder joint irritations.

Work Restrictions / Accommodations

Depending on work duties, the individual may need to be temporarily or permanently reassigned. The individual with a ruptured biceps tendon may be temporarily unable to lift and carry heavy objects, operate equipment, or perform other tasks that require lifting, pushing, or pulling against resistance using the injured arm. If the dominant arm or hand was affected, the individual may be unable to write legibly or type well. Individuals whose dominant arm or hand was affected may require a temporary or permanent reassignment of duties. Individuals with a proximal tendon rupture treated nonsurgically will have a permanent loss of muscle strength. If weight bearing is an important component of the individual's job duties, permanent reassignment is necessary.

Comorbid Conditions

Comorbid conditions that may influence length of disability include impingement syndrome, rotator cuff injuries, tendon degeneration, tendinitis, tendinosis, and osteoarthritis.

Complications

Proximal biceps tendon ruptures are frequently associated with impingement syndrome or rotator cuff tears. Frozen shoulder (adhesive capsulitis) is a potential complication. Left untreated, partial distal biceps tendon rupture can cause median nerve compression.

Factors Influencing Duration

Nonsurgical versus surgical treatment of a proximal tendon rupture, surgical method utilized, job demands, and individual's compliance with therapy and arm use restrictions can affect the length of disability.

Length of Disability

Duration depends on job requirements. Disability may be longer for individuals whose job duties involve pushing, pulling, or lifting against heavy resistance.

Surgical treatment.

Duration in Days

Job Classification	Minimum	Optimum	Maximum
Sedentary work	7	14	21
Light work	7	21	28
Medium work	14	42	Indefinite
Heavy work	21	84	Indefinite
Very Heavy work	21	98	Indefinite

Failure to Recover

If an individual fails to recover within the maximum duration expectancy period, the reader may wish to reference the following questions to assist in better understanding the specifics of an individual's medical case.

Regarding diagnosis:

- Did the individual sustain a traumatic injury to the arm?
- Did the individual report feeling a tearing or popping sensation followed by a sudden, sharp pain in the upper arm?
- Does the individual have difficulty using the arm or is the arm weak, particularly when gripping objects?
- Has the diagnosis been confirmed?
- Is there evidence of other arm injuries?
- Is the upper arm swollen?
- Does bending the elbow reveal a lump?
- When did the rupture occur?
- Did the individual seek out medical treatment in a timely manner?
- Did tests include x-rays, arthrography, ultrasound, and MRI?

Regarding treatment:

- Did the individual suffer a distal biceps tendon rupture? If so, was it treated promptly?
- Did the individual experience a partial or complete rupture?
- Was surgical treatment required? If so, what procedure was performed?
- Has the individual been compliant with physical therapy?
- Has the individual followed guidelines regarding restrictions on arm movements and weight bearing?
- Has the individual been compliant with taking medications and applying ice/heat as prescribed?

Regarding prognosis:

- Was the dominant or nondominant arm affected?
- Was the rupture partial or complete?
- Was the rupture distal or proximal?
- Was surgical or nonsurgical treatment required?
- Was arm strength and mobility completely restored?
- Has the individual developed frozen shoulder or nerve compression?
- Was there a lengthy delay before the individual sought out medical intervention?
- How will use of the arm be affected by complications?

References

Kessler, R.M. Management of Common Musculoskeletal Disorders: Physical Therapy Principles and Methods. Philadelphia: J.B. Lippincott Company, 1990.

Kisner, C., and L. Colby. Therapeutic Exercise Foundations and Techniques. Philadelphia: F.A. Davis Company, 1990.

Malone, Terry R., Thomas McPoil, and Arthur J. Nitz. Orthopedic and Sports Physical Therapy. St. Louis: Mosby, 1997.

Morrey, Bernard. "Biceps Tendon Injury." AAOS Instructional Course Lectures 48 (1999): 405-410.

Travis, Robert, Robert Doane, and Wayne Burkhead. "Tendon Ruptures About the Shoulder." Orthopedic Clinics of North America 31 2 (2000): 313-330.

Yamaguchi, Ken, and Randip Bindra. "Disorders of the Biceps Tendon." Disorders of the Shoulder: Diagnosis and Management. Iannotti, Joseph, and Gerald Williams, eds. Philadelphia: Lippincott, Williams & Wilkins, 1999. 159-190.

Reason for Procedure

A unilateral salpingectomy is used to remove a pregnancy in which a fertilized ovum is implanted in a fallopian tube (ectopic pregnancy). Bilateral salpingectomy is used to treat women who have been diagnosed with chronically infected fallopian tubes (salpingitis) who are not responding to treatment with antibiotics. Surgical removal of the fallopian tubes is also used as partial treatment for some cases of endometriosis and pelvic inflammatory disease.

Description

The salpingectomy procedure is performed in a hospital or outpatient clinic under local or general anesthesia, using one of three methods. Laparoscopy, the most common method, begins with a tiny incision in the abdomen in or near the naval. The surgeon inserts a slender telescope-like instrument, called a laparoscope, through the incision. A second small incision is made just above the pubic hair line, a probe is inserted, and the fallopian tubes are removed.

Another often-used method, the minilaparotomy, requires an incision about two inches long in the lower abdomen and does not employ a viewing instrument. The incision provides access for the removal of the fallopian tubes.

A third less common, more invasive method called laparotomy requires an extensive two- to five-inch incision in the lower abdomen. Two other procedures, magnified visual inspection (culdoscopy) and surgical incision in the vagina (colpotomy), facilitate approaching the fallopian tubes through the vagina rather than through the abdomen. Neither of these two procedures is used very often. Decisions regarding the most appropriate procedural method for a given woman depend on that woman's age, weight, previous lower abdominal surgeries, heart and lung disease history, and other considerations.

Prognosis

Predicted outcome after salpingectomy depends on the purpose of the procedure and the method of procedure (laparoscopy, minilaparotomy, and laparotomy).

When the purpose of the procedure is to treat infected fallopian tubes (salpingitis), removal of the fallopian tubes usually leads to successful outcome--the infection is removed along with the tube. When the purpose of the procedure is to treat endometriosis, removal of a fallopian tube does not usually lead to successful outcome because the inner lining of the uterus (endometrium) has been growing in other places, such as the ovaries, bladder, intestines, and rectum. If the purpose of the procedure is to treat ectopic pregnancy where the ovum is implanted in a fallopian tube rather than in the uterus, removal of the tube leads to successful outcome--the results of the pregnancy are removed with the tube.

Generally, most individuals recover with no problems associated with the anesthesia or the surgery with any of the three methods. Individuals treated with the laparoscopy method recover quicker with fewer problems.

After a salpingectomy, most individuals are advised to avoid strenuous exercise for several days. Most individuals are ready to return to work within a few days (if the procedure type was laparoscopic). Sexual intercourse can be resumed when the individual feels ready (usually within a week).

Rehabilitation

Rehabilitation after a salpingectomy is similar to many other abdominal and pelvic surgeries. Postoperative breathing exercises may be necessary to prevent pulmonary complications. One example is breathing outward (exhaling) into a device called a spirometer that measures the force of breathing outward. Several types of coughing exercises may also be assigned with the same intended goal. Specific exercises to reduce postoperative pain and speed recovery include progressive relaxation and deep breathing techniques. These should be performed several times a day until the pain from inhalation/exhalation is less noticeable.

An example of an exercise that helps increase circulation and prepares the individual for walking is ankle pumps. The individual elevates the feet and repeatedly moves them forward and backward 25 to 50 times. Heel slides are often instructed with the individual long sitting (sitting on a flat surface with both knees straight) and sliding the heel of the affected limb toward the buttock, holding for a count of 20 seconds. Leg raises strengthen the quadriceps and consist of the individual long sitting with the uninvolved knee in a flexed or bent position, while the involved leg is raised to the height of the opposite knee.

Training and exercises related to walking (gait training) are an important component in rehabilitation for the postoperative individual. The final step of the rehabilitation program is to incorporate activities that help the individual return to the home and previous work environment. This may include exercises that resemble the home and/or workplace. Individuals may continue these exercises until recovery from surgery is complete and pain is no longer noticeable when walking or breathing. The physical therapist may need to make modifications for those individuals who have undergone the removal of one or both fallopian tubes. Variations in rehabilitation depend on the extent and residual effects of the procedure and the individual's general health.

Work Restrictions / Accommodations

Extended sick leave may be necessary, depending on whether the procedure was a laparoscopy, minilaparotomy or laparotomy. The length of sick leave will be contingent on the age of the woman, surgical complications, and resulting diagnoses and prognoses. Strenuous physical activities and lifting at work may need to be modified temporarily. Allowances may also have to be made for rest periods at work, for shorter work hours, and/or for fewer work days per week.

Comorbid Conditions

Comorbid conditions that might influence length of disability include obesity, previous abdominal surgeries, heart and lung conditions, and allergy to pain medications.

Procedure Complications

As with any procedure performed under general anesthesia, possibilities exist for the individual to experience a reaction to the anesthesia drugs and to have breathing problems. Some individuals experience complications with the surgery itself, such as bleeding or infection. And on rare occasions, the bowels or blood vessels may be injured during surgery and may require additional surgical repair.

Factors Influencing Duration

Length of disability may be influenced by type of procedure (laparoscopy, minilaparotomy, or laparotomy), reason for the procedure, complications, and job demands related to the surgery and anesthesia.

Specialists

- Gynecologist
- Obstetrician

Length of Disability

Most individuals who are treated with laparoscopies are able to return to work or to resume previous activities with minor restrictions, such as refraining from strenuous exercise or heavy lifting for up to two weeks. Individuals treated with more invasive procedures (minilaparotomies and laparotomies) usually require a longer leave of absence from work and stricter restrictions.

Laparoscopic.

Duration in Days

Job Classification	Minimum	Optimum	Maximum
Sedentary work	3	7	21
Light work	3	7	21
Medium work	7	14	28
Heavy work	7	21	35
Very Heavy work	14	21	35

Open surgery.

Duration in Days

Job Classification	Minimum	Optimum	Maximum
Sedentary work	28	42	56
Light work	28	42	56
Medium work	42	56	70
Heavy work	42	56	70
Very Heavy work	42	56	70

References

Complications in Laparoscopic Treatment of Ectopic Pregnancy. Centre International. 01 Jan 2000. 16 Mar 2001 <http://www.chirurgie-endo.asso.fr/endosurg/6%20GEU/anglais/geu3.htm?tm>.

Ryan, C. Kistner's Gynecology and Women's Health, 7th ed. New York: Mosby, Inc., Co, 1998 16 Mar 2001 <http://home.mdconsult.com/ >.

Salpingitis

Other names / synonyms: Acute Salpingitis, Chronic Salpingitis, Fallopian Tube Abscess, Perisalpingitis, Pyosalpinx, Tubo-Ovarian Abscess, Tubo-Ovarian Inflammatory Disease

614.0, 614.1, 614.2

Definition

Salpingitis refers to inflammation of the fallopian tube. About 3 inches in length, the fallopian tubes connect each ovary with the uterus (womb). The fallopian tube transports an egg from the ovary to the uterus and is the site of fertilization of the egg. When infected, fallopian tubes often develop scar tissue. This scarring can create a blockage that prevents an egg from reaching the uterus. Salpingitis also greatly increases the risk of tubal (ectopic) pregnancy. It is often seen in individuals with pelvic inflammatory disease (PID).

Inflammation of a fallopian tube is usually caused by an infection that has spread upward from the vagina, cervix, or uterus. The most common infections are chlamydia and gonorrhea, both sexually transmitted diseases. Salpingitis can also result from an infection following childbirth, miscarriage, or abortion. An inflammation of the abdominal lining (peritonitis) or even a blood-borne infection such as tuberculosis can also cause salpingitis.

Mucus and other secretions normally help prevent the spread of any infections coming from the cervix or vagina. During ovulation and menstruation, these defenses are less effective. If menstrual blood flows backwards from the uterus into the fallopian tubes, it can carry infectious organisms with it. This may explain why symptoms of salpingitis begin immediately after menstruation more often than at other times.

More than 100,000 women in the US cannot become pregnant each year as a result of scarring in the fallopian tube.

Diagnosis

History: Symptoms include severe lower abdominal and pelvic pain on both sides of the body, frequent urination, headache, and a vague feeling of being sick (malaise), nausea with possible vomiting, and often an abnormal vaginal discharge. Since the abdomen is very tender, the woman may report that she is most comfortable lying on her back with her legs bent at the knee. Even though it can seriously damage the

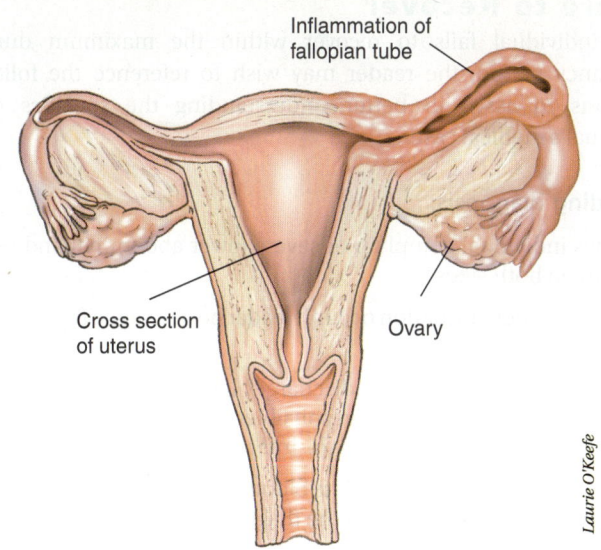

fallopian tubes, infection caused by chlamydia may produce only minor symptoms or no symptoms at all.

Physical exam: The exam may determine the location and nature of the pain. Although a vaginal examination may be very painful, it can reveal the presence of any abnormal vaginal or cervical discharge and any evidence of infection on the cervix itself. A fever may or may not be present.

Tests: Cultures are done to identify the organisms responsible for the infection. Although quick lab tests done in the doctor's office (using stains, dyes, and microscope) can identify many organisms, they may be slightly less accurate. More than one organism may be present simultaneously and could be overlooked. Therefore, many doctors prefer to use both the rapid lab test (to get a faster diagnosis) and the cultures to increase the chance of an accurate diagnosis.

Infection may be confirmed by a complete blood test (CBC) that indicates a high number of white blood cells. A urinalysis and urine culture may also be done to rule out a urinary tract infection. A pregnancy test may be needed to rule out a tubal pregnancy.

A laparoscopy may be done to confirm the diagnosis and rule out conditions with similar symptoms such as tubal pregnancy or appendicitis. Laparoscopy is a surgical procedure where a small, lighted microscope is inserted through a tiny incision into the abdomen. This allows the doctor to visually examine the fallopian tubes and surrounding area.

Treatment

Treatment usually includes antibiotics, pain medication, increased fluids, and bed rest. Because more than one organism may be responsible for the infection, several antibiotics may be given at the same time. Since the symptoms may go away before the infection is completely cured, it is very important that the complete course of antibiotics is finished as prescribed. Individuals should be reevaluated after treatment begins to be sure the antibiotics are effective. All sexual partners should be examined for sexually transmitted diseases and promptly treated as well. Untreated salpingitis can further develop into PID.

Surgery may be necessary to correct complications (drain abscesses) or to remove damaged tubes that do not respond to antibiotic therapy (salpingectomy). This sometimes involves removing the uterus and ovaries as well (hysterectomy with salpingo-oophorectomy).

Prognosis

A favorable outcome is directly related to the promptness of appropriate treatment. Infections sometimes persist despite treatment and can result in persistent backache, abdominal pain, pelvic pain, frequent heavy menstrual periods, and pain during sexual intercourse.

Differential Diagnosis

Conditions with similar symptoms include appendicitis, ectopic pregnancy, ruptured cyst, endometriosis, acute urinary tract infection, regional enteritis, and ulcerative colitis.

Specialists

- General Surgeon
- Gynecologist
- Infectious Disease Physician
- Obstetrician

Work Restrictions / Accommodations

Work responsibilities may need to be adjusted depending on the individual's job requirements. If a surgical procedure was necessary, light or sedentary work may be appropriate

Comorbid Conditions

Endometriosis or sexually transmitted disease may lengthen disability.

Complications

Pus may collect within the fallopian tube (pyosalpinx), sometimes followed by fluid collecting in the fallopian tube (hydrosalpinx). Pus collecting within the abdominal cavity can cause a pelvic abscess. Abscesses may need to be surgically drained.

Factors Influencing Duration

Length of disability depends on the severity and extent of the infection, and the method and response to treatment.

Length of Disability

Medical treatment.

Duration in Days

Job Classification	Minimum	Optimum	Maximum
Sedentary work	7	14	28
Light work	7	14	28
Medium work	7	14	28
Heavy work	7	14	28
Very Heavy work	7	14	28

Percutaneous or transvaginal aspiration.

Duration in Days

Job Classification	Minimum	Optimum	Maximum
Sedentary work	3	7	14
Light work	3	7	14
Medium work	3	7	14
Heavy work	7	14	14
Very Heavy work	7	14	14

Salpingectomy, laparoscopic.

Duration in Days

Job Classification	Minimum	Optimum	Maximum
Sedentary work	3	7	21
Light work	3	7	21
Medium work	7	14	28
Heavy work	7	21	35
Very Heavy work	14	21	35

Salpingo-oophorectomy or abdominal hysterectomy.

Duration in Days

Job Classification	Minimum	Optimum	Maximum
Sedentary work	28	42	56
Light work	28	42	56
Medium work	42	56	70
Heavy work	42	70	84
Very Heavy work	42	84	98

Failure to Recover

If an individual fails to recover within the maximum duration expectancy period, the reader may wish to reference the following questions to assist in better understanding the specifics of an individual's medical case.

Regarding diagnosis:

- Does individual complain of severe lower abdominal and pelvic pain on both sides?
- Does frequent urination occur? Headache or a vague feeling of being sick (malaise)?
- Is there abnormal vaginal discharge? If so, were cultures taken to identify the organism(s) responsible for the infection? What organism(s) is responsible for the infection?
- Has individual had a complete blood count (CBC)? Was a laparoscopy performed to confirm the diagnosis?

Regarding treatment:

- Is individual taking antibiotics exactly as prescribed? Are antibiotics treating the infection successfully?
- Were all sexual partners examined and treated?
- Were the tubes damaged to the point of requiring removal? Does individual require removal of the uterus and tubes?

Regarding prognosis:

- Was antibiotic therapy appropriate for the organism(s) identified? Is additional antibiotic therapy recommended?
- Have any associated conditions or complication developed such as abscess or pelvic inflammatory disease that could impact length of recovery?
- Has adequate time elapsed for recovery?
- Has individual developed an abscess? Does it need to be surgically drained?
- Has individual developed pelvic inflammatory disease? If so, was it addressed in the treatment plan?

References

"Pelvic Inflammatory Disease." Centers for Disease Control and Prevention 1998 27 Feb 2001 <http://192.215.104.222/obgyn/cobra/cobra/TEXT/PROTOCOL/Pid.htm>.

"Salpingitis." InteliHealth 24 Feb 2000 27 Feb 2001 <http://www.intelihealth.com/IH/ihtIH/WSIHW000/9339/23819.html>.

Pelvic Inflammatory Disease (PID) Salpingitis. Erie County Department of Health. 1995. 22 Feb 2001 <http://www.noah-health.org/english/nycounty/erie/pid.html>.

Ryan, C. Kistner's Gynecology and Women's Health, 7th ed. New York: Mosby, Inc., Co, 1998 16 Mar 2001 <http://home.mdconsult.com/ >.

Salpingo-oophorectomy

Other names / synonyms: Excision of Fallopian Tube and Ovary

65.4, 65.6, 65.61, 65.62

Definition

Salpingo-oophorectomy is a surgical procedure involving the removal of one or both the fallopian tubes (salpingectomy) and one or both ovaries (oophorectomy). In a unilateral salpingo-oophorectomy procedure, only one fallopian tube and one ovary are removed. In the bilateral procedure, both fallopian tubes and both ovaries are removed. In women under the age of 40, an attempt is made whenever possible to preserve ovarian function by removing only one ovary or a part of one ovary.

In 1997, 366,000 bilateral salpingo-oophorectomies were performed in the US with over half of the procedures performed on women between the ages of 45 and 64. Of the 82,000 unilateral salpingo-oophorectomies reported, two-thirds were performed on women between the ages of 15 and 44.

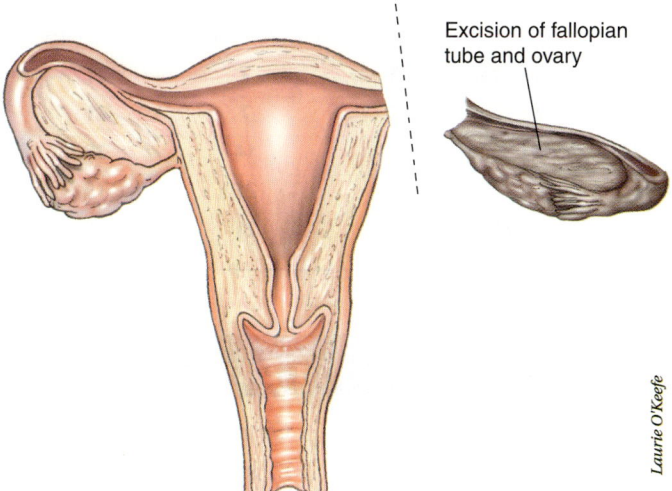

Excision of fallopian tube and ovary

Laurie O'Keefe

Reason for Procedure

A salpingo-oophorectomy may be performed to remove fluid-filled sacs (cysts), benign tumors (fibromas or teratomas), or abscesses. It is also done to treat chronic inflammations of the fallopian tubes (chronic salpingitis or tuberculosis salpingitis), pelvic inflammatory disease, endometrial cells in the pelvic cavity (endometriosis), and breast and ovarian cancer. The procedure is used to remove the results of a pregnancy that develops in a fallopian tube rather than the uterus (ectopic pregnancy).

Salpingo-oophorectomy may also be performed with a hysterectomy as a part of the treatment for uterine cancer or for treatment of a cancerous tumor derived from placental tissue (choriocarcinoma). Salpingo-oophorectomy is used in breast cancer cases when the physician considers that a reduction in the amount of hormones produced by the ovaries (estrogens) may slow the growth of the cancer. Besides treating existing ovarian cancer, the procedure is sometimes used to remove healthy ovaries as a preventive (prophylactic) measure in reducing the risk of ovarian cancer in high-risk women.

Description

The salpingo-oophorectomy procedure is performed in a hospital or outpatient clinic under local or general anesthesia. Laparoscopy is the most common method and begins with a tiny incision in the abdomen in or near the naval. The surgeon inserts a slender telescope-like instrument (laparoscope) through the incision. A second small incision is made just above the pubic hairline and a probe inserted to locate and remove the ovaries and fallopian tubes.

Another often-used method is called the minilaparotomy. This requires an incision about 2 inches long in the lower abdomen and does not employ a viewing instrument. The incision provides access for the removal of the ovaries and fallopian tubes.

A third, less common, more invasive method is called laparotomy and requires an extensive 2- to 5-inch incision in the lower abdomen.

Two other procedures called magnified visual inspection (culdoscopy) and surgical incision in the vagina (colpotomy), respectively, facilitate reaching the ovaries and fallopian tubes through the vagina rather than the abdomen. Neither of these procedures is often used.

Decisions regarding the most appropriate method to be used depend on the woman's age, weight, previous lower abdominal surgeries, heart and lung conditions, and other considerations.

Prognosis

Predicted outcome after salpingo-oophorectomy depends on the purpose for the procedure (removal of cysts, benign tumors, abscesses and treatment of ovarian cancer, endometriosis, or pelvic inflammatory diseases), the method of the procedure (laparoscopy, minilaparotomy, and laparotomy), and whether the procedure was unilateral or bilateral.

If the purpose for the procedure is to remove cysts, benign tumors, and abscesses located in or on the ovaries or fallopian tubes, removal of the ovaries and fallopian tubes (in most cases) leads to successful outcome. If the purpose of the procedure is to treat endometriosis where the inner lining of the uterus (endometrium) grows in or on the fallopian tubes and ovaries as well as in the uterus, removal of the tubes and ovaries leads to successful outcome. If, however, endometrial growth is occurring at other body sites such as the intestines, bladder, and rectum then treatment with salpingo-oophorectomy is not completely successful.

If the purpose of the procedure is treatment of ovarian cancer, the success of the procedure depends on the stage of the cancer. If the cancer has spread outside the ovaries and fallopian tubes, a salpingo-oophorectomy provides only partial treatment. It delays the spread of the cancer and alleviates symptoms but is not a cure. Similarly, if the purpose for the procedure is treatment of pelvic inflammatory disease and the inflammation is present at sites other than the fallopian tubes and ovaries, the treatment is not completely successful.

In general, most individuals recover with no problems associated with the anesthesia or the surgery with any of the three methods. Individuals treated with the laparoscopy method recover quicker with fewer problems. Whether the procedure is unilateral or bilateral usually does not affect outcome because the effect of the procedure and the healing from the surgery occur at much the same rate for removal of one or both fallopian tubes and ovaries. However, whether one or both ovaries are removed, hormonal complications for premenopausal women may arise.

Specialists

- Gynecologist
- Obstetrician

Work Restrictions / Accommodations

Extended sick leave may be necessary depending on whether the method was a laparoscopy, minilaparotomy, or laparotomy. The length of sick leave is contingent on the age of the woman, surgical complications, and resulting diagnoses and prognoses. Strenuous physical activities and lifting at work may need to be modified temporarily. Allowances may also have to be made for rest periods at work, shorter work hours, and/or fewer workdays per week.

Comorbid Conditions

Comorbid conditions that may influence length of disability include obesity, previous lower abdominal surgeries, heart and lung conditions, and allergy to pain and anesthesiology medications.

Procedure Complications

As with any procedure performed under general anesthesia, reaction to the anesthesia and breathing problems are possible complications. Some individuals experience complications with the surgery itself such as bleeding, infection, or bands of scar tissue (adhesions). On rare occasions, the bowels or blood vessels may be injured during surgery and require additional surgical repair.

Longer-term complications occur when ovaries are removed prior to menopause. When unilateral salpingo-oophorectomy is used for premenopausal women, normal hormone production continues in the remaining ovary. However, when bilateral salpingo-oophorectomy is used for premenopausal women, normal hormone production is halted. This causes acute menopause, a condition that often requires hormone replacement therapy (HRT). Because estrogen levels of premenopausal women are higher than postmenopausal women, premenopausal women require a much higher dose of estrogen or hormone replacement than women entering menopause naturally.

Another complication of the removal of both fallopian tubes and both ovaries occurs for premenopausal women considering becoming pregnant. After the procedure, the woman is sterile.

Factors Influencing Duration

Length of disability may be influenced by type of procedure (laparoscopy, minilaparotomy, or laparotomy), reason for the procedure, and complications related to the surgery and anesthesia. Most individuals are ready to return to work within a few days (in laparoscopic procedures).

Length of Disability

Most individuals treated with laparoscopies can return to work or resume previous activities with minor restrictions such as refraining from strenuous exercise or heavy lifting for up to 2 weeks. Individuals treated with more invasive procedures (minilaparotomies and laparotomies) usually require a longer leave of absence from work and stricter restrictions.

Laparoscopic.

Duration in Days

Job Classification	Minimum	Optimum	Maximum
Sedentary work	3	7	21
Light work	3	7	21
Medium work	7	14	28
Heavy work	7	21	35
Very Heavy work	14	21	35

Open surgery.

Duration in Days

Job Classification	Minimum	Optimum	Maximum
Sedentary work	28	42	56
Light work	28	42	56
Medium work	42	56	70
Heavy work	42	70	84
Very Heavy work	42	84	98

References

Ableoff, Martin D., et al. Clinical Oncology, 2nd ed. Philadelphia: Churchill Livingstone, 2000 4 Feb 2001 <http://home.mdconsult.com/ >.

Turkington, Carol A. Salpingo-oophoretomy. Gale Research, Inc. & Midlife Women's Network. 01 Jan 2000. 4 Feb 2001 <http://www.buildingbetterhealth.com/article/gale/100084011>.

Sarcoidosis

Other names / synonyms: Besnier-Boeck Disease, Boeck's Sarcoid, Lofgren's Syndrome, Schaumann's Disease

135

Definition

Sarcoidosis is characterized by collections of inflammatory cells (white blood cells). These collections are called granulomas. Granulomas occur primarily in the lungs, often in the skin and eye, and less frequently in other body organs.

The disease is temporary and causes no lasting damage in most individuals. In some individuals, however, the disease is fatal.

The disease first affects lymph glands in the chest. Early lung involvement causes inflammation of the air pockets (alveoli) within the lung (alveolitis). Although this inflammation affects pulmonary function, the inflammation is reversible. If the disease advances, the inflammation develops into scarring (fibrosis). Fibrotic damage is permanent.

Although the cause of sarcoidosis is unknown, it may be an autoimmune disease. In an autoimmune disease, the body's own immune system causes the disease and its symptoms.

Sarcoidosis occurs mainly between the ages of 20 and 40 years. In the United States, the incidence is 5 cases per 100,000 person for whites, and 40 cases per 100,000 for blacks. White females develop the disease at the same rate as white males. Black females, however, have twice the rate of disease as black males. There is a higher incidence of disease in individuals of Scandinavian, German, Irish, Japanese and Puerto Rican descent. In Scandinavia, the incidence is 64 cases per 100,000 persons.

Diagnosis

History: Symptoms vary depending on the organs involved and the extent of involvement. Some individuals have no symptoms. Symptoms, when present, typically include a dry cough, shortness of breath, pain in the eye or visual disturbances, and painful joints. There can be generalized symptoms of fatigue, fever, aching muscles, or loss of appetite.

Physical exam: Sarcoidosis is often recognized by three physical signs: enlarged lymph nodes in the chest, a red raised rash (erythema nodosum), and inflammation in the eye (uveitis). Eye inflammation may cause redness, pain, decreased vision, and inflammatory cells and nodules within the eye. There may also be enlargement of the liver and spleen and signs specific to involvement of other organs. Involvement of the heart may be evidenced by abnormal rhythm (arrhythmia) or enlargement (cardiomyopathy). Involvement of the central nervous system (CNS) may be evidenced by paralysis, particularly of the facial muscles (Bell's palsy).

Tests: Chest x-ray will show enlarged lymph nodes and/or infiltrates of the lungs. Biopsy is often not necessary, but may be performed on tissue from bronchia, skin, lymph nodes, conjunctivae, salivary glands, or liver. Microscopic examination of biopsied tissue may show the collections of white blood cells (granulomas).

Blood tests typically show elevated calcium, liver enzymes, and gamma-globulin. Blood angiotensin-converting enzyme (ACE) is elevated in 60% of individuals with sarcoidosis.

Pulmonary function tests may be used to detect decreased lung function. If the heart is involved, an electrocardiogram (ECG) may be performed to check heart function.

Treatment

The decision to treat depends on the individual's symptoms, the organs involved, and the extent of involvement. Individuals with disease involving the lungs, skin, liver, or joints are treated based on their symptoms. Mild symptoms typically require no treatment. Individuals with more significant symptoms or those with disease involving the eye, heart, or central nervous system do require treatment.

Corticosteroid drugs are prescribed to reduce inflammation, relieve symptoms, and prevent organ damage. Treatment is continued for up to 1 year, during which time the drug is gradually tapered off or taken only every other day. If an individual can't take corticosteroids or doesn't respond to the drug, a stronger immunosuppressant drug is given. A topical steroid may be added to the oral corticosteroids to treat eye involvement. Treatment specific to other organ damage is also given. The individual should follow a low-calcium, low-salt diet.

Severe fibrosis of an organ has been treated, rarely, with organ transplant. Radiation has also been used to treat localized central nervous system involvement.

When treatment is completed, the individual should be checked every 3 months for 1 to 2 years. Chest x-ray and pulmonary function tests are typically used to monitor disease activity and response to treatment.

Prognosis

The predicted outcome for sarcoidosis is variable. Generally, the prognosis is excellent. Most people recover fully within 2 to 3 years without treatment. Individuals taking corticosteroids typically begin to see improvement within 2 to 3 weeks. Approximately 15% to 20% of individuals develop permanent lung damage, and 5-7% will die from lung failure. Permanent lung damage is not reversible with drug therapy. Lung transplant with a matched donor lung is the only strategy that returns a healthy lung to an individual with permanent lung damage and failure. Limited references to the effect of radiation on localized CNS lesions demonstrate some success.

Differential Diagnosis

Many diseases have similar lesions or symptoms: tuberculosis, Hodgkin's disease, malignancies or metastatic cancer, collagen disorders, parasitic infection, idiopathic hemosiderosis, infectious mononucleosis, enlarged pulmonary arteries, pulmonary eosinophilia, berylliosis, chronic inhalation of coal dust or silica, brucellosis, Q fever, biliary cirrhosis, Wegener's granulomatosis, drug reactions, and other granulomatous lung diseases, such as lymphomatoid granulomatosis, Churg-Strauss syndrome, necrotizing sarcoid granulomatosis, and bronchocentric granulomatosis.

Specialists

- Cardiologist
- Dermatologist
- Internist
- Occupational Medicine Physician
- Ophthalmologist
- Pulmonologist

Rehabilitation

Rehabilitation of sarcoidosis is dependent on the region of the body affected. If the individual has a lung affected by the disease, the disorder is first treated then followed by pulmonary rehabilitation as needed for the recovery period. Physical therapy improves ventilation of the individual experiencing sarcoidosis through the use of breathing exercises. Techniques to strengthen the muscles used in breathing include having the individual assume a relaxed sitting position while leaning forward and resting the forearms on the thighs or a pillow in the lap.

Once breathing returns, focus is then placed on strength and endurance by adding gradual strengthening exercises that incorporate aerobic-type activity into the rehabilitation program. By building endurance, the individual increases the ability to work and the resistance to fatigue. As endurance increases without shortness of breath, active upper and lower extremity exercises are initiated that use very light resistance in addition to light aerobic activities like brisk walking and low-resistance biking. Frequency of the program may vary somewhat depending on the individual's general health.

The rehabilitation of individuals with sarcoidosis may need to be modified depending on the region of the body most affected, especially in cases where the central nervous system is involved.

Work Restrictions / Accommodations

Sarcoidosis is generally not debilitating. The individual's lungs should be protected by avoiding exposure to smoke, dust, and chemicals. Additional work restrictions depend on the location of the lesions and the extent of damage to the affected tissues or organs. If the lungs or heart are affected, appropriate work accommodations may be required until the symptoms subside. Long-term accommodations may be required if the disease relapses, persists for long periods or causes permanent damage to essential tissues and organs.

Comorbid Conditions

Presence of other lung disorders, such as pneumoconiosis due to chronic inhalation of dust, or infectious disease, such as tuberculosis, may lengthen disability. Conditions that would contraindicate corticosteroid use may complicate treatment and prolong recovery. Contraindications to corticosteroid use include diabetes, hypertension, and peptic ulcers.

Complications

Complications of sarcoidosis depend upon the organ affected, the extent of disease, and the time to resolution. Lesions in the muscles, heart, lungs, liver, spleen, central nervous system or eyes may be expected to result in more complications than lesions of the skin or lymph nodes. For example, heart involvement can lead to congestive heart failure and serious arrhythmias. Eye involvement may lead to blindness, although this is rare.

Sarcoidosis and the corticosteroid drugs leave a person vulnerable to certain infections: tuberculosis, aspergillar fungus balls, candidiasis, and cryptococcosis.

Factors Influencing Duration

The length of disability is influenced by the size and location of the lesions, the organs or tissues affected and the response to treatment.

Length of Disability

Length of disability is variable. Disability may be permanent.

Duration in Days

Job Classification	Minimum	Optimum	Maximum
Sedentary work	7	14	42
Light work	7	14	42
Medium work	7	14	42
Heavy work	7	14	56
Very Heavy work	7	14	56

Failure to Recover

If an individual fails to recover within the maximum duration expectancy period, the reader may wish to reference the following questions to assist in better understanding the specifics of an individual's medical case.

Regarding diagnosis:

- Does the individual have symptoms suggestive of sarcoidosis, such as shortness of breath, persistent cough, or a rash on the face, arms or shins, eye irritation, weight loss, fatigue, night sweats, fever, and malaise?
- Does the individual have an ethnic background (black, Scandinavian, German, Irish or Puerto Rican) that puts them at increased risk of developing the disease?
- Did the symptoms arise between the ages of 20 and 40 years old?
- Were the findings in the physical exam consistent with the characteristic findings in sarcoidosis (enlarged chest lymph nodes, rash, eye inflammation)?
- Were other conditions with similar features ruled out?

Regarding treatment:

- Based on the severity of symptoms was the appropriate treatment administered? Were associated organ specific symptoms addressed in the treatment plan? Were the corticosteroids tapered off appropriately?
- Has the individual been monitored every 3 months following completion of treatment?
- Has the individual made appropriate lifestyle changes (diet, smoking cessation etc)?
- Were other more aggressive treatments (radiation therapy or organ transplant) indicated?

Regarding prognosis:

- Has sufficient time passed since diagnosis?
- Did the individual suffer any permanent damage from advanced disease?
- Does the individual have any conditions (other lung disorders) that may complicate treatment or impact recovery?
- Did the individual suffer any opportunistic infections (tuberculosis, aspergillar fungus balls, candidiasis, and cryptococcosis) associated with the disease or corticosteroid use that impacted recovery and prognosis?

References

Baughman, Robert. "Sarcoidosis." Griffith's 5-minute Clinical Consult. Dambro, Mark, and Jo Griffith, eds. Philadelphia: Lippincott, Williams & Wilkins, 1999. 964-965.

Du Bois, R.M. "Sarcoidosis." Conn's Current Therapy 2000, 52nd ed. Rakel, Robert, ed. Philadelphia: W.B. Saunders Company, 2000. 224-228.

Kisner, C., and L. Colby. Theraputic Exercise Foundations and Techniques. Philadelphia: F.A. Davis Company, 1990.

Sarcoidosis. National Heart, Lung, and Blood Institute. 01 Jul 1995. 28 Sept 2000 <http://www.nhlbi.nih.gov/health/public/lung/other/sarcoidosis/index.htm>.

Scully, Rosemary M., and Marylou R. Barnes. Physical Therapy. Philadelphia: J.B. Lippincott Company, 1989.

Simon, Harvey. "Management of Sarcoidosis." Primary Care Medicine, 3rd ed. Goroll, Allan, Lawrence May, and Albert Mulley Philadelphia: Lippincott-Raven, 1995. 279-285.

Scalenectomy
83.45

Definition

Scalenectomy is a controversial surgical procedure that divides the anterior and/or middle scalene muscle, a superficial muscle in the front of the neck. The muscle may be either divided or a segment of it removed. It is often performed at the same time as a more extensive procedure such as removal of the first rib.

Scalenectomy is part of a surgical treatment for thoracic outlet syndrome (TOS) that has failed conservative treatment or with increasing neurovascular symptoms. TOS is caused by compression of the nerves (brachial plexus) or blood supply (subclavian artery and vein) to the arm. This syndrome is usually marked by pain, tingling, or numbness in the hand or arm, and can include coldness or difficulty using the arm or hand. Thoracic outlet syndrome may also be called anterior scalene syndrome or costoclavicular syndrome, all of which produce similar symptoms.

Thoracic outlet syndrome may be the result of traumatic injury such as whiplash of the neck, or related to posture, anatomy and activity. TOS is slightly more common in woman than men. The incidence of TOS has been reported as much higher in the United States than in other countries.

Reason for Procedure

Scalenectomy is used in the surgical treatment of thoracic outlet syndrome (TOS), either alone or combined with resection of the first rib and/or removal of a cervical rib.

The brachial plexus and subclavian vessels pass between the anterior and middle scalene muscles, and can become compressed between these two muscles. Cutting or removing a segment of the anterior or middle scalene muscle can relieve the compression if it is occurring there. Compression can also occur from the first rib, which forms part of the thoracic outlet along with the scalene muscles, especially if the rib has an abnormal anatomy.

A congenital first rib may also be present and removed during the surgery. Scalenectomy may also be done subsequent to first rib removal if that operation failed to give lasting relief of thoracic outlet syndrome. However, surgery should be reserved for in cases in which appropriate nonoperative treatment over several months has failed, or if there are progressive neurovascular complications.

Description

Scalenectomy involves removing a section of the scalene muscle in the lower neck. It is performed as an inpatient and under general anesthesia.

Removal of the anterior or middle section of the scalene muscle is performed through an incision in the neck above the collarbone (supraclavicular). The muscle is identified, separated from the nerves and vessels (dissected) and a small section removed, creating a larger space for the nerves and vessels exiting the neck. Most commonly, a small part of the anterior scalene muscle is taken. The procedure is sometimes combined with the removal or resection of the first rib or a congenital cervical rib. Removal or scar tissue (adhesions) may be necessary as well, to relieve pressure on the nerves and vessels in the thoracic outlet. The area is sutured closed and a soft dressing is applied.

Prognosis

Various studies report that successful outcome is higher in individuals treated early after onset of thoracic outlet syndrome. The procedure alone, without rib removal (resection), appears to have as good a result as those done in combination in some studies. Those individuals with work related injuries appear to have less successful outcome.

Specialists

- General Surgeon
- Neurosurgeon
- Orthopedic Surgeon
- Vascular Surgeon

Rehabilitation

Most individuals leave the hospital the next day after surgery. A sling is worn for the first 48 hours, including at night. It is important to limit use of the sling after the first 2 days to ensure proper mobility of the shoulder. Exercises to improve shoulder mobility are taught to individuals once they leave the hospital. These exercises may include pendulum swings, where the individual bends from the waist, using a chair for support, and lets the arm swing loosely in a circular motion in each direction. Lifting over 5 pounds is prohibited unless approved by the treating physician.

Physical therapy may be prescribed to improve postural imbalances and muscle weakness in the upper torso that may have contributed to the initial injury. An important aspect of proper upper torso functioning is for the individual to learn proper breathing techniques. Muscles of the chest, shoulders, and rib cage may become tight on both sides (bilaterally) or on a single side (unilaterally) if the individual has poor breathing techniques. Chest mobilization exercises are initiated as soon as tolerated. One goal of chest mobilization is to combine trunk stretching with respiration. An example of a chest mobilization exercise is when the individual sits in a chair and clasps his or her hands behind the head with elbows pressing back, which stretches the chest muscles (pectoralis). From this stretched position, the individual exhales and brings the elbows together while simultaneously slightly bending forward. While moving back to the stretched position, the individual inhales

Stretching of the neck and pectoralis muscles is an important aspect of maintaining flexibility of the neck and upper torso. Neck stretching can be done passively or actively. A stretching program may be maintained for as long as 2 years after surgery to minimize the effects of scar tissue contracture. Once the incision has healed and full range of motion for the shoulder is achieved, the individual may engage in body core strengthening and balance using such equipment as a Swiss Ball.

Return to full function is dependent on the initial cause of injury.

Work Restrictions / Accommodations

Work may be temporarily modified to allow for decreased range of motion in the head or arm.

Conservative management of thoracic outlet syndrome includes restriction of work above shoulder level or with the arm extended forward.

Comorbid Conditions

Because psychiatric conditions may lengthen disability, a psychological evaluation is often recommended before surgery. Coexisting cervical nerve root impingement or other, more distal peripheral nerve entrapment (e.g., carpal tunnel syndrome) may also prolong or worsen disability.

Procedure Complications

Complications of the procedure include infection, nerve damage, collapsed lung (pneumothorax) and failure to relieve symptoms.

Factors Influencing Duration

Complications, extent of ongoing symptoms, and job demands may impact duration of disability.

Length of Disability

Duration of disability depends on relief of symptoms of thoracic outlet syndrome and the relation to job requirements. Heavy lifting may be restricted.

Controversial procedure.

Duration in Days

Job Classification	Minimum	Optimum	Maximum
Sedentary work	7	14	21
Light work	14	21	28
Medium work	21	28	35
Heavy work	28	42	84
Very Heavy work	28	42	84

References

"770 Consecutive Supraclavicular First Rib Resections for Thoracis Outlet Syndrome." Annals of Vascular Surgery. PubMed, 01 Sep 1996 11 Jan 01 <http://www.ncbi.nlm.nih.gov/entrez/query.fcgi>.

"The Treatment of Thoracic Outlet Syndrome: A Comparison of Different Operations." Journal of Vascular Surgery. PubMed, 1989 626-634. 08 Jan 2001 <http://www.ncbi.nlm.nih.gov/entrez/query.fcgi>.

Schwartz, Seymour, MD. Principles of Surgery. New York: McGraw-Hill, 1999.

Thoracic Outlet Syndrome. UCLA Medical School. 01 Jul 2000. 06 Jul 2000 <http://www.surgery.medsch.ucla.edu/gonda/dx_TOS.htm>.

Schizoaffective Disorder

Other names / synonyms: Schizo-Affective Psychosis
295.7, 296, 296.4

Definition

Schizoaffective disorder is a combination of a thought disorder, mood disorder, and anxiety disorder characterized by features of both schizophrenia and a significant emotional disturbance resembling either major depression (depressive type) or mania (bipolar type). The psychotic aspects (fixed, untrue beliefs [delusions]), hearing voices or seeing visions (hallucinations), disorganized speech, disorganized behavior, or severely diminished emotions, speech, or activity are present continuously, with the mood disturbance present for a significant portion of that time.

Manic episodes are associated with sudden elation, euphoria, or extreme irritability. Depressive episodes are characterized by sadness, feeling worthless or hopeless, loss of pleasure and interest in life with thoughts of death or suicide attempts. The illness can last for years, and there is often impairment of occupational and social functioning and basic self-care.

Onset can be any at age from adolescence onward. Schizoaffective disorder affects more women than men.

Diagnosis

History: Individual has a continuous illness with psychotic features combined with an emotional disturbance (mania or major depression) present for a significant part of the overall illness. Delusions or hallucinations are noted for at least 2 weeks, separate and distinct from the mood disturbance. A typical history consists of hearing voices for 2 months, becoming severely depressed for the next 3 months while still hearing the voices, then recovering from depression but continuing to have auditory hallucinations.

DSM-IV criteria require an uninterrupted period of illness with symptoms meeting criterion A for schizophrenia (two or more of the following): delusions, hallucinations, disorganized speech, grossly disorganized or catatonic behavior, or negative symptoms such as flat or bland emotional affect. During that time, delusions or hallucinations must be present for at least 2 weeks in the absence of prominent mood symptoms. At some time during the illness, there must be either a major depressive episode, manic episode, or mixed episode meeting DSM-IV criteria as described. Symptoms must not be due to the direct effects of a substance such as drugs or alcohol or a general medical condition such as endocrine disease.

Physical exam: The exam does not contribute significantly to the diagnosis other than to rule out neurological abnormalities that may suggest another diagnosis. Some individuals with this disorder may have abnormal eye movements (optokinetic nystagmus) when asked to count the stripes on a rotating drum or cloth moved before the eyes. Observation of the individual's orientation, dress, mannerisms, behavior, and content of speech provide essential signs to diagnose the illness.

Tests: Tests are not needed to establish this diagnosis, although personality testing such as the Minnesota Multiphasic Personality Inventory (MMPI or MMPI-2) may be helpful.

Treatment

During the acute psychotic episodes, psychiatric hospitalization is often needed to protect individuals from their own loss of reality, judgment, and impulse control. The manic (bipolar) type of schizoaffective disorder is treated with antipsychotic medications and mood stabilizers such as lithium. With the depressive form of schizoaffective disorder, antidepressant medications and antipsychotics are given. As very few individuals with schizoaffective disorder tend to remain on their oral medications after the first year of treatment, long-acting antipsychotics given by injections deep into the muscle, spaced 2 to 4 weeks apart are often needed.

Benzodiazepines may also be given for anxiety and insomnia in the acute stages. Antiparkinsonian drugs are commonly given to treat side effects of the traditional antipsychotic drugs but are rarely needed with the newer antipsychotic agents. Shock therapy (electroconvulsive therapy) is rarely used and is not generally effective.

Psychotherapy and strengthening of family, social, and occupational support is useful. Social and occupational rehabilitation therapy may help overcome the unemployment, homelessness, and poverty often associated with this disorder. Step-down treatment after hospitalization may include day treatment and residing in a halfway house.

Prognosis

Outcome is highly variable. The illness may later evolve into schizophrenia, bipolar disorder, or major depression.

Differential Diagnosis

Some medical illnesses can cause a mixture of mood and psychotic disturbances. Examples of such illnesses are lupus, thyroid or adrenal gland disorders, epilepsy, or stroke. Another cause is substance abuse either acute intoxication or chronic use. The effects of stimulants can resemble mania but the letdown and crash can resemble the depressed form of schizoaffective disorder. Marijuana use can lead to lack of motivation, resembling the depressed form of schizoaffective disorder.

Specialists

- Psychiatrist
- Psychologist

Work Restrictions / Accommodations

Temporary work accommodations may include reducing or eliminating activities where the safety of self or others is contingent upon a constant and/or high level of alertness, such as driving a motor vehicle, operating complex machinery, or handling dangerous chemicals; introducing the individual to new or stressful situations gradually under individually appropriate supervision; allowing some flexibility in scheduling to attend therapy appointments (which normally should occur during the employee's personal time); promoting planned, proactive management of identified problem areas; and offering timely feedback on job performance issues. It will be helpful if accommodations are documented in a written plan designed to promote timely and safe transition back to full work productivity.

Comorbid Conditions

Current alcohol abuse or drug use or the presence of a personality disorder may lengthen disability.

Complications

There is an increased risk of suicide during depressive episodes. Alcohol and drug abuse can occur. Break with reality secondary to psychotic symptoms can lead to accidental injury, death, homicide, or injury to others. Poor impulse control and lack of judgment during manic episodes may lead to loss of employment, financial or legal problems, divorce, or other problems in society and relationships.

Factors Influencing Duration

The depressed form of schizoaffective disorder can have a longer disability and poorer prognosis than the bipolar type. Family and social supports, job history, job duties, severity of illness, response to treatment, and compliance with treatment may all influence length of disability.

Length of Disability

Maximum disability duration includes hospitalization.

Duration in Days

Job Classification	Minimum	Optimum	Maximum
Any work	14	28	98

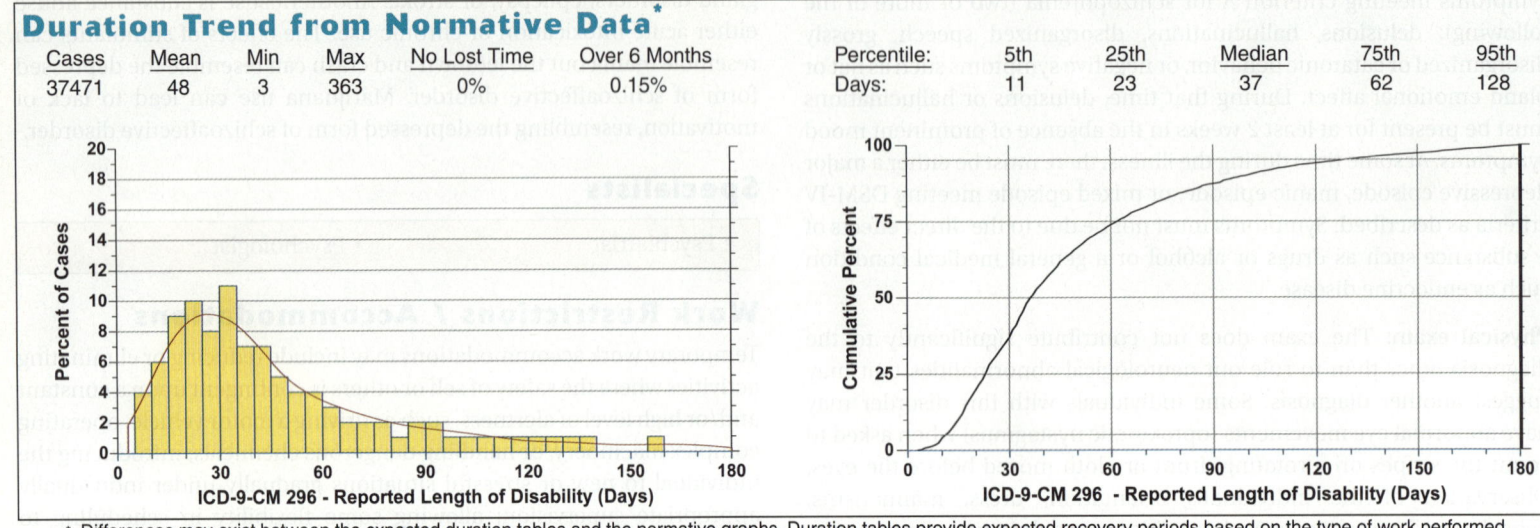

Duration Trend from Normative Data*

Cases	Mean	Min	Max	No Lost Time	Over 6 Months	Percentile:	5th	25th	Median	75th	95th
37471	48	3	363	0%	0.15%	Days:	11	23	37	62	128

* Differences may exist between the expected duration tables and the normative graphs. Duration tables provide expected recovery periods based on the type of work performed by the individual. The normative graphs reflect the actual observed experience of many individuals across the spectrum of physical conditions, in a variety of industries, and with varying levels of case management.

Failure to Recover

If an individual fails to recover within the maximum duration expectancy period, the reader may wish to reference the following questions to assist in better understanding the specifics of an individual's medical case.

Regarding diagnosis:

- Has a diagnosis of schizoaffective disorder been confirmed?
- Have conditions with similar symptoms been ruled out?
- Have conditions directly due to physiological effects of a substance or general medical conditions been identified or ruled out?
- If diagnostic criteria for schizoaffective disorder dictates that the illness has a mixture of both schizophrenia and bipolar disorder symptoms, does individual's diagnosis need to be readdressed?

Regarding treatment:

- Has drug therapy, including antidepressants and lithium, been effective?
- Were antipsychotic (neuroleptic) drugs used while the individual was in a psychotic state? With what response?
- If antipsychotic drugs are causing unpleasant side effects, what alternatives exist?
- Can individual change medications at this point in treatment?
- What long-term therapy regime has physician planned for this individual?

Regarding prognosis:

- If experiencing acute psychotic episodes, is psychiatric hospitalization warranted to protect the individual loss of reality, judgment, and impulse control?
- Would the individual benefit from supervised step-down treatment after hospitalization, such as day treatment or residing in a halfway house?
- What is the individual's current level of occupational functioning?
- To what extent is social dysfunction obvious?
- Is the individual having trouble communicating with co-workers or family members?
- Is the individual experiencing difficulties with self-care such as cooking and personal grooming?
- Is the individual demonstrating increased risk of suicide?
- Is rehabilitation focused on helping the individual regain confidence for self-care and living a fuller life? What more can be done to meet these needs?
- Does the individual have an effective support system in place?
- Is the individual and/or family involved in a psychotherapy experience that helps both the individual and the family members better understand this illness and share coping problems?

References

Long, Philip W., MD. Schizoaffective Disorder. Internet Mental Health. 01 Jan 2000. 10/24/00 <http://www.mentalhealth.com/dis1/p21-ps05.html>.

Mcelroy S.L., P.E. Keck, Jr., and S.M. Strakowski. "An Overview of the Treatment of Schizoaffective Disorder." Journal of Clinical Psychiatry 60 Suppl 5 (1999): 16-21.

Schizoid Personality Disorder
301.20, 301.21

Definition

Schizoid personality disorders are characterized by a lifelong pattern of social withdrawal in day-to-day living, accompanied by lack of vitality, low energy, and decreased spontaneity and expressiveness. Individuals with this disorder are introverted, isolated, lonely, and uncomfortable with human interactions, and may even be described by neighbors as a recluse. Their dress and mannerisms may seem eccentric, their facial expressions bland and unchanging. They often appear aloof and absent-minded, with few friends, and are not prone to small talk or social amenities.

The prevalence of schizoid personality disorder has been reported to be about 7.5% of the general population, but it is not clearly established. A gender ratio of 2:1 (male-to-female) has been reported in some studies.

These individuals will often find work with night shifts or remote work sites, thus minimizing contact with other people. The life histories may reflect solitary interests and success at noncompetitive, isolated, and lonely jobs that others find difficult to tolerate. As they avoid relationships, their sexual lives may exist only in fantasy. Although they do not find pleasure in activities, they may become peripherally involved in health fads, philosophical movements, religious cults, and the metaphysical.

Diagnosis

History: The psychiatric interview and mental status exam are the primary diagnostic methods utilized by the practitioner. In a clinical interview, individuals may appear uneasy, with poor eye contact, and may be anxious to end the interview. DSM-IV criteria for this disorder specify a pervasive pattern of detachment from social relationships and a restricted range of expression of emotions in interpersonal settings, beginning by early adulthood and present in a variety of situations, as indicated by four (or more) of the following: neither desires nor enjoys close relationships, including being part of a family; almost always chooses solitary activities; has little, if any, interest in having sexual experiences with another person; takes pleasure in few, if any, activities; lacks close friends or confidants other than first-degree relatives; appears indifferent to the praise or criticism of others; or shows emotional coldness, detachment, or unresponsiveness (flattened affect).

For the diagnosis to be confirmed, these behaviors cannot occur exclusively during the course of schizophrenia, a mood disorder with psychotic features, another psychotic disorder, or a pervasive developmental disorder, and cannot be due to the direct physiological effects of a general medical condition.

Physical exam: An exam is not helpful in diagnosing this disorder. Observation of the individual's orientation, dress, mannerisms, behavior, and content of speech may assist in diagnosing this illness.

Tests: Psychological testing, such as the Minnesota Multiphasic Personality Inventory (MMPI or MMPI-2) may be helpful in differentiating this disorder from other personality disorders.

Treatment

Individual and group psychotherapy are used to treat schizoid personality disorder, with a treatment approach similar to that used in paranoid personality disorder. One of the more important goals of therapy is to have the individual become comfortable in a social setting, either one-to-one with the therapist or in a group setting. After initial silence, the individual may gradually begin to participate in the group process. It is important for the group leader to protect the individual from criticism for not participating verbally in the group. While the physician needs to communicate concern and caring, the individual's privacy also needs to be respected. Encouraging the individual to maintain usual daily routines may help provide a sense of structure, reassuring him or her that their world will not fall apart if they begin to change. Medications are not generally useful, except as temporary aids in cases of extraordinary anxiety, but small doses of antipsychotics, antidepressants, and psychostimulants have been effective in some individuals.

Prognosis

Many individuals with schizoid personality disorder are able to contribute to society in a limited way, usually in the context of a restricted, well-defined environment. Progression to schizophrenia may occur, usually in the second or third decade.

Differential Diagnosis

A family history of schizophrenia might suggest this is schizophrenia rather than schizoid personality disorder. The two can be distinguished by the thought disorder and delusional thinking seen in schizophrenia. Other Axis I disorders that should be considered are mood disorders, anxiety disorders, dissociative disorders (depersonalization disorders), schizophreniform and brief reactive psychosis, schizotypical personality disorder, paranoid and avoidant types. Personality change due to a general medical condition or side effects of alcohol or drug use may also resemble schizoid personality disorder.

Specialists

- Psychiatrist
- Psychologist

Work Restrictions / Accommodations

Work restrictions and accommodations should be individually determined based on the characteristics of the individual's response to the disorder, the functional requirements of the job and work environment, and the flexibility of the job and work site. The purpose of the restrictions/accommodations is to help maintain the worker's capacity to remain at the workplace without a work disruption or to promote timely and safe transition back to full work productivity.

Comorbid Conditions

Coexisting conditions that may affect recovery and lengthen disability include alcohol and substance abuse, major depressive disorder, and schizotypal, paranoid, and avoidant personality disorders.

Complications

Coexisting psychiatric disorder(s), such as major depression, anxiety disorder, or substance abuse will cause complications. Experiencing lifestyle changes in social settings, living arrangements, or work environment can create additional stress that can complicate schizoid personality disorder.

Factors Influencing Duration

Severity of the disorder, response to treatment, and specific job duties all determine length of disability.

Length of Disability

This condition represents a life-long pattern of behavior. In most cases, no disability is expected.

Failure to Recover

If an individual fails to recover within the maximum duration expectancy period, the reader may wish to reference the following questions to assist in better understanding the specifics of an individual's medical case.

Regarding diagnosis:
- Does the individual's behavior fit the criteria for schizoid personality disorder?
- Has the diagnosis been confirmed?
- Have other psychiatric disorders or underlying medical conditions been ruled out?

Regarding treatment:
- Is the individual currently participating in psychotherapy?
- Has a trust rapport been established with therapist? If not, what can be done to facilitate this relationship?
- Has the individual been involved in group therapy?
- Did group therapy provide the individual with a social network and comfortable environment in which to overcome fears of closeness or feelings of isolation?

Regarding prognosis:
- What is the individual's current level of functioning?
- Has the individual learned to communicate thoughts and feelings directly to others?
- Does the individual do well when working by himself/herself?
- Would accommodations help make the workplace a more appropriate and functional environment for this individual?

References

Schizoid Personality Disorder. Psych Central. 24 Jan 01. 5 Feb 01 <http://www.grohol.com/disorders/sx30t.htm#psych>.

Tasman, Allan, Jeffrey A. Lieberman, and Jerald Kay. Psychiatry, 1st ed. Judy Fletcher Philadelphia: W.B. Saunders Company, 1996 14 Feb 2001 <http://home.mdconsult.com/ >.

Schizophrenia

Other names / synonyms: Schizophrenia Disorder, Schizophrenic Reaction
295, 295.1, 295.2, 295.9

Definition

Schizophrenia is a group of mental disorders characterized by a loss of contact with reality (psychotic behaviors) and by disturbances lasting longer than 6 months in thought, perception, emotions (affect), behavior, and communication.

Although the exact cause is unknown, the consensus is that schizophrenia is fundamentally a physical disease of the brain, associated with an imbalance in two of the complex neurochemical systems in the brain involving the neurochemicals dopamine and glutamate. There are various theories to explain the development of schizophrenia, one being that it is caused by a first or second trimester "insult" (such as maternal malnutrition or exposure to influenza) that leads to dysfunction of part of the brain called the prefrontal cortex. The structural abnormality in the brain is thought to be present at birth, with schizophrenic symptoms becoming manifest in late adolescence when the prefrontal cortex matures. Other risk factors for development of this structural abnormality are intrauterine infections, postnatal complications, and Rh incompatibility in a second or subsequent pregnancy. Other theories hold that genetic factors may play a role, as close relatives of an individual with schizophrenia may have a high risk of developing the disorder. Family problems or poor parenting are not thought to play a role in the development of schizophrenia. However, stress does appear to make things worse for individuals afflicted with this illness.

There are five recognized forms of schizophrenia: catatonic, paranoid, disorganized, undifferentiated, and residual, which are characterized as a constellation of four types of distinctive and predictable symptoms: positive, negative, cognitive, and mood.

Positive symptoms (called "positive" because they add to the individual's experience and behavior) include hearing voices (auditory hallucinations) or seeing visions (visual hallucinations), false personal beliefs (delusions) of being unfairly persecuted (delusions of persecution) or of being someone with great power or fame (delusions of grandiosity), anger, anxiety, and violence. These symptoms are typical of paranoid schizophrenia. Individuals perceive hallucinations and delusions as very real sensory experiences and usually cannot recognize them as being part of the disease process.

Negative symptoms (called "negative" because behavior is taken away) such as inappropriate laughter, incoherence, regressive behavior, emotional flatness, and social withdrawal are typical of disorganized schizophrenia, along with disorganized speech, thought, behavior, and mannerisms. Positive symptoms are also seen in this subtype of schizophrenia.

Catatonic schizophrenia is associated with positive symptoms of excitement, rigidity, and motor disturbances, and negative symptoms of withdrawal, immobility, decreased sensitivity to pain, stupor, and unresponsiveness to surroundings.

Individuals with undifferentiated schizophrenia may have symptoms from more than one of the five forms of the disorder. In residual schizophrenia, the prominent symptoms of the illness have abated, but some features, such as hallucinations (of which auditory are the most common) and emotional flatness, may remain.

Schizophrenia is, in fact, a fairly common disorder, having a relatively even distribution around the world of about 1%. In the United States, 1-1.5% of the population is affected, or about 2 million Americans. The probability of developing schizophrenia jumps to 13% if one parent was afflicted with the disorder, 35% if both parents were afflicted, and 50% if an identical twin has the disease.

Onset is between the ages 16-25 in three-quarters of afflicted individuals, and is uncommon after age 30, and rare after age 40. Overall, schizophrenia occurs equally in men and women, but is more common in men ages 16-25, and more common in ages 25-30 for women.

Diagnosis

No definitive test exists for schizophrenia. Diagnosis is based on a comprehensive assessment of clinical history, symptoms, and signs. According to the Diagnostic and Statistical Manual of Mental Disorders, Fourth Edition (DSM-IV), two or more characteristic symptoms including false personal beliefs (delusions), seeing visions or hearing voices (hallucinations), disorganized speech, disorganized behavior, and negative symptoms are required for a significant portion of a one-month period for this diagnosis, and early signs indicative of the illness (prodromal signs) with social, occupational, or self-care impairments must be evident for a 6-month period that includes the one month of active symptoms.

History: The individual's history reveals continuous signs of mental disturbance (delusions, hallucinations, disorganized speech, grossly disorganized behavior, and emotional flatness) that have been manifested for at least six months. The individual's developmental background, genetic and family history, current stress factors, level of functioning prior to the illness, and course of the illness may be helpful in ruling out other conditions, such as primary mood disorders with psychotic features.

Physical exam: A general physical exam is performed to rule out psychotic disorders due to physical disorders or associated with substance abuse. The physician also looks for signs of emphysema or lung or heart disease because of the high rate of nicotine addiction in schizophrenics. Subtle neurological abnormalities may be suggestive of schizophrenia. Finally, the physician takes note of the individual's presentation during the exam including dress, mannerisms, behavior, content of speech, and style of relating to others.

Tests: Besides psychological tests and a CT scan of the head, which may reveal large ventricles in the brain characteristic of schizophrenia, clinical laboratory tests are used to rule out underlying medical, neurologic, and endocrine disorders that can present as psychoses, such as vitamin deficiencies, uremia, thyrotoxicosis, and electrolyte imbalance.

Treatment

General goals of treatment are to reduce the severity of psychotic symptoms, prevent recurrences of symptomatic episodes and associated deterioration of functioning, and help individuals to function at the highest level possible. The sooner treatment begins, the better. Several large-scale studies have shown that early intervention can forestall the worst long-term outcomes of schizophrenia. Hospitalization, medication, rehabilitation with community support, and psychotherapy are the major components of treatment.

Hospitalization is necessary to treat severe delusions or hallucinations, serious suicidal ideations, inability to care for oneself, or serious problems with drugs or alcohol, while allowing observation by trained mental health professionals to determine whether schizophrenia is the appropriate diagnosis. Hospitalization also allows for the initiation of a mediation regimen under close supervision.

Antipsychotic drugs (neuroleptics) can dramatically improve the functioning of individuals with schizophrenia. Once the troubling symptoms are controlled by the drugs, the individual does not require hospitalization. However, schizophrenics often fail to take their medications as prescribed, and some outpatients are better managed with long-lasting injections of antipsychotic medications that are repeated every 2-3 weeks.

The 30% of individuals with schizophrenia who do not respond to conventional antipsychotic drugs are candidates for atypical antipsychotic drugs.

Antipsychotic drugs affect other neurotransmitter systems including serotonin or have selective affinity for specific dopamine receptor subtypes. Newer atypical antipsychotic drugs currently available are more effective and have fewer adverse effects than conventional antipsychotics. One of the most common and troubling side effects of the older antipsychotic drugs involves abnormal, involuntary movements of the tongue and lips (tardive dyskinesia), but this side effect is much less common with the newer agents.

Electroconvulsive therapy (ECT) is sometimes used to treat catatonic and severely depressed schizophrenic individuals.

Outpatient treatment includes crisis intervention, individual and group psychotherapy, family education and therapy, and rehabilitation and community support services (specifically vocational rehabilitation upon returning to work after recovery from an acute psychotic episode).

Treatment is usually long-term, most often for a lifetime. Studies show that after 10 years of treatment, one-fourth of individuals with schizophrenia recover completely and one-fourth improve modestly. Fifteen percent do not improve, and 10% die.

Prognosis

The predicted outcome of schizophrenia varies considerably from complete recovery to death. Only about 10% of schizophrenics have a good outcome. Most often, there is a gradual decline in functioning after onset of schizophrenia, affecting personal relationships, work, education, and even basic self-care. Some individuals go through periods of improvement and relapse, and others remain disturbed. Complete recovery is unlikely; less than 30% return to work after being hospitalized, 40% attempt suicide, and 10% die from suicide. Excess mortality in schizophrenics is often related to smoking, with higher than expected death rate from diseases of the circulatory, digestive, endocrine, nervous, and respiratory systems. About 50% have a substance abuse problem during their lifetime.

Better outcomes tend to be associated with female gender, family history of affective disorder, absent family history of schizophrenia, good functioning before the onset of illness (premorbid functioning), higher IQ, being married, sudden onset following a stressful incident, fewer prior episodes (both number and length), a pattern of episodes followed by remissions, older age, fewer associated illnesses, paranoid subtype, and symptoms that are predominantly positive (delusions, hallucinations) and not disorganized (thought disorder, disorganized behavior) or negative (emotional flatness, depression). Better quality of the psychiatrist-patient relationship is also associated with better outcome. The course of this condition may also be influenced by cultural and societal complexity, with better outcomes in developing countries.

Differential Diagnosis

Psychoses can also be caused by medical conditions, such as brain tumor, Cushing's disease, or substance abuse. Bipolar disorder and major depression can present with psychotic features and hallucinations similar to the ones in schizophrenia. Other possibilities could be schizophreniform, schizoaffective, delusional, and brief psychotic disorders as well as schizotypal, schizoid, and paranoid personality disorders, which often present with features similar to those of schizophrenia.

Work Restrictions / Accommodations

An individual with schizophrenia returning to work would benefit from a schedule that incorporates flex-time or a part-time position, time off for scheduled medical appointments, scheduled break times that meet the individual's needs rather than following a fixed schedule, a workspace where visual and auditory distractions are minimized, and additional leave after a hospitalization. Individuals would also benefit from the opportunity to phone professionals during the workday, and to meet regularly with the employer, supervisor, and job coach.

Comorbid Conditions

Disability could be lengthened by alcohol use, drug use, stress, depression, or the presence of a personality disorder.

Complications

Alcohol and drug abuse complicate schizophrenia by exacerbating symptoms. About 50% of individuals with schizophrenia can expect to have a substance abuse problem in their lifetime. No one is sure why. Stress, unemployment, poverty, and homelessness are other possible complications. Schizophrenics are three times as likely to smoke as the general population, and are therefore prone to smoking-related health risks including heart disease and cancer.

Use of conventional antipsychotic drugs may cause side effects including muscle stiffness, tremors, weight gain, and an involuntary movement disorder (tardive dyskinesia), most often characterized by puckering or smacking of the lips and tongue and/or writhing of the arms and legs.

Specialists

- Psychiatrist
- Psychologist

Factors Influencing Duration

Negative symptoms (such as regressive behavior, emotional flatness, and social withdrawal) lengthen disability because they are more difficult to treat than positive symptoms (such as hallucinations, delusions, anger, anxiety, violence), and they are often accompanied by intellectual impairment. Lack of insight on the part of the afflicted individual also lengthens disability because such an individual has little incentive to cooperate with treatment and to adhere to a medication regimen. Another negative influence on length of disability is the individual's presence in an unstable or hostile environment. Strength of family and social supports, the quality of the psychiatrist-patient relationship, response to treatment, and specific job duties also influence duration of disability. A recent study suggested that poor level of functioning before the onset of schizophrenia, negative symptoms, and difficulties with thinking and memory were associated with unemployment.

Length of Disability

By definition, symptoms must persist for six months. Disability varies and is contingent on the severity of the condition and on how well hospitalization and medication are able to control the severity of the condition. Disability may be permanent.

First episode.

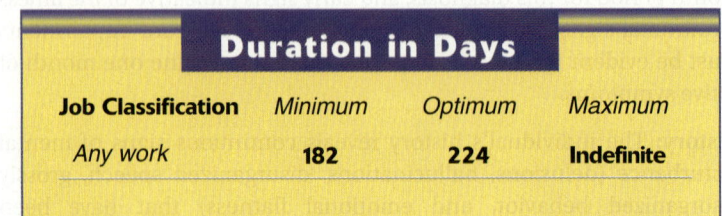

Duration in Days

Job Classification	Minimum	Optimum	Maximum
Any work	182	224	Indefinite

Failure to Recover

If an individual fails to recover within the maximum duration expectancy period, the reader may wish to reference the following questions to assist in better understanding the specifics of an individual's medical case.

Regarding diagnosis:

- Has the individual been experiencing psychotic loss-of-reality symptoms for at least 6 months with increasing difficulty in normal functioning?
- Has the diagnosis been confirmed or does it need to be revisited in light of this criteria?
- Have conditions with similar symptoms been ruled out?

Regarding treatment:

- Since early intervention may forestall the worst long-term outcomes of this devastating brain disorder, was treatment initiated with diagnosis?
- Does current treatment appear to be effective?
- Is a change in treatment plan warranted?
- If individual is experiencing severe delusions, hallucinations, serious suicidal inclinations, inability to care for oneself, or severe problems with drugs or alcohol, can individual be hospitalized until condition can be stabilized?
- Has the individual reported any untoward side effects from antipsychotic medication?
- Has the individual talked with the doctor about these or any other expected side effects?
- Is the individual capable of weighing the risks against the potential benefits that antipsychotic drugs can provide?
- Would individual benefit from changing to one of the newer antipsychotic drugs?
- Does individual understand how important it is to continue medication?
- Is individual capable of maintaining medication regime or would more structured supervision be beneficial?
- Does individual exhibit suicidal tendencies?
- What is being done to protect individual from harming self or others?

Regarding prognosis:

- Is the individual capable of functioning on an independent basis with no threat to self or others?
- Does the individual and/or family know and accept the realistic prognosis of this illness?
- Although no cure is available for schizophrenia, is individual aware that with proper treatment, he/she may still be able to lead a productive and fulfilling life?
- Is individual capable of complying with a long-term medication regime?
- Did psychotherapy help the individual regain the confidence to take care of him/herself and live a fuller life?
- Was individual and family members able to participate in a therapy program that helped them better understand this illness and share coping problems?
- Does the individual have an effective support system in place? If not, what can be done to establish one?

References

"Schizophrenia." Merck Manual of Medical Information - Home Edition, Section 5, Chapter 193. Beers, Mark H., and Robert Berkow, MD, eds. Whitehouse Station, NJ: Merck & Co., Inc, 2000. 1 Jan 2001 <http://www.merck.com/pubs/mmanual/section15/chapter193/193b.htm>.

Schizophrenia: Disease Definition, Natural History, and Epidemiology. Clinical Resources Practice Guidelines. 01 Jan 2000. 18 Aug 2000 <http://www.psych.org/clin_res/pg_schizo_2.cfm>.

Schizophrenia, Paranoid Type
Other names / synonyms: Paranoid Schizophrenia
295.30

Definition

Paranoid schizophrenia is characterized by a mistaken belief (delusion) that the individual is being conspired against or persecuted by others. In general, individuals with paranoid schizophrenia cling strongly to their delusional beliefs despite all evidence to the contrary, and despite the inability of others to verify those beliefs. Delusions are defined as firmly held beliefs that are untrue, not shared by others in the culture, and not easily modifiable. The delusions of a paranoid schizophrenic individual are usually misinterpretations of events or of the individual's senses and revolve around a certain theme that makes perfect sense to the individual. These are not classified as bizarre since these occurrences are possibilities in ordinary life, i.e., being under surveillance by the CIA or FBI. Often the individual hears voices (auditory hallucinations) that support his or her imagined conspiracy.

Compared to other forms of schizophrenia, the thinking of a paranoid schizophrenic individual is not grossly abnormal except for the delusion. Similarly, speech is not as disorganized, emotions are not as flat or inappropriate, and abnormal conditions characterized by stupor, rigidity, flexibility, and mania (catatonia) are not apparent as in other forms of schizophrenia.

Emotions typically experienced by paranoid schizophrenics include anger, hostility, unsociability or standoffishness (aloofness), and argumentativeness. Delusions of grandeur are often followed by delusions of persecution. For instance, a paranoid schizophrenic individual may believe that he or she is Jesus Christ and as such that is being given instructions from God. In the individual's contorted mind, it makes sense that he or she is being watched and persecuted by envious people.

The course of paranoid schizophrenia may be episodic with partial or complete remissions or it may be chronic. In chronic cases, the florid symptoms persist over years, and it is difficult to distinguish discrete episodes. The onset in paranoid schizophrenia tends to occur later in life than in other forms of schizophrenia. The afflicted individual with a high level of social and occupational functioning before the illness is more likely to be married and have children.

Paranoid schizophrenia is the most common form of schizophrenia in most parts of the world. In the US, reports issued by Centers for Disease Control and Prevention (CDC) for 1998 revealed 121,000 diagnoses of paranoid schizophrenia in non-Federal, short-stay hospitals (73,000 men and 47,000 women). Most individuals (62,000) were between the ages of 15 and 44; none were under age 15; 37,000 were between 45 and 64; and 21,000 were 65 or older. Geographic distribution showed the highest prevalences to be in the South and Northeast regions of the US with the lowest prevalences in the West and Midwest (almost equal).

Diagnosis

History: No definitive test exists for paranoid schizophrenia. Diagnosis is based on a comprehensive assessment of clinical history, symptoms, and signs. According to the Diagnostic and Statistical Manual of Mental Disorders, Fourth Edition (DSM-IV), paranoid schizophrenia is diagnosed if certain criteria are met. These are a preoccupation with one or more false personal beliefs (delusions) or frequent auditory hallucinations, and that certain characteristics are not prominent (disorganized speech or catatonic behavior, or flat or inappropriate emotions).

The individual's history reveals delusions and a predominance of auditory hallucinations that are organized around a story of persecution by conspiracy. Emotional (affective) and intellectual (cognitive) functioning remain relatively intact.

Physical exam: A general physical exam is generally not helpful in diagnosis as it is in other forms of schizophrenia. Observation of the individual's orientation, dress, mannerisms, behavior, and content of speech provide signs that may facilitate diagnosis.

Tests: Overall, tests do not establish a diagnosis of paranoid schizophrenia. In addition to psychological tests and a CT of the head (may reveal large ventricles in the brain characteristic of schizophrenia), clinical laboratory tests are used to rule out underlying medical, neurologic, and endocrine disorders that can present as psychoses (e.g., vitamin deficiencies, uremia, thyrotoxicosis, or electrolyte imbalance). Neuropsychological testing is usually normal but personality testing such as the Minnesota Multiphasic Personality Inventory (MMPI or MMPI-2) may reveal paranoid beliefs.

Treatment

General goals of treatment are to reduce the severity of psychotic symptoms, prevent recurrences of symptomatic episodes and associated deterioration of functioning, and help individuals to function at the highest level possible. The sooner treatment begins, the more beneficial. Several large-scale studies have shown that early intervention can forestall the worst long-term outcomes of paranoid schizophrenia. Hospitalization, medication, rehabilitation with community support, and psychotherapy are the major components of treatment.

Hospitalization is necessary in treating severe delusions or hallucinations, serious suicidal ideations, inability to care for oneself, or serious problems with drugs or alcohol while allowing observation by trained mental health professionals to determine whether paranoid schizophrenia is the appropriate diagnosis. Hospitalization also allows the initiation of a medication regimen under close supervision.

Antipsychotic drugs (neuroleptics) can dramatically improve the functioning of individuals with paranoid schizophrenia. Once the troubling symptoms are controlled with drugs, the individual does not require hospitalization. Conventional antipsychotic drugs are characterized by their affinity for the dopamine 2 receptor. Side effects of these drugs include muscle stiffness, tremors, weight gain, and an involuntary movement disorder (tardive dyskinesia) most often characterized by puckering of the lips and tongue and/or writhing of the arms and legs.

Thirty percent of individuals with schizophrenia (all forms included) who do not respond to conventional antipsychotic drugs are candidates for atypical antipsychotic drugs. Antipsychotic drugs affect other neurotransmitter systems including serotonin or have selective affinity for specific dopamine receptor subtypes. Newer atypical antipsychotic drugs currently available are more effective and less likely to cause tardive dyskinesia or other adverse effects than the conventional antipsychotics.

Outpatient treatment for paranoid schizophrenia includes crisis intervention, individual and group psychotherapy, family therapy, and rehabilitation and community support services (specifically, vocational rehabilitation upon return to work after recovery from an acute psychotic episode).

Treatment should be long-term (most often for life). It is important to point out however, that paranoid schizophrenics are difficult to treat. Because they are very suspicious, paranoid schizophrenics tend to evade therapists' open-ended questions. They may also try to avoid hospitalization and medications because they fear a loss of control or other real or imagined dangers.

Prognosis

The prognosis for paranoid schizophrenia is more favorable than for the other forms of schizophrenia. In spite of treatment difficulties, many individuals with paranoid schizophrenia can function quite well. Even though their paranoid views are apparently unshakable, various treatments appear effective in improving social functioning so they do not require lengthy hospitalization. When paranoid schizophrenia is successfully managed, afflicted individuals can enjoy long-term personal, social, and career relationships. In a recent study of 239 individuals hospitalized for paranoid state decades ago before modern medications were available, 27% recovered but 52% did not improve. Poor outcome was associated with seclusive personality, poor functioning before onset of illness, onset 6 months or more before hospitalization, gradual onset, lack of insight, single marital status, and lack of precipitating events.

Differential Diagnosis

Other disorders with psychotic symptoms similar to those seen in paranoid schizophrenia include paranoid personality disorder, schizotypical personality disorder (persecutory type), mood disorder with psychotic features, cocaine or amphetamine abuse, or paranoid traits associated with physical handicap such as hearing impairment.

Specialists

- Psychiatrist
- Psychologist

Work Restrictions / Accommodations

An individual with schizophrenia returning to work would benefit from a schedule that incorporates flex-time or a part-time position, time off for scheduled medical appointments, scheduled break times that meet the individual's needs rather than following a fixed schedule, a workspace where visual and auditory distractions are minimized, and additional leave after a hospitalization. Individuals would also benefit from the opportunity to phone professionals during the workday, and to meet regularly with the employer, supervisor, and job coach.

Comorbid Conditions

Comorbid conditions that may influence length of disability include alcohol use, drug use, stress, depression, or a personality disorder.

Complications

Violence against others and/or suicide are possible complications in response to ideas of being persecuted. Paranoid delusions may lead to loss of relationships and employment.

Factors Influencing Duration

Negative symptoms (regressive behavior, emotional flatness, or social withdrawal) lengthen disability because they are more difficult to treat than positive symptoms (hallucinations, delusions, anger, anxiety, or violence) and are often accompanied by intellectual impairment. Lack of insight on the part of a paranoid schizophrenic individual also lengthens disability, as there is little incentive to cooperate with treatment and adhere to a medication regimen. Another negative influence on length of disability is the individual's presence in an unstable or hostile environment.

Length of Disability

Although the prognosis for paranoid schizophrenia is better than for other forms of schizophrenia, disability varies and is contingent on the severity of the condition and on how well hospitalization and medication can control the severity of the condition. By definition, symptoms must persist for six months. Disability may be permanent.

Duration in Days

Job Classification	Minimum	Optimum	Maximum
Any work	182	224	Indefinite

Failure to Recover

If an individual fails to recover within the maximum duration expectancy period, the reader may wish to reference the following questions to assist in better understanding the specifics of an individual's medical case.

Regarding diagnosis:

- Although thinking is not grossly abnormal, does individual suffer from a mistaken belief of being conspired against and persecuted by others?
- Has diagnosis been confirmed or does it need to be revisited in light of DSM-IV criteria?
- Have conditions with similar symptoms been ruled out?

Regarding treatment:

- Since early intervention may forestall the worst long-term outcomes of this devastating brain disorder, was treatment initiated with diagnosis?
- Does current treatment appear to be effective?
- Is a change in treatment plan warranted?
- If individual is experiencing severe delusions, hallucinations, serious suicidal inclinations, inability to care for oneself, or severe problems with drugs or alcohol, can individual be hospitalized until condition can be stabilized?
- Has the individual reported any untoward side effects from antipsychotic medication?
- Has the individual talked with the doctor about these or any other expected side effects?
- Is the individual capable of weighing the risks against the potential benefits that antipsychotic drugs can provide?
- Would individual benefit from changing to one of the newer antipsychotic drugs?
- Does individual understand how important it is to continue medication?
- Is individual capable of maintaining medication regime or would more structured supervision be beneficial?
- Does individual exhibit suicidal tendencies?
- What is being done to protect individual from harming self or others?

Regarding prognosis:

- Is the individual capable of functioning on an independent basis with no threat to self or others?
- Does the individual and/or family know and accept the realistic prognosis of this illness?
- Although no cure is available for schizophrenia, is individual aware that with proper treatment, he/she may still be able to lead a productive and fulfilling life?
- Is individual capable of complying with a long-term medication regime?
- Did psychotherapy help the individual regain the confidence to take care of him/herself and live a fuller life?

- Was the individual and family members able to participate in a therapy program that helped them better understand this illness and share coping problems?
- Does the individual have an effective support system in place? If not, what can be done to establish one?

References

DSM-IV: Paranoid Schizophrenia. Behavenet.com, American Psychiatric Association. 01 Jan 1994. 9 Sept 2000 <http://www.behavenet.com/capsules/disorders/paranoidschiz.htm>.

Goldman, Lee, J. Claude Bennett, and Russell L. Cecil. Cecil Textbook of Medicine, 21st ed. Philadelphia: W.B. Saunders Company, 1999 14 Feb 2001 <http://home.mdconsult.com/>.

Long, Phillip W., MD. Schizophrenia: European Description. World Health Organization. 01 Jan 1992. 9 Sept 2000 <http://www.mentalhealth.com/icd/p22-ps01.html>.

Stephens, J.H., P. Richard, and P.R. McHugh. "Long-term Follow-up of Patients with a Diagnosis of Paranoid State and Hospitalized, 1913 to 1940." Journal of Nervous and Mental Disease 188 4 (2000): 202-208.

Tasman, Allan, Jeffrey A. Lieberman, and Jerald Kay. Psychiatry, 1st ed. Judy Fletcher Philadelphia: W.B. Saunders Company, 1996 14 Feb 2001 <http://home.mdconsult.com/>.

The PRD Family Guide Encyclopedia of Medical Care - Paranoid Schizophrenia: What You Should Know. HealthSquare.com, New Media Systems, LLC. 01 Jan 1997. 9 Sept 0000 <http://www.healthsquare.com/mc/fgmc2415.htm>.

Schizophreniform Disorder
Other names / synonyms: Brief Reactive Psychosis, Schizophrenia
295.4

Definition

Schizophreniform disorder is a mental disturbance with serious abnormalities in sensory perceptions, thought, speech, attention, mood, behavior, interpretation of everyday life events, and the capacity to enjoy life. Although similar to schizophrenia, schizophreniform disorder is a more acute illness. Lasting for longer than 1 month, but less than 6 months, serious impairment in social and occupational functioning may or may not have occurred, whereas the diagnosis of schizophrenia requires functional impairment and at least 6 months of illness. Schizophreniform disorder is not due to drug or alcohol abuse. It is diagnosed only after ruling out schizoaffective disorder or mood disorders with psychotic features such as bipolar disorder (manic-depression).

Symptoms of this disorder are described as positive or negative. Positive symptoms are an excess of normal functions, such as abnormalities of thinking (delusions), sensory perceptions (hallucinations), language (disorganized speech), or behavior (grossly disorganized or catatonic behavior). Negative symptoms involve a reduction or loss of normal functions, such as a restriction and flattening of emotions, severely reduced speech or thought, and lack of interest in any goal-directed activities.

About 1 person in 1,000 has schizophreniform disorder during their lifetime. It is more common in relatives of those who have either this condition or another mental illness.

Diagnosis

History: History includes at least two of the following: fixed but untrue beliefs (delusions); seeing visions or hearing voices (hallucinations); disorganized speech; grossly disorganized or barely reactive (catatonic) behavior; or diminished emotions, thoughts, or will to pursue any goal. These must have been present for at least 1 month, but less than 6 months. The DSM-IV also requires that schizoaffective disorder and mood disorder with psychotic features are ruled out, and that the disturbance is not due to the direct physiological effects of a drug or medication, or a general medical condition.

Physical exam: An exam does not contribute to this diagnosis. Observation of the individual's orientation, dress, mannerisms, behavior, and content of speech provide signs that may be helpful in diagnosis.

Tests: Psychological tests may be helpful, but do not prove the diagnosis.

Treatment

Initial treatment is hospitalization to establish diagnosis and begin treatment with medication. Hospitalization may also be necessary for patient safety, to address the risk of suicide or homicide, and to take care of basic needs. Antipsychotic drug therapy is helpful for hallucinations and delusions, and to prevent a relapse into psychosis. Anticonvulsants and lithium can also be helpful. Outpatient treatment includes crisis intervention, individual and group psychotherapy, family therapy, and development of social supports. When the individual has recovered sufficiently from the acute psychotic episode, vocational rehabilitation may be needed to provide assistance in returning to work.

Prognosis

Approximately one-third of the individuals with schizophreniform disorder will recover within 6 months. Two-thirds do not recover, becoming chronically ill. At that time, the diagnosis will change to schizophrenia or schizoaffective disorder. In a 40-year follow-up study of this condition, outcome in terms of social and vocational function was intermediate between individuals with schizophrenia and those with mood disorders.

Differential Diagnosis

Disorders with similar symptoms include schizophrenia, schizoaffective disorder, brief psychotic disorder, or a mood disorder with psychotic features. Substance abuse is also one of the most common causes of abrupt onset of psychotic symptoms. Medical conditions with similar symptoms include metabolic and endocrine disorders, partial complex seizures, encephalitis, and brain tumor.

Specialists

- Psychiatrist
- Psychologist

Work Restrictions / Accommodations

Temporary work accommodations may include reducing or eliminating activities where the safety of self or others is contingent upon a constant and/or high level of alertness, such as driving a motor vehicle, operating complex machinery, or handling dangerous chemicals; introducing the individual to new or stressful situations gradually under individually appropriate supervision; allowing some flexibility in scheduling to attend therapy appointments (which normally should occur during the employee's personal time); promoting planned, proactive management of identified problem areas; and offering timely feedback on job performance issues. It will be helpful if accommodations are documented in a written plan designed to promote timely and safe transition back to full work productivity.

Comorbid Conditions

Coexisting conditions that may affect recovery and lengthen disability include drug or alcohol abuse, the presence of a personality disorder, or a superimposed organic mental disorder. However, if the illness has persisted beyond 6 months, the diagnosis should be changed to schizophrenia.

Complications

Complications include injuries, accidents, suicide, and homicide. Alcohol or drug abuse is common. Major mood disorders may also appear.

Factors Influencing Duration

Signs of a favorable outcome are the onset of psychotic symptoms within a month of the first noticeable changes in personality or behavior, feeling surprised and puzzled by the psychotic episode, and having good social and occupational functioning before the disorder started. Negative symptoms usually result in greater disability and are often accompanied by intellectual impairment. Lack of insight is a poor prognostic sign, due to poor cooperation with treatment including stopping the antipsychotic medication. Increased disability is also likely if the individual is in an unstable social environment.

Length of Disability

Maximum disability duration includes hospitalization.

Duration in Days

Job Classification	Minimum	Optimum	Maximum
Any work	28	42	56

Failure to Recover

If an individual fails to recover within the maximum duration expectancy period, the reader may wish to reference the following questions to assist in better understanding the specifics of an individual's medical case.

Regarding diagnosis:

- Does individual meet the DSM-IV criteria for schizophreniform disorder?
- Has a diagnosis of schizophreniform disorder been confirmed?
- If the illness has persisted beyond 6 months, as diagnosis been changed to schizophrenia?
- Have conditions with similar symptoms been ruled out?

Regarding treatment:

- Was treatment initiated with diagnosis?
- Does current treatment appear to be effective? Is a change in treatment plan warranted?
- Has the individual reported any untoward side effects associated with antipsychotic medication?
- Has the individual talked with the doctor about these or any other expected side effects?
- Is the individual capable of weighing the risks against the potential benefits that antipsychotic drugs can provide?
- Would individual benefit from changing to one of the new antipsychotic drugs?
- Does individual understand how important it is to continue medication?
- Is individual capable of maintaining medication regime, or does he/she require more structured supervision?
- If suicidal tendencies are exhibited, what is being done to protect individual from harming self?
- Does the individual exhibit or express violent tendencies towards others? What is being done to protect the individual from harming others?
- Is psychiatric hospitalization warranted until the individual is no longer a threat to self or others?

Regarding prognosis:

- Is individual capable of functioning on an independent basis with no threat to self or others?
- Does the individual exhibit at least two features that indicate a favorable outcome?
- Has the individual received appropriate outpatient care, including crisis intervention, individual and group psychotherapy, family therapy, and the development of social supports?
- Has vocational rehabilitation been offered to provide assistance upon returning to work?

References

Hurst, J.W., ed. Medicine for the Practicing Physician, 4th ed. Stamford: Appleton & Lange, 1996.

Schizophreniform Disorder. Behavioral Health Advisor. 01 Jan 2000. 10 Oct 2000 <http://www.realage.com/Connect/healthadvisor/behavioral/bha/schizdis.htm>.

Sciatica

Other names / synonyms: Neuritis of the Sciatic Nerve, Radiculopathy, Sciatic Neuritis

724, 724.3

Definition

Sciatica is not a disease but a symptom of pain in the distribution of a lumbar nerve root.

The sciatic nerve is the largest nerve in the body, running from the low back (lumbar region) through many smaller branches to the foot. Pain, numbness, tingling, and muscle weakness along the course of the nerve (dermatome distribution) are characteristic of sciatica. Pain may be present in the low back area as well. Sciatica involves the sensory nerves, which cause pain and changes in sensation (paraesthesia) and can also include the nerves that control the muscles (motor nerves) in the back of the thigh and in the lower leg to the foot.

The cause of sciatica is most often pressure on the nerve root by a herniated lumbar disc (radiculopathy). A direct injury to the nerve can also occur from a fall (nerve contusion), fractures of the pelvis, dislocation of the hip (nerve stretch injury), or a wound. Any disease that results in changes in the low back (lumbosacral spine) or in the nerve may cause sciatica. Diabetes may injure the sciatic nerve resulting in sciatica.

Sciatica is the most common symptom of lumbar disc herniation and is found in about 40% of these cases. Smoking increases an individual's risk for disc degeneration and, therefore, sciatica. In addition, sciatica, a symptom, is seen as leg pain referred from the low back, in individuals with no evidence of nerve root or peripheral nerve compression, disease or dysfunction.

Contact the treating physician for more specific diagnostic information when sciatica is the diagnosis provided.

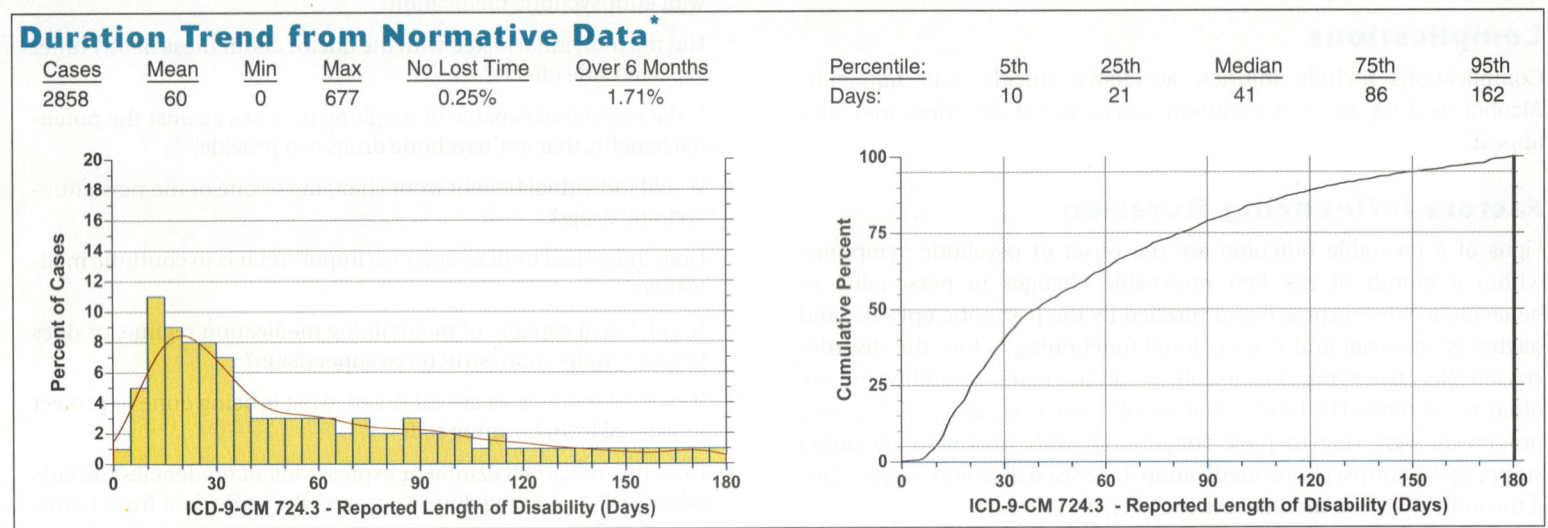

Cases	Mean	Min	Max	No Lost Time	Over 6 Months
2858	60	0	677	0.25%	1.71%

Percentile:	5th	25th	Median	75th	95th
Days:	10	21	41	86	162

* Differences may exist between the expected duration tables and the normative graphs. Duration tables provide expected recovery periods based on the type of work performed by the individual. The normative graphs reflect the actual observed experience of many individuals across the spectrum of physical conditions, in a variety of industries, and with varying levels of case management.

References

Hu, Serina, MD, Ulrich Bueff, MD, and Clifford Tribus, MD. "Disorders, Diseases, and Injuries of the Spine." Current Diagnosis and Treatment in Orthopedics. Skinner, J.B., and Harry B. Skinner, eds. Norwalk: Appleton & Lange, 1995. 185-186.

Scleritis
Other names / synonyms: Leucitis, Sclerotitis
379.0

Definition
Scleritis is an inflammation of the outer white layer of the eye (sclera), commonly associated with autoimmune or collagen vascular diseases such as rheumatoid arthritis, with metabolic disorders, infections, or chemical or physical injuries. Sometimes the cause is unknown. Immediate treatment is needed to keep the condition from spreading to other portions of the eye and creating potentially serious consequences such as cataracts or detachment of the back inner membrane of the eye where images are processed (retinal detachment).

Scleritis also occurs in viral infections of the eye (herpes zoster ophthalmicus) and in a rare condition that involves inflammation of the blood vessels (Wegener's granulomatosis). Chronic inflammation associated with scleritis may potentially perforate the sclera, and cause tissue to thin (necrotizing anterior scleritis).

Scleritis occurs primarily among individuals between 30-60 years of age. Incidence rates are not usually kept, but one study indicates that less than 1% of individuals who visit ophthalmologists have scleritis.

Diagnosis
History: The pain associated with symptoms may be mild at first and increase gradually; it may also be worse at night. Symptoms may vary, ranging from constant and dull, to deep and pulsating, to a severe piercing pain that may radiate to the forehead, brow, or jaw. The individual may complain of sensitivity to light (photophobia), and the eye may tear or appear to bulge (exophthalmia). When scleritis occurs at the back of the eye, vision may gradually decrease or be blurry, and the eye may feel very tender and sore. In about half of scleritis cases, both eyes are affected (bilateral). The individual may have another disease, such as gout or syphilis.

Physical exam: The physical exam will reveal a red or violet patch, or elevated nodule on the eye. Tiny blood vessels of the sclera may be inflamed, making the eye look red. In extreme cases, the tissue of the sclera may have thinned revealing a dark hue to the underlying layer of the eye where blood vessels are found (choroid).

Tests: A microscopic examination of the eye under illumination (biomicroscopy) will determine the extent of inflammation and may show whether the eye's globe has been perforated. A fluorescein dye may be applied to the eye (Seidel sign) to detect abnormal leakage that could be an indication of perforation. Examination and magnification of the eye's interior with an illuminated instrument (ophthalmoscopy) will determine whether the inflammation has spread to the back interior portion of the eye. A scan using high frequency sound waves (ultrasonography) may also reveal abnormalities in the eye's internal structure and aid in the diagnosis. If systemic diseases are suspected as the cause of scleritis, further tests including a complete blood count (CBC) or chest x-ray may be indicated to identify the specific condition.

Treatment
A protective eye shield is applied if a perforation or thinning of the sclera is suspected. In mild cases, systemic non-steroidal anti-inflammatory drugs (NSAIDs) may be given for pain relief. Corticosteroids may be administered orally or as eyedrops to help reduce inflammation and pain. If a perforation occurs in the sclera, surgical repair may be needed. Other drugs may be used to dilate the pupil, protect the iris, and reduce discomfort. In rare cases, depending on underlying conditions, drugs that suppress immune responses may be needed.

Prognosis
Although persistent, scleritis often responds well to corticosteroid drugs. The ultimate outcome for scleritis is difficult to predict since the condition often accompanies an underlying systemic disease. The success of treatment of the underlying condition may be directly linked to the resolution, progression, or recurrences of scleritis. Partial vision loss that may develop as a result of scleritis is usually permanent. In rare cases when the sclera is perforated, the eye may be lost.

Differential Diagnosis
Episcleritis, uveitis, conjunctivitis, keratitis, cerebral tumor, eye trauma, and iritis can resemble scleritis.

Specialists
- Ophthalmologist

Rehabilitation
In extreme cases where vision loss is permanent or severe, the individual may need to be referred to an appropriate agency for the blind.

Work Restrictions / Accommodations
Depending on the severity of the condition and extent of complications, the individual may need special accommodations to compensate for vision loss. In uncomplicated cases, the individual may need only a few days or weeks for recovery. Since the condition tends to recur, additional time off may be needed for medical intervention. If permanent vision loss has occurred, work environments may need to be adjusted to provide for large or high contrast print, or higher illumination. Tasks requiring keen visual acuity may need to be reassigned if vision is permanently impaired.

Comorbid Conditions
Comorbid conditions include rheumatoid arthritis, systemic lupus erythematosus, ankylosing spondylitis, polyarteritis nodosa, relapsing polychondritis, sarcoidosis, syphilis, post-herpes zoster ophthalmicus, tuberculosis, gout, Lyme disease, and hypertension.

Complications
Swelling of the central retina (macular edema) may cause a decrease in vision. Softening of the white portion of the eye (scleromalacia) may occur, especially when scleritis is associated with rheumatoid arthritis. Perforations may also result, leading to possible loss of the eye. While scleritis often responds well to corticosteroid eyedrops, in severe cases use of these drugs may actually increase the risk of perforation. Without prompt treatment, conditions such as cataracts, glaucoma, retinal

detachment, keratitis, uveitis, or optic atrophy could result. Scleritis usually responds to treatment but also tends to recur.

Factors Influencing Duration

Length of disability may be affected by the severity of the condition, response to treatment, or by the presence of an underlying autoimmune disease and the treatment it will require.

Length of Disability

Individuals who experience permanent vision loss may be unable to continue performing tasks that require keen visual acuity.

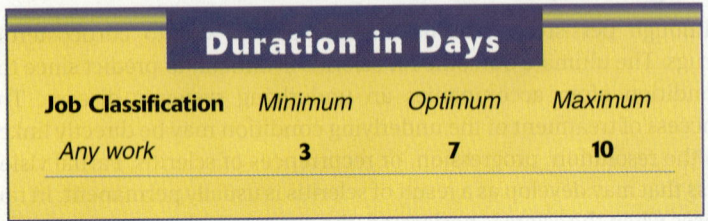

Duration in Days

Job Classification	Minimum	Optimum	Maximum
Any work	3	7	10

Failure to Recover

If an individual fails to recover within the maximum duration expectancy period, the reader may wish to reference the following questions to assist in better understanding the specifics of an individual's medical case.

Regarding diagnosis:

- Has diagnosis of scleritis been confirmed?
- Does the individual have a history of autoimmune disorders such as rheumatoid arthritis that may have caused the condition?
- Have underlying conditions, such as systemic lupus erythematosus, ankylosing spondylitis, polyarteritis nodosa, relapsing polychondritis, sarcoidosis, syphilis, post-herpes zoster ophthalmicus, tuberculosis, gout, Lyme disease, or hypertension, been identified or ruled out?
- Is underlying condition receiving appropriate treatment?
- Has individual experienced any complications from scleritis such as macular edema or scleromalacia?

Regarding treatment:

- Did the individual receive prompt medical treatment after scleritis was apparent?
- Has the inflammation from scleritis spread to other parts of the eye?
- Is there suspicion or evidence of sclera perforation due to use of corticosteroid eyedrops?
- Has surgical repair been performed? Is it anticipated?
- Has drug therapy decreased symptoms? If not, what other treatment options are available?

Regarding prognosis:

- Is underlying condition responding to treatment? If not, what is next in the overall treatment plan?
- Did vision loss occur?
- Is treatment for scleritis (and its underlying condition) being aggressively addressed?
- Does the individual have repeated episodes of scleritis? What is the suspected cause? What can be done to prevent or reduce frequency of recurrences?

References

Adler, Jonathan, and Loice Swisher. Scleritis. eMedicine.com 24 Jan 2001. 13 Feb 2001 < http://www.emedicine.com/emerg/topic521.htm >.

Scleroderma

Other names / synonyms: Dermatosclerosis, Localized Scleroderma, Progressive Systemic Sclerosis

710.1

Definition

Scleroderma is a rare, multisystem, complex disease where the skin hardens and thickens. There are two forms of the disease. When the disease involves the skin and the tissue beneath the skin, it is called localized or limited scleroderma. When the disease also involves internal organs, it is called systemic scleroderma. Localized scleroderma is more common than systemic scleroderma.

The cause of scleroderma is unknown. Various substances such as vinyl chloride, silica dust, and organic solvents have been implicated as causative agents but there is insufficient evidence to link these substances with scleroderma. One hallmark characteristic is the overproduction of collagen, a protein found in skin, bone, tendon, and cartilage. This leads to progressive accumulation of fibrous tissue (fibrosis) in the skin and certain internal organs especially the heart, lungs, and gastrointestinal tract. There is also an autoimmune component of scleroderma, as affected individuals possess antibodies to specific proteins in their cells. In fact, an association exists between certain antibodies and specific clinical subsets of scleroderma.

The usual course of localized scleroderma involves a period of about 2 years during which the skin and underlying tissues harden and stiffen. After that time, the skin symptoms rarely become worse and may even lessen. In rare instances, the hands may become permanently crippled. Localized scleroderma can be subdivided into different forms including morphea and linear scleroderma.

When systemic scleroderma occurs, organ involvement may produce hypertension, lung problems, heart disease, kidney failure, and intestinal tract problems. The final stage of the disease occurs when the kidneys fail and a severe form of high blood pressure (malignant hypertension) develops, which is the main cause of death. Since systemic scleroderma has a large variety of symptoms and signs in each individual, is has been classified into types that include diffuse scleroderma, CREST syndrome, unclassified or transitional form, and overlap syndromes.

Most individuals with scleroderma show symptoms between the ages of 20 and 40. In the US, the yearly incidence of scleroderma is 1 to 20 per million. The incidence is higher in the US than in other countries. Incidence in women is high with the female to male ratio varying between 3 and 8 to one. Scleroderma is a very rare disease with a prevalence rate of 240 per million. Scleroderma appears to be more common in blacks than whites. Blacks, males, and older individuals tend to experience a more rapid progression of the disease. The average annual mortality rate for scleroderma is 1 to 3 per million.

Diagnosis

History: The symptoms and signs of localized scleroderma are thickening and tightening of the skin particularly on the arms, face, or hands that result in a loss of flexibility. These areas also show changes in coloration (pigmentation) of the skin. The individual may complain of puffy hands and feet particularly in the morning. Joint pain and stiffness may occur.

Symptoms and signs of systemic scleroderma include those of localized scleroderma. Most individuals (90%) complain of abnormally cold and numb fingers in response to cold environments caused by an abnormal degree of spasm of the blood vessels (Raynaud's phenomenon). Joint pain, fever, muscle weakness, general discomfort, and swelling are common. Individuals with dysfunction of the canal leading from the throat to the stomach (esophagus) may report heartburn (gastroesophageal reflux), difficulty swallowing, regurgitation of food, and impaired speech (dysphagia). The individual with gastrointestinal involvement may report weight loss (anorexia), nausea, vomiting, bloating, diarrhea, and constipation. Individuals with advanced disease may report shortness of breath.

Physical exam: Skin changes are the hallmark sign of scleroderma. Thickened skin that has lost normal folds, changes in skin pigmentation, spots resembling birthmarks (telangiectasia), and ulcers on the fingertips may be apparent. The hands may display a decreased range of motion. Heart and lung problems may be detected.

Tests: Certain blood tests (ANA studies, RA factor, HLA typing) and removal of a sample of the affected skin (biopsy) for analysis are often performed. The use of diagnostic testing is dependent on the stage and form of the disease. For instance, endoscopy may be performed for gastrointestinal involvement, electroencephalogram (ECG) for heart concerns, and lung function tests for lung involvement.

Treatment

There is no cure for scleroderma. Treatment depends on the severity of the disease and aims to preserve normal body functions and minimize complications. Corticosteroids are sometimes used for skin sclerosis. Antihypertensive medications are used in the treatment of systemic sclerosis. Antibiotics are often prescribed to control the overgrowth of intestinal flora. Other gastrointestinal problems are treated with antacids, prokinetics, and dietary changes. Raynaud's phenomenon is treated with calcium-channel blockers.

Prognosis

In most individuals with localized scleroderma, the disease is self-limited. Hand debilitation can occur in varying degrees.

Systemic scleroderma usually progresses over a period of many years. There may be periods when the disease process seems to be unchanging. Occasionally, the symptoms may lessen (remission) either in certain localized areas or throughout the body. When the disease involves certain internal organs, it becomes life-threatening. Approximately 30% of the individuals with systemic scleroderma die within 5 years of onset.

Differential Diagnosis

Other disorders that have common presenting features are eosinophilic fasciitis and eosinophilia myalgia syndrome.

Specialists

- Dermatologist
- Immunologist
- Rheumatologist

Rehabilitation

Ongoing, home-based physical therapy consisting of stretching, isotonics, and moderate aerobic exercises is usually important to help maintain flexibility and muscle strength.

Work Restrictions / Accommodations

Because of the various symptoms in scleroderma, the work environment accommodations should be considered on an individual basis. In general, work requiring fine motor skills may prove difficult, if not impossible, for individuals with hand debilitation.

Comorbid Conditions

Heart disease, lung disease, kidney disease, gastrointestinal disease, hypertension, and cancer can compound systemic sclerosis and increase the length of disability. Immunodeficiency disorders can cause the individual to be more prone to infection.

Complications

Injury to sclerotic hands can result in infection that can lead to death of the tissue (necrosis). Smoking and exposure to cold temperatures can trigger attacks of Raynaud's phenomenon. Individuals with gastroesophageal reflux are at risk of developing infections of the esophagus. Individuals with scleroderma are twice as likely than the general population to develop cancer especially lung cancer. Depression is common.

Factors Influencing Duration

Length of disability may be influenced by age, disease progression, type of disease (localized or systemic), severity of symptoms, whether or not the individual is in a remission period, and mental health.

Length of Disability

The course of systemic scleroderma varies greatly. Disability duration depends on job requirements and type of scleroderma. Disability may be permanent for individuals who require fine motor skills to perform their duties.

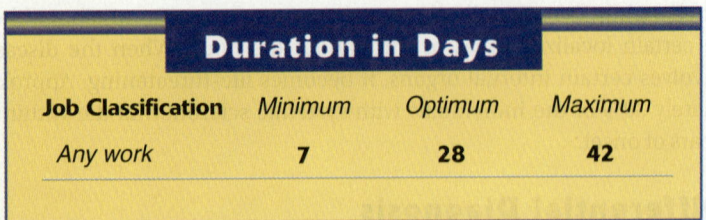

Job Classification	Minimum	Optimum	Maximum
Any work	7	28	42

Failure to Recover

If an individual fails to recover within the maximum duration expectancy period, the reader may wish to reference the following questions to assist in better understanding the specifics of an individual's medical case.

Regarding diagnosis:

- Has diagnosis of scleroderma been confirmed?
- If diagnosis is uncertain, have conditions with similar symptoms been ruled out?
- Has the stage and form (localized or systemic) of the disease been determined?

Regarding treatment:

- Although there is no cure for scleroderma, has treatment been effective in preserving normal body functions?
- Has drug therapy been effective against specific symptoms?
- Is individual participating in an ongoing, home-based physical therapy program in order to help maintain flexibility and muscle strength?
- Have complications (tissue necrosis, Raynaud's phenomenon, esophageal infection) responded to appropriate treatment?
- Has individual been advised to stop smoking? If unable to stop on his/her own, would individual benefit from enrollment in a community stop smoking program?
- Have psychological issues, such as depression, been appropriately addressed through counseling?

Regarding prognosis:

- Is individual compliant with treatment plan? If not, what can be done to enhance compliance?
- Does individual have a coexisting condition (such as heart disease, lung disease, kidney disease, gastrointestinal disease, hypertension, cancer) that may complicate treatment and impact recovery?

References

Anderson, Philip, and Kristin Malaker. "Less Common Disorders." Managing Skin Diseases. Hiscock, Tim, ed. Baltimore: Williams & Wilkins, 1999. 281.

Mayes, MD. "Photopheresis and Autoimmune Diseases." Rheumatic Diseases Clinics of North America 26 1 (2000): viii-ix.

Merkel, Peter. "Measurement of Functional Status, Self-assessment, and Psychological Well-being in Scleroderma." Current Opinion in Rheumatology 10 (1998): 589-594.

Seikowski, K., B. Weber, and U.F. Haustein. "Effect of Hypnosis and Autogenic Training on Acral Circulation and Coping with the Illness in Patients with Progressive Scleroderma." Hautarzt 46 2 (1995): 94-101.

Silman, Alan. "Scleroderma - Demographics and Survival." The Journal of Rheumatology 24 suppl 48 (1997): 58-61.

Steen, Virginia. "Occupational Scleroderma." Current Opinion in Rheumatology 11 (1999): 490-494.

Steen, Virginia. Rheumatic Disease Clinics of North America: Scleroderma. Philadelphia: W.B. Saunders Company, 1996.

Steen, Virginia. Rheumatic Disease Clinics of North America. Philadelphia: W.B. Saunders Company, 1996.

Sclerotherapy

Other names / synonyms: Esophageal Varices Injection, Hemorrhoid Injection, Sclerotherapy of Esophageal Varices, Sclerotherapy of Hemorrhoids, Sclerotherapy of Varicose Veins

39.92, 42.33, 49.42

Definition

Sclerotherapy is a method of treating distended, incompetent veins (varicose veins) that have failed to respond to other, simpler forms of treatment.

Sclerotherapy may be used to treat severe cases of hemorrhoids (varicose veins in the anus), esophageal varices (swollen, easily ruptured veins at the bottom of the esophagus), and distended, superficial veins in the legs.

In sclerotherapy, the vein is injected with an irritating chemical solution (sclerosant). The resulting inflammation in the vein's lining causes the vein to collapse, blocking it. Eventually scar tissue forms, permanently hardening and destroying (obliterating) the vein. Other, healthy veins now take over its work.

Varicose veins tend to run in families, and females are more likely to develop them. In addition, any condition that can result in increased pressure in the veins can cause the development of varicosities. Examples include cirrhosis of the liver or prolonged standing.

Reason for Procedure

Sclerotherapy is used in the treatment of severe varicose veins in the lining of the anus (hemorrhoids), distended veins at the bottom of the esophagus (esophageal varices), and severe varicose veins in the legs.

Without correction, hemorrhoids can cause rectal bleeding and increasing discomfort with bowel movements. A varicose vein that protrudes outside the rectum (prolapsed hemorrhoid) can form blood clots, preventing it from returning to its normal position inside the anus. Strangulation of the vein may occur, resulting in reduced blood supply and extreme pain. Esophageal varices are thin-walled veins that contain blood at a high pressure. If not corrected, esophageal varices can rupture, causing recurrent episodes of profuse bleeding and vomiting of blood (hematemesis). Without correction, large varicose veins in the legs may cause severe bleeding when bumped. Varicose veins may become severe enough to starve tissues of oxygen and nourishment, resulting in leg ulcers.

Description

Sclerotherapy for varicose veins in the leg is done on an outpatient basis without anesthesia. The individual initially stands and the needle is inserted into the vein. The leg is then elevated and the vein is injected with a sclerosing agent, most commonly 23.4% sodium chloride. Pressure is then applied to the leg with bandages. The compression is maintained for 2-3 weeks to allow for the obliteration of the vein.

Prolapsed hemorrhoids are directly injected with the sclerosing agent, usually 5% phenol. This procedure is usually performed with a long needle and an anoscope. Minimal pain is associated with the procedure.

Sclerotherapy of esophageal varices is more difficult. It can be performed using a scope (endoscopy) inserted down the esophagus. This is usually performed under sedation. The veins are identified and injected with the sclerosing agent.

Prognosis

Sclerotherapy for varicose veins in the legs has excellent short-term results. It also has the best cosmetic results of any of the treatments for varicose veins. Recurrence, however, is a possibility.

Sclerotherapy for hemorrhoids combined with dietary counseling is very effective in reducing or eliminating hemorrhoids.

Sclerotherapy for esophageal varices is about 93% successful at stopping bleeding. Since these varices usually result from chronic conditions such as cirrhosis of the liver, there is a chance of recurrence.

Specialists

- Gastroenterologist
- General Surgeon
- Internist
- Proctologist
- Vascular Surgeon

Work Restrictions / Accommodations

Heavy work, lifting, and strenuous physical activities need to be temporarily modified. Periods of prolonged sitting or standing need to be avoided. Individuals who have sclerotherapy for varicose veins may need to elevate legs when sitting.

Individuals who have had leg veins injected must wear special compression stockings for several weeks to prevent immediate recurrence.

Comorbid Conditions

Any bleeding disorder may impact recovery.

Procedure Complications

Sclerotherapy of leg veins is not typically associated with significant complications, although infection is possible. Hemorrhoid injection can be associated with sloughing of the rectal lining, infection, acute inflammation (proctitis), and sensitivity reactions to the sclerosing agent. Sclerotherapy of esophageal varices may be accompanied by significant complications such as perforation of the esophagus, hemorrhage, or infection (mediastinitis).

Factors Influencing Duration

Length of disability may be influenced by the severity of the condition, extent of treatment necessary, response to treatment, or by the presence of complications.

Length of Disability

Hemorrhoids.

	Duration in Days		
Job Classification	Minimum	Optimum	Maximum
Sedentary work	1	2	3
Light work	1	2	3
Medium work	1	3	7
Heavy work	1	4	7
Very Heavy work	1	4	7

Varicose veins.

	Duration in Days		
Job Classification	Minimum	Optimum	Maximum
Sedentary work	3	4	7
Light work	3	4	7
Medium work	7	9	14
Heavy work	7	9	14
Very Heavy work	7	9	14

Esophageal varices.

	Duration in Days		
Job Classification	Minimum	Optimum	Maximum
Sedentary work	14	28	56
Light work	28	42	70
Medium work	42	63	84
Heavy work	56	70	112
Very Heavy work	56	70	112

References

Russel, Thomas. "Anorectum." Current Surgical Diagnosis and Treatment. Way, Lawrence, ed. Norwalk: Appleton & Lange, 1991. 681-699.

Schwartz, Seymour, MD. Principles of Surgery. New York: McGraw-Hill, 1999.

Sebaceous Cyst

Other names / synonyms: Epidermoid Cyst, Follicular Infundibular Cyst

706.1, 706.2

Definition

Sebaceous cyst refers to a slow growing, noncancerous tumor or swelling of the skin.

It is a small sac filled with material from hair follicles, the skin, or an oily substance known as sebum. A sebaceous cyst can occur when the local circulation becomes impaired and blocks the sebaceous glands. Sebaceous cysts are commonly found on the face, ears, back, or genitals. Although harmless, they may grow to a very large size. If infected by bacteria, they can be very painful. In the face, scalp, or back, they are usually related to hair follicles. When found on the scalp, a sebaceous cyst is called a wen.

The two subtypes of sebaceous cysts are epidermoid cysts and milia cysts. Epidermoid cysts contain cells from the outer layer of skin (epidermis). Milia cysts are miniature epidermoid cysts 1 to 2 mm in diameter that usually occur on the face.

The cause (etiology) of sebaceous cysts is unknown. In some cases, it may be from inadequate washing of the skin. Sebaceous cysts are slightly more common in men than in women.

Diagnosis

History: Individuals may report a hard, usually painless lump under the skin. The lumps are usually found on the scalp, face, ear, and genitals.

Physical exam: The exam may reveal a large, smooth nodule under the skin.

Tests: Although not usually necessary, diagnostic evaluation may involve needle aspiration. In this procedure, a needle is inserted into the cyst so that fluid or cells can be withdrawn for microscopic analysis.

Treatment

Most small cysts do not require treatment. Large or painful cysts or cysts that have become infected should be surgically removed. This is usually an outpatient procedure done under local anesthetic. A small incision is made in the skin where the entire cyst is removed. Simply draining a cyst is ineffective because it can grow back unless the entire cyst wall is removed. The surgery is usually done on an outpatient basis under local anesthesia.

Prognosis

If the entire cyst wall is surgically removed, recurrence is rare. Large, painful, or infected cysts that are not treated surgically continue to persist.

Differential Diagnosis

Symptoms of sebaceous carcinoma may be similar to a sebaceous cyst. Other skin cysts or nodules resembling sebaceous cyst include carbuncle, folliculitis, follicular isthmus cyst, pilar cyst, eccrine poroma, and hidradenoma.

Specialists

- Dermatologist
- General Surgeon
- Internist

Work Restrictions / Accommodations

In general, work restrictions or accommodations are not required unless the location of the cyst inhibits motion.

Comorbid Conditions

Comorbid conditions include acne, bacterial and fungal skin infections, and various skin rashes (dermatoses).

Complications

Attempting to drain a cyst rather than surgically removing it can result in infection. Unless the entire cyst wall is removed, the cyst can recur. Spontaneous rupture of the cyst may also occur and lead to infection of the cyst and surrounding skin.

Factors Influencing Duration

Length of disability may be influenced by the location and size of the cyst, the procedure used to remove it, or any infection.

Length of Disability

Surgical excision.

Duration in Days

Job Classification	Minimum	Optimum	Maximum
Any work	1	3	7

Failure to Recover

If an individual fails to recover within the maximum duration expectancy period, the reader may wish to reference the following questions to assist in better understanding the specifics of an individual's medical case.

Regarding diagnosis:

- Does individual report a hard lump under the skin? Is it painful?
- Is cyst located on the scalp, face, ears, back or genitals?
- On exam, does individual have a large, smooth nodule under the skin?
- Was a needle aspiration done?
- Were conditions with similar symptoms ruled out?

Regarding treatment:

- Was cyst large or painful? Did it become infected? Was cyst surgically removed?

Regarding prognosis:

- Can individual's employer accommodate any necessary restrictions?
- Does individual have any conditions that may affect ability to recover?
- Have any complications developed such as infection or a recurrence?

References

Omura, Emily F. "Benign and Malignant Adnexal Tumors." <u>Principles and Practice of Dermatology, 2nd ed.</u> Sams, W. Mitchell, and Peter J. Lynch, eds. New York: Churchill Livingstone, 1996. 241-252.

Sedative, Hypnotic or Anxiolytic Dependence

Other names / synonyms: Antianxiety Drug Dependence, Barbiturate Dependence, Benzodiazepine Addiction, Prescription Drug Abuse, Prescription Drug Dependence, Tranquilizer Dependence

304.1, 305.4

Definition

This is a condition where individuals become dependent on or abuse substances used for their calming effect (sedatives), sleep-inducing effect (hypnotics), and anti-anxiety effect (anxiolytics). These substances (SHAs) include benzodiazepine, carbamate, and barbiturate medications, and are commonly used to treat anxiety, insomnia, muscle tension (spasticity), seizures (convulsions), and to aid in alcohol/drug withdrawal. They are sometimes used to treat high blood pressure (hypertension). Occasionally, an individual who is prescribed one of these medications will abuse it or develop a substance dependence. These medications may also be sold on the street and used for recreational purposes. A physiologic dependence upon the medication, which is being taken as prescribed and necessary, is not in itself considered substance abuse.

Even though up to 90% of hospitalized individuals receive orders for one of the SHAs, and more than 15% of American adults use these medications during any one year, less than 1% of individuals are identified has having abuse or dependence problems associated with their use. An individual is considered to have a substance dependence if he or she develops drug-seeking behavior to the extent that important activities are given up or reduced to obtain the substance, or if the medication is consistently taken in excess of what is prescribed.

Diagnosis

According to the DSM-IV, criteria for the diagnosis of sedative dependence include sedative abuse, defined as a destructive pattern of sedative use, leasing to significant social, occupational, or medical impairment. At least three of the following must have been present when the sedative use was at its worst: tolerance, withdrawal, greater use (using larger amounts or over a longer period) than intended, unsuccessful efforts to cut down or control use, great deal of time spent in use or in recovering from hangovers, reduction in social, occupational or recreational activities because of use, and continued use despite knowing that it caused significant physical or psychological problems. Sedative tolerance is defined as the need for markedly increased amounts of drug for intoxication to occur, or markedly decreased effect with continued use of the same amount of sedative. Sedative withdrawal symptoms include two or more of the following symptoms which develop within several hours to a few days of decreased use: sweating or rapid pulse, increased hand shaking (tremor), sleeplessness (insomnia), nausea or vomiting, restlessness (physical agitation), anxiety, transient sensations of seeing, feeling, or hearing something that isn't there (visual, tactile, or auditory hallucinations or illusions), or major convulsions (grand mal seizures). The individual may also be considered to have sedative withdrawal if sedative is taken to relieve or avoid withdrawal symptoms.

History: The main symptoms of dependence on sedatives, hypnotics, and anxiolytics (SHAs) include a strong desire or craving for the drug, seeking out the drug (often at the expense of other activities), difficulty stopping or cutting down, and continued use despite physical or psychological consequences. Individuals who are addicted to SHAs will suffer withdrawal symptoms if the dose is stopped or reduced too rapidly, which may also include gastrointestinal upset, loss of appetite, and weakness. Severe withdrawal symptoms, which occur mainly with the long-acting barbiturates and tranquilizers, include seizures, confusion (delirium), suspiciousness (paranoia), and uncontrolled rapid or irregular heartbeat (arrhythmia or palpitations).

The possibility of substance abuse or dependency needs to be considered in any situation in which the individual has consistent, ongoing, or deteriorating problems in the presence of continuing use. The clinician needs to develop sensitivity to the diagnostic clues of impairment of social, emotional, occupational, or psychological functioning. Individuals frequently deny that a problem exists despite obvious signs of intoxication.

Physical exam: Signs of sedative dependence, or prolonged use, include slightly decreased heart rate, respiratory rate, and blood pressure. Constant, involuntary, jerking movement of the eyeballs (nystagmus) is the single most useful finding seen in SHA dependence or intoxication. Physical signs of intoxication may include slurred speech, unsteady gait, loss of coordination, impaired thinking, memory, or attention, sluggishness, and tremor. Physical signs of withdrawal are sweating, increased heart rate, increased hand tremor, insomnia, nausea or vomiting, transient hallucinations, psychomotor agitation, anxiety, or seizures. Characteristics of overdose include slow shallow breathing (respiratory depression), clammy skin, low blood pressure (hypotension), stupor, shock, and coma. Death can follow if the low blood pressure and respiratory depression are not treated.

Tests: A polydrug urine screen should be ordered in case the individual is using drugs other than sedatives. Levels of specific SHAs may also be determined. Both blood and urine samples may be used, but urine testing is generally the method of choice. A positive drug screen should always be confirmed by a second test, since it may result in serious consequences for the individual.

Treatment

Recovery from SHA dependence occurs in four phases. The acute phase focuses on alleviating symptoms of physiological withdrawal, and typically lasts for 3 days to 2 weeks or more, since the SHA drugs can stay in the body for fairly long periods after the individual has stopped using them. During the second phase, a one-month period of abstinence, the individual focuses on changing behaviors. The early remission phase can last up to 12 months, and the sustained remission phase lasts as long as the individual abstains from using or abusing these medications.

Treatment during the acute phase requires close observation for at least 72-96 hours for the emergence of withdrawal symptoms while SHAs are withheld. Medication therapy in the acute phase includes the use of benzodiazepines to decrease tremors and reduce or prevent increased blood pressure and heart rate. Medications for other symptoms, such as diarrhea or muscle aches, are given as needed. Most individuals are admitted to a hospital or a specialized unit for the first few days of treatment. Barbiturate detoxification can usually be completed in two weeks, but longer periods may be needed.

Treatment for the one-month abstinence and early remission phases may include education about physical, emotional, and mental aspects of addiction and recovery, identification of stressors and stress management skills, assistance with improved coping skills, assertiveness training, and relaxation training. The individual should be encouraged to avoid people, places and things related to SHA use. Drug urine tests should be monitored periodically. A narcotic antagonist, such as naltrexone, which diminishes the effects of alcohol or sedatives, can be used to help some individuals remain abstinent. The long-term support that self-help groups such as Alcoholics Anonymous provide can be crucial in preventing relapse. Rational Recovery is a self-help group based on cognitive rather than spiritual principles.

Prognosis

Some individuals respond to treatment and stay in remission, while others experience periods of relapse, in which they begin SHA use/abuse after a period of remission, and again meet the criteria for substance dependence. Some individuals are never able to abstain from use, and do not experience any periods of remission. Outcome is improved if the individual seeks treatment early in the disease process and has adequate social support systems in place. However, a significant number of individuals experience at least one relapse after treatment, and some individuals never seek treatment.

Differential Diagnosis

The individual using SHAs may be suffering from a psychiatric disorder along with the substance abuse disorder. Some types of SHA dependence may begin or be continued as a form of self-medication to treat anxiety, depression, or other psychiatric disorders. The most prevalent forms of psychiatric disorders found in those with substance abuse problems are affective disorders, antisocial personality disorder, and alcoholism. SHA dependence needs to be distinguished from SHA use as prescribed for medical conditions, from occasional use for recreational purposes, and from repeated episodes of intoxication. Neurologic disorders such as stroke, TIA, Huntington's chorea, or delirium may share some symptoms and findings with SHA dependence.

Specialists

- Advanced Practice Registered Nurse
- Psychiatrist
- Psychologist

Work Restrictions / Accommodations

Many employers have systems in place for individuals recovering from substance dependence disorders to return to work under special contracts or conditions. These contracts usually provide guidelines for testing blood and urine levels of identified substances, for evaluating work performance, and for treating substance abuse.

Temporary work accommodations may include reducing or eliminating activities where the safety of self or others is contingent upon a constant and/or high level of alertness, such as driving a motor vehicle, operating complex machinery, or handling dangerous chemicals; introducing the individual to new or stressful situations gradually under individually appropriate supervision; allowing some flexibility in scheduling to attend therapy appointments (which normally should occur during the employee's personal time); promoting planned, proactive management of identified problem areas; and offering timely feedback on job performance issues. It will be helpful if accommodations are documented in a written plan designed to promote timely and safe transition back to full work productivity.

Comorbid Conditions

Coexisting conditions that may affect recovery and lengthen disability include psychiatric disorders, such as schizophrenia, major depression, or anxiety disorder, and the abuse or dependence on tobacco, alcohol or other substances.

Complications

Sudden withdrawal of the SHAs can lead to tremors, anxiety, agitation, hallucinations, grand mal seizures, heart arrhythmias, or death. The use of SHAs with similar substances, such as alcohol, multiplies their effect and greatly increases the risk of death. Complications of SHA dependence include pneumonia, sepsis, liver failure, kidney failure, and nervous system dysfunction (peripheral neuropathy) in the arms and legs, in addition to the risk of accidental injury.

Factors Influencing Duration

The individual's readiness to change, severity of the abuse or dependence, success of the treatment program, appropriate patient-treatment matching, stable history of employment, and any physical complications may influence the outcome.

Length of Disability

The maximum expected length of disability includes inpatient hospitalization. Non-hospital detoxification and counseling are becoming more common and most outpatient programs enable the individual to continue working. The acute phase of withdrawal requires close medical supervision.

Detoxification and counseling.

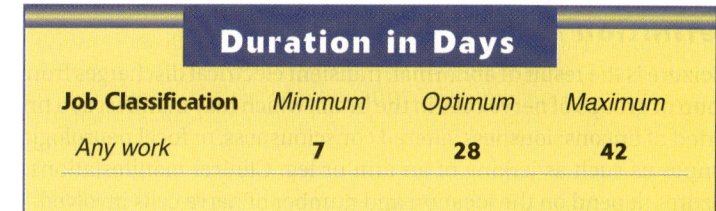

Duration in Days			
Job Classification	Minimum	Optimum	Maximum
Any work	7	28	42

Failure to Recover

If an individual fails to recover within the maximum duration expectancy period, the reader may wish to reference the following questions to assist in better understanding the specifics of an individual's medical case.

Regarding diagnosis:

- Did the individual have a comprehensive psychiatric evaluation, which is essential in developing a treatment plan? If not, what areas were omitted? Would this information affect the current treatment plan? If so, what changes can be made?
- Has diagnosis of SHA dependence been confirmed?

- Was SHA dependence distinguished from SHA use as prescribed for medical conditions, from occasional use for recreational purposes, and from repeated episodes of intoxication?
- Have conditions with similar symptoms been ruled out?
- Have all underlying psychiatric and medical disorders been identified?

Regarding treatment:

- Was detoxification successful? If not, would addition of a longer-acting, less-addictive drug to decrease withdrawal symptoms be beneficial?
- Was treatment approach matched to the particular needs of the individual?
- Were individual's preferences, the medical issues to be addressed, associated psychiatric disorders, and the individual's past response to various forms of treatment taken into consideration?
- Has individual's life focused predominantly on substance use?
- If individual does not meet clinical criteria for hospitalization, would the individual benefit from admission to a residential treatment program?
- Since concurrent use of or withdrawal from other substances can complicate treatment, is the individual being monitored for the presence of other substances?
- Are underlying psychiatric disorders being identified and treated concurrently?
- Did comprehensive rehabilitation program include education about physical, emotional, and mental aspects of addiction and recovery, identification of stressors and stress management skills, assistance with improved coping skills, assertiveness training, and relaxation training?
- While the individual should be encouraged to avoid people, places and things related to SHA use, is individual receiving the long-term support that self-help groups provide?

Regarding prognosis:

- What support system does individual have in place to provide external support and motivation to continue in treatment beyond the initial stage of detoxification?
- Does the individual have the necessary tools, skills, and encouragement to move ahead with his/her life?

References

Compton, W.M., et al. "Substance Dependence and Other Psychiatric Disorders Among Drug Dependent Subjects: Race and Gender Correlates." Am J Addict 9 2 (2000): 113-125.

Frances, Allen. Diagnostic and Statistical Manual of Mental Disorders: 4th ed, text revision. Washington, DC: American Psychiatric Association, 2000.

Hall, Laura Lee. "Making the ADA Work for People with Psychiatric Disabilities." Mental Disorder, Work Disability, and the Law. Bonnie, Richard J., and John Monahan, eds. Chicago: The University of Chicago Press, 1997. 241-280.

Kidorf, M., et al. "Concurrent Validity of Cocaine and Sedative Dependence Diagnoses in Opioid-dependent Outpatients." Drug Alcohol Depend 42 2 (1996): 117-123.

Lader, M. "Iatrogenic Sedative Dependence and Abuse - Have Doctors Learnt Caution?" Addiction 93 8 (1998): 1133-1135.

Long, Philip. Sedative Dependence: Treatment. Mental Health Net. 01 Jan 2000. 08 Feb 2001 <http://www.mentalhealth.com/rx/p23-sb10.html>.

Seizures

Other names / synonyms: Convulsions, Epilepsy, Fits

345, 780.3

Definition

A seizure is the result of abnormal, transient electrical discharges from a group or groups of nerve cells in the brain, which may manifest as a brief period of unconsciousness, altered consciousness, or focal neurological symptoms such as jerking of an arm or leg. Clinical manifestations of seizures depend on the location and number of nerve cells involved.

Seizures are classified as partial, generalized, and unclassified, as defined by the International League Against Epilepsy in 1981. Partial seizures involve only a portion of the brain, and are further classified as either simple, without loss of consciousness, or complex, during which the individual loses consciousness. If the abnormal electrical discharge spreads to involve the entire brain, partial seizures can become generalized. Generalized seizures can range from an episode lasting 10 seconds or less in which the individual stops what they are doing and has a blank stare (absence seizure), to a full-fledged prolonged episode (tonic-clonic or grand-mal seizure) involving body stiffening followed by jerking movements of arms and legs.

Possible causes of seizures may include other medical conditions such as stroke, brain tumor, trauma to the brain, birth defects in the brain, infections, low blood glucose (hypoglycemia), heatstroke, withdrawal from long-term use of alcohol, and drugs or medications. Hysterical individuals may develop episodic symptoms resembling seizures (pseudoseizures). If a seizure occurs only once, it is referred to as an isolated, nonrecurrent seizure. Recurrent seizures are referred to as epilepsy.

Epilepsy is one of the most common diseases of the brain and affects about 1-2% of North Americans. More than 10% of the population will a have a single seizure or a few seizures during their lifetime.

Diagnosis

History: The manifestations of seizures depend on the seizure type. In addition to obtaining history from the individual, it is vital to obtain history from witnesses to the seizure episodes, as description of symptoms during and following an episode is the cornerstone of diagnosis.

In partial seizures, individuals may report chewing movements or smacking of the lips; numbness or tingling of the limbs or face; twitching of the muscles; and distorted, unpleasant perceptions of odor, vision, or time. Generalized seizures may be preceded by an aura of feeling poorly or of an unpleasant odor. During the generalized seizure, which lasts 1-2 minutes, there is loss of consciousness, body stiffening (tonic posturing), and jerking of the limbs (clonic movements), which may cause self-injury or tongue-biting. Loss of control of bowels and bladder may also occur. After the generalized seizure, deep sleep followed by lethargy, headache, confusion, and muscle soreness may be present (post-ictal state). Absence seizures are associated with 10-to-30-second periods of loss of consciousness, with blank stare and fluttering of the eyelids. They may recur several times during the day. Myoclonic seizures are brief and repetitive, and are associated with jerking of the limbs.

Status epilepticus is associated with continuos seizures, and may be fatal if untreated. Epilepsia partialis continua is a rare form of hand or face seizures that may recur several times for seconds or minutes.

Physical exam: The exam during the seizure may reveal tonic-clonic movements or eye movements characteristic of specific seizure types. Following a generalized tonic-clonic seizure, there may be lethargy, sleepiness, confusion, headache, muscle soreness, and weakness on one side of the body that later resolves (Todd's post-ictal paralysis). Careful neurological examination should be done looking for focal abnormalities related to an underlying structural cause of seizure, such as stroke or brain tumor. Physical examination may suggest an underlying medical cause, such as fever and neck stiffness in the case of infection of the spinal fluid and brain coverings (meningitis).

Tests: Electroencephalogram (EEG) should be done to look for abnormal electrical discharges (epileptogenic focus) that can help diagnose the seizure type. However, the history is most important in making the diagnosis, and negative EEG does not rule out the diagnosis of seizure. Various maneuvers (activation procedures) can bring out abnormal electrical discharges on the EEG that would not be seen otherwise, such as doing the EEG when the individual has been awake for 24 hours or more (sleep-deprived EEG), or when breathing rapidly and deeply (hyperventilation), or when lights are flashed in the eyes (photic stimulation). If EEG is still negative, but seizures are strongly suspected clinically, EEG monitoring can be done for longer periods by studying the individual overnight in a sleep laboratory or by hooking up recording equipment during daily activities.

To rule out stroke, brain tumor, or other structural causes of seizures, the brain should be studied by brain MRI or CT in most cases starting in adulthood. Blood tests should be done to check for low glucose, sodium, magnesium, or calcium, or other chemical imbalances that could cause generalized seizures. Drug and alcohol screen may be indicated. A lumbar puncture should be performed if infection is suspected, once brain MRI or CT rules out a structural cause of increased pressure within the brain.

Treatment

Treatment should be aimed at controlling the seizures and treating the underlying disorders, such as brain tumors, infections, and metabolic or endocrine abnormalities. Opinion is divided on whether a first seizure should be treated.

Different anticonvulsant medications may be used to treat different kinds of seizures. Depending on the symptoms of the seizure and how it is controlled, combination therapy may be needed. Once seizures are controlled, medications should be continued for approximately one year. If there are no more seizures and EEG is normal, medications may be cautiously tapered off and discontinued in some individuals. Individuals with uncontrolled seizures should not drive, operate heavy machinery, or work at heights, underwater, or in other potentially dangerous situations.

The vagus nerve stimulator (VNS) is a device that can be used for the treatment of refractory partial epilepsy in adults. The VNS generator is implanted in the upper left side of the chest and can be activated with a magnet at the beginning of the seizure. This action can stop or limit the spread of seizure.

Ten to twenty percent of individuals do not respond to medication therapy. For these individuals, surgery may be an option. Surgery involves resection of the epileptic focus in the brain (corticectomy).

In some individuals, especially children with specific seizure types, dietary modification may improve seizure control. All individuals with seizures should avoid alcohol, drugs, unnecessary medications, undue stress, improper nutrition, and sleep deprivation.

Prognosis

Outcome in seizure disorders varies depending on the seizure type, underlying cause, and response to treatment. In general, outcome is better now that there is a wide range of effective medications. Outcome is good in 60-65% of individuals with new-onset seizures treated with a single drug. Control refers to lack of seizures with use of medication, and remission refers to lack of seizures even when medications are discontinued. Poor seizure control is associated with epilepsy of longer duration, partial seizures, more seizures before treatment, seizures of known cause, abnormal activity on EEG, frequent seizures, or delay in treatment for a year or more. In 20-year follow-up studies, 5-year remission is 50% or better. Although outcome is generally worse in complex partial seizures than in generalized seizures, better outcome in this condition is associated with normal intellectual functioning, and short duration and lower frequency of seizures. Epilepsy may affect life span, with sudden death due to seizure or irregular heart rhythm occurring in 1:2000 to 1:900 individuals with epilepsy.

Specialists

- Neurologist

Differential Diagnosis

Other conditions that present with similar symptoms may include withdrawal from alcohol or illicit drugs, fainting spells (syncope), episodes resembling stroke but which quickly resolve (transient ischemic attacks), and poison ingestion. Pseudoseizures seen in conversion disorder or hysteria resemble the episodic symptoms associated with seizures, but are not associated with abnormal electrical discharges on EEG. Dissociative symptoms associated with certain psychiatric conditions may resemble absence seizures. Spasms or tremors involving the limbs may resemble focal seizures.

Work Restrictions / Accommodations

For jobs that require operating machinery or motor vehicles, or working from heights or in other potentially dangerous situations, special precautions should be taken for those individuals who are at risk of recurrent seizures.

Comorbid Conditions

Comorbid conditions may include illicit drug dependence, alcoholism, structural diseases of the brain underlying the seizure disorder (such as stroke, head injury, or brain tumor), underlying metabolic or endocrine conditions, or brain infections such as meningitis or encephalitis.

Complications

Underlying conditions causing seizures, such as meningitis, brain tumor, stroke, head trauma, brain infections, drug or alcohol abuse, and metabolic or endocrine abnormalities, may cause complications. Self-injury may occur during a seizure, and may be fatal if the individual is behind the wheel or under water. Fear of loss of control coupled with the demands of ongoing medical treatment may affect employment and lead to social isolation. Antiepileptic medications may interfere with medications such as birth control pills, thereby leading to unwanted pregnancy. Use of antiepileptic medications during pregnancy may lead to birth defects, but uncontrolled seizures during pregnancy may pose an additional hazard.

Factors Influencing Duration

Length of disability may be influenced by the individual's response to treatment, frequency of seizures, underlying cause of the seizures, the mental and physical health of the individual, and specific job duties.

Length of Disability

A more specific diagnosis is required to determine disability duration. See specific seizure type for durations. Although seizure control is achieved in most individuals, disability may be permanent in those who do not respond to treatment.

Failure to Recover

If an individual fails to recover within the maximum duration expectancy period, the reader may wish to reference the following questions to assist in better understanding the specifics of an individual's medical case.

Regarding diagnosis:

- Does the individual have partial, generalized, or unclassified seizures?
- Does the individual have any other medical conditions such as stroke, brain tumor, trauma to the brain, birth defects in the brain, infections, hypoglycemia, heatstroke, withdrawal from long-term use of alcohol, and drugs or medications?
- Does the individual have pseudoseizures?
- Did the individual have only one seizure or recurrent seizures?
- Has the individual had a witnessed seizure?
- Does the individual or witness report chewing movements or smacking of the lips; numbness or tingling of the limbs or face; twitching of the muscles; and distorted, unpleasant perceptions of odor, vision, or time with their partial seizure?
- Does the individual have an aura with their grand mal seizure?
- Does the individual have a 1-2 minute loss of consciousness, tonic posturing and clonic movements? Does the individual lose bladder and or bowel control?
- Is the seizure followed by deep sleep then lethargy, headache, confusion, and muscle soreness (post-ictal state)?
- Does the individual have absence seizures with 10-to-30-second periods of loss of consciousness, with blank stare and fluttering of the eyelids?
- Does the individual have myoclonic seizures that are brief and repetitive, and are associated with jerking of the limbs?
- On physical exam was evidence of the underlying cause of the seizure seen such as stroke or meningitis?
- Has the individual had an EEG, MRI, CT scan, comprehensive blood testing and drug and alcohol screen? Was a lumbar puncture done?
- Have conditions with similar symptoms been ruled out?

Regarding treatment:

- Does the individual have an underlying condition? Is it being treated?
- Is the individual being treated with anticonvulsant medications?
- Is the individual a candidate for the vagus nerve stimulator? Has it been implanted?
- Did it become necessary for the individual have a corticectomy done surgically?
- Was the individual advised to avoid alcohol, drugs, unnecessary medications, undue stress, improper nutrition, and sleep deprivation?

Regarding prognosis:

- Is the individual's employer able to accommodate any necessary restrictions?
- Does the individual have any conditions that may affect their ability to recover?
- Does the individual have any complications such as status epilepticus, self-injury, social isolation or side effects of the anticonvulsants?

References

Willmore, James, and James W. Wheless, MD. "Chapter XII: Epilepsy." Dale, D.C., and Daniel D. Federman, MD New York: WebMD Corporation, 2000 Scientific American Medicine. 25 Oct 2000 <http://www.samed.com/sam/forms/index.htm>.

Senile Macular Degeneration

Other names / synonyms: Age-Related Macular Degeneration, ARMD, SMD

362.50, 362.51, 362.52

Definition

Senile macular degeneration (SMD) is a condition where the center of the retina (the macula) deteriorates with age and loses the ability to provide sharply focused, straight-ahead vision. While color and side (peripheral) vision remain intact, a blind area forms in the center of the visual field. Degeneration may occur at different rates in each eye, if both are affected. SMD is one of the leading causes of central vision loss in older age groups.

SMD manifests in two forms. Atrophic or dry macular degeneration is the most common, occurring in 80-90% of all cases of SMD. This form is due to atrophy of pigment cells below the retina, which then damages the central retinal or macular cells. This form of SMD develops very slowly and has no bleeding or drainage from the macula. Dimming or distortion of vision occurs and may be noticed during efforts to read. Both eyes are usually affected to some degree. Severe central vision loss occurs over a period of several years.

Dry SMD may develop into the other form of the disease called exudative or wet macular degeneration. In this form, a protective layer of tissue breaks down between the retina and underlying blood vessels (choroid). Tiny new blood vessels grow beneath the retina and then bleed. The leakage of blood raises the center of the macula while fluid destroys nearby light-sensitive cells. Scar tissue eventually forms when the mound shrinks leaving an elevated mass. Central vision loss may be severe.

SMD is also known as age-related macular degeneration (ARMD) and is more common in whites with light-colored hair and eyes. While aging is considered the major reason for development of the disease, heredity may also play a role. Eye injuries, smoking, high nearsightedness (myopia), antioxidant deficiency, and arteriosclerosis may also contribute to development of the disease.

In an Australian study of 5,147 individuals from age 40 and older, prevalence of early ARMD was 15.1%. Bilaterality of ARMD was strongly age-related, and women appeared to have a higher risk. Early ARMD prevalence rates increased sharply from age 70 in all ethic groups.

Diagnosis

History: Central vision may darken, either suddenly or slowly, or be washed out or blurry. The individual may find it difficult to read in low light or to read low contrast material such as newsprint. Letters may appear smaller with one eye than the other. Straight lines may look wavy. Pain is generally absent.

Physical exam: An ophthalmoscope illuminates the eye's interior (ophthalmoscopy or funduscopy) and may reveal changes in the color (pigmentation) of the macula as well as hemorrhages in and below the retina. Tiny white or yellow deposits (drusen) may be seen beneath the macula. The layer of light-sensitive cells in the macula may show signs of thinning as a result of cell deterioration.

Tests: A refractive exam (refractometry) to determine the presence of visual defects may be done. A microscopic (slit lamp) exam may also be performed to examine the eye's interior. Testing may be done to determine the individual's visual acuity and range of vision. A test card with black and white lines (Amsler grid) help determine how much central vision has been lost. A special dye may be injected and photographically examined to analyze structures in the back of the eye (fluorescein angiography). This test can reveal a membrane containing new blood vessels beneath the retina while pinpointing any areas of active bleeding. A test of pupillary reflex response and retinal photography may also be performed.

Treatment

Lasers are used to treat hemorrhages or the overgrowth of new blood vessels in wet SMD (photocoagulation) primarily to stop progression of the disease. It is unlikely that eyesight will improve. No other specific treatments are known for the condition. Individuals with dry macular degeneration are examined at least twice a year so that any progression to wet macular degeneration may be detected and treated as early as possible. The individual may be taught to perform Amsler grid testing at home for early detection of any vision changes. The individual should receive low vision counseling with prescriptions for any helpful vision devices.

Prognosis

If leakage and bleeding from new blood vessels continue, much of the nerve tissue in the macula will be destroyed. Central vision declines over a period of a few weeks or months and may render the individual legally blind. Peripheral vision and color vision are usually retained. While laser surgery may halt the progression of the disease, at this time there is no known cure or way of improving the lost vision.

Differential Diagnosis

Dry eyes, cataract, diabetic macular edema, cystoid macular edema, serous retinopathy, infections, choroiditis, retinal vascular occlusion, hematologic disorder, hypertensive retinopathy, Stargardt's disease, and fundus flavimaculatus are other possible diagnoses.

Specialists

- Ophthalmologist

Work Restrictions / Accommodations

The individual's ability to perform must be evaluated in light of the job's requirement for visual acuity. Visual aids may be helpful. The individual may need to wear sunglasses or a visor to avoid excessive sun exposure and further damage.

> **Complementary and Alternative Therapies**
>
> Content is intended for awareness only. Treatments may or may not be effective. Scientific evidence may be lacking and some substances have potentially toxic effects. Dr. Presley Reed and the editors do not endorse the use of these therapies in the absence of consultation with a licensed medical professional.
>
> Zinc - May aid cell function and wound healing and help prevent or slow progression of the disease.
>
> Lutein - May provide cell protection that slows or halts formation of the disease.

Comorbid Conditions

Injury, antioxidant deficiency, the aging process, smoking, arteriosclerosis, high myopia, and genetic factors increase risks for both development and acceleration of the disease.

Complications

The progression of dry to wet macular degeneration with the presence of hemorrhages or retinal detachment complicates treatment.

Factors Influencing Duration

Individual reaction to the loss of central sight and any complications may hasten the onset of disability. Some individuals adapt more readily to vision loss and are able to remain relatively independent, however, some individuals may be more dependent on others for most activities of daily living. Low vision training and counseling may be beneficial.

Length of Disability

If permanent loss of vision has occurred, the individual will generally be unable to perform tasks requiring keen visual acuity.

Failure to Recover

If an individual fails to recover within the maximum duration expectancy period, the reader may wish to reference the following questions to assist in better understanding the specifics of an individual's medical case.

Regarding diagnosis:

- Does the individual have dry or exudative macular degeneration?
- What is the individual's age?
- Does the individual have light-colored hair and eyes?
- Does the individual have a family history of macular degeneration?
- Does the individual have a history of eye injuries, smoking, high myopia, antioxidant deficiency, or arteriosclerosis?
- Does the individual report that central vision darkened slowly or suddenly?
- Does the individual find it difficult to read in low light or read low contrast material?
- Does the individual notice letters appear smaller with one eye than the other or straight lines appear wavy?
- On exam are there changes in the pigmentation of the macula? Hemorrhages in and below the retina? Tiny white or yellow deposits beneath the macula? Thinning of the layer of light-sensitive cells in the macula?
- Has the individual had a complete refraction with slit lamp examination? Fluorescein angiography? Pupillary reflex response? Retinal photography? Amsler grid testing?
- Have conditions with similar symptoms been ruled out?

Regarding treatment:

- Does the individual have an eye examination at least twice a year?
- Has the individual had laser photocoagulation?
- Has the individual been trained to use the Amsler grid at home?
- Has the individual received low vision counseling and prescriptions for any helpful vision devices?

Regarding prognosis:

- Is the individual's employer able to accommodate any necessary restrictions?
- Does the individual have any conditions that may affect their ability to recover?
- Does the individual have any complications such as progression of dry to wet macular degeneration? Does the individual have hemorrhages present or retinal detachment?

References

Stein, Harold A., Bernard J. Slatt, and Raymond M. Stein. The Ophthalmic Assistant, 6th ed. St. Louis: Mosby-Year Book, Inc, 1994.

VanNewkirk, M.R., J. Nanjan, and J.J. Wang. "The Prevalence of Age-related Maculopathy: The Visual Impairment Project." Ophthalmology 107 8 (2000): 1593-600.

Sepsis

Other names / synonyms: Septicemia

038, 038.0, 038.1, 038.2, 038.3, 038.4, 038.8, 038.9, 790.7

Definition

Sepsis refers to the whole body's (systemic) response to serious infection. It results from the presence of disease-causing organisms (pathogens), usually bacteria, or the chemicals they produce (toxins) in the bloodstream. The presence of these organisms or toxins can result in inflammatory responses. These include blood vessel dilation, leakage of fluid into tissues, and decline in heart output. The blood pressure then drops severely (septic shock), resulting in cell damage and multiple organ failure, including failure of the heart, liver, lungs, brain, and kidneys. Failure of any of these organs can be fatal. Septic shock is fatal in 60-70% of all cases, even with modern therapeutic measures.

Sepsis may result when pathogens enter the bloodstream due to puncture wounds, deep cuts, burns, infected surgical incisions, gangrene of bowel or any tissue, or the use of intravenous lines and invasive tubes such as bladder catheters.

The incidence of sepsis has been increasing for the last 70 years. This increase is due to the increased use of intravascular catheters and other invasive devices; widespread use of immunosuppressive medications; the AIDS epidemic; the fact that individuals with cancer and diabetes are living longer (predisposing them to more chances of infection); and the emergence of antibiotic-resistant organisms.

Septic shock is the most common cause of death in intensive care units, and the thirteenth most common cause of death in the US. It is estimated that in the US, there are 400,000 cases of sepsis, 200,000 cases of septic shock, and 100,000 deaths from septic shock annually.

Diagnosis

History: The individual will usually complain of fever (febrile) and chills. The individual may complain of shortness of breath and have a feeling of apprehension. There might be specific symptoms suggesting the site of infection (such as abdominal pain if there is gangrene of the intestine), but such localized symptoms are frequently absent. There may be a history of recent surgery, lung infections such as pneumonia, or other severe known infections. There may be a history of recent puncture wound, deep cut, or a burn. The individual might have an invasive tube such as a bladder catheter or an intravenous line, increasing the risk of sepsis.

Physical exam: The individual will usually have a fever, though some individuals may be hypothermic. Examination might suggest the source of the infection. If septic shock develops, blood pressure drops and heart rate rises. There will be abnormal breathing sounds, indicating fluid accumulation in the lungs. Several other common symptoms include rapid, shallow breathing; flushed skin and sweating; weak pulse; decreased urine output; sudden high fever with chills; cold hands and feet with a bluish tinge to the skin (cyanosis); rapid heartbeat; prostration (extreme exhaustion); and changes in mental state reflected as confusion, agitation, disorientation, or coma.

Tests: The infecting organism can often be identified with a blood culture. A blood count may show nonspecific signs of infection. A blood gas analysis may show a low oxygen content in the blood (hypoxemia).

Treatment

Sepsis is generally treated in a hospital intensive care unit (ICU) with intravenous antibiotics directed at the infecting organism. If the source of sepsis is an abscess or dead tissue, surgery is required to drain the abscess (incision and drainage) or to remove the dead tissue (debridement). Less commonly, sepsis is caused by a fungal infection, and can be treated with antifungal medication. Immunosuppressant medications inhibit the body's defense against the infection. Individuals should be taken off these medications. Immunosuppressant medications should not be resumed until the individual has completely recovered from the infection.

When signs of septic shock appear, hospitalization in an ICU is essential. Intravenous antibiotics are used to treat the infection, and intravenous fluids are administered to restore fluid balance, and to maintain the volume of blood for proper circulation. Mechanical respiration may be required to support adequate oxygen supply to the tissues; heart function and oxygenation monitors may be utilized. Blood, urine, and other fluid cultures will be regularly monitored to check for continuing infection.

Prognosis

The predicted outcome for sepsis is variable. If the infection is detected early, it is treatable and the prognosis is good. When a specific infectious site is identified and can be accessed, a good outcome is dependent upon a thorough incision and drainage procedure of the infected area, as well as thorough removal of all dead and infected tissue (debridement). If septic shock and/or end organ failure develop, the prognosis is poor. Septic shock has a high fatality rate.

Differential Diagnosis

Other causes of shock are blood loss (hypovolemic shock), severe vomiting or diarrhea, depressant drug use, heart failure, or severe pancreatitis.

Specialists

- Cardiologist
- Gastroenterologist
- Hepatologist
- Infectious Disease Physician
- Internist
- Nephrologist
- Neurologist
- Pulmonologist
- Urologist

Work Restrictions / Accommodations

If sepsis resolves without complications, no work restrictions or accommodations are necessary. Septic shock requires hospitalization with intensive treatment, followed by a period of convalescence, necessitating prolonged time off from work. Any permanent damage to organs during septic shock may necessitate restrictions or accommodations. Heart damage may necessitate allowing the individual to work fewer hours, and to be permitted to perform more sedentary duties. Kidney damage may require the individual to reduce work hours to allow dialysis treatment. Damage to liver or lungs may require that individuals avoid exposure to certain chemicals or fumes.

Comorbid Conditions

The incidence of sepsis has been increasing due to the increased use of intravascular catheters and other invasive devices, widespread use of immunosuppressive medications, the AIDS epidemic, the fact that individuals with cancer and diabetes are living longer (predisposing them to more chances of infection), and the emergence of antibiotic-resistant organisms.

Complications

Generalized clotting of the blood (disseminated intravascular coagulation) is a serious complication. Organ failure associated with septic shock will complicate the disease. Multiple organ failure (heart, lungs, kidneys, or liver) is usually fatal. Severe metabolic acidosis is associated with poor prognosis.

Factors Influencing Duration

The cause and severity of sepsis will influence the length of disability. The development of septic shock, organ failure, or the presence of drug-resistant organisms will greatly extend the length of disability.

Length of Disability

Duration depends on cause and severity. Disability may be permanent.

Duration in Days

Job Classification	Minimum	Optimum	Maximum
Any work	7	14	42

Failure to Recover

If an individual fails to recover within the maximum duration expectancy period, the reader may wish to reference the following questions to assist in better understanding the specifics of an individual's medical case.

Regarding diagnosis:

- Does individual have fever and chills? Dyspnea? A feeling of apprehension?
- Has individual recently had surgery?
- Has individual recently had pneumonia or other severe infection?
- Has individual had a puncture wound, deep cut, or burn recently?
- Does individual have an indwelling bladder catheter? Intravenous catheter?
- On exam was individual hypotensive? Was tachycardia present?
- Was abnormal breathing or breath sounds present?
- Is the skin flushed? High fever? Cold hands and feet? Cyanosis? Weak pulse?
- Is individual's mental status altered?
- Has individual had blood cultures? CBC? Blood gas analysis?
- Have conditions with similar symptoms been ruled out?

Regarding treatment:

- Was individual hospitalized? Treated with IV antibiotics?
- Was the cause of the sepsis an abscess? Was it drained?
- Was the cause of the sepsis necrotic tissue? Was surgery done to remove it?
- Was it caused by a fungal infection? Was it treated with anti-fungal medication?
- Have catheters and other devices suspected as aggravating the infection been changed or removed?
- Is individual being treated with immunosuppressant medications? Did they consider stopping them until individual has recovered?

Regarding prognosis:

- Is individual's employer able to accommodate any necessary restrictions?
- Does individual have any conditions that may affect ability to recover?
- Has individual had a complication of disseminated intravascular coagulation?
- Have they had any organ failure?

References

Parrillo, Joseph E. "Shock Syndromes Related to Sepsis." Cecil Textbook of Medicine, 20th ed, vol 1. Bennett, J. Claude, and Fred Plum, eds. Philadelphia: W.B. Saunders Company, 1996. 496-501.

Young, Lowell S. "Sepsis Syndrome." Principles and Practice of Infectious Diseases, 4th ed, vol 1. Mandell, Gerald L., John E. Bennett, and Raphael Dolin, eds. New York: Churchill Livingstone, 1995. 690-705.

Septic Shock

Other names / synonyms: Bacteremia, Sepsis, Systemic Inflammatory Response Syndrome

038, 785.59

Definition

Septic shock is a condition of inadequate circulation (due to low blood pressure) to vital organs and tissues that results from an extreme inflammatory response to an overwhelming bacterial infection. If the shock state persists, the inadequate circulation leads to cell damage, metabolic derangements, organ failure, and death.

Gram-negative bacteria are the most common cause of overwhelming infections leading to septic shock. However, recently there has been an increasing incidence of overwhelming infection (sepsis) and septic shock due to gram-positive bacteria and fungal infections. These microorganisms produce various toxic substances that are responsible for triggering a series of events called the inflammatory response.

Gram-negative bacteria (i.e., Escherichia coli, Klebsiella, Enterobacter, Serratia, Pseudomonas, Bacteriodes, Proteus) produce a substance called an endotoxin. Gram positive bacteria (i.e., staphylococcus aureus) produce a toxin known as leukocidin, which is thought to damage white blood cells that are the critical defense factor in our immune system. Both endotoxin and leukocidin increase the viability of the bacteria or fungi. In addition, they are responsible for triggering a series of physiological reactions, which ultimately result in shock and its associated complications (metabolic derangements, organ failure, bleeding disorder, etc).

The probability of infection is related to many factors such as the number of organisms present, their ability to cause disease (virulence), and the individual's degree of resistance (immune function). For example, debilitated individuals or those who have had chest or abdominal surgical procedures have impaired chest wall movement and decreased forces of respiration, which contribute to accumulation of secretions in the lungs and respiratory infections. Victims of trauma are at great risk of developing infections, due to extensive injury, operative procedures, and the gradual depletion of immune defense mechanisms. Likewise, surgery or manipulations of the urinary, biliary (liver, gallbladder and pancreas), or female reproductive organs carry a high risk of overwhelming infection.

Consequently, delineating a single causative factor of septic shock is nearly impossible. The incidence of sepsis and septic shock has increased over the past two decades. Approximately 1 out of 100 hospitalized individuals develop sepsis, and of these 40% develop shock. Septic shock occurs in about 40% of persons with gram-negative bacterial infections and about 20% of those with gram-positive bacterial infections.

Diagnosis

History: Individuals with sepsis may have vague or nonspecific complaints such as fever, chills, fatigue, anxiety, or confusion. In some cases, they may be able to describe a specific area of discomfort or pain, such as sore throat or abdominal pain that may indicate the site of underlying infection. They may report a recent illness, surgery, or procedure that possibly gave rise to the infection.

Physical exam: The most consistent clinical feature in septic shock is alteration in mental function. This may be as subtle as mild disorientation or more severe such as extreme agitation or even obtundation. Rapid (less than 20 per minute), deep respirations (hyperventilation) is also a common finding. The heart rate is usually elevated above 90 beats per minute, and the temperature may be abnormally high or low. The skin may be warm, flushed, and dry early in sepsis. However, as the septic shock progresses, the skin often becomes cool and mottled. Early in septic shock the blood pressure may hover above 100 systolic, but as it progresses and the heart weakens it may drop well below 100 systolic. Local symptoms may point to the source of the underlying infection. For example, a productive cough and chest pain may be present in lung infections. Abdominal pain, nausea, vomiting, and diarrhea may suggest an infection in the abdominal cavity or intestines. Obvious swelling, redness, and pain may indicate soft tissue or bone infections. Often, however, there are no localizing symptoms.

Tests: Blood tests are done to detect evidence of infection and organ system dysfunction. This may include complete blood count (CBC) with differential, chemistry panel with renal function and liver function studies, arterial blood gases (ABGs), coagulation studies, and blood cultures. Additional gram stains and cultures from any exudates or draining wounds will be done to determine a focus of infection. X-ray studies are also done to identify a focus of infection. This may include plain x-rays, computerized tomography (CT) scans, magnetic resonance imaging (MRI) scans, and ultrasound studies of areas in question (head, chest, abdomen, extremity).

Treatment

There are four goals in the management of septic shock: early recognition and resuscitation; reestablishment of blood pressure and circulation to the tissues; provision of optimal supportive care; and timely initiation of treatment to eliminate the source of the infection (septic focus).

The key determinant in survival is early recognition of sepsis and initiation of treatment while the process is readily reversible. Rapid administration of intravenous fluids to help restore and maintain blood pressure is a mandatory first step in the treatment of septic shock.

Individuals with sepsis or septic shock require intensive care monitoring with continuous ECG and frequent assessment of blood pressure, respiratory rate, urine flow (usually by indwelling bladder catheter), neurological status, body temperature, and color. A catheter may be placed through the superior vena cava into the right atrium (central venous pressure catheter) or into the pulmonary artery (pulmonary artery catheter) to continuously measure the pressure and performance in the heart for those with shock of uncertain or mixed etiology or those with severe shock. This serves to guide fluid administration and use of medications to restore and support blood pressure (inotropes and vasoactive drugs).

Supportive care such as assisted ventilation, administration of nutrition support (either intravenous or via gastric tubes), and maintenance of organ function is initiated as appropriate. Eliminating the source of infection may involve one or more of the following: antibiotic administration, drainage of infected wounds or abscesses, clearing lung secretions (bronchoscopy), or surgical resection of infected tissue (i.e., debridement, resection, or removal).

Prognosis

Despite a concerted effort to improve the treatment options and outcome, the mortality rate for septic shock remains at about 35-44%. Furthermore, it is the most common cause of death in intensive care units, and it is the 13th most common cause of death in the US.

Septic shock has a poorer prognosis when it is associated with organ dysfunction, persistent low blood pressure, and evidence of inadequate circulation to the tissues (i.e., altered mental status, low urine output, accumulation of lactic acid).

Differential Diagnosis

Early symptoms can mimic a viral infection with flu-like symptoms or some gastrointestinal upset. Other forms of shock (i.e., cardiogenic shock, hemorrhagic shock) should be considered in the differential diagnosis. Other conditions that produce fever, such as arthritis or side effects from some drugs, may be mistaken for sepsis.

Specialists

- Critical Care Specialist
- Emergency Medicine
- Internist

Work Restrictions / Accommodations

Work restrictions and accommodations are dependent upon the underlying condition and any impairment of organ function.

Comorbid Conditions

Comorbid conditions of diabetes, immune system disorders (AIDS, cancers), chronic lung diseases, multiple trauma, renal failure, or liver failure may impact ability to recover and further lengthen disability.

Complications

Significant complications from sepsis and septic shock include central nervous system (CNS) dysfunction, adult respiratory distress syndrome (ARDS), liver failure, acute renal failure (ARF), and bleeding tendency (disseminated intravascular coagulation (DIC). ARDS occurs in 18%, DIC in about 38%, and renal failure in about 50% of cases of septic shock.

Factors Influencing Duration

The length of disability will be influenced by the severity of the underlying infection, the timeliness of treatment, the individual's response to treatment, and the progression of shock.

Length of Disability

Duration depends on the severity of the underlying condition. Disability may be permanent.

Duration in Days

Job Classification	Minimum	Optimum	Maximum
Any work	14	21	42

Failure to Recover

If an individual fails to recover within the maximum duration expectancy period, the reader may wish to reference the following questions to assist in better understanding the specifics of an individual's medical case.

Regarding diagnosis:

- Has diagnosis of septic shock been confirmed?
- Has source of infection been identified?
- Is infection responding to treatment?
- Has individual experienced any complications related to sepsis or septic shock such as central nervous system (CNS) dysfunction, liver failure, adult respiratory distress syndrome (ARDS) in 18%, acute renal failure (ARF) in about 50%, and disseminated intravascular coagulation (DIC)?
- Does individual have an underlying condition that may impact recovery?

Regarding treatment:

- Were any complications associated with the central venous pressure catheter or pulmonary artery catheter used to administer intravenous fluids?
- Were these measures effective in restoration and support of blood pressure?
- Was infection successfully resolved?
- Were any complications experienced as a result of antibiotic administration, drainage of infected wounds or abscesses, clearing lung secretions (bronchoscopy), or surgical resection of infected tissue (debridement, resection, or removal)?

Regarding prognosis:

- Was shock state resolved before inadequate circulation lead to cell damage, metabolic derangements, or organ failure?
- Did individual experience inadequate tissue perfusion as evidenced by altered mental status, low urine output, or accumulation of lactic acid as a result of inadequate tissue circulation?

References

Clochesy, John M., et al. Critical Care Nursing, 2nd ed. Philadelphia: W.B. Saunders Company, 1996.

Stapczynski, J. Stephan, MD. "Septic Shock." eMedicine.com. 22 Feb. 2001 16 Mar 2001 < http://www.emedicine.com/emerg/topic533.htm >.

Septoplasty

Other names / synonyms: Nasal Septum Correction

21.5

Definition

Septoplasty is a common surgery used to correct structural defects in the bone and soft material (cartilage) that separate the 2 sides of the nasal cavity (nasal septum).

The procedure is used most often to straighten a crooked (deviated) septum resulting from a birth defect or injury. While a deviated septum is very common, surgery usually is required only to correct problems such as breathing difficulties or improper drainage of sinuses that lead to frequent sinus infections. However, a septoplasty also may be performed as part of reshaping the nose (rhinoplasty) in cosmetic or plastic surgery for improving the individual's appearance.

Reason for Procedure

Septoplasty is performed in order to treat a malformed or deviated septum, as this can interfere with breathing and cause snoring. The individual with an uncorrected deviated septum may experience improper drainage during colds or sinus infections, causing these conditions to worsen. Septoplasty may be needed as accompaniment to other intranasal procedures, including removal of a tumor or swollen tissue causing obstruction (polyp, polypectomy).

Description

Blood and urine samples may be collected for laboratory testing (serology) prior to the procedure. X-rays also may be taken of the individual's bone structure. Minor septoplasty procedures are performed with a local anesthetic as an outpatient procedure. More complicated cases are performed under general anesthesia, and may require several days of hospitalization. Typically, the procedure lasts no longer than an hour and a half.

An incision through the outer nose is rarely required, since access often can be gained through the nostril. However, an internal incision likely will be made to the septum to begin the reshaping process. The septum is straightened through partial removal or readjustment of the affected bone and cartilage (surgical reconstruction). In some cases, reshaping of the outer nose (rhinoplasty) may also be done at the same time as the septoplasty.

Material to provide protection and reduce bleeding (nasal packing) may be placed in the affected area and left up to several days following the procedure. The individual may be instructed to avoid strenuous activity for up to a week following the procedure.

Prognosis

Depending on the reason for the procedure, septoplasty has a high success rate in improving and/or correcting the underlying condition. Recovery time may be greatly extended when extreme measures are taken during the procedure, such as complete removal of portions of the septum. Outside bruising may occur if the septoplasty is performed as part of nose reshaping (rhinoplasty). More severe procedures may take as long as a year for complete healing to occur.

Specialists

- Otolaryngologist
- Plastic Surgeon

Work Restrictions / Accommodations

The individual must avoid strenuous work for at least a week following surgery. Depending on the extent of the procedure, recovery may require several days off from work or longer. An individual who continues to experience breathing difficulties from complications may be unable to perform certain work tasks requiring physical endurance.

Comorbid Conditions

An individual with other existing conditions such as swollen tissue causing nasal obstructions (polyps) or tumors may require additional procedures. Individuals who are obese or who smoke or drink alcohol excessively have increased risk of a less favorable surgical outcome. Individuals who take certain prescribed or illegal drugs also may experience less favorable outcomes.

Procedure Complications

The individual may experience an adverse reaction particularly to general anesthetic, if required. Bleeding is also possible following the procedure. In rare cases, a hole might form in the septum (perforation) and cause subsequent difficulty breathing. If infection occurs following the procedure, it's possible that the nose might bend inward. This would require a second surgical correction.

Factors Influencing Duration

Disability time will depend on the procedure's complexity and whether the individual's procedure required local or general anesthesia. Any complications may lengthen the period of disability.

Length of Disability

Duration may vary depending upon local versus general anesthesia.

Duration in Days

Job Classification	Minimum	Optimum	Maximum
Sedentary work	3	10	14
Light work	3	10	14
Medium work	3	14	21
Heavy work	7	14	21
Very Heavy work	7	14	21

References

Cheney, Mack, MD. Facial Surgery, Plastic and Reconstructive. Baltimore: Williams & Wilkins, 1997.

Department of Otolaryngology-Head and Neck Surgery. Septoplasty. University of Washington School of Medicine. 21 Nov 2000. 21 Jan 2001 <http://depts.washington.edu/otoweb/septo.html>.

Shigellosis
Other names / synonyms: Bacillary Dysentery
004, 004.8, 004.9

Definition

Shigellosis, also known as bacillary dysentery, is an infection of the large and small intestines caused by several different species of Shigella bacteria.

Many cases of shigellosis are linked to unsanitary habits such as failure to wash hands after toilet use. The infection primarily associated with the Shigella sonnei form of the bacteria is spread person-to-person or through contamination of food or drinking water. As a result, shigellosis is associated with outbreaks in day-care centers, nursing homes, and institutionalized populations. Infections also may spread indirectly in areas of inadequate waste disposal where flies settle on feces and then on food. Some cases may be caused by the Shigella flexneri strain of bacteria (thought to be sexually transmitted), which can create a chronic form of the disease with symptoms such as arthritis. Dramatically elevated rates of shigellosis in HIV-infected persons point to HIV infection as an important risk factor for shigellosis.

Shigellosis is the most communicable of all bacterial diarrheas. About 300,000 cases are reported in the US annually. In certain areas where sanitation practices may be substandard, the infection is thought to be responsible for up to 10% of diarrhea-related illness.

Diagnosis

History: The illness usually has a sudden onset of symptoms including painful abdominal cramps with frequent, urgent episodes of watery diarrhea. Other symptoms may include fever, chills, headache, muscle aches, loss of appetite (anorexia), nausea, and vomiting. Within days the diarrhea may become mixed with blood, pus, and mucus. The individual becomes progressively weaker. Persistent diarrhea may cause dehydration and weight loss.

The illness occasionally begins with bloody stools. When due to a chronic form of bacterial infection, the individual may also complain of joint pain, eye irritation, and painful urination.

Physical exam: The symptoms could apply to many different conditions, so a physical exam is nonspecific. There may be evidence of fever, abdominal tenderness, or hyperactive bowel sounds. The individual may have signs of dehydration including blood pressure that varies with body position (orthostatic blood pressure), dry mucous membranes, sunken eyes, and decreased skin tension (turgor). Rectal exam may be painful due to inflammation caused by constant diarrhea.

Tests: Direct microscopic examination of stained smears may reveal many leukocytes and red cells in the stool. Diagnosis is confirmed by identifying the infectious organisms in a stool culture.

If toxins are suspected in the blood (sepsis or septicemia), a complete blood count (CBC) may be done to detect the presence of bacteria.

An examination of the inside of the colon through use of a lighted, magnification instrument (colonoscopy) may reveal areas of congested rectal mucosa, small flat irregular blue or purple spots (ecchymoses), and sometimes large areas of ulceration.

Treatment

The illness usually subsides after a week or so, but severe cases may last several weeks. Dehydration is treated by replacing fluids and electrolytes. Antibiotic therapy may be prescribed in severe cases. Anti-motility agents should not be used. Antimicrobial agents may also be prescribed to address the specific form of Shigella bacteria. Antispasmodic drugs are helpful when cramps are severe. Individuals who develop a chronic form of shigellosis with accompanying joint pain may be prescribed nonsteroidal anti-inflammatory medications (NSAIDS), pain relievers (analgesics), or corticosteroids.

Prognosis

Shigellosis is a self-limited disease. While the illness usually subsides after a week or so, severe cases may last several weeks. Most individuals recover completely without any lasting effects. Death, in a few rare cases, is usually the result of unusual strains of the bacteria. A chronic form of the disease, caused by the Shigella flexneri bacteria, may lead to a reactive arthritis such as Reiter's syndrome.

Differential Diagnosis

Conditions with similar symptoms include inflammatory bowel disease (Crohn's disease, ulcerative colitis), irritable bowel syndrome, bowel obstructions, diverticular disease, dyspepsia, intestinal cancer, proctitis, and amebic dysentery or other forms of infective gastroenteritis.

Specialists

- Gastroenterologist
- Infectious Disease Physician
- Internist

Work Restrictions / Accommodations

Extended sick leave may be required for recuperation. If chronic complications develop, individual may be unable to perform strenuous tasks.

Comorbid Conditions

Recovery may be impacted by coexisting conditions associated with dehydration, weakness, and anorexia, and any conditions that compromise the immune system such as AIDS, cancer, and diabetes mellitus.

Complications

Complications include severe dehydration, shock, or collapse. Septicemia, a life-threatening illness, can occur when bacteria multiply rapidly in the blood stream, invading other body organs. In the chronic form of the disease, caused by the Shigella flexneri bacteria, individuals are at risk for developing a type of chronic arthritis (Reiter's syndrome). Some forms of the bacteria might be resistant to antibiotics.

Factors Influencing Duration

Length of disability may be influenced by the severity of symptoms, failure or delay in treatment, response to treatment, or the presence of complications.

Length of Disability

Duration in Days

Job Classification	Minimum	Optimum	Maximum
Sedentary work	3	5	7
Light work	3	5	7
Medium work	3	5	7
Heavy work	3	5	7
Very Heavy work	7	10	14

Failure to Recover

If an individual fails to recover within the maximum duration expectancy period, the reader may wish to reference the following questions to assist in better understanding the specifics of an individual's medical case.

Regarding diagnosis:

- Does individual have painful abdominal cramps with frequent urgent episodes of watery diarrhea or fever, chills, headache, muscle aches, loss of appetite (anorexia), nausea, and vomiting?
- Has the diagnosis of shigellosis been confirmed with a stool culture?
- If the diagnosis is uncertain, have other conditions with similar symptoms such as inflammatory bowel disease (Crohn's disease, ulcerative colitis), irritable bowel syndrome, bowel obstructions, diverticular disease, dyspepsia, intestinal cancer, proctitis, and amebic dysentery or other forms of infective gastroenteritis been ruled out?

Regarding treatment:

- Have the appropriate antimicrobial agents been prescribed? Were associated symptoms treated appropriately with antispasmodic medications or analgesics?
- Have symptoms persisted despite treatment? If so, was individual reevaluated to rule out secondary infection or the possibility of bacterial resistance? Were appropriate adjustments made in antimicrobial therapy?

Regarding prognosis:

- Has adequate time elapsed for recovery (up to several weeks)?
- Have symptoms resolved, persisted, or changed despite treatment? Does diagnosis need to be revisited?
- Has the possibility of chronic shigella been considered? If so, does individual have arthritis symptoms that may suggest the associated condition or Reiter's syndrome? Are these symptoms being addressed in the treatment plan?
- Has individual experienced complications such as dehydration, shock or septicemia that may impact recovery?
- Does individual have any underlying conditions such as HIV, diabetes mellitus, or malnutrition that could impact recovery and prognosis? If so, are these underlying conditions being addressed in the treatment plan?

References

"Antimicrobial Resistance, Data to Assess Public Health Threat from Resistant Bacteria Are Limited." Government Accounting Office Report 28 Apr 1999 11. Electric Library. 29 Aug 2000 <http://www.elibrary.com>.

Shin Splints

Other names / synonyms: Anterior Shin Splints, Medial Tibial Stress Syndrome, Posterior Tibial Shin Splints, Shin Splints

844.9

Definition

Shin splints is a term designated to define musculotendinous inflammation in the lower leg and specifically excludes stress fractures and compartment syndromes. A preferred term is medial tibial stress syndrome because it defines the location and process of the syndrome.

Microtrauma and inflammation is centered most commonly over the inside edge of the tibia (medial tibia) along one origin of the soleus muscle. The broad fibrous attachment of the soleus muscle to the tibia becomes inflamed from repetitive pulling away (microtrauma, avulsions), most often when there has been a significant change in activity or loading of the muscle.

Studies have found that other factors may be involved including faulty posture or foot alignment, muscle fatigue, and tight Achilles tendons. Shin splints are brought on by muscle imbalances, poor conditioning, insufficient shock absorption, or running on the toes. Walking or running mostly on the inside edge of the foot (pronation) rather than the whole foot contributes to shin splints. Running on hard surfaces, worn or improper shoes, and rapid increase of running speed can also bring on shin splints.

Shin splints are most common in individuals who expose their legs to pounding impact during activities such as walking on hard surfaces, running, and jumping. Shin splints primarily affect athletes but can also affect nonathletes, especially individuals exposed to working conditions that involve walking on hard surfaces or over soft surfaces.

Diagnosis

History: Individuals with shin splints (medial tibia syndrome) complain of pain that starts with activity and then may disappear with exertion only to reappear at the end of a workout or when at rest. The pain may be described as aching or soreness initially but can escalate to severe stabbing pain over time. The pain may then continue throughout activity and even force the individual to stop the aggravating task. Eventually, the pain may be constant and not dependent on the activity.

Physical exam: Palpitation of the inside edge of the tibia reveals pain from the middle to lower third of the lower leg. Some swelling may be present. Passive and active ankle motion is not painful but resisted motion replicates the pain (pushing against the examiners hand with the foot).

Tests: Abnormalities resulting from shin splints are not always detected on a plain x-ray. A bone scan may show areas of increased bone formation resulting from the overload placed on this particular region. X-rays of the knee, lower leg, and ankle can identify bony abnormalities such as stress fractures that may complicate shin splints.

Treatment

Conservative treatment of shin splints is aimed at providing rest to the calf muscles, restoring muscle balance, and preventing continued aggravation of the current problem. Providing rest may mean using crutches or a cast to immobilize the foot and ankle, thereby limiting the ability to point the toe during walking. Rest is relative and may mean only a decrease in the intensity or duration of the aggravating activity. It is important to maintain overall conditioning of the lower extremities while providing rest so as not to increase muscle imbalance. Pain control measures include ice massage, anti-inflammatory medications, physical therapy modalities, and rest of the injured leg. A program of calf-stretching exercises helps relieve pain and is an important part of rehabilitation and prevention of additional episodes of shin splints.

Supportive taping can be beneficial if applied by someone experienced in taping techniques for shin splints. Although taping procedures are useful in alleviating shin pain, they should not be used as a way to continue or resume running or other activities too soon. Other preventive measures include use of proper footwear, running or walking on softer surfaces, and increasing mileage and other training goals in a gradual way.

Orthotic devices prescribed by a podiatrist or other healthcare professional including heel lifts can reduce the amount of flat foot (pronation) that places stress on the shin region. By supporting the foot in a better walking position, orthotics can also help prevent recurrence.

Surgical intervention may be indicated in rare cases where the shin splints have recurred at least 2 to 3 times after adequate trials of rest and rehabilitation. Although shin splints are not a compartment syndrome, releasing the band (fascia) around the area of attachment on the soleus to the tibia may be helpful in relieving symptoms (fascial release, fasciotomy). An additional technique splits the soleus at its insertion. This redirects the forces at this point, decreasing the tendency for avulsions.

Specialists

- Exercise Physiologist
- Orthopedist
- Physiatrist
- Physical Therapist
- Sports Medicine Physician

Prognosis

With early, appropriate treatment of inflammation and further preventive measures, most individuals recover fully from shin splints. Modifying factors that caused the pain such as avoiding hard surfaces or changing footwear usually allows for a positive outcome. A solid understanding of what caused the episode of shin splints is important to prevent recurrence.

One study of individuals treated surgically (fascial release, fasciotomy) reported 78% felt they were cured while 93% felt they were functioning above expectations.

Recurrence may occur early during rehabilitation and is due to inadequate rest of the affected area.

Differential Diagnosis

Conditions that present with similar lower leg pain include stress fractures or contusions of the tibia, increased pressure from constricted tissue covering muscles or nerves (compartment syndrome), and irritation of the nerves in the shin.

Rehabilitation

There may be times when physical therapy is needed for successful recovery from shin splints. A physical therapist utilizes various treatments to decrease pain and inflammation followed by stretching and strengthening of key muscles.

Physical therapy using cold treatments can help control inflammation by decreasing the amount of blood flow. These cold treatments also offer some relief from shin pain. Methods of cold treatment include cold packs applied to the affected area or ice massage over the involved site. Heat treatments are also helpful in reducing inflammation and pain. A form of heat treatment includes ultrasound. This uses high frequency sound waves to produce heat that penetrates deep into the involved muscles.

Electrical stimulation is another technique that helps decrease the pain of shin splints. Electrical stimulation can be used in combination with heat or ice.

Strengthening and flexibility programs to correct muscle imbalance are directed by the physical therapist and should be performed regularly. Stretches aimed at the calf muscles are important.

Work Restrictions / Accommodations

The individual recovering from shin splints should avoid repetitive stair climbing, running, and excessive walking on hard or extremely soft surfaces. In severe cases, the amount of time standing may need to be restricted or alternated with periods of sitting. Use of crutches and or a cast will limit upper body dexterity.

Complementary and Alternative Therapies

Content is intended for awareness only. Treatments may or may not be effective. Scientific evidence may be lacking and some substances have potentially toxic effects. Dr. Presley Reed and the editors do not endorse the use of these therapies in the absence of consultation with a licensed medical professional.

Acupuncture -	May stimulate the body's own natural pain relievers.
Massage therapy -	May promote circulation and decrease inflammation.
Arnica -	Applied topically, may help relieve pain and swelling.
Feverfew -	Acts as a pain reliever but should not be used by pregnant or lactating women.

Comorbid Conditions

Conditions that can influence shin splint recovery are related to lower leg alignment. Bowlegs (genu varus) and knock knees (genu valgus) create uneven stress loads on the tibia or shinbone. Fallen arches (pes planus or "flat foot") place additional stress on the inside of the tibia and aggravate symptoms of shin splints. Overweight (obesity) may cause additional stress on the shinbone because of the bone's primary weight-bearing function.

Complications

Pain from shin splints may force the individual to walk on the outside of the foot placing additional stress on other muscles and tendons. Abnormal walking patterns (gait) can lead to back strain. Changed posture or gait can also cause inflammation and arthritic changes in nearby joints (back, hip, knee, or ankle).

Factors Influencing Duration

Factors that may influence disability include age, obesity, response to treatment, severity of the symptoms, and amount of running, walking, or stair climbing required by the individual's occupation.

Length of Disability

Disability may be permanent in individuals who do not respond to conservative treatment and are not candidates for surgical intervention (bleeding disorders, peripheral vascular disease).

Duration in Days

Job Classification	Minimum	Optimum	Maximum
Sedentary work	0	3	7
Light work	1	3	7
Medium work	3	7	14
Heavy work	7	14	28
Very Heavy work	7	14	28

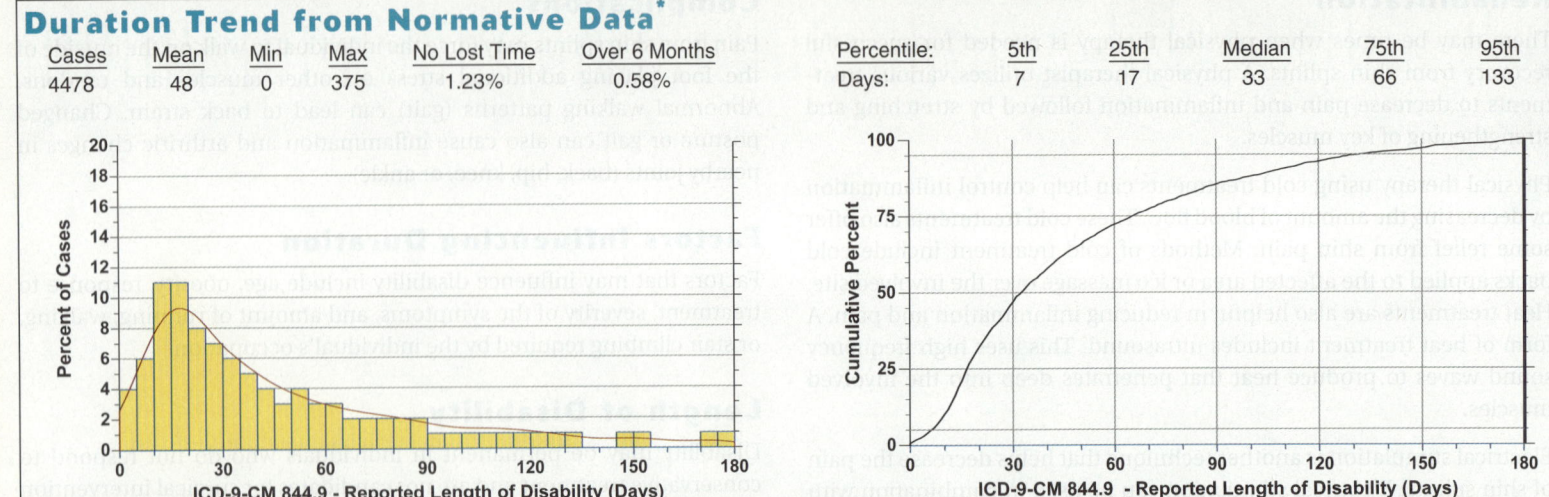

Duration Trend from Normative Data*

Cases	Mean	Min	Max	No Lost Time	Over 6 Months
4478	48	0	375	1.23%	0.58%

Percentile:	5th	25th	Median	75th	95th
Days:	7	17	33	66	133

* Differences may exist between the expected duration tables and the normative graphs. Duration tables provide expected recovery periods based on the type of work performed by the individual. The normative graphs reflect the actual observed experience of many individuals across the spectrum of physical conditions, in a variety of industries, and with varying levels of case management.

Failure to Recover

If an individual fails to recover within the maximum duration expectancy period, the reader may wish to reference the following questions to assist in better understanding the specifics of an individual's medical case.

Regarding diagnosis:

- Did individual complain of pain in the shin area?
- Did the pain begin as aching or soreness and escalate to severe and stabbing?
- Was pain continuous during activity or when at rest?
- Has diagnosis of shin splints been confirmed?
- Has a bone scan been done to evaluate for stress fracture?
- Have x-rays been done on knee, lower leg, and ankle?
- Have other underlying disorders been identified or ruled out, such as muscle imbalances, poor conditioning, improper shoes or running surfaces?

Regarding treatment:

- Have conservative treatments such as rest, analgesics, and ice been effective in relieving symptoms?
- Would individual benefit from physical therapy (deep heat, ultrasound, electrical stimulation, and a good stretching program)?
- Would the individual benefit from consultation with a podiatrist?
- Has individual tried supportive taping?
- Would individual benefit from the use of orthotics?
- Is individual a candidate for surgical intervention?

Regarding prognosis:

- Has recovery required more than 2 months?
- Does the individual have underlying conditions such as obesity, fallen arches, bowed legs or knock knees that could influence recovery from shin splints?
- Is individual realistic about the time needed for a full recovery?
- Has the individual made appropriate modifications in activity, footwear and physical conditions to further recovery?
- Has individual tried to resume activities too soon?

References

Andrish, Jack. "The Leg." Orthopaedic Sports Medicine. DeLee, Jesse C. Jr, and David Drez, eds. Philadelphia: W.B. Saunders Company, 1994. 1603-1607.

Hertling, Darlene, and Rudolph Kessler. Management of Common Musculoskeletal Disorders. Philadelphia: J.B. Lippincott Company, 1990.

Norkin, Cynthia, and Pamela Levangie. Joint Structure and Function. Philadelphia: F.A. Davis Company, 1992.

Steckel, M. Shin Splints. Spinal Health. 01 Jan 2000. 16 Sept 2000 <http://www.spinalhealth.net/inj-shin.html>.

Shock

Other names / synonyms: Anaphylactic Shock, Cardiogenic Shock, Circulatory Collapse, Hypovolemic Shock, Septic Shock, Shock, Toxic Shock Syndrome, Vascular Collapse

785.50, 785.51, 785.59, 958.4

Definition

Shock is a condition in which the blood pressure is inadequate to deliver oxygenated blood to vital organs (brain, heart, lungs, kidneys, and liver). The amount of blood flowing to the organs and their tissues is inadequate to meet the demand of the organs and tissues for oxygen. When shock persists, impaired organ function is followed by irreversible cell damage and death.

Shock may be caused by any condition that dangerously reduces blood flow, including heart problems such as heart attack or heart failure (cardiogenic shock), changes in blood vessels, decreased blood volume (hypovolemic shock), and injuries. Related factors include bleeding, vomiting, diarrhea, inadequate fluid intake, allergic reactions (anaphylactic shock), overwhelming infection (such as septic shock or toxic shock syndrome), diabetes (hyperglycemic hyperosmolar shock), and spinal cord injury (neurogenic shock caused by damage to the nervous system).

While the overall effect (lack of oxygen to tissues and organs) is the same in each of these conditions, the underlying cause and treatment varies. Consequently, shock is categorized according to the underlying pathology. Three broad classifications of shock are related to loss of blood volume (hypovolemic shock), inadequate ability of the heart to pump (cardiogenic shock), or pooling of blood or fluids in the tissues where it is effectively out of circulation (distributive shock due to enlargement [vasodilation] of the veins).

In general, shock occurs when the blood pressure drops below the critical level needed for organ perfusion (usually a mean blood pressure of 60mmHg). However, the exact degree of systemic hypotension necessary to cause shock varies and often is related to pre-existing vascular disease. For example, a modest degree of hypotension may be well tolerated by a young, relatively healthy person, yet cause severe cerebral, cardiac, or renal dysfunction in an older individual with significant arteriosclerosis.

As a result of inadequate perfusion to the brain, heart, lungs, kidney, and other organs and tissues, sudden physical symptoms develop. The most obvious clinical manifestations of shock include mental status changes, changes in blood pressure and heart rate, development of chest pain, shortness of breath and rapid respiratory rate, decreased urine output, and cool, pale, moist skin.

Despite advances in medicine and medical technology, mortality from most forms of shock is high.

Diagnosis

History: If the individual is alert, he/she will usually complain of being dizzy or "lightheaded." Individuals may report that they "blacked out." Witnesses or family members may provide additional information. They may report circumstances that preceded the individual's loss of consciousness, such as chest pain, injury with significant bleeding, vomiting, high fever, or allergic-type reaction.

Physical exam: The exam will sort out symptoms and signs due to shock itself or to the underlying disease process. While thought processes may be preserved, lethargy, confusion, and drowsiness are common. Individuals usually present with cold, moist, and often mottled-blue color (cyanotic) or pale hands and feet. The pulse is usually weak and rapid. However, a slow pulse may occur if there is an underlying heart rhythm disturbance (heart block) or if the shock is at a terminal stage (terminal bradycardia). Sometimes, only femoral or carotid pulses can be felt. A rapid respiratory rate is common in acute shock. In the terminal stage of shock, however, the respiratory center may fail due to inadequate blood flow to the brain (cerebral hypoperfusion) and respirations may cease (apnea). Blood pressure taken by cuff tends to be low (less than 90 mm Hg systolic) or unobtainable, or may decrease further if the individual attempts to stand up (orthostatic hypotension). Fever and chills may be present in shock due to overwhelming infection (septic shock). Signs of blood loss or fluid loss (such as vomiting) may be associated with hypovolemic shock.

Tests: Tests include electrocardiogram (EKG), blood tests and cultures, urine studies, and prothrombin time. Other x-rays and diagnostic tests may be ordered as appropriate for the underlying cause. For example, a trauma victim with evidence of head, chest, abdominal, or extremity injury will need further x-rays and diagnostic tests. If heart failure is suspected, angiography with heart catheterization may be needed.

Treatment

Prompt, aggressive treatment (including resuscitation) is paramount to restoring the blood pressure and preventing organ damage or death. Initial treatment should begin at the site of the incident or on arrival of the victim to the emergency department. This involves ensuring the adequacy of airway and breathing, and controlling any obvious bleeding. The individual is kept warm, with the legs raised slightly to help maintain blood flow to the head and heart (Trendelenburg position), unless the shock is caused by congestive heart failure, in which case the head should be elevated. Fluids should not be given by mouth, although a conscious diabetic suspected to be in insulin shock may be given concentrated sugar in paste form or as sugar-sweetened liquid.

Supplemental oxygen by facemask is provided immediately. If severe shock is present or respirations are inadequate, an artificial airway (endotracheal tube) is inserted to begin assisted ventilation. One or more large (16- to 18-gauge) intravenous lines are inserted in large veins (femoral, internal jugular, or antecubital) to infuse blood or other fluids and to administer any necessary medications. This is especially needed if bleeding (hemorrhage) is suspected.

Sedatives and pain relievers (narcotics) are generally avoided, but severe pain (such as chest pain associated with a heart attack) may be treated with morphine. Treatment may vary based on the underlying cause of the shock, such as treating the allergic reaction in anaphylactic shock, or using antibiotics in septic shock or toxic shock syndrome. However, all shock victims require intensive care monitoring with continuous ECG and frequent assessment of blood pressure, respiratory rate and depth, urine flow (usually by indwelling bladder catheter), neurological status, body temperature, and color. A catheter may be placed through the superior vena cava into the right atrium (central venous pressure catheter) or into the pulmonary artery (pulmonary artery catheter) to continuously measure the pressure in the heart and lungs. This is usually indicated for those with shock of uncertain or mixed cause, or for those with severe shock. This serves to guide fluid administration and use of resuscitative medications (inotropes and vasoactive drugs). A pacemaker may be needed in cardiogenic shock, or other assistive devices may help decrease the workload on the heart, such as intra-aortic balloon counterpulsation or ventricular assist device.

Prognosis

All forms of shock carry a high risk of fatality if there is a delay in treatment or if the shock has progressed to an advanced state. In general, mortality rates range from about 50% in septic shock to as high as 90% in cardiogenic shock. Outcomes are best in those who don't have comorbid conditions, such as advanced age, heart disease, or immune system compromise, and who are treated appropriately in the very early stages of shock.

Differential Diagnosis

Shock is a specific physiological condition with no alternative diagnoses.

Specialists

- Critical Care Specialist
- Emergency Medicine
- General Surgeon
- Internist
- Traumatologist

Work Restrictions / Accommodations

Due to the variable nature of the disorder, work restriction and accommodations are made on an individual basis, once the individual returns to work, according to the type and extent of residual disability. As shock is a life-threatening condition, individuals are hospitalized for treatment, and therefore cannot work until they are stabilized and discharged. Survivors may be permanently disabled.

Comorbid Conditions

Comorbid conditions of vascular disease, bleeding disorders, diabetes, heart disease, immune system dysfunction (such as AIDS), or kidney failure may affect ability to recover and further lengthen disability.

Complications

Shock may be associated with several complications including lack of oxygen to the brain (cerebral ischemia) causing brain damage, heart attack, respiratory failure (adult respiratory distress syndrome), bleeding disorders (disseminated intravascular coagulopathy), kidney (renal) failure, multiple organ failure (multisystem organ failure), and death.

Factors Influencing Duration

Factors that might influence disability include advanced age, any underlying conditions, duration and severity of the shock, and response to treatment interventions.

Length of Disability

Duration depends on cause and treatment. Disability may be permanent. Contact physician for additional case information.

Failure to Recover

If an individual fails to recover within the maximum duration expectancy period, the reader may wish to reference the following questions to assist in better understanding the specifics of an individual's medical case.

Regarding diagnosis:

- Has the underlying cause of shock been determined?
- Has the individual been evaluated for underlying heart failure or infection?
- Is there bleeding, vomiting, diarrhea, inadequate fluid intake, allergic reaction (anaphylactic shock), diabetes (hyperglycemic hyperosmolar shock), or spinal cord injury (neurogenic shock) caused by damage to the nervous system?
- Has individual experienced any complications as a result of shock, such as lack of oxygen to the brain causing brain damage, heart attack, respiratory failure, disseminated intravascular coagulopathy, renal failure, and multiple organ failure?
- Does individual have an underlying condition that may impact recovery?

Regarding treatment:

- Has underlying cause of shock been determined?
- Is it responding to treatment (antibiotics, insulin or blood sugar monitoring, cardiac assistive devices)?
- Were any complications associated with the central venous pressure catheter or pulmonary artery catheter used to monitor or provide fluids and medications?
- Were these measures effective in restoration and support of blood pressure?

Regarding prognosis:

- Was shock state resolved before inadequate circulation lead to cell damage, metabolic derangements, or organ failure?
- Are comorbid conditions present, such as advanced age, heart disease, or immune system compromise?
- Did individual experience inadequate tissue perfusion as evidenced by altered mental status, low urine output, or accumulation of lactic acid as a result of inadequate tissue circulation?

References

Clochesy, John M., et al. Critical Care Nursing, 2nd ed. Philadelphia: W.B. Saunders Company, 1996.

Graber, Mark A. Emergency Medicine: Shock. Virtual Hospital. 20 Jul 1999. 11/25/2000 <http://www.vh.org/Providers/ClinRef/FPHandbook/Chapter01/18-1.html>.

Hypovolemic Shock. HealthCentral. 01 Jan 1999. 11/22/2000 <http://www.healthcentral.com/mhc/top/000167.cfm>.

Shock. Medline Plus. 02 Feb 2000. 11/25/2000 <http://medlineplus.adam.com/ency/article/000039.htm>.

Shoulder Replacement

Other names / synonyms: Shoulder Arthroplasty

81.80, 81.81, 81.82

Definition

Most often, a shoulder arthroplasty is a surgical procedure designed to replace the normal bone of the shoulder with a prosthesis made of metal and polyethylene. What is referred to as the shoulder joint is the connection between the humerus or upper arm bone and a cup-like depression in the scapula or shoulder blade called the glenoid. The glenohumeral joint is a ball-and-socket type joint, similar to that of the hip that is capable of producing arm movement in virtually all directions.

Degenerative arthritis, such as osteoarthritis, rheumatoid arthritis, and post-traumatic arthritis can cause irreparable bone erosion, particularly on the articular surface or area where the two bones are connected and move against one another. To date, arthroplasty is by far the most successful type of treatment for those individuals with arthritic involvement of the glenohumeral joint.

The incidence of shoulder arthroplasty is about 1.78 per 100,000 individuals.

Reason for Procedure

While performed less often than hip or knee replacement, shoulder replacement can restore quality of life for individuals with limited shoulder function due to chronic pain or mechanical dysfunction.

Although the primary indications for this surgery are pain, joint instability, and limited range-of-motion, pain relief is the primary goal. The procedure is performed to relieve pain and stiffness associated with degenerative osteoarthritis, rheumatoid arthritis, or trauma-related arthritis that has failed to respond to medical treatment. The arthroplasty is not performed in individuals without a stable medical status and the necessary motivation to follow through with a substantial physical therapy commitment.

Arthroplasty of the shoulder is a useful treatment for individuals of all ages with unremitting pain and loss of mobility due to arthritic involvement of the shoulder joint; however, individual age and extent of disease may determine which procedure and prosthetic device is most appropriate. Regardless of age, the individual must be motivated to follow through with a substantial physical therapy commitment and must be a good surgical risk.

Description

Initially, either general or local anesthesia will be administered. An incision running across the front of the shoulder from the middle of the collarbone (clavicle) to the middle of the arm bone (humerus) will be made. Scar tissue, which may limit movement, is then removed. The upper end of the humerus is cut using a saw (some of the removed bone may be used as a bone graft to assist with the placement of the implant (prosthesis). The shoulder blade is then prepared for the placement of the artificial socket.

There are two major types of artificial shoulder replacements: the cemented prosthesis and the uncemented prosthesis. The cemented prosthesis is held in place by an epoxy cement that attaches metal to bone. An uncemented prosthesis has a fine mesh of holes on the surface that allows bone to grow into the mesh and attach the prosthesis to the bone. Both types are still widely used. Occasionally, a combination of the two types is used.

The prosthesis is made of two parts: the humeral component is the portion that replaces the ball on the upper end of the humerus, and the glenoid component is the portion that replaces the socket of the scapula. The humeral component is made of metal, and the glenoid component is usually a metal tray (which attaches to the bone) and a plastic cup (which articulates with the ball of the humeral component).

Upon awakening from surgery, a bulky dressing will be on the affected shoulder. A drainage tube may be in place to drain excess fluid from the operative site. For the first few postoperative days, a continuous passive motion (CPM) machine may be used to move the shoulder in order to decrease the possibility of stiffness. The average hospital stay is 3-5 days.

Prognosis

Approximately 90% of individuals experience pain relief following a total shoulder arthroplasty procedure. While the joint usually functions better than the pre-surgery diseased joint, it may not function as well as a healthy normal joint.

Range of motion and strength may also be improved by this procedure, but functional improvement is less predictable than pain relief. Increase in motion is dependent on many factors, including how long the motion had been lost and whether the rotator cuff tendons are intact. Often abduction and flexion do not exceed 90 degrees after shoulder replacement.

Most individuals are very satisfied with their postoperative result.

Specialists

- Orthopedic Surgeon

Rehabilitation

Individuals who undergo total shoulder arthroplasty may require a specific rehabilitation process that begins in the hospital and continues in outpatient physical therapy. The shoulder is immobilized for approximately 5 days, during which the individual maintains range of motion in the neck, wrist, and hand by actively moving these joints in all available directions. Physical therapists teach individuals how to transfer to and from a chair, bed, and bathtub safely. Individuals also learn to use ice in 15-minute increments to reduce swelling and pain at the shoulder. Individuals continue the use of ice packs to reduce pain and swelling after exercise. However, therapists may use hot packs prior to therapy to promote muscle relaxation and pain reduction.

After the period of immobilization, individuals wear a sling, which may be removed for exercise. Therapists begin passive range of motion exercises at this time. These exercises are flexion of the shoulder while the elbow is bent, passive abduction of the shoulder with the arm internally rotated, and passive external rotation to neutral with the arm held at the individual's side. Individuals begin to flex and extend the elbow and supinate and pronate the forearm at this time.

Individuals may then begin self-assisted shoulder flexion and shoulder abduction (shoulder is held in internal rotation). Following this, individuals begin self-assisted shoulder internal rotation and limited external rotation.

The next phase of exercises begins with the therapist may fully stretching the shoulder into flexion, abduction, internal rotation, external rotation, and extension. Individuals may self-stretch into these motions with the use of a cane or broomstick.

The next phase of therapy may include strengthening exercises. Initially, individuals perform isometric exercises in which they use manual resistance and move the shoulder into flexion, abduction, internal rotation, external rotation, and extension. In the final phase of therapy, individuals may begin exercising using resistive elastic tubing. Individuals may need to continue both the stretching and strengthening exercises for 1 year after surgery to ensure the restoration of functional strength and range of motion.

Work Restrictions / Accommodations

Individuals whose jobs require heavy lifting or strenuous activities involving the arm will need permanent reassignment to sedentary duties. Also, the individual will require time off to attend regular physical therapy appointments.

Comorbid Conditions

Conditions that would impact ability to recover and further lengthen disability include rheumatoid arthritis, bursitis, and rotator cuff injury.

Procedure Complications

As with all major surgical procedures, complications can occur. Complications associated with shoulder replacement include: infection, loosening, dislocation, and nerve or blood vessel injury.

Factors Influencing Duration

Factors influencing the length of disability include the underlying disease for which the procedure was performed, the development of complications, individual compliance with therapy and rehabilitation recommendations, the individual's job requirements, and whether the dominant or non-dominant arm was involved. Most individuals will be hospitalized for up to 3-5 days following surgery.

Length of Disability

Duration depends on whether dominant or non-dominant extremity is involved.

Following open, partial or total replacement, individuals can return to sedentary and light work sooner if responsibilities can be performed sitting. This procedure is not compatible with return to moderate or heavy work. Disability may be permanent.

Arthroscopic treatment. Arthroplasty or joint débridement.

Duration in Days

Job Classification	Minimum	Optimum	Maximum
Sedentary work	7	14	21
Light work	14	21	28
Medium work	28	42	56
Heavy work	56	70	84
Very Heavy work	56	70	84

Open, partial or total.

Duration in Days

Job Classification	Minimum	Optimum	Maximum
Sedentary work	28	42	84
Light work	28	56	112
Medium work	Indefinite	Indefinite	Indefinite
Heavy work	Indefinite	Indefinite	Indefinite
Very Heavy work	Indefinite	Indefinite	Indefinite

References

A Patient's Guide to Artificial Shoulder Replacement. Medical Multimedia Group. 22 May 2000. 3 Nov 2000 <http://www.sechrest.com/mmg/reflib/tsr/totshldr.html>.

Kisner, Carolyn, and Lynn Allen Colby. "The Shoulder and Shoulder Girdle." Therapeutic Exercise: Foundations and Techniques. Philadelphia: F.A. Davis Company, 1990. 241-271.

Magee, David J. "Shoulder." Clinical Orthopedic Assessment. Biblis, Margaret M., ed. Philadelphia: W.B. Saunders Company, 1992. 90-142.

Patient Guide to Shoulder Replacement. Johns Hopkins Department of Orthorpaedic Surgery. 2000. 3 Nov 2000 <http://ww2.med.jhu.edu/ortho/sports/shoulder/replacement>.

Shoulder Replacement Surgery. MedFacts. 1996. 3 Nov 2000 <http://www.medfacts.com/surgery.htm>.

Shoulder Replacement. Arthritis Insight.com. 2000. 3 Nov 2000 <http://www.arthritisinsight.com/medical/surgery/shoulder.html>.

Shy Drager Syndrome

Other names / synonyms: MSA, Multiple System Atrophy, PAF with MSA, Progressive Autonomic Failure with Multiple-System Atrophy

333.0

Definition

Shy-Drager syndrome is a progressive, degenerative disorder of the autonomic nervous system (ANS).

The ANS is responsible for controlling many of the involuntary functions of the body, such as heart rate, blood pressure, breathing, swallowing, sweating, and bowel and bladder control. Symptoms of Shy-Drager syndrome occur as nerve cells in the spine and brain that control these functions deteriorate. This results in Parkinson-type movement disorders, such as stiff muscles, moving slowly, and hand tremor, although the most notable symptom is a significant decrease in blood pressure when changing from a reclining or sitting position to a standing position (orthostatic hypotension).

The cause of Shy-Drager syndrome is unknown. This disorder is estimated to affect approximately 25,000 to 100,000 people in the United States, but is often mistaken as Parkinson's disease. Shy-Drager syndrome is primarily seen in men and begins in middle age; however, its occurrence is rare.

Diagnosis

History: Individuals may complain of dizziness, light-headedness, or fainting (syncope), particularly when changing positions, as well as neck or shoulder discomfort when standing. The individual may say that bladder and bowel cannot be controlled (urinary and rectal incontinence), or that constipation is a problem. Additional complaints include dry skin because of inability to perspire, loss of sexual function in males (impotence), involuntary hand tremor, muscle stiffness, and slow movements (bradykinesia). The individual may note slurred speech (dysarthria) and visual impairment.

Individuals may complain of difficulty breathing or periods of interrupted breathing during sleep (sleep apnea) as the disease progresses. The individual may note decreased thinking ability, slow thoughts, and decreased attention span. Other symptoms of disease progression include difficulty swallowing, chewing, and speaking.

Physical exam: Significant decreases in the upper numbers (systolic) of more than 30 mm Hg and the lower numbers of the blood pressure (diastolic) of more than 15 mm Hg are frequently noted. Muscle strength may be decreased in all parts of the body. Application of light pressure with the fingertips (palpation) to the bladder may reveal an enlarged and tender bladder (distension). The individual may have great difficulty when asked to speak, breathe, swallow, walk, etc.

Tests: Testing the level of the hormone (norepinephrine) in the blood whose primary function is to control decreased blood pressure (hypotension) may be useful, but is not diagnostic. Magnetic resonance imaging (MRI) may be useful in identifying changes in the central nervous system.

Treatment

Controlling symptoms of the disorder is the goal of treatment. Anti-Parkinson drugs may be given with caution, since they can cause decreased blood pressure (hypotension). Medications to increase blood pressure, such as alpha-andrenergics or corticosteroids, may be given with careful monitoring for possible side effects. An increase in salt and fluid intake and the use of elastic stockings may be useful in preventing hypotension. Keeping the head elevated during sleep may prevent orthostatic blood pressure changes from occurring upon rising. Urinary incontinence can be treated with drugs and catheterization and constipation may be relieved with an increase in dietary fiber or laxatives. Speech and swallowing difficulties may be improved with the help of a speech pathologist.

Prognosis

The prognosis is poor. Shy-Drager usually ends in death 7 to 10 years after the onset of symptoms. Pneumonia is typically the cause of death, although irregularities in heartbeat may be responsible for death in some individuals.

Differential Diagnosis

Parkinson's disease and other neurological disorders are differential diagnoses for Shy-Drager syndrome.

Specialists

- Neurologist

Work Restrictions / Accommodations

The individual may be restricted from any physical work because of the severe decreases in blood pressure with position changes (orthostatic hypotension). Accommodations may be made for work at a desk, but as the disease progresses and symptoms worsen, the individual will be unable to work.

Comorbid Conditions

Neurological deficits might influence length of disability.

Complications

Severe neurological damage is a complication of Shy-Drager syndrome.

Factors Influencing Duration

The severity of symptoms will influence length of disability.

Length of Disability

Disability may be permanent as symptoms worsen.

Duration in Days

Job Classification	Minimum	Optimum	Maximum
Sedentary work	14	28	Indefinite
Light work	14	28	Indefinite
Medium work	28	42	Indefinite
Heavy work	28	42	Indefinite
Very Heavy work	28	42	Indefinite

Failure to Recover

If an individual fails to recover within the maximum duration expectancy period, the reader may wish to reference the following questions to assist in better understanding the specifics of an individual's medical case.

Regarding diagnosis:

- Has diagnosis of Shy-Drager syndrome been confirmed?
- Does individual complain of dizziness, or of abnormal involuntary activity in breathing, sweating, or eliminating?

Regarding treatment:

- Have symptoms responded to drug therapy? Would change in medication or dose be warranted at this time?
- Is incontinence helped by drugs and catheterization?
- Do dietary modifications address problems with constipation?
- Has individual received a speech therapy consult? Is therapy effective against current speech and swallowing difficulties?
- Is individual a candidate for a pacemaker?

Regarding prognosis:

- Is individual experiencing any complications?
- Is individual realistic about prognosis? Would individual benefit from psychological counseling?
- As disease progresses, will family be able to care for individual in their home? Would individual and/or family benefit from consultation with social worker regarding long-term care?

References

"Disorders of Movement." Merck Manual of Diagnosis and Therapy, 17th ed. Beers, Mark H., and Robert Berkow, MD, eds. Whitehouse Station, NJ: Merck & Co., Inc, 1999. 05 Dec 2000 <http://www.merck.com/mmanual/section14/chapter179/179h.htm>.

Guberman, Alan. An Introduction to Clinical Neurology: Pathophysiology, Diagnosis, and Treatment. Boston: Little, Brown and Company, 1994.

NINDS - Shy-Drager Syndrome Information Page. National Institutes of Health. 27 Jun 2000. 31 Dec 2000 <http://www.ninds.nih.gov/health_and_medical/disorders/shydrger_doc.htm>.

Shy Drager Syndrome. The National Organization for Rare Disorders, Inc. 2000. 12 Feb 2001 <http://www.stepstn.com/cgi-win/nord.exe?proc=Redirect&type=rdb_sum&id=242.htm#general_discussion>.

Sick Sinus Syndrome

Other names / synonyms: Bradycardia-Tachycardia Syndrome, Sinus Node Dysfunction

426.0, 427, 427.81

Definition

Sick sinus syndrome describes abnormalities caused by the malfunction of the natural pacemaker (sinoatrial node) of the heart.

Sick sinus syndrome may present as persistent slow heartbeats (bradycardia). Bradycardia-tachycardia syndrome is another type of sick sinus syndrome in which rapid beating of the atria (also called atrial fibrillation or flutter) alternates with long periods of slow heart rhythms. Sinoatrial block also occurs in sick sinus syndrome and consists of a slight pause in the conduction time of impulses from the heart's sinoatrial node to the atrial tissue. A complete blockage between the heart's natural pacemaker and the atria (sinus arrest) can occur when the impulse from the pacemaker fails to make the upper chambers of the heart contract. Sinus arrest may last for brief or prolonged periods. Often when this occurs, an escape pacemaker lower in the atrium or ventricle takes over.

Sick sinus syndrome occurs in approximately 3 out of every 10,000 individuals, and is most common in the elderly. It affects men and women equally.

Diagnosis

History: Sick sinus syndrome may cause no symptoms. Individuals may, however, complain of dizziness, lightheadedness, fainting, bouts of confusion, palpitations, chest pain, shortness of breath, or fatigue.

Physical exam: Examination reveals that blood pressure may be normal or low. The heart rate (pulse) may be very slow at any time particularly after an episode of abnormally fast heart rate (tachycardia). A slow irregular heart rate or one that varies greatly without any change in the individual's activity level may indicate a diagnosis of sick sinus syndrome. The response of the heart to exercise should be assessed.

Tests: An electrocardiogram (ECG) is performed to detect irregular heartbeat (arrhythmia) characteristic of sick sinus syndrome. Since symptoms are often episodic, individual may wear an ambulatory Holter monitor to continually record the heart's functioning. An intracardiac electrophysiology study (EPS) may be ordered to confirm that the arrhythmia is caused by sick sinus syndrome.

Treatment

If the individual has no symptoms, treatment may not be necessary. When symptoms do present, however, particularly those related to bradycardia, a permanent artificial pacemaker may need to be surgically implanted. In individuals who also have episodes of tachycardia, treatment may include an implanted pacemaker or the prescription of heartbeat regulating (antiarrhythmic) medication.

Prognosis

Sick sinus syndrome progresses slowly. No treatment is necessary as long as the individual is not experiencing symptoms. Even with a permanent artificial pacemaker, the long-term prognosis is excellent.

Differential Diagnosis

Other diseases and conditions that may present with similar irregular heartbeats include hypoglycemia, hypothermia, hypothyroidism, and myxedema coma.

Specialists

- Cardiologist
- Cardiothoracic Surgeon

Work Restrictions / Accommodations

Restrictions depend on work requirements. Current restrictions apply to workplace use of powerful electromagnetic pulses that might interfere with the individual's pacemaker operation. Sources include strong magnetic fields, electrical cables carrying over 10,000 amperes of current, alternating welding currents, powerful radio, TV, and radar transmitter, power tools and assembly line robots, induction furnaces, and electric generating plants or substations. Individual may need to transfer to another area of work or occupation. Safety concerns apply to individuals experiencing dizziness, fainting, or periods of confusion.

Comorbid Conditions

Coexisting conditions that may impact disability include sarcoidosis, amyloidosis, Chagas' disease, cardiomyopathy, coronary artery disease, and high blood pressure (hypertension). Diseases of the heart valves may require more aggressive treatment for sick sinus syndrome.

Complications

Possible complications of sick sinus syndrome include inadequate or inefficient pumping of the heart, heart failure, and injuries sustained by fainting spells and falling.

Factors Influencing Duration

Factors that may influence disability include the presence and severity of symptoms, type of treatment (medication or pacemaker implantation), and the individual's response to treatment.

Length of Disability

Disability is not expected.

Failure to Recover

If an individual fails to recover within the maximum duration expectancy period, the reader may wish to reference the following questions to assist in better understanding the specifics of an individual's medical case.

Regarding diagnosis:

- Has the individual experienced symptoms such as dizziness, fainting, fatigue, shortness of breath, palpitations or chest pain?
- Was an irregular pulse noted on the physical exam?
- Was the diagnosis confirmed on ECG or electrophysiologic studies?
- Have other rhythm disturbances with similar symptoms been ruled out?
- Were other conditions with similar symptoms such as hypoglycemia, hypothermia, hypothyroidism or myxedema coma ruled out?
- Have additional diagnostic studies been done to identify an underlying cause for the rhythm disturbance (echocardiogram, cardiac catheterization)?

Regarding treatment:

- Has the individual had frequent follow-up evaluations to monitor the condition?
- Have symptoms worsened? If so, is insertion of a permanent pacemaker warranted?
- Have any underlying causes been addressed in the treatment plan (i.e., valve replacement)?

Regarding prognosis:

- Have the symptoms persisted despite treatment?
- Is the insertion of a permanent pacemaker warranted?
- Did symptoms persist following pacemaker insertion? If so, was the pacemaker checked for malfunction?
- Does the individual has underlying or associated condition such as sarcoidosis, amyloidosis, Chagas' disease, heart disease, or chronic lung disease that could impact recovery and prognosis?

References

Livingston, Mark, MD, and David Overton. Sinus Bradycardia. eMedicine.com 25 Jul 2000. 16 Aug 2000 <http://www.emedicine.com/emerg/topic534.htm>.

Sick Sinus Syndrome. North American Society of Pacing and Electrophysiology. 2000. 5 Aug 2000 <http://www.naspe.org/your_heart/disorders/sicksinus.html>.

Sickle Cell Anemia
282.5, 282.6, 282.60, 282.61, 282.62

Definition

Sickle cell anemia is an inherited form of anemia that occurs when the sickle cell gene is inherited from both parents. This results in an abnormality of the oxygen-carrying molecule (hemoglobin) in red blood cells that causes the normally round red blood cells to become deformed into a "sickle" shape. This sickle shape causes early destruction of the red blood cells (hemolysis), resulting in chronic anemia. It also causes the red blood cells to become trapped in small blood vessels. This blocks the circulation and causes severe pain and injury to many organs by interfering with their blood supply, or sickle cell crisis. The clinical signs and symptoms of sickle cell anemia occur early in life. There is no known cure.

Sickle cell anemia is seen most often in blacks, but may also be seen in those of eastern Mediterranean, Indian, or Saudi Arabian descent. The sickle cell gene is found in about 8-10% of blacks, and sickle cell anemia in about 0.2%.

Diagnosis

History: Individuals with sickle cell anemia manifest the features of chronic anemia, including pale skin and mucous membranes, fatigue, and decreased exercise capacity. They may also have a yellowing of their eyes and skin (jaundice), frequent infections, and poor wound healing. In addition, there are usually periodic episodes of severe pain in the joints, muscles, chest, or abdomen (sickle crisis).

Physical exam: Physical findings may include a pale complexion (pallor), yellowing of the skin (jaundice), elevated respiratory and heart rates, bleeding (hemorrhages) in the retina, and leg ulcers. The spleen also usually becomes abnormally small over time (autoinfarction).

Tests: The complete blood count (CBC) shows a marked anemia with low numbers of red blood cells together with elevated numbers of white blood cells and platelets. A sickle prep test can demonstrate the sickle shape of the red blood cells. A specific blood test (hemoglobin electrophoresis) can demonstrate the abnormal hemoglobin itself, called hemoglobin-S.

Treatment

There is no cure for sickle cell anemia, so management focuses on prevention and treatment of sickle crises and complications. Individuals are advised to avoid high altitudes and dehydration, treat infections promptly when they occur, and receive preventive vaccinations against pneumococcal pneumonia, haemophilus influenza type b, and meningococcus. For most individuals, the only daily treatment is folic acid supplements, but oral hydroxyurea is sometimes used regularly to reduce the frequency of crises. Treatment of acute crises often requires hospitalization, and consists of rest, pain medications given by injection or through a vein (intravenous), intravenous fluids, oxygen, blood transfusions, and individualized treatments for any infections or complications. Genetic counseling is available for those contemplating pregnancy.

Prognosis

There is no cure for sickle cell anemia, and life expectancy is reduced, with the median age of death being in the forties. Ongoing symptoms of anemia and repeated sickling crises can be expected, as can lasting problems due to permanent organ damage.

Differential Diagnosis

There are other chronic anemias involving abnormal hemoglobins, such as thalassemias or hemoglobin-SC disease, but current testing usually allows for accurate diagnosis. However, a sickle crisis can be confused with an acute gallbladder attack, a kidney stone, appendicitis, heart disease, or various neurologic disorders.

Specialists

- Hematologist

Work Restrictions / Accommodations

Chronic anemia can severely limit the individual's exercise tolerance and capacity for physical exertion. Additional restrictions and accommodations would depend on any long-term complications, such as decreased vision or blindness, physical limitations from strokes, respiratory problems, or chronic pain, and additional time off for treatment of sickle crises and infections can be expected.

Comorbid Conditions

Infections or dehydration for any reason can precipitate a sickle crisis or impact the recovery time.

Complications

Individuals with sickle cell anemia are at risk for damage to major organs because of poor circulation and sickle cell crises. Common complications include gallstones, damage to the spleen (autosplenectomy) with resultant susceptibility to serious infections, damage to the lungs (acute chest syndrome), bones (avascular necrosis), kidneys (papillary necrosis), and heart, strokes, and blindness over time (a result of impaired circulation to the retina and retinal bleeding). All of these complications may occur or become worse during pregnancy.

Factors Influencing Duration

The duration of disability depends on the severity of the chronic anemia, the frequency of sickle crises, and presence of complications, including chronic pain, infections, and permanent complications from any organ damage.

Length of Disability

Duration depends on severity of chronic anemia. Disability will likely be permanent for individuals whose jobs require heavy physical exertion. Chronic pain, visual loss, and organ damage may also result in permanent disability, depending on the extent of the problems.

Without crisis.

Duration in Days

Job Classification	Minimum	Optimum	Maximum
Sedentary work	0	2	7
Light work	0	2	7
Medium work	0	7	14
Heavy work	0	14	21
Very Heavy work	0	14	21

Failure to Recover

If an individual fails to recover within the maximum duration expectancy period, the reader may wish to reference the following questions to assist in better understanding the specifics of an individual's medical case.

Regarding diagnosis:

- Does individual show signs of chronic anemia such as pale skin and mucous membranes, fatigue, and decreased exercise capacity?
- Does individual have yellowing of the eyes and skin (jaundice)? Experience frequent infections? Do wounds heal poorly?
- Have periodic episodes of severe pain in the joints, muscles, chest, or abdomen (sickle crisis) occurred?
- Did exam reveal elevated respiratory and heart rates? Bleeding (hemorrhages) in the retina? Leg ulcers?
- Is spleen abnormally small over time (auto-infarction)?
- Was a complete blood count (CBC) done? Did it show a marked anemia with low numbers of red blood cells and elevated numbers of white blood cells and platelets?
- Did a sickle prep test demonstrate sickle shape of the red blood cells?
- Was a hemoglobin electrophoresis done? Was hemoglobin abnormal (hemoglobin-S)?
- Were other chronic anemias such as thalassemias or hemoglobin-SC disease ruled out?

Regarding treatment:

- Since no cure is available for sickle cell anemia, was individual instructed in how to prevent and treat sickle crisis and complications?
- Has individual avoided high altitudes?
- Are infections being treated promptly?
- Were preventative vaccinations against pneumococcal pneumonia, haemophilus influenza type b, and meningococcus given?
- Does individual take daily folic acid supplements? Oral hydroxyurea?
- Was hospitalization required for acute crises?

Regarding prognosis:

- Has permanent organ damage occurred?
- Have any complications developed such as gallstones or damage to the spleen (autosplenectomy), lungs (acute chest syndrome), bones (avascular necrosis), kidneys (papillary necrosis), or heart?
- Is individual pregnant? Was genetic counseling available?

References

Beutler, Ernest. "Disorders of Hemoglobin." Harrison's Principles of Internal Medicine. Fauci, Anthony S., et al., eds. New York: The McGraw-Hill Companies, Inc, 1998. 645-652.

Schrier, S., MD. "Chapter IV: Hemoglobinopathies and Hemolytic Anemias." Dale, D.C., and Daniel D. Federman, MD, eds. New York: WebMD Corporation, 2000 Scientific American Medicine. 28 Jun 2000 <http://www.samed.com/sam/forms/index.htm>.

Sodipo, J. "Acupuncture and Blood Studies in Sickle-cell Anemia." American Journal of Chinese Medicine 21 1 (1993): 85-89.

Thomas, J.E., et al. "Management of Pain in Sickle Cell Disease Using Biofeedback Therapy: A Preliminary Study." Biofeedback Self Regulation 9 4 (1984): 413-420.

Siderosis

Other names / synonyms: Arc-Welder's Disease, Berylliosis, Lung Aluminosis, Siderosis Pneumoconiosis, Stannosis

503

Definition

Siderosis is a type of occupational lung disease (pneumoconiosis) caused by the inhalation of dust or fumes containing iron or iron oxide particles. It is most commonly seen in arc welders and is also referred to as arc-welders disease. Iron dust and fumes are also found in conjunction with mining, steelmaking, iron or steel rolling, metal polishing, and with ochre pigments. Some airborne dust is often contaminated with other chemical agents. The inhaled iron particles accumulate in the lungs, and while this collection of iron in lungs is visible upon x-ray, it is usually not associated with inflammation or altered lung function. Thus, individuals with siderosis often do not experience any symptoms. Consequently, siderosis is often diagnosed following chest x-rays taken for some other reason.

Diagnosis

History: During a visit to the physician for any unrelated reason, a history of repeated or prolonged exposure to iron or iron oxide dust or fumes will be disclosed.

Physical exam: Physical signs are rare. Abnormal breath sounds may be noted in rare cases.

Tests: Chest x-rays may reveal a net-like (reticular) pattern or, in more severe cases, the presence of small opaque areas (micronodules). Pulmonary function tests (PFT) to evaluate lung volume, capacity, gaseous diffusion, and distribution are usually negative. These tests will utilize spirometry to detect any restriction of normal lung expansion or obstruction of airflow, and the peak flow meter to detect narrowing of the airways. A sample of sputum will reveal the presence of red blood cells (erythrocytes) containing non-hemoglobin iron (siderocytes). The arterial blood gas (ABG) blood test can assess the efficiency of gas exchange in the lungs, and the efficiency of gas absorption into the blood.

Treatment

Siderosis does not normally cause any symptoms, and because there is generally no underlying damage to body tissues, treatment is not required. Avoiding exposure to iron dust or fumes will prevent any further accumulation of particles in the lungs.

Prognosis

Siderosis is a harmless (benign) disease. Most cases never produce symptoms of illness. In rare cases where lung damage does occur, preventing further exposure to iron dust or fumes is highly effective.

Differential Diagnosis

Other non-fibrogenic dust diseases including stannosis (tin), baritosis (barium), and antimony pneumoconiosis also produce an abnormal-appearing chest x-ray without associated symptoms or disease process.

Specialists

- Occupational Medicine Physician
- Pulmonologist

Work Restrictions / Accommodations

Because siderosis does not usually cause any symptoms or tissue injury, work restrictions and/or accommodations are not generally required. Protective clothing, masks, and equipment may be helpful in reducing exposure.

Comorbid Conditions

In the rare cases of lung damage, other types of pneumoconiosis or smoking may lengthen disability.

Complications

Complications do not generally occur.

Factors Influencing Duration

Disability is not expected from siderosis.

Length of Disability

No disability is associated with this diagnosis.

Failure to Recover

If an individual fails to recover within the maximum duration expectancy period, the reader may wish to reference the following questions to assist in better understanding the specifics of an individual's medical case.

Regarding diagnosis:

- Has the diagnosis of siderosis been confirmed?
- Have other lung diseases, such as stannosis (tin), baritosis (barium), and antimony pneumoconiosis been ruled out?
- Has the individual been exposed to other occupational air contaminants?
- Does individual have an underlying condition that may impact recovery?
- Is the individual a tobacco smoker?

Regarding treatment:

- Has individual been provided with protective clothing, mask, and equipment to reduce further exposure?
- Has individual been advised to stop smoking?
- Would enrollment in a community smoking cessation program be beneficial?

Regarding prognosis:

- Has individual been provided with protective clothing, mask, and equipment to reduce further exposure when lung damage has occurred?
- If lung damage has occurred, has individual been advised to stop smoking?

References

Morgan, W.K.C. "Occupational Lung Diseases." <u>Merck Manual of Medical Information.</u> Berkow, Robert, et al., eds. New York: Pocket Books, 1997. 195-201.

Sigmoidoscopy
Other names / synonyms: Coloscopy, Endoscopy of the Distal Colon, Flexible Sigmoidoscopy, Proctoscopy, Proctosigmoidoscopy, Rigid Sigmoidoscopy
45.24, 45.25, 48.23

Definition

Sigmoidoscopy is a procedure that enables a physician to examine the lining of the rectum and lower large intestine (colon or bowel).

The procedure is usually performed in the physician's office or a procedure room, but occasionally it may be performed in the hospital. A soft, bendable scope (sigmoidoscope) about one-half inch in diameter and about 2 feet in length is gently inserted into the anus (rectal opening) and advanced or moved into the rectum and the lower part of the colon (sigmoid colon). The sigmoidoscope, which is equipped with a fiber-optic source for viewing, allows the physician to examine the lining of the lower third of the colon. To further facilitate the examination, the colon is inflated with air, distending or widening the walls to enable the physician to see inflamed tissue, abnormal growths, ulcers, bleeding, and muscle spasms.

Many physicians use the sigmoidoscopy procedure to find the cause of diarrhea, abdominal pain, or constipation. The procedure is recommended for routine screening for colorectal cancer for individuals over 50 years old and for individuals whose families have a history of colorectal cancer.

Sigmoidoscopy is generally not performed in cases of perforation or tear in the bowel, severe diverticulitis, colitis, or inflammatory bowel disease, and in clinically unstable individuals or in individuals who have not followed the dietary restrictions and cleansing routine prescribed prior to the procedure.

According to reports issued by the Centers for Disease Control and Prevention (CDC) in 1998, the number of sigmoidoscopy procedures performed in the US was 69,000. More of the procedures (42,000) were performed on women than on men (27,000).

Reason for Procedure

Many physicians prescribe sigmoidoscopy as a screening test to look for colorectal cancer or for abnormal growths (polyps) in the rectum and last portion of the large intestine (sigmoid and descending colon). These polyps may increase the risk of colorectal cancer.

Sigmoidoscopy is also used to look for painful cracks or slits in the anus (fissures) and painful swellings formed by dilation of blood vessels in the anus (hemorrhoids), to establish the cause of persistent bloody diarrhea and abdominal pain, and to diagnose inflammatory bowel disease. A biopsy taken during a sigmoidoscopy can confirm the findings of other tests, x-rays, or imaging studies.

Description

Sigmoidoscopy is performed in a clinic or in a hospital on an outpatient basis. The individual usually lies on his or her left side on the examining table, and is given pain mediation and a mild sedative to keep him or her comfortable and relaxed during the procedure.

After examining and lubricating the rectal opening, the physician inserts a short, flexible, lighted tube (sigmoidoscope) into the individual's rectum and guides it into the lower portion of the colon. The sigmoidoscope transmits an image of the inside of the colon onto a monitor for examination by the physician. Because the sigmoidoscope is flexible, the physician can move it around the curves of the colon. As the examination progresses, the individual may be asked to change position occasionally to facilitate the passage of the sigmoidoscope through the colon. To improve his or her visualization, the physician may gently infuse air into the colon. The infusion of air sometimes causes individuals to experience a sensation of abdominal fullness, a sensation that should not be painful.

If the sigmoidoscopy procedure reveals any unusual conditions, such as inflammation, ulcer, tumor, or abnormal growth (polyp), the physician may photograph them to provide a permanent record for the individual's medical chart, thereby allowing other physicians to study the case. To better evaluate any areas of suspected abnormality, the physician will take a brushing or biopsy of the colon lining. A brushing involves the passage of a tiny nylon brush though the center of the sigmoidoscope. The brush rubs against the lining of the colon and retrieves bits of tissue for later analysis. Tissue samples for a biopsy or stool samples are collected with tiny metal forceps and suction devices that are introduced through special channels in the sigmoidoscope. Both of these procedures are painless for the individual. If a small polyp is discovered during the procedure, it can usually be removed immediately. This may prevent potential colon cancer and may eliminate the need for major surgery.

Prognosis

Sigmoidoscopy generally provides reliable results in treatment, examination, and diagnosis when performed periodically.

A normal result from a sigmoidoscopy would suggest that the tissue in the lower third of the colon is healthy and that it lacks observable abnormalities. Abnormal results may indicate the following possibilities: inflammation, inflammatory bowel disease, ulcer, tumor, or polyp. Through sigmoidoscopy, the detection and removal of polyps, and thus the possible prevention of colon cancer, are made possible.

Specialists

- Colorectal Surgeon
- Gastroenterologist
- Endocrinologist

Work Restrictions / Accommodations

After a sigmoidoscopy, most individuals are advised to avoid driving or operating machinery for the remainder of the day, because judgment and reflexes are likely to be impaired by the sedation given before and during the procedure. Most individuals are ready to return to work the next day after the procedure.

Comorbid Conditions

Comorbid conditions that may influence length of disability include diverticulitis, colitis, inflammatory bowel disease, allergic reaction to medications used in relation to the procedure, and chronic illnesses, such as heart disease, hypertension, and diabetes.

Procedure Complications

The principal complication of sigmoidoscopy is bleeding (hemorrhage). Bleeding may occur at the site of either a biopsy or polyp removal. Typically minor in degree, such bleeding may stop on its own or be controlled by cauterization. Occasionally, surgery is necessary. It is also possible for the bowel wall to be perforated. Although perforation generally requires surgery, certain cases may be treated with antibiotics and intravenous fluids. Fortunately, both perforation of the colon and bleeding are quite rare.

Factors Influencing Duration

Factors that might influence length of disability include the underlying condition that prompted the procedure and the presence of complications (primarily due to the medications used with the procedure).

Length of Disability

The procedure does not produce a period of disability. Disability duration may, however, be influenced by the underlying condition.

Duration in Days

Job Classification	Minimum	Optimum	Maximum
Any work	0	2	3

References

National Hospital Discharge Survey: Annual Summary 1998. Centers for Disease Control and Prevention (CDC). 01 Sep 2000. 1 Jan 2001 <http://www.cdc.gov/nchs/data/sr13_148.pdf>.

Sigmoidoscopy. National Digestive Information Clearinghouse. 07 Jul 1998. 1 Jan 2001 <http://www.niddk.nih.gov/health/digest/pubs/diagtest/sigmo.htm>.

Silicosis

Other names / synonyms: Occupational Silicosis, Pulmonum Silicosis, Silicosis Pneumoconiosis, Silicosis Pneumonoconiosis, Silicotic Lung Fibrosis

502, 506.4

Definition

Silicosis is a lung disease caused by breathing dust that contains extremely fine particles of crystalline silica. Crystalline silica is a common mineral found in materials such as sand, quartz, concrete, masonry, and rock. As the body tries to eliminate these irritating particles, inflammation causes scarring of the lung tissue (pulmonary fibrosis). The result is less efficient transfer of oxygen and decreased lung capacity.

The four different types of silicosis are chronic simple silicosis, chronic complicated silicosis, subacute silicosis, and acute silicosis. Chronic simple silicosis is generally without symptoms (asymptomatic) and is nonprogressive once exposure ends. It usually follows 10 to 12 years of silica dust exposure and is generally limited to small round spots in the lungs that show on x-ray. Chronic complicated silicosis tends to occur after 20 years or more of exposure. It has progressively worsening symptoms and the areas of lung damage continue to enlarge even after exposure ends. Subacute silicosis tends to occur after 3 to 6 years of heavy silica exposure and resembles chronic complicated silicosis. Acute silicosis can occur after less than 2 years of massive exposure and is clinically distinct from the other forms.

Silicosis primarily affects workers between the ages of 40 and 75. It is a hazard worldwide for individuals in occupations such as quartz mining, metal mining, foundries, pottery, sandblasting, stonecutting, blasting, or tunnel construction. Men tend to acquire silicosis more often than women by nature of professions that are higher risk. The incidence of new cases each year is now decreasing in the US and in other developed nations due to the enforcement of maximum permitted dust levels in industry and through use of protective clothing.

Diagnosis

History: The individual may report a history of exposure to silica dust. Although initially there may be no symptoms, symptoms may eventually include difficulty in breathing, shortness of breath, a cough (either dry or productive), and/or chest tightness.

Physical exam: Auscultation (listening to breath sounds through a stethoscope) may reveal changes in breath sounds indicating obstruction in the upper lobes of the lung. Wheezing only occurs when other conditions such as bronchitis or asthma are present. In chronic complicated silicosis or subacute silicosis, right heart failure and/or a condition known as cor pulmonale may be noted.

Tests: Lung tissue changes due to silicosis are often detected by chest x-ray before they cause any symptoms. Pulmonary function tests evaluate lung function and confirm the presence of lung disorders. These may include spirometry and lung volume measurement (detects any restriction of normal lung expansion or obstruction of air flow), peak flow meter (detects narrowing of the airways), blood gases (assesses efficiency of gas exchange in the lungs), and diffusing capacity (assesses the efficiency of gas absorption into the blood). A CT may also be useful for identifying lung nodules. Sputum (phlegm) may be cultured to rule out tuberculosis.

Treatment

There is no treatment available for silicosis other than reducing symptoms and treating complications. Lung tissue changes due to silicosis are often detected by a chest x-ray before they cause any symptoms. If dust exposure is stopped at this point, further progression of the disease can sometimes be prevented.

The disease is otherwise treated symptomatically. Appropriate medications to control symptoms may include drugs to reduce inflammation (anti-inflammatory), antibiotics to treat or prevent infections, and drugs to widen the airways in the lungs (bronchodilators). Sleeping in a semi-upright position may help drain any fluid in the lungs. Breathing exercises may help improve lung capacity. Because smoking can aggravate the symptoms of silicosis and increase the risk of lung cancer, the individual should be urged to quit smoking. In severe or advanced cases, a lung transplant may be required.

Prognosis

Outcome is dependent on particle size, dust concentration, and duration of dust exposure. If dust exposure can be stopped before symptoms develop, further progression of the disease is sometimes prevented. Lung damage already present is permanent and can result in permanent disability. If silicosis develops at an early age or if complications occur, the outcome is less positive. Although medication cannot treat the underlying disease, it can relieve symptoms and allow a faster recovery. When complications do occur, medication may be helpful for recovery. The extent of recovery, however, will depend on the nature and severity of the complication. Death from silicosis does occur.

Differential Diagnosis

Conditions with similar symptoms include lung diseases (pneumoconiosis) from exposure to other inorganic or nonfibrous dusts (asbestosis, siderosis, stannosis, coal worker's pneumoconiosis, and talcosis). Other diseases with similar symptoms include tuberculosis, sarcoidosis, lung cancer, fungal pneumonia, alveolar proteinosis, and Hodgkin disease.

Specialists

- Pulmonologist

Work Restrictions / Accommodations

When possible, the individual should be removed from all exposure to silica dust. If this is not possible, the individual must be supplied with protective clothing and equipment to prevent further exposure. Specific work restrictions and accommodations are related to the individual's symptoms, the presence of complications, and specific work requirements.

Comorbid Conditions

Coexisting tuberculosis or asthma may impact recovery and lengthen disability. Smoking aggravates the symptoms of silicosis and increases the risk of cancer.

Complications

Complications may include right-sided heart failure (cor pulmonale), progressive massive fibrosis (a variant of silicosis), emphysema, pneumothorax, an increased risk for tuberculosis and other lung infections, lung cancer, and stomach cancer.

Factors Influencing Duration

Length of disability may be influenced by the severity of symptoms or complications, conditions that aggravate the symptoms (asthma, smoking), and the overall health of the individual.

Length of Disability

Duration depends on severity of acute complications and the degree of fibrosis. Those with chronic complicated silicosis, subacute silicosis, or acute silicosis will have a longer disability period than those with chronic simple silicosis. Depending on the extent of lung damage and the physical demands of the job, disability may be prolonged or even permanent. Severe fibrosis may result in permanent disability and/or death.

Duration in Days

Job Classification	Minimum	Optimum	Maximum
Sedentary work	0	7	14
Light work	0	7	14
Medium work	0	14	28
Heavy work	0	84	168
Very Heavy work	0	84	168

Failure to Recover

If an individual fails to recover within the maximum duration expectancy period, the reader may wish to reference the following questions to assist in better understanding the specifics of an individual's medical case.

Regarding diagnosis:

- Does the individual have chronic simple silicosis, chronic complicated silicosis, subacute silicosis, or acute silicosis?
- Does the individual work in quartz mining, metal mining, foundries, pottery, sandblasting, stonecutting, blasting, or tunnel construction?
- Does the individual report a history of exposure to silica dust?
- Does the individual report difficulty breathing, shortness of breath, a dry or productive cough and/or chest tightness?
- On physical exam with auscultation are changes in the breath sounds present?
- Does the individual also have asthma or bronchitis?
- Has the individual had a chest x-ray? Pulmonary function testing?

- Has the individual had arterial blood gasses, sputum culture or a CT?
- Have conditions with similar symptoms been ruled out?

Regarding treatment:
- As there is no treatment for silicosis, is the individual receiving symptomatic treatment?
- Has the individual addressed any correctable factors such as exposure to silica dust and smoking?
- If necessary is the individual being treated with bronchodilators, anti-inflammatory drugs or antibiotics?

- Has the individual tried sleeping in a semi-upright position?

Regarding prognosis:
- Is the individual's employer able to accommodate any necessary restrictions?
- Does the individual have any conditions that may affect ability to recover?
- Does the individual have any complications such as cor pulmonale, progressive massive fibrosis, emphysema, pneumothorax, and an increased risk for tuberculosis and other lung infections, lung cancer, or stomach cancer?

References

Asbestosis and Silicosis Surveillance. Texas Department of Health. 9 Oct 2000 <http://www.tdh.state.tx.us/epidemiology/98annual/reports/silicosis.pdf>.

Dolin, Robert. "Silicosis." *Griffith's 5-minute Clinical Consult*. Dambro, Mark, ed. New York: Lippincott, Williams & Wilkins, 2000. 998-999.

Silicosis and Asbestosis. Professional Health and Safety Consultants, Ltd. 9 Oct 2000 <http://www.healthandsafety.co.uk/silasb.htm>.

Ye, Y., X. Wang, and Y. Zhong. "Clinical Therapeutic Effect of Xifukang in 53 Patients with Silicosis." *Chung Hsi I Chieh Ho Tsa Chih* 10 7 (1990): 420-421.

Sinusitis
Other names / synonyms: Acute Sinusitis, Ethmoidal Sinusitis, Frontal Sinusitis, Maxillary Sinusitis, Sinus Infection
461, 461.0, 461.1, 461.2, 461.3, 461.8, 461.9, 473.2, 473.9

Definition

Sinusitis is an inflammation of the mucosal lining of one or more sinuses. There are 4 pairs of sinuses: above the eyes in the forehead (the frontal sinuses), behind the cheekbones (the maxillary sinuses), behind the nose (the sphenoid sinuses), and between the eyes at the bridge of the nose (the ethmoid sinuses). Sinusitis can be caused by bacterial, fungal, or viral infection, or allergy. Inflammation results in swelling of the mucosal lining, which in turn results in blockage of the small drainage holes to the nose. Because the mucus can't drain properly the sinus cavities fill with mucus, creating an ideal environment for bacteria to multiply and cause infection.

Sinusitis frequently occurs after a cold. An abscess of an upper tooth can also occasionally result in sinusitis. Changes in atmospheric pressure, such as are experienced during airplane flights, can increase the risk of developing sinusitis. Also at increased risk are those who have experienced irritation of the sinuses from chemical fumes such as chlorine or ammonia.

Sinusitis affects approximately 14% of the population. Sinusitis can affect individuals of any age and is equally common in men and women.

Diagnosis

History: Sinusitis is diagnosed mainly by the symptoms reported by the individual. Individuals may report thick yellow/green discharge from the nose, ache in an upper tooth, poor response to nasal decongestants, history of cold or allergic rhinitis, headache (especially upon awakening), or facial pain. The headache and facial pain may be located over the infected sinus.

Physical exam: Physical examination includes tapping with the fingers (percussion) over a sinus and may may show tenderness. A strong light may be directed over the sinuses to observe if there is fluid in them (transillumination of the sinuses).

Tests: Laboratory tests include a CBC (to check for an elevated white blood cell count) and culture of nasal drainage (to identify bacteria, virus, or fungus). Sinus x-rays, cranial CT, or cranial MRI can confirm sinusitis or thickening of sinus membranes.

Treatment

The two goals of treatment are curing the infection and alleviating the symptoms. Decongestants (oral, nose drops, or nasal sprays) may help with sinus drainage. Over-the-counter analgesics may be used for pain. Increasing fluid intake and using a humidifier will increase moisture in the affected sinus and help thin out the mucus allowing it to drain better. Antibiotics are given if the infection is bacterial.

If sinusitis is unresponsive to medical therapy, surgery to clean and drain the sinus (functional endoscopic sinus surgery) may be necessary.

Prognosis

Individuals with uncomplicated sinusitis can expect a full recovery and return to work. Rarely, sinusitis that is complicated by the spread of infection to the facial bones or brain will extend treatment times and require a more lengthy recovery.

Individuals requiring sinus surgery can expect good results and a full recovery.

Differential Diagnosis

The symptoms of sinusitis can be mimicked by the common cold, allergic rhinitis, and impacted or infected teeth. A tumor of the sinus is also possible, though less likely.

Specialists

- Allergist
- Otolaryngologist

Work Restrictions / Accommodations

During the duration of a sinus infection, it is important that the individual have access to adequate amounts of fluids. The individual should avoid irritating fumes and smoke or wear a protective mask. Special air filters called high-efficiency particulate filters and electrostatic filters may be needed to reduce environmental pollutants.

Comorbid Conditions

Asthma and other chronic respiratory diseases (COPD, emphysema) may lengthen disability.

Complications

The persistence of bacteria in the sinuses can lead to chronic sinusitis, spread of infection to the bones of the face (osteomyelitis), the soft tissue of the face (cellulitis), or the brain (meningitis). Other possible complications include abscess formation and blood clot formation in the cavernous sinus (cavernous sinus thrombosis).

Spread of infection to the eyes, mouth, and brain occurs more often in individuals with depressed immunity from AIDS or chemotherapy. Individuals who experience recurrent and prolonged sinus infections may require surgery to permanently improve sinus drainage.

Factors Influencing Duration

The length of disability is influenced by the age and overall health of the individual, the status of their immune system, the existence of chronic underlying medical conditions, deformities of the nose or sinuses, the promptness with which antibiotic therapy was begun, the response to medical therapy and the need for surgical intervention, and the presence of complications.

Length of Disability

Medical treatment.

Duration in Days

Job Classification	Minimum	Optimum	Maximum
Sedentary work	1	3	7
Light work	1	3	7
Medium work	1	3	7
Heavy work	1	3	7
Very Heavy work	1	3	7

Surgical drainage.

Duration in Days

Job Classification	Minimum	Optimum	Maximum
Sedentary work	2	7	14
Light work	2	7	14
Medium work	3	7	14
Heavy work	3	10	21
Very Heavy work	3	10	21

Duration Trend from Normative Data

Cases	Mean	Min	Max	No Lost Time	Over 6 Months
9238	17	0	650	0.62%	0.17%

Percentile:	5th	25th	Median	75th	95th
Days:	6	9	11	17	41

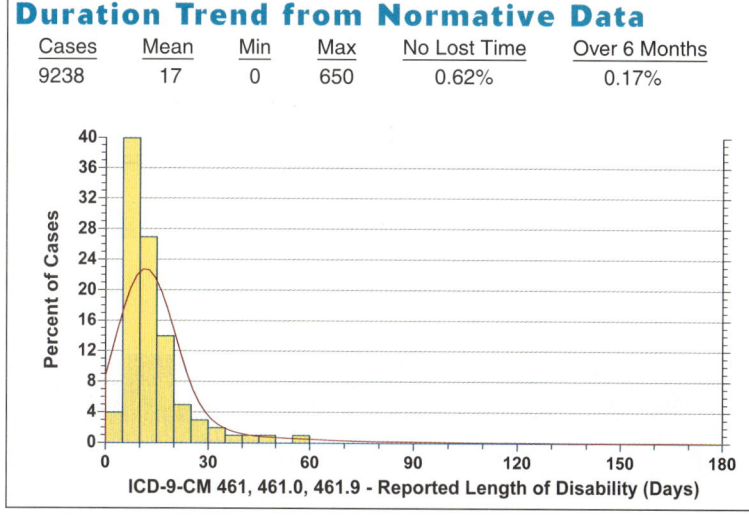
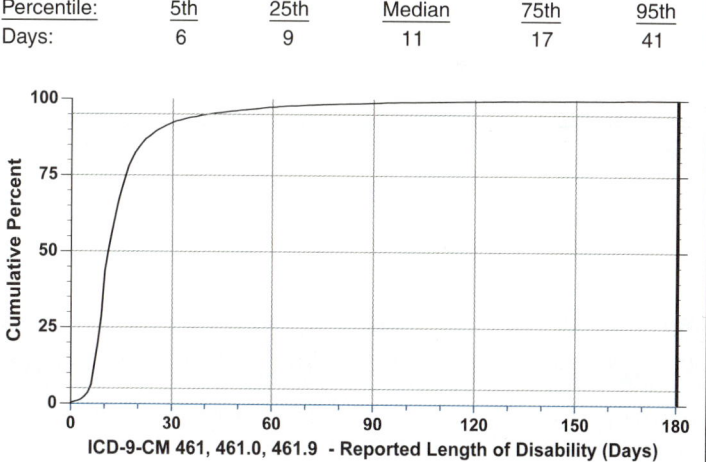

ICD-9-CM 461, 461.0, 461.9 - Reported Length of Disability (Days)

Sinusitis 1929

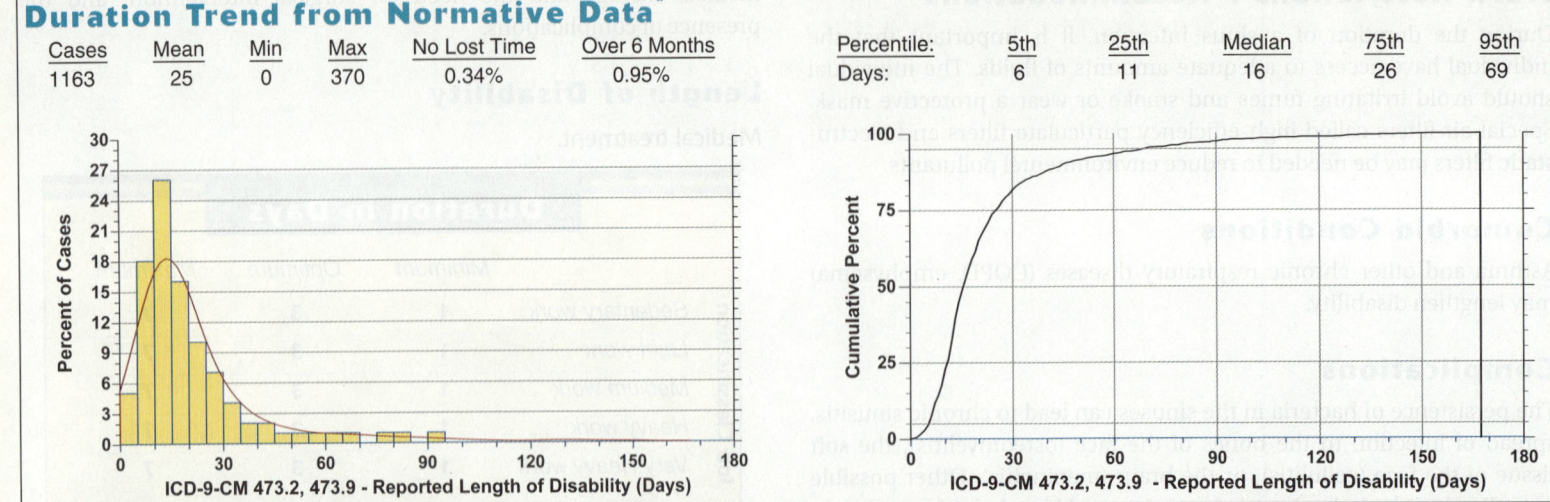

* Differences may exist between the expected duration tables and the normative graphs. Duration tables provide expected recovery periods based on the type of work performed by the individual. The normative graphs reflect the actual observed experience of many individuals across the spectrum of physical conditions, in a variety of industries, and with varying levels of case management.

Failure to Recover

If an individual fails to recover within the maximum duration expectancy period, the reader may wish to reference the following questions to assist in better understanding the specifics of an individual's medical case.

Regarding diagnosis:

- Does individual have a clinical history of a cold or rhinitis?
- Does individual have symptoms suggestive of sinusitis (headache, facial pain, upper tooth ache, or purulent nasal discharge)?
- Were the findings on the clinical exam consistent with the diagnosis of sinusitis?
- Was a nasal culture done? Was the diagnosis confirmed with diagnostic x-rays?
- If the diagnosis was uncertain, were conditions with similar symptoms such as allergy or infected teeth ruled out?

Regarding treatment:

- Was the treatment appropriate for the diagnosis?
- Were symptoms relieved?
- Were appropriate antibiotics administered, as indicated?
- Was surgical intervention needed?

Regarding prognosis:

- Did individual have a full recovery?
- Did individual suffer any complications that may have impacted recovery and prognosis?
- Are there any underlying conditions that may lengthen recovery?

References

Fact Sheet - Sinusitis. National Institute of Allergy and Infectious Diseases. 1999. 12 Jul 2000 <http://www.niaid.nih.gov/factsheets/sinusitis.htm>.

Sinusitis. PlanetRx.com. 1999. 02 Aug 2000 <http://www.planetrx.com/condition/cond_detail/info/83_introduction.html>.

Sjögren's Syndrome

Other names / synonyms: Keratoconjunctivitis Sicca, Sicca Complex, Sicca Syndrome, Sjögren's Disease

710.2

Definition

Sjögren's syndrome is a chronic autoimmune disease that is characterized by the invasion of white blood cells (lymphocytes) into the tear (lacrimal) glands and salivary glands.

The invading lymphocytes promote the destruction of gland tissue leading to dysfunction of the gland. Although the lacrimal and salivary glands are the most commonly affected, Sjögren's syndrome is a whole body (systemic) disease that can affect any organ of the body. As a result, diagnosis is often delayed, and, in all probability, many cases of Sjögren's syndrome are never diagnosed.

Sjögren's syndrome is classified into primary and secondary disease. Primary disease is when the syndrome occurs in the absence of any other autoimmune disorder. Secondary disease refers to Sjögren's syndrome in individuals who have another autoimmune disease, usually scleroderma and rheumatoid arthritis.

The cause of Sjögren's syndrome is unknown, although several viruses have been implicated as triggers for the autoimmune process. Certain individuals may be genetically predisposed to developing Sjögren's syndrome and sex hormones may be involved somehow. The syndrome typically reveals itself in middle age. Ninety percent of the individuals with Sjögren's syndrome are women. Because there is no broadly accepted set of diagnostic criteria for Sjögren's syndrome and the disease often causes variable and nonspecific symptoms in some individuals, the incidence and prevalence are unknown.

Diagnosis

History: The individual may complain of dry eyes (xerophthalmia) and dry mouth (xerostomia). The individual may describe a feeling of sand in the eyes. Individuals may report that swallowing is difficult (pharyngeal dysphagia) and liquids must be taken when eating. Fatigue and fibromyalgia are experienced by half of the individuals with Sjögren's syndrome. Rarely, individuals with Sjögren's syndrome present with other symptoms including joint pain (arthralgia), diarrhea, muscle weakness, headaches, dry cough, or multiple sclerosis-like symptoms.

Physical exam: The individual may have red eyes with evidence of irritation. The individual may blink or rub the eyes excessively. Examination of the mouth and teeth may reveal inadequate saliva production and possibly tooth decay (dental caries). The parotid glands may be enlarged. Exposure of the hands to cold temperatures may cause extreme whitening of the fingers (Raynaud's phenomenon).

Tests: A variety of blood tests would be performed including erythrocyte sedimentation rate (ESR), CBC, antinuclear antibodies, rheumatoid factor, and SS-A and SS-B antibodies. Schirmer's test, for which absorbent paper strips are inserted into the lower eyelid, may be performed to quantify tear production. A rose bengal test, which utilizes a dye to evaluate the cornea, may be performed. Biopsy of a salivary gland or parotid gland may be conducted.

Treatment

There is no cure for Sjögren's syndrome, so treatment is aimed at relieving symptoms and preventing or managing complications. Dry eyes are treated with lubricating eye drops, moisture chamber panels, contact lenses, and/or glasses. Avoidance of drying factors (e.g., hair dryers, medications that cause drying, wind) is important. Blockage of the lower tear ducts (punctal occlusion) with silicone plugs is a method to conserve natural tears. Dry mouth is treated with saliva substitutes or sugar-free lemon hard candy (to stimulate salivation). The individual needs to be meticulous regarding oral hygiene, use mechanical cleaning devices, have frequent dental check ups, and receive fluoride treatments. Humidifiers should be used both at work and at home. Pilocarpine may be used to stimulate tear or saliva production. Analgesics and NSAIDs are used to treat arthralgia or other pains.

Prognosis

Sjögren's syndrome is a chronic, systemic disease for which no cure exists. It can have a substantial impact on quality of life. Strict adherence to treatment guidelines and frequent evaluation by a physician can minimize symptoms and lead to a favorable outcome.

Differential Diagnosis

Mumps, sarcoidosis, parotid tumors, multiple sclerosis, lymphoma, lipoproteinemia, chronic graft-versus-host disease, amyloidosis, human immunodeficiency virus, or hepatitis C virus infection can have similar signs and symptoms. In addition, certain medications (e.g., tricyclic antidepressants, diuretics, antihypertensives) and irradiation can cause dry mouth and eyes.

Specialists

- Immunologist
- Ophthalmologist
- Rheumatologist

Work Restrictions / Accommodations

Individuals should avoid dry surroundings. A humidifier for the office may be necessary. Individuals who work out doors may need to be reassigned to indoor duties in order to avoid wind.

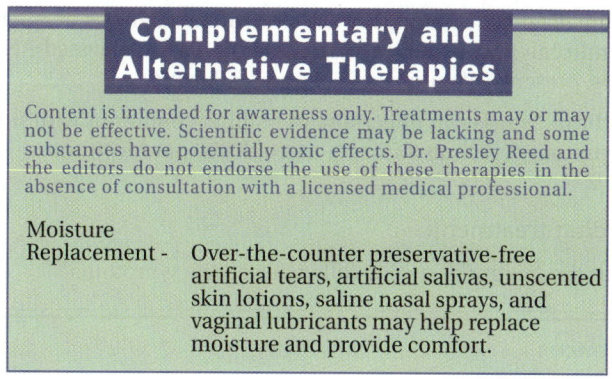

Complementary and Alternative Therapies

Content is intended for awareness only. Treatments may or may not be effective. Scientific evidence may be lacking and some substances have potentially toxic effects. Dr. Presley Reed and the editors do not endorse the use of these therapies in the absence of consultation with a licensed medical professional.

Moisture Replacement - Over-the-counter preservative-free artificial tears, artificial salivas, unscented skin lotions, saline nasal sprays, and vaginal lubricants may help replace moisture and provide comfort.

Comorbid Conditions

Rheumatoid arthritis, scleroderma, and immunodeficiency conditions or diseases (AIDS, certain cancers) may influence the length of disability.

Complications

Tooth decay, chronic oral yeast infection (candidiasis), wasting (atrophy) of the oral mucosa, atrophy of the tongue, small cracks (fissures) on the tongue, irritation and destruction of the membrane that lines the eyelids and exposed surface of the eyeball (conjunctiva), hearing loss, kidney (renal) disease, and skin lesions are potential complications. Individuals with Sjögren's syndrome are at a greater risk of developing malignant lymphoma.

Factors Influencing Duration

Outdoor workers may have a longer disability (in windy, dry environment) than those who work indoors. The severity of symptoms, presence of systemic symptoms, effectiveness of treatment, compliance with treatment recommendations, and development of complications can influence the length of disability.

Length of Disability

If accommodations are not possible, the duration may be longer. In some cases, disability may be permanent for certain work.

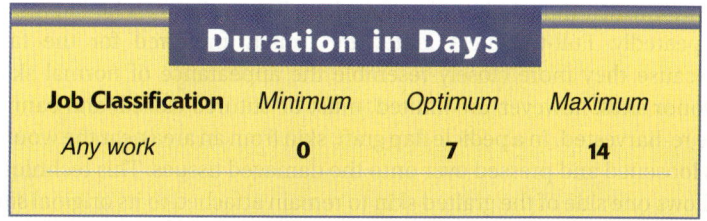

Duration in Days

Job Classification	Minimum	Optimum	Maximum
Any work	0	7	14

Failure to Recover

If an individual fails to recover within the maximum duration expectancy period, the reader may wish to reference the following questions to assist in better understanding the specifics of an individual's medical case.

Regarding diagnosis:

- Did the individual present with characteristic symptoms of dry eyes, dry mouth, difficulty in swallowing, fatigue, or joint and muscle pain?
- Were diagnostic findings consistent with a diagnosis of Sjögren's syndrome (i.e., presence of rheumatoid factor, elevated ANA titers, presence of antigens SS-A and SS-B, etc)?
- If the diagnosis was uncertain, were other conditions with similar symptoms (such as mumps, sarcoidosis, parotid tumors) ruled out?

Regarding treatment:

- Has the treatment successfully relieved the symptoms?
- Has the individual been instructed regarding self-care techniques to help reduce symptoms (such as hard candies to stimulate saliva, meticulous oral hygiene, use of humidifiers)?
- Is the individual complying with the treatment recommendations?
- Would additional counseling and instruction be beneficial?

Regarding prognosis:

- Is individual compliant with treatment plan? What can be done to enhance compliance?
- Have appropriate work accommodations been made to minimize the individual's symptoms (humidifiers)?
- Has the individual suffered any associated complications (such as tooth decay, oral infections, eye inflammation) that could impact recovery and prognosis?
- Does the individual have any underlying conditions, such as rheumatoid arthritis, scleroderma, HIV, or cancer that may impact recovery and prognosis?

References

About Sjögren's Syndrome. Sjögren's Syndrome Foundation, Inc. 2000. 18 Jan 2001 <http://www.sjogrens.com/>.

Bell, Mary, et al. "Sjögren's Syndrome: A Critical Review of Clinical Management." Journal of Rheumatology 26 (1999): 2051-2061.

Cush, John, and Arthur Kavanaugh. "Rheumatic Diseases." Rheumatology Diagnosis and Therapeutics. Cush, John, and Arthur Kavanaugh, eds. Baltimore: Williams & Wilkins, 1999. 147-387.

Manoussakis, Menelaos, and Haralampos Moutsopoulos. "Sjögren's Syndrome." Otolaryngologic Clinics of North America 32 5 (1999): 843-860.

Skin Graft

Other names / synonyms: Allograft, Autograft, Full-Thickness Skin Graft, Pedicle Graft, Split-Thickness Graft

86.6, 86.60, 86.61, 86.62, 86.63, 86.69

Definition

A skin graft is a procedure in which healthy skin is removed (harvested) and is transferred to another area of the body where the skin has been severely damaged by burns, injury, or surgery. New cells grow from the graft, covering the damaged area with fresh skin.

Skin grafts are categorized by the thickness of the donor tissue and the source of the graft. Partial or split-thickness skin grafts (STSGs) contain the outer layer of skin (epidermis) and some but not all of the second layer of skin (dermis), whereas full-thickness skin grafts (FTSGs) contain epidermis, dermis, and various amounts of tissue beneath the skin (subcutaneous tissue).

Split-thickness skin grafts, in which less than the full thickness of skin is removed from the donor site, are used when large areas need to be covered, such as after burns. The donor sites are left to regrow (regenerate), which they do in only a few days. These sites can be harvested repeatedly. Full-thickness grafts are usually preferred for the face because they more closely resemble the appearance of normal skin. Donor sites, however, are limited, must be sutured closed, and cannot be re-harvested. In a pedicle flap graft, skin from an area near the wound is loosened and pressed over onto the damaged tissues. This technique allows one side of the grafted skin to remain attached to its original site, receiving its own blood supply.

Skin grafts can also be categorized by the source of donor tissue. Autografts are taken from the individual receiving the graft, whereas allografts are donated from another person. In either case, if outer skin (epidermis) is allowed to grow in culture to create an increased amount of donor tissue, it is called a cultured autograft or allograft.

The type of skin graft depends on the repair needed and the available blood supply of the damaged area. Skin from an identical twin often makes a successful graft. Skin donated from another person or animal provides a useful temporary cover, but may be eventually rejected by the recipient's body.

Skin grafting is used to cover a wide variety of wounds that cannot be suitably closed surgically. Such wounds arise in a broad population and in all age groups, for a variety of reasons.

Reason for Procedure

Skin grafting is commonly used for the treatment of burns and has become a popular method for treating chronic ulcers (such as venous, pressure, traumatic, and radiation-induced) and skin defects caused by removal of skin cancer and, occasionally, birthmarks.

A skin graft is performed when a damaged area is too large to be repaired by stitching, to restore skin integrity to areas that cannot heal on their own, and in situations where natural healing would result in scars that are unsightly or that might restrict movement. These unsatisfactory consequences of natural healing can be prevented by skin grafting. Furthermore, skin grafting affords early closure of the wound and decreases the risk of wound complications, such as repeated trauma to tissue, and infection.

Description

The procedure for harvesting and grafting skin varies somewhat according to the size, extent of grafting needed to cover the wounded site and the type of cosmetic reconstruction required. For example, extensive facial wounds that involve the nose, lips, or eyes may require skin grafting and a series of plastic surgery interventions to reconstruct normal function and appearance. However, most skin grafting follows a common general procedure.

The size of the wound (recipient site) is measured and a template or pattern of the area to be covered is made. Then a donor site is selected. Although skin can be grafted from any site on the body, care is usually taken to select a site that matches the recipient site in color. Common donor sites are the underside of the wrist, the abdomen or upper thigh. The pattern or template is laid on the donor site and an outline is made. Local anesthesia is injected to the donor site and recipient site. If the area to be grafted is large, general anesthesia may be used. The skin is harvested using a scalpel or a special cutting tool called a dermatome. The donor site is covered with gauze. Any rough edges or fat adhering to the donor skin are removed. If the skin graft must cover an irregular surface, such as a finger, the donor skin may be passed through a mechanical device the produces multiple uniform slits in the skin graft to produce a mesh-like effect that conforms better to the irregular surface. The graft is then anchored into place with stitches and, possibly, staples. A tight dressing (pressure dressing) is applied to minimize lifting and movement of the grafted skin.

Prognosis

The outcome of skin grafting is dependent on the size and condition of area to be covered and the type of graft (split thickness, full thickness, autograft, or allograft). In general, most procedures are successful. Those wounds with small, flat surfaces that are grafted with split-thickness or full-thickness autografts have the best cosmetic and functional outcomes. However, extremely large or complex skin grafting, such as over joints and bony surfaces, or those that require allografts due to lack of suitable donor skin may have greater risk of graft failure and may have poor cosmetic or functional outcomes.

Because additional surgeries may be required, it may take a year to see the final results of the skin graft.

Specialists

- Plastic Surgeon

Rehabilitation

Rehabilitation following a skin graft may be necessary if the graft site is over or near a joint. If this is the case, loss of motion to that particular joint becomes a concern because of the possible scar tissue that may be present and because of any decrease in elasticity seen in the graft compared to the normal skin tissue.

Normally, exercises consisting of passive range of motion provided by a physical therapist are effective to regain and improve skin graft flexibility and joint mobility. Passive range-of-motion exercises begin with the therapist moving the joint with no effort initiated by the individual. This is progressed to active assist range-of-motion exercises in which the individual performs some of the effort in bending and straightening of the joint along with the help of the therapist. As the individual improves with increased motion of the knee joint, the next step of progression is active range-of-motion exercises in which the individual performs all of the motion independently.

In some cases, more than one joint may need to be rehabilitated as in more severe and large surface area burns. If the area of the skin graft has led to joint immobilization for an extended period of time, a gradual strengthening program is implemented by the physical therapist to regain any loss of strength.

Work Restrictions / Accommodations

Vigorous activity should be avoided for 6 weeks after the surgery. The type of work, the location of the wound, and the extent of the surgery will influence any specific work restrictions or special accommodations. For example, skin grafts on hands, feet, fingers, etc. often require splinting to immobilize the extremity. Consequently, these individuals may need temporary job reassignment until there is full return of strength and function. Likewise, special precautions may be needed to keep the grafted area dry, clean and protected from injury (bumps or strains). Follow-up doctor appointments will be necessary after this procedure.

Comorbid Conditions

Comorbid conditions of diabetes mellitus, vascular disease, bleeding disorders or immune suppression may impact ability to recover and further lengthen disability.

Procedure Complications

Complications include death of the grafted tissue (graft failure), collection of fluid (seroma) or blood (hematoma) under the graft (which interferes with the regrowth of blood vessels), and infection of the donor site or the wound (recipient) site.

Factors Influencing Duration

The length of disability will be influenced by size of the damaged tissue area, cause and severity of the wound, extent of the surgery, and if the individual is also the donor of the skin graft.

Length of Disability

Duration depends on underlying cause, site, size, and whether graft is full or partial thickness.

References

Scully, Rosemary M., and Marylou R. Barnes. Physical Therapy. Philadelphia: J.B. Lippincott Company, 1989.

Skin or Subcutaneous Tissue Biopsy

Other names / synonyms: Incisional Biopsy, Punch Biopsy, Shave Biopsy

86.11, 86.2

Definition

A skin or subcutaneous tissue biopsy is a procedure where a skin sample and/or sample of tissue immediately beneath the skin usually from a lesion appearing abnormal in some way, is taken for diagnostic purposes. The four methods used to remove samples are the punch, shave, excisional, and incisional methods. The type of biopsy performed depends on the size and shape of the lesion. The location of the lesion also affects choice of biopsy technique.

A punch biopsy involves the removal of a piece of skin using a sharp, circular punch inserted deep into the skin. The shave biopsy removes only the superficial layer of skin and is used to diagnose diseases that involve only the superficial skin layers or nonpigmented skin cancers such as squamous or basal cell carcinoma. An incisional biopsy removes only part of the lesion and is used on lesions too large for excisional biopsy. An excisional biopsy removes the entire visible or palpable lesion, and can be both diagnostic and therapeutic. An excisional biopsy is best for lesions suspected of being malignant (such as melanoma) as it provides complete assessment, removal of the entire lesion, and easy wound suturing. The excisional biopsy is also good for use on deep skin or subcutaneous tissue, and when the surrounding tissue is necessary for diagnosis.

Reason for Procedure

Indications for performing a skin biopsy include diagnosis of lesions that are suspected of being malignant, fail to heal, increase in size, bleed easily, open and develop sores (ulceration), and lesions or tumors of an uncertain cause. Biopsies are used to diagnose skin conditions and skin cancers such as basal cell cancer, squamous cell cancer, and melanoma. Biopsy may also determine the degree of skin involvement in inflammatory diseases (lupus, hypothyroidism, diabetes, or vascular insufficiency). Excisional biopsy may be therapeutic as the entire lesion and surrounding tissues are removed. Excisional biopsies remove skin cancers, moles, and other small skin lesions.

Description

The area for biopsy is cleansed with an antibacterial solution and a local anesthesia given for pain relief.

In a punch biopsy, the lesion is removed with a special round and hollow (like a straw) scalpel instrument. A rotary motion is used to cut a circle around the lesion into subcutaneous tissue. The "punch" specimen can then be removed and the wound sutured closed. Multiple punch biopsies may be performed.

In a shave biopsy, a scalpel blade is used to "shave" across the top of a lesion, removing a layer of it for pathology. A shave biopsy is only used for benign lesions.

An incisional biopsy is performed by making two parallel elliptical-shaped incisions through the central part of the lesion, extending at each end into normal tissue. The central part of the lesion can then be removed and provides a cross-sectional wedge of tissue for pathology.

In an excisional biopsy, elliptical-shaped incisions are made surrounding the lesion so that the entire lesion and surrounding tissue may be lifted and completely removed. The wound can then be sutured closed.

Prognosis

The predicted outcome is accurate diagnosis or treatment of the lesion. Lesions excessively scratched, infected, crusted, or where the skin has become thickened and leathery (lichenification) may not provide useful pathologic information.

Specialists

- Dermatologist
- General Surgeon
- Plastic Surgeon

Comorbid Conditions

Certain skin conditions may affect results of a skin biopsy. Underlying skin conditions (such as rashes due to allergies or occupational exposures) may prolong disability.

Procedure Complications

Complications of biopsy may include infection and bleeding. A second biopsy may be necessary if inadequate tissue was obtained.

Factors Influencing Duration

Factors that may influence the length of disability include the development of complications, the site of the skin or tissue biopsy, and the underlying disease or condition for which the biopsy was performed.

Length of Disability

Disability depends on the underlying cause for treatment and site. If a lesion is malignant, disability may be permanent.

Duration in Days

Job Classification	Minimum	Optimum	Maximum
Any work	1	2	3

References

Buffington, Sherry, and Clare Brabson. "Specimen Collection and Testing." Nursing Procedures, 3rd ed. Holmes, Nancy, ed. Springhouse, PA: Springhouse Corporation, 2000. 133-165.

Richard, J. Randall. "Punch and Shave Biopsy." Saunders Manual of Medical Practice, 2nd ed. Rakel, Robert E., ed. Philadelphia: W.B. Saunders Company, 2000. 1222-1224.

Sleep Apnea

Other names / synonyms: Central Sleep Apnea, Mixed Sleep Apnea, Obstructive Sleep Apnea, Obstructive Sleep Apnea Syndrome, Obstructive Sleep Apnea-Hypopnea Syndrome

780.57

Definition

Apnea means a pause in breathing. Sleep apnea is a term that describes a group of disorders where breathing stops for a period of time while the individual is asleep.

Everyone takes small pauses occasionally in breathing; however, it is abnormal to stop breathing during sleep for longer than 10 seconds. To qualify as pathologic sleep apnea, the breathing must stop for at least 10 seconds and the episodes must occur least five times per hour.

The three types of sleep apnea are central, obstructive, and mixed. In central apnea, the airflow at the upper airway (e.g., pharynx and nose) and the effort by the diaphragm and other respiratory muscles cease. By contrast, during obstructive apnea, the airflow stops while the effort by the diaphragm and other respiratory muscles continues. In mixed apnea, an initial period of central apnea is followed by a period of obstructive apnea. The most common type of apnea is obstructive sleep apnea. It is also referred to as obstructive sleep apnea syndrome (OSAS). It occurs most often in moderately or severely obese individuals who tend to sleep on their backs (supine).

Individuals with anatomically narrowed airways due to enlarged tonsils and adenoids are predisposed to sleep apnea syndrome. The ingestion of alcohol or sedatives before sleeping or nasal obstruction from any cause such as a cold can worsen the condition. Hypothyroidism and cigarette smoking are additional risk factors for obstructive sleep apnea. Individuals with high blood pressure (hypertension) are also prone to developing sleep apnea. If the condition is severe enough, pulmonary hypertension may occur and the individual may develop right-sided heart failure (cor pulmonale) or myocarditis.

OSAS is most common in men over 40. It occurs in 4% of men and 2% of women between the ages of 30 and 60. Among women, the incidence of OSAS increases after menopause. As individuals age, they commonly gain more weight, which causes the upper airway tissues to sag and become more collapsible. For these reasons, sleep apnea is even more common in older individuals. In others, disturbances in the brain or brain stem interfere with the normal regulation of breathing.

Diagnosis

History: Individuals may complain of morning sluggishness, daytime fatigue, recent weight gain, and impotence. Bed partners may report that the individual has cycles of loud snoring, breath cessation, and restlessness. The apnea is interrupted with a loud snort and gasp before snoring returns to its regular pace. The individual may note personality changes, poor judgment, work-related problems, limited attention, or memory impairment. Other symptoms may include frequent night awakenings, waking unrested in the morning, abnormal daytime sleepiness, headaches, recent weight gain, and lethargy. During the apneic period, the oxygen level in the blood falls dramatically and these persistent low levels of oxygen (hypoxia) cause the daytime symptoms.

Physical exam: The exam may be normal or reveal high blood pressure. The individual may appear sleepy during the exam. The back of the mouth and throat (oropharynx) is often narrowed with excessive soft tissue folds, large tonsils, or a prominent tongue. There may be evidence of a nasal obstruction or poor nasal airflow. The individual may have a short, thick neck (bull neck).

Tests: A test that monitors multiple physiologic parameters during sleep (polysomnography) can help confirm the diagnosis of obstructive sleep apnea and determine the severity and frequency of low blood oxygen level episodes. In addition, monitoring the heart's electrical activity (electrocardiogram [ECG]), measuring blood oxygen levels via oximetry or arterial blood gas levels, and measuring respiratory effort and airflow (pulmonary function tests) may be done.

Treatment

Multiple therapeutic approaches may be tried although no one treatment is considered a panacea. For obesity-related sleep apnea, weight reduction may reduce obstructive episodes, improve blood oxygenation, and reduce daytime drowsiness. Individuals are strictly instructed to avoid alcohol and hypnotic medications. Supplemental oxygen may help raise low blood oxygen levels.

Nasal continuous positive airway pressure (CPAP) or bilevel positive airway pressure (BiPAP) may be used in severe obstructive sleep apnea. Removable dental appliances may be used during sleep to prevent the upper airway from being obstructed by the tongue or other oral structures.

In the few individuals with severe symptoms such as heart or lung abnormalities and who fail to respond to the above measures, surgery may be recommended. Enlarged tonsils and/or adenoids should be removed. One procedure (uvulopalatopharyngoplasty) consists of removing the obstructing soft tissue in the back of the mouth and upper throat. Nasal surgery to realign the nasal septum (nasal septoplasty) or decrease the size of any large nasal bones may be done for those with significant nasal deformities. Creating an airway opening in the neck (tracheostomy) is a surgical procedure that effectively bypasses the obstruction in the mouth and upper throat (oropharynx).

Prognosis

Treatments are generally successful in all but the most severe cases. Uvulopalatopharyngoplasty and nasal septoplasty are effective only 50% of the time in reducing apnea episodes. A tracheostomy is the most effective (radical) surgical procedure for obstructive sleep apnea but carries adverse effects such as scar tissue formation, speech disturbances, and infection. Speech can also be impaired.

Differential Diagnosis

Seizure disorder, narcolepsy, or psychiatric depression should be included in the differential diagnosis.

Specialists

- Internist
- Sleep Disorder Specialist

Work Restrictions / Accommodations

Associated daytime drowsiness and thought and memory problems may present safety concerns. Individuals with these conditions should not have job responsibilities that require operating heavy machinery or driving a vehicle until the condition is corrected. Those who require surgery may need extended leave from work.

Comorbid Conditions

Comorbid conditions of obesity, neurological depression, and lung or heart disorders may impact the ability to recover and further lengthen disability.

Complications

Possible complications include cardiac rhythm abnormalities (eg, sinus arrhythmias, extreme bradycardia, atrial flutter, ventricular tachycardia), high blood pressure (hypertension), heart attack, stroke, morning headache, and slowed thought processing (mentation).

The repeated periods of apnea or decreased breathing (hypopnea) result in insufficient oxygenation of blood. The low blood oxygen levels decrease the amount of oxygen that the brain, heart and other organs receive. This puts stress on these organs and may predispose individuals with sleep apnea to strokes and heart attacks. In addition, low oxygen levels continually wake the individuals, causing them to be sleep deprived and groggy. This sleep deprivation can have serious adverse consequences on daily life activities including driving and job performance.

Factors Influencing Duration

The severity of the disorder, treatment, response to treatment, and job requirements are factors that can influence disability.

Length of Disability

Medical treatment.

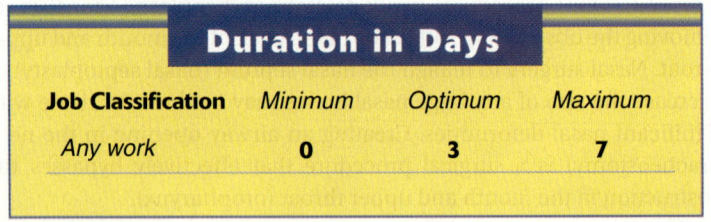

Job Classification	Minimum	Optimum	Maximum
Any work	0	3	7

Failure to Recover

If an individual fails to recover within the maximum duration expectancy period, the reader may wish to reference the following questions to assist in better understanding the specifics of an individual's medical case.

Regarding diagnosis:

- Do factors such as (obesity, sleeping on the back, brain disturbance, alcohol, sedative or cigarette use) place individual at greater risk for sleep apnea?
- Does the individual have associated symptoms such as lethargy, daytime fatigue, or concentration problems?
- Does the bed partner report cycles of loud snoring, breath cessation, and restlessness?
- Did the physical exam reveal associated conditions of hypertension, oral, nasal or pharyngeal obstructions?
- Was a sleep study done to confirm the diagnosis?
- Were additional diagnostic tests done to rule out other conditions with similar symptoms (i.e., seizure disorder, other sleep disorders, psychiatric disturbances)?

Regarding treatment:

- Did the individual receive instructions regarding weight loss, avoidance of alcohol and sedatives and alternative sleeping positions? Were these measures successful in relieving symptoms?
- If not were other more aggressive measures considered (i.e., CPAP, BiPAP, surgical interventions)?

Regarding prognosis:

- Does individual have comorbid conditions such as obesity, psychiatric depression, or lung or heart disorders that may impact recovery and prognosis?
- Did any complications arise such as cardiac rhythm abnormalities (e.g., sinus arrhythmias, extreme bradycardia, atrial flutter, and ventricular tachycardia), hypertension, heart attack, stroke, morning headache, and slowed thought processing (mentation) that could lengthen recovery time?

References

Clochesy, John M., et al. Critical Care Nursing, 2nd ed. Philadelphia: W.B. Saunders Company, 1996.

Social Phobia

Other names / synonyms: Social Anxiety Disorder

300.01, 300.23

Definition

Social phobia is characterized by an excessive fear of humiliation or embarrassment in various social settings such as public speaking, going to parties, urinating in a public restroom (also called shy bladder), and speaking to a date. The individual realizes that his or her fears are excessive and unreasonable. Exposure to the feared social situation may bring on a panic attack with rapid heartbeat and breathing, sweating, and feelings of impending doom. Like panic disorder, social phobia is a common, frequently severe anxiety disorder that can cause significant work and social impairment. Even anticipation of the situation provoking fear can elicit severe distress in the affected individual. Common associated features are hypersensitivity to criticism, difficulty being assertive, or feelings of inferiority.

Studies reveal that phobias are the single most common mental disorders in the US. For social phobia, the onset may be as young as age 5 and as old as 35. In epidemiological studies, females are more often affected than males but in clinical studies, more males are affected. The reason for this discrepancy is not known. Lifetime prevalence is from 3-13%; in outpatient clinics, 10-20% of individuals with anxiety disorders also have social phobia. Social phobia is more prevalent among first-degree relatives of those with this diagnosis than in the general population.

Diagnosis

History: A diagnosis of social phobia excludes conditions where the individual avoids social situations due to embarrassment about another psychiatric condition or a medical condition (e.g., individual is severely handicapped or disfigured from trauma or is morbidly obese).

The DSM-IV-TR (Diagnostic and Statistical Manual of Mental Disorders, 4th Edition, Text Revision, published by the American Psychiatric Association) diagnostic criteria for social phobia include a marked and persistent fear of one or more social or performance situations where individual is exposed to unfamiliar people or possible scrutiny by others. The individual fears that he or she will act in a way (or show anxiety symptoms) that is humiliating or embarrassing but also recognizes that the fear is excessive or unreasonable. Exposure to the feared social situation almost invariably provokes anxiety that may take the form of a panic attack.

The feared social or performance situations are either avoided or endured with intense anxiety or distress. The avoidance, anxious anticipation, or distress in the feared social or performance situation(s) interferes significantly with the individual's normal routine, occupational or academic functioning, or social activities or relationships. Individual may also exhibit marked distress about having the phobia. The fear or avoidance is not due to the direct physiological effects of a substance (drug of abuse or medication) or a general medical condition. It is not better accounted for by another mental disorder such as panic disorder with or without agoraphobia, separation anxiety disorder, body dysmorphic disorder, a pervasive developmental disorder, or schizoid personality disorder. If a general medical condition or another mental disorder is present such as stuttering, trembling in Parkinson's disease, or exhibiting abnormal eating behavior as in anorexia nervosa or bulimia nervosa, the fear associated with social phobia is unrelated to it.

Physical exam: An exam is generally not helpful in diagnosing social phobia. The individual may exhibit increased heart rate or blood pressure if he or she is experiencing anxiety or distress during the interview.

Tests: Tests include laboratory evaluation to rule out organic causes of anxiety such as thyroid and adrenal gland abnormalities. Psychological testing may be helpful in the evaluation of this disorder and could help differentiate a social phobia from avoidant personality disorder.

Treatment

Treatment in its simplest form is the avoidance of the phobic situation. However, in the case of social phobia, it is often impossible or not feasible to avoid the situation causing the anxiety. Psychotherapy and pharmacotherapy used in combination have the best results compared to using either therapy alone. Pharmacotherapy for social phobia involving performance such as stage fright and shy bladder involves the use of antiadrenergic and beta-adrenergic medications. For the generalized type of social phobia, antianxiety agents may be useful. Various studies show that serotonin-specific reuptake inhibitors (SSRIs) and a benzodiazepine are helpful. Psychotherapy involves the use of insight-oriented therapy that enables the individual to seek healthy ways of dealing with the anxiety-provoking stimulus. Hypnosis, supportive (group therapy), and family therapy may also be useful.

Treatment for social phobia usually incorporates behavioral and cognitive methods. Exposure therapy involves the individual gradually being exposed to the dreaded situation. Relaxation training, progressive muscle relaxation, and respiratory control training may be helpful. Many therapists include homework and specific readings (bibliotherapy) for the individual to do between sessions. Since the individual may only spend a few sessions in one-on-one contact with a therapist, this method allows individuals to continue to work on their own with the aid of a printed manual.

Psychodynamic treatment refers to another "talk therapy" where the therapist and individual work together to uncover underlying emotional conflicts. Although this type of therapy may help relieve the stress that contributes to panic attacks, no scientific evidence exists that show this form by itself is effective in overcoming panic disorder or agoraphobia. However, if a phobic disorder occurs along with another emotional disturbance, psychodynamic therapy may be a helpful addition to the overall treatment plan. Therapy groups can also be beneficial.

Prognosis

Only recently has social phobia been recognized as an important mental disorder. Available studies for the course and outcome of this disorder are limited. Duration may be life-long but symptoms can decrease at times especially with treatment.

Differential Diagnosis

It is important to differentiate social phobia from normal shyness or from appropriate fears about certain social situations. For a diagnosis of social phobia, the DSM-IV-TR requires that these symptoms must impair the individual's ability to function appropriately. Schizophrenics may exhibit social phobia and can be differentiated by the presence or absence of psychotic symptoms (delusions, hallucinations) and thought disorder. Individuals with social phobia will have some insight into their fears and often recognize their phobia as irrational. Panic disorder with or without agoraphobia involves many of the same physiologic symptoms experienced by individuals with social phobia and includes sweating, shortness of breath, and a fast pulse or pounding heart (palpitations).

Specialists

- Advanced Practice Registered Nurse
- Internist
- Occupational Therapist
- Physical Therapist
- Psychiatrist
- Psychologist

Work Restrictions / Accommodations

High profile positions with frequent contact on a one-to-one basis will be uncomfortable and may be intolerable for the socially phobic employee. A work environment involving a small group of individuals rather than a large one will be more comfortable for the individual with this disorder. Contact with a large or an unfamiliar group of individuals should be limited. A determination of the phobic situation or object and avoidance of that situation should enable the individual to maintain employment.

Time-limited restrictions and work accommodations should be individually determined based on the characteristics of the individual's response to the disorder, the functional requirements of the job and work environment, and the flexibility of the job and work site. The purpose of the restrictions/accommodations is to help maintain the worker's capacity to remain at the workplace without a work disruption or to promote timely and safe transition back to full work productivity.

Comorbid Conditions

Coexisting conditions that may affect recovery and lengthen disability include panic disorder, specific or simple phobias, agoraphobia, avoidant personality disorder, depression, and substance abuse (especially alcohol dependence).

Complications

The distress associated with social phobia can lead to further psychiatric complications including other anxiety disorders, major depressive disorder, and substance-related disorders. Individuals may self-medicate with marijuana, alcohol, and other mood-altering substances. This complicates the course and prognosis of the disorder. Associated major depression and other anxiety disorders cause complications. Personality disorders are associated with social phobia and are a complicating factor. Often, the exposure to or anticipation of the phobic situation leads to panic attacks. Avoidance of feared social situations can lead to severe impairment in school, work, and relationships.

Factors Influencing Duration

If the phobia involves any object or situation encountered at work or while traveling to work, disability may be affected by the individual's motivation to resolve the phobia. In this case, the individual is forced into a form of exposure therapy on an ongoing, daily basis that is difficult and challenging.

Length of Disability

Length of disability depends on the individual's specific fears and associated psychopathology.

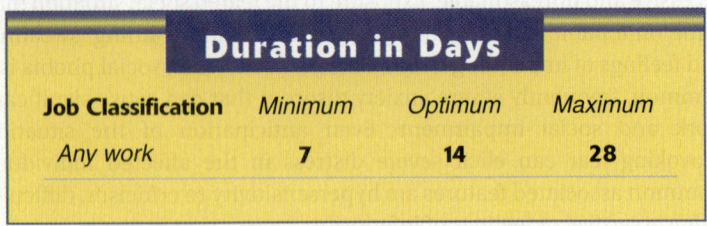

Job Classification	Minimum	Optimum	Maximum
Any work	7	14	28

Failure to Recover

If an individual fails to recover within the maximum duration expectancy period, the reader may wish to reference the following questions to assist in better understanding the specifics of an individual's medical case.

Regarding diagnosis:

- Do the individual's expressed fears meet the criteria for social phobia?
- Has diagnosis been confirmed?
- Is normal functioning significantly impaired?
- What is currently happening in the individual's life that may be triggering or compounding the phobia?
- Have other conditions with similar symptoms been ruled out?

Regarding treatment:

- If not already on medication, would drug therapy be beneficial to this treatment plan?
- If individual is not responding effectively to current medication, what other drug treatment options are available?
- Through cognitive-behavioral therapy, is individual learning to recognize the earliest thoughts and feelings in the panic cycle, eliminate thought patterns that contribute to symptoms, and change his/her behavior?
- Is the individual being taught to cope effectively with symptoms he/she experiences during a panic attack?
- If individual has been avoiding particular places or situations, would the addition of interceptive and invivo exposure be beneficial?
- Is individual involved in a therapy program that includes relaxation techniques? By learning to relax, is the individual able to reduce the anxiety and stress leading to panic attacks?
- Is individual currently involved in a therapy group?
- Would individual also benefit from psychodynamic treatment, in which therapist and individual work together to uncover underlying emotional conflicts?

Regarding prognosis:

- How long has the individual been involved in cognitive-behavioral therapy?
- Would individual benefit from extended therapy?
- Has the individual been involved in current form of treatment for over 6 weeks without a noticeable effect? Has treatment plan been reassessed? What direction will new treatment plan take?
- Since successful treatment of social phobia requires diagnosis and treatment of coexisting conditions, such as substance abuse (both intoxication and withdrawal states) and depression, are these conditions being appropriately addressed?

References

Allen, Francis. Diagnostic and Statistical Manual of Mental Disorders, 4th ed, text revision. Washington, DC: American Psychiatric Association, 2000.

Anxiety Disorders - Phobias. National Institute of Mental Health. 10 Jul 2000. 11 July 2000 <http://www.nimh.nih.gov/anxiety/anxiety/phobia/index.htm>.

Larkin, M. "Hypnosis Makes Headway in the Clinic." Lancet 353 915 (1999): 386.

Let's Talk Facts About Phobias. American Psychiatric Association. 1999. 11 July 2000 <http://www.psych.org/public_info/phobia.cfm>.

Somatization Disorder

Other names / synonyms: Briquet's Disorder, Briquet's Syndrome, Hysteria
300, 300.81, 306

Definition

Somatization disorder falls under the classification of somatoform disorders. These disorders are characterized by physical complaints lacking a known physical (organic) basis. Somatization disorder is characterized by many somatic symptoms that cannot be explained adequately on the basis of physical and laboratory examinations. It begins early in life, affecting mostly women, and is characterized by recurrent multiple complaints involving most organ systems. The physical complaints, often dramatically described, are unexplained, and typically include pain, anxiety and mood related symptoms, gastrointestinal disturbance, and genitourinary symptoms. For a symptom to be significant, the individual may report that it caused him or her to take a medicine, alter his or her life pattern, or see a physician.

Followed long-term, individuals are shown to have an excessive number of surgeries. They develop both anxiety and depression, and have a history of suicidal threats, occupational difficulties, and marital discord. This disorder is considered chronic and is associated with an impairment in the individual's social and occupational functioning.

Somatization disorder is not uncommon. It often begins in the teenage years, and social, ethnic, and cultural factors may be involved in the development of symptoms in this disorder. Though the cause is unknown, it is thought that development of symptoms may be a way of social communication, to avoid obligations, to express emotions, or to symbolize a feeling or belief.

The reported prevalence of the disorder has varied with estimates of 0.1-0.5% of the general population. It has been reported to be more prevalent in rural areas and among the less educated. This disorder is found in about 20% of first-degree female relatives (parents, siblings, or children). Women outnumber men 5-1; the lifetime prevalence of somatization disorder among women may be 1-2% in the general population.

Diagnosis

History: The history will reveal that the symptoms have been present for several years, beginning before age thirty. These individuals have long-term and excessive medical help-seeking behavior probably beginning in adolescence or in the late teens. Their history may reveal repeated surgical operations, drug dependence, marital separation or divorce, and suicide attempts. Their medical history can be long, complicated, and involve many somatic complaints. Family history is important, as somatization disorder is found in about 20% of first-degree female relatives. First-degree male relatives of individuals with somatization disorder show an increased prevalence of both antisocial personality and alcoholism.

The criteria for diagnosis are specific and, during the course of the disorder, the individual must have complained of at least 4 pain symptoms, 2 gastrointestinal symptoms, 1 sexual symptom, and 1 unexplained neurological (pseudoneurological) symptom, none of which is completely explained by physical or laboratory examinations. The specific criteria are given in the DSM-IV and include a history of many physical complaints beginning before age 30 that occur over a period of several years and result in treatment being sought or significant impairment in social, occupational, or other important areas of functioning.

Each of the following criteria must have been met, with individual symptoms occurring at any time during the course of the disturbance: 4 pain symptoms (a history of pain related to at least 4 different sites or functions) such as head, abdomen, back, joints, extremities, chest, rectum, during menstruation, during sexual intercourse, or during urination; 2 gastrointestinal symptoms (a history of at least 2 gastrointestinal symptoms other than pain) such as nausea, bloating, vomiting other than during pregnancy, diarrhea, or intolerance of several different foods; 1 sexual symptom (a history of at least 1 sexual or reproductive symptom other than pain) such as sexual indifference, impotence or premature ejaculation (erectile or ejaculatory dysfunction), irregular periods (menses), excessive menstrual bleeding, vomiting throughout pregnancy); and one pseudoneurological symptom (a history of at least 1 symptom or deficit suggesting a neurological condition not limited to pain, with conversion symptoms such as impaired coordination or balance, paralysis or localized weakness, difficulty swallowing or lump in throat, inability to speak (aphonia), inability to urinate (urinary retention), seeing visions or hearing voices that aren't there (hallucinations), loss of touch or pain sensation, double vision, blindness, deafness, seizures; suddenly forgetting one's identity or whereabouts or feeling unreal (dissociative symptoms), or loss of consciousness other than fainting).

Additionally, after appropriate investigation, each of the symptoms cannot fully be explained by a known general medical condition or the direct effects of a substance (such as the effects of medication, drugs, or alcohol) or, when there is a related general medical condition, the physical complaints or resulting social or occupational impairment are in excess of what would be expected from the history, physical examination, or laboratory findings.

Finally, it is determined that the symptoms are not intentionally faked or produced (as in factitious disorder or malingering).

Physical exam: This is an important part of the diagnosis of somatization disorder. The individual's symptoms, which involve multiple organ systems, require the clinicians to rule out nonpsychiatric (organic) conditions. Close attention should be focused on particular areas of complaints. For example, if one of the complaints is perceived menstrual irregularities (dysmenorrhea), then a pelvic exam would be indicated.

Tests: Tests should include psychological testing and psychiatric evaluation. Exhaustive medical workups are often done to rule out organic causes of the individual's symptoms.

Treatment

Individuals benefit from regular psychotherapy (individual and/or group therapy by a mental health worker or psychiatrist). The goal is to have individuals learn to cope with their symptoms. This may be done by having them identify ways to express their emotions other than by somatic complaints. Supportive primary care physicians may be very effective as the individuals are reassured that their complaints are being understood.

The effectiveness of drug treatment alone in somatization disorder is unknown. However, coexisting mental disorders should be treated with drugs if indicated. Monitoring medication(s) is essential with these individuals, as they are often erratic and unreliable with treatment.

Prognosis

This disorder is chronic and often times debilitating. These individuals continue to seek medical attention for their symptoms, usually at least every year, and tend to have frequent hospitalizations. If they become involved in psychotherapy, their medical help-seeking behaviors and number of hospitalizations can decrease by as much as 50%. However, they tend to resist the idea that their symptoms are rooted in psychological conflicts rather than physical disorders.

Differential Diagnosis

There is always the possibility that the symptoms stem from a bona fide medical disorder, such as multiple sclerosis, myasthenia gravis, systemic lupus erythematosus, acquired immune deficiency syndrome (AIDS), acute intermittent porphyria, hyperparathyroidism, hyperthyroidism, and chronic systemic infections. Panic disorder can be differentiated from somatization disorder by the absence of physical complaints between episodes of panic. Other psychiatric conditions associated with somatization disorder have been discussed under

complications. Munchausen syndrome, malingering, and drug addiction should be considered when the physician is unable to obtain past medical records.

Specialists

- Gastroenterologist
- Gynecologist
- Internist
- Neurologist
- Pain Specialist
- Psychiatrist
- Psychologist
- Urologist

Work Restrictions / Accommodations

Time-limited restrictions and work accommodations are necessary only infrequently, for the most serious cases. In these instances, time-limited restrictions and work accommodations should be individually determined based on the characteristics of the individual's response to the disorder, the functional requirements of the job and work environment, and the flexibility of the job and work site. The purpose of the restrictions/accommodations is to help maintain the worker's capacity to remain at the workplace without a work disruption or to promote timely and safe transition back to full work productivity.

Comorbid Conditions

Alcohol abuse or drug use, or the presence of a personality disorder may lengthen disability.

Complications

About 50% of individuals with somatization disorder have a coexisting mental disorder. Complications might include other personality traits or disorders, especially antisocial personality disorder, and substance abuse or dependence. Major depression, generalized anxiety disorder, and schizophrenia all may present initially with multiple somatic complaints. Some of the most frequent and important complications of this disorder are repeated surgical operations, drug dependence, marital separation or divorce, and suicide attempts. The symptoms associated with major depression, anxiety, and psychosis eventually overshadow the somatic complaints of somatization disorder.

Factors Influencing Duration

Length of disability depends on severity of the illness, presence or lack of bona fide medical conditions, the individual's willingness to seek help through mental health professionals, and the presence of an associated psychiatric condition, substance abuse, or other personality disorder.

Length of Disability

This is a chronic condition. Disability may be intermittent. Duration depends on severity, other psychological and physical conditions, and type of treatment.

Duration in Days

Job Classification	Minimum	Optimum	Maximum
Any work	0	14	28

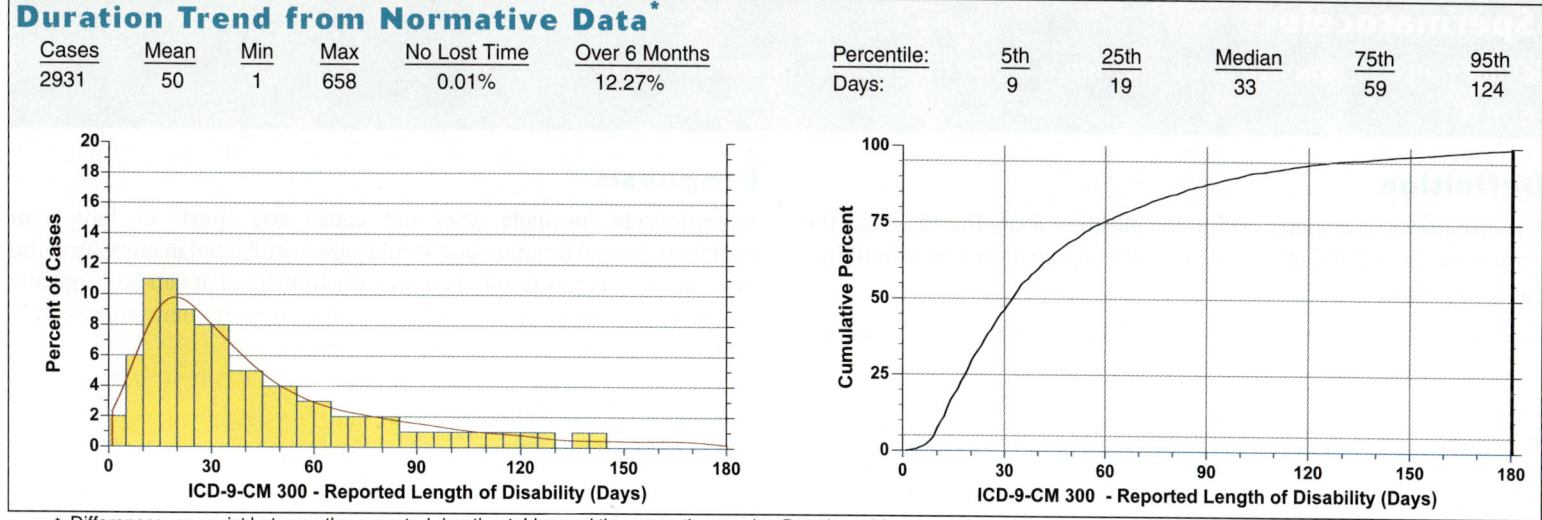

Duration Trend from Normative Data*

Cases	Mean	Min	Max	No Lost Time	Over 6 Months
2931	50	1	658	0.01%	12.27%

Percentile:	5th	25th	Median	75th	95th
Days:	9	19	33	59	124

* Differences may exist between the expected duration tables and the normative graphs. Duration tables provide expected recovery periods based on the type of work performed by the individual. The normative graphs reflect the actual observed experience of many individuals across the spectrum of physical conditions, in a variety of industries, and with varying levels of case management.

Failure to Recover

If an individual fails to recover within the maximum duration expectancy period, the reader may wish to reference the following questions to assist in better understanding the specifics of an individual's medical case.

Regarding diagnosis:

- Does the individual's behavior meet the criteria for somatization disorder?
- Has the diagnosis been confirmed?
- Has an appropriate investigation been made for each physical complaint to rule out an underlying medical condition, or to justify the symptoms?

Regarding treatment:

- What medication is the individual currently taking, and for what condition(s)?
- Is there any overlap of medications?
- Is there any indication of medication overuse or abuse?
- Is the physician aware of all medications that the individual is currently receiving from all participating healthcare providers?
- Does the individual have a therapeutic rapport with the physician? What can be done to facilitate this relationship?
- Is the individual participating in psychotherapy?
- Does current therapy help the individual cope with symptoms and learn to express emotions in ways other than somatic complaints?

Regarding prognosis:

- Because somatization is chronic and often debilitating, is physician supportive and reassuring?
- Does the individual trust primary physician, or is the individual constantly seeking assistance from other healthcare providers?
- Is the individual involved in a solo or group therapy program?
- Has therapy helped individual decrease medical help-seeking behaviors?

References

First, Michael B., ed. Diagnostic and Statistical Manual of mental Disorders. 4th ed. Washington, DC: American Psychiatric Association, 1994.

Somatization Disorder. Merck Manual of Diagnosis and Therapy. 01 Jan 2000. 07 Oct 2000 <http://www.merck.com/pubs/mmanual/section15/chapter186/186b.htm>.

Spermatocele

Other names / synonyms: Cystic Tumor of the Epididymis, Spermatic Cyst

608.1

Definition

A spermatocele is a sperm and fluid collection (cyst) found within the scrotal sac. An individual with this condition may have one or multiple spermatoceles.

Spermatoceles usually lie behind and just above the testicle but are separate from it. They may be very small or may grow as large as a few inches. Trauma, prior vasectomy, or infection of the sperm ducts (epididymis) may be risk factors for spermatocele because of sperm leakage into the scrotal sac. Spermatoceles are harmless with no indication that they may lead to any other more serious condition.

Spermatoceles typically appear after puberty and reach maximum incidence during the fourth and fifth decades of life. They are exceedingly common and identified incidentally in more than 70% of men undergoing scrotal examination using high frequency sound waves (high resolution ultrasonography).

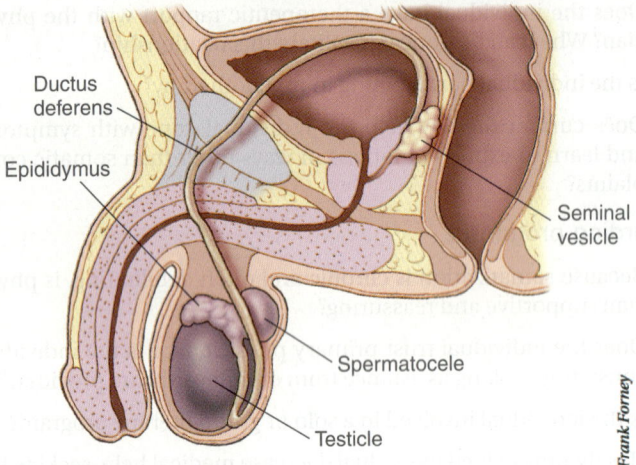

Diagnosis

History: The individual reports the presence of one or more lumps above one or both testicles. These may be accompanied by mild discomfort.

Physical exam: The exam of a spermatocele by touch (palpation) reveals a semifirm mass that can be slightly compressed. The mass is located just above and separate from the testicle.

Tests: A light may be held behind the scrotum (transillumination) and high frequency sound waves applied (ultrasound) to determine the exact location of the mass and whether it is fluid or solid. Fluid may be aspirated from the spermatocele, examined, and then cultured to determine if the cyst is infected with bacteria.

Treatment

No treatment is necessary unless the mass is painful or large enough to consider surgical removal. Spontaneous shrinkage of the cyst may occur if fluid can be withdrawn through a needle inserted into the spermatocele. Additional surgery can be avoided with this procedure.

Prognosis

Spermatocele normally does not cause any short- or long-term problems. Sexual function and fertility are not affected in any way. If the cyst becomes large enough to annoy the individual, it can be surgically removed (spermatocelectomy). Although surgery may successfully remove spermatocele, recurrence is common.

Differential Diagnosis

Conditions with similar symptoms include a collection of fluid within the scrotum (hydrocele), a pooling of blood within the testicular veins (varicocele), abnormal protrusion of tissue into the scrotum (inguinal hernia), twisting (torsion) of the testis, inflammation of the sperm duct (epididymitis), inflammation of the scrotal sac or testis (orchitis), a pooling of blood within the scrotal sac (hematocele), or testicular cancer.

Specialists

- Urologist

Work Restrictions / Accommodations

Lifting and physical activity may be restricted if surgical removal of the spermatocele is required.

Comorbid Conditions

Bleeding disorders, obesity, diabetes mellitus, and immune disorders can result in complications following surgery. The spermatocele can obscure other pathologic conditions within the scrotum or testis such as a hydrocele, varicocele, inguinal hernia, epididymitis, orchitis, hematocele, testicular cancer, or torsion of the testis and may contribute to prolonged recovery if additional surgery is required.

Complications

A serious situation could develop if the spermatocele, a harmless (benign) mass, hides a cancerous (malignant) testicular tumor.

Factors Influencing Duration

The length of disability is influenced by the need for treatment, type of treatment (e.g., aspiration or surgery), response to treatment, and any complications that may occur.

Length of Disability

Medical treatment.

Duration in Days

Job Classification	Minimum	Optimum	Maximum
Any work	0	0	1

Surgical excision including aspiration.

Duration in Days

Job Classification	Minimum	Optimum	Maximum
Any work	3	7	14

Failure to Recover

If an individual fails to recover within the maximum duration expectancy period, the reader may wish to reference the following questions to assist in better understanding the specifics of an individual's medical case.

Regarding diagnosis:

- Does individual have a history of trauma to the testicles, vasectomy, or infection of the sperm ducts (epididymis)?
- Are there one or more lumps above one or both testicles?
- Are these lumps accompanied by mild discomfort?
- Were transillumination and ultrasound done to determine the exact location of the mass? Was the mass fluid or solid?
- Was fluid withdrawn (aspirated) from the spermatocele and cultured to determine if the cyst is infected with bacteria?
- Was the diagnosis of spermatocele confirmed?

Regarding treatment:

- Was fluid withdrawn (aspirated) from the spermatocele resulting in spontaneous shrinkage of the cyst?
- Did needle aspiration successfully shrink the cyst?
- Was surgical excision (spermatocelectomy) required due to the size of the cyst or because the cyst was causing significant discomfort?
- Was surgical excision successful?
- Did any complications occur as a result of surgery?

Regarding prognosis:

- Is this an initial diagnosis or a recurrence of a spermatocele?
- If symptoms have persisted or worsened despite treatment, have other causes been considered?
- Has individual been compliant with the treatment regimen?
- Is it possible that the spermatocele has concealed a cancerous (malignant) testicular tumor?

References

Davis, R.S. "Intratesticular Spermatocele." Urology 51 5A Suppl (1998): 167-169.

Nistal, M., and Paniagua, R. Testicular and Epididymal Pathology. New York: Thieme-Stratton, Inc, 1984.

Spermatocelectomy
63.2

Definition

Spermatocelectomy is the surgical removal of a spermatocele. Spermatoceles are benign harmless cyst-like masses that are found within the scrotum and are filled with fluid and dead sperm cells.

Spermatoceles can be caused by trauma, infection (epididymitis), or congenital abnormalities. Spermatoceles are very common and most often occur without symptoms. Because they are not usually associated with symptoms, spermatoceles rarely require treatment. If they become enlarged enough to cause pain, a spermatocelectomy is performed.

Reason for Procedure

Usually, a spermatocele remains small (less than one-half an inch). Occasionally, a spermatocele can grow to be as large as 6 inches or more. A spermatocelectomy is performed if the spermatocele has grown large enough to cause the individual persistent pain.

Description

Surgery is usually performed on an outpatient basis and requires less than an hour to perform. A general spinal or even local anesthetic can be used for the procedure. The surgery involves making an incision in the scrotum and moving the affected testicle through the incision. The tissue layer covering the testicle and spermatocele is opened. The spermatocele is then dissected free of the epididymis and removed. The procedure can be performed via a micro-surgical technique to insure that there is no inadvertent injury to the epididymal tubules. Finally, the tissue layers and the wound are closed with sutures.

Prognosis

Usually the outcome is good, but because the epididymis is left intact in its normal anatomical position, there is the possibility of another spermatocele at a later time. The recurrence rate is about 5%.

Specialists

- Urologist

Work Restrictions / Accommodations

Most individuals will need to stay off their feet for 3 to 5 days and reduce activity for a week. Heavy lifting or strenuous physical activity may need to be modified temporarily following surgery.

Comorbid Conditions

Any immunosuppressive condition may hinder recovery.

Procedure Complications

As with any surgical procedure, risks of the surgery include bleeding, pain, and postoperative infection. There is the possibility of another duct blocking at a later time. If the epididymis is removed along with the spermatocele, the recurrence rate is lower, but then there is a slight increase in risk of damage to the testicular blood supply.

Factors Influencing Duration

Length of disability may be influenced by complications from surgery.

Length of Disability

Heavy lifting restrictions may be necessary.

Duration in Days

Job Classification	Minimum	Optimum	Maximum
Any work	3	7	14

References

Williams, Richard, MD, and James Donovan, MD. "Urology." *Current Surgical Diagnosis and Treatment*. Way, Lawrence, ed. Norwalk: Appleton & Lange, 1991. 886-949.

Spherocytosis, Hereditary

Other names / synonyms: Chronic Acholuric Jaundice, Chronic Familial Icterus, Chronic Familiar Jaundice, Congenital Hemolytic Anemia, Congenital Hemolytic Icterus, Congenital Hemolytic Jaundice, Congenital Spherocytosis, Globe Cell Anemia, Icterohemolytic Anemia, Minkowski-Chauffard Syndrome, Spherocytic Anemia

282.0

Definition

Hereditary spherocytosis is a type of hemolytic anemia. As in all hemolytic anemias, red blood cells in the peripheral blood are prematurely broken down (hemolyzed) and removed from circulation. When this happens faster than the bone marrow can replace these cells with new ones, the number of red blood cells in the peripheral blood decreases and results in anemia. In hereditary spherocytosis, a defect in the red blood cell membrane gives them a spherical shape making them particularly fragile. The misshapen blood cells cannot pass through the spleen without becoming trapped and broken down.

In spite of the continual hemolytic process, half or more of individuals with hereditary spherocytosis do not show evidence of anemia. Their bone marrow can overproduce red blood cells in order to compensate for the hemolyzed, removed cells. Individuals unable to compensate, however, develop mild to moderate anemia but can be severe in some individuals.

Hereditary spherocytosis periodically develops into an aplastic or hemolytic crisis. An aplastic crisis occurs when the bone marrow stops producing all types of blood cells (i.e., red and white blood cells and platelets) and results in severe anemia. Aplastic crisis is primarily associated with parvovirus B_{19} infection. A hemolytic crisis occurs when many more red blood cells are hemolyzed than can be replaced. A moderate, self-limiting anemia develops. Hemolytic crisis often follows a viral infection.

Approximately 75% of spherocytosis cases are inherited in the form of an autosomal dominant pattern. This means that an individual must inherit only one gene for the disease from either parent. In the remaining 25% of cases, individuals either inherit two genes for the disease, one from each parent (autosomal recessive pattern), or a normal gene has undergone changes (mutation) into a disease gene when passed on to a child (acquired sporadically). Since the hereditary spherocytosis gene has many variations, manifestation also varies considerably.

Hereditary spherocytosis is usually diagnosed in childhood, but sometimes is not diagnosed until adulthood. Adults with this diagnosis usually have a milder form of the disease.

Hereditary spherocytosis is the most common disorder of the red cell membrane. It is most often found in individuals of English or Northern European descent, and affects 1 in 5,000 of this group. It is estimated that 1.4% of this population are silent carriers of the autosomal recessive form. This means they are not affected but may pass the gene to their children.

Diagnosis

History: Severity of symptoms varies considerably. Some individuals may exhibit no symptoms until a significant anemia is precipitated by a viral infection. Other individuals may have yellowing of the skin (jaundice) or symptoms of anemia. Individuals with general symptoms of anemia report fatigue, weight loss, headache, ringing in the ears (tinnitus), heart palpitations, light-headedness when standing up, and the inability to concentrate. There may be a family history of anemia. Because of the increased bile pigment production, gallstones of pigment type are common even in childhood.

Physical exam: The classic physical findings include jaundice and an enlarged spleen (splenomegaly). Other physical findings typically associated with anemia include paleness (pallor), increased heart rate, low blood pressure when standing, and increased breathing rate.

Tests: A complete blood count reveals a decreased number of red blood cells if the individual has anemia. Microscopic examination of a peripheral blood smear shows the classic spherical shape (spherocytes) of some or many of the red blood cells. The concentration of hemoglobin in the red blood cells (mean corpuscular hemoglobin concentration, or MCHC) is often, but not always, increased. A count of immature red blood cells (reticulocyte count) shows an increased number. The most important test is the osmotic fragility test. This test detects the increased tendency of the red blood cells toward hemolysis. Bone marrow examination is not necessary to make this diagnosis.

Treatment

Treatment may not be necessary for mild anemia when the spleen is not enlarged. Supportive treatment such as a blood transfusion is typically needed only during a crisis.

For more significant anemia with an enlarged spleen, surgical removal of the spleen (splenectomy) is the primary treatment. Blood transfusions may be necessary during an aplastic crisis even after splenectomy. Individuals with severe anemia may continue to have symptoms and may require periodic blood transfusions regardless of the crisis state.

All individuals with hereditary spherocytosis should take daily folate supplements to reduce the risk of exaggerating the anemia due to a folate deficiency.

Prognosis

A splenectomy cures the symptoms in most individuals. Although the red cell membrane disorder remains, the spherocytes can remain in the blood longer because the spleen is no longer there to remove them. Even though these cells have a shorter lifespan than normal red blood cells, the bone marrow can usually make more cells in order to compensate. After splenectomy, jaundice usually disappears within 1 to 2 days, the reticulocyte count is back to normal within several days, and the anemia resolves within 2 to 3 months. Red blood cell survival jumps from approximately 10 to 22 days.

Differential Diagnosis

Spherocytes are not seen exclusively in hereditary spherocytosis. They can also occur in ABO transfusion reactions, G6PD deficiency, some malignancies, severe burns, certain infections, some autoimmune hemolytic anemias, and after a transfusion with stored blood.

Specialists

- Hematologist
- Internist

Work Restrictions / Accommodations

Individuals with mild anemia do not typically require work accommodations or restrictions. Individuals with moderate anemia may experience fatigue, breathlessness, or dizziness with exertion. These individuals require a reduction in the physical requirements of work. This reduction may be temporary or permanent depending on the availability of and response to treatment. Individuals in hemolytic or aplastic crisis or those with consistent severe anemia will likely need time off for blood transfusions or recuperation. Time off is needed if a splenectomy or cholecystectomy is required.

Comorbid Conditions

Comorbid conditions that may impact recovery and lengthen disability include other anemias, pregnancy, and liver disease (primary biliary cirrhosis). Infection can precipitate a crisis.

Complications

Primary complications include increasing severity of anemia during crisis times (hemolytic crisis and aplastic crisis) and gallstones with or without inflammation of the gallbladder (cholecystitis). Gallstones are found in 40-80% of adults with hereditary spherocytosis. Incidence of gallstones increases with age but they can be found even in childhood. Individuals with hereditary spherocytosis often have a folate deficiency and if left untreated can eventually exaggerate the anemia. Less common complications include gout, leg ulcers, cardiomyopathy, displacement of bone marrow tissue outside the bone marrow (extramedullary masses), and spinal cord dysfunction.

Factors Influencing Duration

Factors that may influence length of disability include severity of anemia, age at onset, development of complications, and whether splenectomy was required.

Length of Disability

For medical treatment, duration depends on cause. For splenectomy, duration depends on presence of complications.

Medical treatment.

Duration in Days

Job Classification	Minimum	Optimum	Maximum
Sedentary work	7	14	21
Light work	7	14	21
Medium work	7	14	28
Heavy work	7	14	35
Very Heavy work	7	14	42

Surgical treatment (splenectomy).

Duration in Days

Job Classification	Minimum	Optimum	Maximum
Sedentary work	14	21	28
Light work	14	21	28
Medium work	28	35	42
Heavy work	35	42	56
Very Heavy work	35	42	70

Failure to Recover

If an individual fails to recover within the maximum duration expectancy period, the reader may wish to reference the following questions to assist in better understanding the specifics of an individual's medical case.

Regarding diagnosis:

- What age was individual when the condition was diagnosed?
- Has individual had a recent viral infection?
- Does individual have jaundice?
- Does individual report fatigue, weight loss, headache, or tinnitus?

- Does individual have heart palpitations or orthostatic hypotension?
- Is individual unable to concentrate?
- Is there a family history of anemia?
- On exam, were jaundice and splenomegaly present? Pallor?
- Does individual have increased heart and respiratory rates?
- Has individual had a CBC, MCHC, and reticulocyte count?
- Has individual also had an osmotic fragility test?
- Have conditions with similar symptoms been ruled out?

Regarding treatment:
- What is the severity of individual's anemia?
- Has the individual needed transfusions during an aplastic crisis? Because of severe anemia?
- Was a splenectomy necessary?
- Does individual take daily folate supplements?

Regarding prognosis:
- Is individual's employer able to accommodate any necessary restrictions?
- Does individual have any conditions that may affect their ability to recover?
- Has individual had complications such as hemolytic crisis and aplastic crisis?
- Has the individual had gallstones with or without cholecystitis?
- Has the individual had gout, leg ulcers, cardiomyopathy, extramedullary masses, or spinal cord dysfunction? Were other options investigated?

References

Duru, F., and A. Gurgey. "Effect of Corticosteroids in Hereditary Spherocytosis." Acta Paediatrica Japan 36 6 (1994): 666-668.

Ravel, Richard. Clinical Laboratory Medicine, 6th ed. St. Louis: Mosby, 1995.

Spinal Cord Injury

Other names / synonyms: Vertebral Injury
952, 952.0, 952.1, 952.2, 952.3, 952.8, 952.9

Definition

The spinal cord carries all motor and sensory functions between the brain and the rest of the body and injuries may be either complete or incomplete. In complete spinal cord injuries, permanent interruption of the transmission of motor and sensory impulses occurs causing quadriplegia or paraplegia. This is the most severe form of injury and is associated with severe disabilities. Incomplete injuries damage some parts of the spinal cord; however, the cord still remains, at least partially functional.

Injury to the spine is usually caused by compression, bending or shearing forces that can dislocate or fracture the vertebrae and injure the spinal cord. Accumulation of blood, or a displaced vertebra can press on the spinal cord, impairing function. The cord may even be torn or severed, destroying sensation and/or motor function below the site of the injury.

Approximately, 80% of spinal cord injuries occur in persons younger than 40 years of age. Motor vehicle accidents account for 45% of all spinal cord injuries, followed by falls (21.5%), acts of violence (15.5%), and sports injuries (13%). Spinal cord injury can be fatal.

Diagnosis

History: The individual, family member, or others who witness the accident may report what type of injury occurred (fall, flexion, twisting, penetrating). The individual may report feelings of numbness, pain, tingling, burning, or other neurological symptoms experienced immediately following the injury.

Physical exam: The exam focuses first on vital functions. This includes: adequacy of respirations, blood pressure, pulse, examination of level of consciousness and appropriateness of verbal responses to questions. This is followed by an assessment of motor and sensory function in the arms and legs, and reflexes. Presence of back or neck pain or tenderness is evaluated.

Tests: Laboratory tests would include general baseline tests such as complete blood count, blood glucose (to rule out hypoglycemia or insulin shock), arterial blood gases (to assess adequacy of respiration), electrolytes, and toxicology screen. X-rays of the spine may detect fractures or bony abnormalities that may be responsible for spinal injury.

Treatment

A spinal cord trauma is a medical emergency requiring immediate treatment to reduce the long-term effects. The time between the injury and treatment is a critical factor affecting the outcome.

The basic goals of spinal cord injury management are relief of any spinal cord pressure and realignment and stabilization of any fractures or dislocations. This may be accomplished by using traction and/or surgical intervention. The individual must be stabilized before any surgical intervention is done.

Fractures or dislocations to the neck (cervical) vertebrae may be treated initially with skeletal traction. A tight fitting tong (Crutchfield tong) may be placed on the head as a means to apply weighted traction to realign the neck vertebrae. Special beds (Stryker frame, Kinetic therapy bed), which help to maintain spinal alignment, are used until the vertebrae are stabilized. These beds permit safe turning from side to side without disrupting proper alignment of the injured spine. Corticosteroid medications may be administered to reduce swelling in the spinal cord.

Injuries to the spine are either stable or unstable. An unstable injury is one in which it is possible that the vertebrae will shift and cause further damage to the cord, possibly even severing it. Once the individual is physically stable, surgical stabilization, which fastens bones using metal plates, wires, or bone pieces, is often a priority. This may be done by fusing the unstable vertebrae (spinal fusion) or by placing wire or metal stabilizing rods (placement of Harrington or Luque rods). Blood clots or bone fragments may be removed (evacuation of hematoma and/or bone fragments) if they are creating excess pressure on the spinal cord. If the bones are dislocated, the surgeon will attempt reduction putting them back into position under general anesthesia.

Initially, the individual will usually require close monitoring and intervention for life-threatening complications associated with spinal cord injuries. The individual may need respiratory support, blood pressure support, and careful management of fluids and nutrition. Once stable, the individual will receive continued care in a medical or neurological unit. In most instances, the individual will need some form of spinal cord rehabilitation.

Treatment is focused on preventing complications that can be caused by loss of sensation and mobility. Physical therapy can help prevent joints from locking and muscles from becoming permanently contracted. Urinary catheterization and enemas relieve urinary retention and constipation. Diligent skin care and frequent position changes prevent skin breakdown and bedsores.

Prognosis

The outcome depends on the location and the extent of the injury to the spinal cord. Actual damage to the spinal cord can result in loss of sensation and/or mobility below the site of the injury. Paralysis and loss of sensation of part of the body are common outcomes. This may include total paralysis and/or numbness and varying degrees of movement or sensation loss. Death is possible, particularly if there is paralysis of the breathing muscles.

Surgical stabilization is aimed at preventing any additional injury to the spinal cord. In some cases, surgical intervention relieves excess pressure on the spinal cord, and may result in some improvement of neurological function. Surgical intervention to the spine carries a small additional risk (1-4%) of further cord injury.

Recovery of movement or sensation within 1 week usually indicates eventual recovery of most function, although this may take 6 months or more. Losses that remain after 6 months are likely to be permanent.

Differential Diagnosis

Pressure on spinal cord caused by abscess or tumor can present similarly.

Specialists

- Emergency Medicine
- Neurologist
- Neurosurgeon
- Physiatrist

Rehabilitation

Some form of spinal cord rehabilitation is needed for nearly all spinal cord injuries. This may include physical therapy, occupational therapy, respiratory therapy, and psychological therapy. The overall goal of rehabilitation is independent mobility and self-care, successful living at home, and return to gainful employment. The duration and frequency of the rehabilitative process is dictated by degree of injury and disability. Often psychological rehabilitation takes longer than the physical rehabilitation from spinal cord injury.

Some individuals with partial spinal cord injury may only suffer from weakness or paralysis on one side of the body and altered sensation (paresthesia) on the other side. In this case, individuals undergo physical and occupational therapy to strengthen the arms and legs, to learn functional mobility such as walking and transfers, and to learn self-care. Individuals may be ambulatory, however; balance retraining is almost always necessary.

Individuals with spinal cord injury that does not result in quadriplegia or paraplegia may suffer instead from weakness in the arms and legs (quadriparesis) or weakness in the legs and possibly the torso (paraparesis). The rehabilitation of individuals with paresis is contingent upon the severity of the weakness in the arms and legs.

Those with quadriplegia or paraplegia require intensive rehabilitation. If an individual becomes a quadriplegic, there is a lengthy rehabilitation process involved. Therapy goals in the hospital focus on prevention of further illness. Respiratory therapists teach deep breathing exercises and perform chest percussions to keep the lungs clear of mucus. Respiratory therapists routinely assess individuals on ventilators to determine continued need for assisted breathing. Physical therapists establish a routine for changing an individual's position in bed to prevent skin breakdown. Physical therapists teach an individual's family members to be consistent with this routine. Physical therapists stretch all of an individual's joints to maintain flexibility. Occupational therapists assess an individual's potential for self-care. Both occupational and physical therapists focus on increasing sitting tolerance and sitting balance. Psychologists and psychiatrists are a crucial link in the rehabilitation process, helping to focus individuals on attainable goals and treating the depression that occurs after spinal cord injury.

Once individuals are medically stable, individuals are transferred to a rehabilitation hospital for several months. Therapy lasts for several hours each day. Special equipment can increase the independence of individuals with spinal cord injuries. Physical and occupational therapists order wheelchairs with a seat cushion system that maintains correct posture and sitting balance. Adaptive equipment to allow for better grasp is provided to quadriparetics.

Mobility is the goal of physical therapy. Physical therapists teach individuals and their families strategies for rolling, transferring to and from the bed, the wheelchair, the shower, and the car. Wheelchair mobility is a key component to regaining independence. Individuals who have high cord injuries learn to utilize a mouth control system to propel the wheelchair. Other individuals learn to use a joystick control. As wheelchair skills progress, individuals learn to maneuver their wheelchairs outside and to perform activities such as shopping. Slight changes in position, made while sitting in a wheelchair, are taught to prevent skin breakdown.

Achieving independence in self-care is the primary goal of occupational therapists. Occupational therapists teach dressing, grooming, and feeding techniques to individuals with mid-level cervical cord injuries. Individuals with quadriplegia cannot perform self-care.

Both disciplines develop a flexibility program for all joints and teach it to family members. Individuals perform strengthening exercises for arm muscles.

Speech therapists work on communicating strategies for those who are ventilator-dependent, and increasing the volume of speech for all individuals.

Individuals with cord injuries of C5 and below are discharged to outpatient occupational and physical therapy to further address functional gains. This may take place 3 times a week for 4-8 weeks. Individuals with cord injuries of C4 and higher may be eligible for in-home physical and occupational therapy for 3 times a week for 4-8 weeks; these individuals will not be independent in transferring or self-care. In-home therapy should focus on reinforcing family care of the individual.

If an individual becomes a paraplegic, either through illness or injury, a lengthy rehabilitation is involved. While in the hospital, physical therapy focuses on frequently changing an individual's position in bed to prevent skin breakdown, and teaching an individual's family members to comply with the turning schedule. Physical therapists also begin stretching all of an individual's joints to maintain flexibility. Occupational therapists teach self-care strategies at this time. Both occupational and physical therapists will attempt to increase sitting tolerance and sitting balance at this time. Respiratory therapists teach deep breathing exercises and perform chest percussions to keep the lungs clear of mucus. Psychologists and psychiatrists are a crucial link in the rehabilitation process, helping individuals to set attainable goals and treating the depression that occurs after spinal cord injury.

Once individuals are medically stable, they are transferred to a rehabilitation hospital for several months. Therapy lasts for several hours each day. Physical and occupational therapists order equipment that allows individuals their independence. A wheelchair with a seat cushion system that supports correct posture is the most important piece of equipment. Additional equipment such as a sliding board is also ordered. This board allows for safer transfer from the wheelchair to other seating surfaces.

Mobility is the main focus of physical therapy. Crucial to this is wheelchair mobility. Individuals learn to propel a wheelchair on flat surfaces, over curbs, and up and down ramps. Individuals learn to maneuver their wheelchairs outside and to perform activities such as shopping. Physical therapists also teach strategies for rolling, transferring to and from the bed, the wheelchair, the shower, and the car. Individuals also stand in the parallel bars for improved strength and posture. Some of these individuals may learn to walk with forearm crutches; this is done with a combination of weight shifting and upper body momentum. For these individuals, therapists work on safe ambulation in the community.

Occupational therapists teach dressing, grooming, and food preparation techniques to individuals. They make suggestions for changing the home environment to allow for independent self-care.

Both disciplines stretch all joints to maintain flexibility and provide strengthening exercises for any muscles that have movement. Therapists provide a home exercise program based on these exercises that must be followed to maintain function. Therapists also emphasize pressure reliefs, which are changes in position made while sitting, to prevent skin breakdown.

Outpatient physical therapy may be warranted to maximize functional gains and to reinforce the mobility techniques learned in rehabilitation. Also, individuals cleared by their physicians to drive can be assessed for car adaptations and driving school during outpatient physical therapy.

Work Restrictions / Accommodations

Work requirements may need to be adapted if the individual has motor or sensory deficits, such as paraplegia or quadriplegia. See specific diagnosis.

Comorbid Conditions

Obesity and pre-existing pulmonary or cardiovascular disease may contribute to problems of inadequate respiration or instability of blood pressure and pulse, which may slow recovery and lengthen disability.

Complications

Complications of spinal cord injury include: paralysis below the level of injury, loss of sensation, infections, loss of sexual function, deep vein thrombosis, shock, paralysis of breathing muscles, and death.

Factors Influencing Duration

Disability is highly variable as each spinal cord injury is unique. Disability will depend on the site and extent of injury, severity of symptoms, and whether the symptoms are temporary or permanent. The degree of dysfunction and disability varies relative to the level of injury and how much of the cord is spared from trauma. Psychological adjustment to the injury and disability often contributes to the length of disability. Contact physician for additional information to determine disability duration.

Length of Disability

This is a vague diagnosis. Duration depends on location and severity of injury. Contact physician for additional information.

Failure to Recover

If an individual fails to recover within the maximum duration expectancy period, the reader may wish to reference the following questions to assist in better understanding the specifics of an individual's medical case.

Regarding diagnosis:

- Has diagnosis been confirmed?
- Have presence of abscess or tumor been ruled out?
- Has individual experienced any complications from the spinal cord injury such as paralysis below the level of injury, loss of sensation, infections, loss of sexual function, deep vein thrombosis, shock, or paralysis of breathing muscles?
- Does individual have an underlying condition, such as obesity and pre-existing pulmonary or cardiovascular disease that may impact recovery?

Regarding treatment:

- Did individual receive prompt, appropriate treatment immediately following injury?
- Has injury responded appropriately to realignment and stabilization?
- Have corticosteroid medications been administered to reduce swelling and was swelling effectively relieved?
- If originally unstable, has individual's spinal injury now been surgically stabilized?

- If stabilization has been postponed due to individual's health, what is the estimated timeframe before stabilization? Based on what criteria?
- Has the individual been provided respiratory support, blood pressure support, and careful management of fluids and nutrition?
- Has individual received spinal cord rehabilitation?
- Does the individual have the necessary physical assistive devices (i.e., wheelchair, walker, eating utensils) to maximize independence?
- Is the individual receiving physical therapy?
- Does the individual have symptoms of bowel or bladder dysfunction, such as abdominal distention or urinary or fecal incontinence?
- Is family or hired caregiver meticulous in skin care? In position changes?
- Has skin broken down despite prevention?
- What other treatment options or prevention products might be tried?

Regarding prognosis:

- Does the individual have evidence of muscle spasticity or muscle contractures that can interfere with mobility and coordination?
- Did individual experience any improvement of neurological function following surgery?
- Did individual recover movement or sensation within the first week after injury?
- Has it been over 6 months since injury?
- How much dysfunction remains?
- Is individual realistic about prognosis?
- Does the individual demonstrate signs of depression, such as powerlessness, hopelessness, or poor self-image?
- Would individual benefit from psychological counseling?

References

"What Are Spinal Cord Injuries?" Harris, Rob MD, drkoop.com Medical Director. Meeting of the Minds 10 Apr 2000 18July2000 <http://www.drkoop.com/news/special-reports/aans/background.html>.

Hickey, Joanne V. The Clinical Practice of Neurological and Neurosurgical Nursing, 2nd ed. Philadelphia: J.B. Lippincott Company, 1986.

Spinal Cord Stimulation

Other names / synonyms: Dorsal Column Stimulation
03.39

Definition

Spinal cord stimulation (SCS), also known as dorsal column stimulation, is a procedure for relieving chronic, severe pain through electrical stimulation of the spinal cord. This is accomplished by the implantation of an electronic stimulator near the spine to interrupt pain signals to the brain.

The basic SCS unit consists of one or more electrodes implanted in the space just outside of the spinal cord (epidural) and a pulse generator implanted in a pocket underneath the skin (subcutaneous). There are two types of electrodes: percutaneous and plate-type. Percutaneous electrodes are inserted through a needle as an outpatient procedure. Plate electrodes require open surgery for placement, but have a greater inherent stability and, once implanted, are less likely to dislodge.

There are also two types of pulse generator/receiver systems: a totally implantable or a radio frequency system. The totally implantable pulse generator contains a lithium battery as the power source. It can be turned on and off by the individual with a small magnet, however some of the regulation requires outside telemetry. Lithium batteries last between 3 to 4.5 years. The radio frequency system consists of a passive receiver implanted under the skin and a transmitter, which is worn outside of the body, powered by alkaline batteries. The individual has full access to all the features available, including changing the electrode combinations. Both systems present advantages and disadvantages. The decision as to which system is more appropriate is made on an individual basis.

The most common conditions treated with SCS are reflex sympathetic dystrophy (experimental), failed back surgery syndrome (a controversial term), persistent pain of radicular origin (unsuccessfully relieved by surgical intervention and diagnostic studies fail to reveal a specific organic cause outside of nerve damage), phantom limb pain (in which the individual has the sensation of pain in a limb that has been removed by amputation); ischemic pain of vascular origin (in which blood supply to the tissues is decreased) adhesive arachnoiditis (when associated with nervous system), and peripheral neuropathy.

Reason for Procedure

SCS is used to treat individuals with chronic pain whose conditions have failed to respond to other less invasive treatments. More recent uses include treatment of pain caused by angina pectoris, cancer, multiple sclerosis, herpes zoster (shingles), and various types of chronic pain caused by nerve (or spinal cord) damage as a result of trauma.

Description

The individual must first undergo a selection process, in which the doctor ascertains that conservative therapies, such as medication or epidural blocks, have been unsuccessful; determines the underlying reason for the pain; determines that further surgery would not be beneficial; and ensures that the individual has no untreated drug addictions and that the individual is not suffering from any psychological disorders (such as depression or personality disorders) that may interfere with pain management.

The next step is a trial screening, in which the effectiveness of SCS is tested in a reversible process that uses a temporary power source. This device mimics the permanently implanted device. Under local anesthesia, a lead containing 2 to 8 electrodes is placed in the epidural space, near the spinal cord, through an incision or hollow needle placed in the skin. When the electrodes are in place, they are attached to the rest of the components in the system, and a small electric current is conducted through the electrode. The exact placement depends on where the individual experiences pain. The physician determines the exact patterns of stimulation by talking with the individual during implantation about the effects on the individual's pain. The electrode is taped in place to the skin of the back. Following the trial procedure, the individual is instructed on the use of the stimulator system and on how to care for the incision. The individual is instructed to keep a "diary" of pain and daily activities. The trial period may last anywhere from 1 day to several weeks, and is used to determine whether SCS will control the individual's pain and whether the individual is comfortable with the sensation. If the trial period is successful (the individual experiences at least a 50% decrease in pain with no major complications), the temporary stimulator is removed, and a permanent implantation is indicated.

The implantation of the permanent SCS system is similar to the trial procedure. The only differences are that, in order to make the implant permanent, a small incision is made in the back, and the electrode is attached to the covering of the deep muscles in the back (fascia). Because percutaneously inserted electrodes can be dislodged by routine daily activities, better anchoring of the electrodes is often recommended and accomplished through a small laminectomy and suturing of the electrode plate to the dura. This procedure is performed under local anesthesia. A battery pack (generator) or receiver is also implanted through an incision into the fatty layer of either the lower abdomen or the buttocks. The individual usually remains in the hospital for 1 day for observation.

Prognosis

Generally, in properly selected individuals, SCS will produce a 50-70% decrease in pain. Some individuals continue to be relieved of pain up to 20 years after implantation. However, in many, the procedure loses effectiveness over time.

Specialists

- Anesthesiologist
- Neurosurgeon
- Orthopedic Surgeon

Work Restrictions / Accommodations

Immediately after surgery, the individual must avoid lifting, stretching, bending, and twisting movements. The individual must permanently avoid any activities that may cause movements in the leads. The SCS device may not be used while operating a motor vehicle or other heavy equipment; therefore, the individual's need for pain relief must be balanced against such work requirements.

Comorbid Conditions

Existing conditions that may impact ability to recover and may further lengthen disability include chronic infections of the nervous system (e.g., syphilis, herpes simplex, HTLV-I) and chronic fibrotic diseases of the nervous system (e.g., tuberculosis).

Procedure Complications

The individual may experience some discomfort or swelling at the incision sites, which may last for several days. Some individuals also experience pain over the area where the receiver is implanted for several weeks. Risks from the surgery are uncommon, but include infection, bleeding, headaches, and spinal cord injury.

Factors Influencing Duration

Length of disability may be influenced by the underlying condition for which the procedure was done, the effectiveness of the pain relief provided by the procedure, or the presence of complications. Percutaneous electrodes have a shorter disability duration than plate-type electrodes, which require open surgery.

Length of Disability

Duration depends on underlying cause of pain. Heavy and very heavy work is rarely appropriate based on underlying condition for which stimulation is used. In fact, since intractable pain is present, these individuals rarely return to any work. Disability may be permanent.

Duration in Days

Job Classification	Minimum	Optimum	Maximum
Sedentary work	7	14	28
Light work	7	14	28
Medium work	14	28	42
Heavy work	Indefinite	Indefinite	Indefinite
Very Heavy work	Indefinite	Indefinite	Indefinite

References

Patient Guide to Spinal Cord Stimulation. Wake Forest University Baptist Medical Center. 2000. 09 Nov 2000 <http://www.wfubmc.edu/pcc/pain1.htm>.

Spinal Cord Stimulation for the Treatment of Chronic Pain. York Neurosurgical Associates. 2000. 9 Nov 2000 <http://yna.org/New%20Pages/SpinalCordStim.html>.

Spinal Cord Stimulation. Pain Intervention Consultants. 2000. 8 Nov 2000 <http://www.painintervention.com/spinal_cord_stimulation.htm>.

Spinal Cord Stimulation. The American Association of Neurological Surgeons. 1998. 08 Nov 2000 <http://www.neurosurgery.org/pubpages/news/aans98/facts/scs.html>.

Spinal Fusion

Other names / synonyms: Spinal Arthrodesis, Spine Arthrodesis, Spondylosyndesis, Vertebral Fusion
03.09, 80.51, 81.0, 81.00

Definition

Spinal fusion is the surgical immobilization of two or more adjacent bones of the back (vertebra). Multiple bones are made to fuse or grow together to become one solid bone. It is often associated with removal of the intervertebral discs (discectomy) and removal of the lamina (laminectomy).

Approximately 200,000 spinal fusions are performed each year in the US. Forty-eight percent of spinal fusions are in the neck region (cervical spine), 13% are in the midback region (thoracic spine), and 33% are in the lower back region (lumbar spine). Repeat fusions account for 6% of all spinal fusion procedures.

Reason for Procedure

When excess or abnormal motion of the vertebrae causes neurological findings (e.g., numbness, paralysis), or the individual is experiencing pain or other symptoms from spinal disorders, fusion of the vertebrae may be indicated. The purpose is to increase stability, reduce irritation on the affected nerve roots, or reduce compression on the spinal cord. It is also used to correct deformity.

Spinal fusion is an option in the treatment of vertebral inflammation (spondylitis), vertebral dissolution (spondylolysis), vertebral displacement (spondylolisthesis), spinal fractures, scoliosis, or dislocations. Pain attributed to degenerative disease accounts for 97% of cervical spine fusions, 95% of lumbar spine fusions, and 2% of thoracic spine fusions. Scoliosis accounts for 59% of thoracic spine fusions.

Whether or not spine fusion is indicated for "discogenic pain without proven radiculopathy" is controversial (unproven).

Description

Spinal fusions can be either anterior or posterior, depending on the surgical approach and whether the graft and/or instrumentation is affixed to the front (anterior) or back (posterior) side of the spine.

The anterior approach involves cutting into the front side to gain access to the spine. The anterior approach is the most common approach for cervical spine fusions to treat conditions including injury, vertebral degeneration, cancer, infections, and deformities.

The posterior approach gains access to the spine by cutting into the back. Posterior cervical fusions, which are used less frequently than anterior fusions, are used for anterior fusion failure (nonunion, pseudarthrosis), degenerative vertebral instability without compression of the anterior portion, and in some cases of multi-level fusion. Anterior and posterior fusions may be used in combination. This is used most often for degenerative disease, especially when three or more vertebrae will be fused.

For all types of spinal fusion, the segment of the spine is immobilized by using a bone graft to create a bony union (ankylosis) between two or more adjacent vertebrae. The bone grafts are usually obtained from the pelvis or leg at the time of the operation (autograft) but may be obtained from a donor or bone bank (allograft). Screws, wires, rods, hooks, cages, and/or plates are also used. The internal fixation (hardware) is used to hold the segments temporarily rigid while the bone graft establishes a solid union to the vertebrae. In some cervical spine fusions, temporary stability or immobilization is achieved by using a metal halo, which is affixed to the skull by metal pins. This halo is then attached by rods to a well fitting plaster or plastic body jacket. If metal implants are used, external support is not always needed with fusion of the thoracolumbar spine.

Prognosis

Spinal fusion has variable outcome with some individuals experiencing a good to excellent outcome while others experience a poor outcome. Even with successful fusion, back symptoms are not relieved (clinical failure) in 20-60% of the cases. Nonunion occurs in up 20% of all spinal fusions. Surprisingly, in the lumbar spine, clinical results are the same whether or not non-union occurs. Serious complications can have lifelong debilitating effects.

Specialists

- Neurosurgeon
- Occupational Therapist
- Orthopedic Surgeon
- Physical Therapist

Rehabilitation

Modifications may need to be made by the physical therapist for those who have arthritis or other spine conditions. This will vary depending on the level of the spine the spinal fusion was performed.

Work Restrictions / Accommodations

To reduce the risk of complications, the individual may not be allowed to work during the early recovery period. Prolonged sitting, standing, heavy lifting, bending, overhead (spine extension) work, and climbing long flights of stairs may be temporarily restricted. Use of a soft or rigid cervical collar, upper body traction, or halo traction devices may be required for several weeks. These traction devices may severely limit dexterity and mobility. Adjusting worktable height, chair height, and use of foot rests are all beneficial for individuals with back problems. The individual may require frequent breaks. Temporarily working reduced hours may be necessary. Permanent restrictions may include heavy lifting, carrying moderate to heavy loads, and overhead work.

Comorbid Conditions

Arthritis, obesity, diabetes, cancer, and injuries (e.g., vertebral fractures, spinal cord injury, whiplash) sustained during the traumatic event may influence the length of disability. Cigarette smoking decreases the changes of successful spinal fusion. Use of nonsteroidal anti-inflammatory drugs in the early postoperative period decreases the changes of successful spinal fusion.

Procedure Complications

Complications of spinal fusion vary with the surgical approach and the region of the spine. Complications associated with the anterior approach include post thoracotomy pain syndrome, swallowing difficulties, cut (lacerated) aorta, laceration of the tube that conveys urine from the kidney to the bladder (ureter), backwards (retrograde) ejaculation, and abdominal hernias. Those associated with a posterior approach include severe spinal muscle pain, high blood loss, and injury to the vertebral artery and nerves. Complications associated with retrieval of the bone autograft include deep or superficial infection, pelvis fracture (when the bone graft is obtained from the pelvis), vascular injury, collection of blood (hematoma) within tissues, nerve damage, chronic pain at the donor site, and increased blood loss. All spinal fusion procedures carry the additional complications of laceration of the outermost membrane of the spinal cord (dura mater), spinal cord injury, injuries caused by the hardware, hardware loosening and failure, infection, neurologic injury (including paraplegia and quadriplegia), extrusion of the bone graft, fusion failure (pseudarthrosis), vertebral dissolution (spondylolysis), and vertebral displacement (spondylolisthesis).

Factors Influencing Duration

The region of the spine involved, the surgical technique used, the underlying condition for which the fusion was performed, the presence of complications, and an individual's job requirements may influence the length of disability. The individual's preoperative level of physical fitness would also influence the length of disability.

Length of Disability

Duration depends on job requirements. Duration depends on region of spine and approach.

Cervical region of spine. One level fusion.

Job Classification	Minimum	Optimum	Maximum
Sedentary work	42	49	84
Light work	56	63	84
Medium work	70	120	180
Heavy work	84	168	Indefinite
Very Heavy work	84	168	Indefinite

Duration in Days

References

Boden, Scott. The Orthopedic Clinics of North America. Philadelphia: W.B. Saunders Company, 1998.

Kisner, C., and L. Colby. Therapeutic Exercise Foundations and Techniques. Philadelphia: F.A. Davis, 1990.

Spinal Stenosis
724.0, 724.02

Definition

Spinal stenosis is a narrowing of the spinal canal, which refers to the passageways in the middle of the vertebrae and intervertebral discs through which the spinal cord passes. Narrowing of the spinal canal reduces the blood supply to the nerves that supply sensation and motor control to the legs.

Spinal stenosis primarily occurs in the low back (lumbar spine) but may also occur in middle back (thoracic spine) and the neck (cervical spine). It is classified as primary or secondary stenosis. The stenosis may be further classified as central, lateral recess, and/or foraminal, depending on which region(s) of the spinal canal is involved.

Primary stenosis, which is also called constitutional or congenital stenosis, is an inborn (congenital) or developmental abnormality that causes the narrowing.

Secondary or degenerative stenosis is caused by degenerative changes in the spine that occur as part of the natural aging process. Secondary stenosis can also occur as a result of back surgery or trauma. Secondary stenosis is the most common type of spinal stenosis.

Individuals may also have a combined form in which primary stenosis is worsened by the development of secondary stenosis. The combined form occurs in individuals who are born with narrow spinal canals, which undergo further narrowing by acquired degenerative changes.

In the US, 5 out of every 10,000 individuals develop spinal stenosis. The average age of onset of symptoms of degenerative stenosis is 60 years, with men being afflicted twice as often as women. Primary stenosis usually presents at around 30 years of age. Individuals with osteoarthritis, rheumatoid arthritis, scoliosis, spondylolisthesis, achondroplastic dwarfism, Paget's disease, or hunchback (kyphosis) are at an increased risk of developing spinal stenosis.

Diagnosis

History: The chief complaint is pain that is usually located in the calf, buttocks, or back of the thigh and is brought on by walking (neurogenic claudication) or standing. Pain, which frequently affects both legs (bilateral) is most commonly described as aching, but may also present as numbness or weakness. The pain is often sufficiently intense to force individuals to stop walking and to sit in order to seek relief. Others may report that they are more comfortable walking uphill than downhill, or that they can walk farther if they bend forward while they walk. Individuals with severe spinal stenosis may report dysfunction of the bladder or bowel.

Physical exam: With exam, having the individual arch their back to extend the spine may reproduce or worsen the symptoms. Flexing the spine (e.g., sitting, bending over) reduces the symptoms. Straight leg raising may cause pain. Leg deep tendon reflexes may be depressed.

Tests: Either MRI or a myelogram and CT in combination can accurately show the degree and extent of stenosis. A plain x-ray will not show spinal stenosis though it may be suggestive.

Treatment

Analgesics, spinal (epidural) or oral steroids, physical therapy (aerobic conditioning, muscle strengthening, flexibility enhancement, and optimization of body mechanics), and bracing are conservative treatments that may provide symptom relief. However, only surgery can actually enlarge the spinal canal. Surgery is indicated for individuals with moderate to severe symptoms that are not relieved by conservative measures and time. The "decompression" surgery, which may consist of one or more procedures, is performed through an incision in the back. Most frequently, laminectomy is performed in which the lamina of a vertebra are removed. Other surgical options include removal of bone from around a nerve root (foraminotomy) removal of an intervertebral disc (discectomy), and/or fusion of two or more vertebra (arthrodesis). The method of surgical decompression utilized depends on the cause, type, and severity of spinal stenosis; age and overall condition of the individual; and the preference of the surgeon. If a sufficient portion of the joints is removed or the individual has advanced degenerative disease, then it may also become necessary to perform arthrodesis (with or without stabilizing hardware) to stabilize the spine.

Prognosis

Spinal stenosis often runs a gradual course or may be stable for several years. Conservative treatment is effective in reducing pain for half of the individuals, provided their symptoms are mild to moderate. Surgical decompression is successful in eliminating leg pain and allowing individuals to walk in about 80-85% of cases. Since spinal degeneration is a progressive, age-related process, the symptoms of stenosis may recur years later.

Differential Diagnosis

Vascular insufficiency (atherosclerosis of the aorta and/or leg arteries), vertebral disc disease, spinal cord tumor, Paget's disease, diabetes, peripheral neuropathy, and inflammatory spondyloarthropathy (e.g., ankylosing spondylitis) may produce similar signs and symptoms.

Specialists

- Neurologist
- Neurosurgeon
- Orthopedic Surgeon
- Physiatrist
- Physical Therapist

Rehabilitation

The nonoperative treatment of spinal stenosis may involve physical therapy to increase aerobic conditioning, and strength and to teach body mechanics. Flexibility exercises may be tried but may worsen the symptoms.

Depending on the level of the spine, the individual may be instructed in flexion exercises. Exercises to strengthen the spine may be introduced such as sit-ups, which help strengthen the abdominal muscles. Pelvic tilts may be effective in helping strengthen the lumbar spine. Weight resistance exercises may be initiated by the physical therapist to regain strength. For example, leg curls, leg presses, and half knee squats may be introduced. Stationary biking may also be used. Aerobic exercise is a popular form of treatment for spine rehabilitation with the basis for these exercise programs to release the body's own pain relievers (endorphins) as well as increasing strength and endurance of the affected weak muscles. The late phase of the rehabilitation program may include instruction in body mechanics and proper lifting to prevent further injury.

Following surgery for spinal stenosis, therapy may be prescribed by the spine surgeon, with the specific type of therapy determined by the nature of the surgery (decompression alone, or with fusion, one level or multi-level), and by the problems that persist after the surgery. Most of these individuals are older, and thus frequently cardiopulmonary comorbidity is frequent, and must be considered in planning rehabilitation.

Work Restrictions / Accommodations

Work restrictions and special accommodations need to be established on an individual basis. Activities involving standing or walking may need to be limited. Work station modification to permit good posture or seated work may be helpful. Overhead work (spine extension) should be avoided. To reduce the risk of complications, the individual who was treated surgically may not be allowed to work during the early recovery period. Use of analgesics and other medications can affect dexterity and alertness. Drug testing policies will need to be evaluated.

> **Complementary and Alternative Therapies**
>
> Content is intended for awareness only. Treatments may or may not be effective. Scientific evidence may be lacking and some substances have potentially toxic effects. Dr. Presley Reed and the editors do not endorse the use of these therapies in the absence of consultation with a licensed medical professional.
>
> Martial art therapy - Believed to cause an adaptation of the spinal cord to spinal compression rather than a structural change.

Comorbid Conditions

Diabetes, obesity, general debility, cardiopulmonary disorders (common in older individuals) and depression can influence the length of disability. In addition, the underlying cause of stenosis can significantly affect disability.

Complications

Because secondary spinal stenosis is a result of degeneration of the spine, other degenerative changes of the spine may cause complications. Advanced stenosis can cause bowel and bladder dysfunction.

Factors Influencing Duration

The individual's age and overall health and the type of treatment utilized will influence the length of disability.

Length of Disability

Duration depends on severity of pain, and type and success of treatment. Once spinal stenosis becomes evident, the individual is rarely capable of heavy or very heavy work.

Medical treatment.

Job Classification	Duration in Days		
	Minimum	Optimum	Maximum
Sedentary work	1	7	14
Light work	1	14	21
Medium work	1	21	42
Heavy work	1	56	Indefinite
Very Heavy work	1	91	Indefinite

Surgical treatment by laminectomy.

Job Classification	Duration in Days		
	Minimum	Optimum	Maximum
Sedentary work	21	35	91
Light work	28	42	119
Medium work	28	84	182
Heavy work	42	98	Indefinite
Very Heavy work	56	112	Indefinite

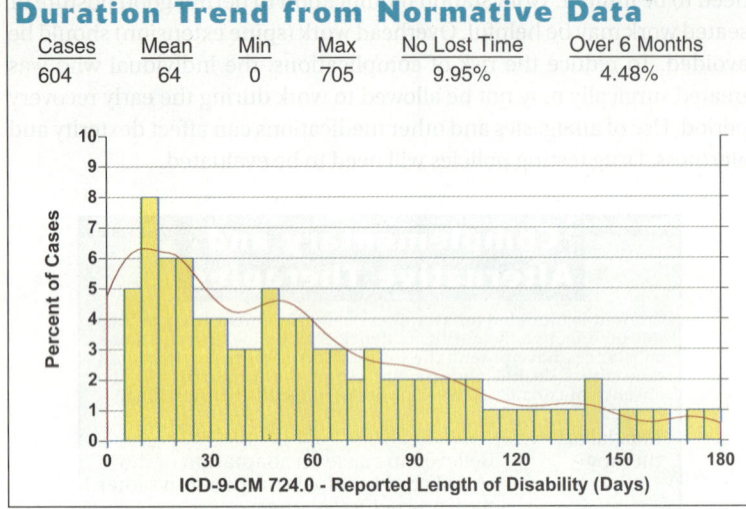

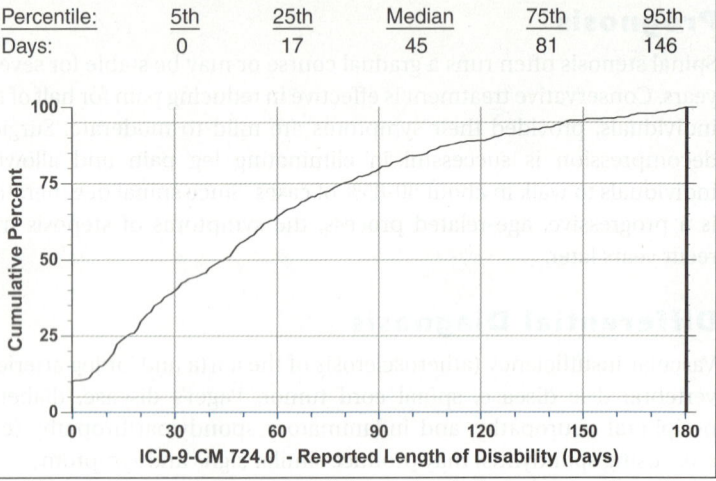

* Differences may exist between the expected duration tables and the normative graphs. Duration tables provide expected recovery periods based on the type of work performed by the individual. The normative graphs reflect the actual observed experience of many individuals across the spectrum of physical conditions, in a variety of industries, and with varying levels of case management.

Failure to Recover

If an individual fails to recover within the maximum duration expectancy period, the reader may wish to reference the following questions to assist in better understanding the specifics of an individual's medical case.

Regarding diagnosis:

- Has diagnosis of spinal stenosis been confirmed?
- Has individual experienced any complications from the spinal stenosis such as sciatica, claudication, or intractable buttock and leg pain?
- Does individual have an underlying condition that may impact recovery?

Regarding treatment:

- Have conservative measures been effective? If not, is surgery indicated?
- Was spinal fusion performed?
- Does a postoperative MRI document persisting nerve compression?
- Do postoperative flexion extension x-rays document spinal instability?

Regarding prognosis:

- Are symptoms severe enough to impair function?
- If surgery was not successful in restoring function, what other treatment options are available to individual?

References

An, Howard, and Thomas Andreshak. "Spinal Stenosis." Principles and Techniques for Spine Surgery. An, Howard, ed. Baltimore: Williams & Wilkins, 1997. 443-460.

Kisner, C., and L. Colby. Therapeutic Exercise Foundations and Techniques. Philadelphia: F.A. Davis, 1990.

Splenectomy

Other names / synonyms: Removal of the Spleen

41.5

Definition

A splenectomy is a procedure that removes the spleen, a large organ in the left upper abdomen. This procedure may be done using a standard open surgery approach through a large incision in the abdomen, or it may be done using a flexible, lighted scope (laparoscope).

Several conditions adversely affect the spleen and may be the underlying reason for a splenectomy. These conditions include cancers of the lymphatic system (lymphoma), cysts on the spleen, enlargement of the spleen, leukemia, traumatic injury to the spleen, a bleeding disorder called idiopathic thrombocytopenia, a hereditary disorder affecting the red blood cells that results in anemia (hereditary spherocytosis), a white blood cell disorder called Felty's syndrome, and a condition in which the body's immune system attacks the red blood cells (autoimmune hemolytic anemia).

Hereditary spherocytosis is a genetically acquired (from family members) disorder. Autoimmune hemolytic anemia has been seen in association with systemic lupus erythematosus, chronic lymphocyte leukemia, or lymphoma. Idiopathic thrombocytopenia purpura (ITP) is an autoimmune disorder in which an antibody binds with platelets, causing them to appear as foreign bodies that are later destroyed by the spleen. Felty's syndrome is often seen in individuals with long-standing, severely deforming rheumatoid arthritis.

Traumatic injuries to the spleen occur following blunt or penetrating trauma to the abdomen. Spontaneous rupture of the spleen can occur during activity in individuals who have enlarged spleens. Likewise, unintentional injury to the spleen may occur during abdominal surgery in individuals with enlarged, fragile spleens.

It is difficult to ascertain the exact incidence and prevalence of the procedure, as there are many different conditions that may warrant a splenectomy.

Reason for Procedure

A splenectomy is usually done on an individual with a diseased, damaged, or enlarged spleen. Removal of an injured and bleeding spleen is done to halt the source of bleeding. In some conditions, the spleen is a factor in the underlying disorder (such as destruction of red blood cells, white blood cells, or platelets). In these cases, removal of the spleen helps to eliminate the source of the blood cell destruction.

Description

A splenectomy is done under general anesthesia. Depending on the surgeon's preference, a standard surgical approach or a laparoscopic approach may be done.

In a standard surgical approach, an incision is made in the upper abdomen. The spleen is located (in the left upper abdomen). The blood vessels supplying blood to the spleen are tied off and cut, and the spleen is lifted out of the abdomen. The surgeon also checks the other organs in the abdomen, looking for injury, tumors, or other conditions. A drainage tube may be placed near the abdominal incision to temporarily drain any accumulated fluid or blood. The abdominal muscles are stitched closed and the skin incision is closed with stitches or surgical staples.

If a laparoscope is used, several small incisions will be made in the abdomen rather than one large incision. The spleen is located by viewing the interior of the abdomen with the scope. Special instruments are passed through the laparoscope to tie and cut the blood supply to the spleen. Another instrument is used to grasp the spleen and draw it up through the laparoscope. The surgeon then uses the laparoscope to view other organs for injury, tumors, or bleeding sites. The laparoscope is withdrawn from the abdomen and the small incisions are closed with a few stitches.

Prognosis

The outcome of the procedure is dependent on the underlying cause for the procedure, the general health of the individual, and the presence of operative complications. For the most part, splenectomy is a highly effective therapy for all of the conditions listed.

In individuals with Felty's syndrome, the procedure is most effective for those who have recurrent infections. In those without recurrent infections, it remains controversial whether a splenectomy is of benefit.

Specialists

- General Surgeon

Work Restrictions / Accommodations

Recovery takes up to 4 weeks for individuals returning to light work, and up to 10 weeks for individuals returning to very heavy work. During the recovery period, lifting should be restricted to less than 25 pounds. No work restrictions or special accommodations are required after an individual has made a complete recovery from splenectomy.

Comorbid Conditions

Comorbid conditions of diabetes, liver disease, heart disease, chronic lung disease, immune suppression, cancer, or bleeding disorders may impact ability to recover and further lengthen disability.

Procedure Complications

The possible complications of surgery include bleeding, infection, and adverse reactions to the anesthesia. Because the spleen plays a major role in fighting infection, after its removal individuals may be at greater risk for developing certain infections. Generally, a vaccine (Pneumovax) is given during the surgical procedure to reduce the potential for developing infections.

Factors Influencing Duration

Any complications, type of work, and underlying reason for the splenectomy may influence the length of disability.

Length of Disability

Duration depends on underlying condition for which splenectomy was performed and presence of complications.

Job Classification	Duration in Days		
	Minimum	Optimum	Maximum
Sedentary work	14	21	28
Light work	14	21	28
Medium work	28	35	42
Heavy work	35	42	56
Very Heavy work	35	42	70

References

Goldman, Lee, and J. Claude Bennett. Cecil Textbook of Medicine, 21st ed. Philadelphia: W.B. Saunders Company, 2000.

Sabiston, David C., and H. Kim Lyerly. Textbook of Surgery, 15th ed. Philadelphia: W.B. Saunders Company, 1997.

Splenomegaly

Other names / synonyms: Enlarged Spleen, Hypersplenism, Spleen Enlargement

789.2

Definition

The term splenomegaly refers to abnormal enlargement of the spleen, an abdominal organ that is part of the lymph system that has many immune system and circulatory functions. The spleen plays a key role in manufacturing antibodies to fight inflammation and infection, cleansing the blood of foreign material, and producing red and white blood cells. Because of its wide variety of functions, the spleen may be affected by many conditions involving the blood or lymph system, by bacterial, viral and parasitic infections, malignancies, and liver disease.

The enlargement may be due to one or more of the following conditions: cirrhosis of the liver, infectious inflammatory diseases such as mononucleosis and hepatitis, chronic infections such as syphilis, tuberculosis, and malaria, diseases of the bone marrow, hemolytic anemias, cancers such as leukemia, lymphoma and Hodgkin's disease, diseases of the metabolic system, cystic fibrosis, biliary atresia, sclerosing cholangitis, Wilson's Disease and Banti's syndrome. However, in nearly 5% of individuals with enlarged spleens, no underlying cause can be determined.

Due to the broad range of conditions that may be associated with splenomegaly, the exact incidence and prevalence of splenomegaly cannot be ascertained.

Diagnosis

History: Individuals may report a history of chronic or acute infectious disease, inflammatory and connective tissue disorders, or liver conditions. They may complain of left upper quadrant abdominal pain; early appetite satisfaction (feeling full immediately upon eating); and recent, unintentional weight loss.

Physical exam: Physical exam may reveal signs and symptoms of an infectious or inflammatory process, such as fever, rapid heart rate, fatigue, tender and/or swollen lymph nodes, and abdominal distention. The edge of the spleen may be felt (palpated) when examining the left upper abdomen. Abnormal swooshing sounds (bruits) may be heard when using a stethoscope to listen (auscultate) over the region of the spleen.

Tests: Laboratory tests include abdominal x-ray, bone marrow examination, splenic scan with technetium, splenic uptake studies, and blood chemistries. A biopsy of the spleen may be done if cancer is suspected; because the spleen tends to bleed profusely, the biopsy is usually done in association with an open surgical exploration of the abdomen (exploratory laparotomy), and partial or total removal of the spleen (splenectomy). A reliable biopsy cannot be obtained via laparoscopic splenectomy, because the tissue is damaged when removed through the laparoscope.

Treatment

Most individuals with splenomegaly require treatment for the underlying disease. Medical interventions such as administration of medications for underlying infections and possible radiation therapy (to shrink the enlarged organ), are used as appropriate. The spleen is surgically removed (splenectomy) only via open abdominal surgery (laparotomy) when medically necessary, when it is markedly enlarged, and when other treatments are not effective. A splenectomy may also be done to assess the rate of disease progress (staging) if it is cancerous.

Prognosis

Outcome can be good (for splenomegaly associated with acute infections that have been adequately treated) or poor (depending upon the underlying disease process and treatment required). Those whose splenomegaly is associated with chronic conditions such as immune depression or cancer tend to have a poorer outcome. However, due to the wide range of conditions associated with splenomegaly, it is impossible to determine the exact outcome for those with splenomegaly. Surgical outcomes following splenectomy are usually good. Those who have underlying bleeding disorders may have more bleeding complications; they usually resolve quickly once the spleen is removed.

Differential Diagnosis

Tumors in the left upper abdomen or fluid in the abdomen (ascites) may mimic splenomegaly and should be considered in the differential diagnosis.

Specialists

- General Surgeon
- Hematologist
- Internist

Work Restrictions / Accommodations

Work restrictions and accommodations are made based on the underlying condition, the type of treatment required, and the individual's physical response to treatment. Anyone with an enlarged spleen is at risk for its accidental rupture and possible hemorrhage. Consequently, strenuous activity, contact sports, and heavy lifting should be avoided until the spleen returns to a normal size or is removed.

Comorbid Conditions

Comorbid conditions of immune suppression, bleeding disorders, anemia, lymphoma, leukemia, or other cancers may influence ability to recover and lengthen disability.

Complications

Complications relate to the underlying condition responsible for the splenomegaly. Spontaneous rupture of an enlarged spleen is rare; however, such ruptures can result in massive bleeding and shock. Enlarged spleens may easily rupture and bleed during laparoscopy. In general, spleens that rupture during laparoscopy are promptly removed (splenectomy), which eliminates the source of the bleeding and minimizes the risk for shock.

Factors Influencing Duration

The individual's age, the underlying condition, the type of treatment required, and the response to the treatment will influence the length of disability.

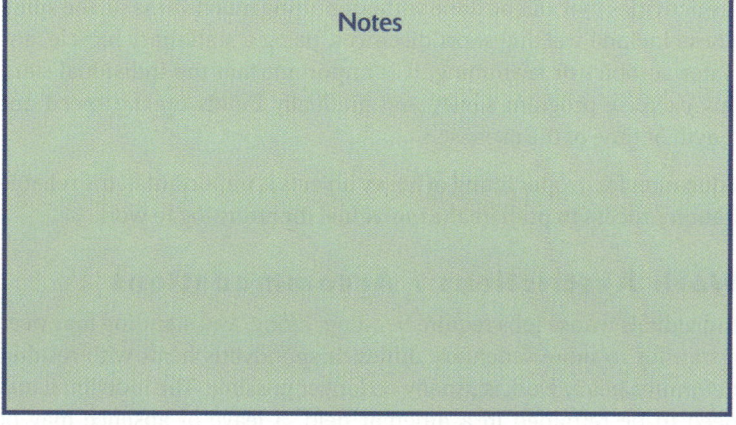

Notes

Length of Disability

Duration depends on cause.

Medical treatment.

Duration in Days

Job Classification	Minimum	Optimum	Maximum
Sedentary work	0	5	10
Light work	0	5	10
Medium work	0	5	10
Heavy work	0	5	10
Very Heavy work	0	5	10

Surgical treatment.

Duration in Days

Job Classification	Minimum	Optimum	Maximum
Sedentary work	14	21	28
Light work	14	21	28
Medium work	28	35	42
Heavy work	35	42	56
Very Heavy work	35	42	70

Failure to Recover

If an individual fails to recover within the maximum duration expectancy period, the reader may wish to reference the following questions to assist in better understanding the specifics of an individual's medical case.

Regarding diagnosis:

- Has diagnosis of splenomegaly been confirmed?
- Have other conditions (tumors in the left upper abdomen or fluid in the abdomen (ascites)) been ruled out?
- Has the cause of spleen enlargement been identified?
- Is underlying condition being appropriately addressed?

Regarding treatment:

- Have medical interventions, such as rest, good nutrition, administration of medications for underlying infections, and possible radiation therapy, been successful?
- If surgical intervene was necessary, for what purpose was the splenectomy performed? Were any complications associated with the procedure?

Regarding prognosis:

- Have underlying conditions responded favorably to treatment?
- If symptoms persist despite treatment, does diagnosis need to be revisited?
- Has condition (for which splenectomy was performed) improved or resolved with removal of spleen?
- What additional therapy may be required?

Splenomegaly

References

Braunwald, Eugene, et al, eds. Harrison's Principles of Internal Medicine, 11th ed. New York: McGraw-Hill Book Company, 1987.

Spondylitis

Other names / synonyms: Ankylosing Spondylitis, Parasitic Spondylitis, Psoriatic Arthritis, Pyogenic Spondylitis, Reiter's Syndrome

720.8, 720.9

Definition

Spondylitis is inflammation of the joints between the vertebrae. It may be either infectious or noninfectious. However, "spondylitis not otherwise specified" is a wastebasket term used by some to describe back pain of unknown etiology. Infection of bone in spine should be called osteomyelitis, while infection of a spinal disc should be called discitis.

Other types of noninfectious spondylitis include psoriatic arthritis, Reiter's syndrome, and the arthritis associated with inflammatory bowel disease (Crohn's disease or ulcerative colitis).

Psoriatic arthritis occurs in some individuals with a chronic skin condition (psoriasis). About 1 in 20 individuals with psoriasis will develop arthritis along with the skin condition. The cause of psoriatic arthritis is not known, but genetic factors may play a role. In general, individuals who have psoriasis have a higher prevalence of arthritis than the general population.

Diagnosis

History: The individual may complain of back pain, hip pain, neck pain, fatigue, morning stiffness, or joint pain. Some may report symptoms of weight loss and night sweats. Symptoms of skin disease (psoriasis) or inflammatory bowel disease may precede or may follow the onset of back symptoms (spondylitis).

Physical exam: The exam may reveal decreased movement in spine, muscle spasms, joint tenderness, and swelling. Eye inflammation may be present, but vision is rarely affected. Skin involvement with psoriasis may be obvious. In Reiter's syndrome, usually, symptoms of conjunctivitis, urethritis, or foot involvement precede the arthritis.

Tests: Erythrocyte sedimentation rate (ESR), hematocrit, blood cultures, and spinal x-rays are performed on all individuals. As in ankylosing spondylitis, the HLA B27 antigen is found with increased frequency in individuals with Reiter's syndrome, psoriatic arthropathy, and enteropathic arthropathy (the arthritis seen associated with Crohn's disease and ulcerative colitis). Other tests used are related to the particular cause of the spondylitis. These may include tuberculin test (PPD) and biopsy for culture and sensitivity to rule out infection (brucellosis, TB, and pyogenic). CT scan is used to evaluate soft tissue changes. MRI may be used for diagnosis and follow-up evaluation.

Treatment

The objective of treatment is to relieve the joint pain and to prevent, delay, or correct deformities. Nonsteroidal anti-inflammatory medications (NSAIDs) such as aspirin are used to reduce inflammation and pain associated with the condition.

Prognosis

The prognosis for the spondylitis associated with psoriasis, inflammatory bowel disease, and Reiter's syndrome is variable. Few individuals progress to total immobility of the joint (ankylosis). However, the course of the disease is unpredictable; remissions and relapses may occur at any stage.

Differential Diagnosis

Other possibilities include spine fractures, a herniated spine disc (vertebral disc), ankylosing spondylitis, rheumatoid arthritis, osteoarthritis, metastatic bone tumor, or muscle abscess.

Specialists

- Anesthesiologist
- Orthopedic Surgeon
- Physiatrist
- Primary Care Provider
- Rheumatologist

Rehabilitation

In general, the treatment of these rheumatologic conditions of the spine is medical (medication) with physical therapy having a minor role. General aerobic conditioning and strengthening exercises may, at times, have a role.

Spine stretching exercises may be introduced to help strengthen the spine and prevent poor posture. Extension exercises may be beneficial as well as exercises to strengthen the lower back and abdominal muscles. Even if symptoms of spondylitis are mild to moderate, there are activities that can be done without putting much stress on the spine. These include walking short distances, using a stationary bicycle, and water aerobics or swimming. It is important that the individual starts any exercise program slowly and gradually builds up the speed and length of time of the exercise.

Education for proper lifting of heavy objects is important in the rehabilitation process to prepare the individual for returning to work.

Work Restrictions / Accommodations

Individuals whose jobs require bending, lifting, and standing may need a transfer to more sedentary duties. If spondylitis heals with residual deformity, heavy work is usually no longer possible. The individual may need to be retrained in a different field. A leave of absence may be required.

Comorbid Conditions

Comorbid conditions of obesity, spinal cord injury may impact ability to recover and further lengthen disability.

Complications

The complications are principally those of the underlying psoriasis or inflammatory bowel disease. Progressive disease may result in abnormal flattening of the lower spine and an exaggeration of the curve of the middle (thoracic) spine.

Factors Influencing Duration

Factors influencing length of disability include underlying cause, extent, and severity of disease at diagnosis, length of time between development of symptoms and diagnosis, treatment required, presence of underlying medical conditions, IV drug abuse, and complications.

Length of Disability

Disability is variable. Depends on specific diagnosis (ankylosing spondylitis, rheumatoid arthritis), severity, response to treatment, region of spine and total amount of spine involvement.

Failure to Recover

If an individual fails to recover within the maximum duration expectancy period, the reader may wish to reference the following questions to assist in better understanding the specifics of an individual's medical case.

Regarding diagnosis:

- Does the individual have any risk factors?
- What symptoms does the individual have?
- What findings were present on physical exam?
- Have an erythrocyte sedimentation rate (ESR), hematocrit, HLA B27 antigen assay, blood cultures, and spinal x-rays been performed to confirm diagnosis?
- Has the individual been evaluated for the possibility of tuberculosis or fungal infection?
- Have conditions such as spine fractures, a herniated spine disc (vertebral disc), rheumatoid arthritis, osteoarthritis, metastatic bone tumor, or muscle abscess been ruled out?

Regarding treatment:

- Is the individual on appropriate rheumatologic medicine under the supervision of a rheumatologist?
- Was surgery necessary?
- Has the individual been receiving physical therapy?
- Have walking aids and assistive devices been made available to the individual?

Regarding prognosis:

- Is there any evidence on the x-rays to suggest another diagnosis?
- Has the individual received training proper lifting of heavy objects?
- Is the individual's employer able to accommodate restrictions if necessary?
- Does the individual have any conditions that might impact recovery?
- Does the individual have any complications?

References

Arnheim, Daniel D. Modern Principles of Athletic Training. St. Louis: Mirror/Mosby Publishing, 1989.

Kessler, R.M. Management of Common Musculoskeletal Disorders: Physical Therapy Principles and Methods. Philadelphia: J.B. Lippincott Co, 1990.

Spondylolisthesis
738.4, 756.12

Definition

Spondylolisthesis describes a condition of forward slippage of one vertebra in the spine over another.

The vertebrae of the spine are stacked one on top of the other and held in place by ligaments, muscles, and discs. The healthy spine is flexible in many directions because of its ability to bend and move without the vertebrae slipping out of position. Spondylolisthesis commonly occurs in the lumbar vertebrae, most often at the level between the fifth lumbar vertebra and the first sacral vertebra.

The three main types of spondylolisthesis are congenital, isthmic, and degenerative. Congenital spondylolisthesis is rare and is found in individuals born with an abnormality of the posterior bones of the spine (the L5-S1 levels). Because of the abnormal orientation of the bones, the normal ability of the spine to resist slippage is diminished and the vertebral body of L5 slips forward on S1. Afflicted individuals usually present with symptoms when they are in their adolescent growth spurt.

The second and most common type is isthmic spondylolisthesis and is caused by another spine condition called spondylolysis where a break occurs in the arch in the posterior segment of the vertebra. The break may be the result of a traumatic episode, a degenerative process, or repeated stress across the area (stress fracture). Spondylolysis is when the break occurs without forward slippage (because of the stability afforded by the ligaments, muscles, and disks of the spine) and spondylolisthesis is when the break is followed by a forward slippage of one bone over the top of another. Spondylolysis is the most common cause of spondylolisthesis.

The third type of spondylolisthesis is the degenerative type and is secondary to arthritis of the spine. As the disc in front of the spine ages, it loses water and some of its ability to resist motion. Degenerative arthritis causes loss of articulate cartilage in the spinal facet joints, leading to increased motion and, ultimately, persisting subluxation of the facet joints, and decreased resistance to forward slippage of one bone on another. The slippage is limited by the structures at the back of the spine that are still intact and by the intact bony restraints of the spine (the pars bone and the facet joint).

Spondylolisthesis can also be caused by a fracture in the spine (traumatic spondylolisthesis) usually in the facet joints connecting one vertebra to another; by destruction of the posterior aspect of the spine through tumor, infection, or osteoporosis (pathological spondylolisthesis); and from spinal surgery (postsurgical spondylolisthesis).

Individuals at risk for spondylolisthesis include those who have spondylolysis, those with an abnormal forward curvature of the lumbar spine (lordosis) especially if they engage in contact sports (football, volleyball, or soccer), certain kinds of gymnastics, or weight lifting. Lower back pain should be evaluated especially in the presence of marked lordosis.

The prevalence of spondylolisthesis in the general population is approximately 2-4% and is about equal in men and women.

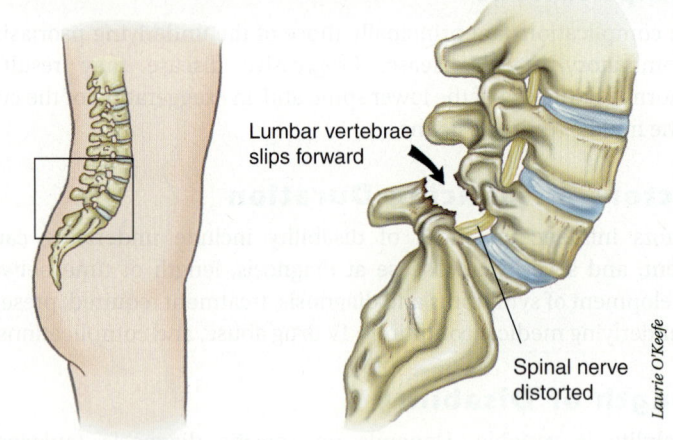

Diagnosis

History: Individuals with spondylolisthesis often present with lordosis, lower back pain, localized tenderness over the spine just above the pelvis, pain in thighs or buttocks, tightness in the hamstrings, and back stiffness.

Individuals with severe grades of slippage may not be able to walk normally and stumble or drag their feet instead. In describing pain, individuals may report that it is aggravated when they arise out of a sitting position, walk up stairs or inclines, get in and out of cars, and lean backward (extension). The pain is relieved at rest when lying flat or leaning forward (flexion).

Physical exam: The physician performs a complete musculoskeletal and neurological back exam to rule out any underlying pathology and determine the extent of nerve involvement. Findings of the exam may reveal decreased sensation and tendon reflexes and weakness of lower leg muscles. Examination of the spine by manual touching and massaging of the areas of concern (palpation) may reveal abnormal spaces between the vertebrae. Findings are also likely to reveal a limited range of motion of the spine, increased pain when leaning backward, relief in pain when leaning forward, clumsy, swayed walking (waddling gait), and tight hamstrings.

Tests: Plain x-rays (radiographs) are adequate to confirm a diagnosis of spondylolisthesis. The amount and percentage of slippage is important and should be measured on a standing lateral x-ray. A change in the percentage of slippage when the individual bends forward or leans backward is an indication that dynamic instability exists. This means that the vertebrae are changing the amount of slippage with spinal motion.

In cases of spondylolysis, the diagnosis may not be evident in plain x-rays. CT and MRI can define the pars defect and can help define nerve root impingement (MRI is better). MRI also helps define the status of the disc at the impaired level and the level adjacent to the slip.

A bone scan helps define how recently a pars fracture may have occurred. Electromyograms (EMGs) and nerve conduction studies check nerve function.

Treatment

Conservative treatment for spondylolisthesis includes rest (not excessive), activity modification (to minimize offending activity), physical therapy (to strengthen trunk muscles, especially the extensors, and to stretch the hamstrings), and analgesics. Corsets or braces are also prescribed when necessary to minimize motion across the area of the slippage and to decrease pain.

Surgical intervention is indicated if conservative therapy fails, pain becomes disabling, the individual becomes unable to function, or a progressive neurological deficit manifests. Age is not a contraindication to surgery. Many elderly individuals seem to benefit a great deal from surgical intervention. The main surgical procedure for treating spondylolisthesis is fusion. In fusion, the surgeon binds two or more bones or levels of the spine to prevent further slippage of the vertebrae. If there is neurologic deficit, in addition to the fusion, a decompression may also be performed. In decompression, the surgeon removes bone and disc tissue compressing lumbar nerve roots. Internal fixation devices, usually pedicle screws, may be used to enhance stability and, thus, chances of successful fusion. Severe grades of slippage may require both anterior and posterior fusion.

Prognosis

Individuals with progressive degenerative changes may continue to have intermittent symptoms. Surgery (fusion, decompression, and debridement) can be curative but some individuals may gain only partial or intermittent relief. Individuals who have sustained an acute fracture with minimal slippage may completely recover if the fracture heals.

Differential Diagnosis

Differential diagnosis can include degenerative lumbar disc disease, spinal stenosis, and degenerative conditions of the spine such as disc disease or arthritis.

Specialists

- Neurosurgeon
- Orthopedic Surgeon
- Physiatrist

Rehabilitation

Rehabilitation for spondylolisthesis varies depending on the severity of the disorder. Lower grades of the spine disorder require minimal therapy that involves exercises. If surgery is indicated for severe and progressive spondylolisthesis, rehabilitation is more involved.

When appropriate, weight resistance exercises may be introduced by the physical therapist to regain strength of the lower extremities affected by the disc disorder. Examples of such exercises include leg curls, leg presses, and half knee squats. Stationary biking and aerobic exercise may be recommended to increase strength and endurance of the affected weak muscles.

Exercises to strengthen the lower back and abdominal muscles may be helpful in preventing future stress and forces on the lumbar spine.

The late phase of the rehabilitation program involves the individual's reinstatement to work or what is also known as work hardening. The exercises are now directed toward work requirements and include instruction in proper lifting to prevent further injury. Back schools are programs available in many rehabilitation programs that focus on managing back disorders and preventing recurrence of symptoms.

Modifications may need to be made by the physical therapist for those individuals with arthritis or other lumbar spine conditions and will vary depending on the degree of spondylolisthesis or type of surgery performed.

Work Restrictions / Accommodations

Work restrictions may include the elimination of overhead work that involves hyperextension of the back. The individual may also be restricted in performing unassisted heavy lifting, repetitive bending, or pushing heavy objects. Some individuals may not be able to perform activities that require twisting at the waist. Use of a rigid corset (orthotic) may be needed to limit motion of the spine. Safety issues should be evaluated as well as drug testing policies since individuals may need to take pain medication.

Individuals with severe pain and hamstring spasm, grade 3 or grade 4 slippage, and individuals who have had spinal fusion are generally restricted to sedentary, light, or moderate work.

Comorbid Conditions

Comorbid conditions that may affect length of disability include obesity or excessive thinness, allergy to treatment medication, and chronic diseases such as heart disease, diabetes, and osteoporosis.

Complications

Progression of the slippage with increased pressure or traction on the spinal nerve roots may complicate treatment.

Factors Influencing Duration

Factors that may influence length of disability include severity of neurological problems, frequency and severity of the pain or weakness, and the ability to modify aggravating activities. Education and compliance with treatment goals are key to management of symptoms. Severe grades of spondylolisthesis may be incompatible with heavy work once symptoms begin.

Length of Disability

Individuals recovering from surgery may not be able to return to work for months or may be permanently disabled for some occupations.

Medical treatment. Grade 1 or Grade 2 spondylolisthesis.

Duration in Days

Job Classification	Minimum	Optimum	Maximum
Sedentary work	0	1	14
Light work	0	3	21
Medium work	0	7	42
Heavy work	0	10	63
Very Heavy work	0	14	91

Surgical treatment by spinal fusion.

Duration in Days

Job Classification	Minimum	Optimum	Maximum
Sedentary work	42	49	84
Light work	56	63	84
Medium work	70	77	112
Heavy work	84	168	Indefinite
Very Heavy work	84	168	Indefinite

Failure to Recover

If an individual fails to recover within the maximum duration expectancy period, the reader may wish to reference the following questions to assist in better understanding the specifics of an individual's medical case.

Regarding diagnosis:

- Has diagnosis been confirmed?
- What type of spondylolisthesis does individual have?
- Have other conditions with similar symptoms been ruled out?
- Does individual have lordosis?
- Does individual engage in contact sports, gymnastics, or weight lifting?
- Where does individual have pain? Lower back, in thighs or buttocks?
- Does the individual have tenderness over the spine above the pelvis?
- Does the individual stumble or drag the feet?
- Is pain relieved when lying flat or leaning forward?

Regarding treatment:

- Have conservative measures been effective in relieving symptoms? Is pain interfering with function?
- Is surgery indicated?
- Did individual undergo internal fixation? If not, upon what was the decision based?

Regarding prognosis:

- Did individual have surgery? Was it successful or did it only bring partial or intermittent relief?
- Were there any complications that could affect recovery?
- Does the individual have an underlying condition that may impact recovery?

References

Canale, Terry. *Campbell's Operative Orthopaedics, 9th ed.* Carlsbad, CA: Mosby, 1998 11 Jan 2001 <http://home.mdconsult.com/ >.

Kessler, R.M. *Management of Common Musculoskeletal Disorders: Physical Therapy Principles and Methods.* Philadelphia: J.B. Lippincott Company, 1990.

Kisner, C., and L. Colby. *Therapeutic Exercise Foundations and Techniques.* Philadelphia: F.A. Davis Company, 1990.

Spondylolisthesis. Allhealth.com. 28 Mar 2000. 10 Jan 2001 <http://www.allhealth.com/ahtools/encyclopedia/article/0,8895,001260,00.html>.

Spondylolisthesis. Spine, Inc. 2000. 09 Jan 2001 <http://www.spine-inc.com/glossary/s/spondylolisthesis.htm>.

Spondylolisthesis. SpineSolver.com. 2000. 08 Jan 2001 <http://www.spinesolver.com/spondylolisthesis.htm#DEFINITION>.

Spondylolysis, Lumbar Region
756.11

Definition

Spondylolysis is a break or fracture in the arch in the posterior segment of a vertebra. The lumbar vertebrae are stacked one on top of the other with the hook-shaped posterior portion forming a joint (facet) with the vertebrae above and below. Ligaments and intervertebral discs and the bony bridge between the anterior sections of the vertebral body all help stabilize the spine

The break may be the result of a traumatic episode, a degenerative process, or repeated stress across the area (stress fracture). Research indications show that the bone fracture occurring in spondylolysis may be associated with an inherited defect in the bone that connects the upper joint of one vertebra to the lower joint of another vertebra (pars interarticularis).

In asymptomatic school children, spondylolysis was found in 4-6% of those surveyed. In certain racial groups such as the Eskimos, the incidence was as high as 50%, suggesting a genetic factor. Incidence goes up with age. It is also higher in individuals involved in sports that place great stress on the back (i.e., gymnastics, weight lifting, and football) and sports where the individual undergoes repeated or constant hyperextension (bending backward) of the lumbar spine.

According to 1998 reports issued by the Centers for Disease Control and Prevention (CDC), the number of cases of spondylolysis diagnosed in the US was 35,000. Twice as many cases were diagnosed in women (24,000) as men (12,000).

Diagnosis

History: Symptomatic individuals with spondylolysis may report acute pain if a recent traumatic fracture occurred. If the fracture is not a recent one, the pain may be felt deep within the lower back and radiate to the buttock and thigh on the affected side. The pain may be relieved with rest. Those individuals with established fractures may experience little or no pain or other symptoms.

Physical exam: The physician performs a complete musculoskeletal exam that often reveals limitation of lumbar flexibility and tight hamstring muscles. Findings of a neurological exam are normal unless infrequent spinal nerve irritation occurs. The forward bend test may be

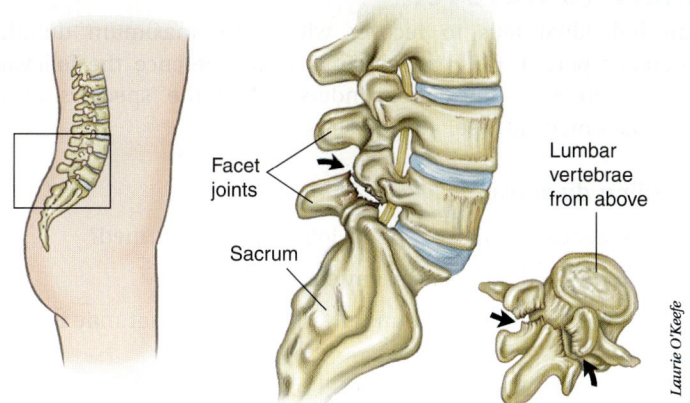

performed. This can detect an abnormal lateral curvature of the spine (scoliosis) since individuals with spondylolysis may also have scoliosis.

Tests: Lateral x-rays (radiographs) of the lower back demonstrate the lesion in 80% of cases, with another 15% visible on oblique films. Because the fracture may involve only one side of the vertebra, oblique views are required from both sides.

In some cases, CT scan and MRI can help define nerve root impingement (MRI is better). MRI can also define the status of the disc at the level of the slip and the level above the slip (where disc herniations are more common). If pain begins after trauma in a young individual, the spondylolysis may represent an acute fracture ("hot" on bone scan) with the ability to heal if the fracture is recognized and a rigid brace is worn for immobilization.

Bone scans are helpful in determining the age of the fracture especially in young individuals. Electromyograms (EMGs) and nerve conduction studies are used to check nerve function.

Treatment

Acute fractures are treated with immobilization using a semirigid brace and cessation of all activities that cause flexion and extension of the lumbar spine. Conservative treatment to control pain includes heat, physical therapy, and medication and is indicated in nonacute but symptomatic fractures.

Individuals with painful spondylolysis, especially when a stress fracture is suspected and the region is "hot" on bone scan, may benefit from a period of immobilization in a body jacket or back brace. Individuals are usually required to wear the braces for 3 to 6 months. Wearing the braces longer than 6 months is not recommended since any desired fusion should have occurred within that timeframe and further wearing of the brace could weaken involved muscles.

Education of the individual should include prevention of injury. Muscle strengthening programs should be included when the acute symptoms subside. Prescribed exercises include those that attempt to increase the strength of the abdominal musculature and the flexibility of the lumbar extensor, hamstring, and quadriceps muscles. Walking and cycling are appropriate exercises during rehabilitation.

Prognosis

Acute fractures that are recognized and treated may heal without complication. For non acute but symptomatic fractures, conservative treatment to control pain (ice and heat, physical therapy, and medication) is generally successful if the fracture is recognized and treated early.

Differential Diagnosis

Differential diagnosis may include degenerative lumbar disc disease, spinal stenosis, and degenerative conditions of the spine such as disc disease, herniated disk, or arthritis.

Specialists

- Neurosurgeon
- Orthopedic Surgeon
- Physiatrist

Rehabilitation

Rehabilitation for spondylolysis to the lumbar region varies involves physical therapy to strengthen the spinal muscles and to stretch the hamstrings.

A flexibility program may be incorporated in rehabilitation of the lumbar spine. The individual may be instructed in several Williams' flexion exercises. Exercises to strengthen the lower back and abdominal muscles may help in preventing future stress and forces on the lumbar spine.

Weight-resistance exercises instructed by the physical therapist helps individuals regain strength of the lower extremities affected by the lumbar spine disorder. Stationary biking and aerobic exercise increase strength and endurance of the affected weak muscles.

The late phase of the rehabilitation program involves the individual's reinstatement to work or what is known as work hardening. These exercises are directed toward work requirements and include instruction of proper lifting to prevent further injury. Back schools are available in many rehabilitation programs and focus on managing back disorders and preventing recurrence of symptoms.

Modifications may need to be made by the physical therapist for those individuals with arthritis or other lumbar spine conditions. This varies depending on the degree of disc disorder or type of surgery performed.

Work Restrictions / Accommodations

For individuals with acute fractures, complete avoidance of overhead work, arching the back, and heavy or unassisted lifting and carrying may be required. Restriction on the frequency and amount of weight involved is prudent. Pushing heavy objects would also aggravate the condition.

Individuals prescribed back braces may require sedentary work during the 3- to 6-month time period when they wear the braces.

Comorbid Conditions

Comorbid conditions that may influence the length of disability include obesity, allergy to treatment medication, and chronic diseases such as heart disease, diabetes, and osteoporosis.

Complications

Bilateral (both sides of the vertebra) defects are likely to lead to a sliding or slipping forward of the vertebrae (spondylolisthesis). This does not occur with unilateral defects.

Factors Influencing Duration

The number and severity of symptoms and frequency of occurrence may influence the length of disability. Occupational situations that require repetitive loading and bending of the spine can increase the likelihood of periods of disability from pain.

Length of Disability

Expected length of disability depends on the individual's work requirements. If the individual is asymptomatic, no disability is expected.

Medical treatment. Acute fractures.

Duration in Days

Job Classification	Minimum	Optimum	Maximum
Sedentary work	1	7	14
Light work	1	14	28
Medium work	42	63	91
Heavy work	42	91	119
Very Heavy work	63	119	182

Failure to Recover

If an individual fails to recover within the maximum duration expectancy period, the reader may wish to reference the following questions to assist in better understanding the specifics of an individual's medical case.

Regarding diagnosis:
- Has diagnosis of lumbar spondylolysis been confirmed?
- Has individual experienced any complications?
- Does individual have an underlying condition that may impact recovery?

Regarding treatment:
- Is condition the result of a fracture?
- Were conservative measures effective in relieving pain?
- Is pain interfering with functional ability?
- Would individual benefit from additional physical therapy?

Regarding prognosis:
- Does pain at the fracture site persist despite treatment?
- Have x-rays verified complete bone union?
- Can individual return to work with accommodations?
- Would a back brace be useful?

References

A Patient's Guide to Low Back Pain: Understanding Spondylolysis and Spondylolisthesis. Medical Multimedia Group. 08 Jun 1998. 10 Jan 2001 <http://www.sechrest.com/mmg/back/spondylo/spondylo.html>.

National Hospital Discharge Survey: Annual Summary 1998. Centers for Disease Control and Prevention (CDC). 01 Sep 2000. 05 Jan 2001 <http://www.cdc.gov/nchs/data/sr13_148.pdf>.

Sprains and Strains

Other names / synonyms: Joint Separation, Muscle Pull, Muscle Tear, Stretched Ligaments, Subluxation, Torn Ligaments
840.8, 840.9, 843, 848

Definition

Sprains are injuries to ligaments and strains are injuries to muscles. They imply a stretching or tearing of tissue and are defined by the amount of damage to the ligament or muscle. When force is applied to across a joint greater than the ligaments can support, a sprain results. The same concept is true for muscle tendon units. When a resistive force greater than a muscle can tolerate is encountered, muscle strains develop.

A first-degree injury is a stretching of the ligament (sprain) or muscle (strain) with the tissue fibers remaining intact. Second-degree sprains and strains show evidence of stretching and tearing of some fibers, but the ligament or muscle remains partially intact. Complete disruption of the ligament or muscle is a third-degree injury.

Ligaments provide stability to joints. By bridging across the joint from bone to bone, they function as hinge. A sprain of the ligament disrupts the joint, allowing it to move outside of its normal range-of-motion (subluxation), or in the case of a third-degree sprain, resulting in a complete dislocation. While a joint is dislocated when all the ligaments involved are torn, a single ligament in a group can have a third-degree sprain with some stability of the joint remaining intact.

Muscles lose strength and function when injured. While first-degree strains may be the result of a bruise (contusion), or over-stretching of the muscle belly, a second-degree strain involves injury to the muscle tendon junction.(musculotendinous junction). Third-degree strains describe a tearing or disruption of the muscle fibers and the sheath (fascia) around it.

A common sprain is of the ankle joint, caused by twisting the joint beyond its normal range of motion. An example of a strain is a quadriceps muscle pull or tear from accelerating quickly when running.

Diagnosis

History: A known injury can result in sprains or strains, but sometimes the actual event is subtle and there may not be any immediate symptoms. The individual may complain of pain, loss of function, change in sensation in the case of muscle strains, or may feel a defect or swelling along the body of the muscle. The individual may have heard a "pop" or "snap" or experienced a sensation of the joint slipping with continued instability or something tearing in ligament injuries. There is usually swelling, lack of function or stability, bruising (ecchymosis) and pain in the affected area.

Physical exam: Inspection reveals swelling of the soft tissue, swelling within a joint (effusion), bruising (ecchymosis), tenderness, inability to use a muscle or changes in joint stability. There may be some deformity of a joint in the case of sprains. Complete muscle tears (third-degree strain) could appear as a ball or knot under the skin. Touching (palpation) the area in either sprains or strains may produce diffuse or point specific pain. In sprains, joints should be tested for laxity, and evaluation of muscle strength is important in strains. The individual may have decreased active and passive motion limited by pain and loss of function. In general, ligamentous sprains are indicated if passive joint motion reproduces complaints, whereas a musculotendinous strain is indicated if resisted joint motion reproduces the complaint. A neurological examination is necessary as the tendons and nerves often lie very close to each other and damage can occur to both.

Tests: Plain x-rays are often used to look for fractures caused by the muscle pulling away from the bone (avulsion fracture). Fractures caused by dislocations may also be seen. Stress x-rays may be needed to evaluate the severity of a sprain. Arthrograms, a test used to view the joint space, are not used as frequently now that MRI is available. MRI can also be useful to determine the integrity of the muscle or ligament.

Treatment

First and second-degree sprains are treated with rest, ice, compression, and elevation (R.I.C.E.) to the injured part. Early movement and/or activity therapy should be explored. If needed, rest may be accomplished with supportive devices such as splints, casts, slings or crutches. Individuals can usually bear partial weight on leg and foot injuries, which promotes normal motion while providing rest. Third-degree sprains are either immobilized or repaired surgically (joint capsulorraphy or ligament repair/reconstruction.) In second-degree sprains, ligament tissue does not grow back together, but immobilization of the area allows scar tissue to form, which will provide joint stability. It is important to regain normal joint function as quickly as possible while guarding against abnormal motion. Physical therapy is very important during the healing process.

First-degree muscle strains repair with little intervention except applications of compression and ice and/or heat. It is important to protect against further injury during this time (with either too little or too much activity). Second-degree strains rarely require surgery, unless complete loss of function has occurred and the other muscles near the injury cannot compensate. Cosmetic deformity is sometimes an indication for surgery (repair torn muscle or tendon.) Third-degree muscle strains sometimes require surgical repair to restore function. Muscle tissue will regenerate and heal, but physical therapy is important to regain the full range-of-motion, muscle length and strength.

Prognosis

With proper rehabilitation, first and second-degree injuries should heal without significant change in function. Third-degree injuries are much more significant and while resolution of pain can be expected over time, there may be a degree of impairment.

Residual lifestyle-limiting symptoms are common 6 to 18 months after an ankle sprain.

Differential Diagnosis

Shin splints (tibial periostitis), fractures or dislocations, infections, bursitis, synovitis, joint deformity and laxity caused by inflammatory joint disease, muscle tumors and cysts all need to be excluded.

Specialists

- Chiropractor
- Exercise Physiologist
- Orthopedic Surgeon
- Physiatrist
- Physical Therapist
- Sports Medicine Physician

Rehabilitation

Control of pain and swelling followed by regaining aerobic conditioning, full motion, flexibility, strength, and endurance of the muscle/joint structures involved are the therapy goals. The final goal is aimed at establishing a home exercise program and returning the individual to full function for work and recreational activities with minimal risk of re-injury.

Application of cold using ice on the injured joint/muscle region may be recommended after the initial sprain or strain if signs of inflammation are present and if activity or movement does not benefit. After this period, heat treatments may be helpful to reduce inflammation and pain and, once appropriate, are beneficial to mildly stretch the muscles that are affected. Forms of heat treatment include ultrasound using high frequency sound waves producing heat penetrating deep into the involved muscles. Electrical stimulation combined with heat or cold treatment is another technique used in physical therapy to relax irritated muscles that may be in spasm. Iontophoresis is another treatment in the rehabilitation of sprains and strains.

Once movement is allowed, passive motion of the involved joint(s) region is permitted and to be used only as tolerated by the individual. Passive range-of-motion exercises begin with the therapist bending and straightening the limb. Each motion is taken until a mild stretch is noted by the individual. This exercise is then progressed to active assist range of motion exercises As the individual improves with increased motion of the involved joint, the next step of progression is active range of motion and requires that the individual perform all of the motion independently.

Joint mobilization techniques are also used by the physical therapist to restore joint motion as well as aid in the stretching of surrounding muscle and tendons. The therapist stabilizes one of the bones with associated muscles comprising the joint while mobilizing the adjoining bone(s) in the direction needed to regain the loss of mobility. Joint mobilization is generally graded in the amount of force used as well as the types of mobilization technique desired per body part.

The instruction of isometric strengthening exercises begins early in the phase of strengthening. Isometric exercise demands that the muscles around the joint contract yet no movement takes place at the joint. Once both range of motion and isometric exercises are tolerated, the individual is progressed to isotonic strengthening involving movement at, and around, the joint. An example of this type of rehabilitation exercise is strengthening with weights using weight equipment/machines and elastic bands.

At the onset, rehabilitation for a strain and or sprain consists of therapy. During this time, the individual is taught exercises to be performed at home. In most cases of a mild strain or sprain, a return to the preinjury level of function should be attained within a few weeks following initiation of the exercise program. Modifications may need to be made by the physical therapist for those individuals who have arthritis, joint irritations, and muscle disorders.

Work Restrictions / Accommodations

A return to activity and early return to work is important in spite of discomfort as this results in better outcomes. Modified duties should be sought, if needed. If the lower extremity is involved, use of assistive devices such as crutches, casts and braces may be necessary. If the upper extremity is involved, restrictions may include little to no use of arm, hand, or shoulder, with limited lifting and carrying. Dexterity may be affected by the injury and use of protective splints. Back strain may be totally incapacitating for a period of time during recovery. Use of medications for management of pain and inflammation may require review of drug policies. Safety issues may need to be evaluated.

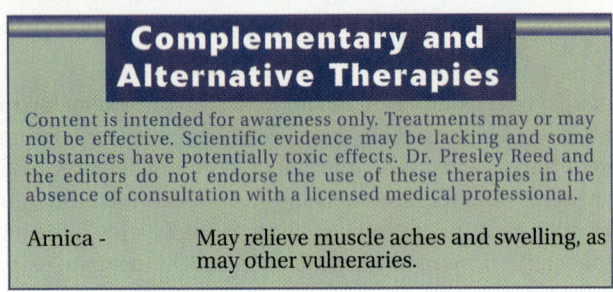

Complementary and Alternative Therapies

Content is intended for awareness only. Treatments may or may not be effective. Scientific evidence may be lacking and some substances have potentially toxic effects. Dr. Presley Reed and the editors do not endorse the use of these therapies in the absence of consultation with a licensed medical professional.

Arnica - May relieve muscle aches and swelling, as may other vulneraries.

Comorbid Conditions

Conditions that may delay recovery include diabetes, inflammatory diseases, neurological disease, hypothyroid conditions, psychosocial conditions, and vascular disease.

Complications

There is often bleeding into the tissues (hematoma) when a sprain or strain occurs. Bleeding into a joint space (hemarthrosis) may require removal (evacuation, aspiration.) Rarely, deposits of calcium in the areas of bleeding in the muscle (myositis ossificans) can lead to stiffness and pain in the muscle. Damage to the surface (articular) cartilage in joints with lax ligaments is possible.

Lack of treatment, especially exercise, often delays recovery because the injury is thought to be slight. Lack of exercise as treatment can result in poor repair and reflex inhibition, which can lead to reinjury during or after the healing phase as a result of the area not being protected.

Factors Influencing Duration

Factors include the location of the injury, the degree of the injury, and how it affects the individual's job performance. Surgery may lengthen the period of disability. Reinsure caused by early return to activity will delay full recovery.

Length of Disability

Length of disability is dependent on the relationship of the injury to job requirements. Return to work that stresses the injured area before complete healing has occurred is likely to cause reinsure and further delay recovery.

For hip sprains and strains, duration depends on severity of injury.

Hip.

Duration in Days

Job Classification	Minimum	Optimum	Maximum
Sedentary work	1	3	14
Light work	7	14	21
Medium work	21	21	28
Heavy work	28	35	42
Very Heavy work	28	42	56

Shoulder. Second degree or moderate. For third degree see rotator cuff tear.

Duration in Days

Job Classification	Minimum	Optimum	Maximum
Sedentary work	1	7	14
Light work	1	7	14
Medium work	7	14	21
Heavy work	14	21	42
Very Heavy work	14	21	56

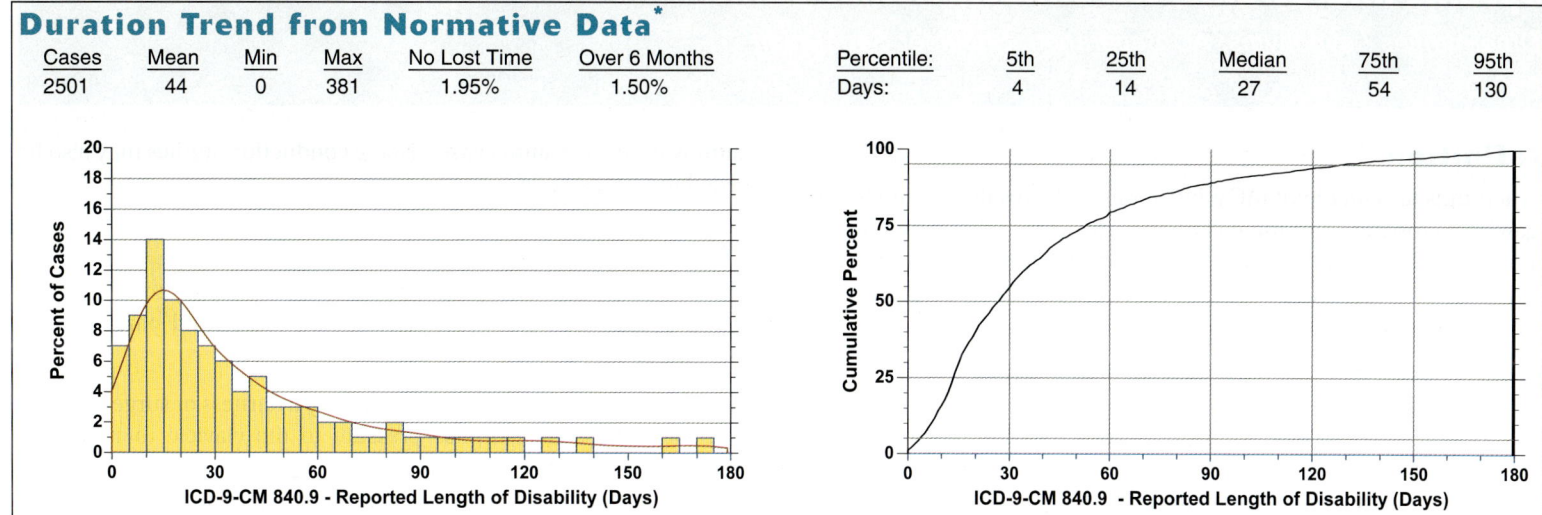

Failure to Recover

If an individual fails to recover within the maximum duration expectancy period, the reader may wish to reference the following questions to assist in better understanding the specifics of an individual's medical case.

Regarding diagnosis:

- Does the individual complain of pain, loss of function or change in sensation?
- Did individual hear a "pop" or "snap"? Experience a sensation of the joint slipping?
- Are swelling, lack of function or stability, and ecchymosis present?
- On exam is soft tissue swelling present? Effusion? Ecchymosis? Tenderness?
- Is individual unable to use a muscle or are there changes in joint stability?
- Is there a ball or a knot under the skin? Joint deformity?
- Is the individual exquisitely tender to palpation?
- Is there any laxity in the joint?
- What were the results of the neurological exam?
- Has the individual had plain x-rays and stress x-rays? MRI?
- Have conditions with similar symptoms been ruled out?

Regarding treatment:

- Is the injury first, second or third degree?
- Has it been treated with rest, ice, compression and elevation (R.I.C.E.)?
- Was it necessary to immobilize the area?
- Was surgery necessary?

Regarding prognosis:

- Is the individual active in physical therapy? Does the individual have a home exercise program?
- Is the individual's employer able to accommodate any necessary restrictions?
- Does the individual have any conditions that may affect ability to recover?
- Does the individual have any complications such as hemarthrosis or myositis ossificans?

References

Braun, B.L. "Effect of Ankle Spain in a General Clinic Population 6 to 18 Months After Medical Evaluation." Archives of Family Medicine 8 2 (1999): 143-148.

Malone, Terry R., Thomas McPoil, and Arthur J. Nitz. Orthopedic and Sports Physical Therapy. St. Louis: Mosby-Year Book, Inc, 1997.

Sprains and Strains, Acromioclavicular Joint

Other names / synonyms: AC Separation, Shoulder Separation

840.0

Definition

An acromioclavicular joint (AC joint) sprain is the result of injury to the ligaments crossing from the collarbone (clavicle) to the acromion, or upper part of the shoulder blade. This is an important joint as it is the only true boney attachment of the arm to the rest of the skeleton. The joint is relatively small and normally fairly rigid.

A sprain of these ligaments results in varying degrees of looseness (laxity) and deformity of the AC joint. Sprains are graded as to the severity of ligament damage and resulting separation of the joint. In grade I AC joint sprains, there has been some stretching of ligament fibers, but no disruption of the joint. In grade II sprains, the damage is greater, resulting in some fibers being torn and minimal disruption or displacement of the joint. Grade III injuries are sprains, which include a complete disruption (dislocation) of the joint because all the ligament fibers are torn (ruptured). Grades IV - VI sprains are much more uncommon, are of much greater severity, and are discussed under acromioclavicular dislocations.

Acromioclavicular sprains occur most often in contact sports, but any impact to the top of the shoulder or fall on an outstretched arm could injure the joint. Either the force of impact is transmitted from the tip of the shoulder across the joint or up the arm to the joint. If the force is greater than the ligaments can accommodate, a sprain results.

Those individuals at greatest risk for an AC dislocation include athletes or workers participating in activities that could result in falls on the shoulder, contact with an object while moving, having an object fall on the shoulder or a fall onto the outstretched hand and arm. This often occurs when an individual tries to prevent or break a fall.

In one study of 1603 shoulder injuries, only 52 were to the AC joint, and of these 52, 85% were classified as sprains.

Sprains and strains of the acromioclavicular joint are often incorrectly confused with shoulder dislocation or glenohumeral dislocation.

Diagnosis

History: Most commonly, individuals will report a direct blow to the tip of the shoulder area, either from a fall or occasionally from a heavy object falling on the shoulder. A fall on the outstretched hand could also cause the injury. Individuals complain of pain, weakness, and a bump on the top of their shoulder. Often the arm is carried across the chest, with pressure under the elbow.

Physical exam: Direct visual examination reveals an asymmetry of the two joints (opposite sides.) There are often abrasions across and somewhat behind the joint. Testing of motion reveals weakness of the forearm, limited active range of motion and painful assisted range of motion of the joint. The high riding tip of the clavicle may be repositioned (reduced) into a normal position by the individual or the doctor, but this maneuver can be painful.

Tests: X-rays of the AC joint, both AP and lateral to establish position of the acromion and clavicle. This is also used to rule out associated fractures. Rarely and MRI or CT scan would be needed to evaluate other anatomy in severe trauma cases. Nerve conduction studies may also be needed in this instance.

Treatment

Minor, or Grade I, injuries are treated with a sling with gradual range of motion and strengthening exercises. Cold therapy and pain medications may be indicated.

Grade II injuries may be treated with a sling, a harness or surgery. Use of a special harness that applies pressure to the clavicle to hold it in position while the ligaments scar over can be effective, but it is not very comfortable. Careful attention must be paid to the skin under the straps to avoid pressure sores and skin infection. Ice, pain medication, and physical therapy are added when appropriate.

Grade III treatment also ranges from a sling, to strapping to surgery. Surgery is more likely to be suggested for those injuries if the individual is intolerant of the strapping device, does not want to have the bump remain on the top of the shoulder, or if the lifestyle demands include heavy overhead work. The surgical procedure is open reduction with internal fixation (ORIF). A metal screw may be inserted or material such as suture, synthetic graft material or wire used to hold the joint in position.

All methods of treatment may require up to 6 to 8 weeks of treatment time. After the dislocation is healed, pain in the joint may be treated with corticosteroid injection.

Prognosis

Normal joint function should return after a Grade I and most Grade II injuries in about 6 - 8 weeks. Grade III dislocations treated surgically (ORIF) will require more extensive therapy for full recovery. Aggressive therapy often cannot begin until 6 weeks after surgery. Chronic pain and decreased joint function does develop in some individuals, especially those who develop degenerative arthritis.

Grade II and III injuries not treated with surgery (ORIF) to reduce the dislocation will leave the individual with a bump on the tip of the shoulder. Surgery will leave a scar about 2 inches long.

Differential Diagnosis

Fractures of the clavicle, especially at the end (distal end), or of the acromion may present with similar symptoms. Acute traumatic bursitis may look like a dislocation.

Specialists

| • Orthopedic Surgeon | • Physiatrist |

Rehabilitation

Rehabilitation of acromioclavicular sprain or strain depends greatly on the severity of the injury. The treatment of a minor acromioclavicular sprain (joint separation caused by stretching of the ligaments) may consist of a sling for comfort for several days. Even if the acromioclavicular joint is not to be exercised, it is important to exercise the fingers, hands, and elbows to prevent stiffness. Once the initial pain and swelling have subsided, the rehabilitation process may warrant the observation and guidance of a physical therapist until the individual progresses to an independent exercise program.

The physical therapist may use cold or warm treatments throughout the period of rehabilitation to control inflammation and pain. Iontophoresis is another treatment in the rehabilitation of acromioclavicular sprain or strain. This technique uses a small electric current to drive anti-inflammatory medication of the same electrical charge into the painful muscle tissues and joint structures.

Strengthening of an acromioclavicular joint following a sprain or strain begins with range of motion to the shoulder in all movements that are pain free. The individual may use a cane or wand to perform these exercises either alone or with a physical therapist. When the movement is pain free, the individual may be progressed to a towel stretch sequence involving the arms raised overhead and stretching behind the back.

The instruction of isometric strengthening exercises begins early in the phase of strengthening. Isometric exercise demands that the muscles around the joint contract yet no movement takes place at the joint.

Once both range of motion and isometric exercises are tolerated, which depends on the extent of the injury from the dislocation, the individual is progressed to isotonic strengthening involving movement at, and around, the acromioclavicular joint. An example of this type of rehabilitation exercise is strengthening with weights. Strength training of this type will also include weight equipment/machines and elastic bands.

Some of the key areas that are emphasized are the trapezius muscles located between the shoulder and neck. The individual exercises the upper trapezius muscle by performing shoulder shrugs against light dumbbell resistance. The front shoulder muscles should also be strengthened. This is done by instructing the individual to perform a rowing motion with light resistance dumbbells while standing upright.

Heavy weightlifting activities should be avoided until the ligament has healed. From this point, a gradual strengthening program is advanced as tolerated. Overhead presses, which also address the muscles on the front of the shoulder, are a good example of strengthening at this phase, as well as variations of dumbbell exercises to forward, backward and sideways motions of the shoulder.

Modifications may need to be made by the physical therapist for those individuals who have arthritis or other joint irritations. If the acromioclavicular sprain or strain requires surgical repair, some restrictions may be placed on the progression of the range of motion and strengthening in certain movements. This varies depending on the degree of the joint separation or type of surgery that was performed.

Work Restrictions / Accommodations

Individuals must avoid lifting, carrying, or overhead work for 6 weeks. They may be restricted by a sling or harness, which limits manual dexterity.

Comorbid Conditions

Degenerative and rheumatoid arthritis, neurological disease, fractures of the clavicle, acromion or scapula or injuries to the rotator cuff could impede recovery from an AC sprain. Damage to nerves and vessels in the area would also complicate recovery.

Complications

If the end of the clavicle is damaged, it may need to be removed surgically to reduce the chance of developing arthritis. There is a small cushion between the bone ends (meniscus) that may be dislodged during the injury and may be an indication for surgery. Any fractures around the shoulder area will complicate recovery.

Skin abrasions are common with this injury and require careful monitoring during treatment to prevent infection. Careful attention must be given to the skin around the bump to observe stretching and tearing (tenting). Treatment may be necessary to prevent further damage to the skin and soft tissue around the bump.

If a metal screw was used during surgery, it may be removed at a later date.

Chronic pain from the injury after conservative or non-operative treatment may be an indication for removal of the end of the clavicle (excision of the distal clavicle).

Skin and bursa infections may develop in the area of an abrasion. Damage to the nerves and vessels in the clavicle area is less likely, but could occur.

Factors Influencing Duration

Dominant verses non-dominant side and degree of separation are important factors in determining disability. Work requirements for manual dexterity, lifting or carrying would increase the disability. Surgical repair of either AC joint would increase disability time, if work responsibilities require two-handed manual dexterity.

Length of Disability

Dominant side injuries require longer disability periods because the individuals will not be able to use their hand above shoulder height, either in sedentary or active jobs. Individuals treated with surgical reconstruction on their dominant shoulder could expect to disabled from heavy lifting and carrying for 2 months.

First-degree or mild.

Duration in Days

Job Classification	Minimum	Optimum	Maximum
Sedentary work	0	3	10
Light work	1	7	10
Medium work	7	21	28
Heavy work	14	21	84
Very Heavy work	14	21	84

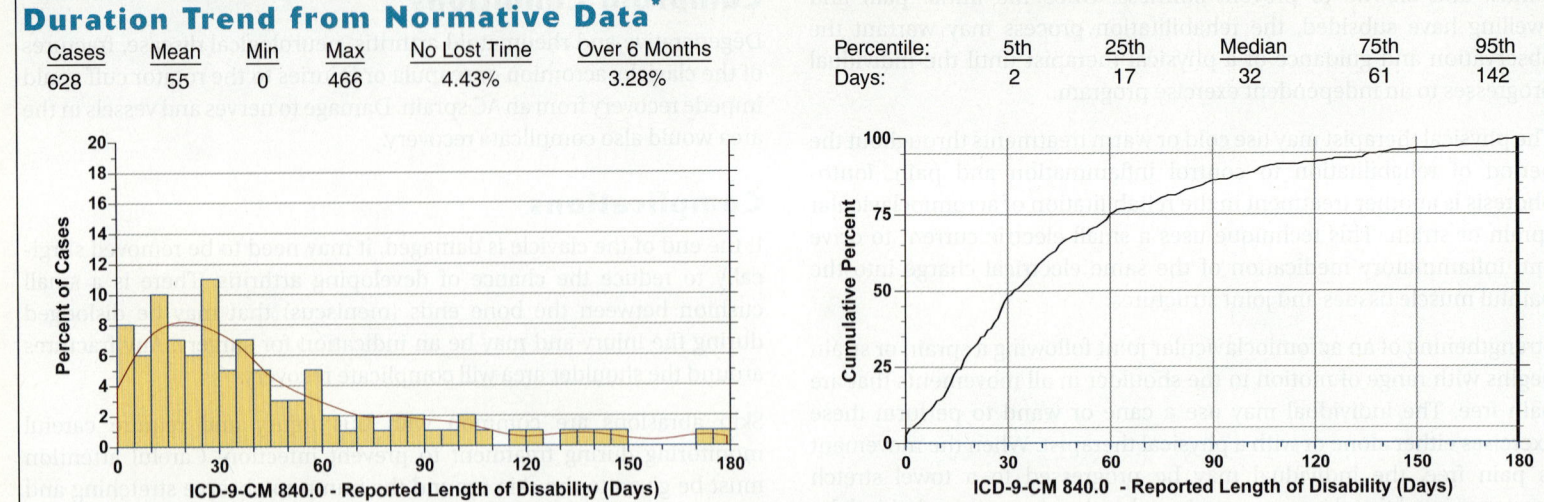

Duration Trend from Normative Data*

Cases	Mean	Min	Max	No Lost Time	Over 6 Months
628	55	0	466	4.43%	3.28%

Percentile:	5th	25th	Median	75th	95th
Days:	2	17	32	61	142

* Differences may exist between the expected duration tables and the normative graphs. Duration tables provide expected recovery periods based on the type of work performed by the individual. The normative graphs reflect the actual observed experience of many individuals across the spectrum of physical conditions, in a variety of industries, and with varying levels of case management.

Failure to Recover

If an individual fails to recover within the maximum duration expectancy period, the reader may wish to reference the following questions to assist in better understanding the specifics of an individual's medical case.

Regarding diagnosis:

- What Grade sprain (I, II ,III) does the individual have?
- What was the mechanism of injury?
- Does the individual complain of pain, weakness, and a bump on the top of the shoulder?
- Is the individual carrying the arm across the chest with support under the elbow?
- On visual exam of both shoulders is asymmetry noted?
- On physical exam, is there weakness of the forearm, limited active range of motion and painful assisted range of motion of the joint?
- Has the individual had an x-ray of the affected area?
- Was it necessary to have a MRI or CT? Nerve conduction studies?
- Have conditions with similar symptoms been ruled out?

Regarding treatment:

- Is the individual's injury Grade I?
- Is the individual being treated with a sling, ice and pain medication?
- Is the individual's injury Grade II?
- Is the individual being treated with a sling or harness?
- Is the individual using ice and pain medication? Was surgery done?
- Is the individual's injury Grade III? Is the individual being treated with a sling or harness? Is the individual using ice and pain medication? Was an open reduction necessary?

Regarding prognosis:

- Is the individual active in rehabilitation?
- Does the individual have a home exercise program?
- Is the individual's employer able to accommodate any necessary restrictions?
- Does the individual have any conditions that may affect ability to recover?
- Does the individual have any complications such as damage to the end of the clavicle or dislodged meniscus dislodged?
- Does the individual have any skin abrasions?
- Does the individual have an infection or damage to nerves and blood vessels?

References

Field L.D., and R.F. Warren. "Acromioclavicular Joint Separations." Shoulder Injuries in the Athlete: Surgical Repair and Rehabilitation. Hawkins, Richard J., and Gary W. Misamore, eds. New York: Churchill Livingstone, 1995. 201-216.

Kessler, R.M. Management of Common Musculoskeletal Disorders: Physical Therapy Principles and Methods. Philadelphia: J.B. Lippincott Company, 1990.

Orthopaedic Sports Medicine. DeLee, Jesse C. Jr., and David Drez, eds. Boston: W.B. Saunders Company, 1990.

Reid, David C. Sports Injury Assessment and Rehabilitation. New York: Churchill Livingstone, 1992. 930-931.

Sprains and Strains, Ankle
845, 845.0, 845.00, 845.01, 845.02, 845.03, 845.09

Definition

An ankle sprain is defined as an injury to the ligaments around the ankle. An ankle strain is an injury to the muscles around the ankle, in which the muscle (or tendon) is overstretched or torn.

Sprains can be categorized by the amount of tearing of the ligament. A first-degree sprain is one in which the ligament fibers are over-stretched but intact. A second-degree sprain is one in which some fibers are actually torn. A third-degree sprain is one in which the ligament is completely torn and nonfunctioning.

Ankle strains are classified in the same manner as sprains, with first-degree indicating over-stretching, second-degree indicating partial tear, and third-degree indicating complete tear (rupture).

An ankle sprain usually occurs as a result of forcibly twisting the ankle or by landing from a jump on a foot that is turned in (inversion) or out (eversion). Basketball has the highest rate of ankle sprains of any sport, but they can also occur in football, soccer, volleyball, skiing, and martial arts.

Strains occur from the same activities and stresses as sprains, but are uncommon about the ankle joint. The tendons that traverse the ankle joint (peroneal tendons laterally; tibialis anterior and posterior tendons medially; extensor tendons anteriorly; and flexor tendons and tendo Achilles posteriorly) are usually strained or ruptured at their point of insertion in the foot, rather than at the ankle level. The only exception to this is the Achilles tendon behind the ankle. This tendon can be strained in the leg, ankle, or foot.

The most common injury is the lateral (inversion) ankle sprain (85% of all ankle sprains). It occurs as a result of rolling over of the foot and ankle with damage to the ligaments connecting the fibula to the talus and calcaneus. There are three ligaments in this area, and another classification system of these sprains (Leach classification) is based on which ligaments are torn (ruptured). A first-degree sprain would be a rupture of the anterior talofibular ligament, the second-degree sprain would be a rupture of both the anterior talofibular and calcaneofibular ligaments, and a third-degree sprain would be ruptures of both of these ligaments plus the posterior talofibular ligament. When the foot is turned out (eversion) during the injury, damage is to the inside (medial) of the ankle. There are four ligaments in this area and these are called the deltoid ligaments. They are much stronger than the lateral ankle ligaments and rarely rupture. Indeed, the bone insertion of these ligaments (medial malleolus) will usually fracture (avulsion fracture) before the ligament ruptures. A much less common sprain occurs to the ligament between the tibia and fibula (syndesmosis). This injury is called diastasis of the tibiofibular syndesmosis and causes significant disability. This injury occurs when force is transmitted from the foot up the center of the ankle joint, such as landing on the foot from a height. Part of the function of ankle ligaments involves a feedback mechanism for balance (proprioception). When the ligaments are sprained, this function is distorted or lost. Strains of the ankle are generally mild (first-degree). They are similar to sprains regarding mechanism of injury, treatment, and prognosis.

Ankle sprains are one of the most common injuries seen in offices and emergency departments. There are 1 million cases reported annually in the US. Every day, 1 person out of 10,000 sprains an ankle. Most sprains result from athletic injuries, accounting for 45% of all athletic injuries.

Diagnosis

History: Individuals with a first-degree sprain or strain may not experience any symptoms until a day or so after injury. Those with a second- or third-degree strain or sprain will describe an injury with a twisting of the ankle and often an audible "pop." Pain and swelling immediately after the injury are more common after a second- and third-degree injury.

The swelling may begin as egg-shaped over the lateral malleolus, but the entire ankle region soon becomes involved. Discoloration may be dramatic. Individuals are most often unable to tolerate any weight bearing on the ankle. Pain over the lower leg, just above the ankle, is more common with a syndesmosis injury. Questions should be directed to history of previous injuries, even if no treatment was sought, as a previous injury could make the ankle unstable and more susceptible to injury.

Physical exam: Local or diffuse swelling and bruising (ecchymosis) is noted. Pain may be localized to the ligaments involved or, more generally, over the lateral, medial, or anterior portion of the ankle. Manual stress of the ligaments may reveal looseness (laxity) of the ankle joint and increased pain. Stress testing of the other ankle is done for comparison (a ruptured ankle ligament will cause the injured ankle to be looser, or more lax, than the uninjured ankle).

Tests: Routine x-rays are done whenever swelling and tenderness are present to rule out damage to the bones, as avulsion fractures are not uncommon. Special x-rays called stress views will allow evaluation of ligament stability. These views involve taking the x-ray while the anesthetized ankle is manually stressed. Stress views of the uninjured ankle are taken for comparison. The spaces between the talus and fibula (or tibia) are measured and compared between the two ankles, with an increased space representing instability. Also, the angle of "tilt" between the top surface of the talus and the bottom surfaces of the tibia and fibula (talar tilt) is measured in the two ankles and compared, with an increase in talar tilt representing instability. A CT scan may be ordered if avulsion fractures or talar dome fractures are suspected. Arthrography to detect ligament and joint capsule tears is useful only in the first 5-7 days after injury, as blood clotting will seal these defects. MRIs are useful for planning surgical reconstruction of ligaments.

Treatment

The emergency treatment of all ankle sprains and strains is rest, ice, compression, and elevation (R.I.C.E.), as well as nonweightbearing with crutches. Early mobilization of the ankle is essential to avoid stiffness. Protective immobilization with a walking cast boot, ankle brace, or cast is usually sufficient treatment for first-degree sprains and first- and second-degree strains. Sometimes, physical therapy modalities to reduce swelling and pain (hydrotherapy, ultrasound) are employed to accelerate recovery.

Conservative treatment with immobilization is sufficient for all deltoid sprains, unless an avulsion fracture of the medial malleolus is present.

In this instance, the fracture is set into the appropriate position surgically and fixated in place with a screw (open reduction with internal fixation). Usually, it is not necessary to repair the deltoid ligament itself; repositioned after fixation of the fracture, it will heal itself. Diastasis of the syndesmosis is surgically repaired by suturing of the ligament (modified Bunnell technique) combined with insertion of a transfixion screw through the tibia and fibula to reposition them together (open reduction with internal fixation). Third-degree strains are treated surgically by sewing (suturing) torn tendon ends together (modified Bunnell technique).

All third-degree and severe second-degree lateral ankle sprains are treated with surgical repair of the torn ligaments (Broström procedure). In severe injuries that are not sufficiently treated, and in which chronic instability develops, special reconstructive procedures (lateral ankle reconstruction) are used. Most of these use tendon or fascia grafts to reconstruct the missing or scarified ligament. These procedures include the Chrisman-Snook procedure, Lee-Evans procedure, and the Watson-Jones procedure.

All of the surgical procedures usually require postoperative casting and nonweightbearing for 6 weeks, followed by intensive physical therapy to reduce pain and swelling and to regain motion and strength. Anti-inflammatory medications are often prescribed to control pain and swelling, training to regain balance (proprioception) is the key to full recovery and is unfortunately sometimes overlooked.

Prognosis

Complete recovery from first-degree sprains and all levels of strains can be expected, even without appropriate treatment. With second- and third-degree sprains, even with appropriate treatment, some individuals will have some subsequent weakness and instability of the ankle (particularly on the lateral side). These individuals may be prone to recurrent injury, and may require an ankle brace for recreational activities and possibly even for normal walking.

Individuals with second- and third-degree sprains treated surgically with primary repair (Broström procedure) will generally have a better functional ankle than those treated nonsurgically with casts or braces. Individuals with chronic injuries treated with lateral ankle stabilization procedures (Crisman-Snook procedure or Watson-Jones procedure) will have a very stable ankle, but may have some residual stiffness in the ankle. This does not usually cause any disability or the need for bracing.

Specialists

- Orthopedic Surgeon
- Physiatrist
- Podiatrist

Complementary and Alternative Therapies

Content is intended for awareness only. Treatments may or may not be effective. Scientific evidence may be lacking and some substances have potentially toxic effects. Dr. Presley Reed and the editors do not endorse the use of these therapies in the absence of consultation with a licensed medical professional.

Acupuncture -	May promote drainage and stimulate healing.
Acupressure -	Said to aid in drainage and stimulate healing.
Chiropractic therapy -	Gentle manipulation and mobilization may help to move the joint back into place.
Arnica -	Used externally, may relieve pain and swelling.
Hydrotherapy -	Ice whirlpool may stimulate injured cells and promote healing. Contrast baths may be used to clear congestion and stimulate healing.
Therapeutic massage -	Performed only after healing has taken place. Massage may increase circulation and prevent or release soft tissues from adhering to bones, tendons, or ligaments.

Differential Diagnosis

Fractures about the ankle may present with similar findings. Pain in the ankle may also come from subluxation of the peroneal tendons or inflammation of the posterior tibial nerve. Gout or infection of the ankle joint should be ruled out.

Rehabilitation

Physical therapy may be necessary for recovery from ankle sprains and strains. Hot packs and ultrasound decrease pain and stiffness prior to therapy sessions. Additionally, physical therapists may use cross-friction massage to injured tendons and ligaments to further promote healing at these areas.

Regaining flexibility is crucial to rehabilitation. Physical therapists may passively stretch the injured ankle and perform joint mobilizations to further increase range of motion. Individuals learn to perform stretches at home such as placing a towel under the ball of the foot and pulling to stretch the Achilles tendon. Stretches are held for thirty seconds, with three to five repetitions being performed. Active flexibility exercises such as making circular motions with the foot or writing the alphabet with the toes also stretch the injured ankle.

Strengthening exercises decrease the risk of recurrent sprains and strains. Therapists may manually resist the foot as an individual plantar-flexes, dorsiflexes, inverts and everts the foot. Elastic tubing with progressively increasing resistances can be used to strengthen the ankle in these motions as well. Standing heel and toe raises can be performed while standing on both feet, or while standing on the injured foot.

Physical therapists focus on normalizing gait after ankle sprains and strains. Individuals with surgical repair of a complete rupture of one or more ligaments or tendons in the ankle are immobilized. Individuals with minor sprains and strains can weight bear partial weight through the injured foot with the use of crutches or a cane. Individuals progress from walking with crutches to walking without assistance. Individuals may walk on a treadmill to facilitate a more fluid gait pattern.

Balance exercises are needed to help retrain the many nerve endings in the ankle that detect joint position. Individuals can start with single leg standing on the injured foot. This can be progressed to walking on a gymnastic mat without wearing shoes and standing on the injured leg while throwing and catching a ball. Individuals can also perform dynamic balance exercises such as running laterally or skipping.

Work Restrictions / Accommodations

Restrictions would include limited weight bearing depending on the severity of the injury. Walking, climbing, and squatting should be limited early in the treatment of ankle sprains.

Use of canes, crutches, or walkers may be necessary. Wearing a cast, boot, or brace is common. Work release time for physical therapy will be necessary. The use of the foot in driving (for gas pedal or clutch, depending on which foot is involved) is prohibited until the individual has returned to full weight bearing in regular shoes.

Comorbid Conditions

Coexisting conditions that may impact recovery and lengthen disability include strain or sprain of the lower leg muscles. Rheumatoid arthritis can cause Achilles bursitis.

Complications

Dislocations, fracture, and soft tissue swelling would complicate the injury. Swelling slows recovery from the injury. Tendon and nerve damage may complicate the injury and treatment. The most common complication after treatment is recurrent instability. Loose bodies may develop from articular cartilage damage at the time of the injury and, if they enlarge, may require surgical removal. Damage to the interosseous talocalcaneal ligament may occur with an ankle sprain and result in chronic subtalar joint pain (sinus tarsi syndrome). Damage to the top of the talus (talar dome) can result in a loosening of the bone and cartilage there (osteochondritis dissecans).

Factors Influencing Duration

Severity of the sprain, amount of swelling, and complications associated with the injury influence the disability period. The work activities involved also influence the length of disability.

Length of Disability

Disability may not occur with first or second-degree sprains or strains.

First or second-degree (mild to moderate) sprain or strain.

Job Classification	Minimum	Optimum	Maximum
Sedentary work	0	3	7
Light work	1	3	7
Medium work	3	7	14
Heavy work	7	14	28
Very Heavy work	7	14	28

Third-degree (severe) sprain or strain (other than Achilles tendon rupture).

Job Classification	Minimum	Optimum	Maximum
Sedentary work	1	3	7
Light work	1	7	28
Medium work	7	14	42
Heavy work	14	21	70
Very Heavy work	14	21	70

Rupture of Achilles tendon.

Job Classification	Minimum	Optimum	Maximum
Sedentary work	1	3	7
Light work	7	14	28
Medium work	28	56	84
Heavy work	42	84	112
Very Heavy work	42	84	112

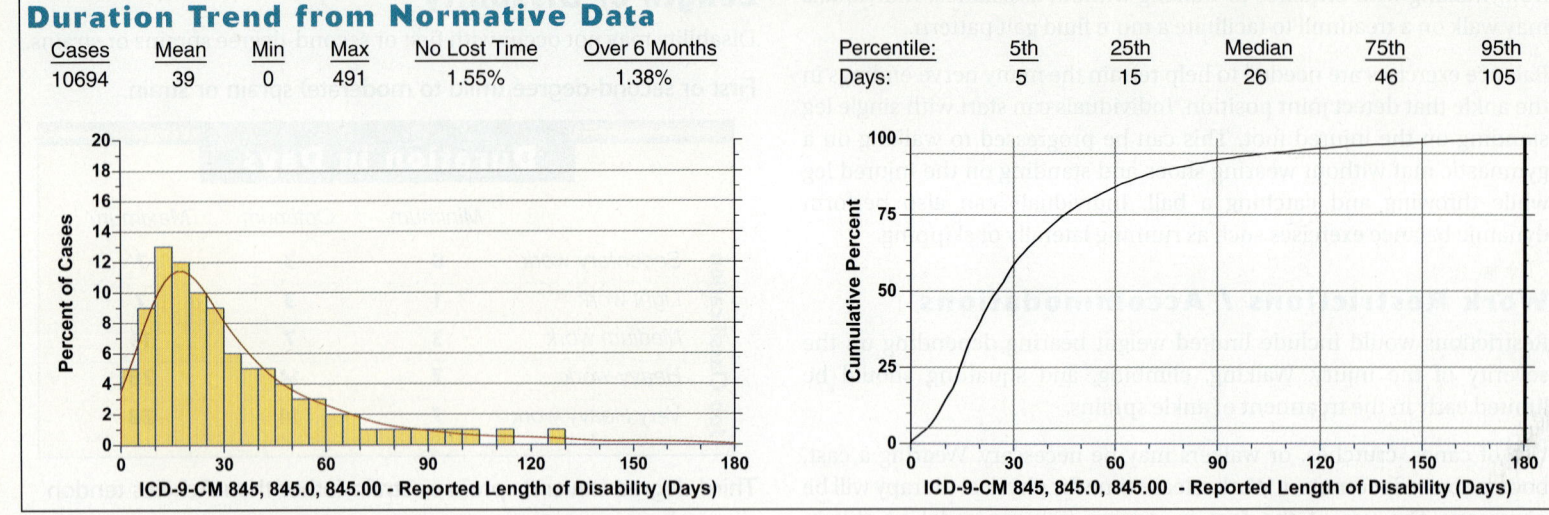

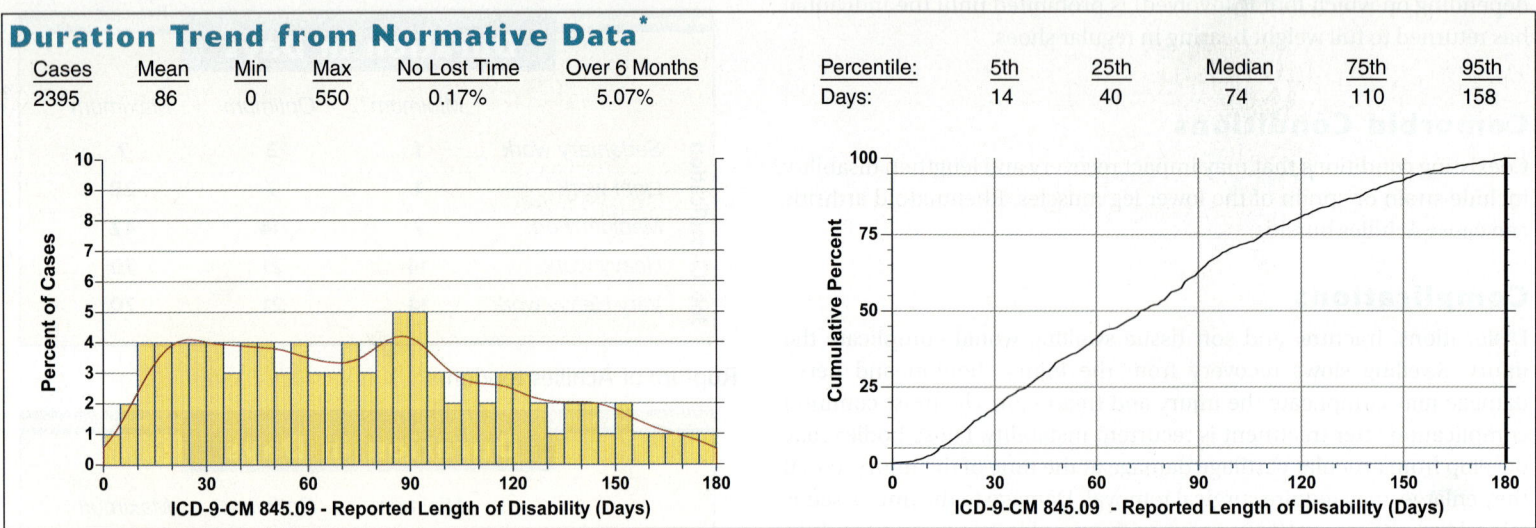

* Differences may exist between the expected duration tables and the normative graphs. Duration tables provide expected recovery periods based on the type of work performed by the individual. The normative graphs reflect the actual observed experience of many individuals across the spectrum of physical conditions, in a variety of industries, and with varying levels of case management.

Failure to Recover

If an individual fails to recover within the maximum duration expectancy period, the reader may wish to reference the following questions to assist in better understanding the specifics of an individual's medical case.

Regarding diagnosis:

- Was diagnosis of ankle sprain/strain confirmed?
- Does pain persist even after a course of treatment?
- Were follow-up x-rays done to rule out fractures missed earlier?
- Does individual have excessive residual swelling?
- Was MRI performed to evaluate soft tissues?
- Did the individual experience any complications?
- Has the individual experienced recurrent instability or chronic subtalar joint pain?
- Does the individual have an underlying condition that may impact recovery?

Regarding treatment:

- Has the individual been compliant with treatments, including rest, ice, compression and elevation (R.I.C.E.), nonweightbearing with crutches and protective immobilization?
- Are elevation, hydrotherapy, and external compression warranted at this time?
- Did individual receive physical therapy?
- Would individual benefit from physical therapy at this point?
- Was avulsion fracture present? Did it require open reduction with internal fixation?
- Was surgical repair successful?
- Were complications a result of the repair procedure?
- Was reconstruction (Chrisman-Snook, Lee-Evans, Watson-Jones) required?
- Did individual receive adequate balance training?

Regarding prognosis:

- To what degree does instability impact function?
- Are appropriate precautions, such as an ankle brace, used to enhance function and prevent reinjury?
- Would individual benefit from a lateral ankle stabilization procedure?
- Although the stiffness resulting from these procedures does not usually cause disability or the need for bracing, does ankle stiffness impact the individual's functional ability? Impact occupational requirements?
- Should consideration be given to more intensive therapy such as aggressive elevation, hydrotherapy treatments, and external compression?
- Has individual been involved in a comprehensive rehabilitation program?

References

Canale, S. Terry. "Ankle Injuries." Campbell's Operative Orthopedics, 9th ed, vol. 2. Canale, S. Terry, ed. St. Louis: Mosby, 1998. 1079-1112.

Lee, M.S., and M.H. Hofbauer. "Evaluation and Management of Lateral Ankle Injuries." Clinics in Podiatric Medicine and Surgery 16 4 (1999): 659-678.

Sprains and Strains, Back
Other names / synonyms: Back Sprain, Back Strain, Lumbago, Lumbar Sprain, Sacral Sprain, Thoracic Sprain
846, 846.0, 846.1, 846.9, 847.1, 847.2, 847.9

Definition

A back sprain involves injury of one or more non-muscular structures (ligament, disc, facet, capsule, etc.) of the back, while a strain involves musculotendinous injury of the back.

Back sprains usually result from over-stretching a ligament, most often due to twisting or heavy lifting or sustained postural loading. Like sprains elsewhere in the body, back sprains are graded from mild to severe, depending upon the degree of damage to the ligament or muscle. In a mild sprain (first-degree), only a few fibers are torn. Moderate sprains (second-degree) result in more fibers being torn and, consequently, some instability about the joint. Acute sprains of this type are usually associated with pain and muscle spasm. In a severe sprain (third-degree), the ligaments are completely disrupted, and joint instability may be severe. Most back sprains are first- or second-degree.

Back strains are most often due to over-stretching or overusing a muscle, and they are usually not as severe as a back sprain. In fact, strains involving the back may not even be felt until the following day. Back strains are most often seen in persons whose occupation or leisure activities involve excessive lifting or torso rotation. Many strains are the result of inadequate warm-up, excessive training, or inadequate healing of a previous muscular injury. Muscular strains are frequent complaints of military personnel who initiate intense training programs immediately prior to semi-annual physical fitness testing.

Back strains and sprains are best avoided by receiving instruction on how to properly lift and move heavy items, realizing one's limitations, and taking the time to stop and ask another person for help when appropriate. Whether an individual has a ligamentous back sprain or a muscular back strain can be differentiated with passive and resisted test movements respectively.

Back pain, usually from strains and sprains, is the second most common complaint seen by physicians. Up to 80% of the population will have back pain at some point in their lives, with the majority suffering from relatively minor sprains and strains. At any given time, 31 million Americans suffer from back pain, and 7 million receive treatment yearly.

Diagnosis

History: Symptoms of an acute sprain or strain include pain and tenderness. If bleeding has occurred, swelling beneath the skin may be present. As a result of the injury and accompanying pain, the individual's movement may be limited, even to the point of requiring temporary immobilization. The pain may be persistent or felt only when the individual moves in a certain way or engages in a specific activity. Strains usually involve exertion of a muscle either for movement or sustained positioning, sprains usually result from the forces induced by movement or positioning on the non-muscular structures of a joint.

Physical exam: The exam may reveal tenderness to the touch or upon pressure, localized swelling, and areas of discoloration along the back and gluteal area. Range of motion will be limited due to pain and muscle spasm, and the involved muscles may be tense. Because back pain can be difficult to diagnose if no history of recent injury or trauma is reported, the physician may try to identify the particular movements or positions that aggravate the pain and determine whether the pain is relieved by lying down.

Tests: Most cases of back strains and sprains do not require any diagnostic tests. Occasionally x-rays or MRI may be necessary to rule out other potential causes of back pain. For example, x-rays of the spine may be taken to rule out fracture.

Treatment

Sprains and strains are treated in the same manner. Activity level should be adjusted according to what the individual can tolerate. Overall, the individual should avoid activities only if they cause the pain to become and stay worse (such as lifting, bending, or twisting). Their activity level should be increased gradually. Bedrest of more than two days is not recommended, as it has been shown to delay recovery. Pain and swelling may be relieved through the application of ice during the first 48-72 hours following injury, and heat, massage, or therapeutic ultrasound thereafter. Nonsteroidal anti-inflammatory drugs are recommended for relief of pain and inflammation. If pain is severe, a mild narcotic may be prescribed for an appropriate short period. In addition, "muscle relaxants" may be prescribed for a short period. Severe sprains and strains are treated with physical therapy, trigger point injections, short-term immobilization with a brace (corset), and use of transcutaneous electrical nerve stimulation (TENS). Exercise tolerance should be explored immediately and instituted within two weeks for the majority of individuals. Passive therapies should be eliminated or restricted severely after one month.

Prognosis

Most first- and second-degree sprains and strains heal on their own without significant functional impairment. There may be an increased potential for injury recurrence, particularly in individuals with more severe injuries or in those who do not allow previous injuries to heal completely.

More severe sprains and strains may heal with excessive scar tissue (fibrosis) and with possible instability, which may result in chronic back pain. However, even most of these individuals will eventually recover, and only 2-4% will have residual chronic back pain.

Differential Diagnosis

Differential diagnoses include back pain due to numerous other causes, especially disc herniation or vertebral compression fracture, as well as diseased internal organs, bone disease, tumor, muscle disease, or psychological stress.

Specialists

- Chiropractor
- Orthopedic Surgeon
- Physiatrist
- Physical Therapist
- Primary Care Provider

Rehabilitation

Therapy may be necessary for individuals who strain the muscles of the back. The first objective of therapy is reduction of pain and muscle spasm. Hot packs and ultrasound are usually applied prior to exercise to relax the strained muscles. Therapists may perform massage to further decrease muscle spasm. More persistent cases of muscle spasm may require mechanical lumbar traction to increase separation of the intervertebral spaces and indirectly promote pain reduction. Ice packs applied after exercise decreases pain and inflammation.

Increasing range of motion in areas that have restrictions is the second objective of rehabilitation. Stretching exercises also maintain the reduction of spasm. Individuals perform lower trunk rotation stretches by lying supine and moving their bent knees from one side to the other. Individuals increase forward bending by lying supine and bringing the knees to the chest. Individuals increase back extension by lying prone and pressing up onto their elbows while allowing their hips to remain on the mat. Individuals stretch the hamstring muscles by sitting, placing one foot on a low stool, and leaning forward. McKenzie hyperextension back exercises are often useful.

Strengthening the back and abdominal muscles prevents future injury. Individuals learn strengthening exercises for the abdominal muscles such as sit-ups. Pelvic tilts also strengthen the lower abdominal muscles. In this exercise, an individual lies supine and flattens the low back against the exercise mat. Individuals learn strengthening exercises for the muscles of the back such as prone extension exercises. In these exercises, individuals lift the upper body or both the upper body and legs from the exercise mat. Treadmill walking is recommended to increase endurance and strength.

Therapy also addresses correct posture and proper body mechanics. Individuals learn strategies for reaching and lifting that protect the back and prevent re-injury.

Work Restrictions / Accommodations

Individuals with severe sprains and/or strains whose jobs require extensive lifting of bending may require temporary reassignment to more sedentary duties.

Complementary and Alternative Therapies

Content is intended for awareness only. Treatments may or may not be effective. Scientific evidence may be lacking and some substances have potentially toxic effects. Dr. Presley Reed and the editors do not endorse the use of these therapies in the absence of consultation with a licensed medical professional.

Acupuncture - May relieve pain.

Acupressure - May relieve pain.

Chiropractic treatment - Manipulation may relieve tension in painful muscles.

Therapeutic massage - Should not be done before a standard medical diagnosis has been made. Then it may be useful in reducing tension in painful muscles, if present. However, typically, back muscles require strengthening, not loosening.

Comorbid Conditions

Comorbid conditions include obesity, alcoholism, hypochondriasis, smoking, and depression.

Complications

Complications of severe injuries include fractures, dislocations, and avulsion injuries (tearing away of a part or structure). An avulsion fracture involves the tearing away of a piece of bone with a ligament at the point of attachment and can result in spinal instability or nerve root or spinal cord injury. Bleeding into a muscle can result in severe pain.

Factors Influencing Duration

Factors include the severity and extent of the injury, the severity of the pain associated with the injury, the method of treatment, the individual's response to treatment and adherence to recommendations, and the individual's job requirements or leisure activities.

Length of Disability

Duration depends on severity.

Cervical spine.

Duration in Days

Job Classification	Minimum	Optimum	Maximum
Sedentary work	1	1	7
Light work	1	3	7
Medium work	3	7	14
Heavy work	3	21	28
Very Heavy work	3	28	42

Lumbar or lumbosacral spine.

Duration in Days

Job Classification	Minimum	Optimum	Maximum
Sedentary work	1	3	7
Light work	1	7	14
Medium work	3	14	28
Heavy work	7	21	42
Very Heavy work	7	28	56

Thoracic spine.

Duration in Days

Job Classification	Minimum	Optimum	Maximum
Sedentary work	1	3	7
Light work	3	7	14
Medium work	7	14	28
Heavy work	7	21	42
Very Heavy work	7	28	56

Duration Trend from Normative Data

Cases	Mean	Min	Max	No Lost Time	Over 6 Months
9734	51	0	491	0.20%	0.79%

Percentile:	5th	25th	Median	75th	95th
Days:	10	18	35	69	143

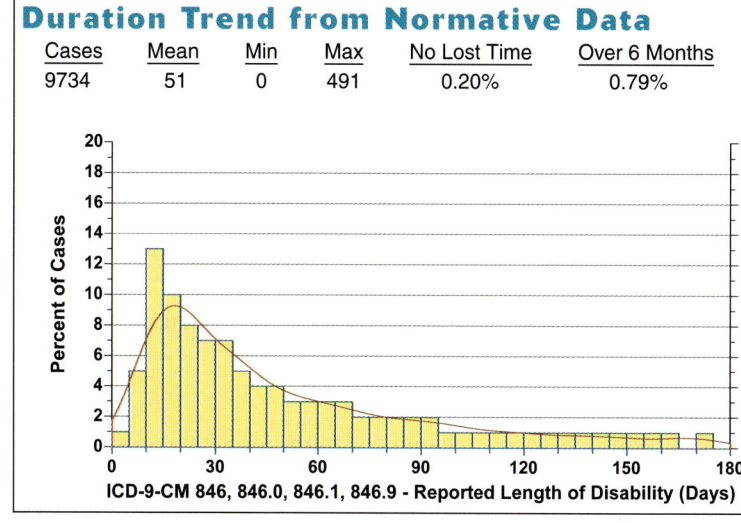
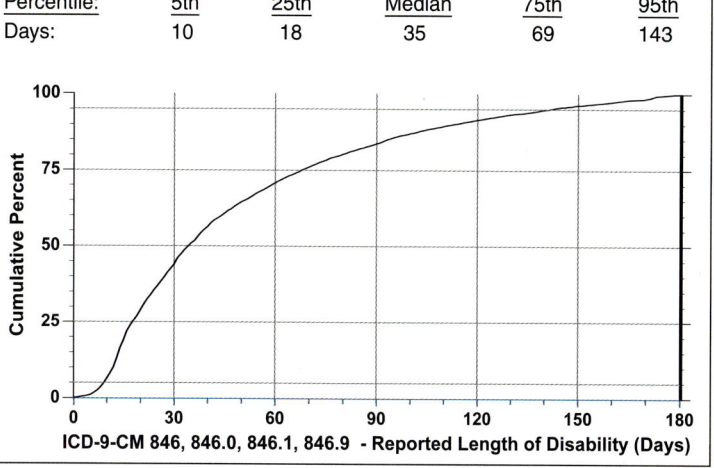

ICD-9-CM 846, 846.0, 846.1, 846.9 - Reported Length of Disability (Days)

Sprains and Strains, Back

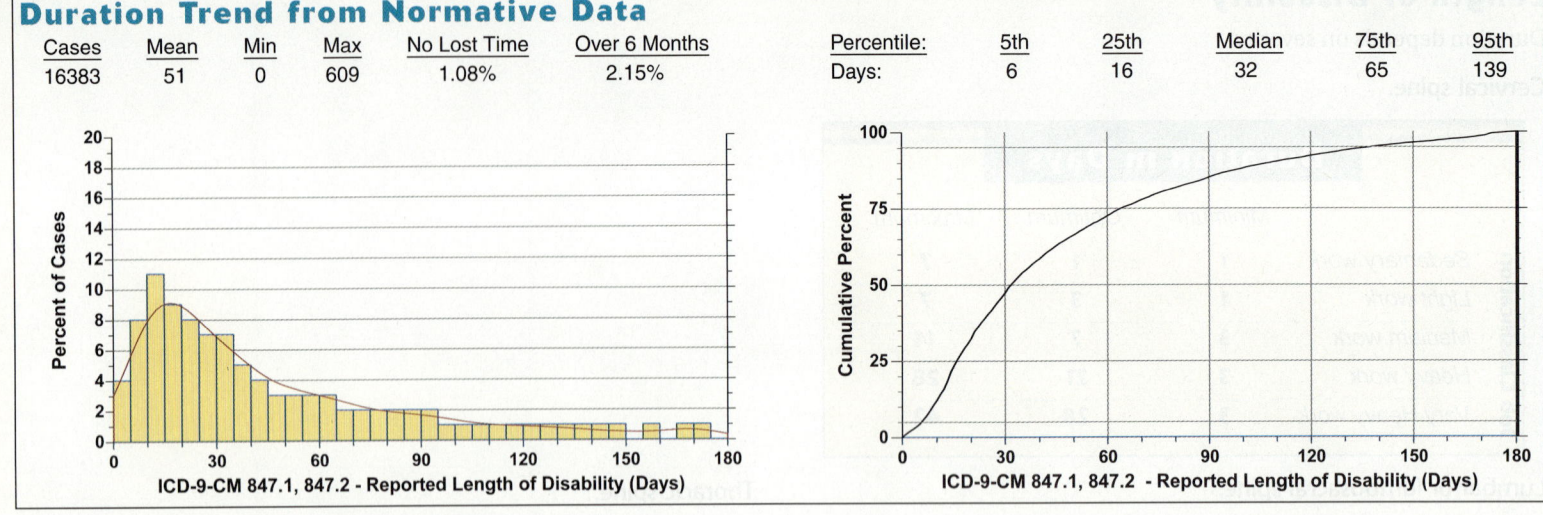

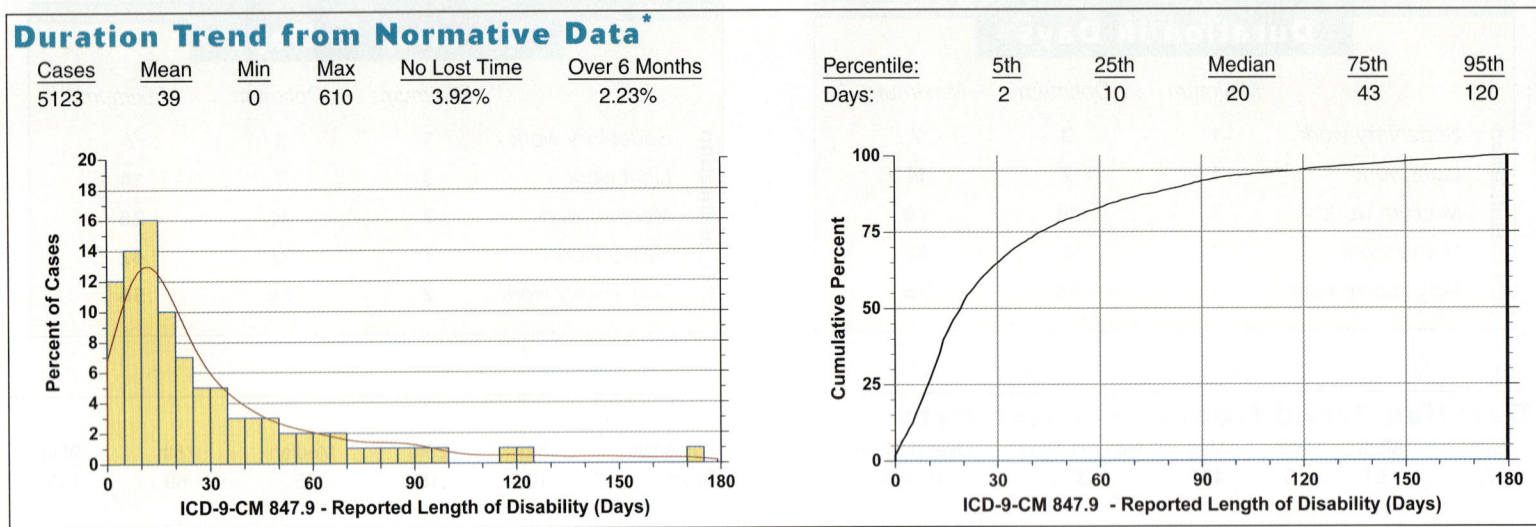

* Differences may exist between the expected duration tables and the normative graphs. Duration tables provide expected recovery periods based on the type of work performed by the individual. The normative graphs reflect the actual observed experience of many individuals across the spectrum of physical conditions, in a variety of industries, and with varying levels of case management.

Failure to Recover

If an individual fails to recover within the maximum duration expectancy period, the reader may wish to reference the following questions to assist in better understanding the specifics of an individual's medical case.

Regarding diagnosis:

- Has diagnosis been confirmed?
- Does individual have continued pain and disability after an adequate course of treatment?
- Have other conditions such as diseased internal organs, bone disease, tumor, muscle disease, or psychological stress, been ruled out?
- Has an MRI been done to rule out disc herniations and fractures?
- Has individual experienced any complications such as fractures, dislocations, avulsion injuries, or bleeding into a muscle?
- Is individual obese?
- Does individual suffer from alcoholism, hypochondriasis, or depression? Is individual a smoker?
- Does individual have an underlying condition that may be impacting recovery?

Regarding treatment:

- Did individual follow recommendations for activity restrictions and limited bed rest?
- Has the individual avoided lifting, bending, or twisting?
- If individual was prescribed bed rest for more than two days, what were the extenuating circumstances?
- Did individual take medications such as nonsteroidal anti-inflammatory drugs or muscle relaxants, as prescribed?
- Did individual ask for more pain relievers or muscle relaxants than injury warranted?
- Was individual able to receive comprehensive rehabilitation?

Regarding prognosis:

- Did individual return to normal activities too soon?
- Was accommodation in the workplace made so that the injury healed completely?
- Has scar tissue or instability resulted in chronic back pain?
- What additional treatment options are available?
- As back pain is one of the most common conditions in which hypochondriasis, somatization, malingering, and seeking of secondary gain is found, has a psychological evaluation been done?
- Would individual benefit from counseling?
- If individual is obese, would weight reduction counseling be appropriate?

References

Campana, Bruce A. "Soft Tissue Spine Injuries and Back Pain." Emergency Medicine, 4th ed, vol. 1. Rosen, Peter, and Roger Barkin, eds. St. Louis: Mosby, 1998. 878-905.

Gunnar, B.J., T.L. Andersson, and A.M. Davis. "A Comparison of Osteopathic Spinal Manipulation with Standard Care for Patients with Low Back Pain." New England Journal of Medicine 341 19 (1999): 1426-1431.

Kisner, Carolyn, and Lynn Allen Colby. "The Spine: Treatment of Acute Problems." Therapeutic Exercise: Foundations and Techniques, 2nd ed. Philadelphia: F.A. Davis Company, 1990. 473-500.

Kisner, Carolyn, and Lynn Allen Colby. "The Spine: Traction Procedures." Therapeutic Exercise: Foundations and Techniques, 2nd ed. Philadelphia: F.A. Davis Company, 1990. 501-518.

Kisner, Carolyn, and Lynn Allen Colby. "The Spine: Posture." Therapeutic Exercise: Foundations and Techniques, 2nd ed. Philadelphia: F.A. Davis Company, 1990. 429-472.

Wood, George W. "Lower Back Pain and Disorders of Intervertebral Disc." Campbell's Operative Orthopedics, 9th ed, vol. 3. Canale, S. Terry, ed. St. Louis: Mosby, 1998. 3014-3092.

Sprains and Strains, Biceps Tendon
840.8

Definition

This is a condition in which the tendon for the biceps muscle is stretched or torn. There are three biceps tendons: two at the shoulder (proximal tendons or the long head and short head of biceps tendons) and one at the elbow (distal biceps tendon). The long head of biceps tendon is the most frequently injured biceps tendon.

Sprains and strains describe minor injuries that are caused by overstretching, overexerting, or long-term overuse of a part of the musculoskeletal system. Sprains and strains occur when the biceps muscle is forced to perform movements that it is not prepared or designed to do. A biceps tendon injury can occur from one stressful incident or gradually from repetitive movements.

The individual may complain of shoulder pain, which can be quite severe. He or she may have pain after a single inciting event or the pain may gradually progress. Edema, muscle spasm, and a reduced ability to move the shoulder are common complaints.

Approximately 3% of shoulder injuries in alpine skiing injuries were due to biceps tendon strains. Individuals with shoulder injuries had a mean age of 35 years, and the male-to-female ratio of these individuals was 3:1.

Diagnosis

History: The individual may complain of shoulder pain, which can be quite severe. He or she may have pain after a single inciting event or the pain may gradually progress. Swelling (edema), muscle spasm, and a reduced ability to move the shoulder are common complaints. A detailed report of how the injury occurred is an important component of the diagnostic process.

Physical exam: Examination with the hands (palpation) may reveal tenderness in the shoulder area and possibly hard knots of muscle indicative of spasm. There may be evidence of edema and bruising. Differential injection tests may also be conducted in which a local anesthetic is injected into specific locations of the shoulder joint. Pain from a biceps tendon injury should be persistent following injection of anesthetic into the space beneath the shoulder blade (subacromial space injection) but relieved by an injection of anesthetic into the joint (intraarticular injection).

Tests: Diagnostic imaging studies are performed primarily to identify any associated injuries because imaging for biceps tendon disorders is nonspecific and difficult. Diagnostic tests may include plain x-rays, arthrography, ultrasound, or MRI.

Treatment

Sprains and strains of the biceps tendons are treated with conservative measures consisting of rest, ice, compression, elevation (R.I.C.E.) and analgesics. An arm sling may be worn to thoroughly rest the arm.

Prognosis

Sprains and strains are minor injuries and a complete recovery can be expected. Most sprains or strains of biceps tendon should resolve between a few days and a few weeks.

Differential Diagnosis

SLAP lesion, partial rupture of biceps tendon, bone fracture, bursitis, bicipital tendonitis, muscle injury, tendinosis, shoulder injuries (e.g., rotator cuff tear), and impingement syndrome can have signs and symptoms that mimic strains and sprains of the biceps tendon.

Specialists

- Orthopedic Surgeon
- Physiatrist
- Physical Therapist

Rehabilitation

The basic goal in the rehabilitation of a sprain and strain of the biceps tendon is to control postoperative pain and swelling followed by regaining full motion, flexibility, strength, and endurance of the muscle/joint structures involved. The final result is aimed at establishing a home exercise program and returning the individual to full function for work and recreational activities with minimal risk of reinjury.

Therapy may begin with the application of cold using ice on the injured area. Heat treatments are helpful to reduce inflammation and pain and once appropriate, are beneficial to mildly stretch the affected muscles. Forms of heat treatment include ultrasound and electrical stimulation.

Once movement is allowed, passive motion of the elbow is permitted only as tolerated by the individual. Passive range-of-motion exercises begin with the therapist bending and straightening the elbow (flexion and extension). Other important movements of the elbow are supination and pronation. Supination is a movement that occurs when the elbow is bent at 90 degrees beginning with the palm of the hand facing down. The hand is then rotated to a position with the palm facing upward. Pronation is the opposite movement of supination and occurs when the palm is rotated back to a position of facing down. This progresses to active assist range of motion exercises.

As the individual improves with increased motion of the elbow joint, the next step of progression is active range of motion. This can be initiated in a warm whirlpool or in conjunction with another form of heat treatment and continued until all movement is restored.

The instruction of isometric strengthening exercises begins early in the phase of elbow strengthening. Isometric exercise demands that the muscles around the elbow joint contract yet no movement takes place at the joint. An example of an isometric exercise for the elbow joint is having the individual push a hand upward against the other hand or other immovable object. Supination and pronation are also strengthened isometrically in this manner.

Once both range of motion and isometric exercises are tolerated, the individual progresses to isotonic strengthening involving movement at and around the elbow joint. An example of this type of rehabilitation exercise is strengthening with weights using weight equipment/machines and elastic bands.

In most cases of a mild strain or sprain of the biceps tendon, a return to the preinjury level of function should be attained within a few weeks following initiation of the exercise program. Modifications may need to be made by the physical therapist for those with arthritis or other elbow/shoulder joint irritations.

Work Restrictions / Accommodations

Depending on work duties, the individual may need to be temporarily reassigned. Activities of the affected arm would be limited if an arm sling is worn. The individual with a sprain or strain of the biceps tendon may be temporarily unable to lift and carry heavy objects, operate equipment, or perform other tasks that require lifting, pushing, or pulling against resistance using the injured arm. If the dominant arm is affected, the individual may be unable to write legibly or type well. Individuals whose dominant arm or hand is affected may require a temporary reassignment of duties.

Comorbid Conditions

Impingement syndrome, rotator cuff injuries, tendon degeneration, tendinitis, tendinosis, and osteoarthritis may influence the length of disability. Other injuries sustained during a traumatic event can lengthen disability.

Complications

Complications are rare but include nerve compression or injury, blood vessel injury, or biceps tendon rupture.

Factors Influencing Duration

The severity of the injury, the individual's compliance with the treatment program, arm use restrictions, and job demands may affect the length of disability.

Length of Disability

First and second-degree (mild to moderate).

Duration in Days

Job Classification	Minimum	Optimum	Maximum
Sedentary work	0	3	7
Light work	1	3	7
Medium work	3	7	14
Heavy work	7	10	21
Very Heavy work	7	21	28

Failure to Recover

If an individual fails to recover within the maximum duration expectancy period, the reader may wish to reference the following questions to assist in better understanding the specifics of an individual's medical case.

Regarding diagnosis:

- Does individual have numbness or tingling in the arm?
- Is the arm cold and discolored?
- Does individual complain of swelling (edema), muscle spasm, and a reduced ability to move the shoulder?
- Have plain x-rays, arthrography, ultrasound, or MRI, been performed?
- Did injection of anesthetic into the subacromial space provide pain relief?
- Have conditions such as SLAP lesion, partial rupture of biceps tendon, bone fracture, bursitis, bicipital tendinitis, muscle injury, tendinosis, shoulder injuries (e.g., rotator cuff tear), or impingement syndrome been ruled out?

Regarding treatment:

- Was individual treated with ice immediately following injury?
- Is individual resting the arm? Is arm in a sling?
- Is individual's pain adequately controlled?
- Was individual treated with heat, ultrasound, or electrostimulation prior to, or in conjunction with, physical therapy?
- Was individual given a home exercise program?

Regarding prognosis:

- If individual is not recovering in a timely manner, has an alternate diagnosis, or has the presence of additional injuries such as, nerve compression or injury, blood vessel injury, or biceps tendon rupture, been considered?
- Have conditions such as impingement syndrome, rotator cuff injuries, tendon degeneration, tendinitis, tendinosis, or osteoarthritis affected recovery?
- Is individual compliant with therapy program and home exercise program?

References

Kessler, R.M. Management of Common Musculoskeletal Disorders: Physical Therapy Principles and Methods. Philadelphia: J.B. Lippincott Company, 1990.

Kisner, C., and L. Colby. Theraeputic Exercise Foundations and Techniques. Philadelphia: F.A. Davis Company, 1990.

Kocher, M.S., and J.A. Feagin. "Shoulder Injuries During Alpine Skiing." American Journal of Sports Medicine 24 5 (1996): 665-669.

Malone, Terry R., Thomas McPoil, and Arthur J. Nitz. Orthopedic and Sports Physical Therapy. St. Louis: Mosby, 1997.

Wedro, Benjamin. "Sprains and Strains." AAEM Emergency Medical and Family Health Guide Plantz, Scott, ed. St. Petersburg: eMedicine.com, Inc, 2000. 27 Dec 2000 <http://emedicine.com/aaem/topic410.htm>.

Yamaguchi, Ken, and Randip Bindra. "Disorders of the Biceps Tendon." Disorders of the Shoulder: Diagnosis and Management. Iannotti, Joseph, and Gerald Williams, eds. Philadelphia: Lippincott, Williams & Wilkins, 1999. 159-190.

Sprains and Strains, Cervical Spine (Neck)
Other names / synonyms: Acceleration Injury, Hyperextension, Soft Tissue Cervical Hyperextension Injury, Whiplash
847, 847.0

Definition

A cervical sprain (whiplash) occurs when muscles around the neck stretch or tear (strain). A strain occurs when the ligaments stretch or tear.

These injuries may often occur during a motor vehicle accident where the individual's car is hit from behind. The sudden acceleration resulting from the collision causes the individual's body to move forward with the head rapidly whipping backward and then forward. This results in injury to many different tissues and structures of the neck including bones, muscles, blood vessels, ligaments, nerves, esophagus, and intervertebral discs. Concussion may also occur. Injuries to the brain stem, bruising of the brain (subdural hematomas), and bleeding (hemorrhage) on the surface of the brain may occur. These multiple injuries give rise to a myriad of symptoms. The extent of injury correlates with the forces of the injury. Extensive complaints with a minimal impact injury, particularly in the context of litigation, suggest symptom magnification behavior overlap.

Other causes of whiplash include a contact sports injury or a blow to the head from a falling object.

Over 1 million such injuries are reported annually in the US. Twenty percent of individuals involved in rear-end collisions report neck pain. Incidence of this injury is significantly higher in women and is a major cause of work absenteeism of young women.

Diagnosis

History: Individual has history of trauma or accident, most commonly a motor vehicle accident. The individual may have had a contact sports injury or blow to the head from a falling object. In mild sprains, pain is mostly in the muscle. This intensifies over several hours and is followed with stiffness and spasm. Individuals may hold their necks rigid or their head tilted to one side because of spasm or to relieve discomfort. Headache, pain in the upper chest and back, and changes in sensation are common in moderate to severe sprains.

Other common symptoms may include headache, dizziness (vertigo), nausea, blurred or double vision, ringing in ears (tinnitus), fatigue, restlessness, loss of libido, insomnia, pain in the jaw or temporomandibular joint (TMJ), and difficulty swallowing (dysphagia). More severe sprains have similar symptoms but resting flat does not relieve the pain. In the most severe cases, symptoms of pain and spasm are intense and signs of instability are present. The individual may be unable to support his or her head.

Physical exam: In any individual with suspected neck sprain, care must be taken during the examination not to increase any instability. Lateral cervical spine x-rays should be taken to rule out a fracture before any neck motion is tested. A neurological assessment of the cervical spine rules out nerve damage. Using the hands to feel areas of the neck region (palpation) helps define the severity of the sprain. Range of motion and stability are tested.

Tests: Cervical spine x-rays are taken to rule out more serious injury but sprains do not show on x-ray. CT and MRI may be warranted to evaluate soft tissue damage. Tests may need to be repeated in 6 months if symptoms do not resolved.

Treatment

Early introduction of movement has been shown to be superior to immobilization. Passive therapies should be limited to those who really require it, and then progress to activity as soon as possible. Conservative treatment may include a soft support collar (may delay recovery) worn for several days. Rigid collars are only used for treatment of fractures occurring at the time of the sprain. Medication to control pain is usually prescribed and may include analgesics and nonsteroidal anti-inflammatory drugs (NSAIDs).

Physical therapy modalities for pain relief are appropriate but most often do not include traction. However, traction may be used for radiculopathy. Early mobilization is valuable in most situations. Surgery is indicated only for treatment of related fractures, instability, or disc herniation. Trigger point injections of anesthetics or steroids may be performed. Pain-induced depression may be treated with antidepressants and psychotherapy. In a small percentage (less than 10%) of individuals, surgery (facet rhizotomy) is necessary as a last resort. This is done to eliminate the chronic pain of radiculopathy. Rhizotomy deadens nerve fibers involved in the relay of pain signals from the joints in the spine to the brain.

Prognosis

Healing of the soft tissue is expected in a few weeks. Most individuals can return to work immediately if not within 6 weeks. Symptoms are still present in 20-70% of the individuals 6 months after injury, however, prognosis is good for these individuals and symptoms eventually resolve.

One-third of individuals report persistent neck pain at 10 years postinjury. Other prolonged symptoms include headache, neck ache, neck stiffness, fatigue, and anxiety (late whiplash syndrome).

Women are more prone to suffer from persistent neck pain than men. Older individuals tend to have more persistent symptoms than younger individuals. Individuals who experienced severe initial neck pain, upper back pain, multiple symptoms, reduced range of motion, neurological deficit, and/or headaches at the back of the head (occipital region) have a poorer prognosis than individuals without these symptoms.

Differential Diagnosis

Chronic symptoms caused by a cervical sprain are similar to degenerative disc or spondylosis. Acute torticollis (wry neck) is an acute unilateral neck pain without a history of injury and may mimic cervical sprains and strains.

Specialists

- Chiropractor
- Exercise Physiologist
- Neurologist
- Orthopedic Surgeon
- Physiatrist

Rehabilitation

Individuals with cervical muscle strain may require therapy. The first objective of therapy is return of pain free range of motion and reduction of muscle spasm, if present. Prior to the employment of passive therapy, activity strategies should be explored that may obviate or reduce the need for passive approaches. Hot packs and ultrasound provide deep heating of the neck musculature. Therapists massage the neck to further reduce muscle spasm. Mechanical or manual traction of the cervical spine may be warranted to decrease persistent muscle spasm. These techniques increase space between the vertebral bodies to provide indirect relief.

The first/primary objective of therapy is to restore range of motion at the neck. Physical therapists may passively stretch the neck into rotation, side bending, flexion, and extension. Individuals learn to actively move the neck in each of these directions to further increase motion. Individuals can increase the stretch of the neck by applying manual overpressure as the neck is moved in each of these directions.

Strengthening exercises prevent reinjury to the neck. Individuals learn gentle isometric exercises. In these, one hand is used for light resistance while the neck is moved into each available direction. Chin tucks also strengthen the neck musculature. This exercise lengthens the spine by bringing the head straight back so that the chin is tucked into the neck. Postural muscles also may require strengthening after a prolonged period of neck immobilization. Backward shoulder rolls and scapular retraction where the shoulder blades are pinched together are examples of postural exercises.

Work Restrictions / Accommodations

Any activity that requires flexion or extension of the neck such as overhead work, lifting, or carrying a heavy object should be restricted. Working at a desk or drafting table may need to be evaluated. Workstation ergonomics need to be addressed. An adjustable chair and proper height of the computer monitor allow for optimal posture and neck positioning. Individuals who spend a great deal of time on the telephone would benefit from a headset.

A work site evaluation is valuable in assessing risk factors for aggravating symptoms during recovery that can be slow. Use of soft support collar may restrict dexterity. Safety and policy drug issues must be evaluated if medication is needed during work time.

Complementary and Alternative Therapies

Content is intended for awareness only. Treatments may or may not be effective. Scientific evidence may be lacking and some substances have potentially toxic effects. Dr. Presley Reed and the editors do not endorse the use of these therapies in the absence of consultation with a licensed medical professional.

Acupuncture -	May relieve pain.
Acupressure -	May relieve pain.
Chiropractic treatment -	May provide symptomatic and functional relief.
Therapeutic massage -	May be useful in reducing tension in painful muscles.

Comorbid Conditions

Fractures, instability, nerve stretch or traction injuries, or disc disruption can complicate treatment. Headaches and referred pain are part of the expected ongoing problems of a cervical sprain but may complicate or prolong treatment. Psychosocial issues may prolong duration.

Complications

Fractures, instability, nerve stretch or traction injuries, or disc disruption can complicate treatment. Headaches and referred pain are part of the expected ongoing problems of a cervical sprain but may complicate or prolong treatment. Complications of cervical strains and sprains include instability, nerve damage, headache, and referred pain.

Factors Influencing Duration

The amount of injury to the supporting structures in the cervical spine and any complications may influence the disability period. Recovery from the sprain and all the problems produced by the injury such as headaches may take several months. Intermittent problems or episodes of pain may occur during recovery.

Length of Disability

Duration depends on severity.

Duration in Days

Job Classification	Minimum	Optimum	Maximum
Sedentary work	1	1	7
Light work	1	3	7
Medium work	3	7	14
Heavy work	3	21	28
Very Heavy work	3	28	42

Duration Trend from Normative Data*

Cases	Mean	Min	Max	No Lost Time	Over 6 Months
16383	53	0	672	1.05%	1.11%

Percentile:	5th	25th	Median	75th	95th
Days:	8	20	37	70	139

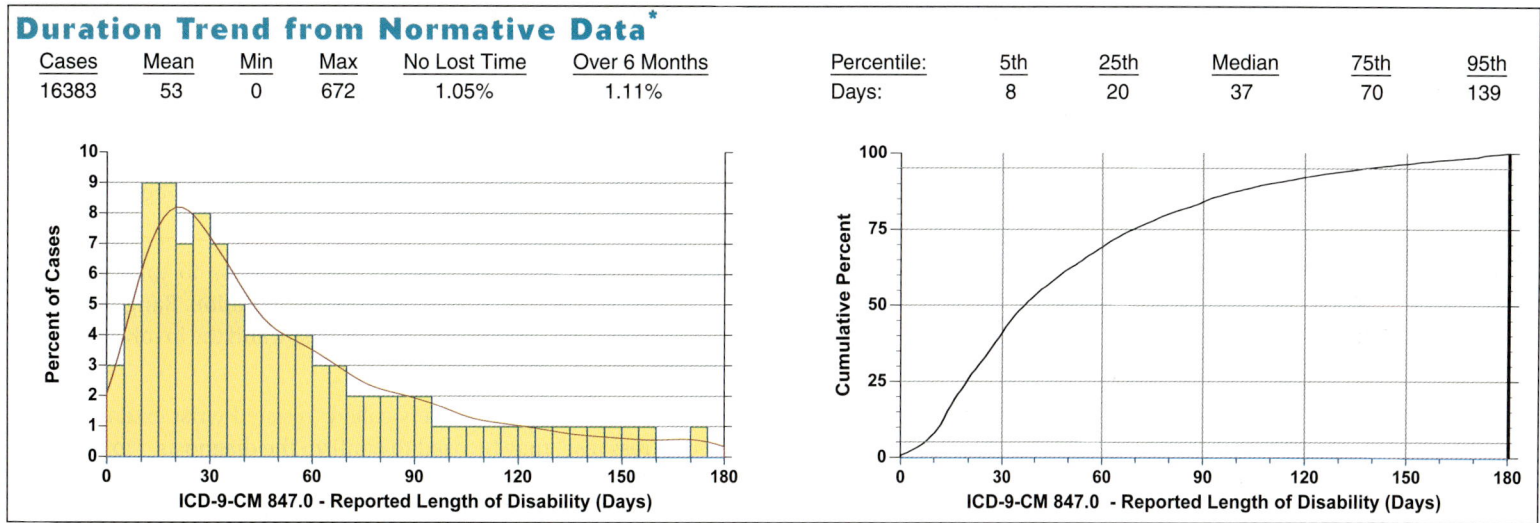

* Differences may exist between the expected duration tables and the normative graphs. Duration tables provide expected recovery periods based on the type of work performed by the individual. The normative graphs reflect the actual observed experience of many individuals across the spectrum of physical conditions, in a variety of industries, and with varying levels of case management.

Failure to Recover

If an individual fails to recover within the maximum duration expectancy period, the reader may wish to reference the following questions to assist in better understanding the specifics of an individual's medical case.

Regarding diagnosis:

- Has diagnosis been confirmed?
- Has degenerative discord spondylosis, or acute torticollis been ruled out?
- If pain and/or stiffness persist after adequate treatment, has MRI been done to rule out disk herniation?
- Has a neurologic evaluation ruled out a pinched nerve (radiculopathy)?
- Was individual involved in a motor vehicle accident recently or in the past?
- Did individual sustain a sports injury or blow to the head from a falling object?
- Does individual hold the neck rigid or the head tilted to one side?
- Does individual exhibit symptoms such as headache, pain in the upper chest and back, changes in sensation, dizziness (vertigo), nausea, blurred or double vision, ringing in ears (tinnitus), fatigue, restlessness, loss of libido, insomnia, pain in the jaw or temporomandibular joint (TMJ), and difficulty swallowing (dysphagia)?
- Does individual have symptoms characteristic of a cervical sprain or strain?
- Is there evidence of symptom magnification behavior?

Regarding treatment:

- Have all aspects of conservative treatment been utilized?
- Has individual worn a soft support collar for several days?
- Were pain medications (analgesics, NSAIDs, antidepressants, anticonvulsants, and cortisone) prescribed to treat pain?
- Were trigger points injected with anesthetics or steroids?
- Has individual participated in a comprehensive, appropriate rehabilitation program?
- Did individual require surgical interventions?

Regarding prognosis:

- How severe was initial injury?
- Was individual able to return to work?
- To what degree do symptoms impact occupational function?

Sprains and Strains, Cervical Spine (Neck) 1983

- Has individual experienced complications such as fractures, instability, nerve stretch or traction injuries, disc disruption, instability, nerve damage, headache, or referred pain?
- Does individual have an underlying condition that may impact recovery?
- What symptoms persist?
- To what degree do symptoms impact individual's ability to perform daily activities?
- Is a psychological evaluation warranted?

References

Campana, Bruce A. "Soft Tissue Spine Injuries and Back Pain." Emergency Medicine, 4th ed, vol. 1. Rosen, Peter, and Roger Barkin, eds. St. Louis: Mosby, 1998. 878-905.

Kisner, Carolyn, and Lynn Allen Colby. "The Spine: Posture." Therapeutic Exercise: Foundations and Techniques, 2nd ed. Philadelphia: F.A. Davis Company, 1990. 429-472.

Sprains and Strains, Elbow
841, 841.0, 841.1, 841.2, 841.3, 841.8, 841.9

Definition

The elbow joint is formed by the joining (articulation) of the humerus (upper arm bone) with the radius and ulna (the 2 bones of the forearm). The radius is located on the thumb side of the forearm, the ulna on the little finger side. An elbow sprain involves a complete or incomplete tear in 1 or more of 3 ligaments (bands of fibrous tissue that connect 2 bones together at a joint). An elbow sprain usually follows a sharp twist. An elbow strain is an overstretching or partial tear in the muscles or tendons that traverse the elbow joint. Both injuries can be the result of overstretching or overuse.

Elbow sprains, like sprains elsewhere in the body, are graded from mild to severe, depending upon the degree of damage to the ligament or muscle. Most elbow sprains are first- or second-degree. In a mild (or first-degree) sprain, only a few fibers are torn. Moderate (or second-degree) sprains result in more fibers being torn and, consequently, some instability about the joint. Acute sprains of this type are usually associated with pain and muscle spasm. In a severe sprain (third-degree), the ligaments are completely disrupted, and joint instability may be severe.

Acute strains occur immediately following muscle overuse or overstretching. Chronic strains occur only after repeated overuse. Usually, strains are not as severe as sprains and may not even be felt until the following day. Both sprains and strains are frequent injuries of persons participating in sports requiring a throwing motion, racquet sports, or golfing. Repetitive use of the forearm and wrist may also result in these injuries. The term "tennis elbow" has been used to describe chronic strain of the lateral side of the elbow, particularly in players of racquet sports. "Tennis elbow" has been a catch-all phrase and has been used to describe over 30 different conditions of the elbow. It currently refers to a chronic strain of the tendon that attaches to the lateral epicondyle of the humerus, often with secondary inflammation of the epicondyle itself (epicondylitis).

Severe elbow sprains result in dislocation of the elbow joint. This is a common injury, accounting for 20% of all joint dislocations. It is seen primarily in younger individuals, particularly those between 5-25 years of age. It accounts for 28% of all elbow injuries.

Diagnosis

History: Individuals will report a sprained elbow with localized pain that is made worse by activity or use, swelling, loss of mobility that may not have occurred immediately, and a black-and-blue discoloration from bleeding into the muscle. There may be a sharp, transient pain, possibly associated with a snapping noise, rapid swelling, and muscle tenderness following several days. Chronic strains cause symptoms of stiffness, soreness, and generalized tenderness that appear several hours following the initial injury.

Physical exam: The exam may reveal tenderness to touch or upon pressure, localized swelling, and areas of discoloration. Range of motion may be limited due to pain and muscle spasm, and the involved muscles may be tense.

Tests: Clinical testing maneuvers called "resisted wrist extension" and "valgus stress test" may be used to confirm the diagnosis. Most cases of elbow strains and sprains do not require any additional diagnostic tests. An x-ray will be taken to rule out fractures. Advanced imaging techniques are not usually indicated and are of limited diagnostic usefulness.

Treatment

Treatment for both sprains and strains is similar and, typically, conservative and nonsurgical. Rest and, in some cases, temporary immobilization with an elastic bandage, splint, or, if severe, a soft cast are typically recommended. Activity level should be adjusted according to what the individual can tolerate. Overall, the individual should avoid activities that aggravate the pain, such as lifting, bending, or twisting, and increase their activity level gradually. Once the acute symptoms resolve, stretching and strengthening exercises may be done. Surgery is rarely indicated. The surgical treatments available are primary repair of ruptured tendons (modified Bunnell technique) or reconstruction of torn ligaments using tendon grafts (Jobe procedure and Andrews procedure).

Pain and swelling may be relieved through the intermittent application of ice during the first 48-72 hours following injury, and heat, massage, or therapeutic ultrasound thereafter. It is also important to elevate the joint above the level of the heart, using pillows when lying down. Nonsteroidal anti-inflammatory drugs are recommended for relief of pain and inflammation. If pain is severe, a mild narcotic may be prescribed for an appropriate short period. In addition, "muscle relaxants" may be prescribed. In some cases, physical therapy may be warranted. Emphasis here will be on regaining full range of motion and the use of warm-up exercises to prevent recurrent injury.

Prognosis

Most first- and second-degree sprains and strains heal on their own without significant functional impairment. More severe sprains may result in a permanent flexion contracture of the elbow, which, fortunately, is usually minor and of little functional consequence. There may be an increased potential for injury recurrence, particularly in individuals with more severe injuries or in those who do not allow previous injuries to heal completely.

Occasionally, torn ligaments do not heal properly and cause recurrent dislocation, necessitating surgical repair. Also, muscle ruptures, where a tendon becomes partially or completely detached, require surgical repair (modified Bunnell technique). Although repair should ideally be carried out within 2-3 days of the injury, delayed repair or reconstruction of older ligament tears generally produces good results. These procedures to reconstruct older ligament tears involve the use of a tendon graft anchored in the bones to replace the torn ligament complex (Jobe procedure, Andrews procedure).

Differential Diagnosis

Differential diagnoses include elbow joint arthrosis in older persons, major tear or rupture, radiohumeral arthritis, soft tissue ectopic calcifications, or an avulsion injury of the medial epicondyle, and fractures of humerus, radius, or ulna.

Specialists

- Orthopedic Surgeon
- Physiatrist
- Sports Medicine Physician

Rehabilitation

Individuals who sustain sprains and strains of the elbow may require therapy. Pain control is the first objective of therapy. Hot packs and ultrasound applied to the elbow provide deep heating. Therapists may perform and teach cross-friction massage of the injured ligaments or tendons to promote healing of these areas. Ice packs may be applied to the elbow after exercising.

Restoration of motion at the elbow, forearm, and wrist is the second goal of therapy. Therapists may passively stretch the elbow and wrist to increase flexion and extension of the forearm to increase rotation. Individuals learn stretching techniques to increase range of motion at the elbow, forearm, and wrist. Individuals stretch the wrist by holding the elbow straight and using their other hand to help bend the wrist into flexion and extension. Individuals stretch the forearm by placing their other hand on the forearm and using it to help turn the forearm in the 2 rotational directions. Elbow flexion and extension are increased with the use overpressure of the noninjured hand to help bend and extend the elbow.

Strengthening exercises restore function and prevent re-injury of the elbow. Initially, the individual will perform isometric exercises of the elbow, forearm, and wrist by manually resisting elbow, forearm, and wrist motions. Strengthening exercises are necessary to restore function and to prevent re-injury. Individuals use light hand weights to strengthen wrist flexion and extension and forearm rotation; individuals place the forearm on a table for support for these exercises. Exercises such as turning a doorknob and turning pages in a book increase the function of the wrist and forearm. Biceps curls and triceps kickbacks with light hand weights increase elbow flexion and extension strength. Individuals squeeze therapy putty to restore hand strength.

Work Restrictions / Accommodations

Restrictions may include little to no use of arm, hand, or shoulder, with limited lifting and carrying. Dexterity may be affected by the injury. Individuals with severe sprains and/or strains with jobs that require extensive lifting may require temporary transfer to more sedentary duties. Use of medications for management of pain and inflammation may require review of drug policies. Safety issues may need to be evaluated.

Complementary and Alternative Therapies

Content is intended for awareness only. Treatments may or may not be effective. Scientific evidence may be lacking and some substances have potentially toxic effects. Dr. Presley Reed and the editors do not endorse the use of these therapies in the absence of consultation with a licensed medical professional.

Acupuncture -	May promote drainage and stimulate healing.
Arnica -	May be used externally to relieve pain and swelling.
Therapeutic massage -	Performed only after healing has taken place. Massage may increase circulation and prevent or release soft tissues from adhering to bones, tendons, or ligaments.

Comorbid Conditions

Comorbidities that could delay healing or lengthen recovery include several types of arthritis conditions. These include osteoarthritis, rheumatoid arthritis, and chronic gouty arthritis.

Complications

Complications of severe injuries include fractures, dislocations, muscle-tendon ruptures, and an avulsion fracture, which involves the tearing away of a piece of bone with a ligament at the point of attachment. Stretch injury to one of the nerves passing by the elbow may occur.

Factors Influencing Duration

Factors include the location, type, and severity of the injury, whether the dominant arm was affected, the severity of the pain associated with the injury, the method of treatment, the individual's response to treatment and adherence to recommendations, and the individual's job requirements.

Length of Disability

Duration in Days

Job Classification	Minimum	Optimum	Maximum
Sedentary work	1	3	7
Light work	1	3	7
Medium work	3	7	14
Heavy work	7	10	21
Very Heavy work	14	21	42

Failure to Recover

If an individual fails to recover within the maximum duration expectancy period, the reader may wish to reference the following questions to assist in better understanding the specifics of an individual's medical case.

Regarding diagnosis:

- Have conditions such as elbow joint arthrosis in older persons, radiohumeral arthritis, soft tissue ectopic calcifications, avulsion injury of the medial epicondyle, and fractures of humerus, radius, or ulna, been ruled out?
- Has diagnosis of elbow strain or sprain been confirmed?
- If pain and/or disability persist after a course of conservative treatment, has an x-ray been done to rule out a fracture or fracture-avulsion that may not have been visible on initial x-rays?
- Has individual experienced any complications such as fractures, dislocations, muscle-tendon ruptures, avulsion fracture, or stretch injury to one of the nerves passing by the elbow associated with elbow strain or sprain?
- Does individual have any underlying conditions such as osteoarthritis, rheumatoid arthritis, or chronic gouty arthritis that could impact recovery?

Regarding treatment:

- Were rest and temporary immobilization with an elastic bandage, splint, or, if severe, a soft cast, recommended?
- Were pain relievers and "muscle relaxants" prescribed?
- Were all conservative options utilized?
- Was individual compliant with treatment as prescribed?
- Were activities such as lifting, bending, or twisting avoided?
- If acute symptoms resolved, did individual begin stretching and strengthening exercises?
- Did individual resume activities too soon?
- Is surgical intervention warranted?
- Would individual benefit from addition of physical therapy, with emphasis on regaining full range of motion and use of warm-up exercises to prevent recurrent injury?

Regarding prognosis:

- Has individual experienced any residual impairment?
- To what degree does impairment impact function?
- Is surgical intervention now warranted?

References

Christian, Claiborne A. "Shoulder and Elbow Injuries." Campbell's Operative Orthopedics, 9th ed, vol. 2. Canale, S. Terry, ed. St. Louis: Mosby, 1998. 1301-1333.

Kisner, Carolyn, and Lynn Allen Colby. "The Elbow and Forearm Complex." Therapeutic Exercise: Foundations and Techniques, 2nd ed. Philadelphia: F.A. Davis Company, 1990. 273-288.

Sprains and Strains, Foot

Other names / synonyms: Sprained Foot
845.1, 845.10, 845.11, 845.12, 845.13, 845.19

Definition

A sprain or strain of the foot is an injury due to a twisting motion or repetitive stress.

Sprains usually involve the joints of the metatarsals and bones of the midfoot (cuboid, navicular) or the hindfoot (calcaneocuboid). Strains are more common in the metatarsal region, involving the tendons, which can be over stressed with a change in activity level. The toe joints are frequently sprained from stubbing the toe, particularly when barefooted.

Strains of the foot may be acute or chronic and result from stress over time. Pressure, poor muscle tone, and excessive weight are risk factors because they stretch the support structures and lead to sprains and strains. In more severe strains and sprains, there are often co-existent tendon ruptures or joint dislocations. A particularly difficult sprain to diagnose is that of the ligament between the bases of the first and second metatarsals (sagittal diastasis), a condition often occurring in football players. A third-degree sprain of the foot may result in dislocation, which is a relatively rare occurrence but one with serious consequences.

Sprains occur more commonly in younger individuals (in the second through fourth decade of life) due to trauma or athletic injuries. Acute strains are also seen more commonly in these individuals, while chronic strains, particularly of the medial musculature (tibialis anterior and posterior) and plantar structures (plantar fascia) are usually seen in middle-aged to older individuals, and more often in females, especially those who are obese.

Diagnosis

History: Individuals will report an increase in activity level or duration that preceded the onset of pain. Individuals may complain of swelling.

Weight bearing is painful, while rest relieves the pain along the forefoot. There may not have been a specific traumatic episode.

Physical exam: Pain is localized over the ligament or tendon involved. Flexion of the toes may cause pain. Swelling and black-and-blue discoloration (ecchymosis) may be present over the injured area.

Tests: X-rays may be taken to rule out any other cause for the symptoms, but are not required.

Treatment

Early treatment for foot sprains and strains follows the acronym R.I.C.E.: rest, ice, compression, and elevation. This treatment is used for the first 2-3 days, followed by modified rest and restricted weight bearing. Anti-inflammatory medications may be used to control pain and swelling. In more chronic cases, taping splints, or prescription in-shoe support devices (orthoses) are useful. Complete tears (third-degree injuries) may require surgical treatment (primary repair or modified Bunnell procedure).

Prognosis

Individuals with simple strains and sprains (first-degree) recover completely after treatment with rest, ice, compression, and elevation (R.I.C.E.). Individuals with partial tears of ligament (sprain) or muscle (strains) recover completely after a period of treatment with taping or splinting. All of these individuals are able to return to work and recreational activities without fear of reinjury. Individuals with complete tears of ligaments or muscles (third-degree injuries) eventually heal after treatment with casting or surgery (primary repair or modified Bunnell procedure), but some individuals develop chronic instability and may need to wear prescription in-shoe supportive devices (orthoses) to prevent re-injury.

Differential Diagnosis

Plantar fasciitis, Morton's neuroma, metatarsalgia, stress fracture, bursitis, or compartment syndrome may present with a similar history. The clinical examination, however, would be very different for each of these diagnoses.

Specialists

- Orthopedic Surgeon
- Physiatrist
- Podiatrist
- Sports Medicine Physician

Rehabilitation

Individuals who suffer foot sprains do not require a lengthy rehabilitation. Therapists first focus on teaching control of pain and swelling. Ice packs may be used as needed to meet this objective. Therapists also instruct the individual to actively roll a golf ball under the foot for self-massage purposes.

Because individuals ambulate with crutches or a cane for a few weeks until pain subsides, therapists focus on correcting gait to eliminate any limp that is present. Individuals may walk on a treadmill to achieve a more fluid gait pattern.

Strengthening the muscles of the toes is necessary to prevent re-injury. Towel crunches are performed in which individuals squeeze the toes around a towel placed on the floor. Individuals can also pick up small objects from the floor with the toes. As there is no period of immobilization, individuals do not require restoration of range of motion.

Work Restrictions / Accommodations

Activity restrictions should include limited or no weight bearing, limited standing, walking, and squatting. Individuals may use ambulation assistive devices (crutches, cane, and walker). Manual dexterity may be affected by the use of these devices. Use of medication would require review of any drug policies. Driving, including using a clutch, is permitted after the individual has returned to normal shoewear.

Complementary and Alternative Therapies

Content is intended for awareness only. Treatments may or may not be effective. Scientific evidence may be lacking and some substances have potentially toxic effects. Dr. Presley Reed and the editors do not endorse the use of these therapies in the absence of consultation with a licensed medical professional.

Exercise - After weight-bearing is allowed, proprioceptive exercises may help re-establish communication with the nerves that provide balance.

Hydrotherapy - Hot and cold contrast baths may decrease swelling.

Comorbid Conditions

Obesity will delay healing and lengthen recovery due to increased stress on the foot in weightbearing.

Complications

Fracture and dislocation complicate the injury. Joint inflammation, degenerative changes in the ligaments and joints are possible complications of the injury. Chronic foot strain may develop as a complication of an acute or sub-acute episode.

Factors Influencing Duration

Extent of the injury, response to treatment, complications, and job demands such as walking, climbing and standing may impact duration of disability.

Length of Disability

First or second-degree (mild to moderate) sprain or strain.

Duration in Days

Job Classification	Minimum	Optimum	Maximum
Sedentary work	1	3	7
Light work	1	3	7
Medium work	3	7	14
Heavy work	3	14	21
Very Heavy work	3	21	28

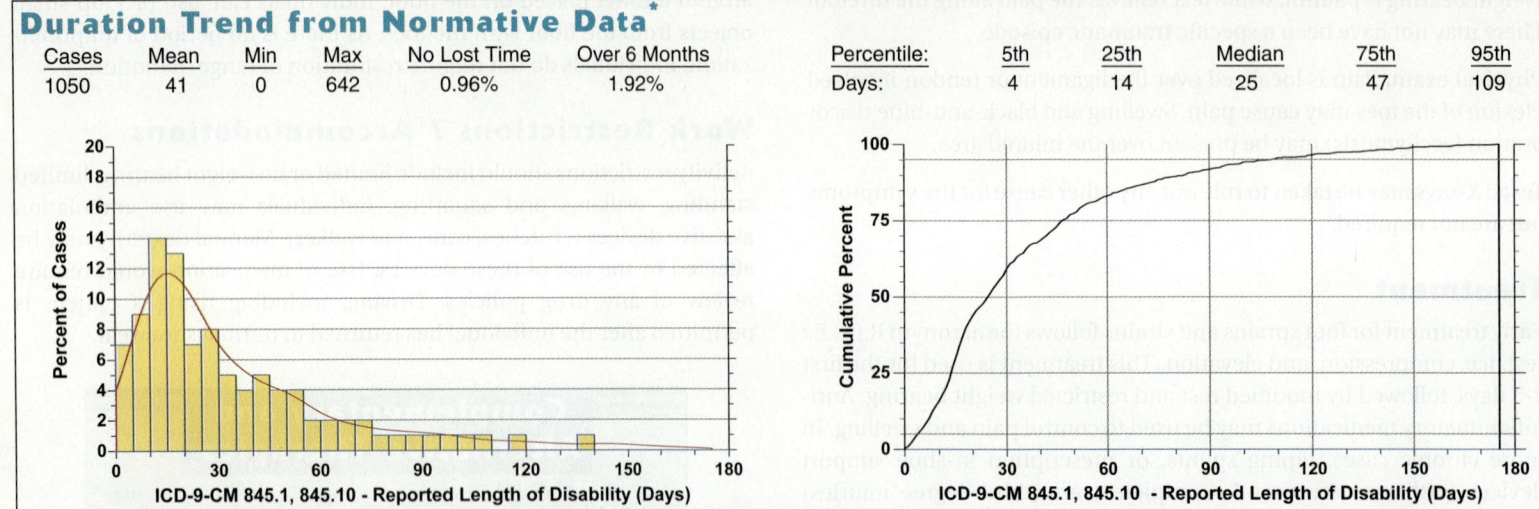

Failure to Recover

If an individual fails to recover within the maximum duration expectancy period, the reader may wish to reference the following questions to assist in better understanding the specifics of an individual's medical case.

Regarding diagnosis:

- Have conditions such as plantar fasciitis, Morton's neuroma, metatarsalgia, stress fracture, bursitis, or compartment syndrome, been ruled out?
- Has diagnosis been confirmed?
- Does the individual have continued pain after treatment?
- Has a bone scan (scintigram) been done to rule out the presence of an occult fracture, particularly in the midfoot area?
- Has individual experienced any complications such as joint inflammation, degenerative changes, associated fracture or dislocation, or chronic foot strain?
- Is individual obese?
- Does individual have an underlying condition that may impact recovery?

Regarding treatment:

- Have all conservative options been utilized?
- Has individual been compliant in following prescribed treatment plan, including rest, ice, compression, and elevation used for the first 2-3 days, followed by modified rest and restricted weight bearing, and anti-inflammatory medications?
- Is surgical intervention warranted?

Regarding prognosis:

- Has individual been compliant with R.I.C.E. treatment, and with taping or splinting if required?
- If symptoms have persisted beyond expected recovery, does diagnosis need to be revisited?
- Have occult fractures been ruled out?
- Would individual with chronic instability benefit from the use of orthotic devices?

References

Geiderman, Joel M. "Orthopedic Injuries: Management Principles." Emergency Medicine, 4th ed, vol. 1. Rosen, Peter, and Roger Barkin, eds. St. Louis: Mosby, 1998. 602-624.

Kisner, Carolyn, and Lynn Allen Colby. "The Ankle and Foot." Therapeutic Exercise: Foundations and Techniques, 2nd ed. Philadelphia: F.A. Davis Company, 1990. 385-408.

Sprains and Strains, Hand or Fingers
842.10, 842.11, 842.12, 842.13, 842.19

Definition

A sprain and strain of the hand is an injury to the ligaments and joint capsule tissue of the hand. A sprain or strain of the fingers is an injury to the ligaments (sprain) or tendons (strain) of the fingers.

The joints of the fingers (interphalangeal joints) are injured more often than are the joints of the hand. Strains are less common than sprains.

The bones of the hand form many small joints, each vulnerable to injury. The system ligaments and joint capsule tissue maintain the joint stability. When these structures are injured (sprained, strained), the joints become loose and possibly deformed. Partial tearing of the ligaments produces pain and swelling while complete disruption leads to loss of stability and dislocation of the joint. Tendon injuries (strains) often happen at the same time because of their close proximity to the joints. When this occurs, individuals experience joint looseness (laxity) and loss of function.

A particularly difficult sprain to treat is that of the ulnar collateral ligament of the thumb also called gamekeeper's thumb. This ligament is frequently seen in skiers and is now known as skier's thumb. The extensor tendons on the top of the hand (dorsum) are the most commonly strained tendons of the hand. These injuries are variable and numerous and classified by the anatomic zone system of Verdan where seven anatomic zones are described (i.e., zone I is the distal interphalangeal joint of the finger and zone VII is the forearm).

Hand injuries are extremely common and affect all age groups. They are often caused by occupational or sports injuries. Although hand injuries account for 6-10% of all emergency department visits, 94% are relatively minor injuries (mostly sprains and strains). Hand injuries account for 19% of all lost work-time injuries and 9% of worker's compensation cases.

Diagnosis

History: Individuals report history of trauma that they may believe to be insignificant. A joint may be painful to the touch (palpation) especially along the sides and feels weak when stressed, as in gripping.

Individuals may also complain of swelling, warmth, and deformity. History of previous injuries is important especially jammed fingers that were never treated. The pain is usually well-localized to the area injured. In severe cases, pain is constant but more commonly felt only when stressing the injured area. Using the hand for lifting, grasping, or typing may be possible but painful.

Physical exam: The joint is loose (lax) with stress testing and may appear deformed with loss of function depending on the severity of the injury. Swelling of the affected joint is common. Touching (palpation) the hand or fingers along the lateral joint margins is painful. Grasping also causes pain.

Tests: Stress view x-rays may be needed to augment plain views. These involve taking x-rays of the hand while stressing the injured joint (often under local anesthesia) then comparing them to stress x-rays of the opposite, uninjured hand. CT or MRI may be necessary to evaluate avulsion fractures resulting in joint surface damage. This is most common with injuries to the thumb and wrist area.

Treatment

First- and second-degree strains and sprains are initially treated with rest, ice, compression, and elevation (R.I.C.E.) for the first 24 hours until swelling subsides. Splints or taping are then used for immobilization. Immobilization should not continue for more than 2 weeks at which time range-of-motion exercises begin. Third-degree sprains and strains often require surgical repair especially if the thumb is involved (skier's thumb). Repair usually includes primary suturing of the ligament, muscle, or tendon (modified Bunnell technique). In some instances, closed reduction is sufficient and followed by immobilization for 3 weeks. Finger sprains sometime require closed reduction with pin fixation. In cases where closed reduction cannot produce a good alignment of the joint or if soft tissue is interposed within the joint preventing reduction, open reduction with internal fixation (ORIF) is necessary.

Prognosis

First- and second-degree sprains and strains of fingers and the hand heal with conservative treatment including rest, splinting, and physical therapy. Third-degree strains and sprains of the hand also usually heal with conservative treatment. Third-degree strains and sprains of the fingers generally heal well regardless of type of treatment but some individuals may have residual stiffness, pain, or instability. Individuals with third-degree strains of the distal interphalangeal joint of the finger may be left with residual crookedness of the finger (swan-neck deformity). Individuals treated with surgical procedures usually heal well but some may have some residual stiffness.

Differential Diagnosis

Arthritis, infection, and fracture may present with similar symptoms. Tendonitis and tendon ruptures should also be ruled out.

Specialists

- Hand Surgeon
- Occupational Therapist
- Orthopedic Surgeon
- Physiatrist

Rehabilitation

Individuals with sprains or strains of the hand or fingers may require outpatient therapy. The individual should see either an occupational therapist or a physical therapist certified as a hand therapist.

Therapy first addresses pain control and the reduction of swelling. To decrease swelling in the hand, individuals learn to position the hand so that it rests above the elbow on a pillow. Hot packs and hot paraffin wax decrease muscle stiffness prior to therapy. Therapists may perform cross-friction massage of the injured ligaments or tendons to promote healing and instruct individuals in self-massage. Ice packs decrease pain and swelling after exercise.

Stretching techniques are necessary to increase range of motion at the wrist and forearm. Therapists may passively stretch the wrist to increase flexion and extension, the forearm to increase rotation, and the hand to increase finger flexion and extension. Individuals stretch the wrist by holding the elbow straight and using their other hand to help bend the wrist into flexion and extension. Individuals stretch the forearm by placing their other hand on the forearm and using it to help turn the forearm in the two rotational directions. Individuals stretch their fingers by making a fist and extending the fingers and adding overpressure with their noninjured hand to increase these motions. Finger and thumb opposition is restored with touching the thumb to each finger.

Strengthening exercises are necessary to restore function and prevent reinjury. Individuals may use light hand weights to strengthen wrist flexion and extension and forearm rotation with the forearm placed on a table for support. Individuals squeeze therapy putty to restore hand strength. The muscles of the fingers are strengthened with pinching therapy putty between the fingers or placing a rubber band around two fingers at a time and spreading them apart. Individuals learn functional exercises such as turning a doorknob and grasping/turning a key. Other exercises are performed that emphasize dexterity such as picking up pegs and placing them in a pegboard.

Work Restrictions / Accommodations

Restrictions may include little to no use of involved hand with limited lifting and carrying. Dexterity is affected by the injury and use of protective splints. Safety issues must be evaluated. Typists, keypad operators, and others with work that requires use of the hands and fingers will need to be away from their typical jobs until the injury heals.

Comorbid Conditions

Arthritis is a comorbid condition that may influence the length of disability.

Complications

Complications include loss of range of motion, chronic stiffness, and discomfort in the involved joints.

Factors Influencing Duration

Factors include the location, type, and severity of the injury, whether the dominant hand was affected, severity of the pain associated with the injury, method of treatment, individual's response to treatment and adherence to recommendations, and individual's job requirements.

Length of Disability

Carpometacarpal joint.

Duration in Days

Job Classification	Minimum	Optimum	Maximum
Sedentary work	1	21	42
Light work	1	21	42
Medium work	1	21	42
Heavy work	42	49	56
Very Heavy work	42	49	56

Interphalangeal joint (finger).

Duration in Days

Job Classification	Minimum	Optimum	Maximum
Sedentary work	1	7	21
Light work	1	7	21
Medium work	1	14	21
Heavy work	2	21	35
Very Heavy work	2	21	35

Interphalangeal joint (thumb).

Duration in Days

Job Classification	Minimum	Optimum	Maximum
Sedentary work	1	21	35
Light work	1	21	35
Medium work	1	28	35
Heavy work	7	42	42
Very Heavy work	7	42	42

Metacarpophalangeal joint (finger).

Duration in Days

Job Classification	Minimum	Optimum	Maximum
Sedentary work	1	14	28
Light work	1	14	28
Medium work	1	21	28
Heavy work	7	28	42
Very Heavy work	7	28	42

Metacarpophalangeal joint (thumb).

Job Classification	Duration in Days		
	Minimum	Optimum	Maximum
Sedentary work	1	21	42
Light work	1	21	42
Medium work	1	21	42
Heavy work	14	42	56
Very Heavy work	14	42	56

Failure to Recover

If an individual fails to recover within the maximum duration expectancy period, the reader may wish to reference the following questions to assist in better understanding the specifics of an individual's medical case.

Regarding diagnosis:

- Was individual diagnosed with a sprain or strain? To the hand or fingers?
- Did the individual have symptoms (swelling, warmth, deformity, loss of strength or function, and joint looseness) consistent with the diagnosis of hand sprain or strain?
- Were other conditions such as arthritis, tendonitis, tendon rupture, infection, and fracture, ruled out?
- Was the diagnosis confirmed with stress x-rays?
- Were other conditions or associated injuries ruled out with MRI or CT?

Regarding treatment:

- Was individual treated with rest, ice, compression, and elevation (R.I.C.E.)?
- Was the treatment appropriate for the type of injury? Splinting, taping, or immobilization following surgery?
- Is the pain well controlled? If not, have alternative pain management techniques been tried?
- Is the individual participating in a rehabilitation program as recommended?
- Would a consultation with a specialist (hand surgeon, orthopedic surgeon, physiatrist or occupational therapist) be beneficial?

Regarding prognosis:

- Has the individual been compliant with physical therapy recommendations?
- Does the individual have any conditions such as peripheral neuropathy, pre-existing rheumatoid or osteoarthritis involving the hand or fingers that may impact ability to recover?
- Did the individual experience any complications such as loss of range of motion, chronic stiffness, pain, infection, or nerve injury that may influence length of disability?

References

Antosia, Robert E., and Everett Lyn. "The Hand." Emergency Medicine, 4th ed, vol. 1. Rosen, Peter, and Roger Barkin, eds. St. Louis: Mosby, 1998. 625-668.

Kisner, Carolyn, and Lynn Allen Colby. "The Wrist and Hand." Therapeutic Exercise: Foundations and Techniques, 2nd ed. Philadelphia: F.A. Davis Company, 1990. 289-316.

Sprains and Strains, Knee
Other names / synonyms: ACL Tear, Sprained Knee
844.0, 844.1, 844.2, 844.8

Definition

The knee is supported by a system of ligaments, cartilages (2 menisci), muscles, and the bone geometry. When an injury occurs to the ligaments of the knee, it is described as a sprain. Injury to the muscle-tendon structures of the knee is a strain.

Both injuries are evaluated based upon the amount of looseness (laxity) of the knee joint. Sprains can occur in any or all of the 4 knee ligaments: the anterior and posterior cruciate ligaments (ACL, PCL), and the medial and lateral collateral ligaments (MCL, LCL). The anterior cruciate ligament (ACL) is the most commonly injured ligament. The degree of sprain is based on the amount of fibers torn, and is judged by the amount of looseness or laxity of the knee.

Sprains are denoted as first, second, or third-degree. This corresponds to the lay classification system of "mild" (first degree), "moderate" (second degree), and "severe" (third degree). Sprains of isolated ligaments may occur, or multiple ligaments may be injured. Sometimes, other structures in the knee may also be injured in association with sprains, such as the famous "terrible triad" ("unhappy triad") of O'Donoghue, in which the ACL, MCL, and medial meniscus are all damaged.

Strains of the many muscle-tendon groups around the knee are evaluated by pain and loss of function and the impact on knee stability. They are also noted to be first, second, or third-degree strains. Often contusions, tendinitis, and bursitis around the knee joint are called knee strains. Strains are often associated with sprains and share the same risk factors and mechanisms of injury.

The knee is the most commonly injured joint in the body, and most injuries are of the ligaments. The majority of cases of sprains and strains result from sports activities, especially football, basketball, and skiing. The injuries also commonly occur in automobile accidents, especially when the flexed knee hits against the dashboard ("dashboard sprain").

Diagnosis

History: Individuals will most often relate a traumatic event. Sometimes, the incident may not seem significant at the time. Individuals may report the onset of pain and swelling, which is important to note as immediate swelling is most often associated with acute ligament tears. Individuals may relate that they felt a "popping" in the knee (reported in 70% of ACL injuries). The mechanism of injury will provide valuable clues to the direction of impact and force to the knee. History of prior injury and treatment is important. Individuals may relate a history of pain in partial ligament tears, but pain is often absent in complete tears. Individuals also complain of the knee "giving way" in 17-65% of cases.

Physical exam: The examiner will touch (palpate) ligament and tendon insertion areas, and pain will be elicited in the affected structures. Areas of localized swelling (effusions) may also be felt on palpation. Pain along the course or attachment to bone (insertion) of a tendon usually indicates strain, whereas such pain on palpation in a ligament area often indicates sprain. Instability or excessive motion of the knee joint is often noted, although sometimes compensatory tightening of the surrounding muscles (physiologic splinting) may prevent detection of this loosening or instability. When observing the individual walking, a limp may be noticed, as can giving way of the knee. Swelling (edema) and bruising (ecchymosis) about the knee joint may be noticed.

Tests: Knee arthrometer (KT-1000) may be done to quantify the degree of laxity. Routine knee x-rays rule out fractures, dislocations, patella-femoral abnormalities, and loose bodies. Stress x-rays may be done. MRI scans will be ordered to examine the ligaments and articular surfaces. There can be both false-positives and false-negatives with MRI scans based on technique and interpretation. Draining fluid from the knee (joint aspiration) is done to decrease pain and evaluate the fluid. Blood in the fluid (aspirant) indicates torn tissue; fat indicates a bone injury. Diagnostic arthroscopy may be necessary to confirm the diagnosis.

Treatment

Mild sprains and strains are treated conservatively with rest from the offending activity, especially avoiding rotational or loading work to the knee. Ice, anti-inflammatory medications, light knee wraps, and muscle strengthening exercises are included in the treatment. Moderate sprains or strains are often treated with braces that restrict but do not eliminate knee motion. It is critical to regain complete extension and flexion of the knee after injury while restricting rotation. Physical therapy modalities to decrease inflammation, strengthen muscles, restore balance and agility are an integral part of the treatment.

Severe (third-degree) sprains often require surgical intervention for repair or reconstruction of the torn tissue. The decision to repair or reconstruct a ligament is based on the amount of instability, the likelihood of increased injury without repair, the number of ligaments injured, and any associated injuries.

Isolated MCL and LCL injuries are usually treated nonsurgically. If the ACL is injured, it is usually treated surgically in younger and athletic individuals, and conservatively in older or sedentary individuals. Most cases of PCL injury require surgery. The surgery involves sewing the ligament back together (end-to-end anastomosis) or anchoring it to bone (ligament-to-bone fixation). These procedures are often performed arthroscopically. Severe strains resulting in torn tendons almost always require surgical repair. This surgery involves suturing of the tendon ends back together (tenoplasty) or anchoring the tendon to bone (tenodesis).

Chronic instability due to ruptures of tendons or ligaments are surgically repaired with procedures known as reconstruction or reconstruction with augmentation (reinforcing the unstable area with a fascia graft or transferred tendon). There are numerous such procedures, including the Slocum, Hughston, Clancy, and Muller procedures.

Prognosis

Isolated injuries to the collateral ligaments, even third-degree injuries, heal well with conservative treatment. If third-degree collateral ligament sprains are associated with other ligament or meniscus damage, they will often require surgery but will heal well. First- and second-degree sprains of ACL and PCL are effectively treated with physical therapy and activity alteration, and recovery can be expected. Third-degree sprains of ACL usually require surgical repair, either primary repair or reconstruction with augmentation. Extensive rehabilitation after such surgery is necessary but recovery can be expected.

Third-degree injuries to PCL in middle-aged or older adults are not treated surgically unless there is gross instability or associated injuries, especially of the meniscus. Recovery from this surgery can be expected, although extensive rehabilitation is necessary.

Regarding strains, full recovery can be expected after physical therapy for first- and second-degree injuries. Third-degree strains involving tendon rupture require surgery (tenoplasty, tenodesis, or a reconstruction with augmentation). Third-degree strains and sprains will require several months for full recovery. Return to limited activity may be expected early in treatment, with an interruption for surgery and eventual return to full activity. Knee braces are often used for all levels of sprains and strains, sometimes only in the early stages of recovery, and often for several months after surgery. Performance braces may be required after recovery to prevent re-injury.

Differential Diagnosis

Patella dislocation, patella-femoral pain syndrome, meniscal tears, tendonitis, gout, and rheumatoid arthritis would present pain and swelling and limited function.

Specialists

- Orthopedic Surgeon
- Physiatrist
- Sports Medicine Physician

Rehabilitation

Individuals who sustain sprains and strains may require therapy. Physical therapy initially focuses on reduction of pain and swelling. Hot packs and ultrasound prior to therapy provide deep heating and pain relief. Therapists may perform and teach cross-friction massage of the injured tendons and ligaments to promote healing. Ice packs are applied to the knee after exercising to decrease pain and swelling.

Individuals learn stretching techniques to increase range of motion. Therapists may passively stretch the knee into flexion and extension. Individuals are instructed to stretch the knee into flexion by sliding the heel of the injured leg up the exercise mat, giving some overpressure with the noninjured leg. Individuals stretch the knee into extension by sitting and placing the noninjured leg under the injured leg to raise it into extension.

Strengthening exercises prevent re-injury of the knee. Individuals perform isometric quadriceps exercises in which the thigh muscles are contracted and held for 5-second intervals. Active strengthening exercises such as straight leg raises, seated knee extensions, and minisquats are also taught. Forwards and lateral step-ups on the injured leg are added as strength increases. Walking on a treadmill is recommended with speed increased as tolerated. Dynamic exercises such as jumping rope or skipping may be added to increase strength once the other exercises become less difficult.

Work Restrictions / Accommodations

Limited to no use of knee for walking, climbing, squatting, or kneeling during early treatment stages will be necessary. This may necessitate use of braces, crutches, canes, or wheelchairs. Individuals will need frequent rest periods with facilities to allow for elevation of the lower extremity. Use of medications for management of pain and inflammation require review of drug policies. Individuals who do not require surgical repair or reconstruction must undergo extensive physical therapy to regain function.

During the recovery phase after surgery, release time for extensive physical therapy may be needed. No squatting, crawling, or kneeling for several months as well as use of a protective brace may be necessary. Avoidance of "at risk" activities would include jumping, twisting, lifting, pushing, or lunging. Avoidance is often facilitated by using a protective or "sport" brace.

Complementary and Alternative Therapies

Content is intended for awareness only. Treatments may or may not be effective. Scientific evidence may be lacking and some substances have potentially toxic effects. Dr. Presley Reed and the editors do not endorse the use of these therapies in the absence of consultation with a licensed medical professional.

Acupuncture -	May promote drainage and stimulate healing.
Arnica -	May relieve pain and swelling.
Hydrotherapy -	Ice whirlpool may stimulate injured cells and promote healing. Contrast baths may also be used to clear congestion and stimulate healing.

Comorbid Conditions

Fractures, associated injuries to the meniscus, dislocations of the patella, dislocation of the knee (which is a limb-threatening injury), and a total disruption of all support structures could complicate recovery and lengthen disability.

Complications

Recurrent effusions, osteoarthritis, and buckling or giving way episodes (chronic instability) with loss of function would be complications of the injury and treatment.

Factors Influencing Duration

Surgical repair of third-degree ligament tears is not performed until swelling has resolved and motion has been restored. This may allow limited work activity early in treatment, with an interruption in work for several weeks following surgery. Disability periods for all sprains and strains depends on the type of injury and associated injuries, treatment plan, work requirements, and ability to modify activities to protect the knee.

Length of Disability

Non-operative treatment. Cruciate ligament.

Duration in Days

Job Classification	Minimum	Optimum	Maximum
Sedentary work	1	3	7
Light work	1	3	7
Medium work	1	7	21
Heavy work	1	14	42
Very Heavy work	1	14	42

Non-operative treatment. Medial or lateral collateral ligament.

Duration in Days

Job Classification	Minimum	Optimum	Maximum
Sedentary work	1	3	7
Light work	1	3	7
Medium work	3	7	21
Heavy work	3	14	42
Very Heavy work	3	14	42

Surgical treatment.

Duration in Days

Job Classification	Minimum	Optimum	Maximum
Sedentary work	21	35	70
Light work	21	63	98
Medium work	182	273	Indefinite
Heavy work	182	273	Indefinite
Very Heavy work	182	273	Indefinite

Failure to Recover

If an individual fails to recover within the maximum duration expectancy period, the reader may wish to reference the following questions to assist in better understanding the specifics of an individual's medical case.

Regarding diagnosis:

- Has diagnosis been confirmed?
- Have conditions such as patella dislocation, patella-femoral pain syndrome, meniscal tears, tendinitis, gout, or rheumatoid arthritis been ruled out?
- If individual has continued pain or stiffness after conservative treatment, was an MRI done to rule out a missed meniscus injury or a fracture of any of the bones involved in the knee joint?
- If imaging results were equivocal, would diagnostic arthroscopy be appropriate?

- Has individual experienced any complications such as recurrent effusions, osteoarthritis, or chronic instability with loss of function?
- Does individual have any underlying condition such as fractures, associated injuries to the meniscus, dislocations of the patella, dislocation of the knee, or a total disruption of all support structures that may impact recovery?

Regarding treatment:

- Has individual been prescribed braces that restrict but do not eliminate knee motion?
- Has individual been enrolled in a comprehensive rehabilitation program with physical therapy modalities to decrease inflammation, strengthen muscles, and restore balance and agility as an integral part of the treatment?
- Is surgical intervention warranted? On what basis? Can procedure be performed arthroscopically?

Regarding prognosis:

- If injury was first- and second-degree sprains of ACL and PCL, has individual been compliant with treatment of physical therapy and activity alteration regimen?
- If not, what can be done to increase compliance?
- If surgical repair or reconstructive surgery was performed, was individual enrolled in a comprehensive, post-surgery, rehabilitation program?
- Has individual been compliant with treatment plan?
- If treated surgically, what were the extenuating circumstances?
- Is individual middle-aged or older?
- If symptoms persist despite treatment, does diagnosis need to be revisited?
- Have workplace accommodations been made to allow for surgery and resultant rehabilitation period?
- Would individual benefit from a performance brace?

References

Antosia, Robert E., and Everett Lyn. "Knee and Lower leg." Emergency Medicine, 4th ed, vol. 1. Rosen, Peter, and Roger Barkin, eds. St. Louis: Mosby, 1998. 786-821.

Miller, Robert H. "Knee Injuries." Campbell's Operative Orthopedics, 9th ed, vol. 2. Canale, S. Terry, ed. St. Louis: Mosby, 1998. 1113-1299.

Sprains and Strains, Rotator Cuff (Capsule)
Other names / synonyms: Glenohumeral Dislocation, Shoulder Dislocation
840.4

Definition

A sprain of the rotator cuff or shoulder capsule is a result of a forceful injury to the ligaments that stabilize the shoulder joint (glenohumeral joint). The injury causes the joint to become loose (lax) and can lead to complete disruption or dislocation, which leads to the sprain.

The glenohumeral joint is the most freely moving joint in the body. The joint is stabilized by several ligaments crossing between the shoulder blade (glenoid of the scapula) and upper arm bone (humeral head).

Sprains of the shoulder capsule are classified by the amount of damage to the ligaments and resulting looseness (laxity) of the joint. Mild stretching without tearing of the ligaments is a grade I sprain. There may be some instability of the joint at this point, but minimal.

With tearing to some fibers of the capsule, along with stretching, the humeral head can slip and almost dislocate, creating a feeling a instability and apprehension. This is a grade II sprain.

Grade III sprains result in complete disruption of the joint capsule and displacement of the humeral out beyond the joint (dislocation). The dislocation can be downward, upward, frontward, or backwards (inferior, superior, anterior, or posterior). Multidirectional instability describes the humeral head moving too far in many directions. The most common direction is anterior, followed by posterior and then infrequently by multidirectional.

Sprains with movement of the humeral head towards the front (anterior) are the result of trauma, usually caused by forced external rotation with the elbow away from the body. This is similar to the throwing motion. Acute posterior sprains and dislocations are rare and are most often the result of a direct blow to the shoulder or outstretched arm. Chronic sprains result from stretched supporting ligaments from repeated injuries that do not heal and changes in the bones that occur when the bones slip out of position (changes in the glenoid lip and humeral head.)

Acute shoulder dislocations are a true emergency because of the possibility of nerve damage while the bones are out of position and require immediate attention, either in a physician's office with x-ray capability, urgent care units, or an emergency room.

Those most likely to sustain a shoulder sprain are individuals exposed to heavy overhead work or heavy lifting or impact to the shoulder area. In one study of 1600 shoulder injuries, 500 were complete dislocations or third-degree sprains.

Diagnosis

History: Individuals will report a traumatic event such as a fall, having their arm jerked backward, or trying to catch something heavy that was slipping. The amount of pain experienced is relative to the grade of sprain. In grade I, individuals will complain of some pain with motion. In grade II, immediate pain will have subsided if the arm bone (humeral head) has returned to a normal position (reduced) and only shoulder motion is painful. Grade III injuries most often present with the individual carrying his arm with the elbow bent and away from his body. Individuals may report a feeling of slipping or tearing in the joint. Pain is immediate and does not subside until the shoulder is repositioned (reduced). If this is a second episode of a grade III sprain or dislocation, the individual may have attempted a self-manipulation or reduction.

Physical exam: A sunken area may be obvious just below the tip of the shoulder (positive sulcus sign) created by the arm bone being out of position. One diagnostic test is to attempt to move the arm through the throwing motion, checking not only the shoulder function, but the individual's level of anxiety (positive apprehension sign). Changes in color, temperature, and sensation and strength may be evident in the arm and hand. Reflexes may be either decreased or accentuated.

Tests: Plain shoulder x-rays, anterior-posterior views (AP), lateral and glenoid views, will demonstrate the position of the humeral head, which defines the direction of any subluxation or dislocation. X-ray examination will also determine the presence of fractures of other bony anatomy of the shoulder (glenoid or humeral head). An MRI is indicated if a tear of the rotator cuff is suspected in association with a sprain.

Treatment

Ligaments do not heal, but the inflammation and pain caused by stretching and tearing is reduced with rest. If bleeding has occurred, scar tissue will form around the ligaments, adding stability and some strength to the joint. Ligaments that are torn away from a bone (avulsed) may reattach themselves if allowed to rest during the healing phase. Rest is relative; motion is often allowed, but not the stress of lifting the arm. Treatment is aimed at reducing further trauma to the joint, regaining motion of the joint, and rehabilitating supporting muscle groups for added stability.

Grade I sprains are treated with relative rest, ice, and NSAIDs as needed. Strengthening of the shoulder muscles can begin when active range of motion (AROM) is achieved. A sling with waist strap is worn initially to rest the shoulder, but wrist motion and gripping exercises are encouraged.

Grade II sprains are treated in a similar manner, with relative rest lasting about 2 weeks allowing scar tissue to form around the ligaments. Strengthening exercises focus on the shoulder stabilizer muscles to help prevent further subluxations. A sling with waist strap is used initially full-time, even in bed, then for activities that put the shoulder at risk.

In grade III sprains, the need for shoulder reduction is urgent, but care must be given to prevent possible nerve and vessel damage from improper manipulation. Most often, no attempt to reduce a first episode dislocation is made without an x-ray examination.

Closed relocation (reduction) is only possible when the muscles around the shoulder are relaxed. Medication for relief of pain and muscle relaxation is usually necessary. Pain relief is immediate and often quite dramatic with reduction.

A sling or sling with waist strap (sling and swath) is worn for up to 6 weeks.

Medication for pain and muscle relaxation are often prescribed. Physical therapy begins after about the first week for joint mobility and strengthening.

There is an indication for reconstructive surgery (shoulder capsulorraphy) in younger individuals who have a higher chance of recurrence. It is almost always indicated after the third dislocation, although some individuals chose to change their lifestyle, reducing the risk of repeated dislocations, instead of undergoing surgery.

Prognosis

Relief of pain and regaining a feeling of stability may come as early as 1-2 weeks as the capsule ligaments heal by scaring and inflammation of the tissues decreases. This is deceptive though, especially in grade II and III injuries. The stretched joint capsule takes about 6 weeks to heal, and the shoulder muscles need about 4 weeks of strengthening to maintain stability. Recovery may then take 6-10 weeks.

In grade III sprains or dislocations, adequate reduction is common, but redislocation is frequent without surgical repair. Fractures associated with a grade III sprain or dislocation often indicate a less optimum recovery because of increased instability of the joint. Individuals may continue to experience apprehension when the arm is placed in a vulnerable position.

Individuals who have recurring episodes of dislocation will have a shorter recovery time after each episode but may not be able to return to overhead activities. They are at greater risk for degenerative arthritis, as well.

Differential Diagnosis

Fractures or dislocations of the acromioclavicular joint may give the same appearance as a grade II or III sprain. Fractures of the glenoid or humeral head may mimic the pain of a sprain, or may have occurred when the shoulder dislocated and then spontaneously reduced. Tears of the glenoid labrum may mimic a capsule sprain by presenting with complaints of instability and pain. Fraying of the biceps tendon at the insertion also causes pain with motion, somewhat similar to a sprain. Muscle bruise and nerve palsy rotator cuff tear should be considered if the diagnosis is unclear.

Specialists

- Orthopedic Surgeon
- Physiatrist
- Physical Therapist

Rehabilitation

Individuals who sustain a sprain of the shoulder capsule may require outpatient physical therapy. In general, rehabilitation occurs in two phases, although specific protocols may vary among physicians. The goals of therapy are to decrease pain, increase stability and regain motion of the joint. Outpatient therapy is gradually reduced, with transition to a home exercise program once goals are achieved.

The first goal of physical therapy involves regaining passive motion when cleared by the physician. Therapists stretch the shoulder into overhead reaching (flexion), reaching out to the side (abduction), backward reaching (extension), and into rotation (internal and external). Passive stretching decreases the risk of frozen shoulder syndrome (adhesive capsulitis) and increases nourishment to the joint. In addition, therapists instruct individuals in pain control techniques. Individuals learn to use heat prior to stretching to help increase muscle flexibility and decrease pain. Individuals also learn to use ice packs after exercise and as needed to control pain and swelling. In addition, therapists may use ultrasound, a deep-heating technique that reaches deeper muscle and bone.

The second goal of physical therapy includes the progression to active range of motion and strengthening of the shoulder stabilizer muscles, often with the assistance of residence training devices and free weights. Individuals learn self-assisted shoulder exercises for flexion, abduction, internal rotation, external rotation, and extension by holding a cane or broomstick and using the non-affected arm to stretch the other shoulder. Individuals may also increase shoulder motion by using overhead pulleys so that by pulling down with the non-affected arm the shoulder with the tear is stretched.

Individuals perform strengthening exercises to correct muscle imbalances and to stabilize the shoulder joint. Initially, individuals perform isometric exercises in which they manually resist the shoulder as it moves into flexion, abduction, internal rotation, external rotation, and extension. Once normal range of motion is restored, individuals may progress to using resistive elastic tubing as the shoulder is moved into each of these directions. Once full strength is established, dynamic strengthening such as playing catch with a medicine ball and performing pushups can begin. If the individual wore a sling upon initial injury, the use of the sling is decreased as strength and stability are regained.

Work Restrictions / Accommodations

Access to ice for control of pain and swelling will allow earlier return to work for nondominant injuries.

Use of a sling or sling and swathe is recommended for grade I and II sprains; and is mandatory for first time dislocations, grade III injuries. This limits manual dexterity and may produce a hazard to the individual or those around him or her.

Pain medication is often prescribed that can affect mental alertness and may require alteration of drug use and testing policies by the employer.

Lifting, carrying, and overhead work will be restricted for several weeks or permanently.

Individuals whose work environment places them at risk for recurrent episodes may be asked to wear a protective harness. Use of the arm overhead is restricted with this device. Wearing the harness may be permanent.

Complications

The more chronic the condition, the more difficult it is to treat. Each time the shoulder capsule is injured, more damage is done to the supporting ligaments, making the shoulder more loose (increased laxity). This, in turn, increases the chance of repeated sprains and onset of impingement syndrome.

Tears of the rotator cuff and a pulling away of its attachment to the arm (avulsion of the greater tuberosity) may occur during a severe sprain. These tears may require early surgical repair.

Any fractures that occur during a grade III sprain (dislocation) shoulder change the anatomy of the shoulder and the mechanical action of the joint. Especially troublesome are fractures of the upper arm bone (humeral head) or shoulder blade (scapula, glenoid). These fractures may require surgical correction to restore normal anatomy, allowing the shoulder to be stable. Stability of the shoulder is critical in preventing recurring sprains of the shoulder capsule.

Nerve or vessel injury from the dislocation will need attention immediately.

Factors Influencing Duration

For surgery, duration depends on open or arthroscopic. Depending on if the nondominant versus dominant side is injured, the individual may be disabled from 1 to 10 weeks. If a surgical reconstruction is necessary for the dominant side, additional recovery time may be needed for individuals who perform heavy work.

Failure to fully rehabilitate the shoulder will lead to repeated injuries and perhaps permanent disability.

Older age individuals may not be able to regain adequate strength and stability to resume strenuous activities that stress the shoulder.

Length of Disability

Following surgical treatment, duration will depend on severity of injury and grade (I, II, or III).

Medical treatment.

Duration in Days

Job Classification	Minimum	Optimum	Maximum
Sedentary work	7	14	28
Light work	21	28	56
Medium work	21	28	56
Heavy work	35	42	84
Very Heavy work	35	63	91

Surgical treatment.

Duration in Days

Job Classification	Minimum	Optimum	Maximum
Sedentary work	7	14	28
Light work	12	21	28
Medium work	42	56	84
Heavy work	70	84	140
Very Heavy work	70	84	140

Failure to Recover

If an individual fails to recover within the maximum duration expectancy period, the reader may wish to reference the following questions to assist in better understanding the specifics of an individual's medical case.

Regarding diagnosis:

- Is the sprain Grade I, II, or III?
- What was the mechanism of injury?
- Does the individual have a chronic sprain?
- Does the individual do overhead work?
- What level of pain does individual have?
- On exam was a deformity noted?
- Is the individual able to move his/her arm? What is the level of anxiety?

- Are the individual's reflexes decreased or accentuated?
- Has the individual had plain x-rays? MRI?
- Have conditions with similar symptoms been ruled out?

Regarding treatment:
- Is the individual giving the affected joint and arm appropriate rest using a sling?
- Is the individual using ice and NSAIDs?
- Is the individual continuing to use the wrist? Doing gripping exercises?
- Was the acute sprain reduced on an emergency basis?
- Was a closed reduction done?
- Was surgery necessary?
- Was medication for pain and muscle relaxation prescribed?
- Was physical therapy started at the appropriate time?

Regarding prognosis:
- Is the individual active in physical therapy? Is the individual doing exercises at home?
- Is the individual's employer able to accommodate any necessary restrictions?
- Is the injury on the dominant or nondominant side?
- If necessary, does individual wear a protective harness?
- Does the individual have any conditions that may affect ability to recover?
- Has the individual developed degenerative arthritis?
- Has the individual had other complications such as repeated strains or impingement syndrome?

References

Himes, J.E. "Shoulder Dislocations." Saunders Manual of Medical Practice. Rakel, R.E, ed. Philadelphia: Harcourt Brace & Company, 1996. 817-818.

Jones, Bill. Essentials of Musculoskeletal Care. Snider, Robert K., ed. Boston: American Academy of Orthopaedic Surgeons, 1997.

Kisner, Carolyn, and Lynn Allen Colby. "The Shoulder and Shoulder Girdle." Therapeutic Exercise: Foundations and Techniques. Philadelphia: F.A. Davis Company, 1990. 241-271.

O'Donoghue, D.H., MD. Treatment of Injuries to Athletes, 4th ed. Philadelphia: W.B. Saunders Company, 1984.

Shoulder Injuries in the Athlete: Surgical Repair and Rehabilitation. Hawkins, Richard J., and Gary W. Misamore, eds. New York: Churchill Livingstone, 1995.

Simon, Robert R., and Steven J. Koenigsknecht. Emergency Orthopedics: The Extremities, 3rd ed. Stamford: Appleton & Lange, 1995.

Sprains and Strains, Wrist
Other names / synonyms: Sprained Wrist
842.0, 842.00, 842.01, 842.02, 842.09

Definition

Sprains and strains of the wrist refer to injuries caused by overstretching or tearing of the wrist joint. If a tendon is injured, the injury is referred to as a strain. If the ligament or joint capsule is injured, the injury is called a sprain. The small wrist bones (carpals) are held in position by their shape (which aligns them in 2 rows) and by supporting ligaments and tendons. Injuries to the ligaments or tendons that cross the joints between the joints of the forearm (radius and ulna) and the carpal bones are also known as wrist sprains or strains.

These injuries usually result from a fall onto an outstretched hand. The position of the hand at impact or rotation of the hand determines the type and severity of injury. More severe injuries involve a disruption of the supporting structures and a dislocation of the carpal joint (scapholunate dissociation, lunate or perilunate dislocation). A stretch injury to the ligaments around the joint of the radius, ulna, and carpal bones can lead to improper mechanics of the wrist joint, with permanent loss of stability.

In the US, wrist injuries account for 2.5% of emergency room visits, and the majority of these are sprains and strains. Athletes and those who participate in recreational sports are at particular risk for these injuries, as are those who use their hands in their occupation with lifting or twisting stresses.

Diagnosis

History: The individual will usually relate a history of injury, but it may often seem insignificant to the individual. The individual often complains of pain, swelling, and weakness.

Physical exam: The physician may notice localized swelling of the wrist and pain on range of motion. Neurovascular examination is usually normal in mild and moderate injuries.

Tests: X-rays with special views to evaluate clinical findings suggestive of fractures of the scaphoid or hook of the hamate are utilized. Stress x-rays of the wrist are taken to evaluate joint instability. The ligaments are well-visualized on MRI examination. Arthrograms are useful to evaluate ligament rupture or joint capsule tear, but are only of benefit in the first 5 days after injury, as blood clotting may fill in defects and provide a false negative reading. Bone scans are useful to rule out carpal fractures. Diagnostic arthroscopy may be used to evaluate carpal instability in severe cases or those unresponsive to therapy.

Treatment

If the injury is minor, there is no loss of stability, and some individuals often do not seek treatment. Other individuals with minor injuries, without clinical or x-ray findings of fracture and/or instability, may be treated with a splint or cast.

Because of the potentially serious nature of wrist injuries, referral to a hand surgeon for evaluation and treatment of all significant injuries is essential. Surgical repair of the ligaments may be necessary to preserve wrist stability. For recent (acute) injuries, sewing (suturing) the torn ligament ends back together is the preferred surgical procedure (primary ligament repair).

For chronic injuries, other procedures that reconstruct and reinforce the torn ligaments are performed. These procedures utilize tendons or grafts of tough connective tissue (fascia lata) to connect the bones together, replacing the torn ligament. These wrist reconstruction procedures include Eliason, Bunnell-Boyes, Regan-Bickel, Lowman, Liebolt, and Hill. This type of surgery may require postoperative splinting or casting to maintain the position of the wrist while healing. If the surgery is simple, just repair of a minor tear, postoperative casting will not be necessary. Nonsteroidal anti-inflammatory drugs may be prescribed to reduce swelling and pain. Application of cold therapy is useful in the first 72 hours after injury to reduce swelling. After the wrist has been immobilized for an adequate period of time to allow healing, gradual return to activity is important to preserve function. Physical therapy administered by an experienced hand therapist is often necessary after significant injuries.

Prognosis

Minor sprains should heal uneventfully. Healing may be delayed and there may be some loss of function in injuries that are under-diagnosed or that require surgical repair. More severe injuries that require splinting or casting usually heal completely. Surgical repair (primary repair of ligament or delayed repair of ligament) is usually successful in restoring function but may have a reduced range of motion postoperatively.

Differential Diagnosis

Fractures of bones of the hands and wrist may clinically resemble wrist sprains and strains. The most common of these is the scaphoid fracture, a fracture that is often difficult to visualize on x-rays and can require extensive surgical repair. Other fractures to be ruled out include those of the radius, ulna, and hook of the hamate, as well as avulsions and avulsion-fractures of ligaments. Other conditions that must be ruled out include rheumatoid arthritis, carpal tunnel syndrome, dislocations of the hand and wrist, and other soft-tissue injuries of the hand.

Specialists

- Occupational Therapist
- Physiatrist
- Physical Therapist

Rehabilitation

Individuals who sustain sprains or strains of the wrist may require outpatient therapy. The individual should be seen by either an occupational therapist or a physical therapist who is a certified hand therapist.

Therapy first addresses pain control and the reduction of swelling. Individuals learn to position the hand so that it rests above the elbow on a pillow to decrease swelling in the hand. Hot packs and hot paraffin wax decrease muscle stiffness prior to therapy. Therapists may perform cross-friction massage of the injured ligaments or tendons to promote healing and instruct individuals in self-massage. Ice packs may help to decrease pain and swelling after exercise.

Individuals learn stretching techniques to increase range of motion at the wrist and forearm. Therapists may passively stretch the wrist to increase flexion and extension, the forearm to increase rotation, and the hand to increase finger flexion and extension. Individuals learn to stretch the wrist by holding the elbow straight and using their other hand to help bend the wrist into flexion and extension. Individuals stretch the forearm by placing their other hand on the forearm and using it to help turn the forearm in the 2 rotational directions. Finger stretches involve making a fist and by extending the fingers and adding overpressure with their noninjured hand to increase these motions. Finger and thumb opposition is restored by touching the thumb to each finger.

Strengthening exercises are necessary to restore function and to prevent re-injury. Individuals may use light hand weights to strengthen wrist flexion and extension and forearm rotation; individuals place the forearm on a table for support for these exercises. Individuals squeeze therapy putty to restore hand strength. The muscles of the fingers should be strengthened by pinching therapy putty between the fingers, or by placing a rubber band around 2 fingers at a time and spreading them apart. Individuals may learn functional exercises such as turning a doorknob and turning the pages of a book.

Work Restrictions / Accommodations

Restrictions may include limited use of the affected hand. Individuals should especially avoid lifting, carrying, and twisting. Use of a cast or splint may affect dexterity and require a review of safety issues. Typists may not be able to type until any casting or splinting is completed and the wrist is healed. Driving may or may not be allowed, depending on the type of immobilization used (driving may be allowed with some wraps or splints but not with a cast). Any tasks requiring manual dexterity or lifting will have to be curtailed until healing is complete and full strength and function of the wrist and hand is regained.

Complementary and Alternative Therapies

Content is intended for awareness only. Treatments may or may not be effective. Scientific evidence may be lacking and some substances have potentially toxic effects. Dr. Presley Reed and the editors do not endorse the use of these therapies in the absence of consultation with a licensed medical professional.

Acupuncture - May promote drainage and stimulate healing.

Acupressure - May aid in drainage.

Arnica - Used externally, may relieve pain and swelling.

Hydrotherapy - Ice whirlpool may stimulate injured cells and promote healing. Contrast baths may also be used to clear congestion and stimulate healing.

Comorbid Conditions

Arthritic conditions such as rheumatoid arthritis and connective tissue conditions such as systemic lupus erythematosus can predispose individuals to strains and sprains, and can lengthen recovery.

Complications

Missed diagnosis, fractures, and dislocations complicate recovery. Surgical complications include infection and stiffness. Inflammatory conditions that weaken supporting tissue may complicate treatment.

Degenerative joint disease of the wrist (osteoarthritis) may result from the injury.

Factors Influencing Duration

Factors include the location, type, and severity of the injury, whether the dominant hand was affected, the severity of the pain associated with the injury, the method of treatment, the individual's response to treatment and adherence to recommendations, and the individual's job requirements.

Length of Disability

For a severe (third-degree) injury, duration depends on whether dominant or non-dominant extremity is involved.

Mild to moderate (first or second-degree).

Duration in Days

Job Classification	Minimum	Optimum	Maximum
Sedentary work	1	3	7
Light work	1	7	14
Medium work	7	14	28
Heavy work	14	21	35
Very Heavy work	21	28	42

Severe (third-degree).

Duration in Days

Job Classification	Minimum	Optimum	Maximum
Sedentary work	1	7	28
Light work	1	14	35
Medium work	14	28	42
Heavy work	21	35	56
Very Heavy work	28	42	70

Duration Trend from Normative Data*

Cases	Mean	Min	Max	No Lost Time	Over 6 Months
1039	60	0	567	4.51%	5.10%

Percentile:	5th	25th	Median	75th	95th
Days:	1	14	31	70	154

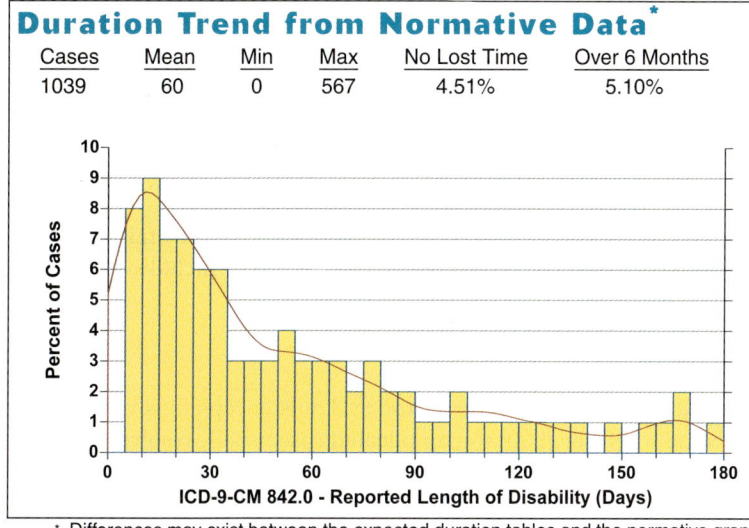
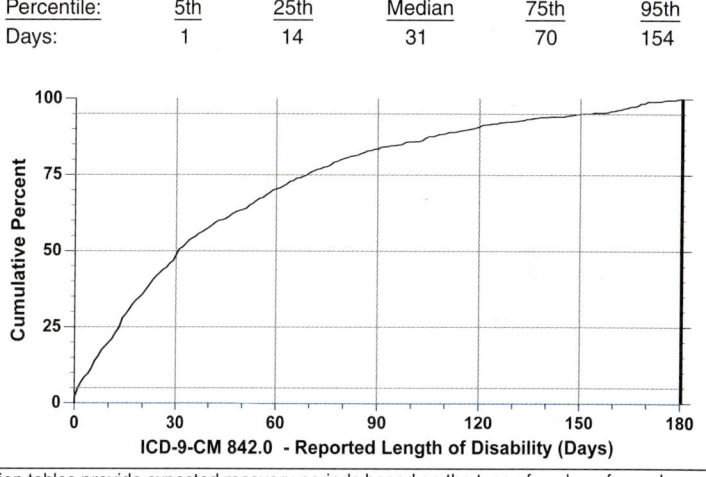

ICD-9-CM 842.0 - Reported Length of Disability (Days)

* Differences may exist between the expected duration tables and the normative graphs. Duration tables provide expected recovery periods based on the type of work performed by the individual. The normative graphs reflect the actual observed experience of many individuals across the spectrum of physical conditions, in a variety of industries, and with varying levels of case management.

Failure to Recover

If an individual fails to recover within the maximum duration expectancy period, the reader may wish to reference the following questions to assist in better understanding the specifics of an individual's medical case.

Regarding diagnosis:

- Has diagnosis been confirmed?
- Have conditions such as rheumatoid arthritis, carpal tunnel syndrome, dislocations of the hand and wrist, and other soft-tissue injuries of the hand been ruled out?
- If pain and stiffness persist despite therapy, has x-ray been done to rule out fracture?
- Has MRI been done to rule out fibrosis or arthritic degeneration?
- Has the individual experienced any complications such as infection, stiffness, inflammatory conditions, or degenerative joint disease?
- Does the individual have any underlying conditions such as rheumatoid arthritis systemic, or lupus erythematosus that may impact recovery?

Regarding treatment:

- Has the individual been evaluated by a hand surgeon?
- Is surgical intervention warranted?
- Would the individual benefit from ligament reconstruction?
- Has the individual received comprehensive rehabilitation? By a hand therapist?

Regarding prognosis:

- Did complications delay diagnosis or treatment?
- Is the individual complying with treatment regimen?
- Is range of motion impaired? How does this impact occupational functioning?

References

Beeson, Michael S. Wrist Dislocations. eMedicine.com. 05 Sep 2000. 9 Oct 2000 <http://www.emedicine.com/emerg/topic149.htm>.

Ritchie, J.V., and D.W. Munter. "Emergency Department Evaluation and Treatment of Wrist Injuries." Emergency Medical Clinics of North America 17 4 (1999): 832-842.

St. Louis Encephalitis
Other names / synonyms: SLE, Viral Meningitis
062.3

Definition

St. Louis encephalitis (SLE) is a viral infection of the brain (encephalitis) that is spread to humans through the bite of infected mosquitoes. Although the virus does not always cause disease, when it does, it can be life threatening.

The SLE virus is part of a group of viruses that are transmitted by blood sucking insects, such as mosquitoes (arboviruses). Birds, especially domestic fowl, can harbor the virus. As the population of infected birds increase, outbreaks of SLE occur. This disease was first identified in St. Louis, hence the name. Although cases average only 193 per year, it is the most prevalent arbovirus in the US.

St. Louis encephalitis is similar to other forms of arboviral encephalitis such as West Nile encephalitis, western equine encephalitis, eastern equine encephalitis, and California encephalitis, which are all found in the US. Similar diseases are also found on other continents such as Japanese B encephalitis. The diseases are typically named for where they are found.

Arboviral infections are usually continuously present (endemic) in specific geographical areas. Individuals who live in these areas often develop immunity to the disease. For instance, once an individual has had St. Louis encephalitis, re-infection is not likely. However, increased travel puts individuals at a higher risk of contracting arboviral viruses from other areas of the world to which they as yet have no immunity.

The very young and the elderly are most susceptible to SLE. The disease, which is more prevalent in the southern portion of the US, occurs most often in the late summer and early fall when mosquito populations are at their highest

Diagnosis

History: Symptoms may include headache, drowsiness, fever, and sore throat. Vomiting and a stiff neck may also occur. The disease progresses rapidly and may involve muscle trembling, mental confusion, convulsions, and coma. The fever may last from 4-10 days.

Physical exam: The exam may reveal some paralysis in the extremities and cranial nerves. Superficial reflexes may be absent.

Tests: A spinal tap may reveal increased pressure in the cerebrospinal fluid pressure and increased protein content. A blood test called HI (hemagglutination-inhibiting) antibody can identify antibodies for an arbovirus group, but not for specific viruses. CT or MRI may also be performed to look for brain lesions.

Treatment

There is no specific treatment for the viral forms of encephalitis such as St. Louis encephalitis. Care is generally supportive.

Severe illness may require hospitalization in order to monitor heart and lung functions. Treatment may include mannitol to reduce intracranial pressure, or anticonvulsants to control convulsions. The airway must be maintained, with administration of supplemental oxygen as needed. If the individual is in a coma, appropriate nutrition must be maintained.

Prevention of St. Louis encephalitis, as with other arboviral diseases, is based on mosquito control. Personal protection includes the use of protective clothing and repellents.

Prognosis

Most individuals who contract the St. Louis encephalitis virus do not become seriously ill. An uncomplicated case usually resolves within 4-10 days.

Others can become seriously ill with a guarded prognosis. Symptoms can worsen at any moment during the course of the disease, even after apparent recovery. Death occurs in up to 30% of elderly individuals.

Differential Diagnosis

Conditions with similar symptoms include aseptic meningitis, lymphocytic choriomeningitis, cerebrovascular accidents, brain tumors, brain abscesses, nonparalytic poliomyelitis, and intoxications. St. Louis encephalitis must also be differentiated from herpes simplex virus, mumps virus, poliovirus, HIV, measles, varicella (chickenpox), infectious mononucleosis, rubella, and vaccination-induced encephalitis.

Specialists

- Infectious Disease Physician
- Neurologist

Rehabilitation

Individuals who contract St. Louis encephalitis may require physical, occupational, and/or speech therapy, contingent upon the symptoms the individual experiences. The frequency and duration of rehabilitation varies with the type and severity of symptoms.

Occupational therapy is most frequently required due to the fatigue associated with this disease. Individuals learn energy conservation techniques, in which activities of daily living such as meal preparation are broken up into smaller components thereby making tasks more manageable. Individuals also learn strategies to complete tasks during the portion of the day that their energy level is highest.

Physical therapy addresses any gait abnormalities that may result. Individuals are assessed for strength deficits that may be contributing to the gait deviation. Individuals learn exercises to strengthen weak musculature (for example, straight leg raises to increase hip flexion strength). Individuals may also engage in treadmill walking to improve the quality of the gait. Individuals may learn to use a cane, a walker, or crutches to normalize the gait pattern. Individuals may also be fitted with orthotic braces for the legs to help with muscular control.

Balance deficits that may be present are addressed through physical and occupational therapy. Individuals may learn exercises to maintain strength in the arms, legs, and trunk. Some examples of exercises are seated leg lifts, arm raises, and bridging exercises in which the buttocks are raised while lying on the back. Individuals learn to perform weight-shifting exercises in standing to aid in balance during walking and transferring. Individuals may perform standing weight shifts during therapy while attending to another task such as putting dishes on a shelf. Individuals improve sitting balance through activities such as weight shifting while sitting on a therapy ball.

Individuals who experience speech impairments attend speech therapy.

Work Restrictions / Accommodations

Accommodations may be required for individuals who have impairments such as difficulty walking, seizures, speech problems, or decreased mental alertness. Because complete recovery can take a long time, the workload may need to be decreased until stamina returns.

Comorbid Conditions

The elderly and individuals with suppressed or weakened immune systems are vulnerable to a more serious illness.

Complications

Complications include paralysis of the arms and legs, bronchial pneumonia, urinary retention, urinary infections, and decubitus ulcers. Mental deterioration, Parkinsonism, and epilepsy may also occur.

Factors Influencing Duration

Length of disability might be influenced by the severity of symptoms, response to treatment, and the presence of complications or residual impairment.

Length of Disability

Duration in Days

Job Classification	Minimum	Optimum	Maximum
Any work	14	28	56

Failure to Recover

If an individual fails to recover within the maximum duration expectancy period, the reader may wish to reference the following questions to assist in better understanding the specifics of an individual's medical case.

Regarding diagnosis:

- Has diagnosis of St. Louis encephalitis been confirmed?
- Has the individual experienced complications such as paralysis of the arms and legs, bronchial pneumonia, urinary retention, urinary infections, and decubitus ulcers that may lengthen disability?
- Does the individual have an underlying condition, weakened immune system or advanced age that may impact recovery?

Regarding treatment:

- Were supportive measures effective in preventing complications?
- Were treatment measures such as hospitalization, mannitol, anticonvulsants, supplemental oxygen, and parental nutrition, effective in preventing or lessening residual impairment?

Regarding prognosis:

- How long has recovery extended past expectation?
- Is this an exacerbation of original symptoms, or have complications developed?
- Does individual use protective clothing and repellents when working in an area known for mosquito infestation?
- Is the individual involved in physical therapy?

References

Brooks, George F., Janet S. Butel, and Stephen A. Morse. Medical Microbiology. Stamford: Appleton & Lange, 1998.

Guccione, Andrew A. "Functional Assessment." Physical Rehabilitation: Assessment and Treatment. O'Sullivan, Susan B., and Thomas J. Schmitz, eds. Philadelphia: F.A. Davis Company, 1994. 193-208.

O'Sullivan, Susan B. "Motor Control Assessment." Physical Rehabilitation: Assessment and Treatment. O'Sullivan, Susan B., and Thomas J. Schmitz, eds. Philadelphia: F.A. Davis Company, 1994. 111-132.

Sarno, Martha Taylor. "Neurogenic Disorders of Speech and Language." Physical Rehabilitation: Assessment and Treatment. O'Sullivan, Susan B., and Thomas J. Schmitz, eds. Philadelphia: F.A. Davis Company, 1994. 633-654.

Stapedectomy

Other names / synonyms: Stapedotomy

19.0, 19.19

Definition

Stapedectomy is a surgical procedure done to restore mobility to the bones in the middle ear that conduct sound to the inner ear. The 3 bones of the middle ear are the hammer (malleus), anvil (incus) and stirrup (stapes). Stapedectomy removes the stapes in whole or part with replacement by a metal or plastic prosthesis.

Stapedectomy is used to treat otosclerosis. Otosclerosis is a condition of the middle ear in which new bone tissue is formed, interfering with the mechanism of the 3 bones conducting sound. It normally occurs in adults between 30 and 50 years of age. In young adults, especially women, conductive deafness occurs between 18 and 40 years of age. Otosclerosis is a chronic disease that frequently runs in families.

Reason for Procedure

The procedure is used for otosclerosis with stapes fixation to overcome a conductive hearing loss. Stapes fixation refers to an overgrowth of bone, which can cause the stapes (stirrup) to become fixed in place to other parts of the middle ear (otosclerosis), usually the eardrum (tympanic membrane), causing deafness. A stapedectomy corrects hearing loss by removing the stapes and replacing it with a prosthesis.

Description

Stapedectomy is ordinarily carried out as outpatient surgery.

If both ears are affected, surgery is done on separate occasions. Stapes surgery is performed through the ear canal under local anesthesia. A small incision may be made in front of the ear to remove tissue for use in the operation. Using an operating microscope, the eardrum is turned forward and the fixed stapes is removed. Tissue is placed over the opening to the inner ear and a wire, Teflon, or metal prosthesis or piston is inserted attached to the incus (the anvil, the second of the 3 middle ear bones). The eardrum is then replaced in its normal position and the ear canal is filled with ointment. The stapes prosthesis allows sound vibrations to again pass from the eardrum to the inner ear fluids. The wound is closed with fine sutures, which usually can be removed about 1 week after surgery.

Prognosis

The individual may expect complete healing of the surgical wound without complications. Hearing should improve immediately. The hearing improvement obtained is usually permanent.

After surgery, the individual should lie flat during the first 24 to 48 hours. The individual should not blow his/her nose for at least 1 week after surgery. Ears should be protected from moisture or cold. Tub baths should be taken instead of showers for 2 weeks after surgery.

Specialists

- Otolaryngologist

Work Restrictions / Accommodations

Individuals with hearing loss may require accommodations in accordance with the impairment. Normal activity may be restricted for several weeks. Individuals should remain relatively immobile. Flying should be restricted for three weeks.

Comorbid Conditions

Meniere disease and chronic ear infections may lengthen recovery from stapedectomy and success of the procedure.

Procedure Complications

Dizziness is normal for a few hours following stapedectomy, and may result in nausea and vomiting. Some unsteadiness is common during the first few postoperative days; dizziness on sudden head movements may persist for several weeks. On rare occasions, dizziness is prolonged. Taste disturbance is not uncommon for a few weeks following surgery. In 5% of the individuals, this disturbance is prolonged. In about 2% of individuals, the hearing may be further impaired due to the development of scar tissue, infection, blood vessel spasm, irritation of the inner ear, or a leak of inner ear fluid (called a fistula). In 1% of individuals, complications in the healing process may be so great that there is severe loss of hearing in the operated ear. This may be to the extent that one cannot obtain benefit from a hearing aid in that ear. For this reason the poorer hearing ear is selected for surgery.

A hole in the eardrum membrane is an unusual complication. It develops in less than 1% of individuals, and is usually due to an infection. Fortunately, should this complication occur, the membrane often heals spontaneously. If healing does not occur, surgical repair may be required. A very rare complication of stapedectomy is temporary weakness of the face. This may occur as a result of an abnormality or swelling of the facial nerve. The surgical site may be subject to excessive bleeding and infection.

Factors Influencing Duration

Individual compliance with after-surgery recommendations can influence length of disability.

Length of Disability

Duration in Days

Job Classification	Minimum	Optimum	Maximum
Sedentary work	4	7	7
Light work	10	10	14
Medium work	10	14	21
Heavy work	21	21	28
Very Heavy work	28	28	28

References

Rowe, Lee, MD. "Otolaryngology." Current Surgical Diagnosis and Treatment. Way, Lawrence, ed. Norwalk: Appleton & Lange, 1991. 843-872.

Stokes-Adams Syndrome

Other names / synonyms: Adams-Stokes Syndrome, Cardiogenic Syncope, Morgagni-Adams-Stokes Syndrome, Stokes-Adams Attacks, Stokes-Adams Syncope with Heart Block, Stokes-Adams-Morgagni Syndrome

426.9

Definition

Stokes-Adams syndrome is a heart disorder characterized by dizziness, labored breathing (dyspnea), and fainting (syncope).

The cause of the fainting spells is an abnormality (atrioventricular block) of the electrical conduction system in the heart that begins with a slow heart rate (bradycardia), which evolves into a complete stoppage of the heart (asystole). Fainting is then caused by loss of oxygen to the brain (cerebral anoxia) after the heart stops beating. Convulsions may occur if the heart stops for longer than 15 seconds. In rare cases, the attendant oxygen loss may cause permanent brain damage.

Risk factors for Stokes-Adams syndrome may include a decreased blood supply (ischemia) to the heart muscle resulting from a heart attack (myocardial infarction or MI), certain prescription drugs, elevated blood potassium levels (hyperkalemia), congenital heart disease, aging (Lenegre's syndrome), diseases of the aortic and mitral valves, and postoperative complications. Infectious diseases that may increase the risk for Stokes-Adams syndrome include acute rheumatic fever, endocarditis, myocarditis, Lyme disease, and almost any other systemic infectious disease such as mononucleosis. Less common risk factors may include infiltrative and connective tissue diseases such as tumors, sarcoidosis, and amyloidosis.

Stokes-Adams syndrome occurs commonly in individuals with certain types of atrioventricular block (third degree atrioventricular block or complete heart block) and it is generally reported in 38-61% of these cases. Atrioventricular block is rarely found in young healthy adults but the incidence increases with age and in individuals who have heart disease. Studies indicate that milder forms of heart block (first degree block) occurs in 5% of men older than 60 years of age, and this figure increases to 10% if cardiac disease is present. Third-degree heart block occurs most often in people greater than seventy years old. Forty percent of elderly individuals who have third-degree block are women.

Diagnosis

History: Individuals may complain of light-headedness or fainting up to several times a day. These spells may occur while the individual is in either a lying or standing position. Usually they will not report any sort of unusual or ill feeling prior to fainting or after regaining consciousness.

Physical exam: The exam will often be normal. The blood pressure may be checked several times in different positions to rule out low blood pressure as a cause of the fainting episodes (postural hypotension). The heart rate may be slow at less than 50 beats a minute (bradycardia) and it may not speed up with exertion.

Tests: The electrical activity of the heart can be recorded (electrocardiogram or ECG) and this may confirm the diagnosis of an electrical conduction block. If not immediately diagnosed, a portable device (Holter monitor) may be worn from which an ECG tracing can be recorded continuously over the period of a day or more. High frequency sound waves (ultrasound) can be used to identify other structural defects that may be associated with conduction abnormalities that are associated with Stokes-Adams syndrome.

Treatment

Stokes-Adams syndrome was the chief impetus for development of a device that monitors and regulates the heart beat (artificial pacemaker) and these have been in use for over 30 years. Surgical implantation of a pacemaker into the heart is still the treatment of choice. In emergency situations, the individual may require the use of electric current to stimulate the heart into a normal beat pattern (cardioversion).

Prognosis

The fainting episodes are usually brief, and most often, the individual will recover immediately. Following pacemaker implantation, the vast majority of individuals show improvement within one month and can usually resume most tasks associated with daily living. The incidence of infection after surgical implantation of a cardiac pacemaker is usually less than 1%. However, the device should be checked regularly to ensure that it is functioning properly.

Differential Diagnosis

Conditions that present with similar symptoms as Stokes-Adams syndrome include low blood pressure attributed to a change in posture (postural hypotension), low hemoglobin in the blood (anemia), blocking of the vessels carrying blood to the brain (diffuse cerebral arteriosclerosis), or general physical debility due to advancing age or other systemic disease.

Specialists

- Cardiologist
- Cardiovascular Surgeon

Rehabilitation

An exercise program may follow pacemaker implantation. Exercise may begin in the coronary care unit of a hospital starting with low-level exercise with the individual positioned on his or her back (supine position). The individual progresses with exercises to sitting and eventually to standing. Progressive walking (ambulating) and eventually stair climbing are an important part of the individual's inpatient exercise program. Intensity is gradually increased until discharge from the hospital.

Phase two usually begins after the individual is discharged from the hospital. Goals are to improve functional capacity by increasing the physical endurance and promoting return to activity. This is done in an outpatient setting such as a rehabilitation center. Individuals typically are also attached to an electrocardiograph (EKG) to record the continuous electrical activity of the heart muscle. A physical therapist keeps a daily log of the individual's blood pressure, heart rate, and cardiac rhythm.

Phase three continues in an outpatient setting such as a rehab center. Individuals may stay involved with an outpatient program for up to a year to accomplish all of the their goals while still at modified work duty. Eventually higher levels of exercise comprise this phase with the addition of recreational activities as tolerated by the individual such as ambulatory exercises on a regular basis.

Phase four of cardiac rehabilitation occurs after discharge from the hospital. Long-term maintenance of physical performance reached to this point is of importance. For the individual with Stokes-Adams syndrome this may consist of walking three or four times a week to help maintain overall endurance and keep high blood pressure under control. Throughout all phases, it is important to allow the heart rate to slowly return to normal after the exercises.

Modifications may need to be made for those individuals participating in a drug treatment for Stokes-Adams syndrome. Adaptations are also made in the case of the condition being associated with coronary heart disease and/or after suffering from a heart attack.

Work Restrictions / Accommodations

There are few, if any, work accommodations that are necessary following implantation of a pacemaker. However, any activity with the potential for creating a significant electromagnetic field should be approached with caution by the individual who has a pacemaker. Generally, this includes avoidance of arc-welding and working directly over combustion engines. If the individual's job requires work within strong electromagnetic interference (EMI), he/she should be monitored during exposure. The initial exposure should be under controlled conditions with an assistant present to prevent sustained exposure should the EMI result in pacemaker inhibition. During the initial exposure, the individual may be monitored with an ambulatory electrocardiogram (ECG) or by monitoring capabilities incorporated within the pacemaker.

Comorbid Conditions

Conditions that decrease blood flow to the atrioventricular (AV) junction in the heart such as heart attack (myocardial infarction or MI) or chronic low blood flow (ischemia) to the heart may affect an individual's ability to alleviate Stokes-Adams syndrome. Trauma to the AV junction resulting from cardiac surgery may have a similar effect. High potassium in the blood stream (hyperkalemia), congenital heart disease, heart valve disease (aortic or mitral valvular disease), diabetes mellitus, breathing abnormality (pulmonary insufficiency), and kidney (renal) disease that requires dialysis may further lengthen disability.

Less commonly, infiltrative and connective tissue diseases of the heart can have detrimental effects.

Complications

Complications of a Stokes-Adams attack may include permanent brain damage (neurological impairment) if there is a prolonged period of low oxygen (anoxia) to the brain. Other complications may include physical harm to the individual as a result of accidents or falling during fainting spells.

Factors Influencing Duration

Factors that might influence the length of disability include the age of the individual, dysfunction or complications of an implanted pacemaker, and complications resulting from surgery.

Length of Disability

Following pacemaker implantation, the individual may have to limit motion of their ipsilateral shoulder and arm. Complete range of motion may be resumed in 2-4 weeks. Durations reflect recovery from procedure only.

Cardiac pacemaker insertion.

Duration in Days

Job Classification	Minimum	Optimum	Maximum
Sedentary work	3	4	7
Light work	3	4	7
Medium work	7	14	21
Heavy work	14	21	28
Very Heavy work	14	21	28

Failure to Recover

If an individual fails to recover within the maximum duration expectancy period, the reader may wish to reference the following questions to assist in better understanding the specifics of an individual's medical case.

Regarding diagnosis:

- Does the individual have any risk factors for Stokes-Adams syndrome, such as ischemia to the heart muscle resulting from a heart attack, certain prescription drugs, hyperkalemia, congenital heart disease, aging (Lenegre's syndrome), diseases of the aortic and mitral valves, rheumatic fever, endocarditis, myocarditis, Lyme disease, or third degree atrioventricular block or complete heart block?
- Did the individual experience frequent episodes of dizziness or syncope?
- Did the physical exam reveal postural hypotension and/or bradycardia?
- Was the diagnosis confirmed with an ECG?

Regarding treatment:

- Was a pacemaker necessary to relieve symptoms?

Regarding prognosis:
- Has the employer made appropriate accommodations to allow the individual to return to work safely (e.g., pacemaker precautions to avoid electromagnetic interference)?
- Does the individual have any existing conditions that could impact recovery such as heart disease, chronic pulmonary disease, diabetes, kidney disease, or electrolyte imbalance?
- Did the individual experience any complications such as stroke or heart attack that could impact recovery and prognosis?

References

Kisner, C., and L. Colby. Therapeutic Exercise Foundations and Techniques. Philadelphia: F.A. Davis Company, 1990.

LeMone, P., and, K.M. Burke. Medical-Surgical Nursing. Upper Saddle River, NJ: Prentice Hall Health, 2000.

Strep Throat
Other names / synonyms: Streptococcal Pharyngitis, Streptococcal Sore Throat, Streptococcal Throat Infection
034, 034.0

Definition

Strep throat is a contagious bacterial infection that is caused by a type of bacteria called group A streptococci. Streptococci are commonly referred to as "strep." The bacterium is spread through the air by a sneeze or cough or by physical contact. The incubation period is generally 3 to 5 days.

In the vast majority of cases, strep throat is a short-lived, uncomplicated infection. It is easily treated with antibiotics. Untreated strep throat, however, can lead to complications including heart and kidney damage. Although very rare, death can occur due to heart or kidney failure.

The infection spreads easily in homes, schools, or other areas where individuals are in close, continued contact with each other. Individuals with a compromised or suppressed immune system are not only at a higher risk for strep throat, but they tend to experience more severe symptoms. Fatigue, smoking, and excessive alcohol consumption reduce immunity and increase an individual's risk of contracting this illness from another infected individual.

Several million cases of strep throat are diagnosed each year. A Canadian study of the epidemiology and clinical features of invasive S. pyogenes infection in a pediatric population over a seven-year period (1984-90) showed an increasing frequency in invasive infections. A reported overall increase in S. pyogenes infections with strep throat was recorded in 4.41-46.54 out of 10,000 outpatients.

Diagnosis

History: Individuals complain of sore throat with pain on swallowing. Other symptoms may include headache, loss of appetite, fatigue, and/or hoarseness. Upon questioning, the individual may reveal contact with another infected individual.

Symptoms of complicated strep disease include persistent sore throat, joint pain (arthritis), skin rash, abdominal pain, and occasionally involuntary movements. Individuals may report the sudden appearance of blood in the urine that indicates kidney involvement. There may also be swelling around the ankles or eyes and shortness of breath or fatigue.

Physical exam: Although 20% of cases have no symptoms (asymptomatic), most individuals experience fever that may be high (over 39 degrees C) and a dry cough. The throat is beefy red upon examination and the tonsils are enlarged. White spots on the throat (collections of pus) may also be present. Lymph nodes in the neck may be tender and enlarged.

Advanced streptococcal infection can also involve the joints especially the knees, ankles, wrists, or elbows and manifest with swollen, painful joints (acute arthritis). The arthritis often moves from one joint to another. A red, raised rash may appear on the skin for short periods of time. If the infection has affected the heart, a heart murmur may be detected. Elevated blood pressure or swelling (edema) may indicate kidney involvement.

Tests: Strep throat is diagnosed by swabbing the throat, then culturing the collected bacteria on a special culture medium called blood agar. Although rapid screening tests are available for strep diagnosis, they have a 5-10% false negative rate so negative results are routinely backed up with the standard blood agar culture. In systemic infection, bacteria may be isolated from blood or the infection may be diagnosed indirectly by the presence of streptococcus-specific antibodies in serum. When kidney disease is suspected, a urinalysis will show blood or protein in the urine, and bacteria may be cultured from either the blood or urine. A kidney biopsy is rarely done to diagnose involvement of the kidneys.

Treatment

Strep throat is treated with antibiotics. The type of antibiotic chosen varies depending on the individual. The antibiotics are usually taken for 10 days. If compliance with a 10-day treatment regimen is difficult, newer antibiotics can provide similar effectiveness with a 5- or 6-day treatment. These newer agents are often more expensive than the standard treatments. In moderate to severe infections, a single dose of antibiotic may be injected.

Nonprescription medications may be used for relief of pain (analgesics) and to reduce fever (antipyretics).

If systemic disease develops, individuals are given antibiotics to treat residual strep throat infection. Anti-inflammatory drugs control joint pain and swelling. For more serious inflammation, corticosteroids may be needed. If rheumatic fever develops, bed rest may be prescribed for 2 to 12 weeks. Prolonged antibiotic therapy may be required to prevent reinfection. When the heart is damaged, preventive antibiotic therapy may be needed prior to any dental or surgical procedures for the rest of the individual's life. Damaged heart valves may require surgical repair (valvuloplasty).

Kidney disease is treated symptomatically. High blood pressure is treated with antihypertensive drugs. Diuretics and a low-salt diet help reduce water retention. For severe complications, kidney dialysis may be needed.

Although once common, removal of the tonsils (tonsillectomy) is rarely performed today.

Prognosis

The prognosis for a treated strep throat is good. Symptoms are usually resolved within 5 to 7 days although prescribed therapy may need to continue for 10 days. Residual effects are not expected in the vast majority of cases.

The predicted outcome for untreated or complicated disease varies. Significant long-term medical problems can develop including rheumatic heart disease and kidney disease (glomerulonephritis). Although very rare, death from heart or kidney failure can occur.

Differential Diagnosis

Conditions with similar symptoms include pharyngitis that is caused by other bacterial and viral infections such as adenoviruses, Epstein-Barr virus, mononucleosis, diphtheria, candidiasis, necrotizing ulcerative gingivostomatitis, and bacterial epiglottitis.

Specialists

- Cardiologist
- Infectious Disease Physician
- Internist
- Nephrologist
- Otolaryngologist

Work Restrictions / Accommodations

Individuals should not return to work until the fever is gone. If work involves strenuous exercise, workload should be slowly increased until normal strength and endurance return.

Comorbid Conditions

Individuals with a compromised immune system are at risk for more serious complications of strep throat and may experience a longer recovery period. There is mounting evidence that smoking (even "passive" smoking) has a harmful effect on the lungs and increases the risk for respiratory infections.

Complications

Suppurative (associated with pus) complications from a strep infection include sinusitis, otitis media, mastoiditis, peritonsillar abscess, and lymph node involvement. Scarlet fever produces a rash caused by bacterial toxins. More serious complications include rheumatic fever or rheumatic heart disease that can damage the valves and muscle of the heart. Another complication is acute glomerulonephritis. This is an inflammation of the kidneys. In severe cases, kidney failure may occur. Strep can also involve the brain (strep meningitis). Other relatively uncommon infections that may be caused by group A streptococci include arthritis, pneumonia, empyema, endocarditis, necrotizing fasciitis, and a toxic shock-like syndrome.

Factors Influencing Duration

Length of disability is determined by the severity of disease at the time of treatment, severity of symptoms, type of treatment, response to treatment, and any complications. Older individuals and those who suffer from inadequate immunity may develop more severe infections.

Length of Disability

Duration depends upon the severity of infection at the initiation of treatment. Other medical complications may prolong disability duration.

Medical treatment without complications.

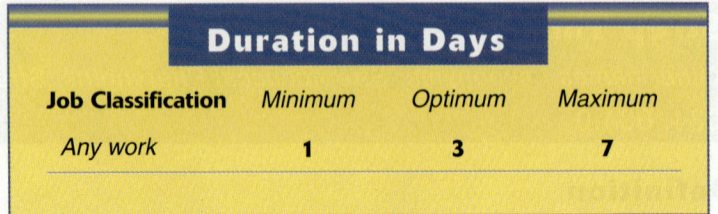

Job Classification	Minimum	Optimum	Maximum
Any work	1	3	7

Failure to Recover

If an individual fails to recover within the maximum duration expectancy period, the reader may wish to reference the following questions to assist in better understanding the specifics of an individual's medical case.

Regarding diagnosis:

- Has diagnosis of streptococcal infection been confirmed by positive culture? Have other conditions such as adenoviruses, Epstein-Barr virus, mononucleosis, diphtheria, candidiasis, necrotizing ulcerative gingivostomatitis), or bacterial epiglottitis, that cause similar symptoms been ruled out?
- Was diagnosis or treatment delayed?
- Has individual experienced complications such as, sinusitis and otitis media?
- If treatment was delayed, did individual experience more serious complications affecting the valves and muscle of the heart, or causing kidney failure?
- Does individual have an underlying condition such as advanced age or a compromised immune system that may impact recovery?

Regarding treatment:

- Is individual taking the medication correctly, at the proper times during the day, and for the required number of days?
- If individual is unable or incapable of complying with medication regimen, is there someone else in the household who could monitor or administer medication?
- Has individual stopped taking antibiotics before completion of the prescribed course due to improvement of symptoms? Why?
- If due to side effects, can an alternate antibiotic be substituted?
- If symptoms persist despite treatment, was culture and sensitivity performed to determine the appropriate antibiotics and to rule-out antibiotic-resistant organisms?
- Has individual stopped taking antibiotics before completion of the prescribed course due to improvement of symptoms? Why? If due to side effects, can an alternate antibiotic be substituted?

Regarding prognosis:

- How much longer than expected has illness persisted?
- Would individual benefit from a different or longer course of antibiotics?
- If individual developed complications, is he/she responding to treatment?
- Would individual benefit from consultation with a specialist (infectious disease specialist, cardiologist, nephrologist)?

References

Burtner, David. "Pharyngitis." Griffith's 5-minute Clinical Consult. Dambro, Mark, ed. Philadelphia: Lippincott, Williams & Wilkins, 2000. 804-805.

Cimolai, N., C. Trombley, and R.J. Adderley. "Invasive Streptococcus Pyogenes Infections in Children." Canadian Journal of Public Health 83 3 (1992): 230-233.

Simon, Harvey. "Infectious Disease." Bacterial Infections of the Upper Respiratory Tract. Dale, D.C., and Daniel D. Federman, MD, eds. New York: WebMD Corporation, 2000 Scientific American Medicine. 20 Aug 2000 <http://www.samed.com/sam/forms/index.htm>.

Strep Demands Immediate Care. United States Food and Drug Administration. 06 May 1998. 20 Aug 2000 <http://www.fda.gov/bbs/topics/CONSUMER/CON00115.html>.

Stress Disorder, Acute
Other names / synonyms: Stress Anxiety, Stress-Related Anxiety Disorder
308.0, 308.3, 308.9

Definition

This disorder is characterized by marked anxiety, feelings of unreality or of being in a dream (dissociative symptoms), and other symptoms that occur within one month after exposure to an extremely stressful trauma (stressor), which could be considered life threatening to the individual or to someone else. The event is frequently re-experienced as a recurrent image, thought, dream, illusion, flashback, feelings of distress with any reminder of the event, or vividly reliving the experience. The individual consistently avoids any reminders of the event, such as specific people or places. Serious anxiety can be manifest as being intensely alert and on guard (hypervigilance), or as sleeplessness, irritability, or difficulty concentrating. Hopelessness can appear along with guilt at having survived the event if others did not. These feelings have a negative impact on relationships or work performance. Decreased emotional responsiveness may be reflected in difficulty enjoying any of life's previous pleasures. Individuals may neglect their basic personal health and even their safety. Impulsiveness and risk-taking behaviors can suddenly appear, in contrast to the individual's usual personality. Acute stress disorder is distinguished from other stress disorders by duration. Symptoms usually last at least 2 days but not more than 4 weeks. If symptoms last longer, a diagnosis of Post-Traumatic Stress Disorder (PTSD) is usually made. Therefore, diagnosing Acute Stress Disorder can identify those who will develop a more chronic condition. Identifying acute stress disorder is also useful because disorganized behavior can leave the individuals unable to care for themselves, thus requiring treatment.

More women than men tend to suffer from anxiety disorders. Genetic factors may play some role, but specific genes have not been identified.

Diagnosis

History: A diagnosis is based on criteria listed in the DSM-IV-TR (Diagnostic and Statistical Manual of Mental Disorders, 4th Edition, Text Revision, published by the American Psychiatric Association). The history, psychiatric interview, and mental status exam of an individual who has experienced or witnessed a traumatic event are used to establish whether the individual's response or behavior meets the diagnostic criteria. The event is one that involved threatened or actual death, serious injury, or threat to physical integrity, and to which the individual's response was intense fear, helplessness, or horror. Either while experiencing or after experiencing the event, the individual has at least three of the following dissociative symptoms: a sense of numbing, detachment, or absence of emotional responsiveness; a reduction in awareness of surroundings or the feeling of being in a daze; feelings of strangeness about the world (derealization); feeling distant from one's own thoughts, feelings, or body (depersonalization); or the inability to recall an important aspect of the trauma (depersonalization).

The traumatic event is persistently reexperienced in at least one of the following ways: recurrent images, thoughts, dreams, illusions, flashbacks; a sense of reliving the experience; or distress when exposed to reminders of the traumatic event. There is marked avoidance of thoughts, feelings, conversations, activities, places, people, or other stimuli that remind the individual of the traumatic event. There are marked symptoms of anxiety or increased arousal, such as difficulty sleeping, irritability, poor concentration, exaggerated alertness (hypervigilance), tendency to jump or flinch at loud noises or sudden movements (exaggerated startle response), or hyperactivity (motor restlessness). The symptoms result in significant distress, impaired relationships, or problems functioning at work or in other activities, but are not merely an exacerbation of a pre-existing psychiatric disorder. The disturbance lasts from a minimum of 2 days to a maximum of 4 weeks, and occurs within 4 weeks of the traumatic event. The diagnosis is not applicable if symptoms are from a drug effect or medical condition; nor is acute stress disorder diagnosed if symptoms could be better explained by a brief psychotic disorder or deterioration of a pre-existing mental disorder.

Physical exam: The exam may show signs of a physical trauma if one occurred, and could show evidence of restlessness or increased startle response.

Tests: Tests do not establish this diagnosis. However, the post-traumatic scales on tests such as the Minnesota Multiphasic Personality Inventory-2 revised may be elevated, and psychological tests may also reveal symptoms related to anxiety.

Treatment

Psychotherapy is usually designed to allow full expression of the emotions and images connected with the trauma. The individual's story may be told and retold, to minimize the chance that he or she will disconnect from the reality of that experience. It may be done as individual or group therapy, or as hypnotherapy. Although psychotherapy is designed to enable individuals to somehow process and integrate this overwhelming experience into their lives, behavioral and cognitive therapies address coping with anxiety symptoms rather than exploring unconscious conflicts. Behavioral therapy aims to gradually increase exposure to the anxiety-provoking situation. Sedating medication and antidepressants may also be helpful.

Prognosis

The majority of individuals experiencing Acute Stress Disorder recover completely. If the disorder lasts more than 4 weeks, a significant percentage develop Post-traumatic Stress Disorder (PTSD). Overall, one-tenth of those with acute stress disorder will remain unchanged or become worse. Decreased functioning following previous stresses, lack of a support system, substance abuse, and the coexistence of other psychiatric disturbances can negatively affect the outcome of the disorder.

Differential Diagnosis

Other possibilities are head trauma, substance abuse, Panic Disorder, Obsessive-compulsive Disorder, dissociative disorders, Borderline Personality Disorder, brief psychotic disorder, major depressive episode, Adjustment Disorder, and malingering. Post-traumatic Stress Disorder is distinguished from Acute Stress Disorder by its longer duration.

Specialists

- Licensed Clinical Social Worker
- Occupational Therapist
- Psychiatrist
- Psychologist

Work Restrictions / Accommodations

Work accommodations may include modifying the work space to decrease noise and visual distractions; introducing the individual to new or stressful situations gradually under appropriate supervision and support; providing some flexibility in work schedule to attend therapy appointments; allowing work-at-home or job-sharing opportunities; allowing break time according to individual needs rather than a fixed schedule; providing praise and positive reinforcement; and allowing workers to phone supportive friends, family members, or professionals during the workday.

If the traumatic event leading to the acute stress disorder occurred at work, accommodations may include placing the individual in a different job environment. Similarly, duties that remind the individual of the event (such as driving in the event of a motor vehicle accident) may be avoided for a time-limited period.

Comorbid Conditions

Alcohol abuse or drug use, or the presence of another psychiatric illness may lengthen disability.

Complications

Individuals may be indifferent to maintaining their health and safety. Impulsive, risk-taking behavior can lead to injury. There is a possibility of progression to post-traumatic stress disorder. Feelings of despair can be severe enough to qualify as a major depressive episode.

Factors Influencing Duration

The intensity and duration of exposure to the traumatic event may influence disability. Factors that negatively influence outcome include previous trauma, poor or marginal levels of functioning prior to the traumatic event, previous or current substance abuse, lack of a support system, reluctance to get appropriate treatment, and the persistence of denial regarding the event or consequences stemming therefrom. These factors tend to result in longer periods of disability. A failure to promptly and decisively settle litigation issues can also be associated with a delayed recovery.

Length of Disability

Duration depends upon response to medications and psychotherapy, the presence of other psychiatric disorders, and the presence of a supportive emotional network.

Duration in Days

Job Classification	Minimum	Optimum	Maximum
Any work	3	7	28

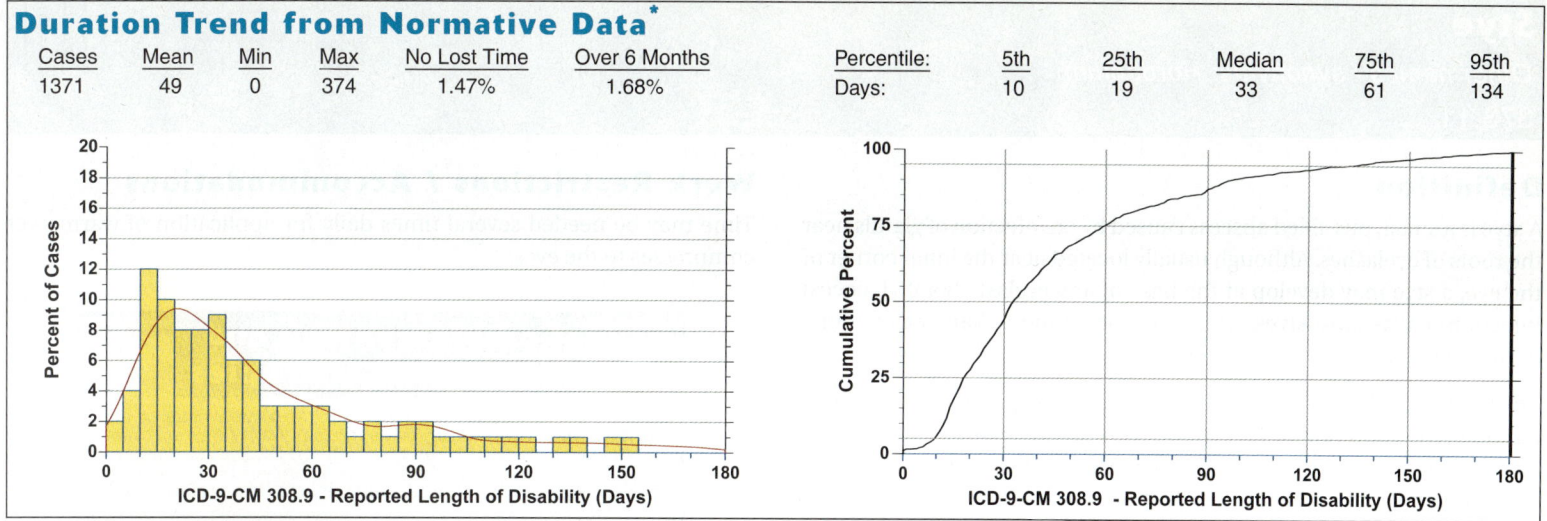

Failure to Recover

If an individual fails to recover within the maximum duration expectancy period, the reader may wish to reference the following questions to assist in better understanding the specifics of an individual's medical case.

Regarding diagnosis:

- Has a diagnosis of Acute Stress Disorder been confirmed?
- Has the stressful event been identified?
- Have underlying medical conditions and other psychiatric disorders been identified or ruled out?
- Does the individual have an underlying condition or experience that may impact recovery?

Regarding treatment:

- Does the individual need more frequent therapeutic encounters?
- Would the individual benefit from the addition of another type of therapy or a change in therapist?
- Has the individual taken medication as prescribed?
- Does the individual experience medication side effects that may interfere with use or benefit from that particular medication?

Regarding prognosis:

- Have symptoms persisted beyond 4 weeks?
- Should diagnosis be changed to Post-traumatic Stress Disorder?
- Are coexisting psychiatric conditions being appropriately addressed?
- Would the individual benefit from substance abuse rehabilitation?
- If a functional support system is not available, would the individual benefit from involvement in group therapy or a community support group?

References

Frances, Allen. Diagnostic and Statistical Manual of Mental Disorders: 4th ed, text revision. Washington, DC: American Psychiatric Association, 2000.

Mental Health: A Report of the Surgeon General. Surgeon General. 01 Jan 2000. 18 Dec 2000 <http://www.surgeongeneral.gov/library/mentalhealth/chapter4/sec2_1.html>.

Stye

Other names / synonyms: Hordeolum

373.11

Definition

A stye is a small, pus-filled abscess caused by an infection of glands near the roots of eyelashes. Although usually located near the inner corner of the eye, a stye may develop at the base of any eyelash. Staphylococcal infections cause most styes, which may occur more than one at a time or in succession.

Most individuals will develop a stye at some point in their lives, although the condition more commonly is found in young adults. Styes often recur particularly in individuals who are subject to stress, which is thought to be a factor in development of the condition. Styes also tend to recur in individuals with blocked glands in the eyelids, chronic eyelid infections, and immune disorders.

Diagnosis

History: Individuals may report pain, redness, blurred vision, and swelling at the site. Pain intensity relates to the amount of lid swelling. Tearing (lacrimation), sensitivity to light (photophobia), or a foreign-body sensation may occur. While external styes are easy to detect, internal styes hidden below the lids are painful but may not be visible.

Physical exam: The exam will reveal a red, swollen lesion, resembling a boil, at the base of an eyelash. Pus may drain from a small yellow area or point.

Tests: Since most styes are caused by staphylococcal infections, culture of the pus inside a stye is rarely required.

Treatment

Warm, wet compresses may be applied 3-4 times daily. If the stye does not begin to resolve within 48 hours, a small incision followed by surgical scraping of the contents (curettage) administered by a medical professional may be needed in the stye to provide drainage for the pus. Antibiotic ointment may be prescribed to promote healing and help prevent recurrence. In difficult cases, oral antibiotics may be prescribed.

Prognosis

Styes usually open and drain within a few days, resolving completely within one week. However, they often recur within a short period of time.

Differential Diagnosis

Conditions with similar symptoms include internal hordeolum, chalazion, blepharitis, eyelid tumor, acute dacryocystitis, papillomas, and xanthelasma.

Specialists

- Ophthalmologist

Work Restrictions / Accommodations

Time may be needed several times daily for application of warm, wet compresses to the eyes.

Complementary and Alternative Therapies

Content is intended for awareness only. Treatments may or may not be effective. Scientific evidence may be lacking and some substances have potentially toxic effects. Dr. Presley Reed and the editors do not endorse the use of these therapies in the absence of consultation with a licensed medical professional.

Hydrotherapy - Warm-to-hot compresses may decrease pain and bring the stye to a head.

Comorbid Conditions

The presence of bacterial blepharitis, which is inflammation of the eyelids, may precede development of styes.

Complications

Complications may include the simultaneous development of more than one stye on the same lid, or the outbreak of bacterial infection of the skin that may progress to underlying tissues (cellulitis).

Factors Influencing Duration

Length of disability may be influenced by the severity of the symptoms, the response to treatment, or the presence of complications.

Length of Disability

While styes typically do not affect visual acuity, they may be painful and distracting for workers engaged in tasks requiring concentration.

Surgical drainage.

Duration in Days

Job Classification	Minimum	Optimum	Maximum
Any work	1	2	3

Failure to Recover

If an individual fails to recover within the maximum duration expectancy period, the reader may wish to reference the following questions to assist in better understanding the specifics of an individual's medical case.

Regarding diagnosis:

- Has diagnosis of stye been confirmed?
- Have other conditions such as internal hordeolum, chalazion, blepharitis, eyelid tumor, acute dacryocystitis, papillomas, and xanthelasma been ruled out?

- Does individual have an underlying condition such as, stress, blocked glands in the eyelids, chronic eyelid infections or immune disorders that may impact recovery or recurrence of styes?

Regarding treatment:

- If symptoms persist despite treatment, has culture and sensitivity been performed to determine the most effective antibiotics and to rule out antibiotic-resistant organisms?
- Does diagnosis need to be revisited?

- Could the condition be related to another disease, such as blepharitis causing inflamed eyelids?

Regarding prognosis:

- Does individual have an underlying condition that may be contributing to the recurrence?
- Is this condition being adequately addressed?
- Would individual benefit from stress-reduction techniques or counseling?

References

McKinley Health Center. STY (Hordeolum). University of Illinois. 27 Aug 1997. 21 July 2000 <http://www.uiuc.edu/departments/mckinley/health-info/dis-cond/misc/sty.html>.

Vaughan, Daniel G., Taylor Asbury, and Paul Riordan-Eva. General Ophthalmology. Stamford: Appleton & Lange, 1995.

Subarachnoid Hemorrhage (Non-traumatic)
430

Definition

A subarachnoid hemorrhage (SAH) refers to the leakage of blood into the subarachnoid space containing the cerebrospinal fluid. The subarachnoid space is located under the middle of three membranes (meninges) that surround the brain and spinal cord. The middle membrane is called the arachnoid.

SAH may occur as a result of head trauma or from a ruptured, dilated blood vessel in the brain (cerebral aneurysm). It is frequently referred to as a "berry" aneurysm because of its shape. SAH may also arise from a complex cluster of thin-walled arteries and veins called an arteriovenous malformation (AVM). The malformation is present at birth (congenital) but bleeding from the lesion usually does not occur until ages 20 to 40 or older. SAH can also be the result of a bleeding disorder such as hemophilia.

Aneurysms and AVMs together account for about 60% of SAHs. Individuals with a history of high blood pressure (hypertension), an infection in the heart (endocarditis), and fluid-filled cysts within the kidneys (polycystic disease of the kidneys) are also at an increased risk for developing SAH.

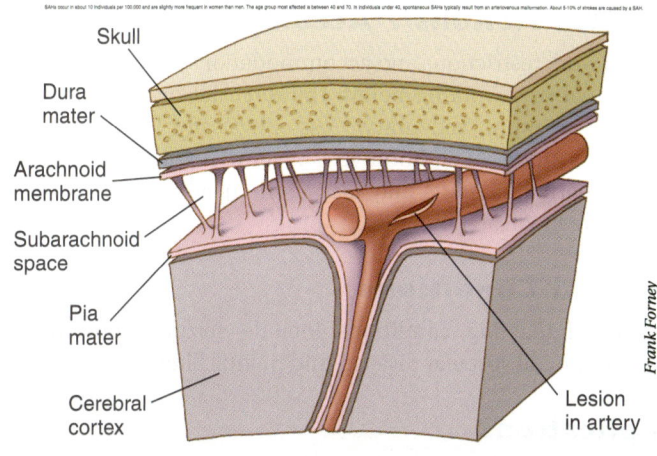

Diagnosis

History: Individuals may report the abrupt onset of a severe, throbbing headache that is localized initially before spreading to other areas. Additional symptoms include dizziness, neck stiffness, nausea, vomiting, drowsiness, sweating, sensitivity to light (photophobia), double vision, weakness on one side of the body (hemiparesis), chills, and decreased consciousness.

Physical exam: The level of consciousness of the individual may vary from alert to comatose. Partial paralysis, dilation of one or both pupils, and/or a rigid (stiff) neck may be present. Blood pressure is often elevated.

Tests: The most frequently used diagnostic test involves the use of a CT to visualize the area affected by the bleeding as well as the source of hemorrhage. The CT is better than the MRI as the MRI may not detect SAH early on. However, CT is not always positive in an individual with a SAH. If results are negative and the history is compelling, a spinal tap is done to look for blood in the cerebrospinal fluid (CSF). This procedure involves inserting a needle into the subarachnoid space in the lower spinal column and removing a small amount of CSF. Intracranial pressure (ICP) is then measured using a screw-type device or catheter with a sensor tip inserted through a burr hole in the skull. Sometimes cerebral angiography is done to identify the exact source of hemorrhage, e.g., AVM or aneurysm.

Treatment

Treatment focuses on first locating the source of hemorrhage and, if possible, surgically repairing the aneurysm or AVM to stop the bleeding. The best time to perform surgery remains controversial. Early surgery (within the first 3 days) reduces the chances of rebleeding while delayed surgery (after 14 days) avoids the time between 3 to 14 days when abnormal contraction of arteries (vasospasm) and its consequences are greatest. In general, individuals who are conscious with a minimal neurologic deficit on arrival do best with early surgery, whereas obtunded individuals do better with delayed surgery.

Ruptured cerebral aneurysms are corrected surgically using one of three procedures: aligning the edges of the ruptured aneurysm to stop the bleeding with stainless steel or cobalt alloy clips (clipping), tying off the bleeding blood vessel with suture (ligation), or wrapping the aneurysm with muscle. The best way to prevent SAH from rupture of a cerebral aneurysm is to diagnose and surgically correct the aneurysm before it ruptures.

Once an aneurysm is treated, follow-up focuses on preventing complications such as rebleeding, cerebral vasospasm, abnormal amounts of CSF collecting around the brain (hydrocephalus), and the effects of elevated intracranial pressure. Vasospasm is treated through administration of large amounts of fluids intravenously (IV) and increasing blood pressure to enhance blood flow to the brain. This increase blood flow ensures an adequate oxygen level to the brain and minimizes damage to the surrounding brain tissue.

An abnormal amount of CSF surrounding the hydrocephalus is typically treated through draining the excess CSF though a shunt into the abdominal or chest cavity or into the heart. If hydrocephalus is not controlled, brain tissue damage can occur as a result of compression of the brain from the excess fluid. Anti-inflammatory medications called steroids and medications to rid the body of excess fluid (diuretics) may also be used in an effort to temporarily control increased intracranial pressure.

Prognosis

The prognosis associated with a SAH is grave. About 50% of individuals die within one year with most deaths occurring early on. Among those individuals who survive SAH, significant neurological deficits are common. If the aneurysm is successfully treated surgically, 50-65% of individuals recover completely but persistent or permanent neurologic deficits are common. Only 30% of individuals return to their prehemorrhage functional level.

Differential Diagnosis

The differential diagnoses include brain tumor, infection, abscess, intracerebral hemorrhage, meningitis, and an acute migrainous attack.

Specialists

- Neurologist
- Neurosurgeon
- Physiatrist

Rehabilitation

The type and length of rehabilitation depend on the severity of residual brain damage as a result of the hemorrhage. Individuals may present with a variety of physical and cognitive disabilities, depending on the severity of the injury. Individuals may need to be treated by physical, occupational, and speech therapists.

Individuals may present with motor control deficits. Physical and occupational therapists treat balance and coordination disorders that may be present. Individuals with impaired coordination perform fine motor coordination exercises in occupational therapy such as picking up pegs and placing them in a pegboard or may work on practical coordination exercises such as fastening buttons or practicing their signatures. Individuals work on gross motor coordination in physical therapy such as kicking a soccer ball that is rolled towards them or throwing beanbags at a target.

Individuals with impaired balance engage in physical and occupational therapy. For example, occupational therapists may work on dynamic sitting balance to promote dressing and grooming abilities. Physical therapists may focus on standing balance to preserve the ability to walk. Individuals may perform exercises in a set of parallel bars, such as walking heel to toe to help improve standing balance. Because individuals with motor control deficits may also have difficulty planning out movements (apraxia) therapists may need to provide cues such as writing down the sequence of common tasks such as getting out of a chair.

The main focus of physical and occupational therapy in the area of motor control is to maximize functional capabilities. Physical therapists teach skills such as getting in and out of bed, walking, or using a wheelchair.

Individuals with poor motor control of the facial muscles may require speech therapy for improved clarity of speech and increased safety in swallowing.

Individuals may also present with perceptual deficits. Occupational and physical therapists provide methods to increase safety, such as a cane to compensate for decreased balance due to double vision. Individuals may require an occupational or physical therapist to assess their homes to remove tripping hazards such as throw rugs.

Individuals may present with persistent fatigue after subarachnoid hemorrhage. Occupational therapists may teach energy conservation techniques. Physical therapy addresses decreased endurance by teaching stretching and strengthening exercises of the arms and legs to improve overall endurance. Individuals may also perform aerobic activity such as walking on a treadmill or riding a stationary bicycle to further increase endurance. For individuals in a persistent vegetative state as a result of subarachnoid hemorrhage, physical and occupational therapists teach family members stretching exercises and positioning techniques to prevent pressure sores and joint contractions.

Individuals may also present with cognitive deficits. Occupational therapists evaluate and treat any deficits that are present.

Vocational counselors work with occupational, physical and speech therapists to replicate job task requirements in therapy. These counselors may help individuals keep future career plans realistic and ease the transition back to work. Vocational counselors may also focus individuals on new careers that may be more appropriate under their current level of disability.

Work Restrictions / Accommodations

Significant work restrictions and accommodations are often required. If the individual was working before the SAH, he or she may require transfer to a more sedentary, less physically and emotionally demanding position. In addition, loss of some cognitive function and/or residual partial paralysis may dictate the need for reassignment or may mandate medical retirement.

Comorbid Conditions

Pre-existing impacting conditions include seizures, obesity, heart disease, peripheral vascular disease, and mental illness.

Complications

Complications include seizures, infection after surgery, long-lasting neurologic deficits, recurrent bleeding (20%), and hydrocephalus. Some SAHs are associated with extension of bleeding into the brain itself, thereby complicating treatment and worsening the prognosis. Another complication of SAH is a low sodium concentration in the blood (hyponatremia) due to the inappropriate release of a hormone called antidiuretic hormone from the pituitary gland. This complication is known as the syndrome of inappropriate antidiuretic hormone (SIADH) secretion.

Factors Influencing Duration

Disability factors include the location and extent of hemorrhage within the brain, underlying cause of the hemorrhage, age and general health of the individual, severity of residual brain damage, and success of treatment measures directed at eliminating the cause of the hemorrhage.

Length of Disability

The length of disability is influenced by individual's job requirements and any comorbid conditions. Excessive physical or emotional stress may not be tolerated. Duration depends on cause and extent of neurological impairment, general health, age, and response to and compliance with treatment and rehabilitation programs. Disability may be permanent.

Duration in Days

Job Classification	Minimum	Optimum	Maximum
Any work	91	182	Indefinite

Failure to Recover

If an individual fails to recover within the maximum duration expectancy period, the reader may wish to reference the following questions to assist in better understanding the specifics of an individual's medical case.

Regarding diagnosis:

- Did subarachnoid hemorrhage (SAH) occur as a result of head trauma or from a ruptured, dilated blood vessel in the brain (cerebral aneurysm)?
- Does individual have a history of high blood pressure (hypertension), an infection in the heart (endocarditis), or fluid-filled cysts within the kidneys (polycystic disease of the kidneys)?
- Did individual exhibit symptoms such as an abrupt onset of a severe, throbbing headache, dizziness, neck stiffness, vomiting, drowsiness, sweating, facial droop, weakness, sensitivity to light (photophobia), chills, and decreased level of consciousness?
- Were the presenting symptoms and clinical history consistent with the diagnosis of subarachnoid hemorrhage?
- Was the diagnosis confirmed with CT, spinal tap and/or cerebral angiogram?
- If the diagnosis was uncertain, were other conditions such as brain tumor, infection, abscess, intracerebral hemorrhage, meningitis, or acute migraine headache ruled out?
- Would individual benefit from consultation with a neurosurgeon?

Regarding treatment:

- Was individual given appropriate stabilization and supportive care (intensive monitoring, bed rest, avoidance of bright lights and noises, blood pressure stabilization)?
- Did individual suffer any deterioration of neurological status, or bleeding or vasospasm?
- Were appropriate medications administered to reduce bleeding and vasospasm?
- Was surgery performed within 3 to 14 days following the initial hemorrhage?

Regarding prognosis:

- Does individual have any persistent or permanent neurological deficits?
- Is the individual involved in rehabilitative therapy?
- What is individual's age and general state of health at time of onset?
- Were there any complications such as seizures, infection after surgery, long-lasting neurologic deficits, recurrent bleeding, hydrocephalus, or syndrome of inappropriate antidiuretic hormone (SIADH) that may have influenced prognosis?
- What was the expected outcome?

References

Boss, Barbara J., Peter M. Sunderland, and Joleen Heath. "Alterations of Neurologic Function." Pathophysiology. McCance, Kathryn L, and Sue E. Heuther, eds. St. Louis: Mosby-Year Book, 1994. 527-586.

Holmes, Nancy, H., managing ed. Handbook of Diseases. Springhouse, PA: Springhouse Corporation, 2000.

O'Sullivan, Susan B. "Stroke." Physical Rehabilitation: Assessment and Treatment. O'Sullivan, Susan B., and Thomas J. Schmitz, eds. Philadelphia: F.A. Davis Company, 1994. 327-360.

Sarno, Martha Taylor. "Neurogenic Disorders of Speech and Language." Physical Rehabilitation: Assessment and Treatment. O'Sullivan, Susan B., and Thomas J. Schmitz, eds. Philadelphia: F.A. Davis Company, 1994. 633-653.

Subarachnoid Hemorrhage (Traumatic)

Other names / synonyms: Post-Traumatic Subarachnoid Hemorrhage

852, 852.0, 852.00, 852.01, 852.02, 852.03, 852.04, 852.05, 852.06, 852.09, 852.1, 852.2, 852.3

Definition

Subarachnoid hemorrhage refers to bleeding into the (potential) space between the middle (arachnoid) and the innermost (pia mater) membranes (meninges) that cover the brain. Hemorrhage into the subarachnoid space can occur secondary to severe blunt head trauma. In blunt head trauma, the brain may be subject to severe twisting and torsion that can shear blood vessels between the arachnoid and pia mater resulting in subarachnoid hemorrhage. Subarachnoid hemorrhage may be concurrent with bleeding elsewhere in the brain (epidural, subdural, or intracerebral hemorrhage). In about 8% of cases of subarachnoid hemorrhage following head trauma, the source of bleeding is a ruptured aneurysm.

The hemorrhage may cause swelling of brain tissue that can increase pressure in the brain. The presence of the blood clot (hematoma) and increased intracranial pressure can obstruct the flow of cerebrospinal fluid resulting in increased fluid in the brain ventricles (hydrocephalus). As pressure within the skull increases, downward displacement of the brain in the spinal canal (herniation) can lead to compression of vital brain structures, leading to coma and death if left untreated.

Diagnosis

History: Traumatic subarachnoid hemorrhage occurs following violent head trauma. History of the accident and whether the injury involved a direct blow, fall, or rotational impact can provide valuable clues to the mechanism of injury. Neurological complications such as loss of consciousness or seizure immediately following the accident suggest a more severe hemorrhage

If the individual remains conscious, other symptoms may be experienced such as severe headache that is often described as "the worst headache if my life." Symptoms associated with the headache may include discomfort from bright light (photophobia), nausea, vomiting, drowsiness, and neck stiffness.

Physical exam: Assessment of patency of airway and adequacy of respiration are the first priorities in examining the unconscious head trauma victim. This is followed by assessment of blood pressure, pulse, and temperature. Trauma to the vital centers of the brain (medulla) can cause wide variations in blood pressure, pulse, respirations, and body temperature. Neurological exam should evaluate level of consciousness, pupil size and reaction, motor responses, and reflexes. A more detailed exam is done to determine if there are signs of other injuries such as trauma to the spinal cord or abdomen.

Tests: Diagnosis is confirmed with CT. A needle puncture of the spinal canal to withdraw cerebrospinal fluid for diagnostic testing (lumbar puncture) may show blood in the cerebral spinal fluid. However, a lumbar puncture is contraindicated if there is evidence of increased intracranial pressure, as this may cause downward displacement of the brain within the spinal canal (herniation) with compression of vital brain structures that can be fatal.

Once the individual's condition is stabilized, the site of the ruptured blood vessel can be determined using an x-ray study of the blood vessels after injection of dye (angiogram) and/or MRI.

Treatment

The first step in treatment consists of general life-support measures such as assisted respiration and intravenous fluid adjustment. High blood pressure must be controlled often through the use of calcium-channel blockers or volume expansion agents. Seizures should be treated with anticonvulsants. Narrowing of arterial walls (vasospasm) following subarachnoid hemorrhage may also respond partially to calcium-channel blockers although there may be harmful side effects in some individuals. Increased pressure within the skull cavity (increased intracranial pressure) may need to be monitored with a probe placed within the ventricular system of fluid-filled chambers within the brain (intraventricular pressure monitor) or relieved by draining the ventricles with a shunt connected to the abdominal cavity (ventriculo-peritoneal shunt) if the ventricles are enlarged (hydrocephalus).

If the source of the bleeding is isolated to the rupture of a weakened vessel (aneurysm) and the location of the bleeding is accessible, surgery to repair the aneurysm may be considered. Surgery is usually delayed until the individual is stabilized. Aneurysms can be surgically blocked off, either by placing a surgical clip at the neck of the aneurysms (neurosurgical clipping) or wrapping the aneurysm with a gauze-like material (neurosurgical wrapping). Vascular malformations (angiomas) can be surgically removed (excision of angioma) if they are accessible. Those that are not surgically accessible are controlled either by dripping or placing a solidifying material through a long tube (catheter) at the site of the angioma (endovascular occlusive procedure), or directing a high intensity x-ray beam (stereotactic radiosurgery) to destroy the angioma. However, traumatic subarachnoid hemorrhage is often associated with widespread brain tissue damage and swelling that may dictate if and when surgical intervention is done.

Prognosis

Approximately one-third of individuals who have suffered a subarachnoid hemorrhage recover fully. Another one-sixth, suffer from some residual disability such as paralysis, mental deterioration, or epilepsy. The rest (up to one-half of all cases) die from either the initial hemorrhage or a recurrent attack.

Both operative and nonoperative management carry the risks of rebleeding, spasm of the artery (vasospasm), and accumulation of excess cerebrospinal fluid (hydrocephalus). Risk of vasospasm is related to severity of subarachnoid hemorrhage on CT, lower level of consciousness as measured by the Glasgow Coma Scale, and presence of associated complications of trauma such as bleeding between the skull and brain (epidural hematoma), between the brain and its outermost covering (subdural hematoma), or within the brain tissue (intracerebral hemorrhage). For each episode of rebleeding or vasospasm, the disability and risk of death increases.

Surgical outcomes vary based on the location of the hemorrhage and any other associated complications such as spasm of the artery, rebleeding, or increased intracranial pressure. In general, the surgical mortality for repair of aneurysms or arteriovenous malformations ranges from 0-8% and the postoperative morbidity ranges from 0-30%.

Differential Diagnosis

Acute subarachnoid hemorrhage occasionally simulates a heart attack because of the associated loss of consciousness and the occasional abnormalities on the ECG. Subarachnoid hemorrhage must be differentiated from and is often associated with intracerebral hemorrhage, bleeding from an aneurysm or cerebral vascular malformation, cerebral contusion and laceration, subdural hematoma, and sometimes brain tumor with hemorrhage. Occasionally migraine or meningitis may resemble the severe headache and stiff neck seen in subarachnoid hemorrhage. CT and x-rays of the cerebral blood vessels (cerebral arteriography) are often necessary to differentiate these possibilities.

Specialists

- Neurologist
- Neurosurgeon
- Physiatrist

Rehabilitation

Traumatic subarachnoid hemorrhage is nearly always associated with head trauma significant enough to cause some degree of brain injury. If the subarachnoid hemorrhage has caused physical and mental deficits, rehabilitation may be necessary to attempt as much recovery as possible. Participants in the rehabilitation program may include physical, occupational, speech, and recreational therapists as well as social workers.

The overall objective for rehabilitation of individuals with traumatic brain injury including subarachnoid hemorrhage is returning them as quickly and as fully as possible to the mainstream of their lives. This requires achieving functional recovery and assisting the individual in coping with remaining disabilities. Goal setting is necessary to optimize the use of time, money, and resources when treating severe subarachnoid hemorrhage. An organized treatment approach from a team of healthcare professionals is necessary for a complete treatment program that combines carryover during daily activities.

Treatment varies for each individual because of the uniqueness of the problems after each head injury. Treatment of the unconscious individual begins with passive range-of-motion exercises of the upper and lower extremity joints. Motivating the individual is important. When regaining consciousness, the individual may still be confused and easily distracted. Because the individual may not recall events that led to the injury, exercises to promote memory return are helpful along with instructing the individual to carry out simple tasks such as receiving an object in his or her hand or instructing the individual to go from a sitting to standing position.

Sequencing of activities by degree of difficulty includes teaching the individual to rise from a chair before instruction in proper walking patterns. Once thought processes begin to return, muscular strength, endurance, and flexibility are addressed. Muscle imbalance is corrected by traditional methods that facilitate the muscles and nervous system working together. The final phase of rehabilitation following traumatic subarachnoid hemorrhage involves the individual's reinstatement to work, as both physical and mental exercises are directed toward specific work requirements.

Work Restrictions / Accommodations

Job requirements may need to be redefined to accommodate any residual physical or mental deficits resulting from the head trauma and subarachnoid hemorrhage.

Comorbid Conditions

Underlying vascular disease, bleeding disorders, heart disease, and high blood pressure may lengthen disability. Subarachnoid hemorrhage following trauma may actually result from rupture of a pre-existing intracranial aneurysm coincident with the trauma,

Complications

Complications from the hemorrhage or resulting surgery may include physical or mental disabilities or seizures. Blockage of pathways that normally recirculate cerebrospinal fluid may cause increased pressure within the skull (hydrocephalus). Hemorrhage recurs approximately 50% of the time in subarachnoid hemorrhage. Lack of adequate blood supply to the brain (delayed cerebral ischemia) may occur in 20-40% of cases, causing death in about half of these cases.

Factors Influencing Duration

Length of disability depends on the extent and severity of neurological deficits resulting from the hemorrhage, other complications associated with the traumatic event, and surgical complications. Psychosocial factors such as depression or lack of an adequate social support system may slow rehabilitation and lengthen disability.

Length of Disability

Disability may be permanent. Intellectual and psychological dysfunction may postpone or prevent return to jobs that have high intellectual demands.

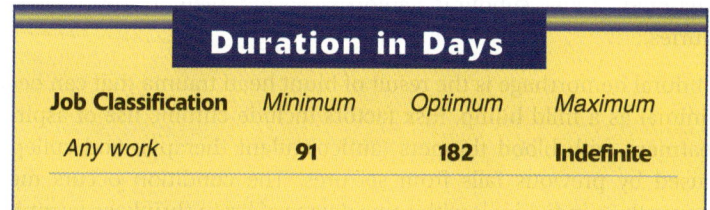

Duration in Days

Job Classification	Minimum	Optimum	Maximum
Any work	91	182	Indefinite

Failure to Recover

If an individual fails to recover within the maximum duration expectancy period, the reader may wish to reference the following questions to assist in better understanding the specifics of an individual's medical case.

Regarding diagnosis:

- Are the signs and symptoms suggestive of traumatic subarachnoid hemorrhage? Is there a history of preceding trauma?
- Has the diagnosis been confirmed by brain CT or MRI?
- Is angiography needed to determine if aneurysm rupture caused the bleeding?
- Are there any complications of the associated trauma?
- Does the individual display signs of postconcussion syndrome such as headache, dizziness, emotional outbursts, tension or nervousness, insomnia, impaired intellectual function, poor judgment, memory lapses, or inability to concentrate?

- Are there signs of increased intracranial pressure or hydrocephalus such as headache, lethargy, forgetfulness, and poor coordination or balance?
- Does the individual display new stroke-like symptoms such as facial droop, muscle weakness, or the inability to talk or walk?
- Has the individual had a follow-up CT of the brain to rule out hydrocephalus or rebleeding?

Regarding treatment:

- Have appropriate life-support measures been instituted?
- Are high blood pressure, seizures, and/or vasospasm being treated with appropriate medications?
- Should increased intracranial pressure be monitored?
- Is shunting needed to correct hydrocephalus?
- Is surgery needed to clip an aneurysm?
- Once the individual is stable, is rehabilitation needed to address deficits?
- Have associated complications of trauma such as fractures been treated appropriately?
- Could the individual benefit from second opinion consultation regarding management?

Regarding prognosis:

- How extensive was the subarachnoid hemorrhage?
- What was the individual's level of consciousness when first seen?
- Are there residual neurologic deficits that would preclude return to work?

References

Cummings, T.J., et al. "The Relationship of Blunt Head Trauma, Subarachnoid Hemorrhage, and Rupture of Pre-existing Intracranial Saccular Aneurysms." Neurological Research 22 2 (2000): 165-170.

Schuster, J.M., et al. "Acute Traumatic Posteroinferior Cerebellar Artery Aneurysms." Neurosurgery 45 6 (2001): 1465-1468.

Subdural Hemorrhage
432.1, 852.2, 852.20, 852.21, 852.22, 852.23, 852.24, 852.25, 852.26, 852.29

Definition

Subdural hemorrhage is bleeding due to trauma that occurs between the outer and middle membranes (meninges) covering the brain. The outer membrane is called the dura, the middle is called the arachnoid, and the inner membrane is known as the pia matter. Subdural hemorrhage, therefore, is bleeding beneath (below) the dura and above the arachnoid. Acute subdural hemorrhages are seen in 15% of head injuries.

Subdural hemorrhage is the result of blunt head trauma that can be as minimal as a mild bump. Risk factors include chronic use of aspirin, treatment with blood thinners (anticoagulant therapy), and epilepsy caused by previous falls from seizures. The condition occurs most frequently in individuals with some degree of brain shrinkage (atrophy) such as chronic alcoholics, individuals over the age of 60, and those with Alzheimer's disease and other degenerative neurologic diseases.

Acute subdural hemorrhage is a life-threatening condition caused by rapid bleeding that requires immediate evaluation and treatment. Subacute and chronic subdural hemorrhages are characterized by slower bleeding. The hematoma expands for days or weeks before the pool of blood is large enough to compress the brain sufficiently to cause symptoms.

Diagnosis

History: Individuals with subdural hemorrhage may present with an unexplained headache, drowsiness, confusion, impaired vision, slurred speech, personality changes, weakness or paralysis on one side of the body, and/or a decreased level of consciousness following a traumatic head injury. The individual may remember sustaining some head trauma within the recent past, but 50% of individuals with suspected chronic subdural hemorrhage offer no history of head trauma.

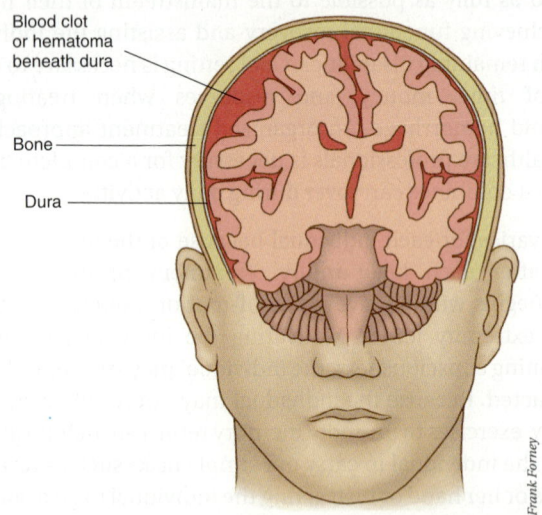

Individuals with suspected subdural hemorrhage may have a history of alcoholism, bleeding disorder, or recent anticoagulation therapy.

Physical exam: An individual's level of consciousness with subdural hemorrhage may range from drowsy and/or confused to comatose. Evidence of trauma to the head may be present. Weakness or paralysis may exist on one side. Speech may be disturbed. The pupils may be unequal in size and react sluggishly to light.

Tests: CT is the standard diagnostic tool used to determine the presence or absence of a skull fracture and/or bleeding within the skull under the dura. If the CT is negative for blood, lumbar puncture is performed to see if blood occurs in the cerebrospinal fluid. MRI is not as useful as CT imaging in the acute phase of injury, but is useful after the initial 48 hours to assess the extent of injury to the brain. Additional diagnostic tests may include an electrocardiogram (ECG), chest x-ray, urinalysis, and blood studies (complete blood count, prothrombin time, erythrocyte sedimentation rate [ESR], blood glucose, electrolytes, type, and crossmatch).

Treatment

Immediate medical treatment for subdural hemorrhage includes establishing a patent airway and maintaining an adequate blood oxygen level and blood pressure. As soon as a definitive diagnosis of subdural hemorrhage is made, the brain is decompressed through opening the skull (craniotomy) to remove any blood or blood clots beneath the dura. Any active bleeding is stopped and the brain examined. Once the individual's condition is stabilized, treatment becomes supportive and focuses on treating any underlying medical conditions

Prognosis

Individuals who have an urgent craniotomy performed to evacuate a subdural hemorrhage often recover with minimal or no significant permanent brain damage. However, some individuals will have a persistent headache, memory loss, difficulty concentrating, and/or seizures.

The mortality rate is related to the time interval between injury and surgery. With acute subdural hematomas, the mortality rate often exceeds 50%, whereas with chronic subdural hematomas, it usually 10% or less.

Differential Diagnosis

Initial differential diagnosis of suspected intracranial hemorrhage focuses on determining the location of the bleeding (epidural, subdural, subarachnoid, or intracerebral). Once the location of bleeding is determined, subdural hemorrhages must be differentiated from epidural hemorrhages, subarachnoid hemorrhages, cerebrovascular disease, hemorrhagic or ischemic stroke, senile dementia, and other diseases with a dementia component.

Specialists

- Cardiologist
- Emergency Medicine
- Endocrinologist
- Internist
- Neurologist
- Neurosurgeon
- Physiatrist
- Radiologist

Rehabilitation

Individuals who sustain a subdural hemorrhage may present with a variety of physical and cognitive disabilities depending on when the hemorrhage is detected. Individuals with early detection will suffer less severe deficits due to surgical intervention that minimizes brain injury. Because subdural hemorrhage is a secondary injury resulting from an initial brain injury such as a contusion, individuals need to be treated by physical, occupational, and speech therapists as well as neuropsychologists, vocational counselors, and social workers.

Individuals may present with motor control deficits. Physical and occupational therapists treat balance and coordination disorders. Individuals with impaired coordination perform fine motor coordination exercises in occupational therapy such as picking up pegs and placing them in a pegboard, or may work on practical coordination exercises such as fastening buttons or practicing their signatures. Individuals work on gross motor coordination in physical therapy such as kicking a soccer ball rolled toward them or throwing beanbags at a target.

Individuals with impaired balance engage in physical and occupational therapy. For example, occupational therapists may work on dynamic sitting balance to promote dressing and grooming abilities. Sitting balance is improved by having an individual sit on a therapy ball while attempting to reach for objects placed at various distances. Physical therapists may focus on standing balance to preserve the ability to walk. Individuals may perform exercises in a set of parallel bars such as walking heel-to-toe to improve standing balance. Because individuals with motor control deficits may also have difficulty planning out movements (apraxia), therapists provide cues such as writing down the sequence of common tasks (e.g., getting out of a chair).

The main focus of physical and occupational therapy in the area of motor control is to maximize functional capabilities. Physical therapists teach skills such as getting in and out of bed, walking, or using a wheelchair. Physical therapists may order equipment such as a trapeze bar that hangs over the bed, crutches or a cane, or self-propelled or power wheelchairs, as appropriate.

Individuals with poor motor control of the facial muscles may require speech therapy for improved clarity of speech and increased safety in swallowing. Speech therapy also strengthens the muscles of the face that improve speech and swallowing.

Individuals may also present with perceptual deficits. Occupational and physical therapists provide methods to increase safety such as a cane to compensate for decreased balance due to double vision. Individuals may require an occupational or physical therapist to assess their homes to remove tripping hazards such as throw rugs. Individuals with hearing loss may require speech therapy. Individuals may present with persistent fatigue due to deficits in the regulatory centers of the brain. Occupational therapists teach energy conservation techniques that make tasks more manageable.

Physical therapy addresses decreased endurance by teaching stretching and strengthening exercises of the arms and legs to improve overall endurance. Individuals may also perform aerobic activity such as walking on a treadmill or riding a stationary bicycle to further increase endurance.

Individuals may have with cognitive deficits due to brain injury. Occupational therapists evaluate and treat any of these deficits.

Work Restrictions / Accommodations

Some individuals who survive a subdural hemorrhage may have a permanent decrease in their thinking and reasoning abilities that prevents them from returning to the job they performed before the injury. These individuals may be retrained in other positions. Individuals recovering from a subdural hemorrhage may also have a change in personality that prevents them from fulfilling the responsibilities of their former position. These individuals may need to be retrained in positions that better accommodate their new personalities. Following evacuation of a chronic subdural hematoma, there may be gradual significant improvement in an individual's neurologic status allowing him or her to resume ordinary or modified work activities.

Individuals suffering damage to the cranial nerves from the initial trauma or the surgical procedure itself may experience a number of conditions including chronic pain, decreased sensation or paralysis in any of the structures above the neck, difficulty swallowing, hearing impairment, visual impairment, and balance disorders. Individuals with chronic pain may find it difficult to concentrate to the degree required by their jobs.

Visual impairment is likely to require major work restrictions and accommodations or a classification of permanent disability. Large computer screens and Braille keyboards may be useful for these individuals. Individuals with hearing loss may require the use of hearing aids and specially equipped telephones. Work restrictions and accommodations for individuals with impairment of their vision, hearing, or balance should focus on providing a safe environment away from moving equipment and other obstacles that could be hazardous. Persistent facial paralysis or palsy may require accommodations if the individual's job requires distinct speech.

Comorbid Conditions

Comorbid conditions that can affect the individual's ability to recover include obesity; history of cigarette, alcohol, or drug abuse; and pre-existing diseases such as bleeding disorders, diabetes, chronic obstructive lung disease, chronic heart disease, and immunosuppressive diseases affecting any of the major body systems.

Complications

Herniation of the brain may occur acutely leading to coma or death. Seizures may be a long-term complication.

Factors Influencing Duration

Factors influencing the length of disability include the number and severity of postoperative complications (i.e., wound infection and adverse reaction to a general anesthetic), extent of brain injury, individual's mental and emotional stability and pre-injury intellect, substance abuse and/or psychiatric status, access to rehabilitation facilities, and strength of the individual's support system. Individuals who experience a subdural hemorrhage as the result of a traumatic head injury often have other major internal and orthopedic injuries that are life-threatening and affect their ability to recover. In some cases, the individual may recover fully from the head injury but be disabled by traumatic injuries to some other body system.

Length of Disability

Rehabilitation on an inpatient and outpatient basis continues until maximum restoration of function or adjustment to loss of function is attained. Disability may be permanent.

Surgical treatment.

Duration in Days

Job Classification	Minimum	Optimum	Maximum
Sedentary work	21	42	Indefinite
Light work	28	42	Indefinite
Medium work	35	56	Indefinite
Heavy work	42	56	Indefinite
Very Heavy work	42	56	Indefinite

Failure to Recover

If an individual fails to recover within the maximum duration expectancy period, the reader may wish to reference the following questions to assist in better understanding the specifics of an individual's medical case.

Regarding diagnosis:

- Has individual had any blunt head trauma?
- Is individual a chronic aspirin user? On anticoagulant therapy? Have brain atrophy?
- Does individual present with an unexplained headache, drowsiness, confusion, impaired vision, slurred speech, personality changes, weakness or paralysis on one side of the body, and/or a decreased level of consciousness following a traumatic head injury?
- Does individual have a history of alcoholism? An altered mental status?
- Is there weakness or paralysis on one side? Is speech disturbed?
- Are individual's pupils unequal in size or react sluggishly to light?
- Was a CT done? A lumbar puncture? Has individual had an ECG, chest x-ray, urinalysis and CBC, prothrombin time, erythrocyte sedimentation rate, blood glucose, electrolytes, blood type, and crossmatch? Was a MRI done later?
- Have conditions with similar symptoms been ruled out?

Regarding treatment:

- Did individual have a craniotomy with blood or clot extraction?
- Is individual receiving supportive treatment?
- Are any underlying conditions being treated?

Regarding prognosis:

- Is individual active in rehabilitation? Is a home exercise program in place?
- Can individual's employer accommodate any necessary restrictions?
- Have any complications developed such as herniation of the brain, prolonged coma, or death? Does individual have seizures?

References

Lewis, Sharon, Margaret Heitkemper, and Shannon Dirksen. Medical-Surgical Nursing. St. Louis: Mosby, 1999.

Weiner, William, and Christopher Goetz. Neurology for the Non-neurologist. Philadelphia: Lippincott, Williams & Wilkins, 1999.

Sunburn
692.71

Definition

Sunburn is a painful burning of the skin caused by overexposure to ultraviolet radiation from the sun or an artificial source (sunlamp, tanning beds). Ultraviolet radiation exposure causes acute, delayed, and temporary skin inflammation. Ultraviolet radiation is comprised of A and B wavelengths, referred to as UVA and UVB, respectively. UVB is 85% responsible for sunburn. Minor sunburn is considered a first degree burn. A severe sunburn that causes blistering is considered a second degree burn.

Sunburn has long been known to prematurely age the skin, causing wrinkling, spotting, and sagging. Now experts believe that each serious sunburn doubles an individual's risk of developing malignant melanoma.

Sunburn is very common although the incidence has decreased in recent years. This decrease is presumably due to the efforts to educate the public about the hazards of sun exposure. Whites are particularly susceptible to sunburn. Individuals who work or recreate outdoors during the hours of 10 am. to 3 p.m., those who sun bathe or use tanning beds, and those who live in or travel to higher altitudes are at an increased risk of developing sunburn. Men are less apt to wear sunscreen than are women, putting them at a higher risk for developing sunburn.

Diagnosis

History: Individuals usually notice reddening of the skin beginning 2 to 4 hours after exposure to ultraviolet radiation. Symptoms, which include swelling and pain, peak at 24 hours. Some individuals may report blistering and peeling skin. Mild cases of sunburn can cause itching. Individuals with severe sunburn may also complain of fever, headache, chills, nausea, and a feeling of discomfort and fatigue (malaise).

Physical exam: An exam reveals a red, swollen (edematous), well-defined area of exposed skin. Most individuals with sunburn seek medical advice only if severe blistering, rash, pain, or fever are involved.

Tests: Tests are not necessary to diagnose sunburn. However, photo testing (irradiation testing) may be performed if a photosensitivity reaction is suspected.

Treatment

Started early and carried out for 2 days, cool baths or compresses and analgesics can help minimize discomfort. Itching can be relieved with antihistamines. The individual should drink ample amounts of fluids to compensate for dehydration, and may benefit from applying a nonprescription hydrocortisone cream or moisturizer three times a day. Application of anesthetic sunburn spray can provide temporary relief from pain. Individuals with severe sunburn benefit from bed rest and burn dressings. Blisters can be drained and the area treated with an antibiotic cream.

Prognosis

Sunburn symptoms resolve in 3 to 5 days.

Differential Diagnosis

Photosensitivity reactions and systemic lupus erythematosus can have similar signs and symptoms.

Specialists

- Dermatologist
- Primary Care Provider

Work Restrictions / Accommodations

Individuals who work outdoors should avoid sun exposure until the sunburn is fully healed. Depending upon the location of the sunburn, use of personal protective equipment (gloves, respirator) may be affected.

Complementary and Alternative Therapies

Content is intended for awareness only. Treatments may or may not be effective. Scientific evidence may be lacking and some substances have potentially toxic effects. Dr. Presley Reed and the editors do not endorse the use of these therapies in the absence of consultation with a licensed medical professional.

Vitamins C and E -	May reduce sunburn reaction.
Aloe vera -	May help as a healing agent; cools skin.

Comorbid Conditions

DNA repair disorders (e.g., xeroderma pigmentosum), systemic lupus erythematosus, dermatomyositis, pemphigus, bullous pemphigoid, actinic lichen planus, erythema multiforme, psoriasis, and eczema may influence the length of disability.

Complications

In serious cases, a sunburn can cause blisters that become infected, which can cause a high fever. Sunburn can trigger outbreaks of herpes simplex lesions, psoriasis, or porphyria. Repeated sunburns are known to increase an individual's risk for developing actinic keratoses and skin cancer.

Factors Influencing Duration

The severity and location of the burn would determine the length of disability, if any. Symptoms may persist for a longer time period in elderly individuals.

Length of Disability

Duration depends on severity and job requirements. Jobs requiring wearing personal protection equipment may cause considerable discomfort and require a longer disability, as would jobs requiring work outdoors.

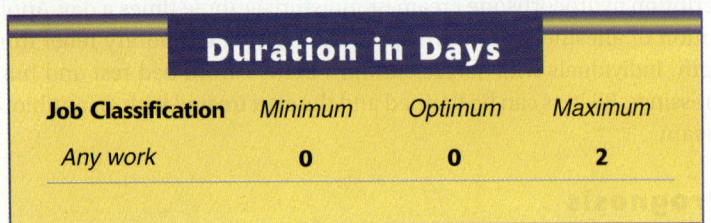

Duration in Days

Job Classification	Minimum	Optimum	Maximum
Any work	0	0	2

Failure to Recover

If an individual fails to recover within the maximum duration expectancy period, the reader may wish to reference the following questions to assist in better understanding the specifics of an individual's medical case.

Regarding diagnosis:

- Has individual recently had an ultraviolet radiation exposure?
- Is individual's skin red, blistering, or peeling? Is there swelling and pain?
- Does individual complain of itching, fever, headache, chills, nausea, or malaise?
- Did individual seek medical care?
- Was irradiation testing performed (if a photosensitivity reaction is suspected)?
- Have conditions with similar symptoms been ruled out?

Regarding treatment:

- Were symptoms treated with cool compresses or baths, analgesics, antihistamines, or nonprescription hydrocortisone cream or moisturizer?
- Is individual drinking adequate fluids?
- Was a topical anesthetic spray used?
- Were bed rest and burn dressings necessary?

Regarding prognosis:

- Can individual's employer accommodate any necessary restrictions?
- Does individual have any conditions that may affect ability to recover?
- Does individual have any complications such as infected blisters, outbreaks of herpes simplex lesions, psoriasis, porphyria, actinic keratoses, and skin cancer?

References

Anderson, Philip, and Kristin Malaker. "Less Common Disorders." *Managing Skin Diseases*. Hiscock, Tim, ed. Baltimore: Williams & Wilkins, 1999. 262-265.

Murphy, Gillian. "The Acute Effects of Ultraviolet Radiation on the Skin." *Photodermatology*. Hawk, J., ed. London: Arnold, 1999. 43-52.

Suture of Skin and Subcutaneous Tissue

Other names / synonyms: Skin Closure, Stitches, Wound Repair
86.5, 86.59

Definition

A suture is a stitch, or a series of stitches, used to close the edges of a wound (laceration) or a surgical incision. Sutures may also be used to hold intravenous lines and surgical drains in place. Several types of suture material, techniques for placing the sutures, and needles that hold the suture material may be used.

Choice of suture material and technique may depend on several factors including the purpose, wound configuration, location, and depth of the wound. Suturing may be percutaneous or dermal (subcuticular). Percutaneous closure passes through both the epidermal and dermal layers of the skin, while in dermal closure, the epidermis is not entered. Sutures may be placed either as a continuous stitch (running) or as an interrupted suture in which every stitch is knotted and cut.

There are a variety of suture materials and sizes that are available. Because suturing can result in inflammation and scarring, the smallest size suture that will maintain closure is chosen. Suture materials may be either absorbable (synthetic, plain gut, chromic gut) or nonabsorbable (nylon and polypropylene, Dacron, metal, silk, and cotton).

Reason for Procedure

Sutures secure the edges of a wound (laceration) or surgical incision, and promote healing of the injured area. Suturing removes "dead space" inside the wound where bacteria and secretions can accumulate, stops excessive bleeding, and provides physical strength to the skin surface that has been injured or cut. Closing the skin also helps prevent infection to the tissue inside. The edges of the wound will seal together, which prevents infection, in about 6 hours if the edges are carefully aligned (opposed) and have not been disturbed following suturing.

Lacerations and cuts as a result of trauma require cleaning and trimming of tissue that cannot be preserved (debridement). Cleansing and debridement decrease the chance of infection and may lessen scarring.

Sutures may be used to hold deep intravenous lines and surgical drains in position. IV lines inserted into the large, deep veins near the heart (central venous catheters) may be placed in critically ill individuals (due to life-threatening medical conditions, or trauma as a result of automobile accidents, burns, or any other severe injury) who require long-term hospitalization and intravenous nutrition (total parenteral nutrition). Specialized IV lines may be positioned into arteries (arterial lines) for blood pressure monitoring in individuals who are critically ill or for monitoring and blood drawing during anesthesia. Arterial lines may be sutured to the skin to help maintain placement. Drains placed during surgery may also be secured to the skin with stitches.

Specialists

- Dermatologist
- Emergency Medicine
- General Surgeon
- Plastic Surgeon
- Primary Care Provider

Description

Suturing can be performed under local or general anesthesia. For traumatic wounds, the wound is cleansed and irrigated with an antibacterial solution, and any tissue that will not survive is removed (débrided). Also, for traumatic wounds prior to suturing, underling structures, nerves, and tendons are assessed for proper functioning. Suture placement will vary with the techniques used, but in general the threaded needle passes into one edge of the skin, through the full depth of the wound, and out the other skin edge. All tissue layers are aligned together as carefully as possible (approximated). Skin sutures are removed after the wound has healed. Internal sutures, made of absorbable material, are used to close subcutaneous (under the skin) tissues. They are left in place permanently and are eventually dissolved by the tissue fluids.

Prognosis

The predicted outcome of suturing is generally good. Suturing allows skin to return to the pre-surgery or pre-injury state, with minimal scar formation.

Work Restrictions / Accommodations

Work restrictions or accommodations depend on the type of work responsibilities and the work environment. The sutured area must remain clean and intact in order to prevent the wound from becoming infected or reopening. Mobility may be impaired if suturing is placed over a joint until healing is completed.

Comorbid Conditions

Comorbid conditions that may affect healing of sutured tissue include obesity, diabetes, and poor nutritional status.

Procedure Complications

Complications of suturing include local inflammation, infection, scarring, and tearing of the skin resulting in separation of the incision (dehiscence).

Factors Influencing Duration

Factors include the severity of the injury, location of the stitches, separation (dehiscence) of the wound, or the development of an infection.

Length of Disability

Duration depends on severity and cause of laceration, its location, underlying cause for the procedure, and the presence of infection.

Duration in Days

Job Classification	Minimum	Optimum	Maximum
Any work	1	1	2

References

Edlich, Richard F., John G. Thacker, and George T. Rodeheaver. "Wound Management and Skin Closure." The Clinical Practice of Emergency Medicine, 2nd ed. Harwood-Nuss, Ann L., ed. Philadelphia: Lippincott-Raven, 1996. 392-403.

Owings, William O. "Wound Management." Saunders Manual of Medical Practice, 2nd ed. Rakel, Robert E., ed. Philadelphia: W.B. Saunders Company, 2000. 1310-1312.

Smith, David J., Kevind C. Chung, and Martin C. Robson. "Wounds and Wound Healing." Essentials of General Surgery, 3rd ed. Lawrence, Peter F., ed. Philadelphia: Lippincott, Williams & Wilkins, 2000. 113-122.

Strohmyer, Lisa L. "Nursing Care of Clients During Medical-surgical Emergencies." Luckmann's Core Principles and Practice of Medical-Surgical Nursing. Polaski, Arlene L., and Suzanne E. Tatro, eds. Philadelphia: W.B. Saunders Company, 1996. 1563-1593.

Sympathectomy

Other names / synonyms: Cervicodorsal Sympathectomy, Endoscopic Sympathectomy, Endoscopic Thoracic Sympathectomy, Endoscopic Transthoracic Sympathectomy, Lumbar Sympathectomy, Sympathetic Block, Thoracic Sympathectomy, Thoracoscopic Sympathectomy

05.2, 05.3

Definition

Sympathectomy is a procedure in which the nerves of the sympathetic nervous system are inactivated, either by surgically cutting them or by destroying them chemically.

The sympathetic nervous system is one of two components of the autonomic nervous system, which regulates the body's involuntary responses that keep the body functioning normally without our conscious input. The sympathetic nervous system controls the body's response to stress ("fight or flight" response). Sympathetic activity increases heart rate, blood pressure, and sweating. It regulates blood flow to different parts of the body by dilating some blood vessels, such as those in the muscles needed to help the individual fight or run away if faced with danger, and constricting others. Sympathetic activity also dilates the bronchi so more oxygen can be taken in, dilates the pupils so more light to enter the eye, and slows digestion.

Sympathetic activity is conveyed to the rest of the body by way of relay centers, called sympathetic ganglia, and sympathetic nerves. There are a number of variations of a sympathectomy procedure in which the fibers to or from one or more ganglia are cut and/or the ganglia themselves are removed. The most common procedure is called a thoracic sympathectomy, in which ganglia located along the spinal column in the region of the chest (thorax) are denervated. Lumbar sympathectomy, which refers to sympathectomy that involves ganglia in the lower back, and cervicodorsal sympathectomy, which refers to sympathectomy that involves ganglia in the neck, are also performed for certain disorders. While thoracic sympathectomies are usually done using a tiny viewing instrument inserted through a small incision (endoscopy), cervicodorsal and lumbar sympathectomies may be done endoscopically or as "open," more invasive procedures. Most sympathectomy procedures are done using general anesthesia.

The most common disorders for which an individual may be a candidate for sympathectomy are excessive sweating (hyperhidrosis) and certain chronic pain disorders such as reflex sympathetic dystrophy (complex regional pain syndrome). Sympathectomy is not a commonly performed procedure, since it is not necessarily a required treatment or the only treatment option for most individuals.

Reason for Procedure

A sympathectomy is used to relieve a variety of disorders, including certain disorders characterized by chronic pain, excessive sweating, or decreased blood flow to the extremities. The most common disorders treated using sympathectomy are excessive sweating (hyperhidrosis) and reflex sympathetic dystrophy (complex regional pain syndrome), which are usually treated via thoracoscopic sympathectomy. Hyperhidrosis is characterized by excessive sweating, usually of the palms, underarms, and sometimes face or feet that is unresponsive to conservative treatments; sympathectomy drastically decreases sweating in these areas. Reflex sympathetic dystrophy (RSD) is a post-traumatic pain syndrome in which the individual experiences severe burning pain and marked hypersensitivity of the skin; sympathectomy is performed to relieve the pain associated with this disorder. Selection of the individual in this disorder requires prior evaluation in a multidisciplinary pain treatment center, including psychological evaluation and testing to rule out contraindicating psychopathology, including depression, somatization, or a personality disorder. Other disorders that may be treated with thoracoscopic sympathectomy are Raynaud's syndrome, frostbite, and arterial insufficiency of the extremities that is not amenable to reconstructive surgery. In each of these cases, the general purpose of the sympathectomy is to improve blood circulation to affected areas, usually the hands and/or feet.

A cervicodorsal sympathectomy is indicated in certain situations to relieve post-traumatic pain complex and restore normal blood supply to the arms. Lumbar sympathectomy is indicated in certain situations to restore normal blood supply to the legs, to relieve leg pain, and to treat non-healing ulcers in the legs or feet.

Description

The most commonly performed sympathectomy procedure is endoscopic sympathectomy in the thoracic region (thoracoscopic sympathectomy). For this procedure, the individual is given general anesthesia and an airway tube is inserted to help the individual breathe. A small hole is made in the upper chest, and the lung on the side being operated on is allowed to collapse (the individual receives enough oxygen via the other lung). A thin tube with a camera on the end (an endoscope) is then inserted into the chest to allow the surgeon to see which nerves are to be cut. One or two additional small holes are made to insert cutting instruments. After the sympathetic nerves are cut, the collapsed lung is then re-expanded and the instruments are removed. Sometimes a small plastic tube is temporarily left in the chest for a few hours to allow any residual fluid or air to escape. The holes are then sewn shut (sutured), and the individual is allowed to awaken. Usually, surgery is performed on one side at a time.

In open cervicodorsal sympathectomy, the individual is also given general anesthesia and an airway tube. An incision is made in the armpit, the muscles are divided, and part of the third rib is removed. As in thoracoscopic sympathectomy, one lung is allowed to collapse. The cervical and dorsal sympathetic nerves are identified and cut. The ribs are then reconstructed and held in place with sutures. The lung is re-expanded, and the muscles and skin are closed with sutures or clips.

In an open lumbar sympathectomy, the individual is given general anesthesia and an airway tube. A large incision is made from the abdomen around to the back just above the buttocks. The muscles are separated, and the appropriate lumbar nerves are located and cut. The muscles and skin are mended with sutures or clips.

Prognosis

The predicted outcome depends upon the underlying disorder for which the sympathectomy was performed. Thoracoscopic sympathectomy in the treatment of hyperhidrosis of the palms has a 92-100% cure rate; success rates for hyperhidrosis of the underarms (axillae) and other areas of the body may be lower in some surgical series. However, in a recent study of lumbar endoscopic sympathectomy for hyperhidrosis of the feet, 98% of individuals were satisfied with the result. In some cases, the sympathetic nerves that are cut during surgery may partially regenerate, leading to recurrence of the problem. Nerve pain and compensatory increased sweating in other areas may lead to poorer outcome after sympathectomy for hyperhidrosis. In a recent study of endoscopic thoracic sympathectomy for axillary hyperhidrosis, 95% were cured of excessive underarm sweating, but all had compensatory sweating, and about half had excessive dryness of the hands.

Reduction of pain in reflex sympathetic dystrophy following sympathectomy depends on how advanced the disease is. Results of sympathectomy in individuals with Raynaud's syndrome and vascular diseases have been unpredictable, and there is currently no way of determining which individuals are the best candidates for sympathectomy.

Specialists

- General Surgeon
- Neurologist
- Neurosurgeon
- Radiologist

Rehabilitation

Individuals who undergo sympathectomy may require rehabilitation services contingent upon the underlying diagnosis. Individuals may require simple stretching and strengthening techniques to regain strength and range of motion that were lost while the individual experienced pain or, in cases of vasomotor dysfunction, to increase blood flow to an area that was experiencing decreased circulation. Individuals may require desensitization training to decrease heightened responses to pain or temperature for individuals with diagnoses such as reflex sympathetic dystrophy (complex regional pain syndrome) or Raynaud's syndrome. Either physical or occupational therapy can address any of the above issues, with the frequency and duration determined by the diagnoses.

Some individuals may require more comprehensive pain management through a pain clinic, particularly if the response to pain is disproportionate to the painful stimulus. Individuals receive physical therapy for pain control. Physical therapists may use body massage or trigger point massage to decrease muscle spasms. Individuals may learn to utilize biofeedback to help decrease any muscle tension and thereby decrease pain. Individuals may also use a TENS unit, which delivers low frequency electrical stimuli via surface electrodes to interrupt the perception of pain. Occupational therapists may teach energy and joint conservation techniques, in which activities of daily living such as meal preparation are broken up into smaller components thereby making tasks more manageable. Psychologists or psychiatrists teach coping skills for better pain management, such as visual imagery or meditation.

Work Restrictions / Accommodations

Work accommodations or restrictions depend on the underlying medical condition and on the individual's work responsibilities. The length of hospital stay varies with the specific sympathectomy procedure and with the individual. Endoscopic sympathectomy for hyperhidrosis of the palms may be done on an outpatient basis. Cervicodorsal and lumbar sympathectomies, done as open procedures (non-endoscopic), can require average hospital stays of approximately 7 days. Following endoscopic sympathectomy, the individual may expect to return to normal activities within a few days. Following open procedures, vigorous exercise should be avoided for 6 weeks following surgery. The individual should not drive for 18 days after hospital discharge.

Comorbid Conditions

Diabetes mellitus, obesity, smoking, atherosclerosis, chronic illness, alcoholism, psychopathology (including depression, somatization and personality disorders), use of certain medications for other conditions (such as sedatives, antihypertensives, muscle relaxants, tranquilizers, sleep inducers, insulin, and narcotics) and the use of mind-altering drugs (such as psychedelics, hallucinogens, marijuana, hypnotics, or cocaine) may lengthen disability. Immunosuppression or bleeding disorders may increase risk of surgical complications.

Procedure Complications

General complications of sympathectomy may include pneumothorax (due to air remaining between the lung and chest wall), bleeding, infection, soreness (at the incision or of the ribs), and treatment failure, including post-sympathetic pain syndrome. In some cases, the sympathetic nerves that are cut during surgery may partially regenerate, leading to recurrence of the problem. Certain complications that may occur are specific to the particular ganglion(s) that are involved in the sympathectomy procedure. The most common complication of thoracoscopic sympathectomy in the treatment of hyperhidrosis is compensatory sweating, which is sweating in other parts of the body, usually back or legs, and occasionally feet; this complication occurs in about 1% of individuals undergoing the procedure. Some individuals (up to 35%) may experience another type of sweating that is increased while eating or smelling certain foods (gustatory sweating). Excessive dryness of the hands is common after surgery to relieve excessive palmar sweating. Another complication is Horner's syndrome, in which the individual develops constriction of the pupil and drooping of the upper eyelid on one side of the face. Less common complications of thoracoscopic sympathectomy include cardiac effects and orthostatic hypotension. Complications specific to lumbar sympathectomy include neuralgia (which usually resolves after 1 to 3 months), impotence, and incisional hernia (which is rare).

Factors Influencing Duration

Factors that may influence the length of disability include the underlying medical condition for which the surgery was performed, whether the procedure was endoscopic or open, complications of surgery or drug therapy, and surgical outcome.

Length of Disability

Duration depends on underlying diagnosis, site (cervical, lumbar, etc.), severity, response to treatment, and duration of symptoms. Cervicodorsal and lumbar sympathectomies, done as open procedures (non-endoscopic), can require average hospital stays of approximately 7 days. Following endoscopic sympathectomy, the individual may expect to return to normal activities within a few days. Following open procedures, vigorous exercise should be avoided for 6 weeks following surgery. The individual should not drive for 18 days after hospital discharge.

Sympathectomy.

Duration in Days

Job Classification	Minimum	Optimum	Maximum
Sedentary work	7	14	21
Light work	7	14	21
Medium work	14	21	28
Heavy work	14	21	28
Very Heavy work	14	21	28

Sympathetic block.

Duration in Days

Job Classification	Minimum	Optimum	Maximum
Sedentary work	3	7	21
Light work	3	7	21
Medium work	7	14	28
Heavy work	7	14	28
Very Heavy work	7	21	35

References

Anguelov, Zlatko, and Kemp Kernstine. Thoracoscopic Sympathectomy for Palm Hyperhidrosis. University of Iowa Health Care. 01 Jul 2000. 9 Nov 2000 <http://uihealthcare.com/NewsEvents/Currents/Vol1Issue3/PalmHyperhidrosis.html>.

Kopelman, D., et al. "The Effect of Upper Dorsal Thoracoscopic Sympathectomy on the Total Amount of Body Perspiration." Surgery Today 30 12 (2000): 1089-1092.

Syncope
Other names / synonyms: Blackout, Fainting, Syncope, Transient Loss of Consciousness
780.2

Definition

Syncope or fainting is a temporary loss of consciousness due to inadequate blood flow to the brain.

There are many causes for syncope including fatigue, pain, dehydration, prolonged or excessive heat exposure (heat exhaustion), low blood sugar (hypoglycemia), diabetes, Parkinson's disease, anemia, emotional disturbances, hyperventilation, exertion, or being in a poorly ventilated room without adequate oxygen. Syncope can be caused by standing still for a long time or by standing up suddenly after sitting or lying down for a long time (postural or orthostatic syncope). This happens because the blood has pooled in the leg veins, reducing the amount available for the heart to pump to the brain. The resultant drop in blood pressure (postural hypotension) is common in the elderly, in diabetics, and in individuals who take certain cardiac medication (antihypertensive or vasodilator). It can also be caused by a shift in body position from lying or sitting to a more vertical position (postural hypotension).

Feeling faint, or fainting, is a common occurrence during pregnancy. During pregnancy, muscles surrounding the blood vessels relax, often lowering the blood pressure.

Another common cause of syncope is overstimulation of the vagus nerve (vasovagal attack). The vagus nerve helps to control breathing and blood circulation. Overstimulation may occur due to severe pain, stress, fear, prolonged coughing, straining to urinate or defecate, or by blowing into a wind instrument.

Serious heart disease such as blood clot in the valves or heart tumor can obstruct blood flow in the heart causing syncope. Another cause of syncope is irregular heart beat (arrhythmias).

Vertebrobasilar insufficiency is a disorder that can temporarily obstruct the blood flowing through the neck to the brain (causing a transient ischemic attack). Syncope can also be caused by a blocked or burst blood vessel (stroke). Pressure on blood vessels caused by osteoarthritis of the bones in the neck can cause a feeling of faintness when the head is suddenly turned.

Syncope can be a symptom of Stokes-Adams syndrome. In this disorder, blood flow to the brain is temporarily inadequate due to an irregular heartbeat (arrhythmia). Interruption of the electrical impulses in the heart (heart block) usually causes the irregular heartbeat.

Syncope is a major cause of morbidity and mortality in older individuals. Pregnant women, workers in hot and enclosed places, workers who stand on their feet all the time, and performers are also at higher risk for syncope. Syncope is a common condition, accounting for 3% of emergency department visits and up to 6% of admissions each year in the US. The Framingham study found that at least 3% of the population will have a syncopal episode within a 26-year period, and that 30% will have recurrences.

Diagnosis

History: The individual may report symptoms such as nausea, sweaty palms, rapid heart rate, dizziness, feeling of extreme weakness, and loss of color in the face before abrupt loss of consciousness. Other symptoms may suggest specific causes. Factors bringing on the fainting spell may include fear or other strong emotion, fatigue, sleep or food deprivation, hot environment, or pain. It is important to determine what the individual was doing before the fainting spell, as syncope at rest, with activity, or in specific situations such as shaving or coughing may suggest different causes. Whether the individual was standing, sitting, or lying down when fainting also helps determine the specific cause. Witnesses to the syncope should report that the loss of consciousness lasted for only a few minutes, with rapid return to full level of consciousness, and without jerking movements during the episode or confusion after the episode that would suggest seizure activity. Medications, medical history, and family history may all contain important clues as to the specific cause of syncope.

Physical exam: Individuals may present with sweaty palms, rapid heart rate, and pale skin. Fever may suggest a precipitating cause, such as urinary infection or pneumonia. Drop in blood pressure and rise in pulse when the individual stands up suggests syncope related to postural changes (postural or orthostatic syncope). Rapid or slow pulse may suggest heart problems causing syncope. The individual should be examined carefully for trauma sustained during the fainting spell. Careful examination of the heart, lungs, and blood vessels may detect abnormalities causing syncope. Neurological examination should be normal; abnormalities may suggest transient ischemic attack or seizure rather than syncope. Specific maneuvers (such as the Hall-Pike maneuver, or carotid sinus massage) may detect specific causes.

Tests: Blood tests should include blood glucose to rule out low blood sugar (hypoglycemia) and blood count to rule out anemia, although stool guaiac examination is more likely to reveal gastrointestinal bleeding causing fainting. Urinalysis and chest x-ray should be done to rule out urinary infection or pneumonia. Cardiac electrophysiology testing, such as EKG, exercise stress test, and Holter monitor are done to rule out any heart abnormalities. Ventilation-perfusion scan should be done if pulmonary embolus is suspected. Head up tilt table test may be necessary to determine cardiovascular reflexes. Brain CT, chest or abdominal CT, and brain MRI are rarely indicated. Electroencephalogram (EEG) should be done if seizure is suspected.

Treatment

Recovery from syncope occurs as soon as normal blood flow is restored to the brain. The individual should be lying down with the legs elevated for 10-15 minutes after regaining consciousness to prevent another attack.

If the individual does not regain consciousness within a minute or two, medical help should be obtained promptly. Emergency care should include protection of the airway and of circulation, and intravenous medications or oxygen may be needed.

Recurrent syncope needs to be evaluated to rule out a more serious underlying condition. Individuals who have had episodes of syncope in the past should be instructed to watch for the warning signs of fainting, such as lightheadedness, dizziness, and nausea. When they experience these warning signs, they should lie down or put their heads between their knees. They should also be careful not to get up suddenly or to remain standing for long periods of time, and should avoid situations or activities that tend to bring on their syncopal attacks.

Syncope originating in the heart may require treatment with anti-arrhythmic drugs, beta-blockers, or pacemaker. Syncope related to disease of the heart valves may require valve replacement.

Specialists

- Cardiologist
- Neurologist
- Endocrinologist

Prognosis

An episode of syncope may be life-threatening if not treated properly. It usually ends with a return to complete consciousness within minutes to hours. Since syncope may be a symptom of an underlying condition, the outcome will depend on the specific diagnosis. Simple fainting (vasovagal syncope) has an excellent outcome, and recurrences are rare. Syncope related to changes in position (postural and orthostatic syncope) and syncope occurring in specific situations, such as shaving or coughing (situational syncope) also have excellent outcomes, but are more likely to recur, and may interfere with quality of life and predispose individuals to secondary injury. Syncope related to heart conditions has a poor outcome, with up to 18-33% of individuals dead in one year. These individuals are usually significantly restricted in daily activities, but may do better after surgery or pacemaker placement. In a study of one-year follow-up in syncope of unknown cause, 2% had sudden death, 20% had recurrent syncope, and 78% had no recurrence.

Differential Diagnosis

Other possibilities include seizure, hypoglycemia, adrenal insufficiency, hyponatremia, drug reaction, alcohol intoxication, subarachnoid hemorrhage, stroke, hyperventilation syndrome, narcolepsy, and panic attacks. There is a wide spectrum of cardiac causes of syncope including various abnormalities of heart rhythm, and structural problems involving the heart or great vessels.

Work Restrictions / Accommodations

Safety considerations may affect whether an individual can perform his or her usual duties if experiencing episodes of syncope. Job duties that require working at heights or in hot, stuffy environments, working with heavy equipment or motor vehicles, standing for long periods, or hazardous occupations may have to be restricted or modified. Depending on the underlying cause of syncope, more modifications or restriction may be necessary.

Comorbid Conditions

Comorbid conditions that may aggravate syncope may include stress, dehydration, low-salt diet, heat exhaustion, pregnancy, drug or alcohol intoxication, urinary or other infection, pneumonia, heart disease, endocrine disturbances, or neurologic conditions.

Complications

Because its onset is usually abrupt, injuries due to falling are a frequent complication. If the individuals do not regain consciousness in a short time, they may develop a seizure. This is especially likely if those around them try to help them to a standing position too quickly.

Factors Influencing Duration

If syncope is due to an underlying cause, the specific diagnosis may influence the length of disability. An individual's job requirements may also determine the length or degree of disability. Age and mental health of the individual may also influence the length of disability.

Length of Disability

No disability is expected for simple vasovagal attack. If syncope is a symptom of an underlying condition, see specific diagnosis for expected length of disability. Neurological and cardiovascular causes may result in disability. Remission is common with syncope. Disability may be permanent for individuals whose job duties require heavy work, heights, prolonged standing, driving, operating heavy machinery, or working in a hot, stuffy environment.

Duration in Days

Job Classification	Minimum	Optimum	Maximum
Any work	X	Y	Z

Duration Trend from Normative Data*

Cases	Mean	Min	Max	No Lost Time	Over 6 Months
1200	41	0	554	1.08%	1.17%

Percentile:	5th	25th	Median	75th	95th
Days:	7	14	24	47	128

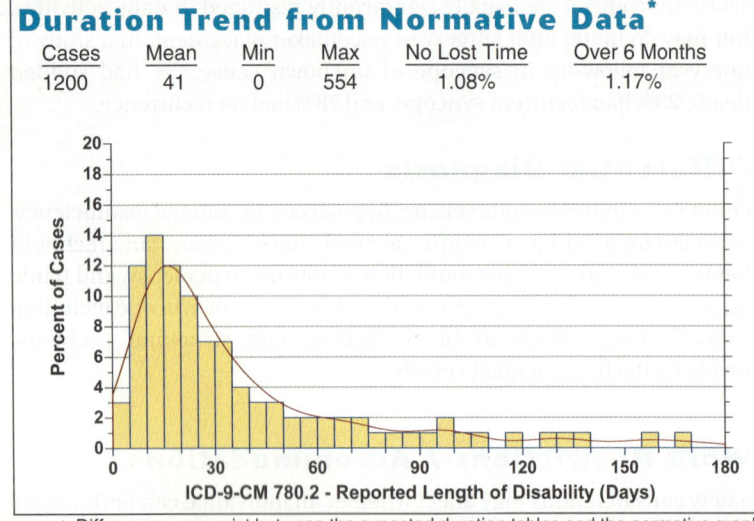
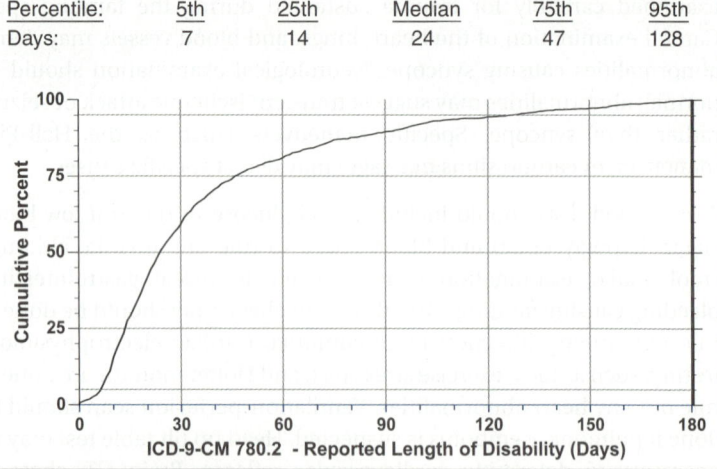

* Differences may exist between the expected duration tables and the normative graphs. Duration tables provide expected recovery periods based on the type of work performed by the individual. The normative graphs reflect the actual observed experience of many individuals across the spectrum of physical conditions, in a variety of industries, and with varying levels of case management.

Failure to Recover

If an individual fails to recover within the maximum duration expectancy period, the reader may wish to reference the following questions to assist in better understanding the specifics of an individual's medical case.

Regarding diagnosis:

- Has diagnosis of syncope been confirmed and other conditions, such as seizure, hypoglycemia, adrenal insufficiency, hyponatremia, drug reaction, alcohol intoxication, subarachnoid hemorrhage, stroke, hyperventilation syndrome, narcolepsy, and panic attacks ruled out?

- Has the cause of syncope been identified?
- Does individual have an underlying condition that may impact recovery?

Regarding treatment:

- Has the cause of syncope been positively identified?
- Is more diagnostic testing or evaluation warranted?
- Is the underlying condition responding to treatment?

Regarding prognosis:
- If underlying condition is not responding to treatment, would individual benefit from consultation with a specialist (cardiologist, neurologist, hematologist, internist, endocrinologist)?
- How often do syncope episodes occur?
- To what extent do they impact functioning?
- Is the individual at risk for secondary injury due to job duties that require working at heights, in hot, stuffy environments, working with heavy equipment or motor vehicles, standing for long periods?

References

Beers, Mark, and Robert Berkow. The Merck Manual of Diagnosis and Therapy. Whitehouse Station, NJ: Merck Research Laboratories, 1999.

Meyer, M.D., and J. Handler. "Evaluation of the Patient with Syncope: An Evidence Based Approach." Emergency Medicine Clinics of North America 177 (1999): 189-201.

Morag, Rumm, and Barry Brenner. Syncope. eMedicine.com 09 Sept 2000. 27 Oct 2000 <http://www.emedicine.com/emerg/topic876.htm>.

NINDS Syncope Information Page National Institute of Neurological Disorders and Stroke. National Institutes of Health. 1 Jan 2000. 8 Aug 2000 <http://www.ninds.nih.gov/health_and_medical/disorders/syncope_doc.htm>.

Synovectomy
80.7, 80.70

Definition

A synovectomy is the surgical removal of the thin membrane lining a joint capsule (synovium).

The joint is opened (arthrotomy) and the synovium is cut away. The procedure can also be performed by means of arthroscopy, utilizing small entrance holes around the joint.

Synovectomy is only a temporary solution to problems of swollen synovium, not a cure. Joint motion, pain and swelling are usually improved and cartilage destruction diminished for about two years. At that time, further surgery may be required. Keep in mind that synovitis is part of other disease processes and the need for synovectomy will depend on the course of the underlying condition, such as rheumatoid arthritis, infection, exposure to toxins, pigmented villonodular synovitis, and hemophilia.

In 1995, there were 116,000 synovectomies on knee joints, and it was the sixth most common musculoskeletal procedure.

Reason for Procedure

Removal of the thin membrane lining a joint capsule (synovium) is done to reduce the symptoms of pain and swelling due to recurrent or persistent synovial inflammation (synovitis). This procedure is usually performed only if the condition is severely disabling, as may occur in severe rheumatoid arthritis, or if the condition has not responded to other, simpler methods of treatment, such as nonsteroidal anti-inflammatory drugs, antirheumatic drugs, or the injection of corticosteroid drugs into the joint itself.

Contraindications for synovectomy include restricted joint motion or significant joint degeneration.

Description

Local, regional or general anesthesia is used depending on the amount of synovium to be removed and the technique employed. The procedure can be performed in an office, outpatient or inpatient setting, depending on the technique.

In an open procedure the joint capsule is exposed through an incision over the affected joint (arthrotomy.) The lining is identified and removed by scraping and cutting. A soft pressure dressing is applied to control swelling. Early limited joint motion is encouraged to prevent scar tissue (adhesions) from forming in the joint.

A synovectomy can also be done arthroscopically. An arthroscope is inserted into the joint space through a small skin incision to visualize the interior of the joint. Small instruments are then inserted through other holes (portals) into the joint to cut away the synovium. An irrigation solution must also be infused into the joint to help clear the area of debris created during the procedure. The result is two or more small incisions used to insert the arthroscope, the irrigation fluid, and the surgical instruments. After the operation, a pressure dressing is applied and the joint is kept mobile to inhibit scarring.

Prognosis

Temporary relief of pain, swelling and decreased range of motion is expected. Synovectomy does not remove the cause of synovitis, so relief of symptoms may not be permanent. Ongoing management of the underlying disease process will influence successful outcome.

Specialists

- Occupational Therapist
- Orthopedic Surgeon
- Physiatrist
- Physical Therapist
- Rheumatologist

Rehabilitation

Individuals who undergo a synovectomy require physical or occupational therapy post-surgery. Individuals are required to wear a compression bandage for several days. Post-surgery the individual is instructed by a therapist at the hospital to elevate the affected limb to decrease pain and swelling. Individuals are also instructed to perform gentle isometric exercises of the immobilized area to preserve strength. Once the bandage is removed, therapy can begin on an outpatient basis. Passive, active-assistive, and active range-of-motion exercises are introduced at this point. Over a period of several weeks, mild resistance exercises are prescribed. Typically, there are restrictions in weight bearing and heavy lifting for approximately two months. For individuals with synovectomy of a lower extremity joint, physical therapy would also instruct in walking with crutches or a walker due to these restrictions.

Work Restrictions / Accommodations

Limited work loading of affected joint is an appropriate restriction. This may include no lifting, gripping, twisting, pushing or pulling, standing, squatting or kneeling, depending on the joint(s) involved. Periods of rest and time for rehabilitation may be necessary.

Individuals may be required to use devices to assist with ambulation such as crutches, canes or walkers. Job requirements may be necessary to accommodate such equipment safely.

Comorbid Conditions

Inflammatory diseases and infection would prolong recovery.

Procedure Complications

Possible complications include infection, bleeding into the joint (hemarthrosis) nerve and vessel damage, damage to bone surface (articular cartilage), and no relief of symptoms.

Factors Influencing Duration

Length of disability may be influenced by the underlying diagnosis, effectiveness of treatment, amount of joint swelling and postoperative pain, the presence of complications, the individual's work requirements, and whether the dominant or nondominant extremity is involved.

Length of Disability

Duration of disability would depend greatly on the management of the underlying cause for synovitis that resulted in synovectomy.

Synovectomy, arthroscopic, knee.

Duration in Days

Job Classification	Minimum	Optimum	Maximum
Sedentary work	5	14	42
Light work	21	35	56
Medium work	35	42	56
Heavy work	35	63	91
Very Heavy work	35	91	119

References

Kisner, Carolyn, and Lynn Allen Colby. "Principles of Treating Soft-tissue, Bony, and Postsurgical Problems." Therapeutic Exercise: Foundations and Techniques. Philadelphia: F.A. Davis Company, 1990. 211-240.

Namba, Robert, and Harry Skinner. "Adult Reconstructive Surgery." Current Diagnosis and Treatment in Orthopedics. Skinner, J.B., and Harry B. Skinner, eds. Norwalk: Appleton & Lange, 1995. 325.

Synovial Cyst

Other names / synonyms: Ganglion, Ganglionic Cyst
727.4, 727.40, 727.41, 727.42, 727.43

Definition

A synovial cyst is a small fluid-filled sac or pouch which, when it develops over a tendon or joint, creates a mass under the skin.

Synovial cysts occur commonly at the wrist, the flexor tendon sheath in the fingers, top of the foot (dorsum), and at the ankle. The size of the sac or cyst can change with activity, and may disappear for a period, only to recur. The mass is often soft but, with time, may become harder to the touch. They may or may not be painful, depending on their size and location.

The risk factors and causes of synovial cysts are unknown although there is some evidence that trauma may be a factor. Synovial cysts are the most common benign soft tissue lesions, accounting for 72% of all such lesions.

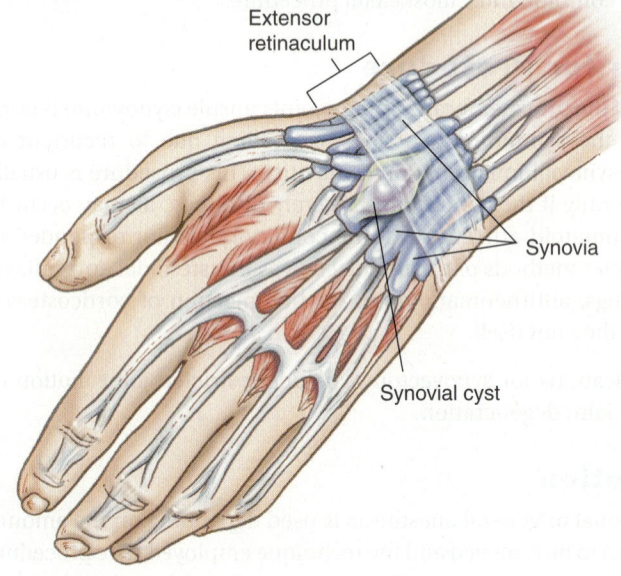

Diagnosis

History: Usually, no precipitating incident will seem significant to the individual. Pain and swelling with activity may be reported. The cyst may change is size with increased activity. While the pain may be present initially (after the cyst forms), the pain usually goes away, and the cyst becomes an asymptomatic lump after a few months. The individual will notice the cyst, whether painful or not, on the limbs, especially the ankle, wrist, fingers, or top of foot. History of trauma is rare.

Physical exam: Palpation of the mass reveals a soft to rigid mass near a joint or over a tendon. A ganglion that cannot be seen (occult) should be suspected for wrist pain without trauma.

Tests: Aspiration of the cyst produces a thick, gelatinous liquid. X-rays may be ordered to rule out tumor or rheumatoid arthritis. Although not usually necessary, MRI is very useful in visualizing the lesion.

Treatment

The ganglion may be drained of its fluid (aspirated) to decrease symptoms, but it usually returns.

Conservative treatment of synovial cysts consists of aspirating the fluid from the sac with a large gauge needle. The sac is then injected with corticosteroid medication to shrink or dissolve it. In longstanding, painful, or recurrent cases, surgical removal of the cyst and its attachment to the tendon or joint capsule (stalk) is necessary. The cyst may also spontaneously rupture, providing relief.

Prognosis

Symptoms of untreated cysts worsen with increased activity. Surgical removal provides complete relief of symptoms, but 10% of cysts recur after surgery. Nonsurgical treatment with draining (aspiration) followed by corticosteroid injection results in relief of symptoms in 35% of cases.

Differential Diagnosis

Rheumatoid arthritis, tumor, tendon rupture, and fracture are possibilities. Other conditions that can have symptoms similar to those of synovial cysts include tumors (benign and malignant), nodules (especially rheumatoid nodules), arthritis conditions (especially rheumatoid arthritis), fractures, and tendon ruptures.

Specialists

- General Surgeon
- Orthopedic Surgeon
- Plastic Surgeon
- Podiatrist

Work Restrictions / Accommodations

No restrictions are necessary for untreated synovial cysts except for cases involving the hand, which may require limiting the use of that hand. If surgery is necessary, time off from work may be necessary until the affected limb heals.

Complementary and Alternative Therapies

Content is intended for awareness only. Treatments may or may not be effective. Scientific evidence may be lacking and some substances have potentially toxic effects. Dr. Presley Reed and the editors do not endorse the use of these therapies in the absence of consultation with a licensed medical professional.

Thread technique - Two sutures are passed through the ganglion, at right angles to each other, and each is tied in a loop. At intervals thereafter, the contents are expelled by massage.

Comorbid Conditions

Diabetes mellitus and peripheral arterial disease can delay healing.

Complications

Synovial cysts on weightbearing surfaces of the foot may make standing or walking painful. Synovial cysts on the palm of the hand may interfere with grasping. Synovial cysts on the top of the foot or ankle may be irritated by shoe pressure.

Factors Influencing Duration

If the dominant hand is affected, the individual's work requirements, and the treatment employed may influence length of disability. There may be recurrent episodes of the ganglion, and each episode may have different disabilities based on symptoms and treatment.

Length of Disability

Duration depends on site and whether dominant or non-dominant limb is involved.

Conservative treatment.

Duration in Days

Job Classification	Minimum	Optimum	Maximum
Sedentary work	1	1	3
Light work	1	1	3
Medium work	1	1	3
Heavy work	1	1	3
Very Heavy work	1	1	3

Aspiration.

Duration in Days

Job Classification	Minimum	Optimum	Maximum
Sedentary work	1	1	3
Light work	1	1	3
Medium work	3	4	7
Heavy work	3	6	7
Very Heavy work	3	6	7

Surgical treatment.

Duration in Days

Job Classification	Minimum	Optimum	Maximum
Sedentary work	1	3	14
Light work	1	3	14
Medium work	7	14	21
Heavy work	14	21	28
Very Heavy work	14	28	42

Duration Trend from Normative Data*

Cases	Mean	Min	Max	No Lost Time	Over 6 Months
1364	35	0	319	0.37%	0.30%

Percentile:	5th	25th	Median	75th	95th
Days:	9	17	27	42	88

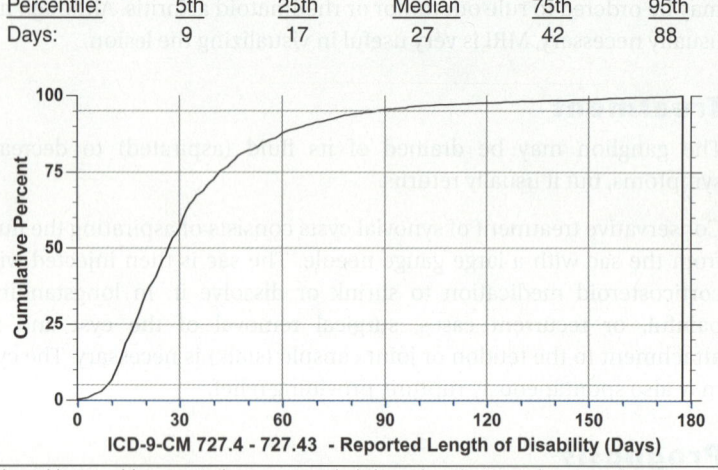

ICD-9-CM 727.4 - 727.43 - Reported Length of Disability (Days)

* Differences may exist between the expected duration tables and the normative graphs. Duration tables provide expected recovery periods based on the type of work performed by the individual. The normative graphs reflect the actual observed experience of many individuals across the spectrum of physical conditions, in a variety of industries, and with varying levels of case management.

Failure to Recover

If an individual fails to recover within the maximum duration expectancy period, the reader may wish to reference the following questions to assist in better understanding the specifics of an individual's medical case.

Regarding diagnosis:

- Has the individual had any trauma to the affected area?
- Where is the individual's cyst located? Is it painful? Is it soft or hard?
- Does the size of the cyst change or did it go away only to return?
- On physical exam, is there a soft to rigid mass near a joint or over a tendon present?
- Has the individual had an x-ray of the affected area? An MRI?
- Has the individual's cyst been aspirated?
- Have conditions with similar symptoms been ruled out?

Regarding treatment:

- Was the individual's cyst drained?
- Was the cyst injected with a corticosteroid? Has it returned?
- Has surgical removal of the cyst become necessary?

Regarding prognosis:

- Is the individual's employer able to accommodate any necessary restrictions?
- Does the individual have any conditions that may affect ability to recover?
- Does the individual have any complications related to the location of the cyst (such as cysts on weight bearing surfaces or the palm of the hand)?

References

Artico, M., et al. "Synovial Cysts: Clinical and Neuroradiological Aspects." Acta Neurochirurgie 139 3 (1997): 176-181.

Steiner, E., et al. "Ganglia and Cysts Around Joints." Radiology Clinics of North America 34 2 (1996): 395-425.

Synovitis
727.00

Definition

Each joint is enclosed in a capsule lined with membrane tissue known as synovium. When the joint lining (synovial lining) becomes irritated and inflamed, a condition known as synovitis develops. The synovium has folds when viewed under the microscope that are filled with blood and lymph vessels. The lining secretes a lubricating fluid called synovial fluid. The result is warmth, tenderness and swelling in and around the joint, which is caused by increased fluid production and swelling of the lining.

Synovitis has many causes including infection, direct joint trauma, allergic reaction, gout, over use syndromes, and inflammatory diseases such as rheumatoid arthritis.

Synovitis can be an acute episode, limited to one joint, or it can be a chronic symptom of a general disease process such as rheumatoid arthritis. It is not a condition specific to either gender. Because synovitis has many possible causes, it is a frequently encountered problem.

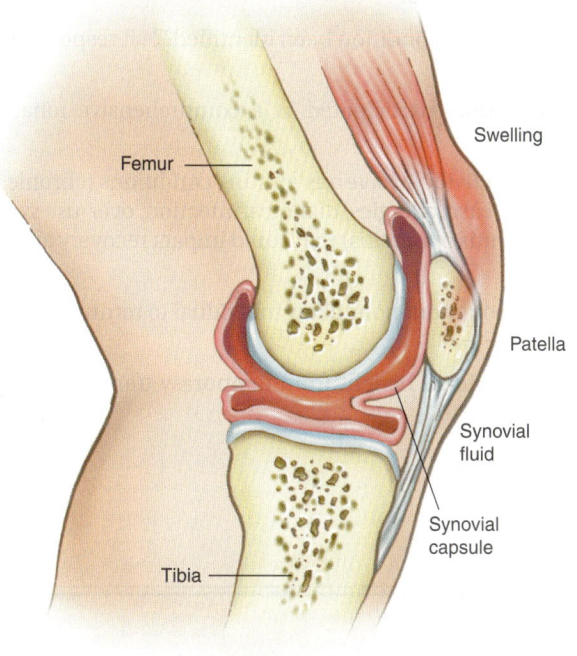

Diagnosis

History: Individuals will complain of pain, swelling, warmth, and stiffness. One joint or several may be involved. Individuals may report relief with heat or cold. The symptoms are often activity related. Individuals must be questioned about known underlying disease.

Physical exam: Joints will appear swollen, red, warm to touch, and have a "boggy" feel to palpation. Motion may be limited and painful.

Tests: Laboratory tests include rheumatoid panel, complete blood count (CBC), urinalysis, joint fluid analysis (following joint aspiration) with gram stain, ESR. Routine x-rays may be indicated to evaluate the joint surface looking for erosion of the articular surface. Nuclear medicine scans may also be valuable.

Treatment

Synovitis is most often treated with anti-inflammatory medications, cold or heat therapy, and rest from aggravating activity. Medication for pain control may be needed. Corticosteroid injections are also used. Splinting for part of the day or night may be helpful.

In destructive synovitis, as found in conditions such as rheumatoid arthritis, surgical removal of the synovium may be required (synovectomy). Destruction of the synovium can also be accomplished with laser therapy/surgery and injections of selectively destructive chemicals (ablation.)

Prognosis

Acute, isolated episodes usually respond well to conservative treatment. In chronic states, the course of the underlying disease will predict the outcome. Synovitis can reoccur when treated surgically by removal of the inflamed synovium (synovectomy) or with chemical or laser destruction (ablation) if the synovium regrows. The underlying disease process may start the abnormal swelling (inflammatory process) of the synovium all over again.

Differential Diagnosis

Infection and joint trauma are other possibilities.

Specialists

- Occupational Therapist
- Orthopedic Surgeon
- Physiatrist
- Physical Therapist
- Rheumatologist
- Sports Medicine Physician

Rehabilitation

The goal of rehabilitation for synovitis is to decrease the inflammation and pain to the inflamed synovial membrane and fluid (synovium) of the affected joint. This allows the physical or occupational therapist to emphasize the rehabilitation on restoring motion and strength to the joint(s) that may be involved. Early in the condition, the therapist instructs the individual to elevate the affected joint, which can help reduce swelling. The therapist also educates the individual on how to avoid pressure from the inflamed bursa by applying an elastic bandage, sling, or soft foam pad to protect the involved area until the swelling goes down.

Rehabilitation offers several possible treatments in controlling the inflammation that results from synovitis. At the initial flare-up of synovitis, the therapist may use cold treatments to control swelling and pain. Electrical stimulation is another technique used to relax muscles around the inflamed joint and decrease pain.

Once the initial pain and inflammation (acute stage of synovitis) have improved, heat is often applied. Treatments in the form of heat are used to help relieve muscle and joint pain and stiffness along with increasing blood flow to help remove inflammation from the synovial membrane. Moist heat packs are one form of heat the physical or occupational therapist utilizes. The pack is used over multiple layers of toweling to achieve a comfortable warming effect. Another form of heat treatment used in physical or occupational therapy includes ultrasound that uses high frequency sound waves producing heat that penetrates deep into the involved synovial membrane and surrounding joint and muscles. Iontophoresis is another popular treatment in the rehabilitation of synovitis.

Once pain and swelling have been greatly reduced, the physical or occupational therapist will perform stretching exercises to help restore full motion to an affected joint and or limb. Passive stretching exercises involve the therapist moving the affected limb with no effort initiated by the individual. The muscles are placed upon a mild stretch. Whenever possible, the individual is instructed in such stretching and repeats it when at home or at work. Modifications may need to be made depending on the location of the affected joint, the stage of the inflammation (i.e., recent flare-up or ongoing pain) and whether surgery was required. However, this condition rarely requires surgical intervention.

Work Restrictions / Accommodations

Limited work (loading) of an affected joint would be an appropriate restriction. Periods of rest and time for rehabilitation would be necessary. Use of medication for control of pain and inflammation will require review of drug policies. Altering job requirements to reduce repetitive activities is helpful.

Comorbid Conditions

Chronic inflammatory diseases would tend to prolong recovery and these conditions are more prone to recurring episodes of synovitis.

Complications

Any chronic inflammatory disease, allergies, diabetes, infection, overuse syndromes and tendonitis or bursitis may complicate synovitis. When the synovitis is chronic, the lining can grow over the articular surface of a joint (pannus) and become destructive to the cartilage.

Factors Influencing Duration

Underlying diagnosis, joint involvement, dominant side, work requirements and tolerance to rehabilitation will affect disability periods.

Length of Disability

This is a vague diagnosis. Duration depends upon the location and severity of the condition. Contact physician for additional information.

Failure to Recover

If an individual fails to recover within the maximum duration expectancy period, the reader may wish to reference the following questions to assist in better understanding the specifics of an individual's medical case.

Regarding diagnosis:

- Did the individual present with pain, swelling and redness of one or more joints?
- Were diagnostic x-rays and blood tests done to confirm the diagnosis?
- Has cause of synovitis been identified?
- Is more than one joint involved?
- Would individual benefit from evaluation by a specialist (rheumatologist, sports medicine specialist)?

Regarding treatment:

- Has enough time passed to allow for conservative measures to resolve symptoms?
- If symptoms persist despite conservative therapy, is more aggressive intervention with laser or surgical treatment now warranted?

Regarding prognosis:

- Has underlying condition been identified? Is it responding well to treatment?
- Has individual participated in a comprehensive rehabilitation program?
- Does the individual have any existing conditions (chronic inflammatory disease, allergies, diabetes, infection, over-use syndromes and tendinitis or bursitis) that could impact recovery and prognosis?
- Would accommodations allow individual to return to present duties?
- Would individual benefit from temporary transfer to a different position?

References

Kessler, R.M. Management of Common Musculoskeletal Disorders: Physical Therapy Principles and Methods. Philadelphia: J.B. Lippincott Company, 1990.

Scully, Rosemary M., and Marylou R. Barnes. Physical Therapy. Philadelphia: J.B. Lippincott Company, 1989.

Syphilis

090, 091, 091.0, 091.1, 091.2, 091.3, 091.4, 091.5, 091.6, 091.7, 091.8, 091.9, 092, 092.0, 092.9, 093.0, 093.1, 093.2, 093.8, 093.9, 094.2, 094.3, 094.8, 094.9, 097, 097.9

Definition

Syphilis is a complex venereal disease caused by the spirochete bacterium, Treponema pallidum. Syphilis is spread by direct contact with a skin ulcer (chancre) of an infected person. This is usually through sexual contact with mucous membranes of the genital area or mouth, but can also be through broken skin on other parts of the body. Therefore, syphilis is unlike other venereal diseases in that it can be transmitted non-sexually.

After entering the body through broken skin, the bacteria quickly move to the lymph nodes where they can spread throughout the body. A pregnant woman can also pass the disease to her unborn child, which may result in stillbirth or with a syphilis-infected infant.

The course of the disease can be divided into 4 stages; primary, secondary, latent, and tertiary. The primary and secondary stages can last 1-2 years during which time the infected person can spread the disease to others. These stages are often unidentifiable because the skin ulcers are usually painless, difficult to identify and pass rather quickly. The individual thinks he/she is cured but the disease progresses to its later stages. In the later 2 phases, latent and tertiary, the disease is no longer contagious. During tertiary syphilis, serious damage to many internal organs of the body, mental disorders, and death can occur. This stage can last for years or decades.

The number of cases of syphilis annually is between 11,000 and 100,000 in the US. Cases are on the decline now possibly due to education about safer sexual practices. The disease is most common in individuals from 15-35 years old. Homosexual men have a particularly high rate of syphilis. Syphilis also plays a role in increasing the risk of acquiring the human immunodeficiency virus (HIV) or AIDS.

Diagnosis

History: Syphilis occurs in 4 stages. The primary stage occurs 10 days to 3 months after exposure. Individuals may complain of painless chancre sores at the site of infection (genital area or the mouth). Individuals may report that the sores heal rapidly. Individuals may also report swollen lymph glands. There may be history of contact with an infected individual.

The secondary stage occurs 2 to 12 weeks after primary stage and lasts for 2 or more years. Individuals may report symptoms of a rash of small open sores that can cover any part the body (most likely the palms of the hands and the soles of the feet), fever, sore throat, fatigue, headache, swollen lymph glands, and hair loss may also occur. Meningitis, hepatitis, arthritis, and inflammation of the bone or eye can also occur during this phase. This phase can also recur at any time and with any severity.

Individuals who are in the latent stage, which occurs 1 year after initial infection and lasts for months to a lifetime, will have no symptoms to report and may believe they are cured. The tertiary stage or late stage may last for years or decades.

Late reactions in syphilis include benign tumors that can occur in any organ of the body, particularly the skin and bones. Individuals may complain of hoarseness and respiratory distress.

Physical exam: In the early stages of syphilis, chancre sores may be identified on the penis or cervix. Swollen, but not tender, lymph glands may be identifiable during the first 2 stages. The late stages of syphilis may reveal tumors (gummas) in the organs, neurological conditions, blindness, or insanity.

Tests: There are several blood tests available for syphilis including the well known Venereal Disease Research Laboratory test (VDRL test). An increasing number of enzyme immunoassays (EIAs) for detecting syphilis antibodies have become available. Treponemal EIAs are an appropriate alternative to the use of combined VDRL/rapid plasma reagin (RPR) and Treponemal pallidum hemagglutination assay (TPHA) tests for screening for syphilis. If treponemal EIA is used for screening, an alternative treponemal test, such as TPHA, should be used for confirmatory testing. The fluorescent treponemal antibody-absorbed test is probably best reserved for specimens giving discrepant results. The most accurate method, however, is a microscopic examination of tissue or fluid from the ulcers for identification of the syphilis bacteria. A spinal tap can also be done in later stages of the disease to diagnose infection of the nervous system.

Individuals diagnosed with syphilis should also be tested for other sexually transmitted diseases including HIV.

Treatment

Treatment in the early stages involves a single injection of an antibiotic. Twenty-four or forty-eight hours after treatment, most individuals can no longer transmit the disease. Individuals should refrain from sexual activity during this time. Partners of individuals with syphilis should also be treated. Individuals who have been exposed to syphilis can be treated by an injection of antibiotic immediately to prevent infection by the bacteria.

In later stages of syphilis, longer treatment with antibiotics is required. Parenteral penicillin continues to be the drug of choice for treatment of all stages of syphilis.

The proper use of condoms can decrease the risk of contracting syphilis. Pregnant women should be tested for syphilis to prevent transmission of the disease to their children. Limiting sexual relationships to a single uninfected partner can decrease the risk of syphilis.

Prognosis

If treated, syphilis can be cured no matter what stage the disease is in. However, serious, irreversible damage can occur to the organs before treatment is sought. Individuals need follow-up care, usually at 3 months, to determine whether or not the infection has been cleared.

The first and second stages of syphilis are self-limiting. About one-third of individuals undergo spontaneous cure during the early phases, one-third will remain in the latent phase, and one-third will develop serious late lesions.

Neurosyphilis (where the bacteria invade the nervous system) can occur in 3-7% of untreated individuals. This results in meningitis, paralysis, mental illness, and degeneration of the spinal nerves. If the blood vessels are affected, a stroke may develop.

Differential Diagnosis

Syphilis is often called the "great imitator" because of the number of diseases that have similar symptoms. Diseases with common skin manifestations include chancroid, genital herpes, skin infections, measles, or rubella. Later stages of the disease may be similar to lymphogranuloma venarum; neoplasms of the skin, liver, lung, stomach, or brain; meningitis and neurological diseases.

Specialists

- Cardiologist
- Neurologist
- Infectious Disease Physician

Work Restrictions / Accommodations

Individuals with open sores found during the first 2 stages of syphilis should be kept away from other employees since this stage is highly contagious through contact with the sores. Depending upon the course of the disease, during the later stages, significant work restrictions may be necessary, as individuals should avoid contact with public. Individuals may be unable to perform duties due to weakness, confusion, or pain in the joints. Reassignment may be necessary.

Comorbid Conditions

Suppression of the immune system and the presence of AIDS can lengthen disability.

Complications

Early treatment of syphilis can result in Jarisch-Herxheimer reaction. This reaction is due to the sudden release of toxins from the syphilis bacteria as they are destroyed. These toxins can aggravate symptoms. Treatment should be continued, however, unless the symptoms become severe, life threatening, or threaten permanent damage. The reaction usually disappears within 24 hours.

The secondary phase of syphilis may cause meningitis, hepatitis, or kidney inflammation.

Progression of the disease to late or tertiary syphilis causes many complications. During this stage damage to the heart, eyes, brain, bones, and joints occurs. A secondary, bacterial infection of the skin ulcers may occur, as well as scarring.

Factors Influencing Duration

The length of disability will be influenced by the stage of the disease and by the specific organs affected by the disease. If the individual is in late-stage syphilis, periods of extended disability may be required.

Length of Disability

Primary, secondary.

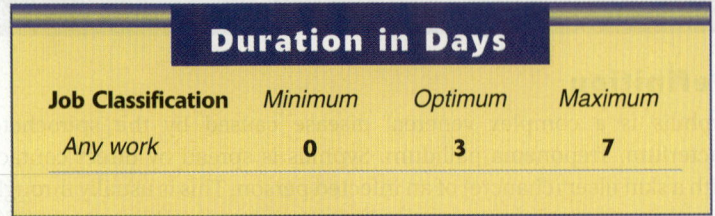

Job Classification	Minimum	Optimum	Maximum
Any work	0	3	7

Early, latent.

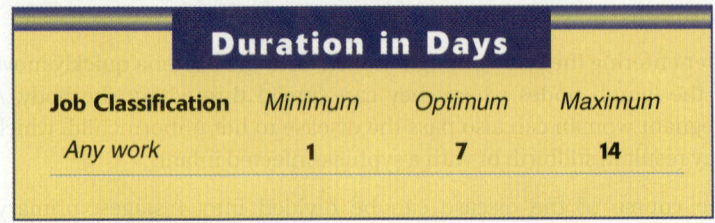

Job Classification	Minimum	Optimum	Maximum
Any work	1	7	14

Failure to Recover

If an individual fails to recover within the maximum duration expectancy period, the reader may wish to reference the following questions to assist in better understanding the specifics of an individual's medical case.

Regarding diagnosis:

- What stage of the disease is individual in?
- Did individual initially have painless chancre sores at the site of infection?
- Were swollen lymph glands present?
- Did a rash develop or small open sores that cover any part the body?
- Does the individual have fever, sore throat, fatigue, headache, and swollen lymph glands?
- Has individual had any hair loss?
- Has individual had meningitis, hepatitis, arthritis, or inflammation of the bone or eye?
- Has individual developed benign tumors in the organs, particularly the skin and bones?
- Does individual complain of hoarseness and respiratory distress?
- On exam did the physician find a chancre on the penis or cervix?
- Were tumors known as gummas found in the organs?
- Does individual have any neurological conditions? Insanity? Blindness?
- Did individual have a VDRL test or antibody testing?
- Was microscopic examination of fluid from the ulcers or tissue done?
- Was individual tested for other sexually transmitted diseases?
- In later stages, was a spinal tap done?
- Have conditions with similar symptoms been ruled out?

Regarding treatment:

- In the early stage, was individual treated with a single injection of penicillin?
- Was the individual's partner also treated?
- In later stages, was individual treated with parenteral penicillin for a longer time period?

Regarding prognosis:

- Is individual's employer able to accommodate any necessary restrictions?
- Is reassignment necessary in order for the individual to return to work?
- Does individual have any conditions that may affect ability to recover?
- Does individual have any complications such as a Jarisch-Herxheimer reaction?
- Does individual have meningitis, hepatitis, or kidney inflammation?
- Does individual have damage to the heart, eyes, brain, bones, and joints?

References

Brooks, G.F., J.S. Butel, and S.A. Morse. Medical Microbiology. Stamford: Appleton & Lange, 1998.

National Institute of Allergy and Infectious Diseases. Fact Sheet: Syphilis. National Institutes of Health. 01 Jul 1998. 01 Jan 2001 <http://www.niaid.nih.gov/factsheets/stdsyph.htm>.

Tierney, L.M., S.J. McPhee, and M.A. Papadakis. Current Medical Diagnosis and Treatment. Stamford: Appleton & Lange, 1998.

Woodward, C., and M.A. Fisher. "Drug Treatment of Common STDs: Part I, Herpes, Syphilis, Urethritis, Chlamydia and Gonorrhea." American Family Physician 60 5 (1999): 1387-1394.

Syringomyelia
336.0

Definition

Syringomyelia describes the condition where a fluid-filled cavity (cyst or syrinx) grows within the spinal cord usually in the neck area (cervical spinal cord). If the cavity forms within the lower brain stem, the condition is referred to as syringobulbia. As the fluid-filled cavity gradually expands, it presses on nerves that serve the hands and arms (in the case of syringomyelia affecting the cervical spinal cord) or the lower extremities (when syringomyelia affects the lumbar spinal cord). As a result, pain, lack of nerve sensation, weakness, and loss of muscle bulk (muscular atrophy) typically occur.

In about half the cases, the disorder is present at birth (congenital) and may be associated with a congenital abnormality of the brain (Chiari I malformation). Although the cause is unknown, taking folic acid during pregnancy may help prevent birth defects such as syringomyelia. The expansion of the cavity often occurs during the teen or young adult years. Symptoms usually begin between the ages of 25 to 40. The disease is more common in men. Syringomyelia can also be caused by spinal cord trauma, infection (meningitis), inflammation (arachnoiditis), or the development of a spinal cord tumor. Some cases of syringomyelia were found in several family members or inherited (familial), but this is rare. In the US, there are 8.4 cases per 100,000 individuals. There are no significant differences in prevalence in other countries.

Diagnosis

History: The individual may have a lack of sensation in the fingers, first noticed as a painless burn or cut or painless ulcers on one or more of the extremities. Decreased or absent sensation to pain, temperature, or touch in a cape-like pattern over the shoulders and back is common and is followed by pain, weakness, and stiffness in the back, shoulders, arms, or legs. Other symptoms may include headaches. In syringobulbia, the individual frequently complains of dizziness and a sensation of spinning (vertigo), jerky eye movements (nystagmus), tongue wasting, facial sensory impairment on one or both sides of the face, other lower cranial nerve palsies, and swallowing difficulty (dysphagia) or slurred speech (dysphasia). Symptoms tend to develop slowly but may come on suddenly with coughing or straining.

Physical exam: The most prominent signs include decreased or absent deep tendon reflexes in the arm and a lack of sensation (dissociated anesthesia) below the level of the syrinx often in the pattern of a cape or shawl. Symptoms are nearly always present on both sides of the body (bilateral) but may be asymmetrical or affect one side only (unilateral). Because of the loss of pain and temperature sensation in the hands and inner forearms, painless ulcers of the extremities may follow trauma.

Tests: CT, photographs of the spinal cord taken after the injection of a contrast material (myelography), MRI, and x-rays of the skull and cervical spine are utilized in making a definitive diagnosis. Nerve conduction velocity testing or electromyography may be used to demonstrate nerve damage.

Treatment

There is no medical treatment for syringomyelia. Surgery is used in an attempt to drain the fluid from the cavity, reduce pain, and stop further progression of neurological symptoms (syringotomy). Congenital syringomyelia may require that pieces of cervical vertebrae in the area of the cavity be removed (cervical laminectomy) in an effort to drain the cavity and decompress the spinal cord. It may be necessary to drain the syrinx with a catheter, drainage tubes, or valves leading to the abdomen.

Prognosis

Approximately half of the individuals with syringomyelia improve significantly after surgery to drain the fluid from the cavity (syringotomy). The other half, although relieved of some pain, eventually become wheelchair-bound. Delay in treatment may result in irreversible spinal cord injury.

Differential Diagnosis

Differential diagnoses include tumors and vascular malformations of the spinal cord. Multiple sclerosis, meningitis, sarcoidosis, vasculitis, or other peripheral neuropathies may present similar symptoms and findings.

Specialists

- Neurologist
- Neurosurgeon
- Occupational Therapist
- Physiatrist

Rehabilitation

Individuals with syringomyelia may require physical and occupational therapy. Individuals may require speech therapy if the tumor is present in the lower brain stem (syringobulbia).

Therapy focuses on educating the individuals about the disease process, improving communication, maintaining range of motion, increasing strength, and improving coordination, balance, and functional abilities such as gait.

Individuals learn about the expected prognosis of the disease and how to prevent secondary problems such as the formation of decubitus ulcers that may result from decreased skin sensation.

To improve communication, speech therapists teach individuals specific lip, tongue, and facial muscle positions to clarify speech.

Because individuals experience weakness and decreased function in their arms and/or legs, a comprehensive stretching program is critical to maintaining range of motion in the joints. Occupational and physical therapists instruct individuals and their family members on how to safely stretch the arms and legs. Individuals learn to stretch the wrist and fingers into flexion and extension to preserve hand function and learn to stretch the hamstrings by lying on the back and bringing the leg up toward the ceiling to promote sitting balance.

The occupational and physical therapists create a strengthening program to maintain functional abilities for the arms and legs. Individuals perform arm exercises such as elbow extensions using light hand weights if crutches or a walker is to be used. Bridging exercises may be performed where the individual lies on the back with the knees bent and lifts the buttocks up from the bed. This promotes the ability to get out of a chair. All strengthening exercises are performed to the individual's tolerance.

Individuals may have impaired coordination with syringomyelia. Occupational therapists assign fine motor coordination exercises such as picking up pegs and placing them in a pegboard, or instruct the individual in practical coordination exercises such as fastening buttons or practicing signatures. In physical therapy, individuals work on gross motor coordination such as kicking a soccer ball rolled toward them or throwing beanbags at a target.

Both sitting and standing balance are important in physical and occupational therapy. The main focus of physical and occupational therapy is to maximize functional capabilities.

Work Restrictions / Accommodations

Work restrictions and accommodations require consideration on an individual, case-by-case basis. The physical environment may need to be adapted if the individual must use a wheelchair for mobility. Individuals may have difficulty with jobs that require physical labor, the ability to walk without difficulty, or fine manipulation with the hands. Alternative job duties may be needed for these individuals. The individual may need breaks to move about in order to avoid becoming stiff and to relieve pressure on the buttocks especially if confined to a wheelchair. Ability to operate equipment depends on the individual's voluntary control of the limbs and the physical requirements of operating specific equipment and machinery. Vocational rehabilitation may be needed.

Comorbid Conditions

Obesity, skin infection, postoperative infections, and permanent neurologic damage are conditions that influence the length of disability. The presence of underlying conditions such as spinal cord trauma or tumor, meningitis, arachnoiditis, arteriovenous malformation, or Chiari Type I malformation may all lengthen disability.

Complications

Neurologic deficits, intense pain, and permanent loss of sensation, loss of voluntary movement, and/or loss of mobility are possible complications. Following surgery, syringomyelia may recur and require additional operations. Injury to the extremities can complicate loss of sensation that protect against temperature extremes or other painful stimuli.

Factors Influencing Duration

Factors influencing length of disability include the pattern and extent of sensory and motor loss and the severity of neurological deficits before surgery. Disability may be permanent.

Length of Disability

Duration depends on age, general state of health, nature and severity of symptoms, response to treatment, and extent of permanent functional loss. Job requirements such as the ability to walk, operate dangerous machinery, and perform physical labor may be jeopardized depending on the remaining functional abilities. The ability to operate equipment and machinery depends on the extent of motor and sensory loss. Disability may be partially reversible, or may be permanent.

Aspiration and drainage.

Duration in Days

Job Classification	Minimum	Optimum	Maximum
Sedentary work	7	14	21
Light work	7	14	21
Medium work	14	21	28
Heavy work	21	28	35
Very Heavy work	21	28	42

Upper cervical laminectomy and occipital craniectomy.

Duration in Days

Job Classification	Minimum	Optimum	Maximum
Sedentary work	28	42	91
Light work	28	42	119
Medium work	28	84	182
Heavy work	42	98	Indefinite
Very Heavy work	56	112	Indefinite

Failure to Recover

If an individual fails to recover within the maximum duration expectancy period, the reader may wish to reference the following questions to assist in better understanding the specifics of an individual's medical case.

Regarding diagnosis:

- Has diagnosis of syringomyelia been confirmed?
- Has extent of nerve damage been assessed?
- Have conditions with similar symptoms been ruled out?
- Has individual experienced any complications related to syringomyelia?
- Does individual have a coexisting condition that may impact recovery?

Regarding treatment:

- Has individual been involved in a comprehensive physical/occupational rehabilitation program?
- If tumor is present in the lower brain stem (syringobulbia), has individual also received speech therapy to improve communication?
- If symptoms are progressing, would individual benefit from surgical intervention (syringotomy)?

Regarding prognosis:

- Has permanent neurological damage already occurred?
- Is individual still a candidate for surgical intervention?
- Would individual benefit from additional or extended physical or occupational therapy?
- If alternative job duties are now indicated, would individual benefit from vocational rehabilitation?

References

Boss, Barbara J. "Alterations of Neurologic Function." Pathophysiology. McCance, Kathryn L., and Sue E. Heuther, eds. St. Louis: Mosby, 1994. 527-586.

Sarno, Martha Taylor. "Neurogenic Disorders of Speech and Language." Physical Rehabilitation: Assessment and Treatment. O'Sullivan, Susan B., and Thomas J. Schmitz, eds. Philadelphia: F.A. Davis Company, 1994. 563-554.

Tachycardia, Paroxysmal Supraventricular

Other names / synonyms: Tachycardia, Paroxysmal Atrial Tachycardia, Paroxysmal Atrioventricular Tachycardia, Paroxysmal Junctional Tachycardia, PSVT

427.0

Definition

Paroxysmal supraventricular tachycardia (PSVT) is a disturbance of the normal heart rhythm (arrhythmia) resulting in a spontaneously occurring and sporadic (paroxysmal) rapid heart rate (tachycardia) of more than 100 beats per minute.

Normally heart chambers (atria and ventricles) contract in a coordinated way. The signal to contract begins in the sinus (sinoatrial - SA) node. It is conducted through the atria (upper heart chambers) and stimulates them to contract. It passes through the atrioventricular (AV) node, then travels throughout the ventricles (larger, lower chambers) and stimulates them to contract. The intermittent and unpredictable (paroxysmal) heart rate disturbance occurs from changes in the electrical conduction pathway of the heart. The types of tachycardia that occur depend on where the change in the conduction pathway is initiated. PSVT can begin in the atria, the SA node, or the AV node.

The two types of PSVT are atrioventricular nodal re-entry tachycardia (AVNRT) and atrioventricular reciprocating tachycardia (AVRT), also known as accessory pathway tachycardia. The AVNRT occurs when there is an abnormal conduction pathway inside or next to the AV node. The AVRT occurs when the AV node is bypassed completely and a "shortcut" conduction pathway is used, manifesting in a condition called Wolff-Parkinson-White (WPW) syndrome.

An underlying lung or heart disease may cause PSVT. PSVT can occur after a heart attack (myocardial infarction) or may occur after lung or heart surgery. The abnormal conduction seen in WPW syndrome, however, may be acquired at birth (congenital). Other risks include excessive smoking, caffeine, and alcohol use; it can also occur with digitalis toxicity.

The most common type of PSVT is AVNRT, which occurs in approximately 50-60% of individuals with PSVT; it is less common in men than women, and often occurs in individuals older than 20 years of age. Of individuals who experience WPW syndrome, 80% have symptoms between 11 and 50 years of age.

Diagnosis

History: Individuals with AVRT may complain of a rapid heartbeat (tachycardia), dizziness, fainting (syncope), shortness of breath, chest pain, chest tightness, or weakness; their skin color may be pale (pallor). Complaints of increased loss of fluid (diuresis) via urination might be made. Individuals with AVNRT may note the sensation of feeling their heart beat (palpitations), a very rapid heart rate, light-headedness, feeling like they will faint (near-syncope), and "neck pounding." Many individuals with either type of PSVT may complain of anxiety or feeling scared.

Physical exam: Symptoms may start and stop suddenly, and can last for a few minutes or as long as a day or two. During an episode of the arrhythmia, heart rate will be greater than 100 beats/minute, with rates of 150 to 250 beats/minute with AVNRT; between episodes, the heart rate will be normal (60-100 beats/minute). The individual will have a rapid pulse and may appear anxious. There will be signs of poor oxygen perfusion. Generally, no other specific physical findings are evident.

Tests: An electrocardiogram (ECG) will confirm the diagnosis. Continuous ambulatory monitoring or a 24-hour Holter monitor may be needed to diagnose PSVT because of the sporadic nature of the disorder.

Treatment

Many individuals with PSVT require no treatment because the irregular heartbeat (arrhythmia) starts and stops spontaneously, and may resolve spontaneously. If symptoms develop or there are underlying cardiac disorders, treatment may be initiated in an attempt to interrupt the arrhythmia and convert back to a normal sinus rhythm. Electrical cardioversion (shock) is successful in converting PSVT in many cases. Individuals are advised to avoid nicotine, caffeine, alcohol, fatigue, and stress, all of which are known to provoke tachycardia.

For those with AVNRT, however, who experience light-headedness or nearly faint (near-syncope), the doctor may initiate measures to interrupt the rapid heart rate (tachycardia) by gently massaging one of the carotid arteries (carotid massage) in the neck and prescribing medications (beta-blocker, calcium-channel blocker). Surgical modification of the electrical conduction pathway may be recommended in some cases. Pacemakers designed to interrupt or override the tachycardia may be an alternative to surgery or the chronic use of medications. Individuals also may learn self-help measures such as coughing, plunging their face in ice water (ice water immersion), or attempting to expel breath while deliberately closing the mouth and nose (Valsalva maneuver).

Individuals with AVRT who experience symptoms such as chest pain, weakness, or fainting (syncope) may also require carotid massage. Carotid artery massage should only be done by a physician because it can cause severe slowing of the heart rate. The doctor may also prescribe medication to try to prevent the arrhythmia from occurring (antiarrhythmics).

Some individuals may not benefit from the above treatments and may require non-surgical removal of the area responsible for generating the arrhythmia. In this procedure, the conduction pathways are identified through electrophysiology studies, and the aberrant pathway can be destroyed by radio frequency waves that are transmitted through a special catheter (radiofrequency catheter ablation, catheter ablation, or RF ablation).

Prognosis

PSVT is generally not life threatening unless other cardiac disorders are present. There is a wide variation in outcome for individuals with PSVT, but most individuals have an excellent outcome, including those who undergo catheter ablation therapy. Success rates for this therapy are estimated at between 94-100%.

Differential Diagnosis

Ventricular tachycardia, sinus tachycardia, atrial flutter, and atrial fibrillation all present with similar symptoms, but an ECG will reveal the correct diagnosis.

Specialists

- Cardiologist

Work Restrictions / Accommodations

Because stress and fatigue are known to trigger an attack, the individual may benefit from a less challenging and stressful job and schedule. Until the arrhythmia is successfully treated, those who have jobs that entail the safety of others, such as pilots, bus or cab drivers, etc., should be placed in a different job at least temporarily. Once the arrhythmia is controlled, no restrictions or accommodations may be required.

Comorbid Conditions

Heart (cardiac) disease, blood vessel (vascular) disease, or panic attacks (anxiety disorder) might influence length of disability.

Complications

Complications of PSVT include atrial fibrillation, other arrhythmias, atrioventricular heart block, congestive heart failure, and sudden death.

Factors Influencing Duration

The individual's age, response to treatment, and adhering to restrictions against nicotine, alcohol, caffeine, fatigue, and stress are factors that might influence length of disability.

Length of Disability

For individuals with medical treatment, duration depends on severity of symptoms, response to treatment, and frequency of occurrence.

Medical treatment.

Duration in Days

Job Classification	Minimum	Optimum	Maximum
Sedentary work	1	3	14
Light work	1	3	14
Medium work	1	7	14
Heavy work	1	14	28
Very Heavy work	1	14	28

Radiofrequency ablation.

Duration in Days

Job Classification	Minimum	Optimum	Maximum
Sedentary work	3	4	7
Light work	3	4	7
Medium work	7	14	21
Heavy work	14	21	28
Very Heavy work	14	21	28

Surgical interruption of aberrant conduction pathway. Catheter ablation.

Duration in Days

Job Classification	Minimum	Optimum	Maximum
Sedentary work	14	21	28
Light work	14	21	28
Medium work	21	28	42
Heavy work	28	42	56
Very Heavy work	28	42	56

Failure to Recover

If an individual fails to recover within the maximum duration expectancy period, the reader may wish to reference the following questions to assist in better understanding the specifics of an individual's medical case.

Regarding diagnosis:

- Does the individual have a history of lung or heart disease?
- Has the individual experienced a recent heart attack (myocardial infarction) or undergone lung or heart surgery?
- Does the individual use nicotine, caffeine, and alcohol?
- Does the individual take the medication digitalis for heart problems?
- Does the individual complain of a rapid heartbeat (tachycardia), dizziness, fainting (syncope), shortness of breath, chest pain or tightness, or weakness?
- Are there complaints of increased loss of fluid (diuresis) via urination?
- Does the individual report the sensation of feeling their heart beat (palpitations), light-headedness, feeling "neck-pounding," or feeling like they will faint (near-syncope)?
- Does the individual report feeling anxious or scared?
- Was an electrocardiogram (ECG) done?
- Was continuous ambulatory monitoring for 24 hours (Holter monitor) required due to the sporadic nature of the disorder?
- Was a diagnosis of PSVT confirmed?

Regarding treatment:

- Did PSVT starts and stop spontaneously?
- If not, did the individual require treatment to interrupt the arrhythmia and convert back to a normal sinus rhythm (electrical cardioversion)? Did that successfully convert PSVT?
- Does the individuals understand the importance of avoiding nicotine, caffeine, alcohol, fatigue, and stress?
- For those who experienced light-headedness or nearly fainting (near-syncope), did the physician initiate carotid massage to interrupt the tachycardia?
- Did the individual require medications (beta-blocker, calcium-channel blocker)?
- Would this individual benefit from placement of a pacemaker?
- Has the individual been instructed on self-help measures such as coughing, ice water immersion, or attempting to expel breath while deliberately closing the mouth and nose (Valsalva maneuver)?
- If no treatments were successful, did the individual require non-surgical removal of the area responsible for generating the arrhythmia via destruction of the aberrant pathway by radiofrequency catheter ablation (catheter ablation or RF ablation)?
- Was this treatment successful?

Regarding prognosis?

- Does the individual have an underlying cardiac disorder?
- Are there any other underlying disorders that could prolong or prevent recovery?
- Is the individual compliant with avoidance of caffeine, alcohol, nicotine, stress, and fatigue?
- Is the individual compliant with all medication regimens?
- Have complications of PSVT developed? If so, how will the complication be treated and what is the expected outcome with treatment?

References

"Paroxysmal Supraventricular Tachycardia." University of Maryland. 20 Feb 2001. <http://umm.drkoop.com/conditions/ency/article/000183.htm>.

Tchou, Patrick, and Richard Trohman. "Supraventricular Tachycardia. Cardiovascular Medicine." Scientific American Medicine Online Dale, D.C., and D.G. Federman New York: WebMD Corporation, 2000 1-14. Scientific American Medicine. 05 Dec 2000 <http://www.samed.com/sam/chapters/01/0105.htm>.

Tarsal Tunnel Release
Other names / synonyms: Posterior Tibial Nerve Decompression
04.44

Definition

Tarsal tunnel release involves relieving pressure on the posterior tibial nerve as it passes along the inside of the ankle, behind the anklebone (medial malleus of the tibia).

The posterior tibial nerve may be trapped by abnormal anatomy or may have pressure applied by inflammation, cysts (ganglions), fatty tumor (lipoma) or other lesions that take up space in the tunnel. Pressure on or irritation of the nerve causes heel pain. This condition is known as tarsal tunnel syndrome.

Reason for Procedure

If conservative treatment of tarsal tunnel syndrome has failed, tarsal tunnel release is often recommended to relieve symptoms of pain and changes in sensation (paraesthesia) in the foot or lower leg. Relief is obtained by relieving pressure on the involved nerve and its branches. It may be also necessary to restore circulation around the nerve that may have been compromised prior to treatment.

Description

Surgery is done under regional or general anesthesia and in an outpatient setting.

The procedure is carried out through an incision along the inner back side of the ankle, along the nerve course. The tunnel is examined and, perhaps, opened. Any abnormalities that may be causing pressure on the nerve are corrected by removing synovitis, ganglions, or lipomas. Any boney obstructions will also be removed. The blood supply to the nerve is checked all along the nerve and any constrictions repaired.

After the wound is closed with sutures, a soft dressing is used to control swelling and weight bearing is restricted for 3 weeks to 6 weeks.

Prognosis

Complete relief of symptoms is reported to be about 90% in individuals with localized symptoms. In those individuals with more generalized symptoms about the foot, 70% report good results. Pain and paraesthesia is often lessened, but not cured, especially if the nerve is hit (percussed.)

Specialists

- Orthopedic Surgeon
- Podiatrist

Rehabilitation

Individuals who undergo tarsal tunnel release may require therapy. Physical therapists first address control of pain and swelling. Heating pads may be applied to the big toe and forefoot to decrease pain and increase muscle flexibility prior to therapy. Ultrasound, which provides deep heating, may be applied to the plantar surface of the foot. Ice packs may be applied to the toes and forefoot as needed to decrease pain and swelling. Individuals also learn to perform scar massage at the surgical site to decrease the risk of forming painful adhesions.

The second goal of physical therapy is to increase the flexibility of the toes, foot, and ankle. Because there is a decrease in the nerve impulse to the foot associated with tarsal tunnel syndrome, the arch may increase and the toes may become clawed. If an increased arch is present, therapists may perform cross-friction massage to the arch of the foot. Therapists may also passively stretch the toes and forefoot into extension and may perform joint mobilizations on the toe joints. Individuals learn to manually stretch the toes and forefoot, and the ankle (into inversion, eversion, plantarflexion, and dorsiflexion). Individuals stretch the ankle into dorsiflexion by placing a towel under the ball of the foot and using it to pull the foot towards them. Individuals also actively move the ankle to further increase range of motion.

The third goal of physical therapy is to strengthen the foot and ankle. Individuals strengthen the muscles of the foot and toes by performing towel crunches performed in which individuals squeeze the toes around a towel placed on the floor. Individuals also engage in picking up small objects from the floor with the toes. Therapists may use manual resistance against the toes as they flex and extend and against the foot as the individual moves the ankle. Elastic tubing with progressively increasing resistances can be used to strengthen the ankle.

The final goal of physical therapy is to regain functional abilities. Because weight bearing will be limited for a period of time after surgery, therapists focus on normalizing an individual's gait pattern once full-weight bearing through the foot is established. Individuals progress from crutches to a cane to walking without assistance during the course of therapy. Treadmill walking may be used to accomplish this goal.

Individuals with an increased arch may need an orthosis to give some cushioning at the arch, and to decrease weight bearing along the lateral border of the foot.

Work Restrictions / Accommodations

Walking, standing, climbing, or squatting may have to be temporarily limited. Immediately after surgery, individuals will not be allowed to put any weight on the foot and will need assistive devices such as crutches, canes, walkers or wheel chairs. Use of these devices may restrict upper body dexterity as well.

Comorbid Conditions

Peripheral neuropathy disease, diabetes, inflammatory diseases, smoking and obesity could complicate recovery from this procedure.

Procedure Complications

Complications include infection, nerve and blood vessel damage, and failure to relieve symptoms.

Factors Influencing Duration

Because weight bearing is restricted during recovery, disability would depend on job requirements. It should be remembered that use of ambulation assistive devices may impair use of the upper extremities as well.

Length of Disability

Job requirements would affect return to work. Even after recovery, activities that require impact to the lower extremity, especially to the foot, may be restricted.

Duration in Days

Job Classification	Minimum	Optimum	Maximum
Sedentary work	3	7	21
Light work	3	7	21
Medium work	3	14	21
Heavy work	7	21	28
Very Heavy work	7	28	42

References

Kisner, Carolyn, and Lynn Allen Colby. "The Ankle and Foot." Therapeutic Exercise: Foundations and Techniques, 2nd ed. Philadelphia: F.A. Davis Company, 1990. 385-408.

Mann, Roger. "Foot and Ankle." Orthopedics Sports Medicine. DeLee, Jesse C., and David Drez, Jr, eds. Philadelphia: Harcourt Brace & Co, 1994. 1832-1833.

Tarsal Tunnel Syndrome

Other names / synonyms: Neuropathy of Distal Tibial Nerve

355.5

Definition

The posterior tibial nerve runs through a narrow tunnel (tarsal tunnel) behind the bony protuberance on the inner side of the ankle and into the foot. The tunnel itself is formed by a dense band of fibrous tissue that supports and strengthens the ankle joint (the flexor retinaculum). Anything that takes up space in the tarsal tunnel will put pressure on the nerve and cause inflammation and pain, a condition called tarsal tunnel syndrome. This syndrome is similar to the carpal tunnel syndrome that occurs in the wrist. Tarsal tunnel syndrome is somewhat uncommon and can be difficult to diagnose.

Causes of the syndrome include an abnormal growth of tissue near the tunnel (tumors, cysts, lipomas, nerve ganglions, scar tissue following trauma), active swelling or bleeding into the tunnel following trauma to the foot or ankle, and the inflammation and swelling of neighboring tendons as a result of rheumatoid arthritis. Individuals with exceptionally flat feet are susceptible to tarsal tunnel syndrome because the flattening (pronation) of the arch causes muscles in the area to compress the nerve. Similarly, obesity is a risk factor because excessive weight can weaken the structure of the foot, resulting in compression of the posterior tibial nerve. Tarsal tunnel syndrome may be related to repetitive motions of the foot during the operation of foot pedals.

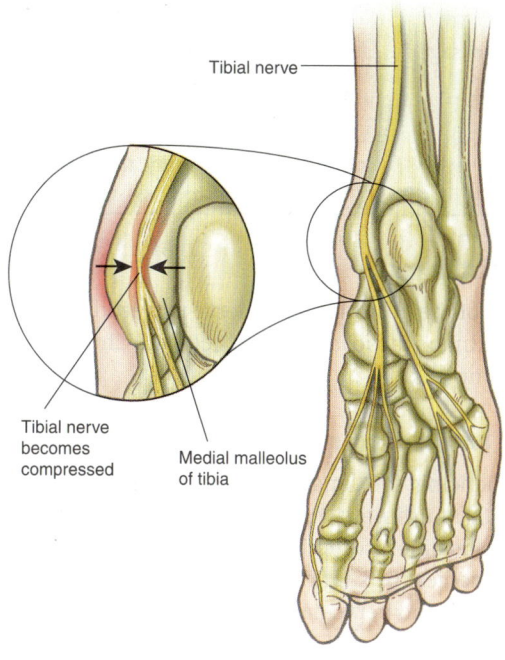

Diagnosis

History: Individuals with tarsal tunnel syndrome experience persistent pain on the sole of the foot that is described as burning and tingling (pins and needles). The pain may radiate to the tips of the toes and up to the lower leg. Typically, this pain is relieved by rest and elevation or by massage. The pain usually worsens as the day progresses (in contrast to the heel pain caused by plantar fasciitis, which is worse in the morning).

Physical exam: Exam of the individual with tarsal tunnel syndrome may reveal few objective signs of nerve compression. Signs of numbness (paresthesia) and muscle weakness may be present. Tapping (percussion) of the area above the tarsal tunnel may cause the individual to feel an uncomfortable tingling sensation that radiates toward the toes (Tinel's sign).

Tests: Electromyography (EMG) may be performed to study nerve function. A nerve conduction velocity (NCV) test can measure how fast the nerve impulses travel along the posterior tibial nerve. If the impulses travel slowly across the ankle, this may confirm a diagnosis of tarsal tunnel syndrome. An x-ray or CT scan of the foot may reveal tumors and other abnormal tissue growth around the tunnel.

Treatment

Medical treatment of tarsal tunnel syndrome includes treatment of underlying causes (trauma, arthritis, and tumors), rest, application of ice, use of nonsteroidal anti-inflammatory medications, and immobilization with a walking foot cast. Injection of the tarsal tunnel with a corticosteroid may give temporary relief of symptoms. Motion control shoes and over-the-counter arch supports may decrease the amount of foot pronation present and help maintain better alignment of the foot and ankle. If the underlying cause of the syndrome is obesity, a weight loss program may be prescribed. Surgical removal of abnormal tissue growths may be necessary to relieve pressure on the nerve. If symptoms last longer than 6 months or muscle weakness develops, surgical release of the posterior tibial nerve (tarsal tunnel release) may be indicated. In this procedure the laciniate ligament is cut, which allows the nerve to expand.

Prognosis

Outcome following medical treatment of tarsal tunnel syndrome is generally good. Surgical removal of tumors and other abnormal tissue growths is also associated with good outcomes. However, surgical outcome following tarsal tunnel release is less satisfactory. One study indicated only 42% of individuals may see improvement in their symptoms following tarsal tunnel release, as measured by nerve conduction studies. If nerves running into the area become bruised or damaged during surgery, they may form a painful spot under the scar (neuroma) or numbness in the foot. Damaged nerves can require many months to regenerate. As the damaged nerves regenerate, the individual may experience an unpleasant tingling sensation in the foot.

Differential Diagnosis

Diabetic neuropathy can also cause nonlocalized pain and paresthesias in the foot. Pain could also be from lumbar disc disease with sciatica or plantar fasciitis.

Specialists

- Orthopedic Surgeon
- Podiatrist

Rehabilitation

Individuals with tarsal tunnel syndrome may require therapy. Ultrasound, which provides deep heating, may be applied to the plantar surface of the foot. Ice packs are applied to the toes and forefoot as needed to decrease pain and swelling.

Because there is a decrease in the nerve impulse to the foot, the arch may increase and the toes may become clawed. Therapists may perform cross-friction massage to the arch of the foot. Therapists may also passively stretch the toes and forefoot into extension and may perform joint mobilizations on the toe joints. Individuals learn to manually stretch the toes and the forefoot (into extension), and the ankle (into dorsiflexion, plantarflexion, inversion, and eversion). Individuals may stretch the ankle by placing a towel under the ball of the foot and using it to pull the foot toward them.

Individuals strengthen the muscles of the foot and toes by performing towel crunches in which individuals squeeze the toes around a towel placed on the floor. Toe and foot muscles are also strengthened by picking up small objects from the floor with the toes.

Therapists may assert manual resistance against the toes as they flex and extend, and against the foot as an individual moves the ankle. Elastic tubing with progressively increasing resistances can be used to strengthen the ankle in these motions as well.

The final goal of physical therapy is to regain functional abilities. If an individual is walking with a cane or crutches, therapists progress individuals to walking without assistance. Therapists focus on normalizing an individual's gait pattern once full-weight bearing through the foot is established; treadmill walking may be used to accomplish this.

Individuals with an increased arch may need an orthosis or shoe insert to provide some cushioning at the arch, and to decrease weight bearing along the outside border of the foot.

Work Restrictions / Accommodations

Individuals with tarsal tunnel syndrome may need to avoid being on their feet for long periods of time until their symptoms are diminished or absent. Individuals operating machines requiring repetitive foot pedaling may need to be reassigned to another position temporarily, if not permanently. Those who experience permanent nerve damage or chronic pain in their feet and whose jobs require them to be on their feet for long periods of the day may need to be reassigned to jobs that would permit them to sit.

Comorbid Conditions

Comorbid conditions that might influence the length of disability for an individual with tarsal tunnel syndrome include diseases and conditions that can affect blood vessels and nerves in the foot. These include diabetes, peripheral vascular disease, peripheral neuropathy, rheumatoid arthritis, and congenital or post-traumatic foot deformities.

Complementary and Alternative Therapies

Content is intended for awareness only. Treatments may or may not be effective. Scientific evidence may be lacking and some substances have potentially toxic effects. Dr. Presley Reed and the editors do not endorse the use of these therapies in the absence of consultation with a licensed medical professional.

Acupressure -	Pressure applied to specific points may relieve pain.
Acupuncture -	May help to relieve discomfort.
Arch taping/ strapping -	Can take tension off the posterior tibial nerve, keeping it from getting inflamed and sore.
Orthotics -	Supporting the foot and arch can take tension off the posterior tibial nerve, reducing the symptoms of tarsal tunnel syndrome. A flattened arch puts strain on the posterior tibial nerve and constricts the tarsal tunnel. A supportive orthotic in the shoe supports the arch and repositions the foot, opening the tarsal tunnel and easing tension on the nerve.
Heel lift -	A length difference in one leg can cause the foot on the longer side to pronate or flatten, constricting the tarsal tunnel and stretching the posterior tibial nerve. Placing a right-sized heel lift in the shoe of the shorter leg can help align the pronated foot, opening the tunnel and easing tension on the nerve.
Hydrotherapy -	Cold compresses or alternating hot and cold compresses can provide relief.
Ice massage -	Ice makes the blood vessels in the sore area become narrower, helping to control the inflammation that is causing the pain.
Ultrasound -	Helps flush the sore area and brings in a new supply of nutrient and oxygen-rich blood.

Complications

Compression of the posterior tibial nerve may lead to permanent nerve damage if treatment is too late or unsuccessful. Chronic foot pain is also a possible complication.

Factors Influencing Duration

Factors influencing the length of disability include the individual's general health and fitness, mental and emotional stability, access to rehabilitation facilities, compliance with recommended treatment, and response to medical or surgical treatment. Persistent obesity, surgical wound infection, and nerve damage are all factors that might influence length of disability.

Length of Disability

Individuals with tarsal tunnel syndrome may be partially or completely disabled for 6-12 months while the posterior tibial nerve regenerates and symptoms subside. Individuals whose jobs require them to use their foot in repetitive pedaling movements or to be on their feet for long periods of time and who cannot be retrained for other positions may be permanently disabled.

Medical treatment.

Duration in Days

Job Classification	Minimum	Optimum	Maximum
Sedentary work	0	3	21
Light work	0	5	21
Medium work	3	7	21
Heavy work	7	14	28
Very Heavy work	7	21	42

Surgical treatment.

Duration in Days

Job Classification	Minimum	Optimum	Maximum
Sedentary work	3	7	21
Light work	3	7	21
Medium work	3	14	21
Heavy work	7	21	28
Very Heavy work	7	28	42

Failure to Recover

If an individual fails to recover within the maximum duration expectancy period, the reader may wish to reference the following questions to assist in better understanding the specifics of an individual's medical case.

Regarding diagnosis:

- Has diagnosis of tarsal tunnel syndrome been confirmed?
- Is the current pain different in any way from the original pain that caused the individual to seek treatment?
- Has the foot been examined by x-ray or CT scan to rule out tumors and other abnormal tissue growth?
- Has muscle weakness in the foot progressed?
- Was a nerve conduction velocity (NCV) test performed to measure how fast the nerve impulses travel along the posterior tibial nerve?
- Has it been repeated to see if the impulses travel faster or slower than at the time of diagnosis?
- Does individual have an underlying condition, such as diabetes, peripheral vascular disease, peripheral neuropathy, rheumatoid arthritis, and congenital or post-traumatic foot deformities, that may be impacting recovery?

Regarding treatment:

- Has the individual complied with all aspects of treatment?
- Are corticosteroid injections indicated?
- Has individual received physical therapy if indicated?
- Did the individual purchase and regularly use whatever motion control shoes or over-the-counter arch supports were prescribed?
- Has individual complied with weight loss goals?
- Would individual benefit from enrollment in a community weight-loss program?
- Has surgical treatment of the syndrome been considered?

Regarding prognosis:

- If symptoms have lasted longer than 6 months, or if muscle weakness has developed, is surgical intervention now warranted?
- Did individual experience complications resulting from surgical procedure?

References

Tarsal Tunnel Syndrome. Chehalem Physical Therapy, Inc. 2000. 2 Jan 2001 <http://www.chehalempt.com/Anklefoot/tarsultun_rehab.htm>.

Tierney, Lawrence, Stephen McPhee, and Maxine Papadakis. Current Medical Diagnosis and Treatment. New York: McGraw-Hill, 2000.

Temporal Arteritis

Other names / synonyms: Giant Cell Arteritis
446.5

Definition

Temporal arteritis is a chronic vascular inflammatory disease of unknown origin occurring in individuals over the age of 50. It may be related to the aging process or it may be a disease where the immune system acts against the individual's own cells (autoimmune disease). Early recognition and treatment is critical to prevent blindness related to inflammation of branches of the ophthalmic artery. Before the eye is affected, headache is the most common symptom.

Temporal arteritis is an inflammation affecting medium- and large-sized oxygen-carrying blood vessels (arteries) resulting from an abnormal accumulation of very large cells (giant cells) in the artery linings. The disease is named temporal arteritis because the temporal artery (a branch of the carotid artery) is frequently affected. The temporal artery and its branches supply the structures of the temporal regions of the head above the cheekbones and directly behind the eyes, commonly referred to as the temple. Temporal arteritis is also called giant cell arteritis because arteries other than the temporal artery can be affected. The arterial inflammation (arteritis) found in temporal arteritis can lead to narrowing of the arteries and eventually complete blockage of the blood supply to the areas served by the arteries.

The American College of Rheumatology criteria for diagnosis require three of the following five conditions: development of symptoms in individuals over age 50, new onset of headache or localized head pain, temporal artery tenderness to palpation, decreased pulsations unrelated to atherosclerosis of cervical arteries, and Westergren erythrocyte sedimentation rate >50.

Fifty percent of individuals diagnosed with temporal arteritis also have a disease called polymyalgia rheumatica that is characterized by pain and stiffness in the encircling bony structures supporting the shoulder (shoulder girdle) and the lower limbs (pelvic girdle) specifically the neck, shoulders, lower back, hips, and thighs.

Some cases of the disease appear to run in families. Association with the HLA-DR4 genetic marker (haplotype) suggests there may be inherited tendencies. Other possible factors that may play some role in causing or predisposing to this disorder include female sex hormones, immunological factors called cytokines, and Chlamydia infection.

In the US, annual incidence rates in individuals age 50 and older range from 10 to 50 per 100,000 individuals. Mean age of onset is 70 and incidence is 1% in individuals over 80. The disease is more common in women than men and is rare in blacks. For unknown reasons, temporal arteritis has a high incidence in northern climates especially Scandinavia and regions of the US with large Scandinavian populations.

Diagnosis

History: Headache is present in more than 85% of individuals, usually in the temporal region on one side. It may worsen at night and is often aggravated by combing the hair or resting head on a pillow. Visual loss may be the first symptom in half the individuals with visual impairment or sudden and painless blindness. Other symptoms may include low-grade fever accompanied by night sweats, scalp tenderness and burning over one or both temples, jaw pain (jaw claudication) that makes opening the mouth and chewing difficult, a general feeling of uneasiness or indisposition (malaise), fatigue, loss of appetite (anorexia), and weight loss. Less common symptoms are dry cough and painful paralysis of the shoulder.

Physical exam: The temporal artery may be tender when touched (palpated) and the arterial pulse may be absent. The vessel may feel lumpy (nodular) or be visibly enlarged. In individuals presenting with blindness, examination with an ophthalmoscope may not reveal changes in the eye for days or even weeks.

Significant findings in medium- and large-sized arteries other than the temporal artery occur in 15% of individuals with temporal arteritis sometimes years after diagnosis and treatment of the disease. If the great artery (aorta) and its major branches are affected, physical examination may reveal unequal pulses in the arms, a heart murmur indicating leakage of blood around the aortic valve (aortic regurgitation), or murmurs (bruits) near the collar bone (clavicle) that result from narrowing of the subclavian artery.

Tests: Several blood tests are usually performed when a diagnosis of temporal arteritis is suspected and include a complete blood count (CBC) to evaluate the presence of anemia, infection, or an inflammatory process. An erythrocyte sedimentation rate (ESR) or measurement of serum alkaline phosphatase levels also helps determine the presence of an inflammatory process. Findings indicating the possibility of temporal arteritis include a very elevated ESR, a normal white blood cell count (suggesting absence of infection), and an elevated alkaline phosphatase level. However, these positive results are also found in a number of other diseases including rheumatoid arthritis, cancer, numerous blood disorders, and liver disease. A definitive diagnosis of temporal arteritis is made from examination of serial biopsies taken from the lining of the temporal artery. More than one tissue sample is required because not all segments of the artery may be involved (skip lesions). Inflammatory changes in the artery lining are found on one side (unilaterally) in 80-85% of individuals with the disease; changes are found on both sides (bilaterally) in 10-15%. Chest x-ray may be a useful screening test for a thoracic aneurysm. Brain MRI, MRI angiography, and ocular pneumoplethysmography may assist in the diagnosis of temporal arteritis.

Treatment

If temporal arteritis is suspected, immediate treatment (even before temporal artery biopsies are performed) with high doses of a corticosteroid is required because blockage (occlusion) of a branch of the ophthalmic artery from inflammation can result in permanent blindness. (The ophthalmic artery supplies blood to the eye, the orbit, and neighboring facial structures.) High-dose steroid therapy is continued for 1 to 2 months. When the disease activity ceases, the daily corticosteroid dosage may be slowly tapered. Low-dose corticosteroid therapy may be required for an additional 1 to 2 years. Adding methotrexate to steroids was shown to be effective in reducing relapses seen with steroid therapy alone.

The ESR is a useful tool in monitoring and tapering corticosteroid therapy. As the ESR begins to drop, so can the daily dosage of corticosteroids. Conversely, a rise in the ESR may require an increase in the daily dosage. Once the disease stabilizes, blood tests are done at 1 to 3 month intervals to insure that the prescribed dosage of corticosteroids is properly controlling the disease. Continued ophthalmologic evaluation is needed to evaluate the effectiveness of treatment and development of any complications involving the eye such as glaucoma or cataract.

Since corticosteroids increase the loss of calcium from bones and may increase the risk of fractures, particularly the vertebrae in the back, individuals on long-term corticosteroid therapy should be given calcium supplements as well as hormones if bone density measurements suggest decreased bone density (osteoporosis). Medications should be given such as histamine blocking agents for protection against gastrointestinal bleeding, a common complication of steroid therapy. Weight gain is another common side effect of long-term corticosteroid therapy and the result of fluid retention. A low salt and/or a potassium-rich diet can help prevent fluid retention. Potassium replacements may also be necessary.

Individuals taking corticosteroids on a long-term basis must be instructed to inform medical personnel about the use of steroids if emergency treatment is required. This information is critical to preventing shock and other life-threatening complications that can occur if corticosteroids are suddenly withdrawn.

Nonsteroidal anti-inflammatory drugs (NSAIDs) are given for relief of painful symptoms such as headache and pain in the jaw.

Prognosis

The prognosis for temporal arteritis is generally good after a course of high-dose corticosteroid therapy for 1 to 2 months followed by low-dose therapy for an additional 1 to 2 years. After the full course of treatment, most individuals go into complete remission. This is maintained even after withdrawal of corticosteroids. The disease may recur, however, and in some individuals it remains active for years. For individuals with other major arteries involved, outcome depends on diagnosis and successful treatment of blood supply blockages and aneurysms that threaten major organs.

Differential Diagnosis

Polymyalgia rheumatica affects half of the individuals diagnosed with temporal arteritis and causes some of the same symptoms such as fever, malaise, weight loss, anemia, and a markedly elevated erythrocyte sedimentation rate (ESR). Polymyalgia rheumatica alone, however, does not cause blindness and responds to low-dose corticosteroid therapy. About 20% of individuals with polymyalgia rheumatica, however, have a positive temporal artery biopsy. Takayasu arteritis is an occlusive arteritis affecting the aorta with vascular symptoms similar to those of temporal arteritis.

Symptoms of fever, malaise, anemia, weight loss, and elevated sedimentation rate are associated with many other diseases such as cancer, blood disorders, and AIDS. Head pain or visual symptoms may be result of brain tumors and other neurological diseases such as migraine, ischemic stroke, and transient ischemic attack. Other ophthalmological diseases that may be confused with temporal arteritis include acute angle-closure glaucoma, iritis, uveitis, orbital infections, retinal artery or vein occlusion, and ultraviolet keratitis. In most cases, a positive temporal artery biopsy leads to definitive diagnosis of temporal arteritis provided that a large enough segment of artery is examined.

Specialists

- Rheumatologist

Rehabilitation

Active range of motion physical therapy where the individual moves the extremities may help individuals with temporal arteritis and polymyalgia rheumatica regain and maintain flexibility and strength while corticosteroid therapy brings these diseases into remission. Exercise can also increase an individual's sense of well-being, which in turn results in an increased appetite and better nutritional status.

If permanent blindness has occurred, the individual requires a wide-range of rehabilitation and supportive interventions to prepare for a life without vision including grief counseling, physical therapy, occupational therapy, and various types of instruction and training (i.e., reading Braille, using a cane or seeing-eye dog, using a voice-activated or Braille computer). In most instances, the individual requires at least some degree of retraining in order to be employable again. Families are also deeply affected by sudden blindness in a loved one and can benefit from talking to a social worker or grief counselor.

Work Restrictions / Accommodations

Generally speaking, no work restrictions or accommodations are required for individuals with temporal arteritis unless permanent blindness has occurred. Some individuals may perform their jobs in spite of persistent pain until the arterial inflammation is brought under control with corticosteroid therapy. Others may require a shortened workday and decreased responsibility in order to return to work before the disease goes into remission. Others may find it impossible to perform their jobs in the presence of pain. Depending on the nature of an individual's job requirements and physical work environment, permanent blindness will most likely require major work restrictions and accommodations or a classification of permanent disability.

Comorbid Conditions

Comorbid conditions influencing the length of disability for individuals with temporal arteritis include diseases, conditions, and medications that weaken the immune system (immunosuppression) and chronic diseases like HIV/AIDS, cancer, or leukemia. Glaucoma is an eye disease characterized by increased pressure in one or both eyes (increased intraocular pressure) and may influence disability since increased intraocular pressure is also a side effect of corticosteroid therapy. Polymyalgia rheumatica commonly accompanies temporal arteritis. Osteoporosis, ulcer disease, and immunosuppression can be aggravated by corticosteroid therapy.

Complications

When untreated, visual loss affects as many as 50% of individuals with temporal arteritis. Up to 75% of individuals having visual disturbance in one eye develop visual loss in the other eye within 3 weeks.

If the great artery (aorta) is involved, the individual may develop a thoracic aortic aneurysm several years after the diagnosis of temporal arteritis. An aortic aneurysm is a condition where the wall of the aorta is weakened and subject to rupture at any time. A ruptured aortic aneurysm is an extreme emergency often resulting in death. Involvement of other arteries in the body can also result in life-threatening conditions such as strokes, heart attack (myocardial infarction), and blockage of the blood supply to other major organs.

When individuals are given high doses of corticosteroids, the body decreases the amount of cortisone it produces. If an individual suddenly stops taking corticosteroids, many side effects can occur and range from a feeling of tiredness to complete physical collapse because the body no longer produces an adequate amount of cortisone on its own. Therefore, under the strict supervision of a physician, the dosage of corticosteroids must be reduced very gradually (a process called tapering) so the body can compensate for the reduction by making its own cortisone again.

Factors Influencing Duration

Factors influencing the length of disability include response to treatment and compliance with corticosteroid therapy, an extremely important factor in recovering from temporal arteritis.

Length of Disability

Length of disability depends on severity of the arteritis, individual's response to treatment, and success of any surgical intervention deemed necessary. Remission is common but disability may be permanent.

Medical treatment.

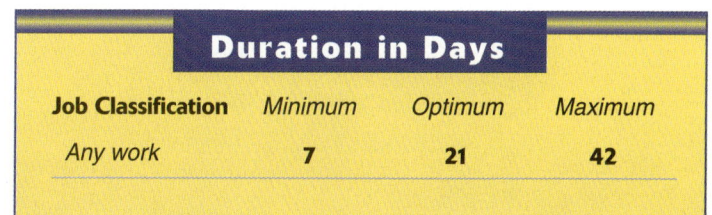

Job Classification	Minimum	Optimum	Maximum
Any work	7	21	42

Temporal Arteritis 2047

Failure to Recover

If an individual fails to recover within the maximum duration expectancy period, the reader may wish to reference the following questions to assist in better understanding the specifics of an individual's medical case.

Regarding diagnosis:

- Have fever and pain persisted? Have any other symptoms developed that would indicate a source of infection?
- Has vision deteriorated in any way?
- Has individual developed muscular weakness or balance problems that might suggest a neurological disease rather than temporal arteritis?
- Is erythrocyte sedimentation rate (ESR) elevated?
- Is individual younger than age 50, making the diagnosis of temporal arteritis unlikely?
- Was temporal artery biopsy positive? If not, are serial temporal artery biopsies needed?

Regarding treatment:

- Was individual's ESR monitored regularly with blood tests?
- Was individual treated with high-dose corticosteroid therapy for 1 to 2 months? Was individual careful to take the steroids at the suggested times of the day, in the correct dosage, and with food to decrease stomach irritation? If the corticosteroid therapy is being tapered, was individual careful about following the physician's directions for decreasing dosage?
- Is individual being followed regularly by an ophthalmologist with adjustment in steroid dosage as indicated?
- Is rehabilitation needed for persistent visual impairment?
- Is individual taking a calcium supplement and exercising?
- Would individual benefit from physical therapy to maintain flexibility and strength until corticosteroid therapy brings the disease into remission?

Regarding prognosis:

- Has individual experienced any complications related to the diagnosis or steroid treatment? Are complications being addressed in the overall treatment plan?
- Does individual have a coexisting condition that may complicate treatment or impact recovery?
- Is visual loss or blindness permanent?
- Has individual received rehabilitation and supportive interventions to prepare for a life without vision? Would individual benefit from grief counseling?
- Does individual have access to assistive devices for the visually impaired?
- Would work accommodations allow individual to continue with present occupation or is retraining required?

References

Afshari, N.A., M.A. Afshari, and S. Lessell. "Temporal Arteritis." International Ophthalmology Clinics 41 1 (2001): 151-158.

Allen, D.T., M.C. Voytovich, and J.C. Allen. "Painful Chewing and Blindness: Signs and Symptoms of Temporal Arteritis." Journal of the American Dental Association 131 12 (2000): 1738-1741.

Atalay, M.K., and D.A. Bluemke. "Magnetic Resonance Imaging of Large Vessel Vasculitis." Current Opinion in Rheumatology 13 1 (2001): 41-47.

Bonnet, F., et al. "A Possible Association Between Chlamydia Psittacci Infection and Temporal Arteritis." Joint Bone Spine 67 6 (2000): 550-552.

Casson, R.J., et al. "Bilateral Ocular Ischemic Syndrome Secondary to Giant Cell Arteritis." Archives of Ophthalmology 119 2 (2001): 306-307.

Connolly, B.P., et al. "Characteristics of Patients Presenting with Central Retinal Artery Occlusion With and Without Giant Cell Arteritis." Canadian Journal of Ophthalmology 35 7 (2000): 379-394.

Hu, Z., et al. "Temporal Arteritis and Fever: Report of a Case and a Clinical Reanalysis of 360 Cases." Angiology 51 11 (2000): 953-938.

Jover, J.A., et al. "Combined Treatment of Giant-cell Arteritis with Methotrexate and Prednisone: A Randomized, Double-blind, Placebo-controlled Trial." Annals of Internal Medicine 134 2 (2001): 106-114.

Mohan, N., and G. Kerr. "Spectrum of Giant Cell Vasculitis." Current Rheumatology Report 2 5 (2000): 390-395.

Nordborg, C., E. Notdborg, and V. Petursdottir. "Giant Cell Arteritis. Epidemiology, Etiology and Pathogenesis." APMIS 108 11 (2000): 713-274.

Tierney, Lawrence, Stephen McPhee, and Maxine Papadakis. Current Medical Diagnosis and Treatment. New York: McGraw-Hill, 2000.

Turbin, R.E., and M.J. Kupersmith. "Giant Cell Crteritis." Current Treatment Options in Neurology 1 1 (1999): 49-56.

Temporomandibular Joint Syndrome

Other names / synonyms: TMJ Dysfunction, TMJ Syndrome

524.60

Definition

Temporomandibular joint syndrome (TMJ) is a disorder that causes persistent pain in the joints at each end of the jawbone. The pain is centered where the muscle comes together with the jaw, in front of the ears (myofascial pain).

The temporomandibular joints play an active role in our speech, chewing capabilities, swallowing, and the facial expressions we make. These joints are prone to various abnormalities, including problems noted at birth, rheumatoid arthritis, or osteoarthritis (inflammation of the joint).

An estimated 10 million individuals in the US develop TMJ pain despite having a normal joint. This is generally caused by muscle spasms in the area resulting from psychological stress, muscle tension, and nocturnal grinding of the teeth (bruxism).

TMJ syndrome affects approximately 4 times as many women as men. It has 2 age peaks, in the early twenties and during perimenopause.

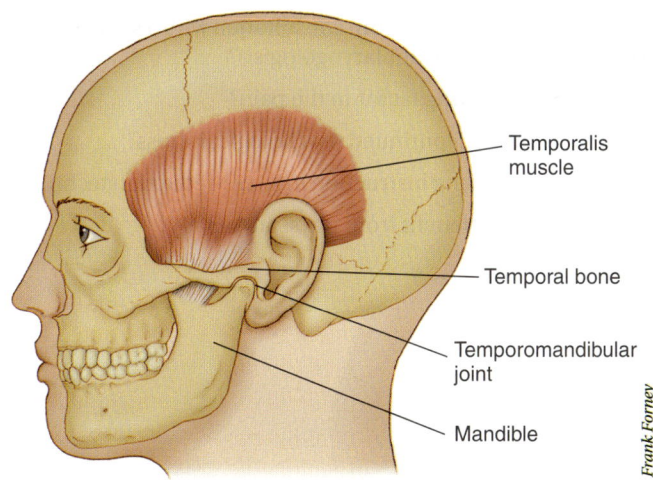

Diagnosis

History: The most common complaints are jaw pain close to the ears and difficulty with jaw movement. The character of the pain may vary from dull to sharp, and may be constant or occasional. Clicking noises in the joint may be heard. A ringing sensation in the ears (tinnitus), as well as hearing problems may be present. Individuals may also complain of earache, headache, or dizziness. A history of dental work, facial trauma, or psychological stress (resulting in nocturnal tooth-grinding) may be reported. The individual should be asked about frequent gum-chewing.

Physical exam: An exam may reveal tenderness in the jaw and lack of mobility. Limitation in jaw movement when opening the mouth may be apparent. Poor dental alignment or missing teeth may be obvious as well. Unusual sounds such as popping or clicking may be noted. There may be evidence of hearing problems. Records of recent dental procedures may be reviewed.

Tests: Laboratory or imaging studies are generally not necessary unless an infection or fracture are suspected.

Treatment

It is important to avoid overuse of the jaw. Gum chewing is eliminated. Jaw clenching or grinding is avoided (if this is done during sleep, a mouth device to stop teeth grinding may be recommended). Local application of heat as well as medications to decrease joint inflammation and pain (nonsteroidal anti-inflammatory drugs, such as ibuprofen) and muscle tension (muscle relaxants such as benzodiazepines) may be beneficial.

Stress may be a contributing factor to the pain. If this is the case, counseling and/or medication to deal with stress may help. In some cases, referral to a physical therapist for treatment such as massage may be given.

Prognosis

Most individuals with TMJ disorders respond well to conservative medical treatment and self-care, including over-the-counter analgesics and warm compresses on the affected muscles. Even if untreated, symptoms generally ease within 2-3 years, but treatment will generally make the individual more comfortable sooner and help prevent the development of dental complications.

Differential Diagnosis

Conditions with similar symptoms might include dental infection, jaw dislocation or fracture, gout, headache (cluster, migraine, or tension), ear or sinus infection, or Lyme disease.

Specialists

- Dentist
- Oral Surgeon
- Otorhinolaryngologist
- Psychologist

Work Restrictions / Accommodations

In jobs requiring extensive verbal communication, such as a tour guide or corporate trainer, work accommodations and/or modifications may be necessary. Since stress is generally implicated in TMJ, transfer to a less stressful position may be appropriate.

> **Complementary and Alternative Therapies**
>
> Content is intended for awareness only. Treatments may or may not be effective. Scientific evidence may be lacking and some substances have potentially toxic effects. Dr. Presley Reed and the editors do not endorse the use of these therapies in the absence of consultation with a licensed medical professional.
>
> | | |
> |---|---|
> | Heat therapy - | Local application of heat may help relieve pain. |
> | Massage therapy - | May help relieve stress and muscle tension. |
> | Spray and stretch - | This medically researched established therapy regimen involves having the individual stretch the jaw open after the skin over the painful area is sprayed with a skin refrigerant or cooled with ice. |

Comorbid Conditions

Arthritis, dental disorders, or immune system disturbances may lengthen disability.

Complications

Complications might include chronic facial pain, and wearing, cracking, or misalignment of the teeth (malocclusion).

Factors Influencing Duration

Factors that might influence the length of disability include whether the condition is complicated by other disorders or if there is joint or cartilage damage.

Length of Disability

In most cases, no disability is expected. Disability may be lengthened for employment in which verbal communication is required, such as teacher or radio announcer.

Duration in Days

Job Classification	Minimum	Optimum	Maximum
Any work	0	0	2

Failure to Recover

If an individual fails to recover within the maximum duration expectancy period, the reader may wish to reference the following questions to assist in better understanding the specifics of an individual's medical case.

Regarding diagnosis:
- Has diagnosis of TMJ been confirmed?
- Have other conditions with similar symptoms been ruled out?
- Does individual have a coexisting condition that may impact recovery?

Regarding treatment:
- Is individual refraining from gum chewing?
- Is individual using a mouthguard at night?
- Has appropriate medication been provided?
- Has medication been effective in relieving symptoms?
- Is individual under continued psychological stress?
- Is individual receiving instruction in stress-reduction techniques?

Regarding prognosis:
- Do symptoms persist despite treatment?
- Would individual benefit from consultation with a specialist (dentist, oral surgeon, otorhinolaryngologist)?
- Is stress a contributing factor to the pain?
- Is individual under continued psychological stress?
- Is individual receiving instruction in stress-reduction techniques?
- Would individual benefit from physical therapy?

References

"Temporomandibular Disorders." Merck Manual of Diagnosis and Therapy, 17th ed. Beers, Mark H., and Robert Berkow, MD, eds. Whitehouse Station, NJ: Merck & Co., Inc, 1999. 05 Jan 2001 <http://www.merck.com/pubs/mmanual/section9/chapter108/108a.htm>.

Tierney, Lawrence, Stephen McPhee, and Maxine Papadakis. Current Medical Diagnosis and Treatment. New York: McGraw-Hill, 2000.

Tendon Release
83.01, 83.13

Definition
Tendon release is a surgical procedure to intentionally cut through or disconnect a tendon (tenotomy.) The procedure normally involves cutting the tendon and allowing it to retract towards the junction of the muscle and tendon. Any tendon could be treated with this procedure, although those in the eye and extremities are the most common.

The procedure is commonly done to relieve tight joints (contractures) or decrease friction irritation. Sometimes the tendon is re-routed (transposed) during the procedure to maintain muscle function. Types of procedures vary from correcting lazy eye syndrome to straightening joints in individuals with chronic diseases who develop contractures to treatment for tennis elbow (lateral epicondylitis.)

Reason for Procedure
This procedure is used to correct shortening in a muscle tendon unit. Tendon release also treats the pain, deformity, and related problems associated with tendon shortening.

Description
Tendon releases are normally done with either regional or local anesthesia, as inpatients or outpatients, depending upon any other problems being addressed during surgery. Generally, an incision is made over the area of tendon attachment, the tendon tissue is cut away from the bone, allowing the tendon to relax or pull back towards the muscle belly. It may not be necessary to release the entire tendon to decrease tension on the muscle tendon unit. If the tendon is to be reattached (transposed) in another location, the incision is larger and the procedure more complicated. Very limited procedures, where the tendon in only lanced or pierced to relieve tension, could be done in a physician's office, under local anesthesia. The wound is closed and dressings applied. Extension splints may be used over joints to promote relaxation of the muscle tendon unit, increasing range of motion.

Prognosis
Outcome is dependent on the underlying condition. Partial to full recovery is expected for most conditions. Compliance with rehabilitation is very important to maintain the surgical outcome.

Specialists
- Neurosurgeon
- Orthopedic Surgeon
- Plastic Surgeon

Rehabilitation
Assistance from a physical therapist and/or occupational therapist who specializes in tendon rehabilitation may be necessary for maximal recovery of function. Careful analyses of the underlying condition as well as the corrective procedures are a determinant in creating an effective therapy schedule. However, the therapy schedule is not rigidly set. Progress is determined by the individual's functional improvement.

The tendons involved and the type of release performed will determine the type and duration of immobilization. Splinting is a common form of immobilization. In the case of tendon release, the affected limb is splinted in the corrected position to maintain movement gained during surgery. For example, if the tendon release is done in the hand, the hand will be splinted with the palm flat (extension) or with the fingers slightly curled (flexion). The type of immobilization influences the amount of early motion the individual is able to achieve. Early mobilization of the limb within the cast also helps reduce the adhesion formation, which can limit motion and slow the progress of therapy.

A conservative amount of tension should be applied to the healing tendons during therapy sessions, especially during the first weeks post surgery. Most tendon release failures occur when adhesions form that restrict the movement of the limb. Active assisted motion can be initiated soon after the release. If the release has been performed on lower body areas, active exercises in the direction of the freed range of motion are necessary to maintain that motion. Exercises such as leg extension in a short arc may be performed. Each exercise, however, must be based on the extent of injury and the current level of function.

Additionally, to maintain proper joint function, exercises for the opposing (antagonist) muscles must also be a part of the exercise plan. For example, in order to exercise the hamstring muscles (antagonist to the quad) the individual lays prone on a table or bench while the therapist applies light resistance. The individual tries to bend the leg to the farthest position attainable without pain. Heat may be applied before or after therapy to help to decrease pain and increase range of motion. Again, exercises must be chosen that fit the extent and location of procedure.

Depending on the causes that necessitated the release, functional recovery varies.

Work Restrictions / Accommodations
Individuals with tendon releases for inflammation, such as tennis elbow, may require temporary reassignment, depending on job requirements. Some reassignments may become permanent, based on recovery and underlying conditions. For example if body position cannot be corrected to accommodate use of work equipment, reassignment would be permanent.

Comorbid Conditions
Inflammatory diseases such as arthritis and neurological diseases such as cerebral palsy are comorbid conditions.

Procedure Complications
Complications from tendon release include infection, nerve and vessel injury, and loss of muscle balance or function.

Factors Influencing Duration
Factors influencing length of disability include reason for procedure, presence of other related diseases, job demands, and complications.

Length of Disability

Disability duration is highly variable. Depending upon the reason for the procedure and the location of the tendon, this procedure may not be compatible with medium or heavy work.

Duration in Days

Job Classification	Minimum	Optimum	Maximum
Sedentary work	7	14	28
Light work	14	28	42
Medium work	28	42	Indefinite
Heavy work	28	42	Indefinite
Very Heavy work	28	42	Indefinite

References

Hunter, James, et al. Rehabilitation of the Hand: Surgery and Therapy, 3rd ed. St. Louis: The C.V. Mosby Company, 1990.

Turek's Orthopaedics. Turek, Samuel, L., and Joseph A. Buckwalter, eds. Philadelphia: Lippincott-Raven, 1994.

Tendon Sheath Incision
83.01

Definition

Incision of a tendon sheath is a procedure to cut through the tissue surrounding a tendon (epitenon, tendon sheath). This is most often necessary to relieve pressure or constriction around a tendon. Often times, the tendon itself is not damaged, but the sheath is enlarged, tight, toughened, and irritating to the tendon, thus preventing normal function of the tendon. Incision of the sheath restores the normal tendon sliding function.

This procedure is often necessary in the treatment of inflammatory disorders, entrapment disorders, or after irritation of the sheath resulting in formation of scar tissue. Inflammatory diseases, cumulative trauma disorders, or changes resulting form fractures and dislocations may cause tenosynovitis, which may lead to the need for tendon sheath incision.

The incision of the sheath can be required anywhere in the body a tendon is affected. In inflammatory disorders like rheumatoid arthritis, the procedure is most often done in the feet and hands. Entrapment disorders like carpal tunnel syndrome and stenosing tenosynovitis occur mostly in the hands and wrists.

Reason for Procedure

This procedure is used to restore tendon function and to relieve symptoms of pain and loss of function caused by entrapment or compression of the tendon in the abnormal sheath.

Tendons that must slide through tight compartments or tunnels are most prone to problems with the tendon sheath. Conditions that cause tenosynovitis such as inflammatory diseases, cumulative trauma disorders, or changes resulting form fractures and dislocations could result in the need for tendon release.

Description

Depending on the tendon involved, local, regional, or general anesthesia may be required. An incision is made over the tendon. The sheath and the tendon are explored, isolating nerve and vessel branches. The sheath is then either cut away (excised) entirely or loosened (released) by making a cut on one side along its length. Tendon function is evaluated with passive motion, and the wound is closed with sutures.

Prognosis

Successful outcome is dependent on the underlying reason for the procedure. Restoration of tendon function is usually possible along with relief of pain and swelling. If there are no other complications (joint contractures, muscle or nerve damage, for example) normal function is expected. There is the possibility of repeated procedures caused by reoccurrence of the underlying disease process.

Specialists

- Orthopedic Surgeon
- Plastic Surgeon

Rehabilitation

Physical therapy after a tendon sheath incision follows the same general procedure no matter the location of the surgery. Pain and edema management, passive and active range of motion to the affected area, light resistance and coordination of the limb, and functional retraining are included in the therapy. The exercises prescribed are limb and degree-of-injury specific.

The first part of therapy is to control swelling (edema) and pain. The individual is required to elevate the limb for at least 10 minutes every hour, as well as to apply ice to the site of injury. If the tendon sheath incision was performed to the hands, the hand should be held overhead and light fist motions made with the injured hand. If the surgery was performed to the leg area, the leg should be elevated higher than the heart while in a reclined position. T.E.N.S. (Transcutaneous Electrical Nerve Stimulation) can be used to help reduce pain associated with the inflammatory response. After the second or third day postsurgery, walking or hand movement may be initiated.

During the range-of-motion phase of therapy, the individual may engage in exercises that help increase limb movement. For example, if the individual is being treated for shin splints, the therapist may start with exercises in which the foot points down or moves side to side. The duration and intensity of each exercise session depends on the underlying cause of the injury. An individual receiving therapy for a hand injury may engage in hand exercises such as opening and closing the hand on an hourly basis. Ice may be used to combat swelling and pain.

Once pain and swelling have subsided, more resistive exercises, such as pointing and flexing the toe using a towel for resistance, can be performed. The goal in this stage is to build muscle strength and flexibility of the affected area. An individual may begin doing more functional activities, such as riding a stationary bike at low resistance or starting to grip objects. In this phase of rehabilitation, the therapist works to build a base for proper biomechanics and limb function. The individual may participate in a supervised therapy sessions quite frequently during this phase. Alternative methods of therapy during this stage may include a whirlpool or full aqua therapy.

One major aspect of therapy is to regain muscle balance in the effected limb. For example, building muscles of the wrist and fingers (including the thumb) is crucial for proper hand function. Further injury occurs when muscle imbalance causes uneven loading to the limb while tasks are performed. Wrist curls may be performed. This exercise can be performed with the palm facing up with the hand curling up toward the ceiling. Exercises are performed in multiple directions. The functional phase can combine several different techniques such as using a balancing platform to build lower body reaction.

Return to normal function depends on proper rehabilitation to both the muscle and tendons involved. Depending on the location and extent of injury, an occupational therapist may be called upon to assess working conditions. The individual may be advised to rotate tasks or take more frequent breaks when the task is repetitive.

Work Restrictions / Accommodations

Work restrictions and accommodations will depend on the tendon(s) involved and the underlying condition necessitating the procedure. Several days are required for the wounds to heal, during which time the area must be kept clean and dry. Initially, any activity that places tension or stress on the tendon will be limited. If there is risk for tendon rupture while any swelling or irritation resolves, use of the affected body part will be restricted for a few weeks. Temporary or permanent reassignment may be required to allow adequate healing and to prevent recurrence.

Comorbid Conditions

Chronic inflammatory conditions such as rheumatoid or psoriatic arthritis or gout may slow and possibly impair recovery.

Procedure Complications

Damage could occur to the tendon, nerves, or blood vessels. Infection and bleeding are also possible complications. Failure to relieve symptoms is another possible complication or poor result.

Factors Influencing Duration

Factors include location of the disorder or condition, whether the dominant or nondominant hand is involved, underlying condition, complications, type of surgery, and the individual's job requirements. Surgery on multiple fingers simultaneously will prolong the disability. During recovery, job requirements that load the tendon muscle unit would be restricted.

Length of Disability

Reoccurrence of the underlying cause for surgery is possible. Restoration of function of the tendon or lack of pain control from the procedure would prolong the disability, perhaps permanently. Individuals who perform heavy or very heavy work may require additional lifting restrictions.

De Quervain's release.

Duration in Days

Job Classification	Minimum	Optimum	Maximum
Sedentary work	1	14	21
Light work	3	14	21
Medium work	7	21	42
Heavy work	21	28	56
Very Heavy work	21	28	56

Trigger finger or thumb.

Duration in Days

Job Classification	Minimum	Optimum	Maximum
Sedentary work	1	14	28
Light work	3	14	28
Medium work	7	21	35
Heavy work	21	28	42
Very Heavy work	21	28	42

References

Buckwalter, Joseph. "Musculoskeletal Tissues and the Musculoskeletal System." Turek's Orthopedics. Turek, Samuel, L., and Joseph A. Buckwalter, eds. Philadelphia: Lippincott-Raven, 1984. 32-33.

Hunter, James, et al. Rehabilitation of the Hand: Surgery and Therapy, 3rd ed. St. Louis: The C.V. Mosby Company, 1990.

Tendonitis

Other names / synonyms: Tendinitis

726.90

Definition

Tendonitis is inflammation of a tendon, the fibrous tissue that connects a muscle to bone. Some tendons are rope-like and others similar to thick sheets. The inflammation is often accompanied by degeneration of the collagen fibers comprising the tendon.

Tendonitis occurs only when there is direct injury to the tendon itself along with partial tearing of the fibers. Tendonitis can be caused from an infection or overload or over-use of the affected tendon. The condition can also be caused by inflammatory diseases such as rheumatoid arthritis, systemic sclerosis, gout, Reiter's syndrome, and diabetes mellitus.

Inflamed tendons are more commonly found in the hand. Other common sites for tendonitis are in the shoulder and knee (rotator cuff tendonitis, patella tendonitis, and iliotibial band tendonitis). Since tendons fail to regenerate quickly because of lack of a rich blood supply, aging may also cause gradual deterioration (tendinosis).

Ongoing (chronic) conditions result from microtrauma or "over-use" of the tendon, with symptoms developing over time. The over-use can be caused from excessive pressure or workload. Repetitive tasks and excessive exercise also may cause tendonitis. Sudden onset (acute) or traumatic tendonitis may be caused by a bruise with bleeding into the tissue (contusion) or muscle-tendon strain.

Tendonitis is a very common condition, prevalent in individuals engaged in sporting events and/or heavy labor.

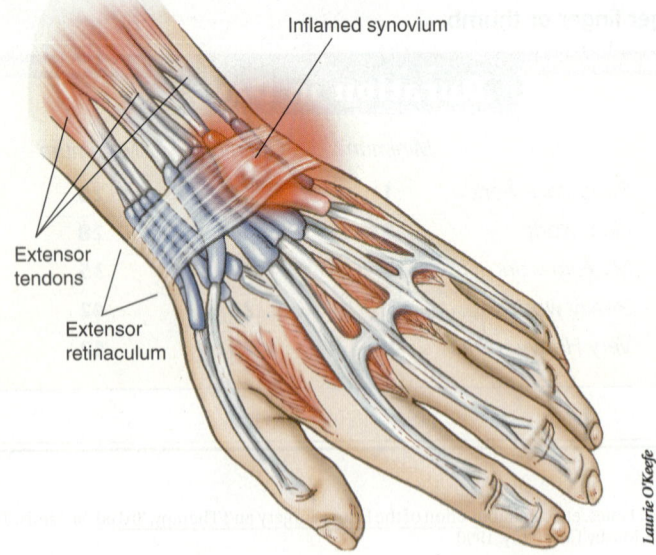

Diagnosis

History: Individuals with tendonitis caused by trauma may have heard or felt a "pop" as the tendon fibers tore. There may be increasing pain. Most individuals, however, report symptoms that begin gradually. Ongoing (chronic) tendonitis creates symptoms including pain during or after activity. Other symptoms may include swelling, stiffness and a sensation of creaking or squeaking with motion.

Individuals with tendonitis of the hand caused by infection may report pain and swelling over the top (dorsum) of the hand. There may be history of a recent bacterial infection, an open wound, or tuberculosis. Individuals may also report previous injuries that may not have been successfully diagnosed and rehabilitated.

Physical exam: Swelling, warmth and tenderness may be evident. A stethoscopic exam may reveal creaking or popping (crepitus) noises along the course of the tendon. Pain accompanying movement may be detected. There may be a visible deformity, such as a torn biceps tendon curling and making a ball under the skin. A neurovascular exam may be necessary to rule out compartment syndrome and nerve injury.

Tests: An x-ray may reveal calcium deposits along the tendon and sheath. Imaging of internal structures using high-powered magnets and computers (magnetic resonance imaging) may be needed to identify tendon tears. Laboratory studies, x-ray, bone scans and compartment pressure measurements may be used to rule out complications or underlying conditions.

Treatment

Tendonitis caused by trauma, especially if it occurs suddenly (acute), generally is treated with rest, cold therapy, compressive dressing and elevation to control swelling (R.I.C.E.). Heat rather than cold therapy might be used for acute forms of the condition, depending on patient response. Nonsteroidal anti-inflammatory drugs (NSAIDs) are prescribed for pain and swelling. Muscle-tendon length might be maintained with gentle stretching. When the onset (acute) episode has passed, rehabilitation for strengthening may be needed to prevent re-injury.

Ongoing (chronic) tendonitis is treated by stopping the aggravating activity, R.I.C.E., NSAIDs and physical therapy to control pain and swelling. With the chronic form, heat may be more effective than cold in therapy. Muscle strengthening may be recommended to restore normal function.

Corticosteroids and/or anesthetics may be injected into the tendon sheath to relieve pain and swelling. In extreme cases, surgery (excision, tenosynovectomy) may be needed to remove inflamed tissue or calcium deposits. Ruptured tendons may require repair through suturing (ruptured tendon repair).

Prognosis

Full recovery likely will occur in ongoing (chronic) cases. In severe cases, traumatic tendonitis with rupture may require surgery (ruptured tendon repair) and take longer to heal. Tendonitis in the hand caused by infection (infective tendonitis) can lead to loss of tendon structure. Repair of the tendon, excision or tenosynovectomy likely will have a good outcome, if damage to the tendon is not extensive. Cases requiring surgery are rare, but individuals with significant tendon damage may experience at least partial loss of function. The recovery period also is likely to be painful.

Differential Diagnosis

Radiculitis, distal nerve compression injury, carpal tunnel syndrome, vascular disorders, myositis ossificans, stress fracture, rheumatoid arthritis, trochanteric bursitis, and chronic compartment syndrome have similar symptoms. Many times, non-specific pain in an arm or leg is called "tendonitis" despite the absence of objective findings to document the diagnosis.

Specialists

- Internist
- Orthopedic Surgeon
- Physiatrist
- Rheumatologist
- Sports Medicine Physician

Rehabilitation

Basic goals in the rehabilitation of tendonitis are to control pain and swelling followed by regaining motion, flexibility, strength, and endurance of the tendon, muscle, and joint structures involved. The final goal is aimed at establishing a home exercise program and returning the individual to full function for work and recreational activities with minimal risk of re-injury.

Application of cold using ice on the injured tendon, muscle, and joint region is performed throughout the duration where pain is intense and disabling. After this period, heat treatments are helpful to reduce inflammation and pain and once appropriate, are beneficial when stretching the tendon and muscle involved. Forms of heat treatment include ultrasound using high frequency sound waves producing heat penetrating deep into the involved tendon and muscle. Electrical stimulation combined with heat or cold treatment is another technique used in physical therapy to relax irritated muscles that may be in spasm. Iontophoresis is another treatment in the rehabilitation of tendonitis.

Once movement is allowed, passive motion of the involved joint(s) region is permitted and to be used only as tolerated by the individual. Passive range-of-motion exercises begin with the therapist bending and straightening the limb. Each motion is taken until a mild stretch is noted by the individual. This is then progressed to active assist range-of-motion. As the individual improves with increased motion of the involved joint, the next step of progression is active range of motion. This can be initiated in a warm whirlpool or in conjunction with another form of heat treatment and continued until all the movement is restored.

Joint mobilization techniques are also used by the physical therapist to restore joint motion affected by tendonitis as well as aid in the stretching of surrounding muscle and tendons. The therapist stabilizes one of the bones with associated muscles comprising the joint while mobilizing the adjoining bone(s) in the direction needed to regain the loss of mobility. Joint mobilization is generally graded in the amount of force used as well as the type of mobilization technique desired per body part.

The instruction of isometric strengthening exercises begins early in the phase of strengthening. Isometric exercise demands that the muscles around the joint contract yet no movement takes place at the joint. An example of an isometric exercise for an elbow joint is the individual pushing his or her hand upward against his or her other hand or other immovable object for a count of ten seconds. Once both range of motion and isometric exercises are tolerated, the individual is progressed to isotonic strengthening involving movement at, and around, the joint. An example of this type of rehabilitation exercise is strengthening with weights using weight equipment/machines and elastic bands.

As the initial pain and swelling subsides and motion becomes pain free, the rehabilitation process may warrant less direct observation and guidance of a physical therapist. The individual, at this point, will then progress to an independent exercise program.

Modifications may need to be made by the physical therapist for those persons who have arthritis or other muscle, joint irritations. If the affected tendon(s) requires surgical repair, some restrictions may be placed on the progression of the range of motion and strengthening in certain movements. This varies depending on the degree or type of surgery that was performed.

Work Restrictions / Accommodations

Restrictions include removing aggravating activities, depending on the tendon involved. This may include avoidance of lifting, carrying, twisting of the wrist or forearm, and overhead work. Use of protective or assistive devices such as crutches or slings may affect dexterity. Safety issues may need to be evaluated. Medication for control of symptoms may require review of drug policies.

Return to sports and work requiring physical activity may need monitoring, as many individuals attempt to resume "normal" activity too soon. This often leads to a cycle of re-injuries.

Comorbid Conditions

Individuals with ongoing (chronic) diseases affecting various portions of the body (systemic) including rheumatoid arthritis and diabetes mellitus may have less chance of permanent recovery, since these conditions may cause tendonitis to continue or recur. Degeneration of tendons found in middle-aged and older individuals can influence disability duration.

Complications

Compartment syndrome and nerve injury may be caused by tissue swelling associated with tendonitis. Inflammation of the lining of the tendon sheath (tenosynovitis) often accompanies tendonitis, and may occur with infection by gonococcal bacteria that is transmitted sexually (gonorrhea). Tendon rupture may occur. When tendon fibers are torn away from the bone, usually from excessive pulling forces, the result is a condition called enthesopathy. Inflammation in tendons of the hand may cause the thumb to extend (de Quervain's disease). Fingers and/or the thumb may be hampered in movement by swelling of the tendons, which creates a sensation of popping (trigger finger).

Factors Influencing Duration

Location of the tendonitis, ability to control aggravating activities, treatment required, and complications might affect the disability period.

Length of Disability

Duration depends on location, severity, and underlying cause. Individuals who must perform repetitive, physically demanding tasks may require extended disability until the condition is resolved.

Duration in Days

Job Classification	Minimum	Optimum	Maximum
Sedentary work	1	3	7
Light work	1	7	14
Medium work	3	14	28
Heavy work	3	14	28
Very Heavy work	3	21	35

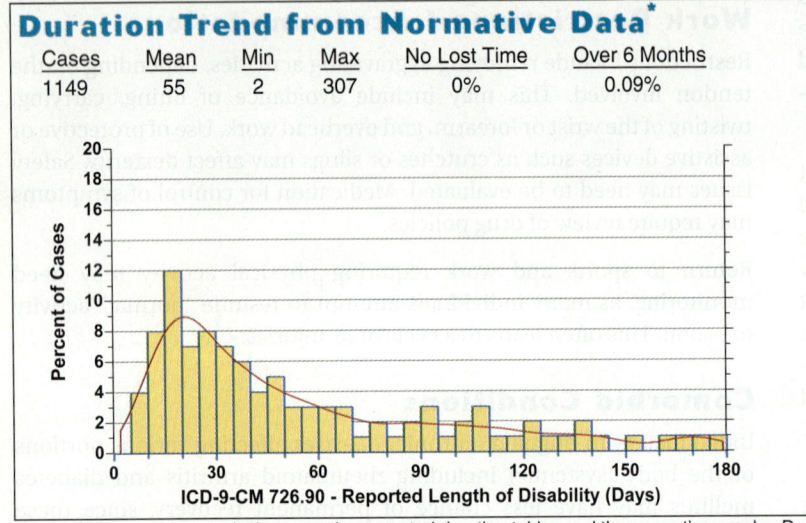
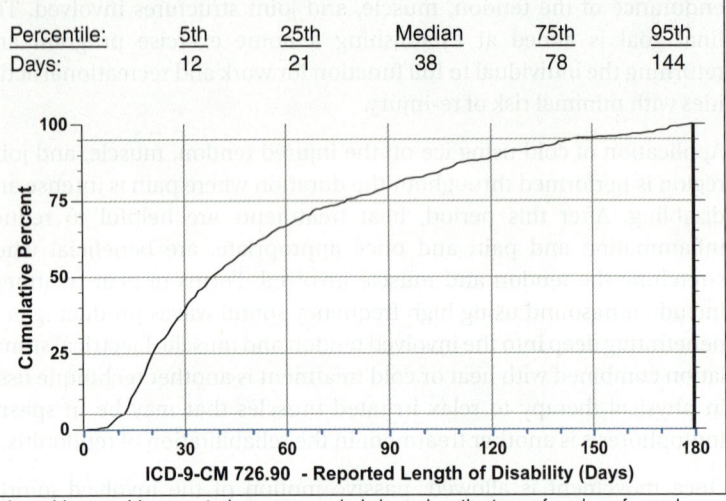

ICD-9-CM 726.90 - Reported Length of Disability (Days)

* Differences may exist between the expected duration tables and the normative graphs. Duration tables provide expected recovery periods based on the type of work performed by the individual. The normative graphs reflect the actual observed experience of many individuals across the spectrum of physical conditions, in a variety of industries, and with varying levels of case management.

Failure to Recover

If an individual fails to recover within the maximum duration expectancy period, the reader may wish to reference the following questions to assist in better understanding the specifics of an individual's medical case.

Regarding diagnosis:

- Does the individual have a history of injury, overload, or over-use of the tendon?
- Does the individual have a history of rheumatoid arthritis, systemic sclerosis, gout, Reiter's syndrome, or diabetes mellitus?
- Does the individual's work or play involve repetitive tasks or excessive exercise?
- Which tendon is involved?
- Does the individual report hearing a pop with an injury?
- Does the individual report a gradual onset of pain during or after activity, swelling, stiffness and a sensation of creaking or squeaking with motion?
- On exam, was swelling, warmth, tenderness, or crepitus evident?
- Is pain with movement detected? Is there a visible deformity?
- Has the individual had an x-ray, MRI, bone scan or compartment pressure measurements?
- Was a neurovascular exam necessary?
- Have conditions with similar symptoms been ruled out?

Regarding treatment:

- Is the individual with an acute injury being treated with rest, ice, compression and elevation (R.I.C.E.)? Is heat, depending on patient response, being used rather than ice?
- Is the individual being treated with NSAIDs?
- Has physical therapy been prescribed?
- Has the individual stopped the aggravating activity?
- Has the individual received an injection of corticosteroids and/or anesthetics?
- Did a tenosynovectomy become necessary?
- Was a ruptured tendon repaired surgically?

Regarding prognosis:
- Is the individual active in physical therapy?
- Does the individual have a home exercise program?
- Does the individual have any conditions that may affect ability to recover?
- Does the individual have any complications such as compartment syndrome, nerve injury tenosynovitis, tendon rupture, enthesopathy, de Quervain's disease or a trigger finger?

References

"Nonarticular Rheumatism: Teninitis and Tenosynovitis." Merck Manual of Diagnosis and Therapy, 17th ed. Beers, Mark H., and Robert Berkow, MD, eds. Whitehouse Station, NJ: Merck & Co, Inc, 1999. 16 Jan 2001 <http://www.merck.com/pubs/mmanual/section5/chapter59/59d.htm>.

Kisner, C., and L. Colby. Therapeutic Exercise Foundations and Techniques. Philadelphia: F.A. Davis Company, 1990.

Tenosynovitis
Other names / synonyms: Tendinitis, Tendonitis, Tendonosynovitis, Tendosynovitis
727.0

Definition

Tenosynovitis (or tendonitis) occurs when the inner (synovial) lining of the tendon sheath of becomes injured or inflamed.

The lining provides nourishment and lubrication to the tendon and is separate from the fibrous outer sheath. The problem occurs most often in the hands and wrists and elbows, and can be caused by injury, calcium deposits, high blood cholesterol levels, rheumatoid arthritis, gout, infection, or repetitive strain or trauma.

Tenosynovitis is often classified as irritative or frictional when there is mild inflammation caused by over-use.

Infective tenosynovitis, although relatively rare, is most common in the tendons of the hand and in the acute stage can create pus (purulent exudate), which compromises the space for the tendon even further. Chronic infective tenosynovitis can be caused by tuberculous and is most common in the forearm and hand.

Woman are more prone to tenosynovitis.

Diagnosis

History: Individuals usually complain of pain, swelling, and limited motion in the affected area. Some individuals may notice a crackling or squeaking noise accompanying use or movement.

Physical exam: Touching (palpation) of the area reveals pain over the tendon, fullness or swelling in the tissue, there may be lumps and a crunching sensation (crepitus.) Testing of the nerves in the area is done by tapping (percussion.) Joints are put through range of motion to create symptoms.

Tests: No tests are necessary for diagnosis although if gout is considered as a cause, uric acid levels may be evaluated. X-rays are sometimes taken to rule out other pathology or to look for tendon calcifications. If nerve entrapment is also suspected, EMG and nerve conduction studies may be ordered for clarification.

Treatment

Treatment usually begins by discontinuing the activity that causes the pain and is often accompanied by oral anti-inflammatory medications and corticosteroid injections to reduce swelling and control the inflammatory reaction. Repeated injections into tendons can weaken the tendon, so injections are limited to 2-3 over several months time. Weight bearing tendons, such as the patella tendon and Achilles tendon, are at greater risk for rupture from injections.

Individuals are often advised to wear a splint for a period to avoid re-injury. Conservative treatment often includes the use of ice packs over the tendon for local pain control and to aid in decreasing inflammation. Acupuncture treatment is successful in some cases of tenosynovitis.

Surgery to incise part or all of the sheath (release of tendon sheath) is necessary when conservative measures fail. Infective tenosynovitis is treated with antibiotic medication and, usually, surgery (irrigation and débridement).

Prognosis

If rest and medical management fail to provide relief, surgery to release the tendon sheath is usually effective. Remission is possible with re-aggravation or flare up of underlying conditions.

Differential Diagnosis

Gout, bursitis, synovitis, tendon entrapment, and nerve entrapment may present with similar findings.

Specialists

- Occupational Therapist
- Orthopedic Surgeon
- Physiatrist
- Physical Therapist
- Rheumatologist
- Sports Medicine Physician

Rehabilitation

Basic goals in the rehabilitation of tenosynovitis are to control pain and swelling followed by regaining motion, flexibility, strength, and endurance of the tendon, muscle, and joint structures involved. The final result is aimed at establishing a home exercise program and returning the individual to full function for work and recreational activities with minimal risk of re-injury.

Application of cold using ice on the injured tendon, muscle, and joint region is performed throughout the duration when pain is intense and disabling. After this period, heat treatments are helpful to reduce inflammation and pain and once appropriate, are beneficial when stretching the tendon and muscle involved. A form of heat treatment includes ultrasound using high frequency sound waves producing heat penetrating deep into the involved tendon and muscle. Electrical stimulation combined with heat or cold treatment is another technique used in physical therapy to relax irritated muscles that may be in spasm. Iontophoresis is another treatment in the rehabilitation of tendonitis.

Once movement is allowed, passive motion of the involved joint(s) region is permitted and is used only as tolerated by the individual. These exercises progress to active assist range-of-motion exercises. As the individual improves with increased motion of the involved joint, the individual then performs all of the motion independently. This can be initiated in a warm whirlpool or in conjunction with another form of heat treatment and continued until all the movement is restored.

Joint mobilization techniques are also used by the physical therapist to restore joint motion affected by tenosynovitis as well as aid in the stretching of surrounding muscle and tendons. The therapist stabilizes one of the bones with associated muscles comprising the joint while mobilizing the adjoining bone(s) in the direction needed to regain the loss of mobility.

The instruction of isometric strengthening exercises begins early in the phase of strengthening. Isometric exercise demands that the muscles around the joint contract yet no movement takes place at the joint. Once both range of motion and isometric exercises are tolerated, the individual is progressed to isotonic strengthening involving movement at, and around, the joint by, for example, utilizing weights and weight equipment/machines and elastic bands.

Job requirements may need to be modified during the rehabilitation process until pain and swelling diminishes. For example, lifting objects that stress the involved joints may need to be limited despite the amount of force needed to accomplish the task. An occupational therapist may fabricate a specific splint for the individual to help immobilize and protect the region of tenosynovitis.

Work Restrictions / Accommodations

Tenosynovitis can affect an individual's ability to perform a number of ordinary functions. Restriction on such activities as gripping, twisting, hammering, lifting, pulling and pushing is common. Adaptive devices or changes in job requirements to decrease stress on the tendons will facilitate earlier return to work. Alternating repetitive tasks and providing rest periods would be part of early treatment. Alteration in job requirements is necessary to prevent re-aggravation.

Comorbid Conditions

Inflammatory conditions, gout, and diabetes are possible comorbid conditions.

Complications

Tendon rupture is a possible complication of chronic tendonitis. The risk of this complication is increased with repeated injections into the tendon due to weakening of the tendon. Injections of steroids into the tendon can be an effective treatment though when limited to less than 3-4 injections over several months.

Factors Influencing Duration

Job requirements, response to treatment, and site of tenosynovitis would affect the length of disability. Injections of corticosteroids sometimes increase pain for several hours to days. Restricted joint motion may limit dexterity and create safety issues at the work site.

Length of Disability

Duration of disability is dependent on location of tendonitis, severity, underlying cause, type of treatment, job requirements and removal of aggravating activities. Remission is common in some tendons, especially in the hand and arm.

Duration in Days

Job Classification	Minimum	Optimum	Maximum
Sedentary work	1	3	7
Light work	1	7	14
Medium work	3	14	28
Heavy work	3	14	28
Very Heavy work	3	21	35

Failure to Recover

If an individual fails to recover within the maximum duration expectancy period, the reader may wish to reference the following questions to assist in better understanding the specifics of an individual's medical case.

Regarding diagnosis:

- Has the individual had an injury, calcium deposits, high blood cholesterol levels, rheumatoid arthritis, gout, infection, or repetitive strain or trauma to the hand, wrist or elbow?
- Does the individual have a history of tuberculosis?
- Does the individual complain of pain, swelling, and limited motion in the affected area?
- Has the individuals noticed a crackling or squeaking noise with use or movement?
- On exam, is the area tender to palpation? Swollen? Crepitus present?
- Did the individual have an x-ray? Uric acid level? EMG and nerve conduction studies?
- Have conditions with similar symptoms been ruled out?

Regarding treatment:

- Has the individual discontinued the activity that causes pain?
- Is the individual using NSAIDs?
- Did the individual have a corticosteroid injection?
- Is the individual using a splint? Using ice? Was acupuncture tried?
- Were antibiotics necessary?
- Did surgery become necessary?

Regarding prognosis:

- Is the individual active in rehabilitation? Is the individual doing exercises at home?
- Is the individual's employer able to accommodate any necessary restrictions?
- Does the individual have any conditions that could affect ability to recover?
- Does the individual have any complications such as tendon rupture?

References

Best, Thomas, and William Garrett. "Basic Science of Soft Tissue." Orthopedic Sports Medicine. DeLee, Jesse, David Drez, and Carl L. Stanitski, eds. Philadelphia: Harcourt Brace & Company, 1993. 32-33.

Iversen, Larry D., and Marc Swiontkowski. Manual of Acute Orthopedic Therapeutics, 4th ed. Boston: Lippincott, Williams & Wilkins, 1995.

Kessler, R.M. Management of Common Musculoskeletal Disorders: Physical Therapy Principles and Methods. Philadelphia: J.B. Lippincott Company, 1990.

Kessler, R.M. Management of Common Musculoskeletal Disorders: Physical Therapy Principles and Methods. Philadelphia: J.B. Lippincott Company, 1990.

Tension Headache
Other names / synonyms: Tension-Type Headache
307.81

Definition

Tension headache is a headache that is mild to moderate in severity, occurs on both sides of the head, does not become worse with physical exertion, and lasts from less than one hour to as long as seven days.

The exact cause of tension headache is unknown, but possible causes are abnormal muscle contractions in the head and neck or lack of reflex in the muscles located near the temples of the head. A tension headache that lasts for more than 15 days per month for up to six months is termed chronic tension headache. Risk factors for tension headache and chronic tension headache include stress, lack of sleep, migraine headaches, mood disorders, and anxiety.

Nearly 60% of the individuals in the United States may experience tension headache during any one year. Less than 3% of the population, however, experiences chronic tension headache.

Diagnosis

History: The individual may complain of a headache that feels like it is "pressing" or "tightening" of the head. The individual may complain of being sensitive to sound (phonophobia) or light (photophobia), but without nausea or vomiting. The individual may also complain of life stressors, lack of sleep, or feeling anxious.

Physical exam: The individual may appear to be in pain and to be anxious. Asking questions about the type and duration of pain and discussion about risk factors aid in the diagnosis.

Tests: No tests are required to diagnose tension headache.

Treatment

Bed rest, relaxation, massage of the head and neck, and hot compresses to the head are often used to relieve pain. Risk factors should be identified and decreased, or alleviated, if possible. Non-narcotic pain relievers (analgesics), tricyclic antidepressants, or muscle relaxants may be prescribed. Non-steroidal anti-inflammatory (NSAIDs) medication or acetaminophen may be useful for some individuals. Sufficient and regular sleep is also advised.

Prognosis

Individuals who take pain relievers as prescribed, follow instructions for bed rest, relaxation, massage, hot compresses, and/or sleep as required, and who try to alleviate stressors have an excellent outcome.

Differential Diagnosis

Differential diagnoses include migraine headache, chronic tension headache, or a combination of migraine and tension headache (mixed headache).

Specialists

- Neurologist

Work Restrictions / Accommodations

A quiet work area without fluorescent lighting may be required temporarily. If the individual's job is stressful, mentally or physically, a temporary assignment to a less stressful job may be required. Time and place may need to be allotted for rest periods and application of hot compresses.

Comorbid Conditions

Mood disorders, anxiety disorders, or migraine headaches may influence length of disability.

Complications

The primary complication of tension headache is migraine headache.

Factors Influencing Duration

The severity of the symptoms and the individual's mental health and response to treatment are factors that might influence length of disability.

Length of Disability

In most cases, no disability is expected.

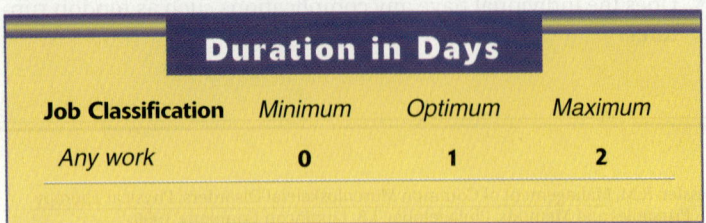

Duration in Days			
Job Classification	Minimum	Optimum	Maximum
Any work	0	1	2

Failure to Recover

If an individual fails to recover within the maximum duration expectancy period, the reader may wish to reference the following questions to assist in better understanding the specifics of an individual's medical case.

Regarding diagnosis:

- Does the individual complain of a headache that feels like it is "pressing" or "tightening" their head? How severe is it? How long has it lasted?
- Does the individual have phonophobia or photophobia?
- Does the individual have any risk factors such as stress, lack of sleep, migraine headaches, mood disorders, or anxiety?
- Does the individual have abnormal muscle contractions in the head and neck?
- Does the individual have a lack of reflex in the muscles located near temples?
- Does the individual have chronic tension headaches?
- On exam, does the individual appear to be in pain? Anxious?
- Have conditions with similar symptoms been ruled out?

Regarding treatment:

- Has the individual tried bed rest, relaxation, massage of the head and neck, or hot compresses to the head to relieve pain?
- Has the individual identified any risk factors?
- Has the individual addressed any correctable risk factors?
- Has the individual been treated with analgesics, tricyclic antidepressants, muscle relaxants, NSAIDs, or acetaminophen?

Regarding prognosis:

- Is the individual's employer able to accommodate any necessary restrictions?
- Does the individual have any conditions that may affect ability to recover?
- Does the individual have any complications such as migraine headache?

References

Beers, Mark, and Robert Berkow, eds. The Merck Manual of Diagnosis and Therapy. Medical Services, USMEDSA, USHH, 1999 30 Nov 2000 <http://www.merck.com/pubs/mmanual/section14/chapter168/168d.htm>.

Welch, K., MA. "Headache. Neurology." Scientific American Medicine Online Dale, D.C., and D.G. Federman New York: WebMD Corporation, 2000 Scientific American Medicine. 28 Dec 2000 <http://www.samed.com/sam/chapters11/1108.htm>.

Tetanus

Other names / synonyms: Lockjaw
037

Definition

Tetanus is a serious, potentially fatal disease of the central nervous system caused when a wound becomes infected by the bacteria Clostridium tetani. The disease is characterized by muscle rigidity and numerous muscle spasms. Often, the first sign is stiffness of the jaw muscles; hence the synonym lockjaw.

Clostridium tetani spores are commonly found in the soil. These bacteria are also found in the intestines of domestic animals, and as a result, soil contaminated with manure is especially likely to contain these spores. The organisms enter the human body through wounds, particularly deep puncture wounds or crushing wounds. The organisms multiply in the wound, producing a poison (neurotoxin) that travels to the central nervous system. There it interferes with the functioning of the nerves that control muscle activity causing severe muscle spasms.

Tetanus has become a rare disease in industrialized countries since the introduction of widespread immunization. There are 40-50 cases reported each year in the US, resulting in about 5 deaths. Of those 40-50 cases, 87% occur in individuals who have not been adequately immunized, and 70% occur in those older than 50 years. On the other hand, tetanus is still a major problem in developing countries, where nearly 1 million people die from tetanus every year. Tetanus has an incubation period of 1-55 days, with more than 80% of cases reporting symptoms within 14 days. The shorter the incubation period, the more serious and life-threatening the disease. In individuals under 50 years, mortality is nearly 100% if symptoms begin within 1-2 days. This risk reduces to 35-40% if the incubation period is greater than 10 days. Worldwide, tetanus is predominantly a disease of underdeveloped countries in warm, damp climates and affects all age groups. Tetanus is one of the target diseases of the World Health Organization Expanded Program on Immunization. Overall annual incidence is 0.5-1 million cases.

Rural populations, particularly farmers, are at an increased risk for infection due to increased contact with soil and manure. In the US, Blacks from the rural South have a greater risk of tetanus. Intravenous drug use, frostbite, skin ulcers, surgical wounds, traumatic wounds, and burns also increase one's risk of tetanus. Those over 50 years of age and women who have recently given birth or had an abortion are also at increased risk. Men and women are affected equally.

Diagnosis

History: The hallmark symptom of tetanus is stiffness of the jaw (trismus or lockjaw), making it difficult or even impossible to open the mouth. Other symptoms include neck stiffness, difficulty swallowing (dysphagia), stiffness in abdominal and back muscles, and contraction of facial muscles into a fixed, excited expression. There may also be a fever, profuse sweating, restlessness, headaches, and painful muscle spasms. Seizures often occur in response to sensory stimuli (noise, light, changes in temperature). Spasms of the respiratory muscles may prevent the individual from being able to breathe adequately.

Physical exam: The exam may reveal a painful or tender wound. However, a wound may not always be present. Muscle rigidity and spasm, increased heart rate (tachycardia), irregular heart beat (arrhythmia), drooling, irritability, and increased blood pressure (hypertension) may be noted. The individual's color may appear bluish or gray (cyanosis) as a result of inadequate oxygen. The individual remains awake and alert throughout the illness.

Tests: No specific laboratory test exists. Although the organism can sometimes be cultured from a wound, a negative culture is not always accurate. Diagnosis is therefore made from observing the symptoms. Electromyography (EMG) may be used to analyze the electrical activity of the muscles. Brain activity can be monitored through electroencephalogram (EEG).

Treatment

Tetanus infection is serious and life threatening. Treatment, usually administered in the intensive care unit of a hospital, includes the administration of tetanus antitoxin or tetanus immune globulin. An open airway must be maintained. Depending on the individual's symptoms, this may be done by different methods. A tube may be inserted into the windpipe (trachea) in a procedure called intubation. In severe cases, an artificial opening in the trachea (tracheostomy) may be required. If the individual is unable to breathe independently, mechanical ventilation may be required. Nutritional support may need to be provided through a feeding tube. The wound is cleaned thoroughly. Damaged tissue may need to be surgically removed (debride). Antibiotics and antitoxins are administered to eradicate the toxin-producing organisms. Anticonvulsants may be necessary to control the seizures. Muscle relaxants may also be prescribed.

Because having tetanus does not grant further immunity against the infection, after recovery the individual should receive the full series of vaccinations.

Prognosis

Recovery is complete if the individual survives the infection. The overall mortality rate ranges from less than 10% to as high as 50%. A short incubation period is associated with a particularly grim prognosis. Mortality approaches 100% in cases with short incubation. High mortality rates are also associated with early onset of convulsions, individuals who require mechanical ventilation, or delay in treatment. Contaminated wounds located on the head and face are more dangerous than wounds located on other parts of the body. The individual's age and severity of symptoms also affect prognosis.

Differential Diagnosis

Conditions with similar symptoms include strychnine poisoning, dental infection, acute drug reaction to phenothiazines, meningoencephalitis, hepatic encephalopathy, rabies, subarachnoid hemorrhage, seizure disorder, alcohol withdrawal, peritonsillar abscess, or hypocalcemic tetany.

Specialists

- Cardiologist
- General Surgeon
- Infectious Disease Physician
- Internist
- Neurologist
- Physiatrist
- Pulmonologist

Work Restrictions / Accommodations

Extended work leave may be required. Upon returning to work, strenuous activity or work requiring heavy lifting may need to be modified until physical stamina returns.

Comorbid Conditions

The elderly and individuals with pre-existing heart disease tend to experience a longer period of disability with a higher rate of mortality.

Complications

Complications include inability to breathe (respiratory arrest), heart failure, blood clots to the lungs (pulmonary emboli), other bacterial infection, dehydration, spinal cord fracture, airway obstruction, suffocation, urinary retention, constipation, pneumonia, destruction of muscle tissue (rhabdomyolysis), coma, and death.

Factors Influencing Duration

Length of disability might be influenced by severity of illness, location of wounds, the promptness and adequacy of treatment, or the presence of complications.

Length of Disability

Duration in Days

Job Classification	Minimum	Optimum	Maximum
Sedentary work	10	14	21
Light work	10	14	21
Medium work	10	14	21
Heavy work	14	21	28
Very Heavy work	14	21	28

Failure to Recover

If an individual fails to recover within the maximum duration expectancy period, the reader may wish to reference the following questions to assist in better understanding the specifics of an individual's medical case.

Regarding diagnosis:
- Has diagnosis of tetanus been confirmed?
- Have other conditions such as strychnine poisoning, dental infection, acute drug reaction to phenothiazines, meningoencephalitis, hepatic encephalopathy, rabies, subarachnoid hemorrhage, seizure disorder, alcohol withdrawal, peritonsillar abscess, or hypocalcemic tetany, that cause similar symptoms to tetanus been ruled out?
- Has individual experienced any complications such as, respiratory arrest, heart failure, pulmonary emboli, other bacterial infection, dehydration, spinal cord fracture, airway obstruction, suffocation, urinary retention, constipation, pneumonia, destruction of muscle tissue, or coma?
- Does individual have an underlying condition such as advanced age or pre-existing heart disease that may impact recovery?

Regarding treatment:
- Was individual hospitalized?
- Did individual receive prompt administration of tetanus antitoxin or tetanus immune globulin?
- Were antibiotics and antitoxins given to eradicate the toxin-producing organisms?
- Were anticonvulsants and muscle relaxants needed to control the seizures?
- Was intubation, tracheostomy, or mechanical ventilation necessary?
- Did individual experience any complications related to these procedures?
- Was surgical débridement of wound required?
- Is wound now healing adequately? If not, what further procedures may be required?

Regarding prognosis:
- Are any of these risk factors (a short incubation period, early onset of convulsions, need for mechanical ventilation, or delay in treatment) relevant to individual's case?
- Where was the wound located?
- Is individual over 50 years of age?

References

"Tetanus." Microsoft® Encarta® Online Encyclopedia. 2000 23 Sep 2000 <http://encarta.msn.com/find/Concise.asp?z=1&pg=2&ti=761556482>.

Abyad, Abdulrazak. "Tetanus." Griffith's 5-minute Clinical Consult. Dambro, Mark, ed. Philadelphia: Lippincott, Williams & Wilkins, 2000. 1060-1061.

Facts About Tetanus For Adults. National Coalition for Adult Immunization. 01 Apr 2000. 23 Sep 2000 <http://www.nfid.org/factsheets/tetanusadult.html>.

Francois, B., M. Clavel, and A. Desachy. "Continuous Intrathecal Injection of Baclofen in Generalized Tetanus. A Therapeutic Alternative." Presse Med 26 22 (1997): 1045-1047.

Simon, Harvey. "Infectious Diseases." Anaerobic Infections. Dale, D.C., and Daniel D. Federman, MD New York: WebMD Corporation, 2000 Scientific American Medicine. 23 Sep 2000 <http://www.samed.com/sam/forms/index.htm>.

Tetanus: Lockjaw. New York State Department of Health. 01 Feb 1999. 23 Sep 2000 <http://www.health.state.ny.us/nysdoh/consumer/tetanus.htm>.

Tetany

Other names / synonyms: Carpopedal Spasm, Muscle Cramps, Muscle Spasm, Parathyroid Tetany
781.7

Definition

Tetany is a state of motor hyperactivity characterized by muscle spasm and cramps, or twitching of the skeletal muscles. The muscles of the mouth, hands, and lower extremities are typically involved, although, all muscles of the body (except for the eye) may be involved.

Tetany is a manifestation of a low calcium level (hypocalcemia), which can be linked to a lack of vitamin D, low magnesium levels (hypomagnesemia), impaired utilization of calcium (such as in renal failure and pancreatitis), decreased function of the parathyroid glands (hypoparathyroidism), excess of bicarbonate in blood (alkalosis). These conditions affect the distribution of calcium in the blood and contribute to low blood calcium levels (hypocalcemia). Less frequently, some drugs or multiple transfusions of blood preserved with citrate can depress calcium levels. All of these conditions alter the mineral balance in the blood that is responsible for normal muscle contraction and nerve conduction.

Tetany is not always a symptom in these disorders. In fact, the exact incidence of tetany is difficult to ascertain since it is a symptom that is sporadically associated with various disturbances and conditions. However, tetany occurs more commonly in chronic or untreated conditions of calcium or magnesium deficiencies, such as in chronic renal failure or chronic pancreatitis. It is seen less commonly in conditions that cause mild or transient fluctuations of calcium or magnesium such as in bicarbonate accumulations or certain medication use.

Surgical removal of parathyroid tumors (parathyroidectomy) can cause functional impairment of the remaining parathyroid gland, resulting in acute hypoparathyroidism and severe calcium deficiencies. While infrequent, this can cause acute life-threatening tetany and possible airway obstruction that requires prompt, emergency treatment.

Diagnosis

History: Individuals may complain of muscle weakness, cramping, twitching, or tingling sensations. They may complain of fatigue or loss of energy.

Physical exam: Individuals are screened for limited range of motion, decreased muscle control, abnormal reflexes, and impaired coordination. Examination also includes physical inspection for symmetry and involuntary movement, measurement of extremities and muscle mass, joint range of motion, examination of gait, and ease of movement. Presence of a facial spasm after tapping the facial nerve (Trousseau's sign) or finger (carpal) spasm after inflating an a blood pressure cuff just above systolic blood pressure (Chvostek's sign) are early signs of low calcium levels that may cause tetany.

Tests: Testing includes serum blood levels for calcium, magnesium, phosphorous, vitamin D, protein (albumin), and thyroid and parathyroid hormone levels. Tetany due to a hormone deficiency is characterized by low serum calcium and high serum phosphorous. Evaluation of muscle electrical activity (electromyography or EMG) and nerve activity (nerve conduction studies) may help differentiating tetany from other neuromuscular diseases.

Treatment

The goal of treatment is to restore the calcium and associated mineral balance within the body. Since tetany is a manifestation of low calcium levels, treatment consists of replacing calcium. Intravenous calcium is given initially to promptly restore the calcium levels. The underlying cause of the calcium deficiency must be determined to guide the ongoing treatment. Administration of oral calcium plus vitamin D, which is necessary for absorption of calcium into the bones, may be needed for long-term control this condition.

Surgical removal of the parathyroid tumors (parathyroidectomy) to treat hyperparathyroidism can infrequently result in acute dysfunction of the remaining parathyroid gland, causing acute hypoparathyroidism and sudden, severe hypocalcemia. The sudden, extreme hypocalcemia can cause life-threatening tetany and possibly airway obstruction. In these cases, immediate treatment with intravenous calcium, and careful monitoring of heart function and airway status are required.

Prognosis

The probable outcome is good if the diagnosis and treatment is made early. Chronic conditions such as renal failure often have persistent imbalances in calcium and magnesium that require long-term treatment to prevent the recurrence of tetany. In these cases, the long-term treatment with calcium and vitamin D replacement has been associated with calcium deposits in the kidneys (nephrocalcinosis).

Differential Diagnosis

Tetany from calcium, magnesium and acid-base balance must be distinguished from the rare disease state of "tetanus" caused by a toxin from an infection caused by Clostridium tetani (prevented by a tetanus shot). Other possible diagnoses include hyperventilation, Parkinson's disease, central nervous system disease, spinal cord lesions, peripheral neuropathy, botulism toxin, cancer, or side effects from hemodialysis or some chemotherapies.

Specialists

- Emergency Medicine
- Endocrinologist
- Internist
- Neurologist

Work Restrictions / Accommodations

With early diagnosis and treatment, accommodations may not be necessary. Severe, prolonged cases of hypoparathyroidism may prevent employment.

Comorbid Conditions

Chronic degenerative neuromuscular diseases, alcoholism, arthritic conditions, use of diuretic medications, malnutrition, malabsorption disorders, herpes zoster, poliomyelitis, pancreatitis, renal disease, or pregnancy may impact recovery and lengthen disability.

Complications

In severe cases, airway obstruction may be a complication of tetany.

Factors Influencing Duration

Treatment of this condition in conjunction with pregnancy, metabolic diseases, alcoholism, or malignancy will lengthen the disability period. Emotional components, impaired mobility, circulatory or respiratory problems will also extend the diagnosis and treatment phases.

Length of Disability

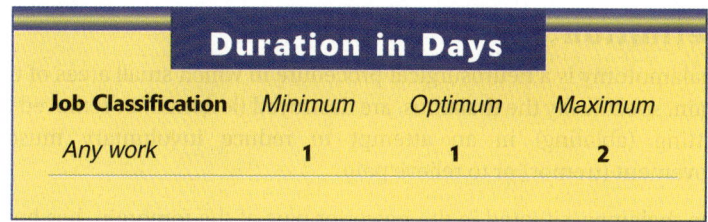

Job Classification	Minimum	Optimum	Maximum
Any work	1	1	2

Failure to Recover

If an individual fails to recover within the maximum duration expectancy period, the reader may wish to reference the following questions to assist in better understanding the specifics of an individual's medical case.

Regarding diagnosis:

- Has the diagnosis of tetany been confirmed by physical exam?
- Have other conditions with similar symptoms such as Parkinson's disease, central nervous system disease, spinal cord lesions, peripheral neuropathy, or side effects from hemodialysis or some chemotherapies, been considered in the differential diagnosis?
- Were blood chemistries done to detect any possible vitamin or mineral deficiencies?
- Has the underlying cause of tetany been discovered?

Regarding treatment:

- Have any underlying causes of tetany been addressed in the treatment plan?
- Has calcium supplementation (either parenteral or enteral) been effective in relieving symptoms?
- If individual's tetany disorder was related to a parathyroidectomy, did individual experience life-threatening complications? If so, was life support intervention administered promptly?
- Has hypocalcemia condition stabilized? Will on-going calcium supplementation be necessary?
- Is individual being monitored for kidney complications?

Regarding Prognosis:

- Was treatment prompt and effective in restoring calcium level and relieving tetany? Has tetany recurred?
- Does individual have an underlying condition that may impact recovery such as chronic degenerative neuromuscular diseases, alcoholism, arthritic conditions, use of diuretic medications, malnutrition, malabsorption disorders, herpes zoster, poliomyelitis, pancreatitis, renal disease, or pregnancy?
- Have underlying conditions been correctly identified and stabilized? If not, what further treatment is necessary?

References

Goroll, Allan H., Albert G. Mulley, and Lawrence A. May. Primary Care Medicine, 3rd ed. New York: Lippincott-Raven, 1995.

Tierney, Lawrence, Stephen McPhee, and Maxine Papadakis, eds. Current Medical Diagnosis and Treatment, 39th ed. New York: Lange Medical Books/McGraw-Hill, 2000.

Thalamotomy

Other names / synonyms: Thalamic Ablation
01.41

Definition

Thalamotomy is a neurosurgical procedure in which small areas of the brain, specifically the thalamus, are destroyed (lesioned) or removed by cutting (ablating) in an attempt to reduce involuntary muscle movement (tremor) or to relieve pain.

The thalamus, situated in the posterior part of the forebrain, has been referred to as "Checkpoint Charlie" because everything that gets inside the brain has to go through the thalamus, which also relays sensory information to the outer layer of the brain (cerebral cortex). The two-part thalamus consists of a myriad of nuclei. The ventral lateral nuclei are involved in controlling movement. Basic sensations, such as pain, may actually reach consciousness (be perceived) within the thalamus. Other sensory impulses, such as temperature, light, touch, and pressure, are processed in the thalamus and then relayed to the cerebral cortex.

Thalamotomy is indicated for individuals who are affected by tremor, Parkinson's disease, or essential tremor. The procedure can also be helpful for other types of tremor such as traumatic stroke, multiple sclerosis tremor, and for other movement disorders, such as dystonia.

Reason for Procedure

Thalamotomy is used to treat individuals who are afflicted with movement disorders. Such movement disorders include tremor-predominant Parkinson's disease and benign essential tremor. These disorders differ in the shaking frequency. Parkinson's disease tremor occurs at a lower shaking frequency when the body is at rest and ceases during purposeful movement. Essential tremor, a relatively common movement disorder without a known cause, has a higher shaking frequency and is most obvious during intentional movement.

Another type of movement disorder treated with thalamotomy is dystonia. Dystonia is characterized by involuntary spasms and muscle contractions and postures. The spasms may affect one part of the body or the whole body. Surgery can provide symptom relief in individuals not receiving benefit from medications.

Thalamotomy can also be helpful for other types of tremor, such as cerebellar tremor, post-traumatic tremor, and multiple sclerosis tremor; for other movement disorders, such as tardive dyskinesia, and chorea; and for pain that has not been responsive to other treatment attempts.

Description

The thalamotomy procedure begins with the definition of the surgical target with computed tomography (CT) and/or magnetic resonance imaging (MRI) scans. The scans are carried out with a special stereotactic frame attached to the individual's head and connected to a computer. Once the appropriate target coordinates have been selected on a computer workstation, the individual is taken to the operating room where a patch of hair is shaved for the application of the local anesthesia. After infiltration with local anesthesia, a 3-4 cm (1-2 inch) incision is made in the scalp and a burr hole is drilled through the skull.

An insulated stimulating electrode is then passed through the burr hole and introduced into the target. The target area is stimulated with very small electrical impulses that may give rise to a variety of different reactions. The purpose of the stimulation is to ascertain that the tip of the probe is in the optimum location in the brain. If the electrical stimulation reduces (almost immediately) the individual's tremor and rigidity, optimum placement of the electrode tip is confirmed. If the electrical stimulation also gives rise to visual, motor, sensory, or other untoward symptoms, indications are that the probe may need repositioning. If symptoms occur even after repositioning, indications are that the surgery cannot be performed safely and that the probe should be removed and the procedure postponed until further re-evaluation.

When the intraoperative stimulation indicates that the tip of the electrode lies in the optimal location (without symptoms), a nonpermanent (temporary) tissue injury (lesion) is created. The creation of a temporary lesion allows for detailed testing of the individual intraoperatively to ensure that no neurologic deficit will be incurred with creation of a permanent lesion. The temporary lesion will allow for assessment of beneficial effect on tremor, rigidity and sluggishness of physical and mental responses (bradykinesia). When all of these conditions are met, a permanent lesion is created at the target site. During the lesioning, the individual is evaluated with a variety of motor, visual and psychological tests to determine whether any adverse effects have developed. If unexpected reactions are observed, further lesioning is stopped immediately.

It is worth noting that the thalamotomy procedure is only mildly painful.

Specialists

- Neurologist
- Neurosurgeon

Prognosis

Clinical studies have shown that tremor is eliminated or alleviated in the majority of individuals after thalamotomy. Hand and arm tremors in about 90% of cases may be permanently eliminated. Younger individuals afflicted with Parkinson's disease, who present with unilateral or marked asymmetry in their symptoms, have been shown to benefit more than older afflicted individuals. This younger group of Parkinson's individuals represents from 5-10% of individuals with Parkinson's.

All in all, the majority of individuals with Parkinson's disease remain tremor free for up to ten years following the thalamotomy procedure. However, other Parkinsonian symptoms, such as difficulty walking and freezing, do not seem to successfully respond to treatment with thalamotomy.

Work Restrictions / Accommodations

Because physical abilities and stage of progression of the disease vary among individuals, work restrictions and accommodations should be evaluated on a case-by-case basis. Consequently, the number and frequency of additional work breaks required after the thalamotomy procedure will vary for each individual.

If the individual's position at work is too physically demanding, he or she may need to be transferred to a more sedentary position. Further restrictions will become necessary as muscle rigidity progresses and the risk of falls increases.

Comorbid Conditions

Comorbid conditions include obesity and pneumonia.

Procedure Complications

The most common complications from the anesthesia are reaction to the medication and breathing problems. Complications from the surgery include bleeding (hemorrhage) and infection. These complications occur in about 2-5% of individuals undergoing the procedure.

The rate of complications for individuals receiving a bilateral thalamotomy is much higher than for individuals receiving a unilateral thalamotomy. Clinical research has shown that more mental and speech problems tend to occur after performance of bilateral thalamotomies.

Factors Influencing Duration

Factors that might influence length of disability include the underlying disease, size of lesion produced during the thalamotomy procedure, and the presence of any complications.

Length of Disability

Duration of disability depends on response to treatment and severity of symptoms due to diagnosis. Disability may be permanent.

Duration in Days

Job Classification	Minimum	Optimum	Maximum
Sedentary work	14	21	28
Light work	14	21	56
Medium work	28	35	84
Heavy work	56	70	112
Very Heavy work	56	70	140

References

Germano, Isabelle. Thalamotomy. Mount Sinai Department of Neurosurgery. 31 Dec 1998. 31 Oct 2000 <http://www.mssm.edu/neurosurgery/Pages/germano/web/Thalamotomy.html>.

Popovic, J.R., and L.J. Kozak. National Hosptial Discharge Survey: Annual Summary, 1998. National Center for Health Statistics. 01 Jan 2000. 23 Oct 2000 <http://www.cdc.gov/nchs/data/sr13_148.pdf>.

Thalassemia

Other names / synonyms: Alpha-Thalassemia Major, Alpha-Thalassemia Trait, Beta-Thalassemia Intermedia, Beta-Thalassemia Major, Beta-Thalassemia Minor, Cooley's Anemia, Mediterranean Anemia

282.4

Definition

Thalassemia is a group of inherited disorders where there is an abnormal production of hemoglobin. Hemoglobin is the protein inside red blood cells that carries oxygen. Each hemoglobin molecule contains four paired protein (globin) chains: two beta-globin chains and two alpha-globin chains.

In thalassemia, there is an inadequate production of one type of globin chain. Consequently, after all the available chains have paired up within the developing red blood cells, there is a shortage of normal hemoglobin and an accumulation of extra chains. The low hemoglobin level reduces the amount of oxygen that can be carried, and the extra chains make the cells fragile and prone to breaking apart (hemolysis). These abnormalities within the red blood cells lead to anemia.

The two main types of thalassemia are beta-thalassemia and alpha-thalassemia, and are categorized according to the type of globin underproduced. The severity of the disease depends on the degree of globin shortage, which, in turn, depends on the genes an individual has inherited.

The most common type of thalassemia is beta-thalassemia where beta-globin is underproduced. The production of beta-globin is controlled by two genes, one inherited from each parent. There are three types of beta-thalassemia. Beta-thalassemia minor occurs when only one gene is defective and the remaining intact gene still produces a sufficient amount of beta-globin. There are typically no symptoms with this type of thalassemia. Beta-thalassemia major occurs when both genes are defective and no beta-globin is produced, resulting in severe anemia. Although both genes are defective, sometimes they produce an amount of beta-globin sufficient to prevent significant anemia. This condition is called beta-thalassemia intermedia.

In alpha-thalassemia, alpha-globin is underproduced. Alpha-globin production is controlled by four genes with each parent contributing two genes. Unlike beta-thalassemia, the genes responsible for alpha-thalassemia are usually missing rather than defective. If only one or two genes are missing, typically there is no disease or symptoms. If three genes are missing, the reduction of alpha-globin is enough to cause significant anemia. This is known as Hemoglobin H disease. Alpha-thalassemia major, a condition incompatible with life, occurs when all four genes are missing. In this case no alpha-globin is produced.

Thalassemia is associated with certain ethnic groups and is found most commonly in people of Mediterranean (Greek or Italian), Southeast Asian, Middle Eastern, or African descent. In the US, 4 of every 100,000 individuals are affected with thalassemia, with the incidence increasing over the last decade because of increased immigration by Southeast Asians to North America.

Diagnosis

History: An individual's symptoms vary according to the degree of anemia. The severe anemia of beta-thalassemia major causes extreme fatigue and shortness of breath. Beta-thalassemia intermedia may cause moderate symptoms, while Hemoglobin H disease may cause moderate to severe symptoms.

Physical exam: Individuals with beta-thalassemia major often present with yellowing (jaundice) of the skin and eyes. An enlarged spleen (splenomegaly) may be discovered upon manipulation (palpate) of the abdomen. Bone deformities and growth retardation may result from an overgrowth of bone marrow. Individuals with beta-thalassemia intermedia and Hemoglobin H disease may have more moderate variations of these physical signs. Individuals with beta-thalassemia minor may have splenomegaly.

Tests: A complete blood count reveals a low hemoglobin and an elevated or near normal red blood cell count. A peripheral blood smear reveals abnormalities in red blood cells. The cells are paler than normal, an indication of the low level of hemoglobin per red blood cell. The cells are also smaller than normal (microcytosis). The size is reflected in a measurement called the mean corpuscular volume or MCV. Although the more severe forms of thalassemia have the most significant drops in hemoglobin levels, even mild forms have red blood cells with a below normal MCV.

Hemoglobin electrophoresis identifies and measures abnormal forms of hemoglobin and helps diagnose the beta-thalassemias. DNA analysis of the genes responsible for alpha-globin production may be used to diagnose the alpha-thalassemias.

Treatment

Treatment for thalassemia includes blood transfusions, surgical removal of the spleen (splenectomy), and iron chelation therapy. Bone marrow transplant using marrow from a matched donor is the most aggressive treatment for thalassemia and the only one considered a cure. The purpose of the transplant is to replace genetically defective bone marrow cells with normal bone marrow cells that help produce normal amounts of both alpha- and beta-globin.

Blood transfusions are the primary treatment for beta-thalassemia major and are given frequently in order to maintain an acceptable hemoglobin level. Hemoglobin H disease also may require transfusions but not as commonly as beta-thalassemia major. In beta-thalassemia intermedia, transfusions are not required to maintain an acceptable hemoglobin level. An individual with this condition, however, is unstable and may over time or quite suddenly develop severe anemia. If transfusion is required, the condition is no longer considered beta-thalassemia intermedia but rather beta-thalassemia major. If the condition improves and no longer requires transfusions, the condition is again categorized as beta-thalassemia intermedia. Folate is usually given along with blood transfusions.

The spleen ordinarily removes red blood cells from circulation, so a splenectomy is often performed to keep red blood cells in circulation longer. This may help reduce the need for transfusions in individuals with beta-thalassemia major and prevent transfusions completely in individuals with beta-thalassemia intermedia. The spleen may be removed through a large abdominal incision (open splenectomy) or through a flexible tube inserted in a small hole in the abdominal wall (laparoscopic splenectomy). Pneumococcal vaccine (vaccine against Streptococcus pneumoniae) should be given regularly to individuals who have had a splenectomy since they are susceptible to infection from this bacterium.

The overgrowth of bone marrow associated with thalassemia causes increased iron absorption. This increased absorption, especially when combined with the iron added to the body through frequent transfusion, causes an overload of iron in body tissues such as the heart, liver, and glands (hematochromatosis). Iron chelation therapy using the drug deferoxamine removes this extra iron from the body. If the iron is not removed, heart failure and death will eventually result. Iron supplements and oxidative drugs such as sulfonamides should be avoided.

Prognosis

The predicted outcome of thalassemia depends on the severity of the disease and the degree to which an individual follows the appropriate prescribed treatment.

Individuals with beta-thalassemia major (the most severe form of thalassemia), can live into their fifties with blood transfusions, iron chelation therapy, and splenectomy. Without iron chelation therapy, however, survival is limited by the degree of iron overload within the heart, with death often occurring between the ages of 20-30. Bone marrow transplant with marrow from a matched donor offers a 54-90% survival rate for adults.

Differential Diagnosis

Beta-thalassemia major is not easily confused with any other disorder. Other types of thalassemia may be confused with iron deficiency anemia or other disorders where hemoglobin production is abnormal (hemoglobinopathy).

Specialists

- Cardiologist
- Endocrinologist
- Hematologist
- Infectious Disease Physician

Work Restrictions / Accommodations

Time off for treatment may be needed. Blood transfusions are required at frequent intervals and require 3 to 4 hours per transfusion. Iron chelation therapy must be taken 5 to 7 times a week. Although the drug is administered through a pump placed under the skin, the process takes up to 12 hours and can cause discomfort. Because individuals with thalassemia may be more susceptible to infection and its complications, work exposure to infection should be limited. Depending on severity, anemia may necessitate reduced physical demands.

Complementary and Alternative Therapies

Content is intended for awareness only. Treatments may or may not be effective. Scientific evidence may be lacking and some substances have potentially toxic effects. Dr. Presley Reed and the editors do not endorse the use of these therapies in the absence of consultation with a licensed medical professional.

Green Tea - Antioxidants (such as green tea) may help improve anemia by protecting the red blood cell and hemoglobin from damage, and decrease risk of infection.

Comorbid Conditions

An individual with thalassemia may also carry a gene responsible for another hemoglobinopathy (e.g., the sickle cell trait). The gene defects responsible for beta-thalassemia minor and sickle cell trait are typically found within the same ethnic groups. Because of this, some people may have both these gene defects. This gene combination produces a condition known as sickle cell thalassemia with symptoms similar to sickle cell anemia.

Viral infection can cause the bone marrow to temporarily slow down or stop making new red blood cells. When this happens, anemia can suddenly worsen.

Complications

Iron overload (hematochromatosis) affects many body organs including the heart, liver, pancreas, and thyroid and may result in diabetes mellitus, hypothyroidism, heart failure, and even death.

Individuals with thalassemia are at increased risk for infection primarily due to iron overload. Many bacteria thrive when iron levels are high. Splenectomy also increases risk of infection particularly of bacterial pneumonia caused by pneumococcus (Streptococcus pneumoniae).

Overgrowth of bone marrow may cause decreased bone density and bone fractures.

Factors Influencing Duration

Length of disability varies with the type of thalassemia and treatment. Laparoscopic splenectomy requires a shorter recovery than open abdominal surgery. The rate of recovery from bone marrow transplant is influenced by risk factors before the transplant including high iron levels, liver disease, and heart disease.

Length of Disability

Disability may be permanent.

Thalassemia major. Medical treatment.

Duration in Days

Job Classification	Minimum	Optimum	Maximum
Sedentary work	0	3	7
Light work	0	3	7
Medium work	7	14	21
Heavy work	Indefinite	Indefinite	Indefinite
Very Heavy work	Indefinite	Indefinite	Indefinite

Thalassemia major. Surgical treatment.

Job Classification	Duration in Days		
	Minimum	Optimum	Maximum
Sedentary work	14	21	28
Light work	14	21	28
Medium work	28	35	42
Heavy work	Indefinite	Indefinite	Indefinite
Very Heavy work	Indefinite	Indefinite	Indefinite

Failure to Recover

If an individual fails to recover within the maximum duration expectancy period, the reader may wish to reference the following questions to assist in better understanding the specifics of an individual's medical case.

Regarding diagnosis:

- Is there a family history of thalassemia? Is individual of Mediterranean (Greek or Italian), Southeast Asian, Middle Eastern, or African descent?
- Has individual had a viral infection that can cause the bone marrow to temporarily slow down or stop making new red blood cells?
- Does individual report fatigue and shortness of breath? Is yellowing (jaundice) of the skin and eyes present?
- On exam, was enlargement of the spleen (splenomegaly), bone deformities, or growth retardation noted?
- Does individual have sickle cell thalassemia?
- Was a complete blood count (CBC) done to determine whether hemoglobin was low?
- Did a peripheral blood smear reveal abnormalities in red blood cells?
- Was hemoglobin electrophoresis required to assist with diagnosing the beta-thalassemias?
- Was DNA analysis done to assist with diagnosing the alpha-thalassemias?
- Was a diagnosis of alpha- or beta-thalassemia confirmed?

Regarding treatment:

- Is individual a candidate for a bone marrow transplant? Is a matched donor available for the transplant? If not, does individual undergo regular blood transfusions?
- Was removal of the spleen (splenectomy) done to keep red blood cells in circulation longer?
- If individual has had a splenectomy, are pneumococcal vaccines given, as required?
- Was chelation therapy done to remove excess iron from the body?
- Does individual understand that, if not removed, excess iron eventually results in heart failure and death?
- Were iron supplements and oxidative drugs such as sulfonamides avoided?
- Have treatments successfully maintained adequate hemoglobin levels?

Regarding prognosis:

- How severe is the disease?
- Was individual compliant with all prescribed medical therapies?
- Are there social, economic, or physical barriers to receiving prescribed medical treatment?
- Has individual met the necessary requirements to receive a bone marrow transplant?
- Has overgrowth of bone marrow occurred causing decreased bone density resulting in bone fractures?
- Has iron overload (hematochromatosis) affected heart, liver, pancreas, or thyroid? As a result, has individual developed diabetes mellitus, hypothyroidism, or heart failure?
- Did a bacterial infection develop secondary to increased iron levels or to splenectomy?
- How will complications be treated and what is expected outcome with treatment?
- How will this disease and its treatments affect the daily activities of individual?

References

Elghetany, M., and Frederick Davey. "Erythrocytic Disorders." Clinical Diagnosis and Management by Laboratory Methods. Henry, John, ed. Philadelphia: W.B. Saunders Company, 1996. 617-663.

Giardini, C., and Guido Lucarelli. "Bone Marrow Transplantation for Beta-Thalassemia." Hematology/Oncology Clinics of North America 13 5 (1999): 1059-1064.

Olivieri, Nancy. "The Beta-Thalassemias." The New England Journal of Medicine 341 2 (1999): 99-109.

Pearson, Howard, Lauren Berman, and Allen Crocker. "Thalassemia Intermedia." U.S. Department of Health and Human Services. 1997. 22 May 2000 <http://sickle.bwh.harvard.edu/thalassemia.pdf>.

Rund, Deborah, and Eliezer Rachmilewitz. "New Trends in the Treatment of Beta-Thalassemia." Critical Reviews in Oncology/Hematology 33 (2000): 105-118.

Schrier, Stanley. "Hemoglobinopathies and Hemolytic Anemias." Dale, D.C., and Daniel D. Federman, MD New York: WebMD Corporation, 2000 Scientific American Medicine. 16 May 2000 <http://www.samed.com/sam/forms/index.htm>.

Thalassemia. Harvard Medical School, Brigham and Women's Hospital, and Massachusetts General Hospital. 10 Oct 1999. 22 May 2000 <http://sickle.bwh.harvard.edu/thalover.html>.

Yamashita, Robert, Dru Foote, and Lina Weissman. "Patient Cultures: Thalassemia Service Delivery and Patient Compliance." Annals of New York Academy of Sciences 850 (1998): 521-522.

Thoracentesis

Other names / synonyms: Pleural Fluid Aspiration, Pleural Tap, Pleurocentesis

34.02, 34.91

Definition

A thoracentesis is a procedure in which a needle is inserted through the chest wall into the pleural space (space between the membranes lining the chest wall and those surrounding the lungs) to remove accumulated pleural fluid. The fluid obtained is analyzed so that appropriate treatment may be prescribed.

The analysis of the fluid will indicate possible causes of accumulated fluids in the pleural cavity (pleural effusion) such as infection, pulmonary hypertension, neoplasms, heart failure, and cirrhosis. If an infection is suspected, a culture of the fluid is often done to determine the presence of microorganisms.

Thoracentesis is often used to relieve symptoms and the effects of increased fluids in the covering of the lungs (pleural effusion). Such conditions causing this might include heart failure, a malignancy, inflammations, infections, or effects associated with pneumonia. Thoracentesis is a not an uncommon procedure.

Reason for Procedure

Thoracentesis is performed to determine the cause of abnormal fluid accumulation (pleural effusion) between the membranes lining the lungs and those lining the chest cavity. As a diagnostic aid, thoracentesis can be used to identify an unknown infection or one that is not responding to treatment.

As a treatment aid, thoracentesis can relieve breathing difficulties by removing the excess fluid caused by pleural effusion.

Description

The procedure is performed while the individual is sitting. Under local anesthesia, a needle is inserted into the body at the upper border of the lower rib. Once pleural fluid is found on aspiration (drawn out by suction), the needle is changed to a needle with a larger bore (inner circumference) so that the fluid can easily be drawn out through connecting tubing and into a container. This procedure is not used if the individual cannot cooperate (as a result of loss of consciousness, fear, compromised mental state, or combativeness) or if the individual has an unstable respiratory or cardiac condition.

Prognosis

Thoracentesis will give the doctor information about the condition of the pleural cavity. It will also indicate the nature of any disease discovered. The procedure may guide the treatment that will be needed.

The use of thoracentesis as treatment for fluids covering the lungs generally relieves the symptoms.

The outcome of tests guides the physician in making an appropriate diagnosis of the underlying cause for the increased fluid.

Specialists

- Pulmonologist
- Thoracic Surgeon

Work Restrictions / Accommodations

Work restrictions or accommodations depend on the individual's job requirements. Strenuous activity or heavy lifting will have to be modified temporarily.

Comorbid Conditions

Pre-existing asthma or allergies may lengthen the recovery period and interfere with some treatment strategies.

Procedure Complications

Possible complications of the procedure include collapsed lung, fluid re-accumulation, pulmonary edema, bleeding, infection, pulmonary edema, and respiratory distress.

Factors Influencing Duration

The underlying cause of the pleural fluid accumulation may influence the length of disability.

Length of Disability

Duration depends on the underlying diagnosis and reflects recovery from procedure only.

Duration in Days

Job Classification	Minimum	Optimum	Maximum
Any work	1	1	2

References

"Thoracentesis." MedlinePlus Health Information. 26 Sep 2000 16 Jan 2001 <http://medlineplus.adam.com/ency/article/003420.htm>.

"Thoracentesis." Health Central, Inc. 01 Oct 2000 4 Jan 2001 <http://www.healthcentral.com/mhc/top/003420.cfm>.

Thoracic Aneurysm

Other names / synonyms: Aneurysm of the Thoracic Aorta, Thoracic Aneurysm, Thoracic Aortic Aneurysm, Thoracic Arch Aneurysm, Thoracic Nonsyphilitic Aneurysm

441.1, 441.2, 441.3, 441.4, 441.5

Definition

A thoracic aneurysm refers to an abnormal, localized vessel wall weakness and ballooning (dilation) in one of the segments of the aorta that are located in the chest.

Aneurysms can occur in any blood vessel, but are more common in arteries than in veins because of higher blood pressure. Some thoracic aneurysms involve a separation in the wall of the vessel (dissecting aneurysm). In other cases, the aneurysm consists of an out-pouching on one side of the arterial wall (saccular aneurysm). Most commonly, the aneurysm extends around the circumference of the vessel (fusiform aneurysm).

Most aneurysms are approximately pea-sized, although they can be as small as a pinhead or as large as an orange. Aneurysms tend to grow at a rate of one-eighth to one-quarter of an inch per year. The likelihood of rupture increases as the aneurysm increases in size. Additionally, as the aneurysm progresses, increasing pressure is exerted against neighboring organs and tissue that may possibly result in potentially lethal complications.

Thoracic aneurysms may be caused by blunt chest trauma. Occasionally, they are a late-stage complication of syphilis. Congenital connective tissue disorders such as Marfan's syndrome and Ehlers-Danlos syndrome are risk factors for thoracic aneurysms.

The thoracic aneurysm accounts for approximately 25% of all aortic aneurysms. The other three-quarters of aortic aneurysms develop in the part of the aorta located in the abdomen (abdominal aortic aneurysms).

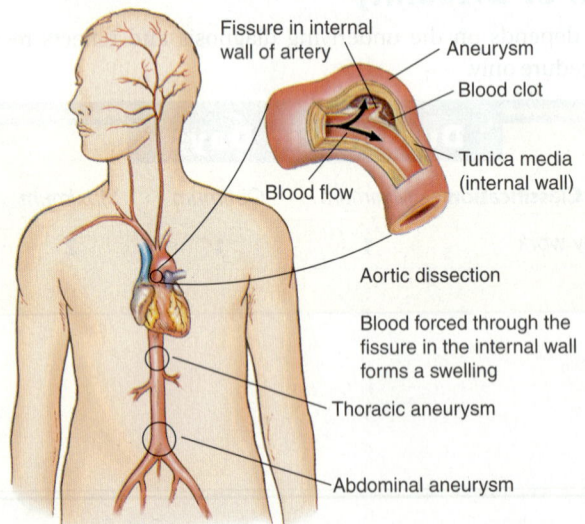

Diagnosis

History: Symptoms associated with the dissecting type of thoracic aneurysm include the sudden onset of a tearing or ripping sensation in the front of the chest extending to the neck, shoulders, lower back, and abdomen, but generally not to the jaw and arm. Additional symptoms may include shortness of breath, fainting, pallor, sweating, the development of a bluish tinge around the mouth and on the nailbeds (cyanosis), increased pulse rate, leg weakness, or transient paralysis.

Symptoms associated with a saccular or fusiform-type thoracic aneurysm vary according to the size and location of the aneurysm, as well as the associated effects of increased pressure and/or rupture on the surrounding structures including the lungs, trachea, larynx, esophagus, and spinal nerves. Symptoms may worsen as the aneurysm continues to enlarge. Individuals may report an aching pain in the shoulders, lower body, or abdomen. They may experience marked respiratory distress and exhibit difficulty breathing, a brassy cough, or wheezing. Hoarseness, loss of voice, or difficulty swallowing may be related to compression of the esophagus.

Physical exam: Nerve pressure may result in a collection of signs noticed upon physical examination including contraction of the pupil, drooping of the eyelid, and recession of the eyeball into the orbit (Horner's syndrome). Abnormal chest wall pulsations and a tugging on the trachea may also be detected.

Tests: A thoracic aneurysm can generally be seen on a chest x-ray. CT, MRI, and ultrasonography scans are useful in determining the size and extent of the aneurysm. An x-ray image of the aorta after a contrast fluid has been injected (contrast aortography) is usually performed if surgery is being considered.

Treatment

Emergency surgery is typically performed on those individuals with a dissecting aneurysm. Additional stabilizing measures may also be necessary. These include the administration of antihypertensive medications, medications to decrease the force of vessel contractions, oxygen for respiratory distress, narcotic analgesics for pain relief, intravenous administration of fluids, and if necessary, whole blood transfusions.

A surgical resection is recommended for aneurysms greater than or equal to six centimeters. However, elective repair is recommended for many individuals whose aneurysm may be prone to rupture even when it is much smaller. Surgical repair of the aneurysm consists of a resection of the aneurysm and restoration of blood flow using a synthetic or composite graft replacement. If aortic valve insufficiency is present, treatment may also involve replacing the aortic valve. Surgery is similar in magnitude to that of open-heart surgery.

Prognosis

Outcome is related to the location and size of the aneurysm and an individual's overall physical health. As an aneurysm enlarges, the risk of rupture increases significantly. Rupture of an aneurysm less than 5 cm wide is uncommon, but the risk increases dramatically when the aneurysm grows larger than 6 cm wide. A ruptured aneurysm results in a poor prognosis; it requires emergency surgery, with mortality of about 50%. The mortality associated with the elective repair of thoracic aneurysm (that is, before rupture) ranges from 10-15%, and the results in survivors are generally good.

Differential Diagnosis

Conditions with similar symptoms may include unstable angina, acute myocardial infarction, pain related to acute chest trauma, abdominal aortic aneurysm, hemothorax, and pneumothorax.

Specialists

- Anesthesiologist
- Cardiologist
- Pulmonologist
- Vascular Surgeon

Work Restrictions / Accommodations

Individual tolerance for physical exercise pre- and postsurgery will dictate the level of physical activity that will be possible. Underlying conditions, effects of surgical repair, or use of postoperative medication may require that individuals be reassigned to a position with less physically demanding requirements. This will require evaluation on an individual, case-by-case basis.

Comorbid Conditions

Comorbid conditions may include obesity, arteriosclerosis, hypertension, cigarette smoking, and endocarditis.

Complications

The major, life-threatening complication of thoracic aneurysm is rupture and the attendant internal bleeding. Bleeding into the pericardium could lead to compression of the heart due to elevated pressure within the thoracic cavity (cardiac tamponade).

Factors Influencing Duration

Factors include the location and size of the aneurysm, whether the aneurysm has ruptured, the age and general health of the individual, and the extent of surgical repair necessary. Underlying cardiovascular diseases such as hypertension or arteriosclerosis and the development of postsurgical complications such as heart attack (myocardial infarction), hemorrhage, thrombosis, or spinal cord ischemia may significantly extend the recovery period and affect rehabilitation potential. In a small percentage of cases, a residual or recurrent aneurysm will be detected after surgery, extending the disability.

Length of Disability

If the job is particularly strenuous and reassignment to a less taxing position is not practical, disability may be permanent. For aneurysmectomy, disability may be permanent.

Non-ruptured.

Duration in Days

Job Classification	Minimum	Optimum	Maximum
Sedentary work	1	3	5
Light work	1	3	5
Medium work	1	3	5
Heavy work	3	5	10
Very Heavy work	3	5	10

Surgical treatment. Aneurysmectomy.

Duration in Days

Job Classification	Minimum	Optimum	Maximum
Sedentary work	56	70	112
Light work	56	84	Indefinite
Medium work	56	105	Indefinite
Heavy work	84	140	Indefinite
Very Heavy work	84	140	Indefinite

Failure to Recover

If an individual fails to recover within the maximum duration expectancy period, the reader may wish to reference the following questions to assist in better understanding the specifics of an individual's medical case.

Regarding diagnosis:

- Has individual experienced blunt chest trauma?
- Does individual have a history of syphilis? History of congenital connective tissue disorders such as Marfan's syndrome or Ehlers-Danlos syndrome?
- Does individual report sudden onset of a tearing or ripping sensation in the front of the chest extending to the neck, shoulders, lower back, and abdomen?
- Does individual complain of shortness of breath, fainting, sweating, development of a bluish tinge around the mouth and on the nailbeds (cyanosis), increased pulse rate, leg weakness, or transient inability to move (paralysis)? Aching pain in the shoulders, lower body, or abdomen?
- Does individual experience marked respiratory distress and exhibit difficulty breathing, a brassy cough, or wheezing? Hoarseness, loss of voice, or difficulty swallowing
- Was a chest x-ray done? CT, MRI, or ultrasonography?
- Was an x-ray of the aorta (contrast aortography) taken, if surgery is considered?
- Was a diagnosis of dissecting, saccular, or fusiform thoracic aneurysm confirmed?

Regarding treatment:

- Did individual undergo emergency surgery to correct a dissecting aneurysm?
- Was surgery required for an aneurysm greater than or equal to 6 cm or for a smaller aneurysm prone to rupture?
- Was removal (resection) of the aneurysm and restoration of blood flow using a synthetic or composite graft replacement performed? Was surgery successful? Any complications?
- Does individual also have aortic valve insufficiency? If so, is replacement of the aortic valve required?

Regarding prognosis:

- What was the location and size of the aneurysm?
- Was aneurysm removed in a timely manner?
- Did any postsurgical complications occur? If so, what were they and what is expected outcome with treatment?
- Did the aneurysm rupture? If so, how severe was the loss of blood? What is expected outcome?

References

"Aneurysms." Merck Manual of Diagnosis and Therapy, 17th ed. Beers, Mark H., and Robert Berkow, MD Whitehouse Station, NJ: Merck & Co., Inc, 1999. 05 Jan 2001 <http://www.merck.com/pubs/mmanual/section16/chapter211/211a.htm>.

Reardon, M.J., et al. "Surgical Management of Primary Aortoesophageal Fistula Secondary to Thoracic Aneurysm." Annals of Thoracic Surgery 69 (2000): 967-970.

Thoracic Disc Disorder with Myelopathy
Other names / synonyms: Thoracic Disc Displacement with Myelopathy, Thoracic Spinal Cord Compression
722.72

Definition

This diagnosis describes a thoracic intervertebral disc herniation with accompanying spinal cord compression. The spinal cord involvement results in nerve impairment affecting the legs and, possibly, bowel and/or bladder control impairment.

A thoracic disc is the least common location for a disc herniation that produces myelopathy and occurs in less than 1% of all symptomatic disc herniations. It occurs twice as frequently in males as in females. The average age at diagnosis is fifty. Most are lower thoracic disc herniations, occurring below the T8 to T9 level. Most cases occur without a history of trauma, and are due to the normal degenerative aging process.

Diagnosis

History: Individuals report pain in the mid-back, sometimes radiating along a rib (radicular pain), which is aggravated by movement and relieved by rest; however, approximately half of all individuals have no pain. There may be a progressive disturbance in gait due to increasing weakness and poor sensation in the legs. Symptoms usually affect one leg more than the other. A "pins-and-needles" sensation (paresthesia) may be reported. Urinary urgency and incontinence are common symptoms. The disorder may develop either acutely over a few weeks or chronically over several years. Most cases occur without a history of trauma, but there might have been a fall landing on the buttocks or feet with a twisting of the spine.

Physical exam: The exam may reveal sensory and motor disturbances in the legs. Individuals will present with mid-back pain. Reflexes in the legs may be overactive, and an abnormal Achilles tendon reflex (clonus) may be present. Babinski's sign, toe extension on stimulation of the bottom of the foot, is an abnormal reflex that may be seen.

Tests: Plain x-rays may show calcification in a thoracic disc, but that disc is usually not causing symptoms. CT scan and/or MRI plus myelography will be diagnostic.

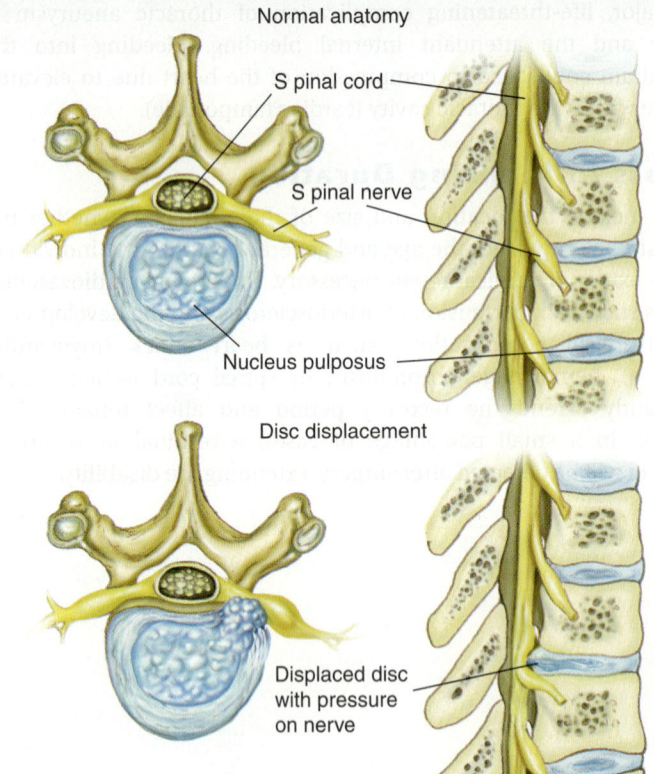

Treatment

This diagnosis is most often treated surgically, if the deficit is severe or progressive. There are several operations to decompress the spinal cord including a discectomy with or without fusion utilizing either the partial rib removal (costotransversectomy) approach or going through the chest (transthoracic).

Prognosis

Without surgery, individuals with mild neurologic deficit may improve with time. With surgery, 70-90% of individuals with myelopathy will improve. However, results of thoracic disc surgery are not as good as the results of cervical or lumbar disc surgery, and approximately 14% of individuals undergoing surgical procedures for thoracic disc problems experience no relief from the surgery. There is also a higher rate of permanent neurologic complication with surgery on the thoracic disc, compared to cervical and lumbar discs. For these reasons, surgery is reserved for cases with severe or progressive neurologic deficit.

Differential Diagnosis

Other causes of pain and spinal cord compression are metastatic cancer, epidural abscess, and Paget's disease. If pain is not present, this condition can be confused with a demyelinating disease in the spinal cord or a muscle disorder such as muscular dystrophy.

Specialists

- Neurologist
- Neurosurgeon
- Orthopedic Surgeon
- Physiatrist

Rehabilitation

Individuals with thoracic disc disorder with myelopathy will likely need rehabilitation under the guidance of a physical therapist. Rehabilitation is an important aspect in regaining mobility in the thoracic region as well as regaining strength to trunk muscles that may have been affected by a resulting myelopathy. Focus is first placed on allowing the thoracic disc herniation to resolve over time. If improvement occurs, rehabilitative exercises are appropriate.

Education in the body mechanics of sitting and making transitions between postures while maintaining lumbar lordosis and avoiding protruded head and neck often helps. Mckenzie protocols to determine which exercise movements to pursue or avoid are appropriate. The individual may be instructed on several methods to stretch the midback. One such stretch is the cat stretch. Swimming is a good exercise for conditioning the thoracic spine, as it will incorporate rotation against mild resistance of the water.

Strengthening of the thoracic muscles may continue with the use of resistance throughout the range of motion. With instruction and supervision by a physical therapist, strengthening is accomplished. Focus is placed on an upper body-strengthening program with resistance lifted within a pain-free range. The therapist will supervise the program initially to ensure the individual is concentrating on the muscle groups being exercised.

Modifications may need to be made by the physical therapist for those who have arthritis or other joint irritations of the thoracic spine.

Work Restrictions / Accommodations

Prolonged standing, walking, or climbing may need to be restricted, if nerve damage to the legs persists. The accommodation may be temporary or permanent. Lifting and carrying may have to be modified due to leg weakness.

Comorbid Conditions

Comorbid conditions that could affect the length of disability and recovery time include obesity and congenital diseases or anomalies of the spine and back.

Complications

Possible complications of this condition include paralysis, incontinence, infection, and bowel and bladder dysfunction (loss of sphincter control and incontinence). Prolonged pain from the thoracotomy (surgical approach) is not uncommon.

Factors Influencing Duration

The severity and duration of spinal cord compression, the number of discs affected, and any complications from surgery might influence the length of disability.

Length of Disability

Disability may be permanent

Surgical treatment. Disc excision and fusion.

Duration in Days

Job Classification	Minimum	Optimum	Maximum
Sedentary work	42	49	84
Light work	56	63	84
Medium work	70	77	112
Heavy work	Indefinite	Indefintie	Indefinite
Very Heavy work	Indefinite	Indefinte	Indefinite

Failure to Recover

If an individual fails to recover within the maximum duration expectancy period, the reader may wish to reference the following questions to assist in better understanding the specifics of an individual's medical case.

Regarding diagnosis:

- Does the individual report mid-back pain? Does it travel along a rib?
- Does the individual have any weakness in a leg?
- Does the individual have any bowel or bladder abnormalities?
- Does the individual have any paresthesias?
- Has the individual had a fall landing on the buttocks or feet with a twisting of the spine?
- Does the individual have any degenerative changes in the area?
- On exam does the individual have mid-back pain? Are the reflexes overactive? Is Babinski's sign present?
- Has the individual had plain x-rays? CT scan with myelography? MRI?
- Have conditions with similar symptoms been ruled out?

Regarding treatment:

- Has the individual undergone a discectomy with or without fusion?

Regarding prognosis:
- Is the individual active in rehabilitation?
- Is the individual's employer able to accommodate any necessary restrictions?
- Does the individual have any conditions that may affect the ability to recover?
- Has the individual had any complications such as paralysis, incontinence, infection, and bowel and bladder dysfunction, or disc calcification?

References

Arnheim, Daniel D. Modern Principles of Athletic Training. St. Louis: Times Mirror/Mosby Publishing, 1989.

Kessler, R.M. Management of Common Musculoskeletal Disorders: Physical Therapy Principles and Methods. Philadelphia: J.B. Lippincott Company, 1990.

Thoracic Outlet Syndrome

Other names / synonyms: Anterior Scalene Syndrome, Brachial Plexus Lesion Disorder, Cervical Rib Syndrome, Thoracic Outlet Compression Syndrome

353.0

Definition

Thoracic outlet syndrome refers to a number of different syndromes that arise from compression of the nerves in the base of the neck (brachial plexus,) or blood vessels (arteries and veins) under the collarbone (subclavian), or under the arm (axillary).

The most frequent of these syndromes is presence of an incomplete extra rib above the normal first rib (cervical rib) that narrows the space under the clavicle and presses on the brachial plexus and fibrous bands of uncertain origin. Cervical ribs are commonly found in asymptomatic individuals and the presence of a cervical rib does not automatically explain local symptoms.

Thoracic outlet syndrome almost always occurs in adulthood, suggesting that this compression or pinching evolves as the muscles and ligaments in this area undergo changes with age and/or use. A majority of individuals with thoracic outlet syndrome are women in early or mid-adult life (female to male ratio 5 to 1) in whom sagging of the shoulders, large breasts, and poor muscular tone may be a cause.

Clavicular abnormalities and certain occupational activities that force prolonged elevation of the arm (hyperabduction of the shoulder) may play an important role. Constriction may also be caused by scar tissue formation from a previous injury. The syndrome is rare, with an annual incidence of 1 in 1 million.

Diagnosis

History: Individuals report pain in the shoulder, arm, and hand, or in all three locations. The hand pain can be severe in the fourth and fifth fingers. Individuals may report that the pain is aggravated by use of the arm and fatigue of the arm is often prominent. Individuals may also have a decrease in sensation in response to stimulation of the sensory nerves or body organs and areas of the organ nerves (hypesthesia).

Physical exam: Physical signs are not commonly seen. Muscle weakness and wasting (atrophy) of the arm muscles and weakness of the grip and other hand movements are rare. There may be tenderness in the area above the clavicle. Symptoms can often be reproduced when the arm is raised or exercised, and the radial pulse in the wrist may diminish or disappear with these maneuvers (Adson's sign). The fingers may turn pale or blue (cyanotic) when the arm is raised overhead.

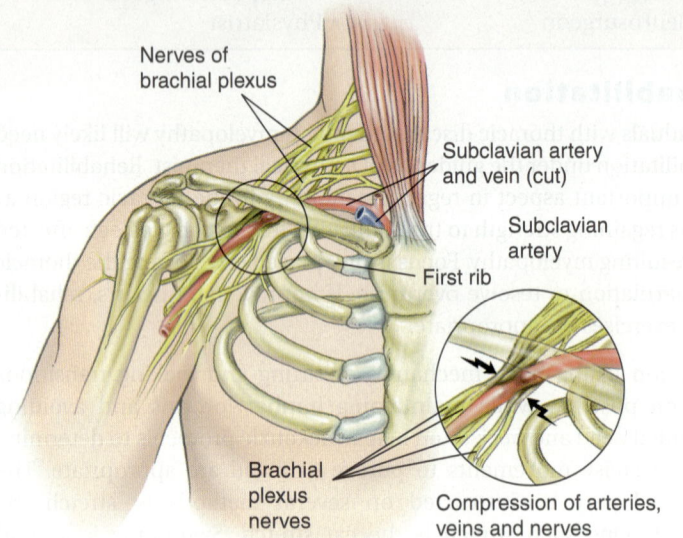

Tests: X-rays of the cervical spine can confirm the presence of a cervical rib or an elongated fibrous band. Nerve conduction studies may reveal areas of decreased sensory potentials. An electromyogram (EMG) can assess nerve damage by measuring the electrical activity of the muscles. Vascular tests such as brachial artery angiography are usually reserved for individuals with suspected arterial blockage, a dilation of the wall of a blood vessel (aneurysm), or an obvious cervical rib. Venography may only be useful in cases where venous thrombosis is observed. Other noninvasive vascular tests using Doppler ultrasonography can help assess vascular status.

Treatment

Conservative treatment directed toward correction of abnormal posture or muscle imbalance should be tried. This may include an exercise program, manual therapy to increase mobility of the shoulder girdle, shoulder braces to improve posture, or changing work habits. Physical activities that aggravate the condition should be avoided. Nonsteroidal anti-inflammatory drugs or muscle relaxants are sometimes useful in relieving pain.

Surgery should be reserved for the few cases in which conservative management has failed to relieve symptoms and when the diagnosis is confirmed. Surgery involves releasing or removing the structures that cause the compression. The procedure could include releasing the scalene muscle (scalenectomy), removal of an accessory rib, or removing all or part of the first rib (rib resection). A second opinion should be obtained in all cases before surgery is performed.

Prognosis

Relief of pressure on the brachial plexus and subclavian artery and vein is usually curative. In general, surgery is usually successful; however, the results of surgery are difficult to evaluate when there are no objective signs or laboratory abnormalities present. Symptoms have also been known to spontaneously disappear. Relief of pain symptoms is usually successfully achieved with nonsteroidal anti-inflammatory drugs or muscle relaxants.

Differential Diagnosis

Thoracic outlet syndrome may be confused with carpal tunnel syndrome, myofascial pain, ulnar neuropathy or entrapment at the elbow, or cervical radiculopathy due to arthritis or disc disease. A superior sulcus tumor of the lung can duplicate the pain of this syndrome. An aneurysm of the subclavian artery can cause compression.

Specialists

- Anesthesiologist
- Neurologist
- Neurosurgeon
- Orthopedic Surgeon
- Psychiatrist
- Thoracic Surgeon

Work Restrictions / Accommodations

Physical activities that must be altered or avoided include awkward postural positions, heavy work, direct load bearing on the shoulder, and working with arms and hands above shoulder height. Individuals most likely to be affected include construction workers, carpenters, repairmen, and others who are required to lift heavy materials throughout the day.

Comorbid Conditions

Other neuropathies causing injury or inflammation of single nerves due to pressure from surrounding ligaments and tissues (entrapment neuropathies) such as carpal tunnel syndrome or cervical radiculopathy) may lengthen disability.

Complications

Symptoms may become severe and, in some cases, blood clots may form in the artery at the shoulder and travel to the hand. Rarely, prolonged pressure on the nerves of the brachial plexus can cause atrophy of the muscles that it innervates.

Factors Influencing Duration

Length of disability will be determined by the severity of symptoms, whether the dominant or nondominant side is affected, whether surgery is required, and outcome of treatment.

Length of Disability

Duration depends on treatment selection (conservative vs. surgical) and outcome.

Medical treatment.

Duration in Days

Job Classification	Minimum	Optimum	Maximum
Sedentary work	0	7	14
Light work	0	7	14
Medium work	0	14	28
Heavy work	0	21	84
Very Heavy work	0	21	84

Surgical treatment, rib resection.

Duration in Days

Job Classification	Minimum	Optimum	Maximum
Sedentary work	21	28	42
Light work	21	28	42
Medium work	28	35	56
Heavy work	28	42	84
Very Heavy work	35	42	84

Surgical treatment, scalenectomy only (controversial procedure).

Duration in Days

Job Classification	Minimum	Optimum	Maximum
Sedentary work	7	14	21
Light work	14	21	28
Medium work	21	28	35
Heavy work	28	42	84
Very Heavy work	28	42	84

Failure to Recover

If an individual fails to recover within the maximum duration expectancy period, the reader may wish to reference the following questions to assist in better understanding the specifics of an individual's medical case.

Regarding diagnosis:

- Does individual have a cervical rib?
- Is there pain in the shoulder, arm, or hand? In the fourth or fifth fingers? Is pain aggravated by use of the arm?
- Does individual have a decrease in sensation in response to stimulation of the sensory nerves?
- Is there any muscle weakness or atrophy?
- Is area above the clavicle tender?

- Are symptoms reproduced when elevating the arm or exercising it? Is the radial pulse absent with arm elevation? Do the finger's become cyanotic?
- Were x-rays done of the cervical spine? Nerve conduction studies? EMG? Has individual had brachial artery angiography? Venography? Doppler ultrasonography?
- Have conditions with similar symptoms been ruled out?

Regarding treatment:

- Is individual in an exercise program? Physical therapy? Use a shoulder brace?
- Has individual changed work habits, if necessary?
- Are physical activities that aggravate the condition being avoided?
- Have NSAIDs or muscle relaxants been given?
- Is surgery recommended? Has individual had a second surgical opinion?

Regarding prognosis:

- Is individual active in physical therapy? Is a home exercise program in place?
- Has individual made the necessary adjustments in physical activities to reduce symptoms?
- Can individual's employer accommodate any necessary restrictions?
- Does individual have any conditions that could affect ability to recover?
- Did any blood clots develop in the artery at the shoulder?

References

Adams R.D., M. Victor, and A.H. Ropper. Principles of Neurology. New York: McGraw-Hill, 1997.

Kenny, R.A., et al. "Thoracic Outlet Syndrome: A Useful Exercise Treatment Option." American Journal of Surgery 165 2 (1993): 282-284.

Kenny, R.A., G.B. Traynor, and D. Withington. "Thoracic Outlet Syndrome: A Useful Exercise Treatment Option." American Journal of Surgery 165 2 (1993): 282-284.

Rowland, Lewis P. Merritt's Textbook of Neurology, 8th ed. Philadelphia: Lea & Febiger, 1989.

Thoracic Spine Pain

Other names / synonyms: Middle Back Pain, Thoracalgia
724.1

Definition

Thoracic spine pain is diagnosed only when the cause of pain in the spine of the upper back (thorax) is unknown. This type of thoracic spine pain (also known as idiopathic thoracic spine pain) is less common than low back pain. Idiopathic means the cause of a disease is unknown.

Pain in the thoracic spine can be the first sign that an individual has an undiagnosed disease or unrecognized injury. A recent blow to the back may have occurred and, if so, should be called a contusion. If heavy lifting was associated with the pain onset, the condition should be called a thoracic strain.

Specific causes for thoracic pain are usually discovered when pain persists and tests are done.

Diagnosis

History: The individual is usually unable to point to a specific area of pain. The individual may have poor posture and report recent overhead activity.

Physical exam: Exam of the thoracic spine determines whether the spine is curved normally. Changes in the degree or angle of the curve can give a different diagnosis. Measurement of chest expansion when breathing in and flexibility of the upper trunk should be normal otherwise another diagnosis may be given, usually ankylosing spondylitis. Lightly pressing with the fingertips (palpation) along the spine may elicit specific sites of pain or abnormalities.

Tests: Radiographic tests of the spine and other organs and laboratory tests rule out diagnoses of cancerous tumors, scoliosis, and other diseases and injuries.

Treatment

Treatment is conservative. Physical modalities and pain relievers may help reduce the pain. Restricted physical activity and spine manipulation may also be helpful in lessening pain. If the thoracic spine pain is a symptom of a diagnosed disease or injury then treatment entirely depends on the nature of the disease or injury.

Prognosis

Whether the individual fully recovers depends on whether the thoracic spine pain is idiopathic (of unknown cause) or whether it is a symptom of an undiagnosed disease or unrecognized injury. If the individual is diagnosed with idiopathic spine pain, he or she is expected to recover completely with time. If thoracic spine pain is caused by a diagnosed illness or injury, treatment for that illness or injury can result in full recovery from thoracic spine pain.

Differential Diagnosis

Other conditions that cause pain in the upper back include referred cervical pain, cardiovascular and respiratory disorders, cancerous tumors, infections, inflammation, metabolic disease, degenerative disc disease, instability, and scoliosis. All these diseases and disorders must be ruled out as the cause of the pain. Stress fracture of the neck or the 7th and 8th ribs also causes thoracic neck pain. Thoracic pain is frequent in fibromyalgia.

Specialists

- Anesthesiologist
- Cardiologist
- Chiropractor
- Internist
- Neurosurgeon
- Orthopedic Surgeon
- Physiatrist
- Physical Therapist
- Pulmonologist
- Rheumatologist

Rehabilitation

The basic goal in the rehabilitation of thoracic spine pain is to decrease discomfort and swelling when present and to regain full motion, flexibility, strength, and endurance of the muscle/soft tissue involved. The final result is aimed at returning the individual to full function for work and recreational activities with minimal risk of reinjury. The method a to achieve this is largely determined in part by the origin and severity of the thoracic spine pain and whether any thoracic joints are involved that cause difficult with movement and function.

If the pain is severe, application of cold using ice on the involved area is performed. After this period, heat treatments are helpful to reduce inflammation and pain and are beneficial to stretch the affected muscles. Forms of heat treatment include ultrasound using high frequency sound waves that produce heat to penetrate deep into the involved muscles. Electrostimulation combined with heat or cold treatment is another technique used in physical therapy to relax irritated thoracic muscles that may be in spasm.

In general, gentle passive stretching of the trunk region affected by the contusion is initiated. An example of stretching is the individual standing with feet apart. The individual side bends his or her trunk to one side (laterally) without any backward (extension) or forward motion (flexion). To stretch tissues of the back portion of the trunk, the individual stands with feet apart and leans forward with the knees straight until a gentle stretch is felt throughout the upper and lower trunk/back. Another technique is called the cat stretch. By placing the chin to the chest, the stretch is felt further along the back of the trunk.

Flexion does not usually benefit the thoracic spine. Education in the body mechanics of sitting and making transitions between postures while maintaining lumbar lordosis and avoiding protruded head and neck often helps. McKenzie protocols to determine which exercise movements to pursue or avoid is appropriate.

Once full range of motion is restored, rehabilitation then focuses on returning general strength to the trunk region as indicated. Sit-ups help strengthen the abdominal muscles. Calisthenics such as push-ups strengthen the muscles in the front upper portion of the trunk. Variations of sit-ups known as cross crunch sit-ups help strengthen the side muscles of the trunk. Physical therapists also instruct resistance exercises through the use of a pulley system that demands a combination of rotation and bending of the trunk and abdominal muscles. Swimming is a good exercise for conditioning the trunk as it incorporates all trunk motions against mild resistance of the water.

If individual has significant soft tissue damage to skin, muscle, and/or ligaments, the healing response may initially take longer with more stretching and strengthening required before return to work. This is especially the case if the rib cage region is involved and breathing is difficult and painful because of the need to expand the chest/rib cage when the individual breathes in (inhalation). Rehabilitation of a fracture to the thoracic spine depends on fracture type, whether there is an associated spinal cord injury, and individual's age and general health. In a thoracic spine fracture without a spinal cord injury, associated damage to muscles and ligaments is a possibility needing appropriate healing and rehabilitation. Once the individual is allowed to return to work, it is important to initially minimize excessive bending, lifting, and twisting of the trunk. Generally speaking, rehabilitation of thoracic spine pain depends greatly on the degree of the tissue injury.

Work Restrictions / Accommodations

Work activities requiring weight bearing on the thoracic spine should be restricted. These include lifting heavy weights, working overhead, and side bending. Restrictions would be appropriate for no more than 90 days, unless a specific disorder is recognized.

Comorbid Conditions

Comorbid conditions that slow full recovery from thoracic spine pain include musculoskeletal disorders, cervicobrachial syndrome, neck pain, obesity, and injuries preventing participation in physical therapy.

Complications

Treatment for thoracic spine pain when the cause is an undiagnosed illness or injury is not effective and may be harmful.

Some diseases with thoracic spine pain as a symptom include musculoskeletal diseases and nonorthopedic conditions such as diseases of the heart, lungs, abdominal organs, and kidneys. The spine is a frequent destination of cancerous tumors that develop in other organs, i.e., cancer with a primary source elsewhere is known as secondary cancer or metastatic cancer.

Factors Influencing Duration

The demands of lifestyle and work influence the recovery from thoracic spine pain. Heavy lifting and vigorous movement of the upper body can aggravate the symptoms. A more extensive degenerative disease process of the discs increases the length of disability.

Length of Disability

This is a vague diagnosis. Duration depends on cause of the pain and treatment. Contact physician to obtain more information on the underlying cause.

Failure to Recover

If an individual fails to recover within the maximum duration expectancy period, the reader may wish to reference the following questions to assist in better understanding the specifics of an individual's medical case.

Regarding diagnosis:

- Can individual point to a specific area of pain?
- Does individual have poor posture?
- Was there a recent injury to the area?
- Does individual have an undiagnosed disease or unrecognized injury?
- On physical exam, were there changes in the normal curvature of the spine?
- Is chest expansion normal? Is flexibility of the upper trunk normal?

- Was there any pain with palpation?
- Has individual had radiographic testing or laboratory testing (MRI, bone scan, sedimentation rate)?
- Have conditions with similar symptoms been ruled out?

Regarding treatment:

- Is the pain idiopathic or secondary to another disease?
- Has individual responded to conservative treatment?
- Was spine manipulation helpful?

Regarding prognosis:

- Is individual active in rehabilitation?
- Can individual's employer accommodate necessary restrictions?
- Does individual have any conditions that may affect ability to recover?
- Are there any other diseases that may be causing the pain?

References

Brukner, P., and K. Khan. "Stress Fracture of the Neck of the Seventh and Eighth Ribs: A Case Report." Clinical Journal of Sports Medicine 6 3 (1996): 204-206.

Cacayorin, E.D., L. Hochhauser, and G.R. Petro. "Lumbar and Thoracic Spine Pain in the Athlete: Radiographic Evaluation." Clinics in Sports Medicine 6 4 (1987): 767-783.

Kessler, R.M. Management of Common Musculoskeletal Disorders: Physical Therapy Principles and Methods. Philadelphia: J.B. Lippincott Company, 1990.

Kisner, C., and L. Colby. Therapeutic Exercise Foundations and Techniques. Philadelphia: F.A. Davis Company, 1990.

Thoracostomy

Other names / synonyms: Open Chest Drainage
34.04, 34.09

Definition

A thoracostomy is the creation of an opening in the chest wall. It is done with an incision or a stab wound using a sharpened, hollow probe (trocar). A thoracostomy is commonly performed for the insertion of a chest tube. This procedure is most often used to evacuate air (pneumothorax), blood (hemothorax), or fluids (pleural effusions, empyema) from the chest cavity.

Generally, pleural effusions are categorized into transudative or exudative effusions Transudative effusions are fluids that have passed through membranes such as in congestive heart failure, cirrhosis, atelectasis, inflammation of the membrane covering the heart (pericardium), or dialysis of the lining of the abdominal cavity. Exudative effusions are fluids that have come from tissues or their capillaries associated with pneumonia, cancer and other tumors, pulmonary embolisms, tuberculosis, related to asbestos exposure, inflammation of the pancreas, traumas, heart injuries, or are drug-induced.

There are an estimated 1 million cases per year in the US.

Reason for Procedure

A thoracostomy and chest tube insertion is done to drain air and fluid out of a portion of the lung so that the entire lung can inflate normally.

Description

Chest tube insertions can be done in an emergency department, hospital room, or the operating room, depending on the situation. A local anesthetic is injected into the skin of the chest. An incision or stab wound is made through the chest wall between the ribs and over the area of lung needing drainage. A gathering stitch (suture) is made around the opening in the skin. A tube (catheter) is inserted into the lung. The gathering suture is pulled tight around the tube. The tube is sutured to the skin near the insertion opening. A chest x-ray is done to confirm the location of the end of the catheter within the lung. The other end of the catheter is placed in a bottle of water and all connections are secured. The bottle is placed on the floor beneath the bed (dependent drainage) and may be connected to a small amount of suction.

Chest tubes are not normally left in place when the individual returns to the job.

Prognosis

The outcome varies considerably with the individual and the underlying disease condition. Thoracostomy is generally considered to be relatively risk-free with a low mortality rate.

Specialists

- Critical Care Specialist
- Pulmonologist
- Thoracic Surgeon

Work Restrictions / Accommodations

Activity may be restricted. Breathing dust, fumes, or irritants should be avoided. A filter mask or respirator may be required depending on the individual's job.

Comorbid Conditions

Asthma, allergies, and pre-existing lung disease may prolong the need for indwelling chest tubes, and lengthen the time necessary for recovery and return to work.

Procedure Complications

Complications from the procedure may include the development of air or gas (pneumothorax) in the outer tissue of the lungs or an inflammation of the covering of the lungs (pleura). Side effects of medications and the development of infections could have an adverse effect on the outcome.

Factors Influencing Duration

The underlying condition and its treatment, the presence of complications, and the individual's response to this procedure will affect the length of disability.

Length of Disability

Length of disability will depend on the individual's response to therapy for the underlying disease.

Duration in Days

Job Classification	Minimum	Optimum	Maximum
Sedentary work	3	14	28
Light work	3	14	28
Medium work	3	21	42
Heavy work	7	21	42
Very Heavy work	7	21	42

References

Abrahamian, Frederick M. "Pleural Effusion." eMedicine.com 01 Feb 2001 13 March 200 <http://www.emedicine.com/emerg/topic462.htm>.

Staton, Gerald W. Jr., MD, and Roland H. Ingram, Jr., MD. "Chapter IX Disorders of the Pleura, Hila, and Mediastinum." Dale, D.C., and Daniel D. Federman, MD New York: WebMD Corporation, 2000 Scientific American Medicine. 13 March 200 <http://www.samed.com/sam/forms/index.htm>.

Thoracotomy
34.02

Definition

A thoracotomy is a surgical procedure where the chest wall (thorax) is opened allowing access to the organs beneath it. A lateral thoracotomy provides access to the lungs, major blood vessels, and esophagus and an anterior thoracotomy provides access to the heart and coronary arteries.

Thoracotomy is performed to allow access to a diseased heart, lung, or other organ in the chest cavity. It can be used to locate a source of bleeding or obtain a biopsy sample.

An emergency thoracotomy may be done to assess damage following a severe chest injury.

Reason for Procedure

Thoracotomy may be needed for lung cancer, other tumors, tuberculosis, lung abscesses, bronchiectasis, emphysema, collapsed lung, gas in the lung (pneumothorax), blood in the lungs (hemothorax), or injuries that have resulted in collapsed lung. It is sometimes performed in emergency situations where traumatic injuries and episodes have occurred.

Air leaks or pneumothorax from injuries may require this procedure. It is also often used in conjunction with heart surgery and in the treatment of recurring pneumothorax or hemothorax or loss of lung volume.

Thoracotomy for open biopsy of the lung, outer covering of the lung (pleura), where nerves and vessels enter or leave (hilum), and dividing part of the thoracic cavity (mediastinum) is the diagnostic gold standard to which all other procedures must be compared. However, other procedures such as thoracoscopy have decreased the need for thoracotomy.

Thoracotomy may be necessary in the emergency room to treat stab or gunshot wounds in the chest and near the heart and lungs.

Description

Several approaches are available to perform a thoracotomy but all are done under a general anesthesia.

In anterior thoracotomy, a vertical incision is made from the base of the neck to the lower end of the breastbone (sternum). The sternum is divided with a saw (sternotomy) and gently pried apart. With the heart exposed, the necessary surgery can be performed. A full-wide thoracotomy is used to gain access to the esophagus, heart, thymus gland, trachea, bronchi, and large blood and lymphatic vessels.

In a lateral thoracotomy, an incision is made between the ribs to allow access to the lungs. The incision is made from back to front along the rib line. The ribs are spread apart and occasionally part of a rib is removed. The lung may be biopsied through the incision.

Following the procedure, a temporary drainage tube is inserted into the pleural cavity (space between the membranes lining the chest wall and the membranes covering the lungs). This allows fluid to drain and prevents the lung from collapsing. If the procedure involved a sternotomy, the sternum is closed with strong stitches or wire. The muscles and overlying skin are closed with stitches.

Specialists

- Critical Care Specialist
- Emergency Medicine
- Pulmonologist
- Thoracic Surgeon

Prognosis

The outcome depends on the type and severity of the problem but many individuals recover uneventfully. Hospital stay is usually 7 to 10 days. The chest tube remains in place until the lung has fully expanded. Pain is managed with medications.

The procedure may be unsuccessful in treating massive traumas reporting to emergency medical facilities.

Work Restrictions / Accommodations

Work restrictions or accommodations depend on the individual's job requirements. Rigorous activities should be avoided until the incision has completely healed.

Comorbid Conditions

Lung, heart, kidney, and liver disease may prolong the recovery and make it more difficult.

Procedure Complications

Complications vary depending on the organ or system being examined and treated. Severe cardiac problems may result in death of the individual. Where lung surgery is involved, complications may include reactions to medications, breathing difficulty, bleeding, infections, blood clots, and pneumonia.

Factors Influencing Duration

Complications or the underlying condition for which the thoracotomy was performed may influence length of disability.

Length of Disability

The length of disability depends on the nature of the underlying disease and disorder. Duration reflects recovery from procedure only.

Duration in Days

Job Classification	Minimum	Optimum	Maximum
Sedentary work	21	28	35
Light work	21	28	35
Medium work	21	28	35
Heavy work	28	35	42
Very Heavy work	28	35	42

References

"Lung Surgery." MedlinePlus Health Information. 26 Sep 2000. 04 Jan 2001 <http://medlineplus.adam.com/ency/article/002956.htm>.

Staton, G.W. Jr., and R.H. Ingram, Jr. "Disorders of the Pleura, Hila, and Mediastinum." Dale, D.C., and Daniel D. Federman, MD New York: WebMD Corporation, 2000 Scientific American Medicine. 15 Jan 2001 <http://www.samed.com/sam/forms/index.htm>.

Threatened Abortion
640.0

Definition

Threatened abortion is a condition in pregnancy before the twentieth week of gestation characterized by uterine bleeding and cramping while the opening of the uterus (cervix) is closed. This stage of abortion may progress to spontaneous incomplete or complete abortion.

The World Health Organization (WHO) estimates that 15% of all pregnancies progress to spontaneous abortion or miscarriage, defined as the naturally occurring delivery or loss of the products of conception before the twentieth week of pregnancy without induction or instrumentation. There are an estimated 600,000 to 800,000 miscarriages each year in the United States.

The most common reason for miscarriage is an abnormality in the developing embryo due to genetic (chromosomal) abnormalities and is the cause in approximately 80% of cases. Less commonly, low progesterone levels can cause miscarriage. Infections, maternal disease states such as diabetes mellitus and hypothyroidism, genital tract abnormalities of the cervix or uterus, pyelonephritis, drug and alcohol abuse, epilepsy, excessive smoking, environmental toxicants, and severe emotional shock or stress can all be causative factors.

Diagnosis

History: Women will report a bloody discharge from the uterus, but the blood loss is usually less than the inevitable abortion. Intermittent abdominal pain is usually not present, but when there is, it can signal the onset of contractions and a miscarriage. History should include onset of bleeding, amount of blood passed, onset of abdominal pain, and history of previous miscarriage.

Physical exam: A pelvic exam is done to check if the opening to the uterus (cervix) is open or closed, to look for evidence of other conditions that may cause bleeding, and to determine if the amniotic sac has ruptured.

Tests: A pregnancy blood test and ultrasound may be done to determine if the embryo or fetus is still present and alive. A complete blood count (CBC) and blood clotting factors are drawn to look for infection or other health conditions that can cause bleeding problems such as a deficiency in blood clotting factor XI (von Wilbrand's disease).

Treatment

Modified bedrest may be recommended. Treatment is applicable in cases where the woman has a treatable condition that is related to the cause of the threatened abortion. If a woman has a divided (septate) uterus, a surgical procedure may be done to correct it (hysteroscopic resection). Removal of a benign tumor of the uterus (leiomyoma) may be performed in the second trimester.

Maternal general diseases such as diabetes mellitus and hypothyroidism and infections should be treated appropriately. The most common cause to be treated is hormone deficiency. Progesterone is the most important hormone for the maintenance of an early human pregnancy and should be administered if deficient. Exposure to environmental toxicants should be avoided.

In individuals with repeated unexplained spontaneous abortion, the father-to-be may be evaluated and treated with white blood cell (leukocyte) immunotherapy. The mother may have antibodies in her blood (antiphospholipid antibodies) that can be associated with reproductive failure. Administration of corticosteroids with low doses of aspirin has resulted in saving the fetus in women who have antiphospholipid antibodies in their blood.

Trauma-focused interventions can help individuals better understand the event, recognize and accept the traumatic experience, and go on with their lives. A physician trained in critical incident stress debriefing (CISD) may help individuals cope. CISD involves a seven-stage process by which the individual describes the event, identifies the most traumatic aspects of it, is educated about normal reactions and coping mechanisms, clarifies ambiguities and prepares for termination of the event.

Prognosis

If there is no dilation of the cervix, the symptoms may subside and the pregnancy may go to full term. If the embryo or fetus is still alive and its attachment to the uterus has not been interrupted despite uterine bleeding and cramping, the pregnancy may continue to delivery.

The condition may progress to profuse or prolonged vaginal bleeding and the cervix may become obliterated (effaced) or opened (dilated) resulting in an inevitable abortion. An incomplete abortion may occur when the uterus is not entirely emptied of its contents. Complete abortion may also occur. This may result in acute stress disorder (ASD) as a consequence of exposure to an extremely traumatic event that arouses intense negative emotions in the person(s) involved.

Differential Diagnosis

Spotting of blood may occur from implantation of the fertilized egg and may be mistaken for a threatened abortion. An incompetent cervix that is unable to carry the products of conception without opening may be present.

Specialists

- Obstetrician

Work Restrictions / Accommodations

Heavy work and lifting may be limited during the time of threatened abortion. Frequent rest periods and light work activities may also be required.

Comorbid Conditions

Other medical conditions of the uterus (such as endometriosis) may further lengthen disability.

Complications

Bleeding may be massive (hemorrhage) and produce anemia or shock, Infection is a possible complication.

Factors Influencing Duration

Factors that might influence disability include the underlying general disease such as diabetes mellitus or hypothyroidism, or poor general health. If bleeding and cramping recurs, the individual may require additional bedrest. The individual may also have residual depression as a result of the loss of the fetus.

Length of Disability

Disability may continue for the duration of the pregnancy. Contact physician for additional information to determine disability duration.

Failure to Recover

If an individual fails to recover within the maximum duration expectancy period, the reader may wish to reference the following questions to assist in better understanding the specifics of an individual's medical case.

Regarding diagnosis:

- Does the individual have a history of miscarriage(s)?
- Were maternal causative factors treated appropriately?
- Were surgical procedures performed for uterine abnormalities prior to the pregnancy?
- When did the bleeding begin and how much blood has passed?
- Does the individual have abdominal pain?
- Did the pelvic exam done by the physician determine whether the opening to the uterus (cervix) is open or closed, if there is evidence of other conditions that may cause bleeding, and whether the amniotic sac has ruptured?
- Was a pregnancy blood test and ultrasound done to determine if the embryo or fetus is still present and living?
- Was the diagnosis confirmed by pelvic exam, ultrasound, and blood tests?

Regarding treatment:

- Has the individual remained on bed rest for an appropriate time period?
- Was a hysteroscopic resection or removal of a leiomyoma required?
- Have any underlying disorders been identified and treated, such as diabetes and hormone deficiencies?
- Is the individual exposed to environment toxins? Has the individual been removed from exposure?
- Has the individual experienced repeated, unexplained spontaneous abortions?
- Does the mother have antiphospholipid antibodies in her blood?
- Would she and the fetus benefit from corticosteroid and low-dose aspirin therapy?

Regarding prognosis:

- Was the individual able to maintain the pregnancy?
- Did she have a partial or complete abortion?
- If the abortion was complete, has psychological counseling been made available to the individual?
- Has the individual experienced a significant loss of blood?
- Is she anemic or did she go into shock from loss of blood?

References

Bowles, Stephen V., et al. "Acute and Post-traumatic Stress Disorder After Spontaneous Abortion." American Academy of Family Physicians. 15 Mar 2000. 3 Jan 2001 <http://www.aafp.org/afp/20000315/1689.html>.

Paizze G.J., et al. "Clinical and Ultrasonographic Implications of Uterine Leiomyomatosis in Pregnancy." Clinical Obstetrics and Gynecology 22 4 (1995): 293-297.

Thrombectomy
Other names / synonyms: Excision of Thrombus, Thromboendarterectomy
38.00, 38.09

Definition

A thrombectomy is a surgical procedure used to remove a blood clot (thrombus) from a vessel. The thrombus obstructs blood flow and may cause tissue death and even loss of a limb if the circulation is not restored promptly.

Thrombosis can occur in veins or arteries. However, thrombectomy in the venous system is rarely done since there is little threat of limb loss and there is a high incidence of recurrent thrombosis post operatively. Consequently, thrombectomy is generally indicated only when there is an arterial thrombosis that is causing severe tissue injury in an extremity (limb-threatening ischemia).

Blood clots that may be removed using this procedure include those arising in the large artery of the hip and thigh (iliofemoral artery) and the artery beneath the clavicle (subclavian artery). The procedure is slightly different depending upon which vessel is involved. Prior to the procedure, an arteriogram is used to determine the exact location and extent of thrombosis.

The blood clot (thrombus) may arise from damage to the inner lining of the blood vessel that results from direct trauma, inflammation or atherosclerosis. Direct trauma to the inner lining of the vessel can occur when a blood vessel is stretched or sheared during vascular interventions (i.e., arteriograms) or from blunt force or crushing injuries to an extremity. In atherosclerosis, the formation of firm, atherosclerotic plaque can cause damage to the inner lining of arteries and precipitate clot formation (thrombosis). Conditions that cause the blood to clot more easily such as dehydration or elevated red blood cell counts (polycythemia), may also be associated with thrombus formation.

Primary polycythemia (polycythemia vera) is a bone marrow disorder that occurs in some individuals over the age of 60 and is more common in men than women. Polycythemia, may also occur secondary to other conditions (secondary polycythemia), particularly those that chronically impair oxygen delivery. This includes smoking, cardiac disease, pulmonary disease, some kidney lesions or exposure to high altitude.

Reason for Procedure

This procedure is used to re-establish blood flow to large arteries that are completely blocked by the blood clot. Sudden blockage of large arteries that supply the legs or arms can cause insufficient tissue oxygenation that quickly leads to tissue death and possible loss of limbs.

Description

In a thrombectomy for iliofemoral thrombosis, local or general anesthesia is administered, and the leg is enclosed in a sterile stockinette. An incision is made near the groin. Vessels around the blood clot are clamped, the artery is partially opened, and the blood clot is partially extracted with forceps. A thrombectomy catheter with a balloon at the tip is then inserted and used to remove the remainder of the blood clot. The vessel and skin surface is closed with stitches.

In a thrombectomy for subclavian thrombosis, general anesthesia is administered. An incision is made along the clavicle. The subclavian artery is opened, and the blood clot is removed. There is generally no need for a thrombectomy catheter. Anticoagulant medications may be administered following the procedure.

Prognosis

When the thrombectomy is done promptly before there has been prolonged loss of blood flow and tissue death (necrosis), the outcome is usually good. Re-occlusion of the vessel is more likely if there are distortions in the blood vessel wall (such as aneurysms or plaque). In these cases, the artery may require a surgically placed bypass graft (femoral artery graft, subclavian artery graft).

Specialists

| • General Surgeon | • Vascular Surgeon |

Work Restrictions / Accommodations

Individuals on anticoagulation therapy need to take caution against cuts and bruises, as they tend to bleed more easily. Temporary transfer to sedentary work may be needed to reduce the risk of injury.

To avoid the risk of recurrent thrombus formation, individuals need to avoid prolonged periods of immobility such as sitting or standing. Those who have occupations that require prolonged standing or sitting (such as bank tellers or desk jobs) may need frequent breaks. Likewise, those in outdoor occupations (construction, landscaping) need to take precautions against dehydration.

Comorbid Conditions

Comorbid conditions of diabetes, atherosclerosis or bleeding disorders may impact ability to recover and further lengthen disability.

Procedure Complications

Complications include artery puncture or tearing, heart attack (from dislodged fragments that travel to the heart or lungs), occlusion of more distal arteries in the affected extremity, bleeding, infection (rare) and swelling of an extremity after the blood flow is restored.

Factors Influencing Duration

Factors that may influence the length of disability associated with this procedure include the severity of the disease, the duration of the thrombosis prior to the procedure, the location of the blood clot, and any underlying medical conditions.

Length of Disability

Individual is anticoagulated for three to six months. Duration is variable and depends on location and severity of thrombosis and complications.

Duration in Days

Job Classification	Minimum	Optimum	Maximum
Sedentary work	14	21	28
Light work	14	21	28
Medium work	28	35	42
Heavy work	91	119	182
Very Heavy work	91	119	182

References

Meeker, Margaret, and Jane Rothrock. Alexander's Care of the Patient in Surgery. St. Louis: Mosby, 1999.

Tierney, Lawrence M., Stephen J. McPhee, and Maxine A. Papadakis, eds. Current Medical Diagnosis and Treatment, 39th ed. New York: Lange Medical Books/McGraw-Hill, 2000.

Thrombocytopenia
Other names / synonyms: Thrombopenia
287.5

Definition

Thrombocytopenia refers to an abnormally low number of platelets in the blood. Platelets are blood cells, produced in the bone marrow, that help form blood clots and stop bleeding. A reduction in the number of platelets may result in bleeding, especially from the smaller blood vessels.

Thrombocytopenia is a symptom of many conditions; it is not a disease. Its causes may be grouped into three categories: decreased platelet production in the bone marrow, increased platelet destruction, and abnormal platelet pooling in the spleen.

Decreased production of platelets can occur when bone marrow activity is impaired. Certain drugs, such as ethanol or many antibiotics, and certain infections, such as HIV or infectious mononucleosis, can impair bone marrow activity and cause thrombocytopenia. Other causes of decreased production include vitamin B_{12} deficiency (pernicious anemia), folate deficiency, aplastic anemia, leukemia, and marrow infiltration (myelophthisic anemia).

Increased destruction is often related to a condition involving the immune system. Immune thrombocytopenia may be associated with certain connective tissue diseases, such as systemic lupus erythematosus (SLE), lymphoproliferative diseases, such as chronic lymphocytic leukemia, or infections, such as the tickborne infection Ehrlichiosis. Certain drugs, particularly the anticoagulant heparin, may also induce it. In immune thrombocytopenia, platelets are destroyed by antibodies created by the individual's own immune system. In posttransfusion thrombocytopenia, platelets are destroyed by antibodies following a blood transfusion.

Nonimmune conditions that increase platelet destruction include mechanical damage, such as that caused by a mechanical heart valve, and use of certain drugs that damage platelets. Thrombotic thrombocytopenic purpura is a serious nonimmune condition in which platelets clump together. It is accompanied by other abnormalities, such as hemolytic anemia and kidney dysfunction. It may be associated with infection. Hemolytic-uremic syndrome (HUS), a similar serious condition, is associated with E. coli infection. Although HUS is rare in adults, it also can cause thrombocytopenia and kidney dysfunction.

Thrombocytopenia may develop during pregnancy, particularly in the third trimester. In many cases, it is believed to be a manifestation of preeclampsia or eclampsia. An enlarged spleen (hypersplenism) can result in thrombocytopenia, sequestering up to 90% of circulating platelets. A variety of conditions may cause hypersplenism, including liver disease. In as many as 50% of cases, the cause of thrombocytopenia is never identified. This is called idiopathic thrombocytopenic purpura.

While thrombocytopenia is a universal symptom in conditions of bone marrow failure, such as aplastic anemia, it has a range of prevalence among other conditions with which it is associated. For example, its reported prevalence in pregnant women is 10%; in individuals with systemic lupus erythematosus, 15%; in individuals using the anticoagulant heparin, 10-15%; in individuals with Ehrlichiosis, 84%; and in individuals with HIV, non-AIDS, 2-90%. Thrombocytopenia is more common among women than men.

Diagnosis

History: Symptoms are dependent on the platelet count. Bleeding only becomes evident when the count drops to a certain point. Individuals usually report bruising, bleeding gums, nosebleeds, excessive bleeding from minor cuts, bloody stools, or prolonged or heavy menstrual bleeding. Headache and dizziness may indicate a risk of brain hemorrhage.

Physical exam: The individual may have small capillary hemorrhages (petechia) or larger bruises (ecchymoses) under the skin. An enlarged spleen may be felt when the physician examines the abdomen by pressing on it with the fingers (palpation).

Tests: A complete blood count (CBC) shows a decrease in the number of platelets. Immature platelets may be seen on a peripheral blood smear. Bone marrow aspiration and biopsy will confirm whether the marrow is involved. Coagulation tests to check platelet function and look for other clotting abnormalities include bleeding time, prothrombin time (PT), partial thromboplastin time (PTT), fibrinogen, and platelet aggregation studies. Additional tests will be performed as needed and may include liver function tests, platelet antibodies, and tests to identify infection such as HIV and Ehrlichiosis, and connective tissue disease, such as systemic lupus erythematosus.

Treatment

Mild to moderate thrombocytopenia may not require treatment. General caution, however, dictates that individuals with thrombocytopenia avoid invasive procedures or injury, if possible, and avoid any drug that may affect platelets, such as aspirin or other nonsteroidal anti-inflammatory drugs (NSAIDs). Treatment may be needed only when the individual has had a traumatic injury or is preparing for surgery.

In more significant thrombocytopenia, treatment is directed at the underlying cause of the thrombocytopenia. For possible drug-induced thrombocytopenia, all drugs that could reduce the numbers of platelets must be discontinued. Only medically necessary drugs should be continued. If the condition is life threatening, intravenous immune globulin should be given. If infection is present, treatment must be directed primarily at clearing the infection. Malignancy-caused thrombocytopenia is treated with appropriate chemotherapy. Removal of the spleen (splenectomy) may be beneficial if the spleen is sequestering platelets.

Immune thrombocytopenia is initially treated with immunosuppressant glucocorticoid drugs until platelet counts return to normal. At that time the glucocorticoids should be gradually tapered off. Individuals with chronic thrombocytopenia may need additional treatment cycles to maintain an adequate platelet count. Individuals with severe bleeding are hospitalized and treated with intravenous glucocorticoids plus high-dose immune globulin (immune globulin increases platelet survival time). If the bleeding is life threatening, platelet transfusions are also given. Splenectomy is beneficial for individuals who do not respond to steroid therapy or require unacceptably high doses to maintain adequate platelets. Although in immune thrombocytopenia the spleen does not sequester platelets, it does produce the antibodies that attack the platelets. Removing the spleen removes the source of the destructive antibodies.

Thrombotic thrombocytopenic purpura, severe thrombocytopenia in pregnancy, and posttransfusion thrombocytopenia are treated with plasma exchange (plasmapheresis). Immune globulin is also given when needed.

Prognosis

Many cases of thrombocytopenia resolve when the offending agent is removed. For example, thrombocytopenia caused by ethanol responds within 10 to 14 days after the removal of ethanol. Once a viral infection is cleared, the platelet count generally rises immediately. In pregnancy, thrombocytopenia resolves following delivery.

In immune thrombocytopenia, immunosuppressant glucocorticoid treatment usually reduces bleeding within one day and raises platelet counts within one to three weeks. Most individuals respond to this treatment, but many will relapse once the treatment has stopped and will require additional treatment cycles. Approximately 90% of individuals with immune thrombocytopenia develop a chronic condition and require ongoing treatment. Splenectomy will bring about partial or complete remission in 80% of individuals with immune thrombocytopenia. Thrombotic thrombocytopenic purpura has a 90% response rate to timely plasma exchange therapy.

Differential Diagnosis

Thrombocytopenia is associated with many conditions, including malignancy, connective tissue disease, particularly systemic lupus erythematosus, infection, such as HIV or Ehrlichiosis, and conditions of bone marrow failure, such as myelofibrosis and aplastic anemia. The differential diagnosis must include these conditions plus others, and also the possible use of any of many drugs associated with thrombocytopenia.

Specialists

- Emergency Medicine
- Immunologist
- Infectious Disease Physician
- Oncologist
- Rheumatologist
- Surgeon

Work Restrictions / Accommodations

Individuals who have significantly decreased platelet counts need a safe work environment, avoiding the risk of personal injury, which could trigger an acute bleed. Where indicated, protective gear, especially to the head, should be worn. Office work or sedentary work would probably be more appropriate than strenuous work involving heavy lifting or other physical exertion. The employer should be aware of the condition so that the appropriate level of care can be obtained quickly in the event of an on-the-job injury. Once the individual's platelet counts have returned to normal, no work restrictions should be needed. Time off will be needed if splenectomy or hospitalization is required.

Complementary and Alternative Therapies

Content is intended for awareness only. Treatments may or may not be effective. Scientific evidence may be lacking and some substances have potentially toxic effects. Dr. Presley Reed and the editors do not endorse the use of these therapies in the absence of consultation with a licensed medical professional.

Chinese herbal medicine -	Zhinu (ZN) -I, -II is said to reduce the number of recurrences. The mechanism of action is not known.
Splenic ultrasound -	A single therapeutic dose of ultrasound directed at the spleen is said to have been effective in immune thrombocytopenia (ITP). The spleen is a major site of clearance of antibody-coated platelets from circulation.

Comorbid Conditions

Thrombocytopenia may be associated with other blood cell diseases, such as aplastic anemia, malignancy, or myeloproliferative disorders.

Disability may also be lengthened if other risk factors for bleeding are present, such as gastrointestinal bleeding, urologic disease, and high blood pressure. Pregnancy may limit the drugs available for safe treatment.

Complications

If the individual's platelet counts drop to a dangerously low level, severe, even life-threatening, bleeding can occur, particularly inside the brain (intracranial hemorrhage). Splenectomy carries a risk of infection.

Factors Influencing Duration

Factors include the underlying cause, severity of the disease, need for and response to treatment, whether or not removal of the spleen is performed, and level of strenuous activity in daily life.

Length of Disability

Contact physician to obtain more information regarding the underlying cause.

Failure to Recover

If an individual fails to recover within the maximum duration expectancy period, the reader may wish to reference the following questions to assist in better understanding the specifics of an individual's medical case.

Regarding diagnosis:

- Does individual have an underlying condition that is causing thrombocytopenia?
- Does individual have idiopathic thrombocytopenic purpura?
- Do individual have bruising, bleeding gums or nosebleeds? Do minor cuts bleed excessively?
- Are stools bloody?
- Have menstrual cycles been prolonged or heavy?
- Any headaches or dizziness?
- On physical exam were petechia or ecchymosis found?
- Was the spleen enlarged on palpation?
- Did the individual have a CBC? Bone marrow biopsy? Coagulation studies?
- Were other diseases such as HIV, Ehrlichiosis and lupus ruled out?
- Have conditions with similar symptoms been ruled out?

Regarding treatment:

- Does the individual have mild to moderate thrombocytopenia? Is the individual avoiding drugs that may affect the platelets?
- Does the individual try to avoid injury or invasive procedures?
- Is the underlying cause of the thrombocytopenia being treated?
- Which type of thrombocytopenia does individual have? Is the treatment appropriate to the type?
- Does the individual respond appropriately to treatment?
- Have platelet transfusions been necessary?
- Has immune globulin been given?
- Did splenectomy become necessary?

Regarding prognosis:

- Is the individual's employer able to accommodate any necessary restrictions?
- Does the individual have any conditions that may affect their ability to recover? Has life-threatening bleeding occurred? Has the individual had multiple infections?

References

Carey, Charles, Hans Lee, and Keith Woeltje. Washington Manual of Medical Therapeutics, 29th ed. Philadelphia: Lippincott-Raven, 1998.

Lee, Richard, et al. Wintrobe's Clinical Hematology, 10th ed. Baltimore: Lippincott, Williams & Wilkins, 1999.

Thrombophlebitis

Other names / synonyms: Nonpuerperal Milk-Leg, Phlebitis, Phlegmasia Alba Dolens, Venous Thrombosis

451, 451.0, 451.1, 451.8, 451.82, 451.83, 451.89

Definition

Thrombophlebitis is a vein inflammation caused by a blood clot. There are several types of thrombophlebitis that can be separated into 2 main categories depending on their tissue depth: those that occur just below the surface of the skin (superficial thrombophlebitis), and those that occur in a deep vein that usually accompanies an artery (deep venous thrombosis or DVT).

Superficial thrombophlebitis may be caused by an intravenous (IV) line or as a result of trauma to the vein. Risks for superficial thrombophlebitis include an increased blood clotting tendency, infection in or near a vein, current or recent pregnancy, varicose veins, blood clots, chemical irritation, or other local irritation of the area. Prolonged sitting, standing, or immobilization may also increase the risk. Superficial thrombophlebitis may occasionally be associated with abdominal cancers (such as carcinoma of the pancreas), deep vein thrombosis, thromboangiitis obliterans, and (rarely) with pulmonary embolus.

Deep vein thrombosis mainly affects the veins in the lower leg and the thigh where a clot has formed (thrombus) in the larger veins of the lower extremities. This thrombus may interfere with circulation in the legs, and it may break off and travel through the blood stream (embolize). The embolus thus created can lodge in the brain, lungs, heart, or other area, causing severe damage to that organ. Risks include prolonged sitting, bedrest, or immobilization; recent surgery or trauma, especially hip surgery, gynecological surgery, heart surgery, or fractures; childbirth within the last 6 months; obesity; and the use of medications such as estrogen and birth control pills. Other risks include a history of malignant tumor, polycythemia vera, changes in the levels of blood clotting factors increasing tendency to clot (hypercoagulability), disseminated intravascular coagulation (DIC), and dysfibrinogenemia. DVT may be associated with, or may cause, pulmonary embolus.

In hospitalized individuals, the incidence of superficial thrombophlebitis is considerably higher than in the general population and ranges between 20-70%. The incidence of DVT is about 80 cases per 100,000 individuals annually. Venous ulceration and venous insufficiency of the lower leg, which are long-term complications of DVT, affect 0.5% of the general population; as many as 5 million people suffer from venous stasis and varying degrees of venous insufficiency. These conditions affect males more than females by a ratio of 1.2 to 1, and usually occur in individuals over the age of 40.

Diagnosis

History: Many individuals are asymptomatic. Those with symptoms may report leg pain, leg swelling (edema), and tender, warm skin over the area of the thrombosis. Individuals may also report a history of recent surgery, prolonged periods of bedrest, inactivity, trauma, and a previous clotting disorder (hypercoagulability).

Physical exam: Skin symptoms may be visible and noticeable to the touch (palpable). For example, in superficial vein thrombophlebitis, the area may appear red and feel warm with a cord-like mass apparent beneath the skin. Additionally, the individual will feel pain during palpation or compression of the affected area. Superficial vein thrombophlebitis is diagnosed solely on the basis of the physical examination. In cases of suspected deep vein thrombosis (DVT), there may be few outward symptoms. Some individuals will, however, have pain when the foot is dorsiflexed or flexed backward (positive Homén's sign).

Tests: No diagnostic procedures are generally needed for superficial thrombophlebitis. Frequent checks of pulse, blood pressure, temperature, skin condition, and circulation should be done. When DVT is suspected, a number of diagnostic procedures may be performed in order to rule out arterial occlusive disease, inflammation of a lymphatic channel (lymphangitis), infection of the subcutaneous tissue beneath the skin (cellulitis), and muscle inflammation (myositis). Tests may also confirm the site and extent of venous occlusion. These tests may include Doppler ultrasound (to identify areas of reduced or obstructed venous blood flow), extremity arteriogram, blood coagulation studies, plethysmography (to identify areas of decreased circulation; it is more sensitive in detecting deep vein thrombosis), phlebography (to confirm the diagnosis as it shows filling defects and diverted blood flow), and contrast venography.

Treatment

Most individuals are treated with medications. Analgesics and nonsteroidal anti-inflammatory drugs (NSAIDs) may be used for inflammation and pain control, anticoagulants for preventing new clot formation, and thrombolytics for dissolving an existing clot. Antibiotics may be used if an infection is present.

Elastic support stockings (and wraps) may be useful in helping reduce pain in some cases. The affected limb may be elevated to reduce swelling (edema), to reduce pain by reducing pressure on it, and to reduce the risk of further damage. Moist heat may also be applied to decrease inflammation and pain.

Surgical intervention including clot removal (thrombectomy), vein stripping, or vein bypass is rarely needed.

Prognosis

Generally the prognosis is positive as thrombophlebitis usually responds to prompt medical treatment. Complete recovery occurs within a relatively short period of time with pharmacological or surgical intervention.

Specialists

- Cardiologist
- Internist
- Vascular Surgeon

Differential Diagnosis

Other conditions that present with similar symptoms include varicose veins; arterial occlusive disease; Achilles tendonitis; arterial insufficiency; arthritis; cellulitis; lymphangitis; extrinsic compression of iliac vein secondary to tumor, hematoma, or abscess; hematoma; lymphedema; muscle or soft tissue injury; neurogenic pain; postphlebitic syndrome; prolonged immobilization or limb paralysis; ruptured Baker cyst; stress fractures or other bony lesions; asymmetric peripheral edema secondary to CHF; liver disease; renal failure; or nephrotic syndrome.

Work Restrictions / Accommodations

Work accommodations may include giving the individual an opportunity to elevate the affected area, and accommodating the need for postural positional changes (e.g., no prolonged standing or sitting). Individuals should avoid sustained periods of inactivity. In more serious cases, time off for rest and recuperation will be necessary.

Comorbid Conditions

Conditions that may impact ability to recover and may further lengthen disability include obesity, hypercoagulability, and polycythemia vera.

Complications

Surgery, stroke, heart attack (myocardial infarction), paralysis, hypertension, and infection are possible complications. A serious, potentially fatal complication that can occur is a pulmonary embolism, wherein the blood clot dislodges from its site of origin and lodges in the blood vessels of the lung.

Factors Influencing Duration

Factors that might influence the length of disability include the specific site, cause, and extent of the blockage, the treatment necessary to relieve the condition, individual response to treatment, concurrent medical conditions, the age and general health of the individual, the ability to ambulate, and the development of complications.

Length of Disability

Medical treatment. Lower extremity, superficial veins.

Duration in Days

Job Classification	Minimum	Optimum	Maximum
Sedentary work	7	14	21
Light work	7	14	21
Medium work	14	21	28
Heavy work	14	21	28
Very Heavy work	14	21	28

Medical treatment. Lower extremity, deep veins.

Duration in Days

Job Classification	Minimum	Optimum	Maximum
Sedentary work	7	14	21
Light work	7	14	21
Medium work	14	21	28
Heavy work	84	112	168
Very Heavy work	84	112	168

Surgical treatment. Ligation and stripping of varicose veins. Lower extremity, superficial veins.

Duration in Days

Job Classification	Minimum	Optimum	Maximum
Sedentary work	7	14	21
Light work	7	14	21
Medium work	14	21	28
Heavy work	21	28	35
Very Heavy work	21	28	35

Surgical treatment. Thrombectomy. Lower extremity, deep veins.

Duration in Days

Job Classification	Minimum	Optimum	Maximum
Sedentary work	14	21	28
Light work	14	21	28
Medium work	28	35	42
Heavy work	91	119	182
Very Heavy work	91	119	182

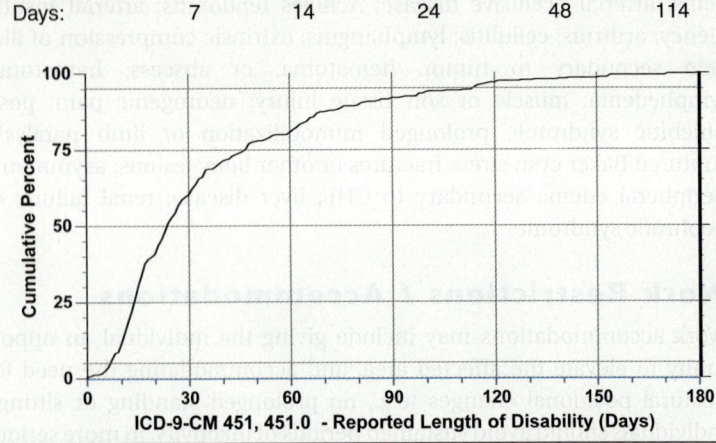

Duration Trend from Normative Data

Cases	Mean	Min	Max	No Lost Time	Over 6 Months
429	43	0	514	0.77%	2.81%

Percentile:	5th	25th	Median	75th	95th
Days:	7	14	24	48	114

ICD-9-CM 451, 451.0 - Reported Length of Disability (Days)

* Differences may exist between the expected duration tables and the normative graphs. Duration tables provide expected recovery periods based on the type of work performed by the individual. The normative graphs reflect the actual observed experience of many individuals across the spectrum of physical conditions, in a variety of industries, and with varying levels of case management.

Failure to Recover

If an individual fails to recover within the maximum duration expectancy period, the reader may wish to reference the following questions to assist in better understanding the specifics of an individual's medical case.

Regarding diagnosis:

- Does individual have superficial thrombophlebitis or deep vein thrombosis (DVT)?
- Did individual have an IV or trauma to the vein?
- Are any risk factors for superficial thrombophlebitis present such as an increased blood clotting tendency, infection in or near a vein, current or recent pregnancy, varicose veins, blood clots, chemical irritation, other local irritation of the area, prolonged sitting, standing, or immobilization?
- Does individual have carcinoma of the pancreas, deep vein thrombosis, thromboangiitis obliterans, or pulmonary embolus?
- Does individual have any risk factor's for DVT such as prolonged sitting, bed rest, or immobilization; recent surgery or trauma especially hip, gynecological, or heart surgery or fractures; childbirth within the last 6 months; obesity; and the use of medications such as estrogen and birth control pills, a history of malignant tumor, polycythemia vera, hypercoagulability, disseminated intravascular coagulation (DIC), and dysfibrinogenemia?
- Is DVT in the lower leg or thigh?
- Does individual report leg pain, edema, and tender warm skin over the area of the thrombosis?
- On physical exam for superficial thrombophlebitis, is the area red and warm with a cord-like mass apparent beneath the skin? Was palpation painful?
- On physical exam for a DVT, does individual have a positive Homén's sign?
- Were Doppler ultrasound, extremity arteriogram, blood coagulation studies, plethysmography, phlebography, and contrast venography done?
- Were conditions with similar symptoms ruled out?

Regarding treatment:

- Is individual being treated with analgesics, NSAIDs, anticoagulants, and thrombolytics? Is antibiotic therapy necessary?
- Does individual wear elastic support stockings or wraps? Use moist heat?
- Does individual elevate the affected limb?
- Was surgical intervention necessary?

Regarding prognosis:

- Can individual employer accommodate any necessary restrictions?
- Does individual have any conditions that may affect ability to recover?
- Have any complications developed such as stroke, myocardial infarction, paralysis, hypertension, infection or pulmonary embolism that may impact recovery and length of disability?

References

Schreiber, Donald, MD. "Deep Venous Thrombosis and Thrombophlebitis." eMedicine.com 01 Mar 2000. 17 March 2000 <http://www.emedicine.com/emerg/topic122.htm>.

Tierney, Lawrence M., Stephen J. McPhee, and Maxine A. Papadakis, eds. Current Medical Diagnosis and Treatment, 39th ed. New York: Lange Medical Books/McGraw-Hill, 2000.

Thymectomy
07.8

Definition

Thymectomy refers to the surgical removal of the thymus gland.

Located in the upper chest behind the breastbone, the thymus forms part of the body's defense (immune) system. Its function is to cause a type of white blood cell (lymphocytes) to become T cells. These T cells are an important part of the body's defense against viruses and other infections.

The most common indication for thymectomy is removal of a tumor in the thymus called a thymoma. Thymectomy is also used to treat myasthenia gravis, an autoimmune condition where the muscles become weak due to the individual's own antibodies attacking the neuromuscular junction. The peak incidence is age between forty and sixty. Thymectomy is performed on men and women equally.

Reason for Procedure

This procedure is used to remove a tumor (thymoma) of the thymus. Tumors of the thymus range from benign or malignant thymomas, lymphomas, and Hodgkin's granulomas.

Thymectomy is also recommended for individuals with myasthenia gravis (with or without thymoma) when medical treatment is unsuccessful. For those who are experiencing increasing side effects from drug therapy of myasthenia gravis, thymectomy provides a means of treating the condition without the use of the offending medication.

Description

Thymectomy is performed in the operating room under general anesthesia. An incision is made over the front of the chest, and the sternum is split (median sternotomy). The thymus and surrounding fatty tissue is then removed. The incision is then closed with stitches. The individual will then spend several days in the hospital recovering. Thymectomy may be followed by treatment with corticosteroid drugs.

Prognosis

Rates of complication and death are low for thymectomy, but are larger with more extensive tumors. Ten-year survival rates for individuals with thymic tumors are about 65% for noninvasive tumors, and 30% for invasive tumors. Death is usually the result of an unresectable tumor that has recurred or spread. Individuals with myasthenia gravis have about a 30% cure rate, and about 75% receive significant reduction in symptoms.

Cough and deep breathing exercises are recommended in the immediate postoperative period until the pain from the surgery has subsided, usually in 2 weeks.

Specialists

- General Surgeon
- Immunologist
- Internist
- Neurologist
- Oncologist
- Radiologist

Work Restrictions / Accommodations

Because of weakness that may persist after thymectomy, an extended work leave may be needed, or the individual may need to be transferred to a more sedentary type of work.

The incision through the sternum to reach the thymus (median sternotomy) can be a painful procedure, and may impact lung function after surgery by not allowing the individual to take a deep breath.

Comorbid Conditions

Diabetes and immune dysfunction would both impair an individual's ability to heal after a thymectomy.

Procedure Complications

The most common complications from thymectomy and median sternotomy include wound infection, postoperative bleeding, injury to nerves in the chest or neck, and infection of the mediastinum (mediastinitis)

Factors Influencing Duration

Factors influencing length of disability include presence of myasthenia gravis, age of individual, severity of symptoms at time of diagnosis, extent of tumor spread, and any complications of the surgery.

Length of Disability

Duration depends on response to treatment. Durations reflect recovery from procedure only.

Duration in Days

Job Classification	Minimum	Optimum	Maximum
Sedentary work	14	21	28
Light work	14	21	28
Medium work	28	28	56
Heavy work	42	42	84
Very Heavy work	42	70	112

References

Schwartz, Seymour, MD. Principles of Surgery. New York: McGraw-Hill, 1999.

Turley, Kevin. "Thoracic Wall, Pleura, Mediastinum, and Lung." Current Surgical Diagnosis and Treatment. Way, Lawrence Norwalk: Appleton & Lange, 1991. 307-348.

Thyroidectomy

Other names / synonyms: Partial Thyroidectomy, Subtotal Thyroidectomy, Total Thyroidectomy

06.2, 06.3, 06.31, 06.39, 06.4, 06.5, 06.6

Definition

A thyroidectomy is the partial (partial thyroidectomy) or complete (total or subtotal thyroidectomy) removal of the thyroid gland. The thyroid gland or a portion of it is cut free and removed.

The thyroid gland is responsible for normal physical growth and development in childhood, as well as maintaining normal energy production and utilization in adults.

The thyroid gland may have to be removed for a number of reasons. Benign and malignant tumors, Graves disease, toxic nodular goiter, large goiters, and thyroid nodules may be treated with thyroidectomy.

Thyroid cancer has an incidence of 40 per 100,000 individuals each year in the US. Low-dose radiation in infancy is a risk factor for developing thyroid cancer later in life. Thyroid nodules are more common in women, but a thyroid nodule in a man is more likely to be cancer.

Graves disease is 6 times more common in women and is more prevalent in young adults.

Reason for Procedure

Thyroidectomy is done to reduce (remove) a thyroid tumor that might be cancerous, to relieve breathing difficulty from an enlarged thyroid gland (goiter), or to treat hyperthyroidism, especially if the individual is pregnant or trying to become pregnant.

Thyroidectomy for known or suspected thyroid cancer involves a total thyroidectomy.

Description

A thyroidectomy may involve removing part or all of the thyroid gland (partial or total thyroidectomy). This surgical procedure is performed in the operating room under general anesthesia. A curved incision is made on the front of the neck and the thyroid gland is located. All (total) or part (lobectomy) of the thyroid gland is then removed. The neck incision is closed with stitches. The individual usually stays in the hospital for 1-2 days. A few blood tests are required after thyroidectomy to ensure proper functioning of the parathyroid glands and the remaining thyroid tissue (if any).

Prognosis

Thyroidectomy for a solitary thyroid nodule reveals cancer in about 20% of individuals. If the nodule was localized to one side of the thyroid gland, then the partial thyroidectomy was sufficient and no further surgery is likely necessary. If the location was more intermediate, or the nodule was quite large, a second surgery for completion of a total thyroidectomy may be performed.

The prognosis of a total thyroidectomy depends on the type of cancer. Papillary thyroid cancer, the most common type, has a favorable prognosis with up to 60% survival 30 years after the surgery. Undifferentiated thyroid cancer has a poor prognosis, with only a 15% survival rate at 10 years after surgery. Follicular cancer of the thyroid is intermediate in prognosis, with a survival rate of about 35% after 30 years. If there is no spread of the tumor, surgery is all that may be necessary. Spread of the tumor will require radioactive iodine treatment after surgery.

Thyroidectomy for hyperthyroidism or Graves disease usually results in a cure, although recurrence is possible and treatment with radioactive iodine may be necessary.

All individuals undergoing a total or subtotal thyroidectomy will require lifelong treatment with thyroid hormone replacement.

The individual must be careful not to engage in active sports for a few weeks after the surgery until the incision has healed.

Specialists

- Endocrinologist
- General Surgeon
- Otolaryngologist

Work Restrictions / Accommodations

Hoarseness, sore throat, or difficulty speaking may require work accommodations. If the individual has cancer, radiation treatment may be required after surgery, requiring frequent absences from work.

Comorbid Conditions

Any disease that would impair an individual's ability to heal would lengthen recovery. An example would be diabetes or an immune disorder.

Procedure Complications

Thyroidectomy is not associated with a high complication rate, although there are a few considerations. Death is rare. Injuries to the parathyroid glands and to the nerves that control the voice box are possible (recurrent laryngeal nerves). These injuries occur in less than 2% of cases. An injury to the parathyroid glands will require treatment with vitamin D and calcium, perhaps even lifelong treatment. Injury to the recurrent laryngeal nerves results in hoarseness.

Transient low functioning of the parathyroid glands (hypoparathyroidism) and hoarseness is common after thyroidectomy. This almost always resolves on its own.

Factors Influencing Duration

The underlying diagnosis for which this procedure was performed as well as the presence of complications may influence length of disability.

Length of Disability

Duration depends on partial verses complete.

Duration in Days

Job Classification	Minimum	Optimum	Maximum
Sedentary work	3	7	14
Light work	3	7	14
Medium work	7	14	21
Heavy work	7	28	42
Very Heavy work	7	28	42

References

Clark, Orlo, MD. "Thyroid and Parathyroid." Current Surgical Diagnosis and Treatment. Way, Lawrence, ed. Norwalk: Appleton & Lange, 1991. 267-285.

Schwartz, Seymour, MD. Principles of Surgery. New York: McGraw-Hill, 1999.

Thyroiditis

Other names / synonyms: Atypical Subacute Thyroiditis, Autoimmune Thyroiditis, Chronic Lymphocytic Thyroiditis, De Quervain's Thyroiditis, Giant Cell Thyroiditis, Granulomatous Thyroiditis, Hashimoto's Disease, Hashimoto's Thyroiditis, Hashitoxicosis, Hyperthyroiditis, Inflammation of the Thyroid, Lymphadenoid Goiter, Lymphocytic Thyroiditis, Painless Thyroiditis, Silent Lymphocytic Thyroiditis, Silent Thyroiditis, Struma Lymphomatosa, Subacute Granulomatous Thyroiditis, Subacute Lymphocytic Thyroiditis, Subacute Thyroiditis, Thyroadenitis

245, 245.0, 245.1, 245.2, 245.3, 245.9

Definition

Thyroiditis refers to either an acute or slowly developing inflammation of the thyroid gland. The thyroid gland is a small gland in the front of the neck, located near the Adam's apple. This gland produces hormones (thyroid hormones) that play an important role in controlling the body's metabolism. When the thyroid becomes inflamed, it can become enlarged (goiter) and overactive (hyperthyroidism), or it can shrink (atrophy) as it loses activity and function (hypothyroidism).

Thyroiditis is often characterized by a period of excessive thyroid hormone production (hyperthyroidism) followed by a period of inadequate thyroid hormone production (hypothyroidism). In some cases, thyroid function is not affected.

There are several types of thyroiditis. The most common type of chronic thyroidism is Hashimoto's disease. Hashimoto's disease is a disease in which the immune system attacks the body's own tissues (an autoimmune disease); in this case the tissues being attacked are the cells of the thyroid gland. As a result, the thyroid gland becomes unable to produce enough hormones. Hashimoto's disease is often not diagnosed until it has suppressed thyroid production, resulting in hypothyroidism. The cause of Hashimoto's thyroiditis is unknown; it can occur in men or women at any age, but is most common among middle-aged to elderly women. In fact, women are 8 times more likely than men to develop this disease, and it tends to run in families. The incidence rate is 1 in 10,000 individuals. Hashimoto's disease is associated with other autoimmune diseases such as diabetes, pernicious anemia, Addison's disease, lupus, chronic hepatitis, hypoparathyroidism, hypopituitarism, vitiligo, and Graves' disease. It is also linked to some genetic conditions including Down syndrome, Turner's syndrome, and Klinefelter's syndrome.

Another type of thyroiditis is called subacute granulomatous thyroiditis. This type of thyroiditis most often follows viral infections such as mumps, influenza, Coxsackie virus, or adenovirus. Subacute granulomatous thyroiditis is characterized by painful thyroid enlargement that can last weeks to months, fever, and a short period of hyperthyroidism followed by a short period of hypothyroidism that usually resolves completely, returning the individual to normal thyroid function. This type of thyroiditis is much less common than Hashimoto's disease, and tends to occur in localized outbreaks (epidemics) due to its association with viral infections. Risk factors for subacute granulomatous thyroiditis include being female, having a recent history of a viral infection, and the presence of other cases in the community. It occurs in young to middle-aged persons, and the incidence rate is 1 in 10,000 individuals.

In rare cases, thyroiditis can be caused by bacterial infection, exposure to radiation, or a condition called Riedel's thyroiditis, which has an unknown cause.

Silent lymphocytic thyroiditis, or painless thyroiditis, also occurs most often in women, typically during or after childbirth (postpartum). It develops when the thyroid gland becomes infiltrated with lymphocytes (a type of white blood cell), and is characterized by an enlarged thyroid gland without associated pain. After several weeks to several months of hyperthyroid symptoms, it resolves completely without permanent damage to thyroid function in about 90% of cases. The cause of silent lymphocytic thyroiditis is unknown, but it is more common in women than men, and tends to run in families; it generally occurs between 13 and 80 years of age. Other risk factors include a history of autoimmune diseases.

Diagnosis

History: Symptoms of thyroiditis will vary depending on the type present. Individuals may complain of pain and a feeling of fullness in the neck due to thyroid enlargement (goiter) and fever. Other common symptoms are actually symptoms of hypothyroidism (hoarse voice, slowed speech, puffiness of the face, swelling of the legs, joint stiffness, dry or thinning hair, constipation, intolerance to cold, unintentional weight gain, fatigue, dry coarse skin, depression) or symptoms of hyperthyroidism (profuse sweating, feeling hot, heat intolerance, restlessness, nervousness, shakiness, difficulty sleeping, tiredness, weakness, diarrhea, frequent bowel movements, bulging eyes, sensitivity to light, unintentional weight loss, increased appetite, menstrual irregularity, confusion). Individuals with subacute granulomatous thyroiditis will often complain of a sore throat although the pain is actually in the thyroid gland.

Physical exam: Exam and palpation of the neck will usually reveal an enlarged thyroid which may or may not be tender, depending on the underlying cause. Physical findings due to hypothyroidism include slow heart rate (bradycardia), cool skin, low body temperature, and sluggish reflexes. Physical findings related to hyperthyroidism include rapid heart rate (tachycardia); irregular heart beat (atrial fibrillation); warm, moist skin; rapid reflexes; and high blood pressure (hypertension).

Tests: Blood tests will reveal abnormal thyroid hormone levels. Blood tests will also show abnormal levels of certain types of blood cells in cases of subacute granulomatous thyroiditis or silent lymphocytic thyroiditis.

A radioactive iodine uptake test is useful in differentiating between the forms of thyroiditis. In this test, the individual is given a small quantity of radioactive chemical (either orally or by injection). The chemical is then absorbed by the thyroid gland whether it is healthy or diseased (depending on the disease process and the type of scan). The radioactivity emitted produces a film image of the thyroid for evaluation of abnormalities.

In Hashimoto's thyroiditis, high levels of immune cells that attack the thyroid (thyroid autoantibodies) are detected. Tests for these include: antithyroid microsomal antibody, antithyroglobulin antibody, and antimitochondrial antibody. Because these levels may also be abnormal in other thyroid conditions such as thyroid cancer or thyrotoxicosis, a small sample of tissue may be removed from the thyroid gland for microscopic examination (biopsy) to confirm the type of thyroiditis present. Other diagnostic tests to determine thyroid function are T4, T3 resin uptake, serum TSH, and T3.

Treatment

Treatment will depend on the type of thyroiditis. Treatment of Hashimoto's disease may be limited to regular observation by the physician if the gland is only slightly enlarged and there is no evidence of thyroid hormone deficiency. Treatment is focused on controlling the symptoms of hypothyroidism. Subacute granulomatous thyroiditis often resolves on its own within a few months. Analgesics and anti-inflammatory medication may be prescribed to reduce inflammation and alleviate pain. During the period when the disease is active, hyperthyroidism may need to be treated with beta-blockers, which can relieve the symptoms of rapid heart rate and excessive sweating. Silent lymphocytic thyroiditis does not require any treatment because it generally resolves on its own. However, symptoms of hyperthyroidism or hypothyroidism may require specific treatment. In the rare cases of bacterial infection, antibiotics may be prescribed.

Prognosis

The prognosis following thyroiditis varies depending on the underlying cause. Hashimoto's disease generally progresses to complete thyroid failure, and subsequent permanent hypothyroidism. However, hypothyroidism generally responds well to treatment, so these individuals are able to function normally. The other types of thyroiditis tend to resolve completely and without treatment. If treatment is indicated, these conditions generally respond well, and total resolution of symptoms is common. Symptoms can recur, but tend to resolve again.

Differential Diagnosis

Thyroiditis shares signs and symptoms with goiter, early Graves' disease, infections of the throat and upper respiratory tract, hemorrhage into a thyroid cyst, subacute systemic illness, and thyroid cancer.

Specialists

- Endocrinologist
- Internist

Work Restrictions / Accommodations

No work restrictions or accommodations should be necessary.

Comorbid Conditions

Individuals with a suppressed or inadequate immune system will have a longer recovery period.

Complications

Thyroiditis is often complicated by hypothyroidism and/or hyperthyroidism.

Factors Influencing Duration

Length of disability may be influenced by the form of thyroiditis, the severity of symptoms, and the individual's response to treatment.

Length of Disability

Duration depends on the type of thyroiditis, symptoms and thyroid function. Hashimoto's disease is progressive and will result in permanent hypothyroidism, which is generally responsive to therapy.

Medical treatment.

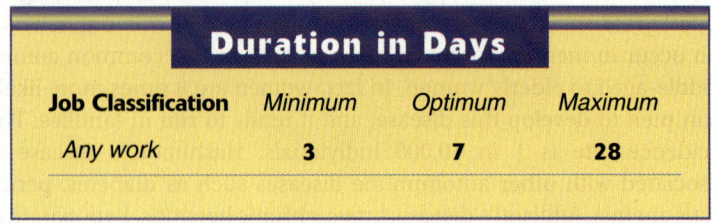

Duration in Days			
Job Classification	Minimum	Optimum	Maximum
Any work	3	7	28

Failure to Recover

If an individual fails to recover within the maximum duration expectancy period, the reader may wish to reference the following questions to assist in better understanding the specifics of an individual's medical case.

Regarding diagnosis:

- Has individual's thyroid gland become enlarged and hyperactive? Atrophied and hypoactive?
- Does individual have any other autoimmune diseases? Does individual have any genetic conditions such as Down syndrome?
- Has individual recently had a baby?
- Has individual recently had a viral illness? A bacterial infection?
- Was there an exposure to radiation or does individual have a condition called Riedel's thyroiditis?
- Does individual complain of pain and a feeling of fullness in the neck and fever? Does individual have a sore throat, hoarse voice, slowed speech, puffy face, swelling of the legs, joint stiffness, dry or thinning hair, constipation, intolerance to heat or cold, unintentional weight gain or loss, fatigue, dry coarse skin, depression, profuse sweating, feeling hot, restlessness, nervousness, shakiness, insomnia, weakness, diarrhea, bulging eyes, sensitivity to light, increased appetite, menstrual irregularity, or confusion?
- On exam, was the thyroid enlarged? Was it tender?
- What was individual's pulse rate? Body temperature? Blood pressure? Reflexes? Was the skin cool or moist?
- Has individual had thyroid function testing including antibodies? Was a radioactive iodine uptake test done? Was a biopsy performed?
- Have conditions with similar symptoms been ruled out?

Regarding treatment:

- Were medications prescribed? If so, is individual compliant with the dosing and usage instructions?

Regarding prognosis:

- Does individual have any conditions that could affect recovery?
- Has individual's thyroiditis been complicated by hypothyroidism and/or hyperthyroidism?

References

Levy, Richard. "Thyroiditis." Griffith's 5-minute Clinical Consult. Dambro, Mark, ed. Philadelphia: Lippincott, Williams & Wilkins, 2000. 1078-1079.

Tics

Other names / synonyms: Chronic Motor Tic Disorder, Chronic Vocal Tic Disorder, Habit Spasm, Tic Disorder, Transient Tic Disorder

307.2, 307.20, 307.23

Definition

A tic is a sudden, rapid, recurrent, nonrhythmic, stereotyped motor movement or vocalization that may be simple and involve only a few muscle groups or complex and involve multiple muscle groups. Many individuals report a sensation of rising tension or a sensation in a part of the body that precedes the motor or vocal tic, and a feeling of relief or tension reduction following the involuntary movement. Although tics are experienced as irresistible, they can be suppressed for varying lengths of time. An individual may feel the need to perform a complex tic until tension is relieved.

Tics occur in bouts of varying frequencies, generally decrease or disappear during sleep, and can change in location, number, frequency, and duration over time. The movements may be simple and resemble shock-like contractions of muscles or muscle groups (myoclonic jerks). More often tics consist of complex movements characterized by head shaking, eye blinking, sniffing, arm waving, touching parts of the body, assuming and holding unusual positions, and cursing or making obscene gestures. In addition to motor tics, vocal tics may also be present such as barking, throat clearing, squealing, repetition of one's own sounds or the sounds of others (echolalia), and explosive, involuntary cursing (coprolalia).

Tics often develop in childhood but also appear in adulthood. Vulnerability to tic disorders is transmitted within families and appears genetic. The specific gene(s) involved are those that affect the ability of the brain to break down chemicals (neurotransmitters) used by nerve cells to communicate with each other, especially the neurotransmitters dopamine, serotonin, and norepinephrine. Not everyone who inherits the genetic vulnerability expresses symptoms. The precise type or severity of tic may be different from one generation to another and can be modified by nongenetic factors. In some cases, tics may follow strep throat, which suggests that autoimmune factors may be involved.

Tics may occur alone or as part of Tourette's syndrome, an inherited neurological disorder characterized by tics and often associated with attention-deficit/hyperactive disorder (ADHD), obsessive-compulsive disorder, or tics. The symptoms of Tourette's syndrome usually appear before age 18. It can affect all ethnic groups and is 3 to 4 times more common in men than women. Approximately 100,000 Americans have full-blown Tourette's syndrome and up to 1 in 200 have partial symptoms such as chronic multiple tics.

Diagnosis

History: A diagnosis is based on criteria listed in the DSM-IV-TR (Diagnostic and Statistical Manual of Mental Disorders, 4th Edition, Text Revision, published by the American Psychiatric Association). The individual may complain of involuntary movements or vocalization and feeling compelled to make such movements or vocalizations in order to relieve perceived tension. These behaviors can be voluntarily suppressed for brief intervals. Transient tic disorder includes motor and/or vocal tics lasting for at least 4 weeks but for no longer than 12 consecutive months. Chronic motor or vocal tic disorder must have duration over 12 months. Tourette's syndrome lasts over 12 months and is further characterized by multiple motor tics and at least one vocal tic during the history of the disorder. Tic disorder cannot be diagnosed if the tics are due to direct physiological effects of a substance such as a stimulant or to a general medical condition such as Huntington's disease.

Physical exam: The exam includes observing the involuntary movements. Simple tics may include head shaking, eye blinking, sniffing, or arm waving. Complex tics may include touching parts of the body, assuming and holding unusual positions, hair twisting, or making obscene gestures. Vocal tics may also be present such as barking, throat clearing, squealing, repetition of one's own sounds (palilalia) or the sounds of others (echolalia), and explosive, involuntary cursing (coprolalia).

Tests: Tests may include head MRI or CT, electroencephalogram (EEG), or blood tests to rule out other conditions possibly confused with tics. However, diagnosis of tics or Tourette's syndrome is primarily on the basis of history and observation of abnormal movements. SPECT brain scan is a research tool that can show abnormal blood flow in the caudate nucleus, a part of the brain involved in controlling movement.

Treatment

When tics are mild and not socially disabling, no treatment is required. Neuroleptic drugs in small doses help reduce the frequency and severity of tics although both short- and long-term side effects may occur. The blood pressure medication clonidine is more effective in reducing motor tics than vocal tics. Relief of nervous tension by sedative or tranquilizing drugs and psychotherapy may be helpful. If the individual also has obsessive-compulsive disorder (common among those with tic disorders), cognitive-behavior therapy may be helpful. Group therapy could also be a useful and cost-effective way to provide cognitive behavioral treatment.

Prognosis

There is no cure for Tourette's syndrome but many individuals with this condition or tic disorder show improvement when they get older. Tics tend to decrease with age, however, associated neuropsychiatric disorders such as depression, panic attacks, mood swings, and antisocial behavior may increase. The primary goal of treatment is not the complete elimination of tics but rather suppression of tics to the point where the individual can function normally. Even without treatment, symptoms can go into remission and then recur but with treatment, many individuals can experience significant reductions in symptoms.

Differential Diagnosis

Drug-induced tardive dyskinesia, tic douloureux, essential myoclonus, chorea, tremor, or partial seizures may also be associated with involuntary movements. Individuals with autism or mental retardation may repeatedly bang their head, rock, or engage in other stereotyped movements, but intelligence is typically not affected by tic disorder or Tourette's syndrome. Schizophrenics may appear to have motor or vocal tics as they respond to vocal hallucinations and is usually not difficult to distinguish from tic disorder.

Specialists

- Advanced Practice Registered Nurse
- Licensed Clinical Social Worker
- Neurologist
- Occupational Therapist
- Psychiatrist
- Psychologist

Work Restrictions / Accommodations

Time-limited restrictions and work accommodations are necessary only infrequently, for the most serious cases. In these instances, time-limited restrictions and work accommodations should be individually determined based on the characteristics of the individual's response to the disorder, the functional requirements of the job and work environment, and the flexibility of the job and work site. The purpose of the restrictions/accommodations is to help maintain the worker's capacity to remain at the workplace without a work disruption or to promote timely and safe transition back to full work productivity. Depending on the type and severity of tic, it may not be safe for individuals with tics to drive, operate heavy machinery, or work at heights.

Comorbid Conditions

Substance abuse, ADHD, obsessive-compulsive disorder, or other psychiatric or neurologic disorders may lengthen disability.

Complications

Stressful situations can aggravate tics. Many individuals with tic disorder are also diagnosed with obsessive-compulsive disorder. Those with Tourette's syndrome may also have learning or sleep disorders. About half of those with Tourette's syndrome have a coexisting obsessive-compulsive disorder, however, only 5% of individuals with obsessive-compulsive disorders have Tourette's syndrome. Severe tics may lead to reactive depression, social withdrawal, or accidental self-injury.

Factors Influencing Duration

The severity of the disorder, effectiveness of treatment, and interference with job requirements influence the length of disability. Medications used to treat tics or ADHD can have side effects that may lengthen disability.

Length of Disability

Duration depends on response to medications and psychotherapy and any other psychiatric disorders. In some individuals with childhood onset, symptoms may disappear by early adulthood while in others the symptoms worsen.

In most cases, no disability is expected.

Duration in Days

Job Classification	Minimum	Optimum	Maximum
Any work	0	1	7

Failure to Recover

If an individual fails to recover within the maximum duration expectancy period, the reader may wish to reference the following questions to assist in better understanding the specifics of an individual's medical case.

Regarding diagnosis:

- Was a diagnosis of tics confirmed?
- Have conditions with similar symptoms been ruled out?
- Does the individual have a coexisting condition that may impact recovery?
- Do stressful situations aggravate tics?

Regarding treatment:

- Would neuroleptic or other medications be beneficial? If not effective, should dosage be modified? Do side effects prevent individual from using or benefiting from that particular medication?
- Does the individual also have obsessive-compulsive disorder?
- Would the individual benefit from more frequent cognitive-behavioral encounters or the addition of group therapy?

Regarding prognosis:

- Do symptoms persist despite treatment?
- Are coexisting disorders being effectively addressed?
- Is the individual participating in appropriate cognitive-behavioral or group therapy?
- Would the individual benefit from evaluation by a neurologist?
- Can the individual continue in present position under appropriate work modifications and accommodations?

References

Evidente, V.G. "Is it a Tic or Tourette's?" Postgraduate Medicine 108 5 (2000): 175-182.

Hall, Laura Lee. "Making the ADA Work for People with Psychiatric Disabilities." Mental Disorder, Work Disability, and the Law. Bonnie, Richard J., and John Monahan, eds. Chicago: The University of Chicago Press, 1997. 241-280.

Tinea

Other names / synonyms: Athlete's Foot, Dermatomycosis, Dermatophytosis, Epidermophytosis, Jock Itch, Microsporosis, Pityriasis Versicolor, Ringworm, Trichophytosis

110, 110.0, 110.1, 110.2, 110.3, 110.4, 110.5, 110.6, 110.8, 110.9, 111, 111.8, 111.9

Definition

Tinea is an infection of skin, hair, and nails caused by a group of fungi (yeasts) called dermatophytes. The body normally hosts a variety of microorganisms including bacteria and mold-like and yeast-like fungi. Some microorganisms are useful to the body while others can multiply rapidly forming infections. Although tinea is the general term for this group of infections, specific names are assigned according to specific sites of infection.

Infection of the scalp is called tinea capitis; infection of the skin under the beard, tinea barbae; infection of general body skin, tinea corporis; infection of the groin, tinea cruris (jock itch); infection of the hands, tinea manuum; infection of the feet, tinea pedis (athlete's foot); infection of the nails, tinea unguium; and infections of the chest, shoulders and back, tinea versicolor.

A certain type of tinea is sometimes called ringworm. Despite the image the term ringworm conveys, no worms or parasites are involved in the infection. The name is derived from the raised circular rash characteristic of that particular tinea infection.

The infections thrive in warm, moist areas. Susceptibility is increased through friction, poor hygiene, prolonged moist skin, and minor skin or nail injuries. It is highly contagious and can be spread by skin-to-skin contact with an infected individual or animal. Tinea is also spread by contact with a contaminated object such as shared towels, shoes, or socks, or prolonged exposure to warm, moist surfaces such as in showers or around swimming pools.

Up to 20% of individuals has a tinea infection sometime during their lives. Tinea barbae (beard) primarily affects men who work with animals. People in hot, humid climates have a greater incidence of tinea corporis (general body skin). Tinea pedis (feet) is the most common tinea infection. It primarily affects men between the ages of 20 and 40 and is associated with sweating, warmth, and tight shoes. Tinea cruris (groin) also primarily affects men. Tinea unguium (nails) affects toenails more often than fingernails. It is associated with diabetes, older age, poor circulation, poorly fitted shoes, and involvement in sports activities. Tinea versicolor is spread by intimate contact or through contaminated towels.

Diagnosis

History: The individual has a history of a red, slightly raised, scaly rash with an elevated border that is circular in some cases. The most common location is between the toes especially for males (athlete's foot). It is also reported in the beard area, the groin area excluding the scrotum or penis (jock itch), under the fingernails or toenails, and on the trunk and shoulders. The rash can be extremely itchy.

Physical exam: The exam reveals the scaly characteristic rash on one or more parts of the body including the scalp, groin, nails, feet, hands, general body skin, and the skin under the beard. As the fungus grows outward, the central area heals and can leave a red ring where the infection is active. Tinea versicolor shows up as scaly and bumpy and can make dark skin appear lighter and light skin appear brownish.

On the skin, the patches grow to about an inch in diameter. Under a beard, an itchy scaly rash may develop. Infections of the groin often show concentric rings. On the feet, dry scaling is apparent. Cracking of the skin between the toes and on the arch of the foot may develop. Nails of the toes or fingers may become red, swollen, and painful. A nonspecific dermatitis may develop at other sites on the hands or feet. Tinea versicolor appears in scaly brownish or white patches. Uncommonly, tinea skin rashes may blister, break open, ooze, and become crusty.

Tests: Diagnosis is primarily based on the appearance of the skin. Identification of the yeast in microscopic examination of skin scrapings using potassium hydroxide (KOH) confirms the diagnosis. Fungal cultures are not routinely performed unless the diagnosis remains in question or the specific identification of yeast is needed in order to choose a drug.

Treatment

Tinea infections of the scalp, the skin under the beard, and nails are treated with an oral antifungal drug, as is infection of the general body skin (tinea corporis). If only one or two patches of rash are present, a topical over-the-counter antifungal cream may be used. Tinea infections of the groin (jock itch), feet (athlete's foot), and hands are also treated with over-the-counter antifungal cream. Topical steroid creams may be used to ease itching. Selenium shampoo may be used for the scalp.

Infected skin should be kept clean and dry. Talcum or medicated powders may be used. Damp compresses help clean blistered or oozing lesions. Because tinea is highly contagious, any clothing, towels, or linen coming in contact with infected skin should be changed and cleaned frequently.

Some oral antifungal drugs must be taken with a fatty meal. Other drugs need stomach acid in order to be absorbed so individuals taking this type of drug should not take antacids, proton pump inhibitors, or histamine H2-receptor blockers.

Prognosis

Without treatment, tinea infection is chronic. With treatment using antifungal drugs, the prognosis for tinea infection is excellent. Cosmetic changes may develop if the infection is not treated immediately, but many of these effects are temporary.

Differential Diagnosis

Viral, bacterial, or Candida infections may resemble a more severe tinea infection. Noninfectious diseases that resemble tinea include psoriasis, seborrhea dermatitis, alopecia, eczema, and contact dermatitis.

Specialists

- Dermatologist
- Infectious Disease Physician
- Internist
- Primary Care Provider

Work Restrictions / Accommodations

Severe infections involving the skin of the hands or feet may require work restrictions until the skin heals. Accommodations may be required if severe foot or hand infections limit the ability of the individual to stand for extended periods of time or to operate machinery. Healthcare workers must take precautions to prevent the spread of infection when the hands are infected.

Complementary and Alternative Therapies

Content is intended for awareness only. Treatments may or may not be effective. Scientific evidence may be lacking and some substances have potentially toxic effects. Dr. Presley Reed and the editors do not endorse the use of these therapies in the absence of consultation with a licensed medical professional.

Hydrotherapy - Soaking area in warm salt water for 5 to 10 minutes may help eliminate the fungus. It may also soften the skin, and may provide better penetration of antifungal medication.

Comorbid Conditions

Secondary bacterial infections such as infection with streptococci or staphylococci may lengthen disability.

Complications

Left untreated, tinea may cause allergic dermatitis to develop. It may also cause hair loss and extensive cracking or eroding of the skin between toes and fingers. Secondary bacterial infections can develop in cracked skin or in hair follicles.

Factors Influencing Duration

Length of disability is influenced by the severity and length of time the infection is present. If the infection occurs on the feet or hands or if skin erosion has occurred, disability may extend until the skin heals, sometimes several weeks.

Length of Disability

No disability is expected.

Failure to Recover

If an individual fails to recover within the maximum duration expectancy period, the reader may wish to reference the following questions to assist in better understanding the specifics of an individual's medical case.

Regarding diagnosis:

- Was diagnosis of tinea confirmed through microscopic examination of skin scrapings using potassium hydroxide (KOH)? Were conditions such as, viral, bacterial, Candida infections, psoriasis, seborrhea dermatitis, alopecia, eczema, and contact dermatitis, ruled out?
- What type of tinea infection does the individual have? On the feet, hands, groin, or under beard?

Regarding treatment:

- Has appropriate antifungal medicine (oral or topical) been used?
- Did individual follow special instructions when taking an oral antifungal drug?

Regarding prognosis:

- Did individual seek prompt treatment?
- Has individual been compliant in prescribed medication regimen?
- Have appropriate environmental or lifestyle changes been made to reduce the likelihood of reinfection? For example, does the individual share towels or shoes? Walk barefoot in public showers or pool areas?
- Has individual experienced any complications such as, allergic dermatitis, hair loss, extensive cracking or eroding of the skin between toes and fingers, secondary bacterial infections of the skin or hair follicles?
- Does individual have an underlying condition that may impact recovery?

References

Chin, James. Control of Communicable Diseases Manual, 17th ed. Washington, DC: American Public Health Association, 2000.

Noble, Sara, Robert Forbes, and Pamela Stamm. "Diagnosis and Management of Common Tinea Infections." American Family Physician 58 1 (1998): 163-174.

Tinnitus

Other names / synonyms: Ringing in the Ears, Tinnitus Aurium
388.3, 388.30, 388.32

Definition

Tinnitus is an annoying sensation of noise in the ear or head when no external sound is actually present. Tinnitus aurium literally means ringing in the ears and is usually associated with hearing loss.

The two types of tinnitus are objective (less common) and subjective (most common). If physicians and others can also hear noise in the affected individual's ear or if the sounds pound or throb (pulsate) in the individual's ear, the condition is called objective tinnitus. If only the affected individual can hear the sounds, the condition is called subjective tinnitus.

Causes of objective tinnitus include abnormalities in the blood vessels within the brain or in front of the ear (arteriovenous malformation or glomus jugulare tumor), spasms of the muscles within the middle ear (stapedius muscle and tensor tympani muscle), temporomandibular joint syndrome (TMJ), and certain dysfunctions of the auditory tube that connects the middle ear with the back of the throat (eustachian tube).

Causes of subjective tinnitus include aging (presbycusis), exposure to loud environmental noise over a period of time or during one extreme incident (noise trauma), stiffening of the middle ear bones (otosclerosis), balance disorders of the inner ear (Ménière's syndrome and labyrinthitis), inflammation and infection of the middle ear (otitis media and mastoiditis), wax or dirt build-up in the ear canal, tumors of the nerves involved in hearing (acoustic neuromas), exposure to drugs such as aspirin that may damage the hearing mechanism (ototoxic drugs), metabolic dysfunction (hyper- or hypothyroidism, hyperlipidemia, zinc deficiency, or vitamin A and/or B deficiency), high blood pressure (hypertension) or high cholesterol and other cardiovascular diseases, skull fracture or closed head trauma, whiplash injury, brain infection (meningitis), multiple sclerosis, Lyme psychological conditions (depression, anxiety), and possibly excessive use of caffeine or other food substances such as aspartame.

Persistent tinnitus can interfere with an individual's ability to perform usual daily activities and can prevent individuals from getting enough sleep. Tinnitus can cause considerable psychological distress and can be incapacitating for some individuals.

Although occasional periods of high-pitched tinnitus lasting several minutes are common in normal-hearing individuals, it is estimated that 1 of every 5 individuals experience some degree of tinnitus and 36 million individuals in the US experience persistent tinnitus that is annoying and bothersome. Nine million individuals are affected so severely they cannot live normal lives. Tinnitus is most prevalent between the ages of 40 and 70, affecting women and men equally. Seventy-five percent of individuals with tinnitus have some degree of permanent damage to the hearing mechanism in the inner ear (sensorineural hearing loss). In a database of over 1,500 individuals with tinnitus, 43% had no known cause and 24% of cases were due to noise exposure.

Diagnosis

History: The individual with tinnitus relates a history of hearing noises not actually present (ringing, buzzing, roaring, clicking, chirping, or hissing) in one or both ears. These noises can be high-pitched or low-pitched, intermittent or constant, with one tone or many tones. Seventy-five percent of individuals with tinnitus report some degree of hearing loss. Thirty-five percent of individuals with tinnitus report feeling dizzy part of the time and some all of the time.

Upon questioning, individuals with tinnitus may relate a history of ear infections or balance disorders, previous ear surgery, exposure to excessive noise, high blood pressure, meningitis, head trauma, a whiplash injury, or depression before and/or since the onset of tinnitus. Some individuals may report sudden onset of tinnitus after taking certain prescription or over-the-counter drugs. An understanding of the individual's work and living environments and activities is necessary to determine exposure to noise trauma.

Physical exam: A thorough medical evaluation is conducted including blood pressure recordings from both arms. Careful assessment of the individual's general mood may reveal signs of depression or anxiety. Pre-existing depression makes it more difficult for an individual to cope with tinnitus, and in some instances, the stress of living with tinnitus can trigger depression. Examination of the ear through an otoscope or microscope may reveal signs of current or treated ear disease.

Tests: Audiometric evaluation (air, bone, and speech discrimination) is performed to identify hearing loss and other diseases and conditions of the hearing mechanism. Brain stem auditory evoked response (BAER) helps evaluate the auditory nerve that may be affected in structural causes of tinnitus associated with sensorineural hearing loss. If a clear-cut diagnosis of ear disease or sensorineural hearing loss cannot be made, other tests and consultations may be ordered to rule out underlying cardiovascular, metabolic, neurological, pharmacological, dental, and psychological abnormalities that might be causing tinnitus. Brain MRI, CT focused on the middle ear, or a type of x-ray called a tomogram of the ear canal may reveal structural causes of tinnitus.

Treatment

Treatment of tinnitus focuses first on medically or surgically treating the underlying cause of the condition including treating depression with nonototoxic antidepressants, antianxiety drugs, and muscle relaxants or psychotherapy, if necessary. Medications taken by the individual are re-evaluated and ototoxic drugs are avoided, if possible (aspirin compounds, aminoglycoside antibiotics, nonsteroidal anti-inflammatory drugs, and heterocycline antidepressants). Surgery may be needed for tinnitus caused by acoustic neuromas, vascular abnormalities, and TMJ syndrome. If the cause of tinnitus cannot be found and/or treated, the focus of treatment changes to helping the individual stop the progression of tinnitus as much as possible and learning how to cope with the condition.

The individual should be instructed to avoid caffeine-containing beverages and food. Excessive noise should be avoided with the use of ear protection, if necessary. The individual is taught to use masking techniques at home and work. Masking is the provision of a low-level noise to block out or mask head noise heard by the individual. This can be accomplished by playing soft music or a tape of nature sounds while resting or sleeping, providing white noise in the workplace, using a hearing aid to amplify sound from the outside and overcome head noise, and wearing a special tinnitus instrument that is a combination hearing aid and tinnitus masker for individuals with both hearing loss and tinnitus.

Prognosis

In many instances, tinnitus resists all types of therapy. Generally speaking, 25% of individuals with tinnitus improve significantly, 50% improve to some degree, and 25% remain unchanged. In some cases, tinnitus may progress in severity as the underlying disease progresses. Improvement usually results from the successful reversal of underlying hearing or medical disorders or the individual's successful use of antidepressants, masking techniques, or special tinnitus instruments. The sensori-neural hearing loss associated with tinnitus may be permanent and irreversible.

Differential Diagnosis

Differential diagnosis for tinnitus includes abnormalities in the blood vessels within the brain or in front of the ear (arteriovenous malformation, arteriovenous shunt, intracranial aneurysm, glomus tumor, or occlusive carotid artery disease), muscle spasms within the middle ear (stapedius muscle and tensor tympani muscle), certain dysfunctions of the auditory tube that connects the middle ear with the back of the throat (eustachian tube), presbycusis, noise trauma, otosclerosis, Ménière's syndrome, labyrinthitis, otitis media, mastoiditis; ototoxic drugs; hyper- or hypothyroidism; hyperlipidemia; zinc deficiency; vitamin A and/or B deficiency, hypertension and other cardiovascular diseases, skull fracture or closed head trauma, whiplash injury, meningitis, multiple sclerosis, TMJ syndrome, and depression and anxiety.

Specialists

- Neurologist
- Otolaryngologist

Rehabilitation

Biofeedback can be useful for individuals whose tinnitus appears related to emotional stress, anxiety, or hysteria. Through visual or auditory signals, the individual learns to relax and exert some degree of control over the autonomic nervous system. This can lower blood pressure, pulse rate, and relax tense muscles.

Physical therapy may be required for individuals with balance disorders. Individuals with persistent balance disorders may benefit from vestibular rehabilitation. This is an exercise program designed to take advantage of the brain's tendency to eventually adapt (habituate) to the repetition of a specific stimulus causing an individual's vertigo.

Individuals visit the physical therapist or occupational therapist during an initial period of and also exercise daily at home. Adaptation may take days or months and requires that individuals be willing to move around despite sensations of imbalance or vertigo (a sensation of rotation or movement of themselves or their surroundings). Although sitting or lying with the head perfectly still may feel more comfortable, this immobility can prolong or even prevent the adaptation process and should be avoided.

Traditional physical therapy addresses the secondary symptoms associated with the inactivity accompanying persistent balance disorders such as decreased strength, loss of range of motion, and increased tension particularly in the cervical and shoulder region that can lead to muscle fatigue and headaches.

Work Restrictions / Accommodations

Individuals with tinnitus must avoid working in excessively noisy environments that can cause additional sensori-neural hearing loss and may need ear protection devices. Since many individuals with tinnitus experience some difficulty with balance, work restrictions and accommodations may be required to protect them and their co-workers (e.g., restrictions on use of certain equipment or working at heights). Accommodations in the phone system may be required for individuals with significant hearing loss. Provision of white noise in the individual's work area may help block out the inner noises.

Complementary and Alternative Therapies

Content is intended for awareness only. Treatments may or may not be effective. Scientific evidence may be lacking and some substances have potentially toxic effects. Dr. Presley Reed and the editors do not endorse the use of these therapies in the absence of consultation with a licensed medical professional.

Gingko biloba -	May help improve hearing loss. In hearing loss associated with aging, 35% of individuals had improvement in tinnitus within 70 days.
Lecithin -	May improve blood flow.
Niacin -	May act as a vasodilator.
Zinc -	May be helpful in cases of tinnitus related to zinc deficiency.

Comorbid Conditions

Comorbid conditions that influence length of disability for individuals with tinnitus include chronic pulmonary or cardiovascular diseases, which increase an individual's risk during surgical procedures that require sedation or a general anesthetic, and diseases and conditions that increase the likelihood of surgical wound infection such as obesity, AIDS, and diabetes.

Complications

Tinnitus itself is not associated with complications although continuing to work or live with excessive environmental noise (i.e., loud music, machinery, tools, and equipment) will most likely increase the degree of sensori-neural hearing loss and, in turn, increase the severity of tinnitus. The frustration of living with tinnitus may bring on or worsen depression or anxiety and individual may have difficulty concentrating.

Factors Influencing Duration

Factors influencing length of disability for tinnitus include the general health and fitness of the individual before onset of the condition; evidence of pre-existing diseases that might interfere with the healing process such as diabetes, HIV/AIDS, or leukemia; individual's general ability to heal; and compliance with a treatment plan. Other factors may be associated with the many diseases and conditions that can cause tinnitus.

Length of Disability

No disability expected, unless job requires auditory discrimination. Length of disability depends on the severity of the individual's tinnitus, strength of the individual's coping mechanisms, degree to which the workplace can be modified to accommodate the individual's needs, response to rehabilitation, and success of medical or surgical treatment of the underlying cause of the tinnitus.

Duration in Days

Job Classification	Minimum	Optimum	Maximum
Any work	0	0	1

Failure to Recover

If an individual fails to recover within the maximum duration expectancy period, the reader may wish to reference the following questions to assist in better understanding the specifics of an individual's medical case.

Regarding diagnosis:

- Does individual report ringing, buzzing, roaring, clicking, chirping, or hissing in one or both ears?
- Does individual have arteriovenous malformation, glomus jugulare tumor, stapedius muscle, tensor tympani muscle spasms, TMJ syndrome, or eustachian tube dysfunction?
- Has individual had exposure to loud environmental noise over a period of time or noise trauma?
- Does individual have otosclerosis, Ménière's syndrome, labyrinthitis, otitis media, mastoiditis, wax or dirt build-up in the ear canal, acoustic neuromas, exposure to ototoxic drugs, hyper- or hypothyroidism, hyperlipidemia, zinc deficiency, vitamin A and/or B deficiency, hypertension, high cholesterol, other cardiovascular diseases, skull fracture, closed head trauma, whiplash injury, meningitis, multiple sclerosis, Lyme, depression, anxiety, and possibly excessive use of caffeine or other food substances such as aspartame?
- Does individual's tinnitus interfere with daily activities or sleep?
- Has the tinnitus caused psychological distress for individual? Is it incapacitating?
- On exam, is there evidence of current or treated ear disease?
- Does individual appear depressed?
- Was blood pressure measured in both arms? Was a complete audiometric evaluation done? Has individual had a brain stem auditory evoked response (BAER)? Has individual had a brain MRI, CT focused on the middle ear, or a tomogram of the ear canal?
- Have conditions with similar symptoms been ruled out?

Regarding treatment:

- What is the underlying cause of individual's tinnitus? Is it being treated?
- Is surgery indicated? Is individual on appropriate medications?
- If necessary, is individual seeing an appropriate mental health professional?
- Has individual been instructed to avoid caffeine-containing beverages and food?
- Does individual wear hearing protection when around any noise?
- Does individual use any masking devices?

Regarding prognosis:

- Is individual active in rehabilitation? Is a home exercise program in place?
- Can individual's employer accommodate any necessary restrictions?
- Does individual have any conditions that may affect ability to recover?

References

Holgers, K.M., A. Axelsson, and I. Pringle. "Gingko Biloba Extract for the Treatment of Tinnitus." Audiology 33 2 (1994): 85-92.

Johnson, Robert M., Robert Brummett, and Alexander Schleuning. "Use of Alprazolam for Relief of Tinnitus: A Double-blind Study." Archives of Otolaryngology - Head and Neck Surgery 119 (1993): 842-845.

Tierney, Lawrence, Stephen McPhee, and Maxine Papadakis. Current Medical Diagnosis and Treatment. New York: McGraw-Hill, 2000.

Tinnitus FAQ. Bixby Organization. 01 Jan 2000. 25 Nov 2000 <http://www.bixby.org/faq/tinnitus/discover.html>.

Toenail, Ingrown
703.0

Definition

An ingrown toenail develops when the edge of a toenail grows into the surrounding skin (the nail fold) of the toe. While some cases of ingrown toenail will not be bothersome, many cases result in inflammation and significant pain.

The most common cause of ingrown toenail is improper trimming of the toenails. Toenails should be trimmed straight across, using specifically designed toenail clippers, and should be just slightly longer than the edge of the toe. Common mistakes include trimming the nails too short and rounding the edges of the nails. Poorly fitting shoes that crowd or place pressure on the toes can also lead to ingrown toenails. Less commonly, ingrown toenails develop when the skin of the nail-fold grows unusually fast and engulfs the edge of the nail. The great toe is usually affected, but any toenail can be come ingrown.

Approximately 5% of the population will develop ingrown toenails each year. Women are affected more often than men because women often wear shoes with high heels and narrow, pointed toes. Neither age nor race contributes to the incidence of this condition. The condition may become serious in those who have diabetes mellitus.

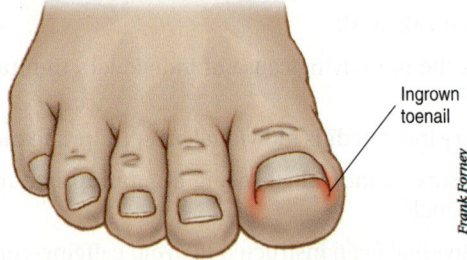

Ingrown toenail

Frank Forney

Diagnosis

History: In mild cases, the individual may not experience symptoms that would prompt a visit to the physician. These cases are often diagnosed incidentally when the individual is examined for some other reason. More commonly, however, the individual will complain of pain and tenderness of the toe.

Physical exam: The skin surrounding the toenail will likely be red and inflamed. The skin may be warm to the touch and swollen; touching the toe will aggravate the pain. The edge of the toenail will be embedded in the skin of the nail fold.

Tests: Diagnosis of ingrown toenail is readily made by symptoms and physical examination findings. Laboratory tests are not normally required.

Treatment

Treatment is directed toward controlling any infection and relieving pain; the condition is likely to recur if preventative measures are not taken. While waiting for medical treatment, soaking the foot in a strong, warm, salt solution several times a day can help relieve the pain. The inflamed area should be covered with a clean, dry dressing. Antibiotics, either topical or oral, will be prescribed if an infection is present.

A wisp of absorbent cotton coated with a glue-like substance that dries to a strong, transparent film (colloidin) can be wedged between nail and inflamed tissue. This redirects nail growth up and away from the affected area.

The edge portion of the nail may need to be trimmed away (excised) to allow the inflamed tissue to heal. This is an outpatient surgical procedure performed using a local anesthetic. If surgical removal is required, the individual will likely be given antibiotic medication to prevent infection while the wound heals. The most permanent cure for ingrown nails involves removing the strip of ingrown nail and applying phenol to the toe tissue from which the nail was removed. The phenol permanently kills the keratin cells, from which nails are formed, and prevents regrowth of toenail in that area.

Individuals with diabetes, poor circulation in the feet, or poor nerve function in the feet should always consult their physician for any foot problems before trying home remedies.

Prognosis

With appropriate treatment, complete recovery is expected. However, unless preventive measures are taken (proper hygiene, nail trimming, and better fitting footwear), the problem is likely to recur. In cases requiring surgery, a second procedure may be needed if the problem recurs.

Differential Diagnosis

Other possibilities include acute or chronic infection of the skin around the toenail (paronychia).

Specialists

- General Surgeon
- Podiatrist

Work Restrictions / Accommodations

If surgery is needed to remove the nail or to drain an abscess, the worker should avoid prolonged periods of standing until healing is complete. Certain footwear (for example, steel-toed boots) will protect the foot and not constrict or place pressure on the healing area. Soft footwear (cloth shoes) may need to be worn temporarily; this may require job accommodations or a job change if specific other footwear is a work requirement. If the individual cannot find footwear that meets job safety requirements and allows adequate room for the toes, a reassignment may be necessary.

Comorbid Conditions

Individuals with diabetes, poor circulation, or nerve damage to the feet are at an increased risk for complications (particularly infection). These individuals will likely have a longer recovery period.

Complications

Untreated ingrown toenails, and ingrown toenails in people with poor hygiene, are prone to infection. In some cases, pus will collect (abscess) in the infected area of the toe, and may need to be surgically drained. If the infection remains untreated or in chronic infectious conditions, the underlying bone can become infected (osteomyelitis).

Factors Influencing Duration

The length of disability will be affected by the severity of symptoms, the development of complications, the response to treatment, and the specific method of treatment. The period of disability will be longer in cases requiring surgical removal of a portion of the toenail.

Length of Disability

Disability is longer for individuals whose job requirements demand standing for extended periods.

Uncomplicated.

Duration in Days

Job Classification	Minimum	Optimum	Maximum
Sedentary work	1	2	3
Light work	1	2	3
Medium work	1	2	7
Heavy work	1	3	7
Very Heavy work	1	3	7

Complicated.

Duration in Days

Job Classification	Minimum	Optimum	Maximum
Sedentary work	2	3	7
Light work	3	3	14
Medium work	3	7	14
Heavy work	14	14	21
Very Heavy work	14	14	21

Duration Trend from Normative Data*

Cases	Mean	Min	Max	No Lost Time	Over 6 Months
801	26	0	366	0.63%	0%

Percentile:	5th	25th	Median	75th	95th
Days:	6	12	18	31	63

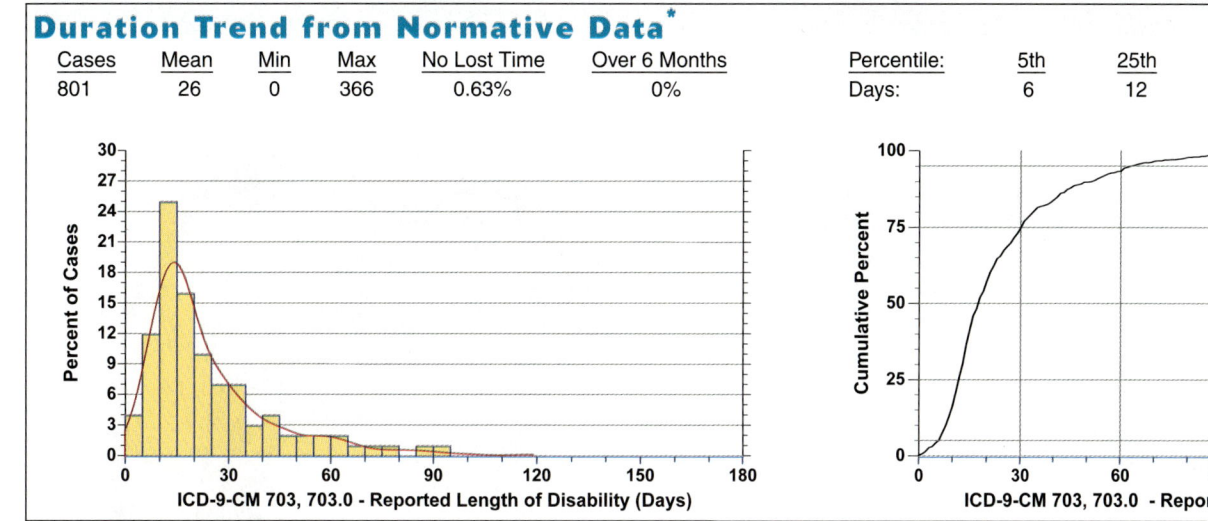

ICD-9-CM 703, 703.0 - Reported Length of Disability (Days)

* Differences may exist between the expected duration tables and the normative graphs. Duration tables provide expected recovery periods based on the type of work performed by the individual. The normative graphs reflect the actual observed experience of many individuals across the spectrum of physical conditions, in a variety of industries, and with varying levels of case management.

Toenail, Ingrown 2101

Failure to Recover

If an individual fails to recover within the maximum duration expectancy period, the reader may wish to reference the following questions to assist in better understanding the specifics of an individual's medical case.

Regarding diagnosis:

- Does individual have a history of infection of the skin around the toenail (paronychia)?
- Does individual trim toenails frequently and properly?
- Do individual's shoes fit properly?
- Does individual complain or redness and pain around the great toe or are other toes also affected? Has the toenail grown into the surrounding skin?

Regarding treatment:

- Was the affected toe soaked in warm, clean water and the edge of the nail trimmed away from the inflamed skin? Was the area of inflammation covered with a clean, dry dressing?
- Does individual understand to avoid footwear that places pressure on the affected toe?
- If there was evidence of infection, were topical or oral antibiotics prescribed?
- Did individual follow antibiotic and treatment regimens?
- Did the symptoms persist with conservative treatment?
- Was excision of the toenail and application of phenol done for persistent symptoms?

Regarding prognosis:

- Was individual compliant with preventive measures such as proper hygiene, nail trimming, and better fitting footwear?
- Is this an initial diagnosis or has the problem recurred?
- Does individual have an underlying disease such as diabetes, poor circulation, or nerve damage to the feet that could cause complications particularly infection? If so, is a longer recovery period required?

References

"Foot Problems." The Merck Manual of Medical Information. Berkow, Robert, Mark Beers, and Andrew Fletcher, eds. New York: Pocket Books, 1997. 279-286.

Foot Facts. American Podiatric Medical Association. 26 Nov 2000 <http://www.apma.org/faq.html>.

Tonsillectomy and Adenoidectomy

Other names / synonyms: Adenotonsillectomy, T&A
28.2, 28.3, 28.6

Definition

Tonsillectomy is a surgical procedure usually needed to remove infected or enlarged tissue masses found at the back of the throat (tonsils), which are thought to aid the body's immune system by filtering bacteria or viruses. Additional tissue masses serving the same purpose are found higher in the throat (adenoids), and often are removed in a procedure called an adenoidectomy. A dual procedure performed at the same time, called an adenotonsillectomy, is commonly referred to as a "T&A."

Tonsillitis or infections of the tonsils and adenoids may lead to the need for a tonsillectomy and adenoidectomy. Enlarged tonsils and adenoids may cause difficulty in breathing or obstruct breathing particularly at night (sleep apnea), leading to numerous adverse health effects that could include high blood pressure (hypertension).

While most procedures are performed on children, adults also may require the surgery. Almost 400,000 tonsillectomies and/or adenoidectomies are performed each year, making them among the most common throat surgeries in the US. In Great Britain, about 70,000 such procedures are performed annually.

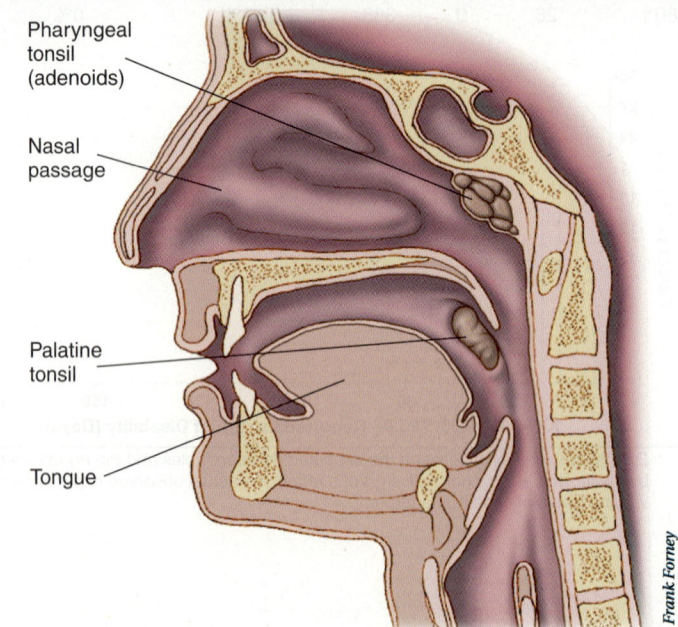

Reason for Procedure

A tonsillectomy and/or adenoidectomy is performed to treat infection, abscesses, or enlargement of the tonsils and/or adenoids that, untreated, could create serious health problems. The procedure is also performed to treat breathing difficulties that may accompany swollen tonsils and adenoids. If adenoids are enlarged, it may be difficult to breathe through the nose.

Recent consensus among the scientific community indicates that tonsils and adenoids play a role in fighting infection. Because of the potential value of this tissue, antibiotic therapy and other remedies likely will be considered first before surgical procedures are considered.

However, ongoing (chronic) problems related to infection or enlargement of the tissue that cannot be resolved in other ways may indicate the need for a tonsillectomy and/or adenoidectomy. The procedures typically are recommended for adults when health problems interfere with breathing, compromise hearing, or cause excessive time away from work. Tonsillectomy may also be necessary for an abscess of the tonsil (quinsy) or if a tonsil is deeply ulcerated or becomes malignant (tonsillar cancer).

Description

General anesthesia is required for a tonsillectomy and/or adenoidectomy. A procedure typically takes about an hour to perform. The individual usually receives fluids given intravenously during the procedure. Methods for removing tissue vary. The application of electrical energy (electrical cauterization) is the most common. A laser or wire used to snare the tissue also may be used.

In a tonsillectomy, the mouth is held open while the exposed tissue located at the back, upper part of the throat (palatine tonsils) is removed. In an adenoidectomy, (usually done at the same time as the tonsillectomy) the adenoid tissue is removed from the part of the throat located behind the nose (nasopharynx). The procedure is commonly done on an outpatient basis, with roughly 6 hours of observation needed following surgery before the individual goes home. If the procedure is done in the hospital, the individual typically remains overnight or for an extra day or two. The individual likely will be advised to stay in bed for several days following the surgery, with full recovery expected within about 3 weeks.

Prognosis

Depending on the severity of the underlying condition, most individuals can expect full recovery from the procedure within several weeks. Procedures typically are very successful at resolving underlying conditions such as ongoing (chronic) infections or airway obstructions.

Specialists

- Otolaryngologist

Work Restrictions / Accommodations

In general, no restrictions or accommodations should be necessary once the individual returns to work. Individuals may need to avoid strenuous activity until fully recovered. If postoperative bleeding or other complications occur, the individual may be returned to surgery, and additional recovery time could be needed. In some cases, the individual may need to be assigned to work tasks that require minimal use of the voice during recovery.

Comorbid Conditions

Bleeding disorders such as sickle cell anemia and use of steroid medications could hamper the individual's ability to recover from surgery.

Procedure Complications

In about 2% of procedures, postoperative bleeding may occur either immediately after or within about 2 weeks of the procedure. In rare cases, a blood transfusion may be required. The individual who experiences difficulty swallowing after a procedure may become dehydrated and could require fluid replacement intravenously. Individuals could experience adverse reactions to anesthesia used for the procedure. Following an adenoidectomy, the individual could experience long-term problems with swallowing.

Factors Influencing Duration

The severity and type of underlying condition, presence of complications, and the extent of the procedure could influence length of disability.

Length of Disability

Individuals who perform physically demanding tasks may need additional recovery time or temporary reassignment to milder tasks until recovery is complete.

Duration in Days

Job Classification	Minimum	Optimum	Maximum
Any work	7	14	21

References

Insight Into Tonsillectomy and Adenoidectomy. American Academy of Otolaryngology - Head and Neck Surgery, Inc. 01 Jan 2000. 21 Jan 2001 <http://www.entnet.org/tonsils.html>.

Tierney, Lawrence, Stephen McPhee, and Maxine Papadakis. Current Medical Diagnosis and Treatment. New York: McGraw-Hill, 2000.

Tonsillitis and Adenoiditis

Other names / synonyms: Adenoid Hypertrophy, Infective Adenoiditis, Infective Tonsillitis, Septic Adenoiditis, Septic Tonsillitis, Suppurative Adenoiditis, Suppurative Tonsillitis, Tonsillar Hypertrophy, Viral Tonsillitis

463, 474, 474.0, 474.1, 474.12

Definition

Tonsillitis is an inflammation of the fleshy tissues that lie on either side of the back of the mouth at the top of the throat (the palatine tonsils). These tissues contain cells that are useful in fighting infection.

Inflammation of the tonsils can be caused by many contagious bacteria or viruses, including Streptococcus bacteria, adenovirus, influenza virus, Epstein-Barr virus, enterovirus, and the herpes simplex virus.

Adenoiditis is an inflammation of the lymphoid tissue at the back of the roof of the mouth (the adenoids). Adenoiditis, or enlarged adenoids (adenoid hypertrophy), is unusual in adults because the adenoids normally shrink and almost disappear as the individual reaches adolescence. Hypertrophy of the adenoids occurs naturally or is caused by chronic inflammation.

Tonsillitis and adenoiditis occur in approximately 19 out of every 1000 men and 22 out of every 1000 women.

Diagnosis

History: Individuals with tonsillitis may report the sudden onset of a sore throat, painful swallowing, and fever. In addition, the individual may experience headache, loss of appetite, chills, malaise, and swollen lymph nodes in the neck and jaw area. Individuals with adenoiditis may report chronic or acute pus-like nasal discharge and chronic mouth breathing. The individual may also experience nasal blockage (obstruction), snoring, sleep disturbances (sleep apnea and restlessness), and ear infections (otitis media).

Physical exam: Exam of the neck and throat of an individual with tonsillitis reveals swollen, red tonsils, often coated with white spots. The lymph nodes in the neck and jaw area may be swollen and tender. Physical exam of an individual with adenoiditis reveals enlarged adenoids and nasal discharge. A rhinoscopy (examination of the nose with a speculum) may be performed.

Tests: A culture of the tonsils may be taken to determine if the tonsillitis is caused by streptococcal bacteria. An x-ray of the side view of the throat may be taken in individuals who may have adenoiditis.

Treatment

Tonsillitis that is caused by a bacterial infection is usually treated with a 10-day course of antibiotics. Supportive treatment includes drinking plenty of fluids, use of a humidifier, and use of over-the-counter medications to relieve pain and/or fever. Tonsillitis that is caused by a viral infection is not treated with antibiotics, but may be treated with antiviral medications. Adenoiditis may be treated with antibiotics.

Surgical removal of the tonsils (tonsillectomy) and adenoids (adenoidectomy) is usually recommended if the tonsils and/or adenoids become chronically infected, if there is an obstruction of the airway, or if the individual experiences excessive snoring or sleep apnea (when breathing momentarily and episodically stops during sleep).

Prognosis

Most cases of tonsillitis heal well. Bacterial infections usually respond favorably to antibiotic therapy. Symptoms of tonsillitis usually lessen in 2-3 days after treatment is begun. If infections recur frequently, surgical removal of the tonsils and adenoids (tonsillectomy and adenoidectomy) may be advised. This surgery is usually successful, with no decrease in immune function.

Differential Diagnosis

Conditions with similar symptoms to tonsillitis include strep throat and other forms of throat infection (pharyngitis). If only one tonsil is enlarged (tonsillar asymmetry), lymphoma or other type of cancer of the tonsil must be ruled out. Adenoid hypertrophy is unusual in adults, and cancer must also be ruled out.

Specialists

- Otolaryngologist
- Primary Care Provider

Work Restrictions / Accommodations

The individual should receive adequate rest and hydration. Work restrictions or accommodations are not usually associated with this condition unless a tonsillectomy/adenoidectomy has been performed. These procedures are usually done on an outpatient basis, and recovery from surgery usually requires 1-2 weeks.

Complementary and Alternative Therapies

Content is intended for awareness only. Treatments may or may not be effective. Scientific evidence may be lacking and some substances have potentially toxic effects. Dr. Presley Reed and the editors do not endorse the use of these therapies in the absence of consultation with a licensed medical professional.

Cool-mist humidifier -	Adds moisture to air, which may soothe the throat and make breathing easier.
Gargling -	A gargle with double-strength tea or warm salt water may offer pain relief.
Echinacea -	Said to be an immune booster.
Hydrotherapy -	A warm, moist towel wrapped around throat may soothe swollen glands.

Comorbid Conditions

Certain comorbid conditions may indicate the need for surgery or additional medical treatment, resulting in prolonged recovery times. Comorbid conditions that may occur include throat infection (pharyngitis), severe nasal obstruction, chronic sinusitis, and right-sided heart failure (cor pulmonale).

Complications

If left untreated, tonsillitis can lead to more serious conditions, such as rheumatic fever and possible accompanying cardiovascular disorders, kidney infections (post-streptococcal glomerulonephritis), or kidney failure. Other complications of untreated tonsillitis include viral or bacterial throat infections (pharyngitis), dehydration due to difficulty swallowing fluids, difficulty breathing (airway obstruction), and abscesses in other parts of the throat (quinsy).

Complications of adenoiditis include right heart failure (cor pulmonale), chronic ear infections (otitis media), airway obstruction, and sleep apnea, in which an individual periodically stops breathing while sleeping.

Factors Influencing Duration

Length of disability may be influenced by the underlying cause (bacterial or viral infection), method of treatment (antibiotics or surgery), response to treatment, or the presence of complications (presence of other infections). If the individual requires a tonsillectomy/adenoidectomy, a more lengthy recuperation period (1-2 weeks) is required.

Length of Disability

Medical treatment.

Duration in Days

Job Classification	Minimum	Optimum	Maximum
Any work	1	3	7

Surgical treatment (tonsillectomy/adenoidectomy).

Duration in Days

Job Classification	Minimum	Optimum	Maximum
Any work	7	14	21

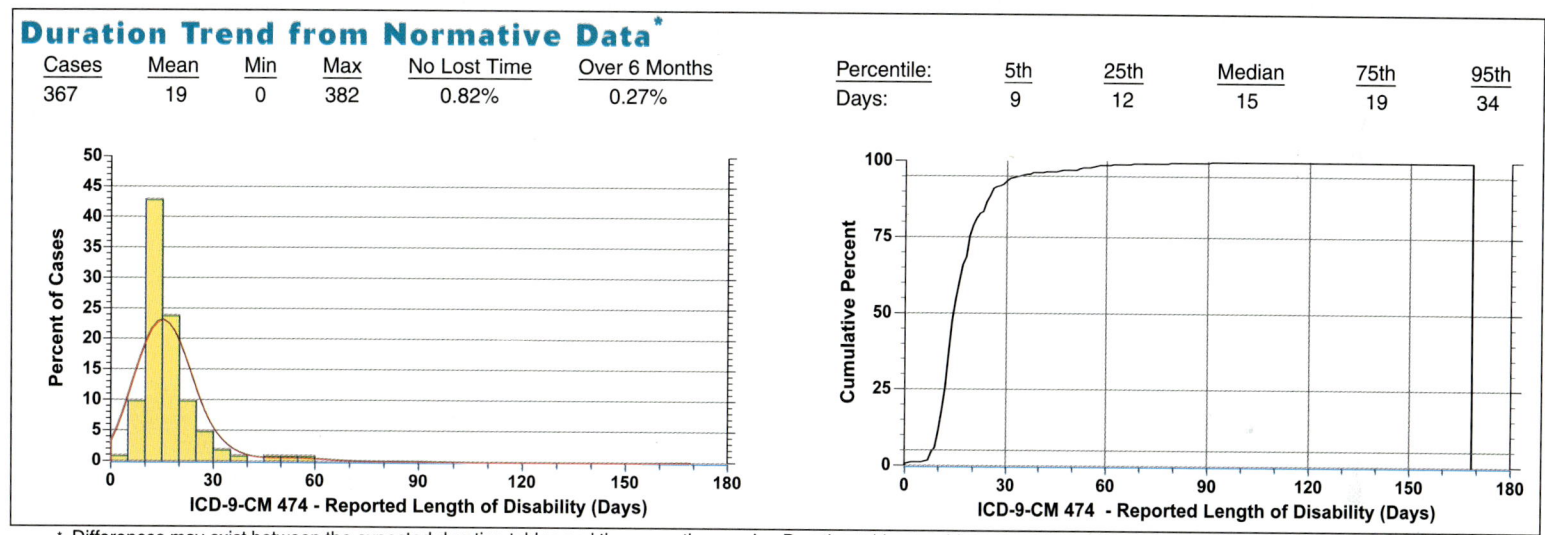

Duration Trend from Normative Data*

Cases	Mean	Min	Max	No Lost Time	Over 6 Months
367	19	0	382	0.82%	0.27%

Percentile:	5th	25th	Median	75th	95th
Days:	9	12	15	19	34

* Differences may exist between the expected duration tables and the normative graphs. Duration tables provide expected recovery periods based on the type of work performed by the individual. The normative graphs reflect the actual observed experience of many individuals across the spectrum of physical conditions, in a variety of industries, and with varying levels of case management.

Tonsillitis and Adenoiditis 2105

Failure to Recover

If an individual fails to recover within the maximum duration expectancy period, the reader may wish to reference the following questions to assist in better understanding the specifics of an individual's medical case.

Regarding diagnosis:

- Did the individual experience symptoms of sore throat, fever, malaise, and/or purulent nasal discharge, ear infections or snoring?
- Has a culture and sensitivity been performed to identify the causative organisms and most appropriate antimicrobial therapy?
- Has diagnosis of tonsillitis and/or adenoiditis been confirmed?
- If not have other conditions with similar symptoms such as strep throat, lymphoma or other cancers been ruled out?

Regarding treatment:

- Has any underlying bacterial infection been treated with the appropriate antibiotics (according to a culture and sensitivity)?
- If the infection was viral, were antiviral medications warranted?
- Has the prescribed medication been taken according to instructions?
- Has surgical intervention been considered (i.e., for chronic infection, or associated snoring or sleep apnea)?

Regarding prognosis:

- Has the infection persisted despite treatment? If so, has culture and sensitivity been done to determine the most effective antibiotic and to rule out antibiotic-resistant organisms? Would extended therapy or change in antibiotics be warranted at this time?
- Was surgery indicated?
- Did the individual experience any complications associated with the infection, such as rheumatic fever, glomerulonephritis, cor pulmonale, throat abscesses, etc., that could impact recovery and prognosis?
- Have these complication been addressed in the treatment plan?
- Does individual have an underlying condition that may impact

References

DerMarderpsoam, Ara, ed. The Review of Natural Products. St. Louis: Facts and Comparisons, 2000.

Tonsillitis and Adenoiditis. American Academy of Otolaryngology - Head and Neck Surgery, Inc. 1999. 12 Jul 2000 <http://www.entnet.org/education/tonsillitis&adenoiditis.html>.

Tooth Extraction

Other names / synonyms: Pulled Tooth, Tooth Removal
23, 23.0, 23.09, 23.1, 23.19

Definition

Tooth extraction is the removal of a tooth from its socket in the bone, either by pulling the tooth (forceps removal) or by cutting out or excising the tooth (oral surgery).

Conditions leading to the need for tooth extraction include badly decayed teeth, broken teeth, crowded teeth, inappropriate contact between teeth when the mouth is closed (malocclusion), and teeth that have become loose because of inflammation of the ligaments and bones that support the teeth (periodontal disease).

According to reports issued by the United States Department of Health and Human Services in May 2000, 7% of young people age 17 or younger and 69% of individuals aged 35 to 44 years have lost at least 1 permanent tooth. Among individuals aged 65 to 74, 26% have lost all their permanent teeth.

Reason for Procedure

Tooth extraction is performed for positional, structural, or economic reasons. Impaction is a common reason for the extraction of wisdom teeth. Extraction is the only known method that will prevent further problems. Teeth may also be extracted to make more room in the mouth prior to straightening the remaining teeth (orthodontic treatment), or because they are so badly positioned that straightening is impossible. Extraction is also used to remove teeth that are so badly decayed or broken that they cannot be restored. In addition, individuals sometimes choose extraction as a less expensive alternative to filling or placing a crown on a severely decayed tooth.

Situations that might warrant oral surgery for tooth extraction rather than extraction with forceps include severely broken teeth and impacted teeth. Sometimes teeth are so severely broken that there is not enough of the tooth above the gum (crown) to be gripped by the forceps. There is also the chance that severely broken teeth may break further or shatter from the pressure of the forceps. Impacted teeth are so badly crowded with other teeth that a forceps extraction could damage the other teeth.

Oral surgery also works better for extracting teeth that have not erupted from the gums.

Description

Tooth extraction can be performed with local anesthesia if the tooth is exposed and appears to be easily removable in one piece. The dentist uses a special instrument (elevator) to grasp the tooth, rock it back and forth to loosen (luxate) it, widen the space in the alveolar bone, and break the tiny elastic fibers (ligaments) that attach the tooth to the bone. Once the tooth is dislocated from the bone, it can be lifted and removed with forceps.

If the tooth is not fully erupted, the dentist may find it necessary to remove some of the overlying gum and bone tissue in order to remove the tooth. If indications are that the extraction is likely to be difficult, the dentist may refer the individual to an oral surgeon, a specialist who is trained to give nitrous oxide, intravenous sedatives, or a general anesthetic to relieve pain. Extracting an impacted tooth or a tooth with curved roots typically requires cutting through gum tissue to expose the tooth. It may also require removing portions of bone to free the tooth. Some teeth must be cut and removed in sections. The extraction site may or may not require one or more stitches to close the cut (incision).

Prognosis

Success of the extraction depends on whether the extraction was performed with forceps or whether oral surgery was necessary. If the extraction is performed with forceps, the wound usually closes and heals in about two weeks. A three-to-six-month period is required for the bone and soft tissue to be completely restructured.

In surgically-performed extractions, the wound is stitched and healing takes about two weeks.

Most extractions result in complete healing without complications.

Specialists

- Dentist
- Oral Surgeon
- Periodontist

Work Restrictions / Accommodations

There are no work restrictions or special accommodations required.

Comorbid Conditions

Comorbid conditions that might influence the length of disability after tooth extraction include medically compromising conditions, such as diabetes mellitus and human immunodeficiency virus (HIV) infection. Also, individuals on medications that cause dry mouth are at higher risk for bacterial infections.

Procedure Complications

Potential complications of tooth extraction include bleeding and infection. Besides infection of the extraction site, infection of the membrane that lines the interior of the heart (endocarditis) is possible in individuals with heart murmurs or with a history of rheumatic fever. (To minimize this risk, these individuals are given antibiotics before and after the procedure.) Complications, such as infection or dry socket may prolong healing time.

In some cases, the underlying support structure of the tooth is involved in the removal of the tooth because the tooth's support structure is very weak and could cave in unless reconstructive surgery is performed at the same time. Occasionally, the alveolar nerve is damaged during extraction of lower molars, causing temporary (and sometimes permanent) numbness in the jaw.

Other complications include jaw fracture, jaw joint pain, and dry socket. Dry socket occurs when a blood clot does not properly form in the empty tooth socket, the bone beneath the socket is painfully exposed to air and food, causing the extraction site to heal more slowly.

Factors Influencing Duration

Factors that might influence the length of disability after tooth extractions include the type of extraction and infections and problems that might occur after treatment such as swelling and bleeding after the extraction and exposure of bone in the socket after a lower back tooth has been removed (dry socket). If oral surgery is necessary to perform the extraction, there may be surgical complications (e.g., general anesthesia complications) in addition to the dental complications.

Length of Disability

Length of disability may be influenced by method of extraction (forceps or surgery) and the presence of complications. After surgical or forceps extraction, most individuals will require at least one day of bed rest following the procedure.

Duration in Days

Job Classification	Minimum	Optimum	Maximum
Any work	1	2	3

References

Dental Review Online: Tooth Extraction. Avant Garde Digital Publications. 01 Dec 1998. 18 Jan 2000 <http://www.dentalreview.com/Tooth_Extraction.htm>.

Ills and Conditions: Tooth Extraction. Blue Shield of California. 01 Jan 2000. 18 Jan 2001 <http://www.mylifepath.com/topic/toothextract>.

Oral Health 2000: Facts and Figures. Office of the Surgeon General, U.S. Department of Health and Human Services. 28 Oct 2000. 6 Feb 2001 <http://www.cdc.gov/nccdphp/oh/sgr2000-fs1.htm>.

Tierney, Lawrence, Stephen McPhee, and Maxine Papadakis. Current Medical Diagnosis and Treatment. New York: McGraw-Hill, 2000.

Torticollis

Other names / synonyms: Loxia, Wryneck

723.5, 754.1

Definition

Torticollis is involuntary, prolonged muscle contractions (dystonia) of the neck that lead to abnormal postures and movement of the head. Torticollis is both a symptom and a disease with many underlying pathologies. The condition may occur without a known cause (idiopathic), it may be genetic (inherited), or acquired secondary to damage to the nervous system or muscles. It may also be psychogenic. Torticollis may be a symptom of a fracture and or dislocation of C1-C2 in the upper cervical spine.

In the US, the incidence of idiopathic torticollis is estimated to be about 3 per 10,000 individuals. Idiopathic torticollis is more common in women than men by a 4.5 to 1 ratio. While torticollis may be found in both children and adults, approximately 90% of cases occur in individuals between the ages of 31 and 60.

Diagnosis

History: The individual may complain of headache, neck pain, stiffness of the neck muscles, and limited range of motion of the neck.

Physical exam: Upon examination, enlargement of the neck muscles and shoulder elevation on the affected side may be observed. A shortening of the neck muscles may be noted. The individual's head will tilt toward the affected side while the chin points to the unaffected side.

Tests: X-rays, MRI, and CT may be used to rule out other diseases or conditions.

Treatment

Torticollis is treated by first identifying the underlying cause. In idiopathic torticollis, heat, cervical spine traction, and massage may be used to treat head and neck pain. Stretching exercises and neck braces may help alleviate muscle spasms. Drug treatments including muscle relaxants and analgesics may be used. At specialized centers, the involved muscle may be injected with botulinum toxin to temporarily paralyze the muscle (for months). If other treatments fail, surgical treatments (selective peripheral denervation or the Bertrand procedure) are sometimes used.

Prognosis

In most individuals, torticollis progresses gradually over a period of months to years. Complete remission sometimes occurs. Remission rates of 12-21% have been reported especially in younger individuals during the first 5 years after onset of the disease. The majority of remissions are only temporary. In many cases, torticollis may persist for life and can result in restricted movement and postural deformity.

Between 80-90% of individuals show significant relief of symptoms following surgery. Physical therapy is usually necessary to stretch muscles that may have shortened due to prolonged periods of involuntary contraction and to strengthen the muscles that are still innervated. After surgery, the mobility of the neck may not return completely to normal and some individuals may experience numbness on the back of the head that extends to the top.

Differential Diagnosis

Other conditions or diseases with similar symptoms include cervical osteomyelitis, retropharyngeal space infection, fractures of the cervical spine, spinal cord neoplasms, tetanus, and a mental disorder with psychogenic torticollis called conversion disorder.

Specialists

- Neurologist
- Neurosurgeon
- Spine Surgeon

Work Restrictions / Accommodations

Work restrictions depend on the severity of the individual's condition (e.g., range of motion). Driving, operating heavy machinery, and any other tasks involving neck and head motions may need to be reduced or eliminated.

Complementary and Alternative Therapies

Content is intended for awareness only. Treatments may or may not be effective. Scientific evidence may be lacking and some substances have potentially toxic effects. Dr. Presley Reed and the editors do not endorse the use of these therapies in the absence of consultation with a licensed medical professional.

Pallidal stimulation - Deep brain stimulation using a quadripolar electrode and a battery-operated programmable pulse generator may be an effective treatment for focal dystonia.

Hypnosis - Hypnobehavioral approach along with hypnotic strategies that includes desensitization, sensory-imaging conditioning, ego-boosting suggestions, and hypnosis-facilitated differential muscle re-training may produce marked reduction of the torticollis and the hypertrophy of the neck muscles as well as a reduced interference of symptoms in daily living.

Comorbid Conditions

Conditions that can impact ability to recover and further lengthen disability include cervical osteomyelitis, cervical osteoarthritis, and cervical disc disease.

Complications

Individuals with prolonged torticollis may develop degenerative osteoarthritis of the cervical spine and an increase in size (hypertrophy) of the sternocleidomastoid muscle.

Factors Influencing Duration

The individual's age, severity of symptoms, and response to treatment are factors that may influence length of disability.

Length of Disability

Disability varies by the cause and severity of the case.

Medical treatment.

Duration in Days

Job Classification	Minimum	Optimum	Maximum
Sedentary work	0	3	14
Light work	0	5	21
Medium work	0	7	28
Heavy work	0	14	42
Very Heavy work	0	28	91

Failure to Recover

If an individual fails to recover within the maximum duration expectancy period, the reader may wish to reference the following questions to assist in better understanding the specifics of an individual's medical case.

Regarding diagnosis:

- Has diagnosis of torticollis been confirmed?
- Has underlying cause been identified?
- How is it being addressed?
- Have conditions with similar symptoms been ruled out?
- Does individual have symptoms of torticollis such as neck pain, stiffness of the neck muscles, or limited range of motion of the neck? Other symptoms?

Regarding treatment:

- Is underlying cause responding to treatment?
- Was massage or heat therapy effective?
- Was the individual placed in traction? With what results?
- Would individual benefit from botulinum toxin injections?

Regarding prognosis:

- Does individual have restricted movement or postural deformity? Has individual had a remission?
- What is the individual's pain level?
- To what level is function impaired?
- Would a more aggressive form of treatment such as surgical intervention be warranted?
- Has individual experienced any complications?
- Does individual have an underlying condition that may impact recovery such as cervical osteomyelitis, cervical osteoarthritis, or cervical disc disease?

References

De Benedittis, G. "Hypnosis and Spasmodic Torticollis - Report of Four Cases: A Brief Communication." International Journal of Clinical Experimental Hypnosis 44 4 (1996): 292-306.

Gildenberg, Philip. Surgery for Spasmodic Torticollis. Houston Stereotactic Center. 2000. 24 Oct 2000 <http://www.stereotactic.net/torticollis.htm>.

Islekel, S., M. Zileli, and B. Zileli. "Unilateral Pallidal Stimulation in Cervical Dystonia." Stereotactic and Functional Neurosurgery 72 2-4 (1999): 248-252.

Ross, Michael, and Susan Dufel, MD. Torticollis. eMedicine.com. 26 Jan 2001. 22 Feb 2001 <http://www.emedicine.com/emerg/topic597.htm>.

Toxic Effects, Arsenic and Compounds

Other names / synonyms: Arsenic Poisoning, Arsenic Salts, Arsenic Trichloride, Arsenic Trioxide, Metallic Arsenic

961.1, 985.1

Definition

Arsenic is a naturally occurring element in the earth's crust. Pure arsenic, a gray-colored metal, is rarely found in the environment. Instead it is usually combined with one or more other elements such as oxygen, chlorine, and sulfur. This combination is referred to as inorganic arsenic. Arsenic combined with carbon and hydrogen is referred to as organic arsenic. The organic forms are usually less toxic than the inorganic forms. While not usually mined, arsenic is instead recovered as a by-product from the smelting of copper, lead, zinc, and other ores. Metal smelter exhaust can release arsenic into the environment. Also present in coal at variable concentrations, arsenic is released into the environment during combustion. Arsenic near acid or acid mist can release the very deadly gas, arsine. Application of pesticides and herbicides containing arsenic has increased environmental dispersion. Twenty-one arsenic compounds are considered to be of concern because of their toxicity and/or presence in the environment.

Fruits and vegetables are sprayed with arsenicals. It is sometimes added to the feed of poultry and other livestock to promote growth, and concentrations are found in many species of fish and shellfish. The average daily human intake of arsenic is about 300 micrograms. Almost all of this is ingested through food and water.

The main use of arsenic in this country is for pesticides. Therefore, the major source of occupational exposure to arsenic-containing compounds is from the manufacture of arsenical herbicides and pesticides. Some products, mostly weed killers, use organic arsenic as the active ingredient. Other pesticides use inorganic forms of arsenic to kill plants, insects, or rodents, or to preserve wood. Persons who manufacture or use these pesticides or who handle treated wood may be exposed to arsenic.

Arsenic is also used in metallurgy, in the production of pigments, glass, most computer chips using silicon-based technology, and in the production of some semiconductors used in LEDs, laser and solar devices.

Diagnosis

Toxicology: Arsenic compounds are irritants of skin, mucous membranes and eyes. Dermatoses, epidermal carcinoma and lung cancer are associated with chronic exposure.

Acute arsenic poisoning is rare and usually is result of ingestion. Initial symptoms include difficulty swallowing, severe abdominal pain, vomiting and diarrhea. Liver, bone marrow, nervous system and cardiovascular effects may be present. Levels of exposure associated with toxicity vary with the particular compound, with trivalent compounds (arsenic trioxide) being the most toxic. Arsenic trichloride is a vesicant and can cause severe respiratory damage upon inhalation. It is rapidly absorbed through the skin and a fatal case following a spill on the skin has been reported.

Chronic intoxication by ingestion is characterized by weakness, loss of appetite, GI disturbances, impaired cognitive function, peripheral neuropathy and skin disorders. Occupational exposure to arsenic compounds can cause hyperpigmentation, hyperkeratoses, as well as dermatitis of both irritant and allergic types. Some organic arsenic compounds (arsanilate) have a selective effect on the optic nerve and can cause blindness. Impaired peripheral circulation and Raynaud's disease have been reported following long term exposure.

In multiple studies, occupational and environmental exposure to inorganic arsenic compounds have been causally associated with cancer of the skin and lungs. Occupational exposure studies of smelter and pesticide workers have shown a close association between exposure to arsenic and lung cancer mortality. An increased risk of lung cancer may also occur in non-occupationally exposed populations living in areas with high atmospheric levels of arsenic resulting from industrial emissions. Epidemiological studies have revealed a close association between arsenic concentrations in drinking water and increased incidence of skin cancers.

Tests: Urinary levels of arsenic can be used as an index of harmful exposure, but dietary factors must be considered before interpreting results. Seafood, especially shellfish, contains significant amounts of organic arsenicals, which are non-toxic but affect the total urinary arsenic levels. The biologic half-life of arsenic in urine is 1-2 days in individuals with normal renal function. Measurement of arsenic in hair or fingernails has been used to detect chronic exposure but levels are not reliable.

Treatment

Treatment must include removal from exposure, decontamination and supportive care. If diagnosis is confirmed, chelation therapy with dimercaprol can be used until arsenic level in the urine is < 50ug/dl. The role of chelation in altering the natural history of chronic sequelae is uncertain.

Prognosis

Prognosis is dependent on the extent and duration of exposure.

Differential Diagnosis

Symptoms and signs of the effects toxic exposure may be similar to other illnesses and exposures, dependent on the organ systems involved.

Specialists

- Medical Toxicologist
- Occupational Medicine Physician

Rehabilitation

Rehabilitation may be required if there are functional deficits. The specific form of rehabilitation will be dependent on the type and extent of functional deficits.

Work Restrictions / Accommodations

Exposure Limits: The Environmental Protection Agency limits the amounts of arsenic released into the environment and used to make pesticides. The maximum contaminant level of drinking water is 0.05

parts per million. The Occupational Safety and Health Administration (OSHA) has set the legal airborne exposure limit (PEL) at 0.10 milligrams per cubic meter averaged over an 8-hour work shift. The National Institute for Safety and Occupational Health (NIOSH) has recommended an airborne exposure limit is 0.002 milligrams per cubic meter not to be exceeded during any 15-minute work period. The American Conference of Governmental Industrial Hygienists (ACGIH) recommends an airborne exposure limit of 0.01 milligrams per cubic meter averaged over an 8-hour work shift.

The individual must have access to information about the health effects of arsenic exposure in the workplace. Respirators, air filters, and protective clothing and eyewear may be needed. Length and levels of arsenic exposure in the work place must be monitored.

Comorbid Conditions

Pre-existing disease may worsen the impact of exposure.

Factors Influencing Duration

Absorbed dose is the primary determinant of severity of toxic effects, and therefore severity and duration of disability. Absorbed dose is dependent on environmental levels, routes of exposure (skin contact, inhalation, ingestion) and duration of exposure. Contact physician for additional information.

Other factors influencing disability include pre-existing disease, age, pregnancy and allergy, all of which affect individual susceptibility to the toxic effect of chemical exposures. Psychological and emotional factors may also play a role in the extent and duration of disability. In some cases, there may be residual permanent disability despite prompt diagnosis and appropriate treatment.

Length of Disability

Absorbed dose is the primary determinant of severity of toxic effects, and therefore severity and duration of disability. Absorbed dose is dependent on environmental levels, routes of exposure (skin contact, inhalation, ingestion) and duration of exposure. In some cases, disability may be permanent. Contact physician for additional information.

Failure to Recover

If an individual fails to recover within the maximum duration expectancy period, the reader may wish to reference the following questions to assist in better understanding the specifics of an individual's medical case.

Regarding diagnosis:

- Has the diagnosis of arsenic poisoning been confirmed?
- Is there a positive history of arsenic exposure in the workplace?
- Is the clinical illness, including the history, physical examination, and laboratory findings, consistent with other case descriptions?
- Are the whole blood and urine levels of arsenic at or near the normal value?
- Is the timing between exposure and clinical onset compatible with the known biologic facts about the hazard?
- Does individual have an underlying condition that may impact recovery?

Regarding treatment:

- If systemic impairment exists, what specific treatments has individual received? Would individual benefit from additional or continued therapy?
- How soon after exposure was appropriate treatment initiated?

Regarding prognosis:

- Was the exposure dose within the range of doses believed to cause such effects? Are there special attributes of this particular individual that make it more or less likely that he or she would be so affected?
- Could arsenic exposure be occurring outside the workplace; i.e., in the home, in the community, or in recreational activities?
- Has the individual recently worked in another organization where arsenic exposure was higher?
- If occupational duties put individual at risk of exposure, is protective gear provided?
- Has individual been instructed in its proper use?

References

Proctor and Hughes' Chemical Hazards of the Workplace, 3rd edition. Hathaway, G.J., et al., eds. New York: Van Nostrand Reinhold, 1991.

Occupational Medicine. LaDou, J., ed. Norwalk, CT: Appleton and Lange, 1990.

Agency for Toxic Substances and Disease Registry Case Studies in Environmental Medicine: Arsenic, Beryllium, Cadmium, Cholinesterase Inhibitors, Lead, Mercury US Department of Health and Human Services, 1993.

Goodman & Gilman's The Pharmacological Basis of Therapeutics Hardman, J.G., and L.E. Lilmbird, eds. New York: McGraw-Hill, 1996.

Toxic Effects, Beryllium

Other names / synonyms: Acute Beryllium Disease, Berylliosis, CBD, Chronic Beryllium Disease

985.3

Definition

Pure beryllium is a hard grayish metal, which occurs naturally as a chemical component of certain kinds of rocks. Two mineral rocks, bertrandite and beryl, are mined for the recovery of beryllium. Very pure gem-quality beryl is better known as either aquamarine or emerald.

Most of the beryllium ore that is mined is processed into beryllium hydroxide, which is further processed into beryllium metal, alloys, and oxide. Pure beryllium metal is used to make aircraft disc brakes, nuclear weapons and reactors, aircraft-satellite-space vehicle structures and instruments, x-ray transmission windows, missile parts, fuel containers, precision instruments, rocket propellants, navigational systems, heat shields, and mirrors. Beryllium oxide is used to make specialty electrical and high technology ceramics, electronic heat sinks, electrical insulators, microwave oven components, gyroscopes, military vehicle armor, rocket nozzles, and laser structural components. Beryllium alloys are used in electrical connectors and relays, springs, precision instruments, aircraft engine parts, nonsparking tools, submarine cable housings, and pivots, wheels, and pinions.

Low level human exposure is common due to low levels of beryllium in the air, food, water and soil. Most of the exposure is from the burning of coal or fuel oil and tobacco smoke and is through inhalation. Ingestion has not been known to cause effects since very little beryllium can leave the digestive tract and enter the bloodstream. Skin and eye contact produces various levels of irritation.

The greatest exposures to beryllium, mostly in the form of beryllium oxide, occur in the workplace. Occupational exposure to beryllium occurs at places where it is mined, processed, and converted into metal, alloys, and chemicals. Workers engaged in machining metals containing beryllium, in reclaiming beryllium from scrap alloys, or in using beryllium products will also be exposed occupationally. Beryllium can be transferred to individuals from workers' clothing.

Diagnosis

Toxicology: Exposure to compounds of beryllium may cause dermatitis, acute pneumonitis and a chronic lung disease (granulomatosis) called berylliosis or chronic beryllium disease (CBD).

Acute inhalation exposure (now rare due to improved working conditions) effects all segments of the respiratory tract with resultant rhinitis, pharyngitis, tracheobronchitis and pneumonitis. In most cases, recovery occurs within 1-6 months, although fatalities due to pulmonary edema have been reported.

Beryllium disease is regarded as chronic if it persists for a year or more and is usually due to granulomas in the lung. Onset may be insidious with only slight cough and fatigue, which can occur as early as one year or as late as 25 years after exposure. Progressive pulmonary insufficiency, anorexia, weight loss, weakness, chest pain, chronic cough are characteristic of advanced disease. There are many similarities between CBD and sarcoidosis, but in sarcoidosis the systemic (non-pulmonary) effects are much more pronounced.

CBD is probably a hypersensitivity phenomenon based on the observations that: 1) CBD patients also show skin hypersensitivity reaction to Beryllium compounds; 2) lymphocytes from CBD patients are transformed with exposure to Beryllium compounds in the test tube (this is the definitive test for making the diagnosis of CBD); 3) CBD patients have decreased helper/suppressor T cell ratios; and 4) there is a lack of a clear dose-response relationship between exposure and severity of disease.

Levels of Beryllium can be measured in blood and urine but urinary levels are highly variable. Elevated levels in blood/urine indicate exposure but do not correlate well with presence of disease.

Treatment

The most important step in the management and treatment of berylliosis is prevention of further exposure. The disease (both acute and chronic) must be promptly recognized, and affected workers removed from further beryllium exposure. Industrial dust suppression is the basis of preventing exposure to beryllium, but its efficiency is imperfect. Chronic beryllium disease (berylliosis) is not curable.

Symptoms and effects are treated as they occur. Respiratory difficulty will be treated immediately with oxygen, bronchodilators or nebulized drugs. Particles of beryllium in the eyes or under the skin will be flushed out or removed.

Treatment of acute berylliosis is generally symptomatic. The lungs often contain fluid (edematous) and blood (hemorrhagic), and mechanical ventilation is necessary in severely affected individuals. In symptomatic individuals with abnormal pulmonary function, corticosteroids may be administered. It is thought that glucocorticoids improve the course of the disease, but these agents may have to be given for the rest of the individual's life. Although corticosteroids have been used in chronic berylliosis, the response is usually unsatisfactory. Marked, sustained improvement with corticosteroids in the treatment of chronic beryllium disease probably means that the individual has sarcoidosis rather than berylliosis.

Prognosis

Prognosis is dependent on the extent and duration of exposure.

Differential Diagnosis

Clinical presentation may be similar to systemic diseases involving the same organ systems. The possibility of exposure to other toxic agents should always be considered.

Specialists

- Medical Toxicologist
- Occupational Medicine Physician

Rehabilitation

Rehabilitation may be required if there are functional deficits. The specific form of rehabilitation will be dependent on the type and extent of functional deficits.

Work Restrictions / Accommodations

Exposure Limits: OSHA has set the legal airborne permissible exposure limit (PEL) at 0.002 milligrams per cubic meter averaged over an 8-hour workshift; 0.005 milligrams per cubic meter as a ceiling limit not to be exceeded during any 15-minute period; and 0.025 milligrams per cubic meter as an acceptable maximum peak, permitted for any 30-minute period above the ceiling limit. NIOSH recommends an airborne exposure limit of 0.0005 milligrams per cubic meter that should not be exceeded at any time. ACGIH (American Conference of Governmental Industrial Hygienists) recommends an airborne exposure limit of 0.002 milligrams per cubic meter averaged over an 8-hour workshift, and 0.01 milligrams per cubic meter as a short-term exposure limit (STEL). Individuals must have access to information about the health effects of beryllium exposure in the workplace. Respirators, air filters, and protective clothing and eyewear may be needed. Length and levels of beryllium exposure in the workplace must be monitored. The individual may need special training to handle the metal, its compounds, and its dust.

Comorbid Conditions

Pre-existing disease will impact the recovery, particularly if it involves the same organ systems affected by the toxic exposure.

Factors Influencing Duration

The levels and length of time exposed, method of exposure, immediacy of treatment, and the individual's response to exposure and treatment will determine length of disability. In some cases, disability may be permanent. Age and the general state of health, and pre-existing disease will affect disability.

Length of Disability

The duration of disability in individuals with CBD depends on the degree of pulmonary insufficiency and the response to treatment. It is highly variable and some degree of permanent disability is not uncommon.

Failure to Recover

If an individual fails to recover within the maximum duration expectancy period, the reader may wish to reference the following questions to assist in better understanding the specifics of an individual's medical case.

Regarding diagnosis:

- Has diagnosis of toxic effects of beryllium been confirmed?
- Is there a positive history of beryllium exposure in the workplace?
- Is the clinical illness, including the history, physical examination, and laboratory findings, consistent with other case descriptions?
- Are the whole blood, urine, and tissue levels of beryllium at or near the normal value?
- Is the timing between exposure and clinical onset compatible with the known biologic facts about the hazard?
- Is the exposure dose within the range of doses believed to cause such effects?
- Does individual have an underlying condition that may impact recovery?

Regarding treatment:

- What specific treatments did individual receive? Would individual benefit from additional or continued therapy?
- If occupational duties put individual at risk of exposure, is protective gear provided?

Regarding prognosis:

- Are there special attributes of the particular individual that make it more or less likely that he or she would be so affected?
- Could beryllium exposure be occurring outside the workplace; i.e., in the home, in the community, or in recreational activities?
- Has the individual recently worked in another organization where beryllium exposure was higher? If occupational duties put individual at risk of exposure, is protective gear provided?
- Has individual been instructed in proper use of protective gear?

References

Proctor and Hughes' Chemical Hazards of the Workplace, 3rd edition. Hathaway, G.J., et al., eds. New York: Van Nostrand Reinhold, 1991.

Occupational Medicine. LaDou, J., ed. Norwalk, CT: Appleton and Lange, 1990.

Agency for Toxic Substances and Disease Registry. Case Studies in Environmental Medicine: Arsenic, Beryllium, Cadmium, Cholinesterase Inhibitors, Lead, Mercury. US Department of Health and Human Services, 1993.

Goodman & Gilman's The Pharmacological Basis of Therapeutics. Hardman, J.G., and L.E. Lilmbird, eds. New York: McGraw-Hill, 1996.

Toxic Effects, Cadmium

Other names / synonyms: Cadmium Metal Exposure, Cadmium Metal Poisoning, Cadmium Oxide Exposure

985.5

Definition

Cadmium metal is used in electroplating, in solder for aluminum, as a constituent of fusible alloys, as a deoxidizer in nickel plating, in engraving, in nickel-cadmium batteries, as pigments in glazes and enamels, in dyeing and printing and in semiconductors and rectifiers. Toxic exposure occurs by inhalation of cadmium oxide fume or dust.

Diagnosis

Toxicology: Cadmium oxide fume is a severe pulmonary irritant; cadmium dust also is a pulmonary irritant but less potent due to larger particle size. Exposure to airborne cadmium is also associated with kidney damage.

Most acute intoxications have been caused by inhalation of concentrations that did not provide warning symptoms of irritation. Following a symptomatic latent period of 4 to 10 hours, there is characteristically nasopharyngeal irritation followed by a feeling of chest constriction or substernal pain with cough and dyspnea. There may also be headache, chills, muscle aches, nausea, vomiting and diarrhea. Pulmonary edema may develop rapidly. In some cases, dyspnea is progressive and may result in death within 7-10 days. Among survivors, the subsequent course is unpredictable; most cases resolve slowly, but respiratory symptoms may linger for several weeks, and impairment of pulmonary function may persist for many months. Repeated exposure to lower levels of cadmium in air has resulted in chronic poisoning characterized by irreversible lung injury of the emphysematous type. Renal tubular damage is also seen with urinary excretion of a specific low molecular weight protein. Clinical evidence of the cumulative effects of cadmium may appear after exposure has ended and the disease tends to be progressive.

The urinary excretion of cadmium bears no relationship to the severity or duration of exposure and can only be used as confirmation of absorption. Excretion of absorbed cadmium is very slow.

Other effects of cadmium exposure are anemia, yellow discoloration of the teeth, rhinitis, nasal septum perforation and damage to the olfactory nerve with loss of smell (anosmia). The long-term ingestion of contaminated food has been associated with a crippling condition among Japanese women called "itai-itai" or "ouch-ouch" disease. It occurs in women after multiple pregnancies and is characterized by back and joint pain, osteomalacia, bone fractures and occasional renal failure.

Occupational exposure to cadmium has been associated with a significant increase in respiratory tract and prostate cancer.

Treatment

Acute cadmium pneumonitis requires anticipatory supportive care. There is no specific treatment. Chronic renal damage is not reversible. There is no data to support chelation therapy as effective and some evidence to suggest it is harmful. Removal from exposure and prevention of complications such as kidney stones and metabolic bone disease are the mainstay of therapy.

Prognosis

Prognosis depends on the degree of end organ damage. Severe cases of exposure can result in death.

Specialists

- Medical Toxicologist
- Occupational Medicine Physician

Differential Diagnosis

Clinical presentation may be similar to systemic diseases involving the same organ systems. The possibility of exposure to other toxic agents should always be considered.

Rehabilitation

Rehabilitation may be required if there are functional deficits. The specific form of rehabilitation will be dependent on the type and extent of functional deficits.

Work Restrictions / Accommodations

Exposure Limits: The Occupational Safety and Health Administration (OSHA) legal airborne permissible exposure limit (PEL) is 0.005 milligrams per cubic meter for cadmium dust or fume averaged over an 8-hour work shift. OSHA has recognized that some processes in certain industries may be unable to achieve the 0.005 milligrams per cubic meter limit through engineering and work practices. These industries must follow SECALs (separate engineering control air limits) of either 0.015 or 0.05 milligrams per cubic meter.

The National Institute of Occupational Safety and Health (NIOSH) recommends that exposure to occupational carcinogens be limited to the lowest feasible concentration.

The American Conference of Governmental Industrial Hygienists (ACGIH) recommended airborne exposure limit is 0.01 milligrams per cubic meter for elemental cadmium and 0.002 milligrams per cubic meter for cadmium compounds (respirable fraction), averaged over an 8-hour work shift.

The individual must have access to information about the health effects of cadmium exposure in the workplace. Respirators, air filters, protective clothing, and eyewear may be needed. Length and levels of cadmium exposure in the workplace must be monitored. The individual may need special training to handle the metal.

Comorbid Conditions

Pre-existing disease will impact the recovery, particularly if it involves the same organ systems affected by the toxic exposure.

Factors Influencing Duration

The levels and length of time exposed, method of exposure, immediacy of treatment, and the individual response to exposure and treatment determine length of disability. In some cases, disability may be permanent. Age, pre-existing disease and mental attitude have an influence on the individual's ability to return to pre-injury functional level.

Length of Disability

Absorbed dose is the primary determinant of severity of toxic effects, and therefore severity and duration of disability. Absorbed dose is dependent on environmental levels, routes of exposure (skin contact, inhalation, ingestion) and duration of exposure. Contact physician for additional information.

Failure to Recover

If an individual fails to recover within the maximum duration expectancy period, the reader may wish to reference the following questions to assist in better understanding the specifics of an individual's medical case.

Regarding diagnosis:

- Are the whole blood and urine levels of cadmium at or near the normal value?
- Is there a positive history of cadmium exposure in the workplace?
- Has the individual recently worked in another organization where cadmium exposure is higher?
- Could cadmium exposure be occurring outside the workplace, i.e., in the home, community, or recreational activities?
- Does the individual have a history of smoking?
- Is the clinical illness including the history, physical examination, and laboratory findings consistent with other case descriptions?
- Are there special attributes of the particular individual that make it more or less likely that he or she would be so affected?
- Is the timing between exposure and clinical onset compatible with the known biologic facts about cadmium exposure?
- Is the exposure dose within the range of doses believed to cause such effects?

Regarding Treatment:

- Was individual removed from exposure?
- Were complications such as kidney stones and metabolic bone disease prevented?

Regarding prognosis:

- Are there alternative ways of constructing the case that better fit the available facts?
- If there is significant uncertainty about the cause, how important is it to be certain?

References

Proctor and Hughes' Chemical Hazards of the Workplace, 3rd edition. Hathaway, G.J., et al., eds. New York: Van Nostrand Reinhold, 1991.

Occupational Medicine. LaDou, J., ed. Norwalk, CT: Appleton and Lange, 1990.

Agency for Toxic Substances and Disease Registry. Case Studies in Environmental Medicine: Arsenic, Beryllium, Cadmium, Cholinesterase Inhibitors, Lead, Mercury. US Department of Health and Human Services, 1993.

Goodman & Gilman's The Pharmacological Basis of Therapeutics. Hardman, J.G., and L.E. Lilmbird, eds. New York: McGraw-Hill, 1996.

Toxic Effects, Carbon Disulfide

Other names / synonyms: Carbon Bisulfide Poisoning, Carbon Disulfide Poisoning, Carbon Sulfide Poisoning, Dithiocarbonic Anhydride Poisoning, Sulphocarbonic Anhydride Poisoning, Weeviltox Poisoning

982.2

Definition

Pure carbon disulfide is a colorless liquid with a pleasant odor similar to chloroform. The impure carbon disulfide used in most industrial processes is a yellowish liquid with an unpleasant odor. The odor properties are not sufficient to provide adequate warning of hazardous concentrations. Carbon disulfide has been an important industrial chemical since the 1800s with many useful properties including the ability to solubilize fats, rubbers, phosphorus, sulfur, and other elements. Carbon disulfide's most important industrial use is in the manufacture of regenerated cellulose rayon (using the viscose process) and cellophane. Another principal industrial use is as a feedstock for carbon tetrachloride production. Carbon disulfide is also used to protect fresh fruit from insects and fungus during shipping, in adhesives for food packaging, and for solvent extraction of growth inhibitors.

Carbon disulfide can be absorbed into the body by inhalation, and through the skin. Individuals most often exposed to carbon disulfide are workers in plants that use carbon disulfide in the manufacturing processes. Prolonged exposure of female workers to low concentrations of carbon disulfide is associated with birth defects in their children. Exposure limit values provide little margin of safety for risk of developmental effects.

Diagnosis

Toxicology: Carbon disulfide toxicity can involve all parts of the nervous system including damage to the cranial nerves and development of peripheral neuropathy with paresthesias and muscle weakness, unsteady gait and dysphagia. There may be permanent axonal neuropathy. In extreme cases of intoxication, a Parkinsonian-like syndrome may occur, characterized by speech disturbances, muscle spasticity, tremor, memory loss, depression and marked psychic symptoms; permanent disability is likely. Psychosis and suicide are established risks after overexposure.

Other reported effects of exposure include multiple ocular effects, GI disturbances, renal damage, hypertension and high frequency hearing loss.

Epidemiologic surveys indicate that overexposure to carbon disulfide is associated with an increase in coronary heart disease.

Treatment

The first step in therapy is to remove the individual from further exposure. Treatment after this depends on the extent of exposure and the organ system affected.

If carbon disulfide exposure is by inhalation, the individual should be moved to fresh air and given artificial respiration, as indicated. Inhalation therapy may be necessary. Following skin contact, the skin should be rinsed with plenty of water, contaminated clothing removed, and the skin rinsed again. Eyes should be liberally flushed with water for several minutes. Contact lenses should be removed if possible.

Prognosis

Prognosis is dependent on the extent and duration of exposure.

Differential Diagnosis

Clinical presentation may be similar to systemic diseases involving the same organ systems. The possibility of exposure to other toxic agents should always be considered.

Specialists

- Medical Toxicologist
- Occupational Medicine Physician

Rehabilitation

Rehabilitation may be required if there are functional deficits. The specific form of rehabilitation will be dependent on the type and extent of functional deficits.

Work Restrictions / Accommodations

Exposure limits: Pregnant women should not be exposed to carbon disulfide.

The Occupational Safety and Health Administration's (OSHA) established airborne permissible exposure limit (PEL) is 20 parts per million (ppm) of carbon disulfide averaged over an 8-hour work shift. OSHA has also set 30 ppm as an acceptable ceiling; and 100 ppm of carbon disulfide as a maximum peak above the acceptable ceiling concentration, not to be exceeded during any 8-hour work period.

The National Institute of Occupational Safety and Health's (NIOSH) recommended exposure limit is 1 ppm averaged over a 10-hour work shift and 10 ppm of carbon disulfide not to be exceeded during any 15-minute work period.

The American Conference of Governmental Industrial Hygienists' (ACGIH) recommended airborne exposure limit is 10 ppm of carbon disulfide averaged over an 8-hour work shift.

Comorbid Conditions

Pre-existing disease will impact the recovery, particularly if it involves the same organ systems affected by the toxic exposure.

Factors Influencing Duration

The level and length of time exposed, method of exposure, individual's response to exposure, immediacy of treatment, and response to treatment may influence the length of disability. In rare instances, disability may be permanent. Age, pre-existing disease, and mental attitude have an effect on the individual's ability to return to pre-injury functional status.

Length of Disability

Absorbed dose is the primary determinant of severity of toxic effects, and therefore severity and duration of disability. Absorbed dose is dependent on environmental levels, routes of exposure (skin contact, inhalation, ingestion) and duration of exposure. In some cases, disability may be permanent. Contact physician for additional information.

Failure to Recover

If an individual fails to recover within the maximum duration expectancy period, the reader may wish to reference the following questions to assist in better understanding the specifics of an individual's medical case.

Regarding diagnosis:

- Has exposure to carbon disulfide been confirmed?
- Is the exposure dose within the range of doses believed to cause such effects?
- Is the timing between exposure and clinical onset compatible with the known biologic facts about the hazard?
- Is the clinical illness including history, physical examination, and laboratory findings consistent with other case descriptions?
- Are there special attributes of the particular individual that make it more or less likely that he or she would be so affected?

Regarding treatment:

- Was treatment timely and appropriate for the type of exposure individual experienced?

Regarding prognosis:

- Is there a positive history of carbon disulfide exposure in the workplace?
- Has the individual recently worked in another organization where carbon disulfide exposure is higher?
- Where there remains significant uncertainty about the cause, how important is it to be certain?
- Are there alternative ways of constructing the case that better fit the available facts?

References

Proctor and Hughes' Chemical Hazards of the Workplace, 3rd edition. Hathaway, G.J., et al., eds. New York: Van Nostrand Reinhold, 1991.

Occupational Medicine. LaDou, J., ed. Norwalk, CT: Appleton and Lange, 1990.

Agency for Toxic Substances and Disease Registry. Case Studies in Environmental Medicine: Arsenic, Beryllium, Cadmium, Cholinesterase Inhibitors, Lead, Mercury. US Department of Health and Human Services, 1993.

Goodman & Gilman's The Pharmacological Basis of Therapeutics. Hardman, J.G., and L.E. Lilmbird, eds. New York: McGraw-Hill, 1996.

Toxic Effects, Carbon Monoxide
Other names / synonyms: Carbonic Oxide Poisoning, Exhaust Gas Poisoning, Flue Gas Poisoning
986

Definition

Carbon monoxide is a colorless, odorless, tasteless, nonirritating gas produced by the incomplete combustion of organic material. It is responsible for more than 5,000 deaths in the US each year. Sources of carbon monoxide include motor vehicle exhaust, improperly vented gas or wood stoves and ovens, and smoke generated by fire. Industrial processes with the potential for high carbon monoxide exposures include fluid catalytic crackers and fluid coking and moving-bed catalytic crackers in refineries; furnace, channel, and thermal operations in carbon black plants; basic oxygen furnaces; and formaldehyde production.

Any fuel-burning appliance not adequately vented and maintained can be a potential source of carbon monoxide including gas appliances (furnaces, ranges, ovens, water heaters, or clothes dryers) fireplaces, wood and coal stoves, space heaters, charcoal grills, automobile exhaust fumes, camp stoves, gas-powered lawn mowers, and power tools.

Carbon monoxide is the leading cause of death from poisoning in the US. In this country, at least 17,000 exposures were reported to regional poison centers in 1998. Several thousand deaths occur each year that can be traced to carbon monoxide poisoning. The number of cases is probably much higher due to an estimated 30% of missed diagnoses from carbon monoxide poisoning and the unreliability of death certificates.

Diagnosis

Toxicology: When inhaled, carbon monoxide combines with the oxygen-carrying substance in the blood (e.g., combines with hemoglobin to form carboxyhemoglobin). By replacing oxygen, carbon monoxide deprives tissues of the necessary oxygen for survival (tissue hypoxia). This is the major pathophysiologic disturbance in carbon monoxide poisoning. At a carbon monoxide concentration of only 0.1%, as many as 50% of the hemoglobin binding sites may be occupied by carbon monoxide. In addition to reducing the oxygen-carrying capacity of the blood, carbon monoxide interferes with release of oxygen to the tissues

History: Symptoms of carbon monoxide poisoning are varied and nonspecific. They are directly related to the duration and concentration of exposure. Individuals may report symptoms that start with frontal headaches and shortness of breath (dyspnea) and progress through a throbbing headache, impaired judgment, nausea, dizziness, visual disturbances, fatigue, confusion, fainting, and seizures. The most common symptoms are headaches, dyspnea, dizziness, and confusion with the latter being the most insidious.

Physical exam: The exam may reveal a rapid pulse (tachycardia), rapid breathing (tachypnea), cardiac arrhythmia, and altered mental status. The notorious cherry-red discoloration of the skin is a truly rare and infrequent finding. The individual may be hyperventilating.

Tests: A correct diagnosis depends on direct spectrophotometric measurement of oxyhemoglobin and carboxyhemoglobin in a blood sample or direct measurement of exhaled carbon monoxide. Levels up to 3% are normal and may reach 15% in heavy smokers. Any levels above 20% are indicative of carbon monoxide exposure. Carboxyhemoglobin levels greater than 20-30% are usually associated with moderate symptoms of intoxication, and levels greater than 50-60% are associated with a serious or fatal outcome. There is considerable variability, however, and levels do not always correlate with symptoms.

Supplemental oxygen before the test and delays between exposure and the test may produce some confusing readings, so diagnosis is most reliable when made on the basis of history, physical findings and routine laboratory tests such as arterial blood gases, CBC and EKG.

Treatment

Carbon monoxide poisoning is treated with 100% oxygen. Hyperbaric oxygen is the treatment of choice with pregnant women, individuals with heart problems, or if there is impaired mental status or coma. Where carbon monoxide poisoning is suspected, the individual should immediately be removed from the site of exposure and given supplemental oxygen in the highest available concentration. Oxygen competes with carbon monoxide for hemoglobin binding sites. Administration of 100% oxygen can reduce the half-life of carboxyhemoglobin to approximately 40 to 60 minutes, thereby restoring normal oxygen saturation within about 2 to 3 hours. It should be noted that it is difficult to deliver 100% oxygen unless the individual has a tube directly inserted into the trachea (endotracheally intubated).

Hyperbaric oxygen (HBO) administered in a sealed chamber can deliver oxygen at a pressure of 2.5 to 3.0 atmospheres and helps speed recovery and reduce neurologic effects. Hyperbaric chambers are not readily available in all locations and situations, thus their use is limited.

Because of concerns about the higher affinity of carbon monoxide for fetal hemoglobin, the recommended threshold for treatment of pregnant women is usually lower.

Prognosis

With low level and brief exposure to carbon monoxide and timely treatment, complete recovery without residual defects is expected. Coma increases the chances of permanent neurologic or psychiatric damage such as memory loss, vision, hearing and speech difficulties, and depression. Some studies showed that 25-40% of individuals died during acute exposure while 15-40% of the survivors suffered immediate or delayed neuropsychological problems and deficits.

Long-term exposure can result in death if the individual is misdiagnosed and/or not removed from further sources of exposure.

Differential Diagnosis

The differential diagnoses include vascular headaches, drug and alcohol use, stroke, food poisoning, sepsis, and psychiatric illness. Carbon monoxide poisoning may also be misdiagnosed as chronic fatigue syndrome, viral or bacterial pulmonary or gastrointestinal infection, a "run-down" condition, an endocrine problem, immune deficiency, a psychiatric/psychosomatic problem, or allergies.

Specialists

- Medical Toxicologist
- Occupational Medicine Physician

Rehabilitation

Rehabilitation may be required if there are functional deficits. The specific form of rehabilitation will be dependent on the type and extent of functional deficits.

Work Restrictions / Accommodations

Exposure limits: The Occupational Safety and Health Administration (OSHA) legal airborne permissible exposure limit (PEL) is 50 parts per million averaged over an 8-hour work shift.

The National Institute of Occupational Safety and Health (NIOSH) recommended airborne exposure limit is 35 parts per million averaged over a 10-hour work shift and 200 parts per million not to be exceeded at any time.

The American Conference of Governmental Industrial Hygienists (ACGIH) recommended airborne exposure limit is 25 parts per million averaged over an 8-hour work shift.

Comorbid Conditions

Pregnancy may lengthen disability due to carbon monoxide exposure. Carbon monoxide exposure creates an additional hazard for the fetus. In individuals with heart problems, low-level exposure to carbon monoxide has been shown to intensify that problem and may accelerate atherosclerosis or hardening of the arteries.

Factors Influencing Duration

The severity of exposure and acute significant neuropsychiatric impairment are important factors in increasing the length of disability. Age, physical condition, pre-existing disease, and mental attitude have an influence on the individual's ability to recovery pre-injury functional capacity. Any residual psychological problems from the carbon monoxide exposure would influence the individual's ability to undergo proper treatment and therapy, thereby increasing the length and level of disability.

Length of Disability

Absorbed dose is the primary determinant of severity of toxic effects, and therefore severity and duration of disability. Absorbed dose is dependent on environmental levels, routes of exposure (skin contact, inhalation, ingestion) and duration of exposure. Contact physician for additional information. Disability may be permanent.

Failure to Recover

If an individual fails to recover within the maximum duration expectancy period, the reader may wish to reference the following questions to assist in better understanding the specifics of an individual's medical case.

Regarding diagnosis:

- Are the whole blood carboxyhemoglobin and the exhaled carbon monoxide levels at or near a normal value?
- Is there a positive history of carbon monoxide exposure in the workplace?
- Has the individual recently worked in another organization where carbon monoxide exposure is higher?
- Could carbon monoxide exposure be occurring outside the workplace, i.e., in the home, community, or recreational activities?
- Does the individual have a history of smoking?
- Is the clinical illness, including the history, physical examination, and laboratory findings consistent with other case descriptions?
- Is the timing between exposure and clinical onset compatible with the known biologic facts about carbon monoxide exposure?
- Is the exposure dose within the range of doses believed to cause such effects?
- Are there special attributes of the particular individual that make it more or less likely that he or she would be so affected?
- Are there alternative ways of constructing the case that better fit the available facts?
- Where there remains significant uncertainty about the cause, how important is it to be certain?

Regarding treatment:

- Has the individual been removed completely from exposure to carbon monoxide?
- Did the individual receive treatment with 100% oxygen via the trachea (endotracheal intubation)?
- Did the individual have access to hyperbaric oxygen chamber?
- Did oxygen therapy resolve symptoms?

Regarding prognosis:

- At what level and for how long was the individual exposed to carbon monoxide?
- If exposure was extensive, has the individual experienced neurological damage, such as memory loss or speech difficulty?
- Have psychiatric disorders resulted, such as depression? If so, how will these complications be treated and what is the expected outcome with treatment?

References

Proctor and Hughes' Chemical Hazards of the Workplace, 3rd edition. Hathaway, G.J., et al., eds. New York: Van Nostrand Reinhold, 1991.

Agency for Toxic Substances and Disease Registry. Case Studies in Environmental Medicine: Arsenic, Beryllium, Cadmium, Cholinesterase Inhibitors, Lead, Mercury. US Department of Health and Human Services, 1993.

Toxic Effects, Chlorinated Hydrocarbon Solvents

Other names / synonyms: 1,1,1-Trichlorethylene Exposure, 1,1,2-Trichlorethylene Poisoning, 1,1-Dichloro-2-Chloroethylene Poisoning, 1-Chloro-2,2-Dichloroethylene Poisoning, Acetylene Trichloride Poisoning, Carbon Bichloride Poisoning, Carbon Dichloride Poisoning, Carbon Tetrachloride Exposure, Chloroform Exposure, Dichloromethane Exposure, Ethinyl Trichloride Poisoning, Ethylene Tetrachloride Poisoning, Ethylene Trichloride Poisoning, Methyl Chloroform Exposure, Methylene Chloride Exposure, Perchlorethylene Poisoning, Percolone Poisoning, Tetrachloroethylene Exposure, Trichloroethylene Poisoning, Trichloroethene Poisoning

982.3

Definition

The addition of chlorine to the carbon-hydrogen chemical backbone increases the stability and decreases the flammability of the resulting compounds. These solvents have characteristic slightly pungent odors. They are used extensively in industry as cleaning, degreasing and thinning agents because of their excellent solvent properties and low flammability relative to other effective solvents. They are also used in the manufacture of other chemicals including plastics and pesticides. Because of their high volatility and low boiling point, workplace exposures may be greater than anticipated. At high temperatures, these substances may decompose yielding highly toxic gases such as phosgene and hydrogen chloride. They are commonly encountered as mixtures with variable toxicity depending on the concentration of individual constituents.

Historically, trichloroethylene was the principal solvent used in vapor degreasing but it is being replaced to a large extent by 1,1,1-trichloroethane, which is somewhat safer. Perchlorethylene has replaced mineral spirits and carbontetrachloride as the primary dry-cleaning solvent because of decreased flammability and toxicity. Methylene chloride is used as a paint stripper and extraction agent. 1,1,1-trichloroethane is used in vapor degreasing and increasingly as a general cleaning and thinning agent. Carbon tetrachloride is still used as a chemical intermediate but most other uses have been phased out due to its liver and kidney toxicity and its potential as a human carcinogen. Use of chloroform is limited also because of its potential as a carcinogen.

Exposure to these compounds in the occupational setting is primarily by inhalation. Skin absorption is variable and usually insignificant, although dermal absorption following prolonged or extensive skin contact can cause systemic toxicity. Chloroform is present in drinking water as a byproduct of chlorination.

Diagnosis

Toxicology: As a class, the chlorinated hydrocarbons are more potent central nervous system depressants (anesthetics), and in causing liver and kidney damage than other organic solvents. Many have been shown to cause cancer in laboratory animals; due to the widespread industrial use, the issue of carcinogenic risk to humans is one of the most controversial issues in regulatory toxicology.

The chlorinated hydrocarbons have been implicated in causing sudden death at high exposure levels probably related to heart arrhythmias (ventricular fibrillation), which results when the heart tissue becomes sensitized by these chemicals to endogenous catecholamines (adrenaline). These solvents are not significant irritants of the skin and mucous membranes, but prolonged contact with the skin can result in sufficient defatting to cause a chronic dermatitis.

Carbon tetrachloride: Its use has declined significantly because of its relative potency as a liver and kidney toxin. It causes significant liver damage at exposure levels not much higher than those causing central nervous system depression. It is probable that the metabolites cause the liver injury, and this may explain why chronic alcoholics are particularly susceptible to poisoning (alcohol induces higher levels of the enzymes which also metabolize the carbon tetrachloride, thus producing higher levels of toxic metabolites).

Methylene chloride: Carbon monoxide is formed during the metabolism of methylene chloride, so exposure by inhalation or dermal absorption can cause elevated levels of carboxyhemoglobin. Simultaneous exposure to environmental carbon monoxide, including cigarette smoke, needs to be considered as additive factors of potential concern.

Trichloroethylene: In combination with even small amounts of ingested alcohol, trichloroethylene can cause a dramatic erythema (redness) predominately affecting the face and upper body. This apparently idiosyncratic Antabuse-like reaction is well recognized among workers and is commonly called "degreaser's flush." Trichloroethylene is also unusual because it is associated with the development of cranial nerve damage, particularly affecting the trigeminal nerve.

Clinical Findings: Acute effects related to central nervous system depression (anesthesia) may include symptoms of dizziness, headache, nausea, vomiting, sleepiness, fatigue, "drunkenness," slurred speech, vertigo, disorientation, depression and loss of consciousness. Respiratory tract irritation may present with sore nose, sore throat and cough.

Chronic effects include dermatitis (red, dry, cracked skin), neurobehavioral dysfunction (headaches, mood changes, memory loss, difficulty concentrating, decreased attention span, and fatigue), liver damage (abdominal pain, nausea, jaundice, abnormal liver function tests) and kidney damage (weakness, fatigue, polyuria, glycosuria, electrolyte abnormalities). Both liver and kidney damage may occur as a result of severe acute poisoning.

Tests: One way of testing for either trichloroethylene or tetrachloroethylene exposure is to measure the amount of the chemical in the exhaled breath. The breath test, if it is performed soon after exposure, can tell if the individual has been exposed to a small amount of trichloroethylene. Because it is stored in the body's fat and slowly released into the bloodstream, tetrachloroethylene can be detected in the breath for weeks following a heavy exposure. Both trichloroethylene and tetrachloroethylene and trichloroacetic acid (TCA), a breakdown product of both chemicals, can be detected in the blood.

These procedures are useful only if the exposure is recent (within weeks or less) because both solvents are rapidly eliminated from the body. In addition, samples of blood and urine tests can be used to identify the chemicals and their breakdown products in individuals suspected of being exposed to both trichloroethylene and tetrachloroethylene.

Treatment

Treatment is non-specific with removal from exposure, decontamination and supportive care.

Prognosis

The prognosis for full recovery from exposure to low levels or brief exposures at high level is good where immediate and appropriate treatment is begun. In cases where severe, irreversible damage has been done to kidney, liver or brain, long-term disability may be anticipated.

Differential Diagnosis

Liver disease, kidney disease, neurological disorders, or lung disease may present with similar signs and symptoms. The industries using chlorinated hydrocarbon solvents often use other organic solvents as well, which may be associated with similar toxicity.

Specialists

- Medical Toxicologist
- Occupational Medicine Physician

Rehabilitation

Rehabilitation may be required if there are functional deficits. The specific form of rehabilitation will be dependent on the type and extent of functional deficits.

Work Restrictions / Accommodations

The Occupational Safety and Health Administration (OSHA) legal airborne permissible exposure limit (PEL) is 100 parts per million trichloroethylene averaged over an 8-hour work shift, 200 parts per million not to be exceeded during any 15-minute work period, and 300 parts per million for 5 minutes in any 2-hour work period. The National Institute of Occupational Safety and Health (NIOSH) recommended airborne exposure limit is 25 parts per million trichloroethylene averaged over a 10-hour work shift. The American Conference of Governmental Industrial Hygienists (ACGIH) recommended airborne exposure limit is 50 parts per million trichloroethylene averaged over an 8-hour work shift and 100 parts per million as a STEL (short-term exposure limit).

The Occupational Safety and Health Administration (OSHA) legal airborne permissible exposure limit (PEL) is 100 parts per million tetrachloroethylene averaged over an 8-hour work shift and 200 parts per million which should not be exceeded at any time. The National Institute of Occupational Safety and Health (NIOSH) recommends that occupational exposure to carcinogens be limited to the lowest feasible concentration. The American Conference of Governmental Industrial Hygienists (ACGIH) recommended airborne exposure limit is 25 parts per million tetrachloroethylene averaged over an 8-hour work shift and 100 parts per million as a STEL (short-term exposure).

Exposed workers should work in well-ventilated areas if possible, immediately wash exposed skin areas, and wear protective gear as indicated.

Comorbid Conditions

Pre-existing disease will impact the recovery, particularly if it involves the same organ systems affected by the toxic exposure.

Factors Influencing Duration

The levels and duration of exposure, method of exposure, immediacy of treatment and the individual response to exposure and treatment determine length of disability. In rare instances, disability may be permanent. Age and the general state of health and pre-existing disease (particularly chronic ethanol abuse) affect duration of disability.

Length of Disability

Absorbed dose is the primary determinant of severity of toxic effects, and therefore severity and duration of disability. Absorbed dose is dependent on environmental levels, routes of exposure (skin contact, inhalation, ingestion) and duration of exposure. Contact physician for additional information.

Other factors influencing disability include pre-existing disease, age, pregnancy and allergy, all of which affect individual susceptibility to the toxic effect of chemical exposures. Psychological and emotional factors may also play a role in the extent and duration of disability. In some cases, there may be residual permanent disability despite prompt diagnosis and appropriate treatment.

Failure to Recover

If an individual fails to recover within the maximum duration expectancy period, the reader may wish to reference the following questions to assist in better understanding the specifics of an individual's medical case.

Regarding diagnosis:

- Has diagnosis of toxic effects of chlorinated hydrocarbon solvents been confirmed?
- Is there a positive history of chlorinated solvent exposure in the workplace?
- Is the clinical illness, including the history, physical examination, and laboratory findings, consistent with other case descriptions?
- Are the whole blood and urine levels of chlorinated solvents and/or their metabolites at or near the normal value?
- Is the timing between exposure and clinical onset compatible with the known biologic facts about the hazard?
- Is the exposure dose within the range of doses believed to cause such effects?
- Has individual experienced any complications related to the toxicity?
- Does individual have an underlying condition that may impact recovery?

Regarding treatment:

- What specific treatments did individual receive?
- Would individual benefit from additional or continued therapy?

Toxic Effects, Chlorinated Hydrocarbon Solvents

Regarding prognosis:

- Are there special attributes of the particular individual that make it more or less likely that he or she would be so affected?
- Could chlorinated solvent exposure be occurring outside the workplace; i.e., in the home, in the community, or in recreational activities?
- Has the individual recently worked in another organization where exposure is higher?
- If occupational duties puts individual at risk of exposure, is protective gear provided?
- Has individual been instructed in its proper use?

References

Proctor and Hughes' Chemical Hazards of the Workplace, 3rd edition. Hathaway, G.J., et al., eds. New York: Van Nostrand Reinhold, 1991.

Occupational Medicine. LaDou, J., ed. Norwalk, CT: Appleton and Lange, 1990.

Agency for Toxic Substances and Disease Registry. Case Studies in Environmental Medicine: Arsenic, Beryllium, Cadmium, Cholinesterase Inhibitors, Lead, Mercury. US Department of Health and Human Services, 1993.

Goodman & Gilman's The Pharmacological Basis of Therapeutics. Hardman, J.G., and L.E. Lilmbird, eds. New York: McGraw-Hill, 1996.

Toxic Effects, Chlorine

Other names / synonyms: Chlorine Gas Poisoning, Chlorine Water Poisoning, Javelle Water Poisoning, Molecular Chlorine Poisoning, NaC10 Poisoning

987.6

Definition

Chlorine is a green-yellow gas with an irritating odor. It is used in metal fluxing, sterilization of water, as a bleaching agent, in the synthesis of chlorinated organic compounds and plastics, and in pulp/paper manufacturing. Exposure is by inhalation.

Diagnosis

Toxicology: Chlorine is a potent irritant of the eyes, mucous membranes and skin; and causes pulmonary irritation. The location and severity of respiratory tract damage is a function of air concentration and duration of exposure. Death at high exposures is from pulmonary edema. Pneumonia is a potential serious complication.

Populations at special risk from chlorine exposure are individuals with pulmonary disease, breathing problems, bronchitis, or chronic lung conditions. Approximately 7,000 exposures to chlorine were reported by regional poison control centers for 1998, the last year that information was available. None of these exposures resulted in death.

History: Symptoms may occur immediately or shortly after exposure. The individual may complain of irritation of the eyes, nose and throat, tearing (lacrimation), coughing, bloody nose, chest pain, or burning of the skin. Pertinent history includes nature and duration of exposure and any previous lung problems.

Physical exam: Signs of respiratory distress such as rapid breathing (tachypnea), bluish skin due to lack of oxygen (cyanosis), difficulty breathing (dyspnea), or fluid in the lungs (pulmonary edema) may be present. Symptoms of pulmonary edema can be delayed up to 48 hours after exposure. A rash may be present on the skin. Shock or coma may occur.

Tests: Pulmonary function tests, chest x-rays, and arterial blood gases may be performed.

Treatment

The individual is removed from exposure. Symptoms and effects are treated as they occur.

Prognosis

Symptoms may increase in the first 2-3 days after exposure, and pulmonary function abnormalities may persist for months. Prolonged symptoms are more likely with pre-existing asthma or other chronic lung disease.

Individuals may not fully recover when exposed to high levels of chlorine for an extended period of time. Permanent damage and irreversible effects may occur. Long-term disability may result. Vision may be permanently affected.

When brief, low-level exposure to the eyes has occurred, prompt ophthalmologic treatment by trained personnel with appropriate medications should leave no permanent injury or impairment. Prompt treatment of skin exposure with dermatological medications and fluids should leave no permanent injury or disability.

Exposure to chlorine gas at 430 parts per million (ppm) for over 30 minutes is lethal. At 1,000 ppm, death may occur within a few minutes. Death is possible from pneumonia, asphyxia, shock, reflex spasm in the larynx, or massive amounts of fluid in the lungs (pulmonary edema).

Differential Diagnosis

Clinical presentation may be similar to systemic diseases involving the same organ systems. The possibility of exposure to other toxic agents should always be considered.

Specialists

- Medical Toxicologist
- Occupational Medicine Physician

Rehabilitation

Rehabilitation may be required if there are functional deficits. The specific form of rehabilitation will be dependent on the type and extent of functional deficits.

Work Restrictions / Accommodations

Exposure limits: The Occupational Safety and Health Administration (OSHA) legal airborne permissible exposure limit (PEL) is 1 ppm of chlorine, not to be exceeded at any time.

The National Institute of Occupational Safety and Health (NIOSH) recommended airborne exposure limit is 0.5 ppm of chlorine that should not be exceeded during any 15-minute work period.

The American Conference of Governmental Industrial Hygienists (ACGIH) recommended airborne exposure limit is 0.5 ppm of chlorine averaged over an 8-hour work shift and 1 ppm of chlorine as a STEL (short-term exposure limit).

The individual must have access to information about the health effects of chlorine gas exposure in the workplace. Respirators, air filters, protective clothing, and eyewear may be needed. Length and levels of chlorine gas exposure in the workplace must be monitored. The individual may need special training to handle the gas.

Comorbid Conditions

Pre-existing disease will impact the recovery, particularly if it involves the same organ systems affected by the toxic exposure.

Factors Influencing Duration

The levels and length of time exposed, method of exposure, immediacy of treatment, and the individual response to exposure and treatment determine the length of disability. Age, physical condition, pre-existing disease, and mental attitude have an influence on the individual's ability to recover pre-injury functional capacity. Smokers may have increased disability duration due to pre-existing lung function abnormalities.

Pulmonary function, lung capacity, exercise capacity, and endurance influence the ability to carry out vigorous and demanding work. Visual impairment both in extent and range influences the ability to carry out intricate detailed work and perform safely in a work environment.

Length of Disability

Absorbed dose is the primary determinant of severity of toxic effects, and therefore severity and duration of disability. Absorbed dose is dependent on environmental levels, routes of exposure (skin contact, inhalation, ingestion) and duration of exposure. Contact physician for additional information. Disability may be permanent.

Failure to Recover

If an individual fails to recover within the maximum duration expectancy period, the reader may wish to reference the following questions to assist in better understanding the specifics of an individual's medical case.

Regarding diagnosis:

- Is or was chlorine present in the exhaled air of the exposed individual?
- Is there a positive history of chlorine exposure in the workplace?
- Has the individual recently worked in another organization where chlorine exposure is higher?
- Could chlorine exposure be occurring outside the workplace, i.e., in the home, community, or recreational activities?
- Does the individual have a history of smoking?
- Is the clinical illness, including the history, physical examination, and laboratory findings, consistent with other case descriptions?
- Is the timing between exposure and clinical onset compatible with the known biologic facts about chlorine exposure?
- Is the exposure dose within the range of doses believed to cause such effects?

Regarding treatment:

- Has the individual been completely removed from exposure to chlorine?
- Does the individual require hospitalization?
- Does the individual require treatment by an ophthalmologist for eye damage?
- Does the individual require measures to assist with breathing?
- Have any complications arisen as a result of the toxicity or of the treatment?

Regarding prognosis:

- Are there special attributes of the particular individual that make it more or less likely that he or she would be so affected?
- Are there alternative ways of constructing the case that better fit the available facts?
- If there is significant uncertainty about the cause, how important is it to be certain?

References

Proctor and Hughes' Chemical Hazards of the Workplace, 3rd edition. Hathaway, G.J., et al., eds. New York: Van Nostrand Reinhold, 1991.

Agency for Toxic Substances and Disease Registry. Case Studies in Environmental Medicine: Arsenic, Beryllium, Cadmium, Cholinesterase Inhibitors, Lead, Mercury. US Department of Health and Human Services, 1993.

Toxic Effects, Chromium

Other names / synonyms: Alpaste Poisoning, Chrome Poisoning, Chromium Element Poisoning, Chromium Fulleride Poisoning

985.6

Definition

Chromium is primarily used for making steel and other alloys. In the form of chromate, it is used in making bricks for metallurgical furnaces. Chromium compounds are employed in chrome plating, the manufacture of pigments, leather tanning, wood treatment, and water treatment.

Workers in industries that produce chromium-containing products are exposed to possible toxic levels. Other occupations that expose workers to chromium are painting, maintenance and servicing of copying machines and disposal of toner powders from these machines, battery makers, candle makers, dye makers, printers, and rubber makers.

Diagnosis

Toxicology: Chromium compounds vary greatly in toxicity depending on the chemical state (valence) and solubility. Health and exposure standards (e.g., ACGIH) are divided into categories: 1) Chromium metal and alloys (including stainless steel); 2) Divalent chromium compounds (e.g., chromous chloride, chromous sulfate); 3) Trivalent compounds (e.g., chromic oxide, chromic sulfate, chromic chloride); 4) Hexavalent compounds (e.g., chromates, dichromates). Certain hexavalent compounds are considered carcinogenic and these compounds tend to be of low solubility in water. Hence the hexavalent compounds are further subdivided into water soluble (e.g., chromic acid) and water insoluble compounds (e.g., zinc chromate).

The metal, divalent and trivalent compounds are relatively non-toxic, probably because of poor absorption via skin/mucous membranes. Unlike Nickel, Chromium metal does not cause allergic dermatitis. Water soluble hexavalent Chromium compounds are severe irritants of the upper respiratory tract, lungs and skin. They are associated with effects such as ulcerations of the skin and nasal mucosa, rhinitis, nosebleed, asthma, pulmonary edema, dermatitis (both irritant and allergic), erosion and discoloration of the teeth, and kidney damage. Exposure to certain water-insoluble compounds appears to be associated with an increased risk of lung cancer.

Skin and mucosal ulcers in exposed workers are readily diagnosed on the basis of job history. A diagnosis of dermatitis requires patch testing for allergy. Airway disease can be diagnosed by improvement following decreased exposure after environmental controls, personal protection or job transfer.

Treatment

Patients with contact dermatitis or true asthma will often require job transfer because of sensitivity to even small exposures. Holes in the skin and nose will heal once exposures are reduced.

Prognosis

The prognosis for recovery is good where the individual has received prompt, effective, and appropriate treatment. Symptoms may disappear when exposure is eliminated and proper worker protection provided.

Exposure to chromium fumes can cause metal fume fever. Severe cases of exposure can cause convulsions and death. Chromium toxicity may cause adverse effects in the kidney (nephritis) and liver, and in the immune system. Chronic exposure has been associated with lung cancer.

Differential Diagnosis

Clinical presentation may be similar to systemic diseases involving the same organ systems. The possibility of exposure to other toxic agents should always be considered.

Specialists

- Medical Toxicologist
- Occupational Medicine Physician

Rehabilitation

Rehabilitation may be required if there are functional deficits. The specific form of rehabilitation will be dependent on the type and extent of functional deficits.

Work Restrictions / Accommodations

Exposure limits: The current national interim primary drinking water regulation for chromium (VI) proposed by EPA is 0.05 milligram per liter (mg/L).

OSHA legal airborne permissible exposure limit (PEL) to chromium is 1 milligram per cubic meter averaged over an 8-hour work shift.

The National Institute of Occupational Safety and Health (NIOSH) recommended airborne exposure limit to chromium is 0.5 milligram per cubic meter averaged over a 10-hour work shift.

The American Conference of Governmental Industrial Hygienists (ACGIH) recommended airborne exposure limit to chromium is 0.5 milligram per cubic meter averaged over an 8-hour work shift.

The individual should avoid skin contact with chromium and wear protective gloves and clothing. All protective clothing (suits, gloves, footwear, and headgear) should be clean, available each day, and put on before work. The individual should also wear impact-resistant eye protection with side shields or goggles. A face shield along with goggles should be worn when working with corrosive, highly irritating or toxic substances.

Where the potential for high exposure exists, a MSHA/NIOSH-approved supplied air respirator with a full face piece operated in a pressure-demand or other positive-pressure mode should be used. For increased protection, it should be used in combination with an auxiliary self-contained breathing apparatus operated in a pressure-demand or other positive-pressure mode.

Exposure to 250 milligrams per cubic meter is immediately dangerous to life and health. If the possibility of exposure above 250 milligrams per cubic meter exists, a MSHA/NIOSH approved self-contained breathing apparatus with a full face piece operated in a pressure-demand or other positive-pressure mode should be used.

Length and levels of chromium exposure in the workplace must be monitored. The individual may need special training to handle the chemical.

Comorbid Conditions

Pre-existing disease will impact the recovery, particularly if it involves the same organ systems affected by the toxic exposure.

Factors Influencing Duration

The levels and length of time exposed, method of exposure, immediacy of treatment, and the individual response to exposure and treatment will determine length of disability.

Other factors influencing disability include pre-existing disease, age, pregnancy and allergy, all of which affect individual susceptibility to the toxic effect of chemical exposures. Psychological and emotional factors may also play a role in the extent and duration of disability. In some cases, there may be residual permanent disability despite prompt diagnosis and appropriate treatment.

Length of Disability

Absorbed dose is the primary determinant of severity of toxic effects, and therefore severity and duration of disability. Absorbed dose is dependent on environmental levels, routes of exposure (skin contact, inhalation, ingestion) and duration of exposure. Contact physician for additional information.

Failure to Recover

If an individual fails to recover within the maximum duration expectancy period, the reader may wish to reference the following questions to assist in better understanding the specifics of an individual's medical case.

Regarding diagnosis:

- Did the individual present with symptoms consistent with the diagnosis of chromium toxicity?
- Did the individual have a known exposure to chromium, such as in the workplace, home, community or during recreation activities?
- Is there a genetic history for the complaint, i.e., liver or kidney abnormalities, gastrointestinal disorders, psychiatric disturbances?
- Is the clinical illness, including the history, physical examination, and laboratory findings consistent with the diagnosis of chromium toxicity?
- Is the exposure dose within the range of doses believed to cause such effects?
- Would the individual benefit from consultation with a specialist?

Regarding treatment:

- Was the treatment appropriate for the type of exposure and severity of symptoms?
- Did symptoms persist?
- Were other more aggressive treatments, such as administering metal complexing agents considered?

Regarding prognosis:

- Did the individual any conditions that may complicate treatment? What was the expected outcome?

References

Proctor and Hughes' Chemical Hazards of the Workplace, 3rd edition. Hathaway, G.J., et al., eds. New York: Van Nostrand Reinhold, 1991.

Agency for Toxic Substances and Disease Registry. Case Studies in Environmental Medicine: Arsenic, Beryllium, Cadmium, Cholinesterase Inhibitors, Lead, Mercury. US Department of Health and Human Services, 1993.

Toxic Effects, Fish and Shellfish

Other names / synonyms: Amnestic Shellfish Poisoning, ASP, Ciguatera Poisoning, Diarrheal Shellfish Poisoning, DSP, Neurologic Shellfish Poisoning, NSP, Paralytic Shellfish Poisoning, PSP, Scombroid Poisoning, Tetraodon Poisoning

988.0

Definition

Humans can become ill from eating certain varieties of poisonous fish or contaminated shellfish. Most cases of fish poisoning are caused by one of three toxins. These toxins are identified as scombroid, ciguatera, and tetraodon poisoning.

Scombroid poisoning occurs when bacterial decomposition produces high levels of histamine in fish flesh after the fish is caught. Commonly implicated species include tuna, mackerel, bonito, skipjack, and mahi-mahi.

Ciguatera poisoning is the most common nonbacterial, fish-borne poisoning in the US. It is caused by consumption of reef fish that feed on certain algae associated with coral reef systems. Species of fish most frequently implicated include grouper, amberjack, red snapper, eel, sea bass, barracuda, and Spanish mackerel. Ciguatoxin and other similar toxins found in this type of poisoning are heat stable and lipid soluble. This means that temperature, gastric acid, or the cooking method does not affect them. The presence of toxin does not affect odor, color, or taste of the fish.

Most ciguatera outbreaks in the US occur in Hawaii and Florida, although tourists may develop symptoms after returning home. Ciguatera poisoning is seldom lethal. Typical incidence of mortality is 0.1% with reported mortality rates of up to 20%. Death usually is attributed to cardiovascular depression, respiratory paralysis, or decrease in the volume of the circulating blood (hypovolemic shock).

Tetraodon poisoning is caused by the ingestion of certain species of puffer fish found in waters of the Far East. These fish contain a potent, heat-stable toxin that affects the human nervous system. Symptoms of tetrodotoxin poisoning occur within minutes after eating the fish. Reports of tetrodotoxin poisoning are rare in the US.

The source of poison in shellfish has been traced to poisonous plankton that the shellfish feed upon during certain times of the year. The term shellfish refers to any aquatic invertebrate animal with a shell, i.e., bivalve mollusks (oysters, mussels, scallops, and clams), mollusks with only one shell or none (abalone, whelk, and conch), and crustacean forms (shrimp and prawns).

The four distinct shellfish-poisoning syndromes are paralytic shellfish poisoning (PSP), neurologic shellfish poisoning (NSP), diarrheal shellfish poisoning (DSP), and amnestic shellfish poisoning (ASP). All four syndromes share common features and primarily involve bivalve mollusks. A separate, unique toxin is responsible for each of the shellfish syndromes. Shellfish are filter feeders and, therefore, accumulate toxins produced by microscopic algae and single cellular algae (diatoms). Toxins responsible for most shellfish poisonings are water-soluble, heat- and acid-stable, and not inactivated by ordinary cooking methods. Toxic outbreaks are often associated with the blooming of single-celled algae. This proliferation (rapid growth) of toxic algae is known as red tide and usually occurs during warmer weather.

Most recent cases of PSP occurred along the northeast Atlantic coast, northwest Pacific coast, or Alaska. Most cases involve recreational shellfish collectors, not commercial vendors. Since 1927, 500 cases of PSP and 30 deaths have been reported in California. Sporadic and continuous outbreaks of NSP occur along the Gulf coast from Florida to Texas.

Fatality rates from PSP, the most severe of the four syndromes, range from 1-12% in isolated outbreaks. The high mortality in some areas is due to poor access to advanced life support capabilities. The mortality rate in the only known outbreak of ASP was 3%. To date, no deaths have been reported for NSP or DSP.

Diagnosis

History: The individual with suspected scombroid poisoning may present with nausea, vomiting, headache, difficulty in swallowing, thirst, itchiness, facial flushing, stomach (epigastric) pain, and hives (urticaria) within a few minutes after eating the fish. Symptoms usually last less than 24 hours.

The individual with ciguatera poisoning may present with abdominal cramps, nausea, vomiting, diarrhea, weakness, numbness, muscle pain, and general itchiness. Itching (pruritus), prickling or tingling (paresthesias), headache, muscle pain (myalgia), reversal of the sensations of hot and cold, and face pain may also occur. Symptoms may develop immediately after eating or may be delayed for as long as 30 hours. They may then increase in frequency and severity over the next 4 to 6 hours and can last 6 to 17 hours.

The individual with suspected tetraodon poisoning may present with dizziness and tingling about the lips and tongue. The first symptoms occur 15 minutes to several hours after ingestion of tetrodotoxin-containing food. Initial symptoms include a sensation of pricking, tingling, or creeping on the lip and tongue (paresthesias) followed by facial and extremity paresthesias and numbness. Salivation, nausea, vomiting, and diarrhea with abdominal pain develop early and can be severe. Severely poisoned individuals may be very weak, have difficulty speaking, and be unable to give a history.

All four shellfish syndromes can produce symptoms from a few minutes to several hours after ingestion of contaminated shellfish. Symptoms often begin within 10 minutes after eating the shellfish. Initially, there is tingling and numbness about the lips with prickly feelings in the fingertips. The throat is often dry. In paralytic shellfish poisoning, the onset is generally noted with paresthesias of the lips, tongue, and gums. Symptom onset is usually within 30 minutes of ingestion. This rapidly progresses to involve the fingers and toes. Other symptoms include a sensation of floating, headache, ataxia, muscle weakness, paralysis, and abnormal nerve sensations on the head. Gastrointestinal (GI) symptoms are less common but may include nausea, vomiting, diarrhea, and abdominal pain.

Physical exam: Examination of individuals with suspected scombroid poisoning may reveal flushing, palpitations, headache, nausea, diarrhea, sense of anxiety or unease, prostration or loss of vision (rare) with diffuse, macular, blanching erythema. Rapid heart rate (tachycardia), wheezing (generally only in histamine-sensitive asthmatics), low blood pressure (hypotension), or high blood pressure (hypertension) may also be noted.

Examination of individuals with suspected ciguatera poisoning may reveal dehydration from GI losses. Neurologic findings are extremely variable from mild to life-threatening. Cardiovascular findings include slow heart rate (bradycardia) and hypotension. Shock may be present.

With suspected tetraodon poisoning, there may be loss of sensory and motor neuron function. Cyanosis, hypotension, and cardiac rhythm disturbances may be noted as well. There may be motor dysfunction with weakness and speech difficulties. Extremity paralysis precedes paralysis of brain parts associated with speech or swallowing. Heart abnormalities (cardiac dysfunction) with hypotension and dysrhythmias (abnormal heart rhythms), central nervous system (CNS) dysfunction (e.g., coma), and seizures may develop. Individuals with severe toxicity may have deep coma, fixed nonreactive pupils, apnea (cessation of breathing), and loss of all brainstem reflexes.

Examination of individuals with suspected shellfish poisoning may reveal volume depletion from GI symptoms common to all shellfish poisoning syndromes. GI problems are noted less often in paralytic shellfish poisoning than in the other syndromes. Paresthesias of the face and extremities are noted only in paralytic and neurologic shellfish poisoning. Amnestic shellfish poisoning is the only shellfish syndrome with cognitive dysfunction as an early finding.

Tests: There are no laboratory tests necessary in suspected scombroid poisoning. In cases where palpitations are a predominant symptom, an electrocardiogram (ECG) may be necessary. Routine laboratory tests (urinalysis, complete blood count, electrolytes, enzymes) may be done when ciguatera poisoning is suspected.

Direct human serum assays for shellfish toxins are not yet available. Routine blood electrolytes, calcium, magnesium and arterial blood gases (ABGs) may be measured to rule out metabolic causes of diffuse sensory and motor nerve abnormalities. Chest and abdominal x-rays and CT may be needed.

Treatment

Symptoms of scombroid poisoning usually subside within 12 hours. If the individual is symptomatic enough to require treatment, antihistamines may be used to counteract the excessive histamine-induced effects. Antihistamines and bronchodilators may be used as needed if advanced life support personnel are involved. The use of activated charcoal may be considered only on very early presentation and if a large amount of fish was ingested. Oxygen and cardiac monitoring may be necessary. Treatment of ciguatera poisoning is largely supportive and symptoms may be treated as they appear. GI decontamination with activated charcoal may be of value if performed within 3 to 4 hours of ingestion. Antiemetics may be needed to control nausea and vomiting. Cool showers and antihistamines can relieve itching. Fluid replacement may be needed to control hypotension. Medications used to treat ciguatera poisoning include antihistamines, analgesics, fever control drugs (antipyretics), and anti inflammatories.

Individuals with tetraodon poisoning may require endotracheal intubation for oxygenation and airway protection when muscle weakness and vomiting are present. No drug has been shown to reverse the effects of tetrodotoxin poisoning. Treatment is symptomatic. Cardiac dysfunction may be treated with intravenous fluids and drugs to control blood pressure (pressors) and irregular heartbeats (antiarrhythmics). If vomiting is present, gastric lavage may not be necessary. Administration of activated charcoal may be done for all symptomatic individuals. Further treatment should focus on supporting cardiovascular function until the toxin is eliminated from the body.

Treatment for all shellfish poisonings is supportive and symptoms may be treated as they appear. Support and maintenance of the airway are of crucial importance in paralytic shellfish poisoning since the greatest danger is respiratory paralysis. Close monitoring for at least 24 hours and aggressive airway management should be done at any sign of respiratory compromise.

Prognosis

The prospects for full recovery of individuals with scombroid and/or ciguatera poisoning are generally excellent. For months afterward, however, unusual sensory phenomena may be severely debilitating. More than 60% of the cases of tetraodon poisoning are fatal within a few hours. Death from tetraodon poisoning can occur within 4 to 6 hours from respiratory muscle paralysis. Survival for more than 24 hours is a good sign of eventual recovery. Death (occurring in less than 10% of the cases) is usually the result of respiratory paralysis.

If the individual survives the first 12 hours of shellfish poisoning, the chances for complete recovery are good. Paralytic shellfish poisoning usually lasts 3 days but muscle weakness may persist for weeks. Severe cognitive dysfunction to the point of interfering with the ability to perform normal daily activities has been noted in a few cases of amnestic shellfish poisoning.

Differential Diagnosis

Conditions presenting with similar symptoms include mushroom poisoning, snake venoms (cobra, coral, and sea), septic shock, sinus bradycardia, ischemic stroke, reaction to heart medications, and arsenic, lithium and mercury poisonings. Botulism, gastroenteritis, and hypocalcemia may also present with similar symptoms.

Specialists

- Medical Toxicologist
- Occupational Medicine Physician

Rehabilitation

Rehabilitation may be required if there are functional deficits. The specific form of rehabilitation will be dependent on the type and extent of functional deficits.

Work Restrictions / Accommodations

Residual sensory phenomena may necessitate temporary reassignment of duties. Residual muscle weakness may require a temporary transfer to a more sedentary position and/or frequent rest breaks.

Individuals with cognitive dysfunction severe enough to interfere with normal daily activities may not be able to return to work until symptoms have resolved.

Comorbid Conditions

Coexisting gastrointestinal diseases, diabetes mellitus, cardiovascular disorders, immunosuppressed conditions, liver diseases (cirrhosis), and kidney disease may worsen the effects of many of the fish and shellfish toxins. In some individuals, asthma may also exacerbate these effects.

Complications

Complications of scombroid and/or ciguatera include residual sensory phenomena that can be severely debilitating. More than 60% of tetraodon poisonings are fatal within a few hours usually a result of respiratory muscle paralysis.

Complications of shellfish poisoning may include residual muscle weakness. Cognitive dysfunction severe enough to interfere with the ability to perform normal daily activities has been noted in amnestic shellfish poisoning.

Hepatitis A, Norwalk virus, Vibrio parahaemolyticus, and Vibrio vulnificus have all been transmitted through shellfish ingestion.

Factors Influencing Duration

The levels, duration, and route of exposure, immediacy of treatment, and the individual response to exposure and treatment determine length of disability. Length of disability may be influenced by the individual's age, general health prior to poisoning, type of poisoning, severity of symptoms, availability of appropriate treatment, individual's response to treatment, development of complications, and residual impairments.

Length of Disability

Absorbed dose is the primary determinant of severity of toxic effects, and therefore severity and duration of disability. Absorbed dose is dependent on environmental levels, routes of exposure (skin contact, inhalation, ingestion) and duration of exposure. Contact physician for additional information. Duration depends on type of poisoning and amount consumed. This condition may be fatal. Disability may be permanent.

Failure to Recover

If an individual fails to recover within the maximum duration expectancy period, the reader may wish to reference the following questions to assist in better understanding the specifics of an individual's medical case.

Regarding diagnosis:

- Are the laboratory values associated with fish and shellfish poisoning at or near the normal value?
- Is the exposure dose within the range of doses believed to cause such effects?
- Is the clinical illness including the history, physical examination, and laboratory findings consistent with other case descriptions?
- Is the timing between exposure and clinical onset compatible with the known biologic facts about the hazard?
- Is there a genetic history for the complaint, i.e., liver or kidney abnormalities, gastrointestinal disorders, or psychiatric disturbances?

Regarding treatment:

- Were symptoms resolved by treatment?
- Was a respirator or other intensive medical intervention required?

Regarding prognosis:

- Does individual suffer from residual complications (sensory impairment, muscle weakness, or cognitive impairment)?
- Are there special attributes of the particular individual that make it more or less likely to be so affected?
- Are there alternative ways of constructing the case that better fit the available facts?
- Was there significant uncertainty about the cause?

References

Proctor and Hughes' Chemical Hazards of the Workplace, 3rd edition. Hathaway, G.J., et al., eds. New York: Van Nostrand Reinhold, 1991.

Occupational Medicine. LaDou, J., ed. Norwalk, CT: Appleton and Lange, 1990.

Agency for Toxic Substances and Disease Registry. Case Studies in Environmental Medicine: Arsenic, Beryllium, Cadmium, Cholinesterase Inhibitors, Lead, Mercury. US Department of Health and Human Services, 1993.

Goodman & Gilman's The Pharmacological Basis of Therapeutics. Hardman, J.G., and L.E. Lilmbird, eds. New York: McGraw-Hill, 1996.

Toxic Effects, Formaldehyde

Other names / synonyms: Formaldehyde Poisoning, Formalin Poisoning, Methanal Poisoning, Methyl Aldehyde Poisoning, Methylene Oxide Poisoning

989.8

Definition

Formaldehyde is a colorless gas with a pungent, suffocating odor. It is often used in an aqueous solution (formalin). The primary uses for formaldehyde are in the production of urea-formaldehyde resins, phenol-formaldehyde resins, plastics, and as a chemical intermediate. Urea-formaldehyde resins and phenol-formaldehyde resins are used primarily as adhesives in the manufacture of particleboard, fiberboard, and plywood and for molding, paper treating and coating, textile treating, surface coating, and foams for insulation. Formaldehyde is a commonly used chemical compound found in as many as 3,000 different building products, and for this reason is one of the most common indoor air pollutants. It is also used in the manufacture of rubber, photographic film, leather, cosmetics, embalming fluids, disinfectants and fumigants. Regional poison control centers reported over 1,500 exposures for 1998, the last year that data were available. No deaths were reported due to these exposures.

Diagnosis

Toxicology: Formaldehyde is an irritant of the eyes and respiratory tract; it causes both primary and sensitization dermatitis. Mild eye irritation with lacrimation and other transient symptoms of mucous membrane irritation have been observed in some people at concentrations as low as 0.1 ppm (the odor of formaldehyde is perceptible to previously unexposed persons at or below 1ppm). For most people, however, a tingling sensation in the eyes, nose, and posterior pharynx is not experienced until air levels reach 2-3 ppm. Some tolerance occurs so that repeated 8 hour exposures at this level are possible. Concentrations of 10 ppm can be withstood for only a few minutes; profuse lacrimation occurs even in those acclimated to lower levels. Between 10-20 ppm it becomes difficult to take a normal breath; burning of the nose and throat becomes more severe and extends to the trachea, producing cough. Upon removal of exposure, lacrimation subsides promptly, but the nasal and respiratory irritation may persist for about an hour. Acute irritation of the respiratory tract from inhalation of high levels of formaldehyde (as in confined space situations) causes pulmonary edema, pneumonitis and death.

Formaldehyde is one of the most common causes of occupational skin disease, causing both irritant and allergic contact dermatitis. Irritant dermatitis results from direct injury to the skin and is characterized by redness and thickening of the affected areas. In more severe cases there may be blistering, scaling and fissures. Dermal sensitization to formaldehyde is a well known phenomenon. Following a 7-10 day latent period, there is typically itching, redness, blistering and scaling in sensitized individuals. Repeated contact tends to cause more severe reactions and sensitization usually persists for life.

A number of studies have suggested that formaldehyde causes asthma and/or exacerbates pre-existing respiratory conditions. Small, transient declines in lung function over the course of a workshift have been the most consistent findings.

Formaldehyde is classified as a human carcinogen and has been linked to nasal and lung cancer with a possible relationship to brain cancer and leukemia

Tests: There are no useful specific tests for exposure or biologic effects. Pulmonary function tests, chest x-rays, bronchoscopy, arterial blood gases, and endoscopy may be performed. Eyes may be examined using a slitlamp and fluorescein dye.

Treatment

The individual should be removed from further exposure to formaldehyde. Symptoms and effects are treated as they occur. Eyes and skin are flushed with copious amounts of water or saline. Antibiotic eyedrops and analgesics may be administered. Respiratory distress can be treated with oxygen, bronchodilators, inhalers, intermittent positive pressure breathing (IPPB).

Prognosis

Effects may worsen up to 20 hours after exposure and persist for several days. Inhalation effects can usually be treated and most individuals will recover fully from brief, low-level exposure to formaldehyde. Short-term exposure to formaldehyde can be fatal, particularly if exposure has occurred in a confined space. However, the odor threshold is low enough that irritation of the eyes and mucous membranes will provide adequete warning before this fatal level is reached in most situations. Ingestion of two tablespoons of formaldehyde in the form of formalin can cause death.

Differential Diagnosis

Clinical presentation may be similar to systemic diseases involving the same organ systems. The possibility of exposure to other toxic agents should always be considered.

Specialists

- Medical Toxicologist
- Occupational Medicine Physician

Rehabilitation

Rehabilitation may be required if there are functional deficits. The specific form of rehabilitation will be dependent on the type and extent of functional deficits.

Work Restrictions / Accommodations

Exposure limits: Once sensitization has occurred (either skin or respiratory tract), the individual may be precluded from working in an area where there is potential for exposure, even at levels below current standards. The Occupational Safety and Health Administration's (OSHA) legal airborne permissible exposure limit (PEL) is 0.75 parts per million (ppm) averaged over an 8-hour work shift and 2 ppm not to be exceeded during any 15-minute work period.

The National Institute of Occupational Safety and Health's (NIOSH) recommended airborne exposure limit is 0.016 ppm averaged over a 10-hour work shift and 0.1 ppm not to be exceeded during any 15-minute work period.

The American Conference of Governmental Industrial Hygienists' (ACGIH) recommended airborne exposure limit is 0.3 ppm, not be exceeded at any time.

Individuals should wear eye protection as well as protective work clothing and equipment in the workplace. Hazard and warning information should be posted in the work area. An education and training program may be needed to communicate all information on the health and safety hazards of formaldehyde for workers who may be potentially exposed to concentrations of 0.1 ppm or greater. This training should increase worker's awareness of specific hazards in their workplace and the control measures employed.

Comorbid Conditions

Previous or pre-existing lung or digestive system disease will worsen effects and complicate treatment and possibly lengthen recovery. Pregnancy may also lengthen disability.

Recovery could be delayed in individuals with hypersensitivity to formaldehyde and products containing formaldehyde. Individuals with asthma or respiratory allergies may be more profoundly affected by exposure to formaldehyde and recovery may be delayed.

Factors Influencing Duration

The levels and length of time exposed, method of exposure, immediacy of treatment, and individual's response to exposure and treatment determine the length of disability. Age, general physical condition, pre-existing medical conditions (particularly lung disease or chronic dermatitis) will influence the individual's ability to recover pre-injury functional capacity and return to work.

Length of Disability

Absorbed dose is the primary determinant of severity of toxic effects, and therefore severity and duration of disability. Absorbed dose is dependent on environmental levels, routes of exposure (skin contact, inhalation, ingestion) and duration of exposure. Contact physician for additional information.

Failure to Recover

If an individual fails to recover within the maximum duration expectancy period, the reader may wish to reference the following questions to assist in better understanding the specifics of an individual's medical case.

Regarding diagnosis:

- Has diagnosis of toxic effects of formaldehyde been confirmed?
- Is the clinical illness including the history, physical examination, and laboratory findings consistent with other case descriptions?
- Are the whole blood and urine levels of formaldehyde and/or its metabolites at or near the normal value?
- Is there a positive history of formaldehyde exposure in the workplace?
- Is the exposure dose within the range of doses believed to cause such effects?
- Is the timing between exposure and clinical onset compatible with the known biologic facts about the hazard?
- Has individual experienced any complications from exposure to formaldehyde?
- Does individual have an underlying condition that may impact recovery such as hypersensitivity to formaldehyde or products containing formaldehyde?
- Does individual smoke?

Regarding treatment:

- Did individual receive prompt and appropriate treatment for the type of formaldehyde exposure?
- Did treatment effectively resolve symptoms? What other treatment options are now warranted?

Regarding prognosis:

- Have symptoms persisted longer than expected?
- Are there special attributes of the particular individual that make it more or less likely that he or she would be so affected?
- Does individual smoke?
- Would individual benefit from enrollment in a smoking cessation program?
- Could formaldehyde exposure be occurring outside the workplace such as in the home, community, or recreational activities?
- Has the individual recently worked in another organization where formaldehyde exposure is higher?
- Are there alternative ways of constructing the case that better fit the available facts?
- Where there remains significant uncertainty about the cause, how important is it to be certain?

References

Proctor and Hughes' Chemical Hazards of the Workplace, 3rd edition. Hathaway, G.J., et al., eds. New York: Van Nostrand Reinhold, 1991.

Agency for Toxic Substances and Disease Registry. Case Studies in Environmental Medicine: Arsenic, Beryllium, Cadmium, Cholinesterase Inhibitors, Lead, Mercury. US Department of Health and Human Services, 1993.

Toxic Effects, Hydrochloric Acid

Other names / synonyms: Chlorhydric Acid Poisoning, Hydrochloride Poisoning, Hydrogen Chloride Poisoning, Muriatic Acid Poisoning, Spirits of Salts Poisoning

983.1, 987.8

Definition

Hydrochloric acid or muriatic acid is the aqueous solution of hydrogen chloride. Hydrogen chloride is a colorless to slightly yellowish gas that can be shipped as a liquefied compressed gas. Both of these have a sharp, irritating odor. Hydrogen chloride is used in the production of chlorinated organic chemicals; production of dyes and intermediates; steel pickling; various mining and oil drilling operations; and as a cleaning and sterilizing agent. It is used in the photographic, textile, brewing, food processing, and rubber industries.

Exposure may occur by inhalation, ingestion, eye or skin contact.

Treatment

There is no specific treatment. Treatment involves removal from exposure, de-contamination and supportive care. Prior to transport to a hospital emergency room following inhalation of hydrogen chloride gas, the individual must be removed from further exposure and placed in fresh air. Cardiopulmonary resuscitation or rescue breathing (CPR) must be performed, if needed. In the event of skin contact, the contaminated clothes must immediately be removed and the skin washed with flowing water for at least 15 minutes. In cases of ingestion, vomiting must not be induced. Instead the individual should be given large amounts of water or milk. Eyes exposed to hydrochloric acid must be washed immediately with large amounts of water for at least 15 minutes, holding the upper and lower lids open. The eyes should continue being irrigated with normal saline.

Prognosis

Prognosis is dependent on the extent and duration of exposure.

Differential Diagnosis

Clinical presentation may be similar to systemic diseases involving the same organ systems. The possibility of exposure to other toxic agents should always be considered.

Specialists

- Medical Toxicologist
- Occupational Medicine Physician

Rehabilitation

Rehabilitation may be required if there are functional deficits. The specific form of rehabilitation will be dependent on the type and extent of functional deficits.

Work Restrictions / Accommodations

Exposure limits: The Occupational Safety and Health Administration's (OSHA) and the National Institute of Occupational Safety and Health's (NIOSH) airborne ceiling exposure limit is 5 parts per million (ppm) that must not be exceeded. The individual must have access to information about the health effects of hydrochloric acid exposure in the workplace. Respirators, air filters, protective clothing, and eyewear may be required. The length and levels of hydrochloric acid exposure in the workplace must be stringently monitored. The individual required to handle the chemical may need special training.

Comorbid Conditions

Pre-existing disease will impact the recovery, particularly if it involves the same organ systems affected by the toxic exposure.

Factors Influencing Duration

The extent of exposure, appropriateness of treatment and extent of toxic damage will impact the duration of disability. Age, general physical condition, and pre-existing disease will also influence the duration of disability and recovery to pre-injury functional capacity and return to work.

Length of Disability

Absorbed dose is the primary determinant of severity of toxic effects, and therefore severity and duration of disability. Absorbed dose is dependent on environmental levels, routes of exposure (skin contact, inhalation, ingestion) and duration of exposure. Contact physician for additional information.

Failure to Recover

If an individual fails to recover within the maximum duration expectancy period, the reader may wish to reference the following questions to assist in better understanding the specifics of an individual's medical case.

Regarding diagnosis:

- Has diagnosis of toxic effects of hydrochloric acid been confirmed?
- Is there a positive history of hydrochloric acid exposure in the workplace?
- Is the timing between exposure and clinical onset compatible with the known biologic facts about the hazard?
- Is the exposure dose within the range of doses believed to cause such effects?
- Is the clinical illness including the history, physical examination, and laboratory findings consistent with other case descriptions?
- Has individual experienced any complications such as pulmonary edema, pneumonitis, perforation of the esophagus or stomach, or peritonitis?
- Does individual have an underlying condition that may impact recovery?

Regarding treatment:

- Was first aid administered? Did individual receive prompt and appropriate treatment?

- Was individual transported to emergency room? If treatment was delayed, did individual experience any complications?
- Has individual stopped smoking?
- Would individual benefit from enrollment in a smoking cessation program?

Regarding prognosis:

- Did individual experience any residual impairment?
- If present, how incapacitating are symptoms?
- Has the individual recently worked in another organization where hydrochloric acid exposure is higher?
- Could hydrochloric acid exposure be occurring outside the workplace such as the home, community, or recreational activities?
- Are there special attributes of the particular individual that make it more or less likely that he or she would be so affected?
- Are there alternative ways of constructing the case that better fit the available facts?
- Where there remains significant uncertainty about the cause, how important is it to be certain?

References

Proctor and Hughes' Chemical Hazards of the Workplace, 3rd edition. Hathaway, G.J., et al., eds. New York: Van Nostrand Reinhold, 1991.

Agency for Toxic Substances and Disease Registry. Case Studies in Environmental Medicine: Arsenic, Beryllium, Cadmium, Cholinesterase Inhibitors, Lead, Mercury. US Department of Health and Human Services, 1993.

Toxic Effects, Hydrofluoric Acid

Other names / synonyms: Anhydrous Hydrofluoric Acid Poisoning, Fluorhydric Acid Poisoning, Fluoric Acid Poisoning, Hydrogen Fluoride Hydrofluoride Poisoning

983.1, 987.8

Definition

Hydrofluoric acid (hydrogen fluoride, HF, or H_2F_2) is a colorless, fuming liquid or colorless gas with a strong irritating odor that is one of the most important fluorine compounds. This property is commonly used to test for the presence of a fluoride. HF is also used extensively in various forms of glass etching such as marking divisions on thermometer tubes and etching designs on glassware. It is also used in ceramic etching such as pottery decoration.

Exposure to hydrogen fluoride and its aqueous solution can occur through inhalation, ingestion, and eye or skin contact. Exposures to potentially toxic levels of hydrogen fluoride may occur where workers are engaged in the manufacture and transportation of hydrogen fluoride or where it is used as an acidizing agent during injection of acid into oil wells. Individuals may also be exposed when the fluorides are liberated during manufacture of fertilizer and the burning of coal and when used to stop fermentation in brewing. Other methods of exposure include the etching of silicon wafers in semiconductor manufacturing, purification of filter paper and graphite, enameling, and the galvanizing of iron.

Anhydrous hydrogen fluoride exposure may occur in the manufacture of chlorofluorohydrocarbons for application in refrigerant fluids, aerosol propellants, specialty solvents, high-performance plastics, and foaming agents. Exposure to HF may also occur in the manufacture and production of fluorosilicone products, pharmaceuticals, and special dyes.

Workers may be exposed to aqueous hydrogen fluoride when removing sand and scale from foundry castings, treating textiles to remove trace metals, and preparing microelectronic circuits and radio parts. Exposure may also occur in the etching, frosting, and polishing of glassware and ceramics; electroplating operations; cleaning sandstone and marble; when used as a pickling agent for stainless steel and other metals; and as a cleaner in the meatpacking industry.

Regional poison control centers reported approximately 2,700 exposure incidents to hydrogen fluoride in 1998, the last year when data were available. Three of these exposures resulted in death.

Diagnosis

Toxicology: Hydrogen fluoride as a gas is a severe respiratory irritant, and in solution it causes severe and painful burns of the skin and eyes.

Inhalation of HF produces transient choking and coughing. After a symptomatic period of several hours up to I-2 days, fever, cough, dyspnea, cyanosis and pulmonary edema may develop. Repeated exposures to excessive concentrations over years have resulted in a crippling fluorosis due to deposition of fluoride in bone.

HF solutions in contact with skin result in marked tissue destruction. Undissociated HF readily penetrates skin and deep tissue where the corrosive fluoride ion can cause necrosis of soft tissues; the tissue damage is excruciatingly painful. Tendonitis and tenosynovitis may result. The process of tissue destruction and neutralization of HF is prolonged for days, unlike other acids, which are rapidly neutralized. Because of the insidious manner of its penetration, a relatively mild or minor exposure can cause a serious burn. Delayed recognition of contact with dilute solutions often results in more severe burns than expected. Severe eye injuries from splashes have been reported.

Symptoms include severe eye, nose and throat irritation; delayed fever, cyanosis and pulmonary edema; severe and painful skin and eye burns from splashes of solutions. Prolonged or repeated exposure to low concentrations of the gas may cause nasal congestion and bronchitis.

Tests: Pulmonary function tests, chest x-rays, and arterial blood gases may be helpful. Endoscopy or bronchoscopy may be needed to evaluate burns in the respiratory and digestive tract. The cornea is examined with a slitlamp using fluorescein dye. Pelvic x-rays may be done to show the early signs of increased bone density from fluoride deposition. These signs are most apparent in the lumbar spine and pelvis. Digital x-rays should be done to evaluate bone integrity if there are burns to the fingers. Electrocardiograms (ECG) may be necessary for cardiac monitoring if burns are significant.

Fluoride concentration in urine is a useful index for exposure to hydrogen fluoride and has been found to average about 4 milligrams/liter in an end-of-shift specimen following an 8-hour exposure to 3 parts per million (ppm) of hydrogen fluoride. Dietary intake of water high in fluoride may increase the urinary fluoride concentration.

Treatment

The high risk of either immediate or delayed onset of pulmonary edema following inhalation of the gas requires that oxygen be administered immediately after a severe exposure. Close observation should be continued for 24-48 hours. The treatment is similar to that of noncardiogenic pulmonary edema from other causes. The value of systemic steroids has not been established.

Persons who have had skin contact with HF should be immediately showered for at least 10 minutes. Contaminated clothing should be removed as quickly as possible. The affected area should be immediately soaked with iced solutions of quaternary ammonium compounds. An iced solution of Epsom salts or a calcium gluconate gel is acceptable for topical therapy. If the burns appear to be deep or if there is exquisite pain, particularly if the concentration of acid was greater than 20%, the painful areas should be cautiously injected with 10% calcium gluconate.

Prognosis

Prognosis for successful recovery varies depending on severity and location of the burn. Effects of mild exposure resolve with treatment.

The prognosis for a successful outcome is poor following fluoride inhalation. Severe inhalation can cause lung damage and chronic lung disease with profound disability. The surface appearance of skin exposed to HF cannot predict the seriousness of the damage, which may be severe and delayed as the fluoride ion aggressively and destructively penetrates deeply into tissues and acts as a serious systemic poison.

The cornea may become opaque with decreased vision, blindness, and total eye destruction. The effect on the level of calcium in the blood can be so profound as to cause death. Repeated exposure via ingestion or inhalation of fluorides can result in mottled teeth, the accumulation of fluoride in bones, osteosclerosis, and kidney and liver damage. Skin lesions take a long time to heal and can result in extensive scarring.

Differential Diagnosis

Clinical presentation may be similar to systemic diseases involving the same organ systems. The possibility of exposure to other toxic agents should always be considered.

Specialists

- Medical Toxicologist
- Occupational Medicine Physician

Rehabilitation

Rehabilitation may be required if there are functional deficits. The specific form of rehabilitation will be dependent on the type and extent of functional deficits.

Work Restrictions / Accommodations

Exposure limits: The Occupational Safety and Health Administration's (OSHA) legal airborne permissible exposure limit (PEL) is 3 parts per million (ppm) averaged over an 8-hour work shift.

The National Institute of Occupational Safety and Health's (NIOSH) recommended airborne exposure limit is 3 ppm averaged over a 10-hour work shift and 6 ppm not to be exceeded during any 15-minute work period.

The American Conference of Governmental Industrial Hygienists' (ACGIH) recommended airborne exposure limit is 3 ppm, not to be exceeded at any time.

Hazard and warning information should be posted in the work area. As part of an ongoing education and training effort, individuals should be given all information on the health and safety hazards of hydrogen fluoride.

Workers should use appropriate personal protective clothing and equipment carefully selected, used, and maintained to be effective in preventing skin contact with hydrogen fluoride. The selection of the appropriate personal protective equipment (e.g., gloves, sleeves, and encapsulating suits) should be based on the extent of the worker's potential exposure to hydrogen fluoride. Nonvented, impact-resistant goggles should be worn when working with fumes, gases, or vapors. A face shield should be worn along with goggles when working with corrosive, highly irritating, or toxic substances.

Where the potential exists for exposure of over 3 ppm of hydrogen fluoride, a Mine Safety and Health Administration/National Institute of Occupational Safety and Health (MSHA/NIOSH)-approved full-face piece respirator with a chemical cartridge specific for hydrogen fluoride should be used. Increased protection may be obtained from full-face piece powered-air purifying respirators.

Comorbid Conditions

Any illness that would predispose the individual to hypocalcemia or hypomagnesemia could have an adverse effect on the ability to recovery and may lengthen disability. Pregnancy may lengthen disability.

Factors Influencing Duration

The levels and length of time exposed, method of exposure, immediacy of treatment, and the individual's response to exposure and treatment determine length of disability. The location of burns has an influence on the individual's ability to recover. Age, general physical condition, and pre-existing disease influence the individual's ability to recover pre-injury functional capacity and return to work.

Length of Disability

Absorbed dose is the primary determinant of severity of toxic effects, and therefore severity and duration of disability. Absorbed dose is dependent on environmental levels, routes of exposure (skin contact, inhalation, ingestion) and duration of exposure. Contact physician for additional information.

Failure to Recover

If an individual fails to recover within the maximum duration expectancy period, the reader may wish to reference the following questions to assist in better understanding the specifics of an individual's medical case.

Regarding diagnosis:

- Did the individual present with symptoms consistent with toxic exposure?
- Were urine and blood fluoride levels tested?
- Is there a positive history of hydrogen fluoride exposure in the workplace?
- Has the individual recently worked in another organization where hydrogen fluoride exposure is higher?
- Would the individual benefit from consultation with an appropriate specialist?
- Were other conditions with similar symptoms considered in the differential diagnosis?

Regarding treatment:

- Was the treatment appropriate for the type of exposure and severity of symptoms?
- Was hospitalization required?

Regarding prognosis:

- Was the exposure mild or significant? What was the expected outcome?
- Did the individual suffer any complications associated with the toxic exposure?
- Were the complications addressed in the treatment plan?
- Did the individual have any conditions that may complicate treatment?
- What was the expected outcome?

References

Proctor and Hughes' Chemical Hazards of the Workplace, 3rd edition. Hathaway, G.J., et al., eds. New York: Van Nostrand Reinhold, 1991.

Occupational Medicine. LaDou, J., ed. Norwalk, CT: Appleton and Lange, 1990.

Agency for Toxic Substances and Disease Registry. Case Studies in Environmental Medicine: Arsenic, Beryllium, Cadmium, Cholinesterase Inhibitors, Lead, Mercury. US Department of Health and Human Services, 1993.

Goodman & Gilman's The Pharmacological Basis of Therapeutics. Hardman, J.G., and L.E. Lilmbird, eds. New York: McGraw-Hill, 1996.

Toxic Effects, Isopropyl Alcohol

Other names / synonyms: 2-Hydroxypropane Poisoning, 2-Propanol Poisoning, Dimethylcarbinol Poisoning, Propanol-2 Poisoning, Sec-propyl Alcohol Poisoning

980.2

Definition

Isopropyl alcohol is a clear, colorless, bitter aromatic liquid that can be mixed with water, alcohol, and other common solvents. A solution of 70% isopropyl alcohol in water is used as a rubbing compound (rubbing alcohol). Isopropanol is a secondary alcohol, which is poisonous if taken internally. It is one of the cheapest alcohols and has replaced ethanol for many uses because of its similar solvent properties. Isopropanol was formerly obtained largely by catalytic reduction of acetone; oxidation of isopropanol is now the major source of acetone.

Isopropyl alcohol is used as a solvent in perfumery and in many personal cosmetic products and preparations. It is externally substituted for industrial methylated and surgical spirits. It is also used in the extraction of alkaloids, in quick-drying oils, in quick-drying inks, as an antiseptic, as a de-icing agent for liquid fuels, as a dehydrating agent, as a window cleaner, as a disinfectant, and in pliable ice packs.

Isopropyl alcohol is an irritant of the skin, eyes, mucous membranes, and upper respiratory tract. Workers in industries where isopropyl alcohol is used may be exposed to harmful levels via inhalation. Ingestion may occur through intentional or accidental consumption of products containing isopropyl alcohol, in place of ethyl alcohol products.

Persons with allergies or who are hypersensitive to alcohol solvents may be adversely affected through skin contact with products containing isopropyl alcohol. Household and cosmetic products that contain isopropanol pose a hazard for accidental ingestion and contribute to allergic and sensitivity reactions. Regional poison control centers in this country reported exposures in excess of twenty thousand.

Diagnosis

History: The individual will have a documented history of recent exposure to isopropyl alcohol. Symptoms of exposure may include dizziness, giddiness, headache, nausea, vomiting, irritation of the skin, eyes, nose, and throat. The individual's eyes may be red and painful. The individual may appear to be inebriated and drunkenness may occur. Repeated skin exposure can cause itching, redness, rash, drying, and cracking. Prolonged skin contact may cause corrosion. Effects may include reduced memory and concentration, personality changes (withdrawal, irritability), fatigue, sleep disturbances, reduced coordination, and/or effects on nerves supplying internal organs (autonomic nerves) and/or nerves to the arms and legs (weakness, "pins and needles").

Physical exam: Pulmonary examination of the individual may reveal irritation of the respiratory tract, respiratory depression, slow or labored breathing (dyspnea), or slurred speech. Flushing, a decrease in pulse rate, unresponsive reflexes, lowered blood pressure, decreased body temperature, a decrease or increase in urine output, abdominal pain, and vomiting of bright red blood (hematemesis) may also be found. Eye examination may reveal corneal burns, blurred vision, and eye damage.

Tests: The amount of isopropyl alcohol in expired air may be measured. Whole blood analysis shows the level of both isopropyl alcohol and its metabolites, and low blood sugar levels. A routine urinalysis will also show the levels of isopropyl alcohol and its metabolites as well as electrolyte levels. Tests of the central nervous system may show a depression.

Treatment

The first step in therapy is to remove the individual from further exposure. Further treatment depends on the extent of exposure and the organ system affected. When isopropyl alcohol has been ingested, the stomach should be emptied, except for very small amounts, via flushing out with water (gastric lavage). Laxatives and activated charcoal may be administered. Vomiting should not be induced; volatile chemicals have a high risk of being aspirated into the individual's lungs during vomiting which increases the medical problems. If the individual is conscious and not convulsing, give 1-2 glasses of water to dilute the chemical. Dehydration and electrolyte changes should be corrected. Blood pressure should be monitored. Kidney dialysis may be necessary.

Following inhalation exposure, the individual should be removed to the fresh air. Respiratory support should be provided along with oxygen and fluids where high-level inhalation exposure has occurred. Where contact with the skin has occurred, flood the affected skin with water, then gently wash all affected skin thoroughly with soap and water.

When isopropyl alcohol has come into contact with the eyes, first check the individual for contact lenses and remove if present. Then flush the eyes with water or normal saline solution for 20-30 minutes, or longer if necessary (lifting the upper and lower lids occasionally).

Prognosis

The prognosis for full recovery is good when immediate and appropriate treatment is begun. Age, general physical condition, and attitude will have an important influence on the progress to recovery. In cases where severe, irreversible damage has been done to kidney and liver, long-term disability may be anticipated. There is an increased incidence of nasal sinus cancer in workers involved in the manufacture of isopropyl alcohol by the strong-acid process.

Differential Diagnosis

Lung disease, gastrointestinal disease, mental disturbances, alcoholism, liver disease, vision problems, and eye diseases may also present with similar signs and symptoms.

Specialists

- Medical Toxicologist
- Occupational Medicine Physician

Rehabilitation

Should poisoning by ingestion have been done intentionally, a psychological counseling and supportive therapy program would be useful. Physical therapy of an indefinite length may be necessary where impaired motor functions are present.

Work Restrictions / Accommodations

Exposure limits: The Occupational Safety and Health Administration (OSHA) has set the legal airborne permissible exposure limit (PEL) at 400 parts per million of isopropyl alcohol averaged over an 8-hour workshift.

The National Institute of Occupational Safety and Health (NIOSH) has recommended an airborne exposure limit of 400 parts per million of isopropyl alcohol averaged over a 10-hour workshift, not to exceed 500 parts per million of isopropyl alcohol during any 15-minute work period.

The American Conference of Governmental Industrial Hygienists (ACGIH) has recommended an airborne exposure limit of 400 parts per million of isopropyl alcohol averaged over an 8-hour workshift not to exceed 500 parts per million of isopropyl alcohol as a STEL (short-term exposure limit).

Comorbid Conditions

Pregnancy may worsen the effects of exposure to isopropyl alcohol. The presence of pre-existing kidney disease, pulmonary insufficiency, or diminished respiratory capacity may lengthen the disability and influence the recovery.

Complications

Heavy use of alcoholic beverages enhances the harmful effect of isopropyl alcohol. Isopropyl alcohol has not been adequately evaluated to determine whether brain or other nerve damage could occur with repeated exposure. However, many solvents and other petroleum-based chemicals that contain it have been shown to cause such damage.

Factors Influencing Duration

The levels, duration, and route of exposure, immediacy of treatment, and the individual response to exposure and treatment determine length of disability. Age, general state of health, excessive use alcoholic beverages, liver and kidney diseases will limit response to treatment and slow recovery.

Length of Disability

Absorbed dose is the primary determinant of severity of toxic effects, and therefore severity and duration of disability. Absorbed dose is dependent on environmental levels, routes of exposure (skin contact, inhalation, ingestion) and duration of exposure. Contact physician for additional information

Failure to Recover

If an individual fails to recover within the maximum duration expectancy period, the reader may wish to reference the following questions to assist in better understanding the specifics of an individual's medical case.

Regarding diagnosis:

- Is the individual exposed to isopropyl alcohol as a solvent, an antiseptic, an extracting agent, a dehydrating agent, or as a disinfectant?
- Does the individual have allergies to alcohol solvents?
- Does the individual complain of dizziness, giddiness, headache, nausea, vomiting, or irritation of the skin, eyes, nose, or throat?
- Does the individual complain of itching, redness, rash, drying, and cracking of the skin?

- Does the individual note memory, concentration, or personality changes (withdrawal, irritability)?
- Does the individual report fatigue, sleep disturbances, reduced coordination, and/or weakness, or "pins and needles" in the extremities?
- Was the amount of isopropyl alcohol in expired air, in blood, and in urine measured?

Regarding treatment:

- Has the individual been removed completely from further exposure?
- If the isopropyl alcohol was ingested, did the individual require stomach pumping (gastric lavage) or administration of laxatives or activated charcoal?
- Following inhalation exposure, was respiratory support required? If so, was it provided quickly?
- Where contact with the skin occurred, was the affected skin flooded with water, then gently washed thoroughly with soap and water?
- If eye contact occurred, were the eyes flushed with water or normal saline solution for at least 20-30 minutes?
- Did treatment resolve all symptoms?

Regarding prognosis:

- What were the level, duration, and route of exposure?
- Was treatment begun immediately and appropriately?
- Has the individual's age, general physical condition, or attitude affected prognosis?
- Does the individual understand that alcoholic beverages enhance the harmful effect of isopropyl alcohol?
- Has the individual experienced severe, irreversible damage to kidneys or liver?
- Are there special attributes of the particular individual that make it more or less likely that he or she would be so affected?
- Are there alternative ways of constructing the case that better fit the available facts?
- Where there remains significant uncertainty about the cause, how important is it to be certain?

References

Proctor and Hughes' Chemical Hazards of the Workplace, 3rd edition. Hathaway, G.J., et al., eds. New York: Van Nostrand Reinhold, 1991.

Occupational Medicine. LaDou, J., ed. Norwalk, CT: Appleton and Lange, 1990.

Agency for Toxic Substances and Disease Registry. Case Studies in Environmental Medicine: Arsenic, Beryllium, Cadmium, Cholinesterase Inhibitors, Lead, Mercury. US Department of Health and Human Services, 1993.

Goodman & Gilman's The Pharmacological Basis of Therapeutics. Hardman, J.G., and L.E. Lilmbird, eds. New York: McGraw-Hill, 1996.

Toxic Effects, Lead (Inorganic Compounds)

Other names / synonyms: Lead Poisoning, Lead Toxicity, Plumbism

961.2, 984, 984.0, 984.9

Definition

The most important uses of lead currently are in storage batteries, paints and ceramic glazes; as a component of solder (auto radiators) and in ammunition. Industries with particularly high potential exposures include construction and remodeling work, lead smelter operations and mines, lead recovery from storage batteries, and radiator repair shops. Other occupations at risk include plumbing, pipe fitting, auto repair, glass or plastic manufacturing, shipbuilding, printing, police work, steel welding, rubber product manufacturing, and firing range instruction.

Exposure to lead occurs by breathing it in (inhalation) or ingestion (oral route), with inhalation the most significant form of occupational exposure. The effects of lead are the same regardless of the route of exposure.

Diagnosis

Toxicology/Clinical Effects: Intense exposure over a brief period may cause a syndrome of acute lead poisoning characterized by abdominal colic, altered bowel habits, fatigue, and hemolytic anemia. In profound cases, a full-blown acute encephalopathy may occur. In milder cases only headache or personality change may be present. Mild liver toxicity and musculoskeletal pains may also occur. Kidney damage (proximal tubular injury) which occurs with childhood poisoning, has not been reported after occupational exposures.

Chronic poisoning is an insidious illness prevalent among individuals overexposed for months to years. Symptoms include arthralgias, headache, weakness, depression, loss of libido, impotence, and vague gastrointestinal complaints. Colic and anemia are usually absent. Although routine examination is often unremarkable, careful assessment of neuropsychiatric function may show diffuse abnormalities of mood, memory and non-verbal intelligence. Nerve conduction and motor function may also be decreased. Assessment of endocrine function, renal function and spermatogenesis may show abnormalities. Late effects include chronic renal failure and brain dysfunction. Hypertension is more common in lead exposed populations.

The diagnosis of lead poisoning requires demonstration of an excess body burden of lead, evidence of organ system impairment consistent with lead and exclusion of other likely causes of the impairment.

Body burden is most easily documented by finding an elevated whole blood lead level (BLL). Normal adult levels are <25ug/dl; symptoms may occur > 40ug/dl and become more frequent and severe as levels increase. One problem with BLL is that it tends to reflect most recent exposure and may inaccurately reflect body burden if exposure has been intermittent or has terminated. Tests that measure lead effect on hemoglobin synthesis such as Zinc Protoporphyrin (ZPP) or Free Erythrocyte Protoporphyrin rise abruptly when BLL reach about 40ug/dl and tend to stay elevated for several months after exposure ceases.

The "gold standard" for body burden is measurement of urinary lead after intramuscular injection of 1 gram of calcium EDTA (a chelating agent also used for treatment of severe poisoning). Urinary levels over 600ug in a 72 hour collection establish an elevated body burden from excessive exposure.

There are no other findings that are either very sensitive or specific for lead poisoning.

Treatment

Removal from exposure is of course essential in all cases of lead intoxication. In acute poisoning, chelation with EDTA should be done if there are severe neurological or gastrointestinal symptoms. The individual should be hospitalized and the treatment should be managed by a physician who has experience with chelation therapy.

Prognosis

Optimal treatment should allow full recovery from lead exposure and its effects, but damage to organs and tissue may not be reversible. The body accumulates lead over a lifetime and normally releases it very slowly. Most body lead (over 95%) is stored in the bones and teeth where it may remain for up to 25 years, however, lead may be released into the blood in times of stress and cause symptoms.

Differential Diagnosis

In mild cases, the symptoms of lead poisoning are very non-specific (e.g., vague GI complaints, headache, weakness), and the diagnosis is often delayed if the exposure history is not obtained. Signs of lead encephalopathy may resemble those of degenerative, metabolic, or other brain diseases such as Alzheimer's disease or other dementia. Physical examination does not easily distinguish lead colic from other abdominal disorders. Long-standing heavy lead exposure results in a pattern of kidney damage difficult to distinguish from the effects of hypertension with signs and symptoms that include hardening of the kidney (nephrosclerosis) and evidence of both glomerular and tubular defects.

Specialists

- Medical Toxicologist
- Occupational Medicine Physician

Rehabilitation

Rehabilitation may be required if there are functional deficits. The specific form of rehabilitation will be dependent on the type and extent of functional deficits.

Work Restrictions / Accommodations

Lead should be removed from the workplace, if possible. If this is not possible, individuals with symptoms or elevated blood lead levels should be reassigned or transferred. Pregnant women should especially be made aware of the risks of lead exposure in the workplace. Parents should avoid bringing contaminated clothing home so as not to inadvertently expose their children.

The OSHA lead standard requires "medical removal protection" if the BLL is above 60 ug/dl or the average of the last 3 levels is above 50 ug/dl. Blood lead levels are repeated every month. When 2 consecutive levels are below 40 ug/dl, the worker may return to the worksite.

Comorbid Conditions

Hypertension may contribute to the renal injury sometimes accompanying lead exposure, and conversely, lead exposure may aggravate the kidney disease associated with essential hypertension. The anemic characteristic of lead intoxication may be worsened by other factors that can cause anemia. Pre-existing kidney and liver diseases slow the elimination of chelated lead from the body and may cause further damage to these organs and result in lengthy rehabilitation and recovery periods. Brain or nerve damage from other causes may exacerbate the signs, symptoms, and complications of lead encephalopathy and peripheral neuropathy.

Factors Influencing Duration

State of general health, age, pre-existing disease and duration of exposure to lead all influence rate and extent of recovery from lead exposure. The effects of lead exposure may be worsened where CNS diseases and disorders are present and prolong the extent and length of recovery. On rare occasions, permanent disability may result from these pre-existing conditions.

Length of Disability

Absorbed dose is the primary determinant of severity of toxic effects, and therefore severity and duration of disability. Absorbed dose is dependent on environmental levels, routes of exposure (skin contact, inhalation, ingestion) and duration of exposure. Contact physician for additional information.

The levels and length of time exposed, method of exposure, immediacy of treatment, and the individual's response to exposure and treatment will determine length of disability. In some cases, disability may be permanent. Age and the general state of health and pre-existing disease will affect disability.

Failure to Recover

If an individual fails to recover within the maximum duration expectancy period, the reader may wish to reference the following questions to assist in better understanding the specifics of an individual's medical case.

Regarding diagnosis:

- Did the individual have a clinical history and presenting symptoms consistent with the diagnosis of lead toxicity?
- Is there a positive history of lead exposure in the workplace?
- Could lead exposure occur outside the workplace, i.e., in the home, community, or recreational activities?
- Has the individual recently worked in another organization where lead exposure was higher?
- Was the diagnosis confirmed with whole blood lead measurements, urine or blood lead content, or measurement of free erythrocyte protoporphyrin (FEP)?
- Would the individual benefit from a consultation with a specialist?

- Were other conditions with similar symptoms considered in the differential diagnosis?

Regarding treatment:

- Was the treatment appropriate for the type of exposure and severity of symptoms?
- Did symptoms persist?
- Were other more aggressive treatments, such as chelation therapy considered?
- Were recommendations and instructions given to the individual regarding avoiding further exposure?
- Has the individual been following the recommendations?

- If not, are there barriers, such as poor understanding, or employment issues, that contribute to poor compliance?

Regarding prognosis:

- What was the expected outcome?
- Did the individual suffer any complications associated with the exposure?
- Were the complications addressed in the treatment plan?
- Does the individual have any pre-existing conditions that influence response to treatment or ability to recover?
- Could the individual benefit from specific consultation depending on the organ system(s) involved?

References

Proctor and Hughes' Chemical Hazards of the Workplace, 3rd edition. Hathaway, G.J., et al., eds. New York: Van Nostrand Reinhold, 1991.

Occupational Medicine. LaDou, J., ed. Norwalk, CT: Appleton and Lange, 1990.

Agency for Toxic Substances and Disease Registry. Case Studies in Environmental Medicine: Arsenic, Beryllium, Cadmium, Cholinesterase Inhibitors, Lead, Mercury. US Department of Health and Human Services, 1993.

Goodman & Gilman's The Pharmacological Basis of Therapeutics. Hardman, J.G., and L.E. Lilmbird, eds. New York: McGraw-Hill, 1996.

Toxic Effects, Mercury

Other names / synonyms: Acrodynia Poisoning, Colloidal Mercury Poisoning, Hydrargyrum Poisoning, Liquid Silver Poisoning, Mad Hatter's Disease Poisoning, Metallic Mercury Poisoning, Pink Disease Poisoning, Quicksilver Poisoning

961.2, 985.0

Definition

Metallic mercury is a liquid at room temperature. It is the most frequent source of mercury poisoning. Mercury also exists commonly as various inorganic salts as well as organic derivatives. Exposure can occur by inhalation of vapor (metallic mercury) or dust (inorganic salts), ingestion or skin absorption (both inorganic and organic forms).

Mercury poisoning is one of the first industrial diseases to be described historically from mining exposures. The use of mercury nitrate in felt hat manufacture caused chronic mercury poisoning and is the source of the phrase "mad as a hatter." Exposure can occur in a number of occupations including dentists and dental technicians, battery workers, caustic soda and chlorine manufacturing, lab technicians, jewelry makers, plastics and instrument manufacturers. Organic mercury is encountered in occupations involving the manufacture and use of disinfectants, fungicides and wood preservatives. Catastrophic poisonings have occurred from ingestion of treated seed grain that was used for flour and from consumption of fish from contaminated water. Inorganic mercury is biotransformed to methyl mercury by aquatic microorganisms with subsequent transfer up the food chain.

In 1998, the American Association of Poison Control Centers reported 4,039 exposures to mercury with 1,385 of these cases in adults older than 19. Sixty-eight individuals had moderate effects, 12 had major effects, and 3 died.

Diagnosis

Toxicology/Clinical Effects: Acute exposure to high concentrations of mercury vapor causes severe respiratory damage, whereas chronic exposure to lower levels is associated primarily with central nervous system damage.

All forms of mercury are irritants of the skin and mucous membranes; allergic dermatitis may also occur. Inhalation of high levels of mercury vapor can cause fulminant chemical pneumonitis. Fumes of mercury can induce the more benign metal fume fever syndrome. Acute poisoning from ingestion is rare but can cause a severe syndrome of gastrointestinal damage followed in several days by salivary gland swelling, and inflammation of the tongue and gums. At high doses, absorption by any route can cause kidney damage which can progress to acute renal failure.

Central nervous system effects are the predominate sequelae of chronic exposure to either inorganic or organic mercury; signs and symptoms may be fulminant or insidious depending on the duration and intensity of exposure. In organic poisoning, peculiar sensory defects are unique including paresthesias, constriction of visual fields, loss of hearing, smell and taste. Inorganic compounds tend to cause personality changes (known as "erethism"), tremor and ataxia. Other effects that are commonly seen with chronic poisoning from inorganic forms include inflammation of the gums, tongue and salivary glands, and skin rash. Kidney damage also occurs especially after intense exposure.

Inhalation of mercury vapor may lead to lung disease including emphysema and interstitial fibrosis. Pink disease (acrodynia) is considered a mercury allergy and usually indicates widespread disease with symptoms of red, swollen hands and feet, itching skin rash, hair loss, sweating, high blood pressure, rapid heart rate, sensitivity to light, irritability, poor appetite, insomnia, poor muscle tone, and constipation or diarrhea.

Toxic effects on the developing fetus have been observed after dietary exposure to organic mercurials.

The diagnosis can be made in the setting of exposure history and consistent clinical findings. Laboratory testing can be helpful to confirm exposure, although blood and urine levels of mercury do not correlate well with observed level of toxicity. Urine levels of mercury are of no value in the diagnosis of organic mercury poisoning; here, blood or hair levels are best used to assess exposure.

Treatment

Treatment begins with removal of the individual from further exposure and supportive care In acute poisoning, treatment with the chelating agent BAL is recommended. In chronic intoxication, the oral chelator D-Penicillamine can be used. The use of EDTA is not recommended. Treatment may be effective in reducing clinical signs and symptoms, but chronic residue in all organ systems may result despite adequate treatment.

Prognosis

Prognosis is dependent on the extent and duration of exposure.

Differential Diagnosis

Clinical presentation may be similar to systemic diseases involving the same organ systems. The possibility of exposure to other toxic agents should always be considered.

Specialists

- Medical Toxicologist
- Occupational Medicine Physician

Rehabilitation

Rehabilitation may be required if there are functional deficits. The specific form of rehabilitation will be dependent on the type and extent of functional deficits.

Work Restrictions / Accommodations

Exposure limits: Mercury contamination has been limited by the Environmental Protection Agency and OSHA to 2 parts of mercury per billion parts of drinking water, 144 per trillion parts of water in rivers, lakes, and streams, and 1 part methylmercury per million parts of seafood and fish. Workplace air is not to contain over 1 milligram of mercury per 10 cubic meters of air. The individual must have access to information about the health effects of mercury in the workplace. Respirators, air filters, protective clothing, and eyewear may be needed. Length and levels of mercury exposure in the workplace must be monitored and reduced, if needed.

Comorbid Conditions

Kidney disease, mental or neurologic disorders, and respiratory diseases or conditions may limit recovery and affect disability prognosis. Pregnancy may lengthen the disability period.

Factors Influencing Duration

Factors that may determine the length of disability include the individual's age, level and duration of exposure, pre-existing disease, general physical and mental condition, and immediacy of treatment.

Length of Disability

Absorbed dose is the primary determinant of severity of toxic effects, and therefore severity and duration of disability. Absorbed dose is dependent on environmental levels, routes of exposure (skin contact, inhalation, ingestion) and duration of exposure. Contact physician for additional information.

Failure to Recover

If an individual fails to recover within the maximum duration expectancy period, the reader may wish to reference the following questions to assist in better understanding the specifics of an individual's medical case.

Regarding diagnosis:

- Has diagnosis of toxic effects of mercury been confirmed?
- Is the clinical illness including history, physical examination, and laboratory findings consistent with other case descriptions?
- Is the whole blood level of mercury at or near the normal value?
- Is the timing between exposure and clinical onset compatible with the known biologic facts about mercury poisoning?
- Is the exposure dose within the range of doses believed to cause such effects?
- Has the individual experienced any complications?
- Does individual have an underlying condition that may impact recovery such as pregnancy, kidney disease, mental or neurologic disorders, or respiratory disease?

Regarding treatment:

- Was treatment effective in resolving symptoms?
- Is individual a candidate for chelation therapy?
- Has individual been under long-term monitoring for delayed effects?
- Has additional treatment been necessary?

Regarding prognosis:

- Was kidney function affected?
- Was hemodialysis required?
- Is there a positive history of mercury exposure in the workplace?
- Has the individual recently worked in another organization where mercury exposure was higher?
- Could mercury exposure be occurring outside the workplace such as in the home, community, or recreational activities?
- Are there special attributes of the particular individual that make it more or less likely that he or she would be so affected?
- Are there alternative ways of constructing the case that better fit the available facts?

References

Proctor and Hughes' Chemical Hazards of the Workplace, 3rd edition. Hathaway, G.J., et al., eds. New York: Van Nostrand Reinhold, 1991.

Agency for Toxic Substances and Disease Registry. Case Studies in Environmental Medicine: Arsenic, Beryllium, Cadmium, Cholinesterase Inhibitors, Lead, Mercury. US Department of Health and Human Services, 1993.

Toxic Effects, Methyl Alcohol

Other names / synonyms: Carbinol Poisoning, Colonial Spirit Poisoning, Columbian Spirits Poisoning, Methyl Alcohol Poisoning, Methyl Hydroxide Poisoning, Monohydroxymethane Poisoning, Pyroxylic Spirit Poisoning, Wood Alcohol Poisoning, Wood Naphtha Poisoning, Wood Spirits Poisoning

980.1

Definition

Methanol is a clear, colorless liquid with a pungent odor at normal temperatures. First discovered in the late 1600s, methanol has been called wood alcohol because it was obtained commercially from the destructive distillation of wood for more than a century. True wood alcohol contained more contaminants including acetone and acetic acid than the chemical-grade methanol available today.

For many years, the largest use for methanol (about 50% of all produced) was in the production of formaldehyde. It is now also used in the production of acetic acid, methyl tert-butyl ether (MTBE), oxindol (used to improve gasoline octane), and other chemical intermediates. Methanol is also a solvent found in paint remover, varnish, and shellac. Methanol is extremely toxic. As little as 2 to 8 ounces can be fatal to an adult. Workers in industries where methyl alcohol is used and produced may be exposed to harmful levels via inhalation or skin contact Historically, methanol poisoning has occurred primarily from intentional ingestion as a substitute for alcoholic beverages or as a contaminant of "moonshine." Two products containing methanol that are most often ingested are antifreeze solutions and windshield washer products.

Approximately 2,500 exposures to methanol and methanol products were reported by regional poison control centers in 1998, the latest year for which information is available. Approximately 15 deaths were reported from the exposures.

Diagnosis

Toxicology: The most important toxic effects of methanol are optic nerve damage, metabolic acidosis and respiratory depression. Typically within 18-48 hours after ingestion, individuals develop nausea, abdominal pain, headache, and slowed breathing. This is accompanied by visual disturbances such as blurred or double vision, changes in color perception, constricted visual fields and complete blindness. One of the most striking features of poisoning is metabolic acidosis, which closely parallels the severity of poisoning. The presence of an asymptomatic latent period following ingestion suggests that methanol must be metabolized before toxic effects occur. Formic acid appears to be the mediator of ocular injury and acidosis as it is formed from methanol by enzymatic breakdown in the body. This also explains why ethanol can be used as an antidote because it has a greater affinity for alcohol dehydrogenase, which is the enzyme responsible for the initial step in metabolism of methanol. The individual variations in the activity of the alcohol dehydrogenase enzyme systems (responsible for the metabolism of both ethanol and methanol) may explain the wide variation in the toxic response to methanol exposure.

Treatment

The first step in therapy is to remove the individual from further exposure. Further treatment depends on the route and extent of exposure and the organ system affected. If ingestion has occurred shortly before presentation (less than one hour), gastric lavage should be performed.

In the event of skin contact, the affected skin is immediately flooded with water and washed with soap and water. In case of eye contact, the individual should first be checked for contact lenses and if present, should be removed. The eye is then promptly irrigated with copious amounts of water for 20 to 30 minutes.

In all cases of potentially severe poisoning, treatment should include hydration, correction of acidosis and administration of folate to increase the oxidation of formic acid. Ethanol administered intravenously is indicated whenever plasma methanol concentrations are higher than 20 mg/dl, when ingested doses are greater than 30 ml, or when there is evidence of acidosis or visual abnormalities. Hemodialysis is indicated when plasma methanol concentrations are greater than 40 mg/dl or when metabolic acidosis is unresponsive to bicarbonate given intravenously.

Prognosis

Prognosis is dependent on the extent and duration of exposure.

Differential Diagnosis

The combination of visual disturbances and metabolic acidosis, together with a history of exposure and the presence of formic acid in the urine, is confirmation of methanol intoxication. Measurement of formic acid in the urine can be done; blood pH is the best method to monitor severe acidosis.

Specialists

• Medical Toxicologist	• Occupational Medicine Physician

Rehabilitation

Rehabilitation may be required if there are functional deficits. The specific form of rehabilitation will be dependent on the type and extent of functional deficits.

Work Restrictions / Accommodations

Exposure limits: The Occupational Safety and Health Administration's (OSHA) legal airborne permissible exposure limit (PEL) is 200 parts per million (ppm) methanol averaged over an 8-hour work shift.

The National Institute of Occupational Safety and Health's (NIOSH) recommended airborne exposure limit is 200 ppm methanol averaged over a 10-hour work shift, not to exceed 800 ppm methanol during any 15-minute work period.

The American Conference of Governmental Industrial Hygienists' (ACGIH) recommended airborne exposure limit is 200 ppm methanol averaged over an 8-hour work shift, not to exceed 250 ppm methanol as a short-term exposure limit (STEL).

Comorbid Conditions

Pregnancy may complicate treatment and recovery. Pre-existing kidney and liver disease, pulmonary insufficiency, or diminished respiratory capacity may lengthen the disability and influence recovery.

Complications

Formic acid is a metabolic product of methanol and can cause a severe increase in acidity (acidosis), visual disturbances leading to blindness, and death.

Factors Influencing Duration

The severity and duration of methanol exposure, method of exposure, immediacy of treatment, and the individual's response to exposure and the effectiveness of treatment influence the length of disability. Age and the general state of health, an individual's job requirements, any complications, and pre-existing disease will affect disability.

Length of Disability

Disability may be permanent where repeated and/or high level exposure occurs. Absorbed dose is the primary determinant of severity of toxic effects, and therefore severity and duration of disability. Absorbed dose is dependent on environmental levels, routes of exposure (skin contact, inhalation, ingestion) and duration of exposure. Contact physician for additional information.

Failure to Recover

If an individual fails to recover within the maximum duration expectancy period, the reader may wish to reference the following questions to assist in better understanding the specifics of an individual's medical case.

Regarding diagnosis:

- Are the whole blood and urine levels of methanol and/or its metabolites at or near the normal value?
- Is the clinical illness including the history, physical examination, and laboratory findings consistent with other case descriptions?
- Is there a positive history of methanol exposure in the workplace?
- Has the individual recently worked in another organization where methyl alcohol exposure is higher?
- Could methanol exposure be occurring outside the workplace, i.e., in the home, community, or recreational activities?

Regarding treatment:

- Has the individual been removed completely from further exposure?
- If ingestion occurred less than one hour before presentation, did the individual require stomaching pumping (gastric lavage)?
- If skin contact occurred, was affected skin immediately flooded with water and washed with soap and water?
- If eye contact occurred, was the eye promptly irrigated with copious amounts of water for at least 20 to 30 minutes?
- If toxicity was severe, did the individual receive intravenous hydration, correction of acidosis, and administration of folate?
- Was kidney dialysis (hemodialysis) required?
- Did treatment successfully resolve all symptoms?

Regarding prognosis:

- Is the timing between exposure and clinical onset compatible with the known biologic facts about the hazard?
- Is the exposure dose within the range of doses believed to cause such effects?
- Are there special attributes of the particular individual that make it more or less likely that he or she would be so affected?
- Are there alternative ways of constructing the case that better fit the available facts?
- Where there remains significant uncertainty about the cause, how important is it to be certain?

References

Proctor and Hughes' Chemical Hazards of the Workplace, 3rd edition. Hathaway, G.J., et al., eds. New York: Van Nostrand Reinhold, 1991.

Agency for Toxic Substances and Disease Registry. Case Studies in Environmental Medicine: Arsenic, Beryllium, Cadmium, Cholinesterase Inhibitors, Lead, Mercury. US Department of Health and Human Services, 1993.

Toxic Effects, Methyl Bromide

Other names / synonyms: Dibromoethane Poisoning, Isobrome Exposure, Methyl Bromide Poisoning, Monobromomethane Exposure

967.3, 987.8

Definition

Methyl bromide is a colorless, odorless gas used as a structural and soil fumigant. It is also used as a methylating agent in the manufacture of other chemicals, and as a solvent to extract oils from nuts, seeds and wool. It is classified as a restricted use pesticide by the EPA and can only be used by certified applicators.

Exposure occurs by inhalation. Methyl bromide has poor warning properties so agents such as chloropicrin (a potent irritant) are added to provide early warning of exposure.

Diagnosis

Toxicology: Methyl bromide is a neurotoxin and causes convulsions; very high acute exposures cause pulmonary edema; chronic exposure causes peripheral neuropathy. The onset of toxic symptoms after acute exposure is delayed--the latent period varying from 30 minutes to several hours. Early symptoms include headache, visual disturbances, nausea and vomiting, and malaise. Some individuals who have recovered from severe intoxication have had persistent central nervous system effects including vertigo, depression, hallucinations, anxiety and inability to concentrate. Skin contact with liquid Methyl bromide produces erythema and edema of the skin. Prolonged contact has caused deeper burns with delayed blistering. It is doubtful that significant skin absorption occurs.

Specific tests: Blood bromide levels can be measured as an index of exposure following Methyl bromide poisoning. They are much lower than the levels associated with intoxication by inorganic bromide salts. The blood level does not appear to correlate with severity of toxicity.

Treatment

There is no specific treatment other than removal from exposure and supportive care including forced diuresis. Hemodialysis may be required if poisoning is severe.

Prognosis

The outcome can vary from complete recovery with minor exposure to death. At brief, low-level exposures and with timely, effective treatment, full recovery is expected. Although treatment may remove bromide from the blood, neuropsychiatric sequelae may persist. With chronic or high level exposure, additional body systems and organs may be compromised resulting in permanent kidney damage, nerve damage, coma, paralysis, and death.

Differential Diagnosis

Clinical presentation may be similar to systemic diseases involving the same organ systems. The possibility of exposure to other toxic agents should always be considered.

Specialists

- Medical Toxicologist
- Occupational Medicine Physician

Rehabilitation

Rehabilitation may be required if there are functional deficits. The specific form of rehabilitation will be dependent on the type and extent of functional deficits.

Work Restrictions / Accommodations

Exposure limits: The Occupational Safety and Health Agency (OSHA) limits the average level of bromomethane in workplace air to 20 ppm for an 8-hour work day over a 40-hour week, and recommends that exposure be reduced as low as possible. Should mental deterioration occur following methyl bromide intoxication, the individual's ability to return to work would be severely compromised. Work restrictions and accommodations would depend on the severity of the poisoning and its permanent after-effects.

Comorbid Conditions

Pre-existing disease will impact the recovery, particularly if it involves the same organ systems affected by the toxic exposure.

Factors Influencing Duration

The level of poisoning and resulting systemic effects will influence the length of disability. There may be long-term pulmonary, kidney, or neurological impairment. Neuropsychiatric problems may result in lengthy disability and resistance to rehabilitation.

Length of Disability

Absorbed dose is the primary determinant of severity of toxic effects, and therefore severity and duration of disability. Absorbed dose is dependent on environmental levels, routes of exposure (skin contact, inhalation, ingestion) and duration of exposure. Contact physician for additional information.

Failure to Recover

If an individual fails to recover within the maximum duration expectancy period, the reader may wish to reference the following questions to assist in better understanding the specifics of an individual's medical case.

Regarding diagnosis:

- Is the whole blood level of bromide at or near the normal value? Has diagnosis of bromide poisoning been confirmed?
- Have underlying medical conditions been identified or ruled out? Is there a genetic history for the complaint; i.e., liver or kidney abnormalities?

- Is the clinical illness, including the history, physical examination, and laboratory findings, consistent with other case descriptions?
- Is the timing between exposure and clinical onset compatible with the known biologic facts about the hazard?

Regarding treatment:

- How soon after exposure was appropriate treatment initiated?
- If systemic impairment exists, what specific treatment has been, or is currently being done?
- Would individual benefit from additional or continued therapy?

Regarding prognosis:

- Was the exposure dose within the range of doses believed to cause such effects?
- Is there a positive history of bromide exposure in the workplace?
- Could bromide exposure be occurring outside the workplace; i.e., in the home, in the community, or in recreational activities?
- Has the individual recently worked in another organization where bromide exposure is higher?
- Are there special attributes of this particular individual that make it more or less likely that he or she would be so affected?
- Are there alternative ways of constructing the case that better fit the available facts?
- Where there remains significant uncertainty about the cause, how important is it to be certain?

References

Proctor and Hughes' Chemical Hazards of the Workplace, 3rd edition. Hathaway, G.J., et al., eds. New York: Van Nostrand Reinhold, 1991.

Occupational Medicine. LaDou, J., ed. Norwalk, CT: Appleton and Lange, 1990.

Agency for Toxic Substances and Disease Registry. Case Studies in Environmental Medicine: Arsenic, Beryllium, Cadmium, Cholinesterase Inhibitors, Lead, Mercury. US Department of Health and Human Services, 1993.

Paul, M., ed. Occupational and Environmental Reproductive Hazards: A Guide for Clinicians. Baltimore: Williams & Wilkins, 1993.

Toxic Effects, Mushrooms

Other names / synonyms: Mushroom Poisoning, Toadstool Poisoning

988.1

Definition

Mushroom poisoning is a toxic, sometimes fatal, effect of eating raw or cooked poisonous mushrooms. The mushrooms that most commonly cause poisoning are Amanita muscaria, A. phalloides (the death cap, or death cup), and the four white Amanita species called destroying angels.

The term toadstool is commonly given to poisonous mushrooms, but for individuals who are not experts in mushroom identification, there are generally no easily recognizable differences between poisonous and nonpoisonous species. Old wives' tales notwithstanding, there is no general rule of thumb for distinguishing edible mushrooms and poisonous toadstools. The toxins involved in mushroom poisoning are produced naturally by the fungi themselves, and each individual specimen of a toxic species should be considered equally poisonous. Most mushrooms that cause human poisoning cannot be made nontoxic by cooking, canning, freezing, or any other means of processing. The only way to avoid poisoning is to avoid consumption of the toxic species.

There are some 70 to 80 species of mushrooms that are poisonous to humans; many of them contain toxic alkaloids (muscarine, agaricin, and phallin). Mushroom poisonings are generally acute and are manifested by a variety of symptoms and prognoses, depending on the amount and species consumed. Because the chemistry of many of the mushroom toxins (especially the less deadly ones) is still unknown and positive identification of the mushrooms is often difficult or impossible, mushroom poisonings are generally categorized by their physiological effects.

There are four categories of mushroom toxins: protoplasmic which destroy cells; neurotoxins, which effect the nervous system; gastrointestinal irritants, which effect the stomach and intestines; and disulfiram-like which are generally less toxic.

Ninety-five percent of all mushroom fatalities in North America are associated with Amanita species mushrooms. Mortality rates are from 10 to 60%. Poisonings in the United States occur most commonly when foragers for wild mushrooms (especially novices) misidentify and consume a toxic species. Other common occurrences are when recent immigrants collect and consume a poisonous American species that closely resembles an edible wild mushroom from their native land, or when mushrooms that contain psychoactive compounds are intentionally consumed by persons who desire these effects. Others at risk are those who commercially grow mushrooms, food handlers, and food preparers.

In 1998 there were 9,839 mushroom exposure incidents in US reported by the American Association of Poison Control Centers. One death was reported in this group of exposures. Eighty-eight percent of reported mushroom exposures were unidentified. One author estimates approximately 5 mushroom exposures per 100,000 population per year.

Diagnosis

History: An individual suspected of eating muscarine-type mushrooms may have watering eyes (lacrimation), contraction of the pupils (miosis), salivation, sweating, vomiting, abdominal cramps and diarrhea. They may also experience a spinning sensation (vertigo), confusion, coma, and occasionally convulsions beginning a few minutes to two hours later. An individual who may have eaten Amanita muscaria will have such symptoms as nausea, vomiting, diarrhea, excessive salivation, perspiration, watering of the eyes, slowed and difficult breathing, dilated pupils, confusion, and excitability.

Symptoms of Amanita species poisoning occur after six to 24 hours and are similar to those of muscarine poisoning. Reduced excretion of urine (oliguria) and absence of urine excretion (anuria) may develop. Jaundice resulting from liver damage is common and develops in two or three days. Within six to 12 hours after eating the Amanita phalloides mushrooms, violent abdominal pain, vomiting, and bloody diarrhea appear, causing rapid loss of fluid from the tissues and intense thirst. Gastrointestinal intestinal (GI) symptoms may be delayed six to 12 hours or more.

Physical exam: The individual should be examined for signs of severe involvement of the liver, kidneys, and central nervous system. Rapid heartbeat (tachycardia) and lowered blood pressure (hypotension) may be present upon exam. Examination may reveal jaundice, bruising (may be present with hepatic failure) and mild abdominal tenderness. There may be bloody diarrhea. There may be nervous system abnormality ranging from confusion and lethargy to coma). Amanita species poisoning can be divided into three stages. The first stage is a latent period of six to 12 hours followed by abdominal cramping, vomiting, and profuse watery diarrhea. In the second stage the individual appears to be improved, however, there is ongoing liver damage that is indicated by elevated laboratory values. The third stage may progress to sudden liver failure with kidney damage.

Tests: Blood tests may be done to indicate liver (hepatic) damage. Blood tests may include prothrombin time (PT) (most reliable indicator for severity of poisoning), aminotransferases, bilirubin, and alkaline phosphatase. A complete blood count (CBC) may be done. The level of electrolytes, blood urea nitrogen (BUN), and creatinine indicates dehydration from vomiting and diarrhea. Glucose levels may be monitored very closely where there may be liver (hepatic) failure. A urinalysis may be done. Blood and/or protein in the urine indicates kidney (renal) involvement. The presence of amylase/lipase (enzymes) indicates an inflammation of the pancreas (pancreatitis).

If a specimen of mushroom ingested is available for analysis, a specialized test may be performed to identify the specific mushroom.

Treatment

Vomiting should be induced immediately in an individual who has eaten an unidentified mushroom. In death cap mushroom poisoning, intensive supportive care for liver (hepatic) and kidney (renal) failure is the primary treatment.

If an individual has eaten, or is suspected of having eaten, a poisonous mushroom, treatment is aggressive since the mortality rate is as high as 60%. The individual may be treated by washing out the stomach (gastric lavage) if vomiting has not already occurred. The first step in detoxifying the mushroom toxin is to remove it from the system. This involves purification of the blood (hemodialysis), filtering impurities from the blood (hemoperfusion) or a forced increase in urine output (diuresis). Activated charcoal may be administered. The toxins of poisonous mushrooms appear to undergo circulation involving the intestine and the liver (enterohepatic) and a repeat dose of activated charcoal may interrupt the cycle and reduce toxicity. Rehydration with an electrolyte solution, monitoring of electrolytes and glucose levels in the blood may be undertaken.

Prognosis

The normal course of the disease varies with the dose and the mushroom species eaten. Although individuals may die within a few hours, complete recovery in 24 hours is usual with appropriate therapy.

Each poisonous species contains one or more toxic compounds, which is unique to few other species. Therefore, cases of mushroom poisonings generally do not resemble each other unless they are caused by the same or very closely related mushroom species. Illness usually begins within a few hours after eating the mushrooms, and recovery usually occurs within 12 hours. Where coma has occurred as a result of poisoning due to Amanita phalloides, death results in more than 50% of the incidents. Death may occur in three to seven days in Amanita species poisoning.

A liver transplant may be necessary and can be life saving for the most severe cases of amatoxin poisoning.

Differential Diagnosis

Clinical presentation may be similar to systemic diseases involving the same organ systems. The possibility of exposure to other toxic agents should always be considered.

Specialists

• Medical Toxicologist	• Occupational Medicine Physician

Rehabilitation

Rehabilitation may be required if there are functional deficits. The specific form of rehabilitation will be dependent on the type and extent of functional deficits.

Work Restrictions / Accommodations

Prevention: Educational programs on the identification of poisonous mushrooms should be provided. Prevention of mushroom poisoning rests upon the avoidance of ingestion of any wild mushrooms not positively identified as edible by a competent authority.

Comorbid Conditions

Pre-existing disease will impact the recovery, particularly if it involves the same organ systems affected by the toxic exposure.

Complications

Liver failure is the most serious complication of amatoxin ingestion. Liver (hepatic) coma and hypoglycemia can complicate liver failure. Progressive hepatic failure can lead to functional kidney failure (hepatorenal syndrome).

Factors Influencing Duration

The levels, duration, and route of exposure, immediacy of treatment, and the individual response to exposure and treatment determine length of disability. Age, health, physical condition all influence how an individual responds to exposure to mushroom poisoning and the ensuing treatment. Long term effects may result where persons in ill health and the elderly are involved.

Length of Disability

Absorbed dose is the primary determinant of severity of toxic effects, and therefore severity and duration of disability. Absorbed dose is dependent on environmental levels, routes of exposure (skin contact, inhalation, ingestion) and duration of exposure. Contact physician for additional information. Length of disability may depend on the type of mushroom involved, the amount consumed, and the course of treatment.

Failure to Recover

If an individual fails to recover within the maximum duration expectancy period, the reader may wish to reference the following questions to assist in better understanding the specifics of an individual's medical case.

Regarding diagnosis:

- Has the individual recently eaten wild mushrooms? If so, what did it look like and when was it ingested?
- Does the individual grow mushrooms commercially, or does the individual work as a food handler or preparer?
- Does the individual report watering eyes (lacrimation), contraction of the pupils (miosis), salivation, sweating, vomiting, abdominal cramps, or diarrhea?
- Has the individual experienced a spinning sensation (vertigo), confusion, or convulsions?
- Were electrolyte levels, blood urea nitrogen (BUN), and creatinine done to determine whether dehydration or kidney damage occurrence?
- Was a specimen of mushroom available for analysis?

Regarding treatment:

- Was vomiting induced immediately?
- Did the individual require pumping of the stomach (gastric lavage) or activated charcoal?
- Did the individual require rehydration with an intravenous electrolyte solution?
- Did the individual require intensive supportive care for liver (hepatic) or kidney (renal) failure?
- Were symptoms completely resolved with treatment?

Regarding prognosis:

- Did the individual receive prompt and appropriate treatment?
- Are there special attributes of the particular individual that make it more or less likely that he or she would be so affected?
- Has the individual developed liver and/or kidney failure?
- Is this individual a candidate for liver transplantation?
- What is the expected outcome for this individual with treatment for complications?

References

Proctor and Hughes' Chemical Hazards of the Workplace, 3rd edition. Hathaway, G.J., et al., eds. New York: Van Nostrand Reinhold, 1991.

Occupational Medicine. LaDou, J., ed. Norwalk, CT: Appleton and Lange, 1990.

Agency for Toxic Substances and Disease Registry. Case Studies in Environmental Medicine: Arsenic, Beryllium, Cadmium, Cholinesterase Inhibitors, Lead, Mercury. US Department of Health and Human Services, 1993.

Goodman & Gilman's The Pharmacological Basis of Therapeutics. Hardman, J.G., and L.E. Lilmbird, eds. New York: McGraw-Hill, 1996.

Toxic Effects, Nickel and Inorganic Compounds

Other names / synonyms: Elemental Nickel Poisoning, Nickel Carbonyl Exposure, Nickel Catalyst Poisoning, Nickel Salts Exposure, Nickel Tetracarbonyl Exposure

985.8

Definition

Nickel is a naturally occurring silvery metal found in the earth's crust in the form of various nickel minerals. Elemental nickel is recovered from mined ore and also recovered from scrap metal. Nickel is ubiquitous in industry because it is used in the manufacture of steel and many alloys. It is used in electroplating, in nickel-cadmium batteries and in ceramics and jewelry manufacture. Manufacture of pure nickel is particularly hazardous because of the potential exposure to the gaseous intermediate nickel carbonyl. Workers engaged in the production, fabrication or welding of nickel alloys may be exposed to nickel dust and fume. In electroplating shops, workers may have respiratory and skin exposure to soluble nickel salts.

Diagnosis

Toxicology: Contact dermatitis, usually due to nickel hypersensitivity, is the most common manifestation of exposure to soluble nickel compounds. Nickel is a common cause of skin allergy in the general population causing redness and vesicles at points of contact in sensitized individuals. Chronic eczematous dermatitis involving the hands and arms may develop in nickel workers, particularly in electroplating shops where there is exposure to liquids and aerosols. Exposure to high levels of aerosols can also cause inflammation of the nose and sinuses, decreased sense of smell, and nasal septal perforation. Nickel fumes may cause an illness resembling metal fume fever.

Exposure to nickel carbonyl is more serious because fulminant pneumonitis and encephalopathy may result. Initial symptoms include headache, fatigue, nausea and vomiting which usually resolve when the individual is removed from exposure. In severe cases, after a delay of hours to days, cough chest pain, and difficulty breathing mark the development of diffuse interstitial pneumonitis, which may progress to adult respiratory distress syndrome (ARDS). Delirium, seizures and coma may occur prior to death.

Exposure to nickel compounds in refining and roasting operations has caused an increase in the rate of nasal and lung cancer.

Tests: The diagnosis of nickel skin allergy can be confirmed by patch testing. In evaluating persons who have been exposed to nickel carbonyl, urine nickel levels greater than 100 ug/L indicate moderate exposure while levels > 500 ug/L indicate severe exposure.

Treatment

Nickel dermatitis should be treated with topical steroids and removal from further exposure. Sensitized workers will usually need to transfer to jobs where there is no potential exposure. Respiratory tract irritation will resolve after removal from exposure. Individuals with significant exposure to nickel carbonyl should be admitted to the hospital to be monitored for the development pulmonary complications and systemic toxicity. Use of the chelating agent Dithiocarb may be helpful when urinary nickel is > 100 ug/L.

Prognosis

Prognosis is dependent on the extent and duration of exposure.

Differential Diagnosis

Clinical presentation may be similar to systemic diseases involving the same organ systems. The possibility of exposure to other toxic agents should always be considered.

Specialists

- Medical Toxicologist
- Occupational Medicine Physician

Rehabilitation

Rehabilitation may be required if there are functional deficits. The specific form of rehabilitation will be dependent on the type and extent of functional deficits.

Work Restrictions / Accommodations

Exposure limits: The Occupational Safety and Health Administration's (OSHA) permissible exposure limit (PEL), time-weighted average (TWA) is 1 milligrams per cubic meter (does not apply to nickel carbonyl).

The National Institute of Occupational Safety and Health (NIOSH) recommended exposure limit (REL) time-weighted average (TWA) is 0.015 milligrams per cubic meter, and it is considered to be a potential carcinogen (causes cancer) (does not apply to nickel carbonyl).

The threshold limit value (TLV) time-weighted average (TWA) is 0.5 milligrams per cubic meter as a confirmed human carcinogen.

The EPA advises no more than 3.5 milligrams of nickel per liter of water for 10 days for adults.

The individual must have access to information about the health effects of nickel exposure in the workplace. Respirators, air filters, and protective clothing and eyewear may be needed. Length and levels of nickel exposure in the workplace must be monitored. The individual may need special training to handle nickel compounds.

Comorbid Conditions

Pre-existing disease will impact the recovery, particularly if it involves the same organ systems affected by the toxic exposure.

Factors Influencing Duration

The levels and length of time exposed, method of exposure, organ systems involved, immediacy of treatment, and the individual's response to exposure and treatment will determine length of disability.

Length of Disability

Absorbed dose is the primary determinant of severity of toxic effects, and therefore severity and duration of disability. Absorbed dose is dependent on environmental levels, routes of exposure (skin contact, inhalation, ingestion) and duration of exposure. Contact physician for additional information.

Other factors influencing disability include pre-existing disease, age, pregnancy and allergy, all of which affect individual susceptibility to the toxic effect of chemical exposures. Psychological and emotional factors may also play a role in the extent and duration of disability. In some cases, there may be residual permanent disability despite prompt diagnosis and appropriate treatment.

Failure to Recover

If an individual fails to recover within the maximum duration expectancy period, the reader may wish to reference the following questions to assist in better understanding the specifics of an individual's medical case.

Regarding diagnosis:

- Has diagnosis of toxic effects of nickel been confirmed?
- Is there a positive history of nickel exposure in the workplace?
- Is the exposure dose within the range of doses believed to cause such effects?
- Is the clinical illness, including the history, physical examination, and laboratory findings, consistent with other case descriptions?
- Are the blood and urine levels of nickel at or near the normal value?
- Is the timing between exposure and clinical onset compatible with the known biologic facts about the hazard?
- Has individual experienced any complications?
- Is individual allergic to nickel?
- Does individual have an underlying condition that may impact recovery?

Regarding treatment:

- Did individual receive prompt, appropriate treatment?
- Have symptoms persisted despite treatment?
- What other treatment options are available?

Regarding prognosis:

- Are there special attributes of the particular individual that make it more or less likely that he or she would be so affected?
- Could nickel exposure be occurring outside the workplace, such as in the home, in the community, or in recreational activities?
- Has the individual recently worked in another organization where nickel exposure is higher?

References

Proctor and Hughes' Chemical Hazards of the Workplace, 3rd edition. Hathaway, G.J., et al., eds. New York: Van Nostrand Reinhold, 1991.

Agency for Toxic Substances and Disease Registry. Case Studies in Environmental Medicine: Arsenic, Beryllium, Cadmium, Cholinesterase Inhibitors, Lead, Mercury. US Department of Health and Human Services, 1993.

Toxic Effects, Organophosphate and Carbamate Pesticides

Other names / synonyms: Carbaryl Exposure, Dichlorvos Exposure, Malathion Exposure, Parathion Exposure, Phorate Exposure, Phosdrin Exposure

989.3

Definition

The organophosphate and carbamate compounds are found in a wide variety of insecticide preparations marketed for home, garden and agricultural use. Since there are so many formulations with different trade names, identification of the active ingredients may be difficult without the help of a Poison Control Center.

Over 80% of the pesticide poisonings in the US are caused by organophosphate and carbamate pesticides, which have in common an inhibition of the enzyme acetylcholinesterase an enzyme that controls the transmission of nerve impulses throughout the body. The use of these compounds has increased markedly since the 1970s when many of the organochlorine insecticides such as DDT were banned. In contrast to the organochlorines, organophosphate and carbamate insecticides degrade rapidly in the environment and do not accumulated or concentrate in the food chain. Thus they have less potential for chronic health effects or environmental contamination. However, organophosphate and carbamate compounds have a greater potential for acute toxicity than the organochlorines, although there is a wide spectrum of potency for acute toxicity in humans among these chemicals. More than 40 of them are currently registered for use, and all run the risk of acute and subacute toxicity.

Many of the toxic "nerve agents" used by the military are similar organophosphate compounds. Exposure to organophosphates and carbamates produces a characteristic, treatable syndrome in humans. Its recognition and timely intervention are of great importance to emergency physicians and affected individuals.

Agricultural exposure is the most common site of organophosphate and carbamate poisoning. Anyone involved in the manufacture, formulation, transport or application of these chemicals is at risk. Most organophosphate and carbamate insecticides are used for crop spraying in commercial agriculture. Approximately 75% of all insecticides are used on three crops: cotton, corn, and soybeans. Poisoning has often occurred among harvest workers who enter a field too soon after crops have been treated. Other occupations at risk include pest control workers, custodial workers, veterinarians, and pet groomers. Accidental exposure to the unsuspecting public can occur near sprayed fields due to wind shifts. Intentional ingestion in a suicide or homicide attempt is not uncommon. Most occupational exposures occur from skin absorption, although inhalation is possible during pesticide manufacture, formulation and application. Although a few cases of mild poisoning from dietary exposure have been reported, hazard to consumers from surface contamination appears to be minimal.

There are approximately 20,000 reported organophosphate exposures per year; however, it is estimated that only 1% of field worker illness from pesticide exposure is reported. According to the 1998 annual report of the American Association of Poison Control Centers, there were 4,332 exposures to carbamates, with one reported death. The same report cited 16,392 exposures to organophosphates, with 11 reported deaths in the US.

Diagnosis

Mechanism of toxicity: All organophosphates and carbamates are inhibitors of the enzyme acetylcholinesterase, an enzyme critical to control nerve impulse transmission from one cell to another throughout the body. When the enzyme is inhibited, there is overstimulation and then paralysis of the secondary cell. The character, duration, and degree of the resulting physiologic effect is directly related to the amount and rate of enzyme inhibition at certain receptor sites in the central and peripheral nervous systems. Some critical mass of enzyme must be inactivated before the signs and symptoms of poisoning are evident.

Clinical Effects: In general, onset of symptoms is more rapid after respiratory exposure than ingestion or skin absorption, ranging from minutes to hours. However, significant variation in onset of symptoms occurs depending on the specific agent and its metabolism as well as variation in the host response. Delayed onset of up to 48 hours has been reported.

In mild poisoning, objective findings may be absent and symptoms are very nonspecific such as weakness, headache and gastrointestinal upset. With more severe poisoning, there are many characteristic findings such as small pupils (miosis), excessive salivation, respiratory distress, hyperactive bowel sounds, generalized muscle weakness and altered consciousness. Death is usually secondary to respiratory failure from increased bronchial secretions, bronchospasm, muscle paralysis and central nervous system depression.

Tests: Specific laboratory diagnosis of organophosphate/carbamate poisoning is possible. Acetylcholinesterase (AChE) activity can be measured in the serum and red blood cells (RBC). The red cell measurement is more specific, as the serum level may be decreased with liver disease or chronic inflammation from any cause. Clinical symptoms generally appear after the RBC activity is depressed by 50% of baseline, but the rate of decline is more important than the absolute level. Some individuals may have mild symptoms when the AChE activity is depressed by 30-50%. AChE levels are not particularly useful in following recovery after acute poisoning (clinical observation is the best guide), but they are essential in the biologic monitoring of occupationally exposed workers.

Treatment

There are four elements to the effective treatment of OP/carbamate poisoning: 1) Supporting respiration with suction, oxygen and intubation as indicated; 2) Decontamination by removal of clothing, washing the skin, hair and fingernails with soap and water (mild intoxication has progressed to life-threatening disease because of continued absorption from clothes or skin). If ingestion is route of exposure, induced vomiting (only before onset of significant symptoms), gastric lavage and administration of charcoal/saline cathartic may be indicated. Health care personnel should be careful to avoid contamination from the patient; 3) Treatment with specific antidotes (poisoning with these chemicals is one of the few examples when antidote therapy can be lifesaving). There are two different drugs that are effective and can be used in combination: a) atropine: massive doses compared to usual use may be required and may help confirm the diagnosis. The use of 50 mg in 24 hours is not unusual. The goal is to titrate the dose vs the individual's signs until a mild "atropinization" is observed (flushing of the skin, dilated pupils, drying of secretions and rapid heartbeat); b) 2-PAM (pralidoxime): this drug is indicated in all significant organophosphate poisonings (usually not necessary with carbamates). To be effective, it must be given within the first 12-24 hours after exposure; and 4) Observation: Symptoms may progress during the first 24-48 hours due to delayed absorption from skin or GI tract.

Prognosis

Long-term follow-up evaluation of workers with acute toxicity and workers with repeated low-dose exposures has shown some evidence of persistent neuro-psychologic impairment with deficits of memory, concentration and brain-wave abnormalities, as well as emotional disturbances with irritability, anxiety and depression. The degree to which these abnormalities are directly due to organophosphate toxicity or to a psychologic reaction to the poisoning episode is difficult to resolve in individual cases.

Differential Diagnosis

Clinical presentation may be similar to systemic diseases involving the same organ systems. The possibility of exposure to other toxic agents should always be considered.

Specialists

• Medical Toxicologist	• Occupational Medicine Physician

Rehabilitation

Rehabilitation may be required if there are functional deficits. The specific form of rehabilitation will be dependent on the type and extent of functional deficits.

Work Restrictions / Accommodations

Exposure limits/Prevention: The Occupational Safety and Health Administration's (OSHA) recommended airborne permissible exposure limits (PEL) range from less than 0.1-15 milligrams per cubic meter, and recommended exposure limits for skin as a time-weighted average (TWA) range from less than 0.1-15 milligrams per cubic meter over an 8-hour workshift.

The National Institute of Occupational Safety and Health's (NIOSH) recommended airborne exposure limit (REL) range from less than 1.0-15 milligrams per cubic meter, and skin exposure limits as a time-weighted averages (TWA) range from less than 0.05-10 milligrams per cubic meter over an 10-hour workshift.

The American Conference of Governmental Industrial Hygienists' (ACGIH) recommended airborne exposure values range from 0.9-10 milligrams per cubic meter for an 8-hour workshift.

Immediately Dangerous to Life or Health (IDLH) values range from 10-250 milligrams per cubic meter.

Where organophosphates and carbamates are manufactured, stored, formulated, or transported workers should wear protective work clothing, wash thoroughly immediately after exposure and at the end of each workshift. Hazard and warning information should be posted in the work area. In addition, as part of an ongoing education and training effort, all information on the health and safety hazards of the organophosphates and carbamates should be communicated to potentially exposed workers.

Skin contact with organophosphates and carbamates should be avoided. Protective gloves and clothing should be worn. Safety equipment suppliers/manufacturers can provide recommendations on the most protective glove/clothing material for the particular operation.

All protective clothing (suits, gloves, footwear, and headgear) should be clean, available each day, and put on before work.

Eye protection should include at least goggles and faceshields when needed. Eye protection is provided where a supplied air respirator is used. Where the potential exists for exposures over the listed values, a MSHA/NIOSH approved supplied-air respirator with a full facepiece operated in the positive pressure mode or with a full facepiece and hood should be used. A helmet in the continuous flow mode or the use of a MSHA/NIOSH-approved self-contained breathing apparatus with a full facepiece operated in pressure-demand or other positive pressure mode may be needed.

Workers who apply pesticides for pest control should wear the protective clothing while engaged in their work. The material of the clothing will vary depending upon the toxicity and form of the pesticide. Shirts, trousers, hats, and chemical resistant footwear as well as chemical resistant gloves are the minimum. If highly toxic materials are being applied, breathing apparatus and full-body chemically resistant clothing, gloves, and boots may be needed.

Comorbid Conditions

Pre-existing disease will impact the recovery, particularly if it involves the same organ systems affected by the toxic exposure.

Factors Influencing Duration

The levels and route of exposure, the type of preparation (lipid or water base) that carried the insecticide and any complications can influence the length of disability. The period of observation can vary from several hours for the asymptomatic individual to at least 48 hours of hospitalization in symptomatic cases. Recovery periods can vary from a few days to almost a year. In rare instances, disability may be permanent. Age, general physical condition and state of health will influence the individual's ability to recover functional capacity and return to work.

Length of Disability

Absorbed dose is the primary determinant of severity of toxic effects, and therefore severity and duration of disability. Absorbed dose is dependent on environmental levels, routes of exposure (skin contact, inhalation, ingestion) and duration of exposure. Contact physician for additional information.

Other factors influencing disability include pre-existing disease, age, pregnancy and allergy, all of which affect individual susceptibility to the toxic effect of chemical exposures. Psychological and emotional factors may also play a role in the extent and duration of disability. In some cases, there may be residual permanent disability despite prompt diagnosis and appropriate treatment.

Failure to Recover

If an individual fails to recover within the maximum duration expectancy period, the reader may wish to reference the following questions to assist in better understanding the specifics of an individual's medical case.

Regarding diagnosis:

- Has diagnosis of toxic effects of organophosphate and carbamate pesticides been confirmed?
- Is there a positive history of organophosphate or carbamate exposure in the workplace?
- Is the clinical illness, including history, physical examination, and laboratory findings, consistent with other case descriptions?
- Are the whole blood and urine levels of the organophosphate or carbamate metabolites and cholinesterase at or near the normal value?
- Is the timing between exposure and clinical onset compatible with the known biologic facts about the hazard?
- Is the exposure dose within the range of doses believed to cause such effects?
- Has individual experienced any complications related to the toxic effects of organophosphate and carbamate pesticides?
- Is individual pregnant or are there special attributes of the particular individual that make it more or less likely that he or she would be so affected?

Regarding treatment:

- Was diagnosis and treatment prompt and adequate?
- Have symptoms resolved?

Regarding prognosis:

- To what extent is function impaired?
- Has the individual recently worked in another organization where organophosphate or carbamate exposure is higher?
- Could organophosphate or carbamate exposure be occurring outside the workplace; i.e., in the home, in the community, or in recreational activities?
- Are there alternative ways of constructing the case that better fit the available facts?

References

Proctor and Hughes' Chemical Hazards of the Workplace, 3rd edition. Hathaway, G.J., et al., eds. New York: Van Nostrand Reinhold, 1991.

Occupational Medicine. LaDou, J., ed. Norwalk, CT: Appleton and Lange, 1990.

Agency for Toxic Substances and Disease Registry. Case Studies in Environmental Medicine: Arsenic, Beryllium, Cadmium, Cholinesterase Inhibitors, Lead, Mercury. US Department of Health and Human Services, 1993.

Goodman & Gilman's The Pharmacological Basis of Therapeutics. Hardman, J.G., and L.E. Lilmbird, eds. New York: McGraw-Hill, 1996.

Toxic Effects, Plants (genus Toxicodendron)

Other names / synonyms: Poison Ivy, Poison Oak, Poison Sumac, Rhus Dermatitis

988.2

Definition

Classic delayed hypersensitivity (allergic) reactions develop following direct contact with a variety of plants but members of the genus Toxicodendron are the most common culprits. Up to two million cases of Toxicodendron dermatitis (poison oak, poison ivy, poison sumac) are reported annually in the US. The oleoresins contained in these plants trigger a delayed hypersensitivity reaction in susceptible individuals. Usually the skin is involved; however, the eyes, airway, and lungs may be affected if exposed to smoke from burning plants.

Toxicodendron species are abundant throughout the US except in desert areas, elevations above 4000 feet, Alaska, or Hawaii. Approximately 50-70% of the US population is susceptible if exposed casually; percentages increase with significant exposure. Approximately 10-15% of the population is extremely sensitive. Toxicodendron dermatitis is the most common cause of contact dermatitis in the US, exceeding all other causes combined. People of color and the elderly tend to be less sensitive.

Diagnosis

History: In individuals who are sensitive to plants such as poison ivy, poison oak, or poison sumac, a reaction appears as a line or streak of rash, usually within 12-48 hours, although the latent period may be as long as 5-6 days. Redness and swelling occur, often followed by blisters and severe itching. In a few days, the blisters may become crusted over and begin to scale off. Morbidity is related to the sensitivity of the individual exposed and degree of exposure, and ranges from localized mild abnormal redness of the skin (erythema) and an itching sensation (pruritus), to diffuse redness, swelling, severe pain, and itching with large fluid-filled sacs (vesicles). The individual may have a history of exposure to the toxic plant.

Physical exam: The dermatitis due to poison ivy, poison oak and poison sumac is highly variable. In mild cases, classic lesions on exposed skin occur after brushing against the plant, or abrasions (excoriations) develop from scratching with contaminated fingernails. Classic characteristics of mild lesions are a linear, abnormally red (erythematous) appearance, possibly filled with fluid (vesicles), which are itching or are mildly painful. In moderate to severe cases there are diffuse areas of abnormal redness (erythema), accumulations of fluid (edema), severe itching (pruritus), pain and/or thin bony prominences (bullae). Lesions appear first on exposed areas; then, secondary lesions may appear on the genitals or other areas to which the oil residue has spread. After 3 days, the skin's moisture inactivates the oleoresin on the skin, so that spread after 3 days is the result of reexposure to dried urushiol on domesticated animals or inanimate objects. The lesions may leak fluid (non-antigenic) until a crust forms. In the majority of cases, the dermatitis resolves without medical treatment and disappears within 2-3 weeks. The most common complication is a secondary infection. Rarely, urticaria or erythema multiforme results from the systemic absorption of the urushiol derivatives.

Tests: Laboratory testing is usually not necessary as part of the evaluation of suspected poison ivy, oak, or sumac exposure. Blood tests may show increased leukocytes (leukocytosis) and eosinophils (eosinophilia) in severe cases.

Treatment

In general symptomatic relief should be provided, and hands, fingernails, and clothing should be decontaminated. Treatment for poison ivy, poison oak, or poison sumac exposure will be guided by the severity of the dermatitis; however, by the time individuals are symptomatic it is usually too late to make any impact. Healing can take from days to 2-3 weeks, depending on severity. For mild dermatitis, calamine lotion, topical cool soaks or compresses, steroid creams or lotions, or antihistamines may be used. For severe dermatitis, corticosteroids may be needed. Topical ground oatmeal paste, baths, or soaks may be used. Analgesics may be taken if necessary for pain.

Prognosis

Individuals exposed to poison ivy, poison oak, or poison sumac may expect healing to take from a few days up to 2-3 weeks depending on severity.

Differential Diagnosis

Symptoms and signs of the effects toxic exposure may be similar to other illnesses and exposures, dependent on the organ systems involved.

Specialists

- Dermatologist

Rehabilitation

Rehabilitation may be required if there are functional deficits. The specific form of rehabilitation will be dependent on the type and extent of functional deficits.

Work Restrictions / Accommodations

The individual should avoid exposure to poison ivy, poison oak, or poison sumac by wearing protective clothing, such as gloves (non-rubber) when handling the plants or working where they are located. Individuals should carefully wash their hands, clean under the fingernails, and wash contaminated clothing with soap.

Complementary and Alternative Therapies

Content is intended for awareness only. Treatments may or may not be effective. Scientific evidence may be lacking and some substances have potentially toxic effects. Dr. Presley Reed and the editors do not endorse the use of these therapies in the absence of consultation with a licensed medical professional.

Ground oatmeal paste -	Applied topically, may help to relieve itching.
Hydrotherapy -	Cool soaks, compresses, or cool baths may help relieve symptoms.

Comorbid Conditions

Pre-existing disease will impact the recovery, particularly if it involves the same organ systems are affected by the toxic exposure.

Factors Influencing Duration

The recovery period from Toxicodendron dermatitis will vary with the severity of exposure and the individual's immunologic status.

Length of Disability

In mild cases, disability will be minimal. Generally, healing will be complete within 2-3 weeks.

Poison oak, poison ivy, and poison sumac.

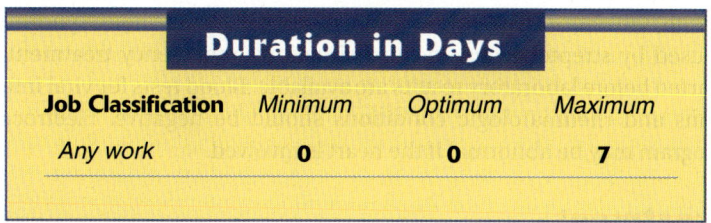

Job Classification	Minimum	Optimum	Maximum
Any work	0	0	7

Failure to Recover

If an individual fails to recover within the maximum duration expectancy period, the reader may wish to reference the following questions to assist in better understanding the specifics of an individual's medical case.

Regarding diagnosis:

- Has diagnosis been confirmed?
- Has suspected plant been identified?
- Is there a positive history of exposure to the suspected plants or plant parts in the workplace?
- Is the clinical illness, including the history, physical examination, and laboratory findings, consistent with other case descriptions?
- Is the timing between exposure and clinical onset compatible with the known biologic facts about the hazard?
- Has individual experienced any complications?
- Does individual have an underlying condition that may impact recovery?

Regarding treatment:

- Are there special attributes of the particular individual that make it more or less likely that he or she would be so affected?
- Did individual require additional treatment?
- If symptoms have not resolved, are systemic steroids indicated?

Regarding prognosis:

- If symptoms persist, what other treatment options are available?
- Could exposure to the suspected plants or plant parts be occurring outside the workplace; i.e., in the home, in the community, or in recreational activities?
- Has the individual recently worked in another organization where exposure to the suspected plants or plant parts is higher?
- Are there alternative ways of constructing the case that better fit the available facts?

References

Proctor and Hughes' Chemical Hazards of the Workplace, 3rd edition. Hathaway, G.J., et al., eds. New York: Van Nostrand Reinhold, 1991.

Agency for Toxic Substances and Disease Registry. Case Studies in Environmental Medicine: Arsenic, Beryllium, Cadmium, Cholinesterase Inhibitors, Lead, Mercury. US Department of Health and Human Services, 1993.

Toxic Shock Syndrome

Other names / synonyms: Menstrual Toxic Syndrome, Staphylococcal Toxic Shock Syndrome, Streptococcal Toxic Shock Syndrome, TSS

040.89, 048.89

Definition

Toxic shock syndrome is a serious but rare, life-threatening disease caused by toxins produced by certain strains of staphylococci or streptococci bacteria. These toxins affect the entire body by causing shock, i.e., the body is unable to move enough blood to all the tissues and organs. Shock typically occurs in three stages that may progress rapidly over a 24- to 72-hour period. During the first stage, symptoms are minimal while the body attempts to compensate for the changes taking place. The second stage progresses more rapidly because the body is no longer able to compensate for the changes. Blood flow decreases to many organs, damaging them. The third stage is usually irreversible since the heart is so extensively damaged that it cannot pump blood through the body. Organ function becomes compromised and death may result.

Reported cases of staphylococcal toxic shock syndrome reached epidemic proportions between 1979 and 1980 with 2-16 cases per 100,000. Reported cases have since declined. The disease is most common in women in their childbearing years and is closely associated with the use of high-absorbency tampons, menstrual sponges, diaphragms, and cervical caps that tend to trap bacteria and cause infection. Cases have also been reported following childbirth, possibly from trauma to the vaginal tissues. Toxic shock syndrome can also occur in men or women as a result of infection of wounds, insect bites, burns, bones, surgical wounds, or respiratory infections. Streptococcal toxic shock syndrome is estimated to affect 10-20 per 100,000 in both men and women ranging in age from 20 to 50 years.

Diagnosis

History: An individual with toxic shock syndrome presents with a sudden onset of high fever, vomiting, and watery diarrhea. This is usually accompanied by a sore throat (pharyngitis), abdominal pain, muscle pain (myalgia), joint pain (arthralgia), feeling lightheaded, headache, and fainting (syncope). A skin rash with flaking skin, inflammation of the mucus membranes of the eye (conjunctivitis), dizziness, and extreme thirst may also occur. The individual may also lose consciousness and depend on a family member or friend to communicate the history and symptoms. The individual may also have had a recent infection. Confusion is more common with staphylococcal toxic shock syndrome. Pain at the site of infection is the most common symptom of streptococcal toxic shock syndrome.

Physical exam: The exam may reveal fever higher than 102 degrees F and low blood pressure (hypotension) accompanied by abnormalities in three or more organ systems, i.e., kidney, liver, heart, lungs, gastrointestinal, muscular, neurological, or hematological. Other findings may include red throat, swelling of the hands, feet and ankles as well as signs of wound or vaginal infections. There may be a rash that first appears on the trunk, then spreads to the arms and legs, and eventually involves the palms and soles. The skin begins to flake off 1 to 2 weeks later.

Tests: Laboratory tests may reveal increased white blood cells (leukocytosis), decreased platelets (thrombocytopenia), decreased red blood cells (anemia), abnormal liver or kidney chemistries or electrolytes, abnormal blood clotting tests, urinalysis positive for bacteria or blood, and positive bacterial cultures of wound pus or vaginal fluid. Blood cultures are usually negative in staphylococcal toxic shock syndrome since the disease is caused by the toxins produced rather than by the infection itself. Blood cultures are positive, however, in more than half of the individuals with streptococcal toxic shock syndrome.

The rapid streptococcal test can be done in 10 to 15 minutes and is positive in more than 85% of individuals with toxic shock syndrome caused by streptococcus. In most situations, emergency treatment is started before laboratory results are available. Blood tests for viral infections and rheumatologic conditions should be negative. Electrocardiogram may be abnormal if the heart is involved.

Treatment

Treatment is immediately begun and usually involves rapid administration of fluids through an IV line, oxygen, heart monitoring, antibiotics, cleaning and draining of the infected area, and removal of the source of toxin (such as tampon). In some cases, pooled human immunoglobulin is given. Kidney, respiratory, or heart complications must be treated promptly. Surgical consultation may be needed for drainage, scraping (debridement), or amputation of a clearly infected area.

Prognosis

With proper treatment most individuals fully recover in 2 to 3 weeks, but in streptococcal toxic shock syndrome, death can occur in up to 30-70% of the cases. Mortality in staphylococcal toxic shock syndrome is usually less than 3%. If shock proceeds to its third stage, all organ systems rapidly deteriorate. Immediate, aggressive treatment yields the most favorable results.

Differential Diagnosis

Shock caused by other conditions such as prolonged bleeding (hemorrhage), drug reaction, trauma, poisoning, myocardial infarction, or dehydration may occur. Other serious diseases with similar symptoms are Rocky Mountain spotted fever, leptospirosis, hepatitis B, and rubeola (measles).

Specialists

- Cardiologist
- Critical Care Specialist
- Emergency Medicine
- Gynecologist
- Infectious Disease Physician
- Nephrologist
- Neurologist
- Primary Care Provider
- Surgeon

Rehabilitation

Rehabilitation therapy depends on any complications that may occur from toxic shock syndrome. Because the organ most susceptible to damage during shock is the heart, an exercise program for strengthening the heart and lungs may be necessary. Toxic shock syndrome also warrants rehabilitation if the condition results in general weakness and/or affects the nervous system. Once initial symptoms (including high fever, headache, and diarrhea) are stabilized and a physician determines no contraindications for physical activity, a gradual strengthening program is initiated by the rehabilitation professional. Aerobic-type activities focus on increasing the individual's ability to work and resistance to fatigue.

Light aerobic activities include brisk walking and low-resistance biking. As endurance increases without symptoms of shortness of breath, the individual begins active upper and lower extremity exercises first using very light resistance and then progressing to moderate resistance using free weights and/or weight machines. Frequency of the program may vary somewhat depending on the individual's general health.

Balance exercises such as side stepping and walking with the eyes closed with and without assistance are useful in addressing any loss of balance and coordination that may result from toxic shock syndrome. The rehabilitation program also varies for individuals as the intensity and progression of exercises depend on the effect they have on the body's organs, especially the kidneys, and the individual's overall health.

Work Restrictions / Accommodations

Extended periods of weakness may prevent heavy physical work. Some mental confusion may persist for a few weeks and may diminish performance in high stress situations. Other accommodations are dependent on the severity of organ damage, if any. With complete recovery, work restrictions should be minimal.

Comorbid Conditions

Comorbid conditions have more influence on the outcome of the disease than on the length of disability. However, individuals with pre-existing heart, kidney, hematologic, or neurologic conditions may have a longer length of disability.

Complications

Due to lack of blood flow, organs can become damaged, initially at the cellular level, and cause kidney failure, brain damage, lung problems, heart damage, or loss of a limb. Release of bacterial toxins into the bloodstream may cause abnormalities in blood clotting that lead to a loss of blood supply to different parts of the body (disseminated intravascular coagulation). Lung problems may lead to extreme difficulty in breathing (adult respiratory distress syndrome or ARDS). In severe cases, death may result.

Factors Influencing Duration

The length of disability may be extended if surgery was necessary to remove gangrenous or infected tissue. Extensive damage to the heart, lungs, and kidneys may also necessitate a longer disability period.

Length of Disability

Duration depends on the severity of symptoms, response to treatment, and complications. Most individuals recover from shock in 2 to 3 weeks. For jobs that require physical strength, disability may be longer due to muscle weakness or heart damage. Jobs that require great amounts of mental concentration may also require longer disability.

Duration in Days

Job Classification	Minimum	Optimum	Maximum
Any work	7	21	42

Failure to Recover

If an individual fails to recover within the maximum duration expectancy period, the reader may wish to reference the following questions to assist in better understanding the specifics of an individual's medical case.

Regarding diagnosis:

- If individual is female, does she have a history of using high-absorbency tampons, menstrual sponges, diaphragms, or cervical caps? Has she given birth recently?
- If individual is male (or female), is there a history of wound infection, insect bite, burns, recent surgery, or respiratory infection?
- Does individual have a fever higher than 102 degrees F and low blood pressure (hypotension)?
- Does individual complain of vomiting and watery diarrhea?
- Was the throat reddened and sore (pharyngitis)?
- Were there complaints of myalgia or arthralgia, and are feet and ankles swollen?
- Did individual experience lightheadedness, headache, or syncope?
- Was there a flaking skin rash, conjunctivitis, or extreme thirst?
- Was individual confused? Complaining of pain? If so, where was the pain located?
- Did the blood reveal infection, decreased clotting ability, and/or anemia?
- Were liver and kidney functions affected?
- Did urinalysis reveal blood or bacteria?
- Was a throat culture done? Did it reveal a streptococcal infection?
- Were blood cultures negative, suggesting staphylococcal TSS, or were they positive, suggesting streptococcal TSS?
- What organisms, if any, did wound or vaginal cultures reveal?

Regarding treatment:

- Was treatment received quickly?
- Did individual receive intravenous fluids, antibiotic therapy and removal of the source of the toxin?
- How did individual respond to treatment?
- Did individual receive surgical consultation? If so, was surgical intervention warranted?
- Has there been kidney, lung, or heart involvement? If so, was consultation from appropriate specialists received (nephrologist, pulmonologist, cardiologist)? Was the damage to the organ(s) temporary and reversible or permanent and irreversible?

Regarding prognosis:

- Did adequate time elapse for recovery (2 to 3 weeks)?
- Based on the type of infection, what was the expected outcome?
- Did individual suffer any complications, such as organ dysfunction, gangrene or coagulopathy that could impact recovery and prognosis?
- Was surgical amputation of a limb performed to treat gangrene?
- Would individual benefit from psychiatric counseling to recover from the trauma of the illness?

References

Hajjeh, Rana A., et al. "Toxic Shock Syndrome in the United States: Surveillance Update, 1979-1996." Emerging Infectious Diseases 5 6 (1999): 6. 05/22/2000 <http://medscape.com/govmt/CDC/EID/1999/v05.n06/e0506.11.hajj/pnt-e0506.11.hajj.html>.

Kisner, C., and L. Colby. Therapeutic Exercise Foundations and Techniques. Philadelphia: F.A. Davis Company, 1990.

Salandy, Dane, and Barry Brenner. Toxic Shock Syndrome. eMedicine.com. 23 May 2000. 12 Sept 2000 <http://www.emedicine.com/emerg/topic600.htm>.

Tierny, Lawrence M., Stephen J. McPhee, and Maxine Papadakis. Current Medical Diagnosis and Treatment. Stamford: Appleton & Lange, 1998.

Toxoplasmosis

Other names / synonyms: Toxo

130, 130.0, 130.1, 130.2, 130.4, 130.5, 130.7, 130.8, 130.9

Definition

Toxoplasmosis is an infection caused by a one-celled organism called Toxoplasma gondii. Individuals infected with this organism may have no symptoms, a mild flu-like illness, or a more severe, sometimes fatal, disease. Typically healthy individuals have few or mild symptoms. Individuals with weakened immune system (such as those with HIV or cancer, transplant recipients, or those who take immunosuppressant drugs) have more significant disease.

The organism is spread through four routes. The first route is through eating undercooked or raw meat, particularly pork, or anything contaminated with its juices. The second route is through hand-to-mouth contact after handling anything contaminated with cat feces, such as cat litter, or garden soil or sand. The third route is from mother to baby during pregnancy. If a woman becomes infected while pregnant or just before becoming pregnant, the infection can spread to the baby. This is called congenital toxoplasmosis. The risk is greatest during the first trimester. In a baby, toxoplasmosis can cause severe disease. Many babies, however, suffer no effects. The fourth route is the least common. The infection can be passed to an individual through an infected body organ during transplantation.

Many people are already immune to toxoplasmosis because of earlier exposure to the organism. People with a weakened immune system may become ill when a past infection becomes reactivated.

In the United States, toxoplasmosis affects more than 60 million people. Males and females are affected equally. Estimates of the number of cases of congenital toxoplasmosis range from 400 to 4,000 per year. Toxoplasmosis is responsible for 750 deaths per year. Half these deaths are attributed to eating infected meat. Toxoplasmosis is the third leading cause of death due to food-borne illness in the United States.

Toxoplasmosis is found worldwide, but is more common in warm climates and lower altitudes. France has a particularly high prevalence of infection. Up to 85% of the population have had infection with Toxoplasma gondii, probably due to the common practice of eating raw meat. Central America also has a high prevalence probably due to the large number of stray cats and the warm climate.

Diagnosis

History: The disease can be divided by infection in the healthy individual, infection in the immunocompromised individual, and ocular (eye) infection.

In healthy individuals, over 80% have no symptoms. If symptoms are present, they may include fever, fatigue, headache, sore throat, muscle or joint pain, swollen lymph glands, and occasional rash.

In the immunocompromised individual (those with HIV or cancer, posttransplant recipients, and those taking immunosuppressant drugs), the symptoms are widespread. It usually affects the central nervous system (brain and spinal cord) and can also affect the lung, heart, and liver. Symptoms include fever, headache, cough, shortness of breath, chest pain, weakness, seizures, psychosis (loss of sense of reality), and cognitive (reasoning, memory) impairment.

Ocular toxoplasmosis usually results from a congenital condition infection of the eye. It typically is without symptoms until an individual is between 20 and 40 years of age. When disease does develop, inflammatory condition (chorioretinitis) may occur, causing visual disturbances such as blurring or island-like gaps in the visual field. It is possible for ocular toxoplasmosis to progress resulting in glaucoma or blindness.

Physical exam: In healthy individuals, lymph nodes in the neck region may be swollen but not tender. Other symptoms may include fever, rash, and muscle tenderness. Abdominal palpation may reveal enlarged spleen or liver.

Immunocompromised individuals may present with inflammation of the tissues surrounding the air passages (interstitial pneumonia), inflammation of the heart (myocarditis), and evidence of neurologic disease, such as altered mental status, seizures, cranial nerve involvement.

An ophthalmic exam of the eye may reveal a whitish gray chorioretinal scar, involving the vascular coat of the eye (choroid) and the retina. Inflammation may prevent a distinct view of the retina.

Tests: Diagnosis depends principally on serologic tests (blood tests) that detect antibodies against T. gondii. Tests for both IgG and IgM antibodies help determine if the antibodies are due to a new or to an old infection. This information is especially important to a pregnant woman. Rarely, the diagnosis is made by finding the organism is blood or tissue in a microscopic examination.

Treatment

Healthy individuals who aren't pregnant or those with chronic latent infections are usually not treated. When symptoms are severe or persistent, or if the individual is pregnant or immunocompromised, the infection is usually treated with a combination of antibiotic drugs. Individuals who are immunocompromised will require drug maintenance treatment for life.

Prognosis

Most individuals have a non-life threatening, self-limited disease. Symptoms, if present, usually resolve within a few months. Rarely, they may last up to a year. If diagnosed early, the survival rate in immunocompromised individuals is greater than 50%. However, recurrence of the infection in these individuals is common. Complications may be fatal. Treatment of infection during pregnancy reduces the risk of congenital toxoplasmosis by 50%.

Differential Diagnosis

Conditions with similar symptoms include cytomegalovirus (CMV), infectious mononucleosis, sarcoidosis, tuberculosis, tularemia, lymphoma, metastatic cancer, herpes simplex, multifocal leukoencephalopathy, fungal encephalitis, vascular stroke, and CNS lymphoma.

Specialists

- Infectious Disease Physician
- Internist
- Primary Care Provider

Rehabilitation

Toxoplasmosis warrants rehabilitation if the condition results in general weakness and/or affects the nervous system including the brain. Once initial symptoms are stabilized, and a physician determines no contraindications for physical activity, the rehabilitation professional initiates a gradual strengthening program. If necessary, respiratory exercises may be instructed for improving ventilation of the individual with breathing difficulties. This is followed with mild strengthening and endurance exercises such as calisthenics. The individual then performs light aerobic activities such as brisk walking and low-resistance biking.

As endurance increases without shortness of breath, active upper and lower extremity exercises are initiated using very light resistance. This progresses to more moderated resistance using free weights and/or weight machines. As the program continues, the frequency of the exercise sessions varies depending on the individual's general health, e.g., individuals with a weakened immune system caused by HIV, cancer, organ transplant, or immunosuppressant drugs may have a more significant case of toxoplasmosis. If tolerated, the individual performs strengthening exercises and aerobic activities on the non-strengthening days of the program.

Balance exercises such as side stepping and walking with the eyes closed with and without assistance are useful in addressing any loss of balance and coordination resulting from toxoplasmosis. The rehabilitation program varies for individuals affected by toxoplasmosis. The intensity and progression of exercises depend on the affected body organs, specifically the kidneys, and the individual's overall health. For example, visual disturbance may require occupational therapy for dealing with decreased vision.

Work Restrictions / Accommodations

Strenuous activity may need to be modified or restricted until physical stamina returns. Visual disturbances due to ocular toxoplasmosis may require accommodations dependent on their severity.

Pregnant women or women who are planning to be pregnant should be tested for toxoplasmosis if their work involves handling of raw meat, soil or sand, or cats. If a woman is already immune, no restrictions regarding the meat, soil, or sand are needed. If a woman is not immune, she should avoid contact with these potential transmitters of infection. If alternate arrangements can't be made, she should wear latex gloves while working outside, especially when working with sand or soil, or when around cats. She should also wear latex gloves when handling raw meat.

Comorbid Conditions

Any condition that weakens the immune system will increase the severity of the disease and prolong disability. Such conditions include HIV-infection, organ transplant, lymphoproliferative disorders, and taking immunosuppressant drugs.

Complications

Complications may include glaucoma, blindness, inflammation of the tissues surrounding the air passages (interstitial pneumonia), inflammation of the heart (myocarditis), inflammation of the brain (encephalitis), partial paralysis, cranial nerve disturbances, and seizures.

Factors Influencing Duration

Length of disability may be influenced by the individual's age, the severity and extent of the disease, and presence of complications.

Length of Disability

Job Classification	Duration in Days		
	Minimum	Optimum	Maximum
Sedentary work	28	42	63
Light work	28	42	63
Medium work	28	42	63
Heavy work	42	42	63
Very Heavy work	42	42	63

Failure to Recover

If an individual fails to recover within the maximum duration expectancy period, the reader may wish to reference the following questions to assist in better understanding the specifics of an individual's medical case.

Regarding diagnosis:

- Did the individual have a history of exposure (i.e., eating undercooked meat, handling cat feces or cat litter, or garden soil) that may put him/her at risk for toxoplasmosis infection?
- Is the individual pregnant?
- Did the individual have flu-like symptoms (fever, fatigue, headache, sore throat, swollen lymph nodes, or rash) that may be consistent with the diagnosis of toxoplasmosis?
- Is the individual immunocompromised (HIV, cancer, posttransplant recipients, taking immunosuppressant drugs)?
- Was there evidence of widespread involvement such as, interstitial pneumonia, myocarditis or neurological impairment?
- Was the diagnosis confirmed with serological tests?
- Was the extent or severity of the infection determined?
- If the diagnosis was uncertain, were other conditions with similar symptoms (cytomegalovirus, mononucleosis) ruled out?

Regarding treatment:

- Was the treatment appropriate for the symptoms and underlying conditions?
- Were antibiotic drugs indicated?
- Did symptoms persist?

Regarding prognosis:

- Did the individual experience any recurrence of infection or complications that may have impacted recovery and prognosis?

References

Chin, James. *Control of Communicable Diseases Manual, 17th ed.* Washington, DC: American Public Health Association, 2000.

Copstead, Lee-Ellen C. *Perspectives on Pathophysiology.* Philadelphia: W.B. Saunders Company, 1994.

Ferri, Fred. *Ferri's Clinical Advisor.* St. Louis: Mosby, 2000.

Hughes, James, and Daniel Colley. "Preventing Congenital Toxoplasmosis." *MMWR* 49 RR02 (2000): 57-75.

Kisner, C., and L. Colby. *Therapeutic Exercise Foundations and Techniques.* Philadelphia: F.A. Davis Company, 1990.

Toxoplasmosis. Centers for Disease Control and Prevention, Division of Parasitic Diseases. 13 Feb 2001. 03 March 2001 <http://www.dpd.cdc.gov/dpdx/HTML/Toxoplasmosis.htm>.

Trabeculectomy

Other names / synonyms: Filtering Surgery, Sclerostomy

12.64

Definition

Trabeculectomy is a surgical procedure used to treat a progressive disease called glaucoma. Individuals with glaucoma generally have high pressure within their eyes (intraocular pressure or IOP). This elevated IOP is associated with the pathological changes that occur in this disease. There is currently no cure for glaucoma so a major goal of therapy is to reduce the individual's IOP in an effort to slow or halt progression of this disease. Trabeculectomy is the term for the surgical removal of a portion of a part of the eye (trabecular meshwork) to facilitate fluid drainage and reduce IOP.

In the normal eye, fluid called the aqueous humor drains from the eye through channels known as the trabecular meshwork. Many individuals with glaucoma have blockage in these drainage channels that prevents normal fluid flow. The reduced rate of drainage causes a buildup of pressure in the eye. Trabeculectomy attempts to resolve this problem by cutting away a small piece of the trabecular meshwork. Fluid is then able to bypass the clogged channels and drain through this new opening.

Trabeculectomy is generally only performed after medication and laser surgery (trabeculoplasty) have failed to control IOP.

There are approximately 2.5 million individuals in the US and 60 million worldwide with the type of glaucoma that can be treated with trabeculectomy.

Reason for Procedure

Trabeculectomy is performed in an effort to reduce the IOP. It is generally performed on individuals with glaucoma who have not responded sufficiently to medication or other surgical procedures (e.g., laser trabeculoplasty or iridectomy). It is also useful in cases where the trabecular meshwork has been irreversibly damaged by repeated episodes of acute glaucoma.

Left untreated, increased pressure within the eye can damage the optic nerve and seriously affect eyesight. Trabeculectomy will not improve eyesight already affected by glaucoma, but it can prevent further damage or slow the progression of this disease.

Description

Trabeculectomy is a surgical procedure usually performed under local anesthesia in an outpatient setting. In adults, general anesthesia is rarely used.

Prior to surgery, individuals may be given a medication to help relieve anxiety. Injections around the eye are first made to numb it. Using a fine surgical blade and aided by a surgical microscope, the surgeon makes a small opening in the (outer white layer of the eye (sclera) and removes a small piece of trabecular meshwork. This allows fluid to bypass the clogged channels of the trabecular meshwork and drain through the new opening. The surgeon looks for a little bubble of fluid (bleb) under the clear layer of tissue (conjunctiva). This bleb is expected and indicates that fluid is now draining through the new channel.

Prognosis

Trabeculectomy is about 80-90% effective at lowering pressure in the eye, however, if the new opening closes, the procedure may need to be repeated. Vision loss prior to the procedure will not be restored and may even be reduced in individuals experiencing complications.

Specialists

- Ophthalmologist

Work Restrictions / Accommodations

Eyesight may be variable for a period of time following the procedure. Duties may need to be reevaluated or temporarily altered. Following this procedure, eye pressure must be monitored regularly as it may rise immediately following the procedure. Eyedrops may be needed periodically throughout the workday. For approximately one month after the procedure, there may be restrictions in driving, reading, bending, or lifting. Strenuous activity needs to be limited during recuperation.

Comorbid Conditions

Trabeculectomy is more successful in individuals who have not had prior eye surgery (i.e., cataract surgery).

Procedure Complications

The primary complication of trabeculectomy is failure of the incision to close properly. Other possible complications include bleeding (hemorrhage), inflammation, infection, loss of too much fluid causing flattening of the eye, worsening of cataracts, swelling of the cornea (clear, outer layer of the eye), or permanent worsening of underlying glaucoma. These complications can result in permanent vision loss.

Factors Influencing Duration

Factors that may influence length of disability include the individual's response to treatment, presence of any other eye disease, or development of complications.

Length of Disability

Duration of disability is longer for individuals performing heavy work or considerable amounts of bending or lifting.

Duration in Days

Job Classification	Minimum	Optimum	Maximum
Sedentary work	3	9	14
Light work	3	9	14
Medium work	14	21	28
Heavy work	14	21	28
Very Heavy work	14	21	28

References

Glaucoma. National Eye Institute. 01 Apr 2000. 21 July 2000 <http://www.nei.nih.gov/publications/glauc-pat.htm>.

Understanding and Living with Glaucoma. Glaucoma Research Foundation. 1999. 20 July 2000 <http://www.glaucoma.org/New%20UG%20Booklet.pdf>.

Trabeculoplasty

Other names / synonyms: Argon Laser Trabeculoplasty

12.59

Definition

Trabeculoplasty (or argon laser trabeculoplasty) is a surgical procedure that uses a laser to treat a progressive disease called glaucoma. Individuals with glaucoma generally have high pressure within their eyes (intraocular pressure or IOP). Elevated IOP is associated with the pathological changes that occur in this disease. As there is currently no cure for glaucoma, one of the major goals of therapy is to reduce the individual's IOP in an effort to slow or halt progression of this disease. Trabeculoplasty is the term for the laser surgery that creates openings in a part of the eye (trabecular meshwork) to facilitate fluid drainage and reduce IOP. It is usually done if medication is not successfully controlling the individual's IOP.

In the normal eye, fluid called the aqueous humor drains from the eye through channels called the trabecular meshwork. The reduced rate of drainage causes a build-up of pressure in the eye. Trabeculoplasty attempts to resolve this problem by poking holes in the trabecular meshwork, allowing improved fluid drainage. Some individuals with glaucoma have blockage in these drainage channels that prevents normal fluid flow.

Approximately 2.5 million Americans and 60 million individuals worldwide have the type of glaucoma that can be treated with trabeculoplasty.

Reason for Procedure

Trabeculoplasty is performed to lower the IOP as a treatment for certain types of glaucoma. This procedure is necessary to help prevent further damage to the optic nerve and subsequent vision loss due to glaucoma. Trabeculoplasty is generally considered when eye drops and oral medications are no longer effective in reducing pressure or when vision starts to be affected despite such therapy. Pressure in the treated eye will gradually decrease over the next month following the procedure.

Description

Trabeculoplasty is often conducted in the ophthalmologist's office or a surgical center. It is an outpatient procedure conducted under local anesthesia. The procedure is generally completed within a matter of minutes.

Prior to surgery, individuals are given eyedrops to numb the eye. The individual then sits facing the laser machine and the eye doctor holds a special lens over the eye. The laser is passed through the lens and reflected onto the trabecular meshwork. The laser passes harmlessly through the tissues of the eye, burning only the parts of the trabecular meshwork where the beam is focused. Approximately 50 to 100 evenly spaced holes are created. These holes allow fluid to flow more efficiently from the eye.

During the procedure, the individual may see bright flashes of red or green light and may experience a slight tingling sensation. After the procedure, the doctor will prescribe eye drops to reduce any inflammation or soreness.

Prognosis

Trabeculoplasty is effective in reducing the IOP of individuals with certain types of glaucoma however it may take several weeks for this reduction to be evident.

Most individuals (85%) benefit from this procedure. In most cases, eye drops or medication is resumed to maintain the proper eye pressure. While trabeculoplasty is effective in getting the pressure down, its effects tend to wear off. More than half of all individuals will experience an increase in pressure within 2 years of the procedure. Once the entire area of the trabecular meshwork is treated, further laser treatments may not be effective.

The long-term effects of laser surgery are unknown.

Specialists

- Ophthalmologist

Work Restrictions / Accommodations

There are no physical restrictions following this procedure. Since vision is stabilized but not improved, visual acuity should be evaluated if the job requires operation of machinery or driving. The individual may need to use eye drops at certain times of the day and a flexible schedule to return to the doctor's office for frequent follow-up visits, particularly in the first month or so following surgery.

Comorbid Conditions

Previous eye surgery may impact recovery.

Procedure Complications

One immediate complication is an immediate but transient increase in IOP. Other complications include iritis, swelling, scarring, or bleeding (hyphema). These complications are less common with laser surgery than conventional surgery.

Factors Influencing Duration

Eye pressure must be checked frequently after this procedure since it will rise at first, then gradually decrease over the next month. Other factors include the individual's response to the procedure and any complications.

Length of Disability

Laser.

Job Classification	Minimum	Optimum	Maximum
Sedentary work	1	2	3
Light work	3	4	7
Medium work	3	4	7
Heavy work	7	9	14
Very Heavy work	7	9	14

References

Glaucoma. National Eye Institute. 21 Jul 2000 <http://www.nei.nih.gov/publications/glauc%2Dpat.htm>.

Understanding and Living with Glaucoma. Glaucoma Research Foundation. 22 Dec 2000. 20 Jul 2000 <http://www.glaucoma.org/searchpageindex/UGbooklet.html>.

Tracheostomy

Other names / synonyms: Mini-Tracheostomy, Percutaneous Tracheostomy, Trach, Tracheotomy

31.1, 31.2

Definition

A tracheostomy is a surgical procedure in which a small opening (ostomy) is created through the neck into the windpipe (trachea). A small, flexible tube (tracheostomy tube) is placed in the opening to provide a protected opening to the airway. A tracheostomy is usually done as a temporary measure to provide access to the airway until the underlying problem is resolved. Once the condition has improved, the tracheostomy tube is removed, and the incision in the neck closes. However, a tracheostomy may be permanent in cases of surgical removal (resection) of the pharynx or larynx, or in those with permanent neurological dysfunction (spinal cord injury, head trauma, or muscular dystrophy).

The most common indications for the procedure are upper airway obstruction (above the level of the larynx) or respiratory failure (either from severe lung conditions or depressed level of consciousness) that require a prolonged period of time on a respirator (mechanical ventilation). Less common indications for a tracheostomy include severe pneumonia (usually aspiration pneumonia), which requires frequent clearing of the airways (suctioning) and administration of medications and humidified oxygen to the trachea and lungs. A tracheostomy is done in rare circumstances for obstructive sleep apnea, a condition that causes intermittent airway obstruction during sleep.

In adults, upper airway obstructions can occur following trauma to the mouth and trachea (i.e., facial fractures). Surgeries to the mouth, pharynx and/or larynx to remove benign or cancerous growths usually require tracheostomies. These cancers are more common in individuals who smoke and ingest alcohol. A tracheostomy may be done as a safety measure for individuals with strokes, severe head trauma, high spinal cord injuries, or neuromuscular disorders (muscular dystrophy) that impair ability to breathe or maintain an open airway. Tracheostomy is one of the most frequently performed surgical procedures in critically ill individuals.

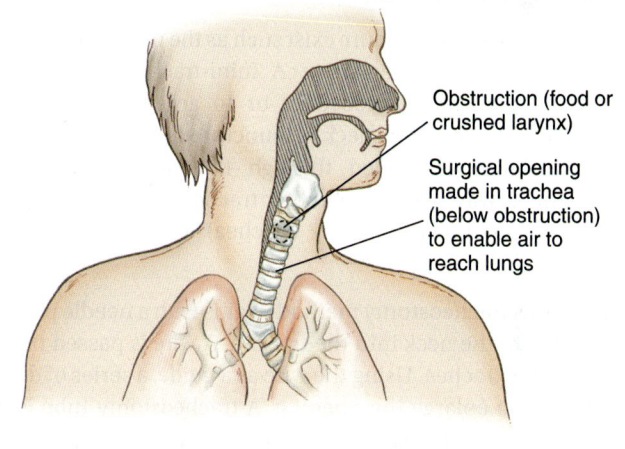

Laurie O'Keefe

Reason for Procedure

Tracheostomy is performed therapeutically for individuals in need of assisted ventilation for an extended period of time (usually greater than 21 days), for control of secretions, to bypass airway obstructions, and for individuals with laryngeal narrowing or closure (stenosis). It is rarely used for the emergency management of an airway obstruction. Instead, individuals needing emergency access to the airway are usually intubated by passing a tube through the larynx to keep the airway open. Converting an intubation to a tracheostomy may facilitate nursing care, feeding and mobility, allow earlier return of speech, and decrease the work of breathing. It also avoids vocal cord paralysis, narrowing of the airway (glottic and subglottic stenosis), infections, tracheal injury, and other complications associated with long-term intubation.

In adults, upper airway obstructions can occur following trauma to the mouth and trachea (i.e., facial fractures). Surgeries to the mouth, pharynx, and/or larynx to remove benign or cancerous growths usually require tracheostomies to bypass the area of injury or surgical site and maintain adequate airflow to the lungs.

A tracheostomy may be done as a safety measure for individuals with strokes, severe head trauma, high spinal cord injuries, or neuromuscular disorders (muscular dystrophy) that impair ability to breathe or maintain an open airway. Tracheostomy provides better long-term access to the upper respiratory system for delivery of respirations, oxygen, and medications when prolonged respiratory support is needed.

A non-emergency (elective) tracheostomy may be used when respiratory problems are anticipated after surgery for cancers involving the larynx or trachea to avoid unnecessary manipulation of the tumor.

Description

Tracheostomy procedures are typically performed in the operating room with the individual under local anesthesia. However, in urgent situations, the procedure may be performed in the emergency department or in the individual's hospital room.

In the standard open surgical procedure, the neck is cleaned with disinfectant solution and sterile towels are applied. A surgical cut is made through the skin and muscle at the base of the neck above the breastbone. The cut is extended deep enough to expose the tough cartilage rings that make up the outer wall of the trachea. Two of these rings are cut, and an endotracheal tube is inserted. Humidified air or oxygen is administered through the tube.

Variations of the general procedure exist such as the mini-tracheostomy and the percutaneous tracheostomy. A mini-tracheostomy is done primarily as an emergency procedure or to access the airway for suctioning. The skin over the neck is punctured, and a solid device called an introducer is guided through the cartilage membrane surrounding the airway. A small diameter tracheostomy tube is placed over the introducer into the airway (trachea) and the introducer is removed.

The percutaneous tracheostomy method begins with a needle puncture through the skin of the neck into the trachea. A wire is passed through the needle into the trachea. Using the wire as a guide, a series of dilating devices are used to enlarge the opening. A tracheostomy tube is then placed over the wire into position in the trachea. The guide wire is then removed.

Prognosis

Mortality rate from tracheostomy is less than 3%. Death is more likely when the procedure is done under emergency circumstances rather than as an elective surgical procedure. Individuals requiring a tracheostomy are usually critically ill, so their outcome may be poor because of their underlying condition.

Specialists

- Emergency Medicine
- General Surgeon
- Otolaryngologist

Rehabilitation

Respiratory therapy may be actively involved in tracheostomy management.

Work Restrictions / Accommodations

Those who return to work with a tracheostomy need to avoid work environments that have airborne irritants, such as fumes, smoke, or dust from soil, wood, or flour products. Accommodations to provide humidified oxygen may be needed on a case-by-case basis. There are no special work restrictions or accommodations for those whose tracheostomy tube has been removed and the surgical site is healed, although there may be restrictions related to underlying conditions.

Comorbid Conditions

Comorbid conditions of immune suppression, bleeding disorders, permanent neurological or neuromuscular dysfunction, or cancer may impact ability to recover and further lengthen disability.

Procedure Complications

Early complications associated with the surgical procedure and insertion of the tracheostomy tube include bleeding, infection, collapsed lung (pneumothorax), and leakage of air into the tissue of the chest or neck (subcutaneous emphysema). Late complications after the procedure include obstruction of the tracheostomy, erosion of the tissue in the trachea (tracheoesophageal fistula), narrowing of the trachea (tracheal stenosis), enlargement (dilatation) of the trachea (ballooned trachea), dislodged tracheostomy tube, and bleeding.

Factors Influencing Duration

Factors that may influence the length of disability include the underlying reason for which the procedure was performed, the type of procedure (mini- vs. standard tracheostomy), and the development of complications.

Length of Disability

Duration depends on the underlying cause.

Duration in Days

Job Classification	Minimum	Optimum	Maximum
Sedentary work	14	21	Indefinite
Light work	14	21	Indefinite
Medium work	14	35	Indefinite
Heavy work	21	35	Indefinite
Very Heavy work	21	42	Indefinite

References

Clochesy, John M., et al. Critical Care Nursing, 2nd ed. Philadelphia: W.B. Saunders Company, 1996.

Goldman, R.K., et al. "Minimally Invasive Surgery. Bedside Tracheostomy and Gastrostomy." Critical Care Clinic 16 1 (2000): 113-130.

Pryor, John P., Patrick M. Reilly, and Michael B. Shapiro. "Surgical Airway Management in the Intensive Care Unit." Critical Care Clinics 16 3 (2000): 473-488.

Susanto, Irawan. Percutaneous Tracheostomy in the ICU. ChestNet. 01 Jan 2000. 9 Mar 2001 <http://www.chestnet.org/education/pccu/vol13/lesson22.html>.

Trachoma

Other names / synonyms: Contagious Granulomatous Conjunctivitis, Egyptian Ophthalmia, Granular Conjunctivitis, Granulomatous Conjunctivitis

076, 076.0, 076.1, 076.9

Definition

Trachoma is an infectious disease caused by the bacteria Chlamydia trachomatis. This disease affects the eyes and is the world's largest cause of preventable blindness.

Trachoma is highly contagious especially in the early stages. It is transmitted from individual to individual by direct contact with eye secretions or through contact with contaminated towels, handkerchiefs, or clothing. Flies attracted to the face and runny noses can also transmit this disease. The initial infection generally strikes young children, however, the infection is then easily passed to other family members. Mothers of infected children are at an increased risk for contracting the disease, as mothers tend to be the primary caretakers. While the initial infection usually occurs in early childhood, progressive damage occurs slowly over the years. By adulthood, repeated infections and progressive scarring can ultimately result in blindness.

Overall, about 10% of the world's population (about 540 million individuals) is at risk of blindness or severe visual impairment due to this disease. Poverty, overcrowding, and poor hygiene are risk factors for this disease. Those who do not have access to clean water or health care are at increased risk.

Trachoma is very rare in the US with cases generally limited to the southwestern part of the country. However, trachoma is the leading cause of preventable blindness worldwide. The World Health Organization estimates that about 6 million individuals have lost their vision to trachoma and 150 million individuals in Africa, Asia, the Middle East, Latin America, and Australia are in need of immediate treatment. Women are affected 2 to 3 times as often as men.

Diagnosis

History: Individual may report contact with an infected individual. The individual may complain of eye (ocular) irritation and discharge from the eyes. In more advanced cases, pain and the sensation of something in the eye (foreign body sensation) may be reported. Some individuals complain of a loss of vision.

Physical exam: The exam may reveal inflammation of the mucus membrane of the eye (conjunctiva). Follicles may be present. Individuals with pain and foreign body sensation may have developed a condition where the eyelashes are turned inward (trichiasis). The inward growing eyelashes rub against the clear, outer layer of the eye called the cornea. If trichiasis is noted, scarring of the cornea may also be observed.

Tests: To confirm the diagnosis of trachoma, the eye is swabbed or the cornea scraped in an effort to obtain a sample for culturing and identification. There are also in-office test kits that identify Chlamydia species, however, these kits are associated with a high rate of false positives so they should be done in addition to not in place of standard bacterial culture.

Treatment

Trachoma is easily treated with antibiotics taken by mouth. Eyedrop formulations may be used in addition to oral medications but should not be used exclusively. With the advent of newer types of antibiotics (macrolide antibiotics), it is now possible to treat this infection with a single dose of medication. However, since this infection is so easily spread from individual to individual, it is necessary to treat not only the individual, but also anyone with whom they have had close contact (i.e., household family members). Simultaneous treatment is necessary to prevent re-infection.

Good personal hygiene (frequent hand and face washing) is also critical to successful treatment. Towels, clothing, and handkerchiefs should not be re-used or shared.

Prognosis

If treated early and effectively with the appropriate antibiotic medications, the prognosis for a full recovery is excellent. The predicted outcome worsens with the length of infection and any complications. Untreated or inadequately treated infections will cause progressive damage and can ultimately lead to blindness.

Differential Diagnosis

Trachoma must be differentiated from inclusion conjunctivitis, which is a milder inflammatory disease also caused by Chlamydia trachomatis infection. Other diseases that cause inflammation of the conjunctiva (conjunctivitis) include allergic conjunctivitis, bacterial conjunctivitis, follicular conjunctivitis, atopic keratoconjunctivitis, viral conjunctivitis, and gonococcal conjunctivitis. Inflammation of the colored part of the eye (iritis) can also cause similar symptoms. Other diseases can cause ulceration of the cornea. Other bacterial ulcers, marginal infiltrates, and herpes infections of the eyes should also be ruled out.

Work Restrictions / Accommodations

For a successful recovery, the individual needs to wash his/her hands and face frequently so will need frequent access to a restroom or washroom. To prevent transmission, close physical contact with others should be avoided until the infection clears. Those whose jobs require such contact (e.g., nurses, physicians, or daycare providers) may require time off from work until the active infection clears. If vision was impaired, tasks requiring close vision, detailed work, or driving should be avoided and reassignment to less visually intensive work may be required.

Complementary and Alternative Therapies

Content is intended for awareness only. Treatments may or may not be effective. Scientific evidence may be lacking and some substances have potentially toxic effects. Dr. Presley Reed and the editors do not endorse the use of these therapies in the absence of consultation with a licensed medical professional.

Berberine - Berberine extracts and decoctions are said to have demonstrated significant antimicrobial activity against a variety of organisms including ocular trachoma infections.

Comorbid Conditions

Individuals with a compromised immune system may be slower to recover.

Complications

Complications of trachoma include inward-turning eyelashes (trichiasis), cloudiness of the cornea (pannus), drooping eyelids (ptosis), ulceration of the cornea, and progressive scarring of the cornea that can result in blindness.

Specialists

- Infectious Disease Physician
- Ophthalmologist

Factors Influencing Duration

The length of disability is influenced by the severity of the infection and length of time the infection was untreated. If complications occur, treatment of the complications may lengthen the period of disability.

Length of Disability

Disability may be permanent for individuals with complicated or advanced disease. Visual impairment and/or blindness may be permanent. Individuals with jobs requiring acute vision may be permanently disabled unless an alternative position can be provided.

Duration in Days

Job Classification	Minimum	Optimum	Maximum
Any work	2	7	10

Failure to Recover

If an individual fails to recover within the maximum duration expectancy period, the reader may wish to reference the following questions to assist in better understanding the specifics of an individual's medical case.

Regarding diagnosis:

- Did the individual present with redness, irritation and discharge from the eye?
- Was a corneal scraping done for culture and sensitivity?
- Was the diagnosis confirmed with a positive eye culture?
- If the diagnosis was uncertain, were other sources of conjunctivitis or iritis ruled out?

Regarding treatment:

- Was infection effectively resolved with antibiotic treatment?
- Has the individual become re-infected?
- Have other individuals, who have had close contact with the infected individual been treated?
- Has the individual received instructions about personal hygiene and measures to prevent spread of infection? Has the individual been compliant with the instructions?

Regarding prognosis:

- Was infection diagnosed and treated in a timely manner? Was individual re-infected by poor hygiene practices?
- Has the individual experienced complications (trichiasis, pannus, ptosis, corneal ulceration or scaring) due to delayed or inadequate treatment? Are the complications being addressed in the treatment plan?
- Does individual have an underlying condition such as a compromised immune system that may impact recovery?

References

"Berberine." Alternative Medical Review 5 2 (2000): 175-177.

Trachoma: A Blinding Disease That Debilitates Families and Communities. International Trachoma Initiative. 2 Oct 2000 <http://www.trachoma.org>.

Traction
93.4, 93.41, 93.42, 93.43, 93.44, 93.45, 93.46

Definition
Traction is the force used to pull on a body part. The force can be applied to the skin, skeleton, head, or trunk and transmits the pull to the bone and muscles.

Traction is usually applied to the spine, pelvis, neck, arms, or legs. The force is generated by weight or force against the weight of the body. The two main types of traction are skin traction and skeletal traction. Of these two types, many specialized forms have been developed to treat conditions in specific parts of the body. With skin traction, weights are attached to the skin, which applies the pulling force to the bone. It is used when light (5 to 7 pounds) or short-term traction is needed. With skeletal traction, pins are attached to the bone so that the pulling force is applied directly to the bone. Skeletal traction is used when skin traction is not possible and when greater weight (25 to 40 pounds) is needed.

Traction is used to treat broken bones (fractures), joint dislocations, and long-term muscle spasms. It is a common, effective treatment especially in injuries sustained during high-energy traumas such as motor vehicle accidents and falls.

Reason for Procedure
Traction relaxes muscle tension and spasm, repositions fracture fragments (reduces a fracture), maintains alignment of bones, maintains length of bones during healing, allows joint motion during fracture healing and reduces swelling, and facilitates joint relocation by reducing muscle spasm.

Use of traction has changed in recent history. For example, it used to be the standard treatment for fractures of the thighbone (femur). The need for prolonged hospitalization, frequent traction adjustments, high risk of incorrect fracture union (malunion), and the development of complications associated with long-term bed rest has made traction a less desirable treatment for femoral fracture in favor of surgery. However, traction is a viable treatment option for individuals not medically stable for surgery or whose femur is broken into many small pieces (comminuted).

Description
Skin traction uses noninvasive means in attaching weights to the skin for applying a pulling force to the underlying bone. Depending on where traction is needed, weights are attached with tape, straps, boots, or cuffs. Skin traction on the fingers may use the weight of the arm hanging by the fingers as the traction force without any added weights. Traction is applied to the trunk with a waist belt attached to ropes and pulleys and is actually a form of skin traction.

Skeletal traction requires insertion of pins or wires into the bone either during open surgery or pierced through the skin. The pins are then rigged to weights by ropes and pulleys. Traction to the head applies a pulling force to the neck and can be accomplished with a neck halter hooked to a rope and pulley system or by tongs inserted directly into the skull that are then hooked onto a rope and pulley system.

Inversion traction places the individual in a partially upside down position. External fixation devices apply a gentle, steady force to encourage bone lengthening in a procedure called an Ilizarov limb lengthening. These devices can also be used to maintain fracture alignment while allowing joint motion. The fixator does not use ropes and pulleys but an outrigging attached to pins inserted through the bones. It is considered a form of skeletal traction.

Traction equipment needs to hang from a bed frame or over a doorframe. It can be used temporarily (e.g., during surgery to maintain body position) or applied for weeks at a time as in a neck fracture. Short periods of manual traction are used during reduction of fractures and dislocations where the physician or assistant manually applies the traction force against the weight of the individual.

Prognosis
Outcome depends on the reason for traction. Traction usually produces very good results. In most cases, traction can successfully realign the ends of a fractured bone and maintain proper bone length, relieve pain, end muscle spasm, relax muscles, and reduce a dislocated joint.

Specialists

• Neurologist	• Physiatrist
• Neurosurgeon	• Physical Therapist
• Orthopedic Surgeon	• Rheumatologist

Work Restrictions / Accommodations
Individuals are not able to work while using the traction device. Upon returning to work, restrictions and accommodations are related to the specific injury or condition for which traction was utilized.

Comorbid Conditions
Circulatory disorders, varicose veins, and skin conditions can be aggravated by traction and may influence length of disability.

Procedure Complications
If traction wrappings are too tight, the nerves and blood vessels can be impaired. Traction wrappings around bony prominences can cause skin pressure sores (lesions). Skin straps may slip resulting in skin injury. Infection can occur around the pins or wires used for skeletal traction. Bone inflammation can occur as a response to the pins used for skeletal traction. Excessive joint separation (overdistraction) can occur if the traction weight is too great. Overdistraction can cause nerve damage. Prolonged bed rest associated with long-term traction can lead to blood clots (deep vein thrombosis), bedsores, lung compromise, and urinary tract infections. Inversion traction can cause heartburn (gastroesophageal reflux), headaches, overstretching of facet joints (hyperextension), and a ruptured aneurysm of the cerebral artery (berry aneurysm). Long-term traction can have a negative emotional effect on the individual.

Factors Influencing Duration

The length of disability depends on whether the traction is an intermittent therapy used at home or in a physical therapy office or if it is part of long-term treatment in a hospital setting.

Length of Disability

Duration depends on site of, reason for, and type of traction. No disability for treatment; see underlying cause for duration.

References

Cole, Andrew, et al. "Zygapophyseal (Facet) Joint Pain: A Functional Approach." Soft Tissue Injuries: Diagnosis and Treatment. Windsor, Robert, and Dennis Lox, eds. Philadelphia: Hanley & Belfus, Inc, 1998. 47-64.

Kram, Derek, and Vasantha Murthy. "Supracondylar Femur Fractures." Treatment and Rehabilitation of Fractures. Hoppenfeld, Stanley, and Vasantha Murthy, eds. Philadelphia: Lippincott, Williams & Wilkins, 2000. 324-332.

Marion, Donald, and Gregory Przybylski. "Injury to the Vertebrae and Spinal Cord." Trauma. Mattox, Kenneth, David Feliciano, and Ernest Moore, eds. New York: McGraw-Hill, 2000. 451-471.

Taylor, Kenneth, and Vasantha Murthy. "Femoral Shaft Fractures." Treatment and Rehabilitation of Fractures. Hoppenfeld, Stanley, and Vasantha Murthy, eds. Philadelphia: Lippincott, Williams & Wilkins, 2000. 306-317.

Transcutaneous Electrical Nerve Stimulation
Other names / synonyms: TENS
93.39

Definition

Transcutaneous electrical nerve stimulation (TENS) is a method of pain control involving transmitting electrical impulses to nerve endings, through the skin and underlying soft tissue. The current is generated in a small battery pack (that can be either worn on a belt or hand held) passed along flexible wires and applied to the skin by surface electrodes or patches. The current delivered can be modified to different wave frequencies, which, in turn, create different sensations: continuous, interrupted, or pulsating; mild or intense; or a mixture of these patterns. Individuals often describe the sensation as vibrating or tingling.

The generated current is similar to other current in the body, but, in TENS, the current travels directly to nerve endings and is different enough to block transmission of pain impulses. It is also thought to stimulate the release of the body's own pain control substance, endorphins.

TENS is used to manage or relieve pain that is caused by chronic injury or illness. TENS can also be used to manage acute pain after surgery or injury. TENS has been used to treat muscle spasm, low back or neck pain, headaches, reflex sympathetic dystrophy, rheumatoid arthritis, phantom limb pain, and pain incurred during labor and delivery. TENS is safe, noninvasive, drug-free, nonaddictive, and has no side effects. Use of TENS can reduce the need for narcotics and other pain controlling drugs.

TENS is contraindicated in persons with demand-type pacemakers.

The TENS is available worldwide. A physicians prescription is required to obtain a TENS unit in the US, and patient education on use of the unit is critical to successful utilization for pain relief.

Reason for Procedure

TENS is used to control or treat pain, usually chronic in nature. Treatment via TENS has advantages over other modalities as it can deliver constant pain control. The effects of other treatments (such as heat) wear off after treatment has ended (removal of the hot pack). TENS is also portable and unobtrusive. TENS may be used throughout the work day. Individuals who suffer from chronic pain who have not benefitted from medication or who cannot take pain medication due to side effects are good candidates for TENS. Additionally, individuals who would like a noninvasive form of pain relief as opposed to steroid injections are good candidates for a trial of TENS.

Description

The therapist, doctor, or nurse should explain to the individual how the unit works and the associated sensations the individual will experience. The parameters for pulse rate and width are set on the TENS unit. The lead wires are plugged into the self-adhesive electrodes, and the electrodes are placed on predetermined sites on the individual's skin. (Electrodes can be placed above the painful site, above and below the painful site, one on the painful area and one on the spine over the corresponding nerve root, over trigger points that refer pain to other areas of the body when touched, or over acupuncture sites.) The wires are then plugged into the TENS unit, the unit is turned on, and the amplitude is set to a comfortable setting within the parameters of the TENS mode that is being used. The time that the TENS unit is left on depends on the mode of TENS that is being used. Fifteen minutes is appropriate for brief intense mode and hyperstimulation mode TENS, 1 hour for burst and low frequency mode TENS, and 24 hours for modulation and conventional mode TENS.

Prognosis

Individuals who utilize TENS according to the prescribed regimen of either the physical therapist or physician are able to reduce or control the pain they experience from the underlying illness or injury. The use of TENS allows individuals to participate in physical and occupational therapy, so that a more complete recovery can occur. TENS allows individuals to resume participation in their daily activities.

Specialists

- Neurologist
- Pain Specialist
- Physiatrist
- Physical Therapist
- Primary Care Provider
- Registered Nurse

Work Restrictions / Accommodations

Because TENS can be worn without interfering in other activities, no work restrictions are required due to its usage.

Comorbid Conditions

Chronic, nonspecific pain conditions such as fibromyalgia may lengthen disability in individuals with other painful conditions such as muscle spasm. Individuals who experience pain in multiple body parts or who experience pain that fluctuates in multiple body parts may not recover as quickly due to an increased inflammatory response in the body.

Procedure Complications

Complications that may result from TENS are mild and reversible. Low frequency and burst mode may not be tolerated because these modes can produce localized muscle contractions. Hyperstimulation mode may not be tolerated due to the production of a noxious stimulus. Skin irritation may result from the use of the electrodes. The TENS should not be used by individuals with a pacemaker, a heart condition, epilepsy, who are pregnant, on infected skin, around the head, or near the carotid artery on the neck.

Factors Influencing Duration

There is no disability associated with the use of the TENS unit itself.

Length of Disability

No disability is expected to result from use of this therapy. Disability may occur as a result of an underlying condition.

References

Foley, Russell A. "Transcutaneous Electrical Nerve Stimulation." Manual for Physical Agents. Hayes, Karen W., ed. Norwalk: Appleton & Lange, 1993. 97-118.

Nelson, Roger M., and Dean P. Currier. Clinical Electrotherapy. Norwalk: Appleton & Lange, 1991.

Transfer of Nerve, Ulnar
Other names / synonyms: Ulnar Nerve Decompression, Ulnar Nerve Transposition
04.6

Definition

Transfer of the ulnar nerve refers to a procedure in which the nerve is repositioned. The nerve is moved from the boney tunnel around the elbow (cubital tunnel) to a new bed in the muscle more in front of the elbow (anterior transposition). This procedure is performed to in cases where conservative treatment for ulnar nerve damage (ulnar neuropathy) has failed.

The procedure decreases the angle the nerve must travel and reduces irritation from compression during elbow bending and maintains important blood supply to the nerve. To further decrease irritation of friction, the bump on the inside border of the elbow (medial epicondyle) may also be removed (medial epicondylectomy) during the procedure.

About one half of the individuals affected with mild neuropathy can be treated successfully with conservative measures. Others will most likely need surgical intervention to prevent irreversible nerve damage and loss of muscle function beyond the elbow.

Ulnar neuropathy is most common in individuals resting their elbow on a hard surface in a flexed position, such as in driving. Other aggravating activities include repetitive motion with a bent (flexed) elbow including keyboarding, sleeping, weightlifting, and pitching a baseball.

Reason for Procedure

Ulnar nerve transfer is carried out to treat ulnar neuropathy at the elbow. Moving the nerve provides relief from irritation caused by compression along the nerve route. The procedure follows failure of conservative management of the neuropathy.

Description

Through an incision along the back inner side of the elbow (posterior medial) the nerve is explored and removed from the boney tunnel, along with its blood supply, and placed in a new space created in the muscle in front of the tunnel. Removal of the inner elbow bump (medical epicondyle) may also be done during the procedure.

Regional or general anesthesia is required for outpatient procedure.

After surgery, a bulky soft dressing is applied, and perhaps a splint to prevent elbow bending (flexion) over the dressing.

Prognosis

Fairly prompt relief of aching should occur, with gradual improvement of feeling (sensation) and decreased symptoms of tingling and burning (paraesthesia). Gripping strength in the hand may take 4-5 months to begin to return, and full function in the small muscles of the hand may take 1.0-1.5 years to return.

Damage to the nerve may be permanent, resulting in little or no improvement of weakness in the small (intrinsic) muscles in the hand.

Specialists

• Hand Surgeon	• Orthopedic Surgeon
• Neurosurgeon	• Physiatrist

Rehabilitation

Gentle mobilization of the elbow, followed by muscle strengthening modalities usually are started 7-10 days after surgery. Rehabilitation following ulnar nerve transfer begins with the goals of controlling postoperative pain and swelling followed by regaining full motion, flexibility, strength, and endurance of the muscle/joint structures of the wrist and elbow. The final result is aimed at returning the individual to full function for work and recreational activities with minimal risk of any reoccurrence of symptoms.

Therapy may begin with cold treatments (ice) on the surgical area. Heat treatments are helpful to reduce inflammation and pain and once appropriate and are beneficial to mildly stretch the muscles that are affected from the ulnar transplant. Forms of heat treatment include ultrasound using high frequency sound waves producing heat penetrating deep into the involved muscles of the upper limb. Electrical stimulation combined with heat or cold treatment is another technique used in physical therapy to relax irritated muscles that may be in spasm.

As postoperative pain subsides, stretching and strengthening exercises of specific wrist and elbow muscles are emphasized. Wrist flexion (bending the wrist by bringing the palm side of the hand to the same of the wrist) and extension (opposite motion) are such exercises. Ulnar deviation is accomplished as the individual brings his or her little finger side of the hand as close to the forearm on that same side as possible. The opposite direction of motion is called radial deviation and is accomplished when the individual brings his or her thumb side of the hand to that same side of the forearm.

Passive range-of-motion exercises for the elbow begin with the therapist bending and straightening the elbow (flexion and extension). Restoring supination and pronation to the elbow is vital in rehabilitation. A supination stretch is described as the elbow bent at 90 degrees beginning with the palm of the hand facing down and then the hand is rotated to a position with the palm facing upward. A pronation stretch is the opposite movement of supination and described as the palm is rotated back to a position of facing down. The therapist may utilize a stretch at the end of each motion to help stretch and improve flexibility of the tendons. As the individual improves with increased motion of the joint, active range of motion exercises follow. Strengthening exercises progress with resistance from a relatively light weight and/or elastic band. Job requirements may need to be modified during the rehabilitation process until pain and swelling diminishes. For example, lifting objects that stress the wrist and elbow joints may need to be limited despite the amount of force needed to accomplish the task.

An occupational therapist may fabricate a specific splint for the individual to help immobilize and protect the region of ulnar nerve transplant. The splint is used initially on a full time basis (if needed) followed by a gradual decrease in frequency and duration until the individual tolerates work demands without discomfort and/or weakness of the upper limb.

Work Restrictions / Accommodations

Individuals recovering from ulnar nerve transfer will have restricted elbow function for several weeks. After return to work, accommodating devices such as phone head sets may be recommended.

Comorbid Conditions

Compression of the ulnar nerve at other sites will compound the neuropathy. Individuals with inflammatory disease may experience more difficult recovery.

Procedure Complications

Infection and bleeding are possible complications to any surgery. This procedure also has the risk of increased nerve damage with loss of function and increased pain.

Factors Influencing Duration

Job requirements and the ability to remove aggravating activities will influence disability. Loss of function of the small (intrinsic) hand muscles would influence disability in jobs requiring dexterity. It takes longer for recovery of the nerve (regeneration) in older individuals.

Length of Disability

Disability may be permanent in individuals without complete recovery or whose job requirements cannot be altered.

Duration in Days

Job Classification	Minimum	Optimum	Maximum
Sedentary work	7	21	42
Light work	7	28	42
Medium work	28	56	Indefinite
Heavy work	28	98	Indefinite
Very Heavy work	42	98	Indefinite

References

Bermat, Michael, MD. Cubital Tunnel Syndrome. 01 Jan 1996. 12 Jan 2001 <http://www.plasticsurgery4u.com/procedure_folder/cubital_tunnel.html>.

Regan, William, and Bernard Morrey. "Entrapment Neuropathies About the Elbow." Orthopedic Sports Medicine, vol. 1. DeLee, Jesse C. Jr., and David Drez, eds. Philadelphia: W.B. Saunders Company, 1994. 856-857.

Transfusion of Blood and Blood Components

Other names / synonyms: Autologous Transfusion, Blood Component Therapy

99.0

Definition

A blood transfusion is the injection (infusion) of compatible blood (whole blood) or blood components (red blood cells, packed red blood cells, white blood cells, gamma globulin, plasma, albumin, platelets, cryoprecipitate, clotting factors) directly into the bloodstream.

The various components of the blood serve a variety of different purposes. Red blood cells are necessary for carrying oxygen to tissues. Packed red blood cells is whole blood in which excess fluid volume has been removed. White blood cells and gamma globulin are necessary for fighting infection. Plasma is the liquid in which all blood components are suspended. Albumin is a protein that helps to maintain the blood pressure. Platelets, cryoprecipitate and other clotting factors are necessary for blood clotting.

Blood given in a transfusion may be the individual's own blood (an autologous transfusion) or it may be from a donor. An exchange transfusion is a type of transfusion in which the individual's entire blood volume is slowly and carefully replaced (exchanged) with donor blood. Before a transfusion can be given, the blood must be cross-matched to ensure compatibility of blood types. The most important blood types are the ABO (blood types A, B, AB, O) and the Rhesus (Rh) blood types (Rh negative or positive). If an incompatible blood type is given, it may result in blood cell destruction. Generally, only blood of the same blood type may be given. Cross matching involves taking a sample of the recipient's blood, identifying the blood group, and matching it with a suitable donor's blood. Cross matching may take up to an hour. In an emergency situation, when there is no time for cross matching, O Rh-negative blood ("universal donor"), plasma protein solution, or an artificial plasma substitute may be given to the individual until tested blood becomes available. Blood is usually transfused into an arm vein. Each unit (approximately one pint) of blood is given over a time period of one to four hours. In an emergency, the blood can be delivered within minutes. The amount of blood given depends upon the condition for which it is required. Usually, when a transfusion is needed, more than one unit is given.

Blood products may be given during hospitalization, as an outpatient, or at home by a home health nurse.

Reason for Procedure

Blood transfusions are performed in order to replace blood lost due to severe bleeding (hemorrhage) after an accident or during an operation. Transfusions are also given to treat chronic anemia that has not responded to medication, other blood disorders (hemophilia, leukemia), or internal bleeding (gastrointestinal bleeding).

In an exchange transfusion, nearly all of the recipient's blood is replaced by donor blood. Babies born with a hemolytic disease (Rh incompatibility) causing abnormally high levels of bilirubin in their blood can suffer brain damage if their blood is not replaced by donor blood. In sickle cell anemia, damaged red blood cells are removed and replaced with healthy donor cells. Transfusion of platelets, cryoprecipitate and other blood clotting factors are given to individuals in order to restore the body's normal coagulating ability (such as hemophilia). Platelet transfusions can also be given to individuals with certain forms of leukemia when there is an abnormal decrease in platelets (thrombocytopenia). White blood cells may be given (rarely) to replace an abnormally low level of white blood cells. Fresh frozen plasma may be given to help increase the blood pressure. Gamma globulin (immune globulin) may be given to help prevent development of certain infections (such as hepatitis B). Depending on the purpose and formulation, gamma globulin may be given as an injection into a muscle (intramuscular, IM) or into a vein (intravenous, IV).

Specialists

- Anesthesiologist
- Emergency Medicine
- General Surgeon
- Hematologist
- Immunologist
- Internist
- Oncologist
- Pathologist
- Registered Nurse

Description

A blood sample will be tested in the laboratory to confirm need. Written consent for a transfusion may be needed. Before the transfusion can be given, access into a vein must be established. A small hollow, plastic tube (catheter) is inserted through the skin directly into a vein (an intravenous catheter, IV catheter). The intravenous catheter is then connected to an intravenous infusion system consisting of tubing and a plastic bag containing a fluid solution that will be dripped into the vein. The solution that is initially hung is usually a plain solution (saline) that is similar to the fluid in the veins. A sample of the individual's blood must be carefully typed and cross-matched (usually done in the blood bank, a part of the laboratory that specializes in identification and preparation of blood components) to assure compatibility. When the blood to be transfused is ready, the blood to be given is carefully checked by two nurses to assure that it is the correct type and product. A special filter and blood tubing are attached to the blood bag (needed for infusion of many, but not all blood products), and the tubing is then inserted into a port on the intravenous tubing. The infusion can then be given. It is allowed to drip in slowly at first and the vital signs are monitored for signs of an infusion reaction. After several minutes, if no reaction occurs, the rate of infusion can be increased. When completed, the blood tubing and bag are removed from the intravenous line and discarded.

Prognosis

The predicted outcome for transfusion of whole blood or packed red blood cells is the return to normal levels. The predicted outcome of infusion of white blood cells and gamma globulin is adequate response to infection or prevention of infection. The predicted outcome of infusion of platelets, cryoprecipitate and other clotting factors is adequate clotting ability. The predicted outcome of infusion of albumin is a rise in the blood pressure.

Work Restrictions / Accommodations

The type of work performed by the individual and the reason for the transfusion will dictate any restrictions or accommodations. If a significant reaction occurred, hospitalization and treatment may require extra time off from work.

Comorbid Conditions

A person who has congestive heart failure may be at risk of heart failure if excess fluid is infused with the transfusion. Individuals with a history of previous transfusion reactions may be at increased risk of reaction (administration of blood that has fewer white blood cells, leukocyte-reduced, may be indicated).

Procedure Complications

Many complications may occur with blood transfusions. One complication that may occur is a reaction to an incompatible blood type (transfusion reaction, ABO incompatibility, hemolytic reaction). Symptoms include chest pain, trouble breathing, fever and chills, and low blood pressure. Life-threatening shock may occur if the transfusion is not stopped and emergency treatment given. Another complication that may occur with transfusion is an allergic reaction to donor blood. This may occur due to an allergic reaction to medications in the donor blood, or to the presence of particles that cause allergic reaction (antigens). This type of reaction may result in anaphylaxis with symptoms such as chills, swelling of the face and larynx, itching and hives, wheezing, nausea and vomiting. Anaphylaxis can result in death unless emergency treatment is initiated. Another complication that can occur is infusion of blood that contains bacteria (usually bacteria such as Pseudomonas or Staphylococcus). This type of reaction may cause fever and chills, vomiting, abdominal cramping and diarrhea, and low blood pressure. Infection with viruses such as hepatitis and HIV is another complication that may occur.

Individuals with impaired heart function (such as heart failure) may not be able to tolerate the fluid volume needed for transfusions and may develop symptoms of fluid volume overload or heart failure. Individuals receiving rapid transfusion of large volumes of blood may be at risk for a severe drop in temperature (hypothermia) because of the low temperature of the blood.

Factors Influencing Duration

Blood transfusions are not disabling unless a transfusion reaction occurs. An adverse reaction to the blood transfusion may occur up to ten days after the transfusion.

Length of Disability

Duration depends on the underlying condition for which the transfusion is administered.

Duration in Days

Job Classification	Minimum	Optimum	Maximum
Any work	2	3	5

References

Hamilton, Sandra, et al. "Intravascular Therapy." Nursing Procedures, 3rd ed. Holmes, H. Nancy, ed. Springhouse, PA: Springhouse, 2000. 272-341.

Sanson, June. "Adult Cardiovascular System Procedures." AACN Guide to Acute Care Procedures in the Home. McNeal, Gloria J., ed. Philadelphia: Lippincott, 2000. 383-431.

Sims, Marion H. "Use of Blood Products." Saunders Manual of Medical Practice, 2nd ed. Rakel, Robert E., ed. Philadelphia: W. B. Saunders Company, 2000. 811-813.

Yawn, David H. "Adverse Reactions to Blood Transfusions." Saunders Manual of Medical Practice, 2nd ed. Rakel, Robert E., ed. Philadelphia: W. B. Saunders Company, 2000. 814-816.

Transient Ischemic Attack

Other names / synonyms: Intermittent Cerebral Ischemia, Mini-Stroke, TIA, Transient Cerebral Ischemia

435, 435.9

Definition

Transient ischemic attack (TIA) refers to a temporary loss of blood supply (ischemia) to a part of the brain, usually due to blockage of the carotid or vertebral arteries in the neck, resulting in a sudden, brief (between 1 - 24 hours) decrease in brain functions, after which normal functions resume. Symptoms will vary with the area of the brain affected. Even a brief interruption to the blood flow can cause a decrease in brain function (neurologic deficit).

Symptoms associated with TIA are similar to those associated with a stroke, except that they disappear completely. TIAs are typically associated with high blood pressure (hypertension) and atherosclerosis, a disease in which fatty deposits (plaque) build up along the interior walls of arteries. Plaque deposits may become large enough to temporarily block blood flow or may promote the formation of blood clots that then occlude that artery or become dislodged, occluding an artery downstream. Less common causes of TIA include blood disorders (sickle cell anemia, polycythemia, or hyperviscosity syndromes where the blood is very thick), spasms of small arteries in the brain, blood vessel abnormalities (such as fibromuscular dysplasia), inflammation of the arteries, systemic lupus erythematosus (SLE), and syphilis.

Typically, alternative (collateral) circulation routes are sufficient to overcome narrow or even blocked arteries. However, as plaque deposits continue to build, these safety factors may become overwhelmed. A TIA is an important warning sign that should be taken seriously and immediately medically evaluated because it may signal an imminent stroke or cerebral hemorrhage.

Health and lifestyle factors that place an individual at risk for having a TIA or stroke include smoking, diabetes, heart disease, increased blood pressure (hypertension), migraine headaches, and heavy use of alcohol. The age at onset varies but incidence rises dramatically after 50 years of age. TIAs occur most commonly in men and among blacks.

Every year, approximately 50,000 Americans experience a TIA; one-third of these individuals will eventually suffer a stroke. One-third of persons having one TIA will have a recurrent TIA, and one-third will have only a single episode of TIA.

Diagnosis

History: Specific symptoms vary depending on the location, degree of vessel involvement, and the extent of collateral circulation. Symptoms usually occur on the same side of the body if more than one body part is involved.

Symptoms typically include a loss of sensation or motor skills, vision disturbances (loss of vision in one eye, decreased visual acuity, double vision), weakness, numbness, tingling, speech difficulty (garbled, slurred, or thick speech), vertigo and problems with balance, incoordination, gait changes (staggering), falling, and an inability to think clearly or understand speech. Individuals may also have elevated blood pressure. Individuals may report episodes that only last a few minutes, but occasionally, continue for one to two hours. Episodes may recur, the individual may later experience a stroke, or in some cases, the individual may experience no further symptoms. Occasionally, the individual may report feelings of burning and prickling in the extremities.

Physical exam: Elevated blood pressure (hypertension) might be found. Speech disturbances, visual changes, or weakness or numbness in the extremities on one side of the body may be noted, as well as loss of sensation or difficulty moving. Less common are facial paralysis, eye pain, and confusion. Listening with a stethoscope (auscultation) over the carotid or other artery may reveal an abnormal sound (bruit) caused by irregular blood flow; this may indicate atherosclerotic plaque or a thrombus in the area.

Tests: To confirm vessel blockage or atherosclerosis, an individual may undergo diagnostic cranial MRI and head CT scans, or cerebral angiography. Doppler ultrasound of the carotids may be performed. These procedures help to locate problem areas and aid in planning the course of treatment for the individual. A complete neurological test may be abnormal during an episode but normal afterwards. An eye examination including pressure (glaucoma) test should be done. A CBC with Protime will rule out hematologic diseases; an ECG and echocardiogram should be done if a heart disorder is suspected.

Treatment

The goal of treatment is to improve the arterial blood supply to the brain and prevent development of stroke. Prompt evaluation within 60 minutes is necessary to identify the cause and determine appropriate treatment. This usually requires hospitalization. Because signs or symptoms are of short duration, individuals may ignore them. However, it is imperative that physicians are made aware of the condition and the symptoms are addressed. Treatment of the underlying cause is essential. Medications are typically prescribed for hypertension, atherosclerosis, and thrombosis to prevent a recurrence or progression of the condition. Aspirin therapy is often the drug of choice. Disorders such as heart disease, diabetes mellitus, and blood disorders should be treated appropriately. If the carotid artery is involved, a procedure may be necessary to remove the blockage (carotid endarterectomy), or if blockage is severe, a vessel graft or resection may be required.

Prognosis

TIAs are generally of short duration; symptoms generally disappear within 24 hours. TIAs should, however, be taken very seriously as a predictor of impending stroke. Approximately one in three individuals who experience a TIA will have a stroke within five years, particularly if the underlying conditions are not addressed.

Medications that help to decrease blood clotting (antiplatelet drugs such as aspirin or ticlopidine) may be taken indefinitely.

Differential Diagnosis

Differential diagnoses include seizure, brain tumor, migraine, and Ménière's disease.

Specialists

- Cardiologist
- Cardiovascular Surgeon
- Neurologist
- Radiologist
- Thoracic Surgeon

Work Restrictions / Accommodations

Given the temporary nature of the episode, work restrictions should be minimal. However, individuals who experience recurrent episodes may require work accommodations, particularly if they operate heavy machinery, work under difficult environmental conditions, or work at unrestricted heights. As such, work accommodations will require consideration on an individual, case-by-case basis. Time off may ne necessary to thoroughly evaluate the underlying reason for TIA.

Comorbid Conditions

Hypertension, diabetes mellitus, atrial fibrillation, and presence of certain blood disorders may lengthen disability.

Complications

The primary complication of a TIA is a stroke.

Factors Influencing Duration

Factors that may influence the length of disability include the underlying chronic disease processes, the age of the individual at diagnosis, and whether surgery is indicated.

Length of Disability

No disability is expected for medical treatment only, but time may be needed for medical evaluation. Length of disability depends on job requirements.

Medical treatment.

Duration in Days

Job Classification	Minimum	Optimum	Maximum
Sedentary work	3	7	10
Light work	3	7	10
Medium work	3	7	10
Heavy work	3	7	10
Very Heavy work	3	7	10

Endarterectomy, carotid artery.

Duration in Days

Job Classification	Minimum	Optimum	Maximum
Sedentary work	14	21	28
Light work	21	28	35
Medium work	28	35	42
Heavy work	42	49	56
Very Heavy work	42	49	56

Duration Trend from Normative Data*

Cases	Mean	Min	Max	No Lost Time	Over 6 Months
456	52	0	404	0.88%	3.31%

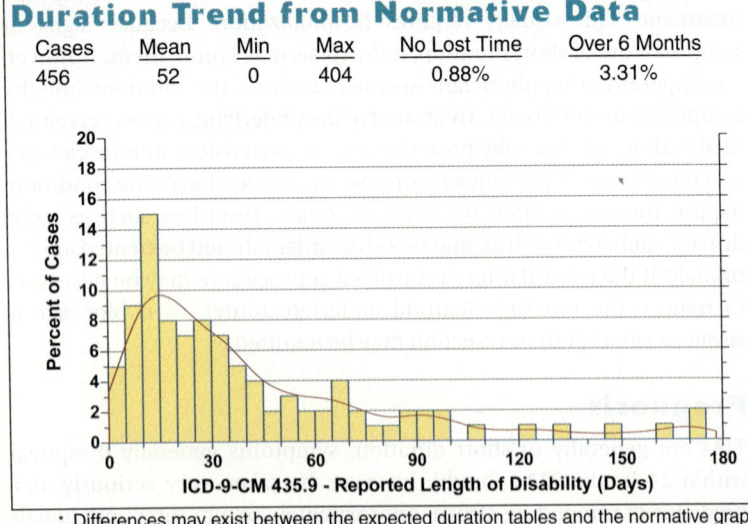

ICD-9-CM 435.9 - Reported Length of Disability (Days)

Percentile:	5th	25th	Median	75th	95th
Days:	6	14	30	60	132

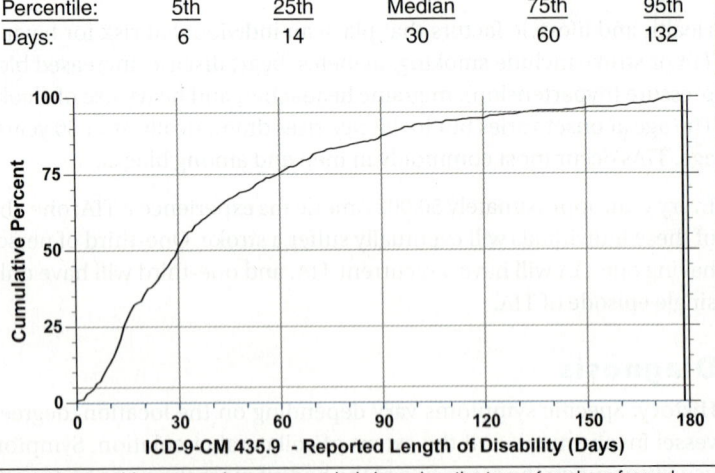

ICD-9-CM 435.9 - Reported Length of Disability (Days)

* Differences may exist between the expected duration tables and the normative graphs. Duration tables provide expected recovery periods based on the type of work performed by the individual. The normative graphs reflect the actual observed experience of many individuals across the spectrum of physical conditions, in a variety of industries, and with varying levels of case management.

Failure to Recover

If an individual fails to recover within the maximum duration expectancy period, the reader may wish to reference the following questions to assist in better understanding the specifics of an individual's medical case.

Regarding diagnosis:

- Did the individual have symptoms suggestive of a TIA such as a transient loss of sensation or motor skills, balance problems, vision disturbances, weakness, numbness, or slurred speech?
- Has the individual experienced any significant lapses in memory?
- Does the individual have a history of high blood pressure?
- Have other blood problems (e.g., polycythemia, sludging) been ruled out?
- Did the physical exam reveal any characteristic neurological findings such as visual disturbances, or alterations in strength or sensation?
- Was a carotid bruit noted?
- Did a Doppler ultrasound of the carotid vessels demonstrate significant narrowing of one or both arteries?
- If the diagnosis was uncertain, were other diagnostic tests, (MRI, CT, angiography) done to rule out other conditions with similar symptoms?
- Was the individual referred to an appropriate specialist (neurologist, neurosurgeon, cardiologist)?

Regarding treatment:

- Was the blood pressure managed effectively with antihypertensive medications?
- Were antiplatelet medications prescribed?
- Was surgery (carotid endarterectomy) indicated?

Regarding prognosis:

- Based on the age, general health, severity of symptoms and type of treatment required, what was the expected outcome?
- Did the individual have any comorbid conditions that may have impacted response to treatment and ability to recovery (primary brain lesion, hypertension, atrial dysrhythmias, bleeding disorders)?
- Did the individual suffer any complications of the condition or treatment (such as stroke) that would impact prognosis?

References

"Transient Ischemic Attack (TIA)." Lycos Health. 1999. 20 Feb 2001 <http://webmd.lycos.com/content/asset/adam_disease_mini_stroke>.

Beers, Mark, and Robert Berkow, eds. The Merck Manual of Diagnosis and Therapy. Medical Services, USMEDSA, USHH, 1999 08 Jan 2001 <http://www.merck.com/pubs/mmanual/section14/chapter174/174b.htm>.

Guidelines for the Management of Transient Ischemic Attacks. American Heart Association. 1998. 09 Jan 2001 <http://www.americanheart.org/Scientific/statements/1994/069401.html>.

Tierney, Lawrence, Stephen McPhee, and Maxine Papadakis. Current Medical Diagnosis and Treatment. New York: McGraw-Hill, 2000.

Transurethral Balloon Dilation of Prostatic Urethra

Other names / synonyms: Transurethral Balloon Dilatation of Prostate, TUBD

60.95

Definition

Transurethral balloon dilation of the prostatic urethra is a nonsurgical method of correcting urinary difficulties (difficulty initiating urination, decreased force and an inability to completely empty the bladder, urinary frequency, urgency, and the need to urinate frequently during the night) caused when an enlarged prostate gland (benign prostatic hypertrophy) obstructs the tube (urethra) through which urine is expelled from the bladder.

Currently, more than 30 million men in the US have urinary tract problems associated with BPH. The incidence of BPH in men in their 50s is 30%, rising to 75% for those age 80 and older.

Reason for Procedure

Transurethral balloon dilatation of the prostatic urethra is a relatively recent development in the treatment of an enlarged prostate (mild benign prostatic hypertrophy). Balloon dilation can help to relieve symptoms caused by benign prostatic hypertrophy (BPH), including difficulty initiating urination, decreased force and an inability to completely empty the bladder (urinary retention), urinary frequency, urgency, and the need to urinate frequently during the night (nocturia).

Advantages of this procedure include low cost, minimal or no hospitalization, and the procedure can be done under local or regional anesthesia. It is a rapid procedure and does not preclude later surgical procedures. Disadvantages are that although this procedure is easily performed, the effectiveness and maximum duration of benefit is highly variable.

Description

The procedure can be done under general, spinal, or local anesthesia, or by intravenous sedation. Using a small, magnified viewing instrument (endoscope) and a fluorescent screen on which the maneuver can be monitored (fluoroscope), a balloon catheter is guided into the prostatic portion of the urethra. The balloon is then inflated for about 5 to 10 minutes. The inflation of the balloon seems to interfere with further subsequent expansion of the prostate tissue.

Prognosis

The effectiveness and duration of benefit are highly variable. Balloon dilation is a fairly new treatment for BPH, and doctors as yet do not know all of its long-term benefits and risks. In many individuals, this treatment seems to work for only a short time. The prognosis appears to be better in individuals younger than 65 years of age, and individuals with prostate gland weight less than 50 grams.

Specialists

- Urologist

Work Restrictions / Accommodations

The individual should refrain from rigorous physical activity during the recovery period.

Comorbid Conditions

Existing conditions that may impact ability to recover and may further lengthen disability include urethral stricture, meatal stenosis, significant middle lobe hypertrophy, neurogenic bladder disease, and malignancies of the prostate.

Procedure Complications

Possible complications of this procedure include temporary dribbling incontinence, hemorrhage, prostatitis, and urinary retention.

Factors Influencing Duration

Length of disability may be influenced by complications of the procedure, pre-existing medical conditions, age of the individual, and continued prostatic obstruction.

Length of Disability

Duration depends on type of anesthesia.

Duration in Days

Job Classification	Minimum	Optimum	Maximum
Any work	1	3	7

References

Hernandez-Graulau, Jose M. Transurethral Balloon Divulsion of Prostate. Department of Urology, New York Medical College. 01 Jan 2000. 13 Jan 2001 <http://www.urological.com/papers/prostate.html>.

Transurethral Incision of Bladder Neck
57.91

Definition

Transurethral incision of the bladder neck is an operative procedure that involves cutting the muscles of the bladder neck. The bladder neck is the lower part of the bladder that connects to the urethra. The muscles may be cut at one or several locations. It is performed with a cystoscopy procedure.

Conditions for which the procedure may be recommended include obstruction of the bladder neck due to benign prostatic hyperplasia or scarring (contracture) that can occur after resection of the prostate. It can also be performed to treat a condition in which there is dysfunction of the bladder neck leading to obstruction (dyssynergia).

Reason for Procedure

This procedure may be used to treat urinary outflow obstruction caused by abnormalities of the bladder neck. In men, the outflow of urine through the bladder neck can become obstructed as a result of benign prostatic hyperplasia, dysfunction of the muscles of the bladder neck (dyssynergia), and a type of scarring (contracture) of the bladder neck that occurs after resection of prostatic tissue. Contracture is due to growth of fibrous connective tissue, which replaces normal muscle tissue of the bladder neck. It results in loss of the normal mobility of the bladder neck.

This procedure is normally only performed if the prostate is small. It can be performed as an alternative method for treating benign prostatic hyperplasia.

Description

Spinal anesthesia is usually used. The individual is positioned on the operating room table on their back with legs up in stirrups (lithotomy position). The opening of the urethra (meatus) is cleansed with a surgical scrub solution, and surgical drapes are placed. A type of cystoscope (resectoscope) is inserted into the urethra. An irrigation system is attached and it is inserted until the bladder neck can be visualized. An instrument called the Colling's knife is extended through the scope to the bladder. Small incisions are made into the wall of the bladder neck at the 11 o'clock and 1 o'clock positions. Sometimes incisions may also be made at the 5 o'clock and 7 o'clock positions. There may be some bleeding for about 24 hours after the surgery, and a urine drainage tube (Foley catheter) may be left in the bladder for 24 hours until the urine is clear.

Prognosis

The predicted outcome of transurethral incision of the bladder neck is relief of urinary symptoms due to obstruction of the bladder neck. The outcome of treatment of benign prostatic hyperplasia is usually good.

Specialists

- Urologist

Work Restrictions / Accommodations

No work restrictions or accommodations are necessary as a result of this procedure.

Comorbid Conditions

A comorbid condition may be renal failure.

Procedure Complications

Complications may include bleeding, infection, perforation of the bladder, incontinence, and stricture.

Factors Influencing Duration

The presence of complications may influence the length of disability.

Length of Disability

Duration in Days

Job Classification	Minimum	Optimum	Maximum
Any work	3	7	9

References

Appell, Rodney A. "Voiding Dysfunction and Incontinence in Men." Atlas of Surgical Techniques in Urology. Whitehead, E. Douglas, ed. Philadelphia: Lippincott-Raven, 1998. 245-246.

Klahr, Saulo. "Obstructive Uropathy." Cecil Textbook of Medicine, 20th ed. Bennett, J. Claude, and Fred Plum, eds. Philadelphia: W.B. Saunders Company, 1996. 589-594.

Nagle, Gratia M. "Genitourinary Surgery." Alexander's Care of the Patient in Surgery, 11th ed. Meeker, Margaret H., and Jane C. Rothrock, eds. St. Louis: Mosby, 1999. 501-598.

Sotolongo, Jose R. "Transurethral Incision of the Bladder Neck." Atlas of Surgical Techniques in Urology. Whitehead, E. Douglas, ed. Philadelphia: Lippincott-Raven, 1998. 259-260.

Stoller, Marshall L. "Retrograde Instrumentation of the Urinary Tract." Smith's General Urology, 15th ed. Tanagho, Emil A., and Jack W. McAninch, eds. New York: Lange Medical Books/McGraw-Hill, 2000. 196-207.

Tanagho, Emil A. "Urinary Obstruction and Stasis." Smith's General Urology, 15th ed. Tanagho, Emil A., and Jack W. McAninch, eds. New York: Lange Medical Books/McGraw-Hill, 2000. 208-220.

Transurethral Removal of Obstruction from Ureter

Other names / synonyms: Transurethral Ureteropyeloscopy, Ureteral Stone-Basketing

56.0

Definition

Transurethral removal of obstruction from the ureter (transurethral ureteropyeloscopy) involves insertion of a lighted fiber optic tube through the urethra and bladder and into the ureter to remove stones that have become lodged in the ureter.

It is most often performed to remove stones (calculi) from the passageway leading from the kidney to the urinary bladder (ureter).

Ureteral stones are formed in the kidneys, generally from calcium (stones can form from many different types of elements, however), which then move into one of the ureters if they are less than one centimeter in diameter. Ureteral stones form due to many causes including excess calcium in the urine (hypercalciuria), certain cancers (myeloma, lung cancer, and metastatic bone cancer), overactivity of the parathyroid gland (hyperparathyroidism), and in people who are immobile for a prolonged period of time. Kidney stones may occur more frequently in people who eat a diet high in salt, in individuals whose occupation may be more sedentary (white collar works and physicians), in individuals who live in a hot climate, in individuals with a family history of kidney stones, and in individuals who take certain medications (certain antihypertensives and antacids).

More than 70% of kidney stones that are under 4 millimeters in size pass through the urinary tract spontaneously, while only 15% of stones larger than 6 millimeters are able to spontaneously pass. Invasive procedures are often required for stones that are unable to spontaneously pass. The most common methods of removing kidney stones are the transurethral methods. Extracorporeal shock wave lithotripsy (ESWL) may be performed to break up stones, allowing spontaneous passage or easier removal using transurethral procedures. Stones in the ureter may also be removed by open surgery.

Reason for Procedure

Transurethral removal of a stone from the ureter relieves the obstruction that is interrupting outflow of urine from the kidney. Removal of the stone relieves the severe pain associated with the presence of a stone lodged in the ureter. Obstruction in the ureters must be relieved to prevent backflow of urine and kidney damage.

Description

Transurethral removal of stones may be done in the doctor's office using local anesthetic or in a hospital with a general or regional anesthetic. An x-ray of the kidney, ureter, and bladder (KUB) is often obtained immediately prior to the procedure to determine the exact location of the stone. A lubricated scope (ureteropyeloscope) is inserted into the urethra and advanced into the bladder. To enable entry into the ureter, a guidewire is inserted using x-ray (fluoroscopy) to advance it into position in the ureter. The ureter is gently pushed open (dilated) using an instrument such as a balloon dilator. The ureteroscope is passed over the guidewire to the area of the stone. Small instruments are inserted through the scope and the stone is grasped by a basket-like instrument and brought out of the body (often called stone-basketing). If needed, the stone may be broken apart by first using a laser beam or high frequency sound waves (ultrasound). Dye may be used to see the stone more clearly. A small stent may be inserted during the procedure to help keep the ureter open (patent).

When the stone is near the upper two-thirds of the ureter it may be pushed up into the kidney where it can be treated using extracorporeal shock wave lithotripsy (ESWL) or retrieved by percutaneous nephrolithotomy.

Prognosis

The predicted outcome of transurethral removal of ureteral obstruction is removal of the obstruction, usually a kidney stone. Removal of the ureteral obstruction will prevent development of kidney damage associated with buildup of urine in the kidney. If buildup of urine has already occurred, removal of the ureteral obstruction will allow thorough drainage of the kidney, and if performed before permanent damage has occurred, allow recovery of kidney function. In some individuals, kidney stones may reoccur.

Specialists

- Urologist

Work Restrictions / Accommodations

Restrictions or accommodations may not be necessary. Time off from work may be needed for treatments such as extracorporeal shock wave lithotripsy (ESWL) needed to help break apart larger stones to allow easy passage from the urinary tract. The presence of kidney stones in the ureter is often very uncomfortable, necessitating hospitalization and use of narcotic pain medications to control the discomfort.

Comorbid Conditions

Comorbid conditions may include kidney damage and decreased kidney functioning.

Procedure Complications

Complications may include infection, perforation of the ureter, bladder, or urethra, and bleeding.

Factors Influencing Duration

The presence of any complications and the individual's reaction to the procedure will determine the length of disability. Recurrence of kidney stones may necessitate repeat procedures.

Length of Disability

Ureteroscopic stone extraction.

Duration in Days

Job Classification	Minimum	Optimum	Maximum
Any work	3	7	14

References

Marberger, Michael, and Georg Ludvik. "Ureteroscopic Stone Removal." Operative Urology. Krane, Robert J., Mike B. Siroky, and John M. Fitzpatrick, eds. New York: Churchill Livingstone, 2000. 93-97.

Nagle, Gratia M. "Genitourinary Surgery." Alexander's Care of the Patient in Surgery. Meeker, Margaret H., and Jane C. Rothrock, eds. St. Louis: Mosby, 1999. 501-598.

Stoller, Marshall L., and Damien M. Bolton. "Urinary Stone Disease." Smith's General Urology, 15th ed. Tanagho, Emil A., and Jack W. McAninch, eds. New York: Lange Medical Books/McGraw-Hill, 2000. 291-320.

Tanagho, Emil A. "Urinary Obstruction and Stasis." Smith's General Urology, 15th ed. Tanagho, Emil A., and Jack W. McAninch, eds. New York: Lange Medical Books/McGraw-Hill, 2000. 208-220.

Transurethral Resection of Prostate

Other names / synonyms: TURP

60.29

Definition

Transurethral resection of the prostate (TURP) refers to a surgical procedure where portions of the prostate gland are removed through the urethra. It is performed in the hospital as an inpatient procedure.

TURP is the most common surgical procedure used to treat benign prostatic hypertrophy (BPH). BPH is a condition that is characterized by an increased size of the prostate gland, leading to symptoms of urinary obstruction (frequency, hesitancy, dribbling). BPH can be diagnosed by a rectal exam or by ultrasonography. It is usually treated initially with medical therapy, reserving TURP for individuals who develop increased symptoms despite treatment.

Benign prostatic hypertrophy is a common condition, affecting about 90% of men by age 80. Symptoms usually begin around age 60-69.

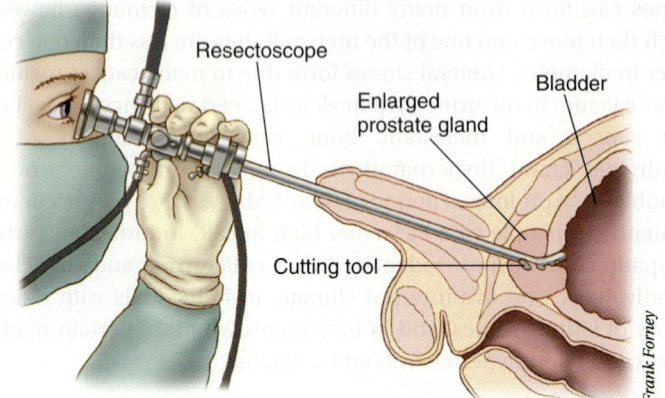

Frank Forney

Reason for Procedure

TURP is most commonly performed for benign prostatic hypertrophy. BPH leads to urinary symptoms of hesitancy, incomplete voiding, increased frequency, and dribbling. Severe cases can lead to urinary retention, hydronephrosis, urinary tract infections, and bladder stones.

Description

TURP is performed in the operating room, usually under regional anesthesia (only part of the body is anesthetized). The individual is positioned on his back with his legs in stirrups. A lubricated scope (resectoscope) is passed up the urethra to the area of the enlarged prostate. An electrocautery loop is then used to cut away as much of the prostate tissue as possible. A urinary catheter is then placed into the urethra. This will stay in place overnight. Most individuals leave the hospital the next day. There is minimal pain associated with this procedure.

Prognosis

TURP is a very effective treatment for BPH. Between 80-90% of individuals experience relief of their urinary symptoms and improved flow. Mortality rates are less than 1% for this procedure, although older individuals may experience more complications.

Specialists

- Urologist

Comorbid Conditions

Conditions that may impair ability to recover include diabetes and immune disorders. Chronic conditions such as heart disease and lung disease may also lengthen disability.

Procedure Complications

Common complications from TURP include postoperative bleeding, clot retention, and urinary tract infection. In addition, a condition called TURP syndrome can result from the absorption of irrigant solution into the bloodstream. TURP syndrome can result in electrolyte imbalances and seizures. Delayed complications can include retrograde ejaculation and impotence.

Factors Influencing Duration

Factors that may influence disability include the individual's age, the development of complications, and response to treatment.

Length of Disability

Duration in Days

Job Classification	Minimum	Optimum	Maximum
Sedentary work	7	9	14
Light work	7	9	14
Medium work	14	16	21
Heavy work	21	24	28
Very Heavy work	21	24	28

References

Hedican, Sean, MD. "Urology." Advanced Surgical Recall. Blackbourne, Lorne, MD, ed. Baltimore: Williams & Wilkins, 1997. 1227-1308.

Schwartz, Seymour, MD. Principles of Surgery. New York: McGraw-Hill, 1999.

Trauma

Other names / synonyms: Injury
959.9

Definition

Trauma is an injury to the body that occurs when a physical force contacts the body. The trauma may be blunt or penetrating. Examples of blunt trauma are motor vehicle collision, fall, and assault with a blunt object. Examples of penetrating trauma are gunfire wounds and stabbings. Thermal trauma occurs in fires, electrical injuries, and hypothermia and frostbite. Exposure to these forces can cause soft tissue injuries, fractures, bleeding, and tearing of vital organs and blood vessels, all of which can result in severe disability and death.

The severity of the injury is related to the force of the impact, duration of impact, body part involved, injuring agent (blast, blunt object, penetrating object), and any associated risk factors (age and pre-existing medical conditions). Trauma from falls from heights and high velocity collisions often result in injury to more than one body part (multiple trauma). Trauma is most often a result of motor vehicle collisions, burns, falls, gunfire, or assault with blunt or penetrating objects.

One of every three individuals in the US experiences a traumatic injury each year. Trauma is the fourth leading cause of death for all ages and is the leading cause of death for those between the ages of 1 and 37. In 1991, 43,536 deaths were caused by motor vehicle crashes and 38,077 were firearm fatalities. Another 12,662 deaths were attributed to falls. Because trauma is a disease of the young and carries the potential for permanent disability, it is responsible for significant loss in productive work years. In 1993, 18.2 million individuals sustained disabling injuries. In economic terms, it is estimated that 115 million days of productivity are lost annually secondary to disabling injuries.

Diagnosis

History: The victim or witnesses report trauma to local ambulance, fire, police, or emergency room personnel. The individual or witnesses may report circumstances of the injury that are helpful in the diagnosis. This may include (as relevant) injury mechanism (fall, gunshot, motor vehicle accident), speed of impact, amount of damage to the vehicles, use of restraints (seatbelts) or helmet, length of the fall, position or condition of the victim at the scene, evidence of blood loss, and any known medical alert information about the individual (i.e., recent or chronic illnesses or history of drug or alcohol use).

Physical exam: The physical assessment of a trauma victim is composed of a primary survey to look for life-threatening injury followed by a secondary survey. In the primary survey, evidence of airway or breathing problems such as pale or bluish complexion, noisy breathing, shallow or slow respirations, foreign objects, and sucking chest wounds may be found. There may be evidence of neurological impairment such as decreased level of consciousness. Hypotension or shock may be present. Pulse may be rapid or weak. Individuals may present with areas of tenderness, bone deformity, bruising, and lacerations.

Tests: X-rays and CT are done as needed. The routine procedure for blunt trauma is to obtain portable radiographs of the cervical spine, chest, and pelvis. Three studies are used to evaluate blunt abdominal or chest trauma: diagnostic peritoneal lavage (DPL), CT scanning, and ultrasonography (US). Management of penetrating abdominal trauma differs from that caused by blunt injury. All gunshot wounds that penetrate the abdomen require surgical exploration (laparotomy) because of the high incidence of significant injury. The surgical exploration serves as a tool for diagnosis as well as treatment of injuries. Urinalysis, complete blood count (CBC), glucose, urea, ammonia, electrolytes, alcohol, blood urea nitrogen (BUN), creatinine, blood type and crossmatch, liver profile, and arterial blood gases may be measured. A spinal tap and tests on cerebral spinal fluid may be done.

Treatment

Trauma assessment and intervention typically occur simultaneously and begin at the scene of the accident. Immediate attention is directed to managing life-threatening conditions such as obstructed airway, lack of breathing, or severe bleeding. Assessment of the need for simple first aid, splinting, and protection of the individual to prevent further injury is then appropriate. Immediate transport to a medical facility with trauma capabilities is the final priority.

Initial care at the trauma center assesses and responds to the need for resuscitation. If airway, breathing, or level of consciousness is inadequate, an artificial airway is inserted (intubation). Supplemental oxygen is given. Treatment of immediate life-threatening injury of the chest and abdomen such as cardiac tamponade, tension pneumothorax, open pneumothorax, flail chest, massive hemothorax, and blunt or penetrating abdominal wound injuries is done. An intravenous drip administers replacement fluids or blood, as indicated. The individual is kept warm with blankets, warming lights, or warm intravenous fluids.

Any fractures with lack of blood supply to the area are treated at this time. Injuries of the hand, neck, and spinal cord are addressed. Tetanus protection is given if needed. Any closed fractures or skin injuries are treated last. The individual is then taken to surgery or the intensive care unit, as appropriate.

Prognosis

The outcome from trauma varies according to the nature and severity of the injury and the promptness of medical attention. In general, better outcomes are reported when trauma injuries are managed within one hour by a comprehensive trauma center. Overall, the death rate for chest injuries is 4-8%. When an additional organ system is also affected, the death rate rises to 10-15%. When multiple organ systems are involved, death rate is 35%.

Death due to trauma occurs in one of three time periods. Immediate death occurs within seconds or minutes of the initial injury. Immediate traumatic deaths result from tearing in the brain, brain stem, spinal cord, heart, aorta, or other large blood vessels. Early death occurs within hours of the injury and results from airway problems, from blood clots in the brain (subdural or epidural hematomas), blood or air in the chest cavity (hemopneumothorax), or other injuries associated with significant blood loss such as lacerations of the spleen, liver or pelvic fractures. Finally, late death occurs following trauma due to complications of infection, multiple organ failure, or severe brain injury.

Differential Diagnosis

An individual may collapse or become unconscious due to other causes such as alcoholic intoxication, poisoning, overdose, cerebrovascular accident, diabetic acidosis, hypovolemic shock, epilepsy, eclampsia, electrolyte imbalance, anaphylaxis, severe sepsis, brain tumors, asphyxia, heat stroke, heart failure, or hysteria.

Specialists

- Emergency Medicine
- Gynecologist
- Internist
- Nephrologist
- Neurosurgeon
- Physiatrist
- Plastic Surgeon
- Pulmonologist
- Urologist
- Vascular Surgeon

Work Restrictions / Accommodations

Restrictions and accommodations depend on the injuries sustained.

Comorbid Conditions

Comorbid conditions include bleeding or immune system disorders, heart disease, diabetes, liver or kidney dysfunction, and chronic lung disease.

Complications

Complications of trauma may include airway obstruction, shock from severe blood loss, sepsis, organ failure, and death.

Factors Influencing Duration

The site and extent of injury, treatment needed, presence of complications, and the individual's response determine length of disability.

Length of Disability

Vague diagnosis. Additional diagnostic information is needed to determine disability duration.

Failure to Recover

If an individual fails to recover within the maximum duration expectancy period, the reader may wish to reference the following questions to assist in better understanding the specifics of an individual's medical case.

Regarding diagnosis:

- Did individual present with a history of some sort of traumatic event (i.e., auto accident, fall, altercation)?
- Was trauma from a blunt force or fall?
- Did individual present with any obvious tissue injury or deformity?
- Did individual sustain blunt trauma to the head, chest, abdomen or pelvis? If so, did individual display any symptoms suggestive of injury to the underlying organs (change in level of consciousness, or shock symptoms)?
- Was a thorough physical exam and diagnostic work up done by a specialist in trauma care?
- Were c-spine x-rays done to rule out fractures or dislocations?
- Was there evidence of internal bleeding detected with a hemoglobin and hematocrit level?
- Was a CT done of the areas of injury to look for injury to underlying structures?
- Were all injuries immediately recognized (in the emergency room or trauma center) or were there injuries that were not discovered until later in the hospital stay?
- If the diagnosis of trauma was uncertain, were other conditions considered in the differential diagnosis?

Regarding treatment:

- Was care rendered by emergency personnel (EMT, RN, paramedic) at the scene of the accident?
- Did individual receive immediate control of life-threatening injuries?
- Was individual treated promptly in an emergency department or trauma center?
- Did individual require urgent surgical intervention?
- Is individual receiving appropriate physical, occupational, and behavioral rehabilitation therapy?

Regarding prognosis:

- Did individual have a severe injury?
- Based on the extent and severity of injuries, what was the expected outcome?
- Did individual receive prompt medical attention by a facility that specializes in trauma care?
- Does individual have any comorbid conditions that may impact ability to recover?
- Did individual suffer any complications that may have impacted length of disability?

References

Harrison's Principles of Internal Medicine, 11th ed. Braunwald, Eugene, et al, eds. New York: McGraw-Hill Book Company, 1987.

Clochesy, John M., et al. Critical Care Nursing, 2nd ed. Philadelphia: W.B. Saunders Company, 1996.

Traveler's Diarrhea
Other names / synonyms: Delhi Belly, Grippe, Intestinal Flu, Montezuma's Revenge, Turista
009.2

Definition

Traveler's diarrhea is caused by fecally contaminated water or foods including raw fruits and vegetables, unbottled juices, unpasteurized milk, and poorly cooked or improperly refrigerated foods. Contaminants are bacteria, protozoa, or viruses. Individuals from industrialized nations typically encounter the disease while visiting countries where waste disposal, water facilities, sanitation, and hygiene practices are substandard. These areas include parts of Mexico, the Caribbean, Central and South America, Africa, Asia, and the Middle East. The organism most likely to cause the disease and which is associated with about half of reported cases is the Escherichia coli bacteria (E. coli). Other bacteria include the protozoa Giardia and the Norwalk virus.

Infections of the gastrointestinal system cause frequent loose stools sometimes accompanied by abdominal cramps, bloating, nausea, and vomiting. Although most cases of traveler's diarrhea are not considered serious, some infections can take a more severe form such as dysentery or cholera.

There is a 40% risk of a visitor from an industrialized country encountering traveler's diarrhea during a trip to a less-developed nation. On a worldwide basis, about 20 million individuals from industrialized nations annually visit less-developed countries. This means almost half of the 5 million US citizens who travel abroad annually to countries with substandard sanitary practices are likely to be infected. Less common outbreaks of diarrhea caused by the same sources also occur within industrialized countries including the US. Bacteria account for almost 80% of traveler's diarrhea, with protozoa and viruses about equally responsible for other outbreaks.

Diagnosis

History: The individual may complain of abdominal cramps, bloating, and frequent watery diarrhea. Nausea, vomiting, and fever may also be reported. The unformed stools do not usually contain blood or mucus. Headache and muscle pain are also common in infections caused by the Norwalk virus.

Physical exam: The reported symptoms are usually enough to make a diagnosis if the individual has just returned from a trip to an underdeveloped area.

A low-grade fever may be present, and the individual may show signs of dehydration if fluids have not been adequately replaced.

Tests: If the condition persists, a stool sample may be taken for microscopic analysis (culture) to identify the specific microorganism causing the condition.

Treatment

Traveler's diarrhea usually resolves on its own within 5 days and only requires drinking plenty of clear liquids (rehydration) to prevent dehydration. For mild diarrhea, over-the-counter medications can provide effective short-term relief by reducing fluid loss from the intestines (antimotility agents), but they should not be taken for more than 48 hours and are not recommended for individuals with fever or blood in their stool. Antibiotics are only effective against bacterial infections and are not usually prescribed unless the infection becomes severe. For prolonged or severe diarrhea, specially formulated oral-hydration salts (ORS) are widely available. The person should continue to eat while experiencing diarrhea, but avoid certain food and liquid irritants such as alcohol, caffeine, raw fruits and vegetables, dairy products, and fatty foods.

Prognosis

Traveler's diarrhea is relatively mild. Approximately 80% of cases resolve on their own within 5 days. The other 20% usually resolves within another week or two. If the condition persists, antibiotic therapy is often successful. Complications such as dehydration or electrolyte imbalance could delay recovery. In rare cases, individuals with weakened immune systems may face severe, prolonged symptoms and possible death.

Differential Diagnosis

Conditions with similar symptoms include bowel obstruction, gastrointestinal disturbances unrelated to infection by microorganisms, colitis, Crohn's disease, irritable bowel syndrome, gastroenteritis, diverticular disease, dyspepsia, intestinal cancer, proctitis, and other chronic illnesses or infections outside the gastrointestinal tract such as a urinary tract infection.

Specialists

- Gastroenterologist
- Internist
- Infectious Disease Physician

Work Restrictions / Accommodations

Strenuous activity may need to be limited until recovery is complete. The individual should also be permitted bathroom breaks, as needed.

Complementary and Alternative Therapies

Content is intended for awareness only. Treatments may or may not be effective. Scientific evidence may be lacking and some substances have potentially toxic effects. Dr. Presley Reed and the editors do not endorse the use of these therapies in the absence of consultation with a licensed medical professional.

Kaolin -	Said to increase the bulk of feces and may be found in many antidiarrheal preparations. Kaolin does not have any antibacterial activity so it should not be used as the sole treatment in infectious diarrheas.
Yogurt -	Said to re-establish normal flora in the intestines.
Berberine -	May have antiprotozoan activity for mild cases of amebiasis.

Comorbid Conditions

Coexisting conditions that could impact recovery include inflammatory bowel disease, suppressed immune system disorders such as AIDS, diabetes, heart disease in the elderly, and conditions requiring immunosuppressive medications.

Complications

Infection with an antibiotic-resistant microorganism is becoming increasingly common. With prolonged diarrhea, dehydration and electrolyte imbalance may occur. Persistent diarrhea can become life-threatening for individuals with weakened immune systems.

Factors Influencing Duration

Length of disability might be influenced by the severity of the illness, response to treatment, presence of complications, and underlying medical conditions that may impact recovery.

Length of Disability

Duration depends on cause.

Duration in Days

Job Classification	Minimum	Optimum	Maximum
Any work	3	7	10

Failure to Recover

If an individual fails to recover within the maximum duration expectancy period, the reader may wish to reference the following questions to assist in better understanding the specifics of an individual's medical case.

Regarding diagnosis:

- Was diagnosis of Traveler's diarrhea confirmed?
- Were other causes of diarrhea ruled out?
- Were appropriate tests conducted to determine the microorganism responsible for the disease?
- Did individual experience untreated or severe dehydration or electrolyte imbalance?

Regarding treatment:

- Was dehydration and electrolyte imbalance successfully avoided or controlled? Did individual require intravenous rehydration?
- Was antibiotic therapy indicated? Did the symptoms resolve following treatment with antibiotics? If not, were repeat culture and sensitivities done to rule out the possibility of antibiotic resistance or secondary infection?
- Were symptoms severe enough to warrant hospitalization?

Regarding prognosis:

- Did the symptoms resolve in approximately 5 days?
- Have tests been performed to rule out an antibiotic-resistant organism?
- Did individual have underlying immune system compromise that could impact recovery and prognosis?
- Did individual experience any complications, such as dehydration or electrolyte imbalance that would prolong recovery?

References

"Traveler Information, Other Infectious Diseases." Traveler's Diarrhea. Travel Health Online. 2000. 29 Aug 2000 <http://www.tripprep.com/travinfo_frame.html>.

Juckett, Gregory. "Prevention and Treatment of Traveler's Diarrhea." American Family Physician 01 Jul 1999 29 Aug 2000 <http://www.aafp.org/afp/990700ap/119.html>.

Spira, Alan. Traveler's Diarrhea. Armchair World. 18 Oct 1997. 29 Aug 2000 <http://www.armchair.com>.

Traveler's Diarrhea. MedicinePlanet.com. 2000. 29 Aug 2000 <http://www.medicineplanet.com>.

Tremor

Other names / synonyms: Asterixis, Ataxic Tremor, Benign Hereditary Tremor, Cerebellar Tremor, Essential Tremor, Intention Tremor, Liver Flap, Parkinsonian Tremor, Physiologic Tremor, Postural Tremor, Resting Tremor, Senile Tremor, Tremor

781.0

Definition

A tremor is an involuntary, regular, shaking or twitching movement resulting from contractions of opposing muscle groups. It can be normal (physiologic) or abnormal (pathologic). A tremor may affect the fingers and hands, head, tongue, jaw, and sometimes the trunk.

Tremors are classified according to their rate, strength, rhythm, distribution in the body, and time of occurrence, i.e., at rest (resting tremor) or during muscular activity (sustention or intention tremors). Tremors that occur during rest are classified as Parkinsonian tremors. The term physiological tremor describes a fine, rapid tremor of outstretched hands and is usually associated with anxiety, stress, fatigue, alcohol withdrawal or hyperthyroid disorder (metabolic derangements), or the effects of certain drugs such as caffeine or corticosteroids. A benign hereditary tremor (or essential tremor) is a slow tremor affecting the hands, head, and voice. It may be isolated to one side of the body and tends to be associated with a family history of tremors. This is the most common tremor.

Several disorders that affect the coordination center of the brain (cerebellum) can result in tremors. Depending on the specific characteristics of the tremor, they may be termed intention, ataxic, or cerebellar tremors. For example, in multiple sclerosis an individual may display a tremor of the arm as it extends to reach for something. This is called an intention tremor. Metabolic disturbances in the brain (encephalopathies) may cause an ataxic or cerebellar tremor characterized by a slow, nonrhythmic movement of an outstretched hand. This is also called asterixis. Since asterixis is most often seen in metabolic disturbances associated with advanced liver disease, it is sometimes referred to as "liver flap."

An individual may display one type of tremor or a combination of multiple types of tremors. For instance, a disorder affecting the liver cells called Wilson's disease is associated with both Parkinsonian tremors and cerebellar tremors.

Tremor may be a frequent feature of some of these disorders yet occurs sporadically in others. For example, tremor is a hallmark finding in essential familial tremor, a disorder that is not well understood but tends to develop in adolescence and may have a hereditary tendency.

Tremor is a common finding in Parkinson's disease, a disorder that usually begins in middle or later life and in some cases, may have a hereditary component. Multiple sclerosis is a neurological disorder more common in females residing in temperate climates of the Northern Hemisphere. It typically arises in the third or fourth decade of life and is frequently associated with intermittent tremors. Prevalence of tremors in other associated conditions such as metabolic derangements, anxiety, or drug effects is sporadic and inconsistent.

Diagnosis

History: The individual complains of involuntary shaking of different body parts such as hands, fingers, legs, feet, limbs, trunk, head, lips, or tongue. The individual may report history of drug or alcohol use or anxiety. They may mention a family history of tremor or other neurologic disease. History should focus on whether the tremor occurs when individual is engaged in voluntary motor activity, at rest, or maintaining a certain posture, and whether it disappears during sleep or is enhanced by stress.

Physical exam: A complete physical exam that includes testing of neurological function, reflexes, coordination, motor strength, and memory is needed for definitive diagnosis of the source of the tremor. Postural tremor is present with the limbs outstretched and usually disappears when the limbs are at rest. Physiologic tremor has a frequency of 8 to 12 per second and is a form of postural tremor seen in normal individuals under certain conditions such as fear, anxiety, or after exercise. It can also occur in hyperthyroidism or poisoning with lead, arsenic, or carbon monoxide. Essential tremor is a form of postural tremor involving the limbs, head, and voice. Resting tremor is lower than physiological tremor with a frequency of 4 to 6 per second and is present at rest and disappears with action. It is often seen in Parkinsonism where it characteristically appears as a "pill rolling" maneuver involving opposing circular movements of the thumb and index finger.

Tests: Electromyographic (EMG) studies may be indicated in some cases. Lab tests may include liver function studies, chemistry panel, and thyroid panel. If a structural cause in the brain is suspected, brain MRI or CT may be necessary.

Treatment

Treatment of tremor depends on its cause. Tremors associated with thyroid disorders, multiple sclerosis, or alcohol withdrawal respond to treatment of the underlying condition and the correction of metabolic derangements.

Antianxiety medications may be useful for tremor associated with anxiety states. Beta-blocker drugs may be effective in treating benign tremors and physiologic tremor due to drugs or acute anxiety states (e.g., stage fright). A variety of medications can manage tremors associated with Parkinson's disease. Levodopa (also called L-dopa) can replace the brain's dwindling supply of dopamine, a substance that helps coordinate muscle activity. Other drugs often used are anticholinergics or an antiviral agent (amantadine) that sometimes reduces the tremor. If unresponsive to medications, alternative treatments include removal of all or part of the thalamus (thalamotomy) or selectively destroying a part of the thalamus using a high-frequency electrical shock (high-frequency thalamic stimulation).

Alcohol, caffeine, and concentrated sugars should be avoided, as they tend to increase anxiety and tremor. Behavioral counseling may be recommended if the source of the tremor is related to drug or alcohol abuse.

Prognosis

Physiologic tremors that occur in various metabolic and toxic states are temporary and usually disappear once the underlying disorder is corrected. Essential tremor is often referred to as a benign essential tremor, but it may be disabling due to coordination problems like spilling of liquids and poor handwriting. Parkinsonian tremors occur in the setting of a chronic and progressive disorder. Current medical and surgical treatment does not cure the disease but may be successful in slowing the progression of the disorder or in alleviating the tremor. Consequently, over time, these types of tremors cause progressive deterioration of muscle coordination and seriously affect the individual's quality of life.

Differential Diagnosis

Multiple sclerosis, Parkinson's disease, Wilson's disease, thyrotoxicosis, stroke, side effects of certain medications, infectious or metabolic brain dysfunction (encephalopathies), tumors or other structural damage involving movement centers in the brain, acute anxiety, alcohol intoxication, and poisoning with lead, arsenic, or carbon monoxide are all potential causes of tremor.

Specialists

- Neurologist
- Psychiatrist

Rehabilitation

Depending on the cause and severity of tremor, physical and/or occupational therapy may be needed to help the individual cope with coordination difficulties. Tremors that occur when the individual is at rest are treated by physical therapy using relaxation techniques such as gentle rocking and/or rotation of the extremities in a sitting position. Other exercises performed in a sitting position include swinging the arms with a gradual increase in speed and amount of movement. The physical therapist may advance this type of exercise by incorporating functional activities used in daily life such as sitting and standing. For example, the individual moves both arms (bilateral) at the same time and in the same pattern (symmetrical patterns) and progresses moving each arm alternately (reciprocal patterns) while maintaining good sitting balance with minimal tremor.

When individuals have significant tremor while maintaining sitting or standing posture, treatment then focuses on techniques such as having the individual sit in a chair with hips tucked back, feet flat on the floor, and elbows supported by a lap table or pillow. The individual then lifts the head and holds it steady. To progress and promote trunk control, the individual uses less support to the elbows from the pillows.

Sitting control is improved by sitting in an armless, backless chair while the therapist applies mild pressure to various regions of the trunk. The individual is instructed to resist the movement created by the therapist. Other exercises include shifting the weight in all directions while sitting and then repeating the same activities in a standing position. Standing exercises are advanced to activities such as placing one foot forward and backward on a straight line and walking between two parallel lines. If job duties require fine motor movements, job reassignment and vocational rehabilitation may be needed.

The rehabilitation program varies for individuals affected by tremors. The type, intensity, and progression of exercises depend on the specific disorder affecting the nervous system.

Work Restrictions / Accommodations

Providing more rest and a calm environment may be helpful. Safety considerations may affect whether an individual can perform his or her usual duties. Duties that require working at heights, with heavy equipment or motor vehicles, or hazardous occupations may have to be restricted or modified. If fine motor skills are required, reassignment may be necessary.

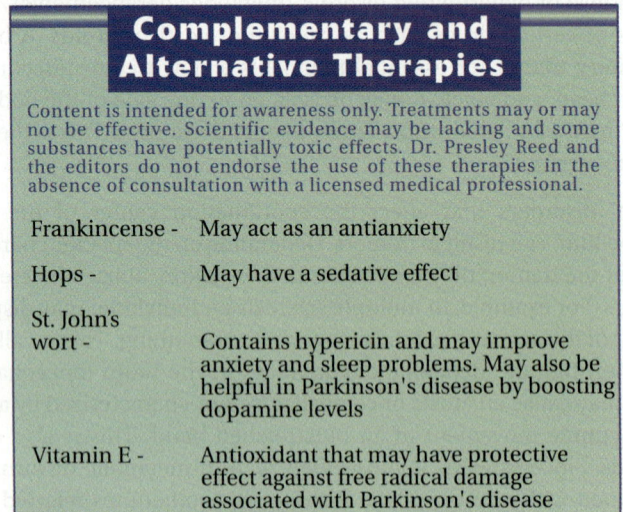

Complementary and Alternative Therapies

Content is intended for awareness only. Treatments may or may not be effective. Scientific evidence may be lacking and some substances have potentially toxic effects. Dr. Presley Reed and the editors do not endorse the use of these therapies in the absence of consultation with a licensed medical professional.

Frankincense -	May act as an antianxiety
Hops -	May have a sedative effect
St. John's wort -	Contains hypericin and may improve anxiety and sleep problems. May also be helpful in Parkinson's disease by boosting dopamine levels
Vitamin E -	Antioxidant that may have protective effect against free radical damage associated with Parkinson's disease

Comorbid Conditions

Comorbid conditions that may lengthen recovery and disability are advanced age, liver failure, or mental or neurological illnesses.

Complications

Complications depend on the underlying disorder causing the tremor. Persistent tremors or those that get progressively worse such as associated with Parkinson's disease can contribute to the development of depression, social withdrawal, sleep disturbances, and fatigue.

Factors Influencing Duration
The severity of the tremor, underlying cause, effectiveness of the treatment, and job requirements affect the length of disability.

Length of Disability
Duration depends on the underlying condition. A more specific diagnosis is needed to determine length of disability.

Failure to Recover
If an individual fails to recover within the maximum duration expectancy period, the reader may wish to reference the following questions to assist in better understanding the specifics of an individual's medical case.

Regarding diagnosis:
- Did individual present with symptoms consistent with the general diagnosis of tremor?
- Was the underlying cause of the tremor determined with a physical exam and diagnostic studies?
- If the diagnosis was uncertain, were all common causes of tremor considered in the differential diagnosis?
- Would individual benefit from consultation with a specialist (neurologist, endocrinologist, physiatrist, internist, psychiatrist)?
- Should EMG, brain MRI or CT, or other tests be done to assist with differential diagnosis?
- Were a recent thyroid panel, liver function studies, and chemistry panel done to rule out functional or metabolic sources of the tremor?
- Has individual complained of nervousness, feelings of anxiety, or depression?

Regarding treatment:
- Was the underlying cause of the tremor addressed in the treatment plan?
- Was the treatment appropriate for the condition?
- Did symptoms persist? If so, were other or more aggressive treatments considered?

Regarding prognosis:
- What was the expected outcome?
- Does individual have any comorbid conditions that may influence the length of disability?
- Is the condition chronic or progressive in nature?
- Does individual have any evidence of depression, social withdrawal or excess fatigue?
- Does individual have access to support groups or behavioral counseling?

References
Beers, Mark H., and Robert Berkow, eds. The Merck Manual of Diagnosis and Therapy, 17th ed. Whitehouse Station, NJ: Merck and Company, Inc, 1999 21Aug 2000 <http://www.merck.com/pubs/mmanual/section14/sec14.htm>.

NINDS Tremor Information Page. National Institute of Neurological Disorders and Stroke. 27 Jun 2000. 11 Nov 2000 <http://www.ninds.nih.gov/health_and_medical/disorders/tremor_doc.htm>.

Trench Mouth
Other names / synonyms: Acute Necrotizing Ulcerative Gingivitis, Stomatitis, Vincent's Angina, Vincent's Infection, Vincent's Stomatitis
101

Definition
Trench mouth is an acute, painful ulceration and infection of the gums (gingivitis). The term trench mouth comes from World War I because this disorder was common among soldiers. Trench mouth occurs when there is an overabundance of normal mouth bacteria. Viruses may be involved in allowing the bacteria to overgrow. This overabundance of bacteria causes an infection that results in inflammation of the gums (gingivitis) and the subsequent development of painful ulcers.

The primary risk factor is poor dental hygiene. Other risk factors include diabetes mellitus, poor nutrition, any other mouth, throat, or tooth infections, smoking, emotional or physical stress, and other infections that weaken the immune system (e.g., HIV and leukemia). Many cases develop in individuals with simple gingivitis (a common, mild gum inflammation) who experience a stressful event such as college exams or changing jobs.

Trench mouth is a rare disease that usually affects young adults between the ages of 15 and 35 although individuals of any age may be affected.

Diagnosis
History: Individuals will complain of onset of painful gums that bleed profusely with any irritation or pressure, foul breath, and a bad taste in the mouth. Eating may be painful. Fever is possible if the infection is extensive. Less commonly, individuals report unintentional weight loss or a sore throat.

Physical exam: The individual may present with red and swollen gums with gum tissue destruction noted between and around the teeth. A grayish-white film caused by decomposed gum tissue may be evident. Ulcers that may be filled with plaque or food debris are present between teeth and on the gums. Fever and swelling of lymph nodes in the head and neck may also be noted.

Tests: Cultures taken from the gums can determine the species of infecting bacteria. Dental or facial x-rays may be used to determine the extent of infection below the gum line and the amount of tissue destruction and also measure any bone loss.

Treatment

Good oral hygiene is vital to treatment and should be immediately initiated. Thorough tooth brushing and flossing must be done as often as possible, preferably 3 to 4 times a day. Saltwater rinses may be soothing to sore gums. Diluted hydrogen peroxide (equal parts 3% hydrogen peroxide and water) can be used to rinse the gums and remove decayed gum tissue. Once the gums have become less tender, a thorough dental cleaning should be performed. The dentist will remove all plaque and tartar from the teeth (scaling) and clean away all dead gum tissue. This cleaning is likely to be painful so the dentist often uses a local anesthetic. After this initial cleaning, the individual may be instructed to continue rinsing with dilute hydrogen peroxide 3 times a day for a few days instead of brushing. If the infection is severe or if the individual has a fever, antibiotics may be prescribed. Pain-relieving medication (analgesics) may also be prescribed to help relieve discomfort.

The individual may be asked to return to the dentist every few days for about 2 weeks for continued cleaning. Professional cleanings continue until healing is well under way. If the gums do not return to their normal shape and position, the dentist may have to surgically reshape them (gingivoplasty).

To prevent recurrences, individuals are instructed in good oral hygiene procedures. Regular visits to the dentist for scaling and cleaning are also important. A good diet, reduction of stress, adequate sleep and exercise, and quitting smoking also help prevent recurrences. Smoking should be stopped and hot or spicy foods avoided.

Prognosis

With early treatment and good follow-up care, trench mouth has a favorable prognosis. If the infection is allowed to progress without treatment or if adequate follow-up is not performed, the disease can result in loss of bone and tissue needed for dental health or spread to the cheeks and lips, destroying these tissues. Ultimately, advanced infection results in tooth loss and its attendant problems.

Systemic disease (sepsis) can develop in untreated cases of trench mouth. The prognosis for these infections depends on the nature and severity of the infections at the beginning of treatment.

Differential Diagnosis

Several types of gingivitis have similar symptoms such as red, inflamed gum tissue. Yeast and fungal infections may share symptoms with trench mouth. Periodontitis should also be ruled out.

Specialists

- Dentist
- Oral Surgeon
- Infectious Disease Physician

Work Restrictions / Accommodations

The individual may need additional breaks to perform oral hygiene. Individuals in contact with the public may need to be temporarily reassigned depending on their symptoms and appearance. Accommodations may need to be made to allow for frequent visits to the dentist until the healing is advanced or completed.

Comorbid Conditions

Immune deficiency and other viral or bacterial infections may lengthen the disability period.

Complications

Advanced, severe, or untreated cases may result in damage to the supporting tissues and underlying bones of the mouth. Such destruction will likely to lead to tooth loss. The bacterial infection (periodontitis) responsible for this disease may spread to other parts of the body, resulting in tissue damage to other structures. Widespread infection (sepsis) can also occur.

Factors Influencing Duration

The length of disability is influenced by the immune status of the individual, severity of disease, and treatment. Individuals with inadequate immunity suffer from systemic disease. Those with complications may have extended disability. Individuals with no access to professional dental care may have more a complicated disease and a longer recovery period.

Length of Disability

There is no disability associated with mild cases of trench mouth. Most individuals who receive adequate treatment fully recover within a few weeks. Severe cases may require hospitalization until the infection is under control.

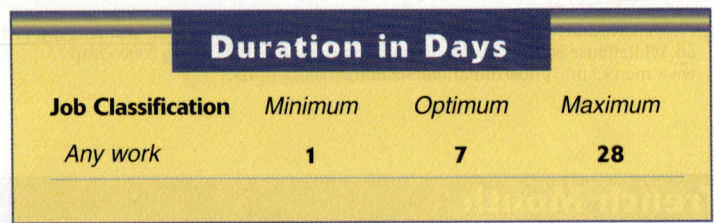

Duration in Days

Job Classification	Minimum	Optimum	Maximum
Any work	1	7	28

Failure to Recover

If an individual fails to recover within the maximum duration expectancy period, the reader may wish to reference the following questions to assist in better understanding the specifics of an individual's medical case.

Regarding diagnosis:

- Did the individual have painful, bleeding gums, mouth ulcers and or foul breath?
- Was a fever or swelling of head and neck lymph nodes noted in the physical exam?
- Was a culture and sensitivity done to detect the causative organism and appropriate antimicrobial treatment?
- Has the diagnosis of trench mouth been confirmed?
- Were other conditions with similar symptoms (other types of gingivitis, yeast and fungal infections, and periodontitis) ruled out?

Regarding treatment:

- Has the individual been compliant with recommendation to rinse the mouth three times daily with hydrogen peroxide? If not, why? What can be done to enhance compliance?
- If antibiotics were prescribed, did the individual complete the entire course of therapy?
- Has the individual kept scheduled appointments for on-going therapy? If not, what can be done to enhance compliance?
- Was gingivectomy indicated?

Regarding prognosis:

- Has the infection persisted or recurred despite treatment?
- Does the individual understand the importance of prevention? Is the individual able to comply with good dental hygiene?
- Has individual experienced any complications such as damage to the supporting tissues or underlying bone of the mouth?
- Has the bacterial infection spread to other parts of the body resulting in tissue damage to other structures?
- Has sepsis occurred?
- Have underlying conditions that may impact recovery (immune deficiency disorders, viral, or bacterial infections) been identified or ruled out?

References

Cohen, Robert. "Mouth and Dental Disorders." The Merck Manual of Medical Information. Berkow, Robert, ed. New York: Pocket Books, 1997. 497-522.

deVlaming, David. "Gingivitis." Griffith's 5-minute Clinical Consult. Dambro, Mark, ed. Philadelphia: Lippincott, Williams & Wilkins, 2000. 432-433.

Trichinosis
Other names / synonyms: Trichinelliasis, Trichinellosis, Trichiniasis
124

Definition

Trichinosis is a parasitic disease of many mammals, including humans, resulting from infection with a worm called Trichinella spiralis. Individuals become infected with Trichinella spiralis after eating undercooked, infected meat. Trichinosis is usually attributed to eating undercooked pork; however, wild game (such as moose, bear, boar, etc.) as well as walrus and seal meat have also been linked to human infection.

When infected meat containing living immature worms (larvae) is eaten, the larvae are deposited into the small intestine where they develop into mature worms. This occurs about one week after eating the infected meat. The adult worms then burrow through the lining of the intestine. Two to three weeks after ingestion, the mature female worms release newborn larvae that travel through the blood vessels to many organ systems. The larvae then settle in muscle tissue where they are encapsulated (encysted) and can remain viable for several years.

The most common sites of infection are the skeletal muscles, particularly the lower leg (gastrocnemius or calf muscle), upper arm (biceps), tongue, and diaphragm, as well as muscles of the lower back, jaw and neck, and the muscles around the eyes. The heart (cardiac muscle) can also be affected, as can the lungs and other organ systems.

Individuals who eat raw or rare pork products, wild game, walrus, or seal meat are at higher risk of infection. Tasting uncooked, homemade sausages for seasoning is another risk factor.

Pork is the meat most commonly associated with trichinosis, and pigs are usually infected when fed uncooked meat scraps. Regulations requiring commercial farmers to sterilize all garbage fed to hogs has substantially reduced the incidence in the US over the past several years. Individuals who raise their own pigs for consumption and who include raw meat scraps in their feed are at increased risk for infection.

Trichinosis occurs throughout the world except in Australia and in some Pacific Islands. It is more common in rural areas than in cities. In the US, there are 50-100 cases of trichinosis reported each year, with the incidence higher in Alaska and in the northeastern portion of the country. While individuals of any age can be infected, most cases are seen in people who are between 20 and 49 years old.

Diagnosis

History: Individuals will often report eating raw or undercooked pork, wild game, walrus, or seal meat within the past week. Complaints of diarrhea, abdominal cramping, headache, muscle soreness, swelling around the eyes, and weakness may be reported. It is important to note that many mild infections may not cause any symptoms at all (asymptomatic).

After the parasite has invaded muscle for several months, symptoms subside except for vague muscle pains or tiredness (lethargy); these symptoms may last up to 6 months.

Physical exam: Clinical signs and symptoms will vary depending on the number of ingested larvae and the phase of the parasitic invasion. Infected muscles will be tender and prone to spasm. Fever may be noted, but tends to come and go. The individual may be sensitive to bright or direct light (photophobia). Inflammation of the mucous membrane of the eye (conjunctivitis) may be noted, and bleeding of certain parts of the eye (subconjunctival hemorrhage, retinal hemorrhage) may occur. Rash, rapid heartbeat (tachycardia), inflammation of the lung(s) (pneumonitis), or bleeding under the fingernails or toenails (splinter hemorrhages) may be present.

If the parasite has spread to other organs, there may be signs of inflammation of the membrane of the brain or spinal cord (meningitis), inflammation of the lungs (pneumonia, pneumonitis), kidney inflammation (nephritis), etc.

Tests: In the second week, there are occasional immature worms in the blood or stomach washings. Between the second and fourth weeks, an increase in the type of white blood cells called eosinophils (eosinophilia) will be noted. Blood tests will also reveal increased levels of certain enzymes (creatine phosphate kinase and lactate dehydrogenase) and certain proteins (gamma globulin).

In the third to fourth weeks, biopsy from swollen or tender skeletal muscle may reveal the encysted larvae. After several weeks, a test that measures the sedimentation rate of red blood cells will reveal an increase in this rate. The parasite is seldom identified from stool samples.

A type of blood test called the bentonite flocculation test is highly sensitive and nearly 100% specific. It becomes positive in about the third week, and reaches its maximum at 2 months. Antibodies can be detected from blood samples, but not until 3-5 weeks after infection. Immunofluorescence tests become positive in the second week, but are less sensitive than the bentonite flocculation test.

An imaging technique called computed tomography (CT) may help the physician see muscle cysts. Another imaging technique called magnetic resonance imaging (MRI) may be indicated to assess neurological involvement, and chest x-rays may be necessary to evaluate the possibility of lung involvement.

Treatment

Most cases resolve spontaneously, and are treated with bedrest and possibly nonprescription medication to reduce fever (antipyretics) and pain (analgesics), as needed.

More severe cases may require hospitalization. Treatment with anti-worm medications may be required. Drugs will not be effective against larvae already encysted within the muscle, but will likely prevent spreading. Additionally, corticosteroids may be used to reduce inflammation, particularly in severe or complicated cases.

In cases of severe heart involvement, implantation of a device to regulate heartbeat (pacemaker) has been required.

Prognosis

The prognosis for trichinosis in otherwise healthy individuals is very good. The infection will often subside on its own. Encysted larvae may remain viable for several years. Five to ten percent of cases are severe, with death resulting in less than 1%. In those severe cases where death occurs, it is a result of cardiac failure or pneumonia (usually occurring during the fourth to eighth week of infection).

There is no clear evidence that ongoing (chronic) trichinosis exists.

Differential Diagnosis

Trichinosis may resemble many other diseases because of its many manifestations. Possibilities include acute rheumatic fever, arthritis, angioedema, botulism, collagen vascular disease, dermatomyositis, encephalitis, eosinophilia-myalgia syndrome, gastroenteritis, idiopathic hypereosinophilic syndrome, idiopathic polymyositis, influenza, meningitis, pneumonitis, polyarteritis nodosa, polymyositis, typhoid fever, and tuberculosis.

Specialists

- Cardiologist
- Infectious Disease Physician
- Internist
- Nephrologist
- Neurologist
- Ophthalmologist
- Pulmonologist

Work Restrictions / Accommodations

In most cases, work restrictions and accommodations will not be required, as most cases are without symptoms.

When symptoms are noted, accommodations and restrictions will depend on the individual's symptoms. For instance, muscle pain and weakness, as well as heart involvement may prevent individuals from performing heavy work. Sensitivity to light may prevent work outdoors or under bright lights, or may require prescription and/or protective sunglasses. Individuals who have been prescribed medication may require frequent breaks over a several-week period in order to take medications at the prescribed times.

Comorbid Conditions

Comorbid conditions include suppression or compromise of the immune system.

Complications

Trichinosis may be complicated by inflammation of the lining of the spinal cord and brain (meningitis), inflammation of the brain (encephalitis), inflammation of the heart (myocarditis) with associated congestive heart failure, brain damage, inflammation of the kidney (nephritis, glomerulonephritis), inflammation of the sinuses (sinusitis), or inflammation of the lungs (pneumonitis).

Factors Influencing Duration

The length of disability will be influenced by the severity of disease and the development of complications, particularly complications of the heart, lungs, or central nervous system. If the individual is immunocompromised, more severe disease and a longer disability period may be expected.

Length of Disability

Most trichinosis infections are short-lived and generally resolve spontaneously without complication. Disability will be longer for those who perform heavy work. Severe and/or complicated infections are associated with longer recovery periods. In some cases, such as with heart damage or brain damage, disability may be permanent. Death occurs in less than 1% of individuals.

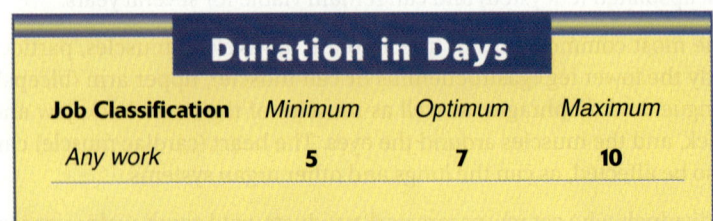

Duration in Days

Job Classification	Minimum	Optimum	Maximum
Any work	5	7	10

Failure to Recover

If an individual fails to recover within the maximum duration expectancy period, the reader may wish to reference the following questions to assist in better understanding the specifics of an individual's medical case.

Regarding diagnosis:

- Did the individual experience symptoms of infection in the skeletal muscles, such as tenderness or muscle spasms?
- Was the individual asymptomatic?

- Were other more serious symptoms noted such as rash, tachycardia, retinal or subconjunctival hemorrhage, or other areas of inflammation or hemorrhage?
- Has the individual recently eaten raw or undercooked meat that could have been affected by Trichinella spiralis?
- Did serological tests reveal eosinophilia or CPK and LDH elevation?
- Were additional diagnostic tests done such as CT scan or MRI to detect extent of muscle or organ system involvement?
- Was a bentonite flocculation test done to confirm the diagnosis?
- If the diagnosis was uncertain, were other conditions with similar symptoms considered in the differential diagnosis (rheumatic fever, arthritis, angioedema, botulism, collagen vascular disease, dermatomyositis, encephalitis, eosinophilia-myalgia syndrome, gastroenteritis, idiopathic hypereosinophilic syndrome, idiopathic polymyositis, influenza, meningitis, pneumonitis, polyarteritis nodosa, polymyositis, typhoid fever, and tuberculosis)?

Regarding treatment:
- Were conservative interventions (bedrest, antipyretics, analgesics) effective in resolving the symptoms?
- If not, was hospitalization and more aggressive therapy needed?
- Did the treatment address other organ system involvement (such as placement of pacemaker, respiratory care, etc.)?

Regarding prognosis:
- Is the individual's employer able to make appropriate work accommodations so the individual can return to work safely?
- Does the individual have any underlying conditions (such as immune system compromise) that could impact recovery and prognosis?
- Has the individual suffered any complications associated with the disease (i.e., meningitis, encephalitis, and myocarditis with associated congestive heart failure, brain damage, nephritis, glomerulonephritis, sinusitis, or pneumonitis) that could impact recovery and prognosis? If so, are the complications being addressed appropriately in the treatment plan?

References

Kelsey, Doris. "Enteric Nematodes of Lower Animals: Zoonoses." Medical Microbiology. Baron, Samuel, ed. New York: Churchill Livingstone, 1991. 1125-1136.

Voorhees, Kenton. "Trichinosis." Griffith's 5-minute Clinical Consult. Dambro, Mark, ed. Philadelphia: Lippincott, Williams & Wilkins, 2000. 1104-1105.

Trichomoniasis
Other names / synonyms: Trich
131, 131.0, 131.00, 131.01, 131.02, 131.03, 131.8, 131.9

Definition

Trichomoniasis is a sexually transmitted disease caused by a one-celled organism called Trichomonas vaginalis. Infection with this organism produces disease ranging from no symptoms to severe inflammation. Trichomoniasis primarily affects women and causes inflammation of the vagina (vaginitis). In men, it can cause inflammation of the prostate, urethra, and seminal vesicles.

Individuals with multiple sex partners are most at risk of developing this infection. It is spread through contact with discharge from the vagina or urethra from an infected individual during sexual intercourse. Even if no symptoms are present, an infected individual can continue to spread the disease as long as he or she carries the organism.

Trichomoniasis is often seen in combination with other sexually transmitted diseases. Up to 40% of individuals with trichomoniasis also have gonorrhea. Trichomoniasis makes an individual more vulnerable to HIV infection when exposed. In individuals already infected with HIV, trichomoniasis increases the likelihood of spreading HIV to a partner.

Approximately 5 million women and men develop trichomoniasis every year. Women, between the ages of 16 and 35 are most commonly affected. An estimated 20% of women have the infection at least once during their reproductive years. Trichomoniasis is present in 30-40% of male sexual partners of infected women. The infection is found worldwide and in all races.

Diagnosis

History: Symptoms usually develop 5 to 28 days after exposure to the infection. Women have a foul-smelling thin, greenish-yellow, foamy vaginal discharge. Often there is pain or burning during urination or sexual intercourse. Some women experience irritation and itching in the vaginal area or lower abdominal pain. Men's symptoms are often absent or mild. They may experience pain or burning during urination or ejaculation.

Some individuals carry the organism for years yet have no symptoms. The infected individual's history includes contact with an infected individual or multiple sexual partners.

Physical exam: The physical exam of a woman confirms vaginal discharge and reveals red vaginal ulcers. The vulva or vagina may be inflamed. Severe cases may also show inflammation of the cervix. In males, inflammation of the prostate, urethra, or seminal vesicles may be detected. There may be a discharge from the urethra in men and women.

Tests: T. vaginalis is identified through examination of vaginal or urethral discharge under a microscope. Because the organism may not be detected in every specimen, several specimens may be needed. The organism may also be cultured from vaginal or urethral discharge. Immunologic blood tests for T. vaginalis are positive in 90% of infected individuals.

Because of the close association of trichomoniasis and other sexually transmitted diseases (STDs), tests for gonorrhea, chlamydia, and other STDs should be performed at the same time.

Treatment

Trichomoniasis is typically treated with an oral antibiotic. The drug is taken either over a period of 7 days or in a single dose. Alcohol must be avoided while taking this medicine because of side effects such as cramping. If initial treatment fails, higher drug concentrations are used for a second round of treatment. Drug treatment should be avoided in the first trimester of pregnancy.

The infected individual should abstain from sex until treatment is completed and symptoms disappear. All sexual partners should be treated at the same time.

Prognosis

The prognosis for treated trichomoniasis is excellent. The cure rate is 90% if all sexual partners are treated at the same time. If any sexual partner is not treated, reinfection is likely.

Some strains of T. vaginalis are resistant to antibiotics. Individuals infected with these strains may have persistent infection.

Differential Diagnosis

In women, similar symptoms are seen in vaginitis caused by yeast (vulvovaginal candidiasis) or bacteria (Gardnerella vaginalis or Mycoplasma hominis). Similar symptoms may also be caused by vaginal exposure to an irritating chemical (chemical vaginitis) or by aging-related changes to the vagina due to lack of estrogen (atrophic vaginitis). Pelvic inflammatory disease may also present with a similar history.

In men, inflammation of the urethra caused by Chlamydia (Chlamydial urethritis) may resemble trichomoniasis.

Specialists

- Gynecologist
- Infectious Disease Physician
- Primary Care Provider
- Urologist

Work Restrictions / Accommodations

No work restrictions or accommodations are required for this diagnosis.

Comorbid Conditions

Pregnancy may delay treatment of the infection until the second trimester. HIV and other sexually transmitted diseases are closely associated with trichomoniasis. These diseases complicate symptoms and treatment and prolong recovery.

Complications

Drug-resistant strains have been reported and infection with these strains may lead to chronic trichomoniasis. Chronic trichomoniasis may cause cellular changes that can be misinterpreted on a Pap smear. Trichomoniasis during pregnancy can cause premature membrane rupture and premature birth.

Factors Influencing Duration

The severity of infection and effectiveness of treatment influence the length of disability. Factors related to reinfection also influence length of disability and include the number of sexual partners, infection status of sexual partners, and condom use.

Length of Disability

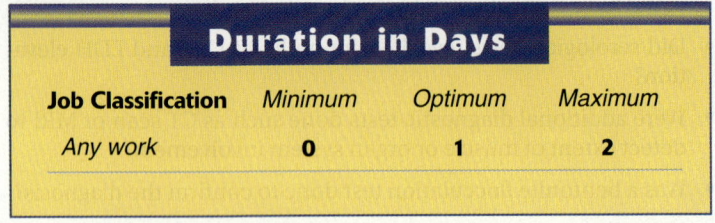

Job Classification	Minimum	Optimum	Maximum
Any work	0	1	2

Failure to Recover

If an individual fails to recover within the maximum duration expectancy period, the reader may wish to reference the following questions to assist in better understanding the specifics of an individual's medical case.

Regarding diagnosis:

- Did the woman present with symptoms of foul-smelling, purulent vaginal discharge and associated burning on urination and sexual intercourse?
- In males, were symptoms of pain or burning during urination or ejaculation noted?
- Was the diagnosis confirmed by positive vaginal or urethral cultures?
- Were other conditions with similar symptoms such as vulvovaginal candidiasis, Gardnerella vaginalis, mycoplasma hominis, chemical vaginitis, and atrophic vaginitis or Chlamydial inflammation of the urethra (in males) ruled out?

Regarding treatment:

- Was a sensitivity test performed to determine the most appropriate antibiotic and to identify antibiotic-resistant organisms?
- Was the individual treated with an appropriate oral antibiotic?
- Did the symptoms persist despite treatment? If so, were appropriate changes or adjustments in the antibiotic therapy made?
- Did individual take all medication as prescribed?
- Was the individual compliant in abstaining from alcohol use during the antibiotic treatment?
- Was the individual instructed to abstain from sex until infection has resolved to prevent disease transmission?
- Were all sexual partners treated as well to prevent disease transmission?

Regarding prognosis:

- Did the infection persist despite treatment?
- Was a repeat culture and sensitivity done to rule out the possibility of antibiotic resistant bacteria?
- Were appropriate adjustments made in the antibiotic treatment?
- Has the individual experienced any complications such as chronic trichomoniasis or epididymitis that may impact recovery and prognosis?
- Does the individual have any existing conditions (pregnancy, HIV or other STDs) that may complicate treatment and impact recovery?

References

Chin, James. Control of Communicable Diseases Manual, 17th ed. Washington, DC: American Public Health Association, 2000.

Trichomoniasis. Centers for Disease Control and Prevention, Division of Sexually Transmitted Diseases. 01 Sep 2000. 27 Sep 2000 <http://www.cdc.gov/nchstp/dstd/Fact_Sheets/FactsTrichomoniasis.htm>.

Trigeminal Neuralgia

Other names / synonyms: Tic Douloureux, Trigeminal Neuralgia
350, 350.1

Definition

Trigeminal neuralgia (tic douloureux) is a very painful disorder of the portion of the fifth cranial nerve known as the trigeminal nerve that supplies sensation to the face. It is characterized by recurrent electric shock-like pains in one or more branches of the trigeminal nerve, each supplying a different portion of the face. Because the sudden, sharp pain causes the individual to wince, the condition is known as tic douloureux or painful twitch.

In most cases, no specific disease of the fifth nerve or central nervous system can be found. The cause of trigeminal neuralgia is unknown. Changes that are associated with death of nerve cells (degenerative changes) or scar tissue (fibrotic changes) have been reported in the trigeminal nerve, but may not be the cause of symptoms. In some cases, the trigeminal nerve may be compressed by a tumor or blood vessels (vascular anomaly) or damaged from dental or surgical procedures, facial injury, or infections. Pain associated with trigeminal neuralgia occasionally occurs in individuals with brain stem damage as a result of multiple sclerosis, or in individuals with blood vessel abnormalities involving the root of the fifth cranial nerve. Some researchers believe that some cases of trigeminal neuralgia may be inherited.

Trigeminal neuralgia is the most frequent of all the painful disorders affecting nerves (neuralgias), but is still relatively rare and affects about 150 per million individuals a year. It can occur at any age but is uncommon before the age of 35. Trigeminal neuralgia is primarily a disorder of middle age and later life, and affects women three times more often than men.

Diagnosis

History: Individuals report a searing or burning pain on one side of the face that occurs in lightening-like jabs in the distribution of one or more branches of the nerve (paroxysm). A paroxysm of pain usually lasts for only seconds or up to 1 or 2 minutes, but may be prolonged for 15 minutes or longer. The bouts of pain may last for days, weeks, or months, then disappear for months or even years.

The individual may occasionally rub or pinch the face or make violent movements of the face and jaw. Watering of the eye on the involved side may occur. The individual may complain of extreme sensitivity of pain or touch receptors in the skin of the face (hyperesthesia). In many cases, there is a trigger zone stimulated by movement such as chewing or talking that sets off a typical paroxysm in the face. Lightly touching the face as in shaving or applying makeup, or even a slight breeze over the affected portion may serve as a trigger. The pain is typically restricted to one or more branches of the nerve and does not spread beyond the nerve. While the pain is occasionally bilateral, in about 5% of cases, paroxysms on both sides at one time are rare.

Physical exam: Physical findings in individuals with trigeminal neuralgia are typically normal. A thorough examination of the teeth, jaw, and sinuses is performed to exclude other causes of pain such as infections of the teeth and nasal sinus. The neurological exam includes an assessment of the pain site of origin and mode of spread of the painful spasm. The trigeminal nerve divides into three main branches. If the first branch (ophthalmic) is affected, shock-like pain is felt along the eye, forehead, and part of the nose. The second or middle nerve branch (maxillary) sends pain along the upper lip, teeth and gum, the side of the nose, the part of the cheek under the eye, and the lower eyelid. Pain from the third branch (mandibular) is felt in the lower lip, teeth, gum, jaw, and outer edge of the tongue. If the individual is examined during an episode of pain, involuntary twitching of the facial muscles along the affected nerve branch may be seen.

Tests: MRI may be done to exclude the possibility of a tumor or blood vessel compressing the trigeminal nerve or to look for changes characteristic of multiple sclerosis. Cerebral angiogram or MRI angiography can delineate abnormalities of the blood vessels.

Treatment

Initial treatment utilizes certain anticonvulsant drugs that suppress the pain and may shorten attacks and encourage remission. Some individuals, however, become resistant to the drug or are unable to tolerate a dose high enough to relieve the pain. Acute episodes can also be relieved with intravenous injection of an anticonvulsant drug.

When medications lose their effectiveness, surgical intervention is an alternative. At present, thermal destruction of the affected nerve branch is the preferred treatment when medication is ineffective. One operative procedure involves injecting the nerve with alcohol. This provides temporary relief from symptoms but pain may return as the nerve regenerates. Other surgical procedures include removing part of the nerve (partial resection) or cutting pathways leading from the nerve (medullary tractotomy). The next step involves attempts to destroy the nerve root using high-frequency currents (thermocoagulation) or by removing part of the nerve (percutaneous ablation). If other treatments fail, neurosurgery can be done to attempt to relieve pressure on the nerve (decompression) or cut part of the nerve (partial rhizotomy). Separating abnormal vessels from the nerve root (microvascular decompression) has become increasingly popular, and is tolerated well even in the elderly. This procedure may become preferred.

Prognosis

Medication frequently provides relief from symptoms. The course of trigeminal neuralgia is characterized by remissions. In most individuals, the sudden attacks of pain are present for several weeks or months and then stop spontaneously. The remission may be short in duration or the pains may be absent for months or years. Attack-free intervals may become shorter as the individual ages but permanent disappearance of symptoms is rare. Trigeminal neuralgia is not fatal but frequent paroxysms may incapacitate an individual. Just the fear of an attack may limit activity.

The outcome of various surgical approaches is unpredictable, but the pain can be so great the individual must be informed of any operations that may provide relief. At present, thermal destruction of the affected nerve branch is the preferred surgical method with a higher success rate than other methods. Individuals with frequent and ongoing attacks may be significantly disabled by the condition. In a recent study of 258 individuals with percutaneous radiofrequency thermal rhizotomy, 87% had excellent or good pain relief at follow-up in less than 6 six months. After 6 months, 83% had excellent or good pain relief, 12% required a second operation, and 10% had unpleasant sensations (anesthesia dolorosa).

Differential Diagnosis

Pain arising from diseases of the teeth, jaw, or sinuses may mimic trigeminal neuralgia. Although the pain of shingles (herpes zoster) or glossopharyngeal neuralgia may be confused with trigeminal neuralgia, herpes zoster is associated with characteristic blisters, and the pain of glossopharyngeal neuralgia should disappear when the tonsillar region is sprayed with local anesthetics. Tumors of the cerebellum may produce pain in the face by compressing the trigeminal nerve but these are usually associated with difficulties in walking, balance, or coordination.

Persistent or remitting neuralgic pains in the head, face, and neck differ from trigeminal neuralgia in that they are not confined to the distribution of the trigeminal nerve. They are classified as atypical facial pain and may be caused by a disturbance of the sympathetic nervous system or a variant of migraine headache. When young adults experience typical symptoms of trigeminal neuralgia, or if both sides of the face are affected, multiple sclerosis should be suspected.

Specialists

- Neurologist
- Neurosurgeon
- Pain Specialist

Rehabilitation

Individuals with trigeminal neuralgia may benefit from nerve desensitization therapy in conjunction with medical management. Those areas of the face experiencing painful responses to pressure or temperature are rubbed with a variety of stimuli such as ice cubes, soft cotton, burlap, and terry cloth. This causes the sensory nerves to accommodate to different stimuli thereby eliciting more normalized responses to pressure or temperature. The physical or occupational therapist instructs the individual to perform this process independently.

Work Restrictions / Accommodations

Some accommodations may be needed if the individual's job involves an activity that triggers the attacks such as headphones or protective gear that touches the face, or working outdoors or in a draft where air currents can trigger facial pain. Accommodations may be needed if the individual experiences side effects from medication.

Comorbid Conditions

Other pre-existing conditions that may affect recovery include sinus infections, dental and gum disease, migraine or other headaches, other neurological conditions, liver problems or bone marrow suppression limiting use of medications, and depression or other psychiatric conditions aggravating response to pain.

Complications

Toxic side effects of the drugs used to control the pain can cause damage to the liver and bone marrow. Surgical procedures can cause numbness of the face or eye that may in itself be unpleasant, and may also lead to complications such as corneal abrasion.

Factors Influencing Duration

Individuals who have frequent attacks may be significantly disabled by the condition. Medications may cause central nervous system effects such as drowsiness and mental impairment when therapy first begins. Recovery from major surgery lengthens the period of disability.

Length of Disability

Duration of disability depends on severity and frequency of symptoms, and on outcome of therapy with anticonvulsants or surgery.

Medical treatment.

Duration in Days

Job Classification	Minimum	Optimum	Maximum
Sedentary work	1	7	14
Light work	1	7	14
Medium work	1	7	14
Heavy work	1	7	14
Very Heavy work	1	7	14

Injection therapy.

Duration in Days

Job Classification	Minimum	Optimum	Maximum
Sedentary work	3	7	21
Light work	3	7	21
Medium work	7	14	28
Heavy work	7	14	28
Very Heavy work	7	21	35

Percutaneous ablation.

Duration in Days

Job Classification	Minimum	Optimum	Maximum
Sedentary work	1	2	7
Light work	1	3	7
Medium work	1	3	7
Heavy work	1	4	7
Very Heavy work	1	4	7

Surgical treatment.

Duration in Days

Job Classification	Minimum	Optimum	Maximum
Sedentary work	7	9	56
Light work	7	9	56
Medium work	14	21	56
Heavy work	14	21	56
Very Heavy work	14	21	56

Duration Trend from Normative Data*

Cases	Mean	Min	Max	No Lost Time	Over 6 Months
16383	42	0	280	0.02%	0.12%

Percentile:	5th	25th	Median	75th	95th
Days:	5	16	30	52	124

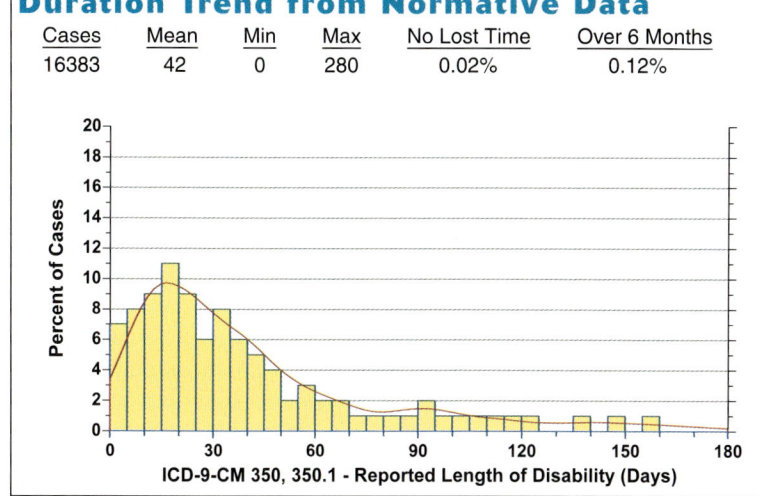
ICD-9-CM 350, 350.1 - Reported Length of Disability (Days)

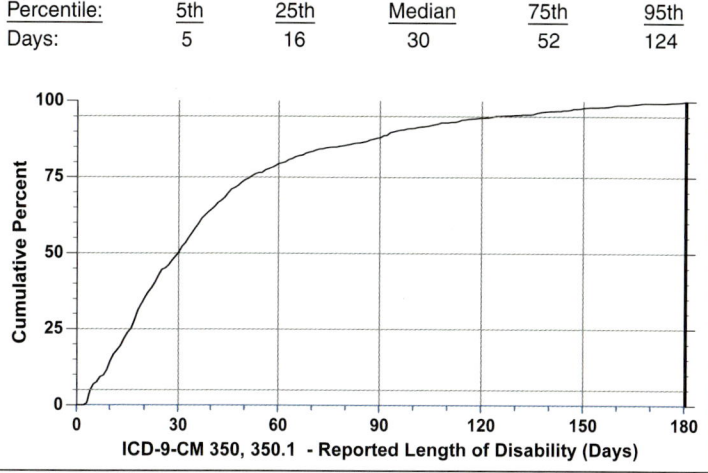
ICD-9-CM 350, 350.1 - Reported Length of Disability (Days)

* Differences may exist between the expected duration tables and the normative graphs. Duration tables provide expected recovery periods based on the type of work performed by the individual. The normative graphs reflect the actual observed experience of many individuals across the spectrum of physical conditions, in a variety of industries, and with varying levels of case management.

Trigeminal Neuralgia

Failure to Recover

If an individual fails to recover within the maximum duration expectancy period, the reader may wish to reference the following questions to assist in better understanding the specifics of an individual's medical case.

Regarding diagnosis:

- Does individual suffer from painful paroxysms of the face, lasting from seconds to 15 minutes or longer?
- Does the pain persist over days, weeks, or months and then disappear?
- Does individual make exaggerated movements of the face and complain of sensitivity to touch and pain? Which parts of the face are affected?
- Does the slightest movement trigger the pain, such as chewing, talking, shaving, applying make-up, or having a breeze touch the face?
- Was an MRI obtained?
- Was there evidence of a tumor or of nerve compression?
- Is there a possibility of multiple sclerosis?
- Was an angiogram or MRI angiography done? If so, were blood vessel abnormalities found?

Regarding treatment:

- What anticonvulsant medication was used? Is the dosage high enough to relieve the pain? Is there another medication, or combination of medications, that would be more beneficial?
- Is individual compliant with the medication regimen?
- Has individual become resistant to the medication?
- Has individual been able to tolerate the dosage?
- Is the use of intravenous medication required?
- Are medications no longer effective for pain control?
- Is surgical intervention required? If so, what procedure is necessary?
- Could individual have multiple sclerosis, especially if individual is a young adult?

Regarding prognosis:

- Is individual getting pain relief with current medications? Do medications need to be re-evaluated?
- Would individual benefit from surgery? Would the benefits of surgery outweigh the risks?
- Would individual benefit from chronic pain management at a specialized pain clinic?
- Would individual benefit from psychological counseling because of fear and anxiety?
- Has the medication caused liver damage or bone marrow damage?
- Has individual experienced post-surgical complications, such as numbness of the face or eye?
- Has a corneal abrasion occurred?
- What treatment(s) will be required for complications?
- What is the expected outcome of the treatment(s)?

References

Adams, C.B. "Trigeminal Neuralgia: Pathogenesis and Treatment." British Journal of Neurosurgery 11 6 (1997): 493-495.

Mathews, E.S., and S.J. Scrivani. "Percutaneous Stereotactic Radiofrequency Thermal Rhizotomy for the Treatment of Trigeminal Neuralgia." Mount Sinai Journal of Medicine 67 4 (2000): 288-299.

Trigger Finger or Thumb

Other names / synonyms: Stenosing Tenosynovitis

727.03

Definition

Trigger finger refers to a sensation when the fingers or thumb feel stuck or temporarily snagged during efforts to straighten or bend the hand.

The condition is caused by swelling often accompanying inflammation that narrows the hand's tunnels (flexor sheath), where tendons glide back and forth to allow movement of the hand and fingers. The tendon itself may develop a knot (nodule) caused by irritation from rubbing against the narrowed tunnel walls of the sheath, similar to a knotted rope repeatedly passing through a constricted area. Once the tendon pulls free of any obstacles, a snapping sensation (triggering) accompanied by pain may then be felt. The snapping movement likely will create more damage to the affected area, resulting in even more inflammation and swelling that creates additional narrowing and interference with hand and finger movement. The cycle of damage could result in the finger or thumb becoming stuck or locked, with movement becoming increasingly more painful and difficult.

The underlying cause of inflammation creating the condition often is not known, but can be associated with diseases such as rheumatoid arthritis and diabetes mellitus. Studies indicate that trigger finger is significantly related to certain occupations and repetitive tasks. One Canadian study indicated a 14% prevalence of trigger finger among workers in a meat-packing plant, with incidence higher among hand tool users.

Diagnosis

History: A sensation of discomfort or pain may begin in the base of the thumb or finger. Individuals may report a snapping or locking of the finger or thumb during grasping and releasing of the hand. Pain and swelling over the palm of the hand may be noted. Often, there is a history of repetitive or sustained activities such as gripping.

Physical exam: A knot in the affected tendon may be detected through touch (palpation), and is usually tender. Finger and thumb movements may be observed through bending and straightening each joint (flexion/extension). Snapping and locking in the affected area may be noted with range-of-motion (ROM) movements.

Tests: X-rays may be used to rule out bone or joint abnormalities, especially if the individual has a history of injury (trauma) to the affected area.

Treatment

The individual may need to wear a splint to reduce swelling and allow hand and finger movement to return to normal. Anti-inflammatory medications to reduce swelling also may be prescribed. The individual may be advised to avoid activities that irritate the affected area. Corticosteroid injections into the tendon sheath are generally tried. If nonoperative treatment fails, surgery may be required to open the tunnel area and allow freer movement of the tendon (open surgical release). In some cases, physical therapy may be required following surgery to restore normal hand movement.

Prognosis

Some cases recover spontaneously; most require steroid injection. About half of cases are resolved with one or two steroid injections, with the other half requiring surgical treatment. Surgery (open surgical release) usually resolves the condition, although recovery may take several weeks. Ongoing (chronic) or recurring problems might result if the condition is caused by an underlying disease creating the inflammation.

Differential Diagnosis

Rheumatoid arthritis, Dupuytren's contracture, tendon rupture, de Quervain's disease (syndrome), and tumors may produce similar symptoms.

Specialists

- Hand Surgeon
- Neurosurgeon
- Occupational Therapist
- Physiatrist
- Physical Therapist
- Rheumatologist

Rehabilitation

Rehabilitation of trigger finger or thumb may involve treating the narrowing or constriction of the tendon sheath in the affected finger. Because the constriction is usually due to inflammation of the sheath (tenosynovitis) that commonly results from overuse or trauma to the underside of the finger, education is as important as rehabilitative techniques.

Treatment varies depending on the severity and duration of the problem. Mild or infrequent symptoms may improve by simply resting the affected hand. Rehabilitation of trigger finger or thumb begins with the goals of decreasing pain and inflammation as well as addressing the cause of the inflammation and restoring of mobility and strength. The therapist may use cold or warm treatments throughout the period of rehabilitation to control inflammation and pain in this region of the wrist.

Methods of cold treatment include cold packs may be applied to the affected area after exercises. Heat treatments can be helpful to reduce inflammation and pain. Forms of heat treatment used in the wrist region include ultrasound that uses high frequency sound waves producing heat that penetrates deep into the involved tissues. Electrical stimulation and iontophoresis are additional techniques used in physical therapy to help decrease pain.

As pain subsides, stretching and strengthening exercises of specific finger or thumb muscles are emphasized. Bending the finger or thumb, as in making a fist (finger flexion) and straightening the joint (finger extension), are examples of such exercises. The therapist may perform each range of motion exercise with the individual in a resting position such as sitting or lying down depending on comfort and therapist preference. Range of motion exercises begin with the therapist moving the finger or thumb with no effort initiated by the individual (passive range of motion). The therapist may utilize a stretch at the end of each motion to help stretch and improve flexibility of the tendon within the tendon sheath. This type of exercise is then progressed to the individual performing some of the motion/effort along with the help of the therapist (active assist range of motion).

As the individual improves with increased motion of the joint, active range of motion is the next step of progression. Strengthening exercises progress with resistance from relatively light resistance putty used in hand rehabilitation. The individual is instructed to squeeze and release the putty a predetermined number of times or to continue the activity throughout a specific duration time.

Job requirements may need to be modified during the rehabilitation process until pain and swelling diminishes. For example, lifting objects that stresses the finger or thumb joints may need to be limited despite the amount of force needed to accomplish the task. An occupational therapist may fabricate a specific splint for the individual to help immobilize and protect the region of tenosynovitis.

As the initial pain and swelling subsides and motion becomes pain free, the rehabilitation process may warrant less direct observation and guidance from a physical therapist. The individual at this point will then progress to an independent exercise program.

Work Restrictions / Accommodations

Restrictions may include limited or no use of the affected hand, which could be protected by a splint. Individuals who require full use of both hands for work tasks may need to be reassigned to other duties until the condition is resolved. If the individual has had surgery, operation of motor vehicles may be restricted for a week or longer. Methods of performing work tasks may need to be evaluated for possible preventive measures to prevent recurrence.

Comorbid Conditions

Individuals diagnosed with trigger finger and who also have rheumatoid arthritis or diabetes mellitus could have extended disability because of ongoing (chronic) or recurring problems with inflammation. Individuals with diabetes mellitus have less chance of a favorable response to steroids used to treat trigger finger, which also could extend time needed for recovery.

Complications

The presence of rheumatoid or osteoarthritis or injury to the hand would complicate treatment. Tendon rupture and tissue wasting could result from injections, although this is unlikely. The triggering condition may recur in the affected area or in another tendon of the hand. The condition may be accompanied by other diseases involving inflammation of the tendons and the immediate area (tendonitis and tenosynovitis).

Factors Influencing Duration

If the dominant hand is involved, ability to perform work tasks such as writing may be hampered. The individual may need to temporarily or permanently cease activities such as repetitive motion that aggravate the condition.

Length of Disability

The individual who relies on full use of both hands, especially for work tasks that involve gripping, may be disabled until recovery occurs.

Medical treatment (including injection).

Duration in Days

Job Classification	Minimum	Optimum	Maximum
Sedentary work	1	7	21
Light work	1	7	21
Medium work	3	7	28
Heavy work	5	7	35
Very Heavy work	5	7	42

Surgical treatment. Tendon sheath incision.

Duration in Days

Job Classification	Minimum	Optimum	Maximum
Sedentary work	1	14	28
Light work	3	14	28
Medium work	7	21	35
Heavy work	21	28	42
Very Heavy work	21	28	42

Failure to Recover

If an individual fails to recover within the maximum duration expectancy period, the reader may wish to reference the following questions to assist in better understanding the specifics of an individual's medical case.

Regarding diagnosis:

- Has diagnosis of trigger finger or thumb been confirmed?
- Have conditions with similar symptoms been ruled out?
- Is trigger finger/thumb associated with an underlying disease, such as rheumatoid arthritis or diabetes mellitus that may impact recovery?

Regarding treatment:

- If underlying cause is known, how is it being managed?
- Were anti-inflammatory medications successful in reducing the swelling? If not, are corticosteroid injections now indicated?
- If surgery was required to open the tunnel area, was it followed by physical therapy to restore normal hand movement?

Regarding prognosis:

- Was condition resolved by surgical intervention?
- Did individual experience any complications as a result of the open surgical release?
- If inflammation was caused by an underlying disease, how is that condition being addressed?
- Is there a chance that chronic inflammation may cause recurring trigger finger problems?
- If related to a certain occupation or repetitive task, will individual be able to avoid that activity?
- Have methods of performing work tasks been evaluated?
- What preventive measures are being taken to avoid recurrence?

References

Kessler, R.M. Management of Common Musculoskeletal Disorders: Physical Therapy Principles and Methods. Philadelphia: J.B. Lippincott Company, 1990.

Patient Education Committee. Trigger Finger. American Society for Surgery of the Hand. 2001. 16 Jan 2001 <http://www.hand-surg.org/brochures/trigger.asp>.

Tubal Ligation

Other names / synonyms: Bilateral Endoscopic Destruction of the Fallopian Tubes, Female Sterilization Surgery, Female Surgical Sterilization, Tied Tubes, Tubal Occlusion, Tubal Sterilization, Tubes Tied

66.2

Definition

Many women use tubal ligation as a permanent method of contraception. The tubal ligation procedure involves surgery that encompasses closure (ligation) of the fallopian tubes to prevent an unfertilized egg from reaching the uterus. The fallopian tubes are paired tubes that connect the ovaries to the uterus and conduct the egg to the uterus. Therefore, when sperm enter the uterus through sexual intercourse, no egg present for fertilization. After the tubal ligation procedure, the ovaries continue to function normally and the eggs released break up and are harmlessly absorbed by the body.

Although tubal ligation is more than 99% effective as a contraceptive, some women have had successful reversals where their fallopian tubes were unblocked and rejoined at a later date. Microsurgical techniques have been successful in restoring fertility in up to 75% of tubal ligation cases. It is important to note that these successful restorations are cases where clips and bands were used to close the tubes rather than more drastic methods such as cauterization. Tubal ligation reversal is very costly and not usually covered by insurance.

In the US, nearly 1 in every 4 married women between the ages of 15 and 44 chooses sterilization as a means of birth control.

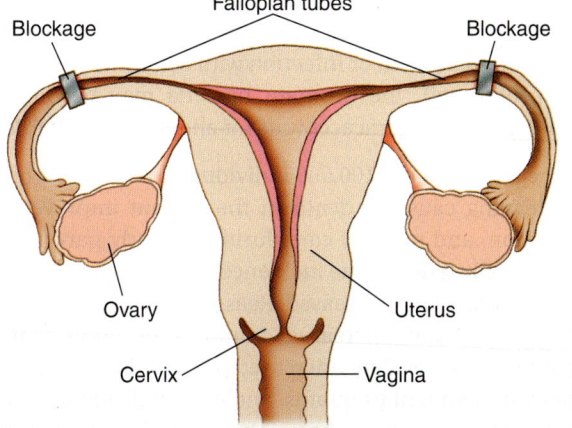

Reason for Procedure

Tubal ligation is performed as a method of contraception because it is very effective and some women are unable to use other methods of contraception. This procedure is performed because the woman may have a health problem that makes pregnancy unsafe or they have a genetic disorder.

Description

The tubal ligation procedure is performed in a hospital or outpatient clinic under local or general anesthesia. Laparoscopy is the most common method and begins with a tiny incision in the abdomen in or near the naval. The surgeon inserts a narrow telescope-like instrument called a laparoscope through the incision. A second small incision is made just above the pubic hairline and a probe is inserted. Once the tubes are found, the surgeon closes them using such techniques as clips, rings, or electric current to cauterize and destroy a portion of the tube (electrocoagulation).

Another method is the mini-laparotomy and requires an incision about 2 inches long in the lower abdomen. It does not employ a viewing instrument. Working from the incision, the surgeon ties and then cuts the tubes.

A third less common more invasive method called laparotomy requires an extensive 2- to 5-inch incision in the lower abdomen. Two other procedures called magnified visual inspection (culdoscopy) and surgical incision in the vagina (colpotomy) facilitate reaching the ovaries through the vagina rather than the abdomen. Neither of these procedures is used very often. Decisions regarding the most appropriate method for a given woman depend on the woman's age, weight, previous lower abdominal surgeries, heart and lung conditions, and other considerations.

Prognosis

Predicted outcome after tubal ligation is good. Most individuals recover with no problems associated with the anesthesia or the surgery. The rate of pregnancy after the procedure is very low (less than 1%).

Specialists

- Gynecologist
- Obstetrician
- Surgeon

Work Restrictions / Accommodations

Most individuals treated with the laparoscopy method can return to work within a few days with the provision that they not engage in heavy lifting or other strenuous work duties for up to 2 weeks. Individuals treated with the laparotomies require more sick leave and a longer restriction on strenuous work duties.

Comorbid Conditions

Comorbid conditions that may influence length of disability include obesity, previous lower abdominal surgeries, heart and lung conditions, and allergy to pain and anesthesiology medications.

Procedure Complications

Although most individuals recover from the tubal ligation procedure with no problems, complications have been reported. Complications related to anesthesia include reaction to anesthesia drugs and breathing problems. Complications related to the surgery include bleeding and infection. On rare occasions, the bowels or blood vessels are injured and may require major surgical repair. An additional complication is possible fertility that could result in pregnancy and stems from incomplete closure of the tubes. Although the rate of pregnancy after tubal ligation is very low, there is a 10-times-greater-than-normal risk that if a pregnancy does occur, the fertilized egg or ovum will be implanted in a fallopian tube rather than the uterus (ectopic). Ectopic pregnancy can be a life-threatening condition.

Factors Influencing Duration

Length of disability may be influenced by whether the tubal ligation was done following delivery, the method used (laparoscopy, minilaparotomy, and laparotomy), and any complications.

Length of Disability

Most individuals can return to work or resume previous activities with minor restrictions. For individuals treated with the more intensive methods such as mini-laparotomy or laparotomy, return to work may be delayed and restrictions are more confining. For duration information, see salpingectomy. Those individuals who perform heavy or very heavy work may require additional lifting restrictions.

Laparoscopic.

Duration in Days

Job Classification	Minimum	Optimum	Maximum
Any work	1	3	7

References

Dott, Andrew, and Caroline Dott. Laparoscopic Surgery. New York Times. 31 May 2000. 25 Jul 2000 <http://www.midlife-passages.com>.

Koop, C. Everett. Tubal Ligation. 01 Jul 2000. 25 Jul 2000 <http://www.drkoop.com/ency/article/002913.htm>.

Simon, Harvey, and Carol Peckham. Female Contraception. Nidus Scientific Publications. 01 Dec 1999. 26 Jul 2000 <http://www.well-connected.com>.

Tierney, Lawrence M., Stephen J. McPhee, and Maxine A. Papadakis, eds. Current Medical Diagnosis and Treatment, 39th ed. New York: Lange Medical Books/McGraw-Hill, 2000.

Tuberculosis, Respiratory

Other names / synonyms: Consumption, TB, White Death, White Plague

011, 011.0, 011.4, 011.8, 011.9, 012, 137

Definition

Tuberculosis (TB) is a chronic infection of the lungs caused by the bacterium Mycobacterium tuberculosis. It is contagious and can be very difficult to treat. The disease is spread through airborne droplets expelled from an infected individual's mouth through coughing, sneezing, or spitting.

If the bacterium is inhaled, the lungs respond by walling off the infected area in nodules known as tubercles. Visible upon x-ray, this stage of TB is termed primary tuberculosis and for most individuals, the immune system stops the disease here. However, 10% of these individuals develop an active TB infection. An active infection occurs when the bacteria spread from the original site into the blood or lymph systems, then move to other areas where they cause infection (extrapulmonary tuberculosis). Although most common in the lung, TB infections can also occur in the skin, kidneys, bones, reproductive, and urinary systems.

Although the body's immune system tries to control the infection instead of being destroyed, the bacteria may instead become inactive (dormant). At a later time (perhaps years), if the individual's immune system becomes impaired (due to leukemia, lymphoma, cancer, steroid therapy, radiation treatment, or infection with certain viruses including HIV, bacteria, or fungi), the dormant bacteria may become active. Activation of dormant bacteria accounts for about 80% of TB infections.

There are 9.8 cases of TB per 100,000 individuals in the US. At one time, TB was the leading cause of death in the US but improvements in hygiene, nutrition, and medical care during the early part of the 20th century dramatically reduced the incidence of TB. Since 1985, however, the number of TB cases has increased. Reasons for this increase include the HIV/AIDS epidemic, increased numbers of immigrants from countries where TB is prevalent, increased poverty, illicit drug use, poor compliance with treatment programs, and more individuals residing in nursing homes. On a worldwide basis, about 8 million new cases of TB are reported each year and about 2 million individuals die every year of the disease. Areas where TB is especially high include sub-Saharan Africa, Southeast Asia, and Eastern Europe.

Diagnosis

History: Individuals with early symptoms may report fatigue, weight loss, fever, night sweats, and loss of appetite. As the disease progresses, there may be chest pain with a productive cough. Sputum also increases and may eventually be streaked with blood. Shortness of breath may indicate damage in the lungs.

Physical exam: Individuals with TB are often chronically ill. Chest sounds may be abnormal. Weight loss and muscle wasting ("consumption") may be present.

Tests: A tuberculin skin test (Mantoux test) is used to identify individuals infected with the TB bacteria 6 to 8 weeks after exposure. A positive test, however, does not indicate that the individual has active TB, only that there has been an infection by the bacteria sometime in the past. Because this test can report false negative with a recent infection (less than 2 to 3 months previously) or in immunocompromised individuals (HIV), it should be repeated if a person has recent exposure to TB.

An x-ray identifies the characteristic lesions in the lungs and may also reveal fluid in the pleural space (pleural effusion) or an enlarged heart (pericarditis). An x-ray of the kidneys using injected dye outlines the kidneys, revealing abnormal masses or cavities that may be caused by TB.

To confirm the diagnosis, a culture is used to identify the TB bacteria. Material for culture may include a sample of material expelled from the lungs (sputum), infected fluid drawn from the chest, abdomen, joint, or around the heart, or a small piece of infected tissue (biopsy). Because TB bacteria grow very slowly, this culture can take up to 4 weeks. Cultures are also used in sensitivity tests to determine what drugs will best combat the bacteria. A polymerase chain reaction (PCR) may be performed on a sample of spinal cord fluid to identify tuberculous meningitis. Tuberculosis of the female reproductive organs may be identified through examination of the pelvis using a laparoscope or from scrapings inside the uterus.

Newer and more rapid DNA tests are beginning to be used for diagnosis. These tests use techniques that amplify the tuberculosis bacterial DNA, and can speed the time for diagnosis to 2 days.

Individuals with TB should also be tested for HIV infection since TB often occurs early in the course of HIV infection.

Treatment

Because the emergence of drug-resistant strains of TB bacteria has made treatment difficult, the disease is typically treated with a combination of antibiotics, i.e., isoniazid and rifampin for 6 to 12 months and pyrazinamide and ethambutol for 2 months. Although individuals with pulmonary TB are usually not contagious after 10 to 14 days of drug therapy, treatment should be continued for 3 months after sputum cultures are negative for the TB bacteria.

More resistant strains of TB are treated for 18 to 24 months with more powerful antibiotics that have more serious side effects. Successful treatment requires cooperation between the individual and health care providers. Individual's compliance is a problem with TB treatment due to the side effects of the drugs. For example, isoniazid and rifampin can cause hepatitis, and ethambutol can cause vision problems. If an individual does not complete treatment, the cure rate decreases and there is an increased risk of developing drug-resistant TB.

In order to prevent the development of active TB, treatment can be given to individuals in close contact with infected individuals and to those with a positive skin test. Individuals with active TB need to take precautions to prevent the spread of the disease by properly covering their mouths and noses when they cough and sneeze and by washing their hands.

Although a vaccine for TB is available, it is not widely used in the US, as its effectiveness is not known.

Prognosis

With appropriate antibiotic therapy, TB can be cured 90% of the time. Individuals with pulmonary TB are usually not contagious after 10 to 14 days of drug treatment. However, a follow-up sputum analysis should be performed to make sure there is no longer any danger of transmission. Treatment should be continued for 3 months after sputum cultures are negative for the TB bacteria. Drugs used to treat TB however, have many side effects and should be constantly monitored.

Relapse of TB often occurs as a result of noncompliance with treatment. With complete and proper treatment, relapse rates are less than 5%.

Individuals infected with resistant strains of TB have a lower cure rate. Strains of TB bacteria resistant to two or more drugs (multidrug-resistant) can have a death rate of 40-60% similar to that for untreated TB.

Differential Diagnosis

Conditions with symptoms similar to pulmonary TB include pneumonia, lung abscess, tumors, and fungal infections of the lung.

Specialists

- Infectious Disease Physician
- Pulmonologist

Rehabilitation

Physical and respiratory therapy applied in conjunction with medications can be important in the overall treatment of the individual with TB. Physical therapy improves ventilation through breathing exercises localized to the area of lung involvement and then followed by a gradual strengthening program. When tolerated, an exercise that promotes both relaxation and a postural alteration for the muscles that aid in breathing begins with the individual assuming a relaxed sitting position while leaning forward and resting the forearms on the thighs or a pillow in the lap.

When hospitalized, the physical therapist and/or respiratory therapist help the individual cough in order to mobilize secretions and clear the airway by having the individual lie in a position that allows for the most effective drainage of secretions. The individual may lie on his or her side with the affected side upward and the head slightly lower than the chest. In addition to proper positioning, the physical therapist uses percussion and vibration techniques to the affected areas to help "shake loose" mucous and secretions. The therapist performs chest percussion with the hands in a cupped position, mildly striking repeatedly over the area of the lung affected by TB.

Once medications are effective and the symptoms of TB subside, and breathing becomes easier, focus is then placed on strength and endurance by incorporating aerobic-type activity into the rehabilitation program. By building endurance, the individual increases the ability to work and the resistance to fatigue. A physical therapist experienced in cardiac and pulmonary rehabilitation keeps a daily log of the individual's blood pressure, heart rate, and cardiac rhythm. As endurance increases without symptoms of shortness of breath, the individual begins active upper and lower extremity exercises using very light resistance in addition to light aerobic activities such as brisk walking and low-resistance biking.

The individual with TB is told that the exercise program can be a lengthy process in order to obtain the maximum benefit of increased pulmonary stamina. Because most individuals with TB are managed with medication, it is important that they let the rehabilitation personnel know what medications they are taking as many of these drugs alter the acute and chronic response to exercise. During the course of rehabilitation, the individual is reminded that a full course of therapy is necessary to kill all the bacteria. Failure to properly complete treatment can create drug-resistant strains of the disease that may render the treatment ineffective.

Work Restrictions / Accommodations

Individuals with pulmonary TB are usually not contagious after 10 to 14 days of drug treatment. However, a follow-up sputum analysis should be performed to make sure there is no longer any danger of transmission. Decreased lung capacity may make strenuous activity difficult. Significant loss of vital organ function due to secondary or opportunistic infections may lengthen disability or require permanent accommodations.

Comorbid Conditions

Dormant TB bacteria may again become activated if the immune system becomes impaired by leukemia, lymphoma, cancer, steroid therapy, radiation treatment, or infection with certain viruses including HIV, bacteria, or fungi. Activation of dormant bacteria accounts for about 80% of TB infections.

Complications

Complications of TB may include collapsed lung and abscess in the lymph nodes. TB that has spread outside the lungs (extrapulmonary tuberculosis) commonly affects the kidney, bones, and joints (tuberculous arthritis). The infection may spread to the prostate, seminal vesicles, and epididymis in men, and to the peritoneum (tuberculous peritonitis) in women. Scarring of the ovaries and fallopian tubes can cause sterility. TB can spread to the heart (tuberculous pericarditis) or the base of the brain (tuberculous meningitis). Delayed treatment can result in irreparable brain damage. Tuberculous meningitis can also result in a brain tumor (tuberculoma).

Factors Influencing Duration

Length of disability may be influenced by the severity and extent of infection, response to treatment, and whether the infection has spread to other body systems. Individuals with a drug-resistant strain of bacteria or those with a weakened immune system may have a longer period of disability. Individuals experiencing drug side effects may also experience extended disability.

Length of Disability

Medical treatment.

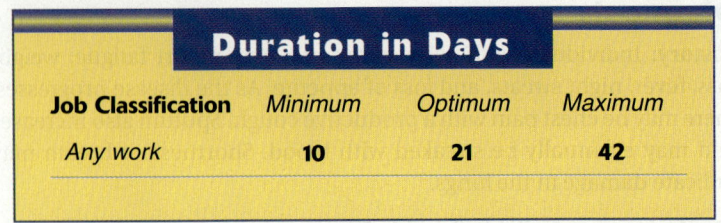

Job Classification	Minimum	Optimum	Maximum
Any work	10	21	42

Failure to Recover

If an individual fails to recover within the maximum duration expectancy period, the reader may wish to reference the following questions to assist in better understanding the specifics of an individual's medical case.

Regarding diagnosis:

- Were symptoms such as fatigue, weight loss, fever, night sweats, and loss of appetite, chest pain or a productive cough present?
- Does individual have a history of past infection or recent exposure to tuberculosis?
- Does individual have underlying immune suppression (i.e., HIV, leukemia, lymphoma, cancer, steroid or radiation treatment)?
- Did individual have a positive Mantoux test? Was the diagnosis confirmed with a sputum culture?
- Were additional diagnostic tests done to rule out the possibility of other organ involvement?
- If the diagnosis is uncertain, were other conditions with similar symptoms (i.e., other lung infections, sarcoidosis or lung cancer) ruled out?

Regarding treatment:

- Did individual receive prompt diagnosis and appropriate antibiotic therapy?
- Has individual been compliant with antibiotic treatment regimen?
- Has individual undergone follow-up cultures to verify effectiveness of treatment?
- Has individual experienced any side effects from the medication?
- Has individual stopped taking medication because of side effects? If so, what alternatives are available?
- Does individual fully understand the importance of completing the whole course of medication?

Regarding prognosis:

- Based on the severity of symptoms, the type of treatment required and the general health of individual, what was the expected outcome?
- Has adequate time elapsed for recovery?
- Has individual completed the full course of medications?
- Have repeat cultures been done to determine if there is drug resistance? Have appropriate changes been made in the medications?
- Does individual have an underlying condition (HIV or other immune suppressing condition) that may impact ability to recover?

References

Brooks, G.F., J.S. Butel, and S.A. Morse. Medical Microbiology. Stamford: Appleton & Lange, 1998.

Scully, Rosemary M., and Marylou Barnes. Physical Therapy. Philadelphia: J.B. Lippincott Company, 1989.

Tularemia

Other names / synonyms: Bacterium Tularense, Deer Fly Fever, Francis' Disease, O'Hara's Disease, Parvovirus B_{19} Infection, Pasteurella Tularensis, Rabbit Fever, Tick Fever

021, 021.0, 021.1, 021.2, 021.3, 021.8, 021.9, 026

Definition

Tularemia is an infection caused by the bacteria Francisella tularensis. It is transmitted from wild animals to humans by direct contact with infected animal tissues, or through the bite of an insect such as a tick or a deer fly. Airborne bacteria can be inhaled into the lungs. Although rare, tularemia may also be transmitted through eating inadequately cooked meat or drinking contaminated water. While most cases of tularemia are characterized by fever, chills, fatigue, and a generalized feeling of illness (malaise), severe cases can result in a widespread, life-threatening disease.

There are several forms of tularemia. The most common form, ulceroglandular tularemia, accounts for about 80% of all cases and is characterized by skin ulcer(s) and swollen lymph glands on the same side as the infection. Glandular tularemia is also characterized by swollen glands but without skin ulcers, indicating the bacteria was probably ingested. Typhoidal tularemia is characterized by a high fever, abdominal pain, and exhaustion. Tularemia involving the lungs is called pneumonic tularemia. Oropharyngeal tularemia involves a sore throat and swollen glands. The most rare form of tularemia, accounting for only about 1% of cases, is oculoglandular tularemia. Probably caused by touching the eye with an infected finger, oculoglandular tularemia causes redness and swelling in the infected eye along with the swollen lymph nodes.

In the US, wild cottontail rabbits are the main source of the disease. Risk factors include geographic location (in the US, more than half of reported cases occur in Arkansas, Missouri, Oklahoma, Tennessee, and Texas), outdoor work, rural residence, handling of wild game, and laboratory work. Hunters, butchers, fur handlers, and laboratory workers are the most commonly infected. In the Midwest, tularemia occurs most frequently in the summer when ticks and deer flies are common. East of the Mississippi River, most cases are seen in the winter when cottontail rabbits are hunted. Men are more commonly affected than women. Elderly individuals and individuals with a compromised immune system are at a higher risk for more severe disease.

In the US, approximately 150-300 cases are seen per year. Worldwide, the incidence is much higher, with nearly 500,000 cases per year.

Diagnosis

History: Includes exposure to wild animals (particularly rabbits), ticks, or deer flies in areas where the disease is known to exist. Symptoms develop within 10 days (usually 2-4 days) of exposure to the bacteria. Individuals who work in a laboratory will report working with animals or bacterial isolates. Symptoms include rapid onset of a high fever, headache, nausea, and weakness. Some individuals will report vomiting and extreme fatigue and/or chills associated with profuse sweating. In most cases a red, itchy blister develops at the site of infection, usually on the finger, arm, eye, or roof of the mouth. The blister, which fills with pus, quickly ulcerates. Swollen and painful lymph nodes may be reported. Difficulty breathing, unproductive or dry cough, and a burning sensation in the chest may be symptoms if tularemia involves the lungs (pneumonic tularemia). Less commonly, there may be abdominal pain and diarrhea. A sore throat is seen in oropharyngeal tularemia. When the eye is involved, typically only one eye is affected. The individual may complain of eye pain, sensitivity to light, tearing, and a discharge from the eye.

Physical exam: The exam may reveal a nonspecific rash on the trunk or extremities, fever of 104-106 degrees F, and an enlarged liver and/or spleen. Listening to the chest might reveal signs of pneumonia. There may be signs of other organs being affected, including the heart, brain, and bones. Delirium may be noted in some cases of pneumonic tularemia. Bacterial infection of the blood (septicemia) and a toxic reaction (toxemia) are characteristics of typhoidal tularemia. Cases of oculoglandular tularemia are associated with inflammation of the mucous membrane of the eye (conjunctivitis) and multiple ulcers. If the individual is a laboratory worker, the infection might only affect the lungs and the lymph nodes, making diagnosis difficult.

Tests: A blood test (serum agglutinins) will be positive after the second week of illness, and may stay positive for years. Blood tests will also reveal antibodies to the bacteria. The level of antibodies will rise steadily, peaking 4-8 weeks after infection. The bacterium can be cultured from an ulcer, sputum, or infected lymph node, confirming the diagnosis. If pneumonic tularemia is suspected, a chest x-ray may be performed to assess lung involvement.

Treatment

Depending on the severity of the infection, treatment may require inpatient care. Fever-reducing drugs (antipyretics) are given until the fever subsides. Antibiotics are usually given, orally or by injection, for 1-2 weeks. Pain medication (analgesics) may be prescribed. Skin ulcers are wrapped in moist bandages, which are changed frequently to prevent the spread of infection. Ulcers in the eye are treated with eye drop antibiotics and possibly eye drop anti-inflammatory medications. If the individual is dehydrated, fluids are given. Treatment of pneumonia is supportive in nature. In severe cases, corticosteroids may be used to reduce inflammation. Abscesses may be drained to relieve some of the discomfort (incision and drainage).

A vaccine is available to high-risk individuals.

Prognosis

When diagnosed early and treated promptly, the prognosis for tularemia is good. Most individuals achieve a full recovery. With treatment, the overall mortality rate is about 1-3%. Mortality rate, however, increases to about 6% for typhoidal-type infections. Severe, complicated, or untreated cases, or individuals with compromised immunity experience, can experience delayed recovery and have a higher incidence of mortality. Individuals who recover from tularemia may have immunity to further infection.

Differential Diagnosis

Conditions with similar symptoms include pyoderma, staphylococcal infections, streptococcal infections, cat-scratch disease, Pasteurella infections, lymphogranuloma venereum, sporotrichosis, plague, toxoplasmosis, legionellosis, Rocky Mountain spotted fever, ehrlichiosis, borreliosis (including Lyme disease), non-typhoid salmonellosis, typhoid fever, brucellosis, Q-fever, psittacosis, tick-borne typhus, viral pneumonia, viral pharyngitis, diphtheric pharyngitis, anthrax, and infectious mononucleosis.

Specialists

- Cardiologist
- Dermatologist
- Gastroenterologist
- Hematologist
- Industrial Hygienist
- Nephrologist
- Neurologist
- Ophthalmologist
- Otolaryngologist
- Pulmonologist
- Rheumatologist

Work Restrictions / Accommodations

Work restrictions may not be required. Complicated cases, severe infections, or infections involving the lungs, heart, or brain may include restrictions as symptoms dictate. Shortness of breath and rapid exhaustion may necessitate restriction from heavy or strenuous work. Individuals who work closely with other people, particularly those who have contact with elderly or immunocompromised individuals, may require extended absence to prevent spreading the infection. Frequent breaks to change bandages may be required until skin ulcers heal. If the eye is involved, tasks requiring keen eyesight, bright lights, or dusty environments should be avoided. Safety glasses and/or sunglasses may be required.

Comorbid Conditions

Elderly individuals and those with a compromised immune system may experience a more severe illness with a longer period of disability.

Complications

The infection can result in pneumonia, lung abscess, respiratory distress syndrome, liver dysfunction, rhabdomyolysis, kidney failure, pericarditis, endocarditis, peritonitis, meningitis, mediastinitis, or osteomyelitis. If another medical condition is present that involves depressed immunity, tularemia will present as a more serious disease.

Factors Influencing Duration

Length of disability will be influenced by severity of the symptoms, response to treatment, and the development of secondary infections. Immunosuppressed and elderly individuals are at greater risk for severe disease, with possibly a longer recovery period.

Length of Disability

Disability may be permanent, particularly if the lungs or heart are involved.

Systemic/pneumonia.

Duration in Days

Job Classification	Minimum	Optimum	Maximum
Sedentary work	7	10	28
Light work	7	10	28
Medium work	7	10	28
Heavy work	14	14	28
Very Heavy work	14	14	28

Failure to Recover

If an individual fails to recover within the maximum duration expectancy period, the reader may wish to reference the following questions to assist in better understanding the specifics of an individual's medical case.

Regarding diagnosis:

- Has individual a history of exposure to wild animals or to ticks?
- Has the diagnosis of tularemia been confirmed with a blood test or culture of the bacteria from an ulcer, sputum, or infected lymph node?
- What form of tularemia did individual have?
- What organ or body system was affected?
- If the diagnosis was uncertain, were other conditions with similar symptoms ruled out (pyoderma, staphylococcal infections, streptococcal infections, cat-scratch disease, Pasteurella infections, lymphogranuloma venereum, sporotrichosis, plague, toxoplasmosis, legionellosis, Rocky Mountain spotted fever, ehrlichiosis, borreliosis, non-typhoid salmonellosis, typhoid fever, brucellosis, Q-fever, psittacosis, tick-borne typhus, viral pneumonia, viral pharyngitis, diphtheric pharyngitis, anthrax, and infectious mononucleosis)?

Regarding treatment:

- Was prompt treatment with antibiotics received?
- Is individual following instructions regarding medication use and dosage, rest, hydration, and/or bandage changing?
- If unable or incapable of following treatment regimen, would individual qualify for outside help? Visiting nurse?
- Has inpatient treatment and/or intravenous antibiotic therapy been considered? If not, why not?

Regarding prognosis:

- Did individual receive prompt diagnosis and treatment?
- Based on the severity of the disease and the general health of individual, what was the expected prognosis?
- Has individual experienced any associated conditions or complications (pneumonia, lung abscess, respiratory distress syndrome, liver dysfunction, rhabdomyolysis, kidney failure, pericarditis, endocarditis, peritonitis, meningitis, mediastinitis, or osteomyelitis) that could impact recovery and prognosis? Are these conditions being addressed in the treatment plan?
- Are there any underlying circumstances such as advanced age or immune system compromise that could impact ability to recover?

References

Case Definitions for Public Health Surveillance - Tularemia. Center for Disease Control. 01 Sep 1996. 14 Sep 2000 <http://www.cdc.gov/epo/dphsi/casedef/tulare97.htm>.

Elders, Greg. "Tularemia." Griffith's 5-minute Clinical Consult. Dambro, Mark, ed. Philadelphia: Lippincott, Williams & Wilkins, 2000. 1116-1117.

Tumor, Benign

Other names / synonyms: Benign Lesion, Benign Mass, Benign Neoplasm, Non-Cancerous Tumor
210, 211, 212, 223, 223.3, 225, 225.0, 225.2, 227, 227.4, 229, 229.9

Definition

A tumor or neoplasm is defined as an abnormal mass of tissue that forms when cells in a specific area reproduce at an increased rate. These cells are derived from normal cells but they undergo changes making them unresponsive to normal controls that help the body limit growth. These cells continue to grow faster than the surrounding tissue and form an abnormal mass of tissue.

Two basic types of tumors are distinguished by their growth patterns and effects on the body and are benign tumors and malignant (cancerous) tumors. Benign tumors grow as well-defined masses. As they grow, they push normal cells out of the way rather than invade the tissue like cancerous tumors. A benign tumor may form a capsule of connective tissue around itself that separates the tumor from adjacent normal cells. Growth of a benign tumor is usually slow and may not increase in size for months or years. Benign tumors do not travel to distant sites in the body (metastasize) like malignant tumors. However, benign tumors may sometimes grow in groups. Although benign tumors are generally localized (restricted to a limited area), they can interfere with normally functioning tissue if they grow large enough to press on nearby structures, block a blood vessel, impinge a nerve, or grow in a vital area of the brain. This can be particularly dangerous in confined spaces such as inside the skull.

It is unclear what causes the development of benign tumors however there are many factors such as environmental exposure, genetics, diet, emotional stress, and others that may be possible causes. In some cases, gender is a factor in the development of certain types of benign tumors. In most cases, benign tumors occur with equal frequency in both genders and can develop in most any region of the body.

Diagnosis

History: Symptoms depend on the site of the growth, the tissue of origin, and size of the growth. Individuals may report noticing a lump or skin change. They may complain of nausea, the sense of fullness, or weight loss if the tumor is in the abdomen and is pressing on the stomach or nearby structures. Tumors can cause pain or nervous system disorder such as dizziness, vision problems, weakness, or headaches by pressing on or disturbing nerve tracts.

Physical exam: Physical findings may vary according to the site and size of the tumor. Examination may reveal a lump or skin change when the tumor is located in the soft tissue or muscle such as the breast, abdomen, muscle, or skin. However, if the tumor is small and located in the deep structures such as the lungs, brain, or other organs, there may be no noticeable physical abnormalities.

Tests: Diagnostic tests that produce images of internal organs include x-ray, ultrasound, CT, and MRI. A mammogram uses low-dose x-ray to identify changes in the breast tissue. Direct inspection of certain internal organs uses an endoscope, a small, lighted tube that is passed into the organ or cavity to be examined. This technique is utilized for examinations of the colon (colonoscopy), stomach and adjacent organs (gastroscopy), bladder (cystoscopy), and abdominal cavity (laparoscopy). These procedures are generally performed if an abnormality is suspected.

Diagnosis is confirmed by a microscopic examination of tumor tissue cells that have been surgically removed (biopsy). Benign tumor (neoplasm) cells retain many of the same features as the tissue they were found in.

Treatment

Treatment of choice is to surgically remove the tumor. The type of surgery required is specific to the location of the tumor and the anatomic area affected by the tumor. If the tumor is located in an inaccessible area, radiation therapy can slow or destroy the production and development of abnormal cells. Some benign tumors such as fatty tumors (lipomas) on the skin produce no symptoms and do not need to be removed.

Prognosis

The outcome following surgical removal of a benign tumor is usually good if the tumor is located in an accessible area. Symptoms are usually relieved with the removal of the tumor. A benign tumor may be incurable if it has infiltrated vital tissue. If the tumor cannot be removed, radiation therapy can slow or destroy the production and development of abnormal cells.

Differential Diagnosis

Malignant tumors, foreign bodies, or pockets of infected material (abscesses) may present with similar symptoms.

Specialists

- Dermatologist
- Endocrinologist
- Gastroenterologist
- General Surgeon
- Gynecologist
- Internist
- Neurologist
- Primary Care Provider
- Urologist

Work Restrictions / Accommodations

The location of the tumor and type of surgical treatment dictate any work restrictions or accommodations needed.

Comorbid Conditions

Comorbid conditions of bleeding disorders or immune suppression may impact the ability to recover from any surgical intervention and lengthen disability. Pre-existing conditions that affect the structure or function of the body part involved (i.e., Parkinson's disease as a pre-existing condition to the development of a benign brain tumor) may impact ability to recover and lengthen disability.

Complications

Complications are determined by the site and extent of the disease. Benign tumors can obstruct passageways, press on nerve tracts causing nervous system disorders, disrupt the function of a vital organ, cause mental and physical disabilities, and may result in death. Brain tumors may have serious complications because of pressure on normal brain tissue. A brain tumor on the lining of the brain (meningioma) even though benign may be incurable when it infiltrates brain tissue or is in a location where it cannot be surgically removed or radiated.

Factors Influencing Duration

Length of disability depends on the type of tumor, location of the tumor, whether treatment is effective, type of treatment required, and individual's response to treatment.

Length of Disability

Vague diagnosis. Disability depends on specific diagnosis, site, stage, grade, and method of treatment. Contact physician for specific diagnosis.

Failure to Recover

If an individual fails to recover within the maximum duration expectancy period, the reader may wish to reference the following questions to assist in better understanding the specifics of an individual's medical case.

Regarding diagnosis:

- Was presence of a tumor determined with a physical exam and diagnostic tests (CT, ultrasound, MRI)?
- Was diagnosis of benign tumor confirmed with a biopsy?
- Were conditions with similar symptoms, such as malignancy, foreign body or abscess, ruled out?
- Was tumor interfering with normal function of adjacent organs or structures?
- Was it accessible for surgical removal or treatment with radiation?

Regarding treatment:

- Was the tumor surgically removed? Was surgeon able to remove all the abnormal tissue?
- If the tumor is inaccessible, has radiation therapy been tried?
- How effective has radiation therapy been in halting or slowing the growth of the tumor?

Regarding prognosis:

- Was the tumor successfully removed?
- If not able to remove all the tissue, what impact does remaining tissue have on function?
- Did surgery impact or alter individual's functional capabilities?
- Has individual received appropriate follow-up care to monitor the status of the tumor?
- Has tumor stopped growing?
- Does individual have an underlying condition (underlying organ dysfunction, bleeding disorder or immune suppression) that may impact recovery?

References

Tierney, Lawrence M., Stephen J. McPhee, and Maxine Papadakis. Current Medical Diagnosis and Treatment, 39th ed. New York: Lange Medical Books/McGraw-Hill, 2000.

Tympanoplasty

Other names / synonyms: Eardrum Repair, Myringoplasty

19.4, 19.5

Definition

Tympanoplasty is a surgical procedure performed on the eardrum (tympanic membrane). There are 3 primary problems that this procedure is used for. These include a hole in the eardrum (perforation), calcium deposits, or a deformity known as a retraction pocket.

The procedure is done in a hospital under general anesthesia and takes 2-3 hours. It may be done through the ear canal (transcanal approach) or via an incision behind the ear (postauricular approach). A membrane (usually fascia) is applied on top (overlay) or underneath the original eardrum (underlay) as a patch or plug to repair the hole.

The most common reason for the surgery is repair of a perforation caused by infection, injury, or previous placement of tubes. Tubes are used to allow drainage and equalize the pressure in the space behind the eardrum. It may also be performed where the perforation in the eardrum did not completely heal via other means.

There are numerous causes for damages to the middle ear. Severe or chronic middle-ear infection is a major cause. Insertion of a sharp object in the ear such as a cotton swab to clean the ear or relieve an itch; an unseen twig on a tree, or hot slag from an industrial site may damage the eardrum. A sudden inward pressure in the ear, such as with a slap; a swimming or diving accident; a nearby explosion, or a sudden outward pressure or suction may also be a causative factor.

Risks for damages to the middle ear and other problems of the eardrum increase with recent middle-ear infections or head injuries.

Reason for Procedure

Tympanoplasty is performed to correct a number of problems: a hole in the eardrum (perforation), calcium deposits, a damaged middle ear, or a deformity known as a retraction pocket. Hearing loss can be treated with the associated repair of the small bones of the middle ear. It may also be performed to repair damage that did not heal following other methods of treatment. The most common reason for tympanoplasty is perforation caused by infection, injury, or previous placement of tubes.

Description

The procedure is performed under general anesthesia and takes 2-3 hours. It may be done through the ear canal (transcanal approach) or via an incision behind the ear (postauricular approach).

In a transcanal approach, an instrument called an ear speculum is placed in the external ear canal, and an operating microscope is positioned. If necessary, the middle ear can be entered through an incision in the eardrum. Depending on the defect, a direct repair of a defect in the eardrum can be performed; or a closure of the defect in the eardrum can be done with a skin or vein graft.

For problems with the small bones (ossicles), as in conductive hearing loss, the surgeon will use an operating microscope to view and repair the chain of small bones (ossicles) using plastic devices or the small bones from a donor.

Hearing is usually tested before and after surgery. Individuals usually leave the hospital the same day. Water in the ear must be avoided. A hair cap should be used when showering for a few weeks to keep the ear dry. No changes in activity or diet are needed following the procedure.

Prognosis

In most cases, tympanoplasty relieves pain and infection symptoms completely. Hearing loss may be minor. Success depends on the size of the area to be repaired, and whether or not there are problems with other parts of the ear. If both eardrums are perforated, the success rate is lower. The procedure can have a less optimistic outcome if the eardrum has become attached to the small bones of the middle ear.

Specialists

- Otolaryngologist

Work Restrictions / Accommodations

Hearing may need to be evaluated if it is important to the individual's job. Loud noise and changes in atmospheric pressure may need to be avoided. Ear protection may be required.

Comorbid Conditions

Smoking; chronic illnesses; and the use of drugs such as antihypertensives, muscle relaxants, tranquilizers, sleep inducers, insulin, sedatives, beta-adrenergic blockers, or cortisone may make surgery more risky. The use of mind-altering drugs, including narcotics, psychedelics, hallucinogens, marijuana, sedatives, hypnotics, or cocaine may make the outcome of surgery and recovery unpredictable.

Procedure Complications

All surgery carries a risk of bleeding, infection, and reactions to pain medicines. The main complication specific to this surgery is a disturbance in taste. This may happen if a certain nerve that runs right behind the eardrum is injured. As with any ear surgery, there are also the risks of dizziness and deafness. Additional risks include incomplete healing of the hole in the eardrum and damage to the small bones in the middle ear, causing hearing loss.

Factors Influencing Duration

The site and size of the perforation, status of the middle ear, the type of surgical approach used, surgical results, and the individual's reaction to the procedure affect length of disability. The state of the individual's health will affect the length of the recovery period.

Length of Disability

Job requirements may influence disability duration.

Duration in Days

Job Classification	Minimum	Optimum	Maximum
Sedentary work	2	3	5
Light work	4	6	7
Medium work	7	10	14
Heavy work	7	10	14
Very Heavy work	7	10	14

References

Beers, Mark H., MD, and Robert Berkow, MD, eds. The Merck Manual of Diagnosis and Therapy, 17th ed. Rahway, NJ: Merck & Co., Inc, 1999. 6 Jan 2000 <http://merck.com/pubs/mmanual>.

Tierney, Lawrence, Stephen McPhee, and Maxine Papadakis. Current Medical Diagnosis and Treatment. New York: McGraw-Hill, 2000.

Tympanum Perforation
Other names / synonyms: Perforated Eardrum, Ruptured Eardrum
384.20

Definition

Tympanum perforation is an injury (opening, erosion, or rupture) to the eardrum (tympanic membrane) as a result of infection, trauma, or the negative pressure associated with underwater diving or flying in an airplane.

The tympanic membrane is a thin, semitransparent membrane, nearly oval in shape stretching across the ear canal that separates the middle ear (tympanum) from the outer ear (external acoustic meatus). It is composed of fibrous tissue and covered with skin on the outside and mucous membrane on the inside. The tympanic membrane vibrates freely with audible sound waves that travel inward from the outside. The handle of the malleus (one of the bones or ossicles of the middle ear) is attached to the center of the tympanic membrane. It receives the vibrations collected by the membrane and transmits them to other bones of the middle ear (the incus and stapes), and eventually to the fluid of the inner ear as part of the hearing process.

The majority of tympanum perforations are related to infection of the middle ear. During an upper respiratory infection, swelling (edema) occurs in the narrow channel (eustachian tube) that connects the tympanum with the back of the throat (nasopharynx). This swelling causes fluid and mucus to accumulate behind the eardrum. When pus-producing bacteria are introduced into this fluid buildup (via the eustachian tube), a middle ear infection occurs (otitis media). As a result of the infection, pressure builds up behind the tympanic membrane, causing severe pain. The membrane sometimes ruptures spontaneously, immediately reducing the pain. In other cases, a physician may make an incision into the membrane (myringotomy) to relieve pressure and pain and drain the infection. A chronic middle ear infection can erode a hole in the eardrum and destroy the structures of the middle ear and mastoid area.

Other causes of tympanum perforation include direct injury from a foreign object such as a cotton-tipped swab being inserted into the ear to relieve irritation, trauma to the ear from a hard slap to the side of the head or a nearby explosion, barotrauma (caused by the sudden change of air pressure during flying or underwater diving), fracture of the base of the skull, and tumor of the middle ear.

Tympanum perforation is a relatively common injury.

Diagnosis

History: The primary symptom of tympanum perforation is hearing loss. An individual may relate a history of upper respiratory infection followed by ear pain, a sharp pain in the ear followed by a sudden decrease in pain and drainage from the ear (clear, containing pus, or bloody), or a chronically draining ear. An individual may also report recent blunt trauma to the side of the head on the affected side or other head trauma, sudden ear pain and hearing loss after insertion of an object into the ear (such as a hairpin, paper clip, or cotton-tipped applicator), or a history of recent air travel or underwater diving. Hearing loss in the affected ear may be partial or complete. Ear noise or buzzing may be present.

Physical exam: An inspection of the ear with an otoscope or microscope shows an opening in the eardrum and may reveal damage to the bones (ossicles) of the middle ear. Crusted blood or drainage of fluid from the middle ear may be present in the ear canal.

Tests: An audiogram may be done to evaluate the extent of hearing loss. An MRI or CT may be ordered to rule out skull fracture or a middle ear tumor, and to gauge the extent of infection in the middle ear and surrounding structures.

Treatment

The goal of treating a tympanum perforation includes providing analgesics for pain relief and antibiotics for the treatment and prevention of infection (oral antibiotics and topical ear drops). A ruptured or perforated tympanic membrane usually heals spontaneously within 2 months. During this time, the individual must prevent moisture from entering the ear as much as possible through use of earplugs when showering and avoidance of swimming and related water activities. The individual is also advised to blow the nose very gently. This helps prevent nasal secretions from being forced into the middle ear through the eustachian tube that can increase the chance of infection.

If the eardrum fails to heal sufficiently within 6 months, a tympanoplasty or myringoplasty may be necessary to repair the perforation. This can include a mastoidectomy to remove infection and other debris from the middle ear and mastoid area. If the ossicles are damaged, a partial or complete prosthesis may be necessary to reconstruct the conductive mechanism. The perforation itself may be closed with a paper graft or tissue (fascia) taken from the temporalis muscle behind the ear.

Prognosis

Most perforations heal by themselves and hearing loss is usually temporary. Successful antibiotic treatment should heal the infection that caused the perforation and prevent further infection before the perforation closes spontaneously or is surgically closed. A ruptured or perforated tympanic membrane usually heals spontaneously within 2 months.

If the eardrum fails to heal sufficiently within 6 months, a tympanoplasty or myringoplasty may be performed to repair the perforation. This can include a mastoidectomy to remove infection and other debris from the middle ear and mastoid area. These surgical procedures are successful in 80-90% of the cases performed, resulting in partial or complete restoration of the hearing mechanism and removal of the infection.

Differential Diagnosis

Tympanum perforation may be caused by a middle ear tumor putting pressure against the inner side of the tympanic membrane. Other underlying causes may be acute or chronic otitis media, acute or chronic infection of the mastoid process (mastoiditis), or a skull fracture.

Specialists

- Emergency Medicine
- Otolaryngologist
- Primary Care Provider

Rehabilitation

Rehabilitation is generally not required for tympanum perforation except in the case of hearing loss. Individuals with permanent conductive hearing loss may require vocational or occupational therapy to help prepare them for a different job. At times, amplification (use of hearing aids) may be required depending on the severity of the hearing loss.

Physical therapy may be required for individuals with balance disorders. Once the initial pain/inflammation of tympanum perforation has resolved, the physical therapist trained in the specialty of vestibular rehabilitation may intervene with vestibular training to help the individual regain balance and coordination. The physical therapist initially begins by evaluating the individual to determine if the balance problem is coming from an inner ear dysfunction or from other areas such as the brain's center for balance. Once this is determined, the therapist establishes a plan of care to treat the individual appropriately. Much of the therapy focuses on balance exercises that challenge the individual's balance with and without the help of visual and sensory stimulus.

Various techniques include walking straight ahead while rotating the head side-to-side and focusing visually on an object. Another technique involves standing on a soft surface (limited sensory stimulus) with the eyes closed (limited visual stimulus) and trying to remain balanced. This is completed first while standing on both legs, then progresses to standing on one leg only. The exercise is timed and advanced in duration, as tolerated. Such techniques increase and retrain balance without the aide of sensory and visual input. The physical therapist may need to modify this program for those individuals with hearing loss because of birth defects, a long-standing infection, or who have undergone surgery.

Work Restrictions / Accommodations

Work restrictions and accommodations for individuals with tympanum perforation are related to the degree of hearing loss the individual experiences. Hearing loss may require long-term or permanent accommodation in the workplace as well as the use of hearing aids. If surgical closure of the perforation is required, flying should be prohibited until the postoperative recovery period is over. The ear must be kept very dry and clean until after the perforation is well healed. This may require protective measures and accommodations in the workplace. Balance disorders can result from disorders of the middle ear and may require work restrictions for the safety of the individual and co-workers. If the perforation was the result of head trauma, other accommodations may be required because of neurological complications.

Comorbid Conditions

Comorbid conditions influencing the length of disability for individuals with tympanum perforation include chronic pulmonary or cardiovascular diseases that increase an individual's risk during surgical procedures requiring a general anesthetic, and diseases and conditions that limit the individual's response to antibiotic therapy or increase the likelihood of surgical wound infection (e.g., obesity, AIDS, and diabetes).

Complications

Complications of a perforated eardrum may include failure to heal spontaneously; persistent ear infection; temporary, long-term, or permanent hearing loss depending on the cause of the perforation; disruption of the reconstruction during the postoperative healing phase; postoperative facial nerve paralysis (rare); and increased pressure in the middle ear. The degree of hearing loss depends on the size and location of the perforation. Since vibrations can still be transmitted to the inner ear by way of the bones of the skull, near total destruction of the tympanic membrane may not produce total deafness.

Factors Influencing Duration

Factors influencing the length of disability for tympanum perforation include the general health and fitness of the individual before the perforation, evidence of pre-existing diseases affecting any of the major body systems (that may interfere with the healing process), individual's general ability to fight infection, presence of antibiotic-resistant organisms, poor compliance with taking the full course of antibiotic therapy, and working or living in a smoke-filled environment.

Length of Disability

Length of disability varies depending on the individual's response to treatment, presence of infection, the individual's response to surgery to close the perforation, and job requirements.

Medical treatment.

Duration in Days

Job Classification	Minimum	Optimum	Maximum
Sedentary work	1	3	7
Light work	1	3	7
Medium work	1	3	7
Heavy work	1	3	7
Very Heavy work	1	3	7

Surgical treatment (tympanoplasty).

Duration in Days

Job Classification	Minimum	Optimum	Maximum
Sedentary work	2	3	5
Light work	4	6	7
Medium work	7	10	14
Heavy work	7	10	14
Very Heavy work	7	10	14

Failure to Recover

If an individual fails to recover within the maximum duration expectancy period, the reader may wish to reference the following questions to assist in better understanding the specifics of an individual's medical case.

Regarding diagnosis:

- Does individual have a history of acute or chronic otitis media, trauma or exposure to recent sudden altitude changes?
- Was diagnosis of tympanum perforation confirmed?
- Was the ear examined with a microscope (rather than an otoscope) for better visualization?
- Was individual seen by appropriate specialists?
- Were additional diagnostic studies performed (such as MRI or CT) to reveal the extent of any infection and rule out the possibility of a skull fracture or tumor?
- Was the cause of the rupture verified and resolved?

Regarding treatment:

- If infection persists despite antibiotic therapy, was individual treated with antibiotics based on the results of culture and sensitivity testing of the ear drainage?
- Is individual still being treated with antibiotics?
- Has individual been compliant with taking the prescribed dose of antibiotic at the prescribed time in the prescribed manner?
- Has individual followed recommended restrictions on activity (flying, underwater diving, insertion of objects into the ear)?
- Has individual kept the ear dry by using earplugs during bathing?
- If eardrum has failed to heal in 6 months, have procedures such as tympanoplasty, myringoplasty, mastoidectomy, paper or tissue graft, or partial or complete prosthesis been performed?
- Will individual's recovery require further treatment? If so, what modality is being considered?

Regarding prognosis:

- Based on the extent of the injury and the type of treatment required what was the expected outcome?
- Has adequate time elapsed for recovery?
- If symptoms persist, has infection been resolved?
- If infection persists despite antibiotic therapy, was individual treated with antibiotics based on the results of culture and sensitivity testing of the ear drainage?
- Did the perforation fail to heal? If so, is surgical intervention warranted? Is tympanoplasty or myringoplasty being considered?
- If healing of the perforation or recovery from surgery is slow, have diabetes, HIV/AIDS, leukemia, and other immunosuppressive diseases been identified or ruled out?
- Has individual experienced complications from the perforated eardrum such as permanent hearing loss, facial nerve paralysis, or increased middle ear pressure?

References

Lewis, Sharon, Margaret Heitkemper, and Shannon Dirksen. Medical-Surgical Nursing. St. Louis: Mosby, 2000.

Umphred, Darcy A. Neurological Rehabilitation. St. Louis: The C.V. Mosby Company, 1990.

Typhoid Fever

Other names / synonyms: Enteric Fever, Paratyphoid, Typhoid

002, 002.0, 002.1, 002.2, 002.3, 002.9

Definition

Typhoid fever is a serious and contagious bacterial infection caused by Salmonella typhi. Entering through the gastrointestinal tract, it spreads through the blood system (bacteremia), inflaming the small and large intestine. Severe cases can be life-threatening.

Typhoid bacteria are shed in the feces and urine of infected individuals. Inadequate hand washing after defecation or urination can contaminate food and water supplies. Livestock and pets infected with the disease also serve as a reservoir for bacterial growth. Humans are subsequently infected by unsanitary handling of the animal's feces or by fecal contamination of water supplies. Flies may spread the disease from feces to food, causing epidemics in areas with poor sanitation practices. Hospital workers who do not take adequate precautions can be infected through the soiled linens of infected individuals.

Although some infected individuals have no symptoms, they are still capable of spreading the disease to others (carriers). In the US, many of the estimated 2,000 carriers are elderly women with chronic gallbladder disease.

Now rare in the US, typhoid is still common in areas with poor sanitation, such as underdeveloped areas of Africa, Asia, and Latin America.

Diagnosis

History: Symptoms of enteric fever include chills, high fever, headache, cough, sore throat, generalized feeling of illness (malaise), abdominal pain, and constipation. Constipation may later turn into "pea soup" diarrhea. Fever plateaus after 7-10 days, leaving individual exhausted.

Physical exam: The exam may reveal an enlarged spleen (splenomegaly) and a slow pulse. In 10% of the cases, a rash (rose spots) occurs on the trunk during the second week of the disease. The fever, which has remained high for 7-10 days, declines to normal during the fourth week. In severe cases, delirium, confusion, and coma may occur. The infection may also cause pneumonia-like symptoms or symptoms similar to a urinary tract infection.

Tests: Blood, feces, and urine may be cultured for the presence of the bacteria Salmonella. Blood samples may indicate a low platelet count and a low white blood cell count. Blood tests (serology) can also look for Salmonella typhi antibodies and antigens (Widal test).

Treatment

The bacterial infection can be treated effectively with a number of antibiotics. When diarrhea is present, fluids and electrolytes must be replaced. Antidiarrheal medicines and narcotics may be used to relieve loss of fluids and cramps.

In severe cases, corticosteroid drugs may be necessary to treat central nervous system symptoms such as seizures, shock, or delirium. If the intestine becomes perforated, emergency surgery will be needed.

Chronic carriers are treated with an extended course of antibiotic therapy to eliminate the bacteria. Treatment of typhoid fever can be complicated by the presence of antibiotic-resistant bacteria. Because the bacterium may be harbored in the biliary tree, gallbladder surgery may be used if antibiotic treatment is ineffective.

Prognosis

With prompt and appropriate treatment, most individuals recover in 2 to 4 weeks. Complication can occur in those who are not treated or in whom treatment is delayed. Untreated and severe situations can result in death. Even with treatment, relapses can occur in up to 15%.

Some individuals become carriers. Although they have no symptoms themselves, they are still capable of spreading the disease to others.

Differential Diagnosis

Conditions with similar symptoms include tuberculosis, infective endocarditis, brucellosis, lymphoma, Q fever, viral hepatitis, malaria, and amebiasis.

Specialists

- Gastroenterologist
- General Surgeon
- Infectious Disease Physician
- Internist

Work Restrictions / Accommodations

Food handlers should be considered unfit for handling food until proven bacteria free. Individuals who suffer intestinal perforations should be given less strenuous work assignments during recovery from the surgery.

Comorbid Conditions

Individuals with inflammatory bowel disease, implants, and prosthetic devices, malnourished individuals, and those with weakened immune systems may develop more severe forms of typhoid fever. Relapse is common in HIV-infected individuals.

Complications

Complications include dehydration, intestinal perforation, hemorrhage, peritonitis, anemia, pneumonia, and inflammation of the liver or spleen. Bacteria in the blood (bacteremia) can result in infection in the bones (osteomyelitis), joints (arthritis), the kidneys (glomerulitis), heart valves (endocarditis), the lining of the brain (meningitis), and in the genital or the urinary tract. Muscle infection can result in abscesses. The infection could also affect the gallbladder and central nervous system.

Factors Influencing Duration

Length of disability may be influenced by the severity of infection at diagnosis, the presence of antibiotic-resistant bacteria, and the development of complications. Serious complications, such as CNS infection, intestinal perforation, or renal failure will require emergency medical care with a delayed recovery time.

Length of Disability

Duration in Days

Job Classification	Minimum	Optimum	Maximum
Sedentary work	14	21	28
Light work	14	21	28
Medium work	14	21	28
Heavy work	21	28	42
Very Heavy work	21	28	63

Failure to Recover

If an individual fails to recover within the maximum duration expectancy period, the reader may wish to reference the following questions to assist in better understanding the specifics of an individual's medical case.

Regarding diagnosis:

- Does individual have chills, high fever, headache, cough, sore throat, generalized feeling of illness (malaise), abdominal pain, and constipation? Did the constipation later turn into diarrhea?
- Was the diagnosis of typhoid fever confirmed by the presence of Salmonella typhi antibodies and antigens in the blood?
- Have other conditions with similar symptoms such as tuberculosis, infective endocarditis, brucellosis, lymphoma, Q fever, viral hepatitis, malaria, and amebiasis, been ruled out?
- Is there evidence of systemic infection or organ system involvement?
- Would individual benefit from consultation with an infectious disease specialist?

Regarding treatment:

- Was individual treated promptly with the appropriate antibiotic therapy?
- Did the symptoms persist despite treatment? Were culture and sensitivity tests done to determine the possibility of antibiotic resistance? Has the antibiotic therapy been adjusted appropriately?
- Is individual a chronic carrier? If so, was the course of antibiotic therapy extended appropriately?
- Was there evidence of biliary involvement? Was surgery indicated?

Regarding prognosis:

- Did adequate time elapse for recovery (2 to 4 weeks)?
- Does individual have an underlying immune suppressive condition that may warrant lifelong suppressive therapy?
- Has individual suffered any associated complications (i.e., intestinal perforation, peritonitis, hemorrhage, organ system involvement) that could impact recovery and prognosis? Have the complications been addressed in the treatment plan?
- If individual is a carrier, has instruction been given regarding prevention of disease transmission?

References

Tierney, Lawrence, Stephen McPhee, and Maxine Papadakis. <u>Current Medical Diagnosis and Treatment</u>. Stamford: Appleton & Lange, 1998.

Typhus Fever

Other names / synonyms: Brill's Disease, Brill-Zinsser Disease, Epidemic Typhus, Flea-Borne Typhus, Louse-Borne Typhus, Mite-Borne Typhus, Murine Typhus, Rat Typhus, Recurrent Typhus, Scrub Typhus, Tsutsugamushi Disease, Typhus

080, 081, 081.0, 081.2, 081.9

Definition

Typhus fever or typhus is an acute infection caused by various species of the bacteria rickettsia.

Forms of typhus fever depend on the particular species of bacteria responsible for the infection. Epidemic typhus is caused by Rickettsia prowazekii and is transmitted from human to human by the body louse. When epidemic typhus recurs several years after the initial attack, this condition is called Brill-Zinsser disease. Native (endemic), mouse (murine), or flea-borne typhus (caused by Rickettsia typhi) is spread to humans by mouse or rat fleas. Mites infected with Rickettsia tsutsugamushi spread scrub typhus or tsutsugamushi disease.

The various forms of typhus have abrupt onsets with incubation periods of 1 to 2 weeks. Epidemic typhus outbreaks typically occur where people are crowded together in unsanitary conditions, i.e., times of war, military camps, or natural disasters. It is more prevalent in the winter months when blankets are shared and more clothing is worn. Epidemic typhus is very rare in the US and Western Europe. Outbreaks still occur in other parts of the world, particularly in the highlands and cold sections or Africa, Asia, Central and South America. The disease is serious and can be fatal, particularly in the elderly. The fatality rate varies considerably and is reported as 1-20%. Without treatment, however, the mortality rate jumps to 40-60%.

Endemic typhus is primarily an urban disease occurring in late summer to early autumn. Control of the rodent population and associated flea problems is essential in managing this disease. About 100 cases of endemic typhus are reported in the US each year, although this form tends to be under-reported. Most cases occur in the Gulf States particularly in south Texas. Less severe than epidemic typhus, the overall mortality rate from this form is 1-2%.

Scrub typhus occurs primarily in Asia and the Western Pacific. Americans are only affected if they travel to parts of the world where this disease exists. Death occurs in up to 30% of untreated individuals.

Typhus is a serious disease and can be fatal particularly in the elderly. Men and women are at equal risk.

Diagnosis

History: Individuals with typhus may present with severe headache, nonproductive cough, nausea, muscle aches (myalgia), chest pain, and a general feeling of illness (malaise). These are followed by a sudden onset of chills, high fever, and extreme fatigue (prostration) that may progress to delirium and stupor. At around 4 to 7 days, a rash may appear on the trunk that spreads across most of the body, but rarely involves the face, palms, and soles.

With scrub typhus, the individual may report a black, crusted bite, tender lymph nodes, eye pain and redness (conjunctivitis), and a short-term rash.

Physical exam: Rash is the major physical finding upon physical examination. The individual may show signs of delirium or stupor. Typhus affects many organs including the intestines, liver, heart, kidneys, and brain. As these organs are affected, corresponding pathology may include constipation, pneumonia, enlargement of the liver or spleen (splenomegaly), kidney damage (renal insufficiency), or slowed heartbeat (bradycardia).

With scrub typhus, the site of the bite becomes a black, crusted area. Lymph nodes may be enlarged not only in the vicinity of the bite (regional) but also throughout the body (generalized adenopathy).

Tests: Blood tests (serologic tests) are used to diagnose typhus fever and exclude other possible diagnoses. Specific tests (complement fixation, immunofluorescence) performed on blood serum drawn 5 to 12 days after onset of symptoms can detect antibodies for the Rickettsia prowazekii.

With scrub typhus, the rickettsial organism may be identified by injecting a laboratory animal with blood drawn during the first few days of illness (mouse inoculation). Although tests identifying antirickettsial antibodies (fluorescein-labeled antirickettsial assays) are preferred over complement fixation tests (tests that determine if antigen-antibody reactions have occurred), a process investigating genetic material (polymerase chair reaction or PCR) is the most sensitive method of diagnosis.

Chest x-rays show evidence of lung involvement. Blood (hematuria) and protein (proteinuria) are usually evident in the urine. In some cases, particularly when scrub typhus is suspected, fluid from the spinal column (cerebrospinal fluid or CSF) may reveal low numbers of mononuclear immune cells. Blood tests can also reveal abnormalities that reflect the involvement of other organs.

Treatment

Typhus fever is treated with antibiotics. Medication may also be prescribed to reduce fever (antipyretics) and relieve muscle aches (analgesics). Severe headaches may require a narcotic pain reliever. Bed rest is necessary for recovery. Any remaining lice, fleas, or mites should be removed and the individual isolated in a clean environment free from rodents. Although relapses may occur, they are usually responsive to antibiotic therapy.

Prognosis

Even though typhus is effectively treated with antibiotics, outcome still depends on age and immunization status. With prompt, appropriate treatment, most individuals recover completely. Although death is uncommon with treatment, vaccination can still change a potentially serious disease into a mild one.

Without treatment, the fever may last 2 weeks followed by a prolonged recovery time and a significantly greater chance of developing complications. The mortality in untreated epidemic typhus can be as high as 60% especially in the elderly. Untreated scrub typhus is associated with a mortality rate of approximately 30%. Endemic typhus has a lower mortality rate of 1-2% in untreated cases.

Differential Diagnosis

Differential diagnoses include any acute feverish (febrile) disease, Rocky Mountain spotted fever, meningococcemia, bacterial meningitis, Boutonneuse fever, measles, rubella, toxoplasmosis, leptospirosis, typhoid fever, Dengue fever, relapsing fever, secondary syphilis, and infectious mononucleosis.

Specialists

- Cardiologist
- Gastroenterologist
- Hematologist
- Infectious Disease Physician
- Internist
- Nephrologist
- Neurologist
- Ophthalmologist
- Pulmonologist

Work Restrictions / Accommodations

In individuals not properly diagnosed or treated, nervous and mental symptoms may persist long after the acute phase subsides. In these cases, work restrictions and accommodations require consideration on a case-by-case basis.

Comorbid Conditions

Individuals with a compromised immune system may experience a longer recovery period.

Complications

Complications associated with typhus vary depending on the organ systems involved. Possible complications include diminished blood volume (hypovolemia), blood vessel inflammation (vasculitis) resulting in obstruction and gangrene, blood clots (thrombosis), circulatory collapse, uremia (a toxic condition associated with renal insufficiency), kidney failure, inflammation of the heart muscle (myocarditis), heart failure, liver infection, pneumonia, respiratory failure, deafness, delirium, coma, inflammation of the spinal column and/or brain (meningoencephalitis, encephalitis), seizures, shock, and death.

Factors Influencing Duration

Factors that may influence the length of disability include the type and severity of typhus, the stage of the disease at beginning of treatment, response to treatment, and development of complications. Elderly individuals have an increased risk of mortality.

Length of Disability

Duration in Days

Job Classification	Minimum	Optimum	Maximum
Any work	7	14	56

Failure to Recover

If an individual fails to recover within the maximum duration expectancy period, the reader may wish to reference the following questions to assist in better understanding the specifics of an individual's medical case.

Regarding diagnosis:

- Did individual experience symptoms of severe headache, nonproductive cough, nausea, muscle aches (myalgia), chest pain, and malaise?
- Was a rash noted on the physical exam?
- Was the diagnosis of typhus fever confirmed with serologic tests by the presence of antibodies for the Rickettsia prowazekii?
- Were other febrile diseases (i.e., Rocky Mountain spotted fever, meningococcemia, bacterial meningitis, Boutonneuse fever, measles, rubella, toxoplasmosis, leptospirosis, typhoid fever, Dengue fever, relapsing fever, secondary syphilis, and infectious mononucleosis) eliminated as causative factors?

Regarding treatment:

- How soon after onset of symptoms was treatment with antibiotics initiated?
- Was individual treated with tetracycline or chloramphenicol?
- What was the response to treatment?
- Is individual following the doctor's orders with regard to bed rest and activity limitations?
- If individual is unable to adequately care for himself/herself, is in-patient care being considered?

Regarding prognosis:

- Have all symptoms resolved? If not, what impairment remains?
- Was individual isolated from the causative fleas, lice, or mites?
- Is it possible that individual was reinfected?
- Would additional antibiotic therapy be appropriate at this time?
- Were underlying conditions such as immunosuppression that may impact recovery identified or ruled out?
- Have complications occurred such organ dysfunction, systemic infection, or shock that can impact recovery and prognosis?

References

Epidemic Louse-Borne Typhyus. World Health Organization. 1997. 22 Sep 2000 <http://www.who.int/inf-fs/en/fact162.html>.

Typhus Fever (Flea-Borne). Virginia Department of Health. 1998. 22 Sep 2000 <http://www.vdh.state.va.us/epi/typhusf.htm>.

Ulcerative Colitis

Other names / synonyms: Idiopathic Proctitis, Rectosigmoiditis, Toxic Megacolon, Ulcerative Enterocolitis, Ulcerative Ileocolitis, Ulcerative Proctitis, Ulcerative Ileocolitis

555, 556, 557

Definition

Ulcerative colitis is a serious, chronic inflammatory disease of the large intestine (colon or bowel) characterized by ulceration and episodes of bloody diarrhea.

The inflammation usually begins in the rectum and lower intestine (sigmoid) and spreads upward to the entire colon. Ulcerative colitis rarely affects the small intestine except, possibly, for the small intestine's lower section (illeum). The inflammation causes the large intestine or colon to empty frequently, resulting in diarrhea. Tiny open sores (ulcers) form in places where the inflammation has killed colon lining cells; the ulcers bleed and produce pus and mucus.

Theories about what causes ulcerative colitis abound, but none have been proven. The most popular theory is that the body's immune system reacts to a virus or a bacterium by causing ongoing inflammation in the intestinal wall.

Individuals with ulcerative colitis have abnormalities of the immune system, but doctors have not ascertained whether these abnormalities are a cause or a result of the disease. Ulcerative colitis is not caused by emotional distress or sensitivity to certain foods or food products, but these factors, as well as a family history of the disease along with stress, have been shown to trigger or aggravate symptoms in some individuals.

An estimated 250,000 Americans have ulcerative colitis. The disease occurs most often in young people (ages 15 to 40), although older individuals sometimes develop the disease. Ulcerative colitis affects males and females equally and appears to run in some families.

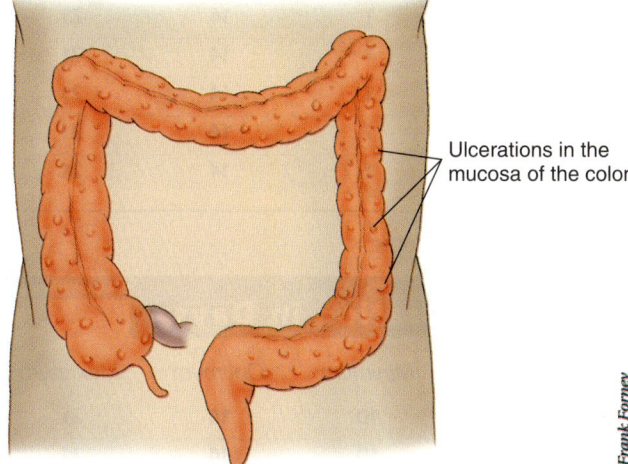

Ulcerations in the mucosa of the colon

Frank Forney

Diagnosis

History: The most common symptoms of ulcerative colitis are abdominal cramps and bloody diarrhea. Afflicted individuals report having to strain to produce stools (tenesmus), repeated bouts of bloody diarrhea alternating with constipation or symptom-free intervals, rectal urgency, fever, nausea and vomiting, a overall feeling of body discomfort (malaise), joint pains (arthralgias), night sweats, and loss of body fluids and nutrients (dehydration).

About half of individuals with ulcerative colitis suffer severe symptoms, such as frequent fever (as high as 104F or 40C), bloody diarrhea (from 10 to 20 bowel movements a day), nausea, and severe abdominal cramps. Other individuals experience less severe problems, such as arthritis, inflammation of the eye, liver disease (fatty liver, hepatitis, cirrhosis, and primary sclerosing cholangitis), osteoporosis, skin rashes, anemia, and kidney stones.

Physical exam: The exam may reveal fever, dehydration, increased heart rate (tachycardia), abdominal tenderness, extreme or unnatural paleness of complexion (pallor), joint tenderness, rebound tenderness on abdominal exam, and anal tenderness upon exam.

Tests: Tests to ascertain the presence of ulcerative colitis include a complete blood count (CBC) with differential, blood iron and ferritin level, C-reactive protein, sedimentation rate, a blood test for liver, kidney, and electrolyte levels (Chem. 20), a liver enzyme test (GGTP), a white-blood-cells-in-the-stool test (fecal leukocytes), a flat plane x-ray of the abdomen, a radiographic x-ray of the colon (barium enema) and an invasive procedure where a scope is placed through the rectal opening and passed up into the colon (endoscopy). There are two kinds of endoscopies: the sigmoidoscopy and the colonoscopy. A sigmoidoscopy is a procedure in which a scope is used to view the sigmoid flexure, a part of the colon that is shaped like the letter s. In a colonoscopy, the entire colon is viewed.

Treatment

Treatment for ulcerative colitis depends on the seriousness of the disease. Most individuals are treated with medication (for minimal symptoms, antidiarrhea medication; for moderate symptoms, sulfa drugs, such as sulfasalazine; for severe disease, medicated enemas and cortisone drugs). In severe cases, an individual may need surgery to remove the diseased colon.

Surgery is the only cure for ulcerative colitis. About 25-40% of individuals with ulcerative colitis must eventually have their colons removed because of massive bleeding, severe illness, rupture of the colon, or risk of cancer. One of several surgeries may be performed. The most common surgery is a proctocolectomy with ileostomy, which is done in two stages. In the proctocolectomy, the surgeon removes the colon and the rectum. In the ileostomy, the surgeon creates a small opening in the abdomen, called a stoma, and attaches the end of the small intestine, called the ileum, to it. This type of ileostomy is called a Brooke ileostomy. Waste will travel through the small intestine and exit the body through the stoma. A pouch is worn over the stoma to collect waste, which the individual empties as needed.

Some individuals, whose symptoms are triggered by certain foods, are able to control the symptoms by avoiding foods that upset their intestines, such as highly seasoned foods or milk sugar (lactose). Vitamin and mineral supplements and iron replacement may be indicated. For individuals with persistent abdominal cramping, eating cooked and skinned fruits and vegetables and eliminating raw fruits and vegetables is recommended. If diarrhea is present, the individual should avoid roughage in his or her diet.

Each individual may experience ulcerative colitis differently, so treatment is adjusted for each individual. Emotional and psychological support is important.

An individual with ulcerative colitis may need medical care for some time with regular doctor visits to monitor his or her condition.

Prognosis

Individuals who are treated with medication (for minimal and moderate symptoms) should not expect a cure but can expect to keep the disease under control if they adhere to their medication regimen, watch their diet, and keep stress to a minimum.

Non-compliance with medical regimens can lead to progression of the disease, dehydration, infection, and overwhelming systemic infections (e.g., sepsis) that have a high mortality. If left to progress untreated over an undetermined period of time, ulcerative colitis will eventually lead to an enlarged colon (toxic megacolon) or colon cancer.

In spite of their compliance with prescribed treatment, some individuals will experience remission periods where the symptoms that can last for months or years will go away. However, most individuals' symptoms eventually return.

Most individuals who are treated with surgery (e.g., proctocolectomy with ileostomy and Brook ileostomy) can expect a cure and a fairly normal, healthy life, provided they learn to live with emptying their ileostomy pouch regularly.

Differential Diagnosis

Ulcerative colitis can be difficult to diagnose because its symptoms are similar to other intestinal disorders, such as irritable bowel syndrome and to another type of inflammatory bowel disease (IBD) called Crohn's disease. Crohn's disease differs from ulcerative colitis as it causes inflammation deeper within the intestinal wall.

Other diseases that have similar symptoms and that need to be distinguished from ulcerative colitis are gastroenteritis, infectious diarrhea, infection of the gastrointestinal tract by amoeba (amebiasis), inflammation of the mesenteric lymph nodes (mesenteric adenitis), lack of blood supply to the small bowel and/or colon (mesenteric ischemia), infection and inflammation of the colon (diverticulitis), HIV, and colitis due to drug ingestion (NSAID induced colitis).

Specialists

- Gastroenterologist
- General Surgeon
- Internist

Work Restrictions / Accommodations

If surgery is performed, individuals will need a change to light, sedentary work for two to four weeks before returning to their usual work responsibilities. Extended work leave may be required for the surgery and for the postoperative therapy and rehabilitation that follow.

If surgery is not performed, individuals will occasionally need extra sick leave for doctor visits and short hospital stays when episodes of abdominal pain, diarrhea, and constipation persist.

Comorbid Conditions

Comorbid conditions that might influence the length of disability include obesity or excessive thinness, allergy to treatment medications, and chronic illnesses, such as heart disease and diabetes.

Complications

Individuals can have many complications, including rectal bleeding, life-threatening blood loss, ulceration through the intestinal wall, enlarged colon (toxic megacolon), cancer of the colon, inflammation of various parts of the eye (conjunctivitis, iritis, uveitis, episcleritis), bone loss (osteoporosis), and arthritis of the knees, ankles, elbows, and wrists. Stress may aggravate the disease. After ten years of active disease, cancer of the colon may be found.

Some individuals have (periods when the symptoms go away) remissions that last for months or even years. However, most individuals' symptoms eventually return. This changing pattern of the disease means one cannot always tell when a treatment has been effective.

Factors Influencing Duration

Disability is influenced by the severity of the individual's symptoms (enlarged colon, colon cancer) and if hospitalization is needed for dehydration and infection.

Length of Disability

Medical treatment.

Duration in Days

Job Classification	Minimum	Optimum	Maximum
Sedentary work	1	14	21
Light work	1	14	21
Medium work	1	14	21
Heavy work	1	14	21
Very Heavy work	1	14	21

Colon resection, laparoscopic.

Duration in Days

Job Classification	Minimum	Optimum	Maximum
Sedentary work	10	14	21
Light work	10	14	21
Medium work	14	21	28
Heavy work	14	35	42
Very Heavy work	14	42	56

Colon resection, open.

Duration in Days

Job Classification	Minimum	Optimum	Maximum
Sedentary work	21	28	42
Light work	21	28	42
Medium work	28	35	56
Heavy work	35	42	56
Very Heavy work	42	42	56

Failure to Recover

If an individual fails to recover within the maximum duration expectancy period, the reader may wish to reference the following questions to assist in better understanding the specifics of an individual's medical case.

Regarding diagnosis:

- What symptoms has individual reported?
- Was individual able to identify factors that trigger or aggravate the symptoms?
- What is individual's age?
- Was individual able to maintain hydration and electrolyte balance?
- On exam, was there fever or evidence of dehydration? Was abdominal or anal tenderness present?
- Were complete blood work-up and stool tests preformed?
- Were x-rays done, both flat plate of the abdomen and barium enema?
- Endoscopy? Results?
- Were similar intestinal diagnoses such as irritable bowel syndrome, Crohn's disease, gastroenteritis, infectious diarrhea, amebiasis, mesenteric adenitis, mesenteric ischemia, diverticulitis, HIV, and colitis due to drug ingestion (NSAID induced colitis) considered?

Regarding treatment:

- Has individual had adequate trials of the various medications?
- Did individual have surgery?
- Is individual able to care for the stoma or does individual need assistance?
- Is individual compliant with the treatment program?
- Is individual involved in a support group?
- If needed, has individual obtained psychological counseling?
- Has the disease progressed?
- Has individual had periods of remission?

Regarding prognosis:

- Is individual active in rehabilitation?
- Is individual's employer able to accommodate sedentary work for a short time as they progress back to their normal work?
- Does individual have any conditions such as include obesity or excessive thinness, allergy to treatment medications, and chronic illnesses, such as heart disease or diabetes that may affect recovery?
- Has individual had any complications?

References

Colitis, Ulcerative (Granulomatous colitis). The University of Illinois at Chicago Medical Center. 23 Feb 2000. 06 Dec 2000 <http://www.healthgate.com/choice/uic/cons/mdx-books/sym/sym92.shtml>.

Rosen, Peter. Emergency Medicine: Concepts and Clinical Practice, 4th ed. Wilmette, IL: Mosby-Year Book, Inc, 1998 01 Mar 2001 <http://home.mdconsult.com/>.

Ultrasound, Diagnostic

Other names / synonyms: Sonography

88.7, 88.71, 88.73, 88.74, 88.75, 88.76, 88.77, 88.78, 88.79

Definition

Diagnostic ultrasound (sonography) is a noninvasive diagnostic imaging technique that uses high frequency sound waves to produce images of structures within the body. The sound waves are sent through the body tissues with a device called a transducer. Objects inside the body reflect a part of the sound waves back to a sensor, where the waves are recorded, analyzed, and displayed for viewing on a screen. Modern sonographic equipment can display live images of moving tissues (real-time viewing), and can also provide 3-dimensional reconstruction information about different structures. The area covered by the ultrasound beam depends on equipment design.

Pulsed Doppler sonography enables the visualization of flow effects in both arteries and veins (vascular systems) as well as in organs. By the use of advanced data processing technology, color Doppler sonography can acquire data rapidly enough to study complex blood flow in the heart and other organs.

Diagnostic ultrasound is painless and safe. Studies have not revealed any negative side effects of this procedure. The capability of ultrasound to visualize internal organs can be enhanced by combining it with endoscopy, an invasive procedure in which the transducer is introduced into a body cavity for better viewing.

Reason for Procedure

Diagnostic ultrasound has a wide variety of uses in general medical practice.

Sonography has become the most frequently used diagnostic technique in the branch of medicine specializing in pregnancy and delivery (obstetrics), since there do not appear to be any adverse biological effects of this procedure. Sonography can be used to visualize a developing baby (fetus), monitor developmental progress, and detect abnormalities in the developing fetus or its environment (placenta).

In gynecology, sonography is most commonly used for the evaluation of pelvic masses and infertility problems. Evaluation of uterine and ovarian disorders is accomplished with a smaller transducer that is inserted into the vagina (transvaginal sonography). Breast ultrasound assesses whether masses seen on mammography are solid or liquid in nature, and may help detect breast cysts in women with dense breasts and normal mammograms.

In general, ultrasonography can be used in the initial evaluation of many abdominal disorders, especially diseases of the gallbladder and biliary tract, as well as blunt abdominal trauma. Real-time sonography allows more consistent and detailed images of the kidneys than do static imaging techniques; for example, Doppler capabilities allow assessment of renal artery stenosis and other blood flow abnormalities. The major blood vessels in the abdomen can also be studied. Lower frequency ultrasound instruments can study the deeper structures in the abdomen and pelvis, and can help diagnose deep vein blood clots (thrombosis).

Ultrasound can be used to guide the physician during other procedures such as needle biopsy or removal of fluid (aspiration). Endoscopic ultrasound is a minimally invasive method helpful in the diagnosis of chronic pancreatitis, and in guiding fine-needle aspiration of masses deep within the chest (mediastinal masses). Regular ultrasound assists the physician performing liver biopsy by visualizing structures in the path of the biopsy needle. Small ultrasound probes can be inserted into the rectum during prostate biopsy to guide the physician and to increase the accuracy of the procedure.

For the evaluation of dynamic effects such as those associated with blood flow, heart function, vascular disorders, or organ perfusion, ultrasound is often superior to other techniques. Echocardiography and 3D-echocardiography help visualize heart structure, function, and volume. A number of superficial organs (less than two inches from the surface of the skin) can be imaged in real time, including the thyroid, testes, breast, carotid arteries, and eye. 3-D sonography can determine volumes of organs and other structures, allowing physicians to determine if organs are enlarged, or if a tumor is changing size in response to treatment.

Sonography provides imaging whenever other methods are considered riskier or even contraindicated because of the individual's condition. It is relatively inexpensive compared to MRI and CT scan. It uses no ionizing radiation, as do CT and plain x-rays. It does not involve the hazards of strong magnetic fields as in MRI. Ultrasonography is much more comfortable for individuals compared to the other imaging methods. While it is thought to be safe and without adverse effects, either to the individual or to the developing baby in the case of obstetrical ultrasound, it should always be done only for valid diagnostic indications. Obstetrical ultrasound merely to determine the sex of the fetus or to "see how the baby is doing" is not recommended.

Description

Ultrasound may be performed in the doctor's office, in a designated unit in a hospital, or at the bedside if necessary, using a portable device. Depending on the area of the body being examined, the doctor may require that the individual take certain steps to prepare for the procedure. These steps may include not eating for a designated period of time (for example in gallbladder evaluation), or that they drink several glasses of water if the pelvis is to be examined.

During the procedure, the individual is generally sitting or lying down. The area being examined is exposed, and a technician applies a gel to the skin in that area, which improves the transmission of the sound waves. The technician or doctor moves the transducer back and forth over the area being examined. As the sound waves echo off the internal structures, they create an image seen on a video monitor. The individual may be asked to hold the breath or change position. There may be several pauses while the images are examined and/or recorded for later examination. In obstetrical ultrasound, the images may be printed out and copies may be given to the individual. The gel is then wiped off and the procedure is over.

In transvaginal ultrasound, the transducer is inserted into the vagina. To help guide the physician performing prostate biopsy, the transducer is inserted into the rectum. In endoscopic ultrasound, the transducer is inserted into the upper gastrointestinal tract.

Prognosis

Diagnostic ultrasound is effective for visualizing internal structures that are within 2 inches of the skin's surface. In instances where the transducer can be inserted into the body, such as into the vagina or rectum, slightly deeper structures can be visualized. This procedure is more effective for visualizing soft tissues or those filled with fluid, and less effective for visualizing bone or air-filled organs.

3D ultrasound determination of large organ volume is precise within a 5% margin of error. Endoscopic ultrasound is reliable in the diagnosis of chronic pancreatitis with good agreement among different experienced endosonographers reviewing the same test. In a large series of blunt abdominal trauma, ultrasound had a sensitivity of 86%, a specificity of 98%, and an accuracy of 97% for detection of injuries within the abdomen.

Specialists

- Gynecologist
- Obstetrician
- Radiologist

Work Restrictions / Accommodations

No work restrictions and accommodations are associated with this procedure.

Comorbid Conditions

There are no comorbid conditions associated with this procedure.

Procedure Complications

Ultrasound is not associated with any complications. In late pregnancy, lying flat on the back on the hard ultrasound table may cause the uterus to compress the large vein (inferior vena cava) in the mother leading blood back to the heart. This may cause her to feel faint or dizzy, which is corrected rapidly by allowing her to sit up or change position.

Factors Influencing Duration

Ultrasound does not result in any disability.

Length of Disability

No disability is expected to result from this procedure. Disability may occur as a result of an underlying condition.

References

Ahmad, M., and T.R. Riley. "Can One Predict When Ultrasound Will Be Useful With Percutaneous Liver Biopsy?" American Journal of Gastroenterology 96 2 (2001): 547-549.

Dolich, M.O., et al. "2,576 Ultrasounds for Blunt Abdominal Trauma." Journal of Trauma - Injury Infection and Critical Care 50 1 (2001): 108-112.

Panelli, F., R.A. Erickson, and V.M. Prasad. "Evaluation of Mediastinal Masses by Endoscopic Ultrasound and Endoscopic Ultrasound-guided Fine Needle Aspiration." American Journal of Gastroenterology 96 2 (2001): 401-408.

Papademetris, X., et al. "Estimation of 3D Left Ventricular Deformation From Echocardiography." Med Image Anal 5 1 (2001): 17-28.

Shiel, William, MD, FACP, chief ed. "Ultrasound." MedicineNet.com. 08 Jul 2000 4 Jan 2001 <http://www.medicinenet.com/script/main/Art.asp?li=MNI&ArticleKey=510>.

Treece, G., et al. "3D Ultrasound Measurement of Large Organ Volume." Med Image Anal 5 1 (2001): 41-54.

Wallace, M.B., et al. "The Reliability of Endoscopic Ultrasound for the Diagnosis of Chronic Pancreatitis: Interobserver Agreement Among Experienced Endosonographers." Gastrointestinal Endoscopy 53 3 (2001): 294-299.

Woo, Joseph. Obstetric ultrasound: a comprehensive guide. ObGyn.Net. 12 Oct 2000. 3/10/01 <http://www.ob-ultrasound.net>.

Ultrasound, Therapeutic
93.39

Definition

Therapeutic ultrasound is the use of ultrasound sound wave technology as an "alternative" type of medicine. Ultrasound technology is principally used for diagnostic purposes. In many medical circles, therapeutic ultrasound is considered an alternative for healing to be used only when traditional treatment methods fail.

Therapeutic ultrasound has gained wide acceptance among sports-medicine specialists as an effective method for generating "deep" heat to treat musculoskeletal injuries and ailments such as back pain, muscle spasms, bursitis, and tendinitis. The same principle of heat generation makes ultrasound one suggested method for treating hypothermia.

It has also been suggested that ultrasound may be helpful in speeding wound and bone healing as it stimulates cell activity and the production of fibroblasts (cells in connective tissue that produce collagen and aid in healing). Occasionally, ultrasound is used to treat plantar warts and to deliver anti-inflammatory drugs through the skin to underlying tissue.

Ultrasound should not be used near pacemakers, prosthetic joints, or other implanted devices.

Reason for Procedure

Ultrasound is capable of sending penetrating heat deeper than any other heating method (e.g., hot packs). Ultrasound can penetrate up to 5 cm below the skin's surface, and heats those structures that contain the most protein, such as muscle. Ultrasound increases blood flow to an injured area and helps promote healing. It can also increase the flexibility of connective tissue such as ligaments and tendons and allow the return of a joint's normal range of motion.

Ultrasound can deliver medicine locally without using invasive procedures such as injections. This technique is known as phonophoresis. Because ultrasound increases the permeability of cell membranes, anti-inflammatory medications such as hydrocortisone or dexamethasone and local anesthetics such as lidocaine can be introduced through the skin. This can help decrease pain and inflammation due to injury.

Description

During the procedure, the individual is told that the sensation of heat should be mild, so if the heat becomes intense, the individual should immediately alert the physical therapist. The frequency of the ultrasound is then selected. If the area being treated is close to the surface of the skin, such as an ankle ligament, the frequency might be 3 MHz. If the area is deeper, such as low back muscles, a frequency of 1 MHz might be selected (waves of 3 MHz are absorbed faster and do not penetrate as deeply as 1 MHz waves, so are more appropriate for superficial targets). A coupling medium such as ultrasound gel is used to allow the transmission of ultrasound waves through the skin. In phonophoresis, a nonsteroidal cream or gel is used as the coupling medium.

For irregularly shaped body parts like fingers, the body part and the ultrasound head can be submerged in water to make the individual more comfortable during treatment. The dosage of the ultrasound is then determined. For more superficial areas, 0.5 Watts/cm2 may be appropriate, and for deeper tissues, 1.5 Watts/cm2 is often used. The ultrasound head is then moved in a circular manner over the treatment site for approximately 5 to 10 minutes. At the end of the ultrasound, the machine is turned off and the ultrasound site wiped clean of any remaining coupling medium.

Prognosis

The healing outcome depends on the nature of the condition treated and the individual's motivation to participate in therapy. Individuals can expect some increase in healing and flexibility in the treated area; however, if the condition is severe or chronic, such as a frozen shoulder, intensive rehabilitation will be needed as an adjunct to ultrasound.

Specialists

- Occupational Therapist
- Physiatrist
- Physical Therapist
- Sports Medicine Physician

Work Restrictions / Accommodations

Any work restrictions are necessitated by the underlying condition and not the ultrasound treatments.

Comorbid Conditions

Individuals with chronic pain conditions such as arthritis or fibromyalgia may recover more slowly than previously healthy individuals.

Procedure Complications

Increased inflammation may be observed in the area being treated. If this occurs, a pulsed mode may be appropriate where the dosage is alternately turned off and on. Individuals may feel pain or irritation over the site of the ultrasound if the technique is applied directly onto the skin. Individuals may experience redness or irritation in response to the anti-inflammatory agent used in phonophoresis.

Factors Influencing Duration

Factors that may influence disability are the individual's response to ultrasound treatment, degree of pain and inflammation present, and the individual's compliance with the physical therapy program.

Length of Disability

No disability is expected for this procedure. Disability may occur as a result of an underlying condition.

References

Hayes, Karen W. "Ultrasound." Manual of Physical Agents. Hayes, Karen W., ed. Norwalk: Appleton & Lange, 1993. 37-48.

Ziskin, MD, et al. "Therapeutic Ultrasound." Thermal Agents in Rehabilitation. Michlovitz, Susan L., ed. Philadelphia: F.A. Davis Company, 1990. 134-169.

Upper Gastrointestinal Series

Other names / synonyms: Barium Swallow, Barium Swallow X-ray, Small Bowel Series, Upper GI Series
87.61, 87.62

Definition

An upper gastrointestinal series is a test that allows visualization of the esophagus, stomach, and first part of the small intestine (duodenum). The test is performed by having the individual swallow a thick barium mixture (also called a barium milkshake). X-rays are then taken as the barium passes through the digestive tract. The barium makes the upper gastrointestinal tract visible under x-ray. The results of an upper gastrointestinal series can reveal conditions such as ulcers, tumors, hiatal hernias, scarring, blockages, and abnormalities of the muscular wall of the gastrointestinal system.

A primary reason for performing an upper gastrointestinal series is peptic ulcer disease. Risk factors for peptic ulcer include the presence of a certain bacterium (H. pylori) in the stomach and smoking tobacco. Other risk factors include increased secretion of acid and the enzyme pepsin by the stomach, reduced production of protective stomach mucus, and intake of medications that aggravate the stomach lining such as aspirin or nonsteroidal anti-inflammatory drugs (NSAIDs).

Individuals whose immune system is deficient (immunodeficiency) are at risk of contracting infections (cytomegalovirus, tuberculosis, syphilis), which can create ulcers in the upper gastrointestinal tract. There is evidence that some individuals may have a genetic predisposition toward development of peptic ulcer disease. However, there is no evidence that psychological stress or excessive alcohol intake are causative factors although they may aggravate an existing ulcer.

Peptic ulcers most commonly occur between 30-55 years of age. Overall, 9% of women and 12% of men will acquire this disease sometime in their lives. There are 500,000 new cases with 4 million recurrences annually.

Reason for Procedure

An upper gastrointestinal procedure is performed so that the esophagus, stomach, and small intestine can be visualized. The purpose of this test is to detect abnormalities of the esophagus, stomach, and small intestine. It is useful in diagnosing swallowing difficulties, heartburn, pain in the upper abdomen, or bleeding from the stomach or esophagus. Also, it can help to diagnose a tumor, ulcer, or hiatal hernia.

Description

The upper gastrointestinal series is typically performed on an outpatient basis. A drug (glucagon) may be given before starting the test to decrease the possibility of gastrointestinal spasm. The individual will be positioned behind x-ray equipment or a fluoroscope during the procedure and they will be asked to swallow approximately 20 ounces of a liquid that contains barium. The barium mixture will have a chalky and unpleasant taste. The barium will be swallowed in an upright position after which the individual will lie on a hard x-ray table. As the stomach fills, the physician may massage (palpate) it to ensure that all parts of the stomach and duodenum are coated so they can be visualized during the procedure. Eventually, the barium coats the esophagus, stomach, and small intestine, which makes them visible on an x-ray or by fluoroscopy. The x-ray table may be tilted so that a series of x-ray or fluoroscopic images can be obtained at different angles through the upper chest and abdomen. The total time required to complete the test once it is started is about 1-2 hours. The individual should be able to return to a normal diet after the test unless other tests are scheduled.

Prognosis

With upper gastrointestinal series, the esophagus, stomach, and upper small intestine will be coated with barium and the shape of these structures will be clearly apparent on x-rays or by fluoroscopy. This procedure helps in diagnosing and determining the appropriate treatment for upper GI cancers, esophageal stricture, hiatal hernia, diverticula, esophageal and stomach ulcers, achalasia, polyps, gastritis, pyloric stenosis, malabsorption syndrome, and duodenal inflammation.

Specialists

- Gastroenterologist
- Radiologist

Work Restrictions / Accommodations

There should be minimal work restrictions after an upper gastrointestinal series. The individual may require ready access to bathroom facilities for 24 hours following the procedure.

Comorbid Conditions

Existing conditions that may impact an individual's ability to recover and further lengthen their disability include severe inflammatory bowel disease, gastritis, diarrhea, or constipation.

Procedure Complications

Complications that might result from upper gastrointestinal series include constipation or diarrhea, bloating, cramping, nausea or vomiting, and abdominal pain. Other complications may include an inflammatory reaction caused by the barium (barium granuloma) or leakage of the barium into the abdominal cavity (intra- and extra-peritoneal extravasation of barium) if the bowel is perforated.

Factors Influencing Duration

The individual may be required to return to the hospital 24 hours after the initial upper GI series for follow-up x-rays. If any suspicious cancer-like masses are seen during upper gastrointestinal series, further tests and treatments may be required.

Length of Disability

In the majority of cases, the length of disability should be no more than a day unless the individual has problems after the test such as diarrhea, cramping, nausea, or vomiting.

Duration in Days

Job Classification	Minimum	Optimum	Maximum
Any work	1	1	1

References

Loeb, S. Illustrated Guide to Diagnostic Tests. Springhouse, PA: Springhouse Corporation, 1994.

Soybel, D.I. "Gastric Outlet Obstruction, Perforation, and Other Complications of Gastroduodenal Ulcer." Therapy of Digestive Disorders. Wolfe, M.M., ed. Philadelphia: W.B. Saunders Company, 2000. 153-168.

Upper Respiratory Infection

Other names / synonyms: Acute Coryza, Cold, Common Cold, Rhinitis, Upper Respiratory Bacterial Infection, Upper Respiratory Tract Infection, URI, URTI, Viral Pharyngitis

460, 465, 465.9

Definition

An upper respiratory infection is a viral or bacterial infection that affects the nose, throat, sinuses, and larynx. These are the most common of all illnesses. The most familiar upper respiratory infections include the common cold, infection of the throat (pharyngitis), tonsils (tonsillitis), the air sinuses behind the nose (sinusitis), and the larynx or voice box (laryngitis).

Colds (known medically as upper respiratory infections) affect the air passages in the head, neck, and chest. For more information, see Cold.

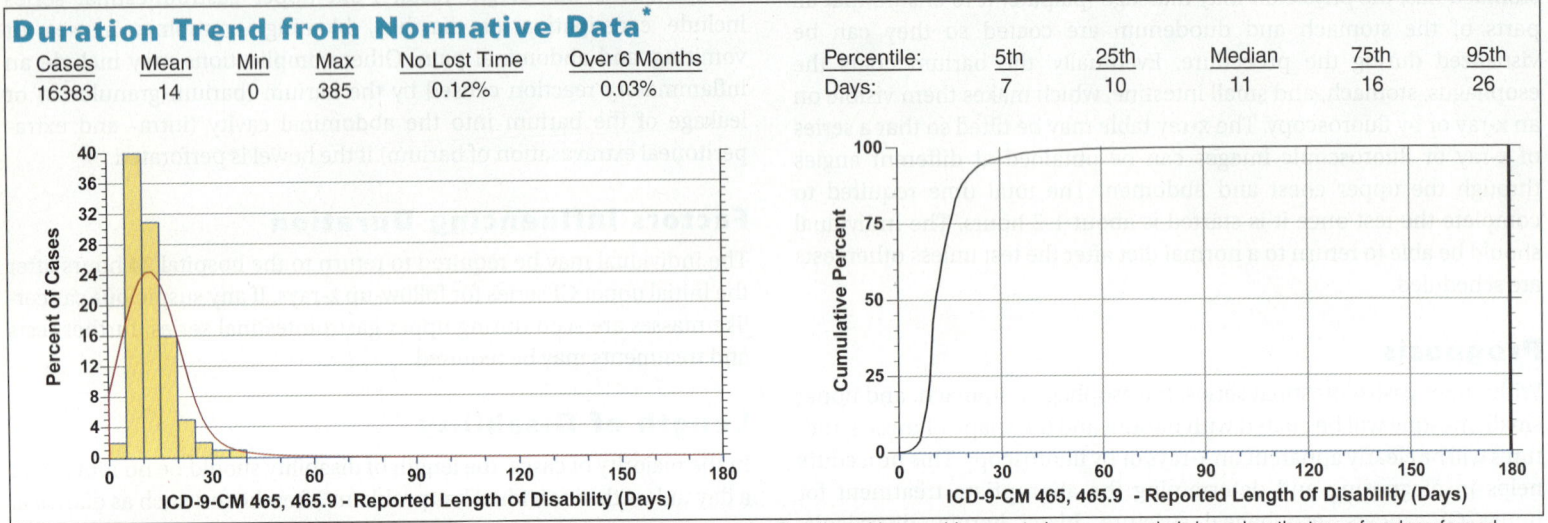

Duration Trend from Normative Data*

Cases	Mean	Min	Max	No Lost Time	Over 6 Months
16383	14	0	385	0.12%	0.03%

Percentile:	5th	25th	Median	75th	95th
Days:	7	10	11	16	26

ICD-9-CM 465, 465.9 - Reported Length of Disability (Days)

* Differences may exist between the expected duration tables and the normative graphs. Duration tables provide expected recovery periods based on the type of work performed by the individual. The normative graphs reflect the actual observed experience of many individuals across the spectrum of physical conditions, in a variety of industries, and with varying levels of case management.

Urethral Catheterization

Other names / synonyms: Foley Catheterization, Indwelling Catheterization, Intermittent Catheterization, Straight Catheterization

57.0, 57.94

Definition

Urethral catheterization is a procedure that involves introducing a flexible, rubber (latex, silicone, or Teflon) tube through the urinary opening (urethra) into the bladder.

There are 2 types of urethral catheterization. A straight or short-term urethral catheterization is a procedure in which the catheter is inserted only long enough to drain the bladder of its contents, and is then promptly removed. An indwelling catheterization is a procedure that inserts a specialized catheter that can be left in the bladder for an extended period of time (days to weeks) for continuous drainage of the bladder into a collection bag.

Straight or short-term catheterization may be done to obtain samples of urine for laboratory analysis in individuals suspected of having urinary tract infection, urinary tract injury, or kidney dysfunction. The most common reason for indwelling urinary catheterization is to monitor the output of urine during surgery or for individuals who are hospitalized with a serious illness, or for individuals who have trauma or obstruction (obstructive uropathy) of the urinary tract. Urinary catheterization may be done in individuals who have urinary incontinence or for those who cannot empty their bladder because of neurological damage.

Older adults may need catheterization if they are at high risk for bladder infection (cystitis) due to incomplete emptying of the bladder associated with prostate enlargement (in men), decreased level of consciousness or immobility. Other risk factors for cystitis include bladder or urethral obstruction, sexual intercourse, insertion of instruments into the urinary tract (catheterization or cystoscopy), pregnancy, diabetes or a history of urinary reflux (reflux nephropathy).

Kidney infection (pyelonephritis) most commonly occurs as a result of lower urinary tract infection (cystitis), particularly in those who have backflow of urine from the bladder into the ureters or kidney pelvis (urinary reflux). The risk of pyelonephritis is increased in those with a history of cystitis, kidney stones, urinary reflux, or urinary tract obstruction. Those who have chronic or recurrent urinary tract infections are also at increased risk and may benefit from catheterization in some cases. Crushing injuries to the pelvis, gunshot wounds, or stab wounds may result in urinary tract trauma and require catheterization.

Obstructive uropathy is a blockage of the normal flow of urine somewhere along the urinary tract. The obstruction increases the pressure to the kidney and can result in acute renal failure. Obstructive uropathy may be caused by kidney stones, narrowing of the urethra, adjacent tumors, scarring of the urethra from previous radiation therapy, urinary tract infections, and cancer. It is more common in those with neuromuscular disorders, diabetes mellitus, benign prostatic hypertrophy, or a history of kidney stones.

Urinary incontinence may occur in those with weakened pelvic muscles or when there is a malfunction of the urethral closure (sphincter). Prior trauma to the urethral area, neurological injury, and some medications may weaken the urethral closure.

Reason for Procedure

Common reasons for the procedure include draining the bladder in individuals who are unable to urinate or unable to control urination, measuring residual urine after urinating, and collecting a urine specimen for culture and sensitivity. Urethral catheterization also allows for diagnostic studies of the lower urinary tract (voiding cystourethrogram and urodynamics). Catheterization can monitor urine output, which is important in intensive care medicine to control fluid balance and detect congestive heart failure, kidney failure, or other disorders affecting urinary output.

Description

Because of anatomical differences, the procedure varies slightly in males and females. In women, the external genital region is cleansed carefully with a disinfectant solution. The external genitalia (labia and external meatus) are spread open to allow direct access to the urethra. A catheter that has been lubricated with a sterile lubricant is slowly inserted into the most forward opening of the 2 openings in the woman's genitals (urethra) and advanced until a flow of urine exits the tube (catheter). In men, the penis is cleansed carefully with a disinfectant solution. A catheter that has been lubricated with a sterile lubricant is slowly inserted into the opening in the penis (urethra) and advanced until a flow of urine exits the tube (catheter).

If the catheter is designed to be left in place (indwelling), a small amount of fluid is inserted via a separate opening (port) in the catheter to inflate a balloon that anchors the catheter gently within the bladder.

Prognosis

Generally, either straight or indwelling urethral catheterization is effective at gathering samples of urine or draining urine from the bladder. While catheterization is a relatively simple procedure, personnel should be trained in the technique to avoid complications. Long-term and serious complications are more common with indwelling catheters, which drain urine for long periods, than with straight catheters, which are removed once the bladder is drained.

Specialists

- Emergency Medicine
- Surgeon
- Urologist

Work Restrictions / Accommodations

Individuals with chronic bladder control problems may need additional restroom facilities or more frequent breaks to visit the restroom. No work restrictions or special accommodations are required once the catheter is removed, except for those related to the underlying condition for which catheterization was performed.

Comorbid Conditions

Comorbid conditions of bladder cancer, kidney failure, or neurological disorders affecting bladder control (neurogenic bladder) may affect ability to recover from the procedure. Bleeding disorders or immunosuppression may increase bleeding or infectious complications of catheterization.

Procedure Complications

Potential complications of the procedure include damage to the tissue of the urethra, bleeding from the urethra or bladder, urinary tract infection, chronic irritation of the bladder, and obstruction of the catheter, causing backflow of urine and possible kidney damage. Some individuals may develop a reaction to the latex material in the catheter. Individuals with known latex sensitivity should have a urethral catheter made of Teflon or silicon to avoid this complication. Catheterization may be associated with release of urinary bacteria into the blood stream, which can cause heart infection (endocarditis) if the bacteria lodge on damaged heart valves. For this reason, individuals with mitral valve prolapse or other heart valve conditions should receive antibiotics before being catheterized.

Factors Influencing Duration

The presence of complications may influence the length of disability.

Length of Disability

No disability is expected for this procedure. Disability may occur as a result of an underlying condition.

References

Eke, N., H. Godfrey, and A. Evans. "Major Surgical Complications From Minor Urological Procedures." Journal of the National Medical Association 92 4 (2000): 196-199.

Godfrey, H., and A. Evans. "Management of Long-term Urethral Catheters: Minimizing Complications." British Journal of Nursing 9 2 (2000): 74-81.

Shapiro, A.J., et al. "Managing the Nondeflating Urethral Catheter." Journal of the American Board of Family Practice 13 2 (2000): 116-119.

Tierney, Lawrence M., Stephen J. McPhee, and Maxine A. Papadakis, eds. Current Medical Diagnosis and Treatment, 39th ed. New York: Lange Medical Books/McGraw-Hill, 2000.

Urethritis
099.4, 099.40, 597

Definition

Urethritis is an inflammation of the urethra, the tube that carries urine from the bladder to the outside of the body. It is usually due to an infection, and may be caused by a variety of organisms, including bacteria and yeasts. It may be caused by the same organisms that cause bladder or kidney infections (e.g., E. coli or Klebsiella), herpes, and some sexually transmitted diseases (e.g., Chlamydia, gonorrhea, and Ureaplasma urealyticum infections). Noninfectious urethritis is often the result of medical catheterization. Urethritis may also develop because of a chemical sensitivity that results in irritation, such as from spermatocides in condoms, contraceptive jelly, cream, or foam. Penetrating trauma to the urethra may also cause urethritis.

Infectious urethritis is considered the most common sexually transmitted syndrome among men in the US. Although women may also develop urethritis, it is primarily a condition of adult men; there is an increased risk among males between 20-35 years old. Unprotected sexual intercourse, multiple sexual partners, and high-risk sexual behaviors are the main risk factors.

Approximately 1 million cases of gonococcal urethritis are diagnosed each year. Urethritis may be associated with other infectious conditions including acute cystitis, orchitis, prostatitis, epididymitis, and proctitis. Noninfectious urethritis occurs in up to 20% of individuals who have been intermittently catheterized as a result of other medical conditions; it is also more common among those using latex catheters as opposed to silicone.

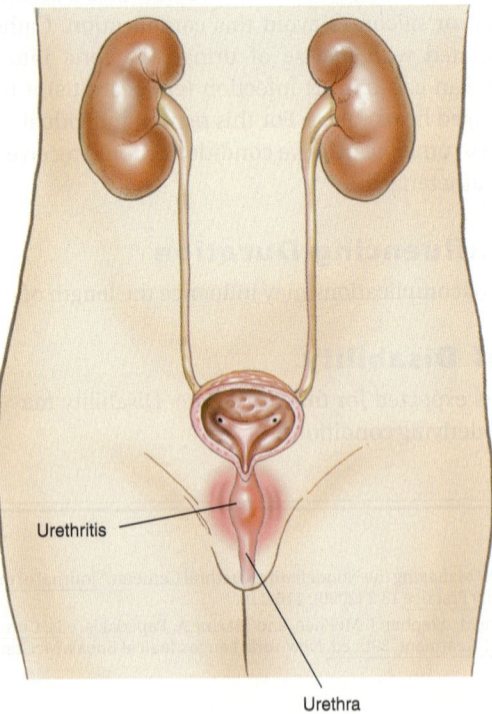

Diagnosis

History: Onset tends to be gradual. Individuals with urethritis complain of a painful, burning sensation with urination (dysuria). The symptoms are usually mild, and in approximately 25% of cases there are no symptoms at all. In these cases, the condition is usually discovered after a partner is diagnosed with a sexually transmitted disease. In severe cases, the pain is sometimes likened to passing small fragments of broken glass. Men may exhibit blood in the urine (hematuria); this is less common in women with urethritis. Pus may also be present in the urine (pyuria), and the individual may experience increased urinary urgency or frequency. In men, intercourse and ejaculation may be painful, and semen may be blood-stained. When caused by a bacterial infection, particularly gonorrhea, there is often a yellow, pus-filled discharge from the penis.

Physical exam: In men, swelling and tenderness may be noted in the testes, epididymis, prostate, or general groin area. In the case of sexually transmitted urethritis caused by gonorrhea or chlamydia, the individual should be examined for evidence of systemic disease. This might include fever, rash, or pain and swelling in the joints. The lymph nodes in the groin area (inguinal) may also be tender and enlarged.

Tests: Triple-void urine specimens will be obtained for urinalysis and culture, and to exclude bladder infection (cystitis). It will also be checked for blood, for white blood cells, or bacterial growth. Urethral discharge may also be cultured to determine the identity of the pathogen causing the urethritis.

Treatment

Urethritis caused by gonorrhea and other bacterial infections is usually successfully treated by antibiotic therapy. Since chlamydia often occurs at the same time as a gonococcal infection (dual infection), effective treatment may also include an effective anti-chlamydial regimen. Because antibiotic-resistant forms of certain infections (penicillin-resistant and tetracycline-resistant) are on the increase, it is necessary that an antibiotic susceptibility test be performed at the same time the infective agent is cultured (culture and sensitivity). Since most urethritis is sexually transmitted, abstinence from sexual intercourse or the use of condoms is recommended throughout the course of treatment. It is imperative that sexual partners are also evaluated and treated. Antibiotic therapy may also be needed if a bacterial infection follows urethritis due to a noninfectious cause. Urethritis caused by trauma or chemical irritants is treated by avoiding the precipitating factors. Analgesic pain relievers and urinary tract-specific analgesics may also be taken concurrently with antibiotics.

Prognosis

With prompt, accurate diagnosis and antibiotic treatment, urethritis usually clears up without any complications. The individual should be instructed concerning the spread of sexually transmitted disease in order to prevent recurrence.

Differential Diagnosis

Conditions with similar symptoms include urinary tract infections, vaginitis, cervicitis, orchitis, prostatitis, urethral stricture, Reiter's syndrome, or Stevens-Johnson syndrome.

Specialists

- Gynecologist
- Urologist

Work Restrictions / Accommodations

Work restrictions or special accommodations are not usually associated with this condition.

Comorbid Conditions

Comorbid conditions include HIV/AIDS and disorders requiring catheterization.

Complications

Complications of gonococcal urethritis in men include inflammation in the epididymis and testes (acute epididymoorchitis), inflammation of the lymph vessels in the penis (penile lymphangitis), inflammation of the prostate gland (prostatitis), and narrowing of a section of the urethra due to scarring (inflammatory urethral stricture). Untreated gonococcal or chlamydial urethritis in women is thought to cause ascending genitourinary infections, which may result in pelvic inflammatory disease (PID), infertility, ectopic pregnancy, and chronic pelvic pain. In both genders, urethritis may proceed up the genitourinary tract to develop bladder infection (cystitis), or kidney infection (pyelonephritis).

Factors Influencing Duration

Length of disability may be influenced by the severity of the symptoms, the underlying cause of the condition, and the response to treatment. Disability may be prolonged if the infective agent does not respond to antibiotic therapy.

Length of Disability

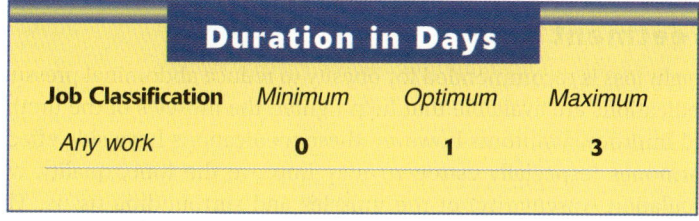

Job Classification	Minimum	Optimum	Maximum
Any work	0	1	3

Failure to Recover

If an individual fails to recover within the maximum duration expectancy period, the reader may wish to reference the following questions to assist in better understanding the specifics of an individual's medical case.

Regarding diagnosis:

- Has diagnosis of urethritis been confirmed with a physical exam?
- Were blood, pus or white cells noted in a urinalysis?
- Was urethral discharge cultured to identify a source of infection?
- Have urinary tract infections and other disorders of the pelvic region been ruled out?

Regarding treatment:

- Were infectious sources of urethritis treated with appropriate antibiotics?
- Do symptoms persist despite treatment?
- Has infective organism been identified?
- Is dual infection present?
- Has culture and sensitivity been done to determine the most effective antibiotic?
- Have antibiotic resistant organisms been ruled out?
- Can antibiotic be administered by injection rather than orally?
- If herpes simplex is the causative organism, would the individual benefit from treatment with an antiviral drug, such as acyclovir?
- Have sexual partners been treated simultaneously to prevent reinfection?
- Have possible chemical irritants (spermatocides) been identified and eliminated?

Regarding prognosis:

- Have symptoms persisted despite treatment?
- Were cultures repeated to rule out the possibility of reinfection or bacterial resistance?
- Has individual been compliant with drug therapy? If not, what can be done to enhance compliance?
- Have chemical irritants been ruled out?
- Has the individual experienced any complications (urinary tract or reproductive infection or inflammation) related to the urethritis that could impact recovery and prognosis?
- Is the individual continuing to engage in unprotected sex?

References

Beers, Mark H., and Robert Berkow. The Merck Manual of Diagnosis and Therapy. Whitehouse Station, NJ: Merck & Co., Inc, 1999.

McKee, K.T. Jr., et al. "Features of Urethritis in a Cohort of Male Soldiers." Clinical Infectious Diseases 30 4 (2000): 736-41.

Urethrocele with Stress Incontinence
618.0, 625.6

Definition

Urethrocele is the sinking (herniation or prolapse) of the female urethra into the front wall of the vagina. The urethra is a small, muscular tube that carries urine from the bladder and normally lies just in front of the vagina. The herniation may be slight and high in the vagina, or large and low with visible bulging at the vaginal entrance.

Urethrocele may be present at birth (congenital) or may be the result of weak pelvic muscles. Stress incontinence (the involuntary discharge of urine due to anatomic displacement and increased abdominal pressure) such as with coughing, sneezing, or laughing is associated with urethrocele. Possible causes of stress incontinence include weak pelvic floor muscles, age-related changes in structural supports, pregnancy, obesity, and incompetent bladder outlet.

Although stress incontinence is a common symptom of urethrocele, urethrocele does not cause stress incontinence. Of women diagnosed with stress incontinence, 75% have urethrocele, however, only half the women diagnosed with moderate to severe urethrocele have stress incontinence.

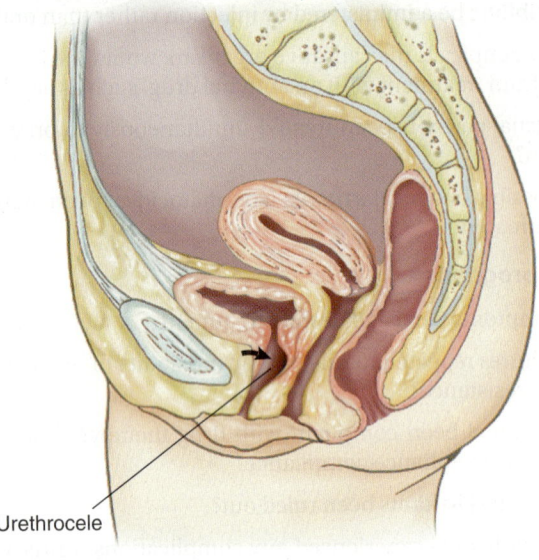

Urethrocele

Diagnosis

History: Individuals may report involuntary leakage of urine with coughing, laughing, sneezing, straining, quick movements, physical activity, or athletics. A large urethrocele may result in urinary frequency, urgency in urination, difficulty emptying the bladder, painful sexual intercourse (dyspareunia), and urinary tract infections.

A woman may be asked to keep a diary to include a record of the times and amount of urine leakage over 24 to 72 hours, fluid intake, and any activity that may be causing the leakage.

Physical exam: A pelvic exam is done to detect any physical conditions that may be linked to incontinence. When the woman is asked to strain, a sliding downward and forward of the urethra and its external opening may be observed. A neurologic exam focusing on the nerves in this area tests reflexes and sensation.

Tests: Tests may include urinalysis and urine culture to rule out infection as the cause of incontinence. With a partially filled bladder, the woman is asked to cough while straining to demonstrate leakage of urine. Up to 20% of women with stress incontinence do not demonstrate incontinence during this test.

The "cotton-tipped applicator test" involves placing a lubricated applicator into the urethra. The angle of the applicator stick at rest is compared to the angle while the woman is straining. A change of more than 30 degrees while straining indicates poor muscle support.

A "pad test" may also be performed with the woman wearing a preweighed sanitary pad during exercise or other activity that usually results in incontinence. The pad is then reweighed to determine the amount of urine lost, if any. Another test involves use of a nontoxic dye in the bladder. A pad stained with dye at the end of the physical activity indicates urine loss.

X-ray studies are most useful for cases of recurrent stress incontinence or for those with no abnormality on cotton-tipped applicator testing or pelvic examination. Urodynamic studies should be performed before any surgical urological corrective procedure.

A urethral pressure profile (UPP) indicates whether an individual would be helped by the standard surgical procedures for stress incontinence. The success rate of surgery is poor in individuals with very low resting urethral closure pressure.

Specialists

- General Surgeon
- Gynecologist
- Urologist

Treatment

Weight loss is recommended for obesity to reduce abdominal pressure. Medications are available that help tighten the muscles of the urethra and improve symptoms however, these medications have side effects. Hormones (especially estrogen) may improve the tone, quality, and circulation (vascularity) of the muscles and surrounding tissue. This treatment uses either an estrogen cream inserted into the vagina, pills taken orally, or skin patches. Vaginal estrogen cream provides relief from symptoms more rapidly than the oral pills, but once symptoms improve, all methods are equally effective.

Isometric exercises (Kegel) can strengthen pelvic floor muscles and reduce or cure stress leakage. Kegel exercises may only provide partial relief for older women or those with severe incontinence.

Weighted cones are used to strengthen the muscles that keep the urethra closed. The cones are inserted into the woman's vagina twice a day. She then substitutes cones of increasing weight to strengthen the muscles. A stiff ring (pessary) is a device inserted into the vagina by a doctor or nurse that helps reposition the urethra and leads to less stress leakage. Although the temporary use of a vaginal pessary may provide relief from incontinence, prolonged use can result in pressure sores and ulcers in the vagina and possible vaginal and urinary tract infections.

Other nonsurgical methods include electrical stimulation of the lower pelvis. This improves continence by stimulating contraction of the urethral muscles. Teflon or collagen can be injected into the area around the urethra. This helps to close the urethra and reduce leakage.

Various surgical procedures involve pulling the bladder up to a more normal position, making an incision in the vagina or abdomen, and securing it with a string attached to the muscle, ligament, or bone. For severe cases of stress incontinence, the bladder may be secured with a wide sling. In rare cases, a doughnut-shaped sac (an artificial sphincter) that circles the urethra is implanted. By pressing a valve under the skin, the sac is deflated and removes pressure from the urethra, allowing passage of urine. Plastic surgery of the urethra (urethroplasty) is performed to correct the prolapsed urethra.

Complementary and Alternative Therapies

Content is intended for awareness only. Treatments may or may not be effective. Scientific evidence may be lacking and some substances have potentially toxic effects. Dr. Presley Reed and the editors do not endorse the use of these therapies in the absence of consultation with a licensed medical professional.

Isometric exercises - Kegel exercises can strengthen pelvic floor muscles and reduce or cure stress leakage. However, these exercises may provide only partial relief for older women or those with severe incontinence.

Prognosis

Any of the various methods of surgical repair (using a string, sling, or implant to raise the prolapsed bladder) is considered the standard treatment for stress incontinence. Correction rate is as high as 75-85% when performed on appropriate candidates. Women with a poorer prognosis may have had previous surgical failures, poor urethral closing pressure at rest, an underlying condition (obesity or diabetes), or combined urinary incontinence (motor-urge and stress incontinence).

Differential Diagnosis

Other types of incontinence may be urge, overflow, or psychogenic (functional) incontinence. Combinations of incontinence are referred to as mixed incontinence, such as stress plus urge incontinence. Transient incontinence is a temporary condition that can be triggered by medications, urinary tract infections, mental problems, severe constipation, and restricted mobility. Urethral tumor and diverticulum are other possible diagnoses.

Work Restrictions / Accommodations

Following surgical repair, responsibilities may need to be largely sedentary. Restrictions may include lifting heavy weights or any work classified as heavy duty.

Comorbid Conditions

Urinary tract infections may coexist with urinary incontinence and increase recovery time. Obesity can have an impact on recovery due to excess weight and pressure on the bladder.

Complications

Although stress incontinence has minor physical complications, it can have major social and psychological effects. Complications from medical therapy are usually side effects from the prescribed medications or local irritation from use of mechanical devices. If surgery is performed, postoperative complications may occur.

Factors Influencing Duration

The particular surgical procedure, any complications, and the individual's job requirements may influence the length of disability.

Length of Disability

Duration depends on severity of incontinence. When medically treated, no disability should be associated with this diagnosis.

Surgical treatment.

Duration in Days

Job Classification	Minimum	Optimum	Maximum
Sedentary work	28	42	56
Light work	28	42	56
Medium work	42	42	56
Heavy work	42	56	70
Very Heavy work	42	56	70

Duration Trend from Normative Data*

Cases	Mean	Min	Max	No Lost Time	Over 6 Months
3126	50	0	221	0.13%	0.16%

Percentile:	5th	25th	Median	75th	95th
Days:	19	35	45	59	96

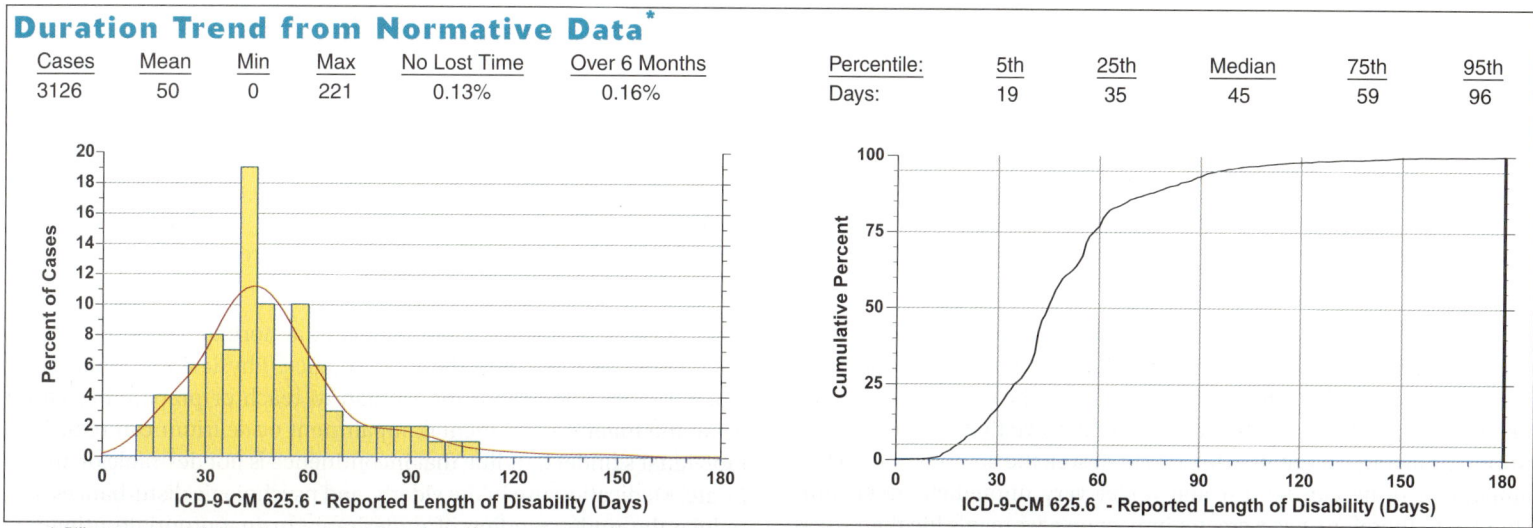

* Differences may exist between the expected duration tables and the normative graphs. Duration tables provide expected recovery periods based on the type of work performed by the individual. The normative graphs reflect the actual observed experience of many individuals across the spectrum of physical conditions, in a variety of industries, and with varying levels of case management.

Failure to Recover

If an individual fails to recover within the maximum duration expectancy period, the reader may wish to reference the following questions to assist in better understanding the specifics of an individual's medical case.

Regarding diagnosis:

- Was diagnosis of stress incontinence confirmed?
- Was the presence of urethrocele confirmed with a pelvic exam?
- Were other causes of incontinence (medications, urinary tract infections, etc.) ruled out?

Regarding treatment:

- Has weight loss or medication been effective in relieving symptoms?
- Has length of medication trial been adequate to gauge effectiveness?
- Has individual been encouraged to perform Kegel exercises to strengthen pelvic floor muscles? Have other strengthening tools been tried?
- Have other nonsurgical treatments such as electrical stimulation or collagen injections been tried?
- Have exercises or other nonsurgical methods been effective in reducing incontinence?
- If nonsurgical methods have failed to reduce symptoms, is surgical intervention now warranted?

Regarding prognosis:

- Is individual an appropriate candidate for surgical intervention?
- Is obesity a factor affecting the outcome of the treatment? If so, how is this being addressed?
- Has individual experienced any complications such as urinary tract infection or bleeding that may impact recovery

References

Urinary Incontinence in Women. National Institute of Diabetes and Digestive Diseases and Kidney Diseases. 11 Feb 1998. 4 July 2000 <http://www.niddk.nih.gov/health/urolog/pubs/uiwomen/uiwomen.htm>.

Beers, Mark H., and Robert Berkow. The Merck Manual of Diagnosis and Therapy. Whitehouse Station, NJ: Merck & Co., Inc, 1999.

Urinary Incontinence in Women

Other names / synonyms: Functional Incontinence, Motor Urge Incontinence, Overflow Incontinence, Sensory Urge Incontinence, Stress Incontinence, Total Urinary Incontinence, Unstable Bladder, Urge Incontinence

625.6, 788.30, 788.31, 788.33, 788.34, 788.35, 788.36, 788.37, 788.39

Definition

Urinary incontinence is the involuntary loss of urine. There are several types of urinary incontinence including stress, urge, overflow, total, and functional. The cause of each type varies. However, there is a great deal of overlap in the conditions, with the result being that one cause may be a factor in more than one type of urinary incontinence.

Stress incontinence results in leakage of urine during coughing, sneezing, jumping, lifting, or even changing position. This is the most common type of urinary incontinence in women. It is often associated with the number of pregnancies and vaginal deliveries, since this creates stretching and weakness of the muscles at the floor of the pelvis, which can allow the urethra to sag. When the urethra sags down, it takes only a small amount of pressure (from either the abdomen or the bladder) to cause a woman to involuntarily loose urine. Sometimes stress incontinence occurs when the urethra itself malfunctions. Loss of estrogen can also affect the urethra and cause stress incontinence. This is a common cause of stress incontinence is women who have passed the menopause.

Urge incontinence, also sometimes called an unstable bladder, results from an abnormal contraction of the bladder muscle (the detrusor muscle). It is not related to position or activity. The woman can feel the need to urinate, but is unable to tighten the valve that controls flow of urine (sphincter) well enough to prevent or stop the flow of urine. A large amount of urine can be lost and under very unpredictable circumstances. It, therefore, has a greater impact on a woman's life than stress incontinence. This condition may coexist with stress incontinence.

Conditions that cause urge incontinence include dysfunction of the nerves that control the bladder (which may be due to strokes or Parkinson's disease) and inflammatory conditions of the bladder. Inflammatory conditions may be due to tumors or stones in the bladder, but it can also occur with acute or chronic inflammatory conditions (cystitis).

Overflow incontinence is seen with a chronically overdistended bladder that never empties, resulting in frequent leakage of urine. This situation may be due to a disorder of the nerves that supply the bladder (as in diabetes), or an obstruction to bladder emptying by urethral narrowing.

Total urinary incontinence is seen when the urethra provides no resistance to the flow of urine. The bladder is unable to store urine, allowing the continuous leak of urine. It can occur with anatomic abnormalities including an abnormal pathway for urine from the bladder (a fistula), an outpouching of the urethra (diverticulum), or an abnormally located ureter (ectopic ureter). Abnormally located ureters are due to a congenital abnormality. Trauma may also result in abnormalities resulting in total urinary incontinence.

Functional incontinence is not related to abnormalities in the urinary tract. Other factors cause the incontinence. Physical immobility may make it more difficult for the woman to reach or prepare herself for using the toilet. Severe mental impairment or delirium can reduce an individual's understanding that incontinence is not desirable or appropriate. Medication use in the elderly, and psychologic disturbances may reduce the understanding of undesirable or inappropriate urination. Medications that may play a role in functional incontinence include antidepressants, antipsychotics, sedative-hypnotics, and narcotic pain medications. Infection also can result in functional incontinence. Diabetes and lack of estrogen also are causes of functional incontinence. Finally, impacted stool may actually result in urinary incontinence (in addition to fecal incontinence).

Accurate statistics about the incidence of urinary incontinence are only available for the elderly. More than 50% of all women 20 to 80 years of age may have urinary incontinence. Fifteen to thirty percent of women over the age of 65 living in retirement communities are incontinent of urine. Each vaginal delivery of a baby makes urinary incontinence more likely, as does increasing age.

Diagnosis

History: With stress incontinence, a woman may report loss of a small amount of urine with sneezing, coughing, laughing, bending, lifting weight, or rising from a sitting to standing position. She may also report the sensation of heaviness in the pelvic area.

With urge incontinence, a woman may report loss of a large amount of urine, frequent voiding, the urge coming too fast to get to the toilet, and the loss of urine at the sound of running water.

In overflow incontinence, there is a report of dribbling urine without being aware of urine loss and the sensation of incomplete emptying of the bladder.

In functional incontinence, the woman may or may not complain of loss of urine, depending on the cause of the functional incontinence. If there is physical disability, there may be a complaint of inability to get to a bathroom on time, the lack of convenient access to a toilet, or the need for assistance in getting on the toilet. If urine loss is due to medication use, the woman may report incontinence. Similarly, women who are postmenopausal, or who have diabetes may report incontinence. In cases of delirium or dementia, it may be the caregivers who note incontinence. Women with psychologic conditions may report urinary urgency and frequency, but without evidence of abnormality. Women who have a stool impaction may report incontinence of both urine and stool.

A voiding diary is kept may be kept. In a voiding diary, factors associated with the incontinence are recorded. Information may include normal voiding, and information about incontinence such as timing (day or nighttime), onset, duration, frequency, possible precipitating events, the presence of blood, and an estimation of the amount of urine lost. Medication use should also be included. The history should reflect any neurologic conditions affecting the bladder and urinary sphincter such as spinal cord injury, stroke, diabetes, Parkinson's disease, or multiple sclerosis. A history of trauma, vaginal surgery, extensive rectal surgery using an incision in the abdomen and perineum, removal of the uterus (radical hysterectomy), radiation therapy, or previous surgical repair of incontinence should be obtained. Other conditions that should be noted include depression, congestive heart failure, and the number of pregnancies.

Physical exam: Abnormalities such as a pouch-like protrusion in the wall of the urethra (urethrocele), pouch-like protrusion of the bladder into the vagina (cystocele), or pouch-like protrusion of the rectum into the back wall of the vagina (rectocele) may be revealed. Other abnormal findings may include redness, vaginal or urethral discharge, or tissue shrinkage (atrophy). The pelvic examination is performed with a full and empty bladder, and during coughing or straining, to check for incontinence and sagging of the urethra (prolapse).

Tests: Tests may include a urinalysis and urine culture. The pad test may be employed to measure involuntary urine loss. Urodynamic test is often performed, including measurements of bladder capacity, sensation, pressures within the bladder when full of urine, pressure changes that occur during urination, voluntary control, and pressure in the urethra (cystometry and urethral pressure profile). Visually inspecting the bladder with fiber-optic video cameras (cystoscopy and urethroscopy) may also be performed.

Treatment

Effective treatment requires a correct diagnosis of the cause of incontinence. Any predisposing conditions should be treated first, such as a chronic cough, urinary infection, or estrogen deficiency.

The treatment of stress incontinence may require exercises to strengthen the pelvic floor (Kegel exercises), biofeedback, electrical stimulation of the pelvic floor muscles, drugs, or surgery.

Surgical procedures include repair of cystocele and bladderneck suspension procedures. There are a variety of bladderneck suspension procedures, involving either an abdominal or vaginal approach, and that may be performed laparoscopically, to repair the urethra. Abdominal approaches include the Marshall-Marchetti or Marshall-Marchetti-Krantz procedures in which the urethra is repositioned through an incision made in the abdomen. Vaginal approaches are repairs made primarily through the wall of the vagina, often referred to as needle suspensions. Vaginal approaches include the Pereyra, Stamey, Raz, Winter, and the Gittes procedures. The pubovaginal sling (placement of an artificial sphincter) and periurethral bulking injections may be applied to compress the urethra and increase resistance to urine leakage.

In the case of overflow incontinence, the cause of incomplete bladder emptying must be surgically removed or corrected if possible. Alpha-blockers therapy, avoidance of anticholinergic drugs, intermittent draining of the bladder with a catheter, or even permanent bladder drainage (suprapubic catheterization) may be recommended.

The treatment of urge incontinence may include antibiotic therapy, topical estrogen therapy or removal of bladder stones or tumors. If urge incontinence is related to neurological diseases, then bladder and bowel training, techniques to assist bladder emptying, urinating according to a schedule, and improvements to aide mobility may be employed. In some cases, management of fluid intake, intermittent catheterization or use of external collection devices is appropriate. If urge incontinence is due to unstable bladder muscles, anticholinergic medications may be beneficial.

Treatment of functional incontinence may include a number of different activities. Functional incontinence that is related to sleeping pills, diuretics, or alcohol, requires restriction or avoidance of the offending substance. Anticholinergic drugs must be avoided. If incontinence is related to sensory deficits, inability to remove clothing quickly or easily, or to access to the toilet, aids such as eyeglasses, hearing aids, easy-to-remove clothing, and convenient toilet facilities should be provided. If incontinence is related to dementia, assisting the individual to the toilet at regularly scheduled times may be attempted.

Incontinence due to stool impaction is treated by relieving the impaction. If incontinence is related to lack of estrogen, medication with estrogen may be recommended. Urinary tract infections causing incontinence are treated with antibiotics.

Prognosis

Outcome of treatment depends on successful treatment of the underlying condition or cause of the incontinence. The great majority of individuals with stress incontinence can be significantly helped. Kegel exercises and electrical stimulation to the pelvic floor may relieve symptoms of stress incontinence in many women. About half of women treated for stress incontinence with surgical correction void normally with no further symptoms in five-year follow-ups. Urge incontinence and overflow incontinence are more likely to recur or become a chronic condition. Treatment of urinary traction infection should relieve all symptoms. Removal of stones from the bladder should also relieve all symptoms of incontinence. Bladder training programs provide great relief.

Incontinence due to dementia and mental health disorders may continue unless there is resolution of the underlying condition.

Estrogen replacement may provide relief of symptoms for women with stress incontinence.

Differential Diagnosis

Incontinence may be due to a abnormalities associated with a number of medical conditions such as stroke, congestive heart failure, neurologic conditions, effects due to lack of estrogen, medications, and stool impaction.

Specialists

- Gynecologist
- Urologist
- Neurologist

Rehabilitation

Rehabilitation procedures such as Kegel exercises, electrical stimulation to the pelvic area, and bladder training programs may be used for treatment of incontinence. Kegel exercises involve tightening the muscles in the pelvis that are used for urination for 10 to 20 seconds, and then relaxing them. This is repeated for several repetitions, at least four times a day in order to build up the strength of muscles in the urethral area. Electrical stimulation to the pelvic area improves functioning of the bladder muscle (detrusor muscle), relieving incontinence in about 52-90% of individuals. Bladder training programs involve a schedule of voiding every two hours. The length of time between voiding is gradually increased when the woman can maintain control between voidings.

Work Restrictions / Accommodations

Lifting should be avoided, as should environments that trigger sneezing or coughing, and changing positions too often. Certain noises (for example, running water) may provoke urination, so workplaces with these noises should be avoided. Individuals at work should have easy access to the toilet. Work restrictions and accommodations may be needed following bladder neck suspension procedures.

Work restrictions and accommodations may also be needed for surgical correction of other problems that contribute to the incontinence. Restrictions and accommodations may include no heavy lifting, shorter workday, and time off for follow-up appointments. In some situations, catheters may be placed in the bladder for several days to a couple of weeks following the procedure. Employees returning to work with catheters in place may need accommodations so that the catheter bag may be emptied and the catheter may be maintained.

Complementary and Alternative Therapies

Content is intended for awareness only. Treatments may or may not be effective. Scientific evidence may be lacking and some substances have potentially toxic effects. Dr. Presley Reed and the editors do not endorse the use of these therapies in the absence of consultation with a licensed medical professional.

Biofeedback - Individuals are taught to regain control over their bladder function through a procedure that detects a physiologic response and gives immediate visual or auditory feedback indicating whether or not the correct response occurred.

Bladder retraining - Gradually increases the voiding interval to an acceptable level.

Comorbid Conditions

Comorbid conditions can include psychiatric conditions, neurologic conditions, endocrine conditions, congestive heart failure, urinary tract infections, stool impaction, and physical mobility limitations.

Complications

Complications may occur as a result of backward flow of urine toward the kidneys (ureteral reflux), enlargement of the urinary drainage system (hydronephrosis), bladder or kidney infection, or chronic kidney failure. Perineal skin damage and infection can result without appropriate preventive skin care.

The inability to control urine can interfere with a woman's enjoyment of social relationships, work, and sexual life. It can lead to social isolation and disability.

Factors Influencing Duration

The type of underlying disorder, obesity, age, diabetes, type of incontinence and character of applied therapy, response to treatment, complications of reconstructive surgery, and job demands may influence length of disability.

Length of Disability

Surgical treatment (Marshall-Marchetti operation).

Duration in Days

Job Classification	Minimum	Optimum	Maximum
Sedentary work	42	49	56
Light work	42	49	56
Medium work	42	49	70
Heavy work	56	63	84
Very Heavy work	56	63	112

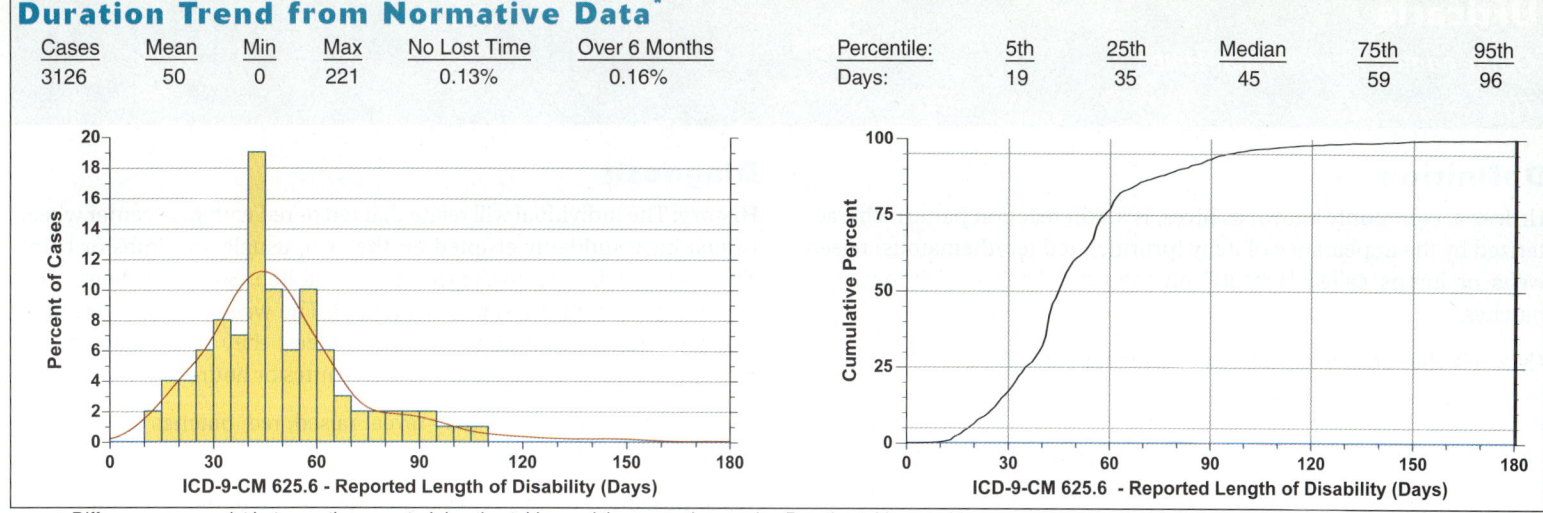

Failure to Recover

If an individual fails to recover within the maximum duration expectancy period, the reader may wish to reference the following questions to assist in better understanding the specifics of an individual's medical case.

Regarding diagnosis:

- Does the individual have a history of multiple childbirths?
- Has the individual gone through menopause?
- Has the individual been referred to an appropriate specialist (urologist, gynecologist)?
- Has the woman kept a "voiding diary" to help identify the circumstances that precipitate incontinence?
- Were any physical abnormalities in the genitourinary system noted on physical exam?
- Was a urodynamic test performed?
- Has the type of incontinence been identified?
- Has the cause of the incontinence been established?

Regarding treatment:

- Has weight loss or medication been effective in relieving symptoms?
- Has a long enough trial of medication been done to gauge effectiveness?
- Has the individual been encouraged to perform Kegel exercises to strengthen pelvic floor muscles? Have other strengthening tools been tried?
- Have other nonsurgical treatments such as electrical stimulation or collagen injections been tried?
- Have exercises or other nonsurgical methods been effective in reducing incontinence?
- If nonsurgical methods have failed to reduce symptoms, is surgical intervention now warranted?

Regarding prognosis:

- Based on the type of treatment required, has adequate time elapsed for complete recovery?
- Have all associated conditions that contribute to the incontinence (mental health, urinary tract infection, estrogen deficiency) been addressed in the treatment plan?
- Would the individual benefit from consultation with an appropriate specialist (psychiatrist, neurologist, gynecologist)?
- Is individual an appropriate candidate for surgical intervention?
- Has the individual experienced any associated complications (reflux, bladder or kidney infection, kidney dysfunction, or perineal excoriation) that could impact recovery and prognosis? If so, are these complications being addressed in the treatment plan?

References

Benson, J. Thomas. "Urinary Incontinence." Textbook of Gynecology, 2nd ed. Copeland, Larry J., and John F. Jarrell, eds. Philadelphia: W.B. Saunders Company, 2000. 1055-1076.

Geriatric Medicine: Urinary Incontinence. Mayo Foundation for Medical Education and Research. 04 Jan 2001. 26 Jan 2001 <http://www.mayo.edu/geriatrics-rst/Incont.html>.

Murphy, Brian S. "Urinary Incontinence." Saunders Manual of Medical Practice, 2nd ed. Rakel, Robert E., ed. Philadelphia: W.B. Saunders Company, 2000. 701-703.

Nagle, Gratia M. "Genitourinary Surgery." Alexander's Care of the Patient in Surgery, 11th ed. Meeker, Margaret H., and Jane C. Rothrock, eds. St. Louis: Mosby, 1999. 501-598.

Presti, Joseph C., Marshall L. Stoller, and Peter R. Carroll. "Urology." Current Medical Diagnosis and Treatment, 39th ed. Tierney, Lawrence M., Stephen J. McPhee, and Maxine A. Papadakis, eds. New York: Lange Medical Books/McGraw-Hill, 2000. 917-958.

Tanagho, Emil A. "Urinary Incontinence." Smith's General Urology, 15th ed. Tanagho, Emil A., and Jack W. McAninch, eds. New York: Lange Medical Books/McGraw-Hill, 2000. 538-554.

Urticaria

Other names / synonyms: Hives

708

Definition

Urticaria, commonly known as hives, is a skin reaction pattern characterized by the appearance of itchy (pruritic), red (erythematous) raised welts or lumps called "wheals" on the skin. They usually occur in batches.

Urticaria that occurs in frequent, recurring episodes over a period of over 6 weeks is called chronic urticaria. In 80-90% of cases, the cause of urticaria is unknown (idiopathic); 3% of afflicted individuals have chronic idiopathic urticaria. Forty to sixty percent of individuals with chronic idiopathic urticaria have an autoimmune cause of their urticaria.

There are three categories of urticaria based on cause: allergic, genetic (hereditary), and physical. Allergic urticaria is usually caused by medications; penicillin is the most common allergen. Virtually any drug can cause allergic urticaria. Aspirin can both cause urticaria, and worsen chronic urticaria in 21-41% of cases. Foods can commonly cause acute urticaria, but rarely cause chronic urticaria. Commonly implicated foods include nuts, fish, shellfish, eggs, milk, chocolate, tomatoes, and fresh berries. Inhalant allergens, especially pollens, mold spores, and animal danders commonly cause allergic urticaria. Allergic urticaria also results from infections (especially viral infections and streptococcal throat infections). Urticaria can be an allergic reaction to insect and spider bites, and develop from skin contact with chemicals, plants, and textiles. Hives may also develop after infections or illnesses (including autoimmune diseases, leukemia, etc.). A type of allergic urticaria also develops with some internal diseases, including rheumatoid arthritis, systemic lupus erythematosus (the initial symptom of the disease in 7-9% of individuals), and polymyositis.

A hereditary form of urticaria occurs, but is rare, accounting for only 2% of all cases of urticaria. This form usually affects the face, and often occurs after minor trauma such as dental work.

The third type of urticaria is physical urticaria. They result from physical factors such as heat, cold, and pressure, and comprise 10-17% of all cases of chronic urticaria. This type of urticaria usually affects young adults, only in the part of the body exposed to the physical stimulation; it is generally of short duration (30-60 minutes). The most common type of physical urticaria is called dermographism, which occurs at the sight of scratching or a tight garment. Another type of physical urticaria is "pressure urticaria," a painful, deep wheal occurring in areas of pressure such as feet, buttocks, and palms. Other less common physical urticaria include "cold urticaria" from exposure to cold and "solar urticaria" from sun exposure. A condition related to urticaria that is sometimes associated with it is "angioedema." This condition is similar to urticaria but involves the deeper dermis and subcutaneous tissue, and usually affects areas with loose subcutaneous tissue such as eyelids or lips.

Up to 15-25% of the population will have urticaria at some point in their lives. Hives are more common in individuals who have experienced other allergic reactions, including hay fever and angioedema.

Diagnosis

History: The individual will relate that red or red with pale center wheals (welts) have suddenly erupted on the skin, usually on limbs or trunk. The welts will blanch to the touch and will itch. Sometimes new welts will develop when the skin is scratched. The welts enlarge, spread, or join together to form large flat raised areas; they can change shape, disappear, and then reappear within minutes or hours.

Physical exam: The exam may reveal raised, red, batches of wheals on various parts of the body.

Tests: Baseline laboratory tests include complete blood count, erythrocyte sedimentation rate, multiphasic screening panel, and a RAST (radio allergosorbent) test for allergies. Other more specialized tests are done to diagnose specific types of urticaria, and may include skin tests (scratch and intradermal tests), skin biopsy, urinalysis, streptococcal throat culture, and tests for physical urticaria including warm water test, stroking test, and ice cube test.

Treatment

There is currently no known permanent cure for chronic idiopathic urticaria; most cases are characterized by periodic flare-ups with symptom-free intervals in between. Most of the time, the urticaria will eventually "burn out" and never return, although this may not happen for months or even years. Thus, symptomatic treatment is necessary. If the urticaria is an allergic reaction, the cause needs to be identified, removed, and avoided, if possible. Diet might need to be modified. Medications (plus their derivatives) need to be identified, avoided, and alternatives substituted. Factors that aggravate urticaria such as alcohol, aspirin, heat, exertion, and stress should be avoided. Cool compresses or soaks to irritated areas, soothing baths, and applying calamine lotion may calm the area, and reduce swelling and pain. Oral antihistamine medications often give quick relief, and are the most effective treatment. A short course of systemic corticosteroid medication may be necessary in severe, resistant episodes of urticaria. The individual should avoiding inflaming the area, and avoid wearing tight clothing.

Prognosis

Most cases of urticaria resolve completely without complications. The wheals can last for several hours. Identifying and avoiding known trigger factors can help prevent allergic reactions in the future. Even if the trigger source cannot be identified, the allergic reactions can lessen in frequency and severity over time without treatment. In rare cases, a medical emergency may arise should anaphylactic shock develop; death is possible if that condition is not treated promptly. Even individuals with anaphylaxis, however, recover completely after treatment of the episode.

Differential Diagnosis

Differential diagnoses include erythema multiforme and erythema nodosum.

Specialists

- Allergist
- Dermatologist
- Immunologist

Work Restrictions / Accommodations

Antihistamines can cause drowsiness and sedation. Work that requires driving or using heavy or dangerous equipment, or other situations where alertness is a safety issue may have to be restricted until treatment is completed. Also, if the urticaria results from exposure to a causative agent in the workplace, avoiding that agent will be necessary, and may require changing work areas.

Complementary and Alternative Therapies

Content is intended for awareness only. Treatments may or may not be effective. Scientific evidence may be lacking and some substances have potentially toxic effects. Dr. Presley Reed and the editors do not endorse the use of these therapies in the absence of consultation with a licensed medical professional.

| Acupuncture - | May help alleviate common allergic symptoms such as skin eruptions. |
| Hypnotherapy - | Hypnotic techniques may help individual relax and alleviate the stress that often accompanies an allergic reaction. |

Comorbid Conditions

Comorbidities include the multitude of conditions and diseases that are associated with the development of urticaria. These include allergies, infections, connective tissue diseases, vasculitis, systemic lupus erythematosus, leukemia, lymphoma, various carcinomas, bites and stings, polymyositis, and rheumatoid arthritis.

Complications

Anaphylaxis and life-threatening airway obstruction, if swelling occurs in the throat, may be associated with urticaria and are medical emergencies.

Factors Influencing Duration

The length of disability may be influenced by the ability to identify and eliminate the causative agent, the effectiveness of the symptomatic treatment, plus the location, extent, and severity of reaction. Antihistamine medication may cause sedation.

Length of Disability

In most cases, no disability is expected. Duration depends on cause, severity of symptoms, and treatment.

Duration in Days

Job Classification	Minimum	Optimum	Maximum
Any work	0	3	7

Failure to Recover

If an individual fails to recover within the maximum duration expectancy period, the reader may wish to reference the following questions to assist in better understanding the specifics of an individual's medical case.

Regarding diagnosis:

- Did the individual present with a skin reaction characterized by raised, red, itchy bumps?
- Does the individual have any known allergies?
- Did the individual report a recent change in diet, medication, cosmetics, soap, etc?
- Was an underlying cause for the skin reaction determined with diagnostic tests such as allergy testing, erythrocyte sedimentation rate (ESR), multiphasic screening panel?
- If the diagnosis is uncertain, were conditions such as erythema multiforme or erythema nodosum ruled out?
- Would individual benefit from consultation with a specialist (allergist, dermatologist, immunologist)?

Regarding treatment:

- Were antihistamines administered? Did the symptoms subside?
- Was the individual instructed to avoid offending allergen(s)?
- Was diet counseling necessary?
- Have medications or conditions (stress, heat, exertion) that could be associated with skin reactions been eliminated?
- Has the individual been compliant with the avoidance recommendations? If not, would additional counseling be beneficial?

Regarding prognosis:

- Did the urticaria subside with treatment? If not, was further investigation done to rule out other skin irritants or causes?
- Does the individual have any underlying skin infections, connective tissue diseases, autoimmune disorders or other conditions that may impact recovery and prognosis? If so, are these conditions being addressed in the treatment plan?

References

Monroe, Eugene W. "Urticaria and Angioedema." Principles and Practice of Dermatology, 2nd ed. Sams, W. Mitchell, and Peter J. Lynch, eds. New York: Churchill Livingstone, 1996. 521-534.

Beers, Mark H., and Robert Berkow. The Merck Manual of Diagnosis and Therapy. Whitehouse Station, NJ: Merck & Co., Inc, 1999.

Uterine Polyps

Other names / synonyms: Endometrial Growths, Endometrial Polyps, Polyp of Corpus Uteri, Uterine Polyps

621.0

Definition

Uterine polyps are growths (tumors) in the lining of the uterus (endometrium). The endometrial tissue normally grows again after it is shed during the menstrual period, but excessive growth can cause polyps to fan out but remain attached to the endometrium by a small stalk resembling a bush or tree. Polyps are usually about the size of a pencil eraser or smaller, but can grow to the size of an orange.

Although the exact cause is unknown, polyps may form spontaneously or as a result of too much estrogen. Uterine polyps may grow faster during pregnancy and with use of estrogen replacement therapy or oral contraceptives. Those present before menopause are unlikely to become cancerous (malignant), but those developing during or after are more likely to become malignant, especially if they grow larger after menopause has passed. They may cease to grow with menopause when estrogen levels drop off.

About 10-24% of women undergoing endometrial biopsy or hysterectomy have had uterine polyps. Uterine polyps are usually rare among women under 20. They are more common with increasing age, peak in the fifth decade, and gradually decline after menopause.

Diagnosis

History: There may be no symptoms, however 50% of individuals report abnormal vaginal bleeding (metrorrhagia). Vaginal bleeding or spotting may be excessively heavy during the regular flow (menorrhagia), may occur between periods, after intercourse or menopause, or during hormone therapy.

Physical exam: On pelvic exam, the uterus may feel lumpy.

Tests: A special water ultrasound (sonohysterogram) uses sterile water to open the uterine cavity to determine if polyps are present. Hysterosalpingogram (HSG) uses dye under pressure to open the uterine cavity, followed by a quick x-ray. A hysteroscope may be used to look inside the uterus to diagnose uterine polyps.

Treatment

Small polyps that do not cause any symptoms usually do not have to be removed, but should be checked every 6 months. If the polyp causes pelvic pain, abnormal menstrual bleeding, or infertility, or if there is a history of miscarriage, a gynecologist may remove it (polypectomy). Small polyps may be removed at the doctor's office by directing a hysteroscope through the vagina and cervical opening to grab the polyp and cut it off. Larger polyps are removed in the operating room under general anesthesia to control possible bleeding. If numerous polyps are found, a hysterectomy may be recommended.

Other ways to treat the polyps or symptoms include shrinking the polyps using gonadotropin-releasing-hormone (GnRH) agonists. Nonsteroidal anti-inflammatory drugs (NSAIDs) or progestins may control bleeding. Destroying endometrial tissue (endometrial ablation) controls bleeding in 70-90% of the cases.

Prognosis

Treatment is successful in most cases. Only a small percentage of polyps may return and need removal again.

Differential Diagnosis

Uterine fibroid (myoma), carcinoma or sarcoma, menstrual dysfunction, vaginitis, vaginal varicosities, cervical disorders such as cervical ectropion, some sexually transmitted diseases, ectopic pregnancy, and retained placental tissue (placental polyp) may have similar symptoms.

Specialists

- Fertility Specialist
- Gynecologist

Work Restrictions / Accommodations

Individuals who have surgery may require a period of limited activity with restrictions on lifting or excessive standing. After removal of a polyp, individuals can usually return to work in a few days. Individuals may experience a little spotting at first but this should not impose any restrictions.

Comorbid Conditions

Comorbid conditions that may influence length of disability include pregnancy, anemia, bleeding disorders, and hormone replacement treatment.

Complications

The polyps may become malignant. They can cause severe bleeding that leads to anemia or shock. The polyps may prevent pregnancy by interfering with the egg and sperm, and may also cause miscarriages if they grow large.

Factors Influencing Duration

Treatment results, complications, age, and job demands influence length of disability.

Length of Disability

Excision and removal, vaginal approach (outpatient).

Duration in Days

Job Classification	Minimum	Optimum	Maximum
Sedentary work	3	7	14
Light work	3	7	14
Medium work	3	10	21
Heavy work	7	10	28
Very Heavy work	7	14	28

Failure to Recover

If an individual fails to recover within the maximum duration expectancy period, the reader may wish to reference the following questions to assist in better understanding the specifics of an individual's medical case.

Regarding diagnosis:

- Has diagnosis of uterine polyp been confirmed by sonohysterogram, hysterosalpingogram (HSG), or hysteroscope?
- Has individual experienced any complications such as severe bleeding leading to anemia or shock?
- Does individual have any underlying conditions, such as pregnancy or hormone replacement treatment that may impact recovery?

Regarding treatment:

- Is the condition so serious that it causes pelvic pain, abnormal menstrual bleeding, infertility, or a history of miscarriage, suggesting individual would benefit from consultation with a gynecologist regarding the best course of action?
- What is/was the procedure of choice: polypectomy or gonadotropin-releasing-hormone (GnRH) agonists?
- Was the treatment performed in an operating room to control bleeding, with the result that individual is experiencing complications relating to surgical procedure?
- Was a hysterectomy required?

Regarding prognosis:

- Have polyps returned despite treatment?
- Particularly with individuals who have entered menopause, is malignancy a possibility?
- Would more aggressive treatment, such as a hysterectomy, now be warranted?

References

Center for Uterine Fibroids: Information About Fibroids. Center for Uterine Fibroids. 2000. 16 Sept 2000 <http://www.fibroids.net/html/frameset.htm>.

Fibroids and Polyps. Ethicon, Inc (Johnson & Johnson). 01 Jan 2000. 20 May 2000 <http://ethiconinc.com/facts/women/fibroids/body.htm>.

Hill, D. Ashley, MD. Associate Director - Department of Obstetrics and Gynecology. Endometrial Polyps. OBGYN.net. 01 Jan 2000. 6 June 2000 <http://www.obgyn.net/women/articles/polyps_dah.htm>.

Ryan, Kenneth, Ross Berkowitz, and Robert Barbieri. "The Uterine Corpus." Kistner's Gynecology and Women's Health. Ryan, Kenneth Linn, ed. St Louis: Mosby, 1999. 121-142.

Uterus, Perforation of

Other names / synonyms: Damage to Uterus

621.8, 637.2, 639.2, 996.32

Definition

Perforation of the uterus is an accidental puncture of the uterus.

Perforation is usually caused by a surgical instrument shaped like a spoon or scoop used for scraping and removing material from an organ (curette) or by an intrauterine device (IUD). There have been some cases of uterine perforation following induced abortion. The instrument penetrates through the uterine wall and may migrate into the abdominal cavity where the bowel or bladder may also be perforated.

A woman's uterus can become perforated during other intrauterine procedures, such as rotating an infant during delivery using forceps, dilation and curettage procedures in which the lining of the uterus is scraped, or during a tubal ligation sterilization procedure. During IUD insertion, perforations can occur when the uterus is abnormally positioned or unusually soft after a birth or abortion. An IUD can also become "lost" within the uterus and the end of the device may pierce the muscular wall of the uterus.

Breast-feeding (lactating) women are at higher risk for perforation of the uterus with an IUD or with D&C and should be carefully monitored. During dilation and curettage procedures, postmenopausal women are at a higher risk for uterine perforation because the cervix narrows and the wall of the uterus become thinner after menopause.

The incidence of uterine perforation from IUD is low; approximately 0.12-0.68/1000 insertions in one study. The incidence of uterine perforation due to induced abortion has been estimated to be about .08% per 1000 abortions.

Diagnosis

History: The woman may report lower abdominal pain, heavy vaginal bleeding, or, if she has an IUD, failure to feel the IUD string. She may also report bloating, rigidity and pain in her abdomen, nausea, vomiting, chills, fever, and irregular heartbeat (tachycardia). Some individuals may not report any symptoms (asymptomatic).

Physical exam: Pelvic examination may reveal heavy vaginal bleeding. ination of the uterus may reveal a softened uterine wall due to birth or abortion. Abdominal distention may be evident upon examination.

Tests: Ultrasound (sonogram) is used to confirm the diagnosis. Blood tests such as a complete blood count (CBC) and sodium, potassium, and chloride (electrolytes) are drawn to detect presence of infection. Radiological studies such as x-rays of the abdominal cavity can reveal a perforated abdominal wall. Laparoscopy may be done to evaluate/confirm possible perforation.

Treatment

Treatment is based on the cause and extent of the perforation. If due to induced abortion procedures, surgical repair of the uterus is indicated. If the bowel becomes perforated, a resection and surgical joining of the bowel segments (anastomosis) may be performed. If due to IUD use, removal of the IUD using an instrument to examine the abdominal cavity (laparoscope) is usually done, unless there is bowel perforation or severe infection (sepsis) present.

Inflammation of the outer membrane of the abdominal wall as a result of bacteria or irritating substance introduced into the abdominal cavity by perforation (peritonitis) may occur if the abdominal wall is penetrated. Broad-spectrum antibiotics are usually administered if symptoms of peritonitis or infection are present. Catheterization of the bladder with follow-up laparoscopy is usually performed to examine extent of the damage to the bladder and assess the need for surgical repair.

Prognosis

If the cause of the perforation is known and treatment is promptly started, full recovery is expected. Surgical repair of damaged organs (repair of the uterus, anastomosis) and removal of IUD are usually successful if there are no complications.

With immediate administration of a broad-spectrum antibiotic, infection usually subsides. If infection is left untreated, sepsis and death can occur.

Differential Diagnosis

Differential diagnoses include other causes of uterine bleeding such as dysfunctional uterine bleeding, leaking of fetal blood cells into the maternal circulation (fetomaternal hemorrhage), postmenopausal bleeding, bleeding during labor (intrapartum hemorrhage) usually caused by placental abnormalities such as placenta previa or abruptio placentae, and excessive bleeding after childbirth (postpartum hemorrhage).

Specialists

- General Surgeon
- Gynecologist
- Obstetrician
- Radiologist
- Urologist

Work Restrictions / Accommodations

Heavy lifting and restrictions on activities may be required if surgical repair surgery has been performed.

Comorbid Conditions

Uterine cancer, uterine fibroid, or encapsulated tumor (fibroma) can further lengthen disability.

Complications

Complications include inflammation of the abdominal lining (peritonitis), bowel or bladder injury, massive bleeding (hemorrhaging), and infection (sepsis). Adhesions and scar tissue can result from surgical repair of the uterus or other organs involved.

Factors Influencing Duration

Factors that may influence the length of disability include the size and cause of the perforation, treatment, the development of serious complications such as infection (sepsis), job demands, and the age and general health of the individual.

Length of Disability

Conservative treatment. Removal of IUD with forceps.

Duration in Days

Job Classification	Minimum	Optimum	Maximum
Sedentary work	1	2	7
Light work	1	2	7
Medium work	1	2	7
Heavy work	1	2	7
Very Heavy work	1	2	7

Laparoscopic treatment.

Duration in Days

Job Classification	Minimum	Optimum	Maximum
Sedentary work	3	7	21
Light work	3	7	21
Medium work	7	14	28
Heavy work	7	21	35
Very Heavy work	14	21	35

Failure to Recover

If an individual fails to recover within the maximum duration expectancy period, the reader may wish to reference the following questions to assist in better understanding the specifics of an individual's medical case.

Regarding diagnosis:

- How did the individual's uterus become perforated? IUD? Surgical procedure? Delivery? Induced abortion?
- Is the individual breastfeeding? Postmenopausal?
- Does the woman report lower abdominal pain, heavy vaginal bleeding, or, if she has an IUD, failure to see the IUD string?
- Does she also report bloating, rigidity and pain in her abdomen, nausea, vomiting, chills, fever, and tachycardia?
- Did pelvic examination reveal heavy vaginal bleeding? Is the uterine wall softened? Was abdominal distention evident?
- Did the individual have an ultrasound done? CBC and electrolytes? Abdominal x-rays?
- Have conditions with similar symptoms been ruled out?

Regarding treatment:

- Was it necessary to repair the perforation surgically?
- Was it necessary to also repair other organs?
- If present, was an IUD removed?

- Did the individual develop peritonitis? Is the individual on antibiotics?

Regarding prognosis:

- Is the individual's employer able to accommodate any necessary restrictions?

- Does the individual have any conditions that may affect their ability to recover?
- Does the individual have any complications such as peritonitis, bowel or bladder injury, hemorrhaging, or sepsis? Does the individual have adhesions or scar tissue?

References

Anderson Kenneth N., Lois E. Anderson, and Walter D. Glauze. Mosby's Medical, Nursing and Allied Health Dictionary. St. Louis: Mosby-Year Book, Inc, 1998.

Lindell, G., and F. Flam. "Management of Uterine Perforations in Connection with Legal Abortion." Acta Obstetrics Gynecology Scandinavica 74 15 (1995): 373-375.

Uveitis
364.0, 364.00, 364.01, 364.10, 364.23, 364.3

Definition

Uveitis is an inflammation in the uveal tract of the eye that includes the circular, colored area surrounding the dark pupil (iris). In this section of the eye, the disease is sometimes called iritis. Most fluids are formed and muscular contractions controlling lens focus take place in the eye's interior in a second structure in the uveal tract (ciliary body). In the ciliary body, the disease is sometimes known as cyclitis. A third major portion of the uveal tract is located at the back of the globe where most of the eye's major blood vessels are concentrated (choroid). Uveitis in this part of the uveal tract is sometimes known as choroiditis.

Almost half of all uveitis cases are linked to problems originating in other parts of the body (systemic diseases) such as infection, immune disorders, or injuries. One or both eyes may be affected. The least serious form of the disease is often related to an injury or immune response (nongranulomatous uveitis). Infection can result in more serious forms of the disease (granulomatous uveitis).

Diagnosis

History: The individual reports blurred vision, sensitivity to light, tearing, and pain depending on what part of the eye is affected. Since many uveitis cases are linked to immune disorders or diseases in other parts of the body, the individual's overall health should be assessed.

Physical exam: In the front portion of the eye, cloudy fluids and a red or swollen iris may indicate uveitis. A small, irregular pupil with decreased light response is another common finding. Decreased visual acuity may also be detected. The most severe inflammation may occur near the area where the clear outer portion of the eye (cornea) joins with the eye's protective covering (sclera) in a zone known as the limbus. Yellow, white, and gray patches may be detected in the back portion of the eye behind the retina where images are processed and sent to the brain.

Tests: An ophthalmoscope and slit lamp exam may reveal swelling, abrasions, particles, or a flare-like effect in fluids indicating uveitis. Sensitivity to light directed into the eye may also be a symptom of the disease. Pressure within the eye (intraocular pressure) should be measured (tonometry).

Treatment

The cause of the uveitis determines treatment. Eyedrops containing cycloplegics ease pain and light sensitivity and are considered a generally safe, early treatment of the disease. Steroids may decrease inflammation but should be used cautiously since they may be associated with increases in intraocular pressure. Follow-up examinations are essential in acute cases.

Prognosis

If treated early, visual problems may be avoided. Complications can cause mild to severe permanent changes of vision. Uveitis may recur even if treated promptly or persist in its chronic state for months or years. Less serious forms of the disease may clear up in a few days or weeks.

Differential Diagnosis

Tumor, acute glaucoma, acute conjunctivitis, trauma, keratitis, corneal abrasion, scleritis, and keratoconjunctivitis are among other diagnoses with symptoms similar to uveitis.

Specialists

- Ophthalmologist
- Rheumatologist

Work Restrictions / Accommodations

Eyedrops may need to be applied during the workday. Individual may need time off from works for frequent eye exams until recovery is complete. With the resolution of acute uveitis, there are no restrictions or accommodations. Chronic uveitis with permanent changes of vision may preclude a return to previous duties if visual acuity is a job requirement.

Comorbid Conditions

Reiter's syndrome or inflammatory bowel disease may lengthen disability.

Complications

Uveitis may result in the iris permanently adhering to the cornea or lens (anterior or posterior synechiae), clouding of the eye fluids (aqueous or vitreous humor), glaucoma, damaged or detached retinas, and cataracts. Infections may spread to other areas of the eye. Complications may also lead to a rise in intraocular pressure that can damage the optic nerve and create permanent vision loss.

Factors Influencing Duration

Individual response to treatment, any complications, underlying cause and its treatment, and recurrence of the uveitis influence length of disability. Uveitis responds slowly to treatment.

Length of Disability

Duration depends on severity, underlying cause, location of inflammation, response to treatment, and side effects of therapy.

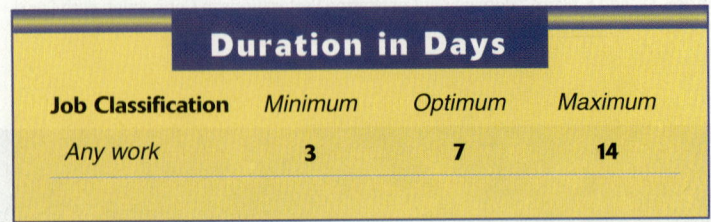

Duration in Days

Job Classification	Minimum	Optimum	Maximum
Any work	3	7	14

Failure to Recover

If an individual fails to recover within the maximum duration expectancy period, the reader may wish to reference the following questions to assist in better understanding the specifics of an individual's medical case.

Regarding diagnosis:

- Does individual have any systemic diseases such as infection, immune disorders, or injuries?
- Were one or both eyes affected?
- Does individual report blurred vision, sensitivity to light, tearing, and pain?
- On exam of the eye, did the physician find cloudy fluids, a red or swollen iris, a small irregular pupil with decreased light response, or decreased visual acuity?
- Was inflammation present in the limbus?
- Were yellow, white, and gray patches seen behind the retina?
- Was ophthalmoscope and slit lamp exam performed? Did exam reveal swelling, abrasions, particles, or a flare-like effect in fluids? Is individual sensitive to light directed into the eye? Was tonometry done?
- Were conditions with similar symptoms ruled out?

Regarding treatment:

- Is individual using eye drops containing cycloplegics? Are steroids being used?
- Is individual attending all follow-up appointments with the doctor?

Regarding prognosis:

- Is individual's employer able to accommodate any necessary restrictions?
- Does individual have any conditions that may affect ability to recover?
- Does individual have any complications such as the iris permanently adhering to the cornea or lens, clouding of the aqueous or vitreous humor, glaucoma, damaged or detached retinas or cataracts?
- Did infections spread to other areas of the eye?
- Does individual have a rise in intraocular pressure that can damage the optic nerve and create permanent vision loss?

References

Beers, Mark H., and Robert Berkow. The Merck Manual of Diagnosis and Therapy. Whitehouse Station, NJ: Merck & Co., Inc, 1999.

Vaginitis

Other names / synonyms: Vaginal Inflammation, Vulvovaginitis

616.1, 616.10, 627.3

Definition

Vaginitis is an inflammation of the lining of the vagina caused by infectious organisms or irritants and is characterized by redness, swelling, itching, and irritation of the vaginal tissues. While almost every woman experiences at least one episode of vaginitis during her lifetime, most have several. Vaginitis is the most common reason an adult female seeks medical attention. The three most common causes of vaginitis are yeast (candidiasis and monilia), bacterial infection (bacterial vaginosis, Gardnerella vaginitis, and nonspecific vaginitis), and parasites (trichomoniasis).

Yeast is normally found in the vagina. When the normal environment of the vagina changes, yeast organisms can flourish. This overgrowth is commonly called a yeast infection (candidiasis or moniliasis) and can be the result of antibiotics, pregnancy, diabetes, birth control pills, or the normal changes during a menstrual period. Sexually transmitted diseases and low estrogen levels accompanying menopause are also associated with increased incidence of yeast infection. Other risk factors include wearing tight, nonbreathing clothing or underwear, excessive douching, and the use of perfumed feminine hygiene sprays. Symptoms of a yeast infection include intense itching, burning, redness, and an odorless, white, "cheesy" discharge.

Bacterial vaginosis, previously called nonspecific vaginitis, is caused by an overgrowth of one or more types of bacteria including streptococcus (normally lives in the vagina without causing inflammation) or E. coli (normally lives in the gastrointestinal tract). Sexually transmitted diseases such as chlamydia and gonorrhea may also cause bacterial vaginosis. Symptoms may include a strong, unpleasant, fishy odor and an abnormal white or gray milky discharge. The exact cause of this bacterial imbalance is unknown although it appears more frequently in women suffering from stress, poor diet, inadequate rest, or emotional upset. This kind of infection is seen in both sexually active and inactive women.

Cytolytic vaginosis is a newly described condition where the organism causing it has not yet been identified. It may, however, be the result of a bacterial overgrowth (lactobacilli). The symptoms worsen during the second half of the menstrual cycle and include burning, itching, vulvar irritation, painful intercourse, and a clumpy, white discharge.

Women visiting undeveloped parts of the world occasionally acquire amebic vaginal infections. Symptoms include a foul-smelling, often bloody discharge that may be accompanied by sores on the vagina.

As the estrogen hormone level is reduced during and after menopause, a woman's vaginal lining becomes thin and dry. This puts her at a higher risk for a vaginal inflammation known as atrophic vaginitis.

Vaginitis can also be caused by an allergic reaction to spermicidal cream, chemicals used in vaginal douches (also in soaps, bath oils, or salts), and laundry detergents or fabric softeners. A woman can also experience allergic vaginitis if her partner uses latex condoms. Other less common causes of vaginitis include cuts or abrasions in the vagina or a foreign body such as a forgotten tampon.

Another cause of vaginitis is called trichomoniasis ("trich"). This is a sexually transmitted disease caused by a one-cell parasite. Characterized by an irritating, frothy, yellow-green discharge with an unpleasant odor, this infection can be transmitted to sexual partners. Between 2 to 3 million Americans are affected yearly.

Diagnosis

History: Symptoms of a yeast infection may include thick white "cheesy" discharge, vaginal itching, painful urination, swelling and redness in the vaginal area, and painful intercourse. With bacterial vaginosis, nearly half of the women have no symptoms. If present, symptoms may include an abnormal white or gray milky discharge with a strong, unpleasant, fishy odor. Itching or vaginal irritation may or may not be present. Trichomoniasis symptoms in women usually occur within 4 to 20 days after exposure and include excessive yellow or green frothy vaginal discharge with a strong unpleasant odor, itching in vaginal and external genital (vulva) area, painful urination or intercourse, and on occasion, lower abdominal pain. Although men with trichomoniasis usually experience no symptoms, they can still infect their sexual partners.

Symptoms of allergic vaginitis include itching, burning, and a nonfoul discharge. History includes use of spermicides, douches, bath oils, deodorants, scented tampons or pads, or new detergents. In atrophic or hormone deficiency vaginitis, there may be complaints about vaginal dryness, discomfort during intercourse, and other menopausal symptoms.

Physical exam: A pelvic exam is performed to collect vaginal secretions for testing, detect other involvement such as cervicitis, and identify other coexisting diseases. If a hormone deficiency exists, the vagina may have a characteristic appearance with loss of folds (rugae).

Tests: A microscopic examination (wet smear) of vaginal secretions is necessary for a correct diagnosis. It may show yeast cells, vaginal cells coated with bacteria (clue cells), or the trichomonas parasite. If the microscopic examination is negative, cultures may be done to identify infectious agents.

Acidity of the vaginal secretions may also be tested. Compared to the normal acidic pH found in the vagina, women with bacterial vaginosis have an alkaline pH. After adding a chemical (potassium hydroxide), vaginal secretions may have a distinctive foul odor (the sniff test).

Because a vaginal discharge can also be associated with cervical or uterine cancer, a Pap smear should be done to rule out cancer. Although a blood test can demonstrate a reduction in estrogen level, a Pap test with maturation index shows more comprehensive changes in cells indicating a pattern of estrogen reduction.

Specialists

- Gynecologist

Treatment

Yeast vaginitis is usually treated with antifungal vaginal creams. Oral antifungal agents are sometimes included to treat chronic or recurring episodes. Bacterial vaginosis and trichomoniasis require specific antibiotic treatment available by prescription. When vaginitis is caused by a sexually transmitted disease, both sex partners should be treated at the same time to prevent reinfection. Over-the-counter products only mask the symptoms of vaginitis without treating the underlying problem and should not be used.

Irritating agents should be avoided in cases of allergic reactions. Appropriate medication may be needed to treat a secondary infection following the removal of a foreign body. Atrophic or hormone deficiency vaginitis can be resolved with estrogen replacement therapy or vaginal estrogen cream.

Prognosis

With proper diagnosis and appropriate specific treatment, full recovery is expected in cases of yeast infections, bacterial vaginosis, and trichomoniasis. Avoidance of irritating agents should resolve allergic reaction. Hormone replacement therapy is usually effective in reducing the inflammation related to decreased estrogen.

Differential Diagnosis

Cervical infections are also associated with abnormal vaginal discharge. Women usually have vaginal discharge during ovulation, but occasionally this discharge become so heavy that it causes concern. Other sexually transmitted diseases can cause vaginal discharge (gonorrhea) or vaginal pain (herpes). A blood-tinged discharge may indicate cancer.

Work Restrictions / Accommodations

Genital itching and discomfort may make sitting for long periods of time uncomfortable. Allowances should be made for adequate break time in order to move around. Some physicians recommend avoiding the wearing of pantyhose until the yeast infection resolves.

Comorbid Conditions

Coexisting conditions that predispose women to yeast infections include pregnancy, diabetes mellitus, and the use of broad-spectrum antibiotics or corticosteroids. Women infected with the human immunodeficiency virus (HIV) may have frequent recurrences or resistant infections. Poor personal hygiene can contribute to the growth of bacteria and fungi. Stool entering the vagina through an abnormal passage from the intestines (fistula) can cause vaginitis.

Complications

Medication to treat bacterial vaginosis and trichomoniasis can cause side effects especially nausea and vomiting. Pelvic inflammatory disease can result in infertility and tubal (ectopic) pregnancy. Data now suggest that women with bacterial vaginosis or trichomoniasis may also have increased risk of premature and low birth weight infants. Sexual partners should be tested and treated as necessary to prevent reinfection.

Factors Influencing Duration

The underlying cause of the vaginitis may influence the length of disability. Pregnancy, uncontrolled diabetes, and the use of oral contraceptives or antibiotics are factors associated with recurring or chronic yeast infections.

Length of Disability

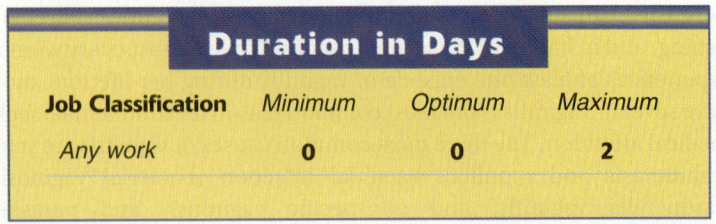

Duration in Days

Job Classification	Minimum	Optimum	Maximum
Any work	0	0	2

Failure to Recover

If an individual fails to recover within the maximum duration expectancy period, the reader may wish to reference the following questions to assist in better understanding the specifics of an individual's medical case.

Regarding diagnosis:

- Is individual pregnant? On antibiotics? Diabetic? Taking birth control pills?
- Does individual have a STD? Is she post-menopausal?
- Does individual typically wear tight, non-breathing clothing? Does she douche excessively? Does she use perfumed feminine hygiene sprays?
- Does individual report intense itching, burning, redness, and an odorless, white, "cheesy" discharge?
- Does individual report a strong, unpleasant, fishy odor and an abnormal white or gray milky discharge?
- Does individual report burning, itching, vulvar irritation, painful intercourse, and a clumpy, white discharge?
- Has individual visited undeveloped parts of the world?
- Does individual have an allergic reaction to spermicidal cream, chemicals used in vaginal douches, soaps, bath oils, salts, laundry detergents or fabric softeners? Does her partner use latex condoms? Does she have cuts or abrasions in the vagina? Is there a forgotten tampon present?
- Did individual have a pelvic exam? Was a microscopic examination (wet smear) of vaginal secretions done? Was a culture done? Was the pH tested? Was a Pap smear done?
- Have conditions with similar symptoms been ruled out?

Regarding treatment:

- Does individual have yeast vaginitis? Is it being treated with antifungal agents?
- Does individual have bacterial vaginosis? Is it being treated with antibiotics?
- Has individual's sexual partner been treated if necessary?
- Does individual have atrophic vaginitis? Is it being treated with estrogen replacement therapy or vaginal estrogen cream?
- Does individual avoid irritating agents?

Regarding prognosis:

- Is individual's employer able to accommodate any necessary restrictions?
- Does individual have any conditions that may affect her ability to recover?
- Does individual have any complications such as side effects from the medication, pelvic inflammatory disease, or the increased risk of premature and low birth weight infants?

References

Neri, A, D. Rabinerson, and B. Kaplan. "Bacterial Vaginosis: Drugs Versus Alternative Treatment." Obstetrical and Gynecological Survey 49 12 (1994): 809-813.

Rosenthal, Sara, MD. The Gynecology Sourcebook. New York: Random House, 1999.

Vagotomy

Other names / synonyms: Gastric Vagotomy, Highly Selective Vagotomy, Parietal Cell Vagotomy, Partial Cell Vagotomy, Proximal Gastric Vagotomy, Proximal Vagotomy, Selective Gastric Vagotomy, Selective Proximal Vagotomy, Selective Vagotomy, Selective Gastric Vagotomy, Truncal Vagotomy

44.00, 44.01, 44.02, 44.03

Definition

Vagotomy is a procedure that surgically interrupts the nerve branches (vagus nerve) in the stomach that stimulate acid production. It is done as a surgical measure to control recurrent peptic ulcers unresponsive to medical treatment and diet or to treat massively bleeding or perforated peptic ulcers. The procedure may also be done in combination with another procedure to treat a complication of peptic ulcer disease called gastric outlet syndrome.

There are several types of vagotomy procedures depending on which nerve branches are surgically severed. Truncal vagotomy interrupts the nerves to the stomach, upper abdominal organs, and upper intestine, and is now used primarily for recurrent ulcer disease after previous stomach (gastric) surgery. Selective gastric vagotomy interrupts only the nerves to the stomach. Since the motility of the stomach is affected by each of these procedures, additional surgical interventions (gastroenterostomy or pyloroplasty) are needed to facilitate stomach emptying. Selective proximal vagotomy, also known as highly selective vagotomy or parietal cell vagotomy, interrupts only the nerves to the acid-producing portion of the stomach, so that stomach motility is unaffected and no additional surgical intervention is needed. Vagotomy can be done as an open surgical procedure, or via laparoscopy or thorascopy.

Peptic ulcer disease is a collective term to describe ulcers that arise in the stomach or first part of the small intestine (duodenum) as a result of an overproduction of acid and pepsin (an enzyme). The incidence of duodenal ulcers is 7 out of 1000 people. They are more common in young adults (age 30 to 40), who have a family history of peptic ulcers, have presence of Helicobacter pylori bacteria in the stomach, have group O blood type, or have chronic use of nonsteroidal anti-inflammatory drugs (NSAIDs). The incidence of gastric ulcers is 8 out of 10,000 people. They are more common in those over 50, and are associated with blood type group A, NSAID use, and chronic gastric inflammation (gastritis).

Non-emergency (elective) vagotomy is performed less often in the past 20 years, as medications used to teat ulcers have become increasingly effective.

Reason for Procedure

A vagotomy is performed to reduce gastric acid production in the treatment of recurrent or bleeding ulcers; or to treat emergent complications of ulcers, such as massive bleeding; or gastric perforations or obstruction between the stomach and the small intestine (gastric outlet obstruction). By reducing the production of gastric acid, the procedure effectively reduces the continued erosion of the stomach lining that leads to ulcers and the complications of bleeding, perforation, or obstruction. Generally, the procedure is done in combination with other procedures that specifically treat the acute problem. To treat gastric outlet obstruction, vagotomy is combined with pyloroplasty, a procedure that widens the opening between the stomach and the small intestine. When ulcers are perforated or bleeding, partial removal of the stomach (gastrectomy) is often combined with vagotomy.

Description

The procedure is performed in the hospital using general anesthesia. Before surgery, the stomach and gastrointestinal tract are visualized with gastroscopy and x-ray procedures, and standard preoperative blood and urine tests are done. Depending on the preference of the surgeon, the procedure can be performed using a flexible, lighted scope (laparoscope), or performed with a standard surgical approach through a large abdominal incision. A tube to drain the stomach (nasogastric tube) and a tube to drain the bladder (urinary catheter) are usually inserted. The surgeon makes an incision in the abdomen between the rib cage and the lower abdomen (over the stomach). The surgeon locates the vagus nerves, and clamps and cuts specific branches depending on which procedure is being done.

Truncal vagotomy involves cutting segments of the 2 vagus nerve branches located where the esophagus joins the stomach. This procedure interrupts vagus nerve supply to the stomach, liver, gallbladder, bile duct, pancreas, small intestine, and half of the large intestine. Since the motility of the stomach is affected, a pyloroplasty or another gastric drainage procedure usually accompanies truncal vagotomy.

Selective vagotomy interrupts only the branch of vagus nerve that supplies the stomach. Parietal cell vagotomy involves cutting only the parts of the vagus nerve that control the acid-secreting cells of the stomach. This procedure avoids the portions of the nerve that influence stomach emptying, so that pyloroplasty is not needed.

The abdominal muscle layers are stitched closed and the abdominal skin is closed with stitches (sutures) or surgical staples.

Prognosis

The surgical procedure is generally effective at reducing gastric acid production. However, over time, 4-11% of individuals have recurrence of ulcers following vagotomy without stomach removal. Ulcers also recur in about 2-3% of individuals who have some portion of their stomach removed. The procedure has a good outcome with a mortality rate of less than 1% when done on individuals who are physically stable (i.e., not in shock). The mortality rate approaches 2% when done as an emergency procedure for individuals with profusely bleeding ulcers or stomach perforation. Approximately 1-2% of individuals have postoperative digestive problems.

Specialists

- General Surgeon

Work Restrictions / Accommodations

No work restrictions or special accommodations are required after an individual has made a complete recovery from a vagotomy. Individuals with dumping syndrome may require more frequent restroom breaks and close proximity to restroom facilities. Depending on the type of vagotomy and any additional surgical procedures performed, individuals will miss varying amounts of time from work, and may be restricted from heavy lifting or other strenuous activities until healing is complete.

Comorbid Conditions

Comorbid conditions of cancer, immune suppression, heart disease, chronic lung disease, diabetes, bleeding disorders, liver disease, or malnutrition may affect ability to recover and further lengthen disability.

Procedure Complications

Complications of this procedure include bleeding, infection, and accidental puncture (perforation) of the stomach. About 20% of individuals have problems with stomach emptying (pylorospasm) after truncal vagotomy, requiring further surgery. Changes in stomach emptying can lead to dumping syndrome, a condition in which the individual experiences palpitations, sweating, nausea, cramps, vomiting, and diarrhea shortly after eating. Difficulty swallowing (dysphagia) may complicate laparoscopic vagotomy. Any abdominal surgery can result in the development of scar tissue (adhesion) around the intestines, which can cause intestinal blockage. These adhesions can occur many years after the surgery and may necessitate additional surgery. As with any procedure done with general anesthesia, there is the risk of reactions to the anesthetic agent or problems with heart rate, blood pressure, or breathing.

Factors Influencing Duration

Factors that might influence disability include advanced age, underlying cause for the procedure, type of vagotomy selected, whether the procedure was done laparoscopically or via standard surgical approach, and whether the procedure was done electively or under emergency conditions.

Length of Disability

If a laparoscopic approach is used, the hospital stay is approximately 1 to 3 days, and individuals can usually return to work in 7 to 10 days. Open procedures and those associated with other surgical procedures may require longer recovery times.

Duration in Days

Job Classification	Minimum	Optimum	Maximum
Sedentary work	7	14	21
Light work	14	21	21
Medium work	14	28	35
Heavy work	14	28	35
Very Heavy work	14	28	35

References

Chang, Tzu-Ming, et al. "Differences in Gastric Emptying Between Highly Selective Vagotomy and Posterior Truncal Vagotomy Combined with Anterior Seromyotomy." Journal of Gastrointestinal Surgery 3 (1999): 533-536.

Goldman, Lee, and J. Claude Bennett. Cecil Textbook of Medicine, 21st ed. Philadelphia: W.B. Saunders Company, 2000.

Vagotonia

Other names / synonyms: Vagus Nerve Disorder

352.3

Definition

Vagotonia refers to a condition of excessive stimulation of the parasympathetic nerve fibers carried by the vagus nerve. The parasympathetic system is part of the autonomic nervous system, which maintains control over involuntary bodily functions. The autonomic nervous system consists of two opposing systems: the sympathetic nervous system, which gears up the body for attack, escape, or other emergency situations, and the parasympathetic nervous system, which maintains bodily functions in a resting state. Parasympathetic nerve fibers within the vagus nerve have wide-reaching effects on many different organ systems, including the heart, lungs, digestive tract, urinary bladder, and sex organs. For example, increased activity in the vagus nerve tends to slow the heart, constrict bronchial passages in the airway, and increase digestive activity.

Because excessive stimulation of the vagus nerve can be associated with a wide variety of clinical conditions, the diagnosis of vagotonia is incomplete at best, and usually refers only to the mechanism underlying a more specific diagnosis. The healthcare provider needs to provide a more complete diagnosis for effective management of the individual case. For example, the effect of vagotonia on the heart may be an abnormally slow heart rhythm (sinus bradycardia; atrioventricular block), which may be associated with fainting (syncope). In the lungs, vagotonia may be manifested as bronchial asthma, and in the intestinal tract as gastric ulcers or irritable bowel syndrome. Contact the physician for more complete diagnostic information.

Valvotomy

Other names / synonyms: Open Mitral Commissurotomy, Valvuloplasty, Valvulotomy

35.0, 35.00, 35.01, 35.02, 35.03, 35.04

Definition

Valvotomy is an open-heart procedure performed to repair a heart valve (aortic, mitral, tricuspid, or pulmonic) that is narrowed (stenosed) because of disease or a congenital abnormality. Although surgical valvotomy may offer relief from symptoms of valvular stenosis (shortness of breath, edema, fatigue, rapid and/or irregular heartbeat, chest pain, fainting spells), the procedure is not considered a cure in most cases. The decision to try and repair a valve rather than replace it depends on the particular valve involved, the cause and severity of the stenosis, and the individual's age and general health.

Congenital heart disease is a common cause of heart valve stenosis. The incidence of congenital heart disease in the US is 1 in 100 newborns and of these, 15-20% have some type of heart valve defect including stenosis. Although the valve is often surgically repaired in infancy or childhood, symptoms can return in adulthood and require additional repair or replacement of the valve. Other causes of heart valve stenosis include coronary artery disease, bacterial endocarditis, and a degenerative calcification process in older adults that damages the valve.

Rheumatic fever/rheumatic heart disease accounts for a large percentage of heart valve stenosis that develops or begins to cause symptoms in adulthood. Found in 1,800,000 Americans, rheumatic fever/rheumatic heart disease occurs more frequently in blacks, Puerto Ricans, Mexicans, and American Indians. The aortic valve is damaged more frequently in men and the mitral valve more frequently in women.

Reason for Procedure

If a heart valve is unable to open freely because of stenosis caused by a congenital abnormality or disease, the amount of blood allowed to pass through the valve is reduced. When this situation develops, the heart is forced to pump harder in an attempt to deliver the necessary amount of blood and oxygen to the body. This extra effort results in changes in blood pressure, circulation, and heart rhythm and can eventually lead to heart failure. During a valvotomy, the leaflets (cusps) of the heart valve are cut so that the opening is enlarged allowing the blood to flow through more normally.

Mitral valvotomy is most often performed on adults with mitral stenosis resulting from rheumatic fever/rheumatic heart disease. When tricuspid valvotomy is performed to repair tricuspid stenosis, the procedure is generally performed at the same time as mitral valvotomy. Tricuspid valvotomy is rarely performed as a separate procedure. Aortic valvotomy is most often done on younger adults with congenitally stenosed aortic valves that may have been repaired in childhood but are again causing symptoms. Aortic valvotomy is rarely performed on older adults with aortic stenosis caused by calcification. These individuals are generally candidates for valve replacement rather than repair. Pulmonic valvotomy is occasionally performed on adults with congenital pulmonary stenosis who are now symptomatic.

Description

After the individual is anesthetized, additional lines may be inserted into various blood vessels to measure central venous pressure and pulmonary artery pressure.

The individual's skin and underlying tissue and muscle are cut (incised) from the notch at the top of the breastbone (sternum) to the bottom of the breastbone (xiphoid process). The breastbone is divided with an electric saw and a sternal retractor inserted and cranked open, separating the two sides of the split sternum and ribs and exposing the heart.

The membrane covering the heart (pericardium) is incised and held back with lengths of surgical thread (suture). The individual is then placed on cardiopulmonary bypass (CPB). During CPB, the individual's blood flow is diverted from the heart and lungs through tubing connected to a heart/lung machine. Anticoagulants are added to the blood to prevent clots from forming on the tubing's artificial surface and traveling to the brain or other vital organs. As blood passes through the heart/lung machine, the pump oxygenator removes carbon dioxide and adds oxygen. The heart/lung machine then pumps the oxygenated blood back to the body through another set of tubing. This artificial circulation allows the cardiovascular surgeon to work in a nearly motionless and bloodless surgical field without endangering the flow of blood and oxygen to the individual's vital organs and other tissues.

During the valvotomy procedure, the heart is opened and the valve or valves are examined. If the cardiovascular surgeon decides the valve can be repaired, a finger or dilating instrument is inserted into the valve to break apart the hardened (calcified) valve structures. Cuts are made or pressure applied in order to separate the leaflets (cusps) of the valve where they have joined. This allows the leaflets to open and close more normally and reduces the degree of narrowing. Increasing the size of the opening into the valve by as little as 1 or 2 square centimeters significantly improves overall blood flow. If the valve cannot be repaired through a valvotomy procedure, the surgeon may decide during surgery to replace the valve with a mechanical or biological replacement valve.

As the individual is gradually removed from CPB, blood returns to the heart and lungs. The anesthesiologist manually reinflates the lungs and the heart may begin to beat again on its own. Once the heart is beating regularly and the individual's blood pressure is stabilized, the individual will be completely removed from CPB. Pacing wires may be stitched to the heart muscle and threaded through the chest wall to the outside. Postoperatively, these can be attached to an external pacemaker if the individual develops an irregular heart rhythm.

Since the individual's blood still contains anticoagulants, the surgeon may need to spend a considerable amount of time controlling bleeding in the surgical field before closing the wound. When bleeding is controlled, the pericardium is closed with sutures. Chest tubes (mediastinal tubes) are inserted through the skin and into the space around the heart (mediastinum). The other ends of the chest tubes are attached to sealed drainage systems that allow blood to drain from the heart cavity without allowing air back in.

Prognosis

Outcome is excellent following mitral valvotomy. Symptoms of congestive heart failure are relieved (pulmonary edema, shortness of breath, limitation of activity, and recurrent blood clots in spite of treatment with blood thinners). Outcome is also excellent for pulmonary valvotomy. Symptoms (shortness of breath with exertion, fainting, chest pain, and right heart failure) are relieved in most cases and recurrence is very rare. Outcome for aortic valvotomy in young adults with congenital aortic valve stenosis is satisfactory. Symptoms are relieved and the individual's activity level increases. Stenosis may recur later in life and a repeat valvotomy or by-valve replacement surgery may be needed. Outcome for aortic valvotomy in older adults with calcified aortic valve stenosis is less satisfactory. Symptoms of heart failure may be relieved for a short time, but recurrence of aortic stenosis is common. These individuals often require eventual aortic valve replacement.

In general, mortality rate for heart valve surgery is 1-3%. The individual's heart may refuse to start beating again after removal from the heart/lung machine despite efforts of medications or a defibrillator. The heart rhythm may go into ventricular fibrillation, a rapid, irregular, and ineffective heartbeat that quickly progresses to cardiac arrest if treatment is unsuccessful. Other causes of disability and/or death during the postoperative period include uncontrollable internal bleeding, overwhelming infection, heart arrhythmia, heart attack, organ failure, irreversible coma caused by stroke, and complete heart failure (cardiac arrest).

Specialists

- Cardiologist
- Cardiovascular Surgeon
- Thoracic Surgeon

Rehabilitation

Cardiac rehabilitation is important in recovery after a valvotomy. Postoperative cardiac individuals can improve their fitness levels substantially with an individually designed exercise program set at a level considered safe for them. Rehabilitation following a cardiac surgery progresses in phases.

Phase one often begins in the hospital. It provides low levels of exercise to help prevent the hazards of bed rest, reduce episodes of low blood pressure when changing positions (orthostatic hypotension), and maintain overall mobility of the body.

Respiratory therapy for the individual with a heart valvotomy begins as soon as the breathing tube (endotracheal tube) is removed. This therapy focuses on preventing lung secretion buildup (that can lead to pneumonia) and reinflating the lungs to their presurgical condition. Respiratory therapists teach individuals pursed lip breathing to increase the airflow to the lungs. Individuals may also use an incentive spirometer, a device that measures and displays the amount of air inspired to help motivate individuals to take deeper breaths. Individuals also learn to produce an effective cough through techniques such as huffing where air is breathed out forcefully while the mouth is open.

Low-level exercise may begin in the coronary care unit of a hospital with the individual first lying on the back (supine position) and progresses to exercises performed while sitting then eventually to standing. Progressive walking (ambulating) and eventually stair climbing are important to the individual's exercise program while hospitalized. Intensity is gradually increased until discharge from the hospital.

Phase two goals are to improve functional capacity by increasing physical endurance and promoting return to activity. This is done in an outpatient setting such as a rehabilitation center. Individuals are usually attached to an electrocardiograph (EKG) monitor. A physical therapist keeps a daily log of the individual's blood pressure, heart rate, and cardiac rhythm.

Phase three continues and may last for several months. Individuals may stay involved with an outpatient program for up to a year in order to accomplish all their goals while still at modified work duty. Higher levels of exercise are eventually added including recreational activities such as swimming and outdoor hiking. Light jogging and cycling are appropriate as long as the individual tolerates the rehabilitation program well. The rehabilitation program may need to be modified because of the various medications prescribed and if any additional medical conditions are present.

Work Restrictions / Accommodations

After 6 postoperative weeks, individuals who have had a successful heart valvotomy without serious postoperative complications or disabilities can usually return to work part-time with few if any restrictions on their activity except for heavy lifting. The number of work hours may gradually increase over the next 6 to 8 weeks until the individual is working a full day. Individuals with residual chronic heart disease or chronic chest pain may require work restrictions and accommodations that help conserve energy and reduce strain on the heart. Other medical problems or permanent disabilities from underlying medical conditions (e.g., diabetes, chronic obstructive lung disease, or chronic renal failure requiring dialysis) or postoperative complications (e.g., partial paralysis or speech impairment because of stroke) may also require work restrictions and accommodations.

Comorbid Conditions

Comorbid conditions include diseases that affect any of the major body systems such as high blood pressure, chronic kidney (renal) disease, bleeding disorders, diabetes mellitus, chronic obstructive lung disease, chronic heart disease, and immunosuppressive diseases. A history of smoking, alcoholism or other substance abuse, and obesity are also comorbidities.

Procedure Complications

Complications after open-heart surgery for repair of heart valves can be life threatening. The most common complication is low cardiac output syndrome as evidenced by low blood pressure, low urine production, and cool extremities. Causes of this syndrome include blood loss, poor pumping by the left ventricle (the heart's pumping chamber), and cardiac tamponade.

Cardiac tamponade is a serious condition that occurs when blood collects between the heart and the pericardium. As the pericardial space fills with blood, it becomes more difficult for the heart to pump effectively. Cardiac tamponade may be treated by attempting to drain the blood through a needle inserted through the chest wall and into the pericardial space (pericardiocentesis). If this is unsuccessful, the individual's chest may be reopened in the operating room where the pericardium is drained and active bleeding controlled.

Arrhythmias are common postoperative complications following open-heart surgery and are treated with antiarrhythmic drugs. If these arrhythmias are unresponsive to drugs, the pacing wires attached to the heart during surgery can be hooked to an external pacemaker that helps establish a normal rhythm. Ventricular fibrillation is a life-threatening arrhythmia that can rapidly progress to complete heart stoppage (cardiac arrest).

Other complications include wound infection, systemic infection, wound separation, gastrointestinal bleeding (as a result of anticoagulation therapy), stroke, heart attack, kidney failure, and death.

Factors Influencing Duration

Factors include previous lung surgery, the number and severity of postoperative complications (i.e., wound infection, bleeding, chronic musculoskeletal pain in the chest area, or an adverse reaction to a general anesthetic), the amount of blood loss during surgery and postoperatively, the number of blood transfusions required, the success of the valvotomy, the individual's nutritional status and mental and emotional stability, access to rehabilitation facilities, and the individual's support system.

Length of Disability

Duration depends on the severity of the underlying condition. In some cases, disability may be permanent.

Duration in Days

Job Classification	Minimum	Optimum	Maximum
Sedentary work	14	28	42
Light work	14	28	42
Medium work	28	49	70
Heavy work	42	70	Indefinite
Very Heavy work	42	70	Indefinite

References

Kisner, C., and L. Colby. Therapeutic Exercise Foundations and Techniques. Philadelphia: F.A. Davis Company, 1990.

Meeker, Margaret, and Jane Rothrock. Alexander's Care of the Patient in Surgery. St. Louis: Mosby, 1999.

Valvuloplasty, Balloon

Other names / synonyms: Cardiological Valvuloplasty, Percutaneous Transluminal Balloon Valvuloplasty, Percutaneous Transseptal Mitral Commissurotomy, PTBV, PTMC

35.96

Definition

Balloon valvuloplasty is an outpatient or short-stay procedure that provides a less traumatic alternative to open-heart surgery for individuals with heart valves that are narrowed (stenosed) because of disease or a congenital abnormality. This is done as part of a procedure where a catheter is threaded from the groin or arm through a blood vessel leading to the heart (cardiac catheterization). The balloon tip is then positioned within the narrowed (stenotic) valve and inflated in order to stretch the valve opening and permit more blood flow through the valve.

Balloon valvuloplasty to treat mitral valve stenosis caused by rheumatic fever/rheumatic heart disease was first performed in the mid-1980s and became a clinically approved technique in 1994. Since then it has been used successfully to relieve pulmonary valve stenosis (a congenital abnormality) and on occasion, symptoms in young adults with congenital aortic valve stenosis. Balloon valvuloplasty may be a last effort to relieve symptoms of heart failure in older adults with severe aortic valve stenosis who are unsuitable candidates for open-heart surgery. The use of balloon valvuloplasty for relieving tricuspid stenosis is still experimental.

Rheumatic fever/rheumatic heart disease accounts for a large percentage of heart valve stenosis developing or causing symptoms in adulthood. Found in 1,800,000 Americans, rheumatic fever/rheumatic heart disease occurs more frequently in blacks, Puerto Ricans, Mexicans, and American Indians. The aortic valve is damaged more frequently in men and the mitral valve more frequently in women. Congenital heart disease is another common cause of heart valve stenosis. In the US, 1 in 100 newborns are affected with this disease and of these, 15-20% have some type of heart valve defect including stenosis. Although the valve is often surgically repaired in infancy or childhood, symptoms can return in adulthood and require additional repair or replacement of the valve. Other causes of heart valve stenosis include coronary artery disease, bacterial endocarditis, and a degenerative calcification process that damages the valve as the individual ages.

Reason for Procedure

If a heart valve is unable to open freely because of stenosis caused by a congenital abnormality or disease, the amount of blood allowed to pass through the valve is reduced. When this situation develops, the heart is forced to pump harder in an attempt to deliver the necessary amount of blood and oxygen to the body. This extra effort results in changes in blood pressure, circulation, and heart rhythm and can eventually lead to heart failure. During a balloon valvuloplasty, the opening is enlarged, allowing the blood to flow through more normally.

Description

Balloon valvuloplasty is performed by specially trained physicians in a special cardiac laboratory equipped with a variety of supplies, monitors, and other equipment. Catheterization is generally performed using a combination of local and general anesthesia.

The artery is punctured with a needle and a guide wire inserted through the needle. The needle is removed and the balloon catheter passed over the guide wire and into the artery. Guided and monitored by a device that x-rays structures deep within the body (fluoroscope), the physician advances the wire and catheter into the correct area of the heart.

Various blood pressure readings are measured within the heart by a machine that translates these pressures into electrical signals (transducer). These values are displayed on a second monitor. The valve diameter is measured after contrast is injected through the catheter and filmed (angiogram). An anticoagulant is injected through the catheter into the heart to prevent clots from forming around the valve or catheter during the procedure.

After the balloon is positioned so that its center is in the ring of tissue that supports the valve leaflets (annulus), it is gently inflated using dilute contrast. This stretches the valve and breaks up any obstructive scar tissue. Careful observation under fluoroscopy is done to ensure that the balloon remains centered, and that it is inflated to its full diameter. This is repeated 2 to 3 times to ensure the maximum effect is achieved. After dilation of the valve is complete, pressures are remeasured to check if the valve is enlarged enough. Balloons of different lengths and diameters may be substituted if the previous dilations did not optimally dilate the valve. A repeat angiogram is performed to document improved valve mobility and filling of arteries with contrast.

A repeat echocardiogram is usually performed soon after the procedure to further document relief of the obstruction and to check for valve leakage.

Prognosis

The immediate outcome for uncomplicated balloon valvuloplasty is excellent in 80-90% of individuals with mitral valve stenosis who do not develop reverse flow of blood leaking out of the valve (regurgitation). Symptoms of congestive heart failure are quickly relieved (pulmonary edema, shortness of breath, recurrent blood clots in spite of treatment with blood thinners, and limitation of activity). The rate of recurrence of stenosis within the first 5 years is low. Mortality rate is approximately 1-3%.

The immediate outcome for balloon valvuloplasty is also excellent for individuals with pulmonary valve stenosis and symptoms are quickly relieved (shortness of breath with exertion, fainting, chest pain, right heart failure). The rate of recurrence of stenosis is very low. Mortality rate is approximately 2-4%.

Outcome for less severe congenital aortic stenosis in young adults is good, with long-term relief of symptoms and few complications. Outcome for balloon valvuloplasty is poor in older adults with severe aortic stenosis resulting from calcification and for those with severely malformed (dysplastic) valves or a very small valve annulus. In these individuals, symptoms of heart failure may be relieved temporarily but the valve quickly narrows again. Such individuals are candidates for aortic valve replacement when (and if) they become suitable candidates for open-heart surgery.

Specialists

- Cardiologist
- Cardiovascular Surgeon
- Thoracic Surgeon

Rehabilitation

Prior to the balloon valvuloplasty procedure, individuals with heart valve disease had restricted daily activities in order to reduce cardiac stress. As a consequence, most individuals experience muscle fatigue due to inadequate muscle oxygenation and metabolism. After the balloon valvuloplasty procedure, some individuals may assume a more active lifestyle. Muscle deconditioning must be overcome so individual can safely engage in activities requiring muscle strength and endurance.

In addition to exercise therapy, an occupational therapist and/or vocational rehabilitation specialist should evaluate whether the individual can return to his or her occupation. Depending on prior level of health and recovery, some individuals may be unable to return to the work force. In either case, the individual should continue with a home exercise program to help reduce further cardiac damage.

For the first week after balloon valvuloplasty, the individual is limited in activity. For example, lifting objects over 15 pounds is usually prohibited. Cardiac rehabilitation begins in an outpatient facility once it is safe for the individual to proceed. Cardiac rehabilitation is a multi-disciplinary program involving exercise, education, and counseling. Professionals assess the individual for functional capacity, risk factors (e.g., poor diet or smoking), and vocational training.

The initial goal of exercise is to increase aerobic or endurance capacity. The individual is closely monitored during subsequent rehabilitation sessions for changes in oxygen uptake and utilization as well as cardiac function. The individual may engage in treadmill walking as tolerated while attached to an electronic heart monitor. Since weight training augments anaerobic (without oxygen) metabolism, it is prohibited until muscle oxygen utilization improves. In addition, the individual is educated on medication, nutrition (a low-fat, low-cholesterol, no added salt diet), stress management, and the safe performance of everyday activities. If needed, programs such as smoking cessation are also implemented. For optimal recovery, the individual must choose a lifestyle that minimizes coronary risk factors. These choices may limit their vocational status and general health.

As aerobic capacity improves, an aqua therapy routine to continue the reconditioning process may be initiated. An aqua program is especially effective if the individual experiences any anxiety about increased functional ability. The support and varying depths of the water allow the therapist more control over the intensity and difficulty of the workout. As functional ability increases, vocational rehabilitation begins concurrent with a progressive exercise program. After exercise therapy, the individual participates in an unsupervised exercise program at home.

If the individual cannot return to work, an occupational therapist may evaluate and modify work conditions. For example, individuals who perform tasks requiring long periods of standing may either have to take more breaks to reduce internal pressure or change to a less taxing job.

Long-term effects (besides occupational changes) include the continual risk for developing bacterial endocarditis (inflammation of the heart lining due to bacteria). Individuals with valvular heart disease should provide their medical history to future physicians and dentists. Preventive antibiotics before dental treatment or any kind of surgery is necessary.

Work Restrictions / Accommodations

Individuals who have had successful balloon valvuloplasty without experiencing serious complications or disabilities may return to work in 1 to 2 weeks. Time should be allocated for physical therapy 3 to 4 days a week. Individuals with residual chronic heart disease or chronic chest pain may require work restrictions and accommodations that conserve their energy and reduce strain on their hearts. Work hours may be limited at the beginning and gradually increased over the next several weeks until the individual works a full day. Other medical problems or permanent disabilities due to underlying medical conditions (i.e., diabetes, chronic obstructive lung disease, chronic renal failure that requires dialysis) or postoperative complications (i.e., partial paralysis or speech impairment from a stroke) may also require work restrictions and accommodations.

Comorbid Conditions

For the individual undergoing balloon valvuloplasty, comorbid conditions that may influence length of disability include previous cardiac surgery, pre-existing diseases affecting any of the major body systems (high blood pressure, chronic renal disease, bleeding disorders, diabetes mellitus, chronic obstructive lung disease, chronic heart disease, and immunosuppressive diseases), history of smoking, alcoholism or other substance abuse, and obesity.

Procedure Complications

Complications during or following balloon valvuloplasty are relatively rare but can include overcorrection of the stenosis that results in leaking (valvular insufficiency or regurgitation) (2-10%), large atrial septal defect (less than 5%), perforation of the left ventricle by the catheter (0.5-4%), cardiac hemorrhage, blood clots in the vessels where catheters were placed (embolism) (0.5-3%), heart attack (0.3-0.5%), life-threatening irregularities in heart rate or rhythm, damage to the heart valve, failure to relieve the stenosis, loss of limb as a result of a femoral artery blood clot cutting off the blood flow, an infection, reaction to the contrast given during angiography, respiratory arrest, kidney (renal) failure, and death. Open-heart surgery may be required to control internal bleeding, repair valvular regurgitation, or close an atrial septal defect. Death occurs in 1 out of 50,000 procedures.

Factors Influencing Duration

Factors influencing the length of disability include the number and severity of procedural complications, amount of blood loss if complications arise, number of blood transfusions, success of the valvuloplasty, individual's nutritional status, mental and emotional stability, access to rehabilitation facilities, and strength of the individual's support system.

Length of Disability

Durations reflect recovery from procedure only. Durations may be affected by level of residual heart valve disease.

Closed.

Duration in Days

Job Classification	Minimum	Optimum	Maximum
Sedentary work	7	9	14
Light work	7	9	14
Medium work	14	21	28
Heavy work	14	21	28
Very Heavy work	21	28	35

References

Cardiac Rehabilitation Programs. American Heart Association. 16 Feb 1994. 20 Dec 2000 <http://www.americanheart.org/Scientific/statements/1994/099402.html>.

Cavanaugh, Bonita. Nurse's Manual of Laboratory and Diagnostic Tests. Philadelphia: F.A. Davis Company, 1999.

Medical Updates on Therapy, Diagnosis and Prevention. American International Health Council. 15 Aug 1999. 20 Dec 2000 <http://www.asca.com/updates/1-5/14.htm>.

Meeker, Margaret, and Jane Rothrock. Alexander's Care of the Patient in Surgery. St. Louis: Mosby, 1999.

Varicocele

Other names / synonyms: Hernia Varicosa, Scrotal Varices, Varicole

456.4

Definition

Varicocele is swelling of the network of veins leading from the testicles (pampiniform plexus) within the scrotum.

Varicoceles are often diagnosed during an infertility checkup. The major risk factor for development of varicocele is the absence of the valves within the veins that prevent backflow of blood. Other risk factors may include inherited or congenital abnormalities of the blood vessels, poor drainage of the spermatic veins, and smoking tobacco. Varicocele occurs in between 8-23% of the general male population. It occurs more frequently in smokers than non-smokers. Approximately 90% of varicoceles occur in the left testicle as a result of the basic anatomy of the left internal spermatic vein. Up to 23% of cases involve both testicles.

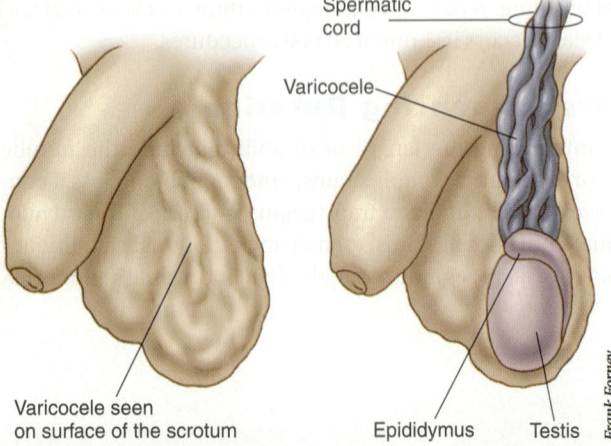

Varicocele seen on surface of the scrotum

Spermatic cord — Varicocele — Epididymus — Testis

Frank Forney

Diagnosis

History: The individual may report a swelling near the scrotum. He may also complain of a heaviness or pulling feeling on one side of the scrotum that is relieved by lying down. There may be a dull pain that increases with heavy lifting or worsens during periods of prolonged standing. Many individuals have no symptoms.

Physical exam: Exam typically reveals a swelling that can be felt on one side of the scrotum. The swelling may become reduced in size or disappear when the individual lies down. The testicle on the same side of the swelling may be soft or shrunken (atrophied). Smaller varicoceles may be detected by having the individual bear down while holding his breath (Valsalva maneuver).

Tests: The history and physical findings of a varicocele are so characteristic that further tests may not be needed. However, a sperm count (spermiogram) may be done to determine if the number of sperm have decreased. Other noninvasive techniques include measurement of the scrotal temperature (scrotal thermography), using high-frequency sound waves to visualize the spermatic veins (sonography), and using sound wave reflection to measure blood flow through the veins (Doppler flow measurement). The most commonly used invasive technique is using x-rays to visualize the varicocele following injection of a radiopaque substance directly into the spermatic veins (spermatic vein retrograde phlebography).

Treatment

Surgery to cut the spermatic vein (high ligation of the spermatic vein) is the usual treatment when the individual has fertility problems or is experiencing discomfort during normal activities. Other treatments to destroy the nonfunctional vein include use of a chemical agent or a balloon that closes the vein (sclerotherapy or balloon catheter embolization, respectively). Both of these procedures are typically done on an outpatient basis.

Prognosis

Surgical treatment (high ligation of the spermatic vein) of varicocele in individuals with low sperm count and motility results in improvement in 70% of cases.

Differential Diagnosis

Conditions that present with similar symptoms as varicocele include blockage of other veins (inferior vena cava; left renal vein) or the presence of abnormal tissue growth within the testicle. A tumor of the kidney (renal tumor) may invade the renal vein and subsequently block the spermatic vein.

Specialists

- General Surgeon
- Urologist

Work Restrictions / Accommodations

Heavy lifting and climbing should be avoided for several days if surgery to cut the spermatic vein (high ligation of the spermatic vein) is used to correct the problem.

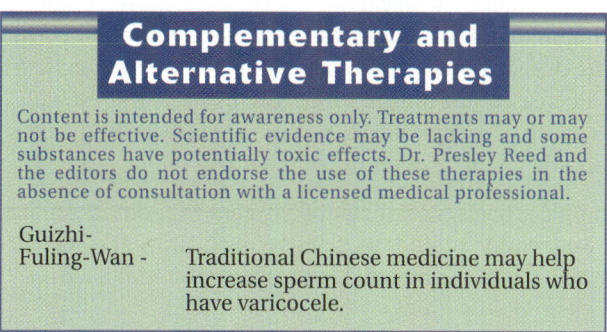

Complementary and Alternative Therapies

Content is intended for awareness only. Treatments may or may not be effective. Scientific evidence may be lacking and some substances have potentially toxic effects. Dr. Presley Reed and the editors do not endorse the use of these therapies in the absence of consultation with a licensed medical professional.

Guizhi-Fuling-Wan - Traditional Chinese medicine may help increase sperm count in individuals who have varicocele.

Comorbid Conditions

Existing conditions that may impact an individual's ability to recover and further lengthen disability include Henoch-Schönlein syndrome vasculitis, polyarteritis nodosa, and rheumatoid arthritis, all of which affect the testicular blood vessels.

Complications

A possible complication of varicocele includes infertility as a result of low sperm count and/or decreased sperm motility. This occurs in 65-75% of individuals. However, varicoceles may arise from obstruction of other connecting veins (left renal vein, inferior vena cava) indicating a more serious problem that needs to be investigated. Varicocele may result in shrinkage (atrophy) of the testicles.

Factors Influencing Duration

The type of surgery used to treat the problem will affect the length of disability. High ligation of the spermatic vein will result in a larger incision in the abdomen than newer, less invasive procedures. Older individuals generally will have longer recovery times than will those who are younger.

Length of Disability

Duration may be longer for heavy and very heavy work.

Intraluminal ablation of spermatic vein (balloon catheter or sclerosing agent).

Duration in Days

Job Classification	Minimum	Optimum	Maximum
Sedentary work	3	4	7
Light work	3	4	7
Medium work	7	9	14
Heavy work	7	9	14
Very Heavy work	7	9	14

Surgical treatment (ligation of spermatic vein).

Duration in Days

Job Classification	Minimum	Optimum	Maximum
Sedentary work	7	9	14
Light work	7	9	14
Medium work	7	14	21
Heavy work	7	14	21
Very Heavy work	7	21	28

Failure to Recover

If an individual fails to recover within the maximum duration expectancy period, the reader may wish to reference the following questions to assist in better understanding the specifics of an individual's medical case.

Regarding diagnosis:

- Does the individual complain of heaviness or a pulling feeling on one side of the scrotum that is relieved by lying down?
- Does he state that there is a dull pain that increases with heavy lifting or worsens during periods of prolonged standing?
- Does the physician note swelling that can be felt on one side of the scrotum?
- Is testicle on the same side of the swelling soft or shrunken (atrophied)?
- Did the physician detect smaller varicoceles after having the individual bear down while holding his breath (Valsalva maneuver)?
- Did the history and physical findings confirm the diagnosis? If not, is a sperm count (spermiogram) required to determine if the number of sperm have decreased?
- Does the physician believe that measurement of the scrotal temperature (scrotal thermography) or x-ray of the vein after injection of radiopaque material (spermatic vein retrograde phlebography) is required?
- Was the diagnosis of varicocele correct?
- Are there other more serious conditions (such as a renal tumor) that are causing symptoms similar to varicocele?

Regarding treatment:

- Was ligation of the spermatic vein done? Did this surgery resolve the varicocele?
- Does the individual require sclerotherapy or balloon catheter embolization?
- Will the procedure be able to be performed on an outpatient basis, or will the individual require hospitalization?

Regarding prognosis:

- What percentage of improvement did the individual attain after ligation of the spermatic vein was done?
- Is this individual a candidate for sclerotherapy or balloon catheter embolization? If so, what percentage of improvement is expected after these procedures?
- Has the individual developed complications?
- Would the individual benefit from counseling for infertility?
- Have any connecting veins been obstructed?
- How will these obstructions be treated, and what is the expected outcome after treatment?

References

Ishikawa, H., et al. "Effects of Guizhi-fuling-wan on Male Infertility with Varicocele." American Journal of Chinese Medicine 24 3-4 (1996): 327-331.

LeMone, P., and K.M. Burke. Medical-Surgical Nursing. Upper Saddle River, NJ: Prentice Hall Health, 2000.

McAninch, J.W. "Disorders of the Testis, Scrotum, and Spermatic Cord." Smith's General Urology. Tanagho, E.A., and J.W. McAninch, eds. Norwalk: Appleton & Lange, 1995. 681-690.

Nistal, M., and R. Paniagua. Testicular and Epididymal Pathology. New York: Thieme-Stratton Inc, 1984.

Varicose Ulcer

Other names / synonyms: Stasis Leg Ulcer, Venous Stasis Ulcer, Venous Ulcer
454.0, 707

Definition

A varicose ulcer is a crater-like, painful eruption on the skin of the lower leg and is associated with varicose veins.

Blood flow in the veins of the legs depends on the correct functioning of the valves in the veins. Valves that do not function properly impede circulation (venous insufficiency), causing malnourished skin tissue the collection of fluids that leads to swelling (edema). This poorly nourished skin tissue cannot heal so even minor breaks in the skin such as a cut or bump become ulcerated.

Risk factors for varicose ulcerations include having a history of varicose veins or of deep venous thrombosis (DVT). It is estimated that more than 300,000 individuals in the US have venous ulcers with the majority being women.

Diagnosis

History: The individual may report recent trauma to the leg such as an insect bite, bump, scratch, or cut. Individual may complain of a very painful sore that won't heal, swelling, skin discoloration, or itching close to the affected area. Some relief may occur with leg elevation but standing worsens the condition.

Physical exam: The exam may reveal brownish pigmentation of the skin and/or thinning and hardening (induration) of the skin near the ulcer. Varicose veins may be seen or felt with light pressure from the fingertips (palpated) close to the ulceration. Swelling (edema) of the affected limb may be evident.

Tests: Tests are generally not required since ulceration is evident. If deep venous thrombosis is suspected, however, a Doppler ultrasound of the affected leg should be done.

Treatment

Treatment includes leg elevation, intermittent warm compresses, and compression dressings soaked with a medication to remove damaged skin. The dressing first requires changing every 2 to 3 days. When the edema decreases and the ulcer begins to heal, the dressing can be changed once or twice a week. If damage done by the ulcer is severe, however, skin grafting may be recommended.

After the ulcer heals, which can take weeks to months, the individual should wear elastic support stockings daily to prevent recurrence of the ulcer. Walking is recommended to promote good circulation.

Prognosis

The outcome for individuals who undergo treatment for varicose ulcers is excellent though the healing process may be lengthy.

Differential Diagnosis

Other possibilities include post-thrombotic syndrome, retroperitoneal vein obstruction, arteriovenous fistula, and congenital venous malformation.

Specialists

- General Surgeon
- Vascular Surgeon

Work Restrictions / Accommodations

Any heavy lifting, prolonged standing, or prolonged sitting will need to be limited. The individual requires time to elevate the leg throughout the workday. Time away for dressing changes at the doctor's office may also be required.

Comorbid Conditions

Diabetes mellitus, cardiovascular conditions, or obesity may lengthen disability.

Complications

Complications include secondary ulceration, fistula with hemorrhage, chronic stasis dermatitis, thrombophlebitis, superficial venous thrombosis, and pulmonary embolism.

Factors Influencing Duration

Factors that may influence the length of disability include age of individual, type of treatment, and response to treatment.

Length of Disability

Medical treatment. Small ulcer.

Duration in Days

Job Classification	Minimum	Optimum	Maximum
Sedentary work	7	14	21
Light work	7	14	21
Medium work	14	21	28
Heavy work	14	21	28
Very Heavy work	14	21	28

Medical treatment. Large, chronic or extensive ulceration.

Duration in Days

Job Classification	Minimum	Optimum	Maximum
Sedentary work	7	28	56
Light work	7	28	56
Medium work	7	28	56
Heavy work	7	28	56
Very Heavy work	7	28	56

Skin graft.

Duration in Days

Job Classification	Minimum	Optimum	Maximum
Sedentary work	14	42	56
Light work	14	42	56
Medium work	28	56	70
Heavy work	28	56	70
Very Heavy work	28	56	70

Failure to Recover

If an individual fails to recover within the maximum duration expectancy period, the reader may wish to reference the following questions to assist in better understanding the specifics of an individual's medical case.

Regarding diagnosis:

- Does individual have a history of varicose veins or DVT?
- Did individual report trauma to the leg such as an insect bite, bump, scratch, or cut?
- Does individual complain of a very painful sore that won't heal, swelling, skin discoloration, or itching close to the affected area?
- Is there is some relief with leg elevation but standing makes it worse?
- On physical exam, is there brownish pigmentation of the skin and/or induration present on the skin near the ulcer? Are varicose veins palpable close to the ulceration? Edema?
- Has individual had a Doppler ultrasound of the affected leg, if necessary?
- Were conditions with similar symptoms ruled out?

Regarding treatment:

- Is individual being treated with leg elevation, intermittent warm compresses, and medicated compression dressings?
- Is skin grafting necessary?
- Does individual wear elastic support stocking daily?

Regarding prognosis:

- Does individual walk on a daily basis?
- Can individual's employer accommodate any necessary restrictions?
- Does individual have any conditions that may affect ability to recover?
- Have any complications developed such as secondary ulceration, fistula with hemorrhage, chronic stasis dermatitis, thrombophlebitis, superficial venous thrombosis, or pulmonary embolism?

References

"Chapter 111. Dermatitis: Stasis Dermatitis." Merck Manual of Diagnosis and Therapy, 17th ed. Beers, Mark H., and Robert Berkow, MD Whitehouse Station, NJ: Merck & Co., Inc, 1999. 30 Dec 2000 <http://www.merck.com/mmanual/section10/chapter111/111h.htm>.

Baron, Edward, and Barbara Ross. Varicose Veins: A Guide to Prevention and Treatment. New York: Facts on File, Inc, 1995.

Varicose Veins

Other names / synonyms: Varices, Varicosis, Varicosities, Varicosity

454, 454.2, 454.9, 456

Definition

Varicose veins (varicosities) are enlarged, twisted veins with nonfunctioning valves located under the skin. The legs are the most common location for varicose veins to develop.

Veins are responsible for carrying blood back to the heart and lungs to be oxygenated. Normal veins in the legs have valves that close, forcing blood toward the heart and preventing it from being pulled down by gravity. Varicose veins develop when these valves leak, allowing blood to remain in the veins and accumulate; the pooling blood causes the vein to become enlarged and twisted. Primary varicose veins occur because of congenitally defective valves or without an exact known cause. Secondary varicose veins occur as the result of some other condition, such as pregnancy.

While causes of varicose veins are not entirely understood, they may include hormonal changes, weakness in the vein walls, abdominal tumors, or a history of deep vein thrombosis or thrombophlebitis. Risk factors include a family history (hereditary risk) of varicose veins, female gender, prolonged standing or sitting, pregnancy, artery and vein abnormalities at birth (congenital anomalies), advanced age, menopause, and obesity.

Varicose veins, the most common type of vascular disease, occur in between 1-10 people in the US. It is estimated that by the time they reach their sixties, 72% of women and 42% of men in the US will have varicose veins.

Diagnosis

History: The individual may complain of pain, swelling, cramping, or aching in the legs; throbbing, burning, or itching of the veins themselves; soreness behind the knee; and ankle swelling. Individuals may also complain of a sensation of fullness or heaviness in the legs, or fatigue after standing for long periods with relief obtained when the leg is elevated.

Physical exam: Diagnosis is based primarily on appearance of the veins. Visible, enlarged veins, brownish discolored ankle skin, and skin ulcers on the legs or above the ankles will be seen. Rapid filling, less than 10-20 seconds, of the varicosities indicates dysfunctional valves. This dysfunction is determined by applying light pressure with the fingertips (palpation) to the primary vein (saphenous vein) in the upper thigh while the individual stands, reclines, elevates the leg to 45 degrees, and then stands again.

Tests: Tests are generally not required for varicose veins. A duplex Doppler ultrasound examination of the extremities is used to observe blood flow and characterize the vessels or if deep venous thrombosis (DVT) is suspected.

Treatment

Treatment may not be required unless the condition is painful or causing skin ulcers. Self-care may decrease symptoms, however. Whenever possible, the individual should elevate the legs, preferably at the level of, or above, the heart. Other helpful measures include wearing elastic stockings or bandages to increase blood flow, avoiding prolonged standing or sitting, and improving circulation by exercising regularly, particularly walking.

Severe varicosities may be treated by injection of a substance into the vein that causes internal scarring (sclerosis), thus blocking the vein (sclerotherapy). This procedure may have to be repeated one or more times.

Surgical correction (vein stripping and ligation) of varicose veins may be done if pain, vein inflammation with formation of blood clots (thrombophlebitis), or skin changes persist; it can also be done for cosmetic reasons. The procedure involves one small incision in the groin, and one in the ankle or calf, through which a wire-like instrument is inserted. As the surgeon pulls back on the wire, the varicosity, along with the wire, is removed; then the veins that join the deeper veins are tied off.

Prognosis

Varicose veins are not curable, but treating early symptoms results in an excellent outcome. Those who undergo sclerotherapy or vein stripping also have excellent outcomes provided they follow postoperative treatment instructions, and no complications develop. The recurrence rate for both sclerotherapy and vein stripping, however, increases with time. No treatment can prevent the occurrence of new varicosities.

Differential Diagnosis

Serious problems such as abdominal tumor or deep thrombophlebitis may first affect venous blood flow in the legs.

Specialists

- Surgeon
- Vascular Surgeon

Work Restrictions / Accommodations

Allowances are required for individuals to elevate their legs. Reducing periods of prolonged standing or sitting are also necessary. Those whose duties require heavy lifting may require a transfer to other duties, since abdominal strain may contribute to varicose veins.

Comorbid Conditions

Blood clotting disorders, poor circulation, high blood pressure (hypertension), and diabetes mellitus may lengthen disability.

Complications

Complications of varicose veins include varicose ulcers, thrombophlebitis, deep venous thrombosis, thrombophlebitis, and pulmonary embolism.

Factors Influencing Duration

The age of the individual, the severity of symptoms, and response to treatment are factors that might influence length of disability.

Length of Disability

Sclerotherapy.

Job Classification	Duration in Days		
	Minimum	Optimum	Maximum
Sedentary work	3	4	7
Light work	3	4	7
Medium work	7	9	14
Heavy work	7	9	14
Very Heavy work	7	9	14

Surgical treatment (ligation and stripping of varicose veins).

Job Classification	Duration in Days		
	Minimum	Optimum	Maximum
Sedentary work	7	14	21
Light work	7	14	21
Medium work	14	21	28
Heavy work	21	28	35
Very Heavy work	21	28	35

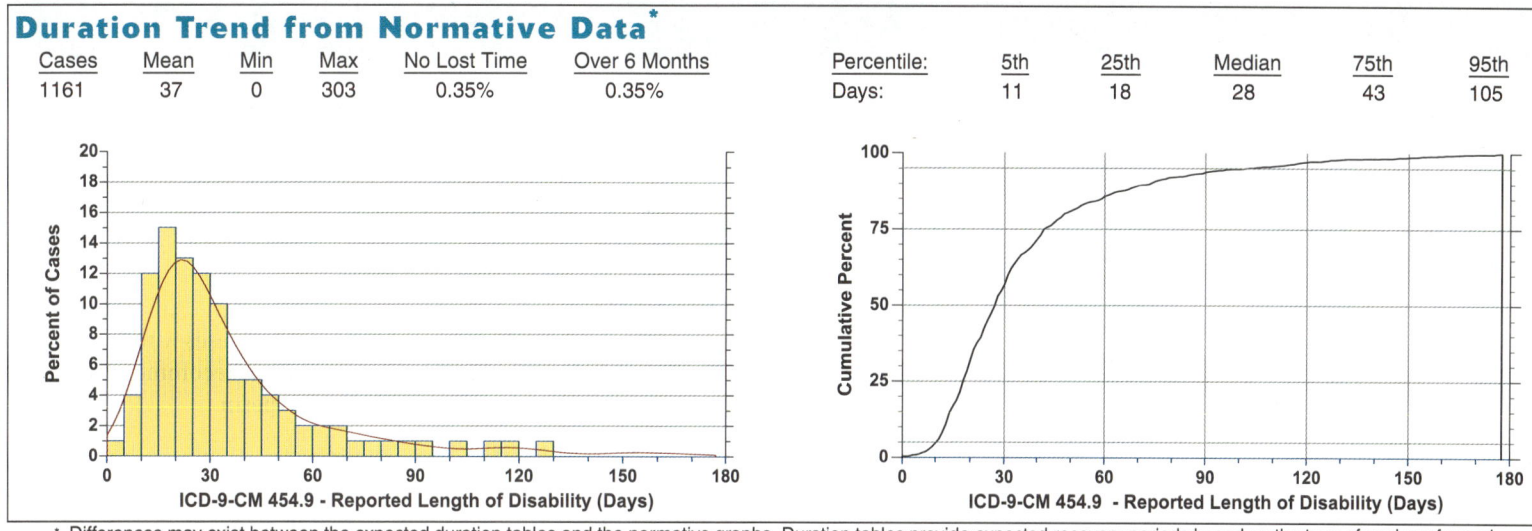

Duration Trend from Normative Data*

Cases	Mean	Min	Max	No Lost Time	Over 6 Months
1161	37	0	303	0.35%	0.35%

Percentile:	5th	25th	Median	75th	95th
Days:	11	18	28	43	105

* Differences may exist between the expected duration tables and the normative graphs. Duration tables provide expected recovery periods based on the type of work performed by the individual. The normative graphs reflect the actual observed experience of many individuals across the spectrum of physical conditions, in a variety of industries, and with varying levels of case management.

Failure to Recover

If an individual fails to recover within the maximum duration expectancy period, the reader may wish to reference the following questions to assist in better understanding the specifics of an individual's medical case.

Regarding diagnosis:

- Are the individual's varicose veins primary or secondary?
- Does the individual have a family history of varicose veins?
- Is the individual female? Pregnant? Menopausal? Obese? Advanced age?
- Does the individual experience prolonged standing or sitting?
- Does the individual have any congenital abnormalities of arteries or veins?
- Does the individual complain of pain, swelling, cramping, or aching in the legs?
- Does the individual have throbbing, burning, or itching of the veins themselves?
- Does the individual have soreness behind the knee and ankle swelling?
- Do legs have a sensation of fullness or heaviness?
- Does the individual have fatigue after standing for long periods?
- Is relief obtained when the leg is elevated?
- On exam, are there visible enlarged veins? Brownish discolored ankle skin?
- Were skin ulcers present on the legs or above the ankles?
- Do the varicosities fill rapidly?
- Was Doppler ultrasound done?
- Have conditions with similar symptoms been ruled out?

Regarding treatment:

- In milder cases, does individual elevate the legs when possible?
- Does the individual wear elastic stockings?
- Does the individual avoid prolonged standing or sitting? Does the individual walk regularly?
- Was sclerotherapy done? Has it been repeated?
- Was vein stripping and ligation done?

Varicose Veins

Regarding prognosis:

- Is individual's employer able to accommodate any necessary restrictions?
- Does individual have any conditions that may affect ability to recover?
- Does individual have any complications such as varicose ulcers, thrombophlebitis, deep venous thrombosis, thrombophlebitis, or pulmonary embolism?

References

Baron, Edward, and Barbara Ross. Varicose Veins: A Guide to Prevention and Treatment. New York: Facts on File, Inc, 1995.

Setness, Peter, ed. "Varicose Veins." Postgraduate Medicine 98 1 (1995): 01 Jan 2001 <http://www.postgradmed.com/issues/1996/pat_note/varicose.htm>.

Vasectomy

Other names / synonyms: Male Contraceptive Procedure
63.7, 63.70, 63.71, 63.72, 63.73

Definition

A vasectomy is a surgical procedure used for male sterilization. This is an elective birth-control procedure for men.

The procedure involves removing a segment of each of the tubes conducting sperm from the testicles (vas deferens). After vasectomy, sperm cell production continues, but the sperm are trapped in the lower end of the vas deferens and eventually dissolve. The length of time for sterilization to occur takes from 1 week to several months, depending upon the frequency of ejaculation.

This procedure is performed on 7% of married men and in over 500,000 men in the US.

Reason for Procedure

This procedure is a birth-control measure that is done to provide permanent sterilization in men.

Description

This procedure is done on an outpatient basis under local anesthesia and takes about 20 minutes to perform.

There are 2 types of vasectomy procedures commonly performed. In the traditional method, a tiny incision is made with a surgical knife (scalpel) in the scrotum. The tubular tissue that produces and contains sperm (vas deferens) is located and pulled through the incision far enough to be cut into 2 pieces. The 2 ends of the vas deferens are then tied with surgical thread (suture) and the ends replaced within the scrotum.

A second approach to performing the vasectomy is called the "no-scalpel vasectomy." In this approach, the vas deferens is pulled through a puncture made by the finger in the thin skin of the scrotum. The vas deferens is pulled through the opening, cut into 2 pieces, and the ends tied and replaced into the scrotum.

The incision from the scalpel or the finger puncture hole contracts and seals itself after the procedure and, therefore, does not require to be sewn or stapled shut. An antibiotic ointment and fluffy dressings within a scrotal support are applied for comfort and to reduce any swelling or bleeding that might occur. The individual should lie on his back as much as possible for up to 48 hours. The application of ice packs for the first 8 hours is helpful. It is essential that the individual have 2 consecutive negative semen analysis tests (absence of sperm in the semen) to determine whether the procedure is effective.

Prognosis

Vasectomy is successful in approximately 90% of cases within 3 months or 12-15 ejaculations. Secondary contraception is recommended until 2 semen analyses demonstrate the absence of sperm.

Specialists

- General Surgeon
- Urologist

Work Restrictions / Accommodations

There should be minimal work restrictions after the surgery. Strenuous activity should be avoided for 1 week. The individual may request a portion of a day off from work for a follow-up doctor's visit to determine if the surgery was effective.

Comorbid Conditions

The presence of scrotal abnormalities, such as hydrocele, may affect recovery.

Procedure Complications

Complications include the formation of blood clots within the scrotum (hematoma) or surgical site infections, each of which occur in up to 3% of cases. Chronic scrotal pain occurs in approximately 1 in 2000 cases. Most post-vasectomy pain is thought to be due to congestion of the tubular structure (epididymis) that becomes swollen with seminal fluid that is not passed through the severed vas deferens. Another complication that occurs in less than 1% of cases is the reopening of the vas deferens (recanalization), leading to presence of sperm in the seminal fluid.

Factors Influencing Duration

Bleeding, scrotum swelling, or infection will increase the length of disability. Most men are able to return to work the day after the surgery.

Length of Disability

Duration in Days

Job Classification	Minimum	Optimum	Maximum
Sedentary work	1	1	3
Light work	1	1	3
Medium work	1	3	7
Heavy work	1	4	7
Very Heavy work	1	4	7

References

Goldstein, Marc. "Surgical Management of Male Infertility and Other Scrotal Disorders." Campbell's Urology, 7th ed. Walsh, Patrick C., et al., eds. Philadelphia: W.B. Saunders Company, 1998. 1331-1377.

Thomas, Michael A. "Contraception." Conn's Current Therapy. Rakel, Robert E., and Edward T. Bope, eds. Philadelphia: W.B. Saunders Company, 2001. 1123-1128.

Vasovagal Syncope

Other names / synonyms: Fainting, Neurally Mediated Syncope, Neurocardiogenic Syncope
780.2

Definition

Vasovagal syncope can be described as a temporary failure of the brain to maintain blood pressure and heart rate. Causes of vasovagal syncope include fear, pain, anxiety, physical and emotional stress, or an unpleasant sight, sound, or smell. Episodes of vasovagal syncope usually begin in adolescence, but they can occur at any age. There is a higher incidence of vasovagal syncope among the elderly.

Diagnosis

History: Individuals may report profuse sweating, nausea, vomiting, feeling dizzy or lightheaded, feeling warm, and pale skin prior to fainting. Individuals may also report previous episodes of fainting.

Physical exam: If physical exam is performed immediately after a fainting episode, shallow and rapid breathing, cool extremities, profuse sweating, and pale skin may be evident. Slow heart beat (bradycardia), change in blood pressure, and heart murmur are also indications for vasovagal syncope.

Tests: Tilt-table testing is usually done to evaluate individuals in unexplained syncope. Not all individuals with vasovagal syncope need the test. During the test, the individual is strapped to a special table and slowly inclined to an angle of between 60 to 80 degrees. In people with vasovagal syncope, this mild stress will result in a drop in the heart rate and blood pressure.

Transcranial Doppler ultrasonography is a noninvasive tool to assess blood flow to the brain. Also electrocardiogram (ECG), complete blood count (CBC) to evaluate anemia, glucose and electrolytes tests, and a pregnancy test may need to be performed.

Treatment

Most individuals don't need to be treated with medications. Many individuals may need education and reassurance. For those with stress-related symptoms and an identifiable stressor, stress reduction therapy including biofeedback may be useful. Individuals should be advised to avoid predisposing factors (such as extreme heat) and to maintain adequate hydration. Medications include antibiotics and selective serotonin reuptake inhibitors (SSRIs). It is believed that vasovagal syncope may be associated with decreased heart rate (bradycardia).

Prognosis

For some individuals, medication therapy may be successful in the prevention of vasovagal syncope. For others, treatment with medication does not lead to prevention and future episodes will continue to occur. Learning coping mechanisms via desensitization therapy including biofeedback can successfully treat stress-induced events.

Differential Diagnosis

Differential diagnoses may include Adams-Stokes attacks, syncope, seizures, low blood glucose (hypoglycemia), irregular heartbeat (arrhythmias), hysterical fainting, cerebral transient ischemic attacks (TIAs), and anxiety attacks.

Specialists

- Cardiologist
- Emergency Medicine
- Internist
- Neurologist

Work Restrictions / Accommodations

Individuals who work with heavy machinery or individuals who climb or work at heights may need to be reassigned to a new position. Individuals may need to work in an environment where there is physical supervision.

Comorbid Conditions

Comorbid conditions may include emotional stress and conditions in which dehydration is prevalent.

Complications

Although some individuals may have some sort of warning, such as dizziness or lightheadedness, some will not. A sudden loss of consciousness can result in falling and hitting the floor, which may result in fractures or other complications, such as severe head injury.

Factors Influencing Duration

Factors influencing length of disability may include individual's response to treatment, emotional status of the individual, frequency of episodes, and cause of vasovagal syncope.

Length of Disability

No disability is expected for simple vasovagal episode. Remission is common in most cases. In cases of repeated episodes, disability may be permanent for individuals who perform heavy work or who work at heights.

Duration in Days

Job Classification	Minimum	Optimum	Maximum
Any work	0	3	7

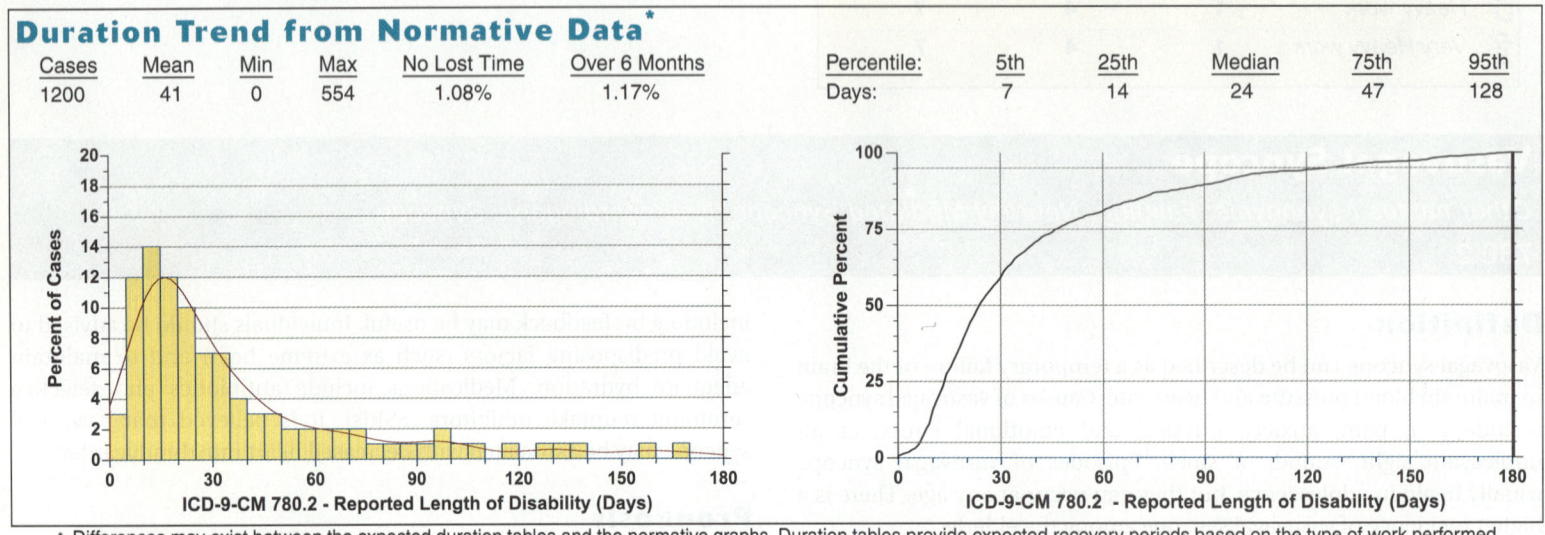

* Differences may exist between the expected duration tables and the normative graphs. Duration tables provide expected recovery periods based on the type of work performed by the individual. The normative graphs reflect the actual observed experience of many individuals across the spectrum of physical conditions, in a variety of industries, and with varying levels of case management.

Failure to Recover

If an individual fails to recover within the maximum duration expectancy period, the reader may wish to reference the following questions to assist in better understanding the specifics of an individual's medical case.

Regarding diagnosis:

- Does individuals report profuse sweating, nausea, vomiting, feeling dizzy or lightheaded, warm, and pale skin prior to fainting?
- Has individual had previous episodes of fainting?
- Does individual have orthostatic hypotension? Dehydration? Pain?
- Has individual been standing for a prolonged time? Does individual have any fear, anxiety, or stress? Witnessed an unpleasant sight, sound, or smell?
- Was a physical exam performed immediately after a fainting episode?
- Did individual have shallow and rapid breathing, cool extremities, profuse sweating, and pale skin?
- Does individual have bradycardia, a change in blood pressure, or heart murmur?
- Did individual have tilt-table testing? Transcranial Doppler ultrasonography? Were ECG, CBC, glucose, electrolyte, and pregnancy tests performed?
- Have conditions with similar symptoms been ruled out?

Regarding treatment:

- Has individual been treated with medications such as beta-blockers, mineralocorticoids, SSRIs, or vasopressors?
- Has individual received education and reassurance?
- If needed, has individual undergone stress reduction therapy including biofeedback? Does individual try to avoid predisposing factors?
- Do frequent episodes of syncope occur with no response to treatment? Has a permanent cardiac pacemaker been considered?

Regarding prognosis:

- Can individual's employer accommodate any necessary restrictions?
- Does individual have any conditions that may affect ability to recover?
- Has individual had any complications such as injuries from falling?

2250   The Medical Disability Advisor—Fourth Edition

References

Fauci, A., Eugene Braunwald, and Kurt Isselbacher. Harrison's Principles of Internal Medicine. New York: McGraw-Hill, 1998.

NINDS Syncope Information Page. National Institute of Neurological Disorders and Stroke. 27 Jun 2000. 22 Aug 2000 <http://www.ninds.nih.gov/health_and_medical/disorders/syncope_doc.htm>.

Vena Cava Interruption

Other names / synonyms: Insertion of Bird Cage Filter, Insertion of Greenfield Filter, Insertion of Vena Caval Umbrella, Interruption Inferior Vena Cava

38.7

Definition

A vena cava interruption is a surgical procedure designed to trap dislodged blood clots (thrombi) in the inferior vena cava, which is the large vein returning blood to the heart after it has circulated through the legs and lower torso. Trapping thrombi coming from veins in the legs prevents them from traveling to the heart and then to the lungs where they could cause a potentially fatal blockage of lung circulation (pulmonary embolism).

In the past, the procedure involved completely closing off (ligating) the inferior vena cava. This was a lengthy surgical procedure, often ineffective. Today, a much simpler and more effective method of vena caval interruption involves inserting a filtering device called a Greenfield, bird cage, or umbrella filter through a large vein in the leg or neck and positioning it in the inferior vena cava. The bird cage and umbrella filters resemble these objects in shape except the umbrella filter resembles an umbrella without the material. These filters are designed to trap large clots (thrombi) and prevent them from traveling to the lungs where they may cause life-threatening pulmonary emboli.

Approximately 90% of pulmonary emboli arise from clots in the deep veins of the lower limbs (deep vein thrombosis). Risk factors for deep vein thrombosis and pulmonary embolism include prolonged sitting, bed rest, immobilization, recent surgery (especially hip surgery) or trauma, gynecological surgery, heart surgery, fractures of the pelvis or femur, childbirth within the last 6 months, obesity, smoking, and the use of medications such as estrogen and birth control pills. Risks also include a history of cancer, a blood disorder called polycythemia vera, and changes in the levels of blood clotting factors making the blood more likely to clot (hypercoagulability). Deep venous thrombosis occurs in approximately 2 out of 1,000 individuals. The condition is most commonly seen in adults over age 60. A pulmonary embolism affects as many as 5 of 10,000 individuals in the US each year.

Reason for Procedure

Vena cava interruption treats individuals who continue to have blood clots even when given blood thinners (anticoagulants) or those who cannot be given these drugs because of the risk of bleeding complications. Vena cava interruption is also used for individuals with multiple small pulmonary clots (emboli) that result in pulmonary insufficiency or pulmonary hypertension, for those with infected (septic) emboli and failure to improve on anticoagulants and antibiotics, and for individuals who have undergone previous surgery (pulmonary embolectomy) to remove a blood clot. Approximately 90-95% of all pulmonary emboli originate in veins drained by the inferior vena cava, so diverting blood flow or preventing blood clots from traversing this vessel protects against pulmonary embolism.

In a recent study of 137 individuals, 140 Greenfield filters were placed for various reasons, which include the inability to tolerate anticoagulants (41%), recurrent pulmonary emboli despite treatment with anticoagulants (23%), cancer with deep vein thrombosis and/or pulmonary embolus (12%), complications of anticoagulants (9%), clot prevention in multiple trauma with pelvic and/or long bone fractures (9%), clot prevention in hip surgery (4%), and deep vein thrombosis with free-floating clot (4%).

Description

Insertion of a filter for vena caval interruption is usually performed using local anesthesia with intravenous injection of sedative. The area around the vein in the groin (femoral vein) or neck (jugular vein) is cleansed with a disinfectant solution, shaved if necessary, and numbed with local anesthetic. The vein is punctured and the device inserted through the vein using a long flexible tube (catheter). Using continuous x-ray (fluoroscopy) for guidance, the device is advanced and anchored in the large vein in the torso (inferior vena cava) where it will filter blood coming from the legs and lower torso to the heart and lungs. If the procedure is done on an outpatient basis, the individual is monitored for 6 to 12 hours then allowed to return home.

Prognosis

Current methods of vena cava interruption are generally effective in reducing the short-term incidence of pulmonary emboli. Mortality from the procedure itself is negligible. After filter placement, deep venous thrombosis occurs in 6-32% of individuals, inferior vena cava thrombosis in 4-11%, and pulmonary embolus in 2-3%, depending on the type of filter used. In a recent study, about 40% of individuals died within a year due to causes unrelated to the filter or recurrent clot formation.

Specialists

• General Surgeon	• Vascular Surgeon

Work Restrictions / Accommodations

Possible work restrictions and accommodations include decreased work activity, extended leave, and increased rest periods. The individual should avoid driving or operating machinery for 24 hours, strenuous exercise or lifting for 2 days, and prolonged standing or sitting for one to 4 weeks following the operation. Temporary reassignment to work that complies with these restrictions may be necessary.

Comorbid Conditions

Comorbid conditions of paralysis or chronic immobility, cancer, or multiple organ failure may affect ability to recover and further lengthen disability. Allergy to contrast dye may hinder fluoroscopic guidance of the filter as it is placed in the inferior vena cava. Smoking or other risk factors for thrombosis may worsen outcome.

Procedure Complications

Complications of vena caval interruption using a filter device include dislodgement and movement (migration) of the filter causing obstruction of blood flow, misplacement of the filter, perforation of adjacent structures such as the duodenum or ureter, and bleeding. In a recent study, thrombosis at the insertion site occurred in 23-36%. Operative morbidity ranges from 4-16%, with reported complications including lung collapse (pneumothorax), air embolism, and tearing of the jugular vein.

Factors Influencing Duration

Factors that may influence the length of disability include age and general health of the individual, location of the clot, another underlying medical or surgical condition, and individual's previous history of emboli.

Length of Disability

Individual is anticoagulated for three to six months.

Duration in Days

Job Classification	Minimum	Optimum	Maximum
Sedentary work	28	35	42
Light work	28	35	42
Medium work	42	49	56
Heavy work	84	112	168
Very Heavy work	84	112	168

References

Clochesy, John M., et al. Critical Care Nursing, 2nd ed. Philadelphia: W.B. Saunders Company, 1996.

Rojas, R.G.A., et al. "Use of Greenfield Filter in Suprarenal Position." Cir Ciruj 64 4 (1996): 102-107.

Venous Embolism and Thrombosis
325, 453, 671.9

Definition

A venous thrombosis is a blood clot that originates in a vein and does not move. An embolus results when the blood clot breaks away from where it originates and travels through the bloodstream. Thrombosis is frequently accompanied by inflammation of the vein (phlebitis), which is known as thrombophlebitis. The terms thrombosis and thrombophlebitis often are interchanged, and generally refer to the same condition.

Thrombosis can occur in veins near the surface of the skin (superficial thrombophlebitis) or in deeper veins (deep vein thrombosis--DVT) and occurs because of damage to the blood vessel and increased blood coagulation components (hypercoagulability). Emboli rarely develop with superficial thrombophlebitis, but the primary concern with DVT is possible entry of an embolus into the lung (pulmonary embolus), which can be fatal.

There are several factors that add to the risk of venous thrombosis formation. These include intravenous (IV) catheters, medication inserted through the catheters that can irritate the vein, blood disorders, birth control pills (oral contraceptives), varicose veins, and pregnancy. Other factors put individuals at risk of not only venous thrombosis formation, but of embolus formation as well. These include prolonged bed rest, such as for recovery after surgery or for a lengthy illness, and after prolonged sitting, particularly after traveling long distances. Heart failure, trauma, abdominal cancers, and stroke may also add to the risk of thrombosis and embolus formation.

Individuals who undergo surgery for orthopedic problems experience venous thrombosis greater than 50% of the time, and 10-40% of individuals who undergo chest or abdominal surgery experience venous thrombosis. Serious complications occur in approximately 3% of individuals who have DVT.

Diagnosis

History: An individual with superficial thrombophlebitis may complain of redness, tenderness, and a feeling of warmth near the thrombus. If DVT is present, the individual may complain of all of the above, as well as skin discoloration and pain with standing or walking, which is relieved with leg elevation. An individual with a pulmonary embolus may complain of an abrupt onset of shortness of breath and rapid breathing (tachypnea), as well as of feeling anxious and of chest pain.

Physical exam: Light pressure applied with the fingertips (palpation) will reveal a hardened (indurated), line-like vein and redness (erythema) or warmth at the site with superficial thrombophlebitis. Superficial veins may be noticeable with DVT, and palpation over the veins in the groin, behind the knee (popliteal), or inside the thigh may reveal tenderness. Deep calf tenderness also may be demonstrated. With PE, rapid respirations are evident and the individual may appear anxious, even panic stricken.

Tests: Non-invasive tests used to diagnosis venous thrombosis are duplex ultrasonography and impedance plethysmography (IPG). If neither of these tests confirms the diagnosis, a venography may be required. This test involves the insertion of a catheter into a vein through which dye is inserted. The ability of the dye to travel throughout the veins is then monitored on x-ray. One test for pulmonary embolus is the lung perfusion scan. This test, in which a radioisotope is injected into a vein, determines the efficacy of pulmonary and venous blood flow via computer. The definitive diagnostic test for PE is pulmonary arteriography, in which dye is injected into the arm and then observed via x-ray as it travels through the lungs.

Treatment

Superficial thrombophlebitis is treated with bed rest, leg elevation, warm compresses applied to the affected limb, and nonsteroidal anti-inflammatory drugs (NSAIDs). Treatment of DVT may require hospitalization because medications that decrease coagulation of the blood (anticoagulants) and destroy thrombi (thrombolytics) must be administered. Leg elevation is required, and the individual will be placed on bed rest. When the individual is allowed to be out of bed, elastic stockings may be required to facilitate circulation and prevent swelling. Individuals may be required to take anti-coagulants on a regular basis, to prevent the possibility of thromboembolism.

Prognosis

The prognosis (outcome) for individuals who are treated with anticoagulant therapy is very good, especially for those whose thrombosis was the result of a reversible cause, such as surgery. Individuals who complete 3 months of therapy after a reversible cause of venous thrombosis have a recurrence rate of approximately 3% annually. For those with underlying conditions, such as cancer, the annual rate of recurrence can be as great as fifteen percent. If the condition is not treated, however, 20-30% of superficial thrombophlebitis cases may develop deep vein thrombosis, and 40-50% of individuals with deep vein thrombosis may experience pulmonary embolus.

Twenty-five percent of individuals who have compromised heart and lung function and experience a pulmonary embolism die. Death is unlikely for those with normal heart and lung function, unless greater than 50% of the lung vasculature is involved.

Differential Diagnosis

Differential diagnoses for venous thrombosis include tears, bleeding, or trauma of the muscles, lymphedema, arthritis, tendonitis, nerve compression, and disorders of the arteries. Differential diagnoses for PE include heart attack (myocardial infarction), cardiac tamponade, and septic shock.

Specialists

- Cardiologist
- Internist
- Pulmonologist

Work Restrictions / Accommodations

Allowances for elevation of the legs and a reduction in periods of prolonged sitting and standing will be required. Individuals taking anticoagulant medication may require transfer if their duties involve the possibility of injury to themselves. Time away for doctor and laboratory appointments will be required.

Comorbid Conditions

Pregnancy, heart failure, and cancer are underlying conditions that might influence length of disability.

Complications

Complications of venous thrombosis include pulmonary embolus, post-thrombotic syndrome, and chronic venous insufficiency. Pulmonary embolus may be complicated by hemorrhage if thrombolytic treatment is used.

Factors Influencing Duration

The age of the individual and response to treatment may influence the length of disability.

Length of Disability

Duration depends on location and organ system affected. Length of disability depends on job requirements and whether complications occur. A more specific diagnosis is required to determine disability duration.

Failure to Recover

If an individual fails to recover within the maximum duration expectancy period, the reader may wish to reference the following questions to assist in better understanding the specifics of an individual's medical case.

Regarding diagnosis:

- Does the individual have a history of blood disorders, heart failure, trauma, abdominal cancer, or stroke?
- Does the individual have a history of varicose veins?
- Has the individual recently had an intravenous (IV) catheter in place? Was any medication inserted through the catheter?
- Is the individual currently pregnant or has the individual recently given birth?
- Does the individual take birth control pills (oral contraceptives)?
- Has the individual been on prolonged bed rest, such as for recovery after surgery or for a lengthy illness?
- Has the individual experienced prolonged sitting, particularly for traveling long distances?
- Has the individual undergone recent orthopedic, chest, or abdominal surgery?
- Does the individual complain of redness, tenderness, and a feeling of warmth near the thrombus?
- If DVT is present, does the individual also complain of skin discoloration and pain with standing or walking, which is relieved with leg elevation?
- Were duplex ultrasonography and impedance plethysmography (IPG) done?
- If neither of these tests confirmed the diagnosis, was a venography done?
- If pulmonary embolus was suspected, was a lung perfusion scan or pulmonary arteriography performed?
- Was a diagnosis of superficial thrombophlebitis or deep vein thrombosis confirmed?

Regarding treatment:

- For superficial thrombophlebitis, was treatment with bed rest, leg elevation, warm compresses applied to the affected limb, and nonsteroidal anti-inflammatory drugs (NSAIDs) given?

- Did the individual require hospitalization for DVT?
- If so, were anticoagulant and thrombolytic medications administered?
- How long was the individual required to be on bed rest?
- Once out of bed, was the individual instructed to wear elastic stockings to facilitate circulation and prevent swelling?
- Will the individual be required to take anticoagulants on a regular basis?
- Is the individual compliant with medication and other treatment regimens?

Regarding prognosis:

- Was the underlying cause of thrombosis a reversible or temporary condition, such as recovery from surgery or pregnancy?
- Does the individual have underlying heart and/or lung disorders?
- Was this an initial diagnosis or was this a recurrence?
- Did the individual seek treatment promptly for superficial thrombophlebitis? If not, has deep vein thrombosis developed?
- Has the individual developed complications such as pulmonary embolus, post-thrombotic syndrome, or chronic venous insufficiency?
- Has thrombolytic therapy caused hemorrhaging, thus complicating pulmonary embolus?
- How will complications be treated and what is their expected outcome with treatment?
- How will the venous thrombosis/embolus and the complications affect the daily activities of the individual?

References

"Venous Thrombosis." Merck Manual of Diagnosis and Therapy, 17th ed. Beers, Mark H., and Robert Berkow, MD Whitehouse Station, NJ: Merck & Co., Inc, 1999 08 Jan 2001 <http://www.merck.com/pubs/mmanual/section16/chapter212/212g.htm>.

Creager, M., and Victor Dzau. "Vascular Diseases of the Extremities." Harrison's Principles of Internal Medicine Fauci, A., et al., eds. New York: The McGraw-Hill Companies, 2000 6. Harrison's Online. 19 Jan 2001 <http://www.harrisonsonline.com/>.

Hirsh, Jack. "Venous Thromboembolism." Dale, D.C., and Daniel D. Federman, MD New York: WebMD Corporation, 2000 Scientific American Medicine. 17 Jan 2001 <http://www.samed.com/sam/forms/index.htm>.

Tierney, Lawrence, Stephen McPhee, and Maxine Papadakis. Current Medical Diagnosis & Treatment. New York: McGraw-Hill, 2000.

Ventilation Pneumonitis

Other names / synonyms: Air Conditioner Lung, Extrinsic Allergic Alveolitis, Humidifier Lung

495.7, 506.9

Definition

Ventilation pneumonitis is a special class of respiratory disease experienced by individuals in office buildings and other locations that rely on forced air ventilation systems and humidifiers in the working environment. Pneumonitis is an inflammation of the lung and its structures due to a wide variety of agents, both biological and particulate. Various biological agents can cause both infectious and noninfectious diseases.

Biological agents are present in the air almost everywhere and are a common factor in office air pollution. They include bacteria, viruses, fungi, pollen, dust mites and other insects, animal dander (tiny scales from hair, feathers, or skin) and molds.

Biological agents can travel through the air and are often invisible. They are usually inhaled, either alone or by attaching themselves to particles of dust, and then enter the respiratory system. Viruses can be carried indoors by people while plants, pets, and insects are potential sources of pollen, dander, and other allergens. Dust mites and other insects can thrive in sofas, stuffed chairs, carpets, and bedding.

Offices can be especially vulnerable to microorganisms because fungi and bacteria find nourishment in inadequately maintained air-circulation systems and dirty washrooms. When biological agents are allowed to flourish in poorly maintained ventilation systems, severe health problems can result that can be experienced by individuals throughout an entire building. Pneumonitis is categorized as acute, subacute, or chronic according to the duration of illness.

A World Health Organization report suggests that as many as 30% of new and remodeled buildings worldwide may generate excessive complaints related to the indoor air quality. In a nationwide random sampling of office workers, 24% perceived air quality problems in their work environments, and 20% believed their work performance was hampered accordingly.

Diagnosis

History: Symptoms of acute pneumonitis disease include chills, cough, fever, difficulty breathing, loss of appetite, nausea, and vomiting. The symptoms may develop 4 to 6 hours following heavy exposure to an inciting agent. In the subacute form, individual reports gradual development of productive cough, difficulty in breathing (dyspnea), fatigue, anorexia, and weight loss. These symptoms may occur in individuals with repeated acute attacks. In chronic disease, the individual often lacks a history of acute episodes. The long-term form of the disease is known by fatigue, cough, weight loss, and difficult breathing during exercise.

Physical exam: The exam varies according to clinical presentation. Fever, rapid breathing (tachypnea), and rales may be noted in both acute and subacute disease. Muscle wasting, weight loss, and tachypnea may be seen in chronic disease. A thickening and widening of the ends of fingers and toes (clubbing) may be noted as well.

Tests: Blood tests such as a complete blood count (CBC) and testing against potential antigens may be performed. Presence of antigens may not indicate disease. Chest x-rays can be taken. High-resolution computerized tomography (HCRT) is of limited value. Pulmonary function tests should be done. An inhalation challenge where the individual develops the typical symptoms indicates presence of the disease. A sample of lung tissue (biopsy) helps confirm the disease.

Treatment

Emphasis on environmental control is the cornerstone of treatment. Measures to minimize antigen exposure usually result in regression of disease but treatment with corticosteroids is required in severe cases. Once the environmental source of inhaled antigen is identified, avoidance is the main treatment. The acute form of disease remits without specific therapy. Corticosteroids may be used to speed recovery in individuals with severe symptoms or significant lung dysfunction.

Prognosis

Recovery is usually complete once the offending agent is identified and removed. In the case of individuals who have contracted the disease from the workplace, permanent resolution of the pneumonitis may not occur without a change of location or change in occupation.

Differential Diagnosis

Pulmonary fibrosis, inhalation fever, organic dust toxic syndrome, and chronic bronchitis may present with similar symptoms.

Specialists

- Internist
- Pulmonologist

Work Restrictions / Accommodations

When complete elimination of allergen exposure is not possible, protective devices may be utilized. An individual with progression of disease in the face of ongoing exposure should be strongly advised to avoid the antigen. This may require drastic measures such as relocation to a new job or home.

Preventive maintenance should be performed routinely in all heating, ventilation, and air conditioning equipment. Water damaged furnishings and carpeting should be removed.

When avoidance of causative antigens cannot be easily achieved, protective devices such as personal respirators may be utilized. Dust respirators do not provide protection and helmet-type air purifying respirators are effective but cumbersome to wear.

Comorbid Conditions

Coexisting lung diseases such as emphysema, asthma, and chronic bronchiolitis seen in smokers may worsen the effects of ventilation pneumonitis and lengthen disability.

Complications

Severe ventilation pneumonitis may result in chronic bronchitis and permanent lung damage. Asthma-like allergies could also develop.

Factors Influencing Duration

Factors include type of and response to treatment and individual's occupation and availability of another job without the presence of the inhaled agent. Age, general state of health, physical condition, and nutritional status may influence the individual's ability to undergo treatment and recovery.

Length of Disability

Duration in Days

Job Classification	Minimum	Optimum	Maximum
Any work	1	3	7

Failure to Recover

If an individual fails to recover within the maximum duration expectancy period, the reader may wish to reference the following questions to assist in better understanding the specifics of an individual's medical case.

Regarding diagnosis:

- Does individual work in a building that relies on forced air ventilation systems and humidifiers? Are they inadequately maintained?
- Does individual have chills, cough, fever, difficulty breathing, loss of appetite, nausea, and vomiting? Did a productive cough gradually develop? Does individual have anorexia and weight loss?
- Does physical exam indicate fever, tachypnea, rales, muscle wasting, weight loss, or clubbing of the fingers and toes?
- Was a complete blood count (CBC) done? Testing against potential antigens? Chest x-ray? Pulmonary function testing? Lung biopsy?
- Has individual had an inhalation challenge?
- Were conditions with similar symptoms such as pulmonary fibrosis, inhalation fever, organic dust toxic syndrome, and chronic bronchitis ruled out?

Regarding treatment:

- Were measures to avoid contact with antigen initiated?
- Were environmental controls initiated?
- Was treatment with corticosteroids necessary?

Regarding prognosis:

- Can individual's employer accommodate any necessary restrictions?
- Does individual have any conditions that may affect ability to recover?
- Have any complications developed such as chronic bronchitis and permanent lung damage? Does individual have asthma-like allergies?

References

Tierney, Lawrence, Stephen McPhee, and Maxine Papadakis. Current Medical Diagnosis & Treatment. New York: McGraw-Hill, 2000.

The Merck Manual of Diagnosis and Therapy. Beers, Mark H., and Robert Berkow, eds. Whitehouse Station, NJ: Merck and Co, Inc., 2000.

Ventricular Fibrillation

Other names / synonyms: Cardiac Arrest, Ventricular Arrhythmia

427.4, 427.41

Definition

Ventricular fibrillation (VF) is serious disruption in the normal rhythm of the heart (arrhythmia). It results from disorganized electrical activity in the lower chambers (ventricles) of the heart, causing the heart to quiver rather than beat. Death can occur in a matter of minutes without cardiopulmonary resuscitation (CPR) or emergency defibrillation and oxygen.

VF is the cause of most cases of sudden cardiac death and often occurs in conjunction with a heart attack (myocardial infarction). Other heart disorders associated with ventricular fibrillation are cardiomyopathy, congestive heart failure, and chronic ventricular arrhythmias. Severe potassium depletion (hypokalemia) and side effects of drugs used to regulate heart rhythm (antiarrhythmics) as well as electrocution, near-drowning, and extreme body temperature decrease (hypothermia) are other causes of VF.

In the US, cause of death was listed as VF in more than 1,500 individuals during the year 1997; however, approximately 225,000 individuals died from sudden cardiac death this same year as a result of VF. The average age of individuals with VF outside of the hospital is 65 years with 70% being men. Sudden cardiac death affects black men 3 times more than white women and 4 times more than white men.

Diagnosis

History: Individuals experiencing an acute myocardial infarction (AMI) may complain of chest pain (angina) and shortness of breath (dyspnea) before VF occurs. Those experiencing VF will lose consciousness and witnesses may see the individual grab his or her chest or left arm before falling to the floor.

Physical exam: The individual is unresponsive without palpable pulse or measurable blood pressure. Bluish discoloration of the skin, lips, and nails (cyanosis) is usually present. The skin may be cold to the touch.

Tests: No tests are warranted or helpful. If the victim happens to be hooked up to an electrocardiogram (ECG), it will show a grossly disorganized pattern devoid of identifiable heartbeats.

Treatment

Basic life support with standard cardiopulmonary resuscitation (CPR) is instituted immediately. As soon as an electrical defibrillator becomes available, the individual is shocked with 200 or more joules. If 3 such shocks are not effective, 1 mg of epinephrine is administered intravenously (IV) and defibrillation is attempted again. Additional drugs may be given and attempts at defibrillation made according to the advanced cardiac life support (ACLS) protocol promulgated by the American Heart Association.

In the emergency room, a tube is inserted into the mouth down to the lungs so oxygen can be administered. Emergency defibrillation (direct current cardioversion, or DC cardioversion) is given. If the individual does not respond well to the first shock, closed-chest cardiac massage and resuscitation (mouth-to-mouth or a manual resuscitator) are performed before administering another shock. If the individual recovers, he or she is monitored and started on antiarrhythmic drugs.

Individuals who do not respond well to drug therapy may need an implantable cardiac defibrillator (ICD). This device is comprised of a power source planted under the skin of the chest or abdomen and patches that are connected to the heart. Newer defibrillators may now be installed via blood vessels. These devices are programmed to recognize and correct a specific arrhythmia by administering an electrical charge. A permanent pacemaker may be implanted in those individuals whose VF was related to a slow heart rhythm.

Prognosis

About 50% of individuals found to be in VF outside the hospital can be resuscitated, but only 25% survive to be discharged from the hospital, often with significant neurologic impairment. Important factors associated with survival to discharge after out-of-hospital are age (60 or older), cardiogenic shock, requirement of 4 or more shocks, absence of an AMI, and unconsciousness upon admission to the hospital. Survival to discharge of individuals who sustain VF while hospitalized following an AMI is better (75-80%).

Cardioversion rates in the absence of heart attack approaches 95%, and these individuals have an excellent prognosis. For individuals with underlying ventricular damage and a heart attack, successful cardioversion rates decrease to 30%, and the mortality rate for these individuals after resuscitation is 70%.

Differential Diagnosis

Other conditions with similar presentation are AMI, congestive heart failure, respiratory arrest, or other cardiac arrhythmias.

Rehabilitation

Individuals who have exhibited ventricular fibrillation may require cardiac rehabilitation both on an inpatient and outpatient basis. Once an individual is deemed medically stable, an EKG-monitored exercise program at a cardiac rehabilitation facility will begin. In addition to exercise under the supervision of a physical and/or occupational therapist, lifestyle changes are addressed as needed such as decreasing fatty foods in the diet, losing weight, or controlling blood pressure. The amount of time for monitored exercise gradually decreases until the individual is able to continue the exercise regimen independently.

EKG-monitored exercise is required for 30-60 minutes, 3-4 times per week, and may last for several weeks until the individual is stable. Individuals learn to self-monitor their pulse and to rate the amount of energy they expend by utilizing a rating of perceived exertion scale. This is a numbered scale that rates exercises from very, very light to very, very hard. Individuals use this scale and their pulse to stay within safe exercise parameters that have been predetermined by their physicians. Individuals attend physical therapy to learn basic conditioning and stretching exercises. Individuals also perform aerobic exercise such as treadmill walking or stationary bicycling. Initial activities may include limited walking, range-of-motion, and treadmill exercises. Eventually, more frequent walks, walk-jog, biking, and arm ergometer exercises may be encouraged. Exercise may become more strenuous as permitted by the physician with a goal of attaining 75-85% maximum intensity while walking, jogging, biking, swimming, performing calisthenics, and/or weight training.

Specialists

- Cardiologist
- Cardiovascular Surgeon

Work Restrictions / Accommodations

Survivors of out-of-hospital VF will frequently have cardiac or neurologic conditions that limit their physical and/or cognitive abilities. Survivors of in-hospital VF following an AMI are likely to have fewer restrictions that are dictated more by the size of the heart attack than presence or absence of VF.

Comorbid Conditions

Coronary artery disease, heart disease, and obesity may lengthen disability.

Complications

The primary complication of VF is death; however, complications among survivors of CPR include fractured ribs, skin burns, bone marrow emboli, pneumothorax, trauma to the heart, and impaired cognitive function.

Factors Influencing Duration

Age, the underlying cause of the VF, and the presence or absence of neurologic deficits influence the length of disability and may cause permanent disability.

Length of Disability

The duration of disability is related to the underlying cause of the VF and the subsequent extent of cardiac damage and neurologic impairment. Disability may be permanent.

Duration in Days

Job Classification	Minimum	Optimum	Maximum
Sedentary work	16	42	Indefinite
Light work	21	42	Indefinite
Medium work	28	56	Indefinite
Heavy work	42	70	Indefinite
Very Heavy work	42	84	Indefinite

Failure to Recover

If an individual fails to recover within the maximum duration expectancy period, the reader may wish to reference the following questions to assist in better understanding the specifics of an individual's medical case.

Regarding diagnosis:

- Does individual have symptoms such as palpitations, dizziness, or chest pain?
- Does individual have a history of heart disease, a recent heart attack, or heart surgery?
- Was there a history of electrocution, near drowning, or hypothermia?
- Does individual take antiarrhythmic drugs?
- Did individual lose consciousness?
- Did witnesses see individual grab his or her chest or left arm before falling to the floor?
- Did the physical exam reveal absence of pulse and blood pressure and loss of consciousness?
- Does individual have a history of implantable cardiac defibrillator?
- Was the diagnosis confirmed with an ECG?
- Did individual receive prompt access to emergency care?

Regarding treatment:

- Was electrical defibrillation and life support (CPR) received promptly?
- Was defibrillation successful in terminating VF?
- Were appropriate diagnostic tests (12-lead ECG, cardiac isoenzymes, etc.) done to determine an underlying cause for the VF?
- Did appropriate specialist (cardiologist, intensivist) evaluate the individual?
- Was care appropriate for the underlying condition?

Regarding prognosis:

- Based on the response to treatment, the underlying condition, and the general health of individual, what was the expected outcome?
- Did individual suffer any associated neurological impairment that could impact recovery and prognosis?
- Did individual suffer any other complications such as rib fractures or pneumothorax that could impact recovery?

References

The Merck Manual of Diagnosis and Therapy. Beers, Mark, and Robert Berkow, eds. Medical Services, USMEDSA, USHH, 1999 1 Jan 2001 <http://www.merck.com/pubs/mmanual/section16/chapter205/205i.htm>.

Watchie, Joanne. Cardiopulmonary Physical Therapy. Philadelphia: W.B. Saunders Company, 1995.

Ventricular Premature Contractions

Other names / synonyms: Premature Ventricular Contraction, PVC

427.69

Definition

Premature ventricular contraction (PVC) is an abnormal heart rhythm (arrhythmia) due to enhanced activity of "pacemaker" cells in a chamber of the heart called the ventricle. There are a number of different types of PVCs, which are classified according to the specific arrhythmia pattern, including their frequency and form. PVCs can also trigger incapacitating or life threatening dysrhythmias.

Premature ventricular beats may occur randomly in healthy individuals without causing noticeable symptoms. They may be associated with stress, fatigue, excess caffeine, alcohol or nicotine consumption, lack of oxygen to tissues or organs (ischemia), low oxygen levels (hypoxia), or electrolyte imbalance (in particular, low potassium - hypokalemia). Both prescription and illicit drugs may be associated with PVCs. The arrhythmia may also be a symptom of a heart attack or other cardiac disease.

PVCs are one of the most common arrhythmias. The prevalence of PVCs increases with age in parallel with increasing prevalence of cardiovascular disease. PVCs without organic heart disease do not, however, seem to increase the risk of sudden incapacitation or mortality. PVCs occur in about 60% of healthy middle-aged males, and in about 80% of individuals who have had one or more heart attacks. It is believed to occur more often in men than in women.

Diagnosis

History: Many individuals have no symptoms and are not aware of the irregular beat. If symptoms do occur, they may include the sensations that the heart has stopped for a second then restarted with a thump, or skipped beats (irregular heartbeats), or given occasional strong, pounding heartbeats (palpitations). Individuals with associated cardiac disease may complain of anxiety, shortness of breath, fatigue, dizziness, or chest discomfort.

Physical exam: Physical findings may include pauses in the pulse that last twice the regular pulse interval (full compensatory pause), or a premature heart sound (either single or double).

Tests: An electrocardiogram (ECG) is necessary to characterize and document the arrhythmia. A blood test to check serum electrolytes is important for determining whether an electrolyte imbalance is causing the arrhythmia. If the individual is taking medication known to cause arrhythmia, blood (serum) drug levels should be obtained. Tests might also be performed if illicit drug use is suspected.

Treatment

Persistent premature ventricular contractions (PVCs) in individuals with heart disease indicate increased risk of sudden arrhythmic death. Various therapeutic options are available including drugs (beta-blockers, antiarrhythmic drugs, calcium channel blockers) or surgically implanted automatic defibrillators. In those without heart disease, however, PVCs may not require any treatment other than correcting an electrolyte imbalance, or avoiding the substance or behavior that precipitated it.

Prognosis

Individuals with structural heart disease have a slightly increased chance of sudden death. Premature ventricular contractions (PVCs) associated with heart attack (myocardial infarction - MI) have a higher mortality rate. Many individuals without cardiac problems recover without treatment, and others do well if the precipitating cause of the arrhythmia, such as electrolyte imbalance, is addressed. Individuals with no underlying heart disease have an outlook similar to that of the general population.

Differential Diagnosis

Conditions with similar symptoms include other arrhythmias such as aberrantly conducted atrial premature complexes or pre-excitation syndromes, ventricular tachycardia and ventricular fibrillation, angina, myocardial infarction, and myocarditis.

Specialists

- Cardiologist
- Critical Care Specialist
- Emergency Medicine

Rehabilitation

Rehabilitation of ventricular premature contractions depends on the cause and extent of the condition. Rehabilitation professionals working with an individual with ventricular premature cardiac heartbeats understand the symptoms by themselves may not be harmful, but are aware that they can be a precursor to 2 more serious types of ventricular contraction irregularities. Physical therapists experienced with cardiac rehabilitation and responsible for producing an exercise program know symptoms can be perceived as skipped beats or fluttering or thumping in the chest known as heart palpitations, and they may cause dizziness or weakness.

In addition to providing a cardiac rehab program to help prevent a condition causing the premature contractions, the physical therapist plays an important role in the counseling factors that can prompt a ventricular arrhythmia. These include stress, exercise, caffeine, tobacco, alcohol, as well as several medications used to treat various heart conditions.

Many types of heart disease are also associated with ventricular contraction disorders (arrhythmias). In the extreme case of a heart attack, blood flow to specific parts of the heart muscle is completely blocked, and that heart tissue dies. If this is the case, the individual experiencing a ventricular premature contraction of this nature participates in an exercise program following 4 progressive phases.

Phase one often begins in the hospital and provides low levels of exercise to prevent complications of bedrest. The individual progresses with exercises to sitting and eventually to standing. Progressive walking (ambulating) and eventually stair climbing are an important part of individual's inpatient exercise program. Intensity is gradually increased until discharge from the hospital.

Phase two goals are to improve functional capacity by increasing physical endurance and to promote return to activity. This is done in an outpatient setting such as a rehabilitation center. Individuals are typically also attached to an electrocardiograph (EKG) monitor to observe any premature contractions during the exercise session. A physical therapist keeps a daily log of the individual's blood pressure, heart rate, and cardiac rhythm.

Phase three continues in an outpatient setting such as a rehab center. Depending on the individual's condition, this phase may last for several months. Individuals may stay involved with an outpatient program for up to a year to accomplish all of the their goals while still at modified work duty. Eventually higher levels of exercise comprise this phase with the addition of recreational activities such as swimming and outdoor hiking. Modifications are made for individuals experiencing ventricular premature contractions after suffering various levels of a heart attack.

Work Restrictions / Accommodations

Work restrictions and accommodations may not be required unless significant underlying heart conditions exist. If this is the case, a less strenuous and/or low-stress assignment may be necessary.

Comorbid Conditions

Presence of psychiatric conditions, substance abuse, stress, or overuse of stimulants (caffeine) may lengthen disability.

Complications

Premature ventricular contractions (PVCs) can progress to ventricular fibrillation. Sudden death occurs more frequently when structural heart disease is present or when PVCs persist after a heart attack.

Factors Influencing Duration

Length of disability may be influenced by severity of symptoms, presence of underlying heart disease, whether the job is strenuous and/or high-stress, compliance with rehabilitation instructions, and response to treatment.

Length of Disability

Disability is not usually associated with this condition.

Failure to Recover

Regarding diagnosis:

- Has diagnosis of ventricular premature contraction been confirmed?
- Has the individual's regular medication regime been evaluated for its potential to cause arrhythmia?
- Is the individual being treated for any underlying cardiac disease?

Regarding treatment:

- Is the individual motivated to effect appropriate lifestyle changes?
- If drug therapy has been unsuccessful, is individual now a candidate for a defibrillator implant?

Regarding prognosis:

- Is the individual motivated to effect appropriate lifestyle changes?
- Has individual recently suffered a myocardial infarction?
- Is individual on drug therapy?
- Has a defibrillator implant been successful?
- Is surgical intervention, such as angioplasty or coronary artery bypass surgery, an option?

References

Kisner, C., and L. Colby. Therapeutic Exercise Foundations and Techniques. Philadelphia: F.A. Davis Company, 1990.

The Merck Manual of Diagnosis and Therapy. Beers, Mark H., and Robert Berkow, eds. Whitehouse Station, NJ: Merck and Co, Inc., 1999.

Ventricular Tachycardia

Other names / synonyms: Torsade De Pointes, V Tach, VT

427.1

Definition

Ventricular tachycardia is an abnormal heart rhythm (arrhythmia) in which the heartbeat is initiated in the lower heart chambers (ventricles) rather than from the sinoatrial node in the right upper heart chamber (right atrium). As a result, the heart beats at an abnormally fast rate of 140 to 220 beats per minute.

Ventricular tachycardia may last as long as several days (sustained) or as little as 30 seconds or less (nonsustained).

Ventricular tachycardia occurs most often in individuals with pre-existing heart disease, such as diseases of the heart valves (e.g., mitral valve prolapse), congenital heart disease, insufficient oxygen to the heart muscle (ischemic heart disease), or disease of the heart muscle (cardiomyopathy). Nonsustained ventricular tachycardia may occur in individuals with no underlying cardiac disease. Ventricular tachycardia can also occur after a heart attack (acute myocardial infarction), or as a result of drug toxicity. A form of ventricular tachycardia associated with drug toxicity (Torsade de Pointes) has an abrupt onset and a poor prognosis. Other risk factors for ventricular tachycardia include rheumatic heart disease, anorexia nervosa, and any affliction that affects the body's metabolism (e.g., diabetes, thyroid abnormalities).

The incidence of ventricular tachycardia is difficult to determine because of the lack of symptoms when it is nonsustained. Sustained ventricular tachycardia occurs in about 3% of individuals who have experienced a myocardial infarction. It is much less common in individuals with coronary artery disease who have not sustained an acute myocardial infarction, and it is uncommonly associated with other forms of cardiac disease with the exception of a certain form of arrhythmia (arrhythmic right ventricular dysplasia). It is estimated that ventricular tachycardia accounts for about half of the sudden deaths (approximately 300,000 per year in the US) that are attributed to cardiac diseases.

Diagnosis

History: The individual may report no symptoms at all (asymptomatic). However, most individuals complain of light-headedness, weakness, chest discomfort, shortness of breath (dyspnea), sensation of the heart beating rapidly or intensely (palpitations), abrupt loss of consciousness (syncope), and/or seizures.

Physical exam: The exam may reveal a pulse that is weak, rapid, or cannot be felt (nonpalpable). There may be inconsistencies in the blood pressure or abnormal (muffled) heart sounds. The individual may appear anxious, agitated, or may lose consciousness.

Tests: Diagnosis is confirmed by recording the electrical activity of the heart (electrocardiogram, or ECG). This record of the electrical activity will show broad and abnormal waves (QT interval prolongation).

Treatment

Individuals who have nonsustained ventricular tachycardia but have no structural damage to the heart muscle or other symptoms may not require drug treatment. Underlying metabolic abnormalities or other cardiac disorders that may be causing the condition should be treated, however. Toxic drug intake should be discontinued if it is causing ventricular tachycardia.

Sustained ventricular tachycardia is a medical emergency that requires immediate intervention to preserve life. Sustained ventricular tachycardia is treated initially with antiarrhythmic drugs. Administration of an electric shock to the heart (electric cardioversion) may be required if a normal heartbeat (rhythm) is not restored quickly with drugs. Striking the individual's chest (thump conversion) may also be used if onset is observed. After normal heart rhythm is restored, the antiarrhythmic drug is usually continued for several months. Treatment of individuals with chronic, recurrent ventricular tachycardia is controversial. A device that shocks the heart into its normal rhythm may be implanted surgically (implantable cardiac defibrillator). Administration of antiarrhythmic drugs may be continued to prevent recurrences.

Definitive but risky surgical treatments have all but ceased due to the availability of implantable defibrillators.

Prognosis

The predicted outcome for individuals who experience nonsustained ventricular tachycardia depends upon the underlying cause for the condition. The outcome is good for individuals who experience ventricular tachycardia as a one-time experience. Complete recovery without lasting adverse reactions may be expected if there is no serious underlying heart disease.

Torsade de Pointes may develop into a sustained condition in which case it can cause fainting (syncope) or sudden death. Torsade de Pointes will lead to cardiac arrest in 50% of cases.

Individuals with sustained ventricular tachycardia who are treated with antiarrhythmic drugs may expect to be free of recurrence of the condition at 6 years in 45-75% of cases. However, sustained ventricular tachycardia can deteriorate into loss of contractile ability by the heart (ventricular fibrillation). This is a medical emergency in which death is a possibility. There is approximately a 30% overall reduction in mortality in individuals with sustained ventricular tachycardia who have an implanted cardiac defibrillator. However, individuals who have a cardiac defibrillator implanted surgically will experience sudden-death mortality in 1-2% of cases on a yearly basis.

Differential Diagnosis

Conditions that present with symptoms similar to ventricular tachycardia include atrial fibrillation and supraventricular tachycardia. The electrocardiogram will probably need expert interpretation in order to differentiate these conditions from ventricular tachycardia.

Specialists

- Cardiologist
- Critical Care Specialist

Work Restrictions / Accommodations

Extended work leave for treatment may be required. Individuals who continue to experience sudden fainting spells (syncope) or dizziness may need limitations on access to unrestricted heights, dangerous machinery, or hazardous work.

Comorbid Conditions

Any condition that may contribute to the severity of the underlying heart condition might impact the individual's ability to recover and further lengthen their disability. Conditions may include diabetes, abnormal functioning of the thyroid gland (thyrotoxicosis), obesity, high blood pressure (hypertension), and high fat or cholesterol in the blood stream (hyperlipidemia or hypercholesterolemia, respectively).

Complications

Possible complications of ventricular tachycardia include progression to a complete lack of organized ventricular contractions (ventricular fibrillation), low blood pressure (hypotension), general organ and cardiovascular system failure (shock), an abnormal condition of the heart characterized by circulatory congestion (congestive heart failure), and death.

Factors Influencing Duration

The length of disability from ventricular tachycardia may be influenced by the underlying cause for the condition, the severity of symptoms, and the type of ventricular tachycardia (i.e., sustained vs. nonsustained), the individual's response to treatment, and the requirements of the job.

Length of Disability

The duration of disability may depend upon the treatment utilized. Individuals who are treated using surgical implantation of a cardiac defibrillator will require longer recovery than those who receive only drug treatment. Individuals who have an implanted cardiac defibrillator may be permanently unable to perform dangerous or heavy physical labor. Permanent disability is possible in severe cases.

Duration in Days

Job Classification	Minimum	Optimum	Maximum
Sedentary work	14	42	Indefinite
Light work	14	42	Indefinite
Medium work	21	56	Indefinite
Heavy work	28	56	Indefinite
Very Heavy work	42	56	Indefinite

Failure to Recover

If an individual fails to recover within the maximum duration expectancy period, the reader may wish to reference the following questions to assist in better understanding the specifics of an individual's medical case.

Regarding diagnosis:

- Does individual complain of light-headedness, weakness, chest discomfort, shortness of breath (dyspnea), sensation of the heart beating rapidly or intensely (palpitations), abrupt loss of consciousness (syncope), and/or seizures?
- Does individual have a history of heart disease or a recent heart attack?
- Are there other underlying conditions that would contribute to ventricular tachycardia?
- Does the physician note a pulse that is weak, rapid, or cannot be felt (nonpalpable)?
- Are there inconsistencies in the blood pressure or abnormal (muffled) heart sounds?
- Does individual appear anxious or agitated?
- Was a recording of the electrical activity of the heart (electrocardiogram, or ECG) obtained?
- Has the diagnosis been confirmed?

Regarding treatment:

- Has the incidence of ventricular tachycardia become more frequent?
- Does individual require drug treatment?
- Have underlying medical conditions been treated?
- Are the appropriate antiarrhythmic drugs being prescribed?
- Is individual taking these exactly as prescribed?
- Would implantation of a cardiac defibrillator be of benefit?

Regarding prognosis:

- Did individual experience nonsustained ventricular tachycardia?
- Did individual recover completely with or without treatment?
- Has individual developed Torsade de Pointes? What can be done for this condition?
- Are antiarrhythmic drugs treating the tachycardia successfully?
- Is individual compliant with the medication regimen?
- Has the condition recurred?
- Does individual have a defibrillator implanted? If so, is it functioning properly?
- Has individual developed any complications? If so, what are they?
- Is individual expected to survive these complications?

References

LeMone, P., and K.M. Burke. Medical-Surgical Nursing. Upper Saddle River, NJ: Prentice Hall Health, 2000.

Tchou, P.J. "Ventricular Tachycardia." Textbook of Cardiovascular Medicine. Topol, E.J., ed. Philadelphia: Lippincott-Raven Publishers, 1998. 1757-1777.

Vertigo

Other names / synonyms: Objective Vertigo, Pathological Vertigo, Physiological Vertigo, Subjective Vertigo, Vertiginous Syndrome

386.1, 386.10, 386.19, 386.2

Definition

Though sometimes inaccurately called "dizziness," vertigo is a unique symptom related to specific diseases of the nervous system (pathologic vertigo) or a mismatch in the body's normal systems of balance and position (physiologic or positional vertigo). Vertigo creates a rotating sensation, which gives individuals the false impression that their surroundings are spinning or moving. Some examples of physiologic vertigo are seasickness, carsickness, and height vertigo.

A sudden (acute) attack of vertigo is usually due to inflammation of the semicircular canals of the inner ear (nonspecific labyrinthitis), possibly of viral origin. Generally, the attack is self-limited. Ongoing (chronic) vertigo occurs almost daily and usually indicates presence of a serious disease.

The principal causes of vertigo are Ménière's disease, adverse reactions to drugs (gentamicin, anticonvulsant intoxication, certain antibiotics, etc.), toxins (notably alcohol intoxication), vestibular neuronitis, multiple sclerosis, vestibular migraine, abnormal connection between the inner and middle ear spaces (perilymphatic fistula), and imbalance created by certain head positions or movement (benign positional vertigo). Head trauma, upper respiratory infection, and hypothyroidism may be associated with the disease. Since balance is partially maintained by receptors in the neck that sense position in space, trauma to the neck can also cause vertigo. Autoimmune disorders such as rheumatoid arthritis, dry eye syndrome (Sjögren's syndrome), ulcerative colitis, Wegener's granulomatosis, scleroderma, allergies, systemic lupus erythematosus, and Cogan's syndrome also may cause symptoms that include vertigo. Autoimmune damage can also be confined to the labyrinth, causing vertigo and hearing loss as isolated symptoms. Steroids and other hormones affect the peripheral vestibular system involved in balance, which may be one mechanism contributing to the symptom of vertigo.

Symptoms involving loss of balance or equilibrium are commonly associated with many disorders. Therefore, incidence of vertigo is not generally known. However, an estimated 25% of individuals who seek medical help for related symptoms are thought to have benign positional vertigo, the most common form. This form of vertigo is estimated to have occurred in about 64 of every 100,000 US citizens. One Japanese study estimated that about 11 of every 100,000 citizens in that country have experienced benign positional vertigo. Vertigo is thought to affect twice as many women than men. The first onset of vertigo typically occurs in individuals who are in their 50s. About 7% of individuals seen in a dizziness clinic have vestibular migraine as a cause of their vertigo.

Diagnosis

History: The individual's primary complaint usually is a sudden sensation that surroundings are spinning or moving (vertigo). Headache, nausea and vomiting, and blurred vision due to jerking eye movements (nystagmus) are common if inflammation of the semicircular canals of the inner ear (labyrinthitis) is the cause. The individual may report problems after use of prescription or other types of drugs. Vertigo may also occur within 24 hours after alcohol intake. Sudden onset may occur while the individual is lying on one side or looking up, with symptoms sometimes resolving in less than a minute. Movement may cause vertigo.

The individual may complain of vertigo after flying or after a prolonged drive in the mountains. Individuals with vertigo caused by sudden rupture of a part of the inner ear (round window of the cochlea) may report symptoms following intense physical exertion such as calisthenics or scuba diving. Other general complaints may include hearing loss, ringing in the ears (tinnitus), falling, or temporary (transient) blindness.

Physical exam: An active or resolving upper respiratory infection may be evident. Exam may reveal the presence of jerky eye movements (nystagmus). Observations of the individual engaged in heel-to-toe walking and touching the nose while the eyes are closed could reveal an unsteady gait, difficulty maintaining equilibrium and poor sense of orientation in space. Special positioning maneuvers designed to bring on symptoms (Dux-Hallpike test and Nylan-Barany maneuvers) may be helpful.

Tests: For definitive diagnosis of the underlying cause of vertigo, tests include audiometry, equilibriometry, brain CT scan, and specific testing of the balancing function of the inner ear (caloric stimulation and electronystagmography). A rare diagnosis of perilymphatic fistula is confirmed with exploratory perforation of the eardrum (tympanotomy). A vascular analysis (angiography) may be needed to determine possible blood flow abnormalities. Neck X-ray or MRI may be indicated to evaluate for musculoskeletal trauma as a cause for vertigo (cervicogenic vertigo). Three-dimensional analysis of eye movement helps determine the type of nystagmus, which in turn may localize the neurological abnormality causing the vertigo.

Treatment

Treatment may involve finding and eliminating the cause of vertigo. For example, cerebellopontine angle tumors may be surgically removed, autoimmune disorders may be treated, and multiple sclerosis may be treated with appropriate medications. If no neurologic or metabolic defect can be identified, bedrest for two to three days is effective as the principal treatment in most cases. In addition, anti-vertiginous and/or anti-nausea drugs may be prescribed. Pain relievers or medications aimed at reducing migraine symptoms may be needed for individuals with headaches.

Positional vertigo is an inconvenience but rarely a serious problem unless the individual's occupation depends on good balance or certain physical maneuvers. In this case, even short episodes of vertigo may be disruptive since the most common treatment is to avoid positions or activities that cause the symptoms.

Individuals with Ménière's disease may be treated with diuretics to reduce fluid in the ears. Decompression chamber therapy also may help restore correct pressure balances in the inner ear. In some conditions, short-term use of steroids may relieve inflammation of nerves in the inner ear. Specific exercises may be recommended for certain types of positional vertigo.

Various surgical options may be considered in extreme, unresolved cases of vertigo including relief of pressure in the inner ear (endolymphatic sac surgery, cochleosacculotomy, and microvascular decompression), removal of certain sensory tissue and nerve fibers (labyrinthectomy), sectioning selected nerves (middle cranial fossa, retrolabyrinthine, retrosigmoid, translabyrinthine), pulling away (avulsion) a selected nerve (singular neurectomy), and sealing the inner ear semicircular canal (posterior semicircular canal occlusion). Other surgical methods of treating vertigo are being investigated, including the creation of openings and antibiotic treatment in the inner ear semicircular canal (Streptomycin perfusion). This technique has shown some early results that appear promising.

Prognosis

Sudden onset (acute) vertigo is usually self-limited, and resolves after several days of bedrest. The prognosis for other types of vertigo varies greatly depending on the underlying cause. In many cases of ongoing (chronic) vertigo, changes in lifestyle may become necessary such as avoiding positions of the head or other body that aggravate or induce symptoms. Chronic diseases, such as autoimmune disorders or multiple sclerosis, that fail to resolve may cause continuing episodes of vertigo for an indefinite time. Success rates for various surgical procedures aimed at resolving or relieving symptoms of more serious forms of vertigo range from 60-90%. There is a slight possibility of permanent hearing loss accompanying these surgical procedures.

Differential Diagnosis

Other possibilities include acute cerebellar lesions, cerebellopontine angle lesions, hyperventilation, Parkinsonism, vitamin B_{12} deficiency, stroke, cervical spondylosis, panic disorder, partial seizures, brain stem ischemia or infarction, perilymphatic fistula, vertebral basilar artery insufficiency, irritation or destruction of nerve pathways, tumor, or multiple sclerosis. Vertigo may be present in association with many other conditions such as Ménière's disease and autoimmune disorders including rheumatoid arthritis. As vertigo is a symptom and not a disease, workup must include a thorough search for the underlying disorder.

Specialists

- Neurologist
- Otolaryngologist

Rehabilitation

Individuals experiencing vertigo are seen by a physical therapist trained in the specialty of vestibular rehabilitation. Once it is determined if the dizziness and balance problem is coming from an inner ear dysfunction or from other areas such as the brain's center for balance, the therapist can establish a plan of care to treat the individual appropriately. Much of the therapy focuses around balance exercises that challenge the individual without stimulating a significant amount of dizziness.

An example of an exercise involves walking straight ahead while rotating the head side to side and focusing visually on an object. Techniques used like this increase the normal amount of sensory and visual input needed for balance compared to simply walking in a straight-forward manner. Modifications may need to be made by the physical therapist for those individuals who have undergone surgery for a condition causing vertigo or who have suffered from some form of head trauma affecting the body's balance.

The Canalith Repositioning Maneuver may be performed by the physical therapist, audiologist, or physician to clear the dislodged calcium crystals from the canal and deposit them back into the part of the inner ear (utricle) where they belong.

Work Restrictions / Accommodations

Work restrictions and accommodations require consideration on an individual basis. Positional vertigo could require adaptation of workstations to make sure the individual is not forced to move the head at certain angles. Tasks requiring good balance or physical maneuvering may need to be reassigned. If the individual experiences permanent hearing loss, other accommodations such as hearing enhancements or amplification may be needed.

Complementary and Alternative Therapies

Content is intended for awareness only. Treatments may or may not be effective. Scientific evidence may be lacking and some substances have potentially toxic effects. Dr. Presley Reed and the editors do not endorse the use of these therapies in the absence of consultation with a licensed medical professional.

Ginger -	May reduce dizziness and vomiting associated with seasickness or motion sickness.
Gingko -	May improve chronic vertigo
Calcium -	Said to be critical to inner ear functioning.
Celery seed -	Has been used in Chinese medicine to treat dizziness.
Magnesium -	Said to be critical to inner ear functioning.
Potassium -	Said to be critical to inner ear functioning.
Pumpkin -	Has been used by some herbalists to treat dizziness.
Scleranthus -	May help mild dizziness related to balance problems.
Acupressure -	Applying pressure to stomach meridian below kneecap may relieve dizziness.
Reflexology -	Working the ear, cervical spine and neck reflexes on the feet may relieve dizziness.

Comorbid Conditions

Some individuals may experience vertigo years after original onset of viral diseases such as mumps or measles that may have damaged the inner ear, creating more severe or prolonged symptoms. The individual may have abnormal anatomic vascular features that compress nerves in the inner ear, leading to continuing damage and/or hearing loss. Any chronic disease causing vertigo, such as multiple sclerosis, autoimmune disorder, stroke, tumor, post-traumatic syndrome, or Ménière's disease, has its own impairments additive to those associated with vertigo. Neurologic disorders affecting other parts of the nervous system involved in balance and spatial orientation, such as peripheral neuropathy or blindness, aggravate balance problems related to vertigo.

Complications

Complications primarily depend on any underlying disease. Some surgical treatments of vertigo must be performed carefully, or injury and loss of hearing may result. Local anesthetics associated with diagnosis and/or treatment also may cause disruption of the inner ear system, leading to possible damage or hearing loss. Autoimmune diseases such as rheumatoid arthritis may both cause and prolong symptoms of vertigo. Certain autoimmune inner ear diseases, such as Sjögren's syndrome and Cogan's disease, may lead to progressive damage to the inner ear and accompanying hearing loss. Depending on the source of vertigo, temporary (transient) blindness could result. Prolonged treatment using some anti-vertiginous medications could result in the individual's inability to adapt naturally to changes in the inner ear system, thus leading to long-term problems with balance. Poor balance associated with vertigo may lead to falls and self-injury.

Factors Influencing Duration

If the individual experiences complications such as hearing loss, ability to perform job tasks requiring keen hearing will be affected. Ability to perform tasks requiring balance and physical maneuvering may also be affected permanently if vertigo is ongoing.

Length of Disability

Duration depends on acute versus chronic form. A more specific diagnosis is required.

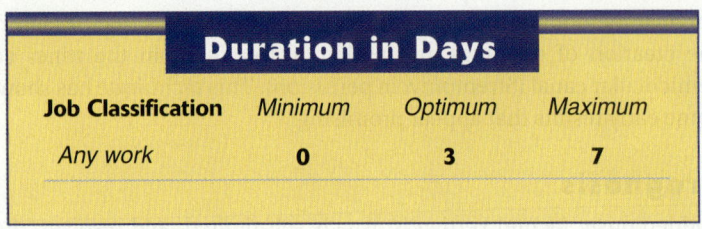

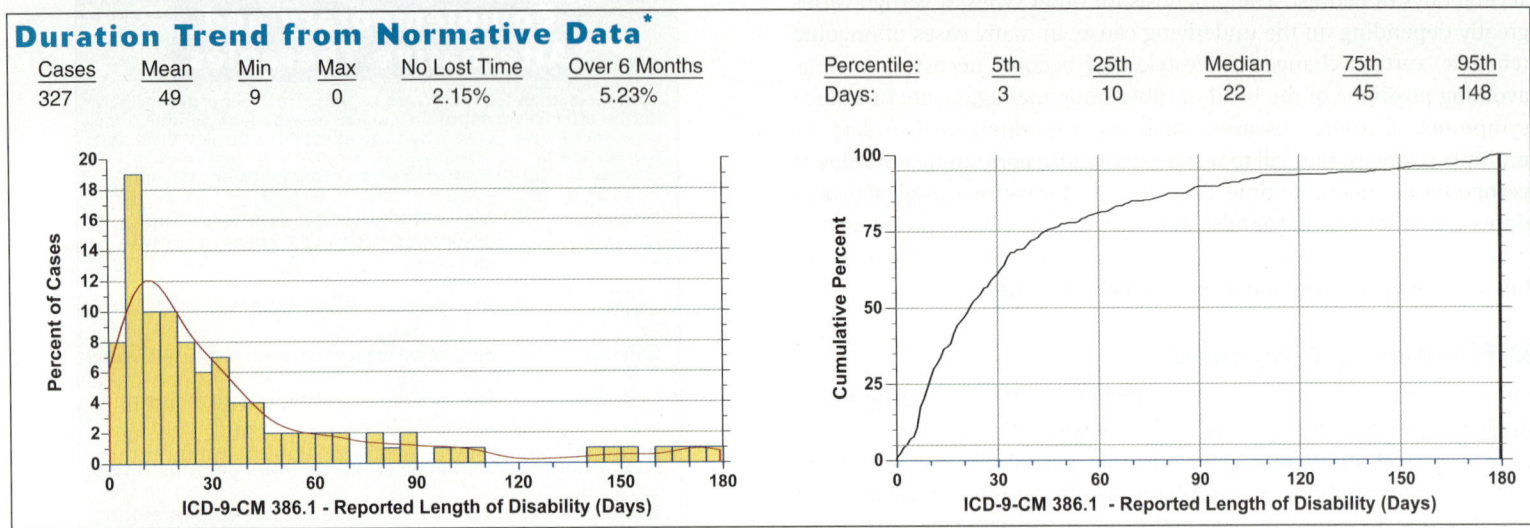

* Differences may exist between the expected duration tables and the normative graphs. Duration tables provide expected recovery periods based on the type of work performed by the individual. The normative graphs reflect the actual observed experience of many individuals across the spectrum of physical conditions, in a variety of industries, and with varying levels of case management.

Failure to Recover

If an individual fails to recover within the maximum duration expectancy period, the reader may wish to reference the following questions to assist in better understanding the specifics of an individual's medical case.

Regarding diagnosis:

- Does the individual have vertigo, a sensation of rotation as if the surroundings are spinning or moving, or nonspecific dizziness, which may have a cardiac, metabolic, or other cause?
- Did the vertigo come on suddenly, suggesting inflammation of the semicircular canals of the inner ear (nonspecific labyrinthitis), or is it chronic, which usually indicates presence of a serious disease?
- Has the underlying condition been identified and confirmed?
- Are additional tests needed, such as audiometry, brain CT, or angiography?

Regarding treatment:

- Has appropriate symptomatic treatment been given, including bedrest, anti-vertiginous and/or anti-nausea drugs, and pain medication for individuals with headaches?
- If vertigo symptoms have not resolved after medical treatment or rest, is the individual considered a candidate for surgical intervention?
- Has the individual received surgical treatments or local anesthetics, which can result in hearing loss?
- Has treatment with anti-vertiginous medications been prolonged, resulting in loss of adaptation to changes in the inner ear system, thus leading to long-term balance problems?
- Are the underlying cause of the vertigo and any complications being treated appropriately?
- If the diagnosis is Ménière's disease, have diuretics been given to reduce fluid in the ears?
- Should decompression chamber therapy be considered to help restore pressure balances in the inner ear?
- Should short-term use of steroids be considered to relieve inflammation of nerves in the inner ear?

- Would specific exercises be helpful for certain types of positional vertigo?

Regarding prognosis:

- Has the underlying cause been identified?
- Is it responding to treatment? Would the individual benefit from evaluation by a specialist (neurologist, neurosurgeon, otolaryngologist, ophthalmologist, internist)?
- To what extent does vertigo affect daily functioning or ability to perform occupational duties?
- Would accommodations such as adaptation of workstation or re-assignment of occupational duties allow the individual to return to work?
- If the individual experiences permanent hearing loss, are accommodations such as hearing enhancements or amplification available?

References

Bamiou, D.E., et al. "Symptoms, Disability and Handicap in Unilateral Peripheral Vestibular Disorders." Scandinavian Audiology 29 4 (2000): 238-244.

Rapoport, A., and M. Sadeh. "Posterior Semicircular Canal Type Benign Paroxysmal Positioning Vertigo." Audiology and Neuro-Otology 6 1 (2001): 50-53.

Vesicourethropexy

Other names / synonyms: Anterior Colporrhaphy, Burch Procedure, Cooper Ligament Colposuspension, Endoscopic Suspension of the Vesical Neck, Fascial Sling Procedure, Lateral Paravaginal Repair, Marshall-Marchetti-Krantz Procedure, Modified Pereyra Procedure, Stamey Technique

59.71

Definition

Vesicourethropexy is a surgical procedure to relieve stress urinary incontinence. It involves repositioning the urethra and bladder neck. It is usually considered after simpler forms of treatment have failed.

The incidence of urinary incontinence is about 5-10% in active older individuals. Stress urinary incontinence is most common in women under age 75. Lack of estrogen after menopause is the largest contributing factor.

Reason for Procedure

This procedure raises the bladder/urethral junction to a normal position in order to return normal pressures within the bladder. It is a remedy for stress urinary incontinence.

Description

Vesicourethropexy is performed in an operating room under general anesthesia and involves a vaginal or abdominal incision. This procedure attempts to lengthen the urethra and raise the bladder neck. A urinary catheter may be inserted into the urethra or through the abdominal wall for a period of time to assist healing.

There is controversy over the best method for the repair with least complications. Success depends on individual selection and the surgeon's skill. Various methods used include anterior colporrhaphy, Cooper ligament colposuspension (Burch procedure), fascial sling procedures, endoscopic suspension of the vesical neck (Stamey technique), Marshall-Marchetti-Krantz procedure, modified Pereyra procedure, and lateral paravaginal repairs.

Prognosis

Vesicourethropexy is a very effective procedure. Complete relief from symptoms can be expected in about 85% of individuals with no recurrence.

Specialists

- Gynecologist
- Urologist

Work Restrictions / Accommodations

Lifting and activity is restricted for a period of time.

Comorbid Conditions

Obesity or chronic cough may lengthen disability and increase recurrence.

Procedure Complications

Wound infection and bleeding are the most common complications. Injury to surrounding structures such as the vagina, ovaries, and intestines is also possible. Injury to the intestines would necessitate immediate repair or colostomy with later repair.

Factors Influencing Duration

The method used, any complications, and individual's response affect the length of disability.

Length of Disability

Duration in Days

Job Classification	Minimum	Optimum	Maximum
Sedentary work	42	49	56
Light work	42	49	56
Medium work	42	49	70
Heavy work	56	63	84
Very Heavy work	56	63	112

References

Andreoli, Thomas, MD, et al. Cecil Essentials of Medicine. Philadelphia: W.B. Saunders Company, 1997.

Kisner, C., and L. Colby. Therapeutic Exercise Foundations and Techniques. Philadelphia: F.A. Davis Company, 1990.

Vesicovaginal Fistula

Other names / synonyms: Cervicovesical Fistula, Ureterovaginal Fistula, Urethrovaginal Fistula, Urethrovesicovaginal Fistula, Uterovesical Fistula

619.0

Definition

A vesicovaginal fistula is an abnormal passage between the bladder and vagina. It is the most common type of fistula.

The fistula may be caused by a hereditary (congenital) defect, injury, infection, spread of a cancerous tumor, radiotherapy of a cancerous growth, or trauma during childbirth. The fistula may form as a complication of removal of the uterus (hysterectomy). Gynecological and urological surgeries can also produce fistulas.

The incidence of vesicovaginal fistulas after hysterectomy is estimated at 0.8 of 1,000 procedures after hysterectomy.

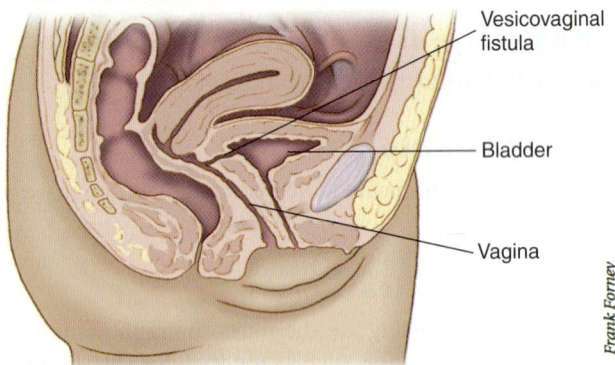

Frank Forney

Diagnosis

History: The woman reports intermittent or continuous loss of urine (incontinence) or watery discharge through the vaginal opening. There may be urinary urgency or voiding more often than every 2 hours (urinary frequency), painful urination, or blood in the urine.

Physical exam: A pelvic examination using a vaginal speculum may reveal the fistula opening on the rear wall of the vagina. Dye may be injected into the bladder with a urinary catheter to help define the fistula.

Tests: Direct visualization of the urinary tract by means of a cystocope inserted into the urethra (cystoscopy) may be done. X-rays of the urinary system (urography) and a radiographic picture of the kidneys and ureters (pyelogram) may be taken to detect the fistula.

Treatment

Vesicovaginal fistulas can be repaired surgically (vesicovaginal closure). The surgical repair may be done through the abdomen (abdominal repair) or the vagina (vaginal repair). Occlusion of the fistula may be done by a transvesical, transperitoneal, vaginal approach or a combination. The procedures for vaginal repair are the flap splitting Latzko techniques. Urinary diversion by insertion of a urinary catheter into the bladder may result in spontaneous healing of the fistula.

Prognosis

The success rate of surgical repair of vesicovaginal fistula is about 90% after a first closure procedure by abdominal, vaginal, or combination repair. Recurrence can occur but most cases are usually successfully closed in a second operation, allowing for a success rate of 100%. A urinary diversion is most successful in individuals with vesicovaginal fistulae resulting from radiation therapy.

Recurrence can occur in these individuals and the method is not as successful as surgical repair. Success rates of occlusion are reported as 86%.

Differential Diagnosis

Possible diagnoses include infiltrating cervical cancer (carcinoma), cervical or uterine growths, or fistula between the ureter and vagina (ureterovaginal fistula).

Specialists

- General Surgeon
- Gynecologist
- Urologist

Work Restrictions / Accommodations

Heavy lifting and activity is restricted after urinary diversion or surgical procedures to avoid excessive pressure.

Comorbid Conditions

Urinary tract infections and vaginal or bladder infections may further lengthen disability.

Complications

Urethral obstruction may complicate treatment with urinary diversion. Excessive damage to cells from radiation therapy may affect the ability to effectively treat the fistula. Difficulties during an operation with a fistula due to bladder injury such as ureteral injury may be higher after laparoscopic hysterectomy compared with traditional hysterectomies. Healing may be inadequate or delayed if blood supply to the fistula is impaired.

Factors Influencing Duration

The type of repair, presence of complications, underlying cause of the fistula, and individual response to treatment affect the length of disability. Surgical repair must be delayed for several months after the original causative surgery is done.

Length of Disability

Surgical treatment.

Duration in Days

Job Classification	Minimum	Optimum	Maximum
Sedentary work	14	21	42
Light work	14	21	42
Medium work	21	28	42
Heavy work	28	42	56
Very Heavy work	28	42	56

Failure to Recover

If an individual fails to recover within the maximum duration expectancy period, the reader may wish to reference the following questions to assist in better understanding the specifics of an individual's medical case.

Regarding diagnosis:

- Is the fistula secondary to a congenital defect, injury, infection, spread of a cancerous tumor, radiotherapy of a cancerous growth, trauma during childbirth, or a complication of a hysterectomy or other gynecological or urological surgeries?
- Does the woman report intermittent or continuous incontinence or watery discharge through the vaginal opening? Is there urinary urgency or urinary frequency, painful urination, or blood in the urine?
- On physical exam, was the fistula opening visible on the rear wall of the vagina?
- Was it necessary to inject dye into the bladder to help define the fistula?
- Has individual had a cystoscopy, urography, or pyelogram?
- Were conditions with similar symptoms ruled out?

Regarding treatment:

- Did individual have urinary diversion done?
- Was occlusion of the fistula done?
- Has individual had surgical repair of the fistula?

Regarding prognosis:

- Can individual's employer accommodate any necessary restrictions?
- Does individual have any conditions that may affect ability to recover?
- Have any complications developed such as urethral obstruction or impaired blood supply to the fistula? Did individual have a laparoscopic hysterectomy?

References

Culligan, Patrick J., and Michael Heit. "Urinary Incontinence in Women." American Academy of Family Physicians. 01 Dec 2000. 24 Jan 2000 <http://www.aafp.org/afp/200001201/2433.html>.

The Merck Manual of Diagnosis and Therapy. Beers, Mark H., and Robert Berkow, eds. Whitehouse Station, NJ: Merck and Co, Inc., 1999.

Vestibular Neuronitis

Other names / synonyms: Acute Peripheral Vestibulopathy, Viral Labyrinthitis

386.12

Definition

Vestibular neuronitis is an inflammation of the vestibular portion of the inner ear characterized by a serious disturbance in balance. The inner ear (a membranous curved cavity located in the temporal bone) is made up of a system of fluid-filled tubes and sacs (the vestibular labyrinth) and the nerves that connect the labyrinth to the brain. The vestibular labyrinth is a critical part of the hearing mechanism and helps maintain an individual's balance by monitoring the directions of the body's motion.

The cause of vestibular neuronitis is unclear, although it may result from a viral infection entering the inner ear from the lining of the brain (meninges), middle ear, or bloodstream. Some of the more common viruses associated with vestibular neuronitis include influenza, measles (rubeola), mumps, German measles (rubella), herpes, hepatitis, polio, and Epstein-Barr. Since it is difficult to determine whether the nerve or labyrinth is the site of the infection, the terms neuronitis and labyrinthitis are used almost interchangeably. Vestibular neuronitis is often called viral labyrinthitis.

Vestibular neuronitis is relatively common given the number of viruses that can cause it.

An epidemiological survey in Japan showed no sexual difference. The peak age distribution was between 40 and 50. In about 30% of all cases, the individual had a common cold prior to the disease.

Diagnosis

History: Individuals with vestibular neuronitis report a sensation of rotation or movement of themselves or their surroundings (vertigo), a rhythmic jerking movement of the eyes (nystagmus), nausea, and vomiting. The degree of vertigo can range from mildly disturbing to incapacitating. The individual may also report a recent or current upper respiratory infection. Ringing in the ears (tinnitus) and hearing loss are not reported.

Physical exam: In the individual with vestibular neuronitis, signs of an upper respiratory infection may be present, but examination of the ears reveals normal (or unchanged) hearing and no signs of infection. These findings suggest viral rather than bacterial labyrinthitis. Neurological examination reveals nystagmus and a balance disturbance. Because balance disturbances can be symptoms of a wide range of diseases and conditions (i.e., trauma, neurological disease, or cardiovascular disease), the physician asks the individual about general health, lifestyle, medical history, current medications, and recent head injuries or infections.

Tests: A wide range of tests may be ordered to help determine the cause of a balance disturbance. An audiogram can assess the individual's hearing. Electronystagmography (ENG) is a test where warm or cold water stimulates the inner ear. Skull x-rays, CT, or MRI of the head help rule out head trauma or cerebral vascular disorders. Electromyography may be ordered to rule out diseases of the neurological system.

Treatment

Treatment of vestibular neuronitis focuses on relief of the nausea and vomiting that accompany the individual's balance disturbance. Pharmacological treatment may include antihistamines, anticholinergics, and sedative-hypnotics. Use of vestibular-suppressant medications is usually only recommended for those with severe nausea and vomiting.

Other treatment includes bed rest to reduce the severity of acute vertigo. Individuals are advised to avoid nicotine, caffeine, and salt, and eliminate situations that may cause stress or anxiety. The individual with vestibular neuronitis should avoid rapid changes in position especially from lying down to standing up, or turning around from one side to the other. The individual should not perform hazardous activities such as driving an automobile, operating dangerous equipment, or climbing a stepladder until the balance disturbance resolves and sedating medication is no longer taken. Normal activities should be resumed as soon as the nausea and vomiting resolves, as physical activity substantially increases the central nervous system's ability to compensate for dysfunction in the labyrinth. Anxiety or depression resulting from this condition may require counseling and treatment with antianxiety or antidepressant medications.

Prognosis

Most cases of vestibular neuronitis resolve within 7 to 10 days. The symptoms of vestibular neuronitis generally peak rapidly and then subside completely. Subsequent attacks may occur over the next 12 to 18 months, but each subsequent attack is less severe and of shorter duration. There is frequently marked suppression of vestibular function on the affected side. As a result, these individuals have a tendency to later develop positional vertigo, a condition where certain head positions and movements can induce violent sensations of vertigo and nystagmus.

Prolonged vertigo can adversely affect all aspects of an individual's life.

Differential Diagnosis

Differential diagnoses for vestibular neuronitis include bacterial infection of the inner ear (bacterial labyrinthitis), endolymphatic hydrops (Ménière's Syndrome), traumatic vertigo following head injury, positioning vertigo (precipitated by changes in head position), perilymphatic fistula, brain stem vascular disease, arteriovenous malformations, tumor of the brain stem and cerebellum, multiple sclerosis, vertebrobasilar migraine, side effects of prescription or nonprescription drugs (including alcohol, tobacco, caffeine, and many illegal drugs), cardiovascular disease, allergies, neurological disorders, and anxiety.

Specialists

- Neurologist
- Otolaryngologist

Rehabilitation

Vestibular rehabilitation helps individuals with persistent or recurrent vertigo. This is an exercise program designed to take advantage of the brain's tendency to eventually adapt (habituate) to the repetition of a specific stimulus causing an individual's vertigo.

Adaptation may take days or months and requires that the individual be willing to move around despite the symptoms of vertigo. Although sitting or lying with the head still is more comfortable, this immobility can prolong or even prevent the adaptation process and should be avoided once the worst of the infection is over.

Traditional physical therapy addresses the secondary symptoms of vestibular neuronitis brought on by inactivity and include decreased strength, loss of range of motion, and increased tension particularly in the cervical and shoulder region that can lead to muscle fatigue and headaches.

Work Restrictions / Accommodations

Work restrictions and accommodations may be required for individuals continuing to experience balance disturbances after recovery from an acute case of vestibular neuronitis. These are for the individual's own protection and the safety of others.

Comorbid Conditions

Comorbid conditions that can influence length of disability include underlying neurological or cardiovascular conditions causing balance disturbances, orthopedic disabilities contributing to instability, and visual impairments contributing to the sensation of vertigo.

Complications

Complications of vestibular neuronitis are related to symptoms exhibited by the individual. Unresolved nausea and vomiting can result in blood electrolyte disturbances. Physical weakness can result from immobility (lying perfectly still provides some relief from vertigo).

Factors Influencing Duration

Factors influencing the length of disability for individuals with vestibular neuronitis include the individual's general fitness and physical and mental health before onset of the condition, general ability to fight infection, and compliance with prescribed treatment and therapy.

Length of Disability

Duration reflects a single attack. Length of disability depends on how quickly the disturbance in balance resolves.

Duration in Days

Job Classification	Minimum	Optimum	Maximum
Any work	7	10	14

Failure to Recover

If an individual fails to recover within the maximum duration expectancy period, the reader may wish to reference the following questions to assist in better understanding the specifics of an individual's medical case.

Regarding diagnosis:

- Did individual present with symptoms such as sensation of rotation or movement of themselves or their surroundings (vertigo), a rhythmic jerking movement of the eyes (nystagmus), nausea, and vomiting? Did individual have recent or current upper respiratory infection?
- Was a thorough physical evaluation and clinical history done to determine the diagnosis?
- Was an audiogram done to determine the cause of a balance disturbance? Electronystagmography (ENG)? Skull x-rays, CT, or MRI? Was electromyography ordered to rule out diseases of the neurological system?
- Were other conditions with similar symptoms ruled out?
- Would individual benefit from consultation with a specialist (otolaryngologist)?

Regarding treatment:

- Were nausea and vomiting relieved? Were antihistamines, anticholinergics, and sedative-hypnotics prescribed?
- Were any underlying respiratory infections addressed in the treatment plan?
- Did individual follow treatment recommendations? Did individual avoid nicotine, caffeine, and salt and eliminate situations that may cause stress or anxiety?
- Did individual return to activity too soon?

Regarding prognosis:

- Has adequate time elapsed for complete recovery?
- Does individual have any comorbid conditions that may influence length of disability?
- Has individual suffered any complications or recurring attacks that may influence ability to recover?

References

Lewis, Sharon, Margaret Heitkemper, and Shannon Dirksen. Medical-Surgical Nursing. St. Louis: Mosby, 2000.

Molony, T.B. "Decision Making in Vestibular Neurectomy." American Journal of Otolaryngology 17 3 (1996): 421-424.

Sekitani, T., Y. Imate, and T. Noguchi. "Vestibular Neuronitis: Epidemiological Survey by Questionnaire in Japan." Acta Oto-laryngologica Supplement 503 (1993): 9-12.

Tierney, Lawrence, Stephen McPhee, and Maxine Papadakis. Current Medical Diagnosis and Treatment. New York: McGraw-Hill, 2000.

Vitamin A Deficiency

Other names / synonyms: Hypovitaminosis A, Retinol Deficiency

264, 264.5, 264.9

Definition

Vitamin A deficiency (hypovitaminosis A) is a nutritional disorder caused when the body lacks vitamin A, a nutrient essential for bone and teeth development and overall growth. One form of vitamin A (retinal) is a component of certain cells in the eye (photoreceptors) that allow us to see. Another form of vitamin A (retinoic acid) keeps the skin and the linings (mucous membranes) of the lungs, intestines, and urinary tract healthy. Certain vitamin A-like medicines (retinoids) are used to treat acne and are being investigated for the treatment of certain types of cancer.

An early sign of vitamin A deficiency is a condition in which the individual has difficulty adjusting from light to dark environments (night blindness, nyctalopia). Later, spots (Bitot's spots) appear on the white of the eye (sclera), and the clear outer layer of the eye (cornea) may harden and scar (xerophthalmia), leading to permanent blindness. The skin and mucous membranes may harden, the skin may become inflamed (dermatitis) and the individual will be more susceptible to infections.

Vitamin A is abundant in dairy products, liver, and eggs. The precursor or building block of vitamin A, beta-carotene, is found in carrots, leafy green vegetables, yellow fruits and vegetables, sweet potatoes, and squash. In most cases, vitamin A deficiency results from a diet that lacks this nutrient. Vitamin A deficiency is also seen in individuals with disorders that prevent nutrient absorption during digestion. In these individuals, vitamin A deficiency occurs even when plenty of foods rich in vitamin A are eaten.

The global risk of vitamin A deficiency has been estimated at approximately 500,000 cases per year. However, vitamin A deficiency is relatively rare in the US and in other developed nations, where most people have access to plenty of nutritious food. It is more common in parts of Asia and Africa where diet consists primarily of rice lacking vitamin A. Regardless of geography, poverty is a risk factor for this disorder, as is old age, because loneliness and depression often result in poor eating habits. Children are also at risk, due to the increased need for vitamin A during growth.

Medical conditions that prevent the body from absorbing nutrients during digestion increase the risk for developing vitamin A deficiency. These include Whipple's disease, tropical sprue, celiac disease (non-tropical sprue), bacterial overgrowth in the intestines, pancreatic disease, cirrhosis of the liver, bile duct obstruction, and amyloidosis. A deficiency of the mineral zinc can contribute to vitamin A deficiency, because zinc helps the body absorb vitamin A from the diet. Alcoholism, eating disorders such as anorexia nervosa or bulimia nervosa, fad diets severely limiting certain foods, and laxative abuse also increase risk.

Diagnosis

History: In the early stages of vitamin A deficiency, individuals complain that they have difficulty adjusting from light to dark environments (night blindness, nyctalopia). Some may also notice that wounds are slow to heal. The mouth, throat, nose, and eyes may be dry and irritated. As the deficiency persists, the eyes become sensitive to light and the eyelids become swollen. The skin may be dry and rough.

Physical exam: Eye examination often reveals an absence of tears. There may be foamy spots (Bitot's spot) on the whites of the eyes (sclera). The clear outer covering of the eye (cornea) may be thickened and scarred, with ulcer formation. In advanced cases, loss of vision may progress to complete blindness in one or both eyes. The skin may be abnormally thickened, with inflammation (dermatitis) and plugs of horny material around the hair follicles (follicular hyperkeratosis). Mucous membranes may be dry, abnormally thickened, or hardened, causing increased susceptibility to infection. The individual may report a recent increase in the number of illnesses.

Tests: A blood test reveals low levels of vitamin A in the blood, which is usually sufficient for definitive diagnosis, in combination with characteristic symptoms and examination results. Night vision threshold testing is also a simple and inexpensive way to make the diagnosis, although other causes of night blindness must be excluded. A therapeutic trial of vitamin A assists in diagnosis.

Treatment

Vitamin A deficiency is treated with oral vitamin A supplements. These supplements are given at higher than normal doses until symptoms resolve. The individual should also be educated on the importance of a well-balanced, nutritious diet, and given a list of foods high in vitamin A and/or the precursor to vitamin A (beta-carotene). Any underlying conditions interfering with vitamin A deficiency should be treated. If vomiting or other digestive conditions prevent absorption of oral vitamin A, it should be given by injection into the muscle. Even after symptoms have resolved, additional daily vitamin A supplements should be given to individuals with absorption problems, as well as to those who may not follow a healthy diet, such as those with alcoholism or eating disorders. During pregnancy and breast feeding, daily doses should not exceed twice the RDA to avoid possible damage to the baby.

Prognosis

In most cases, treatment with vitamin A supplements and a well-balanced diet result in complete resolution of symptoms within 2 months. The inability to adapt from light to dark environments (night blindness, nyctalopia) can be reversed, but vision loss due to scarring is permanent. If an underlying condition is causing or contributing to vitamin A deficiency, that disorder must be treated for a successful outcome. If a healthy, well-balanced diet is not maintained, vitamin A deficiency can recur. In rare cases of very severe vitamin A deficiency, death can occur.

Differential Diagnosis

The diagnosis of vitamin A deficiency is not difficult provided a blood test is abnormal. Other causes of night blindness include retinitis pigmentosa. Other dermatologic conditions could resemble the skin changes seen in this disorder.

Specialists

- Dermatologist
- Dietary Advisor
- Gynecologist
- Internist
- Psychologist
- Pulmonologist
- Urologist

Work Restrictions / Accommodations

In most cases, work restrictions and accommodations are not necessary. If the individual's occupation involves driving, driving at night should be avoided until the deficiency has been reversed. Similarly, jobs requiring keen nighttime/dark vision (police officers, security guards, film developers, etc.) may require temporary reassignment. Individuals with vitamin A deficiency are at increased risk of infection, so they should avoid contact with ill people. Thus, nurses, physicians, and receptionists in a physician's office, etc. may require leave from work or reassignment to a position that does not involve patient contact. If the individual's eyes are sensitive to light, sunglasses may be necessary. The eyes and skin may be unusually sensitive to chemicals and/or fumes, thereby necessitating additional protective clothing or a temporary reassignment to a position not involving contact with irritating agents. In the rare case of permanent blindness or severe visual impairment, disability may be permanent.

Comorbid Conditions

Diseases in which the body's immune system attacks its own organs (autoimmune diseases) such as Sjögren's syndrome and systemic lupus erythematosus may produce more severe symptoms and lengthen the disability period. Individuals with diabetes or those with a weakened or suppressed immune system secondary to AIDS or other conditions may have a longer recovery period. Vitamin A deficiency not sufficiently severe to cause symptoms (subclinical) is common in late pregnancy, especially in women from lower socioeconomic groups.

Complications

Prolonged vitamin A deficiency can result in permanent loss of vision in one or both eyes. In pregnancy, prolonged vitamin A deficiency has been associated with birth defects. Individuals whose diets are lacking vitamin A may also lack other essential nutrients. In such cases, vitamin A deficiency may be complicated by a variety of other nutritional disorders.

Factors Influencing Duration

The length of disability will be determined by the severity of symptoms, the individual's response to treatment, and the presence of an underlying cause or contributing disease. The individual's willingness to follow a healthy diet and access to appropriate foods will also affect the length of disability.

Length of Disability

Little to no disability time should be required. Duration depends on severity. Symptoms usually resolve completely in less than 2 weeks following treatment. If an underlying disease is contributing to or causing the vitamin A deficiency, duration of disability is related to successful treatment of that disease. Vision loss may be permanent, which may cause permanent disability. Rare cases of severe vitamin A deficiency are fatal.

Duration in Days

Job Classification	Minimum	Optimum	Maximum
Any work	0	7	14

Failure to Recover

If an individual fails to recover within the maximum duration expectancy period, the reader may wish to reference the following questions to assist in better understanding the specifics of an individual's medical case.

Regarding diagnosis:

- Do symptoms and examination findings suggest the diagnosis of vitamin A deficiency?
- Could symptoms such as night blindness or skin conditions be caused by other diseases?
- Has the diagnosis of vitamin A deficiency been confirmed by blood test?

Regarding treatment:

- Has the cause of the vitamin A deficiency been identified?
- Is there evidence of a zinc deficiency? Can this be resolved through supplements?
- Does individual have an eating disorder, such as anorexia nervosa or bulimia nervosa? Is there evidence of laxative abuse? Is individual receiving psychological counseling?
- Does individual participate in fad diets that severely limit certain foods? Has individual received nutritional counseling?
- Has individual been instructed to abstain from alcohol?
- Does the individual have an underlying disease that may prevent the body from absorbing vitamins from the diet? If so, is underlying disease being adequately addressed?
- Has the individual been taking supplements as prescribed by the physician?
- As it may take up to 2 months for symptoms to completely resolve, has treatment been of adequate duration?
- Would individual receive more benefit from vitamin A injections?

Regarding prognosis:

- Is the individual following a healthy, balanced diet?
- Do eating disorders and/or laxative abuse continue to prevent adequate nutrition? Would individual benefit from additional psychological counseling?
- Does individual continue to engage in fad diets? Would individual benefit from consultation with a nutritionist?
- Is individual unable to abstain from alcohol? Would individual benefit from enrollment in a community program or support group?
- Does the individual have a coexisting medical condition that may impact recovery? Is this condition being adequately addressed in the overall treatment plan?

References

"Vitamin A Deficiency." Merck Manual of Diagnosis and Therapy, 17th ed. Beers, Mark H., and Robert Berkow, MD, eds. Whitehouse Station, NJ: Merck & Co., Inc., 1999. 3/12/01 <http://www.merck.com/pubs/mmanual/section1/chapter3/3b.htm>.

"Vitamins and Minerals." The Merck Manual of Medical Information. Berkow, Robert, Mark Beers, and Andrew Fletcher, eds. New York: Pocket Books, 1997. 713-729.

Spake, A. "The ABCs of Vitamin A. Veggies Revisited." U.S. News World Report 130 3 (2001): 56.

Vijayaraghavan, K. "Vitamin A Deficiency." Lancet 356 Suppl (2000): s41.

Vitamin B₁ Deficiency

Other names / synonyms: Beriberi, Korsakoff's Psychosis, Thiamine Deficiency, Vitamin B₁ Deficiency, Wernicke-Korsakoff Syndrome, Wernicke's Encephalopathy

265.0, 265.1

Definition

Vitamin B₁ (thiamine) deficiency is a nutritional disorder characterized by nerve, brain, and heart abnormalities. Thiamine is a member of the group of vitamins known as the B-complex vitamins. It is an essential nutrient with a critical role in the metabolism of sugars and starches (carbohydrates). The body uses carbohydrates (particularly the sugar called glucose) for energy, and a lack of thiamine results in an energy shortage. This type of energy shortage has effects on many bodily functions. Early stages of thiamine deficiency are characterized by tiredness (fatigue), irritability, memory impairment, loss of appetite (anorexia), weight loss, sleep disturbances, and abdominal discomfort. Eventually, severe thiamine deficiency (beriberi) develops, resulting in damage to the nerves, brain, and heart.

Nerve abnormalities (dry beriberi) tend to affect the toes, feet, and legs more than other body parts, beginning with a pins-and-needles prickly feeling (paresthesias) in the toes. The prickly feeling gradually progresses to a burning sensation, muscle cramps, loss of muscle mass and function (atrophy), and a condition where the feet, toes and/or wrists are limp and cannot be raised (toe drop, foot drop, wrist drop) because the nerves and muscles do not work properly.

Brain abnormalities (Wernicke-Korsakoff's syndrome or cerebral beriberi) tend to occur when a severe and sudden deficiency of thiamine aggravates a chronic deficiency. For example, this may occur after severe and repeated vomiting or with binge drinking in alcoholics. Cerebral beriberi begins as confusion, inflammation of the vocal cords (laryngitis), and double vision (diplopia) related to incoordination of eye movements (ophthalmoplegia). As memory becomes more and more impaired, Korsakoff's psychosis develops and the individual tends to make up facts and events in order to fill in memory gaps. This process is called confabulation. Wernicke-Korsakoff encephalopathy can result in coma and death if not treated promptly.

Heart abnormalities (wet beriberi) are characterized by a rapid heart rate (tachycardia) and a high output of blood from the heart that causes the skin to be warm and moist. Because of the lack of thiamine, the heart cannot keep up with its own pace and heart failure occurs.

Pork, yeast, whole grain cereals, and legumes are good sources of thiamine. Individuals not eating a sufficient variety of nutritional foods (e.g., on a fad diet) are at an increased risk of developing thiamine deficiency. Certain medical conditions including anorexia nervosa, bulimia nervosa, alcoholism, liver disease, and chronic diarrhea increase risk of thiamine deficiency. Conditions that increase the body's need for thiamine such as hyperthyroidism, pregnancy, and fever also increase the risk for this disease. A large load of sugar or carbohydrate can further deplete thiamine stores in individuals with chronic, borderline deficiency since thiamine is needed to break down (metabolize) carbohydrate. For this reason, individuals in coma of unknown cause should be given intravenous thiamine along with sugar (glucose) to prevent development of Wernicke-Korsakoff syndrome. Diuretic treatment can bring on vitamin B₁ deficiency especially in the elderly.

Thiamine deficiency is a relatively rare condition due to the abundance of thiamine-enriched foods and the wide availability and use of vitamin supplements. It primarily occurs in areas where diet consists primarily of polished rice such as rural parts of Asia and the Pacific Islands.

Diagnosis

History: Symptoms of thiamine deficiency are numerous and most individuals with this condition experience some but not all possible symptoms. Early symptoms may include tiredness (fatigue), abdominal discomfort, sleep disturbances, memory problems, loss of appetite (anorexia), weight loss, and irritability. A pins-and-needles feeling (paresthesias) in the toes, a burning sensation in the feet that may worsen at night, pain in the feet and legs, and muscle cramps in the legs are common symptoms of nerve damage. Mental confusion, inflammation of the vocal cords (laryngitis), and double vision (diplopia) are early symptoms of brain involvement. As the brain becomes more damaged, family members may report increasing confusion and memory loss (amnesia) and a tendency to make up facts and experiences (confabulation) to fill in lost memory. Shortness of breath is a common symptom of heart involvement, as is swelling of the feet and/or legs that indicates fluid retention.

When questioned regarding eating habits, the individual (or family member) may report a diet high in sugars and starches (carbohydrates), particularly rice. However, since thiamine deficiency often occurs in alcoholics and those with eating disorders, description of diet may not be accurate.

Physical exam: On exam and palpation, leg muscles (particularly the calf muscles) may be tender. When squatting, individual may have difficulty returning to a standing position. Leg muscles may weaken and lose function (atrophy). Reflexes and sensation in the hands and particularly the feet may also be decreased. The toes, feet, and/or wrists may droop. Some individuals have a rapid pulse (tachycardia), rapid breathing (tachypnea), high blood pressure (hypertension), and swelling of the feet and ankles. The skin may feel warm and moist. In advanced cases of the disease, there is enlargement of the heart (cardiomegaly) and liver (hepatomegaly).

Tests: Blood tests show impaired red blood cell metabolism (erythrocyte transketolase activity) and abnormally low levels of thiamine. Levels of thiamine are also low in the urine. The definitive test is improvement of symptoms with thiamine administration. Nerve testing (EMG, nerve conduction velocity, somatosensory evoked potential testing) may show signs of nerve involvement (peripheral neuropathy). Electrocardiogram and echocardiogram may show evidence of heart involvement (cardiomyopathy). On brain MRI, the mamillary bodies (a structure selectively affected in Wernicke's encephalopathy) may show signs of shrinkage (atrophy). However, this finding is not specific and can also be seen in Alzheimer's disease and other memory disorders. MRI may also show characteristic abnormalities around the fluid-filled chambers (ventricles) within the brain.

Treatment

Thiamine deficiency is treated with administration of thiamine supplements. In mild cases, this can be done with oral supplements taken at regular intervals for a period of several days until symptoms resolve. In more severe cases, inpatient treatment may be necessary while thiamine is administered intravenously for a few days. Once the individual's symptoms are stabilized, the individual is released from the hospital and oral thiamine supplements are prescribed. In all cases, individual is also given a list of thiamine-rich foods, instruction on the value of a well-balanced healthy diet, and guidance on how to maintain such a diet. Good dietary sources of thiamine include pork, wheat germ, whole grain cereals, brewer's yeast, enriched rice, soymilk, sunflower seeds, beans, pasta, and unroasted peanuts.

If another disease is involved such as alcoholism, anorexia nervosa, bulimia nervosa, or chronic diarrhea, treatment of this disease is important for recovery. If the physician believes that a well-balanced diet will not be maintained, as in malnutrition due to extreme poverty, alcoholism, or eating disorders, dietary supplements may be prescribed for regular use. Prevention of heart and nervous system complications through thiamine supplementation is much easier than reversal of impairments. Some researchers have even advised adding thiamine to alcoholic beverages.

Prognosis

With thiamine supplements and a nutritious, well-balanced diet, the prognosis is excellent and full recovery expected. In rare cases of severe brain impairment, memory loss may be permanent. If untreated, vitamin B_1 deficiency may be fatal, although death from this disorder is very rare.

The prognosis is worse when vitamin B_1 deficiency is related to an underlying disease such as alcoholism, anorexia nervosa, or bulimia nervosa. Characteristics of these underlying conditions are likely to prevent the individual from following a healthy diet and/or taking vitamin supplements on a regular basis.

Differential Diagnosis

Vitamin B_1 deficiency is usually easy to diagnose based on a combination of the individual's symptoms, physical examination findings, and dietary history. However, many conditions share symptoms of this disorder. For example, memory loss, confusion, and irritability are associated with many neurological disorders. Shortness of breath is associated with many diseases of the lungs and is also a classic symptom of heart failure. Heart failure, rapid heartbeat (tachycardia), and rapid breathing (tachypnea) can result from numerous disease processes and are not unique to thiamine deficiency. Fatigue, sleep disturbances, loss of appetite, weight loss, and abdominal discomfort are symptoms common to a wide variety of illnesses.

Specialists

- Cardiologist
- Dietary Advisor
- Internist
- Neurologist
- Psychiatrist

Work Restrictions / Accommodations

Work restrictions and accommodations vary significantly depending on the individual's symptoms, severity of those symptoms, and job requirements. In most cases, tiredness (fatigue) and leg muscle impairment dictate a sedentary position. Jobs requiring moderate or heavy work or physical activity, prolonged standing, or alertness should be avoided, as should driving and operating heavy machinery. Climbing stairs may be difficult. Uncontrolled limpness of the wrists (wrist drop) may make typing, grasping, or any activity requiring fine motor skills difficult or impossible. Confusion or memory problems may necessitate increased supervision if mild, and extended leave or even permanent disability if severe. If the job involves a high level of responsibility such as air traffic controller, physician, or lawyer, extended or permanent leave may be advisable even for mild confusion or memory impairment.

Comorbid Conditions

Individuals with diabetes may have more severe symptoms and a longer recovery period. Alcoholism, eating disorders (anorexia nervosa, bulimia nervosa), chronic gastrointestinal disorders, pregnancy, hyperthyroidism, and fever may all be associated with a prolonged recovery period. Malnutrition or other nutritional disorders may also prolong recovery. Diuretics used to treat heart failure may aggravate thiamine deficiency by increasing its removal (excretion) from the body. Conversely, loss of thiamine related to diuretic use may aggravate heart failure. In a similar way, eating disorders predispose thiamine deficiency that in turn can aggravate the psychiatric symptoms leading to abnormal eating habits.

Complications

Vitamin B_1 deficiency is generally an uncomplicated disease. Individuals whose diets are lacking vitamin B_1 may also lack other essential nutrients. In such cases, vitamin B_1 deficiency may be complicated by a variety of other nutritional disorders. Giving too much B_1 to individuals with cancer who are receiving chemotherapy may promote tumor growth. As B-complex may interfere with absorption of other drugs such as tetracycline, individuals should take these medications at different times from B_1.

Factors Influencing Duration

Duration of disability depends on severity of the disease, response to treatment, and individual's job requirements. If the individual is unable or unwilling to follow dietary and therapeutic instructions, disability may be permanent. If the disorder is related to an underlying illness, treatment and complications of that illness affect the period of disability.

Length of Disability

Duration depends on severity. May be associated with alcoholism. When adequately treated with thiamine supplements and a healthy diet, signs and symptoms usually resolve completely within a period of weeks. Severe cases or individuals with comorbid conditions may have a longer recovery period or even permanent disability. For Wernicke-Korsakoff syndrome, disability may be permanent.

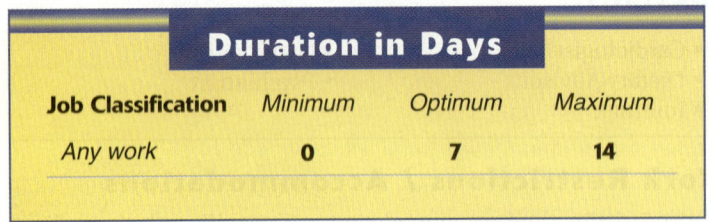

Duration in Days

Job Classification	Minimum	Optimum	Maximum
Any work	0	7	14

Failure to Recover

If an individual fails to recover within the maximum duration expectancy period, the reader may wish to reference the following questions to assist in better understanding the specifics of an individual's medical case.

Regarding diagnosis:

- Does individual eat a diet high in sugars and starches (carbohydrates)? Does individual's diet include sources of thiamine such as pork, yeast, whole grain cereals, and legumes?
- Does individual have a history of anorexia nervosa, bulimia nervosa, alcoholism, liver disease, or chronic diarrhea?
- Are conditions present that increase the body's need for thiamine such as hyperthyroidism, pregnancy, or fever?
- Does individual take medication regularly to eliminate excess fluid (diuretics)?
- Does individual complain of fatigue, abdominal discomfort, sleep disturbances, memory problems, loss of appetite (anorexia), weight loss, and/or irritability? Does individual report a pins-and-needles feeling (paresthesias) in the toes, burning sensation in the feet that may worsen at night, or muscle cramps in the legs?
- Are symptoms suggestive of early brain involvement present such as mental confusion, inflammation of the vocal cords (laryngitis), and double vision (diplopia)?
- Does individual have common symptoms of heart involvement such as shortness of breath or swelling (edema) of the feet and/or legs?
- Were blood tests done for red blood cell metabolism (erythrocyte transketolase activity) function and levels of thiamine?
- Was nerve testing (EMG, nerve conduction velocity, somatosensory evoked potential testing) required? Electrocardiogram (ECG) or echocardiogram? MRI of the brain?
- Was the diagnosis of vitamin B_1 deficiency confirmed?

Regarding treatment:

- Were thiamine supplements administered orally until symptoms resolved?
- If severe deficiency was present, was hospitalization required for intravenous administration of thiamine? When individual was discharged from the hospital, were oral thiamine supplements prescribed?
- Was individual given a list of thiamine-rich foods, instruction on the value of a balanced, healthy diet, and guidance on how to maintain such a diet?
- If an underlying disease is involved such as alcoholism, anorexia nervosa, bulimia nervosa, or chronic diarrhea, was the disease treated adequately?
- Does individual require chemical dependency or psychiatric counseling for underlying conditions?
- Does individual understand the importance of complying with diet and supplemental treatment?

Regarding prognosis:

- Is individual absolutely compliant with eating a nutritious diet and taking thiamine supplements?
- Would individual benefit from hospitalization for alcoholism, anorexia nervosa, or bulimia nervosa, since these conditions are likely to prevent individual from following a healthy diet and/or taking vitamin supplements on a regular basis?
- Does individual have other vitamin deficiencies that could complicate the condition? If individual has cancer and is undergoing chemotherapy, is too much vitamin B_1 being given that may promote tumor growth?
- Because B complex vitamins may interfere with absorption of other drugs such as tetracycline, does individual take other medications at different times?
- Has heart, brain, or nerve involvement occurred? If so, how will this be treated and what is expected outcome with treatment?

inner ear. Specific exercises may be recommended for certain types of positional vertigo.

Various surgical options may be considered in extreme, unresolved cases of vertigo including relief of pressure in the inner ear (endolymphatic sac surgery, cochleosacculotomy, and microvascular decompression), removal of certain sensory tissue and nerve fibers (labyrinthectomy), sectioning selected nerves (middle cranial fossa, retrolabyrinthine, retrosigmoid, translabyrinthine), pulling away (avulsion) a selected nerve (singular neurectomy), and sealing the inner ear semicircular canal (posterior semicircular canal occlusion). Other surgical methods of treating vertigo are being investigated, including the creation of openings and antibiotic treatment in the inner ear semicircular canal (Streptomycin perfusion). This technique has shown some early results that appear promising.

Prognosis

Sudden onset (acute) vertigo is usually self-limited, and resolves after several days of bedrest. The prognosis for other types of vertigo varies greatly depending on the underlying cause. In many cases of ongoing (chronic) vertigo, changes in lifestyle may become necessary such as avoiding positions of the head or other body that aggravate or induce symptoms. Chronic diseases, such as autoimmune disorders or multiple sclerosis, that fail to resolve may cause continuing episodes of vertigo for an indefinite time. Success rates for various surgical procedures aimed at resolving or relieving symptoms of more serious forms of vertigo range from 60-90%. There is a slight possibility of permanent hearing loss accompanying these surgical procedures.

Differential Diagnosis

Other possibilities include acute cerebellar lesions, cerebellopontine angle lesions, hyperventilation, Parkinsonism, vitamin B_{12} deficiency, stroke, cervical spondylosis, panic disorder, partial seizures, brain stem ischemia or infarction, perilymphatic fistula, vertebral basilar artery insufficiency, irritation or destruction of nerve pathways, tumor, or multiple sclerosis. Vertigo may be present in association with many other conditions such as Ménière's disease and autoimmune disorders including rheumatoid arthritis. As vertigo is a symptom and not a disease, workup must include a thorough search for the underlying disorder.

Specialists

- Neurologist
- Otolaryngologist

Rehabilitation

Individuals experiencing vertigo are seen by a physical therapist trained in the specialty of vestibular rehabilitation. Once it is determined if the dizziness and balance problem is coming from an inner ear dysfunction or from other areas such as the brain's center for balance, the therapist can establish a plan of care to treat the individual appropriately. Much of the therapy focuses around balance exercises that challenge the individual without stimulating a significant amount of dizziness.

An example of an exercise involves walking straight ahead while rotating the head side to side and focusing visually on an object. Techniques used like this increase the normal amount of sensory and visual input needed for balance compared to simply walking in a straight-forward manner. Modifications may need to be made by the physical therapist for those individuals who have undergone surgery for a condition causing vertigo or who have suffered from some form of head trauma affecting the body's balance.

The Canalith Repositioning Maneuver may be performed by the physical therapist, audiologist, or physician to clear the dislodged calcium crystals from the canal and deposit them back into the part of the inner ear (utricle) where they belong.

Work Restrictions / Accommodations

Work restrictions and accommodations require consideration on an individual basis. Positional vertigo could require adaptation of workstations to make sure the individual is not forced to move the head at certain angles. Tasks requiring good balance or physical maneuvering may need to be reassigned. If the individual experiences permanent hearing loss, other accommodations such as hearing enhancements or amplification may be needed.

Complementary and Alternative Therapies

Content is intended for awareness only. Treatments may or may not be effective. Scientific evidence may be lacking and some substances have potentially toxic effects. Dr. Presley Reed and the editors do not endorse the use of these therapies in the absence of consultation with a licensed medical professional.

Ginger -	May reduce dizziness and vomiting associated with seasickness or motion sickness.
Gingko -	May improve chronic vertigo
Calcium -	Said to be critical to inner ear functioning.
Celery seed -	Has been used in Chinese medicine to treat dizziness.
Magnesium -	Said to be critical to inner ear functioning.
Potassium -	Said to be critical to inner ear functioning.
Pumpkin -	Has been used by some herbalists to treat dizziness.
Scleranthus -	May help mild dizziness related to balance problems.
Acupressure -	Applying pressure to stomach meridian below kneecap may relieve dizziness.
Reflexology -	Working the ear, cervical spine and neck reflexes on the feet may relieve dizziness.

Comorbid Conditions

Some individuals may experience vertigo years after original onset of viral diseases such as mumps or measles that may have damaged the inner ear, creating more severe or prolonged symptoms. The individual may have abnormal anatomic vascular features that compress nerves in the inner ear, leading to continuing damage and/or hearing loss. Any chronic disease causing vertigo, such as multiple sclerosis, autoimmune disorder, stroke, tumor, post-traumatic syndrome, or Ménière's disease, has its own impairments additive to those associated with vertigo. Neurologic disorders affecting other parts of the nervous system involved in balance and spatial orientation, such as peripheral neuropathy or blindness, aggravate balance problems related to vertigo.

Complications

Complications primarily depend on any underlying disease. Some surgical treatments of vertigo must be performed carefully, or injury and loss of hearing may result. Local anesthetics associated with diagnosis and/or treatment also may cause disruption of the inner ear system, leading to possible damage or hearing loss. Autoimmune diseases such as rheumatoid arthritis may both cause and prolong symptoms of vertigo. Certain autoimmune inner ear diseases, such as Sjögren's syndrome and Cogan's disease, may lead to progressive damage to the inner ear and accompanying hearing loss. Depending on the source of vertigo, temporary (transient) blindness could result. Prolonged treatment using some anti-vertiginous medications could result in the individual's inability to adapt naturally to changes in the inner ear system, thus leading to long-term problems with balance. Poor balance associated with vertigo may lead to falls and self-injury.

Factors Influencing Duration

If the individual experiences complications such as hearing loss, ability to perform job tasks requiring keen hearing will be affected. Ability to perform tasks requiring balance and physical maneuvering may also be affected permanently if vertigo is ongoing.

Length of Disability

Duration depends on acute versus chronic form. A more specific diagnosis is required.

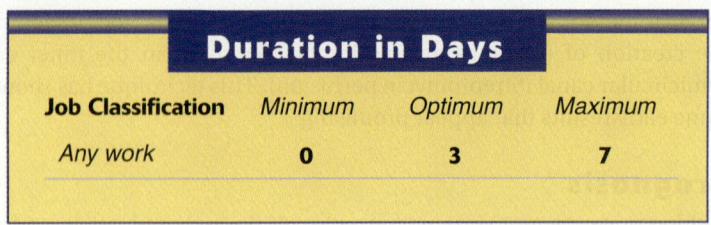

Duration in Days

Job Classification	Minimum	Optimum	Maximum
Any work	0	3	7

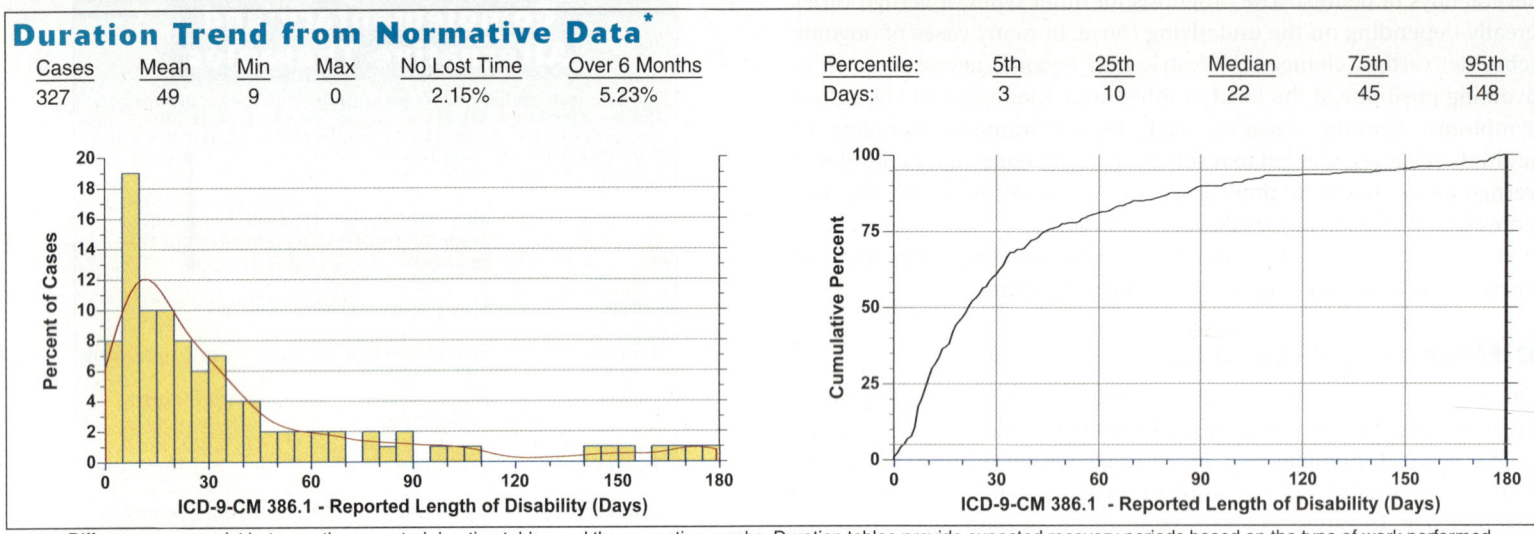

Duration Trend from Normative Data*

Cases	Mean	Min	Max	No Lost Time	Over 6 Months
327	49	9	0	2.15%	5.23%

Percentile:	5th	25th	Median	75th	95th
Days:	3	10	22	45	148

* Differences may exist between the expected duration tables and the normative graphs. Duration tables provide expected recovery periods based on the type of work performed by the individual. The normative graphs reflect the actual observed experience of many individuals across the spectrum of physical conditions, in a variety of industries, and with varying levels of case management.

Failure to Recover

If an individual fails to recover within the maximum duration expectancy period, the reader may wish to reference the following questions to assist in better understanding the specifics of an individual's medical case.

Regarding diagnosis:

- Does the individual have vertigo, a sensation of rotation as if the surroundings are spinning or moving, or nonspecific dizziness, which may have a cardiac, metabolic, or other cause?
- Did the vertigo come on suddenly, suggesting inflammation of the semicircular canals of the inner ear (nonspecific labyrinthitis), or is it chronic, which usually indicates presence of a serious disease?
- Has the underlying condition been identified and confirmed?
- Are additional tests needed, such as audiometry, brain CT, or angiography?

Regarding treatment:

- Has appropriate symptomatic treatment been given, including bedrest, anti-vertiginous and/or anti-nausea drugs, and pain medication for individuals with headaches?
- If vertigo symptoms have not resolved after medical treatment or rest, is the individual considered a candidate for surgical intervention?
- Has the individual received surgical treatments or local anesthetics, which can result in hearing loss?
- Has treatment with anti-vertiginous medications been prolonged, resulting in loss of adaptation to changes in the inner ear system, thus leading to long-term balance problems?
- Are the underlying cause of the vertigo and any complications being treated appropriately?
- If the diagnosis is Ménière's disease, have diuretics been given to reduce fluid in the ears?
- Should decompression chamber therapy be considered to help restore pressure balances in the inner ear?
- Should short-term use of steroids be considered to relieve inflammation of nerves in the inner ear?

References

"Vitamins and Minerals." The Merck Manual of Medical Information. Berkow, Robert, Mark Beers, and Andrew Fletcher, eds. New York: Pocket Books, 1997. 713-729.

Opdenakker, G., et al. "Wernicke Encephalopathy: MR Findings in Two Patients." European Radiology 9 8 (1999): 1620-1624.

Sheedy, D., et al. "Size of Mamillary Bodies in Health and Disease: Useful Measurements in Neuroradiological Diagnosis of Wernicke's Encephalopathy." Alcoholism-Clinical and Experimental Research 23 10 (1999): 1624-1628.

Suter, P.M., and W. Vetter. "Diuretics and Vitamin B1: Are Diuretics a Risk Factor for Thiamin Malnutrition?" Nutrition Reviews 58 10 (2000): 319-233.

Suter, P.M., et al. "Diuretic Use: A Risk for Subclinical Thiamine Deficiency in Elderly Patients." Journal of Nutritional Health Aging 4 2 (2000): 69-71.

Winston, A.P., et al. "Prevalence of Thiamin Deficiency in Anorexia Nervosa." International Journal of Eating Disorders 28 4 (2000): 451-454.

Vitamin B_2 Deficiency

Other names / synonyms: Angular Stomatitis, Cheilosis, Perlèche, Riboflavin Deficiency

266.0

Definition

Vitamin B_2 (riboflavin) deficiency is a nutritional disorder resulting from a lack of dietary riboflavin, an essential vitamin found in dairy products, meats, fish, poultry, yeast, leafy green vegetables, and whole, unrefined or enriched grains. Riboflavin has an important role in the body's metabolism, particularly with respect to energy production. Riboflavin is also required in the early steps of protein synthesis, which affects all body systems. Vitamin B_2 deficiency is often found in conjunction with other B vitamin deficiencies.

Vitamin B_2 deficiency is a rare condition, due to the widespread availability of vitamin enriched products (particularly cereals and bread) and the routine use of vitamin supplements. Individuals who don't eat meat or dairy products (vegans) are at increased risk for vitamin B_2 deficiency. Individuals who follow fad diets (e.g., eating only a few select foods) are at increased risk for developing this disease. Also at increased risk are alcoholics, individuals with eating disorders (anorexia nervosa, bulimia nervosa), those with chronic diarrhea or other chronic gastrointestinal diseases, and individuals with liver or kidney disease. Those who are very poor are also at increased risk, as poverty is associated with an insufficient diet, particularly a lack of animal products. It may occur more frequently in people with cataracts or sickle cell anemia. The nutrient value of vitamin B_2 can be affected by the chemotherapeutic drug Adriamycin, oral contraceptives, tetracycline, and tricyclic antidepressants. Men and women are equally affected.

Diagnosis

History: In most cases, questions regarding normal dietary habits will reveal a diet low in dairy products and animal protein foods. Individuals may complain of soreness around the mouth and throat (ulcers or canker sores), a sore and bright purplish-red tongue, dry and cracking lips (cheilosis), scaly skin on the face and possibly on the scalp as well, and general tiredness (fatigue). Some individuals may complain that their eyes are itchy and sensitive to light (photophobia), and they may also notice a decrease in vision. They may also report migraine headaches.

Physical exam: The physical examination is largely unremarkable. The tongue may be inflamed (glossitis). In some cases, an eye examination will reveal abnormal new vessel growth in the eye (corneal neovascularization or pre-cataracts). In men, the skin of the scrotum may be inflamed.

Tests: A blood test (erythrocyte glutathione reductase activity) can confirm the diagnosis.

Specialists

- Dermatologist
- Dietary Advisor
- Internist
- Ophthalmologist

Treatment

Vitamin B_2 deficiency is treated with vitamin B_2 supplements. These supplements are administered orally, at a dose of approximately 10 times the recommended daily allowance. This dosage is maintained until the individual's symptoms resolve. Because vitamin B_2 works with vitamins B_1, B_3, and B_6, it should be taken as part of a B-complex supplement.

Another important aspect of treatment for this disorder is establishing and maintaining a healthy, well-balanced diet that contains adequate amounts of vitamin B_2. The physician will provide the individual with a list of vitamin B_2-rich foods, and will counsel the individual on good eating habits.

If another disease is involved (alcoholism, anorexia nervosa, bulimia nervosa, chronic diarrhea, etc.) treatment of that disease is important for recovery. In cases where the physician believes that a well-balanced diet will not be maintained (e.g., in cases of malnutrition due to extreme poverty, alcoholism, anorexia nervosa, bulimia nervosa, etc.) dietary supplements may be prescribed for use on a regular basis.

Prognosis

With vitamin B_2 (riboflavin) supplements and a nutritious, well-balanced diet, the prognosis is excellent. The vast majority of individuals who follow this treatment regimen (supplements and diet) will achieve a full recovery.

The prognosis for individuals whose vitamin B_2 deficiency is related to an underlying disease (e.g., alcoholism, anorexia nervosa, bulimia nervosa, etc.) is less positive. Characteristics of these underlying conditions are likely to prevent the individual from following a healthy diet and/or taking vitamin supplements on a regular basis.

Differential Diagnosis

Vitamin B$_2$ deficiency is easily diagnosed based on the history, symptoms, and a blood test. The conditions described for this disorder (e.g., glossitis, seborrheic dermatitis, dry lips and cracked mouth, corneal neovascularization) can occur even without any deficiency in vitamin B$_2$.

Work Restrictions / Accommodations

The signs and symptoms of vitamin B$_2$ deficiency do not generally result in any physical impairment, although they are bothersome and possibly unattractive. In some cases, the individual experiences general tiredness (fatigue), so work requiring strenuous or prolonged physical activity or alertness should be avoided during recovery. A shortened work day may also be helpful during the recovery period. If visual impairment is noticed, jobs requiring keen vision should also be avoided until symptoms resolve.

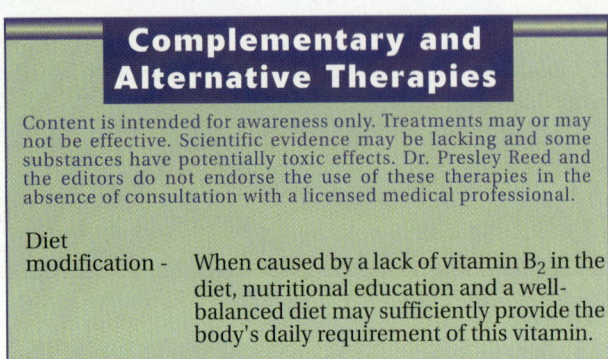

Complementary and Alternative Therapies

Content is intended for awareness only. Treatments may or may not be effective. Scientific evidence may be lacking and some substances have potentially toxic effects. Dr. Presley Reed and the editors do not endorse the use of these therapies in the absence of consultation with a licensed medical professional.

Diet modification - When caused by a lack of vitamin B$_2$ in the diet, nutritional education and a well-balanced diet may sufficiently provide the body's daily requirement of this vitamin.

Comorbid Conditions

Alcoholism, eating disorders, diabetes, chronic gastrointestinal disorders and chronic malnutrition may lengthen disability.

Complications

Individuals whose diets are lacking vitamin B$_2$ may also lack other essential nutrients. In such cases, vitamin B$_2$ deficiency may be complicated by a variety of other nutritional disorders.

Factors Influencing Duration

Factors depend on the severity of the disease, the response to treatment, and the individual's job requirements. If the individual is unable or unwilling to follow dietary and therapeutic instructions, disability may be permanent. In cases where the disorder is related to an underlying illness, treatment of that illness will impact the period of disability.

Length of Disability

Duration depends on severity. When adequately treated with vitamin B$_2$ (riboflavin) supplements and a healthy diet, signs and symptoms usually resolve completely with a period of weeks. Those with severe cases, or individuals with comorbid conditions, may have a longer recovery period.

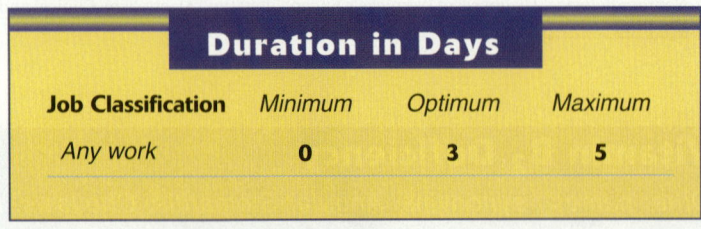

Duration in Days

Job Classification	Minimum	Optimum	Maximum
Any work	0	3	5

Failure to Recover

If an individual fails to recover within the maximum duration expectancy period, the reader may wish to reference the following questions to assist in better understanding the specifics of an individual's medical case.

Regarding diagnosis:

- Is individual a vegan? Does individual follow a fad diet?
- Does individual have anorexia nervosa, bulimia nervosa, or alcoholism?
- Does individual have chronic diarrhea or other chronic gastrointestinal diseases?
- Is there evidence of liver or kidney disease?
- Is individual poverty-stricken?
- Does individual have cataracts or sickle cell anemia?
- Does individual take the chemotherapeutic drug Adriamycin, oral contraceptives, tetracycline, or tricyclic antidepressants?
- Is there soreness around the mouth and throat? Sore and bright purplish-red tongue? Dry and cracking lips? Scaly skin on the face and scalp? Fatigue?
- Does individual complain of itchy eyes and sensitivity to light? Has there been a decrease in vision? Migraine headaches?
- Was glossitis observed on examination? Corneal neovascularization or pre-cataracts? Scrotal skin inflammation?
- Was an erythrocyte glutathione reductase activity done?
- Have conditions with similar symptoms been ruled out?

Regarding treatment:

- Is individual being treated with oral vitamin B$_2$ supplements that are part of a B-complex supplement?
- Has individual been trained in establishing and maintaining a healthy, well-balanced diet containing adequate amounts of vitamin B$_2$?
- Are any underlying conditions being treated?

Regarding prognosis:

- Can individual's employer accommodate any necessary restrictions?
- Does individual have any conditions that may affect ability to recover?
- Have any complications occurred such as other nutritional disorders?

References

Berkow, Robert, Mark Beers, and Andrew Fletcher, eds. "Vitamins and Minerals." The Merck Manual of Medical Information. Berkow, Robert, Mark Beers, and Andrew Fletcher, eds. New York: Pocket Books, 1997. 713-729.

Vitamin B_{12} Deficiency
Other names / synonyms: Cyanocobalamin Deficiency
266.2, 281.1

Definition

Vitamin B_{12} deficiency is a nutritional disorder caused by either a lack of this vitamin in the diet or by the body's inability to use it.

Vitamin B_{12} has many important functions. It is required for the formation and regeneration of red blood cells, it has an important role in maintaining a healthy nervous system, it is required for proper digestion, it aids in the absorption of calcium, and it promotes growth in children. Vitamin B_{12} is only produced by animals, so we need to eat animal products (e.g., meat, dairy products, poultry, fish) to get enough of this vitamin in our diets. In the stomach, acid and enzymes separate the vitamin from the proteins that carry it. The free vitamin is then passed into the small intestine and absorbed into the bloodstream. Some is used immediately, and some is stored in the liver or bone marrow.

Vitamin B_{12} deficiency has 2 possible causes. The most obvious cause is a diet that lacks a sufficient amount of this vitamin. Because vitamin B_{12} is abundant in a wide variety of readily available foods, this type of dietary deficiency is not very common. In fact, it generally only occurs in strict vegetarians (often referred to as vegans) who do not eat meats, dairy products, eggs, or fish. In addition, alcoholics and individuals with eating disorders such as anorexia nervosa or bulimia nervosa tend to have inadequate diets, which put them at risk for this vitamin deficiency.

The other cause of vitamin B_{12} deficiency is the body's inability to use the vitamin once it has been ingested. As described above, this vitamin must be processed in the stomach before it can be utilized. It also has to be absorbed in the small intestine so that it can enter the blood stream. If the stomach does not produce enough of the required acid or enzymes, or if the small intestine does not absorb the nutrient, a deficiency will result. Diseases of the small intestine such as Crohn's disease, or surgical removal of a portion of the small intestine, can result in too little of the vitamin being absorbed. Certain medications such as colchicine (used to treat gout) or Dilantin (used to treat seizures) interfere with vitamin B_{12} absorption, as do acid-reducing drugs that are used to treat ulcers. Excessive alcohol consumption can impair vitamin B_{12} absorption, and individuals with AIDS also have trouble absorbing this nutrient.

Other risk factors include stomach surgery, diseases of the pancreas, or the presence of a fish tapeworm. As we age, our stomachs produce less acid, so less vitamin B_{12} is freed from its carrier protein, and less is available for absorption. Thus, elderly people are at increased risk for this condition. A disease called pernicious anemia can also lead to vitamin B_{12} deficiency, since this disease prevents absorption in the small intestine. Interestingly, pernicious anemia is also a possible complication of vitamin B_{12} deficiency.

Vitamin B_{12} deficiency is an uncommon condition, although the exact incidence of this condition is not known. It affects men and women equally. In addition to those listed above, risk factors also include certain cancers or blood disorders.

Diagnosis

History: Individuals may complain of tiredness (fatigue), shortness of breath, weakness, headaches, heart palpitations, a "pins and needles" (paresthesia) sensation in their extremities, disturbed coordination and balance, decreased appetite, as well as nausea and diarrhea. They may also be aware of depression, confusion, memory loss, disorientation, and nervousness (anxiety).

Physical exam: The individual may be pale or the skin may have a yellowish color (jaundice). The heart rate may be abnormally fast (tachycardia). The exam may detect elevated body temperature (fever), an enlarged liver (hepatomegaly), enlarged spleen (splenomegaly), and a smooth, red, swollen tongue.

Tests: Blood tests will show a low level of vitamin B_{12} in the blood; however, this is not sufficient for a definitive diagnosis. A bone-marrow test can confirm diagnosis. In addition, the doctor may order a Schilling test, a procedure during which the individual is given vitamin B_{12} injections and tablets before tests are run to determine whether the vitamin is being absorbed.

Treatment

The first goal of treatment is to reverse the vitamin deficiency. This is done with vitamin B_{12} supplements (given orally or injected). When a dietary lack of vitamin B_{12} is responsible, the individual will be educated on good sources of this nutrient and the benefits of a well-balanced diet. Individuals who refuse to eat animal products will be prescribed oral vitamin B_{12} supplements for daily use. In cases where an underlying condition is contributing to/causing the vitamin deficiency, treatment of that underlying disease is critical to successful management of vitamin B_{12} deficiency.

Prognosis

Individuals usually see a dramatic improvement in their symptoms and well being within 5-7 days. Some individuals will require vitamin therapy for the remainder of their lives. In severe cases, the individual may be left with permanent neurological problems, including the possibility of paralysis. While rare, death may also occur.

Specialists

- Dietary Advisor
- Gastroenterologist
- Hematologist
- Neurologist
- Primary Care Provider
- Psychiatrist

Differential Diagnosis

Low levels of vitamin B_{12} in the blood can occur in several conditions including folate deficiency megaloblastic anemia, pregnancy, multiple myeloma, certain cancers, severe iron deficiency anemia, or following acute blood loss. In addition, low levels of B_{12} are seen in those who take megadoses of vitamin C, oral contraceptives, and certain other medications.

Work Restrictions / Accommodations

No work restrictions or accommodations should be necessary for most individuals. If the individual is experiencing a loss of balance, working in high places should be avoided. A "pins and needles" feeling in the extremities may make certain tasks difficult, such as standing or walking for a prolonged time, grasping or carrying objects, etc. If the individual's job requires these types of activities, reassignment to a different position may be helpful. In the rare case of paralysis, the individual will require workplace accommodations for a wheelchair, cane, walker, etc. If the individual is depressed, confused, or disoriented, he/she may need extended sick leave for recovery.

Complementary and Alternative Therapies

Content is intended for awareness only. Treatments may or may not be effective. Scientific evidence may be lacking and some substances have potentially toxic effects. Dr. Presley Reed and the editors do not endorse the use of these therapies in the absence of consultation with a licensed medical professional.

Diet modification - When caused by a lack of Vitamin B_{12} in the diet, nutritional education and a well-balanced diet may sufficiently provide the body's daily requirement of this vitamin.

Comorbid Conditions

Comorbid conditions include chronic gastrointestinal disorders, hypothyroidism, and a deficiency of folate, all of which may prolong recovery time.

Complications

Individuals with vitamin B_{12} deficiency are twice as likely as healthy individuals to develop stomach cancer. Some individuals with prolonged vitamin B_{12} deficiency will develop a condition called pernicious anemia. Untreated, this condition can lead to serious neuropathies. Individuals whose diets are lacking vitamin B_{12} may also lack other essential nutrients. In such cases, vitamin B_{12} deficiency may be complicated by a variety of other nutritional disorders.

Factors Influencing Duration

The period of disability will be determined by the type and severity of symptoms, the promptness of treatment, the job description, and the presence of an underlying cause. If symptoms include neurological problems, the disability may be permanent. If another disease is causing/contributing to vitamin B_{12} deficiency, that disease must be successfully treated for full recovery. Individuals who are unable or unwilling to follow a diet containing adequate amounts of vitamin B_{12} may need lifelong supplements; however, this should not affect their ability to work.

Length of Disability

Duration depends on nature and severity of symptoms and duration of symptoms prior to treatment. Most cases will see dramatic improvement in symptoms within 1 week of treatment. If the underlying cause is identified and corrected, full recovery can be expected. Failure of the individual to follow treatment will result in a relapse. For individuals with neurological complications and long duration of symptoms before treatment, disability may be permanent. In rare cases, nerve or brain damage can result in permanent disability or death.

Without complications.

Duration in Days

Job Classification	Minimum	Optimum	Maximum
Sedentary work	0	7	14
Light work	0	7	14
Medium work	0	7	14
Heavy work	0	7	14
Very Heavy work	0	7	14

With neurological complications.

Duration in Days

Job Classification	Minimum	Optimum	Maximum
Sedentary work	0	14	Indefinite
Light work	0	28	Indefinite
Medium work	0	84	Indefinite
Heavy work	0	168	Indefinite
Very Heavy work	0	168	Indefinite

Failure to Recover

If an individual fails to recover within the maximum duration expectancy period, the reader may wish to reference the following questions to assist in better understanding the specifics of an individual's medical case.

Regarding diagnosis:

- Does individual have an underlying condition (folate deficiency megaloblastic anemia, pregnancy, multiple myeloma, certain cancers, severe iron deficiency anemia, acute blood loss) that increases risk of B_{12} deficiency?
- Does individual take megadoses of vitamin C, oral contraceptives or any other medication that could interfere with B_{12} absorption?
- Has diagnosis of vitamin B_{12} deficiency been confirmed by a bone-marrow test?

- Has a Schilling test been done to determine whether the vitamin is being absorbed?
- Has an underlying cause of the deficiency been determined?

Regarding treatment:

- Is individual taking the vitamin supplementation as prescribed?
- Has individual received dietary consultation by a dietitian?
- Has individual been compliant in dietary recommendations?
- Has individual been reevaluated to determine if they are responding appropriately to treatment?

Regarding prognosis:

- Based on the underlying cause of the deficiency, what was the expected prognosis?
- Will this course of treatment resolve the condition, or will individual require lifetime vitamin therapy?
- Has individual experienced associated conditions (such as stomach cancer) or complications (such as neuropathies) that would impact recovery and prognosis?
- If so, how does this impact their occupation and activities?
- Have appropriate accommodations been made so individual can return safely to work?

References

"Vitamin B12 Deficiency." OnHealth. 02 Jan 1998 01 Jan 2001 <http://www.onhealth.webmd.com/conditions/in-depth/item/item%2C2509_1_1.asp>.

Diagnosis and Management of Vitamin B12 Deficiency. College of Physicians and Surgeons of Manitoba. 01 Sep 1995. 01 Jan 2001 <http://www.umanitoba.ca/cgi-bin/colleges/cps/college.cgi/326.html>.

Vitamin C Deficiency
Other names / synonyms: Ascorbic Acid Deficiency, Scurvy
267

Definition

Vitamin C deficiency (scurvy) is a nutritional disorder characterized by bleeding under the gums, skin, and fingernails; depression; tiredness (fatigue); and weakness.

Vitamin C (ascorbic acid) is essential for the formation of the tissue that holds the body's structures together (connective tissue). It also helps the body absorb the essential mineral, iron, and it helps the body recover from burns and wounds. Vitamin C is also a member of the class of chemicals called antioxidants. Antioxidants help protect the body's cells from damage.

Vitamin C is stored in limited quantities in the body. In fact, a healthy adult has about 3 months-worth of vitamin C stored away. Thus, it would take about 3 months without vitamin C for symptoms to begin to appear. Good sources of vitamin C include fruits, especially citrus fruits (e.g., oranges, grapefruits, lemons, limes), tomatoes, potatoes, cabbage, and sweet peppers.

Scurvy used to be a common illness when individuals didn't have access to fresh fruits and vegetables during the winter months. However, modern technology has improved such that the vast majority of people do have access to fresh produce all year. Because these foods are so widely available, scurvy is very rare in the US. Older individuals are at increased risk for this disorder because loneliness often leads to a lack of interest in eating, resulting in poor eating habits. Those who are chronically depressed are also at risk for the same reason. Alcoholics and individuals with eating disorders such as anorexia nervosa or bulimia nervosa are also at increased risk due to poor dietary habits. Certain conditions such as pregnancy, breastfeeding, overactivity of the thyroid gland (hyperthyroidism), inflammatory diseases, surgery, and burns will increase the body's need for vitamin C, thereby increasing the risk of deficiency. This nutritional disorder affects men and women equally.

Diagnosis

History: A dietary history will reveal a lack of fresh or canned fruits and vegetables. Individuals may complain of bleeding gums, loose teeth, bleeding under the fingernails or skin, muscle and joint pain, poor healing of wounds, and easy bruising. The individual may feel tired and/or weak and may also report depression.

Physical exam: Individuals may appear pale and in poor overall health. There may be black and blue marks on the backs of the legs (ecchymoses), tiny bright red spots on the skin (petechia), loose and missing teeth, and bleeding gums. The individual's breath may be foul. Heart rate and blood pressure may fluctuate. There may be wounds or burns that appear to be healing poorly. Severely ill individuals may have fever and convulsions.

Tests: Blood tests can show abnormal red blood cells (anemia) and low or absent levels of vitamin C. Blood tests also often reveal abnormally low levels of iron.

Treatment

Vitamin C deficiency is treated by administering oral vitamin C supplements daily until symptoms disappear. The individual will also be given a list of vitamin C-rich foods, instruction on the value of a well-balanced, healthy diet, and guidance on how to maintain such a diet.

If another disease is involved (alcoholism, anorexia nervosa, bulimia nervosa, depression, etc.) treatment of that disease is important for recovery. In cases where the physician believes that a well-balanced diet will not be maintained (e.g., in cases of alcoholism, anorexia nervosa, bulimia nervosa, etc.), dietary supplements may be prescribed for use on a regular basis.

Prognosis

The prognosis for recovery from vitamin C deficiency is excellent in adults. Vitamin C supplements and a healthy diet will result in a complete recovery in nearly all individuals. In very rare cases, bleeding may occur in the brain, which can result in death.

Differential Diagnosis

Acute blood disorders such as leukemias can mimic some of the physical signs.

Specialists

- Dietary Advisor
- Hematologist
- Primary Care Provider
- Psychologist

Work Restrictions / Accommodations

Vitamin C deficiency is easily treatable and work restrictions or accommodations are not usually necessary. During the recovery period, individuals with muscle or joint pain may have difficulty with certain physical tasks (grasping, typing, strenuous activity, prolonged walking, etc.), which should be avoided until symptoms resolve. Pronounced tiredness and/or weakness may require sick leave.

Comorbid Conditions

Pancreatic or intestinal disease, pernicious anemia, or other vitamin deficiencies may lengthen disability.

Complications

Scurvy may be complicated by severe bleeding into muscles, joints, or organs (such as the brain). Such complications can be fatal, depending on the affected organ, the extent of bleeding, and the promptness of treatment.

Individuals whose diets are lacking vitamin C may also lack other essential nutrients. In such cases, vitamin C deficiency may be complicated by a variety of other nutritional disorders.

Factors Influencing Duration

Inability or unwillingness to follow the recommended diet may lengthen disability.

Length of Disability

Duration depends on severity. Those with jobs requiring heavy work or prolonged exercise may have a longer disability period.

Duration in Days

Job Classification	Minimum	Optimum	Maximum
Any work	0	7	14

Failure to Recover

If an individual fails to recover within the maximum duration expectancy period, the reader may wish to reference the following questions to assist in better understanding the specifics of an individual's medical case.

Regarding diagnosis:

- Does individual have bleeding under the gums, skin, and fingernails? Has individual experienced depression, fatigue, and weakness? Is there muscle or joint pain? Does individual bruise easily? Do wounds heal poorly?
- Is individual older and lonely? Depressed? Alcoholic?
- Does individual have anorexia nervosa or bulimia nervosa?
- Is individual pregnant or breastfeeding?
- Does individual have hyperthyroidism or inflammatory diseases? Had surgery or burns?
- Is individual's diet deficient in fruits and vegetables?
- On exam, does individual appear pale and in poor overall health?
- Are there ecchymosis on the backs of the legs, petechia on the skin, loose and missing teeth, and bleeding gums? Is individual's breath foul?
- Do heart rate and blood pressure fluctuate? Are there wounds or burns that are healing poorly? Does individual have fever and convulsions?
- Did individual have blood testing for vitamin C levels?
- Have conditions with similar symptoms been ruled out?

Regarding treatment:

- Is individual receiving daily oral vitamin C supplements?
- Was individual given instruction on a well-balanced diet? Foods rich in vitamin C? How to maintain such a diet?
- Has an underlying condition been treated? Is individual compliant with the treatment regime?
- If needed, has individual sought help from an appropriate mental health professional?

Regarding prognosis:

- Can individual's employer accommodate any necessary restrictions?
- Does individual have any conditions that may affect ability to recover?
- Have any complications occurred such as severe bleeding into muscles, joints, or organs such as the brain? Does individual have any other nutritional disorders?

References

Berkow, Robert, Mark Beers, and Andrew Fletcher, eds. "Vitamins and Minerals." The Merck Manual of Medical Information. Berkow, Robert, Mark Beers, and Andrew Fletcher, eds. New York: Pocket Books, 1997. 713-729.

Vitamin D Deficiency

Other names / synonyms: Osteomalacia, Rickets
268, 268.0, 268.2, 268.9

Definition

Vitamin D deficiency is a nutritional disorder characterized in adults by softening of the bones. In children it manifests as rickets and in adults as osteomalacia.

Vitamin D is an essential nutrient that increases serum calcium levels by facilitating calcium absorption and mobilizing calcium from bone. It also absorbs calcium and phosphorous from the diet. Without vitamin D, these minerals are not absorbed in sufficient quantities. Because calcium and phosphorous are important in forming and maintaining healthy bones and teeth, a deficiency in vitamin D has a profound effect on these structures.

Vitamin D deficiency is a relatively rare condition since it is found in many foods such as fortified milk, margarine, eggs, liver, fish, and fish oils. The body can also make vitamin D when the skin is exposed to sunlight. A lack of vitamin D in the diet is usually only seen in strict vegetarians (vegans) who avoid all animal products including dairy products and eggs. Individuals who avoid exposure to sunlight or wear protective sunscreen may limit the body's ability to make vitamin D, thereby increasing the need to rely on dietary sources. Another cause of vitamin D deficiency is an inability of the body to absorb the vitamin during digestion (malabsorption) or an inability to process the vitamin once it is absorbed. These individuals may experience a deficiency despite a healthy, balanced diet and normal sun exposure. Certain medications used to treat seizures can also cause vitamin D deficiency.

The risk of developing osteomalacia is higher in those who are housebound, institutionalized, elderly, poor, or required by custom to be completely covered when outdoors. Those with dark skin are also at increased risk. Certain diseases of the kidney, pancreas, liver, intestines, or stomach may also increase the risk of vitamin D deficiency. Alcoholics, individuals with eating disorders such as anorexia nervosa or bulimia nervosa, and those who follow diets that severely limit certain foods (fad diets) have a greater risk of developing vitamin D deficiency. Individuals who abuse laxatives are also at increased risk.

The overall incidence of osteomalacia is 1 in every 1,000 individuals. Pregnancy and breast-feeding increase a woman's need for vitamin D and therefore increase the risk of deficiency. Women are affected slightly more often than men. The recommended daily allowance (RDA) for vitamin D is 400 IU.

Diagnosis

History: Individuals may complain of bone pain particularly around the hips. Muscle weakness is also commonly reported. Some individuals may feel such discomfort and weakness that they choose to remain in bed. Fracturing bones after only minor trauma is also significant history. Individuals may report other symptoms such as tiredness (fatigue), muscle pain, loss of appetite (anorexia), unintentional weight loss, numbness around the mouth, tingling and/or numbness of the extremities (hands, arms, legs, feet), or muscle spasms (tetany) of the hands or feet. Lack of calcium can also cause confusion, memory loss, depression, and hallucinations.

Physical exam: The exam may reveal that the individual has lost inches in height due to collapse of the vertebrae. Reported bone pain is usually dull and spread over a large area (diffuse). Muscle weakness may be evident in the muscles close to the affected bone(s). Questioning the individual on dietary habits may reveal a lack of food sources that are typically rich in vitamin D. Further questioning may also reveal that the individual avoids being outdoors or carefully applies sunscreen before leaving the house.

Tests: Routine blood tests reveal abnormal levels of calcium and phosphate. An x-ray and/or CT of the bone(s) confirm the diagnosis. In most cases, these tests in combination with symptoms and history is sufficient for a definitive diagnosis, however, in unusual cases, a bone biopsy may be necessary to determine the extent of the mineral loss.

Treatment

When vitamin D deficiency is caused by lack of sunlight or poor diet, individuals are given oral vitamin D supplements for up to 4 months. Calcium supplements may also be given.

If the deficiency is due to an underlying condition that prevents absorption or metabolism of vitamin D, successful treatment depends on treatment of the underlying condition. These individuals may require larger doses of vitamin D as well as megadoses of calcium. Depending on the nature of the underlying disease, these supplements may need to be given by injection. Controlled exposure to sunlight or a sunlamp may also be prescribed. Treatment for osteoporosis may also be needed.

All individuals require regular follow-up visits with their doctor to monitor progress.

Prognosis

Individuals whose deficiency is due to inadequate sunlight or poor diet are usually completely cured after 6 months of vitamin D supplements and/or sunlight exposure. If an underlying condition is causing or contributing to vitamin D deficiency, this disorder must be treated for a successful outcome. If a healthy, well-balanced diet is not maintained, vitamin D deficiency can recur.

Differential Diagnosis

Osteoporosis, Paget's disease of bone, and cancer may have similar symptoms. Phosphorous metabolism and absorption disorders can also cause osteomalacia.

Specialists

- Dietary Advisor
- Endocrinologist
- Internist

Work Restrictions / Accommodations

In most cases, work restrictions and accommodations are not necessary. For some individuals, heavy lifting and other strenuous work may need to be discontinued or adjusted. Work schedule flexibility may be required following the diagnosis to accommodate regular examinations at the physician's office. However, if symptoms are severe, individuals may require extended sick leave from work until symptoms begin to subside.

Complementary and Alternative Therapies

Content is intended for awareness only. Treatments may or may not be effective. Scientific evidence may be lacking and some substances have potentially toxic effects. Dr. Presley Reed and the editors do not endorse the use of these therapies in the absence of consultation with a licensed medical professional.

Diet modification -	Vitamin D may aid in balancing the diet and is found in foods such as fortified milk, margarine, eggs, liver, fish, and fish oils. Strict vegetarians (vegans) who avoid all animal products including dairy and eggs can supplement their diets with oral vitamin D and calcium supplements. Consultation with a nutritionist can help ensure that a balanced diet is being consumed.
Light therapy -	Vitamin D is produced in the skin when exposed to ultraviolet light such as sunlight. Individuals who avoid exposure to sunlight or wear too much protective sunscreen may limit the body's ability to make vitamin D, thereby increasing the need to rely on dietary sources. Spending time outdoors or in a sunny window or the prudent use of a sunlamp may help supplement the body's need for vitamin D.

Comorbid Conditions

Malnutrition, pregnancy, and epilepsy may prolong the recovery period.

Complications

Complications of vitamin D deficiency include bone fractures, infection of the bones (osteomyelitis), kidney (renal) failure, renal tubular acidosis, or seizures. In addition, individuals are often deficient in other vitamins and/or minerals as well as vitamin D, complicating the condition.

Factors Influencing Duration

Length of disability depends on the individual's symptoms and severity of those symptoms, response to treatment, underlying illness that may be causing or contributing to the vitamin D deficiency, complications or comorbid conditions, and individual's job requirements. Individuals who perform sedentary work may have a shorter disability period. Recovery also depends on the individual's compliance with the treatment regimen (e.g., use of vitamin supplements, a healthy diet, regular doctor's visits) for the vitamin deficiency and any underlying disease. Individuals who fail to comply with the treatment regimen may have a longer recovery period. Untreated cases can result in permanent disability.

Length of Disability

Duration depends on severity. If the deficiency is treated inconsistently, symptoms may recur, persist, or even worsen. Untreated deficiency can lead to permanent disability.

Duration in Days

Job Classification	Minimum	Optimum	Maximum
Sedentary work	0	7	14
Light work	0	7	14
Medium work	0	7	14
Heavy work	0	14	28
Very Heavy work	0	14	28

Failure to Recover

If an individual fails to recover within the maximum duration expectancy period, the reader may wish to reference the following questions to assist in better understanding the specifics of an individual's medical case.

Regarding diagnosis:

- Has the individual complained of bone pain (particularly in the hips) or fatigue and paresthesias of fingers or hands?
- Does the individual have risk factors for vitamin D deficiency such as inadequate consumption of dairy products (such as vegans, or those with lactose intolerance or those who do not have access to dairy products)?
- Has the individual been housebound or lacked exposure to sunlight? Are they taking any medications that could cause the deficiency?
- Was the vitamin deficiency detected with serological testing? If not, was a bone biopsy indicated?
- If the diagnosis was uncertain, were other conditions with similar symptoms such as osteoporosis, Paget's disease of bone, and cancer, ruled out?

Regarding treatment:

- Were vitamin D and/or calcium supplements prescribed? Is the individual taking the recommended dose at the recommended times?
- Is the individual eating a healthy, balanced diet? Are foods rich in vitamin D being consumed? Would individual benefit from consultation with a nutritionist/dietitian?
- Does the individual spend time outdoors or in a sunny window?
- Is individual also being treated for osteoporosis?

Regarding prognosis:

- Based on the underlying cause, what was the expected outcome?
- Is individual a strict vegetarian? Would individual benefit from consultation with a nutritionist/dietitian?
- Does the individual have any underlying conditions (malnutrition, pregnancy or epilepsy) that could impact recovery?
- Did the individual experience any associated conditions or complications (such as bone fractures, osteomyelitis, renal disorders, or seizures) that could impact recovery and prognosis?

References

"Vitamins and Minerals." *The Merck Manual of Medical Information.* Berkow, Robert, Mark Beers, and Andrew Fletcher, eds. New York: Pocket Books, 1997. 713-729.

National Library of Medicine. "Vitamin D and Related Compounds (Systemic)." *Medline Plus Health Information.* 16 Aug 2000. 26 Dec 2000 <http://www.nlm.nih.gov/medlineplus/druginfo/vitamindandrelatedcompoundssys202597.html>.

Vitamin E Deficiency
269.1

Definition

Vitamin E is an essential nutrient important in protecting the body's cells from damage. It also functions as an antioxidant and decreases low-density lipoprotein (LDL) cholesterol levels. It is important in the formation of red blood cells and assists in the body's use of vitamin K. It also has an important role in nerve function. Vitamin E deficiency is a very rare nutritional disorder characterized by a loss of nerve function (particularly in the legs), muscle weakness, abnormal red blood cells (hemolytic anemia), and decreased reflexes.

There are many sources of vitamin E including vegetable oils, margarine, shortening, leafy-green vegetables, wheat germ, whole grains, beans, seeds, and nuts. In addition to being widely available, the body typically stores about a 1-year supply of this vitamin in fat tissue. The combination of ample reserves and wide availability make pure dietary deficiency of this vitamin highly unlikely. In fact, vitamin E deficiency is very rare and has only been documented in premature infants with a very low birth weight and individuals who fail to absorb fat from their diet.

Since vitamin E is a fat-soluble vitamin, absorption of this nutrient is dependent on absorption of fat. Inability to absorb fat from the diet can occur in certain medical conditions such as cystic fibrosis, insufficiency of the pancreas, chronic blockage of the bile ducts (cholestasis), Crohn's disease, and uncontrolled intestinal diseases. Individuals with these conditions are at increased risk for developing vitamin E deficiency. Individuals with certain eating disorders (anorexia nervosa, bulimia nervosa) or those who drastically limit fat from the diet are also at increased risk of vitamin E deficiency. Additional risks and incidence of this disorder varies with the underlying condition. The recommended daily allowance (RDA) of vitamin E is 30 IU.

Diagnosis

History: In many cases, the individual will not notice any symptoms and the condition is diagnosed incidentally following examination for some other reason. When symptoms are evident, the individual or family members may notice poor coordination and difficulty walking (ataxia). Often, individuals lose the ability to sense the position of their legs. Muscle weakness is also a common complaint. Due to impairment of the muscles that control the eyes, double vision (diplopia) may be reported.

Physical exam: Vitamin E deficiency does not cause many physical signs. The physician may notice brownish discoloration of the skin, muscle weakness, impaired muscle coordination, and slow or absent reflexes.

Tests: A blood test may reveal low levels of vitamin E that confirm the diagnosis. An analysis of the red blood cells may reveal a condition called hemolytic anemia.

Treatment

Vitamin E deficiency is treated with vitamin E supplements. These supplements may be taken by mouth (orally) or injection. Injection is the preferred method of administration if absorption through the gastrointestinal tract is significantly impaired due to an underlying disease.

Prognosis

Vitamin E supplements are successful in relieving symptoms. If nerve damage has occurred, complete recovery may take several months.

Differential Diagnosis

Vitamin E deficiency shares symptoms with several disorders of the central nervous system. Such neurological conditions should be definitively ruled out before a diagnosis of vitamin E deficiency is made.

Specialists

- Hematologist
- Internist
- Neurologist
- Ophthalmologist
- Physical Therapist

Work Restrictions / Accommodations

In many cases, the individual will not have symptoms, so specific work restrictions or accommodations are not required. If symptoms are evident, restrictions and accommodations depend on the particulars of the symptoms, severity of those symptoms, and individual's job requirements. For example, if muscle coordination is impaired, individuals whose jobs require such coordination may need a temporary reassignment. In some cases, extended sick leave may be required (e.g., a surgeon with double vision or loss of muscle coordination; a heavy laborer with severe muscle weakness; a professional dancer with a loss of position sense).

Comorbid Conditions

Chronic liver disease, prior surgical removal of the stomach, alcoholism, and malnutrition may lengthen the recovery period.

Complications

Vitamin E deficiency itself is not associated with complications. However, an underlying disease (e.g., cystic fibrosis, Crohn's disease, or pancreatic insufficiency) may be associated with its own complications.

Factors Influencing Duration

Type and severity of symptoms, the individual's response to treatment, characteristics of the underlying condition, and the individual's job requirements influence disability. Many individuals do not experience symptoms and so will not have a period of disability. When symptoms are present, disability varies significantly depending on the individual's job requirements and responsibilities. Some individuals require extended sick leave during recovery.

Length of Disability

Duration depends on severity.

Duration in Days

Job Classification	Minimum	Optimum	Maximum
Any work	0	3	5

Failure to Recover

If an individual fails to recover within the maximum duration expectancy period, the reader may wish to reference the following questions to assist in better understanding the specifics of an individual's medical case.

Regarding diagnosis:

- Did the individual experience symptoms of muscle weakness or decreased reflexes?
- Has the diagnosis of vitamin E deficiency been confirmed by a blood test? Were certain neurological disorders with similar symptoms ruled out?
- Does the individual have an underlying condition that may impair fat and vitamin E absorption, such as cystic fibrosis, pancreatic disease, cholestasis, or inflammatory bowel disease?
- Has the underlying cause of vitamin E deficiency been identified?

Regarding treatment:

- Are vitamin E supplements being taken as prescribed?
- Would administration by injection be more efficient?

Regarding prognosis:

- Have the symptoms resolved with treatment?
- Has adequate time elapsed for recovery (several months)?
- If the symptoms have persisted, have dosage adjustments been made?
- Have additional nerve studies been done to rule out associated nerve damage?
- Does the individual have any underlying conditions such as chronic liver disease, prior surgical removal of the stomach, alcoholism, or malnutrition that could impact recovery and prognosis?

References

"Vitamins and Minerals." The Merck Manual of Medical Information. Berkow, Robert, Mark Beers, and Andrew Fletcher, eds. New York: Pocket Books, 1997. 713-729.

Meydani, Mohsen, and K.C. Hayes. Nutrient Information: Vitamin E. American Society for Nutritional Sciences. 01 Jan 1999. 01 Jan 2001 <http://www.nutrition.org/nutinfo/content/vie.shtml>.

Vitamin K Deficiency
269.0, 776.0

Definition

Vitamin K deficiency is a nutritional disorder in which the blood fails to clot normally, resulting in excessive bleeding. Vitamin K is a generic term for several related compounds that are essential for normal blood-clotting and bone metabolism. A small amount of this nutrient is stored in the liver and bone, but these reserves will be depleted within 1 week without additional intake.

In adults, vitamin K is obtained in the diet as well as produced by bacteria that normally live in the intestines. Food sources of this vitamin include cooked, dark green vegetables such as spinach, kale, and broccoli; fermented soy products (e.g., natto); kiwi; cabbage; liver; soybean, canola, and olive oils, as well as margarines and mayonnaise made from these oils; alfalfa, oats, wheat, and rye; and fishmeal. Because of the wide availability and the body's ability to produce this nutrient, vitamin K deficiency is very rare in adults.

Vitamin K deficiency occurs in 4 circumstances: in breast-fed infants whose intestines do not contain the necessary bacteria to produce vitamin K, in individuals with diseases that impair the absorption of fat from the diet, in those who combine a lack of vegetable foods with an antibiotic that destroys the intestinal bacteria (eliminating both sources of the vitamin), and in those who need to take medicine (anticoagulants) to reduce clotting in the veins.

Vitamin K is a fat-soluble vitamin, and absorption of this nutrient is dependent upon absorption of fat. Inability to absorb fat from the diet can occur in certain medical conditions such as cystic fibrosis, insufficiency of the pancreas, chronic blockage of the bile ducts (cholestasis), Crohn's disease, and uncontrolled intestinal diseases. Individuals with these conditions are at increased risk for developing vitamin K deficiency. Clotting factors are made in the liver, so certain liver diseases impair this function, hereby increasing one's risk of vitamin K deficiency. Individuals with certain eating disorders (anorexia nervosa, bulimia nervosa) or those who drastically limit fat from the diet are also at increased risk of vitamin K deficiency.

Again, overall, this disorder is very rare in adults. Additional risks and incidence of this disorder will vary with the underlying condition.

Diagnosis

History: The primary symptom of vitamin K deficiency is abnormal bleeding. Common complaints include prolonged bleeding following even minor cuts, bleeding under the skin, or from the nose. Bleeding into the stomach may cause the individual to vomit blood. The individual may also notice blood in the urine or stool.

Physical exam: The exam is often unremarkable. In severe cases, the individual may be weak and pale due to loss of blood. Questioning the individual may reveal use of medications to prevent clotting (anticoagulants) or to prevent infection (antibiotics). A dietary history may also reveal a lack of foods rich in vitamin K.

Tests: A blood test will reveal low levels of a clotting factor called prothrombin. Since prothrombin levels can be low for reasons other than vitamin K deficiency, the diagnosis will usually be confirmed by administering an injection of vitamin K. If the vitamin K injection increases the prothrombin level and stops the bleeding, the diagnosis of vitamin K deficiency is confirmed.

Treatment

Vitamin K deficiency is treated by administering vitamin K supplements. These supplements may be taken by mouth (orally) or they may be injected. Injection is the preferred method of administration if bleeding is severe or absorption through the gastrointestinal tract is significantly impaired due to an underlying disease.

If a poor diet is a contributing factor, the individual will be provided a list of foods rich in vitamin K. Instruction and guidance on the importance of a well-balanced, healthy diet will be provided.

In cases where liver disease is contributing to the vitamin deficiency, a transfusion of plasma may be necessary to replenish clotting factors.

Prognosis

In most cases, a full recovery can be expected. Vitamin K supplements are successful in relieving symptoms for most individuals. If the liver is unable to manufacture clotting factors, transfusions of plasma are effective in replenishing the supply of these factors. Such transfusions may be required periodically, depending on the course of the underlying liver disease. If uncontrolled internal bleeding occurs, the prognosis may be less positive, depending on the site of the bleeding and the promptness of emergency treatment. In severe cases, uncontrolled bleeding can result in shock and even death.

Differential Diagnosis

Conditions that produce similar symptoms include liver damage, anticoagulant therapy, salicylate therapy, other hemorrhagic conditions (scurvy, allergic purpura, leukemia, thrombocytopenia), or hemophilia.

Specialists

- Cardiologist
- Dietary Advisor
- Emergency Medicine
- Gastroenterologist
- Hematologist
- Infectious Disease Physician
- Primary Care Provider

Work Restrictions / Accommodations

In most cases, vitamin K supplements will reverse symptoms quickly and completely, and no work restrictions or accommodations should be necessary. In severe or complicated cases, individuals may require extended sick leave for recovery.

Complementary and Alternative Therapies

Content is intended for awareness only. Treatments may or may not be effective. Scientific evidence may be lacking and some substances have potentially toxic effects. Dr. Presley Reed and the editors do not endorse the use of these therapies in the absence of consultation with a licensed medical professional.

Diet modification - To increase dietary intake of vitamin K, good sources include cooked, dark green vegetables such as spinach, kale, and broccoli; fermented soy products (e.g., natto); kiwi; cabbage; liver; soybean, canola, and olive oils, as well as margarines and mayonnaise made from these oils; alfalfa, oats, wheat, and rye; and fishmeal.

Comorbid Conditions

Chronic liver disease, hemophilia, prior surgical removal of the stomach, alcoholism, and malnutrition may lengthen the recovery period.

Complications

Vitamin K deficiency may be complicated by uncontrolled internal bleeding and possible shock and death. In addition, an underlying disease (e.g., cystic fibrosis, Crohn's disease, pancreatic insufficiency, etc.) may be associated with its own complications.

Vitamin K has also been linked to proper bone metabolism. While this function is not clearly understood, deficiency of vitamin K may contribute to the progression of osteoporosis.

Factors Influencing Duration

Disability will be influenced by the type and severity of symptoms, the individual's response to treatment, the characteristics of the underlying condition, and the individual's job requirements. Many individuals will not experience a period of disability. In others, disability will vary significantly with the individual's job requirements and responsibilities. Some will require extended sick leave during recovery.

Length of Disability

Duration depends on severity.

Duration in Days

Job Classification	Minimum	Optimum	Maximum
Any work	0	3	5

Failure to Recover

If an individual fails to recover within the maximum duration expectancy period, the reader may wish to reference the following questions to assist in better understanding the specifics of an individual's medical case.

Regarding diagnosis:

- Has individual experienced symptoms of spontaneous or excessive bleeding (such as easy bruising, bleeding gums, excessive menstrual bleeding, etc.) that may be associated with vitamin K deficiency?
- Has diagnosis of vitamin K deficiency been confirmed?
- Have other conditions with similar symptoms such as liver damage, anticoagulant therapy, salicylate therapy, other hemorrhagic conditions (scurvy, allergic purpura, leukemia, thrombocytopenia), or hemophilia been ruled out?
- Has cause of vitamin K deficiency (i.e., impaired fat absorption, inadequate intestinal bacterial from antibiotic therapy, anorexia, or bulimia nervosa) been determined?

Regarding treatment:

- Have antibiotics been eliminated in an effort to allow regrowth of intestinal bacterial?
- Is individual taking vitamin K supplements as prescribed?
- If not, would administration by injection be more beneficial?
- If a poor diet is a contributing factor, would individual benefit from consultation with a nutritionist?
- Is inadequate diet due to limited finances?
- Would individual benefit from a community subsidy program?
- If related to an eating disorder, is individual receiving psychological counseling?
- Are underlying medical conditions being adequately managed?
- Would individual benefit from a plasma transfusion?

Regarding prognosis:

- Is individual taking supplements?
- What can be done to enhance compliance?
- Would vitamin K supplementation by injection be more suitable for this individual?
- Does individual have an underlying condition such as liver disease, Crohn's disease, pancreatic insufficiency, cystic fibrosis, hemophilia, prior surgical removal of the stomach, alcoholism, or malnutrition that may impact recovery?
- Are these conditions being addressed appropriately in the treatment plan?
- Does individual need financial assistance in acquiring an adequate diet?

References

"Vitamins and Minerals." The Merck Manual of Medical Information. Berkow, Robert, Mark Beers, and Andrew Fletcher, eds. New York: Pocket Books, 1997. 713-729.

Kohlmeier, Martin, MD, and John W. Suttie. Nutrient Information: Vitamin K. American Society for Nutritional Sciences. 01 Jan 2001. 28 Feb 2001 <http://www.nutrition.org/nutinfo/content/vik.shtml>.

Vitiligo
Other names / synonyms: Acromia, Leucoderma, Piebald
709.01

Definition

Vitiligo is a common skin disorder where patches of skin lose their color (pigmentation).

Characterized by milk-white sharply defined, irregular shaped, flat patches or spots surrounded by the normal skin color, vitiligo occurs most commonly on the face, hands, armpits, and groin. It can range from a single white spot to multiple spots and has a tendency to start as a single spot and eventually grow in size and number. It can also spread from one part of the body to another with spread usually being slow and progressive. Vitiligo results from a loss of the cells that secrete melanin, the substance that gives skin its color. These cells are called melanocytes and they help protect skin from the sun's harmful rays. Consequently, skin areas affected by vitiligo are particularly sensitive to sunlight.

Vitiligo is classified into subtypes based on the distribution of skin lesions. The most common subtype is generalized vitiligo (vitiligo vulgaris) that occurs randomly throughout the whole body. The second most common subtype is the acrofacial subtype that affects the extremities and the face. Less common subtypes affect the extremities (acral vitiligo), one specific body area (localized vitiligo), and areas supplied by certain nerve segments or dermatomes (segmental vitiligo). Vitiligo may affect the retina of the eye in 39% of individuals, but usually does not affect vision. Vitiligo can also affect the nerves of the ears with 16% of individuals having some mild hearing loss.

The exact cause of vitiligo is unknown although genetic, biochemical (hormonal), autoimmune, viral, and chemical causes are suggested. In 30% of individuals, the onset of vitiligo can be precipitated by factors such as emotional stress, physical illness, infection, sunburn, areas of physical pressure (tight clothing, particularly in the belt area), or trauma. It is associated with other skin disorders such as hair loss (alopecia areata), psoriasis, premature graying of the hair, and certain systemic disorders such as thyroid disorders (hypo- and hyperthyroidism), systemic lupus erythematosus (SLE), pernicious anemia, Addison's disease, Grave's disease, or diabetes mellitus.

Although vitiligo can occur at any age, it usually develops in early adulthood, particularly in the second and third decades of life. It affects 1-2% of the population but familial incidence is as high as 20-30%. It is most commonly found in blacks and those living in tropical climates. It is also more noticeable in individuals with darker colored skin because of the contrasting patches. Although vitiligo usually develops gradually over a period of years, about 30% of individuals have a sudden reversal of symptoms (repigmentation).

Diagnosis

History: Aside from loss of skin color, vitiligo has no other symptoms. If vitiligo affects the scalp (vitiligo capitis), the hairs growing out of the affected area also lose their color. Many individuals relate that graying of scalp hair preceded the appearance of the vitiligo.

Physical exam: Loss of pigment is the only skin change that occurs.

Tests: Skin biopsy rules out other skin diseases. In vitiligo, there is a complete lack of melanin production in the nonpigmented areas.

Treatment

Most vitiligo goes untreated. The usual remedy is to mask the white patches with cosmetics and in mild cases, may be all that is necessary.

Giving the individuals photosensitizing compounds then exposing them to ultraviolet light (PUVA phototherapy) has caused the color to return (repigmentation) in more that 50% of cases, but requires many treatments. Steroidal anti-inflammatory (corticosteroid), or 8-methoxypsoralen or trimethylpsoralen medications applied topically as creams, taken orally, or given by injection are effective in mild vitiligo if less than 10% of body surface is involved. If areas of vitiligo are extensive (over 50% of the body), certain chemicals may be used to bleach the pigment from remaining areas of normal skin so as not to be so noticeable (depigmentation). Melanocytes (melanin-forming cells) can also be transplanted from pigmented areas to nonpigmented areas. Very small areas of vitiligo can be treated surgically with a form of tattooing (micropigmentation).

Therapy should take into account the individual's motivation, psychological impact of the disease, and visible extent of the disease. There may be severe psychological effects as a result of this condition particularly among certain cultures where varying skin hues have heightened significance. Counseling may be beneficial.

Prognosis

About 30% of individuals affected with vitiligo undergo a spontaneous repigmentation. Intensive phototherapy has resulted in repigmentation in more than 50% of cases. Results of treatment with steroids are variable with some amount of repigmentation occurring in 10-80% of cases. Bleaching (depigmentation) normal skin in cases of extensive vitiligo is very successful with 80% of individuals satisfied with the results.

Differential Diagnosis

Several diseases of hypopigmentation can resemble vitiligo. These include Vogt-Koyanagi-Harada syndrome, albinism, chemical leukoderma, piebaldism, hypermelanosis of Ito, poliosis, idiopathic guttate hypomelanosis, scleroderma, postinflammatory hypopigmentation, nevus depigmentosus, nevus anemicus, tinea, versicolor, sarcoidosis, and pityriasis alba.

Specialists

- Dermatologist

Work Restrictions / Accommodations

No work restrictions are expected. Some accommodation may be necessary if the individual is in the public eye and is psychologically affected by the perception of disfigurement. Short periods of time off for counseling may be necessary.

> **Complementary and Alternative Therapies**
>
> Content is intended for awareness only. Treatments may or may not be effective. Scientific evidence may be lacking and some substances have potentially toxic effects. Dr. Presley Reed and the editors do not endorse the use of these therapies in the absence of consultation with a licensed medical professional.
>
> Sunscreen - A strong sunscreen with a SPF of 15 or above should be used whenever individual is outdoors. Not only is the depigmented skin more vulnerable to burning and sun damage but also exposure to the sun darkens the adjacent, normal-colored skin, thereby accentuating the blemish.
>
> Artificial tanning solutions - May help to darken the depigmented areas, however, a dermatologist should be consulted before using.

Comorbid Conditions

There are no comorbid conditions that would lengthen disability.

Complications

Because the areas of vitiligo are particularly sensitive to sunlight, careful precautions must be taken to prevent sunburn. Sunscreens that contain high sun protection factor (SPF) must be worn.

Factors Influencing Duration

Disability is not expected unless complications from treatment occur or if individual becomes clinically depressed as a result of the condition and requires some counseling.

Length of Disability

No disability is expected.

Failure to Recover

If an individual fails to recover within the maximum duration expectancy period, the reader may wish to reference the following questions to assist in better understanding the specifics of an individual's medical case.

Regarding diagnosis:

- Does individual have a history of emotional stress, physical illness, infection, sunburn, or trauma?
- Were genetic, biochemical, autoimmune, viral, or chemical causes explored?
- Does individual complain only of loss of skin color?
- If the scalp is affected, does individual relate that graying of scalp hair preceded appearance of the vitiligo? Has the hair growing out of the affected area lost color?

- Was a sample of skin tissue (biopsy) taken to rule out other skin diseases?
- Was the diagnosis of vitiligo confirmed?

Regarding treatment:

- If the vitiligo is mild, are cosmetics used to mask the white patches and/or corticosteroid medications used topically or orally?
- Was PUVA (phototherapy) initiated to cause the color to return (repigmentation)? If so, how many treatments are required?
- If vitiligo is extensive, were chemicals used to bleach the pigment from remaining areas of normal skin?
- Were melanocytes (melanin-forming cells) transplanted from pigmented areas to nonpigmented areas?
- If the vitiligo is confined to a very small area, was surgical treatment with a form of tattooing (micropigmentation) done?
- Were treatments successful?

Regarding prognosis:

- Did individual undergo spontaneous repigmentation or was treatment required?
- How successful were attempts to repigment the skin?
- Was the extent of psychological impact of the disease on individual fully considered?
- Would individual benefit from psychological counseling especially if the vitiligo is extensive or disfiguring?

References

Grimes, Pearl E. "Diseases of Hypopigmentation." Principles and Practice of Dermatology, 2nd ed. Sams, W. Mitchell, and Peter J. Lynch, eds. New York: Churchill Livingstone, 1996. 843-859.

Shah, Rajesh. "Vitiligo Information and Treatment." Homeopathy India Foundation 25 Jul 1999 20 Feb 2001 <http://www.vitiligocure.com>.

Vocational Therapy
93.85

Definition

Vocational therapy is often used in combination with a structured rehabilitation program and is designed to enable the disabled individual to resume productive employment. Individuals who have experienced changes in their mental or physical function due to illness or injury may require vocational therapy to allow them to return to work. Vocational therapy works with individuals and their new physical or mental status to find an appropriate occupational match.

Vocational therapy involves an assessment phase where the individual's skills and aptitudes are evaluated through tests, which is an integral part of vocational therapy. These tests may take several forms and are used to assess an individual's general intelligence level, his of her aptitudes, interests, and work skills. For example, an individual's performance in a series of standardized tests may be compared to a list of essential aptitudes that are grouped by occupations and listed in the Dictionary of Occupational Titles. If a match is obtained and the individual is willing, a job search may be initiated. Another method often used to assess an individual's vocational needs may be a work sample measure. This test measures characteristics such as eye, hand, and foot coordination, dexterity, and size discrimination abilities.

Following completion of the assessment phase, a list of goals is developed and the requirements of specific jobs are assessed. Finally, a determination is made as to whether the individual has the aptitude and skill necessary for a particular job of interest or whether additional training is required. Should additional training be required, the vocational therapist helps determine the types of training necessary.

Vocational training may involve business or vocational instruction, college or university education, and on-the-job training. If the individual qualifies, as in the case of veterans, state and/or federal funds may be used to pay for this training. Additionally, many employers participate in programs that use both state and private funds to cover the wages of the individual in training.

Vocational therapy may also involve re-training. Re-training in computers for example, may be essential for success in today's job market. As such, individuals who have lost jobs as a result of company downsizing, industry elimination, or whose skills are now obsolete are candidates for vocational therapy. Finally, structured workshops are also common methods of training individual with severe disabilities. These workshops focus on topics such as money management, communication skills, and appropriate business attire.

Reason for Procedure

Vocational therapy is used to help an individual develop skills that can be used to obtain employment, maintain income, and achieve some measure of financial stability and self-esteem through regular work. In order to maintain employment, individuals may need to acquire new skills because of a progressive illness such as rheumatoid arthritis, an injury that changes functional level such as a spinal cord injury, or an injury that changes physical work tolerance such as a herniated disc. For these individuals, vocational therapy may direct individuals to technical or college courses.

Vocational therapy can also help individuals with new physical or emotional needs find new employment settings. For example, individuals with psychological illnesses such as schizophrenia may need to gain employment in settings with low distractibility levels. In addition, vocational therapy can help locate part-time job opportunities within the same field for those who cannot tolerate full-time employment but where part-time work is a viable option.

Description

Vocational counselors first ascertain an individual's abilities through intelligence testing, aptitude testing, job skill level, and physical skill level. Counselors help an individual choose career paths that are suited to their interests and abilities. Vocational counselors may consult with other therapy disciplines to ensure that the work being pursued is within the physical and mental capabilities of the individual. Once career paths are chosen, the vocational counselor prepares the individual for job re-entry through simulated interviews, resume and job application workshops, and job re-training (college courses, technical courses, trade school). Vocational counselors also address any concerns the individual may have about entering a new field or a new job description within their original profession.

Prognosis

Individuals can reasonably be expected to re-enter a new profession via vocational counseling. However, individuals with decreased motivation may be less successful in vocational counseling.

Specialists

- Licensed Clinical Social Worker
- Occupational Therapist
- Physical Therapist
- Psychiatrist
- Psychologist
- Vocational Rehabilitation Counselor

Work Restrictions / Accommodations

An individual's employer may need to provide transportation to and from job re-training. Additionally, work hours may need to be adjusted to accommodate for college or technical classes. If work hours cannot be adjusted, the individual requires leave from the current position. Employers may also need to provide funding for classes to allow continued employment.

Comorbid Conditions

There are no comorbid conditions for this procedure.

Factors Influencing Duration

There is no disability associated with the vocational therapy itself. The only factors influencing the length of disability are dictated by the underlying condition that prompted therapy.

Length of Disability

No disability is expected to result from this therapy. Disability may occur as a result of an underlying condition.

References

Trombly, Catherine A., ed. Occupational Therapy for Physical Dysfunction. Baltimore: Williams & Wilkins, 1995.

The Merck Manual of Diagnosis and Therapy. Beers, Mark H., and Robert Berkow, eds. Whitehouse Station, NJ: Merck and Co, Inc., 1999.

Volvulus

Other names / synonyms: Cecal Volvulus, Cecum Volvulus, Colonic Volvulus, Gastric Volvulus, Ileum Volvulus, Sigmoid Volvulus, Splenic Flexure Volvulus, Torsion, Transverse Volvulus

560.2

Definition

Volvulus is an abnormal twisting of a segment or loop of bowel back on itself along its longitudinal axis. The twisting causes intestinal obstruction.

The condition is frequently the result of a prolapsed segment of the membrane that anchors organs to the abdominal wall (mesentery). Volvulus occurs most often in the lower portion of the small intestine (ileum), the first portion of the large intestine (cecum), or the lower portion of the large intestine (sigmoid colon). Volvulus of the middle portion of the large intestine (transverse colon) occurs in only 2-3% of cases of colonic volvulus. In rare cases, volvulus can involve the stomach (gastric volvulus or torsion).

Sigmoid volvulus is the most common form of volvulus and usually occurs when the sigmoid colon is excessively long resulting in a redundant loop. A narrowed base where the sigmoid colon is anchored to the abdominal wall can cause it to stretch and become volvulus. Also, a torque force to the sigmoid colon can initiate the torsion process. When volvulus occurs, the far end of the sigmoid colon then enlarges (hypertrophy) with dilation that extends into the rectum. A vegetarian or high fiber diet with large amounts of coarse vegetables that result in the production of significant intestinal gas or an overload of the sigmoid colon appears to be a risk factor in beginning the twisting process. Certain drugs including psychotropics or sedatives that interfere with

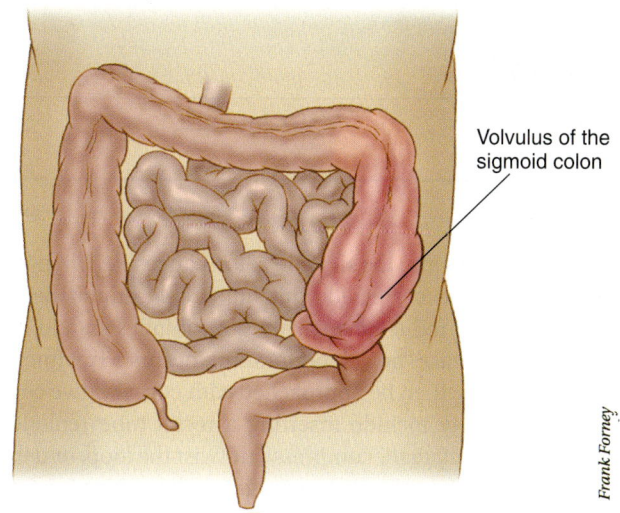

Volvulus of the sigmoid colon

Frank Forney

colonic motility are also a risk factor. Other risk factors may include long-standing constipation, pregnancy, Parkinson's disease, multiple sclerosis, and spinal cord injuries. Volvulus of the ileum may be present at birth as a result of an abnormal rotation that permitted twisting, an internal hernia into which the small bowel may intrude, or a pre-existing intestinal obstruction such as bands of scar tissue (adhesions) that somehow predisposes to secondary volvulus. Volvulus of the cecum is uncommon but is associated with an abnormally moveable area between the distal end of the ileum and the ascending colon. This is generally due to congenitally incomplete retroperitoneal fixation of the cecum or ascending colon. Transverse colon volvulus is caused by distal colon obstruction, elongation, and resulting expansion of the transverse colon causing the potential for volvulus. Splenic flexure volvulus is common after abdominal surgery, distal colon obstruction, or can be due to an abnormally enlarged colon (megacolon). Gastric volvulus is associated with a hernia in the diaphragm or esophageal area.

The incidence of volvulus varies by geographical location. In developing countries, volvulus accounts for 30-40% of intestinal obstructions, while in the US and Europe it accounts for intestinal obstruction in only 3-5% of cases. Individuals with volvulus are usually middle-aged or elderly, but it occurs 15-20 years earlier in developing nations. Sigmoid volvulus is more common in men (63.7%) than women, partially because women have a larger pelvis. Blacks have a higher incidence (67%) than whites (33%).

Diagnosis

History: Individuals will complain of severe gripping abdominal pain, nausea, and vomiting. Superimposed over the severe pain may be waves of severe spasms (colicky pain) as progressive involuntary movements in the intestine (peristaltic activity) in an attempt to move the obstruction along. Some individuals may recall previous subacute episodes of abdominal pain preceding the final acute attack. The individual may also report the inability to pass flatus.

Physical exam: On physical exam, the abdomen is extremely distended, moderately tender, and rigid. Bowel sounds are usually absent.

Tests: X-ray studies (plain or with barium as a contrast medium) and computer-aided x-ray analysis (computerized tomography or CT) can confirm the diagnosis. Examination of the inside of the colon with a flexible, fiber-optic viewing instrument (colonoscopy or sigmoidoscopy) may help to diagnose cecal, transverse, or sigmoid volvulus. A test for serum electrolytes and a complete blood count (CBC) may also be done.

Specialists

- Gastroenterologist
- General Surgeon
- Internist

Treatment

Vomiting and fluid loss into the sigmoid colon can result in hypovolemic shock, which must be corrected with fluid replacement before any attempts are made to reduce the volvulus. Antibiotics should be given prophylactically in case bowel perforation occurs. Treatment of a sigmoid volvulus may then be approached with conservative corrective treatment, which may include inserting a rectal tube (colonoscope, sigmoidoscope) to deflate (decompress), untwist the loop, or deflate (or at least reduce) the bowel prior to surgery. The timing and type of surgery for sigmoid volvulus are determined by suspected lack of blood flow (ischemic) to the bowel or dead (necrotic) bowel tissue, and the success or failure of sigmoidoscopic reduction. Open abdominal surgery is also indicated if the colon does not untwisting (detorsion) or if there is any indication of blood or dark blue/black mucosa on colonoscopy. Surgical removal (resection) of part of a floppy sigmoid colon (colonopexy, sigmoidopexy) with fixation of the base is advisable so that volvulus will not recur.

Correction of an ileum volvulus requires surgery (surgical detorsion). The management of cecal volvulus is more controversial. Reduction of cecal volvulus by barium enema and colonoscopy is possible but runs the risk that a portion of bowel that is dead and decaying (gangrenous) will be left untwisted. The alternative is surgical detorsion with fixation of the cecum to the wall of the pelvic cavity (parietal peritoneum).

Prognosis

Conservative treatment using flexible scoping (colonoscopy, sigmoidoscopy) can successfully reduce sigmoid volvulus in 50-60% of individuals with this condition. However, the volvulus will recur in more than half of these successful cases. Surgical detorsion, bowel resection, and fixation of the bowel corrects volvulus in most individuals with no further recurrence. Surgery without fixation for cecal volvulus may result in recurrence in 12% of cases.

Differential Diagnosis

Conditions that present with similar symptoms as volvulus include development of postoperative adhesions or scar tissue, impaction of feces in the intestine, foreign objects in the bowel, and a condition where the intestine telescopes in on itself (intussusception).

Work Restrictions / Accommodations

No work restrictions or special accommodations are required for conservative treatments, or after simple surgery for those with light work duties. Individuals may require less demanding physical labor upon their return to work until recovery is complete; heavy lifting or climbing may need to be restricted for up to 6 weeks.

Complementary and Alternative Therapies

Content is intended for awareness only. Treatments may or may not be effective. Scientific evidence may be lacking and some substances have potentially toxic effects. Dr. Presley Reed and the editors do not endorse the use of these therapies in the absence of consultation with a licensed medical professional.

Acupuncture - Insertion of needles into certain points on the body may relieve gastric volvulus.

Comorbid Conditions

Existing conditions that may impact an individual's ability to recover and further lengthen the disability include intussusception of the bowel, chronic constipation, and abnormal tissue growth (granulomatous processes).

Complications

Death and decay (gangrene) of the affected portion of bowel is the most common complication if surgery is not performed. Other complications may include puncture (perforation) of the bowel, extreme electrolyte disturbances, and dehydration. Death is a possibility in cases that are left untreated.

Factors Influencing Duration

Length of disability may be influenced by the location of the volvulus, the method of treatment, type of surgery, or complications of surgery. In addition, the presence of tissue death and decay (gangrene) requires surgery to remove (resection) part of the intestine; this increases the risk for development of complications. Conservative treatments may allow for the condition to recur.

Length of Disability

Duration depends on diagnosis for which the procedure is done and whether or not a colostomy is required.

Colon resection. Partial, laparoscopic.

Duration in Days

Job Classification	Minimum	Optimum	Maximum
Sedentary work	10	14	21
Light work	10	14	21
Medium work	14	21	28
Heavy work	14	35	42
Very Heavy work	14	42	56

Colon resection. Partial, open.

Duration in Days

Job Classification	Minimum	Optimum	Maximum
Sedentary work	21	28	42
Light work	21	28	42
Medium work	28	35	56
Heavy work	35	42	56
Very Heavy work	42	42	56

Failure to Recover

If an individual fails to recover within the maximum duration expectancy period, the reader may wish to reference the following questions to assist in better understanding the specifics of an individual's medical case.

Regarding diagnosis:

- Did individual have a clinical history (high-fiber diet, constipation, Parkinson's disease, multiple sclerosis, spinal cord injury, or previous bowel surgery) consistent with the diagnosis of volvulus?
- Did individual present with severe abdominal pain, nausea, vomiting, and inability to pass flatus?
- Was the diagnosis confirmed with abdominal x-rays or CT?
- If the diagnosis was uncertain, were conditions with similar symptoms ruled out (postoperative adhesions or scar tissue, impaction of feces in the intestine, foreign objects in the bowel, or intussusception)?

Regarding treatment:

- Was conservative treatment with insertion of an intestinal tube effective at correcting the condition?
- If not, was surgical correction considered?
- Were other associated conditions or symptoms, such as dehydration or infection, addressed in the treatment plan?

Regarding prognosis:

- Was individual treated promptly?
- Did the volvulus recur?
- Was surgery required?
- What was the expected outcome?
- Does individual have existing conditions (intussusception, chronic constipation, granulomatous processes) or complications (bowel infarct, gangrene, bowel perforation, or fluid and electrolyte disturbances) that may influence the length of disability or recovery?

References

Ballantyne, Garth H., MD. "Laparoscopic Treatment of Volvulus of the Colon." 20 Jan 2000. 20 Jan 2001 <http://www.lapsurgery.com/volvulus.htm>.

LeMone, P., and K.M. Burke. Medical-Surgical Nursing. Upper Saddle River, NJ: Prentice Hall Health, 2000.

Norstein, J. "Treatment of Volvulus and Intussusception." Therapy of Digestive Disorders. Wolfe, M.M., ed. Philadelphia: W.B. Saunders Company, 2000. 636-644.

Wan, Y.G., and L.Y. Yu. "Volvulus of the Stomach Successfully Treated with Acupuncture Report of 9 Cases." Journal of Traditional Chinese Medicine 1 1 (1981): 39-42.

Wandering Atrial Pacemaker
427.89

Definition

Wandering atrial pacemaker is one of a number of possible variations (arrhythmias) in the heart's usual beat. It is usually a normal finding, which occurs in association with sinus arrhythmias. Wandering atrial pacemaker is a condition in which the electrical impulse that triggers heart contractions does not originate from its normal location.

Ordinarily, the beat is initiated from a nucleus of specialized muscle called the sinoatrial (SA) node. In wandering atrial pacemaker, the electrical impulse initiates from other sites in the atrium (upper chamber of the heart) instead.

This condition occurs most often in young people. It is generally considered benign and is usually transitory. Often it is encountered in association with respiratory effort or strain, due to increased vagal tone, for example during the act of lifting heavy weights. Thus, individuals in whom this condition might occur include construction workers, warehouse workers, janitors, and horticulturists or other professions in which digging is involved.

Diagnosis

History: Most individuals have no symptoms.

Physical exam: An abnormal heart rate may be evident.

Tests: Diagnosis is confirmed by recording the electrical activity of the heart (electrocardiogram).

Treatment

Treatment is not usually required for this condition. The heart generally returns to its normal rhythm without intervention.

Prognosis

In most individuals, the heart returns to its normal rhythm without assistance.

Differential Diagnosis

Wandering atrial pacemaker must be distinguished from other arrhythmias. Another disorder of impulse formation is atrioventricular (AV) junctional rhythm. Multifocal atrial arrhythmia may be seen in digitalis toxicity.

Specialists

- Cardiologist

Work Restrictions / Accommodations

There are generally no work restrictions or accommodations associated with this condition.

Complications

Complications are not usually associated with this condition.

Factors Influencing Duration

There is generally no disability associated with this condition, however, it may be brought on by strenuous job activities such as lifting heavy objects.

Length of Disability

There is generally no disability associated with this condition.

Failure to Recover

If an individual fails to recover within the maximum duration expectancy period, the reader may wish to reference the following questions to assist in better understanding the specifics of an individual's medical case.

Regarding diagnosis:

- Has diagnosis of wandering atrial pacemaker been confirmed through electrocardiogram? Is the individual experiencing any symptoms?
- Have other, more dangerous arrhythmias been ruled out?

Regarding treatment:

- Is individual involved in strenuous job activities, weightlifting, or other strenuous activities?
- What modifications can be made to avoid triggering another episode of wandering atrial pacemaker?

Regarding prognosis:

- Has the heart returned to its normal rhythm?
- Does diagnosis need to be revisited?
- Would individual benefit from evaluation by a specialist (internist, cardiologist)?

References

Borgia, J.F., et al. "Wandering Atrial Pacemaker Associated with Repetitive Respiratory Strain." Cardiology 69 2 (1982): 70-73.

Snowberger, P. "Wandering Atrial Pacemaker." RN 54 9 (1991): 36-37.

Warts, Genital

Other names / synonyms: Condylomata Acuminata, HPV, Venereal Verruca, Venereal Wart, Verruca Acuminata

078.19

Definition

Genital warts are viral skin infections caused by a few of the many types of human papillomavirus (HPV). These infections affect warm, moist areas of the genitalia and around the anus.

Spread by sexual contact with an infected partner, genital warts are among the most common of the sexually transmitted diseases. Like many sexually transmitted organisms, HPV causes an infection that may not have visible symptoms (silent infection). Individuals may not even be aware of their infection or the potential risk of transmission to others. Almost half of the women infected with HPV have no obvious symptoms.

Very contagious in its spread between individuals, HPV can also spread to different areas on the same individual. Studies estimate that as many as 40 million Americans are infected with HPV. In addition, every year as many as 1 million new cases of genital warts are diagnosed.

Both men and women can have genital warts. It is more common in individuals with multiple sexual partners and in those who do not use condoms. Because it is spread through skin-to-skin contact, however, even condoms do not guarantee protection from the virus. Up to 45% of individuals with genital warts also have coexisting sexually transmitted diseases such as candidiasis, gonorrhea, and chlamydia.

Diagnosis

History: Individual may complain of painless, flesh-colored, flat- or cauliflower-like warts in the genital area. Warts can occur in the mouths of individuals who have had oral sexual contact with infected individuals. History may or may not include sexual contact with a known infected individual. Such contact may not have been recent, as the incubation period of the virus can range from 2 months to 2 years.

Physical exam: In women, the warts occur on the vulva, labia, or around the anus. A pelvic examination using a device that opens the vagina for visual inspection (speculum) may reveal warts inside the vagina or on the opening to the uterus (cervix). In men, genital warts usually appear on the tip of the penis. Warts may also be found on the shaft of the penis, scrotum, and around the anus. Genital warts often occur in clusters. They can be tiny or accumulate into large masses. If left untreated, genital warts can develop into a fleshy, cauliflower-like lesion. Since up to 45% of individuals with genital warts also have coexisting sexually transmitted diseases, these disease symptoms may also be present.

Tests: An abnormal pap smear (microscopic examination of cells taken from the cervix) may include possible warts. It is important for women with an abnormal Pap smear to undergo further testing to diagnose cervical problems. A procedure called colposcopy uses a magnifying instrument to view the vaginal wall and cervix. A vinegar (acetic acid) solution applied to suspicious areas causes the infected areas to whiten, making them more visible. A small sample of tissue (biopsy) can then be taken from this area and examined under the microscope.

Treatment

Genital warts may sometimes disappear spontaneously (without treatment). However, because there is no way to predict whether warts will grow or disappear, they need to be treated. Small warts and warts in pregnant women can be removed by freezing (cryocautery), burning (electrocautery), or ablation (laser surgery). Large warts or warts that have not responded to other treatment may need to be removed by open or laser surgery.

Several newer, nonsurgical treatments for genital warts are now popular. These include topical and injectable medications. These methods however, are only approved for individuals over 18 and are not indicated for pregnant women or nursing mothers, as they can be absorbed into the body and cause damage to the fetus or child. Although topical medication can cause localized skin irritation in the surrounding skin, these medications are highly effective for genital warts. A group of injectable medications called interferons can be injected into the base of each wart. Although it may require several treatments, these injections are also highly effective.

Women who have had genital warts or whose partners have had genital warts should have frequent pap smears for early identification of precancerous cervical diseases.

Prognosis

Although removing the wart or treating it with injections or creams usually eliminates the skin lesion, it does not thoroughly destroy (eradicate) the virus. Warts often reappear after treatment. Prognosis is favorable if a precancerous cervical condition is discovered and treated early.

Differential Diagnosis

Lesions of syphilis, seborrheic keratoses, and skin cancer may have a similar appearance.

Specialists

- Dermatologist
- Gynecologist
- Urologist

Work Restrictions / Accommodations

Work restrictions or accommodations are not necessary for individuals with genital warts.

Comorbid Conditions

Pregnancy can accelerate the growth and spread of the warts. Immuno-suppressed individuals such as those on chemotherapy or with AIDS may notice dramatic growth and spread of the warts. Other sexually transmitted diseases (candidiasis, gonorrhea, and chlamydia) may coexist but do not generally impact disability.

Complications

Associations have been found between several types of HPV and the development of cancers of the cervix, vulva, anus, and in rare cases, the penis. Genital warts may cause complications in pregnancy such as making the vaginal wall less elastic or causing obstruction during delivery. Infants born to women with genital warts can develop a condition in their throats called laryngeal papillomatosis. This can be a life-threatening condition for the child and requires frequent laser surgery to prevent obstruction of the airway. In immunodeficient individuals (AIDS or undergoing chemotherapy), warts may grow dramatically.

Factors Influencing Duration

Length of disability may be influenced by severity of condition, location of lesions, or type of treatment required.

Length of Disability

For medical treatment, disability depends on site, size or wart, and method of treatment.

Medical treatment.

Duration in Days

Job Classification	Minimum	Optimum	Maximum
Sedentary work	1	1	1
Light work	1	1	1
Medium work	1	1	1
Heavy work	1	1	1
Very Heavy work	1	1	1

Cryotherapy, electrocautery, laser treatment.

Duration in Days

Job Classification	Minimum	Optimum	Maximum
Sedentary work	1	1	2
Light work	1	1	2
Medium work	1	1	2
Heavy work	1	1	2
Very Heavy work	1	1	2

Surgical excision.

Duration in Days

Job Classification	Minimum	Optimum	Maximum
Sedentary work	1	2	7
Light work	1	2	7
Medium work	1	3	7
Heavy work	1	3	7
Very Heavy work	1	3	7

Failure to Recover

If an individual fails to recover within the maximum duration expectancy period, the reader may wish to reference the following questions to assist in better understanding the specifics of an individual's medical case.

Regarding diagnosis:

- Does the individual have multiple sexual partners? Does individual use condoms?
- Does the individual have other STDs?
- Does the individual complain of painless, flesh-colored, flat- or cauliflower-like warts in the genital?
- On exam, were warts present on the vulva, labia, around the anus, inside the vagina, or on the cervix? On the tip or shaft of the penis, scrotum, or around the anus?
- Are the warts in a cluster? Large or small?
- Has the individual had an abnormal Pap smear? Was colposcopy done? Biopsy?
- Were conditions with similar symptoms ruled out?

Regarding treatment:

- Has the individual had small warts treated with cryocautery, electrocautery, or ablation?
- Was it necessary to treat larger warts with open or laser surgery?
- Were warts injected with interferons into the base of each wart?
- Does the individual with warts or a partner with warts have regular Pap smears?

Regarding prognosis:

- Does the individual have any conditions that may affect recovery?
- Have any complications developed such as development of cancers of the cervix, vulva, anus, and in rare cases, the penis?
- Has the individual had complications in pregnancy?

References

Beutner, K.R., et al. "External Genital Warts: Report of the American Medical Association Consensus Conference: AMA Expert Panel on External Genital Warts." Clinics in Infectious Diseases 27 4 (1998): 796-806.

Edwards, Libby, and Peter J. Lynch. "Diseases of the Genitalia." Principles and Practice of Dermatology, 2nd ed. Sams, W. Mitchell, and Peter J. Lynch, eds. New York: Churchill Livingstone, 1996. 959-978.

Warts, Plantar

Other names / synonyms: Human Papillomavirus, Infection of the Feet, Verruca Plantaris

078.10

Definition

Plantar warts are one type of wart caused by the virus called human papillomavirus (HPV). There are over 70 different types of HPV that produce many different types of warts. Plantar warts are caused by HPV types one, two, and four.

Plantar warts differ from other types of warts in that they are generally associated with some degree of pain. This is because the warts tend to occur on the soles of the feet. The pressure of walking forces them to flatten and grow inward instead of making the raised type of lesion many people associate with warts. Transmission of plantar warts is often indirect in nature. For example, if an individual with plantar warts walks barefoot across a damp floor (such as in a locker room or public shower), another person can become infected by walking barefoot on the same floor. Risk factors include skin conditions such as atopic dermatitis, a disease that weakens the immune system (such as HIV infection or lymphomas), treatment with drugs that suppress the immune system, locker room use, and shared showers (such as dormitories and gyms).

Plantar warts are a widespread condition that occurs in about 2% of the population. Women are affected slightly more often than men. Plantar warts can occur at any age, but are more common in young adults.

Diagnosis

History: Individuals with plantar warts often complain of pain on the balls of the feet or the heel. This pain is likely to worsen when the individual stands, walks, or runs and is relieved when weight is taken off the foot. Leg or back pain may be reported, indicating that the individual's posture is distorted in an effort to avoid pressure on the foot.

Physical exam: The exam may reveal singular or grouped lesions on the sole of the foot with disruption of the normal skin markings. The surface is rough and may have black pinpoint dots (thrombosed capillaries). Calluses may be present.

Tests: Visual inspection of the lesions is often sufficient to make the diagnosis of plantar warts. A magnifying glass may be helpful to visualize the orderly, mosaic pattern of the wart (as opposed to a callus).

Treatment

Often treatment is not necessary as plantar warts are generally harmless and usually resolve on their own. Those that are painful or rapidly multiplying can be treated in several ways and treatment varies depending on the severity of the infection and location.

Chemical treatments may be applied to the surface of the wart. These treatments require regular application over a period of up to 12 weeks in order to achieve favorable results. Chemical treatments are effective in about 70% of cases if the individual is compliant with the application regimen. Some warts may be frozen off (cryotherapy). Cryotherapy is uncomfortable but not terribly painful, and frequent treatments (every 1 to 3 weeks) for 3 to 4 months are successful in about 70% of cases. Warts can also be burned off (electrosurgery) with a success rate of about 80%. Laser treatment can also be used to remove warts, but this procedure is generally reserved for those that don't respond to other treatments. Repeated treatments may be necessary and the resulting scab may take a couple of weeks to heal. Very stubborn warts may be injected with an anticancer drug called bleomycin, or with interferon, an agent that boosts the immune system.

Cutting away the wart is not generally recommended, as this method will leave a permanent scar and is no more effective than other, nonscarring methods.

Prognosis

The outcome is good regardless of treatment. In many cases, complete recovery will occur, even without treatment.

Chemical treatments and cryotherapy are effective in about 70% of cases if the individual is compliant with the application regimen. Electrosurgery is a process with a success rate of about 80%. Laser treatment is generally reserved for warts that don't respond to other treatments and is effective in about 70% of cases.

Despite treatment, plantar warts frequently recur.

Differential Diagnosis

Plantar warts may resemble corns (clavi), calluses, other skin diseases with hyperkeratosis, or skin cancer.

Specialists

- Dermatologist
- Podiatrist

Work Restrictions / Accommodations

In general, work accommodations and/or restrictions are not required. If the wart is located in a place that causes painful walking or standing, reassignment to a more sedentary position may be advised until the wart has resolved.

Complementary and Alternative Therapies

Content is intended for awareness only. Treatments may or may not be effective. Scientific evidence may be lacking and some substances have potentially toxic effects. Dr. Presley Reed and the editors do not endorse the use of these therapies in the absence of consultation with a licensed medical professional.

Bleach - Used carefully, may eliminate warts.

Garlic clove - Applied daily for about 2 weeks, may eliminate warts.

Comorbid Conditions

Individuals with a disease that weakens the immune system such as HIV infection or lymphomas, will have a longer recovery period.

Complications

Scarring may occur with overaggressive treatment. A rare type of cancer (epithelioma cuniculatum) is thought to arise from these warts; however, this has not been established.

Factors Influencing Duration

For most cases, disability will not occur. However, when it does occur, severity of symptoms, localization of warts (weightbearing versus nonweightbearing), and rate of healing after treatment will influence length of disability.

Length of Disability

Complete recovery is expected, although recurrence is common. Disability does not always occur but is more likely in individuals with positions that require prolonged standing or walking.

Following cryotherapy, or electrocautery, and surgical excision, duration depends on rate of healing and weight-bearing versus non-weight-bearing location.

Medical treatment.

Duration in Days

Job Classification	Minimum	Optimum	Maximum
Sedentary work	0	2	7
Light work	0	3	7
Medium work	0	7	14
Heavy work	0	14	21
Very Heavy work	0	14	21

Cryotherapy, electrocautery.

Duration in Days

Job Classification	Minimum	Optimum	Maximum
Sedentary work	1	2	7
Light work	7	14	28
Medium work	7	21	28
Heavy work	7	21	28
Very Heavy work	7	21	28

Surgical excision.

Duration in Days

Job Classification	Minimum	Optimum	Maximum
Sedentary work	1	3	7
Light work	1	7	14
Medium work	1	14	21
Heavy work	1	14	21
Very Heavy work	1	21	28

Failure to Recover

If an individual fails to recover within the maximum duration expectancy period, the reader may wish to reference the following questions to assist in better understanding the specifics of an individual's medical case.

Regarding diagnosis:

- Does the individual complain of pain on the balls of the feet or the heel?
- Does exam reveal singular or grouped lesions on the sole of the foot with disruption of the normal skin markings?
- Is the individual's skin rough with black pinpoint dots (thrombosed capillaries)? Are calluses present?
- Were other conditions with similar symptoms eliminated such as corns (clavi), calluses, other skin diseases with hyperkeratosis, and skin cancer?
- Was diagnosis of plantar warts confirmed with visual inspection by a physician?

Regarding treatment:

- Does the individual have severe pain or rapidly multiplying warts that require treatment? Has the individual kept up with treatment frequency? If so, were chemical treatments effective in eliminating warts?
- If warts persisted, was cryotherapy or laser treatment considered? Were repeated treatments necessary?
- Have more aggressive therapies such as injections of bleomycin or interferon been considered?

Regarding prognosis:

- Was the individual compliant with prescribed treatment regimen?
- Does the individual have an underlying condition (immune suppression) that may impact recovery?
- Have the warts recurred despite treatment? If so, were other more aggressive treatments considered?

References

Silko, Gary. "Warts, Plantar." Griffith's 5-minute Clinical Consult. Dambro, Mark, ed. Philadelphia: Lippincott, Williams & Wilkins, 2000. 1174-1175.

Warts. New Zealand Dermatological Society. 24 Nov 1999. 16 Oct 2000 <http://www.dermnet.org.nz/dna/warts/warts.html>.

Warts, Viral

Other names / synonyms: Common Warts, Condyloma Acuminatum, Epidermodysplasia Verruciformis, Flat Warts, Genital Warts, HPV, Human Papillomavirus Infection, Plantar Warts, Venereal Warts, Verruca Plana, Verruca Plantaris, Verruca Vulgaris

078.1, 078.10

Definition

Warts are noncancerous skin growths caused by infection with a virus called human papillomavirus (HPV). There are over 70 types of HPV. Specific features of the wart depend on the type of virus present and the location of the infection. The five most common types of warts are the common wart (verruca vulgaris), the plantar wart (verruca plantaris), the flat wart (verruca plana), genital or venereal wart (condyloma acuminatum), and generalized warts of the skin (epidermodysplasia verruciformis).

The vast majority of warts are painless and harmless, although some types can be painful (plantar warts) and some can increase the risk of cancer (genital warts of the cervix or penis). The wart virus is very contagious and can be spread through direct contact from one part of the body to another. Warts can also be transmitted indirectly in moist warm environments such as locker rooms, bathroom floors, and swimming pools. The risk of transmitting flat warts (warts of the hands or feet) from one individual to another is small. Genital warts are spread through sexual contact.

Risk factors include broken skin, locker room use, the skin condition called atopic dermatitis, use of drugs that suppress the immune system, and current infection with a disease that weakens the immune system (such as HIV or lymphoma). Epidermodysplasia verruciformis will persist for life. Other warts tend to resolve on their own, although they may persist for 5 to 7 years before disappearing.

Warts occur in approximately 7-10% of the population. They predominantly occur on young adults and are rarely seen on children under 3. Although they can occur at any age, frequency declines drastically again when individuals reach adulthood. More women than men are affected.

Diagnosis

History: It can take several months for warts to develop after infection. The individual often does not have any symptoms. In general, the appearance of an unfamiliar lesion prompts the individual to seek medical attention. Some individuals particularly with warts on their feet may report pain that worsens with pressure (e.g., due to walking). Because the wart sheds viral particles, eye symptoms may present including a foreign body sensation, mild secondary viral inflammation of the membrane lining the eyelids (conjunctivitis), and possible corneal involvement.

Physical exam: The appearance of the wart varies depending on the type of HPV responsible and the location of the wart. Common warts (verruca vulgaris) are skin-colored, raised, rough, irregular masses on a broad base and shaped like a cauliflower. Common warts are most commonly found on the hands, especially around the nails and on the fingers. They also frequently infect the scalp, knees, and face.

Skin-colored, round and rough plantar warts (verruca plantaris) may be found on the feet, particularly on the soles of the feet. On close examination, small black spots are seen. These black spots are caused by bleeding within the wart as a result of standing and walking on the wart.

Flat warts (verruca plana) are smaller and smoother than other warts, occur in large numbers (20-100 at a time), are found in a linear arrangement, and are commonly found in the beard area of men, and on the legs and hands of women.

Individuals with genital warts present with warts that are thin, flexible and tall. Generalized skin warts (epidermodysplasia verruciformis) are found on shoulders and hands and are flat and reddish in color.

Tests: In most cases, simple examination of the wart is sufficient for diagnosis. A magnifying glass may help the physician see the mosaic pattern. Definitive diagnosis can be obtained through electron microscopy, immunohistochemical evaluation, or nucleic acid hybridization, but these tests are more academic in nature and not necessary. Human papillomavirus cannot be cultured.

Treatment

No treatment is guaranteed to remove warts. Often treatment is not necessary as warts are generally harmless and usually resolve on their own. Warts that are bothersome, painful, or rapidly multiply can be treated in several ways. Treatment varies depending on the age of the individual, the type of wart, number of warts and their location, and symptomatic problems.

Chemical treatments may be applied to the surface of the wart and must be applied regularly over a period of up to 12 weeks in order to achieve favorable results. Some warts may be frozen off (cryotherapy). Cryotherapy is uncomfortable, but not terribly painful, and can require frequent treatments (every 1 to 3 weeks) for 3 to 4 months. Warts can also be burned off (electrosurgery). Laser treatment can be used to remove warts, but this procedure is generally reserved for warts that don't respond to other treatments. Repeated treatments may be necessary and the resulting scab may take a few weeks to heal. Very stubborn warts may be injected with an anticancer drug called bleomycin or with interferon, an agent that boosts the immune system.

Cutting away the wart is not generally recommended, as this method will leave a permanent scar and is no more effective than other, nonscarring methods.

Prognosis

In most instances, warts resolve completely even without treatment. The rate of recurrence ranges from about 20-70%.

Chemical treatments are effective in about 70% of cases if the individual is compliant with the application regimen. Frequent treatments (every 1 to 3 weeks) of cryotherapy for 3 to 4 months are successful in about 70% of cases. Electrosurgery has a success rate of about 80%.

Differential Diagnosis

Skin lesions may be caused by numerous other conditions. Warts should be differentiated from corns, scar tissue, a skin condition called molluscum contagiosum, the flat warts of syphilis (condyloma lata), hyperkeratosis, moles, cancer, calluses, and skin tags.

Specialists

- Dermatologist
- Gynecologist
- Internist
- Podiatrist
- Primary Care Provider
- Urologist

Work Restrictions / Accommodations

Work restrictions and accommodations are not associated with this condition.

Complementary and Alternative Therapies

Content is intended for awareness only. Treatments may or may not be effective. Scientific evidence may be lacking and some substances have potentially toxic effects. Dr. Presley Reed and the editors do not endorse the use of these therapies in the absence of consultation with a licensed medical professional.

Bleach - Used carefully, may eliminate warts.

Dry ice - May eliminate warts.

Comorbid Conditions

Warts are not generally associated with any disability, as the majority of cases do not present any symptoms. Any condition that weakens the immune system (AIDS) will lengthen the recovery period.

Complications

Possible complications include self-reinfection (autoinoculation). This usually occurs when a wart is picked or scratched, releasing virus particles that can then infect other parts of the body. Scarring can occur if a wart is picked or treated too aggressively. Damage to fingernails can result in abnormal growth and appearance of the nail. Chronic pain may also occur, particularly with plantar warts. Genital warts can be complicated by abnormal growth of the cervical cells (cervical dysplasia), cancer of the cervix, penis or rectum, or obstruction of the male urethra.

Factors Influencing Duration

Disability is not expected, as warts do not generally present symptoms. Recurrence is common.

Length of Disability

Warts generally resolve completely with or without treatment. Duration depends on site, size, and method of treatment.

Cryotherapy.

Duration in Days

Job Classification	Minimum	Optimum	Maximum
Any work	0	3	7

Failure to Recover

If an individual fails to recover within the maximum duration expectancy period, the reader may wish to reference the following questions to assist in better understanding the specifics of an individual's medical case.

Regarding diagnosis:

- Has the diagnosis of warts been confirmed with a physical exam by a physician?
- Have other conditions with similar symptoms been ruled out (corns, scar tissue, flat warts of syphilis (condyloma lata), hyperkeratosis, moles, cancer, calluses, skin tags, and a skin condition called molluscum contagiosum)?

Regarding treatment:

- Did the warts resolve spontaneously? If not, was treatment considered?
- Was chemical treatment effective at eliminating the warts? If not, was the individual compliant with the treatment regimen?
- Did the warts warrant intervention with cryotherapy or laser treatments?
- Were repeat treatments necessary?
- Was more aggressive treatment with injections of bleomycin or interferon considered?

Regarding prognosis:

- Was individual compliant with prescribed treatment regimen?
- Have the warts recurred?
- Is more aggressive therapy being considered? Has it taken longer than 1 to 2 weeks to resolve symptoms?
- Does individual have an underlying condition (such as immune suppression) that may impact recovery?

References

Katz, Stephen. "Viral Skin Infections." The Merck Manual of Medical Information. Berkow, Robert, Mark Beers, and Andrew Fletcher, eds. New York: Pocket Books, 1997. 1076-1080.

Moront, Barbara, and Jeffrey Kessler. "Warts." Griffith's 5-minute Clinical Consult. Dambro, Mark, ed. Philadelphia: Lippincott, Williams & Wilkins, 2000. 1172-1173.

Moront, Barbara, Earl Ang, and Bassem Elsawy. "Condyloma Acuminata." Griffith's 5-minute Clinical Consult. Dambro, Mark, ed. Philadelphia: Lippincott, Williams & Wilkins, 2000. 254-255.

Silko, Gary. "Warts, Plantar." Griffith's 5-minute Clinical Consult. Dambro, Mark, ed. Philadelphia: Lippincott, Williams & Wilkins, 2000. 1174-1175.

Wilson's Disease

Other names / synonyms: Copper Metabolism Disorder, Hepatolenticular Degeneration, Westphal-Struempel Pseudosclerosis, Westphal-Strumpell Pseudosclerosis, Westphal-Strumpell Syndrome

275.1

Definition

Wilson's disease is an inherited disorder in which copper abnormally accumulates in the brain, liver, kidneys, and corneas of the eyes.

Copper is a naturally occurring mineral that the body needs in small amounts to stay healthy. Normally, the liver excretes excess copper through the intestines (gastrointestinal tract) into the feces. In Wilson's disease, the liver is impaired and cannot excrete copper. As a result, copper accumulates in the liver, causing irreversible damage. Eventually the damage causes the liver to slowly release copper into the bloodstream where it travels to other parts of the body. Eventually, the liver, kidneys, brain, and eyes are significantly impaired.

A rare disorder, only 30 individuals per 1 million are afflicted with this disease. The only risk factor is a family history. As a hereditary disease, the accumulation of copper begins at birth. Symptoms usually appear between the ages of 6 to 20, but can appear as late as age forty. However, individuals with a family history can be tested before symptoms develop. If detected before copper has built up to toxic levels, treatment may prevent symptoms from developing.

Diagnosis

History: Symptoms may include a vague feeling of discomfort or illness (malaise), lack of appetite (anorexia), yellowing of the skin (jaundice), vomiting blood, tremor, loss of fine motor skills, rigidity, drooling, difficulty with speech, staggering gait (titubation), early intellectual deterioration, personality changes, and a disorder resembling schizophrenia (schizophreniform disorder).

Physical exam: An eye examination will reveal a golden brown to greenish-looking ring around the individual's cornea (Kayser-Fleischer ring). This ring is a characteristic sign on which the diagnosis of Wilson's disease can be based (a pathognomonic sign). Physical examination findings may include tenderness and swelling of the liver and spleen, fluid build-up in the lining of the abdomen, lack of muscle tone in the face (dystonic facies), and lack of muscle tone in the body (dystonic posture).

Tests: Wilson's disease is usually diagnosed upon definitive lab results. Individuals with this disease have elevated liver and urinary copper levels along with a low serum ceruloplasmin. Although these three results in combination give the diagnosis, removal of small amount of liver tissue for microscopic analysis (liver biopsy) may also be done to assess amount of copper accumulation.

Treatment

Wilson's disease requires treatment with a drug (penicillamine) that binds with the copper, enabling it to be excreted from the body. If started soon after symptoms appear, treatment can sometimes improve liver and brain function. Individuals may respond quite slowly to this treatment, as it sometimes takes up to a year to resolve excess copper build-up. The individual must be monitored every 2 months during the first year, and then every 6 months thereafter. Monitoring consists of acquiring urinary copper levels, serum ceruloplasmin, and serum non-ceruloplasmin levels. Lifetime maintenance therapy is usually required.

Individuals will also need to take vitamin B_6 supplements and follow a low-copper diet (avoiding mushrooms, chocolate, nuts, dried fruit, liver, and shellfish). Taking extra zinc may help block absorption of copper by the intestines.

A liver transplant may be indicated if Wilson's disease progresses to severe, irreversible impairment of the liver.

Family members, especially siblings, should be screened for the disease. If Wilson's disease can be discovered before toxic levels produce symptoms, treatment may prevent symptoms from developing.

Prognosis

Prognosis is good in individuals who are treated with copper-binding medicine, a low copper diet, and vitamin B_6 and zinc supplements before liver or brain damage occurs. Such individuals have a normal life expectancy. If therapy is started soon after symptoms appear, treatment can sometimes improve liver and brain function. If untreated, Wilson's disease is generally fatal, usually by the age 30.

Differential Diagnosis

Conditions with similar symptoms include hepatitis, biliary cirrhosis, cholestasis, schizophrenia, and hemolytic anemia.

Specialists

- Gastroenterologist
- Neurologist
- Ophthalmologist
- Psychiatrist
- Urologist

Rehabilitation

The goal of rehabilitation for Wilson's disease is designing a physical conditioning program for the individual that maintains the body's mobility and strength while improving overall stamina. The proper amount and intensity of rehabilitative exercise is determined by the physical therapist who takes into consideration whether the individual is under medication to limit the symptoms of Wilson's disease by gradually removing excessive copper from the involved tissues. The rehabilitation professional focuses on establishing an independent program because such treatment usually must be continued for life to keep the disease under control. The frequency and duration of the rehabilitation program will vary among individuals with Wilson's disease. Intensity and progression of the exercise will depend on the extent of the disease, which organs are most involved, and the individual's overall health. Rehabilitation professions along with other healthcare professionals take a role in educating the individual about Wilson's disease throughout the course of direct rehabilitation. This includes making sure that the individual understands it is an inherited disorder and that relatives of a person with that diagnosis should be screened. This allows early treatment to prevent or minimize organ damage.

Work Restrictions / Accommodations

Due to possible neurologic impairment with increased risk of falls, a safe environment is essential. Physical condition may require a sedentary position. Intellectual impairment may necessitate a change in job responsibilities. Individuals with advanced liver or brain damage may be permanently disabled and unable to work at all.

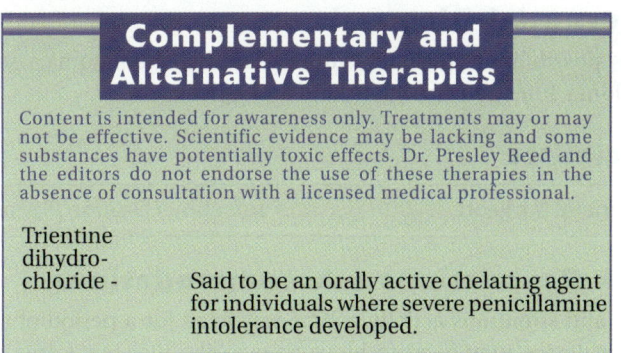

Complementary and Alternative Therapies

Content is intended for awareness only. Treatments may or may not be effective. Scientific evidence may be lacking and some substances have potentially toxic effects. Dr. Presley Reed and the editors do not endorse the use of these therapies in the absence of consultation with a licensed medical professional.

Trientine dihydrochloride - Said to be an orally active chelating agent for individuals where severe penicillamine intolerance developed.

Comorbid Conditions

A psychiatric behavioral disorder may lengthen disability.

Complications

Toxic effects of copper on the liver can progress from inflammation (hepatitis) to permanent scarring, structural damage, and loss of function (cirrhosis). In the brain, accumulations of copper can cause progressive problems ranging from mild intellectual impairment to crippling rigidity, tremor, or dementia.

Factors Influencing Duration

Length of disability may be influenced by the extent of the disease when diagnosed and the response to treatment. The individual usually presents to the clinician after the onset of physical and neurological symptoms. Therefore, it may take several months before improvement in the clinical condition allows the individual to return to work. The other factor that will influence disability is whether or not the individual has any side effects to the therapeutic drugs.

Length of Disability

If Wilson's disease is diagnosed in the early stages, most individuals will respond well to treatment. In cases where the liver, kidneys, or brain are severely impaired, disability may be permanent.

Duration in Days

Job Classification	Minimum	Optimum	Maximum
Any work	42	70	Indefinite

Failure to Recover

If an individual fails to recover within the maximum duration expectancy period, the reader may wish to reference the following questions to assist in better understanding the specifics of an individual's medical case.

Regarding diagnosis:

- Has copper abnormally accumulated in individual's brain, liver, kidneys, and corneas?
- Does individual complain of malaise, anorexia, jaundice, and is vomiting blood?
- Is there a tremor, loss of fine motor skills, or rigidity? Does individual drool and have difficulty with speech?
- Does individual have a staggering gait, early intellectual deterioration, personality changes, and a disorder resembling schizophrenia?
- On exam, is there a golden brown to greenish-looking ring around individual's cornea? Was there tenderness and swelling of the liver and spleen? Fluid build-up in the lining of the abdomen? Lack of muscle tone in the face and body?
- Has individual had blood and urine tests for copper level? Was a serum ceruloplasmin done? Was a liver biopsy done?
- Have conditions with similar symptoms been ruled out?

Regarding treatment:

- Is individual being treated with penicillamine? Being monitored frequently?
- Was lifetime maintenance therapy prescribed?
- Is individual following a low-copper diet?
- Is individual compliant with treatment regime?
- Is a liver transplant indicated?

Regarding prognosis:

- Is individual active in rehabilitation? Is a home exercise program in place?
- Can individual's employer accommodate any necessary restrictions?
- Does individual have any conditions that may affect ability to recover?
- Have any complications occurred such as permanent liver damage and loss of function? Intellectual impairment to crippling rigidity, tremor, or dementia?

References

Scully, Rosemary M., and Marylou R. Barnes. *Physical Therapy.* Philadelphia: J.B. Lippincott Company, 1989.

Walshe, J.M. "Treatment of Wilson's Disease with Trientine (Triethylene Tetramine) Dihydrochloride." *Lancet* 1 8273 (1982): 643-647.

Wound Infection, Postoperative
998.5

Definition
Postoperative wound infection is an infection in the tissues of the incision and operative area. It can occur from 1 day to many years after an operation, but commonly occurs between the fifth and tenth day after surgery. The infection results from contamination of the wound, which is present to some extent in all incisions. A setback in recovery such as malnutrition, cardiac failure, or decreased oxygen to the tissues will weaken the individual and allow the infection to take hold.

There are four categories of wound contamination. They include clean wounds with no gross contamination, lightly contaminated wounds (stomach or biliary surgeries), heavily contaminated wounds (intestinal surgeries), and infected wounds in which there is obvious infection present prior to the surgical incision.

Abdominal surgeries, those lasting over 2 hours, contaminated operations, and the presence of more than three other diagnoses in the individual present the highest risk. Immunosuppressed individuals are also at high risk. Preoperative antibiotics, good isolation techniques and delayed suturing of contaminated or infected wounds will lower the risk of postoperative wound infection.

Diagnosis
History: The individual will complain of increased pain in the incision and operative area. Individuals may report feeling feverish or chilled.

Physical exam: Fever is usually present. The incision may be swollen with tight sutures. Lightly feeling (palpation) the wound may reveal hard areas that are tender and warm. Sutures may be cut to allow further inspection of a portion of the incision. The individual will guard the incision during movement.

Tests: Cultures of wound drainage are taken. A complete blood count (CBC) and sedimentation rate may be done.

Treatment
Antibiotics will be given by mouth or intravenously. The incision may be opened and allowed to drain. Any foul-looking tissue or debris will be removed. If the wound is deep, it may be packed with sterile gauze. Some wounds may be treated with physical therapy using a whirlpool or hot bath (Hubbard tank) to help remove destroyed tissue and foster wound healing. Periodic evaluation of the wound and wound cleansing will be done. When it appears the infection has resolved (approximately 2 weeks) the wound may be closed with stitches or allowed to fill in gradually with scar tissue.

Prognosis
Postoperative wound infections may make any illness more severe and result in a poor surgical outcome. With appropriate treatment (antibiotics and/or wound drainage) the infection may clear and the incision may heal. However, healing will be more prolonged than normally expected for the type of surgery performed. Without treatment there is a substantial risk of the infection spreading systemically causing associated overwhelming infection, tissue deformity and destruction, and possibly death.

Differential Diagnosis
Other possibilities include suture abscess, hematoma, seroma, granuloma, infection elsewhere, and ascites leak.

Specialists
- General Surgeon
- Infectious Disease Physician

Work Restrictions / Accommodations
Lifting and strenuous activity will be restricted for a period of time. A support device may need to be worn over the incisional area during certain activities.

Complementary and Alternative Therapies
Content is intended for awareness only. Treatments may or may not be effective. Scientific evidence may be lacking and some substances have potentially toxic effects. Dr. Presley Reed and the editors do not endorse the use of these therapies in the absence of consultation with a licensed medical professional.

Vitamin A -	May enhance or accelerate wound healing in stomach and skin ulcers.
Vitamin C -	May enhance wound healing for minor surgical wounds and reduce wound inflammation.
Vitamin E -	May reduce inflammation and enhance wound healing and skin repair.
Vitamin K -	May enhance blood clotting and reduce bleeding associated with wounds.
Zinc -	Said to enhance wound healing.
Iron -	Plays a key role in collagen formation, which is needed to repair skin and soft tissue wounds.
Enzymes (proteases) -	Play a key role in protein metabolism and are purported to promote wound healing.

Comorbid Conditions
Comorbid conditions that would influence length of disability include diabetes, vascular disease, cancer, malnutrition, immune suppression, or other areas of infection.

Complications
Wound infection can cause the wound layers to separate, incisional hernias, abscesses, and tissue destruction (gangrene or necrotizing fasciitis), which can result in physical and/or functional deformity. Bacteria from the infection can spread causing an overwhelming, life-threatening, systemic infection (sepsis).

Factors Influencing Duration

The type and extent of the infection, its treatment, the presence of complications, and the individual response to treatment will influence the length of disability. In addition, those of advanced age or those who smoke have prolonged wound healing that might influence the length of disability.

Length of Disability

Duration depends upon site, severity of infection, and infectious agent. Contact physician for additional information.

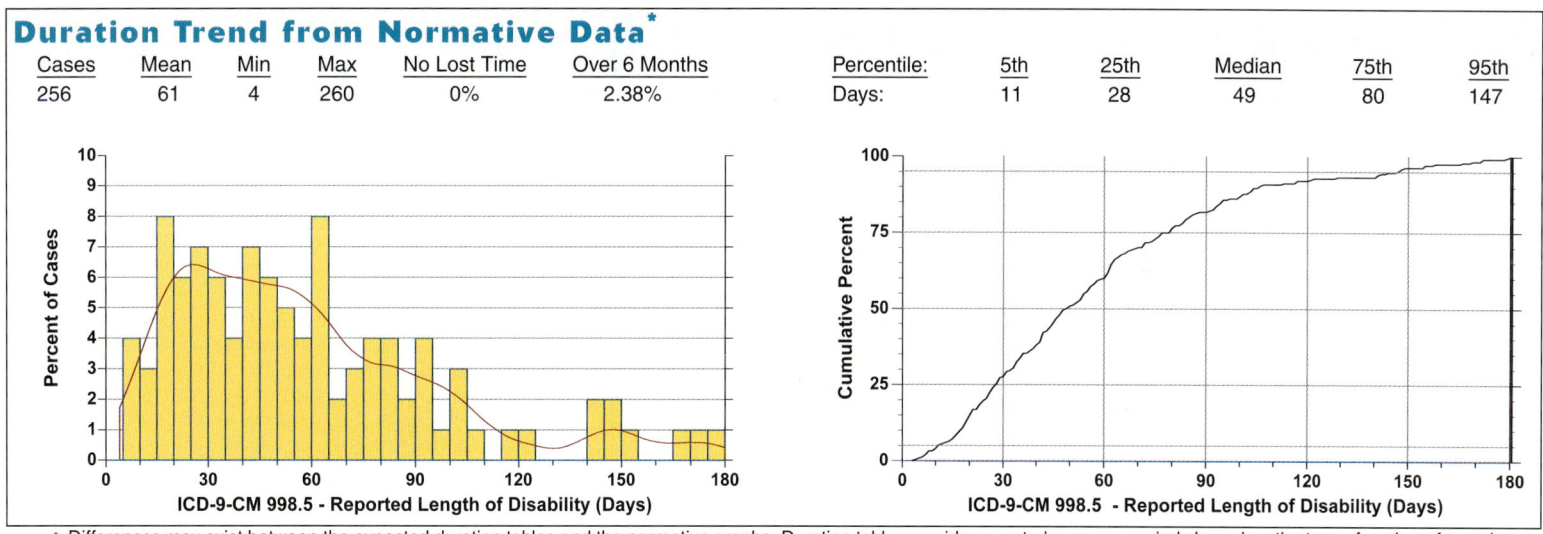

Duration Trend from Normative Data*

Cases	Mean	Min	Max	No Lost Time	Over 6 Months
256	61	4	260	0%	2.38%

Percentile:	5th	25th	Median	75th	95th
Days:	11	28	49	80	147

ICD-9-CM 998.5 - Reported Length of Disability (Days)

* Differences may exist between the expected duration tables and the normative graphs. Duration tables provide expected recovery periods based on the type of work performed by the individual. The normative graphs reflect the actual observed experience of many individuals across the spectrum of physical conditions, in a variety of industries, and with varying levels of case management.

Failure to Recover

If an individual fails to recover within the maximum duration expectancy period, the reader may wish to reference the following questions to assist in better understanding the specifics of an individual's medical case.

Regarding diagnosis:

- Has individual had a recent surgical procedure?
- Does individual have conditions that may place them higher risk for a postoperative wound infection such as abdominal surgery, lengthy surgery, or immune suppression?
- Does individual have symptoms characteristic of a postoperative wound infection such as unusual incisional pain, redness, swelling, drainage, or fever and chills?
- Was an elevated white blood cell count noted?
- Was wound culture positive?
- If the diagnosis was unclear, were other conditions such as suture abscess, hematoma, seroma, granuloma, or other infection considered in the differential diagnosis?

Regarding treatment:

- Have appropriate antibiotics been administered (i.e., antibiotics that are specific for the bacteria that was cultured from the wound)?
- Was the wound opened and allowed to drain?
- Has individual completed the full course of antibiotics?
- Does individual show signs of persistent infection such as redness or drainage around the wound? If so, was the wound re-cultured to determine if the bacteria are resistant to the current antibiotic therapy?

Regarding prognosis:

- Did individual receive prompt treatment?
- Did adequate time elapse for complete recovery?
- Are there signs of systemic infection such as fever, rapid heart rate, chills, and fatigue? If so, was it addressed in the treatment plan?
- Does individual have associated complications such as wound dehiscence, incisional hernias, abscesses, tissue destruction, or systemic infection that may impact recovery and outcome? Were complications addressed promptly and appropriately in the treatment plan?
- Were appropriate specialists consulted (infectious disease specialist, intensivist)?
- Does individual have any underlying conditions (diabetes, vascular disease, cancer, malnutrition, immune suppression, or other areas of infection) that may impact ability to recover? Were these conditions addressed in the treatment plan?

References

Braunwald, Eugene, et al. Harrison's Principles of Internal Medicine, 11th ed. New York: McGraw-Hill Book Company, 1987.

Wound Infection, Postoperative

X-ray

Other names / synonyms: Angiography, Cineradiography, Computed Radiography, Digital Radiography, Fluoroscopy, Interventional Radiography, Mammography, Radiography, Plain X-rays, Tomography, X-ray

87, 88.39

Definition

Radiography is a diagnostic procedure, used to gain a better understanding of what is causing an individual's problems. In radiography, x-rays are used to visualize the interior anatomy of the body. Images are formed because different tissues absorb x-rays differently as they pass through the body. A recording medium is placed on the opposite side of the individual to detect x-ray transmission. This can be a film similar to photographic film, producing a still picture, or it can be electronic detection of the x-rays producing a live (real-time) moving display on a TV monitor.

Radiography is most commonly done as plain film radiography. Since x-rays penetrate straight through the body, structures that overlap each other often cannot be seen clearly with plain x-rays. Tomography is a special technique to provide greater detail of the interior anatomy than plain x-rays. Other special radiography techniques include angiography, mammography, fluoroscopy, interventional radiography, cineradiography, or digital and computed radiography.

Images may be taken in a hospital x-ray department, by mobile units at the bedside or in an operating room, or in facilities outside the hospital. Many office settings have small radiography units.

Reason for Procedure

Radiography is widely used for most medical imaging to discover abnormalities of the lungs, heart, bones, and soft tissues. Radiography has been used for over 100 years, and it can be done at relatively low cost. Mammography involves specialized equipment designed to detect small breast tumors.

Angiography is a way to detect disease in an artery or an abnormality in the organs it supplies. It can be done by injecting an x-ray dye directly into an artery, or intravenously in the special case of digital subtraction angiography. X-ray images in motion (fluoroscopy) can be done in order to find abnormalities in the esophagus or stomach. Cineradiography can take high-speed x-ray pictures to detect abnormalities of swallowing, movements of the heart, or to closely follow an injection of contrast dye through an artery. Interventional radiography is being used for treatment procedures such as percutaneous transluminal angioplasty designed to open up clogged coronary arteries. Such procedures are easier on the individual, lessen the need for surgery, and are relatively inexpensive when compared to most surgical procedures.

Description

Radiography is fast, easy, and non-invasive. X-rays are beamed through the body and hit a recording medium on the other side. The recording medium may be a film similar to photographic film, producing a still picture, or it may be electronic detection of the x-rays producing a live (real-time) moving display on a TV monitor. Images are formed because different tissues absorb x-rays differently as they pass through the body.

Plain x-rays take only minutes to perform, and provide no discomfort to the individual. Real-time images, such as with fluoroscopy or angiography, may take longer.

Prognosis

The outcome depends on the underlying condition. Radiography is a means to diagnose a condition.

Specialists

- Radiologist

Work Restrictions / Accommodations

No work restrictions or accommodations are ordinarily associated with this procedure. Arteriography might require missing that day of work.

Comorbid Conditions

Bleeding disorders may prolong recovery from interventional procedures such as arteriography.

Procedure Complications

Excessive exposure to x-rays can possibly damage some organs that are x-ray sensitive, such as the ovaries and testes, eyes, and the thyroid gland. X-ray exposure can increase the risk of cancer. This risk is minimized by focusing and limiting the x-ray beam, as well as shielding the sensitive organs if possible. Similar precautions are taken for the uterus if a woman could possibly be pregnant.

There are occasionally adverse reactions to x-ray contrast media, if used, which can range from a transient flushing to a life-threatening drop in blood pressure and heart rate. Barium sulfate, a contrast material used to visualize the gastrointestinal tract, can leak out into the abdominal cavity if a perforation of the intestine is present, creating a serious peritonitis. With arteriography, bleeding from the arterial puncture site can occur, as can damage to the artery itself.

Factors Influencing Duration

The underlying condition for which radiography was done will influence length of disability.

Length of Disability

No disability is expected for this procedure. Disability may occur as a result of an underlying condition.

References

Schwartz, Seymour, MD. Principles of Surgery. New York: McGraw Hill, 1999.

Yellow Fever

Other names / synonyms: Jungle Fever, Jungle Yellow Fever, Urban Yellow Fever

060, 060.1, 060.9

Definition

Yellow fever is a viral disease transmitted by mosquitoes and characterized by fever, headache, muscle pain, vomiting, and exhaustion.

Once the yellow fever virus enters the skin, it travels to the lymph nodes where it multiplies. It then enters the blood and spreads to the liver, spleen, kidney, or bone marrow. Infection with yellow fever usually prevents reinfection (life-long immunity).

Yellow fever involves 2 different disease cycles. Jungle yellow fever is transmitted to humans via mosquitos who have bitten infected monkeys. Individuals most likely to catch jungle yellow fever are those who work in the forest such as nut pickers, woodcutters, and road builders.

Urban yellow fever occurs when an infected human moves or travels to a city and a domestic species of mosquito transfers the disease from individual to individual. Those at greatest risk live in crowded conditions. Yellow fever is a preventable disease. Even though it is rare for travelers to endemic areas to contract the disease, many countries in Africa and South America still require vaccination prior to entering the country. Travelers should contact the Centers for Disease Control and Prevention for more information.

Yellow fever was the cause of epidemics in the US in the nineteenth century. Mosquito control has now eliminated the virus in the US and decreased the risk in countries where the disease was once prevalent. Risks still remain, however, because the mosquito has developed an increased resistance to insecticides. Yellow fever is still common in the jungles of Central Africa and Central and South America. About 200,000 individuals are infected worldwide every year. As much as half of infected individuals die from this disease usually near the end of the first week after symptoms appear.

Diagnosis

History: Individuals may report a recent visit to an area where yellow fever is endemic. The period of time between being bitten by an infected mosquito and when symptoms first appear (incubation period) is usually 3 to 6 days, but can be longer. Symptoms include a sudden onset of fever, chills, severe headache, low back pain, generalized muscle aches and pain, decreased appetite, nausea, vomiting, and extreme lack of energy and exhaustion (prostration). The infected individual may also develop a red tongue, flushed face, and reddening of the eyes.

Although symptoms may disappear about the third day, they usually return. If the disease progresses, by the fifth day stomach pain may develop, and bleeding (hemorrhages) from the nose, mouth, under the skin, bladder, and gastrointestinal tract may occur. Urine may contain blood and vomit may be blood-tinged (black vomit). Delirium and seizures followed by coma are common.

Physical exam: The individual may have a fever and initially a fast heart rate (tachycardia). The pulse then slows and becomes weak after a few days. The membrane covering the eye (conjunctiva) may be red and have a discharge (conjunctivitis). The tongue may be coated. If the individual's temperature has fallen only to rise again, the physical exam may reveal yellowing of the skin and whites of the eyes (jaundice) and dark-colored urine. The individual may become dehydrated, blood pressure may fall, and kidney (renal) failure may develop. Delirium, stupor, seizures, and coma may follow.

Tests: Yellow fever may initially be confused with other more common infections. A number of blood and biochemical tests are required in order to make an accurate diagnosis. These include a complete blood count (CBC), bilirubin, serum chemistry detailing liver enzyme levels (ALT, AST), electrolyte levels, coagulation studies (PT, PTT, and clotting time), viral cultures, enzyme-linked immunosorbent assay (ELISA) for identification of viral antigen, and polymerase chain reaction (PCR).

Treatment

Since there is no specific treatment for yellow fever, the goal is to relieve symptoms and prevent or manage complications. Medication may be prescribed to reduce fever (antipyretics) and pain (analgesics) and reduce the risk of gastric bleeding. Antacids and histamine blockers are often prescribed to protect the stomach from bleeding. Intravenous fluids may be given to treat dehydration, maintain blood volume, increase blood pressure, and correct low blood sugar (hypoglycemia). Individuals usually require 1 to 2 weeks of bed rest. Transfusions of whole blood or plasma may be needed to control severe bleeding disorders. Dialysis may be needed if renal failure develops.

Immunizations for yellow fever are often required for entry into certain countries. To avoid being bitten by a mosquito when traveling in areas where yellow fever is found, housing should be screened, insect repellent should be used, and full protective clothing worn.

Prognosis

Most individuals recover from yellow fever in 7 to 8 days with no permanent damage. Weakness may prolong convalescence for 1 to 2 weeks. Initial prognosis is always guarded since a sudden change for the worse is common. Yellow fever kills as many as half of infected individuals. Death usually occurs between the sixth and tenth day of the disease.

Infection with yellow fever usually imparts a lifelong immunity.

Differential Diagnosis

Symptoms are similar to hepatitis, malaria, leptospirosis, dengue fever, and other forms of hemorrhagic fever or jaundice.

Specialists

- Infectious Disease Physician
- Internist

Work Restrictions / Accommodations

Weakness may prolong convalescence.

Comorbid Conditions

Individuals with weakened immune systems may be at increased risk for yellow fever.

Complications

Complications may include liver and kidney failure, irregular heartbeat (arrhythmia), inflammation of the heart muscle (myocarditis), heart failure, secondary bacterial infection, inflammation of the brain (encephalitis), nerve damage, and necrosis of the liver, kidney, or stomach.

Factors Influencing Duration

Length of disability may be influenced by the severity of the disease and any complications that develop.

Length of Disability

The individual may return to work when signs of infection have decreased, appetite returns, and alertness, strength, and feeling of well being will allow. The disease typically runs its course within a week.

Duration in Days

Job Classification	Minimum	Optimum	Maximum
Any work	7	14	56

Failure to Recover

If an individual fails to recover within the maximum duration expectancy period, the reader may wish to reference the following questions to assist in better understanding the specifics of an individual's medical case.

Regarding diagnosis:

- Does the individual have jungle or urban yellow fever?
- Has the individual traveled to an area where yellow fever is endemic?
- Did the individual have a sudden onset of fever, chills, and severe headache?
- Does the individual also have low back pain and generalized muscle aches and pain?
- Does the individual have decreased appetite, nausea, vomiting, and prostration?
- Has the individual developed a red tongue, flushed face, and reddening of the eyes?
- Did the symptoms disappear about the third day, and then reappear?
- Has individual developed stomach pain and hemorrhages from the nose, mouth, under the skin, bladder, and gastrointestinal tract? Is urine and vomit blood-tinged?
- Did the individual develop delirium and seizures, followed by coma?
- On exam, was a fever and tachycardia present?
- Did the pulse then slow and becomes weak after a few days?
- Is the conjunctiva red and have discharge? Is the tongue coated?
- Has the individual's temperature fallen and then risen again?
- Were jaundice and dark-colored urine then present?
- Is the individual dehydrated? Hypotensive? Did renal failure develop?
- Did delirium, stupor, seizures, and coma follow?
- Has the individual had a CBC, bilirubin, liver enzymes, electrolyte levels, coagulation studies, viral cultures, ELISA testing, and polymerase chain reaction?
- Have conditions with similar symptoms been ruled out?

Regarding treatment:

- Has treatment relieved symptoms and prevented or managed complications?
- Was medication given to reduce fever and pain and reduce the risk of gastric bleeding?
- Was the individual given intravenous fluids?
- Were transfusions needed?
- Was dialysis necessary?

Regarding prognosis:

- Is the individual's employer able to accommodate any necessary restrictions?
- Does individual have any conditions that may affect ability to recover?
- Does individual have any complications such as liver and kidney failure, arrhythmias, myocarditis heart failure, encephalitis, nerve damage, or necrosis of the liver, kidney, or stomach?

References

Brooks, George F., Janet S. Butel, and Stephen A. Morse. Medical Microbiology. Stamford: Appleton & Lange, 1998.

Tierney, Lawrence M., Stephen J. McPhee, and Maxine A. Papadakis. Current Medical Diagnosis and Treatment. Stamford: Appleton & Lange, 1998.

Managing Medical Absences

The Interaction Among The ADA, the FMLA, Workers' Compensation and The Disability Benefits Law

Alan M. Koral, Esq.
Vedder, Price, Kaufman & Kammholz
New York, NY

I. INTRODUCTION

Employers and persons handling disability management issues for employers when confronted with issues involving employee absences due to illness or injury traditionally looked to two sources for information about the employer's and the employee's respective rights and obligations: (1) the state workers' compensation law and (2) the employer's own policies and practices, including any applicable collective bargaining agreements. Even then, charting a course of action that accommodated competing interests of employer and employee was never an easy task.

That task was made more complicated by the enactment of state laws prohibiting discrimination against "handicapped" employees and the federal Rehabilitation Act of 1974, which applies to federal contractors and grant recipients. However, while these laws offered certain employee protections, a general lack of awareness about how these laws might affect medical leaves of absence often resulted in their being overlooked by employees, attorneys, (employers) and health care managers.

Managing medical leaves of absence became significantly more complicated with the enactment of the Americans with Disabilities Act of 1990 ("ADA") and the Family and Medical Leave Act of 1993 ("FMLA"). The ADA, FMLA and state workers' compensation laws impose numerous and not always consistent obligations on employers. This legal minefield has created a potential bonanza for plaintiffs' attorneys and has heightened the level of frustration for professionals responsible for dealing with these issues.

More than ever, professionals need a thorough understanding of the principal laws affecting medical leaves, including an understanding of how these laws operate in practice. Parts II through IV of these materials describe the ADA, the state workers' compensation and the FMLA, focusing on those aspects of each law relating to managing medical leaves of absence. Part V describes key areas of interplay between these three laws and suggests practical strategies for employers.

II. THE AMERICANS WITH DISABILITIES ACT

A. Overview

The ADA's employment provisions prohibit discrimination against qualified individuals with disabilities. The ADA also imposes an affirmative obligation on employers to provide "reasonable accommodations" to qualified individuals with disabilities.

B. Employers Covered

1. The ADA's employment provisions apply to all public and private sector employers with 15 or more employees.

2. Note that analogous state laws may have broader coverage. For example, the disability discrimination provisions of the New York Human Rights Law (New York Executive Law Article 15) apply to all New York employers with four or more employees.

C. Protected Individuals

The ADA protects two groups of people: (1) qualified individuals with disabilities and (2) persons associated with individuals with disabilities.

1. Qualified Individuals with Disabilities

a. The ADA defines an individual with a disability as someone whom:

   (1) Has a physical or mental impairment that substantially limits one or more major life activities;

   (2) has "a record of" such an impairment (thereby protecting from discrimination people with a history of a disability which does not currently substantially limit any major life activity, as well as people who are misdiagnosed as having a disability); or

   (3) is "regarded as" having such an impairment (thereby protecting people who are not substantially limited in any major life activity but who, because of common misconceptions or stereotypes, are perceived as having a disability).

b. The following conditions are not considered "disabilities" under the ADA, either because they are specifically excluded (categories 1-4) or because they do not meet the definition of a physical or mental impairment which substantially limits one or more major life activities (categories 5-8):

   (1) current illegal drug use;

   (2) homosexuality and bisexuality;

   (3) transvestitism, transsexualism, pedophilia, exhibitionism, gender identity disorders not resulting from physical impairments, and other sexual behavior disorders;

   (4) compulsive gambling, kleptomania and pyromania;

   (5) temporary, non-chronic impairments;

   (6) pregnancy and other physical conditions which are not the result of a physiological disorder;

   (7) personality traits such as poor judgment, a quick temper, or the tendency to engage in irresponsible behavior; and

   (8) environmental, cultural and economic disadvantages, such as a lack of education, relevant work experience, or training.

c. To be considered a "qualified individual with a disability" protected under the ADA, an individual must:

   (1) meet the skill, experience, education, and other job-related requirements of the position, and

   (2) be able, with or without reasonable accommodation, to perform the "essential functions" of the job in question.

2. Persons "Associated With" Disabled Individuals

a. In addition to protecting qualified individuals with disabilities, the ADA's protection against discrimination also extends to those who have a known association or relationship with a disabled individual. For example, an employer may not refuse to hire or otherwise discriminate against an individual because the person's child, spouse, or "significant other" has a disability.

b. However, unlike an employer's obligations to an employee with a disability, an employer need not provide reasonable accommodation to an employee based upon his or her association with a disabled individual.

D. Prohibition Against Discrimination

The ADA prohibits employers from discriminating against qualified individuals with disabilities because of their disabilities. In other words, if an individual is able safely and effectively to perform the essential functions of the job, with or without reasonable accommodation, the employer may not consider the individual's disability in making employment decisions.

E. Duty of Reasonable Accommodation

1. An employer must provide reasonable accommodation to the known physical or mental limitations of a qualified employee with a disability unless it can show that the accommodation would impose an undue hardship on the business.

2. A "reasonable accommodation" is any modification or adjustment to a job, an employment practice, or the work environment that makes it possible for an individual with a disability to enjoy an equal employment opportunity.

3. Examples of reasonable accommodations:

    a. acquiring equipment or devices that enable the employee to effectively perform the essential functions of the job;

    b. job restructuring -- reallocating or redistributing marginal job functions or altering how an essential job function is performed;

    c. part-time or modified work schedules;

    d. temporarily assigning the employee to a light duty job;

    e. permitting use of accrued paid leave time or unpaid leave;

    f. extending an unpaid leave of absence beyond the time limit in the employer's policy if the requested extension is for a limited period of time and the employee is expected to be able to return to work at the end of the extension; and

    g. reassigning an employee to a vacant position (ordinarily should be considered only when an accommodation is not possible in an employee's present job).

4. Limitations on the duty to accommodate

    a. The duty to accommodate only applies to "the known physical or mental limitations" of the applicant or employee. Accordingly, the duty ordinarily is not triggered unless the individual seeking accommodation advises the employer of the disability and the need for accommodation.

    b. An accommodation need not be the one the employee prefers, as long as it is effective in enabling the employee to perform the essential functions of the job.

    c. An accommodation need not be provided if it would impose an "undue hardship" on the operation of the business.

        (1) An undue hardship is an action that requires "significant difficulty or expense" in relation to the size of the employer, the resources available, and the nature of the operation.

        (2) The concept of undue hardship includes actions which are unduly costly or disruptive or which would fundamentally alter the operation of the business.

F. Health and Safety Concerns ("Direct Threat")

1. The ADA does not require an employer keep an employee with a disability in a job if doing so would pose a "direct threat" to the employee's own health or safety or the health or safety of others.

2. A "direct threat" is a significant risk of substantial harm that cannot be eliminated or reduced to acceptable levels by reasonable accommodation. To establish that a disabled employee poses a direct threat, the employer must be prepared to show:

    a. there exists a high probability that the harm will occur;

    b. the risk is current, not based upon speculation that the individual will be unable to safely perform the job in the future because of the expected continued deterioration of his condition;

    c. the harm anticipated will be substantial;

    d. the employer's determination is based upon objective medical evidence relating to the particular individual, and not on unfounded assumptions, fears, or stereotypes about the limitations or risks posed by a particular type of disability in general; and

    e. the risk cannot be eliminated or reduced to acceptable levels by reasonable accommodation.

G. Job Protection/Reinstatement Obligations

1. The ADA does not specifically require an employer to hold an individual's job open for a particular length of time or to reinstate a qualified employee with a disability who is able to return to work following an extended absence.

2. However, as noted above, an employer's obligation to provide reasonable accommodation to qualified individuals with disabilities may include:

    a. permitting the use of accrued paid leave time or unpaid leave;

    b. permitting a limited extension of an unpaid leave of absence beyond the time limit in the employer's policy if the employee is expected to be able to return to work in the near future;

    c. temporarily assigning the employee to a light duty job; and

    d. reassigning an employee to a vacant position that he or she is able, with or without reasonable accommodation, to perform.

3. In addition, the ADA's prohibition against discrimination effectively requires an employer to ensure that, in administering its medical leave policy, it is not treating employees with disabilities any less favorably than employees whose need for leave does not rise to the level of a disability under the ADA.

H. Restrictions on Medical Inquiries and Examinations

1. The ADA prohibits employers (and their agents) from asking employees about their medical condition or from requiring employees to submit to medical examination unless the inquiry or examination is "job related and consistent with business necessity."

2. The purpose of this prohibition is to prevent employers from taking adverse employment actions based upon medical information, including information about the presence or absence of disabilities, which they have no need to know about.

3. The EEOC has taken the position that an inquiry or examination will be considered job related and consistent with business necessity when an employee:

    a. Is injured on the job;

    b. Suffers an illness or injury that appears to affect the employee's ability to perform essential job functions;

    c. Is returning to work following an extended medical absence;

    d. Requests an accommodation;

    e. Is required to submit to an examination or screening required by other laws.

4. Employers and their agents must treat information obtained from medical inquiries and examinations as confidential.

   a. Documents containing medical information must be kept separate from an employee's regular personnel file. Because workers' compensation claim documents contain medical information, those documents should not be kept in the employee's personnel file, but should instead be kept in a confidential medical file or separate workers' compensation claim file.

   b. Medical information concerning an employee should be communicated to supervisors and managers only on a need-to-know basis.

III. WORKERS' COMPENSATION LAWS

A. Overview

Each State has its own workers' compensation law, and there are considerable variations among the States. Workers' compensation laws (herein after referred to as the "WCL") generally require employers to provide certain benefits to employees suffering work-related injuries or illnesses. These laws also generally prohibit employers from discharging an employee for exercising his or her right to workers' compensation benefits.

B. Employers Covered

Though originally created to provide coverage for employees involved in specified hazardous employment, the WCL now covers all private and public sector employers with one employee or more.

C. Protected Individuals

Typically, any person working for an employer is protected on the first day of employment (with the exception of independent contractors and licensed real estate brokers and sales associates who are characterized in an agreement as independent contractors and who are subject to additional contract terms which provide, in part, for payment of commission on gross sales, broker/associate's choice of location and hours of work, as well as the broker/associate's responsibility for business expenses).

Workers' Compensation is in almost all States the exclusive remedy for injuries sustained by an employee and serves as a bar against action for negligence brought by the employee against the employer and co-workers for such injuries. The exception to this rule is an intentional act by an employer or co-worker causing injury to an employee, in which case the employee would be entitled to seek civil remedies or Workers' Compensation benefits.

D. Injuries and Illnesses Qualifying for Benefits

1. Workers' compensation benefits are paid for illnesses and injuries arising out of and in the course of the employment that temporarily or permanently impair an employee's working abilities.

2. The fact that an injury or illness involves the aggravation of pre-existing condition does not by itself absolve the employer of liability.

3. Any injury that results from the employee's intent to injure himself or another, or that is due solely to the intoxication of the employee from alcohol or a controlled substance while on duty constitutes a non-compensable injury. However, an employee who is injured by the intentional act of a co-worker does qualify for benefits.

4. Also uncompensable are injuries occurring due to travel to and from employment, which are not deemed incidents of employment. However, "special errands" which involve undertaking work or travel not associated with an employee's normal place or time of work and injuries arising from such tasks are compensable.

E. Types of Benefits

1. Medical and rehabilitation benefits

   a. The employer must generally pay for all first aid, medical, and surgical services reasonably necessary to relieve the effects of the work-related injury or illness.

   b. If warranted, the employer must generally also pay for the cost of necessary physical, mental, and vocational rehabilitation.

2. Payment of compensation for disability

   a. Compensation (wage replacement as allowed by the WCL) for disability is typically not allowed for the first seven days of disability.

   b. If the injury results in the employee being disabled for more than a set time period (e.g., fourteen days) not necessarily consecutive, compensation shall be allowed from the date of the disability. This time period varies drastically among the States.

3. Benefits for total disabilities
   A totally disabled person is one whose injury has rendered him or her unable to work at all and unable to have any earning capacity.

   a. Temporary total disability (TTD) benefits

      (1) Are a form of wage replacement and are generally paid while an employee is temporarily unable to work because of a work-related injury or illness.

      (2) TTD benefits may typically be discontinued for any of three reasons:

         (a) the employee is able or released to return to work (either the employee's regular job or a light duty position);

         (b) the employee reaches maximum medical improvement (if the employee cannot return to work with the employer vocational rehabilitation benefits may become payable); or

         (c) the employee resists treatment or otherwise unnecessarily engages in behavior that hinders the employee's recovery.

   b. Permanent total disability (PTD) benefits

      (1) PTD benefits are typically paid for a complete disability which renders the employee without marketable skills because of physical limitation, age, education or work experience except in the field in which the employee can no longer work due to the compensable injury.

      (2) PTD benefits are also payable if an employee suffers a loss of, or the complete loss of use of, essential occupational body parts.

4. Benefits for partial disabilities
   An employee who sustains a partial disability retains some degree of earning capacity. Depending upon the nature of the injury, partial disability awards are in most States non-schedule or schedule awards. Schedule awards are benefits paid for a specific number of weeks depending on which body member is injured as designated by a schedule in the WCL and are usually made after the claimant's condition has stabilized (usually at least six months) when the degree of permanent loss can be established. Non-schedule awards apply for all injuries other than those listed in the Law.

   a. Temporary partial disability (TPD) benefits are usually paid if the job-related injury or disease result in a temporary physical impairment resulting in a decrease of the employee's earning capacity.

   b. Permanent partial disability (PPD) benefits

      (1) PPD benefits are payable only where the employee's earnings are reduced as a result of a non-scheduled injury (injury occurring to a part of the body not listed in Section 15(d)). The employee will not receive an award if he or she can return to work at the same salary.

(2) In some states an employee may receive PPD benefits as set by the Workers' Compensation Board if he or she has no earnings, but is considered only partially disabled.

5. Death benefits

a. Death benefits are payable where an employee dies as a result of a compensable injury suffered in an accident arising out of and in the course of employment or as the result of a compensable occupational disease.

b. Death benefits are payable to an employee's surviving spouse and/or children, whether or not supported by the decedent. Non-marital children and children who prove dependence are also entitled to death benefits.

F. Limited Job Protection/Reinstatement Rights

1. Some states require an employer to hold an injured employee's job open or to reinstate an employee once the employee is able to return to work.

2. Many states prohibit an employer from discharging or otherwise retaliating against an employee for seeking benefits (or testifying in a proceeding) under the WCL.

G. Medical Inquiries and Examinations

1. Unlike the ADA and FMLA, which restrict an employer's access to medical information, the WCL generally permits employers to obtain medical information in a variety of ways:

   a. Written consent from the employee for the health care provider to release to the employer all records relating to the employee's treatment (often included in form report of injury the employee is asked to complete);

   b. Written consent from the employee allowing the employer or its insurance carrier to communicate directly with the health care provider to discuss the nature and extent of the injury, the anticipated duration of any period of disability, the ability to return to work, and any restrictions imposed (also often included in form report of injury the employee is asked to complete);

   c. A written request to the health care provider to make treating records available for inspection and copying;

   d. Industrial Commission or other state agency subpoena for records;

   e. Request for the employee to submit to a medical examination or reexamination by a doctor selected by the employer for purposes of evaluating the basis for the employee's claim, including the nature, extent and probable duration of the injury and the necessity of any work restrictions.

2. The WCL also typically requires the employee to submit to the employer the employee's treating physician's initial report and follow-up treatment reports.

IV. STATE STATUTES GOVERNING LEAVES

Some states have comprehensive statutes governing family and medical leaves. Others, while not having such Laws, have special laws governing certain kinds of medically related leaves. In New York, for example, there are provisions for leaves for bone marrow donation and for adoptive parents' childcare.

V. THE FAMILY AND MEDICAL LEAVE ACT

A. Overview

The FMLA requires covered employers to provide eligible employees with up to 12 weeks of unpaid, job-protected leave each year for qualifying family and medical reasons.

B. Employers Subject to the FMLA

1. All private sector employers with 50 or more employees.

2. All public sector employers regardless of the number of employees.

C. Employees Eligible for FMLA leave

1. General Rule

   a. Employed for 12 months (not necessarily consecutively); and

   b. Worked at least 1,250 hours during the 12-month period preceding the commencement of the leave.

2. Isolated Worksite Exception
Employees who meet the 12 months and 1,250 hours criteria are not entitled to FMLA leave if (a) they work at a worksite with less than 50 employees and (b) the total number of employees at all employer locations within a 75-mile radius of their worksite is less than 50.

D. Qualifying Reasons for FMLA Leave

1. Birth of a child of the employee and to care for the child, provided the leave is completed before the child's first birthday ("birth leave").

2. Placement of a child with employee for adoption or foster care ("placement leave").

3. To care for a child, spouse or parent of the employee who has a serious health condition ("family medical leave").

4. Because of a serious health condition of the employee which renders the employee unable to perform one or more of the essential functions of his or her job ("personal medical leave").

E. Definition of Serious Health Condition

1. A "serious health condition" entitling an employee to FMLA leave is defined as an illness, injury, impairment, or physical or mental condition involving:

   a. Inpatient care (i.e., an overnight stay) in a hospital or other medical care facility, including any period of incapacity or subsequent treatment in connection with such inpatient care; or

   b. Continuing treatment by a health care provider. A serious health condition involving continuing treatment by a health care provider includes:

   (1) A period of incapacity requiring absence from work, school or other regular daily activities for more than three calendar days that also involves:

      (a) Treatment two or more times by a health care provider; or

      (b) Treatment by a health care provider on at least one occasion which results in a regimen of continuing treatment under the provider's supervision (Note -- according to the regulations, the prescription of an antibiotic constitutes a regimen of continuing treatment while the taking of over-the-counter medications, bed rest, and similar activities that can be initiated without a visit to a health care provider are not, by themselves, sufficient to constitute a regimen of continuing treatment).

   or

(2) Any period of incapacity due to pregnancy (including temporary incapacity due to morning sickness).

or

(3) Any period of incapacity or treatment for such incapacity due to a chronic serious health condition, such as asthma, diabetes, or epilepsy, which requires periodic visits to a health care provider for treatment.

or

(4) A period of incapacity that is permanent or long-term due to a condition for which treatment may not be effective, such as Alzheimer's, a severe stroke, or the terminal stages of a disease.

or

(5) A period of absence to receive multiple treatments either for restorative surgery following an injury or for a condition that would likely result in a period of incapacity of more than three consecutive days in the absence of medical intervention or treatment, such as cancer (chemotherapy, radiation, etc.) or kidney disease (dialysis).

2. Alcoholism and Drug Abuse

a. Substance abuse may constitute a serious health condition (if the conditions above are met), thereby allowing an employee to take FMLA leave for substance abuse treatment by a health care provider.

b. However, absences because of substance abuse (rather than for its treatment) do not qualify for FMLA leave.

c. Likewise, the FMLA does not prohibit an employer from disciplining an employee for violating its policy on alcohol and drug use.

F. Length of Leave and Intermittent and Reduced Schedules

1. An eligible employee is entitled to a total of 12 workweeks of FMLA leave during any 12-month period.

2. Leave may be taken:

a. In one 12-week period;

b. In several leaves for different reasons totaling 12 weeks;

c. When medically necessary, family medical leave or personal medical leave may be taken intermittently or as part of a reduced work schedule, up to a maximum of the equivalent of 12 weeks of leave.

3. If leave is being taken intermittently or on a reduced leave schedule, the employer may temporarily transfer the employee to an available alternative position which better accommodates the recurring periods of leave. The temporary transfer cannot result in a cut in the employee's rate of pay or benefits.

4. The following methods exist for determining the 12-month period in which the 12-week leave entitlement occurs:

a. The calendar year;

b. Any fixed 12-month "leave year," such as a fiscal year or a year starting on an employee's anniversary date;

c. The 12-month period measured forward from the date the employee's first FMLA leave begins; or

d. A "rolling" 12-month period measured backward from the date an employee uses any FMLA leave.

5. Unless an employer selects a specific method and communicates the method selected to its employees, the regulations provide that the method that must be used in determining an employee's entitlement to leave is whichever method is most favorable to the employee. Accordingly, the method selected should be clearly set forth in the employer's written FMLA leave policy.

6. Most employers have elected to use the rolling 12-month period measured backward because it is the only one of the three methods which prevents employees from "stacking" two 12-month leaves back to back.

G. Relationship to Paid Leave

1. Generally, the FMLA is unpaid. However, the FMLA permits eligible employees to substitute accrued paid leave for FMLA leave.

2. Accrued paid leave may be substituted for FMLA leave under the following circumstances:

a. The employee may elect or the employer may require an employee to use paid vacation, personal leave, or family leave and charge that leave against an FMLA birth leave, placement leave, or family medical leave, provided that the employer is required to pay family leave only under circumstances permitted by the employer's family leave plan.

b. The employee may elect or the employer may require an employee to use paid vacation, personal leave, or medical or sick leave for an FMLA family medical leave or personal medical leave, provided that the employer is required to pay medical or sick leave only under circumstances permitted by the employer's medical or sick leave plan.

c. An employee on an FMLA leave may receive TTD benefits if the leave is due to a work-related injury or illness. In order to avoid providing injured employees with an incentive not to return to work as soon as they are able, employers should make sure that their paid leave policies do not provide compensation for employees receiving TTD benefits (which, unlike wages, are not taxable income). Otherwise, the employee may end up making more (on an after-tax basis) while on leave than he or she would make working.

3. If an employee elects or is required to substitute accrued paid leave for FMLA leave, the paid leave used may be counted toward the employee's annual 12-week FMLA leave entitlement (provided the employer notifies the employee at the commencement of the leave that it is being counted as FMLA leave).

4. Employers are required to provide group health insurance coverage during FMLA leave under the same terms and conditions that coverage would be provided if the employee were working. If the employee fails to pay the employee share of the premium, coverage may be terminated once the payment is more than 30 days late (provided at least 15 days' notice is given warning the employee that the payment is late and that coverage will terminate if the payment is not made).

H. Employee Notice

1. Employers, through a written leave of absence policy, may require employees to provide advance notice of the need for leave.

a. If the need for a birth leave or a placement leave is foreseeable, the employer may require that at least 30 days' notice be given. If the need for leave is unexpected, the employer cannot require an employee to provide any more notice than is practicable under the circumstances.

b. If the need for a family medical leave or personal medical leave is foreseeable based on planned medical treatment, the employer may require that 30 days' notice must be given. If the need for leave is unexpected, the employer cannot require an employee to provide any more notice than is practicable under the circumstances.

2. If an employee elects to substitute accrued vacation, sick days, or other available paid leave for unpaid FMLA leave, the employer may not require the employee to provide any more advance notice than generally required under the relevant paid leave policy. Accordingly, employers should consider modifying the notice requirements in their paid leave policies so that they are at least as strict as the FMLA's advance notice requirements.

3. If an employee fails to give required 30-day notice when the need for leave is foreseeable, the employee may deny the taking of the leave until 30 days after the given notice.

4. An employee's notification is sufficient if it includes the reason for the leave and the anticipated timing and duration of the leave. The employee does not have to mention the FMLA.

5. The regulations place the burden on the employer to gather sufficient information to determine whether the absence qualifies as FMLA leave and to promptly designate it as leave counting toward the employee's rolling 12-month 12-week FMLA leave entitlement.

6. If the employer has sufficient information to know that the leave is for an FMLA qualifying reason but neglects to notify the employee that the leave will count against the employee's 12-week entitlement, the leave may not later be counted when considering a subsequent request for FMLA qualifying leave. Accordingly, because a workers' compensation absence will almost always constitute a qualifying personal medical leave under the FMLA, employers should make sure that employees who are eligible for FMLA leave and who are absent for work-related injuries are promptly notified that their absence is being counted toward their rolling 12-month FMLA leave entitlement.

I. Responding to Leave Requests

1. Determine the reason for the request and whether the leave is for an FMLA-qualifying reason. Remember that workers' compensation absences normally will also qualify as personal medical leave under the FMLA and need to be treated as such in order to have the absence counted against the employee's rolling 12-month 12-week leave entitlement.

2. Respond to the request within two business days. If the response is initially given verbally, promptly confirm it in writing.

3. If the leave is based on an FMLA-qualifying reason and the employee is eligible for FMLA leave, promptly provide the employee with written notice covering the following items using either the optional Department of Labor form (WH-381) or the employer's own response form:

   a. The leave is designated as and will be counted against the employee's FMLA leave entitlement;

   b. The employee is required to furnish a completed medical certification (and recertifications) and the consequences of failing to do so (include with the notice the Department of Labor Health Care Provider Certification form (WH-380));

   c. Whether the employer's policy requires the employee to substitute any available paid leave and, if not, that the employee may do so if he or she wishes;

   d. The employee's obligation to report periodically on his or her status and intention to return to work, and to promptly report any changes in status affecting the expected return to work date;

   e. The terms and conditions under which any health coverage payments must be made;

   f. Any requirement that the employee present a fitness-for-duty certificate upon his or her return to work;

   g. The restoration rights of the employee (see below);

   h. If the employee is a "key" employee, the consequences of that status (see below); and

   i. The employee's liability, if any, for health insurance premiums if the employee fails to return to work.

J. Job Protection/Reinstatement Obligations

1. General Rule
   At the conclusion of an FMLA leave, the employee must be restored to his or her former position or to an equivalent position with equivalent status, responsibility, pay, benefits, and other conditions of employment.

2. Exceptions

   a. If, at the conclusion of an FMLA leave, an employee is unable to perform the essential functions of the employee's job, the employee has no right to reinstatement under the FMLA. Of course, other laws, such as the ADA, as well as the employer's policies and practices and any applicable collective bargaining agreement, would need to be considered before a decision was made to terminate the employment relationship based upon the employee's inability to return to work after exhausting his or her FMLA leave entitlement.

   b. The taking of an FMLA leave does not provide an employee with any greater right to reinstatement or to other benefits or conditions of employment than if the employee had worked continuously during the leave period. For example, if the employee would have been terminated as part of a reduction in force if he or she had not taken the leave, the employer is not obligated to reinstate the employee at the conclusion of the leave.

3. Highly paid "key" employees may be denied reinstatement if doing so would cause "grievous economic injury" to the employer's operations. In light of the barriers erected by the Department of Labor's regulations implementing the FMLA, it appears that employers will rarely, if ever, be able to deny reinstatement based upon an individual's status as a key employee.

K. Restrictions on Obtaining Medical Information

1. The Department of Labor's model medical certification form (WH-380) should be used. Although the form is optional, the regulations state that an employer may not require more information than what is asked for in the model.

2. If the medical certification is complete, the regulations prohibit the employer from having any direct contact with the employee's health care provider (unless the employee is receiving or seeking workers' compensation benefits, in which case the methods authorized under the Workers' Compensation Act, see above, may be utilized).

3. If the employer has reason to doubt the validity of the certification, the employer may:

   a. Arrange for its doctor to contact the employee's health care provider, with the employee's permission, to clarify any questions and to verify the authenticity of the certification; and/or

   b. Obtain a second opinion at its expense from an independent health care provider it selects to examine the employee.

4. If the second medical opinion conflicts with the first:

   a. The employer may require a third opinion, again at its expense;

   b. The third health care provider must be designated or approved jointly by the employer and the employee;

   c. The third opinion is final and binding on the employer and employee.

5. Although not entirely clear, the regulations appear to prohibit employers from requiring employees returning from an FMLA leave to submit to a return to work medical examination to determine their fitness for duty. Instead, the regulations appear to limit an employer's options to (a) doing nothing or (b) requiring a written certification from the employee's health care provider that the employee is able to return to work.

L. **Discrimination and Retaliation**

1. The FMLA prohibits employers and their agents from interfering with, restraining, or denying the exercise of FMLA rights, and from discriminating against employees for exercising their right to FMLA leave.

2. Examples of unlawful conduct include:

   a. Refusing to approve a leave of absence to which an employee is entitled under the FMLA;

   b. Denying full benefits to an employee on FMLA leave while providing them to employees on other types of unpaid leave;

   c. Basing disciplinary action on the taking of FMLA leave, including the charging of FMLA leave against an employee under a "no fault" attendance policy;

   d. Discriminating against an employee for taking FMLA leave by, for example, using the taking of FMLA leave as a negative factor in promotion or compensation decisions; and

   e. Discharging an employee for taking FMLA leave.

VI. KEY AREAS OF INTERACTION

A. **Differing Definitions of Disability**

1. Not all work-related injuries entitling an employee to workers' compensation benefits are "disabilities" under the ADA.

   a. Many injuries entitling employees to workers' compensation benefits, such as lacerations, sprains, and broken bones, are temporary in nature and, therefore, do not constitute "disabilities" under the ADA.

   b. Some injuries resulting in an award of permanent partial disability (PPD) benefits may not be "disabilities" under the ADA because they do not substantially limit any major life activities. For example, a nuisance value PPD lump sum settlement of $1,500 for "1.5% loss of a leg" may well not involve an impairment, which substantially limits a major life activity.

2. Work-related injuries entitling an employee to workers' compensation TTD benefits normally will be "serious health conditions" under the FMLA. This is because of the seven-day "waiting period" for TTD benefits and the FMLA's definition of "serious health condition" as including any injury involving a period of incapacity exceeding three days and continuing treatment by a health care provider.

3. Not all "serious health conditions" under the FMLA are "disabilities" under the ADA. Examples of protection under the FMLA, but not the ADA, include:

   a. Strep throat resulting in at least three days of incapacity and requiring treatment with an antibiotic;

   b. A broken bone which heals normally and results in no significant permanent impairment; and

   c. Pregnancy and childbirth.

4. Not all "disabilities" under the ADA are "serious health conditions" under the FMLA. Examples of protection under the ADA, but not the FMLA, include:

   a. An employee who is legally blind (an impairment substantially limiting major life activities) but who does not experience periods of incapacity relating to that condition.

   b. An employee who is wrongfully "perceived as" having a disability, such as AIDS or cancer.

B. **Light Duty Assignments**

1. The ADA's duty of reasonable accommodation may require an employer to provide a light duty position for which an employee with a disability is qualified.

   a. The employer should first determine if the employee can perform his or her regular job if certain non-essential functions are reassigned.

   b. If restructuring the employee's current job is not a viable option, the employer may have to consider assigning the employee to an available light duty job. However, if no vacant light duty position is available, the ADA does not require an employer to create one.

2. The WCL typically permits an employer to terminate TTD benefits if an injured employee refuses to accept a medically appropriate light duty assignment.

3. Thus, by offering an injured employee an available light duty assignment, an employer can satisfy its duty to accommodate under the ADA and minimize its workers' compensation liability.

4. However, the FMLA regulations state that an employer is not permitted to require an employee entitled to FMLA leave to accept a light duty position. As long as the employee's serious health condition prevents the employee from performing one or more of the essential functions of his or her regular job, the employee may continue on FMLA leave (up to the 12-week rolling 12-month maximum).

5. As a matter of practice, an employer ordinarily should offer an available light duty position in order to satisfy its duty to accommodate under the ADA. If the employee refuses the offer and elects to remain on FMLA leave, the employer may use the refusal as a basis for terminating the employee's TTD benefits. (Similarly, in the case of an injury or illness which is not work related, an employee's refusal to accept an offered light duty assignment may warrant termination of short-term disability benefits, depending on the language of the employer's STD plan.)

6. Many employers have recognized that an aggressive return to work program, utilizing transitional light duty jobs, is one of the most effective ways of controlling workers' compensation costs. Return to work programs are also regarded as psychologically beneficial to injured employees. The ADA does not require an employer, as part of its duty of reasonable accommodation, to transform a temporary light duty position into a permanent one. Thus, the key for employers is to place a maximum time limit (such as six months) on light duty assignments, and to consistently enforce it to clearly communicate to affected employees the temporary nature of the assignment.

C. **Job Protection/Reinstatement Obligations**

1. The FMLA requires an employer to restore an employee to the same or an equivalent position at the conclusion of an FMLA leave. The FMLA contains no "undue hardship" exception (other than the very limited exception for "key" employees).

2. In contrast, the WCL does not require an employer to reinstate an injured employee when he or she is able to return to work. Rather, it requires only that the employer not discriminate or retaliate against the employee for seeking workers' compensation benefits.

3. Similarly, the ADA does not specifically require an employer to hold an individual's job open for a particular length of time or to reinstate a qualified employee with a disability who is able to return to work following an extended absence. However, the ADA does prohibit an employer from treating a qualified employee with a disability less favorably with regard to leaves and other terms and conditions of employment because of the employee's disability.

4. Furthermore, as noted above, an employer's ADA obligation to provide reasonable accommodation to qualified individuals with disabilities may

include permitting a limited extension of an unpaid leave of absence beyond the time limit in the employer's policy if the employee is expected to be able to return to work in the near future.

5. Because of the FMLA's guarantee of reinstatement, questions of terminating an employee who is unable to return to work for medical reasons ordinarily do not arise unless the employee (a) is not eligible for FMLA leave or (b) has exhausted all available FMLA leave. Unfortunately, because the extent of an employer's duty to accommodate is so hard to define and because of the potential for discrimination claims, employers without well-written policies addressing extended absences often find themselves fruitlessly asking, "How long is long enough?"

6. In order to reduce the risk of liability for discrimination claims (based upon disability or workers' compensation or some other protected status, such as age, sex, race or national origin), many employers have adopted policies which place a specific time limitation (one year is common) on the length of any absence. The advantage of a standard maximum time limitation is that a discrimination claim ordinarily is much easier to defend if the decision to terminate was made pursuant to a uniformly applied policy rather than on an ad hoc basis. However, to be effective, the policy should extend to all types of absences (not just medical), with the exception of military leave of absence mandated by law, and should be consistently applied. Some of the other factors employers should consider in adopting this type of policy include:

   a. Health insurance coverage. Coverage need not be maintained beyond the period of FMLA leave. For administrative convenience, an employer may decide to adopt a set maximum coverage period, such as four months, applicable to all leaves. If the employee wishes to continue coverage, he or she may do so pursuant to COBRA. The employer's health plan will need to be reviewed and revised if necessary to make it consistent with the policy adopted.

   b. Other benefits. Normally employees will not accrue additional paid vacation, sick days or other paid leave time while on an extended leave of absence. Continuing eligibility for other benefits, such as group life insurance or profit sharing, will depend on the terms of the plan document.

   c. Reinstatement rights. Often the employee's right to reinstatement under the policy (following the exhaustion of FMLA leave) is defined as being dependent upon the existence of available job openings.

D. Requests for Reduced Work Schedules

1. Unlike the ADA, the FMLA has no undue hardship limitation. Thus, under the FMLA, leave in the form of a reduced work schedule must be granted to eligible employees provided the reduced schedule leave is medically necessary.

   a. The FMLA permits the transfer of an employee taking a reduced schedule leave to an alternative position, with equivalent pay and benefits, which better accommodates (from the employer's perspective) the reduced work schedule.

   b. The FMLA requires employees needing reduced schedule leave to attempt to schedule their leave so as not to disrupt their employer's operations.

2. If an employee exhausts his or her FMLA leave entitlement but the medical necessity of the reduced leave schedule continues, the question turns to the employer's obligations under the ADA. Questions to be asked might include:

   a. Does the condition constitute a "disability"?

   b. Is the employee a qualified individual with a disability (i.e., is the employee was able, with the requested accommodation, to effectively perform the essential functions of the job)?

   c. Would continuation of the requested accommodation (a reduced or flexible work schedule) constitute an undue hardship?

E. Excessive Absenteeism

1. Courts interpreting the ADA have generally recognized that regular attendance is an "essential function" of most jobs. If an employee's disability results in excessive absenteeism, the employee may not be considered a qualified individual with a disability protected by the ADA, especially if the absences are unpredictable. Thus, the ADA does not necessarily bar the discharge of an employee for excessive absenteeism even if the absences are due to the employee's disability.

2. The FMLA can complicate matters significantly if the absences are due to a serious health condition. As noted above, the FMLA permits eligible employees to take leave on an intermittent basis when medically necessary, regardless of the hardship the intermittent absences may pose for the employer. Furthermore, Department of Labor regulations prohibit employers from counting FMLA leave for disciplinary purposes under attendance policies, including "no fault" policies. Although the employee may be transferred to an alternative position that better accommodates the periods of intermittent leave, often this is not a feasible option.

F. Obtaining Medical Information

1. Of the three laws, the FMLA imposes the most significant restrictions on an employer's ability to obtain medical information. If the absence is not due to a work-related injury or illness (i.e., no workers' compensation) and the employee is not requesting any type of accommodation other than use of FMLA leave to which the employee is entitled, the employer's options are limited and the subject of extensive regulation:

   a. Require the employee to provide a completed medical certification from the employee's health care provider;

      (1) If the certification is incomplete, the regulations do not appear to prohibit the employer from contacting the employee's health care provider directly to obtain the additional information;

      (2) If the certification is complete, the employer may not contact the employee's health care provider directly for more information; however, an employer-selected doctor, with the employee's permission, may contact the employee's health care provider for the purpose of clarifying the information provided and verifying the authenticity of the certification;

   b. In addition, if the employer has reason to doubt the validity of the certification, it may require a second opinion (at its expense) from an independent health care provider that it selects;

   c. If the two opinions conflict, a third and binding opinion may be obtained from a health care provider jointly selected by the employer and the employee;

   d. The employer may require the employee to report periodically (normally no more often than every 30 days) about the employee's status and intention to return to work, and to report immediately any changes in the employee's need for leave;

   e. The employer may require the employee to provide medical recertifications of the continued need for the leave (normally no more often than every 30 days); and

   f. The employer may require the employee to provide a health care provider's certification of the employee's ability to return to work.

2. If the FMLA leave is running concurrently with a workers' compensation absence, the employer and its workers' compensation insurer may utilize the methods of obtaining medical information available to them under the Workers' Compensation Act, notwithstanding the extensive FMLA restrictions which would otherwise apply. However, the employer should continue using FMLA forms and procedures for purposes of assessing the employee's eligibility for FMLA leave.

3. Under the ADA, medical examinations and inquiries must be job related and consistent with business necessity.

   a. Normally an employee's request for an accommodation will warrant the making of medical inquiries and may justify a medical examination;

   b. However, if the only accommodation requested is the use of FMLA leave to which the employee is entitled, the ADA may prohibit the employer from making any medical inquiries or examinations other than those authorized by the FMLA.

Glossary

24-hour urine testing: A test performed on a sample of urine collected for a 24-hour period (the total volume of urine is collected for 24 hours).

abdomen: The lower part of the trunk; the belly.

abdominal: Referring to the abdomen, the belly.

abdominal aorta: The portion of the aorta beginning below the diaphragm and ending where the iliac arteries branch off in the pelvis.

abdominal muscles: The muscles on the front of the belly; the "abs."

abdominal palpation: Part of the physical exam where the physician feels the belly for evidence of disease.

abduction: To move away from the center as in movement of the limbs away from the midline of the body or movement of the fingers or toes away from the midline of the hand or foot.

abductor: A muscle that produces abduction.

abductor pollicis brevis: The short abductor muscle that abducts the thumb. See also abduction.

abductor pollicis longus: The long abductor muscle that abducts the thumb. See also abduction.

ABGs: Arterial blood gases.

ablation: Removal or destruction of a body tissue by surgery, heat, or caustic substance.

abnormal cells: Cells of the body that differ from normal ones of their type. Often refers to cancerous or pre-cancerous cells.

abortifacient: An agent or medicine that causes abortion.

abscess: A localized collection of pus.

absence seizure: A type of seizure where the individual appears to be distant, as if in deep thought. May be accompanied by spasm or twitching.

acalculous: Without stones.

ACE: Angiotensin-converting enzyme. Important in the regulation of blood pressure.

ACE inhibitor: Angiotensin-converting enzyme inhibitor.

acetabulum: The socket of the hip, into which the head of the femur (thigh bone) fits.

acetylcholine: A neurotransmitter released from certain nerve fibers and found in various organs and tissues. This substance helps transmit impulses from nerve to nerve.

acetylcholinesterase: An enzyme that stops the action of acetylcholine. See also acetylcholine.

Achilles tendon: The tendon at the back of the ankle that attaches the large calf muscles (gastrocnemius and soleus) to the heel bone (calcaneus). Currently called calcaneal tendon.

acid: A substance that releases hydrogen ions in solution. The resulting solution turns litmus paper from blue to red, has a pH below seven and is sour in taste. Acids combine with bases to form salts and water, thus neutralizing each other. Acids are vital to chemical processes in cells and tissues. A balance between acids and bases must be maintained for the body to function properly. See also base.

acidosis: A condition where too much acid or too little base in the blood and body tissues occurs. This can result in disorientation, coma, and death if not treated promptly.

acites: An accumulation of fluid in the abdominal cavity. Usually secondary to liver disease. See also ascites.

acoustic: Pertaining to sound or the sense of hearing.

acoustic nerve: The nerve that carries impulses from the ear to the brainstem.

acoustic neuroma: A benign tumor of the acoustic nerve.

acquired: Developed after birth; not hereditary or congenital.

acromioclavicular: Pertaining to the both the acromion and the clavicle (collarbone).

acromioclavicular joint: The joint between the acromion and the lateral end of the clavicle (collarbone).

acromioclavicular ligament: The ligament between the collarbone (clavicle) and acromion.

acromion: The lateral projection of the scapula that forms the point of the shoulder.

ACTH: Adrenocorticotropic hormone.

actinic keratoses: Hard, horny growth on the skin caused by exposure to ultraviolet light, x-rays, or sunlight.

actinotherapy: The use of rays of light (e.g., ultraviolet rays) to treat disease.

action potential: An electrical impulse generated in a neuron or muscle cell when the cell is stimulated.

active range of motion (AROM): Movement of a joint through all degrees of a circle possible for that joint.

acupressure: The practice of applying external pressure at acupuncture points for pain relief or other therapeutic purpose. See also acupuncture.

acupuncture: The Chinese traditional practice of inserting needles at specific body locations to relieve pain, induce anesthesia, or for other therapeutic purpose.

acute: Having a rapid onset and a short course; not chronic.

acute abdomen: An abdominal condition characterized by abrupt onset of severe abdominal pain, usually with signs of peritonitis (such as rigidity of the abdominal muscles). An acute abdomen is usually caused by a localized disease process within the abdominal or pelvic cavity (such as appendicitis, cholecystitis, perforated peptic ulcer, bowel obstruction). An acute abdomen should be evaluated urgently, since immediate surgery may be required.

acute coronary insufficiency: A decrease in the blood flow through the arteries that supply the heart muscle.

acylcarnitine: See carnitine.

ADA-compliant: Refers to dietary guidelines recommended for patients with diabetes.

addiction: Physical dependence on a substance, especially alcohol or other drugs. Deprivation of the substance leads to withdrawal symptoms.

adduction: To move toward the center as in movement of the limbs toward the midline of the body or movement of the fingers and toes toward the midline of the hand or foot.

adductor: A muscle that produces adduction.

adductor pollicis: The muscle that adducts the thumb. See also adduction.

adenocarcinoma: A malignant adenoma (tumor) that grows from the epithelial tissues of a gland. See adenoma, epithelial.

adenoid: A mass of lymphatic tissue located in the back of the nasopharynx (throat); the pharyngeal tonsil. This tissue defends the body from infection via the nasal passages.

adenoma: A benign tumor that grows from the tissues of a gland.

adenovirus: One of a group of related viruses that cause respiratory tract infections.

ADH: Antidiuretic hormone.

adhesion: A fibrous band, usually of scar tissue, binding together parts that are normally separate.

adjuvant: That which assists or enhances, e.g., a drug added to another drug to increase its action.

adjuvant therapy: Refers to treatment, usually of cancer, where one modality is used to increase the effectiveness of another. An example is chemotherapy plus radiation.

adrenal: Pertaining to the area near the kidneys or adrenal glands.

adrenal cortex: The outer layer of the adrenal gland.

adrenal cortical hormones: Hormones secreted by the adrenal cortex including the steroid hormones cortisol and aldosterone and sex hormones (primarily androgens or male sex hormones).

adrenal gland: An endocrine gland located on the upper end of each kidney. The adrenal gland has two major parts, a medulla (inner part) and a cortex (outer layer), each of which secretes a different group of hormones into the blood. See adrenal cortex and adrenal medulla.

adrenal medulla: The inner part of the adrenal gland. The adrenal medulla secretes the adrenergic hormones epinephrine (adrenalin) and norepinephrine.

adrenalin: A hormone secreted by the adrenal medulla, which produces a generalized sympathetic ("fight or flight") response; also called epinephrine. Adrenalin has been synthesized as a drug, and is used to constrict blood vessels (vasoconstrictor) and to dilate bronchial passages (bronchodilator).

adrenergic: Pertaining to epinephrine (adrenalin) or related substances with the same effects. The term is often applied to sympathetic nerve fibers that release the neurotransmitter norepinephrine.

adrenergic receptor: A molecule found on cell membranes that receives adrenergic substances. There are two main types of adrenergic receptors, alpha and beta (which are further classified into alpha 1 and 2, beta 1 and 2 subtypes). Different receptor types are found in varying proportions in different tissues, and are associated with different effects.

adrenocorticotropic hormone (ACTH): See corticotropin.

adrenoglomerulotropin: A hormone secreted by the pineal gland, which is thought to stimulate the adrenal cortex to secrete aldosterone.

adventitia: The outermost coat of an organ (such as a blood vessel wall). The adventitia is composed of connective tissue that merges with the surrounding connective tissue.

aerobic: Pertaining to a microorganism that lives and grows in the presence of oxygen.

aerobic exercise: Exercise that increases the body's consumption of oxygen.

aerosol: Fine droplets or particles of solids or liquids suspended in a gas (such as in air) and dispensed in a fine mist.

affect: The external showing of mood or emotion.

affective disorders: A category of psychiatric disorders characterized by alterations of mood (such as depression or mania). The affective disorders include major depression and bipolar (manic-depressive) disorder.

after-cataract: A cataract that forms in the retained lens or capsule after cataract surgery.

agglutinin: An antibody, present in serum, that causes red blood cells to agglutinate (clump together).

agglutinogen: A substance that stimulates the production of an agglutinin (thereby acting as an antigen).

AHP (Anomalous Head Posture): Refers to the peculiar way an individual holds his or her head when the positioning of the eyes or the musculature controlling eye movement is abnormal.

airborne pathogens: Viruses, bacteria, or other infectious agents that travel through the air.

airborne transmission: The spread of an agent or a disease via the air.

albinism: A hereditary condition characterized by the lack of pigment (color) in the skin, eyes, and hair.

albumin: A simple protein found in many animal tissues, including blood and egg white.

aldosterone: A steroid hormone secreted by the adrenal cortex. It causes sodium to be reabsorbed into the blood and potassium to be excreted into the urine by the kidney. See also mineralocorticoids.

aliquot: A portion of a substance that represents an evenly divided portion of the original amount.

alkali: A substance that turns red litmus paper blue and has a pH over seven. An alkali is a strong base that combines with an acid to form a salt or neutralizes an acid. See also acid, base.

alkaline phosphatase: An enzyme found in several tissues including bone and excreted by the liver. Blood levels of alkaline phosphatase are elevated in certain bone and liver diseases.

alkalosis: Decreased hydrogen ion concentration (increased pH) of the blood and body fluids. Alkalosis may result from either an accumulation of base (alkali) or a loss of acid. See also acid, base, hydrogen ion, pH.

allergen: A substance that triggers an allergic reaction. See also antigen.

allogeneic transplant: A transplant between different members of the same species.

allogenic: Having a different genetic makeup, but belonging to the same species.

allograft: An organ or tissues from a genetically different member of the same species.

aloe vera: An extract from the aloe plant. Often used to soothe superficial burns and injuries.

alopecia: Hair loss.

alpha adrenergic: See adrenergic receptor.

alpha waves: Brain waves on an electroencephalogram (EEG) typical of a normal waking state.

alpha-fetoprotein (AFP): This fetal glycoprotein is excreted along with fetal urine into the amniotic fluid. A small amount crosses the placenta into the mother's circulation where it reaches its peak level at about 30 weeks of pregnancy. This maternal serum level may be checked to detect abnormally high levels of alpha-fetoprotein that may indicate neural tube, abdominal wall, chromosome or kidney, liver or heart abnormalities in the fetus. Low levels may indicate Down's syndrome.

ALS: Amyotrophic lateral sclerosis (Lou Gehrig's disease).

alternative therapy: A treatment or medicine that is not commonly used in conventional Western medicine.

alveolar-capillary membrane: The thin membrane between the air spaces of the lungs (alveoli) and the bloodstream. The site of oxygen-carbon dioxide exchange.

alveolus (plural, alveoli): One of the tiniest air cells of the lungs found at the ends of the smallest airway passages (bronchioles). The pulmonary alveoli are surrounded by capillaries; gas exchange takes place through the alveolar and

capillary walls with oxygen entering the blood, carbon dioxide leaving the blood.

ambulate: To walk or move about.

ambulatory electrocardiographic monitoring: Monitoring of the electrical activity of the heart using a portable monitor. Usually performed for 24 hours.

ameba (or amoeba): A kind of protozoan (single-celled, microscopic animal) characterized by a changeable shape. Amebas of various types live in soil, water, or as parasites.

amebiasis (or amoebiasis): Infection with an ameba.

amino acid: One of a large group of nitrogen-containing organic chemicals. Amino acids are the building blocks from which proteins are made.

amnesia: Loss of memory.

amniocentesis: A procedure to remove a small sample of amniotic fluid for testing. Involves local anesthesia and an ultrasound-guided needle.

amnionitis: An infection of the amniotic fluid.

amphetamines: A class of sympathomimetic drugs that stimulate both the central and peripheral nervous system. Abuse of amphetamines can lead to dependence.

amphiarthrosis: A type of joint in which the bones are connected by cartilage, allowing only slight movement (such as the joints between the vertebral bodies connected by the intervertebral discs).

amplitude: Size or magnitude. The amplitude of a wave is represented by its height above (or depth below) the baseline.

ampulla: A sac-like dilation of a duct or canal.

ampulla of Vater: The area where the pancreatic duct and the common bile duct both end in the duodenal wall. Currently called hepatopancreatic ampulla.

amylase: An enzyme that speeds the breakdown or digestion of starches (complex carbohydrates) into simple sugars. The salivary glands and the pancreas both secrete amylases.

amyloidosis: A condition where amyloid proteins collect in the extracellular tissues of various organs.

amyotrophic: Pertaining to or characterized by muscle atrophy (wasting).

ANA: Antinuclear antibody.

anaerobe: A microorganism that lives and grows without oxygen.

anaerobic: Able to live and grow without oxygen.

anal: Pertaining to the anus.

analgesic: A drug that relieves pain.

analog: In chemistry, a substance that is structurally similar to another substance.

anaphylactic shock: See anaphylaxis.

anaphylaxis: A type of allergic reaction. Mild anaphylaxis is characterized by urticaria (hives) and itching. Severe anaphylaxis is life threatening and is characterized by swelling of tissues (including the larynx), narrowed airways, low blood pressure, and shock (circulatory insufficiency). See also shock.

anasarca: Severe, generalized swelling.

anastomosis: A natural connection between two blood vessels or nerves or a surgically created connection of two tubular structures (such as between two parts of the intestine).

anatomy: The science of the structure of the body and its parts. Anatomy is considered to include histology, the science of the microscopic structure of tissues and cells.

anconeus: A small muscle located on the back of the elbow that helps extend the arm.

androgen: Any of a group of steroid hormones secreted by the adrenal cortex and the testes. Male sex hormones responsible for male sexual characteristics. Testosterone is an example of an androgen.

androgen ablation: Refers to the removal of androgens from the body in order to treat prostate cancer. May involve the administration of antiandrogens or surgical castration.

anecdotal: Based on descriptions of individual cases rather than a controlled study. See also control.

anaerobic bacteria: See anaerobes

anesthesia: Partial or complete loss of sensation, with or without loss of consciousness.

anesthesia dolorosa: Loss of sensation in an area accompanied by pain in that area.

anesthetic: A drug that produces anesthesia.

angina, endurance: Chest pain of cardiac origin that arises with exercise.

angioedema: A condition characterized by the appearance of large areas of edema in the subcutaneous tissues. Can be a reaction to an allergen or can be hereditary.

angiographic embolization: A method of controlling bleeding by placing material in the artery at the site of the hemorrhage. The doctor is guided by dye injected into the arteries and seen via live x-ray.

angiography: X-ray of blood vessels (either arteries, veins, or both) after the injection of dye.

angioma: A tumor made of blood or lymph vessels that are remnants of fetal tissue that developed abnormally. They are usually benign.

angiomyolipoma: An angioma mixed with a myoma and a lipoma. See also angioma, myoma, lipoma.

angioplasty: Reconstruction of a blood vessel, either by surgical procedure or by dilation using a balloon-tipped catheter.

angiotensin: Any of a group of vasoconstrictor hormones whose formation is initiated by the catalytic action of the enzyme renin. These hormones narrow the blood vessels causing blood pressure to rise.

angiotensin-converting enzyme (ACE): An enzyme that speeds the conversion of angiotensin I (a polypeptide) to angiotensin II. See also angiotensin I and II.

angiotensin-converting enzyme inhibitor: A drug that stops the action of angiotensin-converting enzyme (ACE). ACE inhibitors are used in the treatment of high blood pressure (hypertension) and congestive heart failure.

angiotensin I: A polypeptide formed by the catalytic action of the enzyme renin. It has weak vasoconstrictor activity and changes into angiotensin II with the aid of angiotensin-converting enzyme.

angiotensin II: Angiotensin II causes blood vessels to narrow and also stimulates the adrenal cortex to secrete aldosterone, which causes the sodium (salt) level of the blood to elevate. Both these actions raise the blood pressure.

angulation: Displacement of a fracture so that the fragments form an angle with each other.

anhedonia: The inability to feel pleasure while performing acts that are normally pleasurable.

anhydrous: Without water, dry.

aniline dye: Any of a number of synthetic dyes made with an oily liquid derived from benzene.

ankle: The joint above the foot that is the articulation of the tibia and fibula with the talus.

ankylosis: A joint that is stiff, fixed, and unable to move due to changes in the joint itself or the surrounding tissue.

annular: Circular or ring-like in shape (e.g., an annular lesion).

annulus: A structure shaped like a ring.

annulus fibrosus: The fibrous outer portion of an intervertebral disc.

anogenital: Pertaining to both the anus and the genitals.

Anopheles mosquito: The species of mosquito historically linked to the spread of malaria.

anorectal: Pertaining to both the anus and the rectum.

anorexia: Loss of appetite.

anoscope: A funnel-shaped instrument (speculum) used to examine the anus and lower rectum.

antacid: A drug or substance that neutralizes acid (such as stomach acid). See also acid, base.

antagonist: An agent (such as a drug) that opposes or counteracts the action of something else.

antecubital: Pertaining to the front of or the bend of the elbow.

antecubital fossa: The hollow at the front of the elbow that contains several veins and arteries. These veins are commonly used to obtain blood or to give intravenous fluids or medications.

anterior: At or near the front of a structure; the opposite of posterior. In anatomy, anterior refers to the abdominal (ventral) side of the body; also, the palmar (volar) side of the hand and forearm.

anterior chamber: In the eye, the space between the cornea and the iris. The anterior chamber is filled with a transparent liquid, aqueous humor. The place where the iris and cornea meet (at the outer edge of the cornea) is called the angle of the anterior chamber.

anterior cruciate ligament: One of the ligaments of the knee joint. Helps stabilize the knee. this ligament is frequently injured in contact sports.

anterior transperitoneal approach: A surgical incision made through the abdominal wall and extended to the area that will be operated upon.

anterocollis: A forward tilting of the neck caused by spasms of the anterior neck muscles.

anterolateral: Pertaining to the front and toward the outside of the body or of a body structure; anterior and lateral.

anteromedial: Pertaining to the front and toward the middle of the body or of a body structure; anterior and medial.

anteroposterior (AP): From front to back. An AP x-ray is one where the x-ray beam passes through the body from front to back.

anti-: Prefix meaning against.

antiadrenergic: A substance that counteracts the sympathetic nervous system; antisympathetic.

antianginal: A drug or agent that prevents or relieves chest pain and pressure.

antiarrhythmic: A drug or agent that controls or prevents cardiac arrhythmias.

antibiotic: A drug that kills or inhibits the growth of bacteria.

antibiotic resistance: The characteristic of certain bacteria to be resistant to certain antibiotics.

antibiotic sensitivity test: A test to determine what antibiotics a specific bacterial strain is sensitive to.

antibody: A type of protein produced by certain white blood cells (B lymphocytes or plasma cells) in response to a specific antigen (substance recognized as foreign). The antibody combines with the antigen, either neutralizing it or activating other processes that lead to the antigen's neutralization or destruction. This antigen-antibody reaction is part of the immune response. See also immunoglobulin.

anticholinergic: Blocking the action of acetylcholine or related substances. The term is often used to describe drugs or agents that block nerve impulses in cholinergic nerve fibers, especially those of the parasympathetic nervous system. Many commonly used drugs (including phenothiazines and tricyclic antidepressants) have anticholinergic side effects such as dry mouth, constipation, and blurred vision.

anticholinesterase: A drug that inhibits cholinesterases (enzymes that break down acetylcholine), thereby enhancing the action of acetylcholine.

anticoagulant: A drug that inhibits blood clotting; a "blood thinner." Anticoagulants interfere with the production or action of clotting factors (substances in the blood that are required for clotting to take place). See also antiplatelet drug.

anticoagulant therapy: Treatment with anticoagulant medications.

anticonvulsant: A drug that prevents or stops seizures or convulsions.

antidepressant: A drug that alleviates depression.

antidiuretic hormone (ADH): A hormone secreted by the hypothalamus of the brain and stored in the posterior part of the pituitary gland. ADH causes the kidney to decrease water excretion that concentrates the urine. It is also a powerful vasoconstrictor (narrows the blood vessels); for this reason, it is also called vasopressin.

antidromic: Pertaining to an impulse moving along a nerve in the opposite direction from normal. The opposite of orthodromic.

antifungal: A drug that kills or inhibits the growth of fungi.

antifungal drug: A drug that kills or inhibits the growth of fungi.

antigen: A substance (usually a protein) that triggers an immune response. If the immune response is allergic in nature, the antigen is referred to as an allergen.

antihistamine: A drug or agent that blocks the action of histamine. The term usually refers to agents that bind to H1 receptors. See also histamine; histamine receptor.

antihypertensive: A drug that lowers blood pressure.

anti-inflammatory: A drug that decreases inflammation.

antimicrobial: A drug or agent that kills or prevents the growth of microorganisms. An antibiotic is one type of antimicrobial drug.

antimotility agents: A drug or agent that slows the movement of food material and wastes through the digestive tract. Often used to treat diarrhea.

antinuclear antibody (ANA): An autoantibody that reacts against the components of one's own cell center or nuclei. High ANA titers occur in the blood of individuals with certain autoimmune disorders (such as systemic lupus erythematosus).

antioxidant: A substance that inhibits oxidation (chemical combination with oxygen). Many synthetic and natural substances including vitamin C, vitamin E, and beta carotene are antioxidants.

antiparasitic: A drug or agent that kills parasites.

antiperistaltic: A drug or agent that slows movement of food through the intestine or a contraction of the stomach or intestines that propels the contents toward the mouth, as in vomiting.

antiplatelet drug: A drug that inhibits blood clotting by interfering with the aggregation (sticking together) of platelets. Antiplatelet drugs are usually classified as distinct from anticoagulants.

antiprotozoal: A drug or agent that kills protozoa.

antipsychotic: A drug that alleviates the signs and symptoms of psychosis.

antipsychotic drugs: Psychiatric medications used to treat psychosis such as schizophrenia.

antipyretic: A drug that lowers or prevents a fever.

antiretroviral: An agent used against retroviral infections such as HIV.

antiseizure: A drug that prevents seizures or convulsions.

antiseptic: A substance that kills or inhibits the growth of microorganisms on contact when applied to the skin or mucous membranes.

antisympathetic: Counteracting the sympathetic nervous system; antiadrenergic.

antiviral: A drug or agent that destroys or prevents the replication (reproduction) of viruses.

anuria: The absence of urination.

anus: The opening of the rectum, located in the fold between the buttocks.

anxiety: A feeling of apprehension, uneasiness, worry, or dread.

anxiety disorders: A category of psychiatric disorders characterized by prominent symptoms of fear, dread, or anxiety. The anxiety disorders include panic disorder, agoraphobia and other specific phobias, obsessive-compulsive disorder, post-traumatic stress disorder, and generalized anxiety disorder.

anxiolytic: A drug that alleviates anxiety.

aorta: The main trunk artery that emerges from the left ventricle of the heart and branches off to all parts of the body. The aorta rises upward from the heart, curves over to form an arch, descends through the chest, pierces the diaphragm, and continues downward through the abdomen. In the abdomen, the aorta divides into the two common iliac arteries.

aortic: Pertaining to the aorta.

aortic arch: The arch of the aorta; see also aorta.

aortic root: The origin or beginning of the aorta, just above the aortic valve.

aortic valve: An opening composed of folds or flaps that prevents backflow of blood at the junction of the left ventricle and the aorta.

aortic valve disease: Any condition that impairs normal functioning of the aortic valve.

aortography: X-ray of the aorta after injection of dye.

AP: Anteroposterior; from front to back.

aphakic: A condition where the crystalline lens of the eye is absent (e.g., after cataract removal).

aplastic: Characterized by failure of a tissue or body part to develop.

apnea: Absence of breathing.

appendix: A worm-shaped appendage projecting from the blind end of the cecum; also called the vermiform appendix.

apthous: Refers to an ulcer of the mouth. Also known as canker sores.

aqueous: Having the nature of water.

aqueous humor: A transparent fluid that fills the anterior chamber of the eye. Its function is to nourish the cornea and lens and help maintain the shape of the eyeball.

arachnoid: The middle membrane of the meninges (the membranes that enclose the brain and spinal cord) between the pia and the dura.

arachnoiditis: Inflammation of the arachnoid membrane. See also arachnoid.

arch of the aorta: The part of the aorta that curves over the top of the heart between the ascending and descending parts.

AROM: Active range of motion.

arrhythmia: An irregular or abnormal rhythm such as of the heartbeat; cardiac arrhythmia.

arterial blood gases (ABGs): The measurement of the levels of oxygen and carbon dioxide in the blood. The acid-base balance of the body is also revealed.

arterial insufficiency: Refers to the condition where the blood flow to an organ or tissue is not sufficient to meet nutritional needs.

arteriole: A branch of an artery. The smallest arterioles (called terminal arterioles) lead into capillaries.

arteriovenous: Pertaining to an artery and a vein.

arteriovenous (AV) fistula: A direct communication between an artery and a vein without a capillary network in between. AV fistulas are usually of traumatic origin, but are sometimes congenital (AV malformations) or created surgically (AV shunt).

arteriovenous (AV) malformation: See arteriovenous fistula.

arteritis: Inflammation of an artery or arteries.

artery: A blood vessel that carries blood away from the heart to other parts of the body.

arthralgia: Joint pain.

arthrodesis: Surgical fusion of a joint that results in a fixed joint.

arthrofibrosis: A condition where fibrosis affects a joint, limiting the degree of flexion or extension of that joint.

arthropathy: Any disorder of a joint.

arthroscope: An endoscope for examining the inside of a joint. See also endoscope.

arthroscopic surgery: Surgery performed through an arthroscope.

arthrotomy: Incision into a joint; open surgery of a joint.

articular: Pertaining to a joint.

articular cartilage: The cartilage that covers the articular surface of a bone.

articular surface: The part of a bone's surface that comes in contact with another bone.

articulation: A joint.

ascending aorta: The part of the aorta that begins at the heart and rises to meet the aortic arch.

aseptic necrosis: Death of tissue without concomitant infection.

ascites: An abnormal collection of fluid in the abdominal cavity.

ascorbic acid: Vitamin C, a vitamin that occurs naturally and is also synthesized. Ascorbic acid is used in the formation of connective tissue. It is essential in cementing tissues together (such as skin, dentine, cartilage, and bone), and helps in healing and absorbing iron. Deficiency of ascorbic acid is called scurvy.

aseptic: Without infection (clean) or without bacterial infection (e.g., the term aseptic meningitis may refer to a viral meningitis).

ASHD: Atherosclerotic heart disease.

aspergillosis: A pulmonary or systemic infection with the Aspergillus fungi.

Aspergillus: A genus of fungi containing several species that are pathogenic in humans. Responsible for severe pulmonary infections and may cause disseminated infections.

asphyxia: TWhen breathing is impeded causing a decrease in the body's oxygen content and a rise in the carbon dioxide content.

aspiration: (1) Inhalation of liquid or solid material into the lungs. (2) The drawing out by suction (such as removal of fluid from a body cavity with a needle and syringe).

aspiration curettage: An abortion procedure that involves the cutting and suctioning of fetal parts.

aspiration pneumonia: Pneumonia resulting from aspiration of microorganisms or chemical irritants into the lungs.

assay: A test that analyzes a substance to determine its contents and the amount of each. This may be done by chemical, physical, or biological methods.

asterixis: An abnormal jerking movement of muscles that is involuntary and occurs as a result of dorsiflexion and extension of the hand or foot. See also dorsiflexion.

asthenia: Weakness or debility, especially caused by muscular or brain diseases.

astragalus: Obsolete term for the talus, a bone found in the ankle.

astringent: An agent with a constricting effect (i.e., stops bleeding or dries up secretions).

astrocyte: A star-shaped nerve cell with many branches.

asymmetric: When portions of each side of the body are not the same.

asymptomatic: Without symptoms.

asystole: Absence of cardiac contractions; cardiac standstill.

ataxia: Defective muscle coordination evident when voluntary movement is attempted.

atelectasis: The collapse or airless condition of a lung caused by a blockage of an airway or by pressure from outside the lung.

atheroma: In atherosclerosis, a fatty deposit in the wall of an artery.

athlete's foot: A fungus infection of the foot.

atlantoaxial joint: The joint between the atlas and axis (first and second cervical vertebrae).

atlanto-occipital joint: The joint between the atlas (first cervical vertebra) and the base of the skull.

atlas: The first cervical vertebra.

atopic: Pertaining to atopy. See also atopy.

atopy: Pertaining to a group of diseases that are types of inherited allergic conditions with asthma, runny nose, and rash as the principle symptoms.

atria: The smaller upper chambers of the heart. There are two atria: the right atrium and the left atrium. Each pushes blood into the corresponding ventricle.

atrial node: A small rounded structure found in the wall of the right atrium of the heart that is the source of the signal initiating the heartbeat. Also called the sinus node or sinoatrial node.

atrioventricular: Pertaining to an atrium and a ventricle of the heart.

atrioventricular (AV) bundle: See bundle of His.

atrioventricular (AV) node: In the heart, a mass of specialized tissue located in the lower part of the interatrial septum (wall between the two atria), just above the ventricles. The AV node (along with the AV bundle, or bundle of His) conducts electrical impulses between the atria and ventricles. It is also capable of generating electrical impulses when not overridden by the atrial node (the heart's natural pacemaker). See also bundle of His, cardiac conduction, atrial node.

atrium (plural, atria): Either of the two upper chambers of the heart. The right atrium receives deoxygenated blood returning from the body; the left atrium receives oxygenated blood returning from the lungs. See also ventricle.

atrophy: Wasting or decrease in size of a tissue or organ.

atypical depression: Refers to clinical depression accompanied by atypical signs such as increased appetite and increased sleep.

atypical pneumonia: A type of pneumonia that occurs in otherwise healthy young adults. It is usually caused by a virus or mycoplasma organisms. It is a mild form, much like a cold, and may go undetected.

audiometry: A technique for evaluating the sense of hearing; a variation of brainstem auditory evoked potentials. See also evoked potential.

auditory: Pertaining to the sense of hearing.

aura: A subjective symptom experienced by an individual prior to a seizure or migraine. Typical auras include visual auras (sparks, lights) and odors.

auscultation: The act of listening for sounds within the body (such as with a stethoscope).

autoantibody: An antibody against a normal component of one's own tissues.

autogenous: Originating within the individual's own body.

autograft: Transplantation or grafting of a tissue from one place in an individual to another.

autoimmune disease: Disease where the immune system reacts against the body's own tissues. An example is lupus.

autoimmunity: Condition where the immune system reacts against the body's own tissues.

autologous: Originating in an individual's own body.

autologous transplant: Transplantation of tissue from one place in an individual to another.

automatism: Action and behavior that occurs without the person's knowledge or control (e.g., during a hysterical trance).

autonomic: Pertaining to the autonomic nervous system.

autonomic nervous system: The part of the nervous system responsible for regulating involuntary functions (such as respiration, heart rate, blood pressure, and sweating. The autonomic nervous system has two divisions, sympathetic and parasympathetic, that have opposing effects. The sympathetic division is concerned with the body's response to stress; the parasympathetic is concerned with conservation and restoration. The two divisions act cooperatively - stimulation of one is usually associated with inhibition of the other. See also sympathetic nervous system and parasympathetic nervous system.

autonomic synapse: The gap between two nerves of the autonomic nervous system.

autoregulation: Self-regulation (such as the regulation of local blood flow through a tissue or organ in response to local metabolic needs).

autosomal dominant: Hereditary mode of transmitting genetic information in which the trait in question needs to be present in the genome in only one copy in order to be expressed.

autosomal recessive: Hereditary mode of transmitting genetic information in which the trait in question needs to be present in the genome in two copies in order to be expressed.

autotransplantation: See autologous transplant.

AV: Atrioventricular or arteriovenous.

AV node: Atrioventricular node.

avascular: Without blood vessels.

avascular necrosis: Death of bone tissue caused by loss of blood supply.

avulsion: A tearing away of a part or structure.

axial: Pertaining to an axis such as the axis (midline) of the body.

axilla: The armpit.

axillary: Pertaining to the armpit.

axillary artery: A major artery supplying the upper extremity. The axillary artery is the continuation of the subclavian artery; it passes through the region of the shoulder and armpit, and continues into the arm as the brachial artery.

axillary nerve: A branch of the brachial plexus; one of the major nerves of the upper extremity, it supplies the shoulder region.

axillary vein: A major vein of the upper extremity that runs alongside the axillary artery. The axillary vein is the continuation of the brachial vein of the arm; it passes through the region of the shoulder and armpit, and continues into the chest as the subclavian vein.

axis: (1) The second cervical vertebra. (2) An imaginary line that runs through the center of an object or around which an object revolves.

axon: A fiber-like projection of a neuron (nerve cell) that conducts electrical impulses away from the cell body. The axon terminal (end of the axon) releases a chemical neurotransmitter, which conveys the impulse to another neuron or a muscle or gland cell.

azotemia: Excessive amounts of urea in the blood due to kidney failure; uremia.

azygous vein: A large vein that runs upward through the abdomen and chest, just in front and a little to the right of the vertebral column. It receives blood from the walls of the trunk and empties into the superior vena cava.

babesiosis: Infection with a species of the organism *Babesia*. This disease is spread by the bite of a tick.

Babinski's reflex: Dorsiflexion (upward motion) of the big toe when the sole of the foot is stimulated. This is a primitive reflex (normal only in infants). Currently called the plantar reflex.

bacteremia: Bacteria present in the blood.

bacteria: Plural of bacterium.

bacteriocidal agent: An agent that kills bacteria.

bacterium (plural, bacteria): A type of one-celled, microscopic organism Many infectious diseases are caused by bacteria; however, some bacteria are harmless or even helpful such as the bacteria that normally inhabit the human colon. Bacteria come in a variety of shapes including spheres (cocci) and rods. They may also be classified by their staining properties. See Gram's stain, gram-negative, gram-positive.

bacteriuria: The presence of bacteria in the urine.

BAEP: Brainstem auditory evoked potential.

band: In hematology, a band is a type of immature white blood cell. On a complete blood count (CBC) with differential, an elevated percentage of band forms ("left shift") is a sign of bacterial infection. See also complete blood count.

barbiturates: A group of chemicals that belong to the class of sedative-hypnotic drugs.

barium: A chalk-like substance used as a contrast medium for x-rays of the gastrointestinal tract.

baroreceptor: An internal sensory receptor (such as in the wall of a blood vessel) that is stimulated by changes in pressure.

baroreceptor reflex: An autonomic reflex that maintains normal blood pressure. Blood pressure is sensed by baroreceptors (pressure receptors) in the walls of large arteries. This sensory input is conveyed to the cardiac and vasomotor centers in the brainstem, which adjust autonomic output to the heart and blood vessels.

Barrett's esophagus: Metaplasia of the lower esophageal lining. Barrett's esophagus is a complication of reflux esophagitis. As a result of chronic inflammation, the esophageal mucosa is transformed into a different type of mucosa, similar to that of the intestine. May be a precursor to esophageal cancer.

basal cells: A type of small, round cell found in the outer skin that lies between the bases of neighboring cells.

basal ganglia: Masses of gray matter located deep inside the cerebral hemispheres. They are involved in the fine control of movement and posture.

base: A substance that combines with hydrogen ions; especially one that releases hydroxyl ions in solution. Bases combine with acids to form salts and water, thus neutralizing each other. Base also means the lowermost or supporting part of an organ or structure or the proximal end of certain long bones (such as the metacarpals, metatarsals, and phalanges). See also acid, hydrogen ion, hydroxyl ion, salt.

baseline: An observation or measurement that represents the normal background or initial state; used for comparison when measuring the response to a stimulus.

basilar: Pertaining to a base. See also base.

basilar artery: An artery of the brain, formed by the joining of the two vertebral arteries. The basilar artery lies along the underside of the brainstem, and gives off branches to the brainstem, cerebellum, and parts of the cerebral cortex.

basilic vein: A large superficial vein that runs along the medial (inner) side of the arm. Near the shoulder, it is joined by the brachial veins to form the axillary vein.

basophil: A type of granulocyte (white blood cell that contains granules in its cytoplasm), so called because it stains easily with basic (alkaline) dyes. Basophils normally make up 1% or less of the white blood cells in circulation. See also granulocyte.

B-cell: A B-lymphocyte that develops into plasma cells that produce immunoglobulins. B-cells constitute 5-25% of all lymphocytes.

BEAM: Brain electrical activity mapping.

bed: A supporting structure or network (such as a capillary bed).

behavioral modification: Refers to a set of techniques used to change an individual's behavior. See also behavioral therapy.

behavioral therapy: A form of psychotherapy that focuses on the individual's observable behavior (rather than on the mental processes that presumably underlie behavior). The therapist helps the individual change maladaptive behavior by manipulating the environment systematically with respect to the behavior. Also called behavior modification or conditioning therapy.

Bence Jones protein: Proteins found in patients with multiple myeloma. These proteins consist of monoclonal immunoglobulin light chains.

benign: Not progressive or life threatening; not malignant.

benzodiazepines: A class of medications typically prescribed as antianxiety treatment.

Bernstein (acid perfusion) test: A diagnostic test for gastroesophageal reflux. A known concentration of acid is instilled into the esophagus. If the individual's symptoms are reproduced by this procedure, it is an indication that the symptoms are acid-induced.

beta-blocker: A beta-adrenergic blocker. Any of a class of drugs that block adrenergic beta receptors resulting in an antiadrenergic effect. Some beta-blockers act on both beta 1 and beta 2 receptors; some are more specific, blocking primarily one type or the other. See also adrenergic receptor.

beta carotene: A substance that becomes vitamin A.

bibliotherapy: The practice of healing through books.

biceps brachii: A muscle of the arm that helps bend the elbow and turn the hand palm upward.

bicipital groove: A groove in the proximal humerus (bone in the upper arm) for the biceps brachii tendon.

bicuspid valve: An opening with two folds or flaps that prevent the backflow of blood and guard the opening between the left atrium and the left ventricle. Also called the mitral valve.

bicycle ergometer: A machine that measures the amount of energy expended while riding a bicycle.

Bier block: An intravenous regional block. A tourniquet is applied to the limb, and the anesthetic is injected intravenously. Prevented by the tourniquet from entering the systemic circulation, the drug acts only on the regional nerves.

bilateral: Involving or occurring on both sides of the body.

bile: A bitter greenish or yellowish fluid produced by the liver and stored in the gallbladder. After a meal, bile is released into the duodenum where it participates in the digestion and absorption of lipids (fats).

bile duct: A duct that conveys bile. The term usually refers to the common bile duct that receives bile from the hepatic and cystic ducts and conveys it to the duodenum.

bile ducts: The system of ducts that conveys bile from the liver and gallbladder to the duodenum. When used in the singular, the term usually refers to the common bile duct. See also common bile duct.

bile pigments: Constituents of bile that give it its greenish or yellowish color. Bile pigments are breakdown products of hemoglobin from worn out red blood cells. They are carried by the blood to the liver where they are conjugated (chemically altered) and excreted in the bile. Bilirubin is the most abundant bile pigment. See also bilirubin.

bile salts: Constituents of bile necessary for the digestion and absorption of lipids. Bile salts act as detergents, emulsifying the lipids (breaking them up into small globules). Bile salts are also necessary for maintaining the bile in a liquid state; a deficiency of bile salts may lead to stone formation.

biliary: Pertaining to bile or the bile ducts.

biliary ducts: The system of ducts that conveys bile from the liver and gallbladder to the duodenum.

biliary tract: The structures that contain and transport bile (including the small bile canals in the liver, the hepatic and cystic ducts, the gallbladder, and the common bile duct).

bilirubin: A yellowish pigment found in bile, which is the most abundant bile pigment. Bilirubin is a breakdown product of hemoglobin from worn out red blood cells. It is carried by the blood to the liver where it is conjugated (chemically altered) and excreted in the bile. An excess of bilirubin in the blood (hyperbilirubinemia) may result in jaundice (yellow discoloration of the skin and mucous membranes).

bimalleolar: Involving both inner and outer malleoli of the ankle.

bimanual pelvic exam: A variation on the pelvic exam where the physician uses both hands to palpate the structures of the pelvis during a physical exam.

binocular vision: Vision with both eyes. This is what gives us three-dimensional sight.

biochemical: Pertaining to the chemistry of living things.

biofeedback: A technique that trains an individual to gain some control over autonomic functions of the body. Often used in relaxation and pain control.

biomicroscopy: Microscopic examination of living tissue.

bipartite: Having two parts.

biphasic: Consisting of two distinct phases.

bite wing: A type of x-ray of the teeth.

black vomit: Material from the stomach containing blood that has been changed by gastric acid. Also called coffee-ground vomit or emesis

blast: An early precursor form of a cell, usually a blood cell.

Blastomyces dermatitidis: The fungi responsible for the disease blastomycosis.

Blastomycosis: A fungal disease caused by Blastomyces dermatitidis. Characterized by an early pulmonary infection with a later skin, eye, and bone infection.

blepharoptosis: Drooping of the upper eyelid.

blepharospasm: Spasm or twitching of the eyelids.

blister: A collection of fluid within or just below the epidermis.

block: An obstruction or stoppage; a method of anesthesia where the passage of nerve impulses is interrupted by injecting a local anesthetic around a nerve, nerve root, ganglion, or the spinal cord.

blood poisoning: The presence of a large amount of bacteria in the blood.

blood pressure: The pressure exerted by the blood on the inner walls of blood vessels. Blood pressure is highest in the large arteries; it diminishes with distance from the left ventricle, and is lowest in the large veins. However, for ordinary clinical purposes, only arterial pressure is measured. Arterial pressure fluctuates with the cardiac cycle; its highest point corresponds to systole (the systolic pressure), and its lowest point corresponds to diastole (the diastolic pressure). The systolic and diastolic pressures are expressed as two numbers separated by a slash mark (i.e., 120/80; 120 over 80). See also cardiac cycle, diastole, systole.

blood urea nitrogen (BUN): The concentration of urea in the blood. An elevated BUN, accompanied by an elevated serum creatinine, is indicative of renal failure. An elevated BUN with normal creatinine may result from dehydration or from increased protein breakdown (such as after gastrointestinal hemorrhage).

blood vessel: An artery or a vein.

blood-borne: Carried in the bloodstream.

blood-brain barrier: The barrier separating the blood from the central nervous system. In other regions of the body, capillary walls are relatively permeable, allowing many kinds of substances to pass from the blood into the tissues. However, the capillaries of the central nervous system are much less permeable. This is important medically because it prevents many drugs from reaching the brain and spinal cord in therapeutic concentrations.

B-lymphocyte: See lymphocyte.

body: The main part of a bone or organ; the entire individual.

Body Mass Index (BMI): Body mass index correlates to how fat a person is. BMI is calculated by dividing weight in kilograms by height in meters, squared. A BMI of 25 to 29.9 is considered overweight and 30 or above is considered obese.

body mechanics: The science of body movement as applied to activities of daily living, and to the correction and prevention of postural problems.

boil: A furuncle; an acute localized inflammation of the subcutaneous tissue. The inflammation causes blood to clot in the vessels forming a painful "core," which is eventually expelled or reabsorbed. Boils are commonly caused by bacterial infection.

bolus: A mass of medication or fluid given rapidly by IV injection.

bonding: The formation of a close psychological attachment (such as between a parent and infant).

bone cyst: A cyst that appears in the shaft of the long bones, usually in children and usually benign.

bone marrow: A type of connective tissue found in the inner cavities of bones. The cellular elements of blood (red and white blood cells, platelets) are formed in the bone marrow.

bone marrow aspiration: A technique to remove a sample of bone marrow for examination.

bone marrow biopsy: Similar to bone marrow aspiration except that a minor surgical procedure is required to remove the sample of bone.

borborygmi: The rumbling noise caused by gas as it moves through the intestines.

Bouchard's nodes: Small nodules found on the proximal fingers in patients with osteoarthritis.

bougie: A slender, flexible instrument for dilating hollow tube-like organs such as the esophagus.

bowel: A broad term that includes all of the digestive organs, although usually refers to the small and large intestine.

bowel ischemia: Condition where a segment of bowel has less then the normal blood supply.

brachial: Pertaining to the arm (especially the upper arm).

brachial artery: The main artery of the arm (continuation of the subclavian/axillary artery). It runs along the inside of the arm and divides into the radial and ulnar arteries at the bend of the elbow.

brachial plexus: A network of nerves extending from the neck to the armpit that gives rise to the nerves of the arm.

brachial vein: A deep vein of the arm. In each arm, two brachial veins run alongside the brachial artery. Near the shoulder, they merge with the basilic vein (a surface vein of the arm) to form the axillary vein.

brachialis: A muscle of the arm, located under the biceps brachii muscle that helps bend the elbow.

brachiocephalic artery: See brachiocephalic trunk.

brachiocephalic trunk: A branch of the aortic arch; formerly called the innominate (unnamed) artery. The brachiocephalic trunk divides into the right common carotid and right subclavian arteries, which supply blood to the right side of the head and right upper extremity. The left common carotid and left subclavian arteries arise directly from the aorta.

brachiocephalic vein: A large vein formed by the merging of the internal jugular and subclavian veins (which collect blood from the head and upper extremity). The right and left brachiocephalic veins empty into the superior vena cava.

brachioradialis: A muscle located on the lateral side of the forearm that helps bend the elbow.

bradycardia: A slow heart rate (less than 60 beats per minute in an adult). Bradycardia is sometimes normal (i.e., an athletic individual may have a resting heart rate in the 50s); however, it is usually abnormal.

bradykinesia: Extreme slowness of movement.

brain: A large mass of nervous tissue located inside the skull; part of the central nervous system.

brain electrical activity mapping (BEAM): A computerized method for imaging the electrical activity of the brain by converting EEG results to a topographical (map-like) color display.

brainstem: The stem-like lower portion of the brain that connects the higher centers of the brain to the spinal cord. The brainstem contains reflex centers for involuntary functions such as the regulation of blood pressure and respiration.

brainstem auditory evoked potential (BAEP): The response of the brainstem to an auditory stimulus.

BRCA-1: TA marker gene for the propensit to develop breast cancer.

breech: The buttocks.

breech presentation: When the presenting part of the baby is the buttocks instead of the head during birth.

brisement: Breaking by force.

broad ligaments: The supporting ligaments of the uterus.

bronchiole: One of the small air passages of the lungs (less than one millimeter in diameter). The bronchioles are formed by the branching of larger air passages (bronchi). The smallest bronchioles lead into microscopic air sacs called alveoli. See also alveolus and bronchus.

bronchoconstriction: Constriction or narrowing of the bronchi and/or bronchioles due to contraction of the smooth muscle in the bronchial walls.

bronchodilation: Dilation (widening) of the bronchi and/or bronchioles.

bronchodilator: A drug that produces bronchodilation.

bronchospasm: Sudden bronchoconstriction.

bronchus (plural, bronchi): One of the large air passages of the lungs. The trachea (windpipe) divides into two main bronchi (one for each lung) that branch into smaller bronchi. The smallest bronchi subdivide into still smaller passageways called bronchioles. See also bronchiole.

Brook ileostomy: An opening on the abdomen that attaches to an end of small intestine (the ileum).

bruit: A sound (usually abnormal) produced by blood flowing through a blood vessel.

bruxism: Grinding or clenching of the teeth, usually at night. This has the effect of eroding the height of the dental crown.

bubo: An enlarged, inflamed lymph node often discharging pus, which results from infection. Nodes in the groin or axilla are most commonly affected.

BUN: Blood urea nitrogen.

bundle branch: In the cardiac conduction system, either of the two main branches of the bundle of His. The right and left bundle branches run along opposite sides of the interventricular septum and conduct impulses to the right and left ventricles, respectively. See also bundle of His; cardiac conduction.

bundle branch block: Failure of conduction along either of the two bundle branches of the heart's electrical conduction system. Left bundle branch block (LBBB) and right bundle branch block (RBBB) may occur separately or together (complete heart block). See also bundle branch.

bundle of His: A bundle of fibers of the cardiac conduction system; currently called the atrioventricular (AV) bundle. The bundle of His extends from the atrioventricular node to the interventricular septum. There it divides into the right and left bundle branches. See also atrioventricular node, bundle branch, and cardiac conduction.

bursa (plural, bursae): A sac-like structure lined with synovial membrane, usually found in the vicinity of a joint. It contains synovial fluid, which acts to reduce friction between moving parts (such as between a bone and a tendon, or between a ligament and a tendon).

bypass: An alternative passageway surgically created between two blood vessels (i.e., in order to circumvent an obstruction).

C&S: Culture and sensitivity.

C.O. Cardiac output.

CABG: Coronary artery bypass graft.

cachexia: A state of general debility with malnutrition and loss of muscle mass; present in chronic diseases.

cacosmia: A condition when normally pleasant odors are perceived as unpleasant, or when an individual feels ill when exposed to odors.

CAD: Coronary artery disease.

calcaneal tendon: The Achilles tendon.

calcaneal tuberosity: The large, rounded posterior projection of the calcaneus that forms the back of the heel and provides attachment for the Achilles tendon.

calcaneocuboid joint: The joint between the calcaneus and the cuboid bone in the foot.

calcaneofibular ligament: A ligament connecting the calcaneus and fibula; one of the three major ligaments of the outer side of the ankle joint.

calcaneus: The heel bone and the largest of the seven tarsal bones. The calcaneus forms part of the hindfoot.

calcification: Deposition of calcium in tissue.

calcinosis: A condition characterized by the deposition of calcium in various body tissues.

calcium: A metallic chemical element (atomic number 20) denoted by the symbol Ca. Along with phosphorus, it is one of the principal minerals in teeth and bones. It is also found dissolved in the blood in ionized form. Besides the maintenance of bones and teeth, calcium is essential for many body processes, including nerve and muscle function and blood clotting.

calcium-channel blocker: Any of a class of drugs that blocks the movement of calcium into cardiac and smooth muscle cells causing the muscle to relax. Relaxation of cardiac muscle results in decreased strength of contraction and a slower heart rate. Relaxation of smooth muscle in the walls of blood vessels results in vasodilation and lowered blood pressure.

calculus (plural, calculi): An abnormal concretion within the body; a stone. Calculi may be composed of minerals and/or organic compounds produced in the body. For example, many kidney stones (renal calculi) are composed of calcium salts; gallstones (biliary calculi) are composed largely of either cholesterol or bile pigment.

calorie: A unit of heat, commonly used to express the energy content of food.

Campylobacter: A bacteria that causes systemic illness, diarrhea, gastritis, or peptic ulcer disease, depending on the species.

canaliculitis: Inflammation of the lacrimal canaliculus, the duct that drains tears from the eye.

cancellous bone: Spongy bone tissue found in the interior of the bones.

Candida albicans: A yeast-like fungus normally found in the human mouth, intestine, vagina, and on the skin. Although it is part of the normal flora of the human body, it can cause disease under some circumstances.

Candida hypersensitivity syndrome: A controversial diagnosis in which multiple symptoms are attributed to the overgrowth of Candida. The symptoms are presumed to result from a generalized toxic or immunologic reaction. Candida hypersensitivity syndrome is sometimes considered a form of multiple chemical sensitivity.

Candidemia: A systemic infection by a yeast of the Candida genus characterized by the presence of the fungi in the bloodstream.

cannula: A tube inserted into a duct or cavity.

canthoplasty: A surgical procedure on the angle of the eye (canthus).

capillary: Any of the microscopic blood vessels that connect the smallest arterioles (microscopic arteries) with the smallest venules (microscopic veins). Gas exchange between the blood and the tissues occurs through the thin capillary walls.

capillary exchange: The exchange of substances (such as oxygen and carbon dioxide; nutrients and metabolic waste products) between the blood and the tissue fluid, through the capillary walls. See also gas exchange.

carbohydrate: A group of organic chemicals composed only of carbon, hydrogen, and oxygen. Carbohydrates include sugars, starches, glycogen (a starch-like substance found in liver and muscle), and cellulose.

carbon: A non-metallic chemical element (atomic number 6) denoted by the symbol C. It is an important constituent of all organic chemicals.

carbon dioxide: A colorless, odorless gas (CO_2). It is a metabolic waste product and is eliminated from the body primarily via the lungs.

carcinogen: A substance or agent that causes or increases the risk of developing cancer.

carcinoid: A tumor that secretes serotonin. These tumors may grow in the bronchus, intestinal tract, bile ducts, pancreas, or ovary.

carcinoid syndrome: A group of symptoms that occur when a carcinoid tumor produces excess serotonin. Characterized by facial flushing and diarrhea.

carcinoid tumors: A yellow, well defined overgrowth of tissue occurring in the stomach, small intestine, appendix, or colon.

carcinoma: A cancer of epithelial tissue.

cardia: The upper opening of the stomach where it connects with the esophagus.

cardiac: Pertaining to the heart.

cardiac aneurysm: An outpouching of either the atrial or ventricular wall.

cardiac arrhythmia: An abnormal or irregular heartbeat.

cardiac conduction: The conduction of electrical impulses through the heart, resulting in contraction of the cardiac muscle (the heartbeat). The cardiac conduction system consists of nodes (masses) and fibers of specialized tissue. These structures include the sinus node, atrioventricular node, bundle of His, right and left bundle branches, and Purkinje fibers.

cardiac cycle: The interval between the beginning of one heartbeat and the beginning of the next. The cardiac cycle has two phases, systole (the phase of contraction) and diastole (the phase of relaxation).

cardiac enzymes: Enzymes found in myocardial tissue (heart muscle) that are released into the blood when the tissue is damaged or dies. Blood tests for cardiac enzymes are used in the diagnosis of myocardial infarction. Cardiac enzymes include CK (creatine kinase) and LDH (lactic acid dehydrogenase). See also serum enzymes.

cardiac muscle: A type of involuntary muscle found in the walls of the heart; it is responsible for the heart's contractions. It is composed of striated fibers that are branched and interconnected.

cardiac output (C.O.): The volume of blood pumped by the heart per minute. Cardiac output is equal to the stroke volume (volume pumped per cardiac cycle) multiplied by the heart rate (cycles per minute).

cardiac sensitization: Abnormally increased sensitivity of the heart muscle to the initiation of abnormal heart rhythms.

cardiac shunt: An abnormal connection between the chambers of the heart. In a right-to-left cardiac shunt, blood flows directly from the right to the left side of the heart without first passing through the lungs. In a left-to-right cardiac shunt, blood flows directly from the left to the right side of the heart without first being circulated through the body.

cardiac veins: The veins that collect blood from the myocardium (heart muscle). The cardiac veins empty into the coronary sinus, which in turn empties into the right atrium.

cardiogenic: Originating in the heart.

cardioplegia: Arrest of the heartbeat, intentionally caused by drugs and/or body cooling (hypothermia) during open-heart surgery.

cardiopulmonary: Pertaining to both the heart and lungs.

cardiopulmonary bypass: The use of a heart-lung machine to bypass an individual's heart and lungs. The machine oxygenates the blood and pumps it to the body. This provides a bloodless and motionless heart for the surgeon to repair. The heart is restarted after surgery and the blood volume is returned to the body.

cardiorespiratory: Pertaining to both the heart and the entire respiratory system.

cardiovascular: Pertaining to the heart and blood vessels.

cardiovascular system: The organ system concerned with the circulation of blood through the body. It is composed of the heart and blood vessels. See also circulatory system.

carnitine: A substance found primarily in muscle that is necessary for normal energy metabolism. Carnitine transports long-chain fatty acids into the mitochondria (the organelles responsible for cellular energy production).

carotid angiogram: A radiologic procedure to image the carotid arteries. Involves the injection of a radio-opaque dye.

carotid arteries: The large arteries of the neck including the common, external, and internal carotid arteries.

carotid Doppler: A specialized ultrasound study that measures blood flow through the carotid arteries.

carpal: Pertaining to the wrist.

carpal bones: The eight small bones of the wrist.

carpal tunnel: A compartment inside the wrist formed by the carpal bones and the flexor retinaculum (a band of fibrous tissue that stretches across the bones). The median nerve and the flexor tendons of the hand pass through the carpal tunnel.

carpometacarpal (CMC) joints: The joints between the carpal bones of the wrist and the metacarpal bones of the hand.

carpopedal spasm: Spasms of the hands and feet.

carpus: The carpal bones.

cartilage: A type of dense connective tissue that, along with bones, forms the skeleton. In the developing fetus, most of the skeleton is composed of cartilage, which later hardens to form bones. In the adult, the cartilage remains only in certain locations (such as the articular surfaces of bones, intervertebral discs, menisci of the knee, nasal septum, external ear, and portions of the larynx, trachea, and bronchi).

catalyst: A substance that speeds up the rate of a chemical reaction without being changed itself in the process.

cataract: A clouding (opacity) of the lens of the eye.

catatonia: A state of complete inactivity characterized by stupor and/or rigidity.

catatonic schizophrenia: A manifestation of schizophrenia where the individual is unresponsive and remains in a fixed position without moving or speaking.

catecholamines: A group of physiologically active hormones and neurotransmitters in the human body. As hormones, they are responsible for the sympathetic nervous response. They include epinephrine and norepinephrine. See also sympathetic nervous system.

cathartic: A purgative; an agent that produces bowel movements.

catheter: A tube passed into a body cavity for the purpose of removing or injecting fluids, measuring pressures, or performing a variety of other interventions.

catheterization: The process of placing a catheter.

cauda equina: The spinal nerve roots that descend from the lower part of the spinal cord, below the first lumbar vertebrae.

causalgia: A pain syndrome resulting from damage to a major nerve, characterized by severe burning pain and autonomic dysfunction.

cauterization: Destruction of tissue by means of heat, freezing, an electric current, or caustic chemicals; done to destroy diseased tissue or stop bleeding.

cautery: The instrument used to cauterize. See also cauterization.

cavernous sinus thrombosis: Clotting of blood in the cavernous sinus, a dilation of the venous system inside the skull. Can lead to nerve damage and intracerebral infections.

CBC: Complete blood count.

CCU: Coronary care unit.

cecum: A blind pouch that forms the first part of the colon (large intestine). The appendix is located at its lower end.

celiac: Pertaining to the abdomen.

celiac artery: See celiac trunk.

celiac plexus: A network of nerves located in the upper abdomen, just in front of the aorta at the level of the first lumbar vertebra. The celiac plexus supplies sympathetic and sensory nerves to the internal organs of the abdomen.

celiac trunk: A branch of the abdominal aorta. It divides into three major branches, the splenic, hepatic, and left gastric arteries. They supply the organs of the upper abdominal cavity.

cell: The smallest living unit. An individual cell is microscopic; however, all body tissues of plants and animals are made up of cells and cell products. Some organisms (such as bacteria and protozoa) consist of a single cell.

cell body: The main part of a cell that contains the nucleus and organelles.

cell membrane: The membrane that forms the surface of a cell; the outer covering of the cell.

Centers For Disease Control (CDC): The national organization for the monitoring of infectious disease in the United States. Also involved in new research in infectious disease.

central nervous system (CNS): The portion of the nervous system consisting of the brain and spinal cord.

central pain: Pain that results from injury or disease of the central nervous system.

centrifuge: A device that spins test tubes at high speeds. This causes the contents of the tube to separate according to density, with heavier particles settling to the bottom and lighter liquid remaining at the top.

cephalic vein: A large superficial vein that runs along the outer side of the arm. In the region of the shoulder, it merges with the axillary vein to form the subclavian vein.

cerebellum: The part of the brain that lies behind the brainstem and below the cerebrum. It is involved in the maintenance of posture and balance and the coordination of voluntary movement.

cerebral aqueduct: A canal in the brainstem that connects the ventricles (cavities) of the brain.

cerebral arteries: The arteries that supply blood to the cerebral hemispheres of the brain. There are three cerebral arteries (anterior, middle, and posterior) on each side of the brain.

cerebral concussion: A head injury characterized by temporary unconsciousness without evidence of structural damage to the brain. The individual recovers without serious neurological deficits.

cerebral cortex: The outer layer of the cerebrum consisting primarily of gray matter.

cerebral hemispheres: The right and left halves of the cerebrum.

cerebral herniation: Protrusion of part of the brain across or through an opening; usually the result of swelling of the brain.

cerebral infarction: Death of brain tissue due to inadequate blood flow.

cerebrospinal fluid (CSF): A fluid produced within the ventricles (cavities) of the brain. It circulates around the brain and spinal cord (in the subarachnoid space). Its functions are to protect the brain and spinal cord, supply nutrients, and remove waste.

cerebrovascular: Pertaining to the blood vessels that supply the brain.

cerebrum: The largest part of the brain consisting of two hemispheres connected by tracts of fibers. It is involved in all conscious functions including perception, voluntary movement, emotion, memory, language, and reasoning.

cervical: Pertaining to the seven vertebrae of the neck or the cervix (the "neck" of the uterus).

cervical cerclage: A procedure that encircles the cervix of the uterus with sutures or a ring to help prevent habitual abortion due to an incompetent cervix.

cervical extension: The upright posture of the head and neck.

cervical incompetence: A condition where the uterine cervix fails to carry out the function of retaining a fetus within the uterus.

cervical nerves: The first eight pairs of spinal nerves (C1-C8) that exit from the vertebral column in the region of the neck.

cervical nodes: The lymph nodes of the neck.

cervical rib: A short, extra rib associated with a cervical vertebra (usually the seventh cervical vertebra).

cervical spondylotic myelopathy: Refers to muscular dysfunction as a result of abnormal bone growth in the bones of the neck.

cervical stenosis: Narrowing of the spinal canal (the canal containing the spinal cord) in the cervical region of the spine; may be congenital or acquired.

cervicothoracic: Pertaining to both the neck and the chest.

cervicothoracic disc: The intervertebral disc between the seventh cervical vertebra (C7) and the first thoracic vertebra (T1).

cervicothoracic ganglion: A sympathetic ganglion located in the neck; it supplies sympathetic nerve fibers to the head, neck, and upper extremity. Also called the stellate ganglion.

cervix: The neck or any part of an organ shaped like a neck. Usually pertains to the neck of the uterus; the narrow, lower part of the uterus that opens into the vagina.

CFS: Chronic fatigue syndrome.

chalazion: A chronic inflammatory granuloma of one of the small glands of the eyelid.

challenge test: A diagnostic procedure where fluids or a chemical substance is administered and the individual is observed to see whether a physiological response occurs, e.g., an allergen administered to diagnose allergy, a hormone administered to determine whether it produces the normal response, or fluids given to monitor kidney response. (Also called provocation test.)

chancre: A chancre is an ulcer that may appear at the mouth, penis, urethra, eyelid, or conjunctiva. It is red and painless and contains spirochetes. It does not cause a scar; first sign of of syphilis.

chancroid: An ulcer that is contagious and sexually transmitted, but not caused by syphilis. It does cause a scar and may form on the penis, urethra, vulva, or anus. See also Hemophilus ducreyi.

cheilitis: Inflammation of the lips.

cheilosis: Cracking and scaling of the lips.

chem 20: Tests done on the blood including electrolytes, calcium, magnesium, blood urea nitrogen (BUN), creatinine, glucose, alkaline phosphatase (ALP) aspartate transaminase (AST), total and direct bilirubin, total protein, albumin, alanine transaminase (ALT), cholesterol, triglycerides, high density lipids, and low density lipids.

chemical pneumonia: Pneumonia due to the inhalation or aspiration of irritating or toxic chemicals.

chemoexfoliation: Use of chemicals, usually acids, to peel away the top layer of epidermis. A cosmetic procedure.

chemosis: Swelling of the conjunctive (the white of the eyes).

chest tube: A tube inserted through the chest wall for the purpose of draining air or fluid out of the pleural cavity; also called a thoracostomy tube.

CHF: Congestive heart failure.

chlamydia: A type of microorganism that can cause a variety of diseases. Chlamydiae are similar to bacteria but live inside cells as intracellular parasites.

chloride: A salt of hydrochloric acid (HCl) or a negatively charged chlorine ion (Cl-).

chlorine: A chemical element (atomic number 17), denoted by the symbol Cl. A highly reactive gas, chlorine is capable of combining with almost all the other elements.

chloroquine: A white antimicrobial, crystalline powder used to treat malaria, amebic dysentery, or lupus erythematosus.

cholangitis: Inflammation of the biliary ducts.

cholecystenteric: Pertaining to the gallbladder and the intestine.

cholecystenteric fistula: An abnormal passageway between the gallbladder and an adjacent loop of intestine.

cholecystokinin: A hormone manufactured by mucosal cells in the duodenum and secreted into the blood. Cholecystokinin stimulates the release of bile from the gallbladder into the duodenum. It also stimulates the pancreas to secrete digestive enzymes. In this capacity, it is often called pancreozymin.

cholecystostomy: Creation of an opening into the gallbladder through the abdominal wall. The procedure is usually done by means of a percutaneous (through the skin) catheter; however, it can also be done surgically.

choledocholithiasis: Calculi (stones) in the common bile duct.

cholesteatoma: A mass of cholesterol and keratinized epithelial cells in the middle ear.

cholesterol: A wax-like lipid found in animal tissues. Cholesterol is produced by the liver and has a variety of functions in the body. It is an important constituent of cell membranes, a constituent of bile, and used by the body to produce steroid hormones.

cholinergic: A term applied to nerve fibers that release the neurotransmitter acetylcholine. Parasympathetic nerve fibers are cholinergic. Most sympathetic nerve fibers are adrenergic, but some (such as those responsible for sweating) are cholinergic. Acetylcholine is also released by motor nerve fibers that innervate skeletal muscle. Cholinergic also pertains to a drug that stimulates the parasympathetic nervous system. See also autonomic nervous system.

chondrectomy: Surgical excision of cartilage.

chondroblastoma: A rare benign tumor of the epiphysis of a bone (the region where growth takes place).

chondrocalcinosis: A condition where the surface in contact with other bones (articular surface) becomes calcified. This condition resembles gout and affects the joints.

chondromalacia: Softening of articular cartilage, usually of the patella (kneecap).

chondroplasty: Surgical repair or remodeling of cartilage.

Chopart's fracture: An injury, including fracture/dislocation of the midtarsal joints of the foot.

chordae tendineae: In the heart, the fibrous cords that attach the cusps of the mitral and tricuspid valves to the papillary muscles inside the ventricles. See also papillary muscle.

chorea: A movement disorder characterized by an uncontrolled movement of the limbs and/or facial muscles.

chorion: A membrane separate from the embryo that gives rise to the chorionic villi and the placenta.

chorionic villi: Finger-like projections that invade the inner surface of the uterus (endometrium) to become the placenta.

choroid: A layer on the back of the eye that nourishes the retina. It contains blood vessels that supply blood to the retina.

choroiditis: Inflammation of the choroid. See also choroid.

choroidoretinitis: Inflammation of the choroid and retina.

chromaffin tissue: Tissue that stains brown with chromic salts. The adrenal medulla and certain cells of the paraganglia in the brain stain this way.

chromosome: One of the packaged strands of DNA in a cell. The storage area for genetic information.

chronic: Of long duration; usually describes a disease that changes little or progresses slowly. The opposite of acute.

chyle: A milky-white fluid found in the lymphatic system. Consists of fats taken up by the intestines during digestion.

chyme: A mixture of partially digested food and digestive secretions found in the stomach and small intestine after a meal.

ciliary block: A type of nerve block that involves the injection of an anesthetic behind the eye.

ciliary body: Part of the uvea of the eye, located between the iris and the choroid. It contains smooth muscle that, by contracting or relaxing, changes the shape of the lens. This makes it possible for the eye to focus on objects at different distances. The ciliary body also contains cells that secrete the aqueous humor. See also aqueous humor.

cine-: A prefix referring to motion.

cineangiocardiography: Motion-picture photography of the heart and great vessels using fluoroscopy.

circle of Willis: A major communication of arteries at the base of the brain. Branches of the internal carotid arteries form the anterior part of the circle; branches of the basilar artery form the posterior part. Currently called the cerebral arterial circle.

circulatory insufficiency: See shock.

circulatory system: The organ system concerned with the circulation of body fluids. The term is often used synonymously with the cardiovascular system (heart and blood vessels); however, the lymph vessels (which recycle tissue fluid into the bloodstream) may also be considered part of the circulatory system.

circumflex: Winding around (such as the left circumflex artery, a branch of the left coronary artery that winds around the left side of the heart).

circumoral: The area around the mouth.

CIS: Central inhibitory state.

CK: Creatine kinase.

claudication: Lameness or limping that may be a result of inadequate blood supply to and from the legs.

clavicle: The collarbone.

clear lens extraction: A procedure that exchanges a lens with a cataract or deformity for a normal lens. Unlike LASIK and other refractive surgery procedures, the clear lens extraction does not involve changes in the cornea.

climacteric: The physiologic and hormonal changes that occur around menopause.

clinical: Based on or pertaining to the direct observation and treatment of individuals.

closed : Without a wound or incision.

closed reduction: Reduction by nonsurgical methods.

Clostridium: Genus of bacteria that are anaerobic, form spores, and commonly found in soil, human intestinal tracts, and wound infections. Several cause disease in humans such as gas gangrene, colitis, and tetanus.

Clostridium difficile latex assay: A test to detect Clostridium difficile in the feces.

Clostridium tetani: The bacteria that cause lockjaw or tetanus.

clotting factor: A component of blood required for proper clotting.

clubbing: A condition of the fingers or toes characterized by an enlarged, rounded (bulbous) appearance. Clubbing occurs in a variety of diseases, especially those of the lungs.

CMC joints: Carpometacarpal joints.

CNS: Central nervous system.

coagulation test: Refers to any of a variety of tests that measure the blood's ability to clot effectively.

coagulation: Clotting.

coarctation: A narrowing or constriction. Coarctation of the aorta is a congenital narrowing of the aorta.

cobalamin: A chemical compound from which vitamin B12 forms. See also vitamin B12.

cocaine: A central nervous system stimulant derived from coca leaves. Abuse of cocaine results in dependence.

coccus (plural, cocci): A sphere-shaped bacterium.

coccygeal: Pertaining to the coccyx.

coccyx: The small bone at the base of the vertebral column consisting of several fused vertebral segments; the tailbone.

cochlea: A spiral-shaped structure of the inner ear containing the sensory receptors for hearing.

cochleosacculotomy: An operative procedure for Ménière's disease where a shunt is created between the cochlea and the saccule of the inner ear.

cognitive: Pertaining to the mental processes of awareness including perception, thought, and memory.

cognitive therapy: A therapeutic approach that attempts to solve emotional problems by altering the individual's thinking.

cognitive/behavioral therapy: A therapeutic approach that combines cognitive and behavioral therapy. See cognitive therapy, behavioral therapy.

coinfection: Infection by more than one bacteria or virus at the same time.

colic: Painful spasm of a hollow or tubular organ.

colitis: Inflammation of the colon (large intestine).

collagen: A protein that forms the white, non-elastic fibers of tendons, ligaments, skin, and all other connective tissue.

collagen injections: A cosmetic procedure where sterilized collagen proteins are injected into an area of the body to provide shape.

collagen vascular diseases: See connective tissue diseases.

collateral: A side branch of a blood vessel or nerve.

collateral circulation: Overlapping blood supply with branches of one blood vessel communicating with branches of another blood vessel.

collateral ligaments: Ligaments located along the medial and lateral sides of a joint.

colloid: A suspension of fine particles dispersed in a solvent.

colon: The part of the intestine extending from the end of the ileum to the rectum; the large intestine. It includes the cecum, ascending colon, transverse colon, descending colon, and sigmoid colon.

colorectal: Pertaining to both the colon and rectum.

colposcopy: Examination of the vagina and the cervix using a scope.

colpotomy: An operation within the vagina.

comatose: A state of unconsciousness from which the individual cannot be roused.

comminuted fracture: A fracture that is broken into several pieces.

common bile duct: The large duct formed by the merging of the common hepatic duct and the cystic duct that conveys bile to the duodenum.

common carotid artery: The right common carotid arises from the brachiocephalic trunk (a branch of the aorta). The left common carotid arises directly from the aorta. Each common carotid artery divides into an internal and external branch. These provide blood to the head.

common hepatic duct: The biliary duct formed by the merging of the right and left hepatic ducts. The common hepatic duct and the cystic duct join to form the common bile duct, which empties bile into the duodenum.

common iliac artery: The abdominal aorta terminates by dividing into the right and left common iliac arteries. Each common iliac artery then subdivides into an internal and external branch. These provide blood to the pelvis and legs.

common peroneal nerve: One of two large branches of the sciatic nerve (the other is the tibial nerve). Provides sensation and movement to the lower legs.

comorbid: Refers to conditions that exist in conjunction with each other but are unrelated.

complement: A group of serum proteins involved in the immunological destruction of antibody-coated cells.

complementary therapies: Refers to the use of different therapies at the same time to treat a condition.

complete blood count (CBC): A determination of the cellular components in a blood sample. A standard CBC includes a count of red blood cells (RBC), white blood cells (WBC), and platelets. In addition, hemoglobin concentration and hematocrit (the percentage of blood volume made up by RBCs) are measured. A CBC with a differential count also includes a breakdown of the different subtypes of WBCs.

complication: A disorder superimposed upon another that affects the prognosis of the original disorder. For example, a wound infection may be a complication of surgery.

compression fracture: A fracture, especially of the vertebrae, that results from stress on a weakened bone.

concentration: The strength of a substance in a mixture or solution (i.e., the amount of a substance per unit volume of another substance); an increase in the strength of a solution.

concussion: A blow or injury to the head resulting in an alteration in consciousness.

condensing: Making a substance more dense or compact.

conditioned response: An involuntary, learned response to a stimulus that, prior to conditioning, would not elicit the response. In order for conditioning to occur, an initial stimulus must produce a nonconditioned physiological or behavioral response. By pairing this stimulus with a second stimulus, the second stimulus also becomes capable of eliciting the response.

condyle: A rounded protuberance at the end of a long bone that forms an articular surface.

confabulation: The substitution of imagined experiences for gaps in memory.

congenital: Present at birth. May refer to either a hereditary condition or a condition that arises during development of the embryo or fetus.

congenital abnormality: An abnormality present at birth.

congestion: An excessive amount of blood or fluid in an organ or tissue.

conjugation: Joining together; coupling. A type of chemical reaction that takes place in the liver, an essential step in the detoxification and metabolism of drugs and other organic compounds. The compounds are chemically joined to certain other chemicals, allowing them to be excreted harmlessly from the body (i.e., in the urine).

conjunctiva: The mucous membrane that covers the eyeball and the inside of the eyelids.

conjunctival injection: Congestion of the conjunctiva. See also conjunctiva.

connective tissue: Tissue that binds together and supports all the other tissues of the body. The different types of connective tissue include bone, cartilage, fat, and fibrous tissue.

connective tissue diseases: A group of inflammatory disorders (also called collagen vascular diseases) characterized by widespread pathological changes in connective tissue. Examples include systemic lupus erythematosus (SLE), rheumatoid arthritis, polymyositis, ermatomyositis, polymyalgia rheumatica, and scleroderma.

consciousness: State of awareness of one's surroundings.

conservative: A term used to describe treatment that is noninvasive rather than invasive, or medical rather than surgical.

constitutional: Pertaining to the body as a whole rather than a specific part. Constitutional symptoms may include fever, malaise, and myalgias.

contagious: Communicable; able to be transmitted from one individual to another.

contamination: Presence of infectious agents (bacteria or viruses) in an area where they are not normally found.

contractility: The capacity to contract or become shorter in response to a stimulus (such as muscle tissue).

contracture: Fixed shortening of a muscle due to fibrosis.

contraindication: A condition that makes an otherwise suitable treatment inappropriate.

contrast dye: A contrast medium. See contrast medium.

contrast material: A contrast medium. See contrast medium.

contrast medium: A substance impenetrable to x-rays; used in radiology to provide contrast between adjacent anatomical structures. For example, barium (either swallowed or given as an enema) is used for x-rays of the gastrointestinal tract. Other kinds of contrast media are injected into blood vessels (for angiography) and joint cavities (for arthrography). Contrast media are also used in MRI; these substances are characterized by their magnetic properties rather than the ability to absorb x-rays. Also called contrast dye or contrast material.

control: A standard against which experimental observations can be verified. A controlled experiment or study is one that makes use of such a standard. For example, in a placebo-controlled drug study, one group of subjects (the experimental group) receives the active drug, while a comparable group (the control group) receives an inactive substance (placebo). The results for the two groups are then compared. This makes it possible to differentiate between a true pharmacological response and a placebo effect (a response due to the subject's mental "set" or expectation). A greater degree of control is achieved if the study is also double-blind (i.e., if neither the subjects nor the experimenters know who is receiving which treatment). This information is kept in coded form by a third party (such as the pharmacist who formulates the drugs). At the end of the study, the code is broken and the data analyzed.

contusion: An injury where the skin is not broken; a bruise.

conversion disorder: A psychiatric disorder characterized by loss or alteration of physical function that cannot be accounted for by an organic disease process. A conversion symptom is the expression of a psychological need or conflict.

convulsion: An episode of violent, involuntary muscle contractions, as in an epileptic seizure. See also seizure.

COPD: Chronic obstructive pulmonary disease.

coracoacromial: Pertaining to both the coracoid process and the acromion of the scapula (shoulder blade).

coracoclavicular: Pertaining to both the clavicle (collarbone) and the coracoid process of the scapula.

coracoclavicular ligament: The ligament between the clavicle (collarbone) and the coracoid process of the scapula.

coracohumeral: Pertaining to both the humerus (upper arm bone) and the coracoid process of the scapula.

coracoid process: A beak-like projection on the upper anterior surface of the scapula. The coracoid process serves as an attachment for muscles (including biceps brachii) and ligaments.

cornea: The transparent covering of the front of the eyeball. The cornea covers the iris and pupil; its edges are continuous with the sclera (white of eye).

corneocytes: Keratin-filled cells of one of the layers of the cornea.

coronal: Dividing the body (or a body structure) into front and back regions.

coronary: Encircling in the manner of a crown (corona) such as the coronary arteries of the heart.

coronary arteries: The arteries that supply blood to the myocardium (heart muscle); so called because they encircle the heart like a crown (corona). The left main coronary artery divides into a left anterior descending (LAD) and left circumflex branch. The right coronary artery (or in some individuals, the left circumflex) gives off a posterior descending branch. See also left main coronary artery, left anterior descending artery, left circumflex artery, and right coronary artery.

coronary artery bypass graft (CABG): Surgery performed to bypass an obstructed coronary vessel by sewing a new vessel around the obstruction. The internal mammary artery or the saphenous vein are used to provide an alternate route for blood flow to the muscles of the heart.

coronary artery disease: Arteriosclerosis of the coronary arteries. See arteriosclerosis.

coronary care unit (CCU): A hospital area specially equipped for the continuous monitoring and intensive care of individuals with acute myocardial infarction and unstable chest pain.

coronary sinus: A large venous channel in the heart that receives blood from the cardiac veins. The coronary sinus empties into the right atrium.

coronary thrombolysis: Use of thrombolytic (clot-dissolving) agents in the treatment of myocardial infarction.

coronoid fossa: An indentation on the anterior surface of the lower end of the humerus that receives the coronoid process of the ulna to form part of the elbow.

coronoid process: A bony projection of the upper end of the ulna that fits into the coronoid fossa of the humerus.

corpus albicans: A mass of fibrous tissue in the ovary that replaces the corpus luteum after ovulation, forming a whitish scar on the ovary that eventually disappears.

corpus cavernosum: Spongy tissue in the penis that fills with blood to produce an erection.

corpus luteum: A yellow glandular structure that develops in the ovarian follicle after ovulation. If pregnancy occurs, it persists, secreting progesterone. If no pregnancy occurs, it degenerates and is replaced by the corpus albicans.

corrosive esophagitis: A chemical burn of the esophagus caused by ingestion of a corrosive substance such as a strong acid or alkali.

cortex: The outer layer of an organ (such as the cerebral cortex or the adrenal cortex).

cortical bone: The hard, outer portion of a bone.

corticospinal: Pertaining to both the cerebral cortex and the spinal cord.

corticospinal tract: A bundle of nerve fibers that conduct motor impulses from the cerebrum to the spinal cord.

corticosteroid: Any of a group of steroid hormones secreted by the adrenal cortex (including glucocorticoids and mineralocorticoids, but excluding the sex hormones); or any synthetic steroid with activity similar to that of the natural corticosteroid hormones.

corticotropin: A pituitary hormone that stimulates the adrenal cortex to secrete corticosteroid hormones (especially cortisol). Also called adrenocorticotropic hormone (ACTH).

corticotropin releasing hormone (CRH): A hypothalamic hormone that stimulates the pituitary gland to secrete corticotropin.

cortisol: A steroid hormone secreted by the adrenal cortex; also called hydrocortisone. Cortisol plays a role in protein, fat, and carbohydrate metabolism, and helps protects the body against stress. See also glucocorticoids and corticosteroids.

coryza: Acute rhinitis, "runny nose."

costal: Pertaining to a rib or ribs.

costal cartilage: A cartilage that connects the anterior end of a rib to the sternum; a rib cartilage.

costochondral junction: The joint between a rib and its costal cartilage. See also costal cartilage.

costovertebral: Pertaining to both the ribs and vertebrae.

costovertebral angle: The angle between the vertebral column and the twelfth (lowest) rib. The area of the back above the hips and below the ribs.

coumadin: An anticoagulant medication used to inhibit clotting. See anticoagulation.

Coxsackie viruses: A group of viruses (named after Coxsackie, New York, where they were first identified), belonging to the enterovirus category. Coxsackie virus infections may be asymptomatic, but various types are also capable of causing disease, including pleurodynia, meningitis, myocarditis, pericarditis, and a poliomyelitis-like syndrome. See also enteroviruses.

cranial: Pertaining to the cranium, the part of the skull that encloses the brain.

cranial nerves: Twelve pairs of nerves originating in the brain that supply sensory and motor function to the head and neck, as well as autonomic function to internal organs of the trunk.

craniocaudal: Oriented from head to tail.

C-reactive protein: A protein present in the body that helps defend the body from pneumococci bacteria by attacking the outer capsule of the bacteria. Levels are higher when inflammation is present in the body.

creatine kinase (CK): A muscle enzyme (formerly called creatine phosphokinase or CPK). CK occurs in slightly different forms (isoenzymes) in cardiac and skeletal muscle. When muscle tissue is damaged, the enzyme leaks from the damaged cells and enters the blood. Elevated serum CK is a sign of either myocardial infarction/injury or skeletal muscle disease/injury. If necessary, isoenzyme tests can be performed to differentiate between the two.

creatinine: A breakdown product of phosphocreatine (a substance that stores energy in muscle). Elevated serum creatinine is usually a sign of renal failure, but may also occur in muscle disease.

crepitation: A crunching sound or sensation caused by either bone fragments or bony joints grinding together, or by subcutaneous air.

crepitus: A grating sound (such as with joint movement or with movement of the broken ends of a fracture).

CRH: See corticotropin releasing hormone.

cross-sensitization: Sensitization to a substance or stimulus induced by exposure to a different substance or stimulus. For example, allergic cross-sensitization may occur among chemically related substances.

cruciate ligaments: Two ligaments of the knee (one anterior and one posterior) that connect the femur (thigh bone) to the tibia and fibula. The two ligaments cross over each other as they pass through the joint cavity.

cryosurgery: Exposing tissue to extreme cold (less than 20° celsius) by use of a liquid nitrogen probe. This causes tissue destruction to a specific, well-defined area and may be done to control pain, stop bleeding, treat warts, destroy tumors, or produce lesions in the brain to treat disease.

cryptorchidectomy: Surgical removal of undescended testicles.

cryptorchidism: A condition where the testicles fail to descend into the scrotum.

CSF: Cerebrospinal fluid.

CT scan: Computerized (axial) tomography.

cubital: Pertaining to the elbow.

cuboid bone: One of the seven tarsal bones of the foot. Located on the lateral side of the foot, it forms part of the midfoot.

culprit lesion: In coronary artery disease, a stenosis (narrowing) identified as the cause of symptoms.

culture: The cultivation of microorganisms or of tissue cells in special media (nutritive substances) conducive to their growth. Microorganisms are commonly cultured for the purpose of diagnosing infectious disease. A sample of body fluid (such as urine, blood, CSF) or tissue is placed in or on an appropriate culture medium, which is then incubated. If microorganisms grow, they can be identified. In conjunction with a culture, the sensitivity (susceptibility) of bacteria to antibiotics can also be determined (culture and sensitivity testing or C&S).

culture medium (plural, media): A nutritive substance conducive to the growth of microorganisms or tissue cells.

cuneiform bones: The medial, intermediate, and lateral cuneiform bones are three tarsal bones of the foot. They form part of the midfoot.

cuneocuboid joint: The joint between the lateral cuneiform and the cuboid bone of the foot.

cuneonavicular joints: The joints between the three cuneiform bones and the navicular bone of the foot.

curettage: A surgical procedure involving the use of a curette to scrape or clean an area.

curette: A scraping instrument.

cusp: A tapering projection such as a flap or leaflet of a cardiac valve.

cutdown: Surgical exposure of a vein or artery for the purpose of introducing an intravenous or intra-arterial catheter.

CVA: Cerebrovascular accident; stroke.

cyanosis: A bluish or grayish discoloration of the skin due to decreased oxygen in the blood.

cyanotic: A blue, gray, or dark purple discoloration of the skin due to decreased amounts of oxygen-bearing hemoglobin.

cyst: A sac-like or pouch-like structure filled with fluid or solid material. The term usually refers to an abnormal structure (such as a cyst) that may result from obstruction of a duct.

cystic: Pertaining to a cyst, the urinary bladder, or the gallbladder.

cystic duct: The duct of the gallbladder. The cystic duct merges with the common hepatic duct to form the common bile duct.

cystoma: A cystic tumor; a growth containing cysts.

cystometrogram: A graph of results produced when the inner urinary bladder pressure is measured as the bladder is filled (cystometry). The graph compares pressure versus volume levels.

cytology: The science or laboratory study of cells.

cytomegalovirus (CMV): A type of herpes virus that infects human beings and occasionally causes disease.

cytoplasm: The substance of a cell between the nucleus and the cell wall.

cytotoxic: Toxic to cells. A cytotoxic drug is one that kills cells (such as in cancer chemotherapy).

dacryocystoplasty: Surgery on the tear sacs of the eyes.

damping: Decrease in amplitude (such as a wave).

dander: Scales from the hair or feathers of animals that may act as an allergen in sensitive individuals.

DC shock: Direct current shock.

deafferentation: Loss of sensory input due to nerve injury or disease.

debridement: Removal of foreign matter and dead or damaged tissue (such as from a wound).

decompression: Removal of pressure.

decongestant: A drug that relieves congestion or swelling.

deep tendon reflex: An involuntary muscle contraction produced by tapping on a tendon, (e.g., the patellar tendon reflex or "knee jerk").

defibrillation: The process or procedure of stopping fibrillation of the heart (either atrial or ventricular). Defibrillation can be done either with drugs or by applying a direct electrical current (DC shock). See also fibrillation.

deficit: A lack or deficiency or a loss of function.

degenerated disk: Fibrosis of the retinae leading to loss of vision.

degeneration: Deterioration; change of tissue to a less functional form.

dehydration: The condition resulting from excessive loss of body water.

delayed union: Delayed healing of a fracture.

delirium tremens ("DTs"): A severe complication of alcohol withdrawal characterized by delirium, tremulousness, and sometimes convulsions.

delta waves: Brain waves on an electroencephalogram (EEG) characteristic of deep (non-REM) sleep.

deltoid ligament: The ligament of the medial side of the ankle.

deltoid muscle: The muscle covering the tip of the shoulder. It lifts the arm and also helps in bending and straightening the arm at the shoulder joint.

delusion: A false belief held despite obvious evidence to the contrary, and despite not being shared by other members of the culture.

demyelination: Destruction or loss of the outer covering (myelin) from nerve fibers; results in impairment of nerve conduction.

dendrite: A fiber-like projection of a neuron (nerve cell) that conducts electrical impulses toward the cell body.

denervation: Loss of nerve supply.

dental abscess: An abscess of the teeth, gums, or bony structures around the teeth.

dental crown: The part of the tooth covered with enamel. Normally refers to the exposed part of the tooth.

dentine: The inner part of the tooth that provides most of its mass. Largely composed of inorganic substances (hydroxyapatite).

deoxygenation: Removal of oxygen (i.e., from the blood).

deoxyribonucleic acid (DNA): A large, complex organic molecule that is the chemical basis of heredity. The DNA molecule takes the form of linear or circular strands; in double-stranded DNA (the kind ordinarily found in most organisms), the two strands are twisted around each other to form a double helix. DNA encodes the instructions for the synthesis of proteins and RNA; it is also capable of self-replication.

dependence: Physical or psychological craving for a drug.

depolarization: The firing (electrical discharging) of an electrically excitable cell or tissue such as nerve, muscle, or cardiac tissue. Depolarization is followed by a recovery period (repolarization) in which the cell or tissue returns to its original electrical state.

dermatographia: Hives produced by pressure on the skin.

dermatome: (1) An instrument used to cut and slice thin layers of the skin to use for skin grafts. (2) An area of skin innervated by a particular spinal nerve; the sensory territory of a spinal nerve.

dermatophyte: A fungi that causes an infection of the skin, hair, or nails.

dermatophytid: An allergic rash that forms in response to a dermatophyte. Often forms at sites distant to the actual infection.

dermis: The deep layer of skin under the epidermis.

descending aorta: The part of the aorta that descends through the chest and abdomen.

desensitization: (1) The prevention or reduction of allergic reactions by administering graded doses of allergen. (2) In behavioral therapy, a method of treating phobias and related disorders by exposing the individual to anxiety-provoking stimuli. In one type of desensitization, the individual learns relaxation techniques. The individual then applies these techniques during exposure to a very mild anxiety-producing stimulus. This is followed by exposure to progressively stronger stimuli until the individual can tolerate the most extreme stimuli.

devascularization: A decrease of the blood supply to a part of the body.

developmental: Pertaining to development (such as a fetus or a child).

dextrocardia: Abnormal location of the heart in the right side of the chest.

diabetes: A term for disease characterized by excessive urination. Usually refers to diabetes mellitus, a disorder of glucose regulation in the body.

diagnosis: The name of an individual's disease or disorder. The process of determining the cause or nature of an individual's illness. This is done by means of a history (symptoms), physical examination (signs), laboratory tests, and other diagnostic procedures.

dialysis: Passage of a dissolved substance across a membrane. Renal dialysis is a method of providing artificial kidney function. Waste products and other unwanted substances are selectively removed from the blood by passage through a semipermeable membrane (dialysis

membrane). See also hemodialysis and peritoneal dialysis.

diaphragm: (1) A dome-like sheet of muscle that separates the thoracic and abdominal cavities; the main muscle involved in respiration. When the diaphragm contracts, it flattens downward; pressure in the chest cavity decreases, and air is drawn into the lungs. When the diaphragm relaxes, it moves upward; pressure in the chest cavity increases, and air is expelled from the lungs. (2) A contraceptive device consisting of a rubber or plastic cup that fits over the cervix.

diaphysis: The shaft of a long bone.

diarrhea: Frequent, watery bowel movements.

diarthrosis joint: A synovial or hinge joint where the opposing bones move freely.

diastole: The phase of the cardiac cycle when the heart chambers dilate and fill with blood; the period of cardiac relaxation that alternates with contraction (systole). The term usually refers to the ventricles, but may also refer to the atria.

diastolic: Pertaining to or occurring during diastole.

diastolic blood pressure: The pressure in the arteries during the diastolic phase of the cardiac cycle. For example, when the blood pressure is 120/80, the diastolic pressure is 80. See also systolic blood pressure.

diastolic hypertension: Abnormal elevation of the diastolic arterial pressure. See also blood pressure.

diathermy: The use of high frequency oscillating current to generate heat in a body part to warm it for treating a disease or condition.

DIC: Disseminated intravascular coagulation. A disorder of coagulation where clotting factors are used up and bleeding ensues.

differential diagnosis: The process of differentiating between two or more diseases with similar signs and symptoms; a list (usually ranked according to probability) of the possible causes of an individual's symptoms.

differential white blood cell count: See complete blood count.

diffuse: Widely distributed or generalized; not localized.

diffusion: The movement of a solute (dissolved substance) from an area of higher concentration to an area of lower concentration. See also osmosis and filtration.

digit: A finger, thumb, or toe.

dilate: To open, widen, or expand.

dilation: Expansion or increase in diameter of an organ, vessel, or opening.

DIP joints: Distal interphalangeal joints.

diphtheria: An infectious bacterial disease characterized by the formation of a false membrane on the throat and tonsils.

diplopia: Double vision.

direct current (DC) shock: Used to treat cardiac arrhythmia or restart the heart after a cardiac arrest. See also defibrillation.

disc: A flat, round structure such as an intervertebral disc.

disc herniation: Protrusion of the inner part of the intervertebral disk into the area of the spinal cord. May produce neurologic symptoms such as pain, weakness, loss of sensation, or incontinence.

discectomy and fusion: An orthopedic/neurosurgical procedure where a herniated disk is removed and the vertebrae above and below the disk are fused together with metal plates, rods, and screws.

discography: X-ray examination of an intervertebral disc by injecting dye into the disc.

discoid lupus erythematosus: A subcategory of lupus erythematosis characterized by disk-shaped skin lesions.

discoid meniscus: A thickened and wafer-shaped lateral meniscus variant.

dislocation: Displacement of a bone from its normal position in a joint.

disorganized schizophrenia: A severe form of schizophrenia characterized by incoherence, blunted or inappropriate affect, and the absence of delusions.

displaced disc: A herniated intervertebral disc.

displacement: Abnormal position.

dissection: (1) Cutting apart or separating of organs or tissues (i.e., for the purpose of studying their structure). (2) The abnormal separation of tissues (e.g., the layers of an arterial wall, as in a dissecting aneurysm).

disseminated: Distributed over a wide area; scattered throughout the body. The term is usually applied to infectious disease.

disseminated intravascular coagulation: A condition where fibrin is generated in the circulating bloodstream causing widespread clotting and/or bleeding.

distal: The opposite of proximal, in a direction away from the trunk (such as the wrist is distal to the elbow; the foot is distal to the knee).

distal hypospadias: A congenital condition where the urethral opening is on the underside of the end of the penis instead of at the tip.

distal interphalangeal (DIP) joints: The joints between the middle and distal phalanges of the hand or foot.

distal radioulnar (DRU) joint: The joint between the distal radius and distal ulna located just above the wrist.

distention: State of being stretched out or inflated.

diuretic: A drug or agent that increases the production of urine.

diverticulum (plural, diverticula): A sac or outpouching of the wall of a tube-like organ.

DNA: Deoxyribonucleic acid.

DNA analysis: A variety of techniques to analyze an individual's DNA for the presence/absence of certain genes. Often used as a method of matching a DNA sample to a certain individual such as used in forensics.

DNA probe: A small piece of DNA used to identify the presence of a matching sequence in a sample of DNA.

donor tissue: Tissue to be grafted to another area of the body or to another individual.

dopamine: One of several neurotransmitters found in the central nervous system, particularly in the basal ganglia of the brain. Dopamine is also used as a drug to stabilize blood pressure.

Doppler: Pertaining to or using the Doppler effect, an apparent change in the frequency of sound or light waves that occurs when the source of the waves is moving relative to the observer. (When the source and observer are moving toward each other, the frequency increases; when they are moving away from each other, the frequency decreases.)

dorsal: Pertaining to the back or posterior aspect of a body structure; the opposite of ventral. Pertaining to the back of the hand; the opposite of palmar or volar. Pertaining to the top of the foot; the opposite of plantar.

dorsal columns: Tracts of nerve fibers located in the posterior (dorsal) regions of the spinal cord that conduct sensory impulses (touch, pressure, and vibration) to the brain.

dorsal horns: The posterior projections of gray matter in the spinal cord where sensory neurons are located.

dorsal root: The posterior root of a spinal nerve. The dorsal roots carry sensory impulses from the periphery into the dorsal horns of the spinal cord.

dorsal root ganglion: A ganglion (cluster of nerve cell bodies) located on the dorsal root of a spinal nerve. The dorsal root ganglia contain the cell bodies of sensory neurons. See also ganglion.

dorsalis pedis artery: One of the two large arteries that supply the foot (the other is the posterior tibial artery). Pulsation of the dorsalis pedis artery can be felt on the dorsum (top) of the foot.

dorsiflexion: Movement of the foot or toes upward (toward the dorsum of the foot). Dorsiflexion of the foot takes place at the ankle joint.

dorsum: The posterior (back) surface of a body structure. The top of the foot.

double pneumonia: Pneumonia involving both lungs.

double-blind: In a controlled experiment (i.e., comparing a drug to a placebo), a condition in which neither the subjects nor the experimenters know what treatment a given subject is receiving. This information is kept in coded form by a third party, and is revealed at the conclusion of the experiment. The double-blind condition helps prevent the subject's or experimenter's expectations from influencing the outcome. See also control.

Dressler's syndrome: An autoimmune reaction consisting of fever, pericarditis, and sometimes pleuritis, occurring after a myocardial infarction. Also called postmyocardial infarction syndrome.

DRU joint: Distal radioulnar joint.

dry socket: An infection of the socket left when a tooth is removed.

DSM-IV: Diagnostic and Statistical Manual of Mental Disorders, Version IV.

duct: A tubular canal or vessel, especially one that conveys secretions from a gland.

ductal cancer: Breast cancer that is confined to a duct and has not yet spread to other areas of the breast. This is breast cancer at an early stage that can be cured 97% of the time by lumpectomy and radiation.

ductus deferens: See vas deferens.

duodenoscopy: Endoscopy of the duodenum. See also endoscopy and duodenum.

duodenum: The first part of the small intestine. The duodenum is located between the stomach and the jejunum (second part of the small intestine).

dura (mater): The outer membrane covering the spinal cord and brain. See also meninges.

dysarthria: Difficult movement within a joint where two bony surfaces meet.

dysesthesia: Abnormal sensation (such as numbness, tingling, prickling).

dysfunction: Abnormal function.

dyspareunia: Pain during sexual intercourse.

dyspepsia: Indigestion.

dysphagia: Difficulty swallowing.

dysplasia: Abnormal development of a tissue; usually refers to tissue where atypical cells have developed in response to chronic inflammation.

dysplastic nevus: Abnormal growth in a birthmark or mole.

dyspnea: Difficult or labored breathing.

dysregulation: Abnormal or disordered regulation.

dysthymia: Emotion of feeling sad; not as severe as depression.

dystocia: Difficult childbirth.

dystonia: Impaired or abnormal tension (tonicity), e.g., in a muscle.

dystrophy: Disorder resulting from abnormal nutrition or metabolism.

dysuria: Painful or difficult urination.

E. coli: Escherichia coli.

EBV: Epstein-Barr virus.

ecchymosis: Bruise-like discoloration due to rupture of small blood vessels.

ECG: Electrocardiogram.

Echinacea: An herb used as a remedy for certain disorders.

ECHO virus: A virus belonging to the group of viruses known as Enteric Cytopathogenic Human Orphan group. These viruses cause nonbacterial viral meningitis, enteritis, and other infections.

-ectomy: A suffix denoting excision (surgical removal) of any organ or body part.

ectopic: In an abnormal position.

ectropion: A rolling outward of the eyelid.

eczematous lesion: An area of skin that is acutely or chronically inflamed. It may be red, have papules, vesicles, pustules, scales, crusts, or scabs. The lesions may be dry or wet, thickened, and itch or burn.

edema: Swelling or congestion due to an excessive accumulation of fluid in the tissues. Edema may be either localized or systemic.

edematous: A swollen area.

EEG: Electroencephalogram.

effacement: Change in form; usually applied to the shortening and thinning of the cervix of the uterus during labor.

effusion: Abnormal collection of fluid in a body cavity (such as a pleural or pericardial effusion; a joint effusion).

EGD: Esophagogastroduodenoscopy.

Ehlers-Danlos syndrome: An inherited disorder of connective tissue characterized by fragile, hyperelastic skin, and hypermobility of the joints.

ehrlichiosis: An infection with an organism of the genus Ehrlichia. Transmitted by ticks and has similar symptoms to Rocky Mountain spotted fever.

ejection fraction: In cardiology, the percentage of a ventricle's blood volume that is ejected (pumped out) with each heartbeat; the ratio of stroke volume to end-diastolic volume. Ejection fraction is a useful index of ventricular function. See also end-diastolic volume, stroke volume.

EKG: See ECG.

elasticity: The ability to be stretched without breaking.

electrical stimulation: The use of electrical impulses to stimulate a part of the body; often used in chronic pain control.

electrocardiograph: The paper copy of an electrocardiogram.

electrocautery: An instrument used to cauterize consisting of a wire in a holder. The wire is heated to red or white heat by a direct or alternating electrical current.

electrode: An instrument through which electrical current is emitted or received.

electrodesiccation: A means of drying cells and tissues to destroy them by using short high-frequency electric sparks.

Electroencephalographically (EEG): A test used to measure brain activity.

electrolyte: A substance that dissociates into ions (electrically charged particles) when it dissolves, and thus becomes capable of conducting electricity. The ions themselves (i.e., sodium, potassium, chloride, bicarbonate) are also referred to as electrolytes.

electromagnetic radiation: A type of radiation that includes radio waves, microwaves, infra-red, visible light, ultraviolet, x-rays, and gamma rays (in order of increasing energy or decreasing wavelength).

electron: A subatomic particle with negative electric charge; one of the constituents of an atom. The positively charged atomic nucleus (composed of protons and neutrons) is surrounded by the negatively charged electrons. Chemical reactions between atoms or molecules result from the interaction of their electrons.

electron microscope: A microscope that uses a beam of electrons (instead of light) to form an image. An electron microscope provides much greater magnification than a light microscope, making it possible to examine the detailed structure of cellular organelles.

electrophysiology: The study of the relationship between electrical phenomena and body functions. Electrophysiology is concerned with the generation and conduction of electrical currents by body tissues (such as in the heart, nervous system, and muscles); it is also concerned with the effects of electrical stimulation on tissues.

elephantiasis: A condition where the lymphatic vessels are obstructed causing an overgrowth of the skin and tissues beneath the skin, usually affecting the legs and scrotum.

elimination diet: A diet where certain foods are omitted in order to diagnose or treat a food allergy.

ELISA: Enzyme-linked immunosorbent assay.

emaciation: State of being extremely lean, i.e., in starvation.

embolism: Obstruction of a blood vessel by an embolus. See also embolus.

embolus (plural, emboli): A mass of undissolved material carried along in the bloodstream. An embolus may be solid (such as a clot or foreign body), liquid (such as a fat globule), or gaseous (such as an air bubble).

embryo: In prenatal development, the stage between the ovum and the fetus, from the second through the eighth week.

emergency tracheostomy: The emergency placement of a hole in the trachea for administration of oxygen.

EMG: Electromyography.

emollient: An agent that softens the skin.

empirical: Based on practical experience (as opposed to scientific principle).

empyema: Pus in a body cavity, particularly the pleural cavity.

emulsify: To form an emulsion. A mixture of two liquids that are not mutually soluble (such as oil and water). In an emulsion of oil and water, the oil is broken up into tiny globules that are suspended in the water.

encephalopathy: Any disorder of the brain.

enchondroma: A benign tumor made of cartilage. It usually occurs in a place where cartilage is absent such as the long shaft of a bone.

end stage: The final or terminal stage of a disease.

endarteritis: Inflammation of the inner layer of an artery.

end-diastolic: Pertaining to the end of diastole (the phase of cardiac relaxation and filling), just before systole (the phase of contraction) begins.

end-diastolic volume: The volume of blood within a heart chamber (particularly the left ventricle) at the end of diastole when cardiac filling is completed.

endemic: A disease continuously present in a population.

endocardium: The innermost layer of the heart wall, which lines the heart chambers and also forms the heart valves. The endocardium is composed of endothelium (a layer of epithelial cells that lines a body cavity) on a bed of connective tissue. See also endothelium and epithelium.

endocervical canal: The canal through the cervix between the vagina and uterus.

endocrine: Pertaining to the endocrine glands or their secretions (hormones).

endocrine gland: A gland that secretes directly into the bloodstream; a ductless gland. Endocrine glands secrete hormones. See also exocrine gland.

endodontist: A specialist in the biology and pathology of the pulp of the teeth.

endolymphatic sac surgery: A type of surgery on the inner ear.

endometrial: Pertaining to the lining of the uterus, the endometrium.

endometrial carcinoma: Cancer of the lining of the uterus.

endometrium: The mucous membrane that lines the inside of the uterus.

endophthalmitis: Inflammation of the entire eye.

endorphins: A group of neurotransmitters involved in the mediation of pain perception. Released by certain brain cells, endorphins bind to opioid receptors on other brain cells, producing a morphine-like effect; they are sometimes referred to as the brain's natural narcotics. See also narcotic, opioid.

endoscope: An instrument consisting of a tube and an optical system used to examine the inside of a body cavity or organ. The tube may be inserted through either a natural opening or a small incision.

endoscopic cauterization: Cauterization done during endoscopy. See also endoscopy and cauterization.

endoscopic retrograde cholangiopancreatography (ERCP): Contrast x-ray of the biliary and pancreatic ducts. The contrast dye is introduced into the ducts endoscopically via the duodenum.

endoscopy: The use of an endoscope to examine the inside of a body cavity or organ.

endothelium: A layer of epithelial cells lining the heart chambers, blood and lymph vessels, and other body cavities. See also epithelium.

endotoxin: A bacterial poison (toxin) released when certain bacteria die and are broken down.

end-systolic: Pertaining to the end of systole (the phase of cardiac contraction), just before diastole (the phase of relaxation) begins.

end-systolic volume: The volume of blood within a heart chamber (particularly the left ventricle) at the end of systole when cardiac contraction is completed.

enteritis: Inflammation of the intestine (usually the small intestine).

enterohepatic: Pertaining to the intestines and liver.

enterohepatic circulation: Reabsorption of bile constituents (especially bile salts) in the intestine, and re-excretion in the bile. Enterohepatic circulation serves as a recycling mechanism for bile salts.

enteroviruses: A group of viruses (including Coxsackie viruses and polioviruses), which prefers to inhabit the human intestine. Enteroviral infection is usually without symptoms or with mild ones, but can also result in severe disease. See also Coxsackie virus.

enzyme: An organic chemical, usually a protein, that acts as a catalyst for a biochemical reaction. (A catalyst is a substance that speeds up the rate of a chemical reaction without itself being consumed in the reaction.)

Enzyme-linked Immunosorbent Assay: See ELISA.

eosinophil: A type of granulocyte (white blood cell that contains granules in its cytoplasm), so called because it stains easily with eosin (a red dye). Eosinophils normally make up 1-3% of the white blood cells in circulation. The number of eosinophils increases in various conditions including allergic reactions and parasitic infestations. See also granulocyte.

eosinophilia: Increased numbers of eosinophils in the blood.

eosinophilia-myalgia syndrome: A syndrome of eosinophilia and severe generalized muscle pain. An epidemic of the syndrome occurred in 1989 and was traced to the ingestion of contaminated tryptophan.

EP: Evoked potential.

epicardium: The outermost layer of the heart wall; also called the visceral pericardium. See pericardium.

epicondyle: A bony protuberance at the end of a long bone, above a condyle.

epidemic: An outbreak (especially of infectious disease) that spreads rapidly within a population.

epidermis: The outermost layer of skin.

epididymis: A small body located near the testis that contains a convoluted tube ending at the vas deferens. The epididymis is the first part of the duct through which the testis secretes sperm.

epidural: Located outside the dura (the outermost of the membranes that enclose the brain and spinal cord).

epigastrium: The region of the abdomen over the stomach; the upper middle region of the abdomen.

epilepsy: A seizure disorder; has various manifestations ranging from mild absence seizures to grand mal seizures.

epinephrine: A hormone secreted by the adrenal medulla that produces a generalized sympathetic ("fight or flight") response; also called adrenalin. Epinephrine has been synthesized as a drug, and is used as a vasoconstrictor and bronchodilator.

epiphysis: A secondary ossification center at the end of a long bone; all growth of the bone occurs here prior to closure of the epiphyseal growth plate.

episcleritis: Inflammation of the sclera in the layers below the conjunctiva.

episodic: Occurring in distinct episodes.

epithelial membrane: A membrane composed of a layer of epithelial cells on a bed of connective tissue.

epithelium: A type of tissue that covers the external and internal surfaces of the body and forms the lining of body cavities and tubular structures. The skin and mucous membranes; the linings of the thoracic and abdominal cavities; and the linings of the heart and blood vessels are examples of epithelial membranes. Glands are also composed of epithelium. See membrane.

Epstein-Barr virus (EBV): The virus that causes infectious mononucleosis; EBV belongs to the category of herpes viruses.

equilibrium: A state of balance in which all opposing forces are equal.

eradicate: To make extinct.

Erb's point: A point located above the clavicle at the side of the neck. Erb's point lies over the brachial plexus; electrical stimulation at this point causes contraction of various arm muscles.

ERCP: Endoscopic retrograde cholangiopancreatography.

ergometer: A device for measuring work performed or energy expended (i.e., during a cardiac stress test).

ergonomics: The study of how the body expends energy during work.

ergot alkaloids: A group of drugs derived from ergot, a fungus that grows as a parasite on rye.

eructation: Production of gas from the stomach; belching.

eruption: An outbreak (i.e., of a rash).

Erysipelothrix insidiosa: A bacteria widely found in the animal kingdom. Human infection occurs via a wound in individuals who handle animals or animal matter. The disease produced is erysipeloid, a painful, slow spreading, and red swelling of the skin. Currently called Erysipelothrix rhusiopathiae.

erythema: Redness caused by dilation of the capillaries under the skin due to inflammation, a nervous mechanism, or in response to heat, sunburn, or other irritants.

erythrasma: A red-brown eruption in the axilla and groin caused by a bacterial infection.

erythroblastosis fetalis: A hemolytic disease of newborn infants that causes anemia, jaundice, enlargement of the liver and spleen, and generalized edema (hydrops fetalis). The Rh+ infant's red blood cells are destroyed by Rh antibodies produced by the mother, who is Rh-.

erythrocyte: A red blood cell.

erythrocyte sedimentation rate (ESR): A laboratory test used as an indicator of systemic inflammation. The ESR is the speed at which erythrocytes (red blood cells) settle to the bottom of the test tube. An elevated ESR occurs in the presence of inflammation, infection, or cancer.

erythroderma: Abnormally red skin. Also called erythema.

Erythropoietin (EPO): A growth factor for red blood cells; can be manufactured and administered intravenously.

Escherichia coli: A species of gram-negative bacteria normally present in the human colon. Although they do not cause disease in the gastrointestinal tract, they can cause infection if introduced into other areas of the body (such as the urinary tract).

esophageal hiatus: The opening in the diaphragm through which the esophagus passes.

Esophagojejunostomy: A surgical connection of the esophagus to the jejunum.

Esophagomyotomy: The surgical incision of the muscle fibers of the esophagus.

esophagoscopy: Endoscopy of the esophagus. See also endoscopy.

esophagram: An x-ray exam where the individual is observed while swallowing barium to detect esophageal problems.

esophagus: A muscular tube that connects the pharynx (throat) to the stomach. The esophagus carries swallowed food and liquids from the mouth to the stomach.

ESR: Erythrocyte sedimentation rate.

essential fatty acids: Fatty acids essential to proper growth and development. See also fatty acids.

essential tremor: A benign tremor that usually begins in adulthood and affects only the head and arms; often called a familial tremor.

esthesiometer: A device used to measure sensation.

estrogen: Any of a group of steroid hormones (such as estradiol and estrone) that are responsible for female sex characteristics; a female sex hormone. Estrogens are secreted by the ovaries. In addition, androgens (male hormones) are converted to estrogens in body tissues. Drugs with estrogenic activity can also be produced synthetically.

Estrogen Replacement Therapy (ERT): Administration of estrogen after menopause or after removal of the ovaries.

ethmoid bone: One of the bones of the skull located behind the nose. It contains a number of cavities (called air cells) that open into the nasal cavity.

ethmoid sinuses: The air cells of the ethmoid bone.

etiology: The cause of a disease.

eustachian tube: A tube-like channel lined with mucous membrane that connects the middle ear to the pharynx (throat). It allows equalization of pressure between the middle ear and the outside of the body.

eversion: Turning the sole of the foot so that it faces outward (laterally). The opposite of inversion.

evoked potential: The response of nervous tissue or muscle to an applied stimulus. Evoked potentials are used as a technique for assessing the integrity and functioning of the central nervous system. See also action potential.

exacerbation: An increase in severity of a disease or its symptoms; a worsening.

excision: Surgical removal of an organ or tissue.

excretion: Elimination of waste products from the body.

exercise electrocardiography: A technique using electrocardiography to monitor the heart during exercise.

exfoliate: To peel off the outer layer of epidermis, often accomplished through the use of an acid or laser.

exocrine gland: A gland that secretes onto an epithelial surface, either directly or via a duct. See also endocrine gland.

exophthalmos: Bulging eyeballs, possibly due to thyrotoxicosis, eye tumors, swelling behind the eye, leukemia, or aneurysms.

exostosis: A hard growth that develops on the surface of a bone and often involves hardening of muscular attachments.

exotoxin: A poison (toxin) produced by certain microorganisms and released into their surroundings.

extension: The opposite of flexion. The straightening of a joint (such as the knee, elbow, or fingers); increasing the angle between the bones of a joint. The movement of the shoulder or hip in which the arm or leg is raised in a backward direction. Movement of the wrist in the direction of the dorsum of the hand; movement of the thumb away from and parallel to the palm; movement of the toes in the direction of the dorsum of the foot.

extensor: A muscle that extends a joint. See also extension.

extensor digitorum: The extensor muscle of the fingers located in the forearm. It has long tendons that insert on the phalanges of the fingers.

extensor digitorum longus: An extensor (dorsiflexor) muscle of the toes (except the big toe) located in the front of the lower leg. It has long tendons that insert on the distal phalanges of the toes (except the big toe).

extensor hallucis longus: An extensor (dorsiflexor) muscle of the big toe located in the front of the lower leg. It has a long tendon that inserts on the distal phalanx of the big toe.

extensor pollicis brevis: An extensor muscle of the metacarpophalangeal joint at the base of the thumb.

extensor pollicis longus: The extensor muscle of the interphalangeal joint of the thumb.

extensor retinaculum: A band of fibrous tissue that stretches across the dorsum of the wrist, holding the extensor tendons of the hand in position. It acts as a pulley for the extensor tendons.

extensor tendons: The tendons of the extensor muscles of the hand or foot.

external carotid artery: A branch of the common carotid artery. The external carotid supplies structures of the neck, face, jaw, and scalp.

external fixation: The setting of a bone fracture without surgical incision of the skin.

external iliac artery: A branch of the common iliac artery. The external iliac supplies the lower extremity.

external jugular vein: A superficial vein that receives blood from the scalp and face. It descends through the neck and empties into the subclavian vein.

extra-: A prefix meaning outside of.

extra-articular: Outside a joint (i.e., an extra-articular fracture is one that does not involve the articular surface of the bone).

extremity: A limb. The upper extremity is the arm; the lower extremity is the leg.

extrinsic: External.

extrinsic ligaments: Ligaments located outside a joint cavity. See also intrinsic ligaments.

extrinsic muscles: Muscles located outside the part of the body that they control. For example, the extrinsic muscles of the foot are located in the leg and have long tendons that go to the foot. See also intrinsic muscles.

exudate: Material (such as fluid, protein, or cells) that has escaped from blood vessels and accumulated in the tissues or on tissue surfaces, usually as a result of inflammation. Exudates contain a high proportion of protein, cells, and solid matter (as opposed to transudates, which are watery). Pus is an example of an exudate.

facet: A small, smooth area on the surface of a bone that serves as an articular surface.

facet joints: The joints formed between adjacent superior and inferior articular facets of the vertebral column.

fallopian tube: The tube that extends from the outer upper corners of the uterus to the ovary on either side. The ovum moves along this tube toward the uterus. It may be fertilized in the tube by spermatozoa. Also called the uterine tube.

false negative: A test result that indicates an abnormality is not present, when it actually is.

false positive: A test result that indicates an abnormality is present, when it actually is not.

familial: Affecting members of a family; inherited.

familial autonomic dysfunction: A hereditary disease that affects sensory and autonomic function in many organ systems. Also known as familial dysautonomia and Riley-Day syndrome. See autonomic nervous system.

familial adenomatous polyposis: A hereditary disease characterized by the development of numerous polyps in the colon. If untreated, the polyps eventually become malignant.

family history: A record of the state of health or disease of an individual's blood relatives.

fascia: The fibrous membrane that covers, supports, and separates muscles; it also binds the skin to the underlying tissue.

fasciculations: Involuntary muscle twitches due to spontaneous contractions of individual motor units. Fasciculations can be seen under the skin. See also motor unit.

fasciotomy: Surgical incision of fascia.

fasting serum gastrin: A lab test done in the morning prior to eating or drinking that determines the amount of gastrin in the bloodstream. Gastrin is a hormone that stimulates secretion of the glands in the main body of the stomach. It is formed at the pyloric end of the stomach when this area is stimulated by the presence of food in the stomach.

fat embolism: The presence of fat globules in the bloodstream. Usually occurs as a result of a fracture of one of the long bones of the arm or leg.

fatigue: Physical or mental weariness or tiredness that normally occurs after prolonged exertion. Fatigue out of proportion to the degree of exertion may occur as a symptom of disease.

fatty acid: A type of organic chemical, one of the constituents of triglycerides (fats). A fatty acid is composed of a chain of carbon atoms with hydrogen and some oxygen. Three fatty acid molecules combined with one glycerol molecule make up a triglyceride.

febrile: Having or characterized by fever.

fecal: Pertaining to feces.

fecal leukocytes: Leukocytes (white blood cells) in the feces.

fecal-oral transmission: Transmission of disease by oral contact with feces; this may occur, for example, when an individual who prepares food for other people does not wash hands after a bowel movement.

feces: The product of a bowel movement; stools.

Felty's syndrome: Rheumatoid arthritis with splenomegaly and leukopenia.

femoral: Pertaining to the thigh bone (femur) or the thigh.

femoral artery: The major artery of the thigh. The continuation of the external iliac artery, it extends from the groin through the front of the upper thigh. As it reaches the lower thigh, it passes behind the muscles and emerges at the back of the knee where it becomes the popliteal artery.

femoral groove: The groove on the front of the femur where the kneecap slides.

femoral head: The end of the femur that fits into the socket of the hip.

femoral nerve: A major nerve of the lower extremity; a branch of the lumbosacral plexus.

femoral vein: The major deep vein of the thigh. The continuation of the popliteal vein (at the back of the knee), it courses upward through the thigh and groin alongside the femoral artery and continues into the pelvis as the external iliac vein.

femorotibial joint: The joint between the femur and tibia; the hinge of the knee.

femur: The long bone of the thigh.

ferritin: A compound containing iron, phosphorus, and protein that is formed in the intestines. It is the form in which iron is stored in the cells of the liver, spleen, and bone marrow.

fetus: In prenatal development, the stage that begins after the eighth week and ends at birth.

fiberoptic: An optical system where flexible glass or plastic fibers are used to transmit light. The light reflects off the sides of the fibers, making it possible to transmit light around curves and corners. Fiberoptic technology is used in endoscopy. See also endoscopy.

fibrillation: Spontaneous, uncoordinated contractions of individual muscle cells (i.e., ventricular fibrillation).

fibrin: An insoluble plasma protein involved in clotting. It forms sticky strands that trap platelets and other blood cells to form a clot.

fibrinogen: A plasma protein that is the inactive form of fibrin. It is converted to fibrin by the action of an enzyme (thrombin).

fibrocartilage: A type of cartilage containing bundles of fibers.

fibroelastic: Pertaining to connective tissue that contains both elastic and nonelastic fibers.

fibroma: A connective tissue tumor that is fibrous and has an outer capsule enclosing it. Fibromas are irregular in shape, slow of growth, and usually painless. They are found in the outer layer of bones, namely the occiput, pelvis, vertebrae, ribs, long bones, and sternum.

fibromyositis: A term (literally, inflammation of fibrous tissue and muscle) used interchangeably with fibrositis.

fibrosarcoma: A cancerous tumor of the deep connective tissue.

fibrosing mediastinitis: An inflammation and fibrosing of the cavity that separates the lungs and contains the heart, large vessels, trachea, thymus, and connective tissues.

fibrosis: Abnormal formation of fibrous tissue to repair or fill in a disruption in another type of tissue; scar formation.

fibrositis: A term (literally, inflammation of fibrous tissue) used as an "umbrella" for two similar but distinct syndromes, fibromyalgia and myofascial pain syndrome. This usage is not only vague, but also inaccurate, since neither syndrome is characterized by inflammation.

fibrotic: Characterized by fibrosis.

fibrous: Containing fibers that are thread-like or film-like elements.

fibula: One of the two long bones of the lower leg. The fibula is the slender bone located on the lateral side of the leg; the tibia is thicker and located on the medial side. The fibula does not bear weight.

Fick method: A method of determining cardiac output based on theoretical principles developed by the German physician Adolf Fick. See cardiac output.

filtration: The movement of a substance across a membrane from an area of higher hydrostatic (fluid) pressure to an area of lower pressure. See also diffusion and osmosis.

fissure: A crack or slit.

fistula: An abnormal passageway or connection between two organs, or between an organ and the surface of the body.

fixation: Fastening in a fixed position; immobilization.

flaccid: Relaxed, limp, or flabby; without muscle tone.

flagellated: Having one or more flagella.

flagellum (plural, flagella): A hair-like projection on a one-celled organism. A flagellated organism is able to propel itself by rhythmic motions of the flagellum.

flank: The portion of the body on the back between the bottom rib and the top of the iliac crest of the pelvis.

flatulence: Excessive gas in the intestines.

flexion: The opposite of extension. The bending of a joint (such as the knee, elbow, or fingers), decreasing the angle between the bones of a joint. Movement of the shoulder or hip in which the arm or leg is raised in a forward direction; movement of the wrist in the direction of the palm; movement of the thumb across the palm, toward the little finger; movement of the toes in the direction of the sole of the foot; plantar flexion; forward bending of the spine (back or neck); tilting forward of the head; bending the back or neck to the side (lateral flexion).

flexion contracture: Contracture of a flexor muscle so that the joint is permanently flexed.

flexor: A muscle that flexes (bends) a joint.

flexor digitorum longus: A muscle that plantar flexes the toes. Located deep inside the calf, it has long tendons that insert on the distal phalanges of the toes (except the big toe).

flexor digitorum profundus: A flexor muscle of the fingers. Located on the palmar side of the forearm, it has long tendons that insert on the distal phalanges of each finger.

flexor digitorum superficialis: A flexor muscle of the fingers. Located on the palmar side of the forearm, it has long tendons that insert on the middle phalanges of each finger.

flexor hallucis brevis: An intrinsic muscle of the foot that plantar flexes the big toe.

flexor hallucis longus: A plantar flexor of the big toe. It is an extrinsic muscle (located in the calf) with a long tendon that inserts on the distal phalanx of the big toe.

flexor pollicis brevis: An intrinsic muscle of the hand that flexes the thumb.

flexor pollicis longus: A flexor muscle of the thumb. It is an extrinsic muscle (located in the forearm) with a long tendon that inserts on the distal phalanx of the thumb.

flexor retinaculum: A band of fibrous tissue that stretches across the palmar side of the wrist and base of the palm, forming the roof of the carpal tunnel.

flexor tendons: The tendons of the flexor muscles of the hand or foot.

fluorescein eye stain: A staining technique of the eye used to verify corneal abrasions.

flow cytometry: A laboratory method of counting blood cells.

fluctuant: Varying or unstable. For example, an abscess is felt as a fluctuant mass.

fluoroscope: A device consisting of a fluorescent screen and an x-ray tube. When an object is placed between the screen and the tube, its shadow is projected on the screen. This makes it possible to view a motion-picture ("real time") x-ray image.

fluoroscopy: Use of a fluoroscope.

FM: Fibromyalgia.

folate: The ionic form of folic acid.

folic acid: A member of the B vitamin complex found in many foods including legumes, leafy green vegetables, liver, and yeast. Like vitamin B12, folic acid is required for the synthesis of RNA, DNA, and protein; without it, cells cannot divide properly. Folic acid deficiency results in a type of anemia indistinguishable from that of vitamin B12 deficiency.

follicle: A small sac or cavity. In the ovary, a follicle is a sac where the ovum develops.

follicular: Pertaining to a follicle.

folliculitis decalvans: A pustular inflammation of the scalp hair follicles in men; often results in hair loss.

foot drop: Plantar flexion of the foot due to weakness or paralysis of the dorsiflexor muscles, usually a result of injury to the peroneal nerve.

foramen (plural, foramina): A natural opening or hole in a bone forming a passageway for nerves or blood vessels.

foraminotomy: Widening of a foramen, usually referring to a procedure for decompressing a nerve.

forceps: An instrument for grasping or holding; pincers.

forearm: The part of the arm between the elbow and the wrist.

forefoot: The part of the foot containing the metatarsal bones and phalanges; the front part of the foot.

fossa: A shallow concavity or depression.

fracture-dislocation: An injury involving both a fractured bone and a dislocated joint.

free graft: A graft of tissue that has been completely separated from its origin.

free radical: A highly reactive atom or group of atoms having at least one unpaired electron.

frenulum: A thin membrane of tissue usually referring to the membrane underneath the tongue.

frontal: Anterior, towards the front. The forehead bone.

frontal lobes: The anterior portion of the cerebral hemispheres. The frontal lobes play a major role in cognitive and motor functions.

fulminant: Occurring suddenly.

fulminating: Occurring or progressing very rapidly.

functional: A term used to describe a disorder where function is abnormal, but structure is normal. In psychiatry, the term is used synonymously with "psychogenic." In general medicine, functional disorders are not necessarily psychogenic (i.e., a functional heart murmur).

fundoplication: A surgical procedure for the treatment of gastroesophageal reflux. The lower esophageal sphincter is bolstered by wrapping the fundus (upper part of the stomach) around the lower end of the esophagus.

fundus: The portion of a hollow organ that is the largest part, its base, or the part furthest from its opening.

fundusectomy: The removal of the fundus of the stomach.

fungal culture: The growth of a fungus in culture usually for identification of the fungus.

fungus (plural, fungi): A plant or plant-like organism that has no chlorophyll and therefore requires organic matter for its subsistence. Fungi include mushrooms, molds, mildews, and yeasts. Some types of fungi are parasitic and may cause disease.

fusion: The process of uniting or the permanent fixation of a joint, either by surgery (arthrodesis) or as the result of a disease process.

GABA: Gamma aminobutyric acid.

gait analysis: An analysis of an individual's walk.

gallbladder: A sac-like organ located in the right upper abdomen, on the undersurface of the liver. The function of the gallbladder is to store bile.

gamekeeper's thumb: Dislocation or subluxation of the metacarpophalangeal joint of the thumb.

gamma aminobutyric acid (GABA): A neurotransmitter found in the central nervous system.

gamma rays: Electromagnetic radiation with energy higher than that of x-rays. See also electromagnetic radiation.

ganglion (plural, ganglia): (1) A mass of nervous tissue composed primarily of neuron cell bodies (not fibers), and located outside the brain and spinal cord (such as dorsal root ganglion or sympathetic ganglion). The term is also applied to certain masses of gray matter deep inside the brain (the basal ganglia). (2) A cyst developing on a tendon (such as in the wrist); also called a synovial cyst.

gas exchange: The exchange of oxygen and carbon dioxide that takes place in the capillaries. The two gases move in opposite directions across the thin capillary walls. In the lungs, oxygen enters the capillaries while carbon dioxide is eliminated. In all other parts of the body, the capillaries deliver oxygen to the tissues and pick up carbon dioxide. See also capillary exchange.

gastric: Pertaining to the stomach.

gastric acid: Hydrochloric acid secreted in gastric juice by the stomach glands.

gastric juice: The secretions of the glands of the stomach. Gastric juice contains hydrochloric acid, pepsin (a protein-digesting enzyme), mucus, and intrinsic factor.

gastric secretory studies: These studies determine the quality of gastric juice secretion, amount of hydrochloric acid, and the presence of blood, bile, bacteria, and fatty acids.

gastrin: A hormone that stimulates the glands in the main body of the stomach to secrete gastric juice. Gastrin is formed at the pyloric end of the stomach in response to stimulation of this area by the presence of food in the stomach.

gastrinoma: A tumor that produces gastrin.

gastrocnemius: A muscle located in the posterior calf, which plantar flexes the ankle. It joins the soleus muscle to form a common tendon, the Achilles tendon.

gastroenterologist: A physician specializing in diseases of the gastrointestinal tract.

gastroepiploic: Pertaining to the stomach and omentum (the fold of peritoneum that connects the stomach to adjacent organs).

gastroesophageal: Pertaining to the stomach and esophagus.

gastroesophageal junction: The place where the esophagus joins the stomach; the cardia.

gastroesophageal reflux: Backflow of stomach contents into the esophagus.

gastrointestinal: Pertaining to both the stomach and intestine.

gastrointestinal (GI) tract: The digestive tract including the stomach and intestines.

gastroscopy: Endoscopy of the stomach. See also endoscopy.

gelling: To become jelly-like; to congeal and become a semisolid.

gene: The basic unit of heredity. The genes are located on the chromosomes (in the nucleus of each cell) and composed of DNA.

general anesthesia: Anesthesia by which the individual is rendered unconscious.

generalized anxiety disorder: See anxiety disorders.

generalized seizure: A seizure characterized by a general onset throughout the brain.

genetic: Pertaining to the genes; hereditary.

genital: Pertaining to the sexual and reproductive organs.

Gentamicin Perfusion: A destructive treatment for Ménière's disease that involves the instilling of gentamicin into the inner ear.

genu valgum: A deformity of the leg where the lower leg bends outward from the thigh.

gestation: Pregnancy.

GGTP: Gamma glutamyl transpeptidase.

GI: Gastrointestinal.

Giardia lamblia: A flagellated protozoan; an intestinal parasite that can cause disease in humans by interfering with fat absorption in the intestine.

Gilbert's syndrome: An inherited disorder of the liver that may have jaundice as a symptom.

gingiva: The gums.

gingivoplasty: Surgery on the gums.

girdle: An encircling structure or part.

gland: An organ or group of cells that can secrete a substance used by the body.

glans penis: The end of the penis.

glenohumeral joint: The joint formed by the glenoid fossa of the scapula and the head of the humerus; the shoulder joint.

glenoid: Referring to part of the shoulder joint.

glenoid fossa: A shallow concavity in the lateral end of the scapula that receives the head of the humerus; the socket of the shoulder joint.

globulins: A class of proteins that includes immunoglobulins (proteins that act as antibodies).

globus hystericus: The sensation of having a lump in the throat that accompanies hysteria and other neuroses.

glomerulus (plural, glomeruli): A microscopic cluster of capillaries in the kidney that filters the blood.

glossitis: Inflammation of the tongue.

glucagon: A hormone secreted by the alpha cells of the islets of Langerhans in the pancreas. Glucagon counterbalances the effects of insulin by raising the blood sugar level when it begins to fall too low. See also insulin.

glucocorticoids: One of the three categories of steroid hormones secreted by the adrenal cortex. (The other two are mineralocorticoids and sex hormones.) Glucocorticoids play a role in protein, lipid, and carbohydrate metabolism and protect the body against stress. Some also have varying degrees of mineralocorticoid activity. Cortisol is the most important glucocorticoid hormone.

glucose: A simple sugar that serves as the main energy source for the body's cells. Also called dextrose.

glucose tolerance test: A test of glucose metabolism. It is performed by giving the individual a known quantity of glucose, either orally or intravenously. Blood samples are then drawn at specified times and blood glucose levels determined.

glucosuria: Glucose in the urine.

gluteal: Pertaining to the buttocks.

gluten: A protein that can be prepared from wheat, rye, oats, or barley and vegetables such as beans, cabbage, turnips, dried peas, and cucumbers.

gluteus maximus: The large muscle of the buttock.

glycerol: An organic chemical, one of the constituents of triglycerides (fats). One glycerol molecule combined with three fatty acid molecules forms a triglyceride.

glycosaminoglycans: A molecule composed of proteins and sugars; found in connective tissue.

glycosuria: Glucose in the urine. Also called glucosuria.

gonadal: Pertaining to the gonads (ovaries or testes).

gonadotropin-releasing hormone (GnRH) agonist: An agent that simulates the action of GnRH.

gonioscopy: Examination of the angle of the anterior chamber of the eye with a gonioscope.

gonorrhea: A type of sexually transmitted disease caused by the bacteria Neisseria gonorrhoeae.

gradient: A slope or grade or the rate of change of a variable.

graft: Tissue that is transplanted or implanted to repair a defect. A graft may come from a different part of the individual's body, or from a human or animal donor. The term may also be used to refer

Glossary 2343

to an artificial material used for tissue repair (such as a synthetic blood vessel graft).

graft kidney: A kidney transplanted into the individual from another individual or animal.

graft rejection: An immunologic response against grafted tissue or organs; results in death of the grafted tissue. Manifestations are hyperacute, acute, and chronic. May be prolonged or avoided with immunosuppressive medication.

graft vs. host disease: The response of the host's immune system to antigens introduced by the graft tissue. This reaction can cause graft destruction in days to months after transplantation unless immunosuppressive drugs stop the reaction and the graft heals.

gram-negative bacteria: Bacteria that do not take up Gram's stain and are counterstained red.

gram-positive bacteria: Bacteria that take up Gram's stain and are stained purple.

Gram's stain: A method of staining bacteria to make them visible under the microscope.

grand multiparity: Having given birth more than seven times.

granulation tissue: Fleshy tissue containing new capillaries that forms during healing of a gaping wound. The capillaries bring a rich blood supply to the area that later fills in with fibrous scar tissue.

granule: A small, grain-like particle.

granulocyte: A type of white blood cell with granules in its cytoplasm and a lobed nucleus. The three kinds of granulocytes are neutrophils (the most abundant), eosinophils, and basophils. See also basophil, eosinophil, and neutrophil.

granuloma: A nodular collection of white blood cells resulting from a chronic inflammatory response.

gray matter: Nervous tissue containing primarily neuron cell bodies and unmyelinated fibers, so called because of its gray appearance.

great saphenous vein: The longest vein in the body. It extends from the medial side of the foot upward to the thigh where it penetrates to join the femoral vein. Also called the long saphenous vein.

great vessels: The large blood vessels that enter and leave the heart. The great vessels include the superior vena cava and inferior vena cava, the main pulmonary artery and its two major branches (the right and left pulmonary arteries,; the pulmonary veins, and the aorta.

groin: The region between the thigh and the trunk.

guaiac test: A test that checks for the presence of occult blood in vomitus or feces.

guidewire: A long wire used to assist in positioning or moving a catheter.

gumma: A soft tumor seen in the tertiary stage of syphilis. Gummas form in the liver, brain, testes, heart, bone, and skin. They consist of a necrotic center surrounded by inflammation and fibrosis.

Guyon's canal: A compartment on the ulnar side of the wrist through which the ulnar nerve passes.

halitosis: Bad breath.

hallucination: A false perception not accounted for by any external stimulus. Hallucinations may be visual, auditory, or olfactory.

hammer toe deformity: A deformity where the metatarsophalangeal joint is dorsiflexed, while the interphalangeal joints are plantar flexed; also called claw toe.

hamstrings: A group of muscles located in the back of the thigh, which extend the hip and flex the knee.

HDL: High density lipoprotein.

head: The distal end of certain long bones (such as metacarpal and metatarsal bones; phalanges). The proximal end of some long bones (such as the femur, humerus, and radius).

heart block: A disorder where the normal conduction of electrical impulses through the heart is impeded.

heart palpitations: The physical sensation that accompanies an abnormal heart rhythm.

heart-lung machine: A device containing an oxygenator and a mechanical pump; used during cardiopulmonary bypass.

Heberden's nodes: Enlarged nodules on the end joints of the fingers found in rheumatoid arthritis.

Helicobacter pylori (H. pylori): A bacteria that causes constant inflammation of the stomach. It is associated with the majority of gastric and duodenal ulcers.

helminthic: Pertaining to parasitic worms.

hemarthrosis: Blood in a joint space.

hematemesis: Vomiting of blood.

hematocrit: The percentage of total blood volume consisting of red blood cells. To determine hematocrit, a blood sample is centrifuged, so that the red cells separate from the plasma and settle at the bottom. The volume of red cells is then divided by the total volume (red cells + plasma) and expressed as a percentage.

hematologist: A specialist in blood disorders.

hematoma: A localized mass of blood (usually clotted) in the tissues caused by a broken blood vessel.

hematuria: Blood in the urine.

hemi-: A prefix meaning half.

hemiazygous vein: A large vein that runs upward through the abdomen and chest, just in front and a little to the left of the vertebral column. The vein is usually discontinuous in the thoracic region (the lower segment is called the hemiazygous and the upper segment the accessory hemiazygous vein). These vessels collect blood from the walls of the trunk. They communicate with the azygous vein on the opposite side of the vertebral column. In the upper chest, the accessory hemiazygous empties into the left brachiocephalic vein.

hemisection: Cutting in half.

hemodialysis: A method of providing artificial kidney function. The blood is circulated through tubes made of a semipermeable membrane. The tubes are bathed in a dialysis solution that selectively removes waste products and other unwanted substances from the blood. See also dialysis.

hemodynamics: The study of the physical principles involved in the circulation of blood. Hemodynamic measurements include pressures inside the cardiac chambers and great vessels; blood flow rates, including cardiac output (volume of blood pumped by the heart per minute); and vascular resistance (the resistance to flow that arises from friction between the blood and the vessel walls).

hemoglobin: An iron-containing pigment found in red blood cells. Hemoglobin is essential for the transport of oxygen and carbon dioxide in the blood. As the blood passes through the lung capillaries, the hemoglobin molecules bind oxygen. As the blood circulates through the body, the oxygen is released to the tissues. At the same time, hemoglobin binds carbon dioxide from the tissues and releases it to the lungs.

hemoglobin electrophoresis: A test used to diagnose hemoglobinopathies; often used for sickle cell anemia.

hemoglobinopathy: Refers to a disorder affecting the hemoglobin molecule. An example is thalassemia.

hemolysis: Destruction of red blood cells that results in the release of hemoglobin.

hemolytic: Pertaining to the destruction of red blood cells.

hemolytic anemia: Anemia resulting from excessive destruction of red blood cells.

hemopericardium: Blood in the pericardial space. May result from a tumor or an injury to the heart or great vessels.

Hemophilus ducreyi: A bacteria that causes a chancroid. See also chancroid.

hemoptysis: Coughing up or spitting up blood from the respiratory tract. The blood may originate in the oropharynx, larynx, trachea, bronchi, or lungs.

hemorrhage: Abnormal internal or external bleeding. The blood may come from arteries, veins, or capillaries. Arterial blood is bright red and flows in spurts; venous blood is dark and escapes steadily.

hemorrhagic: Pertaining to or characterized by bleeding.

hemostasis: Control of bleeding or of circulation.

heparin: A substance produced by the liver that inhibits blood clotting. Heparin derived from animal tissues is used as an anticoagulant drug.

hepatic: Pertaining to the liver.

hepatic duct: The duct that transports bile from the liver; it joins the cystic duct (of the gallbladder) to form the common bile duct.

hepatic portal system: See portal system.

hepatic portal vein: A large vein that conveys blood from the stomach, small intestine, colon, spleen, pancreas, and gallbladder to the liver. See also portal system and portal vein.

hepatic veins: The veins that receive blood from the liver and empty into the inferior vena cava.

hepatobiliary: Pertaining to the liver and biliary ducts.

hepatomegaly: Enlargement of the liver.

hepatorenal syndrome: Acute renal failure in individuals with liver disease. May result from impaired renal blood flow.

herniate: To rupture through the wall of a cavity containing an organ or part.

herniated disc: A displaced disc; a protrusion of the nucleus pulposus (the soft center of an intervertebral disc) into the spinal canal.

herpes simplex: A virus that commonly causes blisters on the skin or mucous membranes. Herpes simplex type I usually involves the face; the lesions are commonly referred to as cold sores or fever blisters. Herpes simplex type II usually involves the genitals and is sexually transmitted. However, either type can occur in either location.

herpes viruses: A group of viruses that includes herpes simplex, varicella-zoster virus (the cause of chickenpox and herpes zoster), and Epstein-Barr virus (the cause of infectious mononucleosis).

heterologous: Tissue, cells, or blood from another individual or species. An organ or part made of tissues not normally present.

HHV-6: Human herpes virus type 6. See herpes viruses.

hiatus: An opening. For example, the esophageal hiatus is the opening in the diaphragm through which the esophagus passes.

HIDA scan: Hepatobiliary iminodiacetic acid scan (a type of radioisotope scan). A chemical (iminodiacetic acid) tagged with a radioactive isotope is administered intravenously. The chemical is taken up by the liver and excreted in the bile. The scan produces an image of the biliary ducts and gallbladder. See also radioisotope scan.

hidradenitis: A chronic inflammation of the sweat glands. When infected, it is called hidradenitis suppurativa; usually affects the armpits and groin.

high density lipoprotein (HDL): A type of lipoprotein (lipid/protein compound) containing cholesterol; popularly called "good cholesterol." High levels of HDL in the blood are associated with a decreased risk of cardiovascular disease. See also low density lipoprotein.

hindfoot: The rear part of the foot consisting of the calcaneus (heel bone) and talus.

histamine: A biologically active substance normally present in the body that is released from injured cells. It is involved in allergic reactions and the production of pain; it also stimulates secretion of gastric acid. Histamine produces its effects by binding to histamine receptors on the surfaces of cells.

histamine (H2) antagonist: A drug or agent that blocks the action of histamine by binding to H2 receptors. H2 antagonists are used to decrease the secretion of gastric acid. See also histamine and histamine receptor.

histamine (H2) blocker: A histamine (H2) antagonist.

histamine receptor: A molecule found on cell membranes that binds histamine. There are two types, H1 and H2. H1 receptors are found in various tissues; when histamine binds to H1 receptors, it produces a variety of effects such as constriction of smooth muscle in the bronchi and gastrointestinal tract. H2 receptors are found on acid-secreting cells of the stomach lining; when histamine binds to H2 receptors, the cells are stimulated to secrete acid. H1 receptors can be blocked by traditional antihistamines. H2 receptors cannot; however, they can be blocked by another class of drugs (H2 blockers or antagonists).

histologic: Pertaining to the microscopic structure of tissues.

HIV protease inhibitors: Agents that interrupt the replication of the virus by inhibiting the functioning of protease.

homogeneous: The same; uniformity of structure, form, and nature.

hordeolum: An infection of one of the glands of the eyelid.

hormone: A substance secreted into the blood by an endocrine gland. It is carried by the blood to other parts of the body where it regulates the function of other tissues or organs. The term is also applied to substances secreted by scattered endocrine cells (rather than distinct glands) that regulate the function of local tissues.

hormone replacement therapy (HRT): See estrogen replacement therapy.

Horner's syndrome: Constriction of the pupil, drooping of the eyelid, and loss of sweating over the affected side of the face; caused by interruption of the sympathetic nerves in the cervical (neck) region, often by a tumor.

human chorionic gonadotropin (HCG): A hormone secreted by the placenta during pregnancy. It maintains pregnancy by preventing degeneration of the corpus luteum (see also corpus luteum). A pregnancy test is a test for HCG in the blood or urine.

human lymphocyte antigen (HLA): A series of antigens used as indicators for success of a potential transplantation.

human placental lactogen: A hormone secreted by the placenta during pregnancy. During the final stage of pregnancy, it prepares the breasts for milk production.

humerus: The long bone of the upper arm.

hydatidiform: Having the appearance of being composed of vesicles.

hydrocephalus: Accumulation of excess cerebrospinal fluid inside the ventricles of the brain.

hydrochloric acid: The acidic component of gastric juice produced by the parietal cells of gastric glands. The absence of hydrochloric acid is called achlorhydria and is present in pernicious anemia.

hydrogen: A chemical element (atomic number 1), denoted by the symbol H.

hydrogen ion: The positively charged nucleus of a hydrogen atom; a proton. Hydrogen ion is denoted by the symbol H+. Acidity or alkalinity is determined by the concentration of hydrogen ions and expressed in units of pH. See also pH.

hydrops fetalis: Generalized swelling of the body present in erythroblastosis fetalis.

hydrosalpinx: A fluid-filled fallopian tube; often results from pelvic inflammatory disease.

hydroxyl ion: A negatively charged ion composed of a hydrogen and an oxygen atom. Hydroxyl ion is denoted by the symbol OH-. Hydroxyl ions combine with hydrogen ions to form water (H_2O).

hyoid bone: A U-shaped bone located in the neck between the lower jaw and the larynx. It serves as an attachment for muscles of the tongue.

hyper-: A prefix meaning excessive or greater than normal.

hyperbaric oxygen therapy: The administration of pressurized oxygen to treat gas gangrene and carbon monoxide poisoning. The oxygen is delivered at one and one half to three times normal atmospheric pressure.

hypercalcemia: Abnormally high blood calcium.

hypercoagulable: A condition in the body that favors the formation of blood clots.

hyperemesis gravidarum: Excessive vomiting during pregnancy.

hyperemia: More than the usual amount of blood in a part. Redness of the skin that disappears with pressure.

hyperesthesia: Increased sensitivity to sensory stimuli (such as pain or touch).

hyperextension: Extreme or abnormal extension (straightening) of a joint.

hyperhidrosis: Excessive sweating.

hyperlipidemia: Abnormally high blood lipids (fats).

hypernephroma: A kidney adenocarcinoma.

hyperopia: Farsightedness due to the focusing of light rays behind the retina.

hyperpathia: Hypersensitivity to sensory stimuli.

hyperplasia: Increase in size of an organ due to an increase in the number of cells. (In contrast, see hypertrophy.)

hypersensitivity: Abnormal sensitivity to any kind of stimulus; an allergy.

hypertensive encephalopathy: Abnormal brain functioning (encephalopathy) due to hypertension.

hypertrophic cardiomyopathy: Cardiac dysfunction as a result of hypertrophied heart muscle.

hypertrophy: Increase in size of an organ due to an increase in the size of its cells. (In contrast, see hyperplasia.)

hyperventilation: Increased rate and/or depth of breathing, resulting in excessive removal of carbon dioxide from the blood. Symptoms include lightheadedness and paresthesia.

hypervigilance: A state of abnormal alertness.

hyphema: Blood in the anterior chamber of the eye (in front of the iris).

hypnosis: An induced state of altered consciousness in which the individual is highly responsive to suggestion.

hypnotic: Pertaining to sleep or hypnosis; a sedative or anxiolytic drug.

hypo-: A prefix meaning deficient or less than normal.

hypoalbuminemia: Abnormally low blood albumin.

hypocalcemia: Abnormally low blood calcium.

hypocarbia: An abnormally low concentration of carbon dioxide in the blood. See also hyperventilation.

hypogastric: Below the stomach; pertaining to the hypogastrium (the lower middle abdomen, the area above the pubic bone).

hypogastric artery: The internal iliac artery.

hypoglycemia: Abnormally low blood glucose; low blood sugar.

hypogonadism: Abnormally low functioning of the gonads; results in lowered sex hormone concentration with concomitant underdevelopment of secondary sex characteristics.

hypokalemia: Abnormally low blood potassium.

hypomagnesemia: Abnormally low blood magnesium.

hypomania: An alteration of mood similar to mania, but less intense; a mild form of mania. See mania.

hyponatremia: Abnormally low blood sodium.

hypophosphatemia: Abnormally low blood phosphate.

hypoplasia: Underdevelopment of a tissue or organ.

hypoplastic: A structure that underdevelops during embryo formation and is smaller, abnormally shaped, or has impaired function.

hypopyon: The presence of white blood cells in the anterior chamber of the eye.

hyporeflexia: Decreased reflexes.

hypothalamus: A part of the brain located just above the brainstem with multiple functions in regulating the body's internal environment. It secretes a number of hormones (also called releasing and inhibiting factors) that regulate the activity of the pituitary gland, a small endocrine gland attached to the hypothalamus by a stalk. Two other hypothalamic hormones, antidiuretic hormone (ADH) and oxytocin, regulate water balance and stimulate uterine contraction, respectively. The hypothalamus also regulates the autonomic nervous system, as well as appetite, thirst, body temperature, and the sleep/wake cycle. See also pituitary gland, antidiuretic hormone, oxytocin, and autonomic nervous system.

hypothermia: Abnormally low body temperature.

hypotonia: A reduced amount of tone in muscles, arteries, and intraocular pressure.

hypovolemia: Abnormally low blood volume. Hypovolemia may result from hemorrhage or dehydration.

hypovolemic shock: Shock (circulatory insufficiency) caused by loss of circulating blood volume such as due to hemorrhage or dehydration. See also shock.

hypoxemia: Abnormally low concentration of oxygen in the blood.

hypoxia: Abnormally low concentration of oxygen in the tissues.

IABP: Intra-aortic balloon pump.

iatrogenic: Caused by the physician or the treatment (such as iatrogenic disease).

ICU: Intensive care unit.

idiopathic: Of unknown cause.

IFA: Immunofluorescent antiperoxidase antibody stain.

IgE: Immunoglobulin gamma E

ileum: The last segment of the small intestine after the jejunum. The terminal ileum is connected to the cecum (the first part of the colon).

ileus: Intestinal obstruction. Ileus may result from either mechanical blockage (mechanical ileus), intestinal spasm (spastic ileus), or intestinal paralysis (paralytic or adynamic ileus).

iliac arteries: The large arteries of the lower abdomen arising from the division of the abdominal aorta.

iliac crest: The upper margin of the ilium; the highest bony point of the pelvis.

iliac veins: The large veins of the lower abdomen that run parallel to the iliac arteries. The internal and external iliac veins join to form the common iliac vein. The right and left common iliac veins merge to form the inferior vena cava.

ilium (plural, ilia): The wide upper part of the bony pelvis; the hip bone.

IM: Intramuscular.

imaginal exposure: A behavior modification technique where an individual is exposed to a feared stimulus through imagination.

immune complex: A molecule formed by the binding of an antibody to an antigen; also called an antigen-antibody complex.

immune system: The organs, tissues, and cells of the body involved in immunity. These include the lymph nodes and other lymphatic tissues (such as tonsils and adenoids), lymphatic ducts and vessels, spleen, thymus, bone marrow, and white blood cells.

immunity: State of being protected from a disease, especially an infectious disease. Immunity is induced by exposure to a specific antigen (foreign substance or microorganism). This primes the immune system to recognize that antigen, so subsequent exposure results in an immune response.

immunocompetence: The capacity to mount an immune response to an antigen.

immunocompromised: An individual with an immune system that is stressed or inadequate (such as those with AIDS and chronic illnesses, transplant recipients, and the very young and elderly).

immunoglobulin: Any of several structurally related classes of proteins that function as antibodies.

immunological: Pertaining to the immune system or immune response.

immunomodulatory: Having the property of modulating (adjusting) the function of the immune system.

immunosuppressive: Acting to suppress or inhibit the body's immune response. A drug or agent that suppresses or inhibits the body's immune response.

immunotherapy: Treatment that involves modulating or suppressing the immune response.

impaction: Condition of being tightly wedged or driven together.

implantation: Grafting of tissue or an organ into a new location in the body; artificial placement of a device or material into the body.

in vitro fertilization: The fertilization of an egg with sperm done in a laboratory dish. The embryo is later transferred to a uterus.

incarcerated hernia: A hernia that cannot be reduced. An incarcerated hernia may or may not be strangulated (constricted so as to cut off blood supply to the incarcerated tissue).

incarceration: Entrapment (such as a hernia).

incision: An intentional cut made with a knife (e.g., for surgical purposes).

incontinence: Inability to retain urine or feces. This may result from loss of sphincter control or from a nervous system lesion.

incubation period: The time interval between exposure to a disease and the appearance of the first signs or symptoms.

incus: One of the three ossicles (small bones) of the middle ear that helps conduct sound to the inner ear. Also called the "anvil."

indication: A sign or a circumstance that points to the proper treatment of a disease. For example, pain may be an indication for analgesics.

indolent: Inactive; sluggish. For example, an indolent infection is one that neither heals nor progresses.

induced: Made to occur by some influence, drug, or action.

induced hyperthermia: Hyperthermia (fever) caused by external means.

induration: A hardened area, usually slightly raised.

industrial hygiene: The branch of preventive medicine concerned with the health of industrial workers.

infarct: A localized area of tissue death resulting from loss of blood supply.

infarct-avid imaging: A type of radioisotope scan used to detect a recent myocardial infarction.

infarction: Tissue death resulting from loss of blood supply.

infection: Invasion and multiplication of microorganisms in body tissues; disease caused by microorganisms.

infectious: Capable of spreading microorganisms or disease.

infectious mononucleosis: An infection caused by the Epstein-Barr virus; characterized by fever, sore throat, and occasionally splenomegaly.

inferior: Beneath; below; lower in location (such as the inferior surface of a structure is its undersurface). The opposite of superior.

infestation: Condition of being a host to parasites; disease caused by parasites.

infiltration: The process of passing into and being deposited in an organ or tissue such as infiltration of white blood cells into the tissues to fight infection; or infiltration (invasion) of cancer cells.

inflammation: The body's response to tissue injury. Inflammation is a protective response that helps destroy, dilute, or wall off the injurious agent. However, in some cases it may produce more damage than the injury that induces it. Signs and symptoms of inflammation include pain, heat, redness, swelling, and loss of function.

inflammatory bowel disease: Refers to one of the diseases that causes inflammation of the intestines. Crohn's disease and ulcerative colitis are included in this category.

inflammatory mediators: Substances (such as histamine) that are released from cells in response to tissue injury. By their actions on blood vessels, smooth muscle, and other tissues, they produce the signs and symptoms of the inflammatory response.

infraspinatus: A muscle located on the posterior surface of the scapula, below the scapular spine.

Part of the rotator cuff, it rotates and helps stabilize the shoulder joint.

infusion (herbal): A concoction produced by steeping herbs in hot water.

inguinal: Pertaining to the groin.

innervation: The nerve supply of a part of the body.

inpatient: An individual who is hospitalized.

insertion: The distal attachment of a muscle; the attachment of a muscle to a part that moves when the muscle contracts. See also origin.

insertional activity: In electromyography, the short burst of electrical activity that occurs in a muscle when a needle electrode is inserted.

insidious: A term used to describe a disease that comes on in such a way (without symptoms) that the individual is unaware of its onset.

insufficiency: Incompetence or inadequate function.

insufflation: The introduction of vapors or powders into a cavity by blowing them in. Typically refers to the inflation of the abdominal cavity for laparoscopy.

insulin: A hormone secreted by the beta cells of the islets of Langerhans in the pancreas. Insulin promotes the uptake of glucose from the blood into tissues, thus lowering the blood sugar level. Deficiency of insulin results in diabetes mellitus.

insulinoma: An insulin-secreting tumor.

intensive care unit (ICU): A hospital area specially equipped for the continuous monitoring and intensive care of individuals in critical condition. See also coronary care unit (CCU).

intention tremors: Tremors that occur during purposeful activity.

inter-: A prefix meaning between.

interatrial: Located between the atria (i.e., of the heart).

interatrial septum: The wall between the right and left atria of the heart.

intercarpal joints: The joints between carpal bones.

intercarpal ligaments: The ligaments that connect the carpal bones with each other.

intercostal: Between the ribs.

intercuneiform joints: The joints between the cuneiform bones of the foot.

interictal: The period of time between seizures.

intermittent claudication: Severe pain in the calves of the legs while walking; the pain is absent when at rest. It is caused by a temporary interruption in blood flow to the legs such as an arterial spasm.

internal carotid artery: A branch of the common carotid artery. The internal carotid supplies the eyeball and anterior parts of the brain.

internal fixation: Fixation of a fracture or dislocation by means of devices placed into or through the bone (such as pins, rods, or screws).

internal iliac artery: A branch of the common iliac artery; also called the hypogastric artery. The internal iliac arteries supply the anterior abdominal wall, buttocks, genitals, and pelvic organs.

internal jugular vein: A deep vein that receives blood from the brain and eyeball. It descends through the neck alongside the common carotid artery, and merges with the subclavian vein to form the brachiocephalic vein.

internal mammary artery: A branch of the subclavian artery, supplying structures of the chest and anterior chest wall; also called the internal thoracic artery. The internal mammary artery is commonly used as a coronary bypass graft.

interosseous: Situated between bones.

interosseous membrane: A membrane that connects the shafts of two long bones (such as the radius and ulna; the tibia and fibula).

interosseous muscles: A group of intrinsic muscles of the hand or foot that abduct and adduct the fingers or toes.

interpersonal therapy: Therapy centered on relationships between people and social situations.

interphalangeal (IP) joints: The joints between the phalanges of the hand or foot.

intersex: An individual with both male and female characteristics. Discovery of the proper sex requires chromosome analysis and close examination of the anatomy. Also called hermaphrodite.

interstitial: Pertaining to the interstices (spaces) between the cells of an organ or tissue; intercellular. For example, interstitial nephritis is an inflammation of the intercellular connective tissue of the kidney.

interstitial pneumonia: Pneumonia affecting the interstitial tissue of the lungs (the alveolar walls).

intertrigo: Dermatitis in the skin folds.

interventricular: Located between the ventricles (such as of the heart).

interventricular septum: The wall between the right and left ventricles of the heart.

intervertebral: Situated between two adjacent vertebrae.

intervertebral discs: Discs of fibrocartilage between adjacent vertebral bodies.

intervertebral foramina: The openings between adjacent vertebrae through which the spinal nerves emerge.

intestinal polyp: An overgrowth of tissue on the inside of the intestine. May be a precursor to colon cancer.

intestine: The part of the digestive tract extending from the stomach to the anus. It is divided into the small intestine (duodenum, jejunum, and ileum) and the large intestine (colon).

intra-: Prefix meaning within.

intra-aortic balloon counterpulsation: A procedure for supporting circulation in individuals with cardiogenic shock. A balloon-tipped catheter is placed in the aorta. The balloon is connected to a pump synchronized with the ECG. With each heartbeat, the balloon inflates during diastole and deflates during systole. Inflation of the balloon increases the diastolic blood pressure, and helps move blood from the aorta into the coronary, cerebral, and peripheral arteries. This decreases the heart's work load at the same time that it increases blood flow.

intra-aortic balloon pump (IABP): See intra-aortic balloon counterpulsation.

intra-articular: Within a joint (e.g., an intra-articular fracture is one that involves the articular surface of a bone).

intracardiac: Within the heart.

intracerebral hemorrhage: Bleeding that occurs in the cerebral hemispheres of the brain.

intracorneal ring segments (INTACS): Plastic inserts placed in the cornea to correct low levels of nearsightedness.

intracoronary: Within a coronary artery (such as an intracoronary injection).

intracranial: Within the cranium.

intradermal: Within the skin (such as an intradermal injection).

intramural: Within the wall of an organ or vessel.

intramuscular (IM): Within a muscle (such as an intramuscular injection).

intraocular: Within the eye.

intraocular lens: An artificial lens placed inside the eye to correct vision.

intraocular pressure: The pressure within the eye.

intraperitoneal: Within the abdominal cavity.

intrathecal: Within the meninges (the membranous sheath that covers the spinal cord and brain).

intravascular: Within a blood vessel.

intravenous (IV): Within a vein.

intravenous (IV) cholecystogram: A contrast x-ray of the gallbladder obtained after intravenous administration of a dye excreted in the bile.

intravenous immune globulin (IVIG) therapy: Administration of immune globulin to counteract toxins or antigens in the blood.

intrinsic factor: A substance normally present in gastric juice that makes the absorption of vitamin B12 possible. Absence of intrinsic factor results in vitamin B12 deficiency and pernicious anemia.

intrinsic ligaments: Ligaments located within a joint cavity. See also extrinsic ligaments.

intrinsic muscles: Muscles located within the part of the body that they control. For example, the intrinsic muscles of the foot are located in the foot. See also extrinsic muscles.

intubation: Insertion of a tube through the mouth or nose and into the trachea for passage of air.

intussusception: Telescoping of a segment of small intestine within itself; usually occurs at the ileocecal junction.

invasive: (1) A term used to describe a procedure where the body is entered (such as by surgery or by the introduction of needles, tubes, or other devices). (2) Tending to spread (such as an invasive infection or cancer).

inversion: Turning the sole of the foot so that it faces inward (medially). The opposite of eversion.

ion: An electrically charged particle. A negatively charged ion is called an anion; a positively charged particle is a cation.

ionization: The dissociation of chemical compounds (such as salts) into their constituent ions (electrically charged particles).

iontophoresis: The process of transferring ions across a membrane by means of an electrical current; used as a method of delivering medications through skin or mucous membrane to the underlying tissues.

IP joints: Interphalangeal joints.

iridocyclitis: Inflammation of the iris and ciliary body.

iridotomy: Incision of the iris.

iris: The colored membrane of the eye. The iris has an opening in the center (the pupil) through which light passes. By constricting and dilating the pupil, the iris regulates the amount of light that reaches the retina.

iron: A metallic chemical element (atomic number 26) denoted by the symbol Fe (from Latin, ferrum). Iron is an essential component of hemoglobin.

irreducible: Incapable of being reduced or put back into normal position (such as an irreducible fracture or irreducible hernia).

irregular astigmatism: An astigmatism where different parts of the same meridian have different curvatures.

ischemia: Localized deficiency of blood flow due to obstruction of circulation.

islet cells: See islets of Langerhans.

islets of Langerhans: Clusters of endocrine cells, scattered like islands throughout the pancreas. The islets of Langerhans secrete several hormones, all of which are concerned with the regulation of sugar metabolism. The two principle hormones are glucagon (secreted by alpha cells) and insulin (secreted by beta cells). Currently called pancreatic islets.

isoenzyme: One of several forms of an enzyme. For example, the muscle enzyme creatine kinase (CK) is found in slightly different forms in cardiac and skeletal muscle. Although chemically similar, the two forms of CK can be distinguished from each other by isoenzyme tests.

isokinetic: Having the same force. An isokinetic muscle contraction is one where the muscle shortens to produce movement, applying the same force throughout the movement.

isometric: Having the same length. An isometric muscle contraction is one where the muscle is prevented from shortening or lengthening, so that no movement occurs. Pushing against a wall is an example of isometric exercise. See also the opposite isotonic.

isotonic: Having the same tension or tone. An isotonic muscle contraction is one where the same degree of tension is maintained while the muscle shortens to produce movement. See also the opposite isometric.

isotope: Any of several forms of a chemical element that share the same chemical properties, but differ in atomic weight. Some isotopes are radioactive.

isotope scan: See radioisotope scan.

-itis: A suffix denoting inflammation.

IUD: Intrauterine device. A device placed into the uterus to provide contraception.

IV: Intravenous.

IVP: Intravenous pyelogram.

jaundice: Yellow discoloration of the skin, mucous membranes, and sclerae (whites of the eyes) due to excess bilirubin (bile pigment) in the blood. Jaundice may be caused by liver disease, biliary obstruction, or hemolysis (excessive destruction of red blood cells). See also bilirubin.

jejunostomy: A surgically created opening into the jejunum.

jejunum: The middle part of the small intestine between the duodenum and ileum.

Joaquin Valley Fever: A disease caused by breathing in a fungus (Coccidioides immitus) found in the soil in certain parts of the southwestern US, Mexico, and Central and South America.

jock itch: A fungal infection of the groin and perineal area; also called tinea cruris.

joint: The junction between two bones.

joint capsule: A sac or sleeve of fibrous tissue that encloses the ends of bones in a synovial joint. The outer surface of a joint capsule is fibrous and may be blended with ligaments. The inner surface is lined with synovium (synovial membrane).

joint cavity: The space within a joint capsule; it contains synovial fluid.

joint mice: Loose bodies or cartilage in a joint.

joint space: The space between the bones of a joint.

Jones fracture: A diaphyseal fracture of the base of the fifth metatarsal.

jugular veins: The large veins of the neck including the internal jugular, anterior jugular, and external jugular.

Kallman's syndrome: A syndrome of hypogonadism with anosmia (loss of sense of smell). See also hypogonadism.

Kartagener's syndrome: Complete situs inversus (reversal of the location of the body organs). Accompanied by chronic bronchiectasis and sinusitis. It is an autosomal recessive hereditary disorder.

Kawasaki disease: Also known as mucocutaneous lymph node syndrome. Kawasaki disease is characterized by high spiking fevers, conjunctivitis, pharyngitis, strawberry tongue, lymphadenopathy, desquamation of the hands and feet, and the potential complication of coronary artery aneurysms.

keratitis sicca: See keratoconjunctivitis sicca

keratoconjunctivitis sicca: Conjunctivitis and inflammation of the cornea associated with decreased tears.

keratolytic plaster: A substance that causes loosening and shedding of hard or horny growths such as warts.

keratosis pilaris: Lesions of the eyebrows associated with horny overgrowth of epidermis.

ketone: A chemical produced in the body during metabolism of fatty acids.

kidney tubules: Microscopic tubular structures in the kidney through which fluid (filtered from the blood by the glomeruli) is conveyed. As the fluid moves through the tubules, water and other substances pass in or out through the tubule walls. In this way, the composition of the tubular fluid gradually changes until it becomes urine.

kidneys: A pair of organs located in the back of the abdominal cavity that produce urine. The kidneys contain microscopic structures called glomeruli that filter the blood. The filtered fluid then passes into the kidney tubules where it is changed into urine. See also glomeruli and kidney tubules.

kilogram: A metric system unit of mass or weight. A kilogram equals approximately 2.2 pounds.

kindling: A type of time-dependent sensitization involving seizure activity in the central nervous system. Kindling may occur after a single strong stimulus, or after repeated subthreshold stimuli (stimuli below the level normally required to produce a response). Further subthreshold stimuli then result in either convulsions or chronic behavioral changes. See also sensitization.

kinins: A group of protein-like substances found in the body that have a number of biological actions. For example, they dilate small blood vessels, resulting in a local increase in blood flow; they are also involved in the production of pain.

Klippel-Feil syndrome: A congenital abnormality of the spine characterized by a reduction in the number of cervical vertebrae and fusion of cervical vertebrae.

knee arthroplasty: Surgical creation of an artificial knee joint.

KOH: Potassium hydroxide; a strong base.

koilonychia: Deformity of the nails where the surface is concave; associated with iron deficiency.

Koplik's spots: Small reddish areas containing a bluish-white center seen most often near the molars; an early sign of measles.

Kupffer's cells: A cell found in the minute blood vessels of the liver that ingests and digests particles and bacteria. Currently called stellate reticuloendothelial cells.

kyphoscoliosis: An abnormal curvature of the spine characterized by both kyphosis and scoliosis.

kyphosis: Exaggeration of the normal posterior curvature of the thoracic spine, resulting in a hump.

L5-S1 level: Refers to the level of the spine between the sacrum (tailbone) and the lower portion of the lumbar spine.

labia: Literally lips; usually refers to the vagina.

labile: Unstable; changeable (such as labile hypertension or labile mood).

lability: Condition of being labile.

labrum: A lip or lip-like structure.

labyrinth: The inner ear including the vestibule, semicircular canals, and cochlea.

labyrinthectomy: Surgical removal of the labyrinth of the inner ear.

laceration: A nonsurgical wound or cut.

lacinate: A ligament of the foot.

lactase deficiency: A lack of lactase in the intestinal juice. Lactase is an enzyme that splits sugars; it splits lactose into dextrose and galactose. Also called lactose intolerance.

lactic acid: An organic acid involved in many biochemical processes. In aerobic metabolism, it is oxidized to provide energy; however, in anaerobic metabolism, it accumulates as an end product (such as in muscle during heavy exercise).

Lactobacillus acidophilus: A microorganism that is part of the normal flora of the intestinal tract.

Lactobacillus casei: A species of Lactobacillus found in milk and cheese.

LAD: Left anterior descending (branch of the left main coronary artery).

lagophthalmos: A condition where the eyelids cannot completely close over the eye.

lamellar keratoplasty: A technique to change the shape of the cornea. The top curve of the cornea is cut, making a flap. Corneal tissue may be removed, allowing the corneal flap to settle flatter than before (correcting myopia); or the flap may be allowed to bulge, making the corneal surface more rounded (correcting hyperopia).

lamina (plural, laminae): The part of the vertebral arch that projects backward from the pedicle on either side. The two laminae meet in the midline, closing the arch.

lancinating: Sharp or cutting (such as lancinating pain).

laparoscope: An endoscope designed for examination of the abdominal cavity. The laparoscope is inserted into the abdominal cavity through a small incision.

laparoscopic surgery: Surgery performed through a laparoscope. A wide variety of procedures are performed in this manner, including gynecologic procedures and gastrointestinal procedures.

large intestine: The part of the intestine extending from the end of the ileum to the rectum; the colon.

larva: An immature form of an organism (e.g., of an insect or roundworm).

laryngeal: Pertaining to the larynx.

laryngeal spasm: A spasm of the larynx causing severe respiratory distress. The spasm passes in a few seconds. Also called laryngismus.

larynx: The "voice box" located at the upper end of the trachea. Its walls are composed of muscle and cartilage, lined with mucous membrane.

laser: A device that emits focused beams of electromagnetic radiation; used widely for surgery, cauterization, and diagnosis.

Laser interferometer: A device that uses a laser to provide measurements.

LASIK (Laser In Situ Keratomileusis): LASIK is a surgical procedure capable of correcting a wide range of nearsightedness (myopia), farsightedness (hyperopia), and astigmatism.

lassitude: Fatigue; tiredness.

latency: The time between a stimulus and the response. The time between exposure to a disease and the onset of illness.

lateral: Pertaining to the side; away from the midline. In the hand, wrist, and forearm, lateral refers to the radial or thumb side. The opposite of medial.

lateral epicondyle: Refers to a projection on a long bone on the lateral side. May refer to the humerus or the femur.

lateral recti: One of the small muscles that controls movement of the eye.

lateral rotation: Rotation in an outward direction; external rotation.

laterocollis: Tilting of the head to the side caused by spasm of the neck muscles.

lavage: Washing out of a cavity; irrigation.

LBBB: Left bundle branch block.

LDL: Low density lipoprotein.

lead: In electrocardiography, a pair of electrodes (one positive and one negative) for recording electrical activity.

leaflet: A small leaf-like structure (such as the cusp of a heart valve).

Leber's Hereditary Optic Neuropathy (LHON): Hereditary degeneration of the optic nerve with vision loss.

lecithin: A type of phospholipid found in animal tissue.

LEEP: Loop electrosurgical excisional procedure.

left anterior descending artery (LAD): One of the two major branches of the left main coronary artery. The LAD descends along the front of the heart in the groove between the right and left ventricles. It supplies the anterolateral wall of the left ventricle and the interventricular septum. See also left circumflex artery and left main coronary artery.

left circumflex artery: One of the two major branches of the left main coronary artery. The left circumflex artery winds around the left side of the heart to the posterior surface. It supplies the left atrium and the lateral wall of the left ventricle. See also left anterior descending artery and left main coronary artery.

left main coronary artery: One of the two main arteries that supply the myocardium (heart muscle). The left main coronary artery arises from the aorta, just above the aortic valve. It runs for a short distance before dividing into its two major branches, the left anterior descending and left circumflex arteries. See also right coronary artery.

left shift: An elevated percentage of band forms on a differential white blood cell count. See also band and complete blood count.

leiomyofibroma: A leiomyoma that contains hard connective tissue as one of the components. Also known as a fibroid. See also leiomyoma.

leiomyoma: A benign tumor derived from smooth muscle cells.

lens: A transparent body located just behind the iris. The lens focuses light rays on the retina.

lenticular refractive surgery: A type of eye surgery used to improve vision.

leptospirosis: Infection with the Leptospira bacteria; usually characterized by liver and kidney damage.

LES: Lower esophageal sphincter.

lesion: A localized area of diseased or injured tissue.

lethargy: A feeling of general sluggishness, sleepiness, stupor.

leukocyte: A white blood cell.

leukocytopenia: An abnormal decrease in the number of white blood cells.

leukocytosis: An increase in the number of white blood cells.

leukopenia: A decrease of white blood cells, usually below 5,000 per cubic millimeter.

Lhermitte's phenomenon: Electric shock-like pain produced by flexing the neck. Lhermitte's phenomenon is a symptom of a spinal cord lesion.

lichen planopilaris: Hyperkeratosis (horny overgrowth of epithelium) of the scalp associated with lichen planus elsewhere. See lichen planus.

lichen planus: The appearance of shiny flat-topped lesions on the flexor surfaces of the joints, on the male genitalia, and the inside of the cheeks.

lichenification: When skin changes, becoming thick and hard.

ligament: A band or sheet of fibrous connective tissue that binds bones together at a joint. A thickened fold of peritoneum that supports an organ (such as the broad ligaments of the uterus).

ligation: Binding or tying (such as with thread, wire, or suture material). For example, bleeding may be stopped by ligation of a broken blood vessel.

light microscope: A microscope that uses available light and magnifies an image 5 to 1,500 times.

limbic system: A group of deep brain structures involved in emotional responses.

limbus: The edge or border of a part.

linitis plastica: Inflammation and thickening of the stomach lining, usually as a result of cancer.

lipase: An enzyme that catalyzes the breakdown or digestion of lipids (especially triglycerides).

lipid: Any fat or fat-like substance. Lipids include triglycerides (fats), cholesterol, phospholipids, prostaglandins, and waxes.

lipoma: A tumor composed of fat cells.

lipoprotein: A compound molecule consisting of a lipid combined with a protein.

liposuction: A cosmetic procedure that uses a cannula to remove fat cells by suction.

Lisfranc's fracture: Dorsal fracture dislocation of the metatarsal bases of the feet.

lithium carbonate: A salt of the chemical element lithium; used in the treatment of bipolar affective disorder (manic-depressive illness).

livedo reticularis: Blue mottling of the skin of the hands and legs that worsens in the cold and is semipermanent.

liver: The largest organ in the body located in the right upper abdomen. The liver has numerous functions. It plays an important role in carbohydrate, protein, and lipid metabolism. It also secretes bile, manufactures a wide variety of substances necessary for normal body function (including heparin, fibrinogen, plasma proteins, cholesterol, and bile salts), stores certain vitamins, detoxifies drugs, and filters bacteria from the bloodstream.

liver enzymes: Enzymes made by the liver including aspartate transaminase (AST), alanine transaminase (ALT), alkaline phosphatases (ALP), glutamyl transpeptidase (GGT), and lactic dehydrogenase (LDH).

liver function tests: Tests that reveal how well the liver is functioning including a serum bilirubin, alkaline phosphatase, aspartate transaminase (AST), alanine transaminase (ALT), albumin, and globulin.

liver profile: Tests done to screen for liver problems that may include aspartate transaminase (AST), alanine transaminase

(ALT), alkaline phosphatases (ALP), albumin, and total and direct bilirubin.

LLQ: Left lower quadrant.

LMN: Lower motor neuron.

lobar pneumonia: Pneumonia affecting an entire lobe of the lung.

lobe: A part of an organ (such as brain, lung, or liver) or other structure (such as a cell nucleus), demarcated by fairly well-defined boundaries.

lobular cancer: Cancer within a lobe (e.g., of the lung).

lobule: A small lobe or a subdivision of a lobe.

local: Pertaining to or restricted to a limited region (such as local anesthesia); not general.

local anesthesia: Anesthesia limited to a localized area.

local anesthetic: A drug that produces local anesthesia by blocking nerve transmission. It is administered by an injection in the vicinity of the nerve that is to be blocked.

localized: Restricted to a limited region; not generalized.

lockjaw: Tetanus, which causes spasms of the jaw muscles.

loculated: Divided into or containing small spaces or cavities (such as a loculated empyema).

long bone: A bone that is roughly rod-shaped, consisting of a shaft with slightly flaring ends. The humerus, radius, ulna, metacarpals, and phalanges are long bones of the arm and hand.

long thoracic nerve: A branch of the brachial plexus; it supplies the serratus anterior muscle. Injury to this nerve results in "winging" of the scapula.

longitudinal: Lengthwise. The opposite of transverse.

loose bodies: Fragments of cartilage or bone within a joint cavity. They are usually the result of previous trauma and may or may not cause symptoms. Also called joint mice.

lordosis: Exaggeration of the normal anterior curvature (concavity) of the cervical or lumbar spine; swayback.

low density lipoprotein (LDL): A type of lipoprotein (lipid/protein compound) that contains cholesterol; popularly called "bad cholesterol." High levels of LDL in the blood are associated with an increased risk of cardiovascular disease. See also high density lipoprotein.

lower esophageal sphincter: The sphincter at the lower end of the esophagus where the esophagus joins the stomach. It prevents reflux of stomach contents into the esophagus

LP: Lumbar puncture.

L-tryptophan: One of the essential amino acids used in the production of protein in the human body.

lumbago: Dull, aching pain in the lumbar region of the back.

lumbar: Pertaining to the low back (the region of the spine between the thorax and the sacrum).

lumbar discectomy: Surgical removal of the intervertebral disk between two of the lumbar vertebrae. Performed to alleviate problems from a herniated disk.

lumbar nerves: Five pairs of spinal nerves (L1-L5) that exit from the lumbar region of the vertebral column.

lumbosacral: Pertaining to both the lumbar and sacral regions (e.g., of the spine).

lumbosacral disc: The intervertebral disc between the fifth lumbar vertebra (L5) and the sacrum.

lumbosacral plexus: A network of nerves formed by the lumbar and sacral spinal nerves that gives rise to the major nerves of the lower extremity.

lumbricals: A group of intrinsic hand muscles whose function is to make fine adjustments in the position of the fingers.

lumen: The space or passageway within a hollow tube or tube-like structure.

LUQ: Left upper quadrant.

lymph: A clear, often yellowish fluid derived from tissue fluid. The lymph is gathered and transported by lymphatic vessels, filtered through the lymph nodes, and returned via the lymphatic ducts to the bloodstream. See also lymph node, lymphatic duct, and lymphatic vessel.

lymph node: Any of numerous rounded structures composed largely of lymphocytes and located along the course of lymphatic vessels. The lymph nodes filter bacteria and other foreign particles out of the lymph before it reaches the bloodstream. See also lymph and lymphocyte.

lymphadenectomy: Surgical removal of a lymph node.

lymphadenopathy: Inflammation and/or swelling of a lymph node.

lymphangiography: A radiologic technique to determine the flow of lymph through the lymph vessels.

lymphatic: Pertaining to lymph.

lymphatic duct: Either of the two large lymphatic vessels that empty lymph into the bloodstream. The thoracic duct is the larger and longer of the two, coursing upward through the abdomen and chest in front of the spinal column. It receives lymph from all parts of the body except the right half of the upper body; it empties into the junction of the left subclavian and internal jugular veins. The right lymphatic duct is short and located in the right upper chest at the base of the neck. It receives lymph from the right half of the upper body and empties into the junction of the right subclavian and internal jugular veins.

lymphatic system: The organ system concerned with the recycling of lymph and the production of lymphocytes. It consists of the lymphatic vessels and ducts and the lymphoid tissues (including the lymph nodes, tonsils, spleen, thymus, and bone marrow). The lymphatic system is considered part of both the circulatory and immune systems. See also lymph, lymph node, lymphatic duct, lymphatic vessel, lymphocyte, spleen, thymus, tonsil, and bone marrow.

lymphatic vessel: Any of the small or large vessels (ranging from microscopic lymphatic capillaries to the large lymphatic ducts) that collect lymph from the tissues and transport it to the bloodstream. See also lymph and lymphatic duct.

lymphedema: Edema (swelling) resulting from obstruction of lymphatic vessels.

lymphocyte: A type of white blood cell. Some lymphocytes circulate in the blood, while others form the structure of lymphoid organs and tissues such as the spleen and lymph nodes. Different types of lymphocytes play different roles in immunity. B-lymphocytes transform into plasma cells, which produce antibodies; cytotoxic T-lymphocytes attack and kill foreign cells; helper and suppressor T-lymphocytes produce substances that modulate the activities of other immune cells. See also lymphatic system and lymph node.

lymphogranuloma venereum: A sexually transmitted disease caused by Chlamydia trachomatis. Characterized by lymphadenopathy and genital ulcers.

lymphoid: Pertaining to or resembling lymph or the lymphoid tissues. See lymphatic system.

lymphoma: A tumor of lymphatic tissue.

lysis: Destruction, breaking up, or dissolution.

lytic: Relating to a substance that breaks down, dissolves, or decomposes another substance. A substance that relieves or reduces a medical condition.

macrophage: A type of cell found in loose connective tissue and in various organs that assists immunity by ingesting foreign particles and microorganisms.

macula: The portion of the retina that corresponds to the area of sharpest vision.

macular degeneration: Degeneration of the macular area of the retina of the eye; the most common cause of visual impairment in those over age 50; can lead to loss of central vision.

magnesium: A metallic chemical element (atomic number 12) denoted by the symbol Mg. Magnesium is found in body fluids and tissues (including bone, muscle, nervous tissue, and blood), and is essential for the activity of many enzymes.

magnetic resonance imaging (MRI): Technique that uses certain atomic nuclei with odd numbers of protons or neutrons, or both, and subjects them to a strong magnetic field. The nuclei absorb and re-emit electromagnetic energy, which is analyzed and provides image information. This technique is valuable in providing images of the heart, large blood vessels, brain, and soft tissues.

major depression: A mental disease characterized by depressed or irritable mood, pervasive loss of interest in usually pleasurable activities, sleep and appetite disturbances, fatigue, suicidal thoughts, hopelessness, worthlessness, and guilt.

major histocompatibility complex (MHC): The chromosomal region that controls strong transplantation antigens called histocompatibility locus antigens (HLA). In choosing donors of organs to be transplanted, it is essential that the recipient match the HLA type of the donor.

malabsorption: Inadequate absorption of nutrients from the intestine, especially the small intestine.

malaise: A vague feeling of discomfort or illness.

malignant: Life threatening; resistant to treatment (such as malignant hypertension); cancerous, can invade tissue and metastasize.

malingering: Deliberate faking of pain or illness to arouse sympathy; or pretends slow recuperation from a disease once suffered to continue receiving benefits of medical insurance and work absence.

malleolus: Either of the two bony prominences (medial or lateral) of the ankle. The medial malleolus is formed by the distal end of the tibia; the lateral malleolus is the distal end of the fibula.

mallet finger: Flexion deformity of the distal interphalangeal joint of a finger.

malleus: One of the three ossicles (small bones) of the middle ear that helps conduct sound to the inner ear. Also called the "hammer."

malnutrition: Lack of necessary nutrients in the body due to either inadequate diet or inadequate intestinal absorption.

malrotation: Displacement of a long bone fracture such that the distal fragment is rotated around its long axis.

malunion: Healing of a fracture with faulty alignment due to inadequate reduction or fixation.

mammary: Pertaining to the breast.

mandible: The bone of the lower jaw.

mania: A mental state characterized by elevated or irritable mood, along with three or more of the following: grandiosity (inflated self-esteem), decreased need for sleep, extreme talkativeness, flight of ideas or racing thoughts, distractibility, increase in goal-directed activity or psychomotor agitation, and excessive involvement in risky or indiscreet behavior.

manic: Pertaining to or afflicted with mania.

manometry: Measurement of pressure.

manual therapy: Therapy applied to the joints via the hands of the practitioner. An example is chiropractics.

Marfan's syndrome: A hereditary disorder of connective tissue characterized by long extremities (including fingers and toes), hypermobility of joints, flat feet, and dislocation of the lens of the eye. The aorta is often dilated, which may lead to the development of an aortic aneurysm.

mass: A tumor or swelling.

mastoid (process): A bony prominence (part of the temporal bone of skull) located behind the ear. It contains numerous cavities (air cells).

material safety data sheets (MSDS) : Printed information supplied by employers about the known toxicities of industrial chemicals.

Munchausen syndrome: Condition where an individual presents with multiple factitious physical symptoms; associated with multiple hospitalizations. The essential feature is the intentional production of physical symptoms that may be total fabrication. Common complaints include dizziness, blacking out, massive hemoptysis, generalized rashes and abscesses, fevers of unknown origin, and "lupus-like" syndromes.

maxilla: The paired skull bone that forms the upper jaw.

MCP joints: Metacarpophalangeal joints.

MCS: Multiple chemical sensitivity.

McKenzie stretch: Method used to help alleviate the pain of sciatica.

mean corpuscular hemoglobin concentration (MCHC): A percentage measure of concentration of hemoglobin in the average red blood cell.

mean corpuscular volume (MCV): A measure of the volume of red corpuscles expressed in cubic micrometers.

meatal stenosis: Scarring or stricture of the opening of the urethra.

meatotomy: Incision of a meatus (such as the urethral meatus) to enlarge the opening.

meatus: An opening or passage.

mechanical instability: Excessive, abnormal movement of a joint.

mechanical ventilation: Refers to artificial assistance for the work of breathing of an individual.

meconium: A fetus or newborn's first stool. The contents include salts, liquor amnii, mucus, bile, and epithelial cells. It is greenish black to light brown, of mild odor, and tarry.

medial: Pertaining to the middle; near the midline. In the hand, wrist, and forearm, medial refers to the ulnar or little finger side. The opposite of lateral.

medial epicondyle: Refers to a projection on the medial aspect of one of the long bones, typically the humerus or femur.

medial rotation: Rotation in an inward direction; internal rotation.

median cubital vein: A vein located in the antecubital fossa (front of the elbow) that connects the basilic and cephalic veins. It is commonly used as a site for drawing blood.

median nerve: A branch of the brachial plexus; one of the major nerves of the upper extremity.

mediastinum: The wall that separates the two halves of the chest cavity. The mediastinum contains the heart, the great vessels entering and leaving the heart (venae cavae, pulmonary arteries and veins, aorta), and the thymus.

medicamentosa: Concerning drugs.

mediolateral oblique: Refers to a radiologic positioning where the image is obtained at an angle from the medial to lateral side.

medium chain triglycerides: See triglyceride.

medulla: The inner part of an organ (such as the adrenal medulla). The lowest part of the brainstem, continuous with the spinal cord. Also called medulla oblongata.

medullary: Pertaining to bone marrow or to the medulla. See also medulla.

megadose: A dose (e.g., of a vitamin) greatly exceeding the amount required for nutritional balance.

megaloblastic anemia: Anemia characterized by large, abnormal red blood cells (megaloblasts); results from deficiency of vitamin B12 and/or folic acid.

meibomian gland: One of the sebaceous glands between the tarsi and the conjuctiva of the eyelids.

melanoma: A malignant, darkly pigmented mole or tumor of the skin.

melatonin: A hormone, secreted by the pineal gland thought to play a role in the regulation of the ovaries or testes.

melena: Tar-colored stool (bowel movement) due to the presence of partially digested blood.

membrane: A layer of tissue that covers a surface, lines a cavity, or separates one structure from another.

menarche: The initial menstrual period, occurs normally between the 9th and 17th year.

meninges: The three membranes (dura, arachnoid, and pia) that surround the spinal cord and brain. The pia is the thin, innermost membrane, closely covering the brain and spinal cord. The arachnoid is the delicate, web-like middle membrane. The dura is the tough, fibrous outer membrane.

meningitis: Inflammation of the membranes of the spinal cord or brain.

meningoencephalitis: Inflammation of the meninges and the brain. See also meninges.

meniscus: A crescent-shaped fibrocartilage found in certain joints. The knee has two menisci (medial and lateral), also called the semilunar cartilages.

menorrhagia: Excessive bleeding at the time of a menstrual period, either in number of days or amount of blood or both.

menses: Menstruation.

menstruation: Monthly bleeding due to sloughing of the endometrium (lining of the uterus).

mental status examination: A brief screening evaluation of mental function, usually done within the context of the history and physical exam. Mental status includes level of consciousness, orientation (to person, place, and time), affect (mood), thought content and process (such as anxieties, obsessions, delusions), and cognitive function (such as attention, concentration, memory, judgment, abstract thinking). This information is obtained, in part, by observation of the individual's appearance and behavior. The individual is also asked to perform several simple cognitive tasks such as recalling a series of words, serial sevens (counting backward from 100 by sevens), naming recent presidents of the US, interpreting proverbs.

mesencephalon: The midbrain.

mesenteric: Pertaining to the mesentery.

mesenteric emboli: A blood clot in the mesenteric artery; causes intestinal angina due to obstruction of blood flow to the intestines.

mesentery: A fold of the peritoneum that attaches the intestine to the posterior abdominal wall.

metabolic equivalent system units (METs): In cardiac stress testing, the amount of energy expended during different levels of exercise is expressed in METs. The units are multiples of the resting energy expenditure.

metabolism: The sum of all the physical and chemical processes that produce and maintain living substance, and that make energy available for the body's use.

metacarpal bones: The five bones that form the hand (between the wrist and the fingers).

metacarpophalangeal (MCP) joints: The joints between the metacarpal bones of the hand and the proximal phalanges.

metaphysis: The slightly flared region near the end of a long bone.

metaplasia: Conversion of one type of tissue into another type that is abnormal for that location.

metastasis: Spread of disease (such as cancer) from one part of the body to another part; distant from the place of origin.

metastasize: To spread by metastasis.

metastatic: Pertaining to metastasis.

metastatic cancer: Cancer that has spread from its origin to other parts of the body.

metatarsal bones: The five bones of the foot (between the tarsus and the phalanges).

metatarsophalangeal (MTP) joints: The joints between the metatarsal bones of the foot and the proximal phalanges.

metrorrhagia: Bleeding from the uterus especially at any time other than during the menstrual period. May be caused by lesions of the cervix uteri.

METs: Metabolic equivalent system units.

MI: Myocardial infarction.

microbe: A microorganism.

microbiologic culture: Microorganisms grown in or on various media types, typically some form of agar, for purposes of selecting and/or identifying the organisms present.

microbiology: The science that deals with the study of microorganisms.

microkeratome: An instrument used to cut sections of skin for microscopic examination.

microorganism: A microscopic form of life. Microorganisms include viruses, bacteria and bacteria-like organisms (such as Chlamydiae and mycoplasmas), single-celled fungi (such as yeasts), and protozoa.

microscope: An instrument used to obtain an enlarged image of small objects. With a microscope, structural details can be seen that would not otherwise be visible.

microvascular decompression: A technique of decompressing the trigeminal nerve as a treatment for trigeminal neuralgia.

microvasculature: The part of the circulatory system consisting of the small (microscopic) blood vessels.

midcarpal joint: The joint between the proximal and distal row of carpal bones in the wrist.

middle cranial fossa: Refers to a space in the skull where certain structures of the brain are found.

midfoot: The part of the foot between the hindfoot and forefoot. It includes five of the seven tarsal bones (the navicular, cuboid, and three cuneiforms).

midtarsal joint: The joint between the two rows of tarsal bones consisting of both the talonavicular and calcaneocuboid joints; the boundary between the hindfoot and midfoot.

mineralocorticoids: One of the three categories of steroid hormones secreted by the adrenal cortex. The other two are glucocorticoids and sex hormones. Mineralocorticoids play a role in the regulation of fluids and electrolytes. Aldosterone is the most important mineralocorticoid hormone.

minilaparotomy: A small incision made in the abdomen used to diagnose abdominal conditions.

Minnesota Multiphasic Personality Inventory (MMPI): A commonly administered self-report psychiatric test. The MMPI provides scores on a variety of "clinical scales," including hypochondriasis, depression, paranoia, and schizophrenia. A high score on a given scale is an indicator of the corresponding pathological mental function.

mitochondria: Spherical, oval, or rod-shaped structures (organelles) found in the cytoplasm of cells. The mitochondria are the cell's energy generators. Each mitochondrion has a double membrane--an outer membrane and an inner membrane that is folded into the interior of the mitochondrion to provide a large surface area. This surface contains numerous enzymes, and is the site where energy metabolism takes place. Mitochondria also contain their own RNA and DNA; they can replicate (independently of cell replication) and synthesize some of their own proteins.

mitral prolapse: An abnormality of the mitral valve where the valve leaflets bulge into the left atrium during systole. This produces a characteristic clicking sound, sometimes accompanied by a murmur of mitral regurgitation. The condition is usually asymptomatic, but in some cases is associated with non-anginal chest pain and other symptoms.

mitral valve: The flap-like opening between the left aorta and the left ventricle of the heart. Also called the bicuspid valve.

mixed nerve: A nerve that contains both sensory and motor fibers.

mm Hg: Millimeters of mercury, a unit of pressure.

MMPI: Minnesota Multiphasic Personality Inventory.

modality: A method of application of a therapeutic agent, especially a physical agent (as in physical therapy).

Moh's surgery: A type of microscopic surgery done to remove tissue from a basal cell carcinoma lesion that has vague borders.

monocyte: A type of white blood cell, capable of migrating into the tissues and becoming a macrophage.

mononeuropathy: Any disorder involving a single nerve.

mononeuropathy multiplex: Multiple mononeuropathy.

mononuclear: Having one nucleus, particularly a blood cell such as monocyte or lymphocyte.

mononucleotide: A substance produced by hydrolysis of nucleic acid containing phosphoric acid, a glucoside, or a pentoside.

monoplegia: Paralysis of a single limb or a single muscle group.

monozygotic: Derived from the same ovum or egg, as in identical twins.

morbidity: State of being diseased. The number of cases of a disease in a specific population (also referred to as morbidity rate).

morphology: Form or structure.

mortality: State of being mortal. The number of deaths in a specific population (also referred to as mortality rate); the death rate.

mortise: A rectangular recess. In the ankle joint, the distal ends of the tibia and fibula form a mortise into which the talus fits.

motile: Capable of spontaneous movement.

motility: The ability of a cell, organ, or organism to move spontaneously, i.e., gastrointestinal motility (peristalsis).

motor: Pertaining to movement.

motor evoked potential: The response of a muscle to stimulation of the brain or spinal cord.

motor nerve: A nerve composed entirely of motor fibers.

motor neuron: A neuron (nerve cell) that carries impulses away from the brain toward a muscle.

motor unit: A single motor neuron and the muscle cells innervated by its branches.

MS: Multiple sclerosis.

MSDS: Material Safety Data Sheet.

MTP joint: Metatarsophalangeal joint.

mucoid: Resembling mucus.

mucosa: Mucous membrane.

mucous membrane: An epithelial membrane lining a body cavity or passage that communicates with the outside of the body. Mucous membranes secrete mucus. Examples include the linings of the gastrointestinal, respiratory, reproductive, and urinary tracts.

mucus: A viscous or slimy substance secreted by mucous membranes.

multipartite: Having multiple parts.

multiple mononeuropathy: Any disorder involving two or more nerves in an asymmetrical distribution (i.e., both sides of the body not equally affected).

mural: Pertaining to a wall (such as of an organ).

mural fibroid: Fibroid tumor found in the wall of the uterus.

mural thrombus: A blood clot that forms within a heart chamber and is attached to the heart wall.

murine typhus: A disease caused by the Rickettsia typhi organism, transmitted by fleas that live on rats, mice, and other rodents.

murmur: A sound (either normal or abnormal) caused by blood flowing through the chambers of the heart or through a blood vessel. See also bruit.

muscle: An organ that produces movement by contracting (shortening). A type of tissue characterized by the ability to contract.

muscle spindle: A type of sensory receptor found in some muscles that responds to stretching of the muscle.

muscle tone: The state of tension in a resting muscle (i.e., when it is not actively contracting).

muscular dystrophy: Any of a group of inherited degenerative muscle disorders characterized by weakness and wasting. The most well-known type (Duchenne muscular dystrophy) is X-linked, and therefore occurs predominantly in males. Symptoms begin in early childhood, and affected individuals usually do not survive to maturity. Other forms of muscular dystrophy are less severe. Some are begin later in life and do not shorten the life span.

muscularis: The layer of smooth muscle in the wall of a hollow or tubular organ or vessel.

musculocutaneous nerve: A branch of the brachial plexus; one of the major nerves of the upper extremity.

musculoskeletal: Pertaining to both the skeleton and the muscles.

musculoskeletal exam: An exam of the skeleton and muscles.

myalgic encephalomyelitis: A British term for chronic fatigue syndrome.

mycobacterium: A group of acid-fast gram-positive rods that include the organisms causing tuberculosis and leprosy.

mycoplasma: A type of microorganism similar to bacteria, but usually without a cell wall. Unlike chlamydiae, they are able to live and grow outside cells. See also chlamydia.

mycosis: Infection with a fungal organism.

myelin: A fatty substance that forms sheaths around some types of nerve fibers. Myelinated fibers are found in both the central and peripheral nervous system.

myelin sheath: Sheath that surrounds nerve fibers.

myelodyspastic syndrome: A group of disorders in which the bone marrow does not function normally.

myelodysplasia: Defective formation of the spinal cord.

myelofibrosis: Replacement of bone marrow by fibrous tissue.

myeloma: A tumor of bone marrow.

myelopathy: Any disorder of the spinal cord.

myeloproliferative disorders: Disorders characterized by proliferation of bone marrow either in the bone marrow or extra-medullary.

myocardial ischemia: A condition characterized by inadequate blood flow to the heart; leads to angina pectoris and if untreated, to myocardial infarction.

myocardial perfusion scintigraphy: A radiologic procedure used to measure blood flow to the heart muscle.

myocarditis: Inflammation of the myocardium.

myocardium: Heart muscle.

myofascial: Pertaining to muscle and fascia (the fibrous membrane that covers muscles).

myofascial pain syndrome: A muscle disorder (either acute or chronic) characterized by pain and trigger points. Myofascial pain syndrome is commonly precipitated by trauma or muscle overload. See also trigger point.

myofasciitis: A term (literally, inflammation of muscle and fascia) used interchangeably with fibrositis.

myoglobin: A muscle protein similar to hemoglobin. Myoglobin binds oxygen from the blood, stores the oxygen, and transports it within the muscle cell.

myoglobinuria: The presence of myoglobin in the urine; a sign of rhabdomyolysis (breakdown of muscle tissue) or muscle injury. Severe myoglobinuria may lead to acute renal failure due to a toxic effect of myoglobin on the kidneys. See also rhabdomyolysis.

myoma: A tumor composed of muscular tissue.

myometrium: The muscular wall of the uterus.

myositis: Muscle inflammation.

myxoma: A type of connective tissue tumor.

nail root: The proximal portion of the nail underneath the cuticle.

narcotic: A drug or agent that depresses the central nervous system. The term is applied especially to the narcotic analgesics, i.e., the opioids (drugs such as codeine, morphine, and heroin) that produce an opium-like effect. See also opioid.

nasal: Pertaining to the nose.

nasal cannula: A tube used to deliver oxygen through the nose.

nasal septum: The wall between the two nasal passages.

nasogastric (NG) tube: A tube inserted through the nose and into the stomach for the purpose of emptying the stomach, lavaging the stomach, and administering liquid medications.

nasolabial fold: The crease between the nose and the upper lip.

nasolacrimal duct obstruction (NLDO): Obstruction of the duct that drains tears from the eyes.

nasopharynx: The part of the throat located behind the nose. See also oropharynx.

navicular: Scaphoid bones in the wrist and the ankle.

navicular bone: One of the seven tarsal bones of the foot located on the medial side of the foot between the talus and the cuneiforms.

NCV: Nerve conduction velocity.

nebulizer: A device for making a fine spray.

neck: (1) The part of the body between the head and the shoulders. (2) A constricted portion of an organ or structure resembling a neck (such as the neck of the femur).

necrosis: Tissue death.

necrotizing: Causing or characterized by necrosis.

necrotizing fasciitis: An infection of the fascia characterized by death of tissue.

Neisseria gonorrhoeae: The species of bacteria that causes gonorrhea.

neonatologist: A physician specializing in the care and treatment of neonates. A neonate is a newborn infant up to six weeks of age.

neoplasm: A tumor, either benign or malignant.

neoplastic: Pertaining to a tumor or tumor formation.

neovascularization: The growth of new blood vessels.

nephrolithiasis: Formation of kidney stones.

nephropathy: Any disorder of the kidneys.

nephroptosis: A kidney that is lower in the body than normal.

nerve: A bundle of neural fibers (axons and/or dendrites) in the peripheral nervous system (outside the brain and spinal cord). See also tract.

nerve block: A method of anesthesia where the transmission of nerve impulses is interrupted by injecting a local anesthetic around a nerve.

nerve cell growth factors: Proteins necessary for the growth and maintenance of nerve tissue.

nerve conduction velocity (NCV): The speed at which an action potential travels along a nerve.

nerve fiber: An axon or dendrite.

nerve root: The origin of a spinal nerve, as it emerges from the spinal cord.

nervous: Pertaining to nerves or the nervous system; anxious.

nervous system: System made up of the brain, spinal cord, spinal nerves and nerve roots, ganglia, peripheral nerves, and sensory receptors.

neural: Pertaining to nerves or the nervous system.

neuralgia: Severe sharp pain along the course of a nerve.

neurectomy: Surgical removal of a nerve or part of a nerve.

neuritis: Inflammation of a nerve or nerves, usually associated with a degenerative process.

neurocirculatory asthenia: A syndrome of functional nervous and circulatory disturbances.

Symptoms include chest pain, palpitations, shortness of breath, dizziness, and fatigue.

neurodermatitis: Cutaneous inflammation with itching associated with but not entirely due to emotional disturbance.

neuroendocrine: Pertaining to both neurological and endocrine function.

neurogenic: Originating in the nervous system.

neurogenic hypotension: Shock due to loss of vascular tone resulting from injury to the nervous system. See also shock.

neurogenic inflammation: Inflammation of nerves.

neuroleptic drugs: Drugs that cause symptoms that mimic neurological disease.

neuroleptics: See neuroleptic drugs.

neurological: Pertaining to the nervous system.

neurological back exam: Part of a physical exam that examines neurologic complications of spinal disorders.

neurological deficit: Loss of function due to a lesion of the nervous system.

neurolysis: Surgical loosening of adhesions around a nerve or nerve fibers.

neuroma: An unorganized mass of nerve fibers resulting from incision or laceration of a nerve; a tumor of nerve tissue.

neuromuscular: Pertaining to both nerves and muscles.

neuromuscular junction: The point where the axon of a motor neuron terminates on a muscle fiber. Also called myoneural junction.

neuron: A nerve cell.

neuropathic: Pertaining to neuropathy (such as neuropathic pain).

neuropathy: Any disorder of nerves.

neuropsychiatry: A branch of medicine that combines neurology and psychiatry.

neuropsychology: A discipline combining neurology and psychology that deals with the relationship between brain function and cognitive processes or behavior.

neurosis (plural, neuroses): A category of mental disorders characterized by unpleasant or distressing symptoms, but with intact reality testing.

neurotic: Pertaining to or afflicted with neurosis.

neurotoxin: A poison that acts on the nervous system.

neurotransmitter: Any of a variety of substances released by nerve fibers that transmits nerve impulses from the axon terminal (nerve fiber ending) to either another nerve cell or to a muscle or gland. Examples of neurotransmitters include acetylcholine, norepinephrine, dopamine, serotonin, endorphins, and substance P.

neurovascular: Pertaining to both nerves and blood vessels.

neutralization therapy: Therapy that counteracts a harmful effect.

neutrophil: A type of granulocyte (white blood cell that contains granules in its cytoplasm), so called because it stains with neutral dye. Neutrophils are the most abundant type of granulocyte, normally making up 35-65% of the white cells in circulation. Neutrophils are phagocytes (cells that engulf and digest microorganisms and other particles). The number of neutrophils increases in a variety of conditions including bacterial infections. See also granulocyte.

nevus (plural, nevi): An area of skin that is of a different color, usually present at birth (such as a mole or birthmark).

NG tube: Nasogastric tube.

nitrate: Any of a group of drugs (salts of nitric acid) that relax smooth muscle. Nitrates are often used as vasodilators.

nitrous oxide: A gas used as a general anesthetic; laughing gas.

nociceptive: Pertaining to stimulation of pain-sensitive nerve fibers.

nociceptive pain: Pain that arises from stimulation of pain-sensitive nerve fibers such as in bones, joints, soft tissue, and internal organs. It differs in quality from neuropathic pain (which arises from a lesion of the nervous system itself).

nocturia: Excessive urination during the night time hours.

node: A small, rounded organ or structure (such as a lymph node, the sinus node, and atrioventricular node of the heart).

nodule: A small, solid mass or swelling.

non-cardiogenic: Not having an origin with the heart.

noncompliance: The failure of a patient to cooperate by carrying out that portion of the medical care plan under his or her control, i.e., refusal to take medications.

noninvasive: (1) A term used to describe a procedure that does not require entering the body or puncturing the skin. (2) Not tending to spread (such as a noninvasive tumor or infection).

non-ionic: Term denoting a substance not composed of or does not dissociate into ions (charged particles).

non-REM sleep: The stages of sleep not associated with REM (rapid eye movements). See REM.

nonspecific: Not indicative of a particular disease (such as a nonspecific symptom); not directed toward a particular disease (such as a nonspecific treatment).

nonsteroidal anti-inflammatory drug (NSAID): An anti-inflammatory drug that is not a steroid. NSAIDs relieve inflammation by inhibiting the formation of prostaglandins. They also have analgesic (pain-relieving) and antipyretic (fever-reducing) activity.

nonunion: Failure of the fragments of a fracture to unite (knit together).

norepinephrine: A neurotransmitter released from sympathetic nerve fibers. It is secreted as a hormone by the adrenal medulla, and is similar in its actions to epinephrine (adrenalin). In addition, norepinephrine has been synthesized as a drug and is used as a vasoconstrictor.

nosocomial: Pertaining to a hospital or infirmary.

NSAID: Nonsteroidal anti-inflammatory drug.

nuclear scan: The use of radioactive substances injected in the body or inhaled to diagnose certain medical conditions. Such scans are used to diagnose tumors, biliary disease, gastrointestinal bleeding, thyroid function, coronary artery disease, vascular heart disease, and renal dysfunction.

nuclear sclerosis: A variant of cataracts; the most common form of cataract in older individuals.

nuclease: An enzyme that catalyzes the breakdown or digestion of nucleic acids.

nucleic acid: A complex organic chemical found in all living cells. The two most important types of nucleic acid are ribonucleic acid (RNA) and deoxyribonucleic acid (DNA).

nucleoside: A type of sugar (glycoside) formed by the joining of a purine or pyrimidine base with a pentose sugar.

nucleoside analogs: Agents that inhibit the functioning of HIV reverse transcriptase that are needed for the virus to synthesize viral DNA.

nucleus: A membrane-bound organelle found within the cytoplasm of cells that contains the cell's genetic material, and controls cellular metabolism, growth, and reproduction.

nucleus pulposus: The gelatinous center of an intervertebral disc.

nulliparity: The condition of not ever giving birth.

nulliparous: Pertaining to a woman who has never given birth to a child.

nummular dermatitis: A hypersensitivity skin disorder causing characteristic coin-shaped lesions. Also known as nummular eczema.

nystagmus: Constant, involuntary, cyclical movement of the eyeball.

objective: Based on observation (such as a physical exam finding or the results of a diagnostic test); detectable by an observer. The opposite of subjective (a symptom is subjective; a sign is objective).

oblique: Slanted; diagonal.

obstetrician gynecologist: A physician who treats women during pregnancy, delivers infants, and specializes in treatment of disease of the female reproductive organs, including the breasts.

obturator nerve: A branch of the lumbosacral plexus; one of the major nerves of the lower extremity.

occipital: Pertaining to the back of the head.

occlusion: Closure or obstruction (e.g., of an artery).

occult: Hidden or concealed. For example, an occult fracture is one not visible on routine x-rays.

occupational disease: Disease resulting from factors associated with the occupation in which the individual is engaged.

OCG: Oral cholecystogram.

odontoid process: The tooth-like projection from the upper surface of the axis (second cervical vertebra) that acts as a pivot for the atlas (first cervical vertebra).

odynophagia: Painful swallowing.

OKN (optokinetic nystagmus): Concerning the appearance of the twitching of the eye, as in nystagmus when the eyes gaze at moving objects.

olecranon: The upper end of the ulna that forms the point of the elbow.

olecranon fossa: A depression on the posterior surface of the distal humerus that receives the olecranon.

olfactory: Pertaining to the sense of smell.

olfactory cortex: The part of the brain responsible for the perception of odors. Located on the underside of the brain, it is considered part of the limbic system.

olfactory nerves: The nerves responsible for the sense of smell. Their receptors (nerve endings) are located in the mucous membrane of the upper nasal cavity; the nerve fibers pass through a bony plate to terminate in the olfactory bulbs (a pair of structures that are anterior projections of the brain). The olfactory bulbs, in turn, are connected to the olfactory cortex.

oligoastrocytoma: A malignant tumor of the brain consisting of astrocytes.

oligodendroglioma: A malignant tumor occurring principally in the cerebrum consisting mostly of oligodendrocytes.

oliguria: Diminished urine formation.

omentum: A fold of the peritoneum extending from the stomach to adjacent organs.

oncogenes: Tumor genes; when rearranged by various types of toxins, they initiate the growth of tumors.

onset: Beginning or start (such as the onset of a disease).

onychomycosis: Disease of the nails due to a parasitic fungus.

opacification: The process of becoming opaque.

opacity: The property of being opaque. An opaque spot or area (such as on an x-ray film).

opaque: Impenetrable to light or x-rays.

open: Exposed (as a wound or incision).

open reduction: Reduction by surgical methods.

ophthalmological: Pertaining to the study of the eye and its diseases.

ophthalmoscope: An instrument for examining the inside of the eye.

ophthalmoscopy: Examination of the interior of the eye.

opioid: Any natural or synthetic substance with opium-like activity; a narcotic analgesic. Opioids mediate pain perception by binding to opioid receptors on brain cells. They include endorphins (the brain's natural opioids), as well as codeine, morphine, heroin, methadone, and others. See also endorphins and narcotic.

opponens pollicis: The muscle responsible for opposability of the thumb.

opportunistic infection: An infection with a microorganism ordinarily present without causing disease. Disease results from the opportunity provided by altered physiology in the host. For example, opportunistic infections are likely to occur in individuals who are immunosuppressed. The use of broad-spectrum antibiotics may also result in opportunistic infection by suppressing the prevalent bacterial species, allowing other microorganisms to become dominant.

opposability: The ability to move the thumb into contact with the other fingers.

optic: Pertaining to vision.

optic chiasm: The point at which the two optic nerves cross over before entering the brain.

optic nerve: The nerve that carries impulses from the eye toward the brain.

optic radiations: A system of nerve fibers in the brain connecting the visual centers of the thalamus to the visual area of the cerebral cortex.

oral: Pertaining to the mouth.

oral flora: Microorganisms that colonize the mouth.

oral food challenge: See challenge test.

oral surgeon: Physician who performs surgeries of the mouth, especially those related to the jaws and teeth.

oral surgery: Operative procedures pertaining to the mouth and associated structures, especially the jaws and teeth.

organelle: Any of a number of membrane-enclosed structures found within the cytoplasm of cells. Organelles have specific functions (such as the nucleus contains the cell's genetic information and controls its metabolism and reproduction; mitochondria generate energy for cellular processes).

organic: Pertaining to an organ or organs; physical or structural (as opposed to functional); derived from living organisms; denoting chemical compounds that contain carbon.

organism: A living thing.

organization: Conversion of a thrombus (clot) into connective tissue. The process begins when new blood vessels grow into clot; this is followed by infiltration of cells that deposit connective tissue fibers.

orifice: An entrance or outlet; an opening.

origin: The proximal attachment of a muscle; the attachment of a muscle to a part that remains relatively fixed when the muscle contracts.

oropharyngeal: Pertaining to the oropharynx.

oropharynx: The part of the throat located behind the mouth. See also nasopharynx.

orthodontist: A dentist who is an expert in prevention and correction of abnormally positioned or aligned teeth.

orthodromic: Pertaining to an impulse moving along a nerve in the normal direction. The opposite of antidromic.

orthopedics: The branch of medicine concerned with the musculoskeletal system (bones, joints, muscles, and fascia).

orthopedist: A specialist in orthopedics.

orthostatis hypotension: Postural hypotension.

orthotic: Pertaining to an orthosis, a device used to correct misalignment of the joints or alter the mechanics of weightbearing; usually refers to a device that is either added to the outside of a shoe or placed inside the shoe.

orthotic collar: Specialized collar worn around the neck to provide support.

orthotics: The science pertaining to mechanical appliances for orthopedic use.

OS: Oculus sinister; left eye.

oscillopsia: Sensation of oscillation or swinging of the visual field. It is illusory and may be associated with a severe form of labyrinthine nystagmus.

oscilloscope: An instrument that produces a visual display on a cathode ray tube (similar to a TV screen), corresponding to an electronic signal.

osmolarity: The concentration of dissolved particles (molecules and ions) in a solution.

osmosis: The movement of a solvent (such as water) across a semipermeable membrane, from an area of higher to lower concentration (of the solvent). See also diffusion, filtration, and semipermeable membrane.

osmotic fragility test: A test to look for hereditary spherocytosis and thalassemia.

ossicle: A small bone (such as the malleus, incus, or stapes of the middle ear; a sesamoid bone of the foot).

ossification: The process of turning into bone.

osteitis pubis: Inflammation of the pubic bone.

osteoarthritis: Degenerative joint disease.

osteoblastoma: A tumor made of cells that normally form bone.

osteochondroma: A tumor composed of cartilage and bone.

osteochondrosis: A developmental disorder affecting the epiphyses (growth centers) of bones. Osteochondrosis of the spine (Scheuermann's disease) has its onset during adolescence, and is characterized by back pain and kyphosis.

osteogenesis: Ossification, formation, and development of bone taking place in connective tissue or cartilage.

osteoid osteoma: A rare benign tumor that occurs in the young. It is composed of bone made from sheets of bony material that is partially hardened.

osteomalacia: Softening of the bones due to deficiency of calcium and/or vitamin D; results in deformity.

osteonecrosis: Generalized death of bone tissue rather than isolated areas of necrosis.

osteophyte: A bone outgrowth or spur.

osteophyte: A bony excrescence or outgrowth, usually branched in shape.

osteosarcoma: A malignant sarcoma of the bone.

osteotomy: Surgical cutting of bone.

ostium: A small opening, especially into a tubular structure such as a blood vessel.

-ostomy: Suffix denoting an artificial opening between a hollow or tubular organ (such as the intestine) and the surface of the body.

OT: Occupational therapy.

otitis externa: Inflammation of the external ear canal.

otolaryngologist: A specialist in the division of medicine that includes otology (ear), rhinology (nose), and laryngology (throat).

-otomy: Suffix denoting a surgical incision into an organ or structure.

outpatient: An individual who is not hospitalized.

ovaries: Two female organs located in the pelvic cavity. The ovaries contain the reproductive cells (ova); they also secrete estrogens and other sex hormones.

ovum (plural, ova): The female reproductive cell or egg.

oximetry: Measuring of blood oxygen content.

oxygen: A chemical element (atomic number 8) denoted by the symbol O. Most forms of plant and animal life require oxygen for respiration.

oxygenation: Saturation or combination with oxygen, as in the aeration of the blood in the lungs.

oxytocin: A hormone secreted by the hypothalamus and stored in the posterior lobe of the pituitary gland. It promotes contraction of the uterus and ejection of milk from the mammary glands.

P wave: In electrocardiography, the wave produced by depolarization of the atria. The P wave is the electrical equivalent of atrial contraction.

Pneumocystis carinii: An organism that causes a pneumonia in individuals who are immunocompromised.

PA: Posteroanterior.

pacemaker: (1) In cardiology, a specialized group of heart cells that automatically generate electrical impulses. The impulses can spread to other regions of the heart, causing the heart to contract (beat). The heart's normal pacemaker is the sinus node. (2) An artificial pacemaker is a device used to substitute for a defective natural pacemaker by delivering rhythmic electrical stimuli to the heart.

palliate: To ease or decrease the intensity (i.e., of a disease); to relieve temporarily (such as pain) without curing.

palliative: Serving to relieve or alleviate pain with curing it.

palliative therapy: Therapy aimed at the relief of symptoms.

pallidotomy: Surgical destruction of the globus pallidus done to treat involuntary movements or muscular rigidity.

pallor: Paleness.

palpable: Capable of being perceived by touch.

palpate: To examine by touch; to feel.

palpation: Process of examining with the hands; examination by touch.

palpebral fissure width: The width of the opening between the eyelids.

Glossary 2359

palpitate: To cause to throb or beat intensely, such as the heart.

palpitation: The subjective sensation of an excessively rapid or irregular heartbeat.

palsy: Loss of sensory and/or voluntary motor function; paralysis.

pancreas: A glandular organ located behind the stomach in the retroperitoneal space. It is both an exocrine gland (secreting digestive enzymes that are conveyed to the duodenum via the pancreatic duct) and an endocrine gland (secreting insulin and glucagon, hormones that regulate blood sugar levels).

pancreatic duct: The duct that conveys pancreatic juice (containing digestive enzymes) to the duodenum.

pancreatic enzymes: Enzymes (lipase, amylase, ribonucleases, phospholipase A) and precursors of enzymes (trypsin, chymotrypsin, carboxypeptidases) secreted by the acinar cells of the liver. These substances continue the process of fat, starch, and nucleic acid digestion.

pancreatic juice: An alkaline fluid containing digestive enzymes secreted by the exocrine tissue of the pancreas. Pancreatic juice is conveyed to the duodenum (first part of the small intestine) via the pancreatic duct.

pancreatitis: Inflammation of the pancreas.

pancreozymin: A hormone manufactured by mucosal cells of the duodenum and secreted into the blood. Pancreozymin stimulates the pancreas to secrete digestive enzymes. It also stimulates release of bile from the gallbladder into the duodenum. In this capacity, it is usually called cholecystokinin. Pancreozymin and cholecystokinin were once thought to be separate hormones, but are now known to be the same.

pancytopenia: A reduction in all cellular elements of the blood.

panic attack: An acute episode of intense anxiety; also called an anxiety attack. Panic attacks are an essential feature of panic disorder and may also occur in other psychiatric disorders (such as phobias and somatization disorder). They may also occur in certain non-psychiatric medical conditions (such as mitral prolapse or hyperthyroidism).

panic disorder: A disorder characterized by panic attacks.

pannus: Abnormal tissue full of blood vessels that grows over the top of the cornea in response to disease such as trachoma or eczema. Vision is clouded by this tissue.

Pap (Papanicolaou) smear: See Pap test.

Pap (Papanicolaou) test: A test used to detect early stages of cervical cancer. Cells are removed from the vagina and cervix and stained for microscopic analysis.

papillary muscles: In the heart, muscular projections of the inner ventricular walls, which are connected to the cusps of the atrioventricular (mitral and tricuspid) valves. The papillary muscles keep the cusps from turning inside out under the high pressure of ventricular contraction.

papilledema: Swelling of the optic nerve at the point where it enters the eyeball.

papillomavirus: A type of virus that causes papillomas (warts).

papulosquamous lesions: Skin that has pimples and flat scaly patches.

paralytic ileus: Intestinal obstruction due to paralysis of the intestinal smooth muscle.

Paramyxovirus: A subgroup of the myxoviruses similar in physical, chemical, and biological characteristics but differ pathogenetically. Includes parainfluenza, measles, mumps, Newcastle disease, and respiratory syncytial viruses.

paranoid schizophrenia: A type of schizophrenic disorder wherein there are delusions of persecution, grandiosity, jealousy, or hallucinations with persecutory or grandiose content.

paraparesis: Partial paralysis affecting the lower limbs.

paraphimosis: Strangulation of glans penis due to restriction of narrowed or inflamed foreskin.

paraplegia: Paralysis of lower portion of the body and of both legs.

parasite: An organism that lives in, on, or at the expense of another living organism (host) without contributing to the host's survival.

paraspinal, paraspinous: Alongside the spine.

parasympathetic nervous system: The division of the autonomic nervous system concerned with conservation and restoration. The effects of parasympathetic stimulation are opposite to those of the sympathetic nervous system. They include slowing of heart rate, increased blood flow to skin and digestive tract (due to dilation of blood vessels), increased peristalsis (contraction of gastrointestinal smooth muscle), constriction of bronchioles, and constriction of pupils. See also autonomic nervous system and sympathetic nervous system.

parathyroid glands: Four small endocrine glands located on the posterior surface of the thyroid gland in the neck. The parathyroid glands produce parathyroid hormone (also called parathormone or PTH) that regulates calcium and phosphorus metabolism.

parenchyma: The part of the substance of an organ concerned with its specific function, as opposed to its framework.

parenteral: A term denoting any route (i.e., for administering medications) other than the digestive tract. Parenteral routes include intravenous, intra-muscular, subcutaneous, and topical.

paresthesia: Sensation of tingling, prickling, or "pins and needles."

parietal: Pertaining to a wall (i.e., of a body cavity).

parietal bones: The two bones (one on each side) that form the roof and sides of the skull.

parietal lobes: The lobes of the brain that lie underneath the parietal bones.

parietal pericardium: The outermost, fibrous layer of the pericardium.

parietal peritoneum: The serous membrane lining the abdominal and pelvic walls and the underside of the diaphragm.

parietal pleura: The serous membrane extending from the roots of the lungs, covering the heart, and extending backward to the spine.

paronychia: Infection of the skin around the nail.

parotid glands: A gland in the mouth that produces saliva.

paroxysm: A sudden attack or recurrence of a symptom. For example, a paroxysmal tachycardia is characterized by episodes of rapid heart rate that begin and end abruptly.

pars interarticularis: The part of the vertebra between the superior and inferior facets.

partial and total hysterectomy: A partial hysterectomy involves the removal of the uterus, but not the ovaries. A total hysterectomy involves the removal of the body of the uterus including the cervix, and removal of the ovaries.

partial seizure: A seizure that involves only a portion of the brain.

partial thromboplastin time (PTT): A test to measure coagulation.

passive range of motion (PROM): Allowing another individual to move a joint through all of the angles possible to that joint.

patella: The kneecap.

patellar ligament: The ligament that connects the patella to the tibia. It is an extension of the patellar tendon.

patellar reflex: A deep tendon reflex evoked by tapping on the patellar tendon; the "knee jerk" reflex.

patellar tendon: The tendon of the quadriceps femoris muscle (the extensor muscle of the knee). The patella is embedded within the tendon. The tendon extends beyond the patella (as the patellar ligament) to insert on the tibia.

patellectomy: Surgical removal of the kneecap.

patellofemoral: Concerning the patella and femur.

patellofemoral joint: The joint between the patella and femur.

pathergy: Pustular reaction of the skin in response to an intradermal needle prick; used to diagnose Behçet's disease.

pathogen: A microorganism or substance capable of causing disease.

pathological: Diseased or concerning disease.

pathology: The study of the nature and causes of disease; a condition produced by disease.

-pathy: Suffix denoting a disease or disorder.

PAW: Pulmonary artery wedge.

pedicle: The part of the vertebral arch that projects backward from the vertebral body on each side and connects with the lamina.

pedicle graft: Tissue partially lifted and moved to a different location to repair or reconstruct damaged tissue. One end of the graft continues to be attached to the original site, thus preserving the original blood supply.

pedunculated: Having a stalk (such as a polyp).

pelvic: Pertaining to the pelvis, usually the bony pelvis.

pelvic girdle: The bony structure that supports the lower extremities composed of the pelvic and hip bones.

pelvis: The bony basin formed by the hipbones, the sacrum, and the coccyx. The pelvic bones support the vertebral column and articulate with the bones of the lower extremity. The cavity is formed by the pelvic bones and its contents; the lower abdomen.

penetrating keratoplasty: Transplantation of corneal tissue from a donor to replace diseased or scarred corneal tissue that interferes with sight.

penile hypospadias: The condition where the urethral opening is in an abnormal place such as on the underside of the penis.

pepsin: A protein-digesting enzyme secreted by the stomach.

peptic: Pertaining to digestion.

peptic ulcer: An ulcer (usually in the duodenum, stomach, or lower esophagus) induced by the action of digestive secretions.

peptide: An organic chemical composed of two or more amino acids.

percussion: Tapping the body with the fingertips to obtain information about underlying structures. For example, if percussion produces a dull sound, it indicates the presence of either a solid structure or fluid. If percussion produces a hollow, drum-like sound, it indicates the presence of air or gas.

percutaneous: Passing through the skin. For example, in percutaneous aspiration, fluid is withdrawn from a body cavity by passing a needle through the skin.

perforation: A hole or puncture (such as in a hollow organ); also the process (such as ulceration) by which such a hole is produced.

perfusion: The flow of blood (or other substance) through an organ or tissue.

peri-: Prefix meaning around.

perianal: Around the anus.

periapical abscess: Abscess around the apex of the root of a tooth.

periarterial: Around an artery.

periarteritis: Inflammation of the external coat of an artery.

periarthritis: Inflammation of the tissues around a joint.

pericardiocentesis: Puncture of the pericardium (the membranous sac surrounding the heart) for the purpose of withdrawing fluid.

pericardium: The membranes that enclose the heart. The pericardium has two layers, visceral and parietal. Together, these form a double covering consisting of a serous membrane surrounded by a fibrous sac.

pericholecystic: Pertaining to the area around the gallbladder.

perinatologist: A physician specializing in development of the fetus and infact during the prenatal period, beginning after the 28th week of pregnancy through 28 days following birth.

perineum: The region between the external genitals (the vulva in females or the scrotum in males) and the anus.

periodontal: Pertaining to the tissues that surround and support the teeth (including the gums and the bone sockets of the teeth).

periodontal abscess: A localized area of acute or chronic inflammation with pus formation found in the gingival, periodontal pockets, or periodontal ligament.

periodontal pocket: A gingival sulcus enlarged beyond normal limits as a result of poor hygiene.

periodontist: A physician specializing in the branch of dentistry dealing with treatment of diseases of the tissues around the teeth.

periosteum: The fibrous membrane that covers the surfaces of bones (except for the articular surfaces).

periostitis: Inflammation of periosteum, the membrane investing a bone.

peripheral: Located at or pertaining to the periphery; away from the center.

peripheral blood smear: A laboratory test that examines the blood cells under a microscope.

peripheral edema: Swelling of the extremities, in particular the legs.

peripheral nerve: Any nerve outside the central nervous system.

peripheral nervous system (PNS): The part of the nervous system outside the central nervous system. Includes the cranial nerves, spinal nerves and nerve roots, brachial and lumbosacral plexuses, and all of their branches; also the sympathetic and parasympathetic nerves and ganglia.

peripheral neuropathy: Any disorder of a peripheral nerve or nerves.

peripheral resistance: Resistance to blood flow due to constricted arteries in the arms and legs.

peripheral vision: Vision outside of the central focus of sight.

periphlebitis: Inflamed condition of external coat of a vein or tissues around it.

peristalsis: An involuntary, wave-like movement that occurs in hollow tube-like organs, especially those of the digestive tract. The movement is produced by contraction and relaxation of the organ's muscular walls.

peristaltic action: See peristalsis.

peritoneal cavity: The abdominal cavity.

peritoneal dialysis: A method of providing artificial kidney function where the peritoneum (lining of the abdominal cavity) is used as the dialysis membrane. Dialysis fluid is instilled into the peritoneal cavity; waste products and other unwanted substances pass selectively across the membrane, from the blood into the peritoneal fluid. The fluid is then withdrawn. See also dialysis.

peritoneum: The serous membrane that lines the abdominal cavity and covers the surfaces of the abdominal organs.

peroneal: Pertaining to the fibula.

peroneal tubercle: A small elevation on the lateral surface of the calcaneus (heel bone). The tendons of peroneus brevis and longus pass above and below the peroneal tubercle, respectively.

peroneus brevis: A muscle located on the lateral side of the lower leg; an everter of the foot. Its tendon inserts on the base of the fifth metatarsal bone.

peroneus longus: A muscle located on the lateral side of the lower leg; an everter of the foot. Its tendon crosses the sole and inserts on the medial side of the foot.

peroneus tertius: Part of the extensor digitorum longus muscle. Its tendon inserts on the fifth metatarsal and helps evert the foot.

personality disorders: A category of psychiatric disorders characterized by inflexible, maladaptive personality traits.

pes planus: Flat foot.

pessary: A device inserted into the vagina to support the uterus.

PET: Positron emission tomography.

petechiae: Tiny purple spots on the skin caused by minute hemorrhages of capillaries in the skin. May be present in severe fevers or when clotting mechanisms are impaired.

Peyronie's disease: Fibrosis of the penis.

pH: A unit of measurement of acidity or alkalinity. The pH scale extends from zero to 14. A pH of 7 is neutral (neither acid nor alkaline). A pH less than 7 denotes acidity; greater than 7 denotes alkalinity. See also hydrogen ion.

phacoemulsification: The procedure where an ultrasound probe is inserted into the eye and high-frequency sound waves are used to break a cataract apart. The pieces are then removed by suctioning.

phagocytosis: Ingestion and digestion of bacteria and particles by phagocytes.

phalangectomy: Excision of one or more phalanges.

phalanges: Bones of the finger or toe.

phalanx (plural, phalanges): Any of the bones of the fingers or toes.

pharmaceutical: A drug; pertaining to drugs.

pharynx: The throat consisting of the oropharynx and nasopharynx (the parts of the throat located behind the mouth and nose, respectively).

phenothiazine: Any of a group of antipsychotic drugs. Phenothiazines are also used to enhance the effects of analgesics and relieve nausea.

pheochromocytoma: A rare, usually benign tumor, that secretes adrenal medulla hormones (epinephrine and norepinephrine). The increased secretion of these hormones results in hypertension, which may be either continuous or intermittent.

Philadelphia chromosome: Abnormal chromosome 22 in which there is a translocation of the distal portion of its long arm to chromosome 9. Found in leukocyte cultures of many individuals with chronic myelocytic leukemia.

phimosis: Narrowing of the opening of the foreskin so it cannot be pushed back over the glans penis.

phlebitis: Inflammation of a vein.

phlebography: A study of the structure and function of the veins.

phlegm: Thick mucus, especially from the respiratory tract.

phobia: A persistent, intense, irrational fear of a particular object, activity, or situation. The individual recognizes that the fear is excessive and unreasonable. A phobia is considered a psychiatric disorder if it causes undue distress or interferes with normal functioning. Phobias are classified as anxiety disorders.

phosphate: (1) A salt of phosphoric acid (H_3PO_4). (2) Ions composed of phosphorus and oxygen atoms and carrying a triple negative charge (PO_4^{-3}).

phospholipid: A type of lipid consisting of a fatty acid, a nitrogen base, and phosphate. Phospholipids are an important constituent of cell membranes. Lecithin is an example of a phospholipid.

phosphorus: A non-metallic chemical element (atomic number 15) denoted by the symbol P. Along with calcium, it is one of the principal minerals in teeth and bones. It is also essential for many cellular processes including energy metabolism and storage, and (as a constituent of RNA and DNA) protein synthesis and cell replication.

photocoagulation: The use of light or laser beams to repair retinal detachments or hemorrhages.

photophobia: Intolerance to light; present in measles, rubella, meningitis, and eye inflammation.

phototherapeutic keratectomy: It is a treatment to correct damage caused by a diseased cornea. It uses the same laser treatment as photoreactive keratectomy, but does not alter the refractive state of the eye.

phototherapy: Exposure to sunlight or artificial light for therapeutic purposes; use of light to treat certain conditions.

phrenic: Pertaining to the diaphragm (such as the phrenic artery or nerve); pertaining to the mind (as in schizophrenia--literally, "split mind").

physiatrist: A physician specializing in physical medicine.

physical therapist: Individual who completed an accredited physical therapy program and passed a licensing exam, and who is then legally responsible for evaluating, planning, conducting, and supervising a physical therapy program.

physiological: Pertaining to body function, especially normal body function.

physiology: The science of the function of the body and its parts, including the physical and chemical processes involved.

pia (mater): The innermost of the three membranes that surround the brain and spinal cord. See also meninges.

pinched nerve: A nerve compressed between two structures.

pineal gland: A glandular structure located in the brain. It secretes hormones such as melatonin, whose functions are not well understood. However, it appears to play a role in the regulation of reproduction, fluid and electrolyte balance, and circadian rhythms.

PIP joints: Proximal interphalangeal joints.

pituitary gland: A small endocrine gland attached to the hypothalamus (at the base of the brain) by a narrow stalk. The pituitary gland is divided into anterior and posterior portions (called lobes). The anterior lobe secretes a number of hormones that regulate the activities of other endocrine glands--the adrenal cortex, thyroid, and ovaries or testes. The anterior pituitary is itself regulated by hypothalamic hormones (also called inhibiting and releasing factors). In addition, the hypothalamus secretes two other hormones (antidiuretic hormone and oxytocin) that are stored in the posterior lobe of the pituitary. See also hypothalamus, antidiuretic hormone, and oxytocin.

placebo: An inactive substance used in controlled studies of drugs. One group of individuals receives the active drug, while a similar group receives the placebo; the results in the two groups are then compared. See also control.

placebo effect: A response to treatment (i.e., to a drug) that results from the individual's mental "set" or expectation (as opposed to a pharmacological response resulting from drug action). Placebo effects may occur not only with placebos, but also with active drugs (in addition to the pharmacological response). Non-drug treatments may also have placebo effects.

placenta: A structure that forms in the uterus during pregnancy through which the fetus receives nourishment.

plafond: A ceiling. See tibial plafond.

plantar: Pertaining to the sole of the foot.

plantar flexion: Movement of the foot or toes downward (toward the sole of the foot). Plantar flexion of the foot takes place at the ankle joint; plantar flexion of the toes takes place at the metatarsophalangeal and interphalangeal joints. See also dorsiflexion.

plantar ligament: A strong ligament located in the sole of the foot.

plantar nerves: Branches of the tibial nerve that supply the sole of the foot.

plantar reflex: A deep tendon reflex evoked by tapping on the Achilles tendon; the "ankle jerk" reflex.

plaque: (1) In dermatology, a raised lesion of skin or mucous membrane, greater than one centimeter (or one-half centimeter, according to some authorities) in diameter. (2) A deposit of fatty (atherosclerotic) material in the wall of an artery; also called an atheroma. (3) A gummy deposit on the teeth that provides a medium for the growth of bacteria.

plasma: The fluid portion of blood or lymph; the blood cells and platelets are suspended in the plasma.

plasma cell: A type of cell (derived from B-lymphocytes) that produces antibodies.

plasma protein: Any protein found in blood plasma; albumin is the most abundant.

plasmapheresis: A process where blood is removed from the body and the red cells separated from the other constituents by centrifugation. The red cells are then re-suspended in a saline solution and injected back into the donor (or injected into another individual who requires only red cells rather than whole blood).

-plasty: Suffix denoting surgical repair or reconstruction.

platelet: A disc-shaped cell fragment found in blood. Platelets play an important role in blood clotting.

plethysmograph: Device for finding variations in size or a part due to variations in amount of blood passing through or contained in the part.

pleura: A serous membrane that lines the thoracic (chest) cavity and covers the surface of the lungs. The part that lines the thoracic cavity is called the parietal pleura; the part that covers the lungs is the visceral pleura.

pleural cavity: The space between the parietal and visceral pleurae. Normally these two membranes are closely apposed with virtually no space between them; in other words, the pleural cavity is a potential space. However, the pleural cavity may be converted into an actual space by the leakage of air (pneumothorax) or fluid.

pleural effusion: An accumulation of fluid in the pleural cavity.

pleuritic: Related to or similar to pleuritis (inflammation of the pleura). Pleuritic pain is chest pain that increases with respiratory movements (deep breathing and coughing).

pleurodynia: Sharp, intense pain originating in the chest wall.

plexus: A network (i.e., of nerves or blood vessels).

PMS: Premenstrual syndrome.

pneumatic retinopexy: The injection of air or liquid into the eye to hold a detached retina against the nourishing layer below (choroid) in hopes that it will reattach.

Pneumococcus: The causative organism of a common type of bacterial pneumonia (pneumococcal pneumonia); also called Streptococcus pneumoniae. Pneumococci are gram-positive cocci (spherical bacteria) that occur in pairs.

pneumonectomy: Surgical removal of a lung.

pneumonitis: Inflammation of the lungs; pneumonia.

poisons (toxics): Substances that interfere with normal physiological functions of the body whether inhaled, ingested, injected, or absorbed.

poliomyelitis: Inflammation of the gray matter of the spinal cord; an acute viral disease characterized by fever, sore throat, headache, vomiting, and often stiffness of the neck and back.

poly-: A prefix meaning many or much.

polyarteritis: An inflammatory disease of the medium and small arteries.

polyarteritis nodosa: An inflammatory disease causing damage to small and medium arteries that results in impairment of any organs involved.

polyarthralgia: Pain and swelling in multiple joints.

polyarticular: Affecting many joints.

polycystic kidney disease: A hereditary disease in which multiple cysts are found in the kidneys.

polydipsia: Excessive intake of fluids; excessive thirst.

polygenic: Pertaining to or caused by several genes.

polyhydramnios: The presence of more than the usual amount of fluid in the amniotic sac during pregnancy.

polymerase chain reaction: An early test for HIV that turns positive before the HIV shows up in the blood test.

polymyalgia rheumatica: An inflammatory disorder occurring primarily in older individuals. It is characterized by pain and stiffness of the proximal muscles (those of the neck, trunk, and limb girdles), as well as systemic symptoms (such as fever, malaise, and weight loss). See also connective tissue diseases.

polymyositis: An inflammatory disorder involving primarily skeletal muscle and characterized by weakness of the proximal muscles (those of the neck, trunk, and limb girdles). When accompanied by skin involvement, it is called dermatomyositis. See also connective tissue diseases.

polyneuropathy: Any disorder affecting many nerves.

polyp: A tumor (usually benign) with a stalk.

polypeptide: A short chain of amino acids; a protein fragment.

polyuria: The passage of more urine than is normal.

pompholyx: Deep-seated vesicles of the hands and feet, especially the plams and soles. May be chronic and produce itching. Cause is unknown but may be associated with contact allergy or fungal infection.

popliteal: Pertaining to the back of the knee.

popliteal artery: The continuation of the femoral artery as it passes behind the knee. Below the knee, the popliteal artery divides into the anterior and posterior tibial arteries.

popliteal fossa: The concavity behind the knee.

popliteal vein: A deep vein that runs behind the knee, alongside the popliteal artery. It is formed just below the knee by the union of the anterior and posterior tibial veins and continues upward through the thigh as the femoral vein.

portal: Pertaining to a portal system, especially the hepatic portal system.

portal circulation: The movement of blood through a portal system, especially the hepatic portal system.

portal hypertension: Increased pressure in the hepatic portal vein due to obstruction of blood flow through the liver.

portal system: A system of blood vessels in which blood leaving a capillary bed is carried by veins to a second capillary bed before returning to the heart. The term most often refers to the hepatic portal system, the largest portal system in the body.

portal vein: A vein that conveys blood from a capillary bed to a second capillary bed. The term most often refers to the hepatic portal vein that carries blood from the stomach, small intestine, colon spleen, pancreas, and gallbladder to the liver.

positive guaiac test: A test verifying the presence of blood in gastric juices or feces.

positron: A subatomic particle with the same mass as an electron, but with a positive charge; the antiparticle of an electron.

positron emission tomography (PET): A type of imaging accomplished by administering a natural biochemical substance (such as glucose) that is tagged with positron-emitting radioisotopes. Gamma rays (produced when positrons collide with electrons) are detected and interpreted by a computer to form a tomograms (images of a selected body plane or "slice"). The image reflects the concentration of the tagged substance in the body tissues. PET scans are useful in evaluating the metabolic activity of an organ.

posterior: At or near the back or rear of a structure; the opposite of anterior. In anatomy, posterior refers to the back (dorsal) side of the body; also to the dorsal side of the hand and forearm.

posterior capsular opacification: Opacification of the posterior lens capsule of the eye following cataract extraction; may cause blurred vision.

posterior chamber: In the eye, the space behind the iris and lens.

posterior horns: The dorsal horns of the spinal cord.

posterior semicircular canal occlusion: A surgical treatment for benign paroxysmal positional vertigo; used when conservative treatments fail.

posterior tibial artery: One of the two main arteries that supply blood to the foot. Pulsation of the posterior tibial artery can be felt behind the medial malleolus of the ankle.

posteroanterior (PA): From back to front (e.g., a PA x-ray is one where the x-ray beam passes from back to front).

posterolateral: In back and to the lateral side.

posteromedial: In back and to the medial side.

posthitis: Inflammation of the foreskin.

postmenopausal: Occurring after menopause.

postmortem: Occurring after death. An autopsy is a postmortem examination.

postmyocardial infarction syndrome: Chest pain similar to that of pericarditis appears in the second week following onset of myocardial infarction. An autoimmune reaction consisting of fever, pericarditis, and sometimes pleuritis, occurring after a myocardial infarction. Also called Dressler's syndrome.

postpartum: Occurring after childbirth.

postural drainage: Drainage of secretions from the respiratory tract by positioning the individual so that drainage is assisted by gravity. This position also stimulates coughing, which further assists in the removal of secretion

postural proteinuria: Protein in the urine, usually albumin, related to bodily position; may be transient and benign or a sign of severe renal disease.

potassium: A metallic chemical element (atomic number 19) denoted by the symbol K (from Latin, kalium). It is found in ionized form in body fluids and tissues, and is one of the principal cations (positive ions) of the body. It is essential for many body processes including muscle function (especially cardiac muscle), nerve conduction, and fluid and acid-base balance.

potential acuity meter: An instrument used to examine the eyes.

precapillary sphincter: The smooth muscle of a terminal arteriole (the smallest arteriolar branch that leads into a capillary). Blood flow into a capillary bed is regulated by the contraction and relaxation of the precapillary sphincters.

precordial: Overlying the heart.

prefrontal cortex: An anterior part of the frontal lobe of the brain.

pregnancy test: Chemical tests performed after a missed menstrual period to test for pregnancy; tests may be done at a physician's office or at home.

preictal: The period just prior to a stroke or convulsion.

prenatal: Occurring before birth.

prepatellar bursa: A bursa (synovial sac) located in front of the patella between the patella and the skin.

presbyesophagus: Frequent contractions of the esophagus that do not propel food down to the stomach.

presbyopia: Defect of vision in advancing age involving loss of accommodation or recession of near point; occurs due to loss of elasticity of crystalline lens.

primary: First in time or order. A term used to characterize a disorder that arises spontaneously, not as a result of another disorder. The opposite of secondary.

primary bone cancer: Bone cancer that originates from bone cells, not metastatic.

primary disease: The original underlying disease that afflicts an individual.

primitive reflex: A reflex normally present in infants, but which disappears as the nervous system becomes more mature (such as Babinski's reflex). Presence of a primitive reflex in an adult is a sign of a central nervous system disorder.

PRK (photorefractive keratectomy): Removal of part of the cornea to change its shape.

process: (1) A method or system; a series of actions. (2) A projection or outgrowth (i.e., of a bone).

proctitis: Inflammation of the anus and rectum.

proctocolectomy: Removal of the rectum and part of the colon.

proctoscope: An endoscope for examining the rectum.

proctoscopy: Endoscopy of the rectum.

prodromal phase: The earliest stages of a disease when the first symptoms indicate a disease is developing.

progesterone: A female sex hormone secreted by the ovary and the placenta.

progestin: A corpus luteum hormone that prepares the endomedrium for implantation of the fertilized ovum.

prognosis: The probable outcome of a disease or injury.

prolapse: A falling down or slipping out of place of an organ or part; a protrusion or herniation.

prolapse of intervertebral disk: See disk herniation.

proliferation: The rapid reproduction of new parts or whole cells or organisms.

PROM: Premature rupture of membranes; passive range of motion.

pronation: The movement of rotating the forearm so that the palm faces downward or backward; the movement of rotating the lateral border of the foot upward. The opposite of supination.

pronator: A muscle that pronates (turns a part backward or downward).

prone: Lying face downward.

prophylactic antibiotics: Antibiotics used for the purpose of preventing infection and disease.

prophylaxis: Prevention.

proprioception: The sense or awareness of position and movement of the body.

proptosis: A downward displacement such as the uterus or the eyeball in exophthalmic goiter or in inflammatory conditions of the orbit.

prostaglandins: A group of fatty acids found in the body, which have a number of biological actions. For example, different prostaglandins cause contraction or relaxation of smooth muscle. Prostaglandins also promote blood clotting by causing platelets to stick together, influence the secretion of various hormones, and are involved in the production of pain and inflammation.

prostate: A gland that surrounds the neck of the bladder and the urethra in males. Its secretion forms part of the seminal fluid.

prosthesis: An artificial body part or organ.

prosthetic: Pertaining to a prosthesis; artificial.

prosthodontist: A dentist specializing in the mechanics of making and fitting artificial teeth.

prostration: Total exhaustion.

protease: An enzyme that catalyzes the breakdown or digestion of proteins.

protein: A complex organic chemical composed of a chain or chains of amino acids. Animal and plant tissues are composed largely of protein.

proteinuria: Protein in the urine.

prothrombin: A substance in the blood that reacts with salts and the enzyme thrombokinase to form thrombin.

prothrombin time (PT): A test of clotting time used to evaluate the effect of administration of anticoagulant drugs.

proton: A positively charged elementary particle found in atomic nuclei. A hydrogen nucleus consists of a single proton.

proton pump inhibitor: A medication to decrease the release of gastric acids; used to heal corrosive gastritis.

protozoan (plural, protozoa): A single-celled organism belonging to the animal kingdom.

protuberance: A part that is prominent beyond a surface, like a knob.

provocation test: See challenge test.

proximal: The opposite of distal; in a direction toward the trunk (e.g., the shoulder is proximal to the elbow; the hip is proximal to the knee). In a direction toward the origin (e.g., the stomach is proximal to the intestine).

proximal hypospadias: A congenital condition where the opening of the urethra is at the penoscrotal junction, between the folds of scrotal skin, or in the perineum or the vagina.

proximal interphalangeal (PIP) joints: The joints between the proximal and middle phalanges of the hand or foot.

pruritus: Itching.

PSA: Prostate specific antigen.

pseudarthrosis: A false joint developing after a fracture fails to unite.

pseudo-: A prefix meaning false.

pseudocyst: An encapsulated collection of fluid, resembling a cyst; however, unlike a cyst, it is not lined with epithelium.

pseudoneurological: Giving a false impression of being neurological in nature. For example, pseudoneurological symptoms (such as numbness, double vision, or amnesia) may occur in some psychiatric disorders without organic neurological impairment.

psoralens: (1) A chemical that increases the skin's sensitivity to the sun; found naturally in celery, parsnips, carrots, and limes. (2) A photochemical reagent used to investigate nucleic acid structure and function.

psychoactive: Affecting the mental state. For example, antidepressants, antipsychotics, anxiolytics, and sedatives are psychoactive drugs.

psychodynamic psychotherapy: Freudian psychoanalysis.

psychogenic: Of mental or psychological origin.

psychomotor: Pertaining to the effect of mental processes on physical activity.

psychomotor retardation: A generalized slowing of physical and mental activity (such as in major depression).

psychopathology: The study of the causes and nature of psychiatric disorders; abnormal behavior or mental processes.

psychopharmacological medication: Medication used in the treatment of psychiatric illnesses.

psychophysical: Pertaining to or having both mental and physical manifestations.

psychosis (plural, psychoses): A category of mental disorders characterized by impaired reality testing and bizarre or disorganized behavior.

psychotherapy: A method of treating disease, especially nervous disorders, by mental means rather than physical.

psychotic: Pertaining to or afflicted with psychosis.

PTCA: Percutaneous transluminal coronary angioplasty.

ptosis: Drooping of a body part or organ (such as the eyelid).

pulmonary: Pertaining to the lungs.

pulmonary artery: The large artery (or either of its major branches) that delivers deoxygenated blood from the right ventricle of the heart to the lungs. The pulmonary trunk (main pulmonary artery) divides into a right and a left pulmonary artery (going to the right and left lungs, respectively). These branch further to the lobes of the lungs.

pulmonary artery wedge (PAW): In cardiac catheterization, the position of the catheter tip is such that it occludes a small branch of the pulmonary artery. Measurements (such as pressure and oxygen content) taken with the catheter in wedge position reflect conditions in the pulmonary capillaries.

pulmonary embolus: An embolus (mass of undissolved material in the bloodstream) that travels to the lungs. Pulmonary emboli commonly result from thrombosis (clotting) in the veins of the lower extremities.

pulmonary hypertension: Abnormally high pressure in the pulmonary circulation (such as due to narrowing of the pulmonary artery or its branches).

pulmonary trunk: The main pulmonary artery that exits from the right ventricle. After traveling a short distance, it divides into a right and a left pulmonary artery.

pulmonary vein: Any of the large veins that deliver oxygenated blood from the lungs to the left atrium of the heart.

pulmonic insufficiency: Pulmonic regurgitation.

pulmonic regurgitation: Incomplete closure of the pulmonic valve resulting in regurgitation (backflow) of blood into the right ventricle.

pulmonic stenosis: Narrowing or constriction of the pulmonic valve.

pulmonic valve: An opening with three flaps or cusps that guards the opening leading from the right ventricle to the pulmonary artery.

pulp: The soft part of an organ or structure (such as the pulp of the fingertip).

pulpitis: Inflammation of the pulp of the tooth.

pulse: The rhythmic expansion and recoil of an arterial wall that can be felt with the hand. The pulse results from the surge of blood that enters the arterial system with each heartbeat.

pulse pressure: The difference between the systolic and diastolic arterial blood pressures.

pupil: The opening in the center of the iris that allows light to enter the eye. The pupil dilates in dim light and constricts in bright light.

purine: The end-products of nucleoprotein digestion. Purines break down into uric acid.

Purkinje fibers: Modified cardiac muscle fibers that form the terminal branches of the cardiac conduction system. The Purkinje fibers emerge from the right and left bundle branches and extend to all parts of the ventricular myocardium. Currently called conduction myofibers. See also bundle branch and cardiac conduction.

purpura: Condition with various manifestations and causes characterized by hemorrhages into the skin, mucous membranes, internal organs, and tissues. Skin hemorrhages are red, darken to purple, then brownish-yellow and disappear in 2 to 3 weeks.

purulent: Forming or containing pus.

pus: A whitish or yellowish liquid composed of proteins and dead white blood cells. It is produced as a result of infection or inflammation.

pustule: A raised area of skin containing pus or clear lymph fluid.

PVD: Peripheral vascular disease.

pyelolithotomy: The removal of a kidney stone from the kidney via an incision through the skin.

pyelonephritis: Inflammation of the kidney and pelvis.

pylorus: The opening of the stomach into the duodenum; the gastric outlet.

pyogenic: Pus-producing.

pyridoxine: Vitamin B6, which is essential for the formation of tryptophan and needed to fully use other amino acids.

pyrogen: A substance or agent that produces fever.

Q wave: In electrocardiography, an initial downward stroke of a QRS complex. On a normal ECG, Q waves are either absent (i.e., the initial stroke of the QRS complex is upward) or insignificant (very small. Significant Q waves are seen in individuals who have had a myocardial infarction. See also QRS complex.

QRS complex: In electrocardiography, the waveform produced by depolarization of the ventricles. The QRS complex is the electrical equivalent of ventricular contraction.

quadriceps: Four-headed, as a quadriceps muscle.

quadriceps femoris: A group of four muscles located in the anterior thigh that merge into a common tendon (see patellar tendon). Quadriceps femoris is an extensor of the knee.

quinsy: Abscess of tonsil capsule due to bacterial inflammation.

RA: Rheumatoid arthritis.

radial: Pertaining to the radius (one of the two long bones of the forearm); located on the radial (thumb) side of the hand, wrist, or forearm. See also ulnar.

radial artery: One of the two large arteries that supply blood to the hand. Its pulsations can be felt on the radial (thumb) side of the wrist. The radial artery is commonly used for taking the pulse. See also ulnar artery.

radial deviation: Movement of the wrist in the direction of the thumb. The opposite of ulnar deviation.

radial nerve: A branch of the brachial plexus; one of the major nerves of the upper extremity.

radial styloid: The styloid process of the radius; a pointed projection of the distal end of the radius.

radiate: To spread from a common center. For example, pain arising in the heart may radiate down the arm.

radical: A term used to describe treatment that is intended to cure, rather than palliate. Extremely invasive; the opposite of conservative. For example, in a radical mastectomy, not only the breast tissue but also the underlying muscle and the regional lymph nodes are removed.

radicular: Pertaining to a root (such as a nerve root).

radicular pain: Pain originating in a nerve root.

radiculitis: Inflammation of spinal nerve roots, accompanied by pain and hyperesthesia.

radiculopathy: Any disorder of a nerve root.

radioactive isotope: An element with greater or fewer neutrons in the nucleus than is typical and is capable of emitting radiation.

radiocarpal joint: The joint between the radius and the carpus; part of the wrist.

radioisotope: A radioactive isotope of a chemical element. See isotope.

radioisotope scan: A diagnostic procedure where the individual is given a small quantity of a radioactive chemical, either orally or intravenously. The chemical is absorbed by the organ or tissue that is being examined (such as bone, myocardium, or thyroid gland). The emitted radioactivity is detected by scintillation cameras, producing an image of the organ. Depending on the type of scan, an abnormality may appear as either a defect ("cold spot") or bright area ("hot spot") in the image.

radionuclide angiography: The use of radioactive isotopes to measure blood flow to heart muscle.

radiopaque: A substance that does not allow x-rays or radiation to travel through.

radioulnar joint: Either of two articulations between the radius and ulna. The proximal radioulnar joint is located near the elbow; the distal radioulnar joint is located near the wrist.

radius: One of the two long bones of the forearm. The radius is located on the lateral (thumb) side of the forearm; the ulna is on the medial (little finger) side.

rales: Abnormal sounds (often described as crackles) heard on stethoscope examination of the lungs. Rales may occur during inspiration and/or expiration.

range of motion (ROM): The range or angle (measured in degrees) through which a joint can be moved.

rate of perceived exertion (RPE): The subjective level of exercise an individual perceives rated on a scale of 1 to 10.

Raynaud's disease: A peripheral vascular disorder characterized by abnormal vasoconstriction of extremities when exposed to cold or emotional stress; most common in females age 18 to 30.

rays: Lines that diverge from a common center. The term is sometimes applied to the metacarpal bones of the hand or the metatarsal bones of the foot.

RBBB: Right bundle branch block.

RBC: Red blood cell.

reactive airway dysfunction syndrome (RADS): An asthma-like disorder characterized by chronic bronchial hyper-reactivity after an initial exposure to smoke, dust, or fumes.

receptor: A molecule on a cell membrane that binds a specific drug, hormone, or neurotransmitter, resulting in altered cellular function; a sensory nerve ending. See also adrenergic receptor.

recruitment: In muscle physiology, the activation of increasing numbers of motor units as the stimulus intensity increases.

rectovesical: pertaining to both bladder and rectum.

rectum: The part of the large intestine between the sigmoid colon and the anus.

recumbent: Lying down.

red blood cell (RBC): A type of blood cell containing hemoglobin. Its main function is to carry oxygen and carbon dioxide.

reducible: Able to be placed back into the normal position.

reduction: Restoration to normal position (e.g., of a fractured bone, a dislocated joint, or a hernia).

referred pain: Pain felt at a site away from its place of origin. For example, angina pectoris (pain originating in the heart) often radiates down the left arm.

reflex: An involuntary response to a stimulus.

reflex arc: The nerve pathway between the sensory receptor and the responding muscle in a reflex.

reflex sympathetic dystrophy: A neurovascular complication of stroke characterized by severe shoulder pain and stiffness and swelling and pain in the hand.

reflux : Backward flow. For example, gastroesophageal reflux refers to backflow of stomach contents into the esophagus.

reflux esophagitis: Inflammation of the esophagus due to reflux of stomach acid.

refractive error: Condition where parallel rays of light are not focused on the retina because of a defect in the shape of the eyeball or in refracting media of the eye.

refractive lensectomy: The use of cataract surgery technology to correct refractive errors in the absence of a cataract.

refractometry: Measurement of refractive power of lenses.

refractory: Resistant to treatment.

regional pain syndrome (RPS): A multisymptom syndrome that results from major nerve damage and can cause chronic pain. Also known as reflex sympathetic dystrophy.

regurgitation: Backward flow (e.g., return of stomach contents to the mouth). Backflow of blood through a defective heart valve. Valvular regurgitation is also referred to as valvular incompetence or insufficiency. See also insufficiency.

rehydration: Restoration of fluid volume in an individual who has been dehydrated.

relapse: Recurrence of a disease or symptoms after apparent recovery.

relaxation training: A technique for teaching relaxation where the individual is instructed first to tense and then to relax one muscle group at a time (usually starting with the feet and progressing toward the head).

REM: Rapid eye movement.

remission: A period of time during which the symptoms of a disease lessen or disappear (usually temporarily).

renal: Pertaining to the kidneys.

renal infarction: Death of kidney tissue due to loss of blood flow.

renal parenchyma: The main part of the kidney involving the functioning portion.

renal tubules: See kidney tubules.

renin: An enzyme secreted by specialized cells in the kidney in response to a variety of stimuli (such as low renal blood flow). Renin catalyzes the formation of angiotensin I, which in turn is converted to angiotensin II, a powerful vasoconstrictor. Angiotensin II also stimulates the adrenal cortex to secrete aldosterone, a hormone that promotes sodium

renovascular: Pertaining to the blood vessels of the kidneys.

repigmentation: The use of a medication, often psoralens, to encourage abnormally white skin to take on coloration.

resection: Surgical removal of part or all of an organ or structure.

resectoscope: An instrument used to remove the prostrate through the urethra.

residual schizophrenia: Blunted or inappropriate affect, social withdrawal, eccentric behavior but without prominent psychotic symptoms, as the remains of former psychotic schizophrenia.

resistance: Opposition or the ability to oppose. The immune system provides resistance to infection. A microorganism may be resistant to certain antibiotics.

respirator: A machine that assists or controls breathing for a prolonged period of time.

respiratory membrane: The cells that line the smallest unit of ventilation (alveolus) in the lungs. This membrane allows oxygen to exit the lungs and enter the blood while carbon dioxide leaves the blood and enters the lungs to be exhaled.

respiratory tract: The airways or organs involved in breathing; includes the nose and mouth, pharynx, larynx, trachea, bronchi, and lungs.

restenosis: Recurrent stenosis or narrowing (i.e., of an artery or heart valve).

retention: See also aldosterone and angiotensin.

reticular: Meshed in the form of a network.

reticulocyte: A red blood cell in an immature stage of development containing a network of granules or filaments.

retina: The innermost layer of the eye. The retina contains light-sensitive receptors (rods and cones) that send nerve impulses via the optic nerve to the brain.

retinopathy: A disorder of the retina.

retrocollis: Spasm in the muscles at the back of the neck, pulling the head backward.

retrograde: Moving backward or against the usual direction of flow.

retrolabyrinthine: Situated behind the labyrinth of the ear.

retro-orbital: Behind the eye socket.

retroperitoneal: Located behind the peritoneum, outside the peritoneal cavity. The kidneys and the pancreas are retroperitoneal organs.

retropubic: Behind the pubic bone.

retrosigmoid: Behind the sigmoid portion of the colon.

revascularization: Restoration of blood vessels by medical or surgical means. For example, in coronary artery disease, the heart may be revascularized by either thrombolytic (clot-dissolving) therapy, coronary balloon angioplasty, or coronary bypass surgery; regrowth of blood vessels (such as during wound healing).

RF: Rheumatoid factor.

rhabdomyolysis: Breakdown of skeletal muscle tissue resulting in the excretion of myoglobin (a muscle protein) in the urine.

rheumatoid arthritis: Form of arthritis with inflammation of the joints, stiffness, swelling, and pain.

rheumatoid factor (RF): An antibody found in the blood of most individuals with rheumatoid arthritis. RF also occurs in other connective tissue diseases.

rheumatology: The branch of internal medicine concerned with inflammatory disorders of the joints, muscles, and connective tissue.

rhinolaryngoscopy: A procedure for visually examining the nasal passages and larynx.

rhinorrhea: Thin watery discharge from the nose.

rhinovirus: Any of a group of viruses causing the common cold.

rhizotomy: Surgical interruption of a root (such as a nerve root).

rhytidectomy: Excision of wrinkles by plastic surgery.

rib cartilage: A cartilage that connects the anterior end of a rib to the sternum; a costal cartilage.

ribonucleic acid (RNA): A complex organic molecule similar to DNA in structure, but with some slightly different components (i.e., RNA contains ribose, a type of sugar; DNA contains deoxyribose, a slightly different sugar). RNA is involved in the synthesis of proteins from the instructions encoded in DNA.

Rickettsia: A genus of microorganisms similar to both bacteria and viruses; causative agents of many diseases and carried by arthropods (lice, fleas, ticks, mites).

right coronary artery: One of the two main arteries that supply the myocardium (heart muscle). The right coronary artery arises from the aorta, just above the aortic valve. It runs in the groove between the right atrium and right ventricle, winding around the right side of the heart to the posterior surface. It supplies blood to the right atrium and right ventricle. See also left main coronary artery.

right lymphatic duct: See lymphatic ducts.

risk factor: A characteristic or occurrence associated with an increased probability that a disorder will later develop. For example, diabetes mellitus, hypertension, and smoking are risk factors for coronary artery disease.

RLQ: Right lower quadrant.

RNA: Ribonucleic acid.

ROM: Range of motion.

root of the aorta: The origin of the aorta, just above the aortic valve.

rotation diet: A controversial type of diet prescribed by clinical ecologists for the treatment of food intolerance in individuals with multiple chemical sensitivity. The offending foods are eaten cyclically at specified intervals (such as once every few days) in order to maintain tolerance.

rotator cuff: A group of four muscles (supraspinatus, infraspinatus, teres minor, and subscapularis) that rotate and stabilize the shoulder joint.

Rubella serology: Tests for presence of antibodies for the Rubella virus.

RUQ: Right upper quadrant.

S1: The first heart sound produced by the closure of the atrioventricular valves. S1 marks the beginning of systole.

S2: The second heart sound produced by the closure of the semilunar valves. S2 marks the beginning of diastole.

S3: A third heart sound sometimes heard in children and young adults, but normally disappearing with age. It is a vibration caused by rapid ventricular filling during early diastole (just after the AV valves open).

S4: A fourth heart sound, almost always abnormal. It is a vibration caused by rapid ventricular filling; it occurs later in diastole (during atrial contraction) than S3.

SA node: Sinoatrial node

Saccharomyces boulardii: A live yeast taken orally used to treat diarrhea.

sacral: Pertaining to the sacrum.

sacral nerves: Five pairs of spinal nerves (S1-S5) that exit from the sacral region of the spinal column.

sacrococcygeal: Pertaining to both the sacrum and coccyx.

sacroiliac: Pertaining to the sacrum and ilium.

sacroiliac joints: The joints between the two hipbones (ilia) and the sacrum.

sacroiliitis: Inflammation of the sacroiliac joints.

sacrum: A triangular-shaped bone of the lower spine (between the fifth lumbar vertebra and the coccyx), composed of five fused vertebral segments. Situated between the hipbones, it forms the posterior wall of the pelvis.

sagittal: Dividing the body (or a body structure) into right and left regions.

saline: A solution of salt (sodium chloride) in water.

Salmonella: A group of bacteria (gram-negative rods), several species of which can cause disease. Some produce a mild gastroenteritis; others may produce a severe form of food poisoning.

salt: A chemical compound consisting of a positive ion (other than hydrogen ion) and a negative ion (other than hydroxyl ion). A chemical compound resulting from the interaction of an acid and a base; sodium chloride.

saphenous nerve: A nerve of the lower leg.

saphenous vein: Either of two major superficial veins of the leg.

sarcoma: Cancer that arises from connective tissue such as muscle or bone; may affect bones, bladder, kidneys, liver, lungs, parotids, and spleen.

scalene muscles: A group of three muscles (anterior, middle, and posterior) located in the side of the neck.

scalenus anterior: The anterior scalene muscle.

scalenus medius: The middle scalene muscle.

scalenus posterior: The posterior scalene muscle.

scaling: Removal of calculus (tartar) from teeth.

scalpel: A small, straight surgical knife with a convex edge and a thin sharp blade.

scapula (plural, scapulae): The shoulder blade; a large, flat, triangular bone that overlies the posterior surface of the ribs, forming part of the shoulder girdle. The upper lateral surface of the scapula articulates with the head of the humerus, forming the shoulder joint.

scapular spine: Part of the rotator cuff; it helps stabilize the shoulder joint.

scapulohumeral: Pertaining to both the scapula and the humerus.

schema: Shape, plane, or outline.

Scheuermann's disease: Juvenile osteochondrosis; a developmental disorder of the spine. See osteochondrosis.

schizophreniform: Resembling or having the characteristics of schizophrenia.

Schwann cells: Cells of ectodermal origin that comprise the neurilemma (thin membranous sheath enveloping a nerve fiber).

sciatic nerve: The largest nerve of the body. It arises from the lumbosacral plexus and runs down the back of the thigh, where it divides into two branches (the tibial and common peroneal nerves).

scintillation: Radioactive emissions.

scintillation camera: An instrument that detects and records radioactive emissions.

sclera: The fibrous outer coat of the eyeball; the white of the eye.

scleral buckle: A strap put in place around the outside of an eyeball to press the choroid layer of the eye toward a piece of detached retina in hopes that it will reattach.

scleral spur: A ridge formed by the sclera near its junction with the cornea, where the iris and ciliary body are attached.

sclerosis: Hardening of an organ or tissues.

scoliosis: Lateral (side-to-side) curvature of the spine.

scotoma: Island-like blind gap in the visual field.

scrape cytology: The study of the shape and function of cells scraped from a body part.

scrotum: The pouch containing the testes.

sebaceous: Pertaining to sebum.

sebaceous cyst: A cyst in the skin resulting from obstruction of the duct of a sebaceous gland.

sebaceous gland: An oil-secreting gland of the skin.

seborrhea: Abnormal increase in the secretion of the sebaceous glands.

seborrheic keratoses: A tumor that is darker than the surrounding skin, benign, and common in the elderly.

sebum: The oily secretion of the sebaceous glands.

secondary: Next in time or order. A term used to characterize a disorder that arises from another disorder. The opposite of primary.

secondary bone cancer: Cancer of the bone that did not originate in bone tissue but metastasized (spread) to that location.

secondary gain: An emotional or material advantage that an individual derives from his or her illness.

secretin: A hormone secreted into the blood by mucosal cells of the duodenum. Secretin stimulates the pancreas to produce the alkaline fluid component of pancreatic juice.

secretion: A substance produced by a gland or glandular cell. The process by which secretions are produced.

sedation: State of being calmed through use of sedatives.

sedative: A drug or agent that has a calming effect; a tranquilizer.

sedimentation rate: See erythrocyte sedimentation rate.

segmental pneumonia: Pneumonia affecting a lobule (segment of a lobe) of the lung.

Seidel's sign: A test used to determine whether a foreign object has perforated the cornea.

seizure: A sudden attack of a disease. An episode of epilepsy. The most common type is a grand mal seizure characterized by loss of consciousness and generalized, involuntary muscle contractions (a convulsion). In contrast, a petit mal seizure is characterized by a transient "absence" of consciousness without convulsive movements.

selective serotonin reuptake inhibitor (SSRI): A type of antidepressant drug that acts by inhibiting the reuptake of serotonin (a brain neurotransmitter) into the nerve terminals. Normally, reuptake serves to remove excess serotonin from the synapses. When reuptake is inhibited, the amount of serotonin available for receptor binding is increased. The resulting increase in serotonin activity produces an antidepressant effect.

self-limited: Having a predictable course with spontaneous recovery.

semen: A fluid consisting of sperm plus the secretions of various glands (including the prostate).

semicircular canals: Three tubular structures, part of the labyrinth of the inner ear, which play an important role in maintaining equilibrium.

semilunar valve: Heart valves found between the heart and the aorta and the heart and the pulmonary vein.

seminal: Pertaining to semen.

seminoma: A testicular tumor.

semipermeable membrane: A membrane that permits the passage of a solvent (such as water), but prevents the passage of a solute (dissolved substance).

sensitivity: (1) Ability to feel a sensation or respond to a stimulus. An index of the value of a diagnostic test. The higher the sensitivity of a test, the smaller the proportion of false negative results. See also specificity. (2) The susceptibility of a bacterial infection to an antibiotic. See also culture.

sensitization: A physiological mechanism where exposure to a chemical substance (such as an allergen) or other stimulus results in hyperreactivity to subsequent exposures.

sensory: Pertaining to sensation.

sensory nerve: A nerve that conducts impulses from sense organs (sensory receptors) to the central nervous system.

sensory seizure: Seizure where an individual experiences odd sensations such as in the form of sounds and smells.

sentinel pile: A small sac-like protrusion of skin that forms at the anal opening. It is part of the anal fissure triad of ulcer, hypertrophic papilla, and sentinel pile.

sepsis: The presence of microorganisms or their products in the bloodstream.

septic: Pertaining to sepsis.

septic fever: Fever due to sepsis.

septicemia: Sepsis.

septoplasty: Plastic surgery of the nasal septum.

septum: A wall or partition that separates two cavities.

sequela: A condition following and resulting from a disease.

sequestered: Isolated. For example, in a herniated disc, disc material that has separated from the main part of the disc is said to be sequestered.

serologic: Pertaining to the serum or the study of serum.

serological: Pertaining to serology.

serology: The branch of laboratory medicine that deals with the detection and measurement of antibodies and antigens in the blood.

serosa: A serous membrane.

serotonin: A brain neurotransmitter involved in the modulation of mood, pain perception, and sleep.

serous: Having the nature of serum (such as, serous fluid; producing a serous secretion (such as a serous membrane).

serous membrane: An epithelial membrane lining closed body cavities and covering the organs contained within those cavities. Serous membranes secrete a watery (serous) fluid. Examples include the pleurae, pericardium, and peritoneum. See also membrane.

serratus anterior: A muscle of the chest wall. It rotates the scapula (as in raising the arm laterally above the head).

serum: (1) The watery portion of blood after clotting has taken place. (2) the fluid secreted by a serous membrane.

serum electrolytes: Electrolytes found in the blood that include sodium, potassium, chloride, and carbon dioxide.

serum enzymes: Enzymes found in the blood that include aspartate transaminase (AST), alanine transaminase (ALT), alkaline phosphatases (ALP), glutamyl transpeptidase (GGT), lactic dehydrogenase (LDH), and amylase.

sesamoid bone: A small bone that develops inside a tendon where the tendon passes over a bony prominence. There are two sesamoid bones (medial and lateral) in the sole of the foot near the metatarsophalangeal joint of the big toe. The largest sesamoid bone in the body is the patella (kneecap), which is embedded in the tendon of the quadriceps femoris muscle.

sesamoiditis: Inflammation of the sesamoid bone.

sessile: A growth attached by a broad base, not a stem.

sexually transmitted disease (STD): Disease acquired as a result of sexual intercourse with an infected individual.

Shigella: A gram-negative rod with many species that cause mild GI upset to life-threatening dysentery.

Shigella flexneri: Bacterial organism responsible for acute diarrhea in humans.

Shigella sonnei: Bacterial organism that is a frequent cause of bacillary dysentery.

shigellosis: Disease caused by infection with Shigella.

shock: (1) Failure of the circulatory system to maintain adequate blood flow to vital organs; circulatory insufficiency. Signs and symptoms include hypotension; weak, rapid pulse; cold, clammy skin (in hypovolemic or cardiogenic shock); and mental confusion. (2) The passage through the body of an externally generated electrical current; electrical shock. (3) A sudden disturbance of mental equilibrium; emotional shock.

shoulder abduction: Movement of the arm away from the body at the shoulder joint.

shoulder external rotation: Rotation of the arm at the shoulder so that the elbow points inward.

shoulder girdle: The bony structure that supports the upper extremities; composed of the scapulae (shoulder blades) and clavicles (collar bones).

shoulder internal rotation: Rotation of the arm at the shoulder so that the elbow points outward.

shunt: An abnormal or artificially constructed passageway that diverts flow (i.e., of blood) from one region to another.

shunting: The movement of blood through an abnormal passageway in the heart.

sicca syndrome: A syndrome of dry eyes and dry mouth. It may occur alone or in association with connective tissue diseases.

sick sinus syndrome: Dysfunction of the sinus node of the heart, resulting in a variety of atrial arrhythmias. There may be alternating periods of bradycardia and tachycardia.

siderocyte: A red blood cell that contains iron in a form other than hematin.

sigmoid: Pertaining to the sigmoid flexure of the colon.

sigmoid colon: The S-shaped part of the colon just above the rectum.

sigmoidoscope: An endoscope for examining the sigmoid colon and rectum.

sign: An objective manifestation, usually indicative of a disease or disorder. Signs can be observed by the clinician, as opposed to symptoms, which are perceived only by the affected individual. See also symptom, objective, and subjective.

silent ischemia: Myocardial ischemia (insufficient blood supply to the heart muscle) that occurs without symptoms.

silicone: Any of a group of semiorganic compounds where carbon has been replaced by the chemical element silicon. Silicone is commonly used in prosthetic body parts (such as breast implants).

silver almalgam (alloy): An alloy (mixture) of silver with varying amounts of tin or copper, using mercury as a major component; used in dentistry to fill cavities.

single photon emission computed tomography (SPECT): A type of imaging accomplished by administering a radioisotope that emits gamma rays. The gamma rays are detected by cameras rotated around the individual, and are interpreted by a computer to form tomograms (images of selected body planes or "slices"). This decreases interference from overlapping organs, thereby producing clearer images than conventional radioisotope scans.

sinoatrial (SA) node: See sinus node.

sinoatrial block: Refers to blockage of conduction through the sinoatrial node of the stimulus for the heart to beat.

sinus: A cavity or channel. A cavity within a bone (such as the sinuses of the skull); a widened venous channel (such as the coronary sinus).

sinus bradycardia: A slow heart rate (less than 60 beats per minute) resulting from slow firing of the sinus node.

sinus node: A mass of specialized tissue located in the upper part of the right atrium of the heart; also called the sinoatrial (SA) node. The sinus node is the heart's natural pacemaker; it generates electrical impulses that spread throughout the heart, causing the heart muscle to contract. See also cardiac conduction.

sinus rhythm: Cardiac rhythm generated by the sinus node.

sinus tachycardia: A rapid heart rate (greater than 100 beats per minute) resulting from rapid firing of the sinus node.

sinus tarsi: A channel between the talus and calcaneus formed by opposing grooves on each bone.

sinusoid: Resembling a sinus. A microscopic blood vessel, slightly larger than a capillary (such as the sinusoids of the liver).

sinusoidal: Pertaining to a sinusoid.

sitz bath: A bath to sit in with water at hip level. The water may contain medication.

skeletal muscle: A type of muscle attached to the skeleton (except for a few facial muscles); voluntary muscle. See also muscle.

SLE: Systemic lupus erythematosus.

sleep apnea: The condition where breathing stops repeatedly during sleep, enough to cause the oxygen content of the blood to decrease, or that lasts for more than 10 seconds or occurs more than 30 times nightly.

small bowel barium x-ray: A radiologic study that involves the ingestion of barium; used to diagnose conditions of the small bowel.

small intestine: The portion of the gastrointestinal tract between the stomach and the colon (large intestine). The duodenum, jejunum, and ileum are the three parts of the small intestine.

small saphenous vein: A superficial vein that runs along the lateral side of the foot and up the back of the calf. Behind the knee, it penetrates to join the popliteal vein. Also called the short saphenous vein.

SMAS (superficial muscular aponeurotic system): A matrix of connective tissue and fat in continuity with the platysma muscle and muscles of the face.

smooth muscle: A type of muscle found primarily in blood vessels and in hollow organs such as the digestive tract; involuntary muscle. See also muscle.

sodium: A metallic chemical element (atomic number 11) denoted by the symbol Na (from Latin, natrium). It is found in ionized form in body fluids and tissues, and is one of the principal cations (positive ions) of the body. It is essential for many body processes including muscle function, nerve conduction, and fluid and electrolyte balance. Common table salt is composed of sodium chloride.

soleus: A muscle located in the posterior calf that plantar flexes the ankle. It joins the gastrocnemius muscle to form a common tendon, the Achilles tendon.

solubility: The degree to which a substance dissolves in another substance (usually a liquid).

solute: A substance that is dissolved in another substance. Usually, the solute is the component of a solution that is of lesser quantity. See also solution.

solution: A homogeneous mixture of one or more substances (solutes) whose molecules are dispersed in another substance (solvent). The solvent is usually a liquid (such as water); however, any of the components of a solution may be solids, liquids, or gases. See also solute and solvent.

solvent: A substance in which another substance is dissolved. Usually, the solvent is the component of a solution that is of greatest quantity. See also solution.

sound: (1) Auditory sensations produced by vibrations. (2) Not diseased. (3) Instrument used to explore a cavity or canal.

spasm: A sustained, involuntary muscle contraction. Spasms can occur in either skeletal muscle or smooth muscle (such as a blood vessel spasm).

spastic: Characterized by or produced by spasms or by abnormally increased muscle tone.

spasticity: Abnormally increased muscle tone.

specificity: An index of the value of a diagnostic test. The higher the specificity of a test, the smaller the proportion of false positive results. See also sensitivity.

SPECT: Single photon emission computed tomography.

speculum: An instrument for examination of a canal (such as an anoscope or a vaginal speculum).

spermatic cord: A cord-like structure from which the testis is suspended. It contains veins, arteries, nerves, and the vas deferens.

spermatocele: A cyst of epididymis containing spermatozoa.

spermatozoon (plural, spermatozoa): Sperm.

spherocyte: A red blood cell that assumes a spheroid shape.

sphincter: A circular muscle constricting an orifice. The muscle must relax to allow the orifice to open.

sphincter of Oddi: Smooth muscle fibers surrounding the lower end of the common bile duct and the ampulla of Vater (the common termination of the bile and pancreatic ducts in the duodenal wall). Currently called the sphincter of the hepatopancreatic ampulla.

sphincterotomy: Surgical incision of a sphincter.

sphygmomanometer: An instrument for measuring arterial blood pressure.

spicule: A small, needle-shaped projection or fragment (i.e., of bone).

spinal canal: The tube-like space within the vertebral column that contains the spinal cord.

spinal cord: A column of nervous tissue extending from the base of the skull to the lumbar region of the spine; part of the central nervous system. It serves as a pathway between the brain and the peripheral nervous system. It is also a center for simple reflexes.

spinal nerve: Any of the 31 pairs of nerves that emerge from the spinal cord.

spinal reflex: A reflex where an incoming sensory impulse is switched in the spinal cord to an outgoing motor impulse. Since the reflex arc (pathway) does not involve the brain, spinal reflexes are literally "brainless" responses.

spinal shock: An acute condition that results when the spinal cord is severed and characterized by total sensory loss, flaccid paralysis, and loss of reflexes below the level of the lesion. Over a period of days or weeks, the flaccid paralysis is replaced by spastic paralysis, and the reflexes become hyperactive.

spine: The vertebral column. A bony ridge on the posterior surface of the scapula (the scapular spine).

spinothalamic tracts: Tracts of fibers in the spinal cord that carry pain and temperature sensation to the brain.

spinous process: The bony projection that extends backward from the vertebral arch; the most posterior part of a vertebra.

spirochete: Any member of a group of motile, spiral-shaped bacteria. Syphilis is caused by a spirochete.

spirometry: Measurement of the air capacity of the lungs.

spleen: A lymphoid organ located in the left upper abdomen. Its functions are to filter the blood and to store blood; it can also produce certain white blood cells (lymphocytes and monocytes) if the bone marrow is damaged.

splenic: Pertaining to the spleen.

spontaneous: Occurring without assistance or without apparent cause.

spontaneous abortion: Termination of pregnancy without apparent cause; miscarriage.

spontaneous reduction: Reduction of a fracture or dislocation that occurs without assistance.

sporadic: Occurring occasionally or in scattered instances.

spore: A reproductive cell, usually a single cell, produced by plants for reproduction and by some bacteria for defense. Spores produced by bacteria possess a thick cell wall and can withstand harsh environments.

sports medicine specialist: A physician specializing in the treatment of sports-related injuries and conditions.

sprain: A joint injury where a ligament is stretched or torn.

spreading phenomenon: A feature of multiple chemical sensitivity where sensitization to a specific substance is followed by cross-sensitization to multiple, chemically unrelated substances.

spur: A sharp or pointed outgrowth (i.e., of bone).

sputum: Matter expelled from the respiratory tract by coughing or clearing the throat.

squamous: Scale-like.

squamous epithelium: Epithelial tissue composed of a layer or layers of flat, scale-like cells. The skin is a squamous epithelium.

SSRI: Selective serotonin reuptake inhibitor.

ST segment: In electrocardiography, the segment between the QRS complex and the T wave. The ST segment normally is flat and coincides with the baseline. Depression of the ST segment below the baseline or elevation above the baseline is abnormal.

stabilization: Fixation of a fixed or partial denture so that it will not be displaced.

stage: Refers to how far a disease has advanced.

staging: Evaluation to determine the degree of spread of a cancer.

stapes: One of the three ossicles (small bones) of the middle ear that helps conduct sound to the inner ear. Also called the "stirrup."

Staphylococcus: Any of a group of gram-positive cocci (spherical bacteria) occurring in clusters. Staphylococci are commonly present on skin and mucous membranes. Some species, such as Staphylococcus epidermidis, are ordinarily harmless. Others (such as Staphylococcus aureus) may cause disease, including skin and soft tissue infections (boils and abscesses) and food poisoning.

Starling's law of the heart: The greater the length of cardiac muscle fibers (i.e., the more the fibers are stretched), the greater their force of contraction.

stasis: Stagnation of flow of a body fluid. For example, venous stasis refers to the pooling of blood in the veins (usually of the lower extremities). Venous stasis may result in skin changes (stasis dermatitis) or even ulceration (stasis ulcers).

stasis pigmentation: Discoloration of the legs seen in syndromes where blood is allowed to pool in the legs.

status epilepticus: Seizures resistant to medical treatment.

steatorrhea: Fatty stools. Steatorrhea results from malabsorption of fats (such as in disorders of the pancreas or small intestine).

stellate ganglion: A ganglion (cluster of neuron cell bodies) of the sympathetic nervous system located in the neck near the vertebral column. There are two stellate ganglia, one on each side.

stem cell: A cell in the bone marrow capable of giving rise to all types of blood cells.

stenosis: Narrowing or constriction of an opening or passageway.

stenotic: Narrowed; constricted.

stent: A device used to hold tissue in place or to support a graft or anastomosis (such as a blood vessel or duct) during healing.

stereotactic biopsy: Biopsy performed using stereotactic apparatus. Stereotactic apparatus is used to stabilize the instruments for greater precision.

stereotactic neurosurgery: Neurosurgery performed with the use of a stereotactic apparatus. Stereotactic apparatus is used to stabilize the instruments for greater precision.

sterile: (1) Free from living microorganisms. (2) Not fertile, unable to produce young.

sterile technique: Practices employed during surgical or other invasive procedures to prevent contamination of the body by microorganisms.

sternoclavicular: Pertaining to both the sternum and the clavicle.

sternoclavicular joint: The joint between the medial end of the clavicle and the upper portion of the sternum.

sternocleidomastoid: A muscle of the neck that originates on the sternum and clavicle and inserts on the mastoid process (the bony prominence behind the ear).

sternum: The breastbone.

steroids: A group of lipids (fatty substances) with a molecular structure based on a 17-carbon atom ring. The group includes cholesterol, bile acids, vitamin D, corticosteroids (adrenal cortex hormones), sex hormones, and certain carcinogenic hydrocarbons.

stethoscope: An instrument used for auscultation (listening to sounds within the body).

Stevens-Johnson syndrome: A macular eruption with dark red papules or tubercles usually on the extremities.

stillborn: Dead at birth.

stimulant: Any drug or agent that temporarily increases activity. Stimulants may be classified according to the organ on which they act (such as cardiac stimulants or central nervous system stimulants).

stimulus: Anything that causes a response in a cell, tissue, or organism.

stoma: A mouth or small opening. A surgically created opening between two body cavities or tubes, or between a cavity or tube and the surface of the body.

stomach: A sac-like, distensible organ of the digestive tract located between the esophagus and the duodenum. The stomach lining secretes hydrochloric acid and digestive enzymes that assist in breaking down food.

stomatitis: Inflammation of the mouth.

stone: A concretion of hardened organic and/or mineral matter that may form in a hollow organ (such as a gallstone or kidney stone). Also called calculus.

stool: A bowel movement or the product of a bowel movement.

stool osmolality: The density of feces; the amount of solid dissolved per unit of liquid feces.

strain: An injury caused by overstretching or tearing a muscle or tendon. A ruptured muscle or tendon represents the most severe degree of strain.

strangulation: Constriction, so as to cut off blood supply to the constricted part (such as a strangulated hernia).

Streptococci: Plural of streptococcus.

Streptococcus: Any of a group of gram-positive cocci (spherical bacteria) occurring in chains. Some species of streptococci are ordinarily harmless; others cause disease (such as strep throat).

streptomycin profusion: A destructive treatment for Ménière's disease that involves the instilling of streptomycin into the inner ear.

stress: The effect produced when an organism is acted upon by forces (physical or psychological) that tend to disrupt its equilibrium. A certain amount of stress is necessary for well-being; however, excessive stress can result in disease.

stress EKG: Stress electrocardiography.

stress fracture: A fine hairline fracture that appears without evidence of soft tissue damage.

stress x-rays: X-rays taken while a joint is being stressed (i.e., while a force is being applied to the joint) in order to detect mechanical instability (excessive, abnormal joint movement).

striated muscle: Muscle composed of fibers that appear striated (striped) under the microscope. The striations result from the arrangement of proteins that make up the fibers. Skeletal and cardiac muscle are striated; smooth muscle is not.

stricture: A narrowing or constriction of a tubular or hollow organ (such as the esophagus or the urethra).

stridor: A high pitched, "crowing" sound made when breathing is difficult due to a partially obstructed airway.

stroke: Sudden loss of consciousness that may be accompanied by paralysis as a result of blockage of blood flow to the brain or bleeding within the brain.

stroke volume: The volume of blood ejected from the heart during systole (the phase of cardiac contraction), i.e., the amount of blood pumped with each heartbeat.

structural: Pertaining to structure; anatomical. The opposite of functional.

strychnine: A poisonous substance derived from a tree (Strychnos nux-vomica) native to India. It acts by exciting the central nervous system and is used as a rat poison.

stump: The end of a limb (or other structure) remaining after amputation.

stupor: A state of unconsciousness with no awareness of surroundings or stimuli.

styloid: Resembling a stylus (pointed instrument); pointed.

styloid process: A pointed projection of bone.

sub-: Prefix meaning under or beneath.

subacromial bursa: A bursa (synovial sac) located near the shoulder joint, beneath the acromion of the scapula.

subaortic: Located beneath the aorta or aortic valve.

subarachnoid: Below or under the arachnoid membrane and the pia mater of the covering of the brain.

subarachnoid space: The space between the arachnoid and pia. The subarachnoid space contains cerebrospinal fluid. See also meninges.

subclavian: Under the clavicle (collarbone).

subclavian artery: The stem artery of the upper extremity. Extending outward from the base of the neck, it passes underneath the clavicle and continues through the shoulder/armpit region as the axillary artery. In addition to supplying the upper extremity, the subclavian artery sends branches to parts of the head, neck, and chest wall.

subclavian vein: The major vein (the continuation of the axillary vein) that receives blood from the upper extremity. Accompanying the subclavian artery, it passes underneath the clavicle and merges with the internal jugular vein at the base of the neck to form the brachiocephalic vein.

subcoracoid bursa: A bursa (synovial sac) located near the shoulder joint, beneath the coracoid process of the scapula.

subcutaneous: Under the skin. Subcutaneous tissue consists mostly of connective tissue, including fat and fibrous tissue.

subcutaneous abscess: A collection of fluid under the skin.

subdeltoid bursa: A bursa (synovial sac) located near the shoulder joint, beneath the deltoid muscle.

subdural: Beneath the dura (the outer layer of the meninges); between the dura and the arachnoid membrane.

subendocardial: Beneath the endocardium (lining of the heart).

subgingival curettage: Scraping beneath the gingiva.

subjective: Experienced only by the affected individual and not perceptible to an observer. The opposite of objective. A symptom is subjective; a sign is objective.

sublingual: Under the tongue.

subluxation: (1) Partial or incomplete dislocation of a joint where the articular surfaces are still partially in contact. Subluxation of a joint may be followed by spontaneous reduction. (2) Partial displacement of a tendon from its normal position.

submucosa: The layer of connective tissue beneath a mucous membrane.

submucous fibroid: A uterine fibroid located immediately beneath the endometrium.

submucous resection: Removal of tissue below the mucosa, especially removal of cartilaginous tissue beneath the mucosal tissue of the nose.

subscapular bursa: A bursa (synovial sac) located near the shoulder joint, beneath the scapula. It usually communicates with the joint cavity.

subscapularis: A muscle located on the anterior surface of the scapula; one of the four muscles that make up the rotator cuff.

subserous: Beneath a serous membrane.

subserous fibroid: A uterine fibroid immediately beneath the outer surface of the uterus.

substance P: A peptide (short chain of amino acids) present in certain endocrine cells of the gastrointestinal tract and in nerve cells.

Substance P increases the contraction of gastrointestinal smooth muscle and is also a powerful vasodilator. It functions not only as an intestinal hormone, but also as an inflammatory mediator, and as a neurotransmitter (especially in the transmission of pain sensations).

substernal: Located beneath the sternum (breastbone).

subtalar: Beneath the talus.

subtalar joint: The joint between the talus and calcaneus (heel bone).

subungual: Beneath a fingernail or toenail.

subungual hematoma: A collection of blood under a nail as a result of trauma.

sucralfate: A drug containing a sucrose-aluminum combination that lays a protective covering over a gastric ulcer to encourage healing.

superinfection: A secondary infection caused by a microorganism different from the one that caused the primary infection. A superinfection is usually resistant to the treatment given for the primary infection.

superior: Above; higher in location (such as the superior surface of a structure is its upper surface). The opposite of inferior.

supination: The movement of rotating the forearm so that the palm faces upward or forward. The movement of rotating the medial border of the foot upward. The opposite of pronation.

supinator: A muscle that supinates.

supine: Lying face upward.

supportive treatment: (1) Treatment directed toward stabilization of the individual's condition or toward maintaining stability. (2) Treatment of conditions as they occur, including a any symptoms that are distressing.

suppository: A semisolid substance (usually containing medication) for introduction into the rectum or vagina, where it dissolves.

suppressor T-cell: A suppressor T-lymphocyte. See lymphocyte.

suppressor T-lymphocyte: See lymphocyte.

suppuration: Production of pus.

suppurative: Producing or characterized by pus.

supracondylar: Above the condyles of a long bone.

suprapatellar pouch: An extension of the synovial joint cavity of the knee, upward above the patella between the patellar tendon and the femur.

suprapubic: Pertaining to the area above the pubic bone.

suprarenal: Located above the kidneys. Pertaining to the adrenal glands (that are located on top of the kidneys).

suprascapular: Above the scapula.

suprascapular nerve: A branch of the brachial plexus; the nerve that supplies the supraspinatus and infraspinatus muscles of the rotator cuff.

supraspinatus: A muscle located on the posterior surface of the scapula, above the spine of the shoulder blade

supraventricular: Pertaining to or originating in the portion of the heart above the ventricles. For example, a supraventricular arrhythmia is one that originates in the atria, the atrioventricular (AV) node, or the atrioventricular bundle (bundle of His).

surgical staging: The process of using surgery to examine the extent of a disease for staging purposes.

sustentaculum tali: A shelf-like projection on the medial side of the calcaneus (heel bone); its upper surface carries a facet (the middle talocalcaneal facet) for articulation with the talus.

suture: (1) A thread, wire, or other material used to stitch parts of the body together (such as to close a laceration or a surgical wound). (2) To unite by stitching. (3) An immovable joint between two bones (such as in the skull); a synarthrosis.

sympathetic: Pertaining to the sympathetic nervous system.

sympathetic ganglion: A ganglion (cluster of nerve cell bodies) of the sympathetic nervous system. The sympathetic ganglia are located alongside the vertebral column, forming a chain of ganglia on each side of the spine. See also ganglion.

sympathetic nervous system: The division of the autonomic nervous system concerned with the body's response to stress (the "fight or flight" response). The effects of sympathetic stimulation are opposite to those of the parasympathetic nervous system. They include an increase in heart rate and blood pressure, increased blood flow to skeletal muscles (due to dilation of blood vessels), decreased blood flow to skin and digestive tract (due to constriction of blood vessels), sweating, bronchodilation, and dilation of the pupils. See also autonomic nervous system and parasympathetic nervous system.

sympathetic trunks: Two chains of sympathetic ganglia, one on each side of the spinal column.

symptom: A subjective manifestation, usually indicative of a disease or disorder. Symptoms are experienced only by the individual, as opposed to signs, which can be observed by others. See also sign, objective, and subjective.

symptomatic: Treatment aimed at the relief of symptoms.

synapse: The point of junction between two neurons in a neural pathway, (i.e., between the axon of one neuron and the cell body or dendrite of another neuron).

synarthrosis: An immovable joint where the bones are connected by fibrous tissue.

syncope: Transient loss of consciousness due to decreased blood flow to the brain; fainting.

syncytium: A mass of merged cells with multiple nuclei, but without intervening cell membranes.

syndactylism: A condition where two or more toes or fingers are fused together.

syndesmosis: A type of non-synovial joint where the bones are united by intervening fibrous tissue (such as the tibiofibular syndesmosis, just above the ankle joint). See also synovial joint.

syndrome: A group of signs and symptoms that occur together and are related to each other, but that do not indicate a specific cause of illness. For example, the signs and symptoms of carpal tunnel syndrome are all related to compression of the median nerve; however, there are several possible causes of compression, including trauma, inflammatory disease, and tumor.

syndrome X: Myocardial ischemia (insufficient blood supply to the heart muscle) in an individual with normal coronary arteries (i.e., no coronary artery disease or coronary spasm). Syndrome X is believed to be caused by disease of the smaller (microscopic) coronary blood vessels.

syngeneic: Term that describes individuals or cells that do not have detectable tissue incompatibility.

synovial cyst: A cyst developing on a tendon (such as at the wrist). Also called a ganglion.

synovial fluid: A clear lubricating fluid secreted by a synovial membrane.

synovial joint: A type of joint that contains a joint cavity lined with synovial membrane. Synovial joints permit relatively free movement.

synovial membrane: A connective tissue membrane that lines joint cavities, bursae, and tendon sheaths. Synovial membranes secrete a

lubricating fluid (synovial fluid). See also membrane.

synovial tissue: The tissue inside the joint space that secretes synovial fluid.

synovium: A synovial membrane.

synthesis: The formation of a complex substance from simpler compounds or elements.

synthetic: Manufactured; not of natural origin (such as a synthetic drug).

synthetic bone substitute: A manufactured substance used to replace lost bone tissue.

synthetic patch: A patch made of synthetic material (such as a patch used to repair a ruptured blood vessel).

syringobulbia: The formation of cavities in the brainstem; often accompanied by syringomyelia. The condition may be congenital or it may be associated with trauma or a tumor.

syrinx: An abnormal cavity in the spinal cord or brain, as in syringomyelia/syringobulbia.

systemic: Involving the whole body; not localized.

systemic circulation: The circulation of blood through all parts of the body, excluding the pulmonary circulation. The systemic circuit goes from the left ventricle to the right atrium; the pulmonary circuit goes from the right ventricle to the left atrium.

systole: The phase of the cardiac cycle where the heart chambers contract, ejecting blood. The term usually refers to the ventricles, but may also refer to the atria. Systole alternates with diastole, the phase during which the chambers relax and fill with blood. Systolic pertains to or occurs during systole.

systolic blood pressure: The pressure in the arteries during the systolic phase of the cardiac cycle. For example, when the blood pressure is 120/80, the systolic pressure is 120. See also diastolic blood pressure.

systolic hypertension: Abnormal elevation of the systolic arterial pressure. See blood pressure.

T wave: In electrocardiography, the wave produced by repolarization of the ventricles. See also depolarization.

tabes dorsalis: A gradual wasting caused by sclerosis of the posterior columns of the spinal cord.

tachyarrhythmia: An irregular heart rhythm combined with an abnormally rapid rate.

tachycardia: A rapid heart rate (more than 100 beats per minute in an adult). Tachycardia occurs normally during exercise; however, in a resting individual, it is considered abnormal.

tachypnea: Rapid breathing.

talar: Pertaining to the talus (the bone that acts as the pivot of the ankle).

talar dome: The dome-shaped upper articular surface of the talus.

talectomy: Surgical removal of all or part of the talus.

talocalcaneal: Pertaining to both the talus (ankle pivot) and calcaneus (heel bone).

talocalcaneal joint: The joint between the talus and calcaneus (heel bone). It consists of three articulations (anterior, middle, and posterior).

talofibular ligaments: Two ligaments (anterior and posterior) that connect the fibula and the talus at the ankle joint.

talonavicular joint: The joint between the talus and the navicular bone of the foot.

talus: The uppermost of the seven tarsal bones of the foot; the pivot of the ankle joint. Also called astragalus.

tamponade: Compression resulting from elevated pressure. For example, cardiac tamponade (compression of the heart) results when a large amount of fluid accumulates in the pericardium (the membranous sac around the heart).

tardive dyskinesia: Characterized by slow, rhythmic, stereotypic movements that may be generalized or in single muscle groups; may result from use of certain psychotropic drugs.

tarsal: Pertaining to the ankle or tarsus.

tarsal bones: The seven bones that form the hindfoot (calcaneus and talus) and the midfoot (the navicular, cuboid, and cuneiform bones).

tarsal tunnel: A compartment in the ankle bounded by bone and fibrous tissue. The flexor tendons and the tibial nerve pass through the tarsal tunnel on their way to the foot.

tarsal tunnel syndrome: A syndrome of foot pain, paresthesia, numbness, and/or weakness caused by compression of the tibial nerve in the tarsal tunnel.

tarsometatarsal (TMT) joints: The joints between the tarsal and metatarsal bones of the foot.

tarsorrhaphy: A procedure that unites the edges of the lids at the outer edge in order to the reduce the width of the palpebral fissure.

tarsus: The seven metatarsal bones.

T-cell: A T-lymphocyte. See lymphocyte.

TDS: Time-dependent sensitization.

technetium: A metallic chemical element (atomic number 43) denoted by the symbol Tc. Technetium is used in a wide variety of radioisotope scans. For example, technetium pyrophosphate is used to detect myocardial infarction.

telangiectasia: An area of skin reddened due to the dilation of capillaries and terminal arteries near the surface of the skin.

telescoping: The withdrawal of a portion of a tube into the neighboring segment.

temporal bone: A bone on either side of the skull. The inner ear is enclosed in the temporal bone; behind the ear cavity is the mastoid process.

temporal lobectomy: Removal of the temporal lobe of the brain.

temporal lobes: Two areas of the brain located on each side of the cerebrum. The part of the brain responsible for understanding language is located in the temporal lobe, usually the left temporal lobe.

temporomandibular joints (TMJ): The joints between the mandible (lower jawbone) and the temporal bones of the skull.

tender point: A localized area in muscle or associated connective tissue that produces local pain when pressure is applied to it. Tender points are not palpable (cannot be felt by the examiner), but occur in predictable locations in individuals with fibromyalgia. Compare with trigger point.

tenderness: Pain evoked by touch or pressure.

tendon: Fibrous tissue that connects a muscle to a bone or other structure.

tendon sheath: A membrane lined with synovium that surrounds certain tendons (such as in the hand or foot), allowing the tendons to glide smoothly during movement.

tenesmus: Spasms of the anal or bladder sphincters causing pain, the desire to empty bowel or bladder, and involuntary straining.

Tenon's granulomas: Granulomas that form on Tenon's capsule, a thin layer of connective tissue between the conjunctiva and sclera.

tenosynovectomy: Surgical removal of tendon sheath.

tenosynovitis: Inflammation of a tendon sheath.

tenotomy: Surgical cutting of a tendon.

T.E.N.S.: Transcutaneous electrical nerve stimulation.

tension headache: Headache caused by sustained tension of the muscles of the face, neck, and scalp.

teratoma: A tumor containing embryonic tissues such as teeth or hair.

teres major: A muscle of the shoulder girdle that medially rotates and adducts the arm.

teres minor: A muscle of the shoulder girdle that laterally rotates the arm. One of the four muscles of the rotator cuff.

term: A definite period of duration (such as the nine months of pregnancy).

testes: See testis.

testis (plural, testes): The reproductive glands of the male; the testicles. Located in the scrotum, they secrete male sex hormones and also produce the sperm.

testosterone: A male sex hormone secreted by the testes.

tetany: A condition of increased muscle and nerve irritability, often resulting from hypocalcemia (low blood calcium) or alkalosis (excessive alkalinity of body fluids). It is characterized by intermittent painful muscle spasms, usually of the extremities. The term may also be applied to the generalized, painful muscle contractions caused by certain central nervous system poisons (such as strychnine or tetanus toxin).

TFCC: Triangular fibrocartilage complex.

thalamus: A part of the brain located deep inside the cerebral hemispheres. It functions as a relay center for sensory stimuli and plays an important role in the perception of pain. It is also concerned with the integration of voluntary movements.

thallium: A metallic chemical element (atomic number 81) denoted by the symbol Tl. Thallium is used in radioisotope scans of the myocardium.

thenar: Pertaining to the fleshy area at the base of the thumb.

thenar eminence: The fleshy area of the palm at the base of the thumb.

therapeutic: Pertaining to therapy (treatment); having a healing effect.

therapy: Treatment.

thermography: An imaging technique that maps variations in the body's surface temperature, using either infrared cameras or liquid crystals that change color in response to temperature. The surface temperature of a given body part depends on the amount of local blood flow to the skin. Normally, this is the same on both sides of the body. An asymmetrical thermogram is a sign of either increased or decreased blood flow on one side.

thiamine: Vitamin B1 has an important part in the metabolism of carbohydrates and is essential for normal digestion, appetite, and nervous tissue functioning.

third spacing: Abnormal accumulation of body fluid that is unavailable for circulation, but remains inside the body. Normally there are two "compartments" for body fluid - intracellular (inside cells) and extracellular (inside blood vessels). These two compartments are in equilibrium with each other; fluid can pass back and forth between them freely. However, in certain disease states, large amounts of fluid may accumulate in "third spaces," such as the peritoneal cavity (ascites), the retroperitoneal space, or inside an obstructed loop of bowel. Because this fluid is unavailable for circulation, third spacing may lead to dehydration and hypovolemic shock.

thoracic: Pertaining to the chest (thorax).

thoracic aorta: The part of the descending aorta located in the chest (above the diaphragm).

thoracic cavity: The body cavity located above the diaphragm that contains the heart and lungs; the chest cavity.

thoracic duct: See lymphatic duct.

thoracic nerves: The twelve pairs of spinal nerves (T1-T12) that exit from the vertebral column in the thoracic region.

thoracolumbar: Pertaining to both the thoracic and lumbar regions (i.e., of the spine).

thoracolumbar disc: The intervertebral disc between the twelfth thoracic vertebra (T12) and the first lumbar vertebra (L1).

thorax: The part of the body between the neck and the diaphragm; the chest.

three-vessel disease: Coronary artery disease involving three major coronary arteries (i.e., the left anterior descending, left circumflex, and right coronary arteries).

thrombus: A blood clot that obstructs a blood vessel or a cavity of the heart.

thrombotic occlusion : A clot in a blood vessel that blocks the flow of blood.

thrombocyte: A platelet.

thromboembolism: Obstruction of a blood vessel by a clot carried downstream in the blood. See also embolism.

thrombolysis: The breakup or dissolution of blood clots.

thrombolytic: Pertaining to or causing the breakup of blood clots; clot-dissolving. A drug or agent that dissolves clots.

thrombosis: The formation of clots within the blood vessels.

thrombus (plural, thrombi): A clot that forms within a blood vessel.

thrush: Candidiasis of the oral mucous membranes; a yeast infection of the mouth.

thymoma: Tumor of the thymus.

thymus: A lymphoid organ located in the chest just below the neck. The thymus plays an essential role in the maturation of T-lymphocytes. It attains its largest size by puberty, after which it is gradually replaced by connective tissue.

thyroid: The thyroid gland is an endocrine gland located in the front of the neck. The thyroid secretes thyroid hormones that regulate the body's metabolic rate.

thyroid cartilage: The largest cartilage of the larynx that forms the Adam's apple.

thyroid function test: Tests for evidence of increased or decreased thyroid function.

thyroid gland: An endocrine gland located in the front of the neck. It secretes hormones that regulate the body's rate of metabolism.

thyrotoxicosis: Toxic condition caused by hyperactivity of the thyroid gland.

TIA: Transient ischemic attack.

tibia: One of the two long bones of the lower leg; the shinbone. The tibia is located on the medial side of the leg, the fibula on the lateral side.

tibial nerve: A branch of the sciatic nerve.

tibial plafond: Part of the articular surface of the distal tibia that forms the top of the ankle mortise (the medial and lateral malleoli form the sides).

tibial tubercle: The tibial tuberosity.

tibial tuberosity: A prominence on the front of the tibia, just below the knee; the point of attachment of the patellar ligament.

tibialis anterior: A muscle located in the front of the lower leg that dorsiflexes the ankle.

tibialis posterior: A muscle located deep inside the calf that inverts the foot.

tibiocalcaneal: Pertaining to both the tibia and the calcaneus.

tibiofibular: Pertaining to both the tibia and fibula.

tibionavicular: Pertaining to both the tibia and the navicular bone.

tibiotalar: Pertaining to both the tibia and the talus.

tic: An involuntary muscle contraction, usually involving the face, neck, or shoulder muscles.

Tietze's syndrome: A syndrome of pain and swelling of the costochondral junctions.

tilt table: A table with a footboard for support, to which an individual can be strapped; the table can then be tilted to a nearly upright position. Tilt tables are used in neurological disorders to assist in balance and muscle training, and to enhance circulation to the lower extremities. They are also used in the diagnosis of neurally mediated hypotension.

Tinel's sign: Paresthesia produced by pressing or tapping on an injured nerve.

titer: The concentration of a substance (such as an antibody) in solution.

T-lymphocyte: See lymphocyte.

TMJ: Temporomandibular joint.

TMT joint: Tarsometatarsal joint.

tocolysis: The stoppage of labor, usually to prevent premature birth.

tolerance: A progressive decrease in responsiveness to a drug (or other stimulus), so that the dose (or intensity) has to be increased in order to produce the same effect.

tomography: An x-ray technique designed to focus on a selected tissue plane or "slice."

tonic: Pertaining to, characterized by, or producing normal tension (tone), i.e., of a muscle.

tonic-clonic seizures: A convulsive seizure characterized by spasms and movement of the limbs

tonometry: Measures the tension of a part, especially intraocular tension; used to detect glaucoma.

tonsil: A mass of lymphoid tissue in the pharynx (throat).

tooth abscess: A collection of pus in a tooth.

tooth extraction: Removal of tooth.

tophus (plural, tophi): Urate deposit in the tissues (such as near a joint or in the cartilage of the ear); present in gout.

topical: Pertaining to a localized area (usually an area of skin or mucous membrane). For example, a topical medication is one applied to skin or mucous membrane.

topical anesthetic: A local anesthetic applied to the skin or to mucous membrane.

topography: Description of a part of the body.

torsion: (1) Act of being twisted. (2) State of a tooth when rotated around its long axis. (3) Rotation of the vertical meridians of the eye.

tortuous: Twisting and turning.

total knee replacement: Replacement of the knee joint with an artificial joint.

total parenteral nutrition (TPN): Intravenous nutrition, providing all the nutrients necessary to sustain life and normal growth. Also called hyperalimentation.

total T4: Total thyroxine.

Tourette's syndrome: A neurological disorder that begins during childhood and characterized by tics and involuntary vocalizations that may include swearing.

tourniquet: A constricting band placed on an extremity in order to apply pressure over an artery (to stop bleeding) or a vein (to distend the veins, as in prior drawing of blood).

toxic: (1) Pertaining to a poison or toxin; poisonous. (2) Having the symptoms of severe systemic infection (as in "blood poisoning").

toxic megacolon: A complication of ulcerative colitis where the transverse colon dilates more than 6 cm.

toxin: A poisonous substance, especially one of organic origin.

TPN: Total parenteral nutrition.

trabecula: See trabecular meshwork.

trabecular meshwork: A structure located in the angle of the anterior chamber of the eye (where the cornea and iris meet). It provides a channel for aqueous humor to drain out of the eye into the venous system. Blockage of these channels results in glaucoma.

trachea: The windpipe; the large air passage extending from the larynx into the chest, where it divides into the two main bronchi.

tracheotomy: Incision into the trachea through the overlying skin and muscle.

tract: (1) A course or pathway such as the gastrointestinal tract or urinary tract. (2) A bundle of neural fibers (axons or dendrites) in the central nervous system. See also nerve.

trans-: A prefix meaning across or through.

transcapillary fluid shift: Movement of fluid into or out of the capillaries by passing through the capillary walls. Excessive fluid moving out of the capillaries into the tissues produces edema.

transcutaneous: Through the skin.

transducer: (1) A device that converts energy from one form to another. (2) A device that sends and receives sound waves (such as in ultrasonography).

transfusion reaction: Reactions that occur after a blood transfusion. The most serious is the response of the recipient when incompatible blood is administered and is characterized by massive intravascular clumping and lysis of red blood cells.

transient: Brief; short-lived.

translabyrinthine: Refers to a surgical approach for excision of tumors of the brain and/or inner ear.

transluminal: Through the lumen or channel (i.e., of a blood vessel).

transmural: Extending through or involving the entire thickness of the wall of an organ or cavity.

transrectal ultrasound (TRUS): Ultrasound of the prostate using a rectal probe.

transseptal: Through or across a septum (wall between two cavities).

transtympanic electrocochleography: A test for hearing loss that demonstrates evidence of cochlear involvement. It measures the ratio of the summating potential and the action potential on the nerve in response to auditory stimuli.

transvaginal ultrasound: Ultrasound performed through the vagina.

transverse: Crosswise; at right angles to the long axis of a structure. The opposite of longitudinal.

transverse colon: The part of the colon (large intestine) between the ascending and descending colon; so called because it lies horizontally across the upper abdomen.

transverse process: One of the two bony projections extending laterally from the vertebral arch on either side.

trapezius: A large muscle that extends like a cape over the posterior neck and upper back.

tremor: An involuntary trembling or quivering.

triangular fibrocartilage complex (TFCC): A group of structures in the wrist consisting of the disc of the ulnocarpal joint, along with the ligaments that are attached to it. See also ulnocarpal joint.

triceps brachii: A muscle of the upper arm; an extensor of the elbow.

tricuspid insufficiency: See tricuspid regurgitation.

tricuspid regurgitation: Incomplete closure of the tricuspid valve resulting in regurgitation (backflow) of blood into the right atrium.

tricuspid stenosis: Narrowing or constriction of the tricuspid valve.

tricuspid valve: A flap-like opening between the right atrium and the right ventricle of the heart.

tricyclic antidepressant: A class of antidepressant drugs, so called because their molecular structure incorporates three carbon rings.

trigeminal nerve: The fifth cranial nerve; the sensory nerve of the face.

trigger point: A localized area in muscle or associated connective tissue that produces either local or referred pain when pressure is applied to it. Trigger points are palpable (can be felt by the examiner), and are characteristic of myofascial pain syndrome.

triglyceride: A type of lipid, commonly referred to as a fat. A triglyceride is composed of three fatty acid molecules combined with one glycerol molecule.

trigone: A triangular area at the base of the bladder marked by the two ureteral openings above and the urethral opening below.

trimester: A three-month period of time, usually in reference to pregnancy.

trismus: Contraction of the muscles used for chewing; occurs with mouth infections, tetanus, and inflammation of the salivary glands.

trocar: A pointed surgical instrument contained in a cannula used to puncture a body cavity or tube during insertion of the cannula.

trophoblast: The outermost layer of a developing embryo that implants in the uterine lining; it forms part of the placenta.

trunk: (1) The main part of the body to which the head and limbs are attached; the torso. (2) The main stem portion (usually short) of a blood vessel, nerve, or duct, before any branching occurs. For example, the pulmonary trunk (main stem pulmonary artery) runs a short distance before branching into the right and left pulmonary arteries.

tryptophan: An amino acid and a precursor of the neurotransmitter serotonin. It is used in the treatment of insomnia, depression, and migraine.

TSH: Thyroid stimulating hormone.

TTP: Thrombotic thrombocytopenia purpura.

tubal epithelium: Epithelium that lines the fallopian tubes.

tubercle: A small elevation, nodule, or granuloma.

tubercle bacillus: The microorganism that causes tuberculosis, so called because the typical lesion of tuberculosis is a tubercle or granuloma.

tuberosity: A small elevation on a bone; a tubercle.

tubo-ovarian: Pertaining to both the ovaries and the uterine tubes.

tumor: A mass or swelling. A new growth of cells; a neoplasm, either benign or malignant.

tunica albuginea: The fibrous coat of the testicle or ovary.

tunnel vision: Severe constriction of the visual field caused by advanced glaucoma.

turgor: The presence of normal tension in a cell; usually refers to the tautness and elasticity of the skin.

tympanic membrane: The eardrum.

tympanosclerosis: Scarring of the eardrum.

typoscope: A reading aid device for individuals with amblyopia or cataract.

UA: Urinalysis.

UGI: Upper gastrointestinal.

ulcer: An open lesion on the surface of an organ or membrane formed by the sloughing of necrotic (dead) tissue.

ulceration: The process of ulcer formation.

ulcerative colitis: An inflammatory bowel disease characterized by inflammation of the entire colon; can be hereditary.

ulna: One of the two long bones of the forearm. The ulna is located on the medial (little finger) side of the forearm; the radius on the lateral (thumb) side.

ulnar: Pertaining to the ulna (one of the two long bones of the forearm. Located on the ulnar (little finger) side of the hand, wrist, or forearm.

ulnar artery: One of the two large arteries that supply blood to the hand. Its pulsations can be felt on the ulnar (little finger) side of the wrist. See also radial artery.

ulnar deviation: Movement of the wrist in the direction of the little finger. The opposite of radial deviation.

ulnar nerve: A branch of the brachial plexus; one of the major nerves of the upper extremity.

ulnocarpal joint: The joint between the ulna and the carpal bones. The joint contains a disc of fibrocartilage interposed between the ulna and the carpus.

ultrasonography: Use of ultrasound (high frequency sound) for diagnostic or therapeutic purposes.

ultrasound: High frequency sound, inaudible to the human ear.

ultraviolet light: Rays of light emitted by natural or artificial sources not visible to the human eye.

umbilical cord: The cord, containing blood vessels that connects the fetus with the placenta.

umbilical ring: The opening in the abdominal wall for the umbilical cord; after birth, it closes off with scar tissue.

umbilicus: The navel; the place where the umbilical cord was attached during fetal development.

UMN: Upper motor neuron.

uncal: Concerning the uncus (hooked anterior end of the hippocampal gyrus) of the brain.

undifferentiated schizophrenia: A type of schizophrenic disorder characterized by delusions, incoherence, or grossly disorganized behavior.

unilateral: Involving or occurring on one side of the body.

unimalleolar: Involving one malleolus (either the lateral or the medial malleolus of the ankle).

unmyelinated: Term describing a nerve or nerve fiber without a myelin sheath.

Unna boots: Boot-like dressing made of layers of gauze and Unna's paste; used for the lower extremities for treating chronic ulcers usually caused by varicosities of the leg.

unstable angina: Angina that has changed to a more frequent and more severe form; may be an indication of an impending myocardial infarction.

upper airway: See upper respiratory tract.

upper motor neuron: A nerve cell above the level of the twelfth thoracic vertebra, including nerve cells of the spinal cord and brain.

upper respiratory tract: The parts of the respiratory tract outside the thorax (chest), i.e., the nasal cavity, sinuses, pharynx, larynx, and upper trachea.

urate: A salt of uric acid.

urea: A nitrogen-containing organic compound; the principal end-product of protein breakdown. Urea is formed in the liver and excreted by the kidneys. In renal failure, elevated levels of urea are found in the blood. See blood urea nitrogen.

Ureaplasma urealyticum: A common organism that frequently causes genitourinary infection.

urease: An enzyme that speeds the breakdown of urea.

uremia: Elevated levels of urea in the blood due to kidney failure; also called azotemia.

ureter: The tube that carries urine from the kidney to the bladder; there are two ureters, one for each kidney. The wall of the ureter contains smooth muscle and is lined with mucous membrane.

ureterostomy: Surgical creation of an outlet for drainage of the ureters (such as after removal of the bladder).

urethra: The canal that conveys urine from the bladder to the outside of the body.

URI: Upper respiratory infection.

uric acid: A nitrogen-containing waste product that is excreted in the urine.

urinalysis (UA): Analysis of urine, including chemical tests and microscopic examination.

urinary bladder: A muscular, hollow organ located in the pelvis (lower abdominal cavity) that receives urine from the kidneys via the ureters and releases the urine through the urethra.

urinary retention: Inability to urinate.

urinary tract: The organs and ducts involved in the production and excretion of urine; the kidneys, ureters, bladder, and urethra.

US: Ultrasonography or ultrasound.

uterine sarcoma: Sarcoma of the uterus.

uterine tube: Either of the two ducts (one on each side) that extends from the upper part of the uterus and terminates near the ovary. After ovulation, the ovum enters the uterine tube, which conducts it to the uterus. Fertilization of the ovum takes place in the uterine tube. Also called fallopian tube.

uterus: A female reproductive organ located in the pelvis (lower abdominal cavity) that contains and nourishes the embryo and fetus during pregnancy.

uvea: The middle coat of the eyeball, between the sclera and retina. It includes the iris and ciliary body (the anterior uvea) and the choroid (posterior uvea).

vaccine: A substance containing killed or weakened microorganisms (or products of microorganisms), taken to stimulate the immune system and produce immunity.

vagal: Pertaining to the vagus nerve.

vagina: In females, the passageway between the cervix of the uterus and the outside of the body.

vagus nerve: The tenth cranial nerve. It contains both sensory and motor fibers including parasympathetic fibers that supply various organs of the chest and abdomen.

valve: A structure that permits flow (i.e., of blood) in only one direction.

valvular insufficiency: Incomplete closure of a valve (such as a heart valve), resulting in backflow (regurgitation) of blood.

varicose vein: A dilated, tortuous (twisted) vein.

varix (plural, varices): A dilated, tortuous vessel, usually a vein; a varicose vein.

vas deferens: The duct that conveys sperm from the testis to the urethra. Also called the ductus deferens.

vascular: Pertaining to or composed of blood vessels.

vascular dementia: A dementia that usually affects older individuals caused by years of low blood flow to the brain.

vascular resistance: The amount of mechanical resistance of the arteries to the flow of blood. This resistance consists of degree of constriction and plaque build-up on the artery walls.

vascularized, -ization: To become vascular by developing new blood vessels in a structure.

vasculitis: Inflammation of a blood vessel or vessels.

vasoconstriction: Decrease in blood vessel diameter due to contraction of the smooth muscle in the vessel walls.

vasoconstrictor: A drug or agent that produces vasoconstriction.

vasodilation: Increase in blood vessel diameter due to relaxation of the smooth muscle in the vessel walls.

vasodilator: A drug or agent that produces vasodilation.

vasomotor: Pertaining to changes in blood vessel diameter (i.e., vasoconstriction and vasodilation).

vasopressin: See antidiuretic hormone.

vasopressin therapy: The use of vasopressin to cause the blood pressure to rise by decreasing water loss through the urine and narrowing the blood vessels.

vasopressor: A drug or agent that increases blood pressure by decreasing the diameter of arteries and arterioles; a vasoconstrictor.

vasospasm: Spasm of the smooth muscle in the wall of a blood vessel.

vasovagal: Pertaining to the influence of the vagus nerve (a parasympathetic nerve) on the cardiovascular system. A vasovagal reaction is characterized by bradycardia (slow heart rate) and hypotension (low blood pressure). The hypotension results from the combination of bradycardia and dilation of blood vessels. See also parasympathetic nervous system.

vasovagal reaction: Fainting due to stimulation of the autonomic nervous system.

vegan diet: A diet that excludes all animal products, including milk and eggs.

vegetative: Functioning involuntarily.

vein: A blood vessel that carries blood toward the heart.

vena cava (plural, venae cavae): Either of the two great veins that empty into the right atrium of the heart. The superior vena cava receives blood from the upper part of the body; the inferior vena cava receives blood from the lower part of the body.

Glossary 2379

venous: Pertaining to a vein or veins.

venous return: The return of blood via the veins to the right atrium of the heart.

venous varicosities: Varicose veins; abnormal dilations of superficial veins usually in the legs.

ventilation: Inhalation of air into the lungs; oxygenation of blood.

ventral: Pertaining to the abdomen; the anterior or front side of the body. The opposite of dorsal.

ventral horns: The anterior projections of gray matter in the spinal cord. The ventral horns contain the cell bodies of motor neurons.

ventral root: The anterior root of a spinal nerve. The ventral roots contain the axons of motor neurons, carrying impulses from the ventral horns of the spinal cord toward the periphery.

ventricle: A cavity or chamber. Either of the two lower chambers of the heart. The right ventricle pumps deoxygenated blood into the pulmonary artery, which delivers the blood to the lungs. The left ventricle pumps oxygenated blood into the aorta, which distributes the blood to the rest of the body. See also atrium. Also, any of the four cavities within the brain through which cerebrospinal fluid circulates.

ventricular fibrillation: A cardiac arrhythmia characterized by fibrillation (uncoordinated contractions or quivering) of the ventricular heart muscle. The ventricles are unable to pump blood, resulting in cardiac arrest.

ventricular septal defect (VSD): A congenital defect or hole in the septum between the ventricles of the heart. If large, it must be corrected soon after birth. Small VSDs may be asymptomatic and persist into adulthood.

ventricular tachycardia: An abnormally rapid ventricular rhythm (usually faster than 150 beats per minute) generated within the ventricles.

ventriculography: X-ray of a ventricle after injection of contrast medium.

venule: A microscopic vein.

vertebra (plural, vertebrae): A spinal bone. Each vertebra has a cylindrical body and a posterior arch that (with the body) form a bony ring. The spinal column contains seven cervical (neck), twelve thoracic (chest), and five lumbar (low back) vertebrae. The fifth lumbar vertebra rests on top of the sacrum, a wedge-shaped bone consisting of five fused vertebral segments. Below the sacrum is the coccyx, a smaller wedge-shaped bone consisting of three to five fused segments.

vertebral arch: The posterior part of a vertebra, consisting of two pedicles, two laminae, two superior and two inferior articular processes (which form the facet joints), two transverse processes, and a spinous process.

vertebral artery: A branch of the subclavian artery. The right and left vertebral arteries supply blood to the spinal cord and posterior parts of the brain; they merge on the underside of the brain to form the basilar artery.

vertebral body: The cylindrical anterior portion of a vertebra.

vertebral column: The spine.

vertebral foramen: The space enclosed by the vertebral arch.

vertigo: A sensation of spinning. Sometimes called dizziness; however, dizziness can mean either vertigo or light-headedness.

vesical: Pertaining to a bladder (usually the urinary bladder).

vesicle: A small, fluid-filled sac; a blister.

vessel: A tube, duct, or canal.

vestibular disorder: Disorder that affects the vestibule of the inner ear.

vestibular rehabilitation: An exercise approach to manage dizziness and loss of balance associated with diseases of the inner ear.

vestibule: The part of the inner ear between the cochlea and the semicircular canals. It contains a sensory apparatus that responds to changes in the position of the head.

villous: Having villi (hair-like projections).

viremia: The presence of viruses in the blood.

virulence: Power and degree of pathogenicity possessed by organisms to produce disease.

virus: A simple microorganism that consists of one or two strands of DNA or RNA inside a protein coat. It is too small to be seen with an ordinary light microscope, but can be seen with an electron microscope. It reproduces by entering a cell's nucleus and directing the cell to produce viral proteins.

viscera: Internal organs.

visceral: Pertaining to internal organs.

visceral pericardium: A serous membrane that forms the outer surface of the heart wall; also called the epicardium.

visceral pleura: A loose outer covering of the lungs.

viscosity: Stickiness or "gooeyness" of a liquid.

viscous: Sticky or "gooey" (used to describe a liquid).

viscus (plural, viscera): Organs enclosed by a cavity such as the abdomen.

visual evoked potential (VEP): The response of the brain to a visual stimulus.

visual field: Area within which objects can be seen when the eye is focused in one spot.

visual field defect: A blind area within the visual field.

vital signs: The heartbeat, respiration, blood pressure, and body temperature.

vitamin: A term applied to a number of chemically unrelated organic compounds present in many foods, and are required in trace amounts for the body's normal metabolic functioning.

vitamin B12: A water-soluble vitamin found in animal products; also called cobalamin. Its metabolism is interconnected with that of folic acid. Like folic acid, vitamin B12 is necessary for the synthesis of DNA, RNA, and proteins, and hence for the growth and replication of all body cells. Deficiency results in anemia and neurological lesions. See also cobalamin and folic acid.

vitrectomy: Procedure that removes the contents of the vitreous chamber of the eye and replaces it with sterile physiological saline solution.

vitreous: Pertaining to the vitreous body of the eye.

vitreous cavity: In the eye, the space within the posterior chamber that contains the vitreous humor A transparent jelly-like substance that fills most of the posterior chamber of the eye (the space behind the lens), and helps maintain the shape of the eyeball. Sometimes called the vitreous body.

vitreous humor: Clear watery gel inside the eyeball.

volar: Referring to the palm or the palmar side of the hand and forearm.

volar arch: An arterial arch in the palm that gives off branches to the hand and digits. The deep volar arch is formed by the anastomosis (communication) of the radial and ulnar arteries. The superficial volar arch is usually formed by the ulnar artery alone.

volatile: Easily vaporized or evaporated.

Volkmann's ischemic contracture: A permanent flexion contracture of the wrist and hand caused by pressure or a crushing injury around the elbow.

volvulus: A twisting of the bowel upon itself causing obstruction; usually occurs at sigmoid and ileocecal areas of the intestines.

vulva: The external genital organs of a female.

vulvovaginitis: Inflammation of the vulva and vagina or of the vulvovaginal glands caused by some medications, tight-fitting underclothes, inadequate hygiene, allergies, or infectious agents including bacteria, yeasts, viruses, and parasites.

VZIG: Varicella-Zoster Immune Globulin

walking pneumonia: A mild case of pneumonia that does not require bed rest or hospitalization.

warfarin: Also known as Coumadin, a drug used to inhibit blood clotting. See also anticoagulants.

wasting: Emaciating, causing loss of strength of size.

wasting syndrome: A disease characterized by progressive weight loss that equals or exceeds 15% of the individual's body weight.

water brash: A reflexive increase in salivation in response to gastroesophageal reflux.

wavefront technology: A device used to precisely measure how light waves are bent by the human eye.

WBC: White blood cell.

wheeze: A whistling or sighing breath sound caused by narrowing of the respiratory passages. Wheezing may be heard without a stethoscope or may be audible only with a stethoscope.

white blood cell (WBC): Any of several types of leukocytes including neutrophils, lymphocytes, and monocytes. White blood cells are concerned with the body's defense against disease and/or foreign substances. See neutrophil, lymphocyte, and monocyte.

white matter: Nervous tissue consisting primarily of myelinated fibers; so called because of its white appearance.

Williams' flexion exercises: A treatment protocol for individuals with spondylolysis and spondylolisthesis.

wisdom teeth: The third molars. Often an individual's mouth cannot accommodate these teeth and they must be removed.

withdrawal syndrome: A syndrome that occurs in an addicted individual when the drug of addiction is abruptly stopped or the dosage decreased.

wrist drop: Flexion of the wrist due to weakness or paralysis of the extensor muscles of the wrist; usually results from injury to the radial nerve.

xerostomia: Dry mouth caused by an abnormal decrease in salivary secretion.

x-rays: Electromagnetic radiation of an energy higher than ultraviolet light but lower than gamma rays. Images produced by means of a beam of x-rays. Because of their high energy, x-rays are able to pass through most body tissues to varying degrees depending on the tissue density. The denser the tissue, the more x-rays are absorbed. X-rays that are not absorbed pass through the body to expose a photographic plate. On a developed x-ray image, the lightest areas represent the densest tissues (such as bone), while the darkest areas represent the least dense tissues (such as air-filled lung or gas-filled intestine). See also electromagnetic radiation.

YAG laser capsulotomy: A surgical procedure using the YAG laser to treat an after-cataract.

yeast: Unicellular fungi that reproduce by budding. May cause systemic infections as well as vaginitis. Frequently present in individuals with malignant lymphomas, severe diabetes mellitus, or AIDS.

Yersinia: An organism that causes plague, pseudotuberculosis, mesenteric lymphadenitis, and enterocolitis.

yoga: Exercises aimed at physical postures and regulation of breathing.

Translation of ICD-9 CM to ICD-10

This table provides a correlation between ICD-9 CM codes and ICD-10 codes. Only approximate matches are possible for the following reasons:
(1) According to the World Health Organization, the designations of the ICD-10 codes departed significantly from those of the ICD-9 codes, making impossible a "straightforward translation" between the two[1].
(2) US healthcare institutions and consequentially *The Medical Disability Advisor*, Fourth Edition, use the "Clinical Modification" of the ICD-9 codes.[2] The Clinical Modification notation appends decimal numbers to the ICD-9 code in order to further subcategorize diseases. Thus the difficulties encountered by the World Health Organization are compounded when the "CM" ICD-9 codes are used.
The matches in the following table may at times provide the exact correlation needed for a medical condition; at other times they should at least provide direction for those adapting the ICD-9 classifications used in *The Medical Disability Advisor* to the ICD-10 codes.

ICD-9	Description	ICD-10	Description
002.0	Typhoid Fever	A01.0	Typhoid fever Infection due to Salmonella typhi
002.1	Paratyphoid Fever A	A01.1	Paratyphoid fever A
002.2	Paratyphoid Fever B	A01.2	Paratyphoid fever B
002.3	Paratyphoid Fever C	A01.3	Paratyphoid fever C
002.9	Paratyphoid Fever	A01.4	Paratyphoid fever, unspecified Infection due to Salmonella paratyphi NOS
003.0	Salmonellosis	A02.0	Salmonella enteritis Salmonellosis
003.1	Salmonella Septicemia	A02.1	Salmonella septicaemia
003.8	Salmonella Infections, Other Specified	A02.8	Other specified salmonella infections
003.9	Salmonella Infection, Unspecified	A02.9	Salmonella infection, unspecified
004.8	Shigella Infections, Other Specified	A03.8	Other shigellosis
004.9	Shigellosis	A03.9	Shigellosis, unspecified Bacillary dysentery NOS
005.0	Staphylococcal Food Poisoning	A05.0	Foodborne staphylococcal intoxication
005.1	Botulism	A05.1	Botulism Classical foodborne intoxication due to Clostridium botulinum
005.2	Food Poisoning Due to Clostridium Perfringens	A05.2	Foodborne Clostridium perfringens [Clostridium welchii] intoxication
005.3	Food Poisoning Due to Other Clostridia	A05.3	Foodborne Vibrio parahaemolyticus intoxication
005.4	Food Poisoning Due to Vibrio Parahaemolyticus	A05.3	Foodborne Vibrio parahaemolyticus intoxication
005.8	Food Poisoning, Bacterial, Other	A05.4	Foodborne Bacillus cereus intoxication
		A05.8	Other specified bacterial foodborne intoxications
005.9	Food Poisoning, Unspecified	A05.9	Bacterial foodborne intoxication, unspecified
		T62.9	Noxious substance eaten as food, unspecified
006.0	Amebic Dysentery, Acute, Without Mention of Abscess	A06.0	Acute amoebic dysentery
006.1	Amebiasis, Chronic Intestinal, Without Mention of Abscess	A06.1	Chronic intestinal amoebiasis
006.2	Amebic Nondysenteric Colitis	A06.0	Acute amoebic dysentery
		A06.2	Amoebic nondysenteric colitis
006.3	Amebic Liver Abscess	A06.4	Amoebic liver abscess Hepatic amoebiasis
006.6	Amebic Skin Ulceration	A06.7	Cutaneous amoebiasis
006.8	Amebic Infection of Other Sites	A06.0	Acute amoebic dysentery
		A06.3	Amoeboma of intestine
		A06.8	Amoebic infection of other sites
006.9	Amebiasis	A06.0	Acute amoebic dysentery
		A06.1	Chronic intestinal amoebiasis
		A06.9	Amoebiasis, unspecified
007.1	Giardiasis	A07.1	Giardiasis [lambliasis]
007.3	Intestinal Trichomoniasis	A07.8	Other specified protozoal intestinal diseases
007.8	Protozoal Intestinal Diseases, Other Specified	A07.2	Cryptosporidiosis
		A07.8	Other specified protozoal intestinal diseases
007.9	Protozoal Intestinal Disease, Unspecified	A07.9	Protozoal intestinal disease, unspecified
008.0	Escherichia Coli (E. Coli)	A04.0	Enteropathogenic Escherichia coli infection
		A04.1	Enterotoxigenic Escherichia coli infection
		A04.2	Enteroinvasive Escherichia coli infection
		A04.3	Enterohaemorrhagic Escherichia coli infection
		A04.4	Other intestinal Escherichia coli infections
009.0	Colitis, Enteritis, and Gastroenteritis, Infectious	A09	Diarrhoea and gastroenteritis of presumed infectious origin
		M02.1	Postdysenteric arthropathy
009.1	Colitis, Enteritis, and Gastroenteritis of Presumed Infectious Origin	A09	Diarrhoea and gastroenteritis of presumed infectious origin
009.2	Diarrhea, Infectious	A09	Diarrhoea and gastroenteritis of presumed infectious origin

1. *International Classification of Diseases Translator: Ninth and Tenth Revisions*. World Health Organization. Geneva, 1997, p. 3. The translation table used by permission.
2. *International Classification of Diseases, 9th Revision, Clinical Modification*. Los Angeles: Practice Management Information Corporation, 1999.

ICD-9	Description	ICD-10	Description	(Continued)
009.3	Diarrhea of Presumed Infectious Origin	A09	Diarrhoea and gastroenteritis of presumed infectious origin	
011.0	Tuberculosis of Lung, Infiltrative	A16.2	Tuberculosis of lung, without mention of bacteriological or histological confirmation	
011.4	Tuberculous Fibrosis of Lung	A16.2	Tuberculosis of lung, without mention of bacteriological or histological confirmation	
		J65	Pneumoconiosis associated with tuberculosis Any condition in J60-J64 with tuberculosis, any type in A15-A16	
011.8	Tuberculosis, Pulmonary, Other Specified	A16.1	Tuberculosis of lung, bacteriological and histological examination not done	
		A16.2	Tuberculosis of lung, without mention of bacteriological or histological confirmation	
011.9	Tuberculosis, Respiratory (Unspecified)	A15.0	Tuberculosis of lung, confirmed by sputum microscopy with or without culture	
		A15.1	Tuberculosis of lung, confirmed by culture only	
		A15.2	Tuberculosis of lung, confirmed histologically	
		A15.3	Tuberculosis of lung, confirmed by unspecified means	
		A15.9	Respiratory tuberculosis unspecified, confirmed bacteriologically and histologically	
		A16.0	Tuberculosis of lung, bacteriologically and histologically negative	
		A16.1	Tuberculosis of lung, bacteriological and histological examination not done	
		A16.2	Tuberculosis of lung, without mention of bacteriological or histological confirmation	
		A16.4	Tuberculosis of larynx, trachea and bronchus, without mention of bacteriological or histological confirmation	
		A16.9	Respiratory tuberculosis unspecified, without mention of bacteriological or histological confirmation	
		B90.9	Sequelae of respiratory and unspecified tuberculosis Sequelae of tuberculosis NOS	
021	Tularemia	A21.0	Ulceroglandular tularaemia	
		A21.1	Oculoglandular tularaemia Ophthalmic tularaemia	
		A21.2	Pulmonary tularaemia	
		A21.3	Gastrointestinal tularaemia Abdominal tularaemia	
		A21.7	Generalized tularaemia	
		A21.8	Other forms of tularaemia	
		A21.9	Tularaemia, unspecified	
023.0	Brucella Melitensis	A23.0	Brucellosis due to Brucella melitensis	
023.1	Brucella Abortus	A23.1	Brucellosis due to Brucella abortus	
023.2	Brucella Suis	A23.2	Brucellosis due to Brucella suis	
023.3	Brucella Canis	A23.3	Brucellosis due to Brucella canis	
023.8	Brucellosis, Other	A23.8	Other brucellosis	
023.9	Brucellosis, Unspecified	A23.0	Brucellosis due to Brucella melitensis	
		A23.9	Brucellosis, unspecified	
027.1	Erysipeloid	A26.0	Cutaneous erysipeloid Erythema migrans	
		A26.7	Erysipelothrix septicaemia	
		A26.8	Other forms of erysipeloid	
		A26.9	Erysipeloid, unspecified	
034.0	Strep Throat	J00	Acute nasopharyngitis [common cold]	
		J02.0	Streptococcal pharyngitis Streptococcal sore throat Excludes: scarlet fever (A38)	
		J03.0	Streptococcal tonsillitis	
		J04.0	Acute laryngitis	
		J04.1	Acute tracheitis Tracheitis (acute): . NOS . catarrhal Excludes: chronic tracheitis (J42)	
		J04.2	Acute laryngotracheitis Laryngotracheitis NOS Tracheitis (acute) with laryngitis (acute)	
		J06.9	Acute upper respiratory infection, unspecified	
035	Erysipelas	A46	Erysipelas Excludes: postpartum or puerperal erysipelas (O86.8)	
037	Tetanus	A35	Other tetanus Tetanus NOS Excludes: tetanus: . neonatorum (A33) . obstetrical (A34)	
038.0	Streptococcal Septicemia	A40.0	Septicaemia due to streptococcus, group A	
		A40.1	Septicaemia due to streptococcus, group B	
		A40.2	Septicaemia due to streptococcus, group D	
		A40.8	Other streptococcal septicaemia	
		A40.9	Streptococcal septicaemia, unspecified	
038.1	Staphylococcal Septicemia	A41.0	Septicaemia due to Staphylococcus aureus	
		A41.1	Septicaemia due to other specified staphylococcus	
		A41.2	Septicaemia due to unspecified staphylococcus	
038.2	Pneumococcal Septicemia	A40.3	Septicaemia due to Streptococcus pneumoniae	
038.3	Septicemia Due to Anaerobes	A41.4	Septicaemia due to anaerobes	
038.4	Septicemia Due to Other Gram-negative Organisms	A41.5	Septicaemia due to other Gram-negative organisms	
038.8	Septicemias, Other Specified	A41.3	Septicaemia due to Haemophilus influenzae	
		A41.8	Other specified septicaemia	
038.9	Sepsis, Unspecified	A41.9	Septicaemia, unspecified Septic shock	

ICD-9	Description	ICD-10	Description	(Continued)
039.0	Actinomycotic Infections, Cutaneous	A42.8	Other forms of actinomycosis	
		A43.1	Cutaneous nocardiosis	
		A48.8	Other specified bacterial diseases	
		L08.1	Erythrasma	
039.1	Actinomycotic Infections, Pulmonary	A42.0	Pulmonary actinomycosis	
039.1	Actinomycotic Infections, Pulmonary	A43.0	Pulmonary nocardiosis	
039.2	Actinomycotic Infections, Abdominal	A42.1	Abdominal actinomycosis	
039.3	Actinomycotic Infections, Cervicofacial	A42.2	Cervicofacial actinomycosis	
039.4	Actinomycotic Infections, Due to Madura Foot	B47.0	Eumycetoma Madura foot, mycotic Maduromycosis	
		B47.1	Actinomycetoma	
		B47.9	Mycetoma, unspecified Madura foot NOS	
039.8	Actinomycotic Infections, Other Specified Sites	A42.7	Actinomycotic septicaemia	
		A42.8	Other forms of actinomycosis	
		A43.8	Other forms of nocardiosis	
		B47.9	Mycetoma, unspecified Madura foot NOS	
039.9	Actinomycosis, Unspecified Site	A42.9	Actinomycosis, unspecified	
		A43.9	Nocardiosis, unspecified	
		A48.8	Other specified bacterial diseases	
		B47.0	Eumycetoma Madura foot, mycotic Maduromycosis	
		B47.1	Actinomycetoma	
		B47.9	Mycetoma, unspecified Madura foot NOS	
040.0	Gas Gangrene (Bacillus)	A48.0	Gas gangrene	
040.1	Rhinoscleroma	A48.8	Other specified bacterial diseases	
045.1	Acute Poliomyelitis with Other Paralysis	A80.0	Acute paralytic poliomyelitis, vaccine-associated	
		A80.1	Acute paralytic poliomyelitis, wild virus, imported	
		A80.2	Acute paralytic poliomyelitis, wild virus, indigenous	
		A80.3	Acute paralytic poliomyelitis, other and unspecified	
045.2	Acute Nonparalytic Poliomyelitis	A80.4	Acute nonparalytic poliomyelitis	
		A80.9	Acute poliomyelitis, unspecified	
045.9	Acute Poliomyelitis, Unspecified	A80.3	Acute paralytic poliomyelitis, other and unspecified	
		A80.9	Acute poliomyelitis, unspecified	
047.9	Aseptic Meningitis	A87.8	Other viral meningitis	
		A87.9	Viral meningitis, unspecified	
		G03.0	Nonpyogenic meningitis Nonbacterial meningitis	
052	Chickenpox (Varicella)	B01.8	Varicella with other complications	
		B01.9	Varicella without complication Varicella NOS	
053.9	Herpes Zoster, Unspecified (Shingles without Mention of Complication)	B02.9	Zoster without complication Zoster NOS	
054.0	Eczema Herpeticum	B00.0	Eczema herpeticum Kaposi's varicelliform eruption	
054.1	Genital Herpes	A60.0	Herpesviral infection of genitalia and urogenital tract	
		A60.9	Anogenital herpesviral infection, unspecified	
054.2	Herpetic Gingivostomatitis	B00.2	Herpesviral gingivostomatitis and pharyngotonsillitis	
054.5	Herpetic Septicemia	B00.7	Disseminated herpesviral disease	
054.6	Herpetic Whitlow	B00.8	Other forms of herpesviral infection	
054.7	Herpes Simplex with Other Specified Complications	A60.1	Herpesviral infection of perianal skin and rectum	
		B00.1	Herpesviral vesicular dermatitis	
		B00.2	Herpesviral gingivostomatitis and pharyngotonsillitis	
		B00.8	Other forms of herpesviral infection	
054.8	Herpes Simplex with Unspecified Complication	B00.8	Other forms of herpesviral infection	
054.9	Herpes Simplex, Unspecified	B00.1	Herpesviral vesicular dermatitis	
		B00.9	Herpesviral infection, unspecified	
055.7	Measles with Other Specified Complications	B05.4	Measles with intestinal complications	
		B05.8	Measles with other complications	
055.8	Measles with Unspecified Complication	B05.8	Measles with other complications	
055.9	Measles (Rubeola)	B05.9	Measles without complication	
056.7	Rubella with Other Specified Complications	B06.8	Rubella with other complications	
056.8	Rubella with Unspecified Complications	B06.8	Rubella with other complications	
056.9	Rubella Without Mention of Complication	B06.9	Rubella without complication	
		B09	Unspecified viral infection characterized by skin and mucous membrane lesions	
060.1	Urban Yellow Fever	A95.1	Urban yellow fever	
060.9	Jungle Yellow Fever	A95.9	Yellow fever, unspecified	

Translation of ICD-9 CM to ICD-10

ICD-9	Description	ICD-10	Description	(Continued)
061	Dengue Fever	A89	Unspecified viral infection of central nervous system	
		A90	Dengue fever	
062.1	Encephalomyelitis, Western Equine	A83.1	Western equine encephalitis	
062.2	Encephalitis, Eastern Equine	A83.2	Eastern equine encephalitis	
062.3	Encephalitis, St. Louis	A83.3	St Louis encephalitis	
062.9	Encephalitis, Equine	A83.9	Mosquito-borne viral encephalitis, unspecified	
064	Encephalitis, Viral, Transmitted by Other and Unspecified Arthropods	A85.2	Arthropod-borne viral encephalitis, unspecified	
066.1	Colorado Tick Fever	A93.2	Colorado tick fever	
		A93.8	Other specified arthropod-borne viral fevers	
070.0	Hepatitis, Viral Type A with Hepatic Coma	B15.0	Hepatitis A with hepatic coma	
070.1	Hepatitis, Viral Type A Without Mention of Hepatic Coma	B15.9	Hepatitis A without hepatic coma	
070.2	Hepatitis, Viral Type B with Hepatic Coma	B16.0	Acute hepatitis B with delta-agent (coinfection) with hepatic coma	
		B16.2	Acute hepatitis B without delta-agent with hepatic coma	
		B18.0	Chronic viral hepatitis B with delta-agent	
		B18.1	Chronic viral hepatitis B without delta-agent	
070.3	Hepatitis, Viral Type B Without Mention of Hepatic Coma	B16.1	Acute hepatitis B with delta-agent (coinfection) without hepatic coma	
		B16.9	Acute hepatitis B without delta-agent and without hepatic coma	
		B18.0	Chronic viral hepatitis B with delta-agent	
		B18.1	Chronic viral hepatitis B without delta-agent	
070.5	Hepatitis, Viral Type C Without Mention of Hepatic Coma, Other Specified	B17.0	Acute delta-(super)infection of hepatitis B carrier	
		B17.1	Acute hepatitis C	
		B17.2	Acute hepatitis E	
		B17.8	Other specified acute viral hepatitis	
		B18.2	Chronic viral hepatitis C	
		B18.8	Other chronic viral hepatitis	
070.9	Hepatitis, Viral Without Mention of Hepatic Coma, Unspecified	B18.9	Chronic viral hepatitis, unspecified	
		B19.9	Unspecified viral hepatitis without hepatic coma	
071	Rabies	A82.0	Sylvatic rabies	
		A82.1	Urban rabies	
		A82.9	Rabies, unspecified	
072.7	Mumps with Other Specified Complications (Hepatitis, Polyneuropathy)	B26.8	Mumps with other complications	
072.8	Mumps with Unspecified Complication	B26.8	Mumps with other complications	
072.9	Mumps Without Mention of Complication, Unspecified	B26.9	Mumps without complication	
075	Mononucleosis, Infectious	B27.0	Gammaherpesviral mononucleosis	
		B27.1	Cytomegaloviral mononucleosis	
		B27.8	Other infectious mononucleosis	
		B27.9	Infectious mononucleosis, unspecified	
076.0	Trachoma, Initial Stage	A71.0	Initial stage of trachoma	
076.1	Trachoma, Active Stage	A71.1	Active stage of trachoma	
076.9	Trachoma, Unspecified	A71.9	Trachoma, unspecified	
078.1	Viral Warts	A63.0	Anogenital (venereal) warts	
		B07	Viral warts	
078.3	Cat Scratch Disease	A28.1	Cat-scratch disease	
080	Typhus, Louse-Borne	A75.0	Epidemic louse-borne typhus fever due to Rickettsia prowazekii	
		A75.9	Typhus fever, unspecified	
081.0	Typhus, Murine (Fever)	A75.2	Typhus fever due to Rickettsia typhi Murine (flea-borne) typhus	
081.2	Typhus, Scrub	A75.3	Typhus fever due to Rickettsia tsutsugamushi Scrub (mite-borne) typhus	
081.9	Typhus Fever, Unspecified	A75.0	Epidemic louse-borne typhus fever due to Rickettsia prowazekii	
		A75.9	Typhus fever, unspecified	
082.0	Rocky Mountain Spotted Fever	A77.0	Spotted fever due to Rickettsia rickettsii	
		A77.8	Other spotted fevers	
		A77.9	Spotted fever, unspecified	
082.8	Tick-borne Rickettsioses, Other Specified	A77.0	Spotted fever due to Rickettsia rickettsii	
082.9	Tick-borne Rickettsiosis, Unspecified	A77.9	Spotted fever, unspecified	
084.0	Malaria Fever (Falciparum Malaria)	B50.0	Plasmodium falciparum malaria with cerebral complications	
		B50.8	Other severe and complicated Plasmodium falciparum malaria	
		B50.9	Plasmodium falciparum malaria, unspecified	
084.1	Malaria, Vivax (Benign Tertian)	B51.0	Plasmodium vivax malaria with rupture of spleen	

ICD-9	Description	ICD-10	Description	(Continued)
084.1	Malaria, Vivax (Benign Tertian)	B51.8	Plasmodium vivax malaria with other complications	
		B51.9	Plasmodium vivax malaria without complication	
084.2	Malaria, Quartan	B52.0	Plasmodium malariae malaria with nephropathy	
		B52.8	Plasmodium malariae malaria with other complications	
		B52.9	Plasmodium malariae malaria without complication	
084.3	Malaria, Ovale	B53.0	Plasmodium ovale malaria	
084.4	Malaria, Other	B53.1	Malaria due to simian plasmodia Excludes: when mixed with Plasmodium: . falciparum (B50.-) . malariae (B52.-) . ovale (B53.0) . vivax (B51.-)	
		B53.8	Other parasitologically confirmed malaria, not elsewhere classified Parasitologically confirmed malaria NOS	
084.5	Malaria, Mixed	B50.0	Plasmodium falciparum malaria with cerebral complications	
		B50.8	Other severe and complicated Plasmodium falciparum malaria	
		B50.9	Plasmodium falciparum malaria, unspecified	
		B51.0	Plasmodium vivax malaria with rupture of spleen	
		B51.8	Plasmodium vivax malaria with other complications	
		B51.9	Plasmodium vivax malaria without complication	
		B52.0	Plasmodium malariae malaria with nephropathy	
		B52.8	Plasmodium malariae malaria with other complications	
		B52.9	Plasmodium malariae malaria without complication	
		B53.0	Plasmodium ovale malaria	
084.6	Malaria, Unspecified	B54	Unspecified malaria	
084.7	Malaria, Induced	B54	Unspecified malaria	
084.8	Blackwater Fever	B50.8	Other severe and complicated Plasmodium falciparum malaria	
084.9	Malaria, Other Pernicious Complications of	B50.0	Plasmodium falciparum malaria with cerebral complications	
		B50.9	Plasmodium falciparum malaria, unspecified	
		B52.0	Plasmodium malariae malaria with nephropathy	
		B54	Unspecified malaria	
086.1	Chagas' Disease with Other Organ Involvement	B57.3	Chagas' disease (chronic) with digestive system involvement	
		B57.4	Chagas' disease (chronic) with nervous system involvement	
		B57.5	Chagas' disease (chronic) with other organ involvement	
086.2	Chagas' Disease Without Mention of Organ Involvement	B57.1	Acute Chagas' disease without heart involvement	
086.3	Trypanosomiasis, Gambian	B56.0	Gambiense trypanosomiasis	
086.4	Trypanosomiasis, Rhodesian	B56.1	Rhodesiense trypanosomiasis	
086.5	Trypanosomiasis, African, Unspecified	B56.9	African trypanosomiasis, unspecified Trypanosomiasis NOS,	
088.9	Arthropod-borne Disease, Unspecified	A94	Unspecified arthropod-borne viral fever	
091.0	Syphilis, Genital (Primary)	A51.0	Primary genital syphilis	
		A51.9	Early syphilis, unspecified	
091.1	Syphilis, Primary Anal	A51.1	Primary anal syphilis	
091.2	Syphilis, Primary, Other	A51.0	Primary genital syphilis	
		A51.2	Primary syphilis of other sites	
091.3	Syphilis of Skin or Mucous Membrane, Secondary	A51.3	Secondary syphilis of skin and mucous membranes	
		A63.0	Anogenital (venereal) warts	
091.4	Adenopathy Due to Secondary Syphilis	A51.4	Other secondary syphilis	
091.5	Uveitis Due to Secondary Syphilis	A51.4	Other secondary syphilis	
091.6	Syphilis, Secondary of Viscera and Bone	A51.4	Other secondary syphilis	
091.7	Syphilis, Secondary, Relapse	A51.4	Other secondary syphilis	
		A51.9	Early syphilis, unspecified	
091.8	Syphilis, Secondary, Other Forms of	A51.3	Secondary syphilis of skin and mucous membranes	
		A51.4	Other secondary syphilis	
		A51.9	Early syphilis, unspecified	
091.9	Syphilis, Secondary, Unspecified	A51.4	Other secondary syphilis	
092.0	Syphilis, Early, Latent, Serological Relapse After Treatment	A51.5	Early syphilis, latent Syphilis (acquired) without clinical manifestations, with positive serological reaction and negative spinal fluid test, less than two years after infection.	
092.9	Syphilis, Early, Latent, Unspecified	A51.5	Early syphilis, latent Syphilis (acquired) without clinical manifestations, with positive serological reaction and negative spinal fluid test, less than two years after infection.	
093.8	Syphilis, Cardiovascular, Other Specified	A52.7	Other symptomatic late syphilis	
094.0	Tabes Dorsalis	A52.1	Symptomatic neurosyphilis	
094.1	Paresis, General	A52.1	Symptomatic neurosyphilis	
094.2	Meningitis, Syphilitic	A52.1	Symptomatic neurosyphilis	
094.3	Neurosyphilis, Asymptomatic	A52.2	Asymptomatic neurosyphilis	
094.8	Neurosyphilis, Other Specified	A52.1	Symptomatic neurosyphilis	
		A52.7	Other symptomatic late syphilis	

Translation of ICD-9 CM to ICD-10

ICD-9	Description	ICD-10	Description	(Continued)
094.9	Neurosyphilis, Unspecified	A52.2	Asymptomatic neurosyphilis	
		A52.3	Neurosyphilis, unspecified	
095	Syphilis, Late with Symptoms, Other Forms of	A52.7	Other symptomatic late syphilis	
		O98.1	Syphilis complicating pregnancy, childbirth and the puerperium Conditions in A50-A53	
096	Syphilis, Late, Latent	A52.8	Late syphilis, latent Syphilis (acquired) without clinical manifestations, with positive serological reaction and negative spinal fluid test, two years or more after infection.	
097.9	Syphilis	A51.9	Early syphilis, unspecified	
		A53.9	Syphilis, unspecified Infection due to Treponema pallidum	
098.0	Gonococcal Infection, Acute of Lower Genitourinary Tract	A54.0	Gonococcal infection of lower genitourinary tract without periurethral or accessory gland abscess	
		A54.1	Gonococcal infection of lower genitourinary tract with periurethral and accessory gland abscess	
		A54.8	Other gonococcal infections	
		A54.9	Gonococcal infection, unspecified	
098.1	Gonococcal Infection, Acute of Upper Genitourinary Tract	A54.0	Gonococcal infection of lower genitourinary tract without periurethral or accessory gland abscess	
098.2	Gonococcal Infection, Chronic of Lower Genitourinary Tract	A54.0	Gonococcal infection of lower genitourinary tract without periurethral or accessory gland abscess	
098.4	Gonococcal Infection of Eye	A54.3	Gonococcal infection of eye	
098.6	Gonococcal Infection of Pharynx	A54.5	Gonococcal pharyngitis	
098.7	Gonococcal Infection of Anus and Rectum	A54.6	Gonococcal infection of anus and rectum	
098.8	Gonococcal Infection of Other Specified Sites	A54.8	Other gonococcal infections	
099.0	Chancroid	A57	Chancroid Ulcus molle	
099.3	Reiter's Syndrome (Disease)	M02.3	Reiter's disease	
099.4	Urethritis, Other Nongonococcal	A64	Unspecified sexually transmitted disease	
		N34.1	Nonspecific urethritis Urethritis: . nongonococcal . nonvenereal	
099.8	Other Specified Venereal Disease	A51.0	Primary genital syphilis	
		A56.0	Chlamydial infection of lower genitourinary tract	
		A56.2	Chlamydial infection of genitourinary tract, unspecified	
		A56.3	Chlamydial infection of anus and rectum	
		A56.4	Chlamydial infection of pharynx	
		A56.8	Sexually transmitted chlamydial infection of other sites	
		A63.8	Other specified predominantly sexually transmitted diseases	
		A64	Unspecified sexually transmitted disease	
		I88.8	Other nonspecific lymphadenitis	
099.9	Venereal Disease, Unspecified	A64	Unspecified sexually transmitted disease	
101	Trench Mouth (Vincent's Angina)	A69.0	Necrotizing ulcerative stomatitis	
		A69.1	Other Vincent's infections	
110.0	Tinea (Dermatophytosis)	B35.0	Tinea barbae and tinea capitis	
		L44.8	Other specified papulosquamous disorders	
110.1	Dermatophytosis of Nail	B35.1	Tinea unguium	
110.2	Dermatophytosis of Hand	B35.2	Tinea manuum	
110.3	Dermatophytosis of Groin and Perianal Area	B35.6	Tinea cruris	
110.4	Athlete's Foot (Dermatophytosis of Foot)	B35.3	Tinea pedis	
110.5	Dermatophytosis of the Body	B35.4	Tinea corporis	
		B35.5	Tinea imbricata	
110.6	Dermatophytosis, Deep Seated	B35.8	Other dermatophytoses	
110.8	Dermatophytosis of Specified Sites	B35.8	Other dermatophytoses	
110.9	Dermatophytosis of Unspecified Site	B35.5	Tinea imbricata	
		B35.9	Dermatophytosis, unspecified	
111.8	Dermatomycoses, Other Specified	B36.8	Other specified superficial mycoses	
111.9	Dermatomycosis, Unspecified	B36.9	Superficial mycosis, unspecified	
112.0	Candidiasis of Mouth	B37.0	Candidal stomatitis	
		B37.9	Candidiasis, unspecified	
112.3	Candidiasis of Skin and Nails	B37.2	Candidiasis of skin and nail	
112.5	Candidiasis (Systemic)	B37.8	Candidiasis of other sites	
112.8	Candidiasis of Other Specified Sites	B37.7	Candidal septicaemia	
		B37.8	Candidiasis of other sites	
		B49	Unspecified mycosis	
112.9	Candidiasis, Unspecified Site	B37.9	Candidiasis, unspecified	
114	Coccidioidomycosis	B38.0	Acute pulmonary coccidioidomycosis	
		B38.1	Chronic pulmonary coccidioidomycosis	

2388 *The Medical Disability Advisor—Fourth Edition*

ICD-9	Description	ICD-10	Description	(Continued)
114	Coccidioidomycosis	B38.2	Pulmonary coccidioidomycosis, unspecified	
		B38.3	Cutaneous coccidioidomycosis	
		B38.7	Disseminated coccidioidomycosis	
		B38.8	Other forms of coccidioidomycosis	
		B38.9	Coccidioidomycosis, unspecified	
115.0	Infection by Histoplasma Capsulatum	B39.0	Acute pulmonary histoplasmosis capsulati	
		B39.1	Chronic pulmonary histoplasmosis capsulati	
		B39.2	Pulmonary histoplasmosis capsulati, unspecified	
		B39.3	Disseminated histoplasmosis capsulati	
		B39.4	Histoplasmosis capsulati, unspecified American histoplasmosis	
116.0	Blastomycosis	B40.0	Acute pulmonary blastomycosis	
		B40.1	Chronic pulmonary blastomycosis	
		B40.2	Pulmonary blastomycosis, unspecified	
		B40.3	Cutaneous blastomycosis	
		B40.7	Disseminated blastomycosis	
		B40.8	Other forms of blastomycosis	
		B40.9	Blastomycosis, unspecified	
116.1	Paracoccidioidomycosis	B41.0	Pulmonary paracoccidioidomycosis	
		B41.7	Disseminated paracoccidioidomycosis	
		B41.8	Other forms of paracoccidioidomycosis	
		B41.9	Paracoccidioidomycosis, unspecified	
116.2	Lobomycosis	B48.0	Lobomycosis	
117.2	Chromoblastomycosis	B43.0	Cutaneous chromomycosis	
		B43.8	Other forms of chromomycosis	
		B43.9	Chromomycosis, unspecified	
117.5	Cryptococcosis	B45.0	Pulmonary cryptococcosis	
		B45.1	Cerebral cryptococcosis	
		B45.2	Cutaneous cryptococcosis	
		B45.3	Osseous cryptococcosis	
		B45.7	Disseminated cryptococcosis	
		B45.8	Other forms of cryptococcosis	
		B45.9	Cryptococcosis, unspecified	
122.0	Echinococcus Granulosus Infection of Liver	B67.0	Echinococcus granulosus infection of liver	
122.1	Echinococcus Granulosus Infection of Lung	B67.1	Echinococcus granulosus infection of lung	
122.2	Echinococcus Granulosus Infection of Thyroid	B67.3	Echinococcus granulosus infection, other and multiple sites	
122.3	Echinococcus Granulosus Infection, Other	B67.2	Echinococcus granulosus infection of bone	
		B67.3	Echinococcus granulosus infection, other and multiple sites	
122.4	Echinococcus Granulosus Infection, Unspecified	B67.4	Echinococcus granulosus infection, unspecified	
122.5	Echinococcus Multilocularis Infection of Liver	B67.5	Echinococcus multilocularis infection of liver	
122.6	Echinococcus Multilocularis Infection, Other	B67.6	Echinococcus multilocularis infection, other and multiple sites	
122.7	Echinococcus Multilocularis Infection, Unspecified	B67.7	Echinococcus multilocularis infection, unspecified	
122.8	Echinococcus, Unspecified, of Liver	B67.8	Echinococcosis, unspecified, of liver	
122.9	Echinococcus, Other and Unspecified	B67.9	Echinococcosis, other and unspecified	
124	Trichinosis	B75	Trichinellosis Infection due to Trichinella species	
125.6	Other Specified Filariasis	B74.8	Other filariases	
		B83.8	Other specified helminthiases	
125.9	Filariasis, Unspecified	B74.9	Filariasis, unspecified	
130	Toxoplasmosis	B58.8	Toxoplasmosis with other organ involvement	
		B58.9	Toxoplasmosis, unspecified	
131.0	Trichomoniasis, Urogenital	A59.0	Urogenital trichomoniasis	
131.8	Trichomoniasis, Other Specified Sites	A59.8	Trichomoniasis of other sites	
131.9	Trichomoniasis, Unspecified	A59.9	Trichomoniasis, unspecified	
135	Sarcoidosis	D86.0	Sarcoidosis of lung	
		D86.1	Sarcoidosis of lymph nodes	
		D86.2	Sarcoidosis of lung with sarcoidosis of lymph nodes	
		D86.3	Sarcoidosis of skin	
		D86.8	Sarcoidosis of other and combined sites	
		D86.9	Sarcoidosis, unspecified	
136.1	Behçet's Syndrome	M35.2	Beh‡et's disease	
136.3	Pneumocystis Carinii Pneumonia	B59	Pneumocystosis Pneumonia due to Pneumocystis carinii	
136.4	Psorospermiasis	A07.8	Other specified protozoal intestinal diseases	

ICD-9	Description	ICD-10	Description	(Continued)
136.5	Sarcosporidiosis	A07.8	Other specified protozoal intestinal diseases	
136.9	Infection	B64	Unspecified protozoal disease	
		B89	Unspecified parasitic disease	
		B99	Other and unspecified infectious diseases	
		G04.0	Acute disseminated encephalitis postimmunization	
		G04.8	Other encephalitis, myelitis and encephalomyelitis	
		G36.1	Acute and subacute haemorrhagic leukoencephalitis [Hurst]	
138	Post Poliomyelitis Syndrome	B91	Sequelae of poliomyelitis	
141.0	Neoplasm, Base of Tongue, Malignant	C01	Malignant neoplasm of base of tongue	
141.1	Neoplasm, Dorsal Surface of Tongue, Malignant	C02.0	Dorsal surface of tongue	
141.2	Neoplasm, Tip and Lateral Border of Tongue, Malignant	C02.1	Border of tongue Tip of tongue	
141.3	Neoplasm, Ventral Surface of Tongue, Malignant	C02.2	Ventral surface of tongue	
141.4	Neoplasm, Anterior Two-thirds of Tongue, Malignant, Part Unspecified	C02.3	Anterior two-thirds of tongue, part unspecified	
141.5	Neoplasm, Junctional Zone, Malignant	C02.8	Overlapping lesion of tongue	
141.6	Neoplasm, Lingual Tonsil, Malignant	C02.4	Lingual tonsil	
141.8	Neoplasm, Other Sites of Tongue, Malignant	C02.8	Overlapping lesion of tongue	
141.9	Cancer, Tongue, Unspecified	C02.9	Tongue, unspecified	
145.5	Neoplasm, Palate, Malignant, Unspecified	C05.8	Overlapping lesion of palate	
		C05.9	Palate, unspecified	
		C46.2	Kaposi's sarcoma of palate	
145.9	Cancer, Mouth	C06.9	Mouth, unspecified Minor salivary gland	
146.0	Neoplasm, Tonsil, Malignant	C09.9	Tonsil, unspecified	
146.1	Neoplasm, Tonsillar Fossa, Malignant	C09.0	Tonsillar fossa	
146.2	Neoplasm, Tonsillar Pillars, Malignant	C09.1	Tonsillar pillar (anterior)(posterior)	
146.3	Neoplasm, Vallecula, Malignant	C10.0	Vallecula	
146.4	Neoplasm, Anterior Aspect of Epiglottis, Malignant	C10.1	Anterior surface of epiglottis	
146.5	Neoplasm, Junctional Region, Malignant	C10.8	Overlapping lesion of oropharynx	
146.6	Neoplasm, Lateral Wall of Oropharynx, Malignant	C10.2	Lateral wall of oropharynx	
146.7	Neoplasm, Posterior Wall of Oropharynx, Malignant	C10.3	Posterior wall of oropharynx	
146.8	Neoplasm, Other Specified Sites of Oropharynx, Malignant	C09.8	Overlapping lesion of tonsil	
		C10.4	Branchial cleft	
		C10.8	Overlapping lesion of oropharynx	
146.9	Cancer, Oropharynx, Unspecified	C10.9	Oropharynx, unspecified	
150.0	Neoplasm, Cervical Esophagus, Malignant	C15.0	Cervical part of oesophagus	
150.1	Neoplasm, Thoracic Esophagus, Malignant	C15.1	Thoracic part of oesophagus	
150.2	Neoplasm, Abdominal Esophagus, Malignant	C15.2	Abdominal part of oesophagus	
150.3	Neoplasm, Upper Third of Esophagus, Malignant	C15.3	Upper third of oesophagus	
150.4	Neoplasm, Middle Third of Esophagus, Malignant	C15.4	Middle third of oesophagus	
150.5	Neoplasm, Lower Third of Esophagus, Malignant	C15.5	Lower third of oesophagus	
150.8	Neoplasm, Other Specified Part of Esophagus, Malignant	C15.8	Overlapping lesion of oesophagus	
150.9	Cancer, Esophagus	C15.9	Oesophagus, unspecified	
151.0	Neoplasm, Cardia of Stomach, Malignant	C16.0	Cardia Cardiac orifice	
151.1	Neoplasm, Pylorus, Malignant	C16.4	Pylorus Prepylorus	
151.2	Neoplasm, Pyloric Antrum, Malignant	C16.3	Pyloric antrum	
151.3	Neoplasm, Fundus of Stomach, Malignant	C16.1	Fundus of stomach	
151.4	Neoplasm, Body of Stomach, Malignant	C16.2	Body of stomach	
151.5	Neoplasm, Lesser Curvature, Malignant, Unspecified	C16.5	Lesser curvature of stomach, unspecified	
151.6	Neoplasm, Greater Curvature, Malignant, Unspecified	C16.6	Greater curvature of stomach, unspecified	
151.8	Neoplasm, Other Specified Sites of Stomach, Malignant	C16.8	Overlapping lesion of stomach	
151.9	Cancer, Stomach	C16.9	Stomach, unspecified Gastric cancer NOS	
152.0	Neoplasm, Duodenum, Malignant	C17.0	Duodenum	
152.1	Neoplasm, Jejunum, Malignant	C17.1	Jejunum	
152.2	Neoplasm, Ileum, Malignant	C17.2	Ileum	
152.8	Neoplasm, Other Specified Sites of Small Intestine, Malignant	C17.8	Overlapping lesion of small intestine	
152.9	Cancer, Small Intestine (Including Duodenum)	C17.9	Small intestine, unspecified	
153.0	Neoplasm, Hepatic Flexure of Colon, Malignant	C18.3	Hepatic flexure	
153.1	Neoplasm, Transverse Colon, Malignant	C18.4	Transverse colon	
153.2	Neoplasm, Descending Colon, Malignant	C18.6	Descending colon	
153.3	Neoplasm, Sigmoid Colon, Malignant	C18.7	Sigmoid colon Sigmoid (flexure)	

ICD-9	Description	ICD-10	Description
153.4	Neoplasm, Cecum, Malignant	C18.0	Caecum Ileocaecal valve
153.5	Neoplasm, Appendix, Malignant	C18.1	Appendix
153.6	Neoplasm, Ascending Colon, Malignant	C18.2	Ascending colon
153.7	Neoplasm, Splenic Flexure of Colon, Malignant	C18.5	Splenic flexure
153.8	Neoplasm, Other Specified Sites of Large Intestine, Malignant	C18.8	Overlapping lesion of colon
153.9	Neoplasm, Colon, Malignant, Unspecified	C18.9	Colon, unspecified
154.0	Neoplasm, Rectosigmoid Junction (Colon Cancer), Malignant	C19	Malignant neoplasm of rectosigmoid junction
154.1	Cancer, Rectum	C20	Malignant neoplasm of rectum
154.2	Neoplasm, Anal Canal, Malignant	C21.1	Anal canal
154.3	Neoplasm, Anus, Malignant, Unspecified	C21.0	Anus, unspecified
154.8	Neoplasm, Rectum, Rectosigmoid Junction, and Anus, Malignant, Other	C21.2	Cloacogenic zone
		C21.8	Overlapping lesion of rectum, anus and anal canal
155.0	Hepatocarcinoma (Malignant Neoplasm of Liver, Primary)	C22.0	Liver cell carcinoma
		C22.2	Hepatoblastoma
		C22.3	Angiosarcoma of liver
		C22.4	Other sarcomas of liver
		C22.7	Other specified carcinomas of liver
		C22.9	Liver, unspecified
		C45.7	Mesothelioma of other sites
155.1	Neoplasm, Intrahepatic Bile Ducts, Malignant	C22.1	Intrahepatic bile duct carcinoma
155.2	Angiosarcoma, Hepatic	C22.9	Liver, unspecified
157.0	Neoplasm, Head of Pancreas, Malignant	C25.0	Head of pancreas
157.1	Neoplasm, Body of Pancreas, Malignant	C25.1	Body of pancreas
157.2	Neoplasm, Tail of Pancreas, Malignant	C25.2	Tail of pancreas
157.3	Neoplasm, Pancreatic Duct, Malignant	C25.3	Pancreatic duct
157.4	Neoplasm, Islets of Langerhans, Malignant	C25.4	Endocrine pancreas
157.8	Neoplasm, Other Specified Sites of Pancreas, Malignant	C25.7	Other parts of pancreas
		C25.8	Overlapping lesion of pancreas
157.9	Cancer, Pancreas, Part Unspecified	C25.9	Pancreas, unspecified
162.0	Neoplasm, Trachea, Malignant	C33	Malignant neoplasm of trachea
162.2	Neoplasm, Main Bronchus, Malignant	C34.0	Main bronchus
162.3	Neoplasm, Upper Lobe, Bronchus or Lung, Malignant	C34.1	Upper lobe, bronchus or lung
162.4	Neoplasm, Middle Lobe, Bronchus or Lung, Malignant	C34.2	Middle lobe, bronchus or lung
162.5	Neoplasm, Lower Lobe, Bronchus or Lung, Malignant	C34.3	Lower lobe, bronchus or lung
162.8	Neoplasm, Other Parts of Bronchus or Lung, Malignant	C34.8	Overlapping lesion of bronchus and lung
		C39.8	Overlapping lesion of respiratory and intrathoracic organs [See note 5 on page 182]
162.9	Cancer, Lung	C34.9	Bronchus or lung, unspecified
		C45.7	Mesothelioma of other sites
163.0	Neoplasm, Parietal Pleura, Malignant	C38.4	Pleura
163.1	Neoplasm, Visceral Pleura, Malignant	C38.4	Pleura
163.8	Neoplasm, Other Specified Sites of Pleura, Malignant	C38.4	Pleura
163.9	Cancer, Pleura	C38.4	Pleura
		C45.0	Mesothelioma of pleura
170.0	Neoplasm, Bones of Skull and Face, Malignant, Except Mandible	C41.0	Bones of skull and face
170.1	Neoplasm, Mandible, Malignant	C41.1	Mandible Lower
170.2	Neoplasm, Vertebral Column, Excluding Sacrum and Coccyx, Malignant	C41.2	Vertebral column
170.3	Neoplasm, Ribs, Sternum, and Clavicle, Malignant	C41.3	Ribs, sternum and clavicle
170.4	Neoplasm, Scapula and Long Bones of Upper Limb, Malignant	C40.0	Scapula and long bones of upper limb
		C40.8	Overlapping lesion of bone and articular cartilage of limbs
170.5	Neoplasm, Short Bones of Upper Limb, Malignant	C40.1	Short bones of upper limb
		C40.8	Overlapping lesion of bone and articular cartilage of limbs
170.6	Neoplasm, Pelvic Bones, Sacrum, and Coccyx, Malignant	C41.4	Pelvic bones, sacrum and coccyx
170.7	Neoplasm, Long Bones of Lower Limb, Malignant	C40.2	Long bones of lower limb
		C40.8	Overlapping lesion of bone and articular cartilage of limbs
170.8	Neoplasm, Short Bones of Lower Limb, Malignant	C40.3	Short bones of lower limb
		C40.8	Overlapping lesion of bone and articular cartilage of limbs

ICD-9	Description	ICD-10	Description	(Continued)
170.9	Bone Tumors	C40.9	Bone and articular cartilage of limb, unspecified	
		C41.9	Bone and articular cartilage, unspecified	
172.0	Malignant Melanoma of Lip	C43.0	Malignant melanoma of lip	
172.1	Malignant Melanoma of Eyelid, Including Canthus	C43.1	Malignant melanoma of eyelid, including canthus	
172.2	Malignant Melanoma of Ear and External Auditory Canal	C43.2	Malignant melanoma of ear and external auricular canal	
172.3	Malignant Melanoma of Other and Unspecified Parts of Face	C43.3	Malignant melanoma of other and unspecified parts of face	
172.4	Malignant Melanoma of Scalp and Neck	C43.4	Malignant melanoma of scalp and neck	
172.5	Malignant Melanoma of Trunk, Except Scrotum	C43.5	Malignant melanoma of trunk	
172.6	Malignant Melanoma of Upper Limb, Including Shoulder	C43.6	Malignant melanoma of upper limb, including shoulder	
172.7	Malignant Melanoma of Lower Limb, Including Hip	C43.7	Malignant melanoma of lower limb, including hip	
172.8	Malignant Melanoma of Other Specified Sites of Skin	C43.8	Overlapping malignant melanoma of skin	
		C80	Malignant neoplasm without specification of site	
172.9	Melanoma of Skin, Site Unspecified	C43.9	Malignant melanoma of skin, unspecified	
		C79.8	Secondary malignant neoplasm of other specified sites	
		C80	Malignant neoplasm without specification of site	
173.0	Neoplasm, Skin of Lip, Malignant, Other	C44.0	Skin of lip	
173.1	Neoplasm, Eyelid, Including Canthus, Malignant, Other	C44.1	Skin of eyelid, including canthus	
173.2	Neoplasm, Skin of Ear and External Auditory Canal, Malignant, Other	C44.2	Skin of ear and external auricular canal	
173.3	Neoplasm, Skin of Other and Unspecified Parts of Face, Malignant, Other	C44.3	Skin of other and unspecified parts of face	
173.4	Neoplasm, Scalp and Skin of Neck, Malignant, Other	C44.4	Skin of scalp and neck	
173.5	Neoplasm, Skin of Trunk, Except Scrotum, Malignant, Other	C44.5	Skin of trunk	
173.6	Neoplasm, Skin of Upper Limb, Including Shoulder, Malignant, Other	C44.6	Skin of upper limb, including shoulder	
173.7	Neoplasm, Skin of Lower Limb, Including Hip, Malignant, Other	C44.7	Skin of lower limb, including hip	
173.8	Neoplasm, Other Specified Sites of Skin, Malignant, Other	C44.8	Overlapping lesion of skin	
173.9	Skin Cancer, Unspecified	C44.9	Malignant neoplasm of skin, unspecified	
		C46.0	Kaposi's sarcoma of skin	
		C46.9	Kaposi's sarcoma, unspecified	
174.0	Paget's Disease of Breast	C50.0	Nipple and areola	
174.1	Neoplasm, Female Breast, Central Portion, Malignant	C50.1	Central portion of breast	
174.2	Neoplasm, Female Breast, Upper-inner Quadrant, Malignant	C50.2	Upper-inner quadrant of breast	
174.3	Neoplasm, Female Breast, Lower-inner Quadrant, Malignant	C50.3	Lower-inner quadrant of breast	
174.4	Neoplasm, Female Breast, Upper-outer Quadrant, Malignant	C50.4	Upper-outer quadrant of breast	
174.5	Neoplasm, Female Breast, Lower-outer Quadrant, Malignant	C50.5	Lower-outer quadrant of breast	
174.6	Neoplasm, Female Breast, Axillary Tail, Malignant	C50.6	Axillary tail of breast	
174.8	Neoplasm, Other Specified Sites of Female Breast, Malignant	C50.8	Overlapping lesion of breast	
174.9	Cancer, Breast, Unspecified	C50.9	Breast, unspecified	
175	Malignant Neoplasm of the Male Breast	C50.0	Nipple and areola	
		C50.1	Central portion of breast	
		C50.2	Upper-inner quadrant of breast	
		C50.3	Lower-inner quadrant of breast	
		C50.4	Upper-outer quadrant of breast	
		C50.5	Lower-outer quadrant of breast	
		C50.6	Axillary tail of breast	
		C50.8	Overlapping lesion of breast	
		C50.9	Breast, unspecified	
179	Cancer, Uterus	C55	Malignant neoplasm of uterus, part unspecified	
180.0	Neoplasm, Endocervix, Malignant	C53.0	Endocervix	
180.1	Neoplasm, Exocervix, Malignant	C53.1	Exocervix	
180.8	Neoplasm, Other Specified Sites of Cervix, Malignant	C53.8	Overlapping lesion of cervix uteri	
180.9	Cancer, Cervix, Unspecified	C53.9	Cervix uteri, unspecified	
181	Choriocarcinoma	C58	Malignant neoplasm of placenta	
182.0	Neoplasm, Corpus Uteri, Except Isthmus, Malignant (Endometrial Cancer)	C54.1	Endometrium	
		C54.2	Myometrium	

2392   *The Medical Disability Advisor—Fourth Edition*

ICD-9	Description	ICD-10	Description	(Continued)
182.0	Neoplasm, Corpus Uteri, Except Isthmus, Malignant (Endometrial Cancer)	C54.3	Fundus uteri	
		C54.9	Corpus uteri, unspecified	
182.1	Neoplasm, Isthmus, Malignant	C54.0	Isthmus uteri	
182.8	Neoplasm, Other Specified Sites of Body of Uterus, Malignant	C54.8	Overlapping lesion of corpus uteri	
183.0	Cancer, Ovary	C56	Malignant neoplasm of ovary	
185	Cancer, Prostate	C61	Malignant neoplasm of prostate	
186.9	Neoplasm, Other and Unspecified Testis, Malignant (Testicular Cancer)	C62.1	Descended testis	
		C62.9	Testis, unspecified	
188.0	Neoplasm, Trigone of Urinary Bladder, Malignant	C67.0	Trigone of bladder	
188.1	Neoplasm, Dome of Urinary Bladder, Malignant	C67.1	Dome of bladder	
188.2	Neoplasm, Lateral Wall of Urinary Bladder, Malignant	C67.2	Lateral wall of bladder	
188.3	Neoplasm, Anterior Wall of Urinary Bladder, Malignant	C67.3	Anterior wall of bladder	
188.4	Neoplasm, Posterior Wall of Urinary Bladder, Malignant	C67.4	Posterior wall of bladder	
188.5	Neoplasm, Bladder Neck, Malignant	C67.5	Bladder neck Internal urethral orifice	
188.6	Neoplasm, Ureteric Orifice, Malignant	C67.6	Ureteric orifice	
188.7	Neoplasm, Urachus, Malignant	C67.7	Urachus	
188.8	Neoplasm, Other Specified Sites of Bladder, Malignant	C67.8	Overlapping lesion of bladder [See note 5 on page 182]	
188.9	Cancer, Bladder, Unspecified	C67.9	Bladder, unspecified	
189.0	Cancer, Kidney	C64	Malignant neoplasm of kidney, except renal pelvis	
189.1	Neoplasm, Renal Pelvis, Malignant (Renal Cell Carcinoma)	C65	Malignant neoplasm of renal pelvis	
189.8	Neoplasm, Other Specified Sites of Urinary Organs, Malignant	C68.8	Overlapping lesion of urinary organs	
191.0	Neoplasm, Cerebrum, Except Lobes and Ventricles, Malignant	C71.0	Cerebrum, except lobes and ventricles Corpus callosum Supratentorial NOS	
191.1	Neoplasm, Frontal Lobe, Malignant	C71.1	Frontal lobe	
191.2	Neoplasm, Temporal Lobe, Malignant	C71.2	Temporal lobe	
191.3	Neoplasm, Parietal Lobe, Malignant	C71.3	Parietal lobe	
191.4	Neoplasm, Occipital Lobe, Malignant	C71.4	Occipital lobe	
191.5	Neoplasm, Ventricles, Malignant	C71.5	Cerebral ventricle	
		C71.7	Brain stem Fourth ventricle Infratentorial NOS	
191.6	Neoplasm, Cerebellum, Malignant	C71.6	Cerebellum	
191.7	Neoplasm, Brain Stem, Malignant	C71.7	Brain stem Fourth ventricle Infratentorial NOS	
191.8	Neoplasm, Other Parts of Brain, Malignant	C71.8	Overlapping lesion of brain	
191.9	Glioma	C71.9	Brain, unspecified	
192.1	Meningioma	C70.0	Cerebral meninges	
		C70.9	Meninges, unspecified	
192.8	Neoplasm, Other Specified Sites of Nervous System, Malignant (Glioma)	C72.8	Overlapping lesion of brain and other parts of central nervous system	
192.9	Neoplasm, Nervous System, Malignant, Part Unspecified	C72.9	Central nervous system, unspecified Nervous system NOS	
193	Cancer, Thyroid Gland	C73	Malignant neoplasm of thyroid gland	
194.4	Neoplasm, Pineal Gland, Malignant	C75.3	Pineal gland	
197.0	Neoplasm, Secondary, Lung, Malignant	C78.0	Secondary malignant neoplasm of lung	
197.2	Neoplasm, Secondary, Pleura, Malignant	C78.2	Secondary malignant neoplasm of pleura	
197.4	Neoplasm, Secondary, Small Intestine, Including Duodenum, Malignant	C78.4	Secondary malignant neoplasm of small intestine	
197.5	Neoplasm, Secondary, Large Intestine and Rectum, Malignant	C78.5	Secondary malignant neoplasm of large intestine and rectum	
197.7	Neoplasm, Secondary, Liver, Malignant, Specified As Secondary	C78.7	Secondary malignant neoplasm of liver	
197.8	Neoplasm, Secondary, Digestive Organs and Spleen (Esophagus, Stomach, Liver, Pancreas), Malignant	C78.8	Secondary malignant neoplasm of other and unspecified digestive organs	
198.1	Neoplasm, Secondary, Other Urinary Organs, Malignant (Bladder)	C79.1	Secondary malignant neoplasm of bladder and other and unspecified urinary organs	
198.2	Neoplasm, Skin, Malignant	C79.2	Secondary malignant neoplasm of skin	
198.3	Neoplasm, Secondary, Brain and Spinal Cord, Malignant	C79.3	Secondary malignant neoplasm of brain and cerebral meninges	
		C79.4	Secondary malignant neoplasm of other and unspecified parts of nervous system	
198.4	Neoplasm, Secondary, Other Parts of Nervous System, Malignant (Meninges)	C79.3	Secondary malignant neoplasm of brain and cerebral meninges	
		C79.4	Secondary malignant neoplasm of other and unspecified parts of nervous system	
		C79.8	Secondary malignant neoplasm of other specified sites	
198.5	Neoplasm, Secondary, Bone and Bone Marrow, Malignant	C79.5	Secondary malignant neoplasm of bone and bone marrow	

Translation of ICD-9 CM to ICD-10

ICD-9	Description	ICD-10	Description	(Continued)
198.6	Neoplasm, Secondary, Ovary, Malignant	C79.6	Secondary malignant neoplasm of ovary	
199.1	Cancer	C34.9	Bronchus or lung, unspecified	
		C45.9	Mesothelioma, unspecified	
		C80	Malignant neoplasm without specification of site	
200.1	Lymphosarcoma (Hodgkin's Disease)	C82.1	Mixed small cleaved and large cell, follicular	
		C82.2	Large cell, follicular	
		C82.7	Other types of follicular non-Hodgkin's lymphoma	
		C82.9	Follicular non-Hodgkin's lymphoma, unspecified	
		C83.0	Small cell (diffuse)	
		C83.1	Small cleaved cell (diffuse)	
		C83.3	Large cell (diffuse) Reticulum cell sarcoma	
		C83.5	Lymphoblastic (diffuse)	
		C84.3	Lymphoepithelioid lymphoma	
		C84.4	Peripheral T-cell lymphoma	
		C85.0	Lymphosarcoma	
		C88.3	Immunoproliferative small intestinal disease	
		C94.7	Other specified leukaemias Lymphosarcoma cell leukaemia	
200.2	Burkitt's Tumor or Lymphoma	C83.3	Large cell (diffuse) Reticulum cell sarcoma	
		C83.7	Burkitt's tumour	
200.8	Lymphoma, Other Name Variants	C83.0	Small cell (diffuse)	
		C83.2	Mixed small and large cell (diffuse)	
		C83.3	Large cell (diffuse) Reticulum cell sarcoma	
		C83.4	Immunoblastic (diffuse)	
		C83.8	Other types of diffuse non-Hodgkin's lymphoma	
		C84.3	Lymphoepithelioid lymphoma	
201.0	Hodgkin's Paragranuloma	C81.7	Other Hodgkin's disease	
201.1	Hodgkin's Granuloma	C81.7	Other Hodgkin's disease	
201.2	Hodgkin's Sarcoma	C81.7	Other Hodgkin's disease	
201.4	Hodgkin's Disease, Lymphocytic-histiocytic Predominance	C81.0	Lymphocytic predominance	
201.5	Hodgkin's Disease, Nodular Sclerosis	C81.1	Nodular sclerosis	
201.6	Hodgkin's Disease, Mixed Cellularity	C81.2	Mixed cellularity	
201.7	Hodgkin's Disease, Lymphocytic Depletion	C81.3	Lymphocytic depletion	
201.9	Hodgkin's Disease, Unspecified	C81.9	Hodgkin's disease, unspecified	
		C83.8	Other types of diffuse non-Hodgkin's lymphoma	
202.1	Mycosis Fungoides	C84.0	Mycosis fungoides	
202.8	Non-Hodgkin's Lymphoma	C82.1	Mixed small cleaved and large cell, follicular	
		C82.2	Large cell, follicular	
		C83.1	Small cleaved cell (diffuse)	
		C83.2	Mixed small and large cell (diffuse)	
		C83.3	Large cell (diffuse) Reticulum cell sarcoma	
		C83.5	Lymphoblastic (diffuse)	
		C83.6	Undifferentiated (diffuse)	
		C83.8	Other types of diffuse non-Hodgkin's lymphoma	
		C83.9	Diffuse non-Hodgkin's lymphoma, unspecified	
		C84.4	Peripheral T-cell lymphoma	
		C84.5	Other and unspecified T-cell lymphomas	
		C85.1	B-cell lymphoma, unspecified	
		C85.7	Other specified types of non-Hodgkin's lymphoma	
		C85.9	Non-Hodgkin's lymphoma, unspecified type	
		C96.7	Other specified malignant neoplasms of lymphoid, haematopoietic and related tissue	
		C96.9	Malignant neoplasm of lymphoid, haematopoietic and related tissue, unspecified	
203.0	Multiple Myeloma	C90.0	Multiple myeloma	
208.0	Leukemia, Acute, of Unspecified Cell Type	C95.0	Acute leukaemia of unspecified cell type	
208.1	Leukemia, Chronic, of Unspecified Cell Type	C95.1	Chronic leukaemia of unspecified cell type	
208.2	Leukemia, Subacute, of Unspecified Cell Type	C95.2	Subacute leukaemia of unspecified cell type	
208.8	Leukemia, Other, of Unspecified Cell Type	C95.7	Other leukaemia of unspecified cell type	
208.9	Leukemia, Unspecified	C95.9	Leukaemia, unspecified	
213.0	Neoplasm, Bones of Skull and Face, Benign	D16.4	Bones of skull and face	
213.1	Neoplasm, Lower Jaw Bone, Benign	D16.5	Lower jaw bone	
213.2	Neoplasm, Vertebral Column, Excluding Sacrum and Coccyx, Benign	D16.6	Vertebral column	

ICD-9	Description	ICD-10	Description	(Continued)
213.3	Neoplasm, Ribs, Sternum, and Clavicle, Benign	D16.7	Ribs, sternum and clavicle	
213.4	Neoplasm, Scapula and Long Bones of Upper Limb, Benign	D16.0	Scapula and long bones of upper limb	
213.5	Neoplasm, Short Bones of Upper Limb, Benign	D16.1	Short bones of upper limb	
213.6	Neoplasm, Pelvic Bones, Sacrum, and Coccyx, Benign	D16.8	Pelvic bones, sacrum and coccyx	
213.7	Neoplasm, Long Bones of Lower Limb, Benign	D16.2	Long bones of lower limb	
213.8	Neoplasm, Short Bones of Lower Limb, Benign	D16.3	Short bones of lower limb	
213.9	Neoplasm, Bone and Articular Cartilage, Benign, Site Unspecified	D16.9	Bone and articular cartilage, unspecified	
214	Lipoma	D17.0	Benign lipomatous neoplasm of skin and subcutaneous tissue of head, face and neck	
		D17.1	Benign lipomatous neoplasm of skin and subcutaneous tissue of trunk	
		D17.2	Benign lipomatous neoplasm of skin and subcutaneous tissue of limbs	
		D17.3	Benign lipomatous neoplasm of skin and subcutaneous tissue of other and unspecified sites	
		D17.4	Benign lipomatous neoplasm of intrathoracic organs	
		D17.5	Benign lipomatous neoplasm of intra-abdominal organs	
		D17.6	Benign lipomatous neoplasm of spermatic cord	
		D17.7	Benign lipomatous neoplasm of other sites Peritoneum Retroperitoneum	
		D17.9	Benign lipomatous neoplasm, unspecified	
218	Uterine Leiomyoma	D25.0	Submucous leiomyoma of uterus	
		D25.1	Intramural leiomyoma of uterus	
		D25.2	Subserosal leiomyoma of uterus	
		D25.9	Leiomyoma of uterus, unspecified	
223.3	Neoplasm, Bladder, Benign	D30.3	Bladder Orifice of bladder	
225.0	Neoplasm, Brain, Benign	D33.0	Brain, supratentorial	
		D33.1	Brain, infratentorial	
		D33.2	Brain, unspecified	
225.2	Neoplasm, Cerebral Meninges, Benign (Meningioma, Benign)	D32.0	Cerebral meninges	
		D32.9	Meninges, unspecified Meningioma NOS	
225.3	Benign Neoplasm, Spinal Cord	D33.4	Spinal cord	
227.0	Pheochromocytoma	D35.0	Adrenal gland	
227.4	Neoplasm, Pineal Gland, Benign	D35.4	Pineal gland	
229.9	Tumor, Benign	D11.9	Major salivary gland, unspecified	
		D17.9	Benign lipomatous neoplasm, unspecified	
		D19.9	Mesothelial tissue, unspecified	
		D36.9	Benign neoplasm of unspecified site	
		D48.9	Neoplasm of uncertain or unknown behaviour, unspecified "Growth" NOS Neoplasm NOS New growth NOS Tumour NOS	
230.0	Carcinoma in Situ of Oral Cavity (Tongue)	D00.0	Lip, oral cavity and pharynx	
230.1	Carcinoma in Situ of Esophagus	D00.1	Oesophagus	
230.2	Carcinoma in Situ of Stomach	D00.2	Stomach	
230.3	Carcinoma in Situ of Colon	D01.0	Colon Excludes: rectosigmoid junction (D01.1)	
230.4	Carcinoma in Situ of Rectum	D01.1	Rectosigmoid junction	
		D01.2	Rectum	
230.7	Carcinoma in Situ of Other and Unspecified Parts of Intestine	D01.4	Other and unspecified parts of intestine	
230.8	Carcinoma in Situ of Liver and Biliary System	D01.5	Liver, gallbladder and bile ducts	
231.2	Carcinoma in Situ of Bronchus and Lung	D02.2	Bronchus and lung	
232.0	Carcinoma in Situ of Skin of Lip	D03.0	Melanoma in situ of lip	
		D04.0	Skin of lip	
232.1	Carcinoma in Situ of Eyelid, Including Canthus	D03.1	Melanoma in situ of eyelid, including canthus	
		D04.1	Skin of eyelid, including canthus	
232.2	Carcinoma in Situ of Ear and External Auditory Canal	D03.2	Melanoma in situ of ear and external auricular canal	
		D04.2	Skin of ear and external auricular canal	
232.3	Carcinoma in Situ of Skin of Other and Unspecified Parts of Face	D03.3	Melanoma in situ of other and unspecified parts of face	
		D04.3	Skin of other and unspecified parts of face	
232.4	Carcinoma in Situ of Scalp and Skin of Neck	D03.4	Melanoma in situ of scalp and neck	
		D04.4	Skin of scalp and neck	
232.5	Carcinoma in Situ of Skin of Trunk, Except Scrotum	D03.5	Melanoma in situ of trunk	
		D04.5	Skin of trunk Anal	
232.6	Carcinoma in Situ of Skin of Upper Limb, Including Shoulder	D03.6	Melanoma in situ of upper limb, including shoulder	

ICD-9	Description	ICD-10	Description	(Continued)
232.6	Carcinoma in Situ of Skin of Upper Limb, Including Shoulder	D04.6	Skin of upper limb, including shoulder	
232.7	Carcinoma in Situ of Skin of Lower Limb, Including Hip	D03.7	Melanoma in situ of lower limb, including hip	
		D04.7	Skin of lower limb, including hip	
232.8	Carcinoma in Situ of Other Specified Sites of Skin	D03.8	Melanoma in situ of other sites	
		D04.8	Skin of other sites	
232.9	Carcinoma in Situ of Skin, Site Unspecified	D03.9	Melanoma in situ, unspecified	
		D04.9	Skin, unspecified	
233.0	Carcinoma in Situ of the Breast	D05.0	Lobular carcinoma in situ	
		D05.1	Intraductal carcinoma in situ	
		D05.7	Other carcinoma in situ of breast	
		D05.9	Carcinoma in situ of breast, unspecified	
233.1	Carcinoma in Situ of Cervix Uteri	D06.0	Endocervix	
		D06.1	Exocervix	
		D06.7	Other parts of cervix	
		D06.9	Cervix, unspecified	
233.2	Carcinoma in Situ of Other and Unspecified Parts of Uterus	D07.0	Endometrium	
		D07.3	Other and unspecified female genital organs	
233.3	Carcinoma in Situs of Other and Unspecified Female Genital Organs	D03.8	Melanoma in situ of other sites	
		D07.1	Vulva Vulvar intraepithelial neoplasia [VIN], grade III, with or without mention of severe dysplasia	
		D07.2	Vagina Vaginal intraepithelial neoplasia [VAIN], grade III, with or without mention of severe dysplasia	
		D07.3	Other and unspecified female genital organs	
233.4	Carcinoma in Situ of Prostate	D07.5	Prostate	
233.6	Carcinoma in Situ of Other and Unspecified Male Genital Organs (Testis)	D03.8	Melanoma in situ of other sites	
		D07.6	Other and unspecified male genital organs	
233.7	Carcinoma in Situ of Bladder	D09.0	Bladder	
233.9	Carcinoma in Situ of Other and Unspecified Urinary Organs	D09.1	Other and unspecified urinary organs	
234.8	Carcinoma in Situ of Endocrine (Pineal) Gland	D09.3	Thyroid and other endocrine glands	
		D09.7	Carcinoma in situ of other specified sites	
235.1	Neoplasm of Uncertain Behavior of Digestive and Respiratory Systems, Lip, Oral Cavity and Pharynx	D37.0	Lip, oral cavity and pharynx	
235.2	Neoplasm of Uncertain Behavior of Stomach, Intestines and Rectum	D37.1	Stomach	
		D37.2	Small intestine	
		D37.3	Appendix	
		D37.4	Colon	
		D37.5	Rectum Rectosigmoid junction	
		D37.7	Other digestive organs	
235.8	Neoplasm of Uncertain Behavior of Pleura, Thymus and Mediastinum	D38.2	Pleura	
		D38.3	Mediastinum	
		D38.4	Thymus	
236.0	Neoplasm of Uncertain Behavior of Genitourinary Organs, Uterus	D39.0	Uterus	
236.2	Neoplasm of Uncertain Behavior of Genitourinary Organs, ovary	C56	Malignant neoplasm of ovary	
		D39.1	Ovary	
236.4	Neoplasm of Uncertain Behavior of Genitourinary Organs, Testis	D40.1	Testis	
236.5	Neoplasm of Uncertain Behavior of Genitourinary Organs, Prostate	D40.0	Prostate	
236.7	Bladder Polyps	D41.4	Bladder	
237.1	Pineal Gland Neoplasm	D44.5	Pineal gland	
237.5	Brain and Spinal Cord	D43.0	Brain, supratentorial	
		D43.1	Brain, infratentorial	
		D43.2	Brain, unspecified	
		D43.4	Spinal cord	
237.6	Meninges	D42.0	Cerebral meninges	
		D42.1	Spinal meninges	
		D42.9	Meninges, unspecified	

ICD-9	Description	ICD-10	Description	(Continued)
237.7	Neurofibromatosis	Q85.0	Neurofibromatosis (nonmalignant) Von Recklinghausen's disease	
238.2	Neoplasm of Uncertain Behavior, Skin	D48.5	Skin Anal	
238.4	Polycythemia Vera	D45	Polycythaemia vera	
238.7	Other Lymphatic and Hematopoietic Tissues	C94.4	Acute panmyelosis	
		D47.1	Chronic myeloproliferative disease Myelofibrosis (with myeloid metaplasia) Myeloproliferative disease, unspecified	
		D47.3	Essential (haemorrhagic) thrombocythaemia Idiopathic haemorrhagic thrombocythaemia	
		D47.7	Other specified neoplasms of uncertain or unknown behaviour of lymphoid, haematopoietic and related tissue	
		D47.9	Neoplasm of uncertain or unknown behaviour of lymphoid, haematopoietic and related tissue, unspecified	
239.0	Neoplasms of Unspecified Nature of Digestive System	D37.0	Lip, oral cavity and pharynx	
		D37.1	Stomach	
		D37.2	Small intestine	
		D37.3	Appendix	
		D37.4	Colon	
		D37.5	Rectum Rectosigmoid junction	
		D37.6	Liver, gallbladder and bile ducts	
		D37.7	Other digestive organs	
		D37.9	Digestive organ, unspecified	
		D48.3	Retroperitoneum	
		D48.4	Peritoneum	
239.3	Neoplasm of Unspecified Nature of Breast	D48.6	Breast Connective tissue of breast	
239.4	Neoplasm of Unspecified Nature, Bladder	D41.4	Bladder	
239.5	Neoplasm of Other Genitourinary Organs	D39.0	Uterus	
		D39.1	Ovary	
		D39.2	Placenta Chorioadenoma destruens Hydatidiform mole	
		D39.7	Other female genital organs	
		D39.9	Female genital organ, unspecified	
		D40.0	Prostate	
		D40.1	Testis	
		D40.7	Other male genital organs	
		D40.9	Male genital organ, unspecified	
		D41.0	Kidney	
		D41.1	Renal pelvis	
		D41.2	Ureter	
		D41.3	Urethra	
		D41.7	Other urinary organs	
		D41.9	Urinary organ, unspecified	
239.7	Neoplasm of Unspecified Nature, Endocrine Glands and Other Parts of Nervous System	D42.0	Cerebral meninges	
		D42.1	Spinal meninges	
		D42.9	Meninges, unspecified	
		D43.3	Cranial nerves	
		D43.4	Spinal cord	
		D43.7	Other parts of central nervous system	
		D43.9	Central nervous system, unspecified	
		D44.0	Thyroid gland	
		D44.1	Adrenal gland	
		D44.2	Parathyroid gland	
		D44.3	Pituitary gland	
		D44.4	Craniopharyngeal duct	
		D44.5	Pineal gland	
		D44.6	Carotid body	
		D44.7	Aortic body and other paraganglia	
		D44.8	Pluriglandular involvement Multiple endocrine adenomatosis	
		D44.9	Endocrine gland, unspecified	
240.0	Goiter, Specified As Simple	E04.0	Nontoxic diffuse goitre	
240.9	Goiter	E01.0	Iodine-deficiency-related diffuse (endemic) goitre	
		E01.2	Iodine-deficiency-related (endemic) goitre, unspecified Endemic goitre NOS	
		E04.0	Nontoxic diffuse goitre	

Translation of ICD-9 CM to ICD-10

ICD-9	Description	ICD-10	Description	(Continued)
240.9	Goiter	E04.9	Nontoxic goitre, unspecified	
242.0	Goiter, Toxic Diffuse (Graves' Disease)	E05.0	Thyrotoxicosis with diffuse goitre Exophthalmic or toxic goitre NOS	
		E05.9	Thyrotoxicosis, unspecified	
242.1	Hyperthyroidism	E05.1	Thyrotoxicosis with toxic single thyroid nodule	
		E05.2	Thyrotoxicosis with toxic multinodular goitre	
242.2	Goiter, Toxic Multinodular	E05.2	Thyrotoxicosis with toxic multinodular goitre	
242.3	Goiter, Toxic Nodular, Unspecified	E05.2	Thyrotoxicosis with toxic multinodular goitre	
242.8	Thyrotoxicosis of Other Specified Origin	E05.4	Thyrotoxicosis factitia	
		E05.8	Other thyrotoxicosis	
242.9	Thyrotoxicosis without Mention of Goiter or Other Cause (Hyperthyroidism)	E05.5	Thyroid crisis or storm	
		E05.9	Thyrotoxicosis, unspecified	
243	Congenital Hypothyroidism	E00.0	Congenital iodine-deficiency syndrome, neurological type	
		E00.1	Congenital iodine-deficiency syndrome, myxoedematous type	
		E00.2	Congenital iodine-deficiency syndrome, mixed type	
		E00.9	Congenital iodine-deficiency syndrome, unspecified	
		E03.1	Congenital hypothyroidism without goitre Aplasia of thyroid (with myxoedema)	
		E07.1	Dyshormogenetic goitre	
244.0	Hypothyroidism, Postsurgical	E89.0	Postprocedural hypothyroidism Postirradiation hypothyroidism Postsurgical hypothyroidism	
244.1	Hypothyroidism, Other Postablative	E89.0	Postprocedural hypothyroidism Postirradiation hypothyroidism Postsurgical hypothyroidism	
244.2	Hypothyroidism, Iodine	E01.8	Other iodine-deficiency-related thyroid disorders and allied conditions	
244.3	Hypothyroidism, Other Iatrogenic	E03.2	Hypothyroidism due to medicaments and other exogenous substances	
244.8	Hypothyroidism, Other Specified Acquired	E01.8	Other iodine-deficiency-related thyroid disorders and allied conditions	
		E02	Subclinical iodine-deficiency hypothyroidism	
		E03.2	Hypothyroidism due to medicaments and other exogenous substances	
		E03.3	Postinfectious hypothyroidism	
		E03.4	Atrophy of thyroid (acquired)	
		E03.5	Myxoedema coma	
		E03.8	Other specified hypothyroidism	
244.9	Hypothyroidism, Unspecified (Myxedema)	E03.4	Atrophy of thyroid (acquired)	
		E03.9	Hypothyroidism, unspecified Myxoedema NOS	
		E23.0	Hypopituitarism	
245.0	Thyroiditis, Acute	E06.0	Acute thyroiditis Abscess of thyroid	
245.1	Thyroiditis, Subacute	E06.1	Subacute thyroiditis	
245.2	Hashimoto's Thyroiditis	E06.3	Autoimmune thyroiditis	
245.3	Thyroiditis, Chronic Fibrous	E06.5	Other chronic thyroiditis	
245.9	Thyroiditis, Unspecified	E06.9	Thyroiditis, unspecified	
246.1	Congenital (dyshormonogenic) goiter	E03.0	Congenital hypothyroidism with diffuse goitre Goitre (nontoxic) congenital	
		E07.1	Dyshormogenetic goitre	
250.7	Diabetic Gangrene	L92.1	Necrobiosis lipoidica, not elsewhere classified Excludes: that associated with diabetes mellitus (E10-E14)	
251.1	Hyperinsulinism	E16.0	Drug-induced hypoglycaemia without coma	
		E16.1	Other hypoglycaemia Functional nonhyperinsulinaemic hypoglycaemia	
251.2	Hypoglycemia, Unspecified	E16.1	Other hypoglycaemia Functional nonhyperinsulinaemic hypoglycaemia	
		E16.2	Hypoglycaemia, unspecified	
252.0	Hyperparathyroidism	E21.0	Primary hyperparathyroidism Hyperplasia of parathyroid Osteitis fibrosa cystica generalisata [von Recklinghausen's disease of bone]	
		E21.1	Secondary hyperparathyroidism, not elsewhere classified	
		E21.2	Other hyperparathyroidism	
		E21.3	Hyperparathyroidism, unspecified	
		M85.0	Fibrous dysplasia (monostotic) Excludes: fibrous dysplasia of jaw (K10.8)	
252.1	Hypoparathyroidism	E20.0	Idiopathic hypoparathyroidism	
		E20.8	Other hypoparathyroidism	
		E20.9	Hypoparathyroidism, unspecified	
		E89.2	Postprocedural hypoparathyroidism Parathyroprival tetany	
253.2	Simmonds' Disease (Panhypopituitarism)	E23.0	Hypopituitarism	
253.5	Diabetes Insipidus	E23.2	Diabetes insipidus	
255.0	Cushing's Syndrome	E24.0	Pituitary-dependent Cushing's disease	
		E24.1	Nelson's syndrome	
		E24.2	Drug-induced Cushing's syndrome	

ICD-9	Description	ICD-10	Description	(Continued)
255.0	Cushing's Syndrome	E24.3	Ectopic ACTH syndrome	
		E24.4	Alcohol-induced pseudo-Cushing's syndrome	
		E24.8	Other Cushing's syndrome	
		E24.9	Cushing's syndrome, unspecified	
255.1	Aldosteronism	E26.0	Primary hyperaldosteronism Conn's syndrome	
		E26.1	Secondary hyperaldosteronism	
		E26.8	Other hyperaldosteronism Bartter's syndrome	
		E26.9	Hyperaldosteronism, unspecified	
255.4	Addison's Disease (Corticoadrenal Insufficiency)	E27.1	Primary adrenocortical insufficiency Addison's disease Autoimmune adrenalitis	
		E27.2	Addisonian crisis Adrenal crisis Adrenocortical crisis	
		E27.3	Drug-induced adrenocortical insufficiency	
		E27.4	Other and unspecified adrenocortical insufficiency	
		E27.8	Other specified disorders of adrenal gland	
		E71.3	Disorders of fatty-acid metabolism	
		E89.6	Postprocedural adrenocortical(-medullary) hypofunction	
256.3	Premature Menopause	E28.3	Primary ovarian failure Decreased estrogen	
256.4	Polycystic Ovary Syndrome (Stein-Leventhal Syndrome)	E28.2	Polycystic ovarian syndrome Sclerocystic ovary syndrome Stein-Leventhal syndrome	
264.5	Vitamin A Deficiency with Night Blindness	E50.5	Vitamin A deficiency with night blindness	
264.9	Vitamin A Deficiency, Unspecified	E50.9	Vitamin A deficiency, unspecified Hypovitaminosis A NOS	
		E64.1	Sequelae of vitamin A deficiency	
265.0	Beriberi	E51.1	Beriberi Beriberi	
		S36.0	Injury of spleen	
265.1	Thiamine Deficiency	E51.2	Wernicke's encephalopathy	
		E51.8	Other manifestations of thiamine deficiency	
		E51.9	Thiamine deficiency, unspecified	
		E64.8	Sequelae of other nutritional deficiencies	
265.2	Pellagra	E52	Niacin deficiency [pellagra]	
		E64.8	Sequelae of other nutritional deficiencies	
266.0	Vitamin B2 [riboflavin] Deficiency	E53.0	Riboflavin deficiency Ariboflavinosis	
266.2	Vitamin B12 Deficiency	E53.8	Deficiency of other specified B group vitamins	
		E53.9	Vitamin B deficiency, unspecified	
267	Vitamin C (Ascorbic Acid) Deficiency	E54	Ascorbic acid deficiency	
		E64.2	Sequelae of vitamin C deficiency	
268.0	Rickets, Active	E55.0	Rickets, active	
268.2	Osteomalacia, Unspecified	M83.0	Puerperal osteomalacia	
		M83.1	Senile osteomalacia	
		M83.2	Adult osteomalacia due to malabsorption Postsurgical malabsorption osteomalacia in adults	
		M83.3	Adult osteomalacia due to malnutrition	
		M83.4	Aluminium bone disease	
		M83.5	Other drug-induced osteomalacia in adults	
		M83.8	Other adult osteomalacia	
		M83.9	Adult osteomalacia, unspecified	
268.9	Vitamin D Deficiency, Unspecified	E55.9	Vitamin D deficiency, unspecified Avitaminosis D	
269.0	Vitamin K Deficiency	E56.1	Deficiency of vitamin K	
269.1	Vitamin E Deficiency	E53.8	Deficiency of other specified B group vitamins	
		E56.0	Deficiency of vitamin E	
		E56.8	Deficiency of other vitamins	
269.2	Hypovitaminosis	E56.9	Vitamin deficiency, unspecified	
		E64.8	Sequelae of other nutritional deficiencies	
271.4	Glycosuria, Renal	E74.8	Other specified disorders of carbohydrate metabolism	
272.7	Lipidoses	D76.0	Langerhans' cell histiocytosis, not elsewhere classified Eosinophilic granuloma Hand-Schller-Christian disease Histiocytosis X (chronic)	
		E74.0	Glycogen storage disease Cardiac glycogenosis Disease	
		E75.0	GM2 gangliosidosis	
		E75.2	Other sphingolipidosis	
		E75.3	Sphingolipidosis, unspecified	
		E75.5	Other lipid storage disorders	
		E75.6	Lipid storage disorder, unspecified	
		E77.0	Defects in post-translational modification of lysosomal enzymes Mucolipidosis II [I-cell disease] Mucolipidosis III [pseudo-Hurler polydystrophy]	

Translation of ICD-9 CM to ICD-10

ICD-9	Description	ICD-10	Description	(Continued)
272.7	Lipidoses	E78.2	Mixed hyperlipidaemia	
272.8	Dercum's Disease	E78.8	Other disorders of lipoprotein metabolism	
		E88.2	Lipomatosis, not elsewhere classified	
		E88.8	Other specified metabolic disorders Launois-Bensaude adenolipomatosis Trimethylaminuria	
272.9	Unspecified Disorders of Lipoid Metabolism	E78.9	Disorder of lipoprotein metabolism, unspecified	
273.8	Hypoproteinemia	E77.8	Other disorders of glycoprotein metabolism	
		E88.0	Disorders of plasma-protein metabolism, not elsewhere classified	
		R77.1	Abnormality of globulin Hyperglobulinaemia NOS	
274.0	Gouty Arthropathy (Gouty Arthritis)	M10.0	Idiopathic gout Gouty bursitis Primary gout Urate tophus of heart+ (I43.8*)	
		M10.9	Gout, unspecified	
274.1	Gouty Nephropathy	M10.0	Idiopathic gout Gouty bursitis Primary gout Urate tophus of heart+ (I43.8*)	
274.8	Gout with Other Specified Manifestations	M10.0	Idiopathic gout Gouty bursitis Primary gout Urate tophus of heart+ (I43.8*)	
		M10.9	Gout, unspecified	
274.9	Gout, Unspecified	M10.0	Idiopathic gout Gouty bursitis Primary gout Urate tophus of heart+ (I43.8*)	
		M10.2	Drug-induced gout	
		M10.3	Gout due to impairment of renal function	
		M10.4	Other secondary gout	
		M10.9	Gout, unspecified	
275.1	Wilson's Disease	E83.0	Disorders of copper metabolism Menkes' (kinky hair)(steely hair) disease Wilson's disease	
		H18.0	Corneal pigmentations and deposits Haematocornea Kayser-Fleischer ring Krukenberg's spindle Staehli's line Use additional external cause code (Chapter XX), if desired, to identify drug, if drug-induced.	
276.5	Dehydration	E86	Volume depletion Dehydration	
276.7	Hyperkalemia	E87.5	Hyperkalaemia Potassium [K]	
277.0	Cystic Fibrosis	E84.0	Cystic fibrosis with pulmonary manifestations	
		E84.1	Cystic fibrosis with intestinal manifestations	
		E84.8	Cystic fibrosis with other manifestations	
		E84.9	Cystic fibrosis, unspecified	
277.1	Porphyria	E80.0	Hereditary erythropoietic porphyria Congenital erythropoietic porphyria Erythropoietic protoporphyria	
		E80.1	Porphyria cutanea tarda	
		E80.2	Other porphyria	
277.2	Other Disorders of Purine and Pyrimidine Metabolism	E79.1	Lesch-Nyhan syndrome	
		E79.8	Other disorders of purine and pyrimidine metabolism	
		E79.9	Disorder of purine and pyrimidine metabolism, unspecified	
277.3	Amyloidosis	E85.0	Non-neuropathic heredofamilial amyloidosis	
		E85.1	Neuropathic heredofamilial amyloidosis	
		E85.2	Heredofamilial amyloidosis, unspecified	
		E85.3	Secondary systemic amyloidosis Haemodialysis-associated amyloidosis	
		E85.4	Organ-limited amyloidosis	
		E85.8	Other amyloidosis	
		E85.9	Amyloidosis, unspecified	
278.0	Obesity, Simple	E66.0	Obesity due to excess calories	
		E66.1	Drug-induced obesity	
		E66.8	Other obesity Morbid obesity	
		E66.9	Obesity, unspecified Simple obesity NOS	
278.2	Hypervitaminosis A	E67.0	Hypervitaminosis A	
278.4	Hypervitaminosis D	E67.3	Hypervitaminosis D	
278.8	Hyperalimentation (Hypervitaminosis), Other	E66.2	Extreme obesity with alveolar hypoventilation	
		E67.2	Megavitamin-B6 syndrome	
		E67.8	Other specified hyperalimentation	
		E68	Sequelae of hyperalimentation	
279.4	Autoimmune Disease, Not Elsewhere Classified	M35.9	Systemic involvement of connective tissue, unspecified	
280	Iron Deficiency Anemia	D50.0	Iron deficiency anaemia secondary to blood loss (chronic)	
		D50.1	Sideropenic dysphagia	
		D50.8	Other iron deficiency anaemias	
		D50.9	Iron deficiency anaemia, unspecified	
281.0	Pernicious Anemia	D51.0	Vitamin B12 deficiency anaemia due to intrinsic factor deficiency	
281.1	Vitamin B12 Deficiency Anemia, Other	D51.1	Vitamin B12 deficiency anaemia due to selective vitamin B12 malabsorption with proteinuria	

ICD-9	Description	ICD-10	Description	(Continued)
281.1	Vitamin B12 Deficiency Anemia, Other	D51.2	Transcobalamin II deficiency	
		D51.3	Other dietary vitamin B12 deficiency anaemia	
		D51.8	Other vitamin B12 deficiency anaemias	
		D51.9	Vitamin B12 deficiency anaemia, unspecified	
281.2	Folic Acid Deficiency Anemia	D52.0	Dietary folate deficiency anaemia	
		D52.1	Drug-induced folate deficiency anaemia	
		D52.8	Other folate deficiency anaemias	
		D52.9	Folate deficiency anaemia, unspecified	
282.0	Spherocytosis, Hereditary	D58.0	Hereditary spherocytosis Acholuric (familial) jaundice Congenital (spherocytic) haemolytic icterus Minkowski-Chauffard syndrome	
282.1	Hereditary Elliptocytosis	D58.1	Hereditary elliptocytosis Elliptocytosis (congenital) Ovalocytosis (congenital)(hereditary)	
282.2	Anemias Due to Disorders of Glutathione Metabolism	D55.0	Anaemia due to glucose-6-phosphate dehydrogenase [G6PD] deficiency	
		D55.1	Anaemia due to other disorders of glutathione metabolism	
		D59.2	Drug-induced nonautoimmune haemolytic anaemia	
282.3	Hemolytic Anemias Due to Enzyme Deficiency, Other	D55.2	Anaemia due to disorders of glycolytic enzymes	
		D55.3	Anaemia due to disorders of nucleotide metabolism	
		D55.8	Other anaemias due to enzyme disorders	
		D55.9	Anaemia due to enzyme disorder, unspecified	
282.4	Thalassaemia	D56.0	Alpha thalassaemia	
		D56.1	Beta thalassaemia	
		D56.2	Delta-beta thalassaemia	
		D56.3	Thalassaemia trait	
		D56.8	Other thalassaemias	
		D56.9	Thalassaemia, unspecified	
		D64.8	Other specified anaemias	
282.5	Sickle-Cell Trait	D57.3	Sickle-cell trait Hb-S trait	
282.6	Sickle Cell Anemia	D57.0	Sickle-cell anaemia with crisis	
		D57.1	Sickle-cell anaemia without crisis	
		D57.2	Double heterozygous sickling disorders	
		D57.8	Other sickle-cell disorders	
		D58.2	Other haemoglobinopathies	
282.8	Hemolytic Anemia, Hereditary, Other Specified	D58.8	Other specified hereditary haemolytic anaemias	
282.9	Hemolytic Anemia, Unspecified Hereditary	D58.9	Hereditary haemolytic anaemia, unspecified	
283.0	Hemolytic Anemias, Autoimmune	D59.0	Drug-induced autoimmune haemolytic anaemia	
		D59.1	Other autoimmune haemolytic anaemias	
283.1	Hemolytic Anemias, Non-Autoimmune	D59.1	Other autoimmune haemolytic anaemias	
		D59.2	Drug-induced nonautoimmune haemolytic anaemia	
		D59.3	Haemolytic-uraemic syndrome	
		D59.4	Other nonautoimmune haemolytic anaemias	
283.2	Hemoglobinuria Due to Hemolysis from External Causes	D59.5	Paroxysmal nocturnal haemoglobinuria [Marchiafava-Micheli]	
		D59.6	Haemoglobinuria due to haemolysis from other external causes	
		D59.9	Acquired haemolytic anaemia, unspecified	
283.9	Hemolytic Anemia, Acquired, Unspecified	D59.8	Other acquired haemolytic anaemias	
		D59.9	Acquired haemolytic anaemia, unspecified	
284.0	Aplastic Anemia, Constitutional	D61.0	Constitutional aplastic anaemia	
284.8	Aplastic Anemias, Other Specified	D60.0	Chronic acquired pure red cell aplasia	
		D60.1	Transient acquired pure red cell aplasia	
		D60.8	Other acquired pure red cell aplasias	
		D60.9	Acquired pure red cell aplasia, unspecified	
		D61.1	Drug-induced aplastic anaemia	
		D61.2	Aplastic anaemia due to other external agents	
		D61.8	Other specified aplastic anaemias	
		D61.9	Aplastic anaemia, unspecified	
284.9	Aplastic Anemia, Unspecified	D46.0	Refractory anaemia without sideroblasts, so stated	
		D46.2	Refractory anaemia with excess of blasts	
		D46.3	Refractory anaemia with excess of blasts with transformation	
		D46.4	Refractory anaemia, unspecified	
		D61.3	Idiopathic aplastic anaemia	
		D61.8	Other specified aplastic anaemias	
		D61.9	Aplastic anaemia, unspecified	

Translation of ICD-9 CM to ICD-10

ICD-9	Description	ICD-10	Description	(Continued)
285.1	Anemia, Posthemorrhagic, Acute	D62	Acute posthaemorrhagic anaemia	
285.8	Myelophthisic Anemia	D61.9	Aplastic anaemia, unspecified	
		D64.4	Congenital dyserythropoietic anaemia	
		D64.8	Other specified anaemias	
285.9	Anemia, Unspecified	D58.2	Other haemoglobinopathies	
		D64.8	Other specified anaemias	
		D64.9	Anaemia, unspecified	
286.0	Hemophilia A	D66	Hereditary factor VIII deficiency	
286.1	Hemophilia B	D67	Hereditary factor IX deficiency	
286.3	Hypoprothrombinemia	D68.2	Hereditary deficiency of other clotting factors	
		D68.8	Other specified coagulation defects	
286.9	Other and Unspecified Coagulation Defects	D68.8	Other specified coagulation defects	
		D68.9	Coagulation defect, unspecified	
287.2	Purpura Simplex	D69.2	Other nonthrombocytopenic purpura	
		R23.3	Spontaneous ecchymoses	
287.3	Idiopathic Thrombocytopenic Purpura	D69.3	Idiopathic thrombocytopenic purpura	
		D69.4	Other primary thrombocytopenia	
287.4	Secondary Thrombocytopenia	D69.5	Secondary thrombocytopenia	
287.5	Thrombocytopenia, Unspecified	D69.6	Thrombocytopenia, unspecified	
288.0	Neutropenia (Agranulocytosis)	D70	Agranulocytosis	
289.1	Lymphadenitis, Chronic	I88.1	Chronic lymphadenitis, except mesenteric	
289.2	Lymphadenitis, Nonspecific Mesenteric	I88.0	Nonspecific mesenteric lymphadenitis	
289.3	Lymphadenitis, Unspecified, Except Mesenteric	I88.8	Other nonspecific lymphadenitis	
		I88.9	Nonspecific lymphadenitis, unspecified	
		I89.8	Other specified noninfective disorders of lymphatic vessels and lymph nodes	
289.4	Hypersplenism	D73.1	Hypersplenism	
290.1	Dementia, Presenile	A81.0	Creutzfeldt-Jakob disease Subacute spongiform encephalopathy	
		F03	Unspecified dementia	
		G30.0	Alzheimer's disease with early onset	
		G30.1	Alzheimer's disease with late onset	
		G30.8	Other Alzheimer's disease	
		G30.9	Alzheimer's disease, unspecified	
		G31.0	Circumscribed brain atrophy	
		G31.8	Other specified degenerative diseases of nervous system	
290.2	Dementia, Alzheimer's Type, with Delusions (Late Onset)	F03	Unspecified dementia	
290.9	Unspecified Senile Psychotic Condition	F03	Unspecified dementia	
293.0	Acute Delirium	F05.0	Delirium not superimposed on dementia, so described	
		F05.9	Delirium, unspecified	
293.8	Other Specified Transient Organic Mental Disorders	F05.8	Other delirium	
		F53.1	Severe mental and behavioural disorders associated with the puerperium, not elsewhere classified	
294.0	Amnestic Syndrome	F04	Organic amnesic syndrome, not induced by alcohol and other psychoactive substances	
294.9	Organic Psychosis, Unspecified	F06.9	Unspecified mental disorder due to brain damage and dysfunction and to physical disease	
		F09	Unspecified organic or symptomatic mental disorder	
295.1	Schizophrenia, Disorganized Type	F20.1	Hebephrenic schizophrenia	
295.2	Schizophrenia, Catatonic Type	F20.2	Catatonic schizophrenia	
295.4	Schizophreniform Disorder	F23.1	Acute polymorphic psychotic disorder with symptoms of schizophrenia	
		F23.2	Acute schizophrenia-like psychotic disorder	
295.7	Schizoaffective Disorder	F25.0	Schizoaffective disorder, manic type	
		F25.1	Schizoaffective disorder, depressive type	
		F25.2	Schizoaffective disorder, mixed type	
		F25.8	Other schizoaffective disorders	
		F25.9	Schizoaffective disorder, unspecified	
295.9	Schizophrenia, Unspecified	F20.8	Other schizophrenia	
		F20.9	Schizophrenia, unspecified	
		F23.2	Acute schizophrenia-like psychotic disorder	
296.0	Bipolar Affective Disorder, Single Manic Episode	F30.0	Hypomania	
		F30.1	Mania without psychotic symptoms	
		F30.2	Mania with psychotic symptoms	

ICD-9	Description	ICD-10	Description	(Continued)
296.0	Bipolar Affective Disorder, Single Manic Episode	F30.8	Other manic episodes	
		F30.9	Manic episode, unspecified	
		F31.8	Other bipolar affective disorders	
296.1	Manic Disorder, Recurrent	F32.2	Severe depressive episode without psychotic symptoms	
		F32.3	Severe depressive episode with psychotic symptoms	
		F32.8	Other depressive episodes	
		F32.9	Depressive episode, unspecified	
		F33.1	Recurrent depressive disorder, current episode moderate	
		F33.2	Recurrent depressive disorder, current episode severe without psychotic symptoms	
		F38.1	Other recurrent mood [affective] disorders	
296.2	Depression, Major	F31.0	Bipolar affective disorder, current episode hypomanic	
		F31.1	Bipolar affective disorder, current episode manic without psychotic symptoms	
		F31.2	Bipolar affective disorder, current episode manic with psychotic symptoms	
296.3	Major Depressive Disorder, Recurrent Episode	F31.3	Bipolar affective disorder, current episode mild or moderate depression	
		F31.4	Bipolar affective disorder, current episode severe depression without psychotic symptoms	
		F31.5	Bipolar affective disorder, current episode severe depression with psychotic symptoms	
296.4	Bipolar Affective Disorder, Manic	F31.6	Bipolar affective disorder, current episode mixed	
		F38.0	Other single mood [affective] disorders	
296.5	Bipolar Affective Disorder, Depressed	F34.0	Cyclothymia	
296.6	Bipolar Affective Disorder, Mixed	F30.2	Mania with psychotic symptoms	
		F31.7	Bipolar affective disorder, currently in remission	
		F31.8	Other bipolar affective disorders	
		F31.9	Bipolar affective disorder, unspecified	
		F33.4	Recurrent depressive disorder, currently in remission	
		F33.8	Other recurrent depressive disorders	
		F33.9	Recurrent depressive disorder, unspecified	
		F38.1	Other recurrent mood [affective] disorders	
297.9	Delusional Disorder, Unspecified	F22.0	Delusional disorder	
		F22.9	Persistent delusional disorder, unspecified	
		F23.3	Other acute predominantly delusional psychotic disorders	
298.0	Depressive Psychosis	F32.1	Moderate depressive episode	
		F32.2	Severe depressive episode without psychotic symptoms	
		F32.3	Severe depressive episode with psychotic symptoms	
		F33.3	Recurrent depressive disorder, current episode severe with psychotic symptoms	
298.8	Psychotic Disorder, Brief	F23.8	Other acute and transient psychotic disorders	
		F23.9	Acute and transient psychotic disorder, unspecified	
		F28	Other nonorganic psychotic disorders	
		F44.2	Dissociative stupor	
		F44.9	Dissociative [conversion] disorder, unspecified	
298.9	Psychotic Disorder, Unspecified	F07.0	Organic personality disorder	
		F22.8	Other persistent delusional disorders	
		F23.9	Acute and transient psychotic disorder, unspecified	
		F28	Other nonorganic psychotic disorders	
		F29	Unspecified nonorganic psychosis	
		F44.8	Other dissociative [conversion] disorders	
		F45.2	Hypochondriacal disorder	
		F99	Mental disorder, not otherwise specified	
		R41.0	Disorientation, unspecified	
300.0	Anxiety States	F41.0	Panic disorder [episodic paroxysmal anxiety]	
		F41.1	Generalized anxiety disorder	
		F41.3	Other mixed anxiety disorders	
		F41.8	Other specified anxiety disorders	
		F41.9	Anxiety disorder, unspecified	
300.1	Hysteria	F43.1	Post-traumatic stress disorder	
		F44.0	Dissociative amnesia	
		F44.1	Dissociative fugue	
		F44.2	Dissociative stupor	
		F44.3	Trance and possession disorders	
		F44.4	Dissociative motor disorders	
		F44.5	Dissociative convulsions	

Translation of ICD-9 CM to ICD-10

ICD-9	Description	ICD-10	Description	(Continued)
300.1	Hysteria	F44.6	Dissociative anaesthesia and sensory loss	
		F44.7	Mixed dissociative [conversion] disorders	
		F44.8	Other dissociative [conversion] disorders	
		F44.9	Dissociative [conversion] disorder, unspecified	
		F45.3	Somatoform autonomic dysfunction	
		F45.8	Other somatoform disorders	
		F48.8	Other specified neurotic disorders	
		F50.5	Vomiting associated with other psychological disturbances	
		F50.8	Other eating disorders	
		F68.0	Elaboration of physical symptoms for psychological reasons	
300.2	Phobic Disorders	F40.0	Agoraphobia	
		F40.1	Social phobias	
		F40.2	Specific (isolated) phobias	
		F40.8	Other phobic anxiety disorders	
		F40.9	Phobic anxiety disorder, unspecified	
		F41.8	Other specified anxiety disorders	
		F45.2	Hypochondriacal disorder	
300.3	Obsessive-Compulsive Disorder	F42.0	Predominantly obsessional thoughts or ruminations	
		F42.1	Predominantly compulsive acts [obsessional rituals]	
		F42.2	Mixed obsessional thoughts and acts	
		F42.8	Other obsessive-compulsive disorders	
		F42.9	Obsessive-compulsive disorder, unspecified	
		F63.3	Trichotillomania	
300.4	Dysthymic Disorder	F32.0	Mild depressive episode	
		F32.9	Depressive episode, unspecified	
		F33.0	Recurrent depressive disorder, current episode mild	
		F34.1	Dysthymia	
		F41.2	Mixed anxiety and depressive disorder	
300.5	Nervous Fatigue	F48.0	Neurasthenia	
300.6	Depersonalization Disorder	F48.1	Depersonalization-derealization syndrome	
300.7	Hypochondriasis	F45.2	Hypochondriacal disorder	
300.9	Neurotic Disorders	F34.9	Persistent mood [affective] disorder, unspecified	
		F45.9	Somatoform disorder, unspecified	
		F48.9	Neurotic disorder, unspecified	
		F99	Mental disorder, not otherwise specified	
		R45.7	State of emotional shock and stress, unspecified	
		Z91.4	Personal history of psychological trauma, not elsewhere classified	
		Z91.5	Personal history of self-harm Parasuicide Self-poisoning Suicide attempt	
301.0	Personality Disorder, Paranoid	F60.0	Paranoid personality disorder	
		F61	Mixed and other personality disorders	
301.1	Affective Personality Disorder	F34.0	Cyclothymia	
		F34.1	Dysthymia	
301.3	Personality Disorder, Explosive	F60.3	Emotionally unstable personality disorder	
301.4	Personality Disorder, Obsessive-Compulsive	F60.5	Anankastic personality disorder	
301.5	Histrionic Personality Disorder	F60.3	Emotionally unstable personality disorder	
		F60.4	Histrionic personality disorder	
		F68.1	Intentional production or feigning of symptoms or disabilities, either physical or psychological [factitious disorder]	
301.6	Personality Disorder, Dependent	F60.7	Dependent personality disorder	
301.7	Personality Disorder, Antisocial	F60.2	Dissocial personality disorder	
		F61	Mixed and other personality disorders	
301.8	Other Personality Disorders	F48.8	Other specified neurotic disorders	
		F60.6	Anxious [avoidant] personality disorder	
		F60.8	Other specific personality disorders	
		F61	Mixed and other personality disorders	
		F62.8	Other enduring personality changes	
		F68.8	Other specified disorders of adult personality and behaviour	
301.9	Unspecified Personality Disorders	F07.0	Organic personality disorder	
		F60.2	Dissocial personality disorder	
		F60.9	Personality disorder, unspecified	
		F61	Mixed and other personality disorders	

ICD-9	Description	ICD-10	Description	(Continued)
301.9	Unspecified Personality Disorders	F62.0	Enduring personality change after catastrophic experience	
		F62.1	Enduring personality change after psychiatric illness	
		F62.9	Enduring personality change, unspecified	
		F68.8	Other specified disorders of adult personality and behaviour	
		F69	Unspecified disorder of adult personality and behaviour	
302.2	Pedophilia	F65.4	Paedophilia	
302.3	Transvestism	F64.1	Dual-role transvestism	
		F65.1	Fetishistic transvestism	
302.6	Psychosexual Identity, Disorders of	F64.1	Dual-role transvestism	
		F64.2	Gender identity disorder of childhood	
		F64.8	Other gender identity disorders	
		F64.9	Gender identity disorder, unspecified	
		F66.0	Sexual maturation disorder	
		F66.1	Egodystonic sexual orientation	
		F66.2	Sexual relationship disorder	
302.7	Psychosexual Dysfunction	F52.0	Lack or loss of sexual desire	
		F52.1	Sexual aversion and lack of sexual enjoyment	
		F52.2	Failure of genital response	
		F52.3	Orgasmic dysfunction	
		F52.4	Premature ejaculation	
		F52.6	Nonorganic dyspareunia	
		F52.9	Unspecified sexual dysfunction, not caused by organic disorder or disease	
302.8	Psychosexual Disorders, Other Specified	F52.7	Excessive sexual drive	
		F52.8	Other sexual dysfunction, not caused by organic disorder or disease	
		F65.0	Fetishism	
		F65.1	Fetishistic transvestism	
		F65.3	Voyeurism	
		F65.5	Sadomasochism	
		F65.6	Multiple disorders of sexual preference	
		F65.8	Other disorders of sexual preference	
		F66.2	Sexual relationship disorder	
		F66.8	Other psychosexual development disorders	
302.9	Psychosexual Disorder, Unspecified	F52.9	Unspecified sexual dysfunction, not caused by organic disorder or disease	
		F65.9	Disorder of sexual preference, unspecified	
		F66.9	Psychosexual development disorder, unspecified	
303	Alcohol Dependence Syndrome	G31.2	Degeneration of nervous system due to alcohol	
305.9	Drug Abuse, Unspecified	F55	Abuse of non-dependence-producing substances	
306.0	Musculoskeletal - Psychogenic Paralysis; Psychogenic Torticollis	F44.4	Dissociative motor disorders	
		F45.4	Persistent somatoform pain disorder	
		F45.8	Other somatoform disorders	
306.1	Hyperventilation Syndrome	F44.4	Dissociative motor disorders	
		F45.3	Somatoform autonomic dysfunction	
306.2	Neurocirculatory Asthenia	F45.3	Somatoform autonomic dysfunction	
306.3	Skin	F45.8	Other somatoform disorders	
		F54	Psychological and behavioural factors associated with disorders or diseases classified elsewhere	
306.4	Psychogenic Dyspepsia	F45.3	Somatoform autonomic dysfunction	
		F45.8	Other somatoform disorders	
		F50.5	Vomiting associated with other psychological disturbances	
		F54	Psychological and behavioural factors associated with disorders or diseases classified elsewhere	
306.5	Genitourinary	F45.3	Somatoform autonomic dysfunction	
		F45.8	Other somatoform disorders	
		F52.5	Nonorganic vaginismus	
306.6	Endocrine	F54	Psychological and behavioural factors associated with disorders or diseases classified elsewhere	
306.7	Organs of Special Sense	F44.6	Dissociative anaesthesia and sensory loss	
		F45.8	Other somatoform disorders	
306.8	Other Specified Psychophysiological Malfunction	F45.8	Other somatoform disorders	
306.9	Unspecified Psychophysiological Malfunction	F45.8	Other somatoform disorders	
		F45.9	Somatoform disorder, unspecified	

ICD-9	Description	ICD-10	Description	(Continued)
306.9	Unspecified Psychophysiological Malfunction	F59	Unspecified behavioural syndromes associated with physiological disturbances and physical factors	
307.1	Anorexia Nervosa	F50.0	Anorexia nervosa	
		F50.1	Atypical anorexia nervosa	
		F50.2	Bulimia nervosa	
307.2	Tics	F95.0	Transient tic disorder	
		F95.1	Chronic motor or vocal tic disorder	
		F95.2	Combined vocal and multiple motor tic disorder [de la Tourette]	
		F95.8	Other tic disorders	
		F95.9	Tic disorder, unspecified	
307.5	Eating Disorders	F50.2	Bulimia nervosa	
		F50.3	Atypical bulimia nervosa	
		F50.4	Overeating associated with other psychological disturbances	
		F50.5	Vomiting associated with other psychological disturbances	
		F50.8	Other eating disorders	
		F50.9	Eating disorder, unspecified	
		F98.2	Feeding disorder of infancy and childhood	
		F98.3	Pica of infancy and childhood	
308.0	Predominant Disturbance of Emotions	F43.0	Acute stress reaction	
308.3	Reactions to Stress, Other Acute	F43.0	Acute stress reaction	
		F43.8	Other reactions to severe stress	
308.9	Stress Disorder, Acute	F43.0	Acute stress reaction	
		F43.9	Reaction to severe stress, unspecified	
309.0	Adjustment Disorder with Depressed Mood	F43.2	Adjustment disorders	
309.1	Depressive Reaction, Prolonged	F43.2	Adjustment disorders	
309.2	with Predominant Disturbance of Other Emotions	F43.2	Adjustment disorders	
		F60.3	Emotionally unstable personality disorder	
		F93.0	Separation anxiety disorder of childhood	
309.3	Adjustment Reaction with Predominant Disturbance of Conduct	F43.2	Adjustment disorders	
310.2	Postconcussion Syndrome	F07.2	Postconcussional syndrome	
311	Depressive Disorder, Not Elsewhere Classified	F32.9	Depressive episode, unspecified	
		F53.0	Mild mental and behavioural disorders associated with the puerperium, not elsewhere classified	
314.0	Attention Deficit Disorder	F90.0	Disturbance of activity and attention	
		F90.9	Hyperkinetic disorder, unspecified	
320.1	Pneumococcal Meningitis	G00.1	Pneumococcal meningitis	
		G04.2	Bacterial meningoencephalitis and meningomyelitis, not elsewhere classified	
320.2	Streptococcal Meningitis	G00.2	Streptococcal meningitis	
		G04.2	Bacterial meningoencephalitis and meningomyelitis, not elsewhere classified	
		G04.8	Other encephalitis, myelitis and encephalomyelitis	
320.3	Staphylococcal Meningitis	G00.3	Staphylococcal meningitis	
		G04.2	Bacterial meningoencephalitis and meningomyelitis, not elsewhere classified	
320.8	Meningitis Due to Other Specified Bacteria	G00.8	Other bacterial meningitis	
		G04.2	Bacterial meningoencephalitis and meningomyelitis, not elsewhere classified	
320.9	Meningitis Due to Unspecified Bacterium	G00.9	Bacterial meningitis, unspecified	
		G04.2	Bacterial meningoencephalitis and meningomyelitis, not elsewhere classified	
		G06.2	Extradural and subdural abscess, unspecified	
322.2	Meningitis, Chronic	G03.1	Chronic meningitis	
322.9	Meningitis, Unspecified	G03.2	Benign recurrent meningitis [Mollaret]	
		G03.8	Meningitis due to other specified causes	
		G03.9	Meningitis, unspecified	
		G04.9	Encephalitis, myelitis and encephalomyelitis, unspecified	
		G96.1	Disorders of meninges, not elsewhere classified	
		R29.1	Meningismus	
323.5	Encephalitis Following Immunization Procedures	G04.0	Acute disseminated encephalitis postimmunization	
323.8	Encephalitis, Other Causes of	G04.8	Other encephalitis, myelitis and encephalomyelitis	
323.9	Encephalitis, Unspecified Cause	G04.9	Encephalitis, myelitis and encephalomyelitis, unspecified	
		G37.3	Acute transverse myelitis in demyelinating disease of central nervous system	
		G37.4	Subacute necrotizing myelitis	
		G93.4	Encephalopathy, unspecified	

ICD-9	Description	ICD-10	Description	(Continued)
324.0	Brain Abscess	G04.8	Other encephalitis, myelitis and encephalomyelitis	
		G06.0	Intracranial abscess and granuloma	
325	Phlebitis and Thrombophlebitis of Intracranial Venous Sinuses	G08	Intracranial and intraspinal phlebitis and thrombophlebitis of intracranial or intraspinal venous sinuses and veins	
331.0	Alzheimer's Disease	G30.0	Alzheimer's disease with early onset	
		G30.1	Alzheimer's disease with late onset	
		G30.8	Other Alzheimer's disease	
		G30.9	Alzheimer's disease, unspecified	
		G31.0	Circumscribed brain atrophy	
332.0	Paralysis Agitans	G20	Parkinson's disease	
		G21.8	Other secondary parkinsonism	
332.1	Parkinsonism, Secondary	G21.0	Malignant neuroleptic syndrome	
		G21.1	Other drug-induced secondary parkinsonism	
		G21.2	Secondary parkinsonism due to other external agents	
		G21.3	Postencephalitic parkinsonism	
		G21.9	Secondary parkinsonism, unspecified	
333.0	Shy-Drager Syndrome	G23.0	Hallervorden-Spatz disease Pigmentary pallidal degeneration	
		G23.1	Progressive supranuclear ophthalmoplegia [Steele-Richardson-Olszewski]	
		G23.2	Striatonigral degeneration	
		G23.8	Other specified degenerative diseases of basal ganglia	
		G23.9	Degenerative disease of basal ganglia, unspecified	
		G90.0	Idiopathic peripheral autonomic neuropathy Carotid sinus syncope	
		G90.3	Multi-system degeneration Neurogenic orthostatic hypotension [Shy-Drager]	
333.4	Huntington's Chorea	G10	Huntington's disease Huntington's chorea	
		G25.5	Other chorea	
333.7	Athetoid Cerebral Palsy	G24.2	Idiopathic nonfamilial dystonia	
		G80.3	Dyskinetic cerebral palsy Athetoid cerebral palsy	
336.0	Syringomyelia (Syringobulbia)	G60.8	Other hereditary and idiopathic neuropathies	
		G95.0	Syringomyelia and syringobulbia	
		G95.8	Other specified diseases of spinal cord	
336.1	Vascular Myelopathies	G95.1	Vascular myelopathies	
336.8	Myelopathy, Other	G12.2	Motor neuron disease	
		G31.8	Other specified degenerative diseases of nervous system	
		G95.8	Other specified diseases of spinal cord	
336.9	Myelopathy, Unspecified	G95.2	Cord compression, unspecified	
		G95.9	Disease of spinal cord, unspecified	
337.0	Carotid Sinus Syncope	G90.0	Idiopathic peripheral autonomic neuropathy Carotid sinus syncope	
340	Multiple Sclerosis	G35	Multiple sclerosis	
342.0	Hemiplegia, Flaccid	G81.0	Flaccid hemiplegia	
342.1	Hemiplegia, Spastic	G81.1	Spastic hemiplegia	
342.9	Hemiplegia, Unspecified	G81.9	Hemiplegia, unspecified	
343.9	Cerebral Palsy, Unspecified	G80.0	Spastic cerebral palsy	
		G80.9	Infantile cerebral palsy, unspecified	
344.0	Quadriplegia	G82.3	Flaccid tetraplegia	
		G82.4	Spastic tetraplegia	
344.1	Paraplegia	G82.0	Flaccid paraplegia	
		G82.1	Spastic paraplegia	
		G82.2	Paraplegia, unspecified	
		G83.8	Other specified paralytic syndromes Todd's paralysis (postepileptic)	
344.6	Cauda Equina Syndrome	G83.4	Cauda equina syndrome	
		G95.8	Other specified diseases of spinal cord	
		N31.2	Flaccid neuropathic bladder, not elsewhere classified	
		N31.8	Other neuromuscular dysfunction of bladder	
		N31.9	Neuromuscular dysfunction of bladder, unspecified Neurogenic bladder dysfunction NOS	
344.9	Paralysis, Paraplegia, and Quadriplegia	G82.2	Paraplegia, unspecified	
		G83.9	Paralytic syndrome, unspecified	
345.0	Petit Mal Epilepsy	G40.3	Generalized idiopathic epilepsy and epileptic syndromes	
		G40.7	Petit mal, unspecified, without grand mal seizures	
345.1	Grand Mal Seizure	G40.3	Generalized idiopathic epilepsy and epileptic syndromes	
		G40.4	Other generalized epilepsy and epileptic syndromes	

Translation of ICD-9 CM to ICD-10

ICD-9	Description	ICD-10	Description
345.1	Grand Mal Seizure	G40.6	Grand mal seizures, unspecified (with or without petit mal)
		G40.8	Other epilepsy
345.2	Petit Mal Status, Epileptic Absence Status	G41.1	Petit mal status epilepticus
345.3	Grand Mal Status	G40.8	Other epilepsy
		G41.0	Grand mal status epilepticus Tonic-clonic status epilepticus
		G41.8	Other status epilepticus
		G41.9	Status epilepticus, unspecified
345.4	Partial Epilepsy with Impairment of Consciousness	G40.0	Localization-related (focal)(partial) idiopathic epilepsy and epileptic syndromes with seizures of localized onset
		G40.1	Localization-related (focal)(partial) symptomatic epilepsy and epileptic syndromes with simple partial seizures Attacks without alteration of consciousness
		G40.2	Localization-related (focal)(partial) symptomatic epilepsy and epileptic syndromes with complex partial seizures Attacks with alteration of consciousness, often with automatisms
345.5	Jacksonian Seizure	G40.0	Localization-related (focal)(partial) idiopathic epilepsy and epileptic syndromes with seizures of localized onset
		G40.1	Localization-related (focal)(partial) symptomatic epilepsy and epileptic syndromes with simple partial seizures Attacks without alteration of consciousness
		G40.2	Localization-related (focal)(partial) symptomatic epilepsy and epileptic syndromes with complex partial seizures Attacks with alteration of consciousness, often with automatisms
		G40.5	Special epileptic syndromes
		G40.8	Other epilepsy
345.7	Epilepsia Partialis Continua Kojevnikov's Epilepsy	G40.5	Special epileptic syndromes
		G41.2	Complex partial status epilepticus
		G41.8	Other status epilepticus
345.8	Other Forms of Epilepsy	G40.4	Other generalized epilepsy and epileptic syndromes
		G40.5	Special epileptic syndromes
		G40.8	Other epilepsy
345.9	Epilepsy, Unspecified	G40.3	Generalized idiopathic epilepsy and epileptic syndromes
		G40.8	Other epilepsy
		G40.9	Epilepsy, unspecified
346.0	Migraine Headache, Classical	G43.1	Migraine with aura [classical migraine]
		G43.9	Migraine, unspecified
346.1	Migraine, Common (Sick Headache)	G43.0	Migraine without aura [common migraine]
346.2	Cluster Headache	G43.1	Migraine with aura [classical migraine]
		G43.8	Other migraine Ophthalmoplegic migraine Retinal migraine
		G44.0	Cluster headache syndrome
		G44.8	Other specified headache syndromes
346.8	Migraine Headache, Other Forms of	G43.1	Migraine with aura [classical migraine]
		G43.2	Status migrainosus
		G43.3	Complicated migraine
		G43.8	Other migraine Ophthalmoplegic migraine Retinal migraine
346.9	Migraine Headache, Unspecified	G43.9	Migraine, unspecified
347	Narcolepsy	G47.4	Narcolepsy and cataplexy
348.3	Encephalopathy, Unspecified	G40.9	Epilepsy, unspecified
		G93.4	Encephalopathy, unspecified
		G93.8	Other specified disorders of brain Postradiation encephalopathy
		G96.9	Disorder of central nervous system, unspecified
348.5	Cerebral Edema	G93.6	Cerebral oedema
350.1	Trigeminal Neuralgia	G50.0	Trigeminal neuralgia Syndrome of paroxysmal facial pain Tic douloureux
351.0	Bell's Palsy	G51.0	Bell's palsy Facial palsy
		G51.3	Clonic hemifacial spasm
352.3	Vagotonia	G52.2	Disorders of vagus nerve
353.0	Thoracic Outlet Syndrome	G54.0	Brachial plexus disorders Thoracic outlet syndrome
353.5	Neuralgic Amyotrophy	G54.5	Neuralgic amyotrophy
354.0	Carpal Tunnel Syndrome	G56.0	Carpal tunnel syndrome
354.2	Cubital Tunnel Syndrome (Lesion of Ulnar Nerve)	G56.2	Lesion of ulnar nerve Tardy ulnar nerve palsy
355.5	Tarsal Tunnel Syndrome	G57.5	Tarsal tunnel syndrome
355.6	Morton's Neuroma	G57.6	Lesion of plantar nerve Morton's metatarsalgia
		G57.8	Other mononeuropathies of lower limb Interdigital neuroma of lower limb
		G58.8	Other specified mononeuropathies
356.1	Peroneal Muscular Atrophy	G58.9	Mononeuropathy, unspecified

ICD-9	Description	ICD-10	Description	(Continued)
356.1	Peroneal Muscular Atrophy	G60.0	Hereditary motor and sensory neuropathy	
356.8	Peripheral Neuropathy, Other Specified Idiopathic	G12.2	Motor neuron disease	
		G60.2	Neuropathy in association with hereditary ataxia	
		G60.8	Other hereditary and idiopathic neuropathies	
356.9	Peripheral Neuropathy	G58.9	Mononeuropathy, unspecified	
		G60.0	Hereditary motor and sensory neuropathy	
		G60.3	Idiopathic progressive neuropathy	
		G60.9	Hereditary and idiopathic neuropathy, unspecified	
		G62.9	Polyneuropathy, unspecified	
		G96.8	Other specified disorders of central nervous system	
357.0	Guillain-Barré Syndrome.	G04.9	Encephalitis, myelitis and encephalomyelitis, unspecified	
		G58.9	Mononeuropathy, unspecified	
		G61.0	Guillain-Barr, syndrome	
		G62.9	Polyneuropathy, unspecified	
358.0	Myasthenia Gravis	G70.0	Myasthenia gravis	
		G70.9	Myoneural disorder, unspecified	
358.9	Myoneural Disorders, Unspecified	G70.9	Myoneural disorder, unspecified	
360.0	Endophthalmitis, Purulent	H27.8	Other specified disorders of lens	
		H44.0	Purulent endophthalmitis Panophthalmitis Vitreous abscess	
360.1	Endophthalmitis, Other	H16.2	Keratoconjunctivitis	
		H21.3	Cyst of iris, ciliary body and anterior chamber	
		H44.1	Other endophthalmitis Parasitic endophthalmitis NOS Sympathetic uveitis	
361.8	Retinal Detachment, Other Forms of	H33.4	Traction detachment of retina Proliferative vitreo-retinopathy with retinal detachment	
		H33.5	Other retinal detachments	
361.9	Retinal Detachment	H33.2	Serous retinal detachment	
362.1	Other Background Retinopathy and Retinal Vascular Changes	H35.0	Background retinopathy and retinal vascular changes	
		H35.8	Other specified retinal disorders	
362.3	Retinal Vascular Occlusion	G45.3	Amaurosis fugax	
		H34.0	Transient retinal artery occlusion	
		H34.1	Central retinal artery occlusion	
		H34.2	Other retinal artery occlusions	
		H34.8	Other retinal vascular occlusions	
		H34.9	Retinal vascular occlusion, unspecified	
362.5	Macular degeneration (Senile)	H35.3	Degeneration of macula and posterior pole	
		H35.5	Hereditary retinal dystrophy	
		H35.8	Other specified retinal disorders	
362.8	Other Retinal Disorder	H31.8	Other specified disorders of choroid	
		H34.2	Other retinal artery occlusions	
		H35.6	Retinal haemorrhage	
		H35.8	Other specified retinal disorders	
364.0	Iritis	H20.0	Acute and subacute iridocyclitis	
364.3	Uveitis, Unspecified	H20.8	Other iridocyclitis	
		H20.9	Iridocyclitis, unspecified	
		H57.8	Other specified disorders of eye and adnexa	
365.1	Glaucoma, Chronic (Open-Angle)	H40.1	Primary open-angle glaucoma	
366.1	Cataract, Senile	H25.0	Senile incipient cataract	
		H25.1	Senile nuclear cataract	
		H25.2	Senile cataract, morgagnian type	
		H25.8	Other senile cataract	
		H25.9	Senile cataract, unspecified	
		H26.8	Other specified cataract	
		H26.9	Cataract, unspecified	
366.2	Cataract, Traumatic	H26.1	Traumatic cataract	
366.4	Cataract, Associated with Other Disorders	H26.3	Drug-induced cataract	
		H26.8	Other specified cataract	
366.8	Cataract, Other	H26.8	Other specified cataract	
366.9	Cataract, Unspecified	H26.9	Cataract, unspecified	
		H27.8	Other specified disorders of lens	
367.1	Myopia	H44.2	Degenerative myopia	
		H52.1	Myopia	

ICD-9	Description	ICD-10	Description	(Continued)
367.2	Astigmatism	H52.2	Astigmatism	
370.0	Corneal Ulcer	H16.0	Corneal ulcer Ulcer	
370.2	Superficial Keratitis Without Conjunctivitis	H16.1	Other superficial keratitis without conjunctivitis	
370.5	Intersitial and Deep Keratitis	H16.3	Interstitial and deep keratitis	
370.9	Keratitis, Unspecified	H16.9	Keratitis, unspecified	
372.0	Conjunctivitis, Acute	H10.0	Mucopurulent conjunctivitis	
		H10.1	Acute atopic conjunctivitis	
		H10.2	Other acute conjunctivitis	
		H10.3	Acute conjunctivitis, unspecified	
		H10.8	Other conjunctivitis	
		H10.9	Conjunctivitis, unspecified	
372.1	Conjunctivitis, Chronic	H10.1	Acute atopic conjunctivitis	
		H10.4	Chronic conjunctivitis	
372.4	Pterygium	H11.0	Pterygium	
372.5	Conjunctival Degenerations and Deposits	H11.1	Conjunctival degenerations and deposits	
		H11.8	Other specified disorders of conjunctiva	
		H16.2	Keratoconjunctivitis	
		H57.8	Other specified disorders of eye and adnexa	
373.0	Blepharitis	H01.0	Blepharitis	
		H01.8	Other specified inflammation of eyelid	
373.3	Non Infectious Dermatoses of Eyelid	H01.1	Noninfectious dermatoses of eyelid	
		H02.8	Other specified disorders of eyelid Hypertrichosis of eyelid Retained foreign body in eyelid	
375.5	Stenosis and Insufficiency of Lacrimal Passages	H04.5	Stenosis and insufficiency of lacrimal passages	
377.1	Optic Atrophy	H47.2	Optic atrophy Temporal pallor of optic disc	
377.3	Optic Neuritis	H46	Optic neuritis	
		H47.0	Disorders of optic nerve, not elsewhere classified	
		H53.8	Other visual disturbances	
379.0	Scleritis	H15.0	Scleritis	
		H15.1	Episcleritis	
		H15.8	Other disorders of sclera	
		H16.8	Other keratitis	
		H31.8	Other specified disorders of choroid	
379.5	Nystagmus	H51.8	Other specified disorders of binocular movement	
		H55	Nystagmus and other irregular eye movements	
380.1	Otitis Externa, Infective	H60.0	Abscess of external ear of auricle or external auditory canal	
		H60.1	Cellulitis of external ear	
		H60.2	Malignant otitis externa	
		H60.3	Other infective otitis externa	
		H60.9	Otitis externa, unspecified	
382.0	Otitis Media, Acute Suppurative	H66.0	Acute suppurative otitis media	
382.9	Otitis Media, Unspecified	H66.9	Otitis media, unspecified	
383.0	Mastoiditis, Acute	H70.0	Acute mastoiditis	
		H95.0	Recurrent cholesteatoma of postmastoidectomy cavity	
383.1	Mastoiditis, Chronic	H70.1	Chronic mastoiditis	
383.9	Mastoiditis	H70.9	Mastoiditis, unspecified	
386.0	Endolymphatic Hydrops	H81.0	Mnire's disease Labyrinthine hydrops Mnire's syndrome or vertigo	
		H81.3	Other peripheral vertigo	
386.1	Vertigo	H81.0	Mnire's disease Labyrinthine hydrops Mnire's syndrome or vertigo	
		H81.1	Benign paroxysmal vertigo	
		H81.2	Vestibular neuronitis	
		H81.3	Other peripheral vertigo	
		H81.8	Other disorders of vestibular function	
386.2	Vertigo of Central Origin	H81.4	Vertigo of central origin Central positional nystagmus	
386.3	Labyrinthitis	H83.0	Labyrinthitis	
387.9	Otosclerosis, Unspecified	H80.9	Otosclerosis, unspecified	
388.3	Tinnitus	H93.1	Tinnitus	
389.0	Conductive Hearing Loss	H90.0	Conductive hearing loss, bilateral	
		H90.1	Conductive hearing loss, unilateral with unrestricted hearing on the contralateral side	
		H90.2	Conductive hearing loss, unspecified	
389.1	Sensorineural Hearing Loss	H90.3	Sensorineural hearing loss, bilateral	

ICD-9	Description	ICD-10	Description	(Continued)
389.1	Sensorineural Hearing Loss	H90.4	Sensorineural hearing loss, unilateral with unrestricted hearing on the contralateral side	
		H90.5	Sensorineural hearing loss, unspecified	
389.7	Deaf, Mutism, Not Elsewhere Classifiable	H91.3	Deaf mutism, not elsewhere classified	
389.8	Other Specified Forms of Hearing Loss	H91.0	Ototoxic hearing loss	
		H91.8	Other specified hearing loss	
		H91.9	Hearing loss, unspecified	
389.9	Hearing Loss, Unspecified	H91.8	Other specified hearing loss	
		H91.9	Hearing loss, unspecified	
390	Rheumatic Fever	I00	Rheumatic fever without mention of heart involvement Arthritis, rheumatic, acute or subacute	
391.2	Acute Rheumatic Myocarditis	I01.2	Acute rheumatic myocarditis	
394.0	Mitral Stenosis	I05.0	Mitral stenosis Mitral (valve) obstruction (rheumatic)	
394.1	Rheumatic Mitral Insufficiency	I05.1	Rheumatic mitral insufficiency	
394.2	Mitral Stenosis with Insufficiency	I05.2	Mitral stenosis with insufficiency Mitral stenosis with incompetence or regurgitation	
395.0	Rheumatic Aortic Stenosis	I06.0	Rheumatic aortic stenosis Rheumatic aortic (valve) obstruction	
395.1	Aortic Insufficiency, Rheumatic	I06.1	Rheumatic aortic insufficiency	
398.9	Rheumatic Heart Disease, Chronic	I02.0	Rheumatic chorea with heart involvement	
		I08.1	Disorders of both mitral and tricuspid valves	
		I08.2	Disorders of both aortic and tricuspid valves	
		I08.3	Combined disorders of mitral, aortic and tricuspid valves	
		I08.8	Other multiple valve diseases	
		I09.2	Chronic rheumatic pericarditis	
		I09.8	Other specified rheumatic heart diseases Rheumatic disease of pulmonary valve	
		I09.9	Rheumatic heart disease, unspecified	
401.0	High Blood Pressure, Malignant	I10	Essential (primary) hypertension High blood pressure Hypertension (arterial)(benign)(essential)(malignant)(primary) (systemic)	
401.1	High Blood Pressure, Benign	I10	Essential (primary) hypertension High blood pressure Hypertension (arterial)(benign)(essential)(malignant)(primary) (systemic)	
401.9	Essential Hypertension, Unspecified	I10	Essential (primary) hypertension High blood pressure Hypertension (arterial)(benign)(essential)(malignant)(primary) (systemic)	
402.9	Hypertensive Heart Disease, Unspecified	I11.0	Hypertensive heart disease with (congestive) heart failure	
		I11.9	Hypertensive heart disease without (congestive) heart failure Hypertensive heart disease NOS	
410	Myocardial Infarction (MI), Acute	I21.0	Acute transmural myocardial infarction of anterior wall	
		I21.1	Acute transmural myocardial infarction of inferior wall	
		I21.2	Acute transmural myocardial infarction of other sites	
		I21.3	Acute transmural myocardial infarction of unspecified site	
		I21.4	Acute subendocardial myocardial infarction Nontransmural myocardial infarction NOS	
		I21.9	Acute myocardial infarction, unspecified Myocardial infarction (acute) NOS	
		I22.0	Subsequent myocardial infarction of anterior wall	
		I22.1	Subsequent myocardial infarction of inferior wall	
		I22.8	Subsequent myocardial infarction of other sites S	
		I22.9	Subsequent myocardial infarction of unspecified site	
		I23.6	Thrombosis of atrium, auricular appendage, and ventricle as current complications following acute myocardial infarction	
		I24.0	Coronary thrombosis not resulting in myocardial infarction	
		I51.3	Intracardiac thrombosis, not elsewhere classified	
		M21.9	Acquired deformity of limb, unspecified	
413	Angina Pectoris	I20.0	Unstable angina Angina	
		I20.1	Angina pectoris with documented spasm	
		I20.8	Other forms of angina pectoris Angina of effort Stenocardia	
		I20.9	Angina pectoris, unspecified	
414.0	Coronary Atherosclerosis	I25.1	Atherosclerotic heart disease	
		I25.8	Other forms of chronic ischaemic heart disease	
414.8	Other Specified Forms of Chronic Ischemic Heart Disease	I25.5	Ischaemic cardiomyopathy	
		I25.6	Silent myocardial ischaemia	
		I25.8	Other forms of chronic ischaemic heart disease	
414.9	Ischemic Heart Disease, Chronic	I25.1	Atherosclerotic heart disease	
		I25.8	Other forms of chronic ischaemic heart disease	
		I25.9	Chronic ischaemic heart disease, unspecified Ischaemic heart disease (chronic) NOS	
415.0	Cor Pulmonale, Acute	I26.0	Pulmonary embolism with mention of acute cor pulmonale	
415.1	Embolism, Pulmonary	I26.9	Pulmonary embolism without mention of acute cor pulmonale	

Translation of ICD-9 CM to ICD-10

ICD-9	Description	ICD-10	Description	(Continued)
416.0	Hypertension, Primary Pulmonary	I27.0	Primary pulmonary hypertension Pulmonary (artery) hypertension (idiopathic)(primary)	
416.1	Kyphoscoliotic Heart Disease	I27.1	Kyphoscoliotic heart disease	
416.8	Chronic Pulmonary Heart Diseases, Other	I27.8	Other specified pulmonary heart diseases	
416.9	Cor Pulmonale, Unspecified (Chronic Pulmonary Heart Disease)	I24.9	Acute ischaemic heart disease, unspecified	
		I27.9	Pulmonary heart disease, unspecified	
421.0	Endocarditis, Bacterial, Acute and Subacute	I33.0	Acute and subacute infective endocarditis	
		I42.3	Endomyocardial (eosinophilic) disease Endomyocardial (tropical) fibrosis L"ffler's endocarditis	
		I72.9	Aneurysm of unspecified site	
421.9	Endocarditis, Acute and Unspecified	I33.9	Acute endocarditis, unspecified Endocarditis) Myoendocarditis) acute or subacute Periendocarditis)	
423.2	Pericarditis, Chronic Constrictive	I31.1	Chronic constrictive pericarditis	
424.0	Mitral Valve Prolapse (Barlow's Syndrome, Floppy Mitral Valve)	I34.0	Mitral (valve) insufficiency	
		I34.1	Mitral (valve) prolapse Floppy mitral valve syndrome	
		I34.2	Nonrheumatic mitral (valve) stenosis	
		I34.8	Other nonrheumatic mitral valve disorders	
		I34.9	Nonrheumatic mitral valve disorder, unspecified	
424.1	Aortic Valve Stenosis	I35.0	Aortic (valve) stenosis	
		I35.1	Aortic (valve) insufficiency	
		I35.2	Aortic (valve) stenosis with insufficiency	
		I35.8	Other aortic valve disorders	
		I35.9	Aortic valve disorder, unspecified	
424.9	Endocarditis, Valve Unspecified	I38	Endocarditis, valve unspecified	
425.1	Cardiomyopathy, Hypertrophic Obstructive	I42.1	Obstructive hypertrophic cardiomyopathy Hypertrophic subaortic stenosis	
425.4	Cardiomyopathy, Other Primary	I42.0	Dilated cardiomyopathy	
		I42.2	Other hypertrophic cardiomyopathy Nonobstructive hypertrophic cardiomyopathy	
		I42.5	Other restrictive cardiomyopathy	
		I42.8	Other cardiomyopathies	
		I42.9	Cardiomyopathy, unspecified	
		I51.7	Cardiomegaly	
425.9	Cardiomyopathy, Secondary, Unspecified	I42.7	Cardiomyopathy due to drugs and other external agents	
		I42.9	Cardiomyopathy, unspecified	
426.0	Atrioventricular Block, Complete (Third-Degree)	I44.2	Atrioventricular block, complete Complete heart block NOS Third-degree block	
		I49.8	Other specified cardiac arrhythmias	
426.1	Atrioventricular Block, Other and Unspecified	I44.0	Atrioventricular block, first degree	
		I44.1	Atrioventricular block, second degree	
		I44.3	Other and unspecified atrioventricular block	
		I45.5	Other specified heart block Sinoatrial block Sinoauricular block	
426.2	Left Bundle Branch Hemiblock	I44.4	Left anterior fascicular block	
		I44.5	Left posterior fascicular block	
		I44.6	Other and unspecified fascicular block Left bundle-branch hemiblock NOS	
426.3	Left Bundle Branch Block, Other	I44.7	Left bundle-branch block, unspecified	
426.4	Right Bundle Branch Block	I45.0	Right fascicular block	
		I45.1	Other and unspecified right bundle-branch block	
426.5	Bundle Branch Block, Other and Unspecified	I44.3	Other and unspecified atrioventricular block	
		I45.2	Bifascicular block	
		I45.3	Trifascicular block	
		I45.4	Nonspecific intraventricular block Bundle-branch block NOS	
426.8	Other Specified Conduction Disorders	I45.6	Pre-excitation syndrome Anomalous atrioventricular excitation Atrioventricular conduction: . accelerated . accessory . pre-excitation Lown-Ganong-Levine syndrome Wolff-Parkinson-White syndrome	
		I45.8	Other specified conduction disorders	
426.9	Stokes-Adams Syndrome	I45.8	Other specified conduction disorders	
		I45.9	Conduction disorder, unspecified	
427.0	Tachycardia, Paroxysmal Supraventricular	I47.1	Supraventricular tachycardia	
427.1	Ventricular Tachycardia	I47.2	Ventricular tachycardia	
427.2	Paroxysmal Tachycardia, Unspecified	I47.9	Paroxysmal tachycardia, unspecified	
427.3	Atrial Fibrillation and Flutter	I48	Atrial fibrillation and flutter	
427.4	Ventricular Fibrillation and Flutter	I49.0	Ventricular fibrillation and flutter	
427.5	Cardiac Arrest	I46.0	Cardiac arrest with successful resuscitation	

ICD-9	Description	ICD-10	Description	(Continued)
427.5	Cardiac Arrest	I46.9	Cardiac arrest, unspecified	
427.6	Premature Beats	I49.1	Atrial premature depolarization Atrial premature beats	
		I49.2	Junctional premature depolarization	
		I49.3	Ventricular premature depolarization	
		I49.4	Other and unspecified premature depolarization	
427.8	Cardiac Dysrhythmias, Other Specified	I47.0	Re-entry ventricular arrhythmia	
		I47.1	Supraventricular tachycardia	
		I49.5	Sick sinus syndrome Tachycardia-bradycardia syndrome	
		I49.8	Other specified cardiac arrhythmias	
		I49.9	Cardiac arrhythmia, unspecified	
		R00.1	Bradycardia, unspecified Slow heart beat	
		R00.8	Other and unspecified abnormalities of heart beat	
		R01.2	Other cardiac sounds Cardiac dullness, increased or decreased Precordial friction	
427.9	Arrhythmia	I49.9	Cardiac arrhythmia, unspecified	
		I51.8	Other ill-defined heart diseases Carditis (acute)(chronic) Pancarditis (acute)(chronic)	
428.0	Heart Failure, Congestive	I50.0	Congestive heart failure	
428.1	Heart Failure, Left	I50.1	Left ventricular failure	
428.9	Heart Failure, Unspecified	I46.9	Cardiac arrest, unspecified	
		I50.9	Heart failure, unspecified	
429.9	Heart Disease, Unspecified	I46.1	Sudden cardiac death, so described	
		I50.9	Heart failure, unspecified	
		I51.9	Heart disease, unspecified	
430	Subarachnoid Hemorrhage (Non-Traumatic)	I60.0	Subarachnoid haemorrhage from carotid siphon and bifurcation	
		I60.1	Subarachnoid haemorrhage from middle cerebral artery	
		I60.2	Subarachnoid haemorrhage from anterior communicating artery	
		I60.3	Subarachnoid haemorrhage from posterior communicating artery	
		I60.4	Subarachnoid haemorrhage from basilar artery	
		I60.5	Subarachnoid haemorrhage from vertebral artery	
		I60.6	Subarachnoid haemorrhage from other intracranial arteries Multiple involvement of intracranial arteries	
		I60.7	Subarachnoid haemorrhage from intracranial artery, unspecified	
		I60.8	Other subarachnoid haemorrhage Meningeal haemorrhage Rupture of cerebral arteriovenous malformation	
		I60.9	Subarachnoid haemorrhage, unspecified Ruptured (congenital) cerebral aneurysm NOS	
431	Cerebral Hemorrhage	I61.0	Intracerebral haemorrhage in hemisphere, subcortical Deep intracerebral haemorrhage	
		I61.1	Intracerebral haemorrhage in hemisphere, cortical Cerebral lobe haemorrhage Superficial intracerebral haemorrhage	
		I61.2	Intracerebral haemorrhage in hemisphere, unspecified	
		I61.3	Intracerebral haemorrhage in brain stem	
		I61.4	Intracerebral haemorrhage in cerebellum	
		I61.5	Intracerebral haemorrhage, intraventricular	
		I61.6	Intracerebral haemorrhage, multiple localized	
		I61.8	Other intracerebral haemorrhage	
		I61.9	Intracerebral haemorrhage, unspecified	
432.0	Epidural Hematoma (Non-Traumatic)	I62.1	Nontraumatic extradural haemorrhage Nontraumatic epidural haemorrhage	
432.1	Subdural Hemorrhage	I62.0	Subdural haemorrhage (acute)(nontraumatic)	
432.9	Intracranial Hemorrhage	I62.9	Intracranial haemorrhage (nontraumatic), unspecified	
433.1	Carotid Artery Occlusion	I63.0	Cerebral infarction due to thrombosis of precerebral arteries	
		I63.1	Cerebral infarction due to embolism of precerebral arteries	
		I63.2	Cerebral infarction due to unspecified occlusion or stenosis of precerebral arteries	
		I65.2	Occlusion and stenosis of carotid artery	
		I67.2	Cerebral atherosclerosis	
435	Transient Cerebral Ischemia	G45.0	Vertebro-basilar artery syndrome	
		G45.1	Carotid artery syndrome (hemispheric)	
		G45.2	Multiple and bilateral precerebral artery syndromes	
		G45.4	Transient global amnesia	
		G45.8	Other transient cerebral ischaemic attacks and related syndromes	
		G45.9	Transient cerebral ischaemic attack, unspecified	
		G95.1	Vascular myelopathies	
436	Cerebrovascular Accident (CVA), Acute	I63.8	Other cerebral infarction	

Translation of ICD-9 CM to ICD-10

ICD-9	Description	ICD-10	Description	(Continued)
436	Cerebrovascular Accident (CVA), Acute	I64	Stroke, not specified as haemorrhage or infarction Cerebrovascular accident NOS	
		I66.3	Occlusion and stenosis of cerebellar arteries	
		I67.8	Other specified cerebrovascular diseases	
437.0	Cerebral Atherosclerosis (Cerebrovascular Disease)	G95.1	Vascular myelopathies	
		I63.8	Other cerebral infarction	
		I66.9	Occlusion and stenosis of unspecified cerebral artery	
		I67.2	Cerebral atherosclerosis	
437.1	Cerebrovascular Insufficiency, Acute	I66.9	Occlusion and stenosis of unspecified cerebral artery	
		I67.8	Other specified cerebrovascular diseases	
		I67.9	Cerebrovascular disease, unspecified	
437.2	Hypertensive Encephalopathy	I67.4	Hypertensive encephalopathy	
437.3	Cerebral Aneurysm (Non-Ruptured)	I67.1	Cerebral aneurysm, nonruptured	
437.9	Cerebrovascular Disease, Unspecified	G93.6	Cerebral oedema	
		I67.8	Other specified cerebrovascular diseases	
		I67.9	Cerebrovascular disease, unspecified	
440.0	Arteriosclerosis and Atherosclerosis	I70.0	Atherosclerosis of aorta	
440.1	Atherosclerosis of Renal Artery	I70.1	Atherosclerosis of renal artery	
440.2	Atherosclerosis of Arteries of the Extremities	I70.2	Atherosclerosis of arteries of extremities	
440.8	Atherosclerosis of Other Specified Arteries	I70.8	Atherosclerosis of other arteries	
440.9	Atherosclerosis, Generalized and Unspecified	I70.9	Generalized and unspecified atherosclerosis	
441.0	Aortic Dissection (Dissecting Aneurysm)	I71.0	Dissection of aorta [any part] Dissecting aneurysm of aorta (ruptured) [any part]	
441.1	Thoracic Aneurysm, Ruptured	I71.1	Thoracic aortic aneurysm, ruptured	
441.2	Thoracic Aneurysm	I71.2	Thoracic aortic aneurysm, without mention of rupture	
441.3	Abdominal Aneurysm, Ruptured	I71.3	Abdominal aortic aneurysm, ruptured	
441.4	Abdominal Aneurysm	I71.4	Abdominal aortic aneurysm, without mention of rupture	
441.5	Aortic Aneurysm of Unspecified Site, Ruptured	I71.1	Thoracic aortic aneurysm, ruptured	
		I71.5	Thoracoabdominal aortic aneurysm, ruptured	
		I71.8	Aortic aneurysm of unspecified site, ruptured	
441.6	Thoracoabdominal Aneurysm, Ruptured	I71.2	Thoracic aortic aneurysm, without mention of rupture	
		I71.6	Thoracoabdominal aortic aneurysm, without mention of rupture	
		I71.9	Aortic aneurysm of unspecified site, without mention of rupture	
443.0	Raynaud's Phenomenon	I73.0	Raynaud's syndrome	
		T75.2	Effects of vibration Pneumatic hammer syndrome Traumatic vasospastic syndrome Vertigo from infrasound	
443.1	Buerger's Disease (Thromboangiitis Obliterans)	I73.1	Thromboangiitis obliterans [Buerger]	
443.9	Peripheral Vascular Disease, Unspecified	I73.9	Peripheral vascular disease, unspecified	
444.0	Embolism and Thrombosis, Arterial of Abdominal Aorta	I74.0	Embolism and thrombosis of abdominal aorta	
444.1	Embolism and Thrombosis, Arterial of Thoracic Aorta	I74.1	Embolism and thrombosis of other and unspecified parts of aorta	
444.2	Embolism and Thrombosis, Arterial of Arteries of the Extremities	I74.2	Embolism and thrombosis of arteries of upper extremities	
		I74.3	Embolism and thrombosis of arteries of lower extremities	
		I74.4	Embolism and thrombosis of arteries of extremities, unspecified Peripheral arterial embolism	
444.8	Embolism and Thrombosis, Arterial of Other Specified Artery	I74.5	Embolism and thrombosis of iliac artery	
		I74.8	Embolism and thrombosis of other arteries	
444.9	Embolism and Thrombosis, Arterial and Venous, Unspecified	I74.9	Embolism and thrombosis of unspecified artery	
446.0	Polyarteritis Nodosa	M30.0	Polyarteritis nodosa	
		M30.2	Juvenile polyarteritis	
		M30.8	Other conditions related to polyarteritis nodosa	
446.5	Temporal Arteritis	M31.6	Other giant cell arteritis	
448.0	Osler-Weber-Rendu Disease (Hereditary Hemorrhagic Telangiectasia)	I78.0	Hereditary haemorrhagic telangiectasia Rendu-Osler-Weber disease	
451.0	Thrombophlebitis, of Superficial Veins of Lower Extremities	I80.0	Phlebitis and thrombophlebitis of superficial vessels of lower extremities	
451.1	Thrombophlebitis, of Deep Vessels of Lower Extremities	I80.1	Phlebitis and thrombophlebitis of femoral vein	
		I80.2	Phlebitis and thrombophlebitis of other deep vessels of lower extremities	
451.8	Thrombophlebitis, of Other Sites	I80.8	Phlebitis and thrombophlebitis of other sites	
453.3	Renal Vein Thrombosis	I82.3	Embolism and thrombosis of renal vein	
453.9	Thrombosis and Embolism of Unspecified Site, Other Venous	I82.9	Embolism and thrombosis of unspecified vein	
454.0	Varicose (Stasis) Ulcer	I83.0	Varicose veins of lower extremities with ulcer	

ICD-9	Description	ICD-10	Description	(Continued)
454.2	Varicose Veins of Lower Extremities with Ulcer and Inflammation	I83.2	Varicose veins of lower extremities with both ulcer and inflammation Any condition in I83.9 with both ulcer and inflammation	
454.9	Varicose Veins	I83.1	Varicose veins of lower extremities with inflammation	
		I83.9	Varicose veins of lower extremities without ulcer or inflammation	
455.0	Hemorrhoids, Internal, Without Mention of Complication	I84.2	Internal haemorrhoids without complication	
455.1	Hemorrhoids, Internal Thrombosed	I84.0	Internal thrombosed haemorrhoids	
455.2	Hemorrhoids, Internal, with Other Complication	I84.1	Internal haemorrhoids with other complications	
455.3	Hemorrhoids, External, Without Mention of Complication	I84.5	External haemorrhoids without complication	
455.4	Hemorrhoids, External Thrombosed	I84.3	External thrombosed haemorrhoids	
455.5	Hemorrhoids, External, with Other Complication	I84.4	External haemorrhoids with other complications	
455.6	Hemorrhoids Without Mention of Complication, Unspecified	I84.9	Unspecified haemorrhoids without complication	
455.7	Hemorrhoids, Thrombosed, Unspecified	I84.7	Unspecified thrombosed haemorrhoids Thrombosed haemorrhoids, unspecified whether internal or external	
455.8	Hemorrhoids with Other Complication, Unspecified	I84.8	Unspecified haemorrhoids with other complications Haemorrhoids, unspecified whether internal or external	
455.9	Hemorrhoidal Skin Tags, Residual	I84.6	Residual haemorrhoidal skin tags Skin tags of anus or rectum	
456.0	Esophageal Varices with Bleeding	I85.0	Oesophageal varices with bleeding	
456.1	Esophageal Varices Without Mention of Bleeding	I85.9	Oesophageal varices without bleeding	
456.4	Varicocele	I86.1	Scrotal varices Varicocele	
457.2	Lymphangitis	I89.1	Lymphangitis Lymphangitis	
460	Cold (Upper Respiratory Infection)	J00	Acute nasopharyngitis [common cold]	
		R06.5	Mouth breathing	
461.0	Sinusitis, Maxillary	J01.0	Acute maxillary sinusitis Acute antritis	
461.1	Sinusitis, Frontal	J01.1	Acute frontal sinusitis	
461.2	Sinusitis, Ethmoidal	J01.2	Acute ethmoidal sinusitis	
461.3	Sinusitis, Sphenoidal	J01.3	Acute sphenoidal sinusitis	
461.8	Sinusitis, Acute, Other	J01.4	Acute pansinusitis	
		J01.8	Other acute sinusitis Acute sinusitis involving more than one sinus but not pansinusitis	
461.9	Sinusitis, Unspecified	J01.9	Acute sinusitis, unspecified	
462	Sore Throat (Pharyngitis, Acute)	J02.8	Acute pharyngitis due to other specified organisms	
		J02.9	Acute pharyngitis, unspecified	
		J06.0	Acute laryngopharyngitis	
463	Tonsillitis, Acute	J03.8	Acute tonsillitis due to other specified organisms	
		J03.9	Acute tonsillitis, unspecified	
464.0	Laryngitis	J04.0	Acute laryngitis	
464.3	Epiglottitis	J05.1	Acute epiglottitis	
465.9	Upper Respiratory Infection, Unspecified	J06.9	Acute upper respiratory infection, unspecified	
		J39.9	Disease of upper respiratory tract, unspecified	
466.0	Bronchitis, Acute	J20.0	Acute bronchitis due to Mycoplasma pneumoniae	
		J20.1	Acute bronchitis due to Haemophilus influenzae	
		J20.2	Acute bronchitis due to streptococcus	
		J20.3	Acute bronchitis due to coxsackievirus	
		J20.4	Acute bronchitis due to parainfluenza virus	
		J20.5	Acute bronchitis due to respiratory syncytial virus	
		J20.6	Acute bronchitis due to rhinovirus	
		J20.7	Acute bronchitis due to echovirus	
		J20.8	Acute bronchitis due to other specified organisms	
		J20.9	Acute bronchitis, unspecified	
		J22	Unspecified acute lower respiratory infection	
470	Deviated Nasal Septum	J34.2	Deviated nasal septum	
471.0	Nasal Polyps	J33.0	Polyp of nasal cavity	
471.9	Nasal Polyp, Unspecified	J33.0	Polyp of nasal cavity	
		J33.9	Nasal polyp, unspecified	
473.2	Sinusitis, Chronic	J32.2	Chronic ethmoidal sinusitis	
473.9	Sinusitis, Chronic, Unspecified	J32.9	Chronic sinusitis, unspecified	
		J34.8	Other specified disorders of nose and nasal sinuses	
474.0	Tonsillitis, Chronic	J03.9	Acute tonsillitis, unspecified	
		J35.0	Chronic tonsillitis	
474.1	Hypertrophy of Tonsils and Adenoids	J35.1	Hypertrophy of tonsils	
		J35.2	Hypertrophy of adenoids	
		J35.3	Hypertrophy of tonsils with hypertrophy of adenoids	

Translation of ICD-9 CM to ICD-10

ICD-9	Description	ICD-10	Description	(Continued)
475	Peritonsillar Abscess	J03.9	Acute tonsillitis, unspecified	
		J36	Peritonsillar abscess	
477.0	Allergic Rhinitis Due to Pollen	J30.1	Allergic rhinitis	
477.8	Allergic Rhinitis Due to Other Allergen	J30.2	Other seasonal allergic rhinitis	
		J30.3	Other allergic rhinitis	
477.9	Allergic Rhinitis, Unspecified	J30.0	Vasomotor rhinitis	
		J30.1	Allergic rhinitis	
		J30.3	Other allergic rhinitis	
		J30.4	Allergic rhinitis, unspecified	
478.1	Nasal Septum Perforation	J32.0	Chronic maxillary sinusitis	
		J32.2	Chronic ethmoidal sinusitis	
		J33.9	Nasal polyp, unspecified	
		J34.0	Abscess, furuncle and carbuncle of nose	
		J34.1	Cyst and mucocele of nasal sinus	
		J34.3	Hypertrophy of nasal turbinates	
		J34.8	Other specified disorders of nose and nasal sinuses	
481	Pneumococcal Pneumonia	J13	Pneumonia due to Streptococcus pneumoniae	
		J18.1	Lobar pneumonia, unspecified	
482.0	Pneumonia Due to Klebsiella Pneumoniae	J15.0	Pneumonia due to Klebsiella pneumoniae	
482.1	Pneumonia Due to Pseudomonas	J15.1	Pneumonia due to Pseudomonas	
482.2	Pneumonia Due to Hemophilus Influenzae	J14	Pneumonia due to Haemophilus influenzae	
482.3	Pneumonia Due to Streptococcus	J15.3	Pneumonia due to streptococcus, group B	
		J15.4	Pneumonia due to other streptococci	
482.4	Pneumonia Due to Staphylococcus	J15.2	Pneumonia due to staphylococcus	
482.8	Pneumonia Due to Other Specified Bacteria	A48.1	Legionnaires' disease	
		J15.5	Pneumonia due to Escherichia coli	
		J15.6	Pneumonia due to other aerobic Gram-negative bacteria	
		J15.8	Other bacterial pneumonia	
482.9	Pneumonia, Bacterial, Unspecified	J15.9	Bacterial pneumonia, unspecified	
483	Pneumonia Due to Other Specified Organism	J15.7	Pneumonia due to Mycoplasma pneumoniae	
		J16.0	Chlamydial pneumonia	
		J16.8	Pneumonia due to other specified infectious organisms	
485	Bronchopneumonia, Organism Unspecified	J18.0	Bronchopneumonia, unspecified	
486	Pneumonia, Organism Unspecified	J18.2	Hypostatic pneumonia, unspecified	
		J18.8	Other pneumonia, organism unspecified	
		J18.9	Pneumonia, unspecified	
487.0	Influenza with Pneumonia	J10.0	Influenza with pneumonia, influenza virus identified	
		J11.0	Influenza with pneumonia, virus not identified	
487.1	Influenza with Other Respiratory Manifestations	J10.1	Influenza with other respiratory manifestations, influenza virus identified	
		J11.1	Influenza with other respiratory manifestations, virus not identified	
487.8	Influenza with Other Manifestations	J10.8	Influenza with other manifestations, influenza virus identified	
		J11.8	Influenza with other manifestations, virus not identified	
490	Bronchitis, not Specified As Acute or Chronic	J20.9	Acute bronchitis, unspecified	
		J40	Bronchitis, not specified as acute or chronic	
		J98.0	Diseases of bronchus, not elsewhere classified	
491.0	Chronic Bronchitis, Simple	J41.0	Simple chronic bronchitis	
		J42	Unspecified chronic bronchitis	
491.1	Chronic Bronchitis, Mucopurulent	J41.1	Mucopurulent chronic bronchitis	
491.2	Chronic Bronchitis, Obstructive	J44.1	Chronic obstructive pulmonary disease with acute exacerbation, unspecified	
		J44.8	Other specified chronic obstructive pulmonary disease	
491.8	Bronchitis, Chronic, Other	J41.8	Mixed simple and mucopurulent chronic bronchitis	
		J42	Unspecified chronic bronchitis	
		J44.8	Other specified chronic obstructive pulmonary disease	
491.9	Bronchitis, Chronic, Unspecified	J42	Unspecified chronic bronchitis	
		J98.0	Diseases of bronchus, not elsewhere classified	
492	Emphysema	J43.0	MacLeod's syndrome	
		J43.1	Panlobular emphysema Panacinar emphysema	
		J43.2	Centrilobular emphysema	
		J43.8	Other emphysema	
		J43.9	Emphysema, unspecified	
493.0	Asthma, Extrinsic	J45.0	Predominantly allergic asthma	

ICD-9	Description	ICD-10	Description	(Continued)
493.0	Asthma, Extrinsic	J45.8	Mixed asthma	
493.1	Asthma, Intrinsic	J45.1	Nonallergic asthma	
		J45.8	Mixed asthma	
		J45.9	Asthma, unspecified	
493.9	Asthma, Unspecified	J45.0	Predominantly allergic asthma	
		J45.8	Mixed asthma	
		J45.9	Asthma, unspecified	
		J46	Status asthmaticus Acute severe asthma	
494	Bronchiectasis	J47	Bronchiectasis	
		J98.0	Diseases of bronchus, not elsewhere classified	
495.0	Farmer's Lung	J67.0	Farmer's lung	
495.1	Bagassosis	J67.1	Bagassosis	
495.2	Bird-Fancier's Lung	J67.2	Bird fancier's lung	
495.5	Mushroom Workers' Lung	J67.5	Mushroom-worker's lung	
495.7	Ventilation Pneumonitis	J67.7	Air-conditioner and humidifier lung	
495.8	Other Specified Allergic Alveolitis & Pneumonitis	J67.8	Hypersensitivity pneumonitis due to other organic dusts	
495.9	Hypersensitivity Pneumonitis	J67.9	Hypersensitivity pneumonitis due to unspecified organic dust	
496	COPD (Chronic Obstructive Pulmonary Disease)	J44.0	Chronic obstructive pulmonary disease with acute lower respiratory infection	
		J44.9	Chronic obstructive pulmonary disease, unspecified	
500	Pneumoconiosis, Coal Worker's	J60	Coalworker's pneumoconiosis	
501	Asbestosis	J61	Pneumoconiosis due to asbestos	
502	Silicosis	J62.0	Pneumoconiosis due to talc dust	
		J62.8	Pneumoconiosis due to other dust containing silica	
503	Siderosis	J63.0	Aluminosis (of lung)	
		J63.1	Bauxite fibrosis (of lung)	
		J63.2	Berylliosis	
		J63.3	Graphite fibrosis (of lung)	
		J63.4	Siderosis	
		J63.5	Stannosis	
		J63.8	Pneumoconiosis due to other specified inorganic dusts	
504	Byssinosis	J64	Unspecified pneumoconiosis	
		J66.0	Byssinosis Airway disease due to cotton dust	
		J66.1	Flax-dresser's disease	
		J66.2	Cannabinosis	
		J66.8	Airway disease due to other specific organic dusts	
505	Occupational Asthma (Pneumoconiosis)	J64	Unspecified pneumoconiosis	
506.0	Bronchitis and Pneumonitis Due to Fumes or Vapors	J68.0	Bronchitis and pneumonitis due to chemicals, gases, fumes and vapours	
		J68.4	Chronic respiratory conditions due to chemicals, gases, fumes and vapours	
506.1	Acute Pulmonary Edema Due to Fumes and Vapors	J68.1	Acute pulmonary oedema due to chemicals, gases, fumes and vapours	
506.4	Chronic Respiratory Conditions Due to Fumes and Vapors	J68.4	Chronic respiratory conditions due to chemicals, gases, fumes and vapours	
506.9	Respiratory Conditions Due to Fumes or Vapors, Unspecified	J68.8	Other respiratory conditions due to chemicals, gases, fumes and vapours	
		J68.9	Unspecified respiratory condition due to chemicals, gases, fumes and vapours	
507.0	Pneumonitis Due to Inhalation of Food or Vomitus	J69.0	Pneumonitis due to food and vomit Aspiration pneumonia	
		J95.8	Other postprocedural respiratory disorders	
510.0	Empyema with Fistula	J86.0	Pyothorax with fistula	
510.9	Empyema Without Mention of Fistula	J86.9	Pyothorax without fistula	
511.0	Pleurisy Without Mention of Effusion or Current Tuberculosis	J86.9	Pyothorax without fistula	
		J90	Pleural effusion, not elsewhere classified	
		J92.0	Pleural plaque with presence of asbestos	
		J92.9	Pleural plaque without asbestos	
		J94.1	Fibrothorax	
		J94.8	Other specified pleural conditions	
		J94.9	Pleural condition, unspecified	
		J98.4	Other disorders of lung	
		R09.1	Pleurisy	
511.1	Pleurisy with Effusion, with Mention of Bacterial Cause Other Than Tuberculosis	J90	Pleural effusion, not elsewhere classified	
511.9	Pleural Effusion, Unspecified	J90	Pleural effusion, not elsewhere classified	
		J94.8	Other specified pleural conditions	

Translation of ICD-9 CM to ICD-10

ICD-9	Description	ICD-10	Description	(Continued)
511.9	Pleural Effusion, Unspecified	P28.8	Other specified respiratory conditions of newborn	
512	Pneumothorax	J93.0	Spontaneous tension pneumothorax	
		J93.1	Other spontaneous pneumothorax	
		J93.8	Other pneumothorax	
		J93.9	Pneumothorax, unspecified	
513.0	Lung Abscess	J85.0	Gangrene and necrosis of lung	
		J85.1	Abscess of lung with pneumonia	
		J85.2	Abscess of lung without pneumonia	
514	Pulmonary Edema	J18.2	Hypostatic pneumonia, unspecified	
		J81	Pulmonary oedema Acute	
515	Interstitial Pulmonary Fibrosis	J84.1	Other interstitial pulmonary diseases with fibrosis	
518.0	Lung Collapse	J98.1	Pulmonary collapse Atelectasis	
518.4	Acute Edema of Lungs, Unspecified	J81	Pulmonary oedema Acute	
518.5	Adult Respiratory Distress Syndrome	J80	Adult respiratory distress syndrome	
		J95.1	Acute pulmonary insufficiency following thoracic surgery	
		J95.2	Acute pulmonary insufficiency following nonthoracic surgery	
		J95.3	Chronic pulmonary insufficiency following surgery	
520.6	Impacted Tooth	K00.6	Disturbances in tooth eruption	
		K01.0	Embedded teeth	
		K01.1	Impacted teeth	
520.9	Dental Disorders	K00.2	Abnormalities of size and form of teeth	
		K00.9	Disorder of tooth development	
521.0	Cavities (Dental Caries)	K02.0	Caries limited to enamel	
		K02.1	Caries of dentine	
		K02.2	Caries of cementum	
		K02.3	Arrested dental caries	
		K02.4	Odontoclasia Infantile melanodontia	
		K02.8	Other dental caries	
		K02.9	Dental caries, unspecified	
521.7	Posteruptive Color Changes	K03.6	Deposits [accretions] on teeth	
		K03.7	Posteruptive colour changes of dental hard tissues	
521.9	Disease of Hard Tissues of Teeth, Unspecified	K03.9	Disease of hard tissues of teeth, unspecified	
522.5	Dentoalveolar Abscess	K04.7	Periapical abscess without sinus	
522.7	Periapical Abscess with Sinus	K04.6	Periapical abscess with sinus	
523.0	Gingivitis, Acute	K05.0	Acute gingivitis	
523.1	Gingivitis, Chronic	K05.1	Chronic gingivitis	
523.2	Gingival Recession	K06.0	Gingival recession	
523.3	Periodontitis	K05.2	Acute periodontitis	
523.4	Periodontitis, Chronic	K05.3	Chronic periodontitis	
523.9	Unspecified Gingival and Periodontal Disease	K05.6	Periodontal disease, unspecified	
		K06.9	Disorder of gingiva and edentulous alveolar ridge, unspecified	
524.3	Impacted Tooth with Abnormal Position	K07.3	Anomalies of tooth position	
527.5	Salivary Gland Stones	K11.5	Sialolithiasis	
528.3	Ludwig's Angina	K12.2	Cellulitis and abscess of mouth	
530.0	Achalasia	K22.0	Achalasia of cardia	
530.1	Esophagitis	K20	Oesophagitis Abscess	
		K21.0	Gastro-oesophageal reflux disease with oesophagitis	
		K21.9	Gastro-oesophageal reflux disease without oesophagitis	
530.3	Esophageal Strictures	K22.2	Oesophageal obstruction	
530.5	Esophageal Spasm	K22.4	Dyskinesia of oesophagus C	
530.6	Esophageal Diverticula	K22.5	Diverticulum of oesophagus,	
		Q39.6	Diverticulum of oesophagus	
530.7	Mallory-Weiss Syndrome	K22.6	Gastro-oesophageal laceration-haemorrhage syndrome	
530.9	Unspecified Disorder of Esophagus	K22.9	Disease of oesophagus, unspecified	
535.0	Gastritis	K29.0	Acute haemorrhagic gastritis	
		K29.1	Other acute gastritis	
535.1	Atrophic Gastritis	K29.4	Chronic atrophic gastritis	
		K29.5	Chronic gastritis, unspecified	
535.2	Gastric Mucosal Hypertrophy	K29.6	Other gastritis	
535.3	Alcoholic Gastritis	K29.2	Alcoholic gastritis	
535.4	Gastritis, Other Specified	K29.3	Chronic superficial gastritis	

ICD-9	Description	ICD-10	Description	(Continued)
535.4	Gastritis, Other Specified	K29.6	Other gastritis	
535.5	Unspecific Gastritis and Gastroduodenitis	K29.7	Gastritis, unspecified	
		K29.9	Gastroduodenitis, unspecified	
		K52.9	Noninfective gastroenteritis and colitis, unspecified	
535.6	Duodenitis	K29.8	Duodenitis	
536.0	Achlorhydria, Hypochlorhydria	K31.8	Other specified diseases of stomach and duodenum	
536.8	Dyspepsia	K30	Dyspepsia Indigestion	
		K31.2	Hourglass stricture and stenosis of stomach	
		K31.5	Obstruction of duodenum	
		K31.8	Other specified diseases of stomach and duodenum	
		R10.1	Pain localized to upper abdomen	
537.0	Pyloric Stenosis, Acquired (Adult) Hypertrophic	K31.1	Adult hypertrophic pyloric stenosis	
		K31.8	Other specified diseases of stomach and duodenum	
540.0	Appendicitis, Acute with Generalized Peritonitis	K35.0	Acute appendicitis with generalized peritonitis	
		K65.0	Acute peritonitis	
		K65.8	Other peritonitis	
540.1	Appendicitis, Acute with Peritoneal Abscess	K35.1	Acute appendicitis with peritoneal abscess	
540.9	Appendicitis, Acute Without Mention of Peritonitis	K35.9	Acute appendicitis, unspecified	
541	Appendicitis, Unqualified	K37	Unspecified appendicitis	
		K52.9	Noninfective gastroenteritis and colitis, unspecified	
542	Appendicitis, Other	K36	Other appendicitis	
550.0	Inguinal Hernia, with Gangrene	K40.1	Bilateral inguinal hernia, with gangrene	
		K40.4	Unilateral or unspecified inguinal hernia, with gangrene	
550.1	Inguinal Hernia with Obstruction, Without Mention of Gangrene	K40.0	Bilateral inguinal hernia, with obstruction, without gangrene	
		K40.3	Unilateral or unspecified inguinal hernia, with obstruction, without gangrene	
550.9	Inguinal Hernia, Without Mention of Obstruction or Gangrene	K40.2	Bilateral inguinal hernia, without obstruction or gangrene	
		K40.9	Unilateral or unspecified inguinal hernia, without obstruction or gangrene	
551.0	Femoral Hernia with Gangrene	K41.1	Bilateral femoral hernia, with gangrene	
		K41.4	Unilateral or unspecified femoral hernia, with gangrene	
551.1	Umbilical Hernia with Gangrene	K42.1	Umbilical hernia with gangrene	
		Q79.2	Exomphalos Omphalocele	
551.2	Ventral Hernia with Gangrene	K43.1	Ventral hernia with gangrene Gangrenous	
551.3	Diaphragmatic Hernia with Gangrene	K44.1	Diaphragmatic hernia with gangrene	
551.8	Hernia, Other Specified Sites with Gangrene	K45.1	Other specified abdominal hernia with gangrene	
552.0	Femoral Hernia with Obstruction	K41.0	Bilateral femoral hernia, with obstruction, without gangrene	
		K41.3	Unilateral or unspecified femoral hernia, with obstruction, without gangrene	
552.1	Umbilical Hernia with Obstruction	K42.0	Umbilical hernia with obstruction, without gangrene	
		Q79.2	Exomphalos Omphalocele	
552.2	Ventral Hernia with Obstruction	K43.0	Ventral hernia with obstruction, without gangrene	
552.3	Diaphragmatic Hernia with Obstruction	K44.0	Diaphragmatic hernia with obstruction, without gangrene	
553.0	Hernia, Femoral	K41.2	Bilateral femoral hernia, without obstruction or gangrene	
		K41.9	Unilateral or unspecified femoral hernia, without obstruction or gangrene	
553.1	Hernia, Umbilical	K42.9	Umbilical hernia without obstruction or gangrene	
		Q79.2	Exomphalos Omphalocele	
553.2	Hernia, Ventral	K43.9	Ventral hernia without obstruction or gangrene	
		K46.9	Unspecified abdominal hernia without obstruction or gangrene	
553.3	Hernia, Hiatal	K44.9	Diaphragmatic hernia without obstruction or gangrene	
		K45.8	Other specified abdominal hernia without obstruction or gangrene	
553.8	Hernia of Other Specified Sites	K45.8	Other specified abdominal hernia without obstruction or gangrene	
		K46.9	Unspecified abdominal hernia without obstruction or gangrene	
553.9	Hernia of Unspecified Site	K46.0	Unspecified abdominal hernia with obstruction, without gangrene	
		K46.9	Unspecified abdominal hernia without obstruction or gangrene	
555.0	Regional Enteritis, Small Intestine (Ileitis)	K50.0	Crohn's disease of small intestine	
555.1	Regional Enteritis, Large Intestine	K50.1	Crohn's disease of large intestine	
555.2	Regional Enteritis, Small Intestine with Large Intestine	K50.8	Crohn's disease of both small and large intestine	
555.9	Crohn's Disease	K50.9	Crohn's disease, unspecified	
556	Ulcerative Colitis	K51.0	Ulcerative (chronic) enterocolitis	
		K51.1	Ulcerative (chronic) ileocolitis	
		K51.2	Ulcerative (chronic) proctitis	

ICD-9	Description	ICD-10	Description	(Continued)
556	Ulcerative Colitis	K51.3	Ulcerative (chronic) rectosigmoiditis	
		K51.4	Pseudopolyposis of colon	
		K51.5	Mucosal proctocolitis	
		K51.8	Other ulcerative colitis	
		K51.9	Ulcerative colitis, unspecified	
557.0	Mesenteric Thrombosis	K55.0	Acute vascular disorders of intestine	
		K55.1	Chronic vascular disorders of intestine	
558	Gastroenteritis and Colitis, Non-Infectious	K52.0	Gastroenteritis and colitis due to radiation	
		K52.1	Toxic gastroenteritis and colitis	
		K52.2	Allergic and dietetic gastroenteritis and colitis	
		K52.8	Other specified noninfective gastroenteritis and colitis	
		K52.9	Noninfective gastroenteritis and colitis, unspecified	
560.0	Intussusception	K56.1	Intussusception or invagination of: . bowel . colon . intestine . rectum	
560.1	Paralytic Ileus	K56.0	Paralytic ileus	
		K56.7	Ileus, unspecified	
560.2	Volvulus	K56.2	Volvulus	
560.3	Intestinal Impaction	K56.3	Gallstone ileus	
		K56.4	Other impaction of intestine	
560.8	Intestinal Obstruction, Other Specified	K56.5	Intestinal adhesions [bands] with obstruction	
		K56.6	Other and unspecified intestinal obstruction	
560.9	Bowel Obstruction (Intestinal Obstruction, Unspecified)	K56.6	Other and unspecified intestinal obstruction	
562.0	Diverticulosis of Small Intestine	K57.0	Diverticular disease of small intestine with perforation and abscess	
		K57.1	Diverticular disease of small intestine without perforation or abscess	
		K57.4	Diverticular disease of both small and large intestine with perforation and abscess	
		K57.5	Diverticular disease of both small and large intestine without perforation or abscess	
562.1	Diverticulitis and Diverticulosis of Colon	K57.2	Diverticular disease of large intestine with perforation and abscess	
		K57.3	Diverticular disease of large intestine without perforation or abscess	
		K57.4	Diverticular disease of both small and large intestine with perforation and abscess	
		K57.5	Diverticular disease of both small and large intestine without perforation or abscess	
		K57.8	Diverticular disease of intestine, part unspecified, with perforation and abscess	
		K57.9	Diverticular disease of intestine, part unspecified, without perforation or abscess	
564.0	Constipation	K59.0	Constipation	
		R19.8	Other specified symptoms and signs involving the digestive system and abdomen	
564.1	Irritable Bowel Syndrome	K58.0	Irritable bowel syndrome with diarrhoea	
		K58.9	Irritable bowel syndrome without diarrhoea	
564.2	Dumping Syndrome (Post-Gastric Syndrome)	K91.1	Postgastric surgery syndrome, dumping	
		Z90.3	Acquired absence of part of stomach	
564.3	Vomiting Following Gastrointestinal Surgery	K91.0	Vomiting following gastrointestinal surgery	
564.4	Postoperative Functional Disorders, Other	K91.8	Other postprocedural disorders of digestive system, not elsewhere classified	
564.5	Diarrhea, Functional	K59.1	Functional diarrhoea	
564.8	Disorders of Intestine, Functional, Other Specified	K59.2	Neurogenic bowel, not elsewhere classified	
		K59.3	Megacolon, not elsewhere classified	
		K59.8	Other specified functional intestinal disorders	
		K62.8	Other specified diseases of anus and rectum	
564.9	Intestinal Upset	K59.9	Functional intestinal disorder, unspecified	
565.0	Anal Fissure and/or Ulcer	K60.0	Acute anal fissure	
		K60.1	Chronic anal fissure	
		K60.2	Anal fissure, unspecified	
565.1	Anorectal Fistula	K60.3	Anal fistula	
		K60.4	Rectal fistula	
		K60.5	Anorectal fistula	
566	Perirectal Abscess	K61.0	Anal abscess Perianal abscess	
		K61.1	Rectal abscess Perirectal abscess	
		K61.2	Anorectal abscess	
		K61.3	Ischiorectal abscess	
		K61.4	Intrasphincteric abscess	
567.1	Peritonitis, Pneumococcal	K65.0	Acute peritonitis	
567.2	Abscess, Subdiaphragmatic	K65.0	Acute peritonitis	
		K65.9	Peritonitis, unspecified	
567.8	Peritonitis, Other Specified	K65.8	Other peritonitis	
567.9	Peritonitis, Unspecified	K65.0	Acute peritonitis	

ICD-9	Description	ICD-10	Description	(Continued)
567.9	Peritonitis, Unspecified	K65.9	Peritonitis, unspecified	
568.0	Abdominal Adhesions	K66.0	Peritoneal adhesions	
569.0	Anal and Rectal Polyps	K62.0	Anal polyp	
		K62.1	Rectal polyp	
569.1	Rectal Prolapse	K62.2	Anal prolapse	
		K62.3	Rectal prolapse	
569.3	Hemorrhage of Rectum and Anus	K62.5	Haemorrhage of anus and rectum	
569.8	Other Specified Disorders of Intestine	E41	Severe malnutrition with marasmus	
		K56.6	Other and unspecified intestinal obstruction	
		K59.3	Megacolon, not elsewhere classified	
		K59.8	Other specified functional intestinal disorders	
		K60.4	Rectal fistula	
		K62.8	Other specified diseases of anus and rectum	
		K63.1	Perforation of intestine (nontraumatic)	
		K63.2	Fistula of intestine	
		K63.3	Ulcer of intestine	
		K63.4	Enteroptosis	
		K63.8	Other specified diseases of intestine	
		K63.9	Disease of intestine, unspecified	
		K65.8	Other peritonitis	
		K90.2	Blind loop syndrome, not elsewhere classified	
		K92.8	Other specified diseases of digestive system	
		R11	Nausea and vomiting	
		Z90.4	Acquired absence of other parts of digestive tract	
571.0	Alcoholic Fatty Liver	K70.0	Alcoholic fatty liver	
571.1	Hepatitis, Acute Alcoholic	K70.0	Alcoholic fatty liver	
		K70.1	Alcoholic hepatitis	
571.2	Cirrhosis of the Liver, Alcoholic	K70.2	Alcoholic fibrosis and sclerosis of liver	
		K70.3	Alcoholic cirrhosis of liver Alcoholic cirrhosis NOS	
		K74.6	Other and unspecified cirrhosis of liver	
571.3	Alcoholic Liver Damage, Unspecified	K70.9	Alcoholic liver disease, unspecified	
571.4	Hepatitis, Chronic	K73.0	Chronic persistent hepatitis, not elsewhere classified	
		K73.1	Chronic lobular hepatitis, not elsewhere classified	
		K73.2	Chronic active hepatitis, not elsewhere classified	
		K73.8	Other chronic hepatitis, not elsewhere classified	
		K73.9	Chronic hepatitis, unspecified	
571.5	Cirrhosis of the Liver Without Mention of Alcohol	K74.0	Hepatic fibrosis	
		K74.2	Hepatic fibrosis with hepatic sclerosis	
		K74.3	Primary biliary cirrhosis	
		K74.6	Other and unspecified cirrhosis of liver	
		K76.1	Chronic passive congestion of liver	
		K76.6	Portal hypertension	
571.6	Cirrhosis, Biliary	K74.3	Primary biliary cirrhosis	
		K74.4	Secondary biliary cirrhosis	
		K74.5	Biliary cirrhosis, unspecified	
571.8	Liver Disease, Chronic, Nonalcoholic	K72.1	Chronic hepatic failure	
		K76.0	Fatty (change of) liver, not elsewhere classified	
		R16.2	Hepatomegaly with splenomegaly, not elsewhere classified	
571.9	Liver Disease Without Mention of Alcohol, Chronic, Unspecified	K74.1	Hepatic sclerosis	
		K76.0	Fatty (change of) liver, not elsewhere classified	
		K76.1	Chronic passive congestion of liver	
		K76.9	Liver disease, unspecified	
572.0	Liver Abscess	K75.0	Abscess of liver	
572.2	Hepatic Coma	K72.9	Hepatic failure, unspecified	
572.8	Liver Disease, Chronic, Other Sequelae	K66.0	Peritoneal adhesions	
		K70.4	Alcoholic hepatic failure	
		K72.1	Chronic hepatic failure	
		K72.9	Hepatic failure, unspecified	
		K75.3	Granulomatous hepatitis, not elsewhere classified	
		K76.8	Other specified diseases of liver	

Translation of ICD-9 CM to ICD-10

ICD-9	Description	ICD-10	Description	(Continued)
573.0	Liver Congestion, Passive, Chronic	K76.1	Chronic passive congestion of liver	
573.3	Hepatitis, Unspecified	K65.8	Other peritonitis	
		K71.0	Toxic liver disease with cholestasis	
		K71.1	Toxic liver disease with hepatic necrosis	
		K71.2	Toxic liver disease with acute hepatitis	
		K71.3	Toxic liver disease with chronic persistent hepatitis	
		K71.4	Toxic liver disease with chronic lobular hepatitis	
		K71.5	Toxic liver disease with chronic active hepatitis	
		K71.6	Toxic liver disease with hepatitis, not elsewhere classified	
		K71.7	Toxic liver disease with fibrosis and cirrhosis of liver	
		K71.8	Toxic liver disease with other disorders of liver	
		K71.9	Toxic liver disease, unspecified	
		K75.2	Nonspecific reactive hepatitis	
		K75.3	Granulomatous hepatitis, not elsewhere classified	
		K75.8	Other specified inflammatory liver diseases	
		K75.9	Inflammatory liver disease, unspecified Hepatitis NOS	
573.4	Hepatic Infarction	K76.3	Infarction of liver	
573.8	Liver Disorders, Other Specified	K71.9	Toxic liver disease, unspecified	
		K72.9	Hepatic failure, unspecified	
		K75.8	Other specified inflammatory liver diseases	
		K76.1	Chronic passive congestion of liver	
		K76.4	Peliosis hepatis Hepatic angiomatosis	
		K76.5	Hepatic veno-occlusive disease	
		K76.8	Other specified diseases of liver	
		K76.9	Liver disease, unspecified	
573.9	Liver Disease	K76.8	Other specified diseases of liver	
		K76.9	Liver disease, unspecified	
574.0	Calculus of Gallbladder with Acute Cholecystitis	K80.0	Calculus of gallbladder with acute cholecystitis	
574.1	Calculus of Gallbladder with Other Cholecystitis	K80.1	Calculus of gallbladder with other cholecystitis	
574.2	Calculus of Gallbladder Without Mention of Cholecystitis	K80.2	Calculus of gallbladder without cholecystitis	
		K80.5	Calculus of bile duct without cholangitis or cholecystitis	
		K80.8	Other cholelithiasis	
		R10.4	Other and unspecified abdominal pain	
574.3	Calculus of Bile Duct with Acute Cholecystitis	K80.3	Calculus of bile duct with cholangitis	
		K80.4	Calculus of bile duct with cholecystitis	
574.4	Calculus of Bile Duct with Other Cholecystitis	K80.3	Calculus of bile duct with cholangitis	
		K80.4	Calculus of bile duct with cholecystitis	
574.5	Calculus of Bile Duct Without Mention of Cholecystitis	K80.3	Calculus of bile duct with cholangitis	
		K80.5	Calculus of bile duct without cholangitis or cholecystitis	
575.0	Cholecystitis	K81.0	Acute cholecystitis Abscess of gallbladder	
		K81.9	Cholecystitis, unspecified	
575.1	Cholecystitis, Other Chronic	K81.1	Chronic cholecystitis	
		K81.8	Other cholecystitis	
		K81.9	Cholecystitis, unspecified	
		K82.9	Disease of gallbladder, unspecified	
575.2	Obstruction of Gallbladder	K82.0	Obstruction of gallbladder	
		K82.8	Other specified diseases of gallbladder	
575.4	Perforation of Gallbladder	K82.2	Rupture of cystic duct or gallbladder	
575.8	Other Specified Disorders of Gall Bladder	K81.0	Acute cholecystitis Abscess of gallbladder	
		K82.0	Obstruction of gallbladder	
		K82.8	Other specified diseases of gallbladder	
		K83.0	Cholangitis	
		K83.1	Obstruction of bile duct	
		K83.8	Other specified diseases of biliary tract	
		Z90.4	Acquired absence of other parts of digestive tract	
577.0	Pancreatitis, Acute	K85	Acute pancreatitis	
577.1	Pancreatitis, Chronic	K86.0	Alcohol-induced chronic pancreatitis	
		K86.1	Other chronic pancreatitis	
577.2	Pancreatic Cyst and Pseudocyst	K86.1	Other chronic pancreatitis	
		K86.2	Cyst of pancreas	
		K86.3	Pseudocyst of pancreas	

ICD-9	Description	ICD-10	Description	(Continued)
577.8	Other Specified Diseases of Pancreas	K65.0	Acute peritonitis	
		K86.1	Other chronic pancreatitis	
		K86.8	Other specified diseases of pancreas	
		Z90.4	Acquired absence of other parts of digestive tract	
577.9	Pancreatic Disease, Unspecified	K86.9	Disease of pancreas, unspecified	
578.0	Hematemesis	K92.0	Haematemesis	
		K92.2	Gastrointestinal haemorrhage, unspecified	
578.1	Blood in Stool	K92.1	Melaena	
578.9	Hemorrhage of Gastrointestinal Tract, Unspecified	K92.2	Gastrointestinal haemorrhage, unspecified	
581.9	Nephrotic Syndrome with Unspecified Pathological Lesion in Kidney	N12	Tubulo-interstitial nephritis, not specified as acute or chronic	
584.5	Renal Failure, Acute with Lesion of Tubular Necrosis	N12	Tubulo-interstitial nephritis, not specified as acute or chronic	
		N17.0	Acute renal failure with tubular necrosis	
584.6	Renal Failure, Acute with Lesion of Renal Cortical Necrosis	N17.1	Acute renal failure with acute cortical necrosis	
584.7	Renal Failure, Acute with Lesion of Renal Medullary Necrosis	N17.2	Acute renal failure with medullary necrosis	
584.8	Renal Failure, Acute with Other Specified Pathological Lesion in Kidney	N17.8	Other acute renal failure	
584.9	Renal Failure, Acute, Unspecified	N17.9	Acute renal failure, unspecified	
585	Renal Failure (Kidney Failure), Chronic	N18.0	End-stage renal disease	
		N18.8	Other chronic renal failure	
		N18.9	Chronic renal failure, unspecified	
586	Renal Failure, Unspecified (Uremia)	N18.8	Other chronic renal failure	
		N18.9	Chronic renal failure, unspecified	
		N19	Unspecified renal failure	
587	Renal Sclerosis, Unspecified	N26	Unspecified contracted kidney	
		N28.8	Other specified disorders of kidney and ureter	
590.0	Pyelonephritis, Chronic	N11.0	Nonobstructive reflux-associated chronic pyelonephritis	
		N11.1	Chronic obstructive pyelonephritis	
		N11.8	Other chronic tubulo-interstitial nephritis	
		N11.9	Chronic tubulo-interstitial nephritis, unspecified	
590.1	Pyelonephritis, Acute	N10	Acute tubulo-interstitial nephritis	
590.2	Renal and Perinephric Abscess	N15.1	Renal and perinephric abscess	
590.8	Other Pyelonephritis or Pyonephrosis, Not Specified As Acute or Chronic	N11.1	Chronic obstructive pyelonephritis	
		N12	Tubulo-interstitial nephritis, not specified as acute or chronic	
		N13.6	Pyonephrosis	
		N15.8	Other specified renal tubulo-interstitial diseases	
		N17.2	Acute renal failure with medullary necrosis	
590.9	Kidney Infection, Unspecified	N15.8	Other specified renal tubulo-interstitial diseases	
		N15.9	Renal tubulo-interstitial disease, unspecified	
591	Hydronephrosis	N13.0	Hydronephrosis with ureteropelvic junction obstruction	
		N13.1	Hydronephrosis with ureteral stricture, not elsewhere classified	
		N13.2	Hydronephrosis with renal and ureteral calculous obstruction	
		N13.3	Other and unspecified hydronephrosis	
		N13.6	Pyonephrosis	
592.0	Calculus, Renal (Kidney)	N20.0	Calculus of kidney	
		N20.2	Calculus of kidney with calculus of ureter	
		N20.9	Urinary calculus, unspecified	
592.1	Calculus of Ureter	N20.1	Calculus of ureter Ureteric stone	
		N20.2	Calculus of kidney with calculus of ureter	
592.9	Calculus, Urinary, Unspecified	N20.9	Urinary calculus, unspecified	
594.0	Calculus in Diverticulum of Bladder	N21.0	Calculus in bladder	
594.1	Calculus in Bladder, Other	N21.0	Calculus in bladder	
594.2	Calculus in Urethra	N21.1	Calculus in urethra	
595.0	Cystitis, Acute	N30.0	Acute cystitis	
595.1	Cystitis, Interstitial	N30.1	Interstitial cystitis (chronic)	
596.1	Fistula, Intestinovesical	N32.1	Vesicointestinal fistula	
596.2	Bladder Fistula (Vesical Fistula not Elsewhere Classified)	N32.2	Vesical fistula, not elsewhere classified	
599.0	Urinary Tract Infection (Pyuria), Site not Specified	N39.0	Urinary tract infection, site not specified	
599.3	Caruncle of the Urethra, Benign	N36.2	Urethral caruncle	
599.7	Hematuria	R31	Unspecified haematuria	

Translation of ICD-9 CM to ICD-10

ICD-9	Description	ICD-10	Description	(Continued)
600	Prostatic Hypertrophy	N40	Hyperplasia of prostate	
		N41.1	Chronic prostatitis	
		N42.8	Other specified disorders of prostate	
601.0	Prostatitis, Acute	N41.0	Acute prostatitis	
601.1	Prostatitis, Chronic	N41.1	Chronic prostatitis	
601.2	Abscess of Prostate	N41.2	Abscess of prostate	
601.3	Prostatocystitis	N41.3	Prostatocystitis	
601.8	Inflammatory Diseases of Prostate, Other Specified	N41.1	Chronic prostatitis	
		N41.8	Other inflammatory diseases of prostate	
		N42.8	Other specified disorders of prostate	
601.9	Prostatitis, Unspecified	N41.9	Inflammatory disease of prostate, unspecified	
603.1	Hydrocele, Infected	N43.1	Infected hydrocele	
603.8	Other Specified Types of Hydrocele	N43.2	Other hydrocele	
603.9	Hydrocele, Unspecified	N43.3	Hydrocele, unspecified	
604.0	Orchitis	N45.0	Orchitis, epididymitis and epididymo-orchitis with abscess	
604.9	Epididymitis	N45.9	Orchitis, epididymitis and epididymo-orchitis without abscess	
606	Infertility, Male	N46	Male infertility	
607.1	Balanoposthitis	N48.1	Balanoposthitis	
607.2	Inflammatory Disorders of Penis, Other	N48.2	Other inflammatory disorders of penis	
607.3	Priapism	N48.3	Priapism	
607.8	Penis, Disorders of	N48.1	Balanoposthitis	
		N48.2	Other inflammatory disorders of penis	
		N48.4	Impotence of organic origin	
		N48.5	Ulcer of penis	
		N48.6	Balanitis xerotica obliterans	
		N48.8	Other specified disorders of penis	
		Z90.7	Acquired absence of genital organ(s)	
608.1	Spermatocele	N43.4	Spermatocele	
610.1	Fibrocystic Breast Disease	N60.1	Diffuse cystic mastopathy	
610.2	Fibroadenosis of Breast	N60.2	Fibroadenosis of breast	
610.8	Other Specified Benign Mammary Dysplasia	N60.8	Other benign mammary dysplasias	
610.9	Benign Mammary Dysplasia, Unspecified	N60.9	Benign mammary dysplasia, unspecified	
611.0	Abscess, Breast (Inflammatory Disease of Breast)	N61	Inflammatory disorders of breast	
		N64.0	Fissure and fistula of nipple	
611.1	Gynecomastia (Hypertrophy of Breast)	N62	Hypertrophy of breast Gynaecomastia	
614.0	Salpingitis and Oophoritis, Acute	N70.0	Acute salpingitis and oophoritis	
614.1	Salpingitis and Oophoritis, Chronic	N70.1	Chronic salpingitis and oophoritis	
614.2	Salpingitis and Oophoritis Not Specified As Acute, Subacute, or Chronic	N70.9	Salpingitis and oophoritis, unspecified	
614.3	Pelvic Cellulitis and Parametritis, Acute	N73.0	Acute parametritis and pelvic cellulitis	
614.4	Pelvic Cellulitis and Parametritis, Chronic or Unspecified	N73.1	Chronic parametritis and pelvic cellulitis	
		N73.2	Unspecified parametritis and pelvic cellulitis	
		N73.5	Female pelvic peritonitis, unspecified	
		N73.9	Female pelvic inflammatory disease, unspecified	
614.5	Pelvic Peritonitis, Acute or Unspecified, Female	N73.3	Female acute pelvic peritonitis	
		N73.5	Female pelvic peritonitis, unspecified	
614.6	Pelvic Peritoneal Adhesions, Female	N73.6	Female pelvic peritoneal adhesions	
		N99.4	Postprocedural pelvic peritoneal adhesions	
614.7	Pelvic Peritonitis, Chronic, Female	N73.4	Female chronic pelvic peritonitis	
614.9	Pelvic Inflammatory Disease, Unspecified	N73.2	Unspecified parametritis and pelvic cellulitis	
		N73.9	Female pelvic inflammatory disease, unspecified	
616.0	Cervicitis and Endocervicitis	N72	Inflammatory disease of cervix uteri	
		N88.8	Other specified noninflammatory disorders of cervix uteri	
616.1	Vaginitis and Vulvovaginitis	N76.0	Acute vaginitis	
		N76.1	Subacute and chronic vaginitis	
		N76.2	Acute vulvitis Vulvitis NOS	
		N76.3	Subacute and chronic vulvitis	
		N76.4	Abscess of vulva Furuncle of vulva	
		N76.8	Other specified inflammation of vagina and vulva	
616.2	Cyst of Bartholin's Gland	N75.0	Cyst of Bartholin's gland	
616.3	Bartholin's Gland Infection	N75.1	Abscess of Bartholin's gland	

2424 The Medical Disability Advisor—Fourth Edition

ICD-9	Description	ICD-10	Description	(Continued)
617.0	Endometriosis of Uterus	N80.0	Endometriosis of uterus Adenomyosis	
617.1	Endometriosis of Ovary	N80.1	Endometriosis of ovary	
617.2	Endometriosis of Fallopian Tube	N80.2	Endometriosis of fallopian tube	
617.3	Endometriosis of Pelvic Peritoneum	N80.3	Endometriosis of pelvic peritoneum	
617.4	Endometriosis of Rectovaginal Septum and Vagina	N80.4	Endometriosis of rectovaginal septum and vagina	
617.5	Endometriosis of Intestine	N80.5	Endometriosis of intestine	
617.6	Endometriosis in Scar of Skin	N80.6	Endometriosis in cutaneous scar	
617.8	Endometriosis of Other Specified Sites	N80.8	Other endometriosis	
617.9	Endometriosis, Site Unspecified	N80.9	Endometriosis, unspecified	
618.0	Urethrocele with Stress Incontinence	N81.0	Female urethrocele	
		N81.1	Prolapse of anterior vaginal wall NOS	
		N81.6	Prolapse of posterior vaginal wall	
618.2	Uterovaginal Prolapse, Incomplete	N81.2	Incomplete uterovaginal prolapse	
618.3	Uterovaginal Prolapse, Complete	N81.3	Complete uterovaginal prolapse	
618.4	Uterovaginal Prolapse, Unspecified	N81.4	Uterovaginal prolapse, unspecified	
619.0	Fistula, Vesicovaginal (Female Urinary-Genital Tract Fistula)	N82.0	Vesicovaginal fistula	
		N82.1	Other female urinary-genital tract fistulae	
620.0	Cyst of Ovary, Follicular	N83.0	Follicular cyst of ovary	
620.1	Cyst or Hematoma, Corpus Luteum	N83.1	Corpus luteum cyst	
		N83.8	Other noninflammatory disorders of ovary, fallopian tube and broad ligament	
620.2	Ovarian Cyst, Benign	N83.1	Corpus luteum cyst	
		N83.2	Other and unspecified ovarian cysts	
620.8	Hematosalpinx	N83.3	Acquired atrophy of ovary and fallopian tube	
		N83.5	Torsion of ovary, ovarian pedicle and fallopian tube	
		N83.6	Haematosalpinx	
		N83.8	Other noninflammatory disorders of ovary, fallopian tube and broad ligament	
		N84.8	Polyp of other parts of female genital tract	
		N94.8	Other specified conditions associated with female genital organs and menstrual cycle	
		Q50.3	Other congenital malformations of ovary	
		Z90.7	Acquired absence of genital organ(s)	
621.0	Uterine Polyps (Polyp of Corpus Uteri)	N84.0	Polyp of corpus uteri	
621.8	Other Specified Disorders of Uterus, Nec	N81.4	Uterovaginal prolapse, unspecified	
		N83.8	Other noninflammatory disorders of ovary, fallopian tube and broad ligament	
		N85.8	Other specified noninflammatory disorders of uterus	
		N99.8	Other postprocedural disorders of genitourinary system	
		Z90.7	Acquired absence of genital organ(s)	
622.1	Cervical Dysplasia	N72	Inflammatory disease of cervix uteri	
		N87.0	Mild cervical dysplasia	
		N87.1	Moderate cervical dysplasia	
		N87.2	Severe cervical dysplasia, not elsewhere classified	
		N87.9	Dysplasia of cervix uteri, unspecified	
622.7	Cervical Polyps	N84.1	Polyp of cervix uteri	
625.2	Menorrhagia	N94.0	Mittelschmerz	
625.3	Dysmenorrhea	N94.4	Primary dysmenorrhoea	
		N94.5	Secondary dysmenorrhoea	
		N94.6	Dysmenorrhoea, unspecified	
625.4	Premenstrual Syndrome	N94.3	Premenstrual tension syndrome	
		N94.6	Dysmenorrhoea, unspecified	
625.6	Urinary Incontinence in Women	N39.3	Stress incontinence	
625.9	Unspecified Symptom Associated with Female Genital Organs	N94.8	Other specified conditions associated with female genital organs and menstrual cycle	
626.0	Amenorrhea (Absence of Menstruation)	N91.0	Failure to start menstruation at puberty.	
		N91.1	Absence of menstruation in a woman who had previously menstruated.	
		N91.2	Absence of menstruation NOS	
626.1	Menstruation, Scanty or Infrequent	N91.3	Menstruation which is scanty or rare from the start.	
		N91.4	Scanty and rare menstruation in a woman with previously normal periods.	
		N91.5	Oligomenorrhoea, unspecified	
626.2	Menorrhagia (Excessive or Frequent Menstruation)	N92.0	Excessive and frequent menstruation with regular cycle	
		N92.1	Excessive and frequent menstruation with irregular cycle	
626.4	Menstruation, Irregular	N92.1	Excessive and frequent menstruation with irregular cycle	

Translation of ICD-9 CM to ICD-10

ICD-9	Description	ICD-10	Description	(Continued)
626.4	Menstruation, Irregular	N92.6	Irregular menstruation, unspecified	
626.5	Ovulation Bleeding	N92.3	Ovulation bleeding	
626.6	Metrorrhagia	N92.1	Excessive and frequent menstruation with irregular cycle	
		N93.8	Dysfunctional or functional uterine or vaginal bleeding	
		N93.9	Abnormal uterine and vaginal bleeding, unspecified	
626.8	Uterine Bleeding, Dysfunctional	E30.1	Precocious puberty	
		N71.9	Inflammatory disease of uterus, unspecified	
		N89.7	Haematocolpos with haematometra or haematosalpinx	
		N91.0	Failure to start menstruation at puberty.	
		N92.5	Other specified irregular menstruation	
		N93.8	Dysfunctional or functional uterine or vaginal bleeding	
		N94.8	Other specified conditions associated with female genital organs and menstrual cycle	
		P54.6	Neonatal vaginal haemorrhage	
626.9	Menstrual Disorders	N92.6	Irregular menstruation, unspecified	
		N93.9	Abnormal uterine and vaginal bleeding, unspecified	
627.0	Premenopausal Menorrhagia	N92.4	Excessive bleeding in the premenopausal period	
627.1	Postmenopausal Bleeding	N95.0	Postmenopausal bleeding	
627.2	Menopause	N95.1	Symptoms such as flushing, sleeplessness, headache, lack of concentration, associated with menopause	
627.3	Vaginitis, Postmenopausal Atrophic	N95.2	Postmenopausal atrophic vaginitis	
627.8	Menopausal and Postmenopausal Disorders, Other Specified	N95.8	Other specified menopausal and perimenopausal disorders	
627.9	Menopausal Disorder, Unspecified	N95.9	Menopausal and perimenopausal disorder, unspecified	
628.0	Infertility, Female, Associated with Anovulation	N97.0	Female infertility associated with anovulation	
628.2	Infertility, Female, of Tubal Origin	N97.1	Female infertility of tubal origin	
628.3	Infertility, Female, of Uterine Origin	N97.2	Female infertility of uterine origin	
628.4	Infertility, Female, of Cervical of Vaginal Origin	N97.3	Female infertility of cervical origin	
		N97.8	Female infertility of other origin	
628.8	Infertility, Female, of Other Specified Origin	N97.4	Female infertility associated with male factors	
		N97.8	Female infertility of other origin	
628.9	Infertility, Female, Unspecified	N97.9	Female infertility, unspecified	
629.9	Unspecified Cause	N83.9	Noninflammatory disorder of ovary, fallopian tube and broad ligament, unspecified	
		N94.8	Other specified conditions associated with female genital organs and menstrual cycle	
		N94.9	Unspecified condition associated with female genital organs and menstrual cycle	
		N96	Habitual aborter	
630	Hydatidiform Mole	O01.0	Classical hydatidiform mole	
		O01.1	Incomplete and partial hydatidiform mole	
		O01.9	Hydatidiform mole, unspecified	
633.0	Abdominal Pregnancy	O00.0	Abdominal pregnancy	
633.1	Tubal Pregnancy	O00.1	Tubal pregnancy	
633.2	Ovarian Pregnancy	O00.2	Ovarian pregnancy	
633.8	Ectopic Pregnancy, Other	O00.8	Other ectopic pregnancy	
633.9	Ectopic Pregnancy, Unspecified	O00.9	Ectopic pregnancy, unspecified	
639.2	Uterus, Perforation of (Damage to Pelvic Organs and Tissues by Abnormal Pregnancy)	O08.6	Damage to pelvic organs and tissues following abortion and ectopic and molar pregnancy	
640.0	Threatened Abortion	O20.0	Threatened abortion	
641.1	Placenta Previa with Hemorrhage	O44.1	Placenta praevia with haemorrhage	
641.2	Abruptio Placentae	O45.0	Premature separation of placenta with coagulation defect	
		O45.8	Other premature separation of placenta	
		O45.9	Premature separation of placenta, unspecified	
		O46.8	Other antepartum haemorrhage	
		O46.9	Antepartum haemorrhage, unspecified	
642.0	Benign Essential Hypertension Complicating Pregnancy, Childbirth, and the Puerperium	O10.0	Pre-existing essential hypertension complicating pregnancy, childbirth and the puerperium	
		O10.9	Unspecified pre-existing hypertension complicating pregnancy, childbirth and the puerperium	
642.1	Hypertension Secondary to Renal Disease Complicating Pregnancy, Childbirth and the Puerperium	O10.2	Pre-existing hypertensive renal disease complicating pregnancy, childbirth and the puerperium	
		O10.4	Pre-existing secondary hypertension complicating pregnancy, childbirth and the puerperium	
642.2	Other Pre-existing Hypertension Complicating Pregnancy, Childbirth and the Puerperium	O10.0	Pre-existing essential hypertension complicating pregnancy, childbirth and the puerperium	

ICD-9	Description	ICD-10	Description (Continued)
642.2	Other Pre-existing Hypertension Complicating Pregnancy, Childbirth and the Puerperium	O10.1	Pre-existing hypertensive heart disease complicating pregnancy, childbirth and the puerperium
		O10.2	Pre-existing hypertensive renal disease complicating pregnancy, childbirth and the puerperium
		O10.3	Pre-existing hypertensive heart and renal disease complicating pregnancy, childbirth and the puerperium
642.3	Transient Hypertension of Pregnancy	O16	Transient hypertension of pregnancy
642.4	Preeclampsia and Eclampsia (Toxemia of Pregnancy), Mild or Unspecified	O13	Gestational hypertension NOS Mild pre-eclampsia
		O14.0	Moderate pre-eclampsia
		O14.9	Pre-eclampsia, unspecified
642.5	Preeclampsia, Severe	O14.1	Severe pre-eclampsia
642.6	Eclampsia	O15.0	Eclampsia in pregnancy
		O15.1	Eclampsia in labour
		O15.2	Eclampsia in the puerperium
		O15.9	Eclampsia, unspecified as to time period
642.7	Pre-eclampsia or Eclampsia Superimposed on Pre-Existing Hypertension	O11	Pre-existing hypertensive disorder with superimposed proteinuria
		O15.0	Eclampsia in pregnancy
642.9	Unspecified Hypertension Complicating Pregnancy, Childbirth, and the Puerperium	O13	Gestational hypertension NOS Mild pre-eclampsia
		O16	Transient hypertension of pregnancy
643.0	Morning Sickness (Hyperemesis Gravidarum), Mild	O21.0	Hyperemesis gravidarum, mild or unspecified, starting before the end of the 22nd week of gestation
643.1	Hyperemesis Gravidarum with Metabolic Disturbance	O21.1	Hyperemesis gravidarum, starting before the end of the 22nd week of gestation, with metabolic disturbance
643.2	Late Vomiting of Pregnancy	O21.2	Excessive vomiting starting after 22 completed weeks of gestation
643.8	Other Vomiting Complicating Pregnancy	O21.8	Vomiting due to diseases classified elsewhere, complicating pregnancy
643.9	Unspecified Vomiting of Pregnancy	O21.9	Vomiting of pregnancy, unspecified
644.0	Threatened Premature Labor	O47.0	False labour before 37 completed weeks of gestation
		O47.1	False labour at or after 37 completed weeks of gestation
		O47.9	False labour, unspecified
644.1	Other Threatened Abortion	O47.0	False labour before 37 completed weeks of gestation
		O60	Onset (spontaneous) of delivery before 37 completed weeks of gestation
646.2	Unspecified Renal Disease in Pregnancy Without Mention of Hypertension	O12.1	Gestational proteinuria
		O26.8	Other specified pregnancy-related conditions
		O90.8	Other complications of the puerperium, not elsewhere classified
646.9	Unspecified Complication of Pregnancy	O26.9	Pregnancy-related condition, unspecified
		O95	Obstetric death of unspecified cause
647.5	Rubella	O98.5	Other viral diseases complicating pregnancy, childbirth and the puerperium
648.2	Anemia Complicating Pregnancy	O99.0	Anaemia complicating pregnancy, childbirth and the puerperium
648.6	Cardiovascular Disease in Pregnancy	O99.4	Diseases of the circulatory system complicating pregnancy, childbirth and the puerperium
648.8	Gestational Diabetes (Abnormal Glucose Tolerance in Pregnancy)	O99.8	Other specified diseases and conditions complicating pregnancy, childbirth and the puerperium
650	Pregnancy, Normal (Delivery in a Completely Normal Case)	O80.0	Spontaneous vertex delivery
		O80.8	Other single spontaneous delivery
		O80.9	Single spontaneous delivery, unspecified
651.0	Twin Pregnancy	O30.0	Twin pregnancy
651.1	Triplet Pregnancy	O30.1	Triplet pregnancy
651.2	Quadruplet Pregnancy	O30.2	Quadruplet pregnancy
652.2	Isoimmunization from Other and Unspecified Blood-Group Incompatibility	O32.1	Maternal care for breech presentation
		O80.1	Spontaneous breech delivery
		O83.1	Other assisted breech delivery
656.1	Rh Incompatibility	O36.0	Maternal care for rhesus isoimmunization Anti-D [Rh] antibodies
658.0	Oligohydramnios	O41.0	Oligohydramnios without mention of rupture of membranes
658.1	Premature Rupture of Membranes	O42.0	Premature rupture of membranes, onset of labour within 24 hours
		O42.1	Premature rupture of membranes, onset of labour after 24 hours
		O42.2	Premature rupture of membranes, labour delayed by therapy
		O42.9	Premature rupture of membranes, unspecified
658.2	Delayed Delivery After Spontaneous or Unspecified Rupture of Membranes	O75.6	Delayed delivery after spontaneous or unspecified rupture of membranes

ICD-9	Description	ICD-10	Description	(Continued)
666.0	Third-Stage Hemorrhage	O72.0	Third-stage haemorrhage Haemorrhage associated with retained, trapped or adherent placenta	
667.0	Retained Placenta Without Hemorrhage	O73.0	Retained placenta without haemorrhage	
667.1	Retained Portions of Placenta or Membranes, Without Hemorrhage	O73.1	Retained portions of placenta and membranes, without haemorrhage	
669.7	Cesarean Delivery, Without Mention of Indication	O82.0	Delivery by elective caesarean section	
		O82.1	Delivery by emergency caesarean section	
		O82.2	Delivery by caesarean hysterectomy	
		O82.8	Other single delivery by caesarean section	
		O82.9	Delivery by caesarean section, unspecified	
		O84.2	Multiple delivery, all by caesarean section	
		O84.8	Multiple delivery by combination of methods	
671.9	Venous Complications in Pregnancy and the Puerperium, Unspecified	O22.9	Venous complication in pregnancy, unspecified	
		O87.9	Venous complication in the puerperium, unspecified P	
673.0	Obstetrical Air Embolism	O88.0	Obstetric air embolism	
673.1	Amniotic Fluid Embolism	O88.1	Amniotic fluid embolism	
673.2	Obstetric Blood-clot Embolism	O88.2	Obstetric blood-clot embolism	
673.3	Obstetric Pyemic and Septic Embolism	O88.3	Obstetric pyaemic and septic embolism	
673.8	Other Pulmonary Embolism	O88.8	Obstetric fat embolism	
674.8	Complications of the Puerperium, Other	O88.8	Obstetric fat embolism	
		O90.3	Cardiomyopathy in the puerperium	
		O90.4	Postpartum acute renal failure	
		O90.5	Postpartum thyroiditis	
		O90.8	Other complications of the puerperium, not elsewhere classified	
		O99.4	Diseases of the circulatory system complicating pregnancy, childbirth and the puerperium	
675.0	Infections of Nipple	O91.0	Infection of nipple associated with childbirth	
675.2	Postpartum Mastitis (Nonpurulent Mastitis)	O91.0	Infection of nipple associated with childbirth	
		O91.2	Nonpurulent mastitis associated with childbirth	
675.8	Other Specified Infections of the Breast and Nipple	O92.2	Other and unspecified disorders of breast associated with childbirth	
675.9	Unspecified Infection of the Breast and Nipple	O92.2	Other and unspecified disorders of breast associated with childbirth	
680.1	Carbuncle of Neck	L02.1	Cutaneous abscess, furuncle and carbuncle of neck	
680.2	Carbuncle of Trunk	L02.2	Cutaneous abscess, furuncle and carbuncle of trunk	
680.5	Carbuncle of Buttock	L02.3	Cutaneous abscess, furuncle and carbuncle of buttock	
680.9	Furuncle	L02.9	Cutaneous abscess, furuncle and carbuncle, unspecified	
682.0	Cellulitis and Abscess of Face	J34.0	Abscess, furuncle and carbuncle of nose	
		K12.2	Cellulitis and abscess of mouth	
		L02.0	Cutaneous abscess, furuncle and carbuncle of face	
		L03.2	Cellulitis of face	
682.1	Abscess or Cellulitis of Neck	L02.1	Cutaneous abscess, furuncle and carbuncle of neck	
		L03.8	Cellulitis of Head [any part, except face] Scalp	
682.2	Cellulitis and Abscess of Trunk (Including Breast)	L02.2	Cutaneous abscess, furuncle and carbuncle of trunk	
		L03.3	Cellulitis of trunk	
682.3	Cellulitis and Abscess of Upper Arm and Forearm (Including Axilla)	L02.4	Cutaneous abscess, furuncle and carbuncle of limb	
		L03.1	Cellulitis of other parts of limb	
682.4	Cellulitis and Abscess of Hand, Except Fingers and Thumb (Palmar Abscess)	L02.4	Cutaneous abscess, furuncle and carbuncle of limb	
		L03.1	Cellulitis of other parts of limb	
682.5	Cellulitis and Abscess of Buttock	L02.3	Cutaneous abscess, furuncle and carbuncle of buttock	
		L03.3	Cellulitis of trunk	
682.6	Cellulitis and Abscess of Leg, Except Foot	L02.4	Cutaneous abscess, furuncle and carbuncle of limb	
		L03.1	Cellulitis of other parts of limb	
682.7	Cellulitis and Abscess of Foot, Except Toes	L02.4	Cutaneous abscess, furuncle and carbuncle of limb	
		L03.1	Cellulitis of other parts of limb	
682.8	Cellulitis and Abscess, Other Specified Sites	L02.8	Cutaneous abscess, furuncle and carbuncle of other sites	
		L03.8	Cellulitis of Head [any part, except face] Scalp	
682.9	Cellulitis and Abscess, Other Unspecified Sites	L02.8	Cutaneous abscess, furuncle and carbuncle of other sites	
		L02.9	Cutaneous abscess, furuncle and carbuncle, unspecified	
		L03.8	Cellulitis of Head [any part, except face] Scalp	
		L03.9	Cellulitis, unspecified	

ICD-9	Description	ICD-10	Description	(Continued)
682.9	Cellulitis and Abscess, Other Unspecified Sites	L98.3	Eosinophilic cellulitis [Wells]	
684	Impetigo	L00	Staphylococcal scalded skin syndrome	
		L01.0	Impetigo [any organism] [any site]	
		L01.1	Impetiginization of other dermatoses	
685.0	Pilonidal Cyst with Abscess	L05.0	Pilonidal cyst with abscess	
685.1	Pilonidal Cyst Without Mention of Abscess	L05.9	Pilonidal cyst without abscess	
691.8	Atopic Dermatitis	L20.0	Besnier's prurigo	
		L20.8	Other atopic dermatitis	
		L20.9	Atopic dermatitis, unspecified	
		L21.0	Seborrhoea capitis Cradle cap	
		L21.1	Seborrhoeic infantile dermatitis	
692.0	Contact Dermatitis and Other Eczema Due to Detergents	L24.0	Irritant contact dermatitis due to detergents	
692.1	Contact Dermatitis and Other Eczema Due to Oils and Greases	L24.1	Irritant contact dermatitis due to oils and greases	
692.2	Contact Dermatitis and Other Eczema Due to Solvents	L23.5	Allergic contact dermatitis due to other chemical products	
		L24.2	Irritant contact dermatitis due to solvents	
		L25.3	Unspecified contact dermatitis due to other chemical products	
692.3	Contact Dermatitis and Other Eczema Due to Drugs and Medicines in Contact with Skin	L23.1	Allergic contact dermatitis due to adhesives	
		L23.3	Allergic contact dermatitis due to drugs in contact with skin	
		L24.4	Irritant contact dermatitis due to drugs in contact with skin	
		L25.1	Unspecified contact dermatitis due to drugs in contact with skin	
692.4	Contact Dermatitis and Other Eczema Due to Other Chemical Products	L23.0	Allergic contact dermatitis due to metals	
		L23.1	Allergic contact dermatitis due to adhesives	
		L23.5	Allergic contact dermatitis due to other chemical products	
		L24.2	Irritant contact dermatitis due to solvents	
		L24.5	Irritant contact dermatitis due to other chemical products	
		L25.3	Unspecified contact dermatitis due to other chemical products	
		L85.8	Other specified epidermal thickening	
692.6	Poison Ivy, Oak, Sumac, or Other Plant Dermatitis	L23.7	Allergic contact dermatitis due to plants, except food	
		L24.7	Irritant contact dermatitis due to plants, except food	
		L25.5	Unspecified contact dermatitis due to plants, except food	
692.8	Dermatitis Due to Cosmetics	L23.0	Allergic contact dermatitis due to metals	
		L23.2	Allergic contact dermatitis due to cosmetics	
		L23.4	Allergic contact dermatitis due to dyes	
		L23.5	Allergic contact dermatitis due to other chemical products	
		L23.6	Allergic contact dermatitis due to food in contact with skin	
		L23.8	Allergic contact dermatitis due to other agents	
		L24.2	Irritant contact dermatitis due to solvents	
		L24.3	Irritant contact dermatitis due to cosmetics	
		L24.5	Irritant contact dermatitis due to other chemical products	
		L24.8	Irritant contact dermatitis due to other agents Dyes	
		L25.0	Unspecified contact dermatitis due to cosmetics	
		L25.2	Unspecified contact dermatitis due to dyes	
		L25.3	Unspecified contact dermatitis due to other chemical products	
		L25.4	Unspecified contact dermatitis due to food in contact with skin	
		L25.8	Unspecified contact dermatitis due to other agents	
		L30.2	Cutaneous autosensitization	
		L30.8	Other specified dermatitis	
		L56.0	Drug phototoxic response	
		L56.1	Drug photoallergic response	
		L57.8	Other skin changes due to chronic exposure to nonionizing radiation	
		L58.0	Acute radiodermatitis	
		L58.1	Chronic radiodermatitis	
		L58.9	Radiodermatitis, unspecified	
		L59.0	Erythema	
		L59.8	Other specified disorders of skin and subcutaneous tissue related to radiation	
		L59.9	Disorder of skin and subcutaneous tissue related to radiation, unspecified	
692.9	Eczema	L23.9	Allergic contact dermatitis, unspecified	
		L24.9	Irritant contact dermatitis, unspecified cause	

Translation of ICD-9 CM to ICD-10

ICD-9	Description	ICD-10	Description	(Continued)
692.9	Eczema	L25.9	Unspecified contact dermatitis	
		L28.0	Lichen simplex chronicus	
		L30.0	Nummular dermatitis	
		L30.4	Erythema intertrigo	
		L30.8	Other specified dermatitis	
		L30.9	Dermatitis, unspecified	
693.0	Allergic Dermatitis (Due to Drugs/Medicines)	L27.0	Generalized skin eruption due to drugs and medicaments	
		L27.1	Localized skin eruption due to drugs and medicaments	
694.4	Pemphigus	L10.0	Pemphigus vulgaris	
		L10.1	Pemphigus vegetans	
		L10.2	Pemphigus foliaceus	
		L10.3	Brazilian pemphigus	
		L10.4	Pemphigus erythematosus	
		L10.5	Drug-induced pemphigus	
		L10.8	Other pemphigus	
		L10.9	Pemphigus, unspecified	
695.1	Erythema Multiforme	L51.0	Nonbullous erythema multiforme	
		L51.1	Bullous erythema multiforme	
		L51.2	Toxic epidermal necrolysis	
		L51.8	Other erythema multiforme	
		L51.9	Erythema multiforme, unspecified	
		L98.2	Febrile neutrophilic dermatosis	
695.2	Erythema Nodosum	L52	Erythema nodosum	
		L95.8	Other vasculitis limited to skin	
695.4	Lupus Erythematosus	L93.0	Discoid lupus erythematosus	
		L93.1	Subacute cutaneous lupus erythematosus	
		L93.2	Other local lupus erythematosus	
695.9	Unspecified Erythematous Condition	L53.9	Erythematous condition, unspecified	
696.1	Psoriasis, Other	L40.0	Psoriasis vulgaris	
		L40.1	Generalized pustular psoriasis	
		L40.2	Acrodermatitis continua	
		L40.3	Pustulosis palmaris et plantaris	
		L40.4	Guttate psoriasis	
		L40.8	Other psoriasis Flexural psoriasis	
		L40.9	Psoriasis, unspecified	
696.3	Pityriasis Rosea	L30.5	Pityriasis alba	
		L42	Pityriasis rosea	
		L44.8	Other specified papulosquamous disorders	
698.0	Pruritus Ani (Perianal Itch)	L29.0	Pruritus ani	
		L29.3	Anogenital pruritus, unspecified	
700	Corns and Calluses, Infected	L84	Corns and callosities	
701.0	Addison's Keloid	L90.0	Lichen sclerosus et atrophicus	
		L94.0	Localized scleroderma	
		L94.1	Linear scleroderma	
		L94.3	Sclerodactyly	
701.4	Keloid	L91.0	Keloid scar	
703.0	Toenail, Ingrown	L60.0	Ingrowing nail	
704.8	Folliculitis and Other Specified Diseases of Hair and Hair Follicles	L01.0	Impetigo [any organism] [any site]	
		L08.8	Other specified local infections of skin and subcutaneous tissue	
		L66.3	Perifolliculitis capitis abscedens	
		L73.1	Pseudofolliculitis barbae	
		L73.8	Other specified follicular disorders	
		L73.9	Follicular disorder, unspecified	
706.1	Acne, Other	L70.0	Acne vulgaris	
		L70.1	Acne conglobata	
		L70.3	Acne tropica	
		L70.4	Infantile acne	
		L70.5	Acne, excori	
		L70.8	Other acne	
		L70.9	Acne, unspecified	

ICD-9	Description	ICD-10	Description	(Continued)
706.1	Acne, Other	L73.0	Acne keloid	
706.2	Sebaceous Cyst	L70.0	Acne vulgaris	
		L72.0	Epidermal cyst	
		L72.1	Trichilemmal cyst	
		L72.2	Steatocystoma multiplex	
		L72.8	Other follicular cysts of skin and subcutaneous tissue	
		L72.9	Follicular cyst of skin and subcutaneous tissue, unspecified	
707.0	Decubitus Ulcer	L89	Decubitus ulcer	
707.9	Ulcer of Unspecified Sites, Chronic	L58.1	Chronic radiodermatitis	
		L59.8	Other specified disorders of skin and subcutaneous tissue related to radiation	
		L98.4	Chronic ulcer of skin, not elsewhere classified	
708.5	Sleep Disturbances	L50.5	Cholinergic urticaria	
710.0	Lupus Erythematosus, Systemic	M32.0	Drug-induced systemic lupus erythematosus	
		M32.8	Other forms of systemic lupus erythematosus	
		M32.9	Systemic lupus erythematosus, unspecified	
710.1	Systemic Scleroses	M34.0	Progressive systemic sclerosis	
		M34.1	CR(E)ST syndrome	
		M34.2	Systemic sclerosis induced by drugs and chemicals	
		M34.8	Other forms of systemic sclerosis	
		M34.9	Systemic sclerosis, unspecified	
710.2	Sjögren's Disease (Sicca Syndrome)	M35.0	Sicca syndrome	
710.3	Dermatomyositis	M33.0	Juvenile dermatomyositis	
		M33.1	Other dermatomyositis	
		M33.9	Dermatopolymyositis, unspecified	
710.9	Unspecified Diffuse Connective Tissue Disease	M35.9	Systemic involvement of connective tissue, unspecified	
711.0	Septic Arthritis (Pyogenic)	M00.0	Staphylococcal arthritis and polyarthritis	
		M00.1	Pneumococcal arthritis and polyarthritis	
		M00.2	Other streptococcal arthritis and polyarthritis	
		M00.8	Arthritis and polyarthritis due to other specified bacterial agents	
		M00.9	Pyogenic arthritis, unspecified Infective arthritis NOS	
711.9	Arthritis, Infectious	M00.9	Pyogenic arthritis, unspecified Infective arthritis NOS	
		M02.8	Other reactive arthropathies	
		M02.9	Reactive arthropathy, unspecified	
714.0	Rheumatoid Arthritis	M05.8	Other seropositive rheumatoid arthritis	
		M05.9	Seropositive rheumatoid arthritis, unspecified	
		M06.0	Seronegative rheumatoid arthritis	
		M06.1	Adult-onset Still's disease	
		M06.2	Rheumatoid bursitis	
		M06.3	Rheumatoid nodule	
		M06.8	Other specified rheumatoid arthritis	
		M06.9	Rheumatoid arthritis, unspecified	
		M13.8	Other specified arthritis	
		M15.9	Polyarthrosis, unspecified Generalized osteoarthritis	
		M19.9	Arthrosis, unspecified	
714.1	Felty's Syndrome	M05.0	Rheumatoid arthritis with splenoadenomegaly and leukopenia	
715.0	Osteoarthrosis, Generalized	M15.0	Primary generalized (osteo)arthrosis	
		M15.1	Heberden's nodes (with arthropathy)	
		M15.3	Post-traumatic polyarthrosis	
		M15.8	Other polyarthrosis	
		M15.9	Polyarthrosis, unspecified Generalized osteoarthritis	
715.1	Osteoarthrosis, Localized, Primary	M15.2	Bouchard's nodes with arthropathy	
		M16.0	Primary coxarthrosis, bilateral	
		M16.1	Other primary coxarthrosis, unilateral	
		M17.0	Primary gonarthrosis, bilateral	
		M17.1	Other primary gonarthrosis, unilateral	
		M18.0	Primary arthrosis of first carpometacarpal joints, bilateral	
		M18.1	Other primary arthrosis of first carpometacarpal joint	
		M19.0	Primary arthrosis of other joints	
715.2	Osteoarthrosis, Localized, Secondary	M16.2	Coxarthrosis resulting from dysplasia, bilateral	
		M16.3	Other dysplastic coxarthrosis, unilateral	
		M16.4	Post-traumatic coxarthrosis, bilateral	

Translation of ICD-9 CM to ICD-10

ICD-9	Description	ICD-10	Description	(Continued)
715.2	Osteoarthrosis, Localized, Secondary	M16.5	Other post-traumatic coxarthrosis, unilateral	
		M16.6	Other secondary coxarthrosis, bilateral	
		M16.7	Other secondary coxarthrosis, unilateral	
		M17.2	Post-traumatic gonarthrosis, bilateral	
		M17.3	Other post-traumatic gonarthrosis, unilateral	
		M17.4	Other secondary gonarthrosis, bilateral	
		M17.5	Other secondary gonarthrosis, unilateral	
		M18.2	Post-traumatic arthrosis of first carpometacarpal joints, bilateral	
		M18.3	Other post-traumatic arthrosis of first carpometacarpal joint, unilateral	
		M18.4	Other secondary arthrosis of first carpometacarpal joints, bilateral	
		M18.5	Other secondary arthrosis of first carpometacarpal joint, unilateral	
		M19.1	Post-traumatic arthrosis of other joints	
		M19.2	Other secondary arthrosis	
715.3	Osteoarthrosis, Localized, Not Specified Whether Primary or Secondary	M16.9	Coxarthrosis, unspecified	
		M17.9	Gonarthrosis, unspecified	
		M18.9	Arthrosis of first carpometacarpal joint, unspecified	
		M19.9	Arthrosis, unspecified	
		M24.7	Protrusio acetabuli	
715.8	Osteoarthrosis Involving, or with Mention of More Than One Site, but Not Specified As Generalized	M15.8	Other polyarthrosis	
		M15.9	Polyarthrosis, unspecified Generalized osteoarthritis	
		M19.8	Other specified arthrosis	
715.9	Osteoarthrosis, Unspecified Whether Generalized or Localized	M15.4	Erosive (osteo)arthrosis	
		M19.0	Primary arthrosis of other joints	
		M19.9	Arthrosis, unspecified	
717.0	Meniscus Disorders, Knee	M23.2	Derangement of meniscus due to old tear or injury	
717.1	Meniscus, Medial, Derangement of Anterior Horn	M23.2	Derangement of meniscus due to old tear or injury	
		M23.3	Other meniscus derangements	
717.2	Meniscus, Medial, Derangement of Posterior Horn	M23.2	Derangement of meniscus due to old tear or injury	
		M23.3	Other meniscus derangements	
717.3	Meniscus, Medial, Derangement, Other and Unspecified	M23.3	Other meniscus derangements	
717.4	Meniscus, Lateral, Derangement	M23.3	Other meniscus derangements	
717.5	Meniscus, Derangement, Not Elsewhere Classified	M23.0	Cystic meniscus	
		M23.1	Discoid meniscus (congenital)	
		M23.2	Derangement of meniscus due to old tear or injury	
		M23.3	Other meniscus derangements	
		S83.2	Tear of meniscus	
717.6	Loose Bodies, Knee	M23.4	Loose body in knee	
717.7	Patella Chondromalacia	M22.4	Chondromalacia patellae	
717.9	Unspecified Internal Derangement of Knee	M23.3	Other meniscus derangements	
		M23.8	Other internal derangements of knee	
		M23.9	Internal derangement of knee, unspecified	
718.1	Sesamoid, Joint	M24.0	Loose body in joint	
719.0	Effusion of Joint	M25.4	Effusion of joint	
719.4	Arthralgia	M25.5	Pain in joint	
719.9	Joint Disorder, Unspecified	M16.9	Coxarthrosis, unspecified	
		M25.9	Joint disorder, unspecified	
720.0	Ankylosing Spondylitis	M45	Ankylosing spondylitis	
720.8	Other Inflammatory Spondylopathies	M46.8	Other specified inflammatory spondylopathies	
720.9	Spondylitis, Unspecified	M45	Ankylosing spondylitis	
		M46.5	Other infective spondylopathies	
		M46.9	Inflammatory spondylopathy, unspecified	
		M48.8	Other specified spondylopathies	
721.6	Ankylosing Vertebral Hyperostosis	M48.1	Ankylosing hyperostosis	
722.0	Cervical Intervertebral Disc Displacement Without Myelopathy	M50.1	Cervical disc disorder with radiculopathy	
		M50.2	Other cervical disc displacement	
722.1	Displacement of Thoracic or Lumbar Intervertebral Disc Without Myelopathy	M51.1	Lumbar and other intervertebral disc disorders with radiculopathy	
		M51.2	Other specified intervertebral disc displacement	

ICD-9	Description	ICD-10	Description	(Continued)
722.2	Displacement, Intervertebral Disc Without Myelopathy, Site Unspecified	M51.1	Lumbar and other intervertebral disc disorders with radiculopathy	
		M51.2	Other specified intervertebral disc displacement	
		M51.8	Other specified intervertebral disc disorders	
722.3	Schmorl's Nodes	M51.4	Schmorl's nodes	
722.4	Cervical Intervertebral Disc Degeneration	M50.1	Cervical disc disorder with radiculopathy	
		M50.3	Other cervical disc degeneration	
722.6	Degeneration of Intervertebral Disc, Site Unspecified	M51.3	Other specified intervertebral disc degeneration	
722.7	Intervertebral Disc Disorder with Myelopathy	M50.1	Cervical disc disorder with radiculopathy	
		M96.1	Postlaminectomy syndrome, not elsewhere classified	
722.8	Post-laminectomy Syndrome	M96.1	Postlaminectomy syndrome, not elsewhere classified	
722.9	Disc Calcification	M46.3	Infection of intervertebral disc (pyogenic)	
		M46.4	Discitis, unspecified	
		M50.8	Other cervical disc disorders	
		M50.9	Cervical disc disorder, unspecified	
		M51.2	Other specified intervertebral disc displacement	
		M51.8	Other specified intervertebral disc disorders	
		M51.9	Intervertebral disc disorder, unspecified	
723.1	Neck Pain	M54.2	Cervicalgia	
723.3	Cervicobrachial Syndrome	M53.1	Cervicobrachial syndrome	
723.4	Brachial Neuropathy	M54.1	Radiculopathy Neuritis or radiculitis	
723.5	Torticollis	M43.6	Torticollis	
724.0	Spinal Stenosis	M48.0	Spinal stenosis	
724.1	Thoracic Spine Pain	M54.6	Pain in thoracic spine	
724.2	Low Back Pain (Lumbago)	M54.5	Low back pain	
724.3	Sciatica	M54.3	Sciatica	
724.5	Back Pain	M54.8	Other dorsalgia	
		M54.9	Backache NOS	
724.9	Neuritis or Radiculitis Due to Displacement or Rupture of Intervertebral Disc (Lumbar)	G54.9	Nerve root and plexus disorder, unspecified	
		M43.2	Other fusion of spine	
		M45	Ankylosing spondylitis	
		M47.9	Spondylosis, unspecified	
		M48.9	Spondylopathy, unspecified	
		M53.2	Spinal instabilities	
		M53.8	Other specified dorsopathies	
		M53.9	Dorsopathy, unspecified	
		M54.5	Low back pain	
725	Polymyalgia Rheumatica	M35.3	Polymyalgia rheumatica	
726.0	Adhesive Capsulitis of Shoulder	M75.0	Adhesive capsulitis of shoulder	
726.1	Rotator Cuff Syndrome	M75.1	Rotator cuff syndrome	
		M75.2	Bicipital tendinitis	
		M75.5	Bursitis of shoulder	
		M75.8	Other shoulder lesions	
		M75.9	Shoulder lesion, unspecified	
726.2	Impingement Syndrome	M75.0	Adhesive capsulitis of shoulder	
		M75.3	Calcific tendinitis of shoulder	
		M75.4	Impingement syndrome of shoulder	
		M75.8	Other shoulder lesions	
		M75.9	Shoulder lesion, unspecified	
726.3	Enthesopathy of Elbow Region	M70.2	Olecranon bursitis	
		M70.3	Other bursitis of elbow	
		M77.0	Medial epicondylitis	
		M77.1	Lateral epicondylitis Tennis elbow	
		M77.8	Other enthesopathies, not elsewhere classified	
726.4	Enthesopathy of Wrist and Carpus	M70.1	Bursitis of hand	
		M77.2	Periarthritis of wrist	
		M77.8	Other enthesopathies, not elsewhere classified	
726.5	Enthesopathy of Hip Region	M70.6	Trochanteric bursitis Trochanteric tendinitis	
		M70.7	Other bursitis of hip	
		M76.0	Gluteal tendinitis	

ICD-9	Description	ICD-10	Description	(Continued)
726.5	Enthesopathy of Hip Region	M76.1	Psoas tendinitis	
		M76.2	Iliac crest spur	
		M76.8	Other enthesopathies of lower limb, excluding foot	
726.6	Enthesopathy of Knee	M70.4	Prepatellar bursitis	
		M70.5	Other bursitis of knee	
		M76.4	Tibial collateral bursitis	
		M76.5	Patellar tendinitis	
		M76.8	Other enthesopathies of lower limb, excluding foot	
726.7	Enthesopathy of Ankle and Talus	M76.6	Achilles tendinitis	
		M76.8	Other enthesopathies of lower limb, excluding foot	
		M77.3	Calcaneal spur	
		M77.4	Metatarsalgia	
		M77.5	Other enthesopathy of foot	
726.8	Other Enthesopathies	M70.8	Other soft tissue disorders related to use, overuse and pressure	
		M76.3	Iliotibial band syndrome	
		M76.7	Peroneal tendinitis	
		M76.8	Other enthesopathies of lower limb, excluding foot	
		M76.9	Enthesopathy of lower limb, unspecified	
		M77.8	Other enthesopathies, not elsewhere classified	
		M77.9	Enthesopathy, unspecified	
726.9	Enthesopathy of Unspecified Site	M25.7	Osteophyte	
		M65.8	Other synovitis and tenosynovitis	
		M71.5	Other bursitis, not elsewhere classified	
		M77.9	Enthesopathy, unspecified	
		M89.9	Disorder of bone, unspecified	
727.0	Tenosynovitis and Synovitis	M65.1	Other infective (teno)synovitis	
		M65.3	Trigger finger Nodular tendinous disease	
		M65.4	Radial styloid tenosynovitis	
		M65.8	Other synovitis and tenosynovitis	
		M65.9	Synovitis and tenosynovitis, unspecified	
		M67.3	Transient synovitis	
		M70.8	Other soft tissue disorders related to use, overuse and pressure	
		M70.9	Unspecified soft tissue disorder related to use, overuse and pressure	
727.1	Bunion	M20.1	Hallux valgus (acquired)	
727.2	Repetitive Strain Injury	M70.0	Chronic crepitant synovitis of hand and wrist	
		M70.1	Bursitis of hand	
		M70.2	Olecranon bursitis	
		M70.3	Other bursitis of elbow	
		M70.4	Prepatellar bursitis	
		M70.5	Other bursitis of knee	
		M70.7	Other bursitis of hip	
		M70.8	Other soft tissue disorders related to use, overuse and pressure	
		M70.9	Unspecified soft tissue disorder related to use, overuse and pressure	
727.3	Bursitis, Other	M65.9	Synovitis and tenosynovitis, unspecified	
		M70.4	Prepatellar bursitis	
		M71.1	Other infective bursitis	
		M71.5	Other bursitis, not elsewhere classified	
		M71.8	Other specified bursopathies	
		M71.9	Bursopathy, unspecified	
		M77.8	Other enthesopathies, not elsewhere classified	
727.4	Ganglion and Synovial Cyst, Tendon and Bursa	M67.4	Ganglion of joint or tendon (sheath)	
		M67.8	Other specified disorders of synovium and tendon	
		M71.3	Other bursal cyst	
728.0	Infective Myositis	M60.0	Infective myositis	
728.2	Muscle Atrophy and Muscular Wasting Not Classified Elsewhere	G71.8	Other primary disorders of muscles	
		M62.5	Disuse atrophy NEC	
		M62.8	Other specified disorders of muscle	
728.6	Dupuytren's Contracture (Contracture of Palmar Fascia)	M72.0	Palmar fascial fibromatosis	
728.9	Unspecified Disorder of Muscle, Ligament, and Fascia	M24.2	Instability secondary to old ligament injury	
		M60.9	Myositis, unspecified	

ICD-9	Description	ICD-10	Description	(Continued)
728.9	Unspecified Disorder of Muscle, Ligament, and Fascia	M62.0	Diastasis of muscle	
		M62.8	Other specified disorders of muscle	
		M62.9	Disorder of muscle, unspecified	
		M79.8	Other specified soft tissue disorders	
729.0	Rheumatism, Unspecified, and Fibrositis	M79.0	Rheumatism, unspecified Fibromyalgia	
729.1	Myalgia and Myositis	M60.8	Other myositis	
		M60.9	Myositis, unspecified	
		M79.0	Rheumatism, unspecified Fibromyalgia	
		M79.1	Myalgia	
		M79.2	Neuralgia and neuritis, unspecified	
729.2	Neuralgia, Neuritis, and Radiculitis	M47.2	Other spondylosis with radiculopathy	
		M54.1	Radiculopathy Neuritis or radiculitis	
		M79.2	Neuralgia and neuritis, unspecified	
		M79.6	Pain in limb	
729.5	Pain in Limb	M79.6	Pain in limb	
730.0	Osteomyelitis, Acute	M46.2	Osteomyelitis of vertebra	
		M86.0	Acute haematogenous osteomyelitis	
		M86.1	Other acute osteomyelitis	
		M86.2	Subacute osteomyelitis	
		M86.8	Other osteomyelitis	
		M87.8	Other osteonecrosis	
730.1	Osteomyelitis, Chronic	M86.3	Chronic multifocal osteomyelitis	
		M86.4	Chronic osteomyelitis with draining sinus	
		M86.5	Other chronic haematogenous osteomyelitis	
		M86.6	Other chronic osteomyelitis	
		M86.8	Other osteomyelitis	
		M87.1	Osteonecrosis due to drugs	
		M87.2	Osteonecrosis due to previous trauma	
		M87.3	Other secondary osteonecrosis	
		M87.8	Other osteonecrosis	
		M87.9	Osteonecrosis, unspecified	
730.2	Osteomyelitis, Unspecified	M46.2	Osteomyelitis of vertebra	
		M86.8	Other osteomyelitis	
		M86.9	Osteomyelitis, unspecified	
731.0	Paget's Disease of Bone (Osteitis Deformans without Mention of Bone Tumor)	M88.0	Paget's disease of skull	
		M88.8	Paget's disease of other bones	
		M88.9	Paget's disease of bone, unspecified	
732.7	Osteochondritis Dissecans	M93.2	Osteochondritis dissecans	
733.0	Osteoporosis	M48.5	Collapsed vertebra, not elsewhere classified	
		M48.8	Other specified spondylopathies	
		M81.0	Postmenopausal osteoporosis	
		M81.1	Postoophorectomy osteoporosis	
		M81.2	Osteoporosis of disuse	
		M81.3	Postsurgical malabsorption osteoporosis	
		M81.4	Drug-induced osteoporosis	
		M81.5	Idiopathic osteoporosis	
		M81.6	Localized osteoporosis	
		M81.8	Other osteoporosis Senile osteoporosis	
		M81.9	Osteoporosis, unspecified	
		M85.8	Other specified disorders of bone density and structure	
		M87.2	Osteonecrosis due to previous trauma	
733.4	Aseptic Necrosis of Bone	M87.0	Idiopathic aseptic necrosis of bone	
		M87.8	Other osteonecrosis	
		M87.9	Osteonecrosis, unspecified	
733.6	Costochondritis (Tietze's Disease)	M94.0	Chondrocostal junction syndrome [Tietze]	
733.8	Malunion and Nonunion of Fracture	M84.0	Malunion of fracture	
		M84.1	Nonunion of fracture [pseudarthrosis]	
		M84.2	Delayed union of fracture	
735.0	Hallux Valgus, Acquired	M20.1	Hallux valgus (acquired)	
735.2	Hallux Rigidus, Acquired	M20.2	Hallux rigidus	

Translation of ICD-9 CM to ICD-10

ICD-9	Description	ICD-10	Description	(Continued)
735.2	Hallux Rigidus, Acquired	M20.5	Other deformities of toe(s) (acquired)	
735.4	Hammertoe, Acquired	M20.3	Other deformity of hallux (acquired)	
		M20.4	Other hammer toe(s) (acquired)	
735.9	Unspecified Acquired Deformity of Toe	M20.6	Acquired deformity of toe(s), unspecified	
737.8	Curvature of Spine, Other	M40.3	Flatback syndrome	
		M40.5	Lordosis, unspecified	
		M43.8	Other specified deforming dorsopathies	
737.9	Curvature of Spine, Acquired, Unspecified	M40.2	Other and unspecified kyphosis	
		M43.8	Other specified deforming dorsopathies	
		M43.9	Deforming dorsopathy, unspecified	
738.4	Spondylolisthesis, Acquired or Degenerative	M43.1	Spondylolisthesis	
739.1	Cervical Region	M99.0	Segmental and somatic dysfunction	
		M99.1	Subluxation complex (vertebral)	
		M99.2	Subluxation stenosis of neural canal	
		M99.3	Osseous stenosis of neural canal	
		M99.4	Connective tissue stenosis of neural canal	
		M99.5	Intervertebral disc stenosis of neural canal	
		M99.6	Osseous and subluxation stenosis of intervertebral foramina	
		M99.7	Connective tissue and disc stenosis of intervertebral foramina	
		M99.8	Other biomechanical lesions	
		M99.9	Biomechanical lesion, unspecified	
739.2	Thoracic Region	M99.0	Segmental and somatic dysfunction	
		M99.1	Subluxation complex (vertebral)	
		M99.2	Subluxation stenosis of neural canal	
		M99.3	Osseous stenosis of neural canal	
		M99.4	Connective tissue stenosis of neural canal	
		M99.5	Intervertebral disc stenosis of neural canal	
		M99.6	Osseous and subluxation stenosis of intervertebral foramina	
		M99.7	Connective tissue and disc stenosis of intervertebral foramina	
		M99.8	Other biomechanical lesions	
		M99.9	Biomechanical lesion, unspecified	
739.3	Lumbar Region	M99.0	Segmental and somatic dysfunction	
		M99.1	Subluxation complex (vertebral)	
		M99.2	Subluxation stenosis of neural canal	
		M99.3	Osseous stenosis of neural canal	
		M99.4	Connective tissue stenosis of neural canal	
		M99.5	Intervertebral disc stenosis of neural canal	
		M99.6	Osseous and subluxation stenosis of intervertebral foramina	
		M99.7	Connective tissue and disc stenosis of intervertebral foramina	
		M99.8	Other biomechanical lesions	
		M99.9	Biomechanical lesion, unspecified	
739.4	Sacral Region	M99.0	Segmental and somatic dysfunction	
		M99.1	Subluxation complex (vertebral)	
		M99.2	Subluxation stenosis of neural canal	
		M99.3	Osseous stenosis of neural canal	
		M99.4	Connective tissue stenosis of neural canal	
		M99.5	Intervertebral disc stenosis of neural canal	
		M99.6	Osseous and subluxation stenosis of intervertebral foramina	
		M99.7	Connective tissue and disc stenosis of intervertebral foramina	
		M99.8	Other biomechanical lesions	
		M99.9	Biomechanical lesion, unspecified	
739.5	Pelvic Region	M99.0	Segmental and somatic dysfunction	
		M99.1	Subluxation complex (vertebral)	
		M99.2	Subluxation stenosis of neural canal	
		M99.3	Osseous stenosis of neural canal	
		M99.4	Connective tissue stenosis of neural canal	
		M99.5	Intervertebral disc stenosis of neural canal	
		M99.6	Osseous and subluxation stenosis of intervertebral foramina	
		M99.7	Connective tissue and disc stenosis of intervertebral foramina	
		M99.8	Other biomechanical lesions	
		M99.9	Biomechanical lesion, unspecified	

ICD-9	Description	ICD-10	Description	(Continued)
739.6	Lower Extremities	M99.0	Segmental and somatic dysfunction	
		M99.1	Subluxation complex (vertebral)	
		M99.2	Subluxation stenosis of neural canal	
		M99.3	Osseous stenosis of neural canal	
		M99.4	Connective tissue stenosis of neural canal	
		M99.5	Intervertebral disc stenosis of neural canal	
		M99.6	Osseous and subluxation stenosis of intervertebral foramina	
		M99.7	Connective tissue and disc stenosis of intervertebral foramina	
		M99.8	Other biomechanical lesions	
		M99.9	Biomechanical lesion, unspecified	
739.7	Upper Extremities	M99.0	Segmental and somatic dysfunction	
		M99.1	Subluxation complex (vertebral)	
		M99.2	Subluxation stenosis of neural canal	
		M99.3	Osseous stenosis of neural canal	
		M99.4	Connective tissue stenosis of neural canal	
		M99.5	Intervertebral disc stenosis of neural canal	
		M99.6	Osseous and subluxation stenosis of intervertebral foramina	
		M99.7	Connective tissue and disc stenosis of intervertebral foramina	
		M99.8	Other biomechanical lesions	
		M99.9	Biomechanical lesion, unspecified	
743.3	Congenital Cataract and Lens Anomalies	Q12.0	Congenital cataract	
		Q12.1	Congenital displaced lens	
		Q12.2	Coloboma of lens	
		Q12.3	Congenital aphakia	
		Q12.4	Spherophakia	
		Q12.8	Other congenital lens malformations	
746.3	Congenital Stenosis of Aortic Valve	Q23.0	Congenital stenosis of aortic valve	
746.4	Stenosis of Aortic Valve, Congenital	Q23.1	Congenital insufficiency of aortic valve	
747.1	Coarctation of Aorta	Q25.1	Coarctation of aorta	
		Q25.2	Atresia of aorta	
747.6	Anomalies of Peripheral Vascular System, Other	Q27.1	Congenital renal artery stenosis	
		Q27.2	Other congenital malformations of renal artery	
		Q27.3	Peripheral arteriovenous malformation	
		Q27.4	Congenital phlebectasia	
		Q27.8	Other specified congenital malformations of peripheral vascular system	
		Q27.9	Congenital malformation of peripheral vascular system, unspecified	
		Q28.1	Other malformations of precerebral vessels	
750.4	Esophageal Diverticula	Q39.2	Congenital tracheo-oesophageal fistula without atresia	
		Q39.5	Congenital dilatation of oesophagus	
		Q39.6	Diverticulum of oesophagus	
		Q39.8	Other congenital malformations of oesophagus	
751.0	Meckel's Diverticulum	Q43.0	Meckel's diverticulum	
754.1	Torticollis (Congenital Musculoskeletal Deformities)	Q68.0	Congenital deformity of sternocleidomastoid muscle	
771.0	Congenital Rubella	P35.0	Congenital rubella syndrome	
773.0	Hemolytic Disease Due to Rh Isoimmunization	P55.0	Rh isoimmunization of fetus and newborn	
773.1	Hemolytic Disease Due to ABO Isoimmunization	P55.1	ABO isoimmunization of fetus and newborn	
773.2	Hemolytic Disease Due to Other and Unspecified Isoimmunization	P55.8	Other haemolytic diseases of fetus and newborn	
		P55.9	Haemolytic disease of fetus and newborn, unspecified	
		P61.4	Other congenital anaemias, not elsewhere classified	
776.0	Vitamin K Deficiency of Newborn	P53	Vitamin K deficiency of newborn	
780.2	Vasovagal Syncope	R55	Syncope and collapse	
		R57.9	Shock, unspecified	
780.3	Seizures	R56.0	Febrile convulsions	
		R56.8	Other and unspecified convulsions	
780.4	Dizziness and Giddiness	R42	Dizziness and giddiness	
780.6	Fever	R50.0	Fever with chills	
		R50.1	Persistent fever	
		R50.9	Fever, unspecified	
780.7	Malaise	R53	Malaise and fatigue	
780.9	Amnesia	R41.1	Anterograde amnesia	

ICD-9	Description	ICD-10	Description	(Continued)
780.9	Amnesia	R41.2	Retrograde amnesia	
		R41.3	Other amnesia	
		R41.8	Other and unspecified symptoms and signs involving cognitive functions and awareness	
		R46.4	Slowness and poor responsiveness	
		R48.1	Agnosia	
		R52.0	Acute pain	
		R52.1	Chronic intractable pain	
		R52.2	Other chronic pain	
		R52.9	Pain, unspecified	
		R68.0	Hypothermia, not associated with low environmental temperature	
		R68.8	Other specified general symptoms and signs	
781.0	Tremor (Abnormal Involuntary Movements)	R25.0	Abnormal head movements	
		R25.1	Tremor, unspecified	
		R25.2	Cramp and spasm	
		R25.3	Fasciculation	
		R25.8	Other and unspecified abnormal involuntary movements	
781.7	Tetany	R29.0	Tetany	
782.0	Paresthesia	R20.0	Anaesthesia of skin	
		R20.1	Hypoaesthesia of skin	
		R20.2	Paraesthesia of skin	
		R20.3	Hyperaesthesia	
		R20.8	Other and unspecified disturbances of skin sensation	
782.4	Jaundice	R17	Unspecified jaundice	
784.0	Headache	G44.1	Vascular headache, not elsewhere classified	
		G44.3	Chronic post-traumatic headache	
		G44.4	Drug-induced headache, not elsewhere classified	
		R51	Headache	
784.3	Aphasia	R47.0	Dysphasia and aphasia	
784.7	Nosebleed (Epistaxis)	R04.0	Haemorrhage from nose	
785.1	Palpitations	R00.2	Palpitations	
785.2	Heart Murmur	R01.0	Benign and innocent cardiac murmurs	
		R01.1	Cardiac murmur, unspecified	
785.4	Gangrene	L88	Pyoderma gangrenosum	
		R02	Gangrene, not elsewhere classified	
786.3	Hemoptysis	R04.2	Haemoptysis	
		R04.9	Haemorrhage from respiratory passages, unspecified	
786.5	Pain, Chest	R07.1	Chest pain on breathing	
		R07.2	Precordial pain	
		R07.3	Anterior chest-wall pain NOS	
		R07.4	Chest pain, unspecified	
787.0	Nausea and Vomiting	R11	Nausea and vomiting	
787.9	Digestive System Symptoms, Other	R19.4	Change in bowel habit	
		R19.8	Other specified symptoms and signs involving the digestive system and abdomen	
789.0	Abdominal Pain	R10.0	Acute abdomen	
		R10.1	Pain localized to upper abdomen	
		R10.2	Pelvic and perineal pain	
		R10.3	Pain localized to other parts of lower abdomen	
		R10.4	Other and unspecified abdominal pain	
789.2	Splenomegaly	R16.1	Splenomegaly, not elsewhere classified	
789.3	Abdominal or Pelvic Swelling, Mass, or Lump	R19.0	Intra-abdominal and pelvic swelling, mass and lump	
789.5	Ascites	R18	Ascites	
790.7	Bacteremia	A49.9	Bacterial infection, unspecified	
		R78.8	Finding of other specified substances, not normally found in blood	
791.0	Albuminuria (Proteinuria)	N39.1	Persistent proteinuria, unspecified	
		R80	Isolated proteinuria	
791.5	Glycosuria	R81	Glycosuria	
793.1	Coin Lesion	R91	Abnormal findings on diagnostic imaging of lung	
799.1	Respiratory Arrest	J96.0	Acute respiratory failure	
		J96.1	Chronic respiratory failure	
		J96.9	Respiratory failure, unspecified	

ICD-9	Description	ICD-10	Description	(Continued)
799.1	Respiratory Arrest	R09.2	Respiratory arrest	
799.2	Nervousness	R45.0	Nervousness	
801.0	Closed Without Mention of Intracranial Injury	S02.1	Fracture of base of skull	
801.1	Closed with Cerebral Laceration and Contusion	S02.1	Fracture of base of skull	
801.2	Closed with Subarachnoid, Subdural, and Extradural Hemorrhage	S02.1	Fracture of base of skull	
801.3	Closed with Other and Unspecified Intracranial Hemorrhage	S02.1	Fracture of base of skull	
802.0	Fracture, Nasal Bones, Closed	S02.2	Fracture of nasal bones	
		S07.0	Crushing injury of face	
802.2	Fracture, Mandible (Lower Jaw), Closed	S02.6	Fracture of mandible	
802.4	Fracture, Upper Jaw, Closed	S02.4	Fracture of malar and maxillary bones	
803.0	Fracture, Skull, Closed, Without Mention of Brain Injury	S02.9	Fracture of skull and facial bones, part unspecified	
		S07.1	Crushing injury of skull	
		S07.8	Crushing injury of other parts of head	
		S07.9	Crushing injury of head, part unspecified	
		S09.9	Unspecified injury of head	
803.3	Fracture of Skull Closed with Other and Unspecified Intracranial Hemorrhage	S02.9	Fracture of skull and facial bones, part unspecified	
		S07.1	Crushing injury of skull	
		S07.8	Crushing injury of other parts of head	
		S07.9	Crushing injury of head, part unspecified	
		S09.9	Unspecified injury of head	
805.0	Fracture, Cervical Spine Without Mention of Spinal Cord Injury, Closed	S12.0	Fracture of first cervical vertebra Atlas	
		S12.1	Fracture of second cervical vertebra Axis	
		S12.2	Fracture of other specified cervical vertebra	
		S12.7	Multiple fractures of cervical spine	
		S12.9	Fracture of neck, part unspecified	
805.1	Fracture, Cervical Spine Without Mention of Spinal Cord Injury, Open	S12.0	Fracture of first cervical vertebra Atlas	
		S12.1	Fracture of second cervical vertebra Axis	
		S12.2	Fracture of other specified cervical vertebra	
		S12.7	Multiple fractures of cervical spine	
		S12.9	Fracture of neck, part unspecified	
805.2	Fracture, Thoracic Spine Without Mention of Spinal Cord Injury, Closed	S22.0	Fracture of thoracic vertebra	
		S22.1	Multiple fractures of thoracic spine	
805.3	Fracture, Thoracic Spine Without Mention of Spinal Cord Injury, Open	S22.0	Fracture of thoracic vertebra	
		S22.1	Multiple fractures of thoracic spine	
805.4	Fracture, Lumbar Spine Without Mention of Spinal Cord Injury, Closed	S32.0	Fracture of lumbar vertebra	
		S32.7	Multiple fractures of lumbar spine and pelvis	
		S32.8	Fracture of other and unspecified parts of lumbar spine and pelvis	
805.5	Fracture, Lumbar Spine Without Mention of Spinal Cord Injury, Open	S32.0	Fracture of lumbar vertebra	
		S32.7	Multiple fractures of lumbar spine and pelvis	
		S32.8	Fracture of other and unspecified parts of lumbar spine and pelvis	
805.6	Fracture, Sacrum and Coccyx Without Mention of Spinal Cord Injury, Closed	S32.1	Fracture of sacrum	
		S32.2	Fracture of coccyx	
805.7	Fracture, Sacrum and Coccyx Without Mention of Spinal Cord Injury, Open	S32.1	Fracture of sacrum	
		S32.2	Fracture of coccyx	
805.8	Fracture, Vertebral Column, Unspecified, Without Mention of Spinal Cord Injury, Closed	T08	Fracture of spine, level unspecified	
805.9	Fracture, Vertebral Column, Unspecified, Without Mention of Spinal Cord Injury, Open	T08	Fracture of spine, level unspecified	
806.0	Fracture, Cervical Spine with Spinal Cord Injury, Closed	S12.0	Fracture of first cervical vertebra Atlas	
		S12.1	Fracture of second cervical vertebra Axis	
		S12.2	Fracture of other specified cervical vertebra	
		S12.7	Multiple fractures of cervical spine	
		S12.9	Fracture of neck, part unspecified	

Translation of ICD-9 CM to ICD-10

ICD-9	Description	ICD-10	Description	(Continued)
806.1	Fracture, Cervical Spine with Spinal Cord Injury, Open	S12.0	Fracture of first cervical vertebra Atlas	
		S12.1	Fracture of second cervical vertebra Axis	
		S12.2	Fracture of other specified cervical vertebra	
		S12.7	Multiple fractures of cervical spine	
		S12.9	Fracture of neck, part unspecified	
806.2	Fracture, Thoracic Spine with Spinal Cord Injury, Closed	S22.0	Fracture of thoracic vertebra	
		S22.1	Multiple fractures of thoracic spine	
806.3	Fracture, Thoracic Spine with Spinal Cord Injury, Open	S22.0	Fracture of thoracic vertebra	
		S22.1	Multiple fractures of thoracic spine	
806.4	Fracture, Lumbar Spine with Spinal Cord Injury, Closed	S32.0	Fracture of lumbar vertebra	
		S32.7	Multiple fractures of lumbar spine and pelvis	
		S32.8	Fracture of other and unspecified parts of lumbar spine and pelvis	
806.5	Fracture, Lumbar Spine with Spinal Cord Injury, Open	S32.0	Fracture of lumbar vertebra	
		S32.7	Multiple fractures of lumbar spine and pelvis	
		S32.8	Fracture of other and unspecified parts of lumbar spine and pelvis	
806.6	Fracture, Sacrum and Coccyx with Spinal Cord Injury, Closed	S32.1	Fracture of sacrum	
		S32.2	Fracture of coccyx	
806.7	Fracture, Sacrum and Coccyx with Spinal Cord Injury, Open	S32.1	Fracture of sacrum	
		S32.2	Fracture of coccyx	
806.8	Unspecified, Closed	T08	Fracture of spine, level unspecified	
806.9	Unspecified, Open	T08	Fracture of spine, level unspecified	
807.0	Fracture, Ribs (Single or Multiple)	S22.3	Fracture of rib	
		S22.4	Multiple fractures of ribs	
807.1	Rib(s) Open	S22.3	Fracture of rib	
		S22.4	Multiple fractures of ribs	
807.2	Fracture, Sternum (Closed)	S22.2	Fracture of sternum	
807.3	Sternum, Open	S22.2	Fracture of sternum	
808.2	Fracture, Pubis, Closed	S32.5	Fracture of pubis	
808.3	Fracture, Pubis, Open	S32.5	Fracture of pubis	
808.4	Fracture, Pelvis, Other Specified Part, Closed	S32.3	Fracture of ilium	
		S32.7	Multiple fractures of lumbar spine and pelvis	
		S32.8	Fracture of other and unspecified parts of lumbar spine and pelvis	
808.5	Fracture, Pelvis, Other Specified Part, Open	S32.3	Fracture of ilium	
		S32.7	Multiple fractures of lumbar spine and pelvis	
		S32.8	Fracture of other and unspecified parts of lumbar spine and pelvis	
808.8	Fracture, Pelvis, Unspecified, Closed	S32.5	Fracture of pubis	
		S32.7	Multiple fractures of lumbar spine and pelvis	
		S32.8	Fracture of other and unspecified parts of lumbar spine and pelvis	
808.9	Fracture, Pelvis, Unspecified, Open	S32.5	Fracture of pubis	
		S32.7	Multiple fractures of lumbar spine and pelvis	
		S32.8	Fracture of other and unspecified parts of lumbar spine and pelvis	
812.4	Fracture, Elbow (Distal Humerus)	S42.4	Fracture of lower end of humerus	
		S52.0	Fracture of upper end of ulna	
813.1	Upper End, Open	S52.0	Fracture of upper end of ulna	
		S52.1	Fracture of upper end of radius	
		S52.7	Multiple fractures of forearm	
		S52.8	Fracture of other parts of forearm	
		S52.9	Fracture of forearm, part unspecified	
813.2	Shaft, Closed	S52.2	Fracture of shaft of ulna	
		S52.3	Fracture of shaft of radius	
		S52.4	Fracture of shafts of both ulna and radius	
813.3	Shaft, Open	S52.2	Fracture of shaft of ulna	
		S52.3	Fracture of shaft of radius	
		S52.4	Fracture of shafts of both ulna and radius	
813.4	Fracture, Lower End of Forearm, Closed	S52.5	Fracture of lower end of radius	
		S52.6	Fracture of lower end of both ulna and radius	
		S52.8	Fracture of other parts of forearm	
813.5	Fracture, Lower End of Forearm, Open	S52.5	Fracture of lower end of radius	
		S52.6	Fracture of lower end of both ulna and radius	
		S52.8	Fracture of other parts of forearm	

ICD-9	Description	ICD-10	Description	(Continued)
814.0	Fracture, Carpal Bone(s), Closed	S62.0	Fracture of navicular [scaphoid] bone of hand	
		S62.1	Fracture of other carpal bone(s)	
		S62.8	Fracture of other and unspecified parts of wrist and hand	
814.1	Fracture, Carpal Bone(s), Open	S62.0	Fracture of navicular [scaphoid] bone of hand	
		S62.1	Fracture of other carpal bone(s)	
		S62.8	Fracture of other and unspecified parts of wrist and hand	
815.0	Fracture, Metacarpal Bone(s), Closed	S62.2	Fracture of first metacarpal bone	
		S62.3	Fracture of other metacarpal bone	
		S62.4	Multiple fractures of metacarpal bones	
		S62.8	Fracture of other and unspecified parts of wrist and hand	
815.1	Fracture, Metacarpal Bone(s), Open	S62.2	Fracture of first metacarpal bone	
		S62.3	Fracture of other metacarpal bone	
		S62.4	Multiple fractures of metacarpal bones	
		S62.8	Fracture of other and unspecified parts of wrist and hand	
816.0	Fracture, Phalanges of Hand (One or More), Closed	S62.5	Fracture of thumb	
		S62.6	Fracture of other finger	
		S62.7	Multiple fractures of fingers	
816.1	Fracture, Phalanges of Hand (One or More), Open	S62.5	Fracture of thumb	
		S62.6	Fracture of other finger	
		S62.7	Multiple fractures of fingers	
820.0	Fracture (Transcervical), Neck of Femur, Closed	S72.0	Fracture of neck of femur Fracture of hip NOS	
820.1	Fracture (Transcervical), Neck of Femur, Open	S72.0	Fracture of neck of femur Fracture of hip NOS	
820.2	Fracture (Pertrochanteric), Neck of Femur, Closed	S72.1	Pertrochanteric fracture	
		S72.2	Subtrochanteric fracture	
820.3	Fracture (Pertrochanteric), Neck of Femur, Open	S72.1	Pertrochanteric fracture	
		S72.2	Subtrochanteric fracture	
820.8	Fracture, Neck of Femur, Unspecified Part, Closed	S72.0	Fracture of neck of femur Fracture of hip NOS	
820.9	Fracture, Neck of Femur, Unspecified Part, Open	S72.0	Fracture of neck of femur Fracture of hip NOS	
823.0	Fracture, Upper End of Tibia and Fibula, Closed	S82.1	Fracture of upper end of tibia	
		S82.2	Fracture of shaft of tibia with or without mention of fracture of fibula	
		S82.4	Fracture of fibula alone	
		S82.9	Fracture of lower leg, part unspecified	
823.1	Fracture, Upper End of Tibia and Fibula, Open	S82.1	Fracture of upper end of tibia	
		S82.2	Fracture of shaft of tibia with or without mention of fracture of fibula	
		S82.4	Fracture of fibula alone	
		S82.9	Fracture of lower leg, part unspecified	
823.2	Fracture, Shaft of Tibia and Fibula, Closed	S82.2	Fracture of shaft of tibia with or without mention of fracture of fibula	
823.3	Fracture, Shaft of Tibia and Fibula, Open	S82.2	Fracture of shaft of tibia with or without mention of fracture of fibula	
824.0	Fracture, Ankle, Medial Malleolus, Closed	S82.5	Fracture of medial malleolus	
824.1	Fracture, Ankle, Medial Malleolus, Open	S82.5	Fracture of medial malleolus	
824.2	Fracture, Ankle, Lateral Malleolus, Closed	S82.6	Fracture of lateral malleolus	
824.3	Fracture, Ankle, Lateral Malleolus, Open	S82.6	Fracture of lateral malleolus	
824.4	Fracture, Ankle, Bimalleolar, Closed (Pott's Fracture)	S82.8	Fractures of other parts of lower leg	
824.5	Fracture, Ankle, Bimalleolar, Open	S82.8	Fractures of other parts of lower leg	
824.6	Fracture, Ankle, Trimalleolar, Closed	S82.8	Fractures of other parts of lower leg	
824.7	Fracture, Ankle, Trimalleolar, Open	S82.8	Fractures of other parts of lower leg	
824.8	Fracture, Ankle, Unspecified, Closed	S82.3	Fracture of lower end of tibia with or without mention of fracture of fibula	
		S82.8	Fractures of other parts of lower leg	
824.9	Fracture, Ankle, Unspecified, Open	S82.3	Fracture of lower end of tibia with or without mention of fracture of fibula	
		S82.8	Fractures of other parts of lower leg	
825.0	Fracture, Calcaneus (Heel Bone), Closed	S92.0	Fracture of calcaneus	
825.1	Fracture, Calcaneus (Heel Bone), Open	S92.0	Fracture of calcaneus	
825.2	Fracture of Other Tarsal and Metatarsal Bones, Closed	S92.1	Fracture of talus Astragalus	
		S92.2	Fracture of other tarsal bone(s)	
		S92.3	Fracture of metatarsal bone	
		S92.4	Fracture of great toe	
		S92.9	Fracture of foot, unspecified	
826.0	Fracture, Phalanges of Foot, Closed	S92.4	Fracture of great toe	
		S92.5	Fracture of other toe	
826.1	Fracture, Phalanges of Foot, Open	S92.4	Fracture of great toe	
		S92.5	Fracture of other toe	

ICD-9	Description	ICD-10	Description	(Continued)
827.0	Fracture, Leg (Closed)	S82.7	Multiple fractures of lower leg	
		S92.7	Multiple fractures of foot	
		T02.3	Fractures involving multiple regions of one lower limb	
		T12	Fracture of lower limb, level unspecified	
827.1	Fracture, Leg (Open)	S82.7	Multiple fractures of lower leg	
		S92.7	Multiple fractures of foot	
		T02.3	Fractures involving multiple regions of one lower limb	
		T12	Fracture of lower limb, level unspecified	
831.0	Dislocation, Glenohumeral Joint (Shoulder), Closed	S43.0	Dislocation of shoulder joint Glenohumeral joint	
		S43.1	Dislocation of acromioclavicular joint	
		S43.3	Dislocation of other and unspecified parts of shoulder girdle Dislocation of shoulder girdle NOS	
836.0	Meniscus Tear, Knee (Current)	S83.2	Tear of meniscus	
		S83.3	Tear of articular cartilage of knee, current	
836.1	Tear of Lateral Cartilage or Meniscus of Knee, Current	S83.2	Tear of meniscus	
		S83.3	Tear of articular cartilage of knee, current	
836.2	Tear of Cartilage or Meniscus of Knee (Other), Current	S83.2	Tear of meniscus	
		S83.3	Tear of articular cartilage of knee, current	
836.3	Dislocation, Patella (Kneecap), Closed	S83.0	Dislocation of patella	
836.4	Dislocation, Patella (Kneecap), Open	S83.0	Dislocation of patella	
836.5	Other Dislocation of Knee, Closed	S83.1	Dislocation of knee	
836.6	Dislocation, Knee, Other, Open	S83.1	Dislocation of knee	
838.0	Dislocation, Foot, Unspecified	S93.1	Dislocation of toe(s)	
		S93.3	Dislocation of other and unspecified parts of foot	
839.0	Dislocation, Cervical Vertebra, Closed	S13.0	Traumatic rupture of cervical intervertebral disc	
		S13.1	Dislocation of cervical vertebra Cervical spine NOS	
		S13.2	Dislocation of other and unspecified parts of neck	
		S13.3	Multiple dislocations of neck	
		T03.8	Dislocations, sprains and strains involving other combinations of body regions	
839.1	Dislocation, Cervical Vertebra, Open	S13.0	Traumatic rupture of cervical intervertebral disc	
		S13.1	Dislocation of cervical vertebra Cervical spine NOS	
		S13.2	Dislocation of other and unspecified parts of neck	
		S13.3	Multiple dislocations of neck	
		T03.8	Dislocations, sprains and strains involving other combinations of body regions	
839.8	Dislocations, Multiple and Ill-Defined (Other), Closed	S33.4	Traumatic rupture of symphysis pubis	
		T03.1	Dislocations, sprains and strains involving thorax with lower back and pelvis	
		T03.2	Dislocations, sprains and strains involving multiple regions of upper limb(s)	
		T03.3	Dislocations, sprains and strains involving multiple regions of lower limb(s)	
		T03.4	Dislocations, sprains and strains involving multiple regions of upper limb(s) with lower limb(s)	
		T03.8	Dislocations, sprains and strains involving other combinations of body regions	
		T03.9	Multiple dislocations, sprains and strains, unspecified	
		T09.2	Dislocation, sprain and strain of unspecified joint and ligament of trunk	
		T11.2	Dislocation, sprain and strain of unspecified joint and ligament of upper limb, level unspecified	
		T13.2	Dislocation, sprain and strain of unspecified joint and ligament of lower limb, level unspecified	
		T14.3	Dislocation, sprain and strain of unspecified body region	
839.9	Dislocations, Multiple and Ill-Defined (Other), Open	S33.4	Traumatic rupture of symphysis pubis	
		T03.1	Dislocations, sprains and strains involving thorax with lower back and pelvis	
		T03.2	Dislocations, sprains and strains involving multiple regions of upper limb(s)	
		T03.3	Dislocations, sprains and strains involving multiple regions of lower limb(s)	
		T03.4	Dislocations, sprains and strains involving multiple regions of upper limb(s) with lower limb(s)	
		T03.8	Dislocations, sprains and strains involving other combinations of body regions	
		T03.9	Multiple dislocations, sprains and strains, unspecified	
		T09.2	Dislocation, sprain and strain of unspecified joint and ligament of trunk	
		T11.2	Dislocation, sprain and strain of unspecified joint and ligament of upper limb, level unspecified	
		T13.2	Dislocation, sprain and strain of unspecified joint and ligament of lower limb, level unspecified	
		T14.3	Dislocation, sprain and strain of unspecified body region	
840.0	Sprains and Strains, Acromioclavicular Joint	S43.5	Sprain and strain of acromioclavicular joint	

ICD-9	Description	ICD-10	Description
840.4	Sprains and Strains, Rotator Cuff (Rotator Cuff Tear)	S43.4	Sprain and strain of shoulder joint
840.8	Sprains and Strains, Biceps Tendon (Rupture)	S43.4	Sprain and strain of shoulder joint
		S43.7	Sprain and strain of other and unspecified parts of shoulder girdle
840.9	Sprains and Strains, Arm, Site Unspecified	S43.4	Sprain and strain of shoulder joint
		S43.7	Sprain and strain of other and unspecified parts of shoulder girdle
841.0	Sprains and Strains, Radial Collateral Ligament	S53.2	Traumatic rupture of radial collateral ligament
841.1	Sprains and Strains, Ulnar Collateral Ligament	S53.3	Traumatic rupture of ulnar collateral ligament
841.2	Sprains and Strains, Radiohumeral Joint	S53.4	Sprain and strain of elbow
841.3	Sprains and Strains, Ulnohumeral Joint	S53.4	Sprain and strain of elbow
841.8	Sprains and Strains, Elbow and Forearm, Other Specified Sites	S53.4	Sprain and strain of elbow
841.9	Sprains and Strains, Elbow and Forearm, Unspecified Site	S53.4	Sprain and strain of elbow
842.0	Sprains and Strains, Wrist	S63.3	Traumatic rupture of ligament of wrist and carpus
		S63.5	Sprain and strain of wrist
		S63.7	Sprain and strain of other and unspecified parts of hand
843.0	Sprains and Strains, Iliofemoral Ligament (Groin Strain)	S73.1	Sprain and strain of hip
843.8	Groin Strain (Sprains and Strains of Other Specified Sites of Hip and Thigh)	S73.1	Sprain and strain of hip
		S76.1	Injury of quadriceps muscle and tendon
844.0	Sprains and Strains, Knee	S83.4	Sprain and strain involving (fibular)(tibial) collateral ligament of knee
844.1	Sprains and Strains, Medial Collateral Ligament of Knee	S83.4	Sprain and strain involving (fibular)(tibial) collateral ligament of knee
844.2	Sprains and Strains, Cruciate Ligament of Knee	S83.5	Sprain and strain involving (anterior)(posterior) cruciate ligament of knee
844.8	Sprains and Strains, Specified Site of Knee or Leg	S83.6	Sprain and strain of other and unspecified parts of knee
		S83.7	Injury to multiple structures of knee
844.9	Sprains and Strains, Knee or Leg, Unspecified	S83.6	Sprain and strain of other and unspecified parts of knee
		T79.6	Traumatic ischaemia of muscle
845.0	Sprains and Strains, Ankle	S86.0	Injury of Achilles tendon
		S93.2	Rupture of ligaments at ankle and foot level
		S93.4	Sprain and strain of ankle
845.1	Sprains and Strains, Foot	S93.2	Rupture of ligaments at ankle and foot level
		S93.5	Sprain and strain of toe(s)
		S93.6	Sprain and strain of other and unspecified parts of foot
846.0	Sprains and Strains, Lumbosacral Joint	S33.5	Sprain and strain of lumbar spine
846.1	Sprains and Strains, Sacroiliac Ligament	S33.6	Sprain and strain of sacroiliac joint
846.9	Sprains and Strains, Unspecified Site of Sacroiliac Region	S33.7	Sprain and strain of other and unspecified parts of lumbar spine and pelvis
847.0	Sprains and Strains, Cervical Spine (Neck)	S13.4	Sprain and strain of cervical spine Anterior longitudinal (ligament), cervical Atlanto-axial (joints) Atlanto-occipital (joints) Whiplash injury
		S13.6	Sprain and strain of joints and ligaments of other and unspecified parts of neck
847.1	Sprains and Strains, Thoracic Spine	S23.3	Sprain and strain of thoracic spine
		S29.0	Injury of muscle and tendon at thorax level
847.2	Sprains and Strains, Lumbar Spine	S33.5	Sprain and strain of lumbar spine
847.9	Sprains and Strains, Back	T09.2	Dislocation, sprain and strain of unspecified joint and ligament of trunk
848.8	Abdominal Muscle Strain	S23.5	Sprain and strain of other and unspecified parts of thorax
		T03.0	Dislocations, sprains and strains involving head with neck
		T03.1	Dislocations, sprains and strains involving thorax with lower back and pelvis
		T03.2	Dislocations, sprains and strains involving multiple regions of upper limb(s)
		T03.3	Dislocations, sprains and strains involving multiple regions of lower limb(s)
		T03.4	Dislocations, sprains and strains involving multiple regions of upper limb(s) with lower limb(s)
		T03.8	Dislocations, sprains and strains involving other combinations of body regions
		T03.9	Multiple dislocations, sprains and strains, unspecified
		T11.2	Dislocation, sprain and strain of unspecified joint and ligament of upper limb, level unspecified
		T13.2	Dislocation, sprain and strain of unspecified joint and ligament of lower limb, level unspecified
850	Brain Injury	S06.0	Concussion
		S06.2	Diffuse brain injury
851.0	Cerebral (Cortex) Contusion without Mention of Open Intracranial Wound	S06.2	Diffuse brain injury
		S06.3	Focal brain injury
		S06.8	Other intracranial injuries
852.0	Subarachnoid Hemorrhage Following Injury Without Mention of Open Intracranial Wound	S06.4	Epidural haemorrhage

ICD-9	Description	ICD-10	Description	(Continued)
852.0	Subarachnoid Hemorrhage Following Injury Without Mention of Open Intracranial Wound	S06.5	Traumatic subdural haemorrhage	
		S06.6	Traumatic subarachnoid haemorrhage	
		S06.8	Other intracranial injuries	
852.1	Subarachnoid Hemorrhage Following Injury with Open Intracranial Wound	S06.4	Epidural haemorrhage	
		S06.5	Traumatic subdural haemorrhage	
		S06.6	Traumatic subarachnoid haemorrhage	
		S06.8	Other intracranial injuries	
853.0	Intracranial Hemorrhage Following Injury Without Mention of Open Intracranial Wound, Other and Unspecified	S06.2	Diffuse brain injury	
		S06.3	Focal brain injury	
		S06.8	Other intracranial injuries	
853.1	Intracranial Hemorrhage Following Injury with Open Intracranial Wound, Other and Unspecified	S06.2	Diffuse brain injury	
		S06.3	Focal brain injury	
		S06.8	Other intracranial injuries	
854.0	Brain Injury of Other and Unspecified Nature Without Mention of Open Cranial Wound	S01.8	Open wound of other parts of head	
		S06.0	Concussion	
		S06.1	Traumatic cerebral oedema	
		S06.2	Diffuse brain injury	
		S06.3	Focal brain injury	
		S06.7	Intracranial injury with prolonged coma	
		S06.8	Other intracranial injuries	
		S06.9	Intracranial injury, unspecified	
		S09.7	Multiple injuries of head	
		S09.9	Unspecified injury of head	
854.1	Brain Injury of Other and Unspecified Nature with Open Cranial Wound	S01.8	Open wound of other parts of head	
		S06.0	Concussion	
		S06.1	Traumatic cerebral oedema	
		S06.2	Diffuse brain injury	
		S06.3	Focal brain injury	
		S06.7	Intracranial injury with prolonged coma	
		S06.8	Other intracranial injuries	
		S06.9	Intracranial injury, unspecified	
		S09.7	Multiple injuries of head	
		S09.9	Unspecified injury of head	
860.0	Pneumothorax, Traumatic	S27.0	Traumatic pneumothorax	
860.1	Pneumothorax, Traumatic, with Open Wound into Thorax	S27.0	Traumatic pneumothorax	
860.2	Hemothorax Without Mention of Open Wound into Thorax	S26.0	Injury of heart with haemopericardium	
		S27.1	Traumatic haemothorax	
860.3	Hemothorax, Traumatic	S26.0	Injury of heart with haemopericardium	
		S27.1	Traumatic haemothorax	
865.0	Spleen Injury Without Mention of Open Wound into Cavity	S36.0	Injury of spleen	
865.1	Spleen Injury with Open Wound into Cavity	S36.0	Injury of spleen	
870.0	Puncture Wounds	S01.1	Open wound of eyelid and periocular area with or without involvement of lacrimal passages	
870.1	Laceration of Eyelid, Full-thickness, Not Involving Lacrimal Passages	S01.1	Open wound of eyelid and periocular area with or without involvement of lacrimal passages	
870.2	Laceration of Eyelid Involving Lacrimal Passages	S01.1	Open wound of eyelid and periocular area with or without involvement of lacrimal passages	
		S05.8	Other injuries of eye and orbit	
870.3	Penetrating Wound of Orbit, Without Mention of Foreign Body	S05.4	Penetrating wound of orbit with or without foreign body	
870.4	Penetrating Wound of Orbit, Without Mention of Foreign Body	S05.4	Penetrating wound of orbit with or without foreign body	
870.8	Open Wounds of Ocular Adnexa, Specified, Other	S01.1	Open wound of eyelid and periocular area with or without involvement of lacrimal passages	
870.9	Open Wound of Ocular Adnexa, Unspecified	S05.8	Other injuries of eye and orbit	
		S05.9	Injury of eye and orbit, part unspecified	
871.0	Ocular Laceration Without Prolapse of Intraocular Tissue	S05.0	Injury of conjunctiva and corneal abrasion without mention of foreign body	
		S05.3	Ocular laceration without prolapse or loss of intraocular tissue	

ICD-9	Description	ICD-10	Description	(Continued)
871.1	Ocular Laceration with Prolapse or Exposure of Intraocular Tissue	S05.0	Injury of conjunctiva and corneal abrasion without mention of foreign body	
		S05.2	Ocular laceration and rupture with prolapse or loss of intraocular tissue	
871.2	Rupture of Eye with Partial Loss of Intraocular Tissue	S05.0	Injury of conjunctiva and corneal abrasion without mention of foreign body	
		S05.2	Ocular laceration and rupture with prolapse or loss of intraocular tissue	
		S05.3	Ocular laceration without prolapse or loss of intraocular tissue	
		S05.9	Injury of eye and orbit, part unspecified	
871.3	Avulsion of Eye	S05.7	Avulsion of eye Traumatic enucleation	
871.4	Laceration of Eye, Unspecified	S05.0	Injury of conjunctiva and corneal abrasion without mention of foreign body	
		S05.3	Ocular laceration without prolapse or loss of intraocular tissue	
871.5	Penetration of Eyeball with Magnetic Foreign Body	S05.5	Penetrating wound of eyeball with foreign body	
871.6	Penetration of Eyeball with (Nonmagnetic) Foreign Body	S05.5	Penetrating wound of eyeball with foreign body	
871.7	Ocular Penetration, Unspecified	S05.6	Penetrating wound of eyeball without foreign body	
871.9	Open Wound of Eyeball, Unspecified	S05.0	Injury of conjunctiva and corneal abrasion without mention of foreign body	
		S05.8	Other injuries of eye and orbit	
		S05.9	Injury of eye and orbit, part unspecified	
872.0	Open Wound of External Ear, Without Mention of Complications	S01.3	Open wound of ear	
		S08.1	Traumatic amputation of ear	
872.1	Open Wound of External Ear, Complicated	S01.3	Open wound of ear	
		S08.1	Traumatic amputation of ear	
872.6	Open Wound of Other Specified Parts of Ear, Without Mention of Complications	S01.3	Open wound of ear	
		S09.2	Traumatic rupture of ear drum	
872.7	Open Wound of Other Specified Parts of Ear, Complicated	S01.3	Open wound of ear	
		S09.2	Traumatic rupture of ear drum	
872.8	Open Wound of Ear, Part Unspecified, Without Mention of Complication	S01.3	Open wound of ear	
872.9	Open Wound of Ear, Part Unspecified	S01.3	Open wound of ear	
873.0	Open Wound of Scalp, Without Mention of Complication	S01.0	Open wound of scalp	
		S08.0	Avulsion of scalp	
873.1	Open Wound of Scalp, Complicated	S01.0	Open wound of scalp	
		S08.0	Avulsion of scalp	
873.2	Open Wound of Nose, Without Mention of Complication	S01.2	Open wound of nose	
		S01.8	Open wound of other parts of head	
		S08.8	Traumatic amputation of other parts of head	
873.4	Open Wound of Face, Without Mention of Complication	S01.1	Open wound of eyelid and periocular area with or without involvement of lacrimal passages	
		S01.4	Open wound of cheek and temporomandibular area	
		S01.5	Open wound of lip and oral cavity	
		S01.8	Open wound of other parts of head	
		S08.8	Traumatic amputation of other parts of head	
873.5	Open Wound of Face, Complicated	S01.1	Open wound of eyelid and periocular area with or without involvement of lacrimal passages	
		S01.4	Open wound of cheek and temporomandibular area	
		S01.5	Open wound of lip and oral cavity	
		S01.8	Open wound of other parts of head	
		S08.8	Traumatic amputation of other parts of head	
873.6	Open Wound of Internal Structures of Mouth, Without Mention of Complications	S01.5	Open wound of lip and oral cavity	
		S02.5	Fracture of tooth Broken tooth	
		S03.2	Dislocation of tooth	
		S09.9	Unspecified injury of head	
873.7	Open Wound of Internal Structures of Mouth, Complicated	S01.5	Open wound of lip and oral cavity	
		S02.5	Fracture of tooth Broken tooth	
		S03.2	Dislocation of tooth	
		S09.9	Unspecified injury of head	
873.8	Open Wound of Other and Unspecified Open Wound of Head Without Mention of Complication	S01.7	Multiple open wounds of head	
		S01.8	Open wound of other parts of head	
		S01.9	Open wound of head, part unspecified	
		S08.8	Traumatic amputation of other parts of head	
		S08.9	Traumatic amputation of unspecified part of head	

ICD-9	Description	ICD-10	Description	(Continued)
873.9	Open Wound of Other and Unspecified Open Wound of Head, Complicated	S01.7	Multiple open wounds of head	
		S01.8	Open wound of other parts of head	
		S01.9	Open wound of head, part unspecified	
		S08.8	Traumatic amputation of other parts of head	
		S08.9	Traumatic amputation of unspecified part of head	
874.8	Open Wound of Other and Unspecified Parts of Neck, Without Mention of Complications	S11.7	Multiple open wounds of neck	
		S11.8	Open wound of other parts of neck	
		S11.9	Open wound of neck, part unspecified	
		S18	Traumatic amputation at neck level Decapitation	
874.9	Open Wound of Other and Unspecified Parts of Neck, Complicated	S11.7	Multiple open wounds of neck	
		S11.8	Open wound of other parts of neck	
		S11.9	Open wound of neck, part unspecified	
		S18	Traumatic amputation at neck level Decapitation	
879.0	Open Wound of Breast, without Mention of Complication	S21.0	Open wound of breast	
879.1	Open Wound of Breast, Complicated	S21.0	Open wound of breast	
879.6	Open Wound of Other and Unspecified Parts of Trunk, Without Mention of Complication	N81.8	Other female genital prolapse Deficient perineum Old laceration of muscles of pelvic floor	
		S31.0	Open wound of lower back and pelvis Buttock	
		S31.7	Multiple open wounds of abdomen, lower back and pelvis	
		S31.8	Open wound of other and unspecified parts of abdomen	
		S38.3	Traumatic amputation of other and unspecified parts of abdomen, lower back and pelvis	
		T01.1	Open wounds involving thorax with abdomen, lower back and pelvis	
		T09.1	Open wound of trunk, level unspecified	
		T09.6	Traumatic amputation of trunk, level unspecified	
879.8	Open Wound, Multiple Unspecified Sites, Without Mention of Complication	T01.0	Open wounds involving head with neck	
		T01.8	Open wounds involving other combinations of body regions	
		T01.9	Multiple open wounds, unspecified	
		T05.8	Traumatic amputations involving other combinations of body regions	
		T05.9	Multiple traumatic amputations, unspecified	
		T14.1	Open wound of unspecified body region	
		T14.7	Crushing injury and traumatic amputation of unspecified body region	
882.0	Open Wound, Hand (Except Finger), Without Mention of Complication	S61.8	Open wound of other parts of wrist and hand	
		S61.9	Open wound of wrist and hand part, part unspecified	
882.2	Open Wound, Hand (Except Finger), With Tendon Complication	S61.8	Open wound of other parts of wrist and hand	
		S61.9	Open wound of wrist and hand part, part unspecified	
883.0	Open Wound, Finger, Without Mention of Complication	S61.0	Open wound of finger(s) without damage to nail Open wound of finger(s) NOS Excludes: open wound involving nail (matrix) (S61.1)	
		S61.1	Open wound of finger(s) with damage to nail	
883.1	Open Wound, Finger, With Complication	S61.0	Open wound of finger(s) without damage to nail Open wound of finger(s) NOS Excludes: open wound involving nail (matrix) (S61.1)	
		S61.1	Open wound of finger(s) with damage to nail	
883.2	Open Wound, Finger, With Tendon Involvement	S61.0	Open wound of finger(s) without damage to nail Open wound of finger(s) NOS Excludes: open wound involving nail (matrix) (S61.1)	
		S61.1	Open wound of finger(s) with damage to nail	
896.0	Amputation (Traumatic), Foot (Partial)	S98.0	Traumatic amputation of foot at ankle level	
		S98.3	Combined traumatic amputation of toe(s) and other parts of foot	
		S98.4	Traumatic amputation of foot, level unspecified	
896.1	Amputation (Traumatic), Foot, Unilateral, Complicated	S98.0	Traumatic amputation of foot at ankle level	
		S98.3	Combined traumatic amputation of toe(s) and other parts of foot	
		S98.4	Traumatic amputation of foot, level unspecified	
896.2	Amputation (Traumatic), Foot, Bilateral, without Mention of Complication	T05.3	Traumatic amputation of both feet	
896.3	Amputation (Traumatic), Foot, Bilateral, Complicated	T06.3	Injuries of blood vessels involving multiple body regions	
897.0	Amputation (Traumatic), Leg(s) (Complete) (Partial), Unilateral, Below Knee, without Mention of Complication	S88.1	Traumatic amputation at level between knee and ankle	
897.1	Amputation (Traumatic), Leg(s) (Complete) (Partial), Unilateral, Below Knee, Complicated	S88.1	Traumatic amputation at level between knee and ankle	

ICD-9	Description	ICD-10	Description	(Continued)
897.2	Amputation (Traumatic), Leg(s) (Complete) (Partial), Unilateral, at or Above Knee, without Mention of Complication	S78.0	Traumatic amputation at hip joint	
		S78.1	Traumatic amputation at level between hip and knee	
		S78.9	Traumatic amputation of hip and thigh, level unspecified	
		S88.0	Traumatic amputation at knee level	
897.3	Amputation (Traumatic), Leg(s) (Complete) (Partial), Unilateral, at or Above Knee, Complicated	S78.0	Traumatic amputation at hip joint	
		S78.1	Traumatic amputation at level between hip and knee	
		S78.9	Traumatic amputation of hip and thigh, level unspecified	
		S88.0	Traumatic amputation at knee level	
897.4	Amputation (Traumatic), Leg(s) (Complete) (Partial), Unilateral, Level not Specified, without Mention of Complication	S88.9	Traumatic amputation of lower leg, level unspecified	
		T13.6	Traumatic amputation of lower limb, level unspecified	
897.5	Amputation (Traumatic), Leg(s) (Complete) (Partial), Unilateral, Level not Specified, Complicated	S88.9	Traumatic amputation of lower leg, level unspecified	
		T13.6	Traumatic amputation of lower limb, level unspecified	
897.6	Amputation (Traumatic), Leg(s) (Complete) (Partial), Bilateral [Any Level], without Mention of Complication	T05.4	Traumatic amputation of one foot and other leg [any level, except foot]	
		T05.5	Traumatic amputation of both legs [any level]	
897.7	Amputation (Traumatic), Leg(s) (Complete) (Partial), Bilateral [Any Level], Complicated	T05.4	Traumatic amputation of one foot and other leg [any level, except foot]	
		T05.5	Traumatic amputation of both legs [any level]	
910.9	Other and Unspecified Superficial Injury of Face, Neck, and Scalp, Infected	S00.0	Superficial injury of scalp	
		S00.3	Superficial injury of nose	
		S00.4	Superficial injury of ear	
		S00.5	Superficial injury of lip and oral cavity	
		S00.7	Multiple superficial injuries of head	
		S00.8	Superficial injury of other parts of head	
		S00.9	Superficial injury of head, part unspecified	
		S10.1	Other and unspecified superficial injuries of throat	
		S10.7	Multiple superficial injuries of neck	
		S10.8	Superficial injury of other parts of neck	
		S10.9	Superficial injury of neck, part unspecified	
		T00.0	Superficial injuries involving head with neck	
918.1	Corneal Abrasion	S05.0	Injury of conjunctiva and corneal abrasion without mention of foreign body	
919.0	Abrasions	S90.7	Multiple superficial injuries of ankle and foot	
		T00.2	Superficial injuries involving multiple regions of upper limb(s)	
		T00.3	Superficial injuries involving multiple regions of lower limb(s)	
		T00.6	Superficial injuries involving multiple regions of upper limb(s) with lower limb(s)	
		T00.8	Superficial injuries involving other combinations of body regions	
		T00.9	Multiple superficial injuries, unspecified	
		T11.0	Superficial injury of upper limb, level unspecified	
		T14.0	Superficial injury of unspecified body region	
		T14.6	Injury of muscles and tendons of unspecified body region	
		T30.0	Burn of unspecified body region, unspecified degree	
919.1	Abrasion of Friction Burn, Infected	S90.7	Multiple superficial injuries of ankle and foot	
		T00.2	Superficial injuries involving multiple regions of upper limb(s)	
		T00.3	Superficial injuries involving multiple regions of lower limb(s)	
		T00.6	Superficial injuries involving multiple regions of upper limb(s) with lower limb(s)	
		T00.8	Superficial injuries involving other combinations of body regions	
		T00.9	Multiple superficial injuries, unspecified	
		T14.0	Superficial injury of unspecified body region	
		T14.6	Injury of muscles and tendons of unspecified body region	
		T30.0	Burn of unspecified body region, unspecified degree	
920	Head Injury, Superficial	S00.0	Superficial injury of scalp	
		S00.3	Superficial injury of nose	
		S00.4	Superficial injury of ear	
		S00.5	Superficial injury of lip and oral cavity	
		S00.7	Multiple superficial injuries of head	
		S00.8	Superficial injury of other parts of head	
		S00.9	Superficial injury of head, part unspecified	
		S09.8	Other specified injuries of head	

ICD-9	Description	ICD-10	Description	(Continued)
920	Head Injury, Superficial	S10.0	Contusion of throat	
		S10.8	Superficial injury of other parts of neck	
		S10.9	Superficial injury of neck, part unspecified	
921.0	Black Eye, Not Otherwise Specified	S00.1	Contusion of eyelid and periocular area	
921.1	Contusion of Eyelids and Periocular Area	S00.1	Contusion of eyelid and periocular area	
		S05.8	Other injuries of eye and orbit	
		S09.9	Unspecified injury of head	
921.2	Contusion of Orbital Tissues	S05.0	Injury of conjunctiva and corneal abrasion without mention of foreign body	
		S05.1	Contusion of eyeball and orbital tissues	
		S05.9	Injury of eye and orbit, part unspecified	
921.3	Contusion of Eyeball	S05.1	Contusion of eyeball and orbital tissues	
		S05.8	Other injuries of eye and orbit	
		S05.9	Injury of eye and orbit, part unspecified	
921.9	Contusion of Eye, Unspecified	S05.8	Other injuries of eye and orbit	
		S05.9	Injury of eye and orbit, part unspecified	
922.0	Contusion of Breast	S20.0	Contusion of breast	
922.1	Contusion of Chest Wall	S20.2	Contusion of thorax	
922.2	Contusion of Abdominal Wall	S30.1	Contusion of abdominal wall Flank Groin	
922.3	Contusion of Back	S20.2	Contusion of thorax	
		S30.0	Contusion of lower back and pelvis Buttock	
922.4	Contusion of Genital Organs	S30.1	Contusion of abdominal wall Flank Groin	
		S30.2	Contusion of external genital organs	
922.8	Contusion of Multiple Sites of Trunk	T09.0	Superficial injury of trunk, level unspecified	
922.9	Contusion of Unspecified Part of Trunk	T09.0	Superficial injury of trunk, level unspecified	
923.0	Contusion of Shoulder and Upper Arm	S40.0	Contusion of shoulder and upper arm	
		S40.7	Multiple superficial injuries of shoulder and upper arm	
923.1	Contusion of Elbow and Forearm	S50.0	Contusion of elbow	
		S50.1	Contusion of other and unspecified parts of forearm	
923.2	Contusion of Wrist and Hand(s), Except Finger(s) Alone	S60.2	Contusion of other parts of wrist and hand	
		S60.7	Multiple superficial injuries of wrist and hand	
		S60.8	Other superficial injuries of wrist and hand	
923.3	Contusion of Finger or Thumb	S60.0	Contusion of finger(s) without damage to nail	
		S60.1	Contusion of finger(s) with damage to nail	
		S60.9	Superficial injury of wrist and hand, unspecified	
923.8	Contusion of Multiple Sites of Upper Limb	T11.0	Superficial injury of upper limb, level unspecified	
923.9	Contusion of Unspecified Part of Upper Limb	T11.0	Superficial injury of upper limb, level unspecified	
924.0	Contusion of Hip and Thigh	S70.0	Contusion of hip	
		S70.1	Contusion of thigh	
924.1	Contusion of Knee and Lower Leg	S80.0	Contusion of knee	
		S80.1	Contusion of other and unspecified parts of lower leg	
		S80.7	Multiple superficial injuries of lower leg	
924.2	Contusion of Ankle and Foot, Excluding Toes	S90.0	Contusion of ankle	
		S90.3	Contusion of other and unspecified parts of foot	
924.3	Contusion of Toe (Toenail)	S90.1	Contusion of toe(s) without damage to nail	
		S90.2	Contusion of toe(s) with damage to nail	
924.4	Contusion of Multiple Sites of Lower Limb	T13.0	Superficial injury of lower limb, level unspecified	
924.5	Contusion of Unspecified Part of Lower Limb	T13.0	Superficial injury of lower limb, level unspecified	
924.8	Contusion Multiple Sites, Not Elsewhere Classified	T14.0	Superficial injury of unspecified body region	
924.9	Contusion of Lower Limb	T14.0	Superficial injury of unspecified body region	
		T14.6	Injury of muscles and tendons of unspecified body region	
925	Crushing Injury	S07.0	Crushing injury of face	
		S07.8	Crushing injury of other parts of head	
		S17.0	Crushing injury of larynx and trachea	
		S17.8	Crushing injury of other parts of neck	
		S17.9	Crushing injury of neck, part unspecified	
926.0	Crushing Injury of External Genitalia	S38.0	Crushing injury of external genital organs	
926.1	Crushing Injury of Other Specified Sites of Trunk	S28.0	Crushed chest	
		S38.1	Crushing injury of other and unspecified parts of abdomen, lower back and pelvis	
926.8	Crushing Injury of Multiple Sites of Trunk	T04.1	Crushing injuries involving thorax with abdomen, lower back and pelvis	
926.9	Crushing Injury of Trunk, Unspecified Site	T04.1	Crushing injuries involving thorax with abdomen, lower back and pelvis	
927.0	Crushing Injury of Shoulder and Upper Arm	S47	Crushing injury of shoulder and upper arm	

2448   The Medical Disability Advisor—Fourth Edition

ICD-9	Description	ICD-10	Description	(Continued)
927.1	Crushing Injury of Elbow and Forearm	S57.0	Crushing injury of elbow	
		S57.8	Crushing injury of other parts of forearm	
		S57.9	Crushing injury of forearm, part unspecified	
927.2	Crushing Injury of Wrist and Hand(s), Except Finger(s) Alone	S67.8	Crushing injury of other and unspecified parts of wrist and hand	
927.3	Crushing Injury of Finger(s)	S67.0	Crushing injury of thumb and other finger(s)	
927.8	Crushing Injury of Multiple Sites of Upper Limb	T04.2	Crushing injuries involving multiple regions of upper limb(s)	
927.9	Crushing Injury of Upper Limb, Unspecified Site	T04.2	Crushing injuries involving multiple regions of upper limb(s)	
928.0	Crushing Injury of Hip and Thigh	S77.0	Crushing injury of hip	
		S77.1	Crushing injury of thigh	
		S77.2	Crushing injury of hip with thigh	
928.1	Crushing Injury of Knee and Lower Leg	S87.0	Crushing injury of knee	
		S87.8	Crushing injury of other and unspecified parts of lower leg	
928.2	Crushing Injury of Ankle and Foot, Excluding Toe(s) Alone	S97.0	Crushing injury of ankle	
		S97.8	Crushing injury of other parts of ankle and foot	
928.3	Crushing Injury of Toe	S97.1	Crushing injury of toe(s)	
928.8	Crushing Injury of Multiple Sites of Lower Limb	T04.3	Crushing injuries involving multiple regions of lower limb(s)	
928.9	Crushing Injury of Lower Limb, Unspecified Site	T04.3	Crushing injuries involving multiple regions of lower limb(s)	
929.0	Crushing Injury of Multiple Sites, Not Elsewhere Classified	T04.4	Crushing injuries involving multiple regions of upper limb(s) with lower limb(s)	
		T04.7	Crushing injuries of thorax with abdomen, lower back and pelvis with limb(s)	
		T04.8	Crushing injuries involving other combinations of body regions	
		T04.9	Multiple crushing injuries, unspecified	
929.9	Crushing Injury of Unspecified Site	T14.7	Crushing injury and traumatic amputation of unspecified body region	
930.0	Foreign Body, Cornea	T15.0	Foreign body in cornea	
940.0	Chemical Burns of Eyelids and Periocular Area	T26.5	Corrosion of eyelid and periocular area	
		T26.8	Corrosion of other parts of eye and adnexa	
940.1	Burns of Eyelids and Periocular Area, Other	T26.0	Burn of eyelid and periocular area	
		T26.3	Burn of other parts of eye and adnexa	
		T26.8	Corrosion of other parts of eye and adnexa	
940.2	Alkaline Chemical Burn of Cornea and Conjunctival Sac	T26.6	Corrosion of cornea and conjunctival sac	
940.3	Acid Chemical Burn of Cornea and Conjunctival Sac	T26.6	Corrosion of cornea and conjunctival sac	
940.4	Burn of Cornea and Conjunctival Sac, Other	T26.1	Burn of cornea and conjunctival sac	
940.5	Burn with Resulting Rupture and Destruction of Eyeball	T26.2	Burn with resulting rupture and destruction of eyeball	
		T26.7	Corrosion with resulting rupture and destruction of eyeball	
940.9	Burn of Eye	T26.3	Burn of other parts of eye and adnexa	
		T26.4	Burn of eye and adnexa, part unspecified	
		T26.8	Corrosion of other parts of eye and adnexa	
		T26.9	Corrosion of eye and adnexa, part unspecified	
941.0	Burn of Face, Head and Neck, Unspecified Degree	T20.0	Burn of unspecified degree of head and neck	
		T20.4	Corrosion of unspecified degree of head and neck	
941.1	First Degree Burn (Erythema) of Face, Head and Neck	T20.1	Burn of first degree of head and neck	
		T20.5	Corrosion of first degree of head and neck	
941.2	Second Degree Burn (Blisters, Epidermal Loss) of Face, Head, and Neck	T20.2	Burn of second degree of head and neck	
		T20.6	Corrosion of second degree of head and neck	
941.3	Third Degree Burn (Full-Thickness Skin Loss) of Face, Head, and Neck	T20.3	Burn of third degree of head and neck	
		T20.7	Corrosion of third degree of head and neck	
941.4	Deep Necrosis of Underlying Tissues (Deep Third Degree Burn) of Face, Head, and Neck, without Mention of Loss of Body Part	T20.3	Burn of third degree of head and neck	
		T20.7	Corrosion of third degree of head and neck	
949.0	Burn, Unspecified Degree	T27.3	Burn of respiratory tract, part unspecified	
		T29.4	Corrosions of multiple regions, unspecified degree	
		T30.0	Burn of unspecified body region, unspecified degree	
		T30.4	Corrosion of unspecified body region, unspecified degree	
949.1	First Degree Burn (Erythema)	L59.0	Erythema	
		T27.3	Burn of respiratory tract, part unspecified	
		T29.1	Burns of multiple regions, no more than first-degree burns mentioned	
		T29.5	Corrosions of multiple regions, no more than first-degree corrosions mentioned	
		T30.1	Burn of first degree, body region unspecified	
		T30.5	Corrosion of first degree, body region unspecified	

ICD-9	Description	ICD-10	Description	(Continued)
949.2	Second Degree Burn (Blisters, Epidermal Loss)	T27.3	Burn of respiratory tract, part unspecified	
		T29.2	Burns of multiple regions, no more than second-degree burns mentioned	
		T29.6	Corrosions of multiple regions, no more than second- degree corrosions mentioned	
		T30.2	Burn of second degree, body region unspecified	
		T30.6	Corrosion of second degree, body region unspecified	
949.3	Third Degree Burn (Full-Thickness Skin Loss)	T27.3	Burn of respiratory tract, part unspecified	
		T29.3	Burns of multiple regions, at least one burn of third degree mentioned	
		T29.7	Corrosions of multiple regions, at least one corrosion of third degree mentioned	
		T30.3	Burn of third degree, body region unspecified	
		T30.7	Corrosion of third degree, body region unspecified	
952.0	Cervical Spinal Cord Injury Without Evidence of Spinal Bone Injury	S14.0	Concussion and oedema of cervical spinal cord	
		S14.1	Other and unspecified injuries of cervical spinal cord	
		T91.3	Sequelae of injury of spinal cord	
952.1	Thoracic Spinal Cord Injury Without Evidence of Spinal Bone Injury	S24.0	Concussion and oedema of thoracic spinal cord	
		S24.1	Other and unspecified injuries of thoracic spinal cord	
952.2	Lumber Spinal Cord Injury Without Evidence of Spinal Bone Injury	S34.0	Concussion and oedema of lumbar spinal cord	
		S34.1	Other injury of lumbar spinal cord	
		S44.0	Injury of ulnar nerve at upper arm level	
952.3	Sacral Spinal Cord Injury Without Evidence of Spinal Bone Injury	S34.0	Concussion and oedema of lumbar spinal cord	
		S34.1	Other injury of lumbar spinal cord	
952.4	Injury to Nerves and Spinal Cord, Cauda Equina	S34.3	Injury of cauda equina	
952.8	Spinal Cord Injury Without Evidence of Spinal Bone Injury, Multiple Sites	T06.1	Injuries of nerves and spinal cord involving other multiple body regions	
952.9	Spinal Cord Injury, Unspecified	T09.3	Injury of spinal cord, level unspecified	
953.4	Brachial Plexus Injury	S14.3	Injury of brachial plexus	
957.9	Nerve Injury, Unspecified	T14.4	Injury of nerve(s) of unspecified body region	
		T87.3	Neuroma of amputation stump	
958.0	Air Embolism	T79.0	Air embolism (traumatic)	
		T81.7	Vascular complications following a procedure, not elsewhere classified	
958.1	Fat Embolism	T79.1	Fat embolism (traumatic)	
958.4	Traumatic Shock	T79.4	Traumatic shock	
958.8	Compartment Syndrome	M76.8	Other enthesopathies of lower limb, excluding foot	
		T79.6	Traumatic ischaemia of muscle	
		T79.8	Other early complications of trauma	
		T79.9	Unspecified early complication of trauma	
959.9	Trauma	T06.4	Injuries of muscles and tendons involving multiple body regions	
		T14.0	Superficial injury of unspecified body region	
		T14.9	Injury, unspecified	
		T70.4	Effects of high-pressure fluids	
		T74.1	Physical abuse	
		T74.2	Sexual abuse	
		T74.3	Psychological abuse	
		T74.9	Maltreatment syndrome, unspecified	
960.0	Poisoning by Penicillins	T36.0	Penicillins	
960.1	Poisoning by Antifungal Antibiotics	T36.7	Antifungal antibiotics, systemically used	
		T49.0	Local antifungal, anti-infective and anti-inflammatory drugs, not elsewhere classified	
960.2	Poisoning by Chloramphenicol Group	T36.2	Chloramphenicol group	
960.3	Poisoning by Erythromycin and Other Macrolides	T36.0	Penicillins	
		T36.1	Cefalosporins and other beta-lactam antibiotics	
		T36.3	Macrolides	
		T36.5	Aminoglycosides Streptomycin	
		T36.8	Other systemic antibiotics	
960.4	Poisoning by Tetracycline Group	T36.4	Tetracyclines	
960.5	Poisoning by Cephalosporin Group	T36.0	Penicillins	
		T36.1	Cefalosporins and other beta-lactam antibiotics	
960.6	Poisoning by Antimycobacterial Antibiotics	T36.5	Aminoglycosides Streptomycin	
		T36.6	Rifamycins	
		T36.7	Antifungal antibiotics, systemically used	

ICD-9	Description	ICD-10	Description	(Continued)
960.6	Poisoning by Antimycobacterial Antibiotics	T36.8	Other systemic antibiotics	
		T37.1	Antimycobacterial drugs	
960.7	Poisoning by Antineoplastic Antibiotics	T45.1	Antineoplastic and immunosuppressive drugs	
960.8	Poisoning by Other Specified Antibiotics	T36.0	Penicillins	
		T36.1	Cefalosporins and other beta-lactam antibiotics	
		T36.3	Macrolides	
		T36.5	Aminoglycosides Streptomycin	
		T36.8	Other systemic antibiotics	
		T37.8	Other specified systemic anti-infectives and antiparasitics	
960.9	Poisoning by Unspecified Antibiotic	T36.9	Systemic antibiotic, unspecified	
961.0	Poisoning by Sulfonamides	T37.0	Sulfonamides	
		T37.1	Antimycobacterial drugs	
961.1	Poisoning by Arsenical Anti-Infectives	T37.3	Other antiprotozoal drugs	
		T37.8	Other specified systemic anti-infectives and antiparasitics	
961.2	Poisoning by Heavy Metal Anti-Infectives	T37.3	Other antiprotozoal drugs	
		T37.4	Anthelminthics	
		T37.8	Other specified systemic anti-infectives and antiparasitics	
961.3	Poisoning by Quinoline and Hydroxyquinoline Derivatives	T37.8	Other specified systemic anti-infectives and antiparasitics	
		T49.0	Local antifungal, anti-infective and anti-inflammatory drugs, not elsewhere classified	
		T49.4	Keratolytics, keratoplastics and other hair treatment drugs and preparations	
961.4	Poisoning by Antimalarials and Drugs Acting on Other Blood Protozoa	T37.2	Antimalarials and drugs acting on other blood protozoa	
		T37.8	Other specified systemic anti-infectives and antiparasitics	
961.5	Poisoning by Other Antiprotozoal Drugs	T37.3	Other antiprotozoal drugs	
961.6	Poisoning by Anthelmintics	T37.3	Other antiprotozoal drugs	
		T37.4	Anthelminthics	
		T37.8	Other specified systemic anti-infectives and antiparasitics	
961.7	Poisoning by Antiviral Drugs	T37.5	Antiviral drugs	
961.8	Poisoning by Other Antimycobacterial Drugs	T37.0	Sulfonamides	
		T37.1	Antimycobacterial drugs	
		T37.8	Other specified systemic anti-infectives and antiparasitics	
961.9	Poisoning by Other Unspecified Anti-Infectives	T36.8	Other systemic antibiotics	
		T37.1	Antimycobacterial drugs	
		T37.3	Other antiprotozoal drugs	
		T37.4	Anthelminthics	
		T37.8	Other specified systemic anti-infectives and antiparasitics	
		T37.9	Systemic anti-infective and antiparasitic, unspecified	
		T49.0	Local antifungal, anti-infective and anti-inflammatory drugs, not elsewhere classified	
		T50.6	Antidotes and chelating agents, not elsewhere classified	
962.0	Poisoning by Adrenal Cortical Steroids	T38.0	Glucocorticoids and synthetic analogues	
		T49.0	Local antifungal, anti-infective and anti-inflammatory drugs, not elsewhere classified	
		T50.0	Mineralocorticoids and their antagonists	
962.1	Poisoning by Androgens and Anabolic Congeners	T38.5	Other estrogens and progestogens Mixtures and substitutes	
		T38.7	Androgens and anabolic congeners	
962.2	Poisoning by Ovarian Hormones and Synthetic Substitutes	T38.4	Oral contraceptives Multiple- and single-ingredient preparations	
		T38.5	Other estrogens and progestogens Mixtures and substitutes	
		T38.6	Antigonadotrophins, antiestrogens, antiandrogens, not elsewhere classified	
		T38.7	Androgens and anabolic congeners	
		T44.5	Predominantly beta-adrenoreceptor agonists, not elsewhere classified	
962.3	Poisoning by Insulins and Antidiabetic Agents	T38.3	Insulin and oral hypoglycaemic [antidiabetic] drugs	
962.4	Poisoning by Anterior Pituitary Hormones	T38.8	Other and unspecified hormones and their synthetic substitutes	
962.5	Poisoning by Posterior Pituitary Hormones	T38.8	Other and unspecified hormones and their synthetic substitutes	
962.6	Poisoning by Parathyroid and Parathyroid Derivatives	T50.9	Other and unspecified drugs, medicaments and biological substances	
962.7	Poisoning by Thyroid and Thyroid Derivatives	T38.1	Thyroid hormones and substitutes	
962.8	Poisoning by Antithyroid Agents	T38.2	Antithyroid drugs	
962.9	Poisoning by Other and Unspecified Hormones and Synthetic Substitutes	T38.0	Glucocorticoids and synthetic analogues	
		T38.6	Antigonadotrophins, antiestrogens, antiandrogens, not elsewhere classified	
		T38.8	Other and unspecified hormones and their synthetic substitutes	
		T38.9	Other and unspecified hormone antagonists	
		T42.8	Antiparkinsonism drugs and other central muscle-tone depressants	

Translation of ICD-9 CM to ICD-10

ICD-9	Description	ICD-10	Description	(Continued)
962.9	Poisoning by Other and Unspecified Hormones and Synthetic Substitutes	T45.1	Antineoplastic and immunosuppressive drugs	
		T45.2	Vitamins, not elsewhere classified	
		T50.8	Diagnostic agents	
963.0	Poisoning by Antiallergic and Antiemetic Drugs	T45.0	Antiallergic and antiemetic drugs	
		T49.2	Local astringents and local detergents	
963.1	Poisoning by Antineoplastic and Immunosuppressive Drugs	T38.2	Antithyroid drugs	
		T45.1	Antineoplastic and immunosuppressive drugs	
963.2	Poisoning by Acidifying Agents	T45.8	Other primarily systemic and haematological agents	
		T47.5	Digestants	
		T50.3	Electrolytic, caloric and water-balance agents	
		T50.9	Other and unspecified drugs, medicaments and biological substances	
963.3	Poisoning by Alkalizing Agents	T45.8	Other primarily systemic and haematological agents	
		T47.1	Other antacids and anti-gastric-secretion drugs	
		T50.2	Carbonic-anhydrase inhibitors, benzothiadiazides and other diuretics	
		T50.9	Other and unspecified drugs, medicaments and biological substances	
963.4	Poisoning by Enzymes, Not Elsewhere Classified	T45.3	Enzymes, not elsewhere classified	
		T45.5	Anticoagulants	
		T47.5	Digestants	
		T50.6	Antidotes and chelating agents, not elsewhere classified	
963.5	Poisoning by Vitamins	T45.2	Vitamins, not elsewhere classified	
		T45.8	Other primarily systemic and haematological agents	
		T46.9	Other and unspecified agents primarily affecting the cardiovascular system	
963.8	Poisoning by Other Specified Systemic Agents	T45.8	Other primarily systemic and haematological agents	
		T50.6	Antidotes and chelating agents, not elsewhere classified	
963.9	Poisoning by Unspecified Systemic Agent	T45.9	Primarily systemic and haematological agent, unspecified	
964.0	Poisoning by Iron and Its Compounds	T45.4	Iron and its compounds	
		T45.8	Other primarily systemic and haematological agents	
964.1	Poisoning by Folic Acid	T45.8	Other primarily systemic and haematological agents	
		T50.9	Other and unspecified drugs, medicaments and biological substances	
964.2	Poisoning by Anticoagulants	T45.5	Anticoagulants	
964.3	Poisoning by Vitamin K	T45.7	Anticoagulant antagonists	
964.4	Poisoning by Fibrinolysis-affecting Drugs	T45.3	Enzymes, not elsewhere classified	
		T45.6	Fibrinolysis-affecting drugs	
964.5	Poisoning by Anticoagulant Antagonists and Other Coagulants	T45.7	Anticoagulant antagonists	
964.6	Poisoning by Gamma Globulin	T50.9	Other and unspecified drugs, medicaments and biological substances	
964.7	Poisoning by Natural Blood and Blood Products	T45.8	Other primarily systemic and haematological agents	
964.8	Poisoning by Other Specified Agents Affecting Blood Constituents	T45.8	Other primarily systemic and haematological agents	
964.9	Poisoning by Unspecified Agent Affecting Blood Constituents	T45.9	Primarily systemic and haematological agent, unspecified	
965.0	Poisoning by Opiates and Related Narcotics	T39.3	Other nonsteroidal anti-inflammatory drugs	
		T40.0	Opium	
		T40.1	Heroin	
		T40.2	Other opioids	
		T40.3	Methadone	
		T40.4	Other synthetic narcotics	
		T40.6	Other and unspecified narcotics	
		T48.3	Antitussives	
965.1	Poisoning by Salicylates	T39.0	Salicylates	
965.4	Poisoning by Aromatic Analgesics, Not Elsewhere Classified	T39.0	Salicylates	
		T39.1	4-Aminophenol derivatives	
965.5	Poisoning by Pyrazole Derivatives	T39.2	Pyrazolone derivatives	
965.6	Poisoning by Antirheumatics	T39.3	Other nonsteroidal anti-inflammatory drugs	
		T39.4	Antirheumatics, not elsewhere classified	
		T39.8	Other nonopioid analgesics and antipyretics, not elsewhere classified	
		T39.9	Nonopioid analgesic, antipyretic and antirheumatic, unspecified	
		T45.1	Antineoplastic and immunosuppressive drugs	
		T49.0	Local antifungal, anti-infective and anti-inflammatory drugs, not elsewhere classified	
965.7	Poisoning by Other Non-Narcotic Analgesics	T39.8	Other nonopioid analgesics and antipyretics, not elsewhere classified	

ICD-9	Description	ICD-10	Description	(Continued)
965.7	Poisoning by Other Non-Narcotic Analgesics	T39.9	Nonopioid analgesic, antipyretic and antirheumatic, unspecified	
		T40.4	Other synthetic narcotics	
		T41.1	Intravenous anaesthetics	
		T47.8	Other agents primarily affecting the gastrointestinal system	
965.8	Poisoning by Other Specified Analgesics and Antipyretics	T39.3	Other nonsteroidal anti-inflammatory drugs	
		T40.4	Other synthetic narcotics	
		T40.6	Other and unspecified narcotics	
		T49.0	Local antifungal, anti-infective and anti-inflammatory drugs, not elsewhere classified	
965.9	Poisoning by Unspecified Analgesic and Antipyretic	T39.8	Other nonopioid analgesics and antipyretics, not elsewhere classified	
966.0	Poisoning by Oxazolidine Derivatives	T42.2	Succinimides and oxazolidinediones	
966.1	Poisoning by Hydantoin Derivatives	T42.0	Hydantoin derivatives	
966.2	Poisoning by Succinimides	T42.2	Succinimides and oxazolidinediones	
966.3	Poisoning by Other and Unspecified Anticonvulsants	T42.1	Iminostilbenes	
		T42.3	Barbiturates	
		T42.4	Benzodiazepines	
		T42.5	Mixed antiepileptics, not elsewhere classified	
		T42.6	Other antiepileptic and sedative-hypnotic drugs	
		T45.1	Antineoplastic and immunosuppressive drugs	
966.4	Poisoning by Anti-parkinsonism Drugs	T42.8	Antiparkinsonism drugs and other central muscle-tone depressants	
		T44.3	Other parasympatholytics [anticholinergics and antimuscarinics] and spasmolytics, not elsewhere classified	
		T45.0	Antiallergic and antiemetic drugs	
967.0	Poisoning by Barbiturates	T41.1	Intravenous anaesthetics	
		T42.3	Barbiturates	
967.1	Poisoning by Chloral Hydrate Group	T42.6	Other antiepileptic and sedative-hypnotic drugs	
		T49.0	Local antifungal, anti-infective and anti-inflammatory drugs, not elsewhere classified	
967.2	Poisoning by Paraldehyde	T42.6	Other antiepileptic and sedative-hypnotic drugs	
967.3	Toxic Effects, Methyl Bromide	T42.6	Other antiepileptic and sedative-hypnotic drugs	
967.4	Poisoning by Methaqualone Compounds	T42.6	Other antiepileptic and sedative-hypnotic drugs	
967.5	Poisoning by Glutethimide Group	T42.6	Other antiepileptic and sedative-hypnotic drugs	
967.6	Poisoning by Mixed Sedatives, Not Elsewhere Classified	T42.3	Barbiturates	
		T42.6	Other antiepileptic and sedative-hypnotic drugs	
967.8	Poisoning by Other Sedatives and Hypnotics	T42.4	Benzodiazepines	
		T42.6	Other antiepileptic and sedative-hypnotic drugs	
		T42.7	Antiepileptic and sedative-hypnotic drugs, unspecified	
		T43.5	Other and unspecified antipsychotics and neuroleptics	
967.9	Poisoning by Unspecified Sedative or Hypnotic	T42.7	Antiepileptic and sedative-hypnotic drugs, unspecified	
968.0	Poisoning by Central Nervous System Muscle-tone Depressants	T42.8	Antiparkinsonism drugs and other central muscle-tone depressants	
		T43.5	Other and unspecified antipsychotics and neuroleptics	
		T44.3	Other parasympatholytics [anticholinergics and antimuscarinics] and spasmolytics, not elsewhere classified	
968.1	Poisoning by Halothane	T41.0	Inhaled anaesthetics	
968.2	Poisoning by Other Gaseous Anesthetics	T41.0	Inhaled anaesthetics	
		T41.2	Other and unspecified general anaesthetics	
		T43.2	Other and unspecified antidepressants	
968.3	Poisoning by Intravenous Anesthetics	T41.1	Intravenous anaesthetics	
		T41.2	Other and unspecified general anaesthetics	
		T42.3	Barbiturates	
968.4	Poisoning by Other and Unspecified General Anesthetics	T41.1	Intravenous anaesthetics	
		T41.2	Other and unspecified general anaesthetics	
968.5	Poisoning by Surface and Infiltration Anesthetics	T40.5	Cocaine	
		T41.3	Local anaesthetics	
968.6	Poisoning by Peripheral Nerve and Plexus-Blocking Anesthetics	T41.3	Local anaesthetics	
968.7	Poisoning by Spinal Anesthetics	T41.3	Local anaesthetics	
968.9	Poisoning by Other and Unspecified Local Anesthetics	T41.2	Other and unspecified general anaesthetics	
		T41.3	Local anaesthetics	
		T41.4	Anaesthetic, unspecified	
969.0	Poisoning by Antidepressants	T43.0	Tricyclic and tetracyclic antidepressants	
		T43.1	Monoamine-oxidase-inhibitor antidepressants	
		T43.2	Other and unspecified antidepressants	

ICD-9	Description	ICD-10	Description	(Continued)
969.0	Poisoning by Antidepressants	T46.5	Other antihypertensive drugs, not elsewhere classified	
969.1	Poisoning by Phenothiazine-based Tranquilizers	T43.3	Phenothiazine antipsychotics and neuroleptics	
		T44.3	Other parasympatholytics [anticholinergics and antimuscarinics] and spasmolytics, not elsewhere classified	
		T45.0	Antiallergic and antiemetic drugs	
969.2	Poisoning by Butyrophenone-based Tranquilizers	T43.4	Butyrophenone and thioxanthene neuroleptics	
		T43.5	Other and unspecified antipsychotics and neuroleptics	
969.3	Poisoning by Other Antipsychotics, Neuroleptics, and Major Tranquilizers	T42.4	Benzodiazepines	
		T43.3	Phenothiazine antipsychotics and neuroleptics	
		T43.5	Other and unspecified antipsychotics and neuroleptics	
969.4	Poisoning by Benzodiazepine-Based Tranquilizers	T42.4	Benzodiazepines	
969.5	Poisoning by Other Tranquilizers	T42.6	Other antiepileptic and sedative-hypnotic drugs	
		T42.8	Antiparkinsonism drugs and other central muscle-tone depressants	
		T43.4	Butyrophenone and thioxanthene neuroleptics	
		T43.5	Other and unspecified antipsychotics and neuroleptics	
		T44.3	Other parasympatholytics [anticholinergics and antimuscarinics] and spasmolytics, not elsewhere classified	
969.6	Poisoning by Psychodysleptics (Hallucinogens)	T40.7	Cannabis (derivatives)	
		T40.8	Lysergide [LSD]	
		T40.9	Other and unspecified psychodysleptics [hallucinogens]	
969.7	Poisoning by Psychostimulants	T43.6	Psychostimulants with abuse potential	
		T50.7	Analeptics and opioid receptor antagonists	
969.8	Poisoning by Other Specified Psychotropic Agents	T43.5	Other and unspecified antipsychotics and neuroleptics	
		T43.8	Other psychotropic drugs, not elsewhere classified	
969.9	Poisoning by Unspecified Psychotropic Agent	T43.9	Psychotropic drug, unspecified	
970.0	Poisoning by Analeptics	T44.0	Anticholinesterase agents	
		T48.7	Other and unspecified agents primarily acting on the respiratory system	
		T50.7	Analeptics and opioid receptor antagonists	
970.1	Poisoning by Opiate Antagonists	T50.7	Analeptics and opioid receptor antagonists	
970.8	Poisoning by Other Specified Central Nervous System Stimulants	T50.9	Other and unspecified drugs, medicaments and biological substances	
970.9	Poisoning by Unspecified Central Nervous System Stimulant	T50.9	Other and unspecified drugs, medicaments and biological substances	
971.0	Poisoning by Parasympathomimetics	T44.0	Anticholinesterase agents	
		T44.1	Other parasympathomimetics [cholinergics]	
		T49.5	Ophthalmological drugs and preparations	
		T50.6	Antidotes and chelating agents, not elsewhere classified	
971.1	Poisoning by Parasympatholytics	T38.8	Other and unspecified hormones and their synthetic substitutes	
		T42.8	Antiparkinsonism drugs and other central muscle-tone depressants	
		T43.3	Phenothiazine antipsychotics and neuroleptics	
		T44.3	Other parasympatholytics [anticholinergics and antimuscarinics] and spasmolytics, not elsewhere classified	
		T46.3	Coronary vasodilators, not elsewhere classified	
		T49.2	Local astringents and local detergents	
		T49.5	Ophthalmological drugs and preparations	
971.2	Poisoning by Sympathomimetics	T42.8	Antiparkinsonism drugs and other central muscle-tone depressants	
		T44.3	Other parasympatholytics [anticholinergics and antimuscarinics] and spasmolytics, not elsewhere classified	
		T44.4	Predominantly alpha-adrenoreceptor agonists, not elsewhere classified	
		T44.5	Predominantly beta-adrenoreceptor agonists, not elsewhere classified	
		T44.9	Other and unspecified drugs primarily affecting the autonomic nervous system	
		T46.7	Peripheral vasodilators	
971.3	Poisoning by Sympatholytics	T44.6	Alpha-adrenoreceptor antagonists, not elsewhere classified	
		T44.7	Beta-adrenoreceptor antagonists, not elsewhere classified	
		T44.8	Centrally acting and adrenergic-neuron-blocking agents, not elsewhere classified	
		T46.7	Peripheral vasodilators	
971.9	Poisoning by Unspecified Drug Primarily Affecting Autonomic Nervous System	T44.9	Other and unspecified drugs primarily affecting the autonomic nervous system	
972.0	Poisoning by Cardiac Rhythm	T44.7	Beta-adrenoreceptor antagonists, not elsewhere classified	
		T46.1	Calcium-channel blockers	
		T46.2	Other antidysrhythmic drugs, not elsewhere classified	

ICD-9	Description	ICD-10	Description	(Continued)
972.1	Poisoning by Cardiotonic Glycosides and Drugs of Similar Action	T46.0	Cardiac-stimulant glycosides and drugs of similar action	
972.2	Poisoning by Antilipemic and Antiarteriosclerotic Drugs	T45.5	Anticoagulants	
		T46.6	Antihyperlipidaemic and antiarteriosclerotic drugs	
		T46.7	Peripheral vasodilators	
		T49.3	Emollients, demulcents and protectants	
972.3	Poisoning by Ganglion-Blocking Agents	T44.2	Ganglionic blocking drugs, not elsewhere classified	
		T46.9	Other and unspecified agents primarily affecting the cardiovascular system	
972.4	Poisoning by Coronary Vasodilators	T46.1	Calcium-channel blockers	
		T46.3	Coronary vasodilators, not elsewhere classified	
		T46.6	Antihyperlipidaemic and antiarteriosclerotic drugs	
		T46.7	Peripheral vasodilators	
972.5	Poisoning by Other Vasodilators	T42.8	Antiparkinsonism drugs and other central muscle-tone depressants	
		T44.3	Other parasympatholytics [anticholinergics and antimuscarinics] and spasmolytics, not elsewhere classified	
		T46.1	Calcium-channel blockers	
		T46.3	Coronary vasodilators, not elsewhere classified	
		T46.5	Other antihypertensive drugs, not elsewhere classified	
		T46.7	Peripheral vasodilators	
972.6	Poisoning by Other Antihypertensive Agents	T43.5	Other and unspecified antipsychotics and neuroleptics	
		T44.6	Alpha-adrenoreceptor antagonists, not elsewhere classified	
		T44.8	Centrally acting and adrenergic-neuron-blocking agents, not elsewhere classified	
		T46.1	Calcium-channel blockers	
		T46.4	Angiotensin-converting-enzyme inhibitors	
		T46.5	Other antihypertensive drugs, not elsewhere classified	
972.7	Poisoning by Antivaricose Drugs, Including Sclerosing Agents	T46.8	Antivaricose drugs, including sclerosing agents	
972.8	Poisoning by Capillary-active Drugs	T38.8	Other and unspecified hormones and their synthetic substitutes	
		T44.4	Predominantly alpha-adrenoreceptor agonists, not elsewhere classified	
		T46.9	Other and unspecified agents primarily affecting the cardiovascular system	
972.9	Poisoning by Other and Unspecified Agents Primarily Affecting the Cardiovascular System	T46.9	Other and unspecified agents primarily affecting the cardiovascular system	
973.0	Poisoning by Antacids and Antigastric Secretion Drugs	T47.0	Histamine H2-receptor antagonists	
		T47.1	Other antacids and anti-gastric-secretion drugs	
		T50.3	Electrolytic, caloric and water-balance agents	
973.1	Poisoning by Irritant Cathartics	T47.2	Stimulant laxatives	
973.2	Poisoning by Emollients Cathartics	T47.4	Other laxatives	
		T49.3	Emollients, demulcents and protectants	
		T55	Toxic effect of soaps and detergents	
973.3	Poisoning by Other Cathartics, Including Intestinal Atonia Drugs	T47.3	Saline and osmotic laxatives	
		T47.4	Other laxatives	
973.5	Poisoning by Antidiarrheal Drugs	T47.1	Other antacids and anti-gastric-secretion drugs	
		T47.6	Antidiarrhoeal drugs	
973.6	Poisoning by Emetics	T47.7	Emetics	
973.8	Poisoning by Other Specified Agents Primarily Affecting the Gastrointestinal System	T44.3	Other parasympatholytics [anticholinergics and antimuscarinics] and spasmolytics, not elsewhere classified	
		T47.1	Other antacids and anti-gastric-secretion drugs	
		T47.6	Antidiarrhoeal drugs	
		T47.8	Other agents primarily affecting the gastrointestinal system	
973.9	Poisoning by Unspecified Agents Primarily Affecting the Gastrointestinal System	T47.9	Agent primarily affecting the gastrointestinal system, unspecified	
974.0	Poisoning by Mercurial Diuretics	T50.2	Carbonic-anhydrase inhibitors, benzothiadiazides and other diuretics	
974.1	Poisoning by Purine Derivative Diuretics	T48.6	Antiasthmatics, not elsewhere classified	
		T50.2	Carbonic-anhydrase inhibitors, benzothiadiazides and other diuretics	
974.2	Poisoning by Carbonic Acid Anhydrase Inhibitors	T50.2	Carbonic-anhydrase inhibitors, benzothiadiazides and other diuretics	
974.3	Poisoning by Saluretics	T50.1	Loop [high-ceiling] diuretics	
		T50.2	Carbonic-anhydrase inhibitors, benzothiadiazides and other diuretics	
974.4	Poisoning by Other Diuretics	T47.3	Saline and osmotic laxatives	
		T50.0	Mineralocorticoids and their antagonists	
		T50.1	Loop [high-ceiling] diuretics	
		T50.2	Carbonic-anhydrase inhibitors, benzothiadiazides and other diuretics	

ICD-9	Description	ICD-10	Description	(Continued)
974.5	Poisoning by Electrolytic, Caloric, and Water-Balance Agents	T45.8	Other primarily systemic and haematological agents	
		T50.2	Carbonic-anhydrase inhibitors, benzothiadiazides and other diuretics	
		T50.3	Electrolytic, caloric and water-balance agents	
974.6	Poisoning by Other Mineral Salts, Not Elsewhere Classified	T49.7	Dental drugs, topically applied	
		T50.3	Electrolytic, caloric and water-balance agents	
		T50.9	Other and unspecified drugs, medicaments and biological substances	
		T57.8	Other specified inorganic substances	
974.7	Poisoning by Uric Acid Metabolism Drugs	T45.1	Antineoplastic and immunosuppressive drugs	
		T46.3	Coronary vasodilators, not elsewhere classified	
		T50.4	Drugs affecting uric acid metabolism	
975.0	Poisoning by Oxytocic Agents	T45.5	Anticoagulants	
		T48.0	Oxytocic drugs	
975.1	Poisoning by Smooth Muscle Relaxants	T44.3	Other parasympatholytics [anticholinergics and antimuscarinics] and spasmolytics, not elsewhere classified	
		T48.2	Other and unspecified agents primarily acting on muscles	
		T48.6	Antiasthmatics, not elsewhere classified	
975.2	Poisoning by Skeletal Muscle Relaxants	T42.8	Antiparkinsonism drugs and other central muscle-tone depressants	
		T48.1	Skeletal muscle relaxants [neuromuscular blocking agents]	
975.3	Poisoning by Other and Unspecified Drugs Acting on Muscles	T42.6	Other antiepileptic and sedative-hypnotic drugs	
		T48.2	Other and unspecified agents primarily acting on muscles	
975.4	Poisoning by Antitussives	T40.4	Other synthetic narcotics	
		T48.3	Antitussives	
		T48.4	Expectorants	
975.5	Poisoning by Expectorants	T48.4	Expectorants	
975.6	Poisoning by Anti-Common Cold Drugs	T44.9	Other and unspecified drugs primarily affecting the autonomic nervous system	
		T48.5	Anti-common-cold drugs	
975.7	Poisoning by Antiasthmatics	T44.5	Predominantly beta-adrenoreceptor agonists, not elsewhere classified	
		T45.0	Antiallergic and antiemetic drugs	
		T48.6	Antiasthmatics, not elsewhere classified	
975.8	Poisoning by Other and Unspecified Respiratory Drugs	T41.5	Therapeutic gases	
		T48.7	Other and unspecified agents primarily acting on the respiratory system	
		T59.7	Carbon dioxide	
976.0	Poisoning by Iodine (Local Anti-Infectives and Anti-Inflammatory Drugs)	T36.5	Aminoglycosides Streptomycin	
		T37.8	Other specified systemic anti-infectives and antiparasitics	
		T42.8	Antiparkinsonism drugs and other central muscle-tone depressants	
		T44.5	Predominantly beta-adrenoreceptor agonists, not elsewhere classified	
		T49.0	Local antifungal, anti-infective and anti-inflammatory drugs, not elsewhere classified	
		T49.6	Otorhinolaryngological drugs and preparations	
		T49.8	Other topical agents	
976.1	Poisoning by Antipruritics	T41.3	Local anaesthetics	
		T45.0	Antiallergic and antiemetic drugs	
		T49.0	Local antifungal, anti-infective and anti-inflammatory drugs, not elsewhere classified	
		T49.1	Antipruritics	
976.2	Poisoning by Local Astringents and Local Detergents	T49.2	Local astringents and local detergents	
976.3	Poisoning by Emollients, Demulcents, and Protectants	T47.4	Other laxatives	
		T49.3	Emollients, demulcents and protectants	
		T49.8	Other topical agents	
		T50.9	Other and unspecified drugs, medicaments and biological substances	
976.4	Poisoning by Keratolytics, Keratoplastics, Other Hair Treatment Drugs and Preparations	T45.1	Antineoplastic and immunosuppressive drugs	
		T45.3	Enzymes, not elsewhere classified	
		T46.7	Peripheral vasodilators	
		T49.0	Local antifungal, anti-infective and anti-inflammatory drugs, not elsewhere classified	
		T49.3	Emollients, demulcents and protectants	
		T49.4	Keratolytics, keratoplastics and other hair treatment drugs and preparations	
		T50.9	Other and unspecified drugs, medicaments and biological substances	
976.5	Poisoning by Eye Anti-infectives and Other Eye Drugs	T37.5	Antiviral drugs	
		T44.3	Other parasympatholytics [anticholinergics and antimuscarinics] and spasmolytics, not elsewhere classified	

ICD-9	Description	ICD-10	Description	(Continued)
976.5	Poisoning by Eye Anti-infectives and Other Eye Drugs	T44.9	Other and unspecified drugs primarily affecting the autonomic nervous system	
		T49.0	Local antifungal, anti-infective and anti-inflammatory drugs, not elsewhere classified	
		T49.5	Ophthalmological drugs and preparations	
976.6	Poisoning by Anti-infectives and Other Drugs and Preparations for Ear, Nose, and Throat	T41.3	Local anaesthetics	
		T49.0	Local antifungal, anti-infective and anti-inflammatory drugs, not elsewhere classified	
		T49.6	Otorhinolaryngological drugs and preparations	
976.8	Poisoning by Other Agents Primarily Affecting Skin and Mucous Membrane	T45.3	Enzymes, not elsewhere classified	
		T49.8	Other topical agents	
976.9	Poisoning by Unspecified Agent Primarily Affecting Skin and Mucous Membrane	T49.0	Local antifungal, anti-infective and anti-inflammatory drugs, not elsewhere classified	
		T49.9	Topical agent, unspecified	
977.0	Poisoning by Dietetics	T44.9	Other and unspecified drugs primarily affecting the autonomic nervous system	
		T45.0	Antiallergic and antiemetic drugs	
		T50.5	Appetite depressants	
		T50.9	Other and unspecified drugs, medicaments and biological substances	
977.1	Poisoning by Lipotropic Drugs	T47.5	Digestants	
		T50.6	Antidotes and chelating agents, not elsewhere classified	
		T50.9	Other and unspecified drugs, medicaments and biological substances	
977.2	Poisoning by Antidotes and Chelating Agents, Not Elsewhere Classified	T50.6	Antidotes and chelating agents, not elsewhere classified	
977.3	Poisoning by Alcohol Deterrents	T50.6	Antidotes and chelating agents, not elsewhere classified	
977.4	Poisoning by Pharmaceutical Excipients	T47.4	Other laxatives	
		T50.3	Electrolytic, caloric and water-balance agents	
		T50.9	Other and unspecified drugs, medicaments and biological substances	
977.8	Poisoning by Other Specified Drugs and Medicinal Substances	T45.8	Other primarily systemic and haematological agents	
		T50.8	Diagnostic agents	
977.9	Poisoning by Unspecified Drug or Medicinal Substance	T40.6	Other and unspecified narcotics	
		T49.9	Topical agent, unspecified	
		T50.9	Other and unspecified drugs, medicaments and biological substances	
978.0	Poisoning by BCG Vaccine	T50.9	Other and unspecified drugs, medicaments and biological substances	
978.1	Poisoning by Typhoid and Paratyphoid Vaccine	T50.9	Other and unspecified drugs, medicaments and biological substances	
978.2	Poisoning by Cholera Vaccine	T50.9	Other and unspecified drugs, medicaments and biological substances	
978.3	Poisoning by Plague Vaccine	T50.9	Other and unspecified drugs, medicaments and biological substances	
978.4	Poisoning by Tetanus Vaccine	T50.9	Other and unspecified drugs, medicaments and biological substances	
978.5	Poisoning by Diphtheria Vaccine	T50.9	Other and unspecified drugs, medicaments and biological substances	
978.6	Poisoning by Pertussis Vaccine, Including Combinations with Pertussis Component	T50.9	Other and unspecified drugs, medicaments and biological substances	
978.8	Poisoning by Other and Unspecified Bacterial Vaccines	T50.9	Other and unspecified drugs, medicaments and biological substances	
978.9	Poisoning by Mixed Bacterial Vaccines, Except Combinations with Pertussis Component	T50.9	Other and unspecified drugs, medicaments and biological substances	
979.0	Poisoning by Smallpox Vaccine	T50.9	Other and unspecified drugs, medicaments and biological substances	
979.1	Poisoning by Rabies Vaccine	T50.9	Other and unspecified drugs, medicaments and biological substances	
979.2	Poisoning by Typhus Vaccine	T50.9	Other and unspecified drugs, medicaments and biological substances	
979.3	Poisoning by Yellow Fever Vaccine	T50.9	Other and unspecified drugs, medicaments and biological substances	
979.4	Poisoning by Measles Vaccine	T50.9	Other and unspecified drugs, medicaments and biological substances	
979.5	Poisoning by Poliomyelitis Vaccine	T50.9	Other and unspecified drugs, medicaments and biological substances	
979.6	Poisoning by Other and Unspecified Viral and Rickettsial Vaccines	T50.9	Other and unspecified drugs, medicaments and biological substances	
979.7	Poisoning by Mixed Viral-rickettsial and Bacterial Vaccines, Except Combinations with Pertussis Component	T50.9	Other and unspecified drugs, medicaments and biological substances	
979.9	Poisoning by Other and Unspecified Vaccines and Biological Substances	T37.5	Antiviral drugs	
		T49.9	Topical agent, unspecified	
		T50.9	Other and unspecified drugs, medicaments and biological substances	
980.1	Toxic Effects, Methyl Alcohol	T51.1	Methanol	
980.2	Toxic Effects, Isopropyl Alcohol	T51.2	2-Propanol	
982.2	Toxic Effects, Carbon Disulfide	T65.4	Carbon disulfide	
982.3	Toxic Effects, Chlorinated Hydrocarbon Solvents	T41.0	Inhaled anaesthetics	
		T52.8	Other organic solvents	
		T53.2	Trichloroethylene	
		T53.3	Tetrachloroethylene	

ICD-9	Description	ICD-10	Description	(Continued)
982.3	Toxic Effects, Chlorinated Hydrocarbon Solvents	T53.4	Dichloromethane Methylene chloride	
		T53.6	Other halogen derivatives of aliphatic hydrocarbons	
		T53.7	Other halogen derivatives of aromatic hydrocarbons	
		T53.9	Halogen derivative of aliphatic and aromatic hydrocarbons, unspecified	
983.1	Toxic Effects, Hydrofluoric Acid	T54.2	Corrosive acids and acid-like substances	
		T57.8	Other specified inorganic substances	
		T65.8	Toxic effect of other specified substances	
984.0	Toxic Effects, Inorganic Lead Compounds	N14.3	Nephropathy induced by heavy metals	
		T56.0	Lead and its compounds	
984.9	Toxic Effects, Unspecified Lead Compound	M10.1	Lead-induced gout	
		N14.3	Nephropathy induced by heavy metals	
		T56.0	Lead and its compounds	
985.0	Toxic Effects, Mercury	N14.3	Nephropathy induced by heavy metals	
		T56.1	Mercury and its compounds	
985.1	Toxic Effects, Arsenic	L81.8	Other specified disorders of pigmentation	
		T56.1	Mercury and its compounds	
		T57.0	Arsenic and its compounds	
		T60.2	Other insecticides	
985.3	Toxic Effects, Beryllium	N14.3	Nephropathy induced by heavy metals	
		T56.7	Beryllium and its compounds	
985.5	Toxic Effects, Cadmium	N14.3	Nephropathy induced by heavy metals	
		T56.3	Cadmium and its compounds	
985.6	Toxic Effects, Chromium	N14.3	Nephropathy induced by heavy metals	
		T56.2	Chromium and its compounds	
985.8	Toxic Effects, Nickel	N14.3	Nephropathy induced by heavy metals	
		T56.4	Copper and its compounds	
		T56.5	Zinc and its compounds	
		T56.6	Tin and its compounds	
		T56.8	Other metals	
		T57.8	Other specified inorganic substances	
		T59.8	Other specified gases, fumes and vapours	
		T60.3	Herbicides and fungicides	
		T60.4	Rodenticides	
		T65.8	Toxic effect of other specified substances	
		T65.9	Toxic effect of unspecified substance	
985.9	Metal Fume Fever	T56.9	Metal, unspecified	
986	Toxic Effects, Carbon Monoxide	T58	Toxic effect of carbon monoxide from all sources	
987.6	Toxic Effects, Chlorine Gas	T59.4	Chlorine gas	
987.8	Toxic Effects, Ozone	T41.0	Inhaled anaesthetics	
		T49.4	Keratolytics, keratoplastics and other hair treatment drugs and preparations	
		T52.0	Petroleum products	
		T52.1	Benzene	
		T52.2	Homologues of benzene	
		T52.4	Ketones	
		T52.8	Other organic solvents	
		T53.0	Carbon tetrachloride	
		T53.1	Chloroform Trichloromethane	
		T53.2	Trichloroethylene	
		T53.3	Tetrachloroethylene	
		T53.4	Dichloromethane Methylene chloride	
		T53.6	Other halogen derivatives of aliphatic hydrocarbons	
		T53.7	Other halogen derivatives of aromatic hydrocarbons	
		T54.2	Corrosive acids and acid-like substances	
		T54.3	Corrosive alkalis and alkali-like substances	
		T54.9	Corrosive substance, unspecified	
		T56.2	Chromium and its compounds	
		T57.8	Other specified inorganic substances	
		T59.2	Formaldehyde	
		T59.5	Fluorine gas and hydrogen fluoride	
		T59.6	Hydrogen sulfide	
		T59.7	Carbon dioxide	

2458   The Medical Disability Advisor—Fourth Edition

ICD-9	Description	ICD-10	Description	(Continued)
987.8	Toxic Effects, Ozone	T59.8	Other specified gases, fumes and vapours	
		T59.9	Gases, fumes and vapours, unspecified	
		T60.0	Organophosphate and carbamate insecticides	
		T60.1	Halogenated insecticides	
		T60.8	Other pesticides	
		T65.0	Cyanides	
		T65.3	Nitroderivatives and aminoderivatives of benzene and its homologues	
		T65.4	Carbon disulfide	
		T65.5	Nitroglycerin and other nitric acids and esters	
		T65.8	Toxic effect of other specified substances	
988.0	Toxic Effects, Fish and Shellfish	T61.0	Ciguatera fish poisoning	
		T61.1	Scombroid fish poisoning	
		T61.2	Other fish and shellfish poisoning	
		T61.8	Toxic effect of other seafoods	
		T61.9	Toxic effect of unspecified seafood	
988.1	Toxic Effects, Mushrooms	T62.0	Ingested mushrooms	
988.2	Toxic Effects, Plants, Genus Toxicodendron	T62.1	Ingested berries	
		T62.2	Other ingested (parts of) plant(s)	
		T62.8	Other specified noxious substances eaten as food	
		T64	Toxic effect of aflatoxin and other mycotoxin food contaminants	
988.8	Other Specified Noxious Substances Eaten As Food	T62.8	Other specified noxious substances eaten as food	
		T62.9	Noxious substance eaten as food, unspecified	
988.9	Unspecified Noxious Substances Eaten As Food	T62.9	Noxious substance eaten as food, unspecified	
989.3	Toxic Effects, Organophosphate and Carbamate Pesticides	T60.0	Organophosphate and carbamate insecticides	
		T60.4	Rodenticides	
989.5	Insect or Spider Bites and Stings	T63.0	Snake venom	
		T63.1	Venom of other reptiles	
		T63.2	Venom of scorpion	
		T63.3	Venom of spider	
		T63.4	Venom of other arthropods	
		T63.5	Toxic effect of contact with fish	
		T63.6	Toxic effect of contact with other marine animals	
		T63.8	Toxic effect of contact with other venomous animals	
		T63.9	Toxic effect of contact with unspecified venomous animal	
989.8	Toxic Effects, Formaldehyde	T45.8	Other primarily systemic and haematological agents	
		T47.5	Digestants	
		T49.0	Local antifungal, anti-infective and anti-inflammatory drugs, not elsewhere classified	
		T49.8	Other topical agents	
		T52.1	Benzene	
		T52.8	Other organic solvents	
		T52.9	Organic solvent, unspecified	
		T53.6	Other halogen derivatives of aliphatic hydrocarbons	
		T53.7	Other halogen derivatives of aromatic hydrocarbons	
		T54.1	Other corrosive organic compounds	
		T54.2	Corrosive acids and acid-like substances	
		T55	Toxic effect of soaps and detergents	
		T56.8	Other metals	
		T57.0	Arsenic and its compounds	
		T57.8	Other specified inorganic substances	
		T59.2	Formaldehyde	
		T59.8	Other specified gases, fumes and vapours	
		T60.2	Other insecticides	
		T60.3	Herbicides and fungicides	
		T62.2	Other ingested (parts of) plant(s)	
		T62.8	Other specified noxious substances eaten as food	
		T65.2	Tobacco and nicotine	
		T65.3	Nitroderivatives and aminoderivatives of benzene and its homologues	
		T65.4	Carbon disulfide	
		T65.6	Paints and dyes, not elsewhere classified	
		T65.8	Toxic effect of other specified substances	
		T65.9	Toxic effect of unspecified substance	

ICD-9	Description	ICD-10	Description	(Continued)
991.0	Frostbite of Face	T33.0	Superficial frostbite of head	
		T34.0	Frostbite with tissue necrosis of head	
		T35.2	Unspecified frostbite of head and neck	
991.1	Frostbite of Hand	T33.5	Superficial frostbite of wrist and hand	
		T34.5	Frostbite with tissue necrosis of wrist and hand	
		T35.4	Unspecified frostbite of upper limb	
991.2	Frostbite of Foot	T33.8	Superficial frostbite of ankle and foot	
		T34.8	Frostbite with tissue necrosis of ankle and foot	
		T35.5	Unspecified frostbite of lower limb	
991.3	Frostbite of Other and Unspecified Sites	T33.1	Superficial frostbite of neck	
		T33.2	Superficial frostbite of thorax	
		T33.3	Superficial frostbite of abdominal wall, lower back and pelvis	
		T33.4	Superficial frostbite of arm	
		T33.6	Superficial frostbite of hip and thigh	
		T33.7	Superficial frostbite of knee and lower leg	
		T33.9	Superficial frostbite of other and unspecified sites	
		T34.1	Frostbite with tissue necrosis of neck	
		T34.2	Frostbite with tissue necrosis of thorax	
		T34.3	Frostbite with tissue necrosis of abdominal wall, lower back and pelvis	
		T34.4	Frostbite with tissue necrosis of arm	
		T34.6	Frostbite with tissue necrosis of hip and thigh	
		T34.7	Frostbite with tissue necrosis of knee and lower leg	
		T34.9	Frostbite with tissue necrosis of other and unspecified sites	
		T35.0	Superficial frostbite involving multiple body regions	
		T35.1	Frostbite with tissue necrosis involving multiple body regions	
		T35.2	Unspecified frostbite of head and neck	
		T35.3	Unspecified frostbite of thorax, abdomen, lower back and pelvis	
		T35.4	Unspecified frostbite of upper limb	
		T35.5	Unspecified frostbite of lower limb	
		T35.6	Unspecified frostbite involving multiple body regions	
		T35.7	Unspecified frostbite of unspecified site	
991.9	Unspecified Effect of Reduced Temperature	T69.9	Effect of reduced temperature, unspecified	
992.0	Heat Stroke or Sunstroke	T67.0	Heatstroke and sunstroke	
992.3	Heat Exhaustion, Anhydrotic	T67.3	Heat exhaustion, anhydrotic	
992.4	Heat Exhaustion Due to Salt Depletion	T67.4	Heat exhaustion due to salt depletion	
992.5	Heat Exhaustion	T67.5	Heat exhaustion, unspecified	
993.0	Barotitis Media	T70.0	Otitic barotrauma	
993.1	Barotrauma, Sinus	T70.1	Sinus barotrauma	
993.3	Caisson Disease	T70.3	Caisson disease [decompression sickness] Compressed-air disease Diver's palsy or paralysis	
994.6	Motion Sickness	T75.3	Motion sickness	
995.0	Anaphylactic Shock, Other	T78.0	Anaphylactic shock due to adverse food reaction	
		T78.2	Anaphylactic shock, unspecified	
		T88.6	Anaphylactic shock due to adverse effect of correct drug or medicament properly administered	
995.1	Angioneurotic Edema	T78.3	Angioneurotic oedema	
995.3	Multiple Chemical Sensitivity	T78.4	Allergy, unspecified	
998.5	Wound Infection, Postoperative	T81.4	Infection following a procedure, not elsewhere classified	
		T81.8	Other complications of procedures, not elsewhere classified	
999.4	Anaphylactic Shock Due to Serum	T80.5	Anaphylactic shock due to serum	
V22.0	Supervision of Normal First Pregnancy	Z34.0	Supervision of normal first pregnancy	
V22.1	Supervision of Other Normal Pregnancy	Z34.8	Supervision of other normal pregnancy	
		Z34.9	Supervision of normal pregnancy, unspecified	
V22.2	Pregnant State, Incidental	Z32.1	Pregnancy confirmed	
		Z33	Pregnant state, incidental	
V45.3	Intestinal Bypass or Anastomosis Status	Z98.0	Intestinal bypass and anastomosis status	
V55.1	Gastrostomy	Z43.1	Attention to gastrostomy	

Index of ICD-9 CM

Diagnoses (for Procedures, see page 2499)

002	Typhoid Fever and Paratyphoid Fevers 2204
002.0	Typhoid Fever 2204
002.1	Paratyphoid Fever A 2204
002.2	Paratyphoid Fever B 2204
002.3	Paratyphoid Fever C 2204
002.9	Paratyphoid Fever 2204
003	Salmonella Infections, Other 888, 1866
003.0	Salmonellosis 1866
003.1	Salmonella Septicemia 1866
003.2	Salmonella Infections, Localized 1866
003.8	Salmonella Infections, Other Specified 1866
003.9	Salmonella Infection, Unspecified 1866
004	Dysentery (Shigellosis) 888, 1910
004.8	Shigella Infections, Other Specified 1910
004.9	Shigellosis 1910
005	Other Food Poisoning 286, 888
005.0	Staphylococcal Food Poisoning 888
005.1	Botulism 286, 888
005.2	Food Poisoning Due to Clostridium Perfringens 888
005.3	Food Poisoning Due to Other Clostridia 888
005.4	Food Poisoning Due to Vibrio Parahaemolyticus 888
005.8	Food Poisoning, Bacterial, Other 888
005.9	Food Poisoning, Unspecified 888
006	Amebiasis 109
006.0	Amebic Dysentery, Acute, Without Mention of Abscess 109
006.1	Amebiasis, Chronic Intestinal, Without Mention of Abscess 109
006.2	Amebic Nondysenteric Colitis 109
006.3	Amebic Liver Abscess 109
006.4	Amebic Lung Abscess 109
006.5	Amebic Brain Abscess 109
006.6	Amebic Skin Ulceration 109
006.8	Amebic Infection of Other Sites 109
006.9	Amebiasis 109
007	Protozoal Intestinal Diseases, Other 989
007.1	Giardiasis 989
007.3	Intestinal Trichomoniasis 989
007.8	Protozoal Intestinal Diseases, Other Specified 989
007.9	Protozoal Intestinal Disease, Unspecified 989
008.0	Escherichia Coli (E. Coli) 767
008.00	Escherichia Coli, Unspecified 767
008.09	E. Coli Infections, Other Intestinal 767
009	Dysentery 755
009.0	Colitis, Enteritis, and Gastroenteritis, Infectious 973
009.1	Colitis, Enteritis, and Gastroenteritis of Presumed Infectious Origin 973
009.2	Diarrhea, Infectious 973, 2177
009.3	Diarrhea of Presumed Infectious Origin 973
011	Tuberculosis, Pulmonary 2194
011.0	Tuberculosis of Lung, Infiltrative 2194
011.4	Tuberculous Fibrosis of Lung 2194
011.8	Tuberculosis, Pulmonary, Other Specified 2194
011.9	Tuberculosis, Respiratory (Unspecified) 2194
012	Tuberculosis, Respiratory, Other 2194
015	Tuberculosis of Bones and Joints 1709
015.0	Tuberculosis of Vertebral Column (Pott's Disease) 1709
021	Tularemia 2197
021.0	Tularemia, Ulceroglandular 2197
021.1	Tularemia, Enteric 2197
021.2	Tularemia, Pulmonary 2197
021.3	Tularemia, Oculoglandular 2197
021.8	Tularemia, Other Specified 2197
021.9	Tularemia, Unspecified 2197
023	Brucellosis 306
023.0	Brucella Melitensis 306
023.1	Brucella Abortus 306
023.2	Brucella Suis 306
023.3	Brucella Canis 306
023.8	Brucellosis, Other 306
023.9	Brucellosis, Unspecified 306
026	Rat-bite Fever 2197
027.1	Erysipeloid 831
032.82	Diphtheritic Myocarditis 1428
034	Streptococcal Sore Throat 2005
034.0	Strep Throat 2005
035	Erysipelas 830
036.43	Meningococcal Myocarditis 1428
037	Tetanus 2060
038	Septicemia 1905, 1907
038.0	Streptococcal Septicemia 1905
038.1	Staphylococcal Septicemia 1905
038.2	Pneumococcal Septicemia 1905
038.3	Septicemia Due to Anaerobes 1905
038.4	Septicemia Due to Other Gram-negative Organisms 1905
038.8	Septicemias, Other Specified 1905
038.9	Sepsis, Unspecified 1905
039	Actinomycotic Infections 57
039.0	Actinomycotic Infections, Cutaneous 57
039.1	Actinomycotic Infections, Pulmonary 57
039.2	Actinomycotic Infections, Abdominal 57
039.3	Actinomycotic Infections, Cervicofacial 57
039.4	Actinomycotic Infections, Due to Madura Foot 57
039.8	Actinomycotic Infections, Other Specified Sites 57
039.9	Actinomycosis, Unspecified Site 57

040.0	Gas Gangrene (Bacillus) 967
040.1	Rhinoscleroma 1842
040.89	Toxic Shock Syndrome 2152
042	Acquired Immune Deficiency Syndrome (AIDS) 53
042.0	Human Immunodeficiency Virus Infection with Specified Infections 1126
042.1	Human Immunodeficiency Virus Infection Causing Other Specified Infections 1126
042.2	Human Immunodeficiency Virus Infection with Specified Malignant Neoplasms 1126
042.9	AIDS (Acquired Immunodeficiency Syndrome, Unspecified) 53
043	Human Immunodeficiency Virus Infection Causing Other Specified Conditions 1126
043.0	Human Immunodeficiency Virus Infection Causing Lymphadenopathy 1126
043.1	Human Immunodeficiency Virus Infection Causing Specified Diseases of the Central Nervous System 1126
043.2	Human Immunodeficiency Virus Infection Causing Other Disorders Involving Immune Mechanism 1126
043.3	Human Immunodeficiency Virus Infection Causing Other Specified Conditions 1126
043.9	AIDS-related Complex, Unspecified 53
044	HIV (Human Immunodeficiency Virus) 1126
044.0	Human Immunodeficiency Virus Infection Causing Specified Acute Infections 1126
044.9	HIV (Human Immunodeficiency Virus Infection, Unspecified) 1126
045	Polio (Poliomyelitis, Acute) 1683
045.1	Acute Poliomyelitis with Other Paralysis 1683
045.2	Acute Nonparalytic Poliomyelitis 1683
045.9	Acute Poliomyelitis, Unspecified 1683
047.9	Aseptic Meningitis 205
048.89	Toxic Shock Syndrome 2152
052	Chickenpox (Varicella) 490
052.0	Postvaricella Encephalitis 490
052.1	Varicella (Hemorrhagic) Pneumonitis 490
052.7	Chickenpox with Other Specified Complications 490
052.8	Chickenpox with Unspecified Complication 490
052.9	Chickenpox (Varicella without Mention of Complication) 490
053	Shingles (Herpes Zoster) 1110
053.9	Herpes Zoster, Unspecified (Shingles without Mention of Complication) 1110
054	Herpes Simplex 1108
054.0	Eczema Herpeticum 1108
054.1	Genital Herpes 1108
054.2	Herpetic Gingivostomatitis 1108
054.3	Herpetic Meningoencephalitis 1108
054.4	Herpetic Septicemia 1108
054.42	Dendritic Keratitis 1257
054.43	Herpes Simplex Disciform Keratitis 1108
054.5	Herpetic Septicemia 1108
054.6	Herpetic Whitlow 1108
054.7	Herpes Simplex with Other Specified Complications 1108
054.8	Herpes Simplex with Unspecified Complication 1108
054.9	Herpes Simplex, Unspecified 1108
055	Measles 1858
055.0	Postmeasles Encephalitis 1858
055.1	Postmeasles Pneumonia 1858
055.2	Postmeasles Otitis Media 1858
055.7	Measles with Other Specified Complications 1858
055.8	Measles with Unspecified Complication 1858
055.9	Measles (Rubeola) 1858
056	German Measles (Rubella) 1856
056.0	Rubella with Neurological Complications 1856
056.7	Rubella with Other Specified Complications 1856
056.8	Rubella with Unspecified Complications 1856
056.9	Rubella Without Mention of Complication 1856
060	Yellow Fever 2307
060.1	Urban Yellow Fever 2307
060.9	Jungle Yellow Fever 2307
061	Dengue Fever 656
062	Encephalitis, Mosquito-Borne Viral 827
062.1	Encephalomyelitis, Western Equine 827
062.2	Encephalitis, Eastern Equine 827
062.3	Encephalitis, St. Louis 2000
062.9	Encephalitis, Equine 827
064	Encephalitis, Viral, Transmitted by Other and Unspecified Arthropods 827
066.1	Colorado Tick Fever 541
070	Viral Hepatitis 1081, 1083, 1085, 1091
070.0	Hepatitis, Viral Type A with Hepatic Coma 1081
070.1	Hepatitis, Viral Type A Without Mention of Hepatic Coma 1081
070.2	Hepatitis, Viral Type B with Hepatic Coma 1083
070.3	Hepatitis, Viral Type B Without Mention of Hepatic Coma 1083
070.30	Hepatitis, Viral Type B Without Mention of Hepatic Coma and Hepatitis Delta 1083
070.41	Hepatitis, Viral Type C with Hepatic Coma, Other Specified 1085
070.5	Hepatitis, Viral Type C Without Mention of Hepatic Coma, Other Specified 1085
070.51	Hepatitis, Viral Type C 1085
070.9	Hepatitis, Viral Without Mention of Hepatic Coma, Unspecified 1091
071	Rabies 1773
072	Mumps (Infectious Parotitis) 1404
072.0	Mumps Orchitis 1404
072.1	Mumps Meningitis 1404
072.2	Mumps Encephalitis 1404
072.3	Mumps Pancreatitis 1404
072.7	Mumps with Other Specified Complications (Hepatitis, Polyneuropathy) 1404
072.8	Mumps with Unspecified Complication 1404
072.9	Mumps Without Mention of Complication, Unspecified 1404
074.23	Coxsackie Myocarditis 1428
075	Mononucleosis, Infectious 1390
076	Trachoma 2161

076.0	Trachoma, Initial Stage 2161
076.1	Trachoma, Active Stage 2161
076.9	Trachoma, Unspecified 2161
077.99	Viral Conjunctivitis 556
078.1	Viral Warts 2294, 2296, 2298
078.10	Warts, Viral 2296, 2298
078.19	Warts, Genital 2294
078.3	Cat Scratch Disease 435
080	Typhus, Louse-Borne 2206
081	Typhus, Other 2206
081.0	Typhus, Murine (Fever) 2206
081.2	Typhus, Scrub 2206
081.9	Typhus Fever, Unspecified 2206
082	Tick-borne Rickettsioses 1845
082.0	Rocky Mountain Spotted Fever 1845
082.8	Tick-borne Rickettsioses, Other Specified 1845
082.9	Tick-borne Rickettsiosis, Unspecified 1845
083	Other Rickettsiosis 1845
084	Malaria 1330
084.0	Malaria Fever (Falciparum Malaria) 1330
084.1	Malaria, Vivax (Benign Tertian) 1330
084.2	Malaria, Quartan 1330
084.3	Malaria, Ovale 1330
084.4	Malaria, Other 1330
084.5	Malaria, Mixed 1330
084.6	Malaria, Unspecified 1330
084.7	Malaria, Induced 1330
084.8	Blackwater Fever 1330
084.9	Malaria, Other Pernicious Complications of 1330
086	Trypanosomiasis 479
086.0	Chagas' Disease with Heart Involvement 479
086.1	Chagas' Disease with Other Organ Involvement 479
086.2	Chagas' Disease Without Mention of Organ Involvement 479
086.3	Trypanosomiasis, Gambian 479
086.4	Trypanosomiasis, Rhodesian 479
086.5	Trypanosomiasis, African, Unspecified 479
086.9	Trypanosomiasis, Unspecified 479
088.81	Lyme Disease 1319
088.9	Arthropod-borne Disease, Unspecified 1319
090	Syphilis, Congenital 2033
091	Syphilis, Early, Symptomatic 2033
091.0	Syphilis, Genital (Primary) 2033
091.1	Syphilis, Primary Anal 2033
091.2	Syphilis, Primary, Other 2033
091.3	Syphilis of Skin or Mucous Membrane, Secondary 2033
091.4	Adenopathy Due to Secondary Syphilis 2033
091.5	Uveitis Due to Secondary Syphilis 2033
091.6	Syphilis, Secondary of Viscera and Bone 2033
091.7	Syphilis, Secondary, Relapse 2033
091.8	Syphilis, Secondary, Other Forms of 2033
091.9	Syphilis, Secondary, Unspecified 2033
092	Syphilis, Early, Latent 2033
092.0	Syphilis, Early, Latent, Serological Relapse After Treatment 2033
092.9	Syphilis, Early, Latent, Unspecified 2033
93.0	Physical Therapy 1643
093.0	Aneurysm of Aorta, Specified As Syphilitic 2033
93.01	Functional Evaluation 1643
93.02	Orthotic Evaluation 1643
93.03	Prosthetic Evaluation 1643
93.04	Manual Testing of Muscle Function 1643
93.05	Range of Motion Testing 1643
93.06	Measurement of Limb Length 1643
93.07	Body Measurement 1643
93.09	Diagnostic Physical Therapy Procedure, Other 1643
93.1	Physical Therapy Exercises 1643
093.1	Syphilitic Aortitis 2033
93.11	Assisting Exercise 1643
93.12	Active Musculoskeletal Exercise, Other 1643
93.13	Resistive Exercise 1643
93.14	Training in Joint Movements 1643
93.15	Mobilization of Spine 1643
93.16	Mobilization of Other Joints 1643
93.17	Passive Musculoskeletal Exercise, Other 1643
93.18	Breathing Exercise 1643
93.19	Exercise, Not Elsewhere Classified 1643
93.2	Physical Therapy Musculoskeletal Manipulation, Other 1643
093.2	Syphilitic Endocarditis 2033
93.21	Traction, Manual and Mechanical 1643
93.22	Ambulation and Pit Training 1643
93.23	Orthotic Device Fitting 1643
93.24	Training in Use of Prosthetic or Orthotic Device 1643
93.25	Forced Extension of Limb 1643
93.26	Manual Rupture of Joint Adhesions 1643
93.27	Stretching of Muscle or Tendon 1643
93.28	Stretching of Fascia 1643
93.29	Forcible Correction of Deformity, Other 1643
93.3	Physical Therapy Therapeutic Procedures, Other 1643
93.31	Pool Exercise, Assisted 1643
93.32	Whirlpool Treatment 1643
93.33	Hydrotherapy, Other 1643
93.34	Diathermy 1643
93.35	Heat Therapy, Other (Hot Packs, Paraffin Bath) 1643
93.36	Cardiac Retraining 1643
93.37	Prenatal Training 1643
93.38	Physical Therapy, Combined, Without Mention of the Components 1643
093.8	Syphilis, Cardiovascular, Other Specified 2033
093.9	Syphilis, Cardiovascular, Unspecified 2033
094	Neurosyphilis 986
094.0	Tabes Dorsalis 986
094.1	Paresis, General 986
094.2	Meningitis, Syphilitic 2033

Index of ICD-9 CM

094.3	Neurosyphilis, Asymptomatic 2033
094.8	Neurosyphilis, Other Specified 2033
094.9	Neurosyphilis, Unspecified 2033
095	Syphilis, Late with Symptoms, Other Forms of 986
095.8	Syphilis, Other Specified Forms of Late Symptomatic 986
095.9	Syphilis, Late Symptomatic, Unspecified 986
096	Syphilis, Late, Latent 986
097	Syphilis, Other and Unspecified 2033
097.9	Syphilis 2033
098	Gonorrhea 1010
098.0	Gonococcal Infection, Acute of Lower Genitourinary Tract 1010
098.1	Gonococcal Infection, Acute of Upper Genitourinary Tract 1010
098.13	Gonococcal epididymo-orchitis (Acute) Gonococcal orchitis (Acute) 819
098.2	Gonococcal Infection, Chronic of Lower Genitourinary Tract 1010
098.3	Gonococcal Infection, Chronic of Upper Genitourinary Tract 1010
098.33	Gonococcal Epididymo-Orchitis, Chronic 819
098.4	Gonococcal Infection of Eye 1010
098.5	Gonococcal Infection 1010
098.6	Gonococcal Infection of Pharynx 1010
098.7	Gonococcal Infection of Anus and Rectum 1010
098.8	Gonococcal Infection of Other Specified Sites 1010
099	Venereal Diseases, Other 481
099.0	Chancroid 481
099.3	Reiter's Syndrome (Disease) 1798
099.4	Urethritis, Other Nongonococcal 2218
099.40	Urethritis, Other Nongonococcal, Unspecified 2218
099.8	Other Specified Venereal Disease 481
099.9	Venereal Disease, Unspecified 481
101	Trench Mouth (Vincent's Angina) 2181
110	Dermatophytosis (Tinea) 2095
110.0	Tinea (Dermatophytosis) 2095
110.1	Dermatophytosis of Nail 2095
110.2	Dermatophytosis of Hand 2095
110.3	Dermatophytosis of Groin and Perianal Area 2095
110.4	Athlete's Foot (Dermatophytosis of Foot) 2095
110.5	Dermatophytosis of the Body 2095
110.6	Dermatophytosis, Deep Seated 2095
110.8	Dermatophytosis of Specified Sites 2095
110.9	Dermatophytosis of Unspecified Site 2095
111	Dermatomycosis, Other and Unspecified 2095
111.8	Dermatomycoses, Other Specified 2095
111.9	Dermatomycosis, Unspecified 2095
112	Yeast Infection (Candidiasis) 405
112.0	Candidiasis of Mouth 405
112.1	Candidiasis of Vulva and Vagina 405
112.2	Candidiasis of Other Urogenital Sites 405
112.3	Candidiasis of Skin and Nails 405
112.5	Candidiasis (Systemic) 405
112.8	Candidiasis of Other Specified Sites 405
112.9	Candidiasis, Unspecified Site 405
114	Coccidioidomycosis 525
114.0	Coccidioidomycosis, Primary (Pulmonary) 525
114.1	Coccidioidomycosis, Primary (Extrapulmonary) 525
114.2	Coccidioidal Meningitis 525
114.3	Coccidioidomycosis, Other Forms of Progressive 525
114.4	Coccidioidomycosis, Chronic Pulmonary 525
114.5	Coccidioidomycosis, Unspecified Pulmonary 525
114.9	Coccidioidomycosis, Unspecified 525
115	Histoplasmosis 1121
115.0	Infection by Histoplasma Capsulatum 1121
115.10	Without Mention of Manifestation 1121
115.12	Retinitis 1121
115.13	Pericarditis 1121
115.14	Endocarditis 1121
115.15	Pneumonia 1121
115.5	Infection by Histoplasma Duboisii 1121
115.90	Histoplasmosis Without Mention of Manifestation, Unspecified 1121
116	Blastomycotic Infection 266
116.0	Blastomycosis 266
116.1	Paracoccidioidomycosis 266
116.2	Lobomycosis 266
117.2	Chromoblastomycosis 508
117.5	Cryptococcosis 608
122	Echinococcosis 772
122.0	Echinococcus Granulosus Infection of Liver 772
122.1	Echinococcus Granulosus Infection of Lung 772
122.2	Echinococcus Granulosus Infection of Thyroid 772
122.3	Echinococcus Granulosus Infection, Other 772
122.4	Echinococcus Granulosus Infection, Unspecified 772
122.5	Echinococcus Multilocularis Infection of Liver 772
122.6	Echinococcus Multilocularis Infection, Other 772
122.7	Echinococcus Multilocularis Infection, Unspecified 772
122.8	Echinococcus, Unspecified, of Liver 772
122.9	Echinococcus, Other and Unspecified 772
124	Trichinosis 2183
125	Filarial Infection and Dracontiasis 881
125.6	Other Specified Filariasis 881
125.9	Filariasis, Unspecified 881
130	Toxoplasmosis 2154
130.0	Meningoencephalitis Due to Toxoplasmosis 2154
130.1	Conjunctivitis Due to Toxoplasmosis 2154
130.2	Chorioretinitis Due to Toxoplasmosis 2154
130.3	Myocarditis Due to Toxoplasmosis 1428
130.4	Pneumonitis Due to Toxoplasmosis 2154
130.5	Hepatitis Due to Toxoplasmosis 2154
130.7	Toxoplasmosis of Other Unspecified Sites 2154
130.8	Multisystemic Disseminated Toxoplasmosis 2154
130.9	Toxoplasmosis, Unspecified 2154
131	Trichomoniasis 2185
131.0	Trichomoniasis, Urogenital 2185

131.00	Trichomoniasis, Unspecified Urogenital 2185		150.1	Neoplasm, Thoracic Esophagus, Malignant 356
131.01	Trichomonal Vaginitis 2185		150.2	Neoplasm, Abdominal Esophagus, Malignant 356
131.02	Trichomonal Urethritis 2185		150.3	Neoplasm, Upper Third of Esophagus, Malignant 356
131.03	Trichomonal Prostatitis 2185		150.4	Neoplasm, Middle Third of Esophagus, Malignant 356
131.8	Trichomoniasis, Other Specified Sites 2185		150.5	Neoplasm, Lower Third of Esophagus, Malignant 356
131.9	Trichomoniasis, Unspecified 2185		150.8	Neoplasm, Other Specified Part of Esophagus, Malignant 356
135	Sarcoidosis 1875		150.9	Cancer, Esophagus 356
136	Other and Unspecified Infectious and Parasitic Diseases 244		151	Cancer, Stomach 391
136.1	Behçet's Syndrome 244		151.0	Neoplasm, Cardia of Stomach, Malignant 391
136.3	Pneumocystis Carinii Pneumonia 1663		151.1	Neoplasm, Pylorus, Malignant 391
136.4	Psorospermiasis 1202		151.2	Neoplasm, Pyloric Antrum, Malignant 391
136.5	Sarcosporidiosis 1202		151.3	Neoplasm, Fundus of Stomach, Malignant 391
136.9	Infection 1202		151.4	Neoplasm, Body of Stomach, Malignant 391
137	Late Effects of Tuberculosis 2194		151.5	Neoplasm, Lesser Curvature, Malignant, Unspecified 391
138	Post Poliomyelitis Syndrome 1697		151.6	Neoplasm, Greater Curvature, Malignant, Unspecified 391
140	Neoplasm, Lip, Malignant 338		151.8	Neoplasm, Other Specified Sites of Stomach, Malignant 391
141	Neoplasm, Tongue, Malignant 399		151.9	Cancer, Stomach 391
141.0	Neoplasm, Base of Tongue, Malignant 399		152	Neoplasm, Small Intestine (Include Duodenum), Malignant 389
141.1	Neoplasm, Dorsal Surface of Tongue, Malignant 399		152.0	Neoplasm, Duodenum, Malignant 389
141.2	Neoplasm, Tip and Lateral Border of Tongue, Malignant 399		152.1	Neoplasm, Jejunum, Malignant 389
141.3	Neoplasm, Ventral Surface of Tongue, Malignant 399		152.2	Neoplasm, Ileum, Malignant 389
141.4	Neoplasm, Anterior Two-thirds of Tongue, Malignant, Part Unspecified 399		152.8	Neoplasm, Other Specified Sites of Small Intestine, Malignant 389
141.5	Neoplasm, Junctional Zone, Malignant 399		152.9	Cancer, Small Intestine (Including Duodenum) 389
141.6	Neoplasm, Lingual Tonsil, Malignant 399		153	Cancer, Colon 354
141.8	Neoplasm, Other Sites of Tongue, Malignant 399		153.0	Neoplasm, Hepatic Flexure of Colon, Malignant 354
141.9	Cancer, Tongue, Unspecified 399		153.1	Neoplasm, Transverse Colon, Malignant 354
142	Neoplasm, Major Salivary Glands, Malignant 338		153.2	Neoplasm, Descending Colon, Malignant 354
143	Neoplasm, Gum, Malignant 338		153.3	Neoplasm, Sigmoid Colon, Malignant 354
144	Neoplasm, Floor of Mouth, Malignant 338		153.4	Neoplasm, Cecum, Malignant 354
145	Neoplasm, Other and Unspecified Parts of Mouth, Malignant 338, 366		153.5	Neoplasm, Appendix, Malignant 354
			153.6	Neoplasm, Ascending Colon, Malignant 354
145.5	Neoplasm, Palate, Malignant, Unspecified 338		153.7	Neoplasm, Splenic Flexure of Colon, Malignant 354
145.9	Cancer, Mouth 366		153.8	Neoplasm, Other Specified Sites of Large Intestine, Malignant 354
146	Cancer, Oropharynx (Throat) 369		153.9	Neoplasm, Colon, Malignant, Unspecified 354
146.0	Neoplasm, Tonsil, Malignant 369		154	Cancer, Rectum (Rectosigmoid Junction and Anus) 384
146.1	Neoplasm, Tonsillar Fossa, Malignant 369		154.0	Neoplasm, Rectosigmoid Junction (Colon Cancer), Malignant 384
146.2	Neoplasm, Tonsillar Pillars, Malignant 369		154.1	Cancer, Rectum 384
146.3	Neoplasm, Vallecula, Malignant 369		154.2	Neoplasm, Anal Canal, Malignant 384
146.4	Neoplasm, Anterior Aspect of Epiglottis, Malignant 369		154.3	Neoplasm, Anus, Malignant, Unspecified 384
146.5	Neoplasm, Junctional Region, Malignant 369		154.8	Neoplasm, Rectum, Rectosigmoid Junction, and Anus, Malignant, Other 384
146.6	Neoplasm, Lateral Wall of Oropharynx, Malignant 369			
146.7	Neoplasm, Posterior Wall of Oropharynx, Malignant 369		155	Neoplasm, Liver and Intrahepatic Bile Ducts, Malignant 360
146.8	Neoplasm, Other Specified Sites of Oropharynx, Malignant 369		155.0	Hepatocarcinoma (Malignant Neoplasm of Liver, Primary) 360
146.9	Cancer, Oropharynx, Unspecified 369		155.1	Neoplasm, Intrahepatic Bile Ducts, Malignant 360
147	Neoplasm, Nasopharynx, Malignant 338		155.2	Angiosarcoma, Hepatic 360, 1077
148	Neoplasm, Hypopharynx, Malignant 338		157	Cancer, Pancreas 375
149	Neoplasm, Other and Ill-defined Sites Within the Lip, Oral Cavity, and Pharynx, Malignant 338		157.0	Neoplasm, Head of Pancreas, Malignant 375
			157.1	Neoplasm, Body of Pancreas, Malignant 375
150	Neoplasm, Esophagus, Malignant 356		157.2	Neoplasm, Tail of Pancreas, Malignant 375
150.0	Neoplasm, Cervical Esophagus, Malignant 356		157.3	Neoplasm, Pancreatic Duct, Malignant 375
			157.4	Neoplasm, Islets of Langerhans, Malignant 375

157.8	Neoplasm, Other Specified Sites of Pancreas, Malignant 375
157.9	Cancer, Pancreas, Part Unspecified 375
162.0	Neoplasm, Trachea, Malignant 338
162.2	Neoplasm, Main Bronchus, Malignant 363
162.3	Neoplasm, Upper Lobe, Bronchus or Lung, Malignant 363
162.4	Neoplasm, Middle Lobe, Bronchus or Lung, Malignant 363
162.5	Neoplasm, Lower Lobe, Bronchus or Lung, Malignant 363
162.8	Neoplasm, Other Parts of Bronchus or Lung, Malignant 363
162.9	Cancer, Lung 363
163	Pleural Cancer (Mesothelioma) 377
163.0	Neoplasm, Parietal Pleura, Malignant 377
163.1	Neoplasm, Visceral Pleura, Malignant 377
163.8	Neoplasm, Other Specified Sites of Pleura, Malignant 377
163.9	Cancer, Pleura 377
170	Cancer, Bone (Malignant Neoplasm of Bone and Articular Cartilage) 281, 341
170.0	Neoplasm, Bones of Skull and Face, Malignant, Except Mandible 281
170.1	Neoplasm, Mandible, Malignant 281
170.2	Neoplasm, Vertebral Column, Excluding Sacrum and Coccyx, Malignant 281
170.3	Neoplasm, Ribs, Sternum, and Clavicle, Malignant 281
170.4	Neoplasm, Scapula and Long Bones of Upper Limb, Malignant 281
170.5	Neoplasm, Short Bones of Upper Limb, Malignant 281
170.6	Neoplasm, Pelvic Bones, Sacrum, and Coccyx, Malignant 281
170.7	Neoplasm, Long Bones of Lower Limb, Malignant 281
170.8	Neoplasm, Short Bones of Lower Limb, Malignant 281
170.9	Bone Tumors 281
172	Melanoma, Malignant of Skin 387
172.0	Malignant Melanoma of Lip 387
172.1	Malignant Melanoma of Eyelid, Including Canthus 387
172.2	Malignant Melanoma of Ear and External Auditory Canal 387
172.3	Malignant Melanoma of Other and Unspecified Parts of Face 387
172.4	Malignant Melanoma of Scalp and Neck 387
172.5	Malignant Melanoma of Trunk, Except Scrotum 387
172.6	Malignant Melanoma of Upper Limb, Including Shoulder 387
172.7	Malignant Melanoma of Lower Limb, Including Hip 387
172.8	Malignant Melanoma of Other Specified Sites of Skin 387
172.9	Melanoma of Skin, Site Unspecified 387
173	Neoplasm, Skin, Malignant, Other 387
173.0	Neoplasm, Skin of Lip, Malignant, Other 387
173.1	Neoplasm, Eyelid, Including Canthus, Malignant, Other 387
173.2	Neoplasm, Skin of Ear and External Auditory Canal, Malignant, Other 387
173.3	Neoplasm, Skin of Other and Unspecified Parts of Face, Malignant, Other 387
173.4	Neoplasm, Scalp and Skin of Neck, Malignant, Other 387
173.5	Neoplasm, Skin of Trunk, Except Scrotum, Malignant, Other 387
173.6	Neoplasm, Skin of Upper Limb, Including Shoulder, Malignant, Other 387
173.7	Neoplasm, Skin of Lower Limb, Including Hip, Malignant, Other 387
173.8	Neoplasm, Other Specified Sites of Skin, Malignant, Other 387
173.9	Skin Cancer, Unspecified 387
174	Neoplasm, Female Breast, Nipple and Areola, Malignant (Paget's Disease) 1559
174.0	Paget's Disease of Breast 347, 1559
174.1	Neoplasm, Female Breast, Central Portion, Malignant 347
174.2	Neoplasm, Female Breast, Upper-inner Quadrant, Malignant 347
174.3	Neoplasm, Female Breast, Lower-inner Quadrant, Malignant 347
174.4	Neoplasm, Female Breast, Upper-outer Quadrant, Malignant 347
174.5	Neoplasm, Female Breast, Lower-outer Quadrant, Malignant 347
174.6	Neoplasm, Female Breast, Axillary Tail, Malignant 347
174.8	Neoplasm, Other Specified Sites of Female Breast, Malignant 347
174.9	Cancer, Breast, Unspecified 347
175	Malignant Neoplasm of the Male Breast 347
176	Kaposi's Sarcoma 1253
176.0	Kaposi's Sarcoma, Skin 1253
176.1	Kaposi's Sarcoma, Soft Tissue 1253
176.2	Kaposi's Sarcoma, Palate 1253
176.3	Kaposi's Sarcoma, Gastrointestinal Sites 1253
176.4	Kaposi's Sarcoma, Lung 1253
176.5	Kaposi's Sarcoma, Lymph Nodes 1253
176.8	Kaposi's Sarcoma, Other Specified Sites 1253
176.9	Kaposi's Sarcoma, Unspecified 1253
179	Cancer, Uterus 402
180	Neoplasm, Cervix Uteri, Malignant 351
180.0	Neoplasm, Endocervix, Malignant 351
180.1	Neoplasm, Exocervix, Malignant 351
180.8	Neoplasm, Other Specified Sites of Cervix, Malignant 351
180.9	Cancer, Cervix, Unspecified 351
181	Choriocarcinoma 505
182	Neoplasm, Body of Uterus, Malignant (Uterine Cancer) 402
182.0	Neoplasm, Corpus Uteri, Except Isthmus, Malignant (Endometrial Cancer) 402
182.1	Neoplasm, Isthmus, Malignant 402
182.8	Neoplasm, Other Specified Sites of Body of Uterus, Malignant 402
183	Neoplasm, Ovary and Other Uterine Adnexa, Malignant (Ovarian Cancer) 372
183.0	Cancer, Ovary 372
185	Cancer, Prostate 380
186	Cancer, Testicles 393
186.9	Neoplasm, Other and Unspecified Testis, Malignant (Testicular Cancer) 393
188	Neoplasm, Bladder, Malignant 338
188.0	Neoplasm, Trigone of Urinary Bladder, Malignant 338
188.1	Neoplasm, Dome of Urinary Bladder, Malignant 338
188.2	Neoplasm, Lateral Wall of Urinary Bladder, Malignant 338
188.3	Neoplasm, Anterior Wall of Urinary Bladder, Malignant 338
188.4	Neoplasm, Posterior Wall of Urinary Bladder, Malignant 338
188.5	Neoplasm, Bladder Neck, Malignant 338
188.6	Neoplasm, Ureteric Orifice, Malignant 338
188.7	Neoplasm, Urachus, Malignant 338
188.8	Neoplasm, Other Specified Sites of Bladder, Malignant 338

188.9	Cancer, Bladder, Unspecified 338		199	Neoplasm without Specification of Site, Malignant (Cancer) 338
189	Neoplasm, Kidney and Other and Unspecified Urinary Organs, Malignant 338, 358		199.1	Cancer 338
189.0	Cancer, Kidney 358		200	Lymphosarcoma and Reticulosarcoma 338
189.1	Neoplasm, Renal Pelvis, Malignant (Renal Cell Carcinoma) 358		200.1	Lymphosarcoma (Hodgkin's Disease) 1123
189.8	Neoplasm, Other Specified Sites of Urinary Organs, Malignant 338		200.2	Burkitt's Tumor or Lymphoma 1482
191	Neoplasm, Brain, Malignant (Brain Cancer) 344		200.8	Lymphoma, Other Name Variants 338
191.0	Neoplasm, Cerebrum, Except Lobes and Ventricles, Malignant 344		201	Hodgkin's Disease (Lymphoma) 1123
191.1	Neoplasm, Frontal Lobe, Malignant 344		201.0	Hodgkin's Paragranuloma 1123
191.2	Neoplasm, Temporal Lobe, Malignant 344		201.00	Hodgkin's Paragranuloma, Unspecified Site 1123
191.3	Neoplasm, Parietal Lobe, Malignant 344		201.08	Hodgkin's Paragranuloma, Lymph Nodes of Multiple Sites 1123
191.4	Neoplasm, Occipital Lobe, Malignant 344		201.1	Hodgkin's Granuloma 1123
191.5	Neoplasm, Ventricles, Malignant 344		201.10	Hodgkin's Granuloma, Unspecified Site 1123
191.6	Neoplasm, Cerebellum, Malignant 344		201.18	Hodgkin's Granuloma, Lymph Nodes of Multiple Sites 1123
191.7	Neoplasm, Brain Stem, Malignant 344		201.2	Hodgkin's Sarcoma 1123
191.8	Neoplasm, Other Parts of Brain, Malignant 344		201.20	Hodgkin's Sarcoma, Unspecified Site 1123
191.9	Glioma 214, 344, 999		201.28	Hodgkin's Sarcoma, Lymph Nodes of Multiple Sites 1123
192	Neoplasm, Other and Unspecified Parts of Nervous System, Malignant 214		201.4	Hodgkin's Disease, Lymphocytic-histiocytic Predominance 1123
			201.40	Hodgkin's Disease, Lymphocytic-histiocytic Predominance, Unspecified Site 1123
192.1	Meningioma 1355			
192.8	Neoplasm, Other Specified Sites of Nervous System, Malignant (Glioma) 999		201.48	Hodgkin's Disease, Lymphocytic-histiocytic Predominance, Lymph Nodes of Multiple Sites 1123
192.9	Neoplasm, Nervous System, Malignant, Part Unspecified 214		201.5	Hodgkin's Disease, Nodular Sclerosis 1123
193	Cancer, Thyroid Gland 396		201.50	Hodgkin's Disease, Nodular Sclerosis, Unspecified Site 1123
194	Neoplasm, Other Endocrine Glands and Related Structures, Malignant 338		201.58	Hodgkin's Disease, Nodular Sclerosis, Lymph Nodes of Multiple Sites 1123
194.4	Neoplasm, Pineal Gland, Malignant 1647		201.6	Hodgkin's Disease, Mixed Cellularity 1123
197	Neoplasm, Seccondary, Respiratory and Digestive Systems, Malignant 338, 356, 360, 384, 389		201.60	Hodgkin's Disease, Mixed Cellularity, Unspecified Site 1123
197	Neoplasm, Secondary, Respiratory and Digestive Systems, Malignant 354, 363, 377, 391		201.68	Hodgkin's Disease, Mixed Cellularity, Lymph Nodes of Multiple Sites 1123
197.0	Neoplasm, Secondary, Lung, Malignant 363		201.7	Hodgkin's Disease, Lymphocytic Depletion 1123
197.2	Neoplasm, Secondary, Pleura, Malignant 377		201.70	Hodgkin's Disease, Lymphocytic Depletion, Unspecified Site 1123
197.4	Neoplasm, Secondary, Small Intestine, Including Duodenum, Malignant 389		201.78	Hodgkin's Disease, Lymphocytic Depletion, Lymph Nodes of Multiple Sites 1123
197.5	Neoplasm, Secondary, Large Intestine and Rectum, Malignant 354, 384		201.9	Hodgkin's Disease, Unspecified 1123
197.7	Neoplasm, Secondary, Liver, Malignant, Specified As Secondary 360		201.90	Hodgkin's Disease, Unspecified, Unspecified Site 1123
			201.98	Hodgkin's Disease, Unspecified, Lymph Nodes of Multiple Sites 1123
197.8	Neoplasm, Secondary, Digestive Organs and Spleen (Esophagus, Stomach, Liver, Pancreas), Malignant 356, 391		202	Neoplasms of Lymphoid and Histiocytic Tissue, Malignant 338
198.1	Neoplasm, Secondary, Other Urinary Organs, Malignant (Bladder) 338		202.1	Mycosis Fungoides 1416
			202.8	Non-Hodgkin's Lymphoma 1482
198.2	Neoplasm, Skin, Malignant 387		203	Multiple Myeloma and Immunoproliferative Neoplasms 1399
198.3	Neoplasm, Secondary, Brain and Spinal Cord, Malignant 344		203.0	Multiple Myeloma 1399
198.4	Neoplasm, Secondary, Other Parts of Nervous System, Malignant (Meninges) 1355		203.00	Multiple Myeloma Without Mention of Remission 1399
			208	Leukemia of Unspecified Cell Type 1284
198.5	Neoplasm, Secondary, Bone and Bone Marrow, Malignant 281		208.0	Leukemia, Acute, of Unspecified Cell Type 1284
198.6	Neoplasm, Secondary, Ovary, Malignant 372		208.1	Leukemia, Chronic, of Unspecified Cell Type 1284
198.81	Neoplasm, Secondary, Breast, Malignant 347		208.10	Chronic, Without Mention of Remission 1284
198.82	Neoplasm, Secondary, Genital Organs, Malignant 351, 393		208.11	Chronic, with Remission 1284
198.89	Neoplasm, Secondary, Unspecified Site, Malignant 380, 396, 399, 1647		208.2	Leukemia, Subacute, of Unspecified Cell Type 1284
			208.20	Subacute, Without Mention of Remission 1284
			208.8	Leukemia, Other, of Unspecified Cell Type 1284
			208.9	Leukemia, Unspecified 1284

Code	Description	Code	Description
210	Neoplasm, Lip, Oral Cavity, and Pharynx, Benign 2199	230.7	Carcinoma in Situ of Other and Unspecified Parts of Intestine 389
211	Neoplasm, Other Parts of Digestive System, Benign 2199	230.8	Carcinoma in Situ of Liver and Biliary System 360
212	Neoplasm, Respiratory and Intrathoracic Organs, Benign 2199	231	Carcinoma in Situ of Respiratory System 338, 363
213	Osteoma (Benign Neoplasm of Bone and Articular Cartilage) 1536	231.2	Carcinoma in Situ of Bronchus and Lung 363
213.0	Neoplasm, Bones of Skull and Face, Benign 1536	232	Carcinoma in Situ of Skin 387
213.1	Neoplasm, Lower Jaw Bone, Benign 1536	232.0	Carcinoma in Situ of Skin of Lip 387
213.2	Neoplasm, Vertebral Column, Excluding Sacrum and Coccyx, Benign 1536	232.1	Carcinoma in Situ of Eyelid, Including Canthus 387
		232.2	Carcinoma in Situ of Ear and External Auditory Canal 387
213.3	Neoplasm, Ribs, Sternum, and Clavicle, Benign 1536	232.3	Carcinoma in Situ of Skin of Other and Unspecified Parts of Face 387
213.4	Neoplasm, Scapula and Long Bones of Upper Limb, Benign 1536	232.4	Carcinoma in Situ of Scalp and Skin of Neck 387
213.5	Neoplasm, Short Bones of Upper Limb, Benign 1536	232.5	Carcinoma in Situ of Skin of Trunk, Except Scrotum 387
213.6	Neoplasm, Pelvic Bones, Sacrum, and Coccyx, Benign 1536	232.6	Carcinoma in Situ of Skin of Upper Limb, Including Shoulder 387
213.7	Neoplasm, Long Bones of Lower Limb, Benign 1536	232.7	Carcinoma in Situ of Skin of Lower Limb, Including Hip 387
213.8	Neoplasm, Short Bones of Lower Limb, Benign 1536	232.8	Carcinoma in Situ of Other Specified Sites of Skin 387
213.9	Neoplasm, Bone and Articular Cartilage, Benign, Site Unspecified 1536	232.9	Carcinoma in Situ of Skin, Site Unspecified 387
		233	Carcinoma in Situ of Breast and Genitourinary System 338, 347, 351, 358, 380, 393, 402
214	Lipoma 1290		
214.0	Lipoma of Skin and Subcutaneous Tissue of Face 1290	233.0	Carcinoma in Situ of the Breast 347
214.1	Lipoma of Other Skin and Subcutaneous Tissue 1290	233.1	Carcinoma in Situ of Cervix Uteri 351
214.2	Lipoma of Intrathoracic Organs 1290	233.2	Carcinoma in Situ of Other and Unspecified Parts of Uterus 402
214.3	Lipoma of Intra-Abdominal Organs 1290	233.3	Carcinoma in Situs of Other and Unspecified Female Genital Organs 338
214.4	Lipoma of Spermatic Cord 1290		
214.8	Lipoma of Other Specified Sites 1290	233.4	Carcinoma in Situ of Prostate 380
214.9	Lipoma, Unspecified Site 1290	233.6	Carcinoma in Situ of Other and Unspecified Male Genital Organs (Testis) 393
218	Uterine Leiomyoma 875		
218.0	Submucous Leiomyoma of Uterus 875	233.7	Carcinoma in Situ of Bladder 338
218.1	Intramural Leiomyoma of Uterus 875	233.9	Carcinoma in Situ of Other and Unspecified Urinary Organs 358
218.2	Subserous Leiomyoma of Uterus 875	234	Carcinoma in Situ of Other and Unspecified Sites 338
218.9	Fibroid Tumor of Uterus, Unspecified 875	234.8	Carcinoma in Situ of Endocrine (Pineal) Gland 1647
219	Other Benign Neoplaasm of Uterus 875	235.1	Neoplasm of Uncertain Behavior of Digestive and Respiratory Systems, Lip, Oral Cavity and Pharynx 369
223	Neoplasm, Kidney and Other Urinary Organs, Benign 2199		
223.3	Neoplasm, Bladder, Benign 2199	235.2	Neoplasm of Uncertain Behavior of Stomach, Intestines and Rectum 391
223.81	Benign Neoplasm of Other Specified Sites of Urinary Organs, Urethra 434		
		235.8	Neoplasm of Uncertain Behavior of Pleura, Thymus and Mediastinum 377
225	Neoplasm, Brain and Other Parts of Nervous System, Benign 2199		
225.0	Neoplasm, Brain, Benign 2199	236	Neoplasm of Uncertain Behavior of Genitourinary Organs 338, 358, 372, 380, 393, 402
225.2	Neoplasm, Cerebral Meninges, Benign (Meningioma, Benign) 2199		
		236.0	Neoplasm of Uncertain Behavior of Genitourinary Organs, Uterus 402
225.3	Benign Neoplasm, Spinal Cord 440		
227	Neoplasm, Other Endocrine Glands and Related Structures, Benign 2199	236.2	Neoplasm of Uncertain Behavior of Genitourinary Organs,ovary 372
227.0	Pheochromocytoma 1638	236.4	Neoplasm of Uncertain Behavior of Genitourinary Organs, Testis 393
227.4	Neoplasm, Pineal Gland, Benign 2199		
229	Neoplasm, Other and Unspecified Sites, Benign 2199	236.5	Neoplasm of Uncertain Behavior of Genitourinary Organs, Prostate 380
229.9	Tumor, Benign 2199		
230	Carcinoma in Situ of Digestive Organs 338, 354, 356, 360, 369, 384, 389, 391, 399	236.7	Bladder Polyps 264
		236.90	Neoplasms of Uncertain Behavior or Genitourinary Organs, Kidney and Ureter 358
230.0	Carcinoma in Situ of Oral Cavity (Tongue) 369, 399	237	Neoplasm of Uncertain Behavior of Endocrine Glands and Nervous System 338
230.1	Carcinoma in Situ of Esophagus 356		
230.2	Carcinoma in Situ of Stomach 391	237.1	Pineal Gland Neoplasm 1647
230.3	Carcinoma in Situ of Colon 354	237.5	Brain and Spinal Cord 1355
230.4	Carcinoma in Situ of Rectum 384	237.6	Meninges 1355

237.7	Neurofibromatosis 1469
237.70	Neurofibromatosis, Unspecified 1469
237.71	Neurofibromatosis, Type I (Von Recklinghausen's Disease) 1469
237.72	Neurofibromatosis, Type II 1469
238	Neoplasm of Uncertain Behavior of Other and Unspecified Sites and Tissues 338
238.2	Neoplasm of Uncertain Behavior, Skin 387
238.4	Polycythemia Vera 1689
238.7	Other Lymphatic and Hematopoietic Tissues 1689
239	Neoplasms of Unspecified Nature 338
239.0	Neoplasms of Unspecified Nature of Digestive System 338
239.3	Neoplasm of Unspecified Nature of Breast 338
239.4	Neoplasm of Unspecified Nature, Bladder 264
239.5	Neoplasm of Other Genitourinary Organs 338
239.7	Neoplasm of Unspecified Nature, Endocrine Glands and Other Parts of Nervous System 338
240	Goiter, Simple and Unspecified 1008
240.0	Goiter, Specified As Simple 1008
240.9	Goiter 1008
242	Thyrotoxicosis with or Without Goiter 1017
242.0	Goiter, Toxic Diffuse (Graves_ Disease) 1017
242.00	Goiter, Toxic Diffuse, Without Mention of Thyrotoxic Crisis or Storm 1017
242.01	Goiter, Toxic Diffuse, with Mention of Thyrotoxic Crisis or Storm 1017
242.1	Hyperthyroidism 1159
242.10	Goiter, Toxic Uninodular, Without Mention of Thyrotoxic Crisis or Storm 1159
242.11	Goiter, Toxic Uninodular, with Mention of Thyrotoxic Crisis or Storm 1159
242.2	Goiter, Toxic Multinodular 1159
242.20	Goiter, Toxic Multinodular, Without Mention of Thyrotoxic Crisis or Storm 1159
242.21	Goiter, Toxic Multinodular, with Mention of Thyrotoxic Crisis or Storm 1159
242.3	Goiter, Toxic Nodular, Unspecified 1159
242.30	Goiter, Toxic Nodular, Without Mention of Thyrotoxic Crisis or Storm 1159
242.31	Goiter, Toxic Nodular, with Mention of Thyrotoxic Crisis or Storm 1159
242.8	Thyrotoxicosis of Other Specified Origin 1159
242.80	Thyrotoxicosis of Other Specified Origin Without Mention of Thyrotoxic Crisis or Storm 1159
242.81	Thyrotoxicosis of Other Specified Origin with Mention of Thyrotoxic Crisis or Storm 1159
242.9	Thyrotoxicosis without Mention of Goiter or Other Cause (Hyperthyroidism) 1159
242.90	Thyrotoxicosis Without Mention of Goiter or Other Cause Without Mention of Thyrotoxic Crisis or Storm 1159
242.91	Thyrotoxicosis Without Mention of Goiter or Other Cause with Mention of Thyrotoxic Crisis or Storm 1159
243	Congenital Hypothyroidism 1180
244	Hypothyroidism, Acquired 1180
244.0	Hypothyroidism, Postsurgical 1180
244.1	Hypothyroidism, Other Postablative 1180
244.2	Hypothyroidism, Iodine 1180
244.3	Hypothyroidism, Other Iatrogenic 1180
244.8	Hypothyroidism, Other Specified Acquired 1180
244.9	Hypothyroidism, Unspecified (Myxedema) 1180
245	Thyroiditis 2091
245.0	Thyroiditis, Acute 2091
245.1	Thyroiditis, Subacute 2091
245.2	Hashimoto's Thyroiditis 2091
245.3	Thyroiditis, Chronic Fibrous 2091
245.9	Thyroiditis, Unspecified 2091
246.1	Congenital (dyshormonogenic) goiter 1008
250	Diabetes Mellitus Type II 683, 686, 689–690, 692, 694
250.00	Diabetes Mellitus Type II 686
250.01	Diabetes Mellitus Type I 683
250.1	Diabetes with Ketoacidosis (Diabetic Acidosis) 683
250.3	Diabetes with Other Coma 683
250.4	Diabetic Glomerulosclerosis 690
250.5	Diabetic Retinopathy 694
250.6	Diabetic Neuropathy 692
250.7	Diabetic Gangrene 689
250.8	Diabetes with Other Specified Manifestations 683
250.9	Diabetes with Unspecified Complications 683
251.1	Hyperinsulinism 1144
251.2	Hypoglycemia, Unspecified 1171
252.0	Hyperparathyroidism 1148
252.1	Hypoparathyroidism 1173
253.2	Simmonds' Disease (Panhypopituitarism) 1576
253.5	Diabetes Insipidus 681
255.0	Cushing's Syndrome 613
255.1	Aldosteronism 94
255.4	Addison's Disease (Corticoadrenal Insufficiency) 63
256.3	Premature Menopause 1368
256.4	Polycystic Ovary Syndrome (Stein-Leventhal Syndrome) 1686
264	Vitamin A Deficiency 2270
264.5	Vitamin A Deficiency with Night Blindness 2270
264.9	Vitamin A Deficiency, Unspecified 2270
265.0	Beriberi 2272
265.1	Thiamine Deficiency 2272
265.2	Pellagra 1602
266.0	Vitamin B2 2275
266.2	Vitamin B12 Deficiency 2277
267	Vitamin C (Ascorbic Acid) Deficiency 2279
268	Vitamin D Deficiency 2281
268.0	Rickets, Active 2281
268.2	Osteomalacia, Unspecified 2281
268.9	Vitamin D Deficiency, Unspecified 2281
269.0	Vitamin K Deficiency 2284
269.1	Vitamin E Deficiency 2283
269.2	Hypovitaminosis 1182
270	Disorders of Amino-Acid Transport and Metabolism 1679

271.4	Glycosuria, Renal 1006
272.7	Lipidoses 673
272.8	Dercum's Disease 673
272.9	Unspecified Disorsers of Lipoid Metabolism 673
273.8	Hypoproteinemia 1175
274	Gout 1012
274.0	Gouty Arthropathy (Gouty Arthritis) 1012
274.1	Gouty Nephropathy 1012
274.8	Gout with Other Specified Manifestations 1012
274.9	Gout, Unspecified 1012
275.1	Wilson's Disease 2300
276.5	Dehydration 642
276.7	Hyperkalemia 1146
277.0	Cystic Fibrosis 1693
277.1	Porphyria 1693
277.2	Other Disorders of Purine and Pyrimidine Metabolism 1693
277.3	Amyloidosis 1693
278	Obesity and Other Hyperalimentation 1491
278.0	Obesity, Simple 1491
278.00	Obesity, Unspecified 1491
278.01	Obesity, Morbid 1491
278.2	Hypervitaminosis A 1166
278.4	Hypervitaminosis D 1168
278.8	Hyperalimentation (Hypervitaminosis), Other 1164
279.4	Autoimmune Disease, Not Elsewhere Classified 63
280	Iron Deficiency Anemia 1242
280.0	Iron Deficiency Anemia Secondary to Blood Loss (Chronic) 1242
280.1	Iron Deficiency Anemia Secondary to Inadequate Dietary Iron Intake 1242
280.8	Iron Deficiency Anemias, Other Specified 1242
280.9	Iron Deficiency Anemia, Unspecified 1242
281	Other Deficiency Anemias 133
281.0	Pernicious Anemia 1630
281.1	Vitamin B12 Deficiency Anemia, Other 2277
281.2	Folic Acid Deficiency Anemia 885
282	Hemolytic Anemia, Hereditary 1059
282.0	Spherocytosis, Hereditary 1944
282.1	Hereditary Elliptocytosis 1059
282.2	Anemias Due to Disorders of Glutathione Metabolism 1059
282.3	Hemolytic Anemias Due to Enzyme Deficiency, Other 1059
282.4	Thalassemia 2066
282.5	Sickle-Cell Trait 1922
282.6	Sickle Cell Anemia 1922
282.60	Sickle-Cell Anemia, Unspecified 1922
282.61	Hb-s Disease Without Mention of Crisis 1922
282.62	Hb-s Disease with Mention of Crisis 1922
282.8	Hemolytic Anemia, Hereditary, Other Specified 1059
282.9	Hemolytic Anemia, Unspecified Hereditary 1059
283	Hemolytic Anemias, Acquired 1059
283.0	Hemolytic Anemias, Autoimmune 1059
283.1	Hemolytic Anemias, Non-Autoimmune 1059
283.2	Hemoglobinuria Due to Hemolysis from External Causes 1059
283.9	Hemolytic Anemia, Acquired, Unspecified 1059
284	Aplastic Anemia 171
284.0	Aplastic Anemia, Constitutional 171
284.8	Aplastic Anemias, Other Specified 171
284.9	Aplastic Anemia, Unspecified 171
285.1	Anemia, Posthemorrhagic, Acute 133
285.8	Myelophthisic Anemia 1422
285.9	Anemia, Unspecified 133
286.0	Hemophilia A 1061
286.1	Hemophilia B 1064
286.3	Hypoprothrombinemia 81, 1176
286.9	Other and Unspecified Coagulation Defects 1189
287	Purpura and Other Hemorrhagic Conditions 1760
287.2	Purpura Simplex 1760
287.3	Idiopathic Thrombocytopenic Purpura 1189
287.4	Secondary Thrombocytopenia 1760
287.5	Thrombocytopenia, Unspecified 2083
288.0	Neutropenia (Agranulocytosis) 1477
289.1	Lymphadenitis, Chronic 1322
289.2	Lymphadenitis, Nonspecific Mesenteric 1322
289.3	Lymphadenitis, Unspecified, Except Mesenteric 1322
289.4	Hypersplenism 1154
290	Organic Psychosis 1526
290.1	Dementia, Presenile 1526
290.2	Dementia, Alzheimer's Type, with Delusions (Late Onset) 653
291	Alcoholic Psychoses 1526
291.0	Alcohol Withdrawal Delirium 1526
291.2	Alcoholic Dementia, Other 1526
291.3	Alcohol Withdrawal Hallucinosis 1526
291.4	Alcohol Intoxication, Idiosyncratic 1526
291.9	Alcoholic Psychosis, Unspecified 1526
292	Drug Psychoses 1526
293	Transient Organic Psychotic Conditions 1526
294	Organic Psychotic Conditions, Other 1526
294.0	Amnestic Syndrome 1526
294.9	Organic Psychosis, Unspecified 1526
295	Schizophrenia 1878, 1882, 1885, 1888
295.1	Schizophrenia, Disorganized Type 1882
295.2	Schizophrenia, Catatonic Type 1882
295.30	Schizophrenia, Paranoid Type 1885
295.4	Schizophreniform Disorder 1888
295.7	Schizoaffective Disorder 1878
295.9	Schizophrenia, Unspecified 1882
296	Affective Psychoses 1878
296.0	Bipolar Affective Disorder, Single Manic Episode 260
296.1	Manic Disorder, Recurrent 1339
296.2	Depression, Major 665
296.20	Depression, Major, Single Episode Unspecified 665
296.22	Depression, Major, Single Episode, Moderate 665

296.23	Depression, Major, Single Episode, Severe, Without Mention of Psychotic Behavior 665
296.24	Depression, Major, Single Episode, Severe, Specified as With Psychotic Behavior 665
296.3	Major Depressive Disorder, Recurrent Episode 665
296.30	Depression, Major, Recurrent Episode Unspecified 665
296.32	Depression, Major, Recurrent Episode, Moderate 665
296.33	Depression, Major, Recurrent Episode, Without Mention of Psychotic Behavior 665
296.34	Depression, Major, Recurrent Episode, Specified as With Psychotic Behavior 665
296.4	Bipolar Affective Disorder, Manic 253, 1878
296.5	Bipolar Affective Disorder, Depressed 253, 256
296.6	Bipolar Affective Disorder, Mixed 253, 258
296.7	Bipolar Affective Disorder, Unspecified 253
297	Paranoid States 649
297.9	Delusional Disorder, Unspecified 649
298.0	Depressive Psychosis 670
298.8	Psychotic Disorder, Brief 1749
298.9	Psychotic Disorder, Unspecified 1751
300	Neurotic Disorders 1462, 1475, 1937, 1939
300.0	Anxiety States 1475
300.00	Anxiety State, Unspecified 1475
300.01	Panic Disorder 1475, 1578, 1937
300.02	Anxiety Disorder, Generalized 158, 1475
300.1	Hysteria 1188
300.10	Hysteria, Unspecified 1188
300.11	Conversion Disorder 574
300.12	Psychogenic Amnesia 866
300.14	Multiple Personality Disorder 737
300.15	Dissociative Disorder or Reaction, Unspecified 737
300.16	Factitious Illness with Psychological Symptoms 868
300.19	Factitious Illness with Physical Symptoms 866
300.2	Phobic Disorders 1580, 1639, 1641
300.21	Panic Disorder with Agoraphobia 1580
300.23	Social Phobia 1937
300.29	Phobias, Simple 1639
300.3	Obsessive-Compulsive Disorder 1494
300.4	Dysthymic Disorder 764
300.5	Nervous Fatigue 1462
300.6	Depersonalization Disorder 663
300.7	Hypochondriasis 1169
300.81	Somatization Disorder 1939
300.9	Neurotic Disorders 1462, 1475
301.0	Personality Disorder, Paranoid 1588
301.1	Affective Personality Disorder 862
301.10	Affective Personlity Disorder, Unspecified 862
301.13	Cyclothymic Disorder 862
301.20	Personality Disorder, Schizoid 1881
301.21	Personality Disorder, Introverted 1881
301.3	Personality Disorder, Explosive 862
301.4	Personality Disorder, Obsessive-Compulsive 1496
301.5	Histrionic Personality Disorder 862
301.51	Factitious Illness with Physical Symptoms, Chronic 866
301.59	Other Histrionic Personality Disorder 862
301.6	Personality Disorder, Dependent 661
301.7	Personality Disorder, Antisocial 156
301.8	Other Personality Disorders 661
301.81	Personality Disorder, Narcissistic 1437
301.82	Personality Disorder, Avoidant 237
301.83	Personality Disorder, Borderline 284
301.84	Personality Disorder, Passive-Aggressive 1597
301.9	Unspecified Personlity Disorders 862
302	Psychosexual Disorders 1745
302.2	Pedophilia 1745
302.3	Transvestism 1745
302.6	Psychosexual Identity, Disorders of 1745
302.7	Psychosexual Dysfunction 1745
302.70	Psychosexual Dysfunction, Unspecified 1745
302.8	Psychosexual Disorders, Other Specified 1745
302.9	Psychosexual Disorder, Unspecified 1745
303	Alcohol Dependence Syndrome 87, 90
303.0	Alcoholic Intoxication, Acute Unspecified 87
303.9	Alcoholism 90
303.90	Other and Unspecified Alcohol Dependence, Unspecified 90
303.91	Other and Unspecified Alcohol Dependence, Continuous 90
304.0	Narcotic Dependence (Opioid Type Dependence) 1516
304.00	Narcotic Dependence, Unspecified 1516
304.01	Narcotic Dependence, Continuous 1516
304.02	Narcotic Dependence, Episodic 1516
304.03	Narcotic Dependence, in Remission 1516
304.1	Barbiturate Dependence (Sedative, Hypnotic or Anxiolytic Dependence) 1898
304.2	Cocaine Dependence 522
304.20	Cocaine Dependence, Unspecified 522
304.3	Marijuana (Cannabis) Dependence 1341
304.31	Cannabis Dependence, Continuous 1341
304.32	Cannabis Dependence, Episodic 1341
304.33	Cannabis Dependence in Remission 1341
304.4	Amphetamine Dependence 113
304.7	Addictions, Mixed 60
304.8	Addictions, Mixed (Excluding Opioid Type) 60
304.9	Addictions, Mixed, Unspecified Drug Dependence 60
305.0	Alcohol Abuse, Nondependent 87
305.1	Nicotine Dependence 1479
305.2	Marijuana (Cannabis) Abuse 1341
305.3	Hallucinogen Abuse 1635
305.4	Barbiturate Abuse, and Similarly Acting Sympathomimetic Drugs 1898
305.6	Cocaine Abuse 522
305.7	Amphetamine Abuse 113
305.9	Drug Abuse, Unspecified 1635
306	Physiological Malfunction Arising from Mental Factors 866, 1939

306.0	Musculoskeletal - Psychogenic Paralysis 866
306.1	Hyperventilation Syndrome 1161
306.2	Neurocirculatory Asthenia 1467
306.3	Skin 866
306.4	Psychogenic Dyspepsia 769
306.5	Genitourinary 866
306.6	Endocrine 866
306.7	Organs of Special Sense 866
306.8	Other Specified Psychophysiological Malfunction 866
307.1	Anorexia Nervosa 769
307.2	Tics 2093
307.20	Tic Disorder, Unspecified 2093
307.23	Gilles De La Tourette's Disorder 2093
307.5	Eating Disorders 769
307.51	Bulimia 769
307.81	Tension Headache 1033, 2059
308.0	Predominant Disturbance of Emotions 2007
308.3	Reactions to Stress, Other Acute 2007
308.9	Stress Disorder, Acute 2007
309	Adjustment Reaction 69, 72, 74, 284
309.0	Adjustment Disorder with Depressed Mood 69
309.1	Depressive Reaction, Prolonged 69
309.2	with Predominant Disturbance of Other Emotions 69, 72
309.21	Seperation Anxiety Disorder 284
309.24	Adjustment Disorder with Anxiety or Disturbance of Conduct 72
309.28	Adjustment Reaction with Mixed Emotional Features 69
309.3	Adjustment Reaction with Predominant Disturbance of Conduct 72, 74
309.81	Posttraumatic Stress Disorder 1707
309.9	Unspecified Nonpsychotic Mental Disorder Following Organic Brain Damage 69
310.2	Postconcussion Syndrome 1699
311	Depressive Disorder, Not Elsewhere Classified 665
311.0	Depressive Disorder, Unspecified 665
312.34	Intermittent Explosive Disorder 1217
314.0	Attention Deficit Disorder 232
314.00	Attention Deficit Disorder in Adults 232
314.01	Attention Deficit Disorder with Hyperactivity 232
320	Meningitis, Bacterial 1357
320.1	Pneumococcal Meningitis 1357
320.2	Streptococcal Meningitis 1357
320.3	Staphylococcal Meningitis 1357
320.8	Meningitis Due to Other Specified Bacteria 1357
320.82	Meningitis Due to Gram-negative Bacteria, Not Elsewhere Classified 1357
320.9	Meningitis Due to Unspecified Bacterium 1357
321	Meningitis Due to Other Organisms 1357
321.1	Meningitis in Other Fungal Diseases 1357
321.2	Meningitis Due to Viruses Not Elsewhere Classified 1357
322	Meningitis, Unspecified Cause 1357, 1359
322.2	Meningitis, Chronic 1359
322.9	Meningitis, Unspecified 1357
323	Encephalitis 797
323.5	Encephalitis Following Immunization Procedures 797
323.6	Post Infectious Encephalitis 797
323.8	Encephalitis, Other Causes of 797
323.9	Encephalitis, Unspecified Cause 797
324	Abscess, Intracranial and Intraspinal 289
324.0	Brain Abscess 289
325	Phlebitis and Thrombophlebitis of Intracranial Venous Sinuses 2252
331.0	Alzheimer's Disease 105
332	Parkinson's Disease 1593
332.0	Paralysis Agitans 1593
332.1	Parkinsonism, Secondary 1593
333.0	Shy-Drager Syndrome 1919
333.4	Huntington's Chorea 1132
333.7	Athetoid Cerebral Palsy 452
335.20	Amyotrophic Lateral Sclerosis 125
335.21	Muscular Atrophy, Progressive 230
336.0	Syringomyelia (Syringobulbia) 2035
336.1	Vascular Myelopathies 1420
336.8	Myelopathy, Other 1420
336.9	Myelopathy, Unspecified 1420
337.0	Carotid Sinus Syncope 425
337.2	Complex Regional Pain Syndrome (Reflex Sympathetic Dystrophy) 550
340	Multiple Sclerosis 1401
342	Hemiplegia 1056
342.0	Hemiplegia, Flaccid 1056
342.1	Hemiplegia, Spastic 1056
342.8	Other Specified Hemiplegia 1056
342.9	Hemiplegia, Unspecified 1056
343	Cerebral Palsy, Infantile 452
343.9	Cerebral Palsy, Unspecified 452
344	Other Paralytic Syndromes 246
344.0	Quadriplegia 1583
344.00	Quadriplegia, Unspecified 1583
344.01	Quadriplegia C1-C4 Complete 1583
344.02	Quadriplegia C1-C4, Incomplete 1583
344.03	Quadriplegia C5-C7, Complete 1583
344.04	Quadriplegia C5-C7, Incomplete 1583
344.09	Quadriplegia, Other 1583
344.1	Paraplegia 1583
344.6	Cauda Equina Syndrome 440
344.60	Cauda Equina Syndrome Without Mention of Neurogenic Bladder 440
344.61	Cauda Equina Syndrome with Neurogenic Bladder 440
344.9	Paralysis, Paraplegia, and Quadriplegia 1583
345	Epilepsy 824, 1900
345.0	Petit Mal Epilepsy 1631
345.1	Grand Mal Seizure 824, 1014

Code	Description	Code	Description
345.2	Petit Mal Status, Epileptic Absence Status 824	362.1	Other Background Retinopathy and Retinal Vascular Changes 1829
345.3	Grand Mal Status 1014	362.3	Retinal Vascular Occlusion 1827
345.4	Partial Epilepsy with Impairment of Consciousness 824	362.32	Retinal Occlusion, Arterial Branch 1827
345.5	Jacksonian Seizure 1247	362.35	Central Retinal Vein Occlusion 1827
345.7	Epilepsia Partialis Continua Kojevnikov's Epilepsy 824	362.42	Serous Detachment of Retinal Pigment Epithelium 1829
345.8	Other Forms of Epilepsy 1014	362.5	Macular degeneration (senile) 270
345.9	Epilepsy, Unspecified 824	362.50	Senile Macular Degeneration 1903
346	Migraine Headache 1378	362.51	Senile Macular Degeneration, Nonexudative 1903
346.0	Migraine Headache, Classical 1378	362.52	Senile Macular Degeneration, Exudative 1903
346.1	Migraine, Common (Sick Headache) 1378	362.65	Secondary Pigmentary Degeneration 1829
346.2	Cluster Headache 517	362.74	Retinitis Pigmentosa 1829
346.8	Migraine Headache, Other Forms of 1378	362.8	Other Retinal Disorder 270
346.9	Migraine Headache, Unspecified 1378	363.20	Retinitis (Chorioretinitis) 506
347	Narcolepsy 1439	364.0	Iritis 1240, 2231
348.3	Encephalopathy, Unspecified 799	364.00	Uveitis, Acute or Subacute 2231
348.5	Cerebral Edema 799	364.01	Uveitis, Recurrent 2231
349	Reaction to Spinal or Lumbar Puncture 517	364.10	Uveitis, Chronic 2231
350	Trigeminal Nerve Disorders 2187	364.23	Uveitis, Lens-Induced 2231
350.1	Trigeminal Neuralgia 2187	364.3	Uveitis, Unspecified 1240, 2231
351	Facial Nerve Disorders 246	365	Glaucoma 995, 997
351.0	Bell's Palsy 246	365.01	Open Angle with Borderline Findings 997
352.3	Vagotonia 2237	365.1	Glaucoma, Chronic (Open-Angle) 997
353	Nerve Root and Plexus Disorder 287	365.11	Glaucoma, Primary (Open-Angle) 997
353.0	Thoracic Outlet Syndrome 2074	365.15	Residual Stage of Open Angle Glaucoma 997
353.5	Neuralgic Amyotrophy 1465	365.20	Primary Angle-Closure Glaucoma, Unspecified 995
354	Mononeuritis of Upper Limb 430	365.21	Intermittent Angle-Closure Glaucoma 995
354.0	Carpal Tunnel Syndrome 430	365.22	Glaucoma, Acute (Angle-Closure) 995
354.2	Cubital Tunnel Syndrome (Lesion of Ulnar Nerve) 1473	365.23	Chronic Angle-Closure Glaucoma 995
355.5	Tarsal Tunnel Syndrome 2043	365.24	Residual Stage of Angle-Closure Glaucoma 995
355.6	Morton's Neuroma 1393	366	Cataract 436
356.1	Peroneal Muscular Atrophy 227	366.1	Cataract, Senile 436
356.8	Peripheral Neuropathy, Other Specified Idiopathic 1621	366.2	Cataract, Traumatic 436
356.9	Peripheral Neuropathy 1621	366.4	Cataract, Associated with Other Disorders 436
357.0	Guillain-Barré Syndrome 1022	366.8	Cataract, Other 436
357.2	Diabetic Neuropathy 692	366.9	Cataract, Unspecified 436
358.0	Myasthenia Gravis 1414	367.1	Myopia 1431
358.9	Myoneural Disorders, Unspecified 1414	367.2	Astigmatism 212
359	Muscular Dystrophies and Other Myopathies 227	367.20	Astigmatism, Unspecified 212
360.0	Endophthalmitis, Purulent 808	368.00	Amblyopia 107
360.00	Endophthalmitis, Unspecified Purulent 808	368.01	Amblyopia, Strabismic 107
360.01	Endophthalmitis, Acute 808	369	Blindness and Low Vision 270
360.02	Panophthalmitis 808	369.00	Blindness, Both Eyes (Impairment Level not Further Specified) 270
360.03	Endophthalmitis, Chronic 808	369.4	Blindness, Legal As Defined in U.s. 270
360.1	Endophthalmitis, Other 808	370	Keratitis 1257
360.11	Endophthalmitis (Sympathetic Uveitis), Other 808	370.0	Corneal Ulcer 584
360.13	Endophthalmitis, Parasitic 808	370.00	Corneal Ulcer, Unspecified 584
360.19	Endophthalmitis, Other 808	370.2	Superficial Keratitis Without Conjunctivitis 1257
361	Retinal Detachments and Defects 1823	370.5	Intersitial and Deep Keratitis 1257
361.8	Retinal Detachment, Other Forms of 1823	370.9	Keratitis, Unspecified 1257
361.9	Retinal Detachment 1823		
362.0	Diabetic Retinopathy 694		

Index of ICD-9 CM

371.60	Keratoconus, Unspecified 1259
371.61	Keratoconus, Stable Condition 1259
371.62	Keratoconus, Acute Hydrops 1259
372	Conjunctiva, Disorders of 556
372.0	Conjunctivitis, Acute 556
372.00	Conjunctivitis, Acute, Unspecified 556
372.1	Conjunctivitis, Chronic 556
372.10	Conjunctivitis, Chronic, Unspecified 556
372.30	Conjunctivitis, Unspecified 556
372.39	Conjunctivitis, Other 556
372.4	Pterygium 1754
372.40	Pterygium, Unspecified 1754
372.5	Conjunctival Degenerations and Deposits 1754
373	Inflammation of the Eyelids 268
373.00	Blepharitis, Unspecified 268
373.01	Blepharitis, Ulcerative 268
373.11	Stye 2010
373.3	Non Infectious Dermatoses of Eyelid 268
373.32	Contact Dermatitis of Eyelids 268
375.15	Dry Eyes Syndrome 745
375.30	Dacryocystitis 627
375.32	Dacryocystitis, Acute 627
375.42	Dacryocystitis, Chronic 627
375.5	Stenosis and Insufficiency of Lacrimal Passages 629, 745
375.56	Dacryostenosis 629
377	Disorders of Optic Nerve and Visual Pathways 270
377.1	Optic Atrophy 1519
377.10	Optic Atrophy, Unspecified 1519
377.3	Optic Neuritis 1521
377.30	Optic Neuritis, Unspecified 1521
377.32	Neuritis, Retrobulbar 1521
377.34	Amblyopia, Toxic 107
377.39	Toxic Optic Neuropathy 1521
379.0	Scleritis 1891
379.5	Nystagmus 1487
379.51	Congenital Nystagmus 1487
379.52	Latent Nystagmus 1487
379.53	Visual Deprivation Nystagmus 1487
379.55	Disassociated Nystagmus 1487
379.56	Other Forms of Nystagmus 1487
380.1	Otitis Externa, Infective 1543
380.10	Otitis Externa Infective, Unspecified 1543
380.11	Acute Infection of Pinna 1543
380.12	Acute Swimmer's Ear 1543
380.13	Other Acute Infections of External Ear 1543
380.14	Malignant Otitis Externa 1543
380.15	Chronic Mycotic Otitis Externa 1543
380.16	Other Chronic Infective Otitis Externa 1543
381	Otitis Media and Eustachian Tube Disorders, Nonsuppurative 1545
381.00	Otitis Media, Acute Nonsuppurative, Unspecified 1545
381.01	Otitis Media, Acute Serous 1545
382	Otitis Media, Suppurative and Unspecified 1545
382.0	Otitis Media, Acute Suppurative 1545
382.00	Otitis Media, Acute Suppurative Without Spontaneous Rupture of Ear Drum 1545
382.9	Otitis Media, Unspecified 1545
383	Mastoiditis and Other Related Conditions 1349
383.0	Mastoiditis, Acute 1349
383.1	Mastoiditis, Chronic 1349
383.9	Mastoiditis 1349
384.20	Tympanum Perforation 2202
386.0	Endolymphatic Hydrops 1353
386.00	Ménière's Disease 1353
386.01	Active Ménière's Disease, Cochleovestibular 1353
386.02	Active Ménière's Disease, Cochlear 1353
386.03	Active Ménière's Disease, Vestibular 1353
386.04	Inactive Ménière's Disease 1353
386.1	Vertigo 2262, 2268
386.10	Vertigo, Peripheral, Unspecified 2262
386.12	Vestibular Neuronitis 2268
386.19	Vertigo, Peripheral, Other and Unspecified 2262
386.2	Vertigo of Central Origin 2262
386.3	Labyrinthitis 1267
386.31	Serous Labyrinthitis 1267
386.32	Circumscribed Labyrinthitis 1267
386.33	Suppurative Labyrinthitis 1267
386.34	Toxic Labyrinthitis 1267
386.35	Viral Labyrinthitis 1267
387	Otosclerosis 1549
387.9	Otosclerosis, Unspecified 1549
388.3	Tinnitus 2097
388.30	Tinnitus, Unspecified 2097
388.32	Tinnitus, Objective 2097
389	Hearing Loss 1036
389.0	Conductive Hearing Loss 1036
389.1	Sensorineural Hearing Loss 1036
389.12	Neural Hearing Loss 1036
389.14	Central Hearing Loss 1036
389.7	Deaf, Mutism, Not Elsewhere Classifiable 1036
389.8	Other Specified Forms of Hearing Loss 1036
389.9	Hearing Loss, Unspecified 1036
390	Rheumatic Fever 1833
391	Rheumatic Fever with Heart Involvement 1833
391.2	Acute Rheumatic Myocarditis 1428
394.0	Mitral Stenosis 1387
394.1	Rheumatic Mitral Insufficiency 1385
394.2	Mitral Stenosis with Insufficiency 1385
395.0	Rheumatic Aortic Stenosis 167
395.1	Aortic Insufficiency, Rheumatic 165
396.0	Mitral Valve Stenosis and Aortic Valve Stenosis 167
396.1	Mitral Valve Stenosis and Aortic Valve Insufficiency 1387

396.3	Mitral Valve Insufficiency and Aortic Valve Insufficiency 165, 1385
398	Rheumatic Heart Disease, Other 1836
398.9	Rheumatic Heart Disease, Chronic 1836
401	Hypertension 1112, 1116
401.0	High Blood Pressure, Malignant 1116
401.1	High Blood Pressure, Benign 1112
401.9	Essential Hypertension, Unspecified 1112, 1116
402	Hypertensive Heart Disease 1156
402.9	Hypertensive Heart Disease, Unspecified 1156
405	Hypertension, Secondary 1809
405.91	Hypertension, Renovascular 1809
410	Myocardial Infarction (MI), Acute 1424
410.0	Myocardial Infarction of Anterolateral Wall 1424
410.1	Myocardial Infarction of Other Anterior Wall 1424
410.2	Myocardial Infarction of Inferolateral Wall 1424
410.3	Myocardial Infarction of Inferoposterior Wall 1424
410.4	Myocardial Infarction of Other Inferior Wall 1424
410.5	Myocardial Infarction of Other Lateral Wall 1424
410.6	Myocardial Infarction of True Posterior Wall Infarction 1424
410.7	Myocardial Infarction of Subendocardial Infarction 1424
410.8	Myocardial Infarction of Other Specified Sites 1424
410.9	Myocardial Infarction of Unspecified Site 1424
410.90	Myocardial Infarction of Unspecified Site, Episode of Care Unspecified 1424
410.91	Myocardial Infarction of Unspecified Site, Initial Episode 1424
411.1	Angina, Unstable 144
411.81	Coronary Occlusion Without Myocardial Infarction 180
413	Angina Pectoris 140
413.0	Angina Decubitus 140
413.1	Prinzmetal's Angina 1726
413.9	Angina Pectoris, Unspecified 140
414	Other Forms of Chronic Ischemic Heart Disease 587
414.0	Coronary Atherosclerosis 587
414.00	Coronary Atherosclerosis of Unspecified Type of Vessel, Native or Graft 587
414.01	Coronary Atherosclerosis of Native Coronary Artery 587
414.8	Other Specified Forms of Chronic Ischemic Heart Disease 587
414.9	Ischemic Heart Disease, Chronic 587
415.0	Cor Pulmonale, Acute 576
415.1	Embolism, Pulmonary 789
416.0	Hypertension, Primary Pulmonary 576
416.1	Kyphoscoliotic Heart Disease 576
416.8	Chronic Pulmonary Heart Diseases, Other 576
416.9	Cor Pulmonale, Unspecified (Chronic Pulmonary Heart Disease) 576
420	Pericarditis, Acute 1615
420.90	Pericarditis, Acute 1615
420.91	Pericarditis, Acute Idiopathic 1615
420.99	Pericarditis, Acute, Other 1615
421	Endocarditis, Acute and Subacute 802
421.0	Endocarditis, Bacterial, Acute and Subacute 802
421.9	Endocarditis, Acute and Unspecified 802
422	Myocarditis 1428
422.90	Myocarditis, Acute 1428
423.2	Pericarditis, Chronic Constrictive 1617
424.0	Mitral Valve Prolapse (Barlow's Syndrome, Floppy Mitral Valve) 1385, 1389
424.1	Aortic Valve Stenosis 165, 167
424.9	Endocarditis, Valve Unspecified 802
425	Cardiomyopathy 419
425.1	Cardiomyopathy, Hypertrophic Obstructive 419
425.4	Cardiomyopathy, Other Primary 419
425.9	Cardiomyopathy, Secondary, Unspecified 419
426	Conduction Disorders 1040
426.0	Atrioventricular Block, Complete (Third-Degree) 224, 1920
426.1	Atrioventricular Block, Other and Unspecified 1040
426.11	Atrioventricular Block, Incomplete (First-Degree) 226
426.12	Atrioventricular Block, Second Degree, Incomplete (Mobitz Type I) 223
426.13	Atrioventricular Block, Incomplete (Second-Degree) 223
426.2	Left Bundle Branch Hemiblock 310
426.3	Left Bundle Branch Block, Other 310
426.4	Right Bundle Branch Block 310
426.5	Bundle Branch Block, Other and Unspecified 310
426.8	Other Specified Conduction Disorders 1040
426.9	Stokes-Adams Syndrome 1040, 2003
427	Cardiac Dysrhythmias 178, 220, 1920
427.0	Tachycardia, Paroxysmal Supraventricular 2039
427.1	Ventricular Tachycardia 2260
427.2	Paroxysmal Tachycardia, Unspecified 178
427.3	Atrial Fibrillation and Flutter 220
427.31	Atrial Fibrillation 220
427.4	Ventricular Fibrillation and Flutter 2256
427.41	Ventricular Fibrillation 2256
427.5	Cardiac Arrest 409
427.6	Premature Beats 1719
427.69	Ventricular Premature Contractions 2258
427.8	Cardiac Dysrhythmias, Other Specified 178
427.81	Sick Sinus Syndrome (Sinoatrial Node Dysfunction) 1920
427.89	Wandering Atrial Pacemaker 2293
427.9	Arrhythmia 178
428	Heart Failure 1042
428.0	Heart Failure, Congestive 1042
428.1	Heart Failure, Left 1042
428.9	Heart Failure, Unspecified 1042
429.9	Heart Disease, Unspecified 1042
430	Subarachnoid Hemorrhage (Non-Traumatic) 2011
431	Cerebral Hemorrhage 449
432.0	Epidural Hematoma (Non-Traumatic) 821
432.1	Subdural Hemorrhage 2016
432.9	Intracranial Hemorrhage 1226
433.1	Carotid Artery Occlusion 423

435	Transient Cerebral Ischemia 292
435	Transient Cerebral Ischemia 2169
435.9	Transient Ischemic Attack 2169
436	Cerebrovascular Accident (CVA), Acute 454
437	Other and Ill Defined Cerebrovascular Disease 292
437.0	Cerebral Atherosclerosis (Cerebrovascular Disease) 458
437.1	Cerebrovascular Insufficiency, Acute 458
437.2	Hypertensive Encephalopathy 458
437.3	Cerebral Aneurysm (Non-Ruptured) 445, 458
437.9	Cerebrovascular Disease, Unspecified 458
438.11	Aphasia, Late Effects of Cerebrovascular Disease 169
440	Atherosclerosis 186, 216
440.0	Arteriosclerosis and Atherosclerosis 216
440.1	Atherosclerosis of Renal Artery 216
440.2	Atherosclerosis of Arteries of the Extremities 186, 216
440.20	Atherosclerosis of the Extremities, Unspecified 216
440.21	Atherosclerosis of the Extremities with Intermittent Claudication 216
440.22	Atherosclerosis of the Extremities with Rest Pain 216
440.23	Atherosclerosis of the Extremities with Ulceration 216
440.24	Arteriosclerotic Gangrene 186
440.29	Atherosclerosis of Arteries of the Extremities, Other 216
440.8	Atherosclerosis of Other Specified Arteries 216
440.9	Atherosclerosis, Generalized and Unspecified 216
441	Aortic Aneurysm 3, 160, 163
441.0	Aortic Dissection (Dissecting Aneurysm) 3, 163
441.02	Abdominal Aneurysm, Dissecting 3
441.03	Thoracoabdominal Aneurysm, Dissecting 3
441.1	Thoracic Aneurysm, Ruptured 2070
441.2	Thoracic Aneurysm 2070
441.3	Abdominal Aneurysm, Ruptured 3, 160, 2070
441.4	Abdominal Aneurysm 3, 160, 2070
441.5	Aortic Aneurysm of Unspecified Site, Ruptured 160, 2070
441.6	Thoracoabdominal Aneurysm, Ruptured 3
441.7	Thoracoabdominal Aneurysm 3
441.9	Aortic Aneurysm 160
443	Other Peripheral Vascular Disease 308
443.0	Raynaud's Phenomenon 1781
443.1	Buerger's Disease (Thromboangiitis Obliterans) 308
443.9	Peripheral Vascular Disease, Unspecified 1626
444	Embolism and Thrombosis, Arterial 180
444.0	Embolism and Thrombosis, Arterial of Abdominal Aorta 180
444.1	Embolism and Thrombosis, Arterial of Thoracic Aorta 180
444.2	Embolism and Thrombosis, Arterial of Arteries of the Extremities 180
444.22	Peripheral Thrombosis of Lower Extremity 1623
444.8	Embolism and Thrombosis, Arterial of Other Specified Artery 180
444.9	Embolism and Thrombosis, Arterial and Venous, Unspecified 180
445.8	Other Forms of Epilepsy 824
446	Polyarteritis Nodosa and Allied Conditions 1685
446.0	Polyarteritis Nodosa 1685
446.5	Temporal Arteritis 2045
448.0	Osler-Weber-Rendu Disease (Hereditary Hemorrhagic Telangiectasia) 1528
451	Thrombophlebitis 2086
451.0	Thrombophlebitis, of Superficial Veins of Lower Extremities 2086
451.1	Thrombophlebitis, of Deep Vessels of Lower Extremities 2086
451.8	Thrombophlebitis, of Other Sites 2086
451.82	Thrombophlebitis, of Superficial Veins of Upper Extremities 2086
451.83	Thrombophlebitis, of Deep Vessels of the Upper Extremities 2086
451.89	Thrombophlebitis, Other 2086
453	Venous Embolism and Thrombosis 2252
453.3	Renal Vein Thrombosis 1807
453.8	Thrombosis and Embolism of Other Unspecified Veins 180
453.9	Thrombosis and Embolism of Unspecified Site, Other Venous 180
454	Varicose Veins of Lower Extremities 2244, 2246
454.0	Varicose (Stasis) Ulcer 2244
454.2	Varicose Veins of Lower Extremities with Ulcer and Inflammation 2246
454.9	Varicose Veins 2246
455	Hemorrhoids 1073
455.0	Hemorrhoids, Internal, Without Mention of Complication 1073
455.1	Hemorrhoids, Internal Thrombosed 1073
455.2	Hemorrhoids, Internal, with Other Complication 1073
455.3	Hemorrhoids, External, Without Mention of Complication 1073
455.4	Hemorrhoids, External Thrombosed 1073
455.5	Hemorrhoids, External, with Other Complication 1073
455.6	Hemorrhoids Without Mention of Complication, Unspecified 1073
455.7	Hemorrhoids, Thrombosed, Unspecified 1073
455.8	Hemorrhoids with Other Complication, Unspecified 1073
455.9	Hemorrhoidal Skin Tags, Residual 1073
456	Varicose Veins of Other Sites 2242, 2246
456.0	Esophageal Varices with Bleeding 843
456.1	Esophageal Varices Without Mention of Bleeding 843
456.4	Varicocele 2242
457.2	Lymphangitis 1324
458	Hypotension 1178
458.8	Other Specified Hypotension 1178
460	Cold (Upper Respiratory Infection) 533, 2216
461	Sinusitis, Acute 1928
461.0	Sinusitis, Maxillary 1928
461.1	Sinusitis, Frontal 1928
461.2	Sinusitis, Ethmoidal 1928
461.3	Sinusitis, Sphenoidal 1928
461.8	Sinusitis, Acute, Other 1928
461.9	Sinusitis, Unspecified 1928
462	Sore Throat (Pharyngitis, Acute) 1633
463	Tonsillitis, Acute 2104
464.0	Laryngitis 1279
464.3	Epiglottitis 822
464.30	Epiglottitis, Acute, Without Mention of Obstruction 822

464.31	Epiglottitis, Acute, with Obstruction 822	491.20	Chronic Bronchitis, Obstructive, Without Mention of Acute Exacerbation 302
465	Upper Respiratory Infections, Acute, of Multiple or Unspecified Sites 2216	491.21	Chronic Bronchitis, Obstructive, with Acute Exacerbation 302
465.9	Upper Respiratory Infection, Unspecified 2216	491.8	Bronchitis, Chronic, Other 302
466	Acute Bronchitis 299	491.9	Bronchitis, Chronic, Unspecified 302
466.0	Bronchitis, Acute 299	492	Emphysema 792
466.1	Bronchiolitis, Acute 299	492.0	Emphysematous Bleb 792
470	Deviated Nasal Septum 679	492.8	Emphysema, Other 792
471	Polyp of Nasal Cavity 1441	493	Asthma 209
471.0	Nasal Polyps 1441	493.0	Asthma, Extrinsic 209
471.9	Nasal Polyp, Unspecified 1441	493.00	Asthma, Extrinsic, Without Mention of Status Asthmaticus 209
473.2	Sinusitis, Chronic 1928	493.1	Asthma, Intrinsic 209
473.9	Sinusitis, Chronic, Unspecified 1928	493.2	Asthma, Chronic Obstructive 209
474	Tonsillitis and Adenoiditis 2104	493.9	Asthma, Unspecified 209
474.0	Tonsillitis, Chronic 2104	493.90	Asthma, Unspecified, Without Mention of Status Asthmaticus 209
474.1	Hypertrophy of Tonsils and Adenoids 2104	493.91	Asthma, Unspecified, With Status Asthmaticus 209
474.12	Hypertrophy of Adenoids Alone 2104	494	Bronchiectasis 297
475	Peritonsillar Abscess 36	495	Allergic Alveolitis, Extrinsic 1130, 1150
477	Hay Fever (Allergic Rhinitis) 98	495.0	Farmer's Lung 1150
477.0	Allergic Rhinitis Due to Pollen 98	495.1	Bagassosis 1150
477.8	Allergic Rhinitis Due to Other Allergen 98	495.2	Bird-Fancier's Lung 1150
477.9	Allergic Rhinitis, Unspecified 98	495.5	Mushroom Workers' Lung 1150
478.1	Nasal Septum Perforation 1443	495.7	Ventilation Pneumonitis 2254
478.79	Abscess, Larynx 25	495.8	Other Specified Allergic Alveolitis & Pneumontitis 1150
480	Viral Pneumonia 1667	495.9	Hypersensitivity Pneumonitis 1130, 1150
480.9	Viral Pneumonia, Unspecified 1667	496	COPD (Chronic Obstructive Pulmonary Disease) 511
481	Pneumococcal Pneumonia 1667	500	Pneumoconiosis, Coal Worker's 1662
482	Bacterial Pneumonia, Other 1667	501	Asbestosis 201
482.0	Pneumonia Due to Klebsiella Pneumoniae 1667	502	Silicosis 1662, 1926
482.1	Pneumonia Due to Pseudomonas 1667	503	Siderosis 1924
482.2	Pneumonia Due to Hemophilus Influenzae 1667	504	Byssinosis 328
482.3	Pneumonia Due to Streptococcus 1667	505	Occupational Asthma (Pneumoconiosis) 1498, 1662
482.4	Pneumonia Due to Staphylococcus 1667	506.0	Bronchitis and Pneumonitis Due to Fumes or Vapors 299
482.8	Pneumonia Due to Other Specified Bacteria 1667	506.1	Acute Pulmonary Edema Due to Fumes and Vapors 1756
482.83	Legionnaire's Disease 1282	506.4	Chronic Respiratory Conditions Due to Fumes and Vapors 302, 1926
482.84	Legionnaire's Disease 1282		
482.9	Pneumonia, Bacterial, Unspecified 1667	506.9	Respiratory Conditions Due to Fumes or Vapors, Unspecified 2254
483	Pneumonia Due to Other Specified Organism 1667		
484	Pneumonia in Infectious Diseases Classified Elsewhere 1667	507	Pneumonitis Due to Solids and Liquids 1667
485	Bronchopneumonia, Organism Unspecified 1667	507.0	Pneumonitis Due to Inhalation of Food or Vomitus 1667
486	Pneumonia, Organism Unspecified 1667	510	Empyema 794
487	Influenza 1207	510.0	Empyema with Fistula 794
487.0	Influenza with Pneumonia 1207	510.9	Empyema Without Mention of Fistula 794
487.1	Influenza with Other Respiratory Manifestations 1207	511	Pleurisy 1659
487.8	Influenza with Other Manifestations 1207	511.0	Pleurisy Without Mention of Effusion or Current Tuberculosis 1659
490	Bronchitis, not Specified As Acute or Chronic 302	511.1	Pleurisy with Effusion, with Mention of Bacterial Cause Other Than Tuberculosis 1659
491	Bronchitis, Chronic 302		
491.0	Chronic Bronchitis, Simple 302	511.9	Pleural Effusion, Unspecified 1659
491.1	Chronic Bronchitis, Mucopurulent 302	512	Pneumothorax 1671
491.2	Chronic Bronchitis, Obstructive 302	512.0	Pneumothorax, Spontaneous Tension 1671
		512.8	Pneumothorax, Other Spontaneous 1671

Index of ICD-9 CM

513	Abscess of Lung and Mediastinum 29
513.0	Lung Abscess 29
514	Pulmonary Edema 1756
515	Interstitial Pulmonary Fibrosis 1219
518.0	Lung Collapse 1312
518.4	Acute Edema of Lungs, Unspecified 1756
518.5	Adult Respiratory Distress Syndrome 79
518.81	Respiratory Failure 1821
520	Disorders of Tooth Development and Eruption 657
520.6	Impacted Tooth 1191
520.9	Dental Disorders 657
521	Tooth Disorders 657
521.0	Cavities (Dental Caries) 657
521.7	Posteruptive Color Changes 657
521.9	Disease of Hard Tissues of Teeth, Unspecified 657
522	Diseases of Pulp and Periapical Tissues 660
522.5	Dentoalveolar Abscess 660
522.7	Periapical Abscess with Sinus 991
523.0	Gingivitis, Acute 993
523.1	Gingivitis, Chronic 993
523.2	Gingival Recession 993
523.3	Periodontitis 991, 1619
523.4	Periodontitis, Chronic 1619
523.9	Unspecified Gingival and Periodontal Disease 993
524	Dentofacial Anomalies, Including Malocclusion 1191
524.3	Impacted Tooth with Abnormal Position 1191
524.60	Temporomandibular Joint (TMJ) Syndrome, Unspecified 2049
525.1	Loss of Teeth Due to Accident, Extraction, or Local Periodontal Disease 657
527	Diseases of the Salivary Glands 1865
527.5	Salivary Gland Stones 1865
528.3	Ludwig's Angina 1306
530.0	Achalasia 44
530.1	Esophagitis 847
530.10	Esophagitis, Unspecified 847
530.11	Reflux Esophagitis 847
530.19	Esophagitis, Other 847
530.3	Esophageal Strictures 840
530.5	Esophageal Spasm 839
530.6	Esophageal Diverticula 836
530.7	Mallory-Weiss Syndrome 1333
530.81	Gastroesophageal Reflux 979
530.9	Unspecified Disorder of Esophagus 840
531	Gastric Ulcer 1611
533	Ulcer, Peptic, Site Unspecified 1611
533.0	Peptic Ulcer with Hemorrhage, Acute 1611
533.1	Peptic Ulcer with Perforation, Acute 1611
533.2	Peptic Ulcer with Hemorrhage and Perforation, Acute 1611
533.3	Peptic Ulcer Without Mention of Hemorrhage or Perforation, Acute 1611
533.4	Peptic Ulcer with Hemorrhage, Chronic or Unspecified 1611
533.5	Peptic Ulcer with Perforation, Chronic or Unspecified 1611
533.6	Peptic Ulcer with Hemorrhage and Perforation, Chronic or Unspecified 1611
533.7	Peptic Ulcer Without Mention of Hemorrhage or Perforation, Chronic 1611
533.9	Peptic Ulcer Unspecified As Acute or Chronic, Without Mention of Hemorrhage or Perforation 1611
535	Gastritis and Duodenitis 970
535.0	Gastritis 970
535.1	Atrophic Gastritis 970
535.2	Gastric Mucosal Hypertrophy 970
535.3	Alcoholic Gastritis 970
535.4	Gastritis, Other Specified 970
535.5	Unspecific Gastritis and Gastroduodenitis 970
535.6	Duodenitis 749, 970
536.0	Achlorhydria, Hypochlorhydria 49
536.8	Dyspepsia 49, 759
537.0	Pyloric Stenosis, Acquired (Adult) Hypertrophic 1767
537.81	Pylorospasm 1770
540	Appendicitis, Acute 175
540.0	Appendicitis, Acute with Generalized Peritonitis 175
540.1	Appendicitis, Acute with Peritoneal Abscess 175
540.9	Appendicitis, Acute Without Mention of Peritonitis 175
541	Appendicitis, Unqualified 175
542	Appendicitis, Other 175
550	Hernia, Inguinal 1103
550.0	Inguinal Hernia, with Gangrene 1103
550.00	Inguinal Hernia, Unilateral or Unspecified, with Gangrene 1103
550.01	Inguinal Hernia, Unilateral with Gangrene, Recurrent 1103
550.02	Inguinal Hernia, Bilateral with Gangrene 1103
550.03	Inguinal Hernia, Bilateral with Gangrene, Recurrent 1103
550.1	Inguinal Hernia with Obstruction, Without Mention of Gangrene 1103
550.10	Inguinal Hernia, Unilateral with Obstruction, Without Mention of Gangrene 1103
550.11	Inguinal Hernia, Unilateral with Obstruction, Without Mention of Gangrene 1103
550.12	Inguinal Hernia, Bilateral with Obstruction, Without Mention of Gangrene 1103
550.13	Inguinal Hernia, Bilateral with Gangrene, Recurrent 1103
550.9	Inguinal Hernia, Without Mention of Obstruction or Gangrene 1103
550.90	Inguinal Hernia, Unilateral Without Mention of Obstruction or Gangrene 1103
550.91	Inguinal Hernia, Unilateral Without Mention of Obstruction or Gangrene 1103
550.92	Inguinal Hernia, Bilateral Without Mention of Obstruction or Gangrene 1103
550.93	Inguinal Hernia, Bilateral Without Mention of Obstruction or Gangrene 1103
551	Hernia of Abdominal Cavity, Other, with Gangrene 1097, 1100, 1103, 1106
551.0	Femoral Hernia with Gangrene 1103
551.1	Umbilical Hernia with Gangrene 1106

551.2	Ventral Hernia with Gangrene 1100
551.21	Incisional with Gangrene 1100
551.3	Diaphragmatic Hernia with Gangrene 1097
551.8	Hernia, Other Specified Sites with Gangrene 1103
552.0	Femoral Hernia with Obstruction 1103
552.1	Umbilical Hernia with Obstruction 1106
552.2	Ventral Hernia with Obstruction 1100
552.3	Diaphragmatic Hernia with Obstruction 1097
553.0	Hernia, Femoral 1103
553.00	Femoral Hernia, Unilateral or Unspecified 1103
553.01	Femoral Hernia, Unilateral or Unspecified, Recurrent 1103
553.02	Femoral Hernia, Bilateral 1103
553.03	Femoral Hernia, Bilateral, Recurrent 1103
553.1	Hernia, Umbilical 1106
553.2	Hernia, Ventral 1100
553.20	Hernia, Ventral Unspecified 1100
553.21	Ventral Hernia (Incisional) 1100
553.3	Hernia, Hiatal 1097
553.8	Hernia of Other Specified Sites 1097
553.9	Hernia of Unspecified Site 1097
555	Regional Enteritis 600, 2209
555.0	Regional Enteritis, Small Intestine (Ileitis) 600
555.1	Regional Enteritis, Large Intestine 600
555.2	Regional Enteritis, Small Intestine with Large Intestine 600
555.9	Crohn's Disease 600
556	Ulcerative Colitis 2209
557	Vascular Insufficiency of Intestines 1372, 2209
557.0	Mesenteric Thrombosis 1372
558	Gastroenteritis and Colitis, Non-Infectious 535
558.1	Gastroenteritis and Colitis Due to Radiation 535
558.2	Gastroenteritis and Colitis, Toxic 535
558.9	Gastroenteritis, Non-infectious 535, 696, 975
560	Intestinal Obstruction Without Mention of Hernia 1222
560.0	Intussusception 1222
560.1	Paralytic Ileus 1222
560.2	Volvulus 1222, 2289
560.3	Intestinal Impaction 1222
560.30	Impaction of Intestine, Unspecified Impaction of Colon 1222
560.31	Gallstone Ileus Obstruction of Intestine by Gallstones 1222
560.39	Other Concretion of Intestine, Enterolith, Fecal Impaction, Fecal Reservoir Syndrome 1222
560.8	Intestinal Obstruction, Other Specified 1222
560.81	Intestinal or Peritoneal Adhesions with Obstruction (Post-Operative) (Post-Infection) 1222
560.9	Bowel Obstruction (Intestinal Obstruction, Unspecified) 1222
562	Diverticula of Intestine 739
562.0	Diverticulosis of Small Intestine 739
562.01	Diverticulitis of Small Intestine 739
562.1	Diverticulitis and Diverticulosis of Colon 739
562.10	Diverticulosis of Colon Without Mention of Hemorrhage 739
562.11	Diverticulitis of Colon Without Mention of Hemorrhage 739
564.0	Constipation 558, 1224
564.1	Irritable Bowel Syndrome 1244
564.2	Dumping Syndrome (Post-Gastric Syndrome) 747
564.3	Vomiting Following Gastrointestinal Surgery 1224
564.4	Postoperative Functional Disorders, Other 1224
564.5	Diarrhea, Functional 1224
564.8	Disorders of Intestine, Functional, Other Specified 1224
564.9	Intestinal Upset 1224
565.0	Anal Fissure and/or Ulcer 127
565.1	Anorectal Fistula 154
566	Perirectal Abscess 20, 24, 34
567	Peritonitis 1628
567.1	Peritonitis, Pneumococcal 1628
567.2	Abscess, Subdiaphragmatic 38, 42
567.8	Peritonitis, Other Specified 1628
567.9	Peritonitis, Unspecified 1628
568.0	Abdominal Adhesions 1
569	Other Disorders of Intestines 1728
569.0	Anal and Rectal Polyps 1783
569.1	Rectal Prolapse 1783, 1785
569.3	Hemorrhage of Rectum and Anus 1068
569.41	Rectal Ulcer 127, 1788
569.42	Anal or Rectal Pain 1788
569.49	Proctitis 1728
569.8	Other Specified Disorders of Intestine 1728
571	Liver Disease and Cirrhosis, Chronic 1087, 1089
571.0	Alcoholic Fatty Liver 1087
571.1	Hepatitis, Acute Alcoholic 1087
571.2	Cirrhosis of the Liver, Alcoholic 1087
571.3	Alcoholic Liver Damage, Unspecified 1087
571.4	Hepatitis, Chronic 1089
571.5	Cirrhosis of the Liver Without Mention of Alcohol 515
571.6	Cirrhosis, Biliary 515
571.8	Liver Disease, Chronic, Nonalcoholic 515
571.9	Liver Disease Without Mention of Alcohol, Chronic, Unspecified 515
572.0	Liver Abscess 27
572.2	Hepatic Coma 1079
572.8	Liver Disease, Chronic, Other Sequelae 1079
573.0	Liver Congestion, Passive, Chronic 1298
573.1	Hepatitis in Viral Diseases Classified Elsewhere 1081
573.3	Hepatitis, Unspecified 1298
573.4	Hepatic Infarction 1298
573.8	Liver Disorders, Other Specified 1298
573.9	Liver Disease 1298
574	Cholelithiasis 501
574.0	Calculus of Gallbladder with Acute Cholecystitis 501
574.00	Calculus of Gallbladder with Acute Cholecystitis Without Mention of Obstruction 501
574.1	Calculus of Gallbladder with Other Cholecystitis 501

574.10	Calculus of Gallbladder with Other Cholecystitis, Without Mention of Obstruction 501
574.2	Calculus of Gallbladder Without Mention of Cholecystitis 501
574.20	Calculus of Gallbladder Without Mention of Cholecystitis Without Mention of Obstruction 501
574.3	Calculus of Bile Duct with Acute Cholecystitis 501
574.4	Calculus of Bile Duct with Other Cholecystitis 501
574.5	Calculus of Bile Duct Without Mention of Cholecystitis 501
574.6	Calculus of Gallbladder and Bile Duct with Acute Choleystitis 501
574.8	Calculus of Gallbladder and Bile Duct with Acute and Chronic Cholecystitis 501
575	Other Disorders of Gallbladder 497
575.0	Cholecystitis 497
575.1	Cholecystitis, Other Chronic 497
575.2	Obstruction of Gallbladder 497
575.4	Perforation of Gallbladder 497
575.8	Other Specified Disorders of Gall Bladder 497
577	Diseases of Pancreas 1569, 1573
577.0	Pancreatitis, Acute 1573
577.1	Pancreatitis, Chronic 1573
577.2	Pancreatic Cyst and Pseudocyst 1569, 1573
577.8	Other Specified Diseases of Pancreas 1573
577.9	Pancreatic Disease, Unspecified 1573
578	Gastrointestinal Hemorrhage 982
578.0	Hematemesis 982
578.1	Blood in Stool 982
578.9	Hemorrhage of Gastrointestinal Tract, Unspecified 982
580	Glomerulonephritis, Acute 1001
581	Nephrotic Syndrome 1456
581.0	Nephrotic Syndrome with Lesion of Proliferative Glomerulonephritis 1456
581.1	Nephrotic Syndrome with Lesion of Membranous Glomerulonephritis 1456
581.2	Nephrotic Syndrome with Lesion of Membranoproliferative Glomerulonephritis 1456
581.3	Nephrotic Syndrome with Lesion of Minimal Change Glomerulonephritis 1456
581.8	Nephrotic Syndrome, Other 1456
581.9	Nephrotic Syndrome with Unspecified Pathological Lesion in Kidney 1456
582	Glomerulonephritis, Chronic 1003, 1005
582.1	Glomerulosclerosis, Chronic, with Lesion of Membranes 1005
583.89	Nephritis and Nephropathy, Interstitial 1453
584	Renal Failure, Acute 1802
584.5	Renal Failure, Acute with Lesion of Tubular Necrosis 1802
584.6	Renal Failure, Acute with Lesion of Renal Cortical Necrosis 1802
584.7	Renal Failure, Acute with Lesion of Renal Medullary Necrosis 1802
584.8	Renal Failure, Acute with Other Specified Pathological Lesion in Kidney 1802
584.9	Renal Failure, Acute, Unspecified 1802
585	Renal Failure (Kidney Failure), Chronic 1804
586	Renal Failure, Unspecified (Uremia) 1802, 1804
587	Renal Sclerosis, Unspecified 1005
590	Infections of Kidney 1762, 1764
590.0	Pyelonephritis, Chronic 1764
590.1	Pyelonephritis, Acute 1762
590.2	Renal and Perinephric Abscess 40
590.8	Other Pyelonephritis or Pyonephrosis, Not Specified As Acute or Chronic 1762
590.80	Pyelonephritis (Pyelitis), Unspecified 1762
590.9	Kidney Infection, Unspecified 1762
591	Hydronephrosis 1138
592	Calculus of Kidney and Ureter 335
592.0	Calculus, Renal (Kidney) 335
592.1	Calculus of Ureter 335
592.9	Calculus, Urinary, Unspecified 335
594	Calculus of Lower Urinary Tract 333
594.0	Calculus in Diverticulum of Bladder 333
594.1	Calculus in Bladder, Other 333
594.2	Calculus in Urethra 333
595	Cystitis 616, 619
595.0	Cystitis, Acute 616
595.1	Cystitis, Interstitial 619
596.1	Fistula, Intestinovesical 262
596.2	Bladder Fistula (Vesical Fistula not Elsewhere Classified) 262
596.54	Neurogenic Bladder 1471
597	Urethritis, Not Sexually Transmitted and Urethral Syndrome 2218
599	Other Disorders of Urethra and Urinary Tract 262
599.0	Urinary Tract Infection (Pyuria), Site not Specified 1771
599.3	Caruncle of the Urethra, Benign 434
599.7	Hematuria 1055
600	Prostatic Hypertrophy 1731
601	Prostatitis (Inflammatory Disease of the Prostate) 1734
601.0	Prostatitis, Acute 1734
601.1	Prostatitis, Chronic 1734
601.2	Abscess of Prostate 1734
601.3	Prostatocystitis 1734
601.8	Inflammatory Diseases of Prostate, Other Specified 1734
601.9	Prostatitis, Unspecified 1734
603	Hydrocele 1136
603.1	Hydrocele, Infected 1136
603.8	Other Specified Types of Hydrocele 1136
603.9	Hydrocele, Unspecified 1136
604.0	Orchitis 1524
604.9	Epididymitis 819
604.90	Orchitis and Epididymitis, Unspecified 819
606	Infertility, Male 1206
606.9	Male Infertility, Unspecified 1206
607	Disorders of Penis 1608
607.1	Balanoposthitis 1608
607.2	Inflammatory Disorders of Penis, Other 1608
607.3	Priapism 1608
607.8	Penis, Disorders of 1608
607.84	Impotence of Organic Origin 1198

Code	Description	Code	Description
608.1	Spermatocele 1942	625.2	Menorrhagia 1369
608.89	Male Climacteric 1332	625.3	Dysmenorrhea 1369
610	Mammary Dysplasia, Benign 874	625.4	Premenstrual Syndrome 1724
610.1	Fibrocystic Breast Disease 874	625.6	Urinary Incontinence in Women 2220, 2222
610.2	Fibroadenosis of Breast 874	625.9	Unspecified Symptom Associated with Female Genital Organs 1369
610.8	Other Specified Benign Mammary Dysplasisa 874	626.0	Amenorrhea (Absence of Menstruation) 1369
610.9	Benign Mammary Dysplasia, Unspecified 874	626.1	Menstruation, Scanty or Infrequent 1369
611.0	Abscess, Breast (Inflammatory Disease of Breast) 22	626.2	Menorrhagia (Excessive or Frequent Menstruation) 757, 1369
611.1	Gynecomastia (Hypertrophy of Breast) 1025	626.4	Menstruation, Irregular 1369
611.72	Signs and Symptoms in Breast, Lump or Mass in Breast 874	626.5	Ovulation Bleeding 1369
614.0	Salpingitis and Oophoritis, Acute 1870	626.6	Metrorrhagia 1369
614.1	Salpingitis and Oophoritis, Chronic 1870	626.6	Metrorrhagia (Bleeding Unrelated to Menstrual Cycle) 757
614.2	Salpingitis and Oophoritis Not Specified As Acute, Subacute, or Chronic 1870	626.8	Uterine Bleeding, Dysfunctional 757
614.3	Pelvic Cellulitis and Parametritis, Acute 1604	626.9	Menstrual Disorders 1369
614.4	Pelvic Cellulitis and Parametritis, Chronic or Unspecified 1604	627	Menopausal and Post Menopausal Disorders 757
614.5	Pelvic Peritonitis, Acute or Unspecified, Female 1604	627.0	Premenopausal Menorrhagis 757
614.6	Pelvic Peritoneal Adhesions, Female 1604	627.1	Postmenopausal Bleeding 1703
614.7	Pelvic Peritonitis, Chronic, Female 1604	627.2	Menopause 1368
614.9	Pelvic Inflammatory Disease, Unspecified 1604	627.3	Vaginitis, Postmenopausal Atrophic 2233
616.0	Cervicitis and Endocervicitis 472	627.8	Menopausal and Postmenopausal Disorders, Other Specified 1368
616.1	Vaginitis and Vulvovaginitis 2233	627.9	Menopausal Disorder, Unspecified 1368
616.10	Vaginitis, Nonspecific 2233	628	Female Infertility 1204
616.2	Cyst of Bartholin's Gland 242	628.0	Infertility, Female, Associated with Anovulation 1204
616.3	Bartholin's Gland Infection 242	628.2	Infertility, Female, of Tubal Origin 1204
617	Endometriosis 805	628.3	Infertility, Female, of Uterine Origin 1204
617.0	Endometriosis of Uterus 805	628.4	Infertility, Female, of Cervical of Vaginal Origin 1204
617.1	Endometriosis of Ovary 805	628.8	Infertility, Female, of Other Specified Origin 1204
617.2	Endometriosis of Fallopian Tube 805	628.9	Infertility, Female, Unspecified 1204
617.3	Endometriosis of Pelvic Peritoneum 805	629.9	Unspecified Cause 674
617.4	Endometriosis of Rectovaginal Septum and Vagina 805	630	Hydatidiform Mole 1134
617.5	Endometriosis of Intestine 805	633	Ectopic Pregnancy 775
617.6	Endometriosis in Scar of Skin 805	633.0	Abdominal Pregnancy 775
617.8	Endometriosis of Other Specified Sites 805	633.1	Tubal Pregnancy 775
617.9	Endometriosis, Site Unspecified 805	633.2	Ovarian Pregnancy 775
618	Genital Prolapse 621, 2220	633.8	Ectopic Pregnancy, Other 775
618.0	Urethrocele with Stress Incontinence 621, 2220	633.9	Ectopic Pregnancy, Unspecified 775
618.1	Uterine Prolapse without Mention of Vaginal Wall Prolapse 621, 2220	634	Miscarriage (Spontaneous Abortion) 1381
618.2	Uterovaginal Prolapse, Incomplete 621	634.7	Abortion with Other Specified Complications 1381
618.3	Uterovaginal Prolapse, Complete 621	634.9	Abortion/Miscarriage without Mention of Complication 1381
618.4	Uterovaginal Prolapse, Unspecified 621	634.90	Abortion Without Mention of Complication, Unspecified 1381
619.0	Fistula, Vesicovaginal (Female Urinary-Genital Tract Fistula) 2266	634.92	Abortion Without Mention of Complication, Complete 1381
620.0	Cyst of Ovary, Follicular 1552	637.2	Damage to Pelvic Organs by Abortion 2229
620.1	Cyst or Hematoma, Corpus Luteum 1552	639.2	Uterus, Perforation of (Damage to Pelvic Organs and Tissues by Abnormal Pregnancy) 2229
620.2	Ovarian Cyst, Benign 1552	640	Hemorrhage in Early Pregnancy 2080
620.8	Hematosalpinx 1053	640.0	Threatened Abortion 2080
621.0	Uterine Polyps (Polyp of Corpus Uteri) 2228	640.03	Threatened Abortion, Antepartum Condition or Complication 2080
621.8	Other Specified Disorders of Uterus, Nec 2229	641	Antepartum Hemorrhage, Abruptio Placentae and Placenta Previa 1653
622.1	Cervical Dysplasia 467		
622.7	Cervical Polyps 470		

641.1	Placenta Previa with Hemorrhage 1653
641.11	Hemorrhage from Placenta Previa, Delivered, with or Without Mention of Antepartum Condition 1653
641.13	Hemorrhage from Placenta Previa, Antepartum Condition or Complication, 1653
641.2	Abruptio Placentae 16
641.20	Premature Separation of Placenta 16
641.21	Premature Separation of Placenta, Delivered, with or Without Mention of Antepartum Condition 16
641.23	Premature Separation of Placenta, Antepartum Condition or Complication 16
642.0	Benign Essential Hypertension Complicating Pregnancy, Childbirth, and the Puerperium 1711
642.1	Hypertension Secondary to Renal Disease Complicating Pregnancy, Childbirth and the Puerperium 1711
642.2	Other Pre-existing Hypertension Complicating Pregnancy, Childbirth and the Puerperium 1711
642.3	Transient Hypertension of Pregnancy 1711
642.4	Preeclampsia and Eclampsia (Toxemia of Pregnancy), Mild or Unspecified 1711
642.5	Preeclampsia, Severe 1711
642.6	Eclampsia 1711
642.7	Pre-eclampsia or Eclampsia Superimposed on Pre-Existing Hypertension 1711
642.9	Unspecified Hypertension Complicating Pregnancy, Childbirth, and the Puerperium 1711
643	Excessive Vomiting in Pregnancy 1142
643.0	Morning Sickness (Hyperemesis Gravidarum), Mild 1142
643.03	Morning Sickness (Hyperemesis Gravidarum), Mild, Antepartum Condition or Complication 1142
643.1	Hyperemesis Gravidarum with Metabolic Disturbance 1142
643.2	Late Vomiting of Pregnancy 1142
643.8	Other Vomiting Complicating Pregnancy 1142
643.9	Unspecified Vomiting of Pregnancy 1142
644	Premature Labor (Early or Threatened Labor) 1720
644.0	Threatened Premature Labor 1720
644.03	Early or Threatened Labor, Antepartum Condition or Complication 1720
644.1	Other Threatened Abortion 1720
644.2	Premature Labor (Early Onset of Delivery) 1720
646	Other Complications of Pregnancy, Not Elsewhere Classified 1713
646.2	Unspecified Renal Disease in Pregnancy Without Mention of Hypertension 82
646.9	Unspecified Complication of Pregnancy 1713
647.5	Rubella 1856
648.2	Anemia Complicating Pregnancy 136
648.6	Cardiovascular Disease in Pregnancy 422
648.7	Bone and Joint Disorders of Back, Pelvis, and Lower Limbs in Pregnancy 1713
648.8	Gestational Diabetes (Abnormal Glucose Tolerance in Pregnancy) 988
650	Pregnancy, Normal (Delivery in a Completely Normal Case) 1716
651	Pregnancy, Multiple Gestation 1714
651.0	Twin Pregnancy 1714
651.00	Twin Pregnancy, Unspecified As to Episode of Care or Not Applicable 1714
651.1	Triplet Pregnancy 1714
651.10	Triplet Pregnancy, Unspecified As to Episode of Care or Not Applicable 1714
651.2	Quadruplet Pregnancy 1714
651.20	Quadruplet Pregnancy, Unspecified As to Episode of Care or Not Applicable 1714
651.3	Twin Pregnancy with Fetal Loss and Retention of One Fetus 1714
652.2	Isoimmunization from Other and Unspecified Blood-Group Incompatibility 1831
654.2	Abnormality of Organs ans Soft Tissues of Pelvis, Previous Cesarean Delivery NOS 1713
656	Other Fetal and Placental Problems Affecting Management of Mother 1831
656.1	Rh Incompatibility 1831
658	Other Problems Associated with Amniotic Cavity and Membranes 1722
658.0	Oligohydramnios 1722
658.1	Premature Rupture of Membranes 1722
658.13	Premature Rupture of Membranes, Antepartum Condition or Complication, 1722
658.2	Delayed Delivery After Spontaneous or Unspecified Rupture of Membranes 1722
666.0	Third-Stage Hemorrhage 1651
667	Placenta Accreta (Retained Placenta or Membranes, without Hemorrhage) 1651
667.0	Retained Placenta Without Hemorrhage 1651
667.1	Retained Portions of Placenta or Membranes, Without Hemorrhage 1651
669.7	Cesarean Delivery, Without Mention of Indication 476
671.9	Venous Complications in Pregnancy and the Puerperium, Unspecified 2252
673	Obsterical Pulmonar Embolism 789
673.0	Obstetrical Air Emblism 789
673.1	Amniotic Fluid Embolism 789
673.2	Obstetric Blood-clot Embolism 789
673.3	Obstetric Pyemic and Septic Embolism 789
673.8	Other Pulmonary Embolism 789
674.8	Complications of the Puerperium, Other 419
675	Infections of the Breast and Nipple Associated with Childbirth 1705
675.0	Infections of Nipple 1705
675.2	Postpartum Mastitis (Nonpurulent Mastitis) 1705
675.8	Other Specified Infections of the Breast and Nipple 1705
675.9	Unspecified Infection of the Breast and Nipple 1705
680	Carbuncle and Furuncle 407, 961
680.1	Carbuncle of Neck 407
680.2	Carbuncle of Trunk 407
680.5	Carbuncle of Buttock 407
680.9	Furuncle 407, 961
681	Cellulitis of Finger and Toe 443
682	Abscess, Other Cellulitis and Abscess 17, 32
682.0	Cellulitis and Abscess of Face 17

682.1	Abscess or Cellulitis of Neck 17, 443		706.2	Sebaceous Cyst 1896
682.2	Cellulitis and Abscess of Trunk (Including Breast) 17, 443		707	Chronic Ulcer of Skin 2244
682.3	Cellulitis and Abscess of Upper Arm and Forearm (Including Axilla) 17, 443		707.0	Decubitus Ulcer 632
			707.9	Ulcer of Unspecified Sites, Chronic 632
682.4	Cellulitis and Abscess of Hand, Except Fingers and Thumb (Palmar Abscess) 17, 32		708	Urticaria (Hives) 2226
			708.5	Sleep Disturbances 1152
682.5	Cellulitis and Abscess of Buttock 17		709.01	Vitiligo 2286
682.6	Cellulitis and Abscess of Leg, Except Foot 17		710.0	Lupus Erythematosus, Systemic 1317
682.7	Cellulitis and Abscess of Foot, Except Toes 17		710.1	Systemic Scleroses 1892
682.8	Cellulitis and Abscess, Other Specified Sites 17		710.2	Sjögren's Disease (Sicca Syndrome) 1838, 1930
682.9	Cellulitis and Abscess, Other Unspecified Sites 17, 443		710.3	Dermatomyositis 677
684	Impetigo 1193		710.9	Unspecified Diffuse Connective Tissue Disease 1317
685	Pilonidal Cyst 1645		711.0	Septic Arthritis (Pyogenic) 192
685.0	Pilonidal Cyst with Abscess 1645		711.9	Arthritis, Infectious 192
685.1	Pilonidal Cyst Without Mention of Abscess 1645		714.0	Rheumatoid Arthritis 1838
691.8	Atopic Dermatitis 218		714.1	Felty's Syndrome 1838
692	Contact Dermatitis and Other Eczema 560		715	Osteoarthritis and Allied Disorders 1530
692.0	Contact Dermatitis and Other Eczema Due to Detergents 560		715.0	Osteoarthrosis, Generalized 1530
692.1	Contact Dermatitis and Other Eczema Due to Oils and Greases 560		715.00	Osteoarthrosis, Site Unspecified 1530
			715.1	Osteoarthrosis, Localized, Primary 1530
692.2	Contact Dermatitis and Other Eczema Due to Solvents 560		715.10	Osteoarthrosis, Localized, Primary, Site Unspecified 1530
692.3	Contact Dermatitis and Other Eczema Due to Drugs and Medicines in Contact with Skin 560		715.11	Osteoarthrosis, Localized, Primary, Shoulder Region 1530
			715.12	Osteoarthrosis, Localized, Primary, Upper Arm 1530
692.4	Contact Dermatitis and Other Eczema Due to Other Chemical Products 560		715.13	Osteoarthrosis, Localized, Primary, Forearm 1530
			715.14	Osteoarthrosis, Localized, Primary, Hand 1530
692.6	Poison Ivy, Oak, Sumac, or Other Plant Dermatitis 1673		715.15	Osteoarthrosis, Localized, Primary, Pelvic Region and Thigh 1530
692.71	Contact Dermatitis and Other Eczema Due to Sunburn 316, 2019		715.16	Osteoarthrosis, Localized, Primary, Lower Leg 1530
692.8	Dermatitis Due to Cosmetics 268		715.17	Osteoarthrosis, Localized, Primary, Ankle and Foot 1530
692.81	Contact Dermatitis and Other Eczema Due to Cosmetics 560		715.18	Osteoarthrosis, Localized, Primary, Other Specified Sites 1530
692.82	Radiodermatitis 560, 1780		715.19	Osteoarthrosis, Localized, Primary, Multiple Sites 1530
692.83	Contact Dermatitis and Other Eczema Due to Metals 674		715.2	Osteoarthrosis, Localized, Secondary 1530
692.89	Contact Dermatitis and Other Eczema 674		715.20	Osteoarthrosis, Localized, Secondary, Site Unspecified 1530
692.9	Eczema 560, 674, 778		715.21	Osteoarthrosis, Localized, Secondary, Shoulder Region 1530
693	Dermatitis Due to Substances Taken Internally 96		715.22	Osteoarthrosis, Localized, Secondary, Upper Arm 1530
693.0	Allergic Dermatitis (Due to Drugs/Medicines) 96		715.23	Osteoarthrosis, Localized, Secondary, Forearm 1530
694.4	Pemphigus 1606		715.24	Osteoarthrosis, Localized, Secondary, Hand 1530
695.1	Erythema Multiforme 833		715.25	Osteoarthrosis, Localized, Secondary, Pelvic Region and Thigh 1530
695.2	Erythema Nodosum 835			
695.4	Lupus Erythematosus 1317		715.26	Osteoarthrosis, Localized, Secondary, Lower Leg 1530
695.9	Unspecified Erythematous Condition 833		715.27	Osteoarthrosis, Localized, Secondary, Ankle and Foot 1530
696.0	Psoriatic Arthritis 1740		715.28	Osteoarthrosis, Localized, Secondary, Other Specified Sites 1530
696.1	Psoriasis, Other 1738		715.29	Osteoarthrosis, Localized, Secondary, Multiple Sites 1530
696.3	Pityriasis Rosea 1649		715.3	Osteoarthrosis, Localized, Not Specified Whether Primary or Secondary 1530
698.0	Pruritus Ani (Perianal Itch) 1736			
700	Corns and Calluses, Infected 578		715.30	Osteoarthrosis, Localized, Not Specified Whether Primary or Secondary, Site Unspecified 1530
701.0	Addison's Keloid 1254			
701.4	Keloid 1254		715.31	Osteoarthrosis, Localized, Not Specified Whether Primary or Secondary, Shoulder Region 1530
703.0	Toenail, Ingrown 2100			
704.01	Alopecia Areata 103		715.32	Osteoarthrosis, Localized, Not Specified Whether Primary or Secondary, Upper Arm 1530
704.8	Folliculitis and Other Specified Diseases of Hair and Hair Follicles 887			
			715.33	Osteoarthrosis, Localized, Not Specified Whether Primary or Secondary, forearm 1530
706.1	Acne, Other 887, 1896			

715.34	Osteoarthrosis, Localized, Not Specified Whether Primary or Secondary, Hand 1530
715.35	Osteoarthrosis, Localized, Not Specified Whether Primary or Secondary, Pelvic Region and Thigh 1530
715.36	Osteoarthrosis, Localized, Not Specified Whether Primary or Secondary, Lower Leg 1530
715.37	Osteoarthrosis, Localized, Not Specified Whether Primary or Secondary, Ankle and Foot 1530
715.38	Osteoarthrosis, Localized, Not Specified Whether Primary or Secondary, Other Specified Sites 1530
715.39	Osteoarthrosis, Localized, Not Specified Whether Primary or Secondary, Multiple Sites 1530
715.8	Osteoarthrosis Involving, or with Mention of More Than One Site, but Not Specified As Generalized 1530
715.9	Osteoarthrosis, Unspecified Whether Generalized or Localized 1530
715.96	Osteoarthrosis, Unspecified Whether Generalized or Localized, Lower Leg 1530
717	Derangement of Knee, Internal 1219
717.0	Meniscus Disorders, Knee 1364
717.1	Meniscus, Medial, Derangement of Anterior Horn 1364
717.2	Meniscus, Medial, Derangement of Posterior Horn 1364
717.3	Meniscus, Medial, Derangement, Other and Unspecified 1364
717.4	Meniscus, Lateral, Derangement 1364
717.5	Meniscus, Derangement, Not Elsewhere Classified 1364
717.6	Loose Bodies, Knee 1300
717.7	Patella Chondromalacia 1599
717.83	Old Disruption of Anterior Cruciate Ligament 1219
717.9	Unspecified Internal Derangement of Knee 1219
718.01	Shoulder Region 1853
718.1	Sesamoid, Joint 1300
719	Joint Disorders 1251
719.0	Effusion of Joint 1251
719.4	Arthralgia 190
719.40	Joint Pain, Site Unspecified 190
719.41	Joint Pain, Shoulder Region 190
719.42	Joint Pain, Upper Arm and Elbow 190
719.43	Joint Pain, Forearm and Wrist 190
719.44	Joint Pain, Hand 190
719.45	Joint Pain, Pelvic Region and Thigh 190
719.46	Joint Pain, Lower Leg and Knee 190
719.47	Joint Pain, Ankle and Foot 190
719.49	Joint Pain, Multiple Sites 190
719.9	Joint Disorder, Unspecified 1251
719.90	Disorder of Joint, Unspecified, Site Unspecified 1251
719.91	Disorder of Joint, Unspecified, Shoulder Region 1251
719.92	Disorder of Joint, Unspecified, Upper Arm and Elbow 1251
719.93	Disorder of Joint, Unspecified, Forearm and Wrist 1251
719.94	Disorder of Joint, Unspecified, Hand 1251
719.95	Disorder of Joint, Unspecified, Pelvic Region and Thigh 1251
719.96	Disorder of Joint, Unspecified, Lower Leg and Knee 1251
719.97	Disorder of Joint, Unspecified, Ankle and Foot 1251
719.98	Disorder of Joint, Other Specified 1251
719.99	Disorder of Joint, Unspecified, Multiple Sites 1251
720.0	Ankylosing Spondylitis 152
720.8	Other Inflammatory Spondylopathies 1958
720.9	Spondylitis, Unspecified 1958
721.6	Ankylosing Vertebral Hyperostosis 152
722	Disc Disorders 1221
722.0	Cervical Intervertebral Disc Displacement Without Myelopathy 728
722.1	Displacement of Thoracic or Lumbar Intervertebral Disc Without Myelopathy 1221
722.10	Lumbar Intervertebral Disc Displacement Without Myelopathy 732
722.11	Thoracic Intervertebral Disc Displacement Without Myelopathy 735
722.2	Displacement, Intervertebral Disc Without Myelopathy, Site Unspecified 1221
722.3	Schmorl's Nodes 1221
722.4	Cervical Intervertebral Disc Degeneration 634
722.51	Thoracic or Thoracolumbar Intervertebral Disc Degeneration 640
722.52	Lumbar Intervertebral Disc Degeneration 637
722.6	Degeneration of Intervertebral Disc, Site Unspecified 1308
722.7	Intervertebral Disc Disorder with Myelopathy 634
722.71	Cervical Disc Disorder with Myelopathy 464
722.72	Thoracic Disc Disorder with Myelopathy 2072
722.73	Lumbar Disc Disorder with Myelopathy 1308
722.8	Post-laminectomy Syndrome 1701
722.80	Post-laminectomy Syndrome, Unspecified Region 1701
722.81	Post-laminectomy Syndrome, Cervical Region 1701
722.82	Post-laminectomy Syndrome, Thoracic Region 1701
722.83	Post-laminectomy Syndrome, Lumbar Region 1701
722.9	Disc Calcification 701
722.90	Disc Disorder, Other and Unspecified, Unspecified Region 701
722.91	Disc Disorder, Other and Unspecified, Cervical Region 701
722.92	Disc Disorder, Other and Unspecified, Thoracic Region 701
722.93	Disc Disorder, Other and Unspecified, Lumbar Region 701
723.1	Neck Pain 1448
723.3	Cervicobrachial Syndrome 474
723.4	Brachial Neuropathy 287
723.5	Torticollis 2108
724	Other and Unspecified Disorders of Back 239, 1890, 1952
724.0	Spinal Stenosis 1952
724.02	Spinal Stenosis, Lumbar Region 1952
724.1	Thoracic Spine Pain 2076
724.2	Low Back Pain (Lumbago) 1302
724.3	Sciatica 1890
724.5	Back Pain 239
724.6	Disorders of Sacrum 1302
724.79	Coccygodynia 527
724.8	Other Symptoms Referable to Back 239
724.9	Neuritis or Radiculitis Due to Displacement or Rupture of Intervertebral Disc (Lumbar) 1308
725	Polymyalgia Rheumatica 1691

726	Peripheral and Enthesopathies and Allied Syndromes 248, 278, 325
726.0	Adhesive Capsulitis of Shoulder 66
726.1	Rotator Cuff Syndrome 1850
726.10	Disorders of Bursae and Tendons in Shoulder Region, Unspecified 1850
726.11	Calcifying Tendinitis of Shoulder 1850
726.12	Biceps Tendinitis 248
726.2	Impingement Syndrome 1194
726.3	Enthesopathy of Elbow Region 812, 816
726.31	Epicondylitis, Medial 816
726.32	Epicondylitis, Lateral 816
726.4	Enthesopathy of Wrist and Carpus 812
726.5	Enthesopathy of Hip Region 812
726.6	Enthesopathy of Knee 812
726.64	Patellar Tendinitis 812
726.7	Enthesopathy of Ankle and Tarus 812
726.70	Metatarsalgia 1376
726.71	Achilles Bursitis or Tendinitis 47
726.72	Tibialis Tendonitis 47
726.73	Heel Spur (Calcaneal) 1053
726.8	Other Enthesopathies 812
726.9	Enthesopathy of Unspecified Site 812
726.90	Tendinitis 2054
726.91	Bone Spur (Exostosis) 278
727	Other Disorders of Synovium, Tendon, Bursa 239, 248, 312, 325
727.0	Tenosynovitis and Synovitis 2057, 2191
727.00	Synovitis and Tenosynovitis, Unspecified 2031
727.03	Trigger Finger or Thumb 2191
727.04	Radial Styloid Tenosynovitis 1776
727.05	Other Tenosynovitis of Wrist and Hand 1776
727.1	Bunion 312
727.2	Repetitive Strain Injury 1819
727.3	Bursitis, Other 325
727.4	Ganglion and Synovial Cyst, Tendon and Bursa 2028
727.40	Synovial Cyst, Unspecified 2028
727.41	Ganglion of Joint 2028
727.42	Ganglion of Tendon Sheath 2028
727.43	Ganglion, Unspecified 2028
727.51	Baker's Cyst (Synovial Cyst of Popliteal Space) 239
727.61	Rotator Cuff Tear (Ruptured Rotator Cuff) 1853
727.62	Biceps Tendon, Ruptured (Traumatic and Non-Traumatic) 248
727.64	Flexor Tendons of Hand and Wrist 1776
728.0	Infective Myositis 814
728.12	Traumatic Myositis Ossificans 814
728.2	Muscle Atrophy and Muscular Wasting Not Classified Elsewhere 227
728.6	Dupuytren's Contracture (Contracture of Palmar Fascia) 751
728.71	Plantar Fasciitis (Plantar Fascial Fibromatosis) 1655
728.81	Interstitial Myositis 814
728.85	Muscle Spasm 1409
728.86	Necrotizing Fasciitis 814
728.89	Eosinophilic Fasciitis 814
728.9	Unspecified Disorder of Muscle, Ligament, and Fascia 814
729	Other Disorders of Soft Tissue 1411
729.0	Rheumatism, Unspecified, and Fibrositis 1837
729.1	Myalgia and Myositis 879, 1411
729.2	Neuralgia, Neuritis, and Radiculitis 1465
729.5	Pain in Limb 1562
729.89	Other Musculoskeletal Symptoms Referrable to Limbs 879
730.0	Osteomyelitis, Acute 1537
730.1	Osteomyelitis, Chronic 1537
730.2	Osteomyelitis, Unspecified 1537
731.0	Paget's Disease of Bone (Osteitis Deformans without Mention of Bone Tumor) 1557
731.1	Osteitis Deformans in Diseases Classified Elsewhere 281
732.7	Osteochondritis Dissecans 1534
733	Other Disorders of Bone and Cartilage 235
733.0	Osteoporosis 1540
733.00	Osteoporosis, Unspecified 1540
733.01	Senile Osteoporosis 1540
733.03	Disuse Osteoporosis 1540
733.13	Fracture, Vertebra (Pathological) 956
733.4	Aseptic Necrosis of Bone 235
733.40	Avascular Necrosis 235
733.42	Aseptic Necrosis of Head and Neck of Femur 235
733.6	Costochondritis (Tietze's Disease) 595
733.8	Malunion and Nonunion of Fracture 1335
733.81	Malunion of Fracture 1335
733.82	Nonunion of Fracture 1335
735	Acquired Deformities of Toe 312
735.0	Hallux Valgus, Acquired 312, 1027
735.2	Hallux Rigidus, Acquired 1027
735.4	Hammertoe, Acquired 1029
735.9	Unspecified Acquired Deformity of Toe 1027
736.76	Other Calcaneus Deformity 1053
737	Curvature of Spine 610
737.10	Kyphosis 610
737.20	Lordosis 610
737.30	Scoliosis, Idiopathic 610
737.4	Pott's Curvature 1709
737.8	Curvature of Spine, Other 610
737.9	Curvature of Spine, Acquired, Unspecified 610
738.4	Spondylolisthesis, Acquired or Degenerative 1960
739.1	Cervical Region 492
739.2	Thoracic Region 492
739.3	Lumbar Region 492
739.4	Sacral Region 492
739.5	Pelvic Region 492
739.6	Lower Extremities 492
739.7	Upper Extremities 492
743	Congenital Anomalies of Eye 270

743.3	Congenital Cataract and Lens Anomalies 436		786.06	Tachypnea 761
746.3	Congenital Stenosis of Aortic Valve 167		786.09	Dyspnea (Respiratory Distress) 761
746.4	Stenosis of Aortic Valve, Congenital 165		786.3	Hemoptysis 1067
747.1	Coarctation of Aorta 519		786.5	Pain, Chest 486
747.6	Anomalies of Peripheral Vascular System, Other 188		786.50	Chest Pain, Unspecified 486
747.60	Arteriovenous Aneurysm 188		786.52	Pleurodynia 1661
748.61	Congenital Bronchiectasis 297		787.0	Nausea and Vomiting 1446
750.4	Esophageal Diverticula 836		787.02	Nausea 1446
751.0	Meckel's Diverticulum 1351		787.9	Digestive System Symptoms, Other 696
752.11	Paraovarian Cyst (Embryonic Cyst of Fallopian Tubes and Broad Ligaments) 1590		787.91	Other Symptoms Involving Digestive System 975
			788.30	Incontinence with Physical Activity 2222
754.1	Torticollis (Congenital Musculoskeletal Deformities) 2108		788.31	Urge Incontinence 2222
754.52	Metatarsus Primus Varus 1378		788.33	Stress Incontinence 2222
755.66	Hallux Rigidus, Congenital 1027		788.34	Incontinence Without Sensory Awareness 2222
756.11	Spondylolysis, Lumbar Region 1962		788.35	Urinary Incontinence with Post-Void Dribbling 2222
756.12	Spondylolisthesis 1960		788.36	Urinary Incontinence with Nocturnal Enuresis 2222
771.0	Congenital Rubella 1856		788.37	Urinary Incontinence with Continuous Leakage 2222
773	Hemolytic Disease of Fetus or Newborn, Due to Isoimmunization 1059		788.39	Neurogenic Incontinence 2222
			789	Other Symptoms Involving Abdomen and Pelvis 7
773.0	Hemolytic Disease Due to Rh Isoimmunization 1059		789.0	Abdominal Pain 7
773.1	Hemolytic Disease Due to ABO Isoimmunization 1059		789.2	Splenomegaly 1956
773.2	Hemolytic Disease Due to Other and Unspecified Isoimmunization 1059		789.3	Abdominal or Pelvic Swelling, Mass, or Lump 7
			789.5	Ascites 203
776.0	Vitamin K Deficiency of Newborn 2284		790.7	Bacteremia 1905
780.01	Coma 544		791.0	Albuminuria (Proteinuria) 82
780.03	Persistant Vegetative State 544		791.5	Glycosuria 1006
780.2	Vasovagal Syncope 2024, 2249		793.1	Coin Lesion 532
780.3	Seizures 1900		799.1	Respiratory Arrest 1821
780.4	Dizziness and Giddiness 742		799.2	Nervousness 1463
780.51	Insomnia with Sleep Apnea 1214		800	Fracture 892
780.54	Hypersomnia 1152		801.0	Closed Without Mention of Intracranial Injury 941
780.57	Sleep Apnea 1935		801.09	with Concussion, Unspecified 941
780.6	Fever 872		801.1	Closed with Cerebral Laceration and Contusion 941
780.7	Malaise 1328		801.2	Closed with Subarachnoid, Subdural, and Extradural Hemorrhage 941
780.71	Chronic Fatigue Syndrome 509			
780.79	Other Malaise and Fatigue 1328		801.3	Closed with Other and Unspecified Intracranial Hemorrhage 941
780.9	Amnesia 111		801.5	Open Without Mention of Intracranial Injury 941
781.0	Tremor (Abnormal Involuntary Movements) 2179		801.8	Open with Other and Unspecified Intracranial Hemorrhage 941
781.7	Tetany 2062		802	Fracture, Face Bones 892
782.0	Paresthesia 1591		802.0	Fracture, Nasal Bones, Closed 892
782.4	Jaundice 1249		802.2	Fracture, Mandible (Lower Jaw), Closed 892
784.0	Headache 1033		802.4	Fracture, Upper Jaw, Closed 892
784.3	Aphasia 169		803	Fracture, Skull, Other and Unqualified 892, 941
784.7	Nosebleed (Epistaxis) 1485		803.0	Fracture, Skull, Closed, Without Mention of Brain Injury 941
785.1	Palpitations 1566		803.3	Fracture of Skull Closed with Other and Unspecified Intracranial Hemorrhage 449
785.2	Heart Murmur 1045			
785.4	Gangrene 964		805.0	Fracture, Cervical Spine Without Mention of Spinal Cord Injury, Closed 904
785.50	Shock 1915			
785.51	Cardiogenic Shock 417, 1915		805.00	Fracture, Cervical Spine, Unspecified Level, Without Mention of Spinal Cord Injury, Closed 904
785.59	Septic Shock 1184, 1907, 1915			
786.05	Shortness of Breath 761		805	Fracture, Vertebra 920, 939, 948, 954

805.01	Fracture, First Cervical Vertebra Without Mention of Spinal Cord Injury, Closed **904**
805.02	Fracture, Second Cervical Vertebra Without Mention of Spinal Cord Injury, Closed **904**
805.03	Fracture, Third Cervical Vertebra Without Mention of Spinal Cord Injury, Closed **904**
805.04	Fracture, Fourth Cervical Vertebra Without Mention of Spinal Cord Injury, Closed **904**
805.05	Fracture, Fifth Cervical Vertebra Without Mention of Spinal Cord Injury, Closed **904**
805.06	Fracture, Sixth Cervical Vertebra Without Mention of Spinal Cord Injury, Closed **904**
805.07	Fracture, Seventh Cervical Vertebra Without Mention of Spinal Cord Injury, Closed **904**
805.08	Fracture, Multiple Cervical Vertebra Without Mention of Spinal Cord Injury, Closed **904**
805.1	Fracture, Cervical Spine Without Mention of Spinal Cord Injury, Open **904**
805.10	Fracture, Cervical Spine, Unspecified Level, Without Mention of Spinal Cord Injury, Open **904**
805.11	Fracture, First Cervical Vertebra Without Mention of Spinal Cord Injury, Open **904**
805.12	Fracture, Second Cervical Vertebra Without Mention of Spinal Cord Injury, Open **904**
805.13	Fracture, Third Cervical Vertebra Without Mention of Spinal Cord Injury, Open **904**
805.14	Fracture, Fourth Cervical Vertebra Without Mention of Spinal Cord Injury, Open **904**
805.15	Fracture, Fifth Cervical Vertebra Without Mention of Spinal Cord Injury, Open **904**
805.16	Fracture, Sixth Cervical Vertebra Without Mention of Spinal Cord Injury, Open **904**
805.17	Fracture, Seventh Cervical Vertebra Without Mention of Spinal Cord Injury, Open **904**
805.18	Fracture, Multiple Cervical Vertebra Without Mention of Spinal Cord Injury, Open **904**
805.2	Fracture, Thoracic Spine Without Mention of Spinal Cord Injury, Closed **948**
805.3	Fracture, Thoracic Spine Without Mention of Spinal Cord Injury, Open **948**
805.4	Fracture, Lumbar Spine Without Mention of Spinal Cord Injury, Closed **920**
805.5	Fracture, Lumbar Spine Without Mention of Spinal Cord Injury, Open **920**
805.6	Fracture, Sacrum and Coccyx Without Mention of Spinal Cord Injury, Closed **939**
805.7	Fracture, Sacrum and Coccyx Without Mention of Spinal Cord Injury, Open **939**
805.8	Fracture, Vertebral Column, Unspecified, Without Mention of Spinal Cord Injury, Closed **954**
805.9	Fracture, Vertebral Column, Unspecified, Without Mention of Spinal Cord Injury, Open **954**
806.0	Fracture, Cervical Spine with Spinal Cord Injury, Closed **904**
806.00	Fracture, C1-C4 Level of Vertebral Column with Unspecified Spinal Cord Injury, Closed **904**
806	Fracture, Vertebral Column with Spinal Cord Injury **920, 939, 948, 954**
806.01	Fracture, C1-C4 Level of Vertebral Column with Complete Lesion of Cord, Closed **904**
806.02	Fracture, C1-C4 Level of Vertebral Column with Anterior Cord Syndrome, Closed **904**
806.03	Fracture, C1-C4 Level of Vertebral Column with Central Cord Syndrome, Closed **904**
806.04	Fracture, C1-C4 Level of Vertebral Column with Other Specified Spinal Cord Injury, Closed **904**
806.05	Fracture, C1-C4 Level of Vertebral Column with Unspecified Spinal Cord Injury, Closed **904**
806.06	Fracture, C5-C7 Level of Vertebral Column with Complete Lesion of Cord, Closed **904**
806.07	Fracture, C5-C7 Level of Vertebral Column with Anterior Cord Syndrome, Closed **904**
806.08	Fracture, C5-C7 Level of Vertebral Column with Central Cord Syndrome, Closed **904**
806.09	Fracture, C5-C7 Level of Vertebral Column with Other Specified Spinal Cord Injury, Closed **904**
806.1	Fracture, Cervical Spine with Spinal Cord Injury, Open **904**
806.10	Fracture, C1-C4 Level of Vertebral Column with Unspecified Spinal Cord Injury, Open **904**
806.11	Fracture, C1-C4 Level of Vertebral Column with Complete Lesion of Cord, Open **904**
806.12	Fracture, C1-C4 Level of Vertebral Column with Anterior Cord Syndrome, Open **904**
806.13	Fracture, C1-C4 Level of Vertebral Column with Central Cord Syndrome, Open **904**
806.14	Fracture, C1-C4 Level of Vertebral Column with Other Specified Spinal Cord Injury, Open **904**
806.15	Fracture, C1-C4 Level of Vertebral Column with Unspecified Spinal Cord Injury, Open **904**
806.16	Fracture, C5-C7 Level of Vertebral Column with Complete Lesion of Cord, Open **904**
806.17	Fracture, C5-C7 Level of Vertebral Column with Anterior Cord Syndrome, Open **904**
806.18	Fracture, C5-C7 Level of Vertebral Column with Central Cord Syndrome, Open **904**
806.19	Fracture, C5-C7 Level of Vertebral Column with Other Specified Spinal Cord Injury, Open **904**
806.2	Fracture, Thoracic Spine with Spinal Cord Injury, Closed **948**
806.20	Fracture, T1-T6 Level of Vertebral Column with Unspecified Spinal Cord Injury, Closed **948**
806.21	Fracture, T1-T6 Level of Vertebral Column with Complete Lesion of Cord, Closed **948**
806.22	Fracture, T1-T6 Level of Vertebral Column with Anterior Cord Syndrome, Closed **948**
806.23	Fracture, T1-T6 Level of Vertebral Column with Central Cord Syndrome, Closed **948**
806.24	Fracture, T1-T6 Level of Vertebral Column with Other Specified Spinal Cord Injury, Closed **948**
806.25	Fracture, T7-T12 Level of Vertebral Column with Unspecified Spinal Cord Injury, Closed **948**
806.26	Fracture, T7-T12 Level of Vertebral Column with Complete Lesion of Cord, Closed **948**
806.27	Fracture, T7-T12 Level of Vertebral Column with Anterior Cord Syndrome, Closed **948**
806.28	Fracture, T7-T12 Level of Vertebral Column with Central Cord Syndrome, Closed **948**

806.29	Fracture, T7-T12 Level of Vertebral Column with Other Specified Spinal Cord Injury, Closed 948
806.3	Fracture, Thoracic Spine with Spinal Cord Injury, Open 948
806.30	Fracture, T1-T6 Level of Vertebral Column with Unspecified Spinal Cord Injury, Open 948
806.31	Fracture, T1-T6 Level of Vertebral Column with Complete Lesion of Cord, Open 948
806.32	Fracture, T1-T6 Level of Vertebral Column with Anterior Cord Syndrome, Open 948
806.33	Fracture, T1-T6 Level of Vertebral Column with Central Cord Syndrome, Open 948
806.34	Fracture, T1-T6 Level of Vertebral Column with Other Specified Spinal Cord Injury, Open 948
806.35	Fracture, T7-T12 Level of Vertebral Column with Unspecified Spinal Cord Injury, Open 948
806.36	Fracture, T7-T12 Level of Vertebral Column with Complete Lesion of Cord, Open 948
806.37	Fracture, T7-T12 Level of Vertebral Column with Anterior Cord Syndrome, Open 948
806.38	Fracture, T7-T12 Level of Vertebral Column with Central Cord Syndrome, Open 948
806.39	Fracture, T7-T12 Level of Vertebral Column with Other Specified Spinal Cord Injury, Open 948
806.4	Fracture, Lumbar Spine with Spinal Cord Injury, Closed 920
806.5	Fracture, Lumbar Spine with Spinal Cord Injury, Open 920
806.6	Fracture, Sacrum and Coccyx with Spinal Cord Injury, Closed 939
806.60	Fracture, Sacrum and Coccyx with Unspecified Spinal Cord Injury, Closed 939
806.61	Fracture, Sacrum and Coccyx with Complete Cauda Equina Lesion, Closed 939
806.62	Fracture, Sacrum and Coccyx with Other Cauda Equina Lesion, Closed 939
806.69	Fracture, Sacrum and Coccyx with Other Spinal Cord Injury, Closed 939
806.7	Fracture, Sacrum and Coccyx with Spinal Cord Injury, Open 939
806.70	Fracture, Sacrum and Coccyx with Unspecified Spinal Cord Injury, Open 939
806.71	Fracture, Sacrum and Coccyx with Complete Cauda Equina Lesion, Open 939
806.72	Fracture, Sacrum and Coccyx with Other Cauda Equina Lesion, Open 939
806.79	Fracture, Sacrum and Coccyx with Other Spinal Cord Injury, Open 939
806.8	Unspecified, Closed 939
806.9	Unspecified, Open 939
807.0	Fracture, Ribs (Single or Multiple) 892, 936
807.09	Fracture, Ribs (Multiple) 936
807.1	Rib(s) Open 936
807.2	Fracture, Sternum (Closed) 943
807.3	Sternum, Open 943
808	Fracture, Pelvis 930
808.2	Fracture, Pubis, Closed 930
808.3	Fracture, Pubis, Open 930
808.4	Fracture, Pelvis, Other Specified Part, Closed 930
808.41	Fracture, Ilium, Closed 930
808.42	Fracture, Ischium, Closed 930
808.43	Multiple Pelvic Fractures with Disruption of Pelvic Circle, Closed 930
808.49	Fracture, Pelvis, Other Specified Part, Other (Innominate Bone), Closed 930
808.5	Fracture, Pelvis, Other Specified Part, Open 930
808.51	Fracture, Ilium, Open 930
808.52	Fracture, Ischium, Open 930
808.53	Multiple Pelvic Fractures with Disruption of Pelvic Circle, Open 930
808.59	Fracture, Pelvis, Other Specified Part, Other (Innominate Bone), Open 930
808.8	Fracture, Pelvis, Unspecified, Closed 930
808.9	Fracture, Pelvis, Unspecified, Open 930
810	Fracture, Clavicle 907
810.0	Fracture, Clavicle, Closed 907
810.00	Fracture, Clavicle, Closed, Unspecified Part 907
811	Fracture, Scapula (Shoulder Blades) 892
812.4	Fracture, Elbow (Distal Humerus) 910
812.40	Fracture, Humerus, Lower End (Elbow Fracture), Unspecified Part 910
812.41	Fracture, Humerus, Supracondylar (Elbow Fracture) 910
812.42	Fracture, Humerus, Lateral Condyle (Elbow Fracture) 910
812.43	Fracture, Humerus, Medial Condyle (Elbow Fracture) 910
812.44	Fracture, Humerus, Condyle(s) (Elbow Fracture) 910
812.49	Fracture, Humerus, Lower End (Elbow Fracture), Other 910
812.50	Lower End, Unspecified Part 910
812.51	Supracondylar Fracture of Humerus 910
812.52	Lateral Condyle 910
812.53	Medial Condyle 910
812.54	Condyle(s) Unspecified 910
812.59	Other 910
813	Fracture, Radius and Ulna 933
813.00	Upper End of Forearm, Unspecified 933
813.01	Olecranon Process of Ulna 933
813.02	Coronoid Process of Ulna 933
813.03	Monteggia's Fracture 933
813.05	Fracture of Radius and Ulna, Head of Radius 933
813.1	Upper End, Open 933
813.2	Shaft, Closed 933
813.3	Shaft, Open 933
813.4	Fracture, Lower End of Forearm, Closed 933
813.40	Fracture, Lower End of Forearm, Unspecified, Closed 933
813.41	Fracture, Colles', Closed 933
813.42	Fracture, Distal End of Radius, Other (Alone), Closed 933
813.43	Fracture, Distal End of Ulna (Alone), Closed 933
813.44	Fracture, Radius with Ulna, Lower End, Closed 933
813.5	Fracture, Lower End of Forearm, Open 933
813.50	Fracture, Lower End of Forearm, Unspecified, Open 933
813.51	Fracture, Colles', Open 933
813.52	Fracture, Distal End of Radius, Other (Alone), Open 933
813.53	Fracture, Distal End of Ulna (Alone), Open 933

813.54	Fracture, Radius with Ulna, Lower End, Open 933
813.80	Fracture, Forearm, Unspecified, Closed 933
813.81	Fracture, Radius (Alone), Closed 933
813.82	Fracture, Ulna (Alone), Closed 933
813.83	Fracture, Radius with Ulna, Closed 933
813.90	Fracture, Forearm, Unspecified, Open 933
813.91	Fracture, Radius (Alone), Open 933
813.92	Fracture, Ulna (Alone), Open 933
813.93	Fracture, Radius with Ulna, Open 933
814	Fracture, Carpal Bones 901
814.0	Fracture, Carpal Bone(s), Closed 901
814.00	Fracture, Carpal Bone, Unspecified, Closed 901
814.01	Fracture, Navicular (Scaphoid) of Wrist, Closed 901
814.02	Fracture, Lunate (Semilunar) Bone of Wrist, Closed 901
814.03	Fracture, Triquetral (Cuneiform) Bone of Wrist, Closed 901
814.04	Fracture, Pisiform, Closed 901
814.05	Fracture, Trapezium Bone (Larger Multangular), Closed 901
814.06	Fracture, Trapezoid Bone (Smaller Multangular), Closed 901
814.07	Fracture, Capitate Bone (Os Magnum), Closed 901
814.08	Fracture, Hamate (Unciform) Bone, Closed 901
814.09	Fracture, Carpal Bone(s), Other, Closed 901
814.1	Fracture, Carpal Bone(s), Open 901
814.10	Fracture, Carpal Bone, Unspecified, Open 901
814.11	Fracture, Navicular (Scaphoid) of Wrist, Open 901
814.12	Fracture, Lunate (Semilunar) Bone of Wrist, Open 901
814.13	Fracture, Triquetral (Cuneiform) Bone of Wrist, Open 901
814.14	Fracture, Pisiform, Open 901
814.15	Fracture, Trapezium Bone (Larger Multangular), Open 901
814.16	Fracture, Trapezoid Bone (Smaller Multangular), Open 901
814.17	Fracture, Capitate Bone (Os Magnum), Open 901
814.18	Fracture, Hamate (Unciform) Bone, Open 901
814.19	Fracture, Carpal Bone(s), Other, Open 901
815	Fracture, Metacarpal Bone(s) 922
815.0	Fracture, Metacarpal Bone(s), Closed 922
815.00	Fracture, Metacarpal Bone(s), Site Unspecified, Closed 922
815.01	Fracture, Base of Thumb Metacarpal, Closed 922
815.02	Fracture, Base of Other Metacarpal Bone(s), Closed 922
815.03	Fracture, Shaft of Metacarpal Bone(s), Closed 922
815.04	Fracture, Neck of Metacarpal Bone(s), Closed 922
815.09	Fracture, Multiple Sites of Metacarpus, Closed 922
815.1	Fracture, Metacarpal Bone(s), Open 922
815.10	Fracture, Metacarpal Bone(s), Site Unspecified, Open 922
815.11	Fracture, Base of Thumb Metacarpal, Open 922
815.12	Fracture, Base of Other Metacarpal Bone(s), Open 922
815.13	Fracture, Shaft of Metacarpal Bone(s), Open 922
815.14	Fracture, Neck of Metacarpal Bone(s), Open 922
815.19	Fracture, Multiple Sites of Metacarpus, Open 922
816	Fracture, Phalanges of Hand (One or More) 915
816.0	Fracture, Phalanges of Hand (One or More), Closed 915
816.00	Fracture, Phalanx or Phalanges, Unspecified, Closed 915
816.01	Fracture, Middle or Proximal Phalanx or Phalanges, Closed 915
816.02	Fracture, Distal Phalanx or Phalanges, Closed 915
816.03	Fracture, Phalanges of Hand, Multiple Sites, Closed 915
816.1	Fracture, Phalanges of Hand (One or More), Open 915
816.10	Fracture, Phalanx or Phalanges, Unspecified, Open 915
816.11	Fracture, Middle or Proximal Phalanx or Phalanges, Open 915
816.12	Fracture, Distal Phalanx or Phalanges, Open 915
816.13	Fracture, Phalanges of Hand, Multiple Sites, Open 915
820	Fracture, Femoral Neck 912
820.0	Fracture (Transcervical), Neck of Femur, Closed 912
820.00	Fracture (Transcervical), Neck of Femur, Intracapsular Section, Unspecified, Closed 912
820.01	Fracture (Transcervical), Neck of Femur, Epiphysisr, Closed 912
820.02	Fracture (Transcervical), Neck of Femur, Mid-Cervical Section, Closed 912
820.03	Fracture (Transcervical), Neck of Femur, Base, Closed 912
820.09	Fracture (Transcervical), Neck of Femur, Other Area, Closed 912
820.1	Fracture (Transcervical), Neck of Femur, Open 912
820.10	Fracture (Transcervical), Neck of Femur, Intracapsular Section, Unspecified, Open 912
820.11	Fracture (Transcervical), Neck of Femur, Epiphysis, Open 912
820.12	Fracture (Transcervical), Neck of Femur, Mid-Cervical Section, Open 912
820.13	Fracture (Transcervical), Neck of Femur, Base, Open 912
820.19	Fracture (Transcervical), Neck of Femur, Other Area, Open 912
820.2	Fracture (Pertrochanteric), Neck of Femur, Closed 912
820.20	Fracture (Pertrochanteric), Neck of Femur (Unspecified Trochanteric Section), Closed 912
820.21	Fracture (Pertrochanteric), Neck of Femur (Intertrochanteric Section), Closed 912
820.22	Fracture (Pertrochanteric), Neck of Femur (Subtrochanteric Section), Closed 912
820.3	Fracture (Pertrochanteric), Neck of Femur, Open 912
820.30	Fracture (Pertrochanteric), Neck of Femur (Unspecified Trochanteric Section), Open 912
820.31	Fracture (Pertrochanteric), Neck of Femur (Intertrochanteric Section), Open 912
820.32	Fracture (Pertrochanteric), Neck of Femur (Subtrochanteric Section), Open 912
820.8	Fracture, Neck of Femur, Unspecified Part, Closed 912
820.9	Fracture, Neck of Femur, Unspecified Part, Open 912
821	Fracture, Femur 892
822	Fracture, Patella 892
822.0	Fracture, Patella, Closed 892
823	Fracture, Tibia and Fibula 951
823.0	Fracture, Upper End of Tibia and Fibula, Closed 951
823.00	Fracture, Upper End of Tibia Alone, Closed 951
823.01	Fracture, Upper End of Fibula Alone, Closed 951
823.1	Fracture, Upper End of Tibia and Fibula, Open 951
823.10	Fracture, Upper End of Tibia Alone, Open 951
823.11	Fracture, Upper End of Fibula Alone, Open 951
823.2	Fracture, Shaft of Tibia and Fibula, Closed 951
823.20	Fracture, Shaft of Tibia Alone, Closed 951
823.21	Fracture, Shaft of Fibula Alone, Closed 951

Index of ICD-9 CM

823.22	Fracture, Shaft of Fibula with Tibia, Closed 951
823.3	Fracture, Shaft of Tibia and Fibula, Open 951
823.30	Fracture, Shaft of Tibia Alone, Open 951
823.31	Fracture, Shaft of Fibula Alone, Open 951
823.8	Fracture, Tibia and Fibula, Unspecified Part, Closed 951
823.80	Fracture, Tibia Alone, Unspecified Part, Closed 951
823.81	Fracture, Fibula Alone, Unspecified Part, Closed 951
823.82	Fracture of Tibia and Fibula, Unspecified Part, Closed 951
823.9	Fracture, Unspecified Part of Tibia and Fibula, Open 951
823.91	Fracture, Unspecified Part of Tibia Alone, Open 951
823.92	Fracture, Unspecified Part of Fibula Alone, Open 951
824	Fracture, Ankle 895
824.0	Fracture, Ankle, Medial Malleolus, Closed 895
824.1	Fracture, Ankle, Medial Malleolus, Open 895
824.2	Fracture, Ankle, Lateral Malleolus, Closed 895
824.3	Fracture, Ankle, Lateral Malleolus, Open 895
824.4	Fracture, Ankle, Bimalleolar, Closed (Pott's Fracture) 895
824.5	Fracture, Ankle, Bimalleolar, Open 895
824.6	Fracture, Ankle, Trimalleolar, Closed 895
824.7	Fracture, Ankle, Trimalleolar, Open 895
824.8	Fracture, Ankle, Unspecified, Closed 895
824.9	Fracture, Ankle, Unspecified, Open 895
825	Fracture, Tarsal and Metatarsal Bones (One or More) 898, 918, 925, 928, 945
825.0	Fracture, Calcaneus (Heel Bone), Closed 898
825.1	Fracture, Calcaneus (Heel Bone), Open 898
825.2	Fracture of Other Tarsal and Metatarsal Bones, Closed 918, 925, 928, 945
825.20	Fracture, Talus, Unspecified Bone(s) of Foot [Except Toes] 945
825.21	Fracture, Talus 945
825.22	Fracture, Navicular Bones of Foot 928
825.23	Fracture, Cuboid Bones of Foot 928
825.24	Fracture, Cuneiform Bones of Foot 928
825.25	Fracture, Metatarsal Bones 925
825.29	Fracture, Sesamoid Bones of Foot 918
825.39	Fracture, Tarsal and Metatarsal Bones, Other 918
826	Fracture, Forefoot (Sesamoid, Phalanges) 918
826.0	Fracture, Phalanges of Foot, Closed 918
826.1	Fracture, Phalanges of Foot, Open 918
827.0	Fracture, Leg (Closed) 892
827.1	Fracture, Leg (Open) 892
830	Dislocation, Jaw 705
831	Dislocation, Glenohumeral Joint (Shoulder) 719
831.0	Dislocation, Glenohumeral Joint (Shoulder), Closed 719
831.00	Dislocation, Glenohumeral Joint (Shoulder), Closed, Shoulder Unspecified 719
831.01	Dislocation, Anterior of Humerus 719
831.02	Dislocation, Posterior of Humerous 719
831.03	Dislocation, Inferior of Humerous 719
831.04	Dislocation, Acromioclavicular Joint 708
831.14	Dislocation, Acromioclavicular Joint (Clavicle), Open 708
832	Dislocation, Elbow 705
833	Dislocation, Wrist 705
834	Dislocation of Finger 705
835	Dislocation, Hip 705
836	Dislocation, Femorotibial (Knee) Joint 713, 723
836.0	Meniscus Tear, Knee (Current) 713, 1364
836.1	Tear of Lateral Cartilage or Meniscus of Knee, Current 713, 1364
836.2	Tear of Cartilage or Meniscus of Knee (Other), Current 713, 1364
836.3	Dislocation, Patella (Kneecap), Closed 723
836.4	Dislocation, Patella (Kneecap), Open 723
836.5	Other Dislocation of Knee, Closed 723
836.6	Dislocation, Knee, Other, Open 713
836.60	Dislocation, Knee (Other), Unspecified 713
836.61	Dislocation, Tibia, Anterior, Proximal End 713
836.62	Dislocation, Tibia, Posterior, Proximal End 713
836.63	Dislocation, Tibia, Medial, Proximal End 713
836.64	Dislocation, Tibia, Lateral, Proximal End 713
836.69	Dislocation, Knee, Other, Open 713
837	Dislocation, Ankle 705
838	Dislocation, Foot 716
838.0	Dislocation, Foot, Unspecified 716
838.00	Dislocation, Foot, Unspecified, Closed 716
838.01	Dislocation, Tarsal (Bone), Joint Unspecified, Closed 716
838.02	Dislocation, Midtarsal (Joint), Closed 716
838.03	Dislocation, Tarsometatarsal (Joint), Closed 716
838.04	Dislocation, Metatarsal (Bone), Joint Unspecified, Closed 716
838.05	Dislocation, Metatarsophalangeal (Joint) 716
838.06	Dislocation, Interphalangeal (Joint) of Foot, Closed 716
838.09	Dislocation, Foot, Other (Toe, Phalanx of Foot), Closed (Interphalangeal Joint) 716
838.11	Dislocation, Tarsal (Bone), Joint Unspecified, Open 716
838.12	Dislocation, Midtarsal (Joint) 716
838.13	Dislocation, Tarsometatarsal (Joint), Open 716
838.14	Dislocation, Metatarsal (Bone), Joint Unspecified, Open 716
838.15	Dislocation, Metatarsophalangeal (Joint), Open 716
838.16	Dislocation, Interphalangeal (Joint) of Foot, Open 716
838.19	Dislocation, Foot, Other (Toe, Phalanx of Foot), Open (Interphalangeal Joint) 716
839.0	Dislocation, Cervical Vertebra, Closed 711
839.08	Multiple Cervical Vertebrae 711
839.1	Dislocation, Cervical Vertebra, Open 711
839.40	Dislocation, Vertebra, Open 711
839.61	Dislocation, Sternoclavicular Joint, Closed 726
839.71	Dislocation, Sternoclavicular Joint, Open 726
839.8	Dislocations, Multiple and Ill-Defined (Other), Closed 705
839.9	Dislocations, Multiple and Ill-Defined (Other), Open 705
840	Sprains and Strains of Shoulder and Upper Arm 1960
840.0	Sprains and Strains, Acromioclavicular Joint 1968
840.4	Sprains and Strains, Rotator Cuff (Rotator Cuff Tear) 1853, 1994
840.8	Sprains and Strains, Biceps Tendon (Rupture) 1862, 1964, 1979
840.9	Sprains and Strains, Arm, Site Unspecified 1964

Code	Description	Code	Description
841	Sprains and Strains, Elbow and Forearm 1984	847.9	Sprains and Strains, Back 1975
841.0	Sprains and Strains, Radial Collateral Ligament 1984	848	Sprains and Strains 1964
841.1	Sprains and Strains, Ulnar Collateral Ligament 1984	848.8	Abdominal Muscle Strain 5
841.2	Sprains and Strains, Radiohumeral Joint 1984	850	Brain Injury 292
841.3	Sprains and Strains, Ulnohumeral Joint 1984	850.0	Concussion with No Loss of Consciousness 292
841.8	Sprains and Strains, Elbow and Forearm, Other Specified Sites 1984	850.0	Concussion with No Loss of Consciousness 553
841.9	Sprains and Strains, Elbow and Forearm, Unspecified Site 1984	850.1	Concussion with Brief Loss of Consciousness 292
842.0	Sprains and Strains, Wrist 1997	850.1	Concussion with Brief Loss of Consciousness 553
842.00	Sprains and Strains, Wrist, Unspecified Site 1997	850.2	Concussion with Moderate Loss of Consciousness 292
842.01	Sprains and Strains, Wrist, Carpal Joint 1997	850.2	Concussion with Moderate Loss of Consciousness 553
842.02	Sprains and Strains, Wrist, Radiocarpal Joint 1997	850.3	Concussion with Prolonged Loss of Consciousness and Return to Pre-existing Conscious Level 292
842.09	Sprains and Strains, Wrist, Other (Radioulnar Joint, Distal) 1997	850.3	Concussion with Prolonged Loss of Consciousness and Return to Pre-existing Conscious Level 553
842.1	Sprains and Strains, Hand 1989	850.4	Concussion with Prolonged Loss of Consciousness, Without Return to Pre-existing Conscious Level 292
842.10	Sprains and Strains, Hand, Unspecified Site 1989	850.4	Concussion with Prolonged Loss of Consciousness, Without Return to Pre-existing Conscious Level 553
842.11	Sprains and Strains, Hand, Carpometacarpal Joint 1989	850.5	Concussion with Loss of Consciousness of Unspecified Duration 292
842.12	Sprains and Strains, Hand or Fingers, Metacarpophalangeal Joint 1989	850.5	Concussion with Loss of Consciousness of Unspecified Duration 553
842.13	Sprains and Strains, Hand or Fingers, Interphalangeal Joint 1989	850.9	Concussion, Unspecified 292
842.19	Sprains and Strains, Hand, Midcarpal Joint 1989	850.9	Concussion, Unspecified 553
843	Sprains and Strains, Hip and Thigh 1964	851	Cerebral Laceration and Contusion 447
843.0	Sprains and Strains, Iliofemoral Ligament (Groin Strain) 1020	851.0	Cerebral (Cortex) Contusion without Mention of Open Intracranial Wound 447
843.8	Groin Strain (Sprains and Strains of Other Specified Sites of Hip and Thigh) 1020	851.00	Cerebral Contusion, Without Mention of Open Intracranial Wound, Unspecified State of Consciousness 447
843.9	Unspecified Site of Hip and Thigh 1964	851.01	Cerebral Contusion, Without Mention of Open Intracranial Wound, with No Loss of Consciousness 447
844.0	Sprains and Strains, Knee 1991	851.02	Cerebral Contusion, without Mention of Open Intracranial Wound, with Brief (Less Than One Hour) Loss of Consciousness 447
844.1	Sprains and Strains, Medial Collateral Ligament of Knee 1991	851.03	Cerebral Contusion, without Mention of Open Intracranial Wound, with Moderate (1-24 Hours) Loss of Consciousness 447
844.2	Sprains and Strains, Cruciate Ligament of Knee 1991	851.04	Cerebral Contusion, without Mention of Open Intracranial Wound, with Prolonged (More Than 24 Hours) Loss of Consciousne 447
844.8	Sprains and Strains, Specified Site of Knee or Leg 1991	851.05	Cerebral Contusion, without Mention of Open Intracranial Wound, with Prolonged (More Than 24 Hours) Loss of Consciousne 447
844.9	Sprains and Strains, Knee or Leg, Unspecified 1912	851.06	Cerebral Contusion, Without Mention of Open Intracranial Wound, with Loss of Consciousness of Unspecified Duration 447
845	Sprains and Strains of Ankle and Foot 1971, 1986	851.09	Cerebral (Cortex) Contusion without Mention of Open Intracranial Wound with Concussion, Unspecified 447
845.0	Sprains and Strains, Ankle 1971	851.4	Cerebellar or Brain Stem Contusion Without Mention of Open Intracranial Wound 447
845.00	Sprains and Strains, Ankle, Unspecified Site 1971	851.40	Cerebellar or Brain Stem Contusion Without Mention of Open Intracranial Wound, Unspecified State of Consciousness 447
845.01	Sprains and Strains, Ankle, Deltoid Ligament 1971	851.41	Cerebellar or Brain Stem Contusion Without Mention of Open Intracranial Wound, with no Loss of Consciousness 447
845.02	Sprains and Strains, Ankle, Calcaneofibular Ligament 1971	851.42	Cerebellar or Brain Stem Contusion without Mention of Open Intracranial Wound, with Brief (Less Than One Hour) Loss of 447
845.03	Sprains and Strains, Ankle, Tibiofibular Ligament 1971	851.43	Cerebellar or Brain Stem Contusion without Mention of Open Intracranial Wound, with Moderate (1-24 Hours) Loss of Consc 447
845.09	Sprains and Strains, Ankle, Other (Achilles' Tendon) 1971		
845.1	Sprains and Strains, Foot 1986		
845.10	Sprains and Strains, Foot, Unspecified Site 1986		
845.11	Sprains and Strains, Foot, Tarsometatarsal Joint 1986		
845.12	Sprains and Strains, Foot, Metatarsophalangeal Joint 1986		
845.13	Sprains and Strains, Foot, Interphalangeal Joint 1986		
845.19	Sprains and Strains, Foot, Other 1986		
846	Sprains and Strains, Sacroiliac Region 1975		
846.0	Sprains and Strains, Lumbosacral Joint 1975		
846.1	Sprains and Strains, Sacroiliac Ligament 1975		
846.9	Sprains and Strains, Unspecified Site of Sacroiliac Region 1975		
847	Sprains and Strains, Other and Unspecified Parts of Back 1975, 1981		
847.0	Sprains and Strains, Cervical Spine (Neck) 1981		
847.1	Sprains and Strains, Thoracic Spine 1975		
847.2	Sprains and Strains, Lumbar Spine 1975		

851.44	Cerebellar or Brain Stem Contusion without Mention of Open Intracranial Wound, with Prolonged (More Than 24 Hours) Loss 447
851.45	Cerebellar or Brain Stem Contusion without Mention of Open Intracranial Wound, with Prolonged (More Than 24 Hours) Loss 447
851.46	Cerebellar or Brain Stem Contusion Without Mention of Open Intracranial Wound, with Loss of Consciousness of Unspecifie 447
851.49	Cerebellar or Brain Stem Contusion Without Mention of Open Intracranial Wound with Concussion, Unspecified 447
852	Subarachnoid, Subdural, and Extradural Hemorrhage, Following Injury 2014, 2016
852.0	Subarachnoid Hemorrhage Following Injury Without Mention of Open Intracranial Wound 2014
852.00	Subarachnoid Hemorrhage Following Injury Without Mention of Open Intracranial Wound, Unspecified Loss of Consciousness 2014
852.01	Subarachnoid Hemorrhage Following Injury Without Mention of Open Intracranial Wound with no Loss of Consciousness 2014
852.02	Subarachnoid Hemorrhage Following Injury without Mention of Open Intracranial Wound with Brief (less Than One Hour) Los 2014
852.03	Subarachnoid Hemorrhage Following Injury without Mention of Open Intracranial Wound with Moderate (1-24 hours) Loss of 2014
852.04	Subarachnoid Hemorrhage Following Injury without Mention of Open Intracranial Wound with Prolonged (More Than 24 Hours) 2014
852.05	Subarachnoid Hemorrhage Following Injury without Mention of Open Intracranial Wound with Prolonged (More Than 24 Hours) 2014
852.06	Subarachnoid Hemorrhage Following Injury Without Mention of Open Intracranial Wound with Loss of Consciousness of Unspe 2014
852.09	Subarachnoid Hemorrhage Following Injury Without Mention of Open Intracranial Wound with Concussion, Unspecified 2014
852.1	Subarachnoid Hemorrhage Following Injury with Open Intracranial Wound 2014
852.2	Subdural Hemorrhage Following Injury, Without Mention of Open Intracranial Wound 2014, 2016
852.20	Subdural Hemorrhage Following Injury, Without Mention of Open Intracranial Wound, Unspecified State of Consciousness 2016
852.21	Subdural Hemorrhage Following Injury, Without Mention of Open Intracranial Wound with No Loss of Consciousness 2016
852.22	Subdural Hemorrhage Following Injury, without Mention of Open Intracranial Wound with Brief (Less Than One Hour) loss o 2016
852.23	Subdural Hemorrhage Following Injury, without Mention of Open Intracranial Wound with Moderate (1-24 Hours) loss of Con 2016
852.24	Subdural Hemorrhage Following Injury, without Mention of Open Intracranial Wound with Prolonged (More Than 24 Hours) Lo 2016
852.25	Subdural Hemorrhage Following Injury, without Mention of Open Intracranial Wound with Prolonged (More Than 24 Hours) Lo 2016
852.26	Subdural Hemorrhage Following Injury, Without Mention of Open Intracranial Wound with Loss of Consciousness of Unspecif 2016
852.29	Subdural Hemorrhage Following Injury, Without Mention of Open Intracranial Wound with Concussion, Unspecified 2016
852.3	Subdural Hemorrhage Following Injury with Open Intracranial Wound 2014
853	Intracranial Hemorrhage Following Injury, Other and Unspecified 292
853.0	Intracranial Hemorrhage Following Injury Without Mention of Open Intracranial Wound, Other and Unspecified 292
853.00	Intracranial Hemorrhage Following Injury Without Mention of Open Intracranial Wound, Unspecified State of Consciousness, Other and Unspecified 292
853.0	Intracranial Hemorrhage Following Injury Without Mention of Open Intracranial Wound, Other and Unspecified 1230
853.01	Intracranial Hemorrhage Following Injury Without Mention of Open Intracranial Wound, with No Loss of Consciousness, Other and Unspecified 292
853.02	Intracranial Hemorrhage Following Injury without Mention of Open Intracranial Wound, with Brief (Less Than One Hour) Loss of Consciousness, Other and Unspecified 292
853.03	Intracranial Hemorrhage Following Injury without Mention of Open Intracranial Wound, with Moderate (1-24 Hours) Loss of Consciousness, Other and Unspecified 292
853.04	Intracranial Hemorrhage Following Injury without Mention of Open Intracranial Wound, with Prolonged (More Than 24 Hours) Loss of Consciousness and Return to Pre-existing Conscious Level, Other and Unspecified 292
853.05	Intracranial Hemorrhage Following Injury without Mention of Open Intracranial Wound, with Prolonged (More Than 24 Hours) Loss of Consciousness without Return to Pre-existing Conscious Level, Other and Unspecified 292
853.06	Intracranial Hemorrhage Following Injury Without Mention of Open Intracranial Wound, with Loss of Consciousness of Unspecified Duration, Other and Unspecified 292
853.09	Intracranial Hemorrhage Following Injury Without Mention of Open Intracranial Wound, with Concussion, Unspecified, Other and Unspecified 292
853.1	Intracranial Hemorrhage Following Injury with Open Intracranial Wound, Other and Unspecified 292
853.10	Intracranial Hemorrhage Following Injury with Open Intracranial Wound, Unspecified State of Consciousness, Other and Unspecified 292
853.11	Intracranial Hemorrhage Following Injury with Open Intracranial Wound, with No Loss of Consciousness, Other and Unspecified 292
853.12	Intracranial Hemorrhage Following Injury with Open Intracranial Wound, with Brief (Less Than One Hour) Loss of Consciousness, Other and Unspecified 292
853.13	Intracranial Hemorrhage Following Injury with Open Intracranial Wound, with Moderate (1-24 Hours) Loss of Consciousness, Other and Unspecified 292
853.14	Intracranial Hemorrhage Following Injury with Open Intracranial Wound, with Prolonged (More Than 24 Hours) Loss of Consciousness and Return to Pre-existing Conscious Level, Other and Unspecified 292
853.15	Intracranial Hemorrhage Following Injury with Open Intracranial Wound, with Prolonged (More Than 24 Hours) Loss of Consciousness without Return to Pre-existing Conscious Level, Other and Unspecified 292
853.16	Intracranial Hemorrhage Following Injury with Open Intracranial Wound, with Loss of Consciousness of Unspecified Duration, Other and Unspecified 292

853.19	Intracranial Hemorrhage Following Injury with Open Intracranial Wound, with Concussion, Unspecified, Other and Unspecified 292	865.00	Spleen Injury Without Mention of Open Wound into Cavity, Unspecified 1860
854	Brain Injury of Other and Unspecified Nature 292	865.01	Spleen Injury Without Mention of Open Wound into Cavity, Hematoma Without Rupture of Capsule 1860
854.0	Brain Injury of Other and Unspecified Nature Without Mention of Open Cranial Wound 292	865.02	Spleen Injury Without Mention of Open Wound into Cavity, Capsular Tears, Without Major Disruption of Parenchyma 1860
854.00	Brain Injury of Other and Unspecified Nature Without Mention of Open Cranial Wound, Unspecified State of Consciousness 292	865.09	Spleen Injury Without Mention of Open Wound into Cavity, Other 1860
854	Brain Injury of Other and Unspecified Nature 1230	865.1	Spleen Injury with Open Wound into Cavity 1860
854.01	Brain Injury of Other and Unspecified Nature Without Mention of Open Cranial Wound, with No Loss of Consciousness 292	865.10	Spleen Injury with Open Wound into Cavity, Unspecified 1860
854.02	Brain Injury of Other and Unspecified Nature without Mention of Open Cranial Wound, with Brief (Less Than One Hour) Loss Of Consciousness 292	865.11	Spleen Injury with Open Wound into Cavity and Hematoma Without Rupture of Capsule 1860
854.03	Brain Injury of Other and Unspecified Nature without Mention of Open Cranial Wound, with Moderate (1-24 Hours) Loss Of Consciousness 292	865.12	Spleen Injury with Open Wound into Cavity, and Capsular Tears, Without Major Disruption of Parenchyma 1860
854.04	Brain Injury of Other and Unspecified Nature without Mention of Open Cranial Wound, with Prolonged (More Than 24 Hours) Loss Of Consciousness and Return to Pre-existing Conscious Level 292	865.19	Spleen Injury with Open Wound into Cavity, Other 1860
		870	Open Wound of Ocular Adnexa 1504
		870	Open Wound of Ocular Adnexa 1269
		870.0	Puncture Wounds 1269, 1759
854.05	Brain Injury of Other and Unspecified Nature without Mention of Open Cranial Wound, with Prolonged (More Than 24 Hours) Loss Of Consciousness without Return to Pre-existing Conscious Level 292	870.1	Laceration of Eyelid, Full-thickness, Not Involving Lacrimal Passages 1504
		870.1	Laceration of Eyelid, Full-thickness, Not Involving Lacrimal Passages 1269
854.06	Brain Injury of Other and Unspecified Nature Without Mention of Open Cranial Wound, with Loss of Consciousness of Unspecified Duration 292	870.2	Laceration of Eyelid Involving Lacrimal Passages 1504
		870.2	Laceration of Eyelid Involving Lacrimal Passages 1269
854.09	Brain Injury of Other and Unspecified Nature Without Mention of Open Cranial Wound, with Concussion, Unspecified 292	870.3	Penetrating Wound of Orbit, Without Mention of Foreign Body 1504
		870.3	Penetrating Wound of Orbit, Without Mention of Foreign Body 1759
854.1	Brain Injury of Other and Unspecified Nature with Open Cranial Wound 292	870.4	Penetrating Wound of Orbit, Without Mention of Foreign Body 1504
854.10	Brain Injury of Other and Unspecified Nature with Open Cranial Wound, Unspecified State of Consciousness 292	870.4	Penetrating Wound of Orbit, Without Mention of Foreign Body 1759
854.11	Brain Injury of Other and Unspecified Nature with Open Cranial Wound with No Loss of Consciousness 292	870.8	Open Wounds of Ocular Adnexa, Specified, Other 1504
		870.9	Open Wound of Ocular Adnexa, Unspecified 1504
854.12	Brain Injury of Other and Unspecified Nature with Open Cranial Wound, with Brief (Less Than One Hour) Loss of Consciousness 292	871	Open Wound of Eyeball 1504
		871.0	Ocular Laceration Without Prolapse of Intraocular Tissue 1504
854.13	Brain Injury of Other and Unspecified Nature with Open Cranial Wound with Moderate (1-24 Hours) Loss of Consciousness 292	871	Open Wound of Eyeball 1269
		871.0	Ocular Laceration Without Prolapse of Intraocular Tissue 1269
854.14	Brain Injury of Other and Unspecified Nature with Open Cranial Wound, with Prolonged (More Than 24 Hours) Loss of Consciousness and Return to Pre-existing Conscious Level 292	871.1	Ocular Laceration with Prolapse or Exposure of Intraocular Tissue 1269
		871.2	Rupture of Eye with Partial Loss of Intraocular Tissue 1504
854.15	Brain Injury of Other and Unspecified Nature with Open Cranial Wound, with Prolonged (More Than 24 Hours) Loss of Consciousness without Return to Pre-existing Conscious Level 292	871.3	Avulsion of Eye 1504
		871.4	Laceration of Eye, Unspecified 1504
		871.4	Laceration of Eye, Unspecified 1269
854.16	Brain Injury of Other and Unspecified Nature with Open Cranial Wound, with Loss of Consciousness of Unspecified Duration 292	871.5	Penetration of Eyeball with Magnetic Foreign Body 1504
		871.5	Penetration of Eyeball with Magnetic Foreign Body 1759
854.19	Brain Injury of Other and Unspecified Nature with Open Cranial Wound, with Concussion, Unspecified	871.6	Penetration of Eyeball with (Nonmagnetic) Foreign Body 1504
		871.6	Penetration of Eyeball with (Nonmagnetic) Foreign Body 1759
860.0	Pneumothorax, Traumatic 1671	871.7	Ocular Penetration, Unspecified 1504
860.1	Pneumothorax, Traumatic, with Open Wound into Thorax 1671	871.7	Ocular Penetration, Unspecified 1759
860.2	Hemothorax Without Mention of Open Wound into Thorax 1075	871.9	Open Wound of Eyeball, Unspecified 1504
860.3	Hemothorax, Traumatic 1075	872	Open Wound of Ear 1504
865	Rupture of Spleen, Traumatic 1860	872.0	Open Wound of External Ear, Without Mention of Complications 1504
865.0	Spleen Injury Without Mention of Open Wound into Cavity 1860		

Index of ICD-9 CM 2493

872	Open Wound of Ear 1269		879.0	Open Wound of Breast, without Mention of Complication 1504
872.0	Open Wound of External Ear, Without Mention of Complications 1269		879	Open Wound of Other and Unspecified Sites, Except Limbs 1269
872.02	Open Wound of Auditory Canal 1504		879.1	Open Wound of Breast, Complicated 1504
872.1	Open Wound of External Ear, Complicated 1504		879.6	Open Wound of Other and Unspecified Parts of Trunk, Without Mention of Complication 1504
872.1	Open Wound of External Ear, Complicated 1269		879.8	Open Wound, Multiple Unspecified Sites, Without Mention of Complication 1504
872.6	Open Wound of Other Specified Parts of Ear, Without Mention of Complications 1504		880	Open Wound of Shoulder and Upper Arm 1504
872.69	Open Wound of Other and Multiple Sites of the Ear Without Mention of Complications 1504		880	Open Wound of Shoulder and Upper Arm 1269
872.7	Open Wound of Other Specified Parts of Ear, Complicated 1504		881	Open Wound of Elbow, Forearm, and Wrist 1504
872.8	Open Wound of Ear, Part Unspecified, Without Mention of Complication 1504		881	Open Wound of Elbow, Forearm, and Wrist 1269
872.9	Open Wound of Ear, Part Unspecified 1504		882	Open Wound, Hand (Except Finger) 1504
873	Lacerations (Open Wound of Head) 1504		882.0	Open Wound, Hand (Except Finger), Without Mention of Complication 1269
873.0	Open Wound of Scalp, Without Mention of Complication 1504		882	Open Wound, Hand (Except Finger) 1269
873	Lacerations (Open Wound of Head) 1269		882.0	Open Wound, Hand (Except Finger), Without Mention of Complication 1269
873.0	Open Wound of Scalp, Without Mention of Complication 1269		882.2	Open Wound, Hand (Except Finger), With Tendon Complication 1269
873.1	Open Wound of Scalp, Complicated 1504		882.2	Open Wound, Hand (Except Finger), With Tendon Involvement 1269
873.2	Open Wound of Nose, Without Mention of Complication 1504		883	Open Wound, Finger 1504
873.39	Open Wound of Multiple Sites, Complicated 1504		883.0	Open Wound, Finger, Without Mention of Complication 1269
873.4	Open Wound of Face, Without Mention of Complication 1504		883	Open Wound, Finger 1269
873.43	Open Wound of Lip, Without Mention of Complication 1504		883.0	Open Wound, Finger, With No Mention of Complication 1269
873.44	Open Wound of Jaw, Without Mention of Complication 1504		883.1	Open Wound, Finger, With Complication 1269
873.49	Open Wound of Face, Other and Multiple Sites, Without Mention of Complications 1504		883.1	Open Wound, Finger, Complicated 1269
873.5	Open Wound of Face, Complicated 1504		883.2	Open Wound, Finger, With Tendon Involvement 1269
873.59	Open Wound of Other and Multiple Sites, Complicated 1504		883.2	Open Wound, Finger, With Tendon Involvement 1269
873.6	Open Wound of Internal Structures of Mouth, Without Mention of Complications 1504		884	Multiple and Unspecified Open Wound of Upper Limb 1504
873.60	Open Wound of Mouth, Unspecified Site, Without Mention of Complication 1504		884	Multiple and Unspecified Open Wound of Upper Limb 1269
873.7	Open Wound of Internal Structures of Mouth, Complicated 1504		886.0	Traumatic Amputation of Other Finger(s), Without Mention of Complication
873.8	Open Wound of Other and Unspecified Open Wound of Head Without Mention of Complication 1504		890	Lacerations (Open Wound of Hip and Thigh) 1504
873.9	Open Wound of Other and Unspecified Open Wound of Head, Complicated 1504		890	Lacerations (Open Wound of Hip and Thigh) 1269
874	Open Wound of Neck 1504		891	Lacerations (Open Wound of Knee, Leg, and Ankle) 1504
874	Open Wound of Neck 1269		891	Lacerations (Open Wound of Knee, Leg, and Ankle) 1269
874.8	Open Wound of Other and Unspecified Parts of Neck, Without Mention of Complications 1504		891.0	Lacerations (Open Wound of Knee, Leg, and Ankle), Without Mention of Complication 1269
874.9	Open Wound of Other and Unspecified Parts of Neck, Complicated 1504		892	Lacerations (Open Wound, Foot) 1504
875	Open Wound of Chest 1504		892	Lacerations (Open Wound, Foot) 1269
875	Open Wound of Chest 1269, 1512		892.0	Lacerations (Open Wound, Foot), Without Mention of Complication 1269
876	Open Wound of Back 1504		893	Open Wound of Toe(s) 1504
876	Open Wound of Back 1269, 1510		893	Open Wound of Toe(s) 1269
877	Open Wound of Buttock 1504		894	Multiple and Unspecified Open Wound of Lower Limb 1504
877	Open Wound of Buttock 1269		894	Multiple and Unspecified Open Wound of Lower Limb 1269
878	Open Wound of Genital Organs (External), Including Traumatic Amputation 1504		896	Amputation (Traumatic), Foot (Complete) 118
878	Open Wound of Genital Organs (External), Including Traumatic Amputation 1269		896.0	Amputation (Traumatic), Foot (Partial) 118
879	Open Wound of Other and Unspecified Sites, Except Limbs 1504		896.1	Amputation (Traumatic), Foot, Unilateral, Complicated 118
			896.2	Amputation (Traumatic), Foot, Bilateral, without Mention of Complication 118
			896.3	Amputation (Traumatic), Foot, Bilateral, Complicated 118

Code	Description	Code	Description
897	Amputation (Traumatic), Leg(s) (Complete) (Partial) (Lower Extremity), 121	923.8	Contusion of Multiple Sites of Upper Limb 571
897.0	Amputation (Traumatic), Leg(s) (Complete) (Partial), Unilateral, Below Knee, without mention of Complication 121	923.9	Contusion of Unspecified Part of Upper Limb 571
897.1	Amputation (Traumatic), Leg(s) (Complete) (Partial), Unilateral, Below Knee, Complicated 121	924	Contusion of Lower Limb 562, 566
897.2	Amputation (Traumatic), Leg(s) (Complete) (Partial), Unilateral, at or Above Knee, without Mention of Complication 121	924.0	Contusion of Hip and Thigh 566
897.3	Amputation (Traumatic), Leg(s) (Complete) (Partial), Unilateral, at or Above Knee, Complicated 121	924.00	Contusion of Thigh 566
897.4	Amputation (Traumatic), Leg(s) (Complete) (Partial), Unilateral, Level not Specified, without mention of Complication 121	924.01	Contusion of Hip 566
897.5	Amputation (Traumatic), Leg(s) (Complete) (Partial), Unilateral, Level not Specified, Complicated 121	924.1	Contusion of Knee and Lower Leg 566
897.6	Amputation (Traumatic), Leg(s) (Complete) (Partial), Bilateral 121	924.10	Contusion of Lower Leg 566
897.7	Amputation (Traumatic), Leg(s) (Complete) (Partial), Bilateral 121	924.11	Contusion of Knee 566
905	Venomous Animals and Plants As the Cause of Poisoning and Toxic Reactions 1675	924.2	Contusion of Ankle and Foot, Excluding Toes 566
909	Late Effects of Other and Unspecified External Causes 1675	924.20	Contusion of Foot, Excluding Toes 566
910	Superficial Injury of Face, Neck, and Scalp Except Eye 1031	924.21	Contusion of Ankle 566
910.9	Other and Unspecified Superficial Injury of Face, Neck, and Scalp, Infected 1031	924.3	Contusion of Toe (Toenail) 566
918.1	Corneal Abrasion 580	924.4	Contusion of Multiple Sites of Lower Limb 566
919.0	Abrasions 14	924.5	Contusion of Unspecified Part of Lower Limb 566
919.1	Abrasion of Friction Burn, Infected 14	924.8	Contusion Multiple Sites, Not Elsewhere Classified 562
920	Head Injury, Superficial 1031	924.8	Contusion of Multiple Sites, Not Elsewhere Classified 566
921.0	Black Eye, Not Otherwise Specified 564	924.9	Contusion of Lower Limb 562, 566
921.1	Contusion of Eyelids and Periocular Area 564	925	Crushing Injury 603
921.2	Contusion of Orbital Tissues 564	925.1	Crushing Injury of Face and Scalp 603
921.3	Contusion of Eyeball 564	925.2	Crushing Injury of Neck 603
921.9	Contusion of Eye, Unspecified 564	926	Crushing Injury of Trunk 603
922	Contusion of Trunk 568	926.0	Crushing Injury of External Genitalia 603
922.0	Contusion of Breast 568	926.1	Crushing Injury of Other Specified Sites of Trunk 603
922.1	Contusion of Chest Wall 568	926.11	Crushing Injury of Back 603
922.2	Contusion of Abdominal Wall 568	926.12	Crushing Injury of Buttock 603
922.3	Contusion of Back 568	926.19	Crushing Injury of Trunk, Other (Breast) 603
922.4	Contusion of Genital Organs 568	926.8	Crushing Injury of Multiple Sites of Trunk 603
922.8	Contusion of Multiple Sites of Trunk 568	926.9	Crushing Injury of Trunk, Unspecified Site 603
922.9	Contusion of Unspecified Part of Trunk 568	927	Crushing Injury of Upper Limb 603
923	Contusion of Upper Limb 571	927.0	Crushing Injury of Shoulder and Upper Arm 603
923.00	Contusion of Upper Limb 571	927.00	Crushing Injury of Shoulder Region 603
923.01	Contusion of Scapular Region 571	927.01	Crushing Injury of Scapular Region 603
923.02	Contusion of Axillary Region 571	927.02	Crushing Injury of Axillary Region 603
923.03	Contusion of Upper Arm 571	927.03	Crushing Injury of Upper Arm 603
923.09	Contusion of Shoulder and Upper Arm, Multiple Sites 571	927.09	Crushing Injury of Shoulder and Upper Arm, Multiple Sites 603
923.1	Contusion of Elbow and Forearm 571	927.1	Crushing Injury of Elbow and Forearm 603
923.10	Contusion of Forearm 571	927.10	Crushing Injury of Forearm 603
923.11	Contusion of Elbow 571	927.11	Crushing Injury of Elbow 603
923.2	Contusion of Wrist and Hand(s), Except Finger(s) Alone 571	927.2	Crushing Injury of Wrist and Hand(s), Except Finger(s) Alone 603
923.20	Contusion of Hand(s), Except Finger(s) Alone 571	927.20	Crushing Injury of Hand(s), Except Finger(s) Alone 603
923.21	Contusion of Wrist 571	927.21	Crushing Injury of Wrist 603
923.3	Contusion of Finger or Thumb 571	927.3	Crushing Injury of Finger(s) 603
		927.8	Crushing Injury of Multiple Sites of Upper Limb 603
		927.9	Crushing Injury of Upper Limb, Unspecified Site 603
		928	Crushing Injury of Lower Limb 603
		928.0	Crushing Injury of Hip and Thigh 603
		928.00	Crushing Injury of Thigh 603
		928.01	Crushing Injury of Hip 603
		928.1	Crushing Injury of Knee and Lower Leg 603
		928.10	Crushing Injury of Lower Leg 603

928.11	Crushing Injury of Knee 603
928.2	Crushing Injury of Ankle and Foot, Excluding Toe(s) Alone 603
928.20	Crushing Injury of Foot, Excluding Toe(s) Alone
928.21	Crushing Injury of Ankle 603
928.3	Crushing Injury of Toe 603
928.8	Crushing Injury of Multiple Sites of Lower Limb 603
928.9	Crushing Injury of Lower Limb, Unspecified Site 603
929	Crushing Injury of Multiple and Unspecified Sites 603
929.0	Crushing Injury of Multiple Sites, Not Elsewhere Classified 603
929.5	Late Effects of Accident Due to Natural and Environmental Factors 1675
929.9	Crushing Injury of Unspecified Site 603
930	Foreign Body on External Eye 891
930.0	Foreign Body, Cornea 891
940	Burn Confined to Eye and Adnexa 316
940.0	Chemical Burns of Eyelids and Periocular Area 316
940.1	Burns of Eyelids and Periocular Area, Other 316
940.2	Alkaline Chemical Burn of Cornea and Conjunctival Sac 316
940.3	Acid Chemical Burn of Cornea and Conjunctival Sac 316
940.4	Burn of Cornea and Conjunctival Sac, Other 316
940.5	Burn with Resulting Rupture and Destruction of Eyeball 316
940.9	Burn of Eye 316
941	Burn of Face, Head, and Neck 316, 318
941.0	Burn of Face, Head and Neck, Unspecified Degree 318
941.05	Burn of Nose (Septum), Unspecified Degree 318
941.06	Burn of Scalp (Any Part), Unspecified Degree 318
941.07	Burn of Forehead and Cheek, Unspecified Degree 318
941.08	Burn of Neck, Unspecified Degree 318
941.1	First Degree Burn (Erythema) of Face, Head and Neck 318
941.2	Second Degree Burn (Blisters, Epidermal Loss) of Face, Head, and Neck 316, 318
941.3	Third Degree Burn (Full-Thickness Skin Loss) of Face, Head, and Neck 318
941.4	Deep Necrosis of Underlying Tissues (Deep Third Degree Burn) of Face, Head, and Neck, without Mention of Loss of Body Pa 318
944	Burn of Wrist(s) and Hand(s) 321
944.01	Burn of Single Digit 321
944.02	Burn of Thumb (Nail), Unspecified Degree 321
944.05	Burn of Palm, Unspecified Degree 321
944.06	Burn of Back of Hand, Unspecified Degree 321
944.07	Burn of Wrist, Unspecified Degree 321
944.08	Burn of Wrist(s) and Hand(s), Unspecified Degree 321
949.0	Burn, Unspecified Degree 318
949.1	First Degree Burn (Erythema) 318
949.2	Second Degree Burn (Blisters, Epidermal Loss) 318
949.3	Third Degree Burn (Full-Thickness Skin Loss) 318
950	Injury to Optic Nerve and Pathways 270
952	Spinal Cord Injury, Without Evidence of Spinal Bone Injury 1946
952.0	Cervical Spinal Cord Injury Without Evidence of Spinal Bone Injury 1946
952.02	Myelopathy (Cervical Spine with Anterior Cord Syndrome) 1420
952.1	Thoracic Spinal Cord Injury Without Evidence of Spinal Bone Injury 1946
952.2	Lumber Spinal Cord Injury Without Evidence of Spinal Bone Injury 1946
952.3	Sacral Spinal Cord Injury Without Evidence of Spinal Bone Injury 1946
952.4	Injury to Nerves and Spinal Cord, Cauda Equina 440
952.8	Spinal Cord Injury Without Evidence of Spinal Bone Injury, Multiple Sites 1946
952.9	Spinal Cord Injury, Unspecified 1946
953.4	Brachial Plexus Injury 287
957	Injury to Other and Unspecified Nerves 1460
957.9	Nerve Injury, Unspecified 1460
958	Suicide and Self-Inflicted Injury by Other and Unspecified Means 1675
958.0	Air Embolism 789
958.1	Fat Embolism 789
958.4	Traumatic Shock 1184, 1915
958.8	Compartment Syndrome 547
959.9	Trauma 2175
960	Poisoning by Antibiotics 1675
960.0	Poisoning by Penicillins 1675
960.1	Poisoning by Antifungal Antibiotics 1675
960.2	Poisoning by Chloramphenicol Group 1675
960.3	Poisoning by Erythromycin and Other Macrolides 1675
960.4	Poisoning by Tetracycline Group 1675
960.5	Poisoning by Cephalosporin Group 1675
960.6	Poisoning by Antimycobacterial Antibiotics 1675
960.7	Poisoning by Antineoplastic Antibiotics 1675
960.8	Poisoning by Other Specified Antibiotics 1675
960.9	Poisoning by Unspecified Antibiotic 1675
961	Poisoning by Other Anti-infectives 1675
961.0	Poisoning by Sulfonamides 1675
961.1	Poisoning by Arsenical Anti-Infectives 1675
961.1	Poisoning by Arsenical Anti-Infectives 2110
961.2	Poisoning by Heavy Metal Anti-Infectives 1675
961.2	Poisoning by Heavy Metal Anti-Infectives 2136, 2138
961.3	Poisoning by Quinoline and Hydroxyquinoline Derivatives 1675
961.4	Poisoning by Antimalarials and Drugs Acting on Other Blood Protozoa 1675
961.5	Poisoning by Other Antiprotozoal Drugs 1675
961.6	Poisoning by Anthelmintics 1675
961.7	Poisoning by Antiviral Drugs 1675
961.8	Poisoning by Other Antimycobacterial Drugs 1675
961.9	Poisoning by Other Unspecified Anti-Infectives 1675
962	Poisoning by Hormones and Synthetic Substitutes 1675
962.0	Poisoning by Adrenal Cortical Steroids 1675
962.1	Poisoning by Androgens and Anabolic Congeners 1675
962.2	Poisoning by Ovarian Hormones and Synthetic Substitutes 1675
962.3	Poisoning by Insulins and Antidiabetic Agents 1675
962.4	Poisoning by Anterior Pituitary Hormones 1675
962.5	Poisoning by Posterior Pituitary Hormones 1675

962.6	Poisoning by Parathyroid and Parathyroid Derivatives **1675**	967.4	Poisoning by Methaqualone Compounds **1675**
962.7	Poisoning by Thyroid and Thyroid Derivatives **1675**	967.5	Poisoning by Glutethimide Group **1675**
962.8	Poisoning by Antithyroid Agents **1675**	967.6	Poisoning by Mixed Sedatives, Not Elsewhere Classified **1675**
962.9	Poisoning by Other and Unspecified Hormones and Synthetic Substitutes **1675**	967.8	Poisoning by Other Sedatives and Hypnotics **1675**
963	Poisoning by Primarily Systemic Agents **1675**	967.9	Poisoning by Unspecified Sedative or Hypnotic **1675**
963.0	Poisoning by Antiallergic and Antiemetic Drugs **1675**	968	Poisoning by Other Central Nervous System Depressants and Anesthetics **1675**
963.1	Poisoning by Antineoplastic and Immunosuppressive Drugs **1675**	968.0	Poisoning by Central Nervous System Muscle-tone Depressants **1675**
963.2	Poisoning by Acidifying Agents **1675**	968.1	Poisoning by Halothane **1675**
963.3	Poisoning by Alkalizing Agents **1675**	968.2	Poisoning by Other Gaseous Anesthetics **1675**
963.4	Poisoning by Enzymes, Not Elsewhere Classified **1675**	968.3	Poisoning by Intravenous Anesthetics **1675**
963.5	Poisoning by Vitamins **1164, 1166**	968.4	Poisoning by Other and Unspecified General Anesthetics **1675**
963.8	Poisoning by Other Specified Systemic Agents **1675**	968.5	Poisoning by Surface and Infiltration Anesthetics **1675**
963.9	Poisoning by Unspecified Systemic Agent **1675**	968.6	Poisoning by Peripheral Nerve and Plexus-Blocking Anesthetics **1675**
964	Poisoning by Agents Primarily Affecting Blood Constituents **1675**	968.7	Poisoning by Spinal Anesthetics **1675**
964.0	Poisoning by Iron and Its Compounds **1675**	968.9	Poisoning by Other and Unspecified Local Anesthetics **1675**
964	Poisoning by Agents Primarily Affecting Blood Constituents **1677, 1679, 1681**	969	Poisoning by Psychotropic Agents **1675**
964.0	Poisoning by Iron and Its Compounds **1677**	969.0	Poisoning by Antidepressants **1675**
964.1	Poisoning by Folic Acid **1675**	969.1	Poisoning by Phenothiazine-based Tranquilizers **1675**
964.1	Poisoning by Folic Acid **1679**	969.2	Poisoning by Butyrophenone-based Tranquilizers **1675**
964.2	Poisoning by Anticoagulants **1675**	969.3	Poisoning by Other Antipsychotics, Neuroleptics, and Major Tranquilizers **1675**
964.3	Poisoning by Vitamin K **1681**	969.4	Poisoning by Benzodiazepine-Based Tranquilizers **1675**
964.4	Poisoning by Fibrinolysis-affecting Drugs **1675**	969.5	Poisoning by Other Tranquilizers **1675**
964.5	Poisoning by Anticoagulant Antagonists and Other Coagulants **1675**	969.6	Poisoning by Psychodysleptics (Hallucinogens) **1675**
964.6	Poisoning by Gamma Globulin **1675**	969.7	Poisoning by Psychostimulants **1675**
964.7	Poisoning by Natural Blood and Blood Products **1675**	969.8	Poisoning by Other Specified Psychotropic Agents **1675**
964.8	Poisoning by Other Specified Agents Affecting Blood Constituents **1675**	969.9	Poisoning by Unspecified Psychotropic Agent **1675**
964.9	Poisoning by Unspecified Agent Affecting Blood Constituents **1675**	970	Poisoning by Central Nervous System Stimulants **1675**
965	Poisoning by Analgesics, Antipyretics, and Antirheumatics **1675**	970.0	Poisoning by Analeptics **1675**
965.0	Poisoning by Opiates and Related Narcotics **1675**	970.1	Poisoning by Opiate Antagonists **1675**
965.1	Poisoning by Salicylates **1675**	970.8	Poisoning by Other Specified Central Nervous System Stimulants **1675**
965.4	Poisoning by Aromatic Analgesics, Not Elsewhere Classified **1675**	970.9	Poisoning by Unspecified Central Nervous System Stimulant **1675**
965.5	Poisoning by Pyrazole Derivatives **1675**	971	Poisoning by Drugs Primarily Affecting the Autonomic Nervous System **1675**
965.6	Poisoning by Antirheumatics **1675**	971.0	Poisoning by Parasympathomimetics **1675**
965.7	Poisoning by Other Non-Narcotic Analgesics **1675**	971.1	Poisoning by Parasympatholytics **1675**
965.8	Poisoning by Other Specified Analgesics and Antipyretics **1675**	971.2	Poisoning by Sympathomimetics **1675**
965.9	Poisoning by Unspecified Analgesic and Antipyretic **1675**	971.3	Poisoning by Sympatholytics **1675**
966	Poisoning by Anticonvulsants and Anti-Parkinsonism Drugs **1675**	971.9	Poisoning by Unspecified Drug Primarily Affecting Autonomic Nervous System **1675**
966.0	Poisoning by Oxazolidine Derivatives **1675**	972	Poisoning by Agents Primarily Affecting the Cardiovascular System **1675**
966.1	Poisoning by Hydantoin Derivatives **1675**	972.0	Poisoning by Cardiac Rhythm **1675**
966.2	Poisoning by Succinimides **1675**	972.1	Poisoning by Cardiotonic Glycosides and Drugs of Similar Action **1675**
966.3	Poisoning by Other and Unspecified Anticonvulsants **1675**	972.2	Poisoning by Antilipemic and Antiarteriosclerotic Drugs **1675**
966.4	Poisoning by Anti-parkinsonism Drugs **1675**	972.3	Poisoning by Ganglion-Blocking Agents **1675**
967	Poisoning by Sedatives and Hypnotics **1675**	972.4	Poisoning by Coronary Vasodilators **1675**
967.0	Poisoning by Barbiturates **1675**	972.5	Poisoning by Other Vasodilators **1675**
967.1	Poisoning by Chloral Hydrate Group **1675**		
967.2	Poisoning by Paraldehyde **1675**		
967.3	Toxic Effects, Methyl Bromide **2142**		

972.6	Poisoning by Other Antihypertensive Agents 1675		976.6	Poisoning by Anti-infectives and Other Drugs and Preparations for Ear, Nose, and Throat 1675
972.7	Poisoning by Antivaricose Drugs, Including Sclerosing Agents 1675		976.8	Poisoning by Other Agents Primarily Affecting Skin and Mucous Membrane 1675
972.8	Poisoning by Capillary-active Drugs 1675		976.9	Poisoning by Unspecified Agent Primarily Affecting Skin and Mucous Membrane 1675
972.9	Poisoning by Other and Unspecified Agents Primarily Affecting the Cardiovascular System 1675		977	Poisoning by Other and Unspecified Drugs and Medicinal Substances 1675
973	Poisoning by Agents Primarily Affecting the Gastrointestinal System 1675		977.0	Poisoning by Dietetics 1675
973.0	Poisoning by Antacids and Antigastric Secretion Drugs 1675		977.1	Poisoning by Lipotropic Drugs 1675
973.1	Poisoning by Irritant Cathartics 1675		977.2	Poisoning by Antidotes and Chelating Agents, Not Elsewhere Classified 1675
973.2	Poisoning by Emollients Cathartics 1675		977.3	Poisoning by Alcohol Deterrents 1675
973.3	Poisoning by Other Cathartics, Including Intestinal Atonia Drugs 1675		977.4	Poisoning by Pharmaceutical Excipients 1675
973.5	Poisoning by Antidiarrheal Drugs 1675		977.8	Poisoning by Other Specified Drugs and Medicinal Substances 1675
973.6	Poisoning by Emetics 1675		977.9	Poisoning by Unspecified Drug or Medicinal Substance 1675
973.8	Poisoning by Other Specified Agents Primarily Affecting the Gastrointestinal System 1675		978	Poisoning by Bacterial Vaccines 1675
973.9	Poisoning by Unspecified Agents Primarily Affecting the Gastrointestinal System 1675		978.0	Poisoning by BCG Vaccine 1675
974	Poisoning by Water, Mineral, and Uric Acid Metabolism Drugs 1675		978.1	Poisoning by Typhoid and Paratyphoid Vaccine 1675
			978.2	Poisoning by Cholera Vaccine 1675
974.0	Poisoning by Mercurial Diuretics 1675		978.3	Poisoning by Plague Vaccine 1675
974.1	Poisoning by Purine Derivative Diuretics 1675		978.4	Poisoning by Tetanus Vaccine 1675
974.2	Poisoning by Carbonic Acid Anhydrase Inhibitors		978.5	Poisoning by Diphtheria Vaccine 1675
974.3	Poisoning by Saluretics 1675		978.6	Poisoning by Pertussis Vaccine, Including Combinations with Pertussis Component 1675
974.4	Poisoning by Other Diuretics 1675		978.8	Poisoning by Other and Unspecified Bacterial Vaccines 1675
974.5	Poisoning by Electrolytic, Caloric, and Water-Balance Agents 1675		978.9	Poisoning by Mixed Bacterial Vaccines, Except Combinations with Pertussis Component 1675
974.6	Poisoning by Other Mineral Salts, Not Elsewhere Classified 1675		979	Poisoning by Other Vaccines and Biological Substances 1675
974.7	Poisoning by Uric Acid Metabolism Drugs 1675		979.0	Poisoning by Smallpox Vaccine 1675
975	Poisoning by Agents Primarily Acting on the Smooth and Skeletal Muscles and Respiratory System 1675		979.1	Poisoning by Rabies Vaccine 1675
975.0	Poisoning by Oxytocic Agents 1675		979.2	Poisoning by Typhus Vaccine 1675
975.1	Poisoning by Smooth Muscle Relaxants 1675		979.3	Poisoning by Yellow Fever Vaccine 1675
975.2	Poisoning by Skeletal Muscle Relaxants 1675		979.4	Poisoning by Measles Vaccine 1675
975.3	Poisoning by Other and Unspecified Drugs Acting on Muscles 1675		979.5	Poisoning by Poliomyelitis Vaccine 1675
975.4	Poisoning by Antitussives 1675		979.6	Poisoning by Other and Unspecified Viral and Rickettsial Vaccines 1675
975.5	Poisoning by Expectorants 1675		979.7	Poisoning by Mixed Viral-rickettsial and Bacterial Vaccines, Except Combinations with Pertussis Component 1675
975.6	Poisoning by Anti-Common Cold Drugs 1675			
975.7	Poisoning by Antiasthmatics 1675		979.9	Poisoning by Other and Unspecified Vaccines and Biological Substances 1675
975.8	Poisoning by Other and Unspecified Respiratory Drugs 1675		980	Poisoning by Solid or Liquid Substances, Undetermined Whether Accidentally or Purposely Inflicted 1675
976	Poisoning by Agents Primarily Affecting Skin and Mucous Membrane, Ophthalmological, Otorhinolaryngological, and Dental Drugs 1675			
			980.1	Toxic Effects, Methyl Alcohol 2140
976.0	Poisoning by Iodine (Local Anti-Infectives and Anti-Inflammatory Drugs) 1675		980.2	Toxic Effects, Isopropyl Alcohol 2134
			982.2	Toxic Effects, Carbon Disulfide 2116
976.1	Poisoning by Antipruritics 1675		982.3	Toxic Effects, Chlorinated Hydrocarbon Solvents 2120
976.2	Poisoning by Local Astringents and Local Detergents 1675		983.1	Toxic Effects, Hydrofluoric Acid 2131–2132
976.3	Poisoning by Emollients, Demulcents, and Protectants 1675		984	Toxic Effects, Lead 2136
976.4	Poisoning by Keratolytics, Keratoplastics, Other Hair Treatment Drugs and Preparations 1675		984.0	Toxic Effects, Inorganic Lead Compounds 2136
			984.9	Toxic Effects, Unspecified Lead Compound 2136
976.5	Poisoning by Eye Anti-infectives and Other Eye Drugs 1675		985.0	Toxic Effects, Mercury 2138
			985.1	Toxic Effects, Arsenic 2110

985.3	Toxic Effects, Beryllium 2112		995.1	Angioneurotic Edema 150
985.5	Toxic Effects, Cadmium 2114		995.3	Multiple Chemical Sensitivity 100, 1397
985.6	Toxic Effects, Chromium 2124		995.6	Anaphylactic Shock 131
985.8	Toxic Effects, Nickel 2146		995.60	Anaphylactic Shock, Food Reaction 131
985.9	Metal Fume Fever 1374		995.61	Anaphylactic Shock Due to Peanuts 131
986	Toxic Effects, Carbon Monoxide 2117		995.62	Anaphylactic Shock Due to Crustaceans 131
987.6	Toxic Effects, Chlorine Gas 2122		995.63	Anaphylactic Shock Due to Fruits and Vegetables 131
987.8	Toxic Effects, Ozone 2131–2132, 2142		995.64	Anaphylactic Shock Due to Tree Nuts and Seeds 131
988.0	Toxic Effects, Fish and Shellfish 1675		995.65	Anaphylactic Shock Due to Fish 131
988	Toxic Effect of Noxious Substances Eaten As Food 888		995.66	Anaphylactic Shock Due to Food Additives 131
988.0	Toxic Effects, Fish and Shellfish 2126		995.67	Anaphylactic Shock Due to Milk Products 131
988.1	Toxic Effects, Mushrooms 1675		995.68	Anaphylactic Shock Due to Eggs 131
988.1	Toxic Effects, Mushrooms 2143		995.69	Anaphylactic Shock Due to Other Specified Food 131
988.2	Toxic Effects, Plants, Genus Toxicodendron 1675		996.32	Perforation of Uterus by IUD 2229
988.2	Toxic Effects, Plants, Genus Toxicodendron 2150		998.5	Wound Infection, Postoperative 2302
988.8	Other Specified Noxious Substances Eaten As Food 888		999.4	Anaphylactic Shock Due to Serum 129
988.9	Unspecified Noxious Substances Eaten As Food 888		C58150	Total Abdominal Hysterectomy 1186
989.3	Toxic Effects, Organophosphate and Carbamate Pesticides 2147		E870	Accidental Cut, Puncture, Perforation or Hemorrhage 460
989.5	Insect or Spider Bites and Stings 1675		M8700/0	Pheochromocytoma 1638
989.5	Insect or Spider Bites and Stings 1210		M8850/0	Lipoma 1290
989.8	Toxic Effects, Formaldehyde 2129		M8890/0	Leiomyoma 875
989.81	Toxic Effects of Substances Chiefly Nonmedicinal As to Source, Asbestos 201		M9140/3	Kaposi's Sarcoma 1253
			M9180/0	Osteoma 1536
991.0	Frostbite of Face 959		M9400/3	Astrocytoma 214
991.1	Frostbite of Hand 959		M8090/3	Basal Cell Carcinoma 387
991.2	Frostbite of Foot 959		M8720/3	Melanoma, Malignant 387
991.3	Frostbite of Other and Unspecified Sites 959		M9450/3	Oligodendroglioma 999
991.9	Unspecified Effect of Reduced Temperature 959		M9540/1	Neurofibromatosis 1469
992.0	Heat Stroke or Sunstroke 1051		M9700/3	Mycosis Fungoides 1416
992.3	Heat Exhaustion, Anhydrotic 1049		V22.0	Supervision of Normal First Pregnancy 1716
992.4	Heat Exhaustion Due to Salt Depletion 1049		V22.1	Supervision of Other Normal Pregnancy 1716
992.5	Heat Exhaustion 1049		V22.2	Pregnant State, Incidental 1716
993	Effects of Air Pressure 241		V22	Pregnancy, Normal 1716
993.0	Barotitis Media 241		V27	Outcome of Delivery, Single Liveborn 647
993.1	Barotrauma, Sinus 241		V45.3	Intestinal Bypass or Anastomosis Status 978
993.3	Caisson Disease 331		V55.1	Gastrostomy 984
994.6	Motion Sickness 1395			
995.0	Anaphylactic Shock, Other 129			

Procedures

01.24	Craniotomy 598	14.5	Retinal Detachment Repair, Other 1825
01.25	Craniectomy 596	14.51	Retinal Detachment Repair with Diathermy 1825
01.41	Thalamotomy 2064	14.52	Retinal Detachment Repair with Cryotherapy 1825
02.99	Adrenal Tissue Implant or Transplant (to Brain) 76	14.53	Retinal Detachment Repair with Xenon Arc Photocoagulation 1825
03.09	Laminectomy or Laminotomy 1273, 1951	14.54	Retinal Detachment Repair with Laser Photocoagulation 1825
03.31	Lumbar Puncture 1309	14.55	Retinal Detachment Repair with Photocoagulation of Unspecified Type 1825
03.39	Spinal Cord Stimulation 1949		
04.07	Excision of Morton's Neuroma 855	14.59	Retinal Detachment Repair, Other Type 1825
04.43	Carpal Tunnel Release 428	19.0	Stapes Mobilization 2002
04.44	Tarsal Tunnel Release 2041	19.19	Stapedectomy 2002
04.6	Transposition of Cranial and Peripheral Nerves 2165	19.4	Tympanoplasty (Type I) 2201
05.2	Sympathectomy 2022	19.5	Tympanoplasty, Other (Type II, III, IV, and V) 2201
05.3	Sympathetic Block 2022	20.0	Myringotomy 1434
05.35	Celiac Plexus Block 442	20.01	Myringotomy with Insertion of Tube 1434
06.2	Thyroidectomy 2090	20.09	Myringotomy, Other 1434
06.3	Thyroidectomy, Partial 2090	20.4	Mastoidectomy 1347
06.31	Thyroid, Excision of Lesion 2090	20.41	Mastoidectomy, Simple 1347
06.39	Thyroidectomy, Other Partial 2090	20.42	Mastoidectomy, Radical 1347
06.4	Thyroidectomy, Complete 2090	20.49	Mastoidectomy, Other 1347
06.5	Thyroidectomy, Substernal 2090	20.6	Fenestration of Inner Ear 1434
06.6	Excision of Lingual Thyroid 2090	20.96	Cochlear Implant 529
07.21	Adrenalectomy 77	21.31	Nasal Polypectomy 1440
07.3	Adrenalectomy, Bilateral 77	21.5	Resection of Nasal Septum, Submucous 1909
07.8	Thymectomy 2089	21.8	Nose, Repair and Plastic Operations on 1841
11.49	Keratectomy (PRK) 1256	21.83	Nasal Reconstruction, Total 1841
11.6	Corneal Transplant 582	21.84	Rhinoplasty, Revision 1841
11.60	Corneal Transplant, Not Otherwise Specified 582	21.85	Rhinoplasty, Augmentation 1841
11.61	Keratoplasty, Lamellar, with Autograft 582	21.86	Rhinoplasty, Limited 1841
11.63	Keratoplasty, Penetrating, with Autograft 582	21.87	Rhinoplasty, Other 1841
11.69	Corneal Transplant, Other 582	23	Removal and Restoration of Teeth 2107
11.75	Radial Keratotomy 1775	23.0	Tooth Extraction by Forceps 2107
12.12	Iridotomy 1239	23.09	Tooth Extraction 2107
12.14	Iridectomy 1238	23.1	Tooth Extraction by Surgical Removal 2107
12.59	Trabeculoplasty 2158	23.19	Tooth Extraction 2107
12.64	Trabeculectomy Ab Externo 2156	23.70	Root Canal Therapy 1847
13.1	Cataract Surgery (Intracapsular Extraction of Lens) 439	24.31	Gingivectomy 992
13.2	Cataract Surgery (Extracapsular Extraction of Lens by Linear Extraction Technique) 439	28.2	Tonsillectomy Without Adenoidectomy 2102
		28.3	Tonsillectomy with Adenoidectomy 2102
13.3	Cataract Surgery (Extracapsular Extraction of Lens, Simple Aspiration) 439	28.6	Adenoidectomy Without Tonsillectomy 2102
		30.0	Laryngectomy 1278
13.4	Cataract Surgery (Extracapsular Extraction of Lens, Fragmentation and Aspiration) 439	31.1	Tracheostomy, Temporary 2159
		31.2	Tracheostomy, Permanent 2159
13.5	Cataract Surgery (Extracapsular Extraction of Lens, Other) 439	31.42	Laryngoscopy 1281
		32.29	Lung Excision 1314
13.6	Cataract Extraction, Other 439	32.3	Resection of Lung, Segmental 1314
13.7	Prosthetic Lens, Insertion of 439	32.4	Lobectomy of Lung 1314
14.4	Retinal Detachment Repair (with Sclera Buckling and Implant) 1825	32.5	Pneumonectomy, Complete 1664
14.41	Retinal Detachment Repair with Sclera Buckling with Implant 1825	33.22	Bronchoscopy 305
14.49	Retinal Detachment Repair with Other Scleral Buckling 1825		

33.24	Bronchial Biopsy 304
33.26	Lung Biopsy, Closed 1310
33.27	Lung Biopsy 1310
33.28	Lung Biopsy, Open 1310
34.02	Thoracotomy 2069, 2079
34.04	Chest Tube (Via Thoracostomy) 2078
34.09	Thoracostomy (Open Chest Drainage) 2078
34.24	Pleural Biopsy 1657
34.91	Thoracentesis 2069
35.0	Valvotomy, Closed Heart 2237
35.00	Valvotomy, Closed Heart, Unspecified Valve 2237
35.01	Valvotomy, Closed Heart, Aortic Valve 2237
35.02	Valvotomy, Closed Heart, Mitral Valve 2237
35.03	Valvotomy, Closed Heart, Pulmonary Valve 2237
35.04	Valvotomy, Closed Heart, Tricuspid Valve 2237
35.12	Mitral Commissurotomy 1384
35.2	Heart Valve Replacement 1047
35.20	Heart Valve Replacement, Unspecified Valve 1047
35.21	Heart Valve Replacement, Aortic Valve with Tissue Graft 1047
35.22	Heart Valve Replacement, Aortic Valve, Other 1047
35.23	Heart Valve Replacement, Mitral Valve with Tissue Graft 1047
35.24	Heart Valve Replacement, Mitral Valve, Other 1047
35.25	Heart Valve Replacement, Pulmonary Valve with Tissue Graft 1047
35.26	Heart Valve Replacement, Pulmonary Valve, Other 1047
35.27	Heart Valve Replacement, Tricuspid Valve with Tissue Graft 1047
35.28	Heart Valve Replacement, Tricuspid Valve, Other 1047
35.96	Valvuloplasty, Balloon 2240
36.01	Angioplasty, Coronary Balloon (without Mention of Thrombolytic Agent) 590
36.02	Angioplasty, Coronary Balloon (with Thrombolytic Agent), Single Vessel 590
36.04	Coronary Thrombolysis 593
36.05	Angioplasty, Coronary Balloon (with or without Mention of Thrombolytic Agent) 590
36.1	Coronary Bypass (Anastomosis for Heart Revascularization) 592
36.10	Coronary Bypass 592
36.11	Aortocoronary Bypass of One Coronary Artery 592
36.12	Aortocoronary Bypass of Two Coronary Arteries 592
36.13	Aortocoronary Bypass of Three Coronary Arteries 592
36.14	Aortocoronary Bypass of Four or More Coronary Arteries 592
36.15	Coronary Artery Bypass, Single Internal Mammary 592
36.16	Coronary Artery Bypass, Double Internal Mammary 592
36.19	Bypass Anastomosis for Heart Revascularization, Other 592
37.21	Cardiac Catheterization, Right Heart 411
37.22	Cardiac Catheterization, Left Heart 411
37.23	Cardiac Catheterization, Combined Right and Left Heart 411
37.31	Pericardiectomy 1614
37.80	Pacemaker Insertion, Initial or Replacement (Type of Device not Specified) 414
37.82	Pacemaker Insertion, Initial Insertion of a Single-Chamber Device, Rate Responsive 414
37.83	Pacemaker Insertion, Initial Insertion of Dual-Chamber Device 414
37.86	Pacemaker Insertion, Replacement of Any Type Pacemaker Device with Single-chamber Device, Rate Responsive 414
37.87	Pacemaker Insertion, Replacement of Any Type Pacemaker Device with Dual-chamber Device 414
37.91	Open-chest Cardiac Massage 1514
38.0	Embolectomy 786–787
38.00	Thrombectomy, Unspecified Site 2082
38.05	Embolectomy, Pulmonary 787
38.09	Thrombectomy of Lower Limb Veins 2082
38.1	Endarterectomy 801
38.10	Endarterectomy of Unspecified Site 801
38.16	Endarterectomy of Abdominal Arteries 801
38.18	Endarterectomy of Lower Limb Arteries 801
38.3	Aneurysmectomy (Resection of Vessel with Anastomosis) 138
38.30	Aneurysmectomy with Replacement of Unspecified Site 138
38.31	Aneurysmectomy with Anastomosis of Intracranial Vessels 138
38.32	Aneurysmectomy with Anastomosis of Other Vessels of Head and Neck 138
38.33	Aneurysmectomy with Anastomosis of Upper Limb Vessels 138
38.34	Aneurysmectomy with Anastomosis of Aorta, Abdominal 138
38.35	Aneurysmectomy with Anastomosis of Thoracic Vessel 138
38.36	Aneurysmectomy with Anastomosis of Abdominal Arteries 138
38.37	Aneurysmectomy with Anastomosis of Abdominal Veins 138
38.38	Aneurysmectomy with Anastomosis of Lower Limb Arteries 138
38.39	Aneurysmectomy with Anastomosis of Lower Limb Veins 138
38.4	Aneurysmectomy (Resection of Vessel with Replacement) 138
38.41	Aneurysmectomy with Replacement of Intracranial Vessels 138
38.42	Aneurysmectomy with Replacement of Other Vessels of Head and Neck 138
38.43	Aneurysmectomy with Replacement of Upper Limb Vessels 138
38.44	Aneurysmectomy with Replacement of Aorta, Abdominal 138
38.45	Aneurysmectomy with Replacement of Thoracic Vessel 138
38.46	Aneurysmectomy with Replacement of Abdominal Arteries 138
38.47	Aneurysmectomy with Replacement of Abdominal Veins 138
38.48	Aneurysmectomy with Replacement of Lower Limb Arteries 138
38.49	Aneurysmectomy with Replacement of Lower Limb Veins 138
38.5	Ligation and Stripping of Varicose Veins 1287
38.50	Ligation and Stripping of Varicose Veins, Unspecified Site 1287
38.51	Ligation and Stripping of Intracranial Varicose Vessels 1287
38.52	Ligation and Stripping of Other Varicose Vessels of Head and Neck 1287
38.53	Ligation and Stripping of Upper Limb Varicose Vessels 1287
38.55	Ligation and Stripping of Thoracic Varicose Vessels 1287
38.57	Ligation and Stripping of Abdominal Varicose Vessels 1287
38.59	Ligation and Stripping of Lower Limb Varicose Vessels 1287
38.60	Aneurysmectomy 138
38.7	Vena Cava Interruption 2251
39.1	Portal Systemic Shunt 1695
39.51	Repair of Cerebral Aneurysm 1812
39.56	Repair of Blood Vessel with Tissue Patch Graft 183

39.57	Repair of Blood Vessel with Synthetic Patch Graft 183
39.58	Arterial Graft 183
39.92	Sclerotherapy, Varicose Veins 1895
39.95	Dialysis, Renal 1800
41.0	Bone Marrow Transplant 275
41.00	Bone Marrow Transplant, Unspecified 275
41.01	Autologous Bone Marrow Transplant 275
41.03	Allogeneic Bone Marrow Transplant Without Purging 275
41.31	Bone Marrow Biopsy 273
41.5	Splenectomy 1955
41.91	Aspiration of Bone Marrow for the Donor 275
42.23	Endoscopy of Gastrointestinal Tract 810
42.33	Sclerotherapy, Esophageal Varices 1895
42.4	Esophagectomy 845
42.7	Myotomy of Esophagus 1433
42.91	Ligation of Esophageal Varices 1288
42.92	Dilation of Esophagus 700
43.11	Gastrostomy, Percutaneous 984
43.19	Gastrostomy, Other 984
43.4	Resection of Gastric or Duodenal Ulcer Site 1819
43.5	Gastrectomy, Partial with Anastomosis to Esophagus 968
43.6	Resection of Gastric or Duodenal Ulcer Site 968, 1819
43.7	Gastrectomy, Partial with Anastomosis to Jejunum 968
43.89	Gastrectomy, Partial, Other 968
43.99	Gastrectomy, Total, Other 968
44.00	Vagotomy, Not Otherwise Specified 2235
44.01	Vagotomy, Truncal 2235
44.02	Vagotomy, Highly Selective 2235
44.03	Vagotomy, Other Selective 2235
44.13	Gastroscopy, Other (Endoscopy of Stomach) 810
44.2	Pyloroplasty 1769
44.3	Gastroenterostomy 968, 978
44.39	Gastroenterostomy, Other 968, 978
45.13	Esophagogastroduodenoscopy (Endoscopy of Small Intestine) 850
45.23	Colonoscopy 540
45.24	Sigmoidoscopy 1925
45.25	Biopsy of Large Intestine, Closed (Endoscopy) 1925
45.3	Excision or Destruction of Lesion or Tissue of Small Intestine, Local 857
45.30	Resection of Duodenal Lesion (Open and Endoscopic) 857
45.31	Excision of Lesion of Duodenum, Local, Other 857
45.32	Resection of Duodenal Lesion, Other 857
45.7	Colon Resection (Colectomy) 538
45.71	Resection of Large Intestine, Multiple Segmental 538
45.72	Cecectomy 538
45.73	Hemicolectomy, Right 538
45.74	Resection of Transverse Colon 538
45.75	Hemicolectomy, Left 538
45.76	Sigmoidectomy 538
45.79	Excision of Large Intestine, Partial, Other 538
46.1	Colostomy 543
46.10	Colostomy, Not Otherwise Specified 543
46.11	Colostomy, Temporary 543
46.13	Colostomy, Permanent, Other 543
46.20	Ileostomy, Not Otherwise Specified 543
46.21	Ileostomy, Temporary 543
46.22	Ileostomy, Continent (Kock Pouch) 543
46.3	Enterostomy 811
46.31	Enterostomy, Delayed Opening of 811
46.32	Jejunostomy, Percutaneous 811
46.39	Enterostomy, Other 811
47.0	Appendectomy 174
48.23	Rigid Sigmoidoscopy 1925
48.35	Local Excision of Rectal Lesion or Tissue 10
48.5	Abdominoperineal Resection of Rectum 10
48.81	Incision and Drainage of Ischiorectal and/or Perirectal Abscess 1200
49.0	Incision or Excision of Perianal Tissue 884
49.01	Incision and Drainage of Ischiorectal and/or Perirectal Abscess 1200
49.02	Other Incision of Perianal Tissue 884
49.22	Biopsy of Perianal Tissue 884
49.3	Fissurectomy, Anal 884
49.31	Endoscopic Excision or Destruction of Lesion or Tissue of Anus 884
49.42	Sclerotherapy 1070, 1895
49.44	Hemorrhoid Treatment (Destruction of Hemorrhoids by Cryotherapy) 1070
49.45	Hemorrhoid Treatment 1070
49.46	Hemorrhoid Treatment (Excision of Hemorrhoids) 1070
49.7	Repair of Anus 884
50.11	Liver Biopsy 1297
50.12	Liver Biopsy, Open 1297
51.2	Cholecystectomy 495
51.22	Cholecystectomy 495
51.23	Cholecystectomy 495
52.5	Pancreatectomy, Partial 1568
52.51	Pancreatectomy, Proximal 1568
52.52	Pancreatectomy, Distal 1568
52.53	Pancreatectomy, Radical Subtotal 1568
52.59	Pancreatectomy, Other, Partial 1568
52.6	Pancreatectomy, Total 1568
52.7	Whipple Procedure (Pancreaticoduodenectomy) 1571
52.96	Pancreaticojejunostomy 1572
53.0	Hernia Repair, Inguinal, Unilateral 1094
53.1	Hernia Repair, Inguinal, Bilateral 1094
53.2	Hernia Repair, Femoral, Unilateral 1094
53.3	Hernia Repair, Femoral, Bilateral 1094
53.4	Hernia Repair, Umbilical 1094
53.5	Hernia Repair, Incisional 1094
53.7	Hernia Repair, Hiatal or Diaphragmatic 1094
54.1	Laparotomy 1276

54.11	Laparotomy, Exploratory 1276
54.12	Laparotomy, Reopening of Recent Site 1276
54.19	Laparotomy, Other 1276
54.21	Laparoscopy 1275
54.91	Paracentesis 1582
55.01	Nephrotomy 1293, 1458
55.03	Lithotomy, Percutaneous 1294
55.4	Nephrectomy, Partial 1451
55.5	Nephrectomy, Total 1451
55.6	Kidney Transplant 1261
55.69	Kidney Transplant (Including donor) 1261
55.7	Nephropexy 1455
56.0	Cystoscopy (Removal of Calculus, Ureter) 2173
56.2	Lithotomy, Ureter 1293
57.0	Transurethral Clearance of Bladder 2216
57.19	Lithotomy, Urinary Bladder 1293
57.32	Cystoscopy, Transurethral 624
57.33	Biopsy of Bladder, Closed 624
57.6	Cystectomy, Partial 615
57.7	Cystectomy, Total 615
57.71	Cystectomy, Radical 615
57.85	Cystourethroplasty of Bladder Neck 625
57.91	Incision of Bladder Neck, Transurethral 2172
57.94	Urethral Catheterization, Indwelling 2216
59.5	Marshall-Marchetti Operation 1344
59.71	Vesicourethropexy 2265
59.79	Repair of Stress Incontinence 1344
60.2	Prostatectomy, Transurethral 1729
60.29	Transurethral Resection of Prostate 2174
60.3	Prostatectomy, Suprapubic 1729
60.4	Prostatectomy, Retropubic 1729
60.62	Prostatectomy, Perineal 1729
60.95	Dilation of Prostatic Urethra, Transurethral Balloon 2171
62.8	Orchiectomy 1523
63.1	Ligation of Spermatic Vein for Varicocele 1289
63.2	Spermatocelectomy 1943
63.7	Vasectomy and Ligation of Vas Deferens 2248
63.70	Male Sterility Procedure 2248
63.71	Ligation of Vas Deferens 2248
63.72	Ligation of Spermatic Cord 2248
63.73	Vasectomy 2248
64.0	Circumcision 514
64.2	Cryotherapy, Genital Warts, Male (Destruction of Lesion on Penis) 606
64.97	Insertion of Inflatable Penile Prosthesis 1213
65.2	Ovarian Cyst, Resection of 1555
65.3	Oophorectomy 1501
65.4	Salpingo-Oophorectomy 1873
65.5	Oophorectomy, Bilateral 1501, 1503
65.51	Removal of Both Ovaries At Same Operative Episode 1501
65.52	Removal of Remaining Ovary 1501
65.6	Salpingo-Oophorectomy, Bilateral 1873
65.61	Removal of Both Ovaries and Tubes At Same Operative Episode 1873
65.62	Removal of Ovary and Tube 1873
66.2	Tubal Ligation (Bilateral Endoscopic Destruction of Fallopian Tubes) 2193
66.4	Salpingectomy 1868
66.5	Salpingectomy, Total Bilateral 1868
66.51	Removal of Both Fallopian Tubes At Same Operative Episode 1868
66.52	Removal of Remaining Fallopian Tube 1868
66.6	Salpingectomy, Other 1868
66.61	Excision or Destruction of Legion of Fallopian Tube 1868
66.62	Salpingectomy with Removal of Tubal Pregnancy 1868
66.63	Salpingectomy, Bilateral Partial, Not Otherwise Specified 1868
66.69	Salpingectomy, Partial, Other 1868
67.11	Cervical Biopsy 460
67.2	Cervical Conization 463
67.32	Cervical Cauterization 461
67.39	Cervical Polypectomy 469
68.29	Myomectomy, Uterine (Abdominal Approach) 1430
68.3	Hysterectomy, Subtotal Abdominal 1186
68.4	Hysterectomy, Abdominal 1186
68.5	Hysterectomy, Vaginal 1186
68.6	Hysterectomy, Radical Abdominal 1186
68.7	Hysterectomy, Radical 1186
68.9	Hysterectomy, Other and Unspecified 1186
69.0	Dilation and Curettage 699
69.01	Abortion by Dilation and Curettage for Termination of Pregnancy 11
69.5	Aspiration Curretage of Uterus 208
69.51	Aspiration Curretage of Uterus for Termination Pregnancy 208
69.52	Aspiration Curretage Following Delivery or Abortion 208
69.59	Aspiration Curretage of Uterus, Other 208
70.22	Culdoscopy 610
70.5	Repair of Cystocele and Rectocele 1096
70.51	Repair of Cystocele 1096
70.52	Repair of Rectocele 1096
70.71	Suture of Laceration of Vagina 1096
70.8	Obliteration of Vaginal Vault 1096
71.3	Cryotherapy, Genital Warts (Female) 605
71.71	Suture of Laceration of Vulva or Perineum 1618
73.59	Delivery, Assisted Spontaneous (Normal Vaginal) 647
73.6	Episiotomy 826
74	Cesarean Section and Removal of Fetus 476
74.0	Cesarean Delivery 476
74.1	Cesarean Section, Low Cervical 476
74.4	Cesarean Section, Extraperitoneal 476
74.9	Cesarean Section of Unspecified Type 476
74.99	Cesarean Section, Other of Unspecified Type 476
75.0	Abortion, Intra-Amniotic Injection 13
77.5	Metatarsal Head, Removal 314

Index of ICD-9 CM

77.51	Bunionectomy with Soft Tissue Correction and Osteotomy of the First Metatarsal 314
77.53	Bunionectomy, Other, with Soft Tissue Correction (McBride Operation) 314
77.56	Hammertoe Repair 1816
77.58	Excision, Fusion, and Repair of Toes 860
77.59	Bunionectomy, Other (Mayo or Keller Operation) 314
77.68	Excision of Bone Spur, Foot 852
77.91	Rib Resection 1844
78.0	Bone Graft 272
78.10	Application of External Fixation Device, Unspecified Site 1791
78.6	Removal of Implanted Devices from Bone 1791
78.60	Removal of Implanted Devices from Bone, Unspecified Site 1791
79	Reduction of Fracture or Dislocation 1791
79.02	Reduction of Distal Radial Fracture Without Internal Fixation, Closed 1791
79.03	Reduction of Metacarpal Fracture Without Internal Fixation, Closed 1791
79.04	Reduction of Fracture of Phalanges of Hand Without Internal Fixation 1791
79.06	Reduction of Fracture of Tibia Without Internal Fixation, Closed 1791
79.07	Reduction of Tarsal or Metatarsal Fracture, Closed 1791
79.08	Reduction of Toe (Phalanges of Foot) Fracture without Internal Fixation, Closed 1791
79.09	Reduction of Rib Fracture Without Internal Fixation, Closed 1791
79.13	Reduction of Fracture of Carpals and Metacarpals (Bones of Hand) with Internal Fixation 1791
79.14	Reduction of Fracture of Phalanges of Hand (Fingers) with Internal Fixation, Closed 1791
79.23	Reduction of Fracture of Carpals and Metacarpals (Bones of Hand), Open 1791
79.24	Reduction of Fracture of Phalanges of Hand (Fingers), Open 1791
79.26	Reduction of Tibia or Fibula (Leg) Fracture, Open 1791
79.27	Reduction of Tarsal or Metatarsal (Ankle) Fracture without Internal Fixation, Open 1791
79.33	Reduction of Fracture of Carpal or Metacarpal (Bones of Hand) with Internal Fixation, Open 1791
79.34	Reduction of Fracture of Phalanges of Hand (Fingers) with Internal Fixation, Open 1791
79.36	Reduction of Fracture Tibia or Fibula (Leg) with Internal Fixation, Open 1791
79.37	Reduction of Tarsal or Metatarsal Fracture with Internal Fixation, Open 1791
79.71	Reduction of Humerus (Shoulder) Dislocation, Closed 1791
79.72	Reduction of Radius and Ulna (Elbow) Dislocation, Closed 1791
79.74	Reduction of Hand or Fingers (Phalanges) Dislocation, Closed 1791
79.76	Reduction of Tibia or Fibula (Knee) Dislocation, Closed 1791
79.77	Reduction of Tarsal and Metatarsals (Ankle) Dislocation, Closed 1791
79.84	Reduction of Hand or Fingers (Phalanges) Dislocation, Open 1791
79.87	Reduction of Tarsals and Metatarsals (Ankle) Dislocation, Open 1791
80.2	Arthroscopy 199
80.20	Arthroscopy, Unspecified Site 199
80.21	Arthroscopy, Shoulder 199
80.22	Arthroscopy, Elbow 199
80.23	Arthroscopy, Wrist 199
80.24	Arthroscopy, Hand and Finger 199
80.25	Arthroscopy, Hip 199
80.26	Arthroscopy, Knee 199
80.27	Arthroscopy, Ankle 199
80.28	Arthroscopy, Foot and Toe 199
80.29	Arthroscopy, Other Specified Sites 199
80.51	Discectomy (Excision of Intervertebral Disc) 703, 1951
80.52	Chemonucleolysis of Intervertebral Disc 482
80.59	Discectomy, Automated 703
80.6	Meniscectomy and Meniscus Repair 1361
80.7	Synovectomy 2027
80.70	Synovectomy, Unspecified Site 2027
81	Repair and Plastic Operation on Joint Structures 194, 197
81.0	Spinal Fusion 1951
81.00	Spinal Arthrodesis 1951
81.11	Ankle Arthrodesis 194
81.20	Arthrodesis 194
81.21	Hip Arthrodesis 194
81.22	Knee Arthrodesis 194
81.23	Shoulder Arthrodesis 194
81.26	Wrist Arthrodesis 194
81.45	ACL Repair (Anterior Cruciate Ligament) 1814
81.47	Meniscus Repair of Knee 1361
81.51	Hip Replacement, Total 1119
81.52	Hip Replacement, Partial 1119
81.54	Knee Replacement, Total 1263
81.80	Shoulder Replacement, Total 1917
81.81	Shoulder Replacement, Partial 1917
81.82	Repair of Shoulder Dislocation, Recurrent 1917
81.84	Elbow Replacement, Total 197
81.85	Elbow, Other Repair of 197
82.01	De Quervain's Release 630
82.21	Ganglionectomy (Excision of Ganglion, Wrist) 963
82.35	Dupuytren's Release (Fasciectomy) 753
82.41	Tendon Sheath of Hand, Suture 1817
82.42	Flexor Tendon of Hand, Delayed Suture 1817
82.43	Tendon of Hand, Other, Delayed Suture 1817
82.44	Flexor Tendon of Hand, Other Suture 1817
82.45	Tendon of Hand, Other Suture 1817
82.99	Operations on Muscle, Tendon, and Fascia of Hand 1515
83.01	Tendon Sheath Incision 2051–2052
83.13	Tendon Release 2051
83.14	Fasciotomy 870
83.45	Scalenectomy 1877
83.63	Rotator Cuff Repair 1848
84.01	Amputation, Finger or Thumb 123
84.02	Amputation and Disarticulation of Thumb 123

Code	Description	Code	Description
84.91	Amputation, Unspecified 116	87.36	Mammogram (Xerography of Breast) 1337
85.11	Breast Biopsy 295	87.37	Mammogram, Other 1337
85.12	Biopsy of Breast, Open 295	87.51	Percutaneous Hepatic Cholangiogram 493
85.21	Lumpectomy 295	87.53	Cholangiogram, Intraoperative 493
85.23	Mastectomy, Subtotal 1345	87.54	Cholangiography 493
85.31	Mammoplasty, Reduction 1790	87.59	Cholecystography 500
85.32	Mammoplasty, Reduction, Bilateral 1790	87.61	Barium Swallow 2214
85.34	Mammectomy, Unilateral 1345	87.62	Upper Gastrointestinal Series 2214
85.36	Mammectomy, Bilateral 1345	87.64	Lower Gastrointestinal Series 1305
85.4	Mastectomy 1345	87.73	Intravenous Pyelogram 1233
85.41	Mastectomy, Unilateral 1345	88.32	Arthrography 196
85.42	Mastectomy, Bilateral 1345	88.39	X-ray (Radiography, Diagnostic) 2305
85.43	Mastectomy, Unilateral Extended 1345	88.4	Arteriography 185
85.44	Mastectomy, Bilateral Extended 1345	88.40	Arteriography Using Contrast Material, Unspecified Site 185
85.45	Mastectomy, Unilateral Radical 1345	88.41	Arteriography of Cerebral Arteries 185
85.46	Mastectomy, Bilateral Radical 1345	88.42	Aortography (Arteriography of Aorta and Aortic Arch) 185
85.47	Mastectomy, Unilateral Extended Radical 1345	88.43	Arteriography of Pulmonary Arteries 185
85.48	Mastectomy, Bilateral Extended Radical 1345	88.44	Arteriography of Other Intrathoracic Vessels 185
85.5	Mammoplasty, Augmentation 1338	88.45	Arteriography of Renal Arteries 185
85.50	Mammoplasty, Not Otherwise Specified 1338	88.46	Arteriography of Placenta 185
85.51	Breast Augmentation by Unilateral Injection 1338	88.47	Arteriography of Other Intra-Abdominal Arteries 185
85.52	Breast Augmentation by Bilateral Injection 1338	88.48	Arteriography of Femoral and Other Lower Extremity Arteries 185
85.53	Breast Implant, Unilateral 1338	88.49	Arteriography of Other Specified Sites 185
85.54	Breast Implant, Bilateral 1338	88.5	Angiocardiography 148
86.0	Incision of Skin and Subcutaneous Tissue, Drainage of Abscess or Cyst 1201	88.50	Angiocardiography, Not Otherwise Specified 148
86.01	Aspiration of Superficial Abscess 1201	88.51	Angiocardiography of Venae Cavae 148
86.04	Incision with Drainage of Skin and Subcutaneous Tissue, Other 1201	88.52	Angiocardiography of Right Heart Structures 148
		88.53	Angiocardiography of Left Heart Structures 148
86.09	Incision of Skin and Subcutaneous Tissue, Other 1201	88.54	Angiocardiography, Combined Right and Left Heart 148
86.11	Skin or Subcutaneous Tissue Biopsy 1934	88.55	Coronary Arteriography Using a Single Catheter 586
86.2	Excision of Lesion or Tissue of Skin and Subcutaneous Tissue 854, 856, 1934	88.56	Coronary Arteriography Using Two Catheters 586
		88.57	Coronary Arteriography, Other and Unspecified 586
86.23	Excision of Nail, Nail Bed, or Nail Fold 856	88.7	Ultrasound, Diagnostic 2212
86.24	Chemical Peel of Skin 51	88.71	Diagnostic Ultrasound of Head and Neck 2212
86.25	Dermabrasion 865	88.72	Echocardiography 774
86.3	Excision of Plantar Wart(s) 605–606, 858	88.73	Diagnostic Ultrasound of Other Sites of Thorax 2212
86.5	Suture of Skin and Subcutaneous Tissue 2020	88.74	Diagnostic Ultrasound of Digestive System 2212
86.59	Suture of Skin and Subcutaneous Tissue of Other Sites 2020	88.75	Diagnostic Ultrasound of Urinary System 2212
86.6	Skin Graft 1932	88.76	Diagnostic Ultrasound of Abdomen and Retroperitoneum 2212
86.60	Skin Graft, Free, Not Otherwise Specified 1932	88.77	Diagnostic Ultrasound of Peripheral Vascular System 2212
86.61	Skin Graft, Full-thickness to Hand 1932	88.78	Diagnostic Ultrasound of Gravid Uterus 2212
86.62	Skin Graft to Hand, Other 1932	88.79	Diagnostic Ultrasound, Other 2212
86.63	Skin Graft, Full-thickness to Other Sites 1932	88.91	Magnetic Resonance Imaging of Brain and Brain Stem 1327
86.69	Skin Graft to Other Sites 1932	88.92	Magnetic Resonance Imaging of Chest and Myocardium 1327
86.82	Face Lift (Rhytidectomy) 865	88.93	Magnetic Resonance Imaging of Spinal Canal 1327
86.83	Liposuction (Reduction of Adipose Tissue) 1292	88.94	Magnetic Resonance Imaging of Musculoskeletal 1327
86.92	Electrolysis, Other Epilation of Skin 865	88.95	Magnetic Resonance Imaging of Pelvis, Prostate, and Bladder 1327
86.93	Insertion of Tissue Expander 865		
87	Diagnostic Radiology (Radiography) 2305	88.97	MRI (Magnetic Resonance Imaging of Other and Unspecified Sites) 1327
87.21	Myelography 1419	89.14	Electroencephalogram (EEG) 783

89.15	Nerve Conduction Studies 1459
89.37	Pulmonary Function Tests (Spirometry) 1758
89.38	Nonoperative Measurements and Examinations 1758
89.4	Cardiac Stress Tests and Pacemaker Checks 416
89.41	Cardiac Stress Test Using Treadmill 416
89.42	Masters' Two-Step Stress Test 416
89.43	Cardiovascular Stress Test Using Bicycle Ergometer 416
89.44	Cardiovascular Stress Test, Other 416
89.52	Electrocardiogram (ECG, EKG) 781
92.05	Myocardial Perfusion Scan 1427
92.14	Bone Scan 277
92.2	Radiation Therapy (Therapeutic Radiology and Nuclear Medicine) 1778
92.21	Superficial Radiation 1778
92.22	Orthovoltage Radiation 1778
92.23	Radioisotopic Teleradiotherapy 1778
92.24	Teleradiotherapy Using Photons 1778
92.26	Teleradiotherapy of Other Particulate Radiation 1778
93.08	Electromyography (EMG) 784
93.39	Ultrasound, Therapeutic 2164, 2213
93.4	Skeletal Traction and Other Traction 2163
93.41	Spinal Traction Using Skull Device 2163
93.42	Spinal Traction, Other 2163
93.43	Skeletal Traction, Intermittent 2163
93.44	Skeletal Traction, Other 2163
93.45	Thomas' Splint Traction 2163
93.46	Skin Traction of Limbs, Other 2163
93.8	Rehabilitation Therapy 1796
93.81	Recreation Therapy 1796
93.82	Educational Therapy 1796
93.83	Occupational Therapy 1499
93.85	Vocational Therapy 2288
93.89	Rehabilitation, Not Elsewhere Classified 1796
93.95	Hyperbaric Oxygenation 1141
94.25	Psychopharmacotherapy 1743
94.27	Electroconvulsive Therapy 782
94.3	Psychotherapy, Individual 1742, 1748
94.31	Psychoanalysis 1742
94.33	Cognitive Therapy (Behavior Therapy, Conditioning or Aversion Therapy) 530
94.39	Biofeedback 250
94.44	Psychotherapy, Group 1747
94.6	Alcohol and Drug Detoxification and Rehabilitation 84
94.61	Alcohol Rehabilitation 84
94.62	Alcohol Detoxification 84
94.63	Alcohol Rehabilitation and Detoxification 84
94.64	Drug Rehabilitation 84
94.65	Drug Detoxification 84
94.66	Drug Rehabilitation and Detoxification 84
96.07	Nasogastric Intubation 1444
96.49	Abortion, Therapeutic by Prostaglandin Suppository 13
98.5	Lithotripsy, Extracorporeal Shock Wave 1295
98.51	Extracorporeal Shock-Wave Lithotripsy of the Kidney, Ureter and/or Bladder 1295
98.52	Extracorporeal Shock-Wave Lithotripsy of the Gallbladder and/or Bile Duct 1295
98.59	Extracorporeal Shock-Wave Lithotripsy or Other Sites 1295
99.0	Transfusion of Blood and Blood Components 2167
99.1	Intravenous Therapy 1235
99.25	Chemotherapy 485
99.27	Iontophoresis 1236

Index

A

AAA
- Abdominal Aneurysm 3
- Aortic Aneurysm 160

Abdomen
- Abdominal Aneurysm 3
- Abdominal Muscle Strain 5
- Abdominal Pain 7
- Abruptio Placentae 16
- Abscess, Liver 27
- Abscess, Psoas 38
- Abscess, Renal and Perinephric 40
- Abscess, Subdiaphragmatic 42
- Achlorhydria and Hypochlorhydria 49
- Arterial Embolism and Thrombosis 180
- Arterial Graft 183
- Bladder Fistulas 262
- Calculus, Bladder 333
- Calculus, Renal (Kidney and Ureter) 335
- Cancer, Pancreas 375
- Cancer, Small Intestine (Including Duodenum) 389
- Cardiac Pacemaker Insertion 414
- Cholangiography 493
- Cholecystectomy 495
- Cholecystitis 497
- Cholelithiasis 501
- Colitis 535
- Colostomy and Ileostomy 543
- Compartment Syndrome 547
- Constipation 558
- Culdoscopy 610
- Cystectomy 615
- Cystitis, Acute 616
- Cystourethroplasty of Bladder Neck 625
- Fibroid Tumor of Uterus 875
- Filariasis 881
- Hematuria 1055
- Hernia, Umbilical 1106
- Intestinal Obstruction 1222
- Laparoscopy 1275
- Laparotomy 1276
- Liposuction 1292
- Lithotomy 1293—1294
- Liver Biopsy 1297
- Liver Disease 1298
- Lymphadenitis and Lymphadenopathy 1322
- Meckel's Diverticulum 1351
- Myomectomy, Uterine 1430
- Nausea 1446
- Nephrotic Syndrome 1456
- Nephrotomy 1458
- Ovarian Cyst, Benign 1552
- Pancreatic Pseudocyst 1569
- Pancreatitis 1573
- Paracentesis 1582
- Paraovarian Cyst 1590
- Pelvic Inflammatory Disease 1604
- Peptic Ulcer Disease 1611
- Peritonitis 1628
- Polycystic Ovary Syndrome 1686
- Polycythemia Vera 1689
- Portal Systemic Shunt 1695
- Postmenopausal Bleeding 1703
- Preeclampsia and Eclampsia 1711
- Pregnancy, Normal 1716
- Pyelonephritis, Acute 1762
- Pyelonephritis, Chronic 1764
- Pyloric Stenosis, Acquired (Adult) Hypertrophic 1767
- Pyloroplasty 1769
- Pylorospasm 1770
- Pyuria 1771
- Renal Dialysis 1800
- Resection of Gastric or Duodenal Ulcer Site 1819
- Rupture of Spleen, Traumatic 1860
- Salpingitis 1870
- Salpingo-oophorectomy 1873
- Shigellosis 1910
- Somatization Disorder 1939
- Splenectomy 1955
- Thalassemia 2066
- Thoracic Aneurysm 2070
- Trauma 2175
- Tubal Ligation 2193
- Ulcerative Colitis 2209
- Ultrasound, Diagnostic 2212
- Upper Gastrointestinal Series 2214
- Vesicovaginal Fistula 2266
- Volvulus 2289

Abdominal
- Aneurysm 3
- Appendectomy 174
- Appendicitis 175
- Ascites 203
- Aspiration 207—208
- Botulism 286
- Cancer, Liver 360
- Ectopic Pregnancy 775
- Hernia, Incisional 1100
- Muscle Strain 5
- Pain 7
- Traveler's Diarrhea 2177

Abdominal Actinomycosis
- Actinomycosis 57

Abdominal Aneurysm
- Aneurysmectomy 138

Abdominal Aortic Aneurysm
- Abdominal Aneurysm 3
- Aortic Aneurysm 160
- Arterial Graft 183
- Arteriovenous Aneurysm 188

Abdominal Aortic Aneurysm Repair
- Aneurysmectomy 138

Abdominal Hernia
- Hernia, Inguinal and Femoral 1103

Abdominal Nephrotomy
- Nephrotomy 1458

Abdominal Pain
- Abdominal Adhesions 1
- Abdominal Aneurysm 3
- Abdominal Muscle Strain 5
- Abruptio Placentae 16
- Amebiasis 109
- Calculus, Bladder 333
- Calculus, Renal (Kidney and Ureter) 335
- Cancer, Small Intestine (Including Duodenum) 389
- Celiac Plexus Block 442
- Cholangiography 493
- Cholecystitis 497
- Cholecystography 500

Colitis 535
Colonoscopy 540
Culdoscopy 610
Diarrhea 696
Dysentery 755
Dyspepsia 759
E. Coli 767
Ectopic Pregnancy 775
Endometriosis 805
Endoscopy of Gastrointestinal Tract 810
Esophagogastroduodenoscopy 850
Hepatitis A 1081
Intestinal Obstruction 1222
Intestinal Upset 1224
Irritable Bowel Syndrome 1244
Preeclampsia and Eclampsia 1711
Uterus, Perforation of 2229
Volvulus 2289

Abdominal Pregnancy
Ectopic Pregnancy 775

Abdominal Strain
Abdominal Muscle Strain 5

Abdominal Tap
Paracentesis 1582

Abdominal Ultrasound
Abdominal Aneurysm 3
Aortic Aneurysm 160
Appendicitis 175
Ultrasound, Diagnostic 2212

Abdominal-Wall Strain
Abdominal Muscle Strain 5

Abdomino Endorectal Resection
Abdominoperineal Resection of Rectum 10

Abdominopelvic Abscess
Abscess, Psoas 38
Abscess, Subdiaphragmatic 42

Abdominoperineal
Cancer, Rectum 384
Resection of Rectum 10

Ablatio Placentae
Abruptio Placentae 16

Abnormal Dentition
Dental Disorders 657
Impacted Tooth 1191

Abnormal Spine Curvature
Curvature of the Spine, Acquired 610

Abortion
by Dilation and Curettage for Termination of Pregnancy 11
Hydatidiform Mole 1134
Medical Induction 13
Miscarriage 1381
Threatened Abortion 2080
Uterus, Perforation of 2229

Abortion, Therapeutic
Abortion, Medical Induction 13

Abrasion
Corneal Abrasion 580
Erysipelas 830
Erysipeloid 831
Head Injury, Superficial 1031
Open Wound 1504, 1510, 1512
Open Wound, Back 1510
Open Wound, Chest 1512

Abscess
Actinomycosis 57
Anorectal 20
Anorectal Fistula 154
Bartholin's Gland Cyst 242
Brain Abscess 289
Breast 22
Dentoalveolar Abscess 660
Erysipelas 830
Gingival Abscess 991
Incision and Drainage of Ischiorectal and/or Perirectal Abscess 1200
Incision of Skin and Subcutaneous Tissue, Drainage of Abscess or Cyst 1201
Ischiorectal 24
Larynx 25
Liver 27
Lung 29
Palmar 32
Pelvic Inflammatory Disease 1604
Periodontitis 1619
Perirectal 34
Peritonsillar 36
Pilonidal Cyst 1645
Psoas 38
Renal and Perinephric 40
Root Canal Therapy 1847
Salpingitis 1870
Salpingo-oophorectomy 1873
Sepsis 1905
Stye 2010
Subdiaphragmatic 42
Tonsillectomy and Adenoidectomy 2102

Abscess Drainage
Abscess 17, 20, 22, 24—25, 27, 29, 32, 34, 36, 38, 40, 42
Abscess, Anorectal 20
Abscess, Breast 22
Abscess, Ischiorectal 24
Abscess, Larynx 25
Abscess, Liver 27
Abscess, Lung 29
Abscess, Palmar 32
Abscess, Perirectal 34
Abscess, Peritonsillar 36
Abscess, Psoas 38
Abscess, Renal and Perinephric 40
Abscess, Subdiaphragmatic 42
Anorectal Fistula 154
Brain Abscess 289
Incision and Drainage of Ischiorectal and/or Perirectal Abscess 1200
Incision of Skin and Subcutaneous Tissue, Drainage of Abscess or Cyst 1201
Postpartum Mastitis 1705
Stye 2010

Abscess of Oral Soft Tissue
Gingival Abscess 991
Periodontitis 1619

Abscess of Palm of Hand
Abscess, Palmar 32

Abscess of Tonsil
Abscess, Peritonsillar 36

Abscess of Tooth
Dentoalveolar Abscess 660
Periodontitis 1619

Absence Seizure
Epilepsy 824
Petit Mal Epilepsy 1631
Seizures 1900

Absence Spells
Petit Mal Epilepsy 1631

Abuse
    Addictions, Mixed 60
    Alcohol Intoxication, Acute 87
    Alcoholism 90
    Amphetamine Dependence/Abuse 113
    Cocaine Dependence/Abuse 522
    Marijuana Dependence/abuse 1341
    Posttraumatic Stress Disorder 1707
    Sedative, Hypnotic or Anxiolytic Dependence 1898
AC Separation
    Dislocation, Acromioclavicular Joint 708
    Sprains and Strains, Acromioclavicular Joint 1968
Acanthamoeba Keratitis
    Keratitis 1257
Accelerating Angina
    Angina, Unstable 144
Acceleration Injury
    Sprains and Strains, Cervical Spine (Neck) 1981
Accidental Antepartum Hemorrhage
    Abruptio Placentae 16
Accreta Placenta
    Placenta Accreta 1651
Acetabulum Fracture
    Fracture, Pelvis 930
Acetylene Trichloride Poisoning
    Toxic Effects, Chlorinated Hydrocarbon Solvents 2120
Achalasia
    Dilation of Esophagus 700
    Esophageal Spasm 839
    Myotomy of Esophagus 1433
Ache
    Myalgia and Myositis 1411
Achilles Bursitis
    or Tendinitis 47
Achilles Tendinitis
    Achilles Bursitis or Tendinitis 47
Achilles Tendon
    Achilles Bursitis or Tendinitis 47
    Sprains and Strains, Ankle 1971
Achilles Tendon Rupture
    Sprains and Strains, Ankle 1971
Achilles Tendonitis
    Achilles Bursitis or Tendinitis 47
Achillobursitis
    Achilles Bursitis or Tendinitis 47
Achlorhydria
    and Hypochlorhydria 49
    Dyspepsia 759
Acholuric Jaundice
    Spherocytosis, Hereditary 1944
Achylia
    Achlorhydria and Hypochlorhydria 49
Achylosis
    Achlorhydria and Hypochlorhydria 49
    Dyspepsia 759
ACL
    Repair, Anterior Cruciate Ligament 1814
    Sprains and Strains, Knee 1991

ACL Reattachment
    Repair, Anterior Cruciate Ligament 1814
ACL Reconstruction
    Repair, Anterior Cruciate Ligament 1814
ACL Repair
    Repair, Anterior Cruciate Ligament 1814
ACL Tear
    Sprains and Strains, Knee 1991
Acne
    Carbuncle 407
    Folliculitis 887
Acne Miliaris
    Folliculitis 887
Acquired
    Afibrinogenemia 81
    Cerebral Aneurysm (Non-Ruptured) 445
    Curvature of the Spine, Acquired 610
    Deviated Nasal Septum 679
    Esophageal Diverticula 836
    Hypoprothrombinemia 1176
    Immune Deficiency Syndrome 53
    Pyloric Stenosis, Acquired (Adult) Hypertrophic 1767
    Retinitis Pigmentosa 1829
    Torticollis 2108
Acquired Brain Aneurysm
    Cerebral Aneurysm (Non-Ruptured) 445
Acquired Bronchiectasis
    Bronchiectasis 297
Acquired Curvature of the Spine
    Curvature of the Spine, Acquired 610
Acquired Diverticulum
    Esophageal Diverticula 836
Acquired Hemolytic Anemia
    Hemolytic Anemia 1059
    Spherocytosis, Hereditary 1944
    Thalassemia 2066
Acquired Hypertrophic
    Pyloric Stenosis, Acquired (Adult) Hypertrophic 1767
Acquired Hypertrophic Pyloric Stenosis
    Pyloric Stenosis, Acquired (Adult) Hypertrophic 1767
Acquired Hypertrophic Stenosis
    Pyloric Stenosis, Acquired (Adult) Hypertrophic 1767
Acquired Immune Deficiency Syndrome
    Human Immunodeficiency Virus 1126
Acquired Nasal Septum Deviation
    Deviated Nasal Septum 679
    Septoplasty 1909
Acquired Pyloric Constriction
    Pyloric Stenosis, Acquired (Adult) Hypertrophic 1767
Acquired Pyloric Obstruction
    Pyloric Stenosis, Acquired (Adult) Hypertrophic 1767
Acquired Pyloric Stricture
    Pyloric Stenosis, Acquired (Adult) Hypertrophic 1767
Acquired Spinal Curvature
    Curvature of the Spine, Acquired 610
Acquired Stenosis of Nasolacrimal Duct
    Dacryostenosis 629

Acrodynia Poisoning
   Toxic Effects, Mercury 2138

Acromia
   Vitiligo 2286

Acromioclavicular Joint
   Dislocation, Acromioclavicular Joint 708
   Sprains and Strains, Acromioclavicular Joint 1968

Acromioclavicular Joint Dislocation
   Dislocation, Acromioclavicular Joint 708

Acromioclavicular Joint Sprain
   Sprains and Strains, Acromioclavicular Joint 1968

Acromioclavicular Joint Strain
   Sprains and Strains, Acromioclavicular Joint 1968

Acromion
   Dislocation, Acromioclavicular Joint 708
   Fracture, Clavicle 907
   Rotator Cuff Syndrome 1850
   Sprains and Strains, Acromioclavicular Joint 1968

Acromioplasty
   Impingement Syndrome 1194
   Rotator Cuff Repair 1848
   Rotator Cuff Syndrome 1850

Acrophobia
   Phobias, Specific 1639
   Phobic Disorders 1641

ACTH Syndrome
   Cushing's Syndrome 613

Actinomycotic Infection
   Actinomycosis 57

Action Tremor
   Tremor 2179

Acute
   Adult Respiratory Distress Syndrome 79
   Alcohol Intoxication, Acute 87
   Amebiasis 109
   Aortic Insufficiency 165
   Appendicitis 175
   Asthma 209
   Blastomycosis 266
   Bronchitis, Acute 299
   Cardiac Arrest 409
   Cholecystitis 497
   Compartment Syndrome 547
   Cor Pulmonale, Acute and Chronic 576
   Cystitis, Acute 616
   Dyspnea 761
   Gastritis 970
   Glaucoma, Acute (Angle-Closure) 995
   Hypervitaminosis 1164, 1166, 1168
   Hypervitaminosis A 1166
   Laryngitis 1279
   Leukemia 1284
   Lymphangitis 1324
   Malaria 1330
   Myocardial Infarction 1424
   Myocarditis, Acute 1428
   Neck Pain 1448
   Nephritis, Interstitial 1453
   Neutropenia 1477
   Opioid Type Dependence 1516
   Pancreatitis 1573
   Pharyngitis, Acute 1633
   Pleurisy 1659
   Poisoning 1675, 1677, 1679, 1681
   Porphyria 1693
   Prostatitis 1734
   Pyelonephritis, Acute 1762
   Rehabilitation Therapy 1796
   Renal Dialysis 1800
   Renal Failure, Acute 1802
   Rheumatic Fever, Acute 1833
   Salmonellosis 1866
   Schizophreniform Disorder 1888
   Sinusitis 1928
   Spondylolysis, Lumbar Region 1962
   Sprains and Strains, Foot 1986
   Stress Disorder, Acute 2007
   Toxic Shock Syndrome 2152
   Trachoma 2161
   Trench Mouth 2181

Acute Abdomen
   Abdominal Pain 7

Acute Alcoholic Liver Disease
   Hepatitis, Alcoholic 1087

Acute Articular Rheumatism
   Rheumatic Fever, Acute 1833

Acute Bacterial Endocarditis
   Endocarditis, Bacterial 802

Acute Bacterial Meningitis
   Meningitis, Bacterial 1357

Acute Beryllium Disease
   Toxic Effects, Beryllium 2112

Acute Bronchitis
   Bronchitis, Acute 299

Acute Cerebrovascular Accident
   Cerebrovascular Accident 454

Acute Cerebrovascular Disease
   Cerebrovascular Accident 454

Acute Chronic Retinol Toxicity
   Hypervitaminosis 1164, 1166, 1168
   Hypervitaminosis A 1166

Acute Chronic Vitamin A (Retinol) Toxicity
   Hypervitaminosis A 1166

Acute Coronary Insufficiency
   Angina, Unstable 144

Acute Coryza
   Upper Respiratory Infection 2216

Acute Diarrheal Illness
   Diarrhea 696

Acute Encephalopathy
   Delirium 644

Acute Endocarditis
   Endocarditis, Bacterial 802

Acute Enteritis
   Diarrhea 696

Acute Glaucoma
   Glaucoma, Acute (Angle-Closure) 995

Acute Hypervitaminosis A
   Hypervitaminosis 1164, 1166, 1168
   Hypervitaminosis A 1166

Acute Idiopathic Polyneuritis
   Guillain-Barré Syndrome 1022

Acute Idiopathic Polyradiculitis
   Guillain-Barré Syndrome 1022

Acute Infective Polyneuritis
   Guillain-Barré Syndrome 1022

Acute Infective Polyradiculitis
   Guillain-Barré Syndrome 1022

Acute Inflammatory Demyelinating Polyneuropathy
   Guillain-Barré Syndrome 1022

Acute Inflammatory Polyradiculopathy
   Guillain-Barré Syndrome 1022

Acute Intermittent Porphyria
   Porphyria 1693

Acute Interstitial Nephritis
   Nephritis, Interstitial 1453

Acute Intoxication
   Alcohol Intoxication, Acute 87

Acute Kidney Failure
   Renal Failure, Acute 1802

Acute Kidney Infection
   Pyelonephritis, Acute 1762

Acute Lymphangitis
   Abscess 17, 20, 22, 24–25, 27, 29, 32, 34, 36, 38, 40, 42
   Lymphangitis 1324

Acute Lymphocytic Leukemia
   Leukemia 1284

Acute Middle Ear Disease
   Otitis Media 1545

Acute Myelogenous Leukemia
   Leukemia 1284

Acute Myeloid Leukemia
   Leukemia 1284

Acute Necrotizing Ulcerative Gingivitis
   Trench Mouth 2181

Acute Nonlymphoblastic Leukemia
   Leukemia 1284

Acute Organic Brain Syndrome
   Delirium 644

Acute Pericarditis
   Electrocardiogram 781
   Pericarditis, Acute 1615

Acute Peripheral Vestibulopathy
   Vestibular Neuronitis 2268

Acute Pleuritis
   Pleurisy 1659

Acute Polyneuritis
   Guillain-Barré Syndrome 1022

Acute Poststreptococcal Glomerulonephritis
   Glomerulonephritis, Acute 1001

Acute Posttraumatic Stress Disorder
   Stress Disorder, Acute 2007

Acute Pyelitis
   Pyelonephritis, Acute 1762

Acute Salpingitis
   Pelvic Inflammatory Disease 1604
   Salpingitis 1870

Acute Stress Reaction
   Nervous Breakdown 1462

Acute Ulcerative Gingivitis
   Gingivitis 993

Acute Viral Hepatitis
   Hepatitis A 1081
   Hepatitis B 1083
   Hepatitis, Viral 1091

Acute Vitamin a Toxicity
   Hypervitaminosis 1164, 1166, 1168
   Hypervitaminosis A 1166

Adams-Stokes Syndrome
   Stokes-Adams Syndrome 2003
   Heart Block 1040

Adaptive Colitis
   Irritable Bowel Syndrome 1244

ADD in Adults
   Attention Deficit Disorder in Adults 232

Addiction to Dexedrine
   Amphetamine Dependence/Abuse 113

Addiction to Preludin
   Amphetamine Dependence/Abuse 113

Addiction to Ritalin
   Amphetamine Dependence/Abuse 113

Addictions
   Alcohol and Drug Detoxification and Rehabilitation 84
   Alcoholism 90
   Amphetamine Dependence/Abuse 113
   Cocaine Dependence/Abuse 522
   Marijuana Dependence/Abuse 1341
   Mixed 60
   Nicotine Dependence 1479
   Opioid Type Dependence 1516
   Sedative, Hypnotic or Anxiolytic Dependence 1898

Addictions, Mixed
   Opioid Type Dependence 1516

Addison's Disease
   Addison's Disease 63

Addison's Pernicious Anemia
   Pernicious Anemia 1630

Adductor Muscle Strain
   Groin Strain 1020

Adenitis
   Lymphadenitis and Lymphadenopathy 1322

Adenocarcinoma of the Kidney
   Cancer, Kidney 358

Adenocarcinoma of the Prostate
   Cancer, Prostate 380

Adenoid Hypertrophy
   Tonsillitis and Adenoiditis 2104

Adenoidectomy
   Tonsillectomy and Adenoidectomy 2102
   Tonsillitis and Adenoiditis 2104

Adenoidectomy and Tonsillectomy
   Tonsillectomy and Adenoidectomy 2102

Adenoiditis
   Tonsillitis and Adenoiditis 2104

Index 2511

Adenoma
- Cushing's Syndrome 613
- Hyperparathyroidism 1148
- Rectal Polyps 1783

Adenoma of Prostate
- Prostatic Hypertrophy 1731

Adenoma of the Small Bowel
- Cancer, Small Intestine (Including Duodenum) 389

Adenoma, Benign
- Cancer, Small Intestine (Including Duodenum) 389

Adenomatous Polyps
- Rectal Polyps 1783

Adenopathy
- Lymphadenitis and Lymphadenopathy 1322

Adenotonsillectomy
- Tonsillectomy and Adenoidectomy 2102

Adhesions of the Abdomen
- Abdominal Adhesions 1

Adhesive Capsulitis
- of Shoulder 66

Adipoma
- Lipoma 1290

Adipose Tissue Reduction
- Liposuction 1292

Adipose Tumor
- Lipoma 1290

Adiposity
- Obesity, Simple 1491

Adjustment
- Chiropractic Adjustments and Manipulations 492
- Disorder with Depressed Mood 69
- Reaction with Anxious Mood 72
- Reaction with Predominant Disturbance of Conduct 74

Adjustment Disorder
- Adjustment Reaction with Anxious Mood 72
- Adjustment Reaction with Predominant Disturbance of Conduct 74
- with Depressed Mood 69

Adjustment Disorder with Anxiety
- Adjustment Reaction with Anxious Mood 72

Adjustment Disorder with Anxious Mood
- Adjustment Reaction with Anxious Mood 72

Adjustment Disorder with Conduct Disturbance
- Adjustment Reaction with Predominant Disturbance of Conduct 74

Adjustment Disorder with Disturbance of Conduct
- Adjustment Reaction with Predominant Disturbance of Conduct 74

Adjustment Reaction
- Adjustment Disorder with Depressed Mood 69
- with Anxious Mood 72
- with Predominant Disturbance of Conduct 74

Adjustment Reaction with Anxiety
- Adjustment Reaction with Anxious Mood 72

Adjustment Reaction with Depressed Mood
- Adjustment Disorder with Depressed Mood 69

Adjustment Reaction with Disturbance of Conduct
- Adjustment Reaction with Predominant Disturbance of Conduct 74

Adnexal Mass
- Ovarian Cyst, Benign 1552

Adrenal Crisis
- Addison's Disease 63

Adrenal Failure
- Addison's Disease 63

Adrenal Gland
- Addison's Disease 63
- Adrenal Tissue Implant or Transplant to Brain 76
- Adrenalectomy 77
- Aldosteronism 94
- Cushing's Syndrome 613
- Pheochromocytoma 1638

Adrenal Gland Failure
- Addison's Disease 63

Adrenal Gland Removal
- Adrenalectomy 77

Adrenal Insufficiency
- Addison's Disease 63

Adrenal Medulla
- Pheochromocytoma 1638

Adrenal Tissue Implant
- or Transplant to Brain 76

Adrenal Tissue Transplant to Brain
- Adrenal Tissue Implant or Transplant to Brain 76

Adrenalectomy
- Aldosteronism 94
- Cushing's Syndrome 613

Adrenocortical Insufficiency
- Addison's Disease 63

Adult Hypertrophic Pyloric Stenosis
- Pyloric Stenosis, Acquired (Adult) Hypertrophic 1767

Adult Hypertrophic Stenosis
- Pyloric Stenosis, Acquired (Adult) Hypertrophic 1767

Adult Noninfiltrating Astrocytoma
- Astrocytoma 214

Adult Onset Diabetes Mellitus
- Diabetes Mellitus Type II 686

Adult Pyloric Constriction
- Pyloric Stenosis, Acquired (Adult) Hypertrophic 1767

Adult Pyloric Obstruction
- Pyloric Stenosis, Acquired (Adult) Hypertrophic 1767

Adult Pyloric Stricture
- Pyloric Stenosis, Acquired (Adult) Hypertrophic 1767

Aeropleura
- Pneumothorax 1671

Aerothorax
- Pneumothorax 1671

Aerotitis Media
- Barotitis Media 241

Affective Bipolar Disorder
- Bipolar Affective Disorder 253, 256, 258, 260
- Bipolar Affective Disorder, Depressed 256
- Bipolar Affective Disorder, Mixed 258
- Bipolar Affective Disorder, Single Manic Episode 260

Affective Disorders
- Bipolar Affective Disorder 253, 256, 258, 260
- Bipolar Affective Disorder, Depressed 256
- Bipolar Affective Disorder, Mixed 258
- Bipolar Affective Disorder, Single Manic Episode 260

Depression, Major 665
Manic Disorder, Recurrent 1339
Schizoaffective Disorder 1878

Age-related Macular Degeneration
Senile Macular Degeneration 1903

Aggressive Personality Disorder
Explosive Personality Disorder 862
Intermittent Explosive Disorder 1217

Agoraphobia
Panic Disorder 1578, 1580
Panic Disorder with Agoraphobia 1580
Phobias, Specific 1639
Phobic Disorders 1641

Agranulocytopenia
Neutropenia 1477

Agranulocytosis
Neutropenia 1477

AHPS
Pyloric Stenosis, Acquired (Adult) Hypertrophic 1767

AIDS
Acquired Immune Deficiency Syndrome 53
Human Immunodeficiency Virus 1126
Pneumocystis Carinii Pneumonia 1663

Air Conditioner Lung
Legionnaire's Disease 1282
Ventilation Pneumonitis 2254

Air Emboli
Arterial Embolism and Thrombosis 180

Airway Obstruction
Asthma 209
Bronchitis, Acute 299
Bronchitis, Chronic 302
Bronchoscopy 305
Chronic Obstructive Pulmonary Disease 511
Dyspnea 761
Emphysema 792
Epiglottitis 822

Akinetic Seizures
Petit Mal Epilepsy 1631

Albert's Disease
Achilles Bursitis or Tendinitis 47

Albuminuria
Diabetic Glomerulosclerosis 690

Alcohol
Addictions, Mixed 60
and Drug Detoxification and Rehabilitation 84
Delirium 644
Intoxication, Acute 87
Organic Psychosis 1526
Alcoholism 90

Alcohol Abuse
Addictions, Mixed 60
Alcohol Intoxication, Acute 87
Alcoholism 90
Organic Psychosis 1526
Pancreatitis 1573
Pellagra 1602

Alcohol Addiction
Alcoholism 90

Alcohol Dependence
Addictions, Mixed 60

Alcohol Intoxication, Acute 87
Alcoholism 90
Organic Psychosis 1526

Alcohol Dependence Syndrome
Alcoholism 90

Alcohol Detoxification
Alcohol and Drug Detoxification and Rehabilitation 84
Alcoholism 90
Hepatitis, Alcoholic 1087

Alcohol Detoxification and Rehabilitation
Alcohol and Drug Detoxification and Rehabilitation 84

Alcohol or Substance Abuse Rehabilitation
Alcohol and Drug Detoxification and Rehabilitation 84

Alcohol Overdose
Alcohol Intoxication, Acute 87

Alcohol Rehabilitation
Alcohol and Drug Detoxification and Rehabilitation 84
Alcoholism 90
Hepatitis, Alcoholic 1087

Alcohol Treatment
Alcohol and Drug Detoxification and Rehabilitation 84

Alcohol Withdrawal Protocol
Alcohol and Drug Detoxification and Rehabilitation 84

Alcoholic
Alcoholism 90
Organic Psychosis 1526
Pellagra 1602

Alcoholic Cirrhosis of Liver
Hepatitis, Alcoholic 1087

Alcoholic Gastritis
Gastritis 970

Alcoholic Hepatitis
Hepatitis, Alcoholic 1087

Alcoholic Liver Disease
Hepatitis, Alcoholic 1087

Alcoholic Pellagra
Pellagra 1602

Alcoholism
Alcohol Intoxication, Acute 87
Cirrhosis of the Liver 515
Hepatitis, Alcoholic 1087
Hepatitis, Chronic 1089
Organic Psychosis 1526

Alexia
Aphasia 169

Algodystrophy
Complex Regional Pain Syndrome 550

ALL
Leukemia 1284

Allergen
Anaphylactic Shock 129, 131
Angioedema 150
Atopic Dermatitis 218
Blepharitis 268
Byssinosis 328
Eczema 778

Allergic
Allergy 100
Angioedema 150

Index 2513

Asthma 209
Contact Dermatitis 560
Dermatitis 96, 674
Humidifier Fever 1130
Hypersensitivity Pneumonitis 1150
Insect or Spider Bites and Stings 1210
Pneumoconiosis 1662
Poison Ivy, Oak, Sumac, or Other Plant Dermatitis 1673
Pruritus Ani 1736
Rhinitis 98
Sunburn 2019

Allergic Contact Dermatitis
Allergic Dermatitis 96
Contact Dermatitis 560
Dermatitis 674
Eczema 778
Poison Ivy, Oak, Sumac, or Other Plant Dermatitis 1673
Sunburn 2019

Allergic Dermatitis
Contact Dermatitis 560

Allergic Dermatitis Due to Drugs
Allergic Dermatitis 96
Contact Dermatitis 560

Allergic Dermatitis Due to Medicine Reaction
Allergic Dermatitis 96
Contact Dermatitis 560

Allergic Reaction
Allergy 100
Anaphylactic Shock 129, 131
Insect or Spider Bites and Stings 1210
Toxic Effects, Plants (genus Toxicodendron) 2150
Urticaria 2226

Allergic Toxemia
Multiple Chemical Sensitivity Syndrome 1397

Allergy
Pneumoconiosis 1662

Allergy Syndrome
Allergy 100

Allogeneic Bone Marrow Transplant
Bone Marrow Transplant 275

Allograft
Bone Graft 272
Bone Marrow Transplant 275
Heart Valve Replacement 1047
Skin Graft 1932

Alopecia
Areata 103

Alpaste Poisoning
Toxic Effects, Chromium 2124

Alpha-Thalassemia Major
Thalassemia 2066

Alpha-Thalassemia Trait
Thalassemia 2066

ALS
Amyotrophic Lateral Sclerosis 125

Alveolar Echinococcosis
Echinococcosis 772

Alveolar Hydatid Disease
Echinococcosis 772

Alveolar Process Fistula
Gingival Abscess 991

Periodontitis 1619

Alzheimer Disease with Delusions
Dementia, Alzheimer's Type, with Delusions (Late Onset) 653

Alzheimer's Disease
Alzheimer's Disease 105
Dementia 651, 653
Electroencephalogram 783
Organic Psychosis 1526

Alzheimer's Disease with Delusions
Dementia, Alzheimer's Type, with Delusions (Late Onset) 653

Alzheimer's Sclerosis
Alzheimer's Disease 105
Organic Psychosis 1526

Alzheimer's Type Dementia
Dementia, Alzheimer's Type, with Delusions (Late Onset) 653

Alzheimer's Type Dementia with Delusions
Dementia, Alzheimer's Type, with Delusions (Late Onset) 653

Amblyopia
Toxic 107

Amblyopia Ex Anopsia
Amblyopia, Toxic 107

Amebic Colitis
Amebiasis 109

Amebic Dysentery
Amebiasis 109
Dysentery 755

Amenorrhea
Infertility, Female 1204
Menstrual Disorders 1369
Polycystic Ovary Syndrome 1686

Ametropia
Astigmatism 212

AML
Leukemia 1284

Amnesia
Brain Injury 292
Concussion, Cerebral 553
Organic Psychosis 1526
Postconcussion Syndrome 1699

Amnestic Shellfish Poisoning
Toxic Effects, Fish and Shellfish 2126

Amniorrhexis
Premature Rupture of Membranes 1722

Amoebic Colitis
Amebiasis 109

Amoebic Dysentery
Amebiasis 109

Amoral Personality Disorder
Antisocial Personality Disorder 156

Amphetamine Abuse
Amphetamine Dependence/Abuse 113

Amphetamine Addiction
Abuse 113
Amphetamine Dependence/Abuse 113

Amputation
(Traumatic), Foot 118
(Traumatic), Lower Extremity 121
Bone Tumors 281

Crush Wounds 603
　　　Diabetic Gangrene 689
　　　Excision, Fusion, and Repair of Toes 860
　　　Finger or Thumb 123
　　　Gangrene 964
　　　Gas Gangrene 967
　　　Open Wound 1504, 1510, 1512
　　　Osteomyelitis 1537
　Amyotrophic Lateral Sclerosis
　　　ALS 125
　　　Atrophy, Muscular 227, 230
　　　Atrophy, Muscular (Progressive) 230
　Amyotrophy
　　　Neuralgic Amyotrophy 1465
　Anal
　　　Abscess, Anorectal 20
　　　Abscess, Ischiorectal 24
　　　Abscess, Perirectal 34
　　　Anorectal Fistula 154
　　　Fissure and/or Rectal Ulcer 127
　　　Fissurectomy, Anal 884
　Anal Abscess
　　　Abscess, Anorectal 20
　　　Incision and Drainage of Ischiorectal and/or Perirectal Abscess 1200
　Anal Cellulitis
　　　Abscess, Anorectal 20
　　　Abscess, Ischiorectal 24
　　　Abscess, Perirectal 34
　Anal Fissure
　　　and/or Rectal Ulcer 127
　　　Colonoscopy 540
　　　Fissurectomy, Anal 884
　　　Hemorrhage of Rectum and Anus 1068
　Anal Fissurectomy
　　　Fissurectomy, Anal 884
　Anal Fistula
　　　Anorectal Fistula 154
　Anal Hemorrhage
　　　Hemorrhage of Rectum and Anus 1068
　Anal Ulcer
　　　Anal Fissure and/or Rectal Ulcer 127
　Analytical Therapy
　　　Psychotherapy, Individual 1748
　Anancastic Personality Disorder
　　　Obsessive-Compulsive Personality Disorder 1496
　Anaphylactic Shock
　　　Food Reaction 131
　　　Insect or Spider Bites and Stings 1210
　　　Shock 1915
　Anaphylaxis
　　　Anaphylactic Shock 129, 131
　　　Anaphylactic Shock, Food Reaction 131
　　　Cardiac Arrest 409
　　　Insect or Spider Bites and Stings 1210
　Anaplastic Astrocytoma
　　　Astrocytoma 214
　Anaplastic Carcinoma
　　　Cancer, Thyroid Gland 396
　Anastomosis
　　　Diverticulosis and Diverticulitis of Colon 739

　　　Gastrectomy 968
　　　Resection of Gastric or Duodenal Ulcer Site 1819
　Anatrophic Nephrotomy
　　　Nephrotomy 1458
　Andropause
　　　Male Climacteric 1332
　Anemia
　　　Aplastic Anemia 171
　　　Complicating Pregnancy 136
　　　Folic Acid Deficiency Anemia 885
　　　Hemolytic Anemia 1059
　　　Iron Deficiency Anemia 1242
　　　Myelophthisic Anemia 1422
　　　Pernicious Anemia 1630
　　　Sickle Cell Anemia 1922
　　　Spherocytosis, Hereditary 1944
　　　Thalassemia 2066
　Anemia Gravis
　　　Aplastic Anemia 171
　Anemia in Pregnancy
　　　Anemia Complicating Pregnancy 136
　Aneurysm
　　　Abdominal Aneurysm 3
　　　Angiocardiography 148
　　　Aortic Aneurysm 160
　　　Arterial Graft 183
　　　Arteriovenous Aneurysm 188
　　　Computerized Axial Tomography 552
　　　Craniotomy 598
　　　Aneurysmectomy 138
　　　Osler-Weber-Rendu Disease 1528
　　　Repair of Cerebral Aneurysm 1812
　　　Subarachnoid Hemorrhage (Non-traumatic) 2011
　　　Thoracic Aneurysm 2070
　Aneurysm of Brain Meninges
　　　Cerebral Aneurysm (Non-Ruptured) 445
　Aneurysm of the Thoracic Aorta
　　　Thoracic Aneurysm 2070
　Aneurysm Resection
　　　Aneurysmectomy 138
　Aneurysmectomy
　　　Abdominal Aneurysm 3
　　　Aortic Aneurysm 160
　　　Arteriography 185
　　　Arteriovenous Aneurysm 188
　Angel Dust Abuse
　　　Phencyclidine Abuse 1635
　Anger Attacks
　　　Explosive Personality Disorder 862
　　　Intermittent Explosive Disorder 1217
　Angina
　　　Cardiac Arrest 409
　　　Chest Pain 486
　　　Coronary Arteriography 586
　　　Coronary Balloon Angioplasty 590
　　　Decubitus 140
　　　Electrocardiogram 781
　　　Pectoris 140
　　　Rheumatic Heart Disease, Chronic 1836
　　　Unstable 144
　Angina Attack
　　　Angina Pectoris 140

Index　2515

Angina Pectoris
    Aortic Valve Stenosis 167
    Coronary Atherosclerosis 587

Angina Syndrome
    Angina Pectoris 140

Angioblastic Sarcoma
    Hepatic Angiosarcoma 1077

Angiocardiography
    Atrial Fibrillation 220

Angiodilation
    Impotence 1198

Angioedema
    Allergic Dermatitis 96
    Anaphylactic Shock 129, 131
    Anaphylactic Shock, Food Reaction 131
    Insect or Spider Bites and Stings 1210

Angiogram
    Angiocardiography 148
    Arteriography 185
    Coronary Atherosclerosis 587
    Epilepsy 824
    Hemiplegia 1056
    Hepatic Angiosarcoma 1077

Angiography
    Arteriography 185
    Atherosclerosis and Arteriosclerosis 216
    Cardiac Arrest 409
    Cerebral Aneurysm (Non-Ruptured) 445
    Cerebrovascular Disease 458
    Coronary Arteriography 586
    Endocarditis, Bacterial 802
    Transient Ischemic Attack 2169
    X-ray 2305

Angioneurotic Edema
    Angioedema 150

Angioplastic Sarcoma
    Hepatic Angiosarcoma 1077

Angioplasty
    Angina Pectoris 140
    Coronary Arteriography 586
    Coronary Atherosclerosis 587
    Coronary Balloon Angioplasty 590
    Peripheral Vascular Disease 1626
    Renovascular Hypertension 1809

Angiosarcoma
    Cancer, Liver 360
    Hepatic Angiosarcoma 1077

Angiosarcoma Endothelioblastoma
    Hepatic Angiosarcoma 1077

Angiosarcoma of the Liver
    Cancer, Liver 360
    Hepatic Angiosarcoma 1077

Angle Closure Glaucoma
    Glaucoma, Acute (Angle-Closure) 995

Angular Stomatitis
    Vitamin B_2 Deficiency 2275

Anhydrous Hydrofluoric Acid Poisoning
    Toxic Effects, Hydrofluoric Acid 2132

Ankle
    Arthrodesis 194
    Arthroscopy 199

Avascular Necrosis 235
Dislocation 705, 708, 711, 713, 716, 723, 726
Fracture, Ankle 895
Fracture, Talus 945
Reduction of Fracture or Dislocation 1791
Sprains and Strains 1964, 1968, 1971, 1975, 1979, 1981, 1984, 1986, 1989, 1991, 1994, 1997
Sprains and Strains, Ankle 1971
Tetany 2062

Ankle Fracture
    Fracture, Ankle 895

Ankle Sprain
    Dislocation, Foot 716
    Sprains and Strains, Ankle 1971

Ankle Strain
    Sprains and Strains, Ankle 1971

Ankylosing Spondylitis
    Enthesopathy 812
    Spondylitis 1958

ANLL
    Leukemia 1284

Anogenital Pruritus
    Pruritus Ani 1736

Anomia
    Aphasia 169

Anorectal Abscess
    Abscess, Anorectal 20
    Abscess, Ischiorectal 24
    Abscess, Perirectal 34
    Incision and Drainage of Ischiorectal and/or Perirectal Abscess 1200

Anorectal Hemorrhage
    Hemorrhage of Rectum and Anus 1068

Anorectal Suppuration
    Abscess, Ischiorectal 24

Anorexia Nervosa
    Eating Disorders 769
    Pellagra 1602
    Vitamin B_1 Deficiency 2272
    Vitamin B_{12} Deficiency 2277
    Vitamin B_2 Deficiency 2275

Anterior Colporrhaphy
    Vesicourethropexy 2265

Anterior Cord Syndrome
    Myelopathy 1420

Anterior Cruciate Ligament Repair
    Repair, Anterior Cruciate Ligament 1814

Anterior Knee Pain
    Patella Chondromalacia 1599

Anterior Resection of the Sigmoid Colon
    Colon Resection 538

Anterior Scalene Syndrome
    Thoracic Outlet Syndrome 2074

Anterior Shin Splints
    Shin Splints 1912

Anterior Uveitis
    Iritis 1240

Anterior Y-Plasty of Vesical Neck
    Cystourethroplasty of Bladder Neck 625

Antianxiety Drug Dependence
  Sedative, Hypnotic or Anxiolytic Dependence 1898
Antibiotics
  Abscess, Lung 29
  Infection 1202
  Labyrinthitis 1267
  Lyme Disease 1319
Anticancer Drug Therapy
  Chemotherapy 485
Anticoagulants
  Arterial Embolism and Thrombosis 180
  Atherosclerosis and Arteriosclerosis 216
  Atrial Fibrillation 220
  Cardiomyopathy 419
  Cardiovascular Disease in Pregnancy 422
  Carotid Artery Occlusion 423
  Cerebrovascular Disease 458
  Embolism, Pulmonary 789
  Heart Valve Replacement 1047
  Myocardial Infarction, Acute 1424
  Nosebleed 1485
  Peripheral Vascular Disease 1626
  Thrombophlebitis 2086
  Transient Ischemic Attack 2169
Antihemophilic Factor Deficiency
  Hemophilia A 1061
Antrectomy
  Resection of Gastric or Duodenal Ulcer Site 1819
Anus
  Abdominoperineal Resection of Rectum 10
  Abscess, Anorectal 20
  Abscess, Ischiorectal 24
  Abscess, Perirectal 34
  Anal Fissure and/or Rectal Ulcer 127
  Anorectal Fistula 154
  Cancer, Colon 354
  Cancer, Rectum 384
  Colitis 535
  Colonoscopy 540
  Colostomy and Ileostomy 543
  Cryotherapy, Genital Warts (Female) 605
  Cryotherapy, Genital Warts (Male) 606
  Diarrhea 696
  Endoscopy of Gastrointestinal Tract 810
  Episiotomy 826
  Fissurectomy, Anal 884
  Hemorrhage of Rectum and Anus 1068
  Hemorrhoid Treatment 1070
  Hemorrhoids 1073
  Pruritus Ani 1736
  Rectal Ulcer 1788
  Sclerotherapy 1895
  Sigmoidoscopy 1925
  Warts, Genital 2294
Anxiety
  Cognitive Therapy 530
  Conversion Disorder 574
  Disorder, Generalized 158
  Dysthymic Disorder 764
  Hyperventilation Syndrome 1161
  Nervous Breakdown 1462
  Nervousness 1463
  Neurotic Disorders 1475
  Palpitations 1566
  Phobias, Specific 1639
  Phobic Disorders 1641
  Postconcussion Syndrome 1699
  Posttraumatic Stress Disorder 1707
  Psychoanalysis 1742
  Psychopharmacotherapy 1743
  Psychotherapy, Group 1747
  Psychotherapy, Individual 1748
  Sedative, Hypnotic or Anxiolytic Dependence 1898
  Septic Shock 1907
  Stress Disorder, Acute 2007
Anxiety Depression
  Dysthymic Disorder 764
Anxiety Disorders
  Generalized 158
  Nervous Breakdown 1462
  Neurotic Disorders 1475
Anxiety with Predominant Disturbance of Emotions
  Adjustment Reaction with Predominant Disturbance of Conduct 74
Anxiety-Induced Hyperventilation
  Hyperventilation Syndrome 1161
Anxiolytic Abuse
  Sedative, Hypnotic or Anxiolytic Dependence 1898
Anxiolytic Dependence
  Sedative, Hypnotic or Anxiolytic Dependence 1898
Anxious Mood
  Adjustment Reaction with Anxious Mood 72
Anxiousness
  Nervousness 1463
AODM
  Diabetes Mellitus Type II 686
Aorta
  Aortic Aneurysm 160
  Aortic Dissection 163
  Aortic Insufficiency 165
  Arterial Graft 183
  Cardiac Catheterization 411
  Chest Pain 486
  Coarctation of the Aorta 519
  Coronary Balloon Angioplasty 590
Aortic
  Aneurysm 160
  Aneurysmectomy 138
  Dissection 163
  Insufficiency 165
  Thoracic Aneurysm 2070
  Valve Stenosis 167
  Valvuloplasty, Balloon 2240
Aortic Aneurysm
  Abdominal Aneurysm 3
  Aneurysmectomy 138
  Aortic Dissection 163
  Echocardiography 774
  Thoracic Aneurysm 2070
Aortic Dissection
  Aortic Insufficiency 165
  Coarctation of the Aorta 519
  Echocardiography 774
Aortic Hematoma
  Aortic Dissection 163
Aortic Incompetence
  Aortic Insufficiency 165
  Aortic Valve Stenosis 167
  Mitral Insufficiency 1385

Aortic Insufficiency
　Aortic Valve Stenosis 167

Aortic Regurgitation
　Aortic Insufficiency 165

Aortic Stenosis
　Angina Pectoris 140
　Aortic Insufficiency 165
　Aortic Valve Stenosis 167

Aortic Valve Disorder
　Aortic Dissection 163
　Aortic Insufficiency 165
　Aortic Valve Stenosis 167
　Mitral Insufficiency 1385

Aortic Valve Dissection
　Aortic Dissection 163

Aortic Valve Insufficiency
　Aortic Insufficiency 165
　Aortic Valve Stenosis 167
　Heart Valve Replacement 1047

Aortic Valve Replacement
　Heart Valve Replacement 1047

Aortic Valve Stenosis
　Aortic Insufficiency 165

APCs
　Premature Beats 1719

Aplastic Anemia
　Anemia 133, 136
　Bone Marrow Transplant 275

Apnea
　Insomnia with Sleep Apnea 1214
　Sleep Apnea 1935

Apoplexy
　Cerebral Hemorrhage 449

Appendectomy
　Appendicitis 175

Appendicectomy
　Appendectomy 174

Appendicitis
　Appendectomy 174
　Peritonitis 1628

Appendicovesical Fistula
　Bladder Fistulas 262

Appendix
　Appendectomy 174
　Appendicitis 175

Appendix Rupture
　Appendectomy 174
　Appendicitis 175

Arc-Welder's Disease
　Siderosis 1924

ARF
　Renal Failure, Acute 1802

Argon Laser Trabeculoplasty
　Trabeculoplasty 2158

Ariboflavinosis
　Vitamin B$_2$ Deficiency 2275

Arm
　Amputation 116, 118, 121, 123
　Brachial Neuropathy 287
　Cervicobrachial Syndrome 474
　Compartment Syndrome 547
　Contact Dermatitis 560
　Contusion, Upper Limb 571
　Erythema Nodosum 835
　Folliculitis 887
　Fracture, Elbow (Distal Humerus) 910
　Fracture, Radius and Ulna, Distal 933
　Neuralgic Amyotrophy 1465
　Pain in Limb 1562
　Scleroderma 1892
　Thoracic Outlet Syndrome 2074

Arm Fracture
　Fracture, Elbow (Distal Humerus) 910
　Fracture, Radius and Ulna, Distal 933

ARMD
　Senile Macular Degeneration 1903

Arrest
　Cardiac Arrest 409
　Open-Chest Cardiac Massage 1514

Arrhythmia
　Atrial Fibrillation 220
　Cardiac Arrest 409
　Cardiac Catheterization 411
　Cardiac Stress Test 416
　Electrocardiogram 781
　Mitral Commissurotomy 1384
　Mitral Valve Prolapse 1389
　Myocardial Infarction, Acute 1424
　Palpitations 1566
　Premature Beats 1719
　Prinzmetal's Angina 1726
　Rheumatic Fever, Acute 1833
　Sedative, Hypnotic or Anxiolytic Dependence 1898
　Sick Sinus Syndrome 1920
　Tachycardia, Paroxysmal Supraventricular 2039
　Ventricular Fibrillation 2256
　Ventricular Premature Contractions 2258
　Ventricular Tachycardia 2260
　Wandering Atrial Pacemaker 2293

Arrhythmias
　Premature Beats 1719
　Sick Sinus Syndrome 1920
　Tachycardia, Paroxysmal Supraventricular 2039

Arsenic
　Poisoning 1675, 1677, 1679, 1681
　Toxic Effects, Arsenic and Compounds 2110

Arsenic Poisoning
　Poisoning 1675, 1677, 1679, 1681
　Toxic Effects, Arsenic and Compounds 2110

Arsenic Salts
　Toxic Effects, Arsenic and Compounds 2110

Arsenic Trichloride
　Toxic Effects, Arsenic and Compounds 2110

Arsenic Trioxide
　Toxic Effects, Arsenic and Compounds 2110

Arterial
　Arteriosclerotic Gangrene 186
　Atherosclerosis and Arteriosclerosis 216
　Carotid Artery Occlusion 423
　Cerebrovascular Disease 458
　Embolism and Thrombosis 180
　Graft 183
　Peripheral Vascular Disease 1626

Polyarteritis Nodosa **1685**

Arterial Embolism
and Thrombosis **180**

Arterial Graft
Carotid Artery Occlusion **423**
Coarctation of the Aorta **519**

Arterial Hypertension
Hypertensive Heart Disease **1156**

Arterial Insufficiency
Carotid Artery Occlusion **423**
Peripheral Vascular Disease **1626**

Arterial Patch
Arterial Graft **183**
Carotid Artery Occlusion **423**

Arterial Patch Graft
Arterial Graft **183**

Arterial Thrombosis
Arterial Embolism and Thrombosis **180**

Arteriography
Arteriosclerotic Gangrene **186**
Cerebral Hemorrhage **449**
Cerebrovascular Accident **454**
Subarachnoid Hemorrhage (Traumatic) **2014**
Thrombectomy **2082**
Thrombophlebitis **2086**

Arteriosclerosis
Aortic Dissection **163**
Arteriosclerotic Gangrene **186**
Arteriovenous Aneurysm **188**
Atherosclerosis and Arteriosclerosis **216**
Myocardial Infarction, Acute **1424**

Arteriosclerotic
Atherosclerosis and Arteriosclerosis **216**
Cerebral Aneurysm (Non-Ruptured) **445**
Cerebrovascular Disease **458**
Coronary Atherosclerosis **587**
Gangrene **186**

Arteriosclerotic Brain Aneurysm
Cerebral Aneurysm (Non-Ruptured) **445**

Arteriosclerotic Disease
Atherosclerosis and Arteriosclerosis **216**
Cerebrovascular Disease **458**

Arteriosclerotic Heart Disease
Coronary Atherosclerosis **587**

Arteriosclerotic Obliterans
Atherosclerosis and Arteriosclerosis **216**

Arteriovenous Fistula
Arteriovenous Aneurysm **188**

Arteriovenous Malformation
Arteriovenous Aneurysm **188**
Osler-Weber-Rendu Disease **1528**

Artery Disease
Arterial Graft **183**
Arteriography **185**
Carotid Artery Occlusion **423**
Coronary Atherosclerosis **587**
Embolectomy **786**—**787**
Endarterectomy **801**
Polyarteritis Nodosa **1685**

Artery Occlusion
Arteriosclerotic Gangrene **186**

Atherosclerosis and Arteriosclerosis **216**
Carotid Artery Occlusion **423**

Arthralgia
Joint Disorders **1251**

Arthritis
Behçet's Syndrome **244**
Gout **1012**
Hip Replacement, Total **1119**
Infectious **192**
Lyme Disease **1319**
Metatarsalgia **1376**
Psoriatic Arthritis **1740**
Rheumatoid Arthritis **1838**

Arthritis-Dermatitis Syndrome
Gonorrhea **1010**

Arthrocentesis
Aspiration **207**—**208**
Gout **1012**

Arthrodesis
Bone Graft **272**
Excision, Fusion, and Repair of Toes **860**
Hallux Rigidus **1027**
Hammertoe **1029**
Spinal Fusion **1951**
Spinal Stenosis **1952**

Arthrogram
Arthrography **196**

Arthropathy
Joint Disorders **1251**

Arthroplasty
Avascular Necrosis **235**
Elbow **197**
Hallux Rigidus **1027**
Hammertoe **1029**
Hip Replacement, Total **1119**
Knee Replacement, Total **1263**
Rheumatoid Arthritis **1838**
Shoulder Replacement **1917**

Arthroscopic Repair of Rotator Cuff
Rotator Cuff Repair **1848**

Arthroscopy
Carpal Tunnel Release **428**
Ganglionectomy (Wrist) **963**
Meniscectomy and Meniscus Repair **1361**
Meniscus Disorders, Knee **1364**
Osteochondritis Dissecans **1534**
Patella Chondromalacia **1599**
Rheumatoid Arthritis **1838**
Synovectomy **2027**

Arthrosis
Hallux Rigidus **1027**
Osteoarthritis **1530**

Articular
Joint Disorders **1251**

Articular Rheumatism
Joint Disorders **1251**
Rheumatic Fever, Acute **1833**

Articulation
Joint Disorders **1251**

Artificial Ankylosis
Arthrodesis **194**

Artificial Ear
    Cochlear Implant **529**

Artificial Insemination
    Infertility, Female **1204**

Artificial Kidney Machine
    Renal Dialysis **1800**

Asbestos Pneumoconiosis
    Asbestosis **201**
    Pneumoconiosis **1662**

Asbestos Pneumonoconiosis
    Asbestosis **201**

Ascites
    Abscess, Subdiaphragmatic **42**
    Paracentesis **1582**
    Peritonitis **1628**

Ascorbic Acid Deficiency
    Vitamin C Deficiency **2279**

Aseptic Necrosis
    Avascular Necrosis **235**

ASHD
    Coronary Atherosclerosis **587**

Asocial Personality Disorder
    Antisocial Personality Disorder **156**

ASP
    Toxic Effects, Fish and Shellfish **2126**

Aspermia
    Infertility, Male **1206**

Aspiration
    Bartholin's Gland Cyst **242**
    Bone Marrow Biopsy **273**
    Brain Abscess **289**
    Breast Biopsy **295**
    Cancer, Pleura **377**
    Curettage of the Uterus **208**
    Echinococcosis **772**
    Enthesopathy **812**
    Fibrocystic Breast Disease **874**
    Gout **1012**
    Liver Biopsy **1297**
    Lung Biopsy **1310**
    Pancreatic Pseudocyst **1569**
    Pneumonia **1667**
    Spermatocele **1942**
    Synovial Cyst **2028**
    Synovitis **2031**
    Syringomyelia **2035**

Aspiration Biopsy
    Bone Marrow Biopsy **273**
    Liver Biopsy **1297**
    Lung Biopsy **1310**

Assisted Reproductive Technologies (ART)
    Infertility, Female **1204**
    Infertility, Male **1206**

Assisted Spontaneous Delivery
    Delivery, Spontaneous and/or Assisted Vaginal **647**

Asteatotic Eczema
    Contact Dermatitis **560**
    Dermatitis **674**
    Eczema **778**

Asterixis
    Tremor **2179**

Asthenia
    Malaise **1328**

Asthma
    Bronchoscopic Biopsy **304**
    Chronic Obstructive Pulmonary Disease **511**
    Dyspnea **761**
    Occupational Asthma **1498**
    Pneumoconiosis **1662**
    Pulmonary Function Tests **1758**

Asthmatic Bronchitis
    Asthma **209**
    Emphysema **792**

Asthmatic Dermatitis
    Atopic Dermatitis **218**

Astigmatism
    Cataract **436**, **439**

Astrocytoma
    Cancer, Brain **344**
    Glioma **999**

Ataxic Tremor
    Tremor **2179**

Atelectasis
    Lung Collapse **1312**

Atherosclerosis
    Abdominal Aneurysm **3**
    and Arteriosclerosis **216**
    Angina Pectoris **140**
    Angina, Unstable **144**
    Aortic Dissection **163**
    Arterial Graft **183**
    Arteriosclerotic Gangrene **186**
    Bundle Branch Block **310**
    Carotid Artery Occlusion **423**
    Cerebral Aneurysm (Non-Ruptured) **445**
    Coronary Arteriography **586**
    Coronary Atherosclerosis **587**
    Coronary Balloon Angioplasty **590**
    Coronary Bypass **592**
    Endarterectomy **801**
    Heart Murmur **1045**
    Transient Ischemic Attack **2169**

Athetoid Cerebral Palsy
    Cerebral Palsy **452**

Athlete's Foot
    Atopic Dermatitis **218**
    Tinea **2095**

Athyroidism
    Hypothyroidism **1180**

Atonia Constipation
    Constipation **558**

Atopic Dermatitis
    Allergic Dermatitis **96**
    Contact Dermatitis **560**
    Dermatitis **674**
    Eczema **778**

Atopic Disease
    Allergy **100**

Atrial
    Atrioventricular Block Incomplete (Second-Degree) **223**
    Atrioventricular Block, Complete (Third-Degree) **224**
    Atrioventricular Block, Incomplete (First-Degree) **226**
    Fibrillation **220**

Premature Beats **1719**
Tachycardia, Paroxysmal Supraventricular **2039**
Wandering Atrial Pacemaker **2293**

Atrial Complexes
Premature Beats **1719**

Atrial Fibrillation
Arrhythmia **178**
Mitral Stenosis **1387**

Atrial Flutter
Atrial Fibrillation **220**

Atrial Overdrive Pacing
Cardiac Pacemaker Insertion **414**

Atrial Premature Complexes
Premature Beats **1719**

Atrioventricular Block
Complete (Third-Degree) **224**
Heart Block **1040**
Incomplete (First-Degree) **226**
Incomplete (Second-Degree) **223**
Sick Sinus Syndrome **1920**
Stokes-Adams Syndrome **2003**

Atrioventricular Heart Block
Atrioventricular Block Incomplete (Second-Degree) **223**
Atrioventricular Block, Complete (Third-Degree) **224**
Atrioventricular Block, Incomplete (First-Degree) **226**
Sick Sinus Syndrome **1920**

Atrioventricular Response Block
Atrioventricular Block Incomplete (Second-Degree) **223**

Atrophic Arthritis
Osteoarthritis **1530**

Atrophic Gastritis
Gastritis **970**

Atrophy
Muscular **227, 230**
Muscular (Progressive) **230**
Myalgia and Myositis **1411**
Optic Atrophy **1519**
Paralysis, Paraplegia, and Quadriplegia **1583**

Atrophy of the Muscles
Atrophy, Muscular **227, 230**

Attack
Angina Pectoris **140**
Cerebrovascular Accident **454**
Myocardial Infarction, Acute **1424**
Panic Disorder **1578, 1580**
Syncope **2024**
Transient Ischemic Attack **2169**
Vasovagal Syncope **2249**

Attention Deficit Disorder
Biofeedback **250**
in Adults **232**

Attention Deficit Hyperactivity Disorder
Attention Deficit Disorder in Adults **232**
Psychopharmacotherapy **1743**

Atypical
Psychotic Disorder, Unspecified **1751**

Atypical Pneumonia
Pneumonia **1667**

Atypical Psychosis
Psychotic Disorder, Unspecified **1751**

Atypical Somatoform Disorder
Hypochondriasis **1169**

Atypical Subacute Thyroiditis
Thyroiditis **2091**

Augmentation Mammoplasty
Mammoplasty, Augmentation **1338**

Auto Bone Marrow Transplant Without Purging
Bone Marrow Transplant **275**

Autoerythrocyte Sensitization
Purpura Simplex **1760**

Autograft
Arterial Graft **183**
Bone Graft **272**
Bone Marrow Transplant **275**
Heart Valve Replacement **1047**
Skin Graft **1932**

Autoimmune Hemolytic Anemia
Hemolytic Anemia **1059**

Autoimmune Thrombocytopenic Purpura (primary)
Idiopathic Thrombocytopenic Purpura **1189**

Autoimmune Thyroiditis
Thyroiditis **2091**

Autologous Bone Marrow Transplant
Bone Marrow Transplant **275**
Cancer, Breast **347**

Autologous Transfusion
Transfusion of Blood and Blood Components **2167**

Autonomic Nervous System
Diabetic Neuropathy **692**
Peripheral Neuropathy **1621**
Vagotonia **2237**

AV Block
Atrioventricular Block Incomplete (Second-Degree) **223**
Atrioventricular Block, Complete (Third-Degree) **224**
Atrioventricular Block, Incomplete (First-Degree) **226**
Heart Block **1040**
Sick Sinus Syndrome **1920**
Tachycardia, Paroxysmal Supraventricular **2039**

Avascular Necrosis of Femoral Head
Avascular Necrosis **235**
Hip Replacement, Total **1119**

Avascular Necrosis of Femoral Neck
Hip Replacement, Total **1119**

Avitaminosis D
Vitamin D Deficiency **2281**

Avitaminosis E
Vitamin E Deficiency **2283**

Avitaminosis K
Vitamin K Deficiency **2284**

AVN
Avascular Necrosis **235**

Avulsion Fracture
Fracture, Forefoot (Sesamoid, Phalanges) **918**
Fracture, Midfoot (Cuboid, Cuneiform, Navicular) **928**

Avulsion Injury
Open Wound **1504, 1510, 1512**

Avulsions
Muscle Injury **1406**

Azoospermia
    Infertility, Male 1206

B

Babcock Operation
    Hernia, Incisional 1100

Bacillary Dysentery
    Dysentery 755
    E. Coli 767
    Shigellosis 1910

Bacillus Gangrene
    Gas Gangrene 967

Back
    Ankylosing Spondylitis 152
    Chemonucleolysis of Interveterbral Disc 482
    Curvature of the Spine, Acquired 610
    Degeneration, Cervical Intervertebral Disc 634
    Degeneration, Lumbar Intervertebral Disc 637
    Degeneration, Thoracic or Thoracolumbar Intervertebral Disc 640
    Disc Calcification 701
    Displacement, Cervical Intervertebral Disc Without Myelopathy 728
    Displacement, Lumbar Intervertebral Disc Without Myelopathy 732
    Displacement, Thoracic Intervertebral Disc Without Myelopathy 735
    Enthesopathy 812
    Fracture, Cervical Spine (With or Without Spinal Cord Injury) 904
    Fracture, Lumbosacral Spine (With or Without Spinal Cord Injury) 920
    Fracture, Sacrum 939
    Fracture, Thoracic Spine (With or Without Spinal Cord Injury) 948
    Fracture, Vertebra 954, 956
    Fracture, Vertebra (Pathological) 956
    Intervertebral Disc Disorders 1221
    Laminectomy or Laminotomy 1273
    Low Back Pain 1302
    Lumbar Disc Disorder with Myelopathy 1308
    Lumbar Puncture 1309
    Myalgia and Myositis 1411
    Osteoporosis 1540
    Pain 239
    Physical Therapy 1643
    Post-Laminectomy Syndrome 1701
    Pott's Disease 1709
    Sciatica 1890
    Spinal Cord Injury 1946
    Spinal Cord Stimulation 1949
    Spinal Fusion 1951
    Spinal Stenosis 1952
    Spondylitis 1958
    Spondylolisthesis 1960
    Spondylolysis, Lumbar Region 1962
    Sprains and Strains, Back 1975
    Sprains and Strains, Cervical Spine (Neck) 1981
    Thoracic Spine Pain 2076

Back Injury
    Fracture, Cervical Spine (With or Without Spinal Cord Injury) 904
    Fracture, Lumbosacral Spine (With or Without Spinal Cord Injury) 920
    Fracture, Sacrum 939
    Fracture, Thoracic Spine (With or Without Spinal Cord Injury) 948
    Fracture, Vertebra 954, 956
    Spinal Cord Injury 1946
    Sprains and Strains, Back 1975
    Sprains and Strains, Cervical Spine (Neck) 1981
    Ultrasound, Therapeutic 2213

Back Pain
    Ankylosing Spondylitis 152
    Biofeedback 250
    Chiropractic Adjustments and Manipulations 492
    Degeneration, Cervical Intervertebral Disc 634

Degeneration, Lumbar Intervertebral Disc 637
Displacement, Lumbar Intervertebral Disc Without Myelopathy 732
Myelography 1419
Post-Laminectomy Syndrome 1701
Sciatica 1890
Spondylitis 1958
Spondylolisthesis 1960
Spondylolysis, Lumbar Region 1962
Thoracic Spine Pain 2076

Back Sprain
    Sprains and Strains, Back 1975

Back Strain
    Sprains and Strains, Back 1975

Backache
    Back Pain 239
    Low Back Pain 1302

Background Retinopathy
    Diabetic Retinopathy 694

Bacteremia
    Sepsis 1905
    Septic Shock 1907

Bacterial Endocarditis
    Endocarditis, Bacterial 802

Bacterial Infection
    Abscess, Psoas 38
    Encephalopathy 799
    Endocarditis, Bacterial 802
    Endophthalmitis 808
    Epididymitis 819
    Epiglottitis 822
    Erysipelas 830
    Erysipeloid 831
    Folliculitis 887
    Food Poisoning 888
    Furuncle 961
    Gangrene 964
    Gingival Abscess 991
    Infection 1202
    Legionnaire's Disease 1282
    Lyme Disease 1319
    Pruritus Ani 1736
    Rhinoscleroma 1842
    Rocky Mountain Spotted Fever 1845
    Sepsis 1905
    Shigellosis 1910
    Upper Respiratory Infection 2216
    Vaginitis 2233

Bacterial Keratitis
    Keratitis 1257

Bacterial Labyrinthitis
    Labyrinthitis 1267

Bacterial Meningitis
    Meningitis, Bacterial 1357

Bacterial Pneumonia
    Pneumonia 1667

Bacterium Tularense
    Tularemia 2197

Bacteriuria
    Pyuria 1771

BAEPS
    Evoked Potentials 851

Bagassosis
  Humidifier Fever 1130
  Hypersensitivity Pneumonitis 1150

Balanitis Xerotica Obliterans
  Penis Disorders 1608

Balanoposthitis
  Penis Disorders 1608

Baldness
  Alopecia Areata 103

Balkan Nephropathy
  Nephritis, Interstitial 1453

Balloon
  Cardiac Catheterization 411
  Coronary Balloon Angioplasty 590
  Dilation of Esophagus 700
  Embolectomy 786–787
  Embolectomy, Pulmonary 787
  Thrombectomy 2082
  Transurethral Balloon Dilation of Prostatic Urethra 2171
  Valvuloplasty, Balloon 2240

Balloon Angioplasty
  Coarctation of the Aorta 519
  Coronary Balloon Angioplasty 590

Balloon Dilation of Esophagus
  Dilation of Esophagus 700

Balloon Dilation of Prostatic Urethra
  Transurethral Balloon Dilation of Prostatic Urethra 2171

Balloon Valvotomy
  Valvuloplasty, Balloon 2240

Balloon Valvuloplasty
  Mitral Commissurotomy 1384
  Valvuloplasty, Balloon 2240

Balloon Valvuloplasty for the Heart
  Valvuloplasty, Balloon 2240

Ballooning Mitral Cusp
  Mitral Valve Prolapse 1389

BAN
  Neurofibromatosis 1469

Bancroftian Filariasis
  Filariasis 881

Bang's Disease
  Brucellosis 306

Banti's Syndrome
  Cirrhosis of the Liver 515

Barbiturate Abuse
  Sedative, Hypnotic or Anxiolytic Dependence 1898

Barbiturate Dependence
  Sedative, Hypnotic or Anxiolytic Dependence 1898

Barium Enema
  Bladder Fistulas 262
  Cancer, Colon 354
  Cancer, Rectum 384
  Diverticulosis and Diverticulitis of Colon 739
  Hemorrhage of Rectum and Anus 1068
  Lower Gastrointestinal Series 1305

Barium Swallow
  Cancer, Esophagus 356
  Cancer, Small Intestine (Including Duodenum) 389
  Cancer, Stomach 391
  Dumping Syndrome 747
  Duodenitis 749
  Esophageal Diverticula 836
  Esophageal Spasm 839
  Esophageal Strictures 840
  Hernia, Hiatal 1097
  Upper Gastrointestinal Series 2214

Barium Swallow X-ray
  Esophageal Varices 843
  Esophagitis 847
  Gastritis 970
  Gastroesophageal Reflux 979
  Gastrointestinal Hemorrhage 982
  Upper Gastrointestinal Series 2214

Barlow's Syndrome
  Mitral Insufficiency 1385
  Mitral Valve Prolapse 1389

Barotrauma
  Barotitis Media 241

Barotrauma Otitic
  Barotitis Media 241

Bartholin's Gland Cyst
  Bartholin's Gland Cyst 242

Bartholin's Gland Infection
  Bartholin's Gland Cyst 242

Bartholinitis
  Bartholin's Gland Cyst 242

Barton's Fracture
  Fracture, Radius and Ulna, Distal 933

Basal Cell Carcinoma
  Cancer, Skin 387
  Kaposi's Sarcoma 1253

Basedow's Disease
  Hyperthyroidism 1159

Basilar Hemorrhage
  Cerebral Hemorrhage 449

BCC
  Cancer, Skin 387
  Kaposi's Sarcoma 1253

Beats
  Arrhythmia 178
  Atrial Fibrillation 220
  Atrioventricular Block Incomplete (Second-Degree) 223
  Atrioventricular Block, Complete (Third-Degree) 224
  Heart Block 1040
  Palpitations 1566
  Premature Beats 1719
  Sick Sinus Syndrome 1920
  Stokes-Adams Syndrome 2003
  Tachycardia, Paroxysmal Supraventricular 2039
  Ventricular Fibrillation 2256
  Ventricular Premature Contractions 2258
  Ventricular Tachycardia 2260

Beaver Fever
  Giardiasis 989

Bechterew Syndrome
  Ankylosing Spondylitis 152

Beck-Jianu Gastrostomy
  Gastrostomy 984

Bedsore
  Decubitus Ulcer 632

Index 2523

Bee Sting
- Insect or Spider Bites and Stings 1210
- Poisoning 1675, 1677, 1679, 1681

Behavior Therapy
- Alcohol and Drug Detoxification and Rehabilitation 84
- Borderline Personality Disorder 284
- Cerebral Palsy 452
- Dysthymic Disorder 764
- Eating Disorders 769
- Multiple Chemical Sensitivity Syndrome 1397
- Nicotine Dependence 1479
- Obesity, Simple 1491
- Obsessive-Compulsive Personality Disorder 1496
- Pain, Chronic 1564
- Psychosexual Disorders 1745
- Psychotherapy, Individual 1748
- Sedative, Hypnotic or Anxiolytic Dependence 1898
- Stress Disorder, Acute 2007

Behçet's Disease
- Behçet's Syndrome 244

Behçet's Syndrome
- Behçet's Syndrome 244

Belsey (Mark IV) Operation
- Hernia, Hiatal 1097

Bence-Jones Proteinuria
- Albuminuria 82
- Multiple Myeloma 1399

Bends
- Caisson Disease 331

Benign
- Bladder Polyps 264
- Bone Tumors 281
- Breast Biopsy 295
- Cancer, Brain 344
- Cancer, Ovary 372
- Cancer, Skin 387
- Caruncle of the Urethra, Benign 434
- Fibroid Tumor of Uterus 875
- Osteoma 1536
- Ovarian Cyst, Benign 1552
- Pheochromocytoma 1638
- Prostatic Hypertrophy 1731
- Tumor, Benign 2199

Benign Adenoma of Prostate
- Prostatic Hypertrophy 1731

Benign Bone Tumor
- Bone Tumors 281
- Osteoma 1536

Benign Cyst
- Incision of Skin and Subcutaneous Tissue, Drainage of Abscess or Cyst 1201
- Ovarian Cyst, Benign 1552

Benign Headache
- Headache 1033

Benign Hereditary Tremor
- Tremor 2179

Benign Hypertension
- High Blood Pressure, Benign 1112

Benign Lesion
- Tumor, Benign 2199

Benign Local Pleural Fibroma
- Cancer, Pleura 377

Benign Mass
- Tumor, Benign 2199

Benign Meningioma
- Tumor, Benign 2199

Benign Neoplasm
- Osteoma 1536
- Pheochromocytoma 1638
- Tumor, Benign 2199

Benign Polyps with Prostatic-Type Epithelium
- Bladder Polyps 264

Benign Prostatic Hypertrophy
- Cystoscopy, Transurethral 624
- Prostatectomy 1729
- Prostatic Hypertrophy 1731
- Transurethral Balloon Dilation of Prostatic Urethra 2171
- Transurethral Incision of Bladder Neck 2172
- Transurethral Resection of Prostate 2174

Benign Tumor
- Cervical Polypectomy 469
- Cervical Polyps 470
- Coin Lesion 532
- Hydatidiform Mole 1134
- Hyperparathyroidism 1148
- Lipoma 1290
- Osteoma 1536
- Pheochromocytoma 1638
- Tumor, Benign 2199

Bennett's Fracture
- Fracture, Metacarpal Bones 922

Benzodiazepine Addiction
- Sedative, Hypnotic or Anxiolytic Dependence 1898

Beriberi
- Vitamin B_1 Deficiency 2272

Berry Aneurysm
- Cerebral Aneurysm (Non-Ruptured) 445

Berylliosis
- Pneumoconiosis 1662
- Siderosis 1924
- Toxic Effects, Beryllium 2112

Beryllium Poisoning
- Toxic Effects, Beryllium 2112

Besnier-Boeck Disease
- Sarcoidosis 1875

Beta Thalassemia Major
- Thalassemia 2066

Beta Thalassemia Minor
- Thalassemia 2066

Beta-Thalassemia Intermedia
- Thalassemia 2066

Biceps
- Adhesive Capsulitis of Shoulder 66
- Brachial Neuropathy 287
- Bursitis 325
- Enthesopathy 812
- Impingement Syndrome 1194
- Neuralgic Amyotrophy 1465
- Rotator Cuff Syndrome 1850
- Tendonitis 248

Biceps Tendinitis
- Biceps Tendonitis 248

Biceps Tendon Strain
    Biceps Tendonitis 248

Biceps Tenosynovitis
    Biceps Tendonitis 248

Biduotertian Fever
    Malaria 1330

Big Spleen Syndrome
    Hypersplenism 1154

Bilateral Acoustic Neurofibromatosis
    Neurofibromatosis 1469

Bilateral Endoscopic Destruction of Fallopian Tube
    Tubal Ligation 2193

Bilateral Excision of Ovary
    Oophorectomy, Bilateral 1503

Bilateral Oophorectomy
    Oophorectomy, Bilateral 1503

Bilateral Ovariectomy
    Oophorectomy, Bilateral 1503

Biliary Calculi
    Cholelithiasis 501

Bilirubin
    Jaundice 1249

Billowing Mitral Valve
    Mitral Insufficiency 1385
    Mitral Valve Prolapse 1389

Billroth I Procedure
    Gastrectomy 968

Billroth II Procedure
    Gastrectomy 968

Bilot's Spots
    Vitamin A Deficiency 2270

Bimalleolar Fracture
    Fracture, Ankle 895

Binge Eating Disorder
    Eating Disorders 769

Bing-Horton's Neuralgia
    Cluster Headache 517

Biofeedback
    Anxiety Disorder, Generalized 158

Biopsy 1657
    Astrocytoma 214
    Bone Marrow Biopsy 273
    Breast Biopsy 295
    Bronchoscopic Biopsy 304
    Cancer, Bladder 338
    Cancer, Brain 344
    Cancer, Colon 354
    Cancer, Esophagus 356
    Cancer, Skin 387
    Cancer, Small Intestine (Including Duodenum) 389
    Caruncle of the Urethra, Benign 434
    Cervical Biopsy 460
    Cervical Conization 463
    Colonoscopy 540
    Craniotomy 598
    Cystoscopy, Transurethral 624
    Decubitus Ulcer 632
    Dilation and Curettage 699
    Encephalitis 797
    Endometriosis 805
    Endoscopy of Gastrointestinal Tract 810
    Eosinophilic Fasciitis 814
    Esophageal Strictures 840
    Esophagogastroduodenoscopy 850
    Fibrocystic Breast Disease 874
    Fibroid Tumor of Uterus 875
    Liver Biopsy 1297
    Lung Biopsy 1310
    Mycosis Fungoides 1416
    Non-Hodgkin's Lymphoma 1482
    Peptic Ulcer Disease 1611
    Peripheral Neuropathy 1621
    Pheochromocytoma 1638
    Pineal Gland Neoplasm 1647
    Pleural Biopsy 1657
    Pleurisy 1659
    Pneumocystis Carinii Pneumonia 1663
    Pneumonia 1667
    Postmenopausal Bleeding 1703
    Pott's Disease 1709
    Pyelonephritis, Chronic 1764
    Rectal Polyps 1783
    Rectal Ulcer 1788
    Renal Failure, Acute 1802
    Renal Failure, Chronic 1804
    Sigmoidoscopy 1925
    Skin or Subcutaneous Tissue Biopsy 1934
    Splenomegaly 1956
    Tumor, Benign 2199

Biopsy - Cone
    Cervical Conization 463

Biopsy by Pleural Needle
    Pleural Biopsy 1657

Biopsy of Bone Marrow
    Bone Marrow Biopsy 273

Biopsy of Breast
    Breast Biopsy 295

Biopsy of Pleura
    Pleural Biopsy 1657

Biopsy of Skin or Subcutaneous Tissue
    Skin or Subcutaneous Tissue Biopsy 1934

Bipolar
    Affective Disorder 253, 256, 258, 260
    Affective Disorder, Depressed 256
    Affective Disorder, Mixed 258
    Affective Disorder, Single Manic Episode 260

Bipolar Affective Disorder
    Depressed 256
    Mixed 258

Bipolar Affective Disorder Manic
    Manic Disorder, Recurrent 1339
    Schizoaffective Disorder 1878
    Single Manic Episode 260

Bipolar I Disorder
    Bipolar Affective Disorder, Depressed 256
    Bipolar Affective Disorder, Mixed 258

Bipolar Mood Disorder
    Bipolar Affective Disorder 253, 256, 258, 260
    Bipolar Affective Disorder, Depressed 256
    Schizoaffective Disorder 1878

Bird Fancier's Disease
    Hypersensitivity Pneumonitis 1150

Birth by Vaginal Delivery
    Delivery, Spontaneous and/or Assisted Vaginal 647

Episiotomy 826

Bite
　Dengue Fever 656
　Filariasis 881
　Insect or Spider Bites and Stings 1210
　Lyme Disease 1319
　Rabies 1773
　St. Louis Encephalitis 2000

Black and Blue Mark
　Contusion 562, 564, 566, 568, 571
　Contusion, Lower Limb 566
　Contusion, Trunk 568
　Contusion, Upper Limb 571
　Head Injury, Superficial 1031

Black Eye
　Contusion, Eye 564

Black Lung Disease
　Occupational Asthma 1498
　Pneumoconiosis 1662

Blackout
　Syncope 2024

Blackwater Fever
　Malaria 1330

Bladder
　Calculus, Bladder 333
　Cancer, Bladder 338
　Cauda Equina Syndrome 440
　Cystectomy 615
　Cystitis, Acute 616
　Cystitis, Interstitial 619
　Cystoscopy, Transurethral 624
　Cystourethroplasty of Bladder Neck 625
　Fistulas 262
　Hernia Repair, Vaginal 1096
　Lithotomy 1293–1294
　Marshall-Marchetti Operation 1344
　Neurogenic Bladder 1471
　Polyps 264
　Transurethral Incision of Bladder Neck 2172
　Urethritis 2218
　Vesicovaginal Fistula 2266

Bladder Calculi
　Calculus, Bladder 333

Bladder Calculus
　Calculus, Bladder 333

Bladder Cancer
　Cancer, Bladder 338
　Cystectomy 615

Bladder Carcinoma
　Cancer, Bladder 338

Bladder Catheterization
　Urethral Catheterization 2216

Bladder Examination
　Cystoscopy, Transurethral 624

Bladder Fistula 262
　Vesicovaginal Fistula 2266

Bladder Infection
　Cystitis, Acute 616

Bladder Inflammation
　Cystitis, Acute 616

Bladder Neck Incision
　Transurethral Incision of Bladder Neck 2172

Bladder Neck Reconstruction
　Cystourethroplasty of Bladder Neck 625

Bladder Neck Suspension
　Marshall-Marchetti Operation 1344

Bladder Reconstruction
　Cystourethroplasty of Bladder Neck 625

Bladder Stone
　Calculus, Bladder 333
　Hematuria 1055

Bleed
　Abrasions 14
　Endometriosis 805
　Erythema Multiforme 833
　Idiopathic Thrombocytopenic Purpura 1189
　Menstrual Disorders 1369
　Osler-Weber-Rendu Disease 1528
　Postmenopausal Bleeding 1703
　Resection of Gastric or Duodenal Ulcer Site 1819
　Rupture of Spleen, Traumatic 1860
　Sclerotherapy 1895
　Varicose Ulcer 2244
　Varicose Veins 2246

Bleeding
　Cerebral Hemorrhage 449
　Dysfunctional Uterine Bleeding 757
　Endometriosis 805
　Epidural Hematoma 821
　Esophageal Varices 843
　Gastrectomy 968
　Gastrointestinal Hemorrhage 982
　Gingivitis 993
　Hemophilia A 1061
　Hemophilia B 1064
　Hemothorax, Traumatic 1075
　Hepatic Coma 1079
　Hypovolemic Shock 1184
　Idiopathic Thrombocytopenic Purpura 1189
　Intracranial Hemorrhage 1226, 1230
　Lacerations 1269
　Menstrual Disorders 1369
　Myomectomy, Uterine 1430
　Open Wound 1504, 1510, 1512
　Open Wound, Back 1510
　Open Wound, Chest 1512
　Osler-Weber-Rendu Disease 1528
　Periodontitis 1619
　Portal Systemic Shunt 1695
　Postmenopausal Bleeding 1703
　Puncture Wound 1759
　Rectal Ulcer 1788
　Renal Failure, Chronic 1804
　Repair of Cerebral Aneurysm 1812
　Resection of Gastric or Duodenal Ulcer Site 1819
　Rupture of Spleen, Traumatic 1860
　Sclerotherapy 1895
　Shock 1915
　Subarachnoid Hemorrhage (Traumatic) 2014
　Varicose Ulcer 2244
　Varicose Veins 2246
　Vitamin K Deficiency 2284

Bleeding Esophageal Varix
　Esophageal Varices 843

Bleeding from the Rectum
　Hemorrhage of Rectum and Anus 1068

Hemorrhoid Treatment **1070**
Hemorrhoids **1073**
Rectal Ulcer **1788**

Bleeding Gums
Vitamin C Deficiency **2279**

Blighted Ovum
Hydatidiform Mole **1134**

Blind
Blindness **270**

Blindness
Brain Injury **292**
Myopia **1431**
Optic Atrophy **1519**
Retinitis Pigmentosa **1829**
Scleritis **1891**
Trachoma **2161**

Blister
Cervicitis **472**
Chickenpox **490**
Contact Dermatitis **560**
Dermatitis **674**
Eczema **778**
Erythema Multiforme **833**
Herpes Simplex **1108**
Herpes Zoster **1110**
Impetigo **1193**
Pemphigus **1606**
Poison Ivy, Oak, Sumac, or Other Plant Dermatitis **1673**
Sunburn **2019**

Block
Atrioventricular Block Incomplete (Second-Degree) **223**
Atrioventricular Block, Complete (Third-Degree) **224**
Atrioventricular Block, Incomplete (First-Degree) **226**
Bundle Branch Block **310**
Carotid Artery Occlusion **423**
Celiac Plexus Block **442**
Heart Block **1040**
Retinal Vascular Occlusion **1827**
Sick Sinus Syndrome **1920**
Stokes-Adams Syndrome **2003**

Blockage
Carotid Artery Occlusion **423**
Intestinal Obstruction **1222**
Lung Collapse **1312**
Thrombectomy **2082**
Volvulus **2289**

Blocked Retinal Vessel
Retinal Vascular Occlusion **1827**

Blood
Afibrinogenemia **81**
Albuminuria **82**
Anemia **133, 136**
Aplastic Anemia **171**
Arterial Embolism and Thrombosis **180**
Arterial Graft **183**
Bone Marrow Biopsy **273**
Diabetes Mellitus Type I **683, 686**
Diabetes Mellitus Type II **686**
Diabetic Gangrene **689**
Diabetic Glomerulosclerosis **690**
Diabetic Neuropathy **692**
Diabetic Retinopathy **694**
Folic Acid Deficiency Anemia **885**
Hematosalpinx **1053**
Hematuria **1055**
Hemolytic Anemia **1059**

Human Immunodeficiency Virus **1126**
Hyperinsulinism **1144**
Hyperkalemia **1146**
Hypersplenism **1154**
Hypoglycemia **1171**
Hypoprothrombinemia **1176**
Hypotension **1178**
Hypovolemic Shock **1184**
Idiopathic Thrombocytopenic Purpura **1189**
Iron Deficiency Anemia **1242**
Jaundice **1249**
Leukemia **1284**
Porphyria **1693**
Sepsis **1905**
Shigellosis **1910**
Sickle Cell Anemia **1922**
Transfusion of Blood and Blood Components **2167**

Blood Cancer
Leukemia **1284**

Blood Clot
Arterial Embolism and Thrombosis **180**
Cardiac Arrest **409**
Carotid Artery Occlusion **423**
Coronary Thrombolysis **593**
Craniectomy **596**
Craniotomy **598**
Echocardiography **774**
Embolectomy **786–787**
Embolectomy, Pulmonary **787**
Renal Vein Thrombosis **1807**
Thrombectomy **2082**
Vena Cava Interruption **2251**
Venous Embolism and Thrombosis **2252**

Blood Clotting
Afibrinogenemia **81**
Hemophilia A **1061**
Hemophilia B **1064**
Hypoprothrombinemia **1176**

Blood Component Therapy
Transfusion of Blood and Blood Components **2167**

Blood in the Urine
Cancer, Bladder **338**
Cystoscopy, Transurethral **624**
Hematuria **1055**

Blood Insulin Level
Diabetes Mellitus Type I **683, 686**
Diabetes Mellitus Type II **686**
Hyperinsulinism **1144**
Hypoglycemia **1171**

Blood Poisoning
Sepsis **1905**

Blood Pressure
High Blood Pressure, Benign **1112**
High Blood Pressure, Malignant **1116**
Hypotension **1178**

Blood Sugar
Addison's Disease **63**
Diabetes Mellitus Type I **683, 686**
Diabetes Mellitus Type II **686**
Gestational Diabetes **988**
Glycosuria **1006**
Hypoglycemia **1171**

Blood Sugar Insufficiency
Hypoglycemia **1171**

Blood Thinners
- Arterial Embolism and Thrombosis 180
- Atherosclerosis and Arteriosclerosis 216
- Atrial Fibrillation 220
- Cardiomyopathy 419
- Cardiovascular Disease in Pregnancy 422
- Carotid Artery Occlusion 423
- Cerebrovascular Disease 458
- Embolism, Pulmonary 789
- Myocardial Infarction, Acute 1424
- Peripheral Vascular Disease 1626
- Thrombophlebitis 2086
- Transient Ischemic Attack 2169

Blood Transfusion
- Afibrinogenemia 81
- Aplastic Anemia 171
- Ectopic Pregnancy 775
- Esophageal Varices 843
- Hemolytic Anemia 1059
- Spherocytosis, Hereditary 1944
- Thalassemia 2066
- Transfusion of Blood and Blood Components 2167

Blood Vessel Graft
- Arterial Graft 183

Bloody Nose
- Nosebleed 1485

Bloody Sputum
- Hemoptysis 1067

Body Bruise
- Contusion, Trunk 568

Body Dysmorphic Disorder
- Hypochondriasis 1169

Boeck's Disease
- Sarcoidosis 1875

Boeck's Sarcoid
- Sarcoidosis 1875

Boil
- Carbuncle 407
- Excision of Lesion or Tissue of Skin and Subcutaneous Tissue 854
- Furuncle 961
- Gangrene 964

Bone
- Avascular Necrosis 235
- Echinococcosis 772
- Excision of Bone Spur, Foot 852
- Graft 272
- Marrow Biopsy 273
- Marrow Transplant 275
- Multiple Myeloma 1399
- Osteoarthritis 1530
- Osteochondritis Dissecans 1534
- Osteoma 1536
- Osteomyelitis 1537
- Osteoporosis 1540
- Otosclerosis 1549
- Paget's Disease of Bone 1557
- Plantar Fasciitis 1655
- Repair, Hammertoe 1816
- Scan 277
- Tumors 281
- Vitamin D Deficiency 2281

Bone Fusion
- Arthrodesis 194
- Excision, Fusion, and Repair of Toes 860
- Spinal Fusion 1951

Bone Graft
- Avascular Necrosis 235
- Bone Tumors 281
- Malunion and Nonunion of Fracture 1335
- Rib Resection 1844

Bone Infection
- Osteomyelitis 1537

Bone Inflammation
- Osteomyelitis 1537
- Syphilis 2033

Bone Marrow Biopsy
- Aplastic Anemia 171
- Biopsy 252
- Folic Acid Deficiency Anemia 885
- Multiple Myeloma 1399
- Myelophthisic Anemia 1422
- Non-Hodgkin's Lymphoma 1482
- Pernicious Anemia 1630
- Polycythemia Vera 1689
- Splenomegaly 1956

Bone Marrow Transplant
- Aplastic Anemia 171
- Leukemia 1284
- Multiple Myeloma 1399
- Non-Hodgkin's Lymphoma 1482
- Thalassemia 2066

Bone Scan
- Bone Tumor
- Cauda Equina Syndrome 440
- Costochondritis 595
- Fracture, Pelvis 930
- Fracture, Sacrum 939
- Fracture, Tibia or Fibula 951
- Fracture, Vertebra (Pathological) 956
- Gout 1012
- Osteomyelitis 1537
- Plantar Fasciitis 1655

Bone Scintigraphy
- Bone Scan 277

Bone Spur
- Excision of Bone Spur, Foot 852
- Heel Spur (Calcaneal) 1053
- Plantar Fasciitis 1655

Bone Spur Resection
- Excision of Bone Spur, Foot 852

Bone Transplant
- Bone Graft 272

Bone Tumor
- Bone Scan 277
- Osteoma 1536

Bornholm Disease
- Pleurodynia 1661

Borreliosis
- Lyme Disease 1319

Botulism
- Food Poisoning 888

Bougie Dilation of Esophagus
- Dilation of Esophagus 700

Bowel
- Abdominal Adhesions 1
- Abdominal Pain 7
- Abscess, Anorectal 20

Abscess, Ischiorectal 24
Abscess, Perirectal 34
Anal Fissure and/or Rectal Ulcer 127
Anorectal Fistula 154
Cancer, Colon 354
Cancer, Rectum 384
Colitis 535
Colon Resection 538
Colonoscopy 540
Colostomy and Ileostomy 543
Constipation 558
Diarrhea 696
Diverticulosis and Diverticulitis of Colon 739
Dysentery 755
Gastroenteritis, Non-Infectious 975
Intestinal Obstruction 1222
Irritable Bowel Syndrome 1244
Rectal Polyps 1783
Rectal Ulcer 1788
Sigmoidoscopy 1925
Traveler's Diarrhea 2177
Ulcerative Colitis 2209
Volvulus 2289

Bowel Cancer
Cancer, Colon 354
Cancer, Rectum 384

Bowel Disorders
Abscess, Anorectal 20
Abscess, Ischiorectal 24
Abscess, Perirectal 34
Anal Fissure and/or Rectal Ulcer 127
Anorectal Fistula 154
Cancer, Colon 354
Cancer, Rectum 384
Colitis 535
Constipation 558
Diarrhea 696
Diverticulosis and Diverticulitis of Colon 739
Dysentery 755
Gastroenteritis, Infectious 973
Gastroenteritis, Non-Infectious 975
Gastrointestinal Hemorrhage 982
Hemorrhage of Rectum and Anus 1068
Intestinal Obstruction 1222
Irritable Bowel Syndrome 1244
Rectal Polyps 1783
Rectal Ulcer 1788
Traveler's Diarrhea 2177
Ulcerative Colitis 2209
Volvulus 2289

Bowel Obstruction
Abdominal Adhesions 1
Colon Resection 538
Intestinal Obstruction 1222
Volvulus 2289

Bowel Resection
Abdominoperineal Resection of Rectum 10
Colon Resection 538
Diverticulosis and Diverticulitis of Colon 739

Boxer's Fracture
Fracture, Metacarpal Bones 922

BPH
Prostatic Hypertrophy 1731

BPPE
Bladder Polyps 264

Brachial
Neuralgic Amyotrophy 1465
Neuropathy 287
Scalenectomy 1877
Thoracic Outlet Syndrome 2074

Brachial Neuritis
Brachial Neuropathy 287

Brachial Neuropathy and Radiculopathy
Brachial Neuropathy 287

Brachial Plexopathy
Brachial Neuropathy 287

Brachial Plexus Bundle
Brachial Neuropathy 287
Neuralgic Amyotrophy 1465
Thoracic Outlet Syndrome 2074

Brachial Plexus Compression
Thoracic Outlet Syndrome 2074

Brachial Plexus Dysfunction
Brachial Neuropathy 287

Brachial Plexus Lesion Disorder
Thoracic Outlet Syndrome 2074

Brachial Plexus Neuropathy
Brachial Neuropathy 287

Brachial Radiculopathy
Brachial Neuropathy 287

Bradycardia-Tachycardia Syndrome
Sick Sinus Syndrome 1920

Brain
Abscess 289
Adrenal Tissue Implant or Transplant to Brain 76
Amyotrophic Lateral Sclerosis 125
Astrocytoma 214
Cancer, Brain 344
Carotid Artery Occlusion 423
Cerebral Aneurysm (Non-Ruptured) 445
Cerebral Contusion, Closed 447
Cerebral Hemorrhage 449
Cerebral Palsy 452
Cerebrovascular Accident 454
Cerebrovascular Disease 458
Concussion, Cerebral 553
Echinococcosis 772
Electroencephalogram 783
Encephalitis 797
Encephalopathy 799
Endarterectomy 801
Epidural Hematoma 821
Epilepsy 824
Evoked Potentials 851
Glioma 999
Injury 292
Intracranial Hemorrhage, Closed 1230
Meningioma 1355
Postconcussion Syndrome 1699
Repair of Cerebral Aneurysm 1812
Subarachnoid Hemorrhage (Traumatic) 2014
Tumor, Benign 2199

Brain Aneurysm
Cerebral Aneurysm (Non-Ruptured) 445

Brain Aneurysm Clipping
Repair of Cerebral Aneurysm 1812

Brain Aneurysm Repair
Repair of Cerebral Aneurysm 1812

Index 2529

Brain Attack
    Cerebrovascular Accident 454
Brain Bruise
    Cerebral Contusion, Closed 447
Brain Cancer
    Astrocytoma 214
    Cancer, Brain 344
    Glioma 999
Brain Contusion
    Cerebral Contusion, Closed 447
Brain Dysfunction
    Brain Injury 292
    Encephalopathy 799
    Grand Mal Seizure 1014
    Hepatic Coma 1079
Brain Hemorrhage
    Aspiration 207—208
    Cerebral Hemorrhage 449
    Hemiplegia 1056
Brain Inflammation
    Encephalitis 797
    Equine Encephalitis 827
    General Paresis 986
    Hepatic Coma 1079
    Meningitis, Bacterial 1357
Brain Injury
    Cerebral Palsy 452
    Coma 449, 544
    Concussion, Cerebral 553
    Dementia 651, 653
    Hemiplegia 1056
Brain Meninges Aneurysm
    Cerebral Aneurysm (Non-Ruptured) 445
Brain Stem Auditory Evoked Potentials
    Evoked Potentials 851
Brain Surgery
    Craniectomy 596
    Craniotomy 598
Brain Syndrome
    Postconcussion Syndrome 1699
Brain Syphilis
    General Paresis 986
Brain Tumor
    Astrocytoma 214
    Cancer, Brain 344
    Craniotomy 598
    Dementia 651, 653
    Electroencephalogram 783
    Glioma 999
    Hemiplegia 1056
    Meningioma 1355
    Tumor, Benign 2199
Brass Chills
    Metal Fume Fever 1374
Brass-Founder's Ague
    Metal Fume Fever 1374
Bravais-Jacksonian Epilepsy
    Jacksonian Seizure 1247
Breakbone Fever
    Dengue Fever 656

Breakdown
    Nervous Breakdown 1462
    Neurotic Disorders 1475
Breast
    Abscess, Breast 22
    Biopsy 295
    Cancer, Breast 347
    Fibrocystic Breast Disease 874
    Gynecomastia 1025
    Mammography 1337
    Mammoplasty, Augmentation 1338
    Mastectomy 1345
    Paget's Disease of Breast 1559
    Postpartum Mastitis 1705
    Reduction Mammoplasty 1790
Breast Augmentation Mammoplasty
    Mammoplasty, Augmentation 1338
Breast Cancer
    Breast Biopsy 295
    Cancer, Breast 347
    Mastectomy 1345
    Paget's Disease of Breast 1559
Breast Carcinoma
    Cancer, Breast 347
Breast Cyst
    Fibrocystic Breast Disease 874
Breast Hypertrophy
    Gynecomastia 1025
Breast Infection
    Abscess, Breast 22
Breast Lesion
    Breast Biopsy 295
    Cancer, Breast 347
Breast Mammoplasty
    Mammoplasty, Augmentation 1338
    Reduction Mammoplasty 1790
Breast Neoplasm
    Cancer, Breast 347
Breast Nipple
    Cancer, Breast 347
    Mastectomy 1345
Breast Reduction
    Reduction Mammoplasty 1790
Breathlessness
    Dyspnea 761
Brief Depressive Reaction
    Adjustment Disorder with Depressed Mood 69
Brief Posttraumatic Stress Disorder
    Stress Disorder, Acute 2007
Brief Psychotic Disorder
    Psychotic Disorder, Brief 1749
Brief Reactive Psychosis
    Psychotic Disorder, Brief 1749
    Schizophreniform Disorder 1888
Brill's Disease
    Typhus Fever 2206
Brill-Zinsser Disease
    Typhus Fever 2206

Briquet's Disorder
    Somatization Disorder 1939

Briquet's Syndrome
    Conversion Disorder 574
    Somatization Disorder 1939

Brittle Bone Disease
    Osteoporosis 1540

Brittle Diabetes
    Diabetes Mellitus Type I 683, 686

Broken Ankle
    Fracture, Ankle 895
    Fracture, Talus 945

Broken Arm
    Fracture, Elbow (Distal Humerus) 910
    Fracture, Radius and Ulna, Distal 933

Broken Back
    Fracture, Cervical Spine (With or Without Spinal Cord Injury) 904
    Fracture, Lumbosacral Spine (With or Without Spinal Cord Injury) 920
    Fracture, Sacrum 939
    Fracture, Thoracic Spine (With or Without Spinal Cord Injury) 948
    Fracture, Vertebra 954, 956

Broken Collarbone
    Fracture, Clavicle 907

Broken Elbow
    Fracture, Elbow (Distal Humerus) 910

Broken Fibula
    Fracture, Tibia or Fibula 951

Broken Finger
    Fracture, Fingers and Thumb 915

Broken Foot
    Fracture, Forefoot (Sesamoid, Phalanges) 918
    Fracture, Metatarsal Bones 925

Broken Hand
    Fracture, Metacarpal Bones 922

Broken Hip
    Fracture, Femoral Neck 912

Broken Leg
    Fracture, Tibia or Fibula 951

Broken Neck
    Fracture, Cervical Spine (With or Without Spinal Cord Injury) 904

Broken Pelvis
    Fracture, Pelvis 930

Broken Rib
    Fracture, Rib 936

Broken Skull
    Fracture, Skull (Closed) 941

Broken Spine
    Fracture, Cervical Spine (With or Without Spinal Cord Injury) 904
    Fracture, Lumbosacral Spine (With or Without Spinal Cord Injury) 920
    Fracture, Sacrum 939
    Fracture, Thoracic Spine (With or Without Spinal Cord Injury) 948
    Fracture, Vertebra 954, 956

Broken Thumb
    Fracture, Fingers and Thumb 915

Broken Tibula
    Fracture, Tibia or Fibula 951

Broken Toe
    Fracture, Forefoot (Sesamoid, Phalanges) 918

Broken Vertebra
    Fracture, Cervical Spine (With or Without Spinal Cord Injury) 904
    Fracture, Lumbosacral Spine (With or Without Spinal Cord Injury) 920
    Fracture, Sacrum 939
    Fracture, Thoracic Spine (With or Without Spinal Cord Injury) 948
    Fracture, Vertebra 954, 956

Broken Wrist
    Fracture, Carpal Bones 901

Bromide Compound
    Toxic Effects, Methyl Bromide 2142

Bromide Compound Poisoning
    Toxic Effects, Methyl Bromide 2142

Bronchi
    Asthma 209
    Bronchoscopic Biopsy 304
    Bronchoscopy 305
    Cancer, Lung 363
    Chest Pain 486
    Bronchiectasis 297
    Hypersensitivity Pneumonitis 1150
    Bronchitis, Acute 299
    Bronchitis, Chronic 302
    Pneumonia 1667

Bronchi Dilation
    Bronchiectasis 297

Bronchial
    Asthma 209
    Bronchiectasis 297
    Bronchitis, Acute 299
    Bronchitis, Chronic 302
    Bronchoscopic Biopsy 304
    Bronchoscopy 305
    Cancer, Lung 363
    Pneumonia 1667

Bronchial Biopsy
    Bronchoscopic Biopsy 304
    Bronchoscopy 305

Bronchial Dilatation
    Bronchiectasis 297

Bronchiectasis
    Hemoptysis 1067

Bronchitis
    Acute 299
    Chronic 302
    Chronic Obstructive Pulmonary Disease 511
    Dyspnea 761
    Hemoptysis 1067
    Pulmonary Function Tests 1758

Bronchitis with Bronchospasm or Obstruction
    Bronchitis, Acute 299

Broncho Pneumonia
    Pneumonia 1667

Bronchogenic Cancer
    Cancer, Lung 363

Bronchogenic Carcinoma
    Cancer, Lung 363

Bronchopneumonia
    Pneumonia 1667

Bronchoscopy
    Bronchiectasis 297
    Bronchoscopic Biopsy 304
    Cancer, Esophagus 356

Index   2531

Cancer, Lung 363
Coin Lesion 532
Cryptococcosis 608
Pneumocystis Carinii Pneumonia 1663
Pneumonia 1667
Respiratory Failure 1821

Bronchospasm
Bronchitis, Acute 299
Bronchoscopic Biopsy 304
Bronchoscopy 305
Dyspnea 761

Bronchus
Asthma 209
Bronchiectasis 297
Bronchitis, Acute 299
Bronchitis, Chronic 302
Bronchoscopic Biopsy 304
Bronchoscopy 305
Cancer, Lung 363
Pneumonia 1667

Bronchus Biopsy
Bronchoscopic Biopsy 304

Brown Lung Disease
Byssinosis 328

Brown-Sequard Syndrome
Myelopathy 1420

Brugian Filariasis
Filariasis 881

Bruise
Cerebral Contusion, Closed 447
Contusion 562, 564, 566, 568, 571
Contusion, Lower Limb 566
Contusion, Trunk 568
Contusion, Upper Limb 571
Head Injury, Superficial 1031

Bruise of Lower Limb
Contusion, Lower Limb 566

Bruise of the Arm
Contusion, Upper Limb 571

Bruise of the Leg
Contusion, Lower Limb 566

Bruised Ankle
Contusion, Lower Limb 566

Bruised Arm
Contusion, Upper Limb 571

Bruised Elbow
Contusion, Upper Limb 571

Bruised Foot
Contusion, Lower Limb 566

Bruised Hand
Contusion, Upper Limb 571

Bruised Knee
Contusion, Lower Limb 566

Bruised Leg
Contusion, Lower Limb 566

Bruised Limb
Contusion, Lower Limb 566
Contusion, Upper Limb 571

Bruised Shoulder
Contusion, Upper Limb 571

Bruised Thigh
Contusion, Lower Limb 566

Bruised Wrist
Contusion, Upper Limb 571

Bruises
Muscle Injury 1406

Brunschwig's Gastrostomy
Gastrostomy 984

Brush Biopsy
Bronchoscopic Biopsy 304
Lung Biopsy 1310

Buckle Fracture
Fracture, Radius and Ulna, Distal 933

Bulbar Hemorrhage
Cerebral Hemorrhage 449

Bulge
Displacement, Cervical Intervertebral Disc Without Myelopathy 728
Displacement, Lumbar Intervertebral Disc Without Myelopathy 732
Displacement, Thoracic Intervertebral Disc Without Myelopathy 735

Bulimia
Eating Disorders 769

Bulimia Nervosa
Eating Disorders 769

Bullous
Impetigo 1193

Bunion
Bunionectomy 314
Excision, Fusion, and Repair of Toes 860
Metatarsus Primus Varus 1378

Bunionectomy
Bunion 312

Burch Procedure
Vesicourethropexy 2265

Burkitt's Lymphoma
Non-Hodgkin's Lymphoma 1482

Burns
Skin Graft 1932

Bursa Inflammation
Achilles Bursitis or Tendinitis 47
Bursitis 325

Bursa of Large Toe
Bunion 312

Bursae Inflammation
Achilles Bursitis or Tendinitis 47
Bursitis 325

Bursitis
Achilles Bursitis or Tendinitis 47
Arthralgia 190

Busse-Buschke Disease
Cryptococcosis 608

Bypass
Coronary Bypass 592

Bypass Grafting
Arterial Graft 183

Bypass of Coronary Artery
Coronary Bypass 592

Byssinosis
    Hypersensitivity Pneumonitis 1150
    Pneumoconiosis 1662

Byssinosis Pneumonoconiosis
    Byssinosis 328

C

C Section
    Cesarean Delivery 476

Cabbage
    Coronary Bypass 592

CABG
    Angina Pectoris 140
    Angina, Unstable 144
    Arterial Graft 183
    Coronary Bypass 592

CAD
    Coronary Atherosclerosis 587
    Coronary Bypass 592

Cadmium Metal Exposure
    Toxic Effects, Cadmium 2114

Cadmium Metal Poisoning
    Toxic Effects, Cadmium 2114

Cadmium Oxide Exposure
    Toxic Effects, Cadmium 2114

Cadmium Poisoning
    Toxic Effects, Cadmium 2114

Calcaneal Fracture
    Fracture, Calcaneus 898

Calcaneal Spur
    Excision of Bone Spur, Foot 852
    Heel Spur (Calcaneal) 1053

Calcaneus
    Excision of Bone Spur, Foot 852
    Fracture, Calcaneus 898
    Heel Spur (Calcaneal) 1053

Calcaneus Fracture
    Fracture, Calcaneus 898

Calcification
    Disc Calcification 701

Calcification of Intervertebral Disc
    Disc Calcification 701

Calcium
    Hyperparathyroidism 1148
    Tetany 2062

Calculi
    Calculus, Bladder 333
    Calculus, Renal (Kidney and Ureter) 335
    Cholecystectomy 495
    Cholelithiasis 501
    Cystoscopy, Transurethral 624
    Lithotomy 1293—1294
    Lithotomy, Percutaneous 1294
    Lithotripsy, Extracorporeal Shock Wave 1295
    Nephrotomy 1458
    Pancreaticojejunostomy 1572
    Pyelonephritis, Acute 1762
    Pyelonephritis, Chronic 1764
    Salivary Gland Stones 1865
    Transurethral Removal of Obstruction from Ureter 2173

Calculus
    Bladder 333
    Cholecystectomy 495
    Cholelithiasis 501
    Cystoscopy, Transurethral 624
    Lithotomy 1293—1294
    Lithotomy, Percutaneous 1294
    Lithotripsy, Extracorporeal Shock Wave 1295
    Pyelonephritis, Acute 1762
    Pyelonephritis, Chronic 1764
    Renal (Kidney and Ureter) 335
    Renal Failure, Acute 1802
    Salivary Gland Stones 1865
    Transurethral Removal of Obstruction from Ureter 2173

Calf Pain
    Achilles Bursitis or Tendinitis 47

Callositas
    Corn and Callus, Infected 578

Callosity
    Corn and Callus, Infected 578

Callus
    Corn and Callus, Infected 578

Cancer
    Bladder 338
    Brain 344
    Breast 347
    Cervix 351
    Chemotherapy 485
    Choriocarcinoma 505
    Colon 354
    Esophagus 356
    Kidney 358
    Liver 360
    Lung 363
    Oropharynx 369
    Ovary 372
    Pleura 377
    Prostate 380
    Rectum 384
    Skin 387
    Stomach 391
    Testicle(s) 393
    Thyroid Gland 396
    Tongue 399
    Uterus 402

Cancer of the Adrenal Gland
    Pheochromocytoma 1638

Cancer of the Bladder
    Cancer, Bladder 338

Cancer of the Blood
    Leukemia 1284

Cancer of the Bone
    Bone Tumors 281

Cancer of the Bowel
    Cancer, Colon 354
    Cancer, Rectum 384

Cancer of the Brain
    Astrocytoma 214
    Cancer, Brain 344
    Glioma 999

Cancer of the Breast
    Cancer, Breast 347
    Paget's Disease of Breast 1559

Index   2533

Cancer of the Cervix
   Cancer, Cervix 351
   Hysterectomy 1186

Cancer of the Colon
   Cancer, Colon 354
   Cancer, Rectum 384

Cancer of the Duodenum
   Cancer, Small Intestine (Including Duodenum) 389

Cancer of the Endometrium
   Cancer, Uterus 402

Cancer of the Esophagus
   Cancer, Esophagus 356

Cancer of the Kidney
   Cancer, Kidney 358

Cancer of the Large Intestine
   Cancer, Colon 354
   Cancer, Rectum 384

Cancer of the Liver
   Cancer, Liver 360
   Hepatic Angiosarcoma 1077

Cancer of the Lung
   Cancer, Lung 363
   Cancer, Oropharynx 369

Cancer of the Mouth
   Cancer, Mouth (Other Than Tongue) 366

Cancer of the Nipple
   Paget's Disease of Breast 1559

Cancer of the Oropharynx
   Cancer, Oropharynx 369

Cancer of the Ovary
   Cancer, Ovary 372
   Hysterectomy 1186

Cancer of the Pancreas
   Cancer, Pancreas 375

Cancer of the Penis
   Penis Disorders 1608

Cancer of the Pineal Gland
   Pineal Gland Neoplasm 1647
   Tumor, Benign 2199

Cancer of the Pleura
   Cancer, Pleura 377

Cancer of the Prostate
   Cancer, Prostate 380

Cancer of the Prostate Gland
   Cancer, Prostate 380
   Pineal Gland Neoplasm 1647

Cancer of the Rectum
   Cancer, Colon 354
   Cancer, Rectum 384

Cancer of the Skin
   Cancer, Skin 387
   Kaposi's Sarcoma 1253

Cancer of the Small Intestine
   Cancer, Small Intestine (Including Duodenum) 389

Cancer of the Stomach
   Cancer, Stomach 391

Cancer of the Testicles
   Cancer, Testicle(s) 393

Cancer of the Throat
   Cancer, Oropharynx 369

Cancer of the Thyroid
   Cancer, Thyroid Gland 396

Cancer of the Thyroid Gland
   Cancer, Thyroid Gland 396
   Pineal Gland Neoplasm 1647

Cancer of the Tongue
   Cancer, Tongue 399
   Pineal Gland Neoplasm 1647

Cancer of the Urinary Bladder
   Cancer, Bladder 338

Cancer of the Uterus
   Cancer, Uterus 402
   Hysterectomy 1186

Cancerous Tumor
   Cancer, Colon 354
   Cancer, Kidney 358
   Cancer, Liver 360
   Cancer, Lung 363
   Cancer, Oropharynx 369
   Cancer, Rectum 384
   Cancer, Skin 387
   Cancer, Stomach 391
   Hepatic Angiosarcoma 1077

Candidiasis
   Acquired Immune Deficiency Syndrome 53
   Candidiasis 405
   Vaginitis 2233

Candidosis
   Candidiasis 405

Cannabinosis
   Byssinosis 328

Cannabis Abuse
   Marijuana Dependence/Abuse 1341

Cannabis Dependence
   Marijuana Dependence/Abuse 1341

CAO
   Chronic Obstructive Pulmonary Disease 511

CAPD
   Renal Dialysis 1800

Capgras' Syndrome
   Delusional Disorder 649

Capillaritis
   Purpura Simplex 1760

Capsulitis
   Adhesive Capsulitis of Shoulder 66

Car Sick
   Motion Sickness 1395
   Vertigo 2262

Carbamate Pesticide Poisoning
   Toxic Effects, Organophosphate and Carbamate Pesticides 2147

Carbaryl Exposure
   Toxic Effects, Organophosphate and Carbamate Pesticides 2147

Carbinol Poisoning
   Toxic Effects, Methyl Alcohol 2140

Carbon Bichloride Poisoning
   Toxic Effects, Chlorinated Hydrocarbon Solvents 2120

Carbon Bisulfide Poisoning
   Toxic Effects, Carbon Disulfide 2116

Carbon Dichloride Poisoning
   Toxic Effects, Chlorinated Hydrocarbon Solvents 2120

Carbon Disulfide Poisoning
   Toxic Effects, Carbon Disulfide 2116

Carbon Monoxide Poisoning
   Hyperbaric Oxygenation 1141
   Toxic Effects, Carbon Monoxide 2117

Carbon Sulfide Poisoning
   Toxic Effects, Carbon Disulfide 2116

Carbon Tetrachloride Exposure
   Toxic Effects, Chlorinated Hydrocarbon Solvents 2120

Carbonic Oxide Poisoning
   Toxic Effects, Carbon Monoxide 2117

Carbuncle
   Abscess, Renal and Perinephric 40
   Furuncle 961

Carbuncle of Kidney
   Abscess, Renal and Perinephric 40

Carcinoma
   Cancer, Breast 347
   Cancer, Colon 354
   Cancer, Kidney 358
   Cancer, Liver 360
   Cancer, Lung 363
   Cancer, Oropharynx 369
   Cancer, Rectum 384
   Cancer, Skin 387
   Cancer, Stomach 391
   Hepatic Angiosarcoma 1077

Carcinoma of the Bladder
   Cancer, Bladder 338

Carcinoma of the Cervix
   Cancer, Cervix 351

Carcinoma of the Lung
   Cancer, Lung 363
   Hemoptysis 1067

Carcinoma of the Pancreas
   Cancer, Pancreas 375

Cardiac
   Angina Pectoris 140
   Angina, Unstable 144
   Aortic Insufficiency 165
   Aortic Valve Stenosis 167
   Arrest 409
   Arrhythmia 178
   Atrial Fibrillation 220
   Bundle Branch Block 310
   Cardiogenic Shock 417
   Cardiomyopathy 419
   Catheterization 411
   Coronary Balloon Angioplasty 590
   Coronary Bypass 592
   Heart Block 1040
   Heart Murmur 1045
   Heart Valve Replacement 1047
   Mitral Commissurotomy 1384
   Mitral Insufficiency 1385
   Mitral Valve Prolapse 1389

   Myocardial Infarction, Acute 1424
   Myocardial Perfusion Scan 1427
   Neurocirculatory Asthenia 1467
   Open-Chest Cardiac Massage 1514
   Pacemaker Insertion 414
   Palpitations 1566
   Pericarditis, Acute 1615
   Premature Beats 1719
   Rheumatic Fever, Acute 1833
   Rheumatic Heart Disease, Chronic 1836
   Sick Sinus Syndrome 1920
   Stokes-Adams Syndrome 2003
   Stress Test 416
   Tachycardia, Paroxysmal Supraventricular 2039
   Valvuloplasty, Balloon 2240
   Ventricular Fibrillation 2256
   Ventricular Premature Contractions 2258
   Ventricular Tachycardia 2260
   Wandering Atrial Pacemaker 2293

Cardiac Angina
   Angina Pectoris 140

Cardiac Arrest
   Anaphylactic Shock 129, 131
   Open-Chest Cardiac Massage 1514
   Ventricular Fibrillation 2256

Cardiac Arrhythmia
   Arrhythmia 178
   Atrial Fibrillation 220
   Cardiac Arrest 409
   Palpitations 1566
   Premature Beats 1719
   Sick Sinus Syndrome 1920
   Tachycardia, Paroxysmal Supraventricular 2039
   Ventricular Fibrillation 2256
   Ventricular Tachycardia 2260

Cardiac Catheterization
   Cardiac Arrest 409
   Coarctation of the Aorta 519

Cardiac Condition
   Angina Pectoris 140
   Angina, Unstable 144
   Aortic Insufficiency 165
   Aortic Valve Stenosis 167
   Arrhythmia 178
   Atrial Fibrillation 220
   Atrioventricular Block Incomplete (Second-Degree) 223
   Atrioventricular Block, Complete (Third-Degree) 224
   Atrioventricular Block, Incomplete (First-Degree) 226
   Bundle Branch Block 310
   Cardiac Arrest 409
   Cardiogenic Shock 417
   Cardiomyopathy 419
   Cardiovascular Disease in Pregnancy 422
   Heart Block 1040
   Heart Murmur 1045
   Mitral Insufficiency 1385
   Mitral Valve Prolapse 1389
   Myocardial Infarction, Acute 1424
   Neurocirculatory Asthenia 1467
   Pericarditis, Acute 1615
   Premature Beats 1719
   Rheumatic Heart Disease, Chronic 1836
   Sick Sinus Syndrome 1920
   Stokes-Adams Syndrome 2003
   Tachycardia, Paroxysmal Supraventricular 2039
   Ventricular Fibrillation 2256
   Ventricular Premature Contractions 2258
   Ventricular Tachycardia 2260

Wandering Atrial Pacemaker 2293

Cardiac Decompensation
    Heart Failure, Congestive 1042

Cardiac Dysrhythmia
    Arrhythmia 178
    Atrial Fibrillation 220
    Cardiac Arrest 409
    Premature Beats 1719
    Sick Sinus Syndrome 1920
    Tachycardia, Paroxysmal Supraventricular 2039
    Ventricular Fibrillation 2256
    Ventricular Tachycardia 2260

Cardiac Failure
    Cardiac Arrest 409

Cardiac Insufficiency
    Heart Failure, Congestive 1042

Cardiac Massage
    Open-Chest Cardiac Massage 1514

Cardiac Murmur
    Heart Murmur 1045

Cardiac Neurosis
    Neurocirculatory Asthenia 1467

Cardiac Pacemaker Implantation
    Atrioventricular Block Incomplete (Second-Degree) 223
    Bundle Branch Block 310
    Cardiac Pacemaker Insertion 414
    Carotid Sinus Syncope 425

Cardiac Pain
    Angina Decubitus 140
    Angina Pectoris 140
    Myocardial Infarction, Acute 1424
    Prinzmetal's Angina 1726

Cardiac Radionuclide Imaging
    Myocardial Perfusion Scan 1427

Cardiac Stress Test
    Angina, Unstable 144
    Cardiac Catheterization 411
    Coronary Atherosclerosis 587
    Echocardiography 774
    Electrocardiogram 781
    Heart Failure, Congestive 1042

Cardiac Thrombolytic Therapy
    Coronary Thrombolysis 593

Cardiogenic
    Heart Block 1040
    Shock 417, 1915
    Stokes-Adams Syndrome 2003

Cardiogenic Syncope
    Heart Block 1040
    Stokes-Adams Syndrome 2003

Cardiological Balloon Valvuloplasty
    Valvuloplasty, Balloon 2240

Cardiomegaly
    Hypertensive Heart Disease 1156
    Rheumatic Fever, Acute 1833

Cardiomyopathy
    Cardiac Catheterization 411
    Echocardiography 774
    Electrocardiogram 781
    Premature Beats 1719
    Ventricular Fibrillation 2256

Ventricular Tachycardia 2260

Cardiopathy
    Hypertensive Heart Disease 1156

Cardiopulmonary Resuscitation (CPR)
    Cardiac Arrest 409
    Open-Chest Cardiac Massage 1514
    Ventricular Fibrillation 2256

Cardiorespiratory Arrest
    Cardiac Arrest 409
    Open-Chest Cardiac Massage 1514

Cardiospasm
    Prinzmetal's Angina 1726

Cardiovascular Disease
    Arteriosclerotic Gangrene 186
    Arteriovenous Aneurysm 188
    Atherosclerosis and Arteriosclerosis 216
    Atrioventricular Block, Complete (Third-Degree) 224
    Cardiac Catheterization 411
    High Blood Pressure, Benign 1112
    High Blood Pressure, Malignant 1116
    Hypertensive Heart Disease 1156
    in Pregnancy 422
    Peripheral Vascular Disease 1626

Caries
    Dental Disorders 657

Carotid Artery
    Carotid Sinus Syncope 425
    Endarterectomy 801
    Occlusion 423

Carotid Endarterectomy
    Carotid Artery Occlusion 423
    Cerebrovascular Accident 454
    Endarterectomy 801

Carotid Insufficiency
    Carotid Artery Occlusion 423

Carotid Sinus Hypersensitivity
    Carotid Sinus Syncope 425

Carotid Sinus Syndrome
    Cardiac Pacemaker Insertion 414
    Carotid Sinus Syncope 425

Carpal Bones
    Carpal Tunnel Release 428
    Carpal Tunnel Syndrome 430
    Fracture, Carpal Bones 901

Carpal Tunnel Release
    Carpal Tunnel Syndrome 430

Carpal Tunnel Syndrome
    Carpal Tunnel Release 428
    Nerve Conduction Studies 1459
    Paresthesia 1591

Carpet-Layer's Knee
    Bursitis 325

Carpometacarpal Joint Sprain
    Sprains and Strains, Hand or Fingers 1989

Carpometacarpal Joint Strain
    Sprains and Strains, Hand or Fingers 1989

Carpopedal Spasm
    Tetany 2062

Cartilage Surgery
    Meniscectomy and Meniscus Repair 1361

Caruncle
   of the Urethra, Benign 434

Castration
   Orchiectomy 1523

CAT Scan
   Abscess, Subdiaphragmatic 42
   Aortic Aneurysm 160
   Arteriovenous Aneurysm 188
   Ascites 203
   Astrocytoma 214
   Bladder Fistulas 262
   Bladder Polyps 264
   Brain Abscess 289
   Brain Injury 292
   Bronchiectasis 297
   Calculus, Bladder 333
   Calculus, Renal (Kidney and Ureter) 335
   Cancer, Brain 344
   Cancer, Kidney 358
   Cancer, Liver 360
   Cancer, Lung 363
   Cancer, Oropharynx 369
   Cancer, Ovary 372
   Cancer, Pancreas 375
   Cancer, Pleura 377
   Cancer, Prostate 380
   Cancer, Rectum 384
   Cancer, Small Intestine (Including Duodenum) 389
   Cancer, Stomach 391
   Cancer, Testicle(s) 393
   Cancer, Tongue 399
   Cancer, Uterus 402
   Cauda Equina Syndrome 440
   Celiac Plexus Block 442
   Cerebral Aneurysm (Non-Ruptured) 445
   Cerebral Contusion, Closed 447
   Cerebral Hemorrhage 449
   Cerebral Palsy 452
   Cerebrovascular Accident 454
   Cerebrovascular Disease 458
   Cervical Disc Disorder with Myelopathy 464
   Coarctation of the Aorta 519
   Coin Lesion 532
   Computerized Axial Tomography 552
   Concussion, Cerebral 553
   Crush Wounds 603
   Curvature of the Spine, Acquired 610
   Degeneration, Cervical Intervertebral Disc 634
   Degeneration, Thoracic or Thoracolumbar Intervertebral Disc 640
   Dementia 651, 653
   Dementia, Alzheimer's Type, with Delusions (Late Onset) 653
   Dermatomyositis 677
   Diabetic Gangrene 689
   Dislocation, Sternclavicular Joint 726
   Displacement, Lumbar Intervertebral Disc Without Myelopathy 732
   Echinococcosis 772
   Encephalitis 797
   Encephalopathy 799
   Epidural Hematoma 821
   Epilepsy 824
   Fracture, Cervical Spine (With or Without Spinal Cord Injury) 904
   Fracture, Lumbosacral Spine (With or Without Spinal Cord Injury) 920
   Fracture, Midfoot (Cuboid, Cuneiform, Navicular) 928
   Fracture, Pelvis 930
   Fracture, Radius and Ulna, Distal 933
   Fracture, Sacrum 939
   Fracture, Skull (Closed) 941
   Fracture, Sternum (Closed) 943
   Fracture, Talus 945
   Fracture, Thoracic Spine (With or Without Spinal Cord Injury) 948
   Fracture, Vertebra 954, 956
   Fracture, Vertebra (Pathological) 956
   Glioma 999
   Glomerulonephritis, Chronic 1003
   Grand Mal Seizure 1014
   Heat Stroke 1051
   Hemiplegia 1056
   Hepatic Angiosarcoma 1077
   Myelography 1419
   Pancreatic Pseudocyst 1569
   Patella Chondromalacia 1599
   Postconcussion Syndrome 1699
   Pott's Disease 1709
   Renal Failure, Chronic 1804
   Repair of Cerebral Aneurysm 1812
   Rhinoscleroma 1842
   Rupture of Spleen, Traumatic 1860
   Schizophrenia 1882, 1885
   Seizures 1900
   Sprains and Strains, Ankle 1971
   Subarachnoid Hemorrhage (Non-traumatic) 2011
   Subarachnoid Hemorrhage (Traumatic) 2014
   Syringomyelia 2035
   Thoracic Disc Disorder with Myelopathy 2072
   Torticollis 2108
   Transient Ischemic Attack 2169
   X-ray 2305

Cat Scratch Bartonellosis
   Cat Scratch Disease 435

Cat Scratch Disease
   Chorioretinitis 506

Cat Scratch Fever
   Cat Scratch Disease 435

Cataplexy with Narcolepsy
   Narcolepsy 1439

Cataract
   Surgery 439

Cataract Removal
   Cataract 436, 439
   Cataract Surgery 439

Cataract Surgery
   Cataract 436, 439

Catarrhal Asthma
   Asthma 209

Cathartic Colitis
   Irritable Bowel Syndrome 1244

Catheter
   Angiocardiography 148
   Arteriography 185
   Aspiration Curettage of the Uterus 208
   Cardiac Catheterization 411
   Coronary Arteriography 586
   Coronary Balloon Angioplasty 590
   Cystourethroplasty of Bladder Neck 625
   Dilation and Curettage 699
   Dilation of Esophagus 700
   Embolectomy 786—787
   Embolectomy, Pulmonary 787
   Hydronephrosis 1138
   Intravenous Therapy 1235
   Neurogenic Bladder 1471
   Prostatectomy 1729
   Prostatic Hypertrophy 1731
   Pyelonephritis, Acute 1762
   Sepsis 1905

Transurethral Balloon Dilation of Prostatic Urethra **2171**
Urethral Catheterization **2216**
Vesicourethropexy **2265**

Catheterization
Cardiac Catheterization **411**
Urethral Catheterization **2216**

Cats
Toxoplasmosis **2154**

Cauda Equina Syndrome
Discectomy **703**
Fracture, Sacrum **939**

Causalgia
Complex Regional Pain Syndrome **550**

Cauterization
Cervical Cauterization **461**
Nosebleed **1485**
Tubal Ligation **2193**

Cavities
Dental Disorders **657**

Cavity Inflammation
Abscess, Psoas **38**
Abscess, Subdiaphragmatic **42**
Peritonitis **1628**

CBD
Toxic Effects, Beryllium **2112**

Cecal Volvulus
Volvulus **2289**

Cecum Volvulus
Volvulus **2289**

Celiac Plexus Nerve Block
Celiac Plexus Block **442**

Celiac Plexus Neurolytic Block
Celiac Plexus Block **442**

Cell Vagotomy
Vagotomy **2235**

Cellulitis
Abscess, Palmar **32**
Abscess, Perirectal **34**
Ludwig's Angina **1306**

Cellulitis and Abscess of Oral Soft Tissues
Ludwig's Angina **1306**

Cellulitis of Oral Soft Tissue
Ludwig's Angina **1306**

Cellulitis of the Neck
Ludwig's Angina **1306**

Cellulitis Palm of Hand
Abscess, Palmar **32**

Celothelioma
Cancer, Pleura **377**

Central Bilateral Acoustic NF
Neurofibromatosis **1469**

Central Nervous System
Amyotrophic Lateral Sclerosis **125**
Astrocytoma **214**
Behçet's Syndrome **244**
Botulism **286**
Brachial Neuropathy **287**
Cauda Equina Syndrome **440**
General Paresis **986**

Grand Mal Seizure **1014**
Headache **1033**
Multiple Sclerosis **1401**
Rabies **1773**

Central Sleep Apnea
Sleep Apnea **1935**

Cephalgia
Headache **1033**
Tension Headache **2059**

Cephalic Hemorrhage
Cerebral Hemorrhage **449**

Cereal Pellagra
Pellagra **1602**

Cerebellar
Cerebral Hemorrhage **449**
Tremor **2179**

Cerebellar Hemorrhage
Cerebral Hemorrhage **449**

Cerebellar Tremor
Tremor **2179**

Cerebellum Hemorrhage
Cerebral Hemorrhage **449**

Cerebral
Allergy **100**
Aneurysm (Non-Ruptured) **445**
Brain Abscess **289**
Cerebrovascular Accident **454**
Contusion, Closed **447**
Hemorrhage **449**
Palsy **452**
Repair of Cerebral Aneurysm **1812**

Cerebral Abscess
Brain Abscess **289**

Cerebral Allergy
Allergy **100**

Cerebral Aneurysm
Non-Ruptured **445**
Repair of Cerebral Aneurysm **1812**

Cerebral Aneurysm Clipping
Aneurysmectomy **138**
Repair of Cerebral Aneurysm **1812**

Cerebral Aneurysm Repair
Repair of Cerebral Aneurysm **1812**

Cerebral Apoplexy
Cerebrovascular Accident **454**

Cerebral Beriberi
Vitamin B$_1$ Deficiency **2272**

Cerebral Bruise
Cerebral Contusion, Closed **447**

Cerebral Concussion
Brain Injury **292**
Concussion, Cerebral **553**

Cerebral Contusion
Closed **447**

Cerebral Infarction
Cerebrovascular Accident **454**

Cerebral Ischemia
Cerebrovascular Accident **454**
Cerebrovascular Disease **458**

2538   *The Medical Disability Advisor—Fourth Edition*

Transient Ischemic Attack 2169

Cerebral Parenchymal Hemorrhage
　Cerebral Hemorrhage 449

Cerebral Seizure
　Cerebrovascular Accident 454
　Electroconvulsive Therapy 782

Cerebritis
　Encephalitis 797

Cerebromeningeal Hemorrhage
　Cerebral Hemorrhage 449

Cerebrospinal Fluid Examination
　Aspiration 207—208
　Cryptococcosis 608
　Equine Encephalitis 827
　Glioma 999
　Grand Mal Seizure 1014
　Guillain-Barré Syndrome 1022
　Lumbar Puncture 1309

Cerebrospinal Hemorrhage
　Cerebral Hemorrhage 449

Cerebrovascular
　Accident 454
　Disease 458
　Electroencephalogram 783
　Transient Ischemic Attack 2169

Cerebrovascular Arteriosclerotic Disease
　Cerebrovascular Disease 458

Cerebrovascular Hypertensive Disease
　Cerebrovascular Disease 458

Cerebrum Hemorrhage
　Cerebral Hemorrhage 449

Cervical
　Biopsy 460
　Cancer, Cervix 351
　Cauterization 461
　Cervicitis 472
　Conization 463
　Dislocation, Cervical Vertebra 711
　Displacement, Cervical Intervertebral Disc Without Myelopathy 728
　Dysplasia 467
　Intervertebral Disc Disorders 1221
　Laminectomy or Laminotomy 1273
　Lymphadenitis and Lymphadenopathy 1322
　Neck Pain 1448
　Polypectomy 469
　Polyps 470
　Sprains and Strains, Cervical Spine (Neck) 1981
　Thoracic Outlet Syndrome 2074

Cervical Adenitis
　Lymphadenitis and Lymphadenopathy 1322

Cervical Anaplasia
　Cervical Dysplasia 467

Cervical Atypia
　Cervical Dysplasia 467

Cervical Biopsy
　Cervical Polyps 470

Cervical Cancer
　Cancer, Cervix 351
　Cervical Biopsy 460
　Cervical Conization 463

Cervical Cauterization
　Cervical Dysplasia 467
　Cervical Polyps 470
　Cervicitis 472

Cervical Disc Calcification
　Disc Calcification 701

Cervical Disc Degeneration
　Degeneration, Cervical Intervertebral Disc 634

Cervical Disc Disease
　Degeneration, Cervical Intervertebral Disc 634

Cervical Disc Disorder
　with Myelopathy 464

Cervical Disc Displacement without Myelopathy
　Displacement, Cervical Intervertebral Disc Without Myelopathy 728

Cervical Disc Herniation
　Displacement, Cervical Intervertebral Disc Without Myelopathy 728

Cervical Disc Herniation with Myelopathy
　Cervical Disc Disorder with Myelopathy 464

Cervical Disc Prolapse
　Displacement, Cervical Intervertebral Disc Without Myelopathy 728

Cervical Disc Protrusion
　Displacement, Cervical Intervertebral Disc Without Myelopathy 728

Cervical Dysplasia
　Cervical Biopsy 460
　Cervical Cauterization 461
　Cervical Conization 463

Cervical Electrocoagulation
　Cervical Cauterization 461

Cervical Fracture
　Fracture, Vertebra 954, 956

Cervical Intervertebral Disc
　Degeneration, Cervical Intervertebral Disc 634
　Displacement, Cervical Intervertebral Disc Without Myelopathy 728

Cervical Intervertebral Disc Degeneration
　Degeneration, Cervical Intervertebral Disc 634

Cervical Intervertebral Disc Displacement
　Displacement, Cervical Intervertebral Disc Without Myelopathy 728

Cervical Intervertebral Disc Without Myelopathy
　Displacement, Cervical Intervertebral Disc Without Myelopathy 728

Cervical Lymphadenitis
　Lymphadenitis and Lymphadenopathy 1322
　Shock 1915

Cervical Neoplasia
　Cancer, Cervix 351

Cervical Pain
　Neck Pain 1448

Cervical Polypectomy
　Cervical Cauterization 461

Cervical Polyps
　Cervical Polypectomy 469
　Dilation and Curettage 699

Cervical Radiculitis
　Neck Pain 1448
　Sprains and Strains, Cervical Spine (Neck) 1981

Cervical Radiculopathy
　Cervical Disc Disorder with Myelopathy 464

Cervical Rib Syndrome
  Thoracic Outlet Syndrome 2074
Cervical Spinal Fracture
  Fracture, Cervical Spine (With or Without Spinal Cord Injury) 904
Cervical Spine
  Cervical Disc Disorder with Myelopathy 464
  Chemonucleolysis of Intervertebral Disc 482
  Fracture, Cervical Spine (With or Without Spinal Cord Injury) 904
  Syringomyelia 2035
Cervical Spine Dislocation
  Dislocation, Cervical Vertebra 711
Cervical Spondylosis
  Cervical Disc Disorder with Myelopathy 464
Cervical Spondylotic Myelopathy
  Cervical Disc Disorder with Myelopathy 464
Cervical Sprain
  Sprains and Strains, Cervical Spine (Neck) 1981
Cervical Strain
  Sprains and Strains, Cervical Spine (Neck) 1981
Cervical Vertebra Dislocation
  Dislocation, Cervical Vertebra 711
Cervical Vertebra Fracture
  Fracture, Cervical Spine (With or Without Spinal Cord Injury) 904
Cervicalgia
  Neck Pain 1448
Cervicitis
  Cervical Cauterization 461
Cervicobrachial Neuralgia
  Cervicobrachial Syndrome 474
Cervicobrachialgia
  Cervicobrachial Syndrome 474
Cervicodorsal Sympathectomy
  Sympathectomy 2022
Cervicofacial Actinomycosis
  Actinomycosis 57
Cervicovesical Fistula
  Vesicovaginal Fistula 2266
Cervix
  Abortion by Dilation and Curettage for Termination of Pregnancy 11
  Aspiration Curettage of the Uterus 208
  Cancer, Cervix 351
  Cervical Biopsy 460
  Cervical Conization 463
  Cervical Dysplasia 467
  Cervical Polypectomy 469
  Cervical Polyps 470
  Cervicitis 472
  Cryotherapy, Genital Warts (Female) 605
  Delivery, Spontaneous and/or Assisted Vaginal 647
  Dilation and Curettage 699
  Endometriosis 805
  Gonorrhea 1010
  Hysterectomy 1186
  Placenta Previa 1653
Cesarean
  Birth 476
  Delivery 476
  Placenta Accreta 1651
  Placenta Previa 1653
  Preeclampsia and Eclampsia 1711

CFS
  Chronic Fatigue Syndrome 509
Chagas' Disease
  Myocarditis, Acute 1428
Chalk Addiction
  Amphetamine Dependence/Abuse 113
Chancre
  Chancroid 481
  Syphilis 2033
Change of Life
  Menopause 1368
Cheilosis
  Vitamin B_2 Deficiency 2275
Chemexfoliation
  Acid Peel 51
Chemical
  Allergy 100
  Asbestosis 201
  Bladder Polyps 264
  Esophagitis 847
  Porphyria 1693
  Sinusitis 1928
Chemical AIDS
  Allergy 100
  Multiple Chemical Sensitivity Syndrome 1397
Chemical Hypersensitivity Syndrome
  Allergy 100
  Multiple Chemical Sensitivity Syndrome 1397
Chemical Peel
  Acid Peel 51
Chemically Induced Immune Dysfunction
  Multiple Chemical Sensitivity Syndrome 1397
Chemically Induced Immune Dysregulation
  Allergy 100
  Multiple Chemical Sensitivity Syndrome 1397
Chemonucleolysis of Intervertebral Disc
  Chemonucleolysis of Intervertebral Disc 482
Chemotherapy
  Bone Tumors 281
  Cancer, Bladder 338
  Cancer, Brain 344
  Cancer, Breast 347
  Cancer, Cervix 351
  Cancer, Esophagus 356
  Cancer, Kidney 358
  Cancer, Liver 360
  Cancer, Lung 363
  Cancer, Oropharynx 369
  Cancer, Ovary 372
  Cancer, Pancreas 375
  Cancer, Pleura 377
  Cancer, Prostate 380
  Cancer, Rectum 384
  Cancer, Stomach 391
  Cancer, Testicle(s) 393
  Cancer, Thyroid Gland 396
  Cancer, Tongue 399
  Cancer, Uterus 402
  Choriocarcinoma 505
  Glioma 999
  Hepatic Angiosarcoma 1077
  Leukemia 1284
  Multiple Myeloma 1399

  Mycosis Fungoides 1416
  Neutropenia 1477
  Non-Hodgkin's Lymphoma 1482
  Paget's Disease of Breast 1559
  Polycythemia Vera 1689

Chest
  Hemothorax, Traumatic 1075
  Mitral Commissurotomy 1384
  Paracentesis 1582
  Pericarditis, Acute 1615
  Pericarditis, Chronic Constrictive 1617
  Pleural Biopsy 1657
  Pleurodynia 1661
  Pneumoconiosis 1662
  Pneumonectomy 1664
  Pneumonia 1667
  Pneumothorax 1671
  Respiratory Failure 1821
  Rib Resection 1844
  Thoracentesis 2069
  Trauma 2175

Chest Cardiac Massage
  Open-Chest Cardiac Massage 1514

Chest Injury
  Open Wound, Chest 1512

Chest Pain
  Achalasia 44
  Angina Decubitus 140
  Angina Pectoris 140
  Angina, Unstable 144
  Aortic Dissection 163
  Arrhythmia 178
  Atrial Fibrillation 220
  Cancer, Lung 363
  Cardiac Arrest 409
  Cardiac Stress Test 416
  Coronary Atherosclerosis 587
  Coronary Balloon Angioplasty 590
  Coronary Thrombolysis 593
  Costochondritis 595
  Embolism, Pulmonary 789
  Empyema 794
  Gastroesophageal Reflux 979
  Lung Collapse 1312
  Myocardial Infarction, Acute 1424
  Pericarditis, Acute 1615
  Pleurisy 1659
  Pleurodynia 1661
  Pneumothorax 1671
  Prinzmetal's Angina 1726
  Rheumatic Heart Disease, Chronic 1836

Chest X-ray
  Aortic Valve Stenosis 167
  Asthma 209
  Blastomycosis 266
  Bronchiectasis 297
  Bronchitis, Acute 299
  Bronchitis, Chronic 302
  Byssinosis 328
  Cancer, Lung 363
  Cancer, Pleura 377
  Cardiomyopathy 419
  Chest Pain 486
  Chronic Obstructive Pulmonary Disease 511
  Coin Lesion 532
  Cor Pulmonale, Acute and Chronic 576
  Costochondritis 595
  Dyspnea 761
  Embolism, Pulmonary 789
  Emphysema 792
  Empyema 794
  Erythema Nodosum 835
  Filariasis 881
  Fracture, Rib 936
  Fracture, Sternum (Closed) 943
  Heart Failure, Congestive 1042
  Heart Murmur 1045
  Hemothorax, Traumatic 1075
  High Blood Pressure, Malignant 1116
  Histoplasmosis 1121
  Lung Collapse 1312
  Pneumonia 1667
  Siderosis 1924

CHF
  Heart Failure, Congestive 1042

Chicken Pox
  Chickenpox 490

Chickenpox
  Encephalitis 797
  Herpes Zoster 1110

Childbirth
  Delivery, Spontaneous and/or Assisted Vaginal 647
  Pregnancy Complications 1713
  Ultrasound, Diagnostic 2212

Chlamydial Keratoconjunctivitis
  Keratitis 1257

Chlorhydric Acid Poisoning
  Toxic Effects, Hydrochloric Acid 2131

Chlorine Gas Poisoning
  Toxic Effects, Chlorine 2122

Chlorine Water Poisoning
  Toxic Effects, Chlorine 2122

Chloroform Exposure
  Toxic Effects, Chlorinated Hydrocarbon Solvents 2120

Cholangiocarcinoma
  Cancer, Liver 360
  Hepatic Angiosarcoma 1077

Cholangiogram
  Cholangiography 493

Cholangiography
  Cancer, Pancreas 375
  Cholecystectomy 495

Cholangiosarcoma
  Cancer, Liver 360

Cholangitis
  Jaundice 1249

Cholecystectomy
  Cholangiography 493
  Cholecystitis 497
  Cholelithiasis 501

Cholecystitis
  Cholecystectomy 495
  Duodenitis 749

Cholecystogram
  Cholecystography 500

Cholecystography
  Cholelithiasis 501

Choledocholithiasis
    Cholelithiasis 501
    Jaundice 1249

Cholelithiasis
    Cholangiography 493
    Cholecystectomy 495
    Cholecystitis 497
    Cholecystography 500

Cholestatic Jaundice
    Jaundice 1249

Chondromalacia Knee
    Patella Chondromalacia 1599

Chondromalacia Patella
    Patella Chondromalacia 1599

Chondrosarcoma
    Cancer, Bone 341

Chopart's Fracture
    Fracture, Metatarsal Bones 925

Chorea
    Amyotrophic Lateral Sclerosis 125
    Thalamotomy 2064

Chorioblastoma
    Choriocarcinoma 505

Choriocarcinoma
    Pineal Gland Neoplasm 1647

Chorioepithelioma
    Choriocarcinoma 505

Chorionepithelioma
    Choriocarcinoma 505

Choroiditis
    Chorioretinitis 506

Christmas Disease
    Hemophilia B 1064

Chrome Poisoning
    Toxic Effects, Chromium 2124

Chromium Element Poisoning
    Toxic Effects, Chromium 2124

Chromium Fulleride Poisoning
    Toxic Effects, Chromium 2124

Chromium Poisoning
    Toxic Effects, Chromium 2124

Chromomycosis
    Chromoblastomycosis 508

Chronic
    Amyotrophic Lateral Sclerosis 125
    Ankylosing Spondylitis 152
    Asbestosis 201
    Asthma 209
    Behçet's Syndrome 244
    Bronchiectasis 297
    Bronchitis, Chronic 302
    Cholecystitis 497
    Cirrhosis of the Liver 515
    Compartment Syndrome 547
    Cor Pulmonale, Acute and Chronic 576
    Coronary Atherosclerosis 587
    Cystitis, Interstitial 619
    Diabetes Mellitus Type I 683, 686
    Dyspnea 761
    Emphysema 792
    Gastritis 970
    Glomerulosclerosis 1005
    Hydrocele 1136
    Hypervitaminosis A 1166
    Hypotension 1178
    Laryngitis 1279
    Lupus Erythematosus, Systemic 1317
    Lymphangitis 1324
    Myasthenia Gravis 1414
    Narcolepsy 1439
    Neck Pain 1448
    Neurofibromatosis 1469
    Neutropenia 1477
    Non-Hodgkin's Lymphoma 1482
    Obstructive Pulmonary Disease 511
    Osler-Weber-Rendu Disease 1528
    Osteoarthritis 1530
    Pain, Chronic 1564
    Pancreatitis 1573
    Paralysis, Paraplegia, and Quadriplegia 1583
    Paranoid Personality Disorder 1588
    Pelvic Inflammatory Disease 1604
    Pemphigus 1606
    Pericarditis, Chronic Constrictive 1617
    Pneumoconiosis 1662
    Poisoning 1675, 1677, 1679, 1681
    Posttraumatic Stress Disorder 1707
    Psoriasis 1738
    Purpura Simplex 1760
    Pyelonephritis, Chronic 1764
    Renal Dialysis 1800
    Renal Failure, Chronic 1804
    Rheumatic Heart Disease, Chronic 1836
    Rheumatoid Arthritis 1838
    Salpingitis 1870
    Schizophrenia, Paranoid Type 1885
    Scleroderma 1892
    Sjogren's Syndrome 1930
    Somatization Disorder 1939
    Syphilis 2033
    Thyroiditis 2091
    Tuberculosis, Respiratory 2194

Chronic Acholuric Jaundice
    Spherocytosis, Hereditary 1944

Chronic Active Hepatitis
    Hepatitis, Chronic 1089

Chronic Airway Obstruction
    Asthma 209
    Bronchitis, Chronic 302
    Chronic Obstructive Pulmonary Disease 511

Chronic Ankylosing Spondylitis
    Ankylosing Spondylitis 152

Chronic Aortic Insufficiency
    Aortic Insufficiency 165

Chronic Aseptic Meningitis
    Meningitis, Chronic 1359

Chronic Beryllium Disease
    Toxic Effects, Beryllium 2112

Chronic Bronchi Dilation
    Bronchiectasis 297

Chronic Bronchitis
    Bronchitis, Chronic 302
    Chronic Obstructive Pulmonary Disease 511
    Emphysema 792
    Pneumoconiosis 1662

Chronic Constrictive Pericarditis
    Pericarditis, Chronic Constrictive 1617

Chronic Cystic Mastitis
    Fibrocystic Breast Disease 874

Chronic Depressive Reaction
    Adjustment Disorder with Depressed Mood 69

Chronic Desquamating Eosinophilic Bronchitis
    Asthma 209

Chronic Diffuse Glomerulonephritis
    Glomerulonephritis, Chronic 1003

Chronic Epstein-Barr Virus
    Malaise 1328

Chronic Familial Icterus
    Spherocytosis, Hereditary 1944

Chronic Familiar Jaundice
    Spherocytosis, Hereditary 1944

Chronic Fatigue Syndrome
    Malaise 1328

Chronic Glaucoma
    Glaucoma, Chronic (Open-Angle) 997

Chronic Glomerular Syndrome
    Glomerulonephritis, Chronic 1003

Chronic Granulocytic Leukemia
    Leukemia 1284

Chronic Heart Disease
    Coronary Atherosclerosis 587

Chronic Hepatitis
    Hepatitis C 1085
    Hepatitis, Chronic 1089

Chronic Hypotension
    Hypotension 1178

Chronic Idiopathic Neutropenia
    Neutropenia 1477

Chronic Immune Thrombocytopenic Purpura
    Idiopathic Thrombocytopenic Purpura 1189

Chronic Inflammatory Arthritis
    Rheumatoid Arthritis 1838

Chronic Interstitial Nephritis
    Nephritis, Interstitial 1453

Chronic Ischemic Heart Disease
    Coronary Atherosclerosis 587

Chronic Kidney Failure
    Kidney Transplant 1261
    Renal Failure, Chronic 1804

Chronic Kidney Infection
    Pyelonephritis, Chronic 1764

Chronic Liver Disease
    Cirrhosis of the Liver 515
    Glomerulosclerosis 1005
    Hepatitis, Chronic 1089

Chronic Lymphocytic Leukemia
    Leukemia 1284

Chronic Lymphocytic Thyroiditis
    Thyroiditis 2091

Chronic Mastitis
    Fibrocystic Breast Disease 874

Chronic Membranous Glomerulonephritis
    Glomerulonephritis, Chronic 1003
    Glomerulosclerosis 1005

Chronic Meningitis
    Meningitis, Chronic 1359

Chronic Middle Ear Disease
    Otitis Media 1545

Chronic Mononucleosis
    Malaise 1328

Chronic Motor Tic Disorder
    Tics 2093

Chronic Myelogenous Leukemia
    Leukemia 1284

Chronic Myeloid Leukemia
    Leukemia 1284

Chronic Nephritis
    Nephritis, Interstitial 1453

Chronic Obstructive Lung Disease
    Asthma 209
    Bronchitis, Chronic 302
    Chronic Obstructive Pulmonary Disease 511
    Emphysema 792

Chronic Obstructive Pulmonary Disease
    Asthma 209
    Bronchitis, Chronic 302
    Cor Pulmonale, Acute and Chronic 576
    Dyspnea 761
    Emphysema 792

Chronic Open Angle Glaucoma
    Glaucoma, Chronic (Open-Angle) 997

Chronic Organic Brain Syndrome
    Dementia 651, 653

Chronic Pain
    Biofeedback 250
    Fibromyalgia and Myofascial Pain Syndrome 879
    Myalgia and Myositis 1411
    Post-Laminectomy Syndrome 1701
    Spinal Cord Stimulation 1949
    Sympathectomy 2022

Chronic Persistent Hepatitis
    Hepatitis, Chronic 1089

Chronic Post-Traumatic Stress
    Posttraumatic Stress Disorder 1707

Chronic Progressive Chorea
    Amyotrophic Lateral Sclerosis 125

Chronic Progressive Glomerular Syndrome
    Glomerulonephritis, Chronic 1003

Chronic Pulmonary Disease
    Asthma 209
    Bronchitis, Chronic 302
    Chronic Obstructive Pulmonary Disease 511
    Emphysema 792

Chronic Pyelitis
    Pyelonephritis, Chronic 1764

Chronic Pyelonephritis
    Pyelonephritis, Chronic 1764

Chronic Pyonephrosis
    Pyelonephritis, Chronic 1764

Chronic Renal Artery Stenosis
    Renovascular Hypertension 1809
Chronic Renal Insufficiency
    Renal Failure, Chronic 1804
Chronic Retinol Toxicity
    Hypervitaminosis A 1166
Chronic Rhinitis
    Allergic Rhinitis 98
Chronic Salpingitis
    Pelvic Inflammatory Disease 1604
    Salpingitis 1870
Chronic Septic Meningitis
    Meningitis, Chronic 1359
Chronic Systemic Arthritis
    Rheumatoid Arthritis 1838
    Sjogren's Syndrome 1930
Chronic Toxicity Vitamin A
    Hypervitaminosis 1164, 1166, 1168
    Hypervitaminosis A 1166
Chronic Uremia
    Renal Failure, Chronic 1804
Chronic Vitamin A Toxicity
    Hypervitaminosis 1164, 1166, 1168
    Hypervitaminosis A 1166
Chronic Vocal Tic Disorder
    Tics 2093
Chronic/Acute Aortic Insufficiency
    Aortic Insufficiency 165
Cigarette Addiction
    Nicotine Dependence 1479
Ciguatera Poisoning
    Toxic Effects, Fish and Shellfish 2126
Ciliary Neuralgia
    Cluster Headache 517
Cineradiography
    X-ray 2305
Circulatory Collapse
    Shock 1915
Circumcision
    Penis Disorders 1608
Cirrhosis of Lung
    Interstitial Pulmonary Fibrosis 1219
Cirrhosis of the Liver
    Hepatic Coma 1079
    Liver Disease 1298
    Portal Systemic Shunt 1695
Cirrhosis of the Lung
    Interstitial Pulmonary Fibrosis 1219
Clap
    Gonorrhea 1010
Classic Hemophilia
    Hemophilia A 1061
Classic Migraine
    Migraine Headache 1378
Claudication
    Peripheral Vascular Disease 1626

Claustrophobia
    Phobias, Specific 1639
    Phobic Disorders 1641
Clavicle
    Dislocation, Acromioclavicular Joint 708
    Dislocation, Sternclavicular Joint 726
    Fracture, Clavicle 907
    Reduction of Fracture or Dislocation 1791
    Thoracic Outlet Syndrome 2074
Clavicle Fracture
    Fracture, Clavicle 907
    Reduction of Fracture or Dislocation 1791
Clavus
    Corn and Callus, Infected 578
Claw Toe
    Hammertoe 1029
Clergyman's Knee
    Bursitis 325
Climacteric
    Male Climacteric 1332
    Menopause 1368
Clipping of Cerebral Aneurysm
    Cerebral Aneurysm (Non-Ruptured) 445
    Cerebrovascular Accident 454
    Repair of Cerebral Aneurysm 1812
    Subarachnoid Hemorrhage (Non-traumatic) 2011
    Subarachnoid Hemorrhage (Traumatic) 2014
CLL
    Leukemia 1284
Closed
    Bronchoscopic Biopsy 304
    Fracture, Skull (Closed) 941
    Reduction of Fracture or Dislocation 1791
Closed Biopsy
    Bronchoscopic Biopsy 304
Closed Cerebral Contusion
    Cerebral Contusion, Closed 447
Closed Distal Radius and Ulna Fracture
    Fracture, Radius and Ulna, Distal 933
Closed Femorotibial Joint Dislocation
    Dislocation, Femorotibial (Knee) Joint 713
Closed Head Injury
    Brain Injury 292
    Cerebral Contusion, Closed 447
    Concussion, Cerebral 553
    Fracture, Skull (Closed) 941
    Intracranial Hemorrhage, Closed 1230
Closed Head Injury Syndrome
    Postconcussion Syndrome 1699
Closed Head Trauma
    Fracture, Skull (Closed) 941
Closed Manipulative Reduction
    Reduction of Fracture or Dislocation 1791
Closed Mitral Commissurotomy
    Mitral Commissurotomy 1384
Closed Skull Fracture
    Fracture, Skull (Closed) 941
Clostridial Myonecrosis
    Gas Gangrene 967

Clostridium Infections
   Botulism 286
   Colitis 535
   Food Poisoning 888
   Gangrene 964
   Gas Gangrene 967
   Tetanus 2060

Clot
   Arterial Embolism and Thrombosis 180
   Vitamin K Deficiency 2284

Clot in the Renal Vein
   Renal Vein Thrombosis 1807

Cluster Headache
   Headache 1033

CML
   Leukemia 1284

Coal Worker's Pneumoconiosis
   Occupational Asthma 1498
   Pneumoconiosis 1662

Coarctation
   of the Aorta 519

Coarctation of Aorta
   Coarctation of the Aorta 519

Cobalamin Poisoning
   Poisoning, Vitamin B 1679

Cobalt Poisoning
   Toxic Effects, Nickel and Inorganic Compounds 2146

Cocaine Abuse
   Addictions, Mixed 60
   Cocaine Dependence/Abuse 522
   Nasal Septum Perforation 1443

Cocaine Addiction
   Cocaine Dependence/Abuse 522

Cocaine Dependence
   Abuse 522
   Addictions, Mixed 60

Coccidioidal Granuloma
   Coccidioidomycosis 525

Coccyalgia
   Coccygodynia 527

Coccydynia
   Coccygodynia 527

Coccyx Pain
   Coccygodynia 527

Coccyx Region
   Coccygodynia 527
   Fracture, Sacrum 939

Coccyx Spine Pain
   Coccygodynia 527

Cochlear Implant
   Hearing Loss 1036

Codeine Dependency
   Opioid Type Dependence 1516

Cognitive Behavioral Therapy
   Amphetamine Dependence/Abuse 113
   Chronic Fatigue Syndrome 509
   Cocaine Dependence/Abuse 522
   Cognitive Therapy 530

   Depression, Major 665
   Multiple Chemical Sensitivity Syndrome 1397
   Obsessive-Compulsive Disorder 1494
   Obsessive-Compulsive Personality Disorder 1496
   Pain, Chronic 1564
   Panic Disorder 1578, 1580
   Panic Disorder with Agoraphobia 1580
   Psychotherapy, Individual 1748
   Social Phobia 1937

Cognitive Evoked Potentials
   Evoked Potentials 851

Cognitive Therapy
   Attention Deficit Disorder in Adults 232
   Psychotherapy, Individual 1748
   Rehabilitation Therapy 1796

Cognitive-Behavioral Therapy
   Psychotherapy, Individual 1748

Coin Lesion of Lung
   Coin Lesion 532

Cold
   Bronchitis, Acute 299
   Raynaud's Phenomenon 1781
   Upper Respiratory Infection 2216

Cold Injury
   Frostbite 959

Cold Sore
   Herpes Simplex 1108

Colectomy
   Cancer, Colon 354
   Cancer, Rectum 384
   Colitis 535
   Colon Resection 538

Colitis
   Amebiasis 109
   Diarrhea 696
   Dysentery 755
   Gastroenteritis, Infectious 973
   Gastroenteritis, Non-Infectious 975
   Intestinal Upset 1224
   Traveler's Diarrhea 2177
   Ulcerative Colitis 2209

Collapse of the Lung
   Lung Collapse 1312
   Pneumothorax 1671

Collarbone
   Dislocation, Acromioclavicular Joint 708
   Dislocation, Sternclavicular Joint 726
   Fracture, Clavicle 907
   Paget's Disease of Bone 1557
   Rotator Cuff Tear 1853
   Sprains and Strains, Rotator Cuff (Capsule) 1994
   Thoracic Outlet Syndrome 2074

Collarbone Fracture
   Fracture, Clavicle 907

Collateral Ligament Sprain
   Repair, Anterior Cruciate Ligament 1814
   Shin Splints 1912
   Sprains and Strains, Knee 1991

Collateral Ligament Strain
   Repair, Anterior Cruciate Ligament 1814
   Shin Splints 1912
   Sprains and Strains, Knee 1991

Colles' Fracture
    Fracture, Radius and Ulna, Distal 933
Colloidal Mercury Poisoning
    Toxic Effects, Mercury 2138
Colon
    Abdominoperineal Resection of Rectum 10
    Abscess, Anorectal 20
    Abscess, Ischiorectal 24
    Abscess, Perirectal 34
    Amebiasis 109
    Cancer, Colon 354
    Cancer, Rectum 384
    Colitis 535
    Diarrhea 696
    Diverticulosis and Diverticulitis of Colon 739
    Endoscopy of Gastrointestinal Tract 810
    Gastrointestinal Hemorrhage 982
    Irritable Bowel Syndrome 1244
    Lower Gastrointestinal Series 1305
    Resection 538
    Colonoscopy 540
    Sigmoidoscopy 1925
    Ulcerative Colitis 2209
    Volvulus 2289
Colon Cancer
    Cancer, Colon 354
    Cancer, Rectum 384
    Colon Resection 538
    Colonoscopy 540
    Colostomy and Ileostomy 543
    Constipation 558
    Endoscopy of Gastrointestinal Tract 810
Colon Inflammation
    Colitis 535
    Constipation 558
    Diarrhea 696
    Diverticulosis and Diverticulitis of Colon 739
    Gastroenteritis, Non-Infectious 975
    Shigellosis 1910
    Ulcerative Colitis 2209
Colon Resection
    Colitis 535
Colon Stasis
    Constipation 558
Colonial Spirit Poisoning
    Toxic Effects, Methyl Alcohol 2140
Colonic Volvulus
    Volvulus 2289
Colonoscopy
    Cancer, Colon 354
    Colitis 535
    Constipation 558
    Diverticulosis and Diverticulitis of Colon 739
    Endoscopy of Gastrointestinal Tract 810
    Gastrointestinal Hemorrhage 982
    Hemorrhage of Rectum and Anus 1068
    Rectal Polyps 1783
    Shigellosis 1910
Colorado Tick Virus
    Colorado Tick Fever 541
Colorado Tick-Borne Fever
    Colorado Tick Fever 541
Colorectal Cancer
    Abdominoperineal Resection of Rectum 10

Cancer, Colon 354
Cancer, Rectum 384
Colon Resection 538
Colonoscopy 540
Colostomy and Ileostomy 543
Endoscopy of Gastrointestinal Tract 810
Gastrointestinal Hemorrhage 982
Colorectal Carcinoma
    Cancer, Colon 354
    Cancer, Rectum 384
Coloscopy
    Colonoscopy 540
    Sigmoidoscopy 1925
Colostomy
    Colostomy and Ileostomy 543
    Cancer, Colon 354
    Cancer, Rectum 384
    Cancer, Small Intestine (Including Duodenum) 389
    Colitis 535
    Diverticulosis and Diverticulitis of Colon 739
    Rectal Polyps 1783
    Rectal Ulcer 1788
Colovesical Fistula
    Bladder Fistulas 262
Colposcopic Biopsy
    Cancer, Cervix 351
    Cervical Biopsy 460
    Cervical Dysplasia 467
Columbin Spirits Poisoning
    Toxic Effects, Methyl Alcohol 2140
Coma
    Brain Injury 292
    Cerebral Contusion, Closed 447
    Cerebrovascular Accident 454
    Concussion, Cerebral 553
    Electroencephalogram 783
    Evoked Potentials 851
Comatose
    Coma 449, 544
Commissurotomy
    Mitral Commissurotomy 1384
Common
    Iron Deficiency Anemia 1242
    Joint Disorders 1251
    Warts, Plantar 2296
    Warts, Viral 2298
Common Cold
    Cold 533
    Upper Respiratory Infection 2216
Common Migraine
    Migraine Headache 1378
Common Migraine Headache
    Migraine Headache 1378
Common Warts
    Warts, Viral 2298
Compartment Syndrome
    Fasciotomy 870
Compartmental Syndrome
    Compartment Syndrome 547
Compensated Heart Failure
    Heart Failure, Congestive 1042

Compensation Neurosis
　Factitious Illness with Psychological Symptoms 868

Complete
　Atrioventricular Block, Complete (Third-Degree) 224
　Bundle Branch Block 310
　Sick Sinus Syndrome 1920

Complete Atrioventricular Block
　Atrioventricular Block, Complete (Third-Degree) 224

Complete Bundle Branch Block
　Bundle Branch Block 310

Complete Gastrectomy
　Gastrectomy 968

Complete Heart Block
　Atrioventricular Block, Complete (Third-Degree) 224
　Sick Sinus Syndrome 1920

Complications of Pregnancy
　Abruptio Placentae 16
　Anemia Complicating Pregnancy 136
　Cardiovascular Disease in Pregnancy 422
　Ectopic Pregnancy 775
　Gestational Diabetes 988
　Hydatidiform Mole 1134
　Hyperemesis Gravidarum 1142
　Miscarriage 1381
　Placenta Accreta 1651
　Placenta Previa 1653
　Preeclampsia and Eclampsia 1711
　Pregnancy Complications 1713
　Premature Labor 1720
　Premature Rupture of Membranes 1722
　Rh Incompatibility 1831
　Threatened Abortion 2080
　Uterus, Perforation of 2229

Compression
　Atrophy, Muscular 227, 230
　Bursitis 325
　Carpal Tunnel Release 428
　Carpal Tunnel Syndrome 430
　Cauda Equina Syndrome 440
　Fracture, Vertebra (Pathological) 956
　Myelopathy 1420
　Tarsal Tunnel Release 2041
　Tarsal Tunnel Syndrome 2043
　Tendon Sheath Incision 2052
　Thoracic Outlet Syndrome 2074

Compression Fracture
　Fracture, Lumbosacral Spine (With or Without Spinal Cord Injury) 920
　Fracture, Thoracic Spine (With or Without Spinal Cord Injury) 948
　Fracture, Vertebra (Pathological) 956

Compression of Brachial Plexus
　Thoracic Outlet Syndrome 2074

Compression Syndrome
　Thoracic Outlet Syndrome 2074

Compulsive
　Addictions, Mixed 60
　Obsessive-Compulsive Disorder 1494
　Obsessive-Compulsive Personality Disorder 1496
　Tics 2093

Compulsive Personality Disorder
　Obsessive-Compulsive Personality Disorder 1496

Computed Radiography
　X-ray 2305

Computed Tomography
　Computerized Axial Tomography 552

Concato's Disease
　Pericarditis, Chronic Constrictive 1617

Concussion
　Brain Injury 292
　Cerebral 553

Conduct Disturbance
　Adjustment Reaction with Predominant Disturbance of Conduct 74

Conduction Defect
　Heart Block 1040
　Stokes-Adams Syndrome 2003

Conduction Studies
　Nerve Conduction Studies 1459

Conductive Hearing Loss
　Hearing Loss 1036
　Tympanoplasty 2201

Condyloma Acuminatum
　Penis Disorders 1608

Condylomata Acuminata
　Warts, Genital 2294

Cone Biopsy
　Cancer, Cervix 351
　Cervical Biopsy 460
　Cervical Conization 463

Congenital
　Afibrinogenemia 81
　Aortic Insufficiency 165
　Coarctation of the Aorta 519
　Hypoprothrombinemia 1176
　Pernicious Anemia 1630
　Porphyria 1693
　Spherocytosis, Hereditary 1944
　Spinal Stenosis 1952
　Spondylolisthesis 1960
　Syringomyelia 2035
　Vesicovaginal Fistula 2266
　Wilson's Disease 2300

Congenital Aortic Stenosis
　Aortic Insufficiency 165

Congenital Bronchiectasis
　Bronchiectasis 297

Congenital Deficiency of Clotting Factors
　Afibrinogenemia 81
　Hypoprothrombinemia 1176

Congenital Erythropoietic Porphyria
　Porphyria 1693

Congenital Factor IX Disorder
　Hemophilia B 1064

Congenital Factor VIII Disorder
　Hemophilia A 1061

Congenital Folate Malabsorption
　Folic Acid Deficiency Anemia 885

Congenital Hemolytic Anemia
　Spherocytosis, Hereditary 1944

Congenital Hemolytic Icterus
　Spherocytosis, Hereditary 1944

Congenital Hemolytic Jaundice
　Spherocytosis, Hereditary 1944

Congenital Pernicious Anemia
  Pernicious Anemia 1630

Congenital Prothrombin Deficiency
  Afibrinogenemia 81
  Hypoprothrombinemia 1176

Congenital Spherocytosis
  Spherocytosis, Hereditary 1944

Congenital Erythropoietic Porphyria
  Porphyria 1693

Congestion
  Allergic Rhinitis 98
  Allergy 100
  Cold 533
  Deviated Nasal Septum 679
  Pulmonary Edema 1756
  Rhinoscleroma 1842
  Septoplasty 1909
  Sinusitis 1928
  Upper Respiratory Infection 2216

Congestive
  Cardiomyopathy 419

Congestive Atelectasis
  Adult Respiratory Distress Syndrome 79

Congestive Cardiac Failure
  Heart Failure, Congestive 1042

Congestive Cardiomyopathy
  Cardiomyopathy 419

Congestive Heart Failure
  Aortic Valve Stenosis 167
  Ascites 203
  Cardiac Arrest 409
  Cardiovascular Disease in Pregnancy 422
  Heart Failure, Congestive 1042
  Ventricular Fibrillation 2256

Conization of the Cervix
  Cervical Biopsy 460
  Cervical Conization 463

Conjunctiva
  Conjunctivitis 556
  Dacryostenosis 629
  Pterygium 1754

Conn's Disease
  Aldosteronism 94

Conn's Syndrome
  Aldosteronism 94

Constipation
  Abscess, Perirectal 34
  Endoscopy of Gastrointestinal Tract 810
  Hemorrhoids 1073
  Intestinal Upset 1224
  Rectal Ulcer 1788
  Salmonellosis 1866

Constitutional Hypotension
  Hypotension 1178
  Laryngitis 1279

Constriction
  Cardiomyopathy 419
  Coarctation of the Aorta 519
  Pyloric Stenosis, Acquired (Adult) Hypertrophic 1767
  Raynaud's Phenomenon 1781
  Spinal Stenosis 1952

Constrictive Cardiomyopathy
  Cardiomyopathy 419

Constrictive Pericarditis
  Heart Failure, Congestive 1042
  Pericardiectomy 1614
  Pericarditis, Chronic Constrictive 1617

Consumption
  Tuberculosis, Respiratory 2194

Contact Dermatitis
  Dermatitis 674
  Eczema 778
  Poison Ivy, Oak, Sumac, or Other Plant Dermatitis 1673
  Pruritus Ani 1736
  Radiodermatitis 1780

Contagious Granulomatous Conjunctivitis
  Trachoma 2161

Continent Ileostomy
  Colostomy and Ileostomy 543

Continuous Ambulatory Peritoneal Dialysis
  Renal Dialysis 1800

Contraction
  Abdominal Pain 7
  Achalasia 44
  Aortic Dissection 163
  Arrhythmia 178
  Atrial Fibrillation 220
  Atrioventricular Block Incomplete (Second-Degree) 223
  Atrioventricular Block, Complete (Third-Degree) 224
  Atrioventricular Block, Incomplete (First-Degree) 226
  Cardiac Arrest 409
  Delivery, Spontaneous and/or Assisted Vaginal 647
  Esophageal Spasm 839
  Menstrual Disorders 1369
  Muscle Spasm 1409
  Myalgia and Myositis 1411
  Myotomy of Esophagus 1433
  Open-Chest Cardiac Massage 1514
  Premature Beats 1719
  Premature Labor 1720
  Premature Rupture of Membranes 1722
  Sick Sinus Syndrome 1920
  Thoracic Aneurysm 2070
  Threatened Abortion 2080
  Tics 2093
  Torticollis 2108
  Tremor 2179
  Uterus, Perforation of 2229
  Ventricular Fibrillation 2256
  Ventricular Premature Contractions 2258
  Ventricular Tachycardia 2260
  Wandering Atrial Pacemaker 2293

Controversial Diagnosis
  Chronic Fatigue Syndrome 509
  Complex Regional Pain Syndrome 550
  Fibromyalgia and Myofascial Pain Syndrome 879
  Multiple Chemical Sensitivity Syndrome 1397
  Pain, Chronic 1564

Contusion
  Abdominal Muscle Strain 5
  Cerebral Contusion, Closed 447
  Eye 564
  Head Injury, Superficial 1031
  Lower Limb 566
  Muscle Injury 1406
  Trunk 568
  Upper Limb 571

Conversion Disorder
  Hysteria 1188

Conversion Reaction
  Conversion Disorder 574

Convulsion
  Epilepsy 824
  Equine Encephalitis 827
  Grand Mal Seizure 1014
  Seizures 1900
  St. Louis Encephalitis 2000
  Tetany 2062
  Toxic Effects, Methyl Bromide 2142

Cooley's Anemia
  Thalassemia 2066

Cooper Ligament Colposuspension
  Vesicourethropexy 2265

COPD
  Asthma 209
  Bronchitis, Chronic 302
  Chronic Obstructive Pulmonary Disease 511
  Cor Pulmonale, Acute and Chronic 576

Copper Metabolism Disorder
  Wilson's Disease 2300

Coproporphyria
  Porphyria 1693

Cor Pulmonale
  Acute and Chronic 576

Cord Injury
  Spinal Cord Injury 1946

Cord Stimulation
  Spinal Cord Stimulation 1949

Cork Worker's Lung
  Hypersensitivity Pneumonitis 1150

Corkscrew Esophagus
  Esophageal Spasm 839

Corn
  and Callus, Infected 578

Cornea
  Abrasion 580
  Astigmatism 212
  Foreign Body, Cornea 891
  Keratitis 1257
  Keratoconus 1259
  Radial Keratotomy 1775
  Transplant 582
  Ulcer 584

Corneal Inflammation
  Keratitis 1257

Coronary
  Angina, Unstable 144
  Angiocardiography 148
  Arteriography 586
  Atherosclerosis 587
  Balloon Angioplasty 590
  Bypass 592
  Myocardial Infarction, Acute 1424
  Prinzmetal's Angina 1726
  Thrombolysis 593

Coronary Angiography
  Coarctation of the Aorta 519
  Coronary Arteriography 586

Coronary Atherosclerosis 587

Coronary Angioplasty
  Arteriography 185
  Coronary Atherosclerosis 587
  Coronary Balloon Angioplasty 590

Coronary Arteriography
  Angina, Unstable 144

Coronary Arteriosclerosis
  Coronary Atherosclerosis 587
  Mitral Insufficiency 1385

Coronary Artery
  Angina Pectoris 140
  Angina, Unstable 144
  Arterial Graft 183
  Arteriosclerotic Gangrene 186
  Atherosclerosis and Arteriosclerosis 216
  Atrial Fibrillation 220
  Bundle Branch Block 310
  Cardiac Arrest 409
  Cardiac Catheterization 411
  Cardiogenic Shock 417
  Coronary Atherosclerosis 587
  Coronary Balloon Angioplasty 590
  Coronary Bypass 592
  Coronary Thrombolysis 593
  Myocardial Infarction, Acute 1424
  Premature Beats 1719
  Prinzmetal's Angina 1726
  Sick Sinus Syndrome 1920
  Tachycardia, Paroxysmal Supraventricular 2039
  Ventricular Fibrillation 2256
  Ventricular Premature Contractions 2258
  Ventricular Tachycardia 2260

Coronary Artery Angiography
  Coronary Arteriography 586

Coronary Artery Arteriography
  Coronary Arteriography 586

Coronary Artery Balloon Angioplasty
  Angina Pectoris 140
  Arteriography 185
  Coronary Balloon Angioplasty 590

Coronary Artery Bypass
  Cardiogenic Shock 417
  Coronary Atherosclerosis 587
  Coronary Bypass 592

Coronary Artery Bypass Graft
  Angina Pectoris 140
  Angina, Unstable 144
  Arterial Graft 183
  Coronary Bypass 592

Coronary Artery Disease
  Angina Pectoris 140
  Angina, Unstable 144
  Cardiac Arrest 409
  Cardiac Pacemaker Insertion 414
  Cardiac Stress Test 416
  Carotid Artery Occlusion 423
  Chest Pain 486
  Coronary Atherosclerosis 587
  Coronary Bypass 592
  Echocardiography 774
  Electrocardiogram 781
  Embolectomy 786–787
  Heart Valve Replacement 1047

Index 2549

Coronary Artery Vasospasm
    Prinzmetal's Angina 1726
Coronary Atherosclerosis
    Angina, Unstable 144
    Coronary Arteriography 586
Coronary Balloon Angioplasty
    Angina, Unstable 144
    Cardiac Catheterization 411
    Coronary Atherosclerosis 587
Coronary Bypass
    Angina, Unstable 144
    Arteriography 185
    Coronary Arteriography 586
Coronary Insufficiency
    Angina, Unstable 144
Coronary Occlusion
    Arteriosclerotic Gangrene 186
    Atherosclerosis and Arteriosclerosis 216
    Cardiac Arrest 409
    Myocardial Infarction, Acute 1424
Coronary Thrombosis
    Arterial Embolism and Thrombosis 180
    Myocardial Infarction, Acute 1424
Corpulence
    Obesity, Simple 1491
Corpus Albicans Cyst
    Ovarian Cyst, Benign 1552
Corpus Luteum Cyst
    Ovarian Cyst, Benign 1552
Corpus Uteri
    Uterine Polyps 2228
Correction of External Structure of Nose
    Rhinoplasty 1841
Correction of Hernia
    Hernia Repair 1094, 1096
    Hernia Repair, Vaginal 1096
Corrosive Esophagitis
    Esophagitis 847
Cortex Contusion
    Cerebral Contusion, Closed 447
Cortical Hemorrhage
    Cerebral Hemorrhage 449
Corticoadrenal Insufficiency
    Addison's Disease 63
Coryza
    Cold 533
Cosmetic Surgery
    Face Lift 865
    Liposuction 1292
    Mammoplasty, Augmentation 1338
Costoclavicular Syndrome
    Thoracic Outlet Syndrome 2074
Cotton Dust Asthma
    Byssinosis 328
Cotton Worker's Disease
    Byssinosis 328
    Hypersensitivity Pneumonitis 1150

Cotton-Mill Fever
    Byssinosis 328
Couvelaire Uterus
    Abruptio Placentae 16
Crack Abuse
    Cocaine Dependence/Abuse 522
Cracked Rib
    Fracture, Rib 936
Cramp
    Abdominal Adhesions 1
    Abdominal Pain 7
    Amebiasis 109
    Botulism 286
    Cervicobrachial Syndrome 474
    Colitis 535
    Diarrhea 696
    Endometriosis 805
    Gastroenteritis, Non-Infectious 975
    Metatarsalgia 1376
    Muscle Spasm 1409
    Myalgia and Myositis 1411
    Nausea 1446
    Premature Labor 1720
    Premenstrual Syndrome 1724
    Shigellosis 1910
    Tetany 2062
Cranial Fracture
    Epidural Hematoma 821
    Fracture, Skull (Closed) 941
Craniectomy
    Epidural Hematoma 821
Craniotomy
    Adrenal Tissue Implant or Transplant to Brain 76
    Astrocytoma 214
    Brain Injury 292
    Glioma 999
    Repair of Cerebral Aneurysm 1812
    Thalamotomy 2064
Craniovascular Accident
    Cerebrovascular Accident 454
Crescendo Angina
    Angina, Unstable 144
Cricothyrotomy
    Tracheostomy 2159
Crohn's Disease
    Abdominoperineal Resection of Rectum 10
    Cancer, Colon 354
    Colon Resection 538
    Colonoscopy 540
    Colostomy and Ileostomy 543
    Duodenitis 749
    Fissurectomy, Anal 884
    Hemorrhage of Rectum and Anus 1068
CRPS
    Complex Regional Pain Syndrome 550
CRPS I
    Complex Regional Pain Syndrome 550
CRPS II
    Complex Regional Pain Syndrome 550
CRPS III
    Complex Regional Pain Syndrome 550

Cruciate Ligament
    Repair, Anterior Cruciate Ligament **1814**
    Sprains and Strains, Knee **1991**

Cruciate Ligament Repair
    Repair, Anterior Cruciate Ligament **1814**

Crural Hernia
    Hernia, Inguinal and Femoral **1103**

Crush Injury
    Crush Wounds **603**
    Excision of Nail, Nail Bed, or Nail Fold **856**
    Fasciotomy **870**
    Gangrene **964**

Crushing Injury
    Crush Wounds **603**

Cryoretinopexy
    Retinal Detachment Repair **1825**

Cryosurgery
    Cancer, Skin **387**
    Cervical Cauterization **461**
    Cervical Dysplasia **467**
    Cervical Polyps **470**
    Cryotherapy, Genital Warts (Female) **605**
    Cryotherapy, Genital Warts (Male) **606**
    Hemorrhoid Treatment **1070**
    Sclerotherapy **1895**

Cryotherapy
    Cervical Cauterization **461**
    Cervical Dysplasia **467**
    Cervical Polyps **470**
    Cervicitis **472**
    Excision or Destruction of Plantar Warts **858**
    Genital Warts (Female) **605**
    Genital Warts (Male) **606**
    Retinal Detachment Repair **1825**
    Warts, Plantar **2296**

Cryotherapy, Genital Warts (Female)
    Warts, Genital **2294**

Cryotherapy, Genital Warts (Male)
    Warts, Genital **2294**

Cryptogenic Cirrhosis of Liver
    Cirrhosis of the Liver **515**

Crystal Addiction
    Amphetamine Dependence/Abuse **113**

CSD
    Cat Scratch Disease **435**

C-Section
    Cesarean Delivery **476**

CSF Examination
    Lumbar Puncture **1309**

CT Scan
    Abscess, Subdiaphragmatic **42**
    Aortic Aneurysm **160**
    Arteriovenous Aneurysm **188**
    Ascites **203**
    Astrocytoma **214**
    Bladder Fistulas **262**
    Bladder Polyps **264**
    Brain Abscess **289**
    Brain Injury **292**
    Bronchiectasis **297**
    Calculus, Bladder **333**
    Calculus, Renal (Kidney and Ureter) **335**

Cancer, Brain **344**
Cancer, Kidney **358**
Cancer, Liver **360**
Cancer, Lung **363**
Cancer, Oropharynx **369**
Cancer, Ovary **372**
Cancer, Pancreas **375**
Cancer, Pleura **377**
Cancer, Prostate **380**
Cancer, Rectum **384**
Cancer, Small Intestine (Including Duodenum) **389**
Cancer, Stomach **391**
Cancer, Testicle(s) **393**
Cancer, Tongue **399**
Cancer, Uterus **402**
Cauda Equina Syndrome **440**
Celiac Plexus Block **442**
Cerebral Aneurysm (Non-Ruptured) **445**
Cerebral Contusion, Closed **447**
Cerebral Hemorrhage **449**
Cerebral Palsy **452**
Cerebrovascular Accident **454**
Cerebrovascular Disease **458**
Cervical Disc Disorder with Myelopathy **464**
Coarctation of the Aorta **519**
Coin Lesion **532**
Computerized Axial Tomography **552**
Concussion, Cerebral **553**
Crush Wounds **603**
Curvature of the Spine, Acquired **610**
Degeneration, Cervical Intervertebral Disc **634**
Degeneration, Thoracic or Thoracolumbar Intervertebral Disc **640**
Dementia **651**, **653**
Dementia, Alzheimer's Type, with Delusions (Late Onset) **653**
Dermatomyositis **677**
Diabetic Gangrene **689**
Dislocation, Sternclavicular Joint **726**
Displacement, Lumbar Intervertebral Disc Without Myelopathy **732**
Echinococcosis **772**
Encephalitis **797**
Encephalopathy **799**
Epidural Hematoma **821**
Epilepsy **824**
Fracture, Cervical Spine (With or Without Spinal Cord Injury) **904**
Fracture, Lumbosacral Spine (With or Without Spinal Cord Injury) **920**
Fracture, Midfoot (Cuboid, Cuneiform, Navicular) **928**
Fracture, Pelvis **930**
Fracture, Radius and Ulna, Distal **933**
Fracture, Sacrum **939**
Fracture, Skull (Closed) **941**
Fracture, Sternum (Closed) **943**
Fracture, Talus **945**
Fracture, Thoracic Spine (With or Without Spinal Cord Injury) **948**
Fracture, Vertebra **954**, **956**
Fracture, Vertebra (Pathological) **956**
Glioma **999**
Glomerulonephritis, Chronic **1003**
Grand Mal Seizure **1014**
Heat Stroke **1051**
Hemiplegia **1056**
Hepatic Angiosarcoma **1077**
Myelography **1419**
Pancreatic Pseudocyst **1569**
Patella Chondromalacia **1599**
Postconcussion Syndrome **1699**
Pott's Disease **1709**
Renal Failure, Chronic **1804**
Repair of Cerebral Aneurysm **1812**
Rhinoscleroma **1842**
Rupture of Spleen, Traumatic **1860**
Schizophrenia **1882**, **1885**

Index   2551

Seizures 1900
Sprains and Strains, Ankle 1971
Subarachnoid Hemorrhage (Non-traumatic) 2011
Subarachnoid Hemorrhage (Traumatic) 2014
Syringomyelia 2035
Thoracic Disc Disorder with Myelopathy 2072
Torticollis 2108
Transient Ischemic Attack 2169
X-ray 2305

CTCL
Mycosis Fungoides 1416

CT-Guided Biopsy
Lung Biopsy 1310

CTR
Carpal Tunnel Release 428

CTS
Carpal Tunnel Syndrome 430

Cubital Tunnel Syndrome
Neuropathy of Ulnar Nerve (Entrapment) 1473

Cuboid
Dislocation, Foot 716
Fracture, Midfoot (Cuboid, Cuneiform, Navicular) 928
Sprains and Strains, Foot 1986

Cuboid Bone Fracture
Fracture, Midfoot (Cuboid, Cuneiform, Navicular) 928

Culdocentesis
Aspiration 207—208

Culdoscopy
Salpingo-oophorectomy 1873

Cuneiform Bone Fracture
Fracture, Midfoot (Cuboid, Cuneiform, Navicular) 928

Cup Arthroplasty
Hip Replacement, Total 1119
Shoulder Replacement 1917

Curettage
Abortion by Dilation and Curettage for Termination of Pregnancy 11
Aspiration Curettage of the Uterus 208
Cancer, Skin 387
Cervical Polypectomy 469
Choriocarcinoma 505
Cryotherapy, Genital Warts (Female) 605
Cryotherapy, Genital Warts (Male) 606
Dilation and Curettage 699
Excision or Destruction of Plantar Warts 858
Hydatidiform Mole 1134
Miscarriage 1381
Periodontitis 1619
Pilonidal Cyst 1645
Postmenopausal Bleeding 1703
Warts, Viral 2298

Curretage and Dilation
Dilation and Curettage 699

Curvature of the Spine
Acquired 610

Cushing's Disease
Adrenalectomy 77
Avascular Necrosis 235
Cushing's Syndrome 613

Cushing's Syndrome
Adrenalectomy 77
Avascular Necrosis 235
Cushing's Syndrome 613

Cut
Lacerations 1269
Open Wound 1504, 1510, 1512
Open Wound, Back 1510
Open Wound, Chest 1512
Puncture Wound 1759

Cutanea Tarda
Porphyria 1693

Cutaneomucouveal Syndrome
Behçet's Syndrome 244

Cutaneous T-Cell Lymphoma
Mycosis Fungoides 1416

CVA
Cerebrovascular Accident 454

Cyanocobalamin Deficiency
Vitamin B$_{12}$ Deficiency 2277

Cyanocobalamin Poisoning
Poisoning, Vitamin B 1679

Cyclic Schizophrenia
Schizoaffective Disorder 1878

Cyst
Bartholin's Gland Cyst 242
Excision of Lesion or Tissue of Skin and Subcutaneous Tissue 854
Fibrocystic Breast Disease 874
Ganglionectomy (Wrist) 963
Incision of Skin and Subcutaneous Tissue, Drainage of Abscess or Cyst 1201
Ovarian Cyst, Benign 1552
Ovarian Cyst, Resection of 1555
Paraovarian Cyst 1590
Pilonidal Cyst 1645
Salpingo-oophorectomy 1873
Sebaceous Cyst 1896
Spermatocele 1942
Synovial Cyst 2028

Cyst Drainage
Incision of Skin and Subcutaneous Tissue, Drainage of Abscess or Cyst 1201

Cyst of Corpus Luteum
Ovarian Cyst, Benign 1552

Cyst of Ovary
Ovarian Cyst, Benign 1552

Cyst of Synovial Membrane
Synovial Cyst 2028

Cystectomy
Bladder Polyps 264
Cancer, Bladder 338
Cystitis, Interstitial 619

Cystic
Cystocele or Rectocele 621
Fibrocystic Breast Disease 874
Spermatocele 1942

Cystic Breast
Fibrocystic Breast Disease 874

Cystic Hernia
Cystocele or Rectocele 621

Cystic Hydatid Disease
Echinococcosis 772

Cystic Mastitis
Fibrocystic Breast Disease 874

Cystic Tumor of Epididymis
Spermatocele 1942

Cystitis
- Acute 616
- Cystectomy 615
- Cystoscopy, Transurethral 624
- Hematuria 1055
- Interstitial 619

Cystocele
- or Rectocele 621

Cystocele Repair
- Hernia Repair, Vaginal 1096

Cystoma of Ovary
- Ovarian Cyst, Benign 1552

Cystoplasty
- Cystourethroplasty of Bladder Neck 625

Cystoscopy
- Bladder Fistulas 262
- Bladder Polyps 264
- Cancer, Bladder 338
- Cancer, Prostate 380
- Cystitis, Interstitial 619
- Epididymitis 819
- Hematuria 1055
- Transurethral 624

Cystourethrocele
- Cystocele or Rectocele 621

Cystourethroplasty
- of Bladder Neck 625

Cystourethroscopic Examination
- Cystoscopy, Transurethral 624

Cystourethroscopy
- Cystoscopy, Transurethral 624

Cysts
- Cervical Cauterization 461
- Synovial Cyst 2028

Cytotoxic Cancer Treatment
- Chemotherapy 485

D

D&C
- Abortion by Dilation and Curettage for Termination of Pregnancy 11
- Cervical Polyps 470
- Dilation and Curettage 699
- Dysfunctional Uterine Bleeding 757
- Hydatidiform Mole 1134
- Menstrual Disorders 1369
- Postmenopausal Bleeding 1703
- Uterus, Perforation of 2229

DaCosta's Syndrome
- Neurocirculatory Asthenia 1467

Damage to Uterus
- Uterus, Perforation of 2229

Darling's Disease
- Histoplasmosis 1121

De Costa's Syndrome
- Neurocirculatory Asthenia 1467

De Quervain's Disease
- De Quervain's Release 630
- Radial Styloid Tenosynovitis 1776

De Quervain's Release
- De Quervain's Release 630

- Tendon Sheath Incision 2052

De Quervain's Tenosynovitis
- Radial Styloid Tenosynovitis 1776

De Quervain's Thyroiditis
- Thyroiditis 2091

Deafness
- Cochlear Implant 529
- Hearing Loss 1036
- Stapedectomy 2002

Débridement
- Gangrene 964
- Gas Gangrene 967
- Meniscectomy and Meniscus Repair 1361
- Spondylitis 1958

Decompensated Heart Failure
- Heart Failure, Congestive 1042

Decompression
- Cauda Equina Syndrome 440
- Compartment Syndrome 547
- Nasogastric Intubation 1444
- Peripheral Neuropathy 1621
- Spinal Stenosis 1952
- Spondylitis 1958
- Spondylolisthesis 1960

Decompression Gastrostomy
- Gastrostomy 984

Decompression Illness
- Caisson Disease 331

Decompression Sickness
- Caisson Disease 331

Decreased Protein Level in the Blood
- Hypoproteinemia 1175

Decreased Serum Protein
- Hypoproteinemia 1175

Decubitus
- Angina Decubitus 140
- Ulcer 632

Deep Vein Thrombosis
- Peripheral Thrombosis 1623
- Varicose Ulcer 2244
- Vena Cava Interruption 2251
- Venous Embolism and Thrombosis 2252

Deer Fly Fever
- Tularemia 2197

Deer Tick Fever
- Tularemia 2197

Defibrillation
- Stokes-Adams Syndrome 2003

Deficiency 2275
- Acquired Immune Deficiency Syndrome 53
- Afibrinogenemia 81
- Folic Acid Deficiency Anemia 885
- Hemophilia A 1061
- Hyperparathyroidism 1148
- Hypoparathyroidism 1173
- Hypoprothrombinemia 1176
- Hypovitaminosis 1182
- Iron Deficiency Anemia 1242
- Pellagra 1602
- Pernicious Anemia 1630
- Vitamin A Deficiency 2270

Index 2553

Vitamin B$_1$ Deficiency **2272**
Vitamin B$_{12}$ Deficiency **2277**
Vitamin B$_2$ Deficiency **2275**
Vitamin C Deficiency **2279**
Vitamin D Deficiency **2281**
Vitamin E Deficiency **2283**
Vitamin K Deficiency **2284**

Deficiency of Other Clotting Factors
Afibrinogenemia **81**
Hypoprothrombinemia **1176**

Degeneration
Cervical Intervertebral Disc **634**
Joint Disorders **1251**
Lumbar Intervertebral Disc **637**
Optic Atrophy **1519**
Osteoarthritis **1530**
Patella Chondromalacia **1599**
Senile Macular Degeneration **1903**
Thoracic or Thoracolumbar Intervertebral Disc **640**
Wilson's Disease **2300**

Degeneration of Cervical Disc
Degeneration, Cervical Intervertebral Disc **634**

Degeneration of Disc
Degeneration, Cervical Intervertebral Disc **634**
Degeneration, Lumbar Intervertebral Disc **637**
Degeneration, Thoracic or Thoracolumbar Intervertebral Disc **640**

Degeneration of Lumbar Disc
Degeneration, Lumbar Intervertebral Disc **637**

Degeneration of Thoracic Disc
Degeneration, Thoracic or Thoracolumbar Intervertebral Disc **640**

Degeneration of Thoracolumbar Disc
Degeneration, Thoracic or Thoracolumbar Intervertebral Disc **640**

Degenerative
Degeneration, Cervical Intervertebral Disc **634**
Degeneration, Lumbar Intervertebral Disc **637**
Degeneration, Thoracic or Thoracolumbar Intervertebral Disc **640**
Neck Pain **1448**
Organic Psychosis **1526**
Osteoarthritis **1530**
Patella Chondromalacia **1599**
Spinal Stenosis **1952**
Spondylolisthesis **1960**
Spondylolysis, Lumbar Region **1962**

Degenerative Arthritis
Hallux Rigidus **1027**
Osteoarthritis **1530**
Paget's Disease of Bone **1557**

Degenerative Dementia
Organic Psychosis **1526**

Degenerative Disc Disease
Degeneration, Cervical Intervertebral Disc **634**
Degeneration, Lumbar Intervertebral Disc **637**
Degeneration, Thoracic or Thoracolumbar Intervertebral Disc **640**
Disc Calcification **701**

Degenerative Disease
Degeneration, Cervical Intervertebral Disc **634**
Degeneration, Lumbar Intervertebral Disc **637**
Degeneration, Thoracic or Thoracolumbar Intervertebral Disc **640**
Organic Psychosis **1526**
Osteoarthritis **1530**

Degenerative Disorder of the Cervical Spine
Degeneration, Cervical Intervertebral Disc **634**

Degenerative Joint Disease
Osteoarthritis **1530**

Degenerative Osteoarthritis
Osteoarthritis **1530**

Dehydration
Amebiasis **109**
Constipation **558**
Diarrhea **696**
Dysentery **755**
E. Coli **767**
Gastroenteritis, Infectious **973**
Heat Exhaustion **1049**
Muscle Spasm **1409**
Salmonellosis **1866**

Delayed Opening Enterostomy
Enterostomy **811**

Delhi Belly
Traveler's Diarrhea **2177**

Delirium
Organic Psychosis **1526**

Delirium Tremens
Alcohol and Drug Detoxification and Rehabilitation **84**

Delivery
Cesarean Delivery **476**
Perineorrhaphy **1618**
Spontaneous and/or Assisted Vaginal **647**

Delusional Disorder
Neurotic Disorders **1475**

Delusions
Delusional Disorder **649**
Dementia **651, 653**
Dementia, Alzheimer's Type, with Delusions (Late Onset) **653**
Schizoaffective Disorder **1878**
Schizophrenia **1882, 1885**
Schizophrenia, Paranoid Type **1885**
Schizophreniform Disorder **1888**

Delusions of Misidentification or Impersonation
Delusional Disorder **649**

Demand Pacemaker
Cardiac Pacemaker Insertion **414**

Dementia
Alzheimer's Disease **105**
Alzheimer's Type, with Delusions (Late Onset) **653**
General Paresis **986**
Organic Psychosis **1526**
Parkinson's Disease **1593**
Pellagra **1602**

Dementia Paralytica
General Paresis **986**

Dementia Paretic
General Paresis **986**

Dementia with Delusions
Dementia, Alzheimer's Type, with Delusions (Late Onset) **653**

Dental
Dentoalveolar Abscess **660**
Disorders **657**
Gingivitis **993**
Impacted Tooth **1191**
Ludwig's Angina **1306**
Periodontitis **1619**
Root Canal Therapy **1847**
Tooth Extraction **2107**

Dental Abscess
    Dental Disorders 657
    Dentoalveolar Abscess 660
    Gingival Abscess 991
    Periodontitis 1619
    Tooth Extraction 2107

Dental Caries
    Dental Disorders 657

Dental Cavities
    Dental Disorders 657

Dental Disorders
    Dentoalveolar Abscess 660
    Gingival Abscess 991
    Gingivitis 993
    Impacted Tooth 1191
    Periodontitis 1619

Dental Fistula
    Gingival Abscess 991
    Periodontitis 1619

Dentoalveolar Abscess
    Gingival Abscess 991
    Periodontitis 1619

DEP
    Evoked Potentials 851

Dependence
    Addictions, Mixed 60
    Alcoholism 90
    Amphetamine Dependence/Abuse 113
    Cocaine Dependence/Abuse 522
    Marijuana Dependence/abuse 1341
    Nicotine Dependence 1479
    Opioid Type Dependence 1516
    Sedative, Hypnotic or Anxiolytic Dependence 1898

Dependent
    Personality Disorder 661

Depersonalization Syndrome
    Depersonalization Disorder 663

Depressed
    Adjustment Disorder with Depressed Mood 69
    Bipolar Affective Disorder 253, 256, 258, 260
    Bipolar Affective Disorder, Depressed 256
    Bipolar Affective Disorder, Mixed 258
    Depression, Major 665
    Depressive Psychosis 670
    Dysthymic Disorder 764

Depressed Bipolar Disorder
    Bipolar Affective Disorder, Depressed 256

Depressed Mood
    Adjustment Disorder with Depressed Mood 69

Depression
    Adjustment Disorder with Depressed Mood 69
    Bipolar Affective Disorder, Depressed 256
    Cognitive Therapy 530
    Depressive Psychosis 670
    Dysthymic Disorder 764
    Major 665
    Paget's Disease of Breast 1559
    Parkinson's Disease 1593
    Pernicious Anemia 1630
    Postconcussion Syndrome 1699
    Premenstrual Syndrome 1724
    Psychoanalysis 1742
    Psychopharmacotherapy 1743
    Psychotherapy, Group 1747
    Psychotherapy, Individual 1748
    Schizoaffective Disorder 1878

Depression, Major
    Electroconvulsive Therapy 782

Depressive
    Adjustment Disorder with Depressed Mood 69
    Depression, Major 665
    Psychosis 670

Depressive Disorder
    Depression, Major 665

Depressive Psychosis
    Depression, Major 665

Depressive Reaction
    Adjustment Disorder with Depressed Mood 69

Depressive Reaction (Brief and Chronic)
    Adjustment Disorder with Depressed Mood 69

DEPS
    Evoked Potentials 851

Derangement of Knee
    Internal Derangement of Knee 1219

Dermatitis
    Allergic Dermatitis 96
    Atopic Dermatitis 218
    Contact Dermatitis 560
    Eczema 778
    Insect or Spider Bites and Stings 1210
    Pellagra 1602
    Pityriasis Rosea 1649
    Poison Ivy, Oak, Sumac, or Other Plant Dermatitis 1673
    Psoriasis 1738
    Radiodermatitis 1780
    Sunburn 2019
    Toxic Effects, Plants (genus Toxicodendron) 2150
    Warts, Plantar 2296

Dermatitis Verrucosa
    Chromoblastomycosis 508

Dermatomal Evoked Potentials
    Evoked Potentials 851

Dermatomycosis
    Tinea 2095

Dermatophytosis
    Tinea 2095

Dermatosclerosis
    Scleroderma 1892

Descending Aneurysm
    Aortic Aneurysm 160
    Aortic Dissection 163
    Thoracic Aneurysm 2070

Desert Fever
    Coccidioidomycosis 525

Desert Rheumatism
    Coccidioidomycosis 525

Desquamating Eosinophilic Bronchitis
    Asthma 209

Destruction of Duodenal Lesion
    Excision or Destruction of Duodenal Lesion 857

Detached
    Abruptio Placentae 16

Index   2555

Avoidant Personality Disorder 237

Detached Injury
  Muscle Injury 1406

Detached Personality Disorder
  Avoidant Personality Disorder 237

Detached Retina
  Retinal Detachment 1823, 1825
  Retinal Detachment Repair 1825

Detachment
  Abruptio Placentae 16
  Avoidant Personality Disorder 237
  Retinal Detachment 1823, 1825

Detachment of Placenta
  Abruptio Placentae 16

Detox
  Alcohol and Drug Detoxification and Rehabilitation 84

Detoxification
  Alcohol and Drug Detoxification and Rehabilitation 84

Deviated Nasal Septum
  Septoplasty 1909

Deviated Septum
  Deviated Nasal Septum 679
  Septoplasty 1909

Devil's Grip
  Pleurodynia 1661

Dexedrine Addiction
  Amphetamine Dependence/Abuse 113

Diabetes
  Diabetic Gangrene 689
  Diabetic Glomerulosclerosis 690
  Diabetic Neuropathy 692
  Diabetic Retinopathy 694
  Gas Gangrene 967
  Hypoglycemia 1171
  Mellitus Type I 683, 686
  Mellitus Type II 686

Diabetes Mellitus
  Diabetic Gangrene 689
  Diabetic Glomerulosclerosis 690
  Diabetic Neuropathy 692
  Diabetic Retinopathy 694
  Glomerulosclerosis 1005
  Type I 683, 686
  Type II 686

Diabetes Mellitus Type I
  Diabetes Mellitus Type I 683, 686
  Diabetic Gangrene 689
  Diabetic Glomerulosclerosis 690

Diabetes Mellitus Type II
  Diabetes Mellitus Type II 686
  Diabetic Gangrene 689
  Diabetic Glomerulosclerosis 690

Diabetic
  Diabetes Mellitus Type I 683, 686
  Diabetes Mellitus Type II 686
  Gangrene 689
  Glomerulosclerosis 690
  Neuropathy 692
  Retinopathy 694

Diabetic Eye Disease
  Diabetic Retinopathy 694

Diabetic Kidney Disease
  Diabetic Glomerulosclerosis 690

Diabetic Nephropathy
  Diabetic Glomerulosclerosis 690

Diabetic Nerve Damage
  Diabetic Neuropathy 692

Diabetic Neuropathy
  Paresthesia 1591
  Peripheral Neuropathy 1621

Diabetic Retina Disease
  Diabetic Retinopathy 694

Diabetic Retinopathy
  Blindness 270

Diagnostic Exploration for Stones
  Cholangiography 493
  Cholecystitis 497
  Cholelithiasis 501
  Cystoscopy, Transurethral 624
  Ultrasound, Diagnostic 2212

Diagnostic Peritoneal Lavage
  Aspiration 207–208

Diagnostic Procedures
  Angiocardiography 148
  Arteriography 185
  Arthrography 196
  Aspiration 207–208
  Biopsy 252
  Bone Scan 277
  Bronchoscopic Biopsy 304
  Cardiac Catheterization 411
  Cardiac Stress Test 416
  Cervical Biopsy 460
  Cervical Conization 463
  Cholangiography 493
  Cholecystography 500
  Colonoscopy 540
  Computerized Axial Tomography 552
  Coronary Arteriography 586
  Dilation and Curettage 699
  Echocardiography 774
  Electrocardiogram 781
  Electroencephalogram 783
  Electromyography 784
  Endoscopy of Gastrointestinal Tract 810
  Esophagogastroduodenoscopy 850
  Evoked Potentials 851
  Excision of Lesion or Tissue of Skin and Subcutaneous Tissue 854
  Intravenous Pyelogram 1233
  Laparoscopy 1275
  Laparotomy 1276
  Laryngoscopy 1281
  Liver Biopsy 1297
  Lower Gastrointestinal Series 1305
  Lumbar Puncture 1309
  Lung Biopsy 1310
  Magnetic Resonance Imaging 1327
  Mammography 1337
  Myelography 1419
  Myocardial Perfusion Scan 1427
  Nerve Conduction Studies 1459
  Pleural Biopsy 1657
  Pulmonary Function Tests 1758
  Skin or Subcutaneous Tissue Biopsy 1934
  Thoracentesis 2069
  Transcutaneous Electrical Nerve Stimulation 2164
  Transfer of Nerve, Ulnar 2165

Ultrasound, Diagnostic **2212**
Upper Gastrointestinal Series **2214**
X-ray **2305**

Diagnostic Ultrasound
Arteriosclerotic Gangrene **186**
Arteriovenous Aneurysm **188**
Ascites **203**
Atherosclerosis and Arteriosclerosis **216**
Bladder Fistulas **262**
Cancer, Breast **347**
Cancer, Pancreas **375**
Cancer, Prostate **380**
Cancer, Rectum **384**
Cancer, Thyroid Gland **396**
Cancer, Uterus **402**
Cerebrovascular Disease **458**
Choriocarcinoma **505**
Coccygodynia **527**
Diverticulosis and Diverticulitis of Colon **739**
Echinococcosis **772**
Echocardiography **774**
Ectopic Pregnancy **775**
Fibrocystic Breast Disease **874**
Fibroid Tumor of Uterus **875**
Filariasis **881**
Fracture, Sternum (Closed) **943**
Glomerulonephritis, Chronic **1003**
Goiter **1008**
Hepatic Angiosarcoma **1077**
Ultrasound, Diagnostic **2212**

Diagnostic Ultrasound of Heart
Echocardiography **774**

Diagnostic X-ray
X-ray **2305**

Dialysis
Kidney Transplant **1261**
Nephrectomy **1451**
Nephritis, Interstitial **1453**
Peritonitis **1628**
Poisoning **1675, 1677, 1679, 1681**
Pyelonephritis, Chronic **1764**
Renal Dialysis **1800**
Renal Failure, Chronic **1804**

Dialysis Elbow
Bursitis **325**

Dialysis-Associated Peritonitis
Peritonitis **1628**

Diaphragm Adhesions
Abdominal Adhesions **1**

Diaphragmatic Hernia
Hernia, Hiatal **1097**

Diarrhea
Botulism **286**
Colitis **535**
Duodenitis **749**
Dysentery **755**
Endoscopy of Gastrointestinal Tract **810**
Gastroenteritis, Infectious **973**
Gastroenteritis, Non-Infectious **975**
Intestinal Upset **1224**
Pellagra **1602**
Salmonellosis **1866**
Shigellosis **1910**
Traveler's Diarrhea **2177**
Trichinosis **2183**
Ulcerative Colitis **2209**

Diarrheal Shellfish Poisoning
Toxic Effects, Fish and Shellfish **2126**

Diarrheogenic E. Coli
E. Coli **767**

Dibromethane Poisoning
Toxic Effects, Methyl Bromide **2142**

Dichloromethane Exposure
Toxic Effects, Chlorinated Hydrocarbon Solvents **2120**

Dichlorvos Exposure
Toxic Effects, Organophosphate and Carbamate Pesticides **2147**

Dietary Folic Acid Deficiency Anemia
Folic Acid Deficiency Anemia **885**

Diffuse Cystic Mastopathy
Fibrocystic Breast Disease **874**

Diffuse Esophageal Spasm
Esophageal Spasm **839**

Diffuse Fasciitis with Eosinophilia
Eosinophilic Fasciitis **814**

Diffuse Large Cell Lymphoma
Non-Hodgkin's Lymphoma **1482**

Diffuse Small Cleaved Cell Lymphoma
Non-Hodgkin's Lymphoma **1482**

Digital Cyanosis Syndrome
Raynaud's Phenomenon **1781**

Digital Radiography
X-ray **2305**

Dilation
Abortion by Dilation and Curettage for Termination of Pregnancy **11**
Achalasia **44**
and Curettage **699**
Bronchiectasis **297**
Esophageal Strictures **840**
of Esophagus **700**
Pyloroplasty **1769**
Salivary Gland Stones **1865**
Transurethral Balloon Dilation of Prostatic Urethra **2171**

Dilation and Curettage
Abortion by Dilation and Curettage for Termination of Pregnancy **11**
Cervical Polyps **470**
Menstrual Disorders **1369**
Miscarriage **1381**
Uterus, Perforation of **2229**

Dilation of Prostatic Urethra
Transurethral Balloon Dilation of Prostatic Urethra **2171**

Dimethylcarbinol Poisoning
Toxic Effects, Isopropyl Alcohol **2134**

Disarticulation
Dislocation, Foot **716**

Disc
Calcification **701**
Cervical Disc Disorder with Myelopathy **464**
Chemonucleolysis of Inteveterbral Disc **482**
Discectomy **703**
Degeneration, Cervical Intervertebral Disc **634**
Degeneration, Lumbar Intervertebral Disc **637**
Degeneration, Thoracic or Thoracolumbar Intervertebral Disc **640**
Displacement, Cervical Intervertebral Disc Without Myelopathy **728**
Displacement, Lumbar Intervertebral Disc Without Myelopathy **732**
Displacement, Thoracic Intervertebral Disc Without Myelopathy **735**
Intervertebral Disc Disorders **1221**

Lumbar Disc Disorder with Myelopathy **1308**
Sciatica **1890**
Spinal Fusion **1951**
Thoracic Disc Disorder with Myelopathy **2072**

Disc Bulge
Displacement, Cervical Intervertebral Disc Without Myelopathy **728**
Displacement, Lumbar Intervertebral Disc Without Myelopathy **732**
Displacement, Thoracic Intervertebral Disc Without Myelopathy **735**

Disc Degeneration
Curvature of the Spine, Acquired **610**
Degeneration, Cervical Intervertebral Disc **634**
Degeneration, Lumbar Intervertebral Disc **637**
Degeneration, Thoracic or Thoracolumbar Intervertebral Disc **640**
Dislocation, Cervical Vertebra **711**

Disc Disorder
Cervical Disc Disorder with Myelopathy **464**
Degeneration, Cervical Intervertebral Disc **634**
Degeneration, Lumbar Intervertebral Disc **637**
Degeneration, Thoracic or Thoracolumbar Intervertebral Disc **640**
Disc Calcification **701**
Displacement, Cervical Intervertebral Disc Without Myelopathy **728**
Displacement, Lumbar Intervertebral Disc Without Myelopathy **732**
Displacement, Thoracic Intervertebral Disc Without Myelopathy **735**
Intervertebral Disc Disorders **1221**
Lumbar Disc Disorder with Myelopathy **1308**
Thoracic Disc Disorder with Myelopathy **2072**

Disc Disorder with Myelopathy
Cervical Disc Disorder with Myelopathy **464**
Lumbar Disc Disorder with Myelopathy **1308**
Thoracic Disc Disorder with Myelopathy **2072**

Disc Displacement
Displacement, Cervical Intervertebral Disc Without Myelopathy **728**
Displacement, Lumbar Intervertebral Disc Without Myelopathy **732**
Displacement, Thoracic Intervertebral Disc Without Myelopathy **735**
Intervertebral Disc Disorders **1221**

Disc Displacement Without Myelopathy
Displacement, Cervical Intervertebral Disc Without Myelopathy **728**
Displacement, Lumbar Intervertebral Disc Without Myelopathy **732**
Displacement, Thoracic Intervertebral Disc Without Myelopathy **735**
Intervertebral Disc Disorders **1221**

Disc Herniation
Displacement, Cervical Intervertebral Disc Without Myelopathy **728**
Displacement, Lumbar Intervertebral Disc Without Myelopathy **732**
Displacement, Thoracic Intervertebral Disc Without Myelopathy **735**

Disc Protrusion
Displacement, Cervical Intervertebral Disc Without Myelopathy **728**
Displacement, Lumbar Intervertebral Disc Without Myelopathy **732**
Displacement, Thoracic Intervertebral Disc Without Myelopathy **735**

Disc Rupture
Displacement, Cervical Intervertebral Disc Without Myelopathy **728**
Displacement, Lumbar Intervertebral Disc Without Myelopathy **732**
Displacement, Thoracic Intervertebral Disc Without Myelopathy **735**

Discectomy
Cervical Disc Disorder with Myelopathy **464**
Curvature of the Spine, Acquired **610**
Displacement, Cervical Intervertebral Disc Without Myelopathy **728**
Displacement, Thoracic Intervertebral Disc Without Myelopathy **735**
Spinal Fusion **1951**
Spinal Stenosis **1952**
Thoracic Disc Disorder with Myelopathy **2072**

Disease
Addison's Disease **63**
Alzheimer's Disease **105**
Cat Scratch Disease **435**
Cerebrovascular Disease **458**

Chronic Obstructive Pulmonary Disease **511**
Hypertensive Heart Disease **1156**
Legionnaire's Disease **1282**
Lyme Disease **1319**
Meniere's Disease **1353**
Osler-Weber-Rendu Disease **1528**
Paget's Disease of Bone **1557**
Paget's Disease of Breast **1559**
Parkinson's Disease **1593**
Pelvic Inflammatory Disease **1604**
Peptic Ulcer Disease **1611**
Peripheral Vascular Disease **1626**
Pott's Disease **1709**
Rheumatic Heart Disease, Chronic **1836**
Wilson's Disease **2300**

Dislocated Knee
Dislocation, Femorotibial (Knee) Joint **713**
Dislocation, Patella (Kneecap) **723**

Dislocated Shoulder
Glenohumeral Dislocation **719**

Dislocation
Reduction of Fracture or Dislocation **1791**

Dislocation of Acromioclavicular Joint
Dislocation, Acromioclavicular Joint **708**

Dislocation of Femorotibial Joint
Dislocation, Femorotibial (Knee) Joint **713**

Dislocation of Knee Joint
Dislocation, Femorotibial (Knee) Joint **713**

Dislocation of Kneecap
Dislocation, Patella (Kneecap) **723**

Dislocation of Patella
Dislocation, Patella (Kneecap) **723**

Dislocation of Shoulder
Glenohumeral Dislocation **719**

Dislocation of Sternoclavicular Joint
Dislocation, Sternclavicular Joint **726**

Dislocation Reduction
Reduction of Fracture or Dislocation **1791**

Disorder
Adjustment Disorder with Depressed Mood **69**
Antisocial Personality Disorder **156**
Anxiety Disorder, Generalized **158**
Attention Deficit Disorder in Adults **232**
Avoidant Personality Disorder **237**
Bipolar Affective Disorder **253, 256, 258, 260**
Bipolar Affective Disorder, Depressed **256**
Bipolar Affective Disorder, Mixed **258**
Bipolar Affective Disorder, Single Manic Episode **260**
Borderline Personality Disorder **284**
Cervical Disc Disorder with Myelopathy **464**
Conversion Disorder **574**
Delusional Disorder **649**
Dependent Personality Disorder **661**
Depersonalization Disorder **663**
Dissociative Personality Disorder **737**
Dysthymic Disorder **764**
Explosive Personality Disorder **862**
Intermittent Explosive Disorder **1217**
Intervertebral Disc Disorders **1221**
Lumbar Disc Disorder with Myelopathy **1308**
Manic Disorder, Recurrent **1339**
Narcissistic Personality Disorder **1437**
Neurotic Disorders **1475**
Obsessive-Compulsive Disorder **1494**

    Obsessive-Compulsive Personality Disorder **1496**
    Panic Disorder **1578, 1580**
    Panic Disorder with Agoraphobia **1580**
    Paranoid Personality Disorder **1588**
    Passive-Aggressive Personality Disorder **1597**
    Penis Disorders **1608**
    Posttraumatic Stress Disorder **1707**
    Psychosexual Disorders **1745**
    Psychotic Disorder, Brief **1749**
    Psychotic Disorder, Unspecified **1751**
    Schizoaffective Disorder **1878**
    Schizoid Personality Disorder **1881**
    Schizophreniform Disorder **1888**
    Somatization Disorder **1939**
    Stress Disorder, Acute **2007**
    Thoracic Disc Disorder with Myelopathy **2072**

Disorder of the Vagus Nerve
    Vagotonia **2237**

Disorders of Great Toe
    Hallux Rigidus **1027**

Disorders of the Penis
    Circumcision **514**
    Impotence **1198**
    Penis Disorders **1608**

Disorders of the Pneumogastric Nerve
    Vagotonia **2237**

Displacement
    Cervical Intervertebral Disc Without Myelopathy **728**
    Dislocation, Foot **716**
    Lumbar Intervertebral Disc Without Myelopathy **732**
    Thoracic Intervertebral Disc Without Myelopathy **735**

Displacement of Disc Without Myelopathy
    Displacement, Cervical Intervertebral Disc Without Myelopathy **728**
    Displacement, Lumbar Intervertebral Disc Without Myelopathy **732**
    Displacement, Thoracic Intervertebral Disc Without Myelopathy **735**

Dissecting
    Aortic Dissection **163**
    Thoracic Aneurysm **2070**

Dissecting Aneurysm
    Abdominal Aneurysm **3**
    Aortic Dissection **163**

Dissecting Aortic Hematoma
    Aortic Dissection **163**

Dissecting Hematoma
    Aortic Dissection **163**

Dissecting Thoracic Aneurysm
    Thoracic Aneurysm **2070**

Dissection
    Aortic Dissection **163**
    Myotomy of Esophagus **1433**

Dissection of Aorta
    Aortic Dissection **163**

Dissection of Esophagus
    Myotomy of Esophagus **1433**

Disseminated Gonococcal Disease
    Gonorrhea **1010**

Disseminated Multiple Sclerosis
    Multiple Sclerosis **1401**

Disseminated Periarteritis
    Polyarteritis Nodosa **1685**

Disseminated Sclerosis
    Multiple Sclerosis **1401**

Dissociative Disorder
    Dissociative Personality Disorder **737**
    Hysteria **1188**
    Neurotic Disorders **1475**

Dissociative Identity Disorder
    Dissociative Personality Disorder **737**

Distal Colon
    Abdominoperineal Resection of Rectum **10**
    Cancer, Colon **354**
    Colostomy and Ileostomy **543**
    Sigmoidoscopy **1925**

Distal Humerus Fracture
    Fracture, Elbow (Distal Humerus) **910**

Distal Pancreatectomy
    Pancreatectomy **1568**

Distal Radius and Ulna Fracture
    Fracture, Radius and Ulna, Distal **933**

Distal Sensorimotor Neuropathy
    Peripheral Neuropathy **1621**

Distal Sigmoid
    Abdominoperineal Resection of Rectum **10**
    Sigmoidoscopy **1925**

Distal Splenorenal Shunt
    Portal Systemic Shunt **1695**

Distal Tibial Nerve
    Dislocation, Femorotibial (Knee) Joint **713**

Distal Ulna Fracture
    Fracture, Radius and Ulna, Distal **933**

Disturbance of Conduct
    Adjustment Reaction with Predominant Disturbance of Conduct **74**

Disturbance of Emotions
    Adjustment Reaction with Predominant Disturbance of Conduct **74**

Disuse Atrophy
    Atrophy, Muscular **227, 230**

Dithiocarbonic Anhydride Poisoning
    Toxic Effects, Carbon Disulfide **2116**

Diverticula
    Diverticulosis and Diverticulitis of Colon **739**
    Esophageal Diverticula **836**
    Meckel's Diverticulum **1351**

Diverticular Inflammation
    Diverticulosis and Diverticulitis of Colon **739**

Diverticulitis
    Colon Resection **538**
    Colostomy and Ileostomy **543**
    Diverticulosis and Diverticulitis of Colon **739**
    Gastrointestinal Hemorrhage **982**

Diverticulitis and Diverticulosis of Colon
    Diverticulosis and Diverticulitis of Colon **739**
    Hemorrhage of Rectum and Anus **1068**

Diverticulosis
    and Diverticulitis of Colon **739**

Diverticulum
    Meckel's Diverticulum **1351**

Diverting Colostomy
    Colostomy and Ileostomy **543**

Index   2559

Diverting Ileostomy
    Colostomy and Ileostomy 543
Division of Esophagus
    Myotomy of Esophagus 1433
Dizziness
    and Giddiness 742
    Hypotension 1178
    Iron Deficiency Anemia 1242
    Stokes-Adams Syndrome 2003
    Subarachnoid Hemorrhage (Non-traumatic) 2011
    Tachycardia, Paroxysmal Supraventricular 2039
    Vertigo 2262
Donor
    Adrenal Tissue Implant or Transplant to Brain 76
    Bone Marrow Transplant 275
    Kidney Transplant 1261
    Skin Graft 1932
Dorsal Column Stimulation
    Spinal Cord Stimulation 1949
Dorsal Spine Pain
    Thoracic Spine Pain 2076
Double Vision
    Hyperinsulinism 1144
Drainage
    Abscess, Perirectal 34
    Abscess, Psoas 38
    Abscess, Renal and Perinephric 40
    Carbuncle 407
    Craniectomy 596
    Erysipelas 830
    Gastrostomy 984
    Gingival Abscess 991
    Incision and Drainage of Ischiorectal and/or Perirectal Abscess 1200
    Incision of Skin and Subcutaneous Tissue, Drainage of Abscess or Cyst 1201
    Mastoidectomy 1347
    Myringotomy 1434
    Postpartum Mastitis 1705
    Spondylitis 1958
    Thoracentesis 2069
    Thoracostomy 2078
    Thoracotomy 2079
    Trabeculectomy 2156
    Trabeculoplasty 2158
    Urethral Catheterization 2216
    Vagotomy 2235
Drainage of Abscess
    Abscess, Lung 29
    Incision of Skin and Subcutaneous Tissue, Drainage of Abscess or Cyst 1201
    Salpingitis 1870
Drainage of Abscess by Incision of Skin
    Incision of Skin and Subcutaneous Tissue, Drainage of Abscess or Cyst 1201
Drainage of Cyst
    Incision of Skin and Subcutaneous Tissue, Drainage of Abscess or Cyst 1201
Drainage of Cyst by Incision of Skin
    Incision of Skin and Subcutaneous Tissue, Drainage of Abscess or Cyst 1201
Drainage of Ischiorectal Abscess
    Incision and Drainage of Ischiorectal and/or Perirectal Abscess 1200
Drainage of Middle Ear Cavity
    Myringotomy 1434
Drainage of Perirectal Abscess
    Incision and Drainage of Ischiorectal and/or Perirectal Abscess 1200

Dressler's Syndrome
    Pericarditis, Acute 1615
Drug Abuse
    Addictions, Mixed 60
    Alcohol and Drug Detoxification and Rehabilitation 84
    Amphetamine Dependence/Abuse 113
    Cocaine Dependence/Abuse 522
    Delirium 644
    Human Immunodeficiency Virus 1126
    Marijuana Dependence/abuse 1341
    Palpitations 1566
Drug Allergy
    Allergic Dermatitis 96
    Contact Dermatitis 560
Drug Dependence
    Addictions, Mixed 60
    Alcohol and Drug Detoxification and Rehabilitation 84
    Amphetamine Dependence/Abuse 113
    Cocaine Dependence/Abuse 522
    Marijuana Dependence/abuse 1341
    Opioid Type Dependence 1516
    Sedative, Hypnotic or Anxiolytic Dependence 1898
Drug Detoxification
    Alcohol and Drug Detoxification and Rehabilitation 84
    Amphetamine Dependence/Abuse 113
Drug Rash
    Allergic Dermatitis 96
    Contact Dermatitis 560
Drug Rehabilitation
    Alcohol and Drug Detoxification and Rehabilitation 84
    Amphetamine Dependence/Abuse 113
Drug Treatment Program
    Alcohol and Drug Detoxification and Rehabilitation 84
Drug-Induced Hemolytic Anemia
    Hemolytic Anemia 1059
Drugs
    Addictions, Mixed 60
    Allergic Dermatitis 96
    Amphetamine Dependence/Abuse 113
    Cocaine Dependence/Abuse 522
    Contact Dermatitis 560
    Marijuana Dependence/abuse 1341
    Opioid Type Dependence 1516
    Psychopharmacotherapy 1743
    Sedative, Hypnotic or Anxiolytic Dependence 1898
Drunkenness
    Alcohol Intoxication, Acute 87
    Alcoholism 90
Dry Bronchiectasis
    Bronchiectasis 297
Dry Gangrene
    Arteriosclerotic Gangrene 186
    Gangrene 964
Dry-Eyes Disease
    Sjogren's Syndrome 1930
Dry-Mouth and Dry-Eyes Disease
    Sjogren's Syndrome 1930
DSP
    Toxic Effects, Fish and Shellfish 2126
DSRS
    Portal Systemic Shunt 1695

DUB
  Dysfunctional Uterine Bleeding 757
Duodenal
  Cancer, Small Intestine (Including Duodenum) 389
  Duodenitis 749
  Excision or Destruction of Duodenal Lesion 857
  Peptic Ulcer Disease 1611
  Resection of Gastric or Duodenal Ulcer Site 1819
Duodenal Cancer
  Cancer, Small Intestine (Including Duodenum) 389
Duodenal Inflammation
  Duodenitis 749
Duodenal Lesion Destruction
  Excision or Destruction of Duodenal Lesion 857
Duodenal Lesion Resection
  Resection of Gastric or Duodenal Ulcer Site 1819
Duodenal Ulcer
  Gastrectomy 968
  Peptic Ulcer Disease 1611
  Resection of Gastric or Duodenal Ulcer Site 1819
Duodenal Ulcer Site
  Gastrectomy 968
  Resection of Gastric or Duodenal Ulcer Site 1819
Duodenostomy
  Enterostomy 811
Duodenum
  Cancer, Small Intestine (Including Duodenum) 389
  Dumping Syndrome 747
  Duodenitis 749
  Endoscopy of Gastrointestinal Tract 810
  Enterostomy 811
  Esophagogastroduodenoscopy 850
  Excision or Destruction of Duodenal Lesion 857
  Gastrectomy 968
  Gastroenterostomy 978
  Giardiasis 989
  Peptic Ulcer Disease 1611
  Pyloric Stenosis, Acquired (Adult) Hypertrophic 1767
  Pyloroplasty 1769
  Pylorospasm 1770
  Resection of Gastric or Duodenal Ulcer Site 1819
  Upper Gastrointestinal Series 2214
Duodenum Enterostomy
  Enterostomy 811
Dupuytren's Contracture
  Dupuytren's Contracture 751
Dupuytren's Disease
  Dupuytren's Contracture 751
Dupuytren's Operation
  Dupuytren's Contracture 751
  Dupuytren's Release 753
Dupuytren's Release
  Dupuytren's Release 753
Dysarthria
  Aphasia 169
Dysentery
  Amebiasis 109
  Diarrhea 696
  Shigellosis 1910
Dysfunction
  Encephalopathy 799

Impotence 1198
Pain, Chronic 1564
Psychosexual Disorders 1745
Dysfunctional Bleeding
  Dysfunctional Uterine Bleeding 757
Dysfunctional Uterine Bleeding
  Aspiration Curettage of the Uterus 208
  Dilation and Curettage 699
Dysfunctional Uterine Hemorrhage
  Dysfunctional Uterine Bleeding 757
Dyskinesia
  Esophageal Spasm 839
Dyskinetic Cerebral Palsy
  Cerebral Palsy 452
Dysmenorrhea
  Menstrual Disorders 1369
  Pellagra 1602
Dysmorphic Body Disorder
  Social Phobia 1937
Dysmorphic Disorder
  Social Phobia 1937
Dyspepsia
  Achlorhydria and Hypochlorhydria 49
  Duodenitis 749
  Esophagitis 847
  Esophagogastroduodenoscopy 850
Dysplasia
  Cervical Dysplasia 467
  Fibrocystic Breast Disease 874
Dyspnea
  Abscess, Subdiaphragmatic 42
  Stokes-Adams Syndrome 2003
Dysrhythmia
  Arrhythmia 178
  Premature Beats 1719
Dyssocial Personality Disorder
  Antisocial Personality Disorder 156
Dyssomnia
  Insomnia with Sleep Apnea 1214
Dysspermia
  Infertility, Male 1206
Dyssplenism
  Hypersplenism 1154
Dysthymia
  Dysthymic Disorder 764
Dystrophy
  Complex Regional Pain Syndrome 550
  Retinitis Pigmentosa 1829

E

E Coli
  Traveler's Diarrhea 2177
E. Coli Gastroenteritis
  E. Coli 767
Ear Disorders
  Barotitis Media 241
  Cochlear Implant 529
  Hearing Loss 1036

Index 2561

Labyrinthitis 1267
Mastoiditis 1349
Meniere's Disease 1353
Myringotomy 1434
Otitis Externa, Infective 1543
Otitis Media 1545
Otosclerosis 1549
Stapedectomy 2002
Tinnitus 2097
Tympanum Perforation 2202
Vertigo 2262
Vestibular Neuronitis 2268

Ear Infection
Labyrinthitis 1267
Mastoidectomy 1347
Mastoiditis 1349
Myringotomy 1434
Otitis Externa, Infective 1543
Otitis Media 1545
Tympanum Perforation 2202

Ear Popping
Barotitis Media 241

Eardrum
Barotitis Media 241
Hearing Loss 1036
Myringotomy 1434
Otitis Media 1545
Stapedectomy 2002
Tympanoplasty 2201
Tympanum Perforation 2202

Eardrum Perforation
Tympanoplasty 2201
Tympanum Perforation 2202

Eardrum Repair
Tympanoplasty 2201

Early Labor
Premature Labor 1720

Early Onset of Delivery
Premature Labor 1720

Early or Threatened Labor
Premature Labor 1720

Eastern Equine Encephalitis (EEE)
Equine Encephalitis 827

Easy Bruising Syndrome
Purpura Simplex 1760

Eating Disorder
Enterostomy 811

Eaton's Pneumonia
Pneumonia 1667

Ecchymosis
Contusion 562, 564, 566, 568, 571
Muscle Injury 1406
Purpura Simplex 1760

ECG
Angina Pectoris 140
Angina, Unstable 144
Aortic Dissection 163
Aortic Valve Stenosis 167
Arrhythmia 178
Atrial Fibrillation 220
Atrioventricular Block Incomplete (Second-Degree) 223
Atrioventricular Block, Complete (Third-Degree) 224
Atrioventricular Block, Incomplete (First-Degree) 226

Biofeedback 250
Bundle Branch Block 310
Cardiac Arrest 409
Cardiac Catheterization 411
Cardiogenic Shock 417
Cardiomyopathy 419
Cardiovascular Disease in Pregnancy 422
Cor Pulmonale, Acute and Chronic 576
Coronary Atherosclerosis 587
Costochondritis 595
Electrocardiogram 781
Heart Block 1040
Palpitations 1566
Pleurodynia 1661
Premature Beats 1719
Rheumatic Heart Disease, Chronic 1836
Tachycardia, Paroxysmal Supraventricular 2039

Echo
Echocardiography 774

Echo Stress Testing
Cardiac Stress Test 416

Echocardiography
Aortic Dissection 163
Aortic Insufficiency 165
Aortic Valve Stenosis 167
Atrial Fibrillation 220
Cardiac Arrest 409
Cardiac Catheterization 411
Cardiomyopathy 419
Cardiovascular Disease in Pregnancy 422
Coarctation of the Aorta 519
Coronary Atherosclerosis 587
Endocarditis, Bacterial 802
Heart Murmur 1045
Hypertensive Heart Disease 1156
Mitral Stenosis 1387

Eclampsia
Cesarean Delivery 476
Preeclampsia and Eclampsia 1711

Ecological Illness
Allergy 100

ECT
Electroconvulsive Therapy 782

Ecthyma
Impetigo 1193

Ectopic
Pregnancy 775

Ectopic ACTH Syndrome
Cushing's Syndrome 613

Ectopic Endometrium
Endometriosis 805

Ectopic Pregnancy
Aspiration Curettage of the Uterus 208
Culdoscopy 610
Hematosalpinx 1053
Laparoscopy 1275
Salpingectomy 1868

Eczema
Atopic Dermatitis 218
Contact Dermatitis 560
Dermatitis 674
Erysipelas 830

Eczematous Dermatitis
Eczema 778

Edema
- Abscess, Subdiaphragmatic 42
- Angioedema 150
- Diabetic Glomerulosclerosis 690
- Erysipelas 830
- Glomerulonephritis, Acute 1001
- Joint Disorders 1251
- Nephrotic Syndrome 1456
- Pericarditis, Chronic Constrictive 1617
- Preeclampsia and Eclampsia 1711
- Premenstrual Syndrome 1724
- Pulmonary Edema 1756
- Renal Failure, Acute 1802
- Strep Throat 2005
- Sunburn 2019
- Thrombophlebitis 2086
- Thyroiditis 2091

Edema or Excessive Weight Gain in Pregnancy
- Preeclampsia and Eclampsia 1711

Edematous Laryngitis
- Laryngitis 1279

EEG
- Astrocytoma 214
- Cerebral Palsy 452
- Cerebrovascular Disease 458
- Electroencephalogram 783
- Epilepsy 824
- Narcolepsy 1439
- Petit Mal Epilepsy 1631
- Seizures 1900

EFF
- Eosinophilic Fasciitis 814

Effort Syndrome
- Neurocirculatory Asthenia 1467

EGD
- Endoscopy of Gastrointestinal Tract 810
- Esophagogastroduodenoscopy 850

Egyptian Ophthalmia
- Trachoma 2161

EHEC
- E. Coli 767

Ehrlich's Anemia
- Aplastic Anemia 171

EIEC
- E. Coli 767

EKG
- Chest Pain 486
- Electrocardiogram 781
- Myocardial Infarction, Acute 1424

Elbow
- Arthroplasty, Elbow 197
- Epicondylitis, Medial and Lateral 816
- Fracture, Elbow (Distal Humerus) 910
- Sprains and Strains, Elbow 1984

Elbow Arthroplasty
- Arthroplasty, Elbow 197

Elbow Epicondylitis
- Epicondylitis, Medial and Lateral 816

Elbow Fracture
- Arthroplasty, Elbow 197
- Fracture, Elbow (Distal Humerus) 910

Elbow Replacement
- Arthroplasty, Elbow 197

Elective Abortion
- Abortion by Dilation and Curettage for Termination of Pregnancy 11

Electrical Nerve Stimulator
- Atrophy, Muscular 227, 230
- Transcutaneous Electrical Nerve Stimulation 2164
- Ultrasound, Therapeutic 2213

Electroacupuncture
- Transcutaneous Electrical Nerve Stimulation 2164
- Ultrasound, Therapeutic 2213

Electrocardiogram
- Angina Pectoris 140
- Angina, Unstable 144
- Aortic Dissection 163
- Aortic Valve Stenosis 167
- Arrhythmia 178
- Atrial Fibrillation 220
- Atrioventricular Block Incomplete (Second-Degree) 223
- Atrioventricular Block, Complete (Third-Degree) 224
- Atrioventricular Block, Incomplete (First-Degree) 226
- Bundle Branch Block 310
- Cardiac Arrest 409
- Cardiac Catheterization 411
- Cardiogenic Shock 417
- Cardiomyopathy 419
- Cardiovascular Disease in Pregnancy 422
- Carotid Sinus Syncope 425
- Coarctation of the Aorta 519
- Coronary Atherosclerosis 587
- Dyspnea 761
- Embolism, Pulmonary 789
- Heart Block 1040
- Heart Murmur 1045
- Heat Stroke 1051
- High Blood Pressure, Malignant 1116
- Hypertensive Heart Disease 1156

Electrocardiograph Stress Testing
- Cardiac Stress Test 416

Electrocardiography
- Chest Pain 486
- Coronary Thrombolysis 593
- Electrocardiogram 781
- Heart Failure, Congestive 1042

Electrochemotherapy
- Iontophoresis 1236

Electrocoagulation
- Cervical Cauterization 461
- Gastrointestinal Hemorrhage 982
- Hemorrhage of Rectum and Anus 1068

Electroconvulsive Therapy
- Bipolar Affective Disorder 253, 256, 258, 260
- Bipolar Affective Disorder, Depressed 256
- Bipolar Affective Disorder, Mixed 258
- Bipolar Affective Disorder, Single Manic Episode 260
- Depression, Major 665
- Depressive Psychosis 670
- Psychotic Disorder, Brief 1749
- Schizophrenia 1882, 1885

Electrodiagnostic Study
- Electromyography 784

Electroencephalogram
- Astrocytoma 214
- Cerebral Palsy 452
- Cerebrovascular Disease 458

Index 2563

Encephalitis 797
Epilepsy 824
Equine Encephalitis 827
Fracture, Skull (Closed) 941
Grand Mal Seizure 1014
Hepatic Coma 1079

Electromyography
Amyotrophic Lateral Sclerosis 125
Botulism 286
Brachial Neuropathy 287
Dermatomyositis 677
Guillain-Barré Syndrome 1022

Electroneurography
Electromyography 784

Electronic Ear
Cochlear Implant 529

Electroshock Therapy
Electroconvulsive Therapy 782

Elemental Nickel Poisoning
Toxic Effects, Nickel and Inorganic Compounds 2146

Embedded Teeth
Impacted Tooth 1191

Embolectomy
Cardiogenic Shock 417
Embolism, Pulmonary 789
Pulmonary 787

Embolism
Peripheral Vascular Disease 1626
Pulmonary 789
Venous Embolism and Thrombosis 2252

Embolism and Thrombosis
Peripheral Vascular Disease 1626

Embolus
Angiocardiography 148
Arterial Embolism and Thrombosis 180
Cardiac Arrest 409
Carotid Artery Occlusion 423
Cerebral Hemorrhage 449
Cerebrovascular Accident 454
Embolectomy 786—787
Embolectomy, Pulmonary 787
Embolism, Pulmonary 789
Peripheral Vascular Disease 1626

Embryonal Carcinoma
Pineal Gland Neoplasm 1647

EMG
Amyotrophic Lateral Sclerosis 125
Brachial Neuropathy 287
Electromyography 784
Muscle Injury 1406
Myalgia and Myositis 1411
Nerve Injury 1460
Neuralgia, Neuritis, and Radiculitis 1465
Neuralgic Amyotrophy 1465
Peripheral Neuropathy 1621
Tetany 2062
Thoracic Outlet Syndrome 2074

Emotions
Cognitive Therapy 530
Delusional Disorder 649
Depersonalization Disorder 663
Obsessive-Compulsive Personality Disorder 1496
Organic Psychosis 1526

Psychotherapy, Group 1747
Psychotherapy, Individual 1748
Psychotic Disorder, Unspecified 1751
Schizoaffective Disorder 1878
Schizoid Personality Disorder 1881
Schizophrenia 1882, 1885
Schizophreniform Disorder 1888
Somatization Disorder 1939
Stress Disorder, Acute 2007

Emphysema
Bronchitis, Chronic 302
Chronic Obstructive Pulmonary Disease 511
Lung Excision 1314
Pneumoconiosis 1662
Pulmonary Function Tests 1758

Encephalitis
Aspiration 207—208
Delirium 644
Equine Encephalitis 827
St. Louis Encephalitis 2000

Encephalomyelitis
Encephalitis 797

Encephalopathy
Brain Injury 292
Enterostomy 811
Hepatic Coma 1079

Endarterectomy
Coarctation of the Aorta 519

Endarteritis Deformans
Atherosclerosis and Arteriosclerosis 216

Endocarditis
Bacterial 802
Carotid Artery Occlusion 423
Coarctation of the Aorta 519
Delirium 644
Heart Murmur 1045

Endocervicitis
Cervicitis 472

Endodermal Sinus Tumor
Pineal Gland Neoplasm 1647

Endodontics
Root Canal Therapy 1847

Endogenous Endophthalmitis
Endophthalmitis 808

Endogenous Hyperinsulinism
Hyperinsulinism 1144

Endolymphatic Hydrops
Meniere's Disease 1353

Endometrial
Aspiration Curettage of the Uterus 208
Cancer, Uterus 402
Dilation and Curettage 699
Endometriosis 805
Menstrual Disorders 1369
Postmenopausal Bleeding 1703
Uterine Polyps 2228

Endometrial Cancer
Aspiration Curettage of the Uterus 208
Cancer, Uterus 402

Endometrial Carcinoma
Cancer, Uterus 402

Endometrial Growths
  Uterine Polyps 2228

Endometrial Polyp
  Uterine Polyps 2228

Endometriosis
  Culdoscopy 610
  Endometriosis 805
  Uterine Polyps 2228

Endometrium
  Aspiration Curettage of the Uterus 208
  Cancer, Uterus 402
  Dilation and Curettage 699
  Postmenopausal Bleeding 1703
  Uterine Polyps 2228

Endometrium Disorders
  Cancer, Uterus 402
  Endometriosis 805
  Postmenopausal Bleeding 1703
  Uterine Polyps 2228

Endoscopic
  Bronchoscopic Biopsy 304
  Bronchoscopy 305
  Carpal Tunnel Release 428
  Culdoscopy 610
  Dilation of Esophagus 700
  Endoscopy of Gastrointestinal Tract 810
  Esophagogastroduodenoscopy 850
  Excision or Destruction of Duodenal Lesion 857
  Laryngoscopy 1281
  Ligation of Esophageal Varices 1288
  Lithotomy, Percutaneous 1294
  Lung Biopsy 1310
  Nasal Polypectomy 1440
  Sigmoidoscopy 1925
  Transurethral Balloon Dilation of Prostatic Urethra 2171

Endoscopic (Closed) Biopsy
  Bronchoscopic Biopsy 304

Endoscopic Biopsy
  Biopsy 252
  Bronchoscopic Biopsy 304
  Lung Biopsy 1310

Endoscopic Destruction of Duodenal Lesion
  Excision or Destruction of Duodenal Lesion 857

Endoscopic Exam of Upper Gastrointestinal Tract
  Endoscopy of Gastrointestinal Tract 810
  Esophagogastroduodenoscopy 850

Endoscopic Examination
  Bronchoscopic Biopsy 304
  Bronchoscopy 305
  Colonoscopy 540
  Culdoscopy 610
  Dilation of Esophagus 700
  Endoscopy of Gastrointestinal Tract 810
  Esophagogastroduodenoscopy 850
  Excision or Destruction of Duodenal Lesion 857
  Laryngoscopy 1281
  Ligation of Esophageal Varices 1288
  Lithotomy, Percutaneous 1294
  Lung Biopsy 1310
  Sigmoidoscopy 1925
  Transurethral Balloon Dilation of Prostatic Urethra 2171

Endoscopic Examination of Larynx
  Laryngoscopy 1281

Endoscopic Examination of Pelvic Cavity
  Culdoscopy 610

Endoscopic Examination of the Bronchi
  Bronchoscopy 305

Endoscopic Examination of Trachea
  Laryngoscopy 1281

Endoscopic Excision of Duodenal Lesion
  Excision or Destruction of Duodenal Lesion 857

Endoscopic Gastrostomy
  Gastrostomy 984

Endoscopic Lithotomy
  Lithotomy, Percutaneous 1294

Endoscopic Retrograde Cholangiopancreatography
  Cholangiography 493

Endoscopic Suspension of the Vesical Neck
  Vesicourethropexy 2265

Endoscopic Sympathectomy
  Sympathectomy 2022

Endoscopic Thoracic Sympathectomy
  Sympathectomy 2022

Endoscopic Transthoracic Sympathectomy
  Sympathectomy 2022

Endoscopy
  Bronchoscopic Biopsy 304
  Bronchoscopy 305
  Cancer, Colon 354
  Cancer, Esophagus 356
  Cancer, Pancreas 375
  Cancer, Rectum 384
  Cancer, Small Intestine (Including Duodenum) 389
  Cancer, Stomach 391
  Colitis 535
  Colonoscopy 540
  Culdoscopy 610
  Dilation of Esophagus 700
  Duodenitis 749
  Esophageal Diverticula 836
  Esophageal Spasm 839
  Esophageal Strictures 840
  Esophageal Varices 843
  Esophagitis 847
  Esophagogastroduodenoscopy 850
  Excision or Destruction of Duodenal Lesion 857
  Gastrectomy 968
  Gastritis 970
  Gastroesophageal Reflux 979
  Gastrointestinal Hemorrhage 982
  Gastrostomy 984
  Laryngoscopy 1281
  Ligation of Esophageal Varices 1288
  Lithotomy, Percutaneous 1294
  Nasal Polypectomy 1440
  of Gastrointestinal Tract 810
  Pancreatic Pseudocyst 1569
  Pancreatitis 1573
  Pyloric Stenosis, Acquired (Adult) Hypertrophic 1767
  Pylorospasm 1770
  Rhinoscleroma 1842
  Sigmoidoscopy 1925
  Transurethral Balloon Dilation of Prostatic Urethra 2171

Endoscopy of Colon
  Colonoscopy 540
  Hemorrhage of Rectum and Anus 1068
  Sigmoidoscopy 1925

Index 2565

Endoscopy of the Distal Colon
    Colonoscopy 540
    Sigmoidoscopy 1925
Endoscopy of the Gastrointestinal Tract
    Endoscopy of Gastrointestinal Tract 810
    Esophagogastroduodenoscopy 850
Endosurgical Myotomy
    Myotomy of Esophagus 1433
End-Stage Renal Disease
    Renal Failure, Chronic 1804
End-to-side Portacaval Shunt
    Portal Systemic Shunt 1695
Enlarged Spleen
    Hypersplenism 1154
    Splenectomy 1955
    Splenomegaly 1956
Enlarged Thyroid Gland
    Goiter 1008
    Hyperparathyroidism 1148
    Hyperthyroidism 1159
Enteral Feeding
    Enterostomy 811
Enteric Fever
    Typhoid Fever 2204
Enteritis
    Colitis 535
    Diarrhea 696
    Gastroenteritis, Non-Infectious 975
Enterocele Hernia Repair
    Hernia Repair, Vaginal 1096
Enterocolitis
    Ulcerative Colitis 2209
Enterohemorrhagic E. Coli
    E. Coli 767
Enteroinvasive E. Coli
    E. Coli 767
Enterospasm
    Irritable Bowel Syndrome 1244
Enterostomy
    Gastroenterostomy 978
Enterostomy of Duodenum
    Enterostomy 811
Enterotoxigenic E. Coli
    E. Coli 767
Enterovirulent E. Coli
    E. Coli 767
Enthesitis
    Enthesopathy 812
    Psoriatic Arthritis 1740
Environmental Hypersensitivity
    Multiple Chemical Sensitivity Syndrome 1397
Environmental Illness
    Allergy 100
    Multiple Chemical Sensitivity Syndrome 1397
Environmental Somatization Syndrome
    Allergy 100

EP
    Evoked Potentials 851
Epicondylitis
    Medial and Lateral 816
Epidemic Benign Dry Pleurisy
    Pleurodynia 1661
Epidemic Myalgia
    Pleurodynia 1661
Epidemic Pleurodynia
    Pleurodynia 1661
Epidemic Typhus
    Typhus Fever 2206
Epidermal Necrolysis
    Erythema Multiforme 833
Epidermodysplasia Verruciformis
    Warts, Viral 2298
Epidermoid Cyst
    Sebaceous Cyst 1896
Epidermophytosis
    Tinea 2095
Epididymis Disorders
    Epididymitis 819
    Hydrocele 1136
    Spermatocele 1942
Epidural Hematoma
    Craniectomy 596
    Intracranial Hemorrhage 1226, 1230
Epidural Hemorrhage
    Epidural Hematoma 821
    Intracranial Hemorrhage 1226, 1230
Epiglottis
    Epiglottitis 822
Epilepsy
    Craniotomy 598
    Electroencephalogram 783
    Grand Mal Seizure 1014
    Jacksonian Seizure 1247
    Petit Mal Epilepsy 1631
    Seizures 1900
Epileptic
    Epilepsy 824
    Grand Mal Seizure 1014
    Seizures 1900
Epileptic Convulsions
    Epilepsy 824
    Seizures 1900
Epileptic Fits
    Epilepsy 824
    Seizures 1900
Epileptic Seizure
    Epilepsy 824
    Grand Mal Seizure 1014
    Seizures 1900
Epiphrenic Diverticula
    Esophageal Diverticula 836
Episiotomy
    Perineorrhaphy 1618
Episodic Dyscontrol
    Explosive Personality Disorder 862

Intermittent Explosive Disorder 1217
Epispadias
Penis Disorders 1608
Epistaxis
Nosebleed 1485
Epithelial Carcinoma of the Ovary
Cancer, Ovary 372
Epstein Barr Virus
Hepatitis, Viral 1091
Malaise 1328
Mononucleosis 1390
Equine Encephalitis
Encephalitis 797
Equine Encephalomyelitis
Equine Encephalitis 827
ERCP
Cancer, Pancreas 375
Cholangiography 493
Erectile Dysfunction
Impotence 1198
Insertion of Inflatable Penile Prosthesis 1213
Erosion
Gastritis 970
Nasal Septum Perforation 1443
Peptic Ulcer Disease 1611
Erosive Gastritis
Gastritis 970
Eruptive Psoriasis
Psoriasis 1738
Erysipelotrichosis
Erysipeloid 831
Erythema
Multiforme 833
Nodosum 835
Erythema Migrans
Lyme Disease 1319
Erythema Nodosum
Sarcoidosis 1875
Erythremia
Polycythemia Vera 1689
Erythroblastosis Fetalis
Rh Incompatibility 1831
Erythroplasia
Penis Disorders 1608
Erythropoietic Porphyria
Porphyria 1693
Erythropoietic Protoporphyria
Porphyria 1693
Erythroprosopalgia
Cluster Headache 517
Escherichia Coli
E. Coli 767
Esophageal
Achalasia 44
Cancer, Esophagus 356
Colonoscopy 540
Dilation of Esophagus 700
Diverticula 836

Endoscopy of Gastrointestinal Tract 810
Esophagectomy 845
Esophagitis 847
Esophagogastroduodenoscopy 850
Gastroesophageal Reflux 979
Sclerotherapy 1895
Spasm 839
Strictures 840
Varices 843
Esophageal Achalasia
Achalasia 44
Esophageal Aperistalsis
Achalasia 44
Esophageal Cancer
Cancer, Esophagus 356
Dilation of Esophagus 700
Esophageal Strictures 840
Esophagectomy 845
Esophageal Dilation
Achalasia 44
Dilation of Esophagus 700
Esophageal Diverticula 836
Esophageal Strictures 840
Esophageal Dyskinesia
Esophageal Spasm 839
Esophageal Expansion
Dilation of Esophagus 700
Esophageal Inflammation
Esophagitis 847
Esophageal Reflux
Dilation of Esophagus 700
Esophageal Spasm 839
Esophageal Strictures 840
Esophagitis 847
Esophagogastroduodenoscopy 850
Gastroesophageal Reflux 979
Esophageal Resection
Esophagectomy 845
Esophageal Stenosis
Esophageal Strictures 840
Esophageal Stricture 840
Esophagectomy 845
Esophagogastroduodenoscopy 850
Esophageal Varices
Esophagogastroduodenoscopy 850
Gastrointestinal Hemorrhage 982
Esophageal Varices Injection
Sclerotherapy 1895
Esophageal Varix
Esophageal Varices 843
Ligation of Esophageal Varices 1288
Esophageal Varix Ligation
Ligation of Esophageal Varices 1288
Esophagectomy
Cancer, Esophagus 356
Esophagitis
Dyspepsia 759
Esophageal Diverticula 836
Esophagogastroduodenoscopy 850
Gastrointestinal Hemorrhage 982

Esophagogastroduodenoscopy
    Colonoscopy 540
    Endoscopy of Gastrointestinal Tract 810

Esophagoscopy
    Cancer, Esophagus 356
    Colonoscopy 540
    Endoscopy of Gastrointestinal Tract 810
    Esophagogastroduodenoscopy 850

Esophagospasm
    Esophageal Spasm 839

Esophagus
    Achalasia 44
    Cancer, Esophagus 356
    Dilation of Esophagus 700
    Endoscopy of Gastrointestinal Tract 810
    Esophageal Diverticula 836
    Esophageal Spasm 839
    Esophageal Strictures 840
    Esophageal Varices 843
    Esophagectomy 845
    Esophagitis 847
    Esophagogastroduodenoscopy 850
    Gastroesophageal Reflux 979
    Gastrointestinal Hemorrhage 982
    Mallory-Weiss Syndrome 1333
    Myotomy of Esophagus 1433
    Scleroderma 1892
    Sclerotherapy 1895

Essential Anemia
    Anemia 133, 136

Essential Hypertension
    High Blood Pressure, Benign 1112
    Hypertensive Heart Disease 1156

Essential Tremor
    Tremor 2179

Established Atrial Fibrillation
    Atrial Fibrillation 220

ESWL
    Calculus, Renal (Kidney and Ureter) 335
    Lithotripsy, Extracorporeal Shock Wave 1295

ETEC
    E. Coli 767

Ethinyl Trichloride Poisoning
    Toxic Effects, Chlorinated Hydrocarbon Solvents 2120

Ethmoidal Sinusitis
    Sinusitis 1928

Ethylene Tetrachloride Poisoning
    Toxic Effects, Chlorinated Hydrocarbon Solvents 2120

Ethylene Trichloride Poisoning
    Toxic Effects, Chlorinated Hydrocarbon Solvents 2120

Eustachian Tube Dysfunction
    Barotitis Media 241
    Otitis Media 1545
    Tympanum Perforation 2202

Ewing's Sarcoma
    Cancer, Bone 341

Ex Anopsia
    Amblyopia, Toxic 107

Excessive
    Hyperinsulinism 1144
    Hyperkalemia 1146
    Hyperparathyroidism 1148
    Hypersensitivity Pneumonitis 1150
    Hypersomnia 1152
    Hypersplenism 1154
    Hypertensive Heart Disease 1156
    Hyperthyroidism 1159
    Hyperventilation Syndrome 1161
    Hypervitaminosis 1164, 1166, 1168
    Hypervitaminosis A 1166
    Hypervitaminosis D 1168

Excessive Blood Insulin Level
    Hyperinsulinism 1144

Excessive Daytime Sleepiness
    Hypersomnia 1152

Excessive Parathyroid Hormone Disease
    Hyperparathyroidism 1148

Excision
    Abdominoperineal Resection of Rectum 10
    Adrenalectomy 77
    Appendectomy 174
    Breast Biopsy 295
    Cervical Polypectomy 469
    Cholecystectomy 495
    Chromoblastomycosis 508
    Cryotherapy, Genital Warts (Female) 605
    Cryotherapy, Genital Warts (Male) 606
    Cystectomy 615
    Embolectomy 786—787
    Embolectomy, Pulmonary 787
    Fusion, and Repair of Toes 860
    Gingivectomy 992
    Hysterectomy 1186
    Laryngectomy 1278
    Lung Excision 1314
    Nephrectomy 1451
    of Bone Spur, Foot 852
    Oophorectomy 1501, 1503
    Oophorectomy, Bilateral 1503
    or Destruction of Duodenal Lesion 857
    or Destruction of Plantar Warts 858
    Orchiectomy 1523
    Osteoma 1536
    Pancreatectomy 1568
    Pilonidal Cyst 1645
    Pneumonectomy 1664
    Prostatectomy 1729
    Rectal Polyps 1783
    Rectal Ulcer 1788
    Rib Resection 1844
    Salpingectomy 1868
    Salpingo-oophorectomy 1873
    Sebaceous Cyst 1896
    Skin or Subcutaneous Tissue Biopsy 1934
    Spermatocelectomy 1943
    Splenectomy 1955
    Thrombectomy 2082
    Thymectomy 2089
    Thyroidectomy 2090
    Toenail, Ingrown 2100

Excision of Adrenal Gland
    Adrenalectomy 77

Excision of Anal Fissure
    Fissurectomy, Anal 884

Excision of Anus
    Abdominoperineal Resection of Rectum 10

Excision of Appendix
    Appendectomy 174

Excision of Bladder
    Cystectomy 615
Excision of Blood Clot
    Thrombectomy 2082
Excision of Both Fallopian Tubes
    Salpingectomy 1868
Excision of Breast Lesion
    Breast Biopsy 295
Excision of Cervical Polyps
    Cervical Polypectomy 469
Excision of Distal Sigmoid
    Abdominoperineal Resection of Rectum 10
Excision of Duodenal Lesion
    Excision or Destruction of Duodenal Lesion 857
Excision of Embolism
    Embolectomy 786–787
Excision of Entire Lung
    Pneumonectomy 1664
Excision of Esophagus
    Esophagectomy 845
Excision of Fallopian Tube and Ovary
    Salpingo-oophorectomy 1873
Excision of Fallopian Tubes
    Salpingectomy 1868
Excision of Foot Bone Spur
    Excision of Bone Spur, Foot 852
Excision of Gallbladder
    Cholecystectomy 495
Excision of Gingival Tissue
    Gingivectomy 992
Excision of Intervertebral Disc
    Discectomy 703
Excision of Kidney
    Nephrectomy 1451
Excision of Larynx
    Laryngectomy 1278
Excision of Lesion
    or Tissue of Skin and Subcutaneous Tissue 854
    Skin or Subcutaneous Tissue Biopsy 1934
Excision of Lung
    Lung Excision 1314
    Pneumonectomy 1664
Excision of Nail
    Nail Bed, or Nail Fold 856
Excision of Nail Bed
    Excision of Nail, Nail Bed, or Nail Fold 856
Excision of Nail Fold
    Excision of Nail, Nail Bed, or Nail Fold 856
Excision of Ovary
    Cancer, Ovary 372
    Oophorectomy 1501, 1503
    Oophorectomy, Bilateral 1503
Excision of Pancreas
    Pancreatectomy 1568
Excision of Partial Lung
    Lung Excision 1314

Excision of Penile Foreskin
    Circumcision 514
Excision of Peripheral Neuroma
    Excision of Morton's Neuroma 855
Excision of Plantar Warts
    Excision or Destruction of Plantar Warts 858
Excision of Prostate Gland
    Prostatectomy 1729
Excision of Pulmonary Embolism
    Embolectomy, Pulmonary 787
Excision of Rectum
    Abdominoperineal Resection of Rectum 10
Excision of Rib
    Rib Resection 1844
Excision of Skin Tissue
    Excision of Lesion or Tissue of Skin and Subcutaneous Tissue 854
    Skin or Subcutaneous Tissue Biopsy 1934
Excision of Spermatocele
    Spermatocelectomy 1943
Excision of Spleen
    Splenectomy 1955
Excision of Subcutaneous Tissue
    Excision of Lesion or Tissue of Skin and Subcutaneous Tissue 854
    Skin or Subcutaneous Tissue Biopsy 1934
Excision of Testes
    Orchiectomy 1523
Excision of Testis
    Orchiectomy 1523
Excision of the Uterus
    Hysterectomy 1186
Excision of Thrombus
    Thrombectomy 2082
Excision of Thymus Gland
    Thymectomy 2089
Excision of Thyroid Gland
    Thyroidectomy 2090
Excision of Toes
    Excision of Nail, Nail Bed, or Nail Fold 856
Excision of Total Lung
    Pneumonectomy 1664
Excision of Uterus
    Hysterectomy 1186
Excisional Biopsy
    Excision of Lesion or Tissue of Skin and Subcutaneous Tissue 854
    Skin or Subcutaneous Tissue Biopsy 1934
Excretory Urogram
    Intravenous Pyelogram 1233
Excretory Urography
    Intravenous Pyelogram 1233
Exercise Stress Test
    Cardiac Stress Test 416
Exercise Tolerance Test
    Cardiac Stress Test 416
Exertion Angina
    Angina Pectoris 140

Exhaust Gas Poisoning
　Toxic Effects, Carbon Monoxide 2117

Exhaustion
　Nervous Fatigue 1462

Exogenous Endophthalmitis
　Endophthalmitis 808

Exophthalmic Goiter
　Hyperthyroidism 1159

Exostectomy
　Excision of Bone Spur, Foot 852
　Hammertoe 1029

Exostosis
　Excision of Bone Spur, Foot 852
　Heel Spur (Calcaneal) 1053
　Osteoma 1536

Expansion
　Dilation of Esophagus 700

Exploratory Abdominal Surgery
　Laparotomy 1276

Exploratory Laparotomy
　Laparotomy 1276

Explosive Disorder
　Explosive Personality Disorder 862
　Intermittent Explosive Disorder 1217

Explosive Personality Disorder
　Intermittent Explosive Disorder 1217

Expressive Aphasia
　Aphasia 169

External Hemorrhoids
　Hemorrhoid Treatment 1070
　Hemorrhoids 1073

External Hordeolum
　Stye 2010

Extracorporeal Shock Wave Lithotripsy
　Calculus, Renal (Kidney and Ureter) 335
　Cholelithiasis 501
　Lithotripsy, Extracorporeal Shock Wave 1295

Extraction
　Tooth Extraction 2107

Extradural Hematoma
　Epidural Hematoma 821

Extradural Hemorrhage
　Epidural Hematoma 821

Extrapulmonary Respiration Failure
　Adult Respiratory Distress Syndrome 79
　Respiratory Failure 1821

Extreme Stress Response
　Posttraumatic Stress Disorder 1707

Extremity Varix
　Varicose Veins 2246

Extrinsic Allergic Alveolitis
　Humidifier Fever 1130
　Hypersensitivity Pneumonitis 1150
　Ventilation Pneumonitis 2254

Exudative Bronchitis
　Bronchitis, Acute 299

Eye Burn
　Burn of Eye 316

Eye Contusion
　Contusion, Eye 564

Eye Disorders
　Amblyopia, Toxic 107
　Astigmatism 212
　Blepharitis 268
　Blindness 270
　Cataract 436, 439
　Chorioretinitis 506
　Conjunctivitis 556
　Contusion, Eye 564
　Corneal Abrasion 580
　Corneal Ulcer 584
　Dacryocystitis 627
　Dacryostenosis 629
　Diabetic Retinopathy 694
　Dry Eye Syndrome 745
　Endophthalmitis 808
　Foreign Body, Cornea 891
　Glaucoma, Acute (Angle-Closure) 995
　Glaucoma, Chronic (Open-Angle) 997
　Iridectomy 1238
　Iridotomy 1239
　Iritis 1240
　Keratectomy, Laser Photorefractive 1256
　Keratitis 1257
　Keratoconus 1259
　Myasthenia Gravis 1414
　Myopia 1431
　Nystagmus 1487
　Optic Atrophy 1519
　Optic Neuritis 1521
　Pterygium 1754
　Radial Keratotomy 1775
　Retinal Detachment 1823, 1825
　Retinal Vascular Occlusion 1827
　Retinitis Pigmentosa 1829
　Senile Macular Degeneration 1903
　Stye 2010
　Uveitis 2231

Eye Inflammation
　Iritis 1240
　Keratitis 1257
　Uveitis 2231

F

Face
　Cushing's Syndrome 613
　Erysipelas 830
　Folliculitis 887
　Furuncle 961
　Impetigo 1193
　Lift 865
　Myasthenia Gravis 1414
　Scleroderma 1892
　Sebaceous Cyst 1896
　Sinusitis 1928
　Trigeminal Neuralgia 2187

Facial Burn
　Burn of Head and Neck (Includes Face) 318

Factitious Illness
　with Physical Symptoms 866
　with Psychological Symptoms 868

Factor II Deficiency
　Hypoprothrombinemia 1176

Factor IX Deficiency
- Hemophilia B 1064

Factor IX Hemophilia
- Hemophilia B 1064

Factor VIII Deficiency
- Hemophilia A 1061

Factor VIII Deficiency Hemophilia
- Hemophilia A 1061

Factor VIII Disorder
- Hemophilia A 1061

Failed Back Surgery Syndrome
- Post-Laminectomy Syndrome 1701

Failure
- Adult Respiratory Distress Syndrome 79
- Cor Pulmonale, Acute and Chronic 576
- Renal Failure, Acute 1802
- Renal Failure, Chronic 1804
- Respiratory Failure 1821

Fainting
- Carotid Sinus Syncope 425
- Hyperventilation Syndrome 1161
- Hypoglycemia 1171
- Hypotension 1178
- Stokes-Adams Syndrome 2003
- Syncope 2024
- Vasovagal Syncope 2249

Faintness
- Dizziness and Giddiness 742

Falciparum Malaria
- Malaria 1330

Fallopian Tube
- Ectopic Pregnancy 775
- Endometriosis 805
- Hysterectomy 1186
- Paraovarian Cyst 1590
- Pelvic Inflammatory Disease 1604
- Salpingectomy 1868
- Salpingitis 1870
- Salpingo-oophorectomy 1873
- Tubal Ligation 2193

Fallopian Tube Infarction
- Hematosalpinx 1053

Fallopian Tube Inflammation
- Hematosalpinx 1053

Familial
- Atrophy, Muscular (Progressive) 230
- Cardiomyopathy 419
- Diabetes Mellitus Type I 683, 686
- Hyperthyroidism 1159
- Lipoma 1290
- Myopia 1431
- Neurofibromatosis 1469
- Neutropenia 1477
- Nystagmus 1487
- Obesity, Simple 1491
- Osler-Weber-Rendu Disease 1528
- Osteoporosis 1540
- Sickle Cell Anemia 1922
- Spherocytosis, Hereditary 1944
- Thalassemia 2066
- Wilson's Disease 2300

Familial Cardiomyopathy
- Cardiomyopathy 419

Familial Hemolytic Anemia
- Hemolytic Anemia 1059

Familial Hemorrhagic Telangiectasia
- Osler-Weber-Rendu Disease 1528

Familial Muscular Atrophy
- Atrophy, Muscular (Progressive) 230

Farmer's Lung
- Hypersensitivity Pneumonitis 1150

Fascia
- Dupuytren's Contracture 751
- Dupuytren's Release 753
- Eosinophilic Fasciitis 814
- Fasciotomy 870
- Myalgia and Myositis 1411
- Plantar Fasciitis 1655
- Psoriatic Arthritis 1740

Fascial Inflammation
- Eosinophilic Fasciitis 814
- Plantar Fasciitis 1655
- Psoriatic Arthritis 1740

Fascial Sling Procedure
- Vesicourethropexy 2265

Fascicular Block
- Bundle Branch Block 310

Fasciitis
- Eosinophilic Fasciitis 814
- Plantar Fasciitis 1655

Fasciotomy
- Compartment Syndrome 547
- Dupuytren's Contracture 751
- Gangrene 964

Fat
- Arterial Embolism and Thrombosis 180
- Lipoma 1290
- Liposuction 1292
- Obesity, Simple 1491

Fat Emboli
- Arterial Embolism and Thrombosis 180

Fatigue
- Anemia Complicating Pregnancy 136
- Chronic Fatigue Syndrome 509
- Iron Deficiency Anemia 1242
- Malaise 1328
- Multiple Chemical Sensitivity Syndrome 1397
- Radiation Therapy 1778
- Thyroiditis 2091
- Vitamin B_1 Deficiency 2272

Fatigue Syndrome
- Chronic Fatigue Syndrome 509
- Malaise 1328

Fatty Tumor
- Lipoma 1290

Fear of Crowds
- Phobias, Specific 1639
- Phobic Disorders 1641

Fear of Open Spaces
- Panic Disorder with Agoraphobia 1580

Fecalith
- Constipation 558

Feeding Enterostomy
    Enterostomy 811

Feet
    Contusion, Lower Limb 566
    Diabetic Gangrene 689
    Metatarsalgia 1376
    Morton's Neuroma 1393
    Plantar Fasciitis 1655
    Psoriatic Arthritis 1740
    Sprains and Strains, Foot 1986
    Tarsal Tunnel Release 2041
    Tarsal Tunnel Syndrome 2043
    Tinea 2095
    Warts, Plantar 2296

Female
    Abortion by Dilation and Curettage for Termination of Pregnancy 11
    Abortion, Medical Induction 13
    Abruptio Placentae 16
    Abscess, Breast 22
    Anemia Complicating Pregnancy 136
    Bartholin's Gland Cyst 242
    Cancer, Cervix 351
    Cancer, Ovary 372
    Cancer, Uterus 402
    Caruncle of the Urethra, Benign 434
    Cervical Biopsy 460
    Cervical Cauterization 461
    Cervical Dysplasia 467
    Cervical Polypectomy 469
    Cervical Polyps 470
    Cervicitis 472
    Choriocarcinoma 505
    Cryotherapy, Genital Warts (Female) 605
    Culdoscopy 610
    Cystocele or Rectocele 621
    Dilation and Curettage 699
    Dysfunctional Uterine Bleeding 757
    Ectopic Pregnancy 775
    Endometriosis 805
    Episiotomy 826
    Fibrocystic Breast Disease 874
    Gestational Diabetes 988
    Hematosalpinx 1053
    Hydatidiform Mole 1134
    Hyperemesis Gravidarum 1142
    Hysterectomy 1186
    Infertility, Female 1204
    Mammography 1337
    Menopause 1368
    Menstrual Disorders 1369
    Miscarriage 1381
    Myomectomy, Uterine 1430
    Oophorectomy 1501, 1503
    Ovarian Cyst, Benign 1552
    Ovarian Cyst, Resection of 1555
    Paraovarian Cyst 1590
    Pelvic Inflammatory Disease 1604
    Perineorrhaphy 1618
    Placenta Accreta 1651
    Placenta Previa 1653
    Postmenopausal Bleeding 1703
    Postpartum Mastitis 1705
    Preeclampsia and Eclampsia 1711
    Pregnancy, Multiple Gestation 1714
    Pregnancy, Normal 1716
    Premature Labor 1720
    Premature Rupture of Membranes 1722
    Premenstrual Syndrome 1724
    Rh Incompatibility 1831
    Salpingectomy 1868
    Salpingitis 1870
    Salpingo-oophorectomy 1873
    Threatened Abortion 2080
    Trichomoniasis 2185
    Tubal Ligation 2193
    Urethrocele with Stress Incontinence 2220
    Urinary Incontinence in Women 2222
    Uterine Polyps 2228
    Uterus, Perforation of 2229
    Vaginitis 2233
    Vesicovaginal Fistula 2266

Female Infertility
    Infertility, Female 1204

Female Menopause
    Menopause 1368

Female Sterilization
    Tubal Ligation 2193

Female Urethrocele
    Cystocele or Rectocele 621
    Urethrocele with Stress Incontinence 2220
    Urinary Incontinence in Women 2222

Femoral
    Fracture, Femoral Neck 912

Femoral Head
    Avascular Necrosis 235

Femoral Hernia
    Hernia, Inguinal and Femoral 1103

Femoral Hernia Repair
    Hernia Repair 1094, 1096

Femoral Herniation
    Hernia, Inguinal and Femoral 1103

Femoral Neck
    Fracture, Femoral Neck 912

Femorotibial Joint Dislocation
    Dislocation, Femorotibial (Knee) Joint 713

Femur
    Fracture, Femoral Neck 912
    Hip Replacement, Total 1119

FEV1
    Pulmonary Function Tests 1758

Fever
    Colorado Tick Fever 541
    Dengue Fever 656
    Rheumatic Fever, Acute 1833
    Rocky Mountain Spotted Fever 1845
    Typhoid Fever 2204
    Typhus Fever 2206
    Yellow Fever 2307

Fever Blister
    Herpes Simplex 1108

Fiberoptic Colonoscopy
    Colonoscopy 540

Fibrillation
    Atrial Fibrillation 220
    Ventricular Fibrillation 2256

Fibrinogen Deficiency
    Afibrinogenemia 81

Fibrocystic Breast
    Disease 874

Fibroid Tumor in Uterus
    Dilation and Curettage **699**
    Fibroid Tumor of Uterus **875**

Fibroleiomyoma
    Fibroid Tumor of Uterus **875**

Fibroma
    Prostatic Hypertrophy **1731**

Fibromyalgia
    and Myofascial Pain Syndrome **879**
    Arthralgia **190**
    Myalgia and Myositis **1411**

Fibromyoma of Uterus
    Fibroid Tumor of Uterus **875**

Fibromyositis
    Fibromyalgia and Myofascial Pain Syndrome **879**
    Myalgia and Myositis **1411**

Fibrosing Alveolitis
    Interstitial Pulmonary Fibrosis **1219**

Fibrositis
    Fibromyalgia and Myofascial Pain Syndrome **879**
    Myalgia and Myositis **1411**

Fibrotic Lung Disease
    Interstitial Pulmonary Fibrosis **1219**
    Sarcoidosis **1875**

Fibula Fracture
    Fracture, Tibia or Fibula **951**

Filarial Infestation
    Filariasis **881**

Filtering Surgery
    Trabeculectomy **2156**

Fine Needle Aspiration
    Aspiration **207–208**

Finger
    Amputation **116, 118, 121, 123**
    Amputation, Finger or Thumb **123**
    Fracture, Fingers and Thumb **915**
    Radial Styloid Tenosynovitis **1776**
    Reduction of Fracture or Dislocation **1791**
    Sprains and Strains, Hand or Fingers **1989**
    Trigger Finger or Thumb **2191**

Finger Amputation
    Amputation, Finger or Thumb **123**

Finger Fracture
    Fracture, Fingers and Thumb **915**

Finger Sprain
    Sprains and Strains, Hand or Fingers **1989**

First Degree
    Atrioventricular Block, Incomplete (First-Degree) **226**
    Sprains and Strains, Ankle **1971**
    Sprains and Strains, Back **1975**
    Sprains and Strains, Elbow **1984**
    Sprains and Strains, Foot **1986**
    Sprains and Strains, Hand or Fingers **1989**
    Sprains and Strains, Knee **1991**
    Sprains and Strains, Wrist **1997**
    Sunburn **2019**

First Degree AV Block
    Atrioventricular Block, Incomplete (First-Degree) **226**

First Degree Incomplete AV Block
    Atrioventricular Block, Incomplete (First-Degree) **226**

First Metatarsophalangeal Joint Arthritis
    Hallux Rigidus **1027**

First-Degree AV Block
    Atrioventricular Block, Incomplete (First-Degree) **226**

First-Degree Incomplete AV Block
    Atrioventricular Block, Incomplete (First-Degree) **226**

Fish Rose
    Erysipeloid **831**

Fish-Handler's Disease
    Erysipeloid **831**

Fissure
    Abscess, Perirectal **34**
    Anal Fissure and/or Rectal Ulcer **127**
    Postpartum Mastitis **1705**
    Fissurectomy, Anal **884**

Fissure in Ano
    Anal Fissure and/or Rectal Ulcer **127**

Fissure of Anus
    Anal Fissure and/or Rectal Ulcer **127**

Fissurectomy
    Anal **884**
    Incision and Drainage of Ischiorectal and/or Perirectal Abscess **1200**

Fistula
    Abscess, Perirectal **34**
    Anorectal Fistula **154**
    Bladder Fistulas **262**
    Vesicovaginal Fistula **2266**

Fistula in Ano
    Anorectal Fistula **154**

Fits
    Epilepsy **824**
    Seizures **1900**

Fixation of Kidney
    Nephropexy **1455**

Fixed Rate Pacemaker
    Cardiac Pacemaker Insertion **414**

Flat Warts
    Warts, Viral **2298**

Flax Dresser's Disease
    Byssinosis **328**

Flea-Borne Typhus
    Typhus Fever **2206**

Flexible Colonoscopy
    Colonoscopy **540**

Flexible Sigmoidoscopy
    Sigmoidoscopy **1925**

Flexor Muscle Tendinitis
    Biceps Tendonitis **248**

Floppy Mitral Valve
    Mitral Insufficiency **1385**
    Mitral Valve Prolapse **1389**

Floppy Valve
    Mitral Valve Prolapse **1389**

Flu
    Influenza **1207**

Flue Gas Poisoning
    Toxic Effects, Carbon Monoxide **2117**

Fluid Accumulation in Scrotum
  Hydrocele 1136
Fluid Loss
  Dehydration 642
  Intravenous Therapy 1235
Fluorhydric Acid Poisoning
  Toxic Effects, Hydrofluoric Acid 2132
Fluoric Acid Poisoning
  Toxic Effects, Hydrofluoric Acid 2132
Fluoroscopy
  Cancer, Pancreas 375
  Cystocele or Rectocele 621
  X-ray 2305
Flutter
  Atrial Fibrillation 220
  Premature Beats 1719
  Ventricular Fibrillation 2256
Focal and Segmental Hyalinosis
  Glomerulosclerosis 1005
Focal Glomerulosclerosis
  Glomerulosclerosis 1005
Focal Sclerosis with Hyalinosis
  Glomerulosclerosis 1005
Focal Seizure
  Jacksonian Seizure 1247
Folate Acid Deficiency
  Folic Acid Deficiency Anemia 885
Folate Malabsorption
  Folic Acid Deficiency Anemia 885
Foley Catheterization
  Urethral Catheterization 2216
Folic Acid Deficiency
  Anemia 885
  Anemia Complicating Pregnancy 136
  Vitamin B_{12} Deficiency 2277
Folic Acid Deficiency Anemia
  Anemia Complicating Pregnancy 136
Folic Acid Poisoning
  Poisoning, Vitamin B 1679
Folie a Deux
  Delusional Disorder 649
Follicular Carcinoma
  Cancer, Thyroid Gland 396
Follicular Cysts
  Ovarian Cyst, Benign 1552
Follicular Infundibular Cyst
  Sebaceous Cyst 1896
Follicular Lymphoma
  Non-Hodgkin's Lymphoma 1482
Follicular Predominantly Large Cell Lymphoma
  Non-Hodgkin's Lymphoma 1482
Follicular Small Cleaved Cell Lymphoma
  Non-Hodgkin's Lymphoma 1482
Folliculitis
  Furuncle 961
  Sebaceous Cyst 1896

Food
  Anaphylactic Shock, Food Reaction 131
  Botulism 286
  E. Coli 767
  Gastroenteritis, Infectious 973
  Nausea 1446
  Salmonellosis 1866
  Shigellosis 1910
  Traveler's Diarrhea 2177
Food Reaction
  Anaphylactic Shock, Food Reaction 131
  Nausea 1446
Food-Borne Disease
  Food Poisoning 888
  Toxoplasmosis 2154
  Traveler's Diarrhea 2177
  Trichinosis 2183
Foot
  Amputation (Traumatic), Foot 118
  Arteriosclerotic Gangrene 186
  Bunion 312
  Bunionectomy 314
  Corn and Callus, Infected 578
  Diabetic Gangrene 689
  Dislocation, Foot 716
  Excision of Bone Spur, Foot 852
  Excision of Morton's Neuroma 855
  Excision or Destruction of Plantar Warts 858
  Fracture, Calcaneus 898
  Fracture, Forefoot (Sesamoid, Phalanges) 918
  Fracture, Metatarsal Bones 925
  Fracture, Midfoot (Cuboid, Cuneiform, Navicular) 928
  Hallux Rigidus 1027
  Metatarsalgia 1376
  Morton's Neuroma 1393
  Pain in Limb 1562
  Peripheral Vascular Disease 1626
  Plantar Fasciitis 1655
  Psoriatic Arthritis 1740
  Repair, Hammertoe 1816
  Sprains and Strains, Foot 1986
  Tarsal Tunnel Release 2041
  Tarsal Tunnel Syndrome 2043
  Tinea 2095
  Warts, Plantar 2296
  Warts, Viral 2298
Foot Amputation
  Amputation (Traumatic), Foot 118
Foot Dislocation
  Dislocation, Foot 716
Foot Fracture
  Fracture, Forefoot (Sesamoid, Phalanges) 918
  Fracture, Metatarsal Bones 925
  Fracture, Midfoot (Cuboid, Cuneiform, Navicular) 928
Foot Pain
  Excision of Bone Spur, Foot 852
  Excision of Morton's Neuroma 855
  Excision or Destruction of Plantar Warts 858
  Heel Spur (Calcaneal) 1053
  Metatarsalgia 1376
  Morton's Neuroma 1393
  Pain in Limb 1562
  Sprains and Strains, Foot 1986
  Tarsal Tunnel Syndrome 2043
Foot Phalanges
  Bunion 312

Bunionectomy 314
Corn and Callus, Infected 578
Dislocation, Foot 716
Excision of Nail, Nail Bed, or Nail Fold 856
Excision, Fusion, and Repair of Toes 860
Fracture, Forefoot (Sesamoid, Phalanges) 918
Hallux Rigidus 1027
Hammertoe 1029
Metatarsus Primus Varus 1378
Repair, Hammertoe 1816
Toenail, Ingrown 2100

Foot Sprain
Sprains and Strains, Foot 1986

Foot Strain
Sprains and Strains, Foot 1986

Footballer's Groin
Groin Strain 1020

Foraminotomy
Laminectomy or Laminotomy 1273
Spinal Fusion 1951
Spinal Stenosis 1952

Forearm
Arthroplasty, Elbow 197
Compartment Syndrome 547
Enthesopathy 812
Epicondylitis, Medial and Lateral 816
Fracture, Carpal Bones 901
Fracture, Radius and Ulna, Distal 933
Sprains and Strains, Elbow 1984
Sprains and Strains, Wrist 1997

Forearm Fracture
Fracture, Carpal Bones 901
Fracture, Radius and Ulna, Distal 933

Forefoot
Dislocation, Foot 716
Fracture, Forefoot (Sesamoid, Phalanges) 918
Fracture, Metatarsal Bones 925
Hallux Rigidus 1027
Morton's Neuroma 1393
Sprains and Strains, Foot 1986

Foreign Body on Cornea
Foreign Body, Cornea 891

Foreskin
Circumcision 514
Penis Disorders 1608

Foreskin Removal
Circumcision 514

Formaldehyde
Toxic Effects, Formaldehyde 2129

Formaldehyde Poisoning
Toxic Effects, Formaldehyde 2129

Formalin Poisoning
Toxic Effects, Formaldehyde 2129

Foundry Fever
Metal Fume Fever 1374

Fournier's Gangrene
Gangrene 964

Fracture
Ankle 895
Bone Graft 272
Calcaneus 898
Carpal Bones 901

Cervical Spine (With or Without Spinal Cord Injury) 904
Clavicle 907
Elbow (Distal Humerus) 910
Fasciotomy 870
Femoral Neck 912
Fingers and Thumb 915
Forefoot (Sesamoid, Phalanges) 918
Lumbosacral Spine (With or Without Spinal Cord Injury) 920
Metacarpal Bones 922
Metatarsal Bones 925
Midfoot (Cuboid, Cuneiform, Navicular) 928
Multiple Myeloma 1399
Osteoporosis 1540
Paget's Disease of Bone 1557
Pelvis 930
Radius and Ulna, Distal 933
Reduction of Fracture or Dislocation 1791
Rib 936
Sacrum 939
Skull (Closed) 941
Spondylolysis, Lumbar Region 1962
Sternum (Closed) 943
Talus 945
Thoracic Spine (With or Without Spinal Cord Injury) 948
Tibia or Fibula 951
Vertebra 954, 956
Vertebra (Pathological) 956

Fracture of Acetabulum
Fracture, Pelvis 930

Fracture of Arm
Fracture, Elbow (Distal Humerus) 910
Fracture, Radius and Ulna, Distal 933

Fracture of Bones Within the Pelvis
Fracture, Pelvis 930

Fracture of Cuboid Bone of Foot
Fracture, Midfoot (Cuboid, Cuneiform, Navicular) 928

Fracture of Cuniform Bone of Foot
Fracture, Midfoot (Cuboid, Cuneiform, Navicular) 928

Fracture of Distal Humerus
Fracture, Elbow (Distal Humerus) 910

Fracture of Fibula
Fracture, Tibia or Fibula 951

Fracture of Foot
Fracture, Calcaneus 898
Fracture, Forefoot (Sesamoid, Phalanges) 918
Fracture, Metatarsal Bones 925
Fracture, Midfoot (Cuboid, Cuneiform, Navicular) 928
Fracture, Talus 945

Fracture of Hand
Fracture, Metacarpal Bones 922

Fracture of Hip
Fracture, Femoral Neck 912

Fracture of Humerus
Fracture, Elbow (Distal Humerus) 910

Fracture of Lateral Malleolus
Fracture, Ankle 895

Fracture of Lumbar Spine
Fracture, Lumbosacral Spine (With or Without Spinal Cord Injury) 920

Fracture of Medial Malleolus
Fracture, Ankle 895

Fracture of Navicular Bone
Fracture, Midfoot (Cuboid, Cuneiform, Navicular) 928

Index 2575

Fracture of Phalanges of Foot
  Fracture, Forefoot (Sesamoid, Phalanges) 918
Fracture of Phalanges of Hand
  Fracture, Fingers and Thumb 915
Fracture of Posterior Malleolus
  Fracture, Ankle 895
Fracture of Radius
  Fracture, Radius and Ulna, Distal 933
Fracture of Sesamoid Bone
  Fracture, Forefoot (Sesamoid, Phalanges) 918
Fracture of Spine
  Fracture, Cervical Spine (With or Without Spinal Cord Injury) 904
  Fracture, Lumbosacral Spine (With or Without Spinal Cord Injury) 920
  Fracture, Sacrum 939
  Fracture, Thoracic Spine (With or Without Spinal Cord Injury) 948
  Fracture, Vertebra 954, 956
  Fracture, Vertebra (Pathological) 956
Fracture of Spine with Spinal Cord Injury
  Fracture, Cervical Spine (With or Without Spinal Cord Injury) 904
  Fracture, Lumbosacral Spine (With or Without Spinal Cord Injury) 920
  Fracture, Sacrum 939
  Fracture, Thoracic Spine (With or Without Spinal Cord Injury) 948
Fracture of Spine Without Spinal Cord Injury
  Fracture, Cervical Spine (With or Without Spinal Cord Injury) 904
  Fracture, Lumbosacral Spine (With or Without Spinal Cord Injury) 920
  Fracture, Sacrum 939
  Fracture, Thoracic Spine (With or Without Spinal Cord Injury) 948
Fracture of the Lateral Malleolus
  Fracture, Ankle 895
Fracture of the Medial Malleolus
  Fracture, Ankle 895
Fracture of the Posterior Malleolus
  Fracture, Ankle 895
Fracture of Thoracolumbar Spine
  Fracture, Thoracic Spine (With or Without Spinal Cord Injury) 948
Fracture of Tibia
  Fracture, Tibia or Fibula 951
Fracture of Toe
  Fracture, Forefoot (Sesamoid, Phalanges) 918
Fracture of Ulna
  Fracture, Radius and Ulna, Distal 933
Fracture of Vertebra
  Fracture, Cervical Spine (With or Without Spinal Cord Injury) 904
  Fracture, Thoracic Spine (With or Without Spinal Cord Injury) 948
  Fracture, Vertebra 954, 956
Fracture of Wrist
  Fracture, Carpal Bones 901
  Fracture, Radius and Ulna, Distal 933
Fracture Reduction
  Reduction of Fracture or Dislocation 1791
Fractured Cranium
  Fracture, Skull (Closed) 941
Francis' Disease
  Tularemia 2197
Freudian Analysis
  Psychoanalysis 1742
Freudian Therapy
  Psychotherapy, Individual 1748

Frontal Sinusitis
  Sinusitis 1928
Frost Bite
  Frostbite 959
  Gangrene 964
Frostnip
  Frostbite 959
Frozen Shoulder
  Adhesive Capsulitis of Shoulder 66
Full-thickness Skin Graft
  Skin Graft 1932
Fulminant Hepatitis
  Hepatitis B 1083
  Hepatitis, Viral 1091
Functional Blindness
  Blindness 270
Functional Disorders of Intestine
  Intestinal Obstruction 1222
  Intestinal Upset 1224
  Irritable Bowel Syndrome 1244
Functional Dyspepsia
  Irritable Bowel Syndrome 1244
Functional Incontinence
  Urinary Incontinence in Women 2222
Functional Ovarian Cysts
  Ovarian Cyst, Benign 1552
Fungal Infection
  Folliculitis 887
  Histoplasmosis 1121
  Pruritus Ani 1736
  Tinea 2095
Fungal Keratitis
  Keratitis 1257
Furuncle
  Carbuncle 407
Furunculosis
  Carbuncle 407
  Furuncle 961
Fusiform Aneurysm
  Abdominal Aneurysm 3
  Aortic Aneurysm 160
  Thoracic Aneurysm 2070
Fusion
  Ankylosing Spondylitis 152
  Arthrodesis 194
  Excision, Fusion, and Repair of Toes 860
  Spinal Fusion 1951
Fusion of Toes
  Excision, Fusion, and Repair of Toes 860
FVC
  Pulmonary Function Tests 1758

G

Gallbladder
  Cholangiography 493
  Cholecystectomy 495
  Cholecystitis 497
  Cholecystography 500
  Cholelithiasis 501

2576 The Medical Disability Advisor—Fourth Edition

Gallbladder Calculus
    Cholecystectomy 495
    Cholelithiasis 501

Gallbladder Inflammation
    Cholecystitis 497
    Duodenitis 749

Gallbladder Stones
    Cholelithiasis 501

Gallstones
    Cholecystectomy 495
    Cholecystography 500
    Cholelithiasis 501
    Dyspepsia 759
    Lithotripsy, Extracorporeal Shock Wave 1295

Ganglion Cyst
    Ganglionectomy (Wrist) 963
    Synovial Cyst 2028

Ganglionectomy
    Synovial Cyst 2028
    Wrist 963

Ganglionic Cyst
    Synovial Cyst 2028

Gangrene
    Arteriosclerotic Gangrene 186
    Diabetic Gangrene 689
    Frostbite 959
    Gas Gangrene 967

Gangrenous Lymphangitis
    Lymphangitis 1324

Gas
    Gangrene 967
    Poisoning 1675, 1677, 1679, 1681
    Gastroesophageal Reflux 979
    Toxic Effects, Carbon Monoxide 2117
    Toxic Effects, Chlorine 2122
    Toxic Effects, Formaldehyde 2129
    Toxic Effects, Hydrochloric Acid 2131
    Toxic Effects, Hydrofluoric Acid 2132
    Toxic Effects, Mercury 2138
    Toxic Effects, Methyl Bromide 2142

Gastrectojejunostomy
    Gastroenterostomy 978

Gastrectomy
    Cancer, Stomach 391
    Dumping Syndrome 747
    Duodenitis 749
    Gastritis 970
    Gastroenterostomy 978
    Peptic Ulcer Disease 1611
    Pernicious Anemia 1630
    Resection of Gastric or Duodenal Ulcer Site 1819

Gastrectomy with Anastomosis
    Gastrectomy 968
    Resection of Gastric or Duodenal Ulcer Site 1819

Gastric
    Achlorhydria and Hypochlorhydria 49
    Cancer, Esophagus 356
    Cancer, Stomach 391
    Dyspepsia 759
    Nasogastric Intubation 1444
    Nausea 1446
    Peptic Ulcer Disease 1611
    Portal Systemic Shunt 1695
    Pyloroplasty 1769
    Vagotomy 2235

Gastric Achylia
    Achlorhydria and Hypochlorhydria 49
    Dyspepsia 759

Gastric Cancer
    Cancer, Stomach 391
    Gastrectomy 968
    Gastroenterostomy 978

Gastric Carcinoma
    Cancer, Esophagus 356
    Cancer, Stomach 391

Gastric Decompression
    Nasogastric Intubation 1444

Gastric Inflammation
    Gastritis 970

Gastric Ulcer
    Gastrectomy 968
    Peptic Ulcer Disease 1611
    Resection of Gastric or Duodenal Ulcer Site 1819

Gastric Ulcer Site
    Gastrectomy 968
    Peptic Ulcer Disease 1611
    Resection of Gastric or Duodenal Ulcer Site 1819

Gastric Vagotomy
    Vagotomy 2235

Gastric Volvulus
    Volvulus 2289

Gastritis
    Duodenitis 749
    Esophagogastroduodenoscopy 850
    Gastroenterostomy 978
    Pyloric Stenosis, Acquired (Adult) Hypertrophic 1767

Gastroduodenal Ulcer
    Peptic Ulcer Disease 1611

Gastroduodenitis
    Duodenitis 749

Gastroduodenostomy
    Gastrectomy 968
    Gastroenterostomy 978

Gastroenteritis
    Colitis 535
    Diarrhea 696
    Dysentery 755
    E. Coli 767
    Giardiasis 989
    Infectious 973
    Non-Infectious 975
    Salmonellosis 1866
    Shigellosis 1910
    Traveler's Diarrhea 2177

Gastroenteroanastomosis
    Gastrectomy 968
    Gastroenterostomy 978

Gastroenterostomy
    Gastrectomy 968

Gastroenterostomy Bypass
    Gastrectomy 968
    Gastroenterostomy 978

Gastroesophageal Laceration-Hemorrhage Syndrome
    Mallory-Weiss Syndrome 1333

Gastroesophageal Reflux
    Angina Pectoris 140
    Dyspepsia 759
    Esophageal Diverticula 836
    Esophagitis 847
    Esophagogastroduodenoscopy 850

Gastroesophageal Reflux Disease
    Gastroesophageal Reflux 979

Gastrointestinal Bleeding
    Diverticulosis and Diverticulitis of Colon 739
    Dysentery 755
    E. Coli 767
    Gastrointestinal Hemorrhage 982
    Nasogastric Intubation 1444

Gastrointestinal Distress
    Intestinal Upset 1224
    Somatization Disorder 1939

Gastrointestinal Series
    Lower Gastrointestinal Series 1305
    Upper Gastrointestinal Series 2214

Gastrointestinal Tract
    Colonoscopy 540
    E. Coli 767
    Endoscopy of Gastrointestinal Tract 810
    Esophagogastroduodenoscopy 850
    Gastrointestinal Hemorrhage 982
    Lower Gastrointestinal Series 1305
    Sigmoidoscopy 1925
    Upper Gastrointestinal Series 2214

Gastrojejunosotomy
    Gastrectomy 968

Gastrojejunostomy
    Gastrectomy 968
    Gastroenterostomy 978

Gastroschisis
    Hernia, Umbilical 1106

Gastroscopy
    Cancer, Stomach 391
    Colonoscopy 540
    Dyspepsia 759
    Endoscopy of Gastrointestinal Tract 810
    Esophagogastroduodenoscopy 850

Gastrostomy
    Enterostomy 811

Gender Identity Disorder
    Psychosexual Disorders 1745

General Paralysis of the Insane
    General Paresis 986

Generalized Anxiety Disorder
    Anxiety Disorder, Generalized 158

Generalized Convulsive Epilepsy
    Grand Mal Seizure 1014

Generalized Nonconvulsive Epilepsy
    Petit Mal Epilepsy 1631

Genital
    Candidiasis 405
    Cervicitis 472
    Chancroid 481
    Cryotherapy, Genital Warts (Female) 605
    Cryotherapy, Genital Warts (Male) 606
    Gonorrhea 1010
    Impotence 1198
    Penis Disorders 1608
    Trichomoniasis 2185
    Vaginitis 2233
    Warts, Genital 2294

Genital Herpes
    Herpes Simplex 1108

Genital Warts
    Cryotherapy, Genital Warts (Female) 605
    Cryotherapy, Genital Warts (Male) 606
    Warts, Genital 2294
    Warts, Viral 2298

GERD
    Dyspepsia 759
    Gastroesophageal Reflux 979

Germ Cell Tumor
    Pineal Gland Neoplasm 1647

German Measles
    Rubella 1856

Germinoma
    Pineal Gland Neoplasm 1647

Gestalt Theoretical Psychotherapy
    Psychotherapy, Individual 1748

Gestation
    Pregnancy, Multiple Gestation 1714
    Pregnancy, Normal 1716

Gestational
    Diabetes 988
    Hydatidiform Mole 1134

Gestational Trophoblastic Disease
    Hydatidiform Mole 1134

Gestational Trophoblastic Neoplasia
    Hydatidiform Mole 1134

GI Series
    Lower Gastrointestinal Series 1305
    Upper Gastrointestinal Series 2214

Giant Cell Arteritis
    Temporal Arteritis 2045

Giant Cell Thyroiditis
    Thyroiditis 2091

Giant Hives
    Angioedema 150

Giant Urticaria
    Angioedema 150

Giardiasis
    Duodenitis 749
    Traveler's Diarrhea 2177

Giddiness
    Dizziness and Giddiness 742

Gilchrist's Disease
    Blastomycosis 266

Gilles De La Tourette Syndrome
    Tics 2093

Gingiva
    Abscess 991
    Gingivectomy 992
    Gingivitis 993
    Periodontitis 1619

Gingivectomy
    Periodontitis 1619
Gingivitis
    Gingivectomy 992
    Trench Mouth 2181
Gingivoplasty
    Gingivectomy 992
    Periodontitis 1619
Gingivostomatitis
    Gingivitis 993
Gland Infection
    Bartholin's Gland Cyst 242
    Mumps 1404
    Salivary Gland Stones 1865
Glandular Fever
    Mononucleosis 1390
Glass Addiction
    Amphetamine Dependence/Abuse 113
Glaucoma
    Acute (Angle-Closure) 995
    Behçet's Syndrome 244
    Blindness 270
    Chronic (Open-Angle) 997
    Iridectomy 1238
    Iridotomy 1239
    Trabeculectomy 2156
    Trabeculoplasty 2158
Glenohumeral
    Dislocation 719
    Rotator Cuff Tear 1853
    Shoulder Replacement 1917
    Sprains and Strains, Rotator Cuff (Capsule) 1994
Glenohumeral Arthroplasty
    Shoulder Replacement 1917
Glenohumeral Dislocation
    Sprains and Strains, Rotator Cuff (Capsule) 1994
Glenohumeral Joint
    Glenohumeral Dislocation 719
    Rotator Cuff Tear 1853
    Shoulder Replacement 1917
    Sprains and Strains, Rotator Cuff (Capsule) 1994
Glioblastoma
    Astrocytoma 214
    Cancer, Brain 344
Glioblastoma Multiforme
    Astrocytoma 214
Glioma
    Astrocytoma 214
    Cancer, Brain 344
Globe Cell Anemia
    Spherocytosis, Hereditary 1944
Glomerular Disease
    Glomerulonephritis, Acute 1001
    Kidney Transplant 1261
    Nephritis, Interstitial 1453
Glomerular Proteinuria
    Albuminuria 82
Glomerulonephritis
    Hematuria 1055
    High Blood Pressure, Malignant 1116

Nephritis, Interstitial 1453
Glomerulosclerosis
    Glomerulonephritis, Chronic 1003
Glucosuria
    Glycosuria 1006
Glycosuria
    Diabetes Mellitus Type I 683, 686
    Diabetes Mellitus Type II 686
Golfer's Elbow
    Epicondylitis, Medial and Lateral 816
Gonadectomy
    Orchiectomy 1523
Gonococcal Arthritis
    Gonorrhea 1010
Gonococcal Cervicitis
    Gonorrhea 1010
Gonococcal Infectious Arthritis
    Arthritis, Infectious 192
Gonococcal Proctitis
    Gonorrhea 1010
Gonococcal Urethritis
    Gonorrhea 1010
Gonorrhea
    Trichomoniasis 2185
    Urethritis 2218
Gougerot-Blum Purpura
    Purpura Simplex 1760
Gout
    Arthralgia 190
    Biceps Tendonitis 248
    Bursitis 325
Gouty Arthritis
    Gout 1012
Graft
    Aneurysmectomy 138
    Arterial Graft 183
    Arteriovenous Aneurysm 188
    Arthrodesis 194
    Arthroplasty, Elbow 197
    Bone Graft 272
    Bone Marrow Transplant 275
    Corneal Transplant 582
    Coronary Bypass 592
    Cystourethroplasty of Bladder Neck 625
    Dupuytren's Release 753
    Kidney Transplant 1261
    Repair, Anterior Cruciate Ligament 1814
    Rib Resection 1844
    Rotator Cuff Repair 1848
    Shoulder Replacement 1917
    Skin Graft 1932
    Spinal Fusion 1951
Grand Mal Seizure
    Epilepsy 824
    Seizures 1900
Granular Conjunctivitis
    Trachoma 2161
Granulocytopenia
    Neutropenia 1477

Index   2579

Granulomatous Conjunctivitis
  Trachoma 2161
Granulomatous Thyroiditis
  Thyroiditis 2091
Grave's Disease
  Goiter 1008
  Hyperthyroidism 1159
  Thyroidectomy 2090
Gravid
  Pregnancy, Normal 1716
Great Toe
  Bunion 312
  Bunionectomy 314
  Fracture, Forefoot (Sesamoid, Phalanges) 918
  Gout 1012
  Hallux Rigidus 1027
  Hammertoe 1029
  Toenail, Ingrown 2100
Grief Reaction
  Adjustment Disorder with Depressed Mood 69
Grippe
  Traveler's Diarrhea 2177
Groin Pull
  Groin Strain 1020
Group
  Psychotherapy, Group 1747
Group Psychotherapy
  Avoidant Personality Disorder 237
  Psychotherapy, Group 1747
Group Therapy
  Marijuana Dependence/abuse 1341
  Psychotherapy, Group 1747
GTN
  Hydatidiform Mole 1134
Gum Disease
  Dental Disorders 657
  Gingival Abscess 991
  Gingivectomy 992
  Gingivitis 993
  Impacted Tooth 1191
  Periodontitis 1619
  Trench Mouth 2181
Gum Resection
  Gingivectomy 992
Gums
  Gingivectomy 992
  Gingivitis 993
  Impacted Tooth 1191
  Periodontitis 1619
  Tooth Extraction 2107
  Trench Mouth 2181

H

Habit Spasm
  Tics 2093
Hallux
  Metatarsus Primus Varus 1378
Hallux Abducto Valgus
  Bunion 312

Hallux Limitus
  Hallux Rigidus 1027
Hallux Malleus
  Hammertoe 1029
Hallux Valgus
  Bunion 312
  Bunionectomy 314
  Excision, Fusion, and Repair of Toes 860
Hamartoma Polyps
  Rectal Polyps 1783
Hammer Digit Syndrome
  Hammertoe 1029
Hammer Toe
  Repair, Hammertoe 1816
Hammer Toe Repair
  Repair, Hammertoe 1816
Hammertoe
  Excision, Fusion, and Repair of Toes 860
  Repair, Hammertoe 1816
Hammertoe Repair
  Repair, Hammertoe 1816
Hand
  Abscess, Palmar 32
  Amputation, Finger or Thumb 123
  Cancer, Skin 387
  Carpal Tunnel Release 428
  Contact Dermatitis 560
  Eosinophilic Fasciitis 814
  Erysipeloid 831
  Fracture, Metacarpal Bones 922
  Psoriatic Arthritis 1740
  Radial Styloid Tenosynovitis 1776
  Raynaud's Phenomenon 1781
  Reduction of Fracture or Dislocation 1791
  Repair, Tendon Laceration of Hand 1817
  Scleroderma 1892
  Sprains and Strains, Hand or Fingers 1989
  Thoracic Outlet Syndrome 2074
  Tremor 2179
Hand Burn
  Burn of Wrist and Hand 321
Hand Eczema
  Contact Dermatitis 560
  Dermatitis 674
  Eczema 778
Hand Phalanges
  Amputation, Finger or Thumb 123
  Dupuytren's Contracture 751
  Dupuytren's Release 753
  Excision of Nail, Nail Bed, or Nail Fold 856
  Fracture, Fingers and Thumb 915
  Reduction of Fracture or Dislocation 1791
  Trigger Finger or Thumb 2191
Hand Sprain
  Sprains and Strains, Hand or Fingers 1989
Hand Strain
  Sprains and Strains, Hand or Fingers 1989
Hand Tendon Repair
  Repair, Tendon Laceration of Hand 1817
Hands
  Contact Dermatitis 560
  Dermatitis 674

Dupuytren's Contracture 751
Dupuytren's Release 753
Eczema 778
Eosinophilic Fasciitis 814
Sprains and Strains, Hand or Fingers 1989
Vitiligo 2286
Warts, Viral 2298

Hard Measles
Rubeola 1858

Hardening of the Arteries
Atherosclerosis and Arteriosclerosis 216
Bundle Branch Block 310

Hashimoto's Thyroiditis
Goiter 1008
Hypothyroidism 1180
Thyroiditis 2091

Hashitoxicosis
Thyroiditis 2091

Hay Fever
Allergic Rhinitis 98
Nasal Polyps 1441

HCC
Cancer, Liver 360

Head
Craniectomy 596
Dermatitis 674
Diabetic Neuropathy 692
Postconcussion Syndrome 1699

Head Cold
Cold 533

Head Injury
Brain Abscess 289
Brain Injury 292
Coma 449, 544
Computerized Axial Tomography 552
Concussion, Cerebral 553
Delirium 644
Epilepsy 824
Evoked Potentials 851
Fracture, Skull (Closed) 941
Intracranial Hemorrhage 1226, 1230
Intracranial Hemorrhage, Closed 1230
Postconcussion Syndrome 1699
Pulmonary Edema 1756
Subarachnoid Hemorrhage (Traumatic) 2014
Subdural Hemorrhage 2016
Superficial 1031
Tinnitus 2097

Head Trauma
Brain Injury 292
Cerebral Aneurysm (Non-Ruptured) 445
Cerebral Contusion, Closed 447
Craniectomy 596
Craniotomy 598
Encephalopathy 799
Epidural Hematoma 821
Hemiplegia 1056
Trauma 2175

Headache
Brain Abscess 289
Cerebral Hemorrhage 449
Chiropractic Adjustments and Manipulations 492
Chronic Fatigue Syndrome 509
Cluster Headache 517
Meningioma 1355

Meningitis, Bacterial 1357
Migraine Headache 1378
Pharyngitis, Acute 1633
Pheochromocytoma 1638
Pineal Gland Neoplasm 1647
Polyarteritis Nodosa 1685
Postconcussion Syndrome 1699
Posttraumatic Stress Disorder 1707
Premenstrual Syndrome 1724
Renovascular Hypertension 1809
Rocky Mountain Spotted Fever 1845
Salmonellosis 1866
Sinusitis 1928
St. Louis Encephalitis 2000
Subarachnoid Hemorrhage (Non-traumatic) 2011
Syphilis 2033
Tension Headache 2059
Torticollis 2108

Hearing Loss
Cochlear Implant 529
Mastoidectomy 1347
Mastoiditis 1349
Meniere's Disease 1353
Otitis Media 1545
Otosclerosis 1549
Paget's Disease of Bone 1557

Heart
Arrhythmia 178
Atrial Fibrillation 220
Atrioventricular Block, Incomplete (First-Degree) 226
Block 1040
Bundle Branch Block 310
Cardiac Arrest 409
Cardiac Catheterization 411
Cardiac Pacemaker Insertion 414
Cardiac Stress Test 416
Chest Pain 486
Cor Pulmonale, Acute and Chronic 576
Coronary Atherosclerosis 587
Coronary Bypass 592
Coronary Thrombolysis 593
Echocardiography 774
Electrocardiogram 781
Embolectomy 786—787
Endocarditis, Bacterial 802
Failure, Congestive 1042
Hypertensive Heart Disease 1156
Mitral Commissurotomy 1384
Mitral Insufficiency 1385
Mitral Stenosis 1387
Mitral Valve Prolapse 1389
Murmur 1045
Myocardial Infarction, Acute 1424
Myocarditis, Acute 1428
Open-Chest Cardiac Massage 1514
Palpitations 1566
Paracentesis 1582
Premature Beats 1719
Prinzmetal's Angina 1726
Rheumatic Fever, Acute 1833
Rheumatic Heart Disease, Chronic 1836
Sick Sinus Syndrome 1920
Stokes-Adams Syndrome 2003
Tachycardia, Paroxysmal Supraventricular 2039
Valve Replacement 1047
Valvotomy 2237
Valvuloplasty, Balloon 2240
Ventricular Fibrillation 2256
Ventricular Tachycardia 2260
Wandering Atrial Pacemaker 2293

Index 2581

Heart Arrhythmia
- Arrhythmia 178
- Atrial Fibrillation 220
- Cardiac Arrest 409
- Palpitations 1566
- Premature Beats 1719
- Sick Sinus Syndrome 1920
- Tachycardia, Paroxysmal Supraventricular 2039
- Ventricular Fibrillation 2256
- Ventricular Tachycardia 2260

Heart Attack
- Angina, Unstable 144
- Atrioventricular Block Incomplete (Second-Degree) 223
- Atrioventricular Block, Complete (Third-Degree) 224
- Atrioventricular Block, Incomplete (First-Degree) 226
- Cardiogenic Shock 417
- Coronary Thrombolysis 593
- Electrocardiogram 781
- Myocardial Infarction, Acute 1424
- Ventricular Fibrillation 2256
- Ventricular Premature Contractions 2258

Heart Beats
- Arrhythmia 178
- Atrial Fibrillation 220
- Palpitations 1566
- Premature Beats 1719
- Tachycardia, Paroxysmal Supraventricular 2039
- Ventricular Premature Contractions 2258
- Ventricular Tachycardia 2260

Heart Block
- Arrhythmia 178
- Atrioventricular Block Incomplete (Second-Degree) 223
- Atrioventricular Block, Complete (Third-Degree) 224
- Atrioventricular Block, Incomplete (First-Degree) 226
- Bundle Branch Block 310
- Cardiac Pacemaker Insertion 414
- Electrocardiogram 781
- Sick Sinus Syndrome 1920
- Stokes-Adams Syndrome 2003

Heart Catheterization
- Cardiac Catheterization 411
- Pulmonary Edema 1756

Heart Conduction Defect
- Heart Block 1040
- Stokes-Adams Syndrome 2003

Heart Disease
- Arrhythmia 178
- Atrial Fibrillation 220
- Atrioventricular Block Incomplete (Second-Degree) 223
- Bundle Branch Block 310
- Cardiac Arrest 409
- Cardiomyopathy 419
- Cardiovascular Disease in Pregnancy 422
- Coronary Atherosclerosis 587
- Heart Block 1040
- Heart Murmur 1045
- Hypertensive Heart Disease 1156
- Myocardial Infarction, Acute 1424
- Premature Beats 1719
- Rheumatic Heart Disease, Chronic 1836
- Sick Sinus Syndrome 1920
- Stokes-Adams Syndrome 2003
- Strep Throat 2005
- Tachycardia, Paroxysmal Supraventricular 2039
- Ventricular Fibrillation 2256
- Ventricular Tachycardia 2260

Heart Failure
- Cardiac Arrest 409
- Cardiogenic Shock 417
- Congestive 1042
- Endocarditis, Bacterial 802
- Pulmonary Edema 1756
- Vitamin B$_1$ Deficiency 2272

Heart Murmur
- Bundle Branch Block 310

Heart Palpitations
- Palpitations 1566

Heart Valve
- Aortic Valve Stenosis 167
- Heart Murmur 1045
- Mitral Commissurotomy 1384
- Replacement 1047
- Valvotomy 2237

Heart Valve Prosthesis
- Heart Valve Replacement 1047

Heart Valve Replacement
- Aortic Valve Stenosis 167
- Endocarditis, Bacterial 802
- Rib Resection 1844
- Valvotomy 2237

Heart Valve Stenosis
- Aortic Insufficiency 165
- Aortic Valve Stenosis 167
- Cardiac Catheterization 411
- Mitral Stenosis 1387

Heart Valves
- Aortic Insufficiency 165
- Endocarditis, Bacterial 802
- Rheumatic Heart Disease, Chronic 1836
- Valvuloplasty, Balloon 2240

Heart Valvuloplasty
- Valvotomy 2237
- Valvuloplasty, Balloon 2240

Heartburn
- Dyspepsia 759
- Gastroesophageal Reflux 979
- Peptic Ulcer Disease 1611
- Pylorospasm 1770

Heat
- Stroke 1051

Heat Collapse
- Heat Exhaustion 1049

Heat Prostration
- Heat Exhaustion 1049

Heel
- Fracture, Calcaneus 898
- Gout 1012
- Plantar Fasciitis 1655
- Spur (Calcaneal) 1053

Heel Bone Spur
- Heel Spur (Calcaneal) 1053
- Plantar Fasciitis 1655

Heel Fracture
- Fracture, Calcaneus 898

Heel Pain
- Achilles Bursitis or Tendinitis 47

Heel Spur
    (Calcaneal) 1053
Heller Myotomy
    Myotomy of Esophagus 1433
Heloma
    Corn and Callus, Infected 578
Hemangioendothelial Sarcoma
    Hepatic Angiosarcoma 1077
Hematoma
    Aortic Dissection 163
    Contusion 562, 564, 566, 568, 571
    Craniectomy 596
    Intracranial Hemorrhage 1226, 1230
Hematuria
    Bladder Polyps 264
    Cancer, Bladder 338
    Cancer, Kidney 358
    Cystoscopy, Transurethral 624
Hemicolectomy
    Colon Resection 538
Hemiparalysis
    Hemiplegia 1056
    Subarachnoid Hemorrhage (Non-traumatic) 2011
Hemiparesis
    Hemiplegia 1056
Hemodialysis
    Ascites 203
    Renal Dialysis 1800
    Renal Failure, Chronic 1804
Hemolytic Anemia
    Anemia 133, 136
    Rh Incompatibility 1831
    Sickle Cell Anemia 1922
    Spherocytosis, Hereditary 1944
    Thalassemia 2066
    Vitamin E Deficiency 2283
Hemolytic Disease of the Newborn
    Rh Incompatibility 1831
Hemolytic Jaundice
    Jaundice 1249
Hemophilia
    A 1061
    B 1064
Hemorrhage
    Abruptio Placentae 16
    Anemia 133, 136
    Cerebral Hemorrhage 449
    Compartment Syndrome 547
    Ectopic Pregnancy 775
    Encephalopathy 799
    Epidural Hematoma 821
    Gastrointestinal Hemorrhage 982
    Miscarriage 1381
    of Rectum and Anus 1068
    Osler-Weber-Rendu Disease 1528
    Placenta Accreta 1651
    Repair of Cerebral Aneurysm 1812
    Retinal Vascular Occlusion 1827
    Subarachnoid Hemorrhage (Non-traumatic) 2011
    Subarachnoid Hemorrhage (Traumatic) 2014
Hemorrhage of Anus
    Hemorrhage of Rectum and Anus 1068

Hemorrhage of Rectum
    and Anus 1068
Hemorrhagic Cerebrovascular Accident
    Cerebral Hemorrhage 449
    Coma 449, 544
Hemorrhagic Colitis
    E. Coli 767
Hemorrhagic Stroke
    Cerebral Hemorrhage 449
    Cerebrovascular Accident 454
    Intracranial Hemorrhage 1226, 1230
Hemorrhagic Telangiectasia
    Osler-Weber-Rendu Disease 1528
Hemorrhagic Thrombocytopenia
    Idiopathic Thrombocytopenic Purpura 1189
Hemorrhoid
    Pruritus Ani 1736
    Sclerotherapy 1895
    Treatment 1070
Hemorrhoid Cryosurgery
    Hemorrhoid Treatment 1070
Hemorrhoid Injection
    Hemorrhoid Treatment 1070
    Sclerotherapy 1895
Hemorrhoid Ligation
    Hemorrhoid Treatment 1070
Hemorrhoid Sclerotherapy
    Hemorrhoid Treatment 1070
    Sclerotherapy 1895
Hemorrhoid Treatment
    Hemorrhoids 1073
Hemorrhoidectomy
    Hemorrhoid Treatment 1070
    Hemorrhoids 1073
Hemorrhoids
    Gastrointestinal Hemorrhage 982
    Hemorrhage of Rectum and Anus 1068
    Hemorrhoid Treatment 1070
    Sclerotherapy 1895
Hemothorax
    Thoracostomy 2078
    Traumatic 1075
Hendon Ileostomy
    Colostomy and Ileostomy 543
Hepatic
    Cancer, Liver 360
Hepatic Abscess
    Abscess, Liver 27
Hepatic Angiosarcoma
    Cancer, Liver 360
Hepatic Encephalopathy
    Hepatic Coma 1079
Hepatitis
    A 1081
    Alcoholic 1087
    B 1083
    C 1085
    Chronic 1089
    Hepatic Coma 1079

Index   2583

Jaundice 1249
Liver Disease 1298
Viral 1091

Hepatitis A
Hepatitis, Viral 1091

Hepatitis B
Cancer, Liver 360
Cirrhosis of the Liver 515
Hepatitis, Chronic 1089
Hepatitis, Viral 1091

Hepatitis C
Cancer, Liver 360
Cirrhosis of the Liver 515
Hepatitis, Chronic 1089
Hepatitis, Viral 1091

Hepatocarcinoma
Cancer, Liver 360
Hepatic Angiosarcoma 1077

Hepatocellular Carcinoma
Cancer, Liver 360
Hepatic Angiosarcoma 1077

Hepatocellular Carcinoma (HCC)
Cancer, Liver 360

Hepatocerebral Intoxication
Hepatic Coma 1079

Hepatolenticular Degeneration
Wilson's Disease 2300

Hereditary
Atrophy, Muscular (Progressive) 230
Osler-Weber-Rendu Disease 1528
Porphyria 1693
Pterygium 1754
Reiter's Syndrome 1798
Retinitis Pigmentosa 1829
Spherocytosis, Hereditary 1944
Thalassemia 2066

Hereditary Coproporphyria
Porphyria 1693

Hereditary Hemolytic Anemia
Hemolytic Anemia 1059

Hereditary Hemorrhagic Telangiectasia
Osler-Weber-Rendu Disease 1528

Hereditary Muscular Atrophy
Atrophy, Muscular (Progressive) 230

Hereditary Spherocytic Anemia
Hemolytic Anemia 1059
Spherocytosis, Hereditary 1944

Hereditary Spherocytosis
Anemia 133, 136
Spherocytosis, Hereditary 1944

Hereditary Spherocytosis Anemia
Spherocytosis, Hereditary 1944

Hernia
Incisional 1100
Inguinal and Femoral 1103
Repair 1094, 1096
Repair, Vaginal 1096

Hernia Correction
Hernia Repair 1094, 1096
Hernia Repair, Vaginal 1096

Hernia Repair
Hernia, Hiatal 1097
Hernia, Inguinal and Femoral 1103
Hernia, Umbilical 1106
Vaginal 1096

Hernia Varicosa
Varicocele 2242

Herniated
Cervical Disc Disorder with Myelopathy 464
Displacement, Cervical Intervertebral Disc Without Myelopathy 728
Displacement, Lumbar Intervertebral Disc Without Myelopathy 732
Displacement, Thoracic Intervertebral Disc Without Myelopathy 735
Lumbar Disc Disorder with Myelopathy 1308
Thoracic Disc Disorder with Myelopathy 2072

Herniated Cervical Disc with Myelopathy
Cervical Disc Disorder with Myelopathy 464

Herniated Disc
Cervical Disc Disorder with Myelopathy 464
Chemonucleolysis of Interveterbral Disc 482
Discectomy 703
Displacement, Cervical Intervertebral Disc Without Myelopathy 728
Displacement, Lumbar Intervertebral Disc Without Myelopathy 732
Displacement, Thoracic Intervertebral Disc Without Myelopathy 735
Lumbar Disc Disorder with Myelopathy 1308
Thoracic Disc Disorder with Myelopathy 2072

Herniated Lumbar Disc with Myelopathy
Lumbar Disc Disorder with Myelopathy 1308

Herniated Nucleus Pulposis
Displacement, Cervical Intervertebral Disc Without Myelopathy 728
Displacement, Lumbar Intervertebral Disc Without Myelopathy 732
Displacement, Thoracic Intervertebral Disc Without Myelopathy 735

Herniated Thoracic Disc with Myelopathy
Thoracic Disc Disorder with Myelopathy 2072

Herniation
Cervical Disc Disorder with Myelopathy 464
Cystocele or Rectocele 621
Displacement, Cervical Intervertebral Disc Without Myelopathy 728
Displacement, Lumbar Intervertebral Disc Without Myelopathy 732
Displacement, Thoracic Intervertebral Disc Without Myelopathy 735
Lumbar Disc Disorder with Myelopathy 1308
Thoracic Disc Disorder with Myelopathy 2072
Urethrocele with Stress Incontinence 2220

Herniorrhaphy
Hernia Repair 1094, 1096

Heroin Addiction
Opioid Type Dependence 1516

Herpes
Acquired Immune Deficiency Syndrome 53
Simplex 1108

Herpes Keratoconjunctivitis
Keratitis 1257

Herpes Simplex
Encephalitis 797
Erythema Multiforme 833
Penis Disorders 1608

Herpes Simplex Keratitis
Keratitis 1257

Herpes Zoster
Chickenpox 490

Hiatal Hernia
Dilation of Esophagus 700
Esophageal Diverticula 836

Gastroesophageal Reflux 979
Hernia Repair 1094, 1096
Hernia, Hiatal 1097

Hiatus Hernia
Hernia, Hiatal 1097

High Blood Pressure
Benign 1112
Hypertensive Heart Disease 1156
Malignant 1116

High Blood Sugar
Diabetes Mellitus Type I 683, 686
Diabetes Mellitus Type II 686
Diabetic Gangrene 689
Diabetic Glomerulosclerosis 690
Diabetic Neuropathy 692
Diabetic Retinopathy 694

High Ligation
Ligation and Stripping of Varicose Veins 1287

Highly Selective Vagotomy
Vagotomy 2235

Hill Operation
Hernia, Hiatal 1097

Hip
Ankylosing Spondylitis 152
Arthrodesis 194
Arthroscopy 199
Avascular Necrosis 235
Dislocation 705, 708, 711, 713, 716, 723, 726
Fracture, Femoral Neck 912
Replacement, Total 1119
Sprains and Strains 1964, 1968, 1971, 1975, 1979, 1981, 1984, 1986, 1989, 1991, 1994, 1997

Hip Arthroplasty
Fracture, Femoral Neck 912
Hip Replacement, Total 1119

Hip Fracture
Fracture, Femoral Neck 912
Hip Replacement, Total 1119

Hip Replacement
Avascular Necrosis 235
Psoriatic Arthritis 1740
Total 1119

Histamine Cephalgia
Cluster Headache 517

Histamine Headache
Cluster Headache 517
Headache 1033

Histoplasmosis
Chorioretinitis 506

HIV
Acquired Immune Deficiency Syndrome 53
Candidiasis 405
Cryptococcosis 608
Encephalitis 797
Human Immunodeficiency Virus 1126
Kaposi's Sarcoma 1253
Toxoplasmosis 2154

Hives
Allergic Dermatitis 96
Anaphylactic Shock 129, 131
Anaphylactic Shock, Food Reaction 131
Angioedema 150

Contact Dermatitis 560
Insect or Spider Bites and Stings 1210
Urticaria 2226

Hodgkin's Disease
Bone Marrow Transplant 275

Hofmeister Gastrectomy
Gastrectomy 968
Resection of Gastric or Duodenal Ulcer Site 1819

Holle's Vagotomy
Vagotomy 2235

Hordeolum
Stye 2010

Hormone Therapy
Cancer, Breast 347
Menopause 1368
Paget's Disease of Bone 1557
Panhypopituitarism 1576
Polycystic Ovary Syndrome 1686
Psychosexual Disorders 1745
Threatened Abortion 2080
Thyroiditis 2091

Hormones
Addison's Disease 63
Adrenalectomy 77
Aldosteronism 94
Menopause 1368
Menstrual Disorders 1369
Ovarian Cyst, Benign 1552
Panhypopituitarism 1576
Polycystic Ovary Syndrome 1686
Porphyria 1693
Postmenopausal Bleeding 1703
Premenstrual Syndrome 1724

Horton's Headache
Cluster Headache 517

Hospital Addiction
Factitious Illness with Physical Symptoms 866

Hot Flash
Menopause 1368

Hot Tub Lung
Hypersensitivity Pneumonitis 1150
Legionnaire's Disease 1282

Housemaid's Knee
Bursitis 325

HPV
Warts, Genital 2294
Warts, Plantar 2296
Warts, Viral 2298

Human Immunodeficiency Virus
Acquired Immune Deficiency Syndrome 53

Human Papillomavirus
Cancer, Cervix 351
Cervical Biopsy 460
Cervical Cauterization 461
Cryotherapy, Genital Warts (Female) 605
Cryotherapy, Genital Warts (Male) 606
Excision or Destruction of Plantar Warts 858
Warts, Plantar 2296

Human Papillomavirus Infection
Warts, Viral 2298

Humerus
Epicondylitis, Medial and Lateral 816

Fracture, Elbow (Distal Humerus) 910

Humidifier Lung
Legionnaire's Disease 1282
Ventilation Pneumonitis 2254

Hunner's Ulcer
Cystitis, Interstitial 619

Huntington's Disease
Dementia 651, 653

Hyalinosis
Glomerulosclerosis 1005

Hydatid Disease
Echinococcosis 772

Hydatid Mole
Hydatidiform Mole 1134

Hydatidiform Mole
Choriocarcinoma 505

Hydatidosis
Echinococcosis 772

Hydrargyrum Poisoning
Toxic Effects, Mercury 2138

Hydrocalycosis
Hydronephrosis 1138

Hydrochloric Acid Poisoning
Toxic Effects, Hydrochloric Acid 2131
Toxic Effects, Hydrofluoric Acid 2132

Hydrochloride Poisoning
Toxic Effects, Hydrochloric Acid 2131

Hydrofluoric Acid Poisoning
Toxic Effects, Hydrochloric Acid 2131
Toxic Effects, Hydrofluoric Acid 2132

Hydrogen Chloride Poisoning
Toxic Effects, Hydrochloric Acid 2131

Hydrogen Fluoride Hydrofluoride Poisoning
Toxic Effects, Hydrofluoric Acid 2132

Hydronephrosis
Cystoscopy, Transurethral 624

Hydroperitoneum
Ascites 203

Hydrophobia
Rabies 1773

Hydrops Fetalis
Rh Incompatibility 1831

Hydroureteronephrosis
Hydronephrosis 1138

Hymenoptera
Insect or Spider Bites and Stings 1210

Hyperactivity Disorder
Attention Deficit Disorder in Adults 232

Hyperaldosteronism
Adrenalectomy 77
Aldosteronism 94

Hyperbaric Oxygen (HBO or HBO2)
Hyperbaric Oxygenation 1141

Hyperbaric Oxygen Therapy (HBOT)
Hyperbaric Oxygenation 1141

Hyperbaric Oxygenation
Decubitus Ulcer 632
Diabetic Gangrene 689
Gangrene 964
Gas Gangrene 967
Retinitis Pigmentosa 1829
Toxic Effects, Carbon Monoxide 2117

Hypercalcemia
Hyperparathyroidism 1148
Hypoparathyroidism 1173

Hypercalcuria
Hyperparathyroidism 1148

Hypercortisolism
Cushing's Syndrome 613

Hyperextension
Sprains and Strains, Cervical Spine (Neck) 1981

Hyperglobulinemia
Polycythemia Vera 1689

Hyperkinetic Convulsions
Tetany 2062

Hyperkinetic Heart Syndrome
Neurocirculatory Asthenia 1467

Hypernephroma
Cancer, Kidney 358

Hyperplasia of Prostate
Prostatic Hypertrophy 1731

Hyperplastic Gingivitis
Gingivitis 993

Hyperplastic Polyps
Rectal Polyps 1783

Hyperpotassemia
Hyperkalemia 1146

Hypersensitivity
Allergy 100
Angioedema 150
Humidifier Fever 1130
Insect or Spider Bites and Stings 1210
Pneumonitis 1150

Hypersensitivity Angioedema
Angioedema 150

Hypersensitivity Pneumonitis
Humidifier Fever 1130

Hypersensitivity Reaction
Allergy 100

Hypersensitivity Syndrome
Allergy 100

Hypersplenia
Hypersplenism 1154

Hypersplenism
Splenomegaly 1956

Hypertension
Abruptio Placentae 16
Angina Pectoris 140
Aortic Dissection 163
Arteriovenous Aneurysm 188
Atherosclerosis and Arteriosclerosis 216
Biofeedback 250
Bundle Branch Block 310
Cardiovascular Disease in Pregnancy 422

2586   The Medical Disability Advisor—Fourth Edition

Carotid Artery Occlusion 423
Cerebral Aneurysm (Non-Ruptured) 445
Cerebral Hemorrhage 449
Cerebrovascular Disease 458
Coarctation of the Aorta 519
Cocaine Dependence/Abuse 522
Coronary Atherosclerosis 587
Coronary Bypass 592
Diabetic Glomerulosclerosis 690
Glomerulosclerosis 1005
Guillain-Barré Syndrome 1022
Heart Failure, Congestive 1042
Heart Murmur 1045
High Blood Pressure, Benign 1112
High Blood Pressure, Malignant 1116
Hypertensive Heart Disease 1156
Myocardial Infarction, Acute 1424
Pheochromocytoma 1638
Polyarteritis Nodosa 1685
Polycythemia Vera 1689
Porphyria 1693
Preeclampsia and Eclampsia 1711
Premature Beats 1719
Premature Labor 1720
Pyelonephritis, Chronic 1764
Renal Vein Thrombosis 1807
Renovascular Hypertension 1809
Strep Throat 2005
Subarachnoid Hemorrhage (Non-traumatic) 2011
Thyroiditis 2091
Transient Ischemic Attack 2169

Hypertensive
Heart Disease 1156
High Blood Pressure, Benign 1112
Renovascular Hypertension 1809

Hypertensive Cardiomegaly
Hypertensive Heart Disease 1156

Hypertensive Cardiomyopathy
Hypertensive Heart Disease 1156

Hypertensive Cardiopathy
Hypertensive Heart Disease 1156

Hypertensive Cardiovascular Disease
Hypertensive Heart Disease 1156

Hypertensive Disease
Hypertensive Heart Disease 1156
Renovascular Hypertension 1809

Hypertensive Emergency
High Blood Pressure, Malignant 1116

Hypertensive Kidney Disease
Renovascular Hypertension 1809

Hyperthyroidism
Goiter 1008
Gynecomastia 1025
Thyroidectomy 2090
Thyroiditis 2091

Hyperthyroiditis
Thyroiditis 2091

Hypertrophic Arthritis
Osteoarthritis 1530

Hypertrophic Nonobstructive Cardiomyopathy
Cardiomyopathy 419

Hypertrophic Obstructive Cardiomyopathy
Cardiomyopathy 419

Hypertrophic Stenosis
Pyloric Stenosis, Acquired (Adult) Hypertrophic 1767

Hypertrophy
Bundle Branch Block 310
Cor Pulmonale, Acute and Chronic 576
Gynecomastia 1025
Hypertensive Heart Disease 1156
Myalgia and Myositis 1411
Prostatectomy 1729
Prostatic Hypertrophy 1731
Reduction Mammoplasty 1790
Transurethral Balloon Dilation of Prostatic Urethra 2171

Hyperventilation
Poisoning 1675, 1677, 1679, 1681
Retinal Vascular Occlusion 1827
Syndrome 1161

Hypervitaminosis
A 1166
D 1168

Hypervitaminosis A
Hypervitaminosis 1164, 1166, 1168

Hypnotic Dependence
Sedative, Hypnotic or Anxiolytic Dependence 1898

Hypoalbuminemia
Hypoproteinemia 1175
Nephrotic Syndrome 1456

Hypochlorhydria
Achlorhydria and Hypochlorhydria 49
Dyspepsia 759

Hypochondria
is 1169

Hypochondriacal Neurosis
Hypochondriasis 1169

Hypofibrinogenemia
Afibrinogenemia 81

Hypoglycemia
Delirium 644
Dumping Syndrome 747

Hypogonadism
Male Climacteric 1332

Hypomanic Psychosis
Bipolar Affective Disorder, Single Manic Episode 260
Manic Disorder, Recurrent 1339

Hypoparathyreosis
Hypoparathyroidism 1173

Hypopharyngeal Diverticula
Esophageal Diverticula 836

Hypopituitarism
Panhypopituitarism 1576

Hypopituitarism Syndrome
Panhypopituitarism 1576

Hypoplastic Anemia
Aplastic Anemia 171

Hypoprothrombinemia
Afibrinogenemia 81

Hypospadias
Penis Disorders 1608

Hypostasis
Pulmonary Edema 1756

Index 2587

Hypostatic Pneumonia
    Pulmonary Edema 1756
Hypotension
    Cardiogenic Shock 417
    Carotid Sinus Syncope 425
    Embolectomy, Pulmonary 787
    Laryngitis 1279
    Sepsis 1905
    Septic Shock 1907
    Shock 1915
    Vasovagal Syncope 2249
Hypothyroidism
    Constipation 558
    Goiter 1008
    Hypervitaminosis D 1168
    Obesity, Simple 1491
    Thyroiditis 2091
Hypovitaminosis
    Vitamin A Deficiency 2270
Hypovitaminosis A
    Vitamin A Deficiency 2270
Hypovolemic Shock
    Septic Shock 1907
    Shock 1915
Hysterectomy
    Cancer, Cervix 351
    Cancer, Uterus 402
    Cervical Dysplasia 467
    Choriocarcinoma 505
    Dysfunctional Uterine Bleeding 757
    Endometriosis 805
    Menstrual Disorders 1369
    Oophorectomy 1501, 1503
    Placenta Accreta 1651
    Postmenopausal Bleeding 1703
Hysteria
    Conversion Disorder 574
    Somatization Disorder 1939
Hysterical
    Conversion Disorder 574
    Hysteria 1188
Hysterical Blindness
    Conversion Disorder 574
Hysterical Deafness
    Conversion Disorder 574
Hysterical Paralysis
    Conversion Disorder 574
Hysterical Reaction
    Hysteria 1188
Hysteroscopy
    Fibroid Tumor of Uterus 875

I

I&D
    Incision of Skin and Subcutaneous Tissue, Drainage of Abscess or Cyst 1201
IBD
    Colitis 535
    Colonoscopy 540
IBS
    Irritable Bowel Syndrome 1244

IC
    Cystitis, Interstitial 619
Ice Addiction
    Amphetamine Dependence/Abuse 113
ICH
    Intracranial Hemorrhage, Closed 1230
Icterohemolytic Anemia
    Spherocytosis, Hereditary 1944
Icterus
    Jaundice 1249
IDDM
    Diabetes Mellitus Type I 683, 686
Idiopathic Aldosteronism
    Aldosteronism 94
Idiopathic Anemia
    Anemia 133, 136
    Hemolytic Anemia 1059
Idiopathic Brachial Neuritis
    Neuralgic Amyotrophy 1465
Idiopathic Brachial Plexus Neuropathy
    Neuralgic Amyotrophy 1465
Idiopathic Cardiomyopathy
    Cardiomyopathy 419
Idiopathic Hemorrhagic Sarcoma
    Kaposi's Sarcoma 1253
Idiopathic Hypersomnia
    Hypersomnia 1152
Idiopathic Hypotension
    Hypotension 1178
    Laryngitis 1279
Idiopathic Multiple Pigmented Sarcoma
    Kaposi's Sarcoma 1253
Idiopathic Neutropenia
    Neutropenia 1477
Idiopathic Parkinson's Disease
    Parkinson's Disease 1593
Idiopathic Peripheral Autonomic Neuropathy
    Carotid Sinus Syncope 425
Idiopathic Polyneuritis
    Guillain-Barré Syndrome 1022
Idiopathic Proctitis
    Ulcerative Colitis 2209
Idiopathic Pulmonary Fibrosis
    Interstitial Pulmonary Fibrosis 1219
Idiopathic Seizure Disorder
    Epilepsy 824
    Grand Mal Seizure 1014
Idiopathic Thrombocytopenia
    Idiopathic Thrombocytopenic Purpura 1189
Ileitis
    Colitis 535
    Diarrhea 696
    Gastroenteritis, Non-Infectious 975
Ileocolitis
    Ulcerative Colitis 2209

Ileostomy
    Cancer, Small Intestine (Including Duodenum) 389
    Colitis 535
    Colostomy and Ileostomy 543

Ileovesical Fistula
    Bladder Fistulas 262

Ileum Volvulus
    Volvulus 2289

Ileus
    Intestinal Obstruction 1222

Iliac Crest Tap
    Bone Marrow Biopsy 273

Immune Deficiency Syndrome
    Acquired Immune Deficiency Syndrome 53
    Human Immunodeficiency Virus 1126
    Kaposi's Sarcoma 1253

Immune System
    Acquired Immune Deficiency Syndrome 53
    Anaphylactic Shock 129, 131
    Cellulitis 443

Immune Thrombocytopenic Purpura
    Idiopathic Thrombocytopenic Purpura 1189

Immunosuppression
    Acquired Immune Deficiency Syndrome 53
    Multiple Sclerosis 1401
    Pneumocystis Carinii Pneumonia 1663

Impending Cerebrovascular Accident
    Transient Ischemic Attack 2169

Impending Infarction
    Angina, Unstable 144

Impetigo
    Atopic Dermatitis 218

Implant
    Adrenal Tissue Implant or Transplant to Brain 76

Impotence
    Insertion of Inflatable Penile Prosthesis 1213

Impotence of an Organic Origin
    Penis Disorders 1608

Impulse Control Disorder
    Intermittent Explosive Disorder 1217

Inactive Colon
    Constipation 558

Inactive Rheumatic Fever
    Rheumatic Heart Disease, Chronic 1836

Inadequate Personality Disorder
    Dependent Personality Disorder 661

Incision
    Episiotomy 826
    of Skin and Subcutaneous Tissue, Drainage of Abscess or Cyst 1201
    Postpartum Mastitis 1705
    Sepsis 1905
    Skin or Subcutaneous Tissue Biopsy 1934
    Stye 2010

Incision and Drainage
    Incision of Skin and Subcutaneous Tissue, Drainage of Abscess or Cyst 1201

Incision and Drainage of Ischiorectal Abscess
    Abscess, Anorectal 20
    Incision and Drainage of Ischiorectal and/or Perirectal Abscess 1200

Incision and Drainage of Perirectal Abscess
    Incision and Drainage of Ischiorectal and/or Perirectal Abscess 1200

Incision of Bladder Neck
    Transurethral Incision of Bladder Neck 2172

Incision of Chest Wall
    Thoracostomy 2078

Incision of Ischiorectal Abscess
    Incision and Drainage of Ischiorectal and/or Perirectal Abscess 1200

Incision of Perirectal Abscess
    Incision and Drainage of Ischiorectal and/or Perirectal Abscess 1200

Incision of Skin
    and Subcutaneous Tissue, Drainage of Abscess or Cyst 1201

Incision of Skin and Subcutaneous Tissue, Drainage
    Sepsis 1905

Incision of Skin for Abscess Drainage
    Incision of Skin and Subcutaneous Tissue, Drainage of Abscess or Cyst 1201

Incision of Subcutaneous Tissue
    Incision of Skin and Subcutaneous Tissue, Drainage of Abscess or Cyst 1201

Incision of Tendon Sheath
    Tendon Release 2051
    Tendon Sheath Incision 2052

Incisional
    Skin or Subcutaneous Tissue Biopsy 1934

Incisional Biopsy
    Cancer, Oropharynx 369
    Cancer, Tongue 399
    Skin or Subcutaneous Tissue Biopsy 1934

Incisional Hernia
    Hernia Repair 1094, 1096
    Hernia, Incisional 1100

Incompetence
    Aortic Insufficiency 165
    Aortic Valve Stenosis 167

Incomplete
    Atrioventricular Block, Incomplete (First-Degree) 226
    Bundle Branch Block 310

Incomplete AV Block
    Atrioventricular Block Incomplete (Second-Degree) 223
    Atrioventricular Block, Incomplete (First-Degree) 226

Incomplete Bundle Branch Block
    Bundle Branch Block 310

Incomplete First Degree AV Block
    Atrioventricular Block, Incomplete (First-Degree) 226

Incomplete Second Degree AV Block
    Atrioventricular Block Incomplete (Second-Degree) 223

Incomplete Uterovaginal Prolapse
    Cystocele or Rectocele 621
    Urethrocele with Stress Incontinence 2220
    Urinary Incontinence in Women 2222

Incontinence
    Cystocele or Rectocele 621
    Neurogenic Bladder 1471
    Urethrocele with Stress Incontinence 2220
    Urinary Incontinence in Women 2222

Incontinence in Women
    Urinary Incontinence in Women 2222

Incontinence with Urethrocele
    Cystocele or Rectocele 621

Urethrocele with Stress Incontinence **2220**
Urinary Incontinence in Women **2222**

Indigestion
Achlorhydria and Hypochlorhydria **49**
Angina Pectoris **140**
Dyspepsia **759**
Peptic Ulcer Disease **1611**

Individual Psychotherapy
Psychotherapy, Individual **1748**

Induced Epilepsy
Jacksonian Seizure **1247**

Industrial Bronchitis
Hypersensitivity Pneumonitis **1150**

Indwelling Catheterization
Urethral Catheterization **2216**

Inebriation
Alcohol Intoxication, Acute **87**

Infarction
Angina, Unstable **144**
Myocardial Infarction, Acute **1424**

Infected Calluses
Corn and Callus, Infected **578**

Infected Corn
Corn and Callus, Infected **578**

Infected Corns
Corn and Callus, Infected **578**

Infection
Abscess, Anorectal **20**
Abscess, Breast **22**
Abscess, Larynx **25**
Abscess, Palmar **32**
Abscess, Perirectal **34**
Abscess, Peritonsillar **36**
Abscess, Psoas **38**
Abscess, Subdiaphragmatic **42**
Acquired Immune Deficiency Syndrome **53**
Actinomycosis **57**
Amebiasis **109**
Amputation **116, 118, 121, 123**
Bartholin's Gland Cyst **242**
Behçet's Syndrome **244**
Blastomycosis **266**
Blepharitis **268**
Bone Scan **277**
Brain Abscess **289**
Bronchiectasis **297**
Brucellosis **306**
Candidiasis **405**
Carbuncle **407**
Cardiomyopathy **419**
Cellulitis **443**
Cervicitis **472**
Chancroid **481**
Chromoblastomycosis **508**
Cryptococcosis **608**
Curvature of the Spine, Acquired **610**
Cystitis, Acute **616**
Diabetic Gangrene **689**
E. Coli **767**
Erythema Nodosum **835**
Excision of Nail, Nail Bed, or Nail Fold **856**
Hematuria **1055**
Human Immunodeficiency Virus **1126**
Hydronephrosis **1138**
Impetigo **1193**

Joint Disorders **1251**
Ludwig's Angina **1306**
Malaria **1330**
Myelophthisic Anemia **1422**
Myocarditis, Acute **1428**
Nasal Septum Perforation **1443**
Neutropenia **1477**
Orchitis **1524**
Osteoma **1536**
Osteomyelitis **1537**
Otitis Externa, Infective **1543**
Otitis Media **1545**
Pancreatitis **1573**
Pelvic Inflammatory Disease **1604**
Pericarditis, Acute **1615**
Pericarditis, Chronic Constrictive **1617**
Peritonitis **1628**
Pilonidal Cyst **1645**
Pleurisy **1659**
Polio **1683**
Premature Labor **1720**
Pyelonephritis, Acute **1762**
Rheumatic Fever, Acute **1833**
Rocky Mountain Spotted Fever **1845**
Root Canal Therapy **1847**
Salpingitis **1870**
Sebaceous Cyst **1896**
Sepsis **1905**
Shigellosis **1910**
Sinusitis **1928**
Synovitis **2031**
Syphilis **2033**
Syringomyelia **2035**
Tendonitis **2054**
Tenosynovitis **2057**
Tinea **2095**
Tinnitus **2097**
Tonsillectomy and Adenoidectomy **2102**
Tuberculosis, Respiratory **2194**
Tympanoplasty **2201**
Typhoid Fever **2204**
Wound Infection, Postoperative **2302**

Infection of the Feet
Warts, Plantar **2296**

Infectious
Chickenpox **490**
Dysentery **755**
Endocarditis, Bacterial **802**
Gastroenteritis, Infectious **973**
Giardiasis **989**
Human Immunodeficiency Virus **1126**
Mononucleosis **1390**
Pericarditis, Acute **1615**
Pharyngitis, Acute **1633**
Polyarteritis Nodosa **1685**
Shigellosis **1910**
Spondylitis **1958**
Tonsillitis and Adenoiditis **2104**
Trachoma **2161**
Traveler's Diarrhea **2177**
Tuberculosis, Respiratory **2194**
Tularemia **2197**
Typhoid Fever **2204**
Typhus Fever **2206**
Urethritis **2218**
Warts, Genital **2294**
Yellow Fever **2307**

Infectious Arthritis
Arthralgia **190**
Arthritis, Infectious **192**

Infectious Colitis
    Colitis 535
    Diarrhea 696
    Dysentery 755
    Gastroenteritis, Infectious 973
    Gastroenteritis, Non-Infectious 975
    Gastrointestinal Hemorrhage 982
    Traveler's Diarrhea 2177

Infectious Esophagitis
    Esophagitis 847

Infectious Gastroenteritis
    Dysentery 755
    Gastroenteritis, Infectious 973
    Traveler's Diarrhea 2177

Infectious Glomerulonephritis
    Glomerulonephritis, Acute 1001

Infectious Hepatitis
    Hepatitis A 1081
    Hepatitis, Viral 1091

Infectious Jaundice
    Jaundice 1249

Infectious Mononucleosis
    Hepatitis, Viral 1091
    Mononucleosis 1390

Infectious Penile Lesions
    Penis Disorders 1608

Infectious Periarteritis
    Polyarteritis Nodosa 1685

Infectious Spondylitis
    Spondylitis 1958

Infective
    Abscess, Breast 22
    Pericarditis, Acute 1615
    Pharyngitis, Acute 1633
    Tonsillitis and Adenoiditis 2104

Infective Adenoiditis
    Tonsillitis and Adenoiditis 2104

Infective Mastitis
    Abscess, Breast 22

Infective Otitis Externa
    Otitis Externa, Infective 1543

Infective Pericarditis
    Pericarditis, Acute 1615

Infective Pharyngitis
    Pharyngitis, Acute 1633

Infective Polyneuritis
    Guillain-Barré Syndrome 1022

Infective Tonsillitis
    Tonsillitis and Adenoiditis 2104

Inferior Vena Cava
    Vena Cava Interruption 2251

Infertility
    Culdoscopy 610
    Endometriosis 805
    Female 1204
    Laparoscopy 1275
    Male 1206
    Polycystic Ovary Syndrome 1686
    Ultrasound, Diagnostic 2212
    Varicocele 2242

Inflamed Conjunctiva
    Conjunctivitis 556

Inflamed Vermiform Appendix
    Appendicitis 175

Inflammation of Biceps Tendon
    Biceps Tendonitis 248

Inflammation of Brain
    Encephalitis 797

Inflammation of Cervix
    Cervicitis 472

Inflammation of Colon
    Colitis 535
    Diarrhea 696
    Gastroenteritis, Non-Infectious 975
    Hemorrhage of Rectum and Anus 1068
    Rectal Polyps 1783

Inflammation of Conjunctiva
    Conjunctivitis 556

Inflammation of Duodenum
    Duodenitis 749

Inflammation of Epididymis
    Epididymitis 819

Inflammation of Epiglottis
    Epiglottitis 822

Inflammation of Esophagus
    Esophagitis 847

Inflammation of Eye
    Blepharitis 268
    Chorioretinitis 506
    Conjunctivitis 556
    Dacryocystitis 627
    Iritis 1240
    Keratitis 1257
    Optic Neuritis 1521
    Uveitis 2231

Inflammation of Fallopian Tube
    Salpingitis 1870

Inflammation of Fascia
    Eosinophilic Fasciitis 814
    Plantar Fasciitis 1655

Inflammation of Gallbladder
    Cholecystitis 497

Inflammation of Intestines
    Colitis 535
    Gastroenteritis, Infectious 973
    Irritable Bowel Syndrome 1244

Inflammation of Large Intestine
    Colitis 535
    Diverticulosis and Diverticulitis of Colon 739

Inflammation of Lung Lining
    Humidifier Fever 1130
    Hypersensitivity Pneumonitis 1150
    Pleurisy 1659
    Ventilation Pneumonitis 2254

Inflammation of Membranes Covering Brain
    Meningitis, Bacterial 1357

Inflammation of Membranes Covering Spinal Cord
    Meningitis, Bacterial 1357

Inflammation of Meninges
　Meningitis, Bacterial 1357

Inflammation of Middle Ear
　Otitis Media 1545

Inflammation of Muscle
　Myalgia and Myositis 1411

Inflammation of Pancreas
　Pancreatitis 1573

Inflammation of Peritoneum
　Peritonitis 1628

Inflammation of Plantar Fascia
　Plantar Fasciitis 1655

Inflammation of Prostate Gland
　Prostatitis 1734

Inflammation of Renal Interstitial Tissue
　Nephritis, Interstitial 1453

Inflammation of Skeletal Muscle
　Myalgia and Myositis 1411

Inflammation of Skin
　Allergic Dermatitis 96
　Contact Dermatitis 560
　Poison Ivy, Oak, Sumac, or Other Plant Dermatitis 1673

Inflammation of Testis
　Orchitis 1524

Inflammation of Thyroid
　Thyroiditis 2091

Inflammation of Vagina
　Vaginitis 2233

Inflammation of Vermiform Appendix
　Appendicitis 175

Inflammation with Thrombus
　Thrombophlebitis 2086

Inflammatory Bowel Disease
　Colitis 535
　Colonoscopy 540
　Gastrointestinal Hemorrhage 982
　Hemorrhage of Rectum and Anus 1068

Inflammatory Condition
　Abscess, Breast 22
　Lupus Erythematosus, Systemic 1317

Inflammatory Demyelinating Polyneuropathy
　Guillain-Barré Syndrome 1022

Inflammatory Disease
　Abscess, Breast 22
　Behçet's Syndrome 244
　Bronchitis, Acute 299
　Bronchitis, Chronic 302
　Cervicitis 472
　Guillain-Barré Syndrome 1022

Inflammatory Disease of Breast
　Abscess, Breast 22

Inflammatory Disease of Cervix
　Cervicitis 472

Inflammatory Polyradiculopathy
　Guillain-Barré Syndrome 1022

Inflatable Penile Prosthesis Insertion
　Insertion of Inflatable Penile Prosthesis 1213

Influenza
　Arthralgia 190

Infusion of Antineoplastic Agents
　Chemotherapy 485
　Iontophoresis 1236

Infusion of Chemotherapeutic Agents
　Chemotherapy 485

Infusion Therapy
　Chemotherapy 485
　Intravenous Therapy 1235

Ingrown Toenail
　Toenail, Ingrown 2100

Inguinal Hernia
　Hernia Repair 1094, 1096
　Hernia, Inguinal and Femoral 1103

Inguinal Herniation
　Hernia, Inguinal and Femoral 1103

Inhalation
　Toxic Effects, Chlorine 2122
　Toxic Effects, Formaldehyde 2129
　Toxic Effects, Hydrochloric Acid 2131
　Toxic Effects, Hydrofluoric Acid 2132
　Toxic Effects, Lead (Inorganic Compounds) 2136

Inherited Hemolytic Anemia
　Hemolytic Anemia 1059

Injection
　Chemotherapy 485
　Hemorrhoid Treatment 1070
　Hemorrhoids 1073
　Iontophoresis 1236
　Sclerotherapy 1895

Injured Knee Cartilage
　Meniscus Disorders, Knee 1364

Injury
　Abdominal Muscle Strain 5
　Abrasions 14
　Achilles Bursitis or Tendinitis 47
　Amputation (Traumatic), Foot 118
　Amputation (Traumatic), Lower Extremity 121
　Biceps Tendonitis 248
　Brain Injury 292
　Cerebral Contusion, Closed 447
　Contusion, Eye 564
　Contusion, Lower Limb 566
　Contusion, Trunk 568
　Contusion, Upper Limb 571
　Corneal Abrasion 580
　Crush Wounds 603
　Dislocation, Cervical Vertebra 711
　Fracture, Calcaneus 898
　Fracture, Carpal Bones 901
　Fracture, Cervical Spine (With or Without Spinal Cord Injury) 904
　Fracture, Clavicle 907
　Fracture, Elbow (Distal Humerus) 910
　Fracture, Femoral Neck 912
　Fracture, Fingers and Thumb 915
　Fracture, Forefoot (Sesamoid, Phalanges) 918
　Fracture, Metacarpal Bones 922
　Fracture, Metatarsal Bones 925
　Fracture, Midfoot (Cuboid, Cuneiform, Navicular) 928
　Fracture, Pelvis 930
　Fracture, Radius and Ulna, Distal 933
　Fracture, Rib 936
　Fracture, Sacrum 939
　Fracture, Skull (Closed) 941

    Fracture, Sternum (Closed) 943
    Fracture, Thoracic Spine (With or Without Spinal Cord Injury) 948
    Fracture, Tibia or Fibula 951
    Fracture, Vertebra 954, 956
    Gas Gangrene 967
    Groin Strain 1020
    Head Injury, Superficial 1031
    Nerve Injury 1460
    Paralysis, Paraplegia, and Quadriplegia 1583
    Puncture Wound 1759
    Rotator Cuff Tear 1853
    Spinal Cord Injury 1946
    Sprains and Strains, Ankle 1971
    Sprains and Strains, Back 1975
    Sprains and Strains, Cervical Spine (Neck) 1981
    Sprains and Strains, Elbow 1984
    Sprains and Strains, Foot 1986
    Sprains and Strains, Hand or Fingers 1989
    Sprains and Strains, Knee 1991
    Trauma 2175

Inner Ear Fenestration
    Labyrinthitis 1267

Inner Ear Infection
    Labyrinthitis 1267

Insect Bite
    Anaphylactic Shock 129, 131
    Cellulitis 443
    Erysipelas 830
    Insect or Spider Bites and Stings 1210
    St. Louis Encephalitis 2000

Insect Sting
    Insect or Spider Bites and Stings 1210

Insecticide Poisoning
    Toxic Effects, Organophosphate and Carbamate Pesticides 2147

Insertion
    of Inflatable Penile Prosthesis 1213

Insertion of Bird Cage Filter
    Vena Cava Interruption 2251

Insertion of Greenfield Filter
    Vena Cava Interruption 2251

Insertion of Vena Caval Umbrella
    Vena Cava Interruption 2251

Insipidus
    Diabetes Insipidus 681

Insomnia with Sleep Apnea
    Sleep Apnea 1935

Insufficiency
    Hypoparathyroidism 1173

Insufficient Parathyroid Hormone Disease
    Hypoparathyroidism 1173

Insular Sclerosis
    Multiple Sclerosis 1401

Insulin Dependent Diabetes Mellitus
    Diabetes Mellitus Type I 683, 686

Insulinomas
    Hyperinsulinism 1144

Intention Tremor
    Tremor 2179

Interdigital Neuroma
    Excision of Morton's Neuroma 855

Intermediate Coronary Syndrome
    Angina, Unstable 144

Intermittent
    Explosive Disorder 1217
    Transient Ischemic Attack 2169

Intermittent Catheterization
    Urethral Catheterization 2216

Intermittent Cerebral Ischemia
    Transient Ischemic Attack 2169

Intermittent Claudication
    Peripheral Vascular Disease 1626

Intermittent Explosive Disorder
    Explosive Personality Disorder 862

Intermittent Porphyria
    Porphyria 1693

Interna
    Labyrinthitis 1267

Internal
    Derangement of Knee 1219

Internal Hemorrhoids
    Hemorrhoid Treatment 1070
    Hemorrhoids 1073

Internal Knee Derangement
    Internal Derangement of Knee 1219

Interpersonal Therapy
    Psychotherapy, Individual 1748

Interphalangeal Joint Dislocation
    Dislocation, Foot 716

Interruption of Inferior Vena Cava
    Vena Cava Interruption 2251

Interruption of Superior Vena Cava
    Vena Cava Interruption 2251

Intersphincteric Abscess
    Abscess, Perirectal 34

Interstitial Cystitis
    Cystitis, Interstitial 619

Interstitial Lung Disorders
    Interstitial Pulmonary Fibrosis 1219

Interstitial Myocarditis
    Myocarditis, Acute 1428

Interstitial Nephritis
    Nephritis, Interstitial 1453

Interventional Radiography
    X-ray 2305

Intervertebral Chemonucleolysis
    Chemonucleolysis of Interveterbral Disc 482

Intervertebral Chondrocalcinosis
    Disc Calcification 701

Intervertebral Disc Calcification
    Disc Calcification 701

Intervertebral Disc Chemolysis
    Chemonucleolysis of Interveterbral Disc 482

Intervertebral Disc Degeneration
    Degeneration, Cervical Intervertebral Disc 634
    Degeneration, Lumbar Intervertebral Disc 637
    Degeneration, Thoracic or Thoracolumbar Intervertebral Disc 640

Intervertebral Disc Disorder with Myelopathy
    Thoracic Disc Disorder with Myelopathy 2072
Intervertebral Disc Displacement
    Displacement, Cervical Intervertebral Disc Without Myelopathy 728
    Displacement, Lumbar Intervertebral Disc Without Myelopathy 732
    Displacement, Thoracic Intervertebral Disc Without Myelopathy 735
Intestinal
    Abdominal Pain 7
    Colostomy and Ileostomy 543
    Obstruction 1222
    Rectal Polyps 1783
    Shigellosis 1910
    Upset 1224
Intestinal Blockage
    Intestinal Obstruction 1222
Intestinal Flu
    Traveler's Diarrhea 2177
Intestinal Infection
    E. Coli 767
    Giardiasis 989
Intestinal Inflammation
    Colitis 535
    Diarrhea 696
    Gastroenteritis, Infectious 973
    Gastroenteritis, Non-Infectious 975
Intestinal Neuroses
    Irritable Bowel Syndrome 1244
Intestinal Obstruction
    Colon Resection 538
    Nasogastric Intubation 1444
    Volvulus 2289
Intestinal Parasitism
    Trichinosis 2183
Intestinal Stoma
    Colostomy and Ileostomy 543
Intestinal Volvulus
    Intestinal Obstruction 1222
Intestine
    Abdominal Adhesions 1
    Abdominal Pain 7
    Abdominoperineal Resection of Rectum 10
    Arterial Graft 183
    Endometriosis 805
    Hernia Repair 1094, 1096
    Hernia, Incisional 1100
    Hernia, Inguinal and Femoral 1103
    Hernia, Umbilical 1106
    Intestinal Obstruction 1222
    Intestinal Upset 1224
    Volvulus 2289
Intestines
    Colostomy and Ileostomy 543
    Giardiasis 989
Intolerance
    Allergy 100
Intoxication
    Alcoholism 90
    Poisoning 1675, 1677, 1679, 1681
    Poisoning, Iron 1677
    Poisoning, Vitamin B 1679
Intra-Abdominal Abscess
    Abscess, Psoas 38

Abscess, Subdiaphragmatic 42
Intracapsular Fracture of the Femoral Neck
    Fracture, Femoral Neck 912
Intracerebral Hemorrhage
    Cerebral Hemorrhage 449
    Intracranial Hemorrhage 1226, 1230
Intracoronary Artery Thrombolytic Infusion
    Coronary Thrombolysis 593
Intracranial Abscess
    Brain Abscess 289
Intracranial Aneurysm Clipping
    Repair of Cerebral Aneurysm 1812
Intracranial Aneurysm Repair
    Repair of Cerebral Aneurysm 1812
Intracranial Bleed
    Intracranial Hemorrhage 1226, 1230
    Intracranial Hemorrhage, Closed 1230
Intracranial Hematoma
    Intracranial Hemorrhage, Closed 1230
Intracranial Hemorrhage
    Cerebral Hemorrhage 449
Intramural Pseudodiverticulosis
    Esophageal Diverticula 836
Intraocular Inflammation
    Endophthalmitis 808
Intraocular Pressure
    Glaucoma, Acute (Angle-Closure) 995
    Glaucoma, Chronic (Open-Angle) 997
    Iridotomy 1239
Intrapulmonary Respiratory Failure
    Adult Respiratory Distress Syndrome 79
    Respiratory Failure 1821
Intravenous Pyelogram
    Appendicitis 175
    Bladder Polyps 264
    Cancer, Bladder 338
    Cancer, Kidney 358
    Cancer, Prostate 380
    Diverticulosis and Diverticulitis of Colon 739
Intravenous Therapy
    Sepsis 1905
    Septic Shock 1907
    Shigellosis 1910
    Shock 1915
    Tetanus 2060
Intraventricular Conduction Disorder
    Bundle Branch Block 310
Introverted Personality
    Schizoid Personality Disorder 1881
Intussusception
    Meckel's Diverticulum 1351
Invasive Hydatidiform Mole
    Choriocarcinoma 505
In-Vitro Fertilization (IVF)
    Infertility, Female 1204
Iontophoresis
    Carpal Tunnel Syndrome 430

IPF
  Interstitial Pulmonary Fibrosis 1219
Iridectomy
  Glaucoma, Acute (Angle-Closure) 995
Iridocyclitis
  Iritis 1240
  Uveitis 2231
Iridotomy
  Glaucoma, Acute (Angle-Closure) 995
Iritis
  Uveitis 2231
Iron Deficiency
  Anemia 1242
Iron Deficiency Anemia
  Anemia 133, 136
  Anemia Complicating Pregnancy 136
Irregular Heart Beat
  Arrhythmia 178
  Atrial Fibrillation 220
  Cardiac Arrest 409
  Palpitations 1566
  Premature Beats 1719
  Sick Sinus Syndrome 1920
  Tachycardia, Paroxysmal Supraventricular 2039
  Ventricular Fibrillation 2256
  Ventricular Premature Contractions 2258
  Ventricular Tachycardia 2260
Irritable
  Bowel Syndrome 1244
  Nervousness 1463
  Neurotic Disorders 1475
  Postconcussion Syndrome 1699
  Posttraumatic Stress Disorder 1707
  Premenstrual Syndrome 1724
Irritable Bowel Disease
  Irritable Bowel Syndrome 1244
Irritable Bowel Syndrome
  Constipation 558
Irritable Colon
  Irritable Bowel Syndrome 1244
Irritable Heart
  Neurocirculatory Asthenia 1467
Irritant Contact Dermatitis
  Contact Dermatitis 560
  Dermatitis 674
  Eczema 778
  Radiodermatitis 1780
Ischemic Attack
  Cerebrovascular Accident 454
  Transient Ischemic Attack 2169
Ischemic Heart Disease
  Atrioventricular Block, Complete (Third-Degree) 224
  Coronary Atherosclerosis 587
  Heart Failure, Congestive 1042
  Premature Beats 1719
  Ventricular Tachycardia 2260
Ischiorectal Abscess
  Abscess, Anorectal 20
  Abscess, Ischiorectal 24
  Abscess, Perirectal 34
  Incision and Drainage of Ischiorectal and/or Perirectal Abscess 1200

Ischiorectal Fistula
  Abscess, Anorectal 20
  Abscess, Ischiorectal 24
  Abscess, Perirectal 34
Isobrome Exposure
  Toxic Effects, Methyl Bromide 2142
Isolated Phobia
  Phobias, Specific 1639
IV
  Intravenous Therapy 1235
IV Therapy
  Hypovolemic Shock 1184
  Intravenous Therapy 1235
IVP
  Intravenous Pyelogram 1233

J

Janeway Gastrostomy
  Gastrostomy 984
Jaundice
  Abscess, Subdiaphragmatic 42
  Cholangiography 493
  Cholecystography 500
  Cirrhosis of the Liver 515
  Hepatitis C 1085
  Malaria 1330
  Sickle Cell Anemia 1922
  Spherocytosis, Hereditary 1944
Javelle Water Poisoning
  Toxic Effects, Chlorine 2122
Jaw
  Actinomycosis 57
  Ludwig's Angina 1306
  Temporomandibular Joint Syndrome 2049
Jeep Rider's Disease
  Pilonidal Cyst 1645
Jejunal Syndrome
  Dumping Syndrome 747
Jejunitis
  Colitis 535
  Diarrhea 696
  Gastroenteritis, Non-Infectious 975
Jejunostomy
  Enterostomy 811
Jejunum Feeding Enterostomy
  Enterostomy 811
Jock Itch
  Tinea 2095
Jogger's Heel
  Heel Spur (Calcaneal) 1053
Joint
  Arthrography 196
  Arthroscopy 199
  Aspiration 207–208
  Biopsy 252
  Bone Scan 277
  Disorders 1251
  Hallux Rigidus 1027
  Psoriatic Arthritis 1740
  Rheumatism 1837
  Rheumatoid Arthritis 1838

Synovectomy 2027
Synovial Cyst 2028
Synovitis 2031

Joint Arthralgia
Arthralgia 190
Psoriatic Arthritis 1740
Rheumatoid Arthritis 1838

Joint Arthrodesis
Arthrodesis 194

Joint Arthroplasty
Arthroplasty, Elbow 197
Hip Replacement, Total 1119
Knee Replacement, Total 1263
Shoulder Replacement 1917

Joint Cartilage
Loose Bodies, Knee 1300
Meniscus Disorders, Knee 1364
Osteochondritis Dissecans 1534
Patella Chondromalacia 1599

Joint Disorders
Gout 1012
Hammertoe 1029
Rheumatoid Arthritis 1838

Joint Displacement
Dislocation 705, 708, 711, 713, 716, 723, 726

Joint Endoscopy
Arthroscopy 199

Joint Fusion
Arthrodesis 194
Hallux Rigidus 1027
Hammertoe 1029

Joint Mice
Loose Bodies, Knee 1300

Joint Pain
Ankylosing Spondylitis 152
Arthralgia 190
Hemophilia A 1061
Hemophilia B 1064
Influenza 1207
Knee Replacement, Total 1263
Lyme Disease 1319
Metatarsalgia 1376
Polyarteritis Nodosa 1685
Rheumatic Fever, Acute 1833
Scleroderma 1892
Sickle Cell Anemia 1922
Strep Throat 2005

Joint Replacement
Arthrodesis 194
Arthroplasty, Elbow 197
Avascular Necrosis 235
Hip Replacement, Total 1119
Knee Replacement, Total 1263
Paget's Disease of Bone 1557
Shoulder Replacement 1917

Joint Separation
Dislocation 705, 708, 711, 713, 716, 723, 726

Jones Fracture
Fracture, Metatarsal Bones 925

Junctional Tachycardia
Tachycardia, Paroxysmal Supraventricular 2039

Jungian Therapy
Psychotherapy, Individual 1748

Jungle Fever
Yellow Fever 2307

Jungle Yellow Fever
Yellow Fever 2307

Juvenile Diabetes
Diabetes Mellitus Type I 683, 686

K

Kaposi's Sarcoma
Acquired Immune Deficiency Syndrome 53
Human Immunodeficiency Virus 1126
Kaposi's Sarcoma 1253

KC
Keratoconus 1259

Keller Operation
Bunionectomy 314

Keratectomy, Laser Photorefractive
Astigmatism 212

Keratitis Sicca
Dry Eye Syndrome 745

Keratoconjunctivitis Sicca
Corneal Ulcer 584
Dry Eye Syndrome 745
Foreign Body, Cornea 891
Keratitis 1257
Sjogren's Syndrome 1930

Keratomileusis
Astigmatism 212

Keratoplasty
Corneal Transplant 582

Keratotomy
Astigmatism 212
Radial Keratotomy 1775

Kernicterus
Rh Incompatibility 1831

Kidney
Abscess, Renal and Perinephric 40
Aldosteronism 94
Arterial Graft 183
Calculus, Renal (Kidney and Ureter) 335
Cancer, Kidney 358
Cystoscopy, Transurethral 624
Echinococcosis 772
Glomerulonephritis, Acute 1001
Glomerulonephritis, Chronic 1003
Glomerulosclerosis 1005
Glycosuria 1006
Hydronephrosis 1138
Lithotomy 1293–1294
Nephrectomy 1451
Nephrotic Syndrome 1456
Nephrotomy 1458
Porphyria 1693
Pyelonephritis, Chronic 1764
Renal Dialysis 1800
Renal Failure, Acute 1802
Renal Failure, Chronic 1804
Transplant 1261

Kidney and Ureter
Hydronephrosis 1138

Kidney Dialysis
  Glomerulosclerosis 1005
  Renal Dialysis 1800

Kidney Disease
  Cancer, Kidney 358
  Glomerulonephritis, Chronic 1003
  Hyperkalemia 1146
  Kidney Transplant 1261
  Nephrotic Syndrome 1456
  Peritonitis 1628
  Strep Throat 2005

Kidney Donor
  Kidney Transplant 1261
  Nephrectomy 1451

Kidney Failure
  Diabetic Glomerulosclerosis 690
  Glomerulonephritis, Chronic 1003
  High Blood Pressure, Malignant 1116
  Kidney Transplant 1261
  Nephrectomy 1451
  Polyarteritis Nodosa 1685
  Pyelonephritis, Chronic 1764
  Renal Dialysis 1800
  Renal Failure, Acute 1802
  Renal Failure, Chronic 1804

Kidney Infection
  Abscess, Renal and Perinephric 40
  Pyelonephritis, Acute 1762
  Pyelonephritis, Chronic 1764

Kidney Lithotomy
  Lithotomy 1293–1294
  Nephrotomy 1458

Kidney Neoplasm
  Cancer, Kidney 358

Kidney Recipient
  Kidney Transplant 1261

Kidney Removal
  Cancer, Kidney 358
  Kidney Transplant 1261
  Nephrectomy 1451

Kidney Stone
  Calculus, Renal (Kidney and Ureter) 335
  Hematuria 1055
  Hydronephrosis 1138
  Lithotomy 1293–1294
  Lithotomy, Percutaneous 1294
  Lithotripsy, Extracorporeal Shock Wave 1295
  Nephrotomy 1458
  Transurethral Removal of Obstruction from Ureter 2173

Kidney Surgery
  Kidney Transplant 1261
  Nephrectomy 1451
  Rib Resection 1844

Kidney Transplant
  Abscess, Renal and Perinephric 40
  Diabetic Glomerulosclerosis 690
  Glomerulonephritis, Chronic 1003
  Glomerulosclerosis 1005
  Renal Failure, Chronic 1804

Kissing Disease
  Mononucleosis 1390

Knee
  Arthroscopy 199
  Dislocation 705, 708, 711, 713, 716, 723, 726
  Dislocation, Femorotibial (Knee) Joint 713
  Dislocation, Patella (Kneecap) 723
  Erythema Nodosum 835
  Loose Bodies, Knee 1300
  Meniscectomy and Meniscus Repair 1361
  Meniscus Disorders, Knee 1364
  Patella Chondromalacia 1599
  Repair, Anterior Cruciate Ligament 1814
  Replacement, Total 1263
  Shin Splints 1912
  Sprains and Strains, Knee 1991

Knee Arthroplasty
  Knee Replacement, Total 1263
  Meniscectomy and Meniscus Repair 1361

Knee Bruise
  Contusion, Lower Limb 566
  Patella Chondromalacia 1599

Knee Cap
  Joint Disorders 1251
  Patella Chondromalacia 1599

Knee Contusion
  Shin Splints 1912
  Sprains and Strains, Knee 1991

Knee Derangement
  Internal Derangement of Knee 1219

Knee Dislocation
  Dislocation, Femorotibial (Knee) Joint 713
  Dislocation, Patella (Kneecap) 723

Knee Disorders
  Knee Replacement, Total 1263
  Meniscus Disorders, Knee 1364
  Patella Chondromalacia 1599

Knee Injury
  Dislocation, Patella (Kneecap) 723
  Knee Replacement, Total 1263
  Patella Chondromalacia 1599

Knee Replacement
  Psoriatic Arthritis 1740
  Total 1263

Knee Sprain
  Shin Splints 1912
  Sprains and Strains, Knee 1991

Knee Strain
  Repair, Anterior Cruciate Ligament 1814
  Shin Splints 1912
  Sprains and Strains, Knee 1991

Kneecap
  Dislocation, Patella (Kneecap) 723
  Internal Derangement of Knee 1219
  Patella Chondromalacia 1599

Kneecap Dislocation
  Dislocation, Patella (Kneecap) 723

Kneecap Fracture
  Reduction of Fracture or Dislocation 1791

Kneecap Subluxation
  Dislocation, Patella (Kneecap) 723

Koontz Technique
  Hernia, Incisional 1100

Korsakoff's Psychosis
  Vitamin B_1 Deficiency 2272

Index 2597

Kupffer Cell Sarcoma
  Hepatic Angiosarcoma 1077
Kupffer Cells
  Cancer, Liver 360
Kyphosis
  Curvature of the Spine, Acquired 610
  Osteoporosis 1540
  Pott's Disease 1709

L

Labor
  Premature Labor 1720
Labor in Pregnancy
  Premature Labor 1720
Labyrinthitis
  Tinnitus 2097
Laceration 1269
  Head Injury, Superficial 1031
  Open Wound 1504, 1510, 1512
  Open Wound, Back 1510
  Open Wound, Chest 1512
  Puncture Wound 1759
  Repair, Tendon Laceration of Hand 1817
Lacrimal Sac Infection
  Dacryocystitis 627
Lambliasis
  Giardiasis 989
Laminectomy
  Myelopathy 1420
  or Laminotomy 1273
  Spinal Fusion 1951
  Spinal Stenosis 1952
  Syringomyelia 2035
Laminotomy
  Laminectomy or Laminotomy 1273
  Spinal Fusion 1951
Landry's Ascending Paralysis
  Guillain-Barré Syndrome 1022
Landry's Paralysis
  Guillain-Barré Syndrome 1022
Lap Chole
  Cholecystectomy 495
Laparoscopic Cholecystectomy
  Cholecystectomy 495
  Cholecystitis 497
Laparoscopic Hernia Repair
  Hernia Repair 1094, 1096
  Hernia, Incisional 1100
Laparoscopic Nephropexy
  Nephropexy 1455
Laparoscopic Removal of Gallbladder
  Cholecystectomy 495
Laparoscopy
  Abdominal Adhesions 1
  Adrenalectomy 77
  Appendectomy 174
  Appendicitis 175
  Cancer, Liver 360
  Ectopic Pregnancy 775
  Endometriosis 805

  Hemorrhage of Rectum and Anus 1068
  Myomectomy, Uterine 1430
  Oophorectomy 1501, 1503
  Ovarian Cyst, Benign 1552
  Ovarian Cyst, Resection of 1555
  Paraovarian Cyst 1590
  Polycystic Ovary Syndrome 1686
  Rupture of Spleen, Traumatic 1860
  Salpingectomy 1868
  Salpingitis 1870
  Salpingo-oophorectomy 1873
  Splenectomy 1955
  Splenomegaly 1956
  Tubal Ligation 2193
Laparotomy
  Appendectomy 174
  Appendicitis 175
  Cancer, Ovary 372
  Ectopic Pregnancy 775
  Hepatic Angiosarcoma 1077
  Intestinal Obstruction 1222
  Ovarian Cyst, Resection of 1555
  Peritonitis 1628
  Rupture of Spleen, Traumatic 1860
  Salpingo-oophorectomy 1873
  Splenectomy 1955
  Splenomegaly 1956
Large Cell Immunoblastic Lymphoma
  Non-Hodgkin's Lymphoma 1482
Large Intestine
  Abdominal Adhesions 1
  Abdominoperineal Resection of Rectum 10
  Cancer, Colon 354
  Cancer, Rectum 384
  Colitis 535
  Colon Resection 538
  Diverticulosis and Diverticulitis of Colon 739
  Gastrointestinal Hemorrhage 982
Large Toe Bursa Inflammation
  Bunion 312
  Bunionectomy 314
Laryngeal Abscess
  Abscess, Larynx 25
Laryngectomy
  Cancer, Oropharynx 369
Laryngitis
  Hemoptysis 1067
Larynx
  Abscess, Larynx 25
  Laryngectomy 1278
  Laryngoscopy 1281
Laser Iridotomy
  Iridotomy 1239
Laser Peripheral Iridotomy
  Iridotomy 1239
LASIK
  Astigmatism 212
  Keratectomy, Laser Photorefractive 1256
  Myopia 1431
Late-Onset Paraphrenia
  Delusional Disorder 649
Lateral Epicondylitis
  Epicondylitis, Medial and Lateral 816

Lateral Malleolus Fracture
    Fracture, Ankle 895
Lateral Paravaginal Repair
    Vesicourethropexy 2265
Laxative Colitis
    Irritable Bowel Syndrome 1244
Lazy Colon
    Constipation 558
Lazy Eye
    Amblyopia, Toxic 107
LBBB
    Bundle Branch Block 310
LBS
    Irritable Bowel Syndrome 1244
LC
    Cystitis, Interstitial 619
    Lumbar Puncture 1309
Lead Poisoning
    Poisoning 1675, 1677, 1679, 1681
    Toxic Effects, Lead (Inorganic Compounds) 2136
Lead Toxicity
    Toxic Effects, Lead (Inorganic Compounds) 2136
Left Bundle Branch Block
    Bundle Branch Block 310
Left Heart Catheterization
    Cardiac Catheterization 411
Left Hemicolectomy
    Colon Resection 538
Left Ventricular Failure
    Heart Failure, Congestive 1042
Left Ventricular Hypertrophy
    Hypertensive Heart Disease 1156
Leg
    Amputation 116, 118, 121, 123
    Amputation (Traumatic), Lower Extremity 121
    Arterial Graft 183
    Cellulitis 443
    Chromoblastomycosis 508
    Compartment Syndrome 547
    Contact Dermatitis 560
    Dermatitis 674
    Diabetic Gangrene 689
    Fasciotomy 870
    Folliculitis 887
    Fracture, Tibia or Fibula 951
Leg Bruise
    Contusion, Lower Limb 566
Leg Contusion
    Contusion, Lower Limb 566
Leg Fracture
    Fracture, Tibia or Fibula 951
Leg Ulcer
    Varicose Ulcer 2244
    Varicose Veins 2246
Legal Blindness
    Blindness 270
Legionellosis
    Legionnaire's Disease 1282

Legionnaire's Disease
    Legionnaire's Disease 1282
Legionnaire's Pneumonia
    Legionnaire's Disease 1282
    Pneumonia 1667
Leiomyoma
    Dysfunctional Uterine Bleeding 757
    Fibroid Tumor of Uterus 875
    Hysterectomy 1186
    Menstrual Disorders 1369
    Myomectomy, Uterine 1430
    Rectal Polyps 1783
Lesion
    Cancer, Oropharynx 369
    Cancer, Skin 387
    Cancer, Tongue 399
    Candidiasis 405
    Cervical Biopsy 460
    Cervical Cauterization 461
    Coin Lesion 532
    Erythema Nodosum 835
    Herpes Simplex 1108
    Kaposi's Sarcoma 1253
Lesion Disorder
    Carbuncle 407
    Coin Lesion 532
    Contact Dermatitis 560
    Dermatitis 674
    Eczema 778
    Furuncle 961
    Mycosis Fungoides 1416
    Osler-Weber-Rendu Disease 1528
Lesion Resection
    Excision or Destruction of Duodenal Lesion 857
Leucitis
    Scleritis 1891
Leucoderma
    Vitiligo 2286
Leukemia
    Bone Marrow Biopsy 273
    Bone Marrow Transplant 275
    Chemotherapy 485
Leukocytic Sarcoma
    Leukemia 1284
Leukoderma
    Vitiligo 2286
Leukoerythroblastic Anemia
    Myelophthisic Anemia 1422
Leukoerythroblastosis
    Myelophthisic Anemia 1422
Lichen Aureus
    Purpura Simplex 1760
Lichen Simplex Chronicus
    Contact Dermatitis 560
    Dermatitis 674
    Eczema 778
Lichtenstein Open Mesh Technique
    Hernia, Inguinal and Femoral 1103
Lid Contusion
    Contusion, Eye 564

Ligation
    and Stripping of Varicose Veins 1287
    Subarachnoid Hemorrhage (Non-traumatic) 2011

Ligation and Stripping
    of Varicose Veins 1287

Ligation of Esophageal Varices
    Sclerotherapy 1895

Ligation of Fallopian Tubes
    Tubal Ligation 2193

Ligation of Spermatic Vein
    for Varicocele 1289

Light Therapy
    Vitamin D Deficiency 2281
    Vitiligo 2286

Lightheadedness
    Dizziness and Giddiness 742
    Rupture of Spleen, Traumatic 1860
    Shock 1915
    Tachycardia, Paroxysmal Supraventricular 2039
    Vitamin D Deficiency 2281

Limb
    Amputation 116, 118, 121, 123
    Contusion, Lower Limb 566
    Pain in Limb 1562

Lingual
    Cancer, Oropharynx 369
    Cancer, Tongue 399
    Pineal Gland Neoplasm 1647

Lipoma
    Tumor, Benign 2199

Liquid Nitrogen Treatment
    Cryotherapy, Genital Warts (Female) 605
    Cryotherapy, Genital Warts (Male) 606

Liquid Silver Poisoning
    Toxic Effects, Mercury 2138

Lisfranc's Fracture
    Fracture, Metatarsal Bones 925
    Fracture, Midfoot (Cuboid, Cuneiform, Navicular) 928

Lithotomy
    Nephrotomy 1458
    Percutaneous 1294

Lithotomy, Open
    Lithotomy 1293–1294
    Nephrotomy 1458

Lithotripsy
    Calculus, Bladder 333
    Calculus, Renal (Kidney and Ureter) 335
    Extracorporeal Shock Wave 1295

Liver
    Abscess, Liver 27
    Biopsy 1297
    Cancer, Liver 360
    Cholangiography 493
    Disease 1298
    Echinococcosis 772

Liver Biopsy
    Cancer, Liver 360
    Cirrhosis of the Liver 515
    Hepatic Angiosarcoma 1077
    Hepatitis C 1085
    Hepatitis, Alcoholic 1087

Hepatitis, Chronic 1089
Hepatitis, Viral 1091

Liver Cancer
    Cancer, Liver 360
    Esophagogastroduodenoscopy 850
    Hepatic Angiosarcoma 1077

Liver Cell Cancer
    Cancer, Liver 360

Liver Cell Carcinoma
    Cancer, Liver 360

Liver Cirrhosis
    Cirrhosis of the Liver 515
    Liver Disease 1298

Liver Disease
    Encephalopathy 799
    Esophageal Varices 843
    Gynecomastia 1025
    Hepatitis, Alcoholic 1087
    Hepatitis, Chronic 1089
    Hepatitis, Viral 1091
    Jaundice 1249

Liver Failure
    Hepatic Coma 1079
    Hepatitis C 1085

Liver Flap
    Tremor 2179

Liver Inflammation
    Hepatitis A 1081
    Hepatitis B 1083
    Hepatitis C 1085
    Hepatitis, Alcoholic 1087
    Hepatitis, Chronic 1089
    Hepatitis, Viral 1091

Lobar Pneumonia
    Pneumonia 1667

Lobe Syndrome
    Lung Collapse 1312

Lobectomy
    Cancer, Lung 363
    Echinococcosis 772
    Lung Excision 1314
    Pneumonectomy 1664

Localized Fibrous Tumor of the Pleura
    Cancer, Pleura 377

Localized Scleroderma
    Scleroderma 1892

Lock Jaw
    Tetanus 2060

Lofgren's Syndrome
    Sarcoidosis 1875

Long Myotomy
    Myotomy of Esophagus 1433

Loose Bodies of Knee
    Loose Bodies, Knee 1300

Loose Joint Cartilage
    Loose Bodies, Knee 1300

Loose Stool
    Colitis 535
    Diarrhea 696
    Gastroenteritis, Non-Infectious 975

Lordosis
    Curvature of the Spine, Acquired 610
Loss of Consciousness
    Brain Injury 292
    Carotid Sinus Syncope 425
    Cerebral Contusion, Closed 447
    Cerebral Hemorrhage 449
    Cerebrovascular Accident 454
    Coma 449, 544
    Concussion, Cerebral 553
    Epilepsy 824
    Grand Mal Seizure 1014
    Hepatic Coma 1079
    Syncope 2024
    Vasovagal Syncope 2249
Lou Gehrig's Disease
    Amyotrophic Lateral Sclerosis 125
Louse-Borne Typhus
    Typhus Fever 2206
Low Back Pain
    Ankylosing Spondylitis 152
    Chiropractic Adjustments and Manipulations 492
    Coccygodynia 527
    Degeneration, Lumbar Intervertebral Disc 637
    Displacement, Lumbar Intervertebral Disc Without Myelopathy 732
    Prostatitis 1734
Low Back Syndrome
    Low Back Pain 1302
Low Blood
    Hypoglycemia 1171
    Hypotension 1178
Low Blood Glucose
    Hypoglycemia 1171
Low Blood Pressure
    Anemia Complicating Pregnancy 136
    Coma 449, 544
    Hypotension 1178
Low Blood Sugar
    Coma 449, 544
    Hypoglycemia 1171
Low Grade Astrocytoma
    Astrocytoma 214
Lower Extremity
    Amputation (Traumatic), Lower Extremity 121
    Cancer, Skin 387
    Eosinophilic Fasciitis 814
    Gout 1012
    Varicose Veins 2246
Lower Extremity Varix
    Varicose Veins 2246
Lower Gastrointestinal Tract
    Intestinal Upset 1224
Lower GI Series
    Lower Gastrointestinal Series 1305
Lower Intestinal Bleeding
    Gastrointestinal Hemorrhage 982
Lower Limb
    Amputation (Traumatic), Lower Extremity 121
    Erythema Nodosum 835
    Fracture, Tibia or Fibula 951
    Varicose Veins 2246

Low-Lying Placenta
    Placenta Previa 1653
Loxia
    Torticollis 2108
LP
    Emphysema 792
    Lumbar Puncture 1309
LPI
    Iridotomy 1239
Ludwig's Angina
    Ludwig's Angina 1306
Lues
    Syphilis 2033
Lumbago
    Degeneration, Lumbar Intervertebral Disc 637
    Low Back Pain 1302
    Sprains and Strains, Back 1975
Lumbalgia
    Degeneration, Lumbar Intervertebral Disc 637
Lumbar
    Puncture 1309
    Sciatica 1890
Lumbar Disc Disease
    Degeneration, Lumbar Intervertebral Disc 637
Lumbar Disc Disorder
    Displacement, Lumbar Intervertebral Disc Without Myelopathy 732
    with Myelopathy 1308
Lumbar Disc Displacement with Myelopathy
    Lumbar Disc Disorder with Myelopathy 1308
Lumbar Disc Displacement Without Myelopathy
    Displacement, Lumbar Intervertebral Disc Without Myelopathy 732
Lumbar Disc Herniation
    Displacement, Lumbar Intervertebral Disc Without Myelopathy 732
Lumbar Disc Prolapse
    Displacement, Lumbar Intervertebral Disc Without Myelopathy 732
Lumbar Fracture
    Fracture, Vertebra 954, 956
Lumbar Intervertebral Disc
    Degeneration, Lumbar Intervertebral Disc 637
    Displacement, Lumbar Intervertebral Disc Without Myelopathy 732
Lumbar Intervertebral Disc Degeneration
    Degeneration, Lumbar Intervertebral Disc 637
Lumbar Intervertebral Disc Displacement
    Displacement, Lumbar Intervertebral Disc Without Myelopathy 732
Lumbar Intervertebral Disc Without Myelopathy
    Displacement, Lumbar Intervertebral Disc Without Myelopathy 732
Lumbar Laminectomy
    Laminectomy or Laminotomy 1273
Lumbar Nephrotomy
    Nephrotomy 1458
Lumbar Puncture
    Aspiration 207—208
    Cryptococcosis 608
    Dementia 651, 653
    Encephalitis 797
    General Paresis 986
    Grand Mal Seizure 1014
    Guillain-Barré Syndrome 1022

Myelography 1419

Lumbar Region Spondylolysis
Spondylolysis, Lumbar Region 1962

Lumbar Spinal Cord Compression
Lumbar Disc Disorder with Myelopathy 1308

Lumbar Spine
Curvature of the Spine, Acquired 610
Fracture, Lumbosacral Spine (With or Without Spinal Cord Injury) 920
Syringomyelia 2035

Lumbar Spine Fracture
Fracture, Lumbosacral Spine (With or Without Spinal Cord Injury) 920

Lumbar Sprain
Sprains and Strains, Back 1975

Lumbar Sympathectomy
Sympathectomy 2022

Lumbar Vertebrae
Chemonucleolysis of Interveterbral Disc 482

Lumbar Vertebrae Spondylolysis
Spondylolisthesis 1960
Spondylolysis, Lumbar Region 1962

Lumbosacral Area
Fracture, Lumbosacral Spine (With or Without Spinal Cord Injury) 920

Lumbosacral Pain
Fracture, Lumbosacral Spine (With or Without Spinal Cord Injury) 920
Low Back Pain 1302

Lumbosacral Spinal Fracture
Fracture, Lumbosacral Spine (With or Without Spinal Cord Injury) 920

Lumbosacral Spine
Fracture, Lumbosacral Spine (With or Without Spinal Cord Injury) 920

Lump in the Rectum
Hemorrhoids 1073

Lumpectomy
Breast Biopsy 295
Cancer, Breast 347

Lumpy Jaw
Actinomycosis 57

Lung
Abscess, Lung 29
Asbestosis 201
Asthma 209
Biopsy 1310
Bronchiectasis 297
Bronchitis, Acute 299
Bronchoscopy 305
Cancer, Lung 363
Chest Pain 486
Coin Lesion 532
Collapse 1312
Cor Pulmonale, Acute and Chronic 576
Echinococcosis 772
Emphysema 792
Excision 1314
Hemothorax, Traumatic 1075
Hypersensitivity Pneumonitis 1150
Interstitial Pulmonary Fibrosis 1219
Legionnaire's Disease 1282
Pneumocystis Carinii Pneumonia 1663
Pneumonectomy 1664
Pneumonia 1667
Pneumothorax 1671
Sarcoidosis 1875
Siderosis 1924

Silicosis 1926
Toxic Effects, Chromium 2124
Tuberculosis, Respiratory 2194
Ventilation Pneumonitis 2254

Lung Abscess
Abscess, Lung 29

Lung Aluminosis
Siderosis 1924

Lung Biopsy
Coin Lesion 532

Lung Cancer
Bronchoscopic Biopsy 304
Cancer, Lung 363
Hemoptysis 1067
Lung Excision 1314
Pneumonectomy 1664

Lung Carcinoma
Cancer, Lung 363

Lung Collapse
Pneumothorax 1671

Lung Disease
Asbestosis 201
Asthma 209
Blastomycosis 266
Bronchiectasis 297
Bronchoscopic Biopsy 304
Bronchoscopy 305
Byssinosis 328
Cancer, Lung 363
Cancer, Pleura 377
Chronic Obstructive Pulmonary Disease 511
Coccidioidomycosis 525
Cryptococcosis 608
Emphysema 792
Histoplasmosis 1121
Interstitial Pulmonary Fibrosis 1219
Legionnaire's Disease 1282
Lung Excision 1314
Occupational Asthma 1498
Pneumoconiosis 1662
Pneumonia 1667
Siderosis 1924
Silicosis 1926
Tuberculosis, Respiratory 2194

Lung Edema
Pulmonary Edema 1756

Lung Excision
Pneumonectomy 1664
Rib Resection 1844

Lung Function Tests
Pulmonary Function Tests 1758

Lung Infection
Cancer, Lung 363
Cryptococcosis 608
Humidifier Fever 1130
Lung Biopsy 1310

Lung Lining Inflammation
Pleurisy 1659
Ventilation Pneumonitis 2254

Lung Removal
Pneumonectomy 1664

Lung Water
Pulmonary Edema 1756

Lunger's Elbow
    Bursitis 325
Lupus
    Arthralgia 190
    Erythematosus, Systemic 1317
    Hepatitis, Chronic 1089
Luxation
    Dislocation, Foot 716
LVP
    Intravenous Pyelogram 1233
Lyme Arthritis
    Lyme Disease 1319
Lyme Disease
    Arthralgia 190
Lyme Disease Arthritis
    Lyme Disease 1319
Lymph Follicular Hypertrophy
    Lymphadenitis and Lymphadenopathy 1322
Lymph Gland Infection
    Lymphadenitis and Lymphadenopathy 1322
    Lymphangitis 1324
Lymph Node Aspiration
    Lymphadenitis and Lymphadenopathy 1322
Lymph Nodes
    Cancer, Breast 347
    Cancer, Oropharynx 369
    Cancer, Skin 387
    Cancer, Stomach 391
    Cancer, Testicle(s) 393
    Cancer, Thyroid Gland 396
    Cancer, Tongue 399
    Cat Scratch Disease 435
    Chancroid 481
    Lymphadenitis and Lymphadenopathy 1322
Lymphadenitis
    and Lymphadenopathy 1322
Lymphadenitis and Lymphadenopathy
    Non-Hodgkin's Lymphoma 1482
Lymphadenoid Goiter
    Thyroiditis 2091
Lymphadenopathy
    Chronic Fatigue Syndrome 509
    Lymphadenitis and Lymphadenopathy 1322
Lymphangitis
    Abscess 17, 20, 22, 24–25, 27, 29, 32, 34, 36, 38, 40, 42
    Cellulitis 443
Lymphatic Filariasis
    Filariasis 881
Lymphatic Tissue
    Lymphangitis 1324
    Non-Hodgkin's Lymphoma 1482
Lymphoblastic Lymphoma
    Non-Hodgkin's Lymphoma 1482
Lymphoblastoma
    Non-Hodgkin's Lymphoma 1482
Lymphocytic Thyroiditis
    Thyroiditis 2091
Lymphoid Leukemia
    Leukemia 1284
Lymphoid Polyps
    Rectal Polyps 1783
Lymphoma
    Bone Marrow Biopsy 273
    Bone Marrow Transplant 275
    Cancer, Small Intestine (Including Duodenum) 389
    Cancer, Stomach 391
    Mycosis Fungoides 1416
    Non-Hodgkin's Lymphoma 1482
Lymphomas
    Non-Hodgkin's Lymphoma 1482
Lyssa
    Rabies 1773

M

Machine Operator's Lung
    Hypersensitivity Pneumonitis 1150
Macrocytic Anemia
    Anemia Complicating Pregnancy 136
    Pernicious Anemia 1630
Macronodular Cirrhosis
    Cirrhosis of the Liver 515
Macular Degeneration
    Blindness 270
    Senile Macular Degeneration 1903
Mad Hatter's Disease Poisoning
    Toxic Effects, Mercury 2138
Majocchi's Purpura
    Purpura Simplex 1760
Major
    Depression, Major 665
    Thalassemia 2066
Major Depressive Disorder
    Depression, Major 665
Major Depressive Episode with Psychotic Features
    Depressive Psychosis 670
Major Epilepsy
    Epilepsy 824
    Grand Mal Seizure 1014
Malaise
    Chronic Fatigue Syndrome 509
    Multiple Chemical Sensitivity Syndrome 1397
Malarial Fever
    Malaria 1330
Malathion Exposure
    Toxic Effects, Organophosphate and Carbamate Pesticides 2147
Malayan Filariasis
    Filariasis 881
Male
    Cancer, Prostate 380
    Cancer, Testicle(s) 393
    Circumcision 514
    Climacteric 1332
    Cryotherapy, Genital Warts (Male) 606
    Gynecomastia 1025
    Hemophilia A 1061
    Hemophilia B 1064
    Hydrocele 1136
    Infertility, Male 1206
    Orchiectomy 1523

Orchitis 1524
Prostatectomy 1729
Prostatic Hypertrophy 1731
Prostatitis 1734
Spermatocele 1942
Varicocele 2242
Vasectomy 2248

Male Castration
Orchiectomy 1523

Male Contraceptive Procedure
Vasectomy 2248

Male Infertility
Infertility, Male 1206

Male Menopause
Male Climacteric 1332

Male Sterilization
Vasectomy 2248

Malignancy
Cancer, Bladder 338
Cancer, Brain 344
Cancer, Breast 347
Cancer, Cervix 351
Cancer, Colon 354
Cancer, Esophagus 356
Cancer, Kidney 358
Cancer, Liver 360
Cancer, Lung 363
Cancer, Oropharynx 369
Cancer, Ovary 372
Cancer, Pancreas 375
Cancer, Pleura 377
Cancer, Prostate 380
Cancer, Rectum 384
Cancer, Skin 387
Cancer, Small Intestine (Including Duodenum) 389
Cancer, Stomach 391
Cancer, Testicle(s) 393
Cancer, Thyroid Gland 396
Cancer, Tongue 399
Multiple Myeloma 1399
Paget's Disease of Breast 1559
Pericarditis, Chronic Constrictive 1617
Pineal Gland Neoplasm 1647
Radiation Therapy 1778

Malignant
Astrocytoma 214
Bone Tumors 281
Breast Biopsy 295
Cancer, Bladder 338
Cancer, Brain 344
Cancer, Breast 347
Cancer, Cervix 351
Cancer, Colon 354
Cancer, Esophagus 356
Cancer, Kidney 358
Cancer, Liver 360
Cancer, Lung 363
Cancer, Oropharynx 369
Cancer, Ovary 372
Cancer, Pancreas 375
Cancer, Pleura 377
Cancer, Prostate 380
Cancer, Rectum 384
Cancer, Skin 387
Cancer, Small Intestine (Including Duodenum) 389
Cancer, Stomach 391
Cancer, Testicle(s) 393

Cancer, Thyroid Gland 396
Cancer, Tongue 399
Kaposi's Sarcoma 1253
Paget's Disease of Breast 1559
Pineal Gland Neoplasm 1647

Malignant Hemangioendothelioma
Hepatic Angiosarcoma 1077

Malignant Hypertension
High Blood Pressure, Malignant 1116
Renovascular Hypertension 1809

Malignant Jaundice
Jaundice 1249

Malignant Lymphoma of the Thyroid
Cancer, Thyroid Gland 396

Malignant Melanoma
Cancer, Skin 387

Malignant Neoplasm
Astrocytoma 214
Bone Tumors 281
Cancer, Bladder 338
Cancer, Bone 341
Cancer, Brain 344
Cancer, Breast 347
Cancer, Colon 354
Cancer, Esophagus 356
Cancer, Kidney 358
Cancer, Lung 363
Cancer, Oropharynx 369
Cancer, Ovary 372
Cancer, Pancreas 375
Cancer, Pleura 377
Cancer, Prostate 380
Cancer, Rectum 384
Cancer, Small Intestine (Including Duodenum) 389
Cancer, Stomach 391
Cancer, Testicle(s) 393
Cancer, Thyroid Gland 396
Cancer, Tongue 399
Cancer, Uterus 402
Choriocarcinoma 505
Glioma 999
Paget's Disease of Breast 1559

Malignant Neoplasm of Brain
Astrocytoma 214
Cancer, Brain 344
Glioma 999

Malignant Neoplasm of Breast
Cancer, Breast 347
Paget's Disease of Breast 1559

Malignant Neoplasm of Breast Nipple
Cancer, Breast 347
Paget's Disease of Breast 1559

Malignant Neoplasm of Bronchus
Cancer, Lung 363

Malignant Neoplasm of Duodenum
Cancer, Small Intestine (Including Duodenum) 389

Malignant Neoplasm of Rectosigmoid Junction
Cancer, Colon 354
Cancer, Rectum 384

Malignant Neoplasm of Rectum
Cancer, Colon 354
Cancer, Rectum 384

Malignant Neoplasm of Trachea
    Cancer, Lung 363
    Cancer, Oropharynx 369

Malignant Neoplasm of Uterus
    Cancer, Uterus 402
    Choriocarcinoma 505

Malignant Pheochromocytoma
    Pheochromocytoma 1638

Malignant Retinopathy
    Diabetic Retinopathy 694

Malleolar Fracture
    Fracture, Ankle 895

Malleolus
    Fracture, Ankle 895
    Sprains and Strains, Ankle 1971

Mallet Toe
    Hammertoe 1029

Malleus
    Hammertoe 1029
    Hearing Loss 1036

Mallory-Weiss Syndrome
    Esophagogastroduodenoscopy 850
    Mallory-Weiss Syndrome 1333

Mallory-Weiss Tear
    Mallory-Weiss Syndrome 1333

Malnutrition
    Amblyopia, Toxic 107
    Enterostomy 811

Malta Fever
    Brucellosis 306

Malunion of Fracture
    Malunion and Nonunion of Fracture 1335

Mammary Abscess
    Abscess, Breast 22

Mammary Dysplasia
    Fibrocystic Breast Disease 874

Mammillary Fistula
    Abscess, Breast 22

Mammogram
    Abscess, Breast 22
    Cancer, Breast 347
    Fibrocystic Breast Disease 874
    Mammography 1337

Mammography
    Breast Biopsy 295
    X-ray 2305

Mammoplasty
    Augmentation 1338
    Reduction Mammoplasty 1790

Mandible
    Ludwig's Angina 1306

Mania
    Antisocial Personality Disorder 156
    Bipolar Affective Disorder 253, 256, 258, 260
    Bipolar Affective Disorder, Mixed 258
    Bipolar Affective Disorder, Single Manic Episode 260
    Electroconvulsive Therapy 782
    Intermittent Explosive Disorder 1217
    Manic Disorder, Recurrent 1339

    Psychopharmacotherapy 1743
    Schizoaffective Disorder 1878

Manic Depressive Illness
    Bipolar Affective Disorder 253, 256, 258, 260
    Bipolar Affective Disorder, Depressed 256
    Schizoaffective Disorder 1878

Manic Disorder
    Bipolar Affective Disorder, Single Manic Episode 260
    Recurrent 1339

Manic-Depressive Illness Depressed Type
    Bipolar Affective Disorder, Depressed 256

Manipulation
    Chiropractic Adjustments and Manipulations 492
    Degeneration, Cervical Intervertebral Disc 634
    Degeneration, Thoracic or Thoracolumbar Intervertebral Disc 640
    Neck Pain 1448
    Reduction of Fracture or Dislocation 1791

Manipulative Reduction
    Reduction of Fracture or Dislocation 1791

March Seizure
    Jacksonian Seizure 1247

Marginal Gingivitis
    Gingivitis 993

Marie-Struempel Disease
    Ankylosing Spondylitis 152

Marie-Strumpell Disease
    Ankylosing Spondylitis 152

Marie-Strumpell Spondylitis
    Ankylosing Spondylitis 152

Marijuana Abuse
    Addictions, Mixed 60
    Marijuana Dependence/abuse 1341

Marijuana Dependence
    abuse 1341
    Addictions, Mixed 60

Marshall-Marchetti-Krantz Procedure
    Marshall-Marchetti Operation 1344
    Vesicourethropexy 2265

Massage
    Degeneration, Thoracic or Thoracolumbar Intervertebral Disc 640
    Displacement, Cervical Intervertebral Disc Without Myelopathy 728
    Displacement, Lumbar Intervertebral Disc Without Myelopathy 732
    Groin Strain 1020
    Muscle Spasm 1409
    Myalgia and Myositis 1411
    Open-Chest Cardiac Massage 1514
    Physical Therapy 1643
    Salivary Gland Stones 1865
    Tachycardia, Paroxysmal Supraventricular 2039
    Torticollis 2108

Mastectomy
    Cancer, Breast 347
    Paget's Disease of Breast 1559

Mastitis
    Abscess, Breast 22
    Cellulitis 443
    Fibrocystic Breast Disease 874
    Postpartum Mastitis 1705

Mastoid Empyema
    Mastoiditis 1349
    Tympanum Perforation 2202

Index

Mastoid Excision
    Mastoidectomy 1347
Mastoid Process Abscess
    Mastoiditis 1349
    Tympanum Perforation 2202
Mastoidectomy
    Hearing Loss 1036
Mastoiditis
    Brain Abscess 289
    Tympanum Perforation 2202
Maxillary Sinusitis
    Sinusitis 1928
Mayo Operation
    Bunionectomy 314
    Hernia, Umbilical 1106
Mcbride Bunionectomy
    Bunionectomy 314
Measles
    Encephalitis 797
    Rubella 1856
    Rubeola 1858
Meckel's Diverticulum
    Meckel's Diverticulum 1351
Media
    Otitis Externa, Infective 1543
Medial Epicondylitis
    Epicondylitis, Medial and Lateral 816
Medial Malleolus
    Fracture, Ankle 895
    Sprains and Strains, Ankle 1971
Medial Malleolus Fracture
    Fracture, Ankle 895
Medial Tibial Stress Syndrome
    Shin Splints 1912
Median Nerve Compression
    Carpal Tunnel Release 428
    Carpal Tunnel Syndrome 430
Medical Emergency
    Abscess, Larynx 25
    Anaphylactic Shock 129, 131
    Anaphylactic Shock, Food Reaction 131
    Aortic Aneurysm 160
    Aortic Dissection 163
    Botulism 286
    Brain Abscess 289
    Brain Injury 292
    Cardiac Arrest 409
    Cerebrovascular Accident 454
    Compartment Syndrome 547
    Dislocation, Femorotibial (Knee) Joint 713
    Embolectomy, Pulmonary 787
    Embolism, Pulmonary 789
    Endophthalmitis 808
    Epiglottitis 822
    Fracture, Femoral Neck 912
    Gas Gangrene 967
    Heat Stroke 1051
    Hemothorax, Traumatic 1075
    High Blood Pressure, Malignant 1116
    Hypoglycemia 1171
    Hypovolemic Shock 1184
    Intracranial Hemorrhage 1226, 1230

    Intracranial Hemorrhage, Closed 1230
    Pulmonary Edema 1756
    Spinal Cord Injury 1946
    Subdural Hemorrhage 2016
    Toxic Shock Syndrome 2152
    Tracheostomy 2159
    Trauma 2175
    Ventricular Fibrillation 2256
Medical Termination of Pregnancy
    Abortion, Medical Induction 13
Medically Induced Abortion
    Abortion, Medical Induction 13
Medically Induced Therapeutic Abortion
    Abortion, Medical Induction 13
Mediterranean Anemia
    Thalassemia 2066
Mediterranean Fever
    Brucellosis 306
Medullary Carcinoma
    Cancer, Thyroid Gland 396
Megacolon
    Ulcerative Colitis 2209
Megaesophagus
    Achalasia 44
Megaloblastic Anemia
    Anemia 133, 136
Melanoma
    Cancer, Skin 387
Meleney's Synergistic Gangrene
    Gangrene 964
Membranous
    Arthroplasty, Elbow 197
    Bronchitis, Acute 299
    Nephrotic Syndrome 1456
    Pericardiectomy 1614
    Pleurisy 1659
    Renal Failure, Chronic 1804
Membranous Bronchitis
    Bronchitis, Acute 299
Membranous Colitis
    Colitis 535
Membranous Glomerulonephritis
    Nephritis, Interstitial 1453
Memory Loss
    Amnesia 111
    Concussion, Cerebral 553
    Delirium 644
    Vitamin B_1 Deficiency 2272
Menadione
    Poisoning, Vitamin K 1681
Menaquinone
    Poisoning, Vitamin K 1681
Ménière's Disease
    Meniere's Disease 1353
    Tinnitus 2097
    Vertigo 2262
Ménière's Syndrome
    Meniere's Disease 1353

Meningeal Hemorrhage
   Cerebral Hemorrhage 449
   Subarachnoid Hemorrhage (Non-traumatic) 2011

Meningioma
   Tumor, Benign 2199

Meningitis
   Aspiration 207–208
   Bacterial 1357
   Delirium 644
   Hemiplegia 1056

Meningococcal Meningitis
   Meningitis, Bacterial 1357

Meniscal Injury
   Meniscus Disorders, Knee 1364

Meniscectomy
   and Meniscus Repair 1361

Meniscectomy and Meniscus Repair
   Meniscus Disorders, Knee 1364

Meniscus
   Disorders, Knee 1364
   Internal Derangement of Knee 1219
   Meniscectomy and Meniscus Repair 1361

Meniscus Disorders of Knee
   Internal Derangement of Knee 1219
   Meniscectomy and Meniscus Repair 1361
   Meniscus Disorders, Knee 1364

Meniscus Lesion
   Meniscus Disorders, Knee 1364

Meniscus of Knee
   Internal Derangement of Knee 1219
   Meniscectomy and Meniscus Repair 1361
   Meniscus Disorders, Knee 1364

Meniscus Repair
   Meniscectomy and Meniscus Repair 1361
   Meniscus Disorders, Knee 1364

Meniscus Shaving
   Meniscectomy and Meniscus Repair 1361

Meniscus Tear
   Arthrography 196

Menopause
   Caruncle of the Urethra, Benign 434
   Cervical Polypectomy 469
   Cystocele or Rectocele 621
   Goiter 1008
   Menstrual Disorders 1369
   Osteoporosis 1540

Menorrhagia
   Aspiration Curettage of the Uterus 208
   Dilation and Curettage 699
   Menstrual Disorders 1369

Menstrual
   Disorders 1369
   Dysfunctional Uterine Bleeding 757
   Premenstrual Syndrome 1724

Menstrual Disorders
   Dysfunctional Uterine Bleeding 757
   Infertility, Female 1204

Menstrual Migraine
   Premenstrual Syndrome 1724

Menstrual Molimen
   Premenstrual Syndrome 1724

Menstrual Toxic Syndrome
   Toxic Shock Syndrome 2152

Menstruation
   Dysfunctional Uterine Bleeding 757
   Menstrual Disorders 1369
   Paranoid Personality Disorder 1588
   Passive-Aggressive Personality Disorder 1597

Mercury Poisoning
   Poisoning 1675, 1677, 1679, 1681
   Toxic Effects, Mercury 2138

Mesenteric Abscess
   Abscess, Psoas 38
   Abscess, Subdiaphragmatic 42

Mesenteric Adhesions
   Abdominal Adhesions 1

Mesenteric Thrombosis
   Mesenteric Thrombosis 1372

Mesenteric Venous Thrombosis
   Mesenteric Thrombosis 1372

Mesothelioma
   Cancer, Pleura 377

Metabolic Encephalopathy
   Organic Psychosis 1526

Metacarpal
   Fracture, Metacarpal Bones 922
   Reduction of Fracture or Dislocation 1791
   Trigger Finger or Thumb 2191

Metacarpal Bone Fracture
   Fracture, Metacarpal Bones 922
   Reduction of Fracture or Dislocation 1791
   Trigger Finger or Thumb 2191

Metallic Arsenic
   Toxic Effects, Arsenic and Compounds 2110

Metallic Mercury Poisoning
   Toxic Effects, Mercury 2138

Metastatic Endophthalmitis
   Endophthalmitis 808

Metatarsal Bone Fracture
   Bunion 312
   Bunionectomy 314
   Dislocation, Foot 716
   Fracture, Metatarsal Bones 925
   Fracture, Midfoot (Cuboid, Cuneiform, Navicular) 928
   Hallux Rigidus 1027
   Hammertoe 1029
   Metatarsalgia 1376
   Metatarsus Primus Varus 1378
   Morton's Neuroma 1393
   Reduction of Fracture or Dislocation 1791
   Repair, Hammertoe 1816
   Sprains and Strains, Foot 1986

Metatarsalgia
   Morton's Neuroma 1393

Metatarsophalangeal Joint Dislocation
   Dislocation, Foot 716

Meth Addiction
   Amphetamine Dependence/Abuse 113

Methamphetamine Addiction
　Amphetamine Dependence/Abuse 113

Methanal Poisoning
　Toxic Effects, Formaldehyde 2129
　Toxic Effects, Methyl Alcohol 2140

Methyl Alcohol Poisoning
　Toxic Effects, Methyl Alcohol 2140

Methyl Aldehyde Poisoning
　Toxic Effects, Formaldehyde 2129

Methyl Bromide Poisoning
　Toxic Effects, Methyl Bromide 2142

Methyl Chloroform Exposure
　Toxic Effects, Chlorinated Hydrocarbon Solvents 2120

Methyl Hydroxide Poisoning
　Toxic Effects, Methyl Alcohol 2140

Methylene Chloride Exposure
　Toxic Effects, Chlorinated Hydrocarbon Solvents 2120

Methylene Oxide Poisoning
　Toxic Effects, Formaldehyde 2129

Metrorrhagia
　Dysfunctional Uterine Bleeding 757
　Menstrual Disorders 1369

Mexican Typhus
　Typhus Fever 2206

MF
　Mycosis Fungoides 1416

MG
　Myasthenia Gravis 1414

MI
　Coronary Atherosclerosis 587
　Coronary Balloon Angioplasty 590
　Coronary Thrombolysis 593
　Myocardial Infarction, Acute 1424
　Ventricular Fibrillation 2256

Mice
　Loose Bodies, Knee 1300
　Typhus Fever 2206

Microsporosis
　Tinea 2095

Middle
　Myringotomy 1434
　Otitis Media 1545

Middle Back Pain
　Thoracic Spine Pain 2076

Middle Ear Infection
　Otitis Media 1545

Middle Ear Inflammation
　Otitis Media 1545

Middle Ear Otitis Media
　Otitis Media 1545

Middle Lobe Syndrome
　Lung Collapse 1312

Mid-esophageal Diverticula
　Esophageal Diverticula 836

Midfoot
　Dislocation, Foot 716
　Fracture, Midfoot (Cuboid, Cuneiform, Navicular) 928

Sprains and Strains, Foot 1986

Migraine Headache
　Biofeedback 250
　Headache 1033

Migraine Headache with Aura
　Migraine Headache 1378

Migraine Headache Without Aura
　Migraine Headache 1378

Migrainous Neuralgia
　Cluster Headache 517

Mild Brain Injury
　Postconcussion Syndrome 1699

Miller-Fisher's Syndrome
　Guillain-Barré Syndrome 1022

Miner's Elbow
　Bursitis 325

Mini-laparotomy
　Salpingo-oophorectomy 1873

Mini-Stroke
　Transient Ischemic Attack 2169

Mini-Tracheostomy
　Tracheostomy 2159

Minkowski-Chauffard Syndrome
　Spherocytosis, Hereditary 1944

Minor Epilepsy
　Petit Mal Epilepsy 1631

Minor Head Injury
　Head Injury, Superficial 1031

Minor Postpartum Puerperal Infection
　Postpartum Mastitis 1705

Minor Puerperal Infection
　Postpartum Mastitis 1705

Mite-borne Typhus
　Typhus Fever 2206

Mitral Commissurotomy
　Mitral Stenosis 1387

Mitral Insufficiency
　Heart Murmur 1045
　Mitral Stenosis 1387
　Mitral Valve Prolapse 1389

Mitral Regurgitation
　Mitral Insufficiency 1385
　Mitral Valve Prolapse 1389

Mitral Stenosis
　Mitral Insufficiency 1385

Mitral Valve Disorder
　Mitral Insufficiency 1385
　Mitral Valve Prolapse 1389

Mitral Valve Insufficiency
　Endocarditis, Bacterial 802
　Heart Valve Replacement 1047
　Mitral Insufficiency 1385
　Mitral Valve Prolapse 1389

Mitral Valve Obstruction
　Mitral Stenosis 1387

Mitral Valve Prolapse
  Endocarditis, Bacterial 802
  Mitral Insufficiency 1385
  Ventricular Tachycardia 2260
Mitral Valve Repair
  Cardiomyopathy 419
  Mitral Commissurotomy 1384
  Mitral Insufficiency 1385
Mitral Valve Replacement
  Heart Valve Replacement 1047
  Mitral Insufficiency 1385
  Mitral Stenosis 1387
  Mitral Valve Prolapse 1389
Mitral Valve Stenosis
  Mitral Insufficiency 1385
  Mitral Stenosis 1387
  Valvuloplasty, Balloon 2240
Mixed
  Addictions, Mixed 60
  Bipolar Affective Disorder, Mixed 258
Mixed Hernia
  Hernia, Hiatal 1097
Mixed Sleep Apnea
  Insomnia with Sleep Apnea 1214
  Sleep Apnea 1935
MMEF
  Pulmonary Function Tests 1758
MMK Operation
  Marshall-Marchetti Operation 1344
Mobitz Type I
  Atrioventricular Block Incomplete (Second-Degree) 223
  Heart Block 1040
Mobitz Type II
  Atrioventricular Block Incomplete (Second-Degree) 223
  Heart Block 1040
Modified Pereyra Procedure
  Vesicourethropexy 2265
Modified Puestow Procedure
  Pancreaticojejunostomy 1572
Modified Radical Mastoidectomy
  Mastoidectomy 1347
Moist Gangrene
  Gangrene 964
Molar Pregnancy
  Hydatidiform Mole 1134
Molecular Chlorine Poisoning
  Toxic Effects, Chlorine 2122
Molimen
  Premenstrual Syndrome 1724
Monday Chest-Tightness
  Byssinosis 328
Monday Feeling
  Byssinosis 328
Monday Fever
  Byssinosis 328
  Metal Fume Fever 1374
Moniliasis
  Candidiasis 405
  Vaginitis 2233

Monobromomethane Exposure
  Toxic Effects, Methyl Bromide 2142
Monohydroxymethane Poisoning
  Toxic Effects, Methyl Alcohol 2140
Montezuma's Revenge
  Traveler's Diarrhea 2177
Morgagni-Adams-Stokes Syndrome
  Stokes-Adams Syndrome 2003
Morning Sickness
  Hyperemesis Gravidarum 1142
Morton's Neuralgia
  Morton's Neuroma 1393
Morton's Neuroma
  Excision of Morton's Neuroma 855
  Morton's Neuroma 1393
Mosquitoes
  Filariasis 881
  Yellow Fever 2307
Motion Sickness
  Nausea 1446
Motor
  Amyotrophic Lateral Sclerosis 125
  Evoked Potentials 851
  Motion Sickness 1395
Motor Aphasia
  Aphasia 169
Motor Neuron Disease
  Amyotrophic Lateral Sclerosis 125
  Atrophy, Muscular (Progressive) 230
Motor Seizure
  Cerebral Palsy 452
  Epilepsy 824
  Grand Mal Seizure 1014
  Jacksonian Seizure 1247
  Petit Mal Epilepsy 1631
  Seizures 1900
Motor Sickness
  Motion Sickness 1395
Motor Urge Incontinence
  Urinary Incontinence in Women 2222
Mountain Fever
  Colorado Tick Fever 541
Mouth
  Behçet's Syndrome 244
  Candidiasis 405
  Periodontitis 1619
MPD
  Dissociative Personality Disorder 737
MS
  Multiple Sclerosis 1401
MSA
  Shy Drager Syndrome 1919
Mucous
  Allergic Rhinitis 98
  Irritable Bowel Syndrome 1244
Mucous Colitis
  Irritable Bowel Syndrome 1244

Index 2609

Mucous Membrane
    Abrasions 14
    Nasal Polypectomy 1440
    Toxic Effects, Chlorine 2122
Mucous Polyp of Cervix
    Cervical Polyps 470
Multiforme
    Allergic Dermatitis 96
    Glioma 999
    Pemphigus 1606
    Radiodermatitis 1780
    Urticaria 2226
Multilocular Echinococcosis
    Echinococcosis 772
Multiple
    Addictions, Mixed 60
    Allergy 100
    Cauda Equina Syndrome 440
    Cerebral Palsy 452
    Kaposi's Sarcoma 1253
    Myeloma 1399
    Pregnancy, Multiple Gestation 1714
    Sclerosis 1401
Multiple Chemical Intolerance
    Allergy 100
Multiple Chemical Sensitivity
    Allergy 100
Multiple Cognitive Deficits
    Dementia 651, 653
Multiple Gestation
    Pregnancy, Multiple Gestation 1714
    Premature Labor 1720
Multiple Idiopathic Hemorrhagic Sarcoma
    Kaposi's Sarcoma 1253
Multiple Myeloma
    Bone Marrow Transplant 275
Multiple Myelomatosis
    Multiple Myeloma 1399
Multiple Nerve Root Compression
    Cauda Equina Syndrome 440
    Cerebral Palsy 452
Multiple Personality Disorder
    Dissociative Personality Disorder 737
Multiple Pregnancy
    Pregnancy, Multiple Gestation 1714
Multiple Sclerosis
    Hemiplegia 1056
    Optic Neuritis 1521
Multiple Substance Abuse
    Addictions, Mixed 60
Multiple System Atrophy
    Shy Drager Syndrome 1919
Multiple Vitamin Deficiencies
    Hypovitaminosis 1182
Mumps
    Encephalitis 797
    Orchitis 1524
Munchausen's Syndrome
    Factitious Illness with Physical Symptoms 866

Muriatic Acid Poisoning
    Toxic Effects, Hydrochloric Acid 2131
Murine Typhus
    Typhus Fever 2206
Murmur
    Abdominal Aneurysm 3
    Aortic Dissection 163
    Aortic Insufficiency 165
    Aortic Valve Stenosis 167
    Endocarditis, Bacterial 802
    Heart Murmur 1045
    Hypertensive Heart Disease 1156
    Mitral Insufficiency 1385
    Mitral Stenosis 1387
    Mitral Valve Prolapse 1389
    Palpitations 1566
    Pernicious Anemia 1630
    Renal Failure, Chronic 1804
    Rheumatic Fever, Acute 1833
    Rheumatic Heart Disease, Chronic 1836
    Shock 1915
    Sickle Cell Anemia 1922
    Strep Throat 2005
    Thoracic Aneurysm 2070
    Tooth Extraction 2107
Muscle
    Atrophy, Muscular 227, 230
    Atrophy, Muscular (Progressive) 230
    Biopsy 252
    Electromyography 784
    Fasciotomy 870
    Myalgia and Myositis 1411
    Spasm 1409
    Ultrasound, Therapeutic 2213
Muscle Atrophy
    Amyotrophic Lateral Sclerosis 125
    Atrophy, Muscular 227, 230
    Atrophy, Muscular (Progressive) 230
    Paralysis, Paraplegia, and Quadriplegia 1583
    Peripheral Neuropathy 1621
    Syringomyelia 2035
Muscle Contraction
    Esophageal Spasm 839
    Grand Mal Seizure 1014
    Muscle Spasm 1409
Muscle Contraction Headache
    Headache 1033
Muscle Cramps
    Muscle Spasm 1409
    Tetany 2062
Muscle Disorders
    Electromyography 784
    Myalgia and Myositis 1411
Muscle Inflammation
    Myalgia and Myositis 1411
Muscle Spasm
    Muscle Injury 1406
    Neck Pain 1448
    Sprains and Strains, Back 1975
    Tetany 2062
Muscle Wasting
    Atrophy, Muscular 227, 230
    Neuralgic Amyotrophy 1465
    Paralysis, Paraplegia, and Quadriplegia 1583

Muscular Atrophy
    Atrophy, Muscular 227, 230
    Atrophy, Muscular (Progressive) 230
Muscular Rheumatism
    Fibromyalgia and Myofascial Pain Syndrome 879
    Myalgia and Myositis 1411
Musculoskeletal Disorders
    Curvature of the Spine, Acquired 610
    Dermatomyositis 677
    Disc Calcification 701
    Dislocation, Cervical Vertebra 711
    Low Back Pain 1302
    Lyme Disease 1319
    Myalgia and Myositis 1411
    Neck Pain 1448
    Post-Laminectomy Syndrome 1701
    Rehabilitation Therapy 1796
    Spondylolisthesis 1960
    Spondylolysis, Lumbar Region 1962
    Thoracic Spine Pain 2076
    Transcutaneous Electrical Nerve Stimulation 2164
    Ultrasound, Therapeutic 2213
Mushroom Poisoning
    Toxic Effects, Mushrooms 2143
Mushroom Worker's Lung
    Hypersensitivity Pneumonitis 1150
MVT
    Mesenteric Thrombosis 1372
MVV
    Pulmonary Function Tests 1758
Myalgia
    and Myositis 1411
    Chronic Fatigue Syndrome 509
    Fibromyalgia and Myofascial Pain Syndrome 879
    Pneumonia 1667
Myalgic Encephalomyelitis
    Malaise 1328
Myasthenia Gravis Crisis
    Myasthenia Gravis 1414
Myelogram
    Cervical Disc Disorder with Myelopathy 464
    Myelography 1419
    Syringomyelia 2035
Myelography
    Cauda Equina Syndrome 440
    Degeneration, Cervical Intervertebral Disc 634
Myeloma
    Bone Marrow Biopsy 273
    Bone Marrow Transplant 275
    Multiple Myeloma 1399
    Renal Failure, Chronic 1804
Myelomatosis
    Multiple Myeloma 1399
Myelopathic Anemia
    Myelophthisic Anemia 1422
Myeloproliferative Disorders
    Polycythemia Vera 1689
Myocardial
    Infarction, Acute 1424
    Myocarditis, Acute 1428
    Perfusion Scan 1427

Myocardial Infarction
    Acute 1424
    Angina Pectoris 140
    Angina, Unstable 144
    Arrhythmia 178
    Atrioventricular Block Incomplete (Second-Degree) 223
    Atrioventricular Block, Complete (Third-Degree) 224
    Atrioventricular Block, Incomplete (First-Degree) 226
    Cardiac Arrest 409
    Cardiac Catheterization 411
    Cardiac Stress Test 416
    Cardiogenic Shock 417
    Carotid Artery Occlusion 423
    Coronary Arteriography 586
    Coronary Atherosclerosis 587
    Coronary Balloon Angioplasty 590
    Coronary Thrombolysis 593
    Electrocardiogram 781
    Heart Block 1040
    Myocardial Perfusion Scan 1427
    Polycythemia Vera 1689
    Pulmonary Edema 1756
Myocardial Infarction, Acute
    Prinzmetal's Angina 1726
Myocardial Inflammation
    Myocarditis, Acute 1428
Myocardial Ischemia
    Angina Pectoris 140
    Angina, Unstable 144
    Coronary Atherosclerosis 587
    Echocardiography 774
    Prinzmetal's Angina 1726
Myocardial Perfusion Imaging
    Myocardial Perfusion Scan 1427
Myocardial Perfusion Scan
    Cardiac Stress Test 416
Myocardiopathy
    Cardiomyopathy 419
Myocarditis
    Acute 1428
    Cardiac Catheterization 411
Myocardium
    Cardiac Stress Test 416
    Cardiomyopathy 419
    Coronary Bypass 592
    Myocardial Infarction, Acute 1424
    Myocardial Perfusion Scan 1427
    Pericardiectomy 1614
Myoclonic Epileptic Seizures
    Grand Mal Seizure 1014
Myofascial Pain Syndrome
    Fibromyalgia and Myofascial Pain Syndrome 879
    Myalgia and Myositis 1411
Myofasciitis
    Fibromyalgia and Myofascial Pain Syndrome 879
    Myalgia and Myositis 1411
Myoma
    Fibroid Tumor of Uterus 875
    Miscarriage 1381
    Myomectomy, Uterine 1430
    Pregnancy, Multiple Gestation 1714
    Pregnancy, Normal 1716
    Prostatic Hypertrophy 1731
    Uterine Polyps 2228

Myomectomy
  Uterine 1430

Myonecrosis
  Gangrene 964

Myopia
  Keratectomy, Laser Photorefractive 1256
  Radial Keratotomy 1775
  Retinal Detachment 1823, 1825
  Retinitis Pigmentosa 1829
  Senile Macular Degeneration 1903

Myositis
  Fibromyalgia and Myofascial Pain Syndrome 879
  Myalgia and Myositis 1411

Myotomy of Esophagus
  Esophageal Diverticula 836

Myringoplasty
  Hearing Loss 1036
  Tympanoplasty 2201

Myringotomy
  Barotitis Media 241
  Hearing Loss 1036
  Mastoiditis 1349
  Otitis Media 1545

Myxedema
  Hypothyroidism 1180

Myxomatous Mitral Valve
  Mitral Insufficiency 1385
  Mitral Valve Prolapse 1389

N

NaClO Poisoning
  Toxic Effects, Chlorine 2122

Nail Bed Excision
  Excision of Nail, Nail Bed, or Nail Fold 856

Nail Excision
  Excision of Nail, Nail Bed, or Nail Fold 856
  Toenail, Ingrown 2100

Narcissism
  Narcissistic Personality Disorder 1437

Narcissistic
  Antisocial Personality Disorder 156
  Personality Disorder 1437

Narcolepsy
  Electroencephalogram 783
  Hypersomnia 1152

Narcotic Abuse
  Addictions, Mixed 60
  Alcohol and Drug Detoxification and Rehabilitation 84
  Opioid Type Dependence 1516

Narcotic Dependence
  Addictions, Mixed 60
  Alcohol and Drug Detoxification and Rehabilitation 84
  Opioid Type Dependence 1516

Narrow Angle Glaucoma
  Glaucoma, Acute (Angle-Closure) 995
  Iridectomy 1238
  Iridotomy 1239

Nasal
  Allergic Rhinitis 98
  Allergy 100
  Cold 533
  Deviated Nasal Septum 679
  Nosebleed 1485
  Polypectomy 1440
  Polyps 1441
  Rhinoplasty 1841
  Rhinoscleroma 1842
  Rubeola 1858
  Septoplasty 1909
  Septum Perforation 1443
  Sinusitis 1928
  Tonsillitis and Adenoiditis 2104
  Upper Respiratory Infection 2216

Nasal Polyp Excision
  Nasal Polypectomy 1440
  Nasal Polyps 1441

Nasal Polypectomy
  Nasal Polyps 1441

Nasal Polyposis
  Nasal Polyps 1441

Nasal Polyps Removal
  Nasal Polypectomy 1440

Nasal Septum
  Deviated Nasal Septum 679
  Nosebleed 1485
  Perforation 1443
  Rhinoplasty 1841
  Rhinoscleroma 1842
  Septoplasty 1909

Nasal Septum Correction
  Septoplasty 1909

Nasal Septum Deviation
  Deviated Nasal Septum 679
  Septoplasty 1909

Nasal Septum Erosion
  Cocaine Dependence/Abuse 522
  Nasal Septum Perforation 1443
  Nosebleed 1485

Nasal Tumor
  Nasal Polyps 1441
  Nasal Septum Perforation 1443
  Nosebleed 1485

Nasogastric Intubation
  Poisoning 1675, 1677, 1679, 1681
  Pyloric Stenosis, Acquired (Adult) Hypertrophic 1767
  Pylorospasm 1770
  Resection of Gastric or Duodenal Ulcer Site 1819

Nasolacrimal Duct Obstruction
  Dacryocystitis 627
  Dacryostenosis 629

Nasopharyngitis
  Cold 533

Natal Teeth
  Impacted Tooth 1191
  Tooth Extraction 2107

Native Artery Gangrene
  Amputation 116, 118, 121, 123
  Arteriosclerotic Gangrene 186

Nausea
  Dyspepsia 759
  Esophagogastroduodenoscopy 850
  Hyperemesis Gravidarum 1142

Motion Sickness 1395
Peptic Ulcer Disease 1611
Pineal Gland Neoplasm 1647
Radiation Therapy 1778
Renal Failure, Acute 1802
Salmonellosis 1866
Sunburn 2019

Navicular
Dislocation, Foot 716
Fracture, Midfoot (Cuboid, Cuneiform, Navicular) 928
Sprains and Strains, Foot 1986

Navicular Bone Fracture
Fracture, Midfoot (Cuboid, Cuneiform, Navicular) 928

Nearsightedness
Keratectomy, Laser Photorefractive 1256
Myopia 1431

Neck
Cancer, Oropharynx 369
Cancer, Skin 387
Cancer, Thyroid Gland 396
Carbuncle 407
Carotid Artery Occlusion 423
Carotid Sinus Syncope 425
Cellulitis 443
Cervical Disc Disorder with Myelopathy 464
Degeneration, Cervical Intervertebral Disc 634
Dislocation, Cervical Vertebra 711
Displacement, Cervical Intervertebral Disc Without Myelopathy 728
Endarterectomy 801
Fracture, Cervical Spine (With or Without Spinal Cord Injury) 904
Furuncle 961
Goiter 1008
Hyperparathyroidism 1148
Hyperthyroidism 1159
Hypoparathyroidism 1173
Pain 1448
Spinal Cord Injury 1946
Sprains and Strains, Cervical Spine (Neck) 1981
Torticollis 2108

Neck Burn
Burn of Head and Neck (Includes Face) 318

Neck Infection
Ludwig's Angina 1306

Neck of Femur
Fracture, Femoral Neck 912

Neck Pain
Biofeedback 250
Brachial Neuropathy 287
Cervical Disc Disorder with Myelopathy 464
Cervicobrachial Syndrome 474
Chiropractic Adjustments and Manipulations 492
Degeneration, Cervical Intervertebral Disc 634
Displacement, Cervical Intervertebral Disc Without Myelopathy 728
Laminectomy or Laminotomy 1273
Spinal Cord Injury 1946
Ultrasound, Therapeutic 2213

Neck Sprain
Neck Pain 1448
Sprains and Strains, Cervical Spine (Neck) 1981

Neck Strain
Neck Pain 1448
Sprains and Strains, Cervical Spine (Neck) 1981

Necrosis
Abscess, Lung 29
Avascular Necrosis 235
Diabetic Gangrene 689
Embolectomy 786—787
Frostbite 959
Gangrene 964
Hip Replacement, Total 1119

Necrotizing Angitis
Polyarteritis Nodosa 1685

Necrotizing Fascitis
Gangrene 964

Necrotizing Periarteritis
Polyarteritis Nodosa 1685

Needle Aspiration
Aspiration 207—208
Biopsy 252
Chancroid 481
Erysipeloid 831
Goiter 1008

Needle Aspiration Biopsy
Cancer, Oropharynx 369
Liver Biopsy 1297
Lung Biopsy 1310
Pleural Biopsy 1657

Needle Aspiration of Bone Marrow
Bone Marrow Biopsy 273

Needle Biopsy
Biopsy 252
Breast Biopsy 295
Cancer, Lung 363
Cancer, Pancreas 375
Cancer, Pleura 377
Cancer, Prostate 380
Cancer, Thyroid Gland 396
Lung Biopsy 1310
Pleural Biopsy 1657

Negative Personality Disorder
Passive-Aggressive Personality Disorder 1597

Neoplasm
Bone Tumors 281
Cancer, Bladder 338
Cancer, Brain 344
Cancer, Breast 347
Cancer, Cervix 351
Cancer, Colon 354
Cancer, Esophagus 356
Cancer, Kidney 358
Cancer, Lung 363
Cancer, Oropharynx 369
Cancer, Ovary 372
Cancer, Pancreas 375
Cancer, Pleura 377
Cancer, Prostate 380
Cancer, Rectum 384
Cancer, Skin 387
Cancer, Small Intestine (Including Duodenum) 389
Cancer, Stomach 391
Cancer, Testicle(s) 393
Cancer, Thyroid Gland 396
Cancer, Tongue 399
Choriocarcinoma 505
Kaposi's Sarcoma 1253
Meningioma 1355
Nasal Polyps 1441
Paget's Disease of Breast 1559
Pineal Gland Neoplasm 1647
Tumor, Benign 2199

Index 2613

Neoplasm of Meninges
    Meningioma 1355
    Tumor, Benign 2199
Neoplastic Pericarditis
    Pericarditis, Acute 1615
Nephrectomy
    Abscess, Renal and Perinephric 40
    Cancer, Kidney 358
Nephritic Abscess
    Abscess, Renal and Perinephric 40
Nephritis
    Abscess, Renal and Perinephric 40
    Interstitial 1453
    Pyelonephritis, Chronic 1764
    Renal Failure, Chronic 1804
Nephrogenic Diabetes Insipidus
    Diabetes Insipidus 681
Nephrolithiasis
    Calculus, Renal (Kidney and Ureter) 335
Nephrolithotomy
    Lithotomy 1293–1294
    Nephrotomy 1458
Nephropathy
    Albuminuria 82
    Diabetic Glomerulosclerosis 690
    Glomerulonephritis, Acute 1001
    Glomerulonephritis, Chronic 1003
    Glomerulosclerosis 1005
    Renal Failure, Chronic 1804
Nephrosis
    Hydronephrosis 1138
    Nephrotic Syndrome 1456
Nephrotic Syndrome
    Albuminuria 82
Nephrotomy
    Lithotomy 1293–1294
Nephroureterectomy
    Nephrectomy 1451
Nephrydrosis
    Hydronephrosis 1138
Nerve
    Biopsy 252
    Carpal Tunnel Syndrome 430
    Cauda Equina Syndrome 440
    Celiac Plexus Block 442
    Conduction Studies 1459
    Diabetic Neuropathy 692
    Electromyography 784
    Fasciotomy 870
    Injury 1460
    Morton's Neuroma 1393
    Optic Atrophy 1519
    Optic Neuritis 1521
    Peripheral Neuropathy 1621
    Sciatica 1890
    Sympathectomy 2022
    Tarsal Tunnel Syndrome 2043
    Transcutaneous Electrical Nerve Stimulation 2164
    Transfer of Nerve, Ulnar 2165
    Trigeminal Neuralgia 2187
    Ultrasound, Therapeutic 2213
    Vagotonia 2237

Nerve Block
    Celiac Plexus Block 442
Nerve Compression
    Atrophy, Muscular 227, 230
    Carpal Tunnel Syndrome 430
    Cauda Equina Syndrome 440
    Nerve Conduction Studies 1459
    Nerve Injury 1460
    Paresthesia 1591
    Tarsal Tunnel Syndrome 2043
Nerve Conduction Studies
    Brachial Neuropathy 287
    Carpal Tunnel Syndrome 430
    Dislocation, Acromioclavicular Joint 708
    Dislocation, Cervical Vertebra 711
    Dislocation, Foot 716
    Fracture, Lumbosacral Spine (With or Without Spinal Cord Injury) 920
    Nerve Injury 1460
    Tetany 2062
Nerve Conduction Velocity Test
    Nerve Conduction Studies 1459
Nerve Damage
    Diabetic Neuropathy 692
    Nerve Conduction Studies 1459
    Nerve Injury 1460
    Optic Atrophy 1519
    Paralysis, Paraplegia, and Quadriplegia 1583
    Peripheral Neuropathy 1621
    Polyarteritis Nodosa 1685
Nerve Disorders
    Electromyography 784
    Parkinson's Disease 1593
    Vitamin E Deficiency 2283
Nerve Inflammation
    Carpal Tunnel Syndrome 430
    Metatarsalgia 1376
    Optic Atrophy 1519
    Optic Neuritis 1521
Nerve Injury
    Paralysis, Paraplegia, and Quadriplegia 1583
Nerve Lesion
    Electromyography 784
    Morton's Neuroma 1393
Nerve Pain
    Brachial Neuropathy 287
    Celiac Plexus Block 442
    Displacement, Lumbar Intervertebral Disc Without Myelopathy 732
    Nerve Injury 1460
    Neuralgia, Neuritis, and Radiculitis 1465
    Sciatica 1890
Nerve Root Compression
    Cauda Equina Syndrome 440
    Laminectomy or Laminotomy 1273
Nerve Transection
    Nerve Injury 1460
Nerve Trauma
    Nerve Injury 1460
Nervous Breakdown
    Neurotic Disorders 1475
Nervous Exhaustion
    Nervous Fatigue 1462

2614 The Medical Disability Advisor—Fourth Edition

Nervous Indigestion
- Dyspepsia 759
- Irritable Bowel Syndrome 1244

Nervous Tension
- Nervousness 1463

Nervousness
- Anxiety Disorder, Generalized 158

Nest of Hair Disease
- Pilonidal Cyst 1645

Neural Hearing Loss
- Hearing Loss 1036

Neuralgia
- Cluster Headache 517
- Morton's Neuroma 1393
- Neuritis, and Radiculitis 1465
- Neurofibromatosis 1469
- Peripheral Neuropathy 1621
- Sciatica 1890
- Trigeminal Neuralgia 2187

Neurally Mediated Syncope
- Vasovagal Syncope 2249

Neurasthenia
- Nervous Fatigue 1462

Neuritis
- Brachial Neuropathy 287
- Neuralgia, Neuritis, and Radiculitis 1465
- Optic Neuritis 1521
- Sciatica 1890

Neurocardiogenic Syncope
- Vasovagal Syncope 2249

Neurodystrophy
- Complex Regional Pain Syndrome 550

Neurofeedback
- Biofeedback 250

Neurofibromatosis
- Curvature of the Spine, Acquired 610

Neurofibromatosis Type I
- Neurofibromatosis 1469

Neurogenic Bladder
- Cauda Equina Syndrome 440
- Cystitis, Acute 616
- Pyelonephritis, Acute 1762

Neurologic Shellfish Poisoning
- Toxic Effects, Fish and Shellfish 2126

Neurological Disorder
- Amyotrophic Lateral Sclerosis 125
- Brain Injury 292
- Epilepsy 824

Neurological Exam
- Antisocial Personality Disorder 156
- Astrocytoma 214
- Cancer, Brain 344
- Delirium 644

Neuroma
- Excision of Morton's Neuroma 855
- Hearing Loss 1036
- Metatarsalgia 1376
- Morton's Neuroma 1393

Neuropathic Bladder
- Neurogenic Bladder 1471

Neuropathy
- Brachial Neuropathy 287
- Diabetic Neuropathy 692
- Neuralgia, Neuritis, and Radiculitis 1465
- Neuralgic Amyotrophy 1465
- Peripheral Neuropathy 1621
- Pernicious Anemia 1630
- Tarsal Tunnel Syndrome 2043

Neuropathy and Radiculopathy
- Neuralgia, Neuritis, and Radiculitis 1465

Neuropathy of Distal Tibial Nerve
- Tarsal Tunnel Syndrome 2043

Neuropsychiatric Symptoms
- Multiple Chemical Sensitivity Syndrome 1397

Neuropsychological Testing
- Alzheimer's Disease 105
- Dementia, Alzheimer's Type, with Delusions (Late Onset) 653

Neuroses
- Nervous Breakdown 1462
- Neurotic Disorders 1475
- Somatization Disorder 1939

Neurosis
- Factitious Illness with Psychological Symptoms 868
- Nervous Breakdown 1462
- Neurocirculatory Asthenia 1467
- Neurotic Disorders 1475
- Obsessive-Compulsive Disorder 1494
- Somatization Disorder 1939

Neurosyphilis
- General Paresis 986
- Psychotic Disorder, Unspecified 1751
- Syphilis 2033

Neurotic
- Disorders 1475
- Nervous Breakdown 1462

Neurotic Depression
- Dysthymic Disorder 764

Neurotic Disorder 1475
- Nervous Breakdown 1462
- Somatization Disorder 1939

Neurotic Disorders
- Somatization Disorder 1939

New-Onset Effort Angina
- Angina, Unstable 144

NF
- Neurofibromatosis 1469

NF1
- Neurofibromatosis 1469

NF2
- Neurofibromatosis 1469

NG Tube
- Gastrointestinal Hemorrhage 982
- Guillain-Barré Syndrome 1022
- Nasogastric Intubation 1444

NG Tube Placement
- Nasogastric Intubation 1444

Niacin
- Pellagra 1602

Niacin Poisoning
- Poisoning, Vitamin B 1679

Nickel
- Contact Dermatitis 560
- Toxic Effects, Nickel and Inorganic Compounds 2146

Nickel Carbonyl Exposure
- Toxic Effects, Nickel and Inorganic Compounds 2146

Nickel Catalyst Poisoning
- Toxic Effects, Nickel and Inorganic Compounds 2146

Nickel Poisoning
- Toxic Effects, Nickel and Inorganic Compounds 2146

Nickel Salts Exposure
- Toxic Effects, Nickel and Inorganic Compounds 2146

Nickel Tetracarbonyl Exposure
- Toxic Effects, Nickel and Inorganic Compounds 2146

Nicotinamide
- Pellagra 1602

Nicotinamide Poisoning
- Poisoning, Vitamin B 1679

Nicotine Dependence
- Raynaud's Phenomenon 1781

Nicotinic Acid Deficiency
- Pellagra 1602

Nicotinic Acid Poisoning
- Poisoning, Vitamin B 1679

NIDDM
- Diabetes Mellitus Type II 686

Night Blindness
- Vitamin A Deficiency 2270

Nine-Day Measles
- Rubeola 1858

Nipple
- Abscess, Breast 22
- Cancer, Breast 347
- Fibrocystic Breast Disease 874
- Gynecomastia 1025
- Mammoplasty, Augmentation 1338
- Mastectomy 1345
- Paget's Disease of Breast 1559
- Postpartum Mastitis 1705
- Reduction Mammoplasty 1790

Nissen Fundoplication
- Hernia, Hiatal 1097

Nocturnal Angina
- Angina Decubitus 140

Nodal Tachycardia
- Tachycardia, Paroxysmal Supraventricular 2039

Nodosum
- Erythema Nodosum 835

Non-A Hepatitis
- Hepatitis C 1085

Nonachalasia Motility Disorder
- Esophageal Spasm 839

Non-B Hepatitis
- Hepatitis C 1085

Nonbacterial Pneumonia
- Pneumonia 1667

Non-Cancerous Growth
- Caruncle of the Urethra, Benign 434
- Cervical Polyps 470
- Laparotomy 1276
- Osteoma 1536
- Ovarian Cyst, Benign 1552
- Tumor, Benign 2199

Non-Cancerous Tumor
- Caruncle of the Urethra, Benign 434
- Cervical Polyps 470
- Excision or Destruction of Duodenal Lesion 857
- Laparotomy 1276
- Ovarian Cyst, Benign 1552
- Tumor, Benign 2199

Non-Congestive Glaucoma
- Glaucoma, Acute (Angle-Closure) 995
- Glaucoma, Chronic (Open-Angle) 997

Non-Gonococcal Infectious Arthritis
- Arthritis, Infectious 192

Non-Hodgkin's Lymphoma
- Bone Marrow Transplant 275
- Non-Hodgkin's Lymphoma 1482

Nonimmune Hemolytic Anemia
- Hemolytic Anemia 1059

Non-Infectious
- Colitis 535
- Diarrhea 696
- Gastroenteritis, Non-Infectious 975
- Spondylitis 1958

Non-Infectious Colitis
- Colitis 535
- Diarrhea 696
- Gastroenteritis, Non-Infectious 975

Non-Infectious Diarrhea
- Colitis 535
- Diarrhea 696
- Gastroenteritis, Non-Infectious 975

Non-Infectious Enteritis
- Colitis 535
- Diarrhea 696
- Gastroenteritis, Non-Infectious 975

Non-Infectious Gastroenteritis
- Colitis 535
- Diarrhea 696
- Gastroenteritis, Non-Infectious 975

Non-Infectious Spondylitis
- Spondylitis 1958

Non-Insulin Dependent
- Diabetes Mellitus Type II 686
- Hyperinsulinism 1144

Non-Insulin Dependent Diabetes Mellitus
- Diabetes Mellitus Type II 686

Nonketotic Diabetes Mellitus
- Diabetes Mellitus Type II 686

Non-Obstructive Bronchitis
- Bronchitis, Chronic 302

Nonproliferative Retinopathy
- Diabetic Retinopathy 694

Non-Psychotic Brain Syndrome
- Postconcussion Syndrome 1699

Nonpsychotic Posttraumatic Brain Syndrome
- Postconcussion Syndrome 1699

Non-Puerperal Milk-leg
   Thrombophlebitis 2086

Nonrestorative sleep
   Chronic Fatigue Syndrome 509

Non-Rheumatic Pericarditis
   Pericarditis, Acute 1615

Non-Ruptured Aneurysm
   Abdominal Aneurysm 3
   Cerebral Aneurysm (Non-Ruptured) 445
   Thoracic Aneurysm 2070

Non-Ruptured Cerebral Aneurysm
   Cerebral Aneurysm (Non-Ruptured) 445

Nonselective Shunt
   Portal Systemic Shunt 1695

Non-Small Lung Cell Carcinoma
   Cancer, Lung 363

Nonspecific Esophageal Motility Disorder
   Esophageal Spasm 839

Non-Suppurative Otitis Media
   Otitis Media 1545

Non-Syphilitic Aneurysm
   Thoracic Aneurysm 2070

Non-Thrombocytopenic Purpura
   Purpura Simplex 1760

Non-Traumatic
   Anal Fissure and/or Rectal Ulcer 127
   Subarachnoid Hemorrhage (Non-traumatic) 2011

Non-Traumatic Subarachnoid Hemorrhage
   Subarachnoid Hemorrhage (Non-traumatic) 2011

Non-Traumatic Tear of Anus
   Anal Fissure and/or Rectal Ulcer 127

Non-Ulcerative Blepharitis
   Blepharitis 268

Normal Delivery
   Pregnancy, Normal 1716

Normal Pregnancy
   Pregnancy, Normal 1716

Normal Vaginal Delivery
   Delivery, Spontaneous and/or Assisted Vaginal 647

North American Blastomycosis
   Blastomycosis 266

Nose
   Allergic Rhinitis 98
   Cancer, Skin 387
   Cold 533
   Contact Dermatitis 560
   Deviated Nasal Septum 679
   Lupus Erythematosus, Systemic 1317
   Nasal Polypectomy 1440
   Nasal Polyps 1441
   Nasal Septum Perforation 1443
   Nasogastric Intubation 1444
   Nosebleed 1485
   Rhinoplasty 1841
   Rhinoscleroma 1842
   Septoplasty 1909
   Sinusitis 1928
   Upper Respiratory Infection 2216

Nose Fracture
   Rhinoplasty 1841

Nose Job
   Rhinoplasty 1841

Nose Surgery
   Rhinoplasty 1841

Nosebleed
   Nasal Septum Perforation 1443
   Nosebleed 1485

NSLCC
   Cancer, Lung 363

NSP
   Toxic Effects, Fish and Shellfish 2126

Nuclear Magnetic Resonance Imaging
   Magnetic Resonance Imaging 1327

Nuclear Medicine Scan
   Bone Scan 277

Nuclear Stress Testing
   Cardiac Stress Test 416

Nucleus Pulposis
   Chemonucleolysis of Interveterbral Disc 482
   Disc Calcification 701
   Displacement, Cervical Intervertebral Disc Without Myelopathy 728
   Displacement, Lumbar Intervertebral Disc Without Myelopathy 732
   Displacement, Thoracic Intervertebral Disc Without Myelopathy 735

Numbness and Tingling
   Carpal Tunnel Syndrome 430
   Paresthesia 1591
   Peripheral Neuropathy 1621
   Peripheral Vascular Disease 1626
   Pernicious Anemia 1630
   Raynaud's Phenomenon 1781
   Spinal Cord Injury 1946
   Spinal Fusion 1951

Nummular Eczema
   Contact Dermatitis 560
   Dermatitis 674
   Eczema 778

Nutcracker Esophagus
   Esophageal Spasm 839

Nutritional Amblyopia
   Amblyopia, Toxic 107

Nystagmus
   Dizziness and Giddiness 742
   Schizoaffective Disorder 1878

O

O'Hara's Disease
   Tularemia 2197

Obese
   Atherosclerosis and Arteriosclerosis 216
   Hyperinsulinism 1144
   Insomnia with Sleep Apnea 1214
   Liposuction 1292
   Obesity, Simple 1491
   Osteoarthritis 1530
   Plantar Fasciitis 1655
   Polycystic Ovary Syndrome 1686
   Rectal Polyps 1783
   Respiratory Failure 1821
   Sleep Apnea 1935

- Transient Ischemic Attack 2169
- Urethrocele with Stress Incontinence 2220
- Urinary Incontinence in Women 2222
- Varicose Ulcer 2244

Obesity
- Atherosclerosis and Arteriosclerosis 216
- Diabetes Mellitus Type II 686
- Dyspnea 761
- Gastroesophageal Reflux 979
- Gestational Diabetes 988
- Gout 1012
- Heart Failure, Congestive 1042
- Hemorrhoids 1073
- Hernia Repair 1094, 1096
- Hernia, Incisional 1100
- Hernia, Inguinal and Femoral 1103
- Hernia, Umbilical 1106
- High Blood Pressure, Benign 1112
- Hyperinsulinism 1144
- Insomnia with Sleep Apnea 1214
- Liposuction 1292
- Osteoarthritis 1530
- Plantar Fasciitis 1655
- Polycystic Ovary Syndrome 1686
- Respiratory Failure 1821
- Simple 1491
- Sleep Apnea 1935
- Sprains and Strains, Foot 1986
- Transient Ischemic Attack 2169
- Urethrocele with Stress Incontinence 2220
- Urinary Incontinence in Women 2222
- Varicose Ulcer 2244

Objective Vertigo
- Vertigo 2262

Obliterans
- Atherosclerosis and Arteriosclerosis 216
- Penis Disorders 1608

Obsession-Compulsion Personality Disorder
- Obsessive-Compulsive Disorder 1494
- Obsessive-Compulsive Personality Disorder 1496

Obsessive Compulsive Disorder
- Obsessive-Compulsive Disorder 1494
- Obsessive-Compulsive Personality Disorder 1496

Obsessive-Compulsive Anxiety Disorder
- Obsessive-Compulsive Disorder 1494

Obsessive-Compulsive Personality Disorder
- Hypochondriasis 1169
- Obsessive-Compulsive Disorder 1494
- Obsessive-Compulsive Personality Disorder 1496

Obstipation
- Constipation 558

Obstructed Tooth Eruption
- Impacted Tooth 1191

Obstruction
- Arteriography 185
- Arteriosclerotic Gangrene 186
- Asthma 209
- Bronchitis, Acute 299
- Bronchitis, Chronic 302
- Calculus, Renal (Kidney and Ureter) 335
- Cancer, Colon 354
- Cancer, Esophagus 356
- Cancer, Lung 363
- Cancer, Rectum 384
- Cancer, Small Intestine (Including Duodenum) 389
- Cancer, Stomach 391
- Carotid Artery Occlusion 423
- Cholangiography 493
- Chronic Obstructive Pulmonary Disease 511
- Coarctation of the Aorta 519
- Compartment Syndrome 547
- Coronary Arteriography 586
- Coronary Atherosclerosis 587
- Coronary Balloon Angioplasty 590
- Coronary Bypass 592
- Coronary Thrombolysis 593
- Cystitis, Acute 616
- Embolectomy 786–787
- Endarterectomy 801
- Esophageal Spasm 839
- Filariasis 881
- Hearing Loss 1036
- Insomnia with Sleep Apnea 1214
- Intestinal Obstruction 1222
- Intravenous Pyelogram 1233
- Lithotomy 1293–1294
- Lung Collapse 1312
- Mitral Stenosis 1387
- Mononucleosis 1390
- Nasal Polypectomy 1440
- Nasal Polyps 1441
- Nephritis, Interstitial 1453
- Nephrotomy 1458
- Osteoma 1536
- Pancreatectomy 1568
- Pancreatitis 1573
- Pineal Gland Neoplasm 1647
- Prostatic Hypertrophy 1731
- Pyelonephritis, Chronic 1764
- Pyloric Stenosis, Acquired (Adult) Hypertrophic 1767
- Pylorospasm 1770
- Rhinoplasty 1841
- Rhinoscleroma 1842
- Sleep Apnea 1935
- Tonsillitis and Adenoiditis 2104
- Tracheostomy 2159
- Transurethral Incision of Bladder Neck 2172
- Transurethral Removal of Obstruction from Ureter 2173
- Volvulus 2289

Obstructive Jaundice
- Jaundice 1249

Obstructive Lung Disease
- Chronic Obstructive Pulmonary Disease 511

Obstructive Pulmonary Disease
- Chronic Obstructive Pulmonary Disease 511

Obstructive Sleep Apnea
- Sleep Apnea 1935

Obstructive Sleep Apnea Syndrome
- Insomnia with Sleep Apnea 1214
- Sleep Apnea 1935

Obtaining Bone Graft
- Rib Resection 1844

Occlusion of Carotid Artery
- Carotid Artery Occlusion 423

Occlusion of the Renal Vein
- Renal Vein Thrombosis 1807

Occlusive Arteriosclerosis
- Atherosclerosis and Arteriosclerosis 216

Occupational
- Allergy 100

    Asbestosis 201
    Dermatitis 674
    Dyspnea 761
    Epicondylitis, Medial and Lateral 816
    Equine Encephalitis 827
    Erysipeloid 831
    Foreign Body, Cornea 891
    Fracture, Skull (Closed) 941
    Hearing Loss 1036
    Heat Exhaustion 1049
    Heat Stroke 1051
    Histoplasmosis 1121
    Pneumoconiosis 1662
    Radiodermatitis 1780
    Repetitive Strain Injury 1819
    Siderosis 1924
    Silicosis 1926
    Therapy 1499
    Vocational Therapy 2288

Occupational Asbestosis
    Asbestosis 201

Occupational Asthma (Unspecified)
    Asthma 209
    Occupational Asthma 1498
    Pneumoconiosis 1662

Occupational Byssinosis
    Byssinosis 328

Occupational Exposure Asthma
    Occupational Asthma 1498
    Pneumoconiosis 1662

Occupational Illness
    Allergy 100
    Brucellosis 306
    Byssinosis 328
    Humidifier Fever 1130
    Hypersensitivity Pneumonitis 1150
    Impingement Syndrome 1194
    Multiple Chemical Sensitivity Syndrome 1397
    Toxic Effects, Chlorinated Hydrocarbon Solvents 2120
    Toxic Effects, Chromium 2124
    Toxic Effects, Hydrofluoric Acid 2132
    Toxic Effects, Lead (Inorganic Compounds) 2136
    Toxic Effects, Mercury 2138
    Toxic Effects, Methyl Alcohol 2140
    Toxic Effects, Nickel and Inorganic Compounds 2146
    Trigger Finger or Thumb 2191
    Ventilation Pneumonitis 2254
    Wandering Atrial Pacemaker 2293

Occupational Therapy
    Alzheimer's Disease 105
    Amyotrophic Lateral Sclerosis 125
    Cerebral Palsy 452
    General Paresis 986
    Impingement Syndrome 1194
    Neurocirculatory Asthenia 1467
    Paralysis, Paraplegia, and Quadriplegia 1583
    Parkinson's Disease 1593
    Physical Therapy 1643
    Radial Styloid Tenosynovitis 1776
    Rehabilitation Therapy 1796

Ocular Ataxia
    Nystagmus 1487

Oligodendroglioma
    Cancer, Brain 344
    Glioma 999

Oligospermia
    Infertility, Male 1206

Omentum Adhesions
    Abdominal Adhesions 1

Omphalocele
    Hernia, Umbilical 1106

One-sided Paralysis
    Hemiplegia 1056

Onychocryptosis
    Toenail, Ingrown 2100

Oophorectomy
    Bilateral 1503
    Cancer, Ovary 372
    Endometriosis 805
    Hysterectomy 1186

Opacity of Eye Lens
    Cataract 436, 439

Open
    Bronchoscopic Biopsy 304
    Enterostomy 811
    Excision or Destruction of Duodenal Lesion 857
    Idiopathic Thrombocytopenic Purpura 1189
    Lacerations 1269
    Nephrotomy 1458
    Neutropenia 1477
    Pleural Biopsy 1657
    Puncture Wound 1759
    Purpura Simplex 1760
    Reduction of Fracture or Dislocation 1791

Open Angle Glaucoma
    Glaucoma, Chronic (Open-Angle) 997

Open Biopsy
    Biopsy 252
    Breast Biopsy 295
    Lung Biopsy 1310

Open Bronchus Biopsy
    Bronchoscopic Biopsy 304

Open Chest Cardiac Massage
    Open-Chest Cardiac Massage 1514

Open Chest Drainage
    Thoracostomy 2078

Open Destruction of Duodenal Lesion
    Excision or Destruction of Duodenal Lesion 857

Open Distal Radius and Ulna Fracture
    Fracture, Radius and Ulna, Distal 933

Open Excision of Duodenal Lesion
    Excision or Destruction of Duodenal Lesion 857

Open Lithotomy
    Lithotomy 1293–1294
    Nephrotomy 1458

Open Liver Biopsy
    Liver Biopsy 1297

Open Lung Biopsy
    Cryptococcosis 608
    Lung Biopsy 1310

Open Manipulative Reduction
    Reduction of Fracture or Dislocation 1791

Open Mitral Commissurotomy
    Mitral Commissurotomy 1384

Valvotomy 2237
Open Pleural Biopsy
    Pleural Biopsy 1657
Open Wound
    Back 1510
    Chest 1512
    Diabetic Gangrene 689
    Gangrene 964
    Lacerations 1269
    Puncture Wound 1759
Operation
    Adrenal Tissue Implant or Transplant to Brain 76
    Amputation 116, 118, 121, 123
    Amputation, Finger or Thumb 123
    Aneurysmectomy 138
    Appendectomy 174
    Arterial Graft 183
    Arthroplasty, Elbow 197
    Arthroscopy 199
    Bone Graft 272
    Breast Biopsy 295
    Bunionectomy 314
    Cardiac Pacemaker Insertion 414
    Carpal Tunnel Release 428
    Cataract Surgery 439
    Cholecystectomy 495
    Circumcision 514
    Cochlear Implant 529
    Colon Resection 538
    Corneal Transplant 582
    Coronary Bypass 592
    Craniectomy 596
    Cystectomy 615
    Cystourethroplasty of Bladder Neck 625
    De Quervain's Release 630
    Discectomy 703
    Dupuytren's Release 753
    Embolectomy 786–787
    Embolectomy, Pulmonary 787
    Esophagectomy 845
    Excision of Bone Spur, Foot 852
    Excision of Morton's Neuroma 855
    Excision of Nail, Nail Bed, or Nail Fold 856
    Excision or Destruction of Duodenal Lesion 857
    Excision, Fusion, and Repair of Toes 860
    Face Lift 865
    Fissurectomy, Anal 884
    Gastrectomy 968
    Gastroenterostomy 978
    Gastrostomy 984
    Heart Valve Replacement 1047
    Hernia Repair 1094, 1096
    Hip Replacement, Total 1119
    Insertion of Inflatable Penile Prosthesis 1213
    Iridectomy 1238
    Kidney Transplant 1261
    Knee Replacement, Total 1263
    Laminectomy or Laminotomy 1273
    Laparoscopy 1275
    Laparotomy 1276
    Laryngectomy 1278
    Ligation and Stripping of Varicose Veins 1287
    Liver Biopsy 1297
    Lung Excision 1314
    Mammoplasty, Augmentation 1338
    Marshall-Marchetti Operation 1344
    Mastectomy 1345
    Meniscectomy and Meniscus Repair 1361
    Mitral Commissurotomy 1384
    Myomectomy, Uterine 1430
    Nasal Polypectomy 1440
    Nephrectomy 1451
    Nephrotomy 1458
    Nerve Injury 1460
    Oophorectomy 1501, 1503
    Open-Chest Cardiac Massage 1514
    Ovarian Cyst, Resection of 1555
    Pancreatectomy 1568
    Pancreaticoduodenectomy 1571
    Paracentesis 1582
    Pericardiectomy 1614
    Prostatectomy 1729
    Pyloroplasty 1769
    Radial Keratotomy 1775
    Reduction of Fracture or Dislocation 1791
    Renal Dialysis 1800
    Repair of Cerebral Aneurysm 1812
    Repair, Anterior Cruciate Ligament 1814
    Repair, Hammertoe 1816
    Resection of Gastric or Duodenal Ulcer Site 1819
    Retinal Detachment Repair 1825
    Rhinoplasty 1841
    Rib Resection 1844
    Rotator Cuff Repair 1848
    Salpingectomy 1868
    Salpingo-oophorectomy 1873
    Scalenectomy 1877
    Septoplasty 1909
    Shoulder Replacement 1917
    Skin Graft 1932
    Spermatocelectomy 1943
    Spinal Cord Stimulation 1949
    Spinal Fusion 1951
    Sympathectomy 2022
    Synovectomy 2027
    Tarsal Tunnel Release 2041
    Tendon Release 2051
    Tendon Sheath Incision 2052
    Thoracentesis 2069
    Thoracostomy 2078
    Thoracotomy 2079
    Thymectomy 2089
    Thyroidectomy 2090
    Tonsillectomy and Adenoidectomy 2102
    Tooth Extraction 2107
    Trabeculoplasty 2158
    Transurethral Balloon Dilation of Prostatic Urethra 2171
    Tubal Ligation 2193
    Tympanoplasty 2201
    Vasectomy 2248
    Vena Cava Interruption 2251
    Vesicourethropexy 2265
Opiate Dependence
    Opioid Type Dependence 1516
Opioid Dependence
    Opioid Type Dependence 1516
Optic
    Atrophy 1519
    Blindness 270
    Cataract 436, 439
    Cataract Surgery 439
    Contusion, Eye 564
    Glaucoma, Chronic (Open-Angle) 997
    Neuritis 1521
    Nystagmus 1487
    Retinal Vascular Occlusion 1827
    Retinitis Pigmentosa 1829
Optic Disorder
    Blindness 270

    Cataract **436, 439**
    Contusion, Eye **564**
    Glaucoma, Chronic (Open-Angle) **997**
    Nystagmus **1487**
    Optic Atrophy **1519**
    Optic Neuritis **1521**
    Retinal Vascular Occlusion **1827**
    Retinitis Pigmentosa **1829**

Optic Nerve Atrophy
    Optic Atrophy **1519**

Optic Nerve Inflammation
    Optic Neuritis **1521**

Optical Iridectomy
    Iridectomy **1238**

Oral
    Behçet's Syndrome **244**

Oral Cancer
    Cancer, Mouth (Other Than Tongue) **366**

Oral Fistula
    Ludwig's Angina **1306**

Oral Herpes
    Herpes Simplex **1108**

Orchidectomy
    Cancer, Testicle(s) **393**
    Orchiectomy **1523**

Orchiectomy
    Cancer, Testicle(s) **393**
    Orchiectomy **1523**

Orchitis
    Mumps **1404**

Organic
    Psychosis **1526**

Organic Brain Syndrome
    Brain Injury **292**
    Organic Psychosis **1526**

Organic Brain Syndrome with Psychotic Features
    Organic Psychosis **1526**

Organic Mental Syndrome
    Organic Psychosis **1526**

Organic Solvents
    Toxic Effects, Carbon Disulfide **2116**
    Toxic Effects, Chlorinated Hydrocarbon Solvents **2120**

Organophosphate Pesticide Poisoning
    Toxic Effects, Organophosphate and Carbamate Pesticides **2147**

ORIF
    Fracture, Ankle **895**
    Fracture, Fingers and Thumb **915**
    Fracture, Metatarsal Bones **925**
    Fracture, Pelvis **930**
    Fracture, Radius and Ulna, Distal **933**
    Fracture, Sacrum **939**
    Fracture, Talus **945**
    Fracture, Thoracic Spine (With or Without Spinal Cord Injury) **948**
    Fracture, Tibia or Fibula **951**
    Fracture, Vertebra **954, 956**

Oropharyngeal
    Cancer, Oropharynx **369**

Oropharyngeal Cancer
    Cancer, Oropharynx **369**

Oropharynx
    Cancer, Oropharynx **369**

Orthostatic Hypotension
    Hypotension **1178**

Os Sacrum Fracture
    Fracture, Sacrum **939**

Osler-Rendu Disease
    Osler-Weber-Rendu Disease **1528**

Osler-Weber-Rendu Syndrome
    Osler-Weber-Rendu Disease **1528**

Osteitis Deformans
    Paget's Disease of Bone **1557**

Osteoarthritis
    Arthralgia **190**
    Arthrodesis **194**
    Arthroplasty, Elbow **197**
    Hip Replacement, Total **1119**
    Joint Disorders **1251**
    Knee Replacement, Total **1263**
    Myelopathy **1420**
    Neck Pain **1448**

Osteoarthrosis
    Osteoarthritis **1530**

Osteoblastoma
    Bone Tumors **281**
    Cancer, Bone **341**

Osteochondrosis
    Osteochondritis Dissecans **1534**

Osteomalacia
    Vitamin D Deficiency **2281**

Osteomyelitis
    Bone Scan **277**

Osteonecrosis
    Avascular Necrosis **235**

Osteophyte
    Bone Spur **278**
    Excision of Bone Spur, Foot **852**

Osteoporosis
    Curvature of the Spine, Acquired **610**
    Fracture, Femoral Neck **912**
    Fracture, Pelvis **930**
    Fracture, Thoracic Spine (With or Without Spinal Cord Injury) **948**
    Fracture, Vertebra (Pathological) **956**

Osteosarcoma
    Bone Tumors **281**
    Cancer, Bone **341**

Osteotomy
    Bunion **312**
    Paget's Disease of Bone **1557**

Ostomy
    Colostomy and Ileostomy **543**

OT
    Occupational Therapy **1499**
    Paralysis, Paraplegia, and Quadriplegia **1583**
    Parkinson's Disease **1593**
    Physical Therapy **1643**

Otitic Barotrauma
    Barotitis Media **241**

Otitis
  Externa, Infective 1543
  Labyrinthitis 1267
  Media 1545

Otitis Externa
  Infective 1543

Otitis Interna
  Labyrinthitis 1267

Otitis Media
  Brain Abscess 289
  Labyrinthitis 1267
  Mastoiditis 1349
  Tympanum Perforation 2202

Otorrhea
  Otitis Externa, Infective 1543

Otosclerosis
  Hearing Loss 1036
  Stapedectomy 2002
  Tinnitus 2097

Otospongiosis
  Otosclerosis 1549

Outlet
  Scalenectomy 1877
  Thoracic Outlet Syndrome 2074

Ovarian
  Cancer, Ovary 372
  Cyst, Benign 1552
  Cyst, Resection of 1555
  Ectopic Pregnancy 775
  Polycystic Ovary Syndrome 1686
  Salpingo-oophorectomy 1873

Ovarian Cancer
  Ascites 203
  Bone Marrow Transplant 275
  Cancer, Ovary 372
  Oophorectomy 1501, 1503

Ovarian Cyst
  Benign 1552

Ovarian Cyst Resection
  Ovarian Cyst, Resection of 1555

Ovarian Cystectomy
  Ovarian Cyst, Resection of 1555

Ovarian Epithelial Cancer
  Cancer, Ovary 372

Ovarian Pregnancy
  Ectopic Pregnancy 775

Ovariectomy
  Cancer, Ovary 372
  Oophorectomy 1501, 1503
  Oophorectomy, Bilateral 1503

Ovary
  Cancer, Ovary 372
  Ectopic Pregnancy 775
  Endometriosis 805
  Hysterectomy 1186
  Ovarian Cyst, Benign 1552
  Ovarian Cyst, Resection of 1555
  Paraovarian Cyst 1590
  Pelvic Inflammatory Disease 1604
  Salpingo-oophorectomy 1873

Overactive Parathyroid Glands
  Hyperparathyroidism 1148

Overactive Thyroid Gland
  Hyperthyroidism 1159

Overanxious Disorder of Childhood
  Anxiety Disorder, Generalized 158

Over-Breathing Syndrome
  Hyperventilation Syndrome 1161

Overdosage
  Poisoning 1675, 1677, 1679, 1681

Overdose
  Cardiac Arrest 409
  Coma 449, 544
  Nasogastric Intubation 1444
  Poisoning 1675, 1677, 1679, 1681
  Poisoning, Iron 1677
  Poisoning, Vitamin B 1679
  Respiratory Failure 1821

Overflow Incontinence
  Prostatic Hypertrophy 1731
  Urinary Incontinence in Women 2222

Overweight
  Obesity, Simple 1491

P

P300
  Evoked Potentials 851

Pacemaker
  Atrioventricular Block Incomplete (Second-Degree) 223
  Bundle Branch Block 310
  Cardiac Pacemaker Insertion 414
  Rheumatic Heart Disease, Chronic 1836
  Stokes-Adams Syndrome 2003
  Wandering Atrial Pacemaker 2293

Pacemaker Implantation
  Cardiac Pacemaker Insertion 414
  Heart Block 1040
  Stokes-Adams Syndrome 2003

Pacemaker Insertion
  Cardiac Pacemaker Insertion 414

PAF with MSA
  Shy Drager Syndrome 1919

Paget's Disease
  Bone Tumors 281
  Curvature of the Spine, Acquired 610
  Paget's Disease of Bone 1557
  Paget's Disease of Breast 1559

Pain
  Abdominal Pain 7
  Abscess, Perirectal 34
  Abscess, Peritonsillar 36
  Abscess, Subdiaphragmatic 42
  Arteriosclerotic Gangrene 186
  Arthralgia 190
  Arthrodesis 194
  Arthroplasty, Elbow 197
  Back Pain 239
  Bone Tumors 281
  Carpal Tunnel Syndrome 430
  Chest Pain 486
  Cluster Headache 517
  Complex Regional Pain Syndrome 550
  Cystitis, Interstitial 619

Degeneration, Lumbar Intervertebral Disc **637**
Dengue Fever **656**
Dentoalveolar Abscess **660**
Eosinophilic Fasciitis **814**
Fibromyalgia and Myofascial Pain Syndrome **879**
Headache **1033**
in Limb **1562**
Low Back Pain **1302**
Metatarsalgia **1376**
Myalgia and Myositis **1411**
Neck Pain **1448**
Nephropexy **1455**
Neuralgia, Neuritis, and Radiculitis **1465**
Optic Neuritis **1521**
Orchitis **1524**
Osteoarthritis **1530**
Osteochondritis Dissecans **1534**
Osteomyelitis **1537**
Otitis Media **1545**
Paget's Disease of Bone **1557**
Pancreatic Pseudocyst **1569**
Pancreatitis **1573**
Paraovarian Cyst **1590**
Paresthesia **1591**
Patella Chondromalacia **1599**
Pelvic Inflammatory Disease **1604**
Pemphigus **1606**
Penis Disorders **1608**
Peptic Ulcer Disease **1611**
Pericarditis, Acute **1615**
Peripheral Neuropathy **1621**
Peripheral Vascular Disease **1626**
Peritonitis **1628**
Pilonidal Cyst **1645**
Pleurisy **1659**
Pleurodynia **1661**
Pneumothorax **1671**
Post-Laminectomy Syndrome **1701**
Pott's Disease **1709**
Psoriatic Arthritis **1740**
Pylorospasm **1770**
Radial Styloid Tenosynovitis **1776**
Raynaud's Phenomenon **1781**
Renal Failure, Acute **1802**
Renovascular Hypertension **1809**
Repetitive Strain Injury **1819**
Rheumatoid Arthritis **1838**
Root Canal Therapy **1847**
Rotator Cuff Repair **1848**
Rotator Cuff Syndrome **1850**
Rotator Cuff Tear **1853**
Rupture of Spleen, Traumatic **1860**
Salivary Gland Stones **1865**
Salpingitis **1870**
Salpingo-oophorectomy **1873**
Sciatica **1890**
Scleritis **1891**
Shoulder Replacement **1917**
Sickle Cell Anemia **1922**
Somatization Disorder **1939**
Spinal Cord Injury **1946**
Spinal Fusion **1951**
Spondylolysis, Lumbar Region **1962**
Sprains and Strains **1964**, **1968**, **1971**, **1975**, **1979**, **1981**, **1984**, **1986**, **1989**, **1991**, **1994**, **1997**
Sprains and Strains, Back **1975**
Sprains and Strains, Elbow **1984**
Sprains and Strains, Hand or Fingers **1989**
Stye **2010**
Synovectomy **2027**
Syringomyelia **2035**

Temporomandibular Joint Syndrome **2049**
Tendon Release **2051**
Tendon Sheath Incision **2052**
Tendonitis **2054**
Thoracic Outlet Syndrome **2074**
Thoracic Spine Pain **2076**
Toenail, Ingrown **2100**
Torticollis **2108**

Pain Behavior
Pain, Chronic **1564**

Pain Dysfunction Syndrome
Myalgia and Myositis **1411**

Pain in Abdomen
Abdominal Pain **7**

Pain in Back
Back Pain **239**
Low Back Pain **1302**
Thoracic Spine Pain **2076**

Pain in Joint
Arthralgia **190**
Joint Disorders **1251**

Pain in Low Back
Cauda Equina Syndrome **440**
Chemonucleolysis of Interveterbral Disc **482**
Low Back Pain **1302**

Pain in Neck
Neck Pain **1448**

Pain in the Head
Headache **1033**
Migraine Headache **1378**

Pain Medication Abuse
Opioid Type Dependence **1516**

Pain Medication Addiction
Opioid Type Dependence **1516**

Painful
Impacted Tooth **1191**
Joint Disorders **1251**
Ligation and Stripping of Varicose Veins **1287**
Warts, Plantar **2296**

Painful Arc Syndrome
Rotator Cuff Syndrome **1850**

Painful Heel
Heel Spur (Calcaneal) **1053**

Painless Thyroiditis
Thyroiditis **2091**

Palmar
Abscess, Palmar **32**
Dupuytren's Contracture **751**
Dupuytren's Release **753**

Palmar Abscess
Abscess, Palmar **32**

Palmar Fascia Contracture
Dupuytren's Contracture **751**
Dupuytren's Release **753**

Palmar Fasciectomy
Dupuytren's Contracture **751**
Dupuytren's Release **753**

Palmar Fasciotomy
Dupuytren's Release **753**

Palpitations
- Anaphylactic Shock, Food Reaction 131
- Atrioventricular Block, Complete (Third-Degree) 224
- Neurocirculatory Asthenia 1467
- Pheochromocytoma 1638
- Phobias, Specific 1639
- Phobic Disorders 1641
- Renovascular Hypertension 1809
- Tachycardia, Paroxysmal Supraventricular 2039

Palsy
- Atrophy, Muscular (Progressive) 230
- Cerebral Palsy 452
- Parkinson's Disease 1593

Pancreas
- Cancer, Pancreas 375
- Diabetes Mellitus Type I 683, 686
- Diabetes Mellitus Type II 686
- Hyperinsulinism 1144
- Pancreatectomy 1568
- Pancreatic Pseudocyst 1569
- Pancreaticoduodenectomy 1571
- Pancreaticojejunostomy 1572
- Pancreatitis 1573

Pancreatectomy
- Cancer, Pancreas 375

Pancreatic
- Cancer, Pancreas 375
- Pancreatitis 1573
- Pseudocyst 1569

Pancreatic Cancer
- Cancer, Pancreas 375
- Celiac Plexus Block 442
- Esophagogastroduodenoscopy 850
- Pancreatectomy 1568
- Pancreaticoduodenectomy 1571
- Pancreaticojejunostomy 1572

Pancreatic Inflammation
- Pancreaticojejunostomy 1572
- Pancreatitis 1573

Pancreaticoduodenectomy
- Cancer, Small Intestine (Including Duodenum) 389

Pancreaticojejunostomy
- Cancer, Pancreas 375
- Pancreaticoduodenectomy 1571

Pancreatitis
- Avascular Necrosis 235
- Cancer, Pancreas 375
- Hypoproteinemia 1175
- Pancreatectomy 1568
- Pancreatic Pseudocyst 1569
- Pancreaticoduodenectomy 1571
- Pancreaticojejunostomy 1572

Panendoscopy
- Esophagogastroduodenoscopy 850

Panic Attack
- Cognitive Therapy 530
- Hyperventilation Syndrome 1161
- Panic Disorder 1578, 1580
- Panic Disorder with Agoraphobia 1580
- Social Phobia 1937

Panophthalmitis
- Endophthalmitis 808

Pap Smear
- Cancer, Cervix 351
- Cervical Biopsy 460
- Cervical Dysplasia 467
- Cervical Polyps 470
- Fibroid Tumor of Uterus 875

Papillary Carcinoma
- Cancer, Thyroid Gland 396

Papillary Necrosis
- Nephritis, Interstitial 1453

Papilloma of Urinary Bladder
- Bladder Polyps 264

PAR
- Allergic Rhinitis 98

Paracentesis
- Ascites 203
- Aspiration 207–208
- Thoracentesis 2069

Paraesophageal Hernia
- Hernia, Hiatal 1097

Paraganglioma
- Pheochromocytoma 1638

Paralysis
- Botulism 286
- Brain Injury 292
- Conversion Disorder 574
- General Paresis 986
- Hemiplegia 1056
- Neuralgia, Neuritis, and Radiculitis 1465
- Paraplegia, and Quadriplegia 1583
- Parkinson's Disease 1593
- Polio 1683
- Rabies 1773
- Spinal Cord Injury 1946
- Spinal Fusion 1951
- St. Louis Encephalitis 2000

Paralysis Agitans
- Parkinson's Disease 1593

Paralytic Dementia
- General Paresis 986

Paralytic Ileus
- Intestinal Obstruction 1222
- Nasogastric Intubation 1444

Paralytic Shellfish Poisoning
- Toxic Effects, Fish and Shellfish 2126

Paralyzed
- Hemiplegia 1056
- Paralysis, Paraplegia, and Quadriplegia 1583
- Parkinson's Disease 1593

Paranoia
- Cocaine Dependence/Abuse 522
- Delusional Disorder 649
- Paranoid Personality Disorder 1588
- Schizophrenia 1882, 1885
- Schizophrenia, Paranoid Type 1885
- Sedative, Hypnotic or Anxiolytic Dependence 1898

Paranoia Personality Traits
- Paranoid Personality Disorder 1588

Paranoid
- Delusional Disorder 649
- Personality Disorder 1588

Paranoid Schizophrenia
    Schizophrenia, Paranoid Type 1885

Paranoid States
    Delusional Disorder 649

Paranoid Type of Schizophrenia
    Schizophrenia, Paranoid Type 1885

Paraovarian
    Cyst 1590

Paraphilia
    Psychosexual Disorders 1745

Paraphilias
    Psychosexual Disorders 1745

Paraphimosis
    Circumcision 514
    Penis Disorders 1608

Paraphrenia
    Delusional Disorder 649

Paraplegia
    Paralysis, Paraplegia, and Quadriplegia 1583
    Spinal Cord Injury 1946

Parasitic Disease
    Trichinosis 2183

Parasitic Spondylitis
    Spondylitis 1958

Parasympathotonia
    Vagotonia 2237

Parathion Exposure
    Toxic Effects, Organophosphate and Carbamate Pesticides 2147

Parathyroid
    Hyperparathyroidism 1148
    Hypoparathyroidism 1173

Parathyroid Adenoma
    Hyperparathyroidism 1148

Parathyroid Hormone Disease
    Hyperparathyroidism 1148
    Hypoparathyroidism 1173

Parathyroid Tetany
    Tetany 2062

Paratyphoid
    Typhoid Fever 2204

Paraumbilical Hernia
    Hernia, Umbilical 1106

Paresis
    Brain Injury 292
    Cerebral Contusion, Closed 447
    Cerebral Palsy 452
    General Paresis 986
    Paralysis, Paraplegia, and Quadriplegia 1583
    Syphilis 2033

Paresthesia
    Anaphylactic Shock, Food Reaction 131
    Carpal Tunnel Release 428
    Carpal Tunnel Syndrome 430
    Cervicobrachial Syndrome 474
    General Paresis 986
    Multiple Sclerosis 1401
    Panic Disorder 1578, 1580
    Panic Disorder with Agoraphobia 1580
    Tarsal Tunnel Release 2041

    Thoracic Disc Disorder with Myelopathy 2072
    Vitamin B_1 Deficiency 2272

Parietal Cell Vagotomy
    Vagotomy 2235

Parkinson's Disease
    Adrenal Tissue Implant or Transplant to Brain 76
    Constipation 558
    Craniotomy 598
    Dementia 651, 653
    Parkinson's Disease 1593
    Thalamotomy 2064

Parkinsonian Tremor
    Parkinson's Disease 1593
    Thalamotomy 2064
    Tremor 2179

Parkinsonism
    Parkinson's Disease 1593
    Psychopharmacotherapy 1743

Parotitis
    Mumps 1404

Paroxysmal
    Allergic Rhinitis 98
    Atrial Fibrillation 220
    Palpitations 1566
    Pheochromocytoma 1638
    Raynaud's Phenomenon 1781
    Tachycardia, Paroxysmal Supraventricular 2039

Paroxysmal Atrial Fibrillation
    Atrial Fibrillation 220

Paroxysmal Atrial Tachycardia
    Arrhythmia 178
    Palpitations 1566
    Tachycardia, Paroxysmal Supraventricular 2039

Paroxysmal Atrioventricular Tachycardia
    Tachycardia, Paroxysmal Supraventricular 2039

Paroxysmal Digital Cyanosis Syndrome
    Raynaud's Phenomenon 1781

Paroxysmal Junctional Tachycardia
    Tachycardia, Paroxysmal Supraventricular 2039

Paroxysmal Nodal Tachycardia
    Tachycardia, Paroxysmal Supraventricular 2039

Paroxysmal Rhinorrhea
    Allergic Rhinitis 98

Paroxysmal Supraventricular Tachycardia
    Tachycardia, Paroxysmal Supraventricular 2039

Paroxysmal Tachycardia
    Tachycardia, Paroxysmal Supraventricular 2039

Paroxysmal Ventricular Tachycardia
    Ventricular Tachycardia 2260

Parsonage-Aldren-Turner Syndrome
    Neuralgic Amyotrophy 1465

Partial
    Cystectomy 615
    Iridectomy 1238
    Lung Excision 1314
    Mastectomy 1345
    Nephrectomy 1451
    Pancreatectomy 1568
    Resection of Gastric or Duodenal Ulcer Site 1819
    Seizures 1900
    Vagotomy 2235

Partial Amputation
    Amputation (Traumatic), Foot **118**

Partial Cell Vagotomy
    Vagotomy **2235**

Partial Cystectomy
    Cystectomy **615**

Partial Excision
    Cystectomy **615**
    Gastrectomy **968**
    Iridectomy **1238**
    Lung Excision **1314**
    Mastectomy **1345**
    Nephrectomy **1451**
    Pancreatectomy **1568**
    Resection of Gastric or Duodenal Ulcer Site **1819**

Partial Excision of Esophagus
    Esophagectomy **845**

Partial Excision of Gastric Ulcer Site
    Gastrectomy **968**
    Resection of Gastric or Duodenal Ulcer Site **1819**

Partial Excision of Lung
    Lung Excision **1314**

Partial Excision of the Iris
    Iridectomy **1238**

Partial Gastrectomy
    Gastrectomy **968**
    Pyloric Stenosis, Acquired (Adult) Hypertrophic **1767**
    Resection of Gastric or Duodenal Ulcer Site **1819**

Partial Hip Arthroplasty
    Hip Replacement, Total **1119**

Partial Hip Replacement
    Hip Replacement, Total **1119**

Partial Hysterectomy
    Hysterectomy **1186**

Partial Lobectomy
    Lung Excision **1314**

Partial Lung Excision
    Lung Excision **1314**

Partial Meniscectomy
    Meniscectomy and Meniscus Repair **1361**

Partial Motor Seizure
    Jacksonian Seizure **1247**
    Seizures **1900**

Partial Nephrectomy
    Nephrectomy **1451**

Partial Pancreatectomy
    Pancreatectomy **1568**

Partial Resection of Large Intestine
    Colon Resection **538**

Partial Resection of the Large Intestine
    Colon Resection **538**

Partial Thenar Atrophy
    Carpal Tunnel Syndrome **430**

Partial Thyroidectomy
    Thyroidectomy **2090**

Parulis
    Gingival Abscess **991**

Parvovirus B_{19} Infection
    Tularemia **2197**

Passive
    Aggressive-Personality Disorder **1597**
    Dependent Personality Disorder **661**
    Pulmonary Edema **1756**

Passive Aggressive Personality Disorder
    Passive-Aggressive Personality Disorder **1597**

Passive Personality Disorder
    Dependent Personality Disorder **661**

Passive Pneumonia
    Pulmonary Edema **1756**

Pasteurella Tularensis
    Tularemia **2197**

Patch Graft
    Arterial Graft **183**

Patchy Hair Loss
    Alopecia Areata **103**

Patella
    Chondromalacia **1599**
    Dislocation, Patella (Kneecap) **723**
    Internal Derangement of Knee **1219**

Patellar
    Patella Chondromalacia **1599**

Patellar Dislocation
    Dislocation, Patella (Kneecap) **723**

Patellar Injury
    Dislocation, Patella (Kneecap) **723**

Patellofemoral Syndrome
    Patella Chondromalacia **1599**

Pathologic Fracture
    Fracture, Vertebra (Pathological) **956**

Pathological
    Fracture, Vertebra (Pathological) **956**
    Myelopathy **1420**

Pathological Cervical Fracture
    Fracture, Vertebra (Pathological) **956**

Pathological Compression Fracture
    Fracture, Lumbosacral Spine (With or Without Spinal Cord Injury) **920**
    Fracture, Vertebra (Pathological) **956**

Pathological Compression Fracture of Spine
    Fracture, Vertebra (Pathological) **956**

Pathological Condition of Spinal Cord
    Myelopathy **1420**

Pathological Fracture of Spine
    Fracture, Vertebra (Pathological) **956**

Pathological Gangrene
    Diabetic Gangrene **689**

Pathological Lumbar Fracture
    Fracture, Vertebra (Pathological) **956**

Pathological Spine Fracture
    Fracture, Vertebra (Pathological) **956**

Pathological Thoracolumbar Fracture
    Fracture, Vertebra (Pathological) **956**

Pathological Vertigo
    Vertigo **2262**

Paul Ileostomy
    Colostomy and Ileostomy **543**

PCP
    Pneumocystis Carinii Pneumonia **1663**

PCP Abuse
    Phencyclidine Abuse **1635**

PE Tube Placement
    Myringotomy **1434**

Pectoris
    Angina Pectoris **140**

Pedicle Graft
    Skin Graft **1932**

Pedis
    Tinea **2095**

Peg
    Gastrostomy **984**

Pelvic
    Culdoscopy **610**
    Inflammatory Disease **1604**
    Menstrual Disorders **1369**
    Salpingitis **1870**
    Salpingo-oophorectomy **1873**

Pelvic Adhesions
    Abdominal Adhesions **1**

Pelvic Cavity
    Culdoscopy **610**

Pelvic Fracture
    Fracture, Pelvis **930**

Pelvic Inflammatory Disease
    Salpingitis **1870**
    Salpingo-oophorectomy **1873**

Pelvic Inflammatory Infection
    Pelvic Inflammatory Disease **1604**
    Salpingitis **1870**

Pelvis
    Culdoscopy **610**
    Fracture, Pelvis **930**
    Hip Replacement, Total **1119**
    Paget's Disease of Bone **1557**
    Paraovarian Cyst **1590**

Pelvis Fracture
    Fracture, Pelvis **930**

Penetrating Chest Wound
    Open Wound, Chest **1512**

Penetrating Keratoplasty
    Corneal Transplant **582**

Penetrating Thoracic Wound
    Open Wound, Chest **1512**

Penile Implant
    Insertion of Inflatable Penile Prosthesis **1213**

Penile Prosthesis
    Impotence **1198**
    Insertion of Inflatable Penile Prosthesis **1213**

Penile Prosthetic Surgery
    Insertion of Inflatable Penile Prosthesis **1213**

Penis
    Candidiasis **405**
    Circumcision **514**
    Cryotherapy, Genital Warts (Male) **606**
    Disorders **1608**
    Infertility, Male **1206**
    Insertion of Inflatable Penile Prosthesis **1213**

Penis, Disorders of
    Impotence **1198**
    Penis Disorders **1608**

Peptic Stricture
    Esophageal Strictures **840**

Peptic Ulcer
    Disease **1611**
    Duodenitis **749**
    Dyspepsia **759**
    Esophagogastroduodenoscopy **850**
    Gastrointestinal Hemorrhage **982**
    Hypovolemic Shock **1184**
    Upper Gastrointestinal Series **2214**

Peptic Ulcer Disease
    Gastrectomy **968**
    Gastroenterostomy **978**
    Upper Gastrointestinal Series **2214**

Perchlorethylene Poisoning
    Toxic Effects, Chlorinated Hydrocarbon Solvents **2120**

Percolone Poisoning
    Toxic Effects, Chlorinated Hydrocarbon Solvents **2120**

Percutaneous
    Coronary Balloon Angioplasty **590**
    Lithotomy, Percutaneous **1294**
    Liver Biopsy **1297**
    Lung Biopsy **1310**
    Paracentesis **1582**
    Valvuloplasty, Balloon **2240**

Percutaneous Balloon Valvotomy
    Valvuloplasty, Balloon **2240**

Percutaneous Balloon Valvuloplasty
    Mitral Commissurotomy **1384**

Percutaneous Biopsy
    Biopsy **252**
    Lung Biopsy **1310**

Percutaneous Endoscopic Gastrostomy
    Gastrostomy **984**

Percutaneous Enterostomy
    Enterostomy **811**

Percutaneous Kidney Stone Surgery
    Lithotomy, Percutaneous **1294**

Percutaneous Lithotomy
    Lithotomy, Percutaneous **1294**

Percutaneous Liver Biopsy
    Liver Biopsy **1297**

Percutaneous Lung Biopsy
    Lung Biopsy **1310**

Percutaneous Nephrolithotomy
    Lithotomy, Percutaneous **1294**

Percutaneous Paracentesis
    Paracentesis **1582**

Percutaneous Tracheostomy
    Tracheostomy **2159**

Percutaneous Transhepatic Cholangiography
    Cholangiography **493**

Percutaneous Transluminal Balloon Valvuloplasty
    Valvuloplasty, Balloon 2240

Percutaneous Transluminal Coronary Angioplasty
    Angina Pectoris 140
    Cardiogenic Shock 417
    Coronary Balloon Angioplasty 590

Percutaneous Transseptal Mitral Commissurotomy
    Valvuloplasty, Balloon 2240

Percutaneous Valvuloplasty
    Valvuloplasty, Balloon 2240

Perennial Allergic Rhinitis
    Allergic Rhinitis 98

Perforated Eardrum
    Barotitis Media 241
    Hearing Loss 1036
    Tympanum Perforation 2202

Perforated Nasal Septum
    Nasal Septum Perforation 1443

Perforated Septum
    Nasal Septum Perforation 1443

Perforated Tympanum
    Tympanum Perforation 2202

Perforated Uterus
    Uterus, Perforation of 2229

Perforation
    Nasal Septum Perforation 1443
    Tympanum Perforation 2202
    Uterus, Perforation of 2229

Perforation of Eardrum
    Tympanum Perforation 2202

Perforation of Tympanic Membrane
    Tympanum Perforation 2202

Perforation of Uterus
    Uterus, Perforation of 2229

Perfusion Scan
    Myocardial Perfusion Scan 1427

Perianal Abscess
    Abscess, Anorectal 20
    Abscess, Ischiorectal 24
    Abscess, Perirectal 34
    Incision and Drainage of Ischiorectal and/or Perirectal Abscess 1200

Periapical
    Dentoalveolar Abscess 660
    Periodontitis 1619

Periapical Abscess
    Dentoalveolar Abscess 660
    Periodontitis 1619

Periapical Abscess with Sinus
    Gingival Abscess 991

Periarteritis
    Polyarteritis Nodosa 1685

Periarteritis Nodosa
    Polyarteritis Nodosa 1685

Periarthritis
    Adhesive Capsulitis of Shoulder 66

Pericardectomy
    Pericardiectomy 1614
    Pericarditis, Chronic Constrictive 1617

Pericardectomy Syndrome
    Pericarditis, Acute 1615

Pericardial
    Pericardiectomy 1614
    Pericarditis, Acute 1615

Pericardial Inflammation
    Pericarditis, Acute 1615

Pericardial Resection
    Pericardiectomy 1614

Pericardiocentesis
    Aspiration 207—208
    Paracentesis 1582
    Pericarditis, Acute 1615

Pericarditis
    Acute 1615
    Echocardiography 774

Perinephric
    Abscess, Renal and Perinephric 40

Perinephric Abscess
    Abscess, Renal and Perinephric 40

Perineum
    Abdominoperineal Resection of Rectum 10
    Cauda Equina Syndrome 440
    Episiotomy 826
    Perineorrhaphy 1618

Periodontitis
    Gingival Abscess 991
    Tooth Extraction 2107

Peripheral
    Morton's Neuroma 1393
    Neuropathy 1621
    Vascular Disease 1626
    Vestibular Neuronitis 2268

Peripheral Arterial Disease
    Peripheral Vascular Disease 1626

Peripheral Arterial Insufficiency
    Peripheral Vascular Disease 1626

Peripheral Arterial Thrombosis
    Peripheral Thrombosis 1623

Peripheral Arteriosclerosis
    Peripheral Vascular Disease 1626

Peripheral Atherosclerosis
    Peripheral Vascular Disease 1626

Peripheral Autonomic Neuropathy
    Peripheral Neuropathy 1621

Peripheral Disease
    Peripheral Vascular Disease 1626

Peripheral Iridectomy
    Iridectomy 1238

Peripheral Nervous System
    Guillain-Barré Syndrome 1022

Peripheral Neuritis
    Peripheral Neuropathy 1621

Peripheral Neuroma
    Excision of Morton's Neuroma 855
    Morton's Neuroma 1393

Peripheral Neuropathy
    Diabetic Neuropathy 692

Peripheral NF
    Neurofibromatosis 1469
Peripheral Ulcerative Keratitis
    Keratitis 1257
Peripheral Vascular Disease
    Arterial Graft 183
Peripheral Vascular Insufficiency
    Peripheral Vascular Disease 1626
Peripheral Vestibulopathy
    Vestibular Neuronitis 2268
Perirectal
    Abscess, Anorectal 20
    Abscess, Ischiorectal 24
    Abscess, Perirectal 34
    Incision and Drainage of Ischiorectal and/or Perirectal Abscess 1200
Perirectal Abscess
    Abscess, Anorectal 20
    Abscess, Ischiorectal 24
    Abscess, Perirectal 34
    Incision and Drainage of Ischiorectal and/or Perirectal Abscess 1200
Perirectal Abscess Drainage
    Incision and Drainage of Ischiorectal and/or Perirectal Abscess 1200
Perirectal Cellulitis
    Abscess, Anorectal 20
    Abscess, Ischiorectal 24
    Abscess, Perirectal 34
Perirenal Abscess
    Abscess, Renal and Perinephric 40
Perisalpingitis
    Salpingitis 1870
Peritoneal
    Abscess, Psoas 38
    Abscess, Subdiaphragmatic 42
    Laparoscopy 1275
    Peritonitis 1628
    Renal Dialysis 1800
Peritoneal Abscess
    Abscess, Psoas 38
    Abscess, Subdiaphragmatic 42
Peritoneal Adhesions
    Abdominal Adhesions 1
Peritoneal Cavity Inflammation
    Ascites 203
    Peritonitis 1628
Peritoneal Dialysis
    Renal Dialysis 1800
Peritoneoscopy
    Laparoscopy 1275
Peritoneum
    Abdominoperineal Resection of Rectum 10
    Ascites 203
    Peritonitis 1628
Peritonitis
    Abscess, Psoas 38
    Abscess, Subdiaphragmatic 42
    Laparotomy 1276
Peritonsillar Abscess
    Abscess, Peritonsillar 36

Peritonsillar Cellulitis
    Abscess, Peritonsillar 36
Perlèche
    Vitamin B_2 Deficiency 2275
Permanent
    Laryngitis 1279
Permanent Gastrostomy
    Gastrostomy 984
Permanent Idiopathic Hypotension
    Hypotension 1178
Permanent Ileostomy
    Colostomy and Ileostomy 543
Permanent Pacemaker
    Cardiac Pacemaker Insertion 414
Pernicious Anemia
    Anemia 133, 136
    Gastroenterostomy 978
Personality Disorder
    Antisocial Personality Disorder 156
    Avoidant Personality Disorder 237
    Borderline Personality Disorder 284
    Dependent Personality Disorder 661
    Dissociative Personality Disorder 737
    Explosive Personality Disorder 862
    Intermittent Explosive Disorder 1217
    Narcissistic Personality Disorder 1437
    Obsessive-Compulsive Disorder 1494
    Obsessive-Compulsive Personality Disorder 1496
    Paranoid Personality Disorder 1588
    Passive-Aggressive Personality Disorder 1597
    Schizoid Personality Disorder 1881
Personality Disorders
    Antisocial Personality Disorder 156
    Avoidant Personality Disorder 237
    Obsessive-Compulsive Personality Disorder 1496
Personality Traits
    Avoidant Personality Disorder 237
    Dependent Personality Disorder 661
    Paranoid Personality Disorder 1588
    Passive-Aggressive Personality Disorder 1597
    Schizoid Personality Disorder 1881
Person-centered Therapy
    Psychotherapy, Individual 1748
Pesticide Poisoning
    Poisoning, Vitamin B 1679
    Toxic Effects, Arsenic and Compounds 2110
Petit Mal Seizure
    Epilepsy 824
    Seizures 1900
Peyronie's Disease
    Impotence 1198
    Penis Disorders 1608
PFTs
    Pulmonary Function Tests 1758
Phalangectomy
    Excision, Fusion, and Repair of Toes 860
Phalanges
    Fracture, Fingers and Thumb 915
    Fracture, Forefoot (Sesamoid, Phalanges) 918

Phalanges of Foot
    Fracture, Forefoot (Sesamoid, Phalanges) 918

Phalanges of Hand
    Fracture, Fingers and Thumb 915

Pharmacologic Stress Test
    Cardiac Stress Test 416

Pharmacotherapy
    Abscess, Psoas 38
    Attention Deficit Disorder in Adults 232
    Avoidant Personality Disorder 237
    Bipolar Affective Disorder 253, 256, 258, 260
    Bipolar Affective Disorder, Single Manic Episode 260
    Dependent Personality Disorder 661
    Premature Labor 1720
    Premenstrual Syndrome 1724
    Prinzmetal's Angina 1726
    Prostatic Hypertrophy 1731
    Prostatitis 1734
    Pruritus Ani 1736
    Psoriasis 1738
    Psoriatic Arthritis 1740
    Psychopharmacotherapy 1743

Pharyngitis
    Acute 1633

Pharyngoesophageal Diverticula
    Esophageal Diverticula 836

Phencyclidine Addiction
    Phencyclidine Abuse 1635

Phencyclidine Dependence
    Phencyclidine Abuse 1635

Pheochromoblastoma
    Pheochromocytoma 1638

Pheochromocytoma
    Adrenalectomy 77

Pheochromocytoma of Adrenal Gland
    Pheochromocytoma 1638

Phimosis
    Circumcision 514
    Penis Disorders 1608

Phlebitis
    Thrombophlebitis 2086
    Venous Embolism and Thrombosis 2252

Phlegmasia Alba Dolens
    Thrombophlebitis 2086

Phobias
    Cognitive Therapy 530
    Phobic Disorders 1641
    Social Phobia 1937
    Specific 1639

Phobic Disorders
    Phobias, Specific 1639
    Social Phobia 1937

Phorate Exposure
    Toxic Effects, Organophosphate and Carbamate Pesticides 2147

Phosdrin Exposure
    Toxic Effects, Organophosphate and Carbamate Pesticides 2147

Photocoagulation
    Cancer, Rectum 384
    Chorioretinitis 506
    Diabetic Retinopathy 694
    Retinal Detachment 1823, 1825
    Retinal Detachment Repair 1825
    Senile Macular Degeneration 1903

Photodermatitis
    Contact Dermatitis 560
    Dermatitis 674
    Eczema 778

Phylloquinone
    Poisoning, Vitamin K 1681

Physical Medicine
    Physical Therapy 1643

Physical Rehabilitation
    Physical Therapy 1643
    Ultrasound, Therapeutic 2213

Physical Therapy
    Adhesive Capsulitis of Shoulder 66
    Amyotrophic Lateral Sclerosis 125
    Ankylosing Spondylitis 152
    Atrophy, Muscular 227, 230
    Atrophy, Muscular (Progressive) 230
    Biceps Tendonitis 248
    Bone Tumors 281
    Bronchiectasis 297
    Cerebral Palsy 452
    Cervical Disc Disorder with Myelopathy 464
    Cervicobrachial Syndrome 474
    Chronic Fatigue Syndrome 509
    Complex Regional Pain Syndrome 550
    Decubitus Ulcer 632
    Disc Calcification 701
    Dislocation, Patella (Kneecap) 723
    Displacement, Thoracic Intervertebral Disc Without Myelopathy 735
    Dupuytren's Contracture 751
    Enthesopathy 812
    Fibromyalgia and Myofascial Pain Syndrome 879
    Fracture, Talus 945
    General Paresis 986
    Guillain-Barré Syndrome 1022
    Headache 1033
    Hemiplegia 1056
    Mastectomy 1345
    Morton's Neuroma 1393
    Muscle Injury 1406
    Muscle Spasm 1409
    Myalgia and Myositis 1411
    Neck Pain 1448
    Neurocirculatory Asthenia 1467
    Otosclerosis 1549
    Paget's Disease of Bone 1557
    Paget's Disease of Breast 1559
    Pain, Chronic 1564
    Paralysis, Paraplegia, and Quadriplegia 1583
    Parkinson's Disease 1593
    Patella Chondromalacia 1599
    Plantar Fasciitis 1655
    Post-Laminectomy Syndrome 1701
    Radial Styloid Tenosynovitis 1776
    Rehabilitation Therapy 1796
    Rheumatoid Arthritis 1838
    Rotator Cuff Syndrome 1850
    Rotator Cuff Tear 1853
    Shoulder Replacement 1917
    Spinal Stenosis 1952
    Spondylolisthesis 1960
    Spondylolysis, Lumbar Region 1962
    Sprains and Strains, Ankle 1971
    Sprains and Strains, Back 1975
    Sprains and Strains, Cervical Spine (Neck) 1981

Sprains and Strains, Elbow 1984
Sprains and Strains, Foot 1986
Sprains and Strains, Wrist 1997
Tarsal Tunnel Release 2041
Tarsal Tunnel Syndrome 2043
Tendonitis 2054
Thoracic Outlet Syndrome 2074
Thoracic Spine Pain 2076
Ultrasound, Therapeutic 2213

Physiologic Tremor
Tremor 2179

Physiological Ovarian Cysts
Ovarian Cyst, Benign 1552

Physiological Vertigo
Vertigo 2262

Physiotherapy
Physical Therapy 1643

Pick's Disease of Pericardium
Pericarditis, Chronic Constrictive 1617

PID
Pelvic Inflammatory Disease 1604
Salpingitis 1870

Piebald
Vitiligo 2286

Pigeon Breeder's Disease
Hypersensitivity Pneumonitis 1150

Pigmentary Retinal Dystrophy
Retinitis Pigmentosa 1829

Pigmentosa
Retinitis Pigmentosa 1829

Piles
Hemorrhoid Treatment 1070
Hemorrhoids 1073

Pilocytic Astrocytoma
Astrocytoma 214

Pilonidal
Cyst 1645

Pilonidal Disease
Pilonidal Cyst 1645

Pinched nerve
Laminectomy or Laminotomy 1273

Pineal Gland Neoplasm
Tumor, Benign 2199

Pineal Gland Tumor
Pineal Gland Neoplasm 1647
Tumor, Benign 2199

Pinealoma
Pineal Gland Neoplasm 1647

Pineoblastoma
Pineal Gland Neoplasm 1647

Pineocytoma
Pineal Gland Neoplasm 1647

Pink Disease Poisoning
Toxic Effects, Mercury 2138

Pink Eye
Conjunctivitis 556

Pins and Needles
Paresthesia 1591

Pituitary Cachexia
Panhypopituitarism 1576

Pituitary Gland
Cushing's Syndrome 613
Hypothyroidism 1180
Panhypopituitarism 1576

Pituitary Insufficiency
Diabetes Insipidus 681
Panhypopituitarism 1576

Pityriasis Versicolor
Tinea 2095

PK
Corneal Transplant 582
Keratectomy, Laser Photorefractive 1256

Placenta
Abruptio Placentae 16
Accreta 1651
Cesarean Delivery 476
Previa 1653

Placenta Accreta
Cesarean Delivery 476

Placenta Disorders
Abruptio Placentae 16
Cesarean Delivery 476
Placenta Accreta 1651
Placenta Previa 1653

Placenta Previa
Cesarean Delivery 476
Placenta Accreta 1651

Placental Abruption
Abruptio Placentae 16
Cesarean Delivery 476

Plain X-rays
X-ray 2305

Plant Dermatitis
Poison Ivy, Oak, Sumac, or Other Plant Dermatitis 1673
Toxic Effects, Plants (genus Toxicodendron) 2150

Plantar
Fasciitis 1655
Morton's Neuroma 1393
Warts, Plantar 2296
Warts, Viral 2298

Plantar Fascia Inflammation
Plantar Fasciitis 1655

Plantar Fasciitis
Excision of Bone Spur, Foot 852
Plantar Fasciitis 1655

Plantar Nerve Lesion
Excision of Morton's Neuroma 855
Morton's Neuroma 1393

Plantar Neuroma
Excision of Morton's Neuroma 855

Plantar Wart
Excision or Destruction of Plantar Warts 858
Warts, Plantar 2296
Warts, Viral 2298

Plaque Psoriasis
Psoriasis 1738

Plasma Cell Myeloma
Multiple Myeloma 1399

Plastic Operation on Bladder And/or Vesical Neck
    Cystourethroplasty of Bladder Neck 625
Plastic Surgery
    Face Lift 865
    Open Wound 1504, 1510, 1512
    Reduction Mammoplasty 1790
    Rhinoplasty 1841
    Septoplasty 1909
Plastic Surgery of the Nasal Septum
    Septoplasty 1909
Plastic Surgery on the Nose
    Rhinoplasty 1841
    Septoplasty 1909
Pleura
    Biopsy 1657
    Cancer, Pleura 377
    Chest Pain 486
    Empyema 794
    Pleurisy 1659
Pleural
    Biopsy 1657
    Cancer, Pleura 377
    Pleurisy 1659
Pleural Abscess
    Empyema 794
Pleural Cancer
    Cancer, Pleura 377
Pleural Fluid Aspiration
    Thoracentesis 2069
Pleural Inflammation
    Pleurisy 1659
Pleural Needle
    Pleural Biopsy 1657
Pleural Tap
    Thoracentesis 2069
Pleurisy with Effusion
    Pleurisy 1659
Pleuritis
    Pleurisy 1659
Pleurocentesis
    Thoracentesis 2069
Pleurodynia
    Pleurisy 1659
Plexus
    Brachial Neuropathy 287
    Celiac Plexus Block 442
    Neuralgic Amyotrophy 1465
    Thoracic Outlet Syndrome 2074
Plumbism
    Toxic Effects, Lead (Inorganic Compounds) 2136
PMS
    Premenstrual Syndrome 1724
Pneumatic Retinopexy
    Retinal Detachment Repair 1825
Pneumatothorax
    Pneumothorax 1671
Pneumococcal Pharyngitis
    Pharyngitis, Acute 1633

Pneumoconiosis
    Byssinosis 328
    Occupational Asthma 1498
Pneumocystosis
    Pneumocystis Carinii Pneumonia 1663
Pneumogastric Nerve Disorder
    Vagotonia 2237
Pneumonectomy
    Bronchiectasis 297
    Cancer, Lung 363
    Cancer, Pleura 377
    Lung Excision 1314
Pneumonia
    Blastomycosis 266
    Bronchoscopic Biopsy 304
    Empyema 794
    Legionnaire's Disease 1282
    Pneumocystis Carinii Pneumonia 1663
Pneumonitis
    Humidifier Fever 1130
    Hypersensitivity Pneumonitis 1150
    Pneumonia 1667
    Ventilation Pneumonitis 2254
Pneumothorax
    Hemothorax, Traumatic 1075
    Lung Collapse 1312
    Thoracostomy 2078
Poison
    Ivy, Oak, Sumac, or Other Plant Dermatitis 1673
    Toxic Effects, Arsenic and Compounds 2110
    Toxic Effects, Cadmium 2114
    Toxic Effects, Chlorine 2122
    Toxic Effects, Chromium 2124
    Toxic Effects, Formaldehyde 2129
    Toxic Effects, Hydrochloric Acid 2131
    Toxic Effects, Hydrofluoric Acid 2132
    Toxic Effects, Mercury 2138
    Toxic Effects, Nickel and Inorganic Compounds 2146
    Toxic Effects, Plants (genus Toxicodendron) 2150
Poison Ivy
    Oak, Sumac, or Other Plant Dermatitis 1673
    Toxic Effects, Plants (genus Toxicodendron) 2150
Poison Oak
    Poison Ivy, Oak, Sumac, or Other Plant Dermatitis 1673
    Toxic Effects, Plants (genus Toxicodendron) 2150
Poison Plant Dermatitis
    Poison Ivy, Oak, Sumac, or Other Plant Dermatitis 1673
Poison Sumac
    Poison Ivy, Oak, Sumac, or Other Plant Dermatitis 1673
    Toxic Effects, Plants (genus Toxicodendron) 2150
Poisoning
    Food Poisoning 888
    Toxic Effects, Arsenic and Compounds 2110
    Toxic Effects, Carbon Disulfide 2116
    Toxic Effects, Carbon Monoxide 2117
    Toxic Effects, Chlorinated Hydrocarbon Solvents 2120
    Toxic Effects, Fish and Shellfish 2126
    Toxic Effects, Lead (Inorganic Compounds) 2136
    Toxic Effects, Methyl Alcohol 2140
    Toxic Effects, Mushrooms 2143
    Toxic Effects, Nickel and Inorganic Compounds 2146
    Toxic Effects, Organophosphate and Carbamate Pesticides 2147
    Toxic Effects, Plants (genus Toxicodendron) 2150

Poisonous Plant
    Poison Ivy, Oak, Sumac, or Other Plant Dermatitis 1673
    Toxic Effects, Mercury 2138

Poker Spine
    Ankylosing Spondylitis 152

Polio
    Curvature of the Spine, Acquired 610
    Post Polio Syndrome 1697

Poliomyelitis
    Arthrodesis 194
    Atrophy, Muscular 227, 230
    Polio 1683
    Post Polio Syndrome 1697

Polya Gastrectomy
    Gastrectomy 968
    Resection of Gastric or Duodenal Ulcer Site 1819

Polycythemia Rubra
    Polycythemia Vera 1689

Polyneuritis
    Guillain-Barré Syndrome 1022
    Peripheral Neuropathy 1621

Polyneuropathy
    Guillain-Barré Syndrome 1022
    Peripheral Neuropathy 1621

Polyp
    Aspiration Curettage of the Uterus 208
    Cancer, Colon 354
    Caruncle of the Urethra, Benign 434
    Cervical Polypectomy 469
    Cervical Polyps 470
    Colonoscopy 540
    Excision or Destruction of Duodenal Lesion 857
    Nasal Polypectomy 1440
    Nasal Polyps 1441
    Postmenopausal Bleeding 1703
    Rectal Polyps 1783
    Uterine Polyps 2228

Polyp Excision
    Aspiration Curettage of the Uterus 208
    Cervical Polypectomy 469
    Colonoscopy 540
    Endoscopy of Gastrointestinal Tract 810
    Nasal Polypectomy 1440

Polyp of Cervix
    Cervical Polypectomy 469
    Cervical Polyps 470

Polyp of Corpus Uteri
    Aspiration Curettage of the Uterus 208
    Uterine Polyps 2228

Polypectomy
    Cervical Polypectomy 469
    Nasal Polypectomy 1440

Polypoid Disease
    Rectal Polyps 1783

Polyps of Rectum
    Colonoscopy 540
    Hemorrhage of Rectum and Anus 1068
    Rectal Polyps 1783

Polyps of Uterus
    Aspiration Curettage of the Uterus 208
    Uterine Polyps 2228

Polypus
    Nasal Polyps 1441

Polysubstance Abuse
    Addictions, Mixed 60

Polysubstance Addiction
    Addictions, Mixed 60

Polysurgical Addiction
    Factitious Illness with Physical Symptoms 866

Porous Bones
    Osteoporosis 1540

Porphyria Cutanea Tarda
    Porphyria 1693

Portacaval Shunt
    Portal Systemic Shunt 1695

Portal
    Cirrhosis of the Liver 515
    Systemic Shunt 1695

Portal Cirrhosis
    Cirrhosis of the Liver 515

Portal Hypertension
    Ascites 203
    Esophageal Varices 843
    Hepatic Coma 1079
    Ligation of Esophageal Varices 1288
    Portal Systemic Shunt 1695

Portal Systemic Encephalopathy
    Hepatic Coma 1079

Portal Systemic Shunt
    Esophageal Varices 843

Portal Vein to Vena Cava Shunt
    Portal Systemic Shunt 1695

Portosystemic Encephalopathy
    Hepatic Coma 1079

Portosystemic Shunt
    Portal Systemic Shunt 1695

Posada's Disease
    Coccidioidomycosis 525

Positional Vertigo
    Vertigo 2262

Post Concussion Syndrome
    Postconcussion Syndrome 1699

Post Gastrectomy Syndrome
    Dumping Syndrome 747

Post Gastric Surgery Syndrome
    Dumping Syndrome 747

Post Hepatic Cirrhosis
    Cirrhosis of the Liver 515

Post Inflammatory Pulmonary Fibrosis
    Interstitial Pulmonary Fibrosis 1219

Post Laminectomy Syndrome
    Post-Laminectomy Syndrome 1701

Post Menopausal Bleeding
    Postmenopausal Bleeding 1703

Post Operative Wound Infection
    Cellulitis 443
    Wound Infection, Postoperative 2302

Post Poliomyelitis Syndrome
    Polio 1683
    Post Polio Syndrome 1697
Post Traumatic Brain Syndrome
    Postconcussion Syndrome 1699
Post Traumatic Stress Disorder
    Neurocirculatory Asthenia 1467
    Posttraumatic Stress Disorder 1707
    Psychotherapy, Group 1747
Post Traumatic Subarachnoid Hemorrhage
    Subarachnoid Hemorrhage (Traumatic) 2014
Post Vagotomy Syndrome
    Dumping Syndrome 747
Post Viral Fatigue Syndrome
    Malaise 1328
Postconcussional Syndrome
    Postconcussion Syndrome 1699
Posterior Malleolar Fracture
    Fracture, Ankle 895
Posterior Malleolus
    Fracture, Ankle 895
Posterior Pituitary Insufficiency
    Diabetes Insipidus 681
Posterior Tibial Nerve Decompression
    Tarsal Tunnel Release 2041
Posterior Tibial Shin Splints
    Shin Splints 1912
Postinfectious Glomerulonephritis
    Glomerulonephritis, Acute 1001
Postmenopausal
    Bleeding 1703
Postnecrotic Cirrhosis
    Cirrhosis of the Liver 515
Postoperative Cholangiography
    Cholangiography 493
Postpartum Mastitis
    Abscess, Breast 22
    Postpartum Mastitis 1705
Postpartum Puerperal Infection
    Postpartum Mastitis 1705
Postrenal Azotemia
    Renal Failure, Acute 1802
Posttraumatic Brain Syndrome
    Postconcussion Syndrome 1699
Posttraumatic Stress
    Disorder 1707
    Stress Disorder, Acute 2007
Postural
    Hypotension 1178
    Laryngitis 1279
    Tremor 2179
Postural Hypotension
    Hypotension 1178
    Laryngitis 1279
    Syncope 2024
Postural Tremor
    Tremor 2179

Pott's Disease
    Pott's Disease 1709
Pott's Fracture
    Fracture, Ankle 895
Pott's Gangrene
    Arteriosclerotic Gangrene 186
Pouteau Fracture
    Fracture, Radius and Ulna, Distal 933
PPS
    Post Polio Syndrome 1697
P-R Interval
    Atrioventricular Block, Incomplete (First-Degree) 226
Predominant Disturbance of Conduct
    Adjustment Reaction with Predominant Disturbance of Conduct 74
Preeclampsia
    Abruptio Placentae 16
    and Eclampsia 1711
    Cesarean Delivery 476
    High Blood Pressure, Malignant 1116
Pregnancy
    Abortion by Dilation and Curettage for Termination of Pregnancy 11
    Abruptio Placentae 16
    Anemia Complicating Pregnancy 136
    Cesarean Delivery 476
    Complications 1713
    Constipation 558
    Cystitis, Acute 616
    Delivery, Spontaneous and/or Assisted Vaginal 647
    Ectopic Pregnancy 775
    Folic Acid Deficiency Anemia 885
    Gestational Diabetes 988
    Goiter 1008
    Hemorrhoids 1073
    Hydatidiform Mole 1134
    Hyperemesis Gravidarum 1142
    Hypotension 1178
    Hypovitaminosis 1182
    Menstrual Disorders 1369
    Miscarriage 1381
    Multiple Gestation 1714
    Nausea 1446
    Normal 1716
    Paraovarian Cyst 1590
    Placenta Accreta 1651
    Placenta Previa 1653
    Preeclampsia and Eclampsia 1711
    Premature Labor 1720
    Premature Rupture of Membranes 1722
    Renal Vein Thrombosis 1807
    Rubella 1856
    Toxoplasmosis 2154
    Ultrasound, Diagnostic 2212
    Vasectomy 2248
Pregnancy Complicated by Diabetes
    Gestational Diabetes 988
    Rh Incompatibility 1831
Pregnancy Complication
    Anemia Complicating Pregnancy 136
    Ectopic Pregnancy 775
    Gestational Diabetes 988
    Hyperemesis Gravidarum 1142
    Preeclampsia and Eclampsia 1711
    Pregnancy, Multiple Gestation 1714
    Rh Incompatibility 1831

Preinfarction Angina
   Angina, Unstable 144

Preinfarction Syndrome
   Angina, Unstable 144

Preludin Addiction
   Amphetamine Dependence/Abuse 113

Premature
   Beats 1719
   Labor 1720
   Rupture of Membranes 1722

Premature Atrial Complexes
   Premature Beats 1719

Premature Atrial Contraction (PAC)
   Arrhythmia 178
   Palpitations 1566

Premature Beats
   Arrhythmia 178

Premature Contractions
   Ventricular Premature Contractions 2258

Premature Delivery
   Premature Labor 1720

Premature Heart Beats
   Premature Beats 1719

Premature Labor in Pregnancy
   Premature Labor 1720

Premature Membrane Rupture
   Premature Labor 1720
   Premature Rupture of Membranes 1722

Premature Rupture of Membranes in Pregnancy
   Premature Labor 1720
   Premature Rupture of Membranes 1722

Premature Ventricular Beats
   Palpitations 1566
   Ventricular Premature Contractions 2258

Premature Ventricular Complexes
   Ventricular Premature Contractions 2258

Premature Ventricular Contraction
   Ventricular Premature Contractions 2258

Premature Ventricular Contraction (PVC)
   Arrhythmia 178
   Ventricular Premature Contractions 2258

Premenstrual Syndrome
   Menstrual Disorders 1369
   Premenstrual Syndrome 1724

Premenstrual Tension
   Menstrual Disorders 1369
   Premenstrual Syndrome 1724

Prerenal Azotemia
   Renal Failure, Acute 1802

Prescription Drug Abuse
   Sedative, Hypnotic or Anxiolytic Dependence 1898

Prescription Drug Dependence
   Sedative, Hypnotic or Anxiolytic Dependence 1898

Presenile Dementia
   Alzheimer's Disease 105

Pressure
   Decubitus Ulcer 632

   Fasciotomy 870
   Hyperbaric Oxygenation 1141
   Hypotension 1178
   Laryngitis 1279
   Nosebleed 1485
   Sinusitis 1928

Pressure Sore
   Decubitus Ulcer 632

Pressure Ulcer
   Decubitus Ulcer 632

Pressure-related Ear Pain
   Barotitis Media 241

Preterm Labor
   Premature Labor 1720

Previa
   Placenta Previa 1653

Priapism
   Penis Disorders 1608

Primary
   Addison's Disease 63
   Alzheimer's Disease 105
   Aplastic Anemia 171
   Cardiomyopathy 419
   Menstrual Disorders 1369
   Spinal Stenosis 1952
   Syphilis 2033

Primary Adrenal Gland Failure
   Addison's Disease 63

Primary Adrenocortical Insufficiency
   Addison's Disease 63

Primary Aldosteronism
   Aldosteronism 94

Primary Atypical Pneumonia
   Pneumonia 1667

Primary Cardiomyopathy
   Cardiomyopathy 419

Primary Dementia
   Alzheimer's Disease 105

Primary Hypertension
   High Blood Pressure, Benign 1112

Primary Polycythemia
   Polycythemia Vera 1689

Primary Thrombocytopenia
   Idiopathic Thrombocytopenic Purpura 1189

Prinzmetal's Angina
   Prinzmetal's Angina 1726

PRK
   Keratectomy, Laser Photorefractive 1256
   Myopia 1431

Procedure
   Abdominoperineal Resection of Rectum 10
   Abortion by Dilation and Curettage for Termination of Pregnancy 11
   Abortion, Medical Induction 13
   Adrenal Tissue Implant or Transplant to Brain 76
   Adrenalectomy 77
   Alcohol and Drug Detoxification and Rehabilitation 84
   Amputation 116, 118, 121, 123
   Amputation, Finger or Thumb 123
   Aneurysmectomy 138
   Angiocardiography 148

Appendectomy 174
Arterial Graft 183
Arteriography 185
Arthrodesis 194
Arthrography 196
Arthroplasty, Elbow 197
Arthroscopy 199
Aspiration 207—208
Aspiration Curettage of the Uterus 208
Biofeedback 250
Bone Graft 272
Bone Marrow Biopsy 273
Bone Marrow Transplant 275
Bone Scan 277
Breast Biopsy 295
Bronchoscopic Biopsy 304
Bunionectomy 314
Cardiac Catheterization 411
Cardiac Pacemaker Insertion 414
Cardiac Stress Test 416
Carpal Tunnel Release 428
Cataract Surgery 439
Celiac Plexus Block 442
Cervical Biopsy 460
Cervical Cauterization 461
Cervical Conization 463
Cervical Polypectomy 469
Cesarean Delivery 476
Chemonucleolysis of Interveterbral Disc 482
Chemotherapy 485
Cholangiography 493
Cholecystectomy 495
Cholecystography 500
Circumcision 514
Cognitive Therapy 530
Colon Resection 538
Colonoscopy 540
Colostomy and Ileostomy 543
Corneal Transplant 582
Coronary Arteriography 586
Coronary Balloon Angioplasty 590
Coronary Bypass 592
Coronary Thrombolysis 593
Craniectomy 596
Craniotomy 598
Cryotherapy, Genital Warts (Female) 605
Cryotherapy, Genital Warts (Male) 606
Culdoscopy 610
Cystectomy 615
Cystoscopy, Transurethral 624
Cystourethroplasty of Bladder Neck 625
De Quervain's Release 630
Delivery, Spontaneous and/or Assisted Vaginal 647
Dilation and Curettage 699
Dilation of Esophagus 700
Discectomy 703
Dupuytren's Release 753
Echocardiography 774
Electrocardiogram 781
Electroconvulsive Therapy 782
Electroencephalogram 783
Electromyography 784
Embolectomy 786—787
Embolectomy, Pulmonary 787
Endarterectomy 801
Endoscopy of Gastrointestinal Tract 810
Enterostomy 811
Esophagectomy 845
Esophagogastroduodenoscopy 850
Excision of Bone Spur, Foot 852
Excision of Lesion or Tissue of Skin and Subcutaneous Tissue 854

Excision of Morton's Neuroma 855
Excision of Nail, Nail Bed, or Nail Fold 856
Excision or Destruction of Duodenal Lesion 857
Excision or Destruction of Plantar Warts 858
Excision, Fusion, and Repair of Toes 860
Face Lift 865
Fasciotomy 870
Fissurectomy, Anal 884
Ganglionectomy (Wrist) 963
Gastrectomy 968
Gastroenterostomy 978
Gastrostomy 984
Gingivectomy 992
Heart Valve Replacement 1047
Hemorrhoid Treatment 1070
Hernia Repair 1094, 1096
Hernia Repair, Vaginal 1096
Hysterectomy 1186
Incision and Drainage of Ischiorectal and/or Perirectal Abscess 1200
Incision of Skin and Subcutaneous Tissue, Drainage of Abscess or Cyst 1201
Insertion of Inflatable Penile Prosthesis 1213
Intravenous Pyelogram 1233
Intravenous Therapy 1235
Iontophoresis 1236
Iridectomy 1238
Kidney Transplant 1261
Knee Replacement, Total 1263
Laminectomy or Laminotomy 1273
Laparoscopy 1275
Laparotomy 1276
Laryngectomy 1278
Laryngoscopy 1281
Ligation and Stripping of Varicose Veins 1287
Ligation of Esophageal Varices 1288
Ligation of Spermatic Vein for Varicocele 1289
Liposuction 1292
Lithotomy 1293—1294
Lithotomy, Percutaneous 1294
Lithotripsy, Extracorporeal Shock Wave 1295
Liver Biopsy 1297
Lower Gastrointestinal Series 1305
Lumbar Puncture 1309
Lung Biopsy 1310
Lung Excision 1314
Magnetic Resonance Imaging 1327
Mammography 1337
Mammoplasty, Augmentation 1338
Marshall-Marchetti Operation 1344
Mastectomy 1345
Mastoidectomy 1347
Meniscectomy and Meniscus Repair 1361
Myelography 1419
Myocardial Perfusion Scan 1427
Myomectomy, Uterine 1430
Myotomy of Esophagus 1433
Myringotomy 1434
Nasal Polypectomy 1440
Nasogastric Intubation 1444
Nephrectomy 1451
Nephropexy 1455
Nephrotomy 1458
Nerve Conduction Studies 1459
Occupational Therapy 1499
Oophorectomy 1501, 1503
Open-Chest Cardiac Massage 1514
Orchiectomy 1523
Ovarian Cyst, Resection of 1555
Pancreatectomy 1568
Pancreaticoduodenectomy 1571
Paracentesis 1582
Pericardiectomy 1614

Perineorrhaphy 1618
Physical Therapy 1643
Pleural Biopsy 1657
Pneumonectomy 1664
Portal Systemic Shunt 1695
Prostatectomy 1729
Psychoanalysis 1742
Psychopharmacotherapy 1743
Psychotherapy, Group 1747
Psychotherapy, Individual 1748
Pulmonary Function Tests 1758
Pyloroplasty 1769
Radial Keratotomy 1775
Radiation Therapy 1778
Reduction Mammoplasty 1790
Reduction of Fracture or Dislocation 1791
Rehabilitation Therapy 1796
Renal Dialysis 1800
Repair of Cerebral Aneurysm 1812
Repair, Anterior Cruciate Ligament 1814
Repair, Hammertoe 1816
Repair, Tendon Laceration of Hand 1817
Resection of Gastric or Duodenal Ulcer Site 1819
Retinal Detachment Repair 1825
Rhinoplasty 1841
Rib Resection 1844
Root Canal Therapy 1847
Rotator Cuff Repair 1848
Salpingectomy 1868
Salpingo-oophorectomy 1873
Scalenectomy 1877
Sclerotherapy 1895
Septoplasty 1909
Shoulder Replacement 1917
Sigmoidoscopy 1925
Skin Graft 1932
Skin or Subcutaneous Tissue Biopsy 1934
Spermatocelectomy 1943
Spinal Cord Stimulation 1949
Spinal Fusion 1951
Splenectomy 1955
Stapedectomy 2002
Suture of Skin and Subcutaneous Tissue 2020
Sympathectomy 2022
Synovectomy 2027
Tarsal Tunnel Release 2041
Tendon Release 2051
Tendon Sheath Incision 2052
Thalamotomy 2064
Thoracentesis 2069
Thoracostomy 2078
Thoracotomy 2079
Thrombectomy 2082
Thymectomy 2089
Thyroidectomy 2090
Tonsillectomy and Adenoidectomy 2102
Tooth Extraction 2107
Trabeculectomy 2156
Trabeculoplasty 2158
Tracheostomy 2159
Traction 2163
Transcutaneous Electrical Nerve Stimulation 2164
Transfer of Nerve, Ulnar 2165
Transfusion of Blood and Blood Components 2167
Transurethral Balloon Dilation of Prostatic Urethra 2171
Transurethral Incision of Bladder Neck 2172
Transurethral Removal of Obstruction from Ureter 2173
Transurethral Resection of Prostate 2174
Tubal Ligation 2193
Tympanoplasty 2201
Ultrasound, Diagnostic 2212
Ultrasound, Therapeutic 2213
Upper Gastrointestinal Series 2214
Urethral Catheterization 2216
Vagotomy 2235
Valvotomy 2237
Valvuloplasty, Balloon 2240
Vasectomy 2248
Vena Cava Interruption 2251
Vesicourethropexy 2265
Vocational Therapy 2288
X-ray 2305

Process Abscess
   Gingival Abscess 991
   Periodontitis 1619

Processus Vaginalis
   Hydrocele 1136

Procidentia
   Rectal Prolapse 1785

Proctitis
   Fissurectomy, Anal 884
   Ulcerative Colitis 2209

Proctoscopy
   Sigmoidoscopy 1925

Proctosigmoidoscopy
   Sigmoidoscopy 1925

Professional Individual Syndrome
   Factitious Illness with Physical Symptoms 866

Profound Anemia
   Anemia 133, 136

Progressive
   Amyotrophic Lateral Sclerosis 125
   Atrophy, Muscular (Progressive) 230
   Myasthenia Gravis 1414
   Pemphigus 1606
   Scleroderma 1892

Progressive Angina
   Angina, Unstable 144

Progressive Chorea
   Amyotrophic Lateral Sclerosis 125

Progressive Muscular Atrophy
   Atrophy, Muscular (Progressive) 230

Progressive Systemic Sclerosis
   Scleroderma 1892

Prolapse
   Cesarean Delivery 476
   Cystocele or Rectocele 621
   Mitral Insufficiency 1385
   Mitral Valve Prolapse 1389
   Nephropexy 1455
   Urethrocele with Stress Incontinence 2220

Prolapsed Hemorrhoids
   Hemorrhoids 1073

Prolapsed Mitral Valve
   Mitral Insufficiency 1385
   Mitral Valve Prolapse 1389

Prolapsed Rectal Blood Veins
   Hemorrhoid Treatment 1070
   Hemorrhoids 1073

Proliferative Arthritis
   Rheumatoid Arthritis 1838

Proliferative Retinopathy
    Diabetic Retinopathy 694
Prolonged
    Atrioventricular Block, Incomplete (First-Degree) 226
    Posttraumatic Stress Disorder 1707
Prolonged P-R Interval
    Atrioventricular Block, Incomplete (First-Degree) 226
PROM
    Premature Rupture of Membranes 1722
Propanol-2 Poisoning
    Toxic Effects, Isopropyl Alcohol 2134
Proporphyria
    Porphyria 1693
Prostate Cancer
    Cancer, Prostate 380
    Cystoscopy, Transurethral 624
Prostate Enlargement
    Prostatic Hypertrophy 1731
Prostate Fibroma
    Prostatic Hypertrophy 1731
Prostate Gland
    Cancer, Prostate 380
    Cystoscopy, Transurethral 624
    Epididymitis 819
    Hematuria 1055
    Orchiectomy 1523
    Prostatectomy 1729
    Prostatic Hypertrophy 1731
    Prostatitis 1734
    Pyuria 1771
    Transurethral Balloon Dilation of Prostatic Urethra 2171
    Transurethral Resection of Prostate 2174
Prostate Gland Inflammation
    Prostatitis 1734
Prostate Myoma
    Prostatic Hypertrophy 1731
Prostatectomy
    Cancer, Prostate 380
    Cystourethroplasty of Bladder Neck 625
    Prostatic Hypertrophy 1731
Prostatic Adenocarcinoma
    Cancer, Prostate 380
Prostatic Cancer
    Cancer, Prostate 380
Prostatic Hyperplasia
    Prostatic Hypertrophy 1731
Prostatic Hypertrophy
    Hernia, Inguinal and Femoral 1103
Prostatic Obstruction
    Prostatic Hypertrophy 1731
Prostatitis
    Epididymitis 819
    Hematuria 1055
Prostatomegaly
    Prostatic Hypertrophy 1731
Prosthesis
    Amputation 116, 118, 121, 123
    Amputation (Traumatic), Foot 118
    Amputation (Traumatic), Lower Extremity 121

Arthroplasty, Elbow 197
    Fracture, Femoral Neck 912
    Hip Replacement, Total 1119
    Insertion of Inflatable Penile Prosthesis 1213
    Knee Replacement, Total 1263
    Otosclerosis 1549
    Shoulder Replacement 1917
    Stapedectomy 2002
Prosthetic Heart Valve Replacement
    Heart Valve Replacement 1047
Prostration
    Motion Sickness 1395
    Sepsis 1905
    Yellow Fever 2307
Proteinuria
    Albuminuria 82
    Nephrotic Syndrome 1456
    Preeclampsia and Eclampsia 1711
Prothrombin Deficiency
    Afibrinogenemia 81
    Hypoprothrombinemia 1176
    Vitamin K Deficiency 2284
Protrusion
    Chemonucleolysis of Interveterbral Disc 482
    Discectomy 703
    Hemorrhoid Treatment 1070
    Hemorrhoids 1073
    Rectal Ulcer 1788
    Sclerotherapy 1895
    Spinal Fusion 1951
Proximal
    Vagotomy 2235
Proximal Gastrectomy
    Gastrectomy 968
    Resection of Gastric or Duodenal Ulcer Site 1819
Proximal Gastric Vagotomy
    Vagotomy 2235
Proximal Motor Polyneuropathy
    Peripheral Neuropathy 1621
Proximal Vagotomy
    Vagotomy 2235
Pruritus Ani
    Anorectal Fistula 154
PSE
    Hepatic Coma 1079
Pseudocyst
    Pancreatic Pseudocyst 1569
    Pancreatitis 1573
Pseudoerysipelas
    Erysipeloid 831
Pseudomembranous Colitis
    Irritable Bowel Syndrome 1244
Pseudoparalytica Gravis
    Myasthenia Gravis 1414
Pseudosclerosis
    Wilson's Disease 2300
Psoas Abscess
    Abscess, Psoas 38
Psoriasis
    Erysipelas 830

Pruritus Ani **1736**
Psoriatic Arthritis **1740**

Psoriatic Arthritis
  Enthesopathy **812**
  Psoriasis **1738**
  Spondylitis **1958**

PSP
  Toxic Effects, Fish and Shellfish **2126**

PSVT
  Tachycardia, Paroxysmal Supraventricular **2039**

Psychiatric Disorder
  Addictions, Mixed **60**
  Adjustment Disorder with Depressed Mood **69**
  Adjustment Reaction with Anxious Mood **72**
  Amphetamine Dependence/Abuse **113**
  Antisocial Personality Disorder **156**
  Anxiety Disorder, Generalized **158**
  Attention Deficit Disorder in Adults **232**
  Avoidant Personality Disorder **237**
  Bipolar Affective Disorder **253, 256, 258, 260**
  Bipolar Affective Disorder, Depressed **256**
  Bipolar Affective Disorder, Mixed **258**
  Bipolar Affective Disorder, Single Manic Episode **260**
  Borderline Personality Disorder **284**
  Conversion Disorder **574**
  Delusional Disorder **649**
  Dementia **651, 653**
  Dementia, Alzheimer's Type, with Delusions (Late Onset) **653**
  Dependent Personality Disorder **661**
  Depersonalization Disorder **663**
  Depression, Major **665**
  Dissociative Personality Disorder **737**
  Dysthymic Disorder **764**
  Eating Disorders **769**
  Explosive Personality Disorder **862**
  Factitious Illness with Physical Symptoms **866**
  Factitious Illness with Psychological Symptoms **868**
  Hypochondriasis **1169**
  Hysteria **1188**
  Intermittent Explosive Disorder **1217**
  Manic Disorder, Recurrent **1339**
  Narcissistic Personality Disorder **1437**
  Obsessive-Compulsive Disorder **1494**
  Obsessive-Compulsive Personality Disorder **1496**
  Panic Disorder **1578, 1580**
  Paranoid Personality Disorder **1588**
  Passive-Aggressive Personality Disorder **1597**
  Phobias, Specific **1639**
  Phobic Disorders **1641**
  Posttraumatic Stress Disorder **1707**
  Psychosexual Disorders **1745**
  Psychotic Disorder, Brief **1749**
  Psychotic Disorder, Unspecified **1751**
  Schizoaffective Disorder **1878**
  Schizophrenia **1882, 1885**
  Schizophrenia, Paranoid Type **1885**
  Social Phobia **1937**
  Stress Disorder, Acute **2007**

Psychoanalytic (Freudian) Therapy
  Psychotherapy, Individual **1748**

Psychoanalytic Psychotherapy
  Narcissistic Personality Disorder **1437**
  Passive-Aggressive Personality Disorder **1597**
  Psychoanalysis **1742**
  Psychotherapy, Individual **1748**

Psychogenic
  Depressive Psychosis **670**
  Hyperventilation Syndrome **1161**
  Multiple Chemical Sensitivity Syndrome **1397**
  Myalgia and Myositis **1411**
  Nausea **1446**
  Somatization Disorder **1939**

Psychogenic Depressive Psychosis
  Depressive Psychosis **670**

Psychogenic Dyspepsia
  Eating Disorders **769**

Psychogenic Hyperventilation
  Hyperventilation Syndrome **1161**

Psychogenic Pain
  Rehabilitation Therapy **1796**
  Somatization Disorder **1939**

Psychogenic Torticollis **866**

Psychological Disorder
  Addictions, Mixed **60**
  Adjustment Disorder with Depressed Mood **69**
  Adjustment Reaction with Anxious Mood **72**
  Amphetamine Dependence/Abuse **113**
  Antisocial Personality Disorder **156**
  Anxiety Disorder, Generalized **158**
  Attention Deficit Disorder in Adults **232**
  Avoidant Personality Disorder **237**
  Bipolar Affective Disorder **253, 256, 258, 260**
  Bipolar Affective Disorder, Depressed **256**
  Bipolar Affective Disorder, Mixed **258**
  Bipolar Affective Disorder, Single Manic Episode **260**
  Borderline Personality Disorder **284**
  Conversion Disorder **574**
  Delusional Disorder **649**
  Dementia **651, 653**
  Dementia, Alzheimer's Type, with Delusions (Late Onset) **653**
  Dependent Personality Disorder **661**
  Depersonalization Disorder **663**
  Dissociative Personality Disorder **737**
  Dysthymic Disorder **764**
  Eating Disorders **769**
  Explosive Personality Disorder **862**
  Factitious Illness with Physical Symptoms **866**
  Factitious Illness with Psychological Symptoms **868**
  Narcissistic Personality Disorder **1437**
  Nervous Breakdown **1462**
  Neurotic Disorders **1475**
  Obesity, Simple **1491**
  Obsessive-Compulsive Personality Disorder **1496**
  Opioid Type Dependence **1516**
  Paranoid Personality Disorder **1588**
  Passive-Aggressive Personality Disorder **1597**
  Phobias, Specific **1639**
  Phobic Disorders **1641**
  Posttraumatic Stress Disorder **1707**
  Psychosexual Disorders **1745**
  Schizophrenia **1882, 1885**
  Stress Disorder, Acute **2007**

Psychological Symptoms
  Chronic Fatigue Syndrome **509**
  Factitious Illness with Psychological Symptoms **868**
  Male Climacteric **1332**

Psychological Treatment
  Cognitive Therapy **530**
  Multiple Chemical Sensitivity Syndrome **1397**
  Pain, Chronic **1564**
  Psychoanalysis **1742**
  Psychotherapy, Group **1747**
  Psychotherapy, Individual **1748**
  Rehabilitation Therapy **1796**

Psychopathy
    Antisocial Personality Disorder 156
Psychopharmacotherapy
    Nervousness 1463
    Posttraumatic Stress Disorder 1707
    Psychopharmacotherapy 1743
Psychophysiological Asthenic Reactions
    Nervous Fatigue 1462
Psychosis
    Dementia, Alzheimer's Type, with Delusions (Late Onset) 653
    Depression, Major 665
    Depressive Psychosis 670
    Hysteria 1188
    Manic Disorder, Recurrent 1339
    Organic Psychosis 1526
    Paranoid Personality Disorder 1588
    Psychopharmacotherapy 1743
    Psychotic Disorder, Brief 1749
    Psychotic Disorder, Unspecified 1751
    Schizoaffective Disorder 1878
    Schizoid Personality Disorder 1881
Psychotherapy
    Adjustment Disorder with Depressed Mood 69
    Adjustment Reaction with Anxious Mood 72
    Antisocial Personality Disorder 156
    Anxiety Disorder, Generalized 158
    Avoidant Personality Disorder 237
    Bipolar Affective Disorder 253, 256, 258, 260
    Bipolar Affective Disorder, Depressed 256
    Bipolar Affective Disorder, Mixed 258
    Bipolar Affective Disorder, Single Manic Episode 260
    Borderline Personality Disorder 284
    Cocaine Dependence/Abuse 522
    Cognitive Therapy 530
    Complex Regional Pain Syndrome 550
    Conversion Disorder 574
    Delusional Disorder 649
    Dependent Personality Disorder 661
    Depression, Major 665
    Depressive Psychosis 670
    Dissociative Personality Disorder 737
    Dysthymic Disorder 764
    Eating Disorders 769
    Explosive Personality Disorder 862
    Fibromyalgia and Myofascial Pain Syndrome 879
    Group 1747
    Individual 1748
    Narcissistic Personality Disorder 1437
    Nervousness 1463
    Neurocirculatory Asthenia 1467
    Neurotic Disorders 1475
    Obsessive-Compulsive Disorder 1494
    Obsessive-Compulsive Personality Disorder 1496
    Pain, Chronic 1564
    Panic Disorder 1578, 1580
    Panic Disorder with Agoraphobia 1580
    Paranoid Personality Disorder 1588
    Parkinson's Disease 1593
    Passive-Aggressive Personality Disorder 1597
    Phobias, Specific 1639
    Phobic Disorders 1641
    Post-Laminectomy Syndrome 1701
    Posttraumatic Stress Disorder 1707
    Psychopharmacotherapy 1743
    Psychosexual Disorders 1745
    Psychotic Disorder, Brief 1749
    Psychotic Disorder, Unspecified 1751
    Rehabilitation Therapy 1796
    Schizoaffective Disorder 1878
    Schizoid Personality Disorder 1881
    Schizophrenia 1882, 1885
    Schizophrenia, Paranoid Type 1885
    Schizophreniform Disorder 1888
    Sedative, Hypnotic or Anxiolytic Dependence 1898
    Social Phobia 1937
    Somatization Disorder 1939
    Sprains and Strains, Cervical Spine (Neck) 1981
    Stress Disorder, Acute 2007
    Temporomandibular Joint Syndrome 2049
    Tics 2093
    Tinnitus 2097
Psychotherapy, Group
    Narcissistic Personality Disorder 1437
    Neurotic Disorders 1475
    Obsessive-Compulsive Disorder 1494
    Obsessive-Compulsive Personality Disorder 1496
    Opioid Type Dependence 1516
    Posttraumatic Stress Disorder 1707
    Psychosexual Disorders 1745
    Psychotic Disorder, Unspecified 1751
    Schizoid Personality Disorder 1881
    Schizophreniform Disorder 1888
    Social Phobia 1937
    Tics 2093
Psychotic Depression
    Depression, Major 665
Psychotic Disorder
    Brief 1749
    Unspecified 1751
Psychotic Reactive Depression
    Depressive Psychosis 670
Psychotropic Drug Therapy
    Chronic Fatigue Syndrome 509
    Dissociative Personality Disorder 737
    Fibromyalgia and Myofascial Pain Syndrome 879
    Manic Disorder, Recurrent 1339
    Narcissistic Personality Disorder 1437
    Nicotine Dependence 1479
    Obsessive-Compulsive Disorder 1494
    Obsessive-Compulsive Personality Disorder 1496
    Organic Psychosis 1526
    Panic Disorder 1578, 1580
    Panic Disorder with Agoraphobia 1580
    Paranoid Personality Disorder 1588
    Phobias, Specific 1639
    Phobic Disorders 1641
    Psychopharmacotherapy 1743
    Psychosexual Disorders 1745
    Psychotic Disorder, Brief 1749
    Psychotic Disorder, Unspecified 1751
    Schizoaffective Disorder 1878
    Schizoid Personality Disorder 1881
    Schizophrenia 1882, 1885
    Schizophrenia, Paranoid Type 1885
    Schizophreniform Disorder 1888
    Sprains and Strains, Cervical Spine (Neck) 1981
    Stress Disorder, Acute 2007
    Tinnitus 2097
PT
    Chronic Fatigue Syndrome 509
    Complex Regional Pain Syndrome 550
    Fibromyalgia and Myofascial Pain Syndrome 879
    Neurocirculatory Asthenia 1467
    Pain, Chronic 1564
    Paralysis, Paraplegia, and Quadriplegia 1583
    Parkinson's Disease 1593

Patella Chondromalacia 1599
Physical Therapy 1643
Plantar Fasciitis 1655
Radial Styloid Tenosynovitis 1776
Rheumatoid Arthritis 1838
Rotator Cuff Tear 1853
Shoulder Replacement 1917
Spondylolisthesis 1960
Spondylolysis, Lumbar Region 1962
Sprains and Strains, Ankle 1971
Sprains and Strains, Back 1975
Sprains and Strains, Cervical Spine (Neck) 1981
Sprains and Strains, Elbow 1984
Sprains and Strains, Foot 1986
Sprains and Strains, Wrist 1997
Tarsal Tunnel Syndrome 2043

PTBV
   Valvuloplasty, Balloon 2240

PTC
   Cholangiography 493

PTCA
   Angina Pectoris 140
   Coronary Balloon Angioplasty 590

PTMC
   Valvuloplasty, Balloon 2240

PTSD
   Posttraumatic Stress Disorder 1707
   Stress Disorder, Acute 2007

Pubovaginal Sling
   Vesicourethropexy 2265

Puerperal Infection
   Postpartum Mastitis 1705

Pulled Abdominal Muscle
   Abdominal Muscle Strain 5

Pulled Groin
   Groin Strain 1020

Pulled Tooth
   Tooth Extraction 2107

Pulmonary
   Angiocardiography 148
   Asbestosis 201
   Asthma 209
   Bronchoscopic Biopsy 304
   Chronic Obstructive Pulmonary Disease 511
   Edema 1756
   Embolectomy, Pulmonary 787
   Embolism, Pulmonary 789
   Emphysema 792
   Function Tests 1758
   Interstitial Pulmonary Fibrosis 1219
   Lung Collapse 1312
   Mitral Insufficiency 1385
   Mitral Valve Prolapse 1389

Pulmonary Abscess
   Abscess, Lung 29

Pulmonary Apoplexy
   Embolism, Pulmonary 789

Pulmonary Collapse
   Lung Collapse 1312

Pulmonary Congestion
   Pulmonary Edema 1756

Pulmonary Disease
   Chronic Obstructive Pulmonary Disease 511
   Cor Pulmonale, Acute and Chronic 576
   Pulmonary Function Tests 1758

Pulmonary Edema
   Anaphylactic Shock, Food Reaction 131

Pulmonary Embolectomy
   Embolectomy, Pulmonary 787
   Embolism, Pulmonary 789

Pulmonary Embolism
   Cardiac Catheterization 411
   Cardiogenic Shock 417
   Cor Pulmonale, Acute and Chronic 576
   Dyspnea 761
   Embolectomy, Pulmonary 787
   Embolism, Pulmonary 789
   Hemoptysis 1067
   Vena Cava Interruption 2251

Pulmonary Emphysema
   Bronchitis, Chronic 302
   Emphysema 792

Pulmonary Fibrosis
   Asbestosis 201
   Interstitial Pulmonary Fibrosis 1219
   Pulmonary Function Tests 1758
   Silicosis 1926

Pulmonary Function Test 1758
   Asthma 209
   Bronchiectasis 297
   Bronchitis, Chronic 302
   Byssinosis 328
   Chronic Obstructive Pulmonary Disease 511
   Cor Pulmonale, Acute and Chronic 576
   Dyspnea 761
   Emphysema 792
   Sarcoidosis 1875
   Siderosis 1924
   Silicosis 1926

Pulmonary Gangrene
   Abscess, Lung 29

Pulmonary Hemorrhage
   Hemoptysis 1067

Pulmonary Hypostasis
   Pulmonary Edema 1756

Pulmonary Infarction
   Embolism, Pulmonary 789

Pulmonary Necrosis
   Abscess, Lung 29

Pulmonary Thromboembolism
   Embolism, Pulmonary 789

Pulmonum Silicosis
   Silicosis 1926

Pulsion Diverticulum
   Esophageal Diverticula 836

Pump Lung
   Adult Respiratory Distress Syndrome 79

Punch Biopsy
   Skin or Subcutaneous Tissue Biopsy 1934

Puncture
   Lacerations 1269
   Lumbar Puncture 1309

Rabies 1773
Sepsis 1905
Tetanus 2060
Wound 1759

Puncture Wounds
Anorectal Fistula 154
Lacerations 1269
Open Wound 1504, 1510, 1512
Open Wound, Back 1510
Open Wound, Chest 1512
Puncture Wound 1759
Sepsis 1905
Tetanus 2060

Pure Progressive Muscular Atrophy
Atrophy, Muscular (Progressive) 230

Purpura
Cesarean Delivery 476
Idiopathic Thrombocytopenic Purpura 1189
Osler-Weber-Rendu Disease 1528
Rocky Mountain Spotted Fever 1845
Simplex 1760
Splenectomy 1955
Thrombocytopenia 2083

Purulent Bronchitis
Bronchitis, Acute 299
Bronchitis, Chronic 302

Pus
Abscess, Anorectal 20
Abscess, Larynx 25
Abscess, Palmar 32
Actinomycosis 57
Anorectal Fistula 154
Brain Abscess 289
Carbuncle 407

Pus in the Urine
Pyuria 1771

Pustular Psoriasis
Psoriasis 1738

PVC
Ventricular Premature Contractions 2258

Pyelonephritic Scarring
Pyelonephritis, Chronic 1764

Pyelonephritis
Acute 1762
Chronic 1764
Hematuria 1055
Nephritis, Interstitial 1453
Pyelonephritis, Acute 1762
Pyelonephritis, Chronic 1764

Pyloric
Peptic Ulcer Disease 1611
Pyloroplasty 1769
Pylorospasm 1770
Stenosis, Acquired (Adult) Hypertrophic 1767

Pyloric Constriction
Pyloric Stenosis, Acquired (Adult) Hypertrophic 1767

Pyloric Obstruction
Pyloric Stenosis, Acquired (Adult) Hypertrophic 1767

Pyloric Stenosis Repair
Pyloroplasty 1769

Pyloric Stricture
Pyloric Stenosis, Acquired (Adult) Hypertrophic 1767

Pylorospasm 1770

Pyloric Valve Dilation
Pyloroplasty 1769

Pyloric Valve Spasm
Pylorospasm 1770

Pyloromyotomy
Pyloroplasty 1769

Pyloroplasty
Duodenitis 749
Peptic Ulcer Disease 1611
Resection of Gastric or Duodenal Ulcer Site 1819

Pyoderma
Impetigo 1193

Pyogenic Spondylitis
Spondylitis 1958

Pyonephrosis
Pyelonephritis, Acute 1762
Pyelonephritis, Chronic 1764

Pyorrhea Alveolaris
Gingival Abscess 991
Periodontitis 1619

Pyosalpinx
Salpingitis 1870

Pyrexia
Fever 872

Pyridoxine Poisoning
Poisoning, Vitamin B 1679

Pyroxylic Spirit Poisoning
Toxic Effects, Methyl Alcohol 2140

Pyuria
Abscess, Renal and Perinephric 40
Calculus, Bladder 333
Cystitis, Acute 616
Nephritis, Interstitial 1453
Orchitis 1524
Pyelonephritis, Acute 1762
Pyelonephritis, Chronic 1764

Q

Quadriplegia
Paralysis, Paraplegia, and Quadriplegia 1583
Spinal Cord Injury 1946

Quadruplets
Pregnancy, Multiple Gestation 1714

Quartan Malaria
Malaria 1330

Queasiness
Nausea 1446

Quicksilver Poisoning
Toxic Effects, Mercury 2138

Quiescent Rheumatic Fever
Rheumatic Heart Disease, Chronic 1836

Quincke's Disease
Angioedema 150

Quincke's Edema
Angioedema 150

Quinsy
Abscess, Peritonsillar 36

R

RA
   Rheumatoid Arthritis **1838**
   Sjogren's Syndrome **1930**
   Sprains and Strains, Rotator Cuff (Capsule) **1994**

Rabbit Fever
   Tularemia **2197**

Rachiotomy
   Laminectomy or Laminotomy **1273**

Radial
   Keratotomy **1775**
   Styloid Tenosynovitis **1776**

Radial Keratotomy
   Myopia **1431**
   Radial Keratotomy **1775**

Radiation Pericarditis
   Pericarditis, Acute **1615**

Radiation Therapy
   Cancer, Bladder **338**
   Cancer, Brain **344**
   Cancer, Breast **347**
   Cancer, Cervix **351**
   Cancer, Colon **354**
   Cancer, Esophagus **356**
   Cancer, Kidney **358**
   Cancer, Liver **360**
   Cancer, Lung **363**
   Cancer, Oropharynx **369**
   Cancer, Ovary **372**
   Cancer, Pancreas **375**
   Cancer, Pleura **377**
   Cancer, Prostate **380**
   Cancer, Rectum **384**
   Cancer, Skin **387**
   Cancer, Stomach **391**
   Cancer, Testicle(s) **393**
   Cancer, Thyroid Gland **396**
   Cancer, Tongue **399**
   Cancer, Uterus **402**
   Cervical Dysplasia **467**
   Choriocarcinoma **505**
   Glioma **999**
   Leukemia **1284**
   Multiple Myeloma **1399**
   Mycosis Fungoides **1416**
   Non-Hodgkin's Lymphoma **1482**
   Paget's Disease of Breast **1559**
   Pineal Gland Neoplasm **1647**
   Radiodermatitis **1780**
   Sarcoidosis **1875**

Radical Cystectomy
   Cystectomy **615**

Radical Gastrectomy
   Gastrectomy **968**
   Resection of Gastric or Duodenal Ulcer Site **1819**

Radical Nephrectomy
   Nephrectomy **1451**

Radical Prostatectomy
   Prostatectomy **1729**

Radiculitis
   Neuralgia, Neuritis, and Radiculitis **1465**

Radiculopathy
   Displacement, Cervical Intervertebral Disc Without Myelopathy **728**
   Displacement, Lumbar Intervertebral Disc Without Myelopathy **732**
   Displacement, Thoracic Intervertebral Disc Without Myelopathy **735**
   Nerve Conduction Studies **1459**
   Neuralgia, Neuritis, and Radiculitis **1465**
   Paresthesia **1591**
   Sciatica **1890**
   Sprains and Strains, Cervical Spine (Neck) **1981**

Radiculopathy and Neuropathy
   Neuralgia, Neuritis, and Radiculitis **1465**

Radiodermatitis
   Contact Dermatitis **560**

Radiography
   X-ray **2305**

Radionuclide Bone Scan
   Bone Scan **277**

Radionuclide Imaging
   Myocardial Perfusion Scan **1427**

Radius and Ulna Fracture
   Fracture, Radius and Ulna, Distal **933**
   Reduction of Fracture or Dislocation **1791**

Rage Attacks
   Explosive Personality Disorder **862**
   Intermittent Explosive Disorder **1217**

Rash
   Impetigo **1193**
   Insect or Spider Bites and Stings **1210**
   Lupus Erythematosus, Systemic **1317**
   Rocky Mountain Spotted Fever **1845**
   Rubella **1856**
   Rubeola **1858**
   Salmonellosis **1866**
   Sarcoidosis **1875**
   Strep Throat **2005**
   Sunburn **2019**
   Syphilis **2033**
   Tinea **2095**
   Typhoid Fever **2204**
   Urticaria **2226**

Rat Typhus
   Typhus Fever **2206**

Rational-emotive Therapy
   Psychotherapy, Individual **1748**

Raynaud's Phenomenon
   Raynaud's Phenomenon **1781**
   Scleroderma **1892**

RBBB
   Bundle Branch Block **310**

Reaction
   Adjustment Disorder with Depressed Mood **69**
   Adjustment Reaction with Anxious Mood **72**
   Allergy **100**
   Anaphylactic Shock, Food Reaction **131**
   Conversion Disorder **574**
   Hysteria **1188**

Reactive
   Asthma **209**
   Depressive Psychosis **670**
   Enthesopathy **812**
   Psychotic Disorder, Brief **1749**

Reactive Airway Disease
   Asthma **209**

Reactive Arthritis
  Enthesopathy 812
  Reiter's Syndrome 1798
Reactive Depression
  Depressive Psychosis 670
  Dysthymic Disorder 764
Receptive Aphasia
  Aphasia 169
Recompression Therapy
  Hyperbaric Oxygenation 1141
Reconstruction
  Arthroplasty, Elbow 197
  Cystourethroplasty of Bladder Neck 625
  Mammoplasty, Augmentation 1338
  Mastectomy 1345
  Paget's Disease of Breast 1559
  Penis Disorders 1608
  Reduction Mammoplasty 1790
  Repair, Anterior Cruciate Ligament 1814
  Transurethral Incision of Bladder Neck 2172
Reconstruction of Bladder Neck
  Cystourethroplasty of Bladder Neck 625
Recreational Therapy
  Rehabilitation Therapy 1796
Rectal
  Abscess, Anorectal 20
  Abscess, Ischiorectal 24
  Abscess, Perirectal 34
  Anorectal Fistula 154
  Cancer, Colon 354
  Cancer, Rectum 384
  Cystocele or Rectocele 621
  Polyps 1783
  Pruritus Ani 1736
  Ulcer 1788
Rectal Cancer
  Abdominoperineal Resection of Rectum 10
  Cancer, Colon 354
  Cancer, Rectum 384
  Endoscopy of Gastrointestinal Tract 810
Rectal Cellulitis
  Abscess, Anorectal 20
  Abscess, Ischiorectal 24
  Abscess, Perirectal 34
Rectal Fistula
  Abscess, Anorectal 20
  Abscess, Ischiorectal 24
  Abscess, Perirectal 34
  Anorectal Fistula 154
Rectal Hemorrhage
  Hemorrhage of Rectum and Anus 1068
Rectal Lump
  Hemorrhoids 1073
Rectal Prolapse
  Cystocele or Rectocele 621
  Rectal Ulcer 1788
Rectal Ulcer
  Anal Fissure and/or Rectal Ulcer 127
Rectocele
  Cystocele or Rectocele 621
Rectocele Repair
  Hernia Repair, Vaginal 1096

Rectosigmoid
  Abdominoperineal Resection of Rectum 10
  Cancer, Rectum 384
  Ulcerative Colitis 2209
Rectosigmoid Junction
  Cancer, Rectum 384
Rectosigmoiditis
  Ulcerative Colitis 2209
Rectovesical Fistula
  Bladder Fistulas 262
Rectum
  Abdominoperineal Resection of Rectum 10
  Abscess, Anorectal 20
  Abscess, Perirectal 34
  Cancer, Colon 354
  Cancer, Rectum 384
  Colonoscopy 540
  Cystocele or Rectocele 621
  Hemorrhage of Rectum and Anus 1068
  Incision and Drainage of Ischiorectal and/or Perirectal Abscess 1200
  Rectal Ulcer 1788
  Ulcerative Colitis 2209
Rectus Femoris Strain
  Groin Strain 1020
Recurrent
  Bronchitis, Chronic 302
  Chronic Fatigue Syndrome 509
  Manic Disorder, Recurrent 1339
  Multiple Chemical Sensitivity Syndrome 1397
  Panic Disorder 1578, 1580
  Panic Disorder with Agoraphobia 1580
  Pott's Disease 1709
  Seizures 1900
  Vestibular Neuronitis 2268
Recurrent Bronchitis
  Bronchitis, Chronic 302
Recurrent Dislocation of Kneecap
  Dislocation, Patella (Kneecap) 723
Recurrent Hypomanic Psychosis
  Manic Disorder, Recurrent 1339
Recurrent Incisional Hernia
  Hernia, Incisional 1100
Recurrent Manic Episodes
  Manic Disorder, Recurrent 1339
Recurrent Peripheral Vestibulopathy
  Vestibular Neuronitis 2268
Recurrent Seizures
  Epilepsy 824
  Seizures 1900
Recurrent Typhus
  Typhus Fever 2206
Red Measles
  Rubeola 1858
Reduction
  Dislocation 705, 708, 711, 713, 716, 723, 726
  Dislocation, Acromioclavicular Joint 708
  Dislocation, Cervical Vertebra 711
  Dislocation, Femorotibial (Knee) Joint 713
  Dislocation, Foot 716
  Dislocation, Patella (Kneecap) 723
  Dislocation, Sternclavicular Joint 726
  Fracture, Ankle 895

Fracture, Calcaneus 898
Fracture, Carpal Bones 901
Fracture, Clavicle 907
Fracture, Elbow (Distal Humerus) 910
Fracture, Femoral Neck 912
Fracture, Fingers and Thumb 915
Fracture, Metacarpal Bones 922
Fracture, Metatarsal Bones 925
Fracture, Midfoot (Cuboid, Cuneiform, Navicular) 928
Fracture, Pelvis 930
Fracture, Radius and Ulna, Distal 933
Fracture, Sternum (Closed) 943
Fracture, Thoracic Spine (With or Without Spinal Cord Injury) 948
Fracture, Vertebra (Pathological) 956
Liposuction 1292
Mammoplasty 1790
of Fracture or Dislocation 1791

Reduction Mammoplasty
Gynecomastia 1025
Reduction Mammoplasty 1790

Reduction of Adipose Tissue
Liposuction 1292

Reduction of Calcaneal Fracture
Fracture, Calcaneus 898
Reduction of Fracture or Dislocation 1791

Reduction of Dislocation
Reduction of Fracture or Dislocation 1791

Reflex Sympathetic Dystrophy
Complex Regional Pain Syndrome 550
Sympathectomy 2022

Reflex Sympathetic Dystrophy Syndrome
Complex Regional Pain Syndrome 550

Reflux
Gastroesophageal Reflux 979
Hernia, Hiatal 1097
Hydronephrosis 1138
Pyelonephritis, Chronic 1764

Reflux Esophagitis
Esophagitis 847

Refraction Error
Astigmatism 212

Refractory Anemia
Aplastic Anemia 171

Regional
Complex Regional Pain Syndrome 550
Myalgia and Myositis 1411

Regional Fibromyalgia
Myalgia and Myositis 1411

Regurgitation
Achalasia 44
Aortic Insufficiency 165
Aortic Valve Stenosis 167
Hernia, Hiatal 1097
Mitral Insufficiency 1385
Mitral Valve Prolapse 1389

Rehab
Alcohol and Drug Detoxification and Rehabilitation 84
Occupational Therapy 1499
Rehabilitation Therapy 1796
Vocational Therapy 2288

Rehabilitation
Addictions, Mixed 60

Alcohol and Drug Detoxification and Rehabilitation 84
Meniscectomy and Meniscus Repair 1361
Meniscus Disorders, Knee 1364
Mitral Commissurotomy 1384
Multiple Sclerosis 1401
Myasthenia Gravis 1414
Myelopathy 1420
Occupational Therapy 1499
Parkinson's Disease 1593
Physical Therapy 1643
Post-Laminectomy Syndrome 1701
Prinzmetal's Angina 1726
Reiter's Syndrome 1798
Repair of Cerebral Aneurysm 1812
Repair, Anterior Cruciate Ligament 1814
Repair, Tendon Laceration of Hand 1817
Respiratory Failure 1821
Rheumatic Fever, Acute 1833
Rotator Cuff Repair 1848
Rotator Cuff Tear 1853
Shoulder Replacement 1917
Stokes-Adams Syndrome 2003
Subarachnoid Hemorrhage (Non-traumatic) 2011
Sympathectomy 2022
Syringomyelia 2035
Therapy 1796
Vocational Therapy 2288

Rehabilitation Therapy
Ultrasound, Therapeutic 2213

Reiter's Disease
Reiter's Syndrome 1798

Reiter's Syndrome
Enthesopathy 812
Reiter's Syndrome 1798
Spondylitis 1958

Reiter's Urethritis
Reiter's Syndrome 1798

Release Procedures
Carpal Tunnel Release 428
De Quervain's Release 630
Dupuytren's Release 753
Epicondylitis, Medial and Lateral 816
Tarsal Tunnel Release 2041
Tendon Release 2051

Removal
Aneurysmectomy 138
Appendectomy 174
Cataract Surgery 439
Cervical Polypectomy 469
Cholecystectomy 495
Circumcision 514
Ganglionectomy (Wrist) 963
Lithotomy 1293–1294
Lithotomy, Percutaneous 1294
Nasal Polypectomy 1440
Nephrotomy 1458
Oophorectomy 1501, 1503
Ovarian Cyst, Resection of 1555
Pheochromocytoma 1638
Pneumonectomy 1664
Poisoning 1675, 1677, 1679, 1681
Rib Resection 1844
Salivary Gland Stones 1865
Splenectomy 1955
Synovectomy 2027
Thymectomy 2089
Toenail, Ingrown 2100
Tonsillectomy and Adenoidectomy 2102

Index 2645

Tooth Extraction 2107
Transurethral Removal of Obstruction from Ureter 2173

Renal
- Abscess, Renal and Perinephric 40
- Calculus, Renal (Kidney and Ureter) 335
- Cancer, Kidney 358
- Dialysis 1800
- Failure, Acute 1802
- Failure, Chronic 1804
- Glomerulonephritis, Acute 1001
- Glomerulosclerosis 1005
- Glycosuria 1006
- Nephritis, Interstitial 1453
- Nephrotic Syndrome 1456
- Renovascular Hypertension 1809
- Vein Thrombosis 1807

Renal and Perinephric Abscess
- Abscess, Renal and Perinephric 40
- Intravenous Pyelogram 1233

Renal Calculus
- Calculus, Renal (Kidney and Ureter) 335
- Lithotomy 1293–1294
- Nephrotomy 1458

Renal Cancer
- Cancer, Kidney 358

Renal Carbuncle
- Abscess, Renal and Perinephric 40

Renal Cell Carcinoma
- Cancer, Kidney 358

Renal Diabetes
- Glycosuria 1006

Renal Dialysis
- Glomerulonephritis, Chronic 1003
- Glomerulosclerosis 1005

Renal Failure
- Acute 1802
- Chronic 1804
- Delirium 644
- Glomerulonephritis, Chronic 1003
- Glomerulosclerosis 1005
- High Blood Pressure, Malignant 1116
- Pulmonary Edema 1756

Renal Glycosuria
- Glycosuria 1006

Renal High Blood Pressure
- Renovascular Hypertension 1809

Renal Insufficiency
- Renal Failure, Acute 1802
- Renal Failure, Chronic 1804

Renal Interstitial Tissue
- Nephritis, Interstitial 1453

Renal Neoplasm
- Cancer, Kidney 358

Renal Stones
- Calculus, Renal (Kidney and Ureter) 335

Renal Vascular Hypertension
- Renovascular Hypertension 1809

Renal Vein Blood Clot
- Renal Vein Thrombosis 1807

Repair
- Anterior Cruciate Ligament 1814
- Excision, Fusion, and Repair of Toes 860
- Hammertoe 1816
- Hernia Repair 1094, 1096
- Hernia, Hiatal 1097
- Hernia Repair, Vaginal 1096
- Ligation of Spermatic Vein for Varicocele 1289
- Meniscectomy and Meniscus Repair 1361
- Mitral Commissurotomy 1384
- Nerve Injury 1460
- of Cerebral Aneurysm 1812
- Perineorrhaphy 1618
- Rectal Ulcer 1788
- Retinal Detachment Repair 1825
- Rotator Cuff Repair 1848
- Sprains and Strains, Ankle 1971
- Sprains and Strains, Elbow 1984
- Sprains and Strains, Foot 1986
- Sprains and Strains, Hand or Fingers 1989
- Sprains and Strains, Knee 1991
- Tendon Laceration of Hand 1817
- Valvuloplasty, Balloon 2240

Repetitive Strain Injury
- Biceps Tendonitis 248
- Bursitis 325
- Carpal Tunnel Syndrome 430
- De Quervain's Release 630
- Epicondylitis, Medial and Lateral 816
- Ganglionectomy (Wrist) 963
- Impingement Syndrome 1194
- Joint Disorders 1251
- Muscle Injury 1406
- Radial Styloid Tenosynovitis 1776
- Tendonitis 2054
- Tenosynovitis 2057

Replacement
- Arthroplasty, Elbow 197
- Heart Valve Replacement 1047
- Hip Replacement, Total 1119
- Knee Replacement, Total 1263
- Shoulder Replacement 1917

Resection
- Abdominoperineal Resection of Rectum 10
- Aneurysmectomy 138
- Arthroplasty, Elbow 197
- Bone Tumors 281
- Colon Resection 538
- of Gastric or Duodenal Ulcer Site 1819
- Ovarian Cyst, Resection of 1555
- Rectal Polyps 1783
- Rectal Ulcer 1788
- Rib Resection 1844
- Thoracic Aneurysm 2070

Respiratory
- Asthma 209
- Bronchiectasis 297
- Bronchoscopic Biopsy 304
- Cold 533
- Empyema 794
- Failure 1821
- Hemoptysis 1067
- Influenza 1207
- Myasthenia Gravis 1414
- Poisoning 1675, 1677, 1679, 1681
- Siderosis 1924
- Silicosis 1926
- Tuberculosis, Respiratory 2194
- Upper Respiratory Infection 2216
- Ventilation Pneumonitis 2254

Respiratory Bacterial Infection
  Upper Respiratory Infection 2216
Respiratory Distress
  Dyspnea 761
  Hyperventilation Syndrome 1161
  Pleurisy 1659
  Respiratory Failure 1821
Respiratory Failure
  Adult Respiratory Distress Syndrome 79
  Cardiac Arrest 409
  Coma 449, 544
  Polio 1683
  Porphyria 1693
Respiratory Infection
  Coccidioidomycosis 525
  Cold 533
  Legionnaire's Disease 1282
  Upper Respiratory Infection 2216
Respiratory Viral Infection
  Cold 533
  Upper Respiratory Infection 2216
Rest Angina
  Angina Decubitus 140
  Angina, Unstable 144
Resting Tremor
  Tremor 2179
Restrictive Cardiomyopathy
  Cardiomyopathy 419
Retained Menstruation
  Dysfunctional Uterine Bleeding 757
Retina
  Chorioretinitis 506
  Detachment 1823, 1825
  Detachment Repair 1825
  Diabetic Retinopathy 694
  Retinitis Pigmentosa 1829
  Senile Macular Degeneration 1903
  Vascular Occlusion 1827
Retinal
  Chorioretinitis 506
  Detachment 1823, 1825
  Detachment Repair 1825
  Diabetic Retinopathy 694
  Retinitis Pigmentosa 1829
  Senile Macular Degeneration 1903
  Vascular Occlusion 1827
Retinal Artery Occlusion
  Retinal Vascular Occlusion 1827
Retinal Attachment
  Diabetic Retinopathy 694
  Retinal Detachment 1823, 1825
  Retinal Detachment Repair 1825
Retinal Attachment by Cryotherapy
  Retinal Detachment Repair 1825
Retinal Attachment Photocoagulation
  Retinal Detachment Repair 1825
Retinal Detachment
  Repair 1825
Retinal Disease
  Chorioretinitis 506
  Diabetic Retinopathy 694
  Renovascular Hypertension 1809

Retinal Detachment 1823, 1825
Retinal Vascular Occlusion 1827
Retinitis Pigmentosa 1829
Senile Macular Degeneration 1903
Sickle Cell Anemia 1922
Retinal Pigmentation
  Retinitis Pigmentosa 1829
Retinal Vein Occlusion
  Retinal Vascular Occlusion 1827
Retinitis
  Chorioretinitis 506
Retinol
  Hypervitaminosis 1164, 1166, 1168
  Hypervitaminosis A 1166
  Vitamin A Deficiency 2270
Retinol Deficiency
  Vitamin A Deficiency 2270
Retinol Toxicity
  Hypervitaminosis 1164, 1166, 1168
  Hypervitaminosis A 1166
Retinopathy
  Diabetic Retinopathy 694
Retrocecal Abscess
  Abscess, Subdiaphragmatic 42
Retromammary Mastitis
  Abscess, Breast 22
Retroperitoneal Abscess
  Abscess, Psoas 38
Retropubic Urethrovesical Resuspension
  Marshall-Marchetti Operation 1344
Revascularization
  Arterial Graft 183
Rh Incompatibility
  Cesarean Delivery 476
  Premature Labor 1720
Rhesus Isoimmunization
  Rh Incompatibility 1831
Rheumatic
  Aortic Valve Stenosis 167
  Fever, Acute 1833
  Heart Disease, Chronic 1836
Rheumatic Aortic Stenosis
  Aortic Valve Stenosis 167
Rheumatic Carditis
  Rheumatic Heart Disease, Chronic 1836
Rheumatic Fever
  Acute 1833
  Aortic Insufficiency 165
  Arthralgia 190
  Atrioventricular Block, Incomplete (First-Degree) 226
  Heart Murmur 1045
  Valvotomy 2237
  Valvuloplasty, Balloon 2240
Rheumatic Heart Disease
  Carotid Artery Occlusion 423
  Chronic 1836
  Endocarditis, Bacterial 802
  Heart Valve Replacement 1047
  Rheumatic Fever, Acute 1833
  Valvotomy 2237

Index 2647

Valvuloplasty, Balloon 2240

Rheumatic Heart Fever
	Rheumatic Fever, Acute 1833

Rheumatism
	Joint Disorders 1251

Rheumatoid
	Arthritis 1838

Rheumatoid Arthritis
	Arthralgia 190
	Arthroplasty, Elbow 197
	Atrioventricular Block Incomplete (Second-Degree) 223
	Biceps Tendonitis 248
	Bursitis 325
	Costochondritis 595
	Ganglionectomy (Wrist) 963
	Hepatitis, Chronic 1089
	Knee Replacement, Total 1263

Rh-Incompatibility
	Rh Incompatibility 1831

Rh-Induced Hemolytic Disease of the Newborn
	Rh Incompatibility 1831

Rhinitis
	Allergic Rhinitis 98
	Cold 533
	Rubella 1856
	Rubeola 1858
	Upper Respiratory Infection 2216

Rhinoplasty
	Rhinoscleroma 1842
	Septoplasty 1909

Rhinorrhea
	Allergic Rhinitis 98
	Cold 533

Rhus Dermatitis
	Poison Ivy, Oak, Sumac, or Other Plant Dermatitis 1673
	Toxic Effects, Plants (genus Toxicodendron) 2150

Rhytidectomy
	Face Lift 865

Rib
	Costochondritis 595
	Resection 1844

Rib Cage Cartilage Inflammation
	Costochondritis 595

Rib Cage Connective Tissue Inflammation
	Costochondritis 595

Rib Resection
	Thoracic Outlet Syndrome 2074

Rib Syndrome
	Costochondritis 595

266.0£Vitamin B$_2$ 2275

Riboflavin Deficiency
	Vitamin B2 Deficiency 2275

Riboflavin Poisoning
	Poisoning, Vitamin B 1679

Ribs
	Chest Pain 486
	Costochondritis 595

Rickets
	Vitamin D Deficiency 2281

Riedel's Thyroiditis
	Thyroiditis 2091

Right
	Bundle Branch Block 310
	Cor Pulmonale, Acute and Chronic 576

Right Bundle Branch Block
	Bundle Branch Block 310

Right Heart Catheterization
	Cardiac Catheterization 411

Right Heart Failure
	Cor Pulmonale, Acute and Chronic 576
	Embolectomy, Pulmonary 787
	Heart Failure, Congestive 1042

Right Hemicolectomy
	Colon Resection 538

Right Sided Heart Failure
	Cor Pulmonale, Acute and Chronic 576
	Heart Failure, Congestive 1042

Right Ventricle Hypertrophy
	Cor Pulmonale, Acute and Chronic 576

Rigid Sigmoidoscopy
	Sigmoidoscopy 1925

Ringing in the Ears
	Tinnitus 2097

Ringworm
	Tinea 2095

Ritalin Addiction
	Amphetamine Dependence/Abuse 113

Ritualized Acts Neurosis
	Obsessive-Compulsive Disorder 1494

RK
	Radial Keratotomy 1775

Rocky Mountain Fever
	Rocky Mountain Spotted Fever 1845

Rolando's Fracture
	Fracture, Metacarpal Bones 922

Root Canal
	Dental Disorders 657
	Dentoalveolar Abscess 660
	Therapy 1847

Root Canal Treatment
	Root Canal Therapy 1847

Rosenbach's Disease
	Erysipeloid 831

Rotator Cuff
	Impingement Syndrome 1194
	Repair 1848
	Sprains and Strains, Rotator Cuff (Capsule) 1994
	Syndrome 1850
	Tear 1853

Rotator Cuff Syndrome with Subacromial Bursitis
	Impingement Syndrome 1194

RP
	Retinitis Pigmentosa 1829

RSD
	Complex Regional Pain Syndrome 550

RSDS
  Complex Regional Pain Syndrome 550
RSI
  Achilles Bursitis or Tendinitis 47
  Repetitive Strain Injury 1819
Rubber Band Ligation
  Esophageal Varices 843
  Hemorrhoid Treatment 1070
  Hemorrhoids 1073
  Ligation of Esophageal Varices 1288
Rubber Band Ligature of Esophageal Varices
  Ligation of Esophageal Varices 1288
Rubella
  Encephalitis 797
Runny Nose
  Allergic Rhinitis 98
Rupture
  Abdominal Aneurysm 3
  Achilles Bursitis or Tendinitis 47
  Aortic Aneurysm 160
  Aortic Dissection 163
  Appendectomy 174
  Appendicitis 175
  Ectopic Pregnancy 775
  Peritonitis 1628
  Premature Rupture of Membranes 1722
  Repair of Cerebral Aneurysm 1812
  Sprains and Strains, Ankle 1971
  Subarachnoid Hemorrhage (Traumatic) 2014
  Thoracic Aneurysm 2070
  Tympanum Perforation 2202
Rupture of Fallopian Tube
  Hematosalpinx 1053
Rupture of Membranes in Pregnancy
  Premature Rupture of Membranes 1722
Rupture of Spleen
  Splenectomy 1955
  Traumatic 1860
Ruptured Eardrum
  Tympanum Perforation 2202
RVT
  Renal Vein Thrombosis 1807

S

Saccular Aneurysm
  Abdominal Aneurysm 3
  Aortic Aneurysm 160
  Thoracic Aneurysm 2070
Sacral Fracture
  Fracture, Sacrum 939
Sacral Sprain
  Sprains and Strains, Back 1975
Sacrum
  Ankylosing Spondylitis 152
  Cauda Equina Syndrome 440
  Fracture, Sacrum 939
  Intervertebral Disc Disorders 1221
Salivary Gland
  Stones 1865
Salmonella
  Salmonellosis 1866

Salmonella Gastroenteritis
  Salmonellosis 1866
Salpingectomy
  Salpingitis 1870
Salpingitis
  Hematosalpinx 1053
  Pelvic Inflammatory Disease 1604
  Salpingectomy 1868
Salpingo-Oophorectomy
  Cancer, Uterus 402
  Endometriosis 805
San Joaquin Fever
  Coccidioidomycosis 525
SAR
  Allergic Rhinitis 98
Sarcoidosis
  Atrioventricular Block Incomplete (Second-Degree) 223
  Sarcoidosis 1875
Sarcoma
  Bone Tumors 281
  Cancer, Bladder 338
  Cancer, Bone 341
  Cancer, Brain 344
  Cancer, Breast 347
  Cancer, Cervix 351
  Cancer, Colon 354
  Cancer, Esophagus 356
  Cancer, Kidney 358
  Cancer, Liver 360
  Cancer, Lung 363
  Cancer, Oropharynx 369
  Cancer, Ovary 372
  Cancer, Pancreas 375
  Cancer, Pleura 377
  Cancer, Prostate 380
  Cancer, Rectum 384
  Cancer, Skin 387
  Cancer, Small Intestine (Including Duodenum) 389
  Cancer, Stomach 391
  Cancer, Testicle(s) 393
  Cancer, Thyroid Gland 396
  Cancer, Tongue 399
  Cancer, Uterus 402
  Glioma 999
  Hepatic Angiosarcoma 1077
  Kaposi's Sarcoma 1253
  Leukemia 1284
  Multiple Myeloma 1399
  Mycosis Fungoides 1416
SBE
  Endocarditis, Bacterial 802
SC Separation
  Dislocation, Sternclavicular Joint 726
Scalene Syndrome
  Scalenectomy 1877
Scalp
  Alopecia Areata 103
  Cancer, Skin 387
  Folliculitis 887
  Impetigo 1193
  Sebaceous Cyst 1896
Scan
  Bone Scan 277
  Myocardial Perfusion Scan 1427

Index 2649

Scapula
    Dislocation, Acromioclavicular Joint 708
Scapular Fracture
    Fracture, Clavicle 907
Scar Tissue
    Abdominal Adhesions 1
    Esophageal Strictures 840
    Excision of Morton's Neuroma 855
    Keloid 1254
Scarlatina
    Strep Throat 2005
Scarlet Fever
    Strep Throat 2005
SCC
    Cancer, Skin 387
Schamberg's Purpura
    Purpura Simplex 1760
Schaumann's Disease
    Sarcoidosis 1875
Schizoaffective
    Disorder 1878
Schizo-Affective Psychosis
    Schizoaffective Disorder 1878
Schizoid
    Personality Disorder 1881
Schizophrenia
    Electroconvulsive Therapy 782
    Paranoid Type 1885
    Schizoaffective Disorder 1878
    Schizophrenia 1882, 1885
    Schizophreniform Disorder 1888
Schizophrenic Reaction
    Schizophrenia 1882, 1885
Schizophreniform
    Schizophrenia 1882, 1885
Schmorl's Nodes
    Intervertebral Disc Disorders 1221
Sciatic Nerve
    Sciatica 1890
Sciatic Neuritis
    Sciatica 1890
SCLC
    Cancer, Lung 363
Scleral
    Retinal Detachment Repair 1825
Scleral Buckle
    Retinal Detachment Repair 1825
Scleral Buckling
    Retinal Detachment Repair 1825
Scleroderma
    Bursitis 325
    Dilation of Esophagus 700
Sclerosis
    Alzheimer's Disease 105
    Amyotrophic Lateral Sclerosis 125
    Atrophy, Muscular 227, 230
    Glomerulosclerosis 1005
    Multiple Sclerosis 1401

Scleroderma 1892
Sclerostomy
    Trabeculectomy 2156
Sclerotherapy
    Esophageal Varices 843
    Hemorrhoid Treatment 1070
    Pneumothorax 1671
    Sclerotherapy 1895
    Trigeminal Neuralgia 2187
    Varicocele 2242
    Varicose Veins 2246
Sclerotitis
    Herpes Zoster 1110
    Rheumatoid Arthritis 1838
    Scleritis 1891
Scoliosis
    Curvature of the Spine, Acquired 610
    Pott's Disease 1709
    Spinal Fusion 1951
Scombroid Poisoning
    Toxic Effects, Fish and Shellfish 2126
Scope
    Arthroscopy 199
Scrapes
    Abrasions 14
    Head Injury, Superficial 1031
Scrotal Varices
    Ligation of Spermatic Vein for Varicocele 1289
    Varicocele 2242
Scrotum
    Cryotherapy, Genital Warts (Male) 606
    Epididymitis 819
    Filariasis 881
    Hydrocele 1136
    Infertility, Male 1206
    Orchiectomy 1523
    Orchitis 1524
    Paracentesis 1582
    Spermatocele 1942
    Varicocele 2242
    Warts, Genital 2294
Scrub Typhus
    Typhus Fever 2206
SCS
    Spinal Cord Stimulation 1949
Scurvy
    Vitamin C Deficiency 2279
Sea Sickness
    Motion Sickness 1395
    Vertigo 2262
Seasonal Rhinitis
    Allergic Rhinitis 98
Sebaceous Cyst
    Incision of Skin and Subcutaneous Tissue, Drainage of Abscess or Cyst 1201
Seborrheic Dermatitis
    Contact Dermatitis 560
    Dermatitis 674
    Eczema 778
    Vitamin B_2 Deficiency 2275
Second Degree
    Atrioventricular Block Incomplete (Second-Degree) 223

Sprains and Strains, Ankle **1971**
Sprains and Strains, Back **1975**
Sprains and Strains, Elbow **1984**
Sprains and Strains, Foot **1986**
Sprains and Strains, Hand or Fingers **1989**
Sprains and Strains, Knee **1991**
Sprains and Strains, Wrist **1997**
Sunburn **2019**

Secondary Aldosteronism
Aldosteronism **94**

Secondary Gain
Multiple Chemical Sensitivity Syndrome **1397**

Secondary Myelofibrosis
Myelophthisic Anemia **1422**

Secondary Peritonitis
Peritonitis **1628**

Second-degree AV Block
Atrioventricular Block Incomplete (Second-Degree) **223**

Second-degree Incomplete AV Block
Atrioventricular Block Incomplete (Second-Degree) **223**

Sec-Propyl Alcohol Poisoning
Toxic Effects, Isopropyl Alcohol **2134**

Secretory Otitis Media
Otitis Media **1545**

Sector Iridectomy
Iridectomy **1238**

Sedative Dependence
Sedative, Hypnotic or Anxiolytic Dependence **1898**

Segmental
Avascular Necrosis **235**
Lung Excision **1314**

Segmental Glomerulosclerosis
Glomerulosclerosis **1005**

Segmental Hyalinosis
Glomerulosclerosis **1005**

Segmental Resection
Abdominoperineal Resection of Rectum **10**
Colon Resection **538**
Lung Excision **1314**

Segmental Resection of Colon
Colon Resection **538**

Seizure **1900**
Alcoholism **90**
Brain Abscess **289**
Brain Injury **292**
Epilepsy **824**
General Paresis **986**
Grand Mal Seizure **1014**
Jacksonian Seizure **1247**
Meningioma **1355**
Meningitis, Bacterial **1357**
Petit Mal Epilepsy **1631**
Postconcussion Syndrome **1699**
Preeclampsia and Eclampsia **1711**
Rabies **1773**

Seizure Disorder
Electroencephalogram **783**
Epilepsy **824**
Seizures **1900**

Seizures
Cocaine Dependence/Abuse **522**

Preeclampsia and Eclampsia **1711**

Selective Gastric Vagotomy
Vagotomy **2235**

Selective Proximal Vagotomy
Vagotomy **2235**

Selective Shunt
Portal Systemic Shunt **1695**

Selective Vagotomy
Vagotomy **2235**

Senile
Alzheimer's Disease **105**
Arteriosclerotic Gangrene **186**
Atherosclerosis and Arteriosclerosis **216**
Dementia, Alzheimer's Type, with Delusions (Late Onset) **653**
Macular Degeneration **1903**
Organic Psychosis **1526**

Senile Arteriosclerosis
Atherosclerosis and Arteriosclerosis **216**

Senile Dementia
Alzheimer's Disease **105**
Dementia **651, 653**

Senile Dementia of Alzheimer's Type with Delusions
Dementia, Alzheimer's Type, with Delusions (Late Onset) **653**

Senile Dementia of the Alzheimer Type
Dementia **651, 653**

Senile Gangrene
Arteriosclerotic Gangrene **186**

Senile Macular Degeneration
Blindness **270**

Senile Organic Psychosis
Organic Psychosis **1526**

Senile Psychosis
Dementia, Alzheimer's Type, with Delusions (Late Onset) **653**

Senile Tremor
Tremor **2179**

Sensation Disturbance
Paresthesia **1591**
Peripheral Neuropathy **1621**
Syringomyelia **2035**

Sensitivity
Allergy **100**

Sensory
Evoked Potentials **851**
Nerve Conduction Studies **1459**

Sensory Aphasia
Aphasia **169**

Sensory Hearing Loss
Hearing Loss **1036**

Sensory Induced Epilepsy
Jacksonian Seizure **1247**

Sensory Urge Incontinence
Urinary Incontinence in Women **2222**

Sensory-Induced Epilepsy
Jacksonian Seizure **1247**

SEPS
Evoked Potentials **851**

Sepsis
- Delirium 644
- Gas Gangrene 967
- Osteomyelitis 1537
- Pyelonephritis, Acute 1762
- Septic Shock 1907

Septic
- Sepsis 1905
- Shock 1907, 1915

Septic Adenoiditis
- Tonsillitis and Adenoiditis 2104

Septic Arthritis
- Arthritis, Infectious 192

Septic Bronchitis
- Bronchitis, Acute 299

Septic Laryngitis
- Hypotension 1178
- Laryngitis 1279

Septic Shock
- Sepsis 1905
- Shock 1915

Septic Tonsillitis
- Tonsillitis and Adenoiditis 2104

Septicemia
- Empyema 794
- Sepsis 1905
- Septic Shock 1907

Septoplasty
- Deviated Nasal Septum 679
- Nosebleed 1485

Septum
- Deviated Nasal Septum 679
- Septoplasty 1909

Serous Cyst of Ovary
- Ovarian Cyst, Benign 1552

Serous Labyrinthitis
- Labyrinthitis 1267

Serous Meningitis
- Aseptic Meningitis 205

Serous Otitis Media
- Otitis Media 1545

Serum Hepatitis
- Hepatitis B 1083

Serum Sickness
- Anaphylactic Shock 129, 131

Sesamoid Bone
- Fracture, Forefoot (Sesamoid, Phalanges) 918

Severe Depression with Psychotic Features
- Depressive Psychosis 670

Sexual Dysfunction
- Impotence 1198
- Psychosexual Disorders 1745

Sexually Transmitted Disease
- Cancer, Cervix 351
- Cervicitis 472
- Chancroid 481
- Cryotherapy, Genital Warts (Female) 605
- Cryotherapy, Genital Warts (Male) 606
- Gonorrhea 1010
- Hepatitis B 1083
- Herpes Simplex 1108
- Human Immunodeficiency Virus 1126
- Pelvic Inflammatory Disease 1604
- Syphilis 2033
- Trichomoniasis 2185
- Urethritis 2218
- Warts, Genital 2294

Sézary Syndrome
- Mycosis Fungoides 1416

Shaking Palsy
- Parkinson's Disease 1593

Shave Biopsy
- Skin or Subcutaneous Tissue Biopsy 1934

Shaving
- Meniscectomy and Meniscus Repair 1361

Sheath Incision
- De Quervain's Release 630
- Tendon Release 2051
- Tendon Sheath Incision 2052

Shepherd Fracture
- Fracture, Talus 945

Shingles
- Chickenpox 490
- Herpes Zoster 1110
- Human Immunodeficiency Virus 1126

Shock
- Anaphylactic Shock 129, 131
- Anaphylactic Shock, Food Reaction 131
- Cardiogenic Shock 417
- Crush Wounds 603
- Ectopic Pregnancy 775
- Gastritis 970
- Hemothorax, Traumatic 1075
- Hypovolemic Shock 1184
- Insect or Spider Bites and Stings 1210
- Septic Shock 1907
- Toxic Shock Syndrome 2152

Shock Lung
- Adult Respiratory Distress Syndrome 79

Shock Syndrome
- Toxic Shock Syndrome 2152

Shock Therapy
- Electroconvulsive Therapy 782

Shockwave
- Lithotripsy, Extracorporeal Shock Wave 1295

Shortness of Breath
- Dyspnea 761
- Empyema 794
- Lung Collapse 1312
- Neurocirculatory Asthenia 1467
- Panic Disorder 1578, 1580
- Panic Disorder with Agoraphobia 1580
- Pericarditis, Chronic Constrictive 1617
- Pneumocystis Carinii Pneumonia 1663
- Pneumonia 1667
- Pneumothorax 1671
- Polycythemia Vera 1689
- Premature Beats 1719
- Pulmonary Edema 1756
- Reduction Mammoplasty 1790
- Renal Failure, Chronic 1804
- Respiratory Failure 1821
- Rheumatic Fever, Acute 1833

Rheumatic Heart Disease, Chronic **1836**

Shoulder
- Adhesive Capsulitis of Shoulder **66**
- Arthrodesis **194**
- Arthroscopy **199**
- Avascular Necrosis **235**
- Biceps Tendonitis **248**
- Brachial Neuropathy **287**
- Enthesopathy **812**
- Glenohumeral Dislocation **719**
- Impingement Syndrome **1194**
- Neuralgic Amyotrophy **1465**
- Replacement **1917**
- Rotator Cuff Repair **1848**
- Rotator Cuff Syndrome **1850**
- Rotator Cuff Tear **1853**
- Sprains and Strains, Rotator Cuff (Capsule) **1994**
- Thoracic Outlet Syndrome **2074**

Shoulder Acromioplasty
- Impingement Syndrome **1194**
- Rotator Cuff Repair **1848**
- Rotator Cuff Syndrome **1850**

Shoulder Arthroplasty
- Glenohumeral Dislocation **719**
- Shoulder Replacement **1917**

Shoulder Dislocation
- Dislocation, Acromioclavicular Joint **708**
- Glenohumeral Dislocation **719**
- Sprains and Strains, Rotator Cuff (Capsule) **1994**

Shoulder Hand Syndrome
- Complex Regional Pain Syndrome **550**

Shoulder Pain
- Adhesive Capsulitis of Shoulder **66**
- Biceps Tendonitis **248**
- Brachial Neuropathy **287**
- Cervicobrachial Syndrome **474**
- Dislocation, Sternclavicular Joint **726**
- Reduction Mammoplasty **1790**
- Rotator Cuff Tear **1853**

Shoulder Replacement
- Avascular Necrosis **235**

Shoulder Separation
- Dislocation, Acromioclavicular Joint **708**
- Sprains and Strains, Acromioclavicular Joint **1968**

Shoulder Tear
- Rotator Cuff Tear **1853**
- Sprains and Strains, Rotator Cuff (Capsule) **1994**

Shoulder-Hand Syndrome
- Complex Regional Pain Syndrome **550**

Shouldice Repair
- Hernia, Inguinal and Femoral **1103**

Shulman's Syndrome
- Eosinophilic Fasciitis **814**

Shunt
- Portal Systemic Shunt **1695**
- Renal Dialysis **1800**
- Subarachnoid Hemorrhage (Non-traumatic) **2011**
- Syringomyelia **2035**

Shy Drager Syndrome
- Hypotension **1178**

Sialolithiasis
- Salivary Gland Stones **1865**

Sicca Complex
- Sjogren's Syndrome **1930**

Sicca Syndrome
- Sjogren's Syndrome **1930**

Sick Building Syndrome
- Humidifier Fever **1130**

Sick Headache
- Migraine Headache **1378**

Sick Sinus Syndrome
- Cardiac Pacemaker Insertion **414**

Sickle Cell
- Anemia **1922**

Sickle Cell Anemia
- Anemia **133, 136**
- Anemia Complicating Pregnancy **136**

Sickle Cell Disease
- Arthralgia **190**
- Avascular Necrosis **235**
- Sickle Cell Anemia **1922**

Sideroblastic Anemia
- Anemia **133, 136**

Siderosis Pneumoconiosis
- Siderosis **1924**

Sideswipe Fracture
- Fracture, Elbow (Distal Humerus) **910**

Side-to-side Portacaval Shunt
- Portal Systemic Shunt **1695**

Sigmoid Volvulus
- Volvulus **2289**

Sigmoiditis
- Colitis **535**
- Diarrhea **696**
- Gastroenteritis, Non-Infectious **975**
- Ulcerative Colitis **2209**

Sigmoidoscopy
- Anorectal Fistula **154**
- Colitis **535**
- Diverticulosis and Diverticulitis of Colon **739**
- Endoscopy of Gastrointestinal Tract **810**
- Gastrointestinal Hemorrhage **982**
- Hemorrhage of Rectum and Anus **1068**
- Rectal Ulcer **1788**

Silent Lymphocytic Thyroiditis
- Thyroiditis **2091**

Silent Thyroiditis
- Thyroiditis **2091**

Silicosis Pneumonoconiosis
- Silicosis **1926**
- Pneumoconiosis **1662**

Silicotic Lung Fibrosis
- Silicosis **1926**

Silicotuberculosis
- Silicosis **1926**

Simmond's Disease
- Panhypopituitarism **1576**

Simple
- Bronchitis, Chronic **302**
- Chancroid **481**
- Cystectomy **615**

Mastectomy 1345
Nephrectomy 1451
Obesity, Simple 1491
Ovarian Cyst, Benign 1552
Phobias, Specific 1639
Phobic Disorders 1641

Simple Glaucoma
Glaucoma, Acute (Angle-Closure) 995
Glaucoma, Chronic (Open-Angle) 997

Simple Marginal Gingivitis
Gingivitis 993

Simple Mastoidectomy
Mastoidectomy 1347

Simple Phobias
Phobias, Specific 1639

Simple Retinopathy
Diabetic Retinopathy 694

Simplex
Purpura Simplex 1760

Single Manic Episode
Bipolar Affective Disorder, Single Manic Episode 260

Single Vitamin Deficiency
Hypovitaminosis 1182

Sinus Infection
Dacryocystitis 627
Sinusitis 1928
Upper Respiratory Infection 2216

Sinus Node Dysfunction
Sick Sinus Syndrome 1920

Sinus Syncope
Carotid Sinus Syncope 425

Sinus Syndrome
Carotid Sinus Syncope 425

Sinusitis
Brain Abscess 289
Deviated Nasal Septum 679
Upper Respiratory Infection 2216

Siriasis
Heat Stroke 1051

Sjögren's Syndrome
Sjogren's Syndrome 1930

Skeletal
Traction 2163

Skeletal Muscle
Traction 2163

Skeletal Traction
Fracture, Cervical Spine (With or Without Spinal Cord Injury) 904
Traction 2163

Skin
Abrasions 14
Biopsy 252
Cancer, Skin 387
Candidiasis 405
Carbuncle 407
Cellulitis 443
Chromoblastomycosis 508
Contact Dermatitis 560
Corn and Callus, Infected 578
Decubitus Ulcer 632
Dengue Fever 656
Dermatitis 674
Dermatomyositis 677
Eczema 778
Erythema Nodosum 835
Excision of Lesion or Tissue of Skin and Subcutaneous Tissue 854
Face Lift 865
Frostbite 959
Gangrene 964
Gas Gangrene 967
Graft 1932
Herpes Simplex 1108
Impetigo 1193
Iontophoresis 1236
Mycosis Fungoides 1416
or Subcutaneous Tissue Biopsy 1934
Pemphigus 1606
Poison Ivy, Oak, Sumac, or Other Plant Dermatitis 1673
Poisoning 1675, 1677, 1679, 1681
Psoriasis 1738
Puncture Wound 1759
Radiodermatitis 1780
Sarcoidosis 1875
Scleroderma 1892
Sebaceous Cyst 1896
Tinea 2095
Toxic Effects, Methyl Alcohol 2140
Toxic Effects, Plants (genus Toxicodendron) 2150
Vitiligo 2286

Skin Biopsy
Cancer, Skin 387
Eczema 778
Erythema Multiforme 833
Skin or Subcutaneous Tissue Biopsy 1934

Skin Cancer
Cancer, Skin 387
Excision of Lesion or Tissue of Skin and Subcutaneous Tissue 854
Kaposi's Sarcoma 1253

Skin Closure
Suture of Skin and Subcutaneous Tissue 2020

Skin Inflammation
Allergic Dermatitis 96
Atopic Dermatitis 218
Contact Dermatitis 560
Dermatitis 674
Eczema 778
Erysipelas 830
Erythema Multiforme 833
Pemphigus 1606
Poison Ivy, Oak, Sumac, or Other Plant Dermatitis 1673

Skin Lesion
Allergic Dermatitis 96
Atopic Dermatitis 218
Blastomycosis 266
Cancer, Skin 387
Carbuncle 407
Cat Scratch Disease 435
Chickenpox 490
Chromoblastomycosis 508
Contact Dermatitis 560
Corn and Callus, Infected 578
Decubitus Ulcer 632
Dermatitis 674
Eczema 778
Erythema Multiforme 833
Excision of Lesion or Tissue of Skin and Subcutaneous Tissue 854
Folliculitis 887
Furuncle 961
Herpes Zoster 1110

2654 *The Medical Disability Advisor—Fourth Edition*

- Lyme Disease **1319**
- Mycosis Fungoides **1416**
- Pemphigus **1606**
- Poison Ivy, Oak, Sumac, or Other Plant Dermatitis **1673**
- Psoriasis **1738**
- Reiter's Syndrome **1798**
- Skin or Subcutaneous Tissue Biopsy **1934**
- Tinea **2095**
- Vitiligo **2286**
- Warts, Genital **2294**
- Warts, Plantar **2296**
- Warts, Viral **2298**

Skin Suture
- Suture of Skin and Subcutaneous Tissue **2020**

Skull
- Craniectomy **596**
- Craniotomy **598**
- Intracranial Hemorrhage **1226, 1230**

Skull Fracture
- Epidural Hematoma **821**
- Fracture, Skull (Closed) **941**
- Intracranial Hemorrhage, Closed **1230**

SLE
- Lupus Erythematosus, Systemic **1317**
- St. Louis Encephalitis **2000**

Sleep Apnea
- Hypersomnia **1152**
- Insomnia with Sleep Apnea **1214**
- Sleep Apnea **1935**
- Tonsillitis and Adenoiditis **2104**

Sleep Disorder
- Hypersomnia **1152**
- Insomnia with Sleep Apnea **1214**
- Narcolepsy **1439**
- Pain, Chronic **1564**
- Pellagra **1602**
- Posttraumatic Stress Disorder **1707**
- Sleep Apnea **1935**

Sleep Epilepsy
- Narcolepsy **1439**

Sleeping Pill Dependence
- Sedative, Hypnotic or Anxiolytic Dependence **1898**

Sliding Hernia
- Hernia, Hiatal **1097**

Slipped Disc
- Cervical Disc Disorder with Myelopathy **464**
- Displacement, Cervical Intervertebral Disc Without Myelopathy **728**
- Displacement, Lumbar Intervertebral Disc Without Myelopathy **732**
- Displacement, Thoracic Intervertebral Disc Without Myelopathy **735**
- Lumbar Disc Disorder with Myelopathy **1308**
- Thoracic Disc Disorder with Myelopathy **2072**

Sluggish Bowels
- Constipation **558**

Small and Large Cell Lymphoma
- Non-Hodgkin's Lymphoma **1482**

Small Bowel Series
- Upper Gastrointestinal Series **2214**

Small Intestinal Cancer
- Cancer, Small Intestine (Including Duodenum) **389**

Small Intestine
- Cancer, Small Intestine (Including Duodenum) **389**
- Cholangiography **493**
- Dumping Syndrome **747**
- Duodenitis **749**
- Dyspepsia **759**
- Esophagogastroduodenoscopy **850**
- Excision or Destruction of Duodenal Lesion **857**
- Gastroenterostomy **978**
- Gastrointestinal Hemorrhage **982**
- Giardiasis **989**
- Meckel's Diverticulum **1351**
- Upper Gastrointestinal Series **2214**

Small Lymphocytic Lymphoma
- Non-Hodgkin's Lymphoma **1482**

Small Noncleaved Cell Lymphoma
- Non-Hodgkin's Lymphoma **1482**

Small-Cell Lung Carcinoma
- Cancer, Lung **363**

SMD
- Senile Macular Degeneration **1903**

Smelter Chills
- Metal Fume Fever **1374**

Smith's Fracture
- Fracture, Radius and Ulna, Distal **933**

Smokeless Tobacco Dependence
- Nicotine Dependence **1479**

Smoking Addiction
- Nicotine Dependence **1479**

Social Anxiety Disorder
- Social Phobia **1937**

Social Phobia
- Cognitive Therapy **530**

Sociopathic Personality Disorder
- Antisocial Personality Disorder **156**

Soft Chancre
- Chancroid **481**

Soft Tissue Cervical Hyperextension Injury
- Sprains and Strains, Cervical Spine (Neck) **1981**

Solar Plexus Block
- Celiac Plexus Block **442**

Soldier's Heart
- Neurocirculatory Asthenia **1467**

Solitary Rectal Ulcer Syndrome
- Rectal Ulcer **1788**

Solution-focused Brief Therapy
- Psychotherapy, Individual **1748**

Solvents
- Allergy **100**
- Toxic Effects, Chlorine **2122**

Somatization Disorder
- Fibromyalgia and Myofascial Pain Syndrome **879**
- Hysteria **1188**
- Psychoanalysis **1742**

Somatoform Disorder
- Conversion Disorder **574**
- Hysteria **1188**
- Somatization Disorder **1939**

Somatosensory Epilepsy
- Jacksonian Seizure **1247**

Somatosensory Evoked Potentials
    Evoked Potentials 851
Sonography
    Ultrasound, Diagnostic 2212
Sore
    Excision of Lesion or Tissue of Skin and Subcutaneous Tissue 854
    Strep Throat 2005
Sore Throat
    Abscess, Peritonsillar 36
    Pharyngitis, Acute 1633
    Salmonellosis 1866
    St. Louis Encephalitis 2000
    Strep Throat 2005
    Tonsillitis and Adenoiditis 2104
Sound Dilation of Esophagus
    Dilation of Esophagus 700
Spasm
    Asthma 209
    Bronchiectasis 297
    Esophageal Spasm 839
    Muscle Spasm 1409
    Myotomy of Esophagus 1433
    Prinzmetal's Angina 1726
    Pylorospasm 1770
    Rabies 1773
    Tetany 2062
    Tics 2093
Spasmodic
    Allergic Rhinitis 98
    Asthma 209
    Pylorospasm 1770
Spastic
    Cerebral Palsy 452
    Irritable Bowel Syndrome 1244
    Neurogenic Bladder 1471
    Paralysis, Paraplegia, and Quadriplegia 1583
Spastic Colitis
    Irritable Bowel Syndrome 1244
Spastic Colon
    Irritable Bowel Syndrome 1244
Specific Phobias
    Phobic Disorders 1641
Speech Therapy
    Cerebral Palsy 452
    Otosclerosis 1549
    Parkinson's Disease 1593
    Rehabilitation Therapy 1796
Speed Addiction
    Amphetamine Dependence/Abuse 113
Spermatic Cord Varicocele
    Varicocele 2242
Spermatic Cyst
    Spermatocele 1942
Spermatocele
    Spermatocelectomy 1943
Sphenoidal Sinusitis
    Sinusitis 1928
Spherocytic Anemia
    Spherocytosis, Hereditary 1944

Spherocytosis
    Hereditary 1944
Spider Bite
    Insect or Spider Bites and Stings 1210
Spinal
    Cord Injury 1946
    Cord Stimulation 1949
    Diabetic Neuropathy 692
    Fracture, Vertebra 954, 956
    Fusion 1951
    Lumbar Puncture 1309
    Meningitis, Bacterial 1357
    Pott's Disease 1709
    Stenosis 1952
Spinal Arthrodesis
    Curvature of the Spine, Acquired 610
    Spinal Fusion 1951
Spinal Cord
    Astrocytoma 214
    Cauda Equina Syndrome 440
    Cervical Disc Disorder with Myelopathy 464
    Displacement, Cervical Intervertebral Disc Without Myelopathy 728
    Displacement, Lumbar Intervertebral Disc Without Myelopathy 732
    Displacement, Thoracic Intervertebral Disc Without Myelopathy 735
    Injury 1946
    Laminectomy or Laminotomy 1273
    Stimulation 1949
    Syringomyelia 2035
Spinal Cord Dysfunction
    Myelopathy 1420
Spinal Cord Injury
    Myelopathy 1420
    Paralysis, Paraplegia, and Quadriplegia 1583
Spinal Cord Syndrome
    Post-Laminectomy Syndrome 1701
Spinal Curvature
    Curvature of the Spine, Acquired 610
Spinal Fracture
    Curvature of the Spine, Acquired 610
    Fracture, Vertebra 954, 956
Spinal Fusion
    Ankylosing Spondylitis 152
    Bone Graft 272
    Cervical Disc Disorder with Myelopathy 464
    Curvature of the Spine, Acquired 610
    Degeneration, Cervical Intervertebral Disc 634
    Degeneration, Lumbar Intervertebral Disc 637
    Dislocation, Cervical Vertebra 711
    Displacement, Cervical Intervertebral Disc Without Myelopathy 728
    Displacement, Thoracic Intervertebral Disc Without Myelopathy 735
    Evoked Potentials 851
    Fracture, Lumbosacral Spine (With or Without Spinal Cord Injury) 920
    Fracture, Thoracic Spine (With or Without Spinal Cord Injury) 948
    Fracture, Vertebra 954, 956
Spinal Inflammation
    Laminectomy or Laminotomy 1273
    Spinal Fusion 1951
Spinal Meningitis
    Meningitis, Bacterial 1357
Spinal Pain
    Back Pain 239
    Disc Calcification 701
    Fracture, Vertebra 954, 956

    Fracture, Vertebra (Pathological) 956
    Intervertebral Disc Disorders 1221
    Laminectomy or Laminotomy 1273
    Low Back Pain 1302
    Myelopathy 1420
    Post-Laminectomy Syndrome 1701
    Spinal Cord Injury 1946
    Spinal Fusion 1951
    Spinal Stenosis 1952
    Spondylolisthesis 1960

Spinal Puncture
    Lumbar Puncture 1309

Spinal Tap
    Aspiration 207–208
    Lumbar Puncture 1309

Spinal Tuberculosis
    Pott's Disease 1709

Spine
    Ankylosing Spondylitis 152
    Arthroscopy 199
    Back Pain 239
    Chiropractic Adjustments and Manipulations 492
    Computerized Axial Tomography 552
    Curvature of the Spine, Acquired 610
    Degeneration, Cervical Intervertebral Disc 634
    Degeneration, Lumbar Intervertebral Disc 637
    Degeneration, Thoracic or Thoracolumbar Intervertebral Disc 640
    Disc Calcification 701
    Discectomy 703
    Dislocation, Cervical Vertebra 711
    Fracture, Vertebra 954, 956
    Fracture, Vertebra (Pathological) 956
    Intervertebral Disc Disorders 1221
    Myelography 1419
    Osteoarthritis 1530
    Pilonidal Cyst 1645
    Pott's Disease 1709
    Spinal Cord Injury 1946
    Spinal Cord Stimulation 1949
    Spinal Fusion 1951
    Spinal Stenosis 1952
    Spondylitis 1958
    Spondylolisthesis 1960
    Thoracic Spine Pain 2076

Spine Arthrodesis
    Spinal Fusion 1951

Spine Disorders
    Curvature of the Spine, Acquired 610
    Fracture, Vertebra 954, 956
    Lumbar Disc Disorder with Myelopathy 1308
    Pott's Disease 1709
    Spinal Cord Injury 1946
    Spinal Stenosis 1952

Spine Fracture
    Fracture, Sacrum 939
    Fracture, Vertebra 954, 956

Spine Pain
    Ankylosing Spondylitis 152
    Back Pain 239
    Diabetic Neuropathy 692
    Discectomy 703
    Dislocation, Cervical Vertebra 711
    Fracture, Vertebra 954, 956
    Fracture, Vertebra (Pathological) 956
    Intervertebral Disc Disorders 1221
    Laminectomy or Laminotomy 1273
    Low Back Pain 1302
    Osteoarthritis 1530
    Pott's Disease 1709
    Sciatica 1890
    Spinal Cord Injury 1946
    Spinal Fusion 1951
    Spondylitis 1958
    Spondylolisthesis 1960
    Thoracic Spine Pain 2076

Spinning
    Dizziness and Giddiness 742

Spirits of Salts Poisoning
    Toxic Effects, Hydrochloric Acid 2131

Spivak's Gastrostomy
    Gastrostomy 984

Spleen
    Echinococcosis 772
    Hypersplenism 1154
    Rupture of Spleen, Traumatic 1860
    Splenectomy 1955
    Splenomegaly 1956

Spleen Enlargement
    Polycythemia Vera 1689
    Splenomegaly 1956
    Thalassemia 2066

Splenectomy
    Hemolytic Anemia 1059
    Hypersplenism 1154
    Rupture of Spleen, Traumatic 1860
    Spherocytosis, Hereditary 1944
    Thalassemia 2066

Splenic Anemia
    Hypersplenism 1154

Splenic Flexure Volvulus
    Volvulus 2289

Splenic Rupture
    Rupture of Spleen, Traumatic 1860

Splenomegaly
    Cholangiography 493
    Hypersplenism 1154
    Typhoid Fever 2204

Splenorenal Shunt
    Portal Systemic Shunt 1695

Split Personality
    Dissociative Personality Disorder 737

Split-Thickness Graft
    Skin Graft 1932

Spondylitis
    Spinal Fusion 1951

Spondyloarthritis
    Ankylosing Spondylitis 152

Spondylodiscitis
    Pott's Disease 1709

Spondylolysis
    Myelopathy 1420
    Spondylolisthesis 1960

Spondylosyndesis
    Spinal Fusion 1951

Spondylotomy
    Laminectomy or Laminotomy 1273
    Spinal Fusion 1951

Spontaneous Abortion
    Miscarriage 1381
Spontaneous Peritonitis
    Peritonitis 1628
Spontaneous Pneumothorax
    Empyema 794
    Pneumothorax 1671
Sportsman's Groin
    Groin Strain 1020
Spotted Fever
    Rocky Mountain Spotted Fever 1845
Sprained Ankle
    Sprains and Strains, Ankle 1971
Sprained Back
    Sprains and Strains, Back 1975
Sprained Elbow
    Sprains and Strains, Elbow 1984
Sprained Foot
    Sprains and Strains, Foot 1986
Sprained Knee
    Repair, Anterior Cruciate Ligament 1814
    Sprains and Strains, Knee 1991
Sprained Neck
    Sprains and Strains, Cervical Spine (Neck) 1981
Sprained Wrist
    Sprains and Strains, Wrist 1997
Spur
    Excision of Bone Spur, Foot 852
    Heel Spur (Calcaneal) 1053
Squamous Cell Carcinoma
    Cancer, Skin 387
    Cancer, Tongue 399
Squint
    Astigmatism 212
SRUS
    Rectal Ulcer 1788
SS
    Mycosis Fungoides 1416
Ssabanejew-Frank Gastrostomy
    Gastrostomy 984
SSEP
    Evoked Potentials 851
St. Louis
    Encephalitis 2000
Stab Wound
    Open Wound 1504, 1510, 1512
    Open Wound, Back 1510
    Open Wound, Chest 1512
Stable Angina
    Angina Pectoris 140
Stamey Technique
    Vesicourethropexy 2265
Stamm-Kader Gastrostomy
    Gastrostomy 984
Stannosis
    Pneumoconiosis 1662
    Siderosis 1924

Stapedectomy
    Hearing Loss 1036
    Otosclerosis 1549
    Stapedectomy 2002
Staphylococcal Pharyngitis
    Pharyngitis, Acute 1633
Staphylococcal Toxic Shock Syndrome
    Toxic Shock Syndrome 2152
Stasis
    Dermatitis 674
    Eczema 778
    Salivary Gland Stones 1865
    Varicose Ulcer 2244
Stasis Dermatitis
    Contact Dermatitis 560
    Dermatitis 674
    Eczema 778
Stasis Leg Ulcer
    Varicose Ulcer 2244
Stasis Syndrome
    Varicose Ulcer 2244
Stasis Ulcer
    Varicose Ulcer 2244
States
    Delusional Disorder 649
Stein-Leventhal Syndrome
    Polycystic Ovary Syndrome 1686
Stenosing Tenosynovitis
    De Quervain's Release 630
    Trigger Finger or Thumb 2191
Stenosing Tenovaginitis
    Trigger Finger or Thumb 2191
Stenosis
    Aortic Insufficiency 165
    Aortic Valve Stenosis 167
    Hydronephrosis 1138
    Mitral Commissurotomy 1384
    Mitral Stenosis 1387
    Pyloric Stenosis, Acquired (Adult) Hypertrophic 1767
    Renovascular Hypertension 1809
    Rheumatic Heart Disease, Chronic 1836
    Spinal Stenosis 1952
Stenosis of Nasolacrimal Duct
    Dacryostenosis 629
Stereotactic Brain Surgery
    Adrenal Tissue Implant or Transplant to Brain 76
Sterilization
    Tubal Ligation 2193
    Vasectomy 2248
Sternal Fracture
    Fracture, Sternum (Closed) 943
Sternal Tap
    Bone Marrow Biopsy 273
Sternoclavicular Joint Dislocation
    Dislocation, Sternclavicular Joint 726
Sternoclavicular Luxation
    Dislocation, Sternclavicular Joint 726
Sternum
    Chest Pain 486

Costochondritis 595
Dislocation, Sternclavicular Joint 726
Fracture, Clavicle 907
Fracture, Sternum (Closed) 943

Stevens-Johnson Disease
Erythema Multiforme 833

Stiff Lung
Adult Respiratory Distress Syndrome 79

Stiffness
Adhesive Capsulitis of Shoulder 66
Neck Pain 1448
Osteoarthritis 1530
Paresthesia 1591
Parkinson's Disease 1593
Rheumatoid Arthritis 1838
Syringomyelia 2035
Tetanus 2060

Stimulant Dependence
Addictions, Mixed 60
Amphetamine Dependence/Abuse 113
Cocaine Dependence/Abuse 522
Marijuana Dependence/Abuse 1341

Stimulation
Electromyography 784
Nerve Conduction Studies 1459
Physical Therapy 1643
Spinal Cord Stimulation 1949
Transcutaneous Electrical Nerve Stimulation 2164
Ultrasound, Therapeutic 2213

Stimulation Myelographic Study
Nerve Conduction Studies 1459

Sting
Anaphylactic Shock 129, 131
Insect or Spider Bites and Stings 1210

Stitches
Suture of Skin and Subcutaneous Tissue 2020

Stokes-Adams Syndrome
Heart Block 1040
Stokes-Adams Syndrome 2003
Syncope 2024

Stokes-Adams-Morgagni Syndrome
Heart Block 1040
Stokes-Adams Syndrome 2003

Stoma
Cancer, Colon 354
Colostomy and Ileostomy 543
Enterostomy 811

Stomach
Abdominal Pain 7
Achlorhydria and Hypochlorhydria 49
Cancer, Stomach 391
Dumping Syndrome 747
Duodenitis 749
Dyspepsia 759
Endoscopy of Gastrointestinal Tract 810
Esophageal Spasm 839
Esophagogastroduodenoscopy 850
Excision or Destruction of Duodenal Lesion 857
Gastrectomy 968
Gastroenterostomy 978
Gastrointestinal Hemorrhage 982
Gastrostomy 984
Hernia, Hiatal 1097
Mallory-Weiss Syndrome 1333

Nausea 1446
Peptic Ulcer Disease 1611
Pyloric Stenosis, Acquired (Adult) Hypertrophic 1767
Pyloroplasty 1769
Pylorospasm 1770
Resection of Gastric or Duodenal Ulcer Site 1819
Upper Gastrointestinal Series 2214

Stomach Adhesions
Abdominal Adhesions 1

Stomach Cancer
Cancer, Stomach 391
Dumping Syndrome 747
Gastrectomy 968

Stomach Flu
Gastroenteritis, Infectious 973
Traveler's Diarrhea 2177

Stomach Inflammation
Gastritis 970

Stomach Pain
Achlorhydria and Hypochlorhydria 49
Dyspepsia 759
Peptic Ulcer Disease 1611

Stomatitis
Trench Mouth 2181

Stone
Calculus, Bladder 333
Calculus, Renal (Kidney and Ureter) 335
Cholelithiasis 501
Salivary Gland Stones 1865

Stool
Colitis 535
Constipation 558
Diarrhea 696
Peptic Ulcer Disease 1611

Straight Catheterization
Urethral Catheterization 2216

Strained Abdominal Muscle
Abdominal Muscle Strain 5

Strained Ankle
Sprains and Strains, Ankle 1971

Strained Back
Sprains and Strains, Back 1975

Strained Knee
Repair, Anterior Cruciate Ligament 1814

Strained Leg
Repair, Anterior Cruciate Ligament 1814

Strained Neck
Sprains and Strains, Cervical Spine (Neck) 1981

Strep Infection
Abscess, Peritonsillar 36
Impetigo 1193
Lymphadenitis and Lymphadenopathy 1322
Pharyngitis, Acute 1633
Rheumatic Fever, Acute 1833
Strep Throat 2005

Strep Throat
Rheumatic Fever, Acute 1833

Streptococcal Pharyngitis
Rheumatic Fever, Acute 1833
Strep Throat 2005

Streptococcal Throat Infection
    Strep Throat 2005
Streptococcal Toxic Shock Syndrome
    Toxic Shock Syndrome 2152
Stress
    Adjustment Disorder with Depressed Mood 69
    Adjustment Reaction with Anxious Mood 72
    Bipolar Affective Disorder 253, 256, 258, 260
    Conversion Disorder 574
    Delirium 644
    Depersonalization Disorder 663
    Disorder, Acute 2007
    Fibromyalgia and Myofascial Pain Syndrome 879
    Gastroenteritis, Non-Infectious 975
    Glycosuria 1006
    Herpes Simplex 1108
    High Blood Pressure, Benign 1112
    Intermittent Explosive Disorder 1217
    Muscle Injury 1406
    Pain, Chronic 1564
    Peptic Ulcer Disease 1611
    Posttraumatic Stress Disorder 1707
    Temporomandibular Joint Syndrome 2049
    Urinary Incontinence in Women 2222
Stress Disorder
    Acute 2007
    Cognitive Therapy 530
    Posttraumatic Stress Disorder 1707
Stress Fracture
    Bone Scan 277
    Fracture, Pelvis 930
    Fracture, Sacrum 939
    Fracture, Tibia or Fibula 951
Stress Incontinence
    Marshall-Marchetti Operation 1344
    Urinary Incontinence in Women 2222
    Vesicourethropexy 2265
Stress Test
    Angina, Unstable 144
    Cardiac Stress Test 416
Stress Ulcer
    Peptic Ulcer Disease 1611
Stress with Predominant Disturbance of Emotions
    Stress Disorder, Acute 2007
Stress-Related Anxiety Disorder
    Stress Disorder, Acute 2007
Strictures
    Dilation of Esophagus 700
    Esophageal Strictures 840
    Esophagectomy 845
Stripping and Ligation of Varicose Veins
    Ligation and Stripping of Varicose Veins 1287
Stroke
    Brain Injury 292
    Cerebral Hemorrhage 449
    Cerebrovascular Accident 454
    Cerebrovascular Disease 458
    Coarctation of the Aorta 519
    Coma 449, 544
    Constipation 558
    Dementia 651, 653
    Electroencephalogram 783
    Endarterectomy 801
    Enterostomy 811
    Epilepsy 824
    Hemiplegia 1056
    Nystagmus 1487
    Polyarteritis Nodosa 1685
    Polycythemia Vera 1689
    Pulmonary Edema 1756
Struma
    Goiter 1008
Struma Lymphomatosa
    Thyroiditis 2091
Student's Elbow
    Bursitis 325
Styloid Tenosynovitis
    Radial Styloid Tenosynovitis 1776
Subacromial Impingement Syndrome
    Impingement Syndrome 1194
Subacute Bacterial Endocarditis
    Endocarditis, Bacterial 802
Subacute Granulomatous Thyroiditis
    Thyroiditis 2091
Subacute Lymphangitis
    Lymphangitis 1324
Subacute Lymphocytic Thyroiditis
    Thyroiditis 2091
Subacute Meningitis
    Meningitis, Bacterial 1357
Subacute Myocarditis
    Myocarditis, Acute 1428
Subacute Thyroiditis
    Thyroiditis 2091
Subarachnoid Hemorrhage
    (Non-traumatic) 2011
    Intracranial Hemorrhage 1226, 1230
Subarachnoid Stroke
    Intracranial Hemorrhage 1226, 1230
Subcortical Hemorrhage
    Cerebral Hemorrhage 449
Subcutaneous Tissue Biopsy
    Skin or Subcutaneous Tissue Biopsy 1934
Subcutaneous Tissue Treatment Procedures
    Excision of Lesion or Tissue of Skin and Subcutaneous Tissue 854
    Incision of Skin and Subcutaneous Tissue, Drainage of Abscess or Cyst 1201
    Skin or Subcutaneous Tissue Biopsy 1934
    Suture of Skin and Subcutaneous Tissue 2020
Subdiaphragmatic Abscess
    Abscess, Psoas 38
    Abscess, Subdiaphragmatic 42
Subdural Hematoma
    Brain Injury 292
    Coma 449, 544
    Craniectomy 596
    Intracranial Hemorrhage 1226, 1230
Subdural Hemorrhage
    Concussion, Cerebral 553
    Intracranial Hemorrhage 1226, 1230
Subjective Vertigo
    Vertigo 2262

Sublingual Infection
　Ludwig's Angina 1306

Subluxation
　Chiropractic Adjustments and Manipulations 492
　Dislocation, Acromioclavicular Joint 708
　Dislocation, Cervical Vertebra 711
　Dislocation, Femorotibial (Knee) Joint 713
　Dislocation, Foot 716
　Dislocation, Patella (Kneecap) 723
　Dislocation, Sternclavicular Joint 726
　Patella Chondromalacia 1599
　Reduction of Fracture or Dislocation 1791

Submammary Mastitis
　Abscess, Breast 22

Submandibular Space Infection
　Ludwig's Angina 1306

Submucous Cystitis
　Cystitis, Interstitial 619

Subphrenic Abscess
　Abscess, Subdiaphragmatic 42

Subphrenic Peritonitis
　Abscess, Psoas 38

Substance Abuse
　Addictions, Mixed 60
　Alcohol Intoxication, Acute 87
　Alcoholism 90
　Amphetamine Dependence/Abuse 113
　Cocaine Dependence/Abuse 522
　Delirium 644
　Marijuana Dependence/abuse 1341
　Nicotine Dependence 1479
　Opioid Type Dependence 1516
　Psychosexual Disorders 1745
　Psychotherapy, Group 1747
　Pulmonary Edema 1756
　Sedative, Hypnotic or Anxiolytic Dependence 1898

Substance Abuse Withdrawal Program
　Alcohol and Drug Detoxification and Rehabilitation 84

Substance Intoxication
　Poisoning 1675, 1677, 1679, 1681

Subtotal Gastrectomy
　Gastrectomy 968
　Resection of Gastric or Duodenal Ulcer Site 1819

Subtotal Pancreatectomy
　Pancreatectomy 1568

Subtotal Resection of the Colon
　Colon Resection 538

Subtotal Thyroidectomy
　Thyroidectomy 2090

Suction Lipectomy
　Liposuction 1292

Sudek's Atrophy
　Complex Regional Pain Syndrome 550

Sugar
　Diabetes Mellitus Type I 683, 686
　Diabetes Mellitus Type II 686
　Hypoglycemia 1171

Sugar Cane Disease (Bagassosis)
　Hypersensitivity Pneumonitis 1150

Sugar Insufficiency
　Hypoglycemia 1171

Sulphocarbonic Anhydride Poisoning
　Toxic Effects, Carbon Disulfide 2116

Sunstroke
　Heat Stroke 1051

Superficial
　Contusion 562, 564, 566, 568, 571
　Nerve Injury 1460

Superficial Head Injury
　Head Injury, Superficial 1031

Superficial Punctate Keratitis
　Keratitis 1257

Superior Mesenteric Cava Shunt
　Portal Systemic Shunt 1695

Superior Vena Cava
　Portal Systemic Shunt 1695
　Vena Cava Interruption 2251

Suppression of Menstruation
　Dysfunctional Uterine Bleeding 757

Suppurative
　Abscess, Psoas 38
　Abscess, Subdiaphragmatic 42
　Pharyngitis, Acute 1633
　Tonsillitis and Adenoiditis 2104

Suppurative Laryngitis
　Hypotension 1178
　Laryngitis 1279

Suppurative Peritonitis
　Abscess, Psoas 38
　Abscess, Subdiaphragmatic 42

Suppurative Pharyngitis
　Pharyngitis, Acute 1633

Supralevator Abscess
　Abscess, Perirectal 34

Supraspinatus Tendon
　Biceps Tendonitis 248
　Rotator Cuff Repair 1848
　Rotator Cuff Syndrome 1850
　Rotator Cuff Tear 1853

Supraspinatus Tendon Repair
　Rotator Cuff Repair 1848

Supraspinatus Tendon Rupture
　Rotator Cuff Tear 1853
　Sprains and Strains, Rotator Cuff (Capsule) 1994

Supraventricular Tachycardia
　Tachycardia, Paroxysmal Supraventricular 2039

Surgery
　Abdominoperineal Resection of Rectum 10
　Abortion by Dilation and Curettage for Termination of Pregnancy 11
　Abscess, Perirectal 34
　Abscess, Psoas 38
　Abscess, Renal and Perinephric 40
　Adrenal Tissue Implant or Transplant to Brain 76
　Adrenalectomy 77
　Amputation 116, 118, 121, 123
　Amputation, Finger or Thumb 123
　Aneurysmectomy 138
　Appendectomy 174
　Arterial Graft 183

Arthroplasty, Elbow 197
Arthroscopy 199
Bone Graft 272
Bunionectomy 314
Cardiac Pacemaker Insertion 414
Carpal Tunnel Release 428
Cataract Surgery 439
Cholecystectomy 495
Circumcision 514
Cochlear Implant 529
Colon Resection 538
Corneal Transplant 582
Coronary Bypass 592
Craniectomy 596
Cystectomy 615
Cystourethroplasty of Bladder Neck 625
De Quervain's Release 630
Discectomy 703
Dupuytren's Release 753
Embolectomy 786–787
Embolectomy, Pulmonary 787
Esophagectomy 845
Excision of Bone Spur, Foot 852
Excision of Morton's Neuroma 855
Excision of Nail, Nail Bed, or Nail Fold 856
Excision or Destruction of Duodenal Lesion 857
Excision, Fusion, and Repair of Toes 860
Face Lift 865
Fissurectomy, Anal 884
Gastrectomy 968
Gastroenterostomy 978
Gastrostomy 984
Gingivectomy 992
Heart Valve Replacement 1047
Hernia Repair 1094, 1096
Hip Replacement, Total 1119
Hysterectomy 1186
Incision and Drainage of Ischiorectal and/or Perirectal Abscess 1200
Insertion of Inflatable Penile Prosthesis 1213
Iridectomy 1238
Iridotomy 1239
Kidney Transplant 1261
Knee Replacement, Total 1263
Laparoscopy 1275
Laparotomy 1276
Laryngectomy 1278
Ligation and Stripping of Varicose Veins 1287
Ligation of Esophageal Varices 1288
Lithotomy 1293–1294
Liver Biopsy 1297
Lung Excision 1314
Mammoplasty, Augmentation 1338
Marshall-Marchetti Operation 1344
Mastectomy 1345
Meckel's Diverticulum 1351
Meniere's Disease 1353
Meningioma 1355
Meniscectomy and Meniscus Repair 1361
Meniscus Disorders, Knee 1364
Menstrual Disorders 1369
Metatarsalgia 1376
Mitral Commissurotomy 1384
Mitral Insufficiency 1385
Morton's Neuroma 1393
Myelopathy 1420
Myomectomy, Uterine 1430
Nasal Polypectomy 1440
Nasal Polyps 1441
Nasal Septum Perforation 1443
Nausea 1446
Nephrectomy 1451

Nephrotomy 1458
Nerve Injury 1460
Neurogenic Bladder 1471
Nosebleed 1485
Nystagmus 1487
Occupational Therapy 1499
Oophorectomy 1501, 1503
Open-Chest Cardiac Massage 1514
Orchiectomy 1523
Osteoma 1536
Osteomyelitis 1537
Ovarian Cyst, Resection of 1555
Paget's Disease of Bone 1557
Paget's Disease of Breast 1559
Pancreatectomy 1568
Pancreatic Pseudocyst 1569
Pancreaticoduodenectomy 1571
Pancreatitis 1573
Paracentesis 1582
Paralysis, Paraplegia, and Quadriplegia 1583
Paraovarian Cyst 1590
Patella Chondromalacia 1599
Pelvic Inflammatory Disease 1604
Penis Disorders 1608
Peptic Ulcer Disease 1611
Pericardiectomy 1614
Pericarditis, Chronic Constrictive 1617
Peritonitis 1628
Pheochromocytoma 1638
Pilonidal Cyst 1645
Pineal Gland Neoplasm 1647
Placenta Accreta 1651
Plantar Fasciitis 1655
Pneumonectomy 1664
Polyarteritis Nodosa 1685
Polycystic Ovary Syndrome 1686
Post-Laminectomy Syndrome 1701
Postmenopausal Bleeding 1703
Postpartum Mastitis 1705
Pott's Disease 1709
Prostatectomy 1729
Prostatic Hypertrophy 1731
Prostatitis 1734
Psoriatic Arthritis 1740
Pterygium 1754
Pulmonary Edema 1756
Puncture Wound 1759
Pyelonephritis, Chronic 1764
Pyloric Stenosis, Acquired (Adult) Hypertrophic 1767
Pyloroplasty 1769
Pylorospasm 1770
Radial Keratotomy 1775
Radial Styloid Tenosynovitis 1776
Rectal Ulcer 1788
Reduction of Fracture or Dislocation 1791
Rehabilitation Therapy 1796
Renal Dialysis 1800
Renal Failure, Chronic 1804
Renal Vein Thrombosis 1807
Renovascular Hypertension 1809
Repair of Cerebral Aneurysm 1812
Repair, Anterior Cruciate Ligament 1814
Repair, Hammertoe 1816
Resection of Gastric or Duodenal Ulcer Site 1819
Retinal Detachment 1823, 1825
Retinal Detachment Repair 1825
Rheumatic Heart Disease, Chronic 1836
Rheumatoid Arthritis 1838
Rhinoplasty 1841
Rhinoscleroma 1842
Rib Resection 1844

Rotator Cuff Repair **1848**
Rotator Cuff Syndrome **1850**
Rotator Cuff Tear **1853**
Rupture of Spleen, Traumatic **1860**
Salivary Gland Stones **1865**
Salpingectomy **1868**
Salpingitis **1870**
Salpingo-oophorectomy **1873**
Scalenectomy **1877**
Sebaceous Cyst **1896**
Septoplasty **1909**
Shoulder Replacement **1917**
Skin Graft **1932**
Spermatocele **1942**
Spermatocelectomy **1943**
Spherocytosis, Hereditary **1944**
Spinal Cord Stimulation **1949**
Spinal Fusion **1951**
Spinal Stenosis **1952**
Splenomegaly **1956**
Spondylitis **1958**
Spondylolisthesis **1960**
Sprains and Strains, Ankle **1971**
Sprains and Strains, Cervical Spine (Neck) **1981**
Sprains and Strains, Elbow **1984**
Sprains and Strains, Foot **1986**
Sprains and Strains, Hand or Fingers **1989**
Sprains and Strains, Knee **1991**
Stokes-Adams Syndrome **2003**
Subarachnoid Hemorrhage (Non-traumatic) **2011**
Subarachnoid Hemorrhage (Traumatic) **2014**
Sympathectomy **2022**
Synovectomy **2027**
Synovial Cyst **2028**
Synovitis **2031**
Syringomyelia **2035**
Tarsal Tunnel Release **2041**
Tendon Release **2051**
Tendon Sheath Incision **2052**
Tenosynovitis **2057**
Thalassemia **2066**
Thoracentesis **2069**
Thoracic Aneurysm **2070**
Thoracic Disc Disorder with Myelopathy **2072**
Thoracic Outlet Syndrome **2074**
Thoracostomy **2078**
Thoracotomy **2079**
Thrombophlebitis **2086**
Thymectomy **2089**
Thyroidectomy **2090**
Tonsillectomy and Adenoidectomy **2102**
Tonsillitis and Adenoiditis **2104**
Tooth Extraction **2107**
Trabeculoplasty **2158**
Transurethral Balloon Dilation of Prostatic Urethra **2171**
Tubal Ligation **2193**
Tympanoplasty **2201**
Varicocele **2242**
Vena Cava Interruption **2251**
Vesicourethropexy **2265**
Wound Infection, Postoperative **2302**

Surgical
    Kidney Transplant **1261**
    Liposuction **1292**
    Nephropexy **1455**
    Thoracentesis **2069**
    Thoracotomy **2079**
    Valvuloplasty, Balloon **2240**
    Vasectomy **2248**
    Vena Cava Interruption **2251**

Surgical Commissurotomy
    Mitral Commissurotomy **1384**

Surgical Correction of Hernia
    Hernia Repair **1094, 1096**

Surgical Fixation of Kidney
    Nephropexy **1455**

Surgical Incision of Chest Wall
    Lung Biopsy **1310**
    Thoracentesis **2069**
    Thoracotomy **2079**

Surgical Removal
    Aneurysmectomy **138**
    Cataract Surgery **439**
    Hysterectomy **1186**
    Iridectomy **1238**
    Iridotomy **1239**
    Keratectomy, Laser Photorefractive **1256**
    Laryngectomy **1278**
    Lithotomy **1293–1294**
    Lung Excision **1314**
    Nephrotomy **1458**
    Pterygium **1754**
    Transurethral Resection of Prostate **2174**
    Tumor, Benign **2199**

Surgical Removal of Aneurysm
    Aneurysmectomy **138**

Surgical Removal of Cataract
    Cataract Surgery **439**

Surgical Removal of Gallstones
    Cholelithiasis **501**

Surgical Removal of Kidney
    Nephrectomy **1451**

Surgical Repair
    Arterial Graft **183**
    Cystocele or Rectocele **621**
    Excision, Fusion, and Repair of Toes **860**
    Fracture, Femoral Neck **912**
    Hernia Repair **1094, 1096**
    Incision and Drainage of Ischiorectal and/or Perirectal Abscess **1200**
    Laminectomy or Laminotomy **1273**
    Malunion and Nonunion of Fracture **1335**
    Meniscectomy and Meniscus Repair **1361**
    Mitral Commissurotomy **1384**
    Repair of Cerebral Aneurysm **1812**
    Repair, Anterior Cruciate Ligament **1814**
    Repair, Hammertoe **1816**
    Repair, Tendon Laceration of Hand **1817**
    Rotator Cuff Repair **1848**
    Tympanoplasty **2201**
    Valvotomy **2237**
    Vesicourethropexy **2265**

Suture
    of Skin and Subcutaneous Tissue **2020**
    Open Wound **1504, 1510, 1512**
    Open Wound, Back **1510**
    Open Wound, Chest **1512**
    Perineorrhaphy **1618**
    Puncture Wound **1759**

Swimmer's Ear
    Otitis Externa, Infective **1543**

Swollen Glands
    Lymphadenitis and Lymphadenopathy **1322**
    Tularemia **2197**

Swollen Lymph Glands
    Lymphadenitis and Lymphadenopathy 1322

Sylvest's Disease
    Pleurodynia 1661

Sympathalgia
    Complex Regional Pain Syndrome 550

Sympathetic Block
    Sympathectomy 2022

Sympathetic Dystrophy
    Complex Regional Pain Syndrome 550

Syncope
    Aortic Valve Stenosis 167
    Carotid Sinus Syncope 425
    Dizziness and Giddiness 742
    Vasovagal Syncope 2249

Syncope with Heart Block
    Atrioventricular Block Incomplete (Second-Degree) 223
    Atrioventricular Block, Complete (Third-Degree) 224
    Sick Sinus Syndrome 1920

Syndrome
    Acquired Immune Deficiency Syndrome 53
    Behçet's Syndrome 244
    Carpal Tunnel Syndrome 430
    Cauda Equina Syndrome 440
    Cervicobrachial Syndrome 474
    Compartment Syndrome 547
    Complex Regional Pain Syndrome 550
    Cushing's Syndrome 613
    Dry Eye Syndrome 745
    Dumping Syndrome 747
    Fibromyalgia and Myofascial Pain Syndrome 879
    Guillain-Barré Syndrome 1022
    Heart Block 1040
    Hyperventilation Syndrome 1161
    Impingement Syndrome 1194
    Malaise 1328
    Mallory-Weiss Syndrome 1333
    Myalgia and Myositis 1411
    Nephrotic Syndrome 1456
    Neuralgic Amyotrophy 1465
    Pain, Chronic 1564
    Polycystic Ovary Syndrome 1686
    Postconcussion Syndrome 1699
    Post-Laminectomy Syndrome 1701
    Premenstrual Syndrome 1724
    Reiter's Syndrome 1798
    Rotator Cuff Syndrome 1850
    Stokes-Adams Syndrome 2003
    Tarsal Tunnel Syndrome 2043
    Temporomandibular Joint Syndrome 2049
    Toxic Shock Syndrome 2152

Syngeneic Bone Marrow Transplant
    Bone Marrow Transplant 275

Synovectomy
    Rheumatoid Arthritis 1838
    Synovitis 2031

Synovial
    Cyst 2028
    Osteoarthritis 1530
    Rheumatoid Arthritis 1838
    Synovectomy 2027
    Synovitis 2031
    Tenosynovitis 2057

Synovitis
    Radial Styloid Tenosynovitis 1776

Synovitis 2031
Tenosynovitis 2057

Syphilis
    Chorioretinitis 506
    General Paresis 986

Syphilitic Meningoencephalitis
    General Paresis 986

Syringobulbia
    Syringomyelia 2035

Syringomyelia
    Curvature of the Spine, Acquired 610

Systemic Arthritis
    Rheumatoid Arthritis 1838

Systemic Inflammatory Response Syndrome
    Septic Shock 1907

Systemic Lupus Erythematosus
    Arthralgia 190
    Avascular Necrosis 235
    Lupus Erythematosus, Systemic 1317

Systemic Scleroderma
    Scleroderma 1892

Systemic Sclerosis
    Scleroderma 1892

Systemic Shunt
    Portal Systemic Shunt 1695

T

T Lymphocytes
    Acquired Immune Deficiency Syndrome 53

T&A
    Tonsillectomy and Adenoidectomy 2102

Tachycardia
    Abscess, Subdiaphragmatic 42
    Arrhythmia 178
    Cardiac Pacemaker Insertion 414
    Cocaine Dependence/Abuse 522
    Mitral Valve Prolapse 1389
    Myelophthisic Anemia 1422
    Neurocirculatory Asthenia 1467
    Palpitations 1566
    Panic Disorder 1578, 1580
    Panic Disorder with Agoraphobia 1580
    Paroxysmal Supraventricular 2039
    Pheochromocytoma 1638
    Phobias, Specific 1639
    Phobic Disorders 1641
    Pneumocystis Carinii Pneumonia 1663
    Porphyria 1693
    Renal Failure, Chronic 1804
    Renovascular Hypertension 1809
    Rheumatic Fever, Acute 1833
    Sepsis 1905
    Septic Shock 1907
    Thyroiditis 2091
    Ventricular Tachycardia 2260

TAH-BSO
    Hysterectomy 1186

Tail Bone Pain
    Coccygodynia 527

Tailbone Pain
    Coccygodynia 527

Talar Fracture
    Fracture, Talus 945
Talk Therapy
    Psychotherapy, Individual 1748
Talus
    Dislocation, Foot 716
    Fracture, Ankle 895
    Fracture, Talus 945
    Sprains and Strains, Ankle 1971
Tampons
    Toxic Shock Syndrome 2152
Tangential Ileostomy
    Colostomy and Ileostomy 543
Tapeworm Infection
    Echinococcosis 772
Tarsal Tunnel
    Release 2041
    Syndrome 2043
    Tendon Sheath Incision 2052
Tarsometatarsal Joint Dislocation
    Dislocation, Foot 716
TB
    Sick Sinus Syndrome 1920
    Tuberculosis, Respiratory 2194
TBI
    Brain Injury 292
Tear
    Anal Fissure and/or Rectal Ulcer 127
    Aortic Dissection 163
    Epicondylitis, Medial and Lateral 816
    Rotator Cuff Tear 1853
Tear Duct Obstruction
    Dacryocystitis 627
Tear Sac Infection
    Dacryocystitis 627
Tear Sac Inflammation
    Dacryocystitis 627
TEE
    Echocardiography 774
Temporary Colostomy
    Colostomy and Ileostomy 543
Temporary Gastrostomy
    Gastrostomy 984
Temporary Ileostomy
    Colostomy and Ileostomy 543
Temporary Loss of Consciousness
    Syncope 2024
    Vasovagal Syncope 2249
Temporary Pacemaker
    Cardiac Pacemaker Insertion 414
Temporomandibular Joint
    Arthroscopy 199
    Syndrome 2049
Temporomandibular Joint Syndrome
    Biofeedback 250
Tender points
    Fibromyalgia and Myofascial Pain Syndrome 879

Tendinitis
    Achilles Bursitis or Tendinitis 47
    Arthralgia 190
    Biceps Tendonitis 248
    Enthesopathy 812
    Tendonitis 2054
    Tenosynovitis 2057
Tendocalcaneal Bursitis
    Achilles Bursitis or Tendinitis 47
Tendon
    De Quervain's Release 630
    Dupuytren's Release 753
    Enthesopathy 812
    Epicondylitis, Medial and Lateral 816
    Fasciotomy 870
    Ganglionectomy (Wrist) 963
    Impingement Syndrome 1194
    Metatarsalgia 1376
    Radial Styloid Tenosynovitis 1776
    Release 2051
    Repair, Tendon Laceration of Hand 1817
    Sheath Incision 2052
    Sprains and Strains, Ankle 1971
    Sprains and Strains, Back 1975
    Sprains and Strains, Elbow 1984
    Synovial Cyst 2028
Tendon Release
    Tendon Sheath Incision 2052
Tendon Sheath Incision
    Tendon Release 2051
    Tenosynovitis 2057
Tendonitis
    Tenosynovitis 2057
Tendosynovitis
    Tenosynovitis 2057
Tennis Elbow
    Epicondylitis, Medial and Lateral 816
Tenosynovitis
    Arthralgia 190
    Radial Styloid Tenosynovitis 1776
    Tendon Sheath Incision 2052
TENS
    Transcutaneous Electrical Nerve Stimulation 2164
Tension
    Headache 2059
    Intermittent Explosive Disorder 1217
    Nervousness 1463
    Pneumothorax 1671
Tension Headache
    Biofeedback 250
    Headache 1033
Teratoma
    Pineal Gland Neoplasm 1647
Termination of Pregnancy
    Abortion by Dilation and Curettage for Termination of Pregnancy 11
    Abortion, Medical Induction 13
    Dilation and Curettage 699
Termination of Pregnancy by Abortion
    Abortion by Dilation and Curettage for Termination of Pregnancy 11
    Abortion, Medical Induction 13
    Aspiration Curettage of the Uterus 208

Tertian Malaria Plasmodium
    Malaria 1330

Testes
    Cancer, Testicle(s) 393
    Infertility, Male 1206
    Orchiectomy 1523
    Orchitis 1524

Testicle
    Cancer, Testicle(s) 393
    Epididymitis 819
    Orchiectomy 1523
    Orchitis 1524
    Varicocele 2242

Testicular
    Cancer, Testicle(s) 393
    Infertility, Male 1206
    Orchiectomy 1523
    Orchitis 1524

Testicular Choriocarcinoma
    Cancer, Testicle(s) 393

Testicular Embryonal Carcinoma
    Cancer, Testicle(s) 393

Testicular Inflammation
    Orchitis 1524

Testicular Seminoma
    Cancer, Testicle(s) 393

Testicular Yolk Sac Tumor
    Cancer, Testicle(s) 393

Testis
    Cancer, Testicle(s) 393
    Hydrocele 1136
    Orchiectomy 1523
    Orchitis 1524

Tetanus
    Puncture Wound 1759

Tetrachloroethylene Exposure
    Toxic Effects, Chlorinated Hydrocarbon Solvents 2120

Tetraodon Poisoning
    Toxic Effects, Fish and Shellfish 2126

Thalamic Ablation
    Thalamotomy 2064

Thalassemia
    Bone Marrow Transplant 275
    Hemolytic Anemia 1059

The Runs
    Diarrhea 696

Thenar Atrophy
    Carpal Tunnel Syndrome 430

Therapeutic
    Abortion, Medical Induction 13
    Excision of Lesion or Tissue of Skin and Subcutaneous Tissue 854
    Intravenous Therapy 1235
    Iontophoresis 1236
    Laryngoscopy 1281
    Transcutaneous Electrical Nerve Stimulation 2164
    Transfer of Nerve, Ulnar 2165
    Ultrasound, Therapeutic 2213

Therapeutic Abortion
    Abortion by Dilation and Curettage for Termination of Pregnancy 11
    Abortion, Medical Induction 13

    Aspiration Curettage of the Uterus 208

Therapeutic Exercise
    Physical Therapy 1643

Therapist-Guided Support Group
    Psychotherapy, Group 1747

Therapy
    Cognitive Therapy 530
    Electroconvulsive Therapy 782
    Intravenous Therapy 1235
    Occupational Therapy 1499
    Physical Therapy 1643
    Radiation Therapy 1778
    Rehabilitation Therapy 1796
    Root Canal Therapy 1847
    Vocational Therapy 2288

Thermic Fever
    Heat Stroke 1051

Thiamine
    Vitamin B_1 Deficiency 2272

Thiamine Poisoning
    Poisoning, Vitamin B 1679

Thigh
    Contusion, Lower Limb 566
    Groin Strain 1020

Third Degree
    Atrioventricular Block, Complete (Third-Degree) 224
    Sick Sinus Syndrome 1920
    Sprains and Strains, Ankle 1971
    Sprains and Strains, Elbow 1984
    Sprains and Strains, Foot 1986
    Sprains and Strains, Hand or Fingers 1989
    Sprains and Strains, Knee 1991
    Sprains and Strains, Wrist 1997

Third-Degree Atrioventricular Block
    Atrioventricular Block, Complete (Third-Degree) 224
    Sick Sinus Syndrome 1920

Third-Degree AV Block
    Atrioventricular Block, Complete (Third-Degree) 224
    Sick Sinus Syndrome 1920

Third-Degree Heart Block
    Atrioventricular Block, Complete (Third-Degree) 224

Thoracalgia
    Thoracic Spine Pain 2076

Thoracentesis
    Aspiration 207–208
    Empyema 794
    Hemothorax, Traumatic 1075
    Histoplasmosis 1121
    Pleurisy 1659

Thoracic
    Aneurysm 2070
    Degeneration, Thoracic or Thoracolumbar Intervertebral Disc 640
    Displacement, Thoracic Intervertebral Disc Without Myelopathy 735
    Fracture, Thoracic Spine (With or Without Spinal Cord Injury) 948
    Intervertebral Disc Disorders 1221
    Outlet Syndrome 2074
    Spinal Cord Injury 1946
    Spine Pain 2076

Thoracic Actinomycosis
    Actinomycosis 57

Thoracic Aneurysm
    Aneurysmectomy 138

Thoracic Aortic Aneurysm
  Aortic Aneurysm 160
  Thoracic Aneurysm 2070

Thoracic Arch Aneurysm
  Thoracic Aneurysm 2070

Thoracic Compression Syndrome
  Thoracic Outlet Syndrome 2074

Thoracic Disc
  Degeneration, Thoracic or Thoracolumbar Intervertebral Disc 640
  Disorder with Myelopathy 2072
  Displacement, Thoracic Intervertebral Disc Without Myelopathy 735
  Intervertebral Disc Disorders 1221
  Thoracic Disc Disorder with Myelopathy 2072

Thoracic Disc Herniation
  Displacement, Thoracic Intervertebral Disc Without Myelopathy 735

Thoracic Disc Prolapse
  Displacement, Thoracic Intervertebral Disc Without Myelopathy 735

Thoracic Intervertebral Disc
  Degeneration, Thoracic or Thoracolumbar Intervertebral Disc 640
  Displacement, Thoracic Intervertebral Disc Without Myelopathy 735
  Intervertebral Disc Disorders 1221

Thoracic Intervertebral Disc Disease
  Degeneration, Thoracic or Thoracolumbar Intervertebral Disc 640

Thoracic Intervertebral Disc Without Myelopathy
  Displacement, Thoracic Intervertebral Disc Without Myelopathy 735

Thoracic Nonsyphilitic Aneurysm
  Thoracic Aneurysm 2070

Thoracic Outlet Compression Syndrome
  Thoracic Outlet Syndrome 2074

Thoracic Outlet Syndrome
  Scalenectomy 1877

Thoracic Outlet Syndrome Surgery
  Scalenectomy 1877

Thoracic Spinal Cord Compression
  Thoracic Disc Disorder with Myelopathy 2072

Thoracic Spine
  Curvature of the Spine, Acquired 610
  Pain 2076

Thoracic Spine Fracture
  Fracture, Thoracic Spine (With or Without Spinal Cord Injury) 948

Thoracic Spine Injury
  Displacement, Thoracic Intervertebral Disc Without Myelopathy 735
  Fracture, Thoracic Spine (With or Without Spinal Cord Injury) 948
  Thoracic Spine Pain 2076

Thoracic Sprain
  Sprains and Strains, Back 1975

Thoracic Sympathectomy
  Sympathectomy 2022

Thoracocentesis
  Thoracentesis 2069

Thoracolumbar
  Fracture, Thoracic Spine (With or Without Spinal Cord Injury) 948
  Spinal Fusion 1951

Thoracolumbar Fracture
  Fracture, Vertebra 954, 956

Thoracolumbar Intervertebral Disc
  Displacement, Thoracic Intervertebral Disc Without Myelopathy 735
  Intervertebral Disc Disorders 1221

Thoracolumbar Intervertebral Disc Degeneration
  Degeneration, Thoracic or Thoracolumbar Intervertebral Disc 640

Thoracolumbar Spine
  Degeneration, Thoracic or Thoracolumbar Intervertebral Disc 640
  Displacement, Thoracic Intervertebral Disc Without Myelopathy 735
  Spinal Fusion 1951

Thoracoscopic Biopsy
  Pleural Biopsy 1657

Thoracoscopic Sympathectomy
  Sympathectomy 2022

Thoracostomy
  Empyema 794
  Pneumothorax 1671

Thoracotomy
  Coin Lesion 532
  Hemoptysis 1067
  Hemothorax, Traumatic 1075
  Thoracentesis 2069

THR
  Arthritis, Infectious 192
  Hip Replacement, Total 1119
  Osteoarthritis 1530
  Sjogren's Syndrome 1930

Threatened or Missed Abortion
  Abortion 2080
  Hydatidiform Mole 1134

Threatened Premature Labor
  Premature Labor 1720

Three-day Measles
  Rubella 1856

Throat
  Abscess, Larynx 25
  Abscess, Peritonsillar 36
  Cancer, Esophagus 356
  Cancer, Oropharynx 369
  Epiglottitis 822
  Esophageal Diverticula 836
  Esophageal Spasm 839
  Esophageal Strictures 840
  Esophageal Varices 843
  Esophagectomy 845
  Esophagitis 847
  Gastroesophageal Reflux 979
  Laryngectomy 1278
  Myasthenia Gravis 1414
  Pharyngitis, Acute 1633
  Rabies 1773
  Strep Throat 2005

Throat Cancer
  Cancer, Oropharynx 369
  Laryngectomy 1278

Throat Infection
  Pharyngitis, Acute 1633
  Strep Throat 2005

Thrombectomy
  Peripheral Vascular Disease 1626
  Renal Vein Thrombosis 1807
  Thrombophlebitis 2086

Thromboclasis
  Coronary Thrombolysis 593

Thrombocytopenia
  Bone Marrow Biopsy 273

Colorado Tick Fever 541

Thrombocytopenic Purpura
Idiopathic Thrombocytopenic Purpura 1189

Thromboembolism
Arterial Embolism and Thrombosis 180
Embolism, Pulmonary 789

Thromboendarterectomy
Thrombectomy 2082

Thrombolysis
Cardiogenic Shock 417
Coronary Thrombolysis 593
Myocardial Infarction, Acute 1424
Peripheral Vascular Disease 1626

Thrombopenia
Thrombocytopenia 2083

Thrombophlebitis
Venous Embolism and Thrombosis 2252

Thrombosis
Arterial Embolism and Thrombosis 180
Arteriovenous Aneurysm 188
Polycythemia Vera 1689
Renal Vein Thrombosis 1807
Retinal Vascular Occlusion 1827
Venous Embolism and Thrombosis 2252

Thrombus
Arterial Embolism and Thrombosis 180
Carotid Artery Occlusion 423
Cerebral Hemorrhage 449
Cerebrovascular Accident 454
Coronary Arteriography 586
Coronary Thrombolysis 593
Embolectomy 786–787
Embolectomy, Pulmonary 787
Thrombectomy 2082
Thrombophlebitis 2086

Thrush
Acquired Immune Deficiency Syndrome 53
Candidiasis 405

Thumb
Amputation, Finger or Thumb 123
De Quervain's Release 630
Fracture, Fingers and Thumb 915
Radial Styloid Tenosynovitis 1776
Sprains and Strains, Hand or Fingers 1989
Trigger Finger or Thumb 2191

Thymus Gland
Myasthenia Gravis 1414
Thymectomy 2089

Thyroadenitis
Thyroiditis 2091

Thyroid
Cancer, Thyroid Gland 396
Cardiomyopathy 419
Thyroidectomy 2090
Goiter 1008
Hyperparathyroidism 1148
Hyperthyroidism 1159
Hypothyroidism 1180
Thyroiditis 2091

Thyroid Gland Enlargement
Goiter 1008

Thyroid Insufficiency
Hypothyroidism 1180

Thyroidectomy
Cancer, Thyroid Gland 396
Goiter 1008

Thyroiditis
Hyperthyroidism 1159

Thyrotoxicosis
Goiter 1008
Gynecomastia 1025

TIA
Endarterectomy 801
Transient Ischemic Attack 2169

Tibia
Fracture, Ankle 895

Tibia-Femur Dislocation
Dislocation, Femorotibial (Knee) Joint 713

Tibial Nerve Compression
Tarsal Tunnel Syndrome 2043

Tic Disorder
Tics 2093

Tic Douloureux
Trigeminal Neuralgia 2187

Tick Diseases
Colorado Tick Fever 541
Encephalitis 797
Insect or Spider Bites and Stings 1210
Lyme Disease 1319
Rocky Mountain Spotted Fever 1845
Tularemia 2197
Typhus Fever 2206

Tick Fever
Rocky Mountain Spotted Fever 1845
Tularemia 2197

Tick Typhus
Rocky Mountain Spotted Fever 1845

Tied Tubes
Tubal Ligation 2193

Tietze's Syndrome
Costochondritis 595

Timorean Filariasis
Filariasis 881

Tinea Pedis
Erysipelas 830
Tinea 2095

Tinnitus
Barotitis Media 241
Meniere's Disease 1353

Tinnitus Aurium
Tinnitus 2097

TIPS
Portal Systemic Shunt 1695

Tissue
Biopsy 252
Infection 1202

Tissue Death
Arteriosclerotic Gangrene 186
Diabetic Gangrene 689
Embolectomy 786–787

Gangrene 964

Tissue Necrosis
Gangrene 964

Tissue Sample
Biopsy 252

Tissue Sampling
Biopsy 252
Breast Biopsy 295
Bronchoscopic Biopsy 304
Cervical Conization 463
Cystoscopy, Transurethral 624
Esophagogastroduodenoscopy 850

TJR
Hip Replacement, Total 1119

TKR
Knee Replacement, Total 1263

TMJ
Biofeedback 250
Temporomandibular Joint Syndrome 2049

Toadstool Poisoning
Toxic Effects, Mushrooms 2143

Tobacco Addiction
Nicotine Dependence 1479

Toe
Amputation 116, 118, 121, 123
Bunion 312
Bunionectomy 314
Excision, Fusion, and Repair of Toes 860
Fracture, Forefoot (Sesamoid, Phalanges) 918
Hammertoe 1029
Nail, Ingrown 2100
Raynaud's Phenomenon 1781
Repair, Hammertoe 1816

Toes
Corn and Callus, Infected 578
Excision of Morton's Neuroma 855
Excision of Nail, Nail Bed, or Nail Fold 856
Excision, Fusion, and Repair of Toes 860

Tomography
X-ray 2305

Tongue
Cancer, Tongue 399
Ludwig's Angina 1306
Pernicious Anemia 1630

Tonic-Clonic Convulsion
Grand Mal Seizure 1014

Tonic-Clonic Seizure
Grand Mal Seizure 1014
Jacksonian Seizure 1247
Seizures 1900

Tonsil
Abscess, Peritonsillar 36
Pharyngitis, Acute 1633
Tonsillectomy and Adenoidectomy 2102
Tonsilitis and Adenoiditis 2104

Tonsil Removal
Tonsillectomy and Adenoidectomy 2102

Tonsillar Hypertrophy
Tonsillitis and Adenoiditis 2104

Tonsillectomy
Abscess, Peritonsillar 36
and Adenoidectomy 2102
Tonsillitis and Adenoiditis 2104

Tonsillitis
Abscess, Peritonsillar 36
and Adenoiditis 2104
Pharyngitis, Acute 1633
Tonsillectomy and Adenoidectomy 2102

Tooth
Dental Disorders 657
Dentoalveolar Abscess 660
Extraction 2107
Gingival Abscess 991
Impacted Tooth 1191
Periodontitis 1619
Root Canal Therapy 1847

Tooth Decay
Dental Disorders 657

Tooth Removal
Tooth Extraction 2107

TOP
Abortion by Dilation and Curettage for Termination of Pregnancy 11

Torn Knee Cartilage
Meniscus Disorders, Knee 1364

Torsade De Pointes
Ventricular Tachycardia 2260

Torsion
Orchiectomy 1523
Volvulus 2289

Torula
Cryptococcosis 608

Torulosis
Cryptococcosis 608

Total
Cystectomy 615
Knee Replacement, Total 1263
Lung Excision 1314
Pneumonectomy 1664

Total Abdominal Hysterectomy
Hysterectomy 1186

Total Allergy Syndrome
Allergy 100
Multiple Chemical Sensitivity Syndrome 1397

Total Excision
Cystectomy 615
Esophagectomy 845
Gastrectomy 968
Pancreatectomy 1568
Pneumonectomy 1664

Total Hip Replacement
Fracture, Femoral Neck 912
Hip Replacement, Total 1119

Total Immune Disorder Syndrome
Multiple Chemical Sensitivity Syndrome 1397

Total Iridectomy
Iridectomy 1238

Total Joint Arthroplasty
Hip Replacement, Total 1119

Total Knee Replacement
Knee Replacement, Total 1263

Total Lobectomy
    Lung Excision 1314
Total Pancreatectomy
    Pancreatectomy 1568
Total Replacement
    Arthroplasty, Elbow 197
    Knee Replacement, Total 1263
Total Thyroidectomy
    Thyroidectomy 2090
Total Urinary Incontinence
    Urinary Incontinence in Women 2222
Toxemia of Pregnancy
    Cesarean Delivery 476
    Preeclampsia and Eclampsia 1711
Toxic
    Shock Syndrome 2152
Toxic Effects
    Arsenic and Compounds 2110
    Beryllium 2112
    Cadmium 2114
    Carbon Monoxide 2117
    Chlorine 2122
    Chromium 2124
    Formaldehyde 2129
    Hydrochloric Acid 2131
    Hydrofluoric Acid 2132
    Insect or Spider Bites and Stings 1210
    Lead (Inorganic Compounds) 2136
    Mercury 2138
    Methyl Bromide 2142
    Nickel and Inorganic Compounds 2146
    Organophosphate and Carbamate Pesticides 2147
    Plants (genus Toxicodendron) 2150
    Poisoning, Iron 1677
    Poisoning, Vitamin B 1679
Toxic Effects of a Substance
    Poisoning 1675, 1677, 1679, 1681
Toxic Effects of Cobalt
    Toxic Effects, Nickel and Inorganic Compounds 2146
Toxic Effects of Insecticides
    Toxic Effects, Organophosphate and Carbamate Pesticides 2147
Toxic Effects of Mercury
    Toxic Effects, Mercury 2138
Toxic Epidermal Necrolysis
    Erythema Multiforme 833
Toxic Goiter
    Goiter 1008
Toxic Megacolon
    Ulcerative Colitis 2209
Toxic Optic Neuropathy
    Amblyopia, Toxic 107
Toxic Shock Syndrome
    Shock 1915
Toxicity
    Allergy 100
    Anaphylactic Shock, Food Reaction 131
    Hypervitaminosis 1164, 1166, 1168
    Hypervitaminosis A 1166
    Hypervitaminosis D 1168
    Toxic Effects, Beryllium 2112
    Toxic Effects, Carbon Disulfide 2116

Toxic Effects, Chlorinated Hydrocarbon Solvents 2120
Toxic Effects, Chromium 2124
Toxic Effects, Hydrochloric Acid 2131
Toxic Effects, Hydrofluoric Acid 2132
Toxic Effects, Lead (Inorganic Compounds) 2136
Toxo
    Toxoplasmosis 2154
Trabeculectomy Ab Externo
    Trabeculectomy 2156
Trach
    Tracheostomy 2159
Trachea
    Abscess, Larynx 25
    Cancer, Lung 363
    Chest Pain 486
    Epiglottitis 822
    Laryngoscopy 1281
    Tracheostomy 2159
Tracheoscopy
    Endoscopy of Gastrointestinal Tract 810
Tracheostomy
    Anaphylactic Shock 129, 131
    Epiglottitis 822
    Polio 1683
    Tetanus 2060
Tracheotomy
    Tracheostomy 2159
Traction
    Reduction of Fracture or Dislocation 1791
Traction Diverticulum
    Esophageal Diverticula 836
Tranquilizer Dependence
    Sedative, Hypnotic or Anxiolytic Dependence 1898
Transcutaneous Electrical Nerve Stimulator
    Transcutaneous Electrical Nerve Stimulation 2164
    Ultrasound, Therapeutic 2213
Transdermal Iontophoresis
    Iontophoresis 1236
Trans-Esophageal Echocardiogram
    Echocardiography 774
Transfusion of Blood
    and Blood Components 2167
    Rh Incompatibility 1831
Transfusion of Blood Components
    Transfusion of Blood and Blood Components 2167
Transient Cerebral Ischemia
    Transient Ischemic Attack 2169
Transient Ischemic Attack
    Cerebrovascular Accident 454
    Cerebrovascular Disease 458
    Endarterectomy 801
Transient Loss of Consciousness
    Syncope 2024
Transient Tic Disorder
    Tics 2093
Transluminal Coronary Angioplasty
    Coronary Balloon Angioplasty 590
Transplant
    Adrenal Tissue Implant or Transplant to Brain 76

  Bone Graft **272**
  Bone Marrow Transplant **275**
  Cancer, Liver **360**
  Cirrhosis of the Liver **515**
  Corneal Transplant **582**
  Heart Failure, Congestive **1042**
  Hepatic Coma **1079**
  Hepatitis B **1083**
  Hepatitis C **1085**
  Hepatitis, Alcoholic **1087**
  Kidney Transplant **1261**
  Renal Failure, Chronic **1804**

Transurethral
  Balloon Dilation of Prostatic Urethra **2171**
  Cystoscopy, Transurethral **624**
  Incision of Bladder Neck **2172**
  Lithotomy **1293–1294**
  Removal of Obstruction from Ureter **2173**

Transurethral Balloon Dilation of Urethra
  Transurethral Balloon Dilation of Prostatic Urethra **2171**

Transurethral Cystoscopy
  Cystoscopy, Transurethral **624**

Transurethral Incision
  of Bladder Neck **2172**

Transurethral Removal of Obstruction
  from Ureter **2173**

Transurethral Resection of Prostate
  Cancer, Prostate **380**
  Prostatic Hypertrophy **1731**

Transurethral Ureteropyeloscopy
  Transurethral Removal of Obstruction from Ureter **2173**

Transvaginal Enterocele Repair
  Hernia Repair, Vaginal **1096**

Transvenous Pacemaker
  Cardiac Pacemaker Insertion **414**

Transverse Colectomy
  Colon Resection **538**

Transverse Volvulus
  Volvulus **2289**

Transverse Wrist Fracture
  Fracture, Radius and Ulna, Distal **933**

Trauma
  Adhesive Capsulitis of Shoulder **66**
  Amputation **116, 118, 121, 123**
  Amputation (Traumatic), Foot **118**
  Amputation (Traumatic), Lower Extremity **121**
  Anorectal Fistula **154**
  Aortic Aneurysm **160**
  Aortic Valve Stenosis **167**
  Arterial Embolism and Thrombosis **180**
  Avascular Necrosis **235**
  Brachial Neuropathy **287**
  Brain Injury **292**
  Cellulitis **443**
  Cerebral Hemorrhage **449**
  Coma **544**
  Computerized Axial Tomography **552**
  Contusion, Eye **564**
  Contusion, Lower Limb **566**
  Contusion, Trunk **568**
  Contusion, Upper Limb **571**
  Corneal Abrasion **580**
  Crush Wounds **603**
  Degeneration, Thoracic or Thoracolumbar Intervertebral Disc **640**

  Depersonalization Disorder **663**
  Displacement, Lumbar Intervertebral Disc Without Myelopathy **732**
  Dissociative Personality Disorder **737**
  Electroencephalogram **783**
  Esophagectomy **845**
  Fracture, Calcaneus **898**
  Fracture, Carpal Bones **901**
  Fracture, Cervical Spine (With or Without Spinal Cord Injury) **904**
  Fracture, Clavicle **907**
  Fracture, Elbow (Distal Humerus) **910**
  Fracture, Femoral Neck **912**
  Fracture, Fingers and Thumb **915**
  Fracture, Forefoot (Sesamoid, Phalanges) **918**
  Fracture, Metacarpal Bones **922**
  Fracture, Metatarsal Bones **925**
  Fracture, Midfoot (Cuboid, Cuneiform, Navicular) **928**
  Fracture, Pelvis **930**
  Fracture, Radius and Ulna, Distal **933**
  Fracture, Rib **936**
  Fracture, Sacrum **939**
  Fracture, Sternum (Closed) **943**
  Fracture, Thoracic Spine (With or Without Spinal Cord Injury) **948**
  Fracture, Tibia or Fibula **951**
  Fracture, Vertebra **954, 956**
  Fracture, Vertebra (Pathological) **956**
  Frostbite **959**
  Gangrene **964**
  Gas Gangrene **967**
  Gastritis **970**
  Hearing Loss **1036**
  Hematuria **1055**
  Hemorrhage of Rectum and Anus **1068**
  Hemothorax, Traumatic **1075**
  Hyperbaric Oxygenation **1141**
  Hypotension **1178**
  Hypovolemic Shock **1184**
  Intervertebral Disc Disorders **1221**
  Intracranial Hemorrhage **1226, 1230**
  Intracranial Hemorrhage, Closed **1230**
  Lacerations **1269**
  Low Back Pain **1302**
  Ludwig's Angina **1306**
  Meniscus Disorders, Knee **1364**
  Myalgia and Myositis **1411**
  Myelopathy **1420**
  Nasal Septum Perforation **1443**
  Nasogastric Intubation **1444**
  Neck Pain **1448**
  Neuralgia, Neuritis, and Radiculitis **1465**
  Neuralgic Amyotrophy **1465**
  Neurogenic Bladder **1471**
  Nosebleed **1485**
  Nystagmus **1487**
  Open Wound **1504, 1510, 1512**
  Open Wound, Back **1510**
  Open Wound, Chest **1512**
  Osteoma **1536**
  Osteomyelitis **1537**
  Pain in Limb **1562**
  Paralysis, Paraplegia, and Quadriplegia **1583**
  Patella Chondromalacia **1599**
  Pericarditis, Acute **1615**
  Pneumothorax **1671**
  Postconcussion Syndrome **1699**
  Renal Failure, Acute **1802**
  Renal Vein Thrombosis **1807**
  Renovascular Hypertension **1809**
  Repair, Tendon Laceration of Hand **1817**
  Respiratory Failure **1821**
  Retinal Detachment **1823, 1825**
  Rupture of Spleen, Traumatic **1860**

Sepsis 1905
Septic Shock 1907
Shock 1915
Spinal Cord Injury 1946
Splenectomy 1955
Sprains and Strains, Ankle 1971
Sprains and Strains, Back 1975
Sprains and Strains, Cervical Spine (Neck) 1981
Sprains and Strains, Elbow 1984
Sprains and Strains, Foot 1986
Sprains and Strains, Hand or Fingers 1989
Sprains and Strains, Knee 1991
Subarachnoid Hemorrhage (Traumatic) 2014
Synovitis 2031
Thoracic Aneurysm 2070
Thoracic Spine Pain 2076
Thrombophlebitis 2086
Tympanum Perforation 2202

Traumatic
- Amputation (Traumatic), Foot 118
- Amputation (Traumatic), Lower Extremity 121
- Pneumothorax 1671
- Posttraumatic Stress Disorder 1707
- Rupture of Spleen, Traumatic 1860
- Splenectomy 1955
- Subarachnoid Hemorrhage (Traumatic) 2014

Traumatic Brain Injury
- Brain Injury 292
- Enterostomy 811
- Grand Mal Seizure 1014
- Intracranial Hemorrhage, Closed 1230

Traumatic Injury
- Amputation, Finger or Thumb 123
- Amputation (Traumatic), Foot 118
- Amputation (Traumatic), Lower Extremity 121
- Brain Injury 292
- Dislocation 705, 708, 711, 713, 716, 723, 726
- Dislocation, Acromioclavicular Joint 708
- Dislocation, Femorotibial (Knee) Joint 713
- Dislocation, Foot 716
- Dislocation, Patella (Kneecap) 723
- Dislocation, Sternclavicular Joint 726
- Hemothorax, Traumatic 1075
- Lacerations 1269
- Pneumothorax 1671
- Rupture of Spleen, Traumatic 1860
- Subarachnoid Hemorrhage (Traumatic) 2014
- Trauma 2175

Traveler's Diarrhea
- Dysentery 755
- E. Coli 767
- Gastroenteritis, Infectious 973
- Giardiasis 989
- Shigellosis 1910
- Traveler's Diarrhea 2177

Treatment Procedure
- Abdominoperineal Resection of Rectum 10
- Abortion by Dilation and Curettage for Termination of Pregnancy 11
- Abortion, Medical Induction 13
- Adrenal Tissue Implant or Transplant to Brain 76
- Adrenalectomy 77
- Alcohol and Drug Detoxification and Rehabilitation 84
- Amputation 116, 118, 121, 123
- Amputation, Finger or Thumb 123
- Aneurysmectomy 138
- Angiocardiography 148
- Appendectomy 174
- Arterial Graft 183
- Arteriography 185
- Arthrodesis 194
- Arthrography 196
- Arthroplasty, Elbow 197
- Arthroscopy 199
- Aspiration Curettage of the Uterus 208
- Biofeedback 250
- Bone Graft 272
- Bone Marrow Biopsy 273
- Bone Marrow Transplant 275
- Bone Scan 277
- Breast Biopsy 295
- Bunionectomy 314
- Cardiac Catheterization 411
- Cardiac Pacemaker Insertion 414
- Carpal Tunnel Release 428
- Cataract Surgery 439
- Celiac Plexus Block 442
- Cervical Biopsy 460
- Cervical Cauterization 461
- Cervical Conization 463
- Cervical Polypectomy 469
- Cesarean Delivery 476
- Chemonucleolysis of Intervetebral Disc 482
- Chemotherapy 485
- Cholangiography 493
- Cholecystectomy 495
- Cholecystography 500
- Circumcision 514
- Cognitive Therapy 530
- Colon Resection 538
- Colonoscopy 540
- Colostomy and Ileostomy 543
- Corneal Transplant 582
- Coronary Arteriography 586
- Coronary Balloon Angioplasty 590
- Coronary Bypass 592
- Coronary Thrombolysis 593
- Craniectomy 596
- Craniotomy 598
- Cryotherapy, Genital Warts (Female) 605
- Cryotherapy, Genital Warts (Male) 606
- Culdoscopy 610
- Cystectomy 615
- Cystoscopy, Transurethral 624
- Cystourethroplasty of Bladder Neck 625
- De Quervain's Release 630
- Dilation and Curettage 699
- Dilation of Esophagus 700
- Discectomy 703
- Dupuytren's Release 753
- Electroconvulsive Therapy 782
- Embolectomy 786–787
- Embolectomy, Pulmonary 787
- Endarterectomy 801
- Enterostomy 811
- Esophagectomy 845
- Esophagogastroduodenoscopy 850
- Excision of Bone Spur, Foot 852
- Excision of Lesion or Tissue of Skin and Subcutaneous Tissue 854
- Excision of Morton's Neuroma 855
- Excision of Nail, Nail Bed, or Nail Fold 856
- Excision or Destruction of Duodenal Lesion 857
- Excision or Destruction of Plantar Warts 858
- Excision, Fusion, and Repair of Toes 860
- Fasciotomy 870
- Fissurectomy, Anal 884
- Ganglionectomy (Wrist) 963
- Gastrectomy 968
- Gastroenterostomy 978
- Gastrostomy 984

Gingivectomy 992
Heart Valve Replacement 1047
Hemorrhoid Treatment 1070
Hernia Repair 1094, 1096
Hernia Repair, Vaginal 1096
Hysterectomy 1186
Incision and Drainage of Ischiorectal and/or Perirectal Abscess 1200
Incision of Skin and Subcutaneous Tissue, Drainage of Abscess or Cyst 1201
Insertion of Inflatable Penile Prosthesis 1213
Iontophoresis 1236
Iridectomy 1238
Kidney Transplant 1261
Knee Replacement, Total 1263
Laminectomy or Laminotomy 1273
Laparoscopy 1275
Laparotomy 1276
Laryngectomy 1278
Laryngoscopy 1281
Ligation and Stripping of Varicose Veins 1287
Ligation of Esophageal Varices 1288
Ligation of Spermatic Vein for Varicocele 1289
Liposuction 1292
Lithotomy 1293–1294
Lithotomy, Percutaneous 1294
Lithotripsy, Extracorporeal Shock Wave 1295
Lumbar Puncture 1309
Lung Excision 1314
Mammoplasty, Augmentation 1338
Marshall-Marchetti Operation 1344
Mastectomy 1345
Mastoidectomy 1347
Meniscectomy and Meniscus Repair 1361
Myelography 1419
Myocardial Perfusion Scan 1427
Myomectomy, Uterine 1430
Myotomy of Esophagus 1433
Myringotomy 1434
Nasal Polypectomy 1440
Nasogastric Intubation 1444
Nephrectomy 1451
Nephropexy 1455
Nephrotomy 1458
Occupational Therapy 1499
Oophorectomy 1501, 1503
Open-Chest Cardiac Massage 1514
Orchiectomy 1523
Ovarian Cyst, Resection of 1555
Pancreatectomy 1568
Pancreaticoduodenectomy 1571
Paracentesis 1582
Pericardiectomy 1614
Perineorrhaphy 1618
Physical Therapy 1643
Pleural Biopsy 1657
Pneumonectomy 1664
Portal Systemic Shunt 1695
Prostatectomy 1729
Psychoanalysis 1742
Psychopharmacotherapy 1743
Psychotherapy, Group 1747
Psychotherapy, Individual 1748
Pulmonary Function Tests 1758
Pyloroplasty 1769
Radial Keratotomy 1775
Radiation Therapy 1778
Reduction Mammoplasty 1790
Reduction of Fracture or Dislocation 1791
Rehabilitation Therapy 1796
Renal Dialysis 1800
Repair of Cerebral Aneurysm 1812
Repair, Anterior Cruciate Ligament 1814
Repair, Hammertoe 1816
Repair, Tendon Laceration of Hand 1817
Resection of Gastric or Duodenal Ulcer Site 1819
Retinal Detachment Repair 1825
Rhinoplasty 1841
Rib Resection 1844
Root Canal Therapy 1847
Rotator Cuff Repair 1848
Salpingectomy 1868
Salpingo-oophorectomy 1873
Scalenectomy 1877
Sclerotherapy 1895
Septoplasty 1909
Shoulder Replacement 1917
Sigmoidoscopy 1925
Skin Graft 1932
Skin or Subcutaneous Tissue Biopsy 1934
Spermatocelectomy 1943
Spinal Cord Stimulation 1949
Spinal Fusion 1951
Splenectomy 1955
Stapedectomy 2002
Suture of Skin and Subcutaneous Tissue 2020
Sympathectomy 2022
Synovectomy 2027
Tarsal Tunnel Release 2041
Tendon Release 2051
Tendon Sheath Incision 2052
Thalamotomy 2064
Thoracentesis 2069
Thoracostomy 2078
Thoracotomy 2079
Thrombectomy 2082
Thymectomy 2089
Thyroidectomy 2090
Tonsillectomy and Adenoidectomy 2102
Tooth Extraction 2107
Trabeculectomy 2156
Trabeculoplasty 2158
Tracheostomy 2159
Traction 2163
Transcutaneous Electrical Nerve Stimulation 2164
Transfusion of Blood and Blood Components 2167
Transurethral Balloon Dilation of Prostatic Urethra 2171
Transurethral Incision of Bladder Neck 2172
Transurethral Removal of Obstruction from Ureter 2173
Tympanoplasty 2201
Ultrasound, Diagnostic 2212
Ultrasound, Therapeutic 2213
Upper Gastrointestinal Series 2214
Urethral Catheterization 2216
Vagotomy 2235
Valvotomy 2237
Valvuloplasty, Balloon 2240
Vasectomy 2248
Vena Cava Interruption 2251
Vesicourethropexy 2265
Vocational Therapy 2288
X-ray 2305

Tremor
    Addictions, Mixed 60
    Adrenal Tissue Implant or Transplant to Brain 76
    Alcoholism 90
    Cerebral Palsy 452
    Electroencephalogram 783
    Encephalitis 797
    General Paresis 986
    Hepatic Coma 1079
    Marijuana Dependence/Abuse 1341
    Myalgia and Myositis 1411
    Nervousness 1463

    Organic Psychosis 1526
    Parkinson's Disease 1593
    Rabies 1773
    Sedative, Hypnotic or Anxiolytic Dependence 1898
    St. Louis Encephalitis 2000
    Syphilis 2033
    Thalamotomy 2064

Trichinella Spiralis Infestation
    Trichinosis 2183

Trichinelliasis
    Trichinosis 2183

Trichinellosis
    Trichinosis 2183

Trichiniasis
    Trichinosis 2183

Trichloroethylene Poisoning
    Toxic Effects, Chlorinated Hydrocarbon Solvents 2120

Trichomoniasis
    Vaginitis 2233

Trichophytosis
    Tinea 2095

Tricuspid Valve Replacement
    Heart Valve Replacement 1047

Trifacial Neuralgia
    Trigeminal Neuralgia 2187

Trigeminal Neuralgia
    Craniotomy 598

Trigger Finger
    or Thumb 2191
    Tendon Release 2051
    Tendon Sheath Incision 2052

Trimalleolar Fracture
    Fracture, Ankle 895

Triplets
    Pregnancy, Multiple Gestation 1714

Trophoblastic Tumor
    Choriocarcinoma 505

Truncal Vagotomy
    Vagotomy 2235

Trunk Injury
    Contusion, Trunk 568

TSS
    Toxic Shock Syndrome 2152

Tsutsugamushi Disease
    Typhus Fever 2206

Tubal
    Ectopic Pregnancy 775
    Hematosalpinx 1053
    Ligation 2193
    Pelvic Inflammatory Disease 1604
    Salpingectomy 1868
    Salpingitis 1870

Tubal Occlusion
    Tubal Ligation 2193

Tubal Pregnancy
    Ectopic Pregnancy 775
    Laparoscopy 1275

Tubal Sterilization
    Tubal Ligation 2193

TUBD
    Transurethral Balloon Dilation of Prostatic Urethra 2171

Tube Feeding
    Enterostomy 811
    Nasogastric Intubation 1444

Tube Ileostomy
    Colostomy and Ileostomy 543

Tube Placement
    Myringotomy 1434

Tuberculosis
    Ascites 203
    Bronchiectasis 297
    Chorioretinitis 506
    Coin Lesion 532
    Hemoptysis 1067
    Pott's Disease 1709
    Respiratory 2194

Tuberculosis of the Spine
    Pott's Disease 1709

Tuberculosis Pericarditis
    Pericarditis, Acute 1615

Tuberculous Spondylitis
    Pott's Disease 1709

Tubes Tied
    Tubal Ligation 2193

Tubo-Ovarian Abscess
    Salpingitis 1870

Tubo-Ovarian Inflammatory Disease
    Salpingitis 1870

Tumescent Liposuction
    Liposuction 1292

Tumor of Adrenal Medulla
    Pheochromocytoma 1638

Tumor of Epididymis
    Cancer, Testicle(s) 393
    Orchiectomy 1523

Tumor of the Adrenal Medulla
    Pheochromocytoma 1638

Tumor of Uterus
    Cancer, Uterus 402
    Choriocarcinoma 505
    Fibroid Tumor of Uterus 875
    Hydatidiform Mole 1134
    Hysterectomy 1186
    Myomectomy, Uterine 1430
    Uterine Polyps 2228

Tunnel Release
    Carpal Tunnel Release 428
    Tarsal Tunnel Release 2041

Tunnel Syndrome
    Carpal Tunnel Syndrome 430
    Tarsal Tunnel Syndrome 2043

Turista
    Traveler's Diarrhea 2177

TURP
    Cancer, Prostate 380
    Prostatectomy 1729

Prostatic Hypertrophy **1731**
Transurethral Resection of Prostate **2174**

Twentieth Century Syndrome
Allergy **100**
Multiple Chemical Sensitivity Syndrome **1397**

Twins
Placenta Previa **1653**
Pregnancy, Multiple Gestation **1714**

Twisted Neck
Sprains and Strains, Cervical Spine (Neck) **1981**
Torticollis **2108**

Tyloma
Corn and Callus, Infected **578**

Tympanic Membrane
Barotitis Media **241**
Myringotomy **1434**
Otitis Media **1545**
Stapedectomy **2002**
Tympanoplasty **2201**
Tympanum Perforation **2202**

Tympanoplasty
Barotitis Media **241**
Hearing Loss **1036**

Tympanoplasty Radical Mastoidectomy
Mastoidectomy **1347**

Type 1 Diabetes
Diabetes Mellitus Type I **683, 686**

Type 2 Diabetes Mellitus
Diabetes Mellitus Type II **686**

Type I Hernia
Hernia, Hiatal **1097**

Type II Hernia
Hernia, Hiatal **1097**

Type III Hernia
Hernia, Hiatal **1097**

Type IV Hernia
Hernia, Hiatal **1097**

Typhoid
Fever **2204**

Typhus
Fever **2206**

U

Ulcer
Anal Fissure and/or Rectal Ulcer **127**
Corneal Ulcer **584**
Decubitus Ulcer **632**
Peptic Ulcer Disease **1611**
Pyloroplasty **1769**
Rectal Ulcer **1788**
Ulcerative Colitis **2209**
Upper Gastrointestinal Series **2214**
Varicose Ulcer **2244**

Ulcer Site
Decubitus Ulcer **632**
Peptic Ulcer Disease **1611**

Ulcer Site Resection
Resection of Gastric or Duodenal Ulcer Site **1819**

Ulcerated
Corneal Ulcer **584**

Radiodermatitis **1780**
Varicose Ulcer **2244**

Ulcerated Cornea
Corneal Ulcer **584**

Ulcerated Esophageal Varices
Esophageal Varices **843**

Ulcerative Blepharitis
Blepharitis **268**

Ulcerative Colitis
Abdominoperineal Resection of Rectum **10**
Cancer, Colon **354**
Colon Resection **538**
Colonoscopy **540**
Colostomy and Ileostomy **543**
Gastrointestinal Hemorrhage **982**
Hemorrhage of Rectum and Anus **1068**

Ulcerative Enterocolitis
Ulcerative Colitis **2209**

Ulcerative Gingivitis
Gingivitis **993**
Trench Mouth **2181**

Ulcerative Ileocolitis
Intestinal Upset **1224**
Ulcerative Colitis **2209**

Ulcerative Proctitis
Ulcerative Colitis **2209**

Ulcers
Behçet's Syndrome **244**
Blastomycosis **266**
Blepharitis **268**
Cancer, Oropharynx **369**
Cancer, Skin **387**
Cancer, Tongue **399**
Candidiasis **405**
Chancroid **481**
Chromoblastomycosis **508**
Cryptococcosis **608**
Dermatitis **674**
Diabetic Gangrene **689**
Duodenitis **749**
Eczema **778**
Erysipelas **830**
Gangrene **964**
Herpes Simplex **1108**
Penis Disorders **1608**
Peripheral Vascular Disease **1626**
Radiodermatitis **1780**
Raynaud's Phenomenon **1781**
Reiter's Syndrome **1798**
Sickle Cell Anemia **1922**
Syphilis **2033**
Trench Mouth **2181**
Tularemia **2197**
Vagotomy **2235**
Varicose Ulcer **2244**

Ulna and Radius Fracture
Fracture, Radius and Ulna, Distal **933**

Ulnar Nerve Decompression
Transcutaneous Electrical Nerve Stimulation **2164**
Transfer of Nerve, Ulnar **2165**

Ulnar Nerve Transposition
Transfer of Nerve, Ulnar **2165**

Ulnar Neuritis
Neuropathy of Ulnar Nerve (Entrapment) **1473**

Ulnar Neuropathy
  Neuropathy of Ulnar Nerve (Entrapment) 1473
  Transcutaneous Electrical Nerve Stimulation 2164
  Transfer of Nerve, Ulnar 2165

Ultrasonic Liposuction
  Liposuction 1292

Ultrasonography
  Dilation and Curettage 699
  Ultrasound, Diagnostic 2212

Ultrasound
  Abscess, Psoas 38
  Abscess, Subdiaphragmatic 42
  Celiac Plexus Block 442
  Diagnostic 2212
  Echocardiography 774
  Ovarian Cyst, Benign 1552
  Placenta Accreta 1651
  Postmenopausal Bleeding 1703
  Pregnancy, Multiple Gestation 1714
  Pregnancy, Normal 1716
  Premature Rupture of Membranes 1722
  Prostatic Hypertrophy 1731
  Pulmonary Edema 1756
  Pylorospasm 1770
  Rectal Ulcer 1788
  Renal Failure, Acute 1802
  Renovascular Hypertension 1809
  Repair of Cerebral Aneurysm 1812
  Retinal Vascular Occlusion 1827
  Rupture of Spleen, Traumatic 1860
  Salivary Gland Stones 1865
  Scleritis 1891
  Spermatocele 1942
  Stokes-Adams Syndrome 2003
  Threatened Abortion 2080

Ultrasound of Heart
  Echocardiography 774
  Stokes-Adams Syndrome 2003

Ultrasound Therapy
  Ultrasound, Diagnostic 2212

Umbilical Hernia
  Hernia Repair 1094, 1096
  Hernia, Umbilical 1106

Underactive Parathyroid
  Hypoparathyroidism 1173

Underactive Thyroid Gland
  Hypothyroidism 1180

Undulant Fever
  Brucellosis 306

Un-emerged Tooth
  Impacted Tooth 1191

Unexplained
  Chronic Fatigue Syndrome 509

Unipolar Depression
  Depression, Major 665

Unrelated Donor Bone Marrow Transplant
  Bone Marrow Transplant 275

Unsolved Fracture
  Fracture, Femoral Neck 912

Unspecified Allergy
  Allergy 100

Unspecified Conduction Defect
  Heart Block 1040

Unspecified Functional Disorders of Intestine
  Intestinal Upset 1224

Unspecified Iridocyclitis
  Iritis 1240
  Uveitis 2231

Unspecified Neurotic Disorder
  Nervous Breakdown 1462
  Neurotic Disorders 1475

Unstable Angina
  Angina Decubitus 140
  Angina, Unstable 144
  Coronary Arteriography 586
  Coronary Balloon Angioplasty 590

Unstable Bladder
  Urinary Incontinence in Women 2222

Unstable Personality Disorder
  Borderline Personality Disorder 284

Upper Arm
  Contusion, Upper Limb 571

Upper Back Pain
  Thoracic Spine Pain 2076

Upper Endoscopy
  Dumping Syndrome 747
  Esophagogastroduodenoscopy 850

Upper Extremity
  Eosinophilic Fasciitis 814

Upper Gastrointestinal Bleeding
  Dumping Syndrome 747
  Gastrointestinal Hemorrhage 982

Upper Gastrointestinal Series
  Duodenitis 749
  Esophageal Varices 843

Upper Gastrointestinal Tract
  Endoscopy of Gastrointestinal Tract 810
  Esophagogastroduodenoscopy 850
  Gastroesophageal Reflux 979
  Gastrointestinal Hemorrhage 982
  Upper Gastrointestinal Series 2214

Upper GI and Small Bowel Series
  Upper Gastrointestinal Series 2214

Upper GI Endoscopy
  Esophagogastroduodenoscopy 850

Upper GI Series
  Cancer, Small Intestine (Including Duodenum) 389
  Cancer, Stomach 391
  Gastroesophageal Reflux 979
  Upper Gastrointestinal Series 2214

Upper Limb
  Biceps Tendonitis 248
  Contusion, Upper Limb 571

Upper Respiratory Bacterial Infection
  Labyrinthitis 1267
  Upper Respiratory Infection 2216

Upper Respiratory Infection
  Bronchitis, Acute 299
  Cold 533

Upper Respiratory Tract Infection
    Cold 533
    Histoplasmosis 1121
    Upper Respiratory Infection 2216
Upper Respiratory Viral Infection
    Cold 533
    Upper Respiratory Infection 2216
Upper Spine Fracture
    Fracture, Cervical Spine (With or Without Spinal Cord Injury) 904
Upper Urinary Tract Infection
    Pyelonephritis, Acute 1762
Upset
    Intestinal Upset 1224
Urban Yellow Fever
    Yellow Fever 2307
Uremia
    Lithotomy 1293–1294
    Pruritus Ani 1736
    Renal Failure, Chronic 1804
Uremic Pericarditis
    Pericarditis, Acute 1615
Ureter
    Calculus, Renal (Kidney and Ureter) 335
    Intravenous Pyelogram 1233
    Lithotomy 1293–1294
    Lithotomy, Percutaneous 1294
    Transurethral Removal of Obstruction from Ureter 2173
    Transurethral Resection of Prostate 2174
    Urethrocele with Stress Incontinence 2220
    Urinary Incontinence in Women 2222
Ureter Obstruction
    Calculus, Renal (Kidney and Ureter) 335
    Transurethral Removal of Obstruction from Ureter 2173
Ureter Stones
    Calculus, Renal (Kidney and Ureter) 335
    Transurethral Removal of Obstruction from Ureter 2173
Ureteral Stone-basketing
    Transurethral Removal of Obstruction from Ureter 2173
Ureterolithotomy
    Lithotomy 1293–1294
Ureterovaginal Fistula
    Vesicovaginal Fistula 2266
Urethra
    Bladder Polyps 264
    Caruncle of the Urethra, Benign 434
    Catheterization 2216
    Cystitis, Acute 616
    Cystocele or Rectocele 621
    Cystoscopy, Transurethral 624
    Cystourethroplasty of Bladder Neck 625
    Gonorrhea 1010
    Transurethral Balloon Dilation of Prostatic Urethra 2171
    Urethritis 2218
    Vesicourethropexy 2265
Urethra Inflammation
    Urethritis 2218
Urethral
    Catheterization 2216
    Cystocele or Rectocele 621
    Vesicourethropexy 2265

Urethral Polyp
    Caruncle of the Urethra, Benign 434
Urethral Prolapse
    Cystocele or Rectocele 621
Urethritis
    Epididymitis 819
    Hematuria 1055
    Reiter's Syndrome 1798
Urethrocele
    Cystocele or Rectocele 621
    Urinary Incontinence in Women 2222
    Vesicourethropexy 2265
    with Stress Incontinence 2220
Urethrovaginal Fistula
    Vesicovaginal Fistula 2266
Urethrovesical Fistula
    Bladder Fistulas 262
Urethrovesicovaginal Fistula
    Vesicovaginal Fistula 2266
Urge Incontinence
    Urinary Incontinence in Women 2222
URI
    Bronchitis, Acute 299
    Cold 533
    Labyrinthitis 1267
    Upper Respiratory Infection 2216
Urinary
    Albuminuria 82
    Cancer, Kidney 358
    Hydronephrosis 1138
    Incontinence in Women 2222
    Intravenous Pyelogram 1233
Urinary Bladder
    Bladder Fistulas 262
    Bladder Polyps 264
    Calculus, Bladder 333
    Cancer, Bladder 338
    Cystectomy 615
    Cystitis, Acute 616
    Cystitis, Interstitial 619
    Cystocele or Rectocele 621
    Cystourethroplasty of Bladder Neck 625
    Marshall-Marchetti Operation 1344
    Neurogenic Bladder 1471
    Transurethral Incision of Bladder Neck 2172
    Tumor, Benign 2199
    Urethral Catheterization 2216
    Urinary Incontinence in Women 2222
    Vesicourethropexy 2265
    Vesicovaginal Fistula 2266
Urinary Bladder Papilloma
    Bladder Polyps 264
Urinary Incontinence
    Cystoscopy, Transurethral 624
    Cystourethroplasty of Bladder Neck 625
    Hernia Repair, Vaginal 1096
    in Women 2222
    Neurogenic Bladder 1471
    Penis Disorders 1608
    Prostatic Hypertrophy 1731
    Urethral Catheterization 2216
    Vesicourethropexy 2265

Index 2677

Urinary Tract
- Abscess, Renal and Perinephric 40
- Calculus, Bladder 333
- Calculus, Renal (Kidney and Ureter) 335
- Cancer, Bladder 338
- Intravenous Pyelogram 1233
- Lithotomy 1293–1294
- Lithotomy, Percutaneous 1294
- Lithotripsy, Extracorporeal Shock Wave 1295
- Pyuria 1771
- Transurethral Balloon Dilation of Prostatic Urethra 2171
- Urethritis 2218

Urinary Tract Infection
- Abscess, Renal and Perinephric 40
- Cystitis, Acute 616
- Nephritis, Interstitial 1453
- Prostatitis 1734
- Pyuria 1771

Urine
- Albuminuria 82
- Calculus, Bladder 333
- Calculus, Renal (Kidney and Ureter) 335
- Diabetes Insipidus 681
- Hematuria 1055
- Pyuria 1771
- Urinary Incontinence in Women 2222

Urolithiasis
- Calculus, Renal (Kidney and Ureter) 335

URTI
- Upper Respiratory Infection 2216

Urticaria
- Angioedema 150

Uterine
- Cancer, Uterus 402
- Cervical Dysplasia 467
- Fibroid Tumor of Uterus 875
- Hysterectomy 1186
- Menstrual Disorders 1369
- Myomectomy, Uterine 1430
- Polyps 2228

Uterine Bleeding
- Hydatidiform Mole 1134
- Menstrual Disorders 1369

Uterine Cancer
- Cancer, Uterus 402

Uterine Fibroidectomy
- Myomectomy, Uterine 1430

Uterine Fibroids
- Fibroid Tumor of Uterus 875

Uterine Leiomyoma
- Fibroid Tumor of Uterus 875

Uterine Myoma
- Fibroid Tumor of Uterus 875

Uterine Myomectomy
- Hysterectomy 1186
- Myomectomy, Uterine 1430

Uterine Sarcoma
- Cancer, Uterus 402

Uterovaginal Prolapse
- Cystocele or Rectocele 621
- Urethrocele with Stress Incontinence 2220

Uterovesical Fistula
- Vesicovaginal Fistula 2266

Uterus
- Abortion by Dilation and Curettage for Termination of Pregnancy 11
- Aspiration Curettage of the Uterus 208
- Cancer, Cervix 351
- Cancer, Uterus 402
- Cervical Biopsy 460
- Dilation and Curettage 699
- Endometriosis 805
- Fibroid Tumor of Uterus 875
- Hysterectomy 1186
- Menstrual Disorders 1369
- Myomectomy, Uterine 1430
- Pelvic Inflammatory Disease 1604
- Perforation of 2229
- Placenta Accreta 1651
- Placenta Previa 1653
- Uterine Polyps 2228

UTI
- Cystitis, Acute 616
- Pyuria 1771

Uveitis
- Behçet's Syndrome 244
- Iritis 1240

V

V Tach
- Achilles Bursitis or Tendinitis 47
- Ventricular Tachycardia 2260

Vagina
- Bartholin's Gland Cyst 242
- Bladder Fistulas 262
- Candidiasis 405
- Cervicitis 472
- Cryotherapy, Genital Warts (Female) 605
- Cystitis, Acute 616
- Cystocele or Rectocele 621
- Delivery, Spontaneous and/or Assisted Vaginal 647
- Episiotomy 826
- Gonorrhea 1010
- Hernia Repair, Vaginal 1096
- Urethrocele with Stress Incontinence 2220
- Vaginitis 2233
- Vesicovaginal Fistula 2266

Vaginal
- Cervicitis 472
- Cystocele or Rectocele 621
- Delivery, Spontaneous and/or Assisted Vaginal 647
- Postmenopausal Bleeding 1703
- Vaginitis 2233

Vaginal Bleeding
- Cervical Polypectomy 469
- Cervical Polyps 470
- Choriocarcinoma 505
- Postmenopausal Bleeding 1703
- Uterine Polyps 2228
- Uterus, Perforation of 2229

Vaginal Delivery
- Delivery, Spontaneous and/or Assisted Vaginal 647

Vaginal Enterocele
- Hernia Repair, Vaginal 1096

Vaginal Inflammation
- Cervicitis 472
- Vaginitis 2233

Vaginal Prolapse
  Cystocele or Rectocele 621
Vaginitis
  Candidiasis 405
  Pruritus Ani 1736
Vagotomy
  Duodenitis 749
  Gastrointestinal Hemorrhage 982
  Peptic Ulcer Disease 1611
  Pyloroplasty 1769
  Pylorospasm 1770
  Resection of Gastric or Duodenal Ulcer Site 1819
Vagus Nerve Disorder
  Vagotonia 2237
Valgus
  Bunion 312
  Metatarsus Primus Varus 1378
Valley Fever
  Coccidioidomycosis 525
Valve
  Aortic Valve Stenosis 167
  Mitral Insufficiency 1385
  Mitral Valve Prolapse 1389
  Pylorospasm 1770
  Valvuloplasty, Balloon 2240
Valve Dilation
  Aortic Valve Stenosis 167
  Valvuloplasty, Balloon 2240
Valve Disorder
  Aortic Valve Stenosis 167
  Echocardiography 774
  Heart Failure, Congestive 1042
  Mitral Insufficiency 1385
  Mitral Stenosis 1387
  Mitral Valve Prolapse 1389
  Pylorospasm 1770
  Rheumatic Fever, Acute 1833
  Rheumatic Heart Disease, Chronic 1836
Valve Repair
  Pyloroplasty 1769
  Rheumatic Heart Disease, Chronic 1836
  Valvotomy 2237
  Valvuloplasty, Balloon 2240
Valve Replacement
  Aortic Valve Stenosis 167
  Heart Valve Replacement 1047
  Rheumatic Heart Disease, Chronic 1836
Valve Spasm
  Pyloroplasty 1769
  Pylorospasm 1770
Valve Stenosis
  Aortic Valve Stenosis 167
  Cardiovascular Disease in Pregnancy 422
  Mitral Stenosis 1387
  Rheumatic Fever, Acute 1833
  Rheumatic Heart Disease, Chronic 1836
  Valvotomy 2237
Valve Treatment Procedures
  Valvotomy 2237
  Valvuloplasty, Balloon 2240
Valvuloplasty
  Balloon 2240

Cardiac Catheterization 411
  Cardiomyopathy 419
  Valvotomy 2237
Valvuloplasty for the Heart
  Valvuloplasty, Balloon 2240
Valvuloplasty of Heart Valves
  Valvuloplasty, Balloon 2240
Valvulotomy
  Valvotomy 2237
Variant Angina
  Prinzmetal's Angina 1726
Varicella
  Chickenpox 490
  Herpes Zoster 1110
Varices
  Esophageal Varices 843
  Hemorrhoid Treatment 1070
  Ligation of Esophageal Varices 1288
  Sclerotherapy 1895
  Varicocele 2242
  Varicose Veins 2246
Varices Injection
  Hemorrhoid Treatment 1070
  Sclerotherapy 1895
Varicocele
  Infertility, Male 1206
Varicocele Repair
  Ligation of Spermatic Vein for Varicocele 1289
Varicocelectomy
  Infertility, Male 1206
  Ligation of Spermatic Vein for Varicocele 1289
Varicole
  Varicocele 2242
Varicose
  Esophageal Varices 843
  Ligation and Stripping of Varicose Veins 1287
  Sclerotherapy 1895
  Ulcer 2244
  Varicocele 2242
  Veins 2246
Varicose Vein Injection
  Hemorrhoid Treatment 1070
  Sclerotherapy 1895
Varicosis
  Varicose Veins 2246
Varicosities
  Esophageal Varices 843
  Varicocele 2242
  Varicose Veins 2246
Varicosity
  Varicose Veins 2246
Variegate Porphyria
  Porphyria 1693
Varix
  Esophageal Varices 843
  Varicocele 2242
  Varicose Veins 2246
Varix of Esophagus
  Esophageal Varices 843

Index 2679

Vascular
    Peripheral Vascular Disease 1626
    Retinal Vascular Occlusion 1827

Vascular Collapse
    Shock 1915

Vascular Dementia
    Dementia 651, 653

Vascular Disease
    Peripheral Vascular Disease 1626

Vascular Disorders of the Penis
    Penis Disorders 1608

Vascular Insufficiency
    Peripheral Vascular Disease 1626

Vascular Occlusion
    Retinal Vascular Occlusion 1827

Vascular Pathological Gangrene
    Diabetic Gangrene 689

Vasomotor Angina
    Angina Pectoris 140

Vasospasm
    Myocardial Infarction, Acute 1424
    Prinzmetal's Angina 1726

Vasospastic Angina
    Prinzmetal's Angina 1726

Vasovagal
    Phobias, Specific 1639
    Phobic Disorders 1641
    Syncope 2024, 2249

Vasovagal Attack
    Syncope 2024
    Vasovagal Syncope 2249

Vasovagal Syncope
    Syncope 2024

VATS
    Lung Biopsy 1310

Vegans
    Vitamin B_{12} Deficiency 2277
    Vitamin B_2 Deficiency 2275
    Vitamin D Deficiency 2281

Vein
    Ligation and Stripping of Varicose Veins 1287
    Ligation of Spermatic Vein for Varicocele 1289
    Renal Vein Thrombosis 1807
    Thrombophlebitis 2086
    Venous Embolism and Thrombosis 2252

Vein Inflammation with Thrombus
    Thrombophlebitis 2086

Vein Stripping
    Ligation and Stripping of Varicose Veins 1287

Vein Thrombosis
    Venous Embolism and Thrombosis 2252

Veins
    Ligation and Stripping of Varicose Veins 1287
    Thrombophlebitis 2086
    Varicose Veins 2246

Vena Cava Interruption
    Embolism, Pulmonary 789

Venereal
    Chancroid 481
    Gonorrhea 1010
    Syphilis 2033
    Warts, Genital 2294

Venereal Sore
    Chancroid 481
    Syphilis 2033

Venereal Verruca
    Warts, Genital 2294

Venereal Warts
    Warts, Genital 2294
    Warts, Viral 2298

Venezuelan Equine Encephalitis (VEE)
    Equine Encephalitis 827

Venous Embolism
    Arterial Embolism and Thrombosis 180

Venous Stasis Ulcer
    Varicose Ulcer 2244

Venous Thrombosis
    Peripheral Thrombosis 1623
    Thrombophlebitis 2086
    Venous Embolism and Thrombosis 2252

Venous Ulcer
    Peripheral Vascular Disease 1626
    Varicose Ulcer 2244

Ventilation Pneumonitis
    Humidifier Fever 1130

Ventral Hernia
    Hernia, Incisional 1100

Ventricle Hypertrophy
    Aortic Valve Stenosis 167
    Cor Pulmonale, Acute and Chronic 576
    Hypertensive Heart Disease 1156

Ventricular
    Fibrillation 2256
    Premature Beats 1719
    Premature Contractions 2258
    Tachycardia 2260
    Tachycardia, Paroxysmal Supraventricular 2039

Ventricular Arrhythmia
    Ventricular Fibrillation 2256

Ventricular Beats
    Premature Beats 1719
    Ventricular Premature Contractions 2258

Ventricular Complexes
    Premature Beats 1719

Ventricular Contractions
    Atrioventricular Block Incomplete (Second-Degree) 223
    Atrioventricular Block, Complete (Third-Degree) 224
    Atrioventricular Block, Incomplete (First-Degree) 226
    Ventricular Premature Contractions 2258

Ventricular Failure
    Heart Failure, Congestive 1042

Ventricular Fibrillation
    Cardiac Arrest 409

Ventricular Premature Complexes
    Premature Beats 1719

Ventricular Premature Contractions
  Premature Beats 1719
Ventricular Tachycardia
  Cardiac Arrest 409
  Tachycardia, Paroxysmal Supraventricular 2039
VEP
  Evoked Potentials 851
VEPS
  Evoked Potentials 851
Verruca Acuminata
  Warts, Genital 2294
Verruca Plana
  Warts, Viral 2298
Verruca Plantaris
  Warts, Plantar 2296
  Warts, Viral 2298
Verruca Vulgaris
  Warts, Plantar 2296
  Warts, Viral 2298
Verrucae Plantaris
  Warts, Plantar 2296
  Warts, Viral 2298
Vertebra
  Back Pain 239
  Chiropractic Adjustments and Manipulations 492
  Discectomy 703
  Fracture, Cervical Spine (With or Without Spinal Cord Injury) 904
  Fracture, Thoracic Spine (With or Without Spinal Cord Injury) 948
  Fracture, Vertebra 954, 956
  Spinal Fusion 1951
Vertebrae
  Ankylosing Spondylitis 152
  Curvature of the Spine, Acquired 610
  Degeneration, Cervical Intervertebral Disc 634
  Degeneration, Lumbar Intervertebral Disc 637
  Degeneration, Thoracic or Thoracolumbar Intervertebral Disc 640
  Disc Calcification 701
  Dislocation, Cervical Vertebra 711
  Displacement, Cervical Intervertebral Disc Without Myelopathy 728
  Displacement, Lumbar Intervertebral Disc Without Myelopathy 732
  Displacement, Thoracic Intervertebral Disc Without Myelopathy 735
  Fracture, Cervical Spine (With or Without Spinal Cord Injury) 904
  Fracture, Lumbosacral Spine (With or Without Spinal Cord Injury) 920
  Fracture, Sacrum 939
  Fracture, Thoracic Spine (With or Without Spinal Cord Injury) 948
  Spinal Fusion 1951
Vertebral
  Fracture, Cervical Spine (With or Without Spinal Cord Injury) 904
  Fracture, Thoracic Spine (With or Without Spinal Cord Injury) 948
  Spinal Fusion 1951
Vertebral Dislocation
  Dislocation, Cervical Vertebra 711
Vertebral Fracture
  Fracture, Cervical Spine (With or Without Spinal Cord Injury) 904
  Fracture, Thoracic Spine (With or Without Spinal Cord Injury) 948
Vertebral Fusion
  Spinal Fusion 1951
Vertebral Injury
  Spinal Cord Injury 1946
Vertiginous Syndrome
  Vertigo 2262

Vertigo
  Barotitis Media 241
  Dizziness and Giddiness 742
  Epilepsy 824
  Labyrinthitis 1267
  Meniere's Disease 1353
  Otosclerosis 1549
  Paget's Disease of Bone 1557
  Syringomyelia 2035
  Toxic Effects, Chromium 2124
  Transient Ischemic Attack 2169
  Vestibular Neuronitis 2268
Vesical Fistula
  Bladder Fistulas 262
Vesical Fundus Resection
  Cystourethroplasty of Bladder Neck 625
Vesicocervicovaginal Fistula
  Vesicovaginal Fistula 2266
Vesicocutaneous Fistula
  Bladder Fistulas 262
Vesicoenteric Fistula
  Bladder Fistulas 262
Vesicoperineal Fistula
  Bladder Fistulas 262
Vesicourethropexy
  Marshall-Marchetti Operation 1344
Vesicovaginal Fistula
  Bladder Fistulas 262
Vesicular Mole
  Hydatidiform Mole 1134
Vessel Graft
  Arterial Graft 183
  Atherosclerosis and Arteriosclerosis 216
  Coronary Bypass 592
  Thoracic Aneurysm 2070
  Transient Ischemic Attack 2169
Vestibular Neuronitis
  Vertigo 2262
Vestibulitis
  Labyrinthitis 1267
Vibration White-finger
  Raynaud's Phenomenon 1781
Video-Assisted Lung Biopsy
  Lung Biopsy 1310
Vincent's Angina
  Trench Mouth 2181
Vincent's Infection
  Trench Mouth 2181
Vincent's Stomatitis
  Trench Mouth 2181
Viral Adenoiditis
  Tonsillitis and Adenoiditis 2104
Viral Bronchitis
  Bronchitis, Acute 299
  Interstitial Pulmonary Fibrosis 1219
Viral Epiglottitis
  Epiglottitis 822
Viral Hepatitis
  Aspiration 207–208

Index 2681

Hepatitis A **1081**
Hepatitis B **1083**
Hepatitis C **1085**
Hepatitis, Chronic **1089**
Hepatitis, Viral **1091**
Jaundice **1249**

Viral Infection
Brachial Neuropathy **287**
Bronchitis, Acute **299**
Cancer, Liver **360**
Cirrhosis of the Liver **515**
Cold **533**
Colitis **535**
Colorado Tick Fever **541**
Conjunctivitis **556**
Dengue Fever **656**
Diarrhea **696**
Duodenitis **749**
Dysentery **755**
Encephalitis **797**
Equine Encephalitis **827**
Esophagitis **847**
Filariasis **881**
Folliculitis **887**
Gastroenteritis, Infectious **973**
Glomerulonephritis, Acute **1001**
Guillain-Barré Syndrome **1022**
Hepatitis A **1081**
Hepatitis B **1083**
Herpes Simplex **1108**
Infection **1202**
Interstitial Pulmonary Fibrosis **1219**
Upper Respiratory Infection **2216**

Viral Keratitis
Keratitis **1257**

Viral Labyrinthitis
Labyrinthitis **1267**
Vestibular Neuronitis **2268**

Viral Meningitis
Meningitis, Bacterial **1357**
Myelopathy **1420**
St. Louis Encephalitis **2000**

Viral Pericarditis
Pericarditis, Acute **1615**

Viral Pharyngitis
Pharyngitis, Acute **1633**
Upper Respiratory Infection **2216**

Viral Pneumonia
Acquired Immune Deficiency Syndrome **53**
Human Immunodeficiency Virus **1126**
Pneumonia **1667**

Viral Tonsillitis
Pharyngitis, Acute **1633**
Tonsillitis and Adenoiditis **2104**
Upper Respiratory Infection **2216**

Viral Warts
Warts, Genital **2294**
Warts, Plantar **2296**
Warts, Viral **2298**

Virus
Acquired Immune Deficiency Syndrome **53**
Atopic Dermatitis **218**
Excision or Destruction of Plantar Warts **858**
Herpes Simplex **1108**
Herpes Zoster **1110**

Influenza **1207**
Myocarditis, Acute **1428**
Polio **1683**

Vision
Amblyopia, Toxic **107**
Astigmatism **212**
Blindness **270**
Cataract **436, 439**
Cataract Surgery **439**
Corneal Ulcer **584**
Diabetic Retinopathy **694**
Endophthalmitis **808**
Evoked Potentials **851**
Glaucoma, Acute (Angle-Closure) **995**
Glaucoma, Chronic (Open-Angle) **997**
Keratectomy, Laser Photorefractive **1256**
Keratoconus **1259**
Migraine Headache **1378**
Neurofibromatosis **1469**
Optic Neuritis **1521**
Parkinson's Disease **1593**
Retinal Detachment **1823, 1825**
Retinal Vascular Occlusion **1827**
Retinitis Pigmentosa **1829**
Scleritis **1891**
Senile Macular Degeneration **1903**

Visual Evoked Potentials
Evoked Potentials **851**

Vitamin A
Deficiency **2270**
Hypervitaminosis **1164, 1166, 1168**
Hypervitaminosis A **1166**
Hypovitaminosis **1182**
Keratitis **1257**

Vitamin A Toxicity
Hypervitaminosis **1164, 1166, 1168**
Hypervitaminosis A **1166**

Vitamin B_1
Deficiency **2272**

Vitamin B_{12} Deficiency
Amblyopia, Toxic **107**
Anemia **133, 136**
Anemia Complicating Pregnancy **136**
Folic Acid Deficiency Anemia **885**
Gastritis **970**
Neuralgia, Neuritis, and Radiculitis **1465**
Neutropenia **1477**
Paresthesia **1591**
Pernicious Anemia **1630**

Vitamin B_3 Deficiency
Pellagra **1602**

Vitamin C
Deficiency **2279**
Myalgia and Myositis **1411**

Vitamin D
Deficiency **2281**
Hyperparathyroidism **1148**
Hypervitaminosis **1164, 1166, 1168**
Hypervitaminosis D **1168**
Hypoparathyroidism **1173**
Otosclerosis **1549**
Paget's Disease of Bone **1557**
Tetany **2062**

Vitamin D Toxicity
Hypervitaminosis **1164, 1166, 1168**

2682 The Medical Disability Advisor—Fourth Edition

Hypervitaminosis D **1168**
Vitamin Deficiencies
    Anemia **133, 136**
    Anemia Complicating Pregnancy **136**
    Hyperemesis Gravidarum **1142**
    Hypoprothrombinemia **1176**
    Malaise **1328**
    Myalgia and Myositis **1411**
    Premenstrual Syndrome **1724**
    Vitamin A Deficiency **2270**
    Vitamin B_2 Deficiency **2275**
    Vitamin C Deficiency **2279**
    Vitamin D Deficiency **2281**

Vitamin E
    Deficiency **2283**
    Hypervitaminosis **1164, 1166, 1168**

Vitamin K
    Deficiency **2284**
    Hypoprothrombinemia **1176**

Vitamin Overdose
    Hypervitaminosis **1164, 1166, 1168**
    Hypervitaminosis A **1166**
    Hypervitaminosis D **1168**
    Poisoning, Vitamin K **1681**

Vitamin Toxicity
    Hypervitaminosis **1164, 1166, 1168**
    Hypervitaminosis A **1166**
    Hypervitaminosis D **1168**
    Poisoning, Vitamin K **1681**

Vitiligo
    Alopecia Areata **103**

Vocational
    Therapy **2288**

Vocational Rehabilitation
    Rehabilitation Therapy **1796**

Vocational Therapy
    Rehabilitation Therapy **1796**

Voice Box
    Abscess, Larynx **25**

Volvulus
    Colon Resection **538**
    Intestinal Obstruction **1222**
    Meckel's Diverticulum **1351**
    Sigmoidoscopy **1925**

Vomiting During Pregnancy
    Hyperemesis Gravidarum **1142**
    Pregnancy, Normal **1716**

Von Bechterew-Struempel Syndrome
    Ankylosing Spondylitis **152**

Von Bechterew-Strümpell Syndrome
    Ankylosing Spondylitis **152**

Von Recklinghausen's Disease
    Meningioma **1355**
    Neurofibromatosis **1469**
    Tumor, Benign **2199**

VPCS
    Arrhythmia **178**
    Atrial Fibrillation **220**
    Cardiac Arrest **409**
    Premature Beats **1719**
    Sick Sinus Syndrome **1920**
    Tachycardia, Paroxysmal Supraventricular **2039**

    Ventricular Fibrillation **2256**
    Ventricular Tachycardia **2260**

VT
    Ventricular Tachycardia **2260**
    Vocational Therapy **2288**

Vulgaris
    Folliculitis **887**
    Pemphigus **1606**
    Warts, Plantar **2296**
    Warts, Viral **2298**

Vulva
    Cryotherapy, Genital Warts (Female) **605**

Vulvovaginal Gland Abscess
    Bartholin's Gland Cyst **242**

Vulvovaginitis
    Candidiasis **405**
    Vaginitis **2233**

W

Waldenström's Disease
    Polycythemia Vera **1689**

Walking Pneumonia
    Pneumonia **1667**

Wandering Nodal Rhythm
    Wandering Atrial Pacemaker **2293**

Wart
    Genital **2294**
    Plantar **2296**
    Viral **2298**
    Excision or Destruction of Plantar Warts **858**
    Penis Disorders **1608**

Warts
    Cervical Dysplasia **467**
    Cryotherapy, Genital Warts (Female) **605**
    Cryotherapy, Genital Warts (Male) **606**

Washing Biopsy
    Bronchoscopic Biopsy **304**

Wasting
    Acquired Immune Deficiency Syndrome **53**
    Amyotrophic Lateral Sclerosis **125**
    Atrophy, Muscular **227, 230**
    Atrophy, Muscular (Progressive) **230**
    Bone Tumors **281**
    Eating Disorders **769**
    Myalgia and Myositis **1411**
    Neuralgic Amyotrophy **1465**
    Optic Atrophy **1519**
    Optic Neuritis **1521**
    Paralysis, Paraplegia, and Quadriplegia **1583**
    Pericarditis, Chronic Constrictive **1617**
    Peripheral Neuropathy **1621**
    Tuberculosis, Respiratory **2194**

Water
    Giardiasis **989**

Water Loss
    Dehydration **642**

Waterhouse-Friderichsen Syndrome
    Addison's Disease **63**

Weaver's Bottom
    Bursitis **325**

Web Eye
- Pterygium 1754

Wedge Resection
- Arthroplasty, Elbow 197
- Lung Excision 1314
- Ovarian Cyst, Resection of 1555
- Pneumonectomy 1664
- Polycystic Ovary Syndrome 1686

Weeviltox Poisoning
- Toxic Effects, Carbon Disulfide 2116

Weight Loss
- Hyperemesis Gravidarum 1142
- Spondylitis 1958

Welder's Ague
- Metal Fume Fever 1374

Wen
- Sebaceous Cyst 1896

Wernicke-Korsakoff Syndrome
- Vitamin B_1 Deficiency 2272

Western Equine Encephalitis (WEE)
- Equine Encephalitis 827

Westphal-Struempel Pseudosclerosis
- Wilson's Disease 2300

Westphal-Strümpell Pseudosclerosis
- Wilson's Disease 2300

Westphal-Strumpell Syndrome
- Wilson's Disease 2300

Wet Bronchiectasis
- Bronchiectasis 297

Wet Gangrene
- Diabetic Gangrene 689
- Gangrene 964

Wet Lung
- Pulmonary Edema 1756

Wheals
- Erythema Multiforme 833
- Urticaria 2226

Whiplash
- Neck Pain 1448
- Scalenectomy 1877
- Spinal Cord Injury 1946
- Sprains and Strains, Cervical Spine (Neck) 1981

Whipple Pancreatoduodenectomy
- Cancer, Small Intestine (Including Duodenum) 389
- Pancreaticoduodenectomy 1571

Whipple Procedure
- Cancer, Pancreas 375
- Cancer, Small Intestine (Including Duodenum) 389
- Pancreatectomy 1568
- Pancreaticoduodenectomy 1571

White Death
- Tuberculosis, Respiratory 2194

White Plague
- Tuberculosis, Respiratory 2194

Wilson's Disease
- Wilson's Disease 2300

Withdrawal
- Alcohol and Drug Detoxification and Rehabilitation 84

Opioid Type Dependence 1516
Sedative, Hypnotic or Anxiolytic Dependence 1898

Witzel Gastrostomy
- Gastrostomy 984

Wood Alcohol Poisoning
- Toxic Effects, Methyl Alcohol 2140

Wood Naphtha Poisoning
- Toxic Effects, Methyl Alcohol 2140

Wood Spirits Poisoning
- Toxic Effects, Methyl Alcohol 2140

Wooden Tongue
- Actinomycosis 57

Worms
- Filariasis 881

Wound
- Crush Wounds 603
- Excision of Lesion or Tissue of Skin and Subcutaneous Tissue 854
- Lacerations 1269
- Open Wound 1504, 1510, 1512
- Open Wound, Back 1510
- Open Wound, Chest 1512
- Puncture Wound 1759
- Suture of Skin and Subcutaneous Tissue 2020
- Tetanus 2060

Wound Repair
- Suture of Skin and Subcutaneous Tissue 2020

Wrist
- Arthrodesis 194
- Arthrography 196
- Arthroscopy 199
- Avascular Necrosis 235
- Carpal Tunnel Release 428
- Carpal Tunnel Syndrome 430
- Cervicobrachial Syndrome 474
- De Quervain's Release 630
- Epicondylitis, Medial and Lateral 816
- Fasciotomy 870
- Fracture, Carpal Bones 901
- Ganglionectomy (Wrist) 963
- Gout 1012
- Nerve Conduction Studies 1459
- Sprains and Strains 1964, 1968, 1971, 1975, 1979, 1981, 1984, 1986, 1989, 1991, 1994, 1997
- Sprains and Strains, Wrist 1997
- Tetany 2062

Wrist Contusion
- Contusion, Upper Limb 571

Wrist Fracture
- Fracture, Carpal Bones 901
- Fracture, Radius and Ulna, Distal 933

Wrist Ganglionectomy
- Ganglionectomy (Wrist) 963

Wrist Sprain
- Sprains and Strains, Wrist 1997

Wrist Strain
- Sprains and Strains, Wrist 1997

Wry Neck
- Torticollis 2108

Wryneck
- Torticollis 2108

X

Xerophthalmia
: Dry Eye Syndrome 745

Xerotic Keratitis
: Keratitis 1257

X-ray
: X-ray 2305

Y

Yeast Infection
: Candidiasis 405
: Tinea 2095
: Urethritis 2218
: Vaginitis 2233

Yellow Jaundice
: Abscess, Liver 27

Hepatitis A 1081
Hepatitis B 1083
Hepatitis C 1085
Jaundice 1249
Liver Disease 1298

Young-Dees-Leadbetter Bladder Neck Reconstruction
: Cystourethroplasty of Bladder Neck 625

Z

Zenker's Diverticulum
: Esophageal Diverticula 836

Zinc Chill
: Metal Fume Fever 1374

Zoster
: Chickenpox 490

Which format works for you?

"Our primary goal is to help people. By presenting common standards that can be shared by doctors, patients and employers, we have redefined disability management. Everyone is treated with respect."

Presley Reed, MD
Editor-in-Chief, **MDA**
Chairman, **Reed**Group

MDA for Windows

- *Easy to use*
- *Hyperlinks between topics*
- *Print pages directly from your computer*
- *Search by code, description or any word in the reference*
- *Bookmark frequently used entries*
- *Only $525*

This software provides today's technology-driven organizations with instantaneous access to the same trusted MDA information with easier search capabilities than the reference text format. Implement this sophisticated yet easy-to-use tool to empower staff to research, analyze, and make decisions more efficiently. The end result is increased productivity, cost savings, and greater satisfaction among your clients.

FOR ORDER INFORMATION PLEASE SEE NEXT PAGE.

MDA Internet

- *NEW Format*
- *Access full content using your web browser via Internet connection*
- *Always up-to-date*
- *Password protected*
- *Easy to use search capabilities*
- *Only $180 per individual per year*

This exciting Internet-based tool provides users with access to the same MDA information with greater convenience. MDA Internet is an economical, yet powerful tool that is globally accessible using any web browser over an Internet connection, the natural combination of full functionality and minimal system overhead. Realize immediate results based on the use of consistent information across your organization.

FOR ORDER INFORMATION PLEASE SEE NEXT PAGE.

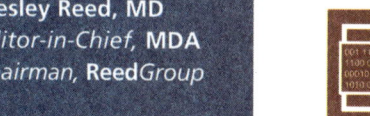

MDA Data License

- *Seamlessly integrate MDA data into your software*
- *Facilitate outcomes reporting*
- *Demonstrate case management effectiveness online*
- *Most effective format to realize the greatest benefits from MDA*
- *Call for more information*

As organizations evolve into an enterprise model, automation and integration become critical factors for success. The MDA Data License is designed for companies that want to maximize their existing technology investment. MDA Data License allows you to integrate the disability duration guidelines database into existing software. The enterprise solution includes MDA for Windows or MDA Internet. The MDA Data License Enterprise Solution gives you the power to benchmark, analyze, and fine-tune your systems-based processing.

TO REQUEST MORE INFORMATION PLEASE SEE NEXT PAGE.

ReedGroup | 4041 Hanover Ave., 2nd Floor ■ Boulder, CO 80305 ■ 800-347-7443 ■ 303-247-1860 ■ 303-247-1863 FAX ■ www.PresleyReed.com

Comprehensive Solutions

MDA Case Manager

As a valued Reed Group customer, you recognize the benefits of the MDA. Imagine the advantages to you and your company in using this tool within a fully integrated software product.

Reed*Group*'s nurse case managers helped design the MDA Case Manager Software to manage absence information and to demonstrate case management effectiveness using its online reports. This flexible, easy to use, and affordable software tool seamlessly integrates the MDA data as a benchmarking tool in the management of medical disability cases, as well as workplace absences. Users can efficiently manage information on employees' medical conditions, treatment, duration, and return to work. Tailor the system to accommodate the various provisions of your company's benefit plan(s):

- Short-term disability
- Long-term disability
- Workers' compensation
- Family Medical Leave
- Paid time off
- Sick leave

Complete Absence Management Services

Reed*Group* can dramatically reduce the duration of employee absence at your company, minimize the costs of lost productivity, and reduce the expense of temporary help. The bottom line is, we'll improve your bottom line!

Reed*Group* has unparalleled experience with 20 years of hands-on client service in medical absence management to improve workplace productivity. Service is customized to each employer's unique needs and requirements for the management of:

- Short-term disability
- Family Medical Leave
- Workers' compensation
- Long-term disability

Reed*Group* uses a four-step methodology to tailor its services to client specifications:

Step 1: **Design** – Reed*Group* carefully listens to ensure a shared understanding of the issues, a common vision of the goals, and a sound strategy for success.

Step 2: **Implementation** – Reed*Group* deploys a customized absence management program that seamlessly integrates with your organization's administrative departments while ensuring objectivity and consistent application of benefits.

Step 3: **Administration** – Reed*Group* actively manages the overall program to ensure on time, on strategy, and on budget results. Reductions in lost time expense range from 10% to 20% for employers.

Step 4: **Evaluation** – Reed*Group* monitors employee absence episodes and provider experience to capture meaningful data to assist the employer in making policy decisions in the future.

Reed*Group*'s service product is designed to enhance an employer's self-insured or fully insured benefit program. As your strategic partner, Reed*Group* provides full turn-key outsourcing service for your organization's absence management program. This process can be accomplished in cooperation with your designated claims fiduciary or insurance company.

Data Analysis

Since its inception, **Reed***Group* has built its products and service on a foundation of research and data analysis for its employer clients. Satisfy your curiosity by comparing your company's absence experience with **Reed***Group*'s proprietary normative database and the MDA benchmarks. **Reed***Group* has special expertise in data analysis, interpretation, reporting, and consulting. Call today to obtain additional information on this valuable **Reed***Group* service.

ReedGroup | 4041 Hanover Ave., 2nd Floor ■ Boulder, CO 80305 ■ 800-347-7443 ■ 303-247-1860 ■ 303-247-1863 FAX ■ www.PresleyReed.com

Order your copies of MDA today

Call today or mail this order form with your payment information to receive your copies of **The Medical Disability Advisor** in the format(s) of your choice. Call about volume order discounts. Please make checks payable to **Reed**Group, Ltd. 30-DAY MONEY BACK GUARANTEE.

ReedGroup
4041 Hanover Ave., 2nd Floor
Boulder, CO 8030
R00MDAT0

# ____	**MDA Reference Text** $425.00 each	$ _____
# ____	**MDA for Windows** $525.00 each	$ _____
# ____	**MDA Internet** $180.00 per individual per year	$ _____

Sales tax in CO 3%, NY 4%, CA 6% — Tax $ _____
Shipping/handling fees: $10 for the first item ($25 in Canada) and $2 for each additional item of the same format. — S/H $ _____
Total $ _____

❏ VISA ❏ Mastercard ❏ American Express ❏ Check
Card Number ____ ____ ____ ____
Exp. Date ___ / ___
Print Cardholder's Name _____
Signature _____

Name: _____
Title: _____
Company: _____
Address: _____
City: _____ State: ____ Zip: ____
Phone: _____ Ext. ____
Department: _____
E-mail: _____

❏ Please add me to **Reed**Group's e-mail newsletter list
❏ Send me more information about MDA Data License
❏ Send me more information about Case Management Software
❏ Send me more information about Reed Management Services

ORDER NOW
800-347-7443
303-247-1860
303-247-1863 FAX

The Medical Disability Advisor

Call **Reed**Group for more information. 800-347-7443 toll free or 303-247-1860

Order your copies of MDA today

Call today or mail this order form with your payment information to receive your copies of **The Medical Disability Advisor** in the format(s) of your choice. Call about volume order discounts. Please make checks payable to **Reed**Group, Ltd. 30-DAY MONEY BACK GUARANTEE.

ReedGroup
4041 Hanover Ave., 2nd Floor
Boulder, CO 8030
R00MDAT0

# ____	**MDA Reference Text** $425.00 each	$ _____
# ____	**MDA for Windows** $525.00 each	$ _____
# ____	**MDA Internet** $180.00 per individual per year	$ _____

Sales tax in CO 3%, NY 4%, CA 6% — Tax $ _____
Shipping/handling fees: $10 for the first item ($25 in Canada) and $2 for each additional item of the same format. — S/H $ _____
Total $ _____

❏ VISA ❏ Mastercard ❏ American Express ❏ Check
Card Number ____ ____ ____ ____
Exp. Date ___ / ___
Print Cardholder's Name _____
Signature _____

Name: _____
Title: _____
Company: _____
Address: _____
City: _____ State: ____ Zip: ____
Phone: _____ Ext. ____
Department: _____
E-mail: _____

❏ Please add me to **Reed**Group's e-mail newsletter list
❏ Send me more information about MDA Data License
❏ Send me more information about Case Management Software
❏ Send me more information about Reed Management Services

ORDER NOW
800-347-7443
303-247-1860
303-247-1863 FAX

The Medical Disability Advisor

Order your copies of MDA today

Call today or mail this order form with your payment information to receive your copies of **The Medical Disability Advisor** in the format(s) of your choice. Call about volume order discounts. Please make checks payable to **Reed**Group, Ltd. 30-DAY MONEY BACK GUARANTEE.

ReedGroup
4041 Hanover Ave., 2nd Floor
Boulder, CO 8030
R00MDAT0

# ____	**MDA Reference Text** $425.00 each	$ _____
# ____	**MDA for Windows** $525.00 each	$ _____
# ____	**MDA Internet** $180.00 per individual per year	$ _____

Sales tax in CO 3%, NY 4%, CA 6% — Tax $ _____
Shipping/handling fees: $10 for the first item ($25 in Canada) and $2 for each additional item of the same format. — S/H $ _____
Total $ _____

❏ VISA ❏ Mastercard ❏ American Express ❏ Check
Card Number ____ ____ ____ ____
Exp. Date ___ / ___
Print Cardholder's Name _____
Signature _____

Name: _____
Title: _____
Company: _____
Address: _____
City: _____ State: ____ Zip: ____
Phone: _____ Ext. ____
Department: _____
E-mail: _____

❏ Please add me to **Reed**Group's e-mail newsletter list
❏ Send me more information about MDA Data License
❏ Send me more information about Case Management Software
❏ Send me more information about Reed Management Services

ORDER NOW
800-347-7443
303-247-1860
303-247-1863 FAX

The Medical Disability Advisor

BUSINESS REPLY MAIL FIRST-CLASS MAIL PERMIT NO. 45-001 BOULDER, CO	NO POSTAGE NECESSARY IF MAILED IN THE UNITED STATES

POSTAGE WILL BE PAID BY ADDRESSEE

ReedGroup
4041 Hanover Avenue, 2nd Floor
Boulder, CO 80305

BUSINESS REPLY MAIL
FIRST-CLASS MAIL   PERMIT NO. 45-001   BOULDER, CO

POSTAGE WILL BE PAID BY ADDRESSEE

NO POSTAGE
NECESSARY
IF MAILED
IN THE
UNITED STATES

ReedGroup
4041 Hanover Avenue, 2nd Floor
Boulder, CO 80305

BUSINESS REPLY MAIL
FIRST-CLASS MAIL   PERMIT NO. 45-001   BOULDER, CO

POSTAGE WILL BE PAID BY ADDRESSEE

NO POSTAGE
NECESSARY
IF MAILED
IN THE
UNITED STATES

ReedGroup
4041 Hanover Avenue, 2nd Floor
Boulder, CO 80305

EVALUATION FORM

The Medical Disability Advisor – Fourth Edition

ReedGroup is committed to the continuous improvement of **The Medical Disability Advisor**. Your satisfaction is important to **Reed**Group. Please take a few moments to complete the following survey about your use of the MDA within your organization. Your input will help us determine which features to integrate into our next edition.

Approximately how many workers does your company employ?

- ❏ 2-99
- ❏ 100-249
- ❏ 250-399
- ❏ 400-999
- ❏ 1,000-17,999
- ❏ 18,000+

Have you used a previous edition of **The Medical Disability Advisor**? ❏ Yes ❏ No

If yes, which edition? ❏ 1st (1991) ❏ 2nd (1994) ❏ 3rd (1997)

Does your company manage medical disability cases for employees? ❏ Yes ❏ No

Does your company manage family medical leave for employees? ❏ Yes ❏ No

FOLD

Please rate **The Medical Disability Advisor**, *Fourth Edition*?

	Excellent	Good	Average	Fair	Poor
Disability Duration Tables	❏	❏	❏	❏	❏
Clinical content	❏	❏	❏	❏	❏
Information clarity	❏	❏	❏	❏	❏
Use of illustrations	❏	❏	❏	❏	❏
Usefulness to your company	❏	❏	❏	❏	❏

The MDA divides information within each topic into subheadings for the reader's convenience. Please let us know which sections are the most and least helpful.

	Most Helpful	Least Helpful
Disability duration tables	❏	❏
Written description of each topic	❏	❏
Diagnosis (history, physical exam, tests)	❏	❏
Prognosis or predicted outcome	❏	❏
Treatment information	❏	❏
Complementary and alternative therapies	❏	❏
Rehabilitation information	❏	❏
Normative data disability duration graphs	❏	❏
Specialists	❏	❏
Co-morbid conditions	❏	❏
Work restrictions and accommodations	❏	❏
Failure to recover questions	❏	❏

FOLD

Please provide a list of ICD-9 clinical or procedure codes you use most frequently._____

Please provide a list of ICD-9 clinical or procedural codes that you would like to see included in the next edition of **The Medical Disability Advisor**._____

Would your company be interested in comparing your disability duration data to **Reed**Group's reference sample database? ❏ Yes ❏ No

Thank you for your time. Your feedback is important to our company. If you have additional questions or comments, please contact **Reed**Group at 800-347-7443 or visit us at www.RGL.net.

OPTIONAL> Contact Name:_____ Title:_____
Company:_____
Address:_____

THANK YOU

Would you like to receive **Reed**Group's periodic email newsletter announcing MDA guideline updates, special offers and other relevant news? If yes, email address:_____

Call **Reed**Group for more information. 800-347-7443 toll free or 303-247-1860

BUSINESS REPLY MAIL
FIRST-CLASS MAIL   PERMIT NO. 45-001   BOULDER, CO

POSTAGE WILL BE PAID BY ADDRESSEE

ReedGroup
4041 Hanover Avenue, 2nd Floor
Boulder, CO 80305

NO POSTAGE
NECESSARY
IF MAILED
IN THE
UNITED STATES

Mailing Instructions

Thank you for responding to this evaluation form. We appreciate your comments and reactions. To return this form to **ReedGroup**, remove it from your MDA book, fold and seal it with a small piece of tape. Do not use staples. Then mail it directly to **ReedGroup**. This is postage paid business reply mail and no stamp is necessary.